DK

ENCYCLOPEDIA *of* ROCK STARS

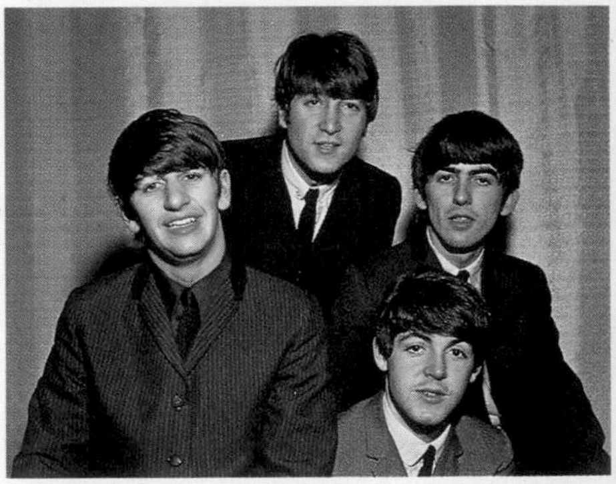

ENCYCLOPEDIA *of* ROCK STARS

DAFYDD REES
& LUKE CRAMPTON

A DK PUBLISHING BOOK

Project Editors
Annabel Martin
Lorna Damms

Senior Art Editor
Karen Ward

DTP
Cooling Brown

Managing Editor
Susannah Marriott

Managing Art Editor
Philip Gilderdale

Production Controller
Antony Heller

This book is dedicated to the memory of Harvey and Archie.

First American Edition, 1996
4 6 8 10 9 7 5 3

Published in the United States by
DK Publishing, Inc.
95 Madison Avenue
New York, New York 10016

Visit us on the World Wide Web at
http://www.dk.com

Published in Great Britain by
Dorling Kindersley Limited.

ISBN 0-7894-1263-2

Reproduced by
Colorlito Rigogliosi S.r.l., Milan, Italy

Printed and bound in the USA
by World Color

Introduction

As a cornerstone of popular western culture, rock music, and its attendant sub-genres, has become the soundtrack to our lives. Since its inception in the 1950s, when it was deemed "devil's music" by some concerned parents, rock has provided successive generations with an absorbing landscape of sounds, memories and events. Each era has yielded performers whose music has influenced subsequent singers and musicians: without Hank Williams and Arthur Crudup, there would likely have been no Elvis Presley; without Little Richard and James Brown, no Prince; without Chuck Berry, Buddy Holly and Lonnie Donegan, no Beatles; no Beatles – one shudders to think. The lineage is clear, the pioneering history almost as compelling and fascinating, triumphant and tragic as the music itself.

As the glory of rock'n'roll has evolved, so too have attempts to document its story, often in an opinionated fashion. All of the different types of truly ground-breaking music created by those already mentioned, together with the likes of Sam Cooke, Bob Dylan, the Beach Boys, the Rolling Stones, Jimi Hendrix et al, right up to present day music heroes such as Oasis, Alanis Morissette and Hootie & the Blowfish, have one thing in common: everyone has a different opinion about who they like and dislike, about which albums they prefer and which they roundly disdain. With the **Encyclopedia of Rock Stars**, however, such subjectivity is abandoned in favor of allowing the history of rock to speak for itself through detailed chronological biographies of its most successful and influential players.

There are two common criticisms of rock history works: first, that "rock" and its predecessor "rock'n'roll" are generic terms, traditionally incorporating a wide range of music styles. The fact that Garth Brooks can happily cover a Kiss song, or that alternative bands of the 1990s can assemble a Carpenters tribute album, testifies to the genre-mixing cultural stew that is commonly coined "rock". The title "Encyclopedia of Rock Stars" continues this all-embracing tradition, hence the inclusion of a diverse selection of artists from punk to funk, pop to rock, country & western to rhythm & blues, folk to rap, surf to mod, reggae to metal, new wave to old hat.

Second, a popular cry from critics and consumers alike questions the inclusion of certain artists to the exclusion of others. Aside from obvious qualifiers (Presley, the Beatles, Michael Jackson), the criteria, always tempered by the book's size, are acts that have either been commercially successful or artistically influential. Many performers have skillfully managed both, making their selection automatic. For the others, we have included artists who have had either a formative influence or maintained consistent critical success, but whose chart impact may have been slight, alongside those who have enjoyed a substantial chart career, but whose biography or career is otherwise limited.

We have also tried to provide a transatlantic balance: in addition to world-conquering acts whose names are familiar to music fans around the globe, we have included a number of performers who are indigenously popular in either the United States or the United Kingdom, traditionally the two most fertile breeding grounds for rock artists.

Within each chronologically compiled biography you will find personal and professional histories, presenting yearly, monthly and often daily diaries. They include the peak position of every UK and US chart single and album; all notable awards, live events, television and radio appearances; discographical information; births, deaths, real names, court cases, lineup changes; and a log of important and sometimes entirely trivial events. With the explosion in media coverage of daily goings-on in the world of music over the past decade, it is inevitable that more information is available to chronicle the 1990s compared to the relatively poorly documented 1950s. This accounts for any imbalance found as the decades progress within each biography. Please refer to the "How To Use" section on page 16 for a more detailed guide to the specific content within each entry.

In attempting to present as much accurate information as space allows, we have tried to confirm each fact as diligently as possible, and, in the process, to dismiss a great deal of misinformation that has always surrounded the history of rock, replacing it with fascinating new information that has either been buried by time, or simply not previously reported.

Universities and colleges now have entire courses devoted to rock music, while the media at large reports daily on the trials and tribulations of the culture's most enduring and more fleeting celebrities. This book attempts to satisfy any inquiring mind, from the most dedicated archivist to the casual music enthusiast. Wherever your level of interest lies, we hope your curiosity is satisfied.

LEARNING CENTER
PARIS JR. COLLEGE

About the authors

Dafydd Rees

Luke Crampton

Born in the UK in the 1950s, Dafydd Rees and Luke Crampton both enjoyed London-based careers in the record trade before co-founding the Media Research & Information Bureau (MRIB) in 1981. During the 1980s MRIB became the largest chart-compiling and music research agency in Europe, numbering among its clients some of the most prestigious names in UK media. MRIB was sold in 1991 when Dafydd and Luke emigrated to America, where they still live, Dafydd on Cape Cod and Luke in Atlanta. They have served as the Official Adjudicator for the annual Ivor Novello Awards (1981–91) and the World Music Awards (1990–93). In addition to writing the rock music history tours for the Tussauds Group's "Rock Circus", the duo have also written 20 books, created successful UK radio and television series, and have featured regularly on radio shows in both the UK and the US. Today Dafydd and Luke continue to work on research projects while constantly updating and developing their "Popular Music Encyclopedia Database" – probably the world's most comprehensive source of historical data on popular music.

1950s

Ike Turner

➢ page 877

9 June 1951 *Rocket 88*, recorded at Sam Phillips' Sun Studio, Memphis, TN, by Ike Turner's Kings Of Rhythm band, hits #1 on the US R&B chart (though credited as a solo cut by the group's lead vocalist and sax player, Jackie Brenston backed by his Delta Cats). Despite failing to cross over to the pop surveys, the single will be cited as the first rock'n'roll recording.

Hank Williams

➢ page 927

31 Dec 1952 With his current hit *I'll Never Get Out Of This World Alive* sitting atop the US Country chart, Hank Williams, the most popular Country artist of the day, dies during the night, age 29, while being driven in his Cadillac, from Montgomery to a New Year's Day concert at the Memorial Auditorium in Canton, OH. Highway patrolman Swann Kitts books the driver, 17-year-old Charles Carr, for speeding, near Rutledge, TN, and remarks that his co-passenger "looks dead". It will not be until the following day when Carr stops for directions in Oak Hill, OH, at 5.30 a.m., that Carr realizes that the father of Country music has indeed passed away.

Elvis Presley

➢ page 669

18 July 1953 Currently employed by the Crown Electric Co., earning $35 a week as a truck driver, Elvis Presley calls at the Memphis Recording Service at 706, Union Avenue, Memphis, TN, and pays $4 to make a private recording (his first ever), covering *My Happiness* and *That's When Your Heartaches Begin*.

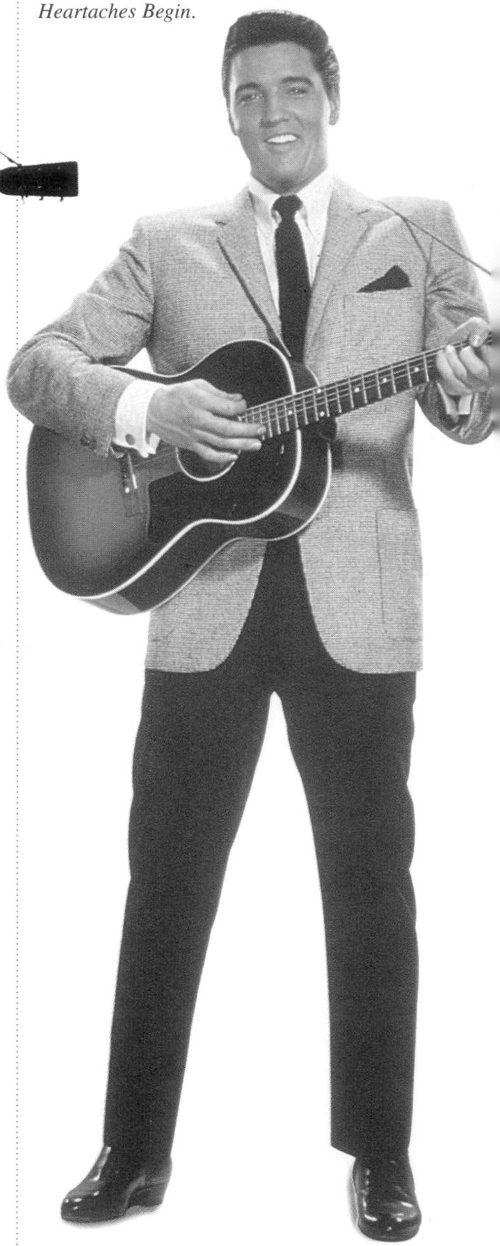

1950 1951 1952 1953 1954

Bill Haley & His Comets ➢ page 379

12 Apr 1954 Bill Haley & His Comets, newly signed to Decca, record *(We're Gonna) Rock Around The Clock* and *Thirteen Women* at the label's Pythian Temple Studios, New York, NY. The first tracks will make music history, not least as the first rock'n'roll release to top the US and UK singles charts.

Little Richard ➢ page 520

14 Sept 1955 Little Richard, having made his first recordings four years earlier, begins a 48-hour session in New Orleans, LA, for Specialty Records. Having covered the blues numbers *Kansas City* and *Directly From My Heart,* and at the suggestion of his producer/manager Robert 'Bumps' Blackwell, Richard records a version of a live number he has written – *Tutti Frutti*.

Jerry Lee Lewis ➢ page 516

4 Dec 1956 Jerry Lee Lewis joins Elvis Presley and Carl Perkins in an impromptu recording session at the Sun Studio in Memphis, TN. Johnny Cash leaves the session early at the insistence of his wife, who wants to go shopping. These historic recordings will become known as "The Million Dollar Quartet".

Paul Anka ➢ page 43

30 Aug 1957 Within a month of its release, Paul Anka's self-penned *Diana* tops the UK chart at the beginning of a nine-week run. Its nine-million-plus worldwide sales will establish the 16-year-old Canadian as one of the first transatlantic pop-teen idols. (Anka's only other single to date, *I Confess,* recorded the previous year, sold a total of 3,000 copies.)

Cliff Richard ➢ page 718

9 Aug 1958 Signed to EMI's Columbia label, 18-year-old Cliff Richard begins a four-week residency at Butlins Holiday Camp, Clacton-On-Sea, Essex, backed by the Drifters (who will change their name to the Shadows in 1959).

Buddy Holly ➢ page 409

3 Feb 1959 At approximately 1.00 a.m., Buddy Holly, Ritchie Valens and the Big Bopper (Jiles Perry Richardson) take off from Mason City, IA, in a light plane due to take them to their next concert date in Fargo, ND. In bad weather and minutes after take-off, the plane crashes in a field some eight miles northwest of the airfield, killing the three stars and pilot Roger Peterson.

1955 ➢ 1956 ➢ 1957 ➢ 1958 ➢ 1959 ➢

1960s

The Beatles

➣ page 74

17 Aug 1960 John Lennon, Paul McCartney, George Harrison, Stuart Sutcliffe and Pete Best, having arrived in Hamburg for their debut German gigs, perform for the first time as the Beatles (during UK dates in the summer they were billed as the Silver Beatles after a brief spell as the Beatals). This is the beginning of a 48-night stint at the Indra club, which will end on October 3rd. They are then moved by promoter Bruno Koschmider into his other club, the Kaiserkeller, where they will play a further 58 nights, sharing the bill with fellow Liverpudlians, Rory Storm & the Hurricanes, whose drummer is Ringo Starr.

Aretha Franklin

➣ page 341

13 Mar 1961 Eighteen-year-old soul singer Aretha Franklin's chart debut, *Won't Be Long*, recorded with the Ray Bryant Combo on Columbia Records, peaks at US #76. It is the first of her 31 US chart singles during the sixties.

The Rolling Stones

➣ page 732

12 Jul 1962 Billed as the Rollin' Stones (a name taken from a Muddy Waters song), Mick Jagger, Keith Richard and Brian Jones (augmented by Ian Stewart, Dick Taylor and future Kinks drummer Mick Avory) make their live debut together at London's Marquee Jazz club.

The Beach Boys

➣ page 68

25 May 1963 *Surfin' USA* becomes the Beach Boys' first top 10 record, hitting US #3. Defining both the burgeoning surf scene and the unique Beach Boys sound, it is Brian Wilson's adaptation of Chuck Berry's *Sweet Little Sixteen* with surf-related lyrics added. Three weeks later, the Wilson-written *Surf City,* which he has given to Jan & Dean, begins a chart ride to US #1.

1960 › 1961 › 1962 › 1963 › 1964 ›

Sam Cooke

➢ page 214

11 Dec 1964 Having spent the previous night at PJ's nightclub, R&B star Sam Cooke checks in to the $3-a-night Hacienda Motel at 9137 South Figuero, Los Angeles, CA, with 22-year-old Elisa Boyer, where he is shot dead by its manager Bertha Franklin. Franklin claims that she shot him in self-defence when he tried to assault her, having previously attempted to rape Boyer.

David Bowie

➢ page 119

8 Mar 1965 David Jones makes his first television appearance on UK-TV's "Gadzooks! It's All Happening", as one of the Mannish Boys, who perform their current single *I Pity The Fool*. He will change his surname to Bowie the following year to avoid confusion with Monkee Davy Jones.

Pink Floyd

➢ page 652

15 Oct 1966 Pink Floyd plays at the "All-Night Rave Pop Op Costume Masque Drag Ball Et Al", on the opening night of the Roundhouse venue in Chalk Farm, London, for which they are paid £15. The **San Francisco Examiner** review of the show is not even aware that Floyd had played, thinking the act to be "a large pick-up band of assorted instruments on a small central platform".

The Grateful Dead

➢ page 368

18 June 1967 Three months after the release of its debut album, the Grateful Dead is the sixth act to play (between Jimi Hendrix and the Who) on the third and final evening of the Monterey International Pop Festival held at the County Fairgrounds, Monterey, CA. After disagreements with music industry executives, they are left out of the film documentary of the event, despite being one of the Festival's main attractions.

James Brown

➢ page 134

5 Apr 1968 Following the assassination of Martin Luther King and riots in 30 US cities, James Brown makes a national TV appeal from the Boston Garden, Boston, MA, urging restraint and more peaceful forms of protest. Its calming effect results in an official commendation from Vice-President Humphrey and a dinner invitation from President Johnson.

Jimi Hendrix

➢ page 400

18 Aug 1969 For $125,000, the highest fee of any attending performer, Jimi Hendrix plays at the Woodstock Music & Art Fair in Bethel, NY, backed by the Gypsy Sons & Rainbows. The set is highlighted by his version of *The Star Spangled Banner*, regarded as a seminal performance and one captured on the subsequently released "Woodstock" film and album.

1965 › 1966 › 1967 › 1968 › 1969 ›

1970s

Elton John

➢ page 462

25 Aug 1970 Elton John makes his live Stateside debut, accompanied by his regular sidemen, bassist Dee Murray and drummer Nigel Olsson, performing at the 20th-anniversary celebrations for Doug Weston's Troubadour club in Los Angeles, CA, and opening for singer-songwriter David Ackles. His critically acclaimed set is witnessed by audience members, including Leon Russell and Quincy Jones. John will later claim that the "awesome" reviews of this performance changed his life.

The Doors

➢ page 277

3 July 1971 The Doors' lead vocalist Jim Morrison, having moved to France, is found dead in a Paris apartment. The cause of death is given as "a heart attack induced by respiratory problems". He is buried six days later in Père Lachaise cemetery, where his grave becomes a graffiti-covered shrine.

Michael Jackson

➢ page 436

14 Oct 1972 Michael Jackson scores his first solo US chart-topping single at age 14 with *Ben*, a ballad written about a rat by American composer Walter Scharf and British lyricist Don Black. Featured in the film of the same name, the song was originally intended for Jackson's contemporary, Donny Osmond.

Stevie Wonder

➢ page 936

6 Aug 1973 En-route from Greenville, NC, to Durham, NC, during a US concert tour, Stevie Wonder is injured when the car he is travelling in crashes into a truck near Winston-Salem, NC. He suffers multiple head injuries, causing the loss of his sense of smell, and lies in a coma for four days, before recovering sufficiently to appear with Elton John in September.

Abba

➢ page 18

6 Apr 1974 With conductor Sven-Olof Walldoff dressed as Napoleon, the infectious Swedish entry *Waterloo*, performed by Abba, wins the Eurovision Song Contest held in Brighton, E. Sussex. (At odds of 20/1, manager, Stig Anderson, has bet the group will win the event.)

The Sex Pistols

➢ page 771

6 Nov 1975 Lining up as Steve Jones, Paul Cook, Glen Matlock and Johnny Rotten, punk pioneers the Sex Pistols play their first gig at the St. Martin's School of Art, London (a performance lasting ten minutes). It will be followed by a series of increasingly controversial concerts around the UK.

Bob Dylan

➢ page 284

25 Nov 1976 Bob Dylan joins the Band at the group's "The Last Waltz" farewell concert held at the Winterland Ballroom, San Francisco, CA. Their joint performances of *Baby Let Me Follow You Down*, *I Don't Believe You (She Acts Like We Never Met)*, *Forever Young* and *I Shall Be Released* will appear in the documentary of the event.

The Bee Gees

➢ page 85

14 Dec 1977 The disco movie "Saturday Night Fever", starring John Travolta, receives its world premiere in New York, NY. With an era-defining soundtrack largely written and performed by the Bee Gees, the double album will become the biggest-selling film soundtrack of all time. Within two weeks the extracted *How Deep Is Your Love* will top the US Hot 100, spending 17 consecutive weeks in the top 10, a **Billboard** record. The group's next five singles (*Stayin' Alive*, *Night Fever*, *Too Much Heaven*, *Tragedy* and *Love You Inside Out*) will all top the US chart.

U2

➢ page 887

18 Mar 1978 After playing pub and club gigs around Dublin, Eire, U2 wins a talent contest sponsored by Guinness Harp Lager at the Limerick Civic Week. Still at school, the group wins £500 and the chance to audition for CBS Ireland (through contest adjudicator, A&R man Jackie Hayden) at Dublin's Keystone Studios.

The Police

➢ page 664

1 Mar 1979 Having completed a 29-date US tour, the Police makes its debut on BBC1-TV's "Top Of The Pops" performing the re-released, Sting-penned hit *Roxanne*. It will become the first of 15 UK top 20 hits over the next five years for the group, reaching #12.

1975 1976 1977 1978 1979

1980s

THE EAGLES

➢ page 288

23 Aug 1982 The Eagles' last album for 12 years, ***Eagles Greatest Hits, Volume 2*** enters the US chart. After a split due to personnel clashes, the group vows not to work together until "hell freezes over" – the title of the 1994 reunion album.

JOHN LENNON

➢ page 511

8 Dec 1980 John Lennon and Yoko Ono leave New York's Record Plant studio at 10.30 p.m. They enter the West 72nd St. entrance of the Dakota building that they live in, and Lennon turns around on hearing a voice say "Mr. Lennon". He is shot four times by 25-year-old Mark David Chapman, before struggling up six stairs to the alcove of the guard area, where he collapses at approximately 10.50 p.m. He is placed in the back seat of Police Officer James Moran's patrol car and driven to the Roosevelt Hospital 15 blocks away, where, at 11.30 p.m., he is pronounced dead. That day, Lennon had autographed Chapman's copy of ***Double Fantasy*** - "John Lennon 1980". Chapman will be sentenced to 20 years to life for Lennon's murder on August 25th, 1981.

BOB MARLEY

➢ page 550

11 May 1981 Having collapsed while jogging in New York's Central Park the previous September and having sought cancer treatment in Germany in December, Bob Marley dies of lung cancer and a brain tumor aged 36, at the Cedars Of Lebanon Hospital, Miami, FL. His body will lie in state at the National Arena in Kingston, Jamaica, on the 21st–22nd.

R.E.M.

➢ page 712

13 Aug 1983 Following seven US stadium dates in July opening for the Police (who are also managed by Copeland), R.E.M.'s singles chart debut, *Radio Free Europe,* peaks at US #78. It is taken from the group's first full-length album, ***Murmur***, on Miles Copeland's I.R.S. label.

1980 › 1981 › 1982 › 1983 › 1984 ›

Marvin Gaye

➢ page 354

1 Apr 1984 Marvin Gaye, who has moved into his parents home at 2101, South Grammercy, Crenshaw, Los Angeles, CA, the previous November, with family and friends concerned about his mental state, is shot by his father (an apostolic minister) during a violent argument. He is pronounced dead at 1.01 p.m. at the California Hospital Medical Center.

Led Zeppelin

➢ page 506

13 July 1985 Performing at the US segment (JFK Stadium, Philadelphia, PA) of the historic "Live Aid" fund-raising rock festival, the remaining members of Led Zeppelin reunite for their first appearance since drummer John Bonham's death five years earlier. Phil Collins (who has already performed at the London event earlier in the day and flown over on Concorde) fills in on drums.

Ray Charles

➢ page175

23 Jan 1986 Ray Charles, whose recording career began in 1949, is inducted by Quincy Jones into the Rock And Roll Hall Of Fame at its inaugural ceremony held at New York's Waldorf-Astoria Hotel.

Dire Straits

➢ page 265

1 Aug 1987 Having won the Best Video category at last year's MTV Music Video Awards in the US, "Money For Nothing" (its song co-written by Mark Knopfler and Sting) becomes the first music video to be broadcast on the premiering MTV Europe satellite network.

The Smiths

➢ page 798

22 Dec 1988 With Morrissey signed as a solo artist to EMI Records, and founding guitarist Johnny Marr already departed from the line-up, the Smiths, comprising Morrissey, Andy Rourke, Mike Joyce and Craig Gannon, reform to play a farewell gig at the Wolverhampton Civic Hall.

Bruce Springsteen

➢ page 815

18 Jan 1989 Bruce Springsteen performs *Crying* as a tribute to Roy Orbison (who has died the month before) at the fourth annual Rock And Roll Hall Of Fame dinner, once again held at New York's Waldorf-Astoria Hotel.

1990s

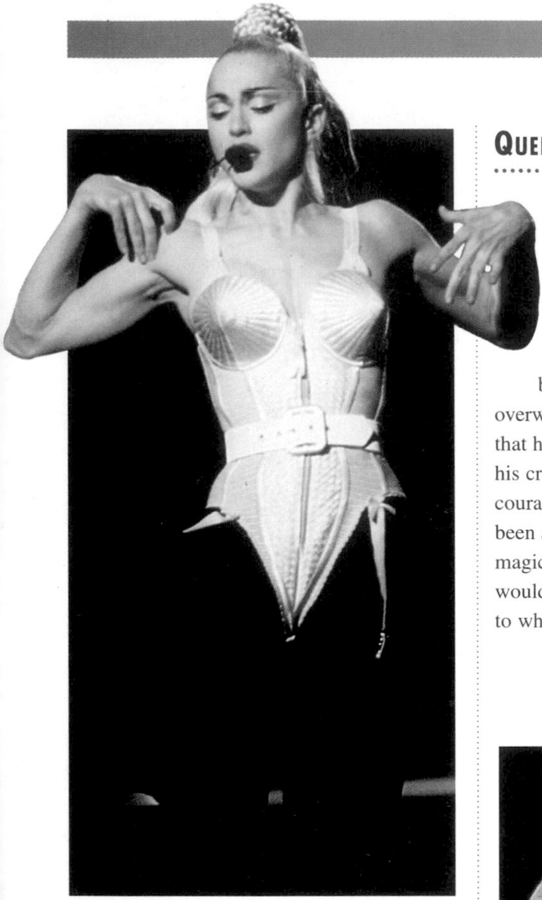

MADONNA

➢ page 540

13 Apr 1990 Promoting her forthcoming album ***I'm Breathless***, Madonna's 54-date worldwide "Blonde Ambition" tour opens at the Chiba Marine Stadium in Tokyo, Japan with the star typically clad in revealing costumes designed by Jean Paul Gaultier. The North American leg will begin on May 4th and 5th at The Summit in Houston, TX, but several subsequent dates will be cancelled when Madonna's vocal chords become infected. On the 29th, police in Toronto, Canada will "review" her third SkyDome show, citing a complaint of lewdness.

QUEEN

➢ page 697

24 Nov 1991 Queen's Freddie Mercury dies of complications from AIDS at his home in Holland Park, London. A statement issued by the group includes the following words: "We have lost the greatest and most beloved member of our family. We feel overwhelming grief that he has gone, sadness that he should be cut down at the height of his creativity, but above all great pride in the courageous way he lived and died. It has been a privilege for us to have shared such magical times. As soon as we are able we would like to celebrate his life in the style to which he was accustomed".

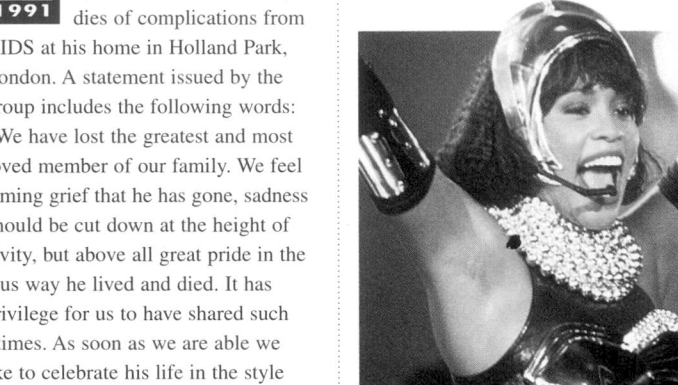

WHITNEY HOUSTON

➢ page 418

28 Nov 1992 *I Will Always Love You*, performed by Whitney Houston and taken from the soundtrack to her film debut "The Bodyguard", hits US #1. Houston's version of the ballad written by Dolly Parton begins a record-breaking 14-week stay atop the US survey. On December 5th it will begin a 10-week run at UK #1, becoming the year's best-selling single worldwide.

1990 ➢ 1991 ➢ 1992 ➢ 1993 ➢

PRINCE/ [symbol]

➢ page 688

7 Jun 1993 On his 35th birthday, Prince issues a statement saying that he is changing his name to [symbol]. With no guidance on the star's preferred pronunciation for the symbol, the media henceforth refers to him as "The Artist Formerly Known As Prince".

NIRVANA

➢ page 618

8 Apr 1994 While installing a burglar alarm, an electrician finds the body of Nirvana's lead singer, Kurt Cobain, in an apartment room above the garage of Cobain's home in Seattle, WA. Cobain has shot himself with a 20-gauge shotgun. His suicide note quotes a lyric from a Neil Young song: "It's better to burn out than to fade away".

OASIS AND BLUR

➢ pages 109 & 622

26 Aug 1995 At the height of a bitter media-fed rivalry between BritPop pioneers Oasis and Blur, and with their record labels having simultaneously released respective singles the week before, Blur's *Country House* enters the UK chart at #1 (the 42nd time a single has arrived in pole position in Britain), outsmarting Oasis' *Roll With It*, which debuts at #2.

TAKE THAT

➢ page 850

13 Feb 1996 Having finally cracked the US market with *Back For Good* the previous year, and positioned as Britain's biggest-selling pop act of the decade to date, Take That holds a press conference confirming that the group is permanently splitting. Telephone help-lines including the Samaritans and Childline report a huge number of calls from distraught teenage girls.

HOW TO USE THIS BOOK

Running alphabetically from A-Z, solo artists are listed by the first letter of their surname, while groups can be found by the first letter of the band name, for example, Elton John is included under the letter section J, as is the group Jethro Tull. Exception: if a solo artist does not have a last name, the entry is listed under the first letter of the chosen performing name, for example, Boy George will be in the B section and Dr. John in the D section. At the beginning of each alphabetical section you will find an index of the included acts for that letter.

If an act's edited history is included in a larger biography, it will be indicated, for example, if you wish to read about Black Flag, the group's entry will indicate, "see Henry Rollins".

Solo artists who were/are members of bands but who have enjoyed significant solo success, for example, Phil Collins from Genesis, will, in addition to the band entry, have their own separate entry, indicated at the close of the band's biography.

All dates and information are as accurate as can be determined. Birth dates are a particularly interesting area of conflicting data, one in which post-fame publicity often seems to make pop stars younger. For example, only when Del Shannon died in 1990 was it generally acknowledged that he was actually born in 1934, though during his commercial peak, it became legend that he arrived in 1939.

EPs in the US (where they have traditionally qualified for the albums chart) are presented in ***bold italic***.

EPs in the UK (where they have traditionally qualified for the singles chart) are in *italic*.

Albums (including LPs, cassettes, 8-tracks, compact discs, mini-discs, etc.) are presented in ***bold italic***.

Locations Each time a town is first mentioned within each entry, there will follow either the relevant abbreviated state in the US (Los Angeles, CA) or abbreviated county in the UK (Wembley, Middx.). If the town is repeated within that entry, the state or county will thereafter not be given.

Chronology Each biographical history is presented chronologically as follows: year, month and date, for example, **1992**, **June** [29]

Publications All magazines, newspapers, books and other literary sources are presented in **bold**.

Singles are presented in *italic*.

CD-ROMs or E-CDs (enhanced multi-media CDs) are presented in ***bold italic***.

SAMPLE ENTRY

BELLY

Tanya Donelly (guitar, vocals); **Tom Gorman** (guitar); **Chris Gorman** (drums); **Gail Greenwood** (bass)

1990

Having already found critical success as a member of alternative quartet Throwing Muses (formed in 1980 with three high-school friends, Kristin Hersh, David Narcizo and Elaine Adamedes (replaced by Leslie Langston in 1985) in Newport, RI who have gone on to sign with the UK-based 4AD label releasing ***Throwing Muses EP*** (1984), ***Throwing Muses*** (1986), *Chains Changed EP* and *The Fat Skier EP* (1987), ***House Tornado*** (1988) and ***Hunkpapa*** (1989), Donelly (b. July 14, 1966, Newport), seeking another outlet for her songwriting ambitions, forms the Breeders with Pixies bassist Kim Deal, again signed to 4AD which now releases its debut set ***Pod***. Recording and performing with both the Breeders and Throwing Muses over the next year, Donelly will contribute to the former's *Safari EP* (to be released in 1992) and the latter's ***The Real Ramona***, before electing to quit both line-ups to form Belly with Chris Gorman (b. July 29, 1967, Buffalo, NY), his brother Tom (b. May 20, 1966, Buffalo) and bassist Fred Abong (who had replaced Langston in Throwing Muses in 1990).

1992

June [29] Once again signed to the loyal 4AD label, Belly's debut effort, the EP *Slow Dust* is released in the UK (to be followed by a further 4-track CD, *Gepetto* issued in November).

1993

Jan [23] *Feed The Tree* debuts at its UK #32 peak.
Feb [13] ***Star***, its 15 songs largely written by Donelly and displaying the group's quirky childlike pop charm, hits UK #2 in its first week behind the Cult's ***Pure Cult***.
Mar [6] *Feed The Tree* tops the US Modern Rock Tracks survey
Apr [10] Re-released *Gepetto (Remix)* bows at its UK #49 peak.
May [1] ***Star***, issued in the US by Sire Records, makes US #59 and will prompt the band's nomination in the Best New Act category for the 1993 Grammy Awards

Broadcasts and other events Television and radio broadcasts, films, videos and general events are presented in "double quotes".
Internet and online events are given in normal text, with web-site addresses indicated in their appropriate lower-case type. Notable television appearances made by artists include the relevant television network abbreviation. These are:

UK: Independent Television – ITV or C4 (Channel Four); British Broadcasting Corporation: BBC1 or BBC2.
US: ABC, CBS, NBC, Fox.
Cable/satellite television: the name of the channel will be indicated, for example, MTV, VH1, Nickelodeon, Sky, HBO, TBS, etc.

Radio appearances will identify the relevant radio station in the UK (for example, BBC Radio 1 (now 1FM) or Capital Radio, and by call-letters in the US (for example, WSB).

Charts The chart peaks of all relevant UK and US pop singles and albums are given in every entry. Every biography, therefore, includes a complete UK/US chart history. Additional chart achievements on specialist surveys (for example R&B, Country, etc.) or other national charts (for example, those in Australia, Germany etc.) are often included where notable. For details of sales achieved see page 952.

Awards Uniquely, all major awards and honors bestowed upon each act are included in each biography. These include, but are not limited to, the annual Grammy Awards, BRIT Awards, Rock And Roll Hall Of Fame, American Music Awards, Ivor Novello Awards, World Music Awards, MTV Video Music (US and Europe), Billboard Music Awards, Oscars, Mercury Music Prize, ASCAP, BMI, Soul Train Music Awards, R&B Foundation, Songwriters Hall Of Fame, Polar Music Prize.

A

ABBA

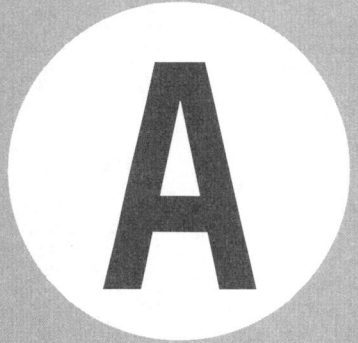

Benny Andersson (keyboards, synthesizer, vocals); **Björn Ulvaeus** (guitar, vocals); **Agnetha Fältskog** (vocals); **Frida Lyngstad** (vocals)

1969

Aug Ulvaeus (b. Apr. 25, 1945, Gothenburg, Sweden), who formed folk band the West Bay Singers with friends from school in 1963, and Andersson (b. Goran Bror Benny Andersson, Dec. 16, 1946, Stockholm, Sweden), former piano player with the Hep Stars (a group which sold more records than the Beatles in Sweden) have met at a party in Västervik, Sweden in 1966, subsequently striking up a songwriting partnership, which has included the formation of a publishing company, Union Songs. Having changed their name to the Hootenanny Singers and been brought to Stockholm at the invitation of Stig Anderson, the duo are signed as the first act on his Polar label. On a Swedish TV show, Ulvaeus meets Fältskog (b. Apr. 5, 1950, Jönköping, Sweden), who has been signed to CBS Sweden as a solo artist at the age of 17, having had a Swedish #1 in 1968 with *I Was So In Love*, before playing Maria Magdalena in the Swedish production of "Jesus Christ Superstar", followed by a summer folk circuit tour throughout the country. Andersson now becomes engaged to Lyngstad (b. Anni-Frid Lyngstad, Nov. 15, 1945, Narvik, Norway), whose German father was thought to have been killed before Lyngstad was born, when his ship sank during World War II, and whose mother died shortly after her birth. (She moved to Eskilstuna, southwest of Stockholm at age two, to be brought up by her grandmother. At ten she entered a local amateur singing contest, and when 11 sang at a Red Cross soirée before fronting her own dance band in her teens, the Anni-Frid Four, which won a television talent contest on September 3rd, 1967 on "Hyland's Corner" with *A Day Off*, which led to a contract with EMI. She is also a veteran of song festivals in Japan and Venezuela.)

1971

Feb [14] After Fältskog and Lyngstad have sung backing vocals on *Hey Old Man* for Andersson and Ulvaeus' forthcoming album ***Happiness***, they decide to perform together so as not to spend time apart, making their first appearance as a group as the Engaged Couples at the Festfolk Quartet nightclub in Gothenburg, but, unhappy with their performance, they abandon plans to continue as a band.

July [7] Ulvaeus and Fältskog marry in Verum, Sweden, with Andersson the wedding organist.

Oct Andersson and Ulvaeus become producer partners at Polar Music.

1972

Feb They submit *Better To Have Loved*, sung by Lena Andersson, as the Swedish entry in the Eurovision Song Contest. It comes third, but will go on to top the Swedish chart.

June *People Need Love* is released in Sweden under the name Björn, Benny, Agnetha & Frida, and hits #2. Anderson begins calling the foursome Abba (after their initials), before realizing it is the name of the largest fish-canning company in Sweden, but successfully negotiates with them to use the moniker. They send a carton of tuna as a gesture of goodwill.

Nov With *She's My Kind Of Girl* selling over 250,000 copies in Japan, Björn & Benny are invited to take part in the World Popular Song Festival in Tokyo.

1973

Jan Andersson, Ulvaeus and Anderson are asked to submit a song for the Swedish entry in the Eurovision Song Contest. They compose *Ring Ring*, which the quartet records and agrees to perform.

Feb [10] *Ring Ring* fails to be chosen as the Swedish entry (it comes in third, as had *Better To Have Loved* the previous year), but is recorded in Swedish,

German, Spanish and English (with lyrics provided by Neil Sedaka and Phil Cody) for a single on which the group is credited as Abba for the first time.
Apr Swedish-sung *Ring Ring* tops all Scandinavian charts, as the group embarks on its first Swedish tour, while an English version hits #1 in Austria, Holland, Belgium and South Africa.
Oct *Ring Ring* is released in Britain, as Abba begins recording its first album at Metronome Studios in Stockholm.

1974

Feb [9] A new Andersson/Ulvaeus/Anderson composition, *Waterloo*, sung in English, wins its heat to represent Sweden in the forthcoming Eurovision Song Contest.
Apr [6] With the accompanying orchestra conducted by Sven-Olof Walldoff dressed as Napoleon, the chirpy, uptempo and instantly catchy *Waterloo* wins the Eurovision Song Contest held in Brighton, E. Sussex. (At odds of 20/1, Stig Anderson has bet on the group to win.)
May [4] *Waterloo* tops the UK chart.
June [15] Abba's debut album ***Waterloo*** reaches UK #28, displaying the clean vocal style of its two female vocalists and the infectious pop writing and natural hit production skills of Andersson and Ulvaeus, a combination which will steer Abba to global success throughout the decade.
July [27] *Ring Ring*, reissued in the UK, makes #32.
Aug [6] *Waterloo* hits US #6 as Abba makes its first US promotion trip, appearing not least on TV's "Mike Douglas Show".
Sept *Waterloo* peaks at US #145.
Oct [26] *Honey Honey* reaches US #27.
Nov The group begins its first European tour at the Falkontheater, Copenhagen, Denmark, playing dates outside Sweden for the first time. The tour also takes in Germany, Austria and Switzerland. *So Long* is issued in the UK, while ***Abba*** peaks at US #174.

1975

Aug [2] Affirmative pop confection *I Do, I Do, I Do, I Do, I Do* makes UK #38, three months after its release.
Oct [25] *S.O.S.*, previously recorded by Fältskog on her solo album ***Eleven Women In One Building***, hits UK #6.
Nov [8] *S.O.S.* reaches US #15, as Abba makes a second promotional US visit.
[15] Abba guests on ABC-TV's "American Bandstand", performing *S.O.S.* and *I Do, I Do, I Do, I Do, I Do*.

1976

Jan [31] *Mamma Mia* tops the UK chart, ending the nine-week reign of Queen's *Bohemian Rhapsody*.
Feb [14] Its parent album ***Abba*** reaches UK #13.
May [1] *I Do, I Do, I Do, I Do, I Do* reaches US #15.
[8] Latin-flavored *Fernando*, already recorded by Lyngstad on her album ***Frida Alone***, hits UK #1. (It also tops the chart in Australia, where they have four other singles in the same Top 30, as they begin a tour. Their popularity will perhaps be greater there than anywhere else: according to record company figures, one in four Australians will own a copy of ***Greatest Hits***.) ***Greatest Hits*** also tops the UK chart, becoming the first of eight consecutive UK #1 Abba albums.
June [18] They give a Royal Performance in Stockholm for Sweden's King and his Queen-to-be, on the eve of the Royal Wedding.
July [4] *Mamma Mia* makes US #32.
Sept [4] *Dancing Queen* becomes their third consecutive UK #1, selling over 850,000 copies.
Nov [20] *Fernando* reaches US #13, as Abba visits for extensive TV appearances.
[27] ***Greatest Hits*** makes US #48.
Dec [3] The Royal Albert Hall box office claims 3½ million applications have been received for 11,212 available tickets for the band's upcoming February 1977 concerts.
[11] *Money Money Money*, taken from the ***Greatest Hits*** album, hits UK #3.

1977

Jan [15] ***Arrival*** tops the UK survey. Like all Abba releases, its songs are written (sometimes with the help of Anderson) and entirely arranged and produced by Andersson and Ulvaeus.
[28] The group begins a tour of Europe and Australia at the Ekeberghallen, Oslo, Norway.
Feb [14] Following Vice Chancellor Sir Robert Megarry's high court injunction against **The Sun**, which has prevented the newspaper from printing revelations that there is alleged friction between Lyngstad and Fältskog over the former's lack of punctuality, Abba performs two sellout concerts on time at the Royal Albert Hall, London during its first UK tour.
Mar "Abba - The Movie" is filmed at the end of an Australian trek.
[29] *Dancing Queen* is certified gold by the RIAA.
Apr [2] *Knowing Me, Knowing You* tops the UK chart.
[4] The RIAA certifies gold sales of ***Arrival***.
[9] Having climbed the chart since December, *Dancing Queen* hits US #1, becoming Abba's biggest US seller and only chart-topper.
[16] ***Arrival*** reaches US #20.
July [23] *Knowing Me, Knowing You* reaches US #14.
Nov [5] *The Name Of The Game* tops the UK chart following an appearance on BBC1-TV's "Top Of The Pops" on the 3rd.
[19] *Money Money Money*, belatedly issued in the US, peaks at #56.

1978

Feb [4] ***The Album***, recorded at the Metronome Studios and featuring Lasse Wellander (guitars), Malando Gassama (percussion), Lars O. Carlsson (saxophone) and string arrangements by Rutger Gunnarsson, enters the UK chart at #1.
[16] "Abba - The Movie", chronicling the group's 1977 Australian tour and featuring many of the songs on ***The Album***, premieres in London.
[18] Acappella-introed *Take A Chance On Me* heads the UK chart, completing a second consecutive #1 hat trick.
Mar [11] *The Name Of The Game* reaches US #12.
May Abba's Polar Studio in Stockholm, one of the most advanced in the world, is completed. The group's US management team, the Scotti Brothers, declares May "Abba Month".
June [12] ***The Album*** sells its millionth copy in Britain.
July [8] *Take A Chance On Me* hits US #3.
[20] ***Greatest Hits*** is certified platinum by the RIAA.
[22] ***The Album*** reaches US #14.
Aug [8] The RIAA confirms *Take A Chance On Me* gold and ***The Album*** platinum.
Oct [6] Andersson and Lyngstad marry in Sweden (both have been wed before).
[7] *Summer Night City* hits UK #5.
Dec [24] Ulvaeus and Fältskog separate and announce they are filing for divorce.

1979

Jan [9] At the "Music For UNICEF Concert", to celebrate the International Year Of The Child, taking place in the General Assembly Hall of the United Nations in New York, NY, Abba sings the ballad *Chiquitita*, donating its royalties from the song to UNICEF. (The show will air on NBC-TV on the 10th.)
Feb [10] *Chiquitita* hits UK #2.
May [12] *Does Your Mother Know?* hits UK #4.
[19] ***Voulez-Vous***, the group's first album to be recorded at Polar Studio, tops the UK chart and will sell over one million copies in five weeks.
July [21] *Does Your Mother Know?* reaches US #19.
Aug [11] Double A-side *Angeleyes/Voulez-Vous* hits UK #3.
Sept [1] *Voulez-Vous* makes US #80, as its parent album ***Voulez-Vous*** reaches US #19.
[13] Abba begins an 18-date North American tour, its first, in Edmonton, AB, Canada set to end at the Maple Leaf Gardens in Toronto, ON, Canada on October 7th.
Oct [13] *Voulez-Vous* B-side, *Angeleyes*, peaks at US #64.
[19] A month of European dates begins in Gothenburg. The tour, highlighted by six sellout performances at Wembley Arena, Wembley, Middx., before a combined audience of 48,000 people, will end on November 15th at the Royal Dublin Society, Main Hall, Dublin, Eire.
Nov [10] *Gimme Gimme Gimme (A Man After Midnight)* hits UK #3 and is their sixth chart single which repeats a key word in its title.
[14] ***Voulez-Vous*** is certified gold by the RIAA.
[17] ***Greatest Hits Vol. 2*** tops the UK survey, as Abba is listed as the biggest-selling group in recording history in the new edition of **The Guinness Book Of Records**.
Dec [22] Anthemic *I Have A Dream*, featuring the choir of the International School of Stockholm, hits UK #2.

1980

Jan [12] *Chiquitita* reaches US #29.
[19] ***Greatest Hits Vol. 2*** makes US #46.
Apr [23] ***Greatest Hits, Volume 2*** is certified gold by the RIAA.
Aug [9] Instant pop classic *The Winner Takes It All* hits UK #1, their first chart-topper in over two years.
Nov [22] ***Super Trouper***, recorded again at the band's own Polar Studio, tops the UK chart with its title cut hitting UK #1 the following week. It includes *The Way Old Friends Do,* recorded live at a November 1979 Wembley Arena concert.

1981

Feb [6] ***Super Trouper*** is certified gold by the RIAA.
[14] Andersson and Lyngstad announce divorce proceedings after he reveals his love for Swedish TV personality Mona Norklit (whom he will marry on New Year's Eve). ***Super Trouper*** reaches US #17.
Mar [14] *The Winner Takes It All* hits US #8, their first US Top 10 hit in over two years.
May [23] *Super Trouper* makes US #45.
July [11] *On And On And On* stops at US #90.
[25] Disco-styled *Lay All Your Love On Me*, released in the UK as a 12"-only single aimed squarely at the dance market, hits #7.
Dec [19] Ballad *One Of Us* hits UK #3, as ***The Visitors*** tops the UK chart. (Polydor International rewards the group with its Golden Gramophone award, an honor usually reserved for the classical field.)

1982

Jan [1] Abba makes its final live appearance, at a concert in Stockholm.
Feb [13] ***The Visitors*** reaches US #29.
Mar The group is informed by Russian authorities that it will not be allowed to tour the Soviet Union because of statements made on US TV supporting Polish Solidarity.
[13] *When All Is Said And Done* makes US #27.
[20] *Head Over Heels* stops at UK #25, the first hint of waning UK popularity.
May [22] Title cut *The Visitors* peaks at US #63.
Aug As individual Abba members move towards increasingly separate personal lives and professional projects, Lyngstad moves to London and releases the solo album ***Something's Going On***, produced by Phil Collins which will spawn the September 4th-peaking UK #43 *I Know There's Something Going On*. The album will reach UK #18 on September 18th and make US #41 in March '83 with the title track also peaking at US #13 on March 26th.
Oct [30] Abba's soap-operatic *The Day Before You Came*, subsequently a 1984 UK #22 hit for UK duo Blancmange, makes UK #32.
Nov During the month the group celebrates its 10th anniversary at Mayfair's Belfry Club, London.
[27] Double anthology ***The Singles: The First Ten Years*** completes the group's run of UK #1 albums in

the '80s and is a huge Christmas seller. It will also make US #63 in the New Year.

Dec [25] *Under Attack* reaches UK #26. Also included on ***The Singles***, this is the final Abba recording.

1983

June [4] After making her acting debut in the Swedish film "Rakenstam", Fältskog begins a solo music career with *The Heat Is On*, which makes UK #35. No official anouncement that Abba has dissolved is forthcoming (though from now on both female vocalists will pursue solo work, while Andersson and Ulvaeus, still writing and producing at Polar Studio, will begin a collaboration with UK lyricist Tim Rice which results in the musical "Chess", in 1985). Fältskog's chart achievements will be: ***Wrap Your Arms Around Me***, produced by Mike Chapman, which reaches UK #18 and US #102, its title ballad making UK #44, and the Russ Ballard-penned UK #63 and US #29 extract *Can't Shake You Loose*, all charting by year's end; ***Eyes Of A Woman***, produced by Eric Stewart, which makes UK #38 in May 1985, and 1988's ***I Stand Alone***, recorded in Malibu, CA, with producer Peter Cetera (UK #72 - Mar [12]) and subsequent duet with him, the US #93 *I Wasn't The One (Who Said Goodbye)*. Lyngstad's remaining chart action will be the January 1984 UK #45 duet with B.A. Robertson, *Time*, and the Steve Lillywhite-produced UK #67 ***Shine***, released later that year.

[26] *Thank You For The Music*, Abba's last UK chart single of the decade and an old airplay and stage favorite from ***Abba - The Album*** in 1978, makes UK #33, while the incomplete ***Thank You For The Music*** compilation reaches UK #17.

1985

Feb [9] Elaine Paige and Barbara Dickson's duet *I Know Him So Well*, from "Chess", begins a four-week tenure at UK #1, following the UK #12 success in January of another "Chess" piece, Murray Head's *One Night In Bangkok* (which will hit US #3 on May 18th).

1986

Jan The group reunites to appear on Swedish TV's "This Is Your Life" tribute to Stig Anderson, singing *Tivedshambo* accompanied by Andersson's accordian.

Apr [7] *I Know Him So Well* is named Best Selling A-Side of 1985 at the 31st annual Ivor Novello Awards, held at the Grosvenor House Hotel, London.

1987

Dec Ulvaeus and Fältskog are investigated in Sweden for alleged tax evasion, while Andersson releases his first solo album ***Klinga Mina Klockor*** on the Mono Music label, which he formed with Ulvaeus in 1986 after the Abba organization had sold its interest in Polar Music to Polydor. During the year, the duo also write six tracks for the eponymously-titled album release by Gemini.

1988

Dec [3] Further retrospective ***Absolute Abba*** peaks at UK #70.

1990

Dec [15] Fältskog marries Swedish surgeon Tomas Sonnenfeld and will subsequently distance herself from the music business, while Lyngstad is becoming increasingly involved with environmental concerns. Andersson and Ulvaeus will spend much of the next year embroiled in legal proceedings against Stig Anderson to collect unpaid royalties.

1991

Aug [13] C4-TV broadcasts "The Story Of Abba", hinting at forthcoming Abba revivalism.

1992

June [11] Andersson and Ulvaeus join U2 onstage in Stockholm for the latter's version of *Dancing Queen*.

Sept [12] Re-issued *Dancing Queen* reaches UK #16, as a rival version by Abbacadabra, masterminded by UK hit production team Mike Stock and Pete Waterman, makes UK #57.

Oct [3] The latest in a stream of Abba anthologies (but the first to be released by Polydor), ***Gold - Greatest Hits*** debuts at UK #1 and will sell over three million units by year's end. It is the climax of a substantial 1992 European Abba revival invoked by UK hit duo Erasure. Their *Abba-Esque E.P.* topped the UK survey on June 13th which in turn inspired Australian-based Abba/Erasure-mimicking outfit Björn Again to succeed as a short-lived, novelty look-a-like singles chart item. Throughout this retro period, Andersson and Ulvaeus continue writing and planning for the 1994 premiere in Stockholm of their new musical "Kristina From Duvemala", based on Wilhelm Moberg's "The Emigrants".

1993

May [12] Disbanded for a decade, the group is named Best Selling Swedish Artist Of The Year at the fifth annual World Music Awards, staged at the Sporting Club in Monte Carlo.

June [5] Further retrospective ***More Abba Gold - More Abba Hits*** bows at its UK #14 peak.

July [31] ***Gold - Greatest Hits*** hits UK #8 (and will debut at its US #63 peak on October 9th).

1994

Dec The US Abba Club Fanzine protests at a segment in the current Australian-based film "Priscilla Queen Of The Desert", in which one of the characters wears a locket containing excrement fictionally and allegedly evacuated by Fältskog. (A more appropriate Antipodean tribute to Abba sees its music featured in the forthcoming movie "Muriel's Wedding", also set Down Under.)

1995

Apr A 66-track, four-CD boxed set ***Thank You For The Music***, containing the group's hits, rare B-sides and previously unreleased tracks, is issued by Polydor.

June [5] Continuing to prove the group's enduring popularity, ***Gold - Greatest Hits*** is certified platinum by the RIAA during a year-plus chart tenure (while the "Abba - Gold" video will be confirmed gold on the 16th).

Sept [14] A 14-track various artists Abba tribute album ***Abbasalutely***, recorded by Australasian indie acts, is released in New Zealand by Flying Nun Records.

1996

Apr [2] ***Gold-Greatest Hits*** now reaches the double-platinum plateau in the US.

ABC

Martin Fry (vocals); **Mark White** (guitar)

1980

Dec Initially positioned in the burgeoning New Romantic movement, the band has been formed in Sheffield, S. Yorks., earlier in the year when Fry (b. Mar. 9, 1958, Manchester, Lancs.), who - at age 18 - has attended Sheffield University to study English Literature, joins White (b. Apr. 1, 1961, Sheffield) and saxophonist Stephen Singleton (b. Apr. 17, 1959, Sheffield), after interviewing them about their group Vice Versa (which has released the 1979 EP *Music 4*) for his fanzine **Modern Drugs**, which he has launched in 1977 aiming to focus on local bands and fashions. Fry is asked to join as lead singer, and at their first gig they are showered with beer bottles. With David Robinson (drums) and Mark Lickley (bass) rounding out the quintet, the band's first live performance as ABC takes place in Sheffield, the group having chosen the name because "the first three letters of the alphabet are known the world over".

1981

Nov [28] Having signed to Phonogram Records for releases via its own Neutron label in the UK (and Mercury in the US), the group's debut *Tears Are Not Enough*, a sturdy pop cut showcasing Fry's earnest and dramatic vocal style, reaches UK #19. (Lickley leaves the line-up after the recording of the first three singles, while David Palmer (b. May 29, 1961, Chesterfield, Derbys.) replaces Robinson for the band's debut album sessions.)

1982

Mar [20] Similarly uptempo *Poison Arrow* hits UK #6.

June [12] *The Look Of Love* hits UK #4.

July [3] ***The Lexicon Of Love***, underpinned by a rich, multi-layered production by Trevor Horn and featuring his studio apprentices and future Art Of Noise members Anne Dudley, Gary Langan and J.J. Jeczalik, enters the UK chart at #1 and will reach US #24 during an eight-month chart stay. Following its release, ABC tours Britain as a prelude to a world trek, during which they will film "Man Trap", an hour-long documentary, with director Julien Temple.

Sept [25] Lush ballad *All Of My Heart* hits UK #5.

1983

Jan [8] *The Look Of Love*, ABC's US chart debut, reaches #18, aided by strong MTV exposure.

Mar [26] *Poison Arrow* reaches US #25.

Nov [12] Previewing their second album, *That Was Then But This Is Now* reaches UK #18. Co-produced by ABC and Gary Langan, ***Beauty Stab***, reflecting Fry and White's view of the current state of Britain, reaches UK #12. With Palmer already departed and Singleton due to quit before the third album, the band is now centered around Fry and White and will be supplemented for touring and future recordings by session musicians.

1984

Jan [28] *S.O.S.* makes UK #39.

Feb [18] *That Was Then But This Is Now* peaks at US #89, as ***Beauty Stab*** climbs to US #69.

Nov [17] Self-produced *(How To Be A) Millionaire* makes UK #49. Fry and White will move to New York, NY and recruit two temporary members, David Yarrith and Eden (b. Fiona Russell-Powell), who, despite the fact that neither can play any instruments or even sing, are stylistically added for dramatic and visual effect.

1985

Apr [13] Ballad *Be Near Me* reaches UK #26.

June [15] *Vanity Kills* charts for a week at UK #70.

Oct ***How To Be A Zillionaire***, with help from Brad Lang on bass and Palmer returning on drums, reaches UK #28 and US #30.

Nov [9] *Be Near Me* becomes ABC's first US Top 10 hit, at #9, spurred by a popular dance remix.

1986

Jan *Ocean Blue* makes UK #51 followed by *(How To Be A) Millionaire* which will reach US #20 on March 22nd and *Vanity Kills* which peaks at US #91 on May 24th.

1987

Jan Following Fry's recovery from a serious year-long illness with Hodgkin's Disease, he and White regroup to begin work on their fourth album.

July [4] Motown-tinged *When Smokey Sings*, a tribute to Smokey Robinson and the first release from sessions with US producer Bernard Edwards, reaches UK #11.

Sept [19] *When Smokey Sings* hits US #5, while *The Night You Murdered Love* climbs to UK #31 one week later.

Oct [24] ***Alphabet City***, featuring the rhythm section of David Clayton on keyboards, Lang on bass and Graham Broad on drums and including the two recent

chart singles, hits UK #7 and will make US #48.
Dec *King Without A Crown* reaches UK #44.

1989

June [3] *One Better World* makes UK #32.
Sept [23] *The Real Thing* peaks at UK #68, as Fry guests on *Mythical Girl*, from producer Arthur Baker's current album.
Oct [28] Self-produced seven-track ***Up*** stops at UK #58.

1990

Apr [14] A revised *The Look Of Love (1990 Mix)* peaks at UK #68.
[21] Greatest hits compilation ***Absolutely*** hits UK #7.
May [7] BBC-TV band-focusing documentary "That Was Then, This Is Now" airs.

1991

Aug [24] Newly signed to Parlophone, its label debut ***Abracadabra*** charts for a week at UK #50, but fails to yield any substantial chart action for its singles, *Love Conquers All* (UK #47 on July 27th or *Say It* (UK #42 on January 11th 1992).

1995

Feb [16] Following the issue of two further compilations in 1993 (***The Remix Collection*** in March and ***Tears Are Not Enough*** in May), ABC's debut set ***Lexicon Of Love*** is certified gold by the RIAA 13 years after its initial release.

PAULA ABDUL

1984

Of Syrian-Brazilian/French-Canadian ancestry, Abdul (b. June 19, 1963, Los Angeles, CA), the second daughter of Harry (once a livestock trader and now owner of a sand and gravel business) and Lorraine (a former assistant to film director Billy Wilder), has grown up in North Hollywood, CA, where she has, at age seven, performed in community theatre groups, spent summers touring in US theatrical productions and begun studying jazz and tap dance techniques from age ten, to win a scholarship to study under Joe Traime at the Bell Lewitzky Company. Attending Van Nuys High School, then Cal State-Northridge College, Abdul has majored in TV and radio studies and has successfully auditioned for (and subsequently choreographed) Los Angeles basketball dance troupe the Laker Girls, earning $50 per game during her freshman year. She decides to take up a full-time career in dance and has already been asked to choreograph a Jacksons/Mick Jagger video for their single *Torture*. This has brought her firmly into the pop dance arena, where she is now asked by A&M Records A&R head John McClain to choreograph for another Jackson (Janet), resulting in the hugely-successful generic dance-step visuals for the Jackson hits *When I Think Of You*, *Nasty* and *What Have You Done For Me Lately*.

1987

Sept [11] She wins the Best Choreography trophy for Janet Jackson's "Nasty" at the fourth annual MTV Video Music Awards, held at the Universal Amphitheatre, Universal City, CA. This further establishes her reputation as the leading American pop dance choreographer, her talent commissioned for video clips promoting Z.Z. Top (she creates the "Velcro Fly" dance step), Duran Duran, Debbie Gibson and even Warren Zevon and Dolly Parton, among others.

1988

Aug [13] Having been signed by Virgin America, her debut release *Knocked Out* makes US #41 and sets the trend for most of her early recordings: commercial pop dance cuts boosted by predictably perfect-timed dance-step promotion videos.
Nov [12] *(It's Just) The Way That You Love Me* stops at US #88.

1989

Feb [11] *Straight Up* tops the US chart, as her debut album ***Forever Your Girl***, with songs written by Elliot Wolff and Jerry Leiber's son Oliver, begins its US chart climb.
Mar [29] *Straight Up* is certified platinum by the RIAA.
Apr [8] *Straight Up* hits UK #3.
[19] Abdul participates in the "Prince's Trust Rock Gala" at the London Palladium with Erasure, Debbie Gibson, T'Pau, Wet Wet Wet and others.
May [20] *Forever Your Girl* hits US #1.
[24] *Forever Your Girl* is certified gold by the RIAA.
June Abdul embarks on the 40-city "Club MTV Live" tour with Tonë Loc, Was (Not Was), Milli Vanilli and Information Society.
[17] *Forever Your Girl* reaches UK #24.
Aug *Knocked Out* makes UK #45.
[30] Still rising on the US survey, *Cold Hearted* is certified gold by the RIAA.
Sept [2] *Cold Hearted* tops the US chart, her third consecutive #1.
[6] She wins Best Dance, Best Female Video, Best Editing and Best Choreography categories for "Straight Up" at the sixth annual MTV Video Music Awards ceremony, at the Universal Amphitheatre, where she is also a performing highlight of the show.
[17] Abdul wins Best Choreography for Fox-TV's "Tracey Ullman Show" at the 41st annual Emmy Awards.
Oct [7] ***Forever Your Girl***, after over 14 months on the survey, hits US #1, where it will stay for ten weeks, becoming Virgin America's biggest-selling album to date.
Dec [2] Reissued *(It's Just) The Way That You Love Me* now hits US #3 and peaks at UK #74.
[17] Abdul participates in the "America Has Heart" benefit at the Universal Amphitheatre, to raise money for the Red Cross Disaster Relief Fund, depleted by Hurricane Hugo and the San Francisco earthquake.
[23] Abdul wins Top Pop Album Artist, Female in **Billboard**'s The Year In Music, one of three #1 feats in this year's round-up.

1990

Jan [22] Abdul collects the Favorite Pop/Rock Female Vocalist, and Favorite Dance Artist trophies, at the 17th annual American Music Awards, and performs *The Way That You Love Me* during the ceremony, held at the Shrine Auditorium, Los Angeles. On returning home to her Studio City condominium, she discovers that thieves have stolen $3,400 worth of jewelry.
Feb [3] ***Forever Your Girl*** returns to US #1, after 81 charted weeks.
[10] *Opposites Attract*, credited with the Wild Pair and including a rap from the Soul Purpose's Derrick Delite, helped by an inventive real life/cartoon-integrated video, tops the US chart.
Mar [8] Abdul's latest awards include Best Female Singer, Best New Female Singer, Best Dressed Female Rock Artist and Sexiest Female Rock Artist in the 1989 **Rolling Stone** Readers' Picks.
[12] *Opposites Attract* is certified gold by the RIAA.
[26] She choreographs the dance routines at the 62nd annual Academy Awards, held at the Dorothy Chandler Pavilion in Los Angeles, the latest commission in her parallel choreographic career, which also now includes a scene in the Kevin Costner movie "Bull Durham", Eddie Murphy's "Coming To America", George Michael's "Monkey" video and other awards shows, including four MTV ceremonies. *Opposites Attract* achieves gold status.
May [5] *Opposites Attract* hits UK #2.
[12] ***Forever Your Girl*** re-enters the UK chart at its #3 peak, having initially charted in April of 1989.
[16] Elliot Wolff wins the Song Of The Year award for *Straight Up* at the seventh annual ASCAP pop awards dinner at the Regent Beverly Wilshire Hotel, Beverly Hills, CA.
June [16] Remix re-shuffle of her debut album, ***Shut Up And Dance (The Dance Mixes)***, hits US #7.
July Abdul is lensed with her idol and dance icon, Gene Kelly, by Annie Leibovitz for **Vanity Fair** magazine. Abdul's star status now includes lucrative sponsorship and advertising deals with Diet Coke and Reebok.
[23] The RIAA certifies US sales of seven million of ***Forever Your Girl*** (it becomes the first debut album to have featured four #1s) and platinum sales of ***Shut Up And Dance (The Dance Mixes)***.
[28] Shep Pettibone remix of *Knocked Out* reaches UK #21.
Sept [25] The RIAA certifies that the "Straight Up" video has reached the 200,000 sales plateau.
Oct [6] *Cold Hearted* makes UK #46.
Nov [10] ***Shut Up And Dance (The Dance Mixes)*** peaks at UK #40.
Dec [9] Driving her Jaguar, Abdul rear ends another car on Laurel Canyon Boulevard, Los Angeles, and is taken to the North Hollywood Medical Center.
[22] Abdul wins Top Pop Album Artist, Female in **Billboard**'s The Year In Music survey.

1991

Feb [20] "Opposites Attract" wins Best Music Video, Shortform at the 33rd annual Grammy Awards, held at New York's Radio City Music Hall.
June [8] Her second album ***Spellbound***, on which she has collaborated extensively with Family Stand founders Peter Lord and V. Jeffrey Smith, tops the US chart. (In doing so, Abdul becomes the first act of the '90s to have two chart-topping albums.)
[15] *Rush Rush* heads the US survey for the first of five weeks.
[22] Benefitting the Pediatric AIDS Foundation, the Disney album ***For Our Children***, to which Abdul has contributed *Good Night My Love (Pleasant Dreams)*, reaches US #31, as ***Club MTV Party To Go - Volume One***, on which she is also featured, reaches US #38.
[24] *Rush Rush* is certified gold by the RIAA.
July [20] *Rush Rush* hits UK #6.
[27] ***Spellbound*** hits UK #4.
Aug [31] *The Promise Of A New Day* bows at its UK #52 peak.
Sept [5] Abdul performs live at the eighth annual MTV Video Music Awards ceremony at the Universal Amphitheatre.
[14] *The Promise Of A New Day* tops the US chart for one week.
Oct She tops a poll (over the likes of Julia Roberts and Michelle Pfeiffer), conducted by PR firm Bruskin Associates, of celebrity women men "would most like to meet under the mistletoe".
Nov While an Illinois judge refuses to dismiss a class action suit brought against Abdul, Virgin Records and its distributor WEA alleging deceptive trade practices, a California federal court orders Virgin to turn over copies of the original recordings of *I Need You* and *Opposites Attract* to vocalist Yvette Marine, who is claiming that she shares lead vocals with Abdul on the cuts. Marine also urges the label and the singer to hold a joint press conference to prove her claims, which were initially filed as a lawsuit on April 8th.
[30] *Blowing Kisses In The Wind* hits US #6.
Dec [4] Abdul receives her star on the Hollywood Walk Of Fame, Hollywood, CA.
[5] Towards the end of a two-month US tour (supported by Color Me Badd), she performs the first of three sold-out nights at the Great Western Forum, Inglewood, CA, collecting gross receipts approaching $1million.

1992

Jan [17] Current fiancé, actor Emilio Estevez, calls Abdul "the most beautiful, talented, sexiest woman I've ever met" on syndicated TV's "The Arsenio Hall Show".
[25] *Vibeology* reaches UK #19.
[27] She collects the Favorite Female Artist, Pop/Rock trophy, at the 19th annual American Music Awards, held at the Shrine Auditorium.
[29] The RIAA certifies sales of three million for ***Spellbound***.
Feb [8] *Vibeology* reaches US #16.
[24] Abdul performs at the Tian He Stadium,

Guangzhou, Japan, before a crowd of 6,000. Her current Far Eastern concert leg include gigs in Yokohoma, Osaka, Tokyo, Hong Kong, Malaysia, Singapore, Manila and Korea).
Mar [14] She is named Humanitarian Of The Year at a Starlight Foundation dinner, in Los Angeles, as rumors abound that she is in talks with producer Karen Poindexter about starring in and choreographing a Broadway revival of "Hair".
Apr [29] Abdul marries Estevez (son of actor Martin Sheen) at a judge's chambers in Santa Monica Superior Court, Santa Monica, CA. Estevez's mother Janet is a witness.
May [9] The well-timed fifth single from ***Spellbound***, *Will You Marry Me?*, featuring Stevie Wonder on harmonica, reaches US #19.
June [13] The second leg of a US tour, again supported by Color Me Badd and sponsored by Kraft Seven Seas salad dressing, opens at the Starplex Amphitheatre, Dallas, TX.
[16] She leaves St. Luke's Hospital, Houston, TX, after being admitted two days earlier with intestinal flu and dehydration, forcing the cancellation of forthcoming dates in Houston and Oklahoma City, OK.
Aug [8] *Will You Marry Me?* charts for a week at UK #73.

1993

May [14] Abdul guests on NBC-TV's "Bob Hope - The First 90 Years".
[24] *The Promise Of A New Day* is cited at the tenth annual ASCAP Pop Awards dinner at the Beverly Hilton Hotel, Los Angeles.
Aug [12] Abdul wins her court case against Marine.
Sept [4] She hosts ABC-TV's "In A New Light '93" AIDS awareness special.

1994

Feb Playboy magazine reports that she is slated to star in her first movie, the musical "12 Bar Blues".
May [10] A statement is issued confirming that Abdul and Estevez are separating.
Aug [20] Press reports claim Abdul is being treating for an eating disorder at a Tulsa, OK clinic.

1995

June [17] *My Love Is For Real*, featuring Ofra Haza, debuts at its UK #28 peak.
July [1] ***Head Over Heels***, variously produced by Rhett Lawrence, Darryl Simmons, Elliot Wolff and Oliver Leiber and featuring contributions from Color Me Badd, Haza and Family Stand, reaches US #18 and debuts at its UK #61 peak. During a UK promo visit, Abdul guests on ITV's "The Brian Conley Show".
[8] *My Love Is For Real* reaches US #28.
Sept [22] Abdul guests on NBC-TV's "The Tonight Show".
[30] *Crazy Cool* makes US #58.
Oct [31] ***Head Over Heels*** is certified gold by the RIAA.
Nov [19] Abdul sings *Luck Be A Lady* at a tribute to Frank Sinatra on his 80th birthday at the Shrine Auditorium.
Dec [9] She appears at the National Council of La Raza awards in Los Angeles, set to air on Fox-TV on the 28th.

AC/DC

Angus Young (guitar); **Malcolm Young** (guitar); **Brian Johnson** (vocals); **Cliff Williams** (bass); **Phillip Rudd** (drums)

1973

Dec [31] Brothers Angus (b. Mar. 31, 1959, Glasgow, Scotland) and Malcolm (b. Jan. 6, 1953, Glasgow) Young debut the hard-rock group at the Chequers club in Sydney, New South Wales, Australia (where the family emigrated, in 1963), with Rob Bailey, Peter Clark and singer Dave Evans. In July the following year, the group records its first single, *Can I Sit Next To You*, for Albert Productions, run by producers Harry Vanda and George Young (both veterans of '60s hitmaking outfit, the Easybeats; Young is also the older brother of Angus and Malcolm). The original line-up disbands shortly thereafter, and the Young brothers, now relocated to Melbourne, Victoria, Australia, recruit the group's roadie, fellow immigrant and veteran of bands the Spectors, the Valentines, Fraternity and Mount Lofty Rangers since the mid-'60s, Bon Scott (b. Ronald Belford, July 9, 1946, Kirriemuir, Angus, Scotland) on vocals. (Scott's convictions on some minor criminal offenses, and a rejection by the Australian Army on the grounds that he is "socially maladjusted", further endear him to the Youngs.) Drummer Rudd (b. May 19, 1954, Melbourne) and bassist Mark Evans (b. Mar. 2, 1956, Melbourne), ex-Buster Brown, complete the line-up. (Original singer Evans will form Rabbit, releasing two albums for CBS in Australia, before joining Hot Cockerel in 1984 and then releasing ***David Evans And Thunder Down Under*** in 1986.)

1974

Nov After gaining a residency at the Hampton Court Hotel in Sydney and touring solidly throughout the year, building a live following for its exuberant hard-rock style, AC/DC has signed to Albert Productions and begins work on its debut album.

1975

Feb Resultant power-charged ***High Voltage*** is released in Australia featuring the single *Dog Eat Dog*.
Dec After touring Australia for much of the year, the group's second album ***TNT*** is released.

1976

Jan On signing to Atlantic Records, the band moves its base to the UK, where early dates are at London's Marquee and other clubs.
Apr First UK single, *It's A Long Way To The Top*, is released.
May [11] AC/DC begins a UK tour, supporting Paul Kossoff's Back Street Crawler, at the Marquee, as ***High Voltage*** is issued in the UK (different to its Australian namesake, the album is a collection of tracks from its first two Australian releases). The nine-date series will end at Reading Town Hall, Reading, Berks.
June [11] The group begins its first headlining UK tour, the 19-date "Lock Up Your Daughters" package, at the City Hall, Glasgow, set to end at London's Lyceum Ballroom, on July 7th. Their image, with Angus Young as a short-trousered, naughty schoolboy, helps attract attention, becoming an enduring and popular visual trademark.
July The band begins a tour of Europe, supporting Rainbow.
Aug AC/DC appears at the annual "Reading Rock Festival", Reading, during a further UK trek which accompanies the release of *Jailbreak*.
Oct The group undertakes its maiden US visit with a club itinerary promoting the recently-issued ***High Voltage***.
Dec *Dirty Deeds Done Dirt Cheap* is released in the UK, as the band returns to Australia for a 26-date, year-end tour and stays for the recording of its next album in Sydney with Vanda and Young.

1977

Feb [18] The group begins a 25-date UK concert trek at Edinburgh University, Edinburgh. Scotland, set to end on March 21st at the Pavilion, Hemel Hempstead, Herts.
June Tired of touring, Evans leaves and Williams (b. Dec. 14, 1949, Romford, Essex), ex-Bandit and Home, is chosen from 50 replies to a **Sounds** ad. (Evans will join Finch, which name-changes to Contraband, then play with a variety of bands, including Swanee, Heaven, Best, Hellcats, Headhunters and Boss, before joining the Party Boys.) Williams' first gigs with the band will be a major European tour supporting Black Sabbath.
July AC/DC begins its second US tour.
Oct [15] ***Let There Be Rock*** climbs to US #154.
Nov [19] ***Let There Be Rock*** reaches UK #17.

1978

May [1] A month-long 20-date UK "Powerage" tour (supported by British Lions) opens at the Town Hall, Middlesbrough, Cleveland, set to end on the 29th at Dundee Caird Hall, Dundee, Scotland, to be punctuated by recordings for the next album.
[15] *Rock'n'Roll Damnation*, the group's first UK hit single, reaches #24.
[20] ***Powerage*** reaches UK #26.
Sept [23] ***Powerage*** peaks at US #133.
Nov [4] ***If You Want Blood, You've Got It***, recorded live in Glasgow during the Powerage tour, reaches UK #13.
[10] The band performs on BBC2-TV's "Rock Goes To College".

1979

Jan *Highway To Hell* recordings begin, with producer Robert John "Mutt" Lange brought in to oversee the sessions midway.
Feb [17] ***If You Want Blood, You've Got It*** peaks at US #113.
Aug [18] ***Highway To Hell*** hits UK #8, as the group supports the Who at Wembley Stadium, Wembley, Middx., on a bill with Nils Lofgren and the Stranglers. The band is midway through yet another European and US tour.
Sept [15] *Highway To Hell* peaks at UK #56.
Nov [10] ***Highway To Hell***, spurred by their current US trek supporting Cheap Trick, Ted Nugent and UFO, reaches US #17, where it will become the band's first million-seller.
Dec During further European dates, a gig in Paris, France, is filmed and will be released as "Let There Be Rock".
[12] *Highway To Hell* makes US #47.

1980

Feb [19] While recording in Britain, Scott and musician friend Alistair Kennear spend the evening at the Music Machine in Camden Town, London, watching groups Protex and the Trendies, while consuming a large amount of alcohol. Kennear drives Scott back to his house in East Dulwich, South London, leaving him asleep in the car.
[20] Kennear returns to the car to find Scott unconscious, and drives him to the nearby King's College Hospital, where he is pronounced dead. The coroner will record a verdict of death by misadventure, stating that Scott had "drunk himself to death".
Mar [1] *Touch Too Much* reaches UK #29.
Apr The group, having announced that Johnson (b. Oct. 5, 1947), former lead singer of UK band Geordie, will replace Scott, begins recording ***Back In Black*** at Compass Point Studios, Nassau, Bahamas.
June Reissued *Dirty Deeds Done Dirt Cheap* (#47), *Whole Lotta Rosie* (#36), *High Voltage (Live Version)* (#48) and *It's A Long Way To The Top (If You Wanna Rock'N'Roll)* (#55) all chart in the UK.
July After preliminary warm-up gigs in Belgium and Holland, AC/DC embarks on its Back In Black world tour in the US, a trek which will take in Europe, Australia (which they have not returned to since 1977) and a first visit to Japan.
Aug [9] Lange-produced ***Back In Black*** tops the UK chart, subsequently regarded as a critical and commercial career peak.
Sept [27] *You Shook Me All Night Long* makes UK #38.
Oct [19] The group begins a 20-date UK tour at the Colston Hall, Bristol, Avon, ending November 12th, the last of three dates at London's Hammersmith Odeon.
Nov [8] *You Shook Me All Night Long* makes US #35 - their first US Top 40 hit.
Dec [13] *Rock'n'Roll Ain't Noise Pollution* reaches UK #15.
[20] ***Back In Black*** hits US #4.

1981

Feb [21] *Back In Black* makes US #37.
May [23] Belatedly issued in the US, ***Dirty Deeds Done Dirt Cheap*** hits #3, as ***High Voltage*** heads to

US #146.
Aug [22] AC/DC headlines the "Monsters Of Rock" festival at Castle Donington, Leics., before a crowd of 65,000.
Dec [5] ***For Those About To Rock (We Salute You)*** hits UK #3.
[26] ***For Those About To Rock (We Salute You)*** tops the US chart.

1982

Feb [20] The extracted *Let's Get It Up* reaches UK #13 and US #44.
July [10] Title cut *For Those About To Rock (We Salute You)* reaches UK #15.

1983

Aug Rudd leaves, exhausted by touring, and is replaced by ex-Tytan and A To Z drummer Simon Wright (b. June 19, 1963), who, like Williams, has responded to an ad in **Sounds**. (Rudd will take up helicopter flying in New Zealand.)
Sept ***Flick Of The Switch*** hits UK #4 and reaches US #15.
Oct [22] *Guns For Hire* peaks at US #84 and will make UK #37 on November 5th.

1984

Jan [25] ***Flick Of The Switch*** is certified gold by the RIAA.
Aug [11] *Nervous Shakedown* reaches UK #35.
[18] AC/DC headlines the "Monsters Of Rock" festival at Castle Donington for the second time, before a crowd of 65,000, as its mini-album ***'74 Jailbreak***, reprising tracks recorded in Australia almost a decade earlier, makes US #76.

1985

Jan [19] The group takes part in the "Rock In Rio" festival at Barra da Tijuca in Rio de Janeiro, Brazil, headlining a bill featuring Ozzy Osbourne, the Scorpions and Whitesnake, before an estimated crowd of 342,000.
July [13] ***Fly On The Wall*** hits UK #7.
[20] *Danger* makes UK #48.
Aug [29] ***Fly On The Wall*** is certified gold by the RIAA.
Sept [7] ***Fly On The Wall*** reaches US #32, as the band undertakes its correspondingly-named tour of the US.

1986

Jan [16-17] The group performs at Wembley Arena, Wembley, during the European leg of the "Fly On The Wall" tour.
[25] *Shake Your Foundations* reaches UK #24.
May [31] ***Who Made Who***, containing old tracks and three new AC/DC songs used on the soundtrack to the Stephen King movie "Maximum Overdrive", reaches UK #11 and makes US #33, as the extracted title cut *Who Made Who* reaches UK #16.
Aug [30] Reissued *You Shook Me All Night Long* makes UK #46.

1987

Dec After a lengthy silence, AC/DC completes new recordings with producers Vanda and Young for ***Blow Up Your Video***.

1988

Jan [23] First extract, the scorching rocker *Heatseeker*, reaches UK #12.
Feb [13] ***Blow Up Your Video*** hits UK #2 and will reach US #12.
Apr [6] ***Blow Up Your Video*** is certified gold by the RIAA.
[9] *That's The Way I Wanna Rock'n'Roll* makes UK #22, as the group begins a major tour to promote the album, with cousin Steve Young replacing Malcolm for the trek. Press reports suggest that Malcolm is trying to kick a chemical dependency habit, though it is also rumored that he wishes to look after his ailing son.
Oct [6] "Who Made Who" video is certified gold by the RIAA.

1989

During an AC/DC sabbatical, Wright is asked to play on Dio's album ***Lock Up The Wolves***, and subsequently leaves to permanently join his band, to be replaced by rock veteran Chris Slade (b. Oct. 30, 1946), ex-Manfred Mann's Earthband, the Firm and Gary Moore.

1990

Apr The group begins recording ***The Razor's Edge***, with producer Bruce Fairbairn, in Vancouver, BC, Canada.
Sept [29] *Thunderstruck*, issued via a new contract with Atco, reaches UK #13.
Oct [4] The RIAA certifies platinum sales for ***If You Want Blood You've Got It***, ***Let There Be Rock*** and ***Powerage*** and sales of three million for ***Dirty Deeds Done Cheap***.
[6] ***The Razor's Edge*** enters at its UK #4 peak.
[23] ***Back In Black*** surpasses RIAA-certified US sales of ten million.
[27] ***The Razor's Edge*** hits US #2, AC/DC's highest-charting US album since 1981.
Nov [2] A 34-date US leg of "The Razor's Edge" world tour begins at Worcester Centrum, MA, with latest recruit Paul Greg on bass.
[11] 21-year-old David Gregory of Boonton, NJ is attacked outside the group's Brendan Byrne Arena, East Rutherford, NJ concert, and will die in Hackensack Hospital on the 12th. A New Jersey state trooper will be cleared of criminal wrongdoing in relation to the incident (though the family will win a $250,000 settlement on March 9th 1992).
Dec [1] *Moneytalks* makes UK #36.
[19] ***'74 Jailbreak*** is certified gold by the RIAA.

1991

Jan [18] Teenagers Curtis Child, Jimmie Boyd and Elizabeth Glausi are killed during a crush in a crowd of 13,294 at the band's Salt Palace Arena, Salt Lake City, UT, concert. (Glausi will die after her parents request her life-support be turned off.)
Feb [9] *Moneytalks* reaches US #24.
[10] The band is cleared of any involvement in causing death at the recent Salt Lake City concert, although negotiations between the group and the victims' relatives will continue.
[26] The RIAA certifies sales of four million copies of ***Highway To Hell***.
Apr [27] *Are You Ready* bows at its UK #34 peak.
May [24] A second string of US dates begins at the Memorial Auditorium, Buffalo, NY.
Aug [17] The band performs before a 72,500 capacity crowd at the first of seven European rock festivals also featuring Metallica and Motley Crue on the annual "Monsters Of Rock" bill held at Castle Donington, with subsequent dates in Budapest, Munich, Basle, Brussels, Gelsenkirchen, Frankfurt and Oldenburg, set to end on September 8th.
Sept [28] During an AC/DC concert at the Tushino Air Field in Moscow, Russia, Johnson tells the audience: "Opera and ballet did not cut the ice in the Cold War years. They used to exchange opera and ballet companies and circuses, but it takes rock and roll to make no more Cold War."
Dec [2] Always a prolific and hard-working live act, AC/DC completes yet another year of touring, playing more than 70 dates (half of them sellouts), and grossing more than $17 million.

1992

Mar [2] The RIAA certifies sales of three million copies of ***The Razor's Edge***.
[26] Copyright owners of the band's *Rags To Riches* 1979 hit file suit in New York against SBK Records and Vanilla Ice alleging illegal sampling use of the recording on the rapper's current ***Extremely Live*** album.
Oct [24] *Highway To Hell (Live)* reaches UK #14 following its performance on BBC1-TV's "Top Of The Pops" the previous week.
[31] The band is featured on ABC-TV's In Concert "Halloween Jam At Universal Studios" special with Black Crowes, En Vogue, Ozzy Osbourne, Slaughter and others.
Nov [7] Performance album ***Live*** bows at its UK #5 peak and will also reach US #15 on Nov [21], while a limited release ***Live: Special Collector's Edition*** debuts at its US #34 pinnacle one week earlier.

1993

Mar [6] *Dirty Deeds Done Dirt Cheap (Live)* charts for a week at UK #68.
July [10] *Big Gun*, featured in new Arnold Schwarzenegger-starring movie "The Last Action Hero", debuts at its UK #23 peak.
[17] *Big Gun* peaks at US #65.
Sept [14] ***Live*** reaches the two million sales plateau, as certified by the RIAA.
Nov [30] The RIAA ratifies multi-platinum sales for ***High Voltage*** (two million) and ***Who Made Who*** (three million). (Following its 1992 world tour, the band has regrouped in Canada to work on its next studio project.)

1995

June [6] The RIAA certifies sales of three million copies for ***For Those About To Rock (We Salute You)***.
Sept [30] *Hard As A Rock* debuts at its UK #33 peak.
Oct [7] ***Ballbreaker***, produced by Rick Rubin and Mike Fraser and seeing the return to the line-up of original drummer Rudd, bows at its UK #6 peak.
[14] ***Ballbreaker*** debuts at its US #4 high. (Meanwhile in Australia, BMG Records release a various artists AC/DC tribute album ***Fuse Box***.)

1996

Jan [12] AC/DC's "Ballbreaker" world tour opens at the Coliseum, Greensboro, NC, before a sellout crowd of 15,899.
May [11] *Hail Caesar* charts for a week at UK #56.
June [1] While St. Martin's Press has recently published Martin Huxley's **AC/DC: The World's Heaviest Rock** biography, the UK leg of the band's current trek begins at the Scottish Exhibition & Conference Centre, Glasgow.

JOHNNY ACE

1952

Sept [27] Having quit school in the tenth grade and following wartime service in the US navy, Ace (b. John Alexander Jr., June 9, 1929, Memphis, TN), the son of a local preacher, has returned to Memphis in the summer of 1949 and joined an R&B/blues combo run by Adolph Duncan, as a pianist, before linking with B.B. King's band. When King moves west to Los Angeles, CA, and the group's singer, Bobby Bland goes into the army, Ace (who has also served time in a Mississippi jail and is estranged from his wife) has taken over vocal duties and renamed the band the Beale Streeters. He has continued to perform under his given name untiil signing with Duke Records (owned by a Houston, TX-based DJ) earlier this year, when he switches to Johnny Ace. With Don Robey, a Houston-based entrepreneur who runs the Texas chitlin circuit, having bought Duke in August, Ace's first single for the label, *My Song*, credited to Johnny Ace with the Beale Streeters, now tops the US R&B chart, where it will remain for nine weeks. It sets a style followed by subsequent releases: a sensitive baritone vocal with subdued jazz, small-group backing, highly popular with black US audiences of the time. (Aretha Franklin will score with her version in 1968.)

1953

Feb *Cross My Heart* hits #3 on the US R&B chart.
July [18] His third single *The Clock* tops the US R&B survey for the first of five weeks. By year's end, Ace will be billed as a solo artist, backed by Robey and the Johnny Otis Band.

1954

Feb *Saving My Love For You* hits US R&B #2, the first of the year's clutch of R&B successes for Ace, which will see *Please Forgive Me* hit US R&B #6 in June and *Never Let Me Go* hit US R&B #9 in October.
Dec After constantly touring the South throughout the year, mainly on a bill with Willie Mae "Big Mama" Thornton, Ace is named Most Programmed Artist Of 1954, following a national DJ poll organised by US music trade weekly, **Cash Box**.
[25] Shortly after 11:00 p.m. and during an intermission at a Negro Christmas Dance at the City Auditorium, Houston, Ace, who has been drinking vodka, fatally shoots himself with a .22 caliber H&R revolver. He had already fired the gun at girlfriend Olivia Gibbs and her friend Mary Carter, but it had not gone off on either occasion. Justice of the Peace Walter Reagan will determine death to be from "playing Russian roulette". (To embellish what is perhaps the first rock'n'roll fatality, stories abound about a hired killer climbing through Ace's dressing room window. Robey seeks to additionally color the tragedy by stating that Ace died on Christmas Eve as midnight approached (although Ace had played a gig in Port Arthur, TX, on the 24th).)

1955

Jan [2] An estimated 5,000 people attend Ace's funeral at the Clayborn Temple AME church in Memphis. Little Junior Parker, Roscoe Gordon and Harold Conner are active pall-bearers, while Don Robey, B.B. King and Willie Mae Thornton are honorary ones.
Feb [12] Posthumously-released *Pledging My Love*, with the Johnny Otis Orchestra, is his most successful cut ever, beginning a ten-week run at US R&B #1.
Mar [19] *Pledging My Love* reaches US #17 and will subsequently become a rock ballad standard. (Ironically, Elvis Presley's version is on the B-side of his current single at the time of his death, more than 20 years later.) The original *Pledging My Love* will resurface in the mid-'80s film "Christine" while Paul Simon will resurrect his name in the song *The Late Great Johnny Ace* for his 1983 album ***Hearts And Bones***.

ACE

Paul Carrack (keyboards, vocals); **Phil Harris** (guitar); **Alan "Bam" King** (guitar, vocals); **Terry "Tex" Comer** (bass); **Fran Byrne** (drums)

1972

Dec Having worked with vocalist Reginald King on an unfulfilled project after Mighty Baby disbanded in 1971, King (b. Sept. 18, 1946, Kentish Town, London), founder of cult '60s mod band the Action, and Harris (b. July 18, 1948, Muswell Hill, London) leave Clat Thyger to form Ace Flash & the Dynamos. They invite Comer (b. Feb. 23, 1949, Burnley, Lancs.), who - after three years with Northern band Warm Dust - has spent a year away from music, and drummer Steven Witherington to join. Calling themselves Ace from January 1973, the band will break into the burgeoning UK "pub-rock" circuit, building a solid following to become one of the movement's most successful combos, particularly after the arrival of Carrack (b. Apr. 22, 1951, Sheffield, Yorks.), also ex-Warm Dust, who will become Ace's featured vocalist from March 1973.

1974

Sept Byrne (b. Mar. 17, 1948, Dublin, Eire), having played with various semi-professional bands in Dublin, including Some People and Rockhouse, before moving to London in October 1973 to join Bees Make Honey, replaces Chico Greenwood, who has in turn replaced Witherington for a short while, and the band signs to the Anchor label (UK).
Dec [7] Ace's debut single *How Long*, from its forthcoming album ***Five A Side***, spurred by instant radio support, reaches UK #20. (Rod Stewart's cover version will make UK #41 in 1982.) The song's theme, often assumed to concern an extra-marital affair, is actually written about rival band Sutherland Brothers & Quiver's attempt to poach Comer.

1975

May [31] *How Long* hits US #3, held off the top by Freddy Fender and John Denver, as its parent album ***Five A Side*** climbs to US #11. The easy-paced melodic song will become a long-term radio staple in the US.
Aug [9] *Rock & Roll Runaway* is its only other US singles chart success, peaking at #71, as the group embarks on a major US tour supporting Yes.

1976

Jan [24] Their sophomore effort, ***Time For Another***, with Poco's Rusty Young guesting on steel guitar, makes US #153.
Mar Harris leaves due to "personal differences", as the band relocates to California.

1977

Feb [19] The band's third album ***No Strings***, featuring ex-John Stewart session guitarist Jon Woodhead, makes US #170.
May [8] The group plays its final gig at the Roundhouse, London, as a projected UK tour is called off. The band splits soon after, with Carrack, Comer and Byrne joining Frankie Miller's band. In the longer term, Byrne will continue playing on the pub circuit with Juice On The Loose, while King and Comer will re-emerge in 1992, gigging with Andy Winfield and Mick Molloy.

1980

May [23] Carrack makes his first solo appearance at London's Venue, promoting ***Nightbird***, his debut solo album on Vertigo. Thereafter, he will enjoy moderate solo success mainly in the US, releasing 1983's ***Suburban Voodoo*** (Epic Records), ***One Good Reason*** (1987) and ***Groove Approved*** (1989 - US #120), both on Chrysalis, join Squeeze for a time (notably for their hit *Tempted*) and then become an integral part of Mike & the Mechanics as one of two lead vocalists.

1996

Feb [3] While Demon Records has collected the highlights from Carrack's overall career with 1987's ***Ace Mechanic*** compilation, and EMI has issued a further Carrack compilation, ***Good Reasons: The Collection*** in January 1994, (by which time he had formed the short-lived Spin 1ne 2wo with Phil Palmer, Rupert Hine, Steve Ferrone and Tony Levin), Carrack, now returning to his solo career, makes UK #63 with ***Blue Views*** which includes *Eyes Of Blue* (which reached UK #40 on January 13th, and a remake of *How Long*, which reaches UK #32 on April 13th).
see also: **SQUEEZE**

ACE OF BASE

Jenny Berggren (vocals); **Linn Berggren** (vocals); **Jonas "Joker" Berggren** (keyboards); **Ulf "Buddha" Ekberg** (keyboards)

1990

Aug [6] Jonas Berggren (b. Mar. 21, 1967, Gothenburg, Sweden), who has acquired equipment through a Swedish government program subsidizing would-be musicians, is booked to perform a late-night gig with his ad-hoc five-piece band, which includes his ex-church-choir singing sisters (and teachers-in-training) Jenny Berggren (b. May 19, 1972, Gothenburg) and Linn Berggren (b. Malin Beggren, Oct. 31, 1970, Gothenburg) at a small nightclub in their hometown, the bleak industrial Swedish city of Gothenburg. When one of the group's members develops stage-fright, Ekberg (b. Dec. 6, 1970, Gothenburg), the keyboardist with the opening band, steps in to deputize. (Ekberg is an ex-skinhead who has weaned himself from membership of a street gang which followed the White Aryan Resistance movement.) Following their performance, the Ace Of Base quartet is born, performing early on under the moniker Tech Noir (named after the discotheque featured in "The Terminator" film).

1991

Initially experimenting with hip-house and industrial techno-based material and rehearsing at a Gothenburg warehouse/studio which they share with car mechanics among others, their first demo, displaying a synthesizer-based pop-reggae meld and including future hits *Wheel Of Fortune* and *All That She Wants*, is rejected by Abba's Polar label in Stockholm. Settled on the Ace Of Base name and supported by the Berggrens' jazz-enthusiast father and teacher mother, the band performs regularly around Gothenburg.

1992

Mar Disappointed with domestic label reaction, Jonas sends their demo cassette to KLF-licensee, Mega Records in Copenhagen, Denmark, which signs Ace Of Base for a down payment of £2,900. *Wheel Of Fortune* makes a swift rise to the top of the Danish singles chart, prompting the band to cut a new version of *All That She Wants*, written by Jonas and Ekberg, with veteran Swedish producer Denniz PoP.
Oct *All That She Wants* release captivates Scandinavian radio and the track hits #1 in Sweden, Norway, Finland and Denmark (where it enters the chart with *Wheel of Fortune* still at #2). Its success leads German label Metronome Musik in Hamburg to sign the band for releases in the rest of Europe and the Far East.

1993

May [22] Already a chart-topper in Germany, *All That She Wants*, an instantly infectious pop-reggae smash, sub-licensed to London Records, hits UK #1.
June [19] ***Happy Nation***, their European-only released debut album enters at its initial UK #21 peak.
Sept [4] *Wheel Of Fortune* reaches UK #20.
Nov [6] Having chart-topped throughout Europe, and with the band now signed to Arista Records in the US, *All That She Wants* hits US #2.
[12] *All That She Wants* is certified platinum by the RIAA for one million US sales.
[20] *Happy Nation* makes UK #42. The album has been variously-produced by Jonas and Ekberg (also its principal songwriters) with PoP, Douglas Carr, the T.O.E.C. team and production duo Adebratt & Ekmann.

1994

Mar [5] *The Sign*, penned by Jonas, hits UK #2.
[12] *The Sign* tops the US Hot 100.
Mar With global success confirmed, Ace Of Base is named Most Successful International Band at the 1993 Echo Awards in Frankfurt, Germany.
Apr [2] ***The Sign***, a repackaging of the European album ***Happy Nation*** but now augmented by four newly-recorded tracks for the North American market, hits US #1 for one week (and will return to the summit for a further week on June 11th). In doing so, Ace Of Base becomes the first Swedish act to top the US Albums chart, a feat not even achieved by its pop forefathers Abba.
[6] Title cut *The Sign* is certified platinum by the RIAA.
[27] Jenny Berggren asleep in the downstairs bedroom of her parents' Gothenberg home awakes shortly before 4:00 a.m. to find 21-year old German Manuela Behrendt hovering over her with a large hunting knife. (Behrendt will be arrested, jailed for one year and banned from Sweden for ten years.)
May [4] Ace Of Base receives the World's Best-selling Pop Newcomers of the Year and Best-selling Scandinavian Recording-artists of the Year trophies at the sixth annual World Music Awards held at the Monte Carlo Sporting Club, at which they also perform *The Sign*.
June [11] The band appears on "The Brian Conley

Show" on ITV, followed by an appearance on BBC2-TV's "The O Zone" the next day.
[18] *Don't Turn Around*, a Diane Warren/Albert Hammond-penned song proving its reggae/pop chops for the second time (Aswad scored with their traditional reggae version in 1988), hits US #4.
[25] *Don't Turn Around* hits UK #5.
[29] *Don't Turn Around* is certified gold by the RIAA.
July [2] ***Happy Nation***, now re-packaged in Europe with the US track listing, finally tops the UK chart.
[25] "The Sign/The Home Video" is certified gold by the RIAA.
Oct [15] *Happy Nation* makes UK #40.
Nov [24] The group appears at the inaugural MTV European Music Awards, staged at the Pariser Platz, Berlin.
Dec [3] *Living In Danger* reaches US #20.
[7] Ace Of Base collects trophies for Top New Artist and Top Single (*The Sign*) at the fifth annual **Billboard** Music Awards held at the Universal Amphitheatre, Universal City, CA. (A spectacular year of global chart domination and multi-platinum recognition is also capped as the group's four members are made Honorary Citizens of Gothenburg later in the month.)

1995

Jan [14] *Living In Danger* debuts at its UK #18 peak.
[30] The group wins the Top Band, Duo or Group/Pop Rock category and Top New Artist category at the 22nd annual American Music Awards held at Los Angeles' Shrine Auditorium.
Apr [5] The RIAA certifies eight million US sales of ***The Sign***.
June [3] Ace Of Base is named Top New Artist (Group) at the inaugural Blockbuster Entertainment Awards held at Hollywood's Pantages Theatre, CA.
Aug [4] *Lucky Love*, the first song from their forthcoming sophomore album, receives its performance premiere at the opening ceremony of the World Games in Gothenburg, an event broadcast live by Eurosport.
Nov [11] *Lucky Love* bows at its UK #20 peak.
Dec [2] With worldwide sales of their debut album now exceeding 19 million, and confirmed by the **Guinness Book Of Records** as the best-selling debut album of all-time, the group's follow-up set ***The Bridge*** debuts at its UK #66 pinnacle.
[16] *Beautiful Life* reaches US #15.

1996

Jan [16] ***The Bridge*** is certified platinum by the RIAA for one million US sales.
[20] ***The Bridge*** reaches US #29.
Feb [3] *Beautiful Life* reaches UK #15.
Feb [6] ***The Sign*** is ratified for nine million US sales by the RIAA.
May [8] The group is named the World's Best-Selling Scandanavian Arist/Group Of The Year at the 1996 World Music Awards held at the Monte-Carlo Sporting Club.
Apr [13] *Lucky Love* reaches US #30.

ADAM & THE ANTS

Adam Ant (vocals); **Marco Pirroni** (guitar); **Kevin Mooney** (bass); **Terry Lee Miall** (drums); **Merrick** (drums)

1976

June [30] **Melody Maker** prints the ad "Beat On A Bass With The B-Sides" in its classified section, placed there by recent Hornsey School of Art, London, attendee Ant (b. Stuart Goddard, Nov. 3, 1954, London), who has been in his first band Bazooka Joe & His Rhythm Hot Shots while still a student at the school.
July [3] Ant meets Andy Warren, who has phoned him two days earlier in response to the ad, outside the Marquee club, London. They form the B-Sides, rehearsing in South Clapham, London, throughout the rest of 1976 and into early 1977 with various personnel, including Lester Square (guitar), Paul Flanagan, Bob Hip and David Tampin (drums), Bid (occasional guitar and vox), and with Warren (bass) and Ant (guitar and vocals). They record a punk version of *These Boots Are Made For Walking*, and then disband.

1977

Apr [23] The Ants, comprising Ant, Warren, Square and Flanagan, make their debut at the Roxy club in Neal Street, London, on a bill which includes Siouxsie & the Banshees.
May [10] Mark Ryan (aka Mark Gaumont) replaces the recently-departed Square, as the Ants make their first appearance at the ICA gallery restaurant, London.
[11] They support X-Ray Spex at the Man In The Moon pub in Chelsea, London, which will lead to a headlining gig there within a fortnight.
June [2] The Angel's drummer Dave Barbe (aka Barbarossa) joins the Ants as they support Desolation Angels at Ant's alumni, Hornsey School of Art.
[20] The group opens for all-girl punkettes, the Slits, in Cheltenham, Glos.
July [5] They film an appearance for the Derek Jarman punk movie "Jubilee", with stand-in Banshees drummer Kenny Morris. (Jarman had seen Ant walking down the King's Road and offered him the role.)
[11] The group plays at the opening of punk venue the Vortex club, on a bill with the Banshees and the Slits.
[14] They record *Plastic Surgery* and *Beat My Guest* at Chappell Studios in London.
[18] Ant dislocates his knee while filming *Plastic Surgery* at London's Theatre Royal, Drury Lane, for "Jubilee".

1978

Jan [23] The band makes its radio debut on BBC Radio 1's "The John Peel Show", performing *Deutscher Girls*, *Lou*, *It Doesn't Matter* and *Puerto Rican*.
[24] They record *Deutscher Girls* and *Plastic Surgery* again for "Jubilee", at AIR Studios, London, with new drummer Johnny Bivouac.
May [14] Bivouac quits after a gig at the Roundhouse, London, with X-Ray Spex.
[15-19] They record demos of *Young Parisians*, *Lady* and *Catch A Falling Star* at Virtual Earth Studios and Chelsea College of Art, London.
June [6] Guitarist Matthew Ashman (b. 1960, Mill Hill, London) makes his debut with the band at a debutante's party at the Hard Rock Café, London.
July [10] The group records its second "John Peel Session", performing *Physical*, *Zerox* and *Friends & Cleopatra*.
[29] They sign a two-single deal with Decca Records.
Sept [9] The band begins a European tour in Leopoldsburg, Belgium, set to end on October 21st at the Titan club in Rome, Italy.
Nov [14] Adam & the Ants record a demo of *Kick* at RAK Studios, London, with Snips producing.

1979

Jan Decca single *Young Parisians* is released, as the band signs to the independent Do It Records.
[11] The group begins its first major UK tour at Brannigans in Leeds, W. Yorks., set to close on February 19th at the Civic Hall, Bishops Stortford, Herts.
[26] The band makes its third "John Peel Session" appearance, performing *Ligotage*, *Tabletalk*, *Animals & Men* and *Never Trust A Man With Egg On His Face*.
July [6] *Zerox/Whip In My Valise*, recorded at London's Roundhouse Studios, is released by Do It Records.
[13] Their 17-date UK Zerox tour begins at the Porterhouse, Retford, Notts., set to end with a sellout date at London's Lyceum Ballroom, on August 5th.
Aug [1] Ant splits his head open at a gig at the Woods, Plymouth, Devon, a wound requiring six stitches.
[12-24] The group records its debut album ***Dirk Wears White Sox*** at the Sound Development Studios, London.
Sept [28-29] They play two sellout shows at London's Electric Ballroom.
Oct [3] Warren leaves to join Square in the Monochrome Set, and is replaced by Lee Gorman. During the month, Sex Pistols' svengali Malcolm McLaren becomes the group's manager and temporarily introduces Jordan, a female acquaintance, on additional vocals while the 12-track ***Dirk Wears White Sox*** is released.

1980

Jan [1] The band plays a sellout New Year's Day gig at the Electric Ballroom, London, marking Gorman's first and last gig with the band.
[14] The UK Independent labels chart is launched in the UK, with ***Dirk Wears White Sox*** at #1 on the albums list.
[24] The current Ants split from Adam, as McLaren pairs Ashman, Gorman and Barbe with girl singer Annabella Lwin forming the new act Bow Wow Wow. (After Bow Wow Wow splits in 1983, the trio will form Chiefs Of Relief, releasing an album in W. Germany. Gorman and Barbe will then team as Atom Age, after which Gorman will run LRG Studios for three years, before linking up with McLaren, producing and writing jingles. Barbe will play briefly in Beats International, before forming Pimp Floyd and drumming for Crazy Little Trees and soul singer Delphi.)
[28] Ant and ex-Models and Siouxsie & the Banshees guitarist Pirroni (b. Apr. 27, 1959, London) meet in a cake shop in Covent Garden and agree to establish a songwriting partnership to create "antmusic". They team up with new manager Falcon Stewart, and recruit drummer/producer Chris Hughes (b. Mar. 3, 1954, London) (later known as Merrick).
Feb [18] Ant, Pirroni and Hughes re-record *Cartrouble* and *Kick!* at Rockfield Studios, Monmouth, Gwent, S. Wales.
Apr [19] The new Ants line-up begins recording the first fruits of the Ant-Pirroni partnership at Matrix Studios, London.
May *Cartrouble* completes the Do It contract, after which Ant and Pirroni sign a publishing deal, having recruited Mooney on bass and Miall (b. Nov. 8, 1958, London) (who had been with Pirroni in the Beastly Cads, later known as the Models, before forming the Music Club), as a second drummer.
[22] A 14-date UK "Ants Invasion" tour, promoting a new flamboyant visual image and a drum/percussion-oriented sound, begins with a sellout date at the Electric Ballroom. The tour will end on July 8th at the Empire Ballroom, London, with special guest, '60s singer Dave Berry.
July [16] The group signs to CBS Records, and begins recording at Rockfield Studios.
Aug Its label debut *Kings Of The Wild Frontier*, produced by Hughes, makes UK #48.
Nov [8] *Dog Eat Dog*, helped by the band's first BBC1-TV "Top Of The Pops" appearance, hits UK #4.

1981

Jan [17] Percussion-heavy *Antmusic* hits UK #2, boosted by a Steve Barron-directed video clip.
[24] ***Kings Of The Wild Frontier*** tops the UK chart.
[31] *Young Parisians*, reissued by Decca, hits UK #9.
Feb [7] Do It reissue *Zerox*, already an Indie chart-topper, makes UK #45.
[14] Another Do It Indie chart-topper *Cartrouble* makes UK #33.
[23] The group takes part in the "25 Years Of British Pop" segment at the Royal Variety Performance held in London.
Mar [7] ***Dirk Wears White Sox*** reaches UK #16.
[14] Reissued *Kings Of The Wild Frontier* hits UK #2. Ant has finally hit a commercial vein, reliant musically upon insistent percussion and boosted visually by swashbuckling pirate images.
May [9] *Stand And Deliver*, promoted with the popular "Dandy Highwayman" video, enters the UK chart at #1, topping Bucks Fizz's *Making Your Mind Up*.

June [6] ***Kings Of The Wild Frontier*** makes US #44, a considerable achievement in the absence of any US chart singles to date.
Sept [19] *Prince Charming* hits UK #1, as the group embarks on the sellout Prince Charming Revue Tour.
Nov [14] ***Prince Charming*** debuts at its UK #2 peak, behind Queen's ***Greatest Hits***. Recent recruit Mooney leaves (later forming Wide Boy Awake), and is replaced by Gary Tibbs (b. Jan. 24, 1958, London), ex-Roxy Music.
Dec [26] ***Prince Charming*** makes US #94.

1982

Jan [9] *Ant Rap* hits UK #3, the sixth straight smash to be produced by Hughes. (Ant, who has recently turned down the lead role in the West End show "Pirates Of Penzance", citing that he's "been through the pirate thing already", will decide to go solo, dismantling the band, but keeping Pirroni as his writing partner. Hughes will become increasingly successful as a producer, notably for Tears For Fears.)
Feb [24] ***Kings Of The Wild Frontier*** wins Best British Album at the inaugural BRIT Awards, at London's Grosvenor House Hotel.
Mar [6] Polydor-reissued *Deutscher Girls*, from the "Jubilee" film soundtrack, reaches UK #13.
[20] *The Antmusic EP (The B-Sides)*, containing old Do It tracks, makes UK #46.
Apr [29] Ant and Pirroni are named Songwriters Of The Year and *Stand And Deliver* is honored as Best Selling A-Side at the 27th annual Ivor Novello Awards lunch, also held at the Grosvenor House Hotel.
June [12] His first release as Adam Ant, *Goody Two-Shoes*, tops the UK chart.
Oct [2] *Friend Or Foe* hits UK #9.
[23] ***Friend Or Foe***, produced by Ant and Pirroni, hits UK #5.
Dec [4] *Desperate But Not Serious* reaches UK #33, breaking his run of Top 10 hits.

1983

Feb [12] *Goody Two-Shoes*, providing a long-awaited US hit, reaches #12.
Mar Ant becomes the first guest VJ on MTV.
[14] ***Friend Or Foe*** is certified gold by the RIAA.
[26] *Desperate But Not Serious*, a minor US follow-up success, peaks at #66, as ***Friend Or Foe*** heads to US #16.
May [16] Curiously, Ant guests on NBC-TV's "Motown 25th Anniversary", alongside many Motown legends.
Nov [12] *Puss'N Boots*, produced by Phil Collins, hits UK #5, and ***Strip***, on which Ant and Pirroni are helped by Richard James Burgess, who plays keyboards, drums and percussion - and produces - reaches UK #20 (and will make US #65).
Dec [17] *Strip*, also produced by Collins, stops at UK #41, after being withdrawn when Ant refuses a request by BBC-TV to change the lyrics of the song and to tone down the accompanying video.

1984

Mar [24] *Strip* makes US #42.
Oct [6] *Apollo 9* reaches UK #13. (By year's end, Ant will record *What's Going On* for the soundtrack to the forthcoming film "Metropolis".)

1985

July [13] Ant, with a new backing band line-up of Pirroni, Chris de Niro (bass) and Bogdan Wiczling (drums), performs at the UK segment of Live Aid at Wembley Stadium, Wembley, Middx., before embarking on a UK tour, which is cancelled after three dates, when Ant is unable to get himself insured.
[20] *Vive Le Rock* makes UK #50.
Sept ***Vive Le Rock***, produced by Tony Visconti, reaches UK #42. It is Ant's last chart entry for five years, following which he will star in a theatrical production of Joe Orton's "Entertaining Mr. Sloane", before he moves to the US and into film and TV acting, where his most noted early roles will be in the film "Slam Dance" and in "The Equalizer" TV series. Pirroni will continue as a successful session musician, not least with his contributions to Sinead O'Connor's 1990 album ***I Do Not Want What I Haven't Got.***
Nov ***Vive Le Rock*** peaks at US #131.

1986

Sept CBS releases the retrospective album ***Hits***, compiled by Pirroni. Ant's only other recording during the year is a collaboration with Stewart Copeland on the theme song to the movie "Out Of Bounds". (His recording career will go on hold while he lives in the US, persisting with his acting career (including the films "World Gone Wild" and Dennis Hopper's "Sunset Heat", and various TV movie roles).)

1990

Mar [3] *Room At The Top*, his recording return on MCA, reaches UK #13 boosted by an appearance on "Top Of The Pops" on February 22nd (and will peak at US #17 on May [5]).
[24] Its parent album, ***Manners And Physique***, produced by André Cymone and featuring longtime cohort Pirroni, makes UK #19 (and will make US #57 on May [5]).
Apr [28] *Can't Set Rules About Love* makes UK #47.

1993

Feb [27] Having contributed to the all-star Peace Choir line-up in March 1991, for the US hit *Give Peace A Chance*, a remake of John Lennon's classic anti-war hymn, and having begun recording tracks for his second MCA project at the Matrix Studios in London with Pirroni and Lee Gorman, Ant plays the first of three sellout dates at the Henry Fonda Theatre in Los Angeles, CA, during his current US tour. (Meanwhile, his acting aspirations show no sign of diminishing. He has now been in over a dozen movies and TV roles, including this year's CBS-TV hit, "Northern Exposure", and is currently working with John Densmore on "Be Bop A Lula", a musical dramatization of Eddie Cochran and Gene Vincent's last night together before Cochran's death.)
Sept [4] Retrospective collection ***Antmusic - The Very Best Of Adam Ant*** hits UK #6.

1994

Aug [19] ***Kings Of The Wild Frontier*** is certified gold by the RIAA. Ant continues his film career, recently and currently appearing in "Desert Wings In Utah", "Drop Dead Rock", "A Lover's Knot", "A Sailor's Tattoo" and "Nomads".

1995

Jan [5] Ant joins Nine Inch Nails onstage for an encore at the Centrum in Worcester, MA, singing *Physical (You're So)*, *Red Scab* and *Beat My Guest*.
Feb [11] *Wonderful*, Ant's first single from an alliance with Capitol Records in the US and EMI Records in the UK, bows at its UK #32 debut. (MCA has refused to release Ant's last project in the UK - the album ***Persuasion***, produced by Chic's Bernard Edwards and Cameo's Larry Blackmon.)
Mar [7] The Los Angeles Fire Department closes the 350-capacity Virgin Megastore on Sunset Boulevard, when 1,300 fans show up for an acoustic performance by Ant.
[22-23] Playing his first UK dates since Live Aid in 1985, Ant performs at London's Shepherd's Bush Empire.
Apr [15] The David Tickle-produced ***Wonderful***, with seven songs penned with former Polecat Boz Boorer, debuts at its UK #24 peak, the same day Ant performs at the Roseland Theater, Portland, OR.
June [3] *Wonderful* reaches US #39 and *Gotta Be A Sin* debuts at its UK #48 peak, as parent album ***Wonderful*** makes US #151. (Ant will cancel the 18 remaining dates of his 70-date US and UK tour, when he is struck down with an upper respiratory infection. Fellow musicians Pirroni and Ruffy also respectively succumb to an ear infection and acute glandular fever.)
Nov [22] Former Ant Matthew Ashman dies after lapsing into a coma, a complication caused by diabetes.

BRYAN ADAMS

1977

Musically influenced by the Beatles, Eddie Cochran and Ray Charles among others, Adams (b. Nov. 5, 1959, Kingston, ON, Canada), who has attended military schools around Europe as the son of a Canadian diplomat father (who has split from his wife in 1971, leaving the boy to be raised during his teens by his mother in Vancouver, BC, Canada), has dropped out of school age 16, knowing his muse lies in a music career and already proficient on both the guitar and piano. Having replaced Nick Gilder as the lead singer for Canadian rock outfit Sweeney Todd in 1976 (cutting the album, ***If Wishes Were Horses***), he now forms a writing partnership with Jim Vallance, drummer with Prism. The duo will write and arrange the tracks *You Walked Away* and *Take It Or Leave It* for Prism's 1980 album ***Armageddon***, and, after signing with Rondor publishing, begin providing hit songs for rock acts, including Bachman-Turner Overdrive, Kiss, Loverboy, Joe Cocker and Bonnie Tyler. Adams and Vallance's own demos receive little response from record companies, however, until A&M offers to record four songs, one of which, *Let Me Take You Dancing*, styled and promoted as a dance record (belying Adam's fervent rock style), is released in November 1979, followed by *Hidin' From Love*, issued next April.

1980

Nov His freshman solo album ***Bryan Adams***, its rhythm section comprising Keith Scott (guitar), Dave Taylor (bass) and Vallance (drums), is released (without the recent dance cut) by A&M.

1982

Mar [20] *Lonely Nights* makes US #84, as its parent album ***You Want It, You Got It***, produced by Bob Clearmountain, climbs to US #118. Adams will spend much of the year gaining a solid live reputation by playing support on US tours by the Kinks, Foreigner and fellow Canadians, Loverboy.

1983

May [28] Piano-led ballad *Straight From The Heart* is his first hit single, at US #10. Its simple, melodic rock structure will become an Adams trademark over future albums. (Adams is in the midst of sellout US dates, supporting Journey.)
June ***Cuts Like A Knife***, featuring Foreigner's Lou Gramm and Chic's Alfa Anderson as backing vocalists, with Mickey Curry taking over from Vallance as Adams' drummer, is a similar chart breakthrough, hitting US #8. The album and live line-up of Scott, Taylor, Curry and Tommy Mandel (keyboards) will support Adams throughout the decade, while Vallance retreats to a co-songwriting role. Touring to promote each album release, Adams will make his first UK concert appearances by year's end.
Aug [6] Extracted title track *Cuts Like A Knife* reaches US #15.
[17] ***Cuts Like A Knife*** is certified platinum by the RIAA.
Oct [29] Fiery *This Time* makes US #24. By year's end, the prolific live performing artist will have spent 283 days on the road.

1985

Jan [19] Uptempo *Run To You* hits US #6, boosted by leafy, autumnal video clip which will become an MTV staple item.
Feb [9] *Run To You*, Adams' first UK hit, reaches #11.
Mar [2] ***Reckless***, co-produced by Adams and Clearmountain, with guest drummer Pat Steward playing on three tracks, hits UK #7.
[14] During his second UK tour, supporting Tina

Turner on her current "Private Dancer" trek, Adams performs at the Wembley Arena, Wembley, Middx.
Apr [6] *Somebody* reaches US #11, and will make UK #35.
June [1] Third extract *Heaven*, also featured some two years earlier on the soundtrack album ***A Night In Heaven***, makes UK #38.
[22] *Heaven*, only released as a single after pressure from US radio, tops the US chart and is his first million-selling single.
July [13] Adams opens the US segment of the "Live Aid" benefit concert at the JFK Stadium, Philadelphia, PA. (He and Vallance have also composed the Northern Lights all-star recording *Tears Are Not Enough* as Canada's contribution to raise money to help combat the famine in Ethiopia.)
Aug [10] ***Reckless*** hits US #1 in its 38th week on chart, helped by Adams' continued exposure as support on Turner's current world tour.
[31] Nostalgic rocker *Summer Of '69* hits US #5 and will make UK #42, as ***You Want It, You Got It*** makes UK #78.
Nov [9] *One Night Love Affair* reaches US #13.
[23] *It's Only Love*, a duet with Tina Turner (written with Vallance over the telephone), reaches UK #29.
Dec The seasonal *Christmas Time* peaks at UK #55.

1986

Jan [18] *It's Only Love* reaches US #15.
Mar *This Time*, from 1983, now reissued in the UK, makes #41, while ***Cuts Like A Knife*** belatedly reaches UK #21.
June [4] Adams joins the two-week Amnesty International "A Conspiracy Of Hope" US tour, also featuring U2, Sting, Peter Gabriel and Lou Reed, at the Cow Palace, San Francisco, CA.
July *Straight From The Heart*, also reissued from 1983, peaks at #51.
Sept [15] "It's Only Love" wins the Best Stage Performance category at the third annual MTV Video Music Awards, broadcast simultaneously from the Universal Amphitheatre, Universal City, CA, and the Palladium, New York, NY.

1987

Feb ***Rock For Amnesty***, on which Adams is featured with Dire Straits, Paul McCartney, Sting and others, makes US #121.
Mar *Heat Of The Night* peaks at UK #50.
Apr [11] ***Into The Fire***, the fourth album to be co-produced by Adams and Clearmountain, hits UK #10, and will peak at US #7.
May [16] *Heat Of The Night* hits US #6 (and is notable as the first-ever commercially-released cassette single in the US).
June [3] He records a live version of the Christmas oldie *Run Rudolph Run* at London's Marquee club, for donation to a charity album.
[5-6] Adams takes part in the fifth annual "Prince's Trust Rock Gala", with Elton John, George Harrison, Ringo Starr and others, at the Wembley Arena, as *Hearts On Fire* makes UK #57.
[8] ***Into The Fire*** is certified platinum by the RIAA.
Aug [8] *Hearts On Fire* reaches US #26.
Sept [11] He performs at the fourth annual MTV Video Music Awards, held at the Universal Amphitheatre.
Oct [3] *Victim Of Love* reaches US #32, and will peak at UK #68.
Dec The Jimmy Iovine-conceived Special Olympics charity album ***A Very Special Christmas***, which includes Adams' *Run Rudolph Run*, makes US #20 and UK #40.

1988

June [11] Adams takes part in "Nelson Mandela's 70th Birthday Tribute" at Wembley Stadium.
July He tops the bill at the "Peace Festival" in East Berlin, E. Germany, attended by 140,000 rock-starved fans.
Dec Concert album recorded in Belgium earlier in the year, ***Live Live Live*** is released, initially only in Japan.

1989

Mar [6] The Greenpeace-supporting album ***Rainbow Warriors***, which features Adams and other artists, is released in the Soviet Union on the Melodiya label.
June Adams takes part in Roskilde Festival '90 in Roskilde, Denmark.

1990

July [21] Adams performs in Roger Waters' music spectacular, "The Wall", at the site of the Berlin Wall in Potzdamer Platz, Berlin, Germany. The event is broadcast live throughout the world, and raises money for the Memorial Fund for Disaster Relief.
Dec Fellow Canadian David Foster's ***River Of Love***, featuring Adams' vocal on its title track, is released in the US.

1991

July [6] Adams takes part in "Rock The Bowl '91" at Milton Keynes Bowl, Milton Keynes, Bucks, on a bill with Z.Z. Top, Thunder and Little Angels.
[13] *(Everything I Do) I Do It For You* tops the UK chart, where it will stay for a record 16 weeks. An instant classic, the ballad was co-written by Michael Kamen, Adams and producer Robert John "Mutt" Lange as the central theme to the current Kevin Costner-starring movie, "Robin Hood : Prince Of Thieves". Kamen had sent Adams an aural impression of harpsichord and lute sounds based on a tune he had originally written in the 1960s. Adams co-penned the lyrics with Lange and fleshed out the instrumentation to complete the song, which was then recorded in London.
[27] *(Everything I Do) I Do It For You* hits US #1, where it will remain for seven weeks, becoming the country's second-biggest selling single to date. It will hit #1 in 16 countries, selling over eight million copies worldwide over the next year and becoming one of the most successful singles of all time. In the immediate absence of a new Adams album, the ***Robin Hood : Prince Of Thieves*** original soundtrack benefits accordingly.
Aug [31] Re-charted ***Reckless*** reaches UK #29.
Sept [12] The RIAA certifies three million sales for *(Everything I Do) I Do It For You.*
[28] *Can't Stop This Thing We Started* reaches UK #12. Adams is honored with the Order Of Canada and the Order Of British Columbia.
Oct [5] Lange-produced ***Waking Up The Neighbours***, which has been released after several false starts involving a number of other producers over the past four years, enters the UK chart at #1.
[12] ***Waking Up The Neighbors*** bows at its US #6 peak.
[24] A ten-date UK tour opens at Dundonald Ice Rink, Belfast, N. Ireland, the first segment of the "Waking Up The Neighbors" world itinerary which will last until the end of 1992.
[29] He breaks the record for the largest all-standing indoor concert attendance in the UK, when 12,000 greet him at the SE&CC, Glasgow, Scotland.
[30] Adams stops midway through *Somebody* during his concert at Whitley Bay Ice Rink, Whitley Bay, Tyne & Wear, when he sees a drunk punching fellow audience members.
Nov [7] Adams invites Slim Whitman to join him on *Rose Marie* during his performance at Wembley Arena.
[8] The still-rising *Can't Stop This Thing We Started* is certified gold by the RIAA.
[16] *Can't Stop This Thing We Started* hits US #2, held off the summit by Prince's *Cream.*
[23] *There Will Never Be Another Tonight* makes UK #32.
Dec [3] *(Everything I Do) I Do It For You* wins the Top World Single, Top Adult Contemporary Single and Top Hot 100 Single categories at the second annual **Billboard** Music Awards, held at the Barker Hangar, Santa Monica Airport, Santa Monica, CA.

1992

Jan [10] Adams guests on NBC-TV's "Late Night With David Letterman", before playing to a 2,500 sellout crowd at the Ritz in New York, his sole US date between the European and Canadian legs of his tour.
[27] He nabs the Favorite Single, Pop/Rock trophy, at the 19th annual American Music Awards, held at the Shrine Auditorium, Los Angeles, CA.
Feb [10-11] The Australian and New Zealand leg of his world trek opens at the Sydney Entertainment Centre, Sydney.
[15] *There Will Never Be Another Tonight* reaches US #31.
[18] In a **USA Today** interview Adams sympathizes with lip-synchers Milli Vanilli and comments: "Who wants to see (the real singers) anyway. They're probably fat and bald."
[25] Adams wins the Best Song Written Specifically For A Motion Picture Or For Television for *(Everything I Do) I Do It For You* at the 34th annual Grammy Awards, held at Radio City Music Hall, New York, though the song will be edged out by *Beauty And The Beast* in a similar nomination at the forthcoming Academy Awards, despite Adams performing live at the ceremony.
[29] *Thought I'd Died And Gone To Heaven* hits UK #8.
Mar [15] North American portion of his non-stop world tour opens at the University of Cincinnati, Cincinnati, OH.
[29] He performs at the 21st annual Juno Awards at the O'Keefe Centre, Toronto, ON, Canada, also collecting Canadian Entertainer and Producer Of The Year trophies.
Apr [15] *(Everything I Do) I Do It For You* receives official recognition of its exceptional success at the 37th annual Ivor Novello Awards, held at the Grosvenor House Hotel, London.
(He is currently starring in an anti-drink-driving Star G.A.S. (Stars Against Alcohol Behind The Wheel) publicity campaign in Germany.)
May [9] *Thought I'd Died And Gone To Heaven* reaches UK #13.
June [18] The German leg of his "Waking Up The Neighbors" tour ends at the Westfalenhalle in Dortmund.
July [9] Adams performs on BBC1-TV's "Top Of The Pops".
[18] During his second European visit in nine months, Adams performs at Wembley Stadium, on a bill including Extreme and Squeeze.
[25] *All I Want Is You* reaches UK #22 on the same day that Adams escapes unhurt from a car accident whilst heading for Vienna, Austria, after a concert in Zurich, Switzerland.
Aug [2] He performs his final European date of the year at "Feile '92", a rock festival held at Thurles Semple Stadium, Tipperary, Eire, together with Christy Moore, Extreme, Kirsty MacColl and others.
Sept [9] He performs *Do I Have To Say The Words?* live at the 1992 MTV Video Music Awards, held at the Pauley Pavilion, Los Angeles.
[26] Power ballad *Do I Have To Say The Words?* bows at its UK #30 peak, while Adams becomes the only native artist in Canadian record history to collect his second Diamond Award (for one million sales of ***Waking Up The Neighbours*** in his home country).
Oct [3] *Do I Have To Say The Words?* reaches US #11, as Adams completes three more months of touring in the US on a bill featuring Steve Miller and Extreme. He will also perform selected year-end dates in December, supported by Mr. Big.
[26] The RIAA certifies sales of three million copies for ***Waking Up The Neighbours***.
Nov [19] ***Reckless*** reaches the RIAA-certified five million sales plateau.

1993

Jan [29-30] South East Asian leg of tour opens in Taipei, Taiwan.
Mar [2] Adams joins George Michael, Sting, James Taylor, Tina Turner, Tom Jones and Herb Alpert at a concert to benefit the world's rain forests at New York's Carnegie Hall.
[3] Adams guests on "Late Night With David Letterman".

[21] ***Waking Up The Neigbours*** is named Best Selling Album (Foreign or Domestic), at the 22nd annual Juno Awards in Toronto.
Apr [3] He embarks on 16-date US tour at the Tri-Cities Coliseum, Kennewick, WA, set to end on the 24th at "Farm Aid V" in Ames, IA.
May [12] Adams is named Best Selling Canadian Artist Of The Year, at the fifth annual World Music Awards in Monte Carlo, Monaco.
June [15] Adams performs *Good Times* and duets with Smokey Robinson on *Bring It On Home To Me* at the "Apollo Theatre Hall Of Fame" concert at the landmark Harlem, New York theatre on an all-star bill. (The show will air on NBC-TV on August 4th.)
Nov [6] Ballad *Please Forgive Me*, extracted from a forthcoming greatest hits compilation ***So Far So Good***, hits UK #2, behind Meat Loaf's *I'd Do Anything For Love (But I Won't Do That)*.
[20] *Please Forgive Me* hits US #7.

1994

Jan [15] ***So Far So Good*** tops the UK chart.
[15-16] Adams plays two shows at Le Let Theatre in Ho Chi Minh City, the first major Western pop star to do so in Vietnam since James Brown in 1971.
[22] *All For Love*, Adams' theme from the movie "The Three Musketeers" recorded in trio with Rod Stewart and Sting, tops the US chart.
[29] *All For Love* hits UK #2, as ***So Far So Good*** peaks at US #6.
Feb [2] *All For Love* is certified platinum by the RIAA.
[11] Sting joins Adams on *All For Love* at the Bushfire benefit concert held at Sydney Football Stadium, Sydney, during the Down Under leg of his current tour.
Apr [3] Adams plays the first of five shows at the SuperBowl, Sun City, South Africa.
May [4] He is named Best Selling Canadian Recording Artist Of The Year at the sixth annual World Music Awards at the Sporting Club, Monte Carlo.
[24] The RIAA certifies sales of three million copies for ***So Far So Good*** the same day Adams plays to a sellout crowd of 12,665 at the Target Center, Minneapolis, MN, during current US dates.
Aug [6] Originally released only in Japan, his 1988 album ***Live! Live! Live!*** bows at its UK #17 peak.
Oct [8] Having sung *O Sole Mio* at Luciano Pavarotti's annual concert in Modena, Italy in September, Adams now performs at "Elvis Presley: The Tribute", an all-star event staged at the Pyramid Arena, Memphis, TN, broadcast live on US pay-per-view TV.
Nov [3] Adams plays the first of a handful of US dates supporting the Rolling Stones at the Sun Bowl, University of Texas, El Paso, TX, before a crowd of 38,732.

1995

Apr [4] Flamenco guitar-based ballad *Have You Ever Really Loved A Woman?*, taken from the movie "Don Juan DeMarco", debuts at its UK #4 peak.
June [3] *Have You Ever Really Loved A Woman?* tops the US chart, as Adams performs at the inaugural Blockbuster Entertainment Awards at Hollywood's Pantages Theatre.
[23] Adams receives the International Award at the annual Nordoff Robbins Music Therapy luncheon at London's Intercontinental Hotel.
Nov [10] Adams and Bonnie Raitt sing their new single, *Rock Steady* (taken from Raitt's forthcoming live album) on CBS-TV's "Late Show With David Letterman".
Dec [2] *Rock Steady* peaks at US #73.

1996

Jan [22] Adams joins compatriot Celine Dion onstage at the annual MIDEM festivities at the Palais Des Festival in Cannes, France, taking a break from working on his first new album in five years, provisionally titled ***18*** (which he is recording with Lange and Kamen in a make-shift studio in nearby St. Tropez, France).
Mar [25] Adams performs his Oscar-nominated song *Have You Ever Really Loved A Woman?* at the 68th Academy Awards ceremony from Los Angeles' Dorothy Chandler Pavilion, accompanied by Kamen on keyboards.
Apr [28] Adams takes part in "Witness : A Concert For Human Rights", also featuring Gloria Estefan, Peter Gabriel and Don Henley, and broadcast live on VH-1 from the Universal Amphitheatre.
May [8] ***Waking Up The Neighbors*** is confirmed quadruple platinum by the RIAA, with ***So Far So Good*** certified at five million.
[25] An 18-month world tour kicks off with a 24-date European-leg (broken by North American media appearances) in Nürburgring, Germany, an initial segment set to end on July 27th at Wembley Stadium.
[30] *Have You Ever Really Loved A Woman?* is named Best Song Included In A Film Or Television Programme at the 41st annual Ivor Novello Awards held at London's Grosvenor House Hotel.
June [1] Adams participates in the 17th annual KISS party staged at Great Woods Center for the Performing Arts, Mansfield, MA as *The Only Thing That Looks Good On Me Is You* debuts at its UK #6 peak.
[4] Following last night's performance on CBS-TV's "Late Show With David Letterman", Adams appears on NBC-TV's "The Today Show", promoting today's release of ***18 Til I Die***, completed with producer and co-writer Lange in southern France and Jamaica and featuring his' stalwart backing musicians, Keith Scott (guitar), Dave Taylor (bass) and Mickey Curry (drums). The album also features guest musicians guitarists Phil Palmer and Paco de Lucia. (The Japanese version of the album includes the additional track *Hey Elvis*.)
July [20] The UK leg of his "Summer Of '96" tour begins at Ibrox Stadium, Glasgow, Scotland.

AEROSMITH

Steven Tyler (vocals, harmonica); **Joe Perry** (lead guitar); **Brad Whitford** (rhythm guitar); **Tom Hamilton** (bass); **Joey Kramer** (drums)

1970

Tyler (b. Steven Tallarico, Mar. 26, 1948, New York, NY), spending his summers at the family-owned Trow-Rico resort in Sunapee, NH, meets Perry (b. Anthony Joseph Perry, Sept. 10, 1950, Boston, MA), working in the local ice-cream parlor, the Anchorage, during his vacation. Perry, playing in the Jam Band, invites Tyler, a veteran of Chain Reaction (who issued one single, *When I Needed You*), William Proud and the Strangeurs and who has released the solo single *You Should Have Been Here Yesterday* on Verve, to a gig at local club The Barn. They decide to form a Cream-style trio with other Jam Band member Hamilton (b. Dec. 31, 1951, Colorado Springs, CO). They have also played together in Pipe Dream and Plastic Glass, with Tyler as drummer. Tyler recruits Kramer (b. June 21, 1950, New York), a friend from Roosevelt High School, who quits the Berklee School of Music in Boston after three weeks to join the band, and guitarist Ray Tabano. The group moves into an apartment at 1325 Commonwealth Ave. in Boston, with Whitford (b. Feb. 23, 1952, Winchester, MA), ex-Justin Tyme, Earth Inc., the Teapot Dome and the Cymbals Of Resistance, soon replacing Tabano, and begins to build a local reputation as a hard-rock act, playing its first gig at Nipmuc Regional High School, performing material by John Lennon, the Rolling Stones and the Yardbirds. They coin their moniker at Kramer's suggestion, after considering the Hookers and Spike Jones.

1971

Local Fenway Theater, Boston manager John O'Toole, who has allowed the band to rehearse in the venue when closed, invites local promoter Frank Connelly to see them. Connelly signs them to a management contract and puts them up in the Sheraton Hotel in Manchester, MA, to rehearse with a view to cutting demos. He then contacts the New York management team of David Krebs and Steve Leber to use their expertise in securing a record deal.

1972

Aug Label boss Clive Davis, at the invitation of Krebs and Leber, sees the band at Max's Kansas City club, New York, and signs them to CBS/Columbia Records for a reported $125,000. (Atlantic Records, also invited to the showcase, turns them down.)

1973

Oct ***Aerosmith***, recorded at Boston's Intermedia Studios with producer Adrian Barber and released to moderate US success, climbs to #166, as the band hits the live circuit, supporting bands ranging from the Mahavishnu Orchestra to Mott The Hoople.
Dec [1] Rock ballad *Dream On*, taken from the album, peaks at US #59.
[17] The group begins recording its second set, at New York's Record Plant Studios (and will spend much of the following year touring the US to promote the resulting March-released ***Get Your Wings***, supporting the Kinks, Mott The Hoople and Sha Na Na).

1975

July [19] *Sweet Emotion* makes US #36, as the group performs at the "Schaefer Music Festival" in New York's Central Park.
Sept [13] The Jack Douglas-produced album ***Toys In The Attic***, boosted by the band's reputation from considerable live work, is their US breakthrough, reaching #11, eventually spending over one year on the survey.
Oct [18] ***Get Your Wings***, co-helmed by Bob Ezrin and Jack Douglas, makes US #74, 18 months after its chart debut.

1976

Apr [3] The band's debut ***Aerosmith*** also re-ascends the US list, now peaking at #21.
[10] Reissued *Dream On* hits US #6.
June [26] ***Rocks***, recorded at the Wherehouse, Waltham, MA, and Record Plant, and critically regarded as an early career high point, hits US #3.
Aug [7] The extracted *Last Child* reaches US #21.
Oct [14] The group makes its live UK debut at the Empire Theatre, Liverpool, Merseyside.
[16] *Home Tonight* makes US #71.

1977

Jan [29] *Walk This Way*, from ***Toys In The Attic*** and inspired by a phrase in the Mel Brooks' film "Young Frankenstein", hits US #10. The band rests from touring for its first extended period in almost five years, to write and prepare the next album.
May [7] *Back In The Saddle* makes US #38.
June The group begins recording ***Draw The Line*** at the Cenacle, an abandoned nunnery in Armonk, NY, and at the favored Record Plant.
Aug The band performs at the "Reading Rock Festival", Reading, Berks.
Nov [19] *Draw The Line* makes US #42.
Dec [13] Its still-rising parent album ***Draw The Line*** is certified platinum by the RIAA.

1978

Jan [28] ***Draw The Line***, featuring the distinctive cartoon work of Al Hirshfeld on the album's cover, reaches US #11, despite poor reviews.
Mar [18] Aerosmith co-headlines the California Jam II festival in Ontario, CA, before an estimated crowd of 350,000, together with Heart, Jean-Michel Jarre, Frank Marino & Mahogany Rush, Dave Mason, Ted Nugent and Santana.
Apr [1] *Kings And Queens* makes US #70.
July [4] The group participates in the Texxas World Music Festival at the Cottonbowl, Dallas, TX (subsequently released as "Aerosmith's Live Texxas

Jam '78" on video in 1989).
Aug [21] The band records *Come Together* with producer George Martin at The Wherehouse, as their contribution to the movie "Sgt. Pepper's Lonely Hearts Club Band", in which they appear as the Future Villain Band.
Sept [30] *Come Together* reaches US #23.
Oct [31] ***Live Bootleg*** is certified gold by the RIAA.

1979

Jan [13] Double performance set ***Live! Bootleg*** reaches US #13.
Feb [3] From the album, *Chip Away The Stone*, recorded at the Civic Auditorium, Santa Monica, CA, in April 1978, makes US #77.
Apr [7] Aerosmith takes part in the California Music Festival, at the Memorial Coliseum, Los Angeles, CA, before a crowd of 110,000, with Van Halen, Cheap Trick, Ted Nugent and the Boomtown Rats.
May The band begins recording ***Night In The Ruts*** at Media Sound and the Record Plant in New York.
July [28] They appear at the "World Series of Rock" concert at the Municipal Stadium, Cleveland, OH, with Journey, Ted Nugent and Thin Lizzy.
Dec Perry leaves the group, citing musical and personality conflicts with Tyler, brought on by an incident after a concert in Cleveland, OH, and is replaced on guitar by Jimmy Crespo, from New York band Flame. (He will form the Joe Perry Project with Ralph Morman (vocals), David Hull (bass) and Ronnie Stewart (drums), which will release ***Let The Music Do The Talking*** (1980) and ***I've Got The Rock'n'Rolls Again*** (1981), before breaking up the band in 1982.)

1980

Jan [19] ***Night In The Ruts***, produced by Aerosmith with Gary Lyons, reaches US #14. The band will embark on a US tour, which is cancelled after a few dates, when Tyler collapses onstage.
Feb [9] Their unlikely revival of the Shangri-Las' 1964 US #5 *Remember (Walkin' In The Sand)* peaks at US #67. Whitford leaves to form his own Whitford-St. Holmes Band with ex-Ted Nugent axeman Derek St. Holmes, Dave Hewitt and Steve Pace. He is replaced by Rick Dufay.

1981

Jan [24] Strong catalog seller ***Aerosmith's Greatest Hits*** makes US #53. (During the month, Tyler will be hospitalised after a serious motorcycle accident.)

1982

Oct [16] Eighth album ***Rock In A Hard Place***, produced by Douglas, Tyler and Tony Bongiovi at the Power Station, New York, and Criteria Studios, Miami, FL, reaches US #32.

1984

Feb [14] Perry and Whitford see Aerosmith backstage at the Orpheum in Boston, and agree to re-join.
Mar After a lengthy hiatus, the original Aerosmith line-up regroups, beginning rehearsals at a Howard Johnson hotel in Boston, with new managers Tim Collins and Steve Barrasso, who had managed the Joe Perry Project. The band will then embark on a major US "Back In The Saddle" reunion tour but, in familiar Aerosmith style, Tyler will collapse during a show in Springfield, IL.

1986

Jan Signed to Geffen Records the previous year for a reported five-album $7 million advance, the group's first new recording in three years, the Ted Templeman-produced ***Done With Mirrors***, recorded at Fantasy Studios in Berkeley, CA, reaches US #36.
May CBS/Columbia-issued ***Classics Live!*** makes US #84.
Sept [27] Run D.M.C.'s *Walk This Way*, an innovative mix of rap and heavy metal, with Tyler and Perry's contribution significantly updating the 1977 original, hits US #4, its double-act video clip having attracted heavy US MTV rotation.
Nov [21] The RIAA certifies sales of two million copies each of ***Aerosmith*** and ***Get Your Wings***.

1987

Sept [5] ***Permanent Vacation***, recorded in Vancouver, BC, Canada, with producer Bruce Fairbairn, becomes Aerosmith's first UK chart success, making #37.
[11] The band performs *Walk This Way* with Run D.M.C. at the fourth annual MTV Video Music Awards, held at the Universal Amphitheatre, Universal City, CA.
Oct [31] *Dude (Looks Like A Lady)*, the group's UK singles bow, makes UK #45.
Nov ***Permanent Vacation*** climbs to US #11, while the group recaptures its onstage reputation during the "Permanent Vacation" tour, which lasts for 12 months, racking up over 150 shows in 42 US states, Japan and Canada.
Dec [12] *Dude (Looks Like A Lady)*, their first US chart single in seven years, reaches US #14.

1988

Feb [17] "Aerosmith's Video Scrapbook" is certified gold by the RIAA.
Apr *Angel* peaks at UK #69. Currently supported on the US leg of their tour by Guns N' Roses, Aerosmith, whose members now reject the chemical and substance abuse excesses of their earlier days, insist on a rider in their contract with the opening act requesting that Guns N' Roses confine drug and alcohol activities to their own dressing room.
[30] *Angel*, confirming a major singles comeback, hits US #3.
Aug [20] *Rag Doll* reaches US #17.
Sept [7] They perform for the second straight year at the fifth annual MTV Video Music Awards, held at the Universal Amphitheatre.
Nov [22] The band's "3x5" video is certified gold by the RIAA.
Dec [21] ***Toys In The Attic*** (at five million) and ***Rocks*** (at three million) are awarded multiplatinum status by RIAA, while retrospective ***Gems*** peaks at US #133.

1989

Feb Whitford produces the fourth album by Boston rock trio the Neighborhoods, winners of the first WBCN "Rock'n'Roll Rumble" in 1979.
Aug [19] Tyler and Perry join Bon Jovi on stage at the Milton Keynes Bowl, Milton Keynes, Bucks., to sing *Walk This Way*.
Sept [12] The group donates instruments and stage clothing for a wall display, called the Aerosmithsonian, at the Hard Rock Café in Boston, in the presence of Mayor Ray Flynn.
[22] Their "Live Texxas Jam '69" video is certified gold by the RIAA.
[23] ***Pump***, again produced by Fairbairn, debuts at its UK #3 peak.
[30] Unabashed *Love In An Elevator*, taken from the album, reaches UK #13.
Oct [28] *Love In An Elevator* hits US #5, spurred by traditionally risqué "sex in an elevator" teasing promo clip.
Nov [8] *Love In An Elevator* is certified gold by the RIAA.
[10] ***Rock In A Hard Place*** is certified gold by the RIAA.
[14] The group embarks on its first European tour in 12 years. David Coverdale will join them on stage at London's Hammersmith Odeon, duetting on *I'm Down* during the nine-date UK leg. ***Pump*** hits US #5.
Dec During extensive North American dates, fans bring canned foods to a hometown Boston Garden concert, which the group passes on as a 20-ton food parcel to the Boston Food Bank.

1990

Feb [10] *Janie's Got A Gun* hits US #4, spurred by a David Fincher-directed promo clip.
[17] As music guests on NBC-TV's "Saturday Night Live", the band also takes part in a "Wayne's World" skit with Mike Myers and Dana Carvey, singing the home-cable spot spoof's title song, which becomes an in-demand bootleg item.
Mar [3] *Dude (Looks Like A Lady)*, reissued in the UK, now reaches UK #20.
[6] Aerosmith are inducted into Hollywood's Rock Walk on Sunset Boulevard, Los Angeles, during three sellout dates at the Great Western Forum, Inglewood, CA.
[8] The band is voted Best Heavy Metal Band in the 1989 **Rolling Stone** Critics' Award Picks.
Apr [19] At Boston's SKC Music Awards, Perry is voted Outstanding Guitarist, Hamilton voted Outstanding Bassist, ***Pump*** Outstanding Pop/Rock Album, *Janie's Got A Gun* Outstanding Song/Songwriter and Aerosmith Outstanding Pop/Rock Band.
[21] *Rag Doll* makes UK #42.
May [5] *What It Takes* hits US #9.
June [29] They play the first of two heavy metal bills, with Metallica, Warrant and the Black Crowes, at the Skydome, Toronto, ON, Canada. (A second gig will be played next day at Silver Stadium, Rochester, NY.)
July [28] Aerosmith performs at the Capital Center, Landover, MD, on the final date of the US part of another world tour.
Aug [18] On the day *The Other Side Of Me* reaches US #22, the group takes part in the "Monsters Of Rock" festival at Castle Donington, Leics., with Whitesnake, Poison, London Quireboys and Thunder, before a crowd of 72,500, with Jimmy Page performing with them for *Train Kept A-Rollin'*.
[20] Page joins the band on stage again at their London Marquee club gig, playing a blues jam which ends with *Immigrant Song*.
[31] The group participates in the Winterthurer Musikfestwochen festival at Winterthur, Switzerland.
Sept [1] *The Other Side* debuts at its UK #46 peak, as the band performs at the "Super Rock '90" festival in Mannheim, Germany, with Whitesnake, Poison, Dio and others.
[7] "Janie's Got A Gun" wins the Best Metal/Hard Rock Video and the Viewers' Choice categories, at the seventh annual MTV Video Music Awards, held again at the Universal Amphitheatre.
[8] Aerosmith headlines the opening night of the Las Vegas, NV, Hard Rock Café, before heading back for the Far East/Australia leg of its marathon "Pump" tour, which will resume in Japan on the 12th. (The 163-date trek will end in Australia the following month, after three million fans have seen the band in 15 countries.)
Nov [1] "Things That Go Pump In The Night" video is certified platinum by the RIAA.
Dec [18] "The Making Of Pump" is confirmed gold by the RIAA.
[22] *What It Takes* wins Top Album Rock Tracks category in **Billboard**'s The Year In Music chart round-up.

1991

Jan [28] Aerosmith is named Favorite Pop/Rock Band, Duo Or Group, and Favorite Heavy Metal/Hard Rock Artist, at the 18th annual American Music Awards, held at the Shrine Auditorium, Los Angeles.
Feb [20] They win Best Rock Performance By A Duo Or Group With Vocal category, for *Janie's Got A Gun*, at the 33rd annual Grammy awards, held at Radio City Music Hall, New York, at which they also perform *Come Together* as part of a tribute to Grammy Living Legend John Lennon.
Mar [3] Tyler and Perry present the 20th annual Juno Awards, at the Queen Elizabeth Theater, Vancouver, for the second consecutive year.
[7] Aerosmith is named Best Band in the annual **Rolling Stone** Readers' Picks music awards.
May The group, having finished its latest tour with a sellout concert at the Miami Arena, Miami, FL on April 22nd, begins work on a new album with producer Fairbairn in Vancouver.
Aug [16] Still signed to Geffen, the band inks a four-album deal with Sony Music which will come into

effect in 1995, and which will reportedly remunerate $10 million in advance payments (per album) and 22% royalties. The average age of band members will be over 45 when the deal kicks in.
Sept [5] "The Other Side" wins the Best Metal/Hard Rock Video category, at the eighth annual MTV Video Music Awards, held again at the Universal Amphitheatre.
Oct [13] The Wang Center Young At Arts Orchestra back Aerosmith on *Dream On* at the Wang Center.
Nov [14] The group is inducted into the Boston Garden Hall Of Fame alongside skating great Sonja Heine, basketball legend Bill Russell and Boston Bruins president and general manager Harry Sinden.
[21] Aerosmith makes a guest appearance, as cartoon characters, performing *Walk This Way* at Moe's Tavern on Fox-TV's "The Simpsons".
[27] They take part in ABC-TV's "MTV 10" anniversary special, offering a pre-taped version of their power ballad *Dream On*, accompanied by a 60-piece orchestra conducted by Michael Kamen.

1992

Jan [25] An exhaustive CBS/Columbia retrospective boxed-set ***Pandora's Box***, including the band's early hits, rare cuts and previously unreleased material, makes US #45 having been certified gold on the 14th by the RIAA, their 13th such sales achievement.
Apr [16] The band wins the Outstanding Rock Band and Outstanding Video ("Sweet Emotion") categories at the Boston Music Awards, held at the Wang Center, Boston.
May [19] They donate $10,000 to supporting a sexually-graphic exhibition, "Corporal Politics", at MIT's List Visual Arts Center, to replace a grant vetoed the previous week by the National Endowment for the Arts' acting chairman.
June [6] Tyler and Perry make guest appearances in "Guns N' Roses Invade Paris!" live Palais Hippodrome de Vincennes concert in Paris, France, broadcast on pay-per-view TV.
July [22] ***Classics Live*** is certified gold by the RIAA.

1993

Apr [7] The group wins the Outstanding Rock Band, Outstanding Male Vocalist (Tyler) and "Right To Rock" categories at the seventh annual Boston Music Awards, at the Wang Center.
[10] *Livin' On The Edge* debuts at its UK #19 peak.
May [1] Bruce Fairbairn-produced ***Get A Grip*** bows at its UK #2 peak, behind Cliff Richard's ***The Album***.
[8] ***Get A Grip*** debuts in pole position on the US chart.
[20] The group films the video for its forthcoming single *Cryin'* at the Central Congregational Church in Fall River, MA, where Lizzie Borden (acquitted of murdering her parents in 1892) used to worship.
June [2] Aerosmith embarks on the US leg of its 16-month world tour at the Kansas Expocentre, Topeka, KS.
[5] *Livin' On The Edge* reaches US #18.
July [3] *Eat The Rich* debuts at its UK #34 peak.
[21] ***Done With Mirrors*** is certified gold by the RIAA.
Aug [26] Aerosmith receives the inaugural star in Boston's Tower Records Walk Of Fame - a 26' brass star bearing the group's name, cemented into the store's landing.
Sept [2] The group performs its Viewers Choice Award winner, *Livin' On The Edge*, at the tenth annual MTV Awards held at the Universal Amphitheatre.
Oct [9] *Cryin'* reaches US #12, as the band guests again on "Saturday Night Live".
Nov [1] *Cryin'* is certified gold by the RIAA, as Columbia reissues the group's first 12 albums, now remastered on compact disc.
[13] *Cryin'* reaches UK #17.
Dec [18] *Amazing* debuts at its UK #57 peak.
[31] The group plays the first of two sellout dates at the Boston Garden.

1994

Jan [22] *Amazing* reaches US #24.
[25-26] During the Central and South American swing of its current tour, including an appearance at the annual Hollywood Rock Festival in Brazil, Aerosmith performs two sellout dates at the Sports Palace, Mexico City, Mexico.
Feb [1] The second US leg of the current tour opens at the Orlando Arena, Orlando Centroplex, Orlando, FL , before a sellout crowd of 11, 648.
[7] The group wins the Pop/Rock Band, Duo Or Group and Heavy Metal/Hard Rock Artist categories at the 21st annual American Music Awards at the Shrine Auditorium.
Mar [1] They perform *Livin' On The Edge* and win the Best Rock Vocal, Duo Or Group category at the 36th annual Grammy Awards at Radio City Music Hall.
Apr [27] The Japanese leg of the tour, set to end on May 13th in Tokyo, opens at the Yokohama Arena, Yokohama.
June [27] CompuServe begins a week-long promotion, during which fans can download Aerosmith music via the Internet. An historic event in the history of music delivery, it marks the first time a major-label band has released an entire audible song, namely the previously unissued *Head First*, via a computer network. With Geffen insisting that the recording will never be made commercially available in any other medium (and will only keep the cut on-line for seven days), it takes fans over one hour to download (though both Geffen and CompuServe waive fees for this unique experiment).
July [2] *Shut Up And Dance* bows at its UK #24 peak.
[30] *Crazy* reaches US #17, as the group plays the second of two dates at the Montreal Forum, Montreal, PQ, Canada, at the start of yet another series of North American dates.
Aug [20] *Sweet Emotion* charts for a week at UK #74.
[30] As the cartoon series "Spider Man" premieres on Fox-TV with its theme written and performed by Perry, Tyler sings *You're So Vain* with Carly Simon at Martha's Vineyard Agricultural Society concert in West Tisbury, MA.
Sept [8] "Cryin" wins Best Video and Best Group Video at the 11th annual MTV Video Music Awards held at Radio City Music Hall.
[11] The band hosts a fundraiser at Whitford's Norwell, MA home for Massachusetts Senator, Edward Kennedy.
Oct [1] The group appears at a promotional event at the Hard Rock Café in San Antonio, TX, set to open in January.
[21] ***Aerosmith's Greatest Hits*** reaches RIAA-certified sales of eight million.
[28] The RIAA certifies ***Classics Live II*** gold, ***Night In The Ruts*** platinum and ***Toys In The Attic*** multi-platinum, with sales of six million.
Nov [5] *Crazy*, coupled with *Blind Man*, debut at its UK #23 peak.
[12] ***Big Ones***, a 13-track best of with two new cuts, *Blind Man* and *Walk On Water*, hits UK #7 in its week of entry.
[19] ***Big Ones*** bows at its US #6 peak.
[24] The group wins the Best Rock Band and Best Rock Act categories at the inaugural MTV European Music Awards held at the Pariser Platz, Berlin, Germany.
[30] Tyler spray cans "Mama Kin's" on the front door of the yet-to-be opened club on Boston's Lansdowne Street, co-owned by Aerosmith and the Lyons Group.
Dec [4-7] A four-date Aerosmith "Cyberspace Tour '94" is launched on the Internet, America OnLine, CompuServe and Prodigy, to benefit the Electronic Frontier Foundation.
[19] The group plays its final date of 1994, which has seen audiences totalling close to a million and grossing in excess of $20 million, at the opening of "Mama Kin's" before a somewhat smaller crowd of 250, aired live on the local W-AAF and W-ZLX radio stations.
[31] *Blind Man* makes US #48.

1995

Jan [12] Tyler and Perry induct Led Zeppelin into the Rock and Roll Hall of Fame at the tenth annual induction dinner, and subsequently perform with Jimmy Page and Robert Plant on *Train Kept A-Rollin'* and a medley comprising *For Your Love, Bring It On Home To Me, Baby Please Don't Go* and *Long Distance Call*, at the post-dinner jam at New York's Waldorf Astoria Hotel.
[13] "Big Ones You Can Look At" video is certified gold by the RIAA.
[19] ***Box Of Fire*** is confirmed gold by the RIAA.
Feb [10] The RIAA also certifies multi-platinum sales of ***Permanent Vacation*** (five million) and ***Pump*** (seven million).
[28] Whitford and Kramer appear at the Massachusetts State House in Boston to pick up the 1995 Commonwealth Award from the Massachusetts Cultural Council and the Massachusetts Advocates for the Arts, Sciences And Humanities.
Mar [1] *Crazy* wins the Best Hard Rock Performance By A Duo Or Group With Vocal category at the 37th annual Grammy Awards held at the Shrine Auditorium.
[26] Tyler celebrates his birthday with brunch at the House of Blues in Cambridge, MA, and joins Perry onstage to perform with the Sons Of Glory.
Nov [7] The RIAA certifies multi-platinum sales of ***Big Ones*** (three million) and ***Get A Grip*** (seven million).
[9] The group plays a 90-minute set as the G Spots at the Middle East Downstairs club in Cambridge.
[21] Garth Brooks' ***Fresh Horses*** is released by Capitol Records (US) including his country re-styling of Aerosmith's *Fever*.

1996

Jan Aerosmith regroups in Miami, FL, with veteran hit producer Glen Ballard (who is coming off recent success with Alanis Morissette) to record a new album scheduled for release later in the year.

a-ha

Morten Harket (lead vocals); **Mags Furuholmen** (keyboards, vocals); **Pal Waaktaar** (guitar, vocals)

1980

Oct Living in the Oslo, Norway suburb of Manglerud, Furuholmen (b. Magne Furuholmen, Nov. 1, 1962, Oslo), his father having played in the Bent Solve Orchestra, and Waaktaar (b. Sept. 6, 1961, Oslo), who have been playing together since childhood, have formed the part-time band Spider Empire in 1977, musically influenced by the Doors and Jimi Hendrix. By 1979, the group has evolved into the four-man outfit Bridges, with Furuholmen, Waaktaar, Viggo Bondi (bass) and Oystein Jevanord (drums). The band now releases *Fakkeltog (Torchlight Procession)* on its own Vakenatt label, with only 1,000 copies pressed. The following year while working on its second release, Waaktaar and Furuholmen meet Harket (b. Sept. 14, 1959, Konigsberg, Norway), who has sung with Mercy, Laelia Anceps and, more recently, soul group Souldier Blue. The trio decides to produce a more commercial form of music, and Bridges dissolves. With Furuholmen coining the new name a-ha, easily memorized as a familiar exclamation in many languages, and recognising the Norwegian market as an ineffectual launch pad for major success, he and Waaktaar will travel to Britain in 1982 (without Harket) to secure label interest, though to little effect.

1983

Jan Undaunted and having completed further demos, the trio relocates to London, where they share an apartment and continue working on self-penned material.
June One particular track, *Lesson One*, impresses John Ratcliff, manager at Rendezvous Studios, where they are recording demos. Ratcliff plays the cut to former record company executive and Everly Brothers collaborator Terry Slater, who becomes their manager, and arranges showcase auditions for record companies at a London rehearsal studio.
Dec They return to Norway for Christmas, having been signed to a worldwide recording contract by

Warner Bros. Records.

1984

Jan *Lesson One*, now re-written by all three band members as *Take On Me*, is recorded in London with producer Tony Mansfield.

Oct *Take On Me* is issued in the UK after a successful Norwegian release, but sells approximately 300 copies.

1985

Apr *Love Is Reason*, also their follow-up in Norway, is issued.

May At Slater's suggestion, a-ha recuts the synthesizer-driven *Take On Me*, this time with Alan Tarney as producer, but it fails to score yet again.

June Disillusioned, the trio elects to spend the summer in Oslo.

July US Warner label issues *Take On Me*, and decides to spend $100,000 on a ground-breaking (and later award-winning) semi-animated video, created by Mike Patterson and Candice Reckinger and directed by Steve Barron, to help catch promotion time on MTV.

Sept a-ha flies to Los Angeles, CA, for a promo visit, as *Take On Me* receives its third UK release.

Oct [19] *Take On Me* tops the US chart, finally realizing its catchy, hook-laden potential on radio.

[26] At the third attempt *Take On Me* finally hits UK #2, lodged behind Jennifer Rush's *The Power Of Love*.

Nov ***Hunting High And Low*** hits UK #2 and US #15, highlighted by Harket's distinctive, smooth, often falsetto vocals and the band's melodic, predominantly synth-based pop style. Seven of its ten tracks are produced by Mansfield.

1986

Jan [25] Waaktaar-penned *The Sun Always Shines On TV* becomes their only UK chart-topper.

Feb [22] *The Sun Always Shines On TV* reaches US #20.

Mar The group begins recording its second album in London.

[17] ***Hunting High And Low*** is certified platinum by the RIAA.

Apr [19] *Train Of Thought*, remixed from their debut album, hits UK #8.

May [7] They perform at the "Montreux Pop Festival", Montreux, Switzerland.

June A 120-date world tour begins in Perth, W. Australia, Australia.

[21] Ballad *Hunting High And Low* hits UK #5.

July a-ha tours Japan, and visits Hawaii to complete work on its sophomore effort.

Sept [15] "Take On Me" wins the Best Concept Video, Best New Artist Video, Best Special Effects, Best Direction, Most Experimental and Viewers' Choice categories, while "The Sun Always Shines On TV" collects the Best Editing and Best Cinematography trophies at the third annual MTV Video Music Awards, broadcast simultaneously from the Universal Amphitheatre, Universal City, CA, and the Palladium, New York, NY. It is a record number of wins by one act for the fledgling ceremony.

Oct [11] Guitar-led *I've Been Losing You* hits UK #8. The largely self-produced, ten-track ***Scoundrel Days*** debuts at UK #2.

Nov [15] ***Scoundrel Days*** makes US #74.

1987

Jan [3] *Cry Wolf*, accompanied by another startling video using state-of-the-art visual trickery, hits UK #5, as the group plays three nights at London's Royal Albert Hall.

Feb A world tour ends at home in Oslo.

Mar [7] *Manhattan Skyline* reaches UK #13 (the band's first single to miss the Top 10), while *Cry Wolf* makes US #50 one week later.

July [11] *The Living Daylights*, a-ha's theme from the new James Bond movie, with lyrics by Waaktaar and music by John Barry, hits UK #5.

1988

Apr [2] *Stay On These Roads*, the title track from the trio's forthcoming album, hits UK #5.

May [14] ***Stay On These Roads***, its ten tracks either written or co-written by Waaktaar, debuts at its UK #2 peak, behind Fleetwood Mac's ***Tango In The Night***.

June [25] *The Blood That Moves The Body* reaches UK #25.

July [2] ***Stay On These Roads*** peaks at US #148.

Sept [10] The extracted *Touchy!* makes UK #11.

Nov [21] The group appears in the "Pop 88" segment at the Royal Variety Performance in London.

1989

Jan [14] *You Are The One* reaches UK #13. (By year's end, Harket will record an anti-pollution single with Björn Eidsvag and star in the movie "Kamilia And The Thief".)

1990

Oct [27] *Crying In The Rain*, the band's remake of the Everly Brothers' 1962 US #6, reaches UK #13.

Nov [3] ***East Of The Sun***, largely written by Furuholmen and Waaktaar, and produced by Chris Neil and Ian Stanley, reaches UK #12.

Dec [15] After 13 consecutive Top 30 singles, the piano-led, mid-tempo *I Call Your Name* stops at UK #44.

1991

Feb [26] Following its recent appearance at the "Rock In Rio II" festival in Brazil, a-ha performs at London's Hammersmith Odeon, during a short UK tour.

Apr [2] a-ha begins a five-date UK tour at the City Hall, Sheffield, S. Yorks.

Oct [26] *Move To Memphis* debuts at its UK #47 peak.

Nov [16] ***Headlines & Deadlines, The Hits Of a-ha***, a six-year retrospective collection, enters at its UK #12 peak, while a parallel video package, "Headlines & Deadlines", is also released.

Dec [2] *Take On Me* is honored for more than one million broadcast performances at the annual BMI Awards, held at London's Dorchester Hotel.

1992

May [14] The group performs at the fourth annual World Music Awards at the Sporting Club, Monte Carlo, Monaco, at which it also collects the World's Best Selling Norwegian Artist trophy.

1993

May [12] a-ha is again named Best Selling Norwegian Artist of the Year at the fifth annual World Music Awards, once more held at the Sporting Club.

[24] The band performs a one-off London show at the Ladbroke Grove Subterania to promote its forthcoming album.

June [12] After a recording hiatus of over two years, *Dark Is The Night* reaches UK #19.

[26] Its parent album ***Memorial Beach***, featuring additional musicians J.B. Bogeberg (bass) and Per Hillestad (drums) bows at its UK #17 peak, as Harket contributes his solo version of Frankie Valli's *Can't Take My Eyes Off You* to the "Coneheads" soundtrack.

Sept [25] *Angel* makes UK #41. With its follow-up *Shapes That Go Together* reaching UK #27 on Mar [24] the following year, frontman Harket elects to pursue a solo career which will begin with the UK #53 *A Kind Of Christmas Card* (Aug [19], 1995), and a second trailer for his debut solo album, *Spanish Steps* released in February the following year.

AIR SUPPLY

Graham Russell (guitar, vocals);
Russell Hitchcock (vocals)

1979

Deciding to form as a vocal duo after meeting in 1976 (while they are both working on a production of "Jesus Christ Superstar" in Melbourne, Victoria, Australia), Hitchcock (b. June 15, 1949, Melbourne) and Russell (b. June 1, 1950, Sherwood, Nottingham, Notts.) have signed to CBS/Columbia Records in July 1977 and recorded their debut album as Air Supply with producer Jimmy Horowitz, at Cherokee Studios in Los Angeles, CA. Its title cut *Love And Other Bruises,* their first Australian chart success at #2, has helped them secure a spot supporting Rod Stewart on the Antipodean and US legs of his 1978 "Footloose And Fancy Free" tour. Taking time off following the concert trek, during which Russell has written *Lost In Love* and *All Out Of Love* while living in Adelaide, S. Australia, Australia, while Hitchcock has returned home to Britain (to compose a rock opera about Robin Hood, called "Sherwood"), Air Supply now signs internationally to Arista Records, recruiting guitarist David Moyse (b. Nov. 5, 1957, Adelaide), keyboardist Frank Esler-Smith (b. June 5, 1948, London), drummer Ralph Cooper (b. Apr. 6, 1951, Coffs Harbour, New South Wales, Australia), Cristan Barker and semi-permanent band members for new album sessions. Current and future members will always revolve around Hitchcock (the consistent lead vocalist) and Russell (the band's main songwriter). Barker soon leaves and guitarist Rex Goh (b. May 5, 1951, Singapore, Singapore) and bassist David Green (b. Oct. 30, 1949, Melbourne) join.

1980

Feb The Russell-penned ballad *Lost In Love* is released in the UK, but interest is divided with a concurrently-released version by Demis Roussos and neither charts.

May [3] *Lost In Love* hits US #3 and establishes a rich harmonic sound, which will always appeal to the more Adult Contemporary tastes of American radio and audiences (the single will become **Billboard**'s Top AC Single Of The Year).

Sept [13] Equally lush ballad *All Out Of Love* hits US #2 and will also reach UK #11.

Oct [10] *All Out Of Love* is certified gold by the RIAA.

Nov [1] ***Lost In Love***, produced by Robie Porter, reaches US #22 and begins a two-year period of non-stop American chart action: *Every Woman In The World* hits US #5 (Jan [31] 1981); *The One That You Love* tops the US chart (and becomes another million-seller) on July [25] 1981. ***The One That You Love*** hits US #10 (Aug [8] 1981, certified platinum by the RIAA on October 7th 1981) reeling off: *Here I Am (Just When I Thought I Was Over You)* (Nov [21] US #5) and *Sweet Dreams* US #5 (Mar [20] 1982). Third Arista album ***Now And Forever*** reaches US #25 on Aug [2] 1982, spawning *Even The Nights Are Better*, reviving an obscure cut by soul trio Bama, which hits US #5 on Sept [4]. *Even The Nights Are Better* makes UK #44 (their second and last UK chart single), while *Young Love* breaks their major hit run in the US, stalling at #38 on Oct [23], the same position achieved by *Two Less Lonely People In The World* on Jan [8] 1983.

1982

Jan [25] They collect the Favorite Band, Duo Or Group, Pop/Rock trophy at the ninth annual American Music Awards, held at the Shrine Auditorium, Los Angeles.

1983

Feb [1] ***Now And Forever*** is certified platinum by the RIAA.

Oct [8] Melodramatic ballad *Making Love Out Of Nothing At All*, written and produced by Jim Steinman, recaptures lost US chart ground, hitting #2.

Nov ***Greatest Hits*** hits US #7. (The album's UK title is ***Making Love ... The Very Best Of Air Supply***.)

Dec [16] *Making Love Out Of Nothing At All* is certified gold by the RIAA.

1985

July [13] After a lengthy chart absence, and with the band now comprising Hitchcock, Russell, Cooper, Esler-Smith and new additions, Don Cromwell (bass), Ken Rarick (keyboards) and Wally Stocker (guitars), *Just As I Am*, produced by Bob Ezrin, reaches US #19.

[29] ***Air Supply*** is certified gold by the RIAA.

Aug [24] *The Power Of Love (You Are My Lady)* peaks at US #68, but will become a global hit for

Jennifer Rush, whose version will become a UK million-seller. Their fifth Arista album, ***Air Supply***, climbs to US #26.

1986

Sept [6] *Lonely Is The Night* makes US #76, and is the only chart success from the Bernard Edwards-produced parent album ***Hearts In Motion***, which peaks at US #84. Following a December 1987 seasonal album, ***Air Supply: The Christmas Album***, the duo will split to work on solo projects for the next two years.

1990

Hitchcock and Russell regroup as a duo and embark on a US tour, to support a new Air Supply album, ***The Earth Is ...***, released via their new deal with Giant Records. Hitchcock will also release the John Boylan-produced single *Caught In Your Web (Swear To Your Heart)*, from the movie "Arachnophobia".

1991

Mar [1] Longtime band member Elser-Smith dies of pneumonia in Melbourne.

1993

Nov [27] While their first, and still most popular American release, *Lost In Love*, was certified by the RIAA for two million US sales on November 25th 1991 and ***Greatest Hits*** certified for five million sales on March 10th, *Goodbye* now makes UK #66, taken from the July-issued ***The Vanishing Race***, produced by Humberto Gatica and supported by a world tour which began on July 10th at the Alameda County Fair, Pleasanton, CA. Following the April 1995 release of ***News From Nowhere*** and a fall promotion tour of Asia (where they remain popular as evidenced by BMG's Hong Kong division issuing a 20-track Air Supply karaoake disc and a two-hour non-music interview video in December 1995), Giant will also release ***Now And Forever - Greatest Hits Live*** in the same month, promoted by a US tour in January 1996 on a bill with ex-Men At Work frontman Colin Hay.

ALABAMA

Randy Owen (vocals, guitar); **Jeff Cook** (keyboards, fiddle); **Teddy Gentry** (bass, vocals); **Mark Herndon** (drums, vocals)

1969

Having grown up in cotton-farm country in Lookout Mountain near Fort Wayne, AL, and between them played in various school and family bands (notably the gospel group the Singing Owens and the Sand Mountain Chicken Pluckers) throughout the '60s, first cousins Owen (b. Dec. 14, 1949, Fort Payne) and Gentry (b. Jan. 22, 1952, Fort Payne) form the Young Country trio with another cousin, Cook (b. Aug. 27, 1949, Fort Payne) who is already a multi-instrumentalist, has been a local radio station deejay since the age of 14 and already fronted his own high-school bands the Viscounts and J.C. & The Chosen Few. Young Country will continue to perform on an ad-hoc basis over the next three years while Cook graduates in Electronics at Alabama Technical College, Owen obtains his degree in English at Jacksonville State University and Gentry works on his grand-father's farm and takes part-time jobs including carpet-laying and movie theater management. Reconvening in 1972 in Anniston, AL as Wild Country, the trio recruits drummer Bennett Vartanian and begins a regular weekend stint at the Canyon Land Amusement Park in Little River Canyon, AL.

1973

Against their families' advice, the group turns professional and relocates to Myrtle Beach, SC where it becomes the house band at the Bowery beach club. The following year, and having gone through four drummers including another cousin Jackie Owen, Wild Country recruits Rick Scott.

1977

July [23] Renamed Alabama and having secured a one-album deal with GRT Records in Nashville, TN, their US Country Chart debut is *I Wanna Be With You Tonight* which will reach #78. Now performing a mix of self-penned and cover material at over 300 gigs/year around the South-eastern states, they travel in a Dodge van named the Blue Goose. Following the messy demise of GRT they are contractually prevented from signing with another label and will manufacture and sell their own records at concerts for the next two years.

1979

Apr [1] Scott leaves the band to be replaced by classically-trained rock drummer Herndon (b. May 11, 1955, Springfield, MA).

Sept [29] Funding the recording of their own album, and originally released on their own Limbo International label, *I Wanna Come Over* has been picked up MDJ Records in Dallas, TX, after the group hired a radio promoter in Atlanta, GA to work the single, and now enters the US Country chart, set to reach #33.

1980

Feb [2] Follow-up, and last to be released by MDJ, *My Home's In Alabama* enters the Country chart on its way to #17. Its success secures the group an appearance on the "New Faces Show" held annually during the Country Radio Seminar in Nashville, which leads to a long-term recording contract with RCA Records negotiated by their manager Larry McBride.

July [19] ***My Home's In Alabama*** becomes the group's first crossover album success, entering the US chart on its way to #71.

Aug [16] Their RCA debut *Tennessee River* tops the US Country chart and begins an historic and unsurpassed string of consecutive US Country #1 singles: during the decade the group will notch up a further 26 chart-toppers, establishing Alabama as the most successful country band of all time. Only one 45, *Tar Top* (which is Owen's nickname), will fail to reach the summit (making #7). (The singles listed hereafter are those which achieve pop crossover success on the Hot 100.)

1981

Mar [28] ***Feels So Right*** produced by the group with McBride and Harold Shedd, begins a 161-week US chart run, during which it will reach #16.

Sept [5] The extracted *Feels So Right* reaches US #20. (The band will sever ties with McBride after he is jailed for fraud, though their successful relationship with producer Shedd will endure throughout the '80s.)

During the year the band performs at a fund-raising event in Fort Payne to benefit local schools. After it becomes apparent that the funds are diverted by the event's promoter, the group decides to hold an annual charity festival under the "June Jam" banner in its home town, the first of which will bow in 1981.

By year's end the band is voted the Country Music Association's (CMA) Instrumental and Vocal Group of the Year, and the Academy of Country Music's (ACM) Vocal Group of the Year.

1982

Mar [6] *Love In The First Degree*, written by Jim Hurt and Tim DuBois, reaches US #15.

[13] ***Mountain Music*** enters the US survey, set to reach #14. A groundbreaking set, it establishes a musical template for future country bands to emulate.

July [3] *Take Me Down* reaches US #18.

Sept [25] *Close Enough To Perfect* penned by Mark Chambers makes US #65.

June [11] *The Closer You Get* reaches US #38.

Nov [12] *Lady Down On Love* peaks at US #76.

The year's awards include Album of the Year (for ***Feels So Right***), Entertainer of the Year and Vocal Group of the Year (ACM), and the CMA's Entertainer of the Year, Instrumental and Vocal Group of the Year.

1983

Jan [17] The group wins the Favorite Band, Duo or Group category at the tenth annual American Music Awards held at Los Angeles' Shrine Auditorium, CA.

Feb [23] Alabama collects the Best Country Performance By A Duo Or Group With Vocal (for ***Mountain Music***) at the 25th annual Grammy Awards. The group's other awards for the year will include Entertainer of the Year and Vocal Group of the Year (ACM), and the CMA's Entertainer of the Year, Vocal Group of the Year and Album of the Year (***The Closer You Get***) which hits US #10 during a 70-week chart-ride.

1984

Jan [16] The group wins Favorite Band, Duo or Group, Favorite Album, Country and Favorite Video Country categories at the 11th annual American Music Awards held at the Shrine Auditorium.

Feb [11] ***Roll On*** enters the US chart set to make #21, [28] Alabama collects the Best Country Performance By A Duo Or Group With Vocal (for ***The Closer You Get***) at the 25th annual Grammy Awards. The group's other awards for the year will include Entertainer of the Year, Album of the Year and Vocal Group of the Year (ACM), and the CMA's Entertainer of the Year honor.

June [16] *When We Make Love* makes US #72.

Oct [25] The RIAA certifies sales of two million copies of ***The Closer You Get***.

1985

Jan [28] Alabama wins the Favorite Band, Duo or Group Country category at the 12th annual American Music Awards again staged at the Shrine Auditorium.

Feb [23] ***40 Hour Week*** begins a 40-week US chart tenure set to make #28.

July [30] The RIAA ratifies multi-platinum sales of ***Feels So Right*** (four million), ***Mountain Music*** (four million) and ***The Closer You Get*** (three million).

Nov [15] ***Alabama Christmas*** is certified platinum by the RIAA.

The year's awards include ACM's Album of the Year (***Roll On***), Entertainer of the Year and Vocal Group Of The Year.

[23] Festive collection, ***Christmas*** enters the US chart, climbing to #75.

1986

Jan [27] Alabama nabs the Favorite Band, Duo or Group Country and Favorite Album Country trophies at the 13th annual American Music Awards held at the Shrine Auditorium.

Mar [1] ***Greatest Hits*** enters the US survey, set to make #24.

July [15] "Alabama's Greatest Video Hits" is certified platinum by the RIAA.

Aug [20] The RIAA certifies sales of two million copies of ***My Home's In Alabama***.

Oct [25] ***The Touch*** begins a 30-week chart ride, making US #42.

Award honors for the year continue with ACM's annual nod for Entertainer of the Year and Vocal Group of the Year.

Nov [29] Their cover of the Carpenters' 1981 US #16 hit *Touch Me When We're Dancing* becomes Alabama's 20th US Country chart-topper.

1987

Jan [6] ***The Touch*** is certified platinum by the RIAA.

[26] Alabama wins the Favorite Band, Duo or Group Country, Favorite Album Country and Favorite Video, Duo Or Group categories at the 14th annual American Music Awards staged at the Shrine Auditorium.

Feb [14] *Deep River Woman*, with Lionel Richie, makes US #71. (In reaching UK #17 the previous month, it will be the only time a record featuring the group will ever chart in the UK.)

Oct [17] ***Just Us*** enters the US survey, set to make #55.

1988

Jan [25] The group wins the Favorite Band, Duo or Group Country category at the 15th annual American Music Awards held again at the Shrine Auditorium.
June [25] Performance set ***Alabama Live*** enters the US chart, set to peak at #76.
Sept [9] ***Just Us*** is certified gold by the RIAA.

1989

Jan [30] Alabama wins the Favorite Band, Duo or Group Country category at the 16th annual American Music Awards held as usual at the Shrine Auditorium.
Feb [18] Variously produced by Barry Beckett, Josh Leo and Larry Lee, ***Southern Star*** begins a 21-week US chart visit, set to make #62.
Oct [25] The RIAA certifies multi-platinum sales of ***40 Hour Week*** (two million), ***Alabama Greatest Hits*** (three million) and ***Roll On*** (three million).

1990

Jan [22] The band nabs the Favorite Band, Duo or Group Country category at the 17th annual American Music Awards held at the Shrine Auditorium.
June [1] During its current US tour with newcomer Clint Black, the band performs at the Patriot Center, George Mason University, Fairfax, VA, a sellout grossing $195,332.
[23] ***Pass It On Down*** makes US #57.
July [26] "Pass It On Down" is certified multi-platinum (100,000 units) by the RIAA.

1991

Jan [28] Alabama wins the Favorite Band, Duo or Group Country category at the 18th annual American Music Awards staged at the Shrine Auditorium.
Apr [13] *Down Home* becomes the band's 30th US Country #1 single.
Dec [14] ***Greatest Hits, Vol.2*** makes US #72.

1992

Jan [27] For the tenth consecutive year, the group collects the Favorite Band, Duo or Group Country trophy at the 19th annual American Music Awards held as always at the Shrine Auditorium.
Nov [28] ***American Pride*** reaches US #46.

1993

Jan [25] Once again, Alabama wins the Favorite Band, Duo or Group Country category at the 20th annual American Music Awards staged at the Shrine Auditorium.
June [24] The RIAA certifies platinum sales of ***American Pride***, ***Pass It On Down*** and ***Southern Star***.
Nov [3] ***Live*** is certified platinum by the RIAA.
[13] Co-produced by the band with Teddy Gentry and longtime helmsmen Leo and Lee, ***Cheap Seats*** makes US #76.

1994

Jan [27] ***Cheap Seats*** is certified gold by the RIAA.
Feb [7] The group is named the Favorite Band Duo Or Group, Country category at the 21st annual American Music Awards held at the Shrine Auditorium.

1995

Jan [30] As ever, Alabama is hailed Favorite Band, Duo or Group/Country adding the Favorite Album Country trophy for ***Read My Mind*** at the 22nd annual American Music Awards staged at its usual venue.
May [27] ***Greatest Hits III*** reaches US #57.
July [31] The RIAA certifies platinum sales of ***Greatest Hits, Volume II*** and multi-platinum sales of ***Greatest Hits*** (four million).
Aug [17] Another US tour kicks off at the Celeste Center, Ohio State Fair, Columbus, OH, grossing $106,835.
Oct [28] ***In Pictures***, co-produced by Emory Gordy Jr. with Alabama, makes US #100.
Nov [21] **Greatest Hits Volume III** is certified platinum by the RIAA.

1996

Jan [11] ***In Pictures*** is confirmed by the RIAA as Alabama's 18th gold album, easily the record for any country band.

THE ALARM

Mike Peters (guitar, vocals); **Dave Sharp** (guitar); **Eddie MacDonald** (bass); **Nigel Twist** (drums)

1981

Sept After playing together for four years in Rhyl, Clwyd, Wales, first as punk band the Toilets, and then as mod group 17 (recording *Don't Let Go* backed with *Bank Holiday Weekend* on the Vendetta label), the quartet, comprising Peters (b. Feb. 25, 1959, Prestatyn, Clwyd, Wales), Sharp (b. Jan. 28, 1959, Salford, Lancs.), MacDonald (b. Nov. 1, 1959, St. Asaph, S. Glamorgan, Wales) and Twist (b. July 18, 1958, Manchester, Lancs.), makes a fresh start as the Alarm, after Dexy's Midnight Runners fire them as support band on a UK tour because they are allegedly not good enough, and after Peters has been inspired by seeing U2 at London's Marquee club, deciding to embrace a similar musical approach. The group now records *Unsafe Building* in a Manchester studio for its own White Cross label, pressing 2,000 copies to sell at gigs and to use as demos for audition, before moving to London in October to continue live work and search for a more permanent record deal.

1982

Aug After support slots for the Jam, U2 and the Beat, and gaining music press support and industry interest, Alarm signs to Miles Copeland's I.R.S. Records.
Oct Its label debut *Marching On* garners good reviews, but few sales.

1983

Oct [15] The band's chart bow, the MacDonald and Peters-penned *68 Guns*, reaches UK #17, helped by the group's first BBC1-TV "Top Of The Pops" appearance.
Nov The band records an album at the Abbey Road and Good Earth studios in London, with producer Alan Shacklock.

1984

Jan [2] The group takes part in "The Big One" peace benefit concert at London's Victoria Apollo.
[28] *Where Were You Hiding When The Storm Broke* reaches UK #22.
Mar [3] Alarm's debut album ***Declaration*** hits UK #6 demonstrating an anthemic rock approach, which will remain in the shadow of U2 and Simple Minds throughout the band's career.
Apr *The Deceiver* peaks at UK #51.
[14] ***Declaration*** makes US #50, as a five-track EP, ***The Alarm***, peaks at US #126, both boosted by a current North American tour.
Nov *The Chant Has Just Begun* stalls at UK #48.

1985

Mar [23] *Absolute Reality* reaches UK #35.
Oct ***Strength***, produced by Mike Howlett and entirely written by MacDonald and Peters, climbs to UK #18.
[5] Extracted title track *Strength* makes UK #40.

1986

Jan [25] *Spirit Of '76*, an affectionate time-warp ode to punk music, reaches UK #22.
Feb [8] *Strength* makes US #61, with parent album ***Strength*** set to peak at US #39 one week later.
May *Knife Edge* makes UK #43.
June Alarm joins the Bangles, the Go-Go's, Bob Marley, R.E.M., Sting and others, contributing unreleased live and studio tracks to ***Live! For Life***, to raise funds for the AMC Cancer Research Center.
July [5] ***Live! For Life*** makes US #105.
[11-12] Alarm supports Queen for two nights at Wembley Stadium, Wembley, Middx.

1987

Oct [24] *Rain In The Summertime*, the first fruits of a fresh recording period, reaches UK #18.
Nov [14] ***Eye Of The Hurricane***, produced by John Porter, debuts at its UK #23 peak and will make US #77.
Dec *Rescue Me*, taken from the album, charts fleetingly at UK #48.

1988

Jan [16] U2-esque *Rain In The Summertime* peaks at US #71.
Feb *Presence Of Love (Laugherne)* makes UK #44 and will stop at US #77 on Apr [16].
July Group embarks on a 2½-month US tour supporting Bob Dylan.
Nov [5] ***Electric Folklore Live***, recorded at the Wang Center, Boston, MA, on April 26th, 1988, debuts at its UK #62 peak.
[12] ***Electric Folklore Live*** peaks at US #167.

1989

Sept [23] *Sold Me Down The River* makes UK #43.
[30] ***Change***, produced by Tony Visconti, bows at its UK #13 peak. (The band also records a Welsh-language version, ***Newid***, only available in their home country.)
Nov ***Change*** makes US #75.
[11] Lush choral effort *A New South Wales*, bemoaning the coal-dust past of their native Wales and featuring the Morriston Orpheus Male Voice Choir, makes UK #31.
[14] The band begins a substantial US tour with the first of two Los Angeles, CA concerts, set to end in New York, NY on December 14th.
[25] Hard-rocking *Sold Me Down The River* makes US #50.

1990

Feb [3] *Love Don't Come Easy* makes UK #48.
[5] The band's "No Frontiers" UK tour ends at London's Brixton Academy.
Oct [27] *Unsafe Building 1990*, an update of their earliest recording, peaks at UK #54.
Nov [24] A 15-track retrospective collection, ***Standards***, charts for a week at UK #47, while a similarly-titled parallel lyrics book is published.
Dec The group releases a cover version of John Lennon's seasonal *Happy Xmas (War Is Over)*.
[2] Sharp plays a solo date at London's Acoustic Room.
[15] ***Standards*** bows at its US #177 peak.

1991

Feb Sharp cuts the solo album ***Hard Travlin'*** at the Hit Factory in New York with producer Bob Johnston, and plays selected acoustic gigs throughout the North-eastern US.
May [4] Midway through a 20-date UK tour, ***Raw***, which will prove to be the Alarm's final studio album, bows at its UK #33 peak and will chart for a week at US #161 on May [18] (its title cut has already stalled at UK #51 on Apr [13]).
June [30] The band performs its last gig at London's Brixton Academy, after which it will split following a decade-long career. Frontman Peters will go on to form the Poets Of Justice, which make its UK tour debut in the summer of 1992, before releasing his ***Breathe*** in October 1994 on the Crai label.

ALICE IN CHAINS

Layne Staley (vocals); **Jerry Cantrell** (guitar); **Mike Inez** (bass); **Sean Kinney** (drums)

1989

Apr Although an earlier unit with the same name was formed by singer Staley (b. Aug. 22, 1967, Bellevue, WA) while he was still attending high school, he has assembled a more permanent Alice In Chains in Seattle, WA, in February 1987, having teamed with Cantrell (b. Mar. 18, 1966, Tacoma, WA) at a local music warehouse facility called the Music Bank. Cantrell has introduced bassist Mike Starr (b. Apr. 4, 1966, Honolulu, HI) with whom he has been in a local metal outfit, Gypsy Rose, who in turn has brought in Kinney (b. May 27, 1966, Seattle) who is dating his sister. The band's self-penned, lyrically-skewed material dealing primarily with death and drug abuse, aptly fused with a grunge metal music bed has led the group's local popularity as one of the darker proponents of the burgeoning Seattle grunge scene, a notoriety which has also brought label attention which now peaks with its signing to Columbia Records.

1990

June The band's first release, the five-track *We Die Young* EP is issued as the group graduates to opening slots for the likes of Poison.
Aug Alice In Chains' debut album***Facelift*** is released in the US.
Sept The band's first headlining tour bows at the Marquee club, Westminster, CA, and will include a sold-out date in October at New York's Cat club.
Nov Further dates ensue with the band opening for Iggy Pop on a US jaunt.
Dec A concert at Seattle's Moore Theatre is filmed by director Josh Taft for subsequent release as "Live Facelift".

1991

Jan [28] Alice In Chains loses out in the Favorite Heavy Metal Artist category at the 18th annual American Music Awards, held at the Shrine Auditorium, Los Angeles, CA. (The band performs *Would?* in Cameron Crowe's filming of the movie "Singles", shot in Seattle.)
Feb [8] The band performs at KNAC Radio's 5th anniversary concert at Long Beach Convention, Long Beach, CA (with Ozzy Osbourne and L.A. Guns), a 13,230 sell-out grossing $192,630, with proceeds benefitting the Children of the Night charity. Later in the month the group will undertake a European tour opening for Megadeth.
May [16] Heavy-metal package tour "Clash of the Titans" opens at the Starplax Amphitheater, Dallas, TX, with Alice In Chains, Anthrax, Megadeth and Slayer on the bill.
July [6] ***Facelift*** finally peaks at US #42.
Aug The group begins a six-month tour as the opening act for Van Halen, and appears on ABC-TV's "In Concert".
Nov Its second EP ***Sap*** is released in the US.
Dec [1] Believing that November has 31 days, Cantrell spends the day hunting with his brother, and completely misses tonight's gig (Columbia will buy him a pocket calendar for Christmas).

1992

Jan Three months of recording begins, helmed by producer Dave Jerden in Los Angeles, CA.
Sept [15] A US tour opening for Ozzy Osbourne and set to end in Norfolk, VA on November 2nd, begins at the Barton Coliseum, Arkansas State Fairgrounds, Little Rock, AR, a gig grossing $200,000. (During the tour Staley will break his leg riding during an off-road vehicle accident.)
[25] During a gig at the State Fair Grandstand, Oklahoma City, OK, there are two stabbings and 20 arrests.
Oct [6] Grimly-themed, drug and hell-obsessed album ***Dirt*** hits US #6.
[24] ***Dirt*** charts for a week at UK #53.

1993

Jan [21] The group appears on BBC1-TV's "Top Of The Pops".
[23] *Would?* debuts at its UK #19 peak.
[30] ***Dirt*** re-charts in the UK at #42.
During the month, Starr performs his last gig with the band at the "Hollywood Festival" in Rio de Janeiro, Brazil. He will be replaced by bassist Mike Inez (b. May 14, 1966, San Fernando, CA) in time for its European tour which kicks off late in the month.
Mar [20] *Them Bones* bows at its UK #26 pinnacle.
June [5] *Angry Chair* enters at its UK #33 peak as the band begins touring as part of this summer's US Lollapalooza caravan trek. (The film soundtrack album to "The Last Action Hero" is also released this month (US) including two new Alice Chains cuts, *What The Hell Have I?* and *A Little Bitter*.)
Aug [10] ***Facelift*** is certified platinum by the RIAA for one million US sales.
Sept [2] "Would?" wins the Best Video From A Film category at the tenth annual MTV Video Music Awards, held in Los Angeles, CA. (With Lollapalooza dates completed, the band re-groups at Seattle's London Bridge Studio, a seven-day residence which will spawn the seven-track EP ***Jar of Flies***.)
Oct [23] *Down In A Hole* becomes the group's fourth consecutive single to climax in its first chart week, at UK #36, as the band undertakes its four continent, six-week "Down In Your Hole" tour.
Dec ***Dirt*** is certified double platinum by the RIAA for two million US sales.

1994

Jan [18] ***SAP*** is confirmed gold by the RIAA.
Feb [5] Paired for UK-only release, ***Jar Of Flies/Sap*** hits #4.
[12] ***Jar Of Flies*** EP enters the US Album chart at #1, with sales in excess of 141,000, becoming the first EP ever to top **Billboard**'s albums survey.
July [25] Alice In Chains pulls out of the opening slot for Metallica's 20-date US "Shit In The Sheds" tour, one day prior to its opening at the Velodrome Field, Cal State Dominguez Hills, CA, when Cantrell and Kinney quit due to Staley's alleged drug problem.
Dec [31] Staley, having formed a parallel ad-hoc unit (initially called the Gacy Bunch and now named Mad Season) with other Seattle musicians, Pearl Jam's Mike McCready, John Baker Saunders and Screaming Trees' Barrett Martin, performs with the band at a New Year's Eve gig in Seattle. (The quartet will release ***Above*** on March 7th the following year.)

1995

Jan [31] ***Dirt*** is certified triple-platinum by the RIAA for three million US sales.
May Kinney, Inez and Cantrell, who have regrouped to work on new material at the end of last year, invite Staley to rejoin the band.
Sept [19] ***Jar Of Flies*** EP is certified by the RIAA for two million sales.
Oct Sony (US) releases the enhanced-CD version ***Jar of Flies*** with multimedia interactive elements added.
[31] Reunited members hold a vinyl-release party (for the forthcoming ***Alice In Chains*** album) at the Weathered Wall club in Seattle.
Nov [11] *Grind* bows at its UK #23 peak.
[18] ***Alice In Chains***, recorded at Seattle's Bad Animal studio and produced by Toby Wright, enters at its UK #37 high, but will drop off the survey after only two weeks.
[25] ***Alice In Chains*** debuts at US #1.

1996

Jan [2] ***Alice In Chains*** is certified platinum by the RIAA for one million US sales. (***Twisted Willie***, a tribute album to Willie Nelson including Kinney performing *Time Of The Preacher* with Johnny Cash and others, and Cantrell's solo version of *I've Seen All Of This World I Care To See* is released in the US.)
Feb [10] *Heaven Beside You* debuts at its UK #35 peak.

ALL ABOUT EVE

Julianne Regan (vocals); **Tim Bricheno** (guitar); **Andy Cousin** (bass); **Mark Price** (drums)

1985

The band, taking its name from Joseph L. Mankiewicz's 1950 film starring Bette Davis, forms in London around the existing long-term partnership of Regan (b. June 30, 1962, Coventry, Warks.,) who has returned to her father's Sligo, Eire birthplace at 16, before relocating to Coventry the following year and becoming a music journalist, and Bricheno (b. July 6, 1963, Huddersfield, Yorks.), and launches its own independent record label Eden, through which a succession of increasingly popular UK singles, including *D For Desire* and the anthemic *In The Clouds*, produced by Bram Tchaikovsky, will be released. With Cousin (b. June 28, 1963, Huddersfield), a friend of Bricheno with whom he has played in Gene Loves Jezebel and X-Mal Deutschland, now rounding out the trio, the group will gig locally for the next 18 months, refining its "hippie-goth" image.

1986

Oct Close links are established with goth-rock band the Mission: Regan adds vocals to their album ***God's Own Medicine***, including the single *Severina*, while the Mission's Wayne Hussey and Simon Hinkler produce All About Eve's *Our Summer*. The band will also be the support act on the Mission's major autumn UK tour.

1987

May [2] *Our Summer* hits UK Independent chart #3. Price (b. Aug. 10, 1959, Nelson, Lancs.), who has had an early taste of stardom wheeling a bicycle up a hill in a UK TV commercial for Hovis bread, joins on drums.
Aug [15] *Flowers In Our Hair* also hits #3 on the UK Independent chart, although the band is already signed to Phonogram Records' Mercury label, which has become aware of the act's burgeoning cult following. During the month the band performs at the annual "Reading Rock Festival", Reading, Berks.
Nov [21] *In The Clouds*, re-released by Mercury, makes UK #47.

1988

Feb [6] *Wild Hearted Woman*, from the debut album ***All About Eve***, makes UK #33.
[27] ***All About Eve***, mainly produced by Paul Samwell-Smith, bows at its UK #7 peak. The album's success coincides with their first large-venue sellout date, at London's Hammersmith Odeon.
Apr [23] *Every Angel*, also from the album and produced by Richard Gottehrer, climbs to UK #30.
Aug [20] Ballad *Martha's Harbour* hits UK #10.
Nov [19] *What Kind Of Fool* reaches UK #29.
Dec The group enters a recording studio in Oxfordshire to begin work on its sophomore project.

1989

Aug [19] Regan plays an acoustic set with Fairport Convention at the latter's annual "Cropredy Festival", Cropredy, Oxon.
Sept [29] *Road To Your Soul*, from a forthcoming album, makes UK #37.
Oct [27] ***Scarlet And Other Stories*** hits UK #9.
Nov [17-18] A short UK tour ends with two nights at London's Hammersmith Odeon.
Dec [23] *December* makes UK #34.

1990

Apr [28] *Scarlet* stops at UK #34, as their video collection "Evergreen" is released.
June [21] Bricheno quits to join Sisters Of Mercy, his interim replacement being Marty Willson-Piper from the Church.
Dec The band begins recording tracks for a new album at the Jam Studios in London and Jacobs Studio in Farnham, Surrey, with producer Warne Livesey.

1991

June [15] *Farewell Mr. Sorrow* bows at its UK #36 peak.
Aug [17] *Strange Way* climbs to UK #50.
Sept [7] ***Touched By Jesus*** enters at its UK #17 pinnacle.
Oct [7] The group embarks on a UK tour at Manchester's Academy, Gtr. Manchester, set to end on the 22nd at London's Brixton Academy. (The band splits from Phonogram, following a recent dispute, allegedly owing the label £750,000, before signing to MCA Records.)
[19] *The Dreamer* makes UK #41.

1992

May The band finishes its MCA debut at Hook End Manor studios.
Nov [7] ***Ultraviolet*** charts for a week at UK #46. The extracted *Phased* (issued as part of an EP) has already peaked at UK #38 on Oct [10], while *Some Finer Day* will chart for a week at UK #57 (Nov [28]).
[20] The group completes a nine-date UK tour at London's Town & Country.

1993

Mar With Mercury having recently issued the retrospective ***Winter Words - Hits And Rarities***, the band dissolves: Cousin will join the Mission; Bricheno forms his own band, CNN while Regan will release a single on Rough Trade under the name Harmony Ambulance, write material with Suede's Bernard Butler before signing a solo deal with Permanent Records in early 1995.)

THE ALLMAN BROTHERS BAND

Duane Allman (guitar); **Gregg Allman** (keyboards, guitar, vocals); **Dickey Betts** (guitar, vocals); **Berry Oakley** (bass); **Butch Trucks** (drums); **Jaimoe Johanson** (drums)

1966

Aug Having formed the Kings together in 1960, veterans of Miami, FL-based bands the Y-Teens, the Shufflers, the Escorts, the House Rockers, and now the Allman Joys, playing teen dances at the YMCA and then Daytona clubs like the Martinique, brothers Duane (b. Howard Duane Allman, Nov. 20, 1946, Nashville, TN) and Gregg Allman (b. Dec. 8, 1947, Nashville), sons of an Army sergeant murdered on Christmas leave during the Korean War, have relocated to Daytona Beach, FL from Lebanon, TN in 1958, and, with bassist Bob Keller and drummer Maynard Portwood, now record demos of *Spoonful*, *Crossroads* and *Shapes Of Things* at Bradley's Barn in Nashville. This occurs after singer J.D. Loudermilk has seen the band at the Briar Patch in Nashville, and recommended them to Buddy Killen at Dial Records.

1967

Feb The Allman Joys disperse, with Duane and Gregg moving to Decatur, GA, where they join the Five Minutes, which includes Paul Hornsby (piano/guitar), Pete Carr (bass) and Johnny Sandlin (drums). The band moves to St. Louis, MO, reverting to the Allman Joys name and then Almanac.
June Almanac moves to Los Angeles, CA, at the suggestion of Bill McEuen, who has seen them in a St. Louis club. The group signs with Liberty Records, renaming to Hour Glass.
Aug The band begins recording its debut album, also named ***Hour Glass*** at Liberty Sound Studios, Los Angeles.
Oct [19-21] Hour Glass supports Eric Burdon & the Animals at the Fillmore West, San Francisco, CA.

1968

Jan The group records its sophomore effort ***Power Of Love***.
Apr A third Hour Glass album is recorded at Rick Hall's Fame Studio in Muscle Shoals, AL, but is rejected by Liberty, and Hornsby, Sandlin and Carr, disillusioned with the label, quit.
June The brothers return to Jacksonville, FL, playing informally with the 31st Of February, a band run by Trucks (b. Jacksonville), who has known the Allmans since touring with the Allman Joys when a member of the Bitter End, occasionally recording demos with them (later issued as ***Duane And Gregg*** in 1973).
Sept The 31st Of February, also comprising guitarist Scott Boyer and bassist David Brown, record at TK Studios in Hialeah, FL. Trucks asks them to help record the group's second album, uncredited as they are still signed to Liberty.
Nov Hall, impressed by Duane's guitar playing, invites him back to Fame as a salaried session man. His contributions to tracks by Wilson Pickett (it is Allman's idea that Pickett record Lennon/McCartney's *Hey Jude*), Arthur Conley, King Curtis and Clarence Carter for Atlantic prompt the label's Jerry Wexler to have him back Aretha Franklin and record material of his own for a projected solo album. (Wexler buys out Duane's contract from Hall for $15,000.) Duane and Gregg are unable to record under their names as they still owe Liberty an album, so Gregg returns to Los Angeles to honor the contract and cut tracks.

1969

Mar Georgia-based Phil Walden, about to form the Atlantic-distributed Capricorn Records, suggests to Duane that he form a band. Allman hires Johanson (b. John Lee Johnson, July 8, 1944, Gulfport, MS), with whom he has worked at Fame and who has toured with Percy Sledge, Otis Redding, Joe Tex and Clifton Chenier, and they go to Jacksonville and recruit old friend Oakley (b. Apr. 4, 1948, Chicago, IL), who has toured with Tommy Roe's back-up band the Romans, to form a Hendrix/Cream-style trio. While there, they begin playing free concerts with Oakley's band Second Coming, which also includes Betts (b. Dec. 12, 1943, West Palm Beach, FL). With Trucks now joining, Walden's hoped-for trio becomes a quintet. Duane, against the wishes of the others, insists on Gregg becoming the group's vocalist. Walden relocates the band to Macon, GA, and puts them on the road throughout the year. (Over the next 2½ years, the group will play over 500 US dates, its first major gig being third on a Blood, Sweat & Tears-headlining bill at the Fillmore East, New York, NY.)
May [11] The band performs at the Piedmont Driving Club, Atlanta, GA, the first of a series of free open-air rock festivals in the area to be headlined by the group.
Sept They make their freshman recordings at Atlantic's New York studios, before becoming the first act to record in Capricorn's own studio.

1970

Feb Their debut album ***Allman Brothers Band***, on Atlantic's Atco label, makes US #188, but is more popular in the South, where the band starts extensive touring, as Duane continues session work between bookings.
Mar [11] King Curtis' *Games People Play*, on which Duane is featured guitarist, wins the Best R&B Instrumental Performance category at the 12th annual Grammy Awards.
July [3] The band plays at the second annual "Atlanta International Pop Festival", alongside Jimi Hendrix, Jethro Tull, B.B. King and others.
Aug [26] Duane starts recording as part of Derek & the Dominos at Miami's Criteria Studios. Eric Clapton has invited him to join after seeing him play with the Allman Brothers, at the recommendation of producer Tom Dowd. A double album is finished in less than ten days. Clapton will later say that Allman was "the catalyst" of this whole project, which will become the ***Layla*** album, and Allman's guitar duetting with Clapton on the title track will become his most famous work outside the Brothers' band.
Sept Dissatisfied with recording results from Capricorn Studios, they move to Atlantic's New York studios, with Adrian Barber producing.
Dec Dowd-produced ***Idlewild South***, named after their Macon farmhouse base, is released, set to make US #38.

1971

Jan [9] The Allman Brothers' first chart single, *Revival (Love Is Everywhere)*, makes US #92.
[28-31] The group plays at the Fillmore West, San Francisco, with Hot Tuna.
Mar [12-13] Switching coasts, the band performs at the Fillmore East in New York, on a bill with Elvin Bishop and Johnny Winter, the latter date being recorded for subsequent album release.
[22] The entire group is arrested in Jackson, AL, for suspected possession of heroin and marijuana.
June [27] As venue regulars, the Allmans headline the last night at the Fillmore East, on a bill with Albert King, the J. Geils Band, the Beach Boys and Mountain.
Aug [17] Duane, and musicians he has worked with on Herbie Mann's ***Push***, play at the funeral of King Curtis, murdered in New York days earlier.
Sept Capricorn-released ***At Fillmore East***, effectively capturing their primal blues rock style and recorded on March 12-13th, reaches US #13.
Oct [25] ***At Fillmore East*** is certified gold by the RIAA.
[29] Returning from wishing Oakley's wife, Linda, a happy birthday, Duane Allman crashes his motorbike in an effort to avoid a truck. After three hours of emergency surgery, he dies in the Macon Medical Center.
Nov [1] The band performs at Duane's funeral, joined by Thom Doucette (harmonica), Dr. John (guitar), Bobby Caldwell (drums) and Delaney Bramlett (vocals).

1972

Apr [2] The group participates in the "Mar Y Sol Festival", Vega Baja, Puerto Rico.
[13] Still rising ***Eat A Peach*** is certified gold by the RIAA.
May ***Eat A Peach***, which includes the last three tracks recorded by Duane, hits US #4.
[13] *Ain't Wastin' Time No More* peaks at US #77, as ***Duane & Gregg Allman*** makes US #129.
Aug [19] *Melissa* stalls at US #86, belying its popularity as a future live favorite and group classic.
Nov [11] Oakley is killed when his motorbike collides with a bus, only three blocks from the site of Duane Allman's death a year before in Macon. He is buried in Macon's Rose Hill cemetery, where Allman also lies.
Dec [21] Still-climbing Duane's ***An Anthology*** is certified gold by the RIAA.
[23] *One Way Out* peaks at US #86. Duane's ***An Anthology*** finally reaches US #28.

1973

Jan Lamar Williams, a friend of Johanson's, replaces Oakley on bass.
Apr The group's first two albums, repackaged together as ***Beginnings***, make US #25.
July [28] The Allman Brothers Band takes part in the largest-ever rock festival before a 600,000 crowd, with the Grateful Dead and the Band, at Watkins Glen Raceway in upstate New York.
Aug [21] Still rising ***Brothers And Sisters*** is certified gold by the RIAA.
[25] Trucks crashes his car in Macon, escaping with a broken leg.
Sept [8] ***Brothers And Sisters***, dedicated to Oakley, tops the US chart, where it will remain for five weeks, and is also the group's UK chart debut at #42.
[25] ***Beginnings*** is certified gold by the RIAA.
[26] The group plays at the Winterland Ballroom, San Francisco, with the Marshall Tucker Band.
Oct [6] ***Win Lose Or Draw*** is certified gold by the RIAA.
[13] *Ramblin' Man* hits US #2, behind Cher's *Half-Breed*.
Nov Gregg Allman's solo ***Laid Back***, produced by

Johnny Sandlin, reaches US #13, while ***Early Allman***, released on the Dial label, peaks at US #171.

1974

Jan [12] The group begins a 12-date European tour at the Odeon Theatre, Birmingham, W. Midlands, set to end in Amsterdam, Holland, on February 11th.
Feb [16] Instrumental *Jessica* peaks at US #65, highlighting Betts' dextrous fret work, as he begins to guide the band's direction.
[23] Gregg Allman's solo single *Midnight Rider* reaches US #19, as he embarks on a solo tour.
Mar [5] ***Laid Back*** is certified gold by the RIAA.
July [20] The band performs at the Knebworth open-air rock festival, Knebworth, Herts., on a bill with the Doobie Brothers and Van Morrison.
Aug Betts' solo album ***Highway Call*** reaches US #19, as he undertakes a US tour backed by country and bluegrass musicians. Duane's ***An Anthology Vol. 2*** also reaches US #49, while Chuck Leavell, Williams and Johanson form the jazz trio We Three, playing local clubs and colleges, followed by a six-week tour.
Sept [23] While the Average White Band are in Los Angeles performing a week of concerts at the Troubadour Club, their drummer, Robbie McIntosh, dies at a local party thrown for Gregg Allman, from a strychnine-based heroin overdose.
Dec Gregg Allman's ***The Gregg Allman Tour*** makes US #50, having been recorded live by the spin-off Gregg Allman Band, which features most of the Brothers Band (but not Betts).

1975

Feb Allman testifies against his former road manager and bodyguard John "Scooter" Herring, on trial for drug trafficking. Herring is sentenced to 75 years in jail, and Allman is ostracized by other band members, who claim he has betrayed their former fraternal loyalty, and vow not to work with him again, despite the fact that Allman has been threatened with a grand jury indictment unless he testifies.
June [30] Allman marries Cher, four days after her divorce from Sonny Bono. They will separate acrimoniously after only ten days, followed by a 3½ year on-again-off-again marriage.
Oct ***Win, Lose Or Draw*** hits US #5.
Nov [15] *Louisiana Lou And Three Card Monty John* makes US #78.
[22] Its A-side *Nevertheless* peaks at US #67.
[25] The group plays a benefit concert for Jimmy Carter's Presidential Campaign Fund at the Civic Center, Providence, RI.

1976

Jan [13] Gregg is subpoenaed in Macon by a federal grand jury investigating an alleged drugs ring.
[24] Double album ***The Road Goes On Forever***, a compilation of their best work to date, reaches US #43.
Mar [6] ***The Road Goes On Forever*** makes UK #54.
July [16] The band goes its separate ways: Allman recording with Cher (***Allman And Woman***) before returning to his own Gregg Allman Band, Betts forming Great Southern, and Trucks studying music at college, while the others, already playing as We Three, form Sea Level with guitarist Jimmy Nalls.
Dec [25] ***Wipe The Windows, Check The Oil, Dollar Gas***, compiling previously unreleased live recordings, makes US #75.

1977

Jan Allman and Betts mend their rift during the Jimmy Carter presidential inauguration celebrations.
Apr Betts signs with Arista Records, after a financial dispute with Capricorn, and forms Great Southern with Dan Toler from Melting Pot, which had opened for the Allmans. Toler in turn recommends fellow Melting Pots Ken Tibbets (bass) and Jerry Thompson (drums).
[23] ***Sea Level*** makes US #43.
May [28] ***Dickey Betts & Great Southern*** reaches US #31.
July [10] Elijah Blue is born to Gregg and Cher, who also release ***Two The Hard Way***, credited as Allman & Woman.
[23] ***Playin' Up A Storm*** by the Gregg Allman Band makes US #42.
Nov While Betts is recording a second album with a new band comprising Toler, drummer Doni Sharbano, bassist David "Rook" Goldflies, keyboardist Michael Workman and drummer/percussionist David Toler, Allman tells Walden that he wants to get the Allman Brothers Band back together.

1978

May [20] Great Southern's ***Atlanta's Burning Down*** reaches US #157.
July The band re-forms with rifts healed after Allman, Trucks and Johanson join Great Southern on stage at a Central Park, New York, concert. Great Southern's Dan Toler (guitar) and Goldflies (bass) complete the new line-up.
Aug The re-formed group plays at the "Capricorn Annual Barbecue" in Macon.
Nov The Allman Brothers Band, minus Leavell and Williams (still with Sea Level, Johanson has quit to join the re-formed Allmans), returns to Criteria Studios with producer Dowd.

1979

Jan [16] Allman and Cher are divorced.
Apr [14] Reunion album ***Enlightened Rogues*** hits US #9 having already been certified gold by the RIAA on March 5th.
May [5] *Crazy Love* reaches US #29.

1980

Jan [18] Capricorn Records announces bankruptcy, leaving the band without a label.
July They sign with Arista Records.
Sept [9] The group performs the first of three UK dates at the Apollo Theatre, Manchester, Gtr. Manchester before playing at London's Rainbow Theatre, with a line-up including Allman, Betts, Johanson, Trucks, Goldflies and Dan Toler.
Oct [4] Their label debut for Arista, ***Reach For The Sky***, produced by the group with Mike Lawler and Johnny Cobb, climbs to US #27.
[11] *Angeline* makes US #58.

1981

Sept [19] *Straight From The Heart* makes US #39. ***Brothers Of The Road***, from which it is taken, reaches US #44 but garners poor reviews. Leavell rejoins them shortly after, but with their style now less fashionable, the band splits again.
Nov ***The Best Of The Allman Brothers Band*** peaks at US #189.

1982

Dec Betts, Leavell and Trucks team with Wet Willie's Jimmy Hall to form the BHLT Band, which will embark on a US tour, augmented by Goldflies on bass and Danny Parks on fiddle.

1983

Jan [25] Band's ex-bassist Williams, a Vietnam veteran, succumbs to Agent Orange-related cancer in Los Angeles.

1984

The BHLT Band splits. Trucks quits to work for a studio and sound company, Leavell completes session work with the Rolling Stones, the Fabulous Thunderbirds, Dave Edmunds and others, and Betts moves to Nashville, where he will form a country band, play on a Hank Williams Jr. album, and co-write Mickey Gilley's country hit *Your Memory Ain't What It Used To Be*.

1986

After a substantial number of club dates across the US, Betts' new band signs with Epic, and will perform gigs during the year with Allman's outfit.
July The Allmans reunite to play at Charlie Daniels' "Volunteer Jam".
Oct [31] The group participates in the "Crackdown On Crack" benefit concert at Madison Square Garden, New York.

1987

May After a four-year break, Gregg Allman returns, signed to Epic Records, with the Gregg Allman Band and a solo album, ***I'm No Angel***, which will reach US #30.
[9] Extracted title cut *I'm No Angel* makes US #49.

1988

Aug Gregg Allman Band's ***Just Before The Bullets Fly*** peaks at US #117.
Nov The Dickey Betts Band's ***Pattern Disruptive***, recorded at Trucks' Pegasus recording studios in Tallahassee, FL, with tracks co-written with actor Don Johnson, peaks at US #187.

1989

Apr The Allman Brothers re-form again with Allman, Betts, Johanson, Trucks and new members Johnny Neel (keyboards), Warren Haynes (guitar) and Allen Woody (bass).
June [28] The group embarks on a 13-date US tour, at Chautauqua Amphitheatre, Chautauqua, NY, ending on July 15th at the Civic Arena, Pittsburgh, PA.
July A four-CD boxed-set retrospective compilation ***Dreams***, produced by Bill Levenson, makes US #103.
Sept [19] Their latest US tour ends at Merriweather Post Pavilion, Columbia, MD.

1990

May Allman is featured on the duet *Imagine Love* for Lori Carson's ***Shelter***.
June [29] An Allman Brothers summer tour opens in Columbia, SC.
Aug [18] ***Seven Turns***, the Allman Brothers' first studio album in nine years, peaks at US #53.
Nov [30] ***I'm No Angel*** is certified gold by the RIAA.

1991

Feb [23] The group performs at American Airlines' "Celebrity Ski For Cystic Fibrosis" charity concert at Crested Butte, CO.
Mar [7] The Allmans are named Comeback Of The Year in the annual **Rolling Stone** Readers' Picks music awards, as they wrap a new album with producer Dowd.
Aug [10] Eight-cut ***Shades Of Two Worlds*** makes US #85.
Oct [9] The band guests on NBC-TV's "The Tonight Show".
Dec [22] "Rush", a movie in which Allman plays drug dealer Will Gaines in a major but silent acting role, opens in US theaters.
[28-31] The band breaks the house record by performing four consecutive sell-outs at the Macon City Auditorium, Macon.

1992

Mar [10-22] The group plays ten dates at the Beacon Theatre, New York.
June [27] Live ***An Evening With The Allman Brothers Band***, recorded at the Macon City Auditorium show on New Year's Eve, debuts at its US #80 peak.
July [3-4] Midway through a four-month US tour, the band grosses $426,011 over two days at Red Rocks Amphitheatre, Denver, CO.
[14] ***Dreams*** is certified gold by the RIAA.
[25] The group performs *Melissa* on the final broadcast of syndicated TV's "The Dennis Miller Show".
Aug [25] ***The Best Of The Allman Brothers Band*** is certified gold and ***The Allman Brothers Band Live At The Fillmore East*** platinum by the RIAA.

1993

Jan [20] The band appears at President Bill Clinton's inauguration festivities at the Shoreham Hotel, Washington, DC, while a further live archive release,

The Fillmore Concerts, is issued by Polydor Chronicles.
Mar [6] Gregg Allman performs with Jonathan Cain at the 16th Bay Area Music Awards, at the Bill Graham Civic Auditorium in San Francisco.
Apr [24] The group makes its first-ever appearance at the 24th annual New Orleans Jazz & Heritage Festival, New Orleans, LA.
May [22] A US tour opens at the Pacific Amphitheatre, Costa Mesa, CA, set to end in Las Vegas, NV, on August 31st.
[29] The Allmans play at the first annual "Laguna Seca Daze" festival at the Laguna Seca Recreation Area, Monterey, CA.
July [31] Betts is arrested at a Saratoga Springs hotel following a shoving match with two policemen, after an argument with his wife. (He will miss much of the tour, seeking help for alcoholism. Zakk Wylde will deputise for him, followed by David Grissom and finally Jack Pearson.)

1994

Apr [1-10] The group plays eight sellout dates at New York's Beacon Theatre.
[24] They perform at the 25th annual New Orleans Jazz & Heritage Festival.
May [21] ***Where It All Begins*** debuts at its US #45 peak.
June [28] The third annual H.O.R.D.E. caravan tour, with the Allmans headlining, opens at the Mud Island Amphitheatre, Memphis, TN, set to end on September 6th at the Garden State Arts Center, Holmdel, NJ.
Aug [14] The Allmans perform at Woodstock II at Winston Farm, Saugerties, NY.
[29] The group guests on CBS-TV's "Late Show With David Letterman".
Oct [11] Gregg performs at the Wang Dang Doodle benefit concert for the Willie Dixon-created Blues Heaven Foundation at Los Angeles' House of Blues club.
Nov [10-11] The band performs at the Sunrise Musical Theatre, Sunrise, in their home state of Florida, during current US dates.

1995

Jan [12] The Allman Brothers are inducted into the Rock and Roll Hall of Fame by Willie Nelson at the tenth annual dinner, also performing *One Way Out* at the post-dinner jam.
May [27] ***2nd Set*** bows at its US #88 peak.
June [22] ***A Decade Of Hits*** is certified platinum by the RIAA.
[30] The second leg of a US tour opens in Concord, CA, set to close on September 10th at the Sandstone Amphitheatre in Bonner Springs, KS.
Sept [2] The group, now comprising Allman, Betts, Jaimoe, Trucks, Woody, Haynes and Marc Quinone, performs *One Way Out* at the Concert for the Rock and Roll Hall of Fame at Cleveland Stadium, Cleveland, OH.

1996

Feb [29] The Allmans perform their most enduring instrumental cut, *Jessica*, which has won the Best Rock Instrumental Performance at the 38th annual Grammy Awards the previous evening at Los Angeles' Shrine Auditorium, on the "Late Show With David Letterman".

MARC ALMOND

1984

June The flamboyant Almond (b. Peter Marc Almond, July 9, 1959, Southport, Lancs.), having completed final UK tour dates at London's Hammersmith Palais with David Ball as the popular electronic pop duo Soft Cell in January, a pairing which has lasted five years and most recently yielded the farewell album ***This Last Night In Sodom***, releases his first solo single, *The Boy Who Came Back*, which peaks at UK #52 (still on the Some Bizzare label). (He has already recorded 1982's ***Untitled*** and the 1983 album ***Torment And Toreros***, while still in Soft Cell, under the off-shoot name Marc & the Mambas.)
Sept *You Have* peaks at UK #57. Almond takes part in a week-long festival at the Bloomsbury Theatre, London, which celebrates the work of French writer George Bataille. (A subsequent mini-album of material from the event, ***Violent Silence***, will be released in French-speaking territories in 1986, and imported into the UK.)
Nov Freshman album ***Vermin In Ermine***, credited to Marc Almond & the Willing Sinners, comprising Richard Riley (guitar), Annie Hogan (piano), Martin McCarrick (cello), Billy McGee (bass) and Stephen Humphries (drums), makes UK #36.

1985

Apr His revival of Donna Summer's disco anthem *I Feel Love (Medley)*, which sees Almond teamed with Bronski Beat, hits UK #3, popular, not least, with the young British gay community who will support much of Almond's work.
Aug [31] *Stories Of Johnny* reaches UK #23.
Oct *Love Letters*, featuring the Westminster City School Choir, peaks at UK #68, as the torch album, ***Stories Of Johnny***, released via a new licensing deal with Phonogram Records, reaches UK #22 and is accompanied by a UK and rest of Europe tour.

1986

Jan A third extract, his version Mel Torme's *The House Is Haunted (By The Echo Of Your Last Goodbye)*, peaks at UK #55.
Feb Almond and the Willing Sinners play a series of dates in Japan.
June *A Woman's Story*, covering an old Cher number (recorded after Almond had heard the original in a London taxi), makes UK #41. (The 12" EP format includes a revival of Procol Harum's *Salty Dog*.)
Oct *Ruby Red* peaks at UK #47.

1987

Feb [14] *Melancholy Rose* charts for a week at UK #71.
Apr [18] ***Mother Fist And Her Five Daughters***, also credited to Marc Almond & the Willing Sinners, makes UK #41.
June He contributes guest vocals to Sally Timms' *This House Is A House Of Tears*, an Almond composition.
Sept Almond is mugged in Barcelona, Spain, by a gang of skinheads who make off with his Dr. Marten boots.
Dec He plays a series of sellout Christmas concerts at London's Astoria Theatre, now backed by La Magia, which retains Annie Hogan, Billy McGee and Steve Humphreys from the Willing Sinners.

1988

Oct [8] Newly signed to EMI's Parlophone imprint, Almond's fourth album ***The Stars We Are***, featuring La Magia, makes UK #41, containing the UK #26 Sept [17]-peaking *Tears Run Rings*, and *Bitter Sweet*, which makes UK #40 on Nov [12].

1989

Jan [28] *Something's Gotten Hold Of My Heart*, a melodramatic duet with the song's original chart-maker Gene Pitney, tops the UK chart for the first of four weeks.
Feb [18] *Tears Run Rings* peaks at US #67, as its parent album ***The Stars We Are*** peaks at US #144 .
Apr *Only The Moment* makes UK #45.

1990

Mar [10] *A Lover Spurned* reaches UK #29.
May *The Desperate Hours* clocks in at UK #45.
June [16] Its parent album ***Enchanted***, produced by Stephen Hague, charts for a week at UK #52.
Nov [17] Almond attends the fifth "Official Marc Almond Convention", held at Heaven in London's Charing Cross.
[28] Almond performs at London's Brixton Academy in a benefit concert for the Terrence Higgins Trust (a British charity promoting awareness of HIV and AIDS), with Everything But The Girl and Working Week. (During the year, Almond has released a commercially-unsuccessful album of Jacques Brel covers, ***Jacques***.)

1991

Oct [5] *Jacky*, reviving Scott Walker's 1968 UK #22, reaches UK #17.
[26] ***Tenement Symphony***, which sees Almond reunited with Soft Cell partner Dave Ball on a handful of tracks, makes UK #48.
Nov [30] Almond participates in the "Red Hot & Dance" AIDS benefit concert in Barcelona, Spain.

1992

Jan [15] Almond is featured on BBC2-TV's "Rapido".
[25] *My Hand Over My Heart* makes UK #33.
May [2] His version of David McWilliams' '60s airplay favorite, *The Days Of Pearly Spencer*, hits UK #4.
[16] ***Tenement Symphony*** re-charts at UK #39.
June [12] Almond performs a one-off concert at Liverpool's Philharmonic Hall.
Sept [30] Following a concert two days earlier in Nottingham, Almond plays at London's Royal Albert Hall.
Oct [18] He attends the sixth official fan club convention, at the London's Astoria Theatre.

1993

Jan Almond continues mixing a live album with producer Gregg Jackman at Sarm West Studios, London.
Apr [3] *What Makes A Man A Man*, extracted from the live set ***12 Years Of Tears - Live At The Royal Albert Hall***, peaks at UK #60.

1995

Apr [20] Almond guests on BBC2-TV's "The O-Zone".
May [13] *Adored And Explored* bows at its UK #25 peak.
July [29] *The Idol* debuts at its UK #44 high.
Nov A two-CD retrospective ***Treasure Box*** is released in the US by EMI.
Dec [13-14] Almond plays two dates at London's Shepherd's Bush Empire.
[30] *Child Star* charts for a week at UK #41.

1996

Feb [10] Almond guests on C4-TV's "The White Room".
Mar [9] ***Fantastic Star*** debuts at its UK #54 peak.
see also: **SOFT CELL**

HERB ALPERT

1958

After serving in the US military, as a trumpeter in the 6th Army band for two years at the Presidio in San Francisco, CA, Alpert (b. Mar. 31, 1935, Los Angeles, CA), the son of immigrants, his father from Russia and his mother from Hungary, who have encouraged his trumpet playing since age eight, has begun his apprenticeship in the record industry as a writer in partnership with insurance salesman Lou Adler. They have early success when they take four demos to Keen Publishing, where Bumps Blackwell invites them to begin an A&R training program at $42 a week and then hires them as staff writers. This leads to writing with Sam Cooke, for whom they pen four consecutive hits, *Love You Most Of All*, *Everybody Likes To Cha Cha Cha*, *Only Sixteen* and *Wonderful World*, under the collective pseudonym Barbara Campbell, Cooke's wife's real name. The following year, Keen rejects Alpert and Adler's song *Baby Talk*, which they then take to Dore Records, who will have a Top 10 US hit with the song as recorded by Jan & Dean. Alpert also records as a vocalist, without success, for RCA Records as Dore Alpert, and secures bit parts in a few Hollywood films, most notably playing drums in the scene when Moses comes down from the mountain in "The Ten Commandments".

1962

Mar Alpert splits with Adler and joins Jerry Moss, who produced him for RCA and is one of the industry's top independent promotion men, to form Carnival Records, which they swiftly change to A&M (based on their surname initials). The label initially operates from Alpert's garage at home and funds itself with $1,000 (secured when Dot Records picks up national distribution for one of Dore Alpert's singles).
Oct Alpert experiments with Sol Lake's tune *Twinkle Star*, re-arranging it as *The Lonely Bull* by double-tracking the trumpet part, thereby creating his trademark sound. He records the cut for $65 and releases it on A&M under the name of the Tijuana Brass.
Dec [8] The Latin-flavored jazz instrumental *The Lonely Bull* hits US #6, selling over 700,000 copies and establishing both Alpert and A&M.

1963

Jan [12] *The Lonely Bull* reaches UK #22, while its parent album ***The Lonely Bull*** rises to US #24.
Mar [30] *Marching Thru Madrid* makes US #96.

1964

Feb [17] The Tijuana Brass, a group of musicians assembled by Alpert to play in concert (on record he uses session players), which will grow into one of the top-grossing live attractions in the US in mid-'60s, is launched in concert in San Francisco, CA, comprising Bob Edmundson (trombone), Lou Pagani (keyboards), John Pisano (rhythm guitar), Tonni Kalash (second trumpet), Nick Ceroli (drums) and Pat Senatore (bass).
Apr [18] *Mexican Drummer Man* makes US #77, as ***Tijuana Brass Vol.2*** reaches US #17.
July [18] *The Mexican Shuffle*, penned by *Lonely Bull* writer Sol Lake, makes US #85.
Dec The BBC Radio program "Newly Pressed" adopts Alpert's *Up Cherry Street* as its theme tune.

1965

May [8] *Whipped Cream* peaks at US #68.
Oct [2] *3rd Man Theme*, B-side of the-still climbing *Taste Of Honey*, makes US #47.
Nov [27] Already on the survey for six months, ***Whipped Cream And Other Delights*** tops the US chart while *A Taste Of Honey*, his first Top 10 single for three years, hits US #7.
Dec [15] ***Whipped Cream And Other Delights*** and the still rising ***Going Places*** are both certified gold by the RIAA.

1966

Jan [29] *Spanish Flea*, written by labelmate Julius Wechter, hits UK #3, re-establishing Alpert in the UK. ***Going Places*** hits UK #4.
Feb [5] *Tijuana Taxi*, the B-side of the still climbing *Zorba The Greek*, makes US #38.
[26] *Zorba The Greek* reaches US #11.
Mar [5] ***Going Places*** finally tops the US chart, where it will stay for six weeks.
[13] Alpert makes a one-off UK appearance at London's Hammersmith Odeon. (The concert will be televised by the BBC on August 4th and 11th.)
[15] *A Taste Of Honey* wins the Record Of The Year, Best Instrumental Performance, Non-Jazz, Best Instrumental Arrangement and Best Engineered Recording categories, at the eighth annual Grammy Awards.
[25] The Tijuana Brass performs at the White House Correspondents' Dinner in Washington, DC.
Apr The group plays at Carnegie Hall, New York, NY.
[2] *Tijuana Taxi* makes UK #37.
[16] *Spanish Flea*, used as the theme for US TV show "The Dating Game", reaches US #27, as ***South Of The Border*** hits US #6, after more than a year on the survey, and ***Herb Alpert's Tijuana Brass Vol.2*** reaches US #17.
[23] *What Now My Love*, the A-side of *Spanish Flea*, reaches US #24.
May [9] ***Herb Alpert's Tijuana Brass, Volume 2***, ***South Of The Border***, ***The Lonely Bull*** and ***What Now My Love*** are certified gold by the RIAA.
[28] ***What Now My Love*** begins a nine-week tenure at US #1 (as Alpert and the Brass becomes the only act in US chart history to place four albums in the Top 10 simultaneously), and ***Whipped Cream And Other Delights*** hits UK #2.
June ***What Now My Love*** reaches UK #18.
July [18] The "Herb Alpert & The Tijuana Brass Show" opens at the Greek Theatre, Los Angeles.
[23] *The Work Song* reaches US #18.
Sept [19] Alpert performs at Monaco Palace for Princess Grace.
Oct [1] *Flamingo* lands at US #28.
[7] The group completes a European tour at the Royal Albert Hall, London.
Dec [17] *Mame* makes US #19.

1967

Jan ***S.R.O.*** hits US #2 and UK #5.
[19] ***S.R.O.*** is certified gold by the RIAA.
Mar [2] *What Now My Love* wins the Best Instrumental Performance (Other Than Jazz) and Best Instrumental Arrangement Of 1966 categories at the ninth annual Grammy Awards.
Apr [1] *Wade In The Water* makes US #37.
May [27] *Casino Royale*, the Bacharach and David-penned theme tune to the spoof James Bond movie, reaches US and UK #27.
June [17] ***Sounds Like*** tops the US chart, before climbing to UK #21.
Aug [5] *The Happening*, an instrumental version of the film theme, which has topped the US survey in a vocal version by the Supremes three months earlier, reaches US #32.
[25] ***Sounds Like*** is certified gold by the RIAA.
Oct [14] *A Banda* makes US #35.
Dec [8] The still rising ***Herb Alpert's Ninth*** is certified gold by the RIAA.

1968

Jan ***Herb Alpert's 9th*** hits US #4, then reaches UK #26.
Feb [10] *Carmen* makes US #51.
Apr [22] Alpert stars in his own CBS-TV special.
May [25] *Cabaret* peaks at US #72.
June [22] Softly swaying ballad *This Guy's In Love With You*, sung by Alpert to his wife Lani Hall on his TV special, tops the US chart, where it will stay for four weeks, becoming Alpert's first vocal hit, his first #1, A&M's first #1 and songwriters Bacharach and David's first #1. It will also be his last chart-topper for more than a decade.
July [19] *This Guy's In Love With You* and the still climbing ***The Beat Of The Brass*** are certified gold by the RIAA.
[27] ***The Beat Of The Brass*** heads the US chart and hits UK #4.
Aug [17] *This Guy's In Love With You* hits UK #3.
Sept [21] *To Wait For Love*, his second vocal hit, peaks at US #51.
Dec [16] ***The Christmas Album*** is certified gold by the RIAA.

1969

Jan [11] *My Favorite Things* makes US #45.
Apr [19] *Zazueira* peaks at US #78.
June [21] A vocal version of the Nilsson song *Without Her* peaks at US #63. (Subsequent releases will revert to trumpet-led instrumentals.)
July [9] *Without Her* makes UK #36.
Aug ***Warm*** reaches US #28 and UK #30.
Nov [4] The Tijuana Brass performs at the Royal Festival Hall, London (to be broadcast on ITV on New Year's Eve). After selling more than 45 million albums, Alpert decides to give up performing, partly due to a tired lip, and will concentrate on studio work and his executive responsibilities with A&M Records.

1970

Jan Alpert is impressed by demo tapes from a brother/sister act, the Carpenters, whom he signs to the label. (They will score 12 million-selling singles for A&M over the next five years.)
Mar [26] ***Warm*** is certified gold by the RIAA.
The Brass Are Comin' makes US #30 and UK #40. Over the next four years, Alpert will release a succession of moderately-successful projects, whose chart achievements will be: ***Greatest Hits*** UK #8 and US #43 (June, certified gold in the US on April 12th 1971), ***Down Mexico Way*** UK #64 (June [27]) and the haunting and spiritual *Jerusalem* US #74 (Nov [7]); 1971's *Jerusalem* UK #42 (Jan) ***Summertime*** US #111 (July) and ***America*** UK #45 (Nov [13]); 1972's ***Solid Brass*** US #135 (June) and in 1973: *Last Tango In Paris* US #77 (Apr [28]) and ***Foursider*** US #196 (Dec).

1974

Apr [19] Alpert begins his first major concert tour in years at Harrah's, Lake Tahoe, NV.
June [15] *Fox Hunt* stalls at US #84, as ***You Smile The Song Begins*** makes US #66.
(Over the next five years, ***Coney Island Number*** will reach US #88 (April 1975), a retrospective collection ***40 Greatest*** will make UK #45 (Nov [12], 1977) and ***Herb Alpert/Hugh Masekela***, a collaboration with the legendary South African trumpeter, will reach US #65 (Mar [25], 1978.)

1979

Oct [20] Already certified gold by the RIAA on September 25th, *Rise*, written by Andy Armer and Alpert's nephew Randy Badazz, and featuring a contemporary disco rhythm far removed from the traditional Alpert feel, boosted by its exposure on daytime TV's "General Hospital", hits US #1, toppling Michael Jackson's *Don't Stop 'Til You Get Enough*.
Nov [24] *Rise* reaches UK #13, as its parent album ***Rise***, produced by Alpert with Badazz, makes UK #37.
Dec [1] ***Rise*** hits US #6.

1980

Jan [19] *Rotation*, also penned by Armer and Badazz, hits US #30, while *Rotation* makes UK #46.
Feb [5] ***Rise*** is certified platinum by the RIAA.
[27] *Rise* wins the Best Pop Instrumental Performance of 1979 category at the 22nd annual Grammy Awards.
July [26] *Beyond* makes US #50.
Aug [23] Repeating his successful new formula, ***Beyond*** reaches US #28 as Alpert enters another five-year period of releasing annual albums and singles to moderate US chart success: *Magic Man* US #79 (Sept [19], 1981), as parent album ***Magic Man*** makes US #61 (Sept). *Route 101* US #37 (Aug [14], 1982) and parent album ***Fandango***, US #100 (Sept [4]). 1983's ***Blow Your Own Horn*** US #120 (Sept) and its spin-offs, *Garden Party* US #81 (Sept [3]) and *Red Hot* US #77 (Dec [24]), ***Bullish*** US #75 (Aug 1984), *Bullish* US #90 (Sept [15]) and 1985's ***Wild Romance***, US #151 (Sept).

1987

Jan Alpert is featured playing cameo trumpet on UB40's current UK #12 hit *Rat In Mi Kitchen*.
Apr ***Keep Your Eye On Me***, mainly produced by Jimmy Jam and Terry Lewis at Flyte Tyme Studios in Minneapolis, MN, is released. Marking another commercial return, it will reach US #18 and UK #79 (Apr [11]).
[4] Dance-hip *Keep Your Eye On Me*, with vocals by Lisa Keith and Terry Lewis, makes US #46.
[18] *Keep Your Eye On Me* reaches UK #19.
June [17] ***Keep Your Eye On Me*** is certified gold by the RIAA.
[20] Dance-styled *Diamonds*, also from the album (and featuring A&M-signed Janet Jackson and Lisa Keith on vocals), tops the US R&B survey and hits US #5 and UK #27.
Sept [5] A third extract, the ballad *Making Love In The Rain*, also with Jackson and Keith on vocals,

peaks at US #35. Alpert, meanwhile, continues to co-run A&M, now just past its 25th birthday and established as one of the largest and most successful independent labels in the world.

1988

Jan [31] Alpert performs the American National Anthem at "Super Bowl XXII" between the Washington Redskins and the Denver Broncos at Jack Murphy Stadium, San Diego, CA.

1989

Oct With Alpert having recently launched his own "Listen" perfume, he and Moss sell A&M Records to the PolyGram conglomerate for $460 million, a remarkable achievement considering their humble beginnings in 1962. Making occasional public performances (including a rendition of *This Guy's In Love With You* with Bacharach at a benefit for "AIDS Project Los Angeles", at the Wiltern Theatre, Los Angeles, in September 1990), Alpert will continue to record, releasing ***North On South St.*** in 1991, ***Midnight Sun*** (his last for A&M in 1992) while yet another retrospective, ***The Very Best Of Herb Alpert***, will peak at UK #34 on Sept [28] later that year.

1996

Apr [23] Having made a rare live performance at the Entertainment Industry's Foundation for Cities in Schools first fundraiser, at the Beverly Hilton Hotel, Los Angeles on April 14th 1993, honoring his partner Jerry Moss (they both then officially left A&M Records on June 18th the same year), Alpert's new label, Almo Sounds (again formed with Moss and distributed through Geffen Records), which has released its first single, Angel Corpus Christi's *Candy* on March 1st earlier this year, now issues his first album in four years, the jazz-phrased ***Second Wind***. Co-produced with Jeff Lorber, it will be promoted with Alpert's first tour in eight years, beginning May 1st in San Francisco, CA.

ALTERED IMAGES

Clare Grogan (vocals); **Tony McDaid** (guitar); **Jim McKinven** (guitar, keyboards); **John McElhone** (bass); **Michael "Tich" Anderson** (drums)

1980

Schoolfriends McDaid, McElhone and Anderson, inspired by the burgeoning post-punk UK indie scene, particularly the Undertones, have invited aspiring actress Grogan (b. Mar. 17, 1962, Scotland) and McKinven to join them in March 1979, performing local club and pub dates as Altered Images in their home town, Glasgow, Scotland, before Grogan begins a six-week stint taking the role of Susan in the Bill Forsyth-directed movie, "Gregory's Girl", in November. A demo tape sent to Siouxsie & the Banshees has secured the group an opening slot on a Banshees Glasgow date in June 1980, followed by a full UK tour support role. They will also participate in the Futurama Festival in Leeds, W. Yorks., in September, which leads to the first of two sessions for the "John Peel Show" on BBC Radio 1, and their signing to Epic Records.

1981

Apr [4] Following a second "John Peel Show" performance in March, *Dead Popstars*, produced by Banshees bassist Steve Severin, causes controversy because of John Lennon's recent death (though recorded prior to it), and makes UK #67.

Oct [31] *Happy Birthday*, the only cut on the forthcoming album to be produced by Martin Rushent, hits UK #2 after a successful BBC1-TV "Top Of The Pops" debut (its 12" single release includes a cover of T. Rex's *Jeepster*). ***Happy Birthday***, otherwise produced by Severin, reaches UK #26 and showcases the band's progression from its raw post-punk roots to a lighter pop style, highlighted by Grogan's adolescent, snappy, high-pitched vocal.

1982

Jan [16] Perky *I Could Be Happy*, from the forthcoming Rushent-produced ***Pinky Blue***, hits UK #7.

Feb Grogan is hit on the head by an exuberant McDaid during an appearance on BBC1-TV's "Swapshop".

Apr [17] Catchy guitar-driven *See Those Eyes* reaches UK#11, spurred by its cult ITV show "The Prisoner"-parodying video clip.

May [22] ***Pinky Blue*** peaks at UK #12.

June [12] Extracted title track, the Grogan-penned *Pinky Blue*, makes UK #35.

July Following the band's recording of Del Shannon's *Little Town Flirt* for the ***Party Party*** soundtrack, McKinven and Anderson leave (the former to re-emerge in One Dove in the '90s) both to be replaced by ex-Restricted Code multi-instrumentalist Stephen Lironi.

1983

Apr [2] Disco-beat, Blondiesque *Don't Talk To Me About Love*, produced by Mike Chapman, hits UK #7.

June ***Bite***, helmed by Chapman and Tony Visconti, reaches UK #16 but proves to be little more than a studio album based around Grogan, effectively making the other band members redundant.

[4] Extracted *Bring Me Closer*, the group's last Top 30 entry, reaches UK #29.

July *Love To Stay* proves to be the band's chart swan song, stopping at UK #46. The group's fashionable teen image of 1981 has become quickly outdated, as 1984's non-charting restrospective, ***Collected Images***, will testify. Their break-up leaves main focus Grogan pursuing a solo acting and recording career, including a co-host slot on ITV's "Night Network" magazine show and roles in a further Forsyth movie, "Comfort And Joy" as well as TV projects "Red Dwarf", "Blott On The Landscape", "The Monocled Mutineer" and "Taggart", and an unsuccessful 1987 London Records solo return (including *Love Bomb* and the unreleased ***Trashman***). With boyfriend Lironi, Grogan will form Universal Love School in 1991 while McElhone will link with two well-received Scottish bands of the late '80s, Hipsway and Texas. A comprehensive Connoisseur Collection hits and oddities round-up, ***The Best Of Altered Images***, brings their career to compact disc in 1992.

AMEN CORNER

Andy Fairweather-Low (vocals, guitar); **Blue Weaver** (organ); **Neil Jones** (guitar); **Clive Taylor** (bass); **Mike Smith** (tenor sax); **Alan Jones** (baritone sax); **Dennis Bryon** (drums)

1966

The group, taking its name from a play by James Baldwin, forms in Cardiff, S. Glamorgan, Wales, its seven members veterans of local Welsh bands: lead singer Fairweather-Low (b. Aug. 8, 1950, Ystrad Mynach, Hengoed, M. Glamorgan, Wales), having been a member of local R&B band the Taffbeats, is in the Sect Maniacs with Alan Jones (b. Feb. 6, 1947, Swansea, W. Glamorgan, Wales); Taylor (b. Apr. 27, 1949, Cardiff) and Neil Jones (b. Mar. 25, 1949, Llanbradach, M. Glamorgan, Wales) are from the Dekkas; Weaver (b. Derek Weaver, Mar. 3, 1949, Cardiff) and Bryon (b. Apr. 14, 1949, Cardiff) are from the Witnesses; and Smith (b. Nov. 4, 1947, Neath, W. Gkamorgan, Wales) is in Lot 13. Gaining a reputation as a strong live R&B band, the twin saxes giving a fatter, more American sound than most UK beat groups of the time, they record a version of Georgie Fame's *Bidin' My Time* at an independent studio in Monmouth, Gwent, Wales, but EMI turns it down.

1967

May The group signs to Decca's Deram imprint.

Aug [26] Its label debut, the slow and bluesy *Gin House Blues*, reaches UK #12.

Oct [28] *World Of Broken Hearts*, with a more mainstream commercial pop sound, reaches UK #24.

Nov [14] The band begins a 15-date, twice-nightly UK package tour, with the Jimi Hendrix Experience, the Move, Pink Floyd, the Nice and others, at the Royal Albert Hall, London, set to end on December 5th at Green's Playhouse, Glasgow, Scotland.

1968

Feb [17] The group's brash cover of American Breed's major US hit *Bend Me, Shape Me* hits UK #3.

Mar The band's debut album ***Round Amen Corner*** reaches UK #26, as the group tours Scotland with Dave Dee, Dozy, Beaky, Mick & Tich and the Love Affair.

Apr [5] They begin a 28-date, twice-nightly UK tour with Gene Pitney, Status Quo, Don Partridge, Simon Dupree & the Big Sound and others, at the Odeon Cinema, Lewisham, London, which will close on May 7th at the Granada Cinema, Walthamstow, London.

May [10] With just two days rest, they begin a ten-date, twice-nightly UK tour, with bill-toppers Herman's Hermits, Dave Berry, the Paper Dolls, John Rowles and the Echoes, at the Town Hall, Birmingham, Warks. It will end on the 19th at the Theatre Royal, Nottingham, Notts.

June [27] The group previews *High In The Sky*, its first single in five months, on BBC Radio 1's "Pop North".

Sept [7] *High In The Sky*, another brash dance single, hits UK #6. (Soon after, the band signs a recording deal with Immediate Records.)

Dec [31] Amen Corner takes part in the "Giant New Year's Eve Gala Pop & Blues Party" at Alexandra Palace, London, with Joe Cocker, John Mayall's Bluesbreakers, the Small Faces and others.

1969

Feb [14] More than 300 fans are injured at an Amen Corner/Love Affair show at the Ice Rink, Paisley, Scotland.

[15] The group's Immediate debut *(If Paradise Is) Half As Nice*, a cover of *Il Paradiso Belavista*, an Italian hit for La Ragazza 77, with English lyrics by Jack Fishman, tops the UK chart, jumping from #19 the previous week.

July [1] Amen Corner headlines the "Pop Proms" concert at the Royal Albert Hall, London, with Marmalade, the Equals and others.

[12] *Hello Suzie*, penned by Roy Wood and featured on his album ***Shazam***, hits UK #4.

Aug The group plays in a club scene in the Christopher Lee, Peter Cushing and Vincent Price horror picture "Scream And Scream Again".

Oct [5] After many months of rumors that Fairweather-Low is leaving the group to pursue a solo career, Amen Corner makes its final appearance, at the Gliderdrome in Boston, Lincs.

Nov [1] ***Explosive Company*** reaches UK #19.

1970

Their final single is a cover of the Beatles' *Get Back*. Fairweather-Low, Weaver, Bryon, Taylor and Neil Jones regroup as Fair Weather, while Alan Jones and Smith will form the nucleus of Judas Jump with Andy Bown.

Aug [29] Fair Weather's *Natural Sinner* hits UK #6, as the group makes its live debut at Scene Two in Scarborough, Yorks, though the band will split by year's end.

1976

Feb [28] A reissued *(If Paradise Is) Half As Nice* makes UK #34. (Fairweather-Low will recut the song in 1992 with Aztec Camera, for inclusion on the **New Musical Express**-issued compilation ***Ruby Trax***.) While he will secure solo success, charting with *Reggae Tune* and *Wide Eyed And Legless* in 1974-75, he will also go on to become an in-demand session player throughout the '80s, eventually joining Eric Clapton's backing band in the early '90s (notably on Clapton's 1992 hit album ***Unplugged***). Weaver and Bryon, with guitarist Alan Kendall, will become the Bee Gees' rhythm section, staying with the trio throughout its glory days in the late '70s and early '80s.

AMERICA

Dewey Bunnell (vocals, guitar); **Gerry Beckley** (vocals, guitar); **Dan Peek** (vocals, guitar)

1970

Oct Bunnell (b. Jan. 19, 1951, Yorks.), Beckley (b. Sept. 12, 1952, Fort Worth, TX) and Peek (b. Nov. 1, 1950, Panama City, FL), having met at Central High School, Bushey Park, Herts., in 1967, and all sons of US air force officers stationed in the UK, their studies now completed, form the central core of acoustic folk-rock quintet Daze in London. Soon becoming a trio and choosing their new name while listening to an Americana jukebox, they audition for Roundhouse venue promoter Jeff Dexter, who books them frequently as the opening act for several major bands (including Elton John and the Who). Warner Bros. Records sign the trio, beating Atlantic and DJM and, as America, they begin recording their debut album with producers Ian Samwell and Jeff Dexter, at Trident Studios in London.

1971

Sept [21] America is featured on the first broadcast of BBC2-TV rock show "The Old Grey Whistle Test".

1972

Jan [22] The Bunnell-penned, easy-flowing, acoustic guitar-led *A Horse With No Name*, showcasing their harmonic vocal skills, becomes an instant UK chart success, hitting #3, and immediately defines the band's long-term style. Its debut album ***America***, though not including the single, reaches UK #14.

Feb The group "returns" to the US hoping to build on its success, making its first concert appearance in the lunchroom of an Ontario college, before embarking on a major North American tour, supporting the Everly Brothers.

Mar [25] Released in the US on the strength of its UK success, *A Horse With No Name* shoots to US #1 (having already been declared gold by the RIAA the previous day) dislodging Neil Young's *Heart Of Gold*, as ***America*** also tops the US chart.

May [7] The group takes part in the Bickershaw Festival, near Wigan, Lancs.

July [1] Beckley-written ballad *I Need You* hits US #9.

Dec [9] The self-produced *Ventura Highway*, appropriately recorded in Los Angeles, CA, with Joe Osborn (bass) and Hal Blaine (drums), hits US #8 (and also makes UK #43).

[18] Still climbing ***Homecoming*** is certified gold by the RIAA.

1973

Jan Aptly-titled ***Homecoming*** hits US #9 and UK #21.

Mar [3] The Peek-written *Don't Cross The River*, featuring Henry Diltz on banjo, makes US #35, as America wins Best New Artist Of 1972 at the 15th annual Grammy Awards.

May [26] *Only In Your Heart* peaks at US #62.

[29] The group begins recording its third album, at the Record Plant in Los Angeles, with guest musicians including Joe Walsh, Carl Wilson and Tom Scott.

Sept [22] Willis Alan Ramsey-penned ballad *Muskrat Love*, the trio's first non-original, peaks at US #67. (It will hit US #4 in 1976 for the Captain & Tennille.)

Nov ***Hat Trick*** reaches US #28 and UK #41.

1974

Apr [17] Returning to London, America begins work with producer George Martin at Air Studios on the forthcoming ***Holiday***.

Oct [30] ***Holiday*** is certified gold by the RIAA.

Nov [9] The Bunnell-penned, fanciful *Tin Man* hits US #4, as ***Holiday*** hits US #3.

1975

Jan [6] Work begins on a second collaboration with Martin and regular sidemen David Dickey (bass) and Willie Leacox (drums), at the Record Plant studios in Los Angeles and San Francisco, CA.

Mar [8] *Lonely People*, also from ***Holiday***, hits US #5.

June [12] Stlill rising ***Hearts*** is certified gold by the RIAA.

[14] *Sister Golden Hair*, written by Beckley, becomes their second US chart-topper, while its parent album ***Hearts*** is on its way to hit US #4.

Sept [27] Piano-led *Daisy Jane*, breaking their US Top 10 chart run, reaches #20.

Dec [20] ***History: America's Greatest Hits***, collecting their most popular material to date, hits US #3 and will remain a popular catalogue item right up to its CD release in the mid-'80s, eventually selling over four million copies.

1976

Jan [17] The uptempo and less harmonious *Woman Tonight* makes US #44.

Feb [7] ***History: America's Greatest Hits*** peaks at UK #60.

[16] Once again with Martin at the helm, America begins recording a new album at the Caribou Ranch Studios, Nederland, CO.

June [5] ***Hideaway*** reaches US #11, having already been confirmed gold by the RIAA on May 19th.

July [10] *Today's The Day*, from ***Hideaway***, reaches US #23.

Sept [11] *Amber Cascades* peaks at US #75.

1977

Mar The Martin-produced ***Harbor***, recorded at Ka Lae Kiki Studios in Kauai, HI, and featuring Larry Carlton on sitar, reaches US #21, but fails to yield hit singles. The band will embark on a US tour by year's end.

May Peek leaves the band (subsequently becoming a born-again Christian and recording solo religious material).

1978

Jan Performance album ***Live*** makes US #129.

Oct [13] Released on the Lamb & Lion label, Peek scores his only US pop hit with *All Things Are Possible*, which makes #78. Its same-titled parent album will go on to garner two Grammy Award nominations in 1980.

1979

Mar [19] Now signed to Capitol Records, sessions begin on their label debut. Beckley and Bunnell are now backed by Dickey and Leacox, with recent additions Mike Woods (lead guitar), Jim Calire (keyboards, sax) and Tom Walsh (percussion).

Apr [21] *California Dreamin'*, from the film "California Dreaming", peaks at US #56.

July [28] ***Silent Letter*** makes US #110, their final collaboration with Martin.

1980

Sept [20] ***Alibi***, recorded with the new production team of Matthew McCauley and Fred Mollin, and with help from Timothy B. Schmit, J.D. Souther and Steve Lukather among others, peaks at US #142.

1982

Oct [16] The duo makes a chart comeback, as the Russ Ballard-written and produced *You Can Do Magic*, hits US #8, their second non-original Top 10 hit.

[30] Its parent set ***View From The Ground***, with support from Carl Wilson, Christopher Cross, Schmit, Jeff Porcaro, Lukather and others, makes US #41. (Beckley and Bunnell are now writing songs with Bill Mumy, best known to TV audiences as William Robinson in the '60s series "Lost In Space".)

Nov [13] *You Can Do Magic*, recorded at Abbey Road Studios, London, peaks at UK #59.

1983

Jan [15] *Right Before Your Eyes*, produced by Bobby Colomby, makes US #45.

July ***Your Move***, produced by Ballard and featuring Stephen Bishop, makes US #81.

Aug [6] The uptempo Ballard/Bunnell-penned *The Border*, with the distinctive sax of Raphael Ravenscroft, makes US #33, their final singles chart appearance of the decade.

1984

Nov ***Perspective***, using three different producers and with material penned with Journey's Steve Perry and Jimmy Webb (for whom Beckley and Bunnell have been featured vocalists on his soundtrack for the animated feature "The Last Unicorn"), peaks at US #185.

1985

June [1] A performance at the Arlington Theatre, Santa Barbara, CA, is recorded for the future ***America In Concert*** release, the band's last album of the decade.

1986

Oct [13] The RIAA certifies platinum sales of ***America*** and four million sales of ***History - America's Greatest Hits***.

1995

Sept [30] Following the 1994 release of a new album ***Hourglass*** on the American Gramaphone label and Beckley's contribution with Robert Lamm and Carl Wilson of *Without Her* to the tribute album ***For The Love Of Harry (Everybody Sings Nilsson)***, Bunnell and Beckley, respectively living in Marin County and San Fernando Valley, CA, and having continued regular touring as America well into the '90s, perform at the 35th anniversary concert of New York's Bitter End night spot, before embarking on a New Year North American tour with Air Supply. (They have also guested on a number of albums, including those by the Beach Boys, Dan Fogelberg and even the Simpsons, while the enduring appeal of their earlier soft-rock hits have now become classic oldies material for US AC radio stations. While Warner Bros. delays the CD release of their most popular albums, Rhino Records has issued ***Encore: More Greatest Hits***, a 16-track round-up of their Capitol highlights, lesser known Warner Bros. album cuts and four new tracks, in 1991.)

TORI AMOS

1988

Aug Having learnt to play the piano from the age of two, Amos (b. Myra Ellen Amos, Aug. 22, 1963, Newton, NC), with Cherokee Indian and Scottish family roots and the daughter of a Methodist minister, attended the Peabody Conservatory in Baltimore, MD, from age five, where she studied under a piano scholarship (and was kicked out at age 11 for playing by ear). Influenced from an early age by the music of Fats Waller, John Lennon and George Gershwin among others, she began playing in bars aroung Washington, DC and Baltimore in her late teens, supported financially by her father. Her first recorded release was *Baltimore*, co-written with her brother Michael and only made available in that city on her own MEA label in 1980. Following a residency at the Hilton Hotel in Myrtle Beach, SC in 1981, Amos began sending demo tapes around the industry attracting the attention of producer Narada Michael Walden who invited her to a recording session in San Francisco, CA in November 1983, a collaboration which bore little fruit. Relocating to Los Angeles, CA the following year and changing her first name to Tori in 1985, Amos has secured a contract with Atlantic Records in 1987 after several rejections from other labels. She is promoted as a scantily-clad rocker, leading the rock outfit Y Kant Tori Read, which now releases the poorly-received ***Y Kant Tori Read***, featuring the singles *The Big Picture* and *Cool On Your Island*. (The band, essentially a studio ensemble, includes future Cult/Guns N' Roses drummer Matt Sorum and ex-Mr. Mister guitarist Steve Farris.)

Sept Al Stewart's ***Last Days Of The Century***, including backing vocals by Amos, is released by Enigma Records (UK). (She will make further cameo appearances over the next two years including three tracks on Stan Ridgway's ***Mosquitos*** (May 1989) and backing vocals on a Sandra Bernhard live album (June 1989). She will also contribute an uncredited vocal to *Distant Storm*, a song featured in the 1990 movie "China O'Brien".)

1991

Oct [21] Having moved to London in February and staying within the WEA group, Amos, now determined on a career as an earnest singer-songwriter/pianist, has signed to its East West imprint, after US Atlantic label co-chairman Doug Morris has asked East West head Max Hole to break her in the UK first. She has recently gigged in London at the Mean Fiddler and Borderline venues, and is quickly becoming the darling of the UK music press. The label now releases a four-track EP *Me And A Gun*, of which the title cut refers autobiographically to a traumatic incident in Los Angeles in 1985 when Amos was raped at gunpoint by a man who had given her a ride home after her performance in a bar.

Nov [30] Another of the EP's cuts, the emotional ballad *Silent All These Years*, gains airplay on BBC Radio 1 and initially makes UK #51, also spurred by a Cindy Palmano-directed video clip.

1992

Jan [21] She performs at the annual Midem festival at the Palais des Festivals, Cannes, France, in the Martinez side bar.

[25] ***Little Earthquakes***, partly produced by her boyfriend Eric Rosse, Davitt Sigerson and Ian Stanley, and showcasing her literate songwriting skills and Kate Bush-esque vocal style, reaches UK #14.

[29] Amos guests on BBC1-TV's "Wogan".

Feb [1] *China* debuts at its UK #51 peak.

[12] Amos begins an eight-date UK tour at King Tut's Wah Wah Hut, Glasgow, Scotland, set to end on the 21st at Sheffield University, Sheffield, S. Yorks.

Mar [28] *Winter*, the CD-single of which includes typically quirky versions of Nirvana's *Smells Like Teen Spirit*, the Rolling Stones' *Angie* and Led Zeppelin's *Whole Lotta Love*, reaches UK #25.

Apr [1] She embarks on another eight-date UK tour at the Guildhall, Southampton, Hants., set to end on the 11th at the Town Hall, Birmingham, W. Midlands, after which she will work on new tracks at Olympic Studios, Barnes, London with producer Stanley.

[23] Amos makes her US network TV debut on NBC-TV's "Late Night With David Letterman".

May [11] During maiden North American club dates, Amos plays to a sellout crowd at the Roxy, Los Angeles.

[30] ***Little Earthquakes*** makes US #54 during a 31-week stay on the survey.

June [8] Amos performs at Hamburg's Stadtpark during a four-date German tour, which sees gigs in Nurburgring, Frankfurt and Stuttgart.

[24] She guests on BBC1-TV's "Summer Scene", followed by an appearance on the network's "Top Of The Pops" on the 25th.

July [4] EP *Crucify* reaches UK #15 and will sell 150,000 copies in the US.

[7] Amos begins a series of North American dates at the Newport Music Hall, Columbus, OH.

Aug [29] Reissued *Silent All These Years* reaches UK #26.

Sept [19] During further US dates she plays in her native North Carolina before a sellout crowd of 624 at the Rialto Theatre, Raleigh, NC, grossing $7,730.

Nov [12] Her performance in Baltimore is recorded to add live rarities (notably her version of *Little Drummer Boy*) to future releases.

Dec [10] Amos guests on BBC2-TV's "Later", and is currently featured on the soundtrack album ***Toys*** (contributing the track *The Happy Worker*). (She is also voted Best New Female Artist in **Rolling Stone**'s annual readers' poll.)

1993

Amos spends the year writing and co-producing her sophomore album (with boyfriend Rosse), much of it prepared in Taos, NM.

1994

Jan [29] *Cornflake Girl* hits UK #4.

Feb [1] She is featured on ITV's "The Beat".

[11] Amos performs on NBC-TV's "The Tonight Show".

[12] Follow-up album, ***Under The Pink*** enters at UK #1.

[19] ***Under The Pink*** debuts at its US #12 peak.

Feb [24] A world tour begins at the Newcastle upon Tyne Theatre, Tyne & Wear set to end on March 7th at the Colston Hall, Bristol, Avon. (Further UK dates will resume on April 21st at the Guildhall, Portsmouth, Hants., including two concerts on April 28-29th at the London Palladium.)

Mar [16] Now living permanently in London, Amos appears on C4-TV's "The Big Breakfast".

[19] *Pretty Good Year* debuts at its UK #7 peak.

[28] She performs on CBS-TV's "Late Show With David Letterman".

Apr [9] *God* makes US #72 (but hits #1 on the Modern Rock Tracks chart).

June [4] *Past The Mission*, featuring Nine Inch Nails' Trent Reznor and recorded at the house in which Sharon Tate was murdered in 1969, reaches UK #31.

[7] "The Under The Pink Tour" North American tour leg opens in Brookville, NY at the Tilles Center, C. W. Post University, a gig grossing $40,680 from 2,034 attendees. (Amos will perform 181 dates during the year including three November concerts in Japan and a final ten shows in Australia in December ending on the 13th in Perth, W. Australia, Australia.)

[15] She is featured on C4's "Naked City". (During the month she is presented with the Visionary Award by the Washington DC Rape Crisis Center.)

Aug [25] Amos is the guest on NBC-TV's "Later With Greg Kinnear".

Sept [3] *Only Saw Today*, coupled with her cover version of John Lennon's *Instant Karma*, bows at its UK #48 peak.

Oct [15] *God* debuts at its UK #44 pinnacle.

Nov [10] ***Under The Pink*** is certified platinum. (Tom Jones' ***The Lead And How To Swing It*** is released featuring a duet with Amos on the Diane Warren-penned *I Wanna Get Back With You*.)

Dec Her version of *Little Drummer Boy*, originally released as a promo CD and in Australia on the EP *Pink Plus* in December 1993, is added to Atlantic Records' Christmas promotion CD ***So This Is Christmas***. (During the year Amos will become a founding sponsor of the RAINN (Rape Abuse and Incest National Network) telephone helpline in the US.)

1995

Jan [6] ***Little Earthquakes*** is certified platinum.

(Sony 550 (US) releases the ***Higher Learning*** movie soundtrack which includes Amos' reading of R.E.M.'s *Losing My Religion*. (During the year she will record a song with the group's Michael Stipe intended for the film soundtrack to "Don Juan DeMarco".)

Feb [24] Amos appears once again on "The Tonight Show".

Mar [1] She presents (with Carly Simon) the Best Male Rock Vocal trophy to Bruce Springsteen at the 37th annual Grammy Awards held at Los Angeles' Shrine Auditorium.

[25] *Let Love Shine* enters at its UK #31 peak.

Apr [8] Atlantic Records' ***Encomium: A Tribute To Led Zeppelin***, featuring *Down By The Seaside*, an Amos/Robert Plant duet, debuts at its US #17 peak.

Oct [7] *Church Of Freedom* charts for a week at UK #54.

[14] Leonard Cohen tribute album ***Tower of Song: The Songs of Leonard Cohen***, including Amos' version of *Famous Blue Raincoat*, charts for a week at US #198.

[16] She performs at the Wharton Center, East Lansing, MI.

1996

Jan [13] Previewing her third album, *Caught A Lite Sneeze* enters at its UK #20 peak and will make US #60 on the 27th.

Feb [3] Her first album following her separation from longtime producer and personal partner Rosse, ***Boys For Pele***, largely recorded in a church in County Wicklow, Eire and featuring the Black Dyke Mills Brass Band, hits UK #2, repeating the same chart peak the following week in the US.

[23] Amos' headlining European leg of the "Dew Drop Inn Tour '96", including three dates at London's Royal Albert Hall begins at the Regent Theatre, Ipswich, Suffolk, to be followed by a 40-city US trek beginning April 9th.

Mar [23] *Talula* enters UK chart at its #22 peak.

Apr [8] Amos makes a return visit to the "Late Show With David Letterman".

LAURIE ANDERSON

1972

After years studying violin and playing in the Chicago Youth Symphony, graduating with a degree in art history from Barnard College and earning her master of fine arts in sculpture from Columbia University, multi-media artist Anderson (b. June 5, 1947, Chicago, IL) begins giving public performances of her work, combining music with mime, speech, graphics, film, sculpture and slides, making her debut performance with "Automotive" on the town green at Rochester, VT, with the townsfolk beeping car, truck and motorcycle horns. A number of subsequent avant-garde events will include a performance on the 59th Street Bridge in New York, NY, playing the violin while wearing skates embedded in blocks of ice, in 1974, and a museum, festival and concert visit to Europe two years later.

1981

May She records an eight-minute monotone-backed track *O Superman* (an extract from her seven-hour work "United States"), selling an initial 1,000 copies by mail order from her Canal Street loft, then as a limited edition of 5,000 for New York independent label One Ten.

Aug *O Superman* is picked up by Warner Bros. Records, which signs her to an album contract.

Oct [24] *O Superman*, despite its length, an odd electronically-treated vocal and atmospheric piece, hits UK #2, backed by strong airplay. Similar success follows around Europe, though mainstream US radio finds it too alternative.

1982

May [8] ***Big Science*** reaches UK #29 and will make US #124.

1983

Feb "America", seven hours long and in four parts, premieres in the US. (Anderson continues with her avant-garde work, but rarely surfaces in the mainstream rock scene.)

1984

Mar ***Mister Heartbreak***, a collaboration with Peter Gabriel, peaks at UK #93 and US #60.

1985

Jan ***United States Live***, recorded at the Brooklyn Academy of Music in February 1983, makes US #192.

1986

May ***Home Of The Brave***, the Nile Rodgers-produced

soundtrack from an Anderson performance film, with contributions from William Burroughs, Bill Laswell and Rodgers, peaks at US #150.

1989

Nov ***Strange Angels*** climbs to US #171, Anderson having recently premiered "Empty Places" at the Brooklyn Academy of Music and embraced the mainstream, filming a TV commercial for Reebok shoes.

1990

Feb [7] She embarks on the "Strange Angels" North American tour in Tempe, AZ. (She will continue to perform in concert - during the summer of 1993 she does shows in Portugal, Spain, Switzerland and Turkey - but her recording career ceases.)

1994

Nov [12] ***Bright Red***, produced by Eno and including a spoken word duet with beau Lou Reed, charts for a week at US #195.

1995

Apr [6-9] Anderson performs at New York's Neil Simon Theater, during the "Nerve Bible" tour. (The current tour features material from ***Bright Red*** and newest album ***The Ugly One With The Jewels***. Her latest book, **Stories From The Nerve Bible** is published along with the CD-Rom title ***Puppet Motel***.)
June [25] AT&T's first televised infomercial, featuring Anderson, airs in the US.

THE ANIMALS

Eric Burdon (vocals); **Alan Price** (keyboards); **Hilton Valentine** (guitar); **Chas Chandler** (bass); **John Steel** (drums)

1962

Burdon (b. May 11, 1941, during an air raid in Walker, Northumberland) joins the Alan Price Combo, a Newcastle-based group playing R&B and rock'n'roll. Price (b. Apr. 19, 1941, Fairfield, Durham) has formed the band in 1960 as the Alan Price Trio with Chandler (b. Bryan Chandler, Dec. 18, 1938, Heaton, Northumberland), with whom Price has briefly played in the Kansas City Five, before they name-change to the Kontors, and Steel (b. Feb. 4, 1941, Gateshead, Northumberland), who has worked in the DeHavilland Aircraft factory in the South, before heading back to Newcastle to join the group. Price had sat in with Burdon's band the Pagans, formed at Newcastle's College of Art & Industrial Design. Valentine (b. May 21, 1943, North Shields, Northumberland), from Whiteley Bay's the Wild Cats, is invited to complete the line-up. They gain a regular slot at Newcastle's Downbeat club and legend has it that local fans call them "the animals" because of their notoriously wild stage act. (Claims are also made that the group in fact gets its name from an army veteran known as "Animal Hog", who ran a gang, which Burdon and Steel were on the fringes of.)

1963

May The group begins a two-month stint at Hamburg's Star Club, Germany.
Dec They record a demo EP for fans, pressing 500 copies which are all sold. The disc reaches London, leading to work offers in the capital.
[27] The band makes its first radio broadcast on BBC Radio's "Saturday Club".
[30] At one of the group's last appearances at Newcastle's Club A-Go-Go, they back US bluesman Sonny Boy Williamson. (In earlier times they have also backed John Lee Hooker and Memphis Slim.)

1964

Jan The group moves to London, and signs with emerging record producer Mickie Most, who has seen them at Club A-Go-Go and will be instrumental in their signing to EMI's Columbia label.
May [2] Their label debut *Baby Let Me Take You Home*, an R&B adaptation of the blues number *Baby Don't You Tear My Clothes*, reaches UK #21.
[9] They begin a 21-date, twice-nightly UK tour, with Chuck Berry, the Swinging Blue Jeans, the Nashville Teens, Karl Denver and others, at the Finsbury Park Astoria, London, ending on the 29th at the Odeon Cinema, Southend, Essex.
June [2] The band begins a ten-day tour of Japan.
July [11] Hailed as an instant pop classic *House Of The Rising Sun*, a Price rearrangement of a traditional folk-blues song, which has almost not been issued when EMI argues that its length (4½ minutes) will prevent radio play, tops the UK chart.
Sept [5] *House Of The Rising Sun* has been released (in shortened form) in the US by MGM Records, and hits #1 after only five weeks on the survey, eventually selling over a million copies.
[14] The group begins its first US tour in York, PA.
[26] *Baby Let Me Take You Home*, previously unsuccessful in the US, is reissued after *Rising Sun*'s success, but it is the B-side *Gonna Send You Back To Walker*, the band's cover of Timmy Shaw's US R&B #41 *Gonna Send You Back To Georgia*, retitled geographically to signify Burdon's birthplace, which becomes a US chart entry, peaking at #57.
Oct [17] *I'm Crying*, penned by Price and Burdon, hits UK #8.
[19] They begin a 28-date, twice-nightly tour with Carl Perkins, the Nashville Teens and Elkie Brooks, at the Odeon Cinema, Liverpool, Lancs., set to close on November 15th at Bournemouth's Winter Gardens, Dorset.
Nov [7] *I'm Crying* reaches US #19. Their debut album ***The Animals*** hits UK #6 and US #7, while *House Of The Rising Sun* is voted Best Disc Of The Year in **New Musical Express** poll.
Dec The group plays a nine-day tour behind the Iron Curtain.

1965

Jan [9] Their revival of John Lee Hooker's *Boom Boom* makes US #43.
[22] As the band prepares to go on stage at Harlem's Apollo Theatre to record the live album ***The Animals At The Apollo***, the US Immigration Department orders the cancellation of the shows.
[30] They guest in the first afternoon edition of BBC Light Programme's "Top Gear".
Feb [27] The Animals' cover of Nina Simone's *Don't Let Me Be Misunderstood* hits UK #3, though their interpretation does not please Ms. Simone.
Apr [3] *Don't Let Me Be Misunderstood* reaches US #15.
[11] The band participates in the annual "**New Musical Express** Poll Winners Concert", at the Empire Pool, Wembley, Middx.
[16] The group begins a Caribbean tour in San Domingo.
[18] "Pop Gear", a film in which they appear with the Beatles, Billy J. Kramer & the Dakotas, Herman's Hermits and the Rockin' Berries, goes on general UK release.
[29] A seven-day tour of Scandinavia begins, without Price, who is ill.
May [1] Their cover of Sam Cooke's *Bring It On Home To Me* hits UK #7.
[5] Due to growing musical disagreement with Burdon, and a dislike of flying which has made US tours anathema to him, Price announces he is leaving.
[8] The band returns from the Scandinavian trek, where Mickey Gallagher, previously with the Unknowns, has filled in for Price. Dave Rowberry (b. Dec. 27, 1943, Newcastle), from the Mike Cotton Sound, takes Price's place full-time.
[30] The group appears on CBS-TV's "The Ed Sullivan Show" at the conclusion of a ten-day US trip.
June ***Animal Tracks*** hits UK #6.
[12] *Bring It On Home To Me* makes US #32, as the US-only ***The Animals On Tour*** peaks at #99.
July [16] The Alan Price Combo, comprising Boots Slade (bass), Roy Mills (drums), John Walters (trumpet), Terry Childs (baritone sax), Steve Gregor (tenor sax) and Pete Kirtley (guitar), takes up residency at Newcastle's Club A-Go-Go, and signs with Decca Records.
Aug [8] The Animals play on the last day of the fifth annual Jazz & Blues Festival, at the Athletic Ground, Richmond, Surrey.
[12] Burdon and Chandler both collapse while performing on "Ready Steady Go!" at the Flamingo Club, London.
[14] *We've Gotta Get Out Of This Place*, a Barry Mann/Cynthia Weil song, hits UK #2, behind the Beatles' *Help!* Written with Paul Revere & the Raiders in mind, Weil will later state that the Animals' cover is her least favorite version of any of her compositions (punk outfit the Angelic Upstarts will also make the UK survey with their interpretation, in 1980).
[25] *We've Gotta Get Out Of This Place* reaches US #13.
[27] Price's debut single *Any Day Now*, credited to the Alan Price Set, is released on Decca (he will successfully launch his solo career, charting 11 hit singles over the next 22 years with Decca, Warner Bros., Jet, Ariola and CBS (duetting with Georgie Fame) labels).
Oct ***Animal Tracks*** is released in the US, set to make #57.
Nov [13] *It's My Life* hits UK #7, while the group is midway through an 11-day tour of Poland.
Dec [5] The band begins a two-week UK radio and TV promotion tour.

1966

Jan [1] *It's My Life* reaches US #23. (Burdon will refuse to renew the group's contract with Mickie Most and EMI because of dissatisfaction over the material on offer, so the group will switch to new producer Tom Wilson, and Decca Records. The US agreement with MGM will be unaffected.)
Feb Steel announces his intention to leave the band, returning to Newcastle, where he will become a successful businessman. Newspaper reports suggest replacements, including the Who's Keith Moon, Viv Prince, formerly with the Pretty Things, and the Nashville Teens' Barry Jenkins. Jenkins (b. Dec. 22, 1944, Leicester, Leics.) gets the job, earning £100 a week for three months, plus a royalty percentage.
[28] The Animals headline at the opening of Tiles club in London's Oxford Street.
Mar [5] Steel makes his final appearance with the group at Birmingham University, Birmingham, Warks., as their Decca debut *Inside Looking Out*, based on a Mississippi prison song, and aired on "Ready Steady Go!" under the title *Rosie* (Burdon and Chandler will subsequently rewrite the lyrics), reaches UK #12.
[15] Jenkins debuts with the Animals at the Paris Olympia, France.
[26] Compilation ***The Best Of The Animals*** enters the US chart, set to hit #6. The group's best-selling US album, it will remain charted for 113 weeks.
Apr [2] *Inside Looking Out* makes US #34.
[13] The group's fifth US tour opens at the Washington Boat Show, Washington, DC, set to end on May 4th at the State Fair, Indianapolis, IN.
May ***The Most Of The Animals***, released in Britain by EMI and anthologizing the Mickie Most-produced singles up to *It's My Life*, hits #4.
June ***Animalisms*** hits UK #4.
[4] Scheduled to fly to Spain, the group stays in the UK to resolve differences which threaten a split.
[25] Their version of the Gerry Goffin/Carole King song *Don't Bring Me Down* hits UK #6.
July [1] The band begins a US tour with Herman's Hermits, Jerry Lee Lewis and Lou Christie, in Honolulu, HI.
[2] *Don't Bring Me Down* reaches US #12.
[28] ***The Best Of The Animals*** is certified gold by the RIAA.
Sept A widening division between Burdon and the others (he is heavily involved with LSD, they are not) prompts the group to split at the end of a US tour. Jenkins remains with Burdon to form the nucleus of a

new group, while the others go their separate ways. Chandler will turn to management, most successfully with Jimi Hendrix in the '60s and Slade in the '70s.
Oct [20] The Animals, now comprising Burdon, Jenkins, former Family member John Weider (b. Apr. 21, 1947, London) on lead guitar, Danny McCullough (b. July 18, 1945, Shepherd's Bush, London) on bass and Tom Parker on organ, embarks on 16-date, twice-nightly UK tour as special guests, with Georgie Fame & the Georgie Fame Band, Chris Farlowe, Geno Washington & the Ram Jam Band and the Paul Butterfield Blues Band, at the Finsbury Park Astoria, London, set to end on November 6th at the Odeon Cinema, Leicester, Leics.
[22] The last single by the original group, but credited to Eric Burdon & the Animals, *See See Rider*, reviving Ma Rainey's 1925 hit, is only issued in the US, and, ironically, is one of their biggest hits, hitting #10. ***Animalization*** (also not issued in Britain) is released, set to make US #20.
Nov [26] *Help Me Girl*, credited to Eric Burdon & the Animals (though it has actually been recorded by Burdon in New York with session players, led by jazzman Benny Golson), reaches UK #14.
Dec [31] *Help Me Girl* reaches US #29.

1967

Jan The original group's final album of the decade, ***Animalisms***, partly recorded on the last US tour (and mostly featuring blues and R&B standards), belatedly reaches US #33. Meanwhile, Burdon relocates to California with his new Animals, with Vic Briggs (b. Feb. 14, 1945, Twickenham, Surrey), ex-Brian Auger & the Trinity, joining on guitar, but without Parker. This group is signed to MGM Records for both the UK and US.
Feb [10] A North American tour starts at Hunter College, New York.
Mar [1] Fans stage a riot at the Coliseum, Ottawa, Canada, while waiting over an hour for the group to appear. The band fails to play at all.
Apr Burdon's solo album, ***Eric Is Here***, recorded at the same time as ***Help Me Girl***, is issued in the US, and will reach #121.
[11] The group embarks on a tour of New Zealand, Australia, Singapore and Hong Kong, with Dave Dee, Dozy, Beaky, Mick & Tich, and Paul & Barry Ryan, in Christchurch, New Zealand. (The Mothers Of Invention's Roy Estrada fills in for McCullough, who is unable to play after breaking his wrist in a fall in Hollywood, CA.)
May [6] First release by the new group, with producer Tom Wilson, is *When I Was Young*, which eschews the traditional Animals R&B sound in favor of psychedelic-flavored hard rock, showing the influence on Burdon of the burgeoning US West Coast scene, and reaches US #15.
[25] The band attends the premiere of the James Mason/Bobby Darin-starring film "Stranger In The House", in which it performs *Ain't That So*.
June ***When I Was Young*** makes UK #45.
[16] The group plays on the opening day of the Monterey International Pop Festival at the County Fairgrounds, Monterey, CA.
July Compilation ***The Best Of Eric Burdon & The Animals, Vol.2*** makes US #71.
Sept [16] *San Franciscan Nights*, celebrating Burdon's new lifestyle, hits US #9.
[24] The group makes its cabaret debut at the Stockton Fiesta, Stockton-on-Tees, Cleveland.
Oct [7] *Good Times*, berating Burdon's hard-drinking past, reaches UK #20.
[19-21] They perform consecutive nights at the Fillmore West on a bill which includes Mother Earth and Hour Glass.
Nov [18] *San Franciscan Nights* hits UK #7, while ***Winds Of Change***, a showcase of the new progressive group style, makes US #42.
Dec [22] The group performs during a five-day "Party Night" festival at London's Roundhouse.

1968

Jan [13] *Monterey*, a tribute to the 1967 festival, reaches US #15.
Mar [2] Two-part single *Sky Pilot*, a controversial attack on the complacency of religion in the face of war (and on which Weider experiments with electric violin), makes UK #40.
Apr [27] *Anything* climbs to US #80.
May ***The Twain Shall Meet*** makes US #79.
June Briggs and McCullough leave, replaced by ex-Big Roll Band and Dantalian's Chariot members, Zoot Money (keyboards) and Andy Summers (b. Andrew Summers, Dec. 31, 1942, Poulton-Le-Fylde, Lancs.) (guitar), as the band becomes Eric Burdon & the New Animals.
July [27] *Sky Pilot* reaches US #14.
Sept ***Every One Of Us*** reaches US #152.
[6] The group begins a series of dates at the Fillmore West, San Francisco, CA, with the Chambers Brothers.
Dec [28] *White Houses*, the band's final US chart single, peaks at #67, as Burdon announces, at the end of US and Japanese tours, that they will disband after a Christmas concert in his home city of Newcastle. (Weider and Jenkins announce they will form Bicycle with members of the Grass Roots, but nothing comes of it. Jenkins joins Heavy Jelly with Jackie Lomax. Briggs and McCulloch record ***Mr. Moon And Mr. Sun***.)

1969

Jan As the group winds up, its revival of Johnny Cash's *Ring Of Fire* makes UK #35, while the double album ***Love Is*** peaks at US #123 (Feb) and compilation ***The Greatest Hits Of Eric Burdon & The Animals*** makes US #153 in April.

1970

Jan Now in Los Angeles, CA, and more interested in looking for movie parts than forming another band, Burdon (at producer Jerry Goldstein's suggestion) teams up with Night Shift, a heavy funk band from Long Beach, CA, which changes its name to War. Together, they will record and tour the US throughout the year.
Sept [28] *Spill The Wine* is certified gold by the RIAA.

1971

Jan Eric Burdon & War begin a European tour, only to have Burdon, suffering from exhaustion, quit midway through and return to the US. War completes the itinerary without him (and will quickly develop into one of the most successful US funk bands of the '70s). When recovered, Burdon realises a long-held ambition, recording ***Guilty*** with blues singer Jimmy Witherspoon. (They will team up again in 1976 for ***Black & White Blues***, released on MCA.)
Sept [4] Burdon performs at an open-air concert in London's Hyde Park on a bill with King Crimson, John Sebastian among others.
Oct Retrospective budget album ***Most Of The Animals*** makes UK #18.

1972

Oct [21] *House Of The Rising Sun*, reissued in the UK on Mickie Most's RAK label, reaches #25.

1973

Aug [23] Burdon performs at the annual Reading Rock Festival, Reading, Berks., with a new back-up trio comprising Aaron Butler (guitar), Randy Rice (bass) and Alvin Taylor (drums), while ***The Best Of The Animals*** peaks at US #188.

1975

Jan Now signed to Capitol Records as the Eric Burdon Band, ***Sun Secrets*** reaches US #51, to be followed by ***Stop*** (with a different line-up), which indeed stops at US #171 in August, following which, the group splits.

1976

Jan The original five Animals get together to play for fun at Chandler's house, and hire a mobile studio to cut an album.

1977

Mar Chandler produces the Burdon solo ***Survivor***, mostly co-written by the singer and ex-New Animals keyboard player Zoot Money, for Polydor in W. Germany (and released in Britain the following year).
Aug ***Before We Were So Rudely Interrupted***, credited to the Original Animals, and taken from the previous year's reunion session, is issued on Chandler's Barn label in the UK and on the Jet label in the US, where it makes US #70.

1982

Oct [23] *House Of The Rising Sun*, reissued for a second time, reaches UK #11.

1983

July The original quintet regroups again for ***Ark*** on the I.R.S. label followed by a lucrative world tour which begins the following month.
Sept [24] *The Night* makes US #48 while ***Ark*** is on its way to US #66.
Dec [31] ***Rip It To Shreds : The Animals Greatest Hits Live*** is recorded at Wembley Arena, by the reunited line-up, but only reaches US #193. The Animals split yet again (Chandler will die on July 17, 1996, having been ill for several months).

1994

Jan [19] Some ten years after the last Animals release during which Burdon has published his autobiography **I Used To Be An Animal, But I'm Alright Now** in 1986, released his own ***Wicked Man*** in 1988, guested on Paul Shaffer's ***Coast To Coast***, singing *Sixteen Tons* in the opening scene of the Tom Hanks/Meg Ryan movie "Joe Versus The Volcano", made a cameo appearance on ABC-TV's "China Beach", toured the US with the Doors' Robby Krieger during the summer of 1990 and embarked on European and North American tours in late 1991 with Brian Auger, The Animals are inducted into the Rock and Roll Hall of Fame by Soul Asylum's Dave Pirner at the ninth annual dinner held at New York's Waldorf-Astoria Hotel.
see also: **FAMILY, POLICE, WAR**

PAUL ANKA

1956

July Already an experienced part-time entertainer (he made his first public appearance at age ten, earning $35 impersonating Johnnie Ray in an amateur talent contest in 1953, at the Ocean Beach club in Gloucester, MA) and budding songwriter while still at high school, Anka (b. July 30, 1941, Ottawa, ON, Canada), the son of Lebanese immigrant restaurateurs Andy and Camy Anka, spends the summer vacation away from his family's restaurant, staying with his uncle Maurice in Los Angeles, CA, working at the Civic Playhouse in an attempt to break into show business.
Sept He takes his composition *I Confess* to nearby Modern Records, whose A&R chief Ernie Freeman records it, backed by the label's *Stranded In The Jungle* hit-makers the Cadets. The disc sells 3,000 copies.
Oct Back at Fisher Park High School in Ottawa, he forms the Bobbysoxers vocal trio with two classmates, and begins work on *Diana*, a song inspired by the family's 18-year-old babysitter Diana Ayoub, for whom the 15-year-old Anka has a passion.

1957

Apr He wins an Easter trip to New York, NY, in a grocery store contest in which he collects more

Campbell's Soup can labels than anyone else. Impressed by the city, he borrows $100 from his father to make a return visit with four songs he has committed to tape. Staying with friends the Rover Boys (who are signed to Paramount Records), he visits, at their suggestion, Don Costa at ABC Records, who signs him to Paramount, impressed by his (then rare) singer/songwriter abilities.

Aug [31] Within a month of its release, *Diana* tops the UK chart, where it will stay for nine weeks. Worldwide sales will top nine million and it becomes one of the top five best-selling singles of all time.

Sept [1] Anka begins "The Biggest Show Of Stars For 1957" package tour with Buddy Holly & the Crickets, Chuck Berry, the Drifters, Frankie Lymon & the Teenagers, the Everly Brothers, Clyde McPhatter and others, at the Brooklyn Paramount Theater, set to end on November 24th at the Mosque, Richmond, VA. (The white artists on the bill are unable to play on several dates because of segregation laws which forbid black and white acts on the same stage.)

[7] *Diana* hits US #2, spending five weeks behind Debbie Reynolds' *Tammy* and instantly transforming Anka into one of America's hottest and youngest teen idols.

Nov [16] *Tell Me That You Love Me*, B-side of the still-climbing *I Love You Baby*, reaches UK #25.

Dec [7] Anka begins his first UK tour at London's Trocadero Theatre.

[14] *I Love You Baby* hits UK #3, helped by a successful "Sunday Night At The London Palladium" ITV spot, and a UK, European and Australian tour.

[21] *I Love You Baby* peaks at US #97.

1958

Jan Anka begins a six-day tour of Australia, playing Melbourne, Sydney and Brisbane, with Buddy Holly & the Crickets and Jerry Lee Lewis.

Feb [24] *You Are My Destiny* hits US #7.

Mar [8] *You Are My Destiny* hits UK #6, the first of several transatlantic Anka chart singles for the year: *Crazy Love* reaches US #19 (May [10]) and UK #26 (May [31]) while its B-side, *Let The Bells Keep Ringing* reaches US #30 (June [21]); *Midnight* peaks at US #69 (Aug [23]) and UK #26 (Sept [27]).

Apr [5] Anka embarks on an 80-day North American tour in Norfolk, VA, co-starring in Irving Feld's "Greatest Show Of Stars" with the Everly Brothers, Sam Cooke and Frankie Avalon, among others.

Oct Anka gives *It Doesn't Matter Anymore* to Buddy Holly, who has expressed interest in recording an Anka song. It will become a 1959 posthumous UK #1 and US #14 for Holly.

[25] *Just Young* peaks at US #80.

1959

Jan [10] *The Teen Commandments*, with George Hamilton IV and Johnny Nash, reaches US #29, while Anka tours the UK again.

Feb [7] Standard *(All Of A Sudden) My Heart Sings*, originally a hit for both Johnnie Johnson and Martha Stewart in 1945, reaches US #15.

[14] *(All Of A Sudden) My Heart Sings* hits UK #10.

Mar He makes his first Hollywood movie, "Girls Town", with Mamie Van Doren and Mel Torme, and will go on to make others, including "The Private Lives Of Adam And Eve", "Look In Any Window" and "The Longest Day", writing themes for them all.

May [2] *I Miss You So* makes US #33.

July [18] Self-penned *Lonely Boy*, from "Girls Town", begins a four-week run at US #1, his second US chart-topper.

Aug Anka makes his first nightclub appearance, at the Sahara Hotel, Las Vegas, NV.

[29] *Lonely Boy* hits UK #3.

Oct [10] *Put Your Head On My Shoulder* hits US #2, set to spend three weeks behind Bobby Darin's *Mack The Knife*, and will hit UK #7 on Nov [21].

1960

Jan [2] *It's Time To Cry* hits US #4.

Feb [27] *It's Time To Cry* reaches UK #28.

Apr [4] *Puppy Love*, written about Annette Funicello, hits US #2, behind Percy Faith's *Theme From A Summer Place* (and will become a global hit a second time with Donny Osmond's cover version in 1972).

[11] *Adam And Eve*, the B-side of *Puppy Love*, peaks at US #90.

[23] *Puppy Love* reaches UK #33.

June He becomes the youngest performer to star at New York's Copacabana nightclub.

[27] *Something Happened*, flip-side of the still-climbing *My Home Town*, makes US #41.

July [4] *My Home Town* hits US #8, as ***Paul Anka Sings His Big 15*** makes its chart bow. It will hit US #4, during a 140-week chart-stay.

Sept [5] *Hello Young Lovers* reaches US #23.

[12] B-side *I Love You In The Same Old Way* makes US #40.

[17] *Hello Young Lovers* stops at UK #44.

Oct [31] *Summer's Gone* reaches US #11.

Dec Live ***Anka At The Copa*** reaches US #23.

1961

Continuing his seamless run of hits, *The Story Of My Love* peaks at US #16 (Feb [20]), *Tonight My Love, Tonight* reaches US #13 (May [1]), *Dance On Little Girl* hits US #10 (July [10]), *Kissin' On The Phone* makes US #35 (Sept [11]), while its B-side *Cinderella* peaks at US #70 (Oct [9]), the same month ***Paul Anka Sings His Big 15, Vol.2*** makes US #72.

Nov [13] ABC-Paramount agrees to terminate his contract early. A week later he will sign a million-dollar contract with RCA Records.

1962

Apr [7] Label debut *Love Me Warm And Tender* reaches US #12, and restores Anka to the UK chart, at #19.

May ***Young, Alive And In Love!*** makes US #61.

July [7] *A Steel Guitar And A Glass Of Wine* reaches US #13.

Aug [4] *A Steel Guitar And A Glass Of Wine* makes UK #41.

[25] Paramount single *I'm Coming Home* stops at US #94.

Sept [22] *Every Night (Without You)* makes US #46, as ***Let's Sit This One Out*** peaks at US #137.

Oct [2] NBC-TV airs the first "Tonight" show, for which Anka writes the theme with host Johnny Carson.

[12] "The Longest Day", for which Anka writes the theme and in which he is one of the many stars, premieres at London's Leicester Square Theatre.

Dec [8] Latin-tempoed *Eso Beso (That Kiss!)*, acknowledging the current bossa nova craze, reaches US #19.

1963

Feb [16] Anka marries Marie Ann Alison DeZogheb, whom he met in Puerto Rico, daughter of Count Charles DeZogheb, a Lebanese businessman, in a chapel at Orly Airport, near Paris, France.

[16] *Love (Makes The World Go 'Round)* reaches US #26.

May [25] Anka-penned *Remember Diana*, belated sequel to his first hit, makes US #39.

June [29] *Hello Jim* peaks at US #97.

July [6] ***Paul Anka's Golden Hits***, a re-recorded version of his ABC-Paramount hits, begins a 33-week US chart stay, although never reaching higher than #65.

Dec [7] The Beatles, appearing on BBC-TV show "Juke Box Jury", vote Anka's new single *Did You Have A Happy Birthday?* a miss.

[14] *Did You Have A Happy Birthday?* stalls at US #89.

1964

May [17] Anka guests on CBS-TV's "The Ed Sullivan Show".

Nov [9] He arrives in London with his wife for a two-week stay, to meet UK songwriters and TV producers.

1965

Jan [16] Anka returns to Britain one day after the release of the Burt Bacharach-penned *To Wait For Love*, his first single recorded in the UK. (His UK TV appearances include ITV's "The Eamonn Andrews Show" and BBC1-TV's "Juke Box Jury".)

1969

Feb [22] Following a quieter three-year period, during which he could assess his favorable financial position in between selected cabaret and film work, *Goodnight My Love* reaches US #27.

Mar ***Goodnight My Love***, Anka's first chart album in five years, makes US #101.

Apr [19] *In The Still Of The Night*, reviving the Five Satins '50s classic, peaks at US #64.

May [10] Frank Sinatra reaches US #27 with *My Way*, a Claude François original called *Comme D'Habitude* onto which Anka has transposed English lyrics. It becomes Sinatra's new signature tune, even though the first attempt at over-writing English lyrics on the French standard was actually made by David Bowie. It also hits UK #5.

June [21] *Sincerely* peaks at US #80.

Dec [6] *Happy* stalls at US #86.

[27] ***Life Goes On*** makes US #194 during a two-week chart stay.

1971

Jan Anka's *She's A Lady* is a UK #12 hit for Tom Jones, and hits #2 in the US, where it sells a million.

Nov [27] Anka, newly signed to Buddah Records, peaks at US #53 with *Do I Love You*.

1972

Jan Buddah album debut ***Paul Anka*** climbs to US #188.

May [6] *Jubilation*, the title track from his forthcoming album, peaks at US #65.

June ***Jubilation*** makes US #192.

1973

June [19] Anka sings *Put Your Head On My Shoulder* on ABC-TV's "American Bandstand's 20th Anniversary Special".

1974

Feb [16] *Let Me Get To Know You*, a one-off hit on the Fame label, stops at US #80.

Aug [14] Still-climbing *(You're) Having My Baby* is certified gold by the RIAA.

[24] *(You're) Having My Baby*, a duet with protegée Odia Coates, whom Anka met when producing the Edwin Hawkins Singers' *Oh Happy Day*, tops the US chart. (Written about his wife's pregnancy, it nonetheless brings the ire of the National Organization of Women, who present him their "Keep Her In Her Place" award.) ***Anka*** hits US #9.

Oct [26] *(You're) Having My Baby* hits UK #6.

Nov [20] ***Anka*** is certified gold by the RIAA.

Dec ***Paul Anka Gold***, a Sire release of original ABC-Paramount hits, makes US #125.

1975

Jan [25] *One Man Woman/One Woman Man*, a second duet with Coates, hits US #7.

May [24] His third collaboration with Coates, *I Don't Like To Sleep Alone*, hits US #8, as parent album ***Feelings*** reaches US #36.

Sept [27] Final Coates pairing, *(I Believe) There's Nothing Stronger Than Our Love*, reaches US #15.

1976

Feb [7] Solo *Times Of Your Life* hits US #7, spurred by its exposure as the tune to a Kodak TV commercial, and is Anka's final Top 10 hit.

[28] ***Times Of Your Life***, featuring the hit and nine tracks from his previous two United Artists albums, makes US #22. Further chart items over the next two years are: *Anytime (I'll Be There)* US #33 (May [15]), ***The Painter*** US #85 (Dec [25]), *Happier* US #60 (Jan [22], 1977) and *My Best Friend's Wife* US #80 (May [7]), while ***The Music Man*** climbs to US #195 (June) and *Everybody Ought To Be In Love* peaks at US #75 (Aug [6]).

Nov [15] ***Times Of Your Life*** is certified gold by the RIAA.

1978

Dec [2] Now re-signed to RCA, Anka makes US #35 with *This Is Love*, while its parent album, the David Wolfert-produced ***Listen To Your Heart***, peaks at US #179 one week later. His remaining RCA chart titles come in 1981 with *I've Been Waiting For You All Of My Life* making US #48 (May [23]) and ***Both Sides Of Love*** stalling at US #171 the following month.

1979

Apr [2] Anka performs the first of four consecutive concerts at the London Palladium, his first UK dates in 18 years.

1983

Sept [3] Now signed to CBS/Columbia Records, Anka reaches US #40 with the lush ballad, *Hold Me 'Til The Mornin' Comes*, penned with compatriot David Foster and featuring backing vocals by Peter Cetera. Parent album ***Walk A Fine Line*** makes US #156. (Based in Las Vegas with his wife and daughters, Anka will continue playing cabaret dates there and at Lake Tahoe, NV, through much of the decade.)

1990

Jan [17] Anka inducts the late Bobby Darin into the Rock and Roll Hall of Fame at the fifth annual dinner, at the Waldorf Astoria Hotel, New York.

Aug [30] Anka receives his certificate of US citizenship with 54 other people during a federal court ceremony in Las Vegas. (He parks his car in a US Immigration and Naturalization Service parking bay and has it towed away.)

1991

Feb [10] Anka joins with 100 celebrities in Burbank, CA, to record *Voices That Care*, a David Foster and fiancée Linda Thompson Jenner-composed and organised charity record to benefit the American Red Cross Gulf Crisis Fund. (He will also become part owner of the National Hockey League's Ottawa Senators in May, and play an ex-con in an episode of NBC-TV's "Perry Mason".)

1993

June [2] Having completed a co-starring role (with Glenne Headly) in "Ganesh" the previous year, the entertainment veteran, still a popular live draw both in Europe and North America, (notably performing at the Royal Albert Hall, London, on November 21st 1992 during an eight-date UK visit, (also appearing on ITV's "Des O'Connor Tonight" on December 23rd not least promoting his most recent album ***Paul Anka Five Decades***, an incomplete retrospective including his first hit, *Diana*, and his latest single, *Freedom For The World*, on which he duets with Israeli vocalist Ofra Haza), Anka is now inducted into the Songwriters Hall of Fame at the 24th annual dinner and induction ceremony, at New York's Sheraton Hotel. In August 1996, Anka will release the bilingual Latin-phrased album, ***Amigos***, featuring guests Julio Iglesias, Celine Dion, Tom Jones, Barry Gibb, Kenny G and others.

ANTHRAX

Joey Belladonna (vocals); **Dan Spitz** (guitar); **Scott Ian** (guitar); **Frank Bello** (bass); **Charlie Benante** (drums)

1983

May The band is initially formed by Ian (b. Scott Rosenfeld, Dec. 31, 1963, Queens, NY) and bassist Dan Lilker (b. Oct. 18, 1964, Queens) in New York, in July 1981, joined by Benante (b. Nov. 27, 1962, Bronx, NY), ex-Overkill guitarist Spitz (b. Jan. 28, 1963, Queens), whose older brother David has played in Black Sabbath, and a number of temporary vocalists (including Neil Turbin and John Donnelly), its members drawn together by their mutual interest in hardcore thrash heavy metal music, comics and skateboarding. Following an 18-month period of non-stop small-town touring through the US, the group persistently courts the attention of Johnny Z (and his partner Marsha Zazula) who signs them to his Megaforce label for its debut release *Soldiers Of Metal* (with Turbin on lead vocals). Building on their growing live notoriety, they will support Manowar and Metallica by year's end.

1984

Feb ***Fistful Of Metal***, notable for some of the fastest metal riff music ever recorded, is released on Megaforce in the US, and licensed to Music For Nations in Europe. As they tour continuously in North America, Ian, needing to play even faster thrash, forms the concurrent splinter group Stormtroopers Of Death (SOD) with Benante, Lilker and Billy Milano (from Method of Destruction). They will play six dates between October and December, and release ***Speak Of English Or Die*** before splitting. Lilker leaves, later joining Nuclear Assault, and the group's roadie Bello (b. Sept. 7, 1965, Bronx), who has previously lived with Benante's family, becomes their permanent bassist.

Aug [12] Working on the EP *Among The Living* in Ithaca, NY, Ian fires Turbin. Matt Fallon joins temporarily, to be permanently replaced by Belladonna (b. Oct. 30, 1960, Oswego, NY), ex-singer with Bible Black. His vocal range and power subsequently give a new polished focus to subsequent recordings.

1985

Feb ***Armed And Dangerous***, a five-track mini-album recorded at Pyramid Studios in New York, including a revival of the Sex Pistols' *God Save The Queen*, arouses interest from Island Records' US division, which signs the band to record its second album, with producer Carl Canedy, again in New York.

1986

Feb ***Spreading The Disease*** is released, with Music For Nations again picking up the European license. The extracted *Madhouse* is issued several times over the ensuing months.

June While ***Spreading The Disease*** makes US #113, the band makes its live UK debut at London's Hammersmith Palais, supporting Onslaught, followed by a European and Scandinavian tour opening for Metallica.

Nov [16-17] They perform two sellout shows at the Hammersmith Odeon, London. The latter part of the year and early 1987 is spent in Miami, FL, and the Bahamas, recording a third album, with producer Eddie Kramer.

1987

Feb [15] The group plays a further sellout Hammersmith Odeon date.

Mar [7] *I Am The Law*, previewing a new album, becomes their UK chart debut, making #32.

Apr [18] ***Among The Living*** receives critical acclaim, charting at UK #18, and will make US #62.

June *Indians* makes UK #44.

Dec [12] *I'm The Man* reaches UK #20, following another UK tour, which has again included sold-out London dates. The following week ***I'm The Man***, including three live cuts from a gig in Dallas, TX, in July 1987, enters the US chart, set to make #53.

1988

Aug The group takes part in the annual Monsters of Rock Festival at Castle Donington, Leics.

[19] ***I'm The Man*** is certified gold by the RIAA, the band's first such award.

Sept [3] *Make Me Laugh* reaches UK #26.

[24] Its parent album ***State Of Euphoria*** reaches UK #12 and will make US #30.

Dec [8] A US tour begins at the Meadowlands Arena, East Rutherford, NJ, set to end on the 27th at the Arizona Veterans Memorial Coliseum & State Fairgrounds, Phoenix, AZ.

1989

Feb [8] ***State Of Euphoria*** is certified gold by the RIAA.

Mar [8] The group begins a six-date UK tour at the Apollo Theatre, Manchester, Gtr. Manchester, ending at London's Hammersmith Odeon, as *Anti-Social* makes UK #44.

May [24] Anthrax's "N.F.V./Oidivnikufesin" video is certified gold by the RIAA.

1990

Jan [24] The band's rehearsal studios in Yonkers, NY, catch fire, causing more than $100,000 worth of damage to the group's equipment.

July [31] ***Among The Living*** is certified gold by the RIAA.

Aug [27] The group begins a tour of Australia at the Thebarton Theatre, Adelaide, S. Australia, Australia.

Sept [1] *In My World* reaches UK #29.

[8] ***Persistence Of Time*** debuts at its UK #13 peak.

[22] ***Persistence Of Time*** reaches US #24.

Oct [21] Anthrax supports Iron Maiden on the latter's "No Prayer On The Road" tour, beginning in Barcelona, Spain. They stay with the trek through to a concert at Wembley Arena, Wembley, Middx., on December 18th.

1991

Jan [12] *Got The Time* reaches UK #16.

[13] A 33-date US tour, again supporting Iron Maiden, begins at the Metro Centre, Halifax, NS, Canada, set to end at the Cow Palace, San Francisco, CA, on March 14th, though Anthrax continues for further concerts without Iron Maiden. (During the trek, Belladonna will sing the national anthem at the US "Hot Rod Mud & Monster Truck Racing Championships" at Madison Square Garden, New York.)

[17] ***Persistence Of Time*** is certified gold by the RIAA.

Feb [20] ***Persistence Of Time*** is nominated for Best Metal Performance at the 33rd annual Grammy Awards, at Radio City Music Hall, New York.

May [16] Multi-act metal package "Clash of the Titans" tour opens at the Starplex Amphitheatre, Dallas, TX, featuring Anthrax, Megadeth, Slayer and Alice In Chains. It will include a sold-out $253,530-grossing date at Madison Square Garden, on June 28th.

July [13] *Bring The Noise*, featuring Public Enemy rapper Chuck D, reaches UK #14.

[20] ***Attack Of The Killers Bs***, comprising B-sides and previously unreleased material, enters at its UK #13 peak reaches US #27.

Sept [24] The band kicks off its "Bring The Noise" US tour with Public Enemy in Poughkeepsie, NY.

Nov [7] ***Attack Of The Killer B's*** is certified gold by the RIAA.

1992

Jan [12] "Bring The Noise", a unique thrash/rap tour outing pairing Anthrax and Public Enemy reaches the UK, highlighted by a London date at the Brixton Academy.

Feb Having signed a multimillion dollar record deal with the Elektra label the previous month, Belladonna announces he is leaving band, although reports having him being fired. (He will subsequently form the band Belladonna with Paul Cook on guitar and Dave Femmia on drums.)

[23] A pre-taped Fox-TV's "Married ... With Children" is broadcast features Ted Bundy winning a dinner date with Anthrax.

Mar The side-band SOD reunites with Ian, Benante, Lilker and Milano in the lineup.

Apr [2] The band holds open auditions for a new lead vocalist at New York's Danceteria.

June After speculation that Scream frontman John

Corabi is to join Anthrax, Elektra announces that ex-Armored Saint singer John Bush (b. Aug. 24, 1963, Los Angeles, CA) is the band's new lead vocalist.
Sept [21] Archive item, SOD's ***Live At The Budokan***, is released in the UK.

1993

Jan [7] *I'm The Man* EP is certified platinum by the RIAA.
May [14] Anthrax begins a six-date club tour at Iguana's, Tijuana, Mexico, set to end on the 24th in New York.
[15] *Only* makes UK #36.
[29] ***The Sound Of White Noise***, Anthrax's first new studio recording in nearly three years and the first to feature Bush, bows at its UK #14 peak.
June [10] Anthrax guests on syndicated TV's "The Arsenio Hall Show".
[12] ***The Sound Of White Noise*** debuts at its US peak, #7, as the group also contributes a track to the soundtrack of Arnold Schwarzenegger's movie "The Last Action Hero".
July [13] ***The Sound Of White Noise*** is certified gold by the RIAA.
[27-29] The group begins a North American tour at the Hara Arena, Dayton, OH.
Sept [11] *Black Lodge* debuts at its UK #53 peak.

1994

Feb [22] Performance set, ***Live: The Island Years***, is released in the US.
May [15] During its current US tour, Anthrax performs at the Hollywood Palladium, Hollywood, CA.
July [9] The Kiss-tribute album, ***Kiss My Ass***, featuring the band's version of *She*, debuts at its US #19.

1995

Oct [17] The group, now comprising Ian, Bello, Bush and Benante (Spitz has left the group prior to the recording of the album), links up with Internet fans on America OnLine.
Nov [11] ***Stomp 442***, produced by the Butcher Brothers and featuring guest guitarist, Pantera's Dimebag Darrell, bows at its US #47 peak.
[28] Bush, Ian and Bello guest on NBC-TV's "Newsradio".
[29] The band plays at the Academy in New York.

THE ARCHIES

Archie Andrews (vocals, lead guitar); **Jughead Jones** (bass guitar); **Veronica Lodge** (organ); **Betty Cooper** (tambourine); **Reggie** (drums); **Hot Dog** (mascot)

1967

CBS-TV commissions Filmation Studios to create an animated Saturday morning show featuring the Archies, a fictional rock group based on the comic book characters originated by cartoonist Bob Montana-based on people he studied with at Haverhill High School, Haverhill, MA, and commissioned by John Goldwater in 1942. (Montana bases Archie partly on himself and partly on then-popular radio show teen Henry Aldrich, Jughead on schoolfriend Richard Linnehan, Veronica on actress Veronica Lake, Betty on schoolfriend Mary Elizabeth Bostwick and Moose on Arnold Daggett.) Don Kirshner is recruited to supervise the music, hiring Jeff Barry (b. Apr. 3, 1939, New York, NY) to produce, who recruits his wife Ellie Greenwich (b. Oct. 23, 1939, Long Island, NY), Toni Wine, Andy Kim, Tony Passalacqua and Ron Dante (b. Carmine Granito, Aug. 22, 1945, Staten Island, New York) as vocalists, with Hugh McCracken, Gary Chester, Artie Butler and Robin McNamara constituting the Archies session band. Archie comic books publish **The Music Man**, showing the group auditioning for Kirshner.

1968

Sept The first "Archies" song, *Bang-Shang-A-Lang* (which launches the cartoon show), is recorded with Dante on lead vocals. His voice becomes identified with the Archies' sound, even though he is never actually seen performing. Greenwich joins in on vocals.
[14] "The Archies" airs for the first time on CBS-TV. (The second series will be renamed "The Archies Comedy Hour".)
Dec [7] Jeff Barry-penned *Bang-Shang-A-Lang*, released on the Calendar label, reaches US #22, as parent album ***The Archies*** makes US #88.

1969

Feb [1] *Feelin' So Good (S.k.o.o.b.y-D.o.o)*, written by Barry with Kim, and with the same vocal pairing as its predecessor, peaks at US #53.
Aug [30] Still-climbing *Sugar Sugar* is already certified gold by the RIAA.
Sept [20] Pure pop confection *Sugar Sugar*, also written by Barry and Kim, and sung by Dante with Wine, begins a four-week stay at US #1, displacing the Rolling Stones' *Honky Tonk Women*. It will become the biggest worldwide seller of 1969, with over six million copies sold. Its parent album ***Everything's Archie*** makes US #66.
Oct [25] Despite "Archie" cartoons being unknown in Britain, *Sugar Sugar* tops the UK chart, where it will stay for eight weeks, selling over 900,000 copies.

1970

Jan [29] Still climbing *Jingle Jangle* is certified for million-plus US sales by the RIAA.
Feb [7] *Jingle Jangle*, the first single on the Kirshner label, once again written by Barry and Kim, and sung as a duet by Dante and Wine, hits US #10. ***Jingle Jangle*** peaks at US #125.
Mar Princess Anne presents Don Kirshner with the Carl-Alan award for *Sugar Sugar* as Best Tune Of 1969.
[28] *Who's Your Baby*, penned by Barry and Kim, and featuring Donna Marie (b. Marie Ladagona, June 28, 1950, Newark, NJ) in Wine's place, who has quit over a royalty dispute with Kirshner, makes US #40.
July [4] Wilson Pickett's version of *Sugar Sugar* reaches US #25.
Aug [1] *Sunshine*, penned by Barry, with Kim and Bobby Bloom on backing vocals, peaks at US #57, as ***Sunshine*** makes US #137.
Nov ***The Archies Greatest Hits*** reaches US #114.

1971

The Archies' last Barry-penned single *A Summer Prayer For Peace* is released. He subsequently quits the Kirshner organization after a follow-up, *Together We Two*, to work for Paramount Pictures in Hollywood, CA. Dante and Ritchie Adams will take over as producers, making the group's final album ***This Is Love*** and single *Strangers In The Morning*. The cartoon series continues as "Archie's TV Funnies" without any music. (Dante, having formed his own studio group the Cuff Links, hitting both the US and UK Top 10 with *Tracy*, will have his greatest successes in the '70s, producing several Barry Manilow albums, before becoming a successful Broadway theater producer, most notably with "Ain't Misbehavin'" and "They're Playing Our Song". In 1975 he will release a new version of *Sugar Sugar*, produced by Manilow.)

1978

Jan The cartoon series ends. During the height of "Archiemania", the Post Cereal group issued Archies records on the back of cereal boxes and an "Archies" restaurant opened in Joliet, IL, serving pre-teens. The group will only ever play live once, at a charity event at St. Theresa's Church, Kennilworth, NJ, with Dante and Marie performing *Sugar Sugar* and *Who's Your Baby*. Remaining a popular oldie, *Sugar Sugar* will be rediscovered as a dance novelty by UK clubs in August 1987, and will re-chart at #91.

JOAN ARMATRADING

1969

Having taught herself to play piano at an early age and taking up the acoustic guitar at the age of 14 (which her mother has bought her from a pawn shop), writing her first song, *When I Was Young*, the same year, but intending to pursue a career in law, Armatrading (b. Dec. 9, 1950, Basseterre, St. Kitts, West Indies), one of five children born to a St. Kitts' native father and Antiguan mother, has settled with her family in Birmingham, Warks., in 1958. Having bought her first album (Van Morrison's ***Astral Weeks***) at age 19, she now meets fellow immigrant Pam Nestor (b. Apr. 28, 1948, Berbice, Guyana), beginning a songwriting and performing partnership. Relocating to London in 1971, the duo will sign a recording and management agreement with Cube Records. With Nestor adding lyrics to Armatrading's music, the resulting Gus Dudgeon-produced ***Whatever's For Us***, a plaintive and thoughtful, mainly acoustic debut highlighted by Armatrading's distinctively earthy but warm vocal range, will be released in November 1972. However, with Nestor concerned that she is largely uncredited on the release the partnership soon dissolves.

1975

Apr Having signed to A&M Records (which has already licensed her Cube debut for US release), ***Back To The Night***, produced by Peter Gage with nine tracks penned by the singer-songwriter (and two residual cuts from the Nestor union), and recorded at Basing Street and Morgan studios in London, is issued to highly favorable reviews but few sales.
June During the month, she performs at a summer concert at London's Hyde Park on a bill with with Don McLean and Caravan.
Nov [13] Armatrading embarks on a 30-date UK tour, supporting labelmates Supertramp, at the Colston Hall, Bristol, Avon, set to end on December 20th at the Kursaal, Southend, Essex.

1976

Oct [23] A collaboration with producer Glyn Johns results in the breakthrough ***Joan Armatrading***, which reaches UK #12. Its mature sound, built around Armatrading's sophisticated songwriting and intricate acoustic guitar work, is due not least to seasoned session musicians, B.J. Cole, Jerry Donahue, Jimmy Jewel and Dave Mattacks.
Nov [13] The extracted ballad *Love And Affection*, with a distinctive Jewel sax solo, hits UK #10, belying its enduring appeal as a popular radio oldie.

1977

June [18] ***Joan Armatrading*** makes US #67, largely on the strength of a spring club-and-college tour of the US.
Oct [1] ***Show Some Emotion***, again entirely self-written and overseen by Johns, and featuring a similar session line-up augmented by David Kemper and Georgie Fame, hits UK #6 and includes future live favorites, *Warm Love* and *Willow* (the latter penned while staying in West Palm Beach, FL).
Dec [24] ***Show Some Emotion*** makes US #52.

1978

July [15] She performs at the Blackbushe Festival, Blackbushe Aerodrome, near Camberley, Surrey, on a bill headlined by Bob Dylan.
Oct [28] ***To The Limit***, on which Armatrading is backed by labelmates the Movies, and which sees a harder rock edge introduced, reaches UK #13, the third album to be produced by Johns. (Armatrading has recently been criticized for writing and performing the theme for "The Wild Geese", an action-adventure film about white mercenaries in South Africa.)
Dec [9] ***To The Limit*** peaks at US #125.

1980

Jan [19] The US-only issued mini-album ***How Cruel*** makes #136 and includes the extracted *Rosie* which makes UK #49 the following month.
May [24] Armatrading begins a 17-date UK/Eire tour at the Gaumont Cinema, Southampton, Hants., to promote her new album ***Me, Myself, I***, set to close on June 25th at the National Stadium, Dublin, Eire.
[31] The Richard Gottehrer-produced ***Me, Myself, I***, featuring seasoned American session support from Marcus Miller, Paul Shaffer and Clarence Clemons, hits UK #5.
Aug [2] The extracted title track, the rock-edged *Me, Myself, I*, reaches UK #21.
[9] ***Me, Myself, I*** reaches US #28.
Sept *All The Way From America* peaks at UK #54.

1981

Sept [19] The Steve Lillywhite-produced ***Walk Under Ladders*** hits UK #6, as the extracted *I'm Lucky* makes UK #46. (The subsequent single *No Love* will make UK #50 on Jan [30], 1982.)
Dec [13] An 11-date UK tour ends at Hammersmith Odeon, London, as ***Walk Under Ladders*** makes US #88. As she will do throughout the decade, Armatrading retreats after each album project and tour, consistently shunning fame's spotlight, preferring to concentrate on songwriting.

1983

Mar [26] Uptempo pop-rocking *Drop The Pilot* reaches UK #11.
Apr The Lillywhite and Val Garay co-produced ***The Key*** hits UK #10 and will reach US #32 spurred, as with each release, by UK and US tours and much critical acclaim.
June [25] *Drop The Pilot* lands at US #78.
Nov Retrospective greatest hits collection ***Track Record*** reaches UK #18 and US #113.

1985

Feb Mike Howlett-produced ***Secret Secrets***, featuring guest keyboardist Joe Jackson, is released, set to make UK #14 and US #73.
Mar *Temptation* peaks at UK #65.

1986

May ***Sleight Of Hand***, written, arranged and produced by Armatrading at her own Bumpkin home studio, and featuring the session line-up of Steve Greetham (bass), Geoff Dugmore (drums), Alex White (keyboards), Ray Cooper (percussion) and Wesley Magoogan (sax), makes UK #34.
June [20] Armatrading performs at the fourth annual Prince's Trust Rock Gala, at Wembley Arena, Wembley, Middx.
Aug ***Sleight Of Hand*** reaches US #68. Celebrating its 25th anniversary in 1987, A&M will issue the 68-minute collection of her greatest Stateside misses, ***Joan Armatrading, Classics*** in the US.

1988

Feb Armatrading begins recording sessions for her new album ***The Shouting Stage***, helped by Mark Knopfler and Big Country's Mark Brzezicki.
June [11] She performs at Nelson Mandela's 70th Birthday Tribute concert at Wembley Stadium, Wembley, on a bill also featuring soundalike freshman Tracy Chapman, who will inadvertently achieve much of what has eluded Armatrading commercially, notably multiplatinum success in the US.
July [16] ***The Shouting Stage***, her second self-produced album, reaches UK #28 and will make US #100.
Aug She embarks on a short US tour.
Oct [16] Armatrading takes part in the "Smile Jamaica" benefit concert, to aid victims of the recent hurricane disaster in the Caribbean, at the Dominion Theatre, London, on a bill also featuring U2 and Keith Richards.

1989

Jan [29] Appearing on BBC Radio 4's "Desert Island Discs", her eight selections include: Mendelssohn's "Violin Concerto in E minor", Ella Fitzgerald's *That Old Black Magic*, Van Morrison's *Madam George*, Mahler's "Symphony #4", Elmer Bernstein's *The Magnificent Seven* film theme, Verdi's "Dies Irae", Muddy Waters' *I'm A Man* and Dvorak's "Symphony #9".

1990

May [26] *More Than One Kind Of Love*, from the forthcoming ***Hearts And Flowers***, spends one week at UK #75.
June [16] The self-produced ***Hearts And Flowers***, once again recorded at her own home studio and featuring jazz saxophonist Andy Shepherd, session players Don Freeman (keyboards), Steve Jansen (drums), Hossam Ramzy (percussion) and Mick Karn (bass), reaches UK #29.
July [8-9] Armatrading plays at the Hammersmith Odeon, during a UK tour to promote her new album.
[14] ***Hearts And Flowers*** peaks at US #161.
Aug [6] Armatrading begins a 14-date US tour at Saratoga Springs Performing Arts Center in Saratoga, NY.
Oct [6] A world trek, interrupted in Australia due to illness, winds up at the King's Trust Concert in Swaziland, an annual event at which she also performed in 1989.

1991

Mar [23] A second greatest hits compilation, ***The Very Best Of Joan Armatrading***, hits UK #9.

1992

Mar Responding to a published Conservative Party celebrity rollcall which has included her name, Armatrading states: "My politics and voting intentions are a personal matter. At no time did I agree to my name being included on a list of Conservative Party supporters. I do not publicly support any political party."
May [23] *Wrapped Around Her* debuts at its UK #56 peak.
June [20] Co-produced and partly co-written with songwriting veteran Graham Lyle, ***Square The Circle*** bows at its UK #34 peak, the same day Armatrading performs at the Carlisle Sands Centre, Carlisle, Northumberland, midway through a month-long UK tour.
Sept [14] During a four-week North American visit, she performs on NBC-TV's "The Tonight Show".
Oct [9] The second segment of her live UK itinerary begins at the Doncaster Dome, Doncaster, S. Yorks. (By year's end, press reports indicate that she has re-teamed with her early collaborator, Pam Nestor.)

1995

June [7] Following a lengthy hiatus, a world tour begins in Belfast, N. Ireland, set to arrive in the UK on September 2nd in Glasgow, Scotland.
[10] After 20 years with A&M, Armatrading's first album for RCA, ***What's Inside***, co-produced with David Tickle and recorded in Los Angeles, CA, with help from the Kronos Quartet, Rolling Stones bass fill-in Darryl Jones and Heartbreaker Benmont Tench, debuts at its UK #48 peak.
Nov [8] Armatrading performs at New York's Beacon Theatre, during her latest US tour.

ARRESTED DEVELOPMENT

Speech (lead vocal); **Aerle Taree** (vocals, clothes designer); **Montsho Eshe** (dancer); **Nadriah** (vocals); **Rasa Don** (drums); **DJ Headliner** (turntables); **Baba Oje** (spiritual adviser)

1987

Speech (b. Todd Thomas, Oct. 25, 1968, Milwaukee, WI), his parents (who have raised the family in Milwaukee and Ripley, TN) - publishers of the **Milwaukee Community Journal** - meets Headliner (b. Timothy Barnwell, July 26, 1967, NJ), a descendant of "salt-water" Africans on the coast of South Carolina (though raised in New Jersey), while both are studying at the Art Institute of Atlanta, GA. (Speech, originally known as DJ Peech, adding the "S" later, has already founded D.L.R. (Disciples of a Lyrical Rebellion), which became Secret Society.) Initially forming a gangsta rap act, they soon turn away from the themes of street violence and begin recruiting other members throughout 1988, to form Arrested Development, eventually inviting Speech's cousin Taree (b. Taree Jones, Jan. 10, 1973, Milwaukee), Eshe (b. Temelca Gaither, Dec. 23, 1974, GA), Nadriah (b. 1959) and Don (b. Donald Jones, Nov. 22, 1968, NJ) to join them in an innovative hip-hop ensemble with a hippie look and an overtly African-American roots consciousness. They all move into the same house in Atlanta, while holding down day jobs moonlighting at small urban community and rural venues. Veteran spiritual adviser Oje (b. May 15, 1932, Laurie, MS), whom Speech met in Milwaukee during his childhood, is asked to join the group after Speech has seen him again on campus at the University of Wisconsin. (The collective will also be augmented by singers Sister Paulette and future solo artiste Dionne Farris, named by her mother Larraine after Dionne Warwick, guitarist Brother Larry and saxophonist Larry Jackson.)

1992

Jan After three years, five months and two days, the band finally signs a recording contract with Chrysalis Records.
May [23] Its debut smash *Tennessee*, uniquely featuring country fiddle samples and led by Speech's impassioned rapping, makes UK #46.
June [16] *Tennessee* is certified gold by the RIAA.
July [18] *Tennessee* hits US #6 aided by hot MTV rotation for its video clip, directed by Milcho.
Sept [18] The still-rising follow-up *People Everyday* is also confirmed gold by the RIAA.
Oct [10] *People Everyday* hits US #8.
Nov [7] *People Everyday* hits UK #2.
Dec [31] The group performs at the "MTV Drops The Ball '93" New Year's celebration from New York's Roseland Ballroom, having appeared earlier in the month on "MTV Unplugged", performing with 17 African musicians age 17 to 60, playing, in their trademark bib overalls and dashkis, to an audience which included innovative rap pioneers the Last Poets and Spike Lee.

1993

Jan [9] *Revolution*, a reggae, rap, R&B and African-chanting fusion from the movie soundtrack to "Malcolm X", peaks at US #90.
[16] The homeless-themed *Mr Wendal*, backed with *Revolution*, hits UK #4.
Feb [13] Their self-produced ***3 Years, 5 Months And 2 Days In The Life Of ...*** album debut hits UK #3. In describing the group's mission, Speech says: "We're a group talking about African struggle. African reality. Our mission is to reach people with what we call life music."
[20] *Mr. Wendal*, aided by heavy MTV video clip rotation, hits US #6.
[24] Increasingly revered as a new breed of rap act, the group collects the Best New Artist and Best Rap Duo Or Group trophies at the 35th annual Grammy Awards, held at the Shrine Auditorium, Los Angeles, CA, at which they also perform.
Mar [1] *Mr. Wendal* is certified gold by the RIAA.
[9] After a slew of recent honors, ***3 Years 5 Months and 2 Days In The Life Of ...*** wins Best Rap Album at the seventh annual Soul Train Music Awards held at the Shrine Auditorium. Performing at the ceremony, the social issues-conscious group invites homeless people to join them onstage. (They have also recently taken top honors in **Rolling Stone**'s and **Village Voice**'s critics' polls.)
[15] The group embarks on the 13-date "Some Vagabonds Named Arrested Development" UK tour,

opening at London's Town & Country club, and set to end on April 25th at Poole Arts Centre, Poole, Dorset.
[20] ***3 Years, 5 Months And 2 Days In The Life Of ...***, highlighted by Speech's poetic lyricism and lilting hip-hop vocal style, finally hits US #7 in its 49th charted week, heading towards three million US sales.
[23] Arrested Development becomes the first rap act to release an album from an "MTV Unplugged" taping, issuing ***Unplugged***, a full-length album documenting their December '92 performance at New York's Ed Sullivan Theater.
[31] The group sweeps the second annual Coca-Cola Atlanta Music Awards at the Fox Theatre, Atlanta, winning in seven categories.
Apr [1] The collective appears on BBC1-TV's "Top Of The Pops".
[3] *Tennessee* re-charts at its UK #18 peak.
[10] ***Unplugged***, featuring one new track *The Gettin'*, debuts at its UK #40 peak.
[24] ***Unplugged*** makes US #60.
[26] The group begins a tour of Australia, set to end on May 10th.
May [26] ***Unplugged*** is certified gold by the RIAA.
June [18] Arrested Development embarks on the 37-date Lollapalooza '93 tour in Vancouver, BC, Canada.
[29] Chrysalis releases the debut album by Gumbo, ***Dropping H20 On The Fiber***, produced by Speech, who also discovered the Milwaukee-based rap group.

1994

Apr [20] The group performs at the University of Illinois, Champaign, IL, opening for Bob Dylan.
May [28] Previewing the band's third album, *Ease My Mind* debuts at its UK #33 peak.
June [25] *Ease My Mind* makes US #45.
July [2] ***Zingalamaduni***, (Swahili for "beehive of culture"), featuring new members Nadirah and Ajile on vocals and Kwesi Asuo aka DJ Kemitsit, debuts at its US #55 peak, having reached UK #16 on June [18].
[23] The group guests on CBS-TV's "Late Show With David Letterman" during current dates on the 1994 WOMAD tour.
Aug [14] The band takes part in Woodstock II at Winston Farm, Saugerties, NY.
Unable to build on its initial success, Arrested Development will dissolve by year's end, notably freeing Speech to begin solo projects.

1995

Feb [8] The RIAA certifies multi-platinum sales of four million for ***3 Years, 5 Months And 2 Days In The Life Of ...***.
Apr [29] The first ex-member to make a solo impact is Farris, whose maiden effort ***Wild Seed - Wild Flower*** makes US #57, spurred by the success of the extracted, Grammy-nominated *I Know* (which will make UK #41 on May [27] and hit US #4 on Aug [19].

1996

Jan [23] Still signed to Chrysalis Records, Speech, having recently contributed to the tribute album ***Inner City Blues - The Music Of Marvin Gaye***, releases his solo debut ***Speech*** (which features sometime ex-member Foley), while his ex-Arrested Development colleagues continue with various ventures: Headliner is preparing his new band's (Nu Breed) debut for later in the year; Taree is writing and recording poetry; Rasa Don has moved back to New Jersey where he is creating a black comic strip; Eshe runs the BAMM management company; Oje is working in community-related affairs; Ajile is working with African dance troupe Fusion, while Farris is preparing her sophomore album.

THE ART OF NOISE

Anne Dudley (keyboards);
J.J. Jeczalik (keyboards, programmer);
Gary Langan (engineer)

1984

Jan Having met through their individual work as part of Trevor Horn's early '80s production team (creators of hits for ABC, Dollar, Frankie Goes To Hollywood and Malcolm McLaren), the original three members Dudley (b. May 7, 1956, London), Jeczalik (b. May 11, 1955) and Langan, all noted arrangers and producers in their own right, get together after working on a strenuous session with Yes. (Only Dudley, who was a pianist on BBC1-TV's "Play School" after leaving college, has previously had chart success as an artist, teaming with actress Joanne Whalley as Cindy & the Saffrons on a remake of the Shangri-Las' *Past, Present And Future*, a UK #56 one year earlier). The initial idea, consistently adhered to, is to release original sound collages, normally instrumental-only, in a faceless - almost groupless - guise. The name, coined by ZTT Records' (to whom the group is signed) Paul Morley, comes from an Italian futurist manifesto.
Apr Their debut release *Beat Box*, issued in the US by Island, becomes a popular dance item and will climb to #10 on the R&B chart.
Nov Largely overseen by the production maestro, the technically proficient ***(Who's Afraid Of) The Art Of Noise*** is released on Horn's ZTT label, set to reach UK #27.

1985

Feb [23] Having again become a club favorite in the US, *Close (To The Edit)*, an original, quirky techno-pop instrumental produced by Horn, hits UK #8.
Apr *Moments In Love* (an edited version of the seven-minute Horn-produced original)/*Beat Box* reaches UK #51 (the former subsequently played at Madonna's wedding to Sean Penn).
Aug ***(Who's Afraid Of) The Art Of Noise*** makes US #85.
Sept [13] "Close To The Edit" wins the Best Editing and Most Experimental categories at the second annual MTV Video Music Awards, held at Radio City Music Hall, New York, NY.
Nov [9] A newly self-sufficient, Horn-less Art Of Noise has left his label, signing to China, on which *Legs* makes UK #69.

1986

Apr [12] *Peter Gunn*, an unlikely collaboration with twang-guitar legend Duane Eddy and an update of his 1959 classic, hits UK #8, spurred by an appearance by all concerned on C4-TV's "The Tube".
July [19] While ***In Visible Silence*** has recently peaked at UK #18 (and will make US #53), a second extract *Paranoimia*, an offbeat collaboration with computerized TV character Max Headroom, makes UK #12. (Its success leads to the group's creation of the theme for Headroom's second UK TV series, and to further involvement with UK TV-theme work ("Krypton Factor 2" and "The Return Of Sherlock Holmes"), and ads for Revlon, Britvic, Bols, Bazique, Martini, Swatch, Barclays Bank, Fabergé, BP, Mars and Brylcreem, among others.)
July [5] While the band is performing its first live concerts, all sellouts, in Japan, the US and a single date in the Britain, *Peter Gunn* makes US #50.
Oct [4] The Dudley and Jeczalik-penned *Paranoimia* reaches US #34.

1987

Feb [24] *Peter Gunn* is named the Best Rock Instrumental Performance, Orchestra, Group Or Soloist at the 29th annual Grammy Awards. (*Peter Gunn* won two Grammys for Henry Mancini at the inaugural awards in 1959.)
July *Dragnet* (released in the US as *Dragnet '88*), recorded as the main theme to the forthcoming Dan Aykroyd/Tom Hanks-starring movie of the same name, peaks at UK #60, as ZTT Records issues ***Daft***, a compilation album of early material.
Oct [10] Their third studio effort ***In No Sense? Nonsense!*** makes UK #55 and will peak at US #134.

1988

Feb Work is completed on a soundtrack contribution to the Fat Boys' film "Disorderlies".
Nov [5] Their latest unorthodox liaison is with Welsh crooner Tom Jones on *Kiss*, a revival of Prince's 1986 US #1, which hits UK #5.
Dec [3] A ten-track retrospective featuring both the ZTT and China successes, ***The Best Of The Art Of Noise*** debuts at its UK #55 peak.

1989

Jan [14] *Kiss* makes US #31, as ***The Best Of The Art Of Noise*** climbs to US #83.
Aug *Yebo*, featuring Mahlathini & the Mahotella Queens, peaks at UK #63. (A reissued version with remixes by Ollie J. and Arkana will be released in February 1995.)

1990

May [5] Dudley conducts the orchestra at the Yoko Ono-organized tribute concert to John Lennon held at the Pierhead, Liverpool, Merseyside.
June [16] *Art Of Love* peaks at UK #67.
July A further China retrospective ***The Ambient Collection*** is released, as the band, always an ad-hoc congregation, splits.
Sept Dudley combines with ex-Killing Joke frontman Jaz Coleman to release ***Songs From The Victorious City***.

1992

Jan [25] *Instruments Of Darkness (All Of Us ...)* makes UK #45. It is taken from ***The Fon Mixes***, a collection of Art Of Noise tracks remixed by different producers and released by China in November 1991.
Feb [29] A second remixed extract, *Shades Of Paranoimia* debuts at its UK #53 peak. The band members' individual careers have blossomed over the past ten years: Dudley's successes as producer/ writer/ arranger/player include hits by Lloyd Cole, Moody Blues, Tom Jones, Rush, Boy George, k.d. lang, a-ha, Paul McCartney, New Edition, Five Star and Phil Collins, with whom she combined for the successful soundtrack to the movie "Buster". Other film-theme work includes "Wilt", "Say Anything", "The Crying Game", "Knight Moves", The Pope Must Die(t)" and "Mighty Quinn", with TV music scored for "Jeeves And Wooster", "Anna Lee" and "Rory Bremner". Jeczalik's production and mixing credits include the Pet Shop Boys, Godley & Creme and McCartney, while Langan's talents have assisted Spandau Ballet, ABC, Billy Idol, Public Image Ltd. and many others. In 1994, Off Beat Records will release a revised 33-minute version of ***The Best Of The Art Of Noise***, sans the group's ZTT hits, but annexed with post-1988 highlights.

ASIA

John Wetton (lead vocals, bass); **Steve Howe** (guitar, vocals); **Geoff Downes** (keyboards, vocals); **Carl Palmer** (drums, percussion)

1981

Jan Having folded his short-lived rock outfit UK, Roxy Music and King Crimson veteran Wetton (b. July 12, 1949, Derby, Derbys.) links with Howe (b. Apr. 8, 1947, London), who has recently left Yes, to form a new band, an initiative prompted by Geffen Records in the US, which is keen to sign a rock supergroup. They approach former Emerson, Lake & Palmer drummer Palmer (b. Mar. 20, 1947, Birmingham, Warks.), and Yes/Buggles keyboards player Downes, as Asia is formed, aimed squarely at supplanting the '70s success of its members' previous bands.

1982

Apr [24] Despite being mauled by UK music critics, their debut album ***Asia***, recorded at the Townhouse Studio, London, and produced by Mike Stone, reaches UK #11.

May [15] Finding a warmer recption in the US where radio readily embraces the familiar grand rock style clearly reminiscent of ELP and Yes, ***Asia*** tops the US chart, where it will reign for two months and eventually sell over four million copies.

June [26] Showcasing Wetton's lead vocal, *Heat Of The Moment*, taken from the album, hits US #4.

July [17] *Heat Of The Moment* makes UK #46, as the band begins stadium-filling live work in the US and around the world.

Sept [18] A second extract *Only Time Will Tell* reaches US #17, and UK #54 a week later.

Dec The band wins the Top Pop New Artist and Top Pop Album categories in **Billboard**'s year-end chart round-up.

1983

Aug Recorded in Canada from February - May at Le Studio in Quebec, PQ and Manta Sound in Toronto, ON, ***Alpha***, supported by another world tour, hits UK #5 and US #6.

Sept [17] *Don't Cry* hits US #10, having already made UK #33 on August 27th. Wetton leaves, and is replaced by Greg Lake (b. Nov. 10, 1948, Bournemouth, Dorset), Palmer's earlier colleague in ELP.

Oct [11] ***Alpha*** is certified platinum by the RIAA.

Nov [26] The second US extract from ***Alpha***, *The Smile Has Left Your Eyes*, makes US #34.

Dec [6] "Asia In Asia", a live TV concert from Budokan Theatre, Tokyo, Japan, has an audience of over 20 million in the US (via MTV), where it is also heard on 285 radio stations. It is Lake's first appearance with the band and proves the peak of the group's live performance career.

1985

Dec [14] By the release of their third album ***Astra***, which now peaks at UK #68, the band line-up, always prone to personnel changes, has seen Howe replaced by Krokus guitarist Mandy Meyer and Wetton rejoin, ousting Lake. Clearly past their commercial apex, the album will also stop at US #67 in early 1986.

1986

Jan [18] *Go* makes US #46. Asia will shortly disband, allowing its members to pursue other projects. Howe will form GTR, a five-piece UK rock band with ex-Genesis guitarist Steve Hackett (which will reach US #14 with *When The Heart Rules The Mind* on July [12], 1986, while ***GTR*** peaks at US #11, followed by *The Hunter* which makes US #85 on Sept [6]). Wetton will record an album with ex-Roxy Music colleague Phil Manzanera (***Wetton Manzanera***), released by Geffen in 1987.

1990

July Wetton, Downes and Palmer receive gold discs at the Soviet Embassy in London for the Asia contribution to the 100,000-selling various artists ***Rock Aid Armenia*** album (released to raise funds for the Life Aid Armenia earthquake victims' fund).

Sept [24-29] Performing a short series of concerts in Japan, the band has reformed with new lead guitarist Pat Thrall (ex-Pat Travers, Go and Automatic Man), principally to record additional songs for the otherwise retrospective ten-track collection ***Then And Now***, which has peaked at US #114 on Sept [15] (with *Days Like These* set to make US #64 on Oct [27]). The line-up will change yet again the following year, when John Payne replaces Wetton and produces ***Aqua*** (the group has persisted with only releasing albums with one word titles beginning with "A") with Downes at the Advision Studios in Brighton, E. Sussex, to be released by FM-Revolver in the UK and by Czar Records in the US, in January 1992. Following a US trek in late 1991, Asia will undertake two short, small-venue UK tours in 1992, highlighted by the one-off appearance of special guest Howe at the July 2nd date at London's Kentish Town Town & Country club, and selected US dates in February 1993. Another new studio effort, ***Aria*** will emerge in May 1994 on Bulletproof Records in Britain with the revised lineup of Downes, Payne, Al Pitrelli (former Danger Danger guitarist) and Mike Sturgis, while the group's most enduring album, the ***Asia*** debut will be certified for four million US sales by the RIAA on February 10th the following year.

see also: **EMERSON LAKE & PALMER, KING CRIMSON, ROXY MUSIC, YES**

THE ASSOCIATES

Billy MacKenzie (vocals);
Alan Rankine (keyboards)

1979

Oct MacKenzie (b. Mar. 27, 1957, Dundee, Scotland) and Rankine (b. Edinburgh, Scotland), having first performed together as cabaret combo the Absorbic Ones in Dundee, in 1976, have formed a succession of ad-hoc bands over the next three years, now emerging as the style-driven Associates on their own Double Hip label, with a version of David Bowie's *Boys Keep Swinging*. With MacKenzie writing lyrics to Rankine's music, they quickly become established as one of the leaders of the energetic Scottish new wave of the early '80s, signing to ex-Polydor Records A&R man Chris Parry's independent Fiction label, which will release their debut album ***The Affectionate Punch*** in August 1980, a set also featuring bassist Michael Dempsey and Australian drummer John Murphy.

1981

Oct Growing interest generated by live appearances has resulted in a five-single deal with Beggars Banquet Records' subsidiary label Situation Two, each self-penned release achieving Top 10 success on the UK Independent singles chart during the year and now assembled as part of an eight-cut mini-album ***Fourth Drawer Down***, which tops the UK Independent chart.

1982

Mar [27] Having established their own Associates label, distributed by WEA, *Party Fears Two*, hits UK #9 and showcases MacKenzie's frantic, high-pitched falsetto vocal style which becomes their trademark sound.

Apr Heaven 17's ambitious British Electric Foundation project ***Music Of Quality And Distinction*** is released featuring MacKenzie's *The Secret Life Of Arabia* and *It's Over*.

May [22] Co-produced by the band with Mike Hedges, the 11-track ***Sulk*** hits UK #10.

June [12] The extracted *Club Country* reaches UK #13.

Aug [21] Following their first major UK tour and by now, the darlings of the style media, the double A-side *18 Carat Love Affair* (featuring part-time band member Martha Ladley), coupled with a revival of Diana Ross' *Love Hangover*, reaches UK #21.

1983

MacKenzie, who has released a solo cut *Ice Cream Factory* under his own name in October the previous year, and Rankine split, the former retaining the rights to the Associates name. (Rankine will release a solo album, ***She Loves Me Not***, in September 1987.)

1984

June [30] After an 18-month lay-off to write new material and now signed directly to WEA, the band, now comprising MacKenzie, Steve Reid, Ian Mackintosh, L. Howard Hughes and Roberto Soave, returns with *Those First Impressions* produced by Heaven 17's Martyn Ware, which makes UK #43.

Sept [15] The Martin Rushent-helmed *Waiting For The Love Boat* peaks at UK #53.

1985

Feb [16] *Breakfast* reaches UK #49, as the MacKenzie-written parent album ***Perhaps*** debuts at UK #23. (Disillusioned by this relative failure, MacKenzie will pursue solo activities, among them cameo collaborations with favored artists, including Yello's *The Rhythm Divine* in August 1987, and work with Paul Haig and Holger Heller.)

1988

Sept MacKenzie re-emerges, still under the Associates name, releasing a UK #56 cover version of Blondie's 1979 chart-topper *Heart Of Glass*, although a projected album, ***The Glamour Chase***, is never issued.

1989

Oct [13] ***The John Peel Sessions***, from a BBC Radio 1 set, is released.

1990

Mar [31] MacKenzie's final Associates album, the Julian Mendelsohn-produced ***Wild And Lonely***, released via his new recording deal with Circa Records and featuring Anne Dudley, Carol Kenyon and Mark Rutherford, charts for a week at UK #71. (WEA simultaneously issues ***Associates Popera: The Singles Collection***, a comprehensive 17-track retrospective, which brings their unique early recordings to compact disc.) MacKenzie will also contribute a song to British Electric Foundation's second effort, ***Music Of Quality & Distinction Volume 2***, in September 1991, while Circa will release his debut solo album, ***Outernational***, 12 months later. Early Associates recordings ***The Radio 1 Sessions*** will also be issued by Nighttracks Records in September 1994.)

THE ASSOCIATION

Terry Kirkman (vocals, assorted instruments);
Jim Yester (vocals, guitar); **Gary Alexander** (vocals, guitar); **Russ Giguere** (vocals, guitar); **Larry Ramos, Jr.** (vocals, guitar); **Brian Cole** (vocals, bass); **Ted Bluechel, Jr.** (vocals, drums)

1965

Nov Kirkman (b. Dec. 12, 1941, Salina, KS), a veteran of California's folk circuit and Alexander (b. Sept. 25, 1943, Chattanooga, TN), old friends now working as arrangers in Los Angeles, CA, join a loose band of musicians who congregate to sing and play on Monday nights after closing at the Troubadour club. Bluechel (b. Dec. 2, 1942, San Pedro, CA), Cole (b. Sept. 8, 1942, Tacoma, WA) and Bob Page become part of this group calling itself the Inner Tubes. In time, its number is pared down to 13 to become the Men, securing a proper date to play the Troubadour. During subsequent rehearsals several members depart. With an upcoming date at the Icehouse, Giguere (b. Oct. 18, 1943, Portsmouth, NH), who is working the lights at the club and has been part of the Inner Tubes, replaces Mike Whalen, who has left to take Barry McGuire's place in the New Christy Minstrels. Page leaves during rehearsals, replaced by Yester (b. Nov. 24, 1939, Birmingham, AL), who, fresh out the Army, joins within a week of returning to Los Angeles. After six months rehearsing, the Association (coined by Kirkman's wife Judy after browsing through a dictionary – the name the Aristocrats had been an earlier suggestion) makes its stage debut at Pasadena's Ice House. *Babe I'm Gonna Leave You* is recorded for Jubilee label in a one-off deal.

1966

Band signs to Valiant Records, having auditioned at the Troubadour, and releases a version of Bob Dylan's *One Too Many Mornings*.

May Sessions with producer Curt Boettcher for their debut album begin at G.S.P. (Gary Paxton's home studio) and Columbia studios in Hollywood, CA.

June [4] Originally cut as a demo for Davon Music, with Alexander on bass, and subsequently given by its writer Tandyn Almer to the group on a six-month exclusive, *Along Comes Mary* enters the Hot 100 at #79, after garnering immediate US radio play despite some interpreting it as a drug hymn.

July [2] The group performs at the County Bowl, Santa Barbara, CA, with the Beach Boys and Sir Douglas Quintet.

[16] *Along Comes Mary* hits US #7.

[22-23] The group plays at San Francisco, CA's Fillmore West with Quicksilver Messenger Service as they embark on their first national tour.

Sept [24] *Cherish*, a soft ballad in contrast to *Mary*, recorded by the New Christy Minstrels but refused a release by writer Kirkman, begins a three-week run at US #1, displacing the Supremes' *You Can't Hurry Love*.

Oct [18] *Cherish* is certified gold by the RIAA.

Nov [19] ***And Then ... Along Comes The Association*** hits US #5.

Dec [24] Alexander's psychedelic *Pandora's Golden Heebie Jeebies*, in stark contrast to *Cherish* and without strong radio support, makes US #35.

1967

Feb [25] *No Fair At All*, written by Yester, peaks at US #51, faring better in the Philippines where it hits #1.

Mar [18] Produced by Yester's brother Jerry, ***Renaissance*** makes US #34.

Apr Warner Bros. buys Valiant Records, and with it the Association's recording contract. Alexander leaves to study meditation in India, and is replaced by New Christy Minstrel Ramos (b. Hilario Ramos Jr., Apr. 19, 1942, Waimea, Kauai, HI).

May [28] The group makes its debut on CBS-TV's "The Smothers Brothers Comedy Hour".

June [16] The band opens the "Monterey International Pop Festival" at the County Fairgrounds, Monterey, CA.

July [1] *Windy*, written by group friend California teen Ruthann Friedman, tops the US chart where it will stay for four weeks, preventing the Music Explosion from achieving its only chart-topper with *Little Bit O' Soul*.

[14] *Windy* is certified gold by the RIAA.

Sept [2] ***Insight Out***, produced by Bones Howe, hits US #8, as *Requiem For The Masses*, B-side of new single *Never My Love*, spends two weeks at anchor position on the Hot 100.

Oct [7] *Never My Love*, penned by Don and Dick Addrisi and returning to the soft style of *Cherish*, hits US #2 for the first of two weeks, unable to dislodge the Box Tops' *The Letter*.

Nov The Association is voted #1 Group Of The Year in the US by the Bill Gavin Radio-Record Congress, ending the Beatles' three-year reign.

[27] *Never My Love* and ***Along Comes ... The Association*** are certified gold by the RIAA.

Dec [28] ***Insight Out*** is certified gold by the RIAA.

1968

Mar [2] Kirkman's *Everything That Touches You* hits US #10.

May [2] The group appears on BBC1-TV's "Top Of The Pops" to promote its new single *Time For Livin'*, and will make two live UK appearances at London's Tottenham Royal and at the annual **New Musical Express** Poll Winners Concert at Empire Pool, Wembley, Middx. They will also play dates in Europe at Bremen, Amsterdam, Brussels and Antwerp.

June [15] ***Birthday***, also produced by Howe, reaches US #23.

[22] *Time For Livin'*, penned by the Addrisi brothers, makes US #39.

[29] *Time For Livin'* reaches UK #23.

Sept [14] *Six Man Band*, an uncharacteristic (and autobiographical) heavy-rock track penned by Kirkman, is their last US Top 50 single, peaking at #47. Soon after, Alexander rejoins, now using his new forename Jules, and they become a seven-man band.

1969

Feb [8] ***Greatest Hits***, a 13-track best of, hits US #4.

Mar [15] *Goodbye Columbus*, title theme to Richard Benjamin/Ali MacGraw movie penned by Yester, peaks at US #80.

Sept [6] ***Goodbye Columbus*** soundtrack, written by Charles Fox and including three Association originals, makes US #99. (Yester's title song will receive a Golden Globe nomination for Best Song.)

Nov [1] ***The Association***, co-helmed by the group with new producer John Boylan, reaches US #32. (The band had been unhappy with Howe's demand that session musicians be used on their recordings, and in turn Howe had been upset that the group had turned down Jim Webb's *MacArthur Park*, which he had written specifically for them.)

1970

July Giguere leaves, and will record the solo album ***Hexagram 16*** and subsequently form the Beechwood Rangers with Bill Martin and Warren Zevon and then Hollywood. He is replaced by Richard Thompson (b. San Diego, CA) (ex-Cosmic Brotherhood, John Klemmer and Richard Thompson Trio), on keyboards.

Aug [22] ***The Association Live***, recorded on April 13th, 1970 at the University of Utah, Salt Lake City, UT, makes US #79.

1971

Aug [21] ***Stop Your Motor*** peaks at US #158.

1972

June [10] A new recording deal with CBS/Columbia Records produces ***Waterbeds In Trinidad***, with material by John Sebastian, John Stewart, Gerry Goffin and Carole King, but is the group's least successful chart album, peaking at US #194.

Aug [2] Cole dies in Los Angeles from an apparent heroin overdose.

1973

Mar Recently signed to the Mums label, a Columbia subsidiary, the one-off Albert Hammond-produced single *Names Tags Numbers Labels* stops at US #91.

1975

The Association, with Bluechel, Ramos and Yester the only original members, teamed with new recruits Maurice Miller (percussion), David Vaught (bass), Dwayne Smith (keyboards) and Art Johnson (guitar), has signed a one single deal with RCA Records, which releases the Jack Richardson-produced *One Sunday Morning*. Alexander invites Giguere to join Bijou, with other founding member Kirkman now writing TV jingles.

1981

Feb [14] Following the success of an HBO-TV special, the original group (with Ric Ulsky in Brian Cole's place), reunited with producer Bones Howe and signed with Elektra Records in a singles deal, makes US #66 with *Dreamer*. (The band will continue to perform around the US regularly until the "Happy Together" tour in 1984, when only Giguere and Ramos remain, taking rights to the Association name with them. With a new line-up featuring Donni Gougeon (keyboards), Paul Holland (bass), Bruce Pictor (drums), and Del Ramos (backing vocals), they will continue to play more than 100 dates a year, and release the 1995 album (under the moniker Association 1995) ***A Little Bit More*** on the On Track Records label). The Yesters will remain active, initially as members of the reformed MFQ, attaining immense popularity in Japan, the only country where their records will be released, and then in the Lovin' Spoonful, with Jerry reuniting with Joe Butler and Steve Boone, and Jim taking founder John Sebastian's place. ***The Association's Greatest Hits*** will be certified multi-platinum by the RIAA with sales of two million on June 1st, 1989.)

RICK ASTLEY

1985

Feb Brought up in Newton-le-Willows, Merseyside, where his early interests included choir singing and playing piano and drums, Astley (b. Feb. 6, 1966, Warrington, Cheshire), has joined his first band, Give Way, as a drummer, while at school in 1982. As lead singer of FBI, a band formed in 1984 with the help of a grant from the UK Government as part of its Enterprise Allowance Scheme, and his repertoire influenced by music heard on visits to Wigan, Lancs.' legendary soul music club, the Pier Casino, Astley is spotted at the Monks Sports and Social Club, Warrington, by Pete Waterman, of the Stock/Aitken/Waterman writing and production hit factory, who offers him apprenticeship studio and vocal work in London. His inauspicious vinyl debut will be singing an uncredited duet on O'chi Brown's *Learning To Live Without Your Love*, released in June the following year on the Magnetic Dance label.

1987

July [27] Following 18 months of rehearsal, grooming and styling with the SAW team at their PWL Studios in London, where he has also been employed as a tape operator, Astley is launched in Britain via a PWL worldwide licensing deal with RCA Records.

Aug [29] His debut single *Never Gonna Give You Up*, a dance-driven soul cut written and produced by SAW, tops the UK chart for the first of five weeks, and becomes Britain's biggest-selling single of the year, before moving on to repeat its chart-topping status in 15 other countries worldwide, including the US, Australia and W. Germany.

Nov [21] *Whenever You Need Somebody* hits UK #3, and marks the start of a six-month non-stop worldwide promotion trek.

[28] His freshman album ***Whenever You Need Somebody*** enters the UK Album chart at #1, and will sell over one million copies in six months. Although underpinned by Stock Aitken & Waterman's ever-present songwriting and dance production, Astley's strong, blue-eyed soul vocal is the album's standout feature.

Dec [12] *When I Fall In Love*, a faithfully-styled revival of Nat "King" Cole's 1957 classic ballad, hits UK #2. The reissue of Cole's original halts its progress to the top, so the single is flipped to give joint promotion (and additional sales) to the double A-side coupling, *My Arms Keep Missing You*.

1988

Feb [8] *Never Gonna Give You Up* is named Best British Single at the seventh annual BRIT Awards, at London's Royal Albert Hall.

Mar [12] After a three-month climb, *Never Gonna Give You Up* tops the US chart for the first of two weeks, knocking George Michael's *Father Figure* off pole position. *Together Forever*, from his debut album, hits UK #2.

Apr Astley undertakes a promotional tour of the Far East and Australia.

June [6] He performs *Never Gonna Give You Up* at the Prince's Trust Rock Gala concert, at the Royal Albert Hall.

[18] *Together Forever* becomes Astley's second US chart-topper, again dislodging George Michael, this time his *One More Try*, as Astley's debut album ***Whenever You Need Somebody*** climbs to hit US #10.

Sept [17] *It Would Take A Strong Man* hits US #10.

Oct [15] *She Wants To Dance With Me* hits UK #6.

Nov [21] Astley takes part in the "Pop 88" segment of the Royal Variety Performance in London.

Dec [10] *Take Me To Your Heart* hits UK #8. (His SAW-steered sophomore album ***Hold Me In Your***

Arms also hits UK #8, as Astley embarks on his first world tour, set to perform 70 shows in 15 countries, including the UK, US, Japan and Australia. In **Billboard**'s year-end chart round-up, Astley wins in the Top Sales Artist, Dance and Top 12" Singles Sales, Dance categories.)

1989

Feb [24] *Never Gonna Give You Up* is certified gold by the RIAA.
[25] Ballad *Hold Me In Your Arms*, one of six Astley-penned cuts from the parent album, hits UK #10, as *She Wants To Dance With Me* hits US #6. ***Hold Me In Your Arms*** climbs towards US #19.
May [27] *Giving Up On Love* makes US #38, as Astley prepares for a three-month US tour.
Aug [26] His cover of the Temptations' *Ain't Too Proud To Beg* peaks at US #89.

1990

Feb [26] ***Hold Me In Your Arms*** is certified gold by the RIAA.
Mar Following a series of disagreements with SAW, Astley, insisting on his creative freedom, successfully extricates himself from the PWL organisation and begins recording his third album, with co-producer Gary Stevenson, at studios in the Isle of Man, UK, Copenhagen, Denmark, and Los Angeles, CA.

1991

Feb [2] After a lengthy absence, his gospel-tinged return, *Cry For Help*, hits UK #7.
Mar [2] ***Free***, featuring tracks co-penned by Astley with either Level 42's Mark King or Climie Fisher's Rob Fisher, and one Michael McDonald cut, *Name Of Love*, and including keyboard help from Elton John, hits UK #9.
[13] The RIAA certifies sales of two million copies for ***Whenever You Need Somebody***.
[29] US promotion includes a performance of *Cry For Help* on syndicated TV's "The Arsenio Hall Show".
[30] *Move Right Out* bows at its UK #58 peak, following his appearance the previous day on TV-AM.
Apr [27] *Cry For Help* hits US #7.
May [11] ***Free*** reaches US #31 (while the extracted *Never Knew Love* will make UK #70 (June [29]), with *Move Right Out* peaking at US #81 (July [6]).

1992

Feb Astley begins work on his fourth album, at Outside Studios, the sessions once again co-produced with Gary Stevenson.

1993

Sept [4] *The Ones You Love*, co-penned with Dave West, debuts at its UK #48 peak.
Oct [16] Maturing as a songwriter and singer with each album, the ten-track ***Body & Soul***, variously co-written by Astley with West, Fisher and Lisa Stansfield among others, charts for a week at US #185.
[23] *Hopelessly* reaches US #28.
Nov [13] *Hopelessly* debuts at its UK #33 peak.

1994

Oct [23] *Hopelessly* is named one of the Most Performed Songs of the year at the annual BMI Awards Ceremony at London's Dorchester Hotel.

ASWAD

Brinsley Forde (vocals); **Tony Gad** (guitar); **Angus "Drummie" Zeb** (drums)

1976

June Having formed in 1975 in London's Ladbroke Grove, Notting Hill area, selecting the arabic word for "black" as its band name, Aswad, initially comprising Forde (former child star of the 1971 BBC-TV children's series "Here Come The Double Deckers"), and Zeb (b. Angus Gaye), plus Donald Benjamin (guitar), Courtney Hemmings (keyboards) and Ras George Levi Oban (bass), signs to Island Records (UK) at the instigation of label head Chris Blackwell, the first British reggae act to secure a major deal, and releases *Back To Africa*, which now tops the UK Reggae listings, taken from the self-penned ***Aswad***, which proves equally popular in the specialist market. Moving to the independent label Grove Muzik in 1978 for *It's Not Our Wish (That We Should Fight)* and supporting the popular "Rock Against Racism" cause, the band will embark on an extensive summer tour of West Africa in the same year becoming the first reggae band to perform in Senegal, before beginning a UK tour at the Woods, Plymouth, Devon on October 2nd set to end on the 31st at Belfast Polytechnic. With Gad (b. Tony Robinson) joining Forde and Zeb as a trimmed down Aswad in 1979, the group's sophomore set, ***Hulet*** will be released by Grove/Island (under a new licensing deal) in June 1980, the same year it also contributes music to the Chrysalis Records (UK)-released soundtrack to the British film "Babylon", which also stars Forde and deals with the pressures of young black life in London.

1982

July [31] Having signed a two-album deal with CBS (UK) and released its label debut ***New Chapter*** in November 1981, Aswad's second CBS effort, ***Not Satisfied***, becomes its first UK chart success, at #50 (packaged with a free 10" dub remix pairing *Unsatisfied* and *Oh Jah*.

1983

Dec Re-signed to Island (now also for releases in the US), their eight-track concert package ***Live And Direct*** charts at UK #57.

1984

Jan [14] The band tops the bill at London's Brixton Academy, for the Greater London Council-sponsored "London Against Racism" concert.
Mar *Chasing For The Breeze*, recorded in Jamaica, peaks at UK #51.
Oct *54-46 (Was My Number)* makes UK #70.
Nov Aswad tours the UK, promoting ***Rebel Souls***, which makes UK #48, and will continue intermittent live work throughout 1985.

1986

Feb [12-14] Aswad hosts a three-day careers course at London's Camden Centre.
June ***To The Top***, released on their own independent Simba label, peaks at UK #71. With a change of management however, they re-sign to Island via the Mango label.

1988

Mar [26] *Don't Turn Around*, a reggae-pop re-styling of an Albert Hammond/Diane Warren song first recorded by Tina Turner, tops the UK chart for the first of two weeks, rewarding the band after over ten years of persistent touring and recording, building its reputation as Britain's premier reggae act.
Apr [9] The parent album ***Distant Thunder***, featuring additional musicians Eddie Thornton (trumpet), Henry Tenyue (trombone), Stanley Andrews (guitar) and saxophonists Alan Williams and longtime cohort Michael Rose among others, debuts at its UK #10 peak, largely due to the band's lilting, melodic reggae style.
June [11] Aswad's treatment of another Hammond/Warren composition, *Give A Little Love*, reaches UK #11.
Sept [24] While *Set Them Free* peaks at UK #70, ***Distant Thunder*** makes US #173, a rare achievement for a reggae release.

1989

Jan [14] Aswad's sixth chart album ***Renaissance***, a semi-retrospective collection released by TV-marketing label Stylus, makes UK #52.
Mar [6] A Greenpeace benefit album ***Rainbow Warriors***, which features Aswad, is released in the USSR on the Melodiya label.
Apr [15] Their reggae adaptation of the Temptations' *Beauty's Only Skin Deep* makes UK #31.
June [16-17] The group takes part in "Cliff Richard - The Event", performed over two days to sold-out 72,000 capacity crowds at Wembley Stadium, Wembley, Middx., and duets with Richard on *Share A Dream With Me*.
July Jackson Browne's ***World In Motion***, to which the group has contributed backing vocals on *When The Stone Begins To Turn*, makes US #45.
Aug [19] *On And On*, reviving US singer/songwriter Stephen Bishop's lilting Caribbean-styled ballad, substituting the "puts on Sinatra and starts to cry" line with "puts on Marley and starts to cry", reaches UK #25.

1990

Apr [16] Aswad participates in "Nelson Mandela - An International Tribute to a Free South Africa" concert at Wembley Stadium.
June [3] They take part in The Big Day, a festival from various locations in Glasgow, Scotland, airing live on C4-TV.
[22-24] The group performs at the "Glastonbury Festival Of Contemporary Performing Arts" near Glastonbury, Somerset.
Sept [8] *Next To You* reaches UK #24.
[9] The band appears at KISS-FM radio station's London launch celebrations.
[29] ***Too Wicked*** makes UK #51.
Oct [6] They perform at the King's Trust benefit concert in Swaziland, on a bill including Joan Armatrading.
Nov [24] *Smile*, featuring Sweetie Irie, peaks at UK #53.

1991

Feb [16] The band begins a 27-date US tour at Municipal Auditorium, Eureka, CA, ending at the Respectable Street Café, West Palm Beach, FL.
Mar [30] Their cover version of the Eagles' *Best Of My Love*, as part of the *Too Wicked* EP (which also includes their treatment of *I Shot The Sheriff*), makes UK #61.
May [1] Aswad is featured in a Bob Marley tribute on BBC-2 TV's "Rapido".

1992

May [23-24] The Reggae Sunsplash US summer tour package, featuring Aswad, performs two dates at the Greek Theatre, Los Angeles, CA, grossing $264,399.
Aug [19-25] The Reggae Sunsplash tour continues with a week of shows in Japan.

1993

May The band records a new album at the Blue Room Complex, with Tommy D producing.
Aug [14] *How Long*, pairing Aswad and Yazz on a revival of Ace's 1974 UK #20, reaches UK #31.
Oct [9] *Dance Hall Mood* debuts at its UK #48 peak.
Dec [1] The group performs live at Tower Records' Piccadilly store in London as part of National AIDS Day.

1994

July [9] Having ended a 17-year on-off association with Island Records, ***Rise And Shine***, released on the Bubblin' label (UK), debuts at its UK #39 peak.
[23] The extracted *Shine* hits UK #5.
Sept [17] *Warriors* debuts at its UK #33 peak.
Nov The group is featured on Music Relief's *What's Going On* benefit single for Rwandan refugees.

1995

Feb [18] *You're No Good* bows at its UK #35 peak.
Mar [9] Ford and Gaye perform with Stevie Wonder on the latter's BBC 1FM radio show from Ronnie Scott's club in London.
July [4] Aswad appears at the Meadow Brook Music Festival at the Oakland University, Rochester, MI, during a current Reggae Sunsplash tour.
[24] The group celebrates its 20th anniversary with a party at the Regency Suite in London Zoo to launch its forthcoming ***Greatest Hits*** compilation.

Aug [5] *If I Was* charts for a week at UK #58.
[12] ***Greatest Hits*** bows at its UK #20 peak.

PATTI AUSTIN

1978

Feb [4] Having performed professionally from the age of five, notably in 1953 at the Apollo Theatre, Harlem, New York, NY (at age four, she had already met future collaborator and producer Quincy Jones at a recording session of her godmother, Dinah Washington, to which her father, trombonist Gordon, was contributing), Austin (b. Aug. 10, 1948, New York) makes US #116 with the Dave Grusin and Larry Rosen-produced ***Havana Candy***. Her first successful album for CTI Records (recorded in August 1977), it follows a commercially unsuccessful spell with United Artists. By age 16, Austin was already a seasoned jazz/soul entertainer, having toured with the likes of Sammy Davis Jr. and made TV appearances backing Bobby Darin, Connie Stevens and Ray Bolger, and, by age 18, she appeared with Quincy Jones singing on the award-winning *The World Goes On* at a song festival in Brazil. This was followed by further touring, with Harry Belafonte and soul diva Roberta Flack, punctuated by regular commercial jingles work.
June Cementing a long-term relationship with Jones, Austin features prominently on his US #15 ***Sounds ... And Stuff Like That!!***, vocalizing on four of seven cuts, including a duet with Luther Vandross on *I'm Gonna Miss You In The Morning*. Increasingly an in-demand session and guest vocalist, Austin will contribute to dozens of projects, including Michael Jackson's ***Off The Wall***, Billy Joel's smash *Just The Way You Are*, and albums by Paul Simon, George Benson, Steely Dan (as a "Babylon Sister" on ***Gaucho***) and many others.

1981

Mar [16] Having recorded for CBS/Columbia Records (though still with CTI, with whom she will continue to record a parallel jazz vocal career throughout the decade, including this year's ***Body Language*** and 1983's ***In My Life***), Austin begins 15 days work on her label debut for Jones' Qwest Records, at Westlake Audio Studios in Los Angeles, CA, with a group of musicians, including Greg Phillinganes, Steve Lukather, Eric Gale, Richard Tee, Bob James and David Foster.
Apr Jones' ***The Dude***, on which Austin sings lead vocal on *Betcha' Wouldn't Hurt Me*, *Somethin' Special*, *Razzamatazz* and *Turn On The Action*, reaches US #13 and UK #19.
July Austin's duet with Japanese singer Yutaka on *Love Light* makes US #81.
Sept [26] The Jones-produced ***Every Home Should Have One***, her Qwest debut, spends a week at UK #99 and will make US #36 on Nov [7].

1982

Jan [16] The extracted *Every Home Should Have One* peaks at US #62.
May [8] Rod Temperton-penned *Baby Come To Me*, a ballad duet with James Ingram, stalls at US #73.
Aug Austin performs at the "Budweiser Superfest", at the Rose Bowl, Pasadena, CA, on a $972,902-grossing R&B bill, which includes Stevie Wonder, Aretha Franklin, Vandross, Jones and Ingram.

1983

Feb [19] After featuring in the top-rated US daytime TV soap drama "General Hospital", *Baby Come To Me* is reissued due to public demand, and after entering the Hot 100 on October 16th, tops the US chart for the first of two weeks, after an 18-week climb.
Mar [1] Still-climbing *Baby Come To Me* is certified gold by the RIAA.
[12] *Baby Come To Me* reaches UK #11.
Apr [16] A remixed version of *Every Home Should Have One* peaks at US #69.
July [9] A further duet with Ingram, *How Do You Keep The Music Playing*, theme from the Burt Reynolds/Goldie Hawn movie "Best Friends", makes US #45.

1984

Feb [25] *It's Gonna Be Special*, from the film "Two Of A Kind", peaks at US #82.
May ***Patti Austin***, once again recorded with the help of top flight session men, including Jerry Hey, Paul Jackson Jr., David Sancious and Preston Glass, with tracks produced by Narada Michael Walden, Glen Ballard, Ollie Brown, Quincy Jones and Ambrosia's David Pack, makes US #87.

1985

Nov ***Gettin' Away With Murder***, produced by Tommy Lipuma, Monte Moir, Russ Titelman, and Jimmy Jam and Terry Lewis, and featuring songs written by the likes of Michael Bolton, Alison Moyet and Randy Goodrum, peaks at US #182. (*The Heat Of Heat* will make US #55 on May [31] the following year.)

1988

June ***The Real Me***, a "torch" album produced by David Pack and featuring such classics as *Smoke Gets In Your Eyes*, *True Love*, *Mood Indigo* and *Cry Me A River*, is issued, her final Qwest release.

1989

Nov [14-17] Recently featured on the cartoon-strip-celebrating album ***Happy Anniversary, Charlie Brown!*** and now signed to Dave Grusin's GRP specialist jazz label, Austin records ***Love Is Gonna Getcha*** at Sunset Sound Studios, Hollywood, CA, with musical assistance from seasoned sessioneer friends Lee Ritenour, Greg Phillinganes, Nathan East and Harvey Mason, among others.

1990

Apr [4] She takes part in the first "New York Rock and Soul Revue" at New York's Beacon Theatre with Phoebe Snow, Michael McDonald and Donald Fagen. (Having featured on many previous Austin projects, Richard Tee invites Austin to contribute to his debut solo album ***Inside You***, and by year's end, she will also be featured on the "Dick Tracy" soundtrack album.)
May [5] Recorded the previous November, ***Love Is Gonna Getcha*** makes US #93.

1991

Mar [1-2] Austin takes part in Donald Fagen's second annual "New York Rock and Soul Revue" at the Beacon Theatre.
Aug [15] She performs *Love Is A Wonderful Thing* on the "International Special Olympics All-Star Gala" broadcast on ABC-TV. (By year's end, her second GRP album, ***Carry On***, produced by Pack, bar one Temperton cut, is released, featuring Michael McDonald, Nathan East, David Benoit and regular co-vocalist Ingram, among others, while Austin will also have recorded a duet featured in the daytime TV soap opera "As The World Turns", with Johnny Mathis.)

1992

July [1] She performs alongside Barbra Streisand, Judy Collins, Vanessa Williams and others at a fundraiser for the Hollywood Women's Political Committee, which raises over $350,000.
Oct [27-28] Their *I'll Keep Your Dreams Alive* duet from the "Freddie FRO7" film having been released in August, Austin opens for George Benson during a five-date UK visit, bowing at Wembley Arena, Wembley, Middx.
Nov [18] She participates in the "Commitment To Life VI" AIDS fundraiser at the Universal Amphitheatre, Universal City, honoring Barbra Streisand and David Geffen and benefitting AIDS Project Los Angeles.

1993

Sept [4] Austin sings *We're All In This Together* on ABC-TV's "In A New Light '93" AIDS awareness special.
Dec [14-19] "The Colors Of Christmas" tour, featuring Austin, Roberta Flack, Peabo Bryson and Jeffrey Osborne, reaches New York's Beacon Theatre.

1994

Apr [22] Austin participates in the seventh annual **Essence** Awards from New York's Paramount, (airing June 6th on Fox-TV).
May Currently touring the US with Ingram, ***That Secret Place*** is released, her last for GRP.
June [24] She performs at New York's Carnegie Hall as part of the 1994 Jazz Festival.
Aug Jazz quartet Fourplay's ***Elixir***, featuring the vocal work of Austin, is released (US).

FRANKIE AVALON

1957

Avalon (b. Francis Avallone, Sept. 18, 1939, Philadelphia, PA), a trumpet-playing prodigy, inspired by the Kirk Douglas movie "Young Man With A Horn", already a local TV celebrity, appearing on the Paul Whiteman-hosted "TV Teen Club" in his pre-teen years and playing with Bobby Boyd & the Jazz Bums during his summer vacation, joins Philadelphia rock group Rocco & the Saints (whose line-up also includes his neighbor Bobby Rydell). Local businessmen Bob Marcucci and Peter De Angelis, scouting artists for their new Chancellor label, see Rocco & the Saints at Mary's Inn in Philadelphia and sign Avalon to a solo contract, recording *Cupid* for his debut. Avalon, while still a member of Rocco & the Saints, also has a brief slot singing *Teacher's Pet* in the film "Disc Jockey Jamboree".

1958

Feb [22] *Dede Dinah*, his first chart success, hits US #7, beginning a rush of chart action, which will see *You Excite Me* make US #49 on May [10], *Ginger Bread*, with backing vocals by the Four Dates, hit US #9 (Sept [6] and UK #30 on Oct [11]), *What Little Girl*, B-side of the still-climbing *I'll Wait For You*, peak at US #79 on Oct [25] with its A-side reaching US #15 on Dec [6].
Apr [5] Avalon embarks on an 80-day North American tour in Norfolk, VA, co-starring in Irving Feld's "Greatest Show Of Stars" with the Everly Brothers, Sam Cooke and Paul Anka, among others.
Dec [25] Alan Freed's ten-day New York Christmas Rock'n'Roll Spectacular bows, featuring Avalon with Eddie Cochran, the Everly Brothers, Chuck Berry, Jackie Wilson, Dion & the Belmonts and others at Loew's State Theater.

1959

Feb [4] Avalon and Jimmy Clanton take over the headlining "Winter Dance Party" tour in Sioux City, IA, following the plane crash which takes the lives of Buddy Holly, Richie Valens and the Big Bopper, dropping other commitments to finish the trek.
Mar [14] *Venus* tops the US chart for the first of five weeks, displacing Lloyd Price's *Stagger Lee*. Avalon's first million-selling single, it will also reach UK #16 on May [23], and is followed by *Bobby Sox To Stockings* hitting US #8 on July [11] and its B-side, *A Boy Without A Girl*, hitting US #10 a week later. *Two Fools* will peak at US #54 on Oct [10] while its A-side, *Just Ask Your Heart*, hits US #7 on Oct [31].

1960

Jan [2] The Marcucci and De Angelis-penned *Why* hits US #1, becoming Avalon's second million-seller and his last #1 released in the '50s. (During its chart run, Avalon films in Racketville, TX, as he begins to pursue a film career in favor of music.)

Swingin' On A Rainbow hits US #9.
[23] *Why* reaches UK #20, beaten out by Anthony Newley's chart-topping cover. (Donny Osmond will also successfully revive the song, in 1972.) Its success is followed by another burst of transatlantic chart activity: *Swingin' On A Rainbow*, flipside of *Why*, makes US #39 (Feb [4]), *Don't Throw Away All Those Teardrops* reaches US #22 on Apr [18], *Don't Throw Away All Those Teardrops* makes UK #37 on May [7] and *Where Are You* reaches US #32 on Aug [1], its B-side, the Glenn Miller-reviving *Tuxedo Junction*, having already peaked at US #82 on June [13].
Sept [18] On his 21st birthday, Avalon receives the $600,000 he has earned before coming of age.
Oct [17] *Don't Let Love Pass Me By* stops at US #85.
[31] A-side *Togetherness* reaches US #26.
Dec [31] *The Puppet Song*, the B-side of *A Perfect Love*, peaks at US #56.

1961

Jan [9] *A Perfect Love* makes US #47, with *All Of Everything* peaking at US #70 on Mar [13], and *Who Else But You* stalling at US #82 on June [5]. Remaining chart success for the year sees *True, True Love* peaking at US #90 on Oct [2], while ***A Whole Lotta Frankie*** makes US #59.

1962

May [19] *You Are Mine* reaches US #26.
Aug [11] *A Miracle* peaks at US #75. (It will be his last chart disc until 1976. He will appear in the movies "The Carpetbaggers", "Voyage To The Bottom Of The Sea", "Panic In The Year Zero", "Survival", "How The West Was Won", "Heat Lightning", "Nine Coaches Waiting" and "The Castilian", and develop a series of "Beach Party" movies for American International Pictures. Towards the end of the decade, during which he will mostly persist with his acting career, he will perform on ITV's "Sunday Night At The London Palladium" on April 30th 1967, and begin filming "The Dark" with Boris Karloff, on location in Southport, Lancs., in November 1969.

1976

Mar [6] Having sung *Dede Dinah* on ABC-TV's "American Bandstand's 20th Anniversary Special" on June 19th, 1973 and after a consistently unspectacular film and TV career, a remake of *Venus* in a topical disco arrangement, makes US #46. (It is not to launch a prolonged comeback on record, and he will continue to work mainly as an actor and, in live work, as a trumpeter.)
Aug [25] CBS-TV four-week variety series "Easy Does It ... Starring Frankie Avalon", in which the star is joined by Annette Funicello, premieres.

1987

Avalon, now living in the San Fernando Valley, CA, with his four sons and four daughters, returns - again with Funicello - to film the affectionately nostalgic "Back To The Beach" movie. (He also appeared performing *Beauty School Dropout* in the 1978 hit movie "Grease".)

1992

While UK retrospective specialist label Castle Communications has released ***The Frankie Avalon Collection*** in May 1990, Avalon, who has recently been added to the Hollywood Walk of Fame (and will attend Funicello's similar unveiling on September 14th, 1993), selling the Twilite Tan tanning product and Zero Pain arthritis treatment via a 1-800 number, and appearing at fundraising charity sports events, is featured playing trumpet on the debut album (***Dead Flowers***) by Edan, a band which includes celebrity offspring, notably Don Everly's son, Edan, and Avalon's own Frankie Jr. The Varese Sarabande label will bring further Avalon material to compact disc with the May 1995 release ***The Best Of Frankie Avalon***.

THE AVERAGE WHITE BAND

Hamish Stuart (vocals, guitar); **Alan Gorrie** (vocals, bass); **Onnie McIntyre** (guitar); **Roger Ball** (alto, baritone saxophone); **"Molly" Duncan** (tenor, soprano saxophone); **Robbie McIntosh** (drums)

1971

Already veterans of Scottish covers bands in the late '60s, ex-Brian Auger's Oblivion Express soul enthusiast Gorrie (b. July 19, 1946, Perth, Tayside, Scotland) and his roommate Duncan (b. Malcolm Duncan, Aug. 24, 1945, Montrose, Angus, Scotland), both living in London, invite Duncan's art school friend Ball (b. June 4, 1944, Dundee, Scotland), and McIntyre (b. Sept. 25, 1945, Lennoxtown, Strathclyde, Scotland), another friend from their music days in Glasgow, Scotland, to form a soul combo with the intention, as Gorrie will later state, "to be the (Detroit) Spinners, but play instruments at the same time". Trumpeter Michael Rosen also features in the initial line-up, but will soon leave, giving the horn section a unique (but Stax-influenced) double sax sound. Although the youngest member of the band, McIntosh (b. 1950, Scotland) is already a much in-demand session player, notably for Ben E. King, and - as another ex-member of Oblivion Express - is Gorrie's first and only choice as the band's drummer. Early gigs reveal the need for a second and stronger vocalist to complement Gorrie, and his choice is ex-Forever More singer/guitarist, Stuart (b. Oct. 8, 1949, Glasgow).

1972

July After playing the European club circuit and US military bases, the Average White Band, a name given to them by Bonnie Bramlett, who is amused that all of the soul band members are white musicians from Scotland, makes its first appearance, at the Lincoln Festival, Lincoln, Lincs.
Oct [21] Chuck Berry's double-entendre *My Ding-A-Ling*, on which McIntyre and McIntosh both play, tops the US chart for the first of two weeks and will also hit UK #1.

1973

Jan [13] They support Eric Clapton at his comeback concert at London's Rainbow Theatre.
The band's blue-eyed R&B/funk style interests MCA Records, which signs them for the album ***Show Your Hand***, and they visit the US for a less than successful tour.
Nov [21] A second, 17-date, North American tour opens at the Whisky, Los Angeles, CA, set to end on December 17th at Massey Hall, Toronto, ON, Canada.

1974

July Now signed to Atlantic Records, the band relocates to the US and records its second album, ***Average White Band***, with producer Arif Mardin, which they will promote on a touring bill headlined by jazz drummer Billy Cobham.
Sept [23] After a week-long booking at the Troubadour Club in Los Angeles, McIntosh dies at a local party thrown for Gregg Allman, from a strychnine-based heroin overdose, when he believes he is snorting cocaine. Gorrie's life is saved by the alertness of Cher, who keeps him conscious. Having auditioned several drummers, the band will replace McIntosh with their longtime friend and ex-Bloodstone, Steve Ferrone (b. Apr. 25, 1950, Brighton, E. Sussex), who will ironically become the only black member of the Average White line-up.

1975

Jan [12] The band plays the first of two benefit concerts in memory of McIntosh, at London's Marquee club.
[14] The still-climbing ***Average White Band*** is certified gold by the RIAA.
Feb [22] Both ***Average White Band***, which fully showcases their self-written, textured, horn-heavy, funk/soul brew, and the extracted instrumental *Pick Up The Pieces*, which has exploded on American radio, hit US #1 in the same week.
Mar [6] *Pick Up The Pieces* is certified gold by the RIAA.
[22] *Pick Up The Pieces* hits UK #6.
[29] ***Average White Band*** also hits UK #6.
Apr Their original MCA album, reissued in the US as ***Put It Where You Want It***, now reaches #39.
May [3] *Cut The Cake* makes UK #31.
June [21] *Cut The Cake* hits US #10.
July [12] Mostly written at Atlantic label boss Ahmet Ertegun's summer home in the Hamptons, Newport, RI, the previous winter, the Mardin-produced ***Cut The Cake***, dedicated to McIntosh, reaches UK #28 and will hit US #4.
[24] ***Cut The Cake*** is certified gold by the RIAA.
Sept [27] Their cover version of the Leon Ware and Pam Sawyer-penned *If I Ever Lose This Heaven* makes #39 in the US, where the band is now permanently based.
Dec [27] *School Boy Crush*, an instant favorite on US R&B stations, reaches US #33 (its opening riff providing the sampled rhythm section for TLC's 1992 US smash, *Ain't 2 Proud 2 Beg*).

1976

May [14] The group embarks on a nine-date UK tour at the Odeon Theatre, Edinburgh, Scotland, set to end on the 29th at the Odeon Theatre, Birmingham, W. Midlands.
Aug [28] ***Soul Searching***, recorded at Atlantic's New York studios and once again overseen by Mardin, hits US #9.
Oct [16] Latin-flavored, Stuart-written extract *Queen Of My Soul* makes US #40, and will reach UK #23 on Oct [30].
Dec [30] ***Soul Searching*** is certified platinum by the RIAA.

1977

Mar [5] Double live album, ***Person To Person***, reaches US #28.
May [20] ***Person To Person*** is certified gold by the RIAA.
Sept [10] ***Benny And Us*** makes US #33, with most lead vocals performed by soul singer Ben E. King. Initially combining to record a one-off cut, *A Star In The Ghetto*, the sessions (on which Luther Vandross was an arranger) proved successful enough to complete an entire album which King will present later in the year at the "Montreux Jazz Festival" in Montreux, Switzerland.

1978

May [6] Named by Stuart to hint at Atlantic's recent merge into the Warner Communications conglomerate, ***Warmer Communications***, their final collaboration with Mardin, reaches US #28.
[16] ***Warmer Communications*** is certified gold by the RIAA.

1979

Mar [8-9] A three-week UK tour climaxes with two nights at the Rainbow Theatre, Finsbury Park, London.
[24] ***Feel No Fret***, self-produced and recorded at Compass Point Studios in the Bahamas, reaches UK #15, where it is their best-selling album since ***Average White Band***, and their first to be released by RCA via a UK-only deal.
Apr [28] The album yields a soulful remake of Bacharach/David's *Walk On By*, which makes US #92 and UK #46.
May [19] ***Feel No Fret***, still on Atlantic in the US (though their final label release), reaches US #32.
Sept [1] The Gorrie-penned *When Will You Be Mine* makes UK #49, as the band negotiates to sign a new American recording contract with Arista (their releases

will continue to be handled by RCA in the UK).
Oct [24] Group performs live on BBC-2 TV's "The Old Grey Whistle Test".

1980

May [31] Insistent, disco-tinged, Gorrie-composed *Let's Go Round Again Pt. 1* reaches UK #12.
June [7] The band takes part in the "Summer Of '80 Garden Party" at the Crystal Palace Concert Bowl, Crystal Palace, London, with Bob Marley & the Wailers, the Q-Tips and Joe Jackson.
[21] ***Shine*** reaches UK #14, becoming the band's second-biggest selling album in Britain.
July [12] Produced in Los Angeles by David Foster, ***Shine*** makes US #116.
[19] *Let's Go Round Again Pt.1* makes US #53.
Aug [2] *For You, For Love*, co-written by Ball with forthcoming Chicago member Bill Champlin, makes UK #46.
[4] The group begins a six-date tour at the Theatre Royal, Nottingham, Notts., their first in Britain for some time, before embarking on further dates in the rest of Europe.
Sept [27] An incomplete Atlantic greatest hits package, also including four unreleased tracks left in the label's vault, ***Volume VIII*** stops at US #182. The band will record one further album, ***Cupid's In Fashion***, for Arista, but its commercial failure will ensure the group's demise. As top-notch musicians and writers, they will all secure steady composition and session work throughout the decade (while Gorrie will record ***Sleepless Nights*** for A&M (US) in 1985).

1989

Aug Re-forming with its core of Gorrie, Ball and McIntyre, the Average White Band has signed to Polydor Records, which releases ***Aftershock***, and will continue to perform at small venues in both the UK and US, while Duncan will re-emerge in 1992, fronting Out Of Order. Stuart, who teamed with Ferrone in 1988 to form half of A&M quartet Easy Pieces, will become the most prominent ex-member, both as an in-demand session player, who also contributes lead vocals to David Foster's 1990 album ***River Of Love***, and as a permanent member of Paul McCartney's touring and recording band, well into the '90s.

1994

Mar [26] *Let's Go Round Again (CCN Remix)* debuts at its UK #56 peak while ***Let's Go Round Again - The Best Of The Average White Band*** will make UK #38 on Apr [2]. The group will continue to perform occasional tours, notably on a US bill with War and Larry Graham & Graham Central Station in October the following year. (Sometimes accused, during their heyday, of borrowing too much from black music history for their recordings, some balance is restored as a number of AWB hits have become popular sampling items for US rap acts, notably TLC and Arrested Development. Gorrie commented on the issue in the sleeve notes to a comprehensive and overdue band retrospective, issued by Rhino Records in the US in 1992: "We've been accused of ripping off black music, which we never tried to do. We worshipped black music and always tried to be original. If we need any vindication (now), then young brothers sampling our stuff today helps us breathe a sigh of relief.")

AZTEC CAMERA

Roddy Frame (vocals, guitar)

1981

Apr At the age of 16, Frame (b. Jan. 29, 1964, East Kilbride, Strathclyde, Scotland), already a teenage veteran of 1978 punk outfit the Forensics, has formed Aztec Camera, which will always revolve around his singer/songwriter creativity, with Dave Mulholland on drums and bassist Campbell Owens. Following a year of performing their innovative brand of melodic but alternative-edged rock in local Scottish towns, they have signed to Glasgow independent label Postcard in December 1980, which now releases the band's debut single, *Just Like Gold*, an immediate UK Independent chart item. It is followed up by a second indie success in August, *Mattress Of Wire*, which is issued to coincide with their first tour of England.

1982

June A new independent label deal is signed with the movement's leading Rough Trade Records in London. Dave Ruffy becomes the band's most permanent drummer. Bernie Clarke also joins (temporarily) on keyboards, co-producing early material with John Brand, including *Pillar To Post*, which becomes another UK Independent chart hit, at #4 in October.

1983

Mar Acoustic guitar-led *Oblivious* becomes their first UK pop chart entry, at #47.
May Highly-rated debut album ***High Land, Hard Rain*** makes UK #22 featuring a collection of Frame originals, sung by him to simple semi-acoustic melodies. The band is signed via a US deal to Sire Records, as the album reaches US #129.
June *Walk Out To Winter* peaks at UK #64.
Aug The band begins a three-month tour of major US venues, supporting Elvis Costello. Frame, still only 19, has to lie about his age in several US states.
Oct Mid-tour, they sign a new multi-album UK record deal with WEA Records.
Dec [3] *Oblivious*, reissued by WEA, reaches UK #18, as Frame prepares songs for a new album.

1984

Sept [15] *All I Need Is Everything*, with an acoustic version of Van Halen's *Jump* on the B-side, makes UK #34.
Oct ***Knife***, produced by Mark Knopfler and subsequently displaying a more textured and sophisticated musical style, reaches UK #14 and will make US #175. The band, now comprising Frame, Owens, Ruffy and Malcolm Ross (b. July 31, 1960) on guitar, begins an extensive world tour to support the release.

1985

Apr US-only released 10" album ***Aztec Camera***, including live tracks recorded at the Dominion Theatre, London, in October 1984, makes #181.

1986

Mar Aztec Camera, now entirely a vehicle for a solo Frame, begins its third album project, in New York, NY, and Boston, MA, assisted by session musicians, including Marcus Miller, Steve Jordan and System's keyboardist David Frank.

1987

June The band begins a UK tour in advance of forthcoming releases and will embark on a US trek in November.
Oct *Deep Wide And Tall*, from the simultaneously-released album ***Love***, fails to chart, while the album initially peaks at UK #49. The nine Frame songs have been overseen by assorted top-drawer producers - Russ Titelman, Tommy LiPuma, David Frank, Michael Jonzun, Rob Mounsey and Frame himself.
Dec ***Love*** peaks at US #193.

1988

Jan Frame returns to Britain for more live dates, before touring Australia.
Mar [12] Lilting ballad *How Men Are* reaches UK #25.
June [11] Uptempo, horn-led, optimistic and catchy *Somewhere In My Heart* hits UK #3, the band's biggest hit to date. It revives UK sales interest in ***Love***, which now peaks at #10 and earns a platinum award. A major UK tour will also culminate in two sold-out dates at London's Royal Albert Hall.
Aug [20] *Working In A Goldmine* makes UK #31.
Oct Reissued *Deep And Wide And Tall* peaks at UK #55.

1990

June [16] ***Stray***, recorded at Dave Edmund's Rockfield Studios, Monmouth, Gwent, Wales, and at the Power Plant, London, produced by Frame with Eric Calvi and introducing a new Aztec Camera, comprising Paul Powell on bass, Gary Sanctuary on keyboards and Frank Tontoh on drums, enters the UK chart at its #22 peak. Paul Carrack, Mick Jones and Edwyn Collins also make guest appearances.
[19] Aztec Camera performs at the Hammersmith Odeon, London, the highlight of a 21-date UK tour. The support act is Frame himself, performing a short acoustic opening to each show.
July *The Crying Scene* stalls at UK #70.
Oct [27] Overtly-political, Frame-penned *Good Morning Britain*, recorded with Big Audio Dynamite frontman Mick Jones taking alternate line vocals with Frame, makes UK #19, as the band finishes a six-month world trek.
Dec ***Red Hot + Blue*** AIDS awareness album is released, featuring the group's Cole Porter cover *Do I Love You?*
[6] During a limited US club-date tour, Aztec Camera performs at the Ritz, New York.
[11] Frame guests on NBC-TV's "Late Night With David Letterman".

1991

June [20] He begins a short acoustic-only UK tour, still under the band name, opening the fourth "Liverpool Festival Of Comedy" at the Hardman House, Liverpool, Merseyside. The tour will also include appearances at the annual Cambridge Folk and Edinburgh Festivals.
Aug [13] Frame performs with Edwyn Collins at Edinburgh's Marco club.

1992

July [25] *Spanish Horses*, featuring Collins on co-vocals, makes UK #52, while Frame continues working on his fifth Aztec Camera album, at the Outside Studios, London. By year's end, the band will also have contributed a duet with Andy Fairweather-Low, covering Amen Corner's *If Paradise Is Half As Nice*, for the **New Musical Express** magazine-released ***Ruby Trax*** compilation.

1993

May [8] *Dream Sweet Dreams* peaks at UK #67.
[25] A UK tour kicks off at Edinburgh's Usher Hall. (Frame will also support Bob Dylan at some of the legend's Hammersmith Labatt's Apollo, London, concerts.)
[29] ***Dreamland***, co-produced by Frame with Ryuichi Sakamoto, bows at its UK #21 peak.

1995

July [14] Frame takes part in the "Phoenix Festival" at Stratford-upon-Avon, Warks.
Nov [26] He finishes an eight-date UK tour at London's Shepherd's Bush Empire, following the release of the Clive Langer/Alan Winstanley-produced ***Frestonia*** (released in the US by Reprise Records).

B

BABYFACE

1983

Nov [12] Nicknamed for his youthful looks by R&B funkster Bootsy Collins, Babyface (b. Kenneth Edmonds, Apr. 10, 1959, Indianapolis, IN), already a guitarist/backing vocalist veteran of mid-'70s R&B combo Manchild (whose only chart presence was the 1977 US R&B #70 cut *Especially For You*), is a member of the six-piece Cincinnati, OH-based funk group the Deele which is signed to Solar Records (US) and now enters the US R&B Singles chart for the first time with *Body Talk* (which eventually hits #3 and makes #74 on the Hot 100), taken from the debut album ***Street Beat*** (which will reach US #78 in April 1984). The line-up includes drummer Antonio "L.A." Reid (b. June 7, 1957, Cincinnati, nicknamed "L.A." after a hat he persistently wears, with whom Babyface will form a songwriting/production partnership which will make its first impression with the release of the band's second album ***Material Thangz*** (US #155 in July 1985).

1987

Apr [4] Still a member of Deele but now signed to Solar as a solo artist, his debut *Lovers* enters the US R&B Singles survey set to reach #42. His first solo album ***Lovers***, co-written and co-produced with Reid and released later in the year, will spawn two further R&B chart singles, *I Love You Babe* and *Mary Mack*.
Aug [29] The Whispers' *Rock Steady*, written and produced by what will become known as the "L.A." Reid & Babyface production team, hits US #7.

1988

Apr [23] *Girlfriend*, written and produced by the duo, and recorded by Pebbles (who will marry Reid the following year), hits US #5.
May ***Eyes of a Stranger***, Deele's final outing which includes its biggest crossover success, *Two Occasions* (US #10 in April), peaks at US #54. (By year's end the pair will relocate to Atlanta, GA, where they establish their new production/record company LaFace Inc., a joint venture with Arista Records.)

1989

Jan [21] Critical in their rapid rise as the hottest R&B songwriting and production team in the US, Bobbys Brown's multi-platinum ***Don't Be Cruel***, largely overseen by Reid and Babyface, tops the US chart (also hitting UK #3).
Mar [4] Sheena Easton's *The Lover In Me*, the pair's next collaboration (this time with regular third cohort and ex-Manchild member Daryl Simmons), hits US #2.
Oct [28] *It's No Crime*, hits US #7, taken from Babyface's sophomore solo effort ***Tender Lover*** which was released in August.

1990

Feb [2] *Tender Lover* reaches US #14.
Mar [3] ***Tender Lover***, co-produced with Reid though largely self-written and self-performed, finally reaches US #14 during a 61-week chart run.
[14] ***Tender Lover*** is named Best R&B/Urban Contemporary Album Of The Year, Male at the fourth annual Soul Train Music Awards held at Los Angeles, CA's Shrine Auditorium.
Apr [28] *Whip Appeal* hits US #6.
June [29] ***Tender Lover*** is certified for two million sales by the RIAA.
Aug [18] *My Kinda Girl* reaches US #30.
Oct [27] Pebbles' *Giving You The Benefit*, again written and produced by Babyface and Reid, hits US #4.
Dec [1] Whitney Houston's *I'm Your Baby Tonight*, written and produced by Reid and Babyface and the latest of the pair's hot R&B/pop nuggets, tops the US chart. (Babyface and Reid will spend the following year working on a dizzying number of songwriting and production projects both for their own LaFace stable and outside R&B acts.)

1992

Aug [15] Beginning an extremely fruitful relationship with the soul quartet Boyz II Men, the Babyface/Reid/Simmons-written and produced cut *End Of The Road* begins the first of a record-breaking 13 weeks atop the US Hot 100. In the same week, TLC's *Baby-Baby-Baby*, released on LaFace and once again penned and produced by the trio, hits US #2.
Sept [19] *Give U My Heart* performed by Babyface with new LaFace signing Toni Braxton and featured in the Eddie Murphy-starring movie "Boomerang", reaches US #29. (In the same week, Bobby Brown's *Humpin' Around*, again co-written and co-produced by Babyface, holds at US #3.)

1993

Feb [24] With Reid, Babyface shares the Producer Of The Year win (with Daniel Lanois and Brian Eno) at the 35th annual Grammy Awards held at the Shrine Auditorium, and also collects the Best R&B Song trophy (for *End Of The Road*) with Reid and Simmons.
Aug [21] Now signed as a solo performer to Epic Records, Babyface's *For The Cool In You* peaks at US #81.
Sept [11] Self-written and produced ***For The Cool In You*** reaches US #16.
Oct [9] *Another Sad Love Song*, the debut hit by Braxton, hits US #7. Her maiden album ***Toni Braxton***, co-written and co-produced by Babyface, will top the US chart in February 1994.

1994

Jan [29] *Never Keeping Secrets* reaches US #15.
Mar [2] ***The Bodyguard*** soundtrack album, for which Babyface was a co-producer, wins the Album Of The Year and Producer(s) Of The Year categories at the 36th annual Grammy Awards, held at Radio City Music Hall, New York, NY.
[15] He wins the Best R&B Album, Male (***For The Cool In You***) category at the eighth annual Soul Train Music Awards held at the Shrine Auditorium.
Apr [23] *And Our Feelings* reaches US #21.
July [16] *Rock Bottom* makes UK #50, his solo UK chart debut.
Aug [27] Boyz II Men's *I'll Make Love To You*, written only by Babyface and marking his creative split from Reid (though their business relationship remains intact at LaFace), begins a record-breaking 14-week tenure at US #1.
Sept [10] Babyface-written, produced and performed *When Can I See You*, a stripped-down acoustic-guitar led ballad, hits US #4 having already been certified gold by the RIAA four days earlier.
[12] He guests on NBC-TV's "The Tonight Show".
Sept Aside from his own solo success, Babyface dominates the R&B/pop scene, particularly in the US where he is currently featured as a writer or producer on hit projects by Gladys Knight (***Just For You***), Boyz II Men (the multi-platinum ***II***), Tevin Campbell (the million-plus selling ***I'm Ready***), Aretha Franklin (her comeback hit *Willing To Forgive*), El DeBarge (***Heart, Mind & Soul***), and on Toni Braxton's multi-platinum ***Toni Braxton***.
Oct [1] *When Can I See You* bows at its UK #35 peak.
Nov [9] ***For The Cool In You*** is certified for two million sales by the RIAA.
[12] *Dream Away*, a duet performed by Babyface with Lisa Stansfield for the movie "The Pagemaster" written by Diane Warren, is released in the US, the same day that Babyface performs live for the first time as a solo artist on a bill with El DeBarge and After Seven, a fund-raising event for the Boarder Baby Project (for which he is also the national spokesman) held in Washington, DC.
Dec [27] He begins his first ever solo concert tour, a five-week US trek opening for Boyz II Men at the Target Center, Minneapolis, MN, a bill which grosses $383,470.

1995

Jan [14] As a songwriter, Babyface collects his 32nd Top 10 US Hot 100 single as Madonna's *Take A Bow*, also featuring him as co-vocalist, hits US #8 (his first being the Whispers' *Rock Steady* in 1987).
[30] Babyface collects the Best Male Artist, Soul/R&B trophy at 22nd annual American Music Awards held at the Shrine Auditorium, at which he also performs *Take A Bow* with Madonna.
Mar [1] He wins the Best Male R&B Vocal Performance category (for *When Can I See You*, which he also performs) and collects the songwriter's award for Best R&B Song (*I'll Make Love To You*) at the 37th annual Grammy Awards, held at the Shrine Auditorium.
[13] Babyface co-hosts the ninth annual Soul Train Music Awards, with Anita Baker and Patti LaBelle, staged at the Shrine Auditorium.
May [16] *Breathe Again* is named Song Of The Year (the most performed song) at the 1995 BMI Pop Awards held at the Beverly Wilshire, Los Angeles, while Babyface is also named Songwriter Of The Year (for the fourth time; he previously took the honor in 1989, 1990 and 1991).
June [20] He performs again on "The Tonight Show".
July [18] After 7's ***Reflections***, with seven cuts produced or penned by Babyface, is released in the US (the group's line-up includes his siblings Kevon and Melvin Edmonds).
[20] Reid's now ex-wife Pebbles' production company Pebbitone files a $10m lawsuit against LaFace and L.A. Reid & Babyface in Los Angeles Superior Court in the latest salvo in legal wranglings surrounding hot LaFace act TLC.
Aug [5] Jon B.'s *Someone To Love*, featuring Babyface, *hits US #10.*
Sept [2] With After 7's *Til You Do Me Right* reaching #40 on the Hot 100, Babyface notches up his 50th Top 40 US hit in just eight years.
Nov [14] Having contributed material to the 1992 ***The Bodyguard*** film soundtrack, ***Waiting To Exhale***, entirely written and produced by Babyface and featuring a host of top R&B talent including Franklin and Braxton is released in the US. Its first single, Whitney Houston's *Exhale (Shoop Shoop)* will immediately top the US Hot 100.

1996

Jan [29] Former business manager Willie Carter files a $10 million breach-of-contract suit in Los Angeles Superior Court against LaFace Records and Reid and Babyface claiming he has not been remunerated for his alleged 5% share ownership of the label.
Feb [10] Babyface's work continues to dominate the US Hot 100 with four records in this week's Top 20: *Exhale (Shoop Shoop)* at #2, Mary J. Blige's *Not Gon' Cry* at #6, Brandy's *Sittin' Up In My Room* at #13 and TLC's *Diggin' On You* at #19, all written and produced solely by Babyface.
[28] Not surprisingly, Babyface collects the trophy for Producer Of The Year at the 38th annual Grammy Awards held at the Shrine Auditorium.

BACHMAN-TURNER OVERDRIVE

Randy Bachman (guitar, vocals); **Blair Thornton** (guitar); **C.F. (Fred) Turner** (bass, vocals); **Robbie Bachman** (drums)

1972

After leaving Guess Who (Canada's most successful band of the '60s) in 1970 and releasing the solo ***Axe***, issued by RCA Records (US) and recorded with guitarists Dan Troiana and Wes Dakus, and drummer Garry Peterson, Randy Bachman (b. Sept. 27, 1943, Winnipeg, MB, Canada) embarks on a new venture, Brave Belt, with brother Robbie Bachman (b. Feb. 18, 1953, Winnipeg), Turner (b. Oct. 16, 1943, Winnipeg) and Chad Allan (also a former member of Guess Who), playing unsuccessfully for two years and recording two non-charting albums (***Brave Belt*** and ***Brave Belt II***) for Reprise Records, before forming

Bachman-Turner Overdrive, with Tim Bachman replacing Allan, its new name partly derived from trucking industry magazine **Overdrive**, with the band appropriately developing a blue-collar image and lyrical inclination.

1973

Aug After 24 record company rejections of their no-frills, solid-rock approach, the band has signed to Mercury Records and its debut set, ***Bachman-Turner Overdrive*** is released. Promoted by regular US touring (the band's hallmark), it climbs to US #70, but Tim Bachman leaves shortly after to concentrate on production, to be replaced on guitar by Thornton (b. July 23, 1950, Vancouver, BC, Canada).

Dec [29] The group's first US chart single *Blue Collar* peaks at #68.

1974

Apr [27] *Let It Ride* reaches US #23.

May [9] Still climbing the US survey, ***Bachman-Turner Overdrive II*** is certified gold by the RIAA.

Aug [10] Down-home rocking *Takin' Care Of Business*, the band's first Top 20 single, reaches US #12, as ***Bachman-Turner Overdrive II*** hits US #4.

Oct [11] ***Bachman-Turner Overdrive*** is certified gold by the RIAA.

[19] ***Not Fragile*** tops the US chart for a week, having been certified gold by the RIAA on August 23rd,

Nov [9] *You Ain't Seen Nothing Yet*, a song only included on ***Not Fragile*** as an afterthought, replaces Stevie Wonder's *You Haven't Done Nothin'* to hit US #1 for a week and become a million-plus seller. Written by Randy for his brother Gary, who has a stutter, and sung appropriately, it is based on Dave Mason's instrumental *Only You Know And I Know*.

Dec [13] ***You Ain't Seen Nothing Yet*** is certified gold by the RIAA.

[21] *You Ain't Seen Nothing Yet* is the band's UK chart debut, hitting #2. By year's end, the group will have undertaken a mini-tour of England, Holland, Belgium and Germany.

1975

Feb [15] *Roll On Down The Highway* reaches UK #22, set to peak at US #14 on Mar [1].

Mar Brave Belt catalog album ***Bachman-Turner Overdrive As Brave Belt*** is reissued by Reprise Records, making US #180.

[1] ***Not Fragile*** reaches UK #12.

May [27] ***Four Wheel Drive*** is certified gold by the RIAA.

July [5] *Hey You* reaches US #21, while ***Four-Wheel Drive*** hits US #5.

Dec [23] Still-rising ***Head On*** is certified gold by the RIAA.

1976

Jan [3] The year's bar-room chart action begins with *Down To The Line* (US #43 on Jan [3]), followed by ***Head On*** (US #23 on Mar [6]), extracted *Take It Like A Man*, which makes US #33 one week later, *Lookin' Out For #1* (US #65, May [15]), *Gimme Your Money Please* (US #70, Oct [2]) and the retrospective ***The Best Of BTO (So Far)***, which reaches US #19 on Oct [9].

[20] The group begins a 29-date US tour in Indianapolis, IN, set to end on February 29th in Richmond, VA.

1977

Apr With Randy Bachman having left to pursue a solo career, replaced by Jim Clench, ***Freeways*** makes US #70.

1978

Mar ***Street Action***, on which the band's name is shortened to BTO, makes US #130. Bachman's solo album ***Survivor***, recorded with Burton Cummings (keyboards), Ian Gardiner (bass) and Jeff Porcaro (drums), is released by Polydor Records but fails to chart.

1979

Apr ***Rock'n'Roll Nights***, also released as BTO, stalls at US #165, having spawned the Mar [31] US #60 *Heartaches*.

May Randy Bachman re-emerges with his new rock outfit Ironhorse, which signed to Scotti Brothers Records, makes US #153 with ***Ironhorse***, with the extracted *Sweet Lui-Louise* reaching US #36 and UK #60, to be followed by ***Everything Is Grey*** (released in May 1980) and its US #89 *What's Your Hurry Darlin'*. In the early '80s, Bachman will form the short-lived Union, signed to Portrait Records (which issues ***On Strike*** in 1981), before returning to solo work.

1984

Sept Having re-formed the band as a trio of Bachman, younger brother Tim and Turner, their comeback album ***Bachman-Turner Overdrive*** is released on the Compleat label and makes US #191 (followed by ***Live! - Live! - Live!*** in August 1986 (on Curb/MCA). (A staple oldie on US radio, *You Ain't Seen Nothin' Yet* will also be resurrected as a popular catchphrase and political rally cry by President Reagan (although he will be unaware of the BTO connection) throughout the decade. The reunion holds, however, and the group will continue to perform as a popular live draw in both the US and Canada, while Randy Bachman will also tour with a re-formed Guess Who.)

1995

Jan [27] ***The Best Of BTO (So Far)*** is certified platinum by the RIAA. While *You Ain't Seen Nothin' Yet* received further UK exposure in the early '90s, as the only disc consistently played by UK parody DJs, Nicey (Harry Enfield) and Smashie (Paul Whitehouse) on the Radio Fab FM comedy spoof of the BBC 1FM station, Randy Bachman re-emerged with the Canadian-only, Sony-released ***Any Road*** in March 1993, featuring Neil Young, guesting on two versions of *Prairie Town*, and Cowboy Junkies' vocalist Margo Timmins, among others.

1996

Apr [16] The Randy Bachman Band performs with Jack Tempchin on electric night at Nashville, TN's Ace of Clubs, during the city's "Tin Pan South" songwriters' week.

BAD COMPANY

Paul Rodgers (vocals); **Mick Ralphs** (guitar); **Boz Burrell** (bass); **Simon Kirke** (drums)

1973

Aug Left without a band after the break-up of Free, rock veterans Kirke (b. July 28, 1949, Shrewsbury, Shrops.) and Rodgers (b. Dec. 17, 1949, Middlesbrough, Cleveland) link up with Ralphs (b. Mar. 31, 1944, Hereford, Hereford & Worcs.), who has recently quit Mott The Hoople, to form Bad Company, the group's name taken from the title of a 1972 Robert Benton-directed film starring Jeff Bridges. Former Boz & the Boz People and King Crimson bassist Burrell (b. Raymond Burrell, Aug. 1, 1946, Lincoln, Lincs.) will join the band in November.

1974

Mar [9] The band makes its live debut, at City Hall, Newcastle-upon-Tyne, Tyne & Wear.

Apr Under the business guidance of Led Zeppelin manager Peter Grant, the band signs to Island Records in the UK, and to Led Zeppelin-owned Swan Song label in the US, and records ***Bad Company*** in ten days in Ronnie Lane's mobile studio.

May [18] The group supports the Who at London's Charlton Athletic Football Club, alongside Lou Reed and Humble Pie.

June [22] Their debut album ***Bad Company***, establishing the band's style of radio-friendly, melodic power-rock and showcasing Rodgers' trademark explosive vocal talent, hits UK #3.

[29] The extracted Ralphs-penned *Can't Get Enough* reaches UK #15.

Sept [28] ***Bad Company*** tops the US chart. Originally intending to tour the US for six weeks, supporting Black Oak Arkansas and the Edgar Winter Group, their rapid rise in popularity has meant their staying an additional two months, now as a bill-topping, stadium-filling draw.

Nov [2] *Can't Get Enough* hits US #5.

1975

Mar [1] Ralphs-written follow-up *Movin' On* reaches US #19.

Apr [12] *Good Lovin' Gone Bad* makes UK #31.

May [3] Their no-frills, band-produced sophomore effort ***Straight Shooter*** hits UK #3 and US #3.

[31] *Good Lovin' Gone Bad* makes US #36.

Sept [20] *Feel Like Makin' Love*, showcasing both Rodgers' distinctive singing and Ralphs' memorable hard-rock guitar hook, and co-written by the pair, hits US #10 and will reach UK #20 on Oct [11].

Dec [31] The group performs at the "Great British Music Festival" at London's Olympia.

1976

Feb [21] ***Run With The Pack*** hits UK #4 and will hit US #5 on Apr [10] while the extracted *Young Blood*, a remake of the Coasters' 1957 US #8, reaches US #20 on May [22], and *Honey Child* peaks at US #59 on Aug [7].

Dec [1] ***Run With The Pack*** is certified platinum by the RIAA.

1977

Mar [15] ***Burnin' Sky*** is certified gold by the RIAA.

[26] ***Burnin' Sky*** climbs to UK #17, set to reach US #15 on Apr [23].

June [11] Title track *Burnin' Sky* stalls at US #78. (The group meets President Jimmy Carter at the White House, having recently been made honorary Colonels of Louisiana by the State of Louisiana.)

1979

Mar [24] ***Desolation Angels***, updating the basic four-piece rock sound with synthesizer and strings and released amid (unfounded) rumors about the band splitting up, hits UK #10. During the month, the group performs at the Wembley Arena, Wembley, Middx., before embarking on a US tour.

May [19] ***Desolation Angels*** hits US #3.

June [16] The Rodgers-penned *Rock'n'Roll Fantasy* reaches US #13.

Aug [25] *Gone, Gone, Gone* peaks at US #56.

1982

Aug [28] After a three-year silence, the quartet returns with ***Rough Diamonds***, reaching UK #15.

Oct ***Rough Diamonds*** reaches US #26.

[16] The extracted Rodgers-written *Electricland* stalls at US #74. Soon after, Rodgers will quit the line-up.

1983

July Confirming a second wave of split rumors, Bad Company officially announces its break-up. (Rodgers will form the Firm with ex-Led Zeppelin guitarist Jimmy Page, drummer Chris Slade and bassist Tony Franklin, releasing 1985's ***The Firm*** and ***Mean Business*** the following year, while Ralphs tours with Pink Floyd's Dave Gilmour, before releasing the 1985 solo album ***Take This***. Burrell and Kirke will both establish their own short-lived rock outfits.)

Dec [8] Rodgers plays alongside Eric Clapton, Jimmy Page and many others in the Ronnie Lane ARMS Appeal concert at New York's Madison Square Garden, having also performed at a similar benefit in London in September.

1986

Jan ***10 From 6***, a ten-track compilation from the

band's six previous albums, makes US #137.
Nov [1] *This Love* makes US #85.
Re-formed minus Rodgers, ***Fame And Fortune***, featuring new vocalist, ex-Ted Nugent band member Brian Howe, makes US #106. It will be followed by ***Dangerous Age***, which will make US #58 in October 1988 (and be certified gold by the RIAA on June 21st 1989), and the extracted Apr [29], 1989-peaking *Shake It Up*.

1990

Mar *Can't Get Enough* enjoys the dubious distinction of becoming the first reissued song used for a UK TV Levi jeans commercial not to concurrently make the UK chart.
July [17] First leg of a lengthy US tour with Damn Yankees begins in Burlington, VT, including latest band recruits Paul Cullen (bass) and Geoffrey Whitehorn (guitar), alongside veterans Kirke and Howe. (Ralphs has taken an extended sabbatical to spend time with his family.)
[28] *Holy Water* makes US #89.
Aug [4] Its parent album ***Holy Water*** reaches US #35.
Dec [5] The RIAA certifies gold sales of *Rock 'N Roll Fantasy* and multi-platinum sales of ***Desolation Angels*** (two million).

1991

Mar [2] Extracted power ballad *If You Needed Somebody* reaches US #16.
June [21] The RIAA confirms sales of two million US copies for ***10 From 6***.
[28] The fourth leg of the US tour with Damn Yankees opens in Omaha, NE, with the latest line-up of Kirke, Ralphs, Howe and David Colwell.
July [4-5] The group, on a bill with Damn Yankees and Tattoo Rodeo, grosses more than $529,000 at the New Pine Knob Theatre, Clarkston, MI.
[29] ***Holy Water*** is certified platinum by the RIAA.
Sept [30] ***Straight Shooter*** is certified multiplatinum by the RIAA for three million sales.
Oct [19] *Walk Through Fire* reaches UK #19.

1992

Oct [10] ***Here Comes Trouble***, produced by Terry Thomas at Livingstone Studios in London, debuts at its US #40 peak.
Nov [7] *How About That* reaches US #38, as the group has recently wound up a short US tour in San Antonio, TX, on the 1st. Its latest line-up sees the more recent trio of Ralphs, Kirke and Howe augmented by ex-Foreigner bassist Rick Wills.
[23] Having formed the Law in 1990 with ex-Who drummer Kenney Jones, and disbanding the unit following the April 1991 release of its only album ***The Law***, Paul Rodgers sings *Dock Of The Bay* at Dan Aykroyd's House of Blues club launch in Cambridge, MA.
Dec [26] *This Could Be The One* peaks at US #87.

1993

Feb [20] Bad Company plays a sole London date at the Town & Country club.
Mar [18] ***Here Comes Trouble*** is certified gold by the RIAA.
May [6] Bad Company embarks on the "Last Rebel Tour", supporting Lynyrd Skynyrd, at the UTC Arena, Chattanooga, TN, set to end on July 11th at the Hilton Hotel, Reno, NV.
[8] ***Tribute To Muddy Waters***, a celebration of Waters' work by a number of notable guitarists (including Jeff Beck, Slash, Gary Moore, Carlos Santana, Dave Gilmour and Brian May), all assembled by Rodgers, who performs lead vocals on each track, makes US #91, set to debut at its UK #9 peak on July [3].
Nov [23] ***The Best Of Bad Company Live ... What You Hear Is What You Get*** is released in the US on East West.
[30] The RIAA certifies sales of five million for their debut album ***Bad Company***.

1994

Jan [14] Having assembled a fresh backing unit, Paul Rodgers & Company, featuring Neal Schon, Todd Jenson and Dean Castronovo, begins a 10-date UK tour at Newport Centre, Newport, Gwent, Wales set to end on the 26th at the Manchester Academy, Manchester, Gtr. Manchester.
Feb [12] Extracted from his 1993 project, Rodgers' *Muddy Water Blues* debuts at its UK #45 peak.

1995

May [11] Bad Company's latest US tour, co-headlining with Ted Nugent, opens at the Sunrise Musical Theatre, Sunrise, FL with the line-up of Robert Hart (vocals), Kirke, Ralphs, Colwell and Wills.
June [24] ***Company Of Strangers*** bows at its US #159 peak.
see also: **FREE; MOTT THE HOOPLE**

BADFINGER

Pete Ham (guitar, piano, vocals); **Tom Evans** (bass, vocals); **Joey Molland** (guitar, keyboards, vocals); **Mike Gibbins** (drums)

1968

July After performing locally in Welsh clubs for a couple of years, and being seen by semi-professional musician Bill Collins, who becomes the group's manager, Ham (b. Apr. 27, 1947, Swansea, W. Glamorgan, Wales), Gibbins (b. Mar. 12, 1949, Swansea), Ron Griffiths (bass), David Jenkins (rhythm guitar) and Terry Gleeson (drums), having auditioned for the Kinks' Ray Davies, are backing UK vocalist David Garrick, playing on his hit *Dear Mrs. Applebee*, when Collins gives a demo tape to Beatles assistant Mal Evans, who in turn gives it to Paul McCartney, who signs them to Apple Records as the Iveys (the name taken from Ivey Place, a road in Swansea). Evans (b. June 5, 1947, Liverpool, Lancs.), who has been in Liverpool group the Calderstones, has replaced Jenkins, who has left to join another band.
Nov The Iveys' debut *Maybe Tomorrow*, produced by Tony Visconti, is released.
Dec Griffiths is asked to leave after a disagreement with Evans and is replaced by Molland (b. June 21, 1948, Liverpool), formerly with the Profiles, the Masterminds, the Merseys and Gary Walker & Rain. Evans switches to bass.

1969

Mar [15] *Maybe Tomorrow* peaks at US #67.
July The proposed ***Maybe Tomorrow*** is withdrawn from both UK and US release schedules, while *No Escaping Your Love* is a Europe-only issue.
Sept The band, now renamed Badfinger, records the McCartney-penned *Come And Get It* and three other tracks during a session produced by the ex-Beatle for the forthcoming Peter Sellers/Ringo Starr movie "The Magic Christian".

1970

Jan [31] *Come And Get It* hits UK #4, taken from parent album ***Magic Christian Music***, which incorporates cuts from ***Maybe Tomorrow***.
Apr [18] *Come And Get It* hits US #7 as ***Magic Christian Music*** makes US #55.
Oct The group begins an eight-week US tour.
Dec [5] *No Matter What* hits US #8 as ***No Dice*** reaches US #28.

1971

Feb [6] *No Matter What* hits UK #5.
Aug [1] Badfinger performs at George Harrison's benefit Concert for Bangladesh at Madison Square Garden, New York, NY.

1972

Feb [5] *Day After Day* hits US #4, one place ahead of Nilsson's cover of the Pete Ham and Tom Evans-written *Without You*, which will go on to top the US chart two weeks later, for a month. ***Straight Up*** reaches US #31.
[26] *Day After Day* hits UK #10, but parent album ***Straight Up*** flops.
Mar [4] *Day After Day* is certified gold by the RIAA.
[11] Nilsson's *Without You* tops the UK chart, where it will stay for five weeks.
Apr [29] *Baby Blue* reaches US #14.

1973

Dec ***Ass*** is the group's final Apple release, making US #122.

1974

Mar Now signed to Warner Bros. Records, ***Badfinger***, produced by Chris Thomas, stalls at US #161, after the label, discovering that a $600,000 advance which had been placed into an escrow account has disappeared, withdraws all copies from the stores and initiates a lawsuit against Badfinger Enterprises. (The group's business manager, Stan Polley, will be accused, amid much rancor, of mishandling their affairs.) Facing a forthcoming US tour, Ham quits the line-up and is replaced by Bob Jackson, only to rejoin a few days later.
Nov ***Wish You Were Here***, released during the US tour, makes US #148. Frustration over management and financial problems sees Molland leave at the end of a UK tour supported by Man.

1975

Jan The group begins work on the tentatively-titled ***Head First***, with producers Kenny Kerner and Richie Wise.
Apr [23] Plagued mainly by the group's ongoing problems, Ham commits suicide, hanging himself in the garage of his London home. The other members subsequently drift apart: Gibbins moves back to Wales (years later he will reappear, playing drums on the Bonnie Tyler hit *It's A Heartache*); Molland forms Blue Goose, then Natural Gas, releasing an eponymously-titled album and opening for Peter Frampton at the height of his ***Frampton Comes Alive!*** success. Evans and Jackson join the Dodgers, releasing a handful of singles.

1978

Molland, laying carpets in Los Angeles, CA, and Evans, insulating pipes in the UK, re-form Badfinger, with Joe Tanzin on guitar and Kenny Harck on drums, and sign to Elektra Records to record ***Airwaves***. Andy Newmark replaces Harck midway through the sessions and, by the time the project is completed, Tanzin has also left. When the record is released, Molland and Evans are the only credited band members.

1979

Mar ***Airwaves*** makes US #125.
Apr [21] *Love Is Gonna Come At Last* peaks at US #69.

1981

Mar The group, now comprising Molland, Evans, Tony Kaye (ex-Yes), Glenn Sherba and Richard Bryans, signs with Radio Records.
[21] *Hold On* peaks at US #56, as its parent album ***Say No More*** reaches US #155.

1983

Nov [23] After the band (which has recently included Steve Craiter) splits once again, at the end of a US tour, Evans, fighting a continuing battle to receive a fair royalty deal for his songs, especially for the multi-million-selling *Without You*, commits suicide in identical circumstances to Ham.

1991

Nov [2] *The Apple EP*, including *Come And Get It* -

available on CD for the first time, charts for a week at UK #60.

1995

Apr Following the compact disc release of ***Magic Christian Music*** and ***No Dice*** (both with bonus tracks), Capitol releases ***The Best Of Badfinger*** in the US. Molland (who released the solo ***After The Pearl*** in 1985) and Gibbins, having successfully sued to recover royalties from the group's Apple recordings during the mid-'80s, subsequently re-formed Badfinger, recording ***Timeless*** in 1989, with Randy Anderson (guitar) and A.J. Nicholas (bass), released on Molland's own Independent Records label. While the band still undertakes occasional US tours, Rhino has released ***The Best Of Badfinger, Volume II***, comprising Warner Bros. material in 1993, while Rykodisc has issued ***Day After Day***, a live album of a 1974 concert. Rykodisc also released a Molland solo album, ***The Pilgrim***, in June 1992.

JOAN BAEZ

1958

July Raised in California, New York, Iraq and Massachusetts, where her father is working at MIT, Baez (b. Jan. 9, 1941, Staten Island, New York, NY), is the second of three daughters of a Mexican physicist father and a Scottish mother who taught English drama. Studying at Boston University's School of Drama, having played local coffee houses Club Mt. Auburn 47, the Ballad Room and the Golden Vanity in Cambridge, MA, and having cut demos (which will emerge in 1964 as ***Joan Baez In San Francisco***) and participated in a recording for local Veritas Records, ***Folksingers 'Round Harvard Square***, she now performs before a crowd of 13,000 as Bob Gibson's special guest at the first Newport Folk Festival, in Newport, RI. (Her performance will be featured on the compilation ***Folk Festival, Vol. 2***.)

1960

She signs to Vanguard Records and releases her maiden album ***Joan Baez***, a collection of traditional folk songs, including a number of Scottish ballads, which will eventually chart at US #15 in 1962 and UK #9 as late as 1965.

1961

Apr Baez meets Bob Dylan for the first time, at Gerde's Folk City in Greenwich Village, New York. She will frequently introduce the 20-year-old folk singer/songwriter (and future boyfriend) onstage during her concert appearances over the next two years.

Oct ***Joan Baez, Vol. 2***, once again distinguished by her sparsely-accompanied, unique vocal style, is released and becomes her first US chart entry, at US #13, confirming the popularity of the burgeoning folk music scene which Baez will pioneer with Dylan.

1962

Oct ***Joan Baez In Concert*** is released, set to hit US #10. It includes her version of *We Shall Overcome*, recorded at the Miles College, Birmingham, AL, a seminal all-purpose protest song with which she will become strongly associated throughout the decade.

1963

May [17] She headlines the first Monterey Folk Festival, Monterey, CA, alongside protegé Dylan.

July Baez appears at the Newport Folk Festival, the first to be held since she debuted there, again introducing Dylan. (She is also currently featured on the compilation albums ***Newport Broadside***, the only time Baez and Dylan will appear together on record, and ***Evening Concerts At Newport Vol. 1***.)

Aug [28] She sings *We Shall Overcome* at a Civil Rights march on Washington, DC.

Nov [9] Baez's debut chart single *We Shall Overcome* peaks at US #90.

Dec Early recordings made at the 1959 Newport Folk Festival, with Bill Wood and Ted Alevizos, are released on ***The Best Of Joan Baez***, for Squire Records, which reaches US #45.

1964

Feb A second performance set, ***Joan Baez In Concert, Part 2***, with sleeve notes by Dylan, hits US #7, and six months later will become her UK chart debut, at #8.

Apr Baez refuses to pay 60% of her income tax in protest at US Government expenditure on armaments. She joins a picket line in Texas, supporting youngsters opposing racial discrimination in employment. She also refuses to appear on ABC-TV's "Hootenanny" because the program refuses to book blacklisted acts.

1965

Jan ***Joan Baez No. 5*** reaches US #12.

May [23] Her romantic liaison with Dylan now over, Baez performs at London's Royal Albert Hall, as *We Shall Overcome* reaches UK #26.

[28] During her stay in London, she leads a Vietnam protest march with Donovan from London's Marble Arch to Trafalgar Square, where the Committee of 100 stages a rally against US policy in Vietnam and where Baez and Donovan also sing.

June ***Joan Baez No. 5*** hits UK #3, becoming her most successful UK album. Baez founds the Institute for the Study of Non-Violence in Carmel, CA, with political mentor, Ira Sandperl, and withholds a further 10% of taxes from the US Government.

July Her 1960 debut album ***Joan Baez*** finally hits UK #9.

Aug [8] Her cover of Phil Ochs' *There But For Fortune* hits UK #8.

Sept [19] Dylan's *It's All Over Now Baby Blue* reaches UK #22.

[29] Baez begins a UK tour at Fairfield Halls, Croydon, Surrey, which will include a performance at the Royal Albert Hall on October 18th.

Oct [9] *There But For Fortune* makes US #50.

Dec She films a segment for the "TNT Awards Show", with Bo Diddley, the Byrds, Ray Charles, Lovin' Spoonful, the Ronettes, Ike & Tina Turner, Roger Miller, Petula Clark and Donovan, singing *100 Miles* and *You've Lost That Lovin' Feelin'*.

1966

Jan [9] *Farewell Angelina*, also penned by Dylan, makes UK #35, as its parent album ***Farewell Angelina*** hits US #10 and UK #5.

[29] ***Joan Baez***, ***Joan Baez Volume 2***, ***Joan Baez In Concert*** are certified gold by the RIAA.

July [31] *Pack Up Your Sorrows*, written by Baez's brother-in-law Richard Farina, who died in a motorcycle crash two months earlier, makes UK #50.

Oct [8] She takes part in a peace festival with the Grateful Dead and Quicksilver Messenger Service at the Outdoor Theater in Mt. Tamalpais State Park, CA.

[16] Baez is one of 124 anti-draft demonstrators arrested for blocking the entrance to the Armed Forces' Induction Center at Oakland, CA, and jailed for ten days.

1967

Aug Because of her strident opposition to the Vietnam War, the Daughters of the American Revolution refuse Baez permission to perform live at Constitution Hall, Washington, DC.

Sept ***Joan*** reaches US #38.

1968

Mar Baez marries draft resister David Harris, leader of Peace & Liberation Commune in Palo Alto, CA, who will spend half of their three-year marriage in jail for draft evasion, in New York. Baez's memoirs **Daybreak** are published in the US.

Aug ***Baptism*** makes US #84.

1969

Jan ***Any Day Now***, a double album consisting wholly of Dylan songs and recorded in Nashville, TN with session guests including David Briggs (keyboards), Norbert Putnam (bass) and Pete Wade (guitar), is released and will reach US #30.

May [10] *Love Is Just A Four-Letter Word* peaks at US #86.

June ***David's Album***, a collection of songs dedicated to her imprisoned husband makes US #36.

July Compilation album ***Joan Baez On Vanguard*** reaches UK #15.

Aug [17] Baez performs on the all-star bill at the Woodstock Music & Art Fair in Bethel, NY.

1970

May ***One Day At A Time*** makes at US #80. (She is also featured on the year's various artists live event compilations ***Woodstock*** and ***Celebration At Big Sur***.)

Aug [30] Baez plays the final day at the Isle of Wight Pop Festival, Godshill, Isle of Wight.

Oct **Daybreak** is published in the UK, while the compilation album ***The First 10 Years*** makes US #73. During the month, Baez will also co-organize and perform at the Big Sur Folk Festival, Big Sur, CA, also featuring the Beach Boys, Linda Ronstadt, Kris Kristofferson and Country Joe McDonald.

1971

Mar [15] Harris is released from jail.

Apr [3] ***The First 10 Years*** charts for a week at UK #41, her first retrospective and last UK chart album.

Oct [2] Her cover of the Band's Civil War story-song *The Night They Drove Old Dixie Down* hits US #3, becoming a million-seller. It is taken from ***Blessed Are***, her final album for Vanguard, which will return her to the US Top 20 at #11.

[22] ***The Night They Drove Old Dixie Down*** is certified gold by the RIAA.

Nov [6] *The Night They Drove Old Dixie Down* hits UK #6.

Dec [18] Her revival of the Beatles' *Let It Be* makes US #49.

(During the year she is also featured on the albums ***Woodstock Two*** and ***Sacco And Vanzetti***.)

1972

Jan ***Carry It On***, Baez's film soundtrack to the movie in which she appears with husband Harris, peaks at US #164.

[31] ***Any Day Now*** and ***Blessed Are*** are certified gold by the RIAA.

May After more than a decade with Vanguard, Baez has signed to A&M Records and released ***Come From The Shadows***, recorded in Nashville with co-producer Norbert Putnam, reaching US #48. (She is also currently featured on the albums ***Silent Running***, ***A Tribute To Woody Guthrie, Part 2***, ***Earl Scruggs: His Family & Friends*** and ***One Hand Clapping***.)

Sept [2] *In The Quiet Morning*, written by her sister Mimi Farina in tribute to Janis Joplin, makes US #69.

Dec [12] ***The Joan Baez Ballad Book*** peaks at US #188.

[16] Baez arrives in Hanoi, N. Vietnam, through the auspices of the Liaison Committee, to distribute Christmas gifts and mail to US prisoners of war.

1973

Apr [4] She performs at the Empire Pool, Wembley, Middx.

May Continuing her anti-war protest, Baez has devoted one side of the album ***Where Are You Now, My Son?*** to a sound documentary of US bombing in Vietnam which makes US #138.

July ***Hits/Greatest & Others*** makes US #163.

1974

May Baez releases ***Gracias A La Vida!***, recorded entirely in Spanish, with Joni Mitchell duetting on the track *Dida*.

1975

Mar [23] Baez participates in an all-star SNACK (Students Need Athletics Culture & Kicks) benefit at San Francisco, CA's Kezar Stadium, to raise funds to make up a shortfall in the San Francisco school system budget, before a crowd of 60,000.
July [26] ***Diamonds And Rust***, featuring songs by Jackson Browne, Janis Ian and John Prine, and her biggest-seller for four years, reaches US #11. (She is also currently featured on ***The Earl Scruggs Revue: Anniversary Special Vol.1***.)
Aug [2] *Blue Sky* peaks at US #57.
Oct [29] Baez joins Dylan as part of his "Rolling Thunder Revue" tour of the US, which launches in Plymouth, MA.
Nov [15] Title track *Diamonds And Rust*, an autobiographical song concerned with Baez's early romantic involvement with Dylan, is her last US chart single, reaching #35.

1976

Mar [20] Live album ***From Every Stage*** reaches US #34 and features her touring band from the previous year, David Briggs (keyboards), Dan Ferguson (guitars), James Jamerson (bass) and Jim Gordon (drums).
Dec [11] ***Gulf Winds*** makes US #62.

1977

Aug [6] ***Blowin' Away***, recorded in Los Angeles, CA, with Wilton Felder, Joe Sample, Larry Knechtel, Donald "Duck" Dunn, Jeff "Skunk" Baxter, Tom Scott and others, and the first result of her signing to Portrait Records, makes US #54. (She is also featured on the compilation album ***Banjoman***.)

1978

Jan [7] A&M compilation ***The Best Of Joan C. Baez*** peaks at US #121.
Feb The movie "Renaldo And Clara", in which Baez appears opposite Bob Dylan, opens in US theaters.
Aug [20] She performs at Wembley Arena, Wembley, her only UK date on a European tour.

1979

May Baez is one of 84 signatories of the open letter to the Socialist Republic of Vietnam, calling for an end to torture in Vietnam and the release of political prisoners. Baez lobbies President Carter to rescue Vietnamese boat people from drowning. The President will send the 7th Fleet to expedite Baez's plea.
Aug [25] ***Honest Lullaby***, produced by Barry Beckett at Muscle Shoals Sound Studios, Muscle Shoals, AL, and released on Portrait, reaches US #113, and is Baez's last chartmaking album. (The following year she will be featured on the album ***Bread & Roses Festival Of Acoustic Music*** and also guest on ***The Amazing Rhythm Aces***.)

1981

Aug On tour in South America, she is greeted with bomb threats and general harassment, having been vocal in opposition to the right-wing coup in Chile. (She also records an album with Grateful Dead, though it will remain released.)

1982

June [12] Still a tireless campaigner for peace causes, Baez (with Jackson Browne, Linda Ronstadt and others) performs for 750,000 people at a rally for nuclear disarmament in Central Park, New York.

1983

During the year, Baez embarks on an 18-city US tour which will end with two shows at New York's Beacon Theatre. The following year she will perform in Europe with Dylan and Santana, but drop out of the tour midway, following organisational disagreements. (She will also be featured on ***The Earl Scruggs Revue: Super Jammin'*** and ***Hard Travellin'***.)

1985

July [13] Baez performs at the American segment of the "Live Aid" benefit at the JFK Stadium in Philadelphia, PA.

1986

June [4] She takes part in the two-week Amnesty International "A Conspiracy Of Hope" concert tour, performing with the Neville Brothers on a bill also featuring Sting, Peter Gabriel, Bryan Adams, Joni Mitchell and Lou Reed, which begins at the Cow Palace, San Francisco.

1987

Sept Her second autobiography **And A Voice To Sing With** is published. She also signs to Gold Castle/Cypress Records (US, released in the UK via Virgin Records) the Alan Abrahams-produced ***Recently***, featuring her interpretations of Peter Gabriel's *Biko*, Mark Knopfler's *Brothers In Arms* and U2's *MLK* amongst others. It is her first album in five years.

1989

Apr ***Diamonds & Rust In The Bullring***, recorded live in Bilbao, Spain, in 1988, is released.
July [18-19] She takes part in the seventh annual "Prince's Trust Rock Gala", with Alexander O'Neal, Van Morrison, Level 42 and others, at the National Exhibition Centre, Birmingham, W. Midlands.
Dec [16] Baez ends a US tour at Universal Amphitheatre, Universal City, CA.

1990

Aug [11] She performs at the "Newport Folk Festival" at Fort Adams State Park, RI, now sponsored by ice-cream entrepreneurs Ben & Jerry, during a short seven-date tour of the North-eastern US. By year's end, Gold Castle will release ***Speaking Of Dreams***, featuring a version of George Michael's *Hand To Mouth*.

1991

Feb [26] Baez performs at a benefit dinner for the Shelter Partnership at the Biltmore Hotel, Los Angeles.
July [21] She sings *You'll Never Walk Alone*, as 13,000 people walk the 6.2 miles through Golden Gate Park, San Francisco, to raise money for AIDS research.
Aug [19] Baez performs *We Shall Overcome* and a Russian protest song over the phone to Radio Free Europe, who later broadcast it to the Soviet Union.
Nov [3] She sings *Amazing Grace* with Kris Kristofferson and Graham Nash at the "Laughter, Love And Music: To Celebrate The Lives Of Bill, Steve And Melissa" memorial concert to Bill Graham at San Francisco's Golden Gate Park Polo Field, before an estimated crowd of 350,000.
Dec Baez takes part in a benefit concert for the Humanitas International Human Rights Committee at Berkeley Community Theater, Berkeley, CA, with Mary-Chapin Carpenter and the Indigo Girls, raising close to $50,000.

1992

Apr [25] As a legendary protest figure for some three decades, Baez continues another year of fundraising, cause-rallying and performance, as she participates in the Sound Action awareness and fundraiser, held to celebrate Earth Day 1992 at the Foxboro Stadium, Foxborough, MA.
Oct [20] Baez plays to a sellout crowd at the Troubadour in Los Angeles.

1993

Apr [10] Using a truck as a stage, Baez performs the first date on a short tour to benefit war-torn Bosnia, singing to refugees in Zagreb, Croatia, prior to a planned televised gig the following night in shell-shocked Sarajevo.
May [21-22] During a short UK concert trip to promote her Virgin Records-released ***Play Me Backwards***, Baez performs at London's Dominion Theatre.
Aug [7] She continues her latest US tour with a performance in New York's Central Park, part of the "Summerstage" series of concerts, as Vanguard sets to release ***Rare, Live & Classic***, a three-CD 60-track anthology reviewing her career from 1958 to 1989, including the previously unreleased duets with Bob Dylan, *Blowin' In The Wind* and *Mama, You Been On My Mind* and tracks from the 1981 sessions with the Grateful Dead.

1994

May [13-15] Baez takes part in Music Midtown, a three day event featuring 70 acts performing at 10th and Peachtree streets in Atlanta, GA.

1995

Apr [10-11, 16-17] Baez's four dates at the Bottom Line in New York are recorded for future release, with guests Mary-Chapin Carpenter, Janis Ian, Mary Black and Kate & Anna McGarrigle.
Sept [26] ***Ring Them Bells***, the live recording of her Bottom Line shows in April, is issued on Angel Records' Guardian imprint.

1996

Feb [9] Now living in Northern California, Baez performs at the Wiltern Theatre, Los Angeles.

ANITA BAKER

1983

June Having replaced lead vocalist Carolyn Crawford in Detroit, MI-based Chapter 8 (a soul outfit formed by Michael J. Powell in 1971) in 1976, Baker (b. Jan. 26, 1958, Toledo, OH) has already recorded US R&B chart entries *I Just Want To Be Your Girl*, *Ready For Your Love*, *Don't You Like It* and ***Chapter 8*** with the group before quitting the line-up in 1980, to settle into an office job in Detroit while simultaneously looking for a solo recording deal, which she finally secures with US independent R&B-based label, Beverly Glen. Her debut solo release is a soaring soul ballad, *No More Tears*, which now makes #49 on the US R&B survey, to be followed by the top five R&B hit *Angel* in October.
Nov Her Beverly Glen-issued maiden effort ***The Songstress*** makes US #139 (and will remain a hot import item in the UK until its 1987 release). Produced by Patrick Moten and label executive Otis Smith, the album features crack session musicians, including Nathan East, Paul Jackson, Jerry Hey, Jim Gilstrap, with strings arranged by Gene Page. It includes a third R&B chart single, the February 1984 #28 *You're The Best Thing Yet*.

1985

Having resolved a contractual dispute with Beverly Glen, Baker signs to Elektra Records, and reunites with producer and Chapter 8 keyboardist Powell to record an album over which they have total creative control.

1986

May [3] Showcasing Baker's seemingly effortless vocal dexterity, ***Rapture*** enters the UK chart on its way to reach #13. Recorded at the Yamaha R&D Studio, Glendale, CA, the eight-track album's guest musicians include Paulinho da Costa, Greg Phillinganes and Sir Gant.
July [26-27] Baker performs two sellout shows at London's Hammersmith Odeon, adding rapturous notices to the reviews already garnered for the album.
Sept [20] ***Rapture*** tops the US R&B chart, having reached US #11.
Nov [1] Soul-swaying *Sweet Love*, co-written by Baker with Louis A. Johnson and Gary Bias, finally gives her a major crossover US hit single, hitting #8. It will reach UK #13 on the 29th.

1987

Feb [14] Remixed *Caught Up In The Rapture* makes US #37.
[21] *Caught Up In The Rapture* makes UK #51, as Baker concentrates on the follow-up to her multiplatinum Elektra debut.
[24] Increasingly regarded as a soul classic, ***Rapture*** wins the Best R&B Vocal Performance, Female category and *Sweet Love* wins the Best R&B Song, as Baker sings *God Bless The Child* at the 29th annual Grammy Awards at the Shrine Auditorium, Los Angeles, CA.
Mar [23] She collects the Best Single, Female trophy at the inaugural Soul Train Music Awards held at the Civic Auditorium, Santa Monica, CA.

1988

Jan [25] With ***Rapture***'s sales success having continued throughout 1987, she wins the Favorite Female Artist, Soul/R&B and Favorite Album, Soul/R&B categories at the 15th annual American Music Awards, held at the Shrine Auditorium.
Mar [2] Baker shares the Best Soul Gospel Performance By A Duo, Group, Choir Or Chorus trophy for her duet on the Winans' *Ain't No Need To Worry* at the 30th annual Grammy Awards.
May [23] *Same Ole Love (365 Days A Year)* makes US #44 over two years after its parent album was originally released.
Oct [8] Previewing her forthcoming project, *Giving You The Best That I Got* makes UK #55.
[22] *No One In The World*, still from ***Rapture***, makes US #44.
[29] Emulating her Elektra debut and once again produced by Powell, her follow-up set ***Giving You The Best That I Got*** debuts at its UK #29 peak.
Nov [12] *Giving You The Best That I Got* tops the US R&B chart.
[19] ***Giving You The Best That I Got*** hits US R&B #1.
Dec [17] Its title ballad *Giving You The Best That I Got* hits US #3.
[24] Baker marries long-time beau Walter Bridgforth, as ***Giving You The Best That I Got*** hits US #1.

1989

Feb [22] Baker wins Best R&B Vocal Performance, Female and Best R&B Song for *Giving You The Best That I Got* at the 31st annual Grammy Awards.
Mar [9] ***Giving You The Best That I Got*** reaches the RIAA-certified three-million sales mark.
Apr [1] *Just Because* reaches US #14.
[12] Baker collects the Best Single, Best Album and Best Song trophies in the R&B/Urban Contemporary trophies at the third annual Soul Train Music Awards, held at the Shrine Auditorium.
May [11] Together with Dick Clark, she co-hosts the 20th annual Songwriters Hall of Fame awards ceremony, held at Radio City Music Hall, New York.

1990

Jan [22] Baker wins the Favorite Female Artist, Soul/R&B category and performs the Gary Taylor-penned *Good Love* at the 17th annual American Music Awards, held at the Shrine Auditorium.
[23] Her "One Night Of Rapture" video set is certified platinum by the RIAA.
Feb [21] Already an awards veteran, she now wins the Best R&B Vocal Performance, Female category for ***Giving You The Best That I Got*** at the 32nd annual Grammy Awards held at the Shrine Auditorium, having won for the single a year earlier.
Apr [16] Baker participates in the "Nelson Mandela - An International Tribute To A Free South Africa" concert at Wembley Stadium, Wembley, Middx., singing *Blowin' In The Wind* with Bonnie Raitt, Mica Paris and Natalie Cole.
May [22-26] She plays to sellout crowds of 23,824, grossing more than $774,000 at Radio City Music Hall, New York.
June [15-16] European dates are highlighted by sellout concerts at the Wembley Arena, Wembley.
[30] Baker begins an extensive "Compositions" tour at the Pine Knob Music Theatre, Clarkston, MI, as *Talk To Me* peaks at UK #68.
July [14] ***Compositions***, mainly recorded live without overdubs, using a rhythm section comprising Greg Phillinganes (keyboards), Nathan East (bass), and Steve Ferrone and Ricky Lawson (drums), bows at its UK #7 peak.
[28] *Talk To Me*, written by Baker, Powell and Vernon Fails, makes US #44.
Aug [25] ***Compositions*** hits US #5 in its sixth week of release.
[28] ***Compositions*** become her third multiplatinum US album.
Sept [19-20, 22-23] Baker performs four dates at the Greek Theatre, Los Angeles.
Oct [13] Graham Lyle/Terry Britten-penned *Soul Inspiration* peaks at US #72.
Nov [3] ***Rubáiyát***, Elektra's 40th anniversary compilation, to which Baker has contributed a cover of *You Belong To Me*, makes US #140.
Dec [1] Baker wins Best Female Artist for ***Compositions*** at the 23rd annual NAACP Image Awards, at the Wiltern Theatre, Los Angeles.
[31] She closes out the year performing in her hometown, selling out the Fox Theatre.

1991

Jan [20] She wins Best R&B Vocal Performance, Female category for ***Compositions*** at the 33rd annual Grammy Awards, at Radio City Music Hall. Baker has now won a NARAS statuette at each of the last five ceremonies.
Apr [4-7] An executive producer for each of her three Elektra album releases, Baker introduces the Taking Care Of Your Own Business seminar (which she has pioneered) at the 15th annual Black Radio Exclusive Conference, held at the Sheraton Hotel, New Orleans, LA.
Dec [18] "Christmas In Washington", featuring Baker and others, airs on NBC-TV.

1992

July [11] "A Call To Action In The War Against AIDS", in which Baker sings *Fairy Tales*, airs on ABC-TV. She is also featured on the current ***Barcelona Gold*** various artists collection (performing *How Fast How Far*), released to celebrate the 1992 Olympics.
[18] Baker attends Whitney Houston and Bobby Brown's nuptials in Mendham, NJ.
Oct [1] She pays $100,000 for Alex Haley's manuscript of **The Autobiography Of Malcolm X**, at the opening of a three-day auction of Haley's literary legacy on his farm near Knoxville, TN.
Nov Baker and her husband file a $1 million defamation lawsuit against Cityscape Detroit, who had protested the demolition by the Bakers of a landmark house of historic note in Detroit, which the couple bought in 1990 and tore down the following year.

1993

Jan [19] The arrival of her first child, Walter Baker Bridgforth, interrupts recording sessions for her fourth Elektra album.
Apr [30] Baker performs at the sixth annual **Essence** Awards.
Nov [20] Frank Sinatra's ***Duets***, to which Baker contributes *Witchcraft*, debuts at its US #2 peak, and will reach UK #31 on Jan [22], 1994.

1994

Jan [11] The RIAA certifies five million sales of ***Rapture***.
July [4] Baker performs at the Hatch Shell in Boston, MA, at the annual Pop Goes The Fourth concert.
Sept [17] *Body And Soul* debuts at its UK #48 peak.
[24] Its parent album ***Rhythm Of Love*** reaches UK #14.
Oct [1] *Body And Soul* reaches US #36, as ***Rhythm Of Love*** debuts at its US #3 peak.
[13] Two days after appearing on NBC-TV's "The Tonight Show", Baker receives a star on the Hollywood Walk of Fame.
Nov [16] "The Walt Disney Company Presents The American Teacher Awards", with Baker performing and acting as one of the presenters, airs live on Disney cable channel from Washington DC's Warner Theater.
Dec [11] Baker participates in the 13th annual "Glad Tidings From D.C." from the National Building Museum, Washington.
[27-31] A West Coast tour opens with sellout dates at the Universal Amphitheatre, Universal City, CA.

1995

Jan [30] Baker nabs the Favorite Female Artist, Soul/R&B trophy at the 22nd annual American Music Awards.
Feb [11] *I Apologize* makes US #74.
Mar [1] Baker and Vince Gill present the Best Album Of The Year award to Tony Bennett at the 37th annual Grammy Awards at the Shrine Auditorium.
[13] Baker, co-hosts with Babyface and Patti LaBelle, the ninth annual Soul Train Music Awards also held at the Shrine Auditorium, picking up Best R&B/Soul Female Single and Best R&B/Soul Female Album trophies in the process.
[20] She guests on syndicated TV's "Oprah Winfrey Show" being interviewed and performing some of her best known songs live.
Apr [29] She performs the first of five sellout dates at New York's Radio City Music Hall. (New York subway travellers will be able to obtain passes decorated with artwork from the ***Rhythm Of Love*** album.)
June [3] Baker wins Top R&B Artist, Female category at the inaugural Blockbuster Entertainment Awards staged at Hollywood's Pantages Theatre, to be broadcast on CBS-TV on the 6th.
Nov [4] Her world tour opens in Wiesbaden, Germany.
[28] New York's Southern District Court hears Elektra's request to establish the validity of her recording contract, after Baker seeks to end her association with the company, claiming that she had to hire her own independent marketing, promotion and publicity team to work on her last album, because personnel changes at the label undermined the company's ability to adequately promote the project. Baker is expected to file suit contesting her contract in California in the New Year.
Dec [31] She gives a New Year's Eve concert at the James L. Knight Center in Miami, FL.

1996

Feb [28] *I Apologize* is named Best R&B Vocal Performance, Female, at the 38th annual Grammy Awards, held at the Shrine Auditorium.
Mar [29] Baker co-hosts and performs *I Apologize* at the tenth annual Soul Train Music Awards, held at the Shrine Auditorium.

LONG JOHN BALDRY

1961

After leaving school, the 6' 7" tall Baldry (b. Jan. 12, 1941, Haddon, Derbys.) has served his musical apprenticeship singing folk, jazz and R&B in London clubs and coffee bars, making his first public appearance at the World Turned Upside Down club in London's Old Kent Road. Subsequently becoming a member of R&B groups led by Cyril Davies and blues singer Ramblin' Jack Elliott for UK and European tours, Baldry, who possesses a powerful, rasping voice, now joins Alexis Korner's Blues Incorporated, contributing not least to Korner's forthcoming album ***R&B From The Marquee***. Returning to the UK after working in Germany with the Horace Silver Quintet at USAF bases there, Baldry will reunite with Cyril Davies as a member of his R&B All-Stars in November the following year, which, signed to Pye Records, will release *Country Line Special* in April 1963 followed by *Preachin' The Blues* in September.

1964

Jan [7] Davies dies of leukemia. Baldry subsequently

takes over as lead singer, forming the Hoochie Coochie Men from the remaining All-Stars members.
May [6] The group appears on the ITV show "Around The Beatles".
July They sign to United Artists Records, releasing *Up Above My Head.*
Dec The Hoochie Coochie Men release their debut album ***Long John's Blues***.

1965

Jan [15] The group joins the Chuck Berry/Moody Blues package tour, after missing the first week due to Baldry's bronchitis. The tour will end on the 31st at the Regal Cinema, Edmonton, London.
Aug [8] The band performs on the final day of the fifth annual National Jazz & Blues Festival at the Athletic Ground, Richmond, Surrey.
Oct After a steady career on the UK R&B club circuit, the Hoochie Coochie Men breaks up. Baldry joins Rod Stewart, Brian Auger and Julie Driscoll in Steampacket.

1966

Sept Steampacket splits, and Baldry joins Bluesology, with Reg Dwight (soon to be called Elton John) on piano.
[23] Baldry embarks on the 12-date Rolling Stones '66 tour as a soloist at the Royal Albert Hall, London, amidst scenes of hundreds of screaming teenagers rushing on to the stage at the start of the Rolling Stones' performance. The tour will end on October 9th at the Gaumont Theatre, Southampton, Hants.

1967

May After Bluesology releases *Cuckoo*, its sixth and final single for United Artists, Baldry leaves to pursue a full-time solo career.
Oct He signs to Pye Records, and uncharacteristically records the ballad *Let The Heartaches Begin.*
Nov [25] The Tony Macaulay and John Macleod-written *Let The Heartaches Begin* tops UK chart.
Scheduled to begin filming in January 1968, it is announced that Baldry will play a business tycoon in 13 one-hour TV shows which will also feature music by Simon Napier-Bell and songs by Macaulay and Macleod.
Dec [9] Baldry guests on BBC1-TV's "Dee Time" having appeared on BBC-TV's "Juke Box Jury" on November 22nd and "Top Of The Pops" on the 23rd.

1968

Jan [20] *Let The Heartaches Begin* climbs to US #88.
May Baldry becomes manager of Bluesology lead singer Stuart A. Brown.
Sept [21] The Mike D'Abo-penned ballad *When The Sun Comes Shinin' Thru*, backed by a 40-piece orchestra, reaches UK #29.
Oct [14] Baldry flies to the US for eight TV dates to promote *When The Sun Comes Shinin' Thru.*
Nov [23] *Mexico*, a Latin-style theme to BBC-TV's coverage of the Mexico Olympics, reaches UK #15.

1969

Mar [1] *It's Too Late Now* reaches UK #21, the last of Baldry's UK hits, all of which have been produced by Macaulay.

1971

June After a period spent performing on the cabaret circuit, and now signed to Warner Bros., he has recorded ***It Ain't Easy***, with one side each produced by ex-colleagues Rod Stewart and Elton John, who owe some of their musical apprenticeship to Baldry. It makes US #83, as he undertakes his first US tour, subsequently choosing to live there.
Sept [25] *Don't Try To Lay No Boogie-Woogie On The King Of Rock And Roll* peaks at US #73. While ***Everything Stops For Tea*** will make US #180 in May 1972, Baldry's only remaining chart success will be a cover version of the Righteous Brothers' *You've Lost That Lovin' Feelin'* , a duet with Kathi McDonald which will peak at US #89 on Aug [25] 1979 (taken from his end-of-decade album ***Out!***, a reference to a period he has spent in a mental institution, which follows a series of non-charting albums he records for the Casablanca and EMI America labels). In 1980 Baldry will relocate to Canada, where he will eventually become a citizen and continue sporadic tours around North America, even into the '90s.

1993

Feb [16] With Baldry currently heard as the voice of the Captain Robotnick character on the Sonic The Hedgehog cartoon and video game and having released a 1986 album, ***Silent Treatment***, via Capitol in the US, UK retrospective specialist label Castle Communications has brought his '60s highlights to compact disk with the 15-track compilation ***The Best Of Long John John Baldry*** (issued in 1991). Baldry now presents Rod Stewart with his award for Outstanding Contribution To British Music at the 12th annual BRIT Awards, at London's Alexandra Palace, as his new Hypertension Records album ***It Still Ain't Easy*** awaits release (already issued in Canada in 1991 on the Stony Plain label).

HANK BALLARD

1953

May Raised by an aunt and uncle in Bessemer, AL, Ballard (b. Henry Ballard, Nov. 18, 1936, Detroit, MI) leaves the local Ford car factory to join the Detroit-based Royals (also featuring Charles Sutton, Lawson Smith and Sonny Woods), a doo-wop group signed to Federal Records, taking over as lead singer from Henry Booth. While the quartet nabs its first US R&B success with the #6 hit *Get It* in August, their name is subsequently changed to the Midnighters to avoid confusion with label-mates the Five Royales.

1954

May [22] The first single to be released under the new moniker is *Work With Me Annie*, written by Ballard (and based on the pop hit *Dance With Me Henry*) which now hits #1 on the US R&B survey despite (or because of) its ripe sexual innuendo which makes radio airplay sparse.
July An equally controversial sequel, *Sexy Ways* hits US R&B #3.

1955

The pattern continues with *Annie Had A Baby* and *Annie's Aunt Fanny* released during the year, also prompting answer records like Etta James' *Roll With Me Henry*. The "Annie" series, unlike the majority of songs currently on the hit parade, has a raunchy, risqué edge to it, which in some ways has opened the door for the early rebellious themes of rock'n'roll.

1959

Jan After a hitless period of four years, they switch to the King label (Federal's parent), now calling themselves Hank Ballard & the Midnighters.
Mar [23] *Teardrops On Your Letter*, already an R&B chart smash (#4), makes the US pop chart at #87. The B-side, recorded on November 11th the previous year, is the Ballard composition *The Twist*, which he claims is based on the Drifters' 1953 song *Whatcha' Gonna Do?* and given to him by the Nightingales, with Ballard making some minor changes.
May [11] *Kansas City* peaks at US #72, eclipsed by a rival #1 version by Wilbert Harrison.

1960

Aug [15] *Finger Poppin' Time*, another dance-creating Ballard composition, is his long overdue pop chart triumph (ultimately selling over a million copies), hitting US #7, one place above Chubby Checker's fast-climbing cover of *The Twist.*
Sept [19] Checker's *The Twist*, with massive national TV promotion behind it, tops the US chart, as Ballard's version, selling well in Checker's wake, reaches US #28.
Nov [21] His follow-up million-seller *Let's Go, Let's Go, Let's Go* hits US #6.

1961

Jan [30] *The Hoochi-Coochi-Coo* reaches US #23, beginning a year of mainly dance-theme fad hits for Ballard which will be: *Let's Go Again (Where We Went Last Night)*, US #39 on Mar [20], and *The Continental Walk*, US #33 on May [15], followed by *The Float*, which climbs to US #92 on June [19], another dance novelty *The Switch-A-Roo*, which reaches US #26 on July [24], *Nothing But Good*, US #49 on Aug [28] and its Sept [11] US #66-peaking B-side, *Keep On Dancing*.

1962

Mar [10] After Chubby Checker has topped the US chart again on Jan [13] with *The Twist,*, Ballard counters with the US #87 *Do You Know How To Twist?*, his final hit. The Midnighters embrace the Islamic religion, and, as black Muslims, refuse to play to white audiences. He splits with the band, stays on the King label as a soloist and begins working with James Brown, eventually becoming a full-time member of Brown's tour revue by 1968.

1972

Nov Following a spell with Silver Fox Records, the first of several label switches, Ballard returns to work with Brown. His recitation on Brown's *Get On The Good Foot* praises him for rescuing Ballard during a self-destructive period. (Ballard will also record a novelty revival of his *Let's Go* hit released as the topical *Let's Go Streaking* in 1974 but without chart success.)

1986

Dec After many years of playing his old hits on the US soul club circuit, he visits the UK to perform at a Christmas show organized by Charly Records, licensee of his King hits in Britain. The critically-acclaimed performance will be released as ***Live At The Palais*** the following spring.

1989

Never the best of friends, Ballard and Checker nevertheless participate, together with Joey Dee, in filming a segment for a feature-length documentary on the Twist, lensed at Lulu's Roadhouse, Kitchener, Canada.

1990

Jan [17] Ballard is inducted into the Rock and Roll Hall of Fame at the fifth annual dinner, at New York's Waldorf Astoria Hotel. He breaks down during his induction speech, as he pays tribute to his wife and manager Theresa McNeil, a fatal victim of a hit-and-run driver in New York three months earlier. In creating *The Twist*, his status as an influential R&B innovator is finally secured, confirmed again on February 26th, 1992, when the non-profit-making organization the Rhythm & Blues Foundation in New York makes a financial award to Ballard, in honor of his contribution to the wider recognition of the genre. (In November 1993, ***Sexy Ways: The Best Of Hank Ballard & the Midnighters*** will be released on the King label, licensed to Rhino Records (US).)

AFRIKA BAMBAATAA

1976

After two years as a teenage lieutenant in a Bronx, New York, NY, street gang called the Black Spades, Bambaataa (b. Kevin Donovan (aka Khayan Aasim), Apr. 10, 1960, South Bronx,) forms Zulu Nation, a Bronx-based grouping of street-wise urban youngsters and Afro-centric culturally and politically-motivated musicians. The music of turntable DJs and rappers at block parties and in clubs is central to the group, and

Bambaataa's reputation as a DJ and Emcee (who has a considerable knowledge of recorded funk history), grows as the momentum of the rap/electro/hip-hop genre he is helping to pioneer develops.

1980

Bambaataa makes his first venture into recorded hip-hop for producer Paul Winfield, with different versions of *Zulu Nation Throwdown* by two rap groups in his collective, Cosmic Force and Soul Sonic Force. Thereafter, Bambaataa joins forces with fledgling New York street-dance label Tommy Boy, run by Tom Silverman.

1982

Feb His debut Tommy Boy release is *Jazzy Sensation* (based on Gwen Guthrie's *Funky Sensation*) by another Zulu Nation rap group, the Jazzy Five, co-produced by Bambaataa and Arthur Baker.
Sept [11] *Planet Rock*, credited to Afrika Bambaataa & the Soul Sonic Force (Emcee G.L.O.B.E., Mr. Biggs and Pow Wow), produced by John Robie and Arthur Baker, and fusing rap with the electronic music of European groups like Tangerine Dream and Kraftwerk (whose *Trans-Europe Express* is a primary inspiration for the track), has become a huge street-selling 12" single hit in New York and other US urban areas, though lack of nationwide airplay restricts it to US #48, (nevertheless earning a gold disk for a million-plus sales) and makes UK #53. (It will have a huge dance record influence on both sides of the Atlantic, with its bass line used on at least 70 American releases in 1983.)

1983

Mar Bambaataa, Baker and Soul Sonic Force follow up with *Looking For The Perfect Beat*, a US and UK Dance chart smash, which also features in the film "Beat Street". (The track will subsequently evolve into the 1988 Bomb The Bass UK #2 hit *Beat Dis*.)

1984

Mar [17] *Renegades Of Funk*, Bambaataa's last Tommy Boy release, cements his position as one of the most influential producers and protagonists of the burgeoning hip-hop genre and also reaches UK #30.
June Switching to New York label Celluloid, Bambaataa releases first album ***Shango Funk Theology***, co-produced with bassist Bill Laswell and featuring Shango - a studio line-up of rappers and funk musicians.
Sept [15] *Unity (Part 1 - The Third Coming)*, on which Tom Silverman has teamed Bambaataa with soul veteran James Brown, makes UK #49.

1985

Feb [2] Time Zone's*World Destruction*, a further liaison with Laswell, which pairs Bambaataa and Public Image Ltd. singer John Lydon, makes UK #44.
Dec [14] Artists United Against Apartheid, a music collective comprising 49 artists including Bambaataa, makes US #38 and UK #21 with *Sun City*.

1986

July [19] Bambaataa takes part in "UK Fresh" at the Capital Music Festival, Wembley Arena, Wembley, Middx.
His connection with Soul Sonic Force severed, following the prosecution of two of its members for armed robbery in the late '70s, he forms Afrika Bambaataa & the Family.

1988

Mar [26] Having released *Bambaataa's Theme* and ***Beware (The Funk Is Everywhere)*** via WEA in 1987, and now signed to EMI Manhattan, he has recorded ***The Light With The Family***, again co-produced by Laswell and featuring guests Boy George, Nona Hendryx and UB40, which includes *Reckless*, with UB40, now reaching UK #17.

1991

Apr [3] Increasingly revered by the new generation of rap artists as one of the genre's original innovators, he appears at "RAP, Portraits And Lyrics Of A Generation Of Black Rockers" with Big Daddy Kane, Queen Latifah and others at the S.O.B., New York.

1996

Feb [9] While EMI has released his 1991 sophomore label effort ***Decade Of Darkness*** (which includes the Oct [19] UK #45-peaking *Just Get Up And Dance*), and Bambaataa has issued the career collection ***Time Zone*** on his own Planet Rock label in 1993, the rap pioneer, who has also recently been a DJ on Hot 97 radio in New York, makes a rare visit to the UK, opening a five-date tour at the Blue Note club in London.

BANANARAMA

Sarah Dallin (vocals); **Keren Woodward** (vocals); **Siobhan Fahey** (vocals)

1981

Jan Dallin (b. Dec. 17, 1961, Bristol, Somerset) and Woodward (b. Apr. 2, 1961, Bristol), former Bristol schoolfriends now living in a flat in London's Tin Pan Alley above a rehearsal hall with Fahey (b. Sept. 10, 1957, London), leave their day jobs (Woodward working at the BBC, Fahey employed in the Decca Records press office and Dallin attending the London College of Fashion) to perform as an unaccompanied vocal trio in pubs and clubs. DJ Gary Crowley, Fahey's former colleague at Decca Records, helps them record demos which leads to a one-off deal with Demon Records (UK) in June resulting in the release of their maiden effort *Ai A Mwana* in September. Produced by former Sex Pistol Paul Cook, its success on the UK Independent chart attracts London Records, which signs them and reissues the single by year's end.

1982

Mar [13] Invited by UK male trio Fun Boy Three to contribute backing vocals to its second single, the resulting *It Ain't What You Do, It's The Way That You Do It* hits UK #4.
May [1] Bananarama's equally deadpan revival of the Velvelettes oldie *Really Sayin' Somethin'*, with Fun Boy Three now backing them, hits UK #5.
July [24] *Shy Boy*, which teams the trio with producers Tony Swain and Steve Jolley, who have presented the song to them as *Big Red Motorbike*, but with new lyrics added, hits UK #4, as the trio tops the bill, with Culture Club, at Capital Radio's "Best Disco In Town" special.
Dec [11] The Barry Blue-produced *Cheers Then*, a ballad which departs from their now-familiar jaunty pop sound, stalls at UK #45.

1983

Mar [19] Their revival of Steam's 1969 US #1 *Na Na Hey Hey Kiss Him Goodbye* hits UK #5, spurring the trio's debut album ***Deep Sea Skiving***, largely overseen by Swain and Jolley, to hit UK #7.
July [16] *Shy Boy* provides their US chart debut peaking at #83, as its parent album ***Deep Sea Skiving*** begins a climb to US #63.
Aug [6] Infectious *Cruel Summer*, accompanied by a synchronized dance-step routine promo video clip in Bananarama tradition, hits UK #8.

1984

Mar [31] *Robert De Niro's Waiting* hits UK #3.
Apr Their sophomore album ***Bananarama***, a further collaboration with producer-writers Swain and Jolley, reaches UK #16.
May [26] *Robert De Niro's Waiting* stalls at US #95, (though the actor reportedly loves the song and contacts the band to arrange a meeting).
June [16] *Rough Justice* reaches UK #23. (During its recording, the band's personal and professional friend Thomas Reilly is shot dead in Belfast, N. Ireland - they attend his funeral.)
July [29] *Cruel Summer*, released in the US after being featured in the movie "The Karate Kid", becomes their first major US chart success, hitting #9, and will spur ***Bananarama*** towards its US #30 peak.
Nov [24] *Hotline To Heaven* stalls at UK #58.
[25] Bananarama gathers with 35 other artists in SARM Studio, Notting Hill, London, to record the historic *Do They Know It's Christmas?*.
Dec [8] Unreleased in the UK, film title theme *The Wild Life* makes US #70.

1985

Sept [14] The Jolley and Swain-written *Do Not Disturb* reaches UK #31.

1986

July [12] *Venus*, a recording of Shocking Blue's 1970 UK #8, and the group's first collaboration with hit production team Stock, Aitken & Waterman, hits UK #8. Largely written and produced by Swain and Jolley, the band's third album ***True Confessions*** is released, set to make UK #46.
Aug [30] *More Than Physical* makes UK #41.
Sept [6] *Venus* tops the US chart (this is the fourth occasion that a remake of a #1 has topped the Hot 100 - Shocking Blue's original hit the top spot on February 7th, 1970), as ***True Confessions*** begins a rise to US #15.
Oct [1] ***True Confessions*** is certified gold by the RIAA.
Nov [8] *More Than Physical* makes US #73.

1987

Jan [24] Co-written by the band with Swain and Jolley, *A Trick Of The Night* stalls at US #76.
Feb [28] *A Trick Of The Night* makes UK #32. The original promotion video clip, directed by BBC1-TV's "In At The Deep End" host (and novice) Chris Searle, is scrapped in favor of a more professional version when the single is released.
Apr [4] Bananarama is in the line-up of Stock, Aitken and Waterman's *Let It Be* single by Ferry Aid, benefitting the Zeebrugge Disaster Fund, which now enters at UK #1.
Aug [1] SAW-helmed *I Heard A rumor* reaches UK #14 as Fahey marries Dave Stewart of Eurythmics at the Chateau Dangu, Normandy, France.
Sept [26] *I Heard A rumor* hits US #4.
Oct [31] *Love In The First Degree* hits UK #3, its funky SAW-contrived B-side, *Mr. Sleeze*, contributing strongly to sales.

1988

Jan [23] *I Can't Help It* reaches UK #20 having already peaked at US #47 on the 9th.
Feb [8] The group performs *Love In The First Degree* at the seventh annual BRIT Awards, at London's Royal Albert Hall, in what will be Fahey's last performance with her colleagues. Relocating to Los Angeles, CA, and France, she retires from the group to enjoy married life, before forming the duo Shakespear's Sister with Marcella Detroit (b. June 21, 1954, Detroit, MI), formerly Marcy Levy, whose musical credits already include co-writing Eric Clapton's 1977 hit, *Lay Down Sally*. Longtime Bananarama friend, Jacqui Sullivan (b. Aug. 7, 1960, London), one-time vocalist with Siren and the Shillelagh Sisters, takes Fahey's place.
[27] ***Wow!*** reaches UK #26, five months after its chart debut, having already made US #44.
Apr [23] *Love In The First Degree* makes US #48.
[30] Further SAW production *I Want You Back* hits UK #5.
Oct [15] *Love, Truth And Honesty* reaches UK #23.
Nov [21] The group takes part in the "Pop 88" segment at the Royal Variety Performance, London.
Dec [3] *Love, Truth And Honesty* stalls at US #89.
[10] *Nathan Jones*, updating the Supremes' 1971 US #16, reaches UK #15, while ***The Greatest Hits Collection*** will peak at US #151.

1989

Jan Shakespear's Sister performs in Leningrad, USSR.
[7] ***The Greatest Hits Collection*** - featuring 18 cuts on CD - hits UK #3.
Mar [11] A novelty cover of the Beatles' *Help!*, recorded with La Na Nee Nee Noo Noo, a parody of Bananarama both vocally and stylistically and featuring Bananarama themselves, with comediennes Dawn French, Jennifer Saunders and Kathy Burke, hits UK #3, with profits from the record going to Comic Relief.
June [24] *Cruel Summer* remix reaches UK #19.
Aug Shakespear's Sister's *You're History* hits UK #7.
Sept [2] Also signed to London Records, the duo's debut album, ***Sacred Heart***, displaying a more experimental rock edge, highlighted by Detroit's vocal histrionics, hits UK #9.
Oct [14] The extracted single *Run Silent* debuts at its UK #54 peak.

1990

Aug [4] Bananarama's *Only Your Love* reaches UK #27, co-written and produced by Youth.
Nov The trio contribute to the ***Rock The World*** benefit album to raise money for the Phoenix House, a London-based rehab centre.

1991

Jan [19] Bananarama's self-written *Preacher Man*, again produced by Youth, reaches UK #20.
Apr [27] Their revival of the Doobie Brothers' *Long Train Running* reaches UK #30.
May [25] Its parent album ***Poplife***, charts for a week at UK #42.
Sept O'Sullivan announces she is quitting the band.
Oct [12] Shakespear's Sister's *Goodbye Cruel World*, produced by Chris Thomas, makes UK #59.

1992

Feb [22] Shakespear's Sister's *Stay* begins an eight-week tenure at UK #1.
[29] Its parent album ***Hormonally Yours***, recorded at George Harrison's Friar Park home studio in Henley-on-Thames, Oxon, debuts at its UK #3 peak. Featuring Fahey and Detroit sharing vocals, but with Detroit also contributing harmonica, guitars and keyboard programming, all 12 tracks are written by the duo (often with help from Steve Ferrera) and also co-produced by them with Alan Moulder (except for *Goodbye Cruel World*).
May [23] Follow-up *I Don't Care* hits UK #7.
July [25] *Goodbye Cruel World* now reaches UK #32.
Sept [5] Having recorded new sessions with equally trimmed duo Stock and Waterman in May, Bananarama's *Movin' On* reaches UK #24, two days after they perform the cut on BBC1-TV's "Top Of The Pops".
[12] ***Hormonally Yours*** makes US #56.
[19] *Stay* hits US #4.
Nov [14] Shakespear's Sister's *Hello (Turn Your Radio On)* reaches UK #14.
[28] Bananarama's *Last Thing On My Mind* debut at its UK #71 peak.

1993

Jan [23] *I Don't Care* makes US #55.
Feb [16] "Stay" wins the Best Video category at the 12th annual BRIT Awards, held at London's Alexandra Palace.
[27] Shakespear's Sister's EP *My 16th Apology* charts for a week at UK #61.
Mar [27] Bananarama's *More, More More*, reviving Andrea True Connection's 1976 UK #5/US #4, reaches UK #24.
Apr [10] A Bananarama double set ***Please Yourself***, featuring ten new cuts (produced and arranged by Stock and Waterman) augmented by six remixes of the group's biggest hits, charts for a week at UK #46. (Meanwhile, the reissued Bluebells' *Young At Heart*, written by Fahey and the Bluebells' Robert Hodgens in 1984 (when it hit UK #8), now tops the UK chart.)
May [26] Fahey and Detroit (together with co-writer Dave Stewart) win the first Outstanding Contemporary Song Collection category (for ***Hormonally Yours***) at the 38th annual Ivor Novello Awards, held at London's Grosvenor House Hotel. (An absent Fahey sends an acceptance message which includes a comment that Shakespear's Sister has split, confirming that "All's well that ends well".)

THE BAND

Robbie Robertson (guitar, vocals);
Richard Manuel (piano, vocals); **Garth Hudson** (organ); **Rick Danko** (bass, vocals);
Levon Helm (drums, vocals)

1964

Helm (b. Mark Lavon Helm, May 26, 1942, Marvell, AR), playing in local Marvell band the Jungle Bush Beaters, has joined Ronnie Hawkins & the Hawks, and, after extensive touring in Canada, in Ontario and Quebec, and US cities near the Canadian/US border, they decided to settle in Toronto, ON, Canada, in 1959. 15-year-old Robertson (b. Jaime Robertson, July 5, 1944, Toronto), already a veteran of local bands Robbie & the Robots, Thumper & the Trombones and Little Caesar & the Consuls, has joined on bass, taking over on guitar from Fred Carter Jr., when he decided to return to the US. Danko (b. Dec. 9, 1943, Simcoe, Canada) joined after opening for Hawkins in 1961, replacing Rebel Paine. Manuel (b. Apr. 3, 1943, Stratford, Canada), from Stratford rock band the Rockin' Revols, also joined that summer. Hudson (b. Aug. 2, 1937, London, Canada), leader of Paul London & the Capers, came on board just before Christmas 1961, but only after Hawkins has agreed to pay him for giving the other band members music lessons. The Hawks, also comprising vocalist Bruce Bruno and saxophonist Jerry Penfound, have split from Hawkins, dissatisfied with the financial set-up. Calling themselves the Levon Helm Sextet, but soon changed to Levon Helm & the Hawks, they have worked for the next 18 months in southern Ontario and colleges and bars in Arkansas, Missouri, Oklahoma and Texas. Now without Bruno and Penfound, the group records its first single *Leave Me Alone* for the Toronto-based Ware label, under the name the Canadian Squires.

1965

Mar A one-off single, the Robertson-penned *The Stones I Throw*, is released by the Atlantic Records subsidiary, Atco. Albert Grossman's secretary Mary Martin suggests that the Hawks might be the band that Grossman's act Bob Dylan is looking for to back him on his proposed electric world tour, a suggestion taken up by Dylan after seeing them perform during a four-month residency at Somers Point, NJ.
Apr [30] Dylan's "Don't Look Back" tour with the Band begins in England.
Sept After his first electric gigs at Forest Hills, New York, NY, and the Hollywood Bowl, Los Angeles, CA, where Dylan has used a plugged-in band comprising Robertson, Helm, Al Kooper and Harvey Brooks, he begins rehearsals with the Hawks in Toronto.

1966

May [26-27] Dylan's world tour culminates in two concerts at London's Royal Albert Hall. (Helm had quit after a concert in Washington, DC on November 28th 1965, unhappy with the nightly booing Dylan's folk fans shower on each night's concert. Mickey Jones takes his place.)

1967

After the tour, Dylan moves to Woodstock, NY, to begin work on editing a documentary of the tour. The group is placed on a weekly retainer with Danko and Manuel helping Dylan with the film. Danko finds a rambling house, painted pink, in nearby West Saugerties, NY. Dylan and the group members begin writing and rehearsing material, with Helm being asked back into the line-up, the results first becoming the celebrated original rock bootleg ***Great White Wonder***, released officially by CBS in 1975 as ***The Basement Tapes***. Grossman signs a deal for them with Capitol (on the contract they are called the Crackers), and they begin work with producer John Simon.

1968

Jan [20] The group takes part in a Woody Guthrie tribute at New York's Carnegie Hall with Dylan, Judy Collins and Richie Havens.
Aug The Band's debut album ***Music From Big Pink*** (named after the house), including some Dylan compositions (*Tears Of Rage*, *This Wheel's On Fire* and *I Shall Be Released*), plus their own originals, reaches US #30.
Sept [28] *The Weight*, featured in the film "Easy Rider", makes US #63, though versions by Aretha Franklin, the Supremes, the Temptations and Jackie DeShannon all chart higher than the Band's original.
Oct [26] *The Weight* reaches UK #21.

1969

Feb The group embarks on live dates, its first since Danko's recovery from a bad auto accident. The Band makes its live debut at the Winterland Ballroom, San Francisco, CA. (Robertson is so nervous that he becomes ill and can only perform under hypnosis, from hypnotist Pierre Claumont.)
Apr [17-19] The Band plays at the Fillmore West, San Francisco, on a bill with the Sons Of Champlin.
Aug [31] They perform on the second day of "Isle Of Wight Festival Of Music", Woodside Bay, near Ryde, Isle of Wight, with Bob Dylan.
Oct Their critically-acclaimed sophomore album ***The Band***, recorded in Hollywood Hills, CA, in a house rented from Sammy Davis Jr., hits US #9 and UK #25 and includes *The Night They Drove Old Dixie Down*, subsequently a hit for Joan Baez (US #3/UK #6).

1970

Jan [3] *Up On Cripple Creek* reaches US #25.
Mar [14] The Robertson-penned *Rag Mama Rag* peaks at US #57, set to make UK #16 on May [2]. (Robertson is responsible for writing the majority of the band's single releases.)
Sept ***Stage Fright***, the title track written about the group's experience returning to performing, recorded at Woodstock Playhouse, engineered by Todd Rundgren and mixed by Glyn Johns, hits US #5 and UK #15.
Oct [19] ***Stage Fright*** is certified gold by the RIAA.
[31] Extracted *Time To Kill* is a minor US chart single, at #77.

1971

Oct ***Cahoots***, the first record to be cut at the Bearsville Studios in Woodstock, reaches US #21, and includes *Life Is A Carnival*, on which Allen Toussaint guests and arranges the horn parts, and *4% Pantomime*, on which Woodstock neighbor Van Morrison (who co-wrote it with Robertson) guests.
Nov [13] *Life Is A Carnival* peaks at US #72.
[27] ***Cahoots*** makes UK #41.
Dec [31] The Band performs one of three concerts at New York's Academy Of Music, newly augmented by a horn section.

1972

Sept Double live album ***Rock Of Ages***, recorded during the earlier Academy Of Music dates, hits US #6.
Nov [2] ***Rock Of Ages*** is certified gold by the RIAA.
[4] The extracted *Don't Do It*, reviving Marvin Gaye's 1964 US #27, makes US #34.

1973

July [28] The group plays its first concert since New Year's Eve 1971, in the "Watkins Glen Festival" with the Allman Brothers Band and the Grateful Dead at the Watkins Glen racetrack in upstate New York.

The Band begins recording ***Moondog Matinee***, a collection of oldies. (The title is taken from Alan Freed's Cleveland radio show, which the group members picked up north of the border in the late '50s.)
Dec [22] *Ain't Got No Home*, the first single to be released from the upcoming oldies album and originally recorded by Clarence "Frogman" Henry, peaks at US #73.

1974

Jan [3] Dylan and the Band begin a six-week tour at Chicago Stadium, Chicago, IL. In addition to backing Dylan, the Band also performs its own set.
Feb Dylan's ***Planet Waves***, to which the Band has contributed, is issued, while the group's own ***Moondog Matinee*** reaches US #28.
July The Band tours with Dylan, and a co-credited live double album, ***Before The Flood***, results, which will hit US #3 and UK #8.
Sept [14] The group plays on a ten-hour concert bill with Crosby Stills Nash & Young and Joni Mitchell at Wembley Stadium, Wembley, Middx.

1975

Mar [23] The Band appears with an all-star line-up at the SNACK (Students Need Athletics Culture & Kicks) benefit at San Francisco's Kezar Stadium, to raise funds to make up for a shortfall in the school system budget.

1976

Jan [31] ***Northern Lights-Southern Cross***, recorded in the group's own Shangri-La Studio in Zuma Beach, CA, reaches US #26.
Apr [3] *Ophelia*, the title inspired by Minnie Pearl's real name, peaks at US #62.
Oct [16] ***The Best Of The Band***, with nine of the album's 12 familiar tracks written by Robertson, makes US #51, as the group decides to stop touring, and - despite good intentions over the next two years - splits. (During the month, Robertson also produces Neil Diamond's ***Beautiful Noise***.)
Nov [25] The Band concludes its career in the grandest style, hosting "The Last Waltz", a remarkable final concert, on Thanksgiving Day at San Francisco's Winterland Ballroom, the site of their first gigs in the spring of 1969. They have invited Paul Butterfield, Bobby Charles, Eric Clapton, Neil Diamond, Bob Dylan, Emmylou Harris, Ronnie Hawkins, Dr. John, Joni Mitchell, Van Morrison, the Staples, Ringo Starr, Muddy Waters, Ron Wood and Neil Young to the event, which is recorded and filmed by Martin Scorsese.

1977

Apr [23] ***Islands***, recorded to honor the group's contract with Capitol, reaches US #64.
Nov [4] Scorsese-lensed "The Last Waltz", critically acclaimed and revered as one of rock's finest films, premieres in New York.

1978

Feb [4] Danko's debut solo album for Arista, ***Danko***, makes US #119.
Apr [29] Warner Bros.-released triple boxed-set ***The Last Waltz***, from their farewell feast, makes UK #39.
June [24] ***The Last Waltz*** reaches US #16. (Each member of the group will continue to perform in the music arena: Helm, who will appear in the Loretta Lynn bio-pic "The Coal Miner's Daughter" in 1980, will form Levon Helm & the RCO Allstars with Steve Cropper, Dr. John and Paul Butterfield, making three albums for ABC between 1977 and 1980, while Danko and Robertson, who similarly appears in a 1980 movie, "Carney", will also move on to solo projects.)

1986

Jan After a number of attempted reunions over the past five years, the latest, with James Weider replacing Robertson, reconvenes for live work.
Mar [6] Manuel, apparently in a fit of depression, hangs himself after a gig at the Cheek to Cheek club in Winter Park, FL. (Robertson will dedicate the future solo cut *Fallen Angel* to him.)

1987

Nov With Robertson having contributed music to the film soundtracks for "Raging Bull", "King Of Comedy" and "The Color Of Money", ***Robbie Robertson***, his long-awaited debut solo album is released. Co-produced with Daniel Lanois and including guests U2, Peter Gabriel, Maria McKee and Danko, among others, it will peak at US #38 and UK #24 (Sept [2] the following year).

1988

Jan [30] Robertson makes his first television appearance for 12 years on NBC-TV's "Saturday Night Live".
Aug [27] His ethereal, partly-spoken *Somewhere Down That Crazy River* reaches UK #15.

1989

Mar With most ex-members increasingly active, Danko and Helm guesting on Ringo Starr's US tour, Robertson contributing to the Greenpeace-supporting ***Rainbow Warriors*** album and the current ***Beauty*** album by Japanese artist Ryuichi Sakamoto, the Band is inducted into the Canadian Hall of Fame at the Juno Awards in Toronto, with Robertson, Danko and Hudson performing together. (During the year, Capitol Records issues the double package retrospective ***To Kingdom Come***, including previously unreleased material.)

1990

July [21] The Band, minus Robertson, takes part in Roger Waters' performance of "The Wall" at the site of the Berlin Wall in Potzdamer Platz, Berlin, Germany. The event is broadcast live throughout the world, and raises money for the Memorial Fund for Disaster Relief.

1991

Oct [19] Having been featured in **Rolling Stone**'s September issue fall fashion layout, Robertson's solo follow-up, ***Storyville***, named after a notorious section of turn-of-the-century New Orleans, LA, debuts at its US #69 peak, having done the same a week earlier at UK #30. Musical guests include Aaron Neville, Blue Nile, Toni Childs, Danko and others. Its release coincides with the rise of Rod Stewart's current single, a cover of *Broken Arrow* from Robertson's 1987 debut album.
Dec [2] The group's sophomore album ***The Band***, from 1969, finally brings the Band its first RIAA-certified platinum disk, confirming US sales exceeding one million. Now comprising Danko, Helm, Hudson, Stan Szelest (on piano), and Weider they continue to work on the first of four albums, part of a new contract with Columbia, although Szelest will shortly pass away, during recording sessions for the group's first album for the label.

1992

Jan [15] Robertson inducts Elmore James into the Rock and Roll Hall of Fame at the seventh annual induction dinner, held at the Waldorf Astoria Hotel, New York, and will perform on NBC-TV's "Saturday Night Live" on the 18th.
Oct [16] With Helm and Hudson featured on recent releases by Michelle Shocked, Jules Shear and Graham Parker, the group performs (still without Robertson) at an all-star Bob Dylan tribute at Madison Square Garden, New York, to celebrate the artist's 30-year recording career.

1993

Nov [20] The Band, now comprising Danko, Helm, Hudson, Weider, Richard Bell (piano) and Randy Ciarlante (drums), chart for a week at US #166, with ***Jericho***, its first new material in 16 years. (During the year Helm's autobiography **This Wheel's On Fire**, in which expands on his longterm feud with Robertson, not least over songwriting credits, is also published.)

1994

Jan [19] Eric Clapton inducts the Band into the Rock and Roll Hall of Fame at the ninth annual dinner held at New York's Waldorf Astoria Hotel, jamming on *The Weight* together, which sees Robertson reunited with the group for the first time in 15 years, although Helm is absent from the night's proceedings.
Aug [13] The group, once again sans Robertson, performs at "Woodstock II" at Winston Farm, Saugerties, NY, where they are joined onstage by Bruce Hornsby, Roger McGuinn, Rob Wasserman and Bob Weir.
Oct [29] ***Music For The Native Americans***, from the Turner Network Television special "The Native Americans" and credited to Robbie Robertson & the Red Road Ensemble, makes US #149.
Dec Capitol releases the three-CD Band boxed-set, ***Across The Great Divide***,which includes the first issue of the group's live performances at Woodstock and Watkins Glen.

1995

Mar [28] Rhino Records (US) releases ***Till The Night Is Gone : A Tribute To Doc Pomus***, including the Band's contribution, *Young Blood*.
Apr [9] The Band records *Not Fade Away* at Bearsville Studios in Woodstock, for inclusion on the 1996 Buddy Holly tribute album, ***notfadeaway: remembering buddy holly***.
July [8-9] The group supports the Grateful Dead at the latter's last ever concerts at Chicago's Soldier Field.
Oct The famed Big Pink house in Saugerties is put on the market by its current owner, Mike Amitin, for $165,000.

1996

Feb [3] With continued interest in the group, including the 1995 releases of ***Live At Watkins Glen*** and "The Band : The Authorized Video Biography", the group performs at the Electric Factory, Philadelphia, PA, sharing the bill with Richie Havens.
Mar [26] Promoting its new studio set, ***High On The Hog***, released by Pyramid Records (US) in February, the Band guests on CBS-TV's "Late Show With David Letterman".

BAND AID

1984

Nov Bob Geldof of the Boomtown Rats sees a graphic BBC1-TV report on the famine suffered by the people of Ethiopia and determines to raise awareness and funds to help their plight. With Ultravox's Midge Ure, he writes a song and devises the idea of producing an all-star benefit record from which nobody (from artists to manufacturer to record shops) takes any profit. Intensive calls around the UK record industry kick-start the project, with all parties agreeing to donate freely to the cause. Geldof sets aside his musical career and the Boomtown Rats effectively cease to be.
[25] 36 artists gather in the SARM Studio, Notting Hill, London, to record the historic *Do They Know It's Christmas?*, including Geldof and Ure with: Bananarama, the Boomtown Rats, Phil Collins, Culture Club (Boy George and Jon Moss), Duran Duran, Frankie Goes To Hollywood, Heaven 17 (Glenn Gregory and Martin Ware), Kool & the Gang (Robert Bell, James Taylor and Dennis Thomas), Annie Lennox, Marilyn, George Michael, Spandau Ballet, Status Quo (Rick Parfitt and Francis Rossi), Sting, U2 (Bono and Adam Clayton), Ultravox, Jody Watley, Paul Weller and Paul Young. The historic recording is produced by Ure.
Dec [7] The record is launched with an Ethiopia Benefit concert at London's Royal Albert Hall, organized by the Save The Children Fund.
[15] *Do They Know It's Christmas?*, released on the Mercury label, enters the UK chart at #1, where it will

remain for five weeks, selling more than three million copies to become the biggest-selling single ever in the UK. (It will sell over 600,000 copies in its first week, 810,000 in its second, and over two million by the end of the month.)
[19] Already climbing the chart in the US, where it has been released on Columbia Records, *Do They Know It's Christmas?* is certified gold for one million sales by the RIAA.

1985

Jan [19] *Do They Know It's Christmas?* reaches US #13. With phenomenal success, the official Band Aid Trust is established as a permanent charity to ensure the swift collection of funds and aid to Africa.
[28] Geldof participates in the recording of USA For Africa's *We Are The World*, the first in a number of similarly-aimed fundraising entertainment industry projects which will also include Canada's contribution, *Tears Are Not Enough*, recorded by the Bryan Adams-led ad-hoc congregation Northern Lights.
Mar [13] Together with co-writer Ure, Geldof receives the Best Selling A-Side award for *Do They Know It's Christmas?* at the 30th annual Ivor Novello Awards luncheon, held at London's Grosvenor House Hotel. By month's end, the first shipment of relief supplies paid for by the Band Aid Trust reaches Ethiopia, accompanied by an ever-present Geldof.
July [13] At 12:01 p.m., Status Quo begins the Live Aid concert extravaganza, organized once again by Geldof and Ure, helped by rock promoters Harvey Goldsmith and Bill Graham, as a follow-up to the Band Aid project. Switching alternately between joint venues, the Wembley Stadium, Wembley, Middx., in the presence of the Prince and Princess of Wales, and the JFK Stadium, Philadelphia, PA, the world's biggest rock acts participate in a worldwide fundraising event. The 16-hour mega-concert includes appearances by Paul Weller, Bob Geldof and the Boomtown Rats, Adam Ant, INXS, Ultravox, Spandau Ballet, Elvis Costello, Nik Kershaw, B.B. King, Sade, Sting, Howard Jones, Bryan Ferry, Paul Young, Alison Moyet, Bryan Adams, U2, the Beach Boys, Dire Straits, Queen, Simple Minds, David Bowie, the Pretenders, the Who, Santana, Pat Metheny, Elton John, George Michael, Madonna, the Thompson Twins, Paul McCartney, Tom Petty, Neil Young, Power Station, Led Zeppelin, Duran Duran, Cliff Richard, Daryl Hall & John Oates, Tina Turner, Bob Dylan, the Rolling Stones' Mick Jagger, Keith Richards and Ronnie Wood, Lionel Richie, Harry Belafonte and Patti LaBelle. Phil Collins makes rock history by performing at Wembley and flying immediately to Philadelphia to play a second set later in the day. Watched by an estimated 1½ to 2 billion people, with telethons in 22 countries, and raising $70 million, Live Aid becomes a defining moment in the rock era.
Sept [13] Geldof receives the Special Recognition trophy at the second annual MTV Video Music Awards, at Radio City Music Hall, New York, NY.
Dec [21] *Do They Know It's Christmas?*, re-charting in the UK, hits #3, now with special Christmas messages by artists including Bowie and McCartney collected on the B-side. It will continue to be seasonally reissued.

1986

Jan [27] Geldof is presented with the Special Award Of Appreciation at the 13th annual American Music Awards, held at the Shrine Auditorium, Los Angeles, CA.
June [14] Geldof is named in H.R.H. the Queen's Birthday Honours List, receiving an honorary knighthood in recognition of his humanitarian activities, and is henceforth Bob Geldof K.B.E. (or "Saint Bob" in the popular press). During a heady period of much award-giving and adulation, including suggestions that he should be honored with the Nobel Peace Prize, Geldof also makes a speech to the United Nations in New York.

1989

Dec [23] A Stock, Aitken and Waterman-conceived re-recording of *Do They Know It's Christmas?*, with Kylie Minogue, Jason Donovan, Chris Rea, Matt Goss, Marti Pellow, Cliff Richard, Sonia and Lisa Stansfield, and credited to Band Aid II, enters the UK chart at #1.

1992

Jan Having raised a total of $144,124,694, the Trust, now closing down, confirms that 2% of the fund was used for administration, 49% given to relief projects and the remaining 49% designated for development. Geldof issues the following press statement: "It seems so long ago that we asked for your help. Seven years. It was only meant to last seven weeks, but I hadn't counted on the fact that hundreds of millions of people would respond and I hadn't reckoned on over $100 million. Seven years. You can count them now in trees and dams and fields and cows and camels and trucks and schools and health clinics, medicines, tents, blankets, clothes, toys, ships, planes, tools, wheat, sorghum, beans, research grants, workshops. Seven years ago I said I did not want to create an institution, but I did not want the idea of Band Aid to die. I did not want the potential of it to cease. There were a few dozen aid agencies and they do great work, but that was not our function. Our idea was to open the avenues of possibility. The possibilities of ending hunger in Africa are there. There can be other Band Aids; there must be others, in new times, in different ways. I once said that we would be more powerful in memory than in reality. Now we are that memory."
see also: **BOOMTOWN RATS, USA FOR AFRICA**

THE BANGLES

Susanna Hoffs (guitar, vocals); **Vicki Peterson** (guitar, vocals); **Michael Steele** (bass, vocals); **Debbi Peterson** (drums, vocals)

1981

Dec After playing in Los Angeles, CA, as the Colours, Vicki Peterson (b. Jan. 11, 1958, Los Angeles), having formed her first band in ninth grade, and needing a drummer, buys a drum kit and recruits sister Debbi (b. Aug. 22, 1961, Los Angeles) to play it, the Peterson sisters have already performed together in the Fans from 1979-1980, and Hoffs (b. Jan. 17, 1959, Los Angeles, CA), graduating from the University of California, Berkeley, CA, and placing a classified ad in the local newspaper **The Recycler** - "Band members wanted: Into the Beatles, Byrds and Buffalo Springfield", become the Supersonic Bangs and then the Bangs. Augmented by bassist Annette Zilinskas (b. Nov. 6, 1964, Van Nuys, CA), they release *Getting Out Of Hand* on their own independent label, Downkiddie, with minimal sales.

1982

Jan They are forced to alter their name to the Bangles because a New Jersey group already records as the Bangs. Gigging around the Los Angeles area leads to local DJ Rodney Bingenheimer including a Bangles song *Bitchin' Summer* on his third ***Rodney On The ROQ*** compilation album on Posh Boy Records. Miles Copeland signs them to a management deal and books them as the opening act for the (English) Beat.
June Their five-song mini-album ***The Bangles*** is issued on Copeland's I.R.S. subsidiary Faulty Products label.

1983

The group signs to CBS/Columbia Records. Zilinskas leaves to join Blood On The Saddle (she will re-surface in 1991 as a member of A&M act the Ringling Sisters), replaced by Steele (b. June 2, 1954), who passes the audition by replying, when asked to describe her dream band, "the Yardbirds with Fairport Convention vocals".

1984

Aug [4] ***All Over The Place***, produced by David Kahne, debuts on the US chart, eventually climbing to #80 during a 30-week stay, and showcases the all-female quartet's clean vocal harmonies (led by Hoffs) and jangling rock-guitar sound which will become its popular trademark. It will peak at UK #86 on Mar [16] the following year.

1985

June Having recently completed its maiden UK tour, the band begins recording sessions for its sophomore Columbia album at the Sunset Sound Factory in Los Angeles.

1986

Feb [1] During a world tour begun in January, the group performs the first of six UK dates at the Portsmouth Polytechnic, Hants., set to end at Warwick University, Warwick, W. Midlands, on the 8th.
Mar [15] *Manic Monday*, written by Prince under the pseudonym Christopher and marking the group's singles chart debut, hits UK #2. ***Different Light*** is released, set to hit US #2 and UK #3 after lengthy chart climbs in both territories. Produced by Kahne, he will conclude, with hindsight, that "the Bangles had a very identifiable vocal sound. Whether they want to sound commercial or not, they can't help it".
Apr [19] *Manic Monday* hits US #2, unable to displace its writer, who is at #1 with *Kiss*. Prince will join the band on stage at a concert in San Francisco, CA, for an encore of *Manic Monday*.
May [24] *If She Knew What She Wants*, inked by Jules Shear, makes UK #31.
June [22] The Bangles support Simple Minds at the "Milton Keynes Bowl Pop Festival", Milton Keynes, Bucks., and will open for Queen at a concert in Eire.
July [12] *If She Knew What She Wants* reaches US #29, and continuing their '60s-tinged musical and visual style, *Going Down To Liverpool*, originally recorded by Katrina & the Waves and featuring Leonard Nimoy in its promotional video, reissued in the UK having appeared on their debut album, makes #56, as the group performs its own headlining sell-out dates in London.
Aug The band embarks on a major US tour.
Sept Hoffs makes her acting debut, starring in her film-maker mother Tamara's "The Allnighter", while Steele takes a sabbatical in Australia.
Nov [15] Written by Liam Sternberg in 1983 and rejected by Toni Basil, *Walk Like An Egyptian*, from ***Different Light***, hits UK #3.
Dec [20] *Walk Like An Egyptian* is the group's biggest US hit, topping the chart for the first of four weeks, toppling Bruce Hornsby's *The Way It Is*, and aided by fun-time "King Tut"-aping video.

1987

Jan [24] *Walking Down Your Street*, the fourth single from ***Different Light***, reaches UK #16.
Feb [2] The RIAA certifies two million sales of ***Different Light***.
[9] They win the Best International Group category at the sixth annual BRIT Awards, at the Grosvenor House Hotel, London.
Apr [18] *Walking Down Your Street* reaches US #11, as Steele-written ballad *Following* peaks at UK #55.
May [1] "The Allnighter" premieres in the US.
Sept [11] Bangles perform at the fourth annual MTV Video Music Awards, held at the Universal Amphitheatre, Universal City, CA.

1988

Feb [6] The group's revival of Simon & Garfunkel's 1966 US #13 *Hazy Shade Of Winter*, produced by Rick Rubin for the soundtrack to the film "Less Than Zero", and issued as a US single on Rubin's Def Jam label, hits #2, behind Tiffany's *Could've Been*.
Mar [12] *Hazy Shade Of Winter* reaches UK #11.
Nov [26] *In Your Room* makes UK #35.
Dec ***Everything***, produced by Davitt Sigerson and

with contributions from David Lindley, Paulinho Da Costa and Vinnie Vincent, reaches US #15 (earning a gold disk).

1989

Jan [7] *In Your Room*, co-written by Hoffs with Billy Steinberg and Tom Kelly, hits US #5.

Apr [1] Penned by the same combination, the ballad *Eternal Flame* becomes the Bangles' second US chart-topper and will hit UK #1 on the 15th.

[17] *Eternal Flame* is certified gold and ***Everything*** platinum by the RIAA.

May [6] ***Everything*** hits UK #5.

June [9] Reissued *Walk Like An Egyptian* peaks at UK #73.

[23] Comprehensive 14-track compilation, ***Bangles' Greatest Hits***, hits UK #4 and makes US #97.

July [1] *Be With You* reaches UK #23, having made US #30 on June [24].

Aug [9] A 15-date US tour begins in Wilkes Barre, PA, set to end September 2nd in Santa Clara, CA.

[21] ***Bangles' Greatest Hits*** is certified gold by the RIAA.

Sept [21] A press statement confirms that the group is splitting, not least allowing Hoffs to pursue a solo career. While *I'll Set You Free* peaks at UK #74 on Oct [14], the re-issued *Walk Like An Egyptian* will make UK #73 on June [9] the following year.

1990

Aug [21] "Walk Like An Egyptian" video is certified gold by the RIAA.

1991

Mar [2] Hoffs' solo debut album ***When You're A Boy*** makes US #83 (and will peak at UK #56 on Apr [6]). Produced by Kahne, the extracted Hoffs/Kelly/Steinberg collaboration *My Side Of The Bed* subsequently reaches US #30 and UK #44. In promoting the album she will support Don Henley on his 1991 US tour. (Peterson will team with River City People's Siobhan Maher to form Kindred Spirit, releasing their debut album in June 1995. Hoffs will contribute a version of Oingo Boingo's *We Close Our Eyes* to the "Buffy The Vampire Slayer" soundtrack and the title track to "Now And Then", with Go-Go's' Jane Wiedlin and Charlotte Caffey, before signing a solo deal with London Records in 1994 and giving birth to a boy, Jackson, with husband M. Jay Roach on February 9th, 1995. ***A Different Light*** will reach the three million US sales plateau on October 7th, 1994.)

BARCLAY JAMES HARVEST

John Lees (guitar, vocals); **Les Holroyd** (bass, vocals); **Stuart "Woolly" Wolstenholme** (keyboards, vocals); **Mel Pritchard** (drums)

1967

June The group has been formed in September 1966 in Oldham, Lancs., where Lees (b. Jan. 13, 1947, Oldham) and Wolstenholme (b. Apr. 15, 1947, Oldham) have both attended art school and played in the six-member blues band Blues Keepers, which includes members of earlier local outfit, Heart & Soul & the Wickeds, which is trimmed to a quartet, including Holroyd (b. Mar. 12, 1948, Bolton, Lancs.) and Pritchard (b. Jan. 8, 1948, Oldham), before changing its name to Barclay James Harvest. Now financially backed by local businessman John Crowther, they rehearse in an 18th-century farmhouse in Diggle on Saddleworth Moor, Lancs., and begin extensive local live work.

1968

Apr Signed to the EMI (UK) subsidiary Parlophone label after cutting demos at Chappell Studios, the band releases its debut single *Early Morning*, which establishes its style of folk and classical-tinged art rock. In June the following year, EMI will launch its "progressive music" label Harvest, tagged after the band, issuing the follow-up, *Brother Thrush.*

1970

June Their debut album ***Barclay James Harvest***, produced by Norman Smith, is released, promoted by a UK tour on which the band is accompanied by an orchestra of classical musicians from the New Symphonia, conducted by Robert John Godfrey. Though considered a pioneering artistic effort, the album, which utilizes woodwind, strings and mellotrons, like all their releases via Harvest, fails to chart.

1971

Aug [28-29] Following the release of ***Once Again*** in February, the band performs to promote its second album of the year, ***BJH And Other Short Stories***, again with orchestral accompaniment, at an August Bank Holiday festival in Weeley, Essex.

1972

Jan [21] The group begins a 28-date UK tour at Birmingham University, Birmingham, W. Midlands, set to end on March 25th at the Bracknell Sports Centre, Berks., before touring the US between March 28th and May 11th.

Oct The six-track ***Baby James Harvest*** is released. (By December, they will have cut two singles, *When The City Sleeps* and *Breathless*, under the pseudonym Bombadil and, having spent much of the year on the road, will retire to the village of Delph, north-east of Oldham, to re-assess their future.)

1973

May *Rock And Roll Woman* is the band's final Harvest release. Splitting with both the label and their original management team, Barclay James Harvest will sign with Kennedy Street Management and secure a recording deal with Polydor Records by year's end (and Capitol Records in the US).

1974

Sept With the band having released *Poor Boy Blues* and *Everyone Is Everybody Else* earlier in the year and taken part in the annual "Reading Rock Festival", Reading, Berks., Lees issues a solo single, covering the Eagles' *Best Of My Love*.

Dec [14] Double album ***Barclay James Harvest Live***, featuring stage versions of their best-known repertoire, including the seven-minute *Mockingbird*, finally rewards seven years of touring, making UK #40.

1975

Oct [25] ***Time Honored Ghosts***, recorded in San Francisco, CA, with producer Elliot Mazer, reaches UK #32.

1976

Oct [30] ***Octoberon***, produced by the band at Strawberry Studios in Stockport, Lancs., reaches UK #19.

1977

Mar [5] ***Octoberon***, their only US chart entry, peaks at #174.

Apr [2] EP *Barclay James Harvest Live* (containing *Rock'n'Roll Star* and *Medicine Man (Parts 1 & 2)*) makes UK #49.

July Harvest releases Lees' solo ***A Major Fancy*** and its extracted single *Child Of The Universe*, recorded in 1972.

Oct [1] ***Gone To Earth*** reaches UK #30, but becomes more commercially successful in Europe, particularly Germany, where it sells over 100,000 copies and elevates the band to superstar status, which they will maintain in Germany and other countries well into the '80s.

1978

Oct [6] ***Harvest XII*** reaches UK #31, as the group's current 14-date UK tour is highlighted by a performance at London's Hammersmith Odeon.

1979

June Wolstenholme announces his desire to pursue a solo career, recording ***Maestro*** for Polydor. The remaining trio recruits Kevin McAlea on keyboards, saxophone and vocals, and Colin Browne on keyboards, guitars and vocals as permanent guest musicians, as the group signs with Handle Artists management.

1980

Feb [2] Holroyd-penned *Love On The Line*, taken from ***Eyes Of The Universe***, makes UK #63, but will reach platinum status in Germany.

Aug [30] The band performs a free concert in front of 175,000 people on the steps of the Reichstag, yards from the Berlin Wall in West Berlin, W. Germany, and filmed for future documentary release.

Oct Polydor releases Wolstenholme's ***Maestro***, but it meets with little success and he will retire from the music business to farm.

Nov [29] *Life Is For Living* peaks at UK #61. By the year's end, the group will have played 52 concerts before 250,000 people in the UK, Germany, France, Belgium, Denmark, Austria, Switzerland, Spain and Portugal.

1981

May [30] Releasing one album a year until 1984, ***Turn Of The Tide*** makes UK #55, while the live in Berlin ***Concert For The People*** will reach UK #15 on Aug [14] 1982. ***Ring Of Changes*** (UK #36 in May 1983) yields their final Singles chart entry in the same month, *Just A Day Away* (UK #68 - Mar [28]), and ***Victims Of Circumstance*** reaches UK #33 in April the following year.

1987

Feb [14] Following the 1986 release of two video projects, "Berlin" and "Victims", ***Face To Face*** peaks at UK #65. Still recording for Polydor, the band is playing to a devoted core audience in the UK, but spends most of its time touring Europe, where it continues to break attendance records and earn gold and platinum sales disks. Their final album of the decade, ***Glasnost (Live)***, recorded at a 1987 concert at Treptower Park, East Berlin, E. Germany, will be released in April 1988.

1990

Sept [15] The group, still touring Europe with great success, performs at the Hammersmith Odeon, in support of its latest album release ***Welcome To The Show***.

1992

Feb [12] The band performs at the Royal Court, Liverpool, Merseyside, to celebrate its 25th anniversary. It is the latest date on a 26-venue UK tour undertaken to support the Polydor-released ***The Best Of Barclay James Harvest***, which has followed 1990's Connoisseur ***Alone We Fly*** retrospective and ***The Harvest Years***, an archive collection released by their debut label in 1991. The tour will end at the Queen Elizabeth Hall in the band's home town of Oldham on May 8th.

1995

Feb [6] Following the release by Polydor of their most recent album, ***Caught In The Light*** in June 1993, a landmark legal battle with the group's former arranger Robert John Godfrey, who is claiming he was the unofficial fifth member of the group, reaches the High Court.

BAUHAUS

Peter Murphy (vocals); **Daniel Ash** (guitar, vocals); **David Jay** (bass, vocals); **Kevin Haskins** (drums)

1978

Dec [31] Having formed earlier in the year in its home town of Northampton, Northants., Bauhaus performs its first public gig at a local pub in Wellingborough, Northants. Haskins (b. July 19, 1960, Northampton), his older brother David (b. Apr. 24, 1957, Northampton), who now calls himself David Jay, both ex-members of punk combo Submerged Tenth, and Ash (b. July 31, 1957, Northampton), who recently played together as the trio Craze, have invited Murphy (b. July 11, 1957, Northampton) to become lead singer and complete their post-punk quartet named 1919, taken from the German art movement which began that year, before settling on the similarly-themed band name Bauhaus.

1979

Aug A one-off deal with independent label Small Wonder in London produces their 12" single debut *Bela Lugosi's Dead*, which fails to chart but will sell consistently in the UK for years, becoming an enduring fixture on the UK Independent chart and a substantial cult release, endearing them to the alternative UK music press and post-punk sub-culture.
Nov Following a gig at the Rock Garden, Covent Garden, London, and a session for John Peel's BBC Radio 1 show, Beggars Banquet signs them to 4AD, its independently-distributed subsidiary label.

1980

Jan *Dark Entries*, a remake of the B-side of *Bela Lugosi*, is released, reinforcing the band's brooding, sonorous style. It will be followed by further UK indie hits, *Terror Couple Kill Colonel* (inspired by a newspaper headline) in July and a cover of T. Rex's *Telegram Sam* in October.
Apr The band undertakes its first European tour of Germany, Holland and Belgium and will embark on its maiden US trek in September.
Nov [15] Its debut album ***In The Flat Field*** charts for a week at UK #72 and will also top the UK Independent chart for two weeks.

1981

Apr [25] Beggars Banquet label-released *Kick In The Eye* makes UK #59.
July [11] *The Passions Of Lovers*, written and recorded in one day, makes UK #56.
Oct [31] *Mask*, a prominent chart breakthrough, reaches UK #30.
Nov Jay teams with poet and painter Ren Halkett (a student of the original Bauhaus movement) to release *Nothing*, while Murphy gets "blown away" appearing in a popular ITV commercial for Maxell Tapes.

1982

Jan The group makes its first UK TV appearance, on BBC2's "Riverside" and also films a scene for the David Bowie and Catherine Deneuve-starring film "The Hunger", performing *Bela Lugosi's Dead* at the Heaven nightclub, London.
Mar [20] EP *Searching For Satori* (including a remixed version of *Kick In The Eye*) reaches UK #45, while *Spirit* will make UK #42 on June [26].
Oct The group, supported by Southern Death Cult, sets out on a UK tour to introduce its forthcoming album.
[30] Having performed the cut on a BBC Radio 1 session, a tongue-in-cheek cover of David Bowie's *Ziggy Stardust* reaches UK #15, spurred by an appearance on BBC1-TV's "Top Of The Pops". ***The Sky's Gone Out*** benefits accordingly, hitting UK #4.

1983

Jan [29] *Lagartija Nick* makes UK #44.
Feb Murphy contracts pneumonia and misses much of the recording of ***Burning From The Inside***.
Apr [23] *She's In Parties* reaches UK #26.
June On its return from dates in Japan, the band begins another UK tour to promote the new album.
July ***Burning From The Inside***, a dysfunctional collection of individual rather than band recordings, reaches UK #13.
[5] Bauhaus' final UK tour date in London ends with lengthy encores and farewells from the group, with a subsequent press release confirming its dissolution.
Oct [29] *The Singles 1981-1983* peaks at UK #52, while a further and more comprehensive retrospective, ***1979-1983***, will make UK #36 in November 1985. Two additional Bauhaus compilations will bring their short career to compact disk, ***Press The Eject And Give Me The Tape*** (released in 1988) and ***Swing The Heartache***, issued the following year. In the short term, Murphy will team with Japan's Mick Karn in Dali's Car for their 1984 album ***Waking Hour***, before embarking on an ongoing solo career (for Beggars Banquet in the UK, licensed to RCA in the US), which will see the issue of: ***Should The World Fail To Fall Apart*** (UK #82 in July 1986), 1988's ***Love Hysteria***, ***Deep*** (US #44 - Apr [21] in 1990) and ***Holy Smoke*** (US #108 - May [2] 1992), as he continues touring into 1992 with his band the Hundred Men. He will return with a solo album, ***Cascades***, in 1995. Ash and Haskins form Tones On Tail, releasing ***Pop*** in March 1984, followed by ***Tones On Tail*** in 1985, before re-grouping with Jay to establish the more commercially-prominent Love & Rockets in 1985. Their debut effort ***Seventh Dream Of Teenage Heaven*** is followed by ***Express***, which makes US #72 in 1987 (though released in 1986, the same year that their third album ***Earth, Sun, Moon*** fails to chart). In 1989, the trio hits US #3 on Aug [5] with *So Alive* (aided by a heavily-rotated stocking-clad, babe-heavy steamy video clip), while its parent album ***Love And Rockets*** subsequently reaches US #14 (and a follow-up single, *No Big Deal*, will stall at US #82 on Sept [30]). Its success will also prompt Bauhaus' ***Swing The Heartache - The BBC Sessions*** to make US #169. Ash embarks on a solo career in 1990 and will peak at US #109 (Apr [6] 1991) with his debut album ***Coming Down***, before releasing ***Foolish Thing Desired*** in March 1993, and rejoining Love & Rockets for the November 1994 album ***Hot Trip To Heaven***. Love & Rockets returns to the US chart on Apr [6], 1996, peaking with ***Sweet F.A.*** at #172.)

THE BAY CITY ROLLERS

Leslie McKeown (vocals); **Eric Faulkner** (guitar); **Stuart "Woody" Wood** (guitar); **Alan Longmuir** (bass); **Derek Longmuir** (drums)

1969

An initial Bay City Rollers line-up has been formed in 1967 around Tynecastle School, Edinburgh, Scotland, student brothers Alan (b. June 20, 1953, Edinburgh) and Derek (b. Mar. 19, 1955, Edinburgh) Longmuir and John Devine, who invited Gordon "Nobby" Clarke to be lead vocalist. Tam Paton, resident bandleader at the Edinburgh Palais, having seen them perform and recognizing their potential, quits his job to manage the teen troupe. He has picked the group's name by sticking a pin in a map of the US, and finding it in Bay City, MI. Principally a Top 20 chart covers band, it begins a 12-month Saturday residency at the local Top Storey club. During several constituent changes, Neil Henderson (b. Glasgow, Strathclyde, Scotland), having played in a number of semi-pro bands, and Archie Marr (b. 1953, Edinburgh) will join on lead guitar and organ respectively in April 1970, followed later in the year by Eric Manclark (b. 1954, Edinburgh).

1971

Oct [30] Signed to Bell Records in the UK by label boss Dick Leahy, their chart debut is a revival of the Gentrys' 1965 US #4 hit *Keep On Dancing*, which, produced by Jonathan King, hits UK #9. It will be followed by *We Can Make Music* in March 1972 and a third effort, *Maana* in June, a single which features their new guitarist Faulkner (b. Oct. 21, 1955, Edinburgh), and wins the Radio Luxembourg Grand Prix Song Contest.

1973

Jan While *Saturday Night* also fails to chart, early members Devine and Clarke leave, replaced by Wood (b. Feb. 25, 1957, Edinburgh) and new lead vocalist McKeown (b. Nov. 12, 1955, Edinburgh).

1974

Mar [9] *Remember (Sha La La)*, the first of several hits to be written and produced by Bill Martin and Phil Coulter, hits #6, restoring UK success.
May [25] Teen-appeal pop ditty *Shang-A-Lang* hits UK #2, helped by strong TV exposure.
Aug [24] With the group's pin-up image, steered by Paton, now firmly aimed at young girl teenagers, *Summerlove Sensation* hits UK #3.
Oct [12] The group's first album ***Rollin'*** tops the UK chart.
[26] *All Of Me Loves All Of You* hits UK #4. A 26-date UK tour follows, accompanied by scenes of teenage-girl fan mania. The national UK press coins "Rollermania" for the craze, identifying the group's tartan stage uniforms as a clothing fad which is quickly adopted by its loyal following (not least, the practice of wrapping tartan scarves around their wrists).

1975

Mar [22] *Bye Bye Baby*, produced by Phil Wainman and reviving an old Four Seasons song, becomes their biggest UK hit, topping the chart for the first of six weeks. Currently at their commercial peak, media reports emerge suggesting that the band do not play instruments on their own recordings.
Apr [1] The "Shang-A-Lang" TV series, featuring the group, premieres on ITV and will run until August 17th, 1977.
May [3] ***Once Upon A Star*** enters the UK chart at #1.
[18] During an appearance at a 47,000-attended "BBC Radio 1 Fun Day" at Mallory Park, near Kirkby Mallory, Leics., 40 girl fans need to be rescued from a lake, having tried to swim out to meet their heroes, who are being ferried from an island in the middle of the racetrack onto the event site. Four fans are taken to hospital, with 35 requiring on-site treatment. The group will leave by helicopter without performing.
July [19] Co-written by Wainman with John Goodison, pop ballad *Give A Little Love* tops the UK chart, where it will remain for three weeks.
Sept [20] The group is launched in the US via a live appearance on Howard Cosell's "Saturday Night Variety Show" on ABC-TV, appropriately singing *Saturday Night*.
Dec [6] *Money Honey*, uncharacteristically written by the band's Faulkner and Wood, hits UK #3.
[16] Still climbing the US chart, *Saturday Night* is certified gold by the RIAA while its parent album, ***Bay City Rollers*** is also confirmed gold by the RIAA on the 31st, prior to its chart peak.

1976

Jan [3] *Saturday Night* tops the US chart for a week. (At the height of the group's US success, they sign a deal to have their faces on cereal boxes.)
[17] UK-only album ***Wouldn't You Like It*** hits UK #3.
[24] US-only ***Bay City Rollers*** reaches US #20.
Apr [3] *Money Honey* hits US #9.
[9] Ian Mitchell (b. Aug. 22, 1958, Scotland) replaces Alan Longmuir, concerned that he is too old to be in the band, with Wood switching to bass.(Longmuir will launch a short-lived solo career with Arista.)
[14] Faulkner reportedly comes close to death after taking a drug overdose at Tam Paton's house, while in a state of exhaustion.
May [1] *Love Me Like I Love You* hits UK #4.
[8] US-only ***Rock'n'Roll Love Letter*** reaches US #31.

June [12] Unreleased in the UK, *Rock And Roll Love Letter*, an earlier album track for its writer Tim Moore, reaches US #28.
Sept [24] At a court case stemming from an earlier incident, McKeown is found not guilty of shooting an air rifle at a girl fan.
[25] The group's revival of Dusty Springfield's *I Only Want To Be With You* hits UK #4 and will make US #12 on Oct [23].
Nov [13] The Jimmy Ienner-produced ***Dedication*** makes US #26, having already hit UK #4 on Oct [9].

1977

Jan [8] *Yesterday's Hero*, written by ex-Easybeats Harry Vanda and George Young, peaks at US #54.
Mar [26] Guy Fletcher and Doug Flett-penned *Dedication* peaks at US #60.
May [28] *It's A Game* reaches UK #16 and will peak at US #23 on July [27].
Aug [13] ***It's A Game***, produced by Harry Maslin, reaches UK #18, while the extracted *You Made Me Believe In Magic* is the Rollers' final single to chart in the UK, having made #34 on Aug [6], but will go on to hit US #10. (By year's end, Mitchell will leave to form the Ian Mitchell Band, to be replaced by guitarist Pat McGlynn (b. Mar. 31, 1958, Edinburgh).
[17] ***It's A Game*** is certified gold by the RIAA.
Oct [26] ***Rock And Roll Love Letter*** is confirmed gold by the RIAA, as the group decides to relocate to the US, where it is now more popular.
Nov [23] ***Dedication*** is certified gold by the RIAA while ***Greatest Hits*** will be confirmed at the same sales plateau on December 7th.

1978

Jan [1] ***Greatest Hits*** makes US #77, while a further chart remnant, *The Way I Feel Tonight*, reaches US #24 one week later.
Oct [28] ***Strangers In The Wild*** makes US #129 but fails to chart in the UK, as the band's commercial demise quickens at a similar speed to its ascent. In the short term, Faulkner leaves for a solo career and will have some success in Japan, McKeown will release the first of a number of solo albums, the reassuring ***All Washed Up*** on the Egotrip label in July 1979, while the remainder of the group will quickly resort to playing smaller venues under the shortened name the Rollers.

1982

May [6] The teenage group's former manager, Paton, is convicted on a charge of gross indecency with boys between the ages of 13 and 19 and is sentenced to three years in jail.

1989

A comprehensive 21-track Japanese-only compact disk collection, ***Memorial***, released by Arista, will remain the most reliable CD retrospective (including an incomplete ***Greatest Hits*** package issued by the US label in 1992).

1990

Having become a regular act on the nostalgia circuit during the mid-'80s, the band is still a major draw in Japan, where various ex-members reunite annually for touring. However, a rival outfit claiming to be the Bay City Rollers embarks on a club tour of the US, which Faulkner says they are doing under false pretences. As the remaining unofficial leader of the Bay City Rollers, he will film a commercial for Skol lager in 1991, encouraging people to "buy me one and we'll cancel the comeback".

1992

July [6] While the group has recently completed a 12-date UK spring tour, David Gates of Gateshead, Northumberland, is given one year's probation and ordered to do 40 hours community service by a magistrate, having been convicted of stealing guitars from the band's van. His solicitor Stephen Mason says, "When he is not trying to save the world from the sounds of the Bay City Rollers he leads a respectable life. On this occasion he had too much to drink." (As Les McKeown's Bay City Rollers, which includes Mitchell, continues gigging into the mid-'90s, another Bay City Rollers, with Longmuir, Wood, Faulkner and Faulkner's girlfriend, Kass, will tour Japan in 1994. (Derek Longmuir, unimpressed with chances of former glory, is now a registered nurse in Edinburgh.)

THE BEACH BOYS

Brian Wilson (bass, keyboards, vocals);
Mike Love (vocals); **Carl Wilson** (guitar, vocals);
Al Jardine (guitar, vocals);
Dennis Wilson (drums, vocals)

1961

Keen music and radio listener Brian Wilson (b. June 20, 1942, Inglewood, CA), son of Murry Wilson, owner of the ABLE (Always Better Lasting Equipment) machine shop, a small company importing lathes and drills from England, and his wife Audree, who have already taken Brian to audition for a group trying to sign to Art Laboe's Original Sound label, living in Los Angeles, CA-suburb Hawthorne, with his brothers Dennis (b. Dec. 4, 1944, Inglewood) and Carl (b. Dec. 21, 1946, Hawthorne), invites cousin Love (b. Mar. 15, 1941, Baldwin Hills, CA), his mother Emily is Murry Wilson's younger sister, and Jardine (b. Sept. 3, 1942, Lima, OH), Brian's classmate at El Camino Junior College, who has broken quarterback Brian's leg during a Hawthorne Cougars football game, to form a singing quintet. Brian is entranced by the close harmony vocals of the Four Freshmen and other similar acts. They perform some early dates, including one at the local Hawthorne High School talent show, as Carl & the Passions, subsequently changing to the Pendletones, playing instruments they are renting, not least with money left for the Wilson brothers by Murry and Audree for food, while they vacation in Mexico.
Sept [15] Jardine has arranged for the group to meet publisher Hite Morgan, for whom he has already auditioned as a past member of a folk group. Morgan and his wife Dorinda, who are, coincidentally, friends of the Wilson parents, invite the Pendletones to their home studio to record a song called *Surfin'*, written by Brian and Love at the prompting of keen surfer Dennis. They also record *Laura*, written by Morgan's son Bruce, and a third cut, *Lavender*. Morgan signs *Surfin'* to his own Guild publishing company.
Oct [3] The group re-records *Surfin'* and *Laura* at World Pacific Studio.
Dec [8] Morgan releases *Surfin'* on his own X label. When RCA threatens suit over the use of X as a label-name, Morgan takes the record to Era's Herb Newman, who picks up distribution through the larger Candix distribution. Candix A&R man Joe Saraceno plays the song to Russ Regan, working at Candix's Buckeye Record Distributors, and between them they coin the Beach Boys name. (The group wants to be called the Pendletones, which the label does not like, and Candix wants to dub them the Surfers, a name already used by another band, as pointed out by Regan.)
[29] The group performs at the Rendezvous Ballroom, on a bill with Dick Dale, the Surfaris and the Challengers, performing two songs during the intermission.
[31] Local radio station KFWB, where Brian Wilson heard the Four Freshmen for the first time, hires them for a show where they debut under their new name the Beach Boys on the bill of "Ritchie Valens' Memorial Dance" at Municipal Auditorium, Long Beach, CA, a date for which they earn $300.

1962

Feb Jardine, discouraged by the lack of money the group has made from *Surfin'* (about $200 each), leaves to study dentistry, and is replaced by David Marks (b. Newcastle, PA), who lives across the street from the Wilsons, on rhythm guitar, with Brian switching to bass. Dennis, originally marginally involved, settles as drummer.
[8] Now gigging regularly at the Rainbow Gardens and Cinnamon Cinder clubs in Los Angeles, the group records *Surfer Girl*, *Surfin' Safari*, *Judy* and *Karate* (aka *Beach Boy Stomp*) at World Pacific.
Mar [25] *Surfin'* peaks at US #75.
May The underfunded Candix label folds. Murry Wilson, who has assumed the role of manager, takes their recordings to Dot, Decca and Liberty Records in search of a new deal, finally interesting Capitol Records' producer Nik Venet with a demo of *Surfin' Safari*.
June [4] Capitol releases *409*, backed with *Surfin' Safari*.
Oct The group begins a week's engagement at Pandora's Box on Sunset Boulevard.
[13] Initial B-side *Surfin' Safari* now reaches US #14, while A-side *409*, a hot rod song, makes US #76.
Nov ***Surfin' Safari***, a mixture of oldies and Brian Wilson songs (mainly written with neighbor Gary Usher), is released, peaking at US #32.

1963

Jan [5] *Ten Little Indians*, from the album, makes US #49.
May [25] *Surfin' USA*, returning to the surf theme and their first Top 10 record, hits US #3. It is Brian Wilson's adaptation of Chuck Berry's *Sweet Little Sixteen* with surf-related lyrics, and is the first single to highlight the vocal harmonies that become the group's trademark.
June [22] *Shut Down*, another hot-rodding song, on the B-side of *Surfin' USA*, makes US #23.
July [6] ***Surfin' USA*** hits US #2 during a 78-week chart ride. Two weeks later, Jan & Dean top the US chart with *Surf City*, a song written for them by Brian.
Aug [17] *Surfin' USA*, the group's UK chart debut, makes #34. Jardine, who has finished his dental studies, is invited back because Brian has been missing so many live dates. Sensing that Murry Wilson wants him out, Marks quits. (Months later he will form David Marks & the Marksmen, signing to A&M, before joining Casey Kasem's Band Without A Name and doing sessions with the Turtles. After a long battle with drugs, Marks will enroll at Berklee School of Music, Boston, MA, and then the New England Conservatory of Music.)
Sept [14] *Surfer Girl*, a slow harmony ballad on a surf theme, hits US #7.
[28] B-side *Little Deuce Coupe*, by now predictably a car/hot rod song, is again a US hit in its own right, reaching #15.
Oct ***Surfer Girl*** and ***Little Deuce Coupe*** are released within four weeks of each other, the former showcasing surf numbers, the latter hot rod and car songs. They are the first Beach Boys albums produced by Brian Wilson. Despite near-simultaneous release, both are major sellers: ***Surfer Girl*** hits US #7, and ***Little Deuce Coupe*** hits US #4.
Dec [21] *Be True To Your School*, from ***Little Deuce Coupe***, hits US #6, as B-side ballad *In My Room* reaches US #23.

1964

Jan The group makes it first overseas tour, a week-long trip to Australia opening in Sydney. On their way home, they play a concert in Hawaii.
Mar [21] *Fun Fun Fun* hits US #5, as the band's clean-cut, all-American visual style is firmly established.
Apr At a recording session at Western Studios for *I Get Around*, Brian fires Murry after they have a fight.
May ***Shut Down Vol. 2*** reaches US #13.
July [3-4] The group headlines "A Million Dollar Party", presented by KPOI, at the International Center Arena, Honoulu, HI, with Jan & Dean, Jimmy Clanton, the Kingsmen, the Rivingtons, Ray Peterson, Jody Miller, Bruce & Terry, Jimmy Griffin, Mary Saenz and Peter & Gordon.
[4] With effortlessly-honed harmonies, *I Get Around* tops the chart and sells over a million. B-side *Don't Worry Baby*, written for the Ronettes but rejected by Phil Spector, peaks at US #24.

Aug ***All Summer Long*** hits US #4.
[29] *I Get Around*, their second UK chart entry, hits #7.
Sept The Beach Boys begin their first major US tour, set to end in Worcester, MA.
[27] They make their debut on CBS-TV's "The Ed Sullivan Show".
Oct [17] *When I Grow Up (To Be A Man)* hits US #9.
[28-29] The Beach Boys record the "TAMI Show (Teen Age Music International Show)" at the Civic Auditorium in Santa Monica, CA, with the Barbarians, Chuck Berry, James Brown, Marvin Gaye, Gerry & the Pacemakers, Lesley Gore, Jan & Dean, Billy J. Kramer & the Dakotas, Smokey Robinson & the Miracles, the Rolling Stones and the Supremes. (The show will open in the UK at the Futurist, Birmingham, Warks., as "Gather No Moss" on August 7th, 1966.)
Nov [1] The group arrives in London for its first UK promotional visit.
[6] They perform *I Get Around*, *When I Grow Up (To Be A Man)* and *Dance Dance Dance* live on ITV's "Ready Steady Go!", and will also make TV appearances on BBC-TV's "Top Of The Pops" and ITV's "Thank Your Lucky Stars" in the next few days.
[14] Two tracks from the EP *Four By The Beach Boys*, *Wendy* and *Little Honda*, reach US #44 and US #65 respectively, as they set out on their second tour of Australia.
Dec [5] ***The Beach Boys Concert***, recorded live in Sacramento, CA and their first #1 album, tops US chart (the first live performance disk to reach the top of the US Album chart), where it will stay for four weeks, while in the UK *When I Grow Up (To Be A Man)* reaches #27.
[7] Brian marries Marilyn Rovell at Los Angeles' City courthouse.
[19] *Dance Dance Dance* hits US #8, as ***The Beach Boys Christmas Album*** is released for the seasonal market.
[23] Brian Wilson suffers a nervous breakdown, the first of three in the next 18 months, on a flight from Los Angeles to Houston, TX, at the start of a two-week tour. Suffering also from partial deafness in one ear, he decides to retire from live performance with the group, and concentrate on writing and producing the records.

1965

Jan Glen Campbell (b. Apr. 22, 1936, Delight, AR) joins as temporary replacement for Brian on live gigs.
Feb [6] *Dance Dance Dance* reaches UK #24.
[18] ***All Summer Long*** and ***The Beach Boys In Concert*** are certified gold by the RIAA.
Mar [25] 22-year-old secretary, Shannon Harris, files a paternity suit against Love before Superior Court Commissioner Frank B. Stoddard. (Her daughter Shawn will marry Dennis Wilson in 1983.)
[27] *Please Let Me Wonder* peaks at US #52.
Apr [9] Bruce Johnston (b. June 27, 1944, Peoria, IL), former member of Bruce & Terry and the Rip Chords, who had met the Beach Boys in 1963 when working as a producer at CBS/Columbia, replaces Campbell to become a full-time Beach Boy, making his debut at a gig in New Orleans, LA.
[10] The group's revival of Bobby Freeman's *Do You Wanna Dance*, the A-side of *Please Let Me Wonder*, reaches US #12.
May [29] Traditionally Brian-produced *Help Me Rhonda* tops the US chart for two weeks, while ***The Beach Boys Today!*** hits US #4.
July [10] *Help Me Rhonda* reaches UK #27.
Aug [28] *California Girls*, on which Brian begins to show the influence of Phil Spector's production style, hits US #3, and ***Summer Days (And Summer Nights!!)*** hits US #2.
Sept [8] The group begins the first of four days of recording sessions for its forthcoming ***Party*** album.
[25] *California Girls* reaches UK #26.
Oct ***Surfin' USA*** is the group's UK Album chart debut, reaching #17.
[1] ***The Beach Boys Today*** is certified gold by the RIAA.
[23] The Sunrays' *I Live For The Sun*, written by Murry Wilson, peaks at US #51.
Nov [3] Band performs *Barbara Ann* and *California Girls* on NBC-TV's "Jack Benny Hour".
[15] ***Surfer Girl*** and ***Surfin' USA*** are certified gold by the RIAA.

1966

Jan [1] *The Little Girl I Once Knew*, another more complex production, reaches US #20. By contrast, ***Beach Boys Party*** is the raw result of impromptu "live-in-the-studio" sessions with friends, and hits US #6.
[18] Brian begins work on what will be regarded as his recording zenith, the ***Pet Sounds*** project.
[29] *Barbara Ann*, a revival of the Regents' 1961 hit and taken from ***Party***, with a guest lead vocal by Dean Torrence (of Jan & Dean), hits US #2, while the Beach Boys tour Japan.
Feb [7] ***Summer Days (And Summer Nights!!)*** is certified gold by the RIAA.
[18] Brian lays down the first track of *Good Vibrations* at Gold Star Studios, on Santa Monica Blvd., Los Angeles.
Mar [12] *Barbara Ann* and parent album ***Beach Boys Party*** both hit UK #3.
Apr [30] Brian Wilson's *Caroline No*, the first solo single by an original Beach Boy, makes US #32.
May [2] The group sings *Help Me Rhonda*, *Their Hearts Were Full Of Spring* and *Little Honda* on NBC-TV's "The Andy Williams Show".
[7] *Sloop John B*, their revival of a 1927 traditional Caribbean tune, hits US #3 and UK #2, selling over a million in the US alone, while the belatedly UK-released ***The Beach Boys Today!*** hits #6.
Painstakingly produced and richly-textured ***Pet Sounds*** is released. The result of many months of Brian's diligent work, the album sets new standards for the group, and is critically acclaimed as its best work yet. It will hit US #10 and UK #2, behind the Beatles' ***Revolver***. Brian has begun the ***Pet Sounds*** project, having been inspired to creatively match the heights of the Beatles' opus ***Rubber Soul***.
June [25] Following a same-titled concert at the Cow Palace in San Francisco the day before, "The Beach Boys' Summer Spectacular", with the Lovin' Spoonful, Percy Sledge, the Byrds and Chad & Jeremy, takes place at the Hollywood Bowl, Hollywood, CA.
Aug Released in the UK a year after its US success, ***Summer Days (And Summer Nights!!)*** peaks at #4, while ***Pet Sounds*** rests two places higher.
[27] Ballad *God Only Knows* hits UK #2, and will become one of the Beach Boys' most covered hits.
Sept [1] Recordings for *Good Vibrations* are completed at United Western Studios.
[17] *Wouldn't It Be Nice* hits US #8.
[24] *Wouldn't It Be Nice* B-side, *God Only Knows*, makes US #39.
Oct The group forms Brother Records, with David Anderle overseeing the operation.
[24] Compilation ***Best Of The Beach Boys*** hits US #8.
Nov [6] The band begins a seven-date, twice-nightly UK tour, with Lulu, David & Jonathan and others, at the Astoria Theatre, Finsbury Park, London, set to end on the 13th at the Birmingham Theatre.
[10] A fire breaks out near Gold Star Studios, the evening that Brian Wilson has been recording a string segment for the track *Fire*. He thinks he is responsible for it, and places the tapes in a vault out of harm's way.
Dec [10] Critically rated the group's best-ever recording, the richly-textured, multi-layered *Good Vibrations*, a track which Brian has been working on for six months, using 17 sessions at four different studios, tops the US chart. (It has already hit UK #1 on Nov [17].) By month's end, the Beach Boys displace the Beatles as World's Best Group in the annual **New Musical Express** poll, while ***Best Of The Beach Boys*** (a different compilation from the earlier US release) hits UK #2, and will remain charted for 142 weeks.
[21] *Good Vibrations* and ***Shut Down - Volume 2*** are both certified gold by the RIAA.

1967

Jan Brian begins working on sessions for an album to further develop the music created on ***Pet Sounds***. The first working title for the project is ***Dumb Angel***, later changed to ***Smile***, though ironically, stress begins to tell on the group, and on Brian in particular, while work is in progress. There is heavy drug abuse, while Brian's ideas and modes of work, such as standing a grand piano in a huge sandbox, become increasingly eccentric as his mental stability deteriorates.
[3] Carl Wilson, having received a US Army draft notice, refuses to be sworn in, saying he is a conscientious objector.
Mar The group files suit in Los Angeles Superior Court against Capitol Records, for alleged non-payment of royalties, and seeking termination of their recording contract. (Brian has already filed a $275,000 lawsuit there against Capitol, for not paying him producer's royalties.)
[2] *Good Vibrations*, nominated in the Best Contemporary (Rock'n'Roll) Recording category, loses to the New Vaudeville Band's *Winchester Cathedral* at the ninth annual Grammy Awards.
Apr ***Surfer Girl***, never previously released in the UK, appears instead of a new album, and reaches UK #13. Carl is arrested in New York by the FBI, and held in custody for five days for refusing to take the Oath of Allegiance and avoiding military call-up. He refuses to report for induction to military service, citing his opposition to the war, and is granted Conscientious Objector status, but refuses to report for assigned alternative civilian duty as a bedpan changer at Los Angeles' Veterans' Hospital. In refusing, he cites that the job would not make use of his talents. (He will be arraigned for trial in June 1967, but the case will drag on for years, until community service in lieu is settled.)
[13] The Beach Boys open a two-week US tour in Starkville, MS, which will end on the 29th in Schenectady, NY.
[25] Brian Wilson guests on CBS-TV's Leonard Bernstein-hosted "Inside Pop - The Rock Revolution" performing *Surf's Up*.
May [2] They begin an eight-date, twice-nightly UK tour at the Adelphi Theatre, Dublin, Eire, with Helen Shapiro, Simon Dupree & the Big Sound, and Terry Reid with Peter Jay's Jaywalkers. The tour will close on the 10th at the ABC Theatre, Edinburgh, Scotland, as the ***Smile*** sessions finally end in disarray, and the Beach Boys will become increasingly notorious in their commercial absence.
[27] Lacking new material, Capitol Records in the UK has extracted the cover version of the Crystals' *Then He Kissed Me* (retitled *Then I Kissed Her*) from ***Summer Days (And Summer Nights!!)***, which hits UK #4.
June The group pulls out of the "Monterey International Pop Festival", Monterey, CA, purportedly because of Carl's draft trial, although there is speculation that they are concerned about how they will be received by the crowd. Otis Redding takes the group's place and Carl is acquitted of draft evasion.
Aug Having established its own Brother Records label, distributed by Capitol, and the cause of much rancor between the two camps, *Heroes And Villains* is released, a track created in similar fashion to *Good Vibrations*. (Brother's first two signings are Redwood and Amy. Redwood's scheduled first single is a 1963 Brian Wilson song *Thinkin 'Bout You Baby*, originally recorded by Sharon Marie and now re-written as *Darlin'*. The record is never released, and Redwood leaves Brother to become Three Dog Night.)
[25] Brian Wilson makes his first concert appearance with the group in over two years, at the International Center, Honolulu, HI.
[26] *Heroes And Villains*, penned with Brian's new writing partner Van Dyke Parks, reaches US #12 and UK #8.
Sept [23] Compilation ***Best Of The Beach Boys, Vol.2*** peaks at US #50. (A separate version with a different track listing will hit UK #3 in November.)
Dec [2] *Wild Honey*, a return to a simpler R&B/rock

sound, makes US #31 and UK #29.
[15] The Beach Boys perform at a UNICEF benefit concert in Paris, France, and there meet Maharishi Mahesh Yogi, who introduces them to transcendental meditation.
[16] ***Smiley Smile***, the Brother label's debut release, peaks disappointingly at US #41, while hitting UK #9. It contains parts of the abandoned ***Smile***, plus some lighter-weight later material, and is carried by the already familiar *Good Vibrations* and *Heroes And Villains*.

1968

Feb [3] *Darlin'* returns the group to both the US and UK Top 20, at #19 and #11 respectively.
Mar [9] R&B-flavored ***Wild Honey*** reaches US #24 and will hit UK #7.
Apr [4] The band is scheduled to open a US college tour, with Buffalo Springfield and Strawberry Alarm Clock, in Nashville, TN, but when word comes that Martin Luther King has been assassinated in nearby Memphis, they cancel the show and subsequently the tour.
[29] Brian and Marilyn Wilson become parents to a daughter, Carnie.
May [4] The group begins an 18-day US tour with the Maharishi at the Singer Bowl, New York, scheduled to end in San Diego, CA, on the 21st, but the concerts are poorly attended and several dates are cancelled. Their live show, based around an old-fashioned greatest hits presentation, is an increasing anachronism in an era of progressive rock concerts. Jardine will comment, "If anybody benefits from this tour, it'll be the florists."
[18] *Friends*, a song inspired by their transcendental meditation conversion, makes US #47 and UK #25.
Aug [17] ***Friends***, again heavily influenced by TM, is their poorest-selling US album yet, peaking at #126.
[28] *Do It Again*, a celebratory return to the group's early sound, tops the UK chart for a week and will reach US #20 on Sept [14].
Oct ***Friends*** fares better in the UK, reaching #13, while compilation ***Best Of The Beach Boys, Vol.3*** hits UK #9 after peaking at US #153.
Dec [1] During a UK tour, the band's performance at the London Palladium is recorded for subsequent album release.
[28] Johnston's first Beach Boys production, *Bluebirds Over The Mountain*, a revival of an oldie by Ersel Hickey, peaks at US #61.

1969

Jan [11] *Bluebirds Over The Mountain*, with lead guitar by Ed Carter, makes UK #33.
Feb The group begins a five-city tour of Texas.
Mar [12] Taken from current album ***20/20***, *I Can Hear Music*, another of the group's revivals (originally by the Ronettes), hits UK #10.
Apr [1] Continuing its legal dispute with Capitol Records, the group sues the label for over $2 million, claiming unpaid royalties and production fees, plus other losses incurred through general mismanagement by the label. ***20/20*** climbs to US #68 and hits UK #3.
[26] *I Can Hear Music* reaches US #24.
May The band holds a press conference to announce the impending end of its Capitol contract, its poor financial situation, and a quest for a new label deal.
July [12] Their final single for Capitol, *Break Away*, which Brian has co-written with Murry, who uses the pseudonym Reggie Dunbar, hits UK #6.
Aug [2] *Break Away* peaks at US #63.
[3] Carl Wilson is indicted in Los Angeles for failing to appear for community service work (as an orderly in a hospital) in lieu of the military. (A mutually acceptable form of community service is found, which means free Beach Boys concerts at hospitals, prisons, and so on.)
[30] US-only album ***Close Up*** makes #136.
Oct [16] Brian and Marilyn Wilson have a second daughter, Wendy.
Nov Murry Wilson sells the "Sea Of Tunes" catalog, comprising all of Brian's songs, to Irving/Almo Music for $700,000.

1970

Jan The group resurrects its Brother Records label as part of a new licensing agreement with Warner/Reprise Records.
Apr [4] US-only *Add Some Music To Your Day* peaks at #64.
June [20] *Cottonfields*, from ***20/20*** and remixed by Capitol for the UK market, with Red Rhodes on pedal steel, hits UK #5, remaining unavailable in the US.
Oct ***Sunflower***, their debut album for Brother/Reprise, peaks at US #151. In the UK, the album remains with EMI (owner of US Capitol), confusingly released on its Stateside label, and reaches #29, while the UK-only compilation ***Greatest Hits***, on Capitol, hits UK #5. In its home territory, the group's live shows take on a new lease of life, as the hip rock crowd re-discovers them in an event-stealing appearance at the "Big Sur Folk Festival", Monterey.
Nov [5] During a four-night stint at the Whisky A-Go-Go, Los Angeles, Brian joins the group on stage for only the second time in five years. His recurring ear problem has caused further damage, and he will not play with the band again for some time.
Dec Dennis' solo single, *Sound Of Free*, written with Daryl Dragon (subsequently of the Captain & Tennille), under the name Dennis Wilson & Rumbo, is released only in the UK.

1971

Jan Former journalist and radio DJ Jack Rieley takes over the group's management, encouraging the band to finish *Surf's Up*, a Brian Wilson song from the abandoned ***Smile*** sessions, of which Brian himself has performed a solo version on the Leonard Bernstein-hosted CBS-TV special "Inside Pop: The Rock Revolution" on April 25th, 1967.
Feb The group performs a sellout concert at New York's Carnegie Hall, to rave reviews. Rieley has prompted a long overdue update of the group's live image, dropping its stage uniforms and lengthening the song sets.
Mar "Two Lane Blacktop" movie co-starring James Taylor and Warren Oates and featuring Dennis opens in US theaters.
Apr [27] The Beach Boys jam with the Grateful Dead at the Fillmore East, New York, NY, on a rendition of *Johnny B. Goode*, cementing new-found favor with the progressive rock audience.
May [1] They perform at a May Day anti-war demo in Washington, DC, before an estimated crowd of 500,000 people. (Later in the year they will also play a benefit for the Berrigan Brothers defense fund.)
June [11] Dennis accidentally puts his right hand through a window pane and severs some nerves. He is replaced for live work by Ricky Fataar, former drummer with South African group Flame, whom the Beach Boys have earlier signed to Brother Records and used for some time as a support band (Carl produced their 1970 debut).
[27] The group plays at the final concert at the Fillmore East, on a bill with J. Geils Band, Country Joe & the Fish, Mountain, Edgar Winter and the Allman Brothers.
Oct An album, originally to be titled ***Landlocked*** because of its ecological theme, but renamed ***Surf's Up*** after the addition of that track, reaches US #29 and UK #15.
Nov [20] The extracted *Long Promised Road*, penned by Carl with manager Rieley, reaches US #89.
Dec The band begins four months of recording sessions at its Brother Studios in Santa Monica.

1972

Jan Johnston leaves the lineup after seven years, citing personality clashes with Rieley, to be replaced by Fataar's former Flame colleague, Blondie Chaplin.
Feb [24] They perform at the "Grand Gala Du Disque", Amsterdam, Holland, and while there tape a TV special.
May [16] The group opens a UK tour in Newcastle, Tyne & Wear, going on to appear at the Lincoln Festival, London's Royal Festival Hall and Crystal Palace, where they are joined on stage by Elton John and the Who's Keith Moon.
June ***Carl And The Passions/So Tough***, with the title resurrecting one of the group's pre-Beach Boys names, reaches US #50 and UK #25. In the US, it is jointly packaged with a reissue of ***Pet Sounds***, US rights to which have reverted to the group from Capitol. After its release, the group has a demountable recording studio transported from Los Angeles to Baambrugge, Holland, at considerable expense, and members take up temporary Dutch residence, while the next album is planned and recorded.

1973

Mar [1] The New York's Joffrey Ballet makes its debut performance of the "Deuce Coupe Ballet", set to the music of the Beach Boys.
Holland, the result of sessions in that country (costing an estimated $250,000), plus a Los Angeles-recorded track, *Sail On Sailor*, added at the insistence of Reprise Records executives concerned about the album's lack of commercial appeal, reaches US #36 and UK #20. It contains a free EP, *Mount Vernon And Fairway*, a musical fairy-tale written by Brian.
[10] *California Saga (On My Way To Sunny Californ-i-a)* makes UK #37.
[17] *Sail On Sailor* is extracted as a US single but stalls at #79.
June [2] *California Saga (On My Way To Sunny Californ-i-a)* stalls at US #84. Shortly after the album's release, Rieley is fired as manager and replaced by Love's brother, Steve.
[4] Murry Wilson, father of Brian, Carl and Dennis, and their original manager, dies from complications following a heart attack.

1974

Jan [26] Double live album ***The Beach Boys In Concert***, recorded during the group's 1972 winter and 1973 summer tours, reaches US #25. Following its release, Chaplin and Fataar leave, and a recovered Dennis, who had considered a full-time solo career, returns on drums. James William Guercio, producer of Chicago and Blood, Sweat & Tears, and owner of Caribou Studios, Nederland, CO, a long-time fan of the group, joins on bass and becomes their part-time manager.
July [27] Elton John's *Don't Let The Sun Go Down On Me*, on which Carl Wilson and Bruce Johnston contribute backing vocals, hits US #2.
Aug [14] The still-climbing ***Endless Summer*** is certified gold by the RIAA.
Sept Double re-package of ***Wild Honey*** and ***20/20*** reaches US #50.
[28] The extracted *Surfin' USA* re-hits US #36.
Oct [4] ***The Beach Boys In Concert*** is certified gold by the RIAA.
[5] Double-album compilation ***Endless Summer***, assembled by Capitol to satisfy nostalgia for the group's '60s classics, tops the US chart for one week (only the second #1 of the group's career), during a 155-week residence.
Nov Double re-package of ***Friends*** and ***Smiley Smile*** reaches US #125.
[30] Chicago's *Wishing You Were Here*, on which Jardine and Carl and Dennis Wilson sing at the invitation of Guercio, reaches US #11.

1975

Apr [30] ***Spirit Of America*** is certified gold by the RIAA.
May Guercio pairs the Beach Boys and Chicago for a 12-city US tour during which 700,000 people will pay $7.5 million to see the bands perform.
[31] *Sail On Sailor* is reissued in the US, two years after first charting, and peaks at #49.
June [21] The group performs at Wembley Stadium, Wembley, Middx., to a rousing reception from 72,000 people, second on the bill to Elton John.
[28] Capitol's second US-only double nostalgia compilation ***Spirit Of America*** hits #8.

Aug [30] Compilation album, ***Good Vibrations - Best Of The Beach Boys*** (of later tracks on Brother/Reprise) reaches US #25.

1976

Jan [2] Dennis Wilson is arrested for carrying a .38 revolver which he has taken from his girlfriend. He is released after the charges are dropped.
[30] The group returns to recording at the Brother Studios with Brian, who, having dropped out of a largely non-productive deal to work with Bruce Johnston and Terry Melcher's Equinox Records, nominally returns as producer on ***15 Big Ones***, a title which refers to the group's 15th anniversary and the number of tracks on the album, mostly nostalgic cover versions.
June [20] Brian films a segment for the forthcoming NBC-TV special on the Beach Boys in which he is arrested for not being able to surf by "Saturday Night Live" alumni Dan Aykroyd and John Belushi, posing as the Surf Police.
July [2] A 44-date US tour begins at the Oakland-Alameda County Stadium, Oakland, CA, set to end on October 3rd at the State Fair, Tulsa, OK.
[3] Brian plays on stage with the Beach Boys for the first time in seven years, at the Anaheim Stadium, Anaheim, CA.
[24] Having not promoted either ***Endless Summer*** or ***Spirit Of America***, Capitol/EMI in the UK has compiled its own Beach Boys collection, released as the TV-advertised ***20 Golden Greats*** which now tops the UK chart for the first of ten weeks, as their new album ***15 Big Ones*** makes UK #31. *Good Vibrations* also re-charts, at UK #18, as a revival of Chuck Berry's *Rock And Roll Music*, from ***15 Big Ones***, makes UK #36.
Aug [5] NBC-TV special "The Beach Boys: It's OK" airs.
[14] *Rock And Roll Music* hits US #5, the group's first US Top 10 hit since *Good Vibrations* a decade earlier.
[28] ***15 Big Ones*** hits US #8.
Sept [1] ***15 Big Ones*** is certified gold by the RIAA.
[18] Brian is a presenter and nominee at CBS-TV's "Don Kirshner's Second Annual Rock Music Awards", broadcast from the Hollywood Palladium, Hollywood.
Oct [2] *It's OK*, a Brian Wilson/Mike Love original from ***15 Big Ones*** which features sax work by Wizzard's Roy Wood, reaches US #29.
Nov [27] Brian sings and appears in sketches on NBC-TV's "Saturday Night Live".
Dec [31] The group, with Brian back in the line-up, plays a show to commemorate the 15th anniversary of its first gig, at the Great Western Forum, Inglewood.

1977

Jan [8] Live tracks recorded at London's Finsbury Park Astoria on August 12th, 1968, and the London Palladium on December 1st the same year, released by Capitol in the US as ***Beach Boys '69: Live In London***, makes US #75.
Feb [19] Having embarked on a solo career for Columbia Records, Johnston wins Song Of The Year for *I Write The Songs* at the 19th annual Grammy Awards.
Mar The group signs to Caribou Records, having just completed an album for Reprise, to whom they still owe one more.
May [7] ***The Beach Boys Love You***, produced by Brian Wilson, charts for a week at UK #28 and will peak at US #53 on the 21st.
July [30] The band plays an exclusive gig for UK CBS Records' (distributors of Caribou Records) annual sales conference in London, having abandoned plans to perform a Wembley concert.
Sept Dennis is the first (original) Beach Boy to release a solo album, ***Pacific Ocean Blue***, on Caribou Records, which climbs to US #96, while Brian Wilson, Love and Jardine reportedly record as the Waves.

1978

Feb [3] ABC-TV's "Dead Man's Curve" biopic, starring Bruce Davison and Richard Hatch as Jan & Dean, and in which Love makes a cameo appearance, airs in the US.
June [24] Movie theme *Almost Summer*, written by Love, Jardine and Brian, and performed by Celebration, featuring Love, reaches US #28.
Sept [30] The Beach Boys' cover of Buddy Holly's *Peggy Sue*, from the forthcoming ***M.I.U.***, peaks at US #59.
Oct [28] ***M.I.U.***, recorded at the Maharishi International University, Fairfield, IA, with Jardine and Ron Altbach producing, and released to fulfill the Reprise contract, makes US #151.

1979

Jan [23] Brian and Marilyn Wilson divorce after 15 years of marriage.
Apr [7] *Here Comes The Night*, with an incongruously strong disco flavor, and their debut release on Caribou, makes US #44, set to reach US #37 two weeks later.
May [12] ***L.A. (Light Album)*** makes UK #32, notable as Johnston returns to the group both as its co-producer (with Curt Becher) and as a performer, and climbs to US #100.
June [9] *Good Timin'*, from the album, makes US #40.
July [21] *Lady Lynda*, written by Jardine about his wife, also from ***L.A. (Light Album)***, is the Beach Boys' first UK Top 10 record since 1970, hitting #6.
Oct [13] Oriental-phrased extract *Sumahama* reaches UK #45.

1980

Jan [13] They participate in a Los Angeles benefit concert for the victims of Kampuchea, along with Starship and the Grateful Dead.
Apr [12] ***Keepin' The Summer Alive*** makes UK #54.
[19] *Goin' On* stalls at US #83.
[26] *Keepin' The Summer Alive* makes US #75.
June [6-7] The group performs two concerts at the Wembley Arena, and will top the bill at the Knebworth Festival, Knebworth, Herts., on the 20th.
July [4] The band gives a free performance to half a million people in Washington, DC, on Independence Day. The July 4th concert will become a regular date on the Beach Boys' calendar throughout the decade.

1981

May Carl reaches US #185 with ***Carl Wilson***, and leaves the line-up to tour with his own Carl Wilson Band. English musician Adrian Baker, a long-time admirer and professional emulator of the Beach Boys' sound, is called in to temporarily fill out group harmonies on live work, while Dennis will fully return to the line-up over the next few months.
Sept [12] Following the medley craze sparked in US and UK by the Star Sound hit *Stars On 45*, Capitol assembles *The Beach Boys Medley*, which links excerpts from their '60s classics, and makes UK #47.
Oct Love's solo ***Looking Back With Love*** is released, but does not chart, and he tours with his own group, the Endless Summer Beach Band. (His two other solo albums, ***First Love*** and ***Country Love***, remain unreleased.)
[3] *The Beach Boys Medley* reaches US #12, the group's first US Top 20 hit for five years.

1982

Jan [30] Double compilation ***Ten Years Of Harmony (1970-1980)*** peaks at US #156, as extracted *Come Go With Me*, a revival of the Del Vikings' oldie, reaches US #18.
Feb Love records in the UK with Adrian Baker, who remains close to the group.
[22] *I Get Around* is certified gold by the RIAA.
Apr Carl returns to the fold, and his own manager, Jerry Schilling, now oversees the group's affairs.
[6] ***The Beach Boys Christmas Album*** is certified gold by the RIAA.
July [17] Further compilation ***Sunshine Dream*** peaks at US #180.
Sept [2] Dennis and Shawn Wilson become parents to son Gage (Murry Wilson's middle name).
[17] Love and Catherine Martinez are married by recently-ordained minister and DJ legend, Wolfman Jack.
Nov [5] Always the band's most brilliant and troubled member, Brian is nominally fired from the group by his former colleagues.

1983

June [4] Carl's solo *What You Do To Me* peaks at US #72.
July [4] The Beach Boys' Independence Day concert in Atlantic City, NJ, will prove to be the last time all three Wilson brothers appear on stage together.
Aug [6] A second UK TV-advertised double album compilation from Capitol, ***The Very Best Of The Beach Boys***, tops UK chart.
Dec [28] Dennis drowns while swimming from his boat in the harbour at Marina Del Rey, CA. (Special dispensation is granted, with the help of President Reagan, who sends his condolences to the Wilson family, for a burial at sea - normally reserved for naval personnel - of the only genuine surfer in the Beach Boys.)

1984

During the year, the Beach Boys make a one-off recording with Frankie Valli & the Four Seasons, *East Meets West*, written by Bob Crewe and Bob Gaudio. It is released on the Seasons' own FBI label in the US.

1985

Jan [15] The band participates in the 50th "American Presidential Inaugural Gala", for President Ronald Reagan, in Washington, DC.
June [22] ***The Beach Boys***, with Stevie Wonder guesting on his own *I Do Love You)*, produced in London by Steve Levine and overseen by Brian, makes US #52 and UK #60.
[29] The extracted Love/Melcher-penned *Getcha Back* reaches US #26.
July [13] The group performs at the "Live Aid" concert in Philadelphia, PA.
Aug [17] *It's Gettin' Late*, also from the album, makes US #82.

1986

July [19] *Rock'n'Roll To The Rescue*, written by Love and Melcher, peaks at US #68. It trailers the double compilation ***Made In The USA***, which reaches US #96, released by Capitol in celebration of the group's 25th anniversary. It contains 20 1962-to-1968 Capitol tracks together with later hits, *Rock And Roll Music*, *Come Go With Me* and *Getcha Back*, and two new Beach Boys' recordings produced by Terry Melcher.
Oct [25] Also from the album, their revival of the Mamas & The Papas' *California Dreamin'*, with electric 12-string guitar played by former Byrd Roger McGuinn, peaks at US #57, as Joan Jett & the Blackhearts' *Good Music*, with backing vocals by the Beach Boys, makes US #83.

1987

Jan Brian Wilson inducts Leiber and Stoller into the Rock and Roll Hall of Fame at the second annual induction dinner, at New York's Waldorf Astoria Hotel, at which Seymour Stein approaches him to record a solo album for Sire.
Sept [12] Invited to co-perform on a remake of *Wipe Out* by rap act the Fat Boys, the resulting combination with the Beach Boys hits UK #2 and US #12.

1988

Jan [20] Elton John inducts the Beach Boys into the Rock and Roll Hall of Fame at the third annual induction dinner held, at the Waldorf Astoria Hotel. Love, in accepting the honor, proceeds to upset the assembled multitude with a rambling and nonsensical speech.
[25] Having never won a Grammy Award, the Beach Boys collect the Special Award Of Merit at the 15th annual American Music Awards, held at the Shrine Auditorium, Los Angeles.
May [26] ***Made In The USA*** is certified gold by the RIAA.
June [12] The Beach Boys and the Four Tops take

part in a sing-off at half-time during the NBA championship game between the Los Angeles Lakers and the Detroit Pistons. The Beach Boys sing for the Lakers, and the Four Tops for the Pistons.

July Now taking a daily six-mile jog along Pacific Coast Highway, Brian releases his first solo album ***Brian Wilson*** on Sire. Having shelved a previous solo debut with the working title ***Sweet Insanity***, this album is partly co-produced and co-written with his therapist Dr. Eugene Landy, who he claims has successfully rehabilitated the Beach Boy using the "milieu" therapy program, (which keeps the pair in round-the-clock electronic communication), it makes US #54 but fails to chart in the UK, despite intense promotion. The typically harmonic highlight *Love And Mercy* is also released.

Sept The Beach Boys, minus Brian, undertake an eight-date US tour. Brian contributes *Goodnight Irene* to the Woody Guthrie/Leadbelly tribute album ***Folkways: A Vision Shared***.

Oct During a UK promotion visit, Brian unexpectedly visits the tenth annual Beach Boys Convention at the Parish Centre, Greenford, Middx.

Nov [5] The Beach Boys, again without Brian, hit US #1 with *Kokomo*, a Caribbean-flavoured pop ditty written by John Phillips, Scott McKenzie, Mike Love and Terry Melcher and featured in the Tom Cruise-starring movie "Cocktail". It is over 24 years since their first hit - the longest span ever achieved in the rock era.

[16] Former manager Stephen Love, Mike's brother, is sentenced to five years probation for embezzling more than $900,000 from the group. (Stephen Love and brother Stan are also sued by Mike Love and a business associate, Michael Seeman, alleging that they kidnapped, assaulted and beat Seeman and extorted $40,000 from him.)

Dec [10] *Kokomo* reaches UK #25.

1989

Jan [10] *Kokomo* is certified platinum by the RIAA.

Apr [17] Landy, Brian's therapist, surrenders his license to practice therapy after an investigation by the California State Board of Medical Quality Assurance into alleged improprieties.

May [27] The Beach Boys and Chicago begin their first tour together since 1975 at the Pacific Amphitheatre, Costa Mesa, CA. Brian sits in on three songs.

June [20] The band, with Brian, begins six further major US dates co-headlining with Chicago.

Aug [26] *Still Cruisin'*, from the Mel Gibson/Danny Glover-starring "Lethal Weapon 2", peaks at US #93.

Sept Brian files a $100-million civil suit at Los Angeles Superior Court, to recover copyrights to songs his father sold to A&M Records and Irving Music for $700,000 in 1969.

Oct ***Still Cruisin'***, an album collecting old and new Beach Boys tracks featured in movies, reaches US #46.

Nov [27] ***Still Cruisin'*** is certified gold by the RIAA.

1990

Apr [19] Brian and Jardine jam at session-drumming legend Hal Blaine's book launch party at the Baked Potato, North Hollywood.

[29] "Summer Dreams: The Story Of The Beach Boys", based on Stephen Gaines' 1986 biography **Heroes & Villains: The True Story Of The Beach Boys**, airs on ABC-TV. (Irving Music will sue producers Leonard Hill for allegedly lying about their intent when requesting the licensing of the Beach Boys' music.)

May [2] As the Beach Boys' legal and financial affairs become increasingly fraught and court-bound, seemingly exacerbated by the interests of those attached to individual band members (not least, Eugene Landy), Stan Love files suit in California Superior Court in Santa Monica, seeking control of Brian Wilson's personal and financial affairs.

[7] Brian Wilson breaks into a press conference in Burbank, CA, called by Stan Love, as he is about to announce his intention to become legal overseer of Brian Wilson's estate and life.

June Various artists compilation ***Smiles, Vibes, And Harmony - A Tribute To Brian Wilson***, an album of cover versions by Sonic Youth, Das Damen, Original Sins, Handsome Dick Manitoba and others, is released on DeMilo Records.

[2] Reissued *Wouldn't It Be Nice* peaks at UK #58.

[7] Brian Wilson files his reply to Stan Love's suit, alleging him to be "a violent thug" motivated by "insatiable greed".

[9] Brian's daughters Wendy and Carnie top the US chart (as two-thirds of Wilson Phillips) with *Hold On*, exactly 25 years after the Beach Boys' *Help Me Rhonda* was at #1.

[17] Brian Wilson files a further $100-million suit against law firm Irell & Manella and attorney Werner Wolfen for fraud and negligence, saying the company helped A&M's publishing company, Almo, defraud him of his publishing rights by making him sign documents when he was incapacitated by a mental breakdown and drug and alcohol problems.

[22] Brian Wilson files suit against Stan Love, alleging he is seeking to do little more than become Wilson's prison guard at a lucrative salary.

[23] A third TV-advertised UK Beach Boys collection ***Summer Dreams***, released by Capitol, hits UK #2.

[29] The extracted *Do It Again* debuts at UK peak, #61.

July [7] ***Pet Sounds***, part of a widely-praised re-mastering of the complete Beach Boys works available for the first time on CD, makes US #162.

[21] *Problem Child*, written and produced by Melcher for the movie "Problem Child", is released.

[28] Brian drops in on "Beach Boys Convention '90" at the Handlery-Stardust Hotel, San Diego, and performs *God Only Knows*, *California Girls*, *Good Vibrations* and a new song, *Spirit Of Rock And Roll*.

Dec [31] The band participates in "Dick Clark's New Year's Rockin' Eve" ABC-TV show.

1991

Jan [28] Brian Wilson plays a solo set at Hollywood's China club.

June [25] The group performs at the Wembley Arena, the climax of a seven-date UK concert visit.

Aug [23] Supported by the Everly Brothers on their current US tour, the band headlines the New York State Fair, Syracuse, NY.

Sept Harper Collins publishes Brian's autobiography (co-written with Greil Marcus) **Wouldn't It Be Nice**.

Oct [10] Wilson is the subject of an interview and documentary on ABC-TV's "Prime Time Live".

[22] ***Two Rooms***, a collection of cover versions of Elton John and Bernie Taupin compositions is released, featuring the Beach Boys' treatment of *Crocodile Rock*.

Dec [2] ***Best Of The Beach Boys*** is certified double platinum by the RIAA for sales of two million copies.

[5] As the result of a Los Angeles court settlement, Landy and Brian Wilson are ordered to stay away from each other, while Wilson is also required to submit his finances to a conservator. A statement issued jointly by Wilson and family members says they have reached agreement that will allow Brian "to receive guidance and assistance, while at the same time allowing him the freedom to live his own life as he chooses".

1992

Feb [5] ***Little Deuce Coupe*** is certified platinum and ***Best Of The Beach Boys Volume 2*** is certified multi-platinum for two million sales by the RIAA.

June [4] With the Beach Boys having participated in the "One To One" benefit honoring Michael Jackson at the State Armory, New York, on the previous evening, Brian performs at Capitol Record's 50th anniversary all-star gala at the Capitol Tower, Los Angeles.

July [31] While Brian has recently received a reported settlement of $10 million from Irving Music in June, the latest round of legal wrangles sees Love suing both him and Irving Music for $50 million in the Los Angeles Superior Court, claiming he has been deprived of royalties and licensing fees for songs he co-wrote with his cousin over the past 30 years, including *California Girls*, *Good Vibrations* and *Fun Fun Fun*.

Sept [5] Having begun their annual US summer tour (traditionally without Brian) in June (America and Poco have opened for them during its early stages), the Beach Boys, supported on this latter leg by David Cassidy, gross $323,400, performing at the New Pine Knob Music Theatre, Clarkston, MI.

Currently without a major recording deal, the band has released a cover version of Sly Stewart's *Hot Fun In The Summertime* from ***Summer In Paradise***, its first studio album in seven years, produced by Melcher on the now independent Brother label in July. By year's end they will also open the Original Beach Boys Café in Hermosa Beach, CA, furnished with group memorabilia, while Carl will continue writing material with America's Gerry Beckley and Chicago's Robert Lamm. Brian continues to record tracks for his sophomore solo album.

1993

June [6] The group embarks on a European tour in Finland, set to end on the 29th at Wembley Arena.

[21] Newly signed to EMI Records in the UK, the Beach Boys release ***Summer In Paradise***.

[29] Capitol releases the long-awaited ***Good Vibrations : 30 Years Of The Beach Boys***, a comprehensive five-CD/cassette boxed-set career retrospective, as the group prepares the annual US summer tour, sponsored under the heading "Tone Soap Presents The Beach Boys". (Brian, meanwhile, contributes vocals to *In My Moon Dreams* for director Paul Bartel's new movie "Shelf Life", duets with daughter Carnie on *Fantasy Is Reality* for Rob Wasserman's ***Trio*** album, sings *Proud Mary* with Carl for a Don Was project, and provides vocals on six songs for Van Dyke Parks' new album ***Voice Of America***.)

Nov [2] ***Good Vibrations : 30 Years Of The Beach Boys*** is certified gold by the RIAA.

1994

Aug [30] The group sings the "Top 10 List" on CBS-TV's "Late Show With David Letterman".

Dec [12] A jury in Los Angeles court finds that Love is due 30% of the $10 million royalty settlement Wilson previously won, for his creative role in helping to write many of the early Beach Boys hits. (After the settlement, Wilson says he will appear with the band in concert again, but expected at three Lake Tahoe concerts, he fails to show up.)

1995

Jan [30] A visibly nervous Brian co-presents, with Don Was, the Soul/R&B Male Artist trophy at the 22nd annual American Music Awards held at the Shrine Auditorium, trying to join in the finale of ***We Are The World***.

Feb [27] Wilson and Love meet at Love's Lake Tahoe home to work on two new songs, one called *Baywatch Nights*, for inclusion in the smash hit TV show "Baywatch", and *Grace Of My Heart*.

Mar [3] Love and the Wilson brothers record two new songs at a Glendale, CA studio, following an impromptu performance of *Do It Again* by Brian and Love earlier in the day at a Malibu Hotel for US syndicated TV's "Entertainment Tonight" crew.

Apr [4] Further compilation ***20 Good Vibrations - The Greatest Hits*** is released in the US, as Brian now performs with the band in Las Vegas. (He also contributes *This Could Be The Night*, and with Carl, Gerry Beckley and Robert Lamm, *Without Her*, to the ***For The Love Of Harry (Everybody Sings Nilsson)*** tribute album.

July [8] New compilation ***The Best Of The Beach Boys*** reaches UK #25.

Aug [11] Brian receives the President's Award from BMI president Frances Preston in recognition of the millions of radio plays of Beach Boys records. He is only the third recipient, and the first pop songwriter. Meanwhile the Beach Boys continue their annual summer tour, this time with Christopher Cross as support act, at the Pine Knob Music Theatre, Clarkston, MI.

[17] Brian appears with his daughters Carnie and Wendy at a benefit for the Children's Health Fund in New York, singing *Do It Again* and solo *The Warmth*

Of The Sun, *God Only Knows* and *California Girls*.
[27] Producer/director Don Was' black and white film about Brian Wilson, "I Just Wasn't Made For These Times", including an extended interview with its subject together with filmed sessions of him updating some of his favorite compositions, having received its premiere at the Sundance Film Festival, now airs on the Disney Channel (US).
Sept [16] The accompanying album, Brian Wilson's ***I Just Wasn't Made For These Times*** debuts at its UK #59 peak, as ***Pet Sounds*** now re-charts at UK #70.
[19] Wilson files suit in Los Angeles Superior Court against his former conservator, attorney Jerome Billet and his firm Billet & Kaplan, alleging negligence resulting in the loss of millions of dollars in court settlements and legal fees. The suit also seeks $10 million in damages for emotional distress.

1996

Feb The Beach Boys, including Brian, join Status Quo onstage at the Brixton Academy.
Mar [2] Status Quo's cover of *Fun Fun Fun*, featuring its originators, bows at its UK #24 peak. (With Brian co-producing, the band begins recording a selection of past hits in a country style in Nashville, TN, with music guests invited to sing lead vocals over its backing harmonies, including Willie Nelson (*The Warmth Of The Sun*), Alabama (*Fun Fun Fun*), Travis Tritt (*Help Me Rhonda*) and Steve Earle (*Shut Down*), among others.)
Apr [20] ***Greatest Hits*** charts for a week at US #198.
May [14] Capitol Records releases ***The Pet Sounds Sessions (Produced By Brian Wilson)***, a four-CD/two-book package featuring backing tracks, vocals without tracks, outtakes and the first true stereo mix of the album. (Its release precedes the much anticipated and much-delayed issue of another three-CD set, ***Smile Era*** which is reportedly being prepared by Brian and songwriter/producer Van Dyke Parks from the original and legendary 1967 ***Smile*** sessions. Curiously, a new 12-track collaboration by the pair, the critically revered ***Orange Crate Art***, mostly written and produced by Parks and entirely sung by Wilson, has been released in 1995 by Warner Bros. Records.)
see also : **Glen CAMPBELL**

THE BEASTIE BOYS

King Ad-Rock (Adam Horovitz) (vocals);
MCA (Adam Yauch) (vocals);
Mike D (Michael Diamond) (vocals)

1981

Yauch (b. Aug. 15, 1967, Brooklyn, New York, NY), adopting the name MCA (Master of Ceremonies Adam), and Diamond (b. Nov. 20, 1965, New York) first teamed up as one half of a hardcore rock band to play at MCA's 15th birthday party. Subsequently recruiting drummer Kate Schellenbach (b. Jan. 5, 1966, New York) and guitarist John Berry, they form the Beastie Boys recording an eight-song rock EP, *Polly Wog Stew*, for release by the New York independent label, Rat Cage Records. With Schellenbach and Berry leaving (they will re-emerge respectively in Luscious Jackson and Thwig), Yauch and and Diamond invite their friend Horovitz (b. Oct. 31, 1966, Manhattan, New York) to complete what will become the permanent trio. Horovitz, the son of playwright and screenwriter Israel Horovitz, has been in local band the Young & the Useless since the age of 14, who released one single *Real Men Don't Use Floss*. They will spend much of 1982 serving their club performance apprenticeship at CBGB's and the Danceteria, New York, night spots, increasingly moving in a hardcore hip-hop direction.

1983

Aug *Cookie Puss*, more a harangue than a song, is released, backed by *Beastie Revolution*, which includes a sample subsequently used on a British Airways commercial, resulting in the group receiving a $40,000 rights payment from the airline.
Oct As the rap portion of their show begins to dominate their performances, they are assisted initially by DJ Double RR (Rick Rubin) to scratch on turntables erected behind them, before engaging the talents of their resident turntable DJ, Doctor Dre, who will go on to become a host of MTV's "Yo! MTV Raps" (not to be confused with N.W.A.'s Dr. Dre).

1984

July Sporting the street fashion of baggy jeans, reversed baseball caps, Adidas trainers, chunky gold chains and hooded sweat-tops, the trio supports Madonna on a US tour.
Oct The group signs to Rubin's fledgling Def Jam label (licensed to CBS/Columbia), which releases the Beastie Boys' first complete rap single, *Rock Hard*.
Nov They appear in the formative rap movie "Krush Groove" with L.L. Cool J., Kurtis Blow, the Fat Boys and other rising rap stars, performing *She's On It*.

1986

Sept On a UK visit as the opening act on Run D.M.C.'s Raising Hell tour, their outrageous stage act and similarly rebellious offstage antics invites a love/hate relationship with UK press.

1987

Mar [7] The trio's debut album, co-produced and written by the trio with Rubin, ***Licensed To Ill*** becomes the first rap album to top the US chart, holding at #1 for seven weeks, as the extracted single, the good-time brat-rant *(You Gotta) Fight For Your Right (To Party)*, hits US #7.
[28] *(You Gotta) Fight For Your Right (To Party)*, despite a BBC ban on the video, reaches UK #11, while the trio appears at a European music trade promotion event in Montreux, Switzerland.
May [30] While on tour in the UK, Horovitz is arrested in Liverpool, Merseyside, on a charge of causing actual bodily harm, when he allegedly hits 20-year-old fan Jo-Anne Clarke with a can of beer, during an audience disturbance following their Royal Court Theatre concert. (He will be acquitted in November, when the case goes to court.) The tabloid press invents lurid stories about their supposed anti-social behaviour, such as laughing at mentally handicapped children. The Volkswagen-logo medallions worn by the trio also cause trouble, as UK fans emulate the style by stealing them from cars.
June [13] *No Sleep Till Brooklyn* makes UK #14, as ***Licensed To Ill*** hits UK #7.
Aug [1] Follow-up *She's On It* hits UK #10.
$350,000 worth of damage is caused as a result of a party held at a Washington, DC residence, after five teenagers attempt to re-create scenes from the boisterous "Fight For Your Right (To Party)" video. Host Gunnar Cole escapes with his life, after being dragged from the house, which is burnt to the ground.
Oct [17] Double A-sided *Girls/She's Crafty* reaches UK #34.
Dec With ***Licensed To Ill*** having sold over four million domestic copies, the group wins the Top New Artist, Pop category in **Billboard**'s annual chart round-up.

1988

Feb [17] "The Beastie Boys" video is certified gold by the RIAA.
Apr [25] *Brass Monkey* makes US #48. (While the group is currently featured in the Run D.M.C. movie "Tougher Than Leather", and during a band hiatus, Horovitz follows a cameo performance in the TV series "The Equalizer" with early movie roles in "The Santa Ana Project" and in Hugh Hudson's "Lost Angels", co-starring with Donald Sutherland.)

1989

Aug [5] Following bitter ructions with Def Jam and now signed to Capitol Records, their sophomore effort ***Paul's Boutique***, named after a Brooklyn store and produced by the Dust Brothers (Matt Dike, John King and Mike Simpson), reaches UK #44, and will make US #14. As its sales quickly diminish, it becomes clear that many of rap's commercial innovators, including the Beasties, Run D.M.C. and Kurtis Blow, have been rapidly superceded by a newer breed of genre superstars, including MC Hammer and L.L. Cool J.
Sept [2] *Hey Ladies* makes US #36.

1990

Mar [8] The group wins Best Album Cover for ***Paul's Boutique*** in **Rolling Stone** magazine's 1989 Critics' Awards.

1992

Mar [11] The group is the subject of a profile on BBC2-TV's imported music show, "Rapido", and will perform a one-off UK date at London's Marquee club on the 15th.
Apr [4] The band performs its first US gig since April 18th, 1991, at the same venue, the Palladium, Los Angeles, CA, on an AIDS benefit bill including the Red Hot Chili Peppers. The trio 'plays' instruments, live for the first time.
[11] *Pass The Mic* debuts at its UK peak, #47.
May [9] Their third outing ***Check Your Head*** debuts at its US peak, #10. Recorded at the band's own G-Son Studios in Attwater, CA, it is released via Capitol on Mike D's own label, Grand Royal, and produced by the group with Mario Caldato.
[11] The trio bows its US tour at the Rave, Milwaukee, WI.
June [16] A UK concert trek, which will include a performance at this year's "Reading Festival", on August 30th, begins at the Newcastle Polytechnic, Newcastle, Tyne & Wear.
July [4] EP *Frozen Metal Head* charts for a week at UK #55.
[18] *So What'cha Want* peaks at US #93. During the month, Yauch marries actress Iona Skye, daughter of '60s folkie Donovan, while songwriters Noah Evans and Miles Kelly file a suit in the US District Court, charging the group with using their song *Time For Livin'* (on the Beastie Boys' recent album) without their permission.
Sept [19] Towards the end of further US live dates, the band donates proceeds from its performance in New Orleans, LA, to Louisiana Choice, which advocates women's rights to choose abortion. By year's end, Horovitz, continuing a parallel acting career, will appear in "Roadside Prophets".

1993

May [22] The group helps out at record store counters in New York to benefit LIFEbeat's CounterAid, a one-day fundraiser for people with HIV and AIDS, as they begin recording a new album in New York.
Sept [9] ***Check Your Head*** is certified platinum by the RIAA.
Dec Horovitz is charged with grand theft and battery for allegedly attacking a TV cameraman and stealing his videotape outside the memorial service for River Phoenix at his Mount Olympus home on November 4th.

1994

Feb [26] Early hardcore material, pre-dating the debut album, collected on the aptly-named Capitol-released, ***Some Old Bullshit***, debuts at its US #46 peak.
Apr The group, wearing matching brown UPS uniforms, plays its first concert in more than a year at a benefit for the Leonard Peltier Defense Fund in Los Angeles. They also contribute *Bennie And The Jets*, with Biz Markie, to the compilation album ***18 Original Hits By 18 Unoriginal Artists***.
May [23] They perform at New York's Madison Square Garden, but have to cancel a subsequent show the following night because of a New York Rangers NHL playoff game.
June [4] ***Ill Communication*** hits UK #10 in its debut week.
[18] Marking an impressive commercial comeback in the fad-affected world of rap, ***Ill Communication*** enters the US chart at #1.

July [9] *Get It Together*, coupled with *Sabotage*, debuts at its UK #19 peak.
[13] "The Skills To Pay The Bills" video is certified gold by the RIAA.
[29] ***Ill Communication*** is certified platinum by the RIAA.
Aug [1] The group plays before its biggest audience of the year, 43,000, at FDR Park in Philadelphia, PA, during the "Lollapalooza '94" tour.
[16] Horovitz attends Madonna's 36th birthday party at the latter's Coconut Grove, FL mansion.
Sept [8] They perform *Sabotage* at the 11th annual MTV Video Music Awards ceremony at New York's Radio City Music Hall.
Oct [3] The group appears on C4-TV's "The Big Breakfast", as the RIAA certifies five million sales of ***Licensed To Ill***.
Nov [26] *Sure Shot* debuts at its UK #27 peak.
Dec [10] They appear as musical guests on NBC-TV's "Saturday Night Live".

1995

Mar [22] "Sabotage/Home Video" is certified gold by the RIAA.
Apr [6] Belying its initial moderate sales, but revived as a strong catalog item, ***Paul's Boutique*** is certified platinum by the RIAA.
June [3] The group is named Top Rap Artist (Duo Or Group) at the inaugural Blockbuster Entertainment Awards at Hollywood's Pantages Theatre. (CBS-TV will broadcast the event on the 6th.)
[10] ***Root Down***, a 10-song EP comprising live versions of tracks from ***Ill Communication***, bows at its US #50 and UK #23 album peak.

1996

Mar Following tour dates in Australia, New Zealand and South-East Asia with Foo Fighters and Sonic Youth, the band's new mini-album, ***The In Sound From Way Out***, including instrumentals and different version of tracks from ***Ill Communication***, is initially released in France through its fan club.
Apr [20] ***The In Sound From Way Out*** debuts at its US #45 peak.
June [15-16] The Beastie Boys host the "Tibetan Freedom Concert" in San Francisco, CA, having also invited A Tribe Called Quest, Beck, Björk, the Fugees, Richie Havens, John Lee Hooker, Biz Markie, Yoko Ono, Pavement, Rage Against The Machine, Smashing Pumpkins and Sonic Youth, among others, in their capacity as co-founders of the benefitting Milarepa Fund.

THE BEATLES

John Lennon (vocals, rhythm guitar);
Paul McCartney (vocals, bass); **George Harrison** (vocals, lead guitar); **Ringo Starr** (vocals, drums)

1957

July [6] The Quarry Men Skiffle Group, after auditioning for Carroll Levis' "TV Star Search Show" at the Empire Theatre, Liverpool, Lancs. a month earlier, are playing the St. Peter's Parish Church Garden Fête, Woolton, Liverpool, when Ivan Vaughan, who had been in the Quarry Men when they were known as the Black Jacks, introduces the group's lead singer, Lennon (b. John Winston Lennon, Oct. 9, 1940, Woolton, Liverpool), to McCartney (b. James Paul McCartney, June 18, 1942, Liverpool), at the end of the band's set. McCartney impresses Lennon with his ability to tune a guitar and his knowledge of rock'n'roll lyrics.
Aug [7] The Quarry Men make their Cavern club debut in Liverpool, but without McCartney, who is at a scout camp in Hathersage, Derbys.
Oct [18] McCartney makes his debut with the group at the New Clubmoor Hall Conservative club in Norris Green, Liverpool.

1958

July [15] Lennon's mother, Julia, dies in a road accident in Liverpool.
Aug Harrison (b. Feb. 24, 1943, Wavertree, Liverpool - only in his '40s would Harrison discover that he was born at 11:42 p.m. on the 24th and not, as legend had dictated, in the early hours of the 25th), who has been at school with McCartney at the Liverpool Institute High (though one year behind), joins the Quarry Men, and the group, now comprising Lennon, McCartney, Harrison and John Lowe, cuts its first record. They pay 17s and 6d to record a demo of Buddy Holly's *That'll Be The Day*, backed with a Harrison/McCartney composition, *In Spite Of All The Danger*.

1959

Aug [29] On the day of the opening of the Casbah Coffee Club, run by Mona Best, in West Derby, Liverpool, Les Stewart and Ken Brown of the scheduled band the Les Stewart Quartet argue, with Stewart walking out. Brown asks Harrison if he knows anyone who can help out, and he brings in Lennon and McCartney. This performance leads to a regular Saturday-night spot at the Casbah, until October 10th, when Brown goes his own way.
Nov [15] Lennon, McCartney and Harrison, now calling themselves Johnny & the Moondogs, participate in the final round of Carroll Levis' "TV Star Search" at the Hippodrome Theatre, Ardwick, Lancs.

1960

Jan Lennon's art-school friend Stuart Sutcliffe (b. June 23, 1940, Edinburgh, Scotland) joins on bass. (They will continue without a regular drummer until the summer.)
May [20] The group, having failed an audition for Larry Parnes to be Billy Fury's backing band, begins a seven-date tour of Scotland at Alloa Town Hall, as the Silver Beetles (after a brief spell as the Beatals), backing Johnny Gentle, another singer from the Parnes talent stable. (Tommy Moore has been added to the line-up on drums. For the tour, McCartney uses the pseudonym Paul Ramon, Sutcliffe calls himself Stuart da Staël and Harrison adopts the forename Carl.)
Aug [12] Pete Best (b. Randolph Peter Best, Nov. 24, 1941, Madras, India), the son of Casbah club owner Mona Best, passes an audition at the Wyvern Social club, and joins the group as its drummer in time for its first visit to Germany.
[17] Having arrived in Hamburg, W. Germany, and playing for the first time as the Beatles, the band begins a 17-day residency at the Indra Club, set to end on October 3rd, before moving to the larger Kaiserkeller club, making 106 appearances in total, playing their last gig on November 30th.
Oct [15] Starr (b. Richard Starkey, July 7, 1940, Dingle, Liverpool), drummer with Rory Storm & the Hurricanes, fills in for Best when the group backs Rory Storm guitarist Wally Eymond on a recording of Gershwin's *Summertime* at the Akustik Studio in Hamburg.
Dec [27] The group plays a gig at the Town Hall, Litherland, Liverpool, to scenes which hint at the adulation they will receive in the future. (Chas Newby substitutes for Sutcliffe, who has stayed behind in Germany.)

1961

Feb [21] The Beatles make their Cavern club debut in Liverpool, at the first of many lunchtime sessions.
Apr [1] They begin a second spell in Hamburg, playing 92 nights at the Top Ten club, through to July 2nd.
Aug German Polydor releases *My Bonnie* by Tony Sheridan & the Beat Brothers. (The name the Beatles is considered too risqué in Germany, as it sounds like the word "peedles", German slang for penis.) Recorded under the auspices of orchestra leader Bert Kaempfert at Harburg Friedrich Ebert Halle in Hamburg, the session also features two other numbers backing Tony Sheridan, plus an Eddie Cantor original, *Ain't She Sweet*, with a Lennon vocal, and a Shadows instrumental pastiche, *Cry For A Shadow*, penned by Lennon and Harrison.
Oct [15] The group appears on the same bill as comedian Ken Dodd at a St. John's Ambulance Brigade star fundraiser at the Albany Cinema, Maghull, Liverpool.
[19] The Beatles and Gerry & the Pacemakers combine forces as one group (the Beatmakers) when they play at Litherland Town Hall.
[28] Raymond Jones calls at Brian Epstein's NEMS record store in Liverpool, to enquire about the availability of the Beatles' German release. Epstein (b. Sept. 19, 1934, Liverpool), unable to trace the record, promises to investigate further. (Beatle historians will question whether Epstein already knew of the Beatles at this time.)
Nov [9] Following up on Jones' enquiry, Epstein sees the group for the first time, at a Cavern lunchtime session.
Dec [9] The Beatles play their first gig in the south of England, at the Palais Ballroom, Aldershot, Hants., on a programme with Ivor Jay & the Jaywalkers, billed as a "Battle Of The Bands - Liverpool v. London". Only 18 people turn up.

1962

Jan [1] The group auditions for Decca Records at the company's West Hampstead studios in London, prior to Brian Poole & the Tremeloes, who are chosen in preference to the Beatles because they are based in the south of England.
[4] The Beatles top the first-ever **Mersey Beat** group popularity poll.
[24] Epstein signs the band and begins to direct their image away from leather jackets towards a smarter stage presentation, with matching suits and respectful bows to the audience.
Feb [1] The Thistle Café in West Kirby, Lancs. is christened "The Beatles Club" for one night, to mark Epstein's debut booking for the group. He reduces his usual commission to 10% of their earnings for the night (£18) to mark the occasion. (Ironically, they never play at the venue again.)
Mar [8] BBC Radio broadcasts "Teenager's Turn (Here We Go)", featuring the Beatles in their first-ever radio appearance. (Over the next few years they will have their own series and various specials on BBC Radio, performing many songs not featured on their albums.)
Apr [10] Sutcliffe, still living in West Germany, is taken ill at his fiancée Astrid Kirchher's mother's house in the Hamburg suburb of Altona, and dies, in his girlfriend's arms, of a brain haemorrhage in an ambulance en route to the hospital.
[13] The group returns to W. Germany for 48 nights at Hamburg's new venue, the Star-Club, a stint which will end on May 31st.
May [8] During a trek around London, visiting UK record companies Oriole, Phillips and Pye, Epstein visits the HMV record store in Oxford Street, which has the facility to transfer tape to acetate. Ted Huntly, the engineer who carries out the job of converting the Beatles' demo tape recorded for Decca to record, sees potential in the songs. He sends Epstein to publisher Ardmore & Beechwood director Sidney Coleman, who arranges a meeting with EMI producer George Martin (b. Jan. 3, 1926, London) the next day.
June [4] Having sufficiently aroused Martin's interest, the Beatles sign a provisional contract with EMI to record demos.
[6] The group makes its debut session at EMI's Abbey Road Studios to record a test for Parlophone, under the direction of Martin's assistant, Ron Richards. They perform *Besame Mucho* and impress Martin with three self-penned compositions, *P.S. I Love You*, *Ask Me Why* and *Love Me Do*.
[9] The Beatles play a Welcome Home night at the Cavern, in front of a record-breaking 900 people.
Aug [14] Long dissatisfied with Best's role in the group, a decision is made by Epstein and the other three Beatles to fire him. Rory Storm drummer Starr, currently playing at Butlin's holiday camp in Skegness, Lincs., is asked to replace him, after Epstein's choice, Johnny Hutchinson of the Big Three, has turned down the invitation.

[15] Best plays his last gig with the group, at the Cavern.
[16] Best is dismissed from the group. (Hutchinson fills in for that night's gig at the Riverpark Ballroom, Chester, Cheshire.)
[18] Starr makes his Beatles debut at the Horticultural Society Dance, Hulme Hall, Port Sunlight, Birkenhead, Lancs.
[23] Lennon marries Cynthia Powell at Mount Pleasant Register Office, Liverpool, with McCartney as best man, and spends his wedding night playing with the Beatles at the local Riverpark Ballroom.
Sept [4] The band's first proper recording session at Abbey Road takes place. They are asked to record Mitch Murray's *How Do You Do It*, which they reluctantly perform. (Gerry & the Pacemakers will hit UK #1 with it the following year.) When they insist on performing their own material, Martin challenges them to come up with a song as good. They record Lennon and McCartney's *Love Me Do*, featured at their audition, which Martin decides has the potential to become their first single.
[11] Martin, unhappy with the results of the previous week's session, has the group return to Abbey Road to re-record *Love Me Do*, with session drummer Andy White taking over from Starr. (They will also record *P.S. I Love You* and an early version of *Please Please Me* at this session.)
Oct [2] Epstein signs the group to a five-year management contract.
[5] The Beatles' debut single *Love Me Do* is released.
[6] The group makes the first of many personal appearances, signing copies of *Love Me Do* at Dawson's Music Shop, Widnes, Lancs.
[12] The Beatles play at the Tower Ballroom, New Brighton, Wallasey, on a bill headed by Little Richard, with Billy J. Kramer & the Contours, the Big Three, the Dakotas and other local groups.
[17] The band makes its maiden television appearance, on the regionally-broadcast "People And Places", live from Granada's Manchester studios, singing *Love Me Do* and *Some Other Guy*.
[28] They make their first major stage appearance, at the Liverpool Empire, on a bill headed by Little Richard, with Craig Douglas, Jet Harris, Kenny Lynch and Sounds Incorporated.
Nov [1-14] The Beatles play a run of 14 nights at the Star-Club.
Dec [18] The group begins its fifth and final club stint in Germany with 13 more dates at the Star-Club, supporting Johnny & the Hurricanes. Ted Taylor of Liverpool group King Size Taylor & the Dominoes records its final performance on New Year's Eve. (It will be released commercially in 1977.)
[27] *Love Me Do* reaches UK #17. (It is later alleged that Epstein purchases 10,000 copies of the record for his NEMS shop, to boost its chart position.)

1963

Jan [3] The band begins its first headlining tour - four nights in Scotland commencing at the Two Red Shoes Ballroom, Elgin, after the first night has been cancelled because of bad weather. (At one date they are billed as "The 'Love Me Do' Boys - The Beatles".)
[19] They make their first national TV appearance, on ITV's "Thank Your Lucky Stars", performing *Please Please Me*.
Feb [2] The Beatles begin their first nationwide tour at Gaumont Cinema, Bradford, Yorks., on a bill headed by Helen Shapiro, with Danny Williams and Kenny Lynch. Their payment for the tour is £80 a week, shared by all four members.
[8] The Beatles, Shapiro and Lynch are asked to leave a Carlisle Golf Club dance at the Crown & Mitre Hotel, because they are wearing leather jackets.
[11] They complete ten new tracks for their debut album ***Please Please Me*** in one session at Abbey Road Studios, in 15 minutes short of ten hours. Lennon's vocal for their cover of the Isley Brothers' *Twist And Shout* is recorded in one take - as an afterthought - to complete the album.
[23] *Please Please Me* hits UK #2. (It will top three of the four UK published record charts.)
Mar [3] The Helen Shapiro-headlining tour ends at the Gaumont Cinema, Hanley, Staffs.
[7] The group joins Gerry & the Pacemakers, the Big Three, Billy J. Kramer & the Dakotas and other local groups for a one-night stand package, "Mersey Beat Showcase", at the Elizabethan Ballroom, Nottingham, Notts. (There will be five more of these through to June 16th, when all the acts are available at the same time.)
[9] The Beatles begin a 21-date, twice-nightly UK tour, supporting Tommy Roe and Chris Montez, at the Granada Cinema, East Ham, London. With their fame rapidly spreading, they eventually top the bill. (Lennon misses three dates because of a heavy cold, and the band plays on as a trio.) The tour will end on the 31st at the De Montfort Hall, Leicester, Leics.
Apr [4] At the request of schoolboy Dave Moores, the group appears at Roxburgh Hall, Stowe School, Bucks., for a fee of £100.
[14] The Beatles see the Rolling Stones perform at the Crawdaddy club in Kingston, Surrey.
[16] They make their BBC-TV debut, on "The 625 Show".
[21] The group appears at the annual "**New Musical Express** Poll Winners' All-Star Concert" at the Empire Pool, Wembley, Middx., before 8,000 fans.
May [4] *From Me To You* (the title inspired by the **New Musical Express**' letters column "From You To Us") tops the UK chart, where it will stay for seven weeks, selling over 650,000 copies. It begins a record-breaking run of 11 consecutive #1s from 11 consecutive releases.
[11] ***Please Please Me*** tops the UK chart. The album showcases a unique and natural combination of songwriting genius, between Lennon and McCartney, who pen eight out of twelve cuts, simple vocal harmony and an excellence in synchronized performing talent demonstrated by all four members, who complement each other under the direction of producer Martin. In changing the panorama of popular music in the short term, this first release sets the stage for their long-term dramatic influence, which will underpin popular culture throughout the decade.
[18] The group begins its third UK tour, supporting Roy Orbison with Gerry & the Pacemakers, at the Adelphi Cinema, Slough, Bucks. Due to audience reaction, the Beatles again become bill-toppers. The 21-date tour will close June 9th at the King George's Hall, Blackburn, Lancs.
[19] Three girls are taken into police custody after climbing - by way of a metal ladder - through a dressing-room window 100' above ground level, at the group's Gaumont Cinema, Hanley, Staffs. show but are released after getting the group's autographs.
June [4] The first in a regular series of radio programs "Pop Go The Beatles" is broadcast on BBC Radio.
[8] *My Bonnie*, credited to Tony Sheridan & the Beatles, charts for a week at UK #48.
Aug [1] A magazine devoted to the group, **Beatles Monthly**, is published for the first time. (It will continue until December 1969, selling 350,000 copies a month at its peak.)
[3] The group plays its final gig at the Cavern after 274 appearances.
Sept [10] The band is honored with the Top Vocal Group Of The Year award at the Variety Club of Great Britain luncheon at London's Savoy Hotel.
[14] Lennon and McCartney-penned instant pop classic *She Loves You* tops the UK chart. (With a reported advance order of 310,000 copies, it will sell 1.6 million in the UK alone and remain Britain's best-selling single, until Wings' *Mull Of Kintyre* overtakes it in 1977.) It will be replaced at #1 by Brian Poole & the Tremeloes' *Do You Love Me*, followed by Gerry & the Pacemakers' *You'll Never Walk Alone*, but will return to the top slot eight weeks later.
Oct [4] The group makes its first live appearance on the new ITV show "Ready Steady Go!", although the band actually mimes to the three songs it performs.
[9] BBC-TV airs "The Mersey Sound" documentary.
[13] The Beatles make their bill-topping debut on ITV's "Sunday Night At The London Palladium". Subsequent press stories report scenes of hysteria amongst fans outside the Palladium, and the term "Beatlemania" is coined.
[17] The band records its first Christmas record, for its fan-club members.
[25] A five-date Swedish tour begins in Karlstad.
Nov [1] The group's first official headlining trek, "Beatles' Autumn Tour", a 33-date, twice-nightly package, with Peter Jay & the Jaywalkers, the Brook Brothers, the Vernons Girls and others, opens at the Odeon Cinema, Cheltenham, Gloucs., as Beatlemania begins to grip the UK. The tour will end December 13th, at the Gaumont Cinema, Southampton, Hants.
[4] The band receives a royal seal of approval from H.R.H. the Queen Mother, Princess Margaret and Lord Snowdon, when it performs at the Royal Variety Performance at London's Prince of Wales Theatre. Lennon creates major headlines when he instructs the audience, "Will the people in the cheaper seats clap your hands. All the rest of you, rattle your jewellery."
[5] The **Daily Mirror** headlines an editorial "Yeah! Yeah! Yeah!" and continues: "You have to be a real sour square not to love the nutty, noisy, happy, handsome Beatles. If they don't sweep your blues away, brother, you're a lost cause. If they don't put a beat in your feet, sister, you're not listening."
[17] John Weightman, headmaster of Clark's Grammar School, Guildford, Surrey issues a directive that pupils with Beatle haircuts will be sent home. "This ridiculous style brings out the worst in boys physically. It makes them look like morons."
[21] In the House of Commons, Sir Charles Taylor (Conservative MP for Eastbourne) asks the Home Secretary whether he would give instructions that the Beatles should no longer receive police protection from their fans, in the London area.
[30] *She Loves You* returns to #1 for two weeks, having passed the one million mark on the 27th, and, with advance orders of 270,000, ***With The Beatles*** tops the UK chart, displacing ***Please Please Me***. (Combined, they will hold the top spot on the chart continuously for 51 weeks, from May 1963 to May 1964.) Once again mixing Lennon and McCartney originals with covers of a few of their favorite American R&B tracks (including *You Really Got A Hold On Me* and *Roll Over Beethoven*), ***With The Beatles*** becomes the first million-selling album in the UK.
Dec [7] All four Beatles appear on the BBC-TV show "Juke Box Jury". They vote the record that they will knock off the top in the US in eight weeks time, Bobby Vinton's *There! I've Said It Again*, a miss.
[14] *I Want To Hold Your Hand* begins a five-week stay at UK #1. (After an initial advance order of 940,000, it will sell 1.5 million copies in the UK and worldwide sales will total 15 million.) It dethrones *She Loves You*, the first time an act has replaced itself at #1. (Lennon will posthumously equal this in 1981, when *Woman* replaces *Imagine* at #1.)
[20] The group wins the World Vocal Group and British Vocal Group categories in the **New Musical Express** poll for 1963.
[22] "The Beatles Come To Town" Pathé News documentary opens in cinemas throughout the UK.
[24] "The Beatles Christmas Show", with Rolf Harris, the Barron Knights, Tommy Quickly, the Fourmost, Billy J. Kramer & the Dakotas and Cilla Black, mixing music and pantomime, opens at London's Finsbury Park Astoria, where it will run until January 11th.
[27] **The Times** music critic William Mann hails Lennon and McCartney as the outstanding English composers of 1963.

1964

Jan [3] The group is seen for the first time on US TV, when NBC-TV's "Jack Paar Show" airs a clip of *She Loves You* from the BBC's "The Mersey Sound".
[15] The band makes its French debut at the Cinéma Cyrano in Versailles, before embarking on a 20-date stint at the Paris Olympia, with Trini Lopez and Sylvie Vartan.
[18] The Beatles make their US chart bow with *I Want To Hold Your Hand*, which enters at #45.

Feb [1] *I Want To Hold Your Hand*, described in a **Billboard** review as a "driving rocker with surf on the Thames sound" and first played on WWDC Radio in Washington, DC, tops the US chart, displacing Bobby Vinton's *There! I've Said It Again*. (The first #1 by a UK act to top the US charts since the Tornados' *Telstar* on December 22nd, 1962, it is the first of three consecutive chart-toppers and 20 US #1s and becomes the fastest-ever UK million-seller in the US.) The Beatles will stay at #1 until May 9th, when *Hello Dolly* topples *Can't Buy Me Love*.
[3] The RIAA certifies *I Want To Hold Your Hand* and ***Meet The Beatles*** gold.
[7] Pan-Am flight PA 101 touches down at 1:20 EDT at New York's John F. Kennedy International Airport, bringing the Beatles to the US, where they experience near-riotous scenes, thanks to major publicity engineered by Capitol Records. (Capitol originally turned down Epstein and the group's first four singles, which were released in the US by Vee-Jay and Swan Records.)
[9] The group, with a flu-stricken Harrison, makes its live US debut, on CBS-TV's "The Ed Sullivan Show", watched by an estimated 73 million viewers. (The crime rate in US cities is reported to have dropped dramatically during the show's broadcast time.) They perform *All My Loving*, *Till There Was You*, *She Loves You*, *I Saw Her Standing There* and *I Want To Hold Your Hand*, and are paid $2,400. Also appearing on the show are Georgia Brown and the children's chorus from the Broadway show "Oliver" (including future Monkee Davy Jones), Tessie O'Shea and Frank Gorshin.
[11] The Beatles' US concert debut takes place at the Washington Coliseum, Washington, DC, with Tommy Roe, the Chiffons and the Caravelles.
[12] The band makes its New York debut at Carnegie Hall. (The New Street Music record store in New York, located next to a barber shop, offers to send buyers of the Beatles album next door for a free Beatle haircut.)
[15] ***Meet The Beatles!*** tops the US chart for the first of 11 weeks.
[16] A second "Ed Sullivan Show" is broadcast, direct from the Deauville Hotel, Miami, FL.
[18] Still in Miami for a concert, the group visits Cassius Clay, preparing for his World Heavyweight bout with Sonny Liston, at his training camp.
[22] The band arrives back from the US at Heathrow Airport. BBC sports program "Grandstand" screens their early-morning return, including an interview with David Coleman, during its afternoon broadcast.
[29] ***Introducing ... The Beatles*** hits US #2, where it will stay for nine weeks, unable to dislodge ***Meet The Beatles!***
Mar [2] Work begins on their first feature film, on location at Marylebone Station, London, based around a typical day in the life of the group.
[14] *Please Please Me* hits US #3, as *My Bonnie* reaches US #26.
[16] Leeds University Law Society elects Starr its vice president.
[19] Prime Minister Harold Wilson presents the Beatles with their award for Show Business Personalities Of The Year For 1963 at the 12th annual Variety Club of Great Britain luncheon, at London's Dorchester Hotel.
[20] The group appears on ITV's live "Ready Steady Go!" show, bringing the program its highest-ever audience rating.
[21] *She Loves You* tops the US survey, while *I Saw Her Standing There* reaches US #14.
[23] Lennon's book of nonsense verse and rhyme, **In His Own Write**, is published in the UK, as the group receives two Carl-Alan Awards from the Duke of Edinburgh at the Empire Ballroom, Leicester Square, London. It is announced that the Beatles have won three Ivor Novello awards - the Most Broadcast Work Of The Year (*She Loves You*), the Highest Certified British Sales (*She Loves You*) and the Special Award For Outstanding Services To British Music, shared with Brian Epstein and George Martin. (*I Want To Hold Your Hand* has the second-highest sales, and *All My Loving* comes second in the Year's Outstanding Song category.)
[25] The group makes its first appearance on BBC-TV's "Top Of The Pops", singing *Can't Buy Me Love*.
[28] The band members' wax images are unveiled at Madame Tussaud's in London. The Australian chart published this week reads: #1 *I Saw Her Standing There*, #2 *Love Me Do*, #3 *Roll Over Beethoven*, #4 *All My Loving*, #5 *She Loves You* and #6 *I Want To Hold Your Hand*.
[31] *Can't Buy Me Love* is certified gold by the RIAA.
Apr [4] *Can't Buy Me Love* simultaneously tops the UK chart, after selling a record 1,226,000 copies in its first week, and in the US it makes a record leap to the top from a #27 chart debut, vaulting over *Twist And Shout* (which moves up one place to hit #2), selling two million copies in its week of release, after advance orders of 1,700,000. Its advance sell-through of one million is the largest in UK record history. *From Me To You* and *Roll Over Beethoven* reach US #41 and #68 respectively. The **Billboard** chart for this week ending reads, without precedent: #1 *Can't Buy Me Love*, #2 *Twist And Shout*, #3 *She Loves You*, #4 *I Want To Hold Your Hand*, #5 *Please Please Me*.
[11] *You Can't Do That* and *There's A Place* make US #48 and #74 respectively.
[13] Still-climbing ***The Beatles' Second Album*** is certified gold by the RIAA.
[18] *Why* peaks at US #88, while ***The Beatles With Tony Sheridan And Their Guests*** and ***Jolly What! The Beatles & Frank Ifield*** make US #68 and #104 respectively.
[23] On the occasion of Shakespeare's 400th birth, Lennon is guest of honor at a Foyle's Literary Lunch at the Dorchester Hotel. His speech consists of, "Thank you very much. You've got a lucky face."
[25] Peter & Gordon's Lennon and McCartney-penned *World Without Love* knocks *Can't Buy Me Love* off the top of the UK chart, as *All My Loving* makes US #45. (The Beatles have a record 14 singles on the US chart.)
[26] The Beatles make their second appearance at the annual **New Musical Express** Poll Winners' Concert at the Empire Pool, Wembley.
[27] Lennon's **In His Own Write** is published in the US. (It receives rave reviews, with **Newsweek** magazine calling him "an unlikely heir to the English tradition of literary nonsense".)
May [2] ***The Beatles' Second Album*** replaces ***Meet The Beatles!*** at US #1, where it will stay for five weeks.
[6] Jack Good-directed "Around The Beatles" airs on ITV.
[9] *Do You Want To Know A Secret* hits US #2, as *Thank You Girl* makes US #35.
[16] *I Want To Hold Your Hand* re-enters the UK chart, at #48.
[18] McCartney is interviewed by David Frost on BBC-TV's "A Degree Of Frost".
[23] Ella Fitzgerald becomes the first artist to chart in the UK with a cover of a Beatles single, when *Can't Buy Me Love* makes UK #34.
[30] *Love Me Do* tops the US chart.
June [3] Starr is rushed to University College Hospital, London, after collapsing at a photo session in Barnes, London, suffering from tonsilitis and pharyngitis.
[4] The group begins its first world tour at K.B. Hallen, Copenhagen, Denmark, with Jimmy Nicol of the Shubdubs (and once of Georgie Fame & the Blue Flames) deputising for Starr for the first five dates.
[6] *P.S. I Love You* hits US #10.
[11] Starr is discharged from hospital and flies out to Australia to join the tour for its June 15th date at the Festival Hall, Melbourne.
[14] In Melbourne, 250,000 people - the largest congregation of Australians ever assembled in one place - gather to meet the group. Meanwhile, thousands of miles away in Sunderland, Tyne & Wear, 12-year-old Carol Dryden is found by an observant railway clerk on a station platform, packed in a tea chest addressed to the Beatles.
[27] Peter & Gordon's *World Without Love* tops the US chart, becoming Lennon and McCartney's first non-Beatle US #1, while an EP, *Four By The Beatles* (#92) and *Sie Liebt Dich* (#97) both make a brief US showing, and *Ain't She Sweet* reaches UK #29.
July [6] "A Hard Day's Night", featuring six new Beatles songs, receives its world premiere at the London Pavilion. (It will receive two Academy Award nominations.)
[10] 200,000 people pack the route from Speke Airport to Liverpool city centre, as the moptops arrive in their home town for a civic reception at the Town Hall, and to attend the northern UK premiere of "A Hard Day's Night".
[23] The group participates in the "Night of a Hundred Stars" midnight charity revue at the London Palladium.
[25] *A Hard Day's Night*, featuring Lennon's double-tracked vocal, tops the UK chart. ***A Hard Day's Night*** hits UK and US #1, and is unique in being the only album comprised entirely of Lennon/McCartney songs. It also features Harrison taking the lead vocal, normally the role of either Lennon or McCartney (or both), on *I'm Happy Just To Dance With You*. (The US version also features four George Martin instrumentals). ***The American Tour With Ed Rudy*** reaches US #20.
Aug [1] *A Hard Day's Night* tops the US chart, as *I'm Happy Just To Dance With You* makes US #95.
[15] *I Should Have Known Better* peaks at US #53.
[19] Their second North American tour, with the Righteous Brothers, Jackie De Shannon, the Exciters and Bill Black's Combo, opens at the Cow Palace, San Francisco, CA. The 26-date tour will end with a charity performance at the Paramount, New York, on September 20th. (The Beatles will be paid a world record fee of $150,000 for a concert at the Municipal Stadium, Kansas City, MO.)
[21] Their performance at the Las Vegas Convention Center, Las Vegas, NV, is stopped twice, due to excessive jelly-baby hurling by fans.
[22] While the Beatles perform at the Hollywood Bowl, Los Angeles, CA, *Ain't She Sweet* reaches US #19, as ***Something New*** hits US #2, where it will stay for nine weeks, behind ***A Hard Day's Night***.
[25] *A Hard Day's Night* is certified gold by the RIAA.
[29] *I'll Cry Instead* reaches US #25.
Sept [5] The McCartney-led *And I Love Her* reaches US #12, as *If I Fell* peaks at US #53.
[15] Police Inspector Carl Bear of Cleveland's Juvenile Bureau stops a Beatles show, after screaming fans invade the stage at the Public Auditorium, Cleveland, OH.
[20] Bob Dylan visits the band backstage on the final date of their US tour at the Paramount, New York.
Oct [3] The group tapes an insert for ABC-TV's "Shindig", at the Granville Theatre, Fulham, London.
[9] The Beatles begin their only UK tour of 1964, a 27-date, twice-nightly UK package, with Mary Wells, Tommy Quickly, Sounds Incorporated and others, at the Gaumont Cinema, Bradford, Yorks., set to end on November 10th at the Colston Hall, Bristol, Somerset.
[10] *Slow Down* reaches US #25.
[13] CBS-TV's "The Entertainers" airs an hour-long documentary on the Beatles' North American tour.
[17] *Matchbox* reaches US #17, as ***The Beatles Vs The Four Seasons*** peaks at US #142.
Dec [2] Starr has his tonsils removed at London's University College Hospital.
[5] ***Song, Pictures And Stories Of The Fabulous Beatles*** makes US #63.
[12] *I Feel Fine*, with advance orders of 750,000, tops the UK chart, and is their fourth consecutive UK million-seller.
[19] ***Beatles For Sale*** hits UK #1, displacing ***A Hard Day's Night***, which has held pole position for 21 weeks. It includes eight new Lennon/McCartney compositions, augmented by six cover versions (including Buddy Holly's *Words Of Love* and formatively influential Chuck Berry's *Rock And Roll Music*, on which Lennon, McCartney and producer Martin all perform on one piano at the same time).
[24] "Another Beatles Christmas Show" opens at London's Hammersmith Odeon, with Freddie & the Dreamers, the Yardbirds, Elkie Brooks, Jimmy Savile, Mike Haslam, Mike Cotton Sound, Sounds Incorporated and Ray Fell. The run will end on January 16th.
[26] *I Feel Fine* tops the US chart, as *She's A Woman* hits

US #4, completing a run of 30 US hits during the year.
[31] *I Feel Fine* and the still-rising ***The Beatles' Story*** are certified gold by the RIAA.

1965

Jan [2] Continuing the practice of an unrelated release pattern in the US, which sees the issue of different album titles, track listings and compilations, ***The Beatles' Story*** hits #7.
[9] Lennon guests on Peter Cook and Dudley Moore's satirical BBC2-TV show "Not Only ... But Also", as ***Beatles '65*** begins a nine-week run at the top of the US chart.
Feb [11] MacLen (Music) Limited signs a deal with Northern Songs.
[23] Filming of the second Beatles feature, provisionally titled "Eight Arms To Hold You", begins in the Bahamas.
Mar [13] *Eight Days A Week* hits US #1, knocking the Temptations' *My Girl* off the top.
[20] *I Don't Want To Spoil The Party* makes US #39.
[27] EP *4 By The Beatles* peaks at US #68.
Apr [11] The Beatles make their third appearance at the annual "**New Musical Express** Poll Winners' Concert" at the Empire Pool, Wembley, before appearing on ITV's "The Eamonn Andrews Show" that evening.
[13] The Beatles win Best Performance By A Vocal Group for *A Hard Day's Night* and Best New Artist of 1964 at the seventh annual Grammy Awards.
[24] *Ticket To Ride* tops the UK chart. Epstein writes to music paper **Melody Maker**, informing it that McCartney plays lead guitar on the record, and wins an album for writing the letter of the week.
May [15] *Yes It Is* makes US #46.
[18] The group appears on "The Best On Record", an NBC-TV special featuring recent Grammy winners.
[22] *Ticket To Ride* knocks Herman's Hermits' *Mrs. Brown, You've Got A Lovely Daughter* off the top in the US.
June [7] BBC Radio airs "The Beatles (Invite You To Take A Ticket To Ride)", the group's final radio session.
[12] ***The Early Beatles*** makes US #43, as it is announced that the Beatles have been included in the Queen's Birthday Honours List, each receiving the MBE (Member of the British Empire). (Protests pour into Buckingham Palace along with returned medals. Colonel Frederick Wragg returns 12 medals and former Canadian MP Hector Dupuis, MBE claims, "The British house of royalty has put me on the same level as a bunch of vulgar numbskulls.")
[20] A nine-date European tour begins at the Palais Des Sports, Paris, France.
[24] Lennon's second book **A Spaniard In The Works** is published in the UK, as the band makes its Italian debut, at Milan's Velodromo Vigorelli.
July [1] **A Spaniard In The Works** is published in the US, as the still-rising ***Beatles VI*** is certified gold by the RIAA.
[3] European tour ends at the Plaza de Toros Monumental, Barcelona, Spain.
[10] ***Beatles VI*** tops the US chart.
[13] Lennon and McCartney win two Ivor Novello Awards, as *Can't Buy Me Love* wins the Most Performed Work Of 1964 and the Highest Certified British Sales categories. (*A Hard Day's Night* is runner-up in the Most Performed Work category and in the Year's Outstanding Theme From Radio, TV Or Film category, and *I Feel Fine* is the runner-up in the Highest Certified British Sales category.) McCartney, the only Beatle to attend the awards ceremony at the Savoy Hotel, London, says, "Thanks. I hope nobody sends theirs back now."
[29] "Help!" premieres at the London Pavilion.
Aug [7] *Help!* takes over the UK #1 spot from the Byrds' *Mr. Tambourine Man*.
[9] Brian Epstein-managed Silkie record a cover of *You've Got To Hide Your Love Away*, with McCartney on guitar, Harrison on tambourine and Lennon producing. (It will reach UK #28 and US #10.)
[11] "Help!" premieres in New York.
[14] ***Help!*** tops the UK chart. The first seven songs (all Lennon/McCartney compositions, with the exception of Harrison's *I Need You*) on the 14-track album have been used in the accompanying film.
[15] Third North American tour begins at Shea Stadium, Flushing, Queens, New York, before a record crowd of 55,600. (With a security force of 2,000 men, the show grosses $304,000, the world record for a pop concert.)
[23] Still-climbing ***Help!*** is certified gold by the RIAA.
[27] The group meets Elvis Presley for the first and only time, at his Bel Air, CA, home on Perugia Way. Lennon, McCartney and Presley join forces on an impromptu version of *You're My World*.
[31] The tour ends at San Francisco's Cow Palace.
Sept [2] *Help!* is certified gold by the RIAA.
[11] With its title cut having topped the US singles survey one week before, ***Help!***, with cover photography by Robert Freeman, begins a nine-week run at US #1.
[12] The Beatles appear on the first "Ed Sullivan Show" of a new season, Sullivan's 18th, singing *I Feel Fine*, *I'm Down*, *Act Naturally*, *Ticket To Ride*, *Yesterday* and *Help!* Also featured on the bill are Cilla Black, Soupy Sales and Allen & Rossi.
[16] *Eight Days A Week* is certified gold by the RIAA.
[25] "The Beatles" cartoon series premieres on ABC-TV. The half-hour episodes comprise two stories each week. The first story is titled "I Want To Hold Your Hand", in which the group, exploring the ocean floor in a diving bell, encounters a lovesick octopus, and the second "A Hard Day's Night", in which the band rehearses in a haunted house.
Oct [9] McCartney-led ballad *Yesterday* tops the US chart. (Over 2,500 cover versions will make it one of the most recorded songs in the history of popular music. When McCartney uses the song in his 1984 film "Give My Regards To Broad Street", he has to apply to the publishers for its use as he no longer holds the copyright.)
[20] *Yesterday* is certified gold by the RIAA.
[23] *Act Naturally* makes US #47.
[26] The Queen presents the Beatles with their MBEs in the Great Throne Room at Buckingham Palace, London, with 182 other recipients. (They later admit to having smoked marijuana in the lavatories.) When the Queen asks Starr, "How long have you been together now?" he replies, "40 years." In responding to a protest which has seen a number of MBE medals returned by disgruntled former recipients, unhappy that they are in the same company as the group, Buckingham Palace will issue the following statement: "Members of Orders can't resign, they can only return their insignias, which they can have back at any time."
Nov Pete Best asks the Manhattan Supreme Court to assume jurisdiction over an $8-million defamation of character suit he has brought against the Beatles and **Playboy** magazine.
Dec [3] The group's final UK tour, a nine-date, twice-nightly package, with the Moody Blues, the Koobas and Beryl Marsden, opens at Glasgow's Odeon Cinema. The tour will finish on the 12th at the Capitol Cinema, Cardiff, Wales.
[13] The band scraps plans to make a third feature film, based on Richard Condon's book **A Talent For Loving**.
[16] "The Music Of Lennon-McCartney", a 50-minute tribute featuring Peter Sellers, Marianne Faithfull, Cilla Black, Peter & Gordon, Lulu, Billy J. Kramer, Esther Phillips and Richard Anthony, airs on ITV in London. (The rest of the UK will see the program the following night.) The Beatles perform *We Can Work It Out*, with Lennon playing the harmonium used by Ena Sharples at the Glad Tidings Mission in ITV soap "Coronation Street", which is brought in from an adjoining studio as they are unable to supply their own.
[18] *Day Tripper/We Can Work It Out* tops the UK chart, as the Beatles spend their third successive Christmas at #1.
[25] Although the band remains innovative with every release, ***Rubber Soul*** marks a distinct creative departure from the pure pop of previous albums and sees the onset of greater songwriting and instrument experimentation, which will develop, encouraged by the ever-present Martin, with each subsequent Beatles album. It tops the UK chart in its first week of release. (On December 18th, 1992, Canadian radio station CFRA will ban the 27-year old ***Rubber Soul*** album cut *Run For Your Life*, on the grounds that a particular lyric, "I'd rather see you dead little girl, than to be with another man", promotes violence against women.)
[26] McCartney, spending Christmas with his father in the Wirral, Cheshire, suffers a 5" cut to his mouth when he falls off a moped.

1966

Jan [3] The band records a spot for NBC-TV 's "Hullabaloo".
[8] *We Can Work It Out*, certified gold by the RIAA two days earlier, and ***Rubber Soul*** both top the US chart. Peter Sellers' comic version of *A Hard Day's Night*, featuring his impression of Sir Laurence Olivier reciting the song as Richard III, reaches UK #14.
[21] Harrison marries Patti Boyd, whom he met on the set of "A Hard Day's Night", at Esher Register Office, Surrey, with McCartney as best man.
[22] *Day Tripper* hits US #5.
[28] The Cavern club closes down, with debts of £10,000.
[29] The Overlanders' version of *Michelle* tops the UK chart, becoming Pye Records' fastest seller since Lonnie Donegan's *My Old Man's A Dustman*.
Mar [1] "The Beatles At Shea Stadium" receives its TV world premiere on BBC1.
[4] Lennon, interviewed by Maureen Cleave in London's **Evening Standard** newspaper, states "We're more popular than Jesus now." (The remark raises little interest in the UK, but has severe repercussions for the group when reprinted in the US before its summer tour.)
[19] Written by Lennon and McCartney with Starr, *What Goes On* makes US #81.
[26] *Nowhere Man* hits US #3 as Peter & Gordon's *Woman*, penned by McCartney under the pseudonym Bernard Webb, reaches UK #22.
Apr [1] *Nowhere Man* is certified gold by the RIAA.
May [1] The Beatles make their last UK concert performance at the annual "**New Musical Express** Poll Winners' Concert" at the Empire Pool, Wembley. Actor Clint Walker presents them with their award.
June [25] *Paperback Writer* tops the UK and US charts, as its promotional film is shown on the final broadcast of "Thank Your Lucky Stars".
[26] During a four-city tour of Germany, the group returns in triumph to Hamburg in an eight-car motorcade escorted by a dozen motorcycle police, playing to a sell-out crowd of more than 7,000 at the Ernst Merck Halle. (It is the band's first visit to the city since the final Star-Club date on December 31st, 1962.)
[30] They play the first of three concerts at the Nippon Budokan Hall, Tokyo, Japan.
July [4] The group performs two shows before a crowd of 80,000 at the Rizal Memorial football stadium, Manila, the Philippines.
[5] After an administrative mix-up which results in the Beatles failing to appear at a presidential reception at the Malacanang Palace with President Ferdinand Marcos and his wife, Imelda, the day before, the group flees an angry crowd at Manila Airport.
[8] ***Yesterday And Today*** is certified gold by the RIAA.
[9] *Rain* makes US #23.
[11] Lennon and McCartney win two more Ivor Novello awards: *We Can Work It Out* has the Highest Certified British Sales Of 1965, while *Yesterday* collects the Outstanding Song Of 1965 trophy at the 11th annual ceremony, held at the BBC Camden Theatre, London.
[14] *Paperback Writer* is certified gold by the RIAA.
[30] ***Yesterday ... And Today*** tops the US chart, but its notorious "butcher" cover (the band posing in white coats amongst bloody cuts of meat and dismembered dolls) is hastily withdrawn, becoming a collector's item.

[31] In an incident repeated in a number of US cities, and two days after US **Datebook** magazine has published Lennon's interview with Maureen Cleave, citizens of Birmingham, AL publicly, burn Beatles records and memorabilia.
Aug [8] The South African Broadcasting Corporation (SABC) bans all Beatles records in response to Lennon's remarks.
[11] The three US TV networks air the Beatles press conference held at the Astor Towers Hotel in Chicago, IL, shortly after the group's arrival for its US tour. Lennon publicly apologizes for his "Jesus" remarks.
[12] The band's fourth and final 14-city North American tour, with the Cyrkle, the Ronettes, the Remains and Bobby Hebb, begins at Chicago's International Amphitheater.
[13] The 14-track ***Revolver*** tops the UK chart. Its closing track *Tomorrow Never Knows* signals a further departure from the three-minute pop song formula, including the use of backward tapes and sitars.
[20] *Yellow Submarine*, featuring Starr on lead vocal, coupled with McCartney-led *Eleanor Rigby*, hits UK #1.
[22] New York police talk teenagers Carol Hopkins and Susan Richmond down from the 22nd floor ledge of the Americana Hotel, after they threaten to jump unless they can get to meet the Beatles. The girls are taken to Roosevelt Hospital for observation.
[29] The final Beatles concert takes place, at Candlestick Park, San Francisco. Their final number after nine years of gigging is Little Richard's *Long Tall Sally*. In the UK, BBC Radio Light Programme broadcasts "The Lennon And McCartney Songbook".
Sept [5] Lennon flies to Celle, Germany, to begin filming the role of Private Gripweed in "How I Won The War".
[10] 11-track version of ***Revolver*** tops the US chart.
[12] Still-climbing *Yellow Submarine* is certified gold by the RIAA.
[17] *Yellow Submarine* hits US #2, as McCartney-produced *Got To Get You Into My Life* hits UK #6 for Cliff Bennett & the Rebel Rousers.
[24] *Eleanor Rigby* reaches US #11.
Nov [9] Lennon meets Yoko Ono for the first time, at a private preview for the "Unfinished Paintings And Objects exhibition at the Indica Gallery in Mason's Yard, London.
[26] The group starts work on a new album at the Abbey Road Studios.
Dec [18] Hayley Mills/Hywel Bennett-starring film "The Family Way", for which McCartney has written the score, premieres in London.
[26] Lennon guests as a men's room attendant on Peter Cook and Dudley Moore's BBC-TV show "Not Only ... But Also".
[31] Harrison is refused admission to Annabel's nightclub in London for not wearing a tie, so he and his party, including wife Patti, Brian Epstein and Eric Clapton, see in the New Year at Joe Lyons' Corner House, Coventry Street, in the West End of London.

1967

Jan [7] Retrospective ***A Collection Of Beatles' Oldies (But Goldies)*** hits UK #7.
[27] The Beatles sign a nine-year contract with EMI Records.
Feb [9] Film clips for *Penny Lane* and *Strawberry Fields Forever* are shown on BBC1-TV's "Top Of The Pops".
[10] *A Day In The Life* is recorded for ***Sgt. Pepper's Lonely Hearts Club Band***. Unprecedented in the popular music era, the group uses 40 session musicians to create the track's orchestral sound.
Mar [2] *Michelle* wins Song Of The Year, *Eleanor Rigby* wins Best Contemporary (Rock'n'Roll) Solo Vocal Performance and ***Revolver*** wins Best Album Cover, Graphic Arts Of 1966 at the ninth annual Grammy Awards.
[11] *Penny Lane/Strawberry Fields Forever* hits UK #2. A run of 11 consecutive UK #1s is stopped by Engelbert Humperdinck's *Release Me*.
[18] *Penny Lane* tops the US chart for one week.
[20] *Penny Lane* is certified gold by the RIAA.
[23] *Michelle* wins the Most Performed Work Of 1966 category, while *Yellow Submarine* wins the Highest Certified British Sales for 1966 trophy at the 12th annual Ivor Novello Awards, held at the Playhouse Theatre, London.
[30] A photo session for ***Sgt. Pepper's Lonely Hearts Club Band***'s sleeve, a montage design created by pop artist Peter Blake, with Michael Cooper as photographer, takes place at Chelsea Manor Studios in Flood Street, London. EMI insists that permission must be granted for use of their photographs by the many famous people selected by the group as an imaginary audience and all those known to be alive are contacted. Mae West rejects the idea of being in a lonely hearts club but is won over by a personal request from the group. Some of Lennon's choice of audience-members (including Jesus Christ, Gandhi and Adolf Hitler) are removed from the final shot. Bob Dylan and Dion are the only two singers featured on the sleeve.
Apr [1] *Strawberry Fields Forever* hits US #8.
[5] McCartney joins Jane Asher in Denver, CO, for her 21st birthday.
May EMI announces that total Beatles record sales currently Top 200 million worldwide.
[18] Lennon and McCartney turn up for a Rolling Stones recording session at Olympic Studios in Barnes, London. They contribute backing vocals to *We Love You*.
[19] The Beatles enter into a business partnership as Beatles and Co. (The company will be renamed Apple Music Limited on November 17th, and then on January 12th, 1968, Apple Corps Limited.)
[20] The BBC announces a ban on ***Sgt. Pepper***'s closing cut *A Day In The Life*, citing that it may encourage drug-taking.
June [8] ***Sgt. Pepper's Lonely Hearts Club Band*** hits UK #1. The landmark project sets new standards in modern music, costing £25,000 to produce and involving 700 hours of studio time. It will be critically revered by some as the seminal album of the rock era and will be seen by others as the climax of the group's career. The sleeve is the first to print lyrics and the inner sleeve has a psychedelic design instead of being plain white. At the group's insistence the album is issued concurrently all over the world and is the first release in the US by Capitol to exactly match a Beatles UK disk.
[19] Having admitted in **Life** magazine that he has taken LSD, McCartney reiterates his claim during an ITV newscast and creates a media furore as intense as that experienced by Lennon the year before.
[25] The recording of the anthemic *All You Need Is Love* at Abbey Road Studios is transmitted worldwide as part of the first global TV link-up, "Our World", to an estimated audience of 400 million. The song features excerpts from the Brandenburg concertos, *La Marseillaise*, *Greensleeves* and *She Loves You*. Martin also uses a segment of Glenn Miller's *In The Mood*, thinking it is out of copyright. (He is later successfully sued for a royalty settlement by Miller's publishers.) In addition to 13 session musicians, friends on backing vocals are Mick Jagger, Keith Richard, Marianne Faithfull, Eric Clapton, Keith Moon, Jane Asher, McCartney's brother Mike McGear, the Walker Brothers' Gary Leeds and Graham Nash and Nash's wife Rose.
July [1] ***Sgt. Pepper's Lonely Hearts Club Band*** tops the US chart.
[22] *All You Need Is Love* hits UK #1.
[24] All four Beatles and Epstein sign a petition calling for the legalization of marijuana, which is published in **The Times** newspaper.
Aug [12] *Baby You're A Rich Man* reaches US #34.
[19] *All You Need Is Love* tops the US survey.
[25] The group attends a conference of the Spiritual Regeneration League at Normal College, Bangor, Wales, to study transcendental meditation with Indian guru Maharishi Mahesh Yogi.
[27] Epstein is found dead in bed at his London home of an apparent drug overdose after a long period of depression. The **New York Times** calls him "the man who revolutionized pop music in our time".
[31] The band announces that it will now manage its own affairs.
Sept [11] The shooting of a TV film "Magical Mystery Tour" begins in Teignmouth, Devon, the same day that *All You Need Is Love* is certified gold by the RIAA.
[27] The Beatles form Apple Publishing Limited.
Oct [7] New York concert promoter Sid Bernstein offers the group $1 million to perform live again. They reject his offer.
[18] The Beatles attend the world premiere of "How I Won The War" at the London Pavilion.
Nov [26] The promotional clip of *Hello Goodbye* airs on CBS-TV's "The Ed Sullivan Show", but is not shown on UK TV due to a Musicians' Union agreement banning miming.
[28] The group records its last fan club record *Christmas Time Is Here Again!*, with all four members taking part, at Abbey Road.
Dec [1] Starr flies to Rome to begin filming "Candy".
[7] The Apple Boutique opens at 94 Baker Street, London.
[9] *Hello Goodbye* begins a seven-week run at UK #1.
[11] Apple Music publishing company signs its first act, Grapefruit.
[15] *Hello Goodbye* is certified gold by the RIAA.
[23] *I Am The Walrus* makes US #56, with vocal contributions from the Mike Sammes Singers and a section from a BBC Radio production of "King Lear", broadcast at the time of recording.
[25] McCartney announces his engagement to Jane Asher.
[26] "Magical Mystery Tour" airs on BBC-TV and is castigated by critics who slur the film's lack of plot and direction. The **Daily Express** TV critic claims never to have seen "such blatant rubbish".
[30] *Hello Goodbye* tops the US chart, as the double EP *Magical Mystery Tour* hits UK #2.

1968

Jan [6] 11-track ***Magical Mystery Tour***, supplementing the six songs used in the film with *Hello Goodbye*, *Strawberry Fields Forever*, *Penny Lane*, *Baby You're A Rich Man* and *All You Need Is Love*, hits US #1.
[7] Harrison begins writing the score for the film "Wonderwall".
[20] ***Magical Mystery Tour*** import album makes UK #31.
[22] Established as a creative and business umbrella for the band's expanding music and merchandising interests, Apple Corps Ltd. opens its offices at 95, Wigmore Street, London, subsequently moving to 3, Savile Row, London. (Future Beatles records will be released on the Apple label.)
Feb [6] Starr guests on Cilla Black's BBC1-TV show "Cilla", for which McCartney has penned the theme tune *Step Inside Love*.
[15] The Harrisons and Lennons fly to India, to study meditation with the Maharishi in Rishikesh. (McCartney, Jane Asher and the Starrs join them four days later. Starr soon becomes bored however, returning to London on March 1st, comparing the retreat centre to a Butlin's holiday camp. The rest of the group departs after the Maharishi has purportedly made amorous advances to actress Mia Farrow, although it seems more likely that this is a mischievous rumor.)
[29] ***Sgt. Pepper*** wins the Album Of The Year, Best Contemporary Album, Best Engineered Recording and Best Album Cover, Graphic Arts categories at the tenth annual Grammy Awards.
Mar [23] Grapefruit's debut single *Dear Delilah* reaches UK #21.
[30] *Lady Madonna*, a rollicking Fats Domino pastiche, tops the UK chart, as *The Inner Light* makes US #96.
Apr [8] *Lady Madonna* is certified gold by the RIAA.
[20] *Lady Madonna* hits US #4.
May [4] Mary Hopkin wins her heat on the ITV talent show "Opportunity Knocks". McCartney sees the performance and makes her the first signing to the Apple label.

[15] Lennon and McCartney appear on NBC-TV's "The Tonight Show", with Joe Garagiola sitting in for Johnny Carson, at which they announce the establishment of Apple.
[17] "Wonderwall" premieres at the Cannes Film Festival, France.
[23] Apple Tailoring opens at 161 New Kings Road, London.
[30] Recording sessions begin for the group's next album.
June McCartney meets future wife Linda Eastman on a US business trip.
[18] The National Theatre's production of "In His Own Write" opens at London's Old Vic Theatre.
July [17] Animated feature "Yellow Submarine" premieres at the London Pavilion. The Beatles make a cameo appearance at the film's end, but do not supply their own voices for their characters.
[20] Appearing on BBC-TV's "Dee Time", Asher announces that her relationship with McCartney is over.
[31] The Apple Boutique in Baker Street closes down, with the remaining stock being given away.
Aug [22] Cynthia Lennon sues John for divorce, citing Yoko Ono (from whom he has become inseparable, adding to the increasingly divisive feelings within the group).
During the month, Starr quits during sessions for the band's new album, but returns a few days later. The incident goes unpublicized.
Sept [8] The band performs *Hey Jude* on ITV's "Frost On Sunday" show.
[13] Still-climbing *Hey Jude* is certified gold by the RIAA.
[14] *Hey Jude*, written by McCartney for Lennon's son Julian, tops the UK chart, becoming the longest-playing #1 ever, at seven minutes and ten seconds.
[21] *Revolution* makes US #12. Madame Tussaud's gives the Beatles' waxworks their fifth change of clothes and hair in four years.
[28] *Hey Jude* begins a nine-week stay at US #1.
[30] Hunter Davies' authorized biography **The Beatles** is published.
Oct [18] Lennon and Ono are taken to Paddington Green police station and charged with obstructing the police in the execution of a search warrant, when cannabis is discovered in the apartment where they are staying.
[19] Lennon and Ono are remanded on bail at Marylebone Magistrates Court and their case adjourned until November 28th.
Nov [8] Cynthia Lennon is granted a divorce because of Lennon's adultery with Yoko Ono.
[28] Lennon pleads guilty to cannabis possession and is fined £150.
Dec [7] A richly diverse and experimental double set, including the use of a full orchestra, ***The Beatles*** tops the UK chart. It is referred to as the ***White Album*** because of its Richard Hamilton-designed plain white sleeve (in marked contrast to the lavish artwork of ***Sgt. Pepper***). For the first time, the Beatles have worked separately on different tracks, as cracks begin to appear in the creative union.
[11] Lennon, Ono and Julian Lennon take part in the Rolling Stones' never-to-be shown TV extravaganza "Rock And Roll Circus".
[28] ***The Beatles*** tops the US chart (while McCartney's production, under the psuedonym Apollo C. Vermouth, of the Bonzo Dog Doo-Dah Band's *I'm The Urban Spaceman* hits UK #5).

1969

Jan [2] Shooting begins at Twickenham Film Studios of the group rehearsing for a back-to-the-roots album (which will evolve into the film and record project ***Let It Be***).
[10] Harrison walks out on the band, albeit temporarily.
[18] A planned Beatles concert at the Roundhouse in London does not materialize.
[30] The group, with Billy Preston guesting on organ, performs for 42 minutes on the roof of the Apple building in Savile Row, before police bring it to a halt, after Stephen King, chief accountant of the nearby Royal Bank of Scotland has rung the police to complain about the noise.
Feb [3] Allen Klein is appointed the Beatles' business manager.
[4] The Beatles appoint New York lawyers Eastman & Eastman as general counsel to Apple (one of the partners is Linda Eastman's father).
[8] ***Yellow Submarine***, a 13-track set principally comprising Martin's film score and containing only six Beatles cuts, hits UK #3. Its sleeve notes include only an extensive preview (by the **Observer**'s Tony Palmer) of ***The Beatles***, originally released a week after ***Yellow Submarine***.
Mar [1] ***Yellow Submarine*** hits US #2, behind the Supremes & the Temptations' ***TCB***.
[12] McCartney marries Linda Eastman at Marylebone Register Office, London.
[20] Lennon marries Yoko Ono in the British Consulate building in Gibraltar.
[25] Lennon and Ono participate in a seven-day "bed-in" promoting world peace, at Amsterdam's Hilton Hotel, ending March 31st.
[31] George and Patti Harrison are fined £250 for cannabis possession. (They had been arrested on McCartney's wedding day.)
Apr [22] Lennon changes his middle name by deed-poll from Winston to Ono in a ceremony on top of the Apple building. The Commissioner of Oaths is Senor Bueño de Mesquita.
[26] *Get Back* debuts at UK #1. As a featured artist, Billy Preston also becomes the only act to receive the label-credit "The Beatles with ...".
May [19] *Get Back* is certified gold by the RIAA.
[22] *Hey Jude* wins the A-Side Which Achieved The Highest Certified British Sales, 1968 category at the 14th annual Ivor Novello Awards, held at London's Royal Gardens Hotel, Kensington.
[24] *Get Back* tops the US chart, as *Don't Let Me Down* makes US #35.
[26] John and Yoko begin another "bed-in", in Room 1742 of Hotel La Reine Queen, Montreal, PQ, Canada, until June 2nd.
June [14] *The Ballad Of John And Yoko*, with only Lennon and McCartney playing on the track, tops the UK chart. It is the first stereo single release by the group and its last UK #1 single.
[16] *The Ballad Of John And Yoko* is certified gold by the RIAA.
July [1] The Lennons are taken to Lawson Memorial Hospital after a car crash in Golspie, Scotland. John receives 17 stitches for a facial wound, Yoko 14 stitches and her daughter Kyoko 4, while Julian suffers from shock.
[12] *The Ballad Of John & Yoko* hits US #8, plagued by radio censorship problems through its use of the word "Christ".
Aug [8] The photo of the group on the zebra crossing outside Abbey Road studios is taken at 10:00 a.m., for use on the sleeve of forthcoming ***Abbey Road***. A policeman holds up traffic as the picture is taken.
[20] The Beatles (with Lennon) are together for the last time in a recording studio, as they complete *I Want You (She's So Heavy)* for ***Abbey Road***.
Sept [20] Klein negotiates a new deal with EMI/Capitol for an increased royalty rate.
[23] Illinois University newspaper **Northern Star** prints a story, headlined "Clues Hint At Beatle Death", which speculates that McCartney has been killed in a car crash in Scotland on November 9th, 1966 (despite the fact that he and then-girlfriend Jane Asher were vacationing in Kenya at the time) and has been replaced by former Beatle-look-a-like competition winner William Campbell, having undergone plastic surgery. (The rumor will mushroom when Detroit radio station WKNR DJ Russ Gibbs breaks the story on air, which will lead to major print articles, which further fuel the story. **Sunday People** journalist Hugh Farmer tracks McCartney down to his farm in Campbeltown, Scotland, and is greeted with the comment, "Do I look dead? I'm as fit as a fiddle.")
Oct [4] ***Abbey Road*** begins an 11-week run at UK #1.
[27] *Something* is certified gold by the RIAA.
Nov [1] ***Abbey Road*** also tops the US survey, where it too will remain for 11 weeks.
[29] Originally charting separately, *Come Together/ Something* tops the US chart.
Dec [6] *Something/Come Together* hits UK #4. It is the first Beatles disk not to make either UK #1 or #2 since *Love Me Do* in 1962. *Something* is also the first Beatles single not penned by Lennon/McCartney, but by Harrison. Frank Sinatra calls it the greatest love song of the last 50 years.
For the first time a Beatles song is licensed for use on a non-Beatles album: *Across The Universe* features on World Wildlife Fund charity album ***No One's Gonna Change Our World***. The falsetto harmonies are performed by teenage Beatles fans Lizzie Bravo and Gayleen Pease, selected from fans waiting for the group outside Abbey Road Studios. **Beatles Monthly** ceases publication after 77 issues, as the Beatles rapidly begin to lose their collective identity and refuse to co-operate for promotion.

1970

Jan [16] The police shut down an exhibition of Lennon's erotic lithographs at a London gallery, for alleged obscenity.
Mar [11] ***Abbey Road*** wins Best Engineered Recording Of 1969 at the 12th annual Grammy Awards.
[17] *Let It Be* is certified gold by the RIAA.
[21] McCartney-led ballad *Let It Be* hits UK #2, held off the top by *Wand'rin' Star*, Lee Marvin's smash from "Paint Your Wagon".
[23] Legendary record producer Phil Spector is called in to remix ***Let It Be*** because the sound is considered too raw for commercial release. (Spector has long wanted to work with the group and, left alone with the master tapes, proceeds to impose his style on the album. He particularly upsets McCartney by adding strings and choir to *The Long And Winding Road.* What began as a back-to-the-roots project finishes as one of their most lavishly-produced sets, involving many hours of mixing.)
[28] Compilation ***Hey Jude*** hits US #2, where it will stay for four weeks, behind Simon & Garfunkel's ***Bridge Over Troubled Water***.
Apr [1] The last session for a Beatles album takes place, with only Starr in attendance. He records drums on three tracks for the forthcoming Spector-helmed ***Let It Be***.
[9] With a rift growing, both financially and artistically, between McCartney and the rest of the group, he quits the Beatles, releasing his debut solo ***McCartney*** almost simultaneously with the group's ***Let It Be***. With Lennon enjoying hits with the Plastic Ono Band, and Starr about to release his debut solo ***Sentimental Journey***, the Beatles are no more. The decision is unanimous amongst the four, but when the story breaks the following day, McCartney is blamed by the press as the "man who broke up the Beatles".
[11] *Let It Be* tops the US chart, having debuted at #6, the highest position ever for any single in its first week of release (*Hey Jude* and *Get Back* are the second and third highest respectively).
May [13] "Let It Be" premieres in New York.
[20] "Let It Be" opens simultaneously at the London Pavilion and Liverpool Gaumont, without any of the group attending. It documents the making of the album and hints at the growing dischord felt by the Beatles during its recording.
[23] ***Let It Be***, released with a picture book in a cardboard box, tops the UK chart. **New Musical Express** calls it a "cardboard tombstone" and a "sad and tatty end to a musical fusion".
[26] ***Let It Be*** is certified gold by the RIAA.
June [13] *The Long And Winding Road/For You Blue* tops US chart. ***Let It Be*** also tops the US chart, as ***The Beatles Featuring Tony Sheridan - In The Beginning (Circa) 1960***, a compilation of early Polydor material recorded in Germany, makes US #117.
Dec [31] McCartney files suit, assigned case number 1970 No. 6315, against the rest of the group, to

dissolve the Beatles & Co. partnership and seeks the appointment of a receiver to handle the group's affairs in the High Court of Justice, Chancery Division, Group B. He also ends links with Allen Klein, who now handles the affairs of the other three.

1971

Jan [16] ***A Hard Day's Night*** re-charts, at UK #30.
[19] The case to dissolve the Beatles' partnership begins in London's High Court. Under oath, Starr says "Paul behaved like a spoilt child."
Mar [3] The South African Broadcasting Corporation lifts its ban on Beatles' music.
[12] A High Court judge declares in McCartney's favor.
Apr [15] ***Let It Be*** wins an Oscar for Best Film Music (Original Song Score) at the 44th annual Academy Awards.
July [24] Having re-entered the chart, ***Help!*** peaks at UK #33.
Aug [3] McCartney announces the formation of his new group, Wings.

1972

Feb [8] The Beatles Fan Club shop is liquidated.
Mar [14] The group is honored at the 14th annual Grammy Awards, receiving the NARAS' Trustees Award "for their outstanding talent, originality and music creativity that have done so much to express the mood and tempo of our times and to bridge the culture gap between several generations".
[31] The Official Beatles Fan Club closes down.
May [21] BBC's Radio 1 begins airing "The Beatles Story".

1973

May [12] Simultaneously released retrospective double albums ***The Beatles 1967-1970*** and ***The Beatles 1962-1966*** hit UK #2 and #3 respectively.
[19] ***The Beatles 1962-1966*** hits US #3.
[26] ***The Beatles 1967-1970*** tops the US chart, a record 15th US chart-topping album for the group.

1974

Jan [8] ***The Early Beatles*** is certified gold by the RIAA.
July [26-28] The Strawberry Fields Forever Fan Club holds the first Beatle Convention, in Boston, MA.
Aug [14] Willy Russell's play "John, Paul, George, Ringo & Bert", with the group's songs interpreted by singer Barbara Dickson, opens at Liverpool's Royal Court Theatre.

1975

Jan [9] The Beatles & Co. partnership is dissolved at a private hearing in the London High Court.

1976

Jan [26] The group's nine-year contract with EMI expires. Shortly thereafter, US promoter Bill Sargent offers the group $30 million to reunite for one concert. They refuse.
Apr [3] *Yesterday*, released as a single in the UK for the first time, hits #8, having been a US success 11 years earlier. The entire back catalog of Beatles singles is re-promoted: *Hey Jude* makes UK #12, *Paperback Writer* reaches UK #23, *Penny Lane/Strawberry Fields Forever* makes UK #32, *Get Back* reaches UK #28 and *Help!* peaks at UK #37. As nostalgia increases, **Beatles Monthly** begins a reissue series from magazine #1.
June [14] Still-climbing ***Rock'n'Roll Music*** is certified platinum by the RIAA.
July [3] ***Rock'n'Roll Music*** reaches UK #11.
[10] ***Rock'n'Roll Music*** hits US #2.
[24] *Back In The USSR* reaches UK #19, while *Got To Get You Into My Life* hits US #7.
Aug [21] ***The Beatles Tapes*** reaches UK #45.
Sept [20] Sid Bernstein, the promoter of the Beatles' New York concerts from 1964 to 1966, takes out full-page advertisements asking the group to reunite for a charity concert.
Nov [20] With Harrison guesting on NBC-TV's "Saturday Night Live", producer Lorne Michaels offers the Beatles the union minimum payment to reunite on the show. Ironically, McCartney is staying with Lennon in New York, and both see the show.
Dec [11] *Ob-La-Di, Ob-La-Da* makes US #49.
[18-19] Europe's first "Christmas Beatles Convention", held at Alexandra Palace in North London, is a commercial disaster.

1977

Jan [10] All outstanding litigation between the Beatles, Apple, Klein and his company ABKCO is settled.
May [26] "Beatlemania", a musical tribute, opens at the Winter Garden Theater, New York.
June [11] ***The Beatles At The Hollywood Bowl***, created by joining together performances at the Hollywood Bowl from August 23rd, 1964, and August 30th, 1965, hits US #2.
[18] ***The Beatles At The Hollywood Bowl*** tops the UK chart. It is a record-breaking 12th UK chart-topping album for the band.
July [30] ***The Beatles Live! At The Star-Club In Hamburg, Germany: 1962*** reaches US #111.
Aug [12] ***The Beatles At The Hollywood Bowl*** is certified platinum by the RIAA.
Oct [18] To celebrate the Queen's silver jubilee, the BPI holds a ceremony at Wembley Conference Centre, Wembley, honoring the best in British music since 1952, at which the Beatles win the Best British Pop Album, 1952-1977 category for ***Sgt. Pepper's Lonely Hearts Club Band***, and Best British Pop Group, 1952-1977 category.
[24] ***Love Songs*** is certified gold by the RIAA.
Dec [10] Double-retrospective ***Love Songs*** reaches US #24 and will hit UK #7 on Jan [28].

1978

Mar [27] "All You Need Is Cash", an affectionate parody of the group's career (featuring the Rutles), premieres on BBC-TV.
Sept [30] *Sgt. Pepper's Lonely Hearts Club Band/With A Little Help From My Friends* peaks at US #71, as Robert Stigwood's film fantasy of the album, starring the Bee Gees, Peter Frampton and others, opens in cinemas (its soundtrack album of cover versions hit US #5 in July).
Oct [21] *Sgt. Pepper's Lonely Hearts Club Band/With A Little Help From My Friends* peaks at UK #63.

1979

May [19] McCartney, Harrison and Starr reunite at a party to celebrate the wedding of Eric Clapton and Harrison's ex-wife, Patti.
Sept [21] United Nations secretary general Kurt Waldheim asks the group to reunite to aid the Vietnamese boat people.
Oct [18] "Beatlemania" opens at the Astoria Theatre, London.
Nov [3] ***Rarities*** makes UK #71.

1980

May [31] ***Rarities***, a different collection from the UK album, reaches US #21.
Dec [8] Lennon, returning from a recording session at the Record Plant, is gunned down by Mark David Chapman in the courtyard of the Dakota building in New York, Lennon's home for the past decade, between 10:45 p.m. and 11:00 p.m. He dies from loss of blood at 11:30 p.m. at the Roosevelt Hospital.

1981

Sept [12] ***Beatles Ballads*** makes UK #17.

1982

May [8] *The Beatles' Movie Medley* reaches US #12, while a more complete film music collection, ***Reel Music***, makes US #19.
[26] ***Reel Music*** is certified gold by the RIAA.
July [3] *The Beatles' Movie Medley* hits UK #10.
Sept [10] The Beatles' Decca audition is released as ***The Complete Silver Beatles***.
Oct [30] *Love Me Do* hits UK #4 on the 20th anniversary of its original release. All their singles will be subsequently re-released on their matching dates, the majority receiving respectable chart placings.
Nov [6] Continuing to repackage past hits, ***20 Greatest Hits*** hits UK #10 and US #50.

1983

Jan [29] *Please Please Me* reaches UK #29.
Feb [8] The Beatles are honored for their Outstanding Contribution To British Music at the second annual BRIT Awards, at London's Grosvenor House Hotel.
Apr [30] *From Me To You* reaches UK #40.
Sept [10] *She Loves You* makes UK #45.
Nov [26] *I Want To Hold Your Hand* peaks at UK #62.

1984

Mar [31] *Can't Buy Me Love* reaches at UK #53.
Apr [9] The Beatle City Exhibition Centre opens in Liverpool.
July [28] *A Hard Day's Night* peaks at UK #52.
Sept [18] The Beatles share the Video Vanguard category (with David Bowie) at the inaugural MTV Video Music Awards, held at Radio City Music Hall, New York, hosted by Dan Aykroyd and Bette Midler.
Oct [4] ***20 Greatest Hits*** is certified gold by the RIAA.
Dec [8] *I Feel Fine* makes UK #65.

1985

Apr [20] *Ticket To Ride* peaks at UK #70.
Aug [10] Much to McCartney's displeasure, Michael Jackson pays $47.5 million for ATV Music and with it the entire Lennon/McCartney catalog.

1986

Mar [13] "The Beatles Live : Ready Steady Go!" video is certified platinum by the RIAA.
Aug [30] *Yellow Submarine/Eleanor Rigby* peaks at UK #63.
Sept [27] *Twist And Shout*, through its exposure in the films "Ferris Bueller's Day Off" and "Back To School", reaches US #23.
Oct [11] ***The Early Beatles***, originally charting in 1965, makes US #197.

1987

Feb [28] *Penny Lane/Strawberry Fields Forever* bows at its UK #65 peak.
Mar [7] On the same day that Lennon and McCartney become the first non-American composers inducted into the Songwriters Hall of Fame at the 18th annual ceremony, held at the Plaza Hotel, New York, the group's back catalog is systematically (and chronologically) released on CD; the Beatles' timeless popularity is underlined as they grace the charts once more: ***Please Please Me*** (UK #32), ***With The Beatles*** (UK #40), ***A Hard Day's Night*** (UK #30) and ***Beatles For Sale*** (UK #45).
May [9] The second batch of Beatles albums released on CD chart: ***Help!*** (UK #61), ***Rubber Soul*** (UK #60) and ***Revolver*** (UK #55).
June [1] ITV airs "It Was Twenty Years Ago Today", a documentary of the making of ***Sgt. Pepper*** and its cultural significance at the time.
[13] ***Sgt. Pepper's Lonely Hearts Club Band*** hits UK #3 on a wave of media nostalgia for the 20th anniversary of the album, still widely regarded as the most important record of the rock era.
July [25] *All You Need Is Love* makes UK #47.
Sept [5] ***The Beatles*** reaches UK #18, while ***Yellow Submarine*** makes UK #60.
Oct [3] ***Magical Mystery Tour*** makes UK #52.
[31] ***Abbey Road*** reaches UK #30 and ***Let It Be*** makes UK #50.
Dec [5] *Hello Goodbye* peaks at UK #63.

1988

Jan [20] The Beatles are inducted into the Rock and Roll Hall of Fame at the third annual dinner, at the Waldorf

Astoria Hotel, New York. McCartney fails to show, still citing business differences with Harrison and Starr.
Mar [19] ***Past Masters Volume One*** and ***Past Masters Volume Two*** make UK #49 and UK #46 respectively. Unlike other recent archive releases, the two-volume CD/Cassette set usefully collects all Beatles recordings which were originally made available commercially in the '60s but did not appear on the group's regular UK album releases.
[26] Extracted from ***Volume Two***, *Lady Madonna* peaks at UK #67.
Apr [9] ***Past Masters - Volume One*** makes US #149.
[16] ***Past Masters - Volume Two*** makes US #121.
May [17] A New York appellate court reinstates punitive damages and claims of fraud and theft against Capitol Records in a nine-year-old $80 million breach of contract suit brought by Harrison, Starr, Ono and Apple Records. A $40 million suit (filed in August 1987), which claims Capitol has deliberately stalled the release of Beatles CDs, is dismissed in Manhattan District Court.
July [22] Worldwide release of ***The Beatles Decca Sessions*** is prevented by lawyers acting on behalf of the remaining members of the group and Yoko Ono.
Sept [10] *Hey Jude* peaks at UK #52.
[23] Acknowledged Beatles authority Mark Lewisohn's book **The Complete Beatles Recording Sessions**, a day-by-day detailed account of the group's studio activity, is published in the UK. It is a companion study to his exhaustive **The Beatles Live**, detailing every live performance by the group, first published in 1986.
Oct [1] BBC Radio 1 airs the first program in a 14-part series called "The Beeb's Lost Beatles Tapes". (It will win the Sony National Radio Award for 1988 as the Best Rock & Pop program on British radio.)
[26] Apple releases "Magical Mystery Tour" on video in the US.

1989

Apr [22] *Get Back* peaks at UK #74.
June [24] Rosanne Cash's version of *I Don't Want To Spoil The Party* (B-side of the Beatles' 1965 *Eight Days A Week*) becomes the first Lennon/McCartney composition to top the US Country chart.
[30] McCartney, Harrison, Starr and Yoko Ono seek injunctions against EMI and Dave Clark, banning the sale of videos of "Ready Steady Go!" featuring the Beatles. The case is settled out of court.
Nov [8] After 116 days in the High Court, ten in the Appeal Court and one at the European Commission (at an estimated total cost of £7 million), all outstanding lawsuits between the Beatles, Apple and EMI/Capitol are said to be resolved.

1990

Apr [12] Asteroids 4147-4150, discovered in 1983 and 1984 by Brian A. Skiff and Dr. Edward Bowell, of the Lowell Observatory in Flagstaff, AZ, are now named Lennon, McCartney, Harrison and Starr, announced by the International Astronomical Union's minor planet centre in Cambridge, MA.
Sept *Michelle* and *Something* are both honored by BMI (who have published a list of the Most Performed Songs 1940-1990) for logging more than four million broadcast performances each, while *Yesterday* has received over five million.

1991

Nov [13] An 83-minute archive video rockumentary, "The Beatles: The First U.S. Visit" (MPI), including their historic "Ed Sullivan Show" appearance, hits US stores.
[29] The wake-up call from Mission Control at the Kennedy Space Center to the crew aboard the latest space shuttle flight is the Beatles' *Twist And Shout*.
Dec [2] At the annual UK BMI Awards at the Dorchester Hotel, London, *Hello Goodbye*, *Love Me Do* and *She Loves You* become the latest Lennon/McCartney compositions to receive awards for accumulating one million broadcast performances each.
[26] Another slew of awards are bestowed upon the group, as the latest sales certifications by the RIAA in the US confirm the following multiplatinum Beatles albums: ***Abbey Road*** (nine million, making it the biggest-selling album released before 1971), ***The Beatles*** (seven million), ***1962-1967*** (five million), ***1967-1970*** (five million), ***Magical Mystery Tour*** (five million), ***Meet The Beatles*** (five million), ***Rubber Soul*** (four million), ***Hey Jude*** (three million), ***Revolver*** (three million), ***Beatles '65*** (two million), ***20 Greatest Hits*** (one million), ***Yellow Submarine*** (one million) and ***Something New*** (one million).

1992

Feb [6] The RIAA certifies sales of eight million for ***Sgt. Pepper's Lonely Hearts Club Band***.
July [27] Celebrating its 25th anniversary as a rock music milestone and tied in with a UK TV documentary, ***Sgt. Pepper's Lonely Hearts Club Band*** hits UK #6.
Oct [17] The 30th anniversary reissue of *Love Me Do* charts for a week at UK #53.
Nov US multi-media company Voyager releases an interactive version of ***A Hard Day's Night*** on CD-ROM for $29.95.

1993

Oct [2] With legal differences resolved, ***The Beatles 1962-1966*** and ***The Beatles 1967-1970***, released worldwide for the first time on CD, debut at their respective UK #3 and #4 peaks.

1994

Feb [13] **The Mail On Sunday** reports that the Beatles will reform for a concert in New York's Central Park, joined by Julian and Sean Lennon, with each Beatle earning $30 million for the one-off gig. McCartney's personal assistant, Jeff Baker, states that the report is an "out and out lie put around by optimistic promoters".
Sept [15] EMI Records pays £78,500 for Lot 804 at a Sotheby's auction - a reel to reel tape owned by 53-year-old retired policeman Bob Molyneux of the July 6th 1957 Quarrymen gig featuring *Puttin' On The Style* and *Baby Let's Play House*.
Dec [10] ***The Beatles Live At The BBC***, collecting 56 songs that the group performed on the British radio station between 1962-65, enters the UK chart at #1.
[24] ***The Beatles Live At The BBC*** debuts at its US #3 peak.

1995

Jan [28] Paul and Linda McCartney and Ono, joined by their children, record Yoko's *Hiroshima Sky Is Always Blue* at McCartney's Mill Studio in Sussex.
Feb [3] ***Live At The BBC*** is certified multi-platinum, for sales of four million, by the RIAA.
Mar [1] ***Abbey Road*** is inducted into NARAS' 22nd annual Hall of Fame at the 37th Grammy Awards.
Apr [1] *Baby It's You*, from ***The Beatles Live At The BBC***, backed with previously unreleased live versions of *Devil In Her Heart*, *Boys* and *I'll Follow The Sun*, debuts at its UK #7 peak.
[22] *Baby It's You* debuts at its US #67 peak, as ***Come Together : America Salutes The Beatles***, a various artists country album with cover art by Lennon, makes US #90 in its week of entry.
[23] The **Sunday Times** reports that Peter Hodgson has found a 1959 tape of the group while clearing out his attic, with 16 songs by the Quarrymen on a tape recorder lent by his grandfather to McCartney.
Nov [19, 22-23] "The Beatles Anthology" airs on ABC-TV. Including extensive new interviews with the remaining trio, edited in with old Lennon interviews, it attempts to build a definitive archival documentary of the Beatles' early years, with personal anecdotes, remembrances and observations, and ends at the conclusion of the first program, with the television premiere of the Beatles first "new" recording since their split: *Free As A Bird* has been assembled around a previously unissued Lennon demo which Ono has passed to McCartney (along with another track, *Real Love*), and to which the remaining members have added a relevant rhythm section and harmony vocal parts, under the guidance of co-producer Jeff Lynne. The TV series, broadcast in six one-hour programs in the UK, is the first salvo in an historic period of renewed Beatles activity which will see the staggered release of three double-CD anthologies which have been diligently researched and assembled by the three remaining Beatles with producer George Martin. Released as a chronological series, each one will include previously unreleased material, out-takes, alternate takes, rehearsals, rare B-sides, studio banter and past hits.
[20] A DJ at a post-Australian Grand Prix party at the Hilton Hotel in Adelaide, Australia becomes the first person to publicly broadcast the new Beatles single *Free As A Bird* at 3:00 p.m. local time. (Harrison attending the party has a copy with him and gives it to the DJ.)
Dec [2] 60 track ***Anthology Volume 1***, encompassing the group's 1958 recordings at the Phillips Sound Recording Service in Liverpool through to 1964, hits UK #2, behind Robson Green & Jerome Flynn's ***Robson And Jerome***.
[9] Having sold 855,000 copies in its week of release, ***Anthology Volume 1*** debuts at US #1, becoming the group's 16th #1 US album, extending its lead over Elvis Presley and the Rolling Stones, who have nine each. (The album also sets a new chart longevity record, the longest span - 31 years and 10 months, between an act's first and last #1 albums.)
[16] Assembled at Mill Studio, the Beatles' first new single *Free As A Bird*, backed with *Christmas Time (Is Here Again)* originally released to fan club members only and alternate takes of *I Saw Her Standing There* and *This Boy*, debuts at its UK #2 peak, behind Michael Jackson's *Earth Song*.

1996

Jan [6] *Free As A Bird* hits US #6 in its week of entry.
[25] The Beatles are named Least Welcome Comeback in **Rolling Stone** magazine's Critics Poll.
Mar [4] The remaining Beatles issue a statement confirming that it has turned down an offer from US and European tour promoters of $225 million for a world tour (which will reportedly be upped to $500 million in a month's time). McCartney says: "The three of us isn't as exciting as the four of us."
[16] A second new single, *Real Love*, originally featured on Lennon's ***Imagine*** soundtrack, backed with a live cut of *Baby's In Black*, a mix of *Yellow Submarine* and an alternate take of *Here, There And Everywhere*, enters the UK chart at its UK #4 high. Despite its chart success, BBC 1FM refuses to add the song to its airplay roster with station controller Matthew Bannister, perhaps oblivious to the group's long association with the broadcasting unit, deeming it "unsuitable for our playlists".
[23] *Real Love* debuts at its US #11 peak.
Apr [6] 45-track ***Anthology Volume 2***, covering the period 1965 to 1968, hits US #1 having also entered in pole position in the UK the week before.
see also: **George HARRISON, John LENNON, Paul McCARTNEY, Ringo STARR**

BEAUTIFUL SOUTH

Paul Heaton (vocals, guitar); **Dave Hemingway** (vocals); **David Rotheray** (guitar); **Briana Corrigan** (vocals); **Sean Welch** (bass); **David Stead** (drums)

1989

June Former Housemartin and committed Northerner, Heaton (b. May 9, 1962, Birkenhead, Lancs.) has formed his new outfit in the spring, sarcastically naming it the Beautiful South, with co-writer and singer Rotheray (Feb. 9 1961, Hull, Humberside), fellow ex-Housemartin Hemingway (b. Sept. 20, 1960, Hull), bassist Welch (Apr. 12, 1960, Enfield, Middx.), female vocalist Corrigan (b. Antrim, Northern Ireland), ex-Anthill Runaways, and drummer, former Housemartin roadie, David Stead (b. Oct. 15, 1962, Huddersfield). Still signed (as were the Housemartins)

to Go! Discs, the group's debut single, the ballad *Song For Whoever*, now hits UK #2, while the band finishes recording its debut album in Milan, Italy.
Nov [4] Largely written by Heaton and Rotheray, ***Welcome To The Beautiful South*** hits UK #2, behind Erasure's ***Wild!*** Its initial album cover, featuring a suicidal girl with the barrel of a gun in her mouth, is replaced by the more consumer-friendly cuddly teddy bear photo set.
Dec [30] Ballad *I'll Sail This Ship Alone* reaches UK #31.

1990

Oct [27] Heaton/Rotheray-penned marital-angst ballad featuring traded vocals by Heaton and Corrigan, *A Little Time* hits UK #1 for a week, aided by a popular domestic scene mini-drama video.
Nov [3] ***Rubáiyát***, Elektra's 40th anniversary compilation, to which the group has contributed its cover of *Love Wars*, makes US #140.
[10] Following experimental dates in the US, where their brand of dour, barbed lyricism and off-beat, UK council-house, leatherette-sofa humor (released on Elektra Records) is largely lost in translation, the second Beautiful South album ***Choke*** immediately hits UK #2, behind the compilation ***Missing You - An Album Of Love***.
[15] An eight-date UK tour begins at the City Hall, Newcastle, Tyne & Wear, set to end on the 25th at the Warrington Parr Hotel, Warrington, Cheshire, and highlighted by a home-town performance at the Hull City Hall on the 17th.

1991

Feb [10] "A Little Time" wins Best Music Video at the 10th annual BRIT Awards, at London's Dominion Theatre. In typical fashion, Heaton's full acceptance speech is "Nice one".
Mar [23] *Let Love Speak Up Itself* peaks at UK #51.
May [15] The group embarks on a four-date UK tour at the De Montfort Hall, Leicester, Leics., set to end on the 19th at the Ulster Hall, Belfast, N. Ireland.
Aug Beautiful South pulls out of the "Cities In The Park" concert in Heaton, Gtr. Manchester.

1992

Jan [18] *Old Red Eyes Is Back* reaches UK #22.
Mar [14] *We Are Each Other* debuts at its UK #30 peak.
Apr [1] Now an 11-piece outfit, including three horn players, the band performs before a sellout crowd at the Troubadour, Los Angeles, CA, during a US club tour. Their typically acerbic set features a cover of the Bee Gees' *You Should Be Dancing*.
[11] The group's third album ***0898***, produced by John Kelly, debuts at its UK #4 peak.
[20] The band begins a nine-date UK tour at the Leisure Centre, Gateshead, Tyne & Wear, set to end on the 30th at London's Brixton Academy.
June [20] *Bell Bottomed Tear* reaches UK #16, as the group performs at the Variety Arts Center in Los Angeles, during a current North American tour.
July Heaton flies back from Japan to appear at Hull Magistrates Court, claiming he is too poor to pay his Poll Tax. He owes over £900 in arrears, but claims he earns £130 a week while the rest of his earnings go into a central account.
Oct [3] *36D* peaks at UK #46.
Nov [17] They wrap up a three-date visit to Germany at the Biskuithalle, Bonn.
[24] Beautiful South plays at the Wembley Arena, Wembley, Middx., as part of a three-date mini-tour which takes in the National Exhibition Centre, Birmingham, W. Midlands and the Sheffield Arena, Sheffield, S. Yorks.

1994

Jan Following an acrimonious split between Heaton and Corrigan, Jacqueline Abbott joins the group on vocals.
Mar [12] *Good As Gold* debuts at its UK #23 peak.
Apr [9] 12-track ***Miaow***, cynically biting as ever, bows at its UK #6 peak.
June [11] Their cover version of Harry Nilsson's 1969 UK #23/US #6 hit, *Everybody's Talkin'* reaches UK #12.
July [14-17] The group takes part in the "Phoenix Festival" at Long Marston, Stratford-upon-Avon.
Sept [3] *Prettiest Eyes* debuts at its UK #37 peak.
Nov [12] *One Last Love Song* debuts at its UK #14 peak.
Dec [3] ***Carry On Up The Charts - The Best Of Beautiful South*** tops the UK chart aided by a limited edition extra CD which comprises rare material and previously unreleased cuts. An enduring chart fixture, it will go on to sell over one million copies in the UK.
[13] The group begins a six-date UK tour at Brixton Academy, set to end on its own turf at the Humberside Ice Arena, Hull on the 20th.

1995

Apr [1] The band appears on BBC2-TV's "Later With Jools Holland".
June [10] The Beatiful South participates in the "Fleadh Festival" in Finsbury Park, London.
Aug [6] They perform at the "T In The Park Festival" at Strathclyde Country Park, Glasgow, Scotland.
Nov [18] *Pretenders To The Throne* debuts at its UK #18 peak, as the group's cover of the Mama Cass hit *Dream A Little Dream Of Me* is featured in the movie "French Kiss".
[20] A seven-date Carry On Around The Country UK tour opens at Cardiff Arena, set to end on the 28th at the G-Mex Centre, Manchester, Gtr. Manchester.
see also: **HOUSEMARTINS**

JEFF BECK

1967

Feb Ex-Wimbledon Art College student Beck (b. June 24, 1944, Wallington, Surrey), already a guitar veteran of early '60s bands Screaming Lord Sutch and the Nightshifts, has quit the Tridents, with whom he played since February 1964, in March the following year, to replace Eric Clapton in the Yardbirds, at the suggestion of future band member Jimmy Page. Having left the seminal rock outfit in November 1966 with a reputation, particularly in the US, as a guitar player of considerable talent, Beck has signed a solo recording deal with EMI's Columbia label in December and now recruits three musicians, ex-Steampacket and Shotgun Express vocalist Rod Stewart, Ron Wood (currently a bass player) and drummer Aynsley Dunbar. Initially backing him on early solo sessions, the trio will become the first incarnation of the Jeff Beck Group.
Mar [3] Together with his sidesmen, Beck is on the support bill for a 32-date Roy Orbison, Small Faces and Paul & Barry Ryan UK package tour, which opens at the Finsbury Park Astoria, London. Set to end on April 9th and having received poor notices, Beck is not asked to complete the tour.
[23] His debut release *Hi-Ho Silver Lining*, written by Scott English, produced by Mickie Most and featuring Beck on both lead guitar and lead vocals, a role he will rarely undertake again, enters the UK chart as a solo recording. Set to reach #14, it will prove unrepresentative of all future work, but will endure as a novelty pop hit and party favorite.
June Billed as a blues/rock outfit, the Jeff Beck Group makes its US debut, at the Fillmore East, New York, NY, to more positive reviews (including **New York Times**' critic Robert Shelton's description of Beck's guitar dexterity as "wild and visionary") than those it recently received in the UK.
Aug [7] His solo follow-up *Tallyman*, written by Graham Gouldman (later of 10cc), reaches UK #30. During its recording, producer Most insists that Beck again performs the lead vocal in preference to Stewart.
[13] The Jeff Beck Group performs at the seventh "National Jazz & Blues Festival", at the Royal Windsor Racecourse, Windsor, Berks.
Sept With Dunbar having left to form his own band, replaced in quick succession by Ray Cook (ex-Tridents) and Mickey Waller, the Group is now augmented by keyboardist Nicky Hopkins and undertakes further US dates.

1968

Mar [23] Third single *Love Is Blue*, an instrumental version of a tune from the "Eurovision Song Contest", and recorded at Most's behest, reaches UK #23.
Aug The Jeff Beck Group releases its debut album ***Truth***, which will climb to #15 in the US, where touring is now concentrated, but fails to chart in the UK. Produced by Most, it has been recorded, mixed and distributed to retail in under two months. (In including one of its tracks, *I Ain't Superstitious*, on his 1993 solo album, ***Lead Vocalist***, Stewart will later recollect: "We didn't know at the time how important this album would become, creating a little bit of rock'n'roll history, influencing musicians and singers. Truly great stuff.") During he month, the band returns to the UK to perform at the eighth "National Jazz & Blues Festival".
Oct [11] A US tour opens in Chicago, IL, notable both for dazzling blues rock performances and bawdy off-stage antics.
Dec [5-8] The group plays at San Francisco's Fillmore West, sharing the bill with Spirit.

1969

July [3] Jeff Beck Group, with Tony Newman having replaced Waller, performs at the Fillmore East, supporting Jethro Tull, before taking part in the annual Jazz Festival in Newport, RI. Seemingly unable to stick to touring commitments, Beck will cancel a scheduled performance at the forthcoming Woodstock Festival in August. (Hopkins will later recall: "Every opportunity was there and we blew it by constantly cancelling out tours. We'd wake up one morning in the States and find Jeff had left the night before and was back in England.")
Aug [2] Jeff Beck Group guests on *Goo Goo Barabajagal (Love Is Hot)* by Donovan, which reaches UK #12 and US #36. While in the US undertaking its current "Beck-ola" tour, Beck and Stewart are invited to form a new rock outfit with Tim Bogert (bass) and Carmine Appice (drums), who are splitting from Vanilla Fudge. Plans are dropped, however, after Beck is hospitalized following a car accident, while Bogert and Appice go on to form Cactus.
Sept [13] Sophomore Jeff Beck Group effort ***Beck-Ola*** makes UK #39 and will go on to peak at #15 in the US, where it is released by Epic. Having completed the album, Stewart and Wood leave to join the Faces.

1971

Nov Following an 18-month period of recuperation from his auto accident, Beck has formed a new backing group, featuring Clive Chaman (bass), Max Middleton (keyboards), Cozy Powell (drums) and Bobby Tench (vocals), which supports him on both the solo-released ***Rough And Ready***, which will peak at US #46, and the accompanying UK and US tour.

1972

May ***Jeff Beck Group*** (sometimes referred to as the "orange" album, as depicted on the cover), produced by Steve Cropper of Booker T. & the MG's, and recorded by the same line-up, is released, set to reach US #19.
Dec [2] Reissued *Hi Ho Silver Lining* reaches UK #17.

1973

Jan Bogert and Appice resurrect the idea of forming a group with Beck, and the thunderous rock trio Beck, Bogert & Appice is born.
Apr ***Jeff Beck, Tim Bogert & Carmine Appice*** reaches US #12 and UK #28. Produced by Don Nix, it includes a version of Stevie Wonder's *Superstition*. During a world tour, they cut a live double album in Japan (***Live In Japan***), where it will be exclusively released.
May In the light of Stewart's current solo success, *I've Been Drinking*, originally the B-side of *Love Is Blue*

from 1968, is re-issued, credited to Jeff Beck & Rod Stewart, and reaches UK #27.

1974

Jan [26] Beck, Bogert & Appice's UK dates are highlighted by the first of two performances at the Rainbow Theatre, London. The union, like so many Beck projects, proves short-term, however, and will soon dissolve.

1975

Apr Taking a non-vocalist direction, he forms an instrumental backing group, comprising Middleton, Philip Chen (bass) and Richard Bailey (drums). This line-up plays on Beck's solo double ***Blow By Blow***. A largely experimental jazz-rock fusion project produced by George Martin, it will hit US #4, re-establishing him as one of the most respected guitarists of the rock era.

1976

June Beck begins a year-long US tour, co-headlining with the Jan Hammer Group.
July [24] Martin-produced ***Wired***, featuring Middleton, Bailey, ex-Mahavishnu Orchestra's Jan Hammer (drums/synthesizer), Wilbur Bascomb (bass) and Narada Michael Walden (drums/keyboards), who also co-writes half of the material, makes UK #38.
Aug [7] ***Wired*** reaches US #16.

1977

May [14] ***Jeff Beck With The Jan Hammer Group Live*** reaches US #23.

1980

Aug [2] After another sabbatical, during which he has recruited Simon Phillips (drums), Mo Foster (bass) and Tony Hymas (keyboards), Beck's ***There And Back***, assisted once again by Hammer, reaches UK #38 and will climb to US #21, as he begins extensive touring with the same line-up through to September 1981.

1981

Sept Beck performs with Eric Clapton at "The Secret Policeman's Other Ball" in London, in aid of Amnesty International, also appearing on the subsequent release ***The Secret Policeman's Other Ball***, which will make UK #69 in December.

1982

Oct [23] The second reissue of *Hi Ho Silver Lining* makes UK #62.

1983

Mar [17] Beck participates in the second annual "Prince's Trust Rock Gala" benefit concert, at the Royal Albert Hall, London, with Eric Clapton, Jimmy Page, Bill Wyman, Carmine Appice, Andy Fairweather Low and Ronnie Lane.
Sept [20-21] Beck joins Clapton, Page, Steve Winwood, Wyman, Charlie Watts, Joe Cocker, Paul Rodgers, Kenny Jones, Fairweather Low, Ray Cooper and Lane (himself an MS sufferer) in a benefit concert at the Royal Albert Hall, in aid of ARMS (Action for Research into Multiple Sclerosis). The second show will be performed in the presence of H.R.H. the Prince and Princess of Wales.
Dec [8] Beck, Clapton, Page and Ry Cooder give another ARMS benefit concert, at Madison Square Garden, New York.

1985

Aug [17] Following a brief tour with Stewart, and a July-peaking collaboration with him on their version of Curtis Mayfield's *People Get Ready* (US #48), Beck releases ***Flash***, which charts at UK #83 and will rise to US #39. With tracks produced by either Nile Rodgers (of Chic) or Arthur Baker, guest performers include Stewart, Hammer, Appice, Hymas and former Wet Willie vocalist Jimmy Hall.

1986

Feb [25] Beck wins Best Rock Instrumental Performance for *Escape* (from ***Flash***) at the 28th annual Grammy Awards.
Nov [21] ***Blow By Blow*** and ***Wired*** are certified platinum by the RIAA, as Beck wraps up work on Mick Jagger's solo album ***Primitive Cool***. (A reported collaboration with Malcolm McLaren has yet to produce results.)

1988

Jan [20] He inducts guitar pioneer Les Paul into the Rock and Roll Hall of Fame at the third annual dinner, held at the Waldorf Astoria Hotel, New York.

1989

Oct Further showcasing his exemplary guitar skills, ***Jeff Beck's Guitar Shop With Terry Bozzio And Tony Hymas***, his tenth solo release on Epic, makes US #49, featuring his longtime keyboardist Hymas and ex-Missing Persons percussionist Bozzio.
[25] Beck teams with Stevie Ray Vaughan on a US arena tour dubbed "The Fire And The Fury", which begins at the Northrop Memorial Auditorium, Minneapolis, MN. The only time they have previously met was at a Columbia Records convention in Hawaii in 1984.
Dec [20] ***Jeff Beck Group*** is certified gold by the RIAA.

1990

Feb [21] ***Jeff Beck's Guitar Shop With Terry Bozzio And Tony Hymas*** wins Best Rock Instrumental Performance at the 32nd annual Grammy Awards, at the Shrine Auditorium, Los Angeles, as Beck prepares to embark on a "Guitar Shop" tour.

1992

Jan [15] Attending the seventh annual Rock and Roll Hall of Fame dinner in New York as a member of the inducted Yardbirds, Beck says of the legendary group: "We paved the way for barbarism - and we set fire to things".
[22] Having worked on the film soundtrack for "The Pope Must Die(t)" in 1991, ***Jeff Beck, Tim Bogert & Carmine Appice*** is finally certified gold (Beck's fourth) in the US. During this year, and still a much in-demand session musician (who contributed, not least, to Mick Jagger's two solo albums during the '80s and Jon Bon Jovi's 1990 ***Blaze Of Glory***), Beck will guest on much of Roger Waters' forthcoming album ***Amused To Death***.
Mar [14] *People Get Ready*, his 1985 one-off reunion with Rod Stewart, belatedly makes UK #49.
June [6] Beck plays on the "Guns N' Roses Invade Paris!" pay-per-view special live from the Hippodrome de Vincennes Stadium in Paris.

1993

Feb [2] Having collaborated together on a version of *Hound Dog* for the 1992 ***Honeymoon In Vegas*** film soundtrack, Epic Soundtrax releases a complete 15-track album of instrumental recordings by Beck with keyboardist Jed Leiber, written as the accompaniment to an A&E cable TV Vietnam-based mini-series, "Frankie's House".
Mar [23] He contributes fret-work to the Paul Rodgers-assembled ***Tribute To Muddy Waters*** released on Victory Music. In reverence to Beck, Rodgers says: "There's Jeff Beck and then there are other guitar players."
Apr [23] Beck performs a one-off showcase event to introduce his forthcoming ***Crazy Legs*** album, at the 1,400-capacity La Cigale, Paris, France, his first full concert date since his 1990 "Guitar Shop" trek.
June [15] He performs on an all-star bill at the first "Apollo Theatre Hall of Fame" concert from the landmark theatre in Harlem, New York, subsequently broadcast on NBC-TV on August 4th.
July [17] During the most prolific release period of his career, Beck's tribute album to Gene Vincent & the Blue Caps (notably their lead guitarist, Cliff Gallup), ***Crazy Legs***, for which he has recruited the services of the UK roots rocking Big Town Playboys (Mike Sanchez (vocals), Adrian Utley (rhythm guitar), Ian Jennings (bass), Clive Denver (drums) and saxophonists, Nick Hunt and Leo Green), charts for a week at US #171.
Nov [27] Reprise-released ***Stone Free: A Tribute To Jimi Hendrix***, to which Beck and Seal contribute *Manic Depression*, reaches US #28.

1994

Jan [19] Beck inducts Rod Stewart into the Rock and Roll Hall of Fame at the ninth annual dinner at New York's Waldorf Astoria Hotel, stating of his love/hate relationship "He loves me and I hate him".
Oct [8] He performs at "Elvis Aaron Presley : The Tribute", a multi-star event staged at the Pyramid Arena, Memphis, TN, and broadcast live on US pay-per-view TV.

1995

Sept [12] ***Jeff Beck With The Jan Hammer Group Live*** is certified gold by the RIAA.
Oct [8] During a current US tour, promoting a new ***Greatest Hits*** collection and sharing the bill with Santana, Beck plays to a sellout 4,877 crowd at the Paramount, New York.
see also: **THE YARDBIRDS**

THE BEE GEES

Barry Gibb (vocals, guitar); **Robin Gibb** (vocals); **Maurice Gibb** (vocals, bass)

1958

Barry Gibb (b. Sept. 1, 1947, Douglas, Isle of Man) and his twin brothers Robin, older by one hour, and Maurice (b. Dec. 22, 1949, Douglas), emigrate from their semi-detached home in Keppel Road, Chorlton-cum-Hardy, Lancs. to Australia with their parents, soon after the birth of latest arrival, Andy. They have already performed for three years at Saturday morning picture shows at the Manchester Gaumont, Whalley Range Odeon and the Palentine Theatre, singing the hits of the day, with Paul Frost and Kenny Oricks, and known as the Rattlesnakes, name-changing later to Wee Johnnie Hayes & the Bluecats. (Their father Hugh is leader of the Mecca-contracted Hughie Gibb Orchestra, their mother Barbara a singer.) The trio's first paid performance at the Gaumont, in 1955, was to mime to Tommy Steele's *Wedding Bells*, but, when their copy of the disk broke on their way to the venue, they had to sing the song live.

1960

Performing on Sundays as the Rattlesnakes at Brisbane's Speedway Circus, they meet race-track organizer Bill Good, who introduces the group to DJ friend Bill Gates, who plays Gibb tapes on his radio show, "Clatter Chatter", on station 4KQ. (As interest in the brothers' music grows, Good names them the B.G.'s after his and Gates' initials, and not because of the Brothers Gibb initials as popularly believed.) This leads to a TV debut on "Anything Goes" and then regular appearances on BTQ7-TV's "Cottie's Happy Hour" show, followed by a six-week residence at Surfer's Paradise, Beachcomber Hotel, Brisbane.

1962

Relocating to Sydney, they perform at the Sydney Stadium on a Chubby Checker headliner, now billing themselves as the Bee Gees. They begin writing, their first composition being *Let Me Love You*, and enjoy their first composing success, for Col Joye, with his Australian chart-topper *Starlight Of Love*.

1963

Jan Following an 18-month residency as the house band at a club in Queensland, the brothers sign to Festival Records, its Leedon subsidiary releasing their debut single *Three Kisses Of Love*. Enjoying their debut chart disk as a group when *Wine And Women* hits #10 in Australia in 1965, the brothers will link with Bill Shepherd (musical director) and Ozzie Byrne (producer) and sign to Spin Records.

1966

Aug Following ten singles of varying Australian chart success, they record their eleventh single, the Barry-penned, piano-led *Spicks And Specks*.

1967

Jan [3] The group returns to the UK on a five-week boat trip, with *Spicks And Specks* now at #1 in Australia.

Feb [24] The Bee Gees sign a five-year management contract with Robert Stigwood (who is in partnership with Brian Epstein) at NEMS Enterprises, following an audition at the Saville Theatre, London, having been turned away by the Grade Organisation. Stigwood will immediately secure them a long-term recording contract with the Polydor label.

Mar Colin Petersen (b. Mar. 24, 1946, Kinearoy, Australia), who, as a child actor, has already appeared in "Cry From The Streets" with Max Bygraves, "Smiley" and "The Scamp", and played in Australian band Steve & the Board, is recruited on drums. Melouney (b. Aug. 18, 1945, Sydney, Australia), whose first Australian chart success has come as a member of the Vibratones, with their cover of the Shadows' *Man Of Mystery*, formed a new band with that group's rhythm guitarist, Tony Barber, called Vince & Tony's Two, and another called Vince Melouney, before joining Billy Thorpe & the Aztecs, who have had seven Australian #1s, has been working in the UK at Simca Motors for four months, when the Gibbs ask him to complete the line-up.

May [11] With music press ads hailing them as "the most significant new musical talent of 1967", the band makes its BBC1-TV "Top Of The Pops" debut singing *New York Mining Disaster*, showcasing their instantly appealing three-part harmonies led, during most of its '60s releases, by Robin's distinctive falsetto.

[27] The group's first UK-recorded single, the two-minutes-and-nine seconds *New York Mining Disaster 1941*, reaches UK #12 and will become a global million-seller.

June [13] The group appears on ITV's "As You Like It".

[29] The band begins a two-week promotional visit to the US.

July [1] *New York Mining Disaster 1941* reaches US #14.

Aug [19] *To Love Somebody*, written by Barry and Robin for Otis Redding, who has visited Barry at New York's Plaza Hotel and requested a brothers Gibb song, but performed by the Bee Gees themselves, makes UK #41 (an enduring composition, it will be successfully covered in 1990 by Jimmy Somerville (UK #8) and Michael Bolton in 1992 (US #11/UK #16).

[26] *To Love Somebody* reaches US #17, as its parent album, co-produced by Stigwood with Byrne, with strings arranged and conducted by Bill Shepherd, ***Bee Gees 1st***, is on its way to hitting UK #8 and US #7.

Oct [11] *Massachusetts*, written by all three brothers and co-produced by them with Stigwood in New York, during the band's first promotional US trip, hits UK #1, as Home Secretary Roy Jenkins rescinds Melouney and Petersen's expulsion orders, due to come into effect on November 30th, when their work permits expire. Jenkins cites the group's value to the UK during its balance-of-payments crisis.

Nov [5] Robin, returning from a weekend in Hastings, Sussex with his girlfriend Molly Hullis, is travelling on a train back to London, which crashes just outside Hither Green station in South-East London, killing 49 and injuring 78. Gibb suffers shock.

[11] *Holiday*, written by Barry and Robin, reaches US #16.

[17] The group turns on the festive illuminations in Carnaby Street, London.

[19] The Bee Gees perform at the Saville Theatre on a bill with the Flowerpot Men and the Bonzo Dog Doo Dah Band.

Dec [9] Psychedelic-tinged, melodramatic *World* hits UK #9, as *Massachusetts* reaches US #11.

[24] The group's Christmas special "How On Earth", filmed at Liverpool Cathedral, Liverpool, Lancs., airs on ITV.

1968

Jan [27] Trio makes its US concert debut, at the Convention Center, Anaheim, CA, and will guest on NBC-TV's "Rowan & Martin's Laugh-In" and CBS-TV's "The Smothers Brothers Show".

Feb [8] With four singles currently in the Danish Top 20, the group flies to Scandinavia to begin a tour.

Mar [2] Piano-led ballad *Words*, despite a six-day halt in sales, following the grant of an ex-partia injunction, hits UK #8 and reaches US #15. Their sophomore album ***Horizontal*** is also released, set to make UK #16 and US #12, highlighting their already-familiar formula for crafting self-written, infectious, harmonic pop gems, often lushly orchestrated and delivered in their instantly-recognizable and unique falsetto vocal style.

[17] They make their debut on CBS-TV's "The Ed Sullivan Show", singing *Words* and *To Love Somebody*.

[27] The band embarks on a 26-date UK tour with Grapefruit, Dave Dee, Dozy, Beaky, Mick & Tich and the Foundations, at the Royal Albert Hall, London, with a 67-piece orchestra.

Apr [20] *Jumbo* peaks at US #57 and, backed with *The Singer Sang His Song*, makes UK #25.

July [27] Robin collapses, as the group prepares to fly to US for its first tour. (He is admitted to a London nursing home the next day, suffering from nervous exhaustion.)

[31] He moves from the nursing home to a health farm in Sussex.

Aug [10] The band begins its re-scheduled US tour in impressive style at Forest Hills Stadium, New York, receiving 13 curtain calls at the end of its performance.

Sept [7] Trio-penned *I've Gotta Get A Message To You*, a fictional account of a man on death row about to be electrocuted, hits UK #1.

[8] The group arrives back in the UK at the end of a US tour and, Barry announces he will be leaving his brothers to pursue a career in movies.

[9] The band flies to Brussels to film a Jean Christophe Averti-directed TV spectacular.

[28] *I've Gotta Get A Message To You* hits US #8, as ***Idea*** hits UK #4 and US #17.

Oct [31] The group begins an 18-date tour of Germany and Austria in Bremen.

Nov [18] The tour is cancelled after a concert in Munich, with six dates remaining, when Barry and Robin are ordered to bed, suffering from acute tonsilitis. (Melouney announces that he is thinking of quitting the band to write and produce. Maurice states that he thinks it "very probable the Bee Gees will be non-existent in two years from now.")

Dec ***Rare, Precious & Beautiful***, a compilation of pre-fame tracks cut in Australia, reaches US #99.

1969

Feb [8] *I Started A Joke* hits US #6, as the band tours Japan.

Mar Despite immense success, the group is prone to internal strife, exacerbated not least by intoxicants, including fame. *First Of May* (UK #6) and *I Started A Joke* (US #6) are the last Bee Gees hits on which Melouney and Petersen appear, while Robin Gibb leaves his brothers for a solo career. (Melouney will go on to form Ashton, Gardner & Dyke, working as its writer and producer.)

[19] Stigwood sues Robin for leaving the group.

Apr [5] Double album ***Odessa***, released in a suede sleeve, hits UK #10 and will climb to US #20.

[18] Maurice marries Scottish-born singer Lulu at Gerrards Cross, Bucks., with twin Robin as best man.

[19] *First Of May* makes US #37.

June [14] *Tomorrow Tomorrow* peaks at US #54.

July [12] Barry and Maurice continue as the Bee Gees, charting with *Tomorrow Tomorrow* at UK #23.

Aug [11] Barry and Maurice begin filming "Cucumber Castle", with guest stars Lulu, Frankie Howerd, Vincent Price, Spike Milligan and others. Barry plays the King Of Cucumber, while Maurice plays the King Of Jelly.

[16] Robin's debut solo, the dramatic ballad *Saved By The Bell*, hits UK #2, behind the Rolling Stones' *Honky Tonk Women*.

Sept Petersen is fired from the Bee Gees, and will sue, citing a five-year contract he signed with the group and Stigwood on July 4th, 1967.

[20] *Don't Forget To Remember*, from "Cucumber Castle", hits UK #2 but will stall at US #73 the following week.

12-track ***Best Of The Bee Gees***, the first of many compilations, hits UK #7 and US #9. Barry produces P.P. Arnold, and goes solo, leaving Maurice as the sole representative of the Bee Gees.

Nov [10] ***Best Of The Bee Gees*** is certified gold by the RIAA.

1970

Feb [14] Robin's *August October* makes UK #45.

[17] Maurice opens in the stage musical "Sing A Rude Song" at Greenwich Theatre, London, playing Bernard Dillon, a jockey who wins the 1910 Derby and the lover of Marie Lloyd, played by Barbara Windsor. (It will transfer to the West End on May 26th.)

Mar [28] Barry and Maurice's atypical, percussion-heavy, calypso-cued *I.O.I.O.* makes UK #49. A second volume of Australian material, ***Rare, Precious & Beautiful Vol. 2***, climbs to US #100.

Apr [4] The Bee Gees' *If Only I Had My Mind On Something Else* stalls at US #91.

[18] With the Bee Gees at a disparate low, Maurice's solo debut *Railroad*, written with brother-in-law Billy Lawrie, is released.

May [9] ***Cucumber Castle*** makes UK #57 and US #94.

July [11] *I.O.I.O.* climbs to US #94.

Nov [14] With compositions already covered by the likes of Janis Joplin, Nina Simone, Frank Sinatra, Andy Williams and Elvis Presley, Engelbert Humperdinck makes US #47 with the Gibb-penned *Sweetheart*, having reached UK #22.

[20] Tin Tin's *Come On Over Again*, produced by Moby Productions (Maurice and Billy Lawrie), is released.

1971

Jan [16] The brothers settle their differences, but have lost much of their UK popularity, reflected by *Lonely Days* only reaching UK #33. About their reunion, Robin tells **Time** magazine: "If we hadn't been related, we would probably never have gotten back together."

[30] US popularity has been less affected by squabbles, as the trio-penned ballad *Lonely Days* hits US #3, while the fully regrouped album ***2 Years On*** makes #32.

Mar [30] *Lonely Days* is certified gold by the RIAA.

Aug [7] Plaintive ballad *How Can You Mend A Broken Heart*, written by Barry and Robin when they reconciled after a 15-month period apart, hits US #1, where it will stay for four weeks, becoming another million-seller and a longterm US radio favorite.

[26] *How Can You Mend A Broken Heart* is certified gold by the RIAA.

Sept [4] A 30-date US tour opens in Boston, MA, set to end on October 3rd in St Louis, MO.

Nov [20] *Don't Wanna Live Inside Myself* peaks at US #53, while its parent album ***Trafalgar*** rises to US #34.

1972

Feb [26] *My World*, written backstage by Barry and Robin at ITV's "The Golden Shot" on which they were appearing, reaches UK #16.

[26] *My World* reaches US #16.

June The Bee Gees undertake a tour of Asia.

Aug [19] The group-penned ballad *Run To Me* hits UK #9, their first UK Top 10 single for three years.

Sept [23] *Run To Me* reaches US #16.

Dec [16] *Alive* makes US #34, taken from ***To Whom It May Concern*** which climbs to US #35.

1973

Feb [19] The band performs at the Royal Festival Hall, accompanied by the London Symphony Orchestra and supported by Colin Blunstone.
[25] They begin a North American tour in Toronto, ON, Canada, set to end on April 1st.
Mar ***Life In A Tin Can*** and a second Polydor retrospective, the 14-track ***Best Of The Bee Gees Vol. 2***, chart in the US (at #69 and #98 respectively).
Apr [7] *Saw A New Morning* climbs to US #94.
June [24] The trio performs at the London Palladium during a current UK tour.

1974

Jan ***A Kick In The Pants Is Worth Eight In The Head*** is rejected by RSO (Robert Stigwood Organisation) Records, to whom the group is now signed, and Atco (RSO's US distributor, as part of WEA, and previous Bee Gees US label). At Stigwood's suggestion, the brothers have recorded sessions with American producer Arif Mardin in London and New York, but the resultant ***Mr. Natural*** stalls at US #178.
Mar [23] The extracted *Mr. Natural* climbs to US #93, and, at a career low, the Bee Gees will perform at the Batley's Variety Club in Batley, W. Yorks, by year's end.

1975

Apr Once again under Mardin's production, the Bee Gees assemble a regular back-up group of Alan Kendall (guitar) and ex-Amen Corner members Dennis Bryon (drums) and Blue Weaver (keyboards), to record ***Main Course*** at Atlantic's New York studios and Criteria Studios in Miami. As an increasingly dominant creative force, Barry has also recently become the principal vocalist of the trio, a role which will become permanent.
Aug [2] Funky and stuttered trio-penned extract *Jive Talkin'*, marking a major new musical direction for the band, hits UK #5.
[9] While the album is immediately embraced by US radio, *Jive Talkin'* tops the US chart.
[21] *Jive Talkin'* is certified gold by the RIAA.
Oct [17] Having separated from Lulu in 1973, Maurice marries Yvonne Spencely (and will renew his wedding vows, following his recovery from alcoholism, on February 23rd, 1992).
Dec [13] *Nights On Broadway*, also from the album, hits US #7.
[23] ***Main Course*** is certified gold by the RIAA.

1976

Mar [20] *Fanny (Be Tender With My Love)*, with strings arranged by Gene Orloff, reaches US #12, as parent album ***Main Course*** finally reaches US #14. Olivia Newton-John is also currently climbing the US survey with her version of a ***Main Course*** appetizer, *Come On Over* (US #23).
Sept [4] Their no holds disco-aimed *You Should Be Dancing*, featuring guest percussion by Stephen Stills, hits US #1. Their third US chart-topper, it was co-produced with Albhy Galuten and Karl Richardson at Criteria Studios, an arrangement and location which proves long-term.
[11] *You Should Be Dancing* hits UK #5.
[15] *You Should Be Dancing* is certified gold by the RIAA.
Nov [13] ***Children Of The World***, on which they were unable to use Atlantic house producer Mardin because RSO had switched distribution from WEA to Polygram, and subsequently co-produced by the band with Galuten and Richardson, after sessions with Richard Perry proved unproductive, hits US #8.
[20] Ballad *Love So Right* hits US #3 and makes UK #41.
Dec [2] The Bee Gees perform at a Madison Square Garden concert, donating the proceeds to the Police Athletic League of New York.
[23] ***Children Of The World*** is certified platinum by the RIAA.
[29] *Love So Right* is confirmed gold by the RIAA.

1977

Jan [21] Compilation ***Bee Gees Gold Volume One*** reaches US #50.
Mar [12] *Boogie Child* reaches US #12.
Stigwood, still head of his own RSO Records and manager of the Bee Gees, is producing a disco-music film, "Saturday Night Fever". He contacts the group, which is recording at the Chateau d'Heronville Studios in France, urgently requesting four songs for the soundtrack to his film project. They finally record five and donate two others. (*Stayin' Alive, How Deep Is Your Love, Night Fever, More Than A Woman, Jive Talkin', You Should Be Dancing, If I Can't Have You* (to be recorded by Yvonne Elliman) and *More Than A Woman* (for Tavares).)
July [30] Double album ***Here At Last ... Bee Gees ... Live*** hits US #8, as their younger sibling Andy hits US #1 with the Barry-penned *I Just Want To Be Your Everything*.
Sept [3] *Edge Of The Universe* reaches US #26.
Nov [22] ***Here At Last ... Bee Gees ... Live*** is certified platinum by the RIAA.
Dec [10] *How Deep Is Your Love*, the smash ballad from "Saturday Night Fever", hits UK #3.
[14] "Saturday Night Fever", starring John Travolta, receives its world premiere in New York. The film, not least through the Bee Gees music, will prove to be the global commercial pinnacle of the disco movement.
[16] Still-climbing *How Deep Is Your Love* is certified gold by the RIAA.
[24] *How Deep Is Your Love* tops the US chart, displacing Debby Boone's *You Light Up My Life* after ten weeks at the top. Eventually selling over one million copies in the US, it will spend 17 consecutive weeks in the Top 10, a **Billboard** Hot 100 record.

1978

Jan [3] ***Bee Gees Gold, Volume 1*** is certified gold by the RIAA.
[21] Soundtrack double album ***Saturday Night Fever***, containing the seven Bee Gees songs, tops the US chart. It will eventually sell over 30 million copies worldwide, and remain the best-selling soundtrack ever.
Feb [4] *Stayin' Alive*, featured in the movie's opening sequence, while character Tony Manero struts down New York City sidewalks, tops the US chart where it will remain for four weeks, displacing Player's *Baby Come Back*, which in turn had taken over from *How Deep Is Your Love*.
[23] Bee Gees win the Best Pop Vocal Performance By A Duo, Group Or Chorus category for *How Deep Is Your Love*, at the 20th annual Grammy Awards.
Mar [4] *Stayin' Alive* hits UK #4 as Andy 's *(Love Is) Thicker Than Water*, co-written by Barry, replaces *Stayin' Alive* at US #1.
[13] *Stayin' Alive* is ratified platinum by the RIAA.
[18] Now at the peak of their commercial career, their disco classic *Night Fever* replaces *(Love Is) Thicker Than Water* at US #1, where it will stay for eight weeks. It is RSO's fifth consecutive US chart-topper, and, in its first week at #1, *Stayin' Alive* is still alive at US #2. The Bee Gees-penned and produced *Emotion* by Samantha Sang also hits US #3. (Such is their current success, many are convinced that Sang does not exist and that the record is the Bee Gees slowed down.)
Apr [29] *Night Fever* also tops the UK survey.
May [2] *Night Fever* is certified platinum by the RIAA.
[6] ***Saturday Night Fever*** hits UK #1, as Tavares' *More Than A Woman* makes US #32.
[12] The Bee Gees are honored with the Special Award, as *How Deep Is Your Love* wins the Best Pop Song and Best Film Music Or Song category, at the 23rd annual Ivor Novello Awards lunch, held at the Grosvenor House Hotel, London.
[13] Elliman's *If I Can't Have You* tops US chart, replacing *Night Fever*.
[27] *If I Can't Have You* hits UK #4 as *More Than A Woman* hits UK #7.
[31] The trio appears on the premiere edition of NBC-TV's "Headliners With David Frost", live from New York, with fellow guests John Travolta and former CIA chief Richard Helms.
June [17] Andy's *Shadow Dancing*, written by all four brothers and produced by the regular Barry Gibb/Galuten/Richardson team, tops the US chart for the first of seven weeks.
July [24] Stigwood-conceived and-critically mauled "Sgt Pepper's Lonely Hearts Club Band" movie (based on the celebrated Beatles album), in which the group acts and sings, premieres in the US.
[29] Its soundtrack ***Sgt. Pepper's Lonely Hearts Club Band*** makes UK #38 but will hit US #5 on Aug [19].
[26] Frankie Valli's *Grease*, the Barry Gibb-penned title tune for the Stigwood-produced John Travolta/Olivia Newton-John film, tops the US chart.
Sept [30] *Grease* hits UK #3.
Oct [7] *Oh Darlin'* by Robin Gibb, from ***Sgt. Pepper***, reaches US #15.
Nov The Bee Gees begin recording ***Spirits (Having Flown)*** at Criteria Studios, with their regular session band of Weaver, Bryon and Kendall, while Chicago's James Pankow, Walter Parazaider and Lee Loughnane provide assistance on horns.
Dec [9] Airy ballad *Too Much Heaven* hits UK #3.
[16] Andy's *(Our Love) Don't Throw it All Away*, written by Barry with Weaver, hits US #9. (By year's end, Barry Gibb will have spent 25 weeks at #1 on the Hot 100 as a writer.)

1979

Jan [6] *Too Much Heaven* tops the US chart.
[9] "The Music For UNICEF Concert", featuring the Bee Gees performing *Too Much Heaven*, staged to celebrate the International Year of the Child, takes place in the General Assembly Hall of the United Nations in New York, to be broadcast the following day on NBC-TV as "A Gift Of Song - The Music For UNICEF Concert".
[12] On the same day that they are presented with a star on the Hollywood Walk of Fame, the trio collects the Favorite Band, Duo Or Group trophy, while ***Saturday Night Fever*** wins the Favorite Album, Soul/R&B category at the sixth annual American Music Awards, held at the Civic Auditorium, Santa Monica, CA.
[30] ***Spirits Having Flown*** is certified platinum by the RIAA.
Feb [9] The organization also confirms platinum sales for *Too Much Heaven*.
[15] The Bee Gees win the Album Of The Year and Best Pop Vocal Performance By A Duo, Group Or Chorus for ***Saturday Night Fever***, Best Arrangement For Voices for *Stayin' Alive* and Best Producer Of The Year categories, at the 21st annual Grammy Awards.
Mar [3] Uptempo *Tragedy* hits UK #1, as disco-moulded parent album ***Spirits (Having Flown)*** tops US chart.
[17] ***Spirits Having Flown*** tops the UK chart.
[24] Highlighting Barry's falsetto more than ever, *Tragedy* hits US #1.
Apr [10] Still-rising *Love You Inside Out* is certified gold by the RIAA.
May [4] *Stayin' Alive* wins the International Hit Of The Year category, while *Night Fever* is named Most Performed Work and Best Selling A-side Of 1978, at the 24th annual Ivor Novello Awards lunch, held once again at the Grosvenor House Hotel.
[5] *Love You Inside Out* reaches UK #13.
[14] *Tragedy* is certified platinum by the RIAA.
June [9] *Love You Inside Out* hits US #1, and is the group's sixth consecutive chart-topper.
Sept They are awarded the Gold Ticket for playing to over 100,000 fans at Madison Square Garden, New York.
Nov [27] The Bee Gees deny US press reports that they are to split.

1980

Jan [12] 20-track double-album compilation ***Bee Gees Greatest*** tops the US chart and hits UK #6.
[18] The band collects the Favorite Band, Duo Or Group, Pop/Rock and Favorite Album, Pop/Rock

trophies at the seventh annual American Music Awards, held at the ABC-TV Studios, Los Angeles, CA.
[26] *Spirits (Having Flown)* reaches UK #16.
Feb [26] ***Bee Gees Greatest*** is certified platinum by the RIAA.
Mar [29] The Bee Gees are sued by songwriter Ron Selle, who claims they stole *How Deep Is Your Love* from an unpublished song he had written years earlier. He will lose the case.
Oct [25] Barbra Streisand's *Woman In Love*, written and produced by Barry, tops the US chart, and will also hit UK #1. (His collaboration with Streisand will yield her US and UK #1 album ***Guilty***, and the further duetted hit single *Guilty* which will hit US #3 and UK #34.)
Dec [6] *Help Me*, a Robin solo, makes US #50.

1981

Feb [25] Barry wins the Best Pop Performance By A Duo Or Group With Vocal with Streisand (for *Guilty*) category, at the 23rd annual Grammy Awards.
Mar [21] *What Kind Of Fool*, by Barry and Streisand, hits US #10.
May [19] *Woman In Love* wins the Best Song Musically Or Lyrically category at the 26th annual Ivor Novello Awards lunch.
Oct [24] Frantic, synthesizer-driven *He's A Liar*, from the forthcoming ***Living Eyes***, reaches US #30.
Nov [14] ***Living Eyes***, with back-up from Jeff Porcaro, Richard Tee, Steve Gadd, Don Felder, Russ Kunkel and Ralph McDonald, peaks at UK #73, a dramatic reversal of fortune after the dizzy heights of the mid-'70s. Also stalling at US #41 on Dec [12], its title cut will peak at US #45 one week earlier.

1982

July [24] Trio-penned *Heart (Stop Beating In Time)* reaches UK #22 for Leo Sayer.
Oct Dionne Warwick's ***Heartbreaker***, produced by Barry and largely written by the three brothers, hits UK 33 and US #25 (and includes the hit singles *Heartbreaker* and *All The Love In The World*).

1983

June [18] *The Woman In You*, previewing the forthcoming ***Staying Alive*** soundtrack, eaches US #24. Robin, having signed a worldwide solo deal with Polydor Records, releases his second solo album ***How Old Are You?***, with the extracted *Another Lonely Night In New York*, peaking at UK #71.
July [16] Having contributed half on the soundtrack's songs, ***Staying Alive***, the sequel to "Saturday Night Fever" begins a US chart rise to #6 (and will reach UK #14), but the backlash against disco prevents a repeat success, particularly for the film. With a lingering image inextricably associated with that era, the group could not be less in vogue and will pursue solo projects for the next four years.
Sept [17] The extracted ballad *Someone Belonging To Someone* makes US and UK #49.
Oct [29] Written by the trio and produced by Barry, *Islands In The Stream*, a pop/country duet by Kenny Rogers and Dolly Parton, tops the US chart (and hits UK #7), taken from Barry's latest production, Rogers' ***Eyes That See In The Dark***, as the band's success is increasingly eclipsed by the brothers' songwriting and Barry's production projects.

1984

July [21] *Boys (Do Fall in Love)*, from Robin's third solo album ***Secret Agent***, makes US #37. (During another year of solo projects, Maurice will complete the soundtrack for the Kathleen Turner-starring movie "A Breed Apart".)
Oct [6] Barry's first solo single *Shine Shine* makes US #37, as its parent album ***Now Voyager*** makes US #72 and UK #85, despite a simultaneously released, complete parallel video package (both featuring a ballad duet with Olivia Newton-John).

1985

During the year, Barry, with Karl Richardson and Albhy Galuten, produces ***Eaten Alive*** for Diana Ross (on which he also co-writes one cut with Michael Jackson), while Robin releases the non-charting ***Walls Have Eyes***.

1986

Mar [8] Extracted Ross single *Chain Reaction*, an uptempo Motown-recalling song written by the Gibb trio, hits UK #1, but only manages US #66.
Barry releases *We Are The Bunburys* under the alias of the Bunburys, co-masterminded with cricket-mad entrepreneur David English, about a group of cricket-playing rabbits, and featuring the help of cricket icon Ian Botham. Ken Kragen becomes the group's new manager.

1987

Apr [15] *Chain Reaction* is named Most Performed Work at the 32nd annual Ivor Novello Awards lunch, at the Grosvenor House Hotel.
Oct [3] *You Win Again* peaks at US #75, as its parent album ***E.S.P.*** climbs to US #96.
[17] The Bee Gees return triumphantly to the UK chart, hitting #1 with the anthemic *You Win Again*, becoming the only band to chart-top in Britain in each of three decades
[24] ***E.S.P.***, their first complete studio release since 1981 and dedicated to the memory of their first producer Ozzie Byrne, hits UK #5. Now freed from both the Stigwood Organisation and its label (having settled a $200-million lawsuit out of court in the early '80s), they are managed by Gary Borman and Harriet Sternberg, and signed to Warner Bros. Records.
Dec [26] The extracted title track *E.S.P.* peaks at UK #51.

1988

Mar [10] Andy Gibb dies in the John Radcliffe Hospital, Oxford, Oxon, five days after his 30th birthday.
Apr [7] *You Win Again* wins Best Contemporary Song category, as the Bee Gees are honored for their Outstanding Contribution To British Music at the 33rd annual Ivor Novello Awards lunch. They are unable to attend the ceremony, mourning the death of their younger brother.
May [14] The group performs at Madison Square Garden as part of Atlantic Records' 40-year anniversary party celebration concert.
June [5-6] The Bee Gees participate in the sixth annual "Prince's Trust Rock Gala", with Eric Clapton, Phil Collins, Peter Gabriel, Elton John and others, at the Royal Albert Hall, London.
[11] Band makes a further live appearance at "Nelson Mandela's 70th Birthday Tribute" at Wembley Stadium, Wembley, Middx.
Sept Both the soundtrack and the Timothy Dalton-starring film "Hawks" fail to score commercially, despite featuring material written and performed by Barry. Still persisting with the Bunburys, Barry has enlisted the help of his brothers and Clapton, among others, to record *Fight (No Matter How Long)*, included on the recently-released 1988 Summer Olympics album ***One Moment In Time***.

1989

Apr [22] *Ordinary Lives* peaks at UK #54.
[29] Its parent album ***One*** reaches UK #29. Co-produced by the trio with Brian Tench, it features a session line-up of Steve Ferrone (drums), Nathan East (bass), Tim Cansfield (guitar) and Peter Vettese (keyboards), while long-time co-hort Kendall is the only remnant evident from their '70s rhythm-section band.
June [24] *One* peaks at UK #71.
July [13] The group appears on NBC-TV's "Late Night With David Letterman".
[31] The Bee Gees begin a US trek in Chicago, IL, with a touring line-up comprising Vic Martin on keyboards, George Perry on bass, Chester Thompson on drums and percussionist Phyllis St. James.
Aug ***One*** makes US #68.
Sept [30] Almost unrivalled in their capacity to bounce back, the Bee Gees hit US #7 with *One*, their first US Top 10 appearance in a decade.

1990

Apr ***Nobody's Child*** a benefit album dedicated to raising awareness and funds for the plight of Romanian orphans is released, including the Bee Gees' live version of *How Can You Mend A Broken Heart?*, recorded at the National Tennis Centre, Melbourne, during concerts on November 17th and 18th, 1989.
Dec [8] Another career anthology, the UK-issued ***The Very Best Of The Bee Gees*** hits UK #8.

1991

Feb [27] A 34-date European tour opens in San Remo, Italy, set to conclude on July 9th at the National Exhibition Centre, Birmingham, W. Midlands.
Apr [6] Moving into the trio's fourth decade of Top 10 UK success, *Secret Love* hits UK #5, and the band joins Status Quo in being the only two groups to achieve a Top 10 placing in four consecutive decades from the '60s onwards. Its parent album ***High Civilization*** debuts at its UK #24 peak.
May [2] The brothers appear on syndicated TV's "The Arsenio Hall Show".
Dec [25] Barry makes a cameo appearance on BBC-1 TV's hit comedy "Only Fools And Horses", waving from the lawn of his Miami home at a passing tourist boat with "Del Boy" on board.

1992

Dec Having inked a worldwide recording deal with Polydor in March, returning the band to the Polygram stable after eight years with Warner Bros., the Bee Gees record sessions for their second album of the decade, at the Mayfair Studios, London, with co-producer Femi Jiya.

1993

June [5] As the group continues to work on its latest album, the Bee Gees make a sole live appearance at KISS Radio's annual fund-raising concert at the Great Woods Center for the Performing Arts, Mansfield, MA, on an all-star bill.
Aug [7] Re-charting ***The Very Best Of Bee Gees*** makes UK #43.
Sept [4] *Paying The Price Of Love* reaches UK #23.
[26] The group takes part in the "Hurricane Relief" benefit concert at Joe Robbie Stadium in Miami.
Nov [20] The Bee Gees top the bill at the 65th Royal Variety Performance at London's Dominion Theatre, performing *Jive Talkin'*, *For Whom The Bell Tolls*, *Massachusetts* and *You Should Be Dancing*, as the 11-track ***Size Isn't Everything***, self-penned and produced as ever, debuts at its US #153 peak.
Dec [4] *Paying The Price Of Love* peaks at US #74.
[25] *For Whom The Bell Tolls* hits UK #4, as ***Size Isn't Everything*** reaches UK #28.
[31] The group takes part in "The Miss Howard Stern New Year's Ever Pageant" broadcast live on pay-per-view TV in the US.

1994

Feb Barry is admitted into a Miami hospital suffering from a heart ailment, resulting in the cancellation of an upcoming tour.
Apr [16] *How To Fall In Love Part 1* debuts at its UK #30 peak.
June [1] The brothers Gibb are inducted into the Songwriters Hall of Fame at the 25th annual ceremony, held at New York's Sheraton Hotel & Towers.

1995

Oct [31] Tribute album, ***Tapestry Revisited : A Tribute To Carole King***, including the Bee Gees' version of *Will You Still Love Me Tomorrow*, is released.

1996

Mar [16] Their songwriting legacy continues to prove its enduring appeal with N-Trance's global smash rap interpretation of *Stayin' Alive* currently #1 in Canada (while the original is also prominently featured in the current hit movie "Grumpier Old Men") and Take

That's final single, their version of *How Deep Is Your Love* currently locked in at the top of the UK chart.

ARCHIE BELL & THE DRELLS

Archie Bell (vocals); **Lee Bell** (vocals); **James Wise** (vocals); **Willie Parnell** (vocals)

1967

Local Houston, TX talent scout Skipper Lee Frazier signs the group, which has comprised Bell (b. Sept. 1, 1944, Henderson, TX), Wise, Parnell and Billy Butler since E.L. Smith Junior High School (as Little Popp & the Fireballs) and then at Phyllis Wheatley Senior High School, after he sees them win a KCOH Radio talent show at the Gold Room in Houston. He sends the vocal quartet into the local Jones studio with Bert Frilot to cut *The Yankee Dance* and *She's My Woman, She's My Girl*, which becomes the group's first release, on the local Ovide label. Parnell soon leaves and is replaced by Joe Cross.

1968

Jan Bell is called up for US army service at Fork Polk, LA, while a third single, *Dog Eat Dog*, is released on Ovide. It will sell 20,000 copies in Texas and Louisiana, before Frazier leases the record to Atlantic.
Mar US DJs flip the single to play the catchy dance number B-side *Tighten Up* instead, which begins to sell.
May ***Tighten Up*** makes US #142.
[18] *Tighten Up*, recorded with the TSU Tornados, tops the US chart. (With Bell still in the army in Germany, Wise has taken the lead vocal role with Charles Gibbs added to the lineup.)
[22] *Tighten Up* is certified gold by the RIAA for one million US sales.
Aug [24] *I Can't Stop Dancing*, recorded in New York, while Bell is on a weekend furlough from his base in Germany, hits US #9. The band is soon teamed with writing and production team Kenny Gamble and Leon Huff, who have seen the group perform at Loretta's High Hat in Longside, NJ, and who will guide the rest of its career which, during the remainder of the decade will see: *Do The Choo Choo*, based on another dance craze, make US #44 (Oct [19]), *There's Gonna Be A Showdown* reach US #21 on Jan [25], 1969, *Love My Baby*, a US #94 peak on Apr [12], marking Bell's return from military service, *Girl You're Too Young*, which makes US #59 on July [19] while parent album ***There's Gonna Be A Showdown*** makes US #163 during August, and *My Balloon's Going Up* reaches US #87 on Oct [4].

1970

Jan [3] *A World Without Music* makes US #90, beginning a decade of uneven chart action for the group, who will fare better in the UK than on their home ground: *Don't Let The Music Slip Away* spends a week at the US Hot 100's anchor position on Apr [18], while *Wrap It Up*, revived by the Fabulous Thunderbirds in 1986, makes US #93 on Dec [12]; *Here I Go Again* reaches UK #11 in November 1972, while the following year *There's Gonna Be A Showdown* makes UK #36 (Feb) and *Dancing To Your Music* peaks at US #61 on May [12], a one-off hit on the Glades label.

1976

Jan The group signs to Gamble and Huff's Philadelphia International Records, as Lucious Larkins replaces Cross.
Mar [20] *Dance Your Troubles Away* peaks at US #95, while *Soul City Walk* reaches UK #13 on June [26]. The band's remaining '70s chart success will be confined to 1977, when *Everybody Have A Good Time* makes UK #43 on June [25] and Archie Bells & the Drells are included on the Philadelphia All-Stars, hit *Let's Clean Up The Ghetto*, which makes US #91 on Aug [27] and UK # 34 on Sept [10], its same-titled album also climbing to US #121 one week later.

1981

Bell begins a solo career, signing to Roger Meltzer and David Morris' Beckett Records, and issues *I Never Had It So Good*. He will subsequently move to WMOT Records the following year, releasing *Touching You*. No longer in demand as a recording artist thereafter, he will continue to perform on the nostalgia circuit throughout the decade. A 1976 Bell & the Drells track, *Don't Let Love Let You Down*, will re-surface to make UK #49 in July 1986, while a 1989 Drells album, ***The Second Time***, will fail to score beyond the US R&B market. (Rhino Records (US) will bring their hits to compact disk in 1993 with the 20-track retrospective ***Tightening It Up: The Best Of Archie Bell & The Drells***.)

BELL BIV DEVOE

Ricky Bell (vocals); **Michael Bivins** (vocals); **Ronnie DeVoe** (vocals)

1990

June [9] Having been three of the founding youngsters in the hit R&B quintet New Edition since 1983, Bell (b. Sept. 18, 1967, Boston, MA), Bivins (b. Aug. 10, 1968, Boston) and DeVoe (b. Nov. 17, 1967, Boston), while continuing to reunite with their independently successful band colleagues for one-off-projects, have formed Bell Biv DeVoe in 1989. Invited to stay on the MCA Records label, which has issued their freshman hit, the group's hip-hop concoction *Poison*, produced by Dr. Freeze, now hits US #3, having already been certified gold by the RIAA on the 1st. It is taken from their debut album ***Poison***, which has hit US #5 on June [2]. With Bell's singing vocal complemented by the rapping of Biv and DeVoe, it showcases a mix of street-corner harmony, cutting-edge new jack swing, soul and hip-hop, which Bell describes as: "mentally hip-hop, smoothed out on the R&B tip, with a pop feel appeal to it". Following the album's release, the trio embarks on a US tour with comedian Sinbad.
Aug [11] *Poison* reaches UK #19.
Sept [8] *Do Me!* hits US #3 and will peak at UK #56, as ***Poison*** has peaked a week earlier at UK #35.
Nov [24] *B.B.D. (I Thought It Was Me?)* makes US #26.
[26] Bell Biv DeVoe collect the Top New Pop Artist at the inaugural **Billboard** Music Awards, held at the Barker Hangar, Santa Monica Airport, Santa Monica, CA, at which the trio also performs.
Dec [19] The group kicks off an 80-city tour at the Onondaga County War Memorial, Syracuse, NY, on a bill with New Edition vocalist Johnny Gill, Keith Sweat and Monie Love.
[31] They guest on ABC-TV's "Dick Clark's New Year's Rockin' Eve".

1991

Jan [28] Bell Biv DeVoe collect the Soul/R&B, Favorite New Artist, Dance Music and Favorite New Artist, Soul/R&B trophies at the 18th annual American Music Awards, held at the Shrine Auditorium, Los Angeles, CA, at which they also perform.
Feb [16] *When Will I See You Smile Again?* peaks at US #63.
Mar [12] They win the Best R&B/Urban Contemporary Album Of The Year, Male category at the fifth annual Soul Train Music Awards, also held at the Shrine Auditorium.
June [10] The group participates in the live pay-per-view cable TV special "James Brown - Living In America".
Aug They contribute to the video of Marvin Gaye's *Mercy Mercy Mercy*, a tie-in between Motown and the Audubon Society to increase awareness of the nation's environmental problems.
Sept [21] Remix set ***WBBD - Bootcity! The Remix Album*** reaches US #18.
Oct [23] ***WBBD - Bootcity! The Remix Album*** becomes the group's second RIAA-certified gold album.
Dec [31] They guest on ABC-TV's "Dick Clark's New Year's Rockin' Eve '93" from Universal Studios, Hollywood, CA.
At the invitation of Motown President Joe Busby, Bivins is asked to assume an A&R role at the helm of his own BIV Entertainment company (licensed through Motown). His first signings are Another Bad Creation and Boyz II Men, both of whom prove instant R&B successes. (Bivins will appear - sitting on a toilet - in the video to Boyz II Men's debut smash *Motownphilly*.) Bell and DeVoe will secure a similar production deal with the Polygram conglomerate the following year.

1992

Jan [27] The group wins the Favorite Band, Duo Or Group, Soul/R&B category at the 19th annual American Music Awards, held at the Shrine Auditorium.
July [18] They attend Whitney Houston and New Edition colleague Bobby Brown's nuptials in Mendham, NJ.
Aug [10] Bivins celebrates his 24th birthday and the unveiling of the Biv 10 Entertainment logo at New York's Country Club.
[15] The Bivins-assembled ad-hoc hip-hop aggregation East Coast Family album, ***East Coast Family Volume One***, released on the Biv label, enters the US chart, set to reach #54.

1993

Jan [9] *Gangsta* reaches US #21.
[11] Reports that the group has been beaten by New York cops turn out to be false.
Apr [7] The trio wins the Outstanding R&B Act category at the Boston Music Awards held at the Wang Center.
July [10] Their sophomore album of original material, ***Hootie Mack*** debuts at its US #19 peak, as the trio launches its own line of clothes licensed to Starter merchandising. They have developed what they call "The Plan", explained by Devoe: "We get the album out. We tour and play hoops for our charities - Boys Clubs and the United Negro College Fund. We do major TV shows, some Club Mental parties by satellite, then a world tour next September (1993) and back to the US. We keep milking the album and work on our movie."
Aug [25] ***Hootie Mack*** is certified gold by the RIAA.
Oct [9] *Something In Your Eyes* debuts at its UK #60 peak.
[16] *Something In Your Eyes* reaches US #38.

1995

Apr [28] The RIAA certifies four million sales of ***Poison***.
see also: **NEW EDITION**

BELLY

Tanya Donelly (guitar, vocals); **Tom Gorman** (guitar); **Chris Gorman** (drums); **Gail Greenwood** (bass)

1990

Having already found critical success as a member of alternative quartet Throwing Muses (formed in 1980 with three high-school friends, Kristin Hersh, David Narcizo and Elaine Adamedes (replaced by Leslie Langston in 1985) in Newport, RI who have gone on to sign with the UK-based 4AD label releasing *Throwing Muses EP* (1984), ***Throwing Muses*** (1986), *Chains Changed EP* and *The Fat Skier EP* (1987), ***House Tornado*** (1988) and ***Hunkpapa*** (1989), Donelly (b. July 14, 1966, Newport), seeking another outlet for her songwriting ambitions, forms the Breeders with Pixies bassist Kim Deal, again signed to 4AD which now releases its debut set ***Pod***. Recording and performing with both the Breeders and

Throwing Muses over the next year, Donelly will contribute to the former's *Safari EP* (to be released in 1992) and the latter's ***The Real Ramona***, before electing to quit both line-ups to form Belly with Chris Gorman (b. July 29, 1967, Buffalo, NY), his brother Tom (b. May 20, 1966, Buffalo) and bassist Fred Abong (who had replaced Langston in Throwing Muses in 1990).

1992

June [29] Once again signed to the loyal 4AD label, Belly's debut effort, the EP *Slow Dust* is released in the UK (to be followed by a further 4-track CD, *Gepetto* issued in November).

1993

Jan [23] *Feed The Tree* debuts at its UK #32 peak.
Feb [13] ***Star***, its 15 songs largely written by Donelly and displaying the group's quirky childlike pop charm, hits UK #2 in its first week behind the Cult's ***Pure Cult***.
Mar [6] *Feed The Tree* tops the US Modern Rock Tracks survey.
Apr [10] Re-released *Gepetto (Remix)* bows at its UK #49 peak.
May [1] ***Star***, issued in the US by Sire Records, makes US #59 and will prompt the band's nomination in the Best New Act category for the 1993 Grammy Awards.
[22] *Feed The Tree* peaks at US #95. Abong is replaced by Greenwood (b. Mar. 10, 1960, Providence, RI).

1994

Feb [21] ***Star*** is certified gold by the RIAA.
Apr [5] Belly is voted Best Modern Rock Act and ***Star*** is named Debut Album Of The Year at the Boston Music Awards held at the Wang Center.

1995

Feb [4] *Now They'll Sleep* debuts at its UK #28 peak.
[25] The group's sophomore set ***King***, produced by Glyn Johns at Compass Point Studios, Bahamas and now featuring shared songwriting material, debuts at its UK #6 peak, released in a limited edition with an A5-size booklet.
Mar [4] ***King*** bows at its US #57 peak.
July [22] *Seal My Fate* enters at its UK #35 pinnacle.

PAT BENATAR

1977

Mar Having studied classical singing in New York, NY, and briefly attending the Juilliard School of Music, Benatar (b. Patricia Andrzejewski, Jan. 10, 1953, Brooklyn, New York), who married her high school sweetheart, G.I., Dennis Benatar and moved for a while to Richmond, VA, (where she worked as a bank clerk and waitress), has been singing off-Broadway in "The Zinger" in 1975 before moving on to perform in cabaret at New York's Catch A Rising Star where she has been spotted by its owner (and her subsequent manager) Rick Newman. Rejected by a number of major labels, she is now signed to Chrysalis Records (keeping her husband's name, although they will later divorce).
June She recruits Neil Giraldo (b. Dec. 29, 1955), former Derringer guitarist, who assembles a backing band comprising Scott St. Clair Sheets (guitar), Roger Capps (bass) and Glen Alexander Hamilton (drums), and begins recording her maiden album ***In The Heat Of The Night*** with producers Mike Chapman and Peter Coleman at MCA Whitney Studios in Glendale, CA, after an earlier pairing with Ron Dante has not worked out.

1980

Mar ***In The Heat Of The Night***, introducing her mainstream, radio-friendly rock style, reaches US #12.
[15] The extracted single *Heartbreaker*, originally recorded by UK singer Jenny Darren, reaches US #23.
June [14] Giraldo-penned *We Live For Love* reaches US #27.
Aug [30] *You Better Run*, her revival of the Young Rascals' 1966 US #20 hit, makes US #42, and her second album ***Crimes Of Passion***, produced this time by Keith Olsen, and with Myron Grombacher replacing Hamilton on drums, is released.
Dec [8] ***In The Heat Of The Night*** is certified platinum by the RIAA.
[20] Rock-driven *Hit Me With Your Best Shot* hits US #9.

1981

Jan ***Crimes Of Passion*** hits US #2.
[26] *Hit Me With Your Best Shot* is certified gold by the RIAA.
Feb [25] Benatar wins the Best Rock Vocal Performance, Female category for ***Crimes Of Passion*** at the 23rd annual Grammy Awards.
Mar [14] *Treat Me Right* reaches US #18.
Aug [1] ***Precious Time***, her UK chart breakthrough, reaches UK #30, though UK hit singles will remain sparse. On the same day, her "You Better Run" video is the second music clip broadcast on the premiering MTV cable network, following Buggles' "Video Killed The Radio Star".
[15] ***Precious Time*** tops the US chart for one week.
Sept [5] *Fire And Ice* reaches US #17.
Oct [31] *Promises In The Dark* makes US #38.

1982

Feb [20] Benatar marries her guitarist/producer Giraldo, on the island of Maui, HI.
[24] Benatar wins Best Rock Vocal Performance, Female for *Fire And Ice* at the 24th annual Grammy Awards.
Nov [13] ***Get Nervous***, produced by Giraldo with Peter Coleman, with Charlie Giordano joining on keyboards in place of Sheets and Giraldo switching from keyboards to guitar, debuts on its way to UK #73.
Dec [11] *Shadows Of The Night*, written by D. L. Byron, reaches US #13.

1983

Jan ***Get Nervous*** hits US #4.
Feb [23] Benatar nabs the Best Rock Vocal Performance, Female for *Shadows Of The Night* trophy at the 25th annual Grammy Awards.
Mar [7] ***Get Nervous*** is certified platinum by the RIAA.
[26] The extracted *Little Too Late* reaches US #20.
May [28] *Looking For A Stranger* makes US #39.
Oct Performance album ***Live From Earth***, recorded in France and California during the group's US and European tour of 1982 and 1983 and including her latest backing band recruit Charlie Giordana on keyboards (who has replaced Sheets), makes UK #60.
Dec [9] Still-climbing ***Live From Earth*** is certified platinum by the RIAA.
[10] *Love Is A Battlefield*, aided by a story-telling Bob Giraldi-directed video clip, hits US #5, while ***Live From Earth*** makes US #13.

1984

Feb [4] *Love Is A Battlefield* becomes her first UK chart single at #49.
[28] Benatar wins the Best Rock Vocal Performance, Female category (for the fourth successive year), for *Love Is A Battlefield*, at the 26th annual Grammy Awards.
Nov ***Tropico*** reaches UK #31.
[6] The RIAA certifies multi-platinum sales of ***Crimes Of Passion*** (four million) and ***Precious Time*** (two million).

1985

Jan [5] *We Belong* hits US #5, taken from ***Tropico***, which reaches US #14.
[9] ***Tropico*** is certified platinum by the RIAA.
Feb [16] *We Belong* reaches UK #22 and *Ooh Ooh Song* makes US #36.
Apr [20] *Love Is A Battlefield*, reissued in the UK, reaches #17.
June [22] Reissued *Shadows Of The Night* makes UK #50.
Aug [24] Her first album ***In The Heat Of The Night*** charts for one week at UK #98.
Sept [14] *Invincible*, her theme from the Helen Slater-starring film "Legend of Billie Jean", hits US #10.
Oct [26] *Invincible* makes UK #53.
Dec ***Seven The Hard Way***, with Donnie Nossov having replaced longtime bassist Capps, reaches US #26 and UK #69.
[14] Artists United Against Apartheid, comprising 49 artists (including Benatar), makes US #38 and UK #21 with *Sun City*.

1986

Jan [18] Sexual politics-themed *Sex As A Weapon* reaches US #28.
Feb [22] *Sex As A Weapon* peaks at UK #67.
Mar [4] ***Seven The Hard Way*** is certified gold by the RIAA.
[8] *Le Bel Age* stops at US #54.

1987

Nov [7] In the absence of new material from Benatar (who is now the mother of a daughter, Haley), a 12-cut compilation, ***Best Shots***, featuring her hit singles, hits #6, her best-performing UK album.
Dec [7] Benatar takes part in "The Gold Medal Celebration" Harry Chapin memorial concert, on what would have been the singer's 45th birthday, at Carnegie Hall, New York. The show, hosted by Harry Belafonte, features contributions from the Hooters (*One Light In A Dark Valley*), Richie Havens (*W-O-L-D*), Judy Collins (*Cat's In The Cradle*), Bruce Springsteen (*Remember When The Music*), Graham Nash (*Sandy*) and others, including Benatar's *Shooting Star*. (A subsequent album, ***Tribute***, documenting the event, will emerge in 1990 on the Relativity label).

1988

July [16] ***Wide Awake In Dreamland*** reaches UK #11, and heads towards US #28.
Aug [6] The extracted *All Fired Up* reaches UK #19, and will do the same in the US on Aug [27].
Oct *Don't Walk Away* makes UK #42.
[12] ***Wide Awake In Dreamland*** is certified gold by the RIAA.

1989

Jan [21] *One Love* peaks at UK #59.
[30] *Love Is A Battlefield* is certified gold by the RIAA.
Nov ***Best Shots*** finally makes US #67.

1990

Dec Benatar records the Charles Brown seasonal standard *Please Come Home For Christmas* specifically for the coalition troops serving in the Persian Gulf.
[20] ***Best Shots*** becomes her ninth RIAA-certified gold album.

1991

May [4] Marking a change in musical direction ***True Love***, a blues-only album produced by Giraldo, debuts at its UK #40 peak.
[10] Benatar embarks on a US tour in Worcester, MA.
[18] ***True Love*** reaches US #37.
[30] Benatar guests on NBC-TV's "The Tonight Show".
June [22] ***For Our Children***, to which Benatar contributes *Tell Me Why*, reaches US #31.

1993

May [20] Benatar plays a sellout date at the Whisky, Los Angeles, performing material from her forthcoming album.
June [19] Marking her rock'n'roll return, ***Gravity's Rainbow***, co-produced by Giraldo and Don Gehman, debuts at its US #85 peak.
Sept [4] Benatar participates in ABC-TV's "In A New Light '93" AIDS awareness special.
Oct [30] *Somebody's Baby* charts for a week at UK

#48. (Chrysalis will release a second collection of career highlights as ***The Very Best Of Pat Benatar*** in April the following year.)

CLIFF BENNETT & THE REBEL ROUSERS

Cliff Bennett (vocals); **Mick King** (lead guitar); **Frank Allen** (bass); **Ricky Winters** (drums); **Sid Phillips** (saxophone, piano)

1961

June Foundry apprentice Bennett (b. June 4, 1940, Slough, Bucks.), having made his first public appearance at a dance in Colnbrook, Middx., has formed the Rebel Rousers in 1959 as a part-time group playing dancehall cover versions of rock hits, in West Drayton, Middx. The group, which has taken its name from the 1958 Duane Eddy hit, *Rebel Rouser*, is unusual for the time in having piano and sax in the line-up. Bennett now quits his job in the family foundry business and turns professional, with the band comprising King, Allen, Phillips and Winters. Signed to EMI Records' Parlophone label, they link with producer Joe Meek for their debut *You Got What I Like*.
Oct Their second single *That's What I Said* also fails to chart, but the group is becoming a big attraction in the UK with its full, US-style R&B sound.

1962

May The band is contracted to play at the Star-Club in Hamburg, W. Germany, for six months but King is unwilling to go, and is replaced on guitar by Bernie Watson from the Savages. On its return the group embarks on its first major UK tour, with Bruce Channel and Frank Ifield.
Nov Watson, often musically at odds with the others, is asked to leave, and is replaced by Dave Wendells from the Crescents, while Mick Burt replaces Winters on drums.
Dec [31] The group begins another season at the Star-Club.

1964

July They sign to a management contract with Brian Epstein's NEMS Enterprises. (The Beatles' manager had seen Bennett during his first stint at the Star-Club.) Allen leaves to replace Tony Jackson in the Searchers, and is replaced by Bobby Thompson from Kingsize Taylor's Band, while Moss Groves is added as a second saxophonist.
Oct [31] Their revival of the Drifters' *One Way Love* is the band's breakthrough UK single hit at #9. Roy Young, erstwhile leader of the Star-Club house band and a regular on "6.5 Special", joins on piano and as a second vocalist.
Dec [26] The band opens in the Brian Epstein presentation "Gerry's Christmas Cracker" at Liverpool's Odeon Cinema, with Gerry & the Pacemakers, the Hollies and Tommy Quickly.

1965

Feb [13] Another Drifters cover, *I'll Take You Home*, makes UK #42.
[16] The group begins a 30-date, twice-nightly package tour, supporting Roy Orbison, with Marianne Faithfull, the Rockin' Berries and others, at the Adelphi Theatre in Slough, Bucks, set to end on March 21st at the Empire Theatre, Liverpool, Lancs.
Apr [2] They participate in the first edition of ITV's "Ready Steady Goes Live!"
May [24] The group takes part in the "British Song Festival" at the Brighton Dome, Brighton, E. Sussex.
June Wendells is fired and Thompson departs to the Rockin' Berries.
July Chas Hodges (b. Charles Hodges, Dec. 28, 1943, London) joins from the Outlaws on lead and bass.
Sept [21] The group performs at the "Pop From Britain" concert at London's Royal Albert Hall with Georgie Fame & the Blue Flames, the Fourmost and the Moody Blues.

1966

Sept [17] *Got To Get You Into My Life*, the Paul McCartney-produced cover version of the Beatles' ***Revolver*** album track, is the group's biggest - but also final - UK chart success, hitting #6 (taken from ***Got To Get You Into Our Lives***).
Oct Budget-priced ***Drivin' You Wild*** reaches UK #25.

1968

June Bennett splits from the Rebel Rousers, which then continues as the Roy Young Band. Bennett forms the Cliff Bennett Band with Mick Green (guitar), Robin MacDonald (bass) and Frank Farley (drums), plus a four-piece brass section. (Green and Farley have both been members of Johnny Kidd & the Pirates.)
Sept A cover of Marvin Gaye's *One More Heartache* is released and, shortly after, the brass section is dropped.
Dec Bennett's version of the Beatles' *Back In The USSR* is released from ***Cliff Bennett Branches Out***.

1969

Mar Green and MacDonald leave to join Engelbert Humperdinck's band, and are replaced by Ken Hensley, ex-Gods, and Paul Bass.
June The group releases *Memphis Streets*, before Farley leaves to get married, and the members go their separate ways.
July Bennett forms Toe Fat with Hensley, Lee Kerslake (drums) and Joe Konas (bass), who is replaced shortly thereafter by John Glasgock. The group makes two EMI albums and stays together for 18 months. They tour the US, where their albums are issued on Motown's Rare Earth label, but find no lasting success.

1971

Bennett signs a new recording deal with CBS, and emerges with a new backing band for ***Rebellion***.

1975

July After a period of obscurity, Bennett has formed Shanghai with his former guitarist Mick Green, plus Brian Alterman (guitar), Speedy Keen (bass) and Pete Kircher (drums). A solid R&B/rock band, and effectively an update of the Rebel Rousers, they release ***Fallen Heroes***.
Unfashionably polished for the dawn of the UK punk era, Shanghai is clearly passé, and will split in December 1976. (Bennett sees no future in a new band and, apart from occasional one-off recordings and appearances, will retire from the full-time music scene, subsequently finding employment in advertising, though he will take part in a Joe Meek tribute at the Odeon Cinema, Lewisham, London, with Screaming Lord Sutch, the Honeycombs, Mike Berry, Heinz, the Moontrekkers, Danny Rivers and the Tornados on June 7th 1991.)

GEORGE BENSON

1963

A child prodigy who won his first singing contest at the age of four, Benson (b. Mar. 22, 1943, Pittsburgh, PA) was already performing on radio as Little Georgie Benson before taking up the guitar at the age of eight, subsequently singing with R&B bands on the chitlin-and-gravy circuit in Pittsburgh, after leaving school. Performing his first paying gig as a guitarist in 1958, he has graduated to guitar session work and some small-label recording with both the Altairs and his own George Benson & His All-Stars (including *It Should Have Been Me* for the Amy label), before now moving to New York, NY, on the recommendation of jazz artist Grant Green, to become a full-time session musician, joining jazz organist Brother Jack McDuff's group, recording for Prestige Records.

1966

Having completed jazz guitar session work for the likes of Herbie Hancock and Wes Montgomery and at the instigation of A&R executive John Hammond, Benson signs to CBS/Columbia Records (US only) as a jazz soloist, recording ***Its Uptown*** and ***Benson Burner*** under his own name (and ***George Benson Cookbook*** and ***Willow Weep For Me*** the following year).

1969

Aug Following a one-off set, ***Giblet Gravy*** for the MGM jazz imprint Verve the previous year, and now signed to A&M Records (having turned down an offer to join Miles Davis' band) which has already issued his label debut ***Shape Of Things To Come***, his first US chart success is ***Tell It Like It Is*** (its guitar work influenced by the style of labelmate Montgomery, who took a jazz guitar album into the US Top 20 in 1967 with ***A Day In The Life***). Benson's album now peaks at US #145.

1970

Having released his final A&M sides on ***The Other Side Of Abbey Road*** in 1970 (a jazz guitar version of the entire Beatles ***Abbey Road*** album), he joins veteran jazz producer Creed Taylor's (who produced Benson's mid-'60s efforts) CTI label, whose workshop approach has resident virtuoso players backing each other on "solo" efforts, releasing ***Beyond The Blue Horizon*** in 1971, followed by ***White Rabbit*** (1972), its title track a cover of Grace Slick's composition, and ***Body Talk*** (1973), variously featuring the likes of Ron Carter (bass), Herbie Hancock (piano), Billy Cobham (drums) and Earl Klugh (guitar).

1974

Feb As a staff musician at CTI Records, Benson has played guitar on the album sessions of almost every act on the label, but now scores in his own right with ***Bad Benson***, which features Carter, pianist Kenny Barron and drummer Steve Gadd among others, and makes US #78.

1975

Nov [22] Benson's first hit single (and only one for CTI) *Supership*, on which he is credited as George "Bad" Benson, reaches UK #30, taken from ***Supership***.

1976

Jan [6-8] Newly signed to Warner Bros. Records, Benson records his debut for the label at Capitol Records Studio, Hollywood, CA, with producer Tommy LiPuma.
July [31] He shoots spectacularly to US #1 with ***Breezin'***. The album initially sells over a million copies, and begins a decade-long shift of emphasis in Benson's records, now encouraged by producer LiPuma to showcase his considerable soul vocal chops.
Aug [21] Collecting highlights from his earlier CTI recordings, ***Good King Bad***, makes US #51.
[28] Benson's first US chart single, a cover of Leon Russell's *This Masquerade*, extracted from ***Breezin'***, hits #10.
Sept [4] Similar archive album ***The Other Side Of Abbey Road***, on A&M, collects further spin-off success from ***Breezin'***, making US #125.
Nov [13] The Bobby Womack-penned Warners album title track *Breezin'* peaks at US #63.
[27] CTI album ***Benson And Farrell*** (a collaboration with jazz flautist Joe Farrell) makes #100.

1977

Feb [19] Benson wins the Record Of The Year for *This Masquerade*, Best Pop Instrumental Performance and Best-Engineered Non-Classical Recording for ***Breezin'***, and Best R&B Instrumental Performance for *Theme From Good King Bad* categories at the 19th annual Grammy Awards.
Mar [12] While Benson undertakes dates in Europe including a show at London's Royal Albert Hall, the

CTI-released album ***George Benson In Concert: Carnegie Hall***, recorded live in 1975, reaches US #122.
[19] Warner Bros. follow-up set, the jazz-soul fused ***In Flight*** hits US #9.
June [25] His update of the Nat "King" Cole/Bobby Darin hit *Nature Boy* makes UK #26.
July [9] ***In Flight*** reaches UK #19, four months after debuting.
[23] *Gonna Love You More* peaks at US #71.
Oct [6] ***In Flight*** is certified platinum by the RIAA.
[8] *The Greatest Love Of All*, the Michael Masser/Linda Creed-penned theme from the Muhammad Ali biopic "The Greatest", released as a one-off by Arista Records, which has soundtrack rights, reaches US #24. (The song will be revived as a US #1 in 1986 by Whitney Houston.)
[22] *The Greatest Love Of All* reaches UK #27.

1978

Feb [18] Double album ***Weekend In L.A.*** charts for a week at UK #47.
Apr [15] ***Weekend In L.A.*** hits US #5.
May [3] ***Weekend In L.A.*** is confirmed platinum by the RIAA.
[22] Benson performs again at the Royal Albert Hall, during a week-long UK tour.
June [10] His revival of the Drifters' *On Broadway*, taken from ***Weekend In L.A.***, hits US #7.

1979

Feb [15] Benson wins the Best R&B Vocal Performance, Male category for *On Broadway* at the 21st annual Grammy Awards.
Mar [6] Still-climbing double album ***Livin' Inside Your Love*** is certified gold by the RIAA.
Apr [14] ***Livin' Inside Your Love*** reaches UK #24.
[21] ***Livin' Inside Your Love*** hits US #7.
[28] The extracted and self-explanatory *Love Ballad* makes US #18, and will also make UK #29 on May [5].

1980

Aug [16] Dance-aimed *Give Me The Night*, Benson's first successful collaboration with UK songwriter Rod Temperton and produced by Quincy Jones, hits UK #7.
Sept [27] *Give Me The Night* becomes Benson's biggest US chart single, hitting #4, while its parent album ***Give Me The Night***, helmed by Jones, hits UK (Sept [6]) and US #3.
Oct [14] ***Give Me The Night*** is certified platinum by the RIAA.
[25] *Love X Love* hits UK #10.
Nov *Love X Love*, also penned by Temperton, peaks at US #61.

1981

Feb [21] *What's On Your Mind* makes UK #45.
[25] Benson wins the Best R&B Vocal Performance, Male for ***Give Me The Night***, Best R&B Instrumental Performance for *Off Broadway* and Best Jazz Vocal Performance, Male for *Moody's Mood* categories at the 23rd annual Grammy Awards.
Sept [26] Benson's duet with Aretha Franklin on *Love All The Hurt Away* makes US #46.
Nov [21] Warner Bros. double compilation set ***The George Benson Collection***, compiled, sequenced and edited by producer LiPuma, reaches UK #19.
Dec [5] Uptempo *Turn Your Love Around* reaches UK #29.

1982

Jan [14] Still-climbing ***The George Benson Collection*** is certified gold by the RIAA.
[30] ***The George Benson Collection*** reaches US #14.
Feb [6] *Turn Your Love Around* restores him to the US Top 10 at #5.
[20] Similarly-styled *Never Give Up On A Good Thing* reaches UK #14 (also peaking at US #52 on Apr [10]).

1983

June [11] *Lady Love Me (One More Time)*, co-written by David Paich and James Newton Howard, reaches UK #11.
[18] *Inside Love (So Personal)* makes US #43. Both are taken from his new Arif Mardin-produced album ***In Your Eyes***, which reaches US #27, and becomes one of his most successful UK albums, hitting #3 during a 53-week chart stay.
July [30] *Feel Like Makin' Love*, his revival of Roberta Flack's 1974 US #1, reaches UK #28.
Aug [24] ***In Your Eyes*** is certified gold by the RIAA.
Sept [10] *Lady Love Me (One More Time)* reaches US #30.
Oct [15] Lush ballad and title track *In Your Eyes* hits UK #7 - his last Top 10 single of the decade.
[22] The RIAA confirms three million sales of ***Breezin'***.
Dec [24] Belatedly-issued *Inside Love (So Personal)* makes UK #57.

1984

Feb [28] Benson wins the Best Pop Instrumental Performance category for *Being With You* at the 26th annual Grammy Awards.

1985

Jan He appears at the "Rock In Rio" festival at Barra da Tijuca, Brazil, before a crowd of 60,000, on a bill with James Taylor.
[26] *20/20* makes US #48.
Feb [23] *20/20* reaches UK #29, taken from the Russ Titelman/Michael Masser-produced ***20/20***, which climbs to US #45 and UK #9.
Apr [27] His update of Bobby Darin's 1960 US #6 hit, *Beyond The Sea (La Mer)*, peaks at UK #60.
Oct [26] UK-compiled, TV-advertised album ***The Love Songs***, featuring all his major hit singles, tops the UK chart for the first of two weeks.
Nov [13] ***20/20*** is certified gold by the RIAA.

1986

Aug [23] *Kisses In The Moonlight* peaks at UK #60.
Sept ***While The City Sleeps ...***, variously produced by Narada Michael Walden, Kashif, Tommy LiPuma and Robbie Buchanan, reaches UK #13 and makes US #77.
Dec [13] *Shiver* is Benson's biggest UK hit single for over three years, reaching #19.

1987

Feb [21] *Teaser* makes UK #45.
July [18] Jazz guitar-returning ***Collaboration***, recorded with fellow jazz guitarist Earl Klugh, makes UK #47 and will reach US #59.

1988

Feb [23] ***Collaboration*** is certified gold by the RIAA.
Sept [3] *Let's Do It Again*, reviving the Staple Singers' 1975 US #1, peaks at UK #56 as ***Twice The Love*** reaches UK #16 (on Sept [10]) and makes US #76.

1989

July [8] ***Tenderly***, continuing Benson's return to his jazz roots, makes UK #52.
Sept [2] ***Tenderly*** tops the US Jazz chart, having peaked at US #140 in August.

1990

Jan [17] Benson inducts Charlie Christian into the Rock and Roll Hall of Fame at the fifth annual induction dinner, at New York's Waldorf Astoria Hotel.
Aug [17] He performs at the "JVC Jazz Festival", Fort Adams State Park, Newport, RI, with B.B. King, Miles Davis and others.
[25] A 14-date US tour starts at the Chautauqua Amphitheatre, Chautauqua, NY, set to end on September 30th at County Park, St. Louis, MO.
Oct ***Big Boss Band***, featuring the Count Basie Orchestra, and reviving such standards as *I Only Have Eyes For You*, *Walkin' My Baby Back Home* and *Skylark*, is released.
Nov [14] Benson begins a short eight-date UK concert visit at Wembley Arena, Wembley, Middx., backed by members of the Royal Philharmonic Orchestra, set to end on the 23rd at the Edinburgh Playhouse, Edinburgh, Scotland.

1991

Feb [20] He wins the Best Jazz Instrumental Performance, Big Band category with the Count Basie Orchestra for *Basie's Bag* at the 33rd annual Grammy Awards, held at Radio City Music Hall, New York, having also played on Quincy Jones' multi Grammy-winning album ***Back On The Block***, guesting on the tracks *Jazz Corner Of The Word*, *Birdland* and *Setembro (Brazilian Wedding Song)*.
July [11-14] Benson takes part in the 16th "North Sea Jazz Festival", at the Congress Centre, the Hague, Holland.
Oct [8-13] He plays at New York's Blue Note club with the Count Basie Orchestra.
[16] Benson performs on the second night of "Guitar Legends", a five-concert series as part of "Expo '92", Seville, Spain.
Nov [9] ***Midnight Moods - The Love Collection***, a 16-track Telstar Records TV-advertised compilation, reaches UK #25.

1992

Aug [11] Benson opens a two-week stint at the Blue Note in Osaka, Japan.
Sept [5] *I'll Keep Your Dreams Alive*, a duet with Patti Austin featured in the movie "Freddie FRO7", charts for a week at UK #68.
Oct [27-28] Benson embarks on a seven-date large-venue UK tour at the Wembley Arena.

1993

June [22] Switching back to soul, Warner Bros. releases ***Love Remembers***, variously produced by David Gamson, Bob James and Stewart Levine, and with much help from his son Steven Benson Hue.
[27] Benson performs at a benefit for the Thurgood Marshall Scholarship Fund in Chicago, IL, as he prepares for a July tour of Holland, Germany, France and Spain.
Sept [10-12] He plays at the the Mountain Winery, Saratoga, CA, during a short tour of California.
[16] Benson guests on NBC-TV's "The Tonight Show".

1994

July [2] He takes part in the "Newport Jazz Festival" at the Saratoga Performing Arts Center, Saratoga Springs, NY.
Sept [27] ***Kermit Unpigged***, featuring a Benson duet with the Muppets, is released on Jim Henson Records in the US.

1996

Mar [19] Having been signed to the specialist jazz GRP label in the US the previous year and now preparing his label debut, Benson performs in a star-studded salute to jazz vibraphonist Lionel Hampton at "Swing Into Spring: A Harlem Tribute To Lionel Hampton" held at New York's Apollo Theater.

BROOK BENTON

1957

After singing with the Camden Jubilee Singers gospel quartet before moving to New York, NY, in 1948, to join the Bill Landford Spiritual Singers, singing R&B with the Sandmen and recording as a soloist on Epic Records, Benton (b. Benjamin Franklin Peay, Sept. 19, 1931, Camden, SC) is working as a truck driver in New York when he meets music publisher and Mercury Records A&R chief Clyde Otis (the first black in such a position at a major label) and joins him as a studio demo singer, also forming a songwriting team with Otis and arranger Belford Hendricks. Scoring his first US chart hit (at #82) with *A Million Miles From Nowhere*, while signed to RCA subsidiary Vik Records the following March, his success as a songwriter also blossoms with Nat King Cole's version of Benton's *Looking Back* hitting US #6 in May 1958 and Clyde McPhatter also hitting US #6 with Benton's *A Lover's Question* in December the same year.

1959

Jan Otis persuades Mercury Records to sign Benton as a vocalist, with himself and Hendricks producing and arranging his recordings.
Apr His first Mercury release *It's Just A Matter Of Time*, written by all three, hits US #3, tops the US R&B chart for ten weeks, and becomes a million-seller. A lush, deep-voiced ballad, it also sets the style for Benton's hit career. (Its B-side *Hurtin' Inside* also peaks at US #78.)
June *Endlessly* reaches US #12 and its B-side *So Close* makes #38.
July [13] *Endlessly* is his UK chart debut, reaching #28.
Aug *Thank You Pretty Baby* makes US #16 and tops the R&B chart for four weeks. (Its B-side *With All Of My Heart* peaks at US #82.)
Nov *So Many Ways* hits US #6, also topping the R&B survey for three weeks.
Dec *This Time Of The Year* peaks at US #66.

1960

Mar *Baby (You Got What It Takes)*, a duet with Dinah Washington, hits US #5, tops the R&B chart for eight weeks, and is another million-seller.
Apr [18] *Hither And Thither And You* peaks at US #58.
May [9] *Hither*'s A-side, *The Ties That Bind*, makes US #37.
June His second duet with Washington, *A Rockin' Good Way (To Mess Around And Fall In Love)*, hits US #7, also topping the R&B ranking for five weeks.
Sept *Kiddio* hits US #7 and is also an R&B survey #1 for nine weeks, while its B-side *The Same One* reaches US #16.
Nov *Kiddio* makes UK #41.
Dec [5] *Fools Rush In*, penned by Johnny Mercer, reaches US #24 while its B-side *You'll Want Me To Want You* will stop at US #93 on the 26th.

1961

Feb [20] *Fools Rush In* makes UK #50.
Apr *Think Twice* reaches US #11, and its B-side *For My Baby* makes #28.
June Compilation album ***Brook Benton Golden Hits***, reaches US #82.
July His revival of the traditional *The Boll Weevil Song* is another million-seller, and also Benton's highest chart-placed US single, hitting #2 for three weeks, unable to dislodge Bobby Lewis' chart-topping *Tossin' And Turnin'*, while peaking at UK #30 - his final UK chart entry.
Sept His treatment of another traditional song *Frankie And Johnny* reaches US #20.
Oct *Frankie*'s B-side *It's Just A House Without You* makes US #45, as ***The Boll Weevil Song & 11 Other Great Hits*** climbs to US #70.

1962

Jan *Revenge* reaches US #15, and its B-side, *The Last Penny*, stops at US #77.
Feb *Shadrack*, a remake of the 1931 song *Shadrack, Meshack, Abednigo*, reaches US #19.
Feb *If You Believe* peaks at US #77.
Mar Film theme *Walk On The Wild Side* makes US #43.
June *Hit Record* is ironically his lowest chart-placed record since his first, stopping at US #45. Benton quickly eschews its gimmick-laden style and returns to blues-ballads.
Oct *Lie To Me*, in his more familiar phrasing, reaches US #13.
Dec B-side *Still Waters Run Deep* peaks at US #89 as ***Singin' The Blues - Lie To Me*** makes US #40.

1963

Jan *Hotel Happiness*, his biggest seller for nearly two years, hits US #3 - but will be his last US Top 10 entry for seven years.
Feb Benton is beaten up in the basement of a St. Louis, MO club, after he refuses to perform a second show because of a rowdy audience.
Mar *Dearer Than Life* peaks at US #59.
Apr *I Got What I Wanted* reaches US #28, as ***Brook Benton's Golden Hits, Volume 2*** climbs to US #82.
July *My True Confession* peaks at US #22.
Oct *Two Tickets To Paradise* reaches US #32.
[13] Benton makes his UK TV debut, second on the bill behind the Beatles, on "Sunday Night At The London Palladium".
[19] He begins a UK "Greatest Record Show Of 1963" tour with Dion, Lesley Gore, Trini Lopez and Timi Yuro at London's Finsbury Park Astoria.

1964

Feb *Going Going Gone* makes US #35. Benton continues to tour the US with great success, earning $25,000 for a week-long stint at the Apollo Theatre in Harlem, New York.
June *Too Late To Turn Back Now/Another Cup Of Coffee* is his last Mercury pairing to make the US top 50, at #43 and #47 respectively.
Aug *A House Is Not A Home* stops at US #75, its sales split with those of Dionne Warwick's version, which climbs to US #71 in the same week.
Oct *Lumberjack* is his last Mercury hit of any consequence, making US #53.
Dec *Do It Right* peaks at US #67.

1965

July Benton leaves Mercury as his last release, *Love Me Now*, spends a week at US #100, and signs to RCA Records.
Dec *Mother Nature, Father Time* makes US #53, but is his only RCA release to chart.

1967

Sept After two barren years and another label change, he has one US chart success on Frank Sinatra's Reprise Records: *Laura (Tell Me What He's Got That I Ain't Got)* makes US #78, regarded by the artist as one of his own favorite recordings.
Oct ***Laura (What's He Got That I Ain't Got)*** makes US #156.
Dec [2] Benton guests on BBC TV's "Dee Time".

1968

Oct Now signed to Atlantic Records subsidiary label Cotillion, and recording in a laid-back soul idiom which updates his earlier style, *Do Your Own Thing* stops at US #99.

1969

July ***Do Your Own Thing*** peaks at US #189.
Aug *Nothing Can Take The Place Of You* reaches US #74.

1970

Feb ***Brook Benton Today*** rises to US #27.
Mar [18] Benton has his first million-seller for almost a decade with what becomes widely regarded as the definitive version of Tony Joe White's soul ballad *Rainy Night In Georgia* hitting US #4 (and R&B #1).
May His version of Frank Sinatra's *My Way* proves an inappropriate follow-up, reaching US #72.
June His strong interpretation of Joe South's *Don't It Make You Want To Go Home* makes US #45.
Aug [22] ***Home Style*** makes US #199.

1971

Jan His duet with the Dixie Flyers on *Shoes*, which makes US #67, proves to be his last hit for Cotillion and also his US chart swan song.

1988

Apr [9] His subsequent moves to MGM, Stax, All Platinum and Olde Worlde later in the '70s, plus a brief tie-up with the Fabergé perfume company when it tried to move into the music business, brought some well-reviewed records (but little sales action), including ***Gospel Truth*** (1972), ***Something For Everyone*** (1973), ***Sings A Love Story*** (1975), ***Mr Bartender*** (1976), ***This Is Brook Benton*** (1976), ***Makin' Love Is Good For You*** (1977), ***Ebony*** (1978) and ***Brook Benton Sings The Standards*** (1984)) but, because his relaxed style and wide repertoire of past hits enjoyed enduring appeal, he has remained in demand on the US club circuit as a ballad singer. While his career highlights have been brought to CD with the 1986 release of both ***16 Golden Classics*** and ***His Greatest Hits***, Benton dies in hospital in New York, aged 56, following an illness.

CHUCK BERRY

1954

Aug [13] Berry (b. Charles Edward Anderson Berry, Oct. 18, 1926, St. Louis, MO), after spending three years in the Algoa Reform School between 1944 and 1947 following an armed robbery conviction, after which he has found work at General Motors, and having served a club apprenticeship since his teenage years, has moved on to residences at the Crank Club, 2742 Vanderventer St., St. Louis, earning $42 a night and Gleeson's Show Place, Cleveland, OH, at $800 a week. He has also married his wife, Themetta, on October 28th, 1948. Joining the club trio the Johnnie Johnson Trio in St. Louis in 1952, with himself on guitar, Johnson on piano and Ebby Harding on drums, they have played evening gigs, while Berry, with a degree in cosmetology and tonsorial skills from the Poro School of Beauty Culture, has also worked by day as a hairdresser and beautician. Recording for the first time, Berry cuts *Oh Maria* and *I Hope These Words Will Find You Well* during sessions for Joe Alexander & the Cubans at the Premier Studios, St. Louis. (They will be released on the Ballad label and be credited to Charles Berryn.)

1955

May Berry meets Muddy Waters, who had seen him at the Cosmopolitan Club in East St. Louis and who puts him in touch with Chess Records, whose Leonard Chess is impressed by Berry's demos of his own songs, one of which is the traditional country tune *Ida Red* (recorded at a cost of $79), and signs him to a record deal.
[21] Berry records *Ida Red*, now rewritten by him as *Maybellene*, in Chicago with Johnnie Johnson on piano, Willie Dixon on bass, Jasper Thomas on drums and Jerome Green playing maracas, laying down his basic style: uptempo blues-based with a country rockabilly infusion, driven by a guitar rhythm - a legendary style which will inspire thousands of artists over the following 30 years and establish Berry as a vital force in the evolution of rock history, not least as the songwriter of all of his influential hits.
Aug [31] *Maybellene* hits US #5 while topping the the R&B chart for nine weeks.
Nov [12] Berry is named Most Promising R&B Artist in **Billboard**'s annual DJ Poll.

1956

June After two non-survey singles, *Roll Over Beethoven* reaches US #29.
Nov [18] Berry performs at the Forum, Wichita, KS, sharing a bill with Bill Haley & the Comets, the Platters, Frankie Lymon, Clyde McPhatter and others.
Dec He appears in the film "Rock Rock Rock", singing *You Can't Catch Me.*

1957

Feb [15] Berry embarks on Irving Feld's "Greatest Show Of 1957" package tour, with Fats Domino, Clyde McPhatter, the Five Satins, LaVern Baker and others, set to end on May 5th.
Apr Berry buys 30 acres of land west of St. Louis, where he will begin building the Berry Park Country Club.
May *School Day* hits US #3 and is a million-seller, also topping the R&B chart.
June [22] *School Day* is his UK chart debut, at #24.
July Berry appears on ABC-TV's "The Big Beat", hosted by DJ Alan Freed.
Aug *Oh Baby Doll*, with Lafayette Leake on piano, Willie Dixon on bass and Fred Below on drums, a

line-up which will play on many of Berry's classic singles, peaks at US #57.
[24] During a current US tour, Berry performs at the Memorial Auditorium, Sacramento, CA, sharing a bill with Louis Jordan & His Orchestra.
Sept He appears in the film "Mr. Rock And Roll", which Alan Freed.
[6] "The Biggest Show Of Stars For 1957 package tour, with Berry. Buddy Holly & the Crickets, Paul Anka, the Drifters, Frankie Lymon & the Teenagers, the Everly Brothers, Clyde McPhatter and others, opens at the Syria Mosque, Pittsburgh, PA, set to close on November 24th at the Mosque, Richmond, VA. (The white artists on the bill are unable to play on several dates because of segregation laws which forbid black and white acts to perform on the same stage.)
Dec *Rock And Roll Music* hits US #8, and continues to confirm his pioneering role in the genre of which he sings.

1958

Mar [17] *Sweet Little Sixteen*, self-penned like the majority of his output, hits US #2 and tops the R&B chart for three weeks, becoming another million-seller and his biggest hit to date.
May [10] *Sweet Little Sixteen* reaches UK #16.
June *Johnny B Goode,* his song later most covered by other artists, hits US #8 and UK #27.
July Appearing at the "Newport Jazz Festival", his performance of *Sweet Little Sixteen* will be seen some months later in "Jazz On A Summer's Day", the documentary film of the event made by Bert Stern.
Aug *Beautiful Delilah* peaks at US #81.
Sept *Carol* reaches US #18.
Nov [17] *Joe Joe Gun*, the B-side of the still-climbing *Sweet Little Rock And Roller*, peaks at US #83.
Dec [1] *Sweet Little Rock And Roller* makes US #47. Both sides of a special seasonal single also make the US chart - *Run Rudolph Run* at #69 and *Merry Christmas Baby* at #71.
[25] "Alan Freed's Christmas Rock & Roll Spectacular", featuring Berry, Bo Diddley, the Everly Brothers and Jackie Wilson in its all-star line-up, opens a 10-day run at Manhattan's Loew's Theater.

1959

Mar *Anthony Boy* peaks at US #60.
May *Almost Grown* makes US #32, its B-side *Little Queenie* (which itself makes #80) featured in the film "Go Johnny Go", in which Berry also sings *Memphis Tennessee* and has a small acting role.
July *Back In The USA* makes US #37.
Dec [1] After performing in El Paso, TX, Berry meets 14-year-old Apache Indian Janice Norine Escalanti, who is, unbeknown to Berry, working as a waitress and prostitute.
[23] Berry is arrested and charged with violating the Mann Act, after he takes Escalanti to work as a hat-check girl in the nightclub he owns in St. Louis, as in the opinion of the police he has transported a minor across a State Line for immoral purposes. Berry allegedly fires her when she is suspected of working as a prostitute. After she reports him to the police, Berry is initally convicted and sentenced to the maximum penalty of five years in jail and fined $2,000. (However, after racist comments by case authority judge George H. Moore Jr. are made public, Berry is freed, prior to a retrial.)

1960

Mar *Too Pooped To Pop* makes US #42, with the B-side *Let It Rock* peaking at US #64.

1961

May [31] The artist's Berryland Amusement Park opens outside St. Louis.

1962

Feb Berry is finally convicted on the Mann Act charge, and begins a three-year stretch in the Indiana Federal Penitentiary in Terre Haute, IN. He will serve two years, and be released in 1964.

1963

June New interest in Berry's music hits the UK as the R&B boom takes hold, with hundreds of groups across the country using his songs as basic repertoire. A compilation album of oldies, simply titled ***Chuck Berry,*** is issued to capitalise on this boom, and climbs to UK #12.
July [27] *Go Go Go,* an earlier US single, makes UK #38. The Rolling Stones also enter the UK chart with their first single, a revival of Berry's *Come On,* which reaches #21.
Aug Renewed interest in Berry begins in the US, where the Beach Boys and Lonnie Mack have just had top five hits with revivals of *Sweet Little Sixteen* (re-written as *Surfin' USA*) and *Memphis Tennessee* (instrumentally, as *Memphis*). With Berry still in jail, Chess Records puts his versions of these songs, plus others, on an album which has audience noise dubbed on, released as ***Chuck Berry On Stage.***
Oct ***Chuck Berry On Stage*** reaches US #29 (his first charted album), and hits UK #6.
Nov [16] Another reissued oldie, *Memphis Tennessee*, backed with *Let It Rock*, eclipses a cover version by Dave Berry to become Chuck's first UK Top 10 single, hitting #6.

1964

Jan Out of prison and in demand (as another boost, the Beatles have just included *Roll Over Beethoven* on their second album), Berry returns to Chess Records' Chicago studio to record new material.
[4] Seasonal *Run Rudolph Run* makes UK #36, while the compilation ***More Chuck Berry*** hits UK #9.
Feb [22] Newly-recorded *Nadine (Is It You?)* reaches UK #27, and will make US #23.
May [9] He begins his first UK tour at the Astoria Theatre, Finsbury Park, London, a 21-date, twice-nightly package, supported by the Animals, the Swinging Blue Jeans, the Nashville Teens, Karl Denver and others, set to end on the 29th at the Odeon Theatre, Southend, Essex.
[23] Berry appears on ITV's "Thank Your Lucky Stars".
June [13] *No Particular Place To Go,* which updates *School Day*'s melody with new car-cruising lyrics, hits UK #3, and will reach US #10. ***His Latest And Greatest*** hits UK #8, while ***Chuck Berry's Greatest Hits*** makes US #34.
Sept [12] *You Never Can Tell* reaches UK #23, and will make US #14.
Oct UK-only album ***You Never Can Tell*** reaches #18.
[28-29] Berry appears in the "TAMI Show (Teenage Music International Show)" at the Civic Auditorium, Santa Monica, CA, together with the Beach Boys, the Supremes and the Rolling Stones among a host of current hot acts.
Nov *Little Marie,* a lyrical sequel to *Memphis Tennessee,* peaks at US #54.
Dec [12] *Promised Land* is found at US #41.

1965

Jan US-only ***St Louis To Liverpool*** climbs to #124.
[8] Backed by the Five Dimensions, Berry begins a 24-date, twice-nightly UK tour, with Long John Baldry and the Moody Blues, at the Odeon Theatre, Lewisham, London, set to close on the 31st at the Regal Theatre, Edmonton, London.
[9] He records several tracks with the Five Dimensions at Pye Studios in London, which will appear on ***Chuck Berry In London***.
[30] *Promised Land* reaches UK #26.
Apr [3] *Dear Dad* peaks at US #95.
June [17-20] Berry takes part in the "First New York Folk Festival" at Carnegie Hall, New York.

1966

June He leaves Chess to sign to Mercury Records for a $150,000 advance, but his time with this label will yield no hits. (He also continues to receive income from his 42-acre Berry Park theme project, which features a guitar-shaped swimming pool, located in Wentzville, MO.)
Aug [7] "Gather No Moss", filmed before a live audience in Santa Monica, CA, premieres in the UK at Birmingham's Futurist Cinema.

1967

Feb [19] Near the end of a London Saville Theatre concert, two fans get on stage, at which point the safety curtain is brought down, almost hitting Berry. Brian Epstein subsequently fires house manager Michael Bullock. He will return to play a further concert the following week (on the 26th).
Mar [17-19] Berry performs at the Fillmore West, San Francisco, sharing the bill with the Grateful Dead.
May ***Chuck Berry's Golden Decade*** peaks at US #191. (During the year, he also records a performance album at the Fillmore Auditorium, San Francisco, CA, with the Steve Miller Band.)

1969

Jan [30] Berry begins a four-day stint at the Fillmore West, San Francisco, on a bill with Mike Bloomfield, Mark Naftalin and Nick Gravenites.
July [5] Berry plays on the final night of the "Pop Proms" at London's Royal Albert Hall, during a current UK tour, with the Who. (Fans storm the stage, leading to a ban on rock music at the venue.)
Sept [13] He appears at the "Toronto Rock'n'Roll Revival Concert" at the Varsity Stadium, University of Toronto, ON, Canada, along with Little Richard, Gene Vincent, Jerry Lee Lewis, Bo Diddley, the Doors, Alice Cooper and John Lennon's Plastic Ono Band.
Dec [25-28] Berry plays year-end concerts at the Fillmore West.

1970

Feb Berry re-signs to Chess and records ***Back Home,*** which includes *Tulane,* later a UK hit for the Steve Gibbons Band.
Mar [19-22] He shares the bill with It's A Beautiful Day at the Fillmore West.

1972

Feb [3] Berry appears at the "Lanchester Arts Festival" at the Coventry Locarno, Coventry, W. Midlands.
June Tracks made in a London studio with members of the Faces backing him, together with cuts from a live show recorded, unknown to Berry, at Lanchester, are packaged as ***The London Chuck Berry Sessions.*** It will eventually hit US #8, and becomes his biggest-selling album.
Aug [5] Berry takes part in the first-ever UK "Rock'n'Roll Revival Show" at Wembley Stadium, Wembley, Middx., with Bill Haley, Little Richard, Jerry Lee Lewis and Bo Diddley.
Sept [13] *My Ding-A-Ling* is certified gold by the RIAA.
Oct [21] The double-entendre, audience-participation novelty number *My Ding-A-Ling,* backed by Onnie McIntyre and Robbie McIntosh of the Average White Band, Dave Kafinetti and Nic Potter and taken from the live portion of the album, tops the US chart for the first of two weeks, becoming a million-plus seller and, ironically, Berry's most successful single ever.
[27] ***The London Chuck Berry Session*** is certified gold by the RIAA.
Nov [25] *My Ding-A-Ling* begins a four-week run atop the UK survey, in spite of efforts by public morality campaigner Mary Whitehouse to have it banned. Double compilation ***Chuck Berry's Golden Decade,*** originally issued in 1967, is reactivated by the success of *My Ding-A-Ling,* and climbs to US #72, while double album ***St. Louie To Frisco To Memphis***, featuring one disk recorded at the Fillmore with the Steve Miller Band, peaks at US #185.

1973

Feb *Reelin' And Rockin'*, also a live album extract, reaches US #27 and UK #18, but will be Berry's last hit single in either country. ***Chuck Berry's Golden Decade, Vol.2*** makes US #110.
Apr [28] Berry, Jerry Lee Lewis and Bruce

Springsteen play at the Cole Field House in Maryland, with Berry backed by Springsteen's band.

Sept ***Bio***, blues-based like most of his '70s Chess recordings and with Berry backed by Elephant's Memory, makes US #175.

1975

Feb [19] Berry begins a nine-date UK tour at the Lewisham Odeon, London, set to end on March 2nd at the Birmingham Odeon.

Mar ***Chuck Berry '75***, on which he duets for the first time on some tracks with his daughter, Ingrid Berry Gibson, is released.

1977

Feb [19] A compilation album of hits ***Motorvatin'***, aided by TV advertising, hits UK #7.

May [3] Berry plays at the Batley Variety Club during a UK tour.

1978

Mar Berry plays himself in the rock'n'roll era film "American Hot Wax", which chronicles the story of DJ Alan Freed.

1979

June [7] He performs at the White House by special request of President Jimmy Carter.

July [10] Berry is sentenced to five months in jail, for income tax evasion in 1973. (Always preferring cash payments for gigs, Berry has developed a long-standing reputation as an aggressive businessman.)

Oct ***Rockit***, with Johnnie Johnson on piano, is released, the only fruit of a new recording deal with Atlantic Records subsidiary Atco.

Nov [19] He is released from jail after serving his sentence in Lompoc Prison Farm, CA.

1980

With the release of ***Rock! Rock! Rock 'N' Roll***, his only original recording of the new decade, Berry will continue to tour throughout the US and Europe over the next four years.

1981

Jan [30] Berry is presented with the Special Award Of Merit at the eighth annual American Music Awards, held at the ABC-TV Studios, Hollywood, CA.

1985

Feb [26] Berry is honored by the NARAS at the 27th annual Grammy Awards with a Lifetime Achievement Award, noting him to be "one of the most influential and creative innovators in the history of American popular music, a composer and performer whose talents inspired the elevation of rock'n'roll to one of music's major art forms".

1986

Jan [23] Keith Richards inducts Berry into the the Rock and Roll Hall of Fame at the inaugural induction dinner at New York's Waldorf Astoria Hotel.

Mar [3] He is also inducted into the Songwriters' Hall of Fame at the 17th annual awards dinner, held at the Hotel Plaza Grand Ballroom, New York.

Oct [16] A special concert at the Fox Theatre in St. Louis, organised by the Rolling Stones' Keith Richards, who leads the backing band, which includes Eric Clapton, Julian Lennon, Linda Ronstadt and Etta James, following a week of rehearsals at Berry's farm in Wentzville, is held to celebrate Berry's 60th birthday and to form the basis of a documentary film.

1987

Oct [8] Berry is awarded his own star on the Hollywood Walk of Fame at 1777 N. Vine St., as the bio-movie about the rock legend, "Hail! Hail! Rock'n"Roll", premieres.

1988

Jan **Chuck Berry: The Autobiography** is published, a revealing account of his personal and musical life, mostly written during his 1979 incarceration.

Mar In Britain to promote both his autobiography and "Hail! Hail! Rock'n'Roll" (to which there is the accompanying ***Hail! Hail! Rock'n'Roll***), Berry plays a London concert at the Hammersmith Odeon, sings *Memphis Tennessee* on ITV chat show "Aspel", and tells a magazine interviewer he may retire "soon".

[2] *Maybellene* is inducted into the NARAS Hall of Fame, at the 30th annual Grammy Awards.

Nov MCA releases ***Chess Box*** an anthology of historic Berry recordings made for Chess between 1955 and 1973.

1989

June Berry becomes one of the first ten people to be inducted into the St. Louis Walk of Fame.

Aug [27] *Johnny B. Goode* is featured on the Voyager Interstellar Record. Berry sings the song at a JPL party after Voyager 2 has encountered the Neptune system.

Nov [3] Berry participates in a 20th anniversary "Rock'n'Roll Revival" concert with the Coasters, Jay & the Americans, the Five Satins, the Skyliners, Bo Diddley and others.

Dec [27] A civil suit for invasion of privacy is filed by Hosana A. Huck, a former cook at the Southern Air restaurant (which Berry bought in 1987), in the St. Charles County Circuit Court, Wentzville, MO, alleging that Berry secretly installed video recording equipment in the ladies' toilets. The suit claims that the resulting tapes, allegedly compiled over a one-year period, "were created for the improper purpose of the entertainment and gratification of the abnormal urination and coprophagous sexual fetishes and sexual predilections of defendant Chuck Berry". Over the next two months, a collective class action suit will be brought by some 200 other women who visited the restaurant during the relevant time period.

1990

Feb [21] *Roll Over Beethoven* is inducted into the NARAS Hall of Fame at the 32nd annual Grammy Awards. The retrospective ***Chuck Berry - The Chess Box*** wins Best Historical Album for its producer Andy McKaie.

June [30] St. Charles County drug-enforcement agents raid Berry Park estate and seize several plastic bags of marijuana, an unspecified quantity of hashish, two rifles, a shotgun, $122,500 in cash, homemade videos of suspected pornography and a box of 8mm films depicting bestiality. The DEA has been surveying Berry since December 1988, after an informant's tip that he was trafficking in cocaine.

July [30] Berry surrenders to police in St. Charles, MO, and is charged with possession of a controlled substance and three counts of child abuse. He is released after posting a $20,000 bond.

Nov [20] Berry is cleared of felony child abuse charges. He pleads guilty to one misdemeanor count of marijuana possession and is placed on two years unsupervised probation, given a six-month jail sentence and ordered to donate $5,000 to a local hospital.

1991

Dec [3] He ends a UK tour with a performance at London's Hammersmith Odeon, returning to the same venue a year later (November 20th) during another UK trek.

1993

Jan [19] He performs *Reelin'n'Rockin'* and *Good Golly Miss Molly* with an all-star band, comprising Little Richard, Stephen Stills, David Pack, Max Weinberg, Nathan East, Greg Phillinganes, and his daughter Ingrid, at "An American Reunion: The Fifty-second Presidential Gala" at the Capital Centre, Landover, MD.

Feb [22] In the latest round of legal wrangles surrounding the controversial rock legend, Berry loses a Supreme Court bid to have some of his litigious battles transferred from State to Federal Court. The Court rejects arguments put forward by Berry's attorneys that he is the victim of a conspiracy to destroy him financially, "tantamount to an economic lynching of a uniquely American cultural icon". (The current issue of **SPY** magazine contains a lengthy investigation into Berry's alleged taste for coprophilia - his wife of 45 years, Themetta, comments, "I never read the papers".)

June [7] Berry attends the ground-breaking ceremony of the Rock and Roll Hall of Fame in Cleveland, OH.

1994

Jan [19] Berry inducts Willie Dixon into the Rock and Roll Hall of Fame at the ninth annual dinner at New York's Waldorf Astoria Hotel, also performing *Roll Over Beethoven* at the post-dinner jam.

May [26] He takes part in the "Apollo Theatre Hall Of Fame" concert, singing with Living Colour's Vernon Reid. (The show will air on NBC-TV on September 6th.)

Sept [16] He performs on CBS-TV's "Late Show With David Letterman".

1995

Sept [2] Berry performs *Johnny B. Goode* and *Rock'n'Roll Music*, backed by Bruce Springsteen & the E. Street Band, at the all-star benefit Concert for the Rock and Roll Hall of Fame at Cleveland Stadium, Cleveland, OH. (He will also donate one of his trademark Gibson guitars to the museum.)

DAVE BERRY

1961

Berry (b. David Grundy, Feb. 6, 1941, Woodhouse, Yorks.), having made his first public appearance in Worksop, Notts., in 1959 in a duo with Malcolm Green, sits in on several occasions with local rock'n'roll outfit the Chuck Fowler Band, and when Fowler joins the army, is contacted by the remaining members to become their new lead singer as Dave Berry & the Cruisers, taking his name from his hero Chuck Berry. The group, comprising Berry, Frank Miles (lead guitar), Alan Taylor (rhythm guitar), John Fleet (bass) and Kenny Slade (drums), becomes a popular attraction in Sheffield, Yorks., via a residency at the Esquire Club, and play other club dates in northern England.

1963

Apr After making their first major appearance at the Gaumont Cinema in Sheffield the previous year, they are spotted by Mickie Most at a Doncaster, Yorks. dancehall date, and he recommends them to Decca's A&R chief Mike Smith, who signs them to the label. They record two tracks with Most producing, *Tongue Twistin'* and *Easy To Cry*, but neither is released.

Sept Their debut single, produced by Mike Smith and the only one on which the Cruisers provide backup - they subsequently back him only on stage - revives Chuck Berry's *Memphis Tennessee*, which charts immediately and brings about the reissue of Berry's original in the UK.

Nov [8] Berry & the Cruisers begin their first UK tour, with Dusty Springfield, the Searchers, Freddie & the Dreamers and Brian Poole & the Tremeloes, in Halifax, Yorks.

[9] Chuck Berry's *Memphis Tennessee* wins the UK chart battle, reaching the Top 10, but Dave Berry's version establishes him at #19.

Dec A remark by George Harrison on UK TV that Elvis Presley's *My Baby Left Me* should be reissued prompts Berry to record it as a follow-up, using top studio players such as Big Jim Sullivan and later members of Led Zeppelin, Jimmy Page and John Paul Jones.

1964

Jan [6] The group begins its second UK tour, on the Rolling Stones' 12-date "Group Scene 1964" package at the Granada Cinema, Harrow, Middx, set to end on the 27th at the Colston Hall, Bristol, Somerset.

Feb [22] *My Baby Left Me* makes UK #37.

May [9] His cover of the Shirelles' *Baby It's You* reaches UK #24.
Sept [5] *The Crying Game*, written by Geoff Stephens and featuring a distinctive guitar part by Jimmy Page, is his first UK Top 10 record, hitting #5. Well-exposed on TV, it also crystallizes the public's image of Berry in performance: black-dressed, slinky, theatrical and mysterious. He will maintain this performing style throughout his career, into the '90s.
Oct Berry breaks with the Cruisers, replacing them with the Frank White Combo - Frank White (lead guitar), Peter Cliff (bass) and John Riley (drums). He keeps the name the Cruisers, and also retains Alan Taylor from the original group.
Dec [5] *One Heart Between Two* makes UK #41, as ***Dave Berry*** is issued in the UK.

1965

Mar [5] The group begins a 14-date, twice-nightly UK tour, supporting the Rolling Stones, at the Regal Cinema, Edmonton, London, set to end on the 18th at the ABC Cinema, Romford, Essex.
Apr [17] Berry makes his acting debut in the role of Bongo Herbert in a touring version of the musical "Expresso Bongo", at the Cliffs Pavilion, Westcliff, Essex.
[25] Berry joins the second half of a Billy Fury tour (with the Pretty Things and the Zephyrs), set to close on May 9th at Bristol's Colston Hall.
May [1] *Little Things*, his cover of a US hit by Bobby Goldsboro, hits UK #5.
[24] Berry takes part in the "British Song Festival" at the Dome, Brighton, Sussex.
July [9] He is part of the UK contingent at the "Knokke Song Festival" in Belgium, and wins the Press Prize, so gaining a sudden high profile in Europe.
Aug [14] *This Strange Effect*, written by the Kinks' Ray Davies, makes UK #37, but is a #1 hit in Holland and Belgium, confirming Berry's continental star status.
Oct [2] Berry stops the show while representing the UK at Holland's annual "Grand Gala Du Disques" at the Congresscentrum, Amsterdam.
Nov Berry re-signs to Decca for three years.

1966

Mar *This Strange Effect* becomes Holland's biggest-selling single ever, with 250,000 copies.
Apr [7] Berry begins a twice-nightly 12-day UK trek with Herman's Hermits, the Mindbenders, Pinkerton's Assorted Colours and David & Jonathan, at the ABC Cinema, Dover, Kent, set to end on the 20th at the ABC Cinema, Edinburgh, Scotland.
Aug [20] After two non-charting UK singles but huge onstage and TV success in Europe, he returns to the UK chart with *Mama*, a cover of a US hit by B.J. Thomas, which hits #5 (and is taken from ***The Special Sound Of Dave Berry***), but will prove his UK chart swan song.

1967

Feb [20] Having recently issued ***One Dozen Berrys***, he marries Dutch girl Marty van Lopik, at the Register Office, Weston-Super-Mare, Somerset.

1968

May [10] He embarks on a ten-date, twice-nightly UK tour to promote ***Dave Berry '68***, with bill-toppers Herman's Hermits, Amen Corner, the Paper Dolls, John Rowles and the Echoes, at Birmingham Town Hall, set to close on the 19th at the Theatre Royal, Nottingham, Notts.

1970

Chaplin House, written and produced by Godley & Creme, is his final Decca release, after which he signs to CBS Records, though there is to be no change in his chart fortunes. (Berry will go on performing in UK clubs and eventually on '60s revival tours. He will also consistently tour Europe, Canada and South Africa throughout the '70s and '80s.)

1980

June [8] After re-recording *Memphis* and *My Baby Left Me* for Decca in 1974 and completing sessions for Chas & Dave in 1976, Berry plays at the Empire Ballroom in London's Leicester Square, on a bill topped by Adam & the Ants, as he continues to perform live.

1992

Sept Having maintained a modest presence on European nostalgia tours and events over the past decade and released ***Hostage To The Beat*** on Butt Records (UK) in 1987, interest in Berry's '60s recordings is revived by the exposure of his most enduring hit, *The Crying Game*, in the Oscar-nominated, Neil Jordan-directed movie "The Crying Game". While Berry's original version is also included on the soundtrack album, Boy George's update now makes UK #22 (and will make US #15 on May [15], 1993).

THE B-52'S

Cindy Wilson (guitar, vocals); **Kate Pierson** (organ, vocals); **Ricky Wilson** (guitar); **Fred Schneider** (keyboards, vocals); **Keith Strickland** (drums)

1976

Oct Friends, Pierson (b. Apr. 27, 1948, Weehawken, NJ), playing in folk-protest band, the Sun Donuts, Schneider (b. July 1, 1951, Newark, GA), a veteran of bands Bridge Mix and Night Soil, studying forestry at the University of Georgia, Athens, GA, and working in Eldorado, a local vegetarian restaurant, Ricky Wilson (b. Mar. 19, 1953, Athens) and Strickland (b. Oct. 26, 1953, Athens), working at local bus stations, and Ricky's sister Cindy (b. Feb. 28, 1957, Athens), making shakes at the Kress's Whirli-Q luncheonette, having dined together at an Athens Chinese restaurant and shared a tropical drink called Flaming Volcano, decide to form a band on their way home, taking its name from the southern US nickname for a bouffant, highly-coiffured "beehive" hairstyle, subsequently adopted as a visual trademark by its two female members.

1977

Feb [14] The group makes its first live performance, at a Valentine Day's houseparty in a greenhouse in Athens.
Dec [12] Having gone to New York, NY, with fellow Athens band, the Fans, and, having dropped off a tape at Max's Kansas City, the band plays its first gig at the new-wave venue in front of an audience of 17. Despite the poor turn-out they are invited back and, not least by developing a highly visual retro stage act featuring boots, mini-skirts and the girls' B-52 hairdos, they become cult favorites at the club.

1978

Aug They finance their own recording of *Rock Lobster* and *52 Girls* with a loan from local Athens record store owner Danny Beard, quickly selling the 2,000 copies pressed, which brings them to the attention of Island Records' boss, Chris Blackwell.

1979

June They begin recording their debut album for Island at Compass Point Studios, the Bahamas, and sign to Warner Bros. Records for releases in the US.
July [8] The B-52's make their UK debut, supported by the Tourists (including pre-Eurythmics Annie Lennox and Dave Stewart), at London's Lyceum Ballroom, at the beginning of a short album-promoting tour.
Aug [4] Their Blackwell-produced debut ***The B52's*** bows at its UK #22 peak, and will make US #59 in August. The post-punk, off-beat dance-rock set features eight original songs (including live favorites *Planet Claire* and *Rock Lobster*) and one cover, the band's version of the Tony Hatch-penned *Downtown*. Hair-stylist La Verne, who created the group's "hairdos" for the cover, is included on the album credits.
[18] *Rock Lobster*, the band's self-financed original reissued by Island, makes UK #37.

1980

Apr The group begins recording ***Wild Planet***, co-self-produced with Rhett Davies, again at Compass Point Studios, following a US tour and dates in Japan and Australia.
May [24] *Rock Lobster* peaks at US #56.
Aug [16] *Give Me Back My Man* peaks at UK #61.
[23] They take part in the "Heatwave Festival" at Mosport Park, Toronto, ON, Canada.
Sept [13] Reinforcing their alternative, quirky pop/rock musical approach, ***Wild Planet*** reaches UK #18, and will do the same Stateside.
Nov [8] *Private Idaho* peaks at US #74.
Dec The band performs three gigs at London's Hammersmith Odeon during a second UK tour.

1981

July In between recording breaks at Skyline Studios, New York, for their forthcoming mini-album ***Mesopotamia***, Strickland, Pierson and Cindy Wilson record two cuts with Adrian Belew and Japanese group the Plastics under the one-off studio name Melon, though these tracks will only ever appear in Japan.
[18] Mini-album ***Party Mix!***, featuring dance-oriented remixes from the first two albums, makes UK #36 and will reach US #55.
Oct [21] ***Wild Planet*** is certified gold by the RIAA.

1982

Feb [27] ***Mesopotamia***, produced by David Byrne of Talking Heads, reaches UK #18, helped by debut UK TV appearance on C4-TV's "The Switch".
Mar [13] ***Mesopotamia*** makes US #35.

1983

May [14] *Future Generation* peaks at UK #63, while the typically eccentric ***Whammy!*** reaches UK #33.
July [30] *Legal Tender* stalls at US #81, as ***Whammy!*** reaches US #29.

1984

While the B-52's take a sabbatical, due, not least, to Ricky Wilson's worsening health, Schneider releases a solo project on the Warner Bros. label under the group name Shake Society, while he, Pierson and Cindy Wilson also make a guest appearance in the Ramones' Live Aid spoof video for *Something To Believe In* in 1985.

1985

Jan The group performs during the "Rock In Rio" festival in Rio de Janeiro, Brazil.
July Recording sessions begin in New York for their sixth album.
Oct [12] Ricky Wilson dies of complications from AIDS.

1986

May [13] ***The B52's*** is certified platinum by the RIAA.
[24] Double A-side reissue of *Rock Lobster* with another early favorite, *Planet Claire*, yields their biggest hit to date, reaching UK #12. ***Bouncing Off The Satellites***, "dedicated to the memory of Ricky Wilson" and given a more synthesizer-driven direction by its producer Tony Mansfield, makes US #85.

1987

Aug [8] ***Bouncing Off Satellites*** debuts at its UK #74 peak, during a two-week chart stay. The group will remain largely inactive over the next 18 months, not least resolving label difficulties which will result in its departure from Island. A book of poetry written by Schneider will be published in 1988.

1989

Mar Always politically active, the group participates in a "Rock Against Fur" benefit at The Palladium,

New York.
May They perform at the "Don't Bungle The Jungle" benefit at the Brooklyn Academy of Music, New York, on a bill with Madonna, and also make a cameo appearance in a similarly retro-styled, Julien Temple-directed movie "Earth Girls Come Easy".
June The group embarks on the "Cosmic Thing Tour", its first for five years, set to end in late August. The augmented stage line-up includes Sara Lee (bass), ex-Gang Of Four and now Raging Hormones, Pat Irwin (keyboards), ex-Raybeats, and Zach Alford (drums).
July [29] ***Cosmic Thing***, the B52's label debut for Reprise Records, and their first recording since Ricky Wilson's death, with the band now a four-piece (featuring Strickland on guitar), initially peaks at UK #75 and begins its US chart rise.
Oct [31] The group begins another major US tour in Atlanta, GA, set to end on February 7th at Radio City Music Hall, New York.
Nov [18] Don Was-produced *Love Shack*, written about a fun-time nightclub in Atlanta, hits US #3, benefitting from a current extensive US tour.
[29] *Love Shack* is certified gold by the RIAA.

1990

Feb [6-8] The group plays three sellout performances at Radio City Music Hall, New York, before crowds of 17,622.
Mar [8] *Love Shack* is voted Best Single Of 1989 in **Rolling Stone** magazine's Music Awards, and the band is named Comeback Of The Year in the magazine's Critics' Awards.
[10] Nile Rodgers-produced *Roam*, with lyrics by band cohort Robert Waldrop, hits US #3, as ***Cosmic Thing*** hits US #4.
[13] The RIAA confirms multi-platinum sales of two million for ***Cosmic Thing***.
[24] *Love Shack* hits UK #2, becoming one of the year's Top 20 bestsellers.
[31] ***Cosmic Thing*** hits UK #9, peaking the next week at #8.
Apr [3] **Roam** is certified gold by the RIAA.
[22] The group participates in "Earth Day" festivities in Central Park, New York, with Daryl Hall & John Oates and others.
May [22] The group's "1979-1989" video collection is certified platinum by the RIAA.
June [2] *Roam* reaches UK #17 and *Deadbeat Club* reaches US #30.
[14] ***Best Of B52's Dance This Mess Around***, a remixed collection of earlier Island highlights, enters the UK chart at peak #36.
[15] A 40-city "Summer Of 1990" tour opens in Middletown, NY, set to close on August 18th at the Aztec Bowl, San Diego, CA.
Aug [13] At a Great Western Forum, Inglewood, CA, concert, they raise $345,000 for various AIDS organizations, before a sellout crowd of 15,921.
[25] *Channel Z* stalls at UK #61.
[27] The group begins a 19-date tour of Australia and Japan at the Entertainment Centre, Melbourne.
Sept [7] "Love Shack" wins the Best Group Video and Best Art Direction categories at the seventh annual MTV Video Music Awards, held at the Universal Amphitheatre, Universal City, CA.
Oct [13] *Candy*, a Was-produced single pairing Pierson with Iggy Pop, charts for a week at UK #67.

1991

Feb [2] *Candy* reaches US #28.
[23] US remix album ***Party Mix - Mesopotamia*** makes US #184, as they contribute a track to the People for the Ethical Treatment of Animals (PETA) album ***Tame Yourself***.
Mar [5] Schneider gives a lecture at the New School for Social Research in New York while Reprise releases his solo debut ***Fred Schneider.***
Sept [8] Pierson guests on Nickelodeon cable channel's "The Adventures Of Pete And Pete".

1992

Mar [26] The band performs at a fundraiser for Democratic Party presidential candidate Jerry Brown, at New York's The Ritz, with actress Kim Basinger subbing for a curiously-absent Cindy Wilson.
July [4] *Good Stuff* reaches UK #21.
[11] Its parent album ***Good Stuff***, produced by Nile Rodgers and Don Was, but recorded by the band (minus the recently-departed Cindy Wilson), debuts at its UK #8 peak.
[18] ***Good Stuff*** reaches US #16.
[20] Schneider co-hosts, with Ice-T, "The Haoui Party: Music People United for AIDS Relief" benefit at the New Music Seminar, at the Roseland Ballroom, New York.
Aug [1] *Good Stuff* reaches US #28.
[16] An extensive US tour, with the line-up of Schneider, Pierson, Julee Cruise (who has replaced Cindy Wilson), Strickland, Sue Hadjopoulos and Pat Irwin, bows at the Mid-Hudson Civic Center, Poughkeepsie, NY, set to end October 28th at Delta Center Arena, Salt Lake City, UT.
Sept [1] *Good Stuff* is certified gold by the RIAA.
[9] B-52's perform live on syndicated TV's "The Arsenio Hall Show".
[19] *Tell It Like It T-I-Is* peaks at UK #61.
Nov [17] The European segment of their current world tour begins at the Falkontheater, Copenhagen, Denmark.

1993

Jan [27] They play a sellout show at the Fox Theatre, Atlanta, during current US dates.
Feb [14-15] The group performs consecutive gigs at London's Brixton Academy, at the beginning of a re-scheduled (from December 1992) seven-date UK tour, originally postponed due to band illness.
May [22] Schneider participates in LIFEbeat's Counteraid benefit, to raise funds for people who have been diagnosed HIV positive and suffering from AIDS. (He will also join Rufus Thomas on disk with *Do The Funky Somethin'* on ***The Godchildren Of Soul: Anyone Can Join*** compilation.)
Sept [30] Pierson is charged with criminal mischief and trespassing during an anti-fur protest at **Vogue**'s New York City offices.

1994

June [11] Featured in the currently playing "The Flintstones" movie, the band's version of *(Meet) The Flintstones*, credited to the B.C. 52's, reaches US #33.
July [6] ***Whammy!*** is certified gold by the RIAA.
[23] *(Meet) The Flintstones* hits UK #3.

1996

May Schneider releases his solo album, ***Just Fred***, a collaboration with the Jon Spencer Blues Explosion, Tar, Six Finger Satellite and producer Steve Albini.

BIG AUDIO DYNAMITE

Mick Jones (guitar, lead vocals); **Don Letts** (effects, vocals); **Dan Donovan** (keyboards); **Leo Williams** (bass); **Greg Roberts** (drums)

1984

Following a "Clash Communiqué" released in September the previous year by his ex-colleagues in the seminal punk band, which states that Jones (b. June 26, 1955, Brixton, London) should leave the group, and having formed a short-lived outfit with Clash drummer Topper Headon, he now begins auditioning members for his new musical project, Big Audio Dynamite with ex-Roxy club DJ and documentary film-maker Don Letts. Still signed to CBS Records in the UK, he negotiates a new CBS/Columbia contract in the US.

1985

Sept After 18 months of recruitment, writing and recording, their first single *The Bottom Line* is released.
Nov Debut album ***This Is Big Audio Dynamite***, co-written by Jones and Letts and produced by Jones, is released, set to make US #103. A marked departure from the proto-punk style of the Clash, its rock-dance feel has been accomplished with much sampling, notably aural segments from movies.

1986

Apr After extensive UK touring, their first hit single (and the first rock hit to feature a sampling technique, with lines taken from the Mick Jagger film "Performance") *E=MC*^{2} climbs to UK #11, and revives sales of the debut album ***This Is Big Audio Dynamite***, which now makes UK #27.
June *Medicine Show*, borrowing Clint Eastwood lines from "A Fistful Of Dollars", reaches UK #29.
July During the recording of a second album in Soho, London, ex-Clash co-founder Joe Strummer wanders into the studio, resulting in him co-producing and co-writing many of the band's new tracks - a reunion which receives considerable music-press interest.
Oct [18] *C'mon Every Beatbox*, taken from it, peaks at UK #51.
Nov ***No.10 Upping St*** (a mock reference to the Prime Minister's London residence) reaches UK #11 and US #119.

1987

Feb [28] *V Thirteen* reaches UK #49. (The rest of the year will be spent touring Europe and the US, where their live achievements will include a record five sold-out nights at the Roxy in Los Angeles, CA, and nine at the Irving Plaza in New York, NY.)
June The band supports U2 on a major European stadium tour. Planet BAD, a "nightclub" hosted by group members, becomes a feature in some of the cities where they play.
Aug On their first visit to South America, they play seven nights in Brazil.

1988

Jan The band begins writing and recording new songs at its Notting Hill, London, base.
June [4] *Just Play Music*, which hits out at the over-sampling on current singles (a trend the band helped launch), peaks at UK #51.
July [9] ***Tighten Up, Vol. '88*** (featuring a cover painting by ex-Clash colleague Paul Simenon), reaches UK #33 and will make US #102.

1989

Sept [16] Jones, who was hospitalized for several months during the previous year with life-threatening viral pneumonia and chickenpox, re-emerges, fully recovered, with B.A.D.'s ***Megatop Phoenix*** (dedicated to his grandmother who passed away earlier in the year), which reaches UK #26, set to make US #87 on Oct [28].

1990

Feb Inspired more than ever by dance music, an enthusiasm which has seen the departure of B.A.D.'s first lineup, Jones assembles a new B.A.D. comprising guitarist Nick Hawkins (b. Feb. 3, 1965, Luton, Beds.), bassist Gary Stonedage (b. Nov. 24, 1962, Southampton, Hants.) and ex-Sigue Sigue Sputnik drummer Chris Kavanagh (b. June 4, 1964, Woolwich, London). (Roberts, Williams and Letts go on to form their own band Screaming Target releasing ***Hometown Hi-Fi*** the following year, while Donovan, recently separated from his wife, actress Patsy Kensit, takes up session work, notably with Sisters Of Mercy.)
Oct [27] *Good Morning Britain*, a collaboration by Aztec Camera's Roddy Frame and Jones, reaches UK #19.
Nov [3] Newly monikered second-phase Big Audio Dynamite II's ***Kool Aid***, also featuring DJ Zonka (b. Michael Custance, July 4, 1962, London), charts for a week at UK #55 (remaining unreleased in the US).

1991

Mar [2] BAD II's *Rush* is included as the B-side on

the UK chart-topping reissue of the Clash's *Should I Stay Or Should I Go* at Jones' insistence (he allegedly objects to the A-side's use as a TV commercial theme for Levi 501s).
Aug [13] BAD II begins a five-date UK tour at the Sheffield Leadmill, Sheffield, S. Yorks., set to end on the 19th at London's Town & Country club.
[17] ***The Globe***, now moving into trance-dance experimentation featuring techno and ambient music beds, charts for a week at UK #63.
[25] Letts' new band, Screaming Target, performs at the annual "Reading Festival", Reading, Berks.
Sept [25-28] BAD II plays at the Sound Factory, New York, with the Farm, during a current North American tour.
Nov [2] ***The Globe*** makes US #76.
[16] The extracted *Rush*, featuring a sample from the Who's *Baba O'Reilly*, peaks at US #32.
Dec [3] The band performs *Rush*, which is also named the Top Modern Rock Track of the year, at the second annual **Billboard** Music Awards held at the Barker Hangar, Santa Monica Airport, CA.

1992

Jan [31] The group performs at London's Town & Country venue at a benefit concert for the Campaign for Nuclear Disarmament.
Mar [7] Title cut *The Globe* peaks at US #72.
Apr [21-22, 24] The "MTV 120 Minutes North American" tour, pairing the acronymous BAD and PIL, visits New York's The Ritz for three nights grossing $146,055 from 7,514 fans.
June [19] The band supports U2 at the "Greenpeace Stop Sellafield" benefit at Manchester's G-Mex.
Sept [5] They take part in the **New Musical Express**' "Viva Eight" show at London's Town & Country.
Oct [3] The group plays at the Joe Robbie Stadium, Miami, FL, during further US dates.

1994

Sept [27] While the Australian-only album ***The Lost Treasures Of B.A.D. I & II*** has been released the previous year, ***The Globe*** is now certified gold by the RIAA.
Oct "Modern Rock Live" US radio show featuring the band broadcasts set live via satellite from Whitfield Street Studios.
Nov [12] *Looking For A Song* debuts at its UK #68 peak. It is taken from the group's simultaneously released 13-track ***Higher Power*** (which samples music by Afrika Bambaataa among others), its last for Sony/Columbia.
Dec [6] The group, now calling itself Big Audio, performs at WFNX's "Miracle On Lansdowne Street" benefit at the Avalon, Boston, MA.

1995

July ***F-Punk***, featuring a current line-up of Jones, Hawkins, Stonadge, Kavanagh, DJ Zonka and Andre Shapps (keyboards), is released in the US on the Radioactive label, co-produced by Shapps with Mike Campbell.
see also: **THE CLASH**

THE BIG BOPPER

1954

Folowing a two-year period in the US Army, and as a DJ on KTRM radio in Beaumont, TX (which he began working for while still attending high school), J. P. Richardson (b. Jiles Perry Richardson, Oct. 24, 1930, Sabine Pass, TX) nicknames himself the Big Bopper after his ample size and will break the record for non-stop dee-jaying when he broadcasts for five days, two hours and eight minutes. A prolific spare-time songwriter, he will send a demo to "Pappy" Dailey, Mercury Records' Houston, TX representative in 1957, which results in a contract to record country & western material. Two hillbilly-style C&W singles, *Beggar To A King* and *Teenage Moon*, are subsequently released in the US, both credited to Jape Richardson.

1958

June He writes a novelty rock song *The Purple People Eater Meets The Witch Doctor*, parodying the current hits by Sheb Wooley and David Seville. Initially released on Bopper's own Texas-based D label, this is quickly taken up by Mercury when the B-side, *Chantilly Lace*, begins gaining airplay.
Aug *Chantilly Lace*, also self-penned, hits US #6, selling over a million copies, and remaining charted for six months.
Dec Both sides of the follow-up, *The Big Bopper's Wedding/Little Red Riding Hood*, chart in the US, at #38 and #72 respectively.

1959

Jan [31] *Chantilly Lace* reaches UK #12. Bopper, who has put together a stage act based on his hits and comic radio persona, joins the "Winter Dance Party", a multi-artist rock tour of Minnesota, Wisconsin and Iowa cities.
Feb [2] After a tour date at Clear Lake, IA, Bopper persuades Waylon Jennings to give him his seat on a light aircraft being chartered by Buddy Holly to the next venue, since his bulk makes sleeping on a tour coach uncomfortable, and he has developed a heavy cold, about which he wishes to consult a doctor.
[3] Just before 1:00 a.m. the plane leaves nearby Mason City Airport in falling snow, then crashes within minutes, killing the pilot and its passengers - the Big Bopper, Holly, and Ritchie Valens.

1960

Jan [18] Posthumous success as a songwriter comes when *Running Bear*, written for fellow Texan Johnny Preston, tops the US chart.
Mar [21] *Running Bear* repeats its US success, hitting UK #1 for two weeks.

1991

Oct [5-6] While Rhino Records (US) has brought Bopper's brief recording career highlights to compact disk with the 1988 release of ***Hellooo Baby: The Best Of The Big Bopper***, his Gibson guitar model LG3, the only surviving instrument of the fatal crash in 1959, is sold at the Red Baron Antique auction, Atlanta, GA.

BIG BROTHER & THE HOLDING COMPANY

See: **JANIS JOPLIN**

BIG COUNTRY

Stuart Adamson (guitar, synthesizer, vocals); **Bruce Watson** (guitar); **Tony Butler** (bass); **Mark Brzezicki** (drums)

1981

June Adamson (b. William Stuart Adamson, Apr. 11, 1958, Manchester, Lancs.), disillusioned with his involvement in UK punk-pop outfit the Skids, returns home to Dunfermline, Fife, Scotland, to form a new band with old friend Bruce Watson (b. Mar. 11, 1961, Timmins, ON, Canada), who quits his job as a cleaner aboard nuclear submarines. They pair with the Jam's Rick Buckler to unsuccessfully demo for Virgin Records, at the London Townhouse, recording *Heart & Soul* and *Angle Park*. Adamson and Watson subsequently form Big Country in September initially recruiting Pete Wishart (a later member of Runrig), his brother Alan, and Clive Parker, ex-Spizz Oil, and securing an offer of a singles-only deal with Ensign Records (UK) in November.

1982

Feb The group's first major gig is supporting Alice Cooper at the Brighton Centre, Brighton, E. Sussex, though after the second night at the Odeon Theatre, Birmingham, W. Midlands, they are dropped from the tour.
Apr Adamson fires the rhythm section and enters the studio with Watson to now record demos for Phonogram, the latest in a line of interested UK labels. They are assisted by studio regulars Mark Brzezicki (b. June. 21, 1957, Slough, Bucks.) and Tony Butler (b. Feb. 3, 1957, Ealing, London), and will subsequently combine to form a permanent rock quartet.
May Big Country signs to Phonogram's Mercury label, and performs at the 101 Club, Clapham, South London.
Aug The group plays its first US gig, supporting the Members at the Peppermint Lounge, New York, NY.
Sept Its debut single *Harvest Home*, produced by Chris Thomas and introducing the band's unique twin-guitar-based bagpipe sound, sells 6,000 copies.
Oct The band completes a tour of Scottish clubs.
Nov They support A Certain Ratio at London's Lyceum Ballroom.
Dec Big Country makes its TV debut on C4-TV's "Whatever You Want", in front of a live audience at Brixton's Ace Club, and supports the Jam for six nights at Wembley Arena, Wembley, Middx.

1983

Jan They open for the Popsicles at the Venue, London.
Feb The band supports U2 at the Hammersmith Palais, London, before embarking on a "Dingwalls UK Tour, playing in Sheffield, Liverpool, Hull and Newcastle.
Mar The group records a session for BBC Radio 1's "John Peel Show".
Apr [16] *Fields Of Fire (400 Miles)*, produced by Steve Lillywhite, hits #10. They complete a 16-date UK trek, including a headlining spot at London's Lyceum Ballroom. The band also makes its first appearance on BBC-TV's "Whistle Test".
May Big Country begins recording its debut album ***The Crossing*** with Lillywhite at the Manor and RAK studios.
June [11] Self-proclaiming *In A Big Country* reaches UK #17. The band starts its first full headlining UK tour, taking in 34 dates, including the Hammersmith Palais.
Aug [6] ***The Crossing*** enters the UK chart at #4, then hits its #3 peak, subsequently remaining on the survey for 80 weeks. It will earn platinum status in the UK, gold in the US and double-platinum in Canada. During the month the band is featured in a live TV broadcast from Sefton Park, Liverpool, Merseyside.
[23] Having performed on the same bill as U2, Simple Minds, Eurythmics and Steel Pulse at Phoenix Park, Dublin, Eire, earlier in the month, Big Country appears at the annual "Reading Rock Festival", Reading, Berks.
Sept The band journeys to New York for a promotional tour, performing two nights at the Ritz Club.
They also appear on a live ITV special from Shepton Mallet, Somerset, and make their directing debut on a documentary for C4-TV's "Play at Home" series.
Oct [1] *Chance* hits UK #9, as the band embarks on a European tour.
Nov ***The Crossing*** is their US chart bow, peaking at #18, as their first North American tour kicks off in Vancouver, BC, Canada.
Dec [3] *In A Big Country*, their US singles debut, reaches #17, as they appear on NBC-TV's "Saturday Night Live".

1984

Jan [19] ***The Crossing*** is certified gold by the RIAA.
[28] *Wonderland* hits UK #8.
Feb [25] *Fields Of Fire (400 Miles)* peaks at US #52.
[28] Big Country performs at the 26th annual Grammy Awards in Los Angeles, CA, where it is nominated in the Best New Group and Best Single categories.

May The band completes a Japanese tour and performs at the "Pink Pop Festival" in Holland.
June *Wonderland* climbs to US #86, while the mini-album ***Wonderland*** makes US #65.
[30] Big Country plays at Wembley Arena, as the special guest of bill-topper Elton John.
Aug The group enters the Polar Studio, Stockholm, Sweden, to record ***Steeltown***, with Steve Lillywhite once again producing.
Oct [6] *East Of Eden* reaches UK #17.
[27] ***Steeltown*** enters the UK chart at #1 and achieves gold status.
Dec [8] *Where The Rose Is Sown* reaches UK #29, while ***Steeltown*** makes US #70.
[13-14] The band plays two sellout gigs at Wembley Arena and the National Exhibition Centre, Birmingham, supported by the Cult.
[24] The group's Christmas Eve gig at the Playhouse, Edinburgh, Scotland, airs live on BBC2-TV.

1985

Jan [26] *Just A Shadow* reaches UK #26.
May Roger Daltrey's solo album ***Under A Raging Moon***, featuring Butler and Brzezicki, with Watson also guesting on one track, is released.
July [13] Big Country participates in the "Live Aid" supergroup finale at Wembley Stadium.
Dec Recording of ***The Seer*** begins, with Robin Millar producing. During the month, the group also opens for Daltrey at New York's Madison Square Garden.

1986

Feb The band contributes the title track to the movie soundtrack to "Restless Natives".
Mar "The Seer" tour, the group's first live itinerary in 14 months, begins in Holland with its subsequent performance on German TV's "Rock Palace" being broadcast throughout Europe. The group sells out two nights at London's Hammersmith Odeon on the UK leg of the trek.
Apr After a lengthy chart absence, *Look Away* becomes their biggest UK hit single, at #7. (The theme to "Restless Natives" is available on the 12" format.) The band plays at the "Soundwave For Greenpeace" benefit at London's Royal Albert Hall, the "Montreux Golden Rose Festival" in Switzerland and also headlines at the "Seinejoke Festival" in Finland.
June [20] The group takes part in the fourth annual "Prince's Trust Rock Gala concert, with Eric Clapton, Phil Collins, Elton John, George Michael, Rod Stewart, Paul Young and others, at the Wembley Arena, before headlining the "Lochem Festival" in Holland.
[28] *The Teacher* reaches UK #28.
July ***The Seer*** hits UK #2, achieving gold status. The band headlines the "Brittany Festival" in France and the three-day "Roskilde Festival" in Denmark.
Aug [9] Big Country supports Queen at Knebworth, Herts., in front of a 200,000 crowd. As part of "The Seer" American tour they then play to 7,000 at the Pier in New York and make TV appearances on "American Bandstand" and "Solid Gold", while ***The Seer*** makes US #59.
Sept "The Seer tour returns to Europe.
[27] *One Great Thing* reaches UK #19, the group's tenth consecutive Top 30 hit.
Oct A performance at Limehouse Studios, London, is broadcast live to US college TV stations.
Dec [6] *Hold The Heart* peaks at UK #55.
[11-12] The group performs two sellout shows at Wembley Arena.

1987

June Big Country supports David Bowie on his UK "Glass Spider" tour, including shows at Cardiff Arms Park, Cardiff, Wales, Slane Castle, Dublin, and two dates at Wembley Stadium.
Dec Their low-key "Under Wraps" trek takes the band to UK clubs and colleges.

1988

Jan Recording of their fourth album ***Peace In Our Time*** begins in Los Angeles, CA, with Peter Wolf at the production desk.
June [5-6] Brzezicki drums alongside Phil Collins at the sixth annual "Prince's Trust Rock Gala" concert, at London's Royal Albert Hall.
[11] Brzezicki plays in the all-star backing band for the "Nelson Mandela 70th Birthday Tribute" concert at Wembley Stadium.
July The band shoots videos for *King Of Emotion* and *Broken Heart* in Australia, with director Richard Lowenstein. They also top the bill with Bryan Adams at the "Peace Festival" in East Berlin, E. Germany, in front of 140,000.
Aug [27] *King Of Emotion* reaches UK #16. Big Country plays a live set at the Soviet Embassy in London, after announcing plans to make a full tour of Russia. The event is broadcast live on BBC Radio 1 and reported on ITV's "News At Ten".
[28] 200,000 see the group perform at the "Soviet Peace Festival" in Tallin, Estonia, with Public Image Ltd.
Oct [8] ***Peace In Our Time*** hits UK #9. Big Country performs in front of the first-ever standing crowd in a Moscow sports stadium, the first Russian concerts to be organized by a private promoter.
Nov The band shoots the video for *Peace In Our Time* in Moscow and Washington.
[12] *Broken Heart (Thirteen Valleys)* makes UK #47. ***Peace In Our Time***, released via the band's new US-only deal with Reprise Records, peaks at US #160.
Dec Stuart Adamson is made an Honorary Patron of the Scottish Prince's Trust.

1989

Jan Three sellout gigs at Hammersmith Odeon conclude the UK leg of their European tour.
Feb [4] *Peace In Our Time* makes UK #39.
Mar Watson joins Fish at a "Lockerbie Disaster Benefit Concert" in Scotland.
May Relentless touring continues in Europe including concerts in Mönchengladbach, W. Germany, and St. Gallen, Switzerland.
July Brzezicki quits the band.
Sept Adamson performs an acoustic set of Big Country numbers at Wet Wet Wet's free concert in Glasgow, Scotland.
Oct Watson joins Fish's solo tour for his Glasgow Barrowlands gig.
Nov Adamson appears at Jerry Lee Lewis' Hammersmith Odeon concert, with Brian May, Van Morrison, John Lodge, Dave Edmunds and others.

1990

Feb Pat Ahern joins Big Country on drums.
May [19] *Save Me* makes UK #41.
[23-24] The group plays two concerts at the Hammersmith Odeon during a UK tour.
[26] Retrospective package ***Through A Big Country - Greatest Hits*** debuts at its UK #2 peak, behind the Carpenters' retrospective ***Only Yesterday***.
June [3] Big Country performs at "The Big Day", an all-day festival from various locations in Glasgow.
July [18] The band takes part in the eighth annual "Prince's Trust Rock Gala" concert, at the Wembley Arena.
[21] *Heart Of The World* makes UK #50.

1991

July The group, now lining up as Adamson, Butler and Watson with Brzezicki helping out as a session musician (he will tour as part of Midge Ure's band in November), begins work on a new album at Rockfield Studios, with Pat Moran producing.
Aug [31] EP *Republican Party Reptile* debuts at its UK #37 peak.
Sept [2-4] They play one-off UK dates at London's Town & Country club.
[28] Its final album for Mercury in the UK and Reprise in the US, ***No Place Like Home*** bows at its UK #28 pinnacle.
Oct [3] The group begins UK tour at London's Town & Country, set to end on 26th at the Coatham Bowl, Redcar.
[19] *Beautiful People* reaches UK #72.

1992

Sept The band, now signed to the Compulsion label in the UK, works on new material at RAK Studios, with Chris Sheldon producing (following earlier sessions in May with producer Dave Bascombe) with its core of Adamson, Watson and Butler augmented by drummer Simon Phillips and keyboardist Colin Berwick.

1993

Mar [18] The group begins a week-long UK tour, to promote its new album ***The Buffalo Skinners***, at the Town & Country club, set to end on the 24th at the Festival Hall, Corby, Northants.
[20] *Alone* reaches UK #24.
Apr [3] ***The Buffalo Skinners*** bows at its UK #25 peak (and will be released in the US on the newly formed Fox label).
May [1] *Ships (Where Were You?)* debuts at its UK #29 peak.
Dec [29] The band plays at Glasgow Barrowlands during a short UK tour.

1994

June [18] Including live performances of past chart hits, ***Without The Aid Of A Safety Net (Live)*** reaches UK #35.

1995

June [10] *I'm Not Ashamed* charts for a week at UK #69, as group takes part in the "Fleadh Festival" in London's Finsbury Park.
[24] ***Why The Long Face*** debuts at its UK #48 peak (and will be issued in the US in November by start-up label, Pure Records).
July [21] During summer festival dates, the band plays at the "Heineken Music Festival" at Roundhay Park, Leeds, Yorks.
Sept [9] *You Dreamer* charts for a week at UK #68.
Oct [5] A 25-date UK tour opens at Motherwell Civic Theatre, set to end on November 6th at Hammersmith's Labatts Apollo Theatre.
Nov [26] The group provides the pre-match entertainment at the Scottish Coca-Cola Cup Final, and later in the day help Glasgow's Lord Provost switch on the Christmas lights in the city's George Square.

BJÖRK

1977

Dec Raised in a hippy commune environment by her mother Hildur and stepfather Saevar Arnason in Iceland's capital city Reykjavik, Björk (b. Björk Gudmundsdóttir, Nov. 21, 1965, Reykjavik), who has learned to play the classical piano and flute from the age of five at her local school, has already had her version of Tina Charles' 1976 hit *I Love To Love* (taped by enthusiastic teachers at the school) played on Iceland's Radio 1 which has led to a record deal for the 11-year old at the local Fálkkin label. Recorded with some of the country's top session talent and including Björk's covers of Syreeta's *Your Kiss Is Sweet* and the Beatles' *Fool On The Hill* among others, with cover-art by her mother and featuring her guitar-playing stepfather, ***Björk*** is released in time for the Christmas market as its performer is successfully promoted in Iceland as a child-prodigy pop singer. (Subsequently inspired by the punk movement, and still attending school, Björk will form two short-lived new wave combos, Exodus in 1979 and Jam 80 the following year.)

1981

Sept With ex-Exodus bassist Jakob Magnusson in the line-up, her new band Tappi Tikarrass, signed to the Spor label, releases its debut mini-album ***Bitid Fast I Vitid*** which will be followed by ***Miranda*** in 1983. Her next group, the punk-goth unit Kukl (formed with future co-Sugarcubes Einar Orn Benediktsson (b. Oct.

29, 1962, Copenhagen, Denmark), Sigtryggur Baldursson (b. Oct. 2, 1962, Stavanger, Norway) and her current boyfriend Thór Eldon Jonson (b. June 2, 1962, Reykjavik), whom she will marry in 1986, will survive for two albums, ***The Eye*** picked up for UK release by Crass Records (1984), followed by ***Holidays In Europe*** two years later.

1986

Sept Comprising Björk (vocals), Benediktsson (trumpet/vocals), Baldursson (drums), Jonson (guitar), Bragi Olafsson (b. Aug. 11, 1962 Reykjavik) (bass) and Einar Mellax (keyboards), to be replaced in 1988 by Margret Ornolfsdottir (b. Nov. 21, 1967, Reykjavik) - who will also marry Jonson in 1989 following his divorce from Björk, the Sugarcubes (under their Icelandic name, Skyurmolarnir) release their debut single *Einn Mol 'A Mann*. Creating an original sound around Björk's distinctively shrieking and earthy lead vocals, the band will receive much critical praise from the alternative music media and, signed to the indie label One Little Indian in the UK (licensed to Elektra in the US), release ***Life's Too Good*** (May 1988, UK #14/US #54), ***Here Today, Tomorrow, Next Week*** (released October 1989, UK #15/US #70) and ***Stick Around For Joy*** (issued February 1992, UK #16/US #95).

1990

Oct Still with the Sugarcubes and having returned to Iceland, Björk's second solo work, ***Gling-Glo***, a set of jazz standards and a collaboration with the jazz be-bop ensemble Trio Gudmundar Ingolfssonar, is released in her homeland on Smekkleysa Records. (Over the past decade, she has also made guest appearances either live or on disk with a variety of other indigenous music projects including those by Stifgrim (1982), Cactus (1983), Rokha Rokha Drum (1984) as its drummer and backing vocalist, the Elgar Sisters (1985) as lead vocalist and as backing singer for singer-songwriter, Megas.)

1991

May [4] Mancunian-based dance act 808 State's *Ooops*, featuring Björk, reaches UK #42.

1992

Sept With One Little Indian set to release the Sugarcubes remix finalé album ***It's It*** the following month, Björk, now intent on a solo career, disbands the group and relocates to London where she rents an apartment in Belsize Park. She will remain with One Little Indian as a solo artist in Britain and with Elektra in the US.

1993

June [19] Her first non-Icelandic solo single, *Human Behaviour* enters at its UK #36 peak.

July [17] Björk's multi-culture-influenced third solo (though first mainstream) album ***Debut***, produced by Nellee Hooper, enters at its UK #3 peak.

Sept [11] *Venus As A Boy* reaches UK #29 as ***Debut*** makes US #61.

Oct [23] Björk and David Arnold's *Play Dead*, released by Island Records and taken from the film soundtrack to "Young Americans", debuts at its UK #12 peak.

Nov [10] She appears on NBC-TV's "Late Night With Conan O'Brien".

Dec [4] *Big Time Sensuality* bows at its UK #17 pinnacle.

[8-9] Björk performs at the "Transmusicales Festival" in Rennes, France.

1994

Jan [25] Björk wins the Best Solo Artist and Object Of Desire categories at the **New Musical Express**' BRAT Awards held in London.

Feb [14] Returning from January dates in Australia, Björk wins the International Female Solo Artist and International Newcomer categories at the 13th annual BRIT Awards held at London's Alexandra Palace, at which she also performs *Satisfaction* with PJ Harvey.

[19] *Big Time Sensuality* peaks at US #88 in its week of entry.

[24] She performs at the Royalty Theatre, London.

[26] Björk appears on BBC2-TV's "Later With Jools Holland".

Mar [19] *Violently Happy* debuts at its UK #13 peak.

Apr [15] She performs on NBC-TV's "The Tonight Show".

July [30] Björk participates in the "Tennents In The Park Festival", Strathclyde Country Park, Glasgow, Scotland.

Aug [1] She appears at the "Feile Festival", Thurles, Tipperary, Eire.

[11] ***Debut*** is certified gold for 500,000 US sales by the RIAA.

[26] She appears on C4-TV's "Passengers".

Oct [28] Madonna's ***Bedtime Stories*** is released containing *Bedtime Story*, co-written with Björk.

Nov [7] Her acoustic set for the "MTV Unplugged" series is broadcast in the US.

1995

Apr [22] Björk appears on C4-TV's "The White Room".

May [6] *Army Of Me*, also featured in the film soundtrack to "Tank Girl", bows at its UK #10 peak. (Her version of Jerome Kern's *Can't Help Lovin' That Man* is currently included on the PolyGram (UK) released collection, ***18 Original Hits By 18 Unoriginal Artists***.)

June [17] She makes another appearance on "Later With Jools Holland".

[23] Songwriter Simon Lovejoy loses a court case held in London alleging that he owned copyright in the track *Crying* (from ***Debut***).

[24] Variously produced by Hooper, Tricky, Howie Bernstein and 808 State's Graham Massey and recorded at Compass Point Studios, Nassau, Bahamas, ***Post*** enters at its UK #2 pinnacle.

July [1] ***Post*** debuts at its US #32 peak.

[22] She participates in the "JAMPAC Benefit", at the Kitsap Pavilion, Bremerton, WA.

Aug [26] *Isobel* bows at its UK #23 peak, while current UK dates are highlighted by her appearance tonight at the "Reading Festival", Reading, Berks. (During the month, and in her second legal wrangling of the year, Björk's label, One Little Indian, is required by a London court to pay Beechwood Music £2,000 and legal costs for using a sample by Scanner on the ***Post*** track *Possibly Maybe*, without permission (a decision which will also necessitate re-pressings of the album).)

Nov [1] During US dates she grosses $68,120 at a gig at the Hollywood Palladium, Hollywood, CA.

[23] Björk is named Best Female Performer at the second annual MTV Europe Music Awards held in Paris, France.

Dec [23] Backed by a 20-piece orchestra, *It's Oh So Quiet*, her version of a 1948 Betty Hutton recording, hits UK #4.

1996

Jan [25] During European dates, she performs at the Wembley Arena, Wembley, Middx.

Feb [19] Björk is named Best International Female Artist at the 15th annual BRIT Awards held at London's Earl's Court Exhibition Centre. The statuette is presented to her by her boyfriend (who has flown in from London) midway through a live concert performance in Hong Kong.

[21] During further Asian dates in Thailand, Björk attacks a TV reporter at Bangkok Airport.

[24] *Hyperballad* bows at its UK #8 peak.

CILLA BLACK

1963

Jan [25] After working as a cloakroom attendant and occasionally guesting with groups (notably Kingsize Taylor & the Dominoes, Faron's Flamingos, the Big Three (at the Zodiac Club) and Rory Storm & the Hurricanes), usually billed as "Swinging Cilla", 19-year old singer Black (b. Priscilla White, May 27, 1943, Liverpool, Lancs.), employed at the BICC Cable firm, makes her Liverpool's Cavern club debut, with Rory Storm & the Hurricanes. (An earlier unannounced performance with the band has taken place at the nearby Iron Door Club after her friend, Pauline Behan, has asked the group if she could sing with them.)

July [25] She makes a recording test for EMI, whose George Martin has spotted her while checking out Gerry & the Pacemakers in Liverpool, and is signed to the company's Parlophone label.

Aug [26] Black makes her first major concert appearance during a week-long residency at the Odeon Cinema, Southport, Lancs., on a bill headed by the Beatles.

[28] She records her debut session for EMI.

Sept [6] Black formally signs a management contract with the Beatles' manager Brian Epstein at her 380 Scotland Road home in Liverpool. She had auditioned for Epstein in a Birkenhead club, backed by the Beatles. (She becomes Black rather than White after a misprint in **Mersey Beat**.)

[27] Her debut single *Love Of The Loved*, an unrecorded song donated by Paul McCartney, is launched with her TV debut on ITV's "Ready Steady Go".

Nov [2] *Love Of The Loved*, released on EMI's Parlophone label, makes UK #35.

Dec [24] She begins a three-week season in the "Beatles' Christmas Show at the Finsbury Park Astoria, London, with the Beatles, Billy J. Kramer, the Fourmost and Rolf Harris, set to close on January 11th.

1964

Feb [29] Her cover of Dionne Warwick's US hit *Anyone Who Had A Heart*, tops the UK chart for the first of four weeks, selling over 900,000 copies in the UK - one of the all-time UK best-selling singles by a female singer, and the first by a British woman since Helen Shapiro's *Walkin' Back To Happiness*. (The week's Top 10 is also the first to feature only UK acts.) She begins a UK tour with Gene Pitney, Billy J. Kramer & the Dakotas and the Swinging Blue Jeans, at the Odeon Cinema, Nottingham, Notts.

May [6] Black is featured on ITV's "Around The Beatles".

[30] *You're My World*, adapted from the Italian ballad *Il Mondo*, becomes Black's second UK #1, beginning a three-week run, as she opens an eight-month season in the "Startime Variety Show at the London Palladium, with the Fourmost, Frankie Vaughan and Tommy Cooper.

July [1] Black, accompanied by the Joe Loss Orchestra, plays at a charity ball at London's Mansion House, in the presence of H.R.H. Princess Margaret and the Lord Chief Justice.

Sept [5] *It's For You*, another Paul McCartney song not recorded by the Beatles and featuring McCartney on piano, hits UK #7, while *You're My World* is her US chart debut and biggest hit, reaching #26.

Oct [3] *It's For You* peaks at US #79.

Nov [2] Black performs in the Royal Variety Show at the London Palladium.

Dec She has a cameo role in Gerry & the Pacemakers' film "Ferry Cross The Mersey", singing *Is It Love?*

1965

Jan [29] Black begins a 22-date, twice-nightly UK tour, with P.J. Proby, the Fourmost, Tommy Roe, Tommy Quickly and Sounds Incorporated, at the ABC Cinema, Croydon, Surrey, set to end on February 21st at the Liverpool Empire.

[30] Her version of the Righteous Brothers' *You've Lost That Lovin' Feelin'*, hits UK #2, outselling the original for its first two weeks, until the Brothers visit the UK for TV promotion and leap to #1.

Mar Her maiden album ***Cilla*** hits UK #5.

[8] She starts a 17-day Australian tour with Freddie &

the Dreamers.
Apr [4] Black makes her US TV debut on CBS-TV's "The Ed Sullivan Show".
[11] She performs at the annual "**New Musical Express** Poll Winners Concert" at the Empire Pool, Wembley, Middx., with a host of other stars.
[18] She makes her "Sunday Night At The London Palladium" ITV debut.
May [15] *I've Been Wrong Before*, penned by novice writer Randy Newman, reaches UK #17.
July [26] Black makes her New York, NY debut as she begins a residency at the Plaza Hotel's Persian Room.
Sept [12] Black appears on a bill with the Beatles on CBS-TV's "The Ed Sullivan Show", singing *September In The Rain* and *Goin' Out Of My Head*.
Oct [2] She represents Britain at the "Grand Gala Du Disques" at the Congresscentrum, Amsterdam, Holland.
[8] Black begins an 18-date, twice-nightly "Star Scene '65 Tour" in association with Radio London, with bill-toppers the Everly Brothers, Billy J. Kramer & the Dakotas and Paddy Klaus & Gibson, at the Granada Cinema, Bedford, Beds., set to end on the 28th at the ABC Cinema, Wigan, Lancs. It will be Black's last tour.
Dec [16] "The Music Of Lennon-McCartney", a 50-minute tribute featuring Black and many other artists, airs on ITV in London. (The rest of the UK sees the program the following night.)
[27] Black makes her stage acting debut in the title role of the Christmas pantomime "Little Red Riding Hood" at the Wimbledon Theatre, Wimbledon, London, which runs through to February 5th.

1966

Feb [5] *Love's Just A Broken Heart* hits UK #5.
Apr [18] Black opens a cabaret season at London's Savoy Hotel.
May [7] *Alfie*, written by Burt Bacharach and Hal David after seeing the Michael Caine movie of the same name, with Bacharach on piano, hits UK #9.
July [2] *Don't Answer Me* hits UK #6, while ***Cilla Sings A Rainbow*** hits #4.
Sept *Alfie* peaks at US #95, in competition with a #32 cover version by Cher. It is Black's last US chart entry.
Nov [3] Black and comedian Frankie Howerd open in the "Way Out In Piccadilly" revue, written by Ray Galton and Alan Simpson with Eric Sykes, at London's Prince of Wales Theatre. (She will leave the show in July 1967.)
[19] *A Fool Am I* reaches UK #13.

1967

Jan [30] Black begins filming "Work ... Is A Four-Letter Word", based on Henry Livings' play "Eh?", with David Warner, Alfred Marks and director Peter Hall.
May [27] Epstein celebrates Cilla's 24th birthday with greetings illuminated at London's Piccadilly Circus, and Birmingham, Bristol and Manchester.
July [1] Black guests on BBC1-TV's "Billy Cotton's Music Hall", as *What Good Am I* reaches UK #24. Shortly afterwards, claiming inattention to her career, Black splits from Epstein's management agency. The disagreements resolved, she returns to him, and is reportedly devastated by his death two months later.
Dec [23] *I Only Live To Love You* makes UK #26.

1968

Jan [30] Her BBC1-TV series is launched, with a new McCartney-penned song *Step Inside Love*, as its theme tune.
Feb [6] Ringo Starr guests on the TV show, duetting with Black on *Act Naturally*.
Apr [13] *Step Inside Love* hits UK #8, her first Top 10 hit for nearly two years.
May *Sher-oo* hits UK #7.
June [15] *Where Is Tomorrow* makes UK #39 in its week of entry.
Dec Compilation ***The Best Of Cilla Black***, collecting her A-side hits to date, reaches UK #21.

1969

Mar [29] *Surround Yourself With Sorrow*, penned by Bill Martin and Phil Coulter, hits UK #3, taken from ***Surround Yourself With Cilla***. Black marries her personal manager, Bobby Willis (a marriage still going strong into the '90s).
Aug [16] *Conversations* hits UK #7.

1970

Jan [10] *If I Thought You'd Ever Change Your Mind*, her cover of Kathe Green's John Cameron-original, reaches UK #20.
Aug ***Sweet Inspiration*** makes UK #42.

1971

Dec [25] Roger Cook/Roger Greenaway-written *Something Tells Me (Something's Gonna Happen Tonight)*, the theme from her new UK TV series, hits UK #3 and is included on ***Images***.

1974

Feb [16] Having released ***Day By Day With Cilla*** the previous year, *Baby We Can't Go Wrong*, the theme from her third UK TV series, makes UK #36, but proves to be her final UK hit single. Having already moved sideways to a "family entertainer" role (the perfect vehicle for her engaging and gregarious Liverpool personality), she will henceforth concentrate on cabaret and TV work (only occasionally releasing middle-of-the-road albums, including ***In My Life*** (this year), ***It Makes Me Feel Good*** (1976) and ***Modern Priscilla*** (1978)).

1983

Feb A TV-advertised retrospective ***The Very Best Of Cilla Black*** returns her to the UK chart after almost a decade, reaching #20.

1994

Oct [18] Having let her entertainment career mostly wane during the late '70s while raising her family, she has returned to the British public consciousness with a vengeance during the '80s, occasionally still singing (and releasing ***Surprisingly Cilla*** in 1985 and ***Love Songs*** in 1987), but mainly hosting top-rated television shows including "Surprise Surprise" and "Blind Date", in the process becoming the UK's first female game-show hostess. Having made a recording comeback in 1993 with the Sony Music (UK)-released ***Through The Years*** (UK #41, Oct [9] and its spin-off singles, *Through The Years* (UK #54, Sept [18]) and *Heart And Soul* (with Dusty Springfield (UK #75, Oct [30]), Black is now honored at BASCA's 20th awards ceremony held at London's Hilton Hotel.

THE BLACK CROWES

Chris Robinson (vocals); **Rich Robinson** (guitar); **Jeff Cease** (guitar); **Johnny Colt** (bass); **Steve Gorman** (drums)

1984

Brothers Chris (b. Christopher Robinson, Dec. 20, 1966, Atlanta, GA) and Rich Robinson (b. Richard Robinson, May 24, 1969, Atlanta), the sons of 1959 US #83 *Boom-A-Dip-Dip* hitmaker Stan Robinson, who, after four years on the road, settled in Atlanta to set up a clothing business with his wife Nancy (née Bradley), a Nashville, TN country singer, make their debut in punk band Mr. Crowe's Garden in Chattanooga, TN. The $50 cheque they are paid for their services bounces. Based in Atlanta, Chris will also enroll at Georgia State University.

1988

After running through six bass players, Colt (b. May 1, 1966, Cherry Point, NC) becomes a permanent fixture. The Robinsons also meet drummer Gorman (b. Aug. 17, 1965, Hopkinsville, KY), who is playing for another band in an adjacent studio to Mr. Crowe's Garden, recording demo sessions, and invite him to join. The group then recruits Cease (b. June 24, 1967, Nashville), in a desire to play harder rock with a two-guitar attack, at a party following a Nashville gig featuring Mr. Crowe's Garden and Cease's current band, Rumble Circus.

1989

May With a settled line-up, dedicated to a uncompromising rock stance and to recording mainly Robinson brothers' songs, the group, having changed its name to the Black Crowes, is signed to Def American by A&R man George Drakoulias, and begins debut recordings with considerable assistance from ex-Allman Brothers Band member Chuck Leavell. Recorded in Atlanta and Los Angeles, CA, all but one of the songs are written by the Robinsons, while the project is produced by Drakoulias.

1990

Mar [24] Having built up a solid cult following through incessant US touring, and benefitting from promising early reviews, ***Shake Your Money Maker*** enters the US chart at #174, at the start of a lengthy chart tenure and multi-platinum US sales.
June [23] The group's debut single *Jealous Again* peaks at US #75.
[29] They play the first of two heavy metal bills, with Aerosmith, Metallica and Warrant at the Skydome, Toronto, ON, Canada. (The second gig will be played the following day at the Silver Stadium in Rochester, NY.)
Aug [7] During a year when they will be on the road for 11 months out of 12, Black Crowes set off on a Heart-supporting North American tour in Winnipeg, MB, Canada, having already opened for Aerosmith and completed a European club tour.
Sept [22] *Hard To Handle*, a remake of Otis Redding's 1968 US #51 original, is their UK singles debut, peaking at #45.
Oct [9] The group makes its US network TV debut on NBC-TV's "Late Night With David Letterman".
[28] Now supporting Robert Plant, they play to a sellout crowd of 6,000 at the Sunken Garden Theatre, San Antonio, TX.
Dec [15] As the group ends the year with a two-month round of 1,000-2,000 seaters in the US, *Hard To Handle* initially makes US #45.

1991

Jan [4] The Black Crowes join the Z.Z. Top tour at the Kiefer U.N.O. Lakefront Arena, New Orleans, LA, augmented by keyboardist Eddie Harsch (b. May 27, 1957, Toronto).
[19] *Twice As Hard* makes UK #47.
Feb [20] They play an impromptu gig with borrowed equipment at the Ritz, Detroit, MI, to benefit the Delta Blues Museum. When they finish their set, they are told that they have been beaten for Best New Artist at the 33rd annual Grammy Awards by Mariah Carey. Rich Robinson says, "I'm relieved. If we'd won, it'd be much too respectable."
Mar [7] The group is named Best New American Band in the annual **Rolling Stone** Readers' Picks and Critics' Picks 1990 music awards. Chris Robinson is also named Best New Male Singer in the Critics' Picks.
[16] The band guests on NBC-TV's "Saturday Night Live".
[25] Following continual comments at the top of its live set by Chris Robinson about commercial sponsorship of tours, and repeated warnings to desist, Z.Z. Top's management drops the group from the tour after the second of three shows at the Omni in Atlanta.
Apr [6] ***Shake Your Money Maker*** finally peaks at US #4 after over a year on the chart and more than three million sales. Taking 54 weeks to reach the top five, it is the slowest to do so since the 59-week climb by Jimi Hendrix's ***Are You Experienced***, which arrived there in 1968.
May [4] Black Crowes perform at the "Memphis In May Beale Street Music Festival" in Memphis, TN.
[11] *She Talks To Angels* reaches US #30.
June [22] *Jealous Again/She Talks To Angels* debuts at its UK #70 peak.
July [31] Robinson receives six months probation after pleading no contest to charges that he spat on

Elizabeth Juergens, a Denver, CO, 7-Eleven customer, in May, after she had allegedly said in front or him : "Who are the Black Crowes?", to which he replied with saliva and a verbal riposte that she would know who they were if she didn't eat so many Twinkies.
Aug [17] The group performs at the annual "Monsters of Rock Festival", Donington Park, Castle Donington, Leics., before a 72,500 capacity crowd, sharing the bill with Metallica, Motley Crue and Queensryche.
[17] Re-activated *Hard To Handle* reaches US #26.
[31] *Hard To Handle* re-charts at UK #39.
Sept [14] ***Shake Your Money Maker*** reaches UK #36.
[24] The band embarks on 20-date UK tour at Colston Hall, Bristol, Avon, set to end on October 19th at London's Hammersmith Odeon. (During the Edinburgh, Scotland gig on the 10th, Chris will jump into the audience to confront coin-throwing hoodlums.)
Oct [26] *Seeing Things* debuts at its UK #72 peak.
Nov [25] Cease is replaced by Marc Ford (b. Apr. 13, 1966, Los Angeles), formerly of Burning Tree (a group which has opened for Black Crowes earlier in the year). Chris Robinson is quoted as saying, "If I have to make a bad analogy, let's say five guys go off to war for 19 months, chances are all of them will not come back. Basically, that's what happened with the Black Crowes. Hope there's no bad blood with Jeff and that he can go off and make the music he wants to make." (Cease, who will go on to form Blackeyed Susan with former Britny Fox singer Dean Davidson, will later claim that he left of his own free will rather than being fired, sharing a mutual dislike of each other with Rich Robinson.)

1992

Apr [11] The group plays its first hometown gig since being thrown off the Z.Z. Top tour, headlining the third annual "Great Atlanta Pot Festival", presented by the National Organization for the Reform of Marijuana Laws, in Piedmont Park.
May [2] *Remedy* bows at its UK #24 peak.
[23] Their sophomore effort, ***Southern Harmony And Musical Companion***, debuts at its UK #2 peak, behind Iron Maiden's ***Fear Of The Dark***.
[27] The group guests on NBC-TV's "The Tonight Show".
[30] ***Southern Harmony And Musical Companion*** enters the US chart in pole position.
June [27] The group performs at the Hordern Pavilion in Sydney, New South Wales, Australia, after selling out four dates in Tokyo, Japan at the start of its "High As The Moon" world tour.
July [11] *Remedy* makes US #48.
[24] Colt is arrested for obstruction of justice while allegedly helping a drunken fan, following the opening of the North American leg of the tour at the Orpheum Theatre, Minneapolis, MN. He opts to pay a fine for the misdemeanor charge.
Sept [1] With the band still constantly on the road, the Falcon Security company files assault charges against Chris Robinson after he allegedly places his foot on the shoulder of a security guard at a Constitution Hall, Washington, DC gig.
[9] They perform live at the ninth annual MTV Video Music Awards, held at the Pauley Pavilion, Los Angeles.
[26] *Thorn In My Pride* peaks at US #80.
Oct [3] *Sting Me* makes UK #42.
[12] Heavy-handed security repeatedly interrupts the group's performance at the Houston Astrodome, and when two speakers topple offstage and injure five fans, the group walks offstage.
[20-21, 23] The Black Crowes play three nights at the Greek Theatre, Los Angeles. During one of them, Chris Robinson tells an audience member in the front row, who is trying to be cool, to "go home and watch VH1. Michael Bolton must be on by now."
[31] ABC-TV airs the "Halloween Jam At Universal Studios" special with the Black Crowes one of the featured acts.
Nov [24] The band's first feature-length video, "Who Killed That Bird Out On Your Window Sill - The Movie", is released in the US.
[28-29] The group ends a brief UK tour at London's Town & Country club.
Dec [5] *Hotel Illness* makes UK #47.

1993

Jan Three Black Crowes, two Wallflowers and two Ju Ju Hounds launch jam band Big Toe at a Sunday night Troubadour, Los Angeles, gig.
Feb [1] Continuing their never-ending tour, the group performs a sellout show at the Johnny Mercer Theatre, Savannah Civic Center, Savannah, GA.
[6] The band plays "An Evening With The Black Crowes" at the Sam Houston Arena, to make up for the abbreviated October 12th show at the Houston Astrodome.
Mar [7] The Black Crowes walk offstage again after finishing their opening number *No Speak No Slave* at the Louisville Gardens, Louisville, KY, following an altercation between two crew members and undercover narcotics officers. One of the crew members, Kevin Wegman of Nice Man Merchandising, is beaten up and spends eight hours in hospital before being arrested.
June [25] The group performs on the Pyramid stage at the "Glastonbury Festival Of Performing Arts", in Glastonbury, Somerset.
July [3-4] They take part in the Torhout and Wechter festivals in Belgium on successive days.
[18] The Black Crowes perform at "The Phoenix 1993 Festival" at Long Marston, Warwick, sandwiched between shows in Switzerland, Norway and Spain.

1994

Aug [11] The group performs a midnight gig at the Dark Horse Tavern in Atlanta under the name Corkscrews of Renown, the night before a Lollapalooza date. (They will also play at New York's CBGB's and Los Angeles' Irving Plaza as Blessed Chloroform.)
Nov [12] ***amorica*** reaches UK #12 in its week of entry.
[19] ***amorica*** debuts at its US #11 peak.
[30] The band plays at the Paradise club in Boston, MA as the O.D. Jubilee Band.
Dec [12] Chris Robinson cyberlinks with fans on American OnLine.

1995

Jan [5] ***amorica*** is certified gold by the RIAA.
[6] UK and Irish tour opens at Newport Centre, Newport, Gwent, Wales, set to end on February 1st at Sheffield City Hall, Sheffield, S. Yorks., before the European leg takes on Germany, France, Belgium, Switzerland, Italy and Spain.
Feb [25] *High Head Blues/A Conspiracy* bows at its UK #25 debut.
Apr [13-14] The band, now augmented full-time by Harsch on keyboards and newcomer Chris Trujillo on percussion, plays hometown sellout dates at the Fox Theatre, Atlanta, during its current US tour.
May [3] The RIAA certifies multi-platinum sales of ***Shake Your Money Maker*** (five million) and ***Southern Harmony And Musical Companion*** (two million).
[10] The Black Crowes play at the Music Hall in Oklahoma City, OK, broadcast live on the Internet, to aid those affected by the bombing of the Alfred P. Murrah Federal Building in Oklahoma City.
July [22] *Wiser Time* bows at its UK #34 debut, as the group supports the Rolling Stones on its current "Voodoo Lounge" tour at the El Molinon Stadium, Gijon, Spain, before a sellout crowd of 45,173.
Aug [18] The "H.O.R.D.E. Festival" tour, which sees the Crowes share the stage with Blues Traveler, Joan Osborne, Ziggy Marley and others, reaches its largest audience, when 27,428 pay $646,773 to see the line-up at the World Music Theatre, Tinley Park, IL.
Sept Capricorn Records releases ***HEMPilation***, a various artists compilation to benefit the National Organization for the Reform of Marijuana Laws, to which the Black Crowes have contributed *Rainy Day Women #12 And 35*.

BLACK FLAG

See: **HENRY ROLLINS**

BLACK SABBATH

Ozzy Osbourne (vocals); **Tony Iommi** (guitar); **"Geezer" Butler** (bass); **Bill Ward** (drums)

1967

Schoolmates Iommi (b. Anthony Iommi, Feb. 19, 1948, Birmingham, Warks.), Ward (b. William Ward, May 5, 1948, Birmingham), Butler (b. Terence Butler, July 17, 1949, Birmingham) and Osbourne (b. John Osbourne, Dec. 3, 1948, Birmingham) form a blues band, first named Polka Tulk but soon changed to Earth. Playing a jazz-blues fusion, they tour exhaustively in the UK and rest of Europe the following year, not least breaking the Beatles' long-held house-attendance record at the Star-Club, Hamburg, W. Germany.

1969

Jan Big Bear Ffolly, combining members from local groups Earth, Bakerloo (of which Spencer Davis Group's Pete York is a member), Tea & Symphony and Locomotive, makes its debut at Birmingham's Opposite Lock.
Feb [6] Big Bear Ffolly makes its London debut at the Marquee club. Prompted by manager Jim Simpson, Earth switches its name to Black Sabbath (the title of an early song by Polka Tulk, originated by Butler's abiding interest in popular black magic novelist Dennis Wheatley) and changes to a suitably-matching macabre image.
Dec After a year's constant touring during which they build a huge live following, the group signs to Philips Records' subsidiary Fontana (UK).

1970

Jan The group's debut release is *Evil Woman (Don't Play Your Games With Me)*, its cover of a 1969 US #19 hit by Minneapolis, MN, based rock quintet, Crow.
Mar [29] The group takes part in a benefit concert for the Campaign for Nuclear Disarmament in London's Victoria Park, with Toe Fat, Liverpool Scene, J.J. Jackson's Dilemma and DJ John Peel.
Apr *Evil Woman* is reissued (again without chart success) on Philips' new "progressive rock" label Vertigo, alongside their first album ***Black Sabbath***, which has been recorded in two days on a £600 budget with producer Rodger Bain. Filled with occult imagery, it climbs to hit UK #8, staying on the survey for five months.
May [24] The group plays at the "Hollywood Music Festival" near Newcastle-under-Lyme, Staffs.
Oct [10] Black Sabbath's second album ***Paranoid***, which features many of their early stage favorites, including *War Pigs*, tops the UK chart for the first of two weeks, while *Paranoid* hits #4. Both will become their most enduring records, and will be regarded as classics in the evolution of heavy-metal rock.
Dec Following a US college tour, ***Black Sabbath***, released in the US on Warner Bros., climbs to #23 (staying charted for 65 weeks), while *Paranoid* reaches US #61.

1971

Mar ***Paranoid*** reaches US #12 during a 65-week chart tenure. With its US and UK popularity thus cemented, the band's exploits become synonymous with the "hard-rock lifestyle": a toxic mixture of drink, drugs, groupies and exhausting tour schedules.
Sept ***Master of Reality***, further extending the group's macabre lyrical themes, hits UK #5 and US #8.

1972

Mar *Iron Man*, belatedly taken from ***Paranoid*** in the

US, charts at #52.
Oct ***Black Sabbath Vol. 4*** hits UK #8 and US #13. The band changes management, replacing Simpson (to his displeasure) with Patrick Meehan, and releases *Tomorrow's Dream*, its first UK single since *Paranoid*.

1974

Jan Their fifth album ***Sabbath Bloody Sabbath***, with keyboard help from Rick Wakeman, hits UK #4 and US #11, while Meehan is replaced as manager by agent Don Arden. The disgruntled Simpson takes action over what he considers an unfairly broken contract with the band, and Osbourne is handed a subpoena as he walks onstage at a US tour date, precipitating an almost two-year enforced hiatus for Sabbath, as legal battles over management rage. Osbourne also begins to isolate himself from the others because of his even harder-drinking lifestyle and an unwillingness to move away from Sabbath's established musical formula.

1975

July Black Sabbath makes its Madison Square Garden, New York, NY, debut.
Sept With legal matters finally resolved and its UK contract (and back-catalog) shifted to NEMS Records, Black Sabbath returns with a major UK tour.
Sept [13] ***Sabotage*** hits UK #7 and will reach US #28.

1976

Jan [31] Double compilation album ***We Sold Our Souls For Rock'n'Roll*** reaches UK #35.
Apr [10] ***We Sold Our Souls For Rock'n'Roll*** makes US #48.
Oct [23] ***Technical Ecstasy***, which returns the band to Vertigo, reaches UK #13. It appears after troubled recording sessions, during which Iommi wanted to experiment with more complex arrangements, overdubs and even a horn section, all against Osbourne's will.
Nov [27] ***Technical Ecstasy*** makes US #51.

1977

Nov Osbourne finally quits after more internal friction. He is replaced on some live dates by ex-Savoy Brown singer, Dave Walker.

1978

Jan Osbourne rejoins, but relations with the rest of the band remain strained.
May [15] The group embarks on a UK tour with Van Halen, set to end on June 16th at Bridlington Spa.
June [24] First UK hit single since *Paranoid*, *Never Say Die*, a taster of the forthcoming album, reaches UK #21.
Oct [7] ***Never Say Die***, recorded at Sounds Interchange in Toronto, ON, Canada, reaches UK #12.
[21] *Hard Road*, taken from it, climbs to #33.
Dec [2] ***Never Say Die*** makes US #69.

1979

Jan With conflict between Osbourne and the band still unresolved, he now leaves permanently to form Blizzard of Oz and embark on a successful solo career.
Mar Sabbath attempts to shed business and legal problems by signing a new management deal with Don Arden while former Rainbow vocalist Ronnie James Dio (b. July 10, 1949, Cortland, NY) is recruited to replace Osbourne as lead singer.
July Butler leaves, replaced for live work by Geoff Nicols from Quartz, but he decides to return in time for the next album recording sessions.

1980

May [7-10] The group plays four nights at London's Hammersmith Odeon during its current UK tour, as ***Heaven & Hell***, introducing Dio's mythology-influenced lyrics, hits UK #9.
July *Neon Knights* is their third consecutive UK hit single, at #22, while ***Heaven And Hell*** reaches US #28.
July ***Black Sabbath: Live At Last***, a previously-unheard onstage recording made in 1975 by the original line-up, is released by NEMS. Disowned by the current band, it nevertheless hits UK #5.
Sept [27] Encouraged by its popularity, NEMS reissues *Paranoid*, which re-charts in the UK at #54, almost ten years after its original success. It also tops the UK Independent chart, sitting oddly among the batch of current new wave records.
Nov Following a successful US tour, Bill Ward leaves, his departure forced by recurring bad health, and is replaced on drums by Vinnie Appice (b. Vincent Appice, Staten Island, NY), younger brother of ex-Vanilla Fudge member Carmine Appice.
Dec [13] *Die Young* makes UK #41.

1981

Nov [14] ***Mob Rules*** reaches UK #12 and US #29, while the extracted title cut *Mob Rules* reaches UK #46. Sabbath experiences more personal bickering as Iommi voices his growing resentment of Dio's influence on the album.

1982

Feb [13] *Turn Up The Night* makes US #37.
May The group is awarded the Gold Ticket for playing to over 100,000 fans at New York's Madison Square Garden.
Nov Dio quits after Iommi accuses him of tampering with the mix of the band's forthcoming live album in order to highlight his vocals. Replaced by Dave Donato, he takes Appice with him to form his own group, Dio.

1983

Jan Double live album ***Live Evil***, recorded on the road in Dallas, TX, San Antonio, TX and Seattle, WA, reaches UK #13 and US #37, though when it appears, the band lacks coherence and seems destined to fold.
June Personnel problems are solved when Ward returns, and Ian Gillan (b. Aug. 19, 1945, Hounslow, Middx.), former vocalist with Deep Purple and his own band Gillan, is persuaded to join.
Aug Black Sabbath headlines the "Reading Festival", Reading, Berks., with its new line-up. Bev Bevan (b. Nov. 24, 1946, Birmingham) of ELO plays drums when Ward is forced by illness to withdraw once again.
Oct ***Born Again***, recorded at the Manor Studios, Shipton-on-Cherwell, Oxon, with Ward back on drums, hits UK #4 and US #39.

1984

Mar [10] Gillan leaves to join the re-forming Deep Purple.

1985

July [13] The original Black Sabbath line-up, including Osbourne, re-forms strictly as a one-off to play at the "Live Aid" benefit concert, at the JFK Stadium, Philadelphia, PA.

1986

Mar ***Seventh Star***, credited to "Black Sabbath with Tony Iommi" (him being the only remaining member of the original band), playing with former Deep Purple vocalist Glenn Hughes (b. Aug. 21, 1952, Penkridge, Staffs.) and newly-recruited musicians, Geoff Nichols (b. Birmingham), Dave Spitz (b. New York) and Eric Singer (b. Cleveland, OH), reaches UK #27 and US #78, but the incarnation shows little sign of maintaining the fan following or success which Black Sabbath achieved in earlier years.
May [13] ***Heaven And Hell*** and ***We Sold Our Soul To Rock 'N' Roll*** are both certified platinum by the RIAA.
Oct [13] The RIAA confirms platinum sales of ***Black Sabbath***, ***Black Sabbath - Volume 4***, ***Master Of Reality*** and ***Sabbath, Bloody Sabbath***.

1987

Sept The Anti-Apartheid Campaign announces it plans to picket Black Sabbath concerts after the group plays a series of July dates in Sun City, South Africa.
Nov [28] ***The Eternal Idol*** charts for a week at UK #66 and will peak at US #168 in January the following year.

1989

Apr [15] Now signed to I.R.S. and joined by ex-Vow Wow's Neil Murray, *Headless Cross* peaks at UK #62.
[29] Parent album ***Headless Cross***, reaches UK #31.
May ***Headless Cross*** makes US #115.
June [27] The group begins a 16-date US tour in Daytona, FL, ending July 16th in Sacramento, CA, with a current line-up of Iommi, Powell, Murray and vocalist Tony Martin.

1990

Sept [1] Its second I.R.S.-released album ***TYR*** debuts at its UK #24 peak.

1991

Sept [5] The group, now comprising Iommi, Butler, Appice and a re-recruited Dio, begins a UK tour at the Corn Exchange, Cambridge, Cambs.

1992

June [13] *TV Crimes* debuts at its UK #33 peak.
July [4] ***Dehumanizer*** reaches UK #28 in its week of entry.
[18] ***Dehumanizer*** debuts at its US #44 pinnacle (having been licensed to Reprise Records).
Sept [1] "The Black Sabbath Story Volume 1: 1970-1978", a definitive long-form home video collection, is released.
[8] The band plays at London's Hammersmith Odeon during the UK leg of its latest tour.
Oct [14] They perform at New York's Beacon Theatre during North American dates.
Nov [14] Judas Priest's Rob Halford makes a one-off appearance fronting Black Sabbath at the Pacific Amphitheatre, Los Angeles, CA, standing in for Dio, who has refused to perform at tonight and tomorrow night's California gigs because Osbourne is re-forming the original Sabbath line-up as part of his farewell solo concert extravaganza on the following night.
[15] Billed as his last-ever live performance, Osbourne's final US date at the Pacific Amphitheatre, Costa Mesa, CA, ends with an original Black Sabbath reunion. A 30-minute Sabbath set features Osbourne, Iommi, Butler and Vinny Appice. (Shortly thereafter, it is announced that Black Sabbath intends to re-form with Osbourne.)

1994

Feb [12] Still signed to I.R.S. (UK), ***Cross Purposes*** makes UK #41 in its week of entry.
[26] ***Cross Purposes*** debuts at its US #122 peak, as the group plays a sellout gig at the Eagles Ballroom, Milwaukee, WI, during its current US tour with Motorhead and Morbid Angel.
Mar [26] Black Sabbath plays at the Festival Hall, Osaka in Japan, during South-East Asian dates.
Oct ***Nativity In Black - A Tribute To Black Sabbath***, including interpretations by Osbourne and Therapy? on *Iron Man*, Sabbath members Butler and Ward with Rob Halford, billed as the Bullring Brummies, on *The Wizard*, and Megadeth and Biohazard, is released.

1995

Jan [31] The RIAA certifies four million sales of the landmark ***Paranoid*** album.
June [17] ***Forbidden*** peaks at UK #71.
July [1] A North American tour opens in Wilkes-Barre, set to end on August 4th at the Aladdin Hotel, Las Vegas, NV. (Powell will quit the band for personal reasons at the end of the trek and head home to England. Drumer Bobby Rondinelli, who played with the group in 1994, will rejoin the band for the European and Asian legs of tour.)
Oct [10] Osbourne and Butler reunite for a tour opening in Toronto.
Nov [10] The group plays at London's Shepherd's Bush Empire, during the its latest six-date UK jaunt.
see also: **DEEP PURPLE, ELECTRIC LIGHT ORCHESTRA, OZZY OSBOURNE**

BOBBY BLAND

1952

Jan A Memphis, TN, resident since his teens, and a gospel and blues vocalist since school days, becoming B.B. King's valet in 1949, Bland (b. Robert Calvin Bland, Jan. 27, 1930, Rosemark, TN), who has grown up listening to the Grand Ole Opry on Nashville, TN's WSM radio station, taken part in the weekly "Amateur Night At Beale" talent show at the Palace Theater in the late '40s and performed live on WDIA in Memphis on the Goodwill and Starlite revues, has been part of a loose musical aggregation, the Beale Streeters (which includes Johnny Ace, Rosco Gordon, Bill Duncan, Earl Forrest and Little Junior Parker), for some three years during which he has made his vinyl debut on Chess Records with his *I Love You Till The Day I Die* appearing on the flip side of the 1951 US R&B chart-topper *Booted* by Rosco Gordon, for whom Bland has also chauffeured. He now makes further recordings (*Loving Blues* and *IOU Blues*) in Memphis with Ike Turner, for the Los Angeles, CA-based Modern label. (*Crying All Night Long* and *Good Lovin'* will also be released to instant obscurity.) He will sign to James Mattis' Duke label, but is drafted into the US army service, stationed at Fort Hood, TX after one release, ironically titled *Army Blues*.

1957

Aug Post-military service, Houston, TX-based entrepreneur Don Robey, who has bought the label from Mattis, has paid Bland $13.80 travel money to get to Houston where he pairs him with bandleader Joe Scott. His bluesy vocal styling gains him the name-tag Bobby "Blue" Bland. After a handful of releases, Bland now scores in the US pop chart with *Farther Up The Road* (a #5 R&B hit) making #43 during a five-month chart ride. Its success breaks him into the nationwide R&B live circuit with Junior Parker as "Blues Consolidated", backed by Parker's band and later by his own 12-piece road band, led by horn player Joe Scott (who arranges Bland's material), and featuring Wayne Bennett, who plays lead guitar on most of them. For the next five years, the package will play 300 shows a year. Most of his hits will be written by these and others of Bland's musicians, under the communal pen-name Deadric Malone.

1960

Feb *I'll Take Care Of You*, his highest-placed entry yet on the R&B chart (#2), crosses to the US pop chart, albeit at #89. (For much of the next decade, most of Bland's singles will be US Hot 100 entries as well as specialist hits.)
Nov *Cry Cry Cry* peaks at US #71.

1961

Mar *I Pity The Fool* reaches US #46, also topping the R&B chart for one week followed by *Don't Cry No More* which will make US #71 (and R&B #2) in August.

1962

Jan *Turn On Your Love Light* brings him into the US Top 30 for the first time, at #28 (and R&B #2).
Mar *Ain't That Loving You* peaks at US #86.
Apr *Who Will The Next Fool Be?* makes US #76.
Sept *Yield Not To Temptation* reaches US #56, while ***Here's The Man*** is his first album-seller (an area where Duke Records is never to become heavily involved), making US #53.
Oct *Stormy Monday Blues* climbs to US #43 and remains charted for three months.

1963

Feb Double A-side *Call On Me/That's The Way Love Is* is Bland's biggest US hit single, some estimates putting its sales at over a million. (Because Duke does not let its sales figures - and thereby its royalty payments - be known, this is never confirmed.) Topping the R&B chart, the two sides march independently up the Hot 100 to reach #22 and #33 respectively.
Aug *Sometimes You Gotta Cry A Little* peaks at US #56, while ***Call On Me/That's The Way Love Is*** (tagged after the double-sided hit, both songs which it contains) is Bland's one major album-seller during the '60s. It reaches #11 during a 26-week chart stay.
Dec *The Feeling Is Gone* peaks at US #91.

1964

Apr *Ain't Nothing You Can Do* is his second biggest selling hit, reaching US #20, to be followed by *Share Your Love With Me*, which makes US #42 in July, ***Ain't Nothing You Can Do*** peaking at US #119 in August and *Ain't Doing Too Bad* which stops at US #49 in November.
Dec [18] Bland performs at Sam Cooke's funeral in Chicago, IL. A reported 200,000 fans file past to pay their respects and, as the sheer numbers get out of hand, the glass doors of the establishment are smashed.

1965

Jan *Blind Man/Black Night* is another double-sided hit, reaching US #78/#99 (*Blind Man* is in competition with fellow bluesman Little Milton's version, which peaks at #86).
Apr [24] *Ain't No Telling* stops at US #93 followed by the US #63 peaking *These Hands (Small But Mighty)* in October.

1966

Feb *I'm Too Far Gone (To Turn Around)* peaks at US #62. He will nab seven further pop hits before the end of the decade: *Good Time Charlie* (US #75, June), *Poverty* (US #65, October),
You're All I Need (US #88, Apr [22], 1967), his revival of Charles Brown's blues classic *Driftin' Blues* (US #96, March 1968), the year in which Joe Scott and guitarist Wayne Bennett leave Bland, and the 1969 singles *Rockin' In The Same Old Boat* (US #59, January), Bland's strongest seller for over four years, *Gotta Get To Know* (US #91. June [14]) and *Chains Of Love* (US #60, October).

1970

Feb [14] *If You've Got A Heart* peaks at US #96.
Dec *Keep On Loving Me (You'll See The Change)* makes US #89.

1972

Mar While *I'm Sorry* has peaked at US #97 on June [19] the previous year, his biggest seller since *Rockin' In The Same Old Boat* is *Do What You Set Out To Do*, which now reaches US #64. It is also his last release for the Duke label, which, following Don Robey's death, is bought by ABC Records, along with its back catalog and artist contracts. Bland is moved to ABC's Dunhill label.
Sept [9] Bland performs at the Ann Arbor Jazz & Blues Festival, Ann Arbor, MI.

1974

Jan Results of his first West Coast recordings for Dunhill (with producer Steve Barri and musical director Mel Jackson, a veteran of US West Coast rock, who widens Bland's repertoire without eroding his roots or style) are on ***His California Album***, which makes US #136. Taken from it is *This Time I'm Gone For Good*, his first US Top 50 entry for nine years, peaking at #42 and charting for 13 weeks.
Mar His revival of the blues standard *Goin' Down Slow* makes US #69.
Aug *Ain't No Love In The Heart Of The City* reaches US #91, but becomes a classic of Bland's later repertoire, and will be a hit cover in 1978 by heavy-rock band Whitesnake. ***Dreamer*** peaks at US #172.
Nov *I Wouldn't Treat A Dog (The Way You Treated Me)*, reaching #88, is his final US hit single, as Dunhill prefers to market him as a sophisticated soul album act.
Dec Bland is teamed with his long-time friend (and one-time employer) B.B. King, also an ABC artist, for ***Together For The First Time ... Live***, which during a 20-week US chart ride, peaks at #43.

1975

Feb [28] ***Together For The First Time ... Live*** is certified gold by the RIAA.
Sept ABC phases out Dunhill and moves Bland to the main label for the C&W-styled ***Get On Down With Bobby Bland***, which makes US #154.

1976

Aug [28] Success of the first Bland/King collaboration album prompts the release of a similar second set, ***Together Again ... Live***, which climbs to US #73. Perhaps to emphasize both men's artistic roots, it is issued on ABC's jazz label, Impulse.

1977

May ***Reflections In Blue*** reaches US #185, to be followed by ***Come Fly With Me*** which will peak at the same position in July 1978.

1979

Oct By the time ***I Feel Good, I Feel Fine*** is released, ABC has been bought by MCA Records, which retains Bland and moves him to the main label. Nevertheless, this is his final US album chart entry, peaking at #187. (He will have five R&B chart albums on MCA, up to ***You've Got Me Loving You*** in 1984.)

1982

For the first time, Bland tours Britain, a country where he has never charted, but where a specialist following of 20 years greets his visit with acclaim.

1985

Dec Signed to a new deal with Malaco Records, he records ***Members Only***. Malaco, based in Jackson, MS, is a fiercely-independent, R&B-oriented label, an '80s equivalent of the musical environment in which Bland first rose to fame. This album and its sequels ***After All*** (1986) and ***Blues You Can Use*** (March 1988) confirm the singer's artistry to be intact even though he has retired from the pop chart mainstream.

1989

Once again credited as Bobby "Blue" Bland, he has his biggest chart success in years when ***Midnight Run*** spends 70 weeks on the US R&B chart, reaching #26.

1990

May [27] Bland performs before a sellout crowd of 5,864 at the Valley Forge Music Fair, Devon, PA.

1991

Mar [15-16] He plays a sellout concert with King at the Circle Star Theatre, San Carlos, CA, during their current US tour.

1992

Jan [15] Now regularly touring annually with B.B. King, Bland is inducted into the Roll and Roll Hall of Fame at the seventh annual dinner, at New York's Waldorf Astoria Hotel. He will also be honored at the Rhythm and Blues Foundation's third annual Pioneer Awards at New York's Rainbow Room on February 26th.

1995

Nov [19] Still touring with B.B. King, having attended blues singer Albert King's funeral in January 1993, and performed at a benefit concert at the Memorial Auditorium, Chattanooga, TN, raising $90,000 for the planned Bessie Smith Hall on March 26th the same year, Bland appears on a "Heavyweights Of Blues" US caravan tour (also featuring Little Milton, Clarence Carter and Johnny Guitar Watson) which makes its last stop of the year at the Grand Olympic Auditorium, Los Angeles, performing to a crowd of 4,050. While MCA Records (US) has issued ***Turn On Your Love Light - The Duke Recordings Volumes 1*** and ***2*** in 1993 and 1994 respectively, Bland, who has recorded some 38 albums in his career, finishes work on a new studio set of standards scheduled for release in 1996.

MARY J. BLIGE

1991

Blige (b. Mary Jane Blige, Jan. 11, 1971, Atlanta, GA), who has been raised in the Bronx, NY, and moved with her family as a young girl to Savannah, GA, where she has sang in a local Pentecostal church choir, has set her sights on an R&B-singing career after her family moves back to New York to live in Yonkers where she has made her first recording, a cover version of Anita Baker's *Caught Up In The Rapture* in a shopping mall karaoke studio. Using this as the basis for her demo, she now comes to the attention of Uptown Records' Andre Harrell who signs her to the MCA-licensed label.

1992

Aug [15] Her maiden effort, *You Remind Me*, featured on the film soundtrack to "Strictly Business", reaches US #29.

[27] *You Remind Me* is certified gold by the RIAA.

Sept [26] ***What's The 411?***, her soul/hip-hop fused debut album, including guests Pasemaster Mase (from De La Soul), Erick Sermon (from EPMD), Grand Puba and Heavy D among others, hits US #6.

Dec [5] *Real Love* hit US #7, having already been certified gold by the RIAA on November 4th, and makes UK #68.

[26] *Reminisce* makes US #57.

1993

Feb [19] The RIAA certifies two million sales of ***What's The 411?***, early confirmation of her stature among a new breed of rising young female R&B vocalists which includes Toni Braxton and Brandy.

[27] Her cover of Rufus & Chaka Khan's 1976 US #5 hit *Sweet Thing* reaches US #28, as *Reminisce* reaches UK #31.

Mar [20] ***What's The 411?*** charts for a week at UK #53.

June [12] *You Remind Me* debuts at its UK #48 peak.

[26] *Love No Limit* makes US #44.

Sept [4] Reissued *Real Love* reaches UK #26.

Dec [4] *You Don't Have To Worry*, sampling James Brown's *Papa Don't Take No Mess*, reaches UK #36.

1994

Feb [12] *You Don't Have To Worry* makes US #63.

[19] A collection of her debut album remixes, ***What's The 411? Remix*** makes US #118.

May [14] *My Love* bows at its UK #29 peak.

Dec [10] *Be Happy*, sampling Curtis Mayfield's *You're Too Good To Me*, reaches US #29 and debuts at its UK #30 high.

1995

Jan [28] ***My Life*** hits US #7 and tops the US R&B survey.

May [13] ***My Life*** makes UK #59.

[28] The RIAA certifies two million sales of ***My Life***.

Apr [15] *I'm Goin' Down* debuts at its UK #12 peak.

[22] *I'm Goin' Down* reaches US #22.

June [3] Method Man's *I'll Be There For You* featuring Blige's cover of *You're All I Need To Get By*, hits US #3.

[30] During US summer dates, she performs at the Starwood Amphitheatre, Antioch, TN, on a $214,506-grossing bill, supporting Boyz II Men and Montell Jordan

July [22] *You Bring Me Joy*, coupled with *I Love You*, makes US #57.

Sept [30] *Mary Jane (All Night Long)* bows at its UK #17 peak.

Oct [5] She takes part in an all-star show at Madison Square Garden, New York, with Wu-Tang Clan, Run DMC, Brandy, Jodeci, Salt-n-Pepa and Notorious B.I.G. among others.

[28] Her version of Aretha Franklin's hit, *(You Make Me Feel Like A) Natural Woman*, also featured in Fox-TV's "New York Undercover", peaks at US #95.

Dec [6] ***My Life*** is named Top R&B Album at the sixth annual **Billboard** Music Awards, broadcast live on Fox-TV from New York's Coliseum.

[16] *(You Make Me Feel Like A) Natural Woman* bows at its UK #23 peak.

1996

Feb [24] *Not Gon' Cry*, featured in the movie "Waiting To Exhale", hits US #2, behind Mariah Carey & Boyz II Men's *One Sweet Day*.

[28] *I'll Be There For You/You're All I Need To Get By* by Method Man featuring Blige, wins the Best Rap Performance, Duo or Group at the 38th annual Grammy Awards held at Los Angeles' Shrine Auditorium.

BLIND FAITH

Eric Clapton (vocals, guitar); **Steve Winwood** (vocals, keyboards); **Rick Grech** (bass); **Ginger Baker** (drums)

1969

Feb Clapton (b. Eric Clapp, Mar. 30, 1945, Ripley, Surrey) and Baker (b. Peter Baker, Aug. 19, 1939, Lewisham, London), remaining together after the demise of Cream in November 1968, join with Winwood (b. May 12, 1948, Birmingham, Warks.), who has just quit Traffic. Grech (b. Nov. 1, 1946, Bordeaux, France) is invited to complete the band, and he leaves Family during a US tour to do so. The music press dubs the line-up an "instant supergroup", while their name is apparently an anticipatory response to this.

June [7] After recording an album, the band makes its live debut, and only-ever UK date, in London's Hyde Park. Donovan joins the group onstage.

July [12] Promoted as "The Ultimate Supergroup", Blind Faith makes its US concert debut at New York's Madison Square Garden. It is the start of a sellout US stadium tour which, despite being financially rewarding, convinces band members that Blind Faith is musically unsatisfying, and that they should split when the tour is completed.

Aug [19] Still-climbing the US chart, ***Blind Faith*** is certified gold by the RIAA (and will finally receive platinum status on Nov [10], 1993).

Sept [20] ***Blind Faith*** tops both the US and UK charts for the first of two weeks. The original UK sleeve, with a picture of a nude 11-year-old girl holding a "phallic" model airplane (photographed by Bob Seidemann), is considered too controversial for use in the US. No single is released from the album as the band completes its US tour, following which Clapton loses interest, and he carries on touring with Delaney and Bonnie. Blind Faith does not play together again, despite manager Robert Stigwood's assertions that the group members will reunite in January 1970. (Grech will stay with Baker in Airforce at the end of 1969, while Winwood will work solo before re-forming Traffic early in 1970.) ***Blind Faith*** will make US #126 when reissued in February 1972.

see also: **Eric CLAPTON, CREAM, FAMILY, TRAFFIC, Steve WINWOOD**

BLONDIE

Debbie Harry (vocals); **Chris Stein** (guitar); **Jimmy Destri** (keyboards); **Gary Valentine** (bass); **Clem Burke** (drums)

1974

Aug The original line-up of Blondie, pairing former beautician and Playboy bunny waitress Harry (b. Deborah Harry, July 1, 1945, Miami, FL), who has also worked at the bar at New York, NY's Max's Kansas City club, with the backing musicians from her earlier female vocal group, the Stilettos, is formed in New York. Harry, who has been raised by adoptive parents Richard and Catherine Harry from the age of three in Hawthorne, NJ, has previously recorded as a member of folk-rock band Wind In The Willows (who released ***Wind In The Willows*** on Capitol Records in July 1968), while the other original members, Stein (b. Jan. 5, 1950, Brooklyn, New York), a graduate of New York's School of Visual Arts, bassist Fred Smith (b. Apr. 10, 1948, New York City) and drummer Billy O'Connor, have played only in local bands. With Czechoslovakian refugee Ivan Kral joining on guitar in October and two female back-up singers, Tish and Snooky, having replaced initial recruits Julie and Jackie, the band's early repertoire is based on the girl group sounds of the '60s. Blondie, having quickly changed from the earlier Angel & the Snake moniker to a name which draws attention to Harry's platinum blonde hair, begins to play the local club circuit, not least at the noted New York punk birthplace, CBGBs.

1975

Oct Ex-Knickers member Destri (b. Apr. 13, 1954, Brooklyn) joins on keyboards. It is the latest in a series of personnel changes among the burgeoning New York new wave bands, which has seen Kral leave to join the Patti Smith Group, ex-Sweet Revenge drummer Burke (b. Clement Burke, Nov. 24, 1955, New York) replace O'Connor (who goes on to law school), and Smith quit to become a member of Television, replaced by Valentine.

1976

Nov Having signed to the Private Stock label, Blondie's debut single *X-Offender* and album ***Blondie***, both produced by ex-Strangeloves member Richard Gottehrer, are released, reflecting a raw, new wave edge.

1977

Jan They make their US West Coast debut at the Whisky A-Go Go in Los Angeles, CA, with an image firmly focused on Harry, followed by a US tour supporting Iggy Pop.

Feb With ***Blondie*** now released in the UK, the group tours behind Television during a short concert visit, which is marred by onstage fights between Stein and Destri.

May [21] Blondie undertakes its second US trek of the year, now supported by Television.

July Valentine leaves to form his own group, the Know, and is replaced by ex-World War II bassist Frank Infante (b. New York), who joins prior to the recording sessions for Blondie's sophomore album.

Oct Having bought Blondie's contract from Private Stock, acquiring rights to all previously-recorded material, Chrysalis releases ***Plastic Letters***, once again produced by Gottehrer.

Nov Infante moves to rhythm guitar, and UK bass player Nigel Harrison (ex-Silverhead) joins.

1978

Mar [18] Blondie's chart career initially breaks in the UK, as *Denis (Denee)*, a pop-punk remake of Randy & the Rainbows' 1963 US #10 *Denise*, hits #2, while ***Plastic Letters*** is on its way to hit UK #10.

Apr [15] ***Plastic Letters*** makes US #72.

May [27] Its second extract *(I'm Always Touched By Your) Presence Dear*, written by Valentine before his departure, hits UK #10. Blondie will spend the summer recording in New York with producer Mike Chapman, who, as one half of the Chinnichap writing and production team, has scored with a succession of '70s UK pop acts, including Mud, the Sweet and Smokie, in a conscious attempt to build a more radio-friendly, commercial sound.

Sept [16] The band's seven-date UK headlining tour climaxes at London's Hammersmith Odeon.

[23] *Picture This*, the first single from the Chapman collaboration, penned by Harry, Stein and Destri, reaches UK #12, spurred by the latest in a parallel series of promotional videos which accompany each single and increasingly focus on Harry as an alternative sex kitten.

Dec [2] *Hanging On The Telephone*, the second single from the forthcoming ***Parallel Lines***, hits UK #5. (By year's end, Harry completes filming "The

Foreigner", directed by Amos Poe, for whom she also acted in the earlier new wave movie "Blank Generation", which also featured the Ramones.)

1979

Feb [3] *Heart Of Glass*, a disco-flavored third single (already a far cry from Blondie's new wave beginnings) also from ***Parallel Lines***, tops the UK chart, where it will stay for four weeks, and sell over a million copies in the UK alone, making it the band's biggest British success.
[17] ***Parallel Lines*** also tops the UK survey for the first of four weeks.
[24] A reactivated ***Blondie*** peaks at UK #75.
Apr [6] Still-climbing *Heart Of Glass* is certified gold by the RIAA.
[28] The group makes its US breakthrough with its first chart disc, *Heart Of Glass* hitting #1, with ***Parallel Lines*** on its way to hit US #6. (A major global success, the album will eventually log over 20 million sales.)
May [26] Stein-penned pop-rock ditty *Sunday Girl* spends the first of three weeks at UK #1.
June With its line-up now settled as Harry, boyfriend Stein, Harrison, Destri and Infante, Blondie wraps up three months of recording under Chapman's direction, at the Electric Lady, Media Sound and Power Station studios in New York.
[6] ***Parallel Lines*** is certified platinum by the RIAA.
Aug [4] *One Way Or Another*, still mining ***Parallel Lines***, reaches US #24.
Sept US label Bomp and London Records in the UK release *Little GTO*, by "the New York Blondes featuring Madame X", the latter being Harry, who is clearly heard on vocals. Chrysalis threatens legal action, and the single is withdrawn.
[29] Continuing the Chapman-helmed pop-rock fusion, ***Eat To The Beat***, featuring guest vocalists Lorna Luft and Donna Destri, tops the UK chart, and will remain on the survey for nine months.
Oct [6] Harry and Stein-penned *Dreaming*, curiously featuring legendary songwriter Ellie Greenwich on backing vocals, hits UK #2.
Nov [24] ***Eat To The Beat*** reaches US #17.
Dec [1] *Dreaming* reaches US #27.
[15] *Union City Blue*, a song also featured in the concurrent Harry-starring motion picture "Union City", reaches UK #13.
[31] Blondie's gig at the Apollo Theatre, Glasgow, Scotland, is broadcast live on BBC-2 TV's "The Old Grey Whistle Test".

1980

Feb [2] *The Hardest Part* stalls at US #84.
Mar [1] *Atomic*, written by Harry and Destri and once again featuring backing vocals from Greenwich, extracted from ***Eat To The Beat***, tops the UK chart for the first of two weeks.
Apr [7] *Call Me* is certified gold by the RIAA.
[19] *Call Me*, a track written and produced by Giorgio Moroder for the soundtrack of the Richard Gere movie "American Gigolo", to which Harry has added lyrics, tops the US chart.
[26] *Call Me* also hits UK #1.
June The film "Roadie", co-starring Meat Loaf and Harry, opens in US theaters, its soundtrack including Blondie's version of Johnny Cash's *Ring Of Fire*.
July *Atomic* makes US #39.
[10] ***Eat To The Beat*** is certified platinum by the RIAA.
Nov [15] *The Tide Is High*, a lilting reggae number written by John Holt and previously recorded by the Paragons, hits UK #1 for the first of two weeks, while ***Autoamerican***, a third album collaboration with Chapman, hits UK #3.

1981

Jan [26] Still-climbing *The Tide Is High* is certified gold and ***Autoamerican*** platinum by the RIAA.
[31] *The Tide Is High* also tops the US survey for one week, as ***Autoamerican*** hits US #7, and the Stein/Harry-penned *Rapture*, highlighted by an innovative Harry rap also excerpted from ***Autoamerican***, with Tom Scott strongly featured on sax, hits UK #5.
Feb Harry announces that she is to record a solo album, produced by Nile Rodgers and Bernard Edwards of Chic.
Mar [28] Having been confirmed gold by the RIAA the day before, *Rapture* hits US #1, where it will remain for two weeks, keeping John Lennon's *Woman* from the top spot.
Aug [8] Harry's solo debut *Backfired* makes UK #32.
[15] Its parent solo album ***Koo Koo***, with a striking H.R. Giger cover, depicting Harry's head pierced by four large pins, and released, as with all Blondie product, on the Chrysalis label, hits UK #6.
Sept [19] The second extract *Backfired* makes US #43, as ***Koo Koo*** makes its way to US #25.
Oct [31] Compilation ***The Best Of Blondie***, simultaneously released with a comprehensive video collection, hits UK #4 and will reach US #30.
Nov [7] Further Harry solo single *The Jam Was Moving* stalls at US #82.

1982

Jan Infante sues the band, claiming he is being excluded from group activities. Following an out-of-court settlement, he will remain in the lineup.
Feb [9] ***Best Of Blondie*** is certified gold by the RIAA.
June [5] Blondie's swan-song album ***The Hunter***, again a Chapman production, hits UK #9.
[12] The extracted *Island Of Lost Souls* reaches UK #11.
July [3] *Island Of Lost Souls* makes US #37, the group's final US chart single.
[10] ***The Hunter*** makes US #33.
[31] *War Child*, taken from ***The Hunter*** stalls at #39.
Aug A projected UK tour is cancelled shortly before the first scheduled gig (at the Apollo Theatre, Glasgow), due to poor ticket sales.
Oct With the group now dissolved, Stein will launch his own Animal label, licensed through Chrysalis, while Harry will initially concentrate on her acting career. (Notable early film roles will include "Videodrome" co-starring James Woods, and the John Waters-directed "Hairspray", though she will also contribute *Rush Rush* (co-written with Moroder) to the soundtrack for "Scarface", and *Feel The Spin* (co-written and produced by Jellybean) for the 1984 rap movie, "Krush Groove".) **Making Tracks: The Rise Of Blondie**, written by Harry and Stein, will also be published. The remaining members will all move towards solo projects and session work, with Destri releasing ***Heart On The Wall*** by year's end.

1983

Apr [20] "Teaneck Tanzi: The Venus Flytrap", a comedy in which Harry stars as a wrestler with Andy Kaufman, opens at the Nederlander Theater, New York. The show ignominiously closes after its opening night. She will mostly withdraw from the entertainment world for three years, to look after Stein, who has become seriously ill.

1986

Dec Harry returns to the UK chart with the Chuck Lorre-penned *French Kissin' (In The USA)*, which hits #8, while her sophomore debut album ***Rockbird***, produced by J. Geils Band's Seth Justman, climbs to US #97 and UK #31. Over the following year, *French Kissin' (In The USA)* peaks at US #57 on Jan [10], *Free To Fall* makes UK #46 in March and *In Love With Love* reaches UK #45 in May, also peaking at US #70 on July [25].

1988

Dec A remix of Blondie's *Denis* makes UK #50.

1989

Jan [14] Its parent album ***Once More Into The Bleach***, an album of updated remixes of earlier Blondie hits, peaks at UK #50.
Feb *Call Me* remix peaks at US #61.
Mar Harry appears in and performs *Bright Side* in CBS-TV's "Wiseguy".
July [12] A Disney press conference announces that Harry will play the Old Woman Who Lived In A Shoe in the Disney Channel's Shelley Duvall-produced "Mother Goose Rock'n'Rhyme".
Oct [3] Harry makes her live comeback in the UK, after a seven-year absence, at the small tex-mex Borderline club in London.
[28] Solo project, credited to Deborah Harry, ***Def, Dumb And Blonde***, produced by Chapman and the Thompson Twins' Tom Bailey, reaches UK #12 and will peak at US #123. Meanwhile, Harry undertakes a US concert tour with a backing band including a fully-recovered Stein (guitar), Leigh Fox (bass), Jimmy Clark (drums), Carla Olla (rhythm guitar) and Suzy Davis (keyboards).
Nov [4] The extracted *I Want That Man* reaches UK #13.

1990

Apr *Sweet And Low* peaks at UK #57.
June [2] Harry performs the first of two dates at the Brixton Academy, London, during a short UK concert visit.
[28] She embarks on the "Escape From New York" package tour with fellow New York, ex-new wave cohorts the Ramones, Tom Tom Club and Jerry Harrison, set to end on August 17th.
Sept [4] Stein is featured on ***Dead City Radio***, a collection of William Burroughs readings, released by Island.

1991

Jan [19] *Well Did You Evah*, which Harry and Iggy Pop have contributed to ***Red Hot + Blue***, an anthology of Cole Porter songs recently released to benefit AIDS education, peaks at UK #42.
Mar [23] A second Blondie retrospective, ***The Complete Picture - The Very Best Of Deborah Harry And Blondie***, augmented by solo highlights, hits UK #3.
July [13] At the beginning of a short UK tour, Harry performs on the "Summer XS" bill at Wembley Stadium, Wembley, Middx. While in the country, she will record sessions in London, reunited with Tom Bailey at the Sugar Shack, and separately with Stein at Air Studios.
Nov [15] Harry's latest acting role, as a telephone-sex operator in "Intimate Stranger", is broadcast on Showtime TV in the US (she has also recently appeared in the movie "The Killbillies"). Burke, sometime drummer with Eurythmics during the '80s, resurfaces in Dramarama, while Harrison is simultaneously holding a post in A&R at Interscope Records and moonlighting as a member of the Brothers Figaro.

1993

Apr [27] Having appeared on ITV's "Satisfaction" on the 8th, Harry guests on Fox-TV's "Tribeca".
July [31] Newly signed to Sire Records, Harry's ***Debravation***, her first solo album in four years (variously produced by Stein, Arthur Baker and Anne Dudley), debuts at its UK #24 peak, led by *I Can See Clearly* (UK #23, July [3]) and followed by *Strike Me Pink* (UK #46 Sept [18]).

1994

Jan Chrysalis releases a Blondie rarities package, ***Blonde And Beyond***, a collection of oddities and rare cuts.
Sept [10] Remix of *Atomic* bows at its UK #19 peak.
Nov ***The Platinum Collection***, a 47-song CD anthology, including the 1975 demo *Once I Had A Love*, re-recorded as *Heart Of Glass*, is released in the US.

1995

Apr [1] Harry debuts her new band, Stein (guitar), former Psychedelic Fur Joe McGinty (keyboards), Greta Brinkman (bass) and Duard Kline (drums), at New York's Don Hill venue, and will perform with the Jazz Passengers two weeks later at S.O.B.'s in New York.
July [8] *Heart Of Glass (Remix)* debuts at its UK #15 high.
[29] ***Beautiful - The Remix Album*** reaches UK #25 in its week of entry.
Oct [28] A remix of *Union City Blue* bows at its UK #31 peak.

BLOOD, SWEAT & TEARS

David Clayton-Thomas (lead vocals); **Steve Katz** (guitar, harmonica, vocals); **Jim Fielder** (bass); **Bobby Colomby** (drums, percussion, vocals); **Fred Lipsius** (piano, alto saxophone); **Dick Halligan** (keyboards, trombone, flute, vocals); **Chuck Winfield** (trumpet, flugelhorn); **Lew Soloff** (trumpet, flugelhorn); **Jerry Hyman** (trombone, recorder)

1967

Dec [16] Having made its live debut at New York, NY's Café Au Go Go in November opening for Moby Grape, and envisioned by ex-Blues Project member Al Kooper (b. Feb. 5, 1944, Brooklyn, New York), Katz (b. May. 9, 1945, New York), Colomby (b. Dec. 20, 1944, New York) and Fielder (b. Oct. 4, 1947, Denton, TX) as an experimental blues/rock/jazz hybrid quartet with a blazing horn section, comprising Lipsius (b. Nov. 19, 1943, New York), Halligan (b. Aug. 29, 1943, Troy, NY), Randy Brecker (b. Nov. 27, 1945, Philadelphia, PA) and Jerry Weiss (May 1, 1946, New York), recruited from the New York session scene, accommodating jazz and serious music forms and players, Blood, Sweat & Tears is launched as the latest signing to CBS/Columbia Records (at the instigation of label boss Clive Davis), in front of 450 guests at the Scene in New York.

1968

Mar [15-17] The group performs at the Avalon Ballroom, San Francisco, CA, on a bill with Son House and John Handy.

June [1] The band's debut, ***The Child Is Father To The Man***, which wraps a selection of Kooper originals and pop cover versions in tight brass and string arrangements, makes US #47, but Kooper and two horn players, Brecker and Weiss, will soon leave the group.

July [13] ***The Child Is Father To The Man*** makes UK #40.

1969

Mar [29] A new line-up, fronted by Clayton-Thomas (b. David Thomsett, Sept. 13, 1941, Surrey), with horn recruits Winfield (b. Feb. 5, 1943, Monessen, PA), Soloff (b. Feb. 20, 1944, Brooklyn) and Hyman (b. May 19, 1947, New York), has recorded ***Blood, Sweat & Tears***, which now tops the US chart for the first of seven weeks, selling over two million copies by year's end, and lays the ground rules for much of the '70s jazz/rock fusion boom.

Apr [12] Their revival of an archive Motown ballad, *You've Made Me So Very Happy*, hits US #2, the first of three million-sellers from the album.

[30] *You've Made Me So Very Happy* reaches UK #35 (the band's only UK hit single), while ***Blood, Sweat & Tears*** makes UK #15.

June [12] *You Made Me So Very Happy* is certified gold by the RIAA.

July [3] The group performs at the "Newport Jazz Festival", Newport, RI, on a bill featuring Johnny Winter and James Brown among others.

[5] *Spinning Wheel*, written by Clayton-Thomas, hits US #2, as the band performs at the "Atlanta Pop Festival", International Raceway, Hampton, GA, before an estimated 125,000 people.

[23] *Spinning Wheel* is certified gold by the RIAA.

Nov Laura Nyro-penned *And When I Die* hits US #2, and will become the third million-selling single from ***Blood, Sweat & Tears***, the first time in RIAA history that three singles from one album have all gone gold.

Dec [2] ***Child Is Father To The Man*** is certified gold by the RIAA.

[20] At the end of an astonishingly, successful year for the band, the **Los Angeles Times** makes the following summary: "Blood, Sweat & Tears may just be the most important new pop music group of the decade. Profound though the influence of the Beatles has been, their work represented an escape from everything B, S & T is bringing into rock; an orchestral sound, warm harmonic concepts and improvized jazz concepts and improvized jazz solos of high caliber."

1970

Jan [14] *And When I Die* is confirmed gold by the RIAA.

Mar [11] ***Blood, Sweat & Tears*** wins the Best Album, Best Arrangements Accompanying A Vocalist (Lipsius for *Spinning Wheel*) and Best Contemporary Instrumental Performance (*Trios Gymnopedies On A Theme* by Erik Satie) categories at the 12th annual Grammy Awards.

June The group embarks on a US State Department-sponsored cultural tour of Eastern Europe, taking in Romania, Poland and Yugoslavia.

July [8] Still-climbing ***Blood Sweat & Tears 3*** is certified gold by the RIAA.

Aug [8] ***Blood, Sweat & Tears 3*** tops the US chart for the first of two weeks and will reach UK #14.

[29] The extracted single, a cover of Goffin-King's *Hi-De-Ho*, makes US #14.

Sept During a UK visit, the band performs at London's Royal Albert Hall.

Nov [7] *Lucretia MacEvil* reaches US #29.

1971

Feb Having scored and recorded the music for the film "The Owl And The Pussycat", the soundtrack album reaches US #186.

Aug ***B, S & T; 4***, recorded in San Francisco, CA, with new horn-playing member Dave Bargeron (b. Sept. 6, 1942, MA), who has replaced Hyman, hits US #10.

[5] ***B, S & T; 4*** is certified gold by the RIAA.

[28] The extracted single *Go Down Gamblin'* makes US #32.

Nov [27] *Lisa, Listen To Me* peaks at US #73. The group plays its first concert with full a symphony orchestra in New Orleans, LA.

Dec [31] Clayton-Thomas and Lipsius make their final appearances with the band, at the Anaheim Convention Center, Anaheim, CA, (the former will launch a solo career, releasing albums for both Columbia, ***David Clayton-Thomas*** (1972), ***Tequila Sunrise*** (1972) and RCA, ***Harmony Junction***).

1972

Jan Blind singer Bobby Doyle (b. Houston, TX), former leader of the Bobby Doyle Trio, which included Kenny Rogers, Georg Wadenius (b. May 4, 1945, Sweden), from Swedish band Made In Sweden, and saxophonist Joe Henderson join the group. The new line-up fails to gel, and the band reorganizes yet again, with Jerry Fisher (b. Mar. 1, 1942, DeKalb, TX) taking over on vocals, and Lou Marini Jr. (b. Charleston, NC) and Larry Willis (b. Dec. 20, 1940, New York) also joining, while original member Halligan quits.

Apr Compilation ***Greatest Hits*** reaches US #19.

Nov [25] *So Long Dixie* reaches #44 in the US, and ***New Blood***, produced by Colomby, peaks at #32.

1973

Apr Clayton-Thomas files a breach of contract lawsuit against his former band members.

Aug [25] ***No Sweat*** peaks at US #72. After Katz, Winfield and Marini leave, the band's personnel becomes extremely fluid, varying from concert to concert, although Jerry LaCroix (b. Oct. 10, 1945) takes over vocal/harmonica duties for a short period, while Tom Malone becomes a more permanent member.

1974

July [13] *Tell Me That I'm Wrong*, with Clayton-Thomas returning as the featured vocalist, peaks at US #83, featured on ***Mirror Image***, which stalls at US #149 in September.

1975

July [12] Their revival of the Beatles' *Got To Get You Into My Life* peaks at US #62, as its parent album ***New City*** makes US #47.

1976

Aug [7] ***More Than Ever***, with guest vocalists Chaka Khan and Patti Austin, is a further commercial disappointment (peaking at US #165), after which the band is dropped by Columbia.

1977

Nov Signed to ABC records, with a revised personnel now comprising Clayton-Thomas (vocals), Dave Bargeron (trombone), Randy Bernson (guitar), Larry Willis (b. New York, NY) (keyboards), Tony Klatka (b. Mar. 6, 1946) (trumpet), Bill Tillman (saxophones, flute), Forrest Buchtel (trumpet, flugelhorn), Mike Stern (guitars), Danny Trifan (bass), Roy McCurdy (drums) and Colomby (percussion), the band releases ***Brand New Day***, produced by Bobby Colomby and Roy Halee. Member changes will continue to afflict the line-up, with Chris Albert (trumpet), Gregory Herbert (saxophone), who will die in February 1988 in Holland at the beginning of a European tour, and Neil Stubenhaus (bass) all spending some time with the group.

1980

Mar Featuring band constituents Clayton-Thomas, Robert Piltch (guitar), Bruce Cassidy (trumpet, flugelhorn), Richard Martinez (keyboards), Bobby Economou (drums), Earl Seymour (saxophones, flute), David Piltch (bass) and Vernon Dorge (saxophones, flute), ***Nuclear Blues***, produced by Jerry Goldstein, is their second and last ABC release. When it fails to chart, the band fades from view for much of the next eight years, although Clayton-Thomas and Colomby (who jointly own the Blood, Sweat & Tears name) will occasionally assemble an aggregation for live work.

1986

Nov [21] The RIAA certifies platinum sales for ***Blood Sweat & Tears Greatest Hits*** and multi-platinum sales for ***Blood Sweat & Tears*** (three million).

1992

July [11-12] With Clayton-Thomas (who, in 1990, has sued the writers of Milli Vanilli's *All Or Nothing* for copyright infringement of his 1969 hit composition *Spinning Wheel*, and who has also inked a solo deal with Zoo Records subsidiary, SRC, in May) and a re-formed Blood, Sweat & Tears having regrouped in July 1988 for a US tour, and increasingly active as a nostalgia troupe, the band performs at "Le Festival Les Heros Sont Immortels", Calais, France.

1993

Mar [12-13] Two reunion concerts are held at New York's Bottom Line to celebrate the silver anniversary of ***Child Is Father To The Man***. Unable contractually to use the name Blood Sweat & Tears, Kooper, Lipsius, Brecker, Fielder, Katz, Soloff and Malone, joined by other musicians, perform as the Child Is Father To The Man Band.

1995

Sept [26] With the Clayton-Thomas led Blood Sweat & Tears still performing (at one of this year's gigs in West Bloomfield, MI, on July 24th, he shocks the audience when he allegedly comments on the weather as being "as hot as the last train going to Auschwitz"), Sony Legacy releases a two-CD ***Greatest Hits*** set in the US. (Clayton-Thomas will be honored with a Hall of Fame induction at the 25th annual Juno Awards held at Coops Coliseum, Hamilton, ON, Canada on March 10th 1996.)

see also: **THE BLUES PROJECT**

MIKE BLOOMFIELD

1967

Apr Bloomfield (b. July 28, 1944, Chicago, IL), who learned blues guitar as a teenager from Chicago giants like Muddy Waters, performed acoustic gigs with Nick Gravenites on vocals and Charley Musselwhite on harmonica before joining the Paul Butterfield Blues Band in 1965, playing with them when they backed Bob Dylan on his "electric" set at the "Newport Folk Festival", Newport, RI, on July 25th. Subsequently invited to contribute lead guitar on Dylan's ***Highway 61 Revisited*** sessions, Bloomfield has now left Butterfield to form Electric Flag, which also includes Barry Goldberg (keyboards), Buddy Miles (drums), Nick Gravenites (vocals), Harvey Brooks (bass), Marcus Doubleday (trumpet), and saxophonists Peter Strazza and Herbie Rich. Bloomfield intends to combine blues with varied musical elements drawn from the others members' distinguished backgrounds.

June [16] Electric Flag makes its live debut at the "Monterey International Pop Festival", County Fairgrounds, Monterey, CA. Its first album ***The Trip***, the soundtrack to an underground Peter Fonda film, is released, subsequently becoming a cult favorite.

1968

June [1] Electric Flag's debut for CBS/Columbia Records, ***A Long Time Comin'***, reaches US #31. Bloomfield quits the squabbling line-up while the album is still on the chart (leaving Miles to organize one more Electric Flag album, ***The Electric Flag***, which will reach US #76 on March 1st, 1969 before the unit splits permanently. Miles will team up with Jimi Hendrix's while Gravenites will join Big Brother & the Holding Company).

Dec [7] Bloomfield's next project is an album of jam sessions, spontaneously recorded with the co-credited Stephen Stills and Blood, Sweat & Tears founder Al Kooper, and issued as ***Super Session***. It will reach US #12.

1969

Feb [6-9] Bloomfield performs at the Fillmore West, San Francisco, CA, on a bill with the Byrds.

Mar [8] Also recorded at the Fillmore West, a second collaboration with Kooper, the double live set ***The Live Adventures Of Mike Bloomfield And Al Kooper***, also featuring Carlos Santana and Elvin Bishop, reaches US #18.

Apr Bloomfield plays live in Chicago with his original idol Muddy Waters, the union subsequently released as ***Fathers And Sons***.

Nov [1] Columbia-issued solo ***It's Not Killing Me*** makes US #127.

1970

Bloomfield writes the score for the movie "Medium Cool" (and will also pen soundtracks to "Steelyard Blues", in collaboration with earlier cohort Gravenites in 1973, and Andy Warhol's "Bad".)

Dec [4] ***Super Session*** is certified gold by the RIAA.

1973

June Increasingly reclusive, he has nevertheless collaborated on ***Triumvirate*** with John Paul Hammond and Dr. John, which makes US #105, again issued by CBS/Columbia.

1974

Nov Bloomfield has briefly reunited with Miles, Goldberg and Gravenites with Roger Troy on bass, as Electric Flag for the Atlantic label, which releases ***The Band Kept Playing***.

1976

June Bloomfield has become a founding member of the MCA label-created quintet KGB, which also includes Ray Kennedy (vocals), Goldberg (keyboards), Rick Grech (bass) and Carmine Appice (drums). It struggles to US #124 with the eponymous ***KGB***, and a disgruntled Bloomfield will leave (along with Grech) before the second and final KGB album ***Motion***, never to play in a band line-up again.

1977

If You Love These Blues, Play 'Em As You Please is released in association with magazine **Guitar Player** as a virtuoso primer for blues guitarists, and is nominated for a Grammy Award. Bloomfield signs to the small Takoma label, and records a series of uncommercial blues/roots albums over the next four years, including ***Analine***, ***Between The Hard Place And The Ground*** and ***Michael Bloomfield***. A 1978 album, ***Count Talent And The Originals***, released on the Clouds label, will reunite him once again with Gravenites and Mark Naftalin.

1981

Feb [15] Shortly before the release of his final album ***Living In The Fast Lane***, and soon after ***Cruisin' For A Bruisin'***, Bloomfield is found dead in his car in San Francisco of an apparently accidental drug overdose. (Following the release by Columbia in 1984 of ***Bloomfield - A Retrospective***, the label will issue ***Essential Blues 1964-1969*** on CD in June 1994.)

KURTIS BLOW

1979

Oct After studying voice at the High School of Music and Art and Communications at New York, NY's City College, and influenced by local rapper DJ Hollywood, Blow (b. Kurt Walker, Aug. 9, 1959, New York, NY) has begun rapping as a DJ in Harlem, New York clubs in 1976. Honing his craft over the next three years at other local venues, including Small's Paradise, and working not least with rap pioneer Grandmaster Flash, he is now offered a deal with Mercury Records, becoming the first rap artist ever to sign to a major label, just as the Sugarhill Gang's *Rapper's Delight* is developing into the first international rap/pop crossover hit.

Dec Blow's debut rap release and one of the genre's earliest, is the seasonal *Christmas Rappin'*, which fails to chart in the US (despite selling some 400,000 copies), but reaches UK #30.

1980

Aug [19] Still climbing the US survey, *The Breaks* is certified gold by the RIAA, the first certified million-selling rap disc.

Sept *The Breaks* makes US #87, but with huge specialist-market sales, particularly in New York, it also hits #4 on the R&B chart. It also marks Blow's recording debut with partner Davy D. (b. David Reeves) on backing tracks and will make UK #47.

Oct ***Kurtis Blow***, produced by J.B. Moore and Robert Ford Jr., and recorded at the Greene Street Studios, New York, reaches US #71.

1981

Aug After finding wider performing success around the US with Davy D. accompanying him at the turntables, he tours Europe and the UK to promote ***Deuce***, which makes US #137. Two more well-received genre-breaking albums over the next four years will confirm Blow as one of the seminal innovators of the burgeoning rap movement: ***Tough***, which peaks at US #167 in October 1982, and ***Ego Trip*** which makes US #83 in October 1984 (and features guest rapper Run of Run D.M.C.). One month later, Blow will appear, together with L.L. Cool J., the Fat Boys, the Beastie Boys and others, in the early rap movie "Krush Groove".

1985

Mar [16] *Party Time* peaks at UK #67.

Apr [27] Novelty rap *Basketball* makes US #71.

June René & Angela's *Save Your Love (For Number 1)*, which features Blow, peaks at UK #66.

Dec [14] Artists United Against Apartheid, comprising 49 artists and including Blow, makes US #38 and UK #21 with *Sun City*.

1986

Feb *If I Ruled The World*, his biggest UK hit, reaches UK #24.

Nov *I'm Chillin'* peaks at UK #64, after which Blow's profile drops, as a new generation of rap artists takes over from the genre's innovators. He will make one further chart appearance when ***Kingdom Blow*** stalls at US #196 on Dec [13] 1987. (Making occasional appearances on US television into the '90s (including a performance of *Christmas Rappin'* on ABC-TV's daytime soap "One Life To Live" on April 24th 1991), Blow will re-emerge to organize and lead popular US caravan tours featuring other rap pioneers, including Grandmaster Flash, Whodini, Sugarhill Gang and Kool Moe Dee under the banner "Old School Reunion Tour".)

BLUE NILE

Paul Buchanan (vocals, synthesizer); **Robert Bell** (synthesizer); **Paul Joseph Moore** (synthesizer)

1983

Buchanan (b. Paul Gerard Buchanan, Apr. 16, 1956, Edinburgh, Scotland), Bell and Moore, all fellow ex-University of Glasgow students, have formed Blue Nile in their home town, Glasgow, Scotland in 1981, initially releasing one single, *I Love This Life* on RSO Records (UK). Dedicated to crafting synthesizer-based, easy-flowing musical collages around Buchanan's songs, they have produced a demo tape (which includes *Tinseltown In The Rain*) which is subsequently used by East Lothian, Scotland-based hi-fi equipment manufacturer, Linn, to test record cutting technology. Linn now offers £250-worth of speakers to the band, and will form its own Linn Records offshoot to specifically and uniquely sponsor and release future Blue Nile material.

1984

May Their debut album ***Walk Around The Rooftops***, recorded entirely in East Lothian and licensed to Virgin Records, offering an impressionist musical landscape, which deeply impresses record reviewers, makes UK #80.

1988

The trio, unimpressed by the demands or potential rewards of the record industry, has spent nearly five years on a follow-up album, meticulously writing and re-recording Buchanan's songs, with Linn's technological recording advances made available to them in their remote East Lothian studio.

1989

Oct [21] Promoted with earnest trade and press ads, quoting enthusiasm for the band from the likes of Phil Collins and Sting, Blue Nile's second album ***Hats***, again released on Linn, debuts at its UK #12 peak, while the slowly-crescendoed *Downtown Lights* has recently made UK #67. Produced by the band, the seven-track, all Buchanan-penned set again wows reviewers, though in interviews the reluctant trio insists on the unimportance of it all.

1990

Apr [7] ***Hats*** peaks at US #108 during a 14-week chart visit, as several cuts, including *Downtown Lights* and *Saturday Night*, become popular modern and college radio items. With some trepidation, the band makes a short spring visit to the US to perform its debut live dates.

Sept [13] After long-time champion of the band, Rickie Lee Jones, has enticed Buchanan and Moore on

stage earlier in the year on her US tour, to help them overcome stage nerves, Blue Nile finally begins its first UK tour, comprising six dates, at the Free Trade Hall, Manchester, Gtr. Manchester, set to end on the 23rd at the Royal Concert Hall, Glasgow, Scotland. The band, augmented by three additional musicians, insists on a no frills, no dry-ice, no T-shirt-merchandising event, allowing the audience to fully concentrate on the group's emotive music.
[29] Second album extract *Headlights On The Parade* stalls at UK #72.
Having recently recorded a duet cover version of *Easter Parade* with Jones, Buchanan, Moore and Bell feature on Robbie Robertson's long-awaited second solo album ***Storyville***.

1991

Jan [19] Released 16 months after its parent album, *Saturday Night* debuts at its UK #50 peak, as the band retreats for another extended recording period (during which Buchanan will reportedly become engaged to actress Rosanna Arquette).

1996

June [1] Following Annie Lennox's recording of *Downtown Lights* for her chart-topping ***Medusa*** album in 1995, Blue Nile returns with its third album in 12 years, ***Peace At Last***, mostly written by Buchanan and revealing a more acoustic-based sound, is released on Warner Bros.

BLUE ÖYSTER CULT

Eric Bloom (lead vocals, lead guitar, keyboards, "stun guitar"); **Donald "Buck Dharma" Roeser** (lead guitar, vocals); **Albert Bouchard** (drums, vocals); **Allen Lanier** (rhythm guitar, keyboards); **Joe Bouchard** (bass, vocals)

1971

Oct Based in Long Island, New York, NY, the band has evolved in 1970 from the Stalk-Forrest Group, itself a hybrid of three outfits, the Cows, Soft White Underbelly and Oaxoa, a group originally launched at Stony Brook University by Roeser (b. Nov. 12, 1947, aka Buck Dharma), Lanier (b. June 25, 1946) and Al Bouchard (b. May 24, 1947, Watertown, NY), along with **Crawdaddy** magazine writer Sandy Pearlman and Richard Meltzer. Pearlman, who has a major influence on the group in his role as mentor, producer and manager, has already delivered two albums featuring vocalist Les Bronstein to the Elektra label (one as Soft White Underbelly, the second as the Stalk-Forrest Group), which rejects both projects. With a five-piece line-up now including Joe Bouchard (b. Nov. 9, 1948, Watertown) and Bloom (b. Dec. 1, 1944), the band signs as Blue Öyster Cult to CBS/Columbia Records and begins recording its debut album at the Warehouse, under producers Murray Krugman and the ever-present Pearlman.

1972

June ***Blue Öyster Cult*** is released, introducing what will become their trademark sound: fast, loud, heavy rock highlighted by Dharma's guitar solos. It reaches US #172, as the group begins extensive US touring as a regular opening act for Alice Cooper.

1973

Apr ***Tyranny And Mutation*** climbs to US #122. Like the first album, it features lyrics by non-member rock writer Meltzer.

1974

June Spurred by strong rock-critic reviews and near constant US touring, ***Secret Treaties*** reaches US #53. It includes *Career Of Evil* written by Patti Smith (Lanier's girlfriend).

1975

Apr Live album ***On Your Feet Or On Your Knees***, recorded in Long Beach, CA, New York, Phoenix, AZ, Portland, OR, Seattle, WA, Vancouver, BC, Canada, and Passaic, NJ, achieves the band's highest US Album-chart placing, at #22.

1976

Aug ***Agents Of Fortune*** is released, containing the band's only sizeable hit single, the uncharacteristically mellow and Byrds-influenced *(Don't Fear) The Reaper*, which reaches US #12, while the album will peak at US #29 and UK #26. The album also includes two further Smith compositions.

1977

July [15] ***On Your Feet Or On Your Knees*** is certified gold by the RIAA.
Dec ***Spectres*** peaks at US #43 and will also be confimed gold by the RIAA on January 19th.

1978

Feb The band embarks on a lengthy 250-date world tour during which it will record selected performances for a second live album release.
Apr [27] The tour's UK segment, incongruously supported by Japan, bows at the Colston Hall, Bristol, Avon, and will include two dates at the Hammersmith Odeon, London, on May 3rd and 4th.
June Two years after its US success, *(Don't Fear) The Reaper* becomes the band's only UK hit single, climbing to #16.
July [17] ***Agents Of Fortune*** is certified platinum by the RIAA.
Oct ***Some Enchanted Evening***, recorded live in Atlanta, GA, Columbus, GA, Little Rock, AR, and Newcastle, Tyne & Wear, makes US #44 and UK #18.

1979

Aug ***Mirrors***, produced by Tom Werman, reaches US #44 and UK #46.
Sept Strings-accompanied extract *In Thee* peaks at US #74.
Nov [1] The band begins 13-date UK tour at the Brighton Centre.

1980

Aug ***Cultosaurus Erectus***, produced by Martin Birch, reaches US #34 and #12 in the UK, where it is their highest chart-placed album. With fantasy novelist Michael Moorcock co-writing one of its tracks, *Black Blade*, the band's metal has become even heavier, with its lyrical imagery now firmly grounded in demonic themes and sinister mysticism.

1981

Aug ***Fire Of Unknown Origin*** reaches US #24 and UK #29. Moorcock again co-writes one track, while the band's previously most prolific songwriter, Al Bouchard, leaves after the climax of a UK tour at the "Monsters Of Rock Festival", Castle Donington, Leics. He is replaced by Rick Downey (b. Aug. 29, 1953), for many years the band's crew chief on the road.
Oct Extracted *Burnin' For You* makes US #40.
Dec [15] Robbie Krieger joins the band on stage at the Country Club in Reseda, CA, playing lead on its version of the Doors' *Roadhouse Blues*.

1982

June The group's third live album ***ETL (Extra-Terrestrial Live)***, recorded in Hollywood, FL, Long Island, NY, Philadelphia, PA, Reseda, CA, and Poughkeepsie, NY, reaches US #29 and UK #39.
Aug During a US tour, the band will open for Journey on a $1,373,010-grossing bill at the Rose Bowl, Pasadena, CA.
Oct Dharma releases his debut solo album ***Flat Out***, for Portrait Records.
Nov [19] ***Fire Of Unknown Origin*** is certified gold by the RIAA.

1983

Dec ***The Revolution By Night***, produced by Bruce Fairbairn, peaks at US #93 and UK #95, while *Shooting Shark*, taken from the album and written by Dharma and Patti Smith, makes US #83 in February the following year.

1986

Mar After a lengthy hiatus, which has seen Lanier quit, the group, now comprising Bloom, Joe Bouchard and Dharma, with new recruits Jimmy Wilcox on percussion and ex-Aldo Nova keyboardist Tommy Zvoncheck, returns with ***Club Ninja***, which makes US #63.

1988

July [13] ***Some Enchanted Evening*** is certified platinum by the RIAA.
Sept The band's 14th album ***Imaginos*** peaks at US #122. Its relative commercial failure will see Joe Bouchard leave the group to form Deadringer, with Neil Smith (ex-Alice Cooper), Dennis Dunaway, Charlie Huhn and Jay Johnson, which will release ***Electrocution Of The Heart*** the following year.

1989

Mar [7] Blue Öyster Cult begins a 13-date UK tour at the Apollo Theatre, Manchester, Gtr. Manchester, set to end on the 20th at the Royal Café, Nottingham, Notts. (In April the following year, CBS will release the incomplete 13-track retrospective collection ***Career Of Evil - The Metal Years***, ending the label's relationship with the band.)

1992

May [11] ***Secret Treaties*** is certified gold by the RIAA.
Oct [13] With their influence clearly evident among a newer generation of heavy metal acts, Blue Öyster Cult, now featuring new bassist Jon Rogers and drummer Chuck Burgi, lacking the support to embark on major arena tours, has settled into a successful second-phase career, playing club tours mainly in the US, but including a one-off UK date tonight at London's Town & Country club. By year's end, the band will have also completed the soundtrack to the horror movie "Bad Channels".

1995

Aug [12] While ***Cult Classic***, an album of new versions of the group's hits, has been released on Herald Records in the US and Fragile in the UK the previous October, the group, still performing on the US club circuit, plays at the first American Association for Nude Recreation's "MusicFest '95" held at a 160 acre nudist park in Turtle Lake Resort, Union City, MI.

THE BLUES PROJECT

Tommy Flanders (vocals); **Steve Katz** (guitar, vocals); **Danny Kalb** (guitar); **Al Kooper** (organ, vocals); **Andy Kulberg** (bass, flute); **Roy Blumenfeld** (drums)

1965

June Kalb (b. Sept. 19, 1942, Brooklyn, NY), who has grown up in suburban Mount Vernon, NY, and played in Dave Van Ronk's Jug Stompers, before forming a duo with bluesologist Sam Charters, has seen Tim Hardin perform at the Night Owl Café, New York, NY, in November 1964, backed by an electric blues trio, including Felix Pappalardi, which has given him the idea to form a similar musical aggregation. Teamed with Blumenfeld, he assembles the Blues Project as an experimental combo playing urban and country blues on electric instruments, using an assortment of folk, jazz, and rock session musicians (including Flanders, Kulberg (b. 1944, Buffalo, NY) John Koerner, Geoff Muldaur and Eric Von Schmidt)

from around New York's Greenwich Village, where they now make a live debut at the Café Au Go Go.
Nov [24-27] The Blues Project takes part in the "Blues Bag" showcase also at the Café Au Go Go, with John Lee Hooker, Muddy Waters and Otis Spann.

1966

Mar They venture outside New York to play in San Francisco, CA, and across the US at college campus gigs, and sign to Verve Folkways Records (US).
Apr [22-23] The group peforms at the Avalon Ballroom, San Francisco, CA with the Great Society.
May [13-14] They take part in the "Laugh Cure Dance Concert" at the Avalon Ballroom, with Quicksilver Messenger Service.
July [23] ***Live At The Café Au Go Go***, recorded at their Bleecker Street home base, makes US #77.
Dec Flanders leaves, and ex-Even Dozen Jug Band Katz (b. May 9, 1945, New York), with whom Kalb has worked in Dave Van Ronk's Ragtime Jug Stompers, and Kooper (b. Feb. 5, 1944, Brooklyn, New York), who has been asked by producer Tom Wilson to play keyboards on their session, and the next day is invited by the group's manager to join the band, take vocals on their sophomore effort ***Projections***.

1967

Feb [10-12] The band performs at the Fillmore West, San Francisco, CA, on a bill with Jimmy Reed.
[17-19] They play further dates at the Fillmore West, this time with the Mothers Of Invention.
Apr *No Time Like The Right Time* is their only US chart single, at #96.
May [13] ***Projections*** makes US #52.
June [18] They open the third and final evening at the "Monterey International Pop Festival" at the County Fairgrounds, Monterey, CA.
Nov [25] ***Live At Town Hall*** reaches US #71, after which Kooper leaves, following disagreements over the band's refusal to record his songs with accompanying horns, and Kalb, heavily drug-dependent, also drops out. Katz will subsequently team with Kooper to form Blood, Sweat & Tears, while Blumenfeld and Kulberg will continue the Blues Project, recruiting Richard Greene and John Gregory, a line-up which will evolve into Sea Train.

1968

Apr [5-7] While ***Planned Obsolescence***, a loose collection of the quintet's final recordings is released, the Blues Project performs on a bill with It's A Beautiful Day, at the Avalon Ballroom, San Francisco.

1969

Aug [16] Retrospective ***Best Of The Blues Project*** makes US #199.

1971

Kalb assembles a new version of the group with Blumenfeld and bassist/sax player Don Kretmar, which signs to Capitol, and records ***Lazarus*** with producer Shel Talmy. Becoming a sextet the following year with the return of Flanders and addition of David Cohen (piano) and Bill Lussenden (guitar), a second Capitol album, ***Blues Project*** will be issued before the unit disbands.

1973

June [24] The original line-up, minus Flanders, reunites for a concert in Central Park, New York, recorded for MCA and subsequently released as ***Reunion In Central Park***. (Katz will go on to form American Flyer in 1976, with Eric Kaz, Doug Yule and Craig Fuller.)

1994

Feb [4] While the original members reunited once more (again minus Flanders) for a single concert on March 17th, 1981 at the Bonds club, New York (during the remainder of the decade, Kalb returned to the East Coast after living in Los Angeles, CA for some years, and cut an acoustic album with ex-Country Joe & the Fish bassist Bruce Barthol, before forming the Danny Kalb Trio with drummer Tom Major and bassist Debbie Hastings), and Rhino Records (US) brought ***The Best Of The Blues Project*** to CD in 1989, a re-formed Blues Project perform at New York's Bottom Line at Al Kooper's 50th birthday celebrations.
see also: **BLOOD, SWEAT & TEARS**

BLUES TRAVELER

John Popper (vocals, harmonica, guitar); **Chan Kinchla** (guitar); **Bobby Sheehan** (bass); **Brendan Hill** (drums)

1988

Having taught himself to play the harmonica from an early age Popper (b. Mar. 29, 1967, Cleveland, OH), who spent much of his childhood in Connecticut and Hill (b. Mar. 27, 1970, London), having met in Princeton High School, NJ, where Popper's music studies and harmonica playing have been guided by Dr. Biancosino, four years earlier when they began performing together in the Blues Band (inspired by the "Blues Brothers" film), have formed the blues-rock outfit Blues Traveler shortly before moving to Brooklyn, NY, in 1987 with avowed Deadhead, Sheehan (b. June 12, 1968, Summit, NJ) and Kinchla (b. Chandler Kinchla, May 29, 1969, Hamilton, ON, Canada), who has turned to playing the guitar after a knee-injury ended a promising football career. With Popper's harmonica playing further nurtured by New School For Social Research teacher Arnie Lawrence, earnest gigging around the New York club circuit has brought the band to the attention of A&M Records, A&R scout, Patrick Clifford which now results in its signing to the label. Fronted by the visually unique lead singer and harmonica virtuoso, Popper (who carries a harmonica pouch which also contains a Swiss Army knife, a sewing kit, watch, flashlight and baton), the group sets out on an exhaustive live schedule around the US, slowly building an increasingly loyal audience which becomes fond of its lengthy jam-oriented blues sets.

1991

Apr [6] Although originally released in 1989, the group's debut album, ***Blues Traveler***, produced by Justin Niebank, finally makes US #136, achieved not least through the band's developing reputation as a hard-working, constantly-touring unit which takes its performance inspiration and style from the Grateful Dead.
Sept [28] ***Travelers And Thieves***, co-produced by the group with Jim Gaines, makes US #125.
Nov [15] The group performs at New York's Madison Square Garden, supporting the Jerry Garcia Band.

1992

Nov During time spent recording the band's third album, Popper is injured after crashing his motorcycle into a Plymouth Duster and will spend the following year in a wheelchair, a restriction which will not, however, prevent him from continuing to perform on stage.

1993

Apr [24] *Save His Soul* debuts at its US #72 peak.

1994

Nov [1] With Popper a frequent solo addition to house-band Paul Shaffer's CBS Orchestra in the past, the band performs on CBS-TV's "Late Show With David Letterman".

1995

June [12] Confirming its burgeoning, notably college-based following, ***Blues Traveler*** is certified gold by the RIAA, some six years after its release.
July [13] Canadian package tour, "Another Roadside Attraction 1995", with Blues Traveler, Tragically Hip, Ziggy Marley, Spirit of the West, Matthew Sweet, Rheostatics, Eric's Trip and the Inbreds, opens at the Thunderbird Stadium, University of British Columbia, Vancouver, BC, grossing $689,551 from a 28,131 crowd.
Aug [3] This year's US package "H.O.R.D.E. (Horizons Of Rock Developing Everywhere) Festival", a multi-act annual roots rock tour which Popper founded in 1992, bows with Blues Traveler, Black Crowes, Ziggy Marley, G. Love & Special Sauce, God Street Wine, Joan Osborne, Chris Whitley and Fiji Mariners at the Riverport Amphitheatre, Maryland Heights, MO grossing $240,590 from 12,693 attendees, a trek set to end on September 3rd at the Shoreline Amphitheatre, Mountain View, CA.
[5] *Run-Around*, from the currently-climbing ***Four***, hits US #8, the band's first chart single.
[17] The RIAA certifies two million US sales of ***Four***.
Sept [9] ***Four***, produced by Michael Barbiero and Steve Thompson and featuring additional musical help from Paul Shaffer and past and present Allman Brothers' Chuck Leavell and Warren Haynes, finally hits US #8.
[13] Popper is detained in South Brunswick, NJ, after police stop his car for an expired registration. They find a concealed dagger and a box of hollow-point bullets (he collects rare and unusual weapons), and charge him with two misdemeanor weapons counts.
[25] Following his arraignment on the above charges which are now turned over to the Middlesex County prosecutor's office, Popper, who has pleaded innocent, emerges from the court to announce: "I love this country and the police did a great job".
[30] Blues Traveler is the music guest on the season premiere of NBC-TV's "Saturday Night Live", filling in for ♀ who has cancelled.
Oct [28] Hollywood Records' John Lennon-tribute album ***Working Class Hero***, including the group's cover of *Imagine*, debuts at its US #94 peak.
Nov [3] Their headlining US tour visits the Fox Theatre, Atlanta, GA, in front of an audience of 4,349. (Released this month, the band's *I Want To Take You Higher* is featured on the pro-marijuana ***Hempilation*** compilation on Capricorn Records.)
[22] The group performs on NBC-TV's "The Tonight Show".

1996

Feb [24] *Run-Around* becomes the longest-charting single (in consecutive weeks) on the US Hot 100 with 49 weeks logged. Only the Four Seasons' *December 1963 (Oh, What A Night)* has enjoyed a longer overall chart stay (54 weeks during two chart runs).
[28] *Run-Around* is named Best Rock Vocal Performance, Duo Or Group at the 38th annual Grammy Awards held at Los Angeles' Shrine Auditorium.
Mar [2] *Hook*, also from ***Four***, reaches US #23.
[12] Philips Media (US) releases ***All Access: The H.O.R.D.E. Festival CD-ROM*** culled from performances on last year's H.O.R.D.E. tour including one by the band.
June [4] While the group prepares to headline its annual summer roots-rock "H.O.R.D.E." caravan tour (beginning on the 6th in Minneapolis, MN), ***Live From The Fall***, a live double-CD is scheduled for release in the US by A&M.

THE BLUETONES

Mark Morriss (lead vocals, guitar); **Adam Devlin** (guitar); **Scott Morriss** (bass); **Ed Chesters** (drums)

1994

Jan Buffalo Springfield fan Mark and younger brother Scott Morriss have grown up in the west London suburb of Hounslow, Middx. Mark has begun writing songs at the age of 14, before studying English, Art and Theatre for A-levels while Scott has attended the local Cranford Community College. Inspired to take up a music career after attending two Stone Roses gigs in May 1989 at the ICA and Dingwalls, Mark and and his brother left home that same year, moving into their own rented home in Hounslow. Subsequently joining Bottle Garden (which plays at local pubs before splitting), the pair recruited Devlin, originally from Staines, Middx., who has attended Gunnersbury Catholic School For Boys in Brentford, Middx., from another local band Perfect Mess to form the Bluetones. From 1991, the band, its members all on the dole, has spent 18 months rehearsing in the garage at their Hounslow home, during which it completes the quartet with the addition of Chesters (ex-Soho) for live gigs, whom they have met at Ruby's (a Carnaby Street disco). While the group's first gig has been on Halloween night, 1993 at the Bacchus wine bar in Kingston, Surrey, the band now plays at London's Bull & Gate pub where it is seen by Neil Burrow who becomes its enthusiastic manager. Spending the rest of the year playing one-off gigs around London (including a summer residency at the Splash club) and signing a publishing deal with Food label boss Andy Ross' publishing company Archaic Music in August, an eight-song demo will be finished on September 18th 1994, followed by sessions at EMI Studios paid for by the publisher. The group's first released track *No. 11*, will be included on indie label, Fierce Panda various artists EP *Return To Splendour* (issued in December), while the band racks up glowing music press reviews with UK tours with Strangelove (in November) and Shed Seven in the last month of the year.

1995

Jan [21] The Bluetones perform at the **New Musical Express**' BRATS Awards bash at London's Astoria.
Feb [2] A four-week UK tour opening for Gaz Coombes & Co begins in Bath, Avon set to end on March 3rd in Brighton, E. Sussex. Having completed a BBC 1-FM Radio session in January for the "John Peel Show" and courted by several major labels, the band releases the Stone Roses-influenced *Slight Return* on its own Superior Quality Recordings label, sold only on 7" vinyl at gigs.
Mar The group signs worldwide with A&M Records after rejecting offers from MCA, EMI, Food, Creation, and Parlophone among others, though UK releases will remain on their own Superior Quality Recording label.
June [17] Hailed as the next big BritPop band by the music media, its chart debut *Are You Blue Or Are You Blind?* debuts at its UK #31 peak, as the band begins its first headlining UK tour supported by Heavy Stereo.
Oct [14] Follow-up single *Bluetonic* reaches UK #19 in its week of entry, promoted by another four-week UK trek.
Dec [16] The Bluetones perform a non-promoted one-off gig in London before dates in Japan where their reputation already precedes them.

1996

Jan The band participates in the **New Musical Express**' "Brat Bus' UK tour with Heavy Stereo, Fluffy and the Cardigans.
Feb [3] Reissued *Slight Return* now now enters at its UK #2 peak.
[24] Their debut album ***Expecting To Fly***, produced by Hugh Jones at Ridge Farm Studios, Redhill, Surrey, enters the UK chart at #1.

BLUR

Damon Albarn (vocals, keyboards);
Graham Coxon (guitar, saxophone);
Alex James (bass); **Dave Rowntree** (drums)

1988

An audience of 15, including his Stanway Comprehensive, Colchester, Essex ex-schoolmate Coxon (b. Mar. 12, 1969, Rintein, near Hannover, W. Germany) and his friend, computer-engineer Rowntree (b. May 8, 1964, Colchester), attend a solo performance given by Albarn (b. Mar. 23, 1968, Whitechapel, London) at Colchester Arts Centre. Dropping plans to proceed as Circus, a unit formed with friend Eddy, Albarn, whose father has been the tour manager for Soft Machine in the '60s (his mother was a stage designer for Joan Littlewood), who attended his first concert in 1974 (to see the Osmonds) and won a regional heat of the "Young Composer of the Year" competition age 15, has already formed the short-lived pop-synth duo Two's A Crowd, and is now attending the East 15 drama school while also working in a London recording studio, which susequently offers him a management deal upon hearing demos he is concurrently recording with £3000 given to him by his grandfather the previous year. Studying for a fine-arts degree at Goldsmith's College, New Cross, London, Coxon, who has played with Rowntree (who has been drumming since the age of 11) in local Colchester bands including Idle Vice and Mr. Pang's Big Bangs, introduces Albarn to college-mate James (b. Nov. 21, 1968, Boscombe, Bournemouth) and the resulting quartet, initially called Seymour, rehearses original material before performing a dozen London gigs the following year. While the band's first official gig in 1990 is at Dingwalls, Camden Town, London (on the bottom of a bill headed by New Fast Automatic Daffodils), they are spotted by Food Records' boss Andy Ross at a subsequent capitol gig at the Powerhaus. (Albarn is also moonlighting as a barman at the Portobello Hotel in London's Notting Hill.)

1990

Mar Further impressed by the band's four-song demo (which includes *Fool* and *She's So High*), Ross and label partner Dave Balfe sign the quartet to Food on the proviso that it changes its name from Seymour to Blur.
Oct Blur's debut release, *She's So High* makes UK #48 as the band embarks on a 21-date UK club tour.

1991

May Stone Roses-influenced *There's No Other Way*, marking the band's first collaboration with producer Stephen Street, hits UK #8.
Aug *Bang* reaches UK #24.
Sept [7] Its parent debut album ***Leisure***, produced by Street, hits UK #7 and will earn a gold disc while Blur undertakes its third UK tour of the year.

1992

Jan [25] *There's No Other Way*, released in the US by SBK Records, peaks at US #82 during a disagreeable 44-date US tour.
Apr [11] Furiously-paced *Popscene*, marking a change in musical direction, bows at its UK #32 peak.
July The band performs at London's Town & Country club, supported by arch-rivals Suede, whose ex-guitarist and future Elastica co-founder, Justine Frischmann, is Albarn's girlfriend. (Tracks recorded later in the year with producer Andy Partridge will be rejected by Food, which insists the band works on alternative material. Matters worsen as the group, notorious for its alcohol binges, splits from its management company following a dispute over unpaid royalties.)

1993

May [1] *For Tomorrow* debuts at its UK #28 peak.
[22] Named after a graffiti scrawl which the band saw on a wall near London's Marble Arch, ***Modern Life Is Rubbish*** debuts at its UK #15 peak, and will earn a gold disc for 100,000 UK sales (and 33,000 in the States). With its lyrically acerbic, parochial social commentary and witty observation, impressed UK music critics liken the band to the Kinks.
July [17] *Chemical World* reaches UK #28.
Aug The band headlines at the annual "Reading Festival", Reading, Berks.
Oct [16] *Sunday Sunday* bows at its UK #26 peak.

1994

Mar [19] *Girls And Boys* hits UK #5 in its week of entry.
May [4] Blur appears on C4-TV's "Naked City".
[7] ***Parklife*** enters at UK #1 on its way to triple-platinum UK sales confirming Blur as a leading light in the emerging BritPop scene.
[29] The group appears on BBC2-TV's "The O Zone".
June [18] *To The End*, with a Pet Shop Boys-remix of *Girls And Boys* on the CD-format, reaches UK #16.
July [23] The band performs on MTV Europe's "MTV Live!".
[31] Blur tops the bill at the "Tennents In The Park Festival", Strathclyde Country Park, Glasgow, Scotland.
Aug [20] *Girls And Boys* makes US #59.
[26] The band appears on C4-TV's "Passengers".
Sept [3] *Parklife*, featuring a narration by actor Phil Daniels, debuts at its UK #10 peak.
[13] ***Parklife***, one of 10 nominees for the third annual Mercury Music Prize, fails to win.
[29] The band performs at the Academy, New York on a $22,500-grossing bill with Pulp.
Oct [7] Playing 76 dates during the year, including the Glastonbury Festival, nine Japanese concert hall dates and seven US concerts, the most attended is tonight's gig at London's Alexandra Palace to a crowd of 7,500.
Nov [12] Blur plays a concert in Milan, Italy.
[19] *End Of A Century* bows at its UK #19 peak.
Dec [4] Blur wins the Best Album (***Parklife***) and Best Alternative/Indie Type Band categories at the seventh annual **Smash Hits** Poll Winners' Party.
[14] Having taped a performance on BBC2-TV's "Later With Jools Holland" a day earlier, Blur members present tonight's BBC1-TV broadcast of "Top Of The Pops".
[16] The group raises £3,000 for an orphanage in India at a secret gig for 400 students in their home town of Colchester at Colchester Sixth Form College, following an appeal from Albarn and Coxon's former music teacher Nigel Hildreth.

1995

Jan [24] Blur wins Best Band, Best Album (***Parklife***), Best Video ("Parklife"), and **New Musical Express** Single Of The Year (*Girls & Boys*) at the **New Musical Express**' BRAT Awards, held at London's New Empire Theatre.
Feb [20] The band collects the Best Single (*Parklife*), Best Video ("Parklife"), Best Album (***Parklife***) and Best British Act trophies at the 13th annual BRIT Awards, held at London's Alexandra Palace.
[23] Albarn plays keyboards (as Dan Abnormal) on BBC1-TV's "Top Of The Pops" for the performing Elastica.
Mar [6] Albarn launches the London indie-format radio station, XFM.
May [18] Blur debuts new songs *Globe Alone* and *Stereotype* at the Dublin Castle pub in Camden Town.
[26] Albarn joins the Rolling Stones on keyboards for its performance of *Hymn To Her* at the Paradiso Club, Amsterdam, Holland.
June [17] Blur performs at London's Mile End Stadium.
During the month Albarn will perform on *I Go To Sleep* with the Pretenders for an "MTV Unplugged" taping and sing *Waterloo Sunset* with the Kinks' Ray Davies on C4-TV's "The White Room".
July [29-30] On a bill grossing £2,997,728, Blur appears with R.E.M., the Cranberries, Radiohead and others at the National Bowl, Milton Keynes, Bucks.
Aug [26] At the height of a bitter media-fed feud between BritPop champs Blur and Oasis, and selling 274,000 copies in its first week, Blur's *Country House* enters the UK chart at #1 (the 42nd time a single has bowed in pole position), outsmarting Oasis' *Roll With It* (at sales of 216,000) which enters at #2.
Sept [9] *Country House (4th Format)* charts for a week at UK #57.
[15] The group performs a rooftop gig at HMV's Oxford Street, London store.
[16] Reactivated debut set, ***Leisure*** makes UK #45.
[23] ***The Great Escape***, again produced by Street and featuring Labour Party politician Ken Livingstone on *Ernold Same*, enters at UK #1.
[25] An 11-date US visit begins in Washington, DC.
Oct [14] ***The Great Escape***, released in the US by

Virgin Records (to whom Blur is now signed in the US), charts for a week at US #150.

Nov [7] Blur wins the Best Album (***The Great Escape***) category at the **Q** Awards held at London's Park Lane Hotel.

[18] The band appears again on BBC2-TV's "Later With Jool Holland".

[21] A 16-date sellout UK tour opens at Belfast Kings Hall set to climax with a pair of concerts at the Wembley Arena, Wembley, Middx.

[13] The group launches its **Blurbook** at a store signing in London's Oxford Street.

[25] *The Universal* bows at its UK #5 peak.

Dec [25] C4-TV broadcasts "Showtime: Blur In Concert".

1996

Feb [24] *Stereotypes* enters the UK chart at its #7 peak.

Mar [5] With a new Blur and an Albarn solo track featured on the recently released ***Trainspotting*** film soundtrack, the band performs in Paris, France. (In an interview with this month's **Q** magazine (made in December of last year), and commenting on the ongoing feud with Oasis, Albarn states: "The only thing we've got in common with Oasis is the fact that we're both doing shit in America". (Blur's most recent album peaked at US #150, while Oasis is currently at #5 on the US album survey with two million-plus Stateside sales.)

MICHAEL BOLTON

1979

Raised on and inspired by the music of Motown, Ray Charles and the blues, Bolton (b. Michael Bolotin, Feb. 26, 1953, New Haven, CT), the youngest son of local Democratic Party official George Bolotin, has taken up the saxophone at the age of seven and guitar at 11, before performing in Connecticut bars at the age of 15 as a member of the Nomads (who were signed to Epic Records (US) for the release of two singles). Having already recorded his solo debut album ***Michael Bolotin*** (released by RCA Records (US) in 1975 and featuring David Sanborn and his future longtime songwriting collaborator Andy Newmark) under his given last name - he will name-change because, as his mother will subsequently confirm, "(Bolotin) sounded too Russian" - a second solo set ***Every Day Of My Life***, a Jack Richardson-produced effort has followed in 1976. Going on to audition for Shelter Records in Los Angeles, CA, he forms the hard rock combo Blackjack with Bruce Kulick (guitar), Jimmy Halsip (bass) and Sandy Germarro (drums) in 1978, which now releases its debut set ***Blackjack***, via Polydor Records, making US #127. A second Blackjack album, ***Worlds Apart***, will fail to score in 1980, leaving Bolton to subsequently secure a solo deal with CBS/Columbia Records.

1983

May [15] *Fools Game* peaks at US #82, as its parent album ***Michael Bolton*** is on its way to US #89. Aimed at the hard-rock market, the Gerry Block/Bolton co-produced project includes a guest appearance by Aldo Nova and is dedicated to Bolton's father.

Oct [8] Bolton secures his first major success as a songwriter as Laura Branigan reaches US #12 with *How Am I Supposed To Live Without You*.

1984

Bolton devotes himself to composition, building up songwriting relationships with the likes of Diane Warren, Eric Kaz, Desmond Child, and Barry Mann and Cynthia Weil, for acts including the Pointer Sisters and Irene Cara.

1985

May His sophomore Columbia album ***Everybody's Crazy*** is released, co-produced with Neil Kernon. Another adult-oriented rock effort, on which Bolton also plays guitar, it will fail to chart, although Starship will subsequently cover the *Desperate Heart* cut co-written with Randy Goodrum.

1987

Dec [12] Co-penned with Eric Kaz, his breakthrough solo hit, the soul-tinged ballad *That's What Love Is All About*, reaches US #19 (Bolton has recently performed the song and his revival of Otis Redding's *(Sittin' On) The Dock Of The Bay* on the syndicated TV show "It's Showtime At The Apollo"). Its parent album ***The Hunger*** begins climbing the US Album survey, featuring a title cut co-written with Journey's Jonathan Cain, who appears on the album with fellow Journeyman Neal Schon. Produced by Keith Diamond, with two cuts separately helmed by Cain and Susan Hamilton, other guests include Schon, James Ingram and the Hawkins Singers and showcasing the full virtuosity of Bolton's four-octave vocal range, it will make US #46 during a 41-week run.

1988

Jan [22] While the Bolton-penned and produced *I Found Someone* hits UK #5 for Cher, he appears on NBC-TV's "Late Night With David Letterman" singing *(Sittin' On) The Dock Of The Bay*.

Mar [26] *(Sittin' On) The Dock Of The Bay*, reviving Redding's 1968 US chart-topper, reaches US #11. In a personal letter to Bolton from Redding's widow Zelma, she calls it "my all-time favorite version of my husband's classic".

Apr Bolton wins the Best Male R&B Vocalist Of The Year trophy, at the annual New York Music Awards.

June [25] *Wait On Love* stalls at US #79, while Bolton is midway through a two-month, cross-country US tour supporting Heart.

Oct Bolton travels to Moscow, USSR, as a member of a US songwriting team (including Warren, Mann, Weil, Cyndi Lauper, Holly Knight, Brenda Russell, Tom Kelly and Billy Steinberg), to collaborate on the album ***Glasnost***, written and performed with USSR counterparts.

Dec Bolton performs four songs (including *I Found Someone*) in front of an audience of his peers, including Lamont Dozier, Carole King, Jimmy Webb and Brian Wilson, at the VH-1 broadcast "Fourth Annual Salute To The American Songwriter" at the Wiltern Theatre, Los Angeles.

1989

June [22] Bolton sings *Georgia On My Mind* and *Yesterday*, and duets with Jeffrey Osborne on *You've Lost That Lovin' Feelin'*, at the Songwriters Hall of Fame, held at Radio City Music Hall, New York (subsequently broadcast on CBS-TV).

July With the transformation from power rocker to R&B-influenced balladeer virtually complete (although he was the opening act for Ozzy Osbourne on a 1988 US tour), ***Soul Provider*** is released, set to hit US #3 during a year's chart tenure. Co-produced with Peter Bunetta, Michael Omartian, Desmond Child and Susan Hamilton, it features an airplay-attracting mix of soul, rock and power ballads, variously co-written with Mann and Weil, Andy Goldmark, Warren, Kaz and others, and once again showcases Bolton's unrestrained vocal power.

Aug He receives two airplay awards at the annual ASCAP Awards for *I Found Someone* and *That's What Love Is All About*.

Sept [16] Title cut *Soul Provider*, featuring Kenny G on saxophone, reaches US #17.

1990

Jan [20] Power ballad *How Am I Supposed To Live Without You*, reviving Laura Branigan's 1983 US #12 cover, tops the Hot 100.

Feb [21] Bolton wins Best Pop Vocal Performance, Male for *How Am I Supposed To Live Without You* at the 32nd annual Grammy Awards held at the Shrine Auditorium, Los Angeles.

Mar [3] *How Am I Supposed To Live Without You*, his UK debut, hits #3.

Apr [14] ***Soul Provider*** hits US #3.

[21] Kiss hits US #8 with *Forever*, which Bolton co-writes with the group's Paul Stanley, while he also features on a newly-released benefit album ***Requiem For The Americas For Save The Children*** (US #166).

May [5] Further power ballad *How Can We Be Lovers* hits US #3.

June [2] *How Can We Be Lovers* hits UK #10.

[29] "Soul Provider - The Videos" is certified gold by the RIAA.

Aug [4] *When I'm Back On My Feet Again*, Warren-penned, hits US #7.

[25] Reissued ***The Hunger*** makes UK #44.

Sept [8] ***Soul Provider*** now hits UK #4.

Oct [6] His retread of Ray Charles' classic *Georgia On My Mind* makes US #36, while the soaring Diane Warren-penned *When I'm Back On My Feet Again* makes UK #44.

[20] Bolton sings the national anthem at the fourth game of the World Series in Oakland, CA.

Dec [28] Bolton ends his most successful career year to date with the first of eight sellout performances at the Universal Amphitheatre, Universal City, CA, supported by Kenny G, which will gross $1,312,710. His 1990 US trek is named Tour Of The Year by **Pollstar** magazine.

1991

Jan Bolton's 15-year marriage to one-time exercise teacher Maureen McGuire ends. He gets custody of their three teenage daughters and lives with them in Westport, CT.

Feb [10] Bolton joins nearly 100 celebrities in Burbank, CA, to record *Voices That Care*, a David Foster and fiancée Linda Thompson Jenner-composed and organized charity record to benefit the American Red Cross Gulf Crisis Fund.

Mar [3] Bolton sings the *Star Spangled Banner* at the New Haven Veterans Memorial Coliseum, New Haven, as part of a special performance by the touring Ice Capades for the families of the Connecticut Guard and Reserve Units in the Persian Gulf.

Apr [8] ***The Hunger*** is certified platinum by the RIAA.

[20] He performs his current single, *Love Is A Wonderful Thing*, on NBC-TV's "Saturday Night Live", prior to beginning a five-month US tour. While on the show, he also sings in an all-star spoof charity troupe, Musicians for Free Range Chickens (in which he is the only genuine star).

The Hunger is his second album to be RIAA-certified platinum (his second) for one million US sales.

May [18] *Love Is A Wonderful Thing* reaches UK #23, as parent album ***Time, Love & Tenderness*** debuts at UK #2, following an appearance on May 3rd on BBC-1 TV's "Wogan" chat show.

[21] *How Am I Supposed To Live Without You* wins the Song Of The Year honor at the 39th annual BMI performance awards, in Los Angeles.

[25] ***Time, Love & Tenderness***, produced by Walter Afanasieff and featuring regular writing partners Warren and Child, Kenny G, as well as a duet with Patti LaBelle and *Steel Bars* (co-penned with Bob Dylan), tops the US chart.

June [1] *Love Is A Wonderful Thing*, co-written with Andy Goldmark, finally hits US #4.

Aug [17] Warren-inked *Time, Love And Tenderness* reaches UK #28, set to hit US #7 on Sept [14].

[25] He performs in front of a 15,315 audience at the Exhibition Stadium, CNE, Toronto, ON, Canada, on a bill with Oleta Adams and Celine Dion.

Oct [4] Bolton duets with Ray Charles on *Georgia On My Mind* during the Fox-TV tribute "Ray Charles: 50 Years In Music".

Nov [9-10] He performs two dates during a short UK concert visit, at the Wembley Arena, Wembley, Middx.

[18] Bolton gives his live TV premiere of his still-climbing *When A Man Loves A Woman* on an "Oprah Winfrey Show" syndicated program, the title-themed "When Your Spouse Is In Love With A Celebrity".

[23] *When A Man Loves A Woman* tops the US chart for a week and will hit UK #8 the following week, during a sellout four-date run at New York's Paramount.
Dec [2] *How Can We Be Lovers* is named as one of the Most Performed Pop Songs Of 1990 at the annual BMI Awards, at the Dorchester Hotel, London.

1992

Jan [27] He wins the Favorite Male Artist, Pop/Rock and Favorite Album, Pop/Rock categories at the 19th annual American Music Awards, held at the Shrine Auditorium.
Feb [9] Bolton sings the US national anthem at the NBA All Star Game.
[11] During his current US tour, Bolton grosses $213,453 at the Myriad Convention Center Arena, Oklahoma City, OK.
[22] *Steel Bars*, penned with Dylan, reaches UK #17.
[25] Bolton collects the Best Pop Vocal Performance, Male for *When A Man Loves A Woman* at the 34th annual Grammy Awards, held at Radio City Music Hall, New York. In his acceptance speech, fellow Grammy winner, composer Irving Gordon (whose *Unforgettable* is named Song Of The Year) aims the following comments at Bolton: "It's nice to have a song accepted that you don't get a hernia when you sing it", further elaborating about performances that "scream, yell or have a nervous breakdown while it talks about tenderness". Backstage, Gordon continues: "I did it in front of Michael Bolton. That's how I feel - it's not necessary to scream your head off to say I love you." Bolton replies: "I don't get a hernia when I sing those notes. For me it's no problem", though **Village Voice** scribe Michael Musto, also a backstager, claims: "I get a hernia listening to it."
Mar [14] Bolton performs at the Starlight Foundation in Los Angeles (honoring Paula Abdul as Humanitarian of the Year), while *Missing You Now* reaches US #12.
[26] ***Michael Bolton*** is certified gold by the RIAA.
Together with co-writer Andy Goldmark and Sony Music Entertainment, Bolton is named in a lawsuit filed on behalf of the Isley Brothers by Three Boys Music Corp., charging the pair with allegedly copying the Isley's 1966 song, titled *Love Is A Wonderful Thing*. Meanwhile, ***Time Love And Tenderness*** is RIAA-certified for five million US sales.
Apr [9] Bolton is honored at the New York Medical College for his efforts in raising funds for their Cancer Research Institute.
May [16] *Missing You Now*, featuring saxophonist Kenny G, reaches UK #28.
June [8] While the court case against Bolton continues, Ronald Isley issues a statement insisting: "There is no doubt in my mind that Michael used my song. It's humiliating that he is being honored while the original writers are ignored." (Bolton has received two awards for *Love Is A Wonderful Thing* in the past three weeks.) "We want him to give back the awards he won. The song he claims is his has the same hook, the same chorus, the same everything as ours. It's not fair." Isley also says he is insulted by a "settlement offer" proposed by a third party, suggesting that the group could write and record a new song with Bolton. Bolton's management company Louis Levin Management responds: "The song is an original and we view the claims to be without merit."
July [13] Bolton's US summer tour, once again supported by Celine Dion, is highlighted by an appearance at the Hollywood Bowl, Los Angeles, which grosses $536,816.
Aug [27-28] Towards the end of further US dates, Bolton performs consecutive gigs at the Arie Crown Theatre, McCormick Place Complex, Chicago, IL.
Oct [1] He appears on NBC-TV's "The Tonight Show".
[28] NBC airs his debut TV special "This Is Michael Bolton", promoting cuts from his forthcoming album and featuring him in concert with saxophonist Kenny G.
[31] Having scored consistently with a hit cover version on each of his multi-platinum albums, Bolton now releases an entire album of his interpretations of golden oldies, collected as ***Timeless (The Classics)***, which immediately hits UK #3.
Nov [12] He appears as a guest on the ITV "TV-AM" couch.
[14] Extracted *To Love Somebody*, a revival of the Bee Gees' 1967 hit, reaches UK #16.
[21] ***Timeless (The Classics)*** tops the US chart for a week.
Dec [6] Bolton performs at the third annual "This Close For Cancer Research Inc." benefit, at Sante's Manor in Milford, CT.
[12] *To Love Somebody* reaches US #11.
[23] He appears on ITV's "Des O'Connor Tonight" show.

1993

Jan [2] *Drift Away*, reviving Dobie Gray's 1973 classic, reaches UK #18.
[16] Bolton attends a benefit for the CityKids Foundation at New York's Planet Hollywood.
[19] Son of a Democrat Party official, Bolton sings *Lean On Me* at the Presidential Inaugural celebration at the Capital Centre, Landover, MD.
[25] He collects the Favorite Male Artist, Pop/Rock and Favorite Adult Contemporary Artist trophies, at the 20th annual American Music Awards, held at the Shrine Auditorium.
Mar [20] *Reach Out I'll Be There*, reviving the Four Tops' 1966 chart-topper, makes UK #37.
May [18] *Love Is A Wonderful Thing*, *Missing You Now* and *Steel Bars* win citations at BMI's 41st annual pop awards dinner, at the Regency Beverly Wilshire Hotel, Los Angeles.
[18-19, 21-22] Bolton performs a four-night series at the Wembley Arena, Wembley.
June [26] He takes part in a benefit for the United Negro College Fund's Ladders of Hope programme at Los Angeles' Dorothy Chandler Pavilion.
Aug [31] Bolton, in the midst of a summer tour, plays at the New York State Fair, Syracuse, NY.
Oct [30] He participates in "A Gala For The President" at Washington's Ford's Theater, broadcast on ABC on November 24th.
Nov [13] *Said I Loved You ... But I Lied*, co-written with producer Robert John "Mutt" Lange, debuts at its UK #15 peak.
[27] ***The One Thing***, variously produced by Bolton, Lange, David Foster and Walter Afanasieff, and largely co-written with either Lange or Warren, debuts at its UK #4 peak.
Dec [4] ***The One Thing*** debuts at its US #3 peak.
[22] *Said I Love You, But I Lied* is certified gold by the RIAA.
[31] Bolton sells out an New Year's Eve concert at the Rosemont Horizon, Rosemont, IL, during current dates.

1994

Jan [22] *Said I Loved You ... But I Lied* hits US #6.
Feb [1] ***The One Thing*** reaches the RIAA-certified three million sales plateau.
[7] Bolton performs *Said I Loved You ... But I Lied* at the 21st American Music Awards again held at the Shrine Auditorium.
[23] His first Australian tour opens at the Entertainment Centre, Sydney, New South Wales, Australia, set to end on March 9th in Perth.
Mar [5] *Soul Of My Soul* reaches UK #32.
Apr [22] Backed by 40-plus members of the Orchestra of New England, Bolton performs at Yale University's Woolsey Hall, New Haven, CT, to benefit the Michael Bolton Foundation.
[23] *Completely* reaches US #32.
[25] In the case brought by the Isley Brothers, Bolton is found guilty, by unanimous verdict, of copyright infringement after 2½ days of deliberation. Angela Winbush, wife of Ronald Isley, had said that had met Bolton at a 1988 Lou Rawls concert, where he professed knowledge of many of the Isleys' songs.
May [2] Bolton holds a press conference in New York insisting he hadn't plagiarize the Isleys, adding that there was "a bit of racial inference" in the decision.
[11] He embarks on another US tour at the North Charleston Coliseum, NC, set to end on September 19th at the Montage Mountain, Scranton, PA.
[21] *Lean On Me* reaches UK #14.
July [26] The RIAA certifies four million sales of ***Timeless (The Classics)***.
Sept [26] The RIAA also confirms multi-platinum sales (six million) of ***Soul Provider***.
Oct [8] Bolton performs *Jailhouse Rock*, backed by Fats Domino and Carl Perkins, at the "Elvis Aaron Presley : The Tribute", a multi-star music event staged at the Pyramid Arena, Memphis, TN, and broadcast live on US pay-per-view TV.
Nov [21] ***Time, Love And Tenderness*** reaches the RIAA-certified eight million sales plateau.

1995

Jan [9] Bolton kicks off the "Recognize Child Abuse" ad campaign by riding on a New York bus.
[30] He collects the Favorite Male Artist, Pop/Rock and Favorite Adult Contemporary Artist trophies at the 22nd annual American Music Awards, held as usual at the Shrine.
Mar [14] Bolton goes to Capitol Hill to protest potential congressional cuts in federal funding for the arts.
Apr [10] Philip Roe is jailed for manslaughter on the grounds of provocation and jailed for seven years at Teeside Crown Court after killing his wife Dulcie, following an argument about her obsession with the singer.
May [31] Bolton is presented with the Hitmaker Award at the 26th annual Songwriters Hall of Fame Awards held at New York's Sheraton Hotel.
July [14] He inaugurates the Meadows Theatre, North Meadows, Hartford, CT.
Sept [12] Bolton performs *Vesti La Giubba* with host Luciano Pavarotti at his War Child charity benefit at Novi Sad Park, Modena, Italy (to be released on ***Pavarotti & Friends*** in March 1996).
[16] Soul-shuffling *Can I Touch You ... There?*, its rhythm track recalling Carly Simon's *Why*, hits UK #6.
[23] *Can I Touch You ... There?* reaches US #27.
[30] ***Greatest Hits 1985-1995***, including 12 hits and five new cuts, including a version of his self-penned *I Found Someone* (a 1987 hit for Cher), bows at its UK #2 peak, behind Blur's ***The Great Escape***.
Oct [7] ***Greatest Hits 1985-1995*** debuts at its US #5 peak.
Dec [2] *A Love So Beautiful* bows at its UK #27 peak.
[6] Bolton performs a medley of hits at the 1995 **Billboard** Music Awards at New York's Coliseum, broadcast live on Fox-TV, as Sony US releases an enhanced CD version of ***Greatest Hits 1985-1995*** with interactive elements.

1996

Feb [17] Bolton embarks on his latest European and Scandinavian tour at the Rudi Sedlmayer Hall, Munich, Germany, set to end on March 30th at the Palatrussardi in Milan, Italy.
Mar [16] Reissued *Soul Provider* enters at its UK #35 peak.
Apr [11] Bolton and Luciano Pavarotti sing *Nessun Dorma* on CBS-TV's "Late Show With David Letterman".

BON JOVI

Jon Bon Jovi (vocals); **Richie Sambora** (guitar); **David Bryan** (keyboards); **Alec John Such** (bass); **Tico Torres** (drums)

1983

Mar The band is formed in Sayreville, NJ, by Bon Jovi (b. John Francis Bongiovi Jr., Mar. 2, 1962, Sayreville), his mother Carol, an ex-Playboy bunny and his father a hairdresser, and Bryan (b. David Bryan Rashbaum, Feb. 7, 1962, New York, NY), who have played together in high school and later in local cover-version bands at local venues, including the Stone Pony and Asbury Park's Fast Lane. They recruit Sambora (b. July 11, 1959, Woodbridge, NJ) and Such

(b. Nov. 14, 1956, Yonkers, NY), ex-Phantom's Opera, who have disbanded their own club act Message in 1982, and Torres (b. Hector Torres, Oct. 7, 1953, New York), whose musical past has included stints with Franke & the Knockouts and performances in strip bars. Bon Jovi, who after leaving high school, has swept the floor for his cousin Tony Bongiovi who was working at the Record Plant, New York, where Bon Jovi subsequently cuts a demo (including the self-penned *Runaway*), has already played in a number of bands, including ten-piece R&B group the Rest (who at one point supported Hall & Oates, Bon Jovi missing his senior prom in order to do so), the Wild Ones, Johnny & the Lechers, the Raze and Atlantic City Expressway, who opened for Bruce Springsteen, the Asbury Jukes and Squeeze, among others.
July [1] The band signs to Phonogram's Mercury label and begins building a solid live reputation on the hard rock circuit (including future slots opening for Z.Z. Top). Recording for its debut album will get underway in the fall.

1984

Apr *Runaway*, the track first recorded by Bon Jovi as a solo effort, which has won inclusion on radio station WDHA's compilation album of unsigned acts, becomes the band's debut chart single, making US #39, while ***Bon Jovi*** is released, set to reach US #43 and UK #71.
July [14] *She Don't Know Me* makes US #48.
Oct During the band's first UK tour, one performance is broadcast by BBC Radio 1.

1985

May [11] ***7800° Fahrenheit*** reaches UK #28, and will make US #37, becoming the group's first gold album.
[25] The extracted *Only Lonely* peaks at US #54.
Aug [17] *In And Out Of Love* peaks at US #69.
[31] *Hardest Part Is The Night* is their UK Singles chart debut, spending a week at #68.

1986

Sept Their major UK chart breakthrough is the hard-rocking but melodic *You Give Love A Bad Name*, which reaches UK #14.
[14] The band opens for .38 Special at the Glens Falls Civic Center, Glens Falls, NY, during a US tour.
Oct [25] ***Slippery When Wet***, recorded at Little Mountain Studios, Vancouver, BC, Canada, with producer Bruce Fairbairn, begins an eight-week stay at US #1 and will go on to sell eight million domestic copies by the end of 1987, one of the biggest-selling rock albums of the decade. It also hits UK #6.
Nov [29] *You Give Love A Bad Name*, penned by Bon Jovi and Sambora with songwriter Desmond Child, tops the US chart, becoming their first million-selling single worldwide.
Dec *Livin' On A Prayer*, written in similar style by the same team, hits UK #4, while ***Bon Jovi*** re-charts at US #77.

1987

Jan ***Slippery When Wet*** returns to US #1, where it will log a further seven weeks.
Feb [14] *Livin' On A Prayer* tops the US chart, where it will stay for three weeks.
[19] ***7800° Fahrenheit*** is certified platinum by the RIAA.
Apr Cowboy-analogized rock ballad *Wanted Dead Or Alive* reaches UK #13.
June [6] *Wanted Dead Or Alive* hits US #7.
Aug [22] Bon Jovi headlines a bill featuring Anthrax, Dio, Cinderella and W.A.S.P., at the annual "Monsters Of Rock" festival, at Castle Donington, Leics., climaxing a year in which it has become the most popular heavy-rock band in the world, as *Never Say Goodbye* reaches UK #21.
Sept [11] *Livin' On A Prayer* wins the Best Stage Performance category at the fourth annual MTV Video Music Awards held, at the Universal Amphitheatre, Universal City, CA.
Dec The group ends the year having played 130 shows in the "Tour Without End", grossing $28,400,000.

1988

Jan [25] They win the Favorite Band, Duo Or Group, Pop/Rock category, at the 15th annual American Music Awards, held at the Shrine Auditorium, Los Angeles.
Apr [18] Their "Breakout" video is certified multi-platinum (100,000 sales) by the RIAA.
[25] The group's manager, Doc McGee, is convicted on drug offenses arising from the 1982 seizure of nearly 40,000lb. of marijuana, smuggled into North Carolina from Colombia. He is sentenced to a five-year suspended prison term, extensive community service and a $15,000 fine. He will, however, continue to manage the band.
Oct [1] Their fourth Mercury-released album ***New Jersey*** hits UK #1, as the extracted single *Bad Medicine* reaches UK #17.
[15] ***New Jersey*** begins a four-week tenure atop the US chart. Repeating the multi-platinum, radio-ready rock formula of the last album, it has once again been helmed by Fairbairn at the Little Mountain Studios.
Nov [19] *Bad Medicine*, once again written by the trio of Bon Jovi, Sambora and Child, also tops the US survey.
Dec [17] Similarly-penned *Born To Be My Baby* reaches UK #22.

1989

Feb [18] *Born To Be My Baby* hits US #3.
Mar Bon Jovi is charged with trespassing after being caught on the ice at New York City's Wollman Skating Rink at 3:30 a.m. with girlfriend Dorothea Hurley and another couple.
[15] At a Meadowlands, East Rutherford, NJ, homecoming concert, the Mayor of Sayreville hands the group the keys to the city, in honor of Bon Jovi Day.
[16] MTV (US) launches a contest to give away Jon Bon Jovi's childhood home in Sayreville.
Apr [29] Bon Jovi marries childhood sweetheart Hurley on the steps of the Graceland Chapel, Las Vegas, NV, in the presence of Reverend George Colton.
May [6] Obligatory rock ballad, the Bon Jovi/Sambora composition *I'll Be There For You* reaches UK #18.
[13] *I'll Be There For You* tops the US chart.
[25] "Slippery When Wet" video is certified multi-platinum (for 200,000 units) by the RIAA.
June Sambora begins a romantic liaison with Cher announcing that "(she's) very cool".
July [10] David F. Pearsall, 18, of Manchester, NH, is charged with theft and released on $1,000 bail, after allegedly stealing Sambora's $2,000 white Kramer guitar at a July 8th concert at Riverfront Park.
[29] *Lay Your Hands On Me* hits US #7.
Aug [11] ***New Jersey*** is released in the USSR. Bon Jovi is paid the maximum allowable license fee, $9,600, from the Russian record company, Melodiya.
[12-13] The group headlines the Moscow Music Peace Festival at Lenin Stadium, with Ozzy Osbourne, Motley Crue, the Scorpions, Cinderella, Skid Row, Drum Madness and Russian talent Gorky Park, Nuance, CCCP and Brigada S. All proceeds go to programmes that fight drug and alcohol abuse in both the US and USSR.
[19] The band headlines a bill, which includes Europe, Vixen and Skid Row, at the Milton Keynes Bowl, Milton Keynes, Bucks., with Aerosmith's Steve Tyler and Joe Perry joining them for an encore of *Walk This Way*.
Sept [2] *Lay Your Hands On Me* reaches UK #18.
[6] Bon Jovi and Sambora perform *Wanted Dead Or Alive* at the sixth annual MTV Video Music Awards, held at the Universal Amphitheatre, Universal City. Their acoustic rendition, in sharp contrast to the group's traditional hard-rocking electric style, gives the cable network's executives the idea of launching a number of acoustic-only showcases, which will evolve into the much-lauded "MTV Unplugged" series of the '90s.
Dec Bon Jovi contributes to the hard-rock compilation album ***Stairway To Heaven/Highway To Hell***, produced by Fairbairn, for the Make A Difference Foundation - Rockers Against Drug And Alcohol Abuse, with Skid Row, the Scorpions and others.
[16] *Living In Sin* hits US #9.
[30] *Living In Sin* makes UK #35.

1990

Feb At the end of another massive global trek, Bon Jovi's 16-month, 237-date world tour ends.
Mar [20] Their "New Jersey" video reaches the RIAA-certified 100,000 sales mark.
Apr Bon Jovi and Bobby Bandiera play at one of three benefits for eight-year-old Tishna Rollo, daughter of producer/engineer John Rollo, who is battling Wilm's Tumor disease, at the Stone Pony, Asbury Park. Sambora's solo *The Wind Cries Mary* is featured in the Andrew Dice Clay movie "The Adventures Of Ford Fairlane".
July Movie "Young Guns II", in which Jon Bon Jovi makes a cameo appearance, having also written its main theme, *Blaze Of Glory*, and the film's entire soundtrack - with contributions from Little Richard, Jeff Beck and Elton John - premieres in US theaters. During a sabbatical from the group, he also writes with Aldo Nova and tours with Southside Johnny. (Aldo Nova is the first signing to Jon Bon Jovi's recently-created Jambco label, which will also sign rock veteran Billy Falcon.)
Aug [25] ***Blaze Of Glory/Young Guns II*** hits UK #2.
Sept [8] *Blaze Of Glory*, Jon Bon Jovi's first solo success, hits US #1, aided by a mountain-top-located promotion clip, heavily rotated on MTV, having already made UK #13. Its parent album ***Blaze Of Glory/Young Guns II*** hits US #3 in only its third week of release.
Nov [15] Bon Jovi is honored with the Silver Clef Award at the third annual Nordoff-Robbins Therapy Centre lunch, at the Roseland Ballroom, New York.
[24] *Miracle*, from "Young Guns II", makes UK #29.
Dec [22] *Miracle* reaches US #12.
[23] For its first gig of the year, the group reassembles for a charity concert to benefit the Monmouth County Arts Council and Holmdel's Sisters of the Good Shepherd at the Count Basie Theatre, Red Bank, NJ.
[31] They perform at an MTV-broadcast New Year's Eve bash at the Tokyo Dome, Japan, with Cinderella, the London Quireboys and Skid Row in support, beginning a 15-date overseas tour.

1991

Jan [19] *Blaze Of Glory* wins Best Original Song at the Golden Globe film awards.
[28] *Blaze Of Glory* wins the Favorite Pop/Rock Single category at the 18th annual American Music Awards, at the Shrine Auditorium, Los Angeles.
Mar [25] Jon Bon Jovi performs the Oscar-nominated *Blaze Of Glory* at the 63rd annual Academy Awards.
July [30] He performs at WHTZ's eighth birthday party in New York, with Mariah Carey, the Black Crowes and Debbie Gibson.
Sept [5] The band is presented with the Michael Jackson Video Vanguard trophy at the eighth annual MTV Video Music Awards, held again at the Universal Amphitheatre.
[28] Sambora's *Ballad Of Youth* enters the US chart, set to reach #63 (having already peaked at UK #59), while his Mercury-released debut album, ***Stranger In This Town*** has peaked at US #36 the week previously (and UK #20 on the 14th).
Dec [18] During an end-of-year US solo tour, Sambora guests on NBC-TV's "Late Night With David Letterman".

1992

Jan [11] ***Two Rooms: Celebrating The Songs Of Elton John And Bernie Taupin***, including Jon Bon Jovi's rendition of *Levon*, reaches US #18.
Feb Having finally split split from McGhee, the band is now self-managed by BJM, based in Red Bank.
May [30] Sambora performs at KISS Radio's 13th anniversary concert at the Great Woods Center for the Performing Arts, Mansfield, MA, also staged to benefit the Genesis Fund, while Bryan completes the score to the forthcoming movie "Netherworld".

June Jon Bon Jovi contributes vocals to *Yeah*, alongside a multi-star vocal cast, a cut on Eddie Murphy's forthcoming R&B album ***Love's Alright***.
Aug The band regroups to begin its first recording sessions in nearly five years, returning to its favored Little Mountain Studios.
Oct [8] They play an unscheduled gig, the first of three, at the After The Gold Rush club, Tempe, AZ, in front of a sellout crowd of 980, to promote their new album.
[24] *Keep The Faith* bows at its UK #5 peak.
[25] The group tapes its MTV "Unplugged" concert, set for broadcast on the 29th.
Nov [5] The band helps MTV Europe celebrate its fifth anniversary with a party at the House Of Commons.
[14] Bob Rock-produced ***Keep The Faith*** enters the UK chart at #1.
[21] ***Keep The Faith*** debuts at its US peak, #5.
[28] *Keep The Faith* reaches US #29.
Dec [20] The band plays two shows at the Count Basie Theatre, Red Bank, to benefit storm relief efforts in Monmouth County.

1993

Jan [9] The group guests on NBC-TV's "Saturday Night Live".
[30] *Bed Of Roses* reaches UK #13.
[31] During last minute squabbles between NBC-TV executives and Garth Brooks, which jeopardize the country star's planned performance of the US national anthem at Superbowl XXVII, held at the Rose Bowl, Pasadena, CA, NBC producers approach audience member Jon Bon Jovi in his seat, asking him to stand in as a last minute replacement. Bon Jovi agrees, but the crisis is resolved and Brooks sings as scheduled.
Feb [8] The group begins a six-month world tour at the Colisée de Quebec, Quebec City, PQ, Canada, set to end on August 8th at the Merriweather Post Pavilion, Columbia, MD.
Mar [6] *Bed Of Roses* hits US #10, where it will stay for six weeks.
[23] The Paul Rodgers-assembled ***Tribute To Muddy Waters***, to which Sambora has contributed fret work, is released on Victory Music.
May [22] Bon Jovi's *In These Arms* hits UK #9, set to reach US #27 on June [12].
Aug [14] *I'll Sleep When I'm Dead* debuts at its US #97 peak and reaches UK #17.
Sept [18] Bon Jovi performs at the Milton Keynes Bowl, Milton Keynes, Bucks.
Oct [16] *I Believe* reaches UK #11.
Dec [20] The group plays its annual Christmas concert at the Count Basie Theatre before a sellout crowd.
[31] It appears on CBS-TV's "Late Show With David Letterman".

1994

Feb [14] Jon Bon Jovi performs *I'll Sleep When I'm Dead* with Dina Carroll at the 13th annual BRIT Awards held at London's Alexandra Palace.
Apr [2] *Dry County* hits UK #9.
Oct [8] Rock ballad *Always* hits UK #2.
[19] The RIAA confirms US sales of two million copies for ***Keep The Faith***.
[22] ***Crossroads***, a 14-track greatest hits collection, enters the UK chart at #1.
[28] The group appears on the "Late Show With David Letterman" without Such, who has decided to leave the band.
Nov [5] ***Crossroads*** debuts at its US #8 peak.
[17] The RIAA certifies multi-platinum sales of ***New Jersey*** (six million).
Dec [5] The band takes part in the Z100 Acoustic Christmas event at New York's Madison Square Garden before a sellout crowd of 17,719, with Weezer, Melissa Etheridge, Indigo Girls, Sheryl Crow, Hole and Toad The Wet Sprocket.
[8] Bon Jovi performs at the Orpheum Theatre, Boston, MA, raising $50,000 for the Greater Boston Food Bank and the KISS Cancer Fund. New England Patriots quarterbacks Drew Bledsoe and Scott Zolak sing backup vocals on *You Give Love A Bad Name*.
[10] *Always* hits US #4.
[15] Sambora and actress Heather Locklear marry in Red Bank, NJ, before flying to Paris, France for a formal wedding on the 17th at the American Cathedral Episcopal Church with family and friends.
[17] Their cover of the seasonal chestnut *Please Come Home For Christmas* debuts at its UK #7 peak.

1995

Feb [1] "Crossroad : The Video" is certified gold by the RIAA.
[18] The group is once again the music guest on "Saturday Night Live".
Mar [4] *Someday I'll Be Saturday Night* hits UK #7.
Apr [5] *Always* is confirmed platinum by the RIAA.
[12] Jon Bon Jovi performs at the sixth annual Carnegie Hall benefit for the Rainforest Foundation.
May [3] The group appears at the seventh annual World Music Awards at the Sporting Club in Monte Carlo, Monaco.
[6] Dozens of fans are injured when 1,000 fans without tickets force their way into a Bon Jovi concert in Jakarta, Indonesia. A riot ensues.
[30] The RIAA certifies multi-platinum sales (two million) of ***Bon Jovi***.
June [17] *This Ain't A Love Song* hits UK #6.
[23-25] During current UK dates, Bon Jovi plays at Wembley Stadium, Wembley, Middx. (During the group's stay in London, they will busk on the South Bank for around 500 fans.)
July [1] The band's first new studio effort in nearly three years, ***These Days*** enters UK chart at #1, the same day it plays the first of two shows in Paris, supporting the Rolling Stones.
[9] A planned concert at the 100,000 capacity Luzhniki Stadium in Moscow, Russia is cancelled because of the crisis in Chechyna.
[15] ***These Days*** bows at its US #9 peak.
[21-23] The group begins a North American tour with three sellout dates at the Jones Beach Theatre, Wantagh, NJ.
Aug [1] The RIAA certifies sales of three million copies of ***Crossroads***.
[12] *This Ain't A Love Song* reaches US #14.
[28] ***These Days*** is certified platinum by the RIAA.
Sept [2] The band performs *Imagine* and, with Eric Burdon, *It's My Life* and *We Gotta Get Out Of This Place*, at the inaugural Concert for the Rock and Roll Hall of Fame at Cleveland Stadium, Cleveland, OH.
[12] ***Blaze Of Glory*** is ratified platinum by the RIAA.
Oct [7] *Something For The Pain* hits UK #8 and peaks at US #76.
[10] The RIAA certifies that the group's most successful album ***Slippery When Wet*** has reached the 12 million sales plateau.
Nov [17] Following a tip-off from a government staff member who had heard he was going to be a guest DJ, Jon Bon Jovi is banned from playing records on Chris Evans' BBC 1FM show on the 21st, because the terms of his work permit do not allow him to be a DJ. He will still be interviewed on the program.
[23] The group collects the Best Rock Act trophy and performs at the second annual MTV Europe Music Awards, held in Paris.
[25] *Lie To Me* bows at its UK #10 peak.
[28] Jon Bon Jovi's solo album ***Blaze Of Glory*** is RIAA-certified for two million sales.
Dec [2] *Lie To Me*, coupled with *Something For The Pain*, peaks at US #88.

1996

Jan Following a successful acting role in "Moonlight And Valentino", Jon Bon Jovi begins filming "The Leading Man" in England.
Feb [19] Bon Jovi is named Best International Group at the 1996 BRIT Awards held at London's Earl's Court Exhibition Centre.
Mar [16] *These Days* hits UK #7.
July [6] The group plays the first of three UK dates on its continuing "These Days" world tour at the Milton Keynes Bowl. (The 22-date European leg of the tour is sponsored by Volkswagen, who simultaneously sell three "Bon Jovi Golf" models at 26,500 Deutsche Marks.

GARY U.S. BONDS

1959

The son of a college professor and a music teacher, Bonds (b. Gary Anderson, June 6, 1939, Jacksonville, FL) has been performing in Norfolk, VA, with his doo-wop group the Turks, when he signs to Frank Guida's local LeGrand Records as a soloist. The studio where he initially records is a poorly-equipped room behind Guida's record store, Frankie's Birdland, but the odd acoustics and makeshift effects combine to create a unique "outdoor" sound. His first single *New Orleans* will be issued nationally, after strong local interest, in September 1960, at which time Guida changes Anderson's name to U.S. Bonds because "buy U.S. Bonds" proves an effective promotional tag, though Anderson himself will not be aware of his new moniker until he hears it on the radio. The single will hit US #6 in November, though the quickly-released follow-up *Not Me* will fail to chart.

1961

Feb *New Orleans* reaches UK #16.
June *Quarter To Three*, with a Guida lyric added to Gene Barge's earlier instrumental *A Night With Daddy G*, and which Bonds later recalls making while he and the band were inebriated, tops the US chart for two weeks and becomes a million-seller.
Aug *Quarter To Three* hits UK #7. The song will become the subject of a lawsuit in 1962, when Chubby Checker is accused of plagiarism for his hit *Dancin' Party*.
Sept *School Is Out* hits US #5, but fails to chart in the UK, as will the balance of Bonds' LeGrand label US successes. Hereafter, his billing is officially adapted to Gary U.S. Bonds, at the request of both himself and the United States Bonds authorities.
Oct *Dance Till Quarter To Three* hits US #6.
Nov *School Is In*, an answer disc to his September hit, reaches US #28.
Dec Bonds performs at the Academy of Music, New York, NY, on a bill also featuring Joey Dee.

1962

Feb *Dear Lady Twist*, exploiting the year's big dance craze, hits US #9.
Apr [21] Bonds begins a 23-date, twice-nightly UK tour, with Johnny Burnette, Gene McDaniels, Mark Wynter, Danny Rivers and others, at St. Andrew's Hall, Glasgow, Scotland, set to end at the Granada Cinema, Walthamstow, London, on May 13th.
May Same craze-oriented *Twist, Twist Señora* hits US #9.
July *Seven Day Weekend* reaches US #27.
Sept His unique sound formula proves to have worn thin on *Copy Cat*, which stalls at US #92. (His hit run now over, Bonds will stay with LeGrand for four more years - turning down in 1963 *If You Wanna Be Happy*, which labelmate Jimmy Soul then takes to US #1. He will continue performing live throughout the next two decades, but will spend more time songwriting with Jerry "Swamp Dogg" Williams and producing Doris Duke, Z.Z. Hill, Johnny Paycheck and others, than recording.)

1969

Nov [29] Bonds takes part in Richard Nader's second "Rock'n'Roll Revival" concert, with Jackie Wilson, Bill Haley & His Comets and a host of other late '50s, early '60s acts, at Madison Square Garden, New York. He will be a regular performer on Nader's bill through the years.

1975

Mar Now signed to Prodigal, Bonds records *Grandma's Washboard Band*, but it fails to restore his chart status.

1978

Performing at a New Jersey club, the Red Baron, he invites audience member Bruce Springsteen, a long-time fan who has performed *Quarter To Three* live frequently, on stage. They become friends and

Springsteen suggests Bonds works with him and his guitarist, Miami Steve Van Zandt, on a comeback album, ***Dedication***, as a shared production.

1981

Apr ***Dedication***, released by EMI America Records, reaches US #22.
June [13] *This Little Girl*, an album track penned by Springsteen, makes UK #43 and will reach US #11.
Aug Bonds' revival of the oldie *Jolé Blon* peaks at US #65 and UK #51, while ***Dedication*** makes UK #43.
Nov [7] His cover of Lennon and McCartney's *It's Only Love* makes UK #43.

1982

June [12] Bonds takes part in a rally for nuclear disarmament, in Central Park, New York, with Jackson Browne, Linda Ronstadt, Bruce Springsteen and James Taylor, before an audience of 750,000.
July ***On The Line***, again produced by Springsteen and Van Zandt, with the E Street Band providing most of the back-up, makes US #52 and UK #55, as his revival of the Box Tops' *Soul Deep* peaks at UK #59.
Aug Springsteen-written *Out Of Work* reaches US #21.

1984

Aug Having put together a backing band, the American Men, and signed to Phoenix Records, Bonds releases ***Standing In The Line Of Fire***.

1992

May [8-9] Although his chart success has waned once more, the reverence and hits generated by the Springsteen association has maintained Bonds' high profile as a live performer, not least as a popular addition to the nostalgia circuit. Together with Ronnie Spector, the Dixie Cups, Lenny Welch and others, he performs at the Radio City Music Hall, New York, at the 20th anniversary concert for WCBS Radio.

BONEY M

Bobby Farrell (vocals); **Marcia Barrett** (vocals); **Liz Mitchell** (vocals); **Maisie Williams** (vocals)

1976

Writer/producer Frank Farian, working as a producer with Peter Meisel's Munich, W. Germany-based Hansa label, records *Baby Do You Wanna Bump?*, using session singers and musicians, a habit he will continue throughout his career. (This causes a furore in 1990, when it is revealed that another Farian creation, Milli Vanilli, has not actually performed on its Grammy-winning debut album.) When *Baby Do You Wanna Bump?* begins selling well in Holland, Farian assembles a group to "perform" in clubs and discos to promote the record further. Although all its members are of West Indian origin, the quartet is already working individually in Germany, Farrell (b. Oct. 6, 1949, Aruba) as a club DJ, Mitchell (b. July 12, 1952, Clarendon, Jamaica) in the German cast of "Hair", taking over from Donna Summer, who by now has achieved worldwide fame with her debut *Love To Love You Baby*, and Barrett (b. Oct. 14, 1948, St. Catherine's, Jamaica) and Williams (b. Mar. 25, 1951, Montserrat, West Indies) both doing session work. Their role is to sing vocals on Farian's electronic disco-style productions, and also to provide a focus for live and TV performances of the records.

1977

Feb *Daddy Cool*, with an electronic dance beat and a stylized female/bass male vocal combination, the basic sound Boney M has established, hits UK #6 and US #65.
Apr Its revival of Bobby Hebb's 1966 smash *Sunny* hits UK #3. ***Take The Heat Off Me*** is issued, set to reach UK #40.
July *Ma Baker* hits UK #2, while making US #96.
Aug [6] Sophomore album ***Love For Sale*** makes UK #13.
Dec *Belfast*, with a curiously socially-aware lyric, hits UK #8.

1978

May [13] Their adaptation of the Melodians' reggae standard *Rivers Of Babylon* shoots to #1 in the UK, where it will stay for five weeks. During its peak-selling week (w/e Apr [17]), the disc has accounted for 14% of total UK singles sales.
July Before performing dates in the Middle East, the band embarks on a tour of France.
Aug *Rivers Of Babylon* reaches US #30, their biggest US hit.
Sept When *Rivers Of Babylon* finally fades, UK radio flips the disc over, its B-side, the traditional *Brown Girl In The Ring*, boosting the record back up to UK #2. Total UK sales are ultimately just shy of two million, making it the country's #2 all-time best-selling single (behind Wings' *Mull Of Kintyre*).
[9] ***Night Flight To Venus***, containing both sides of the recent 45, hits UK #1, where it will stay for four weeks, logging a chart tenure of 65 weeks. The album also makes US #134.
Oct *Rasputin*, taken from the album, and with a disco arrangement parodying Cossack dance music, hits UK #2.
Dec [9] Their update of Harry Belafonte's 1957 hit *Mary's Boy Child* is released for Christmas, arranged by Farian in a medley with his own *Oh My Lord* (which ensures him half the publishing royalties). It rapidly tops the UK chart, staying for four weeks and selling over one million copies, putting it in the UK all-time top five singles sellers. In the US it reaches #85, and is their last US chart entry. (During the month, the band will perform at London's Hammersmith Odeon.)

1979

Mar Revival of *Painter Man*, originally by mid-'60s UK band Creation, hits UK #10.
May Calypso-styled *Hooray! Hooray! It's A Holi-Holiday* hits UK #3.
Sept [15] *Gotta Go Home/El Lute* reaches UK #12.
[17] The group performs at the Empire Pool, Wembley, Middx.
[29] ***Oceans Of Fantasy*** becomes Boney M's second UK chart-topping album.
Nov [26] Group takes part in the "World Of Disco And Rock'n'Roll Segment" at the Royal Variety Performance.

1980

Jan *I'm Born Again*, their first single not to make the UK Top 30, makes #35. Although the compilation, ***The Magic Of Boney M*** will hit UK #1 on May [17], the dance-pop troupe will only log three further original UK chart singles: a revival of the Smoke's 1967 UK hit *My Friend Jack* reaches UK #57 in May, while *Children Of Paradise* peaks at UK #66 on Feb [21], 1981, and the ecologically-themed *We Kill The World (Don't Kill The World)* closes the account on Nov [28] the same year. A second hits collection, ***The Best Of 10 Years***, will reach UK #35 in September 1986.

1992

Dec [26] The band, now featuring vocalist Liz Wells, and still a novelty favorite on the club and cabaret circuit, hits UK #7 with the reviving *Boney M Megamix* (an earlier *Megamix/Mary's Boy Child* peaked at UK #52 in December 1988), while the UK market prepares for a third Boney M retrospective, the TV-advertised ***The Very Best Of Boney M***, released in March 1993. (Still touring around Europe into the mid-'90s, a fourth compilation ***The Greatest Hits*** will reach UK #14 on Apr [10] the following year, one week prior to a remixed *Brown Girl In The Ring ('93)* charts at UK #38 peak.)

THE BONZO DOG DOO-DAH BAND

Vivian Stanshall (vocals, trumpet); **Neil Innes** (vocals, piano); **Rodney Slater** (sax, trumpet); **Roger Ruskin Spear** (sax, kazoo, mechanical objects); **Vernon Dudley Bohay-Nowell** (guitar, banjo); **Sam Spoons** (percussion); **"Legs" Larry Smith** (drums)

1965

Taking its name - Bonzo Dog from a famous cartoon character which appeared in the **Daily Sketch** in the 1920s, then in published adverts in the '30s before being featured in a children's annual from 1935 to 1952 - and Dada Band, a reference to the turn-of-the-century surrealistic art movement, the group is formed by a troupe of art students at Goldsmith's College, Lewisham, London, as a whimsical, '20s-inspired outfit (initially under the "literal" Bonzo Dog Dada Band moniker). Led by Slater (b. Nov. 8, 1944, Lincs.) and Spear (b. June 29, 1943, London), but with an otherwise fluid personnel of up to 30, the number is reduced to a stable seven, comprising Innes (b. Dec. 9, 1944, Essex), Stanshall (b. Mar. 21, 1943, Shillingford, Oxon), Smith (b. Jan. 18, 1944, Oxford, Oxon), Bohay-Newell (b. July 29, 1932, Plymouth, Devon) and Spoons (b. Martin Stafford Ash, Feb. 8, 1942, Bridgewater, Surrey), when they start playing in south London pubs, notably at the Tiger's Head in Catford, Kent.

1966

Apr Moving on to the club and cabaret circuit, where Spear's job is mainly to manage the considerable number of props and gadgets involved in their stage act, they have been signed to EMI's Parlophone label, which releases *My Brother Makes The Noises For The Talkies*, followed by a revival of the Hollywood Argyles' *Alley Oop* in September.

1967

Mar The group begins a two-month Sunday night residency at London's Marquee club.
Oct Now signed to Liberty Records, the group shows an increasingly diversified musical approach, and skills at parody, on its debut album ***Gorilla***, but neither this nor the extracted *Equestrian Statue* chart.
Nov [19] The ensemble plays at London's Savile Theatre, sharing a bill with the Bee Gees, the Flowerpot Men and Tony Rivers & the Castaways.
Dec [26] They appear in the Beatles' TV musical film "Magical Mystery Tour", performing *Death Cab For Cutie*.
[31] The group performs at a New Year's Eve party at the Pink Flamingo in London.

1968

Jan The band begins a residency on the ITV satirical comedy series "Do Not Adjust Your Set", indulging their musical and comic talents through 13 weekly shows.
Apr At the end of the series, Spoons and Bohay-Nowell leave, and Dennis Cowan (b. May 6, 1947, London) joins on bass in preparation for album recording sessions.
Dec *I'm The Urban Spaceman*, an Innes composition pseudonymously produced by Paul McCartney as Apollo C. Vermouth, hits UK #5.
[21] The band appears on BBC-2 TV's "Colour Me Pop".

1969

Jan [18] ***The Doughnut In Granny's Greenhouse***, Monty Python comedian Michael Palin's euphemism for an outside toilet, makes UK #40.
Mar *Mr. Apollo* is released, but does not chart.
Aug [30] ***Tadpoles*** reaches UK #36, as the band performs on the opening day of the "Isle Of Wight Festival Of Music", Woodside Bay near Ryde, Isle of Wight. (Jim Capaldi takes the drummer's seat at the

beginning of their set while Smith is in a nearby pub with the Who's Keith Moon, though he will return midway and take over from the Traffic drummer.)

Nov ***Keynsham***, named after the district of Bristol, Somerset, plugged incessantly on Radio Luxembourg by football pools' entrepreneur Horace Batchelor, is released, followed in quick succession by the extracts *I Want To Be With You* and *You Done My Brain In*.

[6-8] The group opens for Led Zeppelin at the Winterland Ballroom, San Francisco, CA.

1970

Jan The band breaks up, despite being a consistently-popular club and touring attraction. Smith joins Bohay-Nowell and Spoons in Bob Kerr's Whoopee Band, while Spear will become a solo novelty act. Stanshall, Cowan, Spear and "Borneo" Fred Munt form Vivan Stanshall's BiG GRunt.

Aug Compilation album ***The Best Of The Bonzo Dog Doo-Dah Band*** is released in the UK.

1971

Nov Stanshall, Innes and Cowan revive the Bonzo Dog name and, with help from Bubs White (guitars), Andy Roberts (guitars, fiddle), Dave Richards (bass), Dick Parry (saxophone, flute) and Hughie Flint (drums), begin recording ***Let's Make Up And Be Friendly*** in Oxfordshire, which will make US #199 in May the following year. Hereafter, members will move on to solo work. Stanshall and Innes will maintain the highest profiles into the '80s: the former as a TV and radio personality, creator of the thoroughly British movie "Sir Henry At Rawlinson End", Master Of Ceremonies for Mike Oldfield's ***Tubular Bells***, and lyricist for Steve Winwood's ***Arc Of A Diver***; the latter as a composer, songwriter, TV performer, ad-jingle singer, and collaborator with Eric Idle on both ITV's "Rutland Weekend Television" and the Beatles spoof, the Rutles. While a twin compilation album, ***The History Of The Bonzos***, reaches UK #41 on June [22], 1974, Liberty will bring the band's unique brand of entertainment to compact disc in 1990, releasing the double-album retrospective ***Bestiality Of Bonzo Dog Doo Dah Band***.

1995

Mar [5] Having returned to public view through his exposure in Ruddles Ale TV commercials, Stanshall dies in a fire in his London flat.

[21] Steve Winwood sings *Arc Of A Diver* at Stanshall's memorial service at St. Patrick's Church in London's Soho Square.

BOO RADLEYS

Sice (vocals, guitar); **Martin Carr** (guitar); **Tim Brown** (bass); **Rob Cieka** (drums)

1990

Mar Schoolfriends from the age of ten, Carr (b. Nov. 29, 1968, Turso, Highlands, Scotland) and Sice (b. Simon Rowbottom, June 18, 1969, Wallasey, Lancs.) have grown together in the Liverpool, Lancs., suburb of Wallasey, heavily influenced by the music of the Beatles, and, from their mid-teens, by the Jesus & Mary Chain and lately Primal Scream, have formed the Boo Radleys (the name taken from a character in **To Kill A Mockingbird**) with another schoolmate, Brown (b. Feb. 26, 1969, Wallasey) on bass in 1988, playing their first gig at the Victoria bar in New Brighton, Merseyside. After a number of stand-ins, they recruit drummer Steve Hewitt and record a five-track demo in 1989 based around Carr's lyrics, but to no label interest. However, Dandelion Adventure member Mark Waring has passed the tape on to his group's Preston, Lancs.,-based Action Records' label/shop owner Gordon Gibson who signs them up for one album which results in the Boo Radleys now recording the My Bloody Valentine-influenced, guitar-swamped ***Ichabod And I*** debut.

July With the album released by Action, impressed BBC Radio 1 DJ John Peel invites the band to record sessions for his show.

Nov Now signed to indie-staple Rough Trade Records and with Cieka (b. Aug. 4, 1968, Birmingham, W. Midlands) having replaced Hewitt on drums, *Kaleidoscope E*, produced by A.R. Kane's guitarist, Rudi, is released.

1991

Apr The Boo Radleys record another Peel session to promote its second EP, *Every Heaven* (which will be followed by a final Rough Trade release, *Boo! Up EP*, also produced by Alan Moulder, in September). Now identified with the "shoe-gazing", guitar-based indie movement and completing its second album in the autumn, the band's relationship with the label will end as Rough Trade experiences serious financial woes.

1992

Apr [4] With the group signed by enthusiastic Creation Records label boss Alan McGhee, ***Everything's Alright Forever***, its lyrics penned by Carr, is finally released, charting for a week at UK #55.

June [20] *Does This Hurt?*, coupled with *Boo! Forever*, charts for a week at UK #67 though the critically-revered, band favorite *Lazarus* will fail to chart when released in November, while the group undertakes its first US tour opening for Sugar.

1993

Aug [28] Its sophomore set, an ambitious 17-track attempt to reflect much of the pop/rock landscape from the 1960s to the present day and likened by Carr to the Beatles' ***White Album***, the melody-fed ***Giant Step*** debuts at its UK #17 peak.

Oct [23] *Wish I Was Skinny* charts for a week at UK #75, while *Lazarus* opens the group's US chart account making #30 on the Modern Rock singles survey (where Creation licenses to Columbia Records).

Nov Earlier Rough Trade material is released in the UK as ***Learning To Walk***.

1994

Feb [12] *Barney (... & Me)* bows at its UK #48 peak.

June [11] Remixed and reissued *Lazarus* bows at its UK #50 peak as the band prepares to perform at this summer's Creation tenth anniversary celebration "Undrugged" held at London's Royal Albert Hall.

1995

Mar [11] Horns-led *Wake Up Boo!*, featuring *Blues For George Michael* on its CD-single format, bows at its UK #9 peak.

Apr [8] ***Wake Up!***, recorded at a six-week session at the Rockfield Studios in Wales the previous autumn, enters at UK #1 supported by extensive UK tour dates.

May [13] *Find The Answer Within* debuts at its UK #37 peak.

June [17] The group performs on a Blur-headlining concert at London's Mile End Stadium.

July [6] A bill featuring the Boo Radleys, Lush, Elastica, Gene and S*M*A*S*H raises £15,000 for the Shelter charity at a Kentish Town Forum, London benefit.

[29] *It's Lulu* debuts at its UK #25 peak.

Aug [25] Having appeared at the 25th anniversary "Glastonbury Festival Of The Performing Arts" at Worthy Farm in June, the Boo Radleys perform at the annual "Reading Festival", Reading, Berks.

Oct [7] *From The Bench At Belvidere* debuts at its UK #24 peak.

BOOKER T. & THE MG'S

Booker T. Jones (keyboards); **Steve Cropper** (guitar); **Lewis Steinberg** (bass); **Donald "Duck" Dunn** (bass); **Al Jackson Jr.** (drums)

1962

May Jones (b. Nov. 12, 1944, Memphis, TN), who has joined Stax Records as a saxophonist in 1960, though he is a highly proficient multi-instrumentalist, Cropper (b. Oct. 21, 1941, Willow Springs, MO), Jackson (b. Nov. 27, 1935, Memphis) and Steinberg (b. Sept. 13, 1933, Memphis, TN) are all working as regular session musicians in Stax Records' Memphis studio (as well as recording as part of the Mar-Keys), when they record two impromptu tracks at the end of a Sunday session backing Billy Lee Riley. Stax owner, Jim Stewart, likes the bluesy instrumental *Behave Yourself*, and releases it in the US on subsidiary label Volt Records, under the moniker Booker T. & the MG's (which stands for the Memphis Group).

July After DJs begin playing the B-side *Green Onions*, a tight, rhythmic organ-and-guitar instrumental, Stax reissues it as an A-side.

Sept *Green Onions*, hits US #3. (It will not chart in the UK until 1979, though its release the following year will help build a cult following for the band.)

Dec Its parent album, the largely group-penned ***Green Onions*** reaches US #33.

1963

Jan [12] Their second single *Jellybread* peaks at US #82.

Sept [14] *Chinese Checkers* makes US #78.

1964

Feb [22] A sequel to their biggest hit, *Mo-Onions* stalls at US #97.

Mar Steinberg is asked to leave because of unpunctuality for studio sessions, and is replaced by Kings Records distributor employee Dunn (b. Nov. 24, 1941, Memphis), also a former Mar-Keys member and ex-Royal Spades.

Aug ***Green Onions*** is belatedly released in the UK and is their first success, reaching #11.

[15] *Soul Dressing* peaks at US #95.

1965

July [17] *Boot-Leg* returns them to the US chart, peaking at #58. By now, Booker T. & the MG's have become the era-defining R&B backing sound of the Stax/Volt Memphis legend, writing and performing on hits for Rufus Thomas, Wilson Pickett, Otis Redding, Sam & Dave, and others.

1966

Sept [3] *My Sweet Potato* peaks at US #85.

1967

Mar [17] The band begins the 13-date "Soul Sensation '67 UK Tour" at London's Finsbury Park Astoria, alongside Otis Redding, Sam & Dave, Eddie Floyd, Arthur Conley, Carla Thomas and the Mar-Keys, set to end on April 8th at London's Hammersmith Odeon.

June [1] *Green Onions* is certified gold by the RIAA for one million US sales.

[3] *Hip Hug-Her* returns them to US Top 40 success, making #37.

[17] The group performs on the second night of the "Monterey International Pop Festival", County Fairgrounds, Monterey, CA, also backing Otis Redding at the event.

Aug [26] *Slim Jenkin's Place* (originally titled *Slim Jenkin's Joint*, but changed to avoid possible controversy), the B-side of the still-climbing *Groovin'*, peaks at US #70.

Sept [2] ***Back To Back***, with the Mar-Keys, makes US #98.

[23] Their instrumental cover of the Young Rascals' hit *Groovin'* reaches US #21.

[30] ***Hip Hug-Her*** reaches US #35.

1968

June [1] ***Doin' Our Thing*** peaks at US #176.

Aug [31] *Soul Limbo* reaches US #17.

Nov [9] ***Soul Limbo*** makes US #127.

Dec [14] ***The Best Of Booker T. & The MG's*** peaks at US #167.

1969

Jan *Soul Limbo*, the group's UK singles chart debut, reaches #30. The Caribbean-flavored tune will be widely known in later years in the UK as the regular theme to BBC-TV's "Test Match Special" cricket coverage.
Feb [8] *Hang 'Em High*, the theme from the Clint Eastwood movie, returns them to the US Top 10, hitting #9.
May [3] *Time Is Tight*, from Booker T.'s own score for the film "Up Tight", hits US #6. Their soundtrack from the movie makes US #98.
June *Time Is Tight* hits #4 in the UK, where it is their biggest hit.
July [12] An instrumental revival of Simon & Garfunkel's *Mrs. Robinson* makes US #37.
[19] ***The Booker T. Set*** reaches US #53.
Oct [4] *Slum Baby* peaks at US #88. The UK prefers *Mrs. Robinson*'s B-side *Soul Clap '69*, which makes #35.

1970

May ***McLemore Avenue*** makes US #107. The album contains instrumental covers of all the songs on the Beatles' ***Abbey Road***, and the sleeve photo is also similar, showing the MG's walking across the street outside their studio.
July [11] ***McLemore Avenue*** peaks at UK #70.
Aug [15] The extracted George Harrison-penned *Something* makes US #76.
Nov ***Booker T. & The MG's Greatest Hits*** peaks at US #132.

1971

Apr ***Melting Pot*** reaches US #43.
May [22] *Melting Pot*, celebrating ten years of uninterrupted releases on Stax, is their last US hit single, making #45, but stays on the Hot 100 for four months. Tired of the strain of working with the band and a punishing session schedule at the Stax studios, Jones quits soon afterwards, leaving Memphis to live and work in Los Angeles, CA. (He will marry singer Priscilla Coolidge (sister of Rita), sign to A&M Records, and begin a solo career as a songwriter and soul vocalist.)
Aug Cropper also leaves Stax, to open his own TMI recording studio and label in Memphis and work as a producer and session player.

1973

Dunn and Jackson record the album ***MG's*** for Stax, with Bobby Manuel (guitar) and Carson Whitsett (keyboards) taking up the two vacant roles, but it raises little interest.

1975

Oct [1] Jackson is shot dead when he disturbs an intruder at his Memphis home. (He has already been shot in the chest by his wife Barbara, during an incident in July.)

1977

Feb [4] Following the 1976 UK release of ***Union Extended***, consisting of previously-unavailable Booker T. & the MG's tracks, Jones, Cropper and Dunn reunite - as part of an all-star band - to play on the 25th birthday show of ABC-TV's "American Bandstand". The trio stays together, adding drummer Willie Hall (b. Aug. 8, 1950), to record ***Universal Language*** for Asylum Records, which has poor reviews and sales, after which the group splits again. (The following year, Jones will enjoy his biggest commercial success as a producer when he oversees Willie Nelson's million-plus selling ***Stardust***. He will also release the solo albums ***Try And Love Again*** (1978), ***The Best Of You*** (1980) and ***I Want You*** (1981), all released by A&M.)

1980

Jan Due to its inclusion on the soundtrack of the Who film "Quadrophenia", *Green Onions* becomes popular again in the UK, and finally charts 17 years after its US Top 10 success, hitting #7.
June Cropper and Dunn feature in the movie "The Blues Brothers", as members of the starring duo's backing band. (They will continue to work throughout the decade as respected freelance players and producers, working with numerous acts, while Jones continues to have a mildly successful career as a soul vocalist.)

1992

Jan [15] As the cornerstone of the Memphis soul sound of the '60s, Booker T. & the MG's are inducted into the Rock and Roll Hall of Fame at the seventh annual ceremony, held at the Waldorf Astoria Hotel, New York, NY.
Nov [2] Having re-formed with Jones in 1990 for nostalgia tours of the US and Europe, and also worked as the backing band for Japanese artist Masai during 1991, Cropper and Dunn jam at the launch of Dan Aykroyd's House of Blues club in Harvard, MA, alongside Eddie Floyd, Andrew Strong, Charlie Musselwhite and others.

1993

Aug [14] Neil Young, backed by Booker T. & the MG's, whom he has met during last October's Bob Dylan anniversary concert at New York's Madison Square Garden, embarks on the US leg of his world tour at the Marcus Amphitheatre, Milwaukee, WI.

1994

Apr [19] ***That's The Way It Should Be***, the group's first album since 1977's ***Universal Language***, is released by Columbia Records.

1995

Mar [1] The extracted *Cruisin'* nabs the Best Pop Instrumental Performance at the 37th annual Grammy Awards held at the Los Angeles' Shrine Auditorium.
[2] The group receives the Lifetime Achievement Award at the sixth annual Rhythm & Blues Pioneer Awards at the Hollywood Palladium, Hollywood, CA.
Sept [2] They perform *Green Onions* and appropriately act as a general backing band at the Concert for Rock and Roll Hall of Fame at the Cleveland Stadium, Cleveland, OH. (Their most enduring recording is also currently featured on the soundtrack to "Get Shorty", together with *Can't Be Still.*)

THE BOOMTOWN RATS

Bob Geldof (vocals); **Johnnie Fingers** (keyboards, vocals); **Gerry Cott** (guitar); **Pete Briquette** (bass, vocals); **Gerry Roberts** (guitar, vocals); **Simon Crowe** (drums, vocals)

1975

Having interviewed the likes of Elton John and Little Richard for the **New Musical Express** and other publications as a music journalist, Geldof (b. Oct. 5, 1954, Dublin, Eire) forms the Nightlife Thugs, soon changing their name to Boomtown Rats (after a gang featured in the David Carradine-starring movie "Bound For Glory" based on the life of Woody Guthrie) in Dun Laoghaire, a small harbor town near Dublin, enlisting Fingers (b. John Moylett, Sept. 10, 1956, Eire), his cousin Briquette (b. Patrick Cusack, July 2, 1954, Eire), Cott, Roberts (b. June 16, 1954) and Crowe. Initially managing the band, Geldof soon takes over lead vocal duties from Roberts.

1976

Oct Having relocated to the London suburb of Chessington, the Boomtown Rats are signed to Ensign Records, as the new wave of punk music begins to ride the UK music scene. Although more versatile and coherent than many of their punk contemporaries, the band's initial success will be inextricably linked to the rise in popularity of the genre.

1977

June [30] Geldof is attacked during the band's gig at the Music Machine in Camden Town, London.
Sept *Looking After No. 1*, led by Geldof's frantic vocal style, is issued after weeks of UK touring, including support dates with Tom Petty. It reaches UK #11, while their album debut ***The Boomtown Rats*** climbs to UK #18.
Dec The school-themed, pop-punk *Mary Of The Fourth Form* reaches UK #15.

1978

May *She's So Modern* reaches UK #12.
July [9-10] Climaxing an extensive UK tour, the group performs final dates at the Hammersmith Odeon, London. During the month, *Like Clockwork* becomes the group's first Top 10 record, hitting UK #6, while ***A Tonic For the Troops***, produced by Robert "Mutt" Lange, hits UK #8, beginning a 44-week chart tenure.
Nov [7] The band appears on ITV's "Get It Together".
[18] Melodramatic Geldof-penned *Rat Trap*, heralding a more textured departure away from punk, tops the UK chart, where it will stay for two weeks.

1979

Jan [29] San Diego, CA, schoolgirl Brenda Spencer shoots and kills several of her schoolmates. Pressed for a reason, she says: "I don't like Mondays", a quote which proves inspirational to Geldof.
Feb The group undertakes a US tour.
Mar ***A Tonic For The Troops*** makes US #112.
Apr [7] Their first American tour includes an appearance at the "California Music Festival", with Ted Nugent, Aerosmith, Cheap Trick and Van Halen.
May A US tour ends at the Palladium, New York.
July [7] Band members make a personal appearance at the opening of the Virgin Megastore, Oxford Street, London.
[28] *I Don't Like Mondays*, produced by Phil Wainman, hits UK #1 in its second week on the chart, remaining at the top for four weeks, and (aided by a striking Jon Roseman-directed promo video) becomes the Rats' biggest-selling single.
Nov ***The Fine Art of Surfacing***, chiefly the work of Geldof and Fingers, hits UK #7.
Dec *Diamond Smiles* reaches UK #13. ***The Fine Art Of Surfacing*** makes #103 in the US (where the group's recordings are issued by Columbia).

1980

Feb *Someone's Looking At You* hits UK #4, as the band sets off on a lengthy world tour, covering Europe, US, Japan and Australia.
Mar Despite attempts by Brenda Spencer's parents to have *I Don't Like Mondays* banned in the US, and with many US radio stations refusing to playlist the disc, the single becomes their sole US hit, peaking at #73.
May [9] *I Don't Like Mondays* wins the Best Pop Song and Outstanding British Lyric categories at the 25th annual Ivor Novello Awards, held at the Grosvenor House Hotel, London.
Dec [6] A switch to Mercury Records sees the release of reggae-tinged *Banana Republic*, which hits UK #3.

1981

Feb ***Mondo Bongo***, co-produced by the band with Tony Visconti, hits UK #6.
[2] The extracted *The Elephants' Graveyard (Guilty)* reaches UK #26. ***Mondo Bongo*** makes US #116. Cott leaves soon after, and the band continues as a quintet.
Dec [12] *Never In A Million Years* peaks at UK #62, their first single not to breach the Top 30.

1982

Mar 8,000 fans try to get into the 3,000-capacity Athens Sporting Stadium, Athens, Greece, to see the band. After riotous scenes, the group agrees to play two extra shows.
Apr *House On Fire*, with an offbeat arrangement, rekindles interest, reaching UK #24 while its parent

album ***V Deep*** makes UK #64.
June *Charmed Lives* is the group's first single not to chart in the UK.
Aug Geldof is featured in the starring role of "The Wall", a movie based on the 1979 Pink Floyd album of the same title.

1984

Feb [18] *Tonight* peaks at UK #73.
May *Drag Me Down* makes UK #50, and is the Boomtown Rats UK chart swan song for the decade.
Nov Geldof sees a graphic BBC-TV report on famine in Ethiopia and determines to raise funds to help the situation. It is the beginning of the Band Aid relief project to which Geldof will intermittently devote his not inconsiderable energies over the next five years. He temporarily sets aside his musical career, and the Boomtown Rats effectively cease to be.
[25] 36 artists, including Geldof and members of the Boomtown Rats, gather in the SARM studio, Notting Hill, London, to record the historic *Do They Know It's Christmas?*.

1985

Jan [28] Geldof participates in the making of the US equivalent of the Band Aid record, USA For Africa's *We Are The World*.
Mar [13] Together with co-writer Midge Ure, Geldof receives the Best Selling A Side award for *Do They Know It's Christmas?* at the 30th annual Ivor Novello Awards luncheon, held at the Grosvenor House Hotel.
July [13] The Boomtown Rats perform during the UK segment of the Geldof-organized "Live Aid" concert extravaganza, held at Wembley Stadium, Wembley, Middx.

1986

Jan [27] Geldof is presented with the Special Award Of Appreciation at the 13th annual American Music Awards, held at the Shrine Auditorium, Los Angeles, CA.
June [14] Geldof is named in H.R.H. the Queen's Birthday Honours List, receiving an honorary knighthood in recognition of his humanitarian activities, and is now Bob Geldof K.B.E.
Aug He marries his long-time girlfriend, UK TV presenter and writer Paula Yates, in Las Vegas, NV, witnessed by the Eurythmics' Dave Stewart and Annie Lennox. They already have a daughter, Fifi Trixiebelle.
Nov Geldof launches a solo recording career on Mercury Records with *This Is The World Calling*, which reaches UK #25. Solo ***Deep In The Heart Of Nowhere***, mainly produced by Stewart, makes US #130.
Dec [6] ***Deep In The Heart Of Nowhere*** spends a week at UK #79.

1987

Jan [10] *This Is The World Calling* peaks at US #82.
Mar Geldof is listed in the latest edition of **Who's Who**.
Feb *Love Like A Rocket* reaches UK #61. During the year, Geldof continues his efforts for the Band Aid Trust charity, inks a best-selling autobiography, **Is That It?**, and stars in a series of UK TV milk commercials.

1988

May [14] Geldof performs Graham Parker's *You Can't Be Too Strong* at Atlantic Records' 40th birthday celebration, in New York.

1990

July [7] The acoustic-driven, jig-inducing *The Great Song Of Indifference* reaches UK #15, while his well-received sophomore solo effort ***The Vegetarians Of Love*** (which includes the hit), produced by Rupert Hine, reaches UK #21 on Aug [4].

1992

Jan [12] Having lost none of his confrontational zeal, Geldof is arrested after a disturbance on a Boeing 727 plane which has been grounded for five hours on the tarmac at Stansted Airport, Stansted, Essex.
Apr [20] Geldof appears at "A Concert For Life : Freddie Mercury Tribute" benefit held at Wembley Stadium, Wembley.
Aug [16] During a number of summer dates, including the "Gosport Festival" and the "Green Belt Festival", Geldof, together with his backing band the Happy Clubsters, performs at "Womad's 10th Birthday" event, held at the Royal Victoria Park, Bath, Avon.

1993

Jan Still working on new material with producer Hine at Joe's Garage Studio, Geldof's Planet 24 TV production company, having been awarded a £10-million contract, begins broadcasting the UK morning television digest "The Big Breakfast".
Apr Geldof's third solo effort ***The Happy Club***, featuring World Party's Karl Wallinger among other musical guests, is released by Polydor.

1994

May [7] Geldof's *Crazy* charts for a week at UK #65.
July [2] The reissued *I Don't Like Mondays* bows at its UK #38 peak.
[9] ***Loudmouth - The Best Of The Boomtown Rats*** hits UK #10 in its week of entry, although people will be more interested in his private life, as his wife leaves him and subsequently engages in a very public relationship with Michael Hutchence.
see also: **BAND AID**

PAT BOONE

1955

Jan After winning on "Ted Mack's Original Amateur Hour" and "Arthur Godfrey's Talent Scouts" (he will become a regular until 1959 on "Arthur Godfrey & His Friends"), Boone (b. Charles Eugene Boone, June 1, 1934, Jacksonville, FL, the great-great-great-great grandson of western pioneer Daniel Boone) signs to Dot Records. Having married Shirley Foley (with whom he had eloped at 17), daughter of country singer Red Foley, on November 7th, 1953, he has previously cut a number of C&W records for the Republic label in his senior year at David Lipscomb High School, and has had his own radio show, "Youth On Parade", on Nashville's WSIX, before moving to Denton, TX, where he landed a job at Forth Worth TV station WBAP, while also a student of Speech and English at Columbia University, after transferring from North Texas State University.
Feb Boone goes to Chicago, IL, to record for Dot boss Randy Wood, on the understanding that Boone will work for him when the appropriate song materializes.
Apr His first Dot release, a version of Otis Williams & the Charms' R&B song *Two Hearts, Two Kisses*, reaches US #16, the first in a series of R&B originals which Boone will successfully cover and which will define his early chart career.
Sept *Ain't That A Shame*, his rock-styled cover of a Fats Domino song, hits US #1 and is his first million-seller (Domino's original hits US #10 at the same time). Boone will always introduce it on stage as *Isn't That A Shame*, since the English student in him finds the title ungrammatical.
Oct [19] Boone appears on a bill at the Circle Theater, Cleveland, OH, with Elvis Presley.
Nov His cover of the El Dorados' R&B rocker *At My Front Door (Crazy Little Mama)* hits US #7, while ballad B-side *No Arms Can Ever Hold You* makes #26 in its own right.
Dec *Ain't That A Shame*, his UK chart debut, hits #7.

1956

Jan *Gee Whittakers!* reaches US #19.
Mar A contrasting coupling of the ballad *I'll Be Home*, covered from the Flamingos, and rocker *Tutti Frutti* from Little Richard, is his first double-sided US Top 20 hit, at #4 and #12 respectively, making it his second million-seller. (Commenting on Boone's version in **Rolling Stone** in 1990, Little Richard will say, "He did the best he could.")
Apr B-side *Just As Long As I'm With You* makes US #76.
June Another Little Richard cover *Long Tall Sally* hits US #8.
[15] *I'll Be Home* is his second, and all-time biggest, UK hit, topping the chart for the first of six weeks. Because of its lyrics, it will be regularly requested on armed forces radio shows in thhe UK over the next ten years.
Aug His update of Ivory Joe Hunter's *I Almost Lost My Mind* hits US #1, Boone's third million-seller. B-side *I'm In Love With You* reaches #57.
Sept *I Almost Lost My Mind* makes UK #14, with *Long Tall Sally* simultaneously reaching #18.
Oct A further million-seller is *Friendly Persuasion*, title theme to the Gary Cooper-starring movie, which hits US #5, while its B-side, a remake of Joe Turner's *Chains Of Love*, makes US #20.
Nov *Howdy!* reaches US #14.
Deemed ready for a parallel movie career, Boone lands a million-dollar contract with 20th Century Fox to make one film a year for seven years.

1957

Jan [5] Boone finishes a UK tour at the Gaumont State, Kilburn, London, before returning to the US to resume college.
Feb [4] He begins filming "Bernardine". *Don't Forbid Me*, a ballad rejected by Elvis Presley and recorded in 15 minutes by Boone at the end of a session, hits US #1 and becomes his fifth million-seller, while its B-side *Anastasia* makes US #37. In the UK, *Friendly Persuasion* hits #3.
Mar *Don't Forbid Me* stays at UK #2 for five weeks, kept from the top by Dot labelmate Tab Hunter with *Young Love*.
Apr Rocker *Why Baby Why* hits US #5. Ballad B-side, a cover of Lucky Millinder's *I'm Waiting Just For You*, reaches US #27, and is another US million-seller. (Several DJs refuse to play *I'm Waiting Just For You* because of Boone's constant use of black artists' material.)
May *Why Baby Why* reaches UK #17.
June *Love Letters In The Sand* tops the US survey, beginning a five-week run, and proves to be his biggest-selling record (with sales of three million). It is sung in the film "Bernadine", in which he makes his starring movie debut, opposite Terry Moore. Title song *Bernadine*, on the B-side, reaches #14, and the two hits stay on the US chart for 34 and 26 weeks respectively. On the US Album ranking, inspirational EP *A Closer Walk With Thee* reaches #13.
Aug *Love Letters In The Sand* is another long-staying UK hit, holding the #2 spot for seven weeks (behind both Elvis Presley's *All Shook Up* and Paul Anka's *Diana*).
Sept *Remember You're Mine* hits US #6, as B-side *There's A Gold Mine In The Sky* reaches US #20. Released as a double A-side in the UK, *Remember You're Mine/There's A Gold Mine In The Sky* hits UK #5 and is his eighth million-seller. ***Pat*** peaks at US #19, as ***Four By Pat*** hits US #5.
Oct [3] "The Pat Boone Chevy Showroom", a weekly musical series, begins on ABC-TV (and will run until mid-1960).
Pat Boone reaches US #20.
Nov [4] B-side *When The Swallows Come Back To Capistrano* stalls at US #80.
Dec *April Love*, taken from film of the same title, his second starring role (opposite Shirley Jones, later of the Partridge Family, whom he refuses to kiss so as not to upset his wife), tops the US chart for six weeks, becoming another million-seller. (The song is nominated for an Oscar in 1958.) Compilation ***Pat's***

Great Hits hits US #3, while his inspirational ***Hymns We Love*** makes US #21, and the soundtrack album from "April Love" peaks at #12.
[13] Seasonal ***White Christmas*** reaches UK #29. (By year's end, Boone has moved to New Jersey and enrolled at New York's Columbia University.)

1958

Feb *April Love* hits UK #7.
Mar Gospel-rocker *A Wonderful Time Up There* (an oldie originally titled *Gospel Boogie*) hits US #4, and its B-side ballad *It's Too Soon To Know* reaches US #11. This is his tenth million-seller.
May *A Wonderful Time Up There* hits UK #2, while *It's Too Soon To Know* hits UK #7.
[19] B-side *Cherie, I Love You* peaks at US #63.
June *Sugar Moon* hits US #5, peaking just as Boone graduates with a BA degree in Speech and English. His 11th million-seller, this also ends a run of nine consecutive singles which have topped a million in US sales.
July *If Dreams Came True* hits US #7, and the B-side *That's How Much I Love You* makes US #39. *Sugar Moon* hits UK #6.
Sept ***Stardust*** hits US #2.
Oct *For My Good Fortune* reaches US #21, and its B-side *Gee But It's Lonely* (written for Boone by Phil Everly of the Everly Brothers) makes US #31. *If Dreams Came True* reaches UK #16.
Nov *Yes Indeed!* makes US #13.
[3] Boone performs at the Royal Variety Performance in London.
[22] ***Stardust*** hits UK #10.
Dec Boone stars in the film musical "Mardi Gras", from which *I'll Remember Tonight* makes US #34.
[5] *Gee But It's Lonely* reaches UK #30.

1959

Feb *With The Wind And The Rain In Your Hair* reaches US #21. Its B-side, reviving an early Elvis Presley hit, *Good Rockin' Tonight*, climbs to US #49. Meanwhile, *I'll Remember Tonight* reaches UK #18.
Apr *For A Penny* makes US #23, and *With The Wind And The Rain In Your Hair* reaches UK #21.
[20] B-side *The Wang Dang Taffy-Apple Tango* peaks at US #62.
July *Twixt Twelve And Twenty* reaches US #17. The title is taken from a book written by Boone, giving advice to teenagers on the conduct of their lives and loves, which adds greatly to his clean-cut image. *For A Penny* peaks at UK #19.
Aug ***Tenderly*** reaches US #17, while *Twixt Twelve And Twenty* makes UK #18. *Fool's Hall Of Fame* will reach US #29 in October, while *Beyond The Sunset* peaks at US #71 in December, Boone's poorest-selling single to date.

1960

Feb [12] ***Pat's Great Hits*** is certified gold by the RIAA.
Mar [21] *(Welcome) New Lovers* restores him to the US Top 20, at #18, as B-side *Words* stalls at US #94. The year's remaining chart action will see the inspirational *He Leadeth Me* reach UK #12 in May, *Walking The Floor Over You* make US #44 on June [27] (its B-side *Spring Rain* peaking at #50), and *Moonglow* reach US #26 in July. The 1957 album ***Hymns We Love*** belatedly charts at UK #14 on July [25], while *Walking The Floor Over You* makes UK #39 in August (its B-side *Candy Sweet* peaking at US #72 on Aug [22]); *Delia Gone* makes US #66 the following week, while *Dear John* reaches US #44 on Nov [28], its flip-side *Alabam* peaking at US #47 on Dec [5]. By year's end, the Boone-starring movie "Journey To The Centre Of The Earth" is confirmed as one of the year's most successful.

1961

Feb [13] *The Exodus Song (This Land Is Mine)*, which adds Boone's own lyrics to Ernest Gold's film theme, peaks at US #64.
June [19] Sales fortunes revive dramatically with *Moody River*, a deceptively jaunty song with a lyric about suicide, which hits US #1 for a week and sells over a million.
July *Moody River* reaches UK #18.
Sept [18] *Big Cold Wind* makes US #19, as ***Moody River*** makes US #29.
Dec Seasonal album ***White Christmas*** reaches US #39.
[27] *Johnny Will* hits UK #4.

1962

Jan [13] *Johnny Will* makes US #35.
Feb [10] Its B-side *Pictures In The Fire* makes US #77.
[12] Filming begins at Shepperton studios for the Boone-starring "The Main Attraction", with Mai Zetterling.
Mar [3] *I'll See You In My Dreams* climbs to US #32 and UK #27.
Apr He stars in the movie musical "State Fair", with Bobby Darin and Ann-Margret. Soundtrack album ***State Fair*** climbs to US #12.
May [19] *Quando Quando Quando* charts briefly at US #95, and makes UK #41.
June Boone interviews former President Eisenhower, Bobby Kennedy and J. Edgar Hoover for his book "The Young Defenders", which explains Communism to teenagers.
July Boone's last major hit is *Speedy Gonzales*, a song he has heard in the Philippines in 1961, where it was a hit for US singer David Dante, a novelty rock disc featuring the voice of the cartoon character, played by Mel Blanc. It hits US #6 and UK #2 (where it stays for five weeks, behind Frank Ifield's *I Remember You*), and is a chart-topper in many other countries, selling over two million copies worldwide.
Oct *Ten Lonely Guys* makes US #45, while a compilation album, ***Pat Boone's Golden Hits***, makes US #66.
Nov [17] Boone guests on ITV's "Thank Your Lucky Stars" (he will also appear on ITV's "Sunday Night At The London Palladium"), during a UK visit for the premiere of "The Main Attraction".
Dec *The Main Attraction* reaches UK #12, and is Boone's last UK chart single. ***White Christmas*** makes US #116.

1963

Mar The Bossa nova-styled *Meditation* reaches US #91.
June Boone stars in the British-made romantic comedy film "Never Put It In Writing".

1964

Oct *Beach Girl*, in a contemporary surf-music style, makes US #72.
Boone stars alongside Debbie Reynolds and Tony Curtis in "Goodbye Charlie".

1965

Feb With his manager Jack Spina, Boone forms Penthouse, a record production and management corporation whose first signing is Groucho Marx's daughter Melinda.

1966

Feb [6] Boone appears on ITV's "Sunday Night At The London Palladium".
[9] He records four tracks in London with writer/producer Tony Hatch.
Dec Humorously-styled *Wish You Were Here, Buddy* makes US #49. This is his last chart success on Dot Records, which he leaves shortly after, to move briefly to Capitol, and then to Bill Cosby's Tetragrammaton label.

1969

Apr With film roles dwindling following last year's appearance in "The Perils Of Pauline", his final US hit (his 60th, and his sole chart single on Tetragrammaton) is a cover of John Stewart's *July, You're A Woman*, which spends two weeks at #100.

1970

With the hits dried up, his recording career takes a back seat to his TV, cabaret and Christian activities, including tours with his own gospel-based Pat Boone Family Show. His style becomes country-oriented for MGM and Motown's Melodyland country label recordings, and he will also record with his four (now grown) daughters.

1976

Apr [10] Compilation double album ***Pat Boone Originals***, featuring 40 1955-62 Dot label hits, climbs to UK #16, aided by TV advertising.

1977

Oct [15] Boone's third daughter, Debby (b. Sept. 22, 1956, Hackensack, NJ), hits US #1 for ten weeks with *You Light Up My Life*, the theme song from the film of the same title. It becomes the year's biggest hit in the US and sells over two million copies, thus surpassing the achievements of most of her father's records.

1996

Feb [19] Having not attempted a serious musical comeback, despite occasional recordings for ABC, MCA, Hitsville, Motown, and Lamb & Lion, Boone has remained a frequently-seen US TV personality, making guest appearances for example (as ever, in his trademark white buck leather shoes) in an episode of "Moonlighting" in 1987, and alongside early '90s country star Billy Ray Cyrus in 1993. The **Los Angeles Times** now reports that Boone is set to record an album of hard rock covers including material by Van Halen, AC/DC, Guns N' Roses, Metallica and Megadeth.

BOSTON

Tom Scholz (guitar, keyboards); **Brad Delp** (guitar, vocals); **Barry Goudreau** (guitar); **Fran Sheehan** (bass); **Sib Hashian** (drums)

1976

While a product designer for Polaroid, Scholz (b. Mar. 10, 1947, Toledo, OH), a Massachusetts Institute of Technology graduate with a master's degree in mechanical engineering (who, at 6' 6" tall, also played center in the university's basketball squad), has made sophisticated rock demos with musician friends in his spare time, using a self-constructed basement studio in Boston, MA. The recordings sufficiently impress Epic Records to gain a label deal. The debut album, mostly featuring Scholz's basement originals, is completed in Los Angeles, CA, studio sessions with producer John Boylan. Scholz recruits local musicians Delp (b. June 12, 1951, Boston), Goudreau (b. Nov. 29, 1951, Boston), Sheehan (b. Mar. 26, 1949, Boston) and Hashian (b. Aug. 17, 1949, Boston), to tour with him in promoting the project. They are named Boston after their home base.
Dec [4] Hallmaked by Scholz's guitar work and Delp's vocal power, the band's melodic, rock-driven premiere ***Boston*** hits US #3 and will eventually sell over 15 million copies in the US alone, the most commercially-impressive debut in US rock history.
[25] *More Than A Feeling*, subsequently regarded as an adult-oriented rock classic and enduring radio favorite, hits US #5.

1977

Feb [26] ***Boston*** makes #11 in the UK (where it will re-chart in 1981 at #58) in the same week that *More Than A Feeling* reaches UK #22.
Mar [5] *Long Time* climbs to US #22.
June [18] *Peace Of Mind* makes US #38.

1978

Sept [16] Repeating the formula, Boston's sophomore effort ***Don't Look Back*** also tops the US chart, in only its third week (and will hit UK #9 during a ten-week run).
Oct [7] Title cut *Don't Look Back* hits US #4 and makes UK #43.

Nov [4-5] The band makes its major concert debut in its home town, performing two shows at the Boston Garden during a major US tour.

1979

Jan *A Man I'll Never Be* makes US #31, while a third extract, *Feelin' Satisfied*, reaches US #46 in April.
Oct [13] The group performs the first in a series of sellout performances at the Rainbow Theatre, London, at the beginning of a UK tour, set to end on the 26th at the Royal Highland Exhibition, Ingliston, Edinburgh, Scotland.

1980

Oct ***Barry Goudreau***, the guitarist's solo debut released on Portrait, makes US #88. Frustrated by Scholz's disinterest in recording hasty follow-ups, Goudreau will quit Boston (which is often inactive as a performing unit between albums) to form Orion The Hunter in 1982, whose ***Orion The Hunter*** will make US #57 in June 1984.

1986

Nov [1] During ongoing contractual disagreements between Scholz and Epic, ***Third Stage***, released on MCA Records, tops the US chart, as a new-look Boston, with Scholz and Delp now joined by Gary Phil (guitar) and Jim Masdea (drums), resurfaces after a seven-year absence. It reaches UK #37. ***Boston*** and ***Don't Look Back*** both re-chart, at US #98 and US #146 respectively.
[8] *Amanda* becomes Boston's first US chart-topping single.

1987

Feb [14] *We're Ready* hits US #9, while Boston returns to the US large-venue live circuit.
[26] The RIAA certifies four million sales for ***Third Stage***.
Apr [18] *Can'tcha Say (You Believe In Me)/Still In Love* reaches US #20.

1989

With news that he and Delp are recording an album together, Goudreau brings legal proceedings against Scholz, a dispute eventually settled out of court.
Aug [15] Delp guests on *Get Back* during a Ringo Starr concert at the Great Woods Center for the Performing Arts, Mansfield, MA.

1990

Feb [13] The latest round in an acrimonious lawsuit between CBS Records and Scholz begins in the US Federal Court, White Plains, NY. CBS is suing Scholz for reneging on a contract which reportedly required the delivery of ten albums in five years. Scholz is countersuing, claiming millions in unpaid royalties.
Mar [20] After a seven-year legal battle, CBS loses its $20-million lawsuit against Scholz. In going against the record company, the decision also requires that CBS must pay the Boston founder substantial back royalties.

1991

Jan [9-12] While Scholz is not renowned for his prolific output (a factor which undoubtedly helped achieve the multiplatinum success of only three albums in 15 years), ex-Boston members Delp and Goudreau, now joined by Tim Archibald (bass), Brian Maes (keyboards) and Dave Stefanelli (drums), are introduced during Giant Records' first convention, held at the Le Bel-Age Hotel, Los Angeles, CA, as the rock quintet RTZ (an acronym for Return To Zero).
June [29] Delp performs the Boston standard *More Than A Feeling* at a Casino Ballroom, Hampton Beach, NH concert given by blond teen/rock duo, the Nelsons. Meanwhile, Scholz, an avid aviator and inventor (who has registered over ten patented inventions), continues to labor over a forthcoming album for a patient MCA Records.

1992

Mar [28] RTZ's ***Return To Zero*** makes US #169 (and includes *Face The Music* which made US #49 the previous September).
Dec [7] The RIAA certifies six million sales of ***Don't Look Back***.

1994

June [25] Scholz finally re-emerges with Boston's ***Walk On*** featuring additional vocalist Tommy Funderburke, which simultaneously debuts at its US #7 and UK #56 peaks.
July [9] The extracted *I Need Your Love* makes US #51.
Sept [8] ***Walk On*** is certified platinum by the RIAA.
Nov [9] ***Boston*** becomes the third-biggest selling album of all time in the US, when the RIAA certifies sales of 15 million sales.
Dec [12] The group, now comprising Scholz, Delp, who as a sideline fronts his own Beatles covers band, Beatlejuice, Fran Cosmo (vocals), Gary Pihl (guitar), Dave Sikes (vocals, bass) and Curley Smith (drums), performs at the House of Blues club in Cambridge, MA.

1995

May [16] Boston opens its world tour at the Civic Center, Mankato, MN before a sellout crowd of 6,067. (MCA will announce the termination of its contract with the group in the midst of the tour.)

DAVID BOWIE

1964

June From the age of eight, Bowie (b. David Robert Jones, Jan. 8, 1947, Brixton, London) has insisted that he will become "the greatest rock star in England", having heard one of his father's Little Richard singles, and having been given a Selmer saxophone, which he learns to play with lessons from Ronnie Ross (who will be invited by Bowie to perform on Lou Reed's *Walk On The Wild Side* in 1973). Going on to complete a commercial art course at Bromley Technical High School, Bromley, Kent, where Peter Frampton is also studying (both under the tutelage of Frampton's father), Bowie has fronted the Kon-Rads, while schoolfriend George Underwood has formed George & the Dragons. Working at an advertising agency, Bowie has joined with Underwood to form the King Bees, in January, which now releases a one-off UK single, *Liza Jane*, on Decca's Vocalion label, attracting little interest.
Dec Still using his real name, he joins London-based group the Manish Boys who sign to EMI's Parlophone label.

1965

Mar [8] His first TV appearance, performing with the group on its current single *I Pity The Fool*, on "Gadzooks! It's All Happening", goes ahead despite concern over the length of his hair.
June After the Manish Boys fold, he forms the Lower Third, playing summer gigs in UK seaside towns.
Aug The Lower Third records *You've Got A Habit Of Leaving* for Parlophone, but it is subsequently attributed to Davy Jones.
Sept After seeing the Lower Third perform at London's Marquee club, Ken Pitt becomes Jones' manager.

1966

Jan The Lower Third signs to Pye Records, and Jones adopts the surname Bowie for the first time, after Pitt learns that another Davy Jones has been signed as a member of a new made-for-TV US group, the Monkees.
[14] *Can't Help Thinking About Me*, by David Bowie & the Lower Third, is released in the UK by Pye (and on Warner Bros. in the US) and becomes an airplay favorite on the influential pirate station Radio London.
Feb The Lower Third splits, leaving Bowie to continue as a solo artist.
Apr Bowie's debut solo single *Do Anything You Say* is released.
Aug He plays "The Bowie Showboat", a regular Sunday-afternoon slot at the Marquee, backed by the Buzz and broadcast by sponsor Radio London. *I Dig Everything* is released by Pye, after which he is dropped by the label.
Sept Pitt persuades Denny Cordell at Decca Records' new progressive Deram label to sign his client.
Dec *Rubber Band* is the first label release by Bowie.

1967

Apr [14] *The Laughing Gnome*, a novelty performance in an Anthony Newley vocal style, is released, showcasing Bowie's current crooning inclinations (a musical direction which has also inspired him to be the first songwriter to set English lyrics to Claude François' French standard, *Comme D'Habitude*, an idea subsequently taken up by Paul Anka as *My Way*).
June Already wearing make-up, a preference, inspired by Pink Floyd's Syd Barrett, which he will maintain throughout his career, Bowie's debut album ***David Bowie*** is released by Deram, garnering strong reviews but modest sales.
July The extracted *Love You Till Tuesday* is released.
Aug Bowie meets fringe theatrical artist Lindsay Kemp and begins mime and dance lessons under his direction, also appearing in his December-premiering "Pierrot In Turquoise" mime production in Oxford, Oxon.
Dec Bowie works on tracks for BBC's "Top Gear" radio show with producer Tony Visconti, the beginning of a long working partnership.

1968

Apr [24] Apple Records turns down Bowie.
May [20] "The Pistol Shot", in which Bowie has a small part, airs on BBC2-TV.
July He forms a trio named Feathers, with his girlfriend Hermione Farthingale and bassist John Hutchinson. They record privately and play live at London's Middle Earth and other clubs and colleges, but the combo will dissolve within six months.

1969

Feb Bowie and Pitt make a 30-minute film intended for TV, based around tracks from the first album and one new song, *Space Oddity*.
May Bowie co-founds the Beckenham Arts Lab, a performance club in the backroom of a South London pub where he also rehearses.
June He meets Angela Barnett at a King Crimson reception at the Speakeasy club, London. Philips label subsidiary Mercury employee Calvin Lee, having heard *Space Oddity* and convinced it will be a hit, offers Bowie a new record deal.
[20] Bowie signs to Philips and the same day is in Trident Studio, London, re-recording *Space Oddity* with producer Gus Dudgeon.
July [11] His innovative astronomical-themed epic *Space Oddity*, featuring the memorable song character "Major Tom", is released in the UK to coincide with the recent Apollo moon landing. Initially gathering few UK sales, it is also issued in the US on the Mercury imprint.
Aug Bowie wins song festivals in Malta and Italy with *When I Live My Dream*. He organizes and plays in the Beckenham Free Festival, Beckenham, Kent, which 5,000 attend at the recreation ground, and which is later commemorated in his song *Memory Of A Free Festival*.
Sept Following strong airplay and helped by its use as a theme on current BBC-TV astronomy programmes, *Space Oddity* finally hits UK #5.
Oct As an acoustic solo act, he opens for Humble Pie on a UK tour.
Nov Bowie and Angie Barnett move into an apartment in Haddon Hall, Beckenham. ***David Bowie***, produced by Visconti, and featuring the Moody Blues' bassist John Lodge, is released in the UK on Philips, and in the US as ***Man Of Words, Man Of Music*** on Mercury.

1970

Feb He forms a new backing band, Hype, with Visconti on bass, John Cambridge on drums and Mick Ronson on guitar, rehearsing at the Thomas A Becket pub, which makes its live debut at the Roundhouse, Camden Town, London.
Mar *The Prettiest Star*, written for Angie, is issued as a UK single.
[20] Bowie and Angie Barnet (b. Mary Angela Barnetty) are married at Bromley Register Office, Kent.
May [10] Bowie receives a Special Award for Originality for *Space Oddity* at the 15th annual Ivor Novello Awards, held at the Talk Of The Town, London.
June *Memory Of A Free Festival* is issued as a UK single, re-recorded with new band Hype, with Mick "Woody" Woodmansey on drums.
Aug Bowie and Pitt part amicably. Tony DeFries, originally brought in to handle financial affairs, becomes his new manager. Bowie plays sax on Dib Cochran & the Earwigs' *Universal Love*, a group featuring Visconti, Rick Wakeman and Mickey Finn.
Nov Prior to its UK release, the Visconti-produced, Bowie-penned ***The Man Who Sold The World***, featuring Ronson, Woodmansey, guitarist Tim Renwick and bass player Herbie Flowers, is released in the US.

1971

Jan Single *Holy Holy* is released in the UK.
[27] Bowie arrives in US for his first visit. He does not perform live because of work permit restrictions, but attracts publicity when he wears dresses at promotional events in Texas and California.
Mar Bowie sings with Arnold Corns (inspired by Bowie's favorite Pink Floyd track, *Arnold Layne*), a group based around his protegé, dress designer Freddi Burretti (renamed Rudi Valentino), which releases *Moonage Daydream*, but after it fails to sell, the band dissolves.
Apr ***The Man Who Sold The World*** is released in the UK, but with a different sleeve showing Bowie in a dress. This is later withdrawn and copies of the original will become high-priced collectors' items. Demo recordings are made for what will become ***Hunky Dory***.
May [28] A son Duncan Zowie Haywood is born in Bromley Hospital.
June Peter Noone (of Herman's Hermits) reaches UK #12 with the Bowie song *Oh You Pretty Thing*. DeFries negotiates the signing of Bowie to RCA Records worldwide, on the strength of his client's ***Hunky Dory*** demo tapes and the commercial success of *Oh You Pretty Thing*.
[20] He plays a solo acoustic set at the hippy-attended "Glastonbury Fayre Festival", Glastonbury, Somerset.
July Tracks for what will become ***Ziggy Stardust*** are recorded.
Dec The Ken Scott-produced ***Hunky Dory*** is released, featuring Ronson, Woodmansey, Trevor Boulder (bass) and Rick Wakeman (piano). With each album release, and driven by his inventive artistic bent, Bowie will enter new musical territory, failing to repeat any particular creative formula.

1972

Jan *Changes*, his first RCA single, gives him a US chart debut at #66. Bowie declares his bisexuality in an interview in **Melody Maker**.
Feb [11] A lengthy UK tour bows with a performance at the "Lanchester Arts Festival", Coventry, W. Midlands, during which the band, led by guitarist Ronson and with Boulder on bass and Woodmansey on drums, acquires the name the Spiders, and Bowie introduces his latest stage personna, Ziggy Stardust.
Apr [5] Bowie plays Oakland-Alameda County Coliseum, Oakland, CA, as ***Hunky Dory*** makes a belated US chart showing at #93, the first Bowie album chart entry anywhere. *Starman* is released as a single.
June ***The Rise And Fall Of Ziggy Stardust And The Spiders From Mars***, providing a theatrical pseudonym basis for Bowie and the band, proves his UK Album chart breakthrough, at #5, and reaches US #75.
July Continuing his astronomical interest, *Starman* hits UK #10 and US #65.
[8] Bowie walks on stage at London's Royal Festival Hall, at a benefit concert for the Save The Whale campaign, and proclaims, "I'm Ziggy". Lou Reed joins him during the set.
Sept [7] Another extensive UK tour ends at the Top Rank, Hanley, Stoke-on-Trent. Quirky *John I'm Only Dancing* is released in the UK, and reaches #12. ***Hunky Dory*** charts in the wake of ***Ziggy Stardust***, now hitting UK #3. (Mott The Hoople's *All The Young Dudes*, written by Bowie, also hits UK #3.)
[22] A US tour by Bowie and the Spiders begins in Cleveland, OH.
[28] Bowie sells out his first-ever New York, NY show at Carnegie Hall.
Nov RCA reissues ***The Man Who Sold The World*** and the first Philips/Mercury album, now retitled ***Space Oddity***, in both the UK and US, which now chart at UK #26, US #105, and at UK #17, US #16 respectively. *The Jean Genie*, written on the road in the US and recorded in New York, hits UK #2, but stalls at US #71.
Dec [24] Bowie, having returned to the UK by sea at the end of the US tour, plays a Christmas Eve concert at the Rainbow Theatre, London.

1973

Jan *Space Oddity* single is reissued by RCA in the US, this time charting at #15 - his first US Top 20 hit.
[25] Always a fearful flier, he departs aboard the US-bound QE2, on a 100-day world tour.
Feb [14] Bowie performs the opening concert of the US leg at Radio City Music Hall, New York.
Mar ***Images 1966-1967***, comprising material recorded while signed to Deram and produced by Mike Vernon, makes US #144.
Apr [7] ***The Rise & Fall Of Ziggy Stardust (Spiders From Mars)*** makes US #75.
[8] Japanese leg of the tour, which includes a performance at Hiroshima, opens in Tokyo.
[28] Lou Reed's *Walk On The Wild Side*, produced by Bowie and Ronson, reaches US #16 and will hit UK #10.
May [5] ***Aladdin Sane***, with songs written during his first US tour, tops the UK chart and goes on to reach US #17. *Drive-In Saturday* hits UK #3. With a new visual image unveiled with each of his album releases, Bowie's reputation as an innovating musical, theatrical and video force is strengthened with each incarnation.
[12] A week after completing the world tour, he plays to 18,000 fans at Earls Court, London, the fisrt rock act to do so.
July [3] A UK tour closes at Hammersmith Odeon, London, with Jeff Beck joining him on stage. Bowie announces he is to retire from live performing - "This show will stay the longest in our memories, not just because it is the end of the tour, but because it is the last show we'll ever do". Although he is genuinely exhausted, it eventually transpires that the Ziggy Stardust fantasy stage persona is being retired, not Bowie.
[14] *Life On Mars*, issued on the strength of its onstage popularity, hits UK #3, his third space-themed UK smash.
Oct [13] *The Laughing Gnome*, a novelty cut reissued by Deram, hits UK #6.
[18] Bowie films US TV show "The Midnight Special" at the Marquee, with guests the Troggs and Marianne Faithfull.
Nov [3] ***Pin-Ups***, featuring Twiggy on the sleeve and containing revivals of Bowie's favorites songs from the '60s, tops the UK Album chart and will reach US #23. The extracted version of the Merseys' *Sorrow* hits UK #3.
[16] Bowie hosts his first US television special, on NBC-TV.
Dec RCA announces that Bowie has sold 1,056,400 albums and 1,024,068 singles for the label thus far.

1974

Feb Lulu's revival of *The Man Who Sold The World*, featuring Bowie's backing vocals and production, hits UK #3.
Mar [2] *Rebel Rebel* UK #5.
Apr He travels to the US, where he will live and work for two years.
May [11] Melodramatic *Rock And Roll Suicide* makes UK #22.
[25] Returning with a self-penned project, ***Diamond Dogs***, recorded in London and Hilversum, Holland, with Tony Newman and Aynsley Dunbar on drums, Herbie Flowers on bass and Mike Garson on keyboards, with a controversial sleeve painting by Belgian artist Guy Peellaert, and featuring *1984* and *Big Brother* from a musical version of "1984", which George Orwell's widow refuses to sanction, hits UK #1 and US #5. *Rebel Rebel* is released as a US single, and peaks at #64.
June [12] ***The Rise & Fall Of Ziggy Stardust (Spiders From Mars)*** is certified gold by the RIAA.
[14] "Diamond Dogs" North American tour, a highly-choreographed and theatrical stage performance drawing on concepts from the album, opens in Montreal, PQ, Canada.
July [13] *Diamond Dogs* reaches UK #21.
[20] The tour closes at Madison Square Garden, New York.
[26] ***Diamond Dogs*** is certified gold by the RIAA.
Oct [12] His revival of Eddie Floyd's *Knock On Wood* hits UK #10.
Nov ***David Live***, recorded at the Tower, Philadelphia, PA, on the "Diamond Dogs" tour, hits UK #2, held off the top by the Bay City Rollers' ***Rollin'***, and US #8.
[7] ***David Live*** is also confirmed gold by the RIAA.

1975

Jan Bowie initiates legal action to break from manager DeFries, and looks towards a new deal with Michael Lippman.
[26] BBC1-TV's "Omnibus" program broadcasts Alan Yentob's "Cracked Actor", a documentary film about Bowie.
Feb Nicolas Roeg signs him to star in "The Man Who Fell To Earth" movie, to play a title role originally cast for Peter O'Toole.
[1] Stuttering *Changes*, a belated US single release, makes #41.
Mar [8] *Young Americans* reaches UK #18.
[29] In another dramatic style turn, ***Young Americans***, showcasing a new soul/funk fusion, hits UK #2, behind Tom Jones' ***20 Greatest Hits***. It was recorded in Philadelphia with Main Ingredient guitarist Carlos Alomar, Willie Weeks on bass and Luther Vandross on backing vocals. John Lennon plays on two tracks.
Apr [12] ***Young Americans*** hits US #9. Bowie announces a second career retirement. "I've rocked my roll. It's a boring dead end. There will be no more rock'n'roll records or tours from me. The last thing I want to be is some useless fucking rock singer."
May [10] *Young Americans* reaches US #28.
July Bowie begins filming "The Man Who Fell To Earth".
[2] ***Young Americans*** is certified gold by the RIAA.
Sept [6] Its second extract *Fame* reaches UK #17.
[20] Co-written with Lennon and Alomar, *Fame* proves his most successful US single thus far, hitting #1 for the first of two weeks.
Oct [17] *Fame* is also confirmed gold by the RIAA.
Nov [4] Bowie premieres *Golden Years* on US TV's "Soul Train".
[8] *Space Oddity*, reissued in the UK on a three-track single with *Changes* and the previously-unreleased *Velvet Goldmine*, tops the UK chart.
Bowie conducts a satellite interview from his Los Angeles, CA home with UK TV interviewer Russell Harty. (The Spanish government wants to use the satellite "up-time" to announce the death of General Franco, but Bowie refuses to give it up.)

1976

Jan [10] *Golden Years*, from a forthcoming album, hits UK #8 and US #10.
[31] ***Station To Station***, comprising six extended tracks, hits UK #5.
Feb [2] A world tour opens in Vancouver, BC, Canada. After firing him, Bowie sues manager Lippman.
[28] ***Station To Station*** hits US #3 having been certified gold by the RIAA two days earlier.
Mar [18] The film premiere of "The Man Who Fell To Earth" in London is not attended by Bowie, who is on tour in the US.
[21] He is arrested with Iggy Pop and others at a Massachusetts hotel, on suspicion of marijuana possession, and is bailed for $2,000. (The case is adjourned and will be dropped a year later.)
[26] The US leg of the world tour ends in New York. He sails for Europe.
Apr [27] After a trip to Moscow, Bowie is detained for hours on a train at the Russian/Polish border, by customs officers who take exception to Nazi books and mementoes found in his luggage. It is apparently research material for a film on Goebbels.
May [3-8] He performs six shows at Wembley, Middx., his first UK gigs in almost three years.
June [5] *TVC 15* makes UK #33 and US #64, as Bowie and Iggy Pop vacation at Château d'Herouville, France, and go into the studio to work on what will be Pop's ***The Idiot***.
July [10] ***Changesonebowie***, a compilation of past hits selected by Bowie, hits UK #2.
[17] ***Changesonebowie*** hits US #10.
Oct [1] He moves to the Schöneberg district of West Berlin, Germany, to live semi-reclusively for three years. He has gone there with Iggy Pop in a mutual (and successful) attempt to kick an addiction to cocaine.
Nov [16] The final mix of the forthcoming ***Low*** is completed at Hansa Studios in Berlin.

1977

Jan ***Low***, co-produced by Bowie and Visconti, but notable as the first in a trilogy of more experimental collaborations with Brian Eno, is released, introducing a dark, densely-synthesized sound, and hits UK #2 and US #11. Bowie wins the US Academy of Science Fiction Fantasy and Horror Films Best Actor Award for "The Man Who Fell To Earth".
Mar *Sound And Vision*, from the album, hits UK #3 but stalls at US #69.
Apr [5] In an unlikely cultural meeting of the minds, Bowie and Pop guest on "The Dinah Shore Show" on US TV.
Sept [9] He appears on Marc Bolan's ITV show "Marc", singing *Heroes* and a duet with Bolan titled *Standing Next To You*. After the show they tape demos, which will not develop due to Bolan's death one week later.
[11] Bowie records a guest appearance on the seasonal TV broadcast "Bing Crosby's Merrie Olde Christmas", duetting with Crosby on *The Little Drummer Boy*. (Crosby will die a month later, before the show is screened, but the duet will be a UK hit five years hence.)
[20] Bowie attends Bolan's funeral and will set up a Trust Fund for Bolan's son, Rolan.
Oct Co-penned with Eno, *Heroes* reaches UK #24. French-and German-language versions are also released.
[22] ***Heroes***, another recording at the Hansa Studios, Berlin, with major contributions from Brian Eno and Robert Fripp, and featuring long-time side musician Alomar, hits UK #3.
Dec [10] ***Heroes*** makes US #35.

1978

Feb [4] *Beauty And The Beast*, from ***Heroes***, makes UK #39. While Bowie and his wife Angie separate, he begins filming the David Hemmings-directed "Just A Gigolo" in Berlin, with Sydne Rome and Marlene Dietrich.
Mar [29] A world tour starts at the Sports Arena, San Diego, CA, following rehearsals in Dallas, TX, with tour musicians Alomar (guitar), Roger Powell and Sean Mayes (keyboards), George Murray (bass), Dennis Davis (drums) and Simon House (violin).
May [9] The US leg of the tour ends at Madison Square Garden, New York.
[14] Bowie embarks on the European portion in Hamburg, W. Germany.
June [10] RCA's new version of Prokofiev's ***Peter And The Wolf***, which Bowie narrates, with Eugene Ormandy conducting the Philadelphia Orchestra, makes US #136.
[14-16] The UK leg of the tour begins at the City Hall, Newcastle, Tyne & Wear, set to end on July 1st at London's Earls Court.
Sept The 1964 King Bees single *Liza Jane* is reissued in the UK.
[30] Double live album ***Stage***, recorded at the Spectrum, Philadelphia, on April 28th and 29th, hits UK #5.
Nov [11] His global tour recommences in Adelaide, S. Australia, Australia.
[16] The world premiere of "Just A Gigolo" screens in West Berlin.
Dec [2] ***Stage*** makes US #44.
[6] The Japanese concert leg begins in Osaka, set to end in Tokyo on the 12th.
[9] EP *Breaking Glass* peaks at UK #54.

1979

Apr [23] Once again co-written with Eno, *Boys Keep Swinging* premieres on BBC1-TV's "Kenny Everett Video Show".
May *Boys Keep Swinging* hits UK #7.
[20] Bowie selects his favorite records on BBC Radio 1's "Star Special".
June [2] ***Lodger***, recorded at the Mountain Studios, Montreux, Switzerland (where Bowie will subsequently choose to live), hits UK #4.
July [14] ***Lodger*** peaks at US #20.
Aug The extracted *D.J.* reaches UK #29.
Dec Unissued 1975 and 1972 versions of *John I'm Only Dancing (Again) (1975)/John I'm Only Dancing (1972)* make UK #12.
[31] He performs an acoustic version of *Space Oddity* on "The Kenny Everett New Year TV Show".

1980

Feb [8] Divorce becomes final between Bowie and Angie. He gains custody of son Zowie, now known as Joe. Angie receives a £30,000 settlement.
Mar Bowie's interpretation of Brecht/Weill's *Alabama Song*, coupled with an acoustic *Space Oddity* climbs to UK #23.
June Bowie researches the history of John Merrick, the Elephant Man, in London, prior to portraying him on stage in the US.
July [29] He opens in Denver, CO, in title role of "The Elephant Man", breaking the venue's box-office record and receiving strong notices.
Aug [23] *Ashes To Ashes*, a continuation of the "Major Tom" saga introduced in *Space Oddity*, and accompanied as ever by a visually-striking and innovative David Mallet-produced video, becomes Bowie's second UK #1 single.
Sept [23] He takes over the role of John Merrick in "The Elephant Man" from Jeff Hayenga, at the Booth Theatre on Broadway, New York.
[27] Returning to the more accessible rock structure of his early '70s period, ***Scary Monsters And Super Creeps*** hits UK #1 and makes US #12.
Oct He films a cameo appearance for the German movie "Christiane F".
Nov [22] *Fashion* hits UK #5.

1981

Jan [3] He plays his final night in "The Elephant Man" on Broadway.
[10] *Fashion* restores Bowie to the US Hot 100 chart, at #70.
[24] K-tel-compiled 16-track, TV-advertised ***The Best Of David Bowie*** hits UK #3, while *Scary Monsters (And Super Creeps)* reaches UK #20.
Reissues of ***Hunky Dory*** and ***The Rise And Fall Of Ziggy Stardust*** make UK #32 and #33 respectively.
Feb [24] He wins the #1 Male Singer category at the annual UK Rock & Pop Awards, sponsored by the **Daily Mirror**.
Apr [4] *Up The Hill Backwards* makes UK #32.
July In Montreux, Switzerland, where he is now based, Bowie records a vocal for Giorgio Moroder's theme for the forthcoming film "Cat People", and also joins Queen in the studio, where they collaborate on *Under Pressure*.
Aug He takes the title role in Bertolt Brecht's "Baal", in a production filmed by BBC-TV.
Sept [15] ***Changesonebowie*** is certified platinum by the RIAA.
Nov [21] Co-written and co-performed by Queen and Bowie, *Under Pressure*, highlighted by vocal interplay with Freddie Mercury, hits UK #1.
Dec [12] RCA-issued acoustic guitar-led *Wild Is The Wind* reaches UK #24.

1982

Jan [9] *Under Pressure* reaches US #29.
[16] A further hits collection ***Changestwobowie*** makes UK #24 and US #68.
Feb "Christiane F", a huge box-office hit in Germany, is shown in the US, having premiered in the UK in December.
Mar [2] "Baal" airs on BBC-TV.
[13] *Baal's Hymn*, a five-song EP of songs from the play, reaches UK #29.
Aladdin Sane reissue makes UK #49.
He starts filming "The Hunger", a vampire fantasy co-starring Catherine Deneuve and Susan Sarandon.
Apr [10] ***Christiane F*** soundtrack, featuring nine Bowie cuts, makes US #135.
[24] *Cat People (Putting Out Fire)*, the movie theme with Bowie's vocal, makes UK #26.
May [8] *Cat People (Putting Out Fire)* peaks at US #67.
Sept He begins filming "Merry Christmas Mr. Lawrence" in the Pacific, with co-stars Tom Conti and Ryuichi Sakamoto.
Nov Work ends on "Merry Christmas Mr. Lawrence" and he flies to New York for album recording sessions.
Dec [25] His 1977 duet with Bing Crosby, *Peace On Earth-Little Drummer Boy*, hits UK #3.

1983

Jan [27] He signs a new five-year recording contract in New York with EMI America Records, reportedly worth $10 million.
Rare reissue reaches UK #34.
Apr [23] ***Let's Dance***, produced with Nile Rodgers, and guesting co-Chic veterans Bernard Edwards and Tony Thompson, featuring guitarist Stevie Ray Vaughan among others, hits UK #1 and US #4.
The reissued ***Pin-Ups*** and ***The Man Who Sold The World*** make UK #57 and #64 respectively.
May [9] His debut 45 for EMI, the self-penned *Let's Dance*, with a notable guitar part by Vaughan, hits UK #1, where it will stay for three weeks.
[21] *Let's Dance* also tops the US chart, becoming the first Bowie single to make pole position in both the US and UK.
Diamond Dogs reissue makes UK #60.
[30] Prior to touring, he tops the bill of the "US 83 Festival" in San Bernardino, CA, being paid a record fee of $1 million.
June [2] His "Serious Moonlight 83" UK tour opens at Wembley Arena, Wembley. Each show is sold out on the day of announcement.
[16] *Let's Dance* is certified gold by the RIAA, his first since *Fame*.
[27] ***Let's Dance*** is also confirmed platinum by the RIAA.
China Girl, an older song co-penned with Iggy Pop, hits UK #2 (and US #10), despite a BBC ban on its video (which includes a brief nude sex scene).
Reissued ***Heroes*** and ***Low*** make UK #75 and #85 respectively.

July [12] Having recently received the Gold Ticket Award for playing to over 100,000 fans at New York's Madison Square Garden, the "Serious Moonlight 83" North American leg opens in Montreal.
Aug An incomplete nine-track compilation of later RCA highlights, ***Golden Years***, makes UK #33 and US #99.
[3] ***Aladdin Sane*** is certified gold by the RIAA.
Oct *Modern Love* hits UK #2 and US #14.
Nov [24] The Pacific leg of the tour opens in New Zealand.
Ziggy Stardust - The Motion Picture, the album of Bowie's final tour as Ziggy Stardust, reaches UK #17 and US #89. RCA's ***White Light, White Heat*** makes UK #46.
Dec [12] The "Serious Moonlight 83" tour closes in Bangkok, Thailand.

1984

Feb [21] Bowie wins the Best British Male Artist category at the third annual BRIT Awards, at the Grosvenor House Hotel, London.
Mar [10] *Without You* peaks at US #73.
Apr ***Fame And Fashion***, comprising more RCA greatest hits, makes UK #40 and US #147.
[19] *Let's Dance* is named International Hit Of The Year at the 29th annual Ivor Novello Awards lunch, at the Grosvenor House Hotel, London.
May Reissued Deram album ***Love You Till Tuesday*** makes UK #53.
Sept [18] Bowie wins the Best Male Video category for "China Girl" and shares the Video Vanguard Award with the Beatles at the inaugural MTV Video Music Awards, held at Radio City Music Hall, New York, hosted by Dan Aykroyd and Bette Midler.
[28] His 22-minute film "Jazzin' For Blue Jean" airs on C4's "The Tube".
[29] *Blue Jean*, boosted by a Julien Temple-helmed video, hits UK #6.
Oct [6] ***Tonight***, despite lukewarm reviews, tops the UK chart and will reach US #11. Co-produced by Bowie with Hugh Padgham and Derek Bramble (with strings arranged by Arif Mardin), guests include Tina Turner and longtime cohort Iggy Pop.
Nov [3] *Blue Jean* hits US #8.
[21] ***Tonight*** is certified platinum by the RIAA.
Dec [22] *Tonight*, penned with Pop and featuring Turner, charts at #53 in both the UK and the US.

1985

Feb Bowie links with highly-rated jazz fusion group, the Pat Metheny Band, on *This Is Not America*, the theme for the movie "The Falcon And The Snowman" (in which he does not appear). It reaches UK #14.
[26] "David Bowie" wins the Best Video, Short Form category at the 27th annual Grammy Awards.
Mar [23] *This Is Not America* makes US #32.
June *Loving The Alien* reaches UK #19.
[29] Bowie records a revival of Martha & the Vandellas' *Dancing In The Street* with Mick Jagger, for the forthcoming "Live Aid" fundraising event.
July [13] He performs at the historic "Live Aid" benefit concert at Wembley Stadium, Wembley, during which the video clip for *Dancing In The Street* also receives its world premiere.
Sept [7] *Dancing In The Street* enters the UK chart at #1, where it stays for a month, with all income going directly to the Band Aid Trust.
Oct [12] *Dancing In The Street* hits US #7.

1986

Mar His title theme from the Temple-directed movie "Absolute Beginners", in which he has a character part, hits UK #2.
Apr "Absolute Beginners" opens in the UK, to mixed reviews.
May [3] *Absolute Beginners* peaks at US #53.
July *Underground*, the theme from "Labyrinth", a spectacular children's fantasy film in which Bowie plays the Goblin King, reaches UK #21.
Sept [15] The video for "Dancing In The Street" wins the Best Overall Performance category at the third annual MTV Video Music Awards, broadcast simultaneously from the Universal Amphitheatre, Universal City, CA and the Palladium, New York.
Nov He records the theme for the full-length cartoon film "When The Wind Blows", which deals with nuclear holocaust. It makes UK #44.

1987

Mar Bowie performs a short set as part of a press conference at the Players Theatre, Charing Cross, London, at which he announces a new deal with EMI America and a forthcoming world tour. Erstwhile schoolmate Peter Frampton plays guitar.
Apr *Day In-Day Out* reaches UK #17 and US #21. BBC-TV bans the promo video, claiming it "contains disturbing images". Meanwhile, Bowie flies around the world with his new live backing band (including Frampton), holding a series of press conferences/performances to announce dates and venues of the upcoming "Glass Spider" tour.
May [2] With a central rhythm section of Frampton, Alomar and multi-instrumentalist Erdal Kizilcay, and somehow featuring actor Mickey Rourke rapping on the track *Making My Love*, ***Never Let Me Down*** hits UK #6 and will reach US #34, while the "Glass Spider" 1987 world tour, featuring Frampton as lead guitarist, gets underway in Rotterdam, Holland.
[23] *Day-In Day-Out* reaches US #21.
June Guest acts on individual "Glass Spider" tour dates in UK cities include Alison Moyet, Big Country, and Terence Trent D'Arby.
July *Time Will Crawl*, taken from the album, peaks at UK #33.
[8] ***Never Let Me Down*** is certified gold by the RIAA. Bowie is honored with the Silver Clef Award for Outstanding Achievement at the annual Nordoff Robbins Music Therapy lunch in London.
Sept [11] He performs at the fourth annual MTV Video Music Awards, held at the Universal Amphitheatre, Universal City.
[26] Co-penned with Alomar, *Never Let Me Down* makes UK #34 and US #27.
Oct [9] Wanda Lee Nichols alleges that Bowie sexually assaulted her "in a Dracula-like fashion" in a Dallas, TX, hotel room after a "Glass Spider" tour concert.

1988

Apr Bowie plays a benefit gig at the ICA, London, with guitarist Reeves Gabrels.
May "Glass Spider 1" and "2" videos are released, chronicling performances from Bowie's last major trek.
Aug Bowie appears as Pontius Pilate in Martin Scorsese's controversial movie "The Last Temptation Of Christ".
Dec With little back-catalog action and devoid of new material, this month marks the end of the first year that Bowie has not appeared on either the UK Singles or Albums charts since 1971.

1989

Apr Bowie selects small Massachusetts label Rykodisc to reissue his 18 back-catalog albums on compact disc.
May He enthusiastically returns to a two-guitar, bass and drums line-up for his new band, Tin Machine, and enlists Gabrels and Tony and Hunt Sales (with whom he worked in 1977 on an Iggy Pop album).
[31] Tin Machine makes its live debut at the first International Music Awards, in New York, playing *Heaven's In Here*.
June [3] Tin Machine's eponymous debut album which includes a version of John Lennon's *Working Class Hero*, hits UK #3 and begins its rise to US #28.
[14] Tin Machine makes its US stage debut at the World Ballroom, New York.
Bowie is confirmed as musical director of the forthcoming film, "The Delinquents", starring Kylie Minogue, though his actual involvement will diminish. Tin Machine tour dates begin at the Kilburn National Ballroom, London, while ***Tin Machine*** reaches US #28.
July [1] Hinting at commercial failure for the Tin Machine project, extracted *Under The God* stalls at UK #52.
Sept [9] Tin Machine's *Tin Machine*, twinned with a live cover version of Bob Dylan's *Maggie's Farm*, stalls at UK #48.
Oct First Rykodisc collection, ***Sound + Vision***, anthologizing past hits and unreleased rarities, peaks at US #97.

1990

Jan [23] Bowie holds a London press conference to announce his forthcoming, and final, global concert tour, "The Sound And Vision World Tour 1990", set to begin on March 3rd in Quebec, PQ, Canada, during which he will invite each local audience to decide on the "greatest hits" running order of each show, a process organized via voting polls through local radio stations.
Feb [12] Sexual-assault suit by Nichols against Bowie is dismissed by a Dallas Federal judge (although Bowie admits spending the night with her).
[21] ***Sound + Vision*** wins Best Album Package at the 32nd annual Grammy Awards, at the Shrine Auditorium, Los Angeles.
Mar [19] UK leg of the world tour bows.
[31] Not to be confused with earlier volumes, a new retrospective hits collection, ***Changesbowie***, debuts at UK #1, and will remain charted for 26 weeks.
Apr [2] Bowie is honored with the Outstanding Contribution To British Music trophy at the 35th annual Ivor Novello Awards luncheon, held at the Grosvenor House Hotel, London.
[14] Fashionably-updated *Fame 90*, included on the multiplatinum selling ***Pretty Woman*** soundtrack album, remixed by Jon Gass and featuring Queen Latifah, reaches UK #28. Bowie's RCA-catalog albums are finally made available on CD, now licensed to EMI in the UK but to Rykodisc in the US. Demand for them and the original artwork vinyl albums, also once again available, returns most titles to the chart, ***Hunky Dory***, ***The Man Who Sold The World*** and ***Space Oddity*** making UK #39, #66 and #64 respectively.
May [19] ***Changesonebowie*** reaches US #39.
[26] While *Pink Rose*, a Bowie collaboration with Adrian Belew, is released in the US on Atlantic, the popularity of his "Sound & Vision Tour" is highlighted by a $1,117,086 box-office take for one performance, supported by Lenny Kravitz, at Dodger Stadium, Los Angeles.
June [21] U2's Bono joins Bowie onstage at the Richfield Coliseum, Cleveland, OH, singing *Gloria*.
[23] The most in-demand UK reissue proves to be ***The Rise And Fall Of Ziggy Stardust***, which makes UK #25.
July [14] Reissued ***The Rise And Fall Of Ziggy Stardust*** makes US #93.
[28] Rereleased ***Aladdin Sane*** charts for a week at UK #43, while ***Pinups*** peaks at UK #52.
Aug [4-5] Further UK dates include two open-air concerts at Milton Keynes Bowl, Milton Keynes, Bucks. (By the tour's end, Bowie will have played 110 shows in 15 countries.)
Oct [27] Reissued ***Diamond Dogs*** charts for a week at UK #67.

1991

Mar [29] ***Changesbowie*** is certified platinum by the RIAA.
May [4] ***Young Americans*** and ***Station To Station*** re-chart at UK #54 and UK #57 respectively while ***Low*** charts for a week at UK #64 on Sept [7].
June [2] Bowie joins Morrissey onstage during his encore at the Great Western Forum, Inglewood, CA, duetting on Marc Bolan's *Cosmic Dancer*.
July [7] Bowie guest stars in HBO-TV's "Dream On" as film director Sir Rowland Moorecock.
Aug [13] With Tin Machine, Bowie plays his first live session for Radio 1 in 19 years, performing on the Mark Goodier evening show.
[14] Tin Machine appears on BBC-1 TV's "Wogan", performing *You Belong In Rock n' Roll*, which will peak at UK #33 on the 24th.
Sept [6] The band is featured on ABC-TV's "In

Concert".
[14] ***Tin Machine II*** enters at its UK #23 peak (and will peak at US # 126 the following week). Although the album remains on both surveys for only three weeks, an undaunted Bowie takes the rock troupe on a second round of concert dates in the UK and US.
Nov [2] The extracted *Baby Universal* reaches UK #48, the same day that Tin Machine's UK tour opens at the Civic Hall, Wolverhampton, W. Midlands.
[23] During month-end US dates, Tin Machine performs on NBC-TV's "Saturday Night Live".

1992

Feb [27] Bowie attends Elizabeth Taylor's 60th birthday party celebrations at Disneyland, Anaheim, CA.
Apr Rykodisc reissues ***Scary Monsters*** with four additional tracks.
[20] Bowie performs at "A Concert For Life : Freddie Mercury Tribute", a fundraising AIDS benefit honoring the late Queen vocalist.
[24] He marries 36-year-old Somalian veteran model Iman in a civil ceremony at the City Hall, Lausanne, Switzerland. (They will marry in a church ceremony in Florence, Italy, on June 6th.)
Aug As Bowie reunites for sessions with producer Nile Rodgers, he inks a recording deal with fledgling US label Savage.
[22] *Real Cool World*, featured in the Kim Basinger-voiced cartoon caper "Cool World" movie, charts for a week at UK #53.
Sept Bowie appears on the front cover of **Architectural Digest** (the first human to do so since 1988). This issue includes a pictorial guide through his home in Mustique and a short interview in which he says: "My ambition is to make music so incredibly uncompromised that I will have absolutely no audience left whatsoever, and then I'll be able to spend the entire year on the island." True to his word, Bowie has recently released a final Tin Machine album, the live ***Oy Vey Baby***, in August (its title, a pun on U2's current release, ***Achtung Baby***).
Nov [1] Bowie attends a rally for Presidential nominee Bill Clinton at the Brendan Byrne Arena, East Rutherford, NJ.
Dec "Twin Peaks: Fire Walk With Me", David Lynch's feature-length movie, including a cameo role by Bowie, opens in the US (and follows his 1991 acting foray, "The Linguine Incident", co-starring Rosanna Arquette).

1993

Feb Instrumentalist Philip Glass releases ***Low***, a symphonic treatment of Bowie and Eno's 1977 album collaboration, featuring the names and photographs of all three artists on its front cover.
Apr [3] *Jump They Say* hits UK #9.
[17] ***Black Tie White Noise***, Bowie's first solo album since 1987, debuts at UK #1. His label debut for Savage Records, it reunites him both co-producer Nile Rodgers and with early career guitar sidesman, Mick Ronson.
[24] ***Black Tie White Noise*** debuts at its US #39 peak.
[30] Aged 46, Ronson dies of liver cancer in England. Bowie issues a short statement: "I miss him terribly."
May [12] Bowie guests on NBC-TV's "Late Night With David Letterman".
[29] A third compilation in the series, ***Changesbowie*** bows at UK #56.
June Financially-strapped Savage Records goes under, therefore unable to service Bowie's current album and leaving the artist in search of a new recording contract.
[12] Title track *Black Tie White Noise*, featuring Al B. Sure!, debuts at its UK #36 peak.
Oct [23] *Miracle Goodnight* debuts at its UK #40 peak.
Nov [20] ***The Singles Collection***, released by EMI, bows at its UK #9 peak. (Rykodisc releases a two-CD set, ***The Singles: 1969-1993 Featuring His Greatest Hits***, in the US.)
Dec [1] Bowie participates in the "Concert Of Hope" at Wembley Arena, with George Michael, Annie Lennox, k.d. lang and Simply Red.
[4] *Buddha Of Suburbia* debuts at its UK #35 peak. It is the title theme to the simultaneously released ***Buddha Of Suburbia***, Bowie's first complete television soundtrack (and includes music guest Lenny Kravitz).

1994

May [7] Performance album ***Santa Monica '72***, released on the Trident label (UK) peaks at UK #74.
June [23] Bowie hooks up to American OnLine in New York to promote "Jump : The David Bowie Interactive CD-ROM".
Dec He becomes a patron of War Child, the music industry charity set up to raise funds for a music centre for children in Bosnia.

1995

June [13] Bowie films on location in New York as Andy Warhol for the forthcoming film "Basquiat". (He will also attend the graduation of his son, Duncan Jones, from Wooster College, Wooster, OH.)
Sept [14] He embarks on six-week US "Outside Tour" at the Meadows Music Theatre, Hartford, CT, supported by Nine Inch Nails, a bill grossing $251,025 from 10,838 attendees. The tour will end on October 29th at the Great Western Forum.
[23] From his forthcoming album, *The Heart's Filthy Lesson* debuts at its UK #35 peak.
Oct [7] Newly signed to Virgin Records (worldwide), ***Outside***, with Bowie assuming seven different character roles in a concept album based around a bizarre murder, and marking a collaborative reunion with producer Brian Eno, hits UK #8 in its week of entry.
[14] *The Heart's Filthy Lesson* bows at its US #92 high, as ***Outside*** debuts at its US #21 peak.
Nov [7] Bowie and Eno receive the Inspiration Award at the annual **Q** Awards at London's Park Lane Hotel, the same day ***Sound + Vision*** is certified gold by the RIAA in the US.
[14-15, 17-18] "The Outsiders" UK tour, with Morrissey opening for Bowie, opens at Wembley Arena, set to end on December 8th at Manchester's Nynex Arena.
[23] He performs *The Man Who Sold The World* at the second annual MTV Europe Music Awards held in Paris, France.
Dec [2] *Strangers When We Meet*, backed with *The Man Who Sold The World (Live)*, bows at its UK #39 peak the same day Bowie appears on BBC2-TV's "Later With Jools Holland".
[18] Savage Records files a $100 million breach-of-contract suit against Bowie, his management company Isolar and BMG in New York Supreme State Court, charging that they "engaged in a fraudulent common scheme which was intended to and actually did destroy (the) plaintiffs' business causing (the) plaintiffs to lose their exclusive rights over Bowie albums and videos and suffer monetary damages in excess of $20 million".
[31] Bowie guests on C4-TV's "The White Room New Year Special" with Oasis, Stevie Wonder, PM Dawn, Pulp and Jimmy Cliff.

1996

Jan [17] David Byrne inducts Bowie into the Rock and Roll Hall of Fame at the 11th annual dinner held at New York's Waldorf Astoria Hotel.
Feb [19] Bowie receives the Outstanding Contribution To British Music honor at the 15th annual BRIT Awards at London's Earl's Court, at which he also performs with the Pet Shop Boys.
Mar [2] Taken from ***Outside***, *Hallo Spaceboy* enters at its UK #12 peak.

THE BOX TOPS

Alex Chilton (guitar, vocals); **Gary Talley** (guitar); **John Evans** (organ); **Bill Cunningham** (bass, piano); **Danny Smythe** (drums)

1967

Mar Memphis Central High School student Chilton (b. Dec. 28, 1950, Memphis, TN) has been recommended by Jimmy Newman, a mutual friend, as a talented vocalist to join Ronnie & the Devilles, a white soul group formed in Memphis, initially comprising Ronnie Jordan (keyboardist), Evans and Smythe (a three-time winner on the "Ted Mack Amateur Hour" radio broadcast), together with Russ Caccamisi (bass) and Richard Malone (lead guitar). With Jordan having left early on, the group has already cut a few sides at American Recording Studios (including covers of Floyd Cramer's *Last Date* and Thomas Wayne's *Tragedy*) for producer Chips Moman's private label, Youngstown Records. Dan Penn, a writer/producer working at the studio, now introduces the group to a Wayne Thompson composition, *The Letter*, which they duly record under Penn's direction, prior to line-up changes which will see Caccamisi leave to study engineering on a college scholarship (and eventually work for Rank Xerox), replaced on bass by Evans. Cunningham (b. Jan. 23, 1950, Memphis) is recruited as a new keyboard player and Malone, whose air force father has been transferred to San Diego, CA, is replaced by Talley (b. Aug. 17, 1947, Memphis), from local band the In Crowd. Bell Records executives, in town from New York to collect some Purify Brothers recordings, sign the group, whose name is changed by manager Roy Mack to the Box Tops.
July Bell subsidiary label Mala releases *The Letter* (which clocks in at 1 minute and 58 minutes), and the group performs the song live on the local "The Jerry Blavet Show".
Sept [23] With Chilton still a high-school student, *The Letter* tops the US chart, where it will stay for four weeks.
[25] *The Letter* is certified gold by the RIAA.
Oct [21] *The Letter* hits UK #5, while the Box Tops open selected concert dates for the Beach Boys (having already supported Wilson Pickett, Carla Thomas and the Staples Singers during a regional tour of the Carolinas). Further line-up changes have seen session men enlisted for the recording of their debut album, with Evans quitting to enroll at Memphis State University (partly avoiding the draft), Cunningham switching to keyboards and Rick Allen (b. Jan. 28, 1946, Little Rock, AR) joining on bass. (Evans will reappear as a member of the Maffers in 1973.)
Dec *Neon Rainbow* reaches US #24. Smythe now quits, replaced by Thomas Boggs (b. July 16, 1947, Wynn, AR), while Chilton's contract is renegotiated by his father.

1968

Feb [3] ***The Letter/Neon Rainbow*** makes US #87.
Apr *Cry Like A Baby*, featuring a distinctive electric sitar solo by Reggie Young, hits US #2 and UK #15.
May [2] Its title hit *Cry Like A Baby* is certified gold by the RIAA.
[17] With the line-up temporarily settled as Chilton, Allen, Cunningham, Talley and Boggs, the Box Tops make their New York debut, at the Space Club.
June *Choo Choo Train* reaches US #26.
[2] ***Cry Like A Baby*** makes US #59.
Oct Gospel-flavored *I Met Her In Church* makes US #37.

1969

Feb *Sweet Cream Ladies, Forward March* reaches US #28.
[22] ***The Box Tops Super Hits*** makes US #45.
May Bob Dylan-inked *I Shall Be Released* peaks at US #67. Further personnel upheavals see Allen leave, Cunningham return to bass, and Jerry Riley join to

replace original guitarist Talley, while Boggs quits, to be replaced by Bobby Gudiotti.
Aug The group returns to the US Top 20 with *Soul Deep* (#18), which is also their third and last UK hit #22. Constantly on the road in the US, the band cancels a scheduled UK tour.
Sept [27] ***Dimensions*** makes US #77.
Nov *Turn On A Dream* peaks at US #58. By year's end Chilton has married and fathered a son, and Cunningham has quit (he will earn a degree in music before going on to play string bass in the President Orchestra in the '70s), replaced by Swain Scharfer.

1970

Mar Their final chart hit *You Keep Tightening Up On Me* (US #92) is released on Bell. Dogged by a volatile and ever-changing line-up, the band splits. Chilton returns to Memphis to form Big Star with its co-songwriter and guitarist Chris Bell (b. Jan. 12, 1951, Memphis), also enlisting bassist Andy Hummel (b. Jan. 26, 1951, Memphis) and drummer Jody Stephens (b. Oct. 4, 1952, Memphis). Attempting to combine Beatle-style harmonies with a punchy guitar style (subsequently termed "power pop"), they will sign to Terry Manning's Memphis-based Ardent label in 1972 and record ***#1 Record*** and ***Radio City*** in 1974, before splitting in 1975.

1978

July Big Star's ***#1 Record/Radio City*** is released in the UK for the first time, as a double package. Previously unavailable and recorded prior to Big Star's demise, ***Third Album*** also belatedly appears on the UK Aura label. US label Ryko will bring Big Star and Chris Bell recordings to compact disc in March 1992. (Chilton will subsequently release two solo albums, ***One Day In New York*** and ***Like Flies On Sherbert***, and play occasional club dates.)
Dec [28] Bell is killed in the early hours in an car accident, when his Triumph TR6 hits a telephone pole on Poplar Avenue, Memphis.

1989

Nov [12] The Box Tops reunite for a one-off benefit gig for Nashville Cares at the Ace of Clubs, Nashville, TN, with a line-up of Chilton, Evans (who now manages a music store in West Memphis, AR), Talley (currently a Nashville session guitarist and photographer), Cloud (bass), Gene Houston (drums) and Jay Spell (additional keyboards). (Cunningham now owns an import clothing store in Washington, DC; Smythe is an award-winning commercial artist living in Memphis; Allen lives in Memphis and plays with local oldies band the GTOs, and Boggs is part-owner of Huey's, a popular bar in downtown Memphis, and still plays drums with country outfit, the Settlers. In July 1995, Ardent Records (US) announces the imminent release of the "lost" Alex Chilton album ***1969***, recorded between Box Tops and Big Star projects in Memphis in late 1969.

BOY GEORGE

1986

July George (b. George O'Dowd, June 14, 1961, Eltham, Kent), who - at age 15 - modelled hairstyles for **The Hairdressers' Journal** and was expelled from Eltham Green High School, having made his final album ***From Luxury To Heartache*** with the globally-successful Culture Club, which is in the process of disbanding, makes a brief appearance at an anti-apartheid concert on London's Clapham Common. He has lost his familiar chubbiness, arrives inexplicably covered in flour and introduces himself as "your favorite junkie". Within a week, his brother, fearing for George's life, leaks the story of the singer's heroin addiction to the press. The pop star, who had publicly denounced drugs, is now himself an addict.
[12] The police arrest George, his friend Marilyn and several others for possession of drugs. No sooner have the headlines slipped off the front pages than New York keyboardist Michael Rudetski, who played on the final Culture Club album and was signed up for another, dies of a drug overdose in George's home. (Rudetski's parents later take unsuccessful legal action against George for contributing to their son's death.) Subsequently appearing in court on the drugs charge, George tells the court he will undertake Dr. Meg Patterson's electronic "black box" treatment to cure his addiction.

1987

Feb Publicly stating that he is cured on BBC1-TV chat show "Wogan", George confirms Culture Club's split and discusses his ambitions for a solo career.
Mar George's remake of Bread's *Everything I Own*, a copy of Ken Boothe's 1974 reggae-style chart-topper, hits UK #1.
May George sings Blue Mink's 1969 UK # hit *Melting Pot* on the last ever C4-TV show "The Tube".
June [13] *Keep Me In Mind* reaches UK #29.
[27] His debut solo album, the mostly self-penned ***Sold***, co-produced by Glenn Skinner and Stewart Levine, peaks at UK #29 in its week of entry.
July The extracted title track *Sold* reaches UK #24.
Aug ***Sold*** makes US #145.
Nov Fourth track from the album, *To Be Reborn*, co-written with Lamont Dozier, climbs to UK #13.

1988

Feb [20] *Live My Life*, from the film soundtrack to "Hiding Out", makes US #40.
Mar *Live My Life* peaks at UK #62.
June *No Clause 28*, a song about the British government's decision to ban the promotion of homosexuality by local authorities, peaks at UK #57.
Oct *Don't Cry* peaks at UK #60.

1989

Jan [22] Appearing on BBC Radio's "Desert Island Discs", George selects *Blowin' In The Wind* (Marlene Dietrich), *It Must Be Love* (Madness), *If I Were Your Woman* (Gladys Knight), *Life's A Gas* (Marc Bolan), *Stormy Weather* (Elizabeth Welch), *When A Man Loves A Woman* (Ella Fitzgerald), *Woman To Woman* (Shirley Brown) and *War Baby* (Tom Robinson).
Mar *Don't Take My Mind On A Trip* peaks at UK #68.
Apr Its parent album ***High Hat***, having failed to make the UK survey, peaks at US #126.
Nov George's new band, Jesus Loves You, makes UK #68 with *After The Love*, on his own recently-formed label, More Protein.

1991

Feb [23] Now a member of the Hare Krishna movement (he recorded an album with Asha Bhosle in Bombay, India the previous year), his *Bow Down Mister*, with a Krishna-promoting sleeve and lyrics, debuts at its UK #69 peak.
Apr [13] Jesus Loves You's ***The Martyr Mantras*** spends a week at UK #60.
Nov George appears at Butlin's Holiday Camp, Bognor Regis, W. Sussex, with Jesus Loves You (on a bill also featuring Jools Holland, Bad Manners and Limahl).
Dec [1] He performs at the "Red Hot & Dance" AIDS benefit concert.

1992

Sept [10] George appears on BBC-1 TV's "Top Of The Pops", performing *The Crying Game*.
[26] *The Crying Game* reaches UK #22. Produced by the Pet Shop Boys, his cover of the 1964 Dave Berry UK #5 is the title theme to the hit movie "The Crying Game". George has only agreed to record the song after seeing rushes from the Neil Jordan film.
Dec [12] Jesus Loves You's *Sweet Toxic Love* charts for a week at UK #65.
[13] He appears on BBC-2 TV's "The Ozone", during the month when his More Protein label will fold.

1993

May [15] *The Crying Game* reaches US #15, as George continues working on his autobiography, **Take It Like A Man**, with writer Spencer Bright.
June [19] PM Dawn's *More Than Likely*, featuring George, makes UK #40.
Oct [16] ***At Worst ... The Best Of ...***, a career collection comprising George's material with Culture Club, Jesus Loves You and his solo work, reaches UK #24.
Dec [4] ***At Worst ... The Best Of ...*** peaks at US #169.
[16] He plays a one-off London concert at Hammersmith's Labatts Apollo.
[31] George performs on New Year's Eve at New York's Beacon Theatre.

1994

Mar [12] ***The Devil In Sister George***, a further compilation of tracks from Culture Club, Jesus Loves You and solo George, reaches UK #26 in its week of entry.
May [30] George performs live on ITV's "21 Years Of Virgin Records".
Aug [30] A California woman's paternity suit against George is thrown out of a British court.

1995

Jan [19] George appears at the "Commitment To Life VIII" AIDS benefit, honoring Elton Johns, Tom Hanks and Ron Meyer at the Universal Amphitheatre, Universal City, CA.
Apr [1] His cover of Iggy Pop's *Funtime* bows at its UK #45 peak.
[24] George's autobiography **Take It Like A Man** is published by HarperCollins.
June [3] ***Cheapness And Beauty***, produced by 24-year-old Jessica Corcoran, whom George had discovered through her production of Shed Seven's *Dolphin* single, makes UK #44.
[24] George takes part in the "Gay Pride Festival in London's Victoria Park.
July [8] *Il Adore* makes UK #50.
Aug Kirk Brandon begins a High Court action against George, following the latter's assertion in his autobiography that they had an affair and alluded to in the track *Unfinished Business* on ***Cheapness And Beauty***.
Oct [21] *Same Thing In Reverse* charts for a week at UK #56.
Nov [17] George performs at the Limelight in New York during his current US tour. (He reportedly finances it himself after severing ties with Virgin, citing the company's lack of support in the US for his latest album.)
see also: **CULTURE CLUB**

BOYZ II MEN

Wanya Morris (vocals); **Michael McCary** (vocals); **Shawn Stockman** (vocals); **Nathan Morris** (vocals)

1990

Having formed at Philadelphia, PA's High School of Creative and Performing Arts in 1988, Wanya Morris (b. July 29, 1973, Philadelphia), Nathan Morris (b. June 18, 1971, Philadelphia), McCary (b. Dec. 16, 1972, Philadelphia) and Stockman (b. Sept. 26, 1972, Philadelphia), who have performed at talent shows in Delaware and New Jersey, meet New Edition/Bell Biv DeVoe vocalist Michael Bivins, who is appearing at a radio-sponsored show at Philadelphia's Civic Center. As he leaves the stage they begin singing for him. Two months later he invites them to dinner at Sylvia's in New York, before signing them as the second act to his newly-formed Biv Entertainment company, which has a licensing deal with Motown.

1991

Aug [24] The quartet's freshman R&B album ***Cooleyhighharmony***, comprising one side of hip-hop tinged dance cuts and another of soulful, harmony-filled ballads, hits US #3.

Sept [7] The extracted double-era inspired *Motownphilly* hits US #3, during a 24-week stay on the Hot 100.
Oct [31] *Motownphilly* is certified platinum by the RIAA.
Dec [14] Ballad *It's So Hard To Say Goodbye To Yesterday*, showcasing the quartet's deft harmony skills, hits US #2, where it will stay for four weeks behind Michael Jackson's *Black Or White*.
[24] *It's So Hard To Say Goodbye To Yesterday* is certified gold by the RIAA.

1992

Jan [11] The group wins the Best New Artist category at the 24th annual NAACP Image Awards, held at the Wiltern Theatre, Los Angeles, CA.
[25] They participate in TNT cable-TV's "Super Bowl Saturday Night".
[27] The Boyz win the Favorite New Artist, Soul/R&B category at the 19th annual American Music Awards, held at the Shrine Auditorium, Los Angeles.
Feb [25] Boyz II Men win the Best R&B Performance By A Duo Or Group With Vocal category for ***Cooleyhighharmony*** at 34th annual Grammy Awards, at Radio City Music Hall, New York, at which they also perform (in their trademark '50s high-school matching garb) and present the Best Rap Duo Or Group trophy (with Color Me Badd).
Mar [7] *Uhh Ahh*, a track currently featured on the "White Men Can't Jump" film soundtrack, reaches US #16.
[12] They nab the Best R&B/Soul New Artist trophy at the sixth annual Soul Train Music Awards, also held at the Shrine Auditorium.
Apr [1] The group embarks on Hammer's "Too Legit To Quit" tour in Hampton, VA.
[10] ***Cooleyhighharmony*** tops sales of four million in the US, becoming the biggest-selling record by an R&B group in pop history.
May [2] *Please Don't Go* peaks at US #49, despite a 20-week stay on the Hot 100.
[16] The group guests on NBC-TV's "Bob Hope's America Red White & Beautiful - The Swimsuit Edition".
[25] Tour manager Khalil Rountree is killed by gunfire after a scuffle in an elevator on the 26th floor of the Guest Quarters Suite Hotel in Chicago, IL. Their assistant tour manager, Quadree El-Amin, is also wounded during the shootings by three assailants, which result in Boyz II Men cancelling some of their forthcoming dates as support act to Hammer.
Aug [1-2] The quartet performs at KMEL Radio's "Summer Jam '92" at the Shoreline Amphitheatre, Mountain View, CA. Billed as the largest rap festival ever, two sellout crowds totalling 36,308 pay some $1,093,512.
[15] Mournful ballad *End Of The Road*, featured in the Eddie Murphy movie "Boomerang", and in just its fifth week on the survey, hits US #1, where it will remain for a record 13 weeks (an achievement initially superceded by Whitney Houston's 14-week tenure with *I Will Always Love You* the following year).
Sept Boyz II Men are featured on Norman Brown's ***Just Between Us***.
[16] *End Of The Road* is certified platinum by the RIAA.
Oct [17] The group guest stars on NBC-TV's "Out All Night".
[24] They appear on BBC1-TV's "Going Live!" during a promotional visit to the UK. (They also guest on "Dance Energy House Party", "Top Of The Pops" and "The O Zone".)
[31] *End Of The Road* begins a three-week run atop the UK chart.
Nov [7] ***Cooleyhighharmony*** hits UK #7.
Dec [9] The group wins the Top Singles Artists - Duo/Group, Top Singles Artists, Top Single (*End of The Road*) and the Top 40 Radio Monitor Tracks (*End Of The Road*) categories at the third **Billboard** Music Awards, held at the Universal Amphitheatre, Universal City, CA.
[17] The RIAA certifies five million sales of ***Cooleyhighharmony***.
[18] Boyz II Men guests on CBS-TV's "Keep Christmas With You", starring Kenny Rogers.
[26] *Motownphilly* reaches UK #23.
[31] The quartet appears on "MTV Drops The Ball '93" from New York's Roseland Ballroom.

1993

Jan [16] Boyz II Men win the Best Vocal Group category at the 25th annual NAACP Image Awards, at the Civic Auditorium, Pasadena, CA, as *In The Still Of The Nite (I'll Remember)*, reviving the Five Satins' '50s classic and featured in the ABC-TV mini-series "The Jacksons", hits US #3.
[20] They perform *Cooleyhighharmony* at MTV's "1993 Rock & Roll Inaugural Ball" in Washington, DC.
[25] They collect the Favorite Single, Pop/Rock and Favorite Band, Soul/R&B trophies, at the 20th annual American Music Awards, held at the Shrine Auditorium.
[27] *In The Still Of The Nite (I'll Remember)* is certified platinum by the RIAA.
Feb [23] The group is the musical guest on NBC-TV's "The Tonight Show".
[24] They nab the Best R&B Vocal Duo Or Group trophy for *End Of The Road* at the 35th annual Grammy Awards, held at the Shrine Auditorium.
Mar [6] *In The Still Of The Nite (I'll Remember)* reaches UK #27.
[9] Adding to its already bulging trophy cabinet, the band nabs the Best R&B/Soul Group Single, R&B/Soul Song Of The Year and R&B Music Video of the year statuettes at the seventh annual Soul Train Music Awards, also held at the Shrine Auditorium.
Apr [20] Intended to include cover versions of the Beatles' *Yesterday* and Marvin Gaye's *Mercy Mercy Me*, the release of ***MTV: Live And Unplugged***, documenting their 1992 performance on the show, is permanently cancelled by Motown.
May [12] The group performs *End Of The Road* at the fifth annual World Music Awards from the Sporting Club, Monte Carlo, Monaco, at which they are named International New Group Of The Year.
Dec [9] Their still-rising seasonal collection ***Christmas Interpretations*** is certified platinum by the RIAA.
[18] ***Christmas Interpretations*** reaches US #19.

1994

Jan [8] The extracted *Let It Snow* reaches US #32.
[15] A revised version of their debut album, billed as ***Cooleyhighharmony (International Edition)*** peaks at US #154.
Aug [13] The group begins a pre-album release promotional tour of Europe.
[27] Written and produced by Babyface, *I'll Make Love To You* begins a record-breaking 14 weeks at US #1, tying Whitney Houston's recent historic achievement with *I Will Always Love You*.
Sept [8] The group performs at the 11th annual MTV Video Music Awards held at New York's Radio City Music Hall.
[10] *I'll Make Love To You* hits UK #5.
[17] Recorded at Granny's House studio in Reno, NV, ***II***, including a version of *Yesterday*, which McCary and Nathan Morris used to sing in their school choir, debuts at US #1, the first Motown album to do so since Stevie Wonder's ***Songs In The Key Of Life***. (The album variously produced by Babyface, Dallas Austin, Tim Kelly and Bob Robinson and Jimmy Jam and Terry Lewis, will sell six million copies in the US by year's end.)
Oct [1] ***II*** reaches UK #17.
[6] *I'll Make Love To You* is certified platinum by the RIAA.
Nov [8] The group guests on NBC-TV's "The John Larroquette Show".
[26] *On Bended Knee*, a ballad written by producers Jam and Lewis, debuts at its UK #20 peak.
Dec [3] *On Bended Knee* replaces *I'll Make Love To You* at US #1.
[31] Boyz II Men, currently on tour with Babyface, perform to a sellout crowd of 16,500 at New York's Madison Square Garden.

1995

Jan [11] "Then II Now" video is certified gold by the RIAA.
[25] *On Bended Knee* is confirmed platinum by the RIAA.
[30] The group wins the Pop/Rock and Soul/R&B single for *I'll Make Love To You* and Band, Duo Or Group, Soul/R&B categories at the 22nd annual American Music Awards at the Shrine Auditorium, also performing *On Bended Knee*.
Mar [1] *I'll Make Love To You* now wins Best R&B Performance By A Duo Or Group and ***II*** Best R&B Album for Boyz II Men at the 37th annual Grammy Awards also held at the Shrine Auditorium.
[13] They complete the hat-trick, when *I'll Make Love To You* is named Best R&B/Soul Single, Group, Band Or Duo and ***II*** Best R&B/Soul Album, Group, Band Or Duo at the ninth annual Soul Train Awards at the Shrine Auditorium. Once again they perform at the event.
[18] *Thank You* reaches US #21.
Apr [22] *Thank You* debuts at its UK #26 peak, as the group performs at an Earth Day benefit in Washington, DC.
June [3] Having recently bought their own recording studio (to be renamed Stonecreek Recording) in Gladwyne, PA, they perform at the inaugural Blockbuster Entertainment Awards at Hollywood's Pantages Theatre, as well as collecting trophies for Top R&B Group and Top CD.
[12] The RIAA certifies multi-platinum sales (eight million) of ***II***.
[17] *The Water Runs Dry* hits US #2.
[22] Boyz II Men is honored at the second annual VH-1 Honors ceremony at Shrine Auditorium, as *The Water Runs Dry* is certified gold by the RIAA.
July [8] *The Water Runs Dry* bows at its UK #24 peak.
[10] The group's Springfield, IN concert is cancelled after members of its backing band are injured in an auto accident following their Deer Creek Music Center show the night before.
[24] Boyz II Men and the now-disbanded New Kids On The Block play a benefit basketball game at UMass-Boston, Clark Athletic Center, Boston, MA.
Aug [31] Their "From Then II Now" video is certified platinum by the RIAA.
Sept [3] The group sings the US national anthem at the opening of the expansion Jacksonville Jaguars' NFL debut, against the Houston Oilers, in Jacksonville, FL.
Oct [7] *Vibin'* makes US #56.
[8] They perform at Oriole Park Camden Yards in Baltimore, MD, in welcoming Pope John Paul II, who is there to celebrate mass with 50,000 attending Catholics.
[9] L.L. Cool J.'s new single *Hey Lover*, featuring uncredited chorus work from the Boyz, is released in the US.
[10] The group guests at Mariah Carey's New York Madison Square Garden sellout concert.
[21] Boyz II Men are featured on the inaugural MTV series "Bootleg", which focuses on the backstage goings on of various acts in concert.
[24] Motown releases ***II - Yo Te Voy A Amar***, including ten English language originals from ***II*** plus four new Spanish-language recordings of existing cuts.
Nov [23] "Boyz II Men: Going Home" premieres on the Disney cable channel (US).
Dec [2] *One Sweet Day*, a duet with Mariah Carey co-written by them all with co-producer Walter Afanasieff, debuts at US #1, on its way to a record-breaking 16 weeks at the summit.
[9] *One Sweet Day* debuts at its UK #6 peak.
[30] Hastily packaged ***The Remix Collection*** reaches US #17.

1996

Jan [6] *I Remember* makes US #46, as Stockman's debut solo single (he is still in the group) *Visions Of A Sunset*, featured in the film soundtrack to "Mr. Holland's Opus", is released in the US. O.J. Simpson calls a Los Angeles radio station and, in requesting

One Sweet Day, dedicates the current hit to his murdered wife, Nicole.
[30] By now perennial winners, Boyz II Men collect the Favorite Band Duo Or Group and Favorite Album Soul/R&B trophies at the 23rd American Music Awards, held at the Shrine Auditorium.
Feb [13] The group and Sony Music Entertainment president Tommy Mottola announce a joint venture, giving the group its own Stonecreek Recordings label based in Philadelphia.
[28] Together with Carey they perform their current US chart-topper, *One Sweet Day* at the 38th annual Grammy Awards, held at the Shrine Auditorium.
Mar [6] Boyz II Men breaks its own record (14 weeks, previously shared with Whitney Houston) as its *One Sweet Day* duet with Carey logs its 15th consecutive week atop the US chart (it will also hold on for one more week in pole position, the longest in US chart history).
[15] Boyz II Men visits Roosevelt Junior High School in New Bedford, MA, after 13-year-old pupil Peter Schinas wins the national "Fox Rocks Your School" promotion sponsored by the Fox-TV network. The prize: a special appearance by Boyz II Men.
[29] They are honored with the Sammy Davis Jr. Award for Outstanding Achievements in the Field of Entertainment, presented to them by Bill Cosby, at the tenth annual Soul Train Music Awards, held at the Shrine Auditorium.

PAUL BRADY

1976

Brady (b. May 19, 1947, Strabane, County Tyrone, N. Ireland), raised in Strabane, N. Ireland, began performing in his teens in R&B bands playing keyboards and rhythm guitar on cover material, notably with the Kult while still attending college in Dublin, Eire. Influenced by the Irish folk boom, he has joined the Johnstons in 1967 recording seven albums until splitting from them in 1972. Subsequently linking up with popular Irish roots band Planxty, he teams with the band's Andy Irvine to now release the critically praised ***Andy Irvine & Paul Brady***, soon followed by another folk collaboration, ***The High Part Of The Road*** with Tommy Peoples. His solo recording career will begin with the issue of the still folk-based ***Welcome Here Kind Stranger*** in 1978.

1981

Moving away from folk towards a pop/rock direction, Brady has secured a one-album deal with WEA Records in the UK which now releases the self-penned ***Hard Station***, co-produced by Brady with Hugh Murphy, which includes the Irish chart-topper, *Crazy Dreams* (which will become a much- covered song by the likes of Dave Edmunds and Roger Chapman).

1983

May Now signed to Polydor Records, Brady's ***True For You***, co-produced with Neil Dorfsman is released, again to much critical praise. Becoming a favorite recording and performing artist with his more famous contemporaries, Brady opens for the likes of Dire Straits, and Eric Clapton, while Tina Turner will cover the album's *Steel Claw*.

1984

Oct Mark Knopfler's soundtrack album ***Cal***, featuring collaborations with Brady, is released in the UK.
Nov A one-off live album for Demon Records, ***Full Moon***, recorded at the Half Moon pub, Putney, London on April 4th, is released in the UK.

1986

Moved to Polydor's sister label, Mercury Records, ***Back To The Centre*** is released, produced by Ian Maidman and featuring Clapton, U2's Larry Mullen and Loudon Wainwright III.

1987

Apr Following the Ireland-only issue of the collaborative set ***Molloy, Brady, Peoples*** on Mulligan Records (with Matt Molloy and Tommy People,) early in the year, Brady's increasingly well-received string of self-written solo albums continues with the release of ***Primitive Dance***, followed by ***Paradise Is Here*** (1989), both supported by UK club tours.

1990

Dec [12] Brady performs the first of three concerts at the Harlesden Mean Fiddler, London, set to end on the 17th.

1991

Apr [6] During a largely chart-less UK and US career (though in Ireland, all of his albums will top the album chart), ***Trick Or Treat***, helmed by Steely Dan producer Gary Katz, spends one week at UK #62 and includes a host of admiring talent including Bonnie Raitt (who will include two Brady covers on her next release, ***Luck Of The Draw***) and Toto's Jeff Porcaro and David Paich.

1992

Apr Polygram imprint, Fontana releases the Brady compilation, ***Songs & Crazy Dreams***.

1995

May [15] Mercury (UK) releases ***Spirits Colliding***, on which the singer-songwriter also plays guitars, keyboards, mandolin, bouzouki, whistle, bass and percussion, and which features songs co-written with Mark Nevin and John Prine.
[28] A UK tour is highlighted by a performance at the London Palladium.

1996

Jan [13] *The World Is What You Make It* bows at its UK #67 peak.

BILLY BRAGG

1982

Following four years of dead-end jobs after leaving school, Bragg (b. Steven William Bragg, Dec. 20, 1957, Barking, Essex) has formed punk/R&B outfit Riff Raff in 1977, which records the EP *I Wanna Be A Cosmonaut* for the Chiswick label, released in May 1978. After the band has split by in 1980 (when the independent label Geezer released the last of four Riff Raff singles *New Home Town*), an unemployed Bragg has signed up for the British army in 1981 and been posted to a tank division. Immediately finding army life unsuitable, he has bought himself out of the military after only 90 days. Set on a career in music, he now begins to tour the UK via bus and train, playing small venues and working men's clubs as a solo singer/songwriter, developing his style as a working-class, politically-motivated, folk/punk protest performer.

1983

July Having been offered three afternoons of studio time to record demos of his songs for Chappell music publishing, the promising results are collected as the two-track mini-album ***Life's A Riot With Spy Vs. Spy*** and released on Utility. The short set, showcasing Bragg's abrasive cockney vocal style and raw guitar technique, immediately attracts positive reviews from the alternative UK music press.
[27] He makes his UK radio debut on BBC Radio 1's "John Peel Show".
Oct Bragg signs to the Go! Discs label (UK), which also licenses the rights to his mini-album premiere.

1984

Jan [5] Bragg performs at the ICA Theatre, London, on a bill with Bronski Beat and the Redskins. Promoted by an energetic tour schedule (economic not least because he performs only with his guitar), ***Life's A Riot With Spy Vs Spy*** reaches UK #30, having topped the UK Independent Albums chart for two months and ultimately selling 150,000 copies.
July Bragg begins recording sessions for his sophomore album, at the Berry Street Studio, London.
Aug He embarks on a well-received, small-venue US concert trek.
Sept [14] He headlines a Greater London Council-sponsored event at the Porchester Hall, London, billed as "Ken Livingstone's Camp Party". During the month, and as a vocal supporter of a number of left-wing political causes, Bragg performs several "Food For The Miners" benefit shows.
Oct [19] He is arrested with others during an anti-apartheid sit-down outside South Africa House, Trafalgar Square, London.
Brewing Up With Billy Bragg (described by Bragg as "a puckish satire on contemporary mores") reaches UK #16. Produced by Edward De Bono, the self-written 11-track set features only two other musicians, Dave Woodhead (trumpet) and Kenny Craddock (organ).

1985

Feb [23] Kirsty McColl's version of Bragg's song *A New England*, originally featured on ***Life's A Riot***, hits UK #7.
Mar [23] EP *Between The Wars* marks his own UK Singles chart debut, making #15.

1986

Jan *Days Like These* makes UK #43.
[25] A seven-date "Red Wedge In Concert '86" trek, a politically-active group of musicians formed by Bragg and including Paul Weller and the Communards, touring to raise funds in support of the electioneering Labour Party, opens at the Apollo Theatre, Manchester, Gtr. Manchester, set to end on the 31st at the City Hall, Newcastle, Tyne & Wear.
July *Levi Stubbs' Tears* reaches UK #29.
Oct *Talking With The Taxman About Poetry*, its title taken from the Soviet poet Mayakovsky, hits UK #8.
Nov [2] He is arrested and charged with criminal damage after cutting an air-base fence in Norfolk, UK, during an anti-nuclear demonstration.
Greetings To The New Brunette, featuring Smiths guitarist Johnny Marr and MacColl, makes UK #58.

1987

June [20] Double album ***Back To Basics***, including tracks from ***Life's A Riot*** and the *Between The Wars* EP, climbs to UK #37, as Red Wedge, represented by Bragg, Jerry Dammers, Matt Johnson (The The) and Dr. Robert (Blow Monkeys), launches its pre-election pamphlet, **Move On Up**, at Ronnie Scott's, with guest of honor Labour Party leader Neil Kinnock.

1988

May [21] With his cover version of the Beatles' *She's Leaving Home*, Bragg, with featured pianist Cara Tivey, enjoys a surprise UK chart-topper as one side of a double A-side benefit record for the Childline charity (its more-broadcast flip being Wet Wet Wet's version of *With A Little Help From My Friends*). Both songs are featured on the compilation album ***Sergeant Pepper Knew My Father***.
Sept *Waiting For The Great Leap Forwards* peaks at UK #52.
Nov [5] ***Workers Playtime*** marks a modest US chart debut at #198, having made UK #17 on Oct [1].

1989

Feb [22] Bragg makes his US network TV debut on NBC-TV's "Late Night With David Letterman". (During his current US tour, Bragg will also play a benefit concert for the Pittson Coal Company in Norton, VA.)

1990

Apr [21] Bragg takes part in an "Earth Day" benefit concert at the Merriweather Post Pavilion, Columbia, MD.

May [12] ***The Internationale*** peaks at UK #34 and features Bragg's version of the Sandino national anthem *Nicaragua Nicaraguita*.
June [3] He participates in "The Big Day", from the Custom House Quay, Glasgow, Scotland, broadcast live on C4-TV.
Bragg tours Eastern Europe with 10,000 Maniacs' Natalie Merchant and R.E.M.'s Michael Stipe.
July *The Internationale* is released as an EP in the US on his own Utility label, licensed to Elektra.
Aug [25] He takes part in the annual "Reading Festival", Reading, Berks.
Sept Bragg and Merchant record as the Lemon Jeffersons at Fort Apache Studios in Boston, MA.
[24] ***Tom's Album***, a collection of ten different interpretations of Suzanne Vega's *Tom's Diner*, including one by Bragg backed by R.E.M., is released.
Nov [3] ***Rubáiyát***, Elektra's 40th anniversary compilation, to which he contributes a cover of *Seven And Seven Is*, peaks at US #140.
[29] Bragg performs at a benefit for the Terrence Higgins Trust at London's Brixton Academy.

1991

Apr [20] He takes part in the "Earth Day 1991 Concert" at Foxboro Stadium, Foxborough, MA, with Jackson Browne, Rosanne Cash, Bruce Cockburn, Bruce Hornsby & the Range, Indigo Girls and others.
June [9] BBC2-TV's "Great Journeys", with Bragg and Andy Kershaw travelling to Bolivia and Chile to unearth 17th-century silver routes, airs.
July [13] *Sexuality*, co-written and produced by Johnny Marr, and featuring a full rhythm section, reaches UK #27.
Sept [7] *You Woke Up My Neighbourhood* debuts at its UK #54 peak.
[28] Bragg's seventh album ***Don't Try This At Home*** hits UK #8 upon release.
Oct [12-13] Bragg performs at London's Town & Country venue during a 15-date UK tour, set to end on the 31st at the Cambridge Corn Exchange, Cambs.
Nov [17] ***Revolution No. 9***, a compilation of cover versions of Beatles hits to which Bragg has contributed *Revolution*, is released to raise funds for Oxfam's Cambodian Aid Appeal.
Dec [10] Towards the end of a US concert visit, Bragg plays at the Wiltern Theatre, Los Angeles, CA.
[29-31] He closes the year with three dates at the Hackney Empire, London.

1992

Jan [13] Bragg appears on ITV's "Stage 1".
Feb [6] He performs on a bill with Merchant at the University of New Hampshire, Durham, NH.
Mar [7] EP *Accident Waiting To Happen* reaches UK #33.
Apr [2] Bragg plays at the "Artists Against Racism" concert at the Hackney Empire.
July [12] He participates in a Woody Guthrie Tribute concert, celebrating the folk legend's birth 80 years ago, held in Central Park, New York, NY.

1993

Feb [12] Bragg takes part at the "Burnsall Strikers Benefit" at Camden Centre, London.
July [17] He performs on the Mean Fiddler stage at the Phoenix Festival at Long Marston, Stratford-upon-Avon.
Aug [28] He takes part in a benefit for the Shake-A-Leg charity at Fort Adams State Park, Newport, RI, duetting with Natalie Merchant on *Summertime* and *Bread And Circus*.

1994

June [21] Appearing on BBC2-TV's "Newsnight" and commenting on George Michael's court loss, Bragg says that Michael "would have got a better result if he'd sued his hairdresser".

1995

Nov [21] Having not released an album since 1991, but performed on the acoustic stage at this summer's 25th anniversary "Glastonbury Festival", Bragg plays at Tramps in New York, his first gig in the city in four years.

TONI BRAXTON

1990

Sept [29] Growing up singing in church choirs with her four younger sisters, Braxton (b. Oct. 7, 1968, Severn, MD) has learnt to play the piano and has begun writing songs as a teenager, her tastes influenced by the music of Quincy Jones, Stevie Wonder, Whitney Houston and Chaka Khan and has also successfully entered a number of talent contests. While studying teacher-training at Bowie State University, she has joined with her siblings, Tamar (now age 12), Trina (14), Towanda (15) and Traci (18) to form the Braxtons who, signed to Arista Records, now make their chart debut with *Good Life* entering the US R&B chart set to reach #79. Following a successful audition for hot R&B production team, L.A. Reid and Babyface in 1991, Braxton goes on to sign as a solo artist to their LaFace Records (co-owned by Arista), based in Atlanta, GA.

1992

Sept [19] While preparing her debut album, *Give U My Heart* performed by Babyface and co-vocalist Braxton, a song featured in the Eddie Murphy-starring movie "Boomerang", now reaches US #29, spurred by her television debut alongside Babyface on the US-TV syndicated "Arsenio Hall Show".

1993

Jan [16] *Love Shoulda Brought You Home*, her solo debut also featured on the "Boomerang" soundtrack, reaches US #33.
July [31] Her maiden album ***Toni Braxton*** enters the US chart. Supervised by L.A. Reid and Babyface with assorted producers Vincent Herbert, Tim Thomas and Ted Bishop, Bo Watson, Vassal Benford, Ronald Spearman and Ernesto Philips, the soul-drenched set reveals a mature, enticing talent which immediately garners positive radio and media attention.
Sept [18] *Another Sad Love Song*, co-written by Babyface and Daryl Simmons, makes UK #51.
Oct [5] *Another Sad Love Song* is certified gold by the RIAA.
[9] *Another Sad Love Song* hits US #7.
Dec [4] Braxton makes her UK television debut on ITV's "Des O'Connor Tonight".
[7] Still rising on the US survey, *Breathe Again* is also certified gold by the RIAA.
[10] Braxton performs her final live concert of the year at the Paramount, New York on a bill grossing $297,372 from 8,760 attendees.

1994

Jan [7] US tour dates resume at the Fox Theatre, Detroit, MI.
[22] *Breathe Again*, written by Babyface, hits US #3.
Feb [5] *Breathe Again* hits UK #2.
[7] Braxton performs *Another Sad Love Song* at the 21st annual American Music Awards held at the Shrine Auditorium, Los Angeles, CA, at which she also collects trophies for the Top Soul/R&B New Artist and Top Adult Contemporary New Artist.
[8] She guests with Lou Rawls and Queen Latifah on Fox-TV's "Roc".
[26] ***Toni Braxton*** finally tops the US chart eight months after release.
Mar [1] Braxton wins the Best New Artist and Best R&B Vocal Performance, Female (*Another Sad Love Song*) categories at the 36th annual Grammy Awards held in New York's Radio City Music Hall, at which she also performs with Kenny G.
[15] *Breathe Again* is named Best R&B Single, Female, and ***Toni Braxton*** is hailed R&B Album Of The Year at the eighth annual Soul Train Awards, staged at the Shrine Auditorium.
Apr [16] Reissued *Another Sad Love Song* reaches UK #15.
[30] ***Toni Braxton*** hits UK #4.
May [4] Capping a slew of recent awards, Braxton is named the World's Best-selling R&B Newcomer Of The Year at the sixth annual World Music Awards held at the Sporting Club, Monte Carlo, Monaco.
[28] *You Mean The World To Me* hits US #7.
July [9] *You Mean The World To Me* bows at its UK #30 peak.
[13] *You Mean The World To Me* is certified gold by the RIAA.
[25] "The Hit Video Collection", collecting her promo clips to date, is also certified gold by the RIAA.
Sept Braxton signs a management deal with Stiefel/Phillips Entertainment.
Dec [3] *Love Shoulda Brought You Home*, with *The Christmas Song* as its B-side, debuts at its UK #33 peak.
[17] She appears on ABC-TV's "Christmas At Home With The Stars".
[24] *I Belong To You*, coupled with *How Many Ways*, reaches US #30.

1995

Jan [30] Braxton wins the Top Album, Soul/R&B category for ***Toni Braxton*** at the 22nd annual American Music Awards, held at the Shrine Auditorium.
Mar [1] Confirming the endurance of her debut recordings which have already collected honors at last year's event, *Breathe Again* nabs the Best Female R&B Vocal Performance at the 37th annual Grammy Awards held at the Shrine Auditorium.
May [16] *Breathe Again* is named Song Of The Year at the 1995 BMI Pop Awards held at the Beverly Wilshire Hotel, Los Angeles, CA.
[30] The RIAA certifies sales of seven million copies of ***Toni Braxton*** (its worldwide tally will top ten million by year's end).
Oct [24] The Babyface-produced film soundtrack, ***Waiting To Exhale*** is released in the US including the new Braxton cut, *Let It Flow*. (Meanwhile Braxton begins work on her sophomore album which will be variously produced, not least by Babyface and R. Kelly, a project scheduled for release in June the following year.)

1996

June [18] Braxton's sophomore set, and the extracted first single *You Make Me High*, is set for release.

BREAD

David Gates (guitar, vocals); **James Griffin** (guitar, vocals); **Larry Knechtel** (bass, keyboards); **Mike Botts** (drums)

1968

Griffin (b. Memphis, TN), who already has the Warner Bros.-released solo ***Summer Holiday*** to his credit, teams with Gates (b. Dec. 11, 1940, Tulsa, OK), a songwriter (who penned the Murmaids' 1963 #3 US hit *Popsicles And Icicles*), producer and session musician, who first recorded with Leon Russell for Lee Hazlewood's East West label in the late '50s before moving to Los Angeles, CA, in the early '60s. Settled on the west coast, Gates has linked with Robb Royer who, as a member of the Pleasure Faire with Michele Cochrane, Tim Hallinan and Steve Cohn, has released an eponymously-titled album for Uni, produced by Gates. Together with Griffin, they take their pop-folk, harmony demos to Elektra Records, a folk label which has moved into rock with acts like the Doors, but has not previously signed a pure pop band.

1969

Nov [8] Choosing the band name Bread, having been stuck in traffic behind a Wonder Bread truck, their debut album ***Bread***, featuring session drummer Jim Gordon, reaches US #127, but fails to chart in the UK.

1970

Aug [6] Still-climbing *Make It With You* is certified gold by the RIAA.
[22] Gates-penned ballad *Make It With You*, from their sophomore effort ***On The Waters***, tops the US chart for one week and will hit UK #5 in September. The album will reach US #12 and UK #34.
Nov [14] Reissued follow-up ballad *It Don't Matter To Me*, taken from ***Bread***, hits US #10.

1971

Feb *Let Your Love Go*, from the group's new album ***Manna***, reaches US #28.
Mar ***Manna*** reaches US #21. Griffin and Royer's lyrics to the song *For All We Know*, from the movie "Lovers And Other Strangers", win an Oscar for Best Film Song of 1970, with Griffin using the alias Arthur James and Royer being credited as Robb Wilson.
May *If*, from ***Manna***, hits US #4, further defining Bread's hallmark sound: lushly-orchestrated, pure, melodic pop ballads, showcasing Gates' commercial songwriting instincts and his crystal-clear treble vocal, a combination which proves irresistible to US radio both now and in future decades.
Line-up changes during the year will see full-time drummer Botts (b. Sacramento, CA) join, as the group begins touring, while Royer quits, replaced by multi-instrumentalist Larry Knechtel (b. Bell, CA), a former member of Duane Eddy's Rebels and already a legendary Los Angeles session musician. (He has played bass on the Byrds' *Mr. Tambourine Man*, piano on Simon & Garfunkel's *Bridge Over Troubled Water*, and has been part of a session trio comprising Joe Osborn (bass) and Hal Blaine (drums), which has played on million-selling records by the Beach Boys, the Monkees, the 5th Dimension, Johnny Rivers, the Association, Paul Revere & the Raiders and countless others.)
Aug Hard-rocking *Mother Freedom*, the first release to feature Knechtel, makes US #37.
Nov [27] Continuing Gates' Top 10 ballad streak, which will always prove to be the band's strongest suit, *Baby I'm-A Want You* hits US #3, and makes UK #14.

1972

Jan [7] *Baby I'm-A Want You* is certified gold by the RIAA.
Mar Recorded in Hollywood, produced, arranged and largely written by Gates, ***Baby I'm-A Want You*** hits US #3 and UK #9, as a second ballad extract, *Everything I Own*, hits US #5 and UK #32.
[9] ***Baby I'm-A Want You*** is certified gold by the RIAA.
June Bitter-sweet Gates love song, *Diary* reaches US #15.
Sept Concert-themed *Guitar Man* reaches US #11 and UK #16, featuring a memorable guitar solo by Knechtel.
Oct The first of many compilations, ***Best Of Bread*** hits UK #7.
Nov Recorded with the same line-up and continuing the successful Gates-led formula, Bread's fifth album ***Guitar Man*** reaches US #18.
[21] ***Guitar Man*** is confirmed gold by the RIAA.
Dec The extracted *Sweet Surrender* reaches US #15.
[21] ***Manna*** and ***On The Waters*** are both certified gold by the RIAA.

1973

Mar Gates-written ballad *Aubrey*, the third single from ***Guitar Man***, reaches US #15. The group disbands amid rumors of a disagreement between Gates and Griffin, who is apparently concerned that his compositions have not been released as singles.
Apr [10] The still-climbing ***The Best Of Bread*** is certified gold by the RIAA.
May ***Best Of Bread*** hits US #2 during a two-year chart tenure. Gates and Griffin will embark on solo careers, while Botts works with Linda Ronstadt and Knechtel returns to sessions, although illness will force him to temporarily retire.
Oct Remaining with Elektra, Gates' debut solo album ***First***, entirely and not surprisingly written and recorded in the Bread tradition, is released, set to make US #107. It includes the mini-opus *Clouds*, an ambitious seven-minute single.
Nov Gates' *Sail Around The World* stalls at US #50.

1974

July Further compilation ***Best Of Bread Volume II*** reaches US #32 and UK #48, while Griffin, signed to Polydor, releases ***James Griffin***, co-produced and co-written with early Bread colleague Royer.
Oct [26] Ken Boothe's reggae treatment of *Everything I Own* hits UK #1.
Dec [24] ***The Best Of Bread : Volume II*** is certified gold by the RIAA.

1975

Feb Gates' ballad *Never Let Her Go*, indistinguishable from earlier Bread outings, peaks at US #29, while his sophomore effort ***Never Let Her Go***, assisted by Knechtel, climbs to US #102 and will reach UK #32 on May [31].
Mar [8] A predominantly-spoken cover version of *If* by actor Telly Savalas tops the UK chart (the Bread original never even made the survey).
Apr [29] Gates embarks on a four-date UK tour, with Larry Knechtel, Dean Parks, Jim Gordon and Carol Carmichael backing him, at the New Theatre, Southport, Mersyside, set to end on May 4th at the Birmingham Odeon, W. Midlands.

1977

Jan After commercially-modest solo careers, Gates and Griffin bury the hatchet, and Bread has re-formed (with Knechtel and Botts). The resulting Gates-helmed ***Lost Without Your Love*** reaches US #26 and UK #17, while the mournful ballad title track hits US #9 and UK #27.
Feb [17] ***Lost Without Your Love*** is certified gold by the RIAA.
May Mid-tempo, harmony-drenched *Hooked On You* peaks at US #60.
Nov [26] TV-advertised, 20-track compilation album ***The Sound Of Bread***, selling prodigiously in the UK, ultimately achieving double-platinum status, hits #1 for the first of three weeks, knocking the Sex Pistols' ***Never Mind The Bollocks - Here's The Sex Pistols*** from the top spot. A similar US compilation fails to chart. (The group dissolves permanently, with Gates once again becoming the most commercially-active member. Griffin, who will resume his solo career and record an album with the Hollies' Terry Sylvester, released in 1981 by Polydor, subsequently sues Gates when the latter tours using the band's name, which they co-own. A judge orders the group not to record, perform or collect royalties until the case is resolved. Litigation will finally end in 1984.)

1978

Feb Gates' title theme to the Neil Simon hit movie "Goodbye Girl" reaches US #15.
June [2-3] Gates begins an 11-date UK tour, with Knechtel, Gordon and Parks, at the Birmingham Odeon, Birmingham, W. Midlands, set to end on the 14th at the Hammersmith Odeon, London.
July [29] Largely a retrospective Gates release, ***Goodbye Girl***, including previously-issued solo material which features both Knechtel and Botts, debuts at its UK #28 peak and will sneak to US #165, containing the US #30 *Took The Last Train*. Co-written with Knechtel, the mid-tempo Moog synthesizer-driven pop ditty is, after a stream of non-charting ballad releases, ironically, Gates' only solo UK chart appearance, making #50.

1980

Feb Gates' Elektra chart swan song *Where Does The Lovin' Go?* makes US #46, taken from ***Falling In Love Again***, another self-produced and self-written album featuring Knechtel and Botts.

1981

Oct Now signed to Arista Records, Gates, still recording in the familiar Bread style with sidesman Knechtel, releases ***Take Me Now***, which includes the US #62 title cut. The album will be his final recording of the decade.

1987

Mar [14] As further evidence of the enduring appeal of Gates' early compositions, a second cover of *Everything I Own*, now recorded by Boy George, hits UK #1 for the first of two weeks.
Nov [28] Following the resolution of their legal dispute, the 1985 US release ***Anthology Of Bread***, co-produced by Gates and Griffin, is now followed by a further retrospective, ***The Collection - Bread and David Gates***, which peaks at UK #84.

1995

Aug [9] Griffin, who has moved to Nashville, TN, and initially formed Dreamer, before teaming with ex-Eagle and Poco-player, Randy Meisner, and *I Can Help*-hitmaker Billy Swan as Black Tie (who score a US country hit with a revival of Buddy Holly's *Learning The Game* on the independent Bench label), has formed the Remingtons with Richard Mainegra and Rick Yancey, both ex-Cymarron (releasing ***Blue Frontier*** on BMG Records in 1992). Meanwhile, the other slices of Bread have been less visible, with Gates retiring to run a 800-acre ranch in Northern California, and Knechtel, after 14 years on a neighboring cattle ranch, also moving to Nashville, cutting new-age albums, including ***Urban Gypsy*** and ***Mountain Moods***, and playing in Elvis Costello's band (notably on 1991's ***Mighty Like A Rose***), while Botts has continued session work, jingle writing and working on children's albums. With Gates having returned to the recording scene with the September 1994 release of ***Love Is Always Seventeen*** (featuring Billy Dean and Knechtel) on the Discovery label (US), the group's enduring appeal, not least on AC and oldies radio in the US, is confirmed with ***Anthology Of Bread*** now being certified platinum by the RIAA.

ELKIE BROOKS

1964

Oct [19] Having sung professionally since the age of 15, Brooks (b. Elaine Bookbinder, Feb. 25, 1945, Salford, Lancs.), sister of Billy J. Kramer & the Dakotas' drummer Tony Mansfield and who made her recording debut for Decca with a revival of Etta James' *Something's Got A Hold On Me* (released in August), now begins a 28-date, twice-nightly UK tour, with the Animals, Carl Perkins, the Nashville Teens and others, at the Odeon Cinema, Liverpool, Lancs., set to end on November 15th at the Winter Gardens, Bournemouth, Dorset.

1965

May [25] Brooks participates in the "British Song Contest" at the Dome, Brighton, E. Sussex.
June After two more singles for Decca, she moves to EMI's HMV label for *He's Gotta Love Me*, the first of three releases for the label. (Brooks spends the next few years performing extensive studio and stage vocal back-up work, as well as being a featured singer with both the Eric Delaney and Humphrey Lyttleton bands. She will also record a one-off single for NEMS Records, *Come September*, released in April 1969.)

1970

Encouraged by Pete Gage (whom she will later marry), Brooks joins Dada, a large UK jazz-rock fusion band, sharing lead vocals with Paul Korda on their only album ***Dada***, recorded for Atco.

1972

Apr Dada fragments, with several of its members, including Brooks, Gage and Korda's replacement Robert Palmer, regrouping as rock/blues outfit Vinegar Joe, who record an eponymous album for Island Records on which Brooks and Palmer are featured as joint vocalists.

1974

Mar [9] After much live acclaim, particularly in Europe, but modest sales for two further albums, ***Rock And Roll Gypsies*** and ***Six-Star General***, Vinegar Joe plays its final UK gig, at St. Paul's College, Cheltenham, Gloucs., followed by a two-week tour of Yugoslavia. Brooks subsequently releases a solo single, *Rescue Me*, on Island, but - like all her output to date - it fails to chart. At the invitation of southern boogie band Wet Willie, she moves to Macon, GA, to spend a year touring with them as a backing vocalist.

1975

Oct Having returned to the UK, she has signed to A&M Records as a soloist, now releasing ***Rich Man's Woman***, which is warmly reviewed by critics as a mature vocal set.
Dec Alan Seifert becomes Brooks' manager.

1977

Apr Former managers John Sherry and Miles Copeland sue Brooks for £13,000 in the High Court, claiming she has broken the terms of a five-year contract signed in 1972.
May *Pearl's A Singer*, produced and part-written by veteran duo Jerry Leiber and Mike Stoller, provides her breakthrough, hitting UK #8.
Sept Its parent album ***Two Days Away***, produced by Leiber/Stoller, makes UK #18.
Oct Ellie Greenwich-penned *Sunshine After The Rain* hits UK #10.

1978

Mar Lush Mike Batt-produced ballad *Lilac Wine* reaches UK #16.
Apr [30] Brooks begins a 29-date UK tour at the Liverpool Empire. The tour, which includes eight shows at the London Palladium, will end June 1st at the Gaumont Theatre, Ipswich, Suffolk.
June ***Shooting Star***, produced by David Kershenbaum, peaks at UK #20, while her revival of Neil Young's *Only Love Can Break Your Heart* makes UK #43.
Dec [2] *Don't Cry Out Loud*, once again produced by Leiber and Stoller, and written by Peter Allen and Carole Bayer Sager, reaches UK #12.
[3-4] Brooks performs at the Dominion Theatre, London.

1979

May *The Runaway* makes UK #50. (It is her last hit single for almost three years, as her next six singles releases will fail to chart.)
Oct ***Live And Learn***, a second Leiber/Stoller album production, makes UK #34.
Dec [21] Having married her sound engineer Trevor Jordan a year previously, she gives birth to a son, Jermaine.

1980

Oct [28] Brooks begins a 27-date UK tour at the Empire, Sunderland, Tyne & Wear, set to close on November 27th at the Guildhall, Portsmouth, Hants.

1982

Feb Compilation ***Pearls***, comprising hit singles to date, plus new material, is Brooks' biggest UK seller, hitting #2. *Fool (If You Think It's Over)*, reviving Chris Rea's original, reaches UK #17.
May *Our Love*, from the forthcoming ***Pearls II***, makes UK #43.
Aug Her revival of the Moody Blues' *Nights In White Satin* makes UK #33.
Dec ***Pearls II***, produced by Gus Dudgeon and concentrating mainly on well-known cover material, hits UK #5. An example, her version of Rod Stewart's *Gasoline Alley*, peaks at UK #52 in February 1983, while the next five years will also see her final A&M album ***Minutes*** make UK #35 in 1984, and a collection of movie standards recorded for EMI as ***Screen Gems*** also reach UK #35, in January the following year.

1987

Jan A move to the fledgling Legend Records brings about a major UK chart revival, as *No More The Fool* (written by Russ Ballard) hits #5.
Feb [7] ***No More The Fool***, produced by Ballard, hits UK #5, while a TV-advertised compilation album, ***The Very Best Of Elkie Brooks***, anthologizing her A&M hits, hits UK #10. Meanwhile *Break The Chain*, written and produced by Ballard, makes UK #55 in April, and a cover of Bob Seger's *We've Got Tonight* peaks at UK #69 on July [11].

1994

Apr [16] Having signed to Legacy Records, Brooks made UK #57 with ***Bookbinder's Kid*** on June [18], 1988, and reached #58 with a TV-advertised album for Telstar, ***Inspirations***, on Nov [25], 1989, and still a popular draw on the UK concert-hall circuit, her latest project, a blues covers album, ***Nothin' But The Blues***, peaks at UK #58 in its week of entry.

GARTH BROOKS

1984

The youngest of six children born to Colleen Carroll, a successful country singer in the '50s who was signed to Capitol Records and a regular on Red Foley's "Ozark Jubilee" ABC-TV show, Brooks (b. Troyal Garth Brooks, Feb. 7, 1962, Tulsa, OK), his family having moved to Yukon, OK when Brooks was five, having played four sports at high school and attended Oklahoma State University on an athletic scholarship (for the javelin), majoring in advertising and marketing, has played in a bluegrass band, and worked as a bouncer at the Stillwater, OK, club Tumbleweeds, where he met Sandy Mahl, with whom he will live for two years before getting married in 1986. Now set to follow his muse as a country singer, Brooks makes his first visit to Nashville, TN, but, despondent having spoken with royalty collecting agency ASCAP's Merl Littlefield, returns to Oklahoma after only 23 hours, and will not permanently relocate to the Country capitol until 1987, when he and Sandy find work in a boot store while Brooks hones his performance skills playing at local clubs. With his brother becoming his manager, his sister Betsy Smittle will become the bassist in his backing band, Stillwater.

1988

With the help of new managers Bob Doyle and Pam Lewis, Brooks is signed to Capitol Records, having been finally discovered at Nashville's Bluebird Café by the label's Len Scholds, after filling in for a no-show performer who was originally second on the bill.

1989

Mar [25] Co-penned by the singer, his debut *Much Too Young (To Feel This Damn Old)* enters the US Country chart on its way to hit #8.
May Capitol releases Brooks' freshman effort ***Garth Brooks***. Produced by Allen Reynolds, the partly self-written set impresses genre critics and showcases the singer's classic country-vocal style.
Dec [12] Ballad *If Tomorrow Never Comes*, again co-penned by Brooks, and an early career highlight, tops the US Country chart.
[14-17] Already a hot live draw, Brooks' four-night sellout stand at the Fox Theatre, Detroit, MI, nets $718,899.

1990

May [12] ***Garth Brooks***, a Country chart-topper, crosses over to the the US Album survey on its way to #13 and will stay charted well into 1993.
July [14] Brooks performs at a country jamboree at the 11th annual "Bull Run Country Music Festival", Bull Run Regional Park, Washington, DC, on the same day that *The Dance* begins a three-week stay atop the US Country chart.
Sept [22] His sophomore effort ***No Fences*** enters the US Album survey. Once again produced by Reynolds, it will eventually hit US #3, stay charted for over two years and become the biggest-selling country album of all time. Its success will not only elevate Brooks to replace Randy Travis as the forerunner of the "new country" genre, but will also be largely credited for opening the crossover floodgates for a host of fresh young country voices, both on US radio and at retail.
Oct [6] The extracted *Friends In Low Places* tops the US Country chart.

1991

Jan [12] Brooks takes part in the "World's Largest Country Music Show" at the Suncoast Dome, St. Petersburg, FL, before a sellout crowd of 37,313, the same day that *Unanswered Prayers* becomes his third straight US Country chart-topper.
[28] He nabs the Favorite Single, Country trophy at the 18th annual American Music Awards, held at the Shrine Auditorium, Los Angeles, CA.
Feb [1] He performs on a bill with the Judds at the Palace of Auburn Hills, Auburn Hills, MI, grossing $382,552.
Mar [25] ***No Fences*** receives NARM's 1990 Best Seller Country Album, Male award.
Apr [6] As *Two Of A Kind* hits #1 on the US Country survey, ***No Fences*** is confirmed as the fastest-selling triple-platinum country album since the inception of multi-million selling awards in 1984. During the month, the video for his current single *Thunder Rolls* is banned by The Nashville Network, Country Music Television and the syndicated PBS programme New Country Video, all of whom object to the graphic depiction of domestic violence in the clip.
[24] He collects six trophies at 26th annual Academy of Country Music Awards in Los Angeles, including Entertainer Of The Year, Top Male Singer and Top Album (***No Fences***).
May [26] Brooks participates in the "F.A.R.M. Fest '91" benefit at the Myriad Convention Center, Oklahoma City, OK, to benefit Oklahoman farmers, before a sellout crowd of 14,230.
June [22] Controversial *The Thunder Rolls*, a popular live number, tops the US Country chart but, like Brooks' other singles to date, fails to crack the Hot 100.
Aug [22] He performs at the New York State Fair, Syracuse, NY, grossing $278,078.
Sept [28] ***Ropin' The Wind*** debuts at US #1 and will become his third mainstay on the US Album survey.
Oct [2] Brooks performs at the 25th annual Country Music Awards held at the Grand Ole Opry, Nashville, and wins the Entertainer Of The Year, Single Of The Year, Album Of The Year and Music Video Of The Year trophies. "Garth Brooks" video is also certified multi-platinum with sales of 200,000 units by the RIAA on the same day.
[12] He sings *Unchained Melody* at the wedding of his keyboardist, David Gant, to Susan Polly in Elkhorn, TN.
[17] Brooks performs on NBC-TV's "The Tonight Show".
Nov [2] Brooks guest stars on NBC-TV's "Empty Nest".
[7] He performs at the 12,000-seat Middle Tennessee State University show in Murfreesboro, TN, a show which has sold out in 21 minutes.
[16] His cover of Billy Joel's *Shameless* tops the US Country chart.
[26] More than 10,000 cans of food are donated in Jackson, MS, by fans hoping to get tickets to Brooks' December 6th show. They have been asked to bring ten cans each to a grocery store in exchange for a

lottery envelope, ten of which hold concert tickets.
Dec [3] At the second annual **Billboard** Music Awards, held at the Barkar Hangar, Santa Monica Airport, Santa Monica, CA, Brooks wins the Top Albums Artist, Hot Country Singles, Top Country Album, Top Country Albums Artist and Top Country Artist categories.
[14] With his Stillwater tour band including James Garver (lead guitar), Smittle (bass), Steve McClure (steel guitar), Ty England (acoustic guitar/vocals), Gant (keys/fiddle) and Mike Palmer (drums), Brooks' sellout performance at the Charlotte Coliseum, NC, grosses $345,480, a house record.
[26] Brooks is featured on ABC-TV's "Entertainers '91", saluting the year's Top 20 entertainers. (During the year, his phenomenal live popularity has seen $7,110,642 garnered from 48 shows, in front of 479,607 people. The record-breaking ***Ropin' The Wind*** becomes the first album to be simultaneously certified gold (500,000), platinum (1 million), double platinum, triple platinum and quadruple platinum by the RIAA, due to the extraordinary speed of the title's sales.)

1992

Jan [9] Brooks guests again on "The Tonight Show".
[17] NBC-TV airs the "This Is Garth Brooks" special, which attracts 28 million viewers.
[19] He donates $25,000 to the cerebral palsy telethon, after seeing the show and matching ten cents for every dollar raised locally.
[27] Brooks bows out of the 19th annual American Music Awards, held at the Shrine Auditorium, at which he wins the Favorite Male Artist, Country, Favorite Single, Country and Favorite Album, Country categories, to take care of his three-month pregnant wife. (Subsequently admitting to adulterous behavior during early touring, Brooks will make a number of emotional speeches at future awards ceremonies, thanking his wife Sandy, with whom he is completely reconciled, for standing by him.)
Feb [1] *Shameless* charts for one week at UK #71.
[8] ***No Fences*** finally hits US #3, as ***Garth Brooks*** finally reaches its US peak at #13.
[15] ***Ropin' The Wind*** debuts at its UK #41 peak, although his extraordinary US success will not be repeated in country-resistant Europe (with the exception of Eire).
[25] Brooks adds the Best Country Vocal Performance, Male honor for ***Ropin' The Wind*** to his bulging trophy cabinet at the 34th annual Grammy Awards, from New York's Radio City Music Hall.
Mar [5] He headlines the Academy of Country Music's sponsored Country Radio Seminar's 23rd annual "Super Faces Show", at the Opryland Hotel, Nashville.
[14] Brooks, currently appearing on the front cover of **Time** magazine and quoted in an official press release from rock legends Kiss saying, "My biggest influence through junior high was Kiss. That was my thing", is the musical guest on NBC-TV's "Saturday Night Live".
Apr [29] Brooks, now considered both a country legend and sex-symbol (despite his thinning hair and less-than-matinee idol looks), performs at the 27th annual Academy of Country Music Awards.
June [2] Another North American tour begins, at the McNichols Sports Arena, Denver, CO, before a sellout 18,225 crowd.
[8] A daughter Taylor Mayne Pearl Brooks, named after heroes James Taylor and Minnie Pearl and the state of Maine, where she was conceived, is born in Nashville to Sandy and Garth. Brooks says, "After this, nothing else matters." He will subsequently tell a Nashville audience - "Retirement, just getting out for good, is very much in the picture right now. This daughter needs a father, and my wife needs a partner to help raise her."
[22] 198,000 calls jam and knock out local telephone lines at 10:15 a.m. in Phoenix, AZ, as ticket demand for his forthcoming July 19th concert reaches fever pitch.
Aug [20] Dr. Homer Hardy Jr., a Tulsa, OK doctor, files a $35-million lawsuit against the Southwestern Bell telephone company, alleging that his wife died because he could not reach emergency 911 on July 18th, due to a phone-line jam caused by intense ticket demand for Brooks' forthcoming concert.
[21] Brooks returns to his native Oklahoma to perform before a sellout crowd of 14,585 at the Myriad Convention Center Arena.
[25] To tie in with the release of his ***Beyond The Season*** Christmas album, Brooks announces the launch of a fundraising campaign for the Feed the Children Charity.
Sept [5] Having broken the house record at the New York State Fair in Syracuse, NY, three days earlier, Brooks plays to a sellout crowd at the Meadowlands Arena, East Rutherford, NJ, having sold the 19,927 available tickets in 17 minutes.
[19] With his *The Dance* voted the third most popular country song of all time by readers of **Country America** magazine, his first festive album ***Beyond The Season*** hits US #2.
[21] New album ***The Chase*** is premiered on the Westwood One radio network.
[22] Brooks is interviewed by Jane Pauley on NBC-TV's "Dateline".
Oct [8] He breaks another house record, this time at the Humphrey Coliseum, Mississippi State University, Starkville, MS.
[10] ***The Chase*** debuts at US #1 and will be certified for five million US sales in just eight weeks.
[26] Brooks participates in TNN cable-TV's "Hats Off To Minnie - America Honors Minnie Pearl" special.
Nov [22] Brooks ends a ten-date Southern swing during the month, grossing more than $1.5 million, with a sellout show at the Carolina Coliseum, University of South Carolina, Columbia, SC.
Dec [9] Brooks wins the Top Country Singles Artist, Top Country Artist, Top Country Album Artist, Top Country Album, Top Billboard 200 Album Artist, Top Billboard 200 Album, Top Pop Artist and Top Billboard 200 Album Artist (Male) categories at the 1992 **Billboard** Music Awards, at the Universal Amphitheatre, Universal City, CA.
[12] Brooks ends his seven-month US tour at the Palace of Auburn Hills, before a sellout crowd of 23,464, having played more than 80 SRO shows and grossing in excess of $20 million.
[18] He guests on Kenny Rogers' CBS-TV "Christmas In The Ozarks" special. (By year's end, Brooks signs a 20-year deal with Liberty Records (renamed from Capitol).)

1993

Jan [25] He collects the Favorite Male Artist, Country trophy at the 20th annual American Music Awards, held at the Shrine Auditorium.
[29] Brooks performs two sellout benefit concerts at the Great Western Forum, Inglewood, CA, grossing $724,420 for various charities.
[31] After last-minute squabbles with NBC-TV executives who are reluctant to show the video of Brooks' *We Will Be Free*, a song which has gained favor not least from the gay community (his sister Betsy is a self-proclaimed lesbian), as part of the programme at Superbowl XXVII between the Buffalo Bills and the Dallas Cowboys at the Rosebowl, Pasadena, CA, Brooks sings the national anthem as previously agreed. (NBC had approached audience member Jon Bon Jovi to stand in as a last-minute replacement if necessary.) Hearing-impaired actress Marlee Matlin signs the anthem. The previous time Books had sung it was at an Oklahoma City horse show in the mid-'80s.
Feb [16] Brooks is featured on NBC-TV's "Academy Of Country Music's Hits" special.
[17] He wins the Male Vocalist and Best Album (***Ropin' The Wind***) categories at the inaugural German American Country Music Federation awards in Nashville.
[22-23] Brooks appears at the "Livestock Show & Rodeo", Houston, TX.
Mar [4] He is named Best Country Artist in **Rolling Stone**'s Readers' Picks Music Awards .
[29] Brooks guests on ABC-TV's annual Academy Awards night "The Barbara Walters Special".
May [12] He is named the World's Best-Selling Country Artist Of The Year at the fifth annual World Music Awards, at the Sporting Club, Monte Carlo, Monaco.
[14] Brooks guests on NBC-TV's "Bob Hope - The First 90 Years".
July [9] Terry Currier, co-owner of record store Music Millenium, organizes the Garth Brooks Bar-B-Q, where his CDs are placed on a grill and cooked, in response to Brooks' stance on the sale of second-hand CDs.
Sept [18] Once again helmed by Reynolds, ***In Pieces*** debuts at US #1.
[23-25] He performs three sellout dates at Texas Stadium, Irving, TX, during his current US tour.

1994

Jan [29] *Red Strokes*, coupled with *Friends In Low Places* reaches UK #13.
Feb [7] Brooks wins the Best Male Artist, Country category at the 21st annual American Music Awards, held again at the Shrine Auditorium.
[12] ***In Pieces*** bows at its UK #2 peak, behind Tori Amos' ***Under The Pink***.
Mar [1] He performs *Standing Outside The Fire* at the 36th annual Grammy awards at New York's Radio City Music Hall.
[30] Brooks plays the first of eight sellout dates at The Point Depot, Dublin, Eire.
Apr [22] During a current tour of Europe and Scandinavia, Brooks performs before a crowd of more than 7,000 at the Spektrum, Oslo, Norway.
[23] *Standing Outside The Fire* reaches UK #28.
May [4] Brooks is named the World's Best Selling Country Artist Of The Year at the sixth annual World Music Awards, at the Sporting Club in Monte Carlo.
[6] "This Is Garth Brooks, Too!" airs on NBC-TV.
July [13] Brooks performs *Hard Luck Woman*, included on the ***Kiss My Ass*** tribute album, with Kiss on "The Tonight Show".
[14] He performs with the Hollywood Bowl Orchestra at the Hollywood Bowl as part of the 1994 World Cup festivities.
Nov [29] The RIAA certifies six million sales of his debut set ***Garth Brooks***.
Dec [31] Collecting his chart successes to date, ***The Hits*** makes UK #54.

1995

Jan [7] ***The Hits*** tops the US chart.
[18] "Garth Brooks - The Hits - Live From Texas Stadium" airs on NBC-TV. Brooks invites fans to call him toll-free between 4:00 p.m. and 6:00 p.m. from the Eastern and Central time zones on 1-800-GARTH-TX.
[19] He takes part in the "Commitment To Life VIII" AIDS benefit honoring Elton John, Tom Hanks and Ron Meyer at the Universal Amphitheatre, Universal City.
[30] Brooks wins the Male Artist/Country category at the 22nd annual American Music Awards, staged at the Shrine Auditorium.
Feb [17] The RIAA certifies multi-platinum sales for ***The Chase*** (six million), ***Ropin' The Wind*** (11 million) and ***No Fences*** (13 million), once again confirming Brooks as the biggest-selling country artist of all-time.
[18] *The Dance*, coupled with *Friends In Places*, debuts at its UK #36 peak.
Mar [7] The RIAA certifies three million sales of "The Garth Brooks Collection".
[14] Brooks goes to Capitol Hill to protest potential congressional cuts in federal funding for the Arts.
[23] He wins the International Album (***In Pieces***), International Male Vocalist and Best Touring Act categories at the inaugural Great British Country Music Awards held in Birmingham, W. Midlands.
May [10] Brooks performs live at the 30th annual Academy of Country Music Awards from Universal Studios, Universal City.
June [1] Having shipped nearly ten million copies and bringing new meaning to the word "limited", CEMA ceases production of ***The Hits***.
[30] Brooks buries the master of ***The Hits*** beneath his Hollywood Walk of Fame star, which he accepts at

11:30 a.m., in front of Capitol's offices on the corner of Sunset and Vine.

July [21] Songwriter Guy Thomas files a $5 million lawsuit in Los Angeles against Brooks claiming copyright infringement of his composition *Conviction Of The Heart* (which Thomas co-wrote with Kenny Loggins - who is not suing) by Brooks' *Standing Outside The Fire*.

Sept [28] ***The Hits*** is RIAA-certified with eight million sales.

Nov [14] The RIAA also confirms multi-platinum sales of ***In Pieces*** (six million) and ***Beyond The Season*** (three million).

[23] Brooks performs *The Fever* live on Fox-TV's NFL Thanksgiving Day special.

Dec [2] ***Fresh Horses***, Brooks' first studio album in two years with eight of the 10 songs co-penned by him, reaches UK #22 (released on the Parlophone label) in its week of entry. Brooks claims to have listened to some 4,700 songs to find cover worthy material for the project, which includes his version of Aerosmith's *Fever* (with reworked lyrics).

[9] ***Fresh Horses*** debuts at its US #2 peak, behind the Beatles' ***Anthology 1***.

Jan [30] He collects the Favorite Male Country Artist and Favorite Country Album (for ***The Hits***) statuettes at the 23rd annual American Music Awards, held at the Shrine Auditorium. However, when also named the Favorite Artist, he leaves the trophy on the podium, later explaining that he cannot accept it, feeling instead that the award should have gone to Hootie & The Blowfish.

Feb [12] He performs *Like We've Never Had A Broken Heart* with Trisha Yearwood on US-TV's syndicated "Crook & Chase".

[17] *She's Every Woman* bow at its UK #55 peak.

Mar [4] Brooks sends a letter (which will appear in a full-page ad in **Billboard** on the 23rd) asking US radio stations to synchronize a sympathetic music tribute at 9:02 a.m. ET to commemorate the one year anniversary of the Alfred P. Murrah Federal Building bombing in Oklahoma City on April 19th.

[13-17] Brooks begins a 77-city world tour with five shows at the Omni, Atlanta, GA, where 80,000 tickets have sold in 2½ hours, breaking the previous house record held by Elvis Presley.

BROS

Matt Goss (vocals); **Luke Goss** (drums); **Craig Logan** (bass)

1980

Having participated in two school groups, the Goss twins (b. Sept. 29, 1968, Lewisham, London, Matt older by 20 minutes, and two months premature), their father a London police detective and their mother a cabaret singer, formed, at age 12, Caviar, their most serious venture to date. They met Logan (b. Apr. 22, 1969, Kirkcaldy, Fife. Scotland) in the dinner line, borrowed 50p and asked him to join the band. They will continue to write and practice throughout their student days, convinced that they will become major teen stars, subsequently leaving school in 1984, when they begin playing, initially under the name Gloss, in working men's clubs and similar venues around South London. Writing over 20 original songs, they team up with their subsequent producer, co-writer and publisher Nicky Graham in 1985, who introduces them to Thom Watkins, manager of the Pet Shop Boys.

1987

Apr With Watkins behind them, the trio signs a worldwide deal with CBS Records, which puts together a marketing plan to launch the teen-act in the fall.

Aug Their first single *I Owe You Nothing* is released in the UK, but initially fails to chart.

1988

Feb *When Will I Be Famous* is their first hit, at UK #2, taking four months to peak. It causes controversy over the extent of vocal involvement by backing singer Dee Lewis.

Mar *Drop The Boy* hits UK #2, as the trio starts to receive widespread media coverage in teen mags and youth TV programs in the UK, in true teenage-idol tradition. Their faces adorn a horde of cash-in fan publications, and their UK fan club receives applications for membership at the rate of 3,000 a week.

Apr [9] ***Push***, produced by Graham and with Andy Richards on keyboards, debuts at its UK #2 peak, behind the compilation album ***Now! That's What I Call Music 11***. All of its songs are credited to "The Brothers", though, at the very least, they are co-penned by producer Graham.

May The trio appears at the "Montreux Rock Festival" in Montreux, Switzerland, televised around the world. The Bros segment is the most often repeat-screened during UK TV coverage.

June [25] *I Owe You Nothing*, astutely reissued with a facelift remix, gives Bros its first UK chart-topper within two weeks of re-release. It coincides with their first headlining UK tour (sponsored by Pepsi Cola for £250,000), which starts on the 23rd and runs for 11 sellout dates.

July [16] *When Will I Be Famous?*, the group's only US chart record, peaks at #83, as its parent album ***Push*** pulls up at US #171.

Sept Typically up-beat, slickly-produced *I Quit* hits UK #4.

Dec *Cat Among The Pigeons*, coupled with their seasonal cover of *Silent Night*, hits UK #2.

1989

Jan Logan leaves the band amid much reported acrimony.

Feb [13] The group wins the Best British Newcomer category at the eighth annual BRIT Awards, at London's Royal Albert Hall.

May [4] The Goss twins promise Logan that they will not touch the group's estimated £5 million assets until the dispute over compensation is settled, which it ultimately is, to Logan's satisfaction.

July [29] *Too Much* bows at its UK #2 peak, behind Sonia's *You'll Never Stop Me Loving You*.

Oct [7] *Chocolate Box* hits UK #9 in its week of entry.

[28] Its parent album ***The Time*** debuts at its UK #4 peak.

Dec *Sister* hits UK #10, as Bros wins the **Smash Hits** Readers' Poll, Worst Group category.

1990

Mar *Madly In Love* confirms their commercial downturn, peaking at UK #14 with only four weeks on the survey. With a change of management, to Elton John's John Reid Enterprises, following another court action (during which it is claimed that the band is broke due to lifestyle excesses), Bros retreats from the British media glare to spend the last months of the year recording in the US with members of Quincy Jones' Qwest stable, in search of a new non-teeny bop direction. (Meanwhile, Logan will successfully link with UK singer Kim Appleby, both romantically and as co-songwriter and producer of her debut solo hits.)

1991

Oct [12] ***Changing Faces*** bows at its UK #18 peak, but will quickly fall off the survey. (*Are You Mine?* fleetingly made #12 on July [13], with *Try* reaching UK #27 on Oct [5]). Having failed to secure any hits in the US, and clearly out of fashion in the UK, the band's 15 minutes is up, although Luke Goss will return in 1993 as leader of Luke Goss & the Band Of Thieves, peaking at UK #52 on June [12] with *Sweeter Than The Midnight Rain*, Matt Goss will have his first solo hit with *If You Were Here Tonight* on Apr [27], 1996 and Logan will be named international marketing manager at EMI Records in Sept 1995.

BOBBY BROWN

1985

Nov [25] Brown (b. Robert Baresford Brown, Feb. 5, 1969, Roxbury, MA), having first performed at the age of three when his mother pushed him on stage during the intermission of a James Brown concert in Boston, MA, has already earned his musical spurs as one fifth of the smash R&B pop-teen act New Edition, which he co-founded in 1981. Following the success of the act's current ***All For Love*** platinum (US) album, he becomes the first member of the unit to decide on a solo career, signing to MCA Records.

1986

Dec As the extracted *Girlfriend* tops the US R&B chart, his debut album ***King Of Stage***, produced by Bobby Louil Siolas Jr., enters the US chart, set to reach #88. It will yield *Girlfriend* (which peaks at US #57 on Jan [24] the following year) and the US R&B #31 hit *Girl Next Door*.

1988

Jan Brown completes the recording of his second album, mainly helmed by hot hitmaking writing/production duo L.A. Reid and Babyface, but also with hip-hop specialist Gene Griffin and soul-ballad producer Larry White, enabling Brown to display his full range of funk, R&B, rap, dance, soul and ballad qualities.

Aug *Don't Be Cruel*, written by Reid, Babyface and Darryl Simmons, makes UK #42.

Oct [15] *Don't Be Cruel* hits US #8, having topped the US R&B chart on July [23].

1989

Jan [10] The still-rising *My Prerogative* is certified gold by the RIAA.

[14] Co-written by Brown and Griffin, *My Prerogative*, boosted by a feverish Brown dance-displaying, MTV hotly-rotated video clip, hits US #1 (having topped the US R&B chart on Oct [15]) and UK #6.

[19] *Don't Be Cruel* is also confirmed gold by the RIAA.

[21] Having already topped the US R&B Album ranking for 11 weeks, ***Don't Be Cruel*** hits US #1, during a 97-week chart tenure. It will also hit UK #3 (on July [22]), its mix of light hip-hop fused with aggressive dance and soul numbers proving popular worldwide.

[25] Wowing fans with his non-stop dancing antics, Brown is arrested at the Municipal Auditorium, Columbus, GA, for an overtly sexually suggestive performance. He will be fined $652 under the Anti-Lewdness Ordinance for giving a "sexually explicit performance harmful to minors on city property, whether the performers are clothed or not".

Mar [18] Co-penned by L.A. Reid and Darnell Bristoll, *Roni* hits US #3, his third US Top 10 single in a row.

Apr Reissued *Don't Be Cruel* reaches UK #13.

[12] He wins the Best R&B/Urban Contemporary Album Of The Year, Male category at the third annual Soul Train Music Awards, held at the Shrine Auditorium, Los Angeles, CA.

[25] Brown wins Act of the Year, R&B Act, Top Male Vocalist, Top Rock Single (for *My Prerogative*) at the third SKC Boston Music Awards, at the Wang Center in his hometown of Boston.

May Having recently cancelled 20 concerts on the final leg of his US tour, amid much criticism, the toe-tapping *Every Little Step* hits UK #6.

June [10] Once again helped by an up-beat, precision-timed, dance-busting video, *Every Little Step* hits US #3. (His trademark dancing abilities will bridge the gap between Michael Jackson and next year's hot-foot sensation, MC Hammer.)

[16] *Every Little Step* is certified gold by the RIAA.

[30] Police rush to a near-riot scene at the HMV store in Oxford Street, London, and close off the street, as 4,000 fans try to get Brown's autograph during a personal appearance. Six fans are hospitalized and one given the kiss of life.

Aug [5] Trailering the MCA-synergized movie project "Ghostbusters II", in which he has a cameo role playing a doorman, Brown's *On Our Own*, taken from the soundtrack, hits US #2, having already hit UK #4, while the reissued ***King Of Stage*** now makes UK #40.
[12] At a Walt Disney press conference, it is announced that Brown will play the Three Blind Mice in their cable channel's Shelley Duvall-produced "Mother Goose Rock'n'Rhyme", alongside Paul Simon (Simple Simon), Art Garfunkel (Rhymeland bartender), Little Richard (Old King Cole) and others.
[25] *On Our Own* is certified platinum by the RIAA.
Sept [6] Brown performs at the annual MTV Video Music Awards, at the Universal Amphitheatre, Universal City, CA.
Nov [4] Remixed *Rock Wit'Cha* hits US #7, having peaked at UK #33.
[14] *Rock Wit' Cha* is ratified gold by the RIAA.
Dec [2] While a belated UK release of *Roni* climbs to UK #21, a remix album of hit extracts from ***Don't Be Cruel***, ***Dance ... Ya Know It!*** fills in between studio projects, hitting US #9 and UK #26.
[23] He wins Top Pop Singles Artist, Male, Top Pop Album Artist, Male and Top Black Artist categories in **Billboard**'s The Year In Music statistical round-up.

1990

Jan [12] Brown is scheduled to be presented with the Martin Luther King Jr. Musical Achievement Award at Symphony Hall in Boston, during a Tony Bennett/ Count Basie Orchestra concert, but fails to show up.
[16] ***Dance! ... Ya Know It!*** is certified platinum by the RIAA.
[22] He collects the Favorite Male Artist, Pop/Rock and Favorite Album, Soul/R&B trophies at the 17th annual American Music Awards, held at the Shrine Auditorium.
[27] MCA Music Video issues "His Prerogative", a collection of video hits from the past 18 months.
Feb [17] ***Dance! ... Ya Know It!*** hits US #9.
[21] *Every Little Step* wins the Best R&B Vocal Performance, Male category at the 32nd annual Grammy Awards, at the Shrine Auditorium.
Mar [8] Brown is named Best New Male Singer and Best R&B Artist in **Rolling Stone**'s Readers' Picks for 1989, and Best R&B Artist in the Critics' Awards.
[9] "His Prerogative" video is certified multi-platinum with sales of 100,000 units by the RIAA.
[14] He performs at the fourth annual Soul Train Awards, at the Shrine Auditorium.
Apr [19] He wins the Outstanding Male Vocalist and Outstanding R&B Act category at the fourth annual SKC Boston Music Awards, at the Wang Center.
June [5] Brown plays the first of eight sellout nights at the Wembley Arena, Wembley, Middx., during his current world tour, as the MCA UK-issued *Free Style Mega-Mix*, mixed by Rita Liebrand (the sister of mix-master Ben Liebrand), reaches UK #14.
July [21] His duet with Glenn Medeiros *She Ain't Worth It* tops the US chart and will also reach UK #12.

1991

Jan [16] Brown inducts Wilson Pickett into the Roll and Roll Hall of Fame, at the annual awards dinner, held at the Waldorf Astoria Hotel, New York.
Feb [10] Brown joins with nearly 100 celebrities in Burbank, CA, to record *Voices That Care*, a David Foster and fiancée Linda Thompson Jenner-composed and organized charity record to benefit the American Red Cross Gulf Crisis Fund.
Mar [17-18] He participates in the American Music Awards Concert Series at the Yokohama Arena, Yokohama, Japan.
Apr Having already established his own Bosstown recording studio in Atlanta, GA, where he is now based, Brown forms the Bosstown label and continues recording the follow-up to ***Don't Be Cruel***.
Aug He contributes to a video of Marvin Gaye's *Mercy Mercy Mercy*, a tie-up between Motown and the Audubon Society to increase awareness of the nation's environmental problems.

1992

Mar [19] Brown wins the Outstanding Male Vocalist award at the first annual Coca-Cola Atlanta Music Awards, held at the Fox Theatre, Atlanta, GA.
Apr [19] He is cited by Metro Police for operating an uninsured car (a 1991 Porsche registered to his girlfriend, Whitney Houston) and driving without a license on Route 138 in Canton, MA.
July [18] Brown marries Houston at her New Jersey estate in Mendham. (In a March 1993 interview in **Details**, his former colleague in New Edition and invited guest, Ronald DeVoe says: "They got to the part about 'til death do you part, and Bobby was laughing.")
Aug [29] *Humpin' Around* reaches UK #19.
Sept [5] ***Bobby***, repeating the successful formula of its multiplatinum predecessor, with production assistance once again from L.A. Reid/Babyface and Teddy Riley, debuts at its UK #11 peak.
[9] He performs *Humpin' Around* live at the ninth annual MTV Video Music Awards held at the Pauley Pavilion, Los Angeles.
[12] *Humpin' Around* hits US #3, as ***Bobby*** bows at its US #2 peak.
[26] Brown is the musical guest on NBC-TV's "Saturday Night Live" season-opener.
Oct [13] *Humpin' Around* is certified gold by the RIAA.
[24] *Good Enough* makes UK #41.
Dec [26] Having made UK #41 on Oct [24], the Reid, Babyface and Simmons-penned *Good Enough* hits US #7.
[29] He begins a major US tour in Charleston, WV, set to end in Tampa, FL on February 28th.
[31] New Year's Eve "MTV Drops The Ball '93" festivities, featuring Brown and others, airs on the US cable network.

1993

Jan [22] *Good Enough* is certified gold by the RIAA.
[25] He collects the Favorite Male Artist, Soul/R&B trophy at the 20th annual American Music Awards, held at the Shrine Auditorium, which he also co-hosts with Wynonna Judd and Gloria Estefan.
Feb [19] The RIAA certifies two millon sales of ***Bobby***.
[20] *Get Away* reaches US #14.
Mar [4] A daughter, Bobbi Kristina Houston Brown, is born to Whitney and Bobby Brown.
Apr [7] Brown wins Act Of The Year, Outstanding R&B album (***Bobby***) and Outstanding R&B Vocalist at the Boston Music Awards, at the Wang Center.
[26] Brown and Queline Young are fined $850 for public lewdness for simulating the sex act at a January 13th Augusta-Richmond County Civic Center gig. He still awaits trial in an assault case.
[27] MCA issues ***B. Brown Posse*** on Brown's new Triple B label, a various artists album overseen by Brown and featuring his sister Coop, and ***NBA Jam Session***, both albums released under the auspices of Brown.
[28] The RIAA certifies seven million sales of ***Don't Be Cruel***.
May [15] *That's The Way Love Is* makes US #57.
[31] Brown performs at the Neal Blaisdell Arena, Honolulu, HI, his last show for a while before taking time off because of high blood pressure and throat problems, causing the cancellation of the European leg of his tour.
June [19] *That's The Way Love Is* debuts at its UK #56 peak.
Sept [30] Brown and Houston are stopped in their limousine at Kennedy International Airport, New York, by nine police officers with guns, looking for drug couriers.
Nov [23] MCA (US) releases ***Remixes In The Key Of B***.

1994

Jan [22] Brown and Houston's first duet *Something In Common* debuts at its UK #16 peak.
Apr [11] Charges against Brown and his bodyguards, William Brinson and Christopher Harvest, for beating Lee Rucker in Atlanta 1992 are dropped by the alleged victim. No reason is given.
[26] Brown is arrested and charged in the beating of a nightclub patron at the Mannequin in Orlando, FL. He is released on $5,000 bail.
May [3] He attends the birthday celebrations of soul legend James Brown at the Civic Center, Augusta, GA.
June [25] *Two Can Play That Game* bows at its UK #38 peak.
Sept [28] One week after an initial separation from Houston (though subsequent press reports will indicate an early reunion), Brown is a witness to the fatal drive-by shooting of Steven Sealy, his sister's fianceé, shot while getting into Brown's Bentley outside the Biarritz Lounge in Roxbury.

1995

Apr [8] *Two Can Play That Game* hits UK #3.
July [8] *Humpin' Around* hits UK #8.
Aug [5] ***Two Can Play That Game*** reaches UK #24 in its week of entry.
[18] He allegedly kicks a security guard at Le Montrose Suite Hotel in Los Angeles and is issued with a citation for misdemeanor battery.
Oct [14] Reissued *My Prerogative* bows at its UK #17 peak.

1996

Feb [3] Reworked *Every Little Step (Remix)* enters at UK #25 peak.
Apr [22] Brown is booked for DUI in Atlanta, unable to recite the alphabet. The woman in the car with him is not Whitney Houston.
see also: **NEW EDITION**

JAMES BROWN

1955

Nov Abandoned by his mother at age four and raised by an aunt, Handsome "Honey" Washington, in her bordello at 944, Twiggs Avenue in Augusta, GA, Brown (b. May 3, 1933, Barnwell, SC, various birthdates (notably 1928) and places will be listed in print, the confusion arising from Brown's occasional use of fake I.D.) quit school in the seventh grade, where he had formed his first singing group the Cremona Trio. After delinquent teenage years in Augusta, including a hard labor stretch in a state corrective institution at age 16 for petty theft (he was originally sentenced to serve 8 to 16 years but was transferred to the Alto Reform School, Alto, GA, to serve a reduced four-year sentence), Brown was released on parole after three years and one day (not least because, as a proficient baseball player, he could pitch for a team in nearby Toccoa, GA). Linking up with a young local pianist, Bobby Byrd, Brown spends a brief period staying in Byrd's grandmother's family home in Toccoa before coming under the wing of Little Richard's manager, Clint Brantley, who offers him a room above his Two Spot nightclub in Macon, GA, where Brown, working days at the Lawson Motor Company, becomes a temporary member of the house band. While his musical apprenticeship has also included playing drums and organ for Bill Johnson, the Four Steps of Rhythm, the Gospel Starlighters and others, Brown has joined Byrd's gospel troupe, the Three Swanees, which becomes the Swanee Quintet, then the Swanees, whose line-up also includes Sylvester Keels and Nafloyd Scott, a unit which evolves into Brown's long-term backing band, the Famous Flames. Based in Macon, the secular combo plays live gigs around Georgia, in a style which blends gospel with raucous jump blues-based R&B. At Brantley's instigation, Brown and the Famous Flames now record an acetate dub of a Brown and Johnny Terry composition, *Please, Please, Please* at Macon radio station WIBB, supervised by DJ Hamp Swain, who begins playing the cut on air while Brantley sends copies to Duke

Records' Don Robey in Houston and the Chess Brothers in Chicago.

1956

Jan [23] King Records executive Ralph Bass, having heard the song on an Atlanta Radio station, signs Brown with the Famous Flames to the Federal label (a subsidiary of Syd Nathan's Cincinnati, OH-based King parent) for $200.

Feb [4] Brown, with a Famous Flames line-up of Byrd (piano, backing vocals), Scott (guitar) and backing vocalists Keels, Johnny Terry and Nashpendle Knox, re-records *Please, Please, Please* (supplemented by Wilbert "Lee Diamond" Smith and Ray Felder (tenor saxes), Clarence Mack (bass), and Edison Gore (drums) at King Studios in Cincinnati).

Apr The impassioned *Please, Please, Please*, credited to James Brown & the Famous Flames, makes the US R&B chart (#6), mainly on regional sales in Georgia and bordering states, where it benefits from the group's rapidly-growing touring popularity. (It will continue to sell steadily, eventually logging over one million US sales, wherever Brown takes his live show, but will never cross over to the US Top 100.)

1957

Apr The initial line-up of the Famous Flames disbands during a period when nine follow-up singles will fail to register sales.

1958

Sept [18] Given one last chance by the Federal/King stable, Brown cuts four tracks at the Belltone Studios, New York, NY, under producer Andy Gibson and arranger Gene Redd, including the self-written, gospel-inflected *Try Me (I Need You)*.

1959

Jan *Try Me (I Need You)* becomes his first national success, reaching #48 and topping the R&B chart for a week on its way past one million sales. On the strength of its success, Universal Attractions booking agency owner Ben Bart takes a special interest in the young star. With Bart's guidance, not least on the business front, Brown forms a revamped and permanent backing band (still called the Famous Flames, and led by tenor saxophonist J.C. Davis) and takes a unique, innovative and unprecedented R&B show on the road, mixing calculated stage hysteria with absolute musical precision. (This live brew will break box-office records in all the major R&B venues around the US between 1959 and 1962.)

1960

June *Think*, originally recorded by the Five Royales and written by the quintet's Lowman Pauling, is Brown's second US crossover hit, reaching #33, his third US million-selling single.

[27] *You've Got The Power*, featuring female vocalist Bea Ford, peaks at US #86. Brown begins to release singles at the rate of one every two or three months - a practice he will continue for the next ten years, and which satisfies a demand fuelled by constant touring. Of the initial batch, *This Old Heart* makes US #79 (September 1960 - his last for Federal), *The Bells*, reviving Billy Ward & His Dominoes' death song (#68 - his first hit on parent King label, in December 1960), *Bewildered* (#40, March 1961), *I Don't Mind* (#47, June 1961), *Baby You're Right* (#49, September 1961) and *Lost Someone* (#48, January 1962). Though none are UK hits, many pass into repertoires of groups spearheading the UK beat boom in the mid-'60s.

1962

May *Night Train*, a personalization of the old Jimmy Forrest hit on which Brown name-checks his regular tour venues, hits US #35. Follow-up chartmakers in 1962 are *Shout And Shimmy* (#61, July), *Mashed Potatoes USA* (#82, September) and *Three Hearts In A Tangle* (#93, December).

Oct [24] His now-legendary stage act at Harlem's Apollo Theatre, New York, is taped for a live album.

1963

Feb [9] *Every Beat Of My Heart* spends a week at US #99.

June Brown's first US Top 20 hit revives the schmaltzy, but intense, ballad *Prisoner Of Love*, a hit for Perry Como, Billy Eckstine and the Ink Spots in 1946, which reaches #18. ***Live At The Apollo***, recorded the previous October, is released and sells in unprecedented quantities for an R&B album (over a million within the year), peaking at US #2. It will be regarded as a seminal bench mark in the evolution of live albums.

Aug *These Foolish Things*, another old standard updated with gospel fervor, peaks at US #55.

Sept Brown embarks on "The Biggest Show Of Stars For '63" package tour with Marvin Gaye, the Drifters, Jimmy Reed, Martha & the Vandellas, Inez Foxx, Ruby & the Romantics, the Crystals, Doris Troy and Major Lance. He also forms Fair Deal Records with Bart, following Syd Nathan's decision to allow Brown the opportunity to establish his own Try Me label and Jim Jam Music publishing unit.

Nov Brown joins Ben E. King, the Coasters, the Falcons and Otis Redding on a "Saturday Night At The Apollo" bill in Harlem, New York.

Dec *Signed, Sealed And Delivered* reaches US #77.

1964

Feb [15] Reissued *Please, Please, Please* stalls at US #95.

Mar *Oh Baby Don't You Weep*, a major seller, reaches US #23.

Apr Restricted by arrangements at King, and determined to build upon the huge audience-crossover success of such hits as ***Live At The Apollo***, Brown and Bart, through Fair Deal, and, ignoring King, send a set of new recordings to Mercury subsidiary Smash. King issues live ***Pure Dynamite! Live At The Royal***, recorded at the Royal Theater, Baltimore, MD, which hits US #10.

May The first two releases on Smash, *Caldonia* and *The Things That I Used To Do*, only reach US #95 and #99 respectively, but a further live album, ***Showtime***, makes #61. Third single *Out Of Sight* climbs to US #24, pioneering a new Brown style, with a hard, rhythmic, dance-funk base and a stripped-down, phrase-shouting song structure. Brown quickly develops this "funk" sound into a blend which will revolutionize the whole R&B idiom, and power his future hits. (King wins a lawsuit preventing Fair Deal from leasing any further product to Smash, which will result in no new Brown releases between July 1964 and July 1965.)

June [20] "The Summer Shower Of Stars" package tour, featuring Brown, Solomon Burke, Garnett Mimms, Otis Redding and Joe Tex, performs at the Donnelly Theatre, Boston, MA.

Oct [28-29] Brown records the "TAMI Show (Teen Age Music International Show)" at the Civic Auditorium in Santa Monica, CA, also featuring the Barbarians, Chuck Berry, the Beach Boys, Marvin Gaye, Gerry & the Pacemakers, Lesley Gore, Jan & Dean, Billy J. Kramer & the Dakotas, Smokey Robinson & the Miracles, the Rolling Stones and The Supremes. (In a more bizarre teaming, he will appear in the Frankie Avalon movie "Ski Party", lip-synching an early recording of *I Got You*.)

Dec After the success of *Out Of Sight*, King Records accedes to Brown's demands for greater creative and marketing freedom, and he returns to the label with *Have Mercy Baby*, which reaches US #92. The new deal also allows him to continue sending productions to Smash (but only instrumentals, normally with Brown at the organ).

[18] Brown tries to attend the funeral of Sam Cooke in Chicago, but fans rush the limousine and he drives away rather than cause further disruption.

1965

June [5] Instrumental album ***Grits And Soul*** on Smash reaches US #124.

Sept Teamed with new band leader Nat Jones, Brown develops his legendary *Out Of Sight* rhythm pattern into *Papa's Got A Brand New Bag*, which gives him his first US Top 10, at #8, tops the R&B chart for eight weeks and becomes another million-seller. It is also his UK chart debut, reaching #25. The historic recording, taped at the Arthur Smith Studios in Charlotte, NC, in February, features members of his current backing group, including Maceo Parker, St. Clair Pinckney, Al Clark and Eldee Williams (tenor saxes), Jimmy Nolen and Alphonso Kellum (guitars), Melvin Parker (drums), Lucas "Fats" Gander (organ) and Joe Dupars, Ron Tooley and Levi Rasbury (trumpets).

Dec Equally influential to future R&B generations, *I Got You (I Feel Good)* hits US #3 and spends six weeks at R&B #1, selling over a million (Brown had originally produced the song, initially known as *I Found You*, for Yvonne Fair in 1962). An instrumental version of *Try Me* reaches US #63, taken from the Smash-label instrumental album ***James Brown Plays James Brown Yesterday And Today***.

1966

Jan [8] ***Papa's Got A Brand New Bag*** reaches US #26.

Feb A reissue of a 1960 Federal release, *I'll Go Crazy*, peaks at US #73, while an instrumental version of *Lost Someone* stalls at US #94.

Mar *I Got You (I Feel Good)* reaches UK #29.

[5] ***I Got You (I Feel Good)*** makes US #36.

[11] ITV's "Ready Steady, Go!" is entirely devoted to Brown's music, following which, he performs two London gigs the same evening.

[15] Brown wins Best R&B Recording Of 1965 for *Papa's Got A Brand New Bag* at the eighth annual Grammy Awards.

Apr *Ain't That A Groove Part 1* makes US #42.

May The slow, intense, orchestra-backed ballad (conducted by Sammy Lowe) *It's A Man's Man's Man's World*, co-written by Brown and Betty Newsome, hits US #8, and R&B #1 for two weeks, another million-seller, as Brown makes his prime-time debut on CBS-TV's "The Ed Sullivan Show".

June [18] Instrumental ***James Brown Plays New Breed*** makes US #101.

July *It's A Man's Man's Man's World* reaches UK #13.

[10] Civil disturbance occurs when fans are unable to get into Brown's Los Angeles Sports Arena concert, Los Angeles, CA.

Aug *Money Won't Change Part 1* peaks at US #53. Using his newly-acquired Lear jet, Brown flies to Washington, DC, to discuss the "Don't Be A Drop Out" campaign with Vice President Hubert Humphrey.

Oct [15] ***It's A Man's Man's Man's World*** reaches US #90.

[30] Brown makes a return appearance on "The Ed Sullivan Show".

Nov *Don't Be A Drop-Out*, recorded to support the US "Stay In School" campaign, reaches US #50.

Dec [10] ***Handful Of Soul*** makes US #135.

[21] Band begins a one-week stint at the Westbury Music Fair, Westbury, NY.

1967

Feb *Bring It Up* reaches US #29.

Mar A revival of Wilbert Harrison's *Kansas City* peaks at US #55.

Apr *Think*, a duet with backing singer Vicki Anderson, revives Brown's own 1960 hit and anchors at US #100.

June [2] Brown begins a one-week engagement at the Apollo Theatre, Harlem.

[3] ***Raw Soul*** peaks at US #88, while *Let Yourself Go* reaches US #46.

July [22] ***James Brown Plays The Real Thing*** makes US #164.

Aug [12] ***Live At The Garden*** reaches US #41. Alfred Ellis replaces Jones as the Famous Flames' leader and Brown's chief musical collaborator. The two define their musical path in a new direction unrelated to any other R&B or pop trend, building a funk genre with the rhythm section (usually highlighting "funky drummer" Clyde Stubblefield and guitarist Nolen), with vocals and lyrics used as rhythmic addenda rather than the focal point of the recordings. First example *Cold Sweat* hits US #7, with three weeks at R&B #1, and tops a million sales.

Oct [28] ***Cold Sweat*** reaches US #35.

Nov *Get It Together (Part 1)* reaches US #40. (By year's end, Brown has bought radio station WJBE, Knoxville, TN, and will purchase WEBB, Baltimore, MD, and WRDW, Augusta, GA.)

1968

Jan *I Can't Stand Myself (When You Touch Me)* reaches US #28, while its B-side *There Was A Time* will make US #36 the following month.

Feb [15] With his studio band currently comprising Ellis, Rasbury, DuPars and Waymond Reed, Parker, Pinckney, Nolen and Kellum, Bernard Odum and Stubblefield, Brown cuts the self-inked *I Got The Feelin'* at the Vox Studios, Los Angeles.

Apr [5] After the assassination of Martin Luther King and riots in 30 US cities, Brown makes a national TV appeal from the Boston Garden, Boston, MA, urging restraint and more constructive channelling of justified anger. Its calming effect results in an official commendation from Vice President Humphrey. (He will further use his position constructively, playing for American troops in Vietnam later in the year.)

I Got The Feelin', another million-seller, hits US #6 and tops the R&B chart for two weeks.

May [4] ***I Can't Stand Myself*** reaches US #17.

[8] Brown attends a dinner at the White House, Washington, at the invitation of President and Mrs. Johnson.

June *Licking Stick, Licking Stick*, the epitome of funk minimalism written by Brown, long-time cohorts Byrd and Ellis, and featuring the first white member of Brown's backing band, bassist Tim Drummond, reaches US #14. Released at the same time (and reaching US #52) is the contrasting *America Is My Home*, another spoken narration, which affirms Brown's social conscience and patriotism.

[15] ***I Got The Feelin'*** reaches US #135.

Aug *I Guess I'll Have To Cry, Cry, Cry*, the last hit to be credited to James Brown & the Famous Flames, peaks at US #55. Hereafter Brown is listed alone, though the Flames will continue to back him.

[31] ***James Brown Plays Nothing But Soul*** makes US #150.

Oct *Say It Loud - I'm Black And I'm Proud* provides another million-seller, hitting US #10, and tops the R&B chart for six weeks. (Much of US black youth now looks to him as a heroic figurehead, a true star who has risen from a deprived background and fulfilled the classic American dream simply via raw talent.)

Dec *Goodbye My Love* makes US #31.

[28] ***Live At The Apollo, Vol. 2*** makes US #32 during a nine-month chart tenure.

1969

Jan Brown begins a US tour in San Bernardino, CA, set to end on February 10th at the Memorial Auditorium, Dallas, TX. During the month he will also perform at President Nixon's inaugural celebrations in Washington.

Mar *Give It Up Or Turnit A Loose* climbs to US #15, and spends two weeks at R&B #1.

May *I Don't Want Nobody To Give Me Nothin' (Open Up The Door, I'll Get It Myself)* reaches US #20.

[31] ***Say It Loud - I'm Black And I'm Proud*** peaks at #53.

July [3] Brown performs at the "Newport Jazz Festival", Newport, RI, alongside several rock and blues acts, including Blood, Sweat & Tears and Johnny Winter.

[19] ***Gettin' Down To It*** peaks at US #99.

[23] Los Angeles declares James Brown Day, in honor of his sellout concert at the Great Western Forum, Inglewood, CA. Mayor Sam Yorty is late to hand Brown the proclamation, so the singer walks out (though the concert goes ahead).

Aug Introducing the new Popcorn dance-craze, *Mother Popcorn (You Got To Have A Mother For Me)* becomes another million-seller, reaching US #11 and R&B #1 (for two weeks), while the wholly instrumental *The Popcorn* makes #30.

Sept [6] At the end of a Memphis, TN, concert Brown announces his intention to retire from the road after the next Independence Day.

Instrumental *Lowdown Popcorn* reaches US #41.

[27] The equally non-vocal ***James Brown Plays And Directs The Popcorn*** makes US #40.

Oct *World* reaches US #37.

[4] ***It's A Mother*** peaks at #26.

Nov *Let A Man Come In And Do The Popcorn (Part 1)* climbs to US #21.

Dec Largely instrumental *Ain't It Funky Now* reaches US #24.

1970

Jan *Let A Man Come In And Do The Popcorn (Part 2)* reaches US #40.

Mar *It's A New Day* reaches US #32.

Apr *Funky Drummer* makes US #51 (belying its subsequent popularity as one of the most sampled songs of the hip-hop generation of the late-'80s), while the instrumental ***Ain't It Funky*** reaches US #43.

May *Brother Rapp* reaches US #32.

June ***Soul On Top***, recorded by Brown with the Louie Bellson Orchestra, climbs to US #125. The Famous Flames break up and Brown revamps his backing band as the JB's, retaining Byrd and incorporating members of Cincinnati band the Pacesetters, including brothers William "Bootsy" and Phelps "Catfish" Collins, and later more experienced players, including Fred Wesley and Alfred Ellis.

July ***It's A New Day So Let A Man Come In*** peaks at US #121.

Aug The pure funk *Get Up, I Feel Like Being A Sex Machine*, one of his most distinctive and enduringly-influential releases, reaches US #15 and is Brown's first million-seller of the decade.

Oct *Get Up, I Feel Like Being A Sex Machine* restores him to the UK chart after a four-year break, peaking at #32.

Nov *Super Bad*, another million-seller, reaches US #13 and tops the R&B chart for two weeks, while the live ***Sex Machine*** makes US #29.

[19] Brown marries Deirdre Jenkins at her home in Barnwell, SC.

1971

Jan *Get Up, Get Into It, Get Involved* makes US #34.

Mar *Soul Power* reaches US #29. Instrumental *Spinning Wheel* reaches US #90, and the live ***Super Bad***, US #61.

May *I Cried* makes US #50, while ***Sho Is Funky Down Here*** peaks at US #137.

July [1] Brown signs with Polydor Records in a deal which brings to the label his entire back catalog of recordings from the previous two decades, together with the license for his own People label.

Escape-ism, a monolog spoken by Brown over a JB's rhythm track, reaches US #35.

Aug He turns the summer's fashion craze into a dancefloor number as the People-released *Hot Pants (She Got To Use What She Got To Get What She Wants)* reaches US #15, tops the R&B chart, and is another million-seller. Brown parts from many of the JB's, including Ellis, who is replaced as leader by Fred Wesley, and Collins, who moves with other JB members to George Clinton's Parliament/Funkadelic collective.

Sept His Polydor debut *Make It Funky* reaches US #22 and tops the R&B survey for two weeks.

Oct ***Hot Pants*** reaches US #22.

Nov *My Part: Make It Funky Part 3*, a variation on the previous single, peaks at US #68.

Dec *I'm A Greedy Man* makes US #35. *Hey America* reaches UK #47.

1972

Feb Double live album ***Revolution Of The Mind - Live At The Apollo, Vol.3*** reaches US #39. The JB's single *Gimme Some More* reaches US #67. Written and produced by Brown, it is released on People.

Mar *Talking Loud And Saying Nothing* reaches US #27 and spends a week at R&B #1. *King Heroin*, a harrowing anti-drug message narrated by Brown, makes US #40.

June *There It Is* makes US #43, while *Pass The Peas* by the JB's (featuring Brown uncredited) creeps to US #95.

July Brown's revival of Bill Doggett's 1956 million-seller *Honky Tonk* climbs to US #44.

Aug ***James Brown Soul Classics***, a compilation of previous hits, reaches US #83, while ***There It Is***, with new material, makes #60.

[12] Brown performs at "The Festival of Hope" to benefit the Nassau Society of Crippled Children & Adults, at Roosevelt Raceway, Garden City, New York.

Sept [19] The still-climbing *Get On The Good Foot* is certified gold by the RIAA.

Oct [21] *Get On The Good Foot* peaks at US #18, his first million-seller in over a year, and resides atop the R&B chart for four weeks.

Dec [9] *I Got A Bag Of My Own* makes US #44.

[11] After a concert in Knoxville, TN, Brown is arrested while talking to fans about drug abuse and is charged with disorderly conduct, when an informant tells police that he is trying to incite a riot. Brown threatens Knoxville with a million-dollar lawsuit, and the incident is hastily written off as a "misunderstanding".

1973

Feb [3] *What My Baby Needs Now Is A Little More Lovin'*, with Brown duetting with his new protegée, Lyn Collins, makes US #56.

Mar [3] *I Got Ants In My Pants (And I Want To Dance)* reaches US #27, while the double-album set ***Get On The Good Foot*** makes US #68.

Brown and Wesley of the JB's score the soundtrack to the movie "Black Caesar", starring Fred Williamson. The subsequent album by Brown (now billed on album sleeves as "The Godfather Of Soul") reaches US #31.

Apr [14] *Down And Out In New York City*, extracted from it, makes US #50.

June Brown's oldest son Teddy is killed in a car accident in upstate New York.

[9] *Think*, a third version of his 1960 hit, peaks at US #77.

July [14] *Doing It To Death*, credited to Wesley & the JB's, but written and produced by Brown (playing incognito), reaches US #22 and tops the R&B chart for two weeks, selling over a million.

Aug [4] The JB's, currently comprising Wesley (trombone), Nolen and Hearlon "Cheese" Martin (guitars), Fred Thomas (bass), John "Jabo" Starks (drums) and John Morgan (tambourine), join Brown to record *The Payback*, the title cut to a movie which, unlike the song, is subsequently canned.

Sept Brown and Wesley's score for a second movie, "Slaughter's Big Rip-Off" (starring Jim Brown), is released, set to make US #92.

[22] Extracted *Sexy, Sexy, Sexy* makes US #50.

1974

Jan [19] *Stoned To The Bone* peaks at US #58.

Apr [18] The still-rising *The Payback* is certified gold by the RIAA following the same certification of its also-climbing parent album ***The Payback*** on March 18th.

May [11] *The Payback* reaches US #26, during a three-month chart spell, and hits R&B #1 for two weeks while the double album ***The Payback*** reaches US #34.

Aug [17] *My Thang* reaches US #29, and tops the R&B chart for two weeks.

Sept Double album ***Hell*** makes US #35.

[6] Brown performs at the "Ann Arbor Blues & Jazz Festival" at the Griffin Hollow Amphitheater, St. Clair College, Windsor, ON, Canada.

[28] *Papa Don't Take No Mess* reaches US #31, and spends a week at R&B #1.

Dec [28] Double A-side *Funky President (People It's Bad)/Coldblooded* peaks at US #44.

1975

Mar [15] *Reality* makes US #80, while album ***Reality*** makes #56. Brown's billing is now the "Minister Of New Super Heavy Funk". (This fails to impress the US Treasury Department's tax division, which is claiming that "the hardest-working man in show business" has been working overtime and owes $4.5 million in unpaid taxes from 1969/70.)
June [14] *Sex Machine, Part 1* (an updated re-recording of *Get Up, I Feel Like Being A Sex Machine)* makes US #61. ***Sex Machine Today*** reaches US #103.
Oct ***Everybody's Doing The Hustle And Dead On The Double Bump*** limps to US #193.

1976

Sept Tight-funked *Get Up Offa That Thing* reaches UK #22 (his first UK hit for almost five years), while its parent album ***Get Up Offa That Thing*** makes US #147. (The single will make US #45 on Oct [9].)

1977

Jan [14] During European dates, Brown performs at London's Hammersmith Odeon.
Feb [12] *Body Heat* makes UK #36.
Mar [12] *Body Heat* peaks at US #88, his last US Hot 100 entry for nearly nine years. Its parent album ***Body Heat*** reaches US #126.
Aug [18] Brown attends Elvis Presley's funeral at Graceland in Memphis, TN.
Sept [29] The JB's, frequently rumored to be at odds with Brown over peremptory treatment and disputed wages, walk out mid-tour in Hallandale, FL, complaining of underpayment, though most will return.

1978

Jan Brown is forced to sell WJBE to help restore his financial position.
Sept [2] ***Jam/1980s*** makes US #121.
Dec [14] Brown performs at the Hammersmith Odeon, London, during a short European tour which also sees dates in Amsterdam, Holland, and Hamburg, W. Germany and Dusseldorf, W. Germany among other cities.

1979

Mar [10] Brown performs at the Grand Ole Opry, Nashville, TN.
Sept [1] ***The Original Disco Man*** (the title a jibe at the style which has supplanted his own as the US dancefloor mainstay) makes US #152.
Richmond County Superior Court finds Brown guilty of unpaid rent, breach of contract and punitive damages regarding a property in Augusta.
Dec He ends the year with a tour of Japan.

1980

Apr Radio station WRDW is sold by auction.
June [20] "The Blues Brothers" movie, in which Brown makes a cameo appearance playing a manic singing-and-dancing preacher, opens in the US.
Aug Double live album ***James Brown ... Live/Hot On The One***, recorded in Tokyo, Japan, reaches US #170.
Nov ***Live And Lowdown At The Apollo, Vol.1*** peaks at US #163.

1981

Jan [17] He returns to the UK chart with a revamp of *The Payback*, now issued as *Rapp Payback (Where Iz Moses?)*, recorded for Florida's TK Records and licensed in Britain to RCA. A popular dancefloor release, it reaches UK #39.
Nov Brown, having appeared at the 15th annual "Montreux Jazz Festival", visits the UK for concert dates.

1982

Mar Island Records signs Brown, but scheduled sessions at the Compass Point Studios in the Bahamas, with Sly Dunbar and Robbie Shakespeare producing, prove fruitless.

1983

July *Bring It On ... Bring It On*, another independent production, makes UK #45.
Dec [18] Jimmy Nolen, Brown's former lead guitarist, dies in Atlanta (from a heart attack), aged 47.

1984

Sept Brown teams with electro-rapper Afrika Bambaataa for the one-off *Unity (The Third Coming)*, which makes UK #49.

1985

May With Brown's formidable catalog now yielding cult favorites in UK clubs, turntable remixer DJ Froggy is commissioned by Polydor to produce a medley of snatches from 12 of them. The subsequent *Froggy Mix* reaches UK #50 and is unique in being a recording entirely featuring Brown, but one he has not actually recorded.
June *Get Up, I Feel Like Being A Sex Machine*, reissued in the UK after 15 years, reaches #47.

1986

Jan [23] Brown is inducted into the Roll and Roll Hall of Fame at the inaugural ceremony, held at the Waldorf Astoria Hotel, New York.
Feb [15] *Living In America* hits UK #5.
Mar [1] *Living In America*, written and produced by Dan Hartman, and the theme from the film "Rocky IV", recorded by Brown at the specific request of Sylvester Stallone hits US #4, his first million-seller in 13 years.
Get Up, I Feel Like Being A Sex Machine re-enters the UK chart, this time reaching #46.
Oct [18] *Gravity* peaks at UK #65 and US #93, as ***Gravity***, with duets from Alison Moyet and Steve Winwood, makes US #156 and UK #85.

1987

Feb [24] Brown wins Best R&B Performance, Male for *Living In America* at the 29th annual Grammy Awards.
Oct [31] TV-advertised hits compilation ***The Best Of James Brown - Godfather Of Soul*** reaches UK #17.

1988

Jan *She's The One*, recorded in the early '70s but not issued at the time, is released by Polydor to satisfy the UK demand for new Brown material. Remixed by Tim Rogers, it makes UK #45.
Mar [7] Brown visits the UK to be presented with a special award for 20 years of innovation in dance-music, by the assembled delegates at the World DJ Convention at London's Royal Albert Hall. (Brown's influence is extended to a new generation of dance music enthusiasts as his archive material becomes the most extensively used, albeit in sound-bite form, in the increasingly successful DJ practice of scratching, mixing and sampling.) His unannounced and dramatic stage entrance to accept the award earns a five-minute standing ovation.
Apr [7] Brown turns himself into authorities in Aiken County, SC. He is charged with assault with intent to murder, as well as aggravated assault and battery. He is released on a $15,000 bond. His wife Adrienne announces that she will file for a legal separation.
[9] Adrienne is arrested at Bush Field Airport, Augusta, GA, after allegedly receiving nasal spray bottles containing PCP (a depressant drug) from a courier. She is released on $1,550 bond.
[28] Adrienne files a request to drop the assault charges and the legal separation.
May *The Payback Mix*, a sampled medley (by mixing team Coldcut) of snippets from Brown oldies and some by former associates like the JB's and Bobby Byrd, reaches UK #12.
[10] Adrienne is charged with criminal mischief and arson in a Bedford, NH hotel room, and PCP is confiscated from her. Brown claims his wife set fire to some of his clothes.
[19] He is released on a $24,000 bond after spending the night in jail, following a car chase in Aiken County, SC, near his home. His fifth arrest in ten months, he is charged with assault, possession of PCP and illegal weapons and resisting arrest. (Brown is a member of the President's Council Against Drugs.)
[20] Adrienne is arrested again, at Bush Field and once more, PCP is found in her possession.
[25] She pleads innocent in Merrimack District Court to causing the Bedford hotel fire.
[30] Brown announces that, despite loving her, he is divorcing his wife.
June *I'm Real*, recorded by Brown with production team Full Force, reaches UK #31.
[3] Adrienne's attorney asks for the dismissal of a Richmond County, GA, traffic misdemeanor charge, citing diplomatic immunity. (US Representative D. Douglas Bernard Jr., on James Brown Appreciation Day in 1986, called Brown "our number one ambassador").
[7] Adrienne is indicted in Augusta, on two counts of PCP possession.
[16] She is arrested at her Beech Island home. After waiving extradition, she is jailed in Richmond County.
[20] Adrienne is released from jail after posting a $30,000 total property bond, on condition that she remains in the four-county area and submits to drug tests and counselling.
[25] ***I'm Real***, containing new material, reaches UK #27 but only US #96.
July [21] Brown, having returned from a European tour, pleads no contest to PCP possession and guilty to carrying a gun and resisting arrest, in Aiken circuit court, and receives a two-year suspended sentence and $1,200 fine.
I Got You (I Feel Good), backed with Martha & the Vandellas' *Nowhere To Run*, reissued because of their exposure in film "Good Morning Vietnam", peaks at UK #52.
Aug [5] Brown is admitted to Crawford Long Hospital, Atlanta, for lower jaw surgery to correct a degenerative disorder.
He guests with Aretha Franklin on *Gimme Your Love*, which makes US R&B #41.
Dec [15] As the climax to months of conflict with law regulators, not least involving a car chase through two states, Brown is finally sentenced to a six-year jail term.

1989

July [19] Brown is moved from the minimum-security State Park Correctional Facility in Columbia, SC, to the medium-security Stevenson Correctional Institution after having $40,000 in cheques and cash discovered in his prison cell.

1990

Jan [19] Brown becomes eligible for work release.
Apr [12] Having already served 15 months of his term, Brown is transferred from State Park to Lower Savannah Work Center, Aiken County. He will earn at least the minimum $3.80 an hour counselling youths about drug abuse.
May [15] Brown sings a medley of hits and lectures students in the Job Training Partnership Act on the importance of education, at Jack's Beauty College in North Augusta, SC. It is his first appearance as a community liaison officer and counsellor with the Aiken-Barnwell Counties Community Action Commission in a prison work-release programme.
[31] Brown is interviewed for the C4-TV programme "The Word".
Dec [25] While on a 72-hour furlough from the work center, he plays two three-song sets (*I Got You, Please Please Please Me* and *Living In America*) for the troops at Fort Jackson, Columbia, SC.

1991

Feb [27] Brown is released from Lower Savannah Work Center on parole, eight days prior to his eligibility date. (Brown's parole term is scheduled to end on October 23rd, 1993, at which point he will begin a five-year period on probation and submit to a drug-testing and substance-abuse program. He is also not allowed to drive.) Following an intended two-week vacation at his Beech Island home, Brown announces that he has plans for albums, concert tours, movies and documentaries to reinstate his reputation for hard work. On being released, he is quoted as saying: "I feel good."

May [7] Boxed-set ***Star Time***, a 72-song collection from his 35-year career, is released, bringing much of his catalog to compact disc.

June [10] Live pay-per-view US cable TV special "James Brown - Living In America", featuring Hammer, C&C Music Factory, Bell Biv Devoe, En Vogue and others, airs.

July [4] He performs at the Wembley Arena, Wembley, Middx., during UK dates.

Aug Brown sues shoe manufacturer Kenneth Cole over an ad referring to his recent incarceration, which has included the line: "Two great things with sole under lock and key." He seeks $5 million in compensatory damages.

[14] Brown attends an Atlanta Falcons football practice in Suwanee, GA, running a play at half-back, while wearing his street clothes.

Sept [7] He sings *Move On* during a "Party For Richard Pryor" tribute, which is set to air on CBS-TV on Nov [23].

Nov [16] ***Sex Machine - The Very Best Of James Brown*** debuts at its UK #19 peak.

[23] Reissued *Get Up, (I Feel Like Being A Sex Machine)* peaks at UK #69.

Dec [1] Brown performs at the Wembley Arena.

1992

Jan [27] He receives the Award Of Merit at the 19th American Music Awards, in Los Angeles. The inscription reads "When this unique artist exploded on the scene, his energy and captured the music public and inspired so many of his fellow artists. Now, over three decades later, the Godfather of Soul continues to excite the world with his vibrant performances."

Feb [25] Brown receives NARAS' 1992 Lifetime Achievement Award, at the 34th annual Grammy Awards, held at New York's Radio City Music Hall (while ***Star Time*** wins the Best Album Notes Grammy category).

[27] He guests on NBC-TV's "Late Night With David Letterman".

Apr [27] Brown files a $10-million lawsuit in Columbia, SC, against the Molson & AC&R company, claiming that it used his vocal and signature song *I Feel Good* in television commercials without his permission, causing the star mental distress and emotional injury.

May [4] He meets with New York Mayor David Dinkins to propose an arts festival in New York this summer, "to make people feel good" after the controversial Rodney King verdict in Los Angeles.

[30] Brown performs at KISS Radio's 13th anniversary concert, at the Great Woods Center for the Performing Arts, Mansfield, MA, to benefit the Genesis Fund.

June [5] He performs at the Greek Theatre, Los Angeles. (During his visit, he is inducted into Hollywood's Rock Walk.)

[15] Attorneys for Brown tell a Washington federal judge that distributor 20th Century Fox failed to ask permission to use a film footage clip of a 1965 performance of the singer in the recent soul film "The Commitments". Brown seeks $3 million in restitution but will lose the suit.

[20] Polydor issues the previously-unreleased 17-track ***Love Power Peace - Live At The Olympia, Paris 1971***, marking Brown's only live recording with the original JB's.

July [11] He participates in the Capital Radio "Coca-Cola Music Festival", at the Lee Valley Park Showground, Waltham Abbey, Essex.

Aug [13] In the latest round of legal tussles, PolyGram sues Brown, asking a federal judge to declare that it owns the rights to *I Got You (I Feel Good)*, after the label was sued by Molson & AC&R for selling them the rights for a recent TV ad, after Brown had sued them for using it without his permission.

Oct [24] *I Got You (I Feel Good)* remix, credited to James Brown vs. Dakeyne, charts for a week at UK #72.

Nov Having started a new label, Brown Stone Records, in partnership with industry veteran Harry Stone in August, Brown opens his own West Coast office, James Brown West Inc., in Hollywood, CA, to be run by Vonny Hilton Sweeney.

1993

Feb [25] Hammer presents James Brown with the Lifetime Achievement trophy at the fourth annual Rhythm & Blues Foundation Pioneer Awards, held at the Hollywood Palace, Los Angeles.

Mar [9] Scotti Bros. releases ***Universal James***, Brown's first original studio recording of the decade, with ten tracks written and produced either by (C&C Music Factory's) Clivilles & Cole or (Soul II Soul's) Jazzie B.

[11] Brown receives the Lifetime Achievment Award at the National Association Of Black Owned Broadcasters' awards dinner at the Sheraton Hotel, Washington.

[19] He performs at Radio City Music Hall, having guested on "Late Night With David Letterman" the previous day.

Apr [17] *Can't Get Any Harder* debuts at its UK #59 peak.

May [3] Celebrating his 60th birthday, PolyGram brings several key titles from the soul legend's catalog to compact disc, not least ***Hot Pants***, ***Revolution Of The Mind (Live At The Apollo Vol. 3)***, ***Sex Machine*** and ***There It Is***, complete with updated liner notes and bonus cuts.

Sept [15] Brown attends a ceremony in Steamboat Springs, CO, to dedicate the James Brown Soul Center of the Universe Bridge.

Nov [20] Part of Ninth Street in Augusta is renamed James Brown Boulevard.

1994

Feb [24] Brown is honored by the South Carolina house and Representative Ralph Anderson for his work since being released from prison.

Apr [15] Brown performs before a crowd of 4,281 at New York's Radio City Music Hall.

[30] He participates in an all-star version of *Get On Up* at the end of the opening night of the House of Blues on Sunset Boulevard, Los Angeles, with Bruce Springsteen, Magic Johnson, Woody Harrelson, Jeffrey Osborne, Jim Belushi, Dan Aykroyd and Steve Cropper among others.

May [3] He celebrates what is probably his 61st birthday at the Civic Center, Augusta, with Hammer, Bobby Brown, Simply Red, Tone Loc and Sharon Stone, among others.

Aug [28] Brown strikes a cyclist while driving in Augusta, and is cited for not yielding the right of way.

Dec [9] He files for divorce, after surrendering the day before for allegedly assaulting his wife.

1995

Mar [9] Magistrate in Aiken County drops the criminal domestic violence charge against Brown, filed by his wife.

Sept [2] He performs *It's A Man's Man's Man's World* and *I Feel Good* at the Concert for the Roll and Roll Hall of Fame at the Cleveland Stadium, Cleveland, OH.

Oct [31] Brown is once again arrested, on charges of battering his wife. County Sheriff's office had received a call from her at 4:20 a.m. asking for medical assistance.

1996

Jan [6] Following months of attempts at drug rehabilitation, and two days after cosmetic surgery, Brown's wife Adrienne dies age 47 at a Beverly Hills, CA health-care facility.

Feb [20] Brown guests on CBS-TV's "Late Show With David Letterman".

July [19] Brown is among headlining entertainment scheduled to perform during the 1996 Centennial Olympic Games in Atlanta which begin today.

JACKSON BROWNE

1966

Apr Already a proficient pianist, folk-oriented singer, songwriter and guitarist, Browne (b. Oct. 9, 1948, Heidelberg, W. Germany), son of US army parents, becomes an active member of the folk-rock fraternity at the Paradise club in Los Angeles, CA. Invited to join the Nitty Gritty Dirt Band, he does not stay long but leaves two of his songs, *Melissa* and *Holding*, for inclusion on their 1967 Liberty Records (US) debut album, ***Nitty Gritty Dirt Band***. Signed as a songwriter in January the following year to Nina Music, the publishing arm of Elektra Records, he picks up a number of gigs on the New York, NY club circuit including playing guitar for Nico at the Dome and Electric Circus venues and also backing Tim Buckley. She will also cover three of his compositions for her in-progress ***Chelsea Girl***, while demo cuts recorded for his publisher will subsequently emerge on bootleg albums.

1968

Now signed to Elektra Records as a recording artist, Browne returns to Los Angeles, but the results of his attempts to record an album at Paxton Lodge Ranch Studio, are never issued. The label lets him go, signing instead Steve Noonan, to whose debut album Browne contributes five songs. His songs are also recorded by acts like Tom Rush, who cuts *Shadow Dream Song* on his ***The Circle Game*** for Elektra (and will also cover *These Days* and *Jamaica Say You Will*).

1971

Oct Browne signs with record entrepreneur David Geffen's fledgling Asylum label. He has sent a demo tape and an 8" x 10" photo of himself to the company. Impressed, Geffen's secretary urges her boss to visit Browne at his Echo Park, Los Angeles, home (which he shares with Longbranch Pennywhistle members J.D. Souther and future Eagle Glenn Frey).

1972

Mar His debut album, ***Jackson Browne*** (sometimes called ***Saturate Before Using*** - a legend printed on the sleeve), recorded with assistance from Russ Kunkel (drums), Leland Sklar (bass) and Craig Doerge (keyboards), along with David Crosby (harmony vocals), and Albert Lee and the Byrds' Clarence White (guitars), peaks at US #53 and establishes his literate, self-written folk-rock melodic style which will distinguish all future recordings.

May [6] His first single, *Doctor My Eyes*, from the album, hits US #8 (a cover version by the Jackson 5 will hit UK #9 in 1973). Browne supports Joni Mitchell on a US tour and later accompanies her on European dates.

Sept Browne tours the US with labelmates and friends the Eagles, as *Rock Me On The Water* makes US #48. The Eagles' *Take It Easy*, co-written by Browne with Frey, reaches US #12 (Browne's own version will appear on his second album).

1973

Nov Self-produced, ***For Everyman***, sees multi-instrumentalist David Lindley joining a backing band which includes Doerge, Doug Haywood (bass) and Jim Keltner (drums). It reaches US #43, while the extracted *Red Neck Friend* (said to concern masturbation), peaks at #85. Browne appears on the sleeve of the Eagles album, ***Desperado***, for which he has co-written *Doolin' Dalton*.

1974

Jan The second single from the album, coupling *Ready Or Not* and *Take It Easy*, is released, while Browne co-writes *James Dean* for the third Eagles' follow-up, ***On The Border***.

Dec Co-produced with Al Schmitt, Browne's third effort, ***Late For The Sky***, with a sleeve in the style of French painter Magritte, reaches US #14. It features his friend Lindley (guitar, violin), plus Jai Winding

(keyboards), Doug Haywood (bass, vocals) and Larry Zack (drums), together with longtime musician friends Dan Fogelberg, Don Henley and Souther on backing vocals. The extracted US singles are *Walking Slow* and *Fountain Of Sorrow*.
[24] ***Late For The Sky*** is certified gold by the RIAA.

1976

Mar [25] Browne's wife Phyllis commits suicide.
Nov [16] ***Jackson Browne*** is confirmed gold by the RIAA, following the similar certification of ***For Everyman*** on October 8th the previous year.
Dec [18] As lyrically refined as ever, ***The Pretender***, with help from Bonnie Raitt, Lowell George, David Crosby, Jeff Porcaro and Graham Nash and produced by Jon Landau, hits US #5. It also marks Browne's UK chart debut, reaching #26.

1977

Mar Mournful ballad, *Here Come Those Tears Again*, from the album, makes US #23.
Apr [12] ***The Pretender*** is certified platinum by the RIAA.
Aug Browne undertakes a lengthy US tour with a familiar backing band of Lindley, Kunkel, Leland Sklar (bass), Doerge, Danny Kortchmar (guitar) and Haywood, with backing vocalist Rosemary Butler.
June Lengthy title track, *The Pretender*, reaches US #58.

1978

Feb Unique live "road" album, ***Running On Empty***, chronicling Browne's US summer tour and recorded on stage, in hotel rooms, dressing rooms, and on the tour bus, hits US #3, also reaching UK #28.
Apr Its title track, *Running On Empty*, recorded at the Merriweather Post Pavilion, Columbia, MD, reaches US #11.
Aug Browne's revival of the 1960 Maurice Williams & the Zodiacs hit, *Stay*, featuring vocal sparring with Lindley and again taken from the live set, reaches US #20 and UK #12.
[25] ***Running On Empty*** is confirmed platinum by the RIAA.

1979

Aug [4] Browne joins Emmylou Harris, Nicolette Larson, Michael McDonald, Bonnie Raitt, Linda Ronstadt and members of Little Feat in a benefit concert for Lowell George's widow, at the Great Western Forum, Inglewood, CA. The 20,000 crowd raises over $230,000.
Sept [19-23] Browne and Raitt join Bruce Springsteen, Carly Simon and the Doobie Brothers, among others, in a series of anti-nuclear concerts as MUSE (Musicians United For Safe Energy), held at Madison Square Garden, New York, NY. The concerts were actually instigated by Browne and Raitt.

1980

Jan Triple-album set, ***No Nukes***, documenting last September's MUSE concert series, reaches US #19. Co-produced by Browne, John Hall and Raitt, it features US stars such as James Taylor, the Doobie Brothers and Tom Petty, and includes three Browne tracks, not least another version of *Stay*, with Springsteen.
Mar [20] 28-year-old Joseph Riviera holds up the Asylum Records office in New York, demanding to see either Browne or the Eagles, wanting them to finance his trucking operation. He surrenders when told that neither act is in the office since both live in California.
Sept [13] ***Hold Out***, co-produced with Greg Ladanyi and dedicated to Browne's second wife Lynne Sweeney, tops the US chart, and also makes UK #44. While the eight minute-plus title cut is co-written with Doerge, the extracted *Boulevard* reaches US #19.
[15] ***Hold Out*** is ratified platinum by the RIAA.
Nov Further extract *That Girl Could Sing* makes US #22.

1982

During a European visit, Browne performs at the "Lisdoonarva Music Festival" in Ireland, the "Glastonbury Fayre" in England and makes an appearance at the 16th annual "Montreux Jazz Festival", in Montreux, Switzerland.
June [12] Always politically active, he now takes part in a rally for nuclear disarmament, in Central Park, New York, with Ronstadt, Springsteen, Gary U.S. Bonds and James Taylor, before an audience of 750,000.
Sept [3-5] Browne performs to a crowd of 400,000 at the "US Festival", financed by Apple Computers founder Steve Wozniak, in San Bernadino, CA, during a three-day event also featuring the Cars, Fleetwood Mac and the Grateful Dead.
Oct Self-produced and co-written with Kortchmar, *Somebody's Baby*, from the soundtrack of the movie "Fast Times At Ridgemont High", becomes Browne's biggest US hit to date, at #7.

1983

Sept Now without Lindley (replaced by Rick Vito, later with Fleetwood Mac), but retaining long-standing sidesmen Kunkel, Doerge, Haywood and bassist Bob Glaub, Browne hits US #8 with the harder rock-edged ***Lawyers In Love***, his first album in three years. Also featuring Raitt, Kortchmar and Waddy Wachtel, it makes UK #37, while the extracted title track peaks at US #13. Further excerpt, *Tender Is The Night*, will reach US #25 in November, while *For A Rocker* will peak at US #45 the following February.
Nov [8] ***Lawyers In Love*** is certified gold by the RIAA.

1985

Dec [14] Artists United Against Apartheid, comprising 49 artists including Browne, makes US #38 and UK #21 with *Sun City*.

1986

Jan [18] Browne duets with Clarence Clemons, Springsteen's sax player, on *You're A Friend Of Mine* (with additional vocals by Browne's girlfriend, actress Daryl Hannah), which reaches US #18.
Apr Browne expresses his criticism of US foreign policy and his support of Amnesty International in the self-produced ***Lives In The Balance***, which reaches US #23 and UK #36.
[19] *For America* reaches US #30.
June [15] Browne takes part in the Amnesty International concert broadcast on MTV from Giants Stadium, East Rutherford, NJ, with the Police, U2, Peter Gabriel and Bryan Adams.
July [5] Impassioned love-themed *In The Shape Of A Heart* stalls at US #70 and will reach UK #66 in the UK in October, the first instance of a Browne release scoring better in the UK, helped perhaps by a well-received "Lives In The Balance" autumn British tour.
[8] ***Lives In The Balance*** is certified gold by the RIAA.

1988

June [11] Browne performs at "Nelson Mandela's 70th Birthday Tribute" concert held at Wembley Stadium, Wembley, Middx., an event shown on TV throughout the world, leading a star band on a song written specifically for the occasion. On his return to the US, Browne embarks on a six-week tour in support of the Christic Institute, a non-profitmaking organization whose lawsuit against a group of US covert operatives is currently on appeal.

1989

May [16] ***For Everyman*** and ***Late For The Sky*** are certified platinum by the RIAA.
June [17] ***World In Motion***, dedicated to Browne's mother Bea Koeppel, who died of cancer in 1988, reaches UK #39.
July [28] A 16-date US tour begins at the Mud Island Amphitheatre, Memphis, TN, as ***World In Motion*** makes US #45. During the tour, which will end on August 27th at the Open Air Theatre, San Diego, CA, Browne is joined on stage by Springsteen for an encore of *Stay* at a concert at Bally's Grandstand Under The Stars, Atlantic City, NJ, and will also perform with Neil Young and others at the "Paha Sapa Music Festival" on South Dakota's Pine Ridge Reservation, to benefit the Oglala Lakota Sioux.

1990

Apr [16] Browne appears at the "Nelson Mandela - An International Tribute For A Free South Africa" concert at Wembley Stadium, Wembley, singing two songs with Johnny Clegg.
Aug [31] He joins Stevie Wonder and Bonnie Raitt to sing *Amazing Grace* at the memorial service for Stevie Ray Vaughan at Laurel Land Memorial Park, Dallas, TX.
Oct [12-13] He joins Crosby, Stills & Nash, Peter Gabriel, Sinead O'Connor, Sting and many others, performing at the Amnesty International benefit, "From Chile ... An Embrace Of Hope", at the National Stadium, Santiago, Chile.
[26] Browne performs at Neil Young's fourth annual Bridge School benefit at the Shoreline Amphitheatre, Mountain View, CA, with Young, Elvis Costello, Steve Miller and Edie Brickell.
Nov [16-17] He joins Springsteen and Raitt in two all-acoustic benefit concerts at the Shrine Auditorium, Los Angeles, raising more than $600,000 for the Christic Institute, to finance a lawsuit claiming that the US Government sanctioned illegal arms sales and drugs trafficking to finance covert operations during the Iran-Contra affair.
Dec [16] Browne and Raitt perform at a concert in Sioux Falls, ND, to commemorate the 100th anniversary of the massacre at Wounded Knee.

1991

Jan [16] The Byrds are joined by Browne and Don Henley for a rendition of *Feel A Whole Lot Better* at the annual Roll and Roll Hall of Fame post-induction dinner jam, at the Waldorf Astoria Hotel, New York.
July [19] He participates in the "Telluride Midsummer Music Festival" at the Town Park, Telluride, CO.
Aug [14] Browne and Jennifer Warnes guest on syndicated TV's "The Arsenio Hall Show", to sing and promote *Golden Slumbers* from Disney's ***For Our Children***, an album raising money for the AIDS Pediatric foundation.
Oct [7] Browne performs at a "Ban The Dam Jam" at Beacon Theatre, New York, with David Byrne, Indigo Girls and Bruce Cockburn.
Nov [3] He sings *For A Dancer* at "Laughter, Love And Music : To Celebrate The Lives Of Bill, Steve And Melissa", a tribute to the late concert promoter Bill Graham at San Francisco, CA's Golden Gate Park Polo Fields, before an estimated 350,000 crowd.
[21] Browne takes part in the Second Annual Hollywood Hunger Banquet for Oxfam America, held at the Sony Studios, Culver City, CA, for which he is, along with others including Crosby Stills & Nash, Joni Mitchell, Al Jarreau and David Byrne, a member of the Honorary Banquet Committee. Upon arrival, guests (having paid $150 a ticket) are selected randomly to receive meals proportionate to worldwide food distribution: 15% are given a gourmet dinner, 25% eat simple fare with the remaining 60% offered only rice and water.

1992

Jan [4] The Chieftains' festive ***The Bells Of Dublin***, to which Browne contributes *The Rebel Jesus*, peaks at US #107.
[30] He participates in the "Friends Of Smitty" benefit at Palace Theatre, Burbank, CA, for session keyboardist and songwriter William Smith, who has recently suffered a stroke.
Apr [14] "Free To Laugh", a comedy and music special for Amnesty International featuring Browne and others, airs on the Lifetime cable channel.
June [30] Browne duets with the Indigo Girls on NBC-TV's "The Tonight Show" and is featured on their current album.

Sept [23] Browne allegedly assaults girlfriend Daryl Hannah, an event which will apparently lead to the demise of their relationship.
Oct [10] Browne takes part in the "All Our Colors - The Good Road Concert", with Santana, Steve Miller, John Lee Hooker and others, at the Shoreline Amphitheatre, Mountain View, CA.
Nov [11] He joins Crosby Stills & Nash, Raitt and Jimmy Buffett to perform a benefit concert for the victims of Hurricane Iniki in Hawaii.

1993

Jan He takes part in a benefit for UCLA Environmental Science and Engineering Program at the Universal Amphitheatre, Universal City.
Nov [6] Featuring guests Henley, Crosby, Warnes and Luis Conte and co-produced by Browne with Scott Thurston (and one track with Don Was), ***I'm Alive***, much of it said to chronicle the break-up of his relationship with Hannah, debuts at its UK #35 peak.
[10] Browne guests on CBS-TV's "Late Show With David Letterman".
[13] ***I'm Alive*** debuts at its US #40 peak.
Dec [6] *Doctor My Eyes* is used as a wake-up call for NASA's current space-flight crew on board Endeavour.

1994

Feb [18] Browne plays to a sellout crowd at the Paramount, New York, during two-month US tour.
May [24] He gives 15-year-old Clarissa J. Markiewicz of Buffalo, NY, a plaque and performs a 45-minute concert for her, as part of a contest held by Scholastic Inc. and Elektra Entertainment.
June [12-14] Browne performs at London's Royal Albert Hall.
[25] *Everywhere I Go* charts for a week at UK #67.
July [22] His latest US tour opens at the Mann Music Center, Philadelphia, PA, set to end on August 30th at the Summer Pops Bowl Amphitheatre, San Diego, CA.

1995

Mar Giant Records (US) releases the soundtrack to ***Bye Bye Love***, including Browne and Timothy Schmit's cover of the Everly Brothers' *Let It Be*.
Sept [2] Browne sings *Songs Of Freedom*, *Emancipation* and *Redemption Song* and, with Melissa Etheridge, *Wake Up Little Susie*, at the Concert for the Roll and Roll Hall of Fame at Cleveland Stadium, Cleveland, OH.
Oct [7] He performs at the sixth annual "Music Festival", an event founded by Browne in 1990, at Verde Valley School, Sedona, AZ, in support of the school's Native American Scholarship Fund.
Nov [5] Browne takes part in an all-star cast concert performance of "The Wizard Of Oz", playing the role of the Scarecrow, at New York's Avery Fisher Hall, with the proceeds benefitting the Children's Defense Fund. (The show premieres on the TNT network on the 22nd.)

1996

Feb [15] Browne guests on "The Tonight Show".
Mar [2] Unusually for Browne, each track on his latest release ***Looking East***, which enters at its US #36 peak, is co-written in ensemble with Jeff Young, co-producers Kevin McCormick, and Thurston and Mark Goldenberg. It also features music guests Bonnie Raitt, Valerie Carter, Ry Cooder, David Lindley, Sir Harry Bowens and the ever-present Crosby. Its release also marks the first time Elektra has simultaneously issued a same-titled multimedia (E-CD) version which visually follows the songwriting and recording process of some of the album's tracks.
[9] ***Looking East*** bows at its UK #47 peak.

THE BUCKINGHAMS

Dennis Tufano (lead vocals, guitar); **Carl Giammarese** (guitar); **Nick Fortune** (bass); **Marty Grebb** (keyboards); **Jon-Jon Poulos** (drums)

1965

Giammarese (b. Aug. 21, 1947, Chicago, IL) and Fortune (b. Nicholas Fortuna, May 1, 1946, Chicago), members of the Centuries, playing the Chicago dance circuit and teen clubs and having already recorded *Love You No More* for the local Spectra-Sound label, and Tufano (b. Sept. 11, 1946, Chicago) and Poulos (b. Mar. 31, 1947, Chicago), members of the Pulsations, team up together retaining the name the Pulsations, adding Dennis Miccoli on keyboards. Auditioning for "All Time Hits", a variety show on local TV station WGN, they secure a 13-week contract as the Buckinghams, a name suggested by a security guard at the station, who learns that WGN wants to give them a British-sounding moniker. They revive the Drifters/Searchers' hit, *Sweets For My Sweet*, on Spectra-Sound, before signing to the larger - but still local - USA label, all the while building a large following in the Chicago area.

1966

Dec [31] After three singles, *I'll Go Crazy*, *I Call Your Name*, and *I've Been Wrong*, have failed to catch on nationally, *Kind Of A Drag*, having captured radio attention around the US, enters the Hot 100 at #90.

1967

Feb [18] *Kind Of A Drag*, written by Jim Holvay, of fellow Chicago group the Mob, tops the US chart, knocking the Monkees' *Daydream Believer* from #1, and becomes a million seller. The group's contract is bought from USA by CBS Records, which teams them with producer/manager Jim Guercio, whom the Buckinghams have already met through his cousin, Burt Jesperson, one of the group's roadies. (At the time he is brought in to the produce the band, Guercio is in Los Angeles, CA, playing bass for UK duo Chad & Jeremy.)
Mar Grebb (b. Sept. 2, 1946, Chicago) replaces Miccoli, who has been fired at the beginning of the year.
Apr [8] Lloyd Price-revived classic, *Lawdy Miss Clawdy*, released by USA as by the Falling Pebbles, but subsequently credited to the Buckinghams, to compete with their CBS debut, makes US #41.
[23] ***Kind Of A Drag***, compiled by USA from earlier recordings, makes US #109.
May [13] *Don't You Care*, on Columbia, adding a fuller, brassier sound to the smooth vocal/keyboard blend introduced on *Kind Of A Drag*, hits US #6. It is again written by Holvay, along with fellow Mob player Gary Beisbier, and produced by Guercio.
June [18] The group appears on CBS-TV's "The Smothers Brothers Comedy Hour".
Aug [4] The band begins its only nationwide US package tour in Hartford, CT, with Gene Pitney, the Easybeats, the Happenings, the Fifth Estate and the Music Explosion.
[12] Taken from ***Time And Charges***, *Mercy Mercy Mercy*, a brass-backed vocal version of jazzman Cannonball Adderley's early 1967 US #11 instrumental original, hits US #5.
[19] ***Time And Charges*** makes US #58.
Oct [14] *Hey Baby (They're Playing Our Song)*, another Beisbier/Holvay original, reaches US #12.

1968

Jan [27] *Susan*, with a topical cacophonous psychedelic bridge, reaches US #11.
Mar [30] ***Portraits*** makes US #53.
June [29] *Back In Love Again*, written by Grebb, and with new producer Jimmy Wisner, peaks at US #57 - their final hit single. Disillusioned with CBS over musical differences and producer selection (Guercio has left over publishing and management differences), the band continues, fulfilling outstanding commitments, without support from the label. (Guercio goes on to develop the Buckinghams' brass-rock sound, with even greater success, with fellow CBS acts Chicago and Blood, Sweat & Tears.)
Oct [12] Appropriately-titled ***In One Ear And Gone Tomorrow***, mainly self-penned, makes US #161.

1969

July [19] Compilation album, ***Greatest Hits***, the Buckinghams' US chart swan song, makes #73, as Grebb leaves, going on to form the Fabulous Rhinestones with Kal David and Harvey Brooks. He is replaced by John Turner.

1970

The Buckinghams call it a day, as Tufano and Giammarese team as a duo, Poulos goes into management and Fortune becomes a session player in Chicago. (After the Fabulous Rhinestones break up, Grebb will become an integral part of Bonnie Raitt's band.)

1973

June [2] Tufano and Giammarese, now signed to Ode Records, return to the US chart with the Lou Adler-produced *Music Everywhere*, making #68.

1980

Mar [26] Poulos dies of drug-related heart failure.
July Tufano, Giammarese and Fortuna (reverting to his given name), at the behest of Chicago's WLS programme director John Guerin, re-form the Buckinghams for the annual ChicagoFest, adding John Cammelot (keyboards) and Tom Osfar (drums). (They will appear at the festival again the following summer, and begin playing dates in the Chicago area.)

1985

Apr The group, now with Giammarese on lead vocals, Fortuna, Cammelot, and Tom Scheckel (b. Nov. 19, 1954, Chicago) on drums (Tufano has decided to pursue an acting career in Los Angeles, CA), joins the nostalgia-aimed "Happy Together Tour" with the Turtles, the Grass Roots, Gary Lewis and the Mamas And The Papas, performing at the Abbey, Lake Geneva, WI, as the local Red label releases *Veronica* and its parent album, ***A Matter Of Time***.

1994

Jan [8] The Buckinghams, still playing more than 100 US dates a year, with a line-up of Giammarese, Fortuna, Scheckel, Bruce Soboroff (b. Aug. 31, 1952, Chicago) (keyboards) and Bob Abrams (b. Feb. 24, 1955, Ohio) (lead guitar), perform on the "Salute To The '60s" bill (also featuring Gary Puckett and the Association), at the Star Plaza Theatre, Merriville, IN, to a crowd of 1,902.

TIM BUCKLEY

1966

July Having been raised in Amsterdam, NY, but moving with his parents to southern California at age nine, Buckley (b. Timothy Buckley III, Feb. 14, 1947, Washington, DC), who has performed with California C&W bands including Princess Ramona & the Chreokee Riders, the Bohemians (which he formed) and Harlequin 3 (both of the latter units with bassist Jim Fielder and drummer Larry Beckett), and as a solo singer/guitarist in Los Angeles, CA folk clubs, is spotted by Frank Zappa's manager, Herb Cohen, at the It's Boss venue. Cohen arranges a showcase for Buckley at the Night Owl Café in New York, attended by Elektra Records' Jac Holzman, who promptly offers Buckley a recording deal.
Oct His warmly-received debut album, ***Tim Buckley***, produced by Holzman, introduces a distinctive folk/rock style, highlighted by his versatile tenor vocal.

1967

Apr [25] During a month in which he performs several dates at New York, NY's Café Au Go Go (one of which is attended by George Harrison and Brian Epstein), Buckley is featured in the Leonard Bernstein-hosted CBS-TV documentary "Inside Pop - The Rock Revolution".

Nov [18] After a further spell in New York, playing with ex-Velvet Underground singer Nico and others, his sophomore album, ***Goodbye And Hello***, produced by Jerry Yester of the Lovin' Spoonful, and featuring his regular musical coterie of Lee Underwood, Jim Fielder and Carter Collins, makes US #171. The album also includes his best-known and most-covered song (notably by Blood, Sweat & Tears), *Morning Glory*.

1968

Mar [8] Buckley plays on the opening night of the Fillmore East, New York, on a bill including Albert King and Big Brother & the Holding Company.

July [19-21] He performs at the Avalon Ballroom, San Francisco, with the Velvet Underground.

Oct He tours the UK, appearing on several TV shows, and recording a six-song session for BBC Radio 1's "Top Gear" show. (Tracks recorded during this visit will be released in 1990 as ***Dream Letter: Live In London***.)

1969

June [7] The jazz-oriented ***Happy Sad***, produced by both Yester and Zal Yanovsky, makes US #81.

1970

Feb Buckley moves to Cohen and Zappa's Straight Records for ***Blue Afternoon***, which is a minor US chartmaker, at #192.

Oct ***Lorca***, recorded for Elektra to fulfil contractual obligations, contains material in an experimental free-form jazz style, rendering it wholly uncommercial.

1971

Jan ***Starsailor*** further develops Buckley's jazzy, avant-garde experimentations. It fails to chart but introduces another revered cut, *Song To The Siren* (revived in 1983 by This Mortal Coil (UK #66). Disillusioned by its poor reception, however, he withdraws from the music arena for over a year.

1972

Oct After working as a chauffeur and taxi driver and also making a cameo appearance in the movie "The Christian Licorice Store", Buckley records ***Greetings From L.A.*** for Warner Bros., in an unaccustomed funk-rock style, produced by Jerry Goldstein (ex-Strangeloves). Sexually charged and more accessible than his previous two albums, it is once again both well-received and non-charting.

1973

Dec ***Sefronia***, on Frank Zappa and Herb Cohen's new label, Discreet Records, combines new Buckley compositions with revivals of oldies, including the Jaynettes' 1963 hit, *Sally Go Round The Roses*.

1974

Aug Buckley tours Europe, playing at the Knebworth Festival, Knebworth, Herts., and performing on BBC2-TV's "Old Grey Whistle Test".

Nov ***Look At The Fool***, another funk-based set, is less well received.

1975

Apr Buckley returns to live work in the US, touring Texas and California, and begins work on a retrospective double album (to be recorded live on stage), movie screenplays and a novel.

June [29] He dies in a Santa Monica, CA hospital from an overdose of heroin and morphine, having taken the drug cocktail at a friend's house, apparently believing it to be cocaine. (UCLA grad student Richard Keeling will be arraigned on October 2nd for allegedly supplying Buckley with the heroin.) (Anthology specialists Rhino Records will issue an 11-track compilation, ***Best Of Tim Buckley***, in 1983.)

BUCKS FIZZ

Cheryl Baker (vocals); **Jay Aston** (vocals); **Mike Nolan** (vocals); **Bobby G** (vocals)

1981

Mar Bucks Fizz is formed by experienced session singers in London, to represent the UK in the 26th annual "Eurovision Song Contest" with the purpose-penned *Making Your Mind Up*. Baker (b. Rita Crudgington, Mar. 8, 1954, London) has already entered in 1978 with Co-Co, which lost the contest, but nevertheless gained a #13 UK hit with its entry *Bad Old Days*. Aston (b. May 4, 1961, London), Nolan (b. Dec. 7, 1954, Dublin, Eire) and G (b. Robert Gubby, Aug. 23, 1953, London), a self-employed builder who auditions after placing an ad in **The Stage** in a last ditch attempt for a career in showbiz, have no previous chart pedigree. They sign to RCA Records.

Apr [4] The bubbly quartet wins the "Eurovision Song Contest" held at the Royal Dublin Society Hall, Dublin, Eire, with the perky *Making Your Mind Up*, which subsequently shoots to #1 in the UK, where it will stay for three weeks. Co-written by Andy Hill, the song's success ensures that the group will stay together, not least under his songwriting and production guidance.

June Similarly-styled follow-up *Piece Of The Action* reaches UK #12.

Sept *One Of Those Nights*, a slower, smoother sound, reaches UK #20, while their debut album ***Bucks Fizz*** reaches UK #14.

Dec The group asks the Labour Party to withdraw its electioneering political badges, which are enscribed with the legend "The Tories Have A Worse Record Than Bucks Fizz". RCA claims that "they are insulting a very talented group".

1982

Jan [16] Co-penned by Hill and ex-King Crimson lyricist Pete Sinfield, *The Land Of Make Believe* tops the UK chart.

Apr [17] *My Camera Never Lies* also hits UK #1, the group's third and final chart-topper.

May Sophomore effort, the Hill-produced ***Are You Ready?***, hits UK #10.

July Ballad *Now Those Days Are Gone*, highlighting close-harmony vocals, hits UK #8.

1983

Jan Co-written by Hill and his production partner Nicola Martin, *If You Can't Stand The Heat* hits UK #10.

Mar *Run For Your Life* reaches UK #14.

Apr ***Hand Cut*** reaches UK #17.

June Richly-produced Abba pastiche *When We Were Young* hits UK #10.

Oct *London Town* breaks their UK Top 20 chart run, stalling at #34.

They perform in the presence of H.R.H. Queen Elizabeth the Queen Mother at the Royal Variety Performance, London.

Dec 12-track ***Greatest Hits***, including the hit singles to date, reaches UK #25.

1984

Jan *Rules Of The Game* peaks at UK #57.

[19-21] The group performs cabaret dates at Baileys, Watford, Herts.

Sept *Talking In Your Sleep*, a cover of the 1983 US #3 hit by Detroit group the Romantics, reaches UK #15.

Nov *Golden Days* peaks at UK #42, while ***I Hear Talk*** reaches UK #66.

Dec Bobby G makes UK #65 with the self-penned theme song for the BBC1-TV series "Big Deal", issued on the BBC's own label. Shortly after leaving a gig in Newcastle, Tyne & Wear, the Bucks Fizz tour bus crashes in icy conditions. The group and entourage suffer various degrees of injury, most notably Nolan, who is taken to hospital in a comatose state, believed to be brain-damaged. (He will regain consciousness, recover and eventually return to performing.)

1985

Jan The title track *I Hear Talk* makes UK #34.

July *You And Your Heart So Blue* makes UK #43.

Sept *Magical* peaks at UK #57.

Nov Bobby G's *Big Deal* is reactivated due to a new season of the TV series and now peaks at UK #46.

Aston leaves amidst much rancor, selling the story of her alleged affair with producer Andy Hill to a national newspaper. Shelley Preston (b. May 14, 1960), who has been working in nightclubs in Sri Lanka, is chosen from over 1,000 auditioning girls as her replacement.

1986

July A label switch from RCA to Polydor is followed by the euphoric, tribal-sounding *New Beginning (Mamba Seyra)*, sung partly in Swahili, which hits UK #8, the group's first Top 10 hit in three years.

Sept Their brisk revival of Stephen Stills' *Love The One You're With* makes UK #47.

Nov *Keep Each Other Warm* makes UK #45, while the aptly-titled ***The Writing On The Wall*** stalls at UK #89 in December.

1988

Nov The group, recording again for RCA, returns to the UK chart with *Heart Of Stone* (subsequently a global hit for Cher in 1990), which makes #50.

1991

Apr Having dissolved in 1989, the band reunites for occasional live projects, including the Jet label-released ***Bucks Fizz Live At The Fairfield Hall Croydon***. Baker remains the most prominent member, having successfully pursued a career in television, hosting a number of UK kids' programs (most notably "Eggs'n'Baker" on BBC1-TV).

BUFFALO SPRINGFIELD

Stephen Stills (vocals, guitar); **Neil Young** (vocals, guitar); **Richie Furay** (vocals, guitar); **Bruce Palmer** (bass); **Dewey Martin** (vocals, drums)

1966

Apr [1] The group is formed with members who have been variously linked in earlier projects: Stills (b. Jan. 3, 1945, Dallas, TX) and Furay (b. May 9, 1944, Yellow Springs, OH) have released a single and an album (***They Call Us The Au Go Go Singers*** on the Roulette label) as part of folk outfit Au Go Go Singers (an East Coast version of the New Christy Minstrels), in New York, NY, during 1964 having first met in October that year while playing in a prior group, the New Choctawquins. (Still has subsequently relocated to Los Angeles, CA, to form the short-lived Buffalo Fish with future Monkee Peter Tork.) Young (b. Nov. 12, 1945, Toronto, ON, Canada), who has previously fronted Neil Young & The Squires and Palmer (b. September 1946, Liverpool, NS, Canada), who was a member of the Toronto-based Jack London & the Sparrows, have both played in Detroit, MI combo the Mynah Birds, recording one album for Motown in 1965. Prime mover Stills, who first met Young on April 18th the previous year, now invites them all to Los Angeles to investigate teaming up, where they are joined by ex-Dillards drummer and session veteran Martin (b. Dewayne Midkiff, Sept. 30, 1942, Chesterville, ON, Canada) and, briefly, by bass player Ken Koblun, a former colleague of Young's in the Squires, who subsequently returns to Canada. (Young and Palmer have travelled from Toronto to Los

Angeles to meet Stills in a 1953 Pontiac hearse.)
[15] The group, now calling itself Buffalo Springfield named after a steamroller they have spotted doing road repairs, makes its live debut at the Orange County Fairgrounds in San Bernardino, CA.
May Having heard the band perform, and suitably impressed, the Byrds' Chris Hillman persuades Elmer Valentine, the owner of the local Whisky A-Go-Go, to sign the group as the house band for six weeks.
July [18] Following further reputation-enhancing gigs opening for Johnny Rivers and the Turtles, the band has signed to Atlantic Records subsidiary Atco Records for a $22,000 advance at the instigation of label boss Ahmet Ertegun, and now begins work on its debut album at the Gold Star studios in Los Angeles.
[25] The group opens for the Rolling Stones at the Hollywood Bowl, Hollywood, CA.
[31] Their debut single, *Nowadays Clancy Can't Even Sing*, written by Young and sung by Furay, is released in the US.
Aug During the month, the group makes its TV debut on ABC-TV's "Hollywood Palace".
Oct [22] Buffalo Springfield opens for Love at the Whisky A-Go-Go.
Nov [11-13] They play three dates at the San Francisco's Fillmore Auditorium with Country Joe & the Fish.
Dec [2-3] The group performs at the Avalon Ballroom, San Francisco, on a bill with the Daily Flash and the Congress Of Wonders.
[20] The band's debut album ***Buffalo Springfield***, featuring seven cuts written by Stills and five by Young, is released.

1967

Feb The group performs at a concert sponsored by CAFF (Community Action For Facts & Freedom) with the Byrds, the Doors and Peter, Paul & Mary, held at the Valley Center.
Mar [25] Stills, inspired to write a song about the repression of Los Angeles youth by the police following a scene he witnessed on Sunset Boulevard on December 5th the previous year, has penned *For What It's Worth*, which now becomes the group's only major hit, at US #7 and hailed as an era-defining statement. ***Buffalo Springfield***, which does not include the hit, makes US #80. In the UK, the album sleeve and label both suggest that the US hit is included even though it is omitted, featuring instead Stills' *Baby Don't Scold Me* (later something of a collector's item, being replaced by *For What It's Worth* on all subsequent pressings).
[11] The group appears at the Longshoremen's Hall, San Francisco, supported by Peter Whea & the Breadmen.
Apr [7] The band plays alongside Jefferson Airplane at the University of San Francisco.
[11-16] They play a series of dates at the Rock Garden in San Francisco.
[28] Buffalo Springfield performs at the Fillmore West, San Francisco, on a bill with the Steve Miller Band.
Palmer is deported from the US for a visa infringement involving drugs, but will intermittently rejoin, his bass slot otherwise being variously filled by Love's Ken Forsi, Koblun, Jim Fielder (later in Blood, Sweat & Tears), Bob West and even the group's manager, Dick Davies.
May Their sophomore album ***Stampede*** is recorded but never released (subsequently appearing as a bootleg), and features Koblun, Fielder and ex-Daily Flash guitarist Doug Hastings, who is recruited for a short period, while Young, who rarely sees eye to eye with Stills, temporarily leaves (heading to London to work with Jack Nitzsche and Andrew Loog Oldham).
June [16] With a line-up comprising Stills, Furay, Martin, Palmer, Hastings and additional guest vocalist David Crosby (from the Byrds), the band performs on the opening evening of the "Monterey International Pop Festival", County Fairgrounds, Monterey, CA. (Crosby's appearance with the band exacerbates an already-strained relationship with Roger McGuinn, which will result in his departure from the Byrds).
Aug [1-3] The group plays the Fillmore Auditorium with Richie Havens and Muddy Waters.
[5] *Bluebird*, written by Stills and featuring banjo player Charlie Chin (later in Cat Mother & the All Night Newsboys), peaks at US #58.
Sept The band begins recording a new album, once again joined by Young.
Oct [21] *Rock'n'Roll Woman*, another Stills composition, makes US #44.
Dec [21-23] Buffalo Springfield performs three further dates at the Fillmore West.

1968

Jan [6] ***Buffalo Springfield Again*** reaches US #44. Its sleeve lists people who have inspired or influenced the group, including Hank B. Marvin of the Shadows (the inspiration for Young's early guitar playing).
[20] The extracted Young-penned song *Expecting To Fly* makes US #98, but the group destabilizes as it attempts to record a fourth album. Palmer, having returned in September, has once again been deported, replaced permanently by the group's recording engineer, Jim Messina (b. Dec. 5, 1947, Maywood, CA).
May [5] The group finally implodes after a final gig in Long Beach, Los Angeles, supporting Iron Butterfly, and the members quickly fan out to launch other projects: Stills will form Crosby, Stills & Nash (after assisting Al Kooper to complete the album ***Super Session***); Palmer begins a short-lived solo career (recording ***The Cycle Is Complete*** in 1971 for the Verve-Forecast label); Young will achieve parallel success as both a solo artist for Reprise Records and as a fourth annex to Crosby, Stills & Nash, while Furay will go on to form Poco. With its successful offshoots, Buffalo Springfield will be revered in hindsight as a seminal folk-rock experiment.
Oct [26] Third Buffalo Springfield album to be released ***Last Time Around***, assembled after the split by Messina from the group's final sessions, makes US #42. Extracted *On The Way Home* stalls at US #82, by which time Messina has joined Furay in the newly-launched Poco.
Nov Martin assembles a touring band as Buffalo Springfield, comprising Randy Fuller (ex-Bobby Fuller Four) (guitar, vocals), Bill Darnell (lead guitar) and Stephen Leferer (bass). Stills bulldozes the idea, instigating legal action preventing use of the band's name. (Martin will subsequently form Dewey Martin's Medicine Ball with Fuller, Darnell, Peter Bradstreet (keyboards), Terry Gregg (bass) and Buddy Emmons (steel guitar), recording for Uni and RCA, before returning to early '70s session work, subsequently joining the Village in 1976).

1969

Mar [15] Compilation ***Retrospective/The Best Of Buffalo Springfield***, peaks at US #42.

1973

Dec A double anthology ***Buffalo Springfield*** reaches US #104 in the wake of the success achieved by Stills, Young, Furay and Messina in their various post-Springfield projects.

1974

July [6] A concert planned by Asylum Records at the Los Angeles Memorial Coliseum, featuring the Byrds, Buffalo Springfield and Crosby Stills Nash & Young, fails to materialize.

1986

Aug [18] On the US syndicated radio show, "Rockline", Young announces that the Buffalo Springfield are having regular meetings to see whether a reunion is possible.

1987

After Palmer and Martin have formed a tribute combo, touring as Buffalo Springfield Revisited with Young soundalike Frank Wilks and guitarist Stan Endersby in 1985, a revised line-up, featuring Bob Frederickson (guitar) and Harlan Spector (keyboards) alongside Palmer, Martin and Wilks, is assembled for live work. Martin will leave temporarily, to play with Rick Roberts and Randy Meisner, but rejoins following a number of reunions at Stephen Stills' house with Furay, Palmer and Young.

1988

May [12] The group appears at Madison Square Garden, New York, as part of Atlantic Records' 40th anniversary celebration concert. (***Retrospective*** will be certified platinum by the RIAA on April 12th the following year.)

1991

Dec [31] Buffalo Springfield, featuring Martin, ex-Crazy Horse guitarist/vocalist Michael Curtis, lead guitarist Bill Darnell and former Al Stewart sideman, bassist/vocalist Robin Lamble, performs old and new material to celebrate New Year at the Rio Suite Hotel & Casino in Las Vegas, NV, as the group continues to play on the small-venue nostalgia circuit.
see also: **CROSBY STILLS NASH & YOUNG; POCO; NEIL YOUNG**

JIMMY BUFFETT

1970

Sept Having studied at Auburn University and majored in history and journalism at the University of Southern Mississippi, Hattiesburg, MS, and having become a freelance journalist (including a stint at **Billboard** magazine), Buffett (b. Dec. 25, 1946, Pascagoula, AL) has moved to Nashville, TN, in 1969, in an attempt to secure a recording deal as a country singer, duly signing with Andy Williams' Barnaby label, which now releases his debut album ***Down To Earth***, reputedly selling only 324 copies. Tapes of Buffett's planned sophomore album ***High Cumberland Jubilee*** are misplaced the following year by Barnaby, delaying its release indefinitely. He will subsequently quit the label and leave Nashville by year's end.

1972

Buffett relocates to Key West, FL, after a gig falls through at a Miami, FL club, initially teaming with Jerry Jeff Walker. Buffett buys a 50' ketch, makes it his home and begins the seafaring lifestyle for which he will later become famous and which will influence much of his songwriting. By night, he plays local bars, including the Green Parrot and Ernest Hemingway's old haunt, Sloppy Joe's.

1973

Mar Signed to ABC/Dunhill Records, Buffett releases ***A White Sport Coat And A Pink Crustacean*** (a play on the title of an old Marty Robbins hit), introducing his self-written wryly humorous, buccaneer-themed, story-telling style, which will distinguish subsequent hits.
Oct Buffett records ***Living And Dying*** at the Woodland Sound Studio in Nashville, with producer Don Gant.

1974

Apr ***Living And Dying In 3/4 Time*** reaches US #176. He appears in the movie "Rancho Deluxe", for which he also scores the music (and contributes six tracks to the non-charting soundtrack album on United Artists).
July [13] Self-penned and reassuringly-themed *Come Monday*, his first US hit single, reaches #30.

1975

Apr *A1A* (the designation of a beach access road off US Route 1 in Florida) makes US #25. Previously touring alone, Buffett forms a permanent backing unit, the Coral Reefer Band, initially comprising Roger Bartlett (guitar), Harry Dailey (bass), Phillip Fajardo (drums) and Greg Taylor (harmonica).

1976

Mar [27] ***Havana Daydreamin'***, on ABC Records, reaches US #65. Following its success, the previously "lost" second Barnaby album ***High Cumberland Jubilee*** re-surfaces.

1977

July His nautically-themed ***Changes In Latitudes, Changes In Attitudes***, produced by Norbert Putnam, charts a course to US #12.
[23] The extracted alcohol-exhalting *Margaritaville* hits US #8.
Nov [5] Title track *Changes In Latitudes, Changes In Attitudes* draws the line at US #37.
Dec [14] ***Changes In Latitudes, Changes In Attitudes*** is certified platinum by the RIAA.

1978

May He makes a cameo appearance in the film "FM", singing *Livingston Saturday Night*, which is included on the soundtrack album (making US #5 and UK #37).
[10] The still-climbing ***Son Of A Son Of A Sailor*** is also certified platinum by the RIAA.
[20] ***Son Of A Son Of A Sailor***, once again helmed by Putnam, hits US #10, and is a second million-seller. With songs written aboard his latest vessel, Euphoria II (which is moored in Nassau, Bahamas), it features his current musical crew of Ken Buttrey (drums), Dailey (bass), Tim Krekel (guitar), Jay Spell (piano), "Fingers" Taylor (harmonica) and Mike Utley (organ).
June [17] *Cheeseburger In Paradise*, taken from the album, makes US #32.
Sept [9] *Livingston Saturday Night* peaks at US #52.
Nov [10] The still-rising ***You Had To Be There*** is confirmed gold by the RIAA.
Dec [9] *Mañana* peaks at US #84.
[16] A live double album ***You Had To Be There***, recorded at the Fox Theatre, Atlanta, GA, and the Maurice Gusman Cultural Center, Miami, makes US #72.

1979

May [1-17] Buffett records the forthcoming ***Volcano*** at Air Studios, Montserrat, West Indies.
Oct [13] ***Volcano***, his maiden voyage for MCA Records following the closure of ABC, erupts at US #14. It features musical guests James Taylor, Russ Kunkel (drums) and Dave Loggins and recent backing-band addition, keyboardist Andy McMahon.
Nov [3] *Fins* makes US #35, while a further extract *Volcano* will peak at US #66 on Jan [19] and the Buffett/Utley-penned ballad *Survive* will climb to US #77 on Mar [29] the following year.
Dec [27] ***Volcano*** is certified gold by the RIAA.

1981

Mar [28] *It's My Job* peaks at US #57 (curiously, Buffett's only singles chart entry of the decade). Its parent album ***Coconut Telegraph*** makes US #30. Touring less, Buffett spends even more time at sea in the Caribbean aboard Euphoria II. He also becomes chairman of the Save The Manatee committee, dedicated to the protection of the endangered marine animal. (In 1992 he will sue the Florida Audubon Society for independent control of the Save the Manatee committee, which he has chaired since its inception).

1982

Feb [13] ***Somewhere Over China*** reaches US #31. Buffett opens a store in Key West, named Margaritaville, in which he sells the tropical shirts which have become synonymous with his image. He launches **The Coconut Telegraph**, a regular newsletter for his fans, which will maintain a consistent mail-out of 4,000 copies.

1984

Oct Following the US #59 success of ***One Particular Harbor*** the previous November, ***Riddles In The Sand*** reaches US #87. His range of "Caribbean Soul" tropical-design shirts is distributed to retail outlets across the US.

1985

Aug ***Last Mango In Paris*** makes US #53. A competition accompanies its release, offering a trip on Buffett's ketch as the prize. 100,000 people enter and five winners receive a free cruise. Meanwhile, Buffett's song *Turning Around* is used on the soundtrack of the film "Summer Rentals".
Dec A 13-track retrospective ***Songs You Know By Heart - Jimmy Buffett's Greatest Hit(s)***, with chart singles and favorite album tracks, including the typical *Why Don't We Get Drunk*, *Boat Drinks* and *Grapefruit - Juicy Fruit*, peaks at US #100. A video is made for *Who's The Blonde Stranger*, in which Florida Governor Bob Graham makes a guest appearance. Buffett completes the script for a projected movie to be titled "Margaritaville". (Buffett becomes campaign singer for Tony Tarracino in his successful bid to become mayor of Key West.)

1986

July ***Floridays***, recorded variously in Memphis, Fort Lauderdale and Los Angeles, and co-produced by Buffett with long-time cohort Mike Utley, reaches US #66.

1988

July Having spent much of the previous year writing a children's book with his daughter Savannah Jane (who has also played mini-conga on ***Floridays***), editing **The Coconut Telegraph** and running the "Margaritaville" restaurant and clothing stores, his new album ***Hot Water***, recorded at Buffett's own Shrimpboat Sound Studios in Key West, having been released to coincide with a major 31-city US tour from late June to mid-August, peaks at US #46.

1989

June [30] He embarks on an 18-date US tour at the Palace of Auburn Hill, Auburn Hills, MI, which will end on July 27th in Birmingham, AL.
July ***Off To See The Lizard*** peaks at US #57.
Oct As his first novel "Tales From Margaritaville" hits **The New York Times** best-seller list, Buffett continues his "Off To See The Lizard Tour '89", backed by the Coral Reefer Band and with the Neville Brothers in support. He has also become an investor in a Florida Minor League baseball team.

1990

Jan [21] As "The Lizard" tour continues at Barton Coliseum, Arkansas State Fairgrounds, Little Rock, AR, Buffett will team with Glenn Frey to write a musical, "Rules Of The Road", in between touring and recording commitments.
Apr [22] On "Earth Day 1990", and as its board committee member, Buffett spends the day performing and promoting environmental awareness.
Aug [19] A three-month "Jimmy's Jump Up" tour, with Little Feat supporting, ends at the Saratoga Performing Arts Center at Saratoga Springs, NY.
Dec [1] A further live album ***Feeding Frenzy*** makes US #68.

1991

Jan [25] During a short New Year tour, Buffett plays before a 32,693 capacity crowd at the Suncoast Dome, St. Petersburg, FL.
Feb [10] Buffett joins nearly 100 celebrities in Burbank, CA, to record *Voices That Care*, a David Foster and fiancée Linda Thompson Jenner-composed and organized charity record to benefit the American Red Cross Gulf Crisis Fund.
Mar Buffett encounters four Cuban exiles who have swum up to his house in Florida, seeking political asylum. He hands them over to local authorities after offering them refreshments.
June [22] During his annual summer concert trek with current Coral Reefers Peter Mayer (guitar), Jim Mayer (bass), Utley and Jay Oliver (keyboards), Roger Guth (drums), Robert Greenidge (steel drum) and Brie Howard (percussion), Buffett performs before a sellout audience of 17,919 at the Hollywood Bowl, Hollywood, CA.

1992

Apr [22] Buffett plays an acoustic show at Tennessee Performing Arts Center, Nashville, to benefit the W.O. Smith Nashville Community School.
May [5] He guests on NBC-TV's "The Tonight Show".
[26-27, 29-30] During his current "Recession Recess Tour", Buffett breaks the house record at the Riverbend Music Center, Cincinnati, OH, grossing more than $1,626,000 before crowds of 71,671.
June [5] The RIAA certifies multi-platinum sales (two million) of ***Songs You Know By Heart***.
[13] A second retrospective collection ***Boats Beaches Bars And Ballads***, the maiden voyage for his newly-formed Margaritaville Records, docks at US #68. (The critically-acclaimed debut album by his own discovery, New Orleans, LA group Evangeline, will be the label's second release.)
Sept [12] Buffett's second book, the novel **Where Is Joe Merchant**, which revolves around a search in the Caribbean for a missing rock star, tops the **New York Times** best-seller list.
[16] ***Feeding Frenzy*** is certified gold by the RIAA.
Oct [2] Buffett is the featured guest on the syndicated TV talk show, "Whoopi Goldberg".
Nov [11] He joins Crosby Stills & Nash, Bonnie Raitt and Jackson Browne to play a charity show for the victims of the recent Hurricane Iniki in Hawaii.

1993

May [25] Issued by Buffett & Various Artists, ***Margaritaville Cafe Light Night Menu*** (recorded at Buffett's own establishment) is released on his own Margaritaville label.
June [3] Buffett embarks on his annual US tour at the Shoreline Amphitheatre, Mountain View, CA, set to end on September 4th, with the last of three dates at the Great Woods Center for the Performing Arts, Mansfield, MA.
[12] ***Before The Beach*** enters at its US #169 peak, during a two-week stay on the chart.

1994

June [11] ***Fruitcakes*** bows at its US #5 high, as Buffett plays the second of two sellout shows at the Coca-Cola Star Lake Amphitheatre, Burgettstown, PA, during a US tour lasting from April to July.
Aug [1] He takes part Paul Simon's fifth annual "Back At The Ranch" benefit in Montauk Point, NY.
[25] Buffett's Grumman G-44 Widgeon twin-engine sea plane crashes in the waters of Maddaket Harbor off Nantucket shortly after 3:00 p.m., capsizing in four feet of water. He is taken to Nantucket Cottage Hospital, but released approximately two hours later.
Oct [27] ***Boats Beaches Bars And Ballads*** is certified by the RIAA for sales of two million.
Nov [15] Frank Sinatra's ***Duets II*** album, with Sinatra and Buffett singing *Witchcraft*, is released by Capitol.
Dec [19] ***Fruitcakes*** is certified platinum by the RIAA.

1995

Aug [4] The latest leg of a US tour opens with a sellout performance at the World Music Theatre, Tinley Park, IL.
[19] With other projects including a musical adaptation of Herman Wouk's **Don't Stop The Carnival**, two children's books, **The Jolly Mon** and **Trouble Dolls** (both written with his daughter) and running his two restaurant/store/club complexes in New Orleans and Key West, his new album ***Barometer Soup*** debuts at its US #6 peak.
Oct [5] ***Barometer Soup*** is certified gold by the RIAA.
[12] Buffett guests on NBC-TV's "The Tonight Show".
Nov The Margaritaville label releases ***The Parakeet Album : Songs Of Jimmy Buffett***, a covers collection of Buffett favorites sung by children.

1996

Jan [16] With Island Records boss Chris Blackwell and U2's Bono on board (Buffett and Bono have been guests at Blackwell's Jamaican estate and at his Pink Sands resort on Harbour Island), Buffett makes an emergency landing of his sea-plane, the Flying Boat, after Jamaican police open fire on the aircraft as it takes off from Montego Bay, Jamaica. An anonymous tip-off had incorrectly identified the plane as carrying drugs. Bullets are lodged in the craft but with no injuries to any party.

SOLOMON BURKE

1955

Dec A former boy preacher, Burke (b. 1936, Philadelphia, PA), gospel broadcaster since his teens on "Solomon's Temple" and soloist in his family's own Philadelphia church, the House Of God For All People (his grandmother Eleanora Moore dreamt of his birth and founded Solomon's Temple: The House Of God For All People Church), signs to Bess Berman's Apollo Records in New York, NY, after being discovered at a Liberty Baptist Church gospel talent show by Viola Williams, the wife of local DJ Kae Williams, and makes his first recording, *Christmas Presents From Heaven*.

1957

Burke initially quits the business after Apollo fails to pay him. He studies at Eccles Mortuary College, where he becomes a Doctor of Mortuary Science, which in turn leads him to join his aunt's A. V. Berkley Funeral Home in Philadelphia.

1960

Dec Having recorded for Artie Singer's Singular Records, after Babe Shivian has pleaded with him to return to the music arena in 1958, Burke now signs to Atlantic Records at the suggestion of **Billboard** magazine's Paul Ackerman.

1961

Nov [20] His second Atlantic release, the C&W song *Just Out Of Reach (Of My Two Empty Arms)* climbs to US #24 - one of the first country/R&B hybrids, and one of the first definable hits in the distinguished '60s soul genre in which Atlantic is to be a prime mover.

1962

Mar [17] *Cry To Me*, written by Burke's new producer Bert Berns, reaches US #44, and will be covered subsequently by the Rolling Stones, among others.
July [21] The double A-sided *Down In The Valley/I'm Hanging Up My Heart For You* charts in the US at #71 and #85 respectively.
Sept [15] Country-phrased *I Really Don't Want To Know*, makes US #93.

1963

June *If You Need Me*, a song given to Burke while on tour by its co-writer and fellow R&B singer, Wilson Pickett, competes with Pickett's own version, reaching #37 against the latter's #64. By year's end, *Can't Nobody Love You* makes US #66 (August) and *You're Good For Me* reaches US #49 (December).

1964

Feb [29] Another C&W oldie, *He'll Have To Go*, climbs to US #51, followed by *Goodbye Baby (Baby Goodbye)*, a US #33 in June, the gospel-flavored *Everybody Needs Somebody To Love* (later used by Burke as a fundraiser march for his church), which reaches US #58 in August, and *Yes I Do* (US #92 in October) while *The Price*, which Burke wrote about his own disintegrating marriage, makes US #57 in December.

1965

May [1] His biggest US hit is *Got To Get You Off My Mind*, reaching #22 which also spends four weeks atop the R&B survey.
June [14] Burke arrives in the UK for a promotional visit, during which he will appear on "Ready Steady Goes Live!" and "Thank Your Lucky Stars".
July [17] *Tonight's The Night*, written with Don Covay and coupled with a cover of Bob Dylan's *Maggie's Farm*, is his last US Top 30 entry, at #28 (also hitting R&B #2).
Aug Compilation album, ***The Best Of Solomon Burke***, is one of only two albums during his entire career to make the US survey, peaking at #141.
Sept [4] With the rise to chart status of other solo soul singers with styles approximating his own (many also on Atlantic), Burke's sales decline, as *Someone Is Watching* peaks at only US #89. (His next three singles, *Only Love (Can Save Me Now)*, *Baby Come On Home* and *I Feel A Sin Coming On*, will only reach #94, #96 and #97 respectively, through 1965-66.)

1967

Feb [25] *Keep A Light In The Window Till I Come Home* is Burke's best-seller for two years, reaching US #64.
July [22] *Take Me (Just As I Am)*, recorded at Stax in Memphis, TN, continues his resurgence, making US #49.

1968

June Burke peaks at US #68 with *I Wish I Knew (How It Would Feel To Be Free)*. He soon finds out, being released from his Atlantic contract.

1969

June [8] Having signed a new recording deal with Bell Records, his cover of Creedence Clearwater Revival's *Proud Mary*, only three months after the original has been a million seller, nevertheless peaks at US #45. It is, however, Burke's only hit for Bell, and he will find it difficult to maintain with other labels the consistency he managed at Atlantic.
July ***Proud Mary*** tops his only other Album chart entry by one place, reaching #140.

1971

May [1] Now signed to MGM Records, he re-charts in the US after a two-year absence, with *The Electronic Magnetism (That's Heavy, Baby)*, which peaks at #96.

1972

Apr [29] Also on MGM (where his releases vary greatly in quality, much of the material offered him being sub-standard), *Love's Street And Fool's Road*, a song from the movie "Cool Breeze", reaches US #89.

1975

Mar [29] After three years, and a brief spell on the Dunhill label, Burke has switched labels again - to Chess Records - returning with the Barry White-styled *You And Your Baby Blues*, which makes US #96. Hereafter, Burke semi-retires from secular performing and recording to concentrate on his religious duties as bishop of his church. (This will remain his foremost activity through to the '90s, with most album releases being gospel or inspirational led, though he will make occasional US tours as part of "The Soul Clan", an aggregation of soul singers who first made their names with the Atlantic group of labels during the '60s, including Eddie Floyd, Joe Tex, Ben E. King and Wilson Pickett.)

1993

Feb [25] Burke receives the Pioneer Award from the Rhythm and Blues Foundation at Los Angeles, CA's Palace Theatre.

1995

Mar [28] Rhino Records (US) releases ***Till The Night Is Gone : A Tribute To Doc Pomus***, to which Burke contributes. Now the owner of a chain of West Coast mortuaries, he will go on to win the Best Soul Album category for ***Live At The House Of Blues***, at the W.C. Handy Awards in Memphis, later in the year while George Nierenberg's film biography of the soul pioneer, "Sweet Inspiration" is set for release in 1996.

DORSEY BURNETTE

1956

Nov Burnette (b. Dec. 28, 1932, Memphis, TN), having played stand-up double bass in his younger brother's rockabilly outfit, the Johnny Burnette Trio, since 1953, which has signed to Coral Records in April 1956, following a succession of triumphs on the "Ted Mack Amateur Hour" TV showcase in New York, NY, where he has taken temporary work as an electrician, and recently toured the Northeastern US on a package with Carl Perkins and Gene Vincent, now drops out of live work with the trio, and is replaced on stage dates by Tony Austin.

1957

Dec Following the demise of the Johnny Burnette Trio, the Burnettes have relocated in Los Angeles, CA, where they soon secure their first songwriting success, penning *Waiting In School*, a US #18 hit for Ricky Nelson, to be followed by a second hit, *Believe What You Say* (US #4 in May 1958). Each brother will also write independently for Nelson, Dorsey inking *It's Late* (US # 9 in 1959) and the non-charting *A Long Vacation*.

1959

Dec Having recorded *My Honey* for Imperial Records in 1958 as the Burnette Brothers, and with Johnny now embarking on a successful solo career, Dorsey signs to Era Records for his own recording deal.

1960

Mar Burnette secures his first hit with *Tall Oak Tree*, an ecology-shaded song already rejected by Nelson, which reaches US #23.
Aug *Hey Little One* makes US #48.

1961

Mar [27] Now successfully launched as independent artists, the brothers, under the name the Texans, peak at US #100 with *Green Grass Of Texas*, a one-off recording for the Infinity label.
Nov Dorsey moves to the Dot label, making a permanent musical switch to country and western.

1968

Following a mid-decade period with the Reprise label, Burnette signs to Liberty Records as a country performer, although *The Greatest Love* will be his only remaining pop chart entry, reaching US #67 in February 1969. He will then move to Capitol Records in 1972, beginning a four-year spell of country hits, including ten C&W chart singles and the albums ***Here And Now*** and ***Dorsey Burnette***, also achieving success as a writer for Jerry Lee Lewis and Glen Campbell. He is voted 1973's Most Promising Newcomer by the Academy of Country Music (despite a 20-year recording career) and will join Motown's country label, Melodyland, in 1975, signing to Calliope Records two years later to record ***Things I Treasure***.

1979

Aug [19] Burnette dies of a heart attack at Canoga Park, CA. (Continuing his father's musical heritage, Dorsey's son Rocky (b. June 12, 1953, Memphis, TN) will launch a successful career with EMI-America, scoring a major hit in 1980 with *Tired Of Toein' The Line*).

JOHNNY BURNETTE

1952

After attending high school with Elvis Presley, Burnette (b. Mar. 25, 1934, Memphis, TN) has temporarily worked as a Mississippi bargeman and tried to earn an additional living as both a boxer and a singer. He persuades his older brother Dorsey (b. Dec. 28, 1932, Memphis) and their neighbor Paul Burlison (b. Feb. 4, 1929, Brownsville, TN), a member of local band the Memphis Four, to form a trio which he will front.

1953

With Johnny on guitar and lead vocals, Dorsey on stand-up bass and Burlison on lead guitar, the Johnny Burnette Trio begins to play Memphis dates, notably as a regular rockabilly act at the Hideaway club. Their debut single, *You're Undecided*, recorded for Von Records in Boonsville, MS, is also released.

1955

When Presley becomes successful on the local Sun label, the trio auditions for its founder Sam Phillips, but he finds their sound too similar to Elvis and rejects them.

1956

Mar Seeing Presley on television, Burnette takes the trio to New York, NY, and works part time in a factory, while the band joins auditions for the "Ted Mack Amateur Hour" TV showcase.

Apr The Johnny Burnette Trio becomes the show's winners for three successive weeks, earning a tour and a spot in the final (to be held in September). The group also attracts interest from New York record companies, and signs to Coral.

May [7] The trio records *Tear It Up* and other tracks with producer Bob Thiele, at the Pythian Temple Studio, New York.

July [2-5] They tape further sessions at Bradley's Barn Studio, Nashville, TN, while *Oh Baby Babe* and *The Train Kept A-Rollin'* are released.

Sept Narrowly failing to win the "Amateur Hour" final, they join a three-month tour of the Northeastern US, with Carl Perkins and Gene Vincent.

Nov With Dorsey replaced by Tony Austin for stage work, the Johnny Burnette Trio films a spot in the Alan Freed movie "Rock Rock Rock", singing *Lonesome Train*, which is also their next single.

1957

Sept After record company apathy and poor promotion see two more singles fail to hit, the trio splits. Burlison leaves the music arena and returns to Memphis, while the brothers head for Los Angeles, CA.

Dec The brothers have their first songwriting success with *Waiting In School* for Ricky Nelson (US #18), followed by a second hit, *Believe What You Say* (US #4 in May 1958). (Johnny will also pen *Just A Little Too Much*, a US #9 hit for Nelson in July 1959.)

1958

Oct With the duo having recorded *My Honey* for Imperial Records as the Burnette Brothers earlier in the year, Johnny signs as a solo singer to Freedom Records, a new subsidiary of the successful Liberty label, which will release three non-charting singles. When the label is closed the following year, he records directly for Liberty under the production of Snuff Garrett.

1960

July Burnette's first collaboration with Garrett, *Dreamin'*, makes US #11 and will hit UK #5 in October.

Dec *You're Sixteen* hits US #8, becoming a million seller.

1961

Feb *You're Sixteen* hits UK #3.

Mar *Little Boy Sad* reaches US #17, also making UK #12 in May.

[27] Now successfully launched as solo artists, the brothers, under the name the Texans, peak at US #100 with *Green Grass Of Texas*, a one-off recording for the Infinity label.

June Johnny's first ballad release after three uptempo hits, *Big, Big World*, climbs to US #58, but is not released in the UK.

Sept *Girls*, released only as a UK single, reaches #37.

Nov *God, Country And My Baby*, a mock-patriotic song, is his final US chart entry, at #18.

1962

Apr [21] Burnette embarks on 23-date, twice-nightly UK package tour with Gary U.S. Bonds, Gene McDaniels, Mark Wynter, Danny Rivers and others, at St. Andrews Hall, Glasgow, Scotland, set to end on May 13th at the Granada Cinema, Walthamstow, London.

May *Clown Shoes*, written by P.J. Proby, is his final UK hit, at #35.

July Burnette moves briefly to Chancellor Records, which releases *I Wanna Thank Your Folks* and *Remember Me*.

1963

Nov [1] He begins a UK tour in Birmingham, W. Midlands, after releasing two singles, *All Week Long* and *Sweet Suzie* via Capitol earlier in the year.

1964

Aug [1] Having recently formed his own Magic Lamp label following a short spell with the small Sahara Records, Burnette falls from his boat while fishing on Clear Lake, CA, and is drowned. (His son Billy (b. May 8, 1953, Memphis), will become a successful songwriter and session musician, and joins Fleetwood Mac in 1987, following Lindsay Buckingham's departure.)

KATE BUSH

1975

While still attending St. Joseph's Convent Grammar School where she has started playing the piano at the age of 11, Bush (b. Catherine Bush, July 30, 1958, Bexleyheath, Kent), the daughter of a physician, enters into discussions with EMI's record label and publishing division (which will result in advances of £3,000 and £500 respectively), after Dave Gilmour of Pink Floyd has heard her songs *The Man With The Child In His Eyes*, *Berlin* and *Maybe* (made available after a friend of her parents, Ricky Hopper, has paid for demo studio recordings) and passed them on to the company's Bob Mercer. EMI encourages Bush to develop her songwriting and take voice, dance (with Lindsay Kemp) and mime (with Adam Darius) classes which will hone her overall style. Meanwhile, she gains live experience playing South London pub gigs with her K.T. Bush Band, comprising her brother Paddy and future boyfriend Del Palmer.

1978

Jan *Wuthering Heights*, with lyrics inspired by Emily Brontë's novel (Bush shares Brontë's birthday), is issued in the UK with a major artist-launch publicity campaign, despite EMI's concern that the record is not radio friendly. Originally scheduled for release the previous November, its initial airing on London's Capital Radio prompts an enthusiastic listener response which has convinced EMI to distribute the single to retail.

Feb [16] Bush is featured on BBC1-TV's "Top Of The Pops".

Mar [11] *Wuthering Heights* hits UK #1, where it will remain for four weeks. Startlingly different among its chart contemporaries, its lush orchestral backing, supporting Bush's unique soprano vocal style, immediately establishes her as a major new UK talent.

Apr [1] Her Andrew Powell-produced, self-written maiden album ***The Kick Inside***, crafted during the previous three years and recorded in 1977, including work by Gilmour, hits UK #3 on its way to a million-plus UK sales.

July [8] Follow-up single, the piano-led ballad *The Man With The Child In His Eyes*, with lyrics Bush wrote when she was 14, hits UK #6.

Nov [17] Bush appears on BBC2-TV's "Sounds Like Friday: Leo Sayer".

[25] Melodramatic *Hammer Horror* peaks at UK #44.

Dec [2] Her sophomore album, ***Lionheart***, further showcasing Bush as an innovative and literate songwriter and performer, hits UK #6.

1979

Mar [3] After an initial US chart failure with *Wuthering Heights*, *The Man With The Child In His Eyes* peaks at US #85.

Apr [3] A 28-date "Tour Of Life", a 2½ hour-long act, strong on dance, image and theatrical choreography (including 17 costume changes), which will play throughout Europe, opens at the Empire Theatre, Liverpool, Merseyside, with the UK segment set to climax at the London Palladium. Exhausted by the experience, Bush will not tour again.

[14] *Wow*, a re-recording of a track on her second album, reaches UK #14.

May [4] Bush wins the Outstanding British Lyric category for *The Man With The Child In His Eyes* at the 24th annual Ivor Novello Awards, held at the Grosvenor House Hotel, London.

[12] Bush, with Steve Harley, Peter Gabriel and other friends, headlines a benefit concert at the Hammersmith Odeon, London, for the family of her lighting director Billy Duffield, killed in a stage accident.

Oct [13] EP *Kate Bush On Stage*, featuring four live tracks from the benefit show, hits UK #10. Bush devises and records a 30-minute special, including a guest appearance by Gabriel, for broadcast on BBC2-TV.

1980

Mar [15] Gabriel's *Games Without Frontiers*, with Bush guesting on vocals, hits UK #4 and will make US #48.

May [24] *Breathing*, relating the horror of nuclear fallout, reaches UK #16.

Aug [2] *Babooshka* hits UK #5, aided by a dramatic video, becomes Bush's biggest hit since *Wuthering Heights*. With her visually creative leanings, Bush is one of the first major UK acts to embrace the burgeoning promo-video medium.

Sept [20] ***Never For Ever***, self-written as ever, and co-produced with Jon Kelly, enters the UK chart at #1.

Nov [1] Extracted *Army Dreamers* reaches UK #16.

Dec [13] Seasonal *December Will Be Magic Again* makes UK #29.

1981

July [25] Percussion-heavy *Sat In Your Lap* reaches UK #11.

Oct Video "Live At The Hammersmith Odeon" is issued.

Nov Bush attends Abbey Road Studios' 50th birthday party.

1982

Aug [14] *The Dreaming*, the title track from Bush's forthcoming album, featuring the unlikely help of animal impressionist Percy Edwards and Australian singer/painter Rolf Harris (on didgeridoo), makes UK #48.

Sept [25] Self-arranged and produced at the Advision and Odyssey Studios, ***The Dreaming***, hits UK #3. Musical guests include long-time supporter Gilmour, Asia keyboardist Geoff Downes, her brother Paddy, and long-time beau Palmer on bass.

Nov *There Goes A Tenner*, from the album, becomes her first single not to chart in the UK.

1983

June Bush begins upgrading her home studio at her

350-year-old South London farmhouse, resulting in a self-contained 48-track facility.

July US-only mini-album, ***Kate Bush***, reaches US #148.

Dec EMI releases "The Single File" a retrospective video collection.

1985

Aug [31] Having typically remained out of the public eye for two years, Bush hits UK #3 with the breathless, drum-led *Running Up That Hill*, which becomes her biggest seller since *Wuthering Heights*.

Sept [28] ***Hounds Of Love***, launched by EMI with a party at the London Planetarium, enters the UK chart at #1. Once again produced by Bush, it features orchestral arrangements by Michael Kamen and includes musical guest John Williams on cello.

Nov [2] *Cloudbusting*, also from the album and featuring actor Donald Sutherland in its innovative video, reaches UK #20.

[30] *Running Up That Hill*, finally giving Bush her US breakthrough, reaches #30.

Dec ***Hounds Of Love*** makes US #30, her first significant US album success.

1986

Mar [8] The extracted title track, *Hounds Of Love*, reaches UK #18.

May [17] *The Big Sky*, featuring Youth on bass, makes UK #37.

June Recent project-related video package, "Hair Of The Hound", is issued.

Nov [15] *Experiment IV*, promoted with a self-directed video, reaches UK #23, as *Don't Give Up*, a ballad duet with Peter Gabriel, hits UK #9.

1987

Jan [17] ***The Whole Story***, an incomplete anthology of Bush's best-known work, hits UK #1, and becomes her best-selling album. A video version is also a #1 success on the UK video survey. The album makes US #76.

Feb [9] Bush wins Best British Female Artist at the sixth annual BRIT Awards, at the Grosvenor House Hotel, London.

Mar [28] Bush makes a rare live appearance, performing *Running Up That Hill* and *Let It Be* with Gilmour and Gabriel at "The Secret Policeman's Third Ball" in London.

Apr [25] *Don't Give Up* peaks at US #72.

1988

New Bush song, *This Woman's Work*, is included by producer John Hughes in his film "She's Having A Baby".

1989

Sept [30] *The Sensual World*, featuring Davey Spillane on Uillean pipes, debuts at UK #12, but then falls to #15, spending only four weeks in the Top 40.

Oct [28] Its parent album, ***The Sensual World***, recorded variously in Dublin, the Abbey Road Studios, London, and at her home studio, hits UK #2 and will reach US #43 and reflects a softer, folk-edged musical approach, featuring the Trio Bulgarka, punk violinist Nigel Kennedy, Gilmour, and orchestral arrangements once again by Kamen.

Dec [9] Soft, ethereal ballad, *This Woman's Work*, reaches UK #25.

1990

Mar [17] Third ***Sensual World*** extract, *Love And Anger*, makes UK #38.

Oct [26] EMI, with whom Bush has been signed for 15 years, issues a comprehensive career boxed set, ***This Woman's Work***, comprising all of her recordings to date.

Nov Currently recording her eighth album, Bush appears at her fan club convention and announces that she hopes to tour (she has not done so since 1979), following the album's 1991 release.

1991

Dec [14] Following a year without the expected album release, and appearances on Roy Harper's ***Once*** and the TV documentary "Bringing It All Back Home", *Rocket Man*, Bush's contribution to the ***Two Rooms : Celebrating The Songs Of Elton John And Bernie Taupin*** tribute, reaches UK #12, as she will make a rare TV appearance on BBC1-TV's "Wogan" on the 16th.

1993

Sept [18] *Rubberband Girl* debuts at its UK #12 peak.

Nov [13] Bush's first album in four years, ***The Red Shoes*** (its title taken from Michael Powell's classic film), featuring Jeff Beck, Eric Clapton, her earliest supporter David Gilmour and [SYMBOL], bows at its UK #2 peak.

[20] ***The Red Shoes*** debuts at its US #28 high.

[27] *Moments Of Pleasure* enters at its UK #26 peak.

Dec [25] *Rubberband Girl* bows at US #88 chart pinnacle.

1994

Apr [23] Title cut *The Red Shoes* reaches UK #21.

July [30] *The Man I Love*, accompanied by Larry Adler on harmonica and released by Mercury Records, debuts at its UK #27 peak.

Nov [19] *And So Is Love*, featuring Clapton on guitar, reaches UK #26 in its week of entry.

During the year, Bush makes a 50-minute movie for home video release, "The Line, The Cross And The Curve".

BUSH

Gavin Rossdale (vocals, guitar);
Nigel Pulsford (guitar); **Dave Parsons** (bass);
Robin Goodridge (drums)

1992

Influenced by the music of the Sex Pistols, X-Ray Spex, Steel Pulse and the Pixies, and after three years performing in other bands, frontman and part-time painter Rossdale (b. Oct 30), forms Bush in London with Pulsford (b. Apr 11), Parsons (b. July 2), and Goodridge (b. Sept 10), who are also all painters. Performing its first gig together in an outdoor car park, the quartet will spend the next two years performing at small UK clubs, before London-based DJ Gary Crowley passes the group's demo tape on to George Michael's ex-manager Rob Kahane at Trauma Records in the US. Kahane visits Bush during demo sessions in a Harlesden, London studio, and, signs the band, offering the members complete freedom to record its debut album (which will be completed with veteran producers Clive Langer and Alan Winstanley).

1994

Dec [10] With both album rock and alternative radio stations following the lead taken by KROQ in Los Angeles, CA, Bush's debut *Everything Zen*, recorded in one take, enters the US Modern Rock singles chart on its way to #2, supported by its first US club date tour (including a bottom-of-the-bill appearance at New York, NY's CBGB venue) and a Matt Mahurin-directed video clip.

1995

May [20] US tour dates kick off as the band appears at "96X Fest", held at the Strawberry Banks, Hampton, VA.

July [17] Bush's debut album, ***Sixteen Stone***, which is still climbing the US chart, is certified platinum by the RIAA.

Aug [12] Bush appears at "X-Fest" at the Deer Creek Music Center, Noblesville, IN, promoted by WRZX-FM, also featuring Weezer, Sponge, Quicksand, Ned's Atomic Dustbin and Teenage Fan Club on a bill grossing $219,944 from 20,133 attendees.

[19] Mid-way through its first headlining US tour, Bush performs an acoustic set on WBCN Boston, followed by a sold-out show at the Memorial Auditorium, Worcester, MA (the tour will close on October 13th at the Balch Fieldhouse, Boulder CO).

Oct The movie soundtrack album to "Mallrats" is released in the US including a new cut by Bush.

Nov [4] *Comedown*, spurred by another critically-praised video clip, reaches US #30. During the month, Interscope releases the Enhanced-CD, ***Little Things*** which includes previously unreleased tracks, samples of 12 new songs, music video clips, interviews and a video game.

Dec [1] An eight-date UK mini-tour ends at London's Astoria 2 Theatre.

[16] Bush is the music guest on NBC-TV's "Saturday Night Live".

1996

Jan [22] Still rising on the US survey and still without any chart action in its home country, ***Sixteen Stone*** is now certified by the RIAA for three million US sales.

Feb [1] Bush returns to the US for a further three-month concert visit beginning at the Cumberland County Coliseum, Portland, ME, before returning to London to record its sophomore album.

[3] ***Sixteen Stone***, licensed via Trauma to Interscope Records, hits US #4.

[24] *Glycerine* reaches US #28.

Apr [13] The group guests on the premiere of the Roseanne-produced Fox-TV "Saturday Night Special".

May [4] Still-climbing *Machinehead* now makes US #43.

JERRY BUTLER

1957

A resident of Chicago, IL, since age three, Butler (b. Dec. 8, 1939, Sunflower, MS) has spent several years in church choirs, notably the Northern Jubilee Gospel Singers, and has sung with local doo-wop group the Quails, when he and close friend Curtis Mayfield (introduced in Mayfield's mother's church), singing with the Alphatones, meet a Tennessee R&B group named the Roosters in Chicago, and join forces with them.

Dec Renamed the Impressions, with Butler as lead singer, the group auditions for Ewart Abner's Falcon Records, a subsidiary of leading Chicago R&B label Vee-Jay, and is signed.

1958

Apr Their first recording session produces the group's own ballad composition, *For Your Precious Love*, the song which most impressed Abner at the audition.

July *For Your Precious Love* reaches US #11, though the group is disconcerted to find Abner has credited "The Impressions Featuring Jerry Butler" on the record label, clearly emphasising the soloist.

Sept Two more singles follow, neither charting, and both with soloist-plus-group billing at the label's insistence. Butler, sensing the others' antagonism, decides to leave. Abner subsequently decides to retain him as a solo act, and drops the group, which promptly disbands (though Mayfield remains at the Vee-Jay studios as a session musician and writer and, three years later will re-form the Impressions as a trio, with original member Sam Gooden and previous Roosters member Fred Cash, finding major US chart success in the '60s).

1960

Dec After several solo records, two hits on the R&B chart, and a move to Vee-Jay after the subsidiary labels close, Butler is reunited with Mayfield on *He Will Break Your Heart*, a major US hit (#7) which they have co-written and on which Mayfield supplies backing vocals and guitar.

1961

Apr *Find Another Girl*, a similar collaboration,

reaches US #27.
Aug *I'm A-Telling You*, again with Mayfield's back-up, makes US #25.
Dec Sensing the chance to broaden his audience appeal, Butler records *Moon River*, Henry Mancini's song from the movie "Breakfast At Tiffany's", which reaches US #11, two weeks in advance of the composer's original. This success launches him as a purveyor of (usually R&B-oriented) sophisticated ballads throughout the decade, and ensures him regular lucrative live engagements on the US supper-club circuit.

1962

Sept *Make It Easy On Yourself*, a Burt Bacharach/Hal David song which becomes another standard (and a hit for the Walker Brothers in 1965), reaches US #20.
Nov *You Can Run (But You Can't Hide)* makes US #63, while *Theme From Taras Bulba (The Wishing Star)* will anchor the Hot 100 in December.

1963

Apr *Whatever You Want* peaks at US #68.

1964

Jan *Need To Belong*, a Curtis Mayfield song, climbs to US #31.
Apr *Giving Up On Love* makes US #56.
July *I Don't Want To Hear It Anymore*, one of the earliest hits written by Randy Newman, stalls at US #95, but many radio DJs play the B-side, Butler's own song *I Stand Accused*, which makes US #61 (much covered, it will be a US #42 hit for Isaac Hayes in 1970).
Nov After hearing the ballad *Let It Be Me* in the Bahamas, Butler has recorded it as a duet with Vee-Jay girl, Betty Everett, and it becomes his biggest US hit to date, at #5. Their album of duets, ***Delicious Together***, reaches US #102.

1965

Jan *Smile*, a second ballad duet with Everett, makes US #42.
Mar Solo single, *Good Times*, peaks at US #64.
June [25] During a visit to the UK, Butler appears on ITV's "Ready Steady Go!" though UK chart success will consistently elude him.
July [3] He performs on ITV's "Thank Your Lucky Stars".

1966

Mar His revival of *For Your Precious Love* peaks at US #99, but Vee-Jay is in no position to promote it, since the company is badly in debt and about to crash.
Aug Now dubbed "The Ice Man" by Philadelphia DJ George Woods (a tag which stays with him hereafter), because of his super-cool stage presence and cool vocal style, Butler signs a new contract with Mercury Records.

1967

Feb Butler's label debut, *I Dig You Baby*, reaches US #60.
Nov *Mr. Dream Merchant* is his first solo US Top 40 for four years, at #38.

1968

Jan *Lost* finds its way to US #62.
Feb ***Mr. Dream Merchant***, his first solo chart album, makes US #154.
Mar ***Jerry Butler's Golden Hits Live***, featuring on stage versions of earlier hits, reaches US #178. While performing at Prep's nightclub in Philadelphia, Butler meets songwriting/production team Kenny Gamble and Leon Huff, and they agree to work together.
July First fruit of the Philadelphia recording sessions is *Never Give You Up*, a Gamble/Huff/Butler composition, which makes US #20.
Nov *Hey, Western Union Man*, a further collaboration by the trio climbs to US #16, and tops the R&B chart.

1969

Jan Gamble and Huff-produced ***The Ice Man Cometh*** (including the two recent hits) reaches US #29, while a third extract, *Are You Happy?*, peaks at US #39.
Apr *Only The Strong Survive*, a final single from ***The Ice Man Cometh***, hits US #4 (also topping the R&B survey for two weeks), attracting cover versions from Elvis Presley and others.
[24] *Only The Strong Survive* is certified gold by the RIAA.
July From new Philadelphia sessions, *Moody Woman* reaches US #24.
Oct *What's The Use Of Breaking Up* makes US #20.
Dec *Don't Let Love Hang You Up* reaches US #44, while Butler's second Gamble/Huff-produced album, ***Ice On Ice***, containing this and the two previous hits, makes US #41.

1970

Jan Two more ***Ice On Ice*** tracks are US chart singles: *Got To See If I Can't Get Mommy (To Come Back Home)* (#62), and *I Could Write A Book* (#46).
July Compilation album, ***The Best Of Jerry Butler***, rounding up his Mercury singles to date, reaches US #167. This also marks the end of Butler's Philly period, as Gamble and Huff, thanks largely to their huge success with him, have launched their own Philadelphia International label, and major companies are sending artists like Wilson Pickett and Archie Bell & the Drells to work with the duo. With his own credibility at an all-time high, Butler establishes the Songwriters' Workshop in Chicago, backed by music publisher Chappell, which gives creative opportunities to young writers like Chuck Jackson, Marvin Yancy, Terry Callier and Brenda Lee Eager - who will in turn provide Butler with a fund of material for future recordings.
Aug *Where Are You Going*, recorded for the film soundtrack to "Joe", charts briefly at US #95, while ***You And Me*** peaks at #172.

1971

Jan A duet with fellow Chicago artist Gene Chandler, *You Just Can't Win (By Making The Same Mistake)*, credited to Gene & Jerry, makes US #94.
Mar Solo single, *If It's Real What I Feel*, reaches US #69. It is taken from ***Jerry Butler Sings Assorted Sounds*** (most of them courtesy of the Songwriters' Workshop), which makes US #186.
Apr Another duet with Chandler, ***Gene & Jerry - One & One***, reaches US #143.
July *How Did We Lose It Baby* stalls at US #85.
Oct Another Workshop-originated album, ***The Sagittarius Movement***, is released, peaking at US #123, but remaining charted for 22 weeks. The excerpted *Walk Easy My Son* makes US #93.

1972

Mar *Ain't Understanding Mellow*, a duet with young protegée Eager (discovered in a Chicago choir run by the Reverend Jesse Jackson, to whose charitable endeavors in the city Butler is a regular contributor), reaches US #21, staying charted for almost five months. Eager also becomes a member of his vocal backing group, Peaches.
Apr [6] *Ain't Understanding Mellow* becomes Butler's second RIAA-certified gold record.
June His revival of *I Only Have Eyes For You*, from ***The Spice Of Life***, reaches US #85, while the album peaks at US #92.
Sept A second duet with Eager, *(They Long To Be) Close To You*, and the solo *One Night Affair* are Butler's final Mercury chart entries, peaking at US #91 and #52 respectively. He subsequently concentrates on the Workshop, his music publishing activities and the running of two small talent-showcase labels, Fountain and Memphis, in Chicago.

1975

Jan Butler's contract with Mercury expires, and he is approached by Abner, who first recorded him, now president of Motown Records.
Apr Signed to Motown, his label debut, ***Love's On The Menu***, fails to chart.

1977

May ***Suite For The Single Girl*** reaches US #146, while the extracted *I Wanna Do It To You* makes US #51.
July Motown teams Butler with Thelma Houston, in anticipation of repeating past duetting successes. ***Thelma And Jerry*** reaches US #53.

1979

Jan Butler has reunited with Gamble and Huff, signing to their Philadelphia International label. The renewed liaison does not repeat the earlier chart triumphs, but ***Nothing Says I Love You Like I Love You*** reaches US #160. It proves to be his final US chart entry outside the R&B field. Hereafter, in addition to short-lived recording stints with Fountain Records and the CTI label in the early '80s, Butler will concentrate on business affairs and still-lucrative live performances.

1983

Butler reunites with Mayfield and various members of the Impressions, for a 30-city "Silver Anniversary" US tour, sponsored by Budweiser beer, to celebrate the 25th birthday of *For Your Precious Love*. (Its success will prompt Butler and other erstwhile Impressions to occasionally reunite for further live dates over the next few years, billed as "The Love Reunion".)

1994

Mar [2] After a number of years spent on the periphery of the music arena (duetting with Aretha Franklin, for example, in 1985 for US TV ads promoting McDonald's new lettuce-and-tomato hamburger), and having sought and won political office in Chicago in 1986, Butler occasionally emerging for concert engagements (including reunion shows in 1993 with the Impressions billed as "An Evening Of Love Songs With The Dells And The Impressions"), is honored with the Pioneer Award at the fifth annual Rhythm and Blues Foundation ceremonies at New York, NY's Roseland Ballroom. Later in the day, he also guests on CBS-TV's "Late Show With David Letterman", with Bonnie Raitt and Ben E. King. (A class-action suit in Atlanta, GA, federal court in front of Judge Clarence Cooper, in which a number of popular '60s acts, including Butler, seek back-dated pension fund remuneration from allegedly unscrupulous record labels, will begin on September 21st the following year.)

PAUL BUTTERFIELD

1965

Vocalist and harmonica player Butterfield (b. Dec. 17, 1942, Chicago, IL) forms a racially-integrated R&B band, the Paul Butterfield Blues Band, in Chicago. Personnel include the ex-rhythm section of a band previously fronted by bluesman Howlin' Wolf, who are Smokey Smothers (guitar), Jerome Arnold (bass) and Sam Lay (drums), plus Butterfield's former University of Chicago classmate, Elvin Bishop (b. Oct. 21, 1942, Tulsa, OK) (guitar). Signed to Elektra Records, Smothers leaves and they bring in Mike Bloomfield (b. July 28, 1944, Chicago) on guitar, while Mark Naftalin joins on keyboards during the recording of the first album.
July [25] Amongst their first live gigs outside Chicago is a spot on the "Newport Folk Festival", Newport, RI, where their electric blues set is ill-received by many acoustic folk music purists. They impress Bob Dylan, however, who invites them to back him on stage later the same day. This, Dylan's first-ever non-acoustic set, proves equally controversial.

1966

Jan ***The Paul Butterfield Blues Band***, recorded in New York, NY, makes US #123.
Mar [25-27] The group performs at the Fillmore West, San Francisco, CA, sharing a bill with the

Quicksilver Messenger Service.
June Band contributes five tracks to a seminal Elektra various artists album, ***What's Shakin'***, alongside the Lovin' Spoonful, Eric Clapton, Tom Rush and Al Kooper.
Oct [20] They begin a 16-date, twice-nightly tour at London's Finsbury Park Astoria, with Georgie Fame, Chris Farlowe, Geno Washington and special guests the Animals. During the trek, which will end on November 6th at the Leicester Odeon, Leics., they also record with John Mayall.
Dec With Billy Davenport replacing Lay on drums, ***East West***, the title track of which lasts over 13 minutes and includes Eastern instrumental influences, peaks at US #65. Bloomfield leaves after its release, to form Electric Flag.

1967

Jan EP *Bluesbreakers With Paul Butterfield*, featuring Mayall, is released in the UK by Decca Records.
[20-22, 27-29] The Butterfield Blues Band returns for a succession of dates at the Fillmore West, San Francisco.
June [17] The group performs on the second day of the "Monterey International Pop Festival" at the Monterey County Fairgrounds, Monterey, CA.
Aug [22] The band supports Cream, again at the Fillmore West, at the start of the UK rock trio's US tour.

1968

Mar [30] A considerably changed group, retaining only Butterfield, Bishop and Naftalin from previous line-ups, is heard on ***The Resurrection Of Pigboy Crabshaw*** (a title that refers to Bishop's nickname), which reaches US #52. In addition to a fresh rhythm section, the group now includes three horn players.
May [24-26] The band appears at the Avalon Ballroom, San Francisco, on a bill with the MC5 and the Psychedelic Stooges.
July [2] They open a series of dates at the Fillmore West, sharing the bill with Creedence Clearwater Revival.
Aug [15] The band performs at the "Woodstock Music & Art Fair", and will later be heard briefly on the three-album set ***Woodstock***.
Sept [28] ***In My Own Dreams***, by the same line-up (with Naftalin credited as Naffy Markham), reaches US #79.

1969

Mar [27-30] The Butterfield Blues Band returns again to play at the Fillmore West, now sharing a bill with Mike Bloomfield & Friends.
Dec [6] After further personnel changes, Butterfield is the only original group member on his band's fifth album ***Keep On Moving***, produced by Jerry Ragavoy, which peaks at US #102.

1970

Dec [14, 16-20] Having returned to their favored venue in March, they share an unlikely billing at the Fillmore West with Ravi Shankar.

1971

Feb Double performance album ***Live***, produced by Todd Rundgren and recorded at the Troubadour in Los Angeles, CA, after yet more personnel changes, reaches US #72.
Sept A final studio album for Elektra, ***Sometimes I Just Feel Like Smilin'***, reaches US #124, after which, tired of touring, Butterfield breaks up the band and moves to live in Woodstock, NY.

1972

June Retrospective double album ***Golden Butter - The Best Of The Paul Butterfield Blues Band*** peaks at US #136.
An Offer You Can't Refuse, featuring Butterfield's earliest recordings from 1963 with Smokey Smothers' band in Chicago, is released by the specialist UK blues label, Red Lightnin'.

1973

Feb After a quiet period in Chicago, Butterfield forms a new group, Better Days, and signs to Rundgren's Bearsville Records. With a line-up including Geoff Muldaur and guitarist Amos Garrett, plus guests like Bobby Charles (writer of Bill Haley's *See You Later, Alligator*), sax player David Sanborn (b. July 30, 1945, Tampa, FL), and Muldaur's wife Maria, ***Better Days*** peaks at US #145.
Nov The outfit's sophomore album ***It All Comes Back*** reaches US #156, after which the group splits.

1976

Feb ***Put It In Your Ear***, featuring Butterfield accompanied mainly by session musicians, including Levon Helm, and produced by Henry Glover, is released by Bearsville.
Nov [25] He makes a guest appearance in the Band's spectacular farewell concert in San Francisco, and is later seen in Martin Scorsese's movie of the event, "The Last Waltz". (He duets on *Mystery Train* with Helm, plays harmonica for Muddy Waters on *Mannish Boy*, and joins an all-star cast on *I Shall Be Released*.)

1981

After a long absence, during which he has attempted without much success to work with Helm and Rick Danko (ex-members of the Band) in both the RCO All-Stars and the Danko-Butterfield Band, Butterfield tries to restart his recording career. During sessions for ***North South*** for Bearsville, recorded in Memphis with producer Willie Mitchell, he is stricken with peritonitis, entailing two operations which long delay the album's completion. He returns to live work after its release, but the album fails to sell and he will not regain his lost popularity.

1987

May [4] After a lengthy recording silence was broken in 1986 with the US release of ***The Legendary Paul Butterfield Rides Again*** on Amherst Records, Butterfield, a heavy drinker for most of his adult life, is found dead in his North Hollywood, CA, apartment.

THE BUZZCOCKS

Pete Shelley (guitar, vocals); **Howard Devoto** (vocals); **Steve Diggle** (guitar, bass); **Steve Garvey** (bass); **John Maher** (drums)

1976

July [20] The Buzzcocks makes its debut supporting the Sex Pistols and the Damned at the Free Trade Hall, Manchester, Gtr. Manchester. The group has been formed by philosophy student and Iggy & the Stooges fan Devoto (b. Howard Trafford), who, after travelling to see the Sex Pistols at High Wycombe, Bucks., in February and then promoting a Pistols gig in Manchester two months later, teams with Shelley (b. Apr. 17, 1955), ex-member of the Jets Of Air, whom Devoto met at the Bolton Institute of Higher Education, Bolton, Lancs. Diggle, whom they saw at a Manchester gig, and Maher, recruited from a **Melody Maker** ad they placed, complete the initial quartet.
Aug [29] The group makes its London debut at the Screen On The Green, Islington, London, on a seminal punk bill with the Sex Pistols and the Clash.
Sept [21] The band plays in the 100 Club punk festival with the Damned and the Vibrators, and receives widespread UK rock press attention.
Oct The group records an 11-track demo at the Stockport Studios.
Dec [28] Having played some gigs on the Sex Pistols-led "Anarchy In The UK Tour", the Buzzcocks begin recording with producer Martin Hannett at Indigo Sound Studio.

1977

Jan EP *Spiral Scratch* is released on their own independent New Hormones label, set up by Devoto and Shelley with a £500 loan, subsequently becoming a prototype punk-era collectors' item.
Mar Having played just 11 gigs with the group, Devoto leaves, forming Magazine (who will score five UK chart albums for Virgin Records between 1978 and '81), before launching a solo career in 1983 with ***Jerky Versions Of The Dream***). With Diggle switching from bass to guitar, Shelley recruits Garth Smith from Jets Of Air as the new bassist, a revised line-up which will make its first appearance supporting the Clash at the Coliseum, Harlesden, London.
May [1] As its support act, the Buzzcocks embark on the Clash's "White Riot" tour, bowing at the Roxy, London.
Aug [16] They sign to EMI's United Artists label on the day Elvis Presley dies.
Oct Their first UA single *Orgasm Addict*, produced by Martin Rushent, is released.
Nov Smith is fired for extreme unreliability during their first UK tour as headliners, and is replaced on bass by Steve Garvey.

1978

Feb [25] *What Do I Get*, the group's first UK hit, makes #37. (The single's release had been held up for two weeks after a row breaks out between EMI, United Artists and the group's management, after it was claimed that EMI had tried to sub-contract the pressing of the B-side because of its title, *Oh Shit*.)
Apr [1] Their major-label album debut ***Another Music In A Different Kitchen*** reaches UK #15, comprising an era-defining collection of short burst punk-pop cuts, largely written and sung by Shelley.
May [5] The group undertakes a 19-date "Entertaining Friends" tour, with the Slits and Penetration, at Liverpool University, set to end on June 6th at the Edinburgh Odeon, Edinburgh, Scotland.
[13] *I Don't Mind* peaks at UK #55.
July [22] *Love You More* makes UK #34.
[29] The group guests on ITV's "Revolver".
Oct [1] 26-date tour begins at the New Theatre, Oxford, Oxon., set to end on the 31st at Portsmouth Guild Hall, Portsmouth, Hants.
[14] ***Love Bites*** reaches UK #13.
Nov [4] Biggest UK hit *Ever Fallen In Love (With Someone You Shouldn't Have)* reaches #12, as the group embarks on the "Beating Hearts" tour with the Subway Sect. (The song will be successfully covered in 1987 by the Fine Young Cannibals, hitting UK #9.)
[14] The band appears on BBC2-TV's "The Old Grey Whistle Test".
Dec [16] *Promises* reaches UK #20.

1979

Jan During a break from recording and touring, Shelley produces Alberto Y Lost Trios Paranoias, while Maher assists Patrick Fitzgerald with his debut album.
Mar [17] *Everybody's Happy Nowadays* reaches UK #29, as the group plays concerts in Europe and a five-date UK tour (including a performance at the Hammersmith Odeon, London, which will be recorded and subsequently released as ***Entertaining Friends***).
Aug [4] *Harmony In My Head*, a Diggle song premiered on BBC Radio 1's "John Peel Show", makes UK #32.
Sept [15] EP *Spiral Scratch*, reissued to meet fans' demand in the UK, reaches #31. The group embarks on its first US tour, promoting ***Going Steady***, a compilation of UK singles.
Oct [13] ***A Different Kind Of Tension*** reaches UK #26 in a three-week stay on the chart, while the band tours the UK with Joy Division.

1980

May The Buzzcocks make their first live appearance of the year, at Manchester Polytechnic, Manchester.
Sept [13] *Are Everything/Why She's A Girl From The Chainstore* stalls at UK #61, while a UK "Tour Of Instalments" dissolves after only a few dates.

1981

Feb Following two non-charting singles and a loss of career momentum, the band splits when each member receives a solicitor's letter stating that Shelley wishes to sever all commitments to the Buzzcocks. (Shelley, initially backed by Garvey, will start a solo career which will include 1981's Rushent-produced ***Homosapien*** released via Island Records, ***XL-1***, which makes UK #42 in July 1983, the extracted *Telephone Operator* having reached UK #66 in March, and ***Heaven And Sea*** in 1986, while Diggle and Meyer will launch a new band, Flag of Convenience, in September, initially signed to Sire, but switching to the small independent label, MCM in 1985.)

1987

July EMI-issued retrospective ***Singles - Going Steady***, originally released in August 1985, brings their greatest hits to compact disc.

1989

May Diggle's band, the now-acronymed FOC, tours Europe, only to discover that posters promoting the gigs are using the Buzzcocks name. Diggle name-changes to Buzzcocks FOC for the group's July-released single *Sunset*. This leads to Diggle and Shelley deciding to re-form the unit, providing it is with the original line-up. Garvey, now living in New York, NY, and Maher, owner of a Volkswagen repair shop in Manchester, agree, and the group embarks on its first dates since 1980.

Nov [7] The Buzzcocks plays its first US date in a decade in Providence, RI.

1990

Aug [25] The group appears at the annual "Reading Festival", Reading, Berks.

Oct [3] A nine-date UK tour begins at the Cliff Pavilion, Southend, Essex, set to end on the 13th at the UEA, Norwich, Norfolk.

1991

Apr With the group augmented by ex-Smiths' drummer Mike Joyce, the Planet Pacific label releases the Buzzcocks' first new recording in ten years, the four-track EP *Alive Tonight*.

June [16-17] The band plays at London's Town & Country club.

Aug [3] Sharing a bill with Orchestral Manoeuvres In The Dark, the Wonder Stuff, the Soup Dragons and the Railway Children, the Buzzcocks participate in the "Cities In The Park Festival" at Heaton Park, Prestwich, Gtr. Manchester.

Dec [5-6] The band plays at the Palace, Hollywood, CA, before two sellout crowds of 1,637, during a short US tour.

1992

Sept [7] They participate in the final day of the **New Musical Express**/Spastic Society 40th anniversary celebrations at the Town & Country club.

1993

May [11] A UK tour commences at the Market Tavern, Kidderminster, Hereford & Worcs., set to close on June 27th at the Northampton Roadmenders club, Northampton, Northants., coinciding with the release of a new album, ***Trade Test Transmissions***, on Essential Records (UK).

1994

Aug [6] The group, currently Shelley, Diggle, Tony Barber (bass) and Phil Barker (drums), takes part in "Madstock!" at London's Finsbury Park following live UK summer appearances including the "Phoenix Festival", Long Marston, Stratford-Upon-Avon, Warks., held July 14-17th.

1995

June [15] EMI releases boxed set retrospective ***Product***, containing the band's entire United Artists output, including three albums, all the singles and B-sides and a 24-minute live gig recorded at the London Lyceum in 1979. (During the year, Shelley contributes *Better Off Without A Wife* to the Tom Waits tribute album ***Step Right Up - The Songs Of Tom Waits***.)

1996

Jan [23] Re-energized not least by latent respect from the latest crop of new punk acts in the US (most notably Green Day), and newly signed to I.R.S. Records, the Buzzcocks releases ***French***, a 23-cut live album recorded at L'Arapho Club in Paris, France in April the previous year. This will be quickly followed by a new studio set recorded at Fantasy Studios, Berkeley, CA with producer (and Green Day engineer) Neil King. As Sheeley points out: "The thing that surprises me is the whole list of bands that say the Buzzcocks were why they got into music. Now it's about time we showed them how to do it properly."

THE BYRDS

Roger McGuinn (vocals, guitar); **Gene Clark** (vocals, percussion); **David Crosby** (vocals, guitar); **Chris Hillman** (vocals, bass); **Michael Clarke** (drums)

1964

Jim McGuinn (b. James McGuinn III, July 13, 1942, Chicago, IL), who has worked with the Limeliters, the Chad Mitchell Trio (with whom he toured South America for the State Department), Judy Collins and Bobby Darin (the latter as a writer at New York, NY's Brill Building), and Clark (b. Harold Eugene Clark, Nov. 17, 1944, Tipton, MO), who, at 13, formed his own band, the Sharks, playing with the Surf Riders before joining the New Christy Minstrels, meet at the Troubadour club in Los Angeles, CA, where McGuinn has opened for Hoyt Axton and Roger Miller, and start working as a duo at the Folk Den. Having seen them perform, Crosby (b. David Van Cortland, Aug. 14, 1941, Los Angeles), ex-Les Baxter's Balladeers, persuades the duo to let him sing harmony with them. Crosby introduces McGuinn and Clark to producer Jim Dickson, for whom he has already recorded solo, and the trio records *The Only Girl I Adore*. Shortly thereafter they form the Jet Set, cutting *You Movin'* and *The Only Girl*, with session players Hal Blaine and Larry Knechtel. Drummer Clarke (b. June 3, 1944, New York), whom Crosby has seen playing with Dino Valenti in Big Sur, CA, and bluegrass prodigy Hillman (b. Dec. 4, 1942, Los Angeles), ex-Scottsville Squirrel Barkers, the Golden State Boys (who become the Blue Diamond Boys), and finally the Hillmen with Vern and Rex Gosdin and Don Parmley, who has just made some recordings with Dickson, are also recruited. Elektra boss Jac Holzman shows interest, and the newly-formed group records a series of demos (which will emerge in 1969 as ***Preflyte*** and reach US #84), including *Please Let Me Love You*, which Holzman releases on Elektra as by the Beefeaters.

Nov [10] McGuinn, Hillman and Crosby sign to CBS/Columbia Records, after being recommended to the label by Miles Davis.

[19] They change their name to the Byrds on Thanksgiving Day.

1965

Jan [20] Now resident at Los Angeles club Ciro's, the band records Bob Dylan's *Mr. Tambourine Man*, produced by Doris Day's son Terry Melcher (ex-the Rip Chords and Bruce & Terry with Beach Boy Bruce Johnston) and producer of CBS act Paul Revere & the Raiders, with Blaine (drums), Knechtel (bass), Jerry Cole (rhythm guitar), Leon Russell (electric piano) and McGuinn (lead guitar), at Columbia's Hollywood Studios.

May [11] The Byrds make their network TV debut on NBC-TV's "Hullabaloo".

June [26] *Mr. Tambourine Man*, recorded in a harmony-rich arrangement with McGuinn's distinctive 12-string Rickenbacker guitar (musical elements which will define much of the Byrds' output), considerably different from Dylan's original, tops the US chart, and is a global million-seller.

July [24] *Mr. Tambourine Man* also tops the UK survey, dislodging the Hollies' *I'm Alive*.

Aug [4] The group arrives in the UK for a 14-day stay of TV, radio and ballroom dates, touring with Them and Kenny Lynch, but much of it is cancelled when McGuinn contracts a viral infection.

[7] ***Mr. Tambourine Man***, establishing their position as frontrunners in the folk-rock movement, hits US #6 and will hit UK #7 (their only UK Top 10 album).

[17] The Byrds' scheduled show at the 4,000-seat theatre at the Guildhall, Portsmouth, Hants., is called off because of lack of support. The 250 fans who bought tickets are given their money back.

[21] Two-minute long *All I Really Want To Do*, another Dylan song, hits UK #4, and #40 in the US (where Cher's version is the bigger hit).

Sept [16] The group performs *Feel A Whole Lot Better* and *The Bells Of Rhymney* on the season premiere of ABC-TV's "Shindig".

Dec [4] After quickly recording its sophomore album ***Turn! Turn! Turn!***, the group releases the title track as its third single. Adapted by folk singer Pete Seeger from a Bible passage (in **Ecclesiastes**), it tops the US chart and reaches UK #26.

The Byrds film a segment for the "TNT Award Show", alongside Joan Baez, Bo Diddley, Ray Charles, the Lovin' Spoonful, the Ronettes, Ike & Tina Turner, Roger Miller, Petula Clark and Donovan, singing *Mr. Tambourine Man* and *Turn! Turn! Turn!*

1966

Feb [26] Double A-side *Set You Free This Time* (penned by Clark)/*It Won't Be Wrong* (co-written by McGuinn) is a minor US hit, the former reaching #79, and the latter #63.

Mar [1] Clark announces his decision to leave the group, reportedly (although he later partially denies it) due to his fear of flying. He is not replaced, as the group still includes three vocalists. (He will go on to form the Gene Clark Group with the Grass Roots' Joel Larson, the Leaves' Bill Reinhardt and the Modern Folk Quartet's Chip Douglas.)

Turn! Turn! Turn!, with Jim Dickson producing, is released, set to reach US #17 and UK #11.

May [21] *Eight Miles High* runs into some airplay bans by broadcasters who "hear" drug connotations, though the group insists the song is about the experience of being at 40,000' in an aircraft. Written by McGuinn, Crosby and Clark, it has been recorded before the latter's departure, and soars to US #14 and UK #24.

June [22] The Gene Clark Group plays at Hollywood's Whisky A Go-Go club.

[25] The Byrds appear at "The Beach Boys Summer Spectacular", with the Lovin' Spoonful, Percy Sledge and Chad And Jeremy.

July [30] *5D (Fifth Dimension)*, written by McGuinn, makes US #44.

Sept ***Fifth Dimension***, with Allen Stanton producing, makes US #24.

Clark rejoins for a 12-day stint at the Whisky A Go-Go.

Oct [1] ***Fifth Dimension*** reaches UK #27.

[29] *Mr. Spaceman*, extracted from the album and again written by McGuinn, makes US #36.

Nov [28] The group begins recording sessions for its fourth album, with producer Gary Usher and guests Clarence White and Vern Gosdin on guitars and Hugh Masekela on trumpet.

Dec Clark's debut solo single *Echoes* is released in the US.

1967

Feb The band performs at a concert sponsored by CAFF (Community Action For Facts & Freedom) with Peter, Paul & Mary, Buffalo Springfield and the

Doors at the Valley Center, and will also undertake a UK tour which will include an appearance at their fan club gathering at the Roundhouse, London.

Mar [4] *So You Want To Be A Rock'n'Roll Star*, co-written by McGuinn and Hillman and said to have been inspired by the overnight success of the Monkees, with a standout trumpet solo by Masekela, reaches US #29. McGuinn, now a follower of the Subud religious cult, decides he wishes to be known henceforth as Roger McGuinn.

[10] Clark plays the Ash Grove folk club, Hollywood, with Clarence White and the Gosdin Brothers.

[31] The Byrds open a weekend stay at the Fillmore West with Moby Grape.

Apr [25] "Inside Pop - The Rock Revolution", an analysis by Leonard Bernstein featuring McGuinn with other luminaries, airs on CBS-TV.

May [6] *My Back Pages* marks a return to the Dylan songbook, and takes the group to US #30, while its parent album, the Usher-produced ***Younger Than Yesterday***, climbs to US #24 and UK #37.

June [17] The Byrds take part in the "Monterey International Pop Festival" at the County Fairgrounds, Monterey, CA. (Crosby joining Buffalo Springfield on stage the day before has caused much consternation to McGuinn.)

July [1] From ***Younger Than Yesterday***, *Have You Seen Her Face* (written by Hillman) reaches US #74. B-side *Don't Make Waves* is the theme to a movie starring Tony Curtis as a swimming pool salesman (and will appear as the B-side to their next single release in the UK).

Aug [19] *Lady Friend*, written by Crosby, peaks at US #82.

Oct Crosby leaves, unhappy that the group has chosen to record Goffin and King's *Goin' Back* in preference to his *Triad*. (*Triad* will appear on Jefferson Airplane's ***Crown Of Creation*** in 1968.) He agrees to be bought out, spending his proceeds on a yacht. After numerous meetings with McGuinn, Clark is briefly re-recruited to replace Crosby, while an early retrospective, ***Greatest Hits***, hits US #6.

[22] The group appears on CBS-TV's "The Smothers Brothers Comedy Hour".

Nov After just three days of recording, Clark leaves again. (He will initially release ***Gene Clark With The Gosdin Brothers*** for CBS, prior to linking with Doug Dillard for ***The Fantastic Expedition Of Dillard And Clark*** (1969) and ***Through The Morning - Through The Night*** (1970), before resuming a solo career in 1971 with ***Gene Clark*** and 1973's ***Roadmaster*** (all released by A&M).)

Dec [2] *Goin' Back*, a 1966 UK #10 for Dusty Springfield, makes US #89. Clarke now decides to quit, relocating to Hawaii. Much of his work on the forthcoming album has already been done by session drummer Jim Gordon, leaving McGuinn and Hillman to complete the project.

[7] The Byrds opens a series of dates at the Fillmore West, San Francisco, with Electric Flag in support.

1968

Jan McGuinn and Hillman re-sign with CBS, and hire Hillman's cousin, ex-Rising Sons Kevin Kelley (b. 1945, CA), as the trio embarks on a tour of the US college circuit.

Feb Singer/guitarist Gram Parsons (b. Cecil Connor, Nov. 5, 1946, Winter Haven, FL), ex-the Shilohs and International Submarine Band, is recruited to play keyboards.

[15] The Byrds perform on the Grand Ole Opry, at the Ryman Auditorium, Nashville, TN.

Apr ***The Notorious Byrd Brothers*** nests at US #47 and UK #12. The sleeve shows McGuinn, Hillman and Clarke looking out of the windows of a stable, while a fourth window, which contains a horse, is rumored to represent the way McGuinn regards Crosby. During this period, the quartet (of McGuinn, Hillman, Kelley and Parsons) is joined by occasional members, pedal steel guitarist Sneaky Pete Kleinow and banjo player Doug Dillard, the next album also featuring contributions from John Hartford (banjo, guitar) and ex-Kentucky Colonels Clarence White (guitar).

June [8] *You Ain't Going Nowhere*, from the forthcoming album, goes to US #74 and UK #45 - the group's first UK hit in over two years.

July [29] On the eve of the South African leg of the group's world tour, Parsons, refusing to play to segregated audiences, checks out of his London hotel and quits the band, to be replaced for the tour by ex-Byrds roadie, Carlos Bernal.

Aug [4-5] The group appears at the "Newport Pop Festival" in Costa Mesa, CA, alongside the Grateful Dead, Steppenwolf, Sonny & Cher, Canned Heat, Jefferson Airplane and many more.

Sept ***Sweetheart Of The Rodeo*** appears, having been delayed because Parsons (who has influenced the group towards country-rock music and sung lead on many original tracks) is threatened with legal action if his voice can be heard on the album. (He still owes an International Submarine Band album.) His vocal having been erased and substituted either by Hillman or McGuinn, the album reaches US #77, but fails to chart in the UK (though it will subsequently be regarded as one of the most influential albums of the '60s, laying the foundations for the early '70s country-rock genre).

Oct Returning from a tour, McGuinn finds himself the only remaining Byrd, as Hillman quits, soon to team up with Gram Parsons to form the Flying Burrito Brothers, as will Kleinow. Kelley joins Tim Buckley's band, while the other occasional group members also depart. McGuinn recruits Clarence White (b. June 6, 1944, Lewiston, ME), who has been in Nashville West and the second incarnation of the Gene Clark Group, on guitar. He recommends Nashville West veterans, Gene Parsons (b. Apr. 9, 1944) (who has also played with White in Cajun Gib & Gene) on drums, and John York (b. Aug. 3, 1946, White Plains, NY), a member of Clark's group, completing a sixth incarnation of the Byrds.

1969

Feb Clarke joins Hillman and Gram Parsons in the Flying Burrito Brothers.

[6-9] The Byrds play at the Fillmore West, San Francisco, with Mike Bloomfield, Pacific Gas & Electric, Nick Gravenites and Mark Naftalin.

Mar New line-up's debut *Bad Night At The Whiskey* fails to chart. (Its B-side *Drug Store Truck Driving Man*, co-written by McGuinn and Parsons prior to the latter's departure, will become better known.)

May [24] The Bob Johnston-produced ***Dr. Byrds & Mr. Hyde*** reaches UK #15, having already peaked at US #153 in April.

June A version of Dylan's *Lay Lady Lay*, coupled with *Old Blue*, from ***Dr. Byrds***, fails to chart.

[12-15] The Byrds headline a bill comprising Pacific Gas & Electric and Joe Cocker & the Grease Band at the Fillmore West, San Francisco.

[21] The group appears at the "Newport '69" festival held at San Fernando Valley State College, Devonshire Downs, CA.

Aug [31] The Byrds perform at the "New Orleans Pop Festival" at the Louisiana International Speedway, Gonzales, LA.

Sept Double A-side *I Wasn't Born To Follow* (performed on the soundtrack of the movie "Easy Rider"), and *Child Of The Universe* (from ***Dr. Byrds*** and also the "Candy" movie soundtrack) is released. York leaves to join the Sir Douglas Quintet.

Oct Skip Battin (b. Feb. 2, 1934, Gallipolis, OH), formerly half of Skip & Flip with Gary "Flip" Paxton, takes York's place.

Dec [6] *The Ballad Of Easy Rider* brakes at US #65.

1970

Jan Melcher-produced ***The Ballad Of Easy Rider*** reaches US #36. A version of the title track credited solely to McGuinn has previously appeared on the ***Easy Rider*** soundtrack album, alongside *I Wasn't Born To Follow* and the McGuinn solo *It's Alright Ma (I'm Only Bleeding)*.

[2-4] The Byrds return to the Fillmore West on a bill with Fleetwood Mac.

[7] *Jesus Is Just Alright*, from ***The Ballad Of Easy Rider***, spends a week at US #97.

[14] ***The Ballad Of Easy Rider*** makes UK #41.

June [27] The group performs at the "Bath Festival of Blues & Progressive Music", Shepton Mallet, Somerset. (The entrance fee for the weekend is £2 10s.)

Nov With an unusually stable line-up, the double album set ***Untitled*** is released, set to reach US #40 and UK #11.

1971

Feb *Chestnut Mare*, written with New York psychologist Jacques Levy for "Gene Tryp", a C&W musical version of Henrik Ibsen's "Peer Gynt" from the album, makes UK #19 but fails in the US (where the Byrds' singles chart flight is now permanently grounded).

May *I Trust (Everything Is Gonna Work Out Right)*, from the forthcoming ***Byrdmaniax***, is released, as the group undertakes a UK tour.

Aug ***Byrdmaniax*** reaches US #46.

Oct Further extract *Glory Glory* is released.

1972

Jan ***Farther Along*** peaks at US #152, featuring the current single *America's Great National Pastime* (co-written by Battin and Kim Fowley).

July Final Byrds recording sessions take place at Columbia, three of the cuts eventually appearing on McGuinn's first solo album.

Aug Gene Parsons quits for a solo career (and will eventually join the Flying Burrito Brothers in 1974), initially signing to Reprise.

Sept Battin is fired (eventually joining New Riders Of The Purple Sage), and is replaced by ex-session drummer John Guerin, before a major re-shuffle brings in temporary drummers Daryl Dragon (b. Aug. 27, 1942, Los Angeles) (ex-Beach Boys) and Jim Moon.

Dec Compilation album ***Best Of The Byrds - Greatest Hits Vol. 2*** peaks at US #114. Having recorded ***White Light*** in 1971, Clark releases a second solo album, ***Roadmaster***, on A&M, which features all five original Byrds on two tracks.

1973

Jan With the original group of McGuinn, Hillman, Crosby, Clark and Clarke re-formed for a new album released on the Asylum label, ***Byrds*** reaches US #20, although the reunion proves shortlived.

Feb [24] The Byrds make their final live appearance, at the Capitol Theatre in Passaic, NJ, after which McGuinn dissolves the band. McGuinn and White are the only remaining members. Hillman returns for the date, with his Manassas colleague Joe Lala filling in on drums.

Apr [14] ***Byrds*** makes UK #31.

May [19] Retrospective double album ***History Of The Byrds*** makes UK #47, as McGuinn makes his post-Byrds solo debut at New York's Academy of Music.

July [14] White is killed by a drunk driver while loading equipment after a gig in Palmdale, CA.

McGuinn's debut solo album for CBS ***Roger McGuinn*** makes US #137.

Sept [8] Reissued by CBS, ***Preflyte***, the album of demos, which reached US #84 when released by Together Records in 1969, makes US #183.

[19] Gram Parsons dies of heart failure in mysterious circumstances, in Joshua Tree, CA.

1974

Ex-Byrds members remain active: in the short-term, Clark's solo career resumes with the Asylum album ***No Other*** (US #144) (he will also record ***Firebyrd*** for Takoma Records and ***Two Sides To Every Story*** for RSO in the '80s), while McGuinn's sophomore effort ***Peace On You*** makes US #92. Crosby has returned to varying combinations of the Crosby, Stills, Nash & Young family, while Hillman, already a veteran of Manassas (formed by Stephen Stills in 1971), has formed the Souther Hillman Furay band with J.D. Souther and Richie Furay in September 1973, which releases ***Souther Hillman Furay*** during this year, followed by ***Trouble In Paradise*** in 1975.

1975

Nov McGuinn joins Bob Dylan's "Rolling Thunder Revue" touring troupe, having released his third solo set ***Roger McGuinn Band*** (US #165).

1976

Hillman's solo album ***Slippin' Away*** makes US #153, while McGuinn releases ***Cardiff Rose***, produced by Mick Ronson and featuring a pick-up band of Ronson (guitars), Rob Stoner (bass) and Howie Wyeth (drums), all of whom also played on the recent Dylan sojourn. (Clarke re-emerges to form Firefall, which will release a number of albums on Atlantic Records).

1977

May With McGuinn having recently issued ***Thunderbyrd*** (including a version of Tom Petty's *American Girl*), and Hillman having made US #188 with ***Clear Sailin'***, the pair re-teams with Clark for a package tour of Europe, on which each performs as a soloist.

1979

Feb Reunited as a formal trio, McGuinn Clark & Hillman play at the Venue, London, during a brief visit to promote ***McGuinn Clark & Hillman***, which makes US #39, with the extracted *Don't You Write Her Off* climbing to US #33. During a subsequent US tour, they will be joined on stage at a concert in San Francisco by Crosby. This Byrds' off-shoot will also release the US #136 ***City*** in 1980, when McGuinn and Hillman will pair-off to record ***McGuinn/Hillman***.

1984

Hillman now forms the successful country act the Desert Rose Band, with Herb Pedersen, J.D. Maness, John Jorgensen, Bill Bryson and Steve Duncan, which will continue to be popular to the end of the decade.

1986

Nov [21] ***The Byrds' Greatest Hits*** is certified platinum by the RIAA.

1987

Clark cuts ***So Rebellious A Lover***, the first of two folk albums with Carla Olson. He also joins Clarke, who, having left Firefall, is sued by Crosby, McGuinn and Hillman for illegally using the Byrds name for his current touring outfit.

1988

McGuinn and Hillman link with Crosby to make an impromptu performance at the Ash Grove, Los Angeles. (In between the McGuinn, Clark and Hillman projects, McGuinn has made occasional tours with his wife, and manager, Camilla, and has guested on other artists' records, notably strumming his 12-string electric guitar on the Beach Boys' 1986 US #57 version of the Mamas & The Papas' standard *California Dreamin'*, and is also set to guest on Elvis Costello's forthcoming 1989 album ***Spike***.)

1989

Jan Crosby, McGuinn and Hillman play three California club dates as the Byrds, to establish their legal right to the band's moniker and to keep Gene Clark and Michael Clarke from touring with that name. McGuinn and Hillman contribute *You Ain't Going Nowhere* to the Nitty Gritty Dirt Band's Grammy-winning album ***Will The Circle Be Unbroken Volume Two***.

Feb [20] Arista Records president Clive Davis announces the signing of Roger McGuinn, at a pre-Grammy dinner at the Beverly Hills Hotel. McGuinn plays a short set for the assembled multitude.

Apr [7] McGuinn joins Crowded House on *Mr. Tambourine Man*, *Eight Miles High* and *So You Want To Be A Rock'n'Roll Star* in concert in Los Angeles. The tracks will be released under the name *Byrdhouse* on a CD EP.

1990

Feb [24] McGuinn, Crosby and Hillman sing *He Was A Friend Of Mine*, *Turn! Turn! Turn!* and *Mr. Tambourine Man*, the latter with Dylan, at the "Roy Orbison All-Star Tribute", Universal Amphitheatre, Universal City, CA.

Aug [6-8] McGuinn, Crosby and Hillman record four songs, including McGuinn's *He Was A Friend Of Mine*, Dylan's *Paths Of Victory* and Julie Gold's *From A Distance*, at Treasure Isle Recorders in Nashville, TN.

Nov [17] The definitive 90-track, four-CD box set ***The Byrds***, including the four recently-recorded cuts, makes US #151.

1991

Jan [16] The Byrds are inducted into the Rock and Roll Hall of Fame at the sixth annual dinner, at the Waldorf Astoria Hotel in New York. During the ceremony, Crosby announces "an airstrike has just started on Baghdad", heralding the on-set of the Gulf War. The traditional post-dinner jam features the group playing with Don Henley and Jackson Browne.

Mar [9] McGuinn's ***Back From Rio***, his first solo album in 13 years, with contributions from Elvis Costello, Michael Penn, Tom Petty and Dave Stewart, makes US #44.

May [24] Gene Clark dies of natural causes at his Sherman Oaks, CA home.

Oct [16] McGuinn sings *Mr. Tambourine Man* with Tom Petty at the "Bob Dylan 30th Anniversary Concert Celebration" at New York's Madison Square Garden, and also joins Eric Clapton, George Harrison and Petty in backing Dylan on *My Back Pages*.

1993

Dec [19] Michael Clarke dies of liver failure in Treasure Island, FL. (He had been scheduled to play a New Year's Eve gig, fronting his own Michael Clarke's Byrds.)

1994

Sept A tribute album to Arthur Alexander including McGuinn's version of *Anna* is released in the US.

see also: **CROSBY, STILLS, NASH & YOUNG**

C

J. J. CALE

1964

Having taken up guitar at school in Tulsa, OK, and been a member of high school and semi-professional bands like Johnny Cale & the Valentines, Cale (b. Jean Jacques Cale, Dec. 5, 1938, Oklahoma, OK), who has quit the US air force in the late '50s, travels to Los Angeles, CA, with friend Leon Russell, to make a career in the music business, initially working as a recording engineer with, among others, producer Snuff Garrett. He also performs at the Whisky A-Go-Go (the venue's manager renames him J.J. Cale), where he shares the stage - on Johnny Rivers' night off - with Billy Lee Riley. Temporarily moving to Nashville, TN, to become a country singer and songwriter, Cale makes little progress, despite touring for a while with the Grand Ole Opry road company and playing behind the likes of Red Sovine and Little Jimmy Dickens, and subsequently returns to Los Angeles. He re-teams with Russell and other Oklahoma friends Carl Radle and Chuck Blackwell. While singing in bars and developing his songwriting skills, he gains further studio experience as an arranger, producer and guitarist, working not least with Delaney & Bonnie.

1967

Having released an original version of *After Midnight* in 1965, Cale records a psychedelic rock album with Russell and others, ***A Trip Down Sunset Strip***, released under the name the Leathercoated Minds. He is also signed to Liberty Records and records a number of singles under the production guidance of Garrett, before returning to Oklahoma to build and record in his own home studio in 1968.

1969

Cale is signed to the fledgling Shelter Records, established by Leon Russell and producer Denny Cordell (who has been introduced to Cale's home demo tapes by Radle).

1970

Sept [29] Recording begins at Nashville's Moss Rose Studio for his first solo album, sessions which will end on June 9th the following year at the Bradley Barn Studio in Mount Juliet, TN.

Dec [12] Eric Clapton's cover version of *After Midnight* reaches US #18.

1972

Jan Cale's debut album for Shelter ***Naturally*** makes US #51. Produced by his friend and manager Audie Ashworth, the 12-song self-penned album introduces Cale's unique unlabored, husky vocal and rootsy guitar style, which will effortlessly impress critics and distinguish all subsequent recordings.

Apr Extracted *Crazy Mama* makes US #22. Cale builds a 16-track recording studio in Nashville, named Crazy Mama's.

June Cale's new version of *After Midnight* reaches US #42.

Nov *Lies*, recorded at the Muscle Shoals Studio, AL, climbs to US #42.

1973

Jan ***Really*** makes US #92, while the similarly laid-back, sparse, bluesy ***Okie*** will peak at US #128 the following June.

1976

Oct ***Troubadour***, still produced by Ashworth and including the subsequent drug-culture standard *Cocaine* (which Clapton will take to US #30 in 1980 as the B-side to *Tulsa Time*), makes UK #53 and peaks at US #84.

Dec The extracted *Hey Baby* charts briefly at US #96.

1979

Sept His fifth album ***5***, featuring stalwart Radle and keyboardist David Briggs, makes US #136 and UK #40. In common with all releases, publicity-shy Cale refrains from any concerted touring or media promotion for the album.

1981

Mar Rarely departing from his economic trademark style, which mixes blues, country, jazz and rock'n'roll, Cale will release three albums during the next three years, retaining his traditional backing musicians and co-producer Ashworth: ***Shades***, featuring Leon Russell, reaches US #110 and UK #44, while ***Grasshopper*** peaks at US #149 and UK #36 in April 1982, and ***8*** makes UK #47 in September the following year.

1984

Mar Cale writes the score for the film "La Femme De Mon Pote" ("My Best Friend's Girl"), starring Isabelle Huppert, released as ***La Femme De Mon Pote*** in June.

July Mercury Records, now licensees of Cale's catalog, brings his career highlights to CD for the first time with the issue of the 14-track ***Special Edition***.

1986

Aug Cale, with Peer Rabin and the Munich Factory, writes the music for the German film "50/50".

1988

July UK retrospective specialist label Knight Records releases a second Cale compilation, ***Nightriding: J.J. Cale***.

1990

Apr [21] After a lengthy recording hiatus and scatttered live outings, mainly in the US, during which he is based in a mobile home commuting between Los Angeles and his Nashville studio, Cale's mostly self-written and self-produced ***Travel-Log*** on the Silvertone label, makes US #131, supported by a US tour.

1992

Sept [26] Having recently produced John Hammond's ***Got Love If You Want It***, Cale's ***Number 10***, bringing his total original studio album releases to a half-score, debuts at its UK #58 peak, his second recording for Silvertone (licensed in the US to BMG). With the album recorded at his San Diego, CA retreat, the reclusive Cale comments on his immediately identifiable style: "I'm always trying to move in another direction, but my records always end up sounding the same."

1993

Aug [5] Cale, making a rare live appearance, plays the "Edmonton Folk Festival", Edmonton, Canada.

1994

Aug [14] Cale performs at the Center Stage, Atlanta, GA, during a short tour to promote his latest album ***Closer To You***.

Nov [6-8] He plays the Labatt's Apollo, Hammersmith, London, as **Pulse** publishes an interview with him, in which he comments on soundalike Mark Knopfler, "My hope is that someday he covers one of my songs, instead of sounding like them".

1996

Aug Mercury Records' Chronicles imprint releases a two-CD anthology in the US.

JOHN CALE

1963

A musical prodigy who first composed for the BBC at age eight, Cale (b. Dec. 4, 1940, Garnant, Dyfed, Wales), having studied classical piano as a child and later viola and piano at London's Guildhall School of Music, moves to New York, NY's Eastman Conservatory to study avant-garde music on a scholarship from the Leonard Bernstein Foundation. He studies with LaMonte Young, John Cage and Xenakis. (An ensemble project with Young, "The Dream Academy", will influence his work with the Velvet Underground.) Cale meets Lou Reed, an apprentice songwriter, at a New York party. Reed plays Cale demos of songs (including *Heroin*), and invites him to join him in a new band. This becomes the Velvet Underground, for which Cale plays the viola, bass and keyboards.

1968

Mar Having recorded two albums (***The Velvet Underground And Nico*** and ***White Light/White Heat***) with the band, personality clashes between Cale and Reed come to a head, and Cale is fired, to be replaced by Doug Yule.

1970

Signed to CBS/Columbia, he records his first solo album ***Vintage Violence***, a baroque rock'n'roll mixture, and produces the second Stooges album ***Funhouse***. (The CBS/Columbia deal is also as a staff producer, a role he will later repeat when signing to other companies.)

1971

Mar Cale returns to the avant-garde arena with the release of ***Church Of Anthrax***, a collaboration with Terry Riley (sax and keyboards).

1972

Academy In Peril is issued on Reprise Records, during a year when he also supplies the music for the movie "Caged Heat".

1973

Featuring a musical contribution from Little Feat, Cale turns rock'n'roll into chamber music for what critics hail as his best work, ***Paris 1919***.

1974

Feb He signs as a house producer with Island Records, and produces fellow ex-Velvet Underground alumna Nico's ***The End***.

June [1] Cale appears with Brian Eno, Kevin Ayers, Robert Wyatt, Nico and others in a concert organized by Island at London's Rainbow Theatre. A recording of the event, ***June 1st, 1974 (A.C.N.E.)***, is released by Island.

Sept ***Fear*** is released, featuring Roxy Music members Phil Manzanera and Eno.

1975

Apr ***Slow Dazzle*** is issued, including appearances by Eno and a live Manzanera/Chris Spedding backing band.

Nov Similar personnel feature on ***Helen Of Troy***, with Phil Collins also guesting on drums.

1976

Having helmed New York rock poet Patti Smith's debut album, ***Horses***, in 1975, Cale produces the eponymous debut album for the Modern Lovers, led by Jonathan Richman and including Jerry Harrison (later of Talking Heads) on keyboards.

1977

Feb ***Guts*** is released. Unhappy with a particular live performance from his support band, he takes revenge at one gig by decapitating a live chicken on stage, after which the band walks off in protest. The incident becomes the inspiration for the subsequent 12" EP release *Animal Justice*, issued on the Illegal label and featuring *Chickenshit*.

1978

Dec [28] Cale performs at New York's CBGBs. (Part of the concert will be heard on 1991's ***Even Cowgirls Get The Blues*** album, along with another CBGBs concert, recorded on December 31st, 1979.)

1979

Cale forms a new band comprising George Scott, ex-Contortions (bass), Doug Brawne (drums), Joe Bidewell (keyboards), Mark Aaron (guitar) and Deerfrance (vocals), with which he tours Europe and the US.

1980

Sabotage Live, recorded on stage in Paris, is issued on the independent Spy Records label.

1981

Mar Newly signed to A&M Records, Cale releases ***Honi Soit***, his first studio recording in four years, which reaches US #154, his only chart entry.

1982

Aug Back on Island via its licensed imprint, Ze Records, ***Music For A New Society***, a return to near one-man efforts of early albums, is well received. Cale begins to tour, performing both solo (playing guitar and piano) and with a new band.

1983

June A second Ze effort, ***Caribbean Sunset***, is released to little attention, while the live performance ***John Cale Comes Alive*** emerges on the same label in September.

1985

Nov Now signed to Beggars Banquet, ***Artificial Intelligence*** is released, coinciding with Nico's ***Camera Obscura***, produced by Cale.

1987

July Cale surprises the New Music Seminar, New York, by turning up with Spedding and other old colleagues in his best-received live band for years.

1989

Jan [7-8] He teams with Lou Reed for two work-in-progress shows at St. Ann's Church, Brooklyn Heights, New York, as a tribute to the late Andy Warhol.

1990

May [26] A further collaboration with Reed, ***Songs For 'Drella***, inspired by and dedicated to Warhol, and released on Sire Records, makes US #103, having reached UK #22 on the 5th.

June Cale joins members of the Velvet Underground, playing together for the first time since 1969, as they attend the opening of the Cartier Foundation's Andy Warhol retrospective at Jouy en Josas, outside Paris, France, performing *Heroin*. Cale's own ***Words For The Dying*** is released on the Opal label.

1991

Apr [24] Cale appears at the tenth anniversary of "The Arts At St. Ann's" series celebration, at St. Ann's Church, Brooklyn Heights, an event also featuring Aaron Neville and Dr. John, among others.

1992

Nov [22] Cale performs at London's Royal Festival Hall, in addition to making an appearance on BBC2-TV's "The Late Show : Later".

1993

Jan [19] Newly signed to Rykodisc, Cale appears on NBC-TV's "The Tonight Show" to promote his latest album ***Fragments Of A Rainy Season***. He tells program host Jay Leno that the remaining Velvets plan to re-unite. When pressed for a reason, Cale responds: "Money".

1994

Oct [8] Following a duet with Suzanne Vega of Hector Zazou's *The Long Voyage* and the Rhino Records (US) release of the double CD anthology, ***Seducing Down The Door***, drawing on his recorded work for Columbia, Reprise, Island, I.R.S., A&M, Ze, PVC, Opal and Sire, Cale performs *Heartbreak Hotel* at the "Elvis Aaron Presley : The Tribute", a multi-star music event staged at the Pyramid Arena, Memphis, TN, and broadcast live on US pay-per-view TV.

see also: **VELVET UNDERGROUND**

CAMEO

Larry Blackmon (vocals, drums); **Tomi Jenkins** (vocals); **Nathan Leftenant** (vocals)

1977

Sept [10] The band was formed as the New York City Players in 1974 by Larry "Mr. B" Blackmon (b. May 29, 1956, New York, NY), who had already been in a number of R&B groups, including the Mighty Gees, Concrete Wall and East Coast. With their name changed to the more manageable Cameo in 1976, the group's reputation is established via an unremitting 200-gigs-a-year touring schedule. While the original nucleus of Blackmon with vocalists Jenkins and Leftenant will endure, a variable ensemble numbering up to 13 (including Wayne Cooper, Eric Curham, Gary Dow, Gregory Johnson, Anthony Lockett and Leftenant's brother Arnett) will be common during the band's early career. Now signed to Casablanca Records subsidiary Chocolate City, Cameo, are currently touring as the support act on Parliament/Funkadelic Mothership's 1977-78 concert trek, while the Blackmon-produced ***Cardiac Arrest*** gives the band its first chart success, reaching US #116.

1978

Apr [22] ***We All Know Who We Are***, also helmed by Blackmon, who will continue as producer on all projects, spends 23 weeks on the US chart, peaking at #58, while ***Ugly Ego*** makes US #83 on December 16th.

1980

July [17] The still-climbing ***Cameosis*** is certified gold by the RIAA.

Aug [16] Now issuing at least one gold-certified album per year, with each release advancing the unique Cameo funk/soul meld, ***Secret Omen*** has climbed to #46 in September 1979 (and certified gold on December 4th), while ***Cameosis*** reaches US #25, and is their biggest-selling record to date during a six-month chart stay. ***Feel Me*** will rise to US #44 in January 1981, while ***Knights Of The Sound Table*** also stops at US #44 in July of the same year. It is their first UK album release, though their seventh in US (the previous six have all been hot UK import items). ***Alligator Woman*** reaches US #23 in May 1982 and, following a label switch to Blackmon's own Atlanta Artists label, ***Style*** peaks at US #53 in June 1983.

1981

Jan [27] ***Feel Me*** is certified gold by the RIAA while ***Knights Of The Sound Table*** will reach a similar sales plateau on August 6th, with ***Alligator Woman*** achieving gold ratification on July 16th the following year.

Sept [20] Cameo performs at London's Town & Country club, also broadcast live on BBC2-TV's all-night "Rock Around The Clock".

1984

May [5] *She's Strange*, helped by an Amos Poe-directed video clip, gives the group its first R&B/dance/pop crossover hit in the US, making #47, and is the group's UK chart debut, at #37. ***She's Strange*** subsequently reaches US #27.

[30] ***She's Strange*** is confirmed gold by the RIAA.

June Cameo undertakes its first UK concert tour.

1985

July [13] *Attack Me With Your Love*, from the forthcoming ***Single Life***, peaks at UK #65.

Sept Produced, as ever, by Blackmon and showcasing his distinctive funk vocal, ***Single Life*** makes US #58 and peaks at UK #66.

Oct The extracted title track *Single Life* becomes Cameo's first Top 20 entry, reaching UK #15. It also spends longer at the top of the UK Dance chart than any other record during the year. It hits US R&B #2, but fails to cross over.

Nov [11] ***Single Life*** is certified gold by the RIAA.

Dec Cameo returns to the UK for a full headlining tour, which includes three sellout shows at London's Hammersmith Odeon. *She's Strange* is reissued as a UK single, climbing to #22.

1986

Mar Atypical ballad *A Goodbye* peaks at UK #65.

Sept [20] The group performs at London's Town & Country during BBC2's live "Rock Around The Clock" all-night broadcast.

Oct Co-penned by Blackmon and Jenkins, *Word Up* hits UK #3, and will be Cameo's biggest international smash.

[4] *Word Up* tops the US R&B ranking as will its parent album, three weeks later.

Nov ***Word Up!***, the group's 12th and most successful album, hits UK #7 and US #8.

[22] *Word Up* hits US #6.

Dec A UK tour gains a high music media profile, not least due to the prominent red codpiece (designed by fashion guru Jean-Paul Gaultier), which forms part of Blackmon's stage garb. *Candy*, from ***Word Up!***, reaches UK #27.

[9] ***Word Up*** becomes Cameo's first RIAA-certified platinum disc.

1987

Mar [21] Having topped the US R&B chart in January, *Candy* reaches US #21.

[23] Cameo wins the Best Single, Group Or Band and Album Of The Year, Group categories at the inaugural Soul Train Music Awards, held at the Santa Monica Civic Center, Santa Monica, CA.

May *Back And Forth*, also from the album but remixed for single release, reaches UK #11.

[30] *Back And Forth* makes US #50.

Nov Continuing to work in his own Atlanta Artists studio with several protegé acts, Blackmon makes a surprise appearance as guest vocalist on Ry Cooder's ***Get Rhythm*** while *She's Mine*, a final extract from ***Word Up!***, reaches UK #35.

1988

Jan [25] Cameo wins the Favorite Band, Duo Or Group, Soul/R&B category at the 15th annual American Music Awards, held at the Shrine Auditorium, Los Angeles, CA.

Oct [29] *You Make Me Work* peaks at UK #74 and will rise to US #85 on Nov [19].

Dec Its parent album ***Machismo*** climbs to US #56, having beefed out at UK #86 on Nov [26].

[19] ***Machismo*** is certified gold by the RIAA.

1990

July [21] While Blackmon has produced tracks for Eddie Murphy's ***So Happy*** the previous year, Cameo's 14th album ***Real Men Wear Black*** makes US #84.

1992

Feb Blackmon is appointed to an R&B A&R post with Warner Bros. Records in Los Angeles.

Mar [17] Newly signed to Reprise Records, Cameo releases ***Emotional Violence***. While Leftenant has left, core members Blackmon and Jenkins are joined by longtime associate member Charlie Singleton.

May [30] The group performs at the KISS Radio 13th anniversary concert at the Great Woods Center for the Performing Arts, Mansfield, MA, to benefit the Genesis Fund charity.

June [6] They appear at an "Earth Pledge Concert" on the Great Lawn of New York's Central Park.

1995

Mar [8] Following the Mercury (US) release of ***The Best Of Cameo*** in May 1993. and having separated from Warner Bros/Reprise in both his A&R role and for Cameo product, Blackmon, still under the guise of his formative funk unit, has issued ***In The Face Of Funk*** on his own Way 2 Funky label in 1994 and has assembled the latest lineup of Cameo to perform as part of a 31-city touring "Funkfest '95" caravan, opening tonight in Westbury, NY.

GLEN CAMPBELL

1960

One of 12 children in a musical family, Campbell (b. Apr. 22, 1936, Delight, AR), who was given his first guitar, bought by his father for $5.00 from a Sears-Roebuck catalog, at the age of four, having left school in 1953 to join a band in Wyoming, but ending up having to sell his guitar and hitchhike home, joined his uncle's the Dick Bills Band, a western swing combo, in Albuquerque, NM, in 1954, gaining live touring experience, before forming his own group, Glen Campbell & the Western Wranglers, in 1958, which made regular appearances on the daily Albuquerque radio show "K Circle B" and weekly TV shows "Hoffman Hayride" and "Country Store", until 1959. Following 18 months of road gigs, and having married Billie Campbell in Carlsbad, NM, he now decides, at the urging of Albuquerque DJ Jerry Naylor, to settle in Los Angeles, CA, where he seeks session work as a guitarist. He also becomes a studio and stage member of the Champs for seven months, when the group's leader, Dave Burgess, drops out, playing at local venues including the Crossbow Club.

1961

Dec [15] Campbell guests on Dick Clark's "American Bandstand" TV show, singing his debut single *Turn Around, Look At Me*.

[25] *Turn Around, Look At Me*, for the small Los Angeles label Crest, written by Eddie Cochran's former partner Jerry Capehart, peaks at US #62.

1962

Sept [1] Newly signed to Capitol Records, Campbell makes US #76 with *Too Late To Worry - Too Blue To Cry*. He records his freshman album ***Big Bluegrass Special***, which the company will take six months to issue, losing any commercial momentum gained by the success of the single.

1963

Oct The Folkswingers, an instrumental quartet of session players with Campbell on guitar, makes US #132 with ***12 String Guitar!*** During the year, Campbell plays on 586 record sessions (later reckoning that only three hit singles emerge from them).

1965

Jan Still an in-demand session musician and also a regular player on ABC-TV's "Shindig" music show, he temporarily joins the stage line-up of the Beach Boys, replacing Brian Wilson, but leaves when Bruce Johnston joins the group on a permanent basis. (It is Campbell's lead guitar which has been heard on most of the Beach Boys' hits to date.)

Oct [30] A cover of Donovan's *The Universal Soldier* outsells the original and returns Campbell to the US chart after a three-year absence, peaking at #45.

1966

Dec Having demanded that Capitol gives him a chance to record and release on his own terms, Campbell has a US Country chart hit (#18) with a revival of Jack Scott's *Burning Bridges*.

1967

Aug [5] A cover of John Hartford's *Gentle On My Mind* makes US #62.

Dec [16] *By The Time I Get To Phoenix*, an evocative ballad - about the end of a relationship, written by 21-year-old Jimmy Webb, gives Campbell his first US Top 30 hit, reaching #26. ***Gentle On My Mind***, produced by Al De Lory is also his US album chart debut, and will eventually hit #5 on the back of later successes. (It is voted Album Of The Year by the Academy of Country Music.) Following its release, Campbell embarks on a US tour supporting the Righteous Brothers.

1968

Jan [21] Campbell guests on CBS-TV's "The Smothers Brothers Comedy Hour".

Feb [24] *Hey Little One* peaks at US #54.

[29] Campbell wins the Best Vocal Performance, Male and Best Contemporary Male Solo Vocal Performance for *By The Time I Get To Phoenix*, and Best C&W Recording and Best C&W Solo Vocal Performance, Male for *Gentle On My Mind* categories at the tenth annual Grammy awards. (*Gentle On My Mind*'s writer, John Hartford, also wins Grammys for Best Folk Performance for his version of the song and Best C&W Song.)

May [25] *I Wanna Live* makes US #36.

June [15] ***Hey Little One*** makes US #26, his third album to achieve a gold disc for half a million sales.

[23] Campbell hosts "The Summer Brothers Smothers Show", the summer replacement for "The Smothers Brothers Comedy Hour", which will air until September 8th.

Aug [10] *Dreams Of The Everyday Housewife* makes US #32.

Sept [7] ***By The Time I Get To Phoenix***, some eight months after its chart debut, now reaches US #15.

Oct [12] ***A New Place In The Sun*** reaches US #24.

Nov [2] Reissued *Gentle On My Mind* makes US #39.

[23] His first duet with Capitol labelmate Bobbie Gentry, *Mornin' Glory*, peaks at US #74, as its parent album ***Bobbie Gentry And Glen Campbell*** reaches US #11.

[21] ***Wichita Lineman*** tops the US chart for the first of five weeks and achieves gold status.

1969

Jan [10] *Hey Little One* is certified gold by the RIAA.

[11] Extracted *Wichita Lineman*, a further collaboration with writer Webb, hits US #3.

[22] *Wichita Lineman* is confirmed gold by the RIAA.

[29] "The Glen Campbell Goodtime Hour" program debuts on CBS, and will run for three seasons until June 13th, 1972.

Mar [8] Another duet with Gentry, reviving the Everly Brothers' *Let It Be Me*, makes US #36.

[12] ***By The Time I Get To Phoenix*** wins Album Of The Year, and *Wichita Lineman* wins Best Engineered Recording at the 11th annual Grammy Awards.

[15] *Wichita Lineman* is his UK chart debut, hitting #7.

Apr [12] *Galveston*, an anti-war song penned by Webb some six years earlier, hits US #4.

May [3] ***Galveston***, continuing a long association with arranger/producer Al De Lory, hits US #2, behind the Original Cast recording of ***Hair***.

[31] *Where's The Playground, Susie*, also written by Webb, reaches US #26, as *Galveston* reaches UK #14.

June He files a lawsuit against Starday Records for releasing demos which he had recorded in the early part of his career.

Aug Campbell breaks new career ground when he stars alongside John Wayne in the movie "True Grit".

[23] *True Grit*, the movie's title song, sung by Campbell, sticks at US #35.

Sept [19] ***Glen Campbell Live*** is certified gold by the RIAA.

Oct [14] *Galveston* is certified gold by the RIAA.

Nov [29] *Try A Little Kindness* reaches US #23, as ***Glen Campbell - Live*** makes US #13. (During the year Campbell is named Most Promising New Male Star by **Photoplay** magazine, Top Male Star Of The Future by **Box Office** magazine, Top Male Star by the Cowboy Hall of Fame, Top Male Vocalist by both **Billboard** and **Cashbox**, Jukebox Artist Of The Year by the Music Operators of America, TV Performer Of The Year by the nation's television editors, Top Male Vocalist, Top TV Personality and Album Of The Year winner by the Academy of Country And Western Music and named Honorary Chairman of the National Arthritis Foundation.)

1970

Jan [24] His revival of the Everly Brothers' *All I Have To Do Is Dream*, once again in duet with Gentry, hits UK #3.

[31] Campbell makes his UK album debut with ***Glen Campbell - Live***, which peaks at #16.

Feb [14] *Try A Little Kindness* makes UK #45.

[19] *Try A Little Kindness* is certified gold by the RIAA.

[28] *Honey Come Back*, penned by Webb, reaches US #19.

Apr [4] *All I Have To Do Is Dream* reaches US #27. ***Try A Little Kindness*** climbs to US #12, as Campbell makes his Las Vegas, NV, cabaret debut at the International Hotel.

May [5] Campbell co-stars with the 5th Dimension in a US TV special.

[9] His update of Edwin Hawkins' gospel song *Oh Happy Day* makes US #40, previewing a fully inspirational album, ***Oh Happy Day***, which reaches US #38.

June [6] *Honey Come Back* hits UK #4, as ***Try A Little Kindness*** makes UK #37.

July Soundtrack album from the movie "Norwood" (Campbell's second film role, playing Norwood Pratt) climbs to US #90.

Aug [15] Mac Davis-written *Everything A Man Could Ever Need* peaks at US #52.

Oct [31] His remake of Conway Twitty's *It's Only Make Believe* hits US #10, as *Everything A Man Could Ever Need* makes UK #32.

Nov ***The Glen Campbell Goodtime Album***, based on his TV show, reaches US #27.

[18] Campbell appears at a Royal Command Performance in London.

Dec *It's Only Make Believe* hits UK #4, as ***The Glen Campbell Album*** reaches UK #16. (By year's end, Campbell will be appointed to the National Reading Council by President Nixon, made Honorary Chairman for the Christmas Seal Drive in Arkansas, appointed a Kentucky Colonel by Governor Louie B. Nunn and made Honorary Mayor of Studio City, CA.)

1971

Apr [17] His revival of Roy Orbison's *Dream Baby* makes US #31 and will be his last UK chart single for four years, at UK #39.

May ***Glen Campbell's Greatest Hits*** makes US #39.

July [24] *The Last Time I Saw Her*, written by Gordon Lightfoot, peaks at US #61, followed by ***The Last Time I Saw Her***, which stalls at US #87.

Nov [6] Capitol teams Campbell with labelmate Anne Murray on an Al De Lory arrangement blending covers of *I Say A Little Prayer* and *By The Time I Get To Phoenix* (sung by Murray and Campbell respectively), which climbs to US #81. The companion album ***Anne Murray/Glen Campbell***, released to coincide with a US tour by the duo, peaks at US #128.

Dec [18] ***Glen Campbell's Greatest Hits*** hits UK #8 - his first UK Top 10 album (and longest chart stayer, at 113 weeks). (During the year, Campbell is named to the State Committee, National Library Week for Arkansas, becomes a contributing editor to "Merit Who's Who Among American High School Students" and will perform at the "Salute To Agriculture" show at the White House for President Nixon and headline the Royal Command Performance before H.R.H. Queen Elizabeth II.)

1972

May [15] ***Glen Campbell's Greatest Hits*** is certified gold by the RIAA.

Sept [30] *I Will Never Pass This Way Again* peaks at US #61.

Dec ***Glen Travis Campbell*** makes US #148, while the extracted *One Last Time* climbs to US #78 on Jan [20]. ***I Knew Jesus (Before He Was A Star)*** will make US #154 in June 1973, having spawned *I Knew Jesus (Before He Was A Star)*, a US #45 hit in May. 1974 will see *Houston (I'm Comin' To See You)* peaking at US #68 on Mar [2] with ***Reunion*** (re-teaming Campbell with Webb, who offers eight new compositions) making US #166 in November. (By year's end, Campbell will be named #1 Vocalist and #1 TV Musical Show in the annual Motion Picture Daily-Television Today poll voted on by the nation's television editors, be given his own Hollywood Walk of Fame Star in front of Grauman's, named Entertainment's Man Of The Year In Golf by the All-American Collegiate Golf Foundation, had his guitar placed on permanent display in the Country Music Hall of Fame in Nashville, hosted the Country Music Awards, made honorary chairman of the Los Angeles City Schools Annual Festival Of Music and sing *By The Time I Get To Phoenix* at the personal request H.R.H. Elizabeth, the Queen Mother at the Royal Film Performance.)

1973

During the year Campbell makes his debut at New York, NY's Carnegie Hall, narrates NBC-TV's "The Incredible Flight Of The Snow Goose", tours the UK once again and is made Honorary Chairman of the National Migraine Foundation.

1974

He is named Entertainer Of The Year by the Great Britain Country Music Association, stars in NBC-TV's "Homecoming", named Chancellor's Lecturer in the Division of Music and Theatre and seen the initiation of the Glen Campbell Scholarship Program for the University of California, crowned King at New Orleans' Mardi Gras and toured the UK, Japan and Australia.

1975

Sept [5] Still-climbing *Rhinestone Cowboy* is certified gold by the RIAA.
[6] After a 14-year chart career, *Rhinestone Cowboy*, his cover of the Larry Weiss original, gives Campbell his first US #1. (A subsequent Sylvester Stallone/Dolly Parton starring film, "Rhinestone", will be based on the song.)
Oct [18] ***Rhinestone Cowboy***, produced by Dennis Lambert and Brian Potter, reaches US #17 and earns a gold disc.
Nov [8] *Rhinestone Cowboy* returns him to the UK chart, hitting #4, as ***Rhinestone Cowboy*** makes UK #38.
Dec [31] ***Rhinestone Cowboy*** is certified gold by the RIAA. (*Rhinestone Cowboy* will also be named Song and Single Of The Year at the Academy of Country Music Awards, which Campbell hosts. During the year he also deputizes for Johnny Carson on NBC-TV's "The Tonight Show" twice, co-hosts the "Mike Douglas" show, films six "Glen Campbell Music Shows" for BBC-TV, tours the UK again and plays his first dates in New Zealand - nine SRO dates grossing $350,000.)

1976

Jan [17] *Country Boy (You Got Your Feet In LA)*, written by Lambert and Potter, reaches US #11.
[31] Campbell wins the Favorite Single, Pop/Rock and Favorite Single, Country categories at the third annual American Music Awards, held at the Santa Monica Civic Auditorium, Santa Monica, CA.
May [8] A medley covering Hamilton, Joe Frank & Reynolds' *Don't Pull Your Love* and the Casinos' *Then You Can Tell Me Goodbye* reaches US #27.
[15] ***Bloodline***, once again helmed by Lambert and Potter, makes US #63.
July [4] Campbell appears in "Salute By Satellite" TV special in the role of Bicentennial Ambassador of Goodwill. (He will also star in the NBC-TV special, "Hi, I'm Glen Campbell", the CBS-TV special, "Glen Campbell Down Home, Down Under" and sing *True Grit* in ABC-TV's "All Star Tribute To John Wayne".
Nov [27] TV-advertised compilation ***20 Golden Greats*** tops the UK chart for the first of six weeks.
Dec [10] ***That Christmas Feeling*** is certified gold by the RIAA.
[11] US equivalent ***The Best Of Glen Campbell*** makes US #116. (In another year filled with honors, Campbell is named Honorary Chairman of the Save Your Vision Week by the Arkansas Optometric Association and Entertainer Of The Year by the Greater Reno Chamber of Commerce.

1977

Jan [31] He wins the Favorite Album, Country category at the fourth annual American Music Awards, held at the Santa Monica Civic Auditorium.
Apr [2] Campbell begins a 14-date UK tour at London's Royal Festival Hall (with Jimmy Webb and the Royal Philharmonic Orchestra), set to end on the 17th at the Usher Hall, Edinburgh, Scotland.
[20] Still-climbing *Southern Nights* is certified gold by the RIAA.
[23] Allen Toussaint-penned *Southern Nights* reaches UK #28, as its parent album ***Southern Nights***, co-produced by Campbell with Gary Klein, makes UK #51. (These are his final UK hits, although he will remain a popular live performer in the UK.)
[30] *Southern Nights* hits US #1.
May [21] ***Southern Nights*** reaches US #22.
Aug [20] His cover of Neil Diamond's *Sunflower* makes US #39.
Oct [5] ***Southern Nights*** is also ratified gold by the RIAA.

1978

Jan [21] ***Live At The Royal Festival Hall***, with the Royal Philharmonic Orchestra, peaks at US #171.
Dec [9] *Can You Fool* makes US #38.
[23] With all song selections delivered by Micheal Smotherman, ***Basic***, co-produced by the artist with Tom Thacker, peaks at US #164.

1980

June [28] A duet with Rita Coolidge on *Somethin' 'Bout You Baby I Like* makes US #42.

1981

Feb [14] *I Don't Want To Know Your Name* peaks at US #65.
Mar ***It's The World Gone Crazy*** makes US #178, following which Campbell leaves Capitol after 20 years.
Aug [29] Newly signed to Mirage and marking a return to country music which will endure well into the '90s, *I Love My Truck* brakes at US #94, his final Hot 100 showing of the decade.

1982

His weekly 30-minute "The Glen Campbell Music Show" airs on US syndicated TV, while Campbell signs to Atlantic America, an Atlantic Records country imprint, releasing ***Old Home Town***, the first in an ongoing series of genre specific albums which will include ***Letter To Home*** (1984) and ***It's Just A Matter Of Time*** (1985).

1988

Sept Having cut the inspirational ***No More Night*** for the Word label in 1987, Campbell continues down the country road with a two-album deal with MCA Records: ***Still Within The Sound Of My Voice*** now completes one year on the US Country chart, and is followed by the November release of ***Light Years***.

1989

Aug [5] ***The Complete Glen Campbell***, a UK-only compilation on the TV-advertising Stylus label, makes UK #47, while the recording veteran returns to the Capitol Records stable, signed to its Nashville division under the direction of label head and sometime Campbell producer Jimmy Bowen.

1990

Walkin' In The Sun, released on Capitol's Nashville label, continues Campbell's success on the US Country chart. By year's end, *By The Time I Get To Phoenix* is honored as one of the BMI's "Most Performed Songs Between 1940-1990", having logged over four million performances.

1991

Jan Campbell embarks on "The Goodtime Glen Campbell Music Show" US tour, with John Hartford and Nicolette Larson, coinciding with the release of ***Unconditional Love***, co-produced by Bowen and Jerry Crutchfield.
Dec [2[***Glen Campbell's Greatest Hits*** is certified platinum by the RIAA before
Galveston and ***Gentle On My Mind*** reach the same sales plateau on the 26th.

1992

Jan [8] ***By The Time I Get To Phoenix*** is certified platinum by the RIAA.
Feb [12] The RIAA certifies multi-platinum sales for ***Wichita Lineman*** (two million).
Apr [9] He co-hosts the 23rd gospel Dove Awards, in Nashville, TN, with Marilyn McCoo.
Sept [28] In common with many country veterans, Campbell begins a month-long stint in the genre's newest live mecca, Branson, MO, having recently undertaken a 25th anniversary tour of the UK and Eire.
Dec [30] Campbell starts a four-day appearance at Harrah's Casino Hotel, Reno, NV.

1993

Jan [19] Crutchfield-produced ***Somebody Like That*** is released on the resurrected EMI Records imprint, Liberty.
Sept [27] Campbell makes a guest appearance at Jimmy Webb's Avery Fisher Hall concert in New York.
Oct [1] CBS-TV's "A Day In The Life Of Country Music", featuring one day (May 7th) in the life of several country artists including Campbell, airs.

1994

Mar [23] Campbell takes part in "Rhythm Country And Blues - The Concert", to benefit the Country Music Foundation and the Rhythm And Blues Foundation, at the Universal Amphitheatre, Universal City, CA.
Apr Campbell's autobiography **Rhinestone Cowboy** is published by Villard Books.
June The 2,200-seat Glen Campbell Goodtime Theatre opens in Branson, MO.

CAN

Damo Suzuki (vocals); **Irmin Schmidt** (keyboards, vocals); **Holger Czukay** (bass, vocals); **Michael Karoli** (guitar, violin); **Jaki Liebezeit** (drums)

1969

Aug Already a classical musical veteran who has conducted the Vienna Symphony Orchestra among others, Schmidt (b. May 29, 1937, Berlin, Germany) has also studied ethnic music under the avant-garde, modern classical composer Karlheinz Stockhausen in the early '60s, before a 1966 visit to New York, NY prompted him to form an experimental rock band which fuses classical, art-rock and electronic elements. Back in Cologne, West Germany, Schmidt has teamed with avant-garde electronic composer, multi-instrumentalist musician and Stockhausen collaborator, Czukay (b. Mar. 24, 1938, Danzig, Germany), who has also been inspired to move towards a rock direction while teaching in Switzerland in 1966, encouraged to do so by one of his students, Karoli (b. Apr. 29, 1948, Straubing, West Germany). This trio, joined by Liebezeit (b. May 26, 1938, Dresden, Germany) and flautist David Johnson, has played its first improvisational performance in June 1968 in Cologne under the name Inner Space, before changing its name to Can by the end of the year, by which time, US-born singer Malcolm Mooney has become its first lead vocalist, with Johnson departing. With Czukay having already released ***Canaxis 5***, a one-off side-project album with Rolf Dammers earlier in the year, Can's debut LP, ***Monster Movie*** is now issued by the Munich Music Factory label in a limited edition of 500 copies. In October, the band plays a well-received residency at a theatre in Zurich, Switzerland, with Mooney subsequently suffering a nervous breakdown and returning to his home country.

1970

May Impressed by the album, the German division of United Artists Records signs the band and re-releases ***Monster Movie***. Can finds its new lead vocalist in Suzuki (b. Kenji Suzuki, Jan. 16, 1950, Japan), after Liebezeit and Czukay have spotted the singer street-busking in Munich, West Germany. Switching to sister label, Liberty Records, the group's sophomore album, ***Soundtracks***, collecting Can themes already used in movie scores including music from the film "Deep End", is released in September, and also includes the avant-garde 14-minute opus, *Mother Sky*.

1971

Feb Taking its title from a natural monument near Ibiza, the largely free-form double-LP ***Tago Mago*** is released in Germany. By year's end, the group sets up its own studio, named after its first band moniker, Inner Space, in a disused movie theater in the German town of Weilerwist, a facility which will become its long-term recording base.

1972

Feb During the month, Can performs at the Sporthalle, Cologne, before heading to London in April for its first British gigs to promote the belated UK release of ***Tago Mago***.

Aug Karoli is temporarily sidelined suffering from a perforated ulcer.

Nov The expansive ***Ege Bamyasi Okraschoten*** is issued including their most accessible rock cut, *Spoon*, which has provided Can with its only German #1 hit the previous year.

1973

June With albums now simultaneously released in both Germany and the UK on United Artists, ***Future Days*** is issued, receiving the group's best notices to date. It also marks Suzuki's final work with Can (he will become a Jehovah's Witness and retire from the music industry until resurfacing in the German group Dunkelziffer, releasing ***In The Night*** in 1984).

1974

Jan With remaining group members sharing vocal duties, the band plays a seven-hour concert in Berlin, before heading to the UK in February for its third tour in three years, a visit which will include its UK-TV bow on BBC2's "Old Grey Whistle Test". Further dates follow in France before the group records ***Soon Over Babaluma*** during the summer, set for release in November with lead vocals alternating between Schmidt and Karoli. During the year, United Artists (UK) also issues a collection of previously unreleased Can recordings as ***Limited Edition***.

1975

Sept Having split with United Artists (which has recently issued the German-only ***Can - The Classic German Rock Scene*** compilation), the group has signed to Virgin Records in the UK (licensed to Polydor Records in the US), which now releases ***Landed***, self-produced, as always, by the band.

Nov During a European tour, Can performs at London's Drury Lane Theatre, joined onstage by Tim Hardin for a version of *The Lady Came From Baltimore*.

1976

Oct [9] Written by Pink Floyd's Dave Gilmour, *I Want More* is the group's only UK or US chart success, reaching UK #26. It taken from the simultaneously released ***Flow Motion*** which features Gilmour playing guitar on three tracks, an album supported by another well-received European concert trek.

1977

May With the group now augmented by ex-Traffic members, bassist Rosko Gee and Gahanian percussionist Reebop Kwaku-Baah, the R&B-tinged ***Saw Delight*** is released, marking a distinct change in musical direction. Following a promotional European tour, Czukay quits the band, leaving the remaining members to record ***Out Of Reach***, which will be issued in July the following year, three months before United Artists collects catalog items for the release of the ***Cannibalism*** compilation (with sleeve-notes by the Buzzcocks' lead singer, Pete Shelley).

1979

July With the group now officially split, its final album, ***Can***, with Czukay having returned for editing duties, emerges on Harvest Records in Germany. Subsequently revered as influential pioneers of avant-garde, ethnic, ambient and electronic art-rock music genres, each of the band's core members will embark on productive solo careers: Karoli will become an in-demand session player and release the 1984 solo album ***Deluge***; Liebezeit forms the Phantom Band initially issuing ***Phantom Band*** (1980) followed by ***Freedom Of Speech*** (1981) and ***Nowhere*** (1984) before entering session work for the likes of Eurythmics, Brian Eno and Jah Wobble (and work with his former Can band-mates); Schmidt, who records five soundtrack albums between 1978 and 1983, will release ***Music at Dusk*** in 1987, while Czukay will become the most prominent and prolific solo artist, recording ***Movies*** (1980), ***On The Way To The Peak Of Normal*** (1982), ***Full Circle***, featuring Liebezeit and Wobble (1982), ***Snake Charmer***, co-credited to U2's The Edge and Wobble (1983), ***Der Osten Ist Rot*** ("The East Is Rotten"), ***Rome Remains Rome*** (1987) and ***Flight And Premonition***, a collaboration with David Sylvian in 1988.

1989

Oct After the original lineup of Czukay, Schmidt, Karoli, Liebezeit and Mooney has reformed Can some two years earlier, the group has signed to Mercury Records (UK) which now releases ***Rite Time***, thought the reunion proves short-lived. Czukay will reemerge in 1991 with Karoli, Liebezeit and vocalist Sheldon Angel for the album ***Radio Wave Surfer*** for Virgin Records, while Schmidt records ***Impossible Holidays*** for Mute Records (UK), released in November 1992. Mute will also bring Can selections to compact disc with the issue of ***Cannibalism 2*** (1990) and ***Cannibalism 3*** the following year. With Schmidt continuing work on an opera of Mervyn Peake's **Gormenghast**, scheduled for release in 1996, Spoon Records releases the comprehensive Can CD retrospective ***Anthology 1968-1993*** in 1994.

CANDLEBOX

Kevin Martin (vocals); **Peter Klett** (guitar); **Bardi Martin** (bass); **Scott Mercado** (drums)

1992

Lyricist Kevin Martin (b. Apr 9, 1969, Elgin, IL), has moved from Texas to Seattle, WA in 1985 where he first met Mercado (b. Nov 11, 1964, San Francisco, CA), though they have not teamed up musically until May 1991, when they formed the short-lived combo Uncle Duke. Subsequently recruiting Klett (Dec. 26, 1969, Bellevue, WA) in September and Bardi Martin (June 12, 1969, Olympia, WA), no relation to Kevin, in December, the quartet, named Candlebox after a phrase in a song by Midnight Oil, has recorded an eight-song demo in 48 hours which the band has issued on cassette in May, selling the 600 copies pressed in two months. Maverick Records A&R scout Guy Oseary, who will also sign Alanis Morissette, attends a showcase performance and now signs the band to the Madonna-owned label, placing them in the studio to record their debut album with producer Kelly Gray.

1994

May [7] *You* peaks at US #78.

Aug [27] Released in July the previous year, the guitar-fuelled ***Candlebox***, including two cuts taken directly from the group's original demo, finally hits US #7 while the band performs at the 1994 "Reading Festival", Reading, Berks.

Oct [1] *Far Behind*, its B-side featuring the band's live cover of Jimi Hendrix' *Voodoo Chile*, reaches US #18.

Nov [23] The group appears on CBS-TV's "Late Show With David Letterman".

Dec [17-18] Candlebox performs its last US tour dates of the year with consecutive gigs at the Memorial Hall, Kansas City, KS grossing $113,387 from an audience of 6,306. (During the month, the band will also play on the second night of KROQ's annual "Almost Acoustic Christmas" event held at the Universal Amphitheatre, Universal City, CA.)

1995

Jan [5] The RIAA certifies three million sales of ***Candlebox***.

Aug [27] Candlebox's sophomore set ***Lucy***, co-produced by Gray and Jon Plum at Seattle's London Bridge Studio, reaches US #11.

Oct [26] While Candlebox has recently completed a European tour, Hollywood Records (US) John Lennon tribute album, ***Working Class Hero*** including the band's cover of *Steel And Glass*, debuts at its US #94 peak.

[26] A US tour gets underway at the Roy Wilkins Auditorium, St. Paul Civic Center, MN, a gig grossing $52,459 from 2,761 fans.

Dec [11] The group holds a chat-session on **America Online**.

CANNED HEAT

Bob "The Bear" Hite (vocals, harmonica); **Al "Blind Owl" Wilson** (guitar, harmonica, vocals); **Henry Vestine** (guitar); **Larry Taylor** (bass); **Fito De La Parra** (drums)

1966

Evolving from a jug band, the group, taking its name from a Tommy Johnson song, begins to play electric blues and boogie in Los Angeles, CA (in clubs including Ash Grove), through the influence of its joint lead singers, Hite (b. Feb. 26, 1945, Torrance, CA), a 300lb (hence his nickname) blues expert and archivist, and Wilson (b. July 4, 1943, Boston, MA), with Vestine (b. Dec. 25, 1944, Washington, DC), Frank Cook, who has played with Charlie Haden, Chet Baker and Elmo Hope, and ex-Kaleidscope Stuart Brotman completing the line-up. (Brotman does not stay long, and is briefly replaced by Mark Andes (b. Feb. 19, 1948, Philadelphia, PA), before Taylor (b. Samuel Taylor, June 26, 1942, Brooklyn, New York, NY), having once played piano with Chuck Berry under the name Lafayette Leake and, at age 14, having played with Jerry Lee Lewis, becomes the group's permanent bass player.

1967

June [17] An appearance on the second day of the "Monterey International Pop Festival", County Fairgrounds, Monterey, CA, leads to a contract with Liberty Records.

Aug [10-13] The group performs at the Avalon Ballroom, San Francisco, CAsharing the bill with Moby Grape and Vanilla Fudge.

Nov [18] Their debut album, ***Canned Heat***, reaches US #76.

1968

Sept *On The Road Again*, originally recorded by the Memphis Jug Band in the late '20s, travels to US #16 and hits UK #8. The band tours the UK and Europe, with Fito de la Parra (b. Adolpho de la Parra, Feb. 8, 1946, Mexico City, Mexico) replacing Cook on

drums. (Cook has been on vacation in Mexico, where he meets de la Parra and tells him he can take his place in the band.)
[2] The band performs at London's Revolution club at the start of its first UK visit.
Oct [3-5] The group shares a bill with Gordon Lightfoot at San Francisco's Fillmore West, as ***Boogie With Canned Heat*** hits UK #5 after 21 weeks on chart.
[26] ***Boogie With Canned Heat*** reaches US #16, eight months into a 12-month chart stay.

1969

Jan *Going Up The Country*, a reworking of Henry Thomas' 1928 blues tune *Going Down South*, reaches US #11 (the band's biggest US hit) and UK #19.
[25] Double album ***Living The Blues*** makes US #18. One disc comprises live recordings, while the other is dominated by the extended *Refried Boogie*. De la Parra is arraigned in Southfield, Detroit, MI, after the arrest of 28 people on narcotics charges.
Apr The extracted *Time Was* peaks at US #67.
Aug [1-2] The band appears at the Fillmore East, New York, on a bill with Jefferson Airplane, before playing the "Woodstock Music & Art Fair" in Bethel, NY.
[30] ***Hallelujah*** makes US #37, as Harvey Mandel (b. Mar. 11, 1946, Detroit, MI) replaces Vestine on guitar.

1970

Jan ***Vintage Canned Heat***, compiling early pre-Liberty tracks, reaches US #173, while a more contemporary compilation, ***Canned Heat Cookbook (The Best Of Canned Heat)***, makes US #86.
Feb *Let's Work Together*, a cover of Wilbert Harrison's original, hits UK #2.
Mar ***Canned Heat Cookbook*** becomes a major UK seller, hitting #8.
July Live ***Canned Heat '70 Concert*** reaches UK #15, while their revival of Cleveland Crochet's oldie *Sugar Bee* makes UK #49.
Sept [3] While his band colleagues wait for him at the airport, due to fly to Berlin, W. Germany, Wilson dies, aged 27, of a drug overdose, having suffered from deep depression. He is found with a bottle of downers in the garden of Hite's house in Topanga Canyon, CA.
[13] Despite Wilson's death, the band begins its planned European tour at the Free Trade Hall, Manchester, Gtr. Manchester. Joel Scott Hill joins the group in Paris, France.
Oct ***Future Blues*** reaches US #59 and UK #27 marking the band's last UK chart album.
Nov *Let's Work Together* climbs to US #26.

1971

Apr ***Hooker'n'Heat***, pairing the band with blues legend John Lee Hooker, who had been asked to record with the band by Hite, when they met at Portland Airport, reaches US #73.
July ***Canned Heat Concert***, recorded live in Europe, peaks at US #133.

1972

Apr *Rockin' With The King*, with Little Richard guesting on piano and vocals, rolls to US #88. ***Historical Figures And Ancient Heads*** reaches US #87.

1974

Many Rivers To Cross, produced by Barry Beckett and Roger Hawkins at Muscle Shoals Studios, AL, is released by Atlantic. (As the blues boom abates, Canned Heat falls from wide audience favor, and by the end of the decade, it is mainly performing in bars, minor clubs and at low-key festivals, while Taylor and Mandel will hook up with John Mayall's band.)

1981

Apr [5] Hite dies from a heart attack, aged 36, after being taken ill in between sets at the Palamino Club in North Hollywood, CA. (Shortly thereafter, Canned Heat embarks on a major tour of Australia.)

1992

Nov [19] While Vestine is now playing in the Rent Party Band, along with former Sunray member Byron Case, Canned Heat (who still regularly feature in '60s revival package tours in the US, not least as part of "An Evening Of California Dreamin'" in the late '80s, and who also guested on John Lee Hooker's 1989 album ***The Healer***), now comprising de la Parra, Taylor, Junior Watson (guitar), a returned Mandel and James Thornbury (flute, guitar, harmonica), performs at London's Town & Country Club.

1994

Aug [16] The group's new album, ***Internal Combustion***, its first since the 1990 ***Reheated***, is released in US by the River Road Record label. (Canned Heat's current line-up comprises Vestine, de la Parra, Watson, Thornbury and Ron Shumake.)

THE CAPTAIN & TENNILLE

Daryl Dragon (keyboards); **Toni Tennille** (vocals)

1971

Sept Dragon (b. Aug. 27, 1942, Los Angeles, CA), son of conductor Carmen Dragon, meets Tennille (b. Catheryn Antoinette Tennille, May 8, 1943, Montgomery, AL) at the Marines Memorial Theatre, San Francisco, CA, where she is appearing in the musical "Mother Earth", which she has co-written. Tennille, the daughter of a professional singer father and local television personality mother, is currently a member of the South Coast Repertory Company having played classical piano as a teenager. Dragon (a regular in the Beach Boys' stage band, and a short-time drummer with the Byrds, who was also a member of Natalie Cole's early '60s jazz combo, the Malibu Music Men) is a keyboard player in the house band. After "Mother Earth" closes in 1972, the duo tours with the Beach Boys - Dragon on keyboards and Tennille on back-up vocal harmonies, while Dragon also co-writes tracks for the group with Dennis Wilson. Mike Love dubs Dragon "Captain Keyboard" because of the naval officer's cap he invariably wears on stage.

1973

Sept Following their tour with the Beach Boys, the duo is performing regularly at the Smoke House restaurant in Encino, CA, when, unable to interest any record labels in their material, they organize and pay for the recording of their own first single *The Way I Want To Touch You* (a ballad written by Tennille while on the Beach Boys trek.) They also spend $250 to have 500 copies pressed on their own label, Butterscotch Castle.

1974

Feb [14] Dragon and Tennille are married in Virginia City, NV, on St. Valentine's Day, while driving through 22 states promoting their debut single. A&M Records becomes interested and signs the duo to a recording contract, re-releasing *The Way I Want To Touch You.*

1975

June [21] Their first hit, the jaunty pop Neil Sedaka/Howard Greenfield-penned *Love Will Keep Us Together*, hits US #1 for the first of four weeks, eventually selling over two million copies.
July [1] *Love Will Keep Us Together* is certified gold by the RIAA.
Aug [1] Their still-rising debut album ***Love Will Keep Us Together*** is also confirmed gold by the RIAA.
[2] ***Love Will Keep Us Together*** hits US #2.
[16] *Love Will Keep Us Together* makes UK #32.
Sept [13] Spanish-sung version of the same hit, *Por Amor Viviremos*, makes US #49.
Nov [29] *The Way I Want To Touch You* is re-released (for a second time) as a follow-up, hitting US #4.
Dec [17] *The Way I Want To Touch You* is certified gold by the RIAA.

1976

Feb [7] *The Way I Want To Touch You* reaches UK #28.
[28] *Love Will Keep Us Together* wins the Record Of The Year category at the 18th annual Grammy Awards. It will also be named Best International Single at the Juno Awards (Canada's equivalent of the Grammys).
Mar [27] *Lonely Night (Angel Face)* hits US #3.
Apr [8] *Lonely Night (Angel Face)* is ratified gold by the RIAA.
May [1] Self-produced ***Song Of Joy***, further showcasing the duo's appealing mix of light pop and ballads, hits US #9.
July [10] *Shop Around*, their revival of the Miracles' first major chart success, hits US #4.
They are invited to sing at a White House dinner in honor of H.R.H. Queen Elizabeth II.
Aug [13] *Shop Around* is certified gold by the RIAA.
Sept [20] ABC-TV premiers "The Captain And Tennille" prime-time musical variety show.
[23] ***Song Of Joy*** is certified platinum by the RIAA.
Nov [20] *Muskrat Love*, written by Willis Alan Ramsey, hits US #4, confirmed gold by the RIAA on December 8th.

1977

Mar [14] "The Captain And Tennille" airs for the last time on ABC-TV.
Apr [11] The still-climbing ***Come In From The Rain*** is certified gold by the RIAA.
May [7] *Can't Stop Dancin'*, featuring Tennille's sisters, Melissa and Louisa, on backing vocals, reaches US #13.
[28] ***Come In From The Rain*** reaches US #18.
July [2] The extracted title track *Come In From The Rain* peaks at US #61.
Dec [13] Still-rising ***Captain & Tennille's Greatest Hits*** is confirmed gold by the RIAA.

1978

Feb [4] ***Captain & Tennille's Greatest Hits*** package makes US #55.
May [20] *I'm On My Way* peaks at US #74.
Aug [26] ***Dream*** climbs no higher than US #131, despite spending 30 weeks on the survey.
Nov [18] Having peaked at UK #63 one week earlier, a further Sedaka/Greenfield-penned ballad, *You Never Done It Like That*, hits US #10.

1979

Jan [27] *You Need A Woman Tonight* makes US #40. By mutual consent, the duo leaves A&M and signs a new deal with Casablanca Records.

1980

Feb [9] ***Make Your Move*** reaches US #23.
[11] Still-rising ballad *Do That To Me One More Time* is certified gold by the RIAA.
[16] *Do That To Me One More Time*, written by Tennille, tops the US chart and will prove to be the duo's final chart-topper and million-selling single.
Mar [15] *Do That To Me One More Time* hits UK #7.
[29] *Love On A Shoestring* peaks at US #55, as ***Make Your Move***, the duo's only UK chart album, makes #33.
June [7] *Happy Together (A Fantasy)* peaks at US #53 and is the duo's last hit single. It is followed by a period of re-assessment, during which Tennille elects to pursue a solo career.
Aug [5] ***Make Your Move*** is certified gold by the RIAA.

1995

Having recorded ***More Than You Know*** for the Mirage label in 1984, ***Moonglow*** two years later, and ***All Of Me***, an album of standards from 1929 to 1948 released on Gaia Records (US #198 in 1987), and having appeared in the stage show "Stardust" in 1991, Tennille has issued ***Never Let Me Go***, a further set of '30s and '40s standards, on the Bay Cities label (US) in 1992, before reuniting with the Captain to now record an album reworking their past hits.

CAPTAIN BEEFHEART & THE MAGIC BAND

Captain Beefheart (vocals); **Alex St. Clair** (guitar); **Jeff Cotton** (guitar); **Jerry Handley** (bass); **John French** (drums)

1966

Having appeared regularly as a child on TV, displaying a prodigious talent for clay sculpting, Don Van Vliet (b. Jan. 15, 1941, Glendale, CA), a high-school friend in Lancaster, CA of Frank Zappa (with whom he formed an unsuccessful band, the Soots), having already played in late '50s R&B bands including the Blackouts and the Omens, adopted the name Captain Beefheart, from his idea for a movie, "Captain Beefheart Meets The Grunt People", and has formed the first incarnation of his Magic Band in 1964. Based in Los Angeles, CA, Beefheart and the group are now signed to A&M Records, where they are produced by David Gates (later of Bread). (The complete recordings will appear 20 years later as ***The Legendary A&M Sessions***, but originally just two singles, *Diddy Wah Diddy* and *Frying Pan/Moonchild*, are released, before they are dropped by A&M.)

May [20-22] Beafheart & the Magic Band joins Love and Big Brother & the Holding Company to perform at the Avalon Ballroom, San Francisco, CA, returning for an August 26th-27th booking later in the year.

Oct [28-30] The group performs at San Francisco's Fillmore Auditorium.

1967

Apr *Safe As Milk* is recorded for Buddah Records, with a band that includes Ry Cooder and Antennae Jim Semens (Jeff Cotton) on guitars. During the recording, Beefheart (with a multi-octave vocal range) destroys a high-quality studio microphone simply by singing into it. Cooder leaves soon after, causing plans to appear at the "Monterey International Pop Festival" to be abandoned, but Semens becomes a regular Beefheart sideman.

July [27-30] The band performs another engagement at the Avalon Ballroom.

Sept [29-30] The group opens for the Doors also at the Avalon.

1968

Jan [19] The band performs at the Middle Earth during a handful of London dates.

Dec *Strictly Personal* is released by Blue Thumb Records (and on Liberty in the UK), but the quality is marred for Beefheart by unauthorized post-production work from Blue Thumb's Bob Krasnow.

1969

Oct Signed to Straight Records, and now assuming artistic control over the recording sessions, Beefheart produces the double set ***Trout Mask Replica***, which, despite not charting in US, is destined for cultural landmark status. Written in less than one day but recorded over a year, it features the first assemblage of the definitive Magic Band line-up, including Zoot Horn Rollo (Bill Harkleroad) on guitar, Rockette Morton (Mark Boston) on guitar and bass, and the Mascara Snake on clarinet.

Nov Beefheart is featured on Zappa's ***Hot Rats***.

Dec [6] ***Trout Mask Replica*** reaches UK #21.

1970

May [22-24] The group takes part in the "Hollywood Music Festival" at Newcastle-under-Lyme, Staffs.

1971

Jan ***Lick My Decals Off, Baby*** is another UK chartmaker, at #20.

Feb Beefheart & the Magic Band make their New York live debut at Ungano's.

May [29] ***Mirror Man***, featuring the remaining material recorded for, but not released by, Buddah Records in 1968, and featuring Semens, Handley, Drumbo and St. Clair, much to Beefheart's displeasure, makes UK #49.

1972

Feb After falling out with Zappa, ***The Spotlight Kid*** appears on Reprise, and is Beefheart's US chart debut, reaching #131.

[19] ***The Spotlight Kid***, recorded by Beefheart with Rollo (ex-surf band, the Nightbeats), Taj Mahal, Ed Marimba, Rockette, Bassus Ophelius, Winged-Eel Fingerling, John "Drumbo" French, Ted Cactus and Rhys Clark, makes UK #44.

May [5-7] The group appears at the "Bickershaw Festival", Wigan, Lancs., with the Grateful Dead and Country Joe & the Fish.

1973

Dec ***Clear Spot***, now featuring the latest Magic Band recruits Marimba, Orejon, Milt Holland and Russ Titelman, peaks at US #191.

1974

May ***Unconditionally Guaranteed*** charts at US #192 and is Beefheart's last album with the existing Magic Band, as Rollo and Morton leave to form their own group, Mallard. A new deal is signed, with Virgin Records in the UK, and with Mercury in US.

Nov ***Blue Jeans And Moonbeams***, is poorly received, despite a new line-up: the Captain, Jeff Morris Tepper, Bob West, Mark Gibbons, Micheal Smotherman, Gene Pello, Jimmy Caravan and Ty Grimes.

1975

July [5] Beefheart appears with Pink Floyd, Steve Miller and Roy Harper at the "Knebworth Festival", Knebworth, Herts.

Nov Reunited with Zappa, singing with the Mothers Of Invention, he tours and contributes to ***Bongo Fury***. Thereafter, Beefheart temporarily retires, returning to the Mojave Desert, CA, to paint.

1978

Nov Breaking a long silence, ***Shiny Beast (Bat Chain Puller)*** is released by Warner Bros. in the US, while its UK release is delayed until Virgin wins a suit to enforce its own rights to Beefheart material. The Magic Band has changed once again, now including Tepper, Bruce Malbourne Fowler, Eric Drew Feldman, Richard Redus, Robert Arthur Williams and Art Tripp III.

1980

Sept ***Doc At the Radar Station***, recorded with Drumbo, Gary Lucas, Redrus and Tripp, is released internationally on Virgin, coinciding with a successful tour of the US and Europe by Beefheart, and an unprecedented appearance on NBC-TV's "Saturday Night Live".

1982

Sept [25] ***Ice Cream For Crow***, featuring Hatsize Snyder, Cliff Martinez, Williams, Lambourne Fowler and mainstay Drumbo, returns him to the UK chart, at #90 (and is issued via Epic Records in the US).

Nov [11] Beefheart makes another rare TV appearance, on NBC's "Late Night With David Letterman".

1986

After a long silence, and an eventual announcement that the ever esoteric and eclectic artist is leaving music to concentrate on painting at the Mojave Desert home he shares with his wife Jan, Beefheart exhibits in London, while Virgin will begin issuing the majority of his back-catalog on CD the following year. (In 1995, photographer/director Anton Corbijn will produce a movie based on Beefheart, "Some Yoyo Stuff".)

CARAVAN

Pye Hastings (vocals, guitar); **David Sinclair** (keyboards); **Richard Sinclair** (bass, vocals); **Richard Coughlan** (drums)

1968

Jan Having toured as the Wilde Flowers with Kevin Ayers, Robert Wyatt and Hugh Hopper (who leave to form Soft Machine), the Canterbury-based UK band re-emerges as Caravan, comprising Hastings (b. Jan. 21, 1947, Banffshire, Scotland), cousins David (b. Nov. 24, 1947, Herne Bay, Kent) and Richard Sinclair (b. June 6, 1948, Herne Bay) and Coughlan (Sept. 2, 1947, Herne Bay). Releasing their debut effort ***Caravan*** on MGM's Verve imprint in October, its gentle rock eccentricity establishes the group as a significant English underground band, popular not least on the UK college circuit.

1970

Sept During a hectic touring schedule, the band, now signed to Decca Records, releases ***If I Could Do It All Again, I'd Do It All Over You***, co-produced by the band with their manager, Terry King.

1971

May ***In The Land Of Grey And Pink***, produced by David Hitchcock, is released on Decca's progressive Deram label and is distinguished by the 22-minute *Nine Feet Underground*, which consumes side two of the album.

Aug [7] David Sinclair announces that he is leaving to join Robert Wyatt's Matching Mole. He will be replaced by jazz-rock keyboardist Steve Miller, ex-DC & the MB's and Delivery.

[28-29] The group takes part in the "Weeley Festival", Weeley, Essex.

1972

May [19] ***Waterloo Lily*** is released, the band's fourth album to receive critical approval, yet still commercially restricted to their devoted cult following.

July Geoff Richardson (b. July 15, 1950) joins the line-up on electric violin, while Stuart Evans (bass) and Derek Austin (keyboards) join briefly for a tour of Australia.

Nov Richard Sinclair leaves to form Hatfield & the North, taking Miller with him. His interim replacement is John Perry.

1973

Oct David Sinclair rejoins Caravan for ***For Girls Who Grow Plump In The Night***, which features brass and orchestral arrangements. The planned album sleeve, depicting a naked, pregnant woman, is vetoed by Decca, but a compromise is reached on the retail version: the woman, still clearly pregnant, wears flimsy nightwear.

1974

Apr ***Live Caravan And The New Symphonia*** is released, recorded six months earlier with the New Symphonia Orchestra, conducted by Martyn Ford at London's Drury Lane Theatre Royal. It features much earlier material reworked for the orchestral arrangements.

July Mike Wedgwood (b. May 19, 1950), ex-Kiki Dee and Curved Air, replaces Perry.

1975

Aug [30] Spooneristically-titled ***Cunning Stunts*** charts at UK #50 after the band performs at the annual "Reading Festival", Reading, Berks. Jan Schelhaas, ex-the National Head Band and Gary Moore's band, joins on keyboards, and Dek Messecar replaces Wedgwood, who leaves for a solo career in the US.

Oct [18] ***Cunning Stunts***, on Miles Copeland's BTM label, reaches US #124 and is the band's only international success.

1976

May [15] ***Blind Dog At St. Dunstan's***, on the BTM label, makes UK #53.
Nov Decca issues compilation album ***The Canterbury Tales***, to coincide with a UK tour.

1977

Aug ***Better By Far***, produced by Tony Visconti, is released on Arista. The band retires from live work for a year, as the Sinclair cousins and Schelhaas work with Camel for an extended period.

1980

Nov ***The Album*** is released on manager Terry King's Kingdom label, with David Sinclair back in the line-up.

1982

June The four original members (the Sinclairs, Hastings and Coughlan) re-form for the first time in 11 years, with Mel Collins joining on saxophone, for Caravan's final recording, ***Back To Front***, also released on Kingdom.

1990

Sept [28] While the remainder of the '80s only yielded a number of retrospectives (including ***Collection: Caravan*** (1984), ***And I Wish I Weren't Stoned Don't Worry*** (1985), ***The Best Of Caravan*** (1987) and ***Canterbury Collection*** (1987)), Caravan holds a nostalgic reunion gig at the Buckingham High School. (The following year, Richard Sinclair will also assemble various ex-members of both Caravan and Camel, touring UK clubs as Caravan of Dreams.)

MARIAH CAREY

1988

Singing since the age of four (her parents, a Venezuelan aerospace-engineer father and opera-singing mother, divorced when she was three), Carey (b. Mar. 27, 1970, New York, NY), whose mother, Indiana-born Irish-American Patricia (having named her daughter after *They Call The Wind Mariah*, from the Lerner and Loewe musical "Paint Your Wagon", from which came *Wand'rin Star* by Lee Marvin - UK #1 the day Carey was born) has been a vocal coach and former New York City opera singer, has begun writing songs with Ben Margulies while still attending Harborfields High school at 16, having been weaned on the music of Aretha Franklin, Minnie Riperton and Stevie Wonder. While working as a waitress and coat-check girl in New York, she wins an audition to be back-up singer for Brenda K. Starr, who passes Carey's demo tape to CBS/Columbia Records president, Tommy Mottola, who now signs her. (Subsequently marrying the label executive, Carey will say: "We have a very, very special relationship. I admire him and respect him enormously.") She will spend much of the following year commuting between the Tarpan Studios, San Rafael, CA, and the Sky Line and the Hit Factory studios in New York, recording tracks for her debut release.

1990

Apr Columbia launches Carey with an invitation-only soirée in New York, at which she sings three songs accompanied by Richard Tee on piano.
June Carey makes TV appearances on NBC-TV's "The Tonight Show" and Fox-TV's "The Arsenio Hall Show". (She has already created a stir singing the national anthem before the first game of the NBA finals.)
[30] Her maiden album ***Mariah Carey*** enters the US chart at #80. Largely co-penned by Carey and Margulies, and co-produced by Narada Michael Walden, Rhett Lawrence, Ric Wake and Carey, reviews of the ten-track project confirm that Columbia has firmly placed their young high-pitched diva between Whitney Houston and Anita Baker.
Aug [1] The still-climbing *Vision Of Love* is certified gold by the RIAA.
[4] Hot airplay cut, *Vision Of Love*, co-penned with Margulies, tops the US chart for the first of four weeks.
Sept [15] *Vision Of Love* hits UK #9, as parent album ***Mariah Carey*** debuts at its UK #6 peak.
Oct [27] Carey is the musical guest on NBC-TV's "Saturday Night Live".
Nov [10] Ballad follow-up *Love Takes Time* begins a three-week hold on US #1, having been confirmed gold by the RIAA on the 6th.
[20] Carey makes her second appearance on "The Tonight Show".
Dec [1] *Love Takes Time* makes UK #37.

1991

Feb [2] House-remixed version of the uptempo *Someday* makes UK #38.
[12] *Someday* is certified gold by the RIAA.
[20] From five nominations, Carey wins Best Pop Vocal Performance, Female, for *Vision Of Love* and Best New Artist at the 33rd annual Grammy Awards, at Radio City Music Hall, New York.
[23] "Mariah Carey : The First Vision", a mini-collection of video clips from her debut project, enters the US and UK video charts.
Mar [2] ***Mariah Carey***, after 36 weeks on the survey, hits US #1, and is on its way to six platinum RIAA US sales awards.
[7] Carey is named Best New Female Singer in the annual **Rolling Stone** Readers' Picks music poll.
[9] *Someday*, once again co-written with Margulies, becomes Carey's third consecutive US #1.
[12] Carey collects the Best New R&B/Urban Contemporary Artist, Best R&B/Urban Contemporary Single, Female, and Best R&B/Urban Contemporary Album, Female (for ***Mariah Carey***) trophies at the fifth annual Soul Train Awards, at the Shrine Auditorium, Los Angeles, CA.
[26] Her collection of video clips to date, "The First Vision" is certified platinum by the RIAA.
May [25] Ballad *I Don't Wanna Cry* tops the Hot 100.
June [1] *There's Got To Be A Way* debuts at its UK #54 peak.
Sept [5] Carey sings *Emotions* at the eighth annual MTV Video Music Awards ceremony, held at the Universal Amphitheatre, Universal City, CA.
[13] The RIAA certifies multi-platinum sales of ***Mariah Carey*** (six million).
Oct [5] Her sophomore album, ***Emotions***, reuniting many of the original cast from her debut set, bows at its US #4 peak.
[12] *Emotions* becomes her fifth consecutive US chart-topper, and will become her fourth RIAA-certified gold single on the 15th.
Nov [9] *Emotions* reaches UK #17.
[16] She performs live on "Saturday Night Live".
Dec [3] Carey wins the Hot 100 Singles Artist, Top Pop Artist, Top Pop Album and Top AC Artist categories at the second annual Billboard Music Awards, held at Santa Monica Airport's Barker Hangar, Santa Monica, CA.
[26] She is featured on "Entertainers '91", saluting the year's Top 20 entertainers, on ABC-TV.

1992

Jan [22] Carey's stepfather, Joseph Vian, of Lake Hiawatha, NJ, files papers in Manhattan Federal Court seeking compensatory and punitive damages, claiming that he supported her emotionally and paid for her Manhattan apartment, a car and dental work in her early career years on the understanding that she would repay him when she became successful. Vian also claims that Carey "actively sought to break up the marriage" between him and her natural mother, Patricia Carey, who has recently filed for divorce.
[23] Carey appears live via satellite on BBC1-TV's "Top Of The Pops".
[25] *Can't Let Go* hits US #2 and will reach UK #20 the following week.
[27] She wins the Favorite Female Artist, Soul/R&B category at the 19th annual American Music Awards, held at the Shrine Auditorium.
Feb [15] ***Emotions*** hits UK #4.
[25] Carey sings *Won't You Talk To Me* at the 34th annual Grammy Awards, at Radio City Music Hall, New York.
Mar [20] Songwriters Sharon Taber and Randy Gonzalez file a copyright infringement suit in Central District Federal Court in Los Angeles alleging that Carey's *Can't Let Go* was based on their composition *Right Before My Eyes*. (Various motions will result in the suit not being heard until April 1996.)
Apr [11] *Make It Happen* hits US #5, also peaking at UK #17 on the 25th.
[27] Carey guests on BBC1-TV's "Wogan".
May [20] She performs on MTV's "Unplugged" series in New York, backed by producer Walter Afanasieff (piano), Dan Shea (keyboards), Vernon Black (guitar), Randy Jackson (bass), Gigi Gonaway (drums), Sammy Figueroa (percussion), Ren Klyce (celeste, timpanis) and David Cole (piano). Traditionally uncomfortable with live performance, Carey will subsequently confirm that her MTV appearance was a turning point in her career: "It was the first time I did that many songs in front of an audience. I had to learn in the public eye, and I'm still learning."
June [20] Plucked from the recent MTV appearance, her live version of Jacksons' 1970 US #1 ballad, *I'll Be There,* featuring backing singer Trey Lorenz on vocals, tops the US chart, with proceeds going to AmFAR, the United Negro College Fund, Hale House and the T.J. Martell Foundation. (Carey will shortly begin producing Lorenz's freshman album, ***Trey Lorenz***).
July [4] *I'll Be There* hits UK #2, as ***MTV Unplugged (EP)***, a seven-track mini-album documenting the earlier broadcast, hits US #3.
[18] ***MTV Unplugged (EP)*** debuts at its UK #3 peak.
Dec [7] ***MTV Unplugged (EP)*** becomes the first MiniDisc title to be pressed for commercial release by Sony, as the electronics/software giant introduces MiniDisc players and recording titles to the consumer market in the US.
[9] Carey wins the Hot 100 Singles Artist (Female) and Top 200 Album Artist (Female) categories, at the third annual **Billboard** Music Awards, held at the Universal Amphitheatre.
[17] She sings carols at a children's Christmas party sponsored by New York's Police Athletic League.

1993

Jan [25] Carey collects the Favorite Female Artist, Pop/Rock and Favorite Album, Adult Contemporary trophies at the 20th annual American Music Awards, held at the Shrine Auditorium, before beginning work in New York on a gospel pop album for release later in the year.
Apr [26] Lawsuit filed by her stepfather is thrown out of a New York court by Federal District Court Judge Michael B. Mukasey.
May [18] *Can't Let Go*, *Emotions* and *Make It Happen* receive citations at the BMI's 41st annual pop awards dinner, at the Regency Beverly Wilshire Hotel, Los Angeles.
June [5] Carey weds Sony Music president, Tommy Mottola, at the St. Thomas Episcopal Church, Manhattan, with Barbra Streisand, Bruce Springsteen, Ozzy Osbourne, Billy Joel, Robert DeNiro and others in attendance.
July [14] She invites Albany Police Athletic League band members onstage in Schenectady, NY, for the taping of an NBC-TV special, singing *I'll Be There*.
Sept [4] *Dreamlover* hits UK #9.
[11] *Dreamlover* tops the US chart as ***Music Box*** enters the UK chart at #1.
[22] ***Dreamlover*** is certified platinum by the RIAA.
Nov [3] Carey's "Tentative" tour opens in Miami, FL.
[13] *Hero* hits UK #7.
[25] Carey's NBC-TV special airs.
Dec [10] She performs at New York's Madison Square Garden, dedicating *Hero* to the three men who subdued Long Island Railroad gunman Colin Ferguson. (She will donate proceeds from the sale of the single to the families of the victims.)
[15] Still-climbing *Hero* is certified platinum by the

RIAA.
[25] *Hero* tops the US chart, as ***Music Box*** finally reaches the US summit.

1994

Feb [9] Carey guests on ITV's "Des O'Connor Tonight".
[19] Her cover version of Harry Nilsson's 1972 transatlantic chart-topper, *Without You* debuts at UK #1.
Mar [19] *Without You*, coupled with *Never Forget You*, hits US #3, the same day Carey guests on CBS-TV's "Late Show With David Letterman".
[22] *Without You* is certified gold by the RIAA.
June [25] *Anytime You Need A Friend* reaches US #12 and UK #8.
Sept [17] Updating the Lionel Richie/Diana Ross 1981 US chart-topper, *Endless Love*, recorded with Luther Vandross, debuts at its UK #3 peak.
[27] The RIAA certifies sales of eight million copies of ***Mariah Carey*** and four million copies of ***Emotions***.
Oct [1] *Endless Love* hits US #2, behind Boyz II Men's *I'll Make Love To You*.
[17] "Here Is Mariah Carey" video is certified platinum by the RIAA.
[28] *Endless Love* is confirmed gold by the RIAA.
Nov [24] She is named Best Female Artist at the inaugural MTV European Music Awards held at the Pariser Platz, Berlin, Germany.
Dec [4] Carey wins the Best Female Solo Singer at the seventh annual **Smash Hits** Poll Winner's Party.
[7] She accepts her Top Female Artist trophy via satellite from New York, at the fifth annual **Billboard** Music Awards, held at the Universal Amphitheatre, Universal City.
[8] Carey helps raise $700,000 at the Fresh Air Fund benefit at the Cathedral of St. John the Divine in New York. One of the charity's children's camps in Fishkill, NY will be named Camp Mariah in her honor.
[13] ***MTV Unplugged*** is certified multi-platinum by the RIAA for three million sales.
[17] Festive collection ***Merry Christmas*** hits US #3, as the extracted *All I Want For Christmas Is You* hits UK #2. (In selling 200,000 units of ***Merry Christmas*** in its week of release in Japan, its becomes the best-selling one-week album in Japanese recording history. By Christmas 1995, the album will surpass ***The Bodyguard*** as Japan's best-selling foreign album ever, at 2.7 million sold.)
[24] ***Merry Christmas*** reaches UK #32.
[27] The RIAA certifies multi-platinum (three million) sales of ***Merry Christmas***.

1995

Jan [19] ***Music Box*** is certified multi-platinum by the RIAA, with sales of eight million.
[30] Carey wins the Favorite Female Artist/Pop Rock category at the 22nd annual American Music Awards.
May [3] She attends the seventh annual World Music Awards at the Sporting Club in Monte Carlo, Monaco, set to air on ABC-TV on the 30th.
June [3] Carey wins the category for Top Pop Artist (Female) at the inaugural Blockbuster Entertainment Awards at Hollywood's Pantages Theatre, set to air on CBS-TV on the 6th.
Aug [1] St. Martin's Press publishes Chris Nickson's biography **Mariah Carey: Her Story**.
Sept [23] *Fantasy*, heavily sampling Tom Tom Club's *Genius Of Love*, debuts at its UK #4 peak.
[30] *Fantasy* bows at US #1, creating US chart history in becoming the first single by a female artist to do so.
Oct [7] Largely co-produced as always by Carey and Afanasieff and featuring Babyface among its guests, ***Daydream*** enters the UK chart at #1.
[10] Carey sings to a sellout crowd at New York's Madison Square Garden, with guests Boyz II Men.
[21] ***Daydream*** debuts at US #1.
Nov [7] The RIAA certifies sales of two million copies of *Fantasy*.
[28] ***Daydream*** is confirmed multi-platinum by the RIAA, with sales of four million.
Dec [2] Co-written by Carey and Afanasieff with the soul quartet, *One Sweet Day*, a duet with Boyz II Men, debuts at US #1, beginning a record-breaking 16 weeks at the summit. It is also Carey's tenth US chart-topping single in five years.
[7] 6,000 fans attend a personal appearance by Carey at Tower Records' Piccadilly Circus store in London, beating the record of 4,000 held by Barry Manilow.
[9] *One Sweet Day* debuts at its UK #6 peak.

1996

Jan [17] Carey inducts Gladys Knight & the Pips into the Rock and Roll Hall of Fame at the 11th annual dinner at New York's Waldorf Astoria.
[6] O.J. Simpson calls a Los Angeles radio station and, in requesting *One Sweet Day*, dedicates the current hit to his murdered wife, Nicole.
[30] She performs *Fantasy* and is named Favorite Female Artist, Pop/Rock and Favorite Female Artist, Soul/R&B at the 23rd American Music Awards, staged at the Shrine Auditorium.
Feb [7] Carey guests on ITV's "Des O'Connor Tonight".
[17] Her cover of Journey's 1982 US #2 *Open Arms* hits UK #4 in its week of entry.
[28] Together with Boyz II Men she performs their current US chart-topper, *One Sweet Day* at the 38th annual Grammy Awards, held at the Shrine Auditorium, though she goes home empty-handed, despite receiving five nominations.
Mar [6] Carey and Boyz II Men break the latter's own record (14 weeks, previously shared with Whitney Houston) as *One Sweet Day* logs its 15th consecutive week atop the US chart (it will also hold on for one more week in pole position, the longest in US chart history).
May [4] *Always Be My Baby* tops the US chart, bringing Carey level with Whitney Houston and Madonna as the only female artists with 11 US chart-toppers.

BELINDA CARLISLE

1985

May [10] After three successful albums, including the multiplatinum ***Beauty And The Beat***, and seven US hit singles, including the million-selling *We Got The Beat*, the new wave all-girl quintet the Go-Go's hold a press conference to announce the break-up of the band. Carlisle (b. Aug. 17, 1958, Hollywood, CA), an ex-high school cheerleader named after her mother's favorite film, "Johnny Belinda", remains signed to I.R.S. Records, and prepares a solo career and album with the assistance of ex-Go-Go colleague Charlotte Caffey.

1986

May [9] Fully recuperated from the excesses indulged in as a Go-Go, Carlisle performs her first solo concert in Cleveland, OH.
Aug [9] *Mad About You* hits US #3, while her maiden album ***Belinda*** reaches US #13.
Oct [11] Second extract *I Feel The Magic* reaches US #82, as Carlisle tours the US as the support act to Robert Palmer, followed by a three-month club tour of her own.
Nov [24] ***Belinda*** is certified gold by the RIAA.

1987

Oct Now signed domestically to MCA Records (and Virgin in the UK), her sophomore album ***Heaven On Earth*** is released. Completing her musical transition to pure pop rock, the set is produced by Rick Nowels and features guest musicians including Thomas Dolby, Caffey, Ellen Shipley and Michelle Phillips.
Dec [5] Co-penned by Nowels and Shipley, *Heaven Is A Place On Earth* tops the US chart for one week, spurred by a promo video clip directed by actress Diane Keaton.

1988

Jan [15] Still-climbing ***Heaven On Earth*** is certified platinum by the RIAA.
[16] *Heaven Is A Place On Earth* tops the UK chart for two weeks, while ***Heaven On Earth*** peaks at US #13.
Mar [1] Carlisle guests on NBC-TV's "Late Night With David Letterman".
[19] Further album excerpt *I Get Weak*, written by Diane Warren, hits US #2 and UK #10.
May Carlisle sets out on her first major solo headlining tour, starting in the US and Canada.
June [18] She makes a promotional visit to Japan, while *Circle In The Sand* hits US #7 and UK #4, and its parent album ***Heaven On Earth*** hits UK #4.
Aug Her debut US release *Mad About You* is re-issued by I.R.S. in the UK and climbs to #67.
[13] *I Feel Free*, reviving Cream's 1967 UK #11, peaks at US #88.
Sept Carlisle undertakes her first UK tour, including three sold-out dates at London's Hammersmith Odeon, as *World Without You* makes UK #34.
Dec *Love Never Dies* peaks at UK #54.

1989

Mar [6] Greenpeace-fundraising ***Rainbow Warrors*** album is released, featuring a contribution from Carlisle.
Oct *Leave A Light On*, a second Nowels/Shipley composition, hits UK #4.
Nov [4] Nowels-helmed ***Runaway Horses***, featuring fellow Go-Go's Caffey, Valentine and Schock guesting on *Shades Of Michaelangelo*, and contributions from George Harrison and Bryan Adams, hits UK #4 during an 18 month chart ride.
Dec [5] Still-climbing ***Runaway Horses*** is certified gold by the RIAA.
[9] *Leave A Light On*, featuring George Harrison on slide guitar, reaches US #11.
[16] Its parent album ***Runaway Horses*** makes US #37.
[30] *La Luna* makes UK #38.

1990

Mar [3] *Summer Rain* reaches US #30.
[10] *Runaway Horses* makes UK #40.
[28] The Go-Gos regroup for a one-off benefit concert at the Universal Amphitheatre, Universal City, CA, for the California Environmental Protection Initiative Of 1990. (This event will lead to a temporary reunion later in the year.)
May [2] Carlisle announces she is pulling out of a $35,000 appearance at the Frontier Days Rodeo in Cheyenne, WY, on July 23rd, citing maltreatment of livestock at such events as her reason.
June [2] *Vision Of You* peaks at UK #41.
Nov [3] *(We Want) The Same Thing* hits UK #6.
[9] The reunited Go-Go's guest on NBC-TV's "Late Night With David Letterman" on the eve of a comeback US tour.

1991

Jan [26] Still mining ***Runaway Horses***, *Summer Rain* peaks at UK #23.
Feb Carlisle contributes *Bless The Beasts And Childiren* to the various artists album ***Tame Yourself***, benefitting People for the Ethical Treatment of Animals (PETA).
Oct [8] She guests on "Late Night With David Letterman".
[19] *Live Your Life Be Free* reaches UK #12.
[26] Her fourth solo album ***Live Your Life Be Free*** debuts at its UK #7 peak.
Nov [23] *Do You Feel Like I Feel* reaches UK #29 having peaked at US #73 one week earlier.

1992

Jan [18] *Half The World* makes UK #35.
Apr [27] Married to actor James Mason's son, Morgan, Carlisle gives birth to James Duke Mason in Los Angeles.
Aug [28] During a brief visit to the UK, she guests on BBC1-TV's "Summer Scene".
Sept [12] *Little Black Book*, penned with Shakespear's Sister's Marcella Detroit, reaches UK #28.
[26] Rounding up her hits to date, ***The Best Of Belinda Carlisle Volume 1*** tops the UK chart.
Oct [4] Carlisle appears on BBC2-TV's "The O Zone".

1993

Sept [23] Carlisle guests on CBS-TV's "Late Show With David Letterman".
Oct [2] *Big Scary Animal*, the first track from her new album ***Real***, reaches UK #12.
[23] ***Real*** debuts at its UK #9 peak, as Carlisle contributes guest vocals on the Lemonheads' new album, ***Come On Feel The Lemonheads***.
Dec [4] *Lay Down Your Arms* reaches UK #27.

1996

Jan Having reunited with the Go-Go's once again in 1994 (for their ***Return To The Valley Of The Go-Go's*** and an accompanying tour), Carlisle signs a new solo deal with Chrysalis Records, and begins work on her label debut.
see also: **THE GO GO'S**

ERIC CARMEN

1975

Nov Carmen (b. Aug. 11, 1949, Cleveland, OH), classically trained at the Cleveland Institute of Music and already a veteran of Cleveland-based early '60s combos the Fugitives, the Harlequins, the Sounds of Silence and Cyrus Erie, became lead singer of 1968's *It's Cold Outside* chartmakers the Choir, formed with Wally Bryson (b. July 18, 1949, Gastonia, NC) and Dave Smalley (b. July 10, 1949, Oil City, UT) on guitar and Jim Bonfanti (b. Dec. 17, 1948, Windber, PN) on drums, from previous outfit, the Outsiders. Evolving into the Quick and finally settling as the Raspberries, signed to Capitol Records in 1971, the group, directed by Carmen's Beatles/Beach Boys-influenced songwriting and vocal skills, released its debut album ***The Raspberries*** (US #51) and ***Fresh*** (US #36) in 1972, followed by 1973's ***Side 3*** (US #128) (after which Smalley and Bonfanti leave to form Dynamite and are replaced by Mike McBride, ex-Cyrus Erie, on drums, and bassist Scott McCarl). Having notched up six US Hot 100 chart 45s (including the gold-certified #5 smash *Go All The Way* in 1972), the Raspberries' final single hit *Overnight Sensation (Hit Record)* made US #18 in November 1974, becoming their most enduring legacy on US radio. Following poor sales of their final release ***Starting Over*** in April of this year, the band splits, leaving Carmen free to pursue a solo career with Arista Records, which now releases his freshman effort ***Eric Carmen.***

1976

Mar Lushly-orchestrated, self-penned dramatic ballad *All By Myself*, based on a Rachmaninoff melody from his Piano Concerto No. 2 in C Minor, hits US #2, while the self-written, Jimmy Ienner-produced ***Eric Carmen***, recorded at O.D.O. Sound Studios, New York, NY, peaks at US #21.
Apr [21] *All By Myself* is certified gold by the RIAA.
[29] Carmen appears on BBC1-TV's "Top Of The Pops" performing *All By Myself*.
May *All By Myself* reaches UK #12, spurred by a UK promotional visit. ***Eric Carmen*** spends a week on the UK chart at #58.
June Ten-track retrospective ***The Best Of The Raspberries Featuring Eric Carmen*** makes US #138.
July *Never Gonna Fall In Love Again*, also based on Rachmaninoff (his 2nd Symphony), makes US #11. (Irish singer Dana's version has already made UK #31 in March.)
Sept *Sunrise* makes US #34.
Oct He begins recording a follow-up album in London, with producer Gus Dudgeon.

1977

Feb Disagreements lead Dudgeon to quit the project, leaving Carmen as sole producer.
Oct His sophomore effort, the self-written ***Boats Against The Current*** climbs to US #45.
[27] ***Eric Carmen*** is certified platinum by the RIAA.
Nov Extracted perky pop-tinged *She Did It* peaks at US #23, while the recent album's title cut *Boats Against The Current* moors at US #88 in December.

1978

Dec *Change Of Heart* makes US #19, as its parent album ***Change Of Heart***, further showcasing Carmen's talent for crafting melodic pop-rock nuggets, peaks at US #137. His final chart appearance of the decade will be a remake of the Four Tops' 1964 smash *Baby I Need Your Lovin'*, which makes US #62 the following February.

1980

July *It Hurts Too Much* reaches US #75, while his final original album for Arista, ***Tonight You're Mine***, makes US #160.

1985

Mar After a five-year recording hiatus, and newly signed to Geffen Records, *I Wanna Hear It From Your Lips* peaks at US #35. It previews a second album titled ***Eric Carmen***, co-produced by Bob Gaudio and Don Gehman, which makes US #128, also yielding the US #87 *I'm Through With Love* in April.

1988

Feb [13] Franke Previte/John DeNicola-penned *Hungry Eyes*, an instant airplay favorite featured on the RCA soundtrack to the smash movie "Dirty Dancing", hits US #4, Carmen's first Top 10 hit in 11 years.
June Arista Records releases ***The Best Of Eric Carmen*** compilation, which rises to US #59, as the artist embarks on "Dirty Dancing The Concert Tour" with Bill Medley, Merry Clayton and the Contours.
Aug [13] *Make Me Lose Control* hits US #3, taking his record sales to over 15 million worldwide.
Oct [15] *Reason To Try*, used by NBC-TV for coverage of the 1988 Summer Olympics and taken from ***One Moment In Time***, peaks at US #87.

1992

While Cramen has not released a new studio set since 1985, Rhino Records releases his debut solo effort ***Eric Carmen*** on compact disc, having added additional versions of *Sunrise* and *All By Myself*.

KIM CARNES

1975

After working as a demo session and jingle singer in Los Angeles, CA, in the late '60s, Carnes (b. July 20, 1946, Pasadena, CA), left the New Christy Minstrels with her husband Dave Ellingson and, as Kim & Dave, recorded *Nobody Knows*, the theme song to the 1971 movie "Vanishing Point", for Jimmy Bowen's Amos label in Los Angeles. Bowen, who was introduced to the pair by Mike Settle, signed them to a publishing deal and they worked as staff writers, not least with Glenn Frey and J.D. Souther. While Amos eventually issued her maiden album ***Rest On Me*** in 1974 (featuring back-up players including James Burton and ex-Cricket Glen D. Hardin), Carnes was signed to A&M Records by David Anderle, which now releases her label debut ***Kim Carnes***, a largely self-penned pop/rock/country meld, produced by Mentor Williams and featuring top sessioneers David Foster, Jim Keltner, Dean Parks and Leland Sklar, among others.

1977

Kim and Dave composition *Love Comes From Unexpected Places* wins the "Tokyo Song Festival". ***Sailin'*** is released, produced by Jerry Wexler and Barry Beckett.

1978

July Her duet with Gene Cotton on her self-penned ballad *You're A Part Of Me* reaches US #36.

1979

Mar At the instigation of label executive Jim Mazza, Carnes has become the first artist signed to the new EMI America label, and now reaches US #56 with *It Hurts So Bad*. Carnes and Ellingson have also written all the songs for Kenny Rogers' ***Gideon***, which makes US #12.

1980

May Her ballad duet with Rogers, *Don't Fall In Love With A Dreamer*, hits US #4.
July Her revival of the Miracles' *More Love* hits US #10, taken from ***Romance Dance***, a more rock-directed affair produced by George Tobin which waltzes to US #57.
Oct A second extract, her remake of the Box Tops' 1968 hit *Cry Like A Baby* makes US #44.
Dec [15] Carnes begins recording her second album for EMI America, at Los Angeles' Record One Studio.

1981

May [16] *Bette Davis Eyes*, revitalizing a 1974 Jackie DeShannon ***New Arrangement*** album track with an arrangement by Bill Cuomo, tops the US chart for the first of nine weeks, displacing EMI America labelmate Sheena Easton's *Morning Train*. (During its run, and after its first five chart-topping weeks, it is nudged from #1 by Stars On 45's *Stars On 45* for one week, but returns to top spot for a further four weeks.) It will also hit UK #10.
June [16] *Bette Davis Eyes* is certified gold by the RIAA.
[27] Rock-driven, synthesizer-heavy ***Mistaken Identity***, produced by Val Garay and featuring musical guests Danny Kortchmar, Waddy Wachtel and Wendy Waldman, tops the US chart for the first of four weeks and reaches UK #26.
July [16] ***Mistaken Identity*** is certified platinum by the RIAA.
Sept *Draw Of The Cards* folds at US #28 and UK #49.
Nov *Mistaken Identity* reaches US #60.
Dec [18] Carnes and Tina Turner perform at Rod Stewart's Great Western Forum, Inglewood, CA concert, broadcast live to an estimated 35 million people.

1982

Feb [24] Having topped the charts in 21 territories, *Bette Davis Eyes* wins both the Record Of The Year and Song Of The Year categories, at the 24th annual Grammy Awards.
Aug *Voyeur* reaches US #29 (and UK #68 in October), while the Garay-produced parent set ***Voyeur*** peaks at US #49.

1983

Jan Carnes/Ellingson-penned *Does It Make You Remember* reaches US #36.
Nov *Invisible Hands* reaches US #40, as the Keith Olsen-produced ***Café Racers*** drives to US #97.

1984

Feb *You Make My Heart Beat Faster (And That's All That Matters)* peaks at US #54.
[28] ***Flashdance***, to which Carnes contributes *I'll Be Here Where The Heart Is*, wins Best Album Of Original Score Written For A Motion Picture Or A Television Special, at the 26th annual Grammy Awards.
June *I Pretend* reaches US #74.
Nov Richard Marx co-written ballad *What About Me?*, sung in a trio with Kenny Rogers and James Ingram, makes US #15.

1985

Jan A duet with Barbra Streisand, *Make No Mistake, He's Mine*, reaches US #51. (Co-written by Carnes, the song will become a 1987 US Country chart-topper for Ronnie Milsap and Kenny Rogers.) Meanwhile, the Nile Rodgers-produced Carnes solo single *Invitation To Dance*, featured in the film "That's

Dancing!", makes US #68. With *What About Me?* also still charting, Carnes becomes the only artist ever to hold simultaneous positions on the US chart as a soloist, in a duet and as one of a trio.
[28] Carnes joins 44 other artists at A&M's Hollywood studios to record *We Are The World* under the fundraising collective name USA For Africa.
June Self-penned *Crazy In The Night (Barking At Airplanes)* reaches US #15, taken from the Bill Cuomo co-produced ***Barking At Aeroplanes***, which lands at US #48.
Aug *Abadabadango* makes US #67.

1986

June [7] *Divided Hearts* makes US #79. Reuniting Cross with producer Val Garay and featuring long-time cohorts Craig Krampf and Waddy Wachtel, its parent album ***Light House*** shines at US #116.

1988

July Having lost ground in the pop/rock field and newly signed to MCA Records, the country-oriented ***View From The House***, produced by former label boss Jimmy Bowen, is released, featuring the Country chart extract *Speed Of The Sound Of Loneliness*, with Lyle Lovett on backing vocals.

1991

June [2] Having contributed *Everybody Needs Someone* to the 1990 film soundtrack to "Impulse", the CBS-TV series "Sunday Dinner", to which Carnes has contributed the title theme, premieres in the US.

1995

Jan [14] After working on the 1992 Michael Berger/Tim Rice musical "Tycoon", and recording ***Checkin' Out The Ghosts***, a new Joey Carbone-produced studio set for Japanese label Teichiku Records the same year, ***Gypsy Honeymoon***, a Carnes hit retrospective with three new tracks produced by Don Dixon, has been released by EMI America in February 1993. Still touring the US, notably as the opening act for Kenny Rogers, Carnes joins him tonight at the Star of the Desert Arena, Jean, NV, performing with the Nevada State Symphony at the venue's opening event.

MARY-CHAPIN CARPENTER

1987

July Carpenter (b. Feb. 21, 1958, Princeton, NJ), who as a child lived with her parents in Tokyo, Japan, has moved with them to Washington, DC in 1974 (where she will be permanently based, eschewing the Country capital of Nashville), before gradutating from Brown University with a degree in American Civilization. Beginning her music career as a folk singer playing in clubs and bars around Washington, Carpenter's burgeoning local reputation gains her first award, a Wammie for Best Live Performer in 1986. Entering the studio for the first time that same year to cut an album's worth of demo recordings with her guitarist friend, and future longterm producer, John Jennings, the results impress Columbia Records which signs her to the label and now releases (only in the US) her maiden album, the critically well-received ***Hometown Girl*** which will sell around 20,000 copies. Overseen by Jennings, its mostly self-written folk/country mix includes one of the first cover versions of Tom Waits' *Downtown Train*.

1990

Jan [20] Carpenter's sophomore set ***State Of The Heart***, mixing uptempo country rock with mood-filled ballads, makes US #183, its success in the Country field (including her US Country chart debut, *How Do*) earning her the accolade of the Academy of Country Music's Top New Female Artist at the end of the year.
Nov [3] Her third album, ***Shooting Straight In The Dark*** enters the US chart, its sales slowly buoyed by the success of the extracted cajun-based *Down At The Twist And Shout* (featuring top Cajun act, Beausoleil), which will become a US Country #2 smash the following summer.

1992

Feb [25] Carpenter collects the trophy for Best Country Vocal Performance, Female (for *Down At The Twist And Shout*) at the 34th annual Grammy Awards, held at New York, NY's Radio City Music Hall.
Mar [14] ***Shooting Straight In The Dark*** finally peaks at US #70.
July [1] She takes part in a fundraiser for the Hollywood Women's Political Committee, raising over $350,000, with Barbra Streisand, Chynna Phillips, Patti Austin, Vanessa Williams and Judy Collins.
Oct [24] ***Come On Come On***, including the Mark Knopfler-penned Country hit *The Bug*, reaches US #31 during a two-year plus chart tenure. (At year's end, Carpenter will be voted the Country Music Association's Female Vocalist Of The Year.)
Nov [14] Shawn Colvin's ***Fat City***, featuring Carpenter (her friend since 1988) as one of its guests, debuts at its US #142 peak.

1993

Jan [17] Carpenter performs *You Ain't Goin' Nowhere* with Rosanne Cash and Shawn Colvin at "The Bob Dylan 30th Anniversary Celebration" held at New York's Madison Square Garden.
Feb [24] *I Feel Lucky* (her US Country #4 hit the previous summer) is named Best Country Vocal Performance, Female at the 35th annual Grammy Awards, held at Los Angeles, CA's Shrine Auditorium.
Mar [27] *Passionate Kisses*, written by Lucinda Williams, makes US #57.
Nov [20] *He Thinks He'll Keep Her* charts for a week at UK #71.

1994

Mar [1] Having recently been once again voted the CMA's Female Vocalist Of The Year, Carpenter, for the third consecutive year, nabs the Best Country Vocal Performance, Female trophy (for *Passionate Kisses*) at the 36th annual Grammy Awards, staged at Radio City Music Hall.
[15] Her second album ***State Of The Heart*** is certified gold by the RIAA.
Oct [22] ***Stones In The Road***, produced as ever by Jennings and including guest musicians Lee Roy Parnell, Branford Marsalis and Paul Brady, debuts at its US #10 peak.
[29] ***Stones In The Road*** reaches UK #26, encouraged by a UK concert visit where Carpenter's cult following now sits alongside those earned by the likes of Lyle Lovett and Nanci Griffith.
Nov [5] *Shut Up And Kiss Me* peaks at US #90.
[10] Carpenter appears on NBC-TV's "The Tonight Show".
[19] *Shut Up And Kiss Me* becomes Carpenter's first US Country Singles chart-topper.
[21] Her current US tour reaches the Fox Theatre, Atlanta, GA, a bill grossing $102,245 from 4,402 fans.
Dec [6] Carpenter appears at BT's tenth Anniversary Concert at the London Arena, on a mixed bill with Kylie Minogue, East 17, Dave Stewart, Belinda Carlisle, the Kinks and others.
[10] She guests on BBC2-TV's "Later With Jools Holland".
[13] With ***Stones In The Road*** certified for one million US sales a week earlier, the RIAA also confirms platinum sales of ***Shooting Straight In The Dark*** and three million sales of ***Come On, Come On***.

1995

Jan [7] *One Cool Remove*, a duet with Colvin, debuts at its UK #40 peak.
[30] She is the music guest on CBS-TV's "Late Show With David Letterman". (During the month she also plays at a Governors' Ball at the White House in Washington.)
Mar [1] Carpenter performs at the 37th annual Grammy Awards held at the Shrine Auditorium and collects trophies for Best Female Country Performance (*Shut Up And Kiss Me*) and Best Country Album (***Stones In The Road***).
[23] Carpenter is named Best International Female Vocalist at the inaugural Great British Country Music Awards held in Birmingham, W. Midlands, though she is unable to attend, performing tonight at the Sioux City Convention Center Auditorium, IA, in front of 3,740 fans.
Apr [10] Carpenter and the McGarrigle sisters join Joan Baez in concert at New York's Bottom Line where the folk veteran is recording four nights for subsequent release as ***Ring Them Bells***.
May [5-6] A five-date UK tour is highlighted by two nights at London's Apollo Theatre.
[28] She headlines the "Songs For The Heartland" benefit concert at the Oklahoma Civic Center, raising money for families of victims in the recent Oklahoma City bomb disaster.
June [3] *Shut Up And Kiss Me* bows at its UK #35 peak.
July [26] Carpenter's PBS-TV special "In The Spotlight" airs in the US, including duet performances with Joan Baez and Colvin.
Sept [30] She records a duet version of *Wishing* with Kevin Montgomery (whose father Bob co-wrote the song) at the Javelina Studios, Nashville, TN, for inclusion in the forthcoming Buddy Holly tribute set ***notfadeaway***, due for release in January 1996. (During the month, and after twelve years under the wing of Studio One Artists Agency, Carpenter signs a new management deal with Borman Entertainment in Los Angeles.)
Oct [28] Her six-month US tour which began in March, broken only by selected European dates in May, finally ends at the Jack Breslin Student Events Center, Michigan State University, East Lansing, MI, as the John Lennon tribute album, ***Working Class Hero***, featuring Carpenter's version of *Grow Old With Me*, bows at its US #94 peak.
Dec [1] "Tony Bennett: Here's To The Ladies", including a duet by the host with Carpenter on *Honeysuckle Rose*, airs on CBS-TV.

1996

Jan [9] Columbia Records (US) releases the film soundtrack ***Dead Man Walking*** including a new cut by Carpenter written specifically for the project.

THE CARPENTERS

Karen Carpenter (vocals, drums);
Richard Carpenter (keyboards, vocals)

1963

Richard (b. Oct. 15, 1946, New Haven, CT), having relocated with the Carpenter family from New Haven to Downey, CA, a few months after his sister Karen's (b. Mar. 2, 1950, New Haven) 13th birthday, and performing with her at a Sunday-afternoon talent show in Furman Park, Downey, is asked by choir director Vance Hayes to play the organ at the Downey Methodist Church. During the next three years, Karen learns to play the drums under the guidance of Bill Douglass at Drum City in Hollywood, CA, while Richard meets Wes Jacobs at California State University, Long Beach, CA, and suggests they form a jazz trio with Karen. Frank Poole, choir director at Cal State, hears them and suggests they audition for top session bassist Joe Osborn, who has set up his own Magic Lamp label.

1966

May [13] Karen is signed to the company, which promptly releases 500 copies of *Looking For Love*, credited to her but featuring Richard and Jacobs, in June. The trio goes on to perform *The Girl From Ipanema* and *Iced Tea* at the County of Los Angeles Department of Parks and Recreation annual "Battle Of The Bands" contest at the Hollywood Bowl, where they are spotted by Neely Plumb, West Coast A&R

director of RCA, who signs them as the Richard Carpenter Trio in September. However, despite cutting 11 tracks with producer Rick Jarrard, they are soon dropped by the label.

1967

Jacobs quits the trio to study at the Juillard faculty in New York, NY, before moving on to play tuba with the Detroit Symphony Orchestra. Poole introduces new choir member John Bettis to Richard and the pair find employment at Disneyland, working the Coke Corner stand. They form the Summerchimes, comprising choir members themselves, Danny Woodhams, Gary Sims and Karen, who is still attending high school. Recording nine tracks at the United Audio Studios in Orange County in May, the group name changes to Spectrum, adding Leslie Johnston on vocals.

1968

Having played one-off gigs at the local Troubadour and Whisky A Go-Go clubs, and another opening for Steppenwolf at the Blue Law venue, Spectrum folds midway through the year, with Richard and Karen deciding to record all subsequent vocal parts on their own, producing demos at Joe Osborn's home, which are subsequently hawked by the duo's manager, Ed Sulzer. By year's end Karen and Richard win the preliminary rounds of the nationally-televised "Your All-American College Show" competition, representing Long Beach State.

1969

Apr [22] Having seen the duo performing on the broadcast, John and Tom Bahler of the group Going Thing, who are currently recording jingles for the Ford Motor Company, ask Karen and Richard to join their band. Linking with them and signing a deal with the J. Walter Thompson advertising agency, the duo's earlier demo tapes have come to the attention of A&M Records founder Herb Alpert, who now signs them to the label.
Nov Debut album ***Offering*** is released.

1970

Feb [26] At the request of songwriter Burt Bacharach, the duo opens a benefit performance for the Reiss-Davis Clinic, performing a medley of Bacharach/Hal David songs.
May [9] Their first single, a cover of the Beatles' *Ticket To Ride*, makes US #54.
July [25] *(They Long To Be) Close To You*, a little-known Bacharach/David composition recorded by Dionne Warwick seven years earlier, hits US #1.
Aug [12] *(They Long To Be) Close To You* is certified gold by the RIAA.
Sept ***Close To You***, featuring old friend Osborn and session drummer supreme Hal Blaine joining with Richard as the album's rhythm section, enters the US chart at the beginning of an 87-week chart run, which will climax at #2. The album further showcases the duo's easy-paced, effortlessly-harmonious melodic style which will become their popular trademark.
Oct [10] *(They Long To Be) Close To You* hits UK #6.
[31] Further ballad *We've Only Just Begun*, originally penned by Paul Williams and Roger Nichols for a Crocker Citizens Bank TV commercial, hits US #2.
Nov [13] *We've Only Just Begun* and ***Close To You*** are both confirmed gold by the RIAA.

1971

Feb [6] *We've Only Just Begun* makes UK #28, as ***Close To You*** is on its way to UK #23.
Mar [13] *For All We Know*, from the movie "Lovers And Other Strangers" hits US #3 (and will subsequently win an Oscar for Best Song Of The Year). Their debut album ***Offering***, retitled ***Ticket To Ride***, peaks at US #150.
[16] The duo wins the Best Contemporary Vocal Performance By A Group category for *Close To You* and Best New Artist Of 1970, at the 13th annual Grammy Awards.
Apr [12] *For All We Know* is certified gold by the RIAA.
June [5] ***Carpenters***, produced by Jack Daugherty, enters the US chart and will hit #2.
[7] ***Carpenters*** is certified gold by the RIAA.
[19] Paul Williams-penned extract *Rainy Days And Mondays* also hits US #2.
July Karen is appointed National Youth Chairman of the American Society.
[20] Having spent the first half of the year touring the world, the Carpenters launch their own NBC-TV series, "Make Your Own Kind Of Music". Featuring regulars Al Hirt and Mark Lindsay (ex-Paul Revere & the Raiders), it will run until September 7th.
[21] *Rainy Days And Mondays* is ratified gold by the RIAA.
Sept [24] The duo performs at the Royal Albert Hall, London.
Oct [16] *Superstar*, a Leon Russell/Bonnie Bramlett-penned song which Richard had seen Bette Midler perform on NBC-TV's "The Tonight Show", hits US #2.
[18] Still-climbing *Superstar* is certified gold by the RIAA.
Nov [13] *Superstar*, backed with *For All We Know*, reaches UK #18, as ***The Carpenters*** heads towards UK #12.

1972

Jan [1] *Merry Christmas Darling*, a Richard Carpenter tune penned to lyrics written some 20 years earlier by Frank Pooler, makes UK #45.
[15] *Bless The Beasts And Children*, from the film of the same name, and the B-side of *Superstar*, peaks at US #67.
Feb [26] *Hurting Each Other*, originally recorded by Ruby & the Romantics, hits US #2.
[29] *Hurting Each Other* is certified gold by the RIAA.
Mar [14] The Carpenters win the Best Pop Vocal Performance By A Group category for ***The Carpenters*** at the 14th annual Grammy Awards.
Apr ***Ticket To Ride*** reaches UK #20.
June [10] *It's Going To Take Some Time*, penned by Carole King, reaches US #12.
July Now settled into a familiar Daugherty-produced recording pattern wrapping the rhythm section of Richard, Osborn, Blaine (occasionally supplemented by Karen on drums) and guitarists Tony Peluso and Tim May around Karen's distinctive and angelic vocals, ***A Song For You*** enters the US chart, and will peak at #4.
[10] ***A Song For You*** is confirmed gold by the RIAA.
Aug [26] *Goodbye To Love*, featuring a distinctive fuzz-guitar solo by Peluso, hits US #7.
Sept The Carpenters tour the UK.
Nov [11] *Goodbye To Love*, released in the UK as a double A-side with *I Won't Last A Day Without You*, hits #9, while ***A Song For You*** reaches UK #13.

1973

Apr [21] *Sing*, written for "Sesame Street" by Joe Raposo, hits US #3.
May [17] *Sing* is certified gold by the RIAA.
June ***Now And Then***, highlighted by the oldies medley comprising *Fun Fun Fun*, *The End Of The World*, *Da Doo Ron Ron*, *Deadman's Curve*, *Johnny Angel*, *The Night Has A Thousand Eyes*, *Our Day Will Come* and *One Fine Day*, interspersed with Peluso's "DJ", hits #2 in both the US and the UK.
[7] ***Now And Then*** is certified gold by the RIAA.
July [28] Richard/Bettis-penned ballad *Yesterday Once More* also hits US #2.
Aug [13] The RIAA certifies *Yesterday Once More* gold.
[18] *Yesterday Once More* hits UK #2, behind Gary Glitter's *I'm The Leader Of The Gang (I Am)*.
Nov [10] Further Richard/Bettis-written song *Top Of The World* hits UK #5.
Dec [1] *Top Of The World* tops the US chart. ***The Singles 1969-1973***, featuring 12 hits, is released (and will eventually top both the US and UK surveys), becoming one of the most successful hit collections of the decade.
[11] *Top Of The World* is certified gold by the RIAA.

1974

Feb [19] The Carpenters win the Favorite Band, Duo Or Group category, at the inaugural American Music Awards, held at the Aquarius Theater, Hollywood, CA.
Mar [30] Cajun standard *Jambalaya (On The Bayou)*, backed with *Mr. Guder*, reaches UK #12.
May [1] The duo performs, at the request of President Nixon, at a White House state dinner honoring West German Chancellor Willy Brandt.
[25] *I Won't Last A Day Without You*, penned by Paul Williams and Roger Nichols, reaches US #11.
June [15] Reissued in the UK, *I Won't Last A Day Without You* makes #32.

1975

Jan [25] *Please Mr. Postman*, their cover of the Marvelettes 1961 chart-topper, hits US #1.
Feb [11] *Please Mr. Postman* is confirmed gold by the RIAA.
[15] *Please Mr. Postman* hits UK #2, behind Pilot's *January*.
May [17] Once again written by Richard and Bettis, *Only Yesterday* hits UK #7 and will peak at US #4 the following week.
June ***Horizon***, arranged and produced by Richard, reaches US #13, confirmed gold by the RIAA four days later.
July [5] ***Horizon*** tops the UK chart.
Aug Reissued ***Ticket To Ride*** makes UK #35.
Sept [20] *Solitaire*, inked by Neil Sedaka, reaches US #17 and UK #32.
Nov [1] Following five years of constant recording and touring, Karen, now weighing only 90lb, due to an extensive slimming program, is taken ill and takes two months off to recuperate, forcing the cancellation of a scheduled UK tour.
Dec [27] She sends Christmas greetings to her UK fans in the form of *Santa Claus Is Comin' To Town*, which makes UK #37.

1976

Apr [17] Their update of Herman's Hermits' 1967 smash, *There's A Kind Of Hush (All Over The World)* reaches UK #22 and peaks at US #12 the following week.
July [10] *I Need To Be In Love* makes UK #36.
[14] Still-climbing ***A Kind Of Hush*** is certified gold by the RIAA.
[24] *I Need To Be In Love* reaches US #25. The Richard-produced ***A Kind Of Hush*** makes US #33 and hits UK #3.
Sept [25] Originally a hit for Wayne King in 1931, the duo's treatment of *Goofus* peaks at US #56, breaking a run of 17 consecutive Top 30 hits.
Dec The Carpenters are presented with 21 gold discs while visiting London. They have to leave them behind at Heathrow Airport, however, because they are too heavy to take on as excess baggage.

1977

Jan Performance album ***Live At The Palladium*** reaches UK #28.
July [2] *All You Get From Love Is A Love Song* makes US #35.
Aug Richard Carpenter receives substantial, but undisclosed, damages in the UK High Court, for a **Daily Mail** article alleging that the duo could not write their own songs.
Oct ***Passage*** makes US #49, but reaches UK #12.
Nov [12] The extracted *Calling Occupants Of Interplanetary Craft (The Recognized Anthem Of World Contact Day)*, a cover of a song by Canadian band Klaatu, hits UK #9, and makes US #32 on the 26th.

1978

Feb [18] *Sweet Sweet Smile*, written by Juice Newton, makes UK #4 (and US #44 on Apr [15]).
Dec [23] *I Believe You* stalls at US #68. A second hit retrospective, ***The Singles 1974-78***, a UK-only release, hits #2, while the seasonal ***Christmas Portrait***

makes US #145. During the month, the duo performs at their alma mater with the Long Beach State Choir.

1979

Richard checks into the Menninger Clinic, Topeka, KS, for six weeks (he has been heavily reliant on quaaludes since taking them to help him sleep following their 1974 European tour), after which he decides to take a year off. Karen, in the meantime, embarks on a solo project in New York, with producer Phil Ramone. The album remains unfinished as she rejoins Richard to commence work on a new album, titled ***Made In America***.

Mar [12] The duo signs a new recording deal with A&M.

1980

Apr [26] The Carpenters' "Music, Music, Music" special airs on ABC-TV.

Aug [31] Karen, whose health problems are currently being treated by Dr. Steven Levenkorn in New York, marries real estate developer Thomas Burris at the Beverly Hills Netherlands Hilton Hotel. (They will divorce in 1983).

1981

Jan [16] ***Christmas Portrait*** is certified gold by the RIAA.

Aug [1] *Touch Me When We're Dancing*, previously a minor hit in 1979 for Muscle Shoals session band Bama, returns the duo to the US Top 20, reaching #16. ***Made In America*** makes US #52, but climbs to UK #12.

Oct [17] *(Want You) Back In My Life Again* peaks at US #72.

1982

Jan [16] *Those Good Old Dreams* makes US #63.

Apr Karen makes what will prove to be her final recording sessions.

May [8] *Beechwood 4-5789*, a remake of another Marvelettes smash, stalls at US #74. (It will be the duo's last US Hot 100 chart entry.)

Dec [17] Karen makes her last singing appearance, at Buckley School in Sherman Oaks, CA, a performance attended by her godchildren.

1983

Feb [4] Found unconscious at her parents' Downey home, Karen is rushed to the Downey Community Hospital where she dies, aged 32, of cardiac arrest at 9:51 a.m. The Los Angeles coroner gives the cause of death as "heartbeat irregularities brought on by chemical imbalances associated with anorexia nervosa".

June [25] Karen Carpenter is remembered in a tribute at the First Congregational Church of Long Beach.

Oct *Make Believe It's Your First Time* peaks at UK #60.

Nov ***Voice Of The Heart*** makes US #46 and UK #6.

1984

Oct ***Yesterday Once More***, a UK-only TV-advertised album, hits UK #10. (During the year, Richard marries Mary Rudolph at the Downey United Methodist Church. They will have two daughters - Kristi Lynn, born in 1987, and Traci Tatum, born in 1989.)

1985

Jan ***An Old-Fashioned Christmas*** spends a week on the US chart at #190.

June [26] Richard begins work on his self-produced solo debut ***Time***, to be released by A&M in October 1987. (He will sing lead vocals on the majority of the tracks, with Dusty Springfield guesting on *Something In Your Eyes* and Dionne Warwick helping on *In Love Alone*.)

1989

Jan [1] CBS-TV movie "The Karen Carpenter Story", with Cynthia Gibb in the title role, tops the US ratings.

1990

Jan [13] Reissued ***The Singles 1969-1973*** and ***The Singles 1974-1978*** re-chart in UK, reaching #24 and #42 respectively. ***Lovelines***, rounding up previously-unissued Carpenters material, also charts for a week at UK #73.

Apr [7] Confirming the enduring appeal of their radio friendly hits, a fresh TV-advertised compilation, ***Only Yesterday***, tops the UK chart, during a three-month stay in the Top 10.

Sept *For All We Know* and *We've Only Just Begun* are honored by the BMI as two of its "Most Performed Songs Between 1940-1990", having each logged more than three million performances.

Dec [29] Re-released *Close To You*, now paired with the festive *Merry Christmas Darling*, reaches UK #25.

1991

Sept [3] While the seasonal ***Christmas Portrait*** has returned to the US chart, making #159 on Jan [5], a comprehensive four-CD boxed-set career retrospective, ***From The Top***, comprising the duo's hits and previously-unreleased material, is released by A&M.

1992

Nov [19] The RIAA certifies four million sales of ***The Singles 1969-1973***.

1993

Feb [13] Re-released *Rainy Days And Mondays* bows at its UK #63 peak, as ***Only Yesterday*** re-charts, reaching UK #15 on Jan [16].

1994

Oct [1] The Karen & Richard Carpenter Performing Arts Center at Cal State University, Long Beach is opened.

[15] ***Interpretations*** reaches UK #29 in its week of entry, as ***If I Were A Carpenter***, a retro-hip tribute album featuring alternative updates of the duo's hit by the likes of Babes In Toyland, Sonic Youth, Shonen Knife, Cracker, Matthew Sweet, Sheryl Crow and Grant Lee Buffalo, is released.

Dec [24] *Tryin' To Get The Feeling Again* debuts at its UK #44 peak, during a two-week chart stay. A Richard Carpenter-compiled Japanese-only compilation ***22 Hits Of The Carpenters*** will be released in Japan on November 10th the following year (where the Carpenters remain enormously popular), reaching the one million sales plateau within three months of release.

THE CARS

Ric Ocasek (vocals, guitar); **Benjamin Orr** (vocals, bass guitar); **Elliot Easton** (guitar); **Greg Hawkes** (keyboards); **David Robinson** (drums)

1976

Dec [31] Having played guitar since the age of ten and dropped out of Bowling Green State University, Ocasek (b. Richard Otcasek, Mar. 23, 1949, Baltimore, MD) and "Upbeat" TV show house band teen-veteran Orr (b. Benjamin Orzechowski, Aug. 9, 1955, Cleveland, OH), who have been songwriting and performing partners for almost a decade in Cleveland, New York, NY, Woodstock, NY, and Ann Arbor, MI, and now resident in Cambridge, MA, have formed the Cars earlier in the year with Hawkes, who - in 1970 - played on album by Milkwood, a folk group fronted by Ocasek and Orr, Easton (b. Elliot Shapiro, Dec. 18, 1953, Brooklyn, New York), who - in 1974 - joined with Ocasek and Orr in Boston, MA-based combo, Cap'n Swing, and ex-Modern Lovers and DMZ drummer Robinson (b. Apr. 2, 1953). The group now makes its live debut at a New Year's Eve show at the Pease Air Force Base, Portsmouth, NH.

1977

Feb The Cars begin playing regularly at Boston club, the Rat, and are noted by Fred Lewis, who becomes their manager.

Mar Lewis arranges a spot opening Bob Seger's concert at Boston's Music Hall, while a demo tape of *Just What I Needed* becomes Boston's WCOZ and WBCN radio stations' #1 request. Supporting dates for the J. Geils Band, Foreigner and Nils Lofgren soon follow.

Nov Having been seen at Holy Cross College, Boston, they are signed to Elektra Records, which teams them with producer Roy Thomas Baker, set to begin recording their debut album in England in early '78.

1978

Sept [16] Their debut single *Just What I Needed* reaches US #27.

Nov The group undertakes a mini-tour of UK, Belgium, France and Germany.

[25] *My Best Friend's Girl*, the first picture-disc single commercially available in the UK, hits #3.

[30] The band plays to a 1,500 sellout crowd at London's Lyceum Ballroom during a UK visit.

Dec [23] *My Best Friend's Girl* makes US #35.

1979

Jan The Cars are voted Best New Band of the Year in **Rolling Stone**'s annual Readers' Poll.

Feb [15] A Taste Of Honey beats out the Cars, among others, to win the Best New Artist category at the 21st annual Grammy Awards.

Mar [24] Their debut album ***The Cars*** freewheels to US #18, 39 weeks after its chart debut. The rock/pop-art set will spend 139 weeks on chart, becoming a million-seller.

[31] *Just What I Needed* reaches UK #17.

Apr [14] ***The Cars*** reaches UK #29.

July [14] ***Candy-O***, its sleeve designed by legendary pin-up artist Alberto Vargas, reaches UK #30. Once again helmed by Baker, it is largely written by Ocasek, whose quirky lead vocal style, offset by the band's new-wave rhythm edge, has already established the Cars' trademark sound.

[28] *Let's Go* peaks at UK #51.

Aug The band plays to an audience of 500,000 in Central Park, New York.

[25] ***Candy-O*** hits US #3.

Sept [8] *Let's Go* reaches US #14.

Nov [24] Second sophomore album extract *It's All I Can Do* makes US #41.

1980

Sept [20] Retaining Baker's production skills, ***Panorama*** hits US #5.

Oct [15] ***Panorama*** is certified platinum by the RIAA.

[18] *Touch And Go* reaches US #37.

1981

The band buys the Intermedia Studio, Boston, relaunching it as Synchro Sound, not least to record future Cars albums. During the year, all of the group's members involve themselves with other ancillary projects - Ocasek produces Suicide, the New Models, the Peter Dayton Band, Bebe Buell and Romeo Void; Robinson helms singles for the Vinny Band and Boys Life, and Easton produces the Dawgs.

1982

Jan [9] ***Shake It Up***, recorded at Synchro Sound, hits US #9, while *Shake It Up* hits US #4 on Feb [27]. A further excerpt, *Since You're Gone*, makes US #41 on May [8] and UK #37 on June [12], the band's first UK chart success in three years.

[20] ***Shake It Up*** is certified platinum by the RIAA.

Sept [3-5] The Cars perform at the "US Festival", an event financed by Apple Computers founder Steven Wozniak, in San Bernardino, CA, to 400,000 people, along with Jackson Browne, Fleetwood Mac, the Grateful Dead, Eddie Money, Police, Santana, Talking Heads and many others.

1983

Mar The band's central creative force, Ocasek, releases his freshman solo album ***Beatitude*** on Geffen Records, which reaches US #28.

[19] The extracted *Something To Grab For* makes US #47. (Ocasek produces Bad Brains, while Easton will

oversee recordings for the Peter Bond Set and Jules Shear during the year.)

1984

Apr [28] *You Might Think* hits US #7. (Its computer-generated video will win first prize in the first "International Music Video Festival" in St. Tropez, France.) ***Heartbeat City***, co-produced by the band with Robert John "Mutt" Lange and once again principally written by Ocasek, hits US #3.
May [12] The Cars are the musical guests on NBC-TV's "Saturday Night Live".
July [7] *Magic* reaches US #12.
Sept [18] "You Might Think" wins the Video Of The Year category at the inaugural MTV Video Music Awards held at New York's Radio City Music Hall, hosted by Dan Aykroyd and Bette Midler.
[29] Synthesizer-steered ballad *Drive*, written by Ocasek but with a lead vocal by Orr, is the Cars' most successful single to date, hitting US #3 and eventually becoming a million-seller.
Oct [13] *Drive* hits UK #5, their first UK Top 10 success for six years, as ***Heartbeat City*** reaches UK #25.
Dec [22] *Hello Again* reaches US #20.

1985

Mar [30] *Why Can't I Have You?* makes US #33.
Apr [6] Easton's solo ***Change No Change*** makes US #99.
July [15] The RIAA certifies three million sales of ***Heartbeat City***.
Aug [31] Repromoted in the UK following its dramatic use during "Live Aid" (providing mood backing for African famine film footage), *Drive* re-charts and hits #4. Ocasek donates all subsequent *Drive* royalties to the Band Aid Trust.
Nov 13-track compilation ***The Cars' Greatest Hits*** reaches UK #27 and US #12.

1986

Jan [11] *Tonight She Comes* hits US #7, while *I'm Not The One* makes US #32 on Mar [22].
[16] ***The Cars Greatest Hits*** is certified platinum by the RIAA.
Nov [15] Ocasek's solo *Emotion In Motion* reaches US #15, as his sophomore effort ***This Side Of Paradise***, co-produced with both Chris Hughes and Ross Cullum, heads to US #31.

1987

Jan [24] Ocasek's *True To You* peaks at US #75.
Feb [14] Orr's *Stay The Night* reaches US #24, as his debut Elektra-released solo tryout ***The Lace***, co-produced with Larry Klein and Mike Shipley and featuring co-driver Easton, makes US #86.
Sept [5] The Cars return with the Ocasek-written and-produced ***Door To Door***, which opens at its UK #72 peak.
[11] The band performs at the fourth annual MTV Video Music Awards, held at the Universal Amphitheatre, Universal City, CA.
Oct [21] ***Door To Door*** is certified gold by the RIAA.
[24] The extracted *You Are The Girl* reaches US #17, as ***Door To Door*** closes at US #26.
Nov [21] *Strap Me In* is restricted to US #85.

1988

Feb [1] A press release confirms that, after six studio albums, the band is dissolving.
[13] The final Cars US chart single of the decade *Coming Up You* peaks at US #74.

1989

Jan Ocasek's son Christopher releases a solo album, before going on to form Glamour Camp.
Aug [23] Ocasek marries long-time belle, Czechoslovakian model Paulina Porizkova, on the Caribbean island of St. Bart's.

1990

Apr [22] Ocasek makes his first solo public appearance at the "Earth Day" festivities in Central Park, New York, on a bill with the B-52's, Hall & Oates and others.

1991

Aug [8] Newly signed to Warner Bros. Records and promoting his latest solo project, the Nile Rodgers co-produced ***Fireball Zone*** (a title coined by novelist Thomas Pynchon relating to the hottest spot in a war where rockets fall, with cover-work by Porizkova), Ocasek appears on the first night of a Billy Joel benefit concert at the Indian Field Ranch, Montauk, Long Island.

1993

Sept [21] Having produced an album for Black 47 in 1992, Ocasek's much-delayed fourth solo effort ***Quick Change World***, co-produced with Mike Shipley, is released by Warner Bros. (While Hawkes, Orr and Robinson have retreated from the music industry, Easton, hopeful for a Cars reunion ("We're going through a mending process right now"), continues performing with his Band Of Angels.)

1994

May The Cars, minus Orr, meet for a rehearsal.
Aug [27] Weezer's album ***Weezer***, produced by Ocasek, enters the US chart set to reach #16 and platinum certification.
Dec [18] Orr returns with a six-piece band at the Rat in Boston.

1995

Apr [5] The RIAA certifies multi-platinum sales for ***Candy-O*** (three million) and their debut set ***The Cars*** (six million).
Nov Two-CD ***The Cars Anthology - Just What I Needed***, with previously unreleased demos, B-sides and other rare cuts, is released in the US on Rhino Records. (A further Rhino-released anthology, ***Prototypes : Raw Hits And Rare Tracks***, will be issued in May 1996. Ocasek continues to live in New York producing, Orr lives in Vermont, working with his band simply called Orr, Easton lives in Los Angeles, CA, having worked with Brian Wilson and Andy Paley, Hawkes has recorded two CDs of synthesizer and sound effects, while Robinson remains musically inactive.)

JOHNNY CASH

1950

An avid country music fan since childhood, having written his first song at age 12, Cash (b. J. R. Cash, Feb. 26, 1932, Kingsland, AR, he will only be called John during his teen years), son of cotton farmer Ray Cash, raised on a Federal Government resettlement colony in Dyess, AR, joins the US air force after graduating from Dyess High School and working at a Pontiac, MI auto factory, and is stationed in Germany, where he learns to play guitar and write songs, and forms a group called the Landsberg Barbarians, with five other servicemen who also have backgrounds in country music. (Claiming, early in his career, that he has come from Cherokee Indian ancestry, Cash's roots are actually to be found in 17th-century Scotland.) In 1953, his first published song *Hey Porter* is printed in the service newspaper **Stars And Stripes**.

1954

July [3] He leaves the US Air Force and moves to Memphis, TN.
Aug Working around Memphis as an electrical appliance door-to-door salesman, and enrolled in a radio announcers' course part-time, Cash meets the Tennessee Three, a trio of part-time musicians who work as mechanics at the same garage as Cash's brother, Roy, and have played with him in the Delta Rhythm Ramblers. He begins to rehearse and play small local gigs with the combo, which comprises Marshall Grant (guitar), Luther Perkins (guitar) and Red Kernodle (steel guitar). Kernodle will soon leave.
[7] Cash marries Vivian Liberto, whom he met three weeks before entering the service and with whom he corresponded daily throughout his German posting.

1955

Encouraged by Elvis Presley's success at Sam Phillips' Sun Records, Cash, Grant and Perkins try to audition for Phillips as a gospel act. Phillips insists they can only succeed commercially singing country. Grant moves to bass, while Perkins switches from acoustic to electric guitar. Sun signs the trio, largely on the strength of Cash's voice and his songs *Hey Porter* and *Cry Cry Cry*. (Phillips names his new artist, now known as John Cash, Johnny Cash.)
May [24] Daughter Rosanne is born. (During the '80s, she will become a major country artist in her own right, having done back-up singing and solo spots in her father's stage show during the '70s.)
June [21] His first single *Hey Porter/Cry Cry Cry* is released.
Aug [5] Cash makes his first major live appearance since signing with Sun, at Memphis' Overton Park Shell on a bill with Elvis Presley.
Sept *Cry Cry Cry* hits #1 in Memphis, and the group supports Elvis Presley on local gigs and features in a 15-minute radio show on KWEM, Memphis (sponsored by Cash's employer).
Nov *Cry Cry Cry* makes the US Country chart at #14 for a week.
Dec Cash plays a guest slot on the "Louisiana Hayride" show in Shreveport, LA, (becoming a weekly regular the following month), and plays live gigs around the Mid-South with Carl Perkins, supporting Presley, George Jones and others.

1956

Jan Cash quits his day job to concentrate on performing.
Mar The double-sided *So Doggone Lonesome/Folsom Prison Blues* hits #5 on the Country survey. Bob Neal, Presley's ex-caretaker, becomes Cash's manager.
May *I Walk The Line* is released. Written by Cash and originally performed on "Louisiana Hayride" as a slow ballad, Phillips insists on speeding up the tempo, and it becomes Cash's first crossover success.
July [7] He appears on the "Grand Ole Opry" in Nashville, TN.
Nov [10] *I Walk The Line* reaches US #17, having lodged at #2 on the Country chart for several weeks.
Dec [4] Carl Perkins and his group are recording a session at Sun Studios, with Jerry Lee Lewis guesting on piano. Cash is also present, but his wife draws him away to go shopping. Presley, in Memphis for Christmas, arrives and the three of them settle down to an impromptu session, mostly singing gospel songs and recent hits.

1957

Jan *There You Go* hits #2 on the Country ranking. Cash is in demand for live appearances all over the US, having toured Florida, Colorado, California, and even Ontario, Canada.
[19] He appears on CBS-TV's "Jackie Gleason Show", having already been seen regularly on "The Jimmy Dean Show".
July [1] *Next In Line* makes US #99.
Sept Cash undergoes throat surgery in a Memphis hospital and is ordered not to sing for a month.
Oct [21] *Home Of The Blues* reaches US #88 and #5 on Country chart. ***Johnny Cash With His Hot & Blue Guitar***, the only album released by Sun while Cash is with the label (there will be six more after he leaves), is released.

1958

Mar [31] Pop-oriented *Ballad Of A Teenage Queen* reaches US #14 and tops the Country chart. Produced and written by Jack Clement, whom Phillips has paired with Cash to widen the singer's appeal to a teenage audience, the original trio recording has dubbed male and female back-up voices added to give the pop/rock feel.

June [30] *Come In Stranger*, B-side of *Guess Things Happen That Way*, peaks at US #66.
July [28] *Guess Things Happen That Way* reaches US #11 and also tops the Country survey.
Aug [1] Cash's Sun contract expires, and he and the Tennessee Two sign to CBS/Columbia Records. He ends his residency on the "Grand Ole Opry" and moves his family, band and manager Neal from Memphis to Los Angeles, CA.
Sept [15] *The Ways Of A Woman In Love*, penned by Charlie Rich and released by Sun upon Cash's departure, reaches US #24.
Nov [10] His first CBS/Columbia single, *All Over Again* makes US #38.
[24] B-side *What Do I Care?* peaks at US #52.
Dec [15] Sun single *I Just Thought You'd Like To Know*, B-side of *It's Just About Time*, climbs to US #85.

1959

Jan His debut CBS/Columbia album ***The Fabulous Johnny Cash*** is his first US Album chart entry, reaching #19.
[12] *It's Just About Time* makes US #47.
Feb [16] *Don't Take Your Guns To Town* reaches US #32.
June [1] *Frankie's Man Johnny* peaks at US #57.
Aug [10] *Katy Too* (on Sun) makes US #66.
Sept [21] Double A-sided *I Got Stripes* and *Five Feet High And Rising* reach US #43 and #76 respectively. The latter is themed on the 1937 flood evacuation of the Dyess Colony, where the Cash brood was then living, having been one of 600 families selected by the US government to reclaim swampland near the Mississippi River a year earlier.
Oct [4] "The Rebel", for which Cash supplies the weekly theme *The Ballad Of Johnny Yuma*, premieres on ABC-TV.
Dec [28] Seasonal *The Little Drummer Boy* peaks at US #63. (Cash recruits his own drummer boy, signing up W.S. Holland, who will remain with him for 30 years.)

1960

Jan [1] Cash plays the first of many free (and notable) jailhouse shows, in the San Quentin prison. Incarcerated country singer Merle Haggard is in the captive audience.
Mar [14] *Straight A's In Love* (on Sun) peaks at US #84.
July [25] *Second Honeymoon* climbs to US #79, while double A-side on Sun *Down The Street To 301/Honky-Tonk Girl* makes US #85/#92.

1961

Jan [9] *Oh Lonesome Me* climbs to US #93.
Constantly on the road, and beginning to rely heavily on drink and pills, Cash becomes estranged from his family, which by now includes four daughters. He spends time on the bohemian folk scene in New York, NY's Greenwich Village.
Dec [11] *Tennessee Flat-Top Box* makes US #84.

1962

Sept [15] *Bonanza!* climbs to US #94.

1963

Feb [9-18] Cash plays a series of dates at US Air Force bases in the UK, his first visit to the country since 1959.
May ***Blood, Sweat And Tears*** reaches US #80, his second chart album in almost five years.
July [27] *Ring Of Fire*, a brass-flavored Mexican/western arrangement, climbs to US #17. It is co-written by Merle Haggard and June Carter (b. June 24, 1929), an established country performer. Carter and Cash begin playing as a duo.
Sept ***Ring Of Fire - The Best Of Johnny Cash*** reaches US #26.
Nov [30] *The Matador*, styled similarly to *Ring Of Fire*, makes US #44.

1964

Mar [21] *Understand Your Man* makes US #35. Cash becomes an erratic and unreliable performer as he starts to overlook scheduled live dates.
Aug ***I Walk The Line***, featuring six newly-recorded versions of his old Sun hits, reaches US #53.
Nov [28] His version of Bob Dylan's *It Ain't Me Babe* peaks at US #58.
Dec ***Bitter Tears (Ballads Of The American Indian)***, a collection of Indian protest songs penned with Peter La Farge, makes US #47.

1965

Feb [11] ***Ring Of Fire*** is certified gold by the RIAA.
Mar [13] *Orange Blossom Special* peaks at US #80, while its parent ***Orange Blossom Special*** heads to a US #49 peak in April.
June [12] *It Ain't Me Babe* opens his UK chart account, reaching #28.
[17-20] Cash takes part in the first "New York Folk Festival" at Carnegie Hall, New York.
(By year's end, he is arrested for transporting amphetamines across the US/Mexican border as well being sued by the US Government for accidentally burning 508 acres of national forest while under the influence.)

1966

Mar [26] *The One On The Right Is On The Left*, a tongue-twisting novelty, makes US #46.
May [7] Cash begins a ten-date UK tour at the Empire Theatre, Liverpool, Lancs., with the Statler Brothers and June Carter, set to end on the 22nd at the Granada Cinema, Walthamstow, London.
July [9] *Everybody Loves A Nut* makes US #96, as parent set ***Everybody Loves A Nut*** peaks at US #88, set to reach UK #28 on the 23rd.

1967

Already a legendary substance abuser, and staying in a small town in Georgia, Cash is found near death, requiring urgent medical attention from a local policeman. Vivian divorces him.
July [14] ***I Walk The Line*** is certified gold by the RIAA.
Aug Compilation ***Johnny Cash's Greatest Hits, Volume 1*** reaches US #82 and will stay on chart for 71 weeks.

1968

Jan [27] *Rosanna's Going Wild* peaks at US #91.
Feb [29] Cash and Carter win Best C&W Performance Duet, Trio Or Group (Vocal or Instrumental) for *Jackson* at the tenth annual Grammy awards.
Mar Cash marries June Carter, having proposed to her on stage.
May [4] ***From Sea To Shining Sea*** makes UK #40. Cash starts a 13-date UK tour at the Free Trade Hall, Manchester, Lancs., set to end on the 19th at the Newcastle Odeon, Tyne & Wear.
July [6] A new version of *Folsom Prison Blues*, originally recorded in the mid-'50s for Sun, is issued to trailer ***Johnny Cash At Folsom Prison*** and climbs to US #32. ***Old Golden Throat*** makes UK #37.
Aug Live ***Johnny Cash At Folsom Prison***, a recording of a concert at the jail, is a major crossover success for Cash. It reaches US #13 (eventually spending 122 weeks on chart) and hits UK #8 (with a 53-week tenure). Cash will subsequently comment: Prisoners are the greatest audience that an entertainer can perform for. We bring them a ray of sunshine and they're not ashamed to show their appreciation."
Oct [21] Cash wins Best Album for ***Johnny Cash At Folsom Prison*** at the annual Country Music Awards.
[25] He embarks on a twice-nightly UK tour at the Odeon Cinema, Manchester, with Carl Perkins, the Statler Brothers, Carter and the Tennessee Three, set to end at the Birmingham Empire, W. Midlands, on November 3rd. (Cash turns down an opportunity to appear in the Rolling Stones' "Rock'n'Roll Circus" film documentary to be filmed in December.)

1969

Feb [17] Cash records in Nashville with Bob Dylan. *Girl From The North Country*, included on Dylan's ***Nashville Skyline*** (for which Cash writes the liner notes), is the only duet released from the session.
[22] *Daddy Sang Bass* makes US #42, written by Carl Perkins about the Cash family (and referencing "little brother" Jack Cash, who has died after falling onto an electric saw).
Mar [12] Cash wins Best Country Vocal Performance, Male for *Folsom Prison Blues* and Best Album Notes for ***Johnny Cash At Folsom Prison*** at the 11th annual Grammy Awards.
Apr ***Then Holy Land***, gospel music with a narration, reaches US #54.
June [7] Cash begins his own ABC-TV series, "The Johnny Cash Show", with regulars the Carter Family, the Statler Brothers, Carl Perkins and the Tennessee Three (Bob Wotton replaces Luther Perkins, who died in a house fire in 1968).
Aug [14] Still-climbing *A Boy Named Sue* is named gold by the RIAA.
[23] Live ***Johnny Cash At San Quentin***, the soundtrack to an ITV documentary of the same title, focusing on a Cash concert in the penitentiary, tops the US Album chart for the first of four weeks and is later a million-seller.
[23] The extracted *A Boy Named Sue*, a humorous tongue-in-cheek narrative song written by Shel Silverstein, hits US #2 and is also a million-seller.
Oct [18] *A Boy Named Sue* hits UK #4. ***Johnny Cash At San Quentin*** hits UK #2 (and will stay charted for 114 weeks).
Dec [6] Double A-side *Blistered/See Ruby Fall* makes US #50, as *Get Rhythm*, the original 1956 B-side of *I Walk The Line*, is reissued by Sun and peaks at US #60. ***Greatest Hits, Volume 1*** reaches UK #23 and will stay charted for six months.

1970

Jan [29] Still-climbing ***Hello, I'm Johnny Cash*** is certified gold by the RIAA.
Feb [28] His version of Tim Hardin's *If I Were A Carpenter*, duetted with Carter, makes US #36 as *Rock Island Line* on Sun peaks at US #93.
Mar ***Hello, I'm Johnny Cash*** hits both US and UK #6.
[11] *A Boy Named Sue* wins Best Country Vocal Performance, Male and Best Country Song (for its writer, Shel Silverstein), while Cash's annotation for Dylan's ***Nashville Skyline*** wins Best Album Notes at the 12th annual Grammy Awards.
Apr [17] Cash performs at the White House at the invitation of President Nixon. (The Commander-in-Chief supposedly makes a special request for *Okie From Muskogee* and *Welfare Cadillac*, but Cash respectfully declines and sings *A Boy Named Sue* instead.)
May He wins four awards at the inaugural UK Country Music Award ceremony held at London's Royal Lancaster Hotel.
[23] *What Is Truth?* reaches US #19.
June [27] *What Is Truth?* reaches UK #21.
July ***The World Of Johnny Cash*** climbs to US #54 and hits UK #5.
Oct [3] *Sunday Morning Coming Down*, penned by Kris Kristofferson, makes US #46.
Dec ***The Johnny Cash Show*** reaches UK #18.

1971

Jan [9] *Flesh And Blood*, from the ***I Walk The Line*** movie soundtrack album, makes US #54.
Mar [16] Cash and Carter win the Best Country Performance By A Duo Or Group category for *If I Were A Carpenter* at the 13th annual Grammy Awards.
Apr [3] *The Man In Black*, an archetypal Cash narrative song, peaks at US #58.
May "The Johnny Cash Show" airs for the last time on ABC-TV. The Cashes travel to Israel to film "Gospel Road", about Christianity and modern-day life in the Holy Land.
June [10] *Kate* peaks at US #75.
Aug ***Man In Black***, including a duet with evangelist Billy Graham, makes US #56 and will reach UK #18 the following month. "The Man In Black" will become Clash's nomenclature.
[17] He performs the first of three UK concerts, at the Belle Vue, Manchester.
Nov Documentary "In The Footsteps Of Jesus" airs

on US TV. ***The Johnny Cash Collection (His Greatest Hits, Volume II)*** reaches US #94, as ***Johnny Cash*** makes UK #43.
Dec [23] ***The World Of Johnny Cash*** is certified gold by the RIAA.

1972

After appearing with Kirk Douglas in the western "A Gunfight", Cash will guest-star on NBC-TV's "Columbo" opposite Ida Lupino, among half-a-dozen guest acting roles.
May *A Thing Called Love*, with the Evangel Temple Choir, hits UK #4, while ***A Thing Called Love*** reaches US #112 and UK #8.
Oct Compilation ***Star Portrait*** makes UK #16, while ***Johnny Cash: America (A 200-Year Salute In Story And Song)*** climbs to US #176.

1973

Mar ***Any Old Wind That Blows*** peaks at US #188. Cash joins evangelist Graham on stage and sings a duet with Cliff Richard at Wembley Stadium, Wembley, Middx.

1976

May [29] Novelty song *One Piece At A Time* reaches US #29.
July [24] *One Piece At A Time* makes UK #32, as parent album ***One Piece At A Time*** makes US #185, his final solo US pop chart entry.
Aug Cash starts a new four-week summer series, "The Johnny Cash Show", on CBS-TV, originating from the "Grand Ole Opry" in Nashville, featuring country music guest stars.
[14] ***One Piece At A Time*** makes UK #49.
Oct [9] Compilation ***The Best Of Johnny Cash*** makes UK #48.

1977

Jan [31] Cash is honored with the Special Award Of Merit at the fourth annual American Music Awards, held at the Civic Auditorium, Santa Monica, CA.
Oct [25] ***The Johnny Cash Portrait/His Greatest Hits, Volume 2*** is certified gold by the RIAA.

1978

Sept [2] ***Itchy Feet - 20 Foot-tapping Greats***, Cash's final mainstream chart album, reaches UK #36.

1979

Mar Cash performs at the Wembley Conference Centre, Wembley, with the Tennessee Five, the Carter Family and the Tennessee Trumpets, during his latest UK tour.

1980

Oct [13] Cash is inducted into the Country Music Association Hall of Fame.

1981

Apr [23] Carl Perkins and Jerry Lee Lewis, in Germany appearing in different music festivals, join Cash on stage in Stuttgart. Their performance is recorded and later released as ***The Survivors***.

1985

Sept [28] Known collectively as the Highwaymen, Cash has teamed with Waylon Jennings, Willie Nelson and Kris Kristofferson on ***The Highwayman***, which tops the US Country chart and makes US #92. (The extracted title track *The Highwayman*, penned by Jimmy Webb and recorded in the previous decade by its writer, topped the US Country singles ranking on August 17th.)

1986

Jan [27] As a Highwayman, Cash wins the Favorite Video, Duo Or Group, Country and Favorite Video Single, Country categories at the 13th annual American Music Awards, held at the Shrine Auditorium, Los Angeles.
Feb [25] *The Highwayman* wins the Best Country Song category at the 28th annual Grammy Awards.
July Cash joins Jerry Lee Lewis, Carl Perkins and Roy Orbison for ***Class Of '55 (Memphis Rock & Roll Homecoming)*** which makes US #87.
Nov [21] The RIAA certifies two million sales each of ***Johnny Cash At Folsom Prison***, ***Johnny Cash At San Quentin*** and ***Johnny Cash's Greatest Hits***.

1987

Feb [24] ***Interviews From The Class Of '55 Recording Sessions*** wins the Best Spoken Word Or Non-Musical Recording category at the 29th annual Grammy Awards.
Mar ***1958-1986: The CBS Years*** anthologizing a selection of hits is released.
May Cash debuts for Mercury with ***Johnny Cash Is Coming To Town***, including the subsequent live favorite *The Night Hank Williams Came To Town*.

1988

Dec [17] ***Water From The Wells Of Home***, featuring a cast including Paul McCartney, the Everly Brothers, Waylon Jennings, Emmylou Harris, Hank Williams Jr., daughter Rosanne Cash (who has recently topped the US Country chart with a version of her father's '60s composition *Tennessee Flat Top Box*), and son John Carter Cash, is released, featuring *That Old Wheel*, a duet with Hank Williams Jr. ***Classic Cash***, featuring re-recordings of several of his best-known hits, is released.
[19] Cash is admitted into a Nashville hospital for double bypass open-heart surgery.
UK label Red Rhino releases ***'Til Things Are Brighter***, a various artists tribute of Cash material to benefit AIDS research, featuring Michelle Shocked, Brendan Croker, the Mekons and others.
(During the year the Country Music Foundation in Nashville organizes an exhibition to commemorate Cash's career.)

1989

Mar *Ballad Of A Teenage Queen*, recorded with daughter Rosanne and the Everly Brothers, and its parent ***Boom Chicka Boom*** make further US Country chart inroads, as Cash is bestowed with the Aggie Award, the highest honor awarded by the Songwriters Guild of America.

1990

Oct [18] Cash, who is once again featured as one of the Highwaymen on ***Highwaymen 2***, begins a five-date UK tour, at the Liverpool Empire, set to end on the 23rd at the Bournemouth International Centre.
Nov [21] He sings *A Love Song To America*, written by Sgt. Jeffrey Grantham (serving with the 831st Supply Squadron in the Persian Gulf), on the TNN network's "Nashville Now".
Dec [5] Cash is honored by NARAS as a Grammy Living Legend.

1991

Mar [27] Cash, on a promotional visit to the UK, performs two songs on TV-AM's "Good Morning Britain", as his new album ***The Mystery Of Life*** is issued via his ongoing record deal with Mercury.
Oct [2] Cash takes part in the "25th Annual Country Music Awards", which airs on CBS-TV.
Nov [20] He begins another short UK tour at the Plymouth Pavilions, Plymouth, Devon.

1992

Jan [15] He is inducted into the Rock and Roll Hall of Fame, at the seventh annual dinner, held at New York's Waldorf Astoria Hotel.
[22] Cash places a note in the Western Wall of the old city of Jerusalem (superstition dictates that God reads notes left in its cracks).
Apr [10] The Highwaymen embark on a six-date UK tour, at the Wembley Arena, set to end on the 29th at the City Hall, Sheffield, S. Yorks.
Aug Cash participates in the third annual "Back To The Ranch" concert, in Montauk, Long Island, NY, with Paul Simon, Waylon Jennings, Kris Kristofferson and Willie Nelson.
Oct [16] He performs *It Ain't Me Babe* with June Carter, at the Bob Dylan 30th anniversary celebration at New York's Madison Square Garden.
[26] "Hats Off To Minnie - America Honors Minnie Pearl", to which Cash contributes, airs on the TNN network.
Dec [19] Cash completes a three-month US tour at the Keswick Theater, Glenside, PA.

1993

Jan [16] Having made ongoing cameo appearances in a string of US TV movies, including "Murder In Coweta County" (with Andy Griffith), "The Baron And The Kid" (inspired by his 1981 hit "The Baron"), "The Last Days Of Frank & Jesse" and "The Pride Of Jesse Hallam", he now guest stars on CBS-TV's Jane Seymour-led "Dr Quinn, Medicine Woman".
Mar [5-6] Cash performs at the Trump Castle, Atlantic City, NJ, during current US dates.
May [22] He guests on CBS-TV's "Willie Nelson The Big Six-O" birthday celebrations.
June In an odd-ball move, Cash signs a deal with the traditionally rap/metal label Def American, and begins work on a new album with producer Rick Rubin.

1994

Feb [13] Cash embarks on a tour of New Zealand and Australia in Christchurch, New Zealand.
May [21] Rubin-helmed, critically revered ***American Recordings*** makes US #110.
July [9] Cash appears on BBC2-TV's "Later With Jools Holland".
Aug [27] UK-only retrospective ***The Man In Black - Definitive Collection*** debuts at its UK #15 peak.
Sept [12] ***Red Hot + Country***, including Cash's interpretation of Neil Young's *Forever Young*, is released.
Nov [19] Cash leaves Branson, MO, cutting short an engagement at the Shenandoah South Theatre, saying "I have no plans to come back at all. I don't think I'm doing myself or my fans a favor by being here."

1995

Jan [26] Cash is named Best Country Artist and Comeback Of The Year in the **Rolling Stone** 1995 Critics' Picks.
Feb [16] ***The Johnny Cash Portrait*** is certified platinum and ***The Johnny Cash Show*** gold by the RIAA.
Mar [1] ***American Recordings*** wins Best Contemporary Folk Album at the 37th annual Grammy Awards held at Los Angeles' Shrine Auditorium.
[3] Cash leaves the stage during a show at London's Royal Albert Hall, suffering from a bad reaction to facial surgery, before cancelling the rest of his 12-date UK tour. He flies to California to a pain management clinic.
[23] Cash is named All-Time Favorite Artist at the inaugural Great British Country Music Awards held in Birmingham, W. Midlands.
May [1] The Highwaymen guest on CBS-TV's "Late Show With David Letterman", before embarking on a US tour the following month.
Aug [3] Cash performs at the Westbury Music Fair, Westbury, NY, with June Carter and the Carter Family, John Carter Cash and Kris Kristofferson.
Sept [2] He sings *Folsom Prison Blues* and, with John Mellencamp, *Ring Of Fire* at the Concert for the Rock and Roll Hall of Fame at Cleveland Stadium, Cleveland, OH.

1996

Jan [9] ***Dead Man Walking*** soundtrack, with a Cash track written specifically for the movie, is released (US). Cash will begin recording his next album, again with Rubin as producer, in February in Los Angeles, backed by members of Tom Petty's Heartbreakers and the recently disbanded folk-rock combo, the Jayhawks.

DAVID CASSIDY

1970

Sept [25] Having made his stage debut in the chorus of a 1960 summer stock production of "The Pyjama Game" and worked with the Los Angeles Theater Company in "And So To Bed", during his senior year at Rexford High School in 1967, Cassidy (b. Apr. 12, 1950, New York, NY), son of actor Jack Cassidy and stepson of actress Shirley Jones, subsequently moved to New York, taking an $80-per-week job in the mailroom of a textile firm, while auditioning and taking acting classes at night. Going on to play Dorothy Loudon's son in "The Fig Leaves Are Falling" during its five-day run in 1968, a CBS Films scout flew him to Los Angeles, CA for a screen test. Failing to interest CBS, he was nevertheless signed by a Universal talent agent who secured him small but regular TV drama roles in "Adam 12", "Bonanza" "The FBI", "Ironside", "Marcus Welby MD" and "The Mod Squad", which led to his being casted as Keith Partridge in the "The Partridge Family", which now premieres on ABC-TV. The Partridge Family, comprising Shirley (Shirley Jones), Keith (Cassidy), Laurie (Susan Dey), Danny (Danny Bonaduce), Christopher (Jeremy Gelbwaks) and Tracy (Suzanne Crough), is loosely based on real-life family singing group, the Cowsills.

Oct Signed to Bell Records, the Partridge Family chart-debuts in the US with the Tony Romeo-penned *I Think I Love You*, with Cassidy the featured lead singer, backed by top Los Angeles, CA, session singers Ron Hicklin, Jackie Ward, Tom and John Bahler and musicians Tommy Tedesco, Larry Knechtel, Larry Carlton and Hal Blaine. ***The Partridge Family Album***, produced by Wes Farrell, is issued, and hits US #4. (As with the Archies, Farrell will recruit top writing talent, including Neil Sedaka, Barry Mann and Cynthia Weil, and Tommy Boyce and Bobby Hart.)

Nov [21] *I Think I Love You* tops the US chart for the first of three weeks, ultimately selling over one million copies.

1971

Mar [27] *Doesn't Somebody Want To Be Wanted* hits US #6, and will become another million-seller. With the TV show not yet broadcast in the UK, *I Think I Love You* still reaches #18. ***The Partridge Family Up To Date*** is released, on its way to hit US #3.

June [12] *I'll Meet You Halfway* hits US #9.

Sept [25] *I Woke Up In Love This Morning* reaches US #13. Third album ***The Partridge Family Sound Magazine*** hits US #9.

Dec [25] Having signed a solo deal with Bell, *Cherish*, Cassidy's first US release and a revival of the Association's chart-topper, hits US #9, already certified gold by the RIAA on the 16th.

1972

Jan [8] Family album ***Up To Date*** makes UK #46.

[22] Family single *It's One Of Those Nights (Yes Love)* reaches US #20.

Mar As "The Partridge Family" reaches UK TV, *It's One Of Those Nights (Yes Love)* boosts the Family's chart fortunes, peaking at UK #11.

Apr [1] Cassidy's second solo single *Could It Be Forever* peaks at US #37.

[22] ***The Partridge Family Shopping Bag*** enters the UK chart, where it will climb to #14. In the US, it reaches US #18.

[29] Partridge Family's *Am I Losing You* peaks at US #59.

May Cassidy is launched as a solo act in the UK with *Could It Be Forever*, using *Cherish* as its B-side, and hits UK #2, while its parent album ***Cherish*** reaches US #15.

[11] He is featured bare-chested on the cover of **Rolling Stone**.

June Solo album ***Cherish*** hits UK #2.

[30] ***Cherish*** is certified gold by the RIAA.

July [1] Cassidy's solo revival of the Young Rascals' *How Can I Be Sure* reaches US #25.

Aug [19] The Partridge Family's revival of Sedaka's *Breaking Up Is Hard To Do* hits UK #3 at the height of the TV show's UK popularity, and makes US #28.

Sept [30] *How Can I Be Sure* tops the chart for the first of two weeks in the UK where constant media coverage confirms his status as a major teen idol.

Oct [14] R&B-flavored solo *Rock Me Baby*, a deliberate attempt to harden his teeny-bop musical image, makes US #38, his last solo US hit single for 18 years. Meanwhile, ***Greatest Hits*** by the Partridge Family reaches US #21.

Dec *Rock Me Baby* climbs to UK #11.

[9] Seasonal ***Christmas Card*** makes UK #45, and is the Partridge Family's final charting album in the UK.

1973

Jan [27] The Family's update of Gene Pitney's *Looking Through The Eyes Of Love* makes US #39 and will hit UK #9.

The Wes Farrell-produced solo ***Rock Me Baby*** hits UK #2, after peaking at US #41.

Mar [17-18] Cassidy performs four shows in two days at the Empire Pool, Wembley, Middx., during a UK tour.

[21] BBC-TV bans teenybopper acts appearing live on "Top Of The Pops", after a riot following Cassidy's performance.

Apr Cassidy from now on concentrates his solo recording career in the UK, where his fan following is strongest. The Tony Romeo-penned ballad *I Am A Clown*, backed with *Some Kind Of A Summer*, hits UK #3.

[21] The Partridge Family's US chart swan song is *Friend And Lover*, at #99.

June The final Partridge Family UK hit, reviving the Ronettes' *Walking In The Rain*, hits #10.

Oct [27] Double A-side *Daydreamer/The Puppy Song* tops the UK chart, boosted by Cassidy's arrival at Heathrow Airport, lip-synching to the song as he walks down the plane's steps captured live on TV.

Dec [15] ***Dreams Are Nothin' More Than Wishes***, a US non-charter, is Cassidy's most successful UK solo album, topping the survey for one week. (Produced by Rick Jarrard, the album features songs by Nilsson, Michael McDonald and Kim Carnes, who, with husband Dave Ellingson, is a member of Cassidy's live band.)

1974

Feb [19] Cassidy co-hosts the inaugural American Music Awards with Michael Jackson, at the Aquarius Theater, Hollywood, CA.

May [26] Tragedy occurs during a UK concert at the White City Stadium, London, when, in the frenzied crowd, over 1,000 fans have to be treated by attendant ambulance workers. Six girls are taken to hospital, and 14-year-old Bernadette Whelan dies four days later from heart failure. Cassidy admits he is shaken by the tragedy and feels some responsibility.

June [1] *If I Didn't Care* hits UK #9.

Aug [10] His revival of Lennon/McCartney's *Please Please Me* ("The Beatles wrote the soundtrack to my youth" is Cassidy's most notable quote of the time) climbs to UK #16. Solo ***Cassidy Live*** hits UK #9.

[31] "The Partridge Family" airs for the last time.

1975

Feb He signs a worldwide solo recording contract with RCA Records, which will bring no US chart success, but will bear fruit internationally.

Aug [9] His first RCA single *I Write The Songs*, penned by Beach Boy Bruce Johnston and backed with *Get It Up For Love*, reaches UK #11, as parent album ***The Higher They Climb***, with help from members of the Beach Boys, the Turtles and America, peaks at UK #22, his final Album-chart action of the decade. (Two further Cassidy sets, ***Home Is Where The Heart Is*** and ***Gettin' It In The Street*** will be released by RCA.)

Nov [22] A revival of the Beach Boys' *Darlin'* reaches UK #16.

1978

Nov [2] Cassidy returns to US TV-series work (he has guest-starred on "The Love Boat" and "Fantasy Island"), starring as policeman Dan Shay in NBC-TV's "David Cassidy - Man Undercover". (The show will air until August 2nd, 1979.)

(During the year Cassidy stars in a production of John Van Druten's "Voice Of The Turtle" at West Point, NY, with his wife, actress Kay Lenz. They will perform the play again the following year, at the Westport County Playhouse, CT. He is nominated for Best Actor in a Television Drama for his role in a "Police Story" episode, "A Chance To Live".)

1981

May He stars in a West Coast run of George M. Cohan's musical "Little Johnny Jones". (When the show reaches Broadway, Donny Osmond takes over the role.) Cassidy will go on to replace Andy Gibb in Tim Rice and Andrew Lloyd Webber's Broadway version of "Joseph And His Amazing Technicolor Dream Coat" between May and September 1983, and will complete a road tour of "Jesus Christ Superstar" the following year, before retreating with his new wife, Meryl Tanz (he and Lenz divorced in 1981) to his Santa Barbara, CA home to breed horses.

1985

Mar [16] Newly signed to MLM/Arista Records, and teamed with producer Alan Tarney, Cassidy's comeback single *The Last Kiss*, with vocal help from George Michael, hits UK #6.

June [8] *Romance (Let Your Heart Go)* peaks at UK #54.

[15] Its parent set ***Romance*** reaches UK #20.

1986

Nov UK label Starblend releases ***David Cassidy - His Greatest Hits Live***, recorded at a London's Royal Albert Hall concert in October 1985.

1987

He takes over the role of The Rock Star from Cliff Richard in the West End production of Dave Clark's musical "Time", at London's Dominion Theatre. On his return to the US, Cassidy makes the feature film "Instant Karma".

1988

June [21] Cassidy is named in a Los Angeles paternity suit. (During the year he will cut demos for MCA Records which fail to secure a further comeback contract.)

1989

Apr [12] DJs Mark Thompson and Brian Phelps, the morning drive team at Los Angeles station KLOS, are wondering out loud what has happened to Cassidy, on his 39th birthday, their curiosity instantly gratified by Cassidy, who calls to tell them. They invite him to the studio and he sings three new songs on the air. Cassidy subsequently hears from three interested record companies, one of which, Enigma, signs him.

1990

Sept [15] Asia's ***Then And Now***, featuring the Cassidy/John Wetton-penned *Prayin' For A Miracle*, makes US #114.

Oct [11] Cassidy makes his first-ever live TV appearance, on syndicated TV's "The Arsenio Hall Show".

Nov [17] Confounding pop historians, his second recording comeback, *Lyin' To Myself*, reaches US #27, as its parent album ***David Cassidy*** makes US #136.

1991

Feb [8] Cassidy and his wife, songwriter Sue Schrifin, become parents to a son, Beau Devlin.

[10] Cassidy joins with nearly 100 celebrities in Burbank, CA, to record *Voices That Care*, a David Foster and fiancée Linda Thompson Jenner-composed and-organized charity record to benefit the American

Red Cross Gulf Crisis Fund.
Mar "Spirit Of '76", in which Cassidy plays a time traveler destined for 1776, but instead returning to 1976 and the disco boom, is released in cinemas throughout the US.
Sept [7] Cassidy is named Most Unwelcome Comeback in the annual **Rolling Stone** Readers' Picks music awards.
[14] Cassidy embarks on his first US tour in 15 years, bowing in Hersheypark, PA, with ex-Partridge Family brother Danny Bonaduce opening. (When Nickelodeon cable channel broadcasts "The Partridge Family", Cassidy, Bonaduce and Shirley Jones will actively promote the re-runs.)

1994

Sept [7] NBC-TV's "The John Larroquette Show", for which Cassidy has penned the theme, premieres. (Cassidy will also host a retro-video '70s show for US cable network VH1 the following year.)

CAST

John Power (lead vocals, guitar); **Liam Tyson** (guitar); **Peter Wilkinson** (bass); **Keith O'Neil** (drums)

1994

Aug Following the breakup of the much-lauded La's in 1991 (a Byrds/R.E.M.-influenced pop quintet which has scored an international hit with *There She Goes* in 1990, taken from its only album ***The La's***), the group's bassist John Power (b. Sept. 14, 1967) has formed Cast, a Liverpool, Merseyside-based quartet with a similar music brief to the La's, switching himself to lead guitar and lead vocals. Linking with managers Robert Swerdlow and Dave Nicoll, the band's demo tape has been hawked around UK record labels. Polydor Records' director of A&R UK, Paul Adam, who has first seen the group open for Shed Seven at London's Venue in New Cross earlier in the year (having attended the gig to see the latter combo), signs the band to Polydor worldwide after seeing it now perform at the Princess Charlotte Club in Leicester, Leics.

1995

July [15] *Finetime* debuts at its UK #17 peak.
Sept [30] *Alright* reaches UK #13 in its week of entry.

1996

Jan [20] *Sandstorm* hits UK #8 again in its first week.
Feb [10] Cast's debut album ***All Change***, produced by John Leckie and featuring the three hit singles, hits UK #8. (The 12-track album is entirely written by Power and benefits from glowing support from Oasis' Noel Gallagher.)
Mar [30] Following a three-month European tour, the band performs its first US gig at the 91X-sponsored Radiohead show in San Diego, CA.
Apr [2] ***All Change*** is released by A&M in the US. Its first US extract, *Alright* is also featured on forthcoming Winona Ryder-starring film soundtrack to "Boys" (on A&M Records).
[22] Following its debut shows in Japan, Cast begins a US club tour.

NICK CAVE

1980

Oct Raised in rural Warracknabeal in Victoria, Australia, Cave (b. Nicholas Edward Cave, Sept. 22, 1957, Wangaratta, Australia), the son of a librarian mother and English Literature teacher father, has sung in his local church choir before attending boarding school and forming his first band, Boys Next Door in 1977 with friend and multi-instrumentalist Mick Harvey (b. Sept. 29, 1958, Rochester, Australia), bassist Tracy Pew and drummer Phil Calvert in Caulfield, Melbourne, Australia, with ex-Young Charlatans guitarist Rowland S. Howard (b. Oct. 24, 1959, Melbourne) joining the following year. Releasing its first single, a cover of Nancy Sinatra's *These Boots Are Made For Walking* in May 1978, the band has signed to the native Mushroom label the following year, issuing the pop-based, Cave-lyricized ***Door Door*** album in May, preceding its second and final set, the mini-album ***Hee Haw***, released by the indie Missing Link Records in December 1979. With all five members relocating to London earlier this year, they have changed their name to Birthday Party and determined on a raw aggressive, post-punk direction, led by Cave's distinctively ranting vocal style and dark, goth-housed, provocative lyrics. A slot on BBC Radio 1's John Peel Show" earns the band a deal with the alternative UK indie label 4AD Records which now releases the Birthday Party's freshman album ***The Birthday Party***.

1982

July Following the release of the critically praised ***Prayers On Fire*** in May the previous year, and a UK tour which has seen Pew, detained for drug-possession, replaced by ex-Magazine bassist Barry Adamson (b. June 1, 1958, Manchester, Lancs.), the group has also cut a one-off album, ***The Tuff Monks*** under the same moniker as part of an ad-hoc outfit with members of the Go-Betweens, released in Australia only in February on the Au Go Go label. The Birthday Party's final album, ***Junkyard*** now peaks at UK #73. With Calvert leaving to join the Psychedelic Furs in October (and Harvey switching to drums), the group will release the four-track EP *Bad Seed* in February the following year (providing Cave with the new name of his backing unit, the Bad Seeds, which takes root in Berlin, West Germany by March 1993) and its last hurrah, *Mutiny EP* in October. With Howard leaving to form Crime & the City Solution, Cave, backed by Harvey, Adamson, and Einstürzende Neubauten guitarist Blexa Bargeld (b. Jan. 12, 1959, Berlin), is signed to another UK indie label, Mute Records.

1984

May [21] Nick Cave & the Bad Seeds perform at Berlin's The Loft club.
June Including the preview single, their cover of Elvis Presley's 1969 US #3 and UK #2 hit *In The Ghetto*, Nick Cave & the Bad Seeds' ***From Her To Eternity*** reaches UK #40. Ex-Die Haut drummer Thomas Wylder (b. Oct. 9, 1959, Zurich, Switzerland) becomes the Bad Seed's skins-man. During the year, Cave's collaboration with Lydia Lunch, ***Honeymoon In Red*** is released.

1985

June [15] The Presley-obsessing ***The First Born Is Dead***, lyrically led, as always, by Cave, spends a week at UK #53.

1986

Aug [30] Including unique versions of Glen Campbell's *By The Time I Get To Phoenix* and Jimi Hendrix' *Hey Joe* among others, the covers album ***Kicking Against The Pricks*** spends one week at UK #89, and includes the UK Independent Chart #1 extract *The Singer*.
Nov Having gone on to play with the Saints, ex-Birthday Party member Pew dies from an epileptic fit at the age of 28.
Dec The double EP, ***Your Funeral...My Trial*** is released.

1988

Oct [1] With Roland Wolf having replaced Adamson and ex-Cramps guitarist Kid Congo Powers (b. Brian Tristan, Mar. 27, 1961, La Puente, CA) recruited as the latest Bad Seed, the self-produced ***Tender Prey*** spends a week at UK #67. During the year, Cave's first book, **King Ink**, a collection of poems and lyrics, is published by Black Spring, while Cave & the Bad Seeds contribute three cuts to the film soundtrack ***Gas Food Lodging***.

1989

Mar With Cave having already appeared in his 1987 film "Wings Of Desire", Wim Wender's latest movie, "Ghosts Of The Civil Dead", also featuring Cave (as a prison inmate) and the band, now premieres, accompanied by its soundtrack written by Cave, Harvey and Bargeld. During the year, Black Spring issues Cave's second book, the novel **And The Ass Saw The Angel**, while he enters a detox facility to rid himself of a long-held addiction to heroin and subsequently relocates to Sao Paulo, Brazil where he meets his future wife Viviane.

1990

Apr [28] Recorded in Brazil with the Bad Seeds, Cave's first album of the decade, the stripped down, mostly acoustic-based ***The Good Son***, also featuring a strings section, charts for a week at UK #47. (As with all his albums, the set is released in the US by Elektra Records, though none will chart.)

1991

Nov [26] A Leonard Cohen tribute album, ***I'm Your Fan***, to which Cave and the Bad Seeds have contributed their cover of *Tower Of Song*, is released. During the year, Cave's acting ambitions see him paired with Brad Pitt in "Johnny Suede", while he also contributes *(I'll Love You) Till The End Of Time* to Wenders' latest project, "Until The End Of The World".

1992

Apr [11] With Powers exiting for Conway Savage (b. July 27, 1960, Foster, Australia) and Wolf replaced by ex-Triffid, Martyn P. Casey (b. July 10, 1960, Chesterfield, Derbys.) *Straight To You/Jack The Ripper* charts for a week at UK #68.
May Its parent album, ***Henry's Dream***, produced by David Briggs, reaches UK #29.
Dec [12] A duet cover of Louis Armstrong's *What A Wonderful World* by Cave and Shane MacGowan spends a week at UK #72.

1993

July The film soundtrack album to Wenders' "Faraway, So Close", featuring two Cave & the Bad Seeds cuts, is released.
Sept [18] The performance set, ***Live Seeds*** spends a week at UK #67.

1994

Apr [9] *Do You Love Me* charts for a week at UK #68.
[30] Co-produced by Cave, the band and Tony Cohen, its parent album ***Let Love In*** climbs to UK #12.
Aug [25] This year's Lollapalooza caravan tour, including Cave &The Bad Seeds on the bill, reaches the Aztec Bowl, San Diego University, CA.

1995

Oct [14] *Where The Wild Roses Grow*, an unlikely Antipodean duet with Kylie Minogue, debuts at its UK #11 peak. Of the collaboration, Cave says: "I've always wanted to write Kylie a song, to have her sing something sad and slow."

1996

Feb [17] Drawing the strongest notices of his career, ***Murder Ballads***, a typically dark set devoted to homicide and featuring guests PJ Harvey, MacGowan and Kylie Minogue and co-produced by Cave, the Seeds, Cohen and Victor Van Vugt, peaks at UK #8 in its week of entry.
Mar [9] The extracted *Henry Lee*, with Harvey, spends a week at UK #36.

CHAD & JEREMY

Chad Stuart (vocals, guitar);
Jeremy Clyde (vocals, guitar)

1964

July Stuart (b. Dec. 10, 1941, UK) and Clyde (b. Mar. 22, 1941, UK, who claims to be related to the Duke of Wellington) have met at the Central School of Drama in London. Both guitar players, the pair formed an acoustic folk-pop duo in 1963, and began writing together, with Stuart underscoring Clyde's lyrics. After signing to UK independent label Ember Records and appearing on ITV's "Ready Steady Go!", Chad & Jeremy have already secured their only UK chart success *Yesterday's Gone*, a #37 title in December 1963, and, amidst the euphoria for British acts following the Beatles' success in the US, *Yesterday's Gone*, licensed by World Artists Records, now climbs to US #21.

Oct *A Summer Song* hits US #7, after failing to score in the UK. (When previewed on BBC-TV's "Juke Box Jury", it had been voted a miss, but panellist Ringo Starr predicted that, "it will do well in the States".) Chad & Jeremy move to Hollywood, realizing that their best chance of enduring success may lie in the US. The duo embarks on the "Memphis Special" tour with Johnny Rivers.

Nov Their debut album ***Yesterday's Gone***, including both hits, reaches US #22.

Dec They record a guest spot (as the Redcoats pop singers) for CBS-TV's "Dick Van Dyke Show".

1965

Jan Their update of the standard *Willow, Weep For Me* makes US #15, after further well-received appearances on US TV shows like "Hullabaloo".

Mar [1] Recommended by William Morris talent agency employee Jerry Brandt to sign with manager Allen Klein, they secure a deal with CBS/Columbia Records and begin recording with label staffer Lor Crane at the label's New York studio.

Apr ***Chad & Jeremy Sing For You*** reaches US #69, while the extracted *If I Loved You*, revived from the musical "Carousel", makes US #23.

[23] Close to splitting, after a period of constant touring in 1964, the duo cancels a one-nighter US tour with Gene Pitney, when Stuart is stricken with glandular fever.

May *What Do You Want With Me* peaks at US #51.

June *Before And After*, written by Van McCoy, makes US #17.

[1] The duo begins a four-week US tour.

July Their version of Lennon/McCartney's *From A Window*, issued by World Artists, peaks at US #97, while Billy J. Kramer's version makes US #23.

Aug Columbia follow-up, *I Don't Wanna Lose You Baby*, another Van McCoy tune, reaches US #35, as their debut Columbia album ***Before And After*** makes #37.

[24] Clyde opens in the musical "Passion Flower Hotel" at London's Prince of Wales Theatre.

Sept [25] BBC1-TV broadcasts "The Dick Van Dyke Show", filmed the previous December.

Nov Their update of the ballad standard *I Have Dreamed*, from the musical "The King And I", makes US #91.

Dec *I Don't Wanna Lose You Baby*, a third Van McCoy composition, reaches US #77.

1966

Jan The duo reaches the final of the "San Remo Song Festival".

Apr [3] The movie "The Great St. Trinian's Train Robbery", in which Clyde has a cameo role, goes on general release in the UK.

May ***The Best Of Chad & Jeremy*** and ***More Chad & Jeremy***, compiling their early Ember/World Artists tracks, are issued in the US on Capitol, and chart at US #49 and #144 respectively. *Distant Shores*, written by James William Guercio, who will become the duo's manager before moving onto greater success with the Buckinghams, Chicago and Blood Sweat & Tears, also makes US #30.

June [25] They perform at the "The Beach Boys Summer Spectacular", on a bill with the Byrds, the Lovin' Spoonful and others, in Anaheim, CA.

Oct ***Distant Shores***, produced by Larry Marks, climbs to US #61 while the self-penned extract *You Are She* makes #87, their final US singles chart entry.

Dec Chad & Jeremy appear in an episode of "Batman", in which Catwoman steals their voices and threatens to use her voice-eraser machine, unless her demands of $22.5 million for their return are met.

1967

Nov Critically-praised ***Of Cabbages And Kings***, which makes US #186, is a five-movement piece scored and arranged by Stuart, and produced by Gary Usher. Following the release of ***The Ark*** in 1968 and their work on the ***Three In The Attic*** movie soundtrack the following year, Chad & Jeremy will announce a permanent split. Stuart will move to Sun Valley, ID, to compose music, while Clyde will immerse himself in acting, his most prominent early stage role taken in "Conduct Unbecoming" in London's West End. He will continue to be seen in UK TV roles throughout the next three decades. The duo will reunite for ***Chad Stewart & Jeremy Clyde***, released on the Rocshire label in 1983, and will participate in occasional nostalgia package tours towards the end of the decade, not least in the "British Invasion" oldies trek of the US in 1986.

THE CHAMBERS BROTHERS

George Chambers (bass, vocals); **Willie Chambers** (guitar, vocals); **Lester Chambers** (harmonica, vocals); **Joe Chambers** (guitar, vocals); **Brian Keenan** (drums)

1954

The Chambers family moves from Mississippi to Los Angeles, CA, where George Chambers (b. Sept. 26, 1931, Flora, MS), home after a tour of US army duty in Korea, organizes brothers Willie (b. Mar. 3, 1938, Flora), Lester (b. Apr. 13, 1940, Flora), and Joe (b. Aug. 24, 1942, Scott County, MS), who have already sung together at their local Mount Calvary Baptist Church in Lee County, MS as teenagers, into a gospel group (which in its early days also includes Major (b. Mar 19, 1927, Flora). Although George will sing professionally, they will play almost exclusively to church congregations for several years. Also becoming members of the Interdenominational Singers Alliance, the brothers will cut two gospel sides, *I Trust In God* and *Just A Little More Faith* for Randy Strickland's Proverb label by deacade's end.

1961

George meets Ed Pearl, owner of Los Angeles' famous Ash Grove coffee house and, after an audition, they make their club debut at the venue. Inevitably, the Chambers are influenced by the coffee house folk scene, and begin to add folk numbers to their gospel set.

1965

July Now favorites in the folk field, they get a wild reception at the "Newport Folk Festival", Newport, RI. They are beginning to add pop and blues songs to their repertoire, with Lester being taught harmonica by blues legend Sonny Terry, and the rest of the band picking up rock guitar styles.

Aug Having signed to Vault Records in Los Angeles (after ABC shareholders have allegedly been reluctant to sign a black act to the label), they record ***People Get Ready***, a set of rough soul-blues, highlighted by the title track and *Your Old Lady*.

1966

The Chambers Brothers Now is issued, for which the brothers have brought in ex-Manfred Mann drummer Keenan (b. Jan. 28, 1944, New York, NY), who has played in London groups from age 17, after being sent to school in the UK, returning to New York on his 20th birthday.

1967

Apr [28-29] The band performs at the Avalon Ballroom, San Francisco, on a bill with Iron Butterfly.

Dec Newly signed to CBS/Columbia Records, their label debut ***The Time Has Come*** is issued in the US. Picking up rock and "progressive" FM airplay, it will eventually hit US #4, earning a gold disc by December 1968.

1968

Jan [11-13] The group performs at San Francisco's Fillmore West.

Now selling out clubs and auditoriums around the country, they play in a network-TV showcase for new performers, and are invited back. Their cross-cultural influences and "black hippie" image make them highly popular with the new white counter-culture.

June [18-23] They share the bill with the Quicksilver Messenger Service at the Fillmore West.

July [5] They appear at the Hollywood Bowl with Steppenwolf and bill-toppers, the Doors.

Aug [4-5] The group plays at the "Newport Pop Festival" in Costa Mesa, CA, alongside the Byrds, Jefferson Airplane, Steppenwolf and many others.

Sept *The Time Has Come Today*, from ***The Time Has Come***, reaches US #11.

[6-11] They make another appearance at the Fillmore West, this time with Eric Burdon & the Animals.

Dec ***A New Time - A New Day*** climbs to US #16, while their extracted revival of Otis Redding's *I Can't Turn You Loose* makes #37.

[4] ***The Time Has Come*** is certified gold by the RIAA.

1969

Jan Vault Records issues one of its older tracks, the group's update of the Isley Brothers' *Shout*, which reaches US #83.

Feb [2] The group guests on CBS-TV's "The Smothers Brothers Comedy Hour".

July *Wake Up*, used on the soundtrack of the movie "The April Fools", makes US #92.

1970

Feb ***Love, Peace And Happiness***, a double set, of which one record has been recorded live at New York's Fillmore East, peaks at US #58. Title track *Love, Peace And Happiness* is their last US chart single, making a brief showing at #96.

Aug [28] The group begins its second tour of Europe.

Dec A double album of material recorded between 1965-66 ***The Chambers Brothers' Greatest Hits***, released by Vault, peaks at US #193.

1971

Mar ***New Generation*** reaches US #145.

Dec Columbia issues its own version of ***The Chambers Brothers' Greatest Hits***, which makes US #166.

1972

Mar The group has temporarily broken up by the time the album ***Oh My God!*** is released, and drummer Keenan joins Genya Ravan's band. Reforming in 1974 to record ***Unbonded*** for Avco Records, they will release ***Right Move*** the following year, before dissolving once more.

1989

Nov Having occasionally reunited for ad-hoc recording projects and tours, the Chambers Brothers (now comprising George, Joe and Willie - Keenan has recently died from a heart attack and Lester runs a music production company in Orlando, FL) participate in an "Earthquake Relief" benefit concert alongside John Fogerty, Bonnie Raitt, Neil Young, Los Lobos and others, staged in recently quake-blasted San Francisco, CA.

THE CHAMPS

Chuck Rio (tenor saxophone); **Dave Burgess** (rhythm guitar); **Buddy Bruce** (lead guitar); **Cliff Hils** (bass); **Gene Alden** (drums)

1957

Dec [26] Burgess (b. Lancaster, CA), an A&R employee at Challenge Records in Los Angeles, CA, deciding his own instrumental *Train To Nowhere* has hit potential, has recorded it while working at Gold Star Studios with a group, for singer Jerry Wallace. A flip-side cut is needed, and Rio (b. Daniel Flores, Rankin, TX) suggests his Latin-flavored *Tequila*, written while on a trip to Tijuana. The resulting disc is released on Gene Autry's Challenge label, under the moniker the Champs, a name which Burgess has shortened from the name of Autry's horse, Champion.

1958

Jan US radio DJs dismiss the A-side, preferring to take a shot of *Tequila*.
Mar [17] *Tequila* tops the US chart for the first of five weeks, having hit #1 only two weeks after entering. It passes one million sales in the US and is also a US R&B chart-topper for four weeks.
Apr *Tequila* hits UK #5, while back home, the Champs must tour to capitalize on the record's success. Hils and Bruce do not want to work live and are replaced by Dave Norris (b. Springfield, MA) on guitar and Joe Burness on bass.
June The follow-up *El Rancho Rock* climbs to US #30. Burness leaves and Van Norman takes his place.
Aug *Midnighter*, the B-side of *El Rancho Rock*, makes US #94. Flores and Alden leave, to make way for Jimmy Seals (b. Oct. 17, 1941, Sidney, TX) on sax and Dash Crofts (b. Aug. 14, 1940, Cisco, TX) on drums, while Dean Beard joins on piano.
Sept *Chariot Rock* climbs to US #59.

1959

May [4] *Tequila* wins the Best R&B Performance Of 1958 category at the inaugural Grammy Awards presentation.

1960

Feb Confounding rumors that the Champs is a spent force, the group rearranges the original hit formula to come up with *Too Much Tequila*, making US #30. The group continues, with personnel interruptions: Beard leaves and is not replaced; Norman dies in a car crash, his place being taken by Bobby Morris (b. Tulsa, OK); and Burgess, deciding that playing live is keeping him from his work at Challenge, brings in session guitarist Glen Campbell (b. Apr. 22, 1936, Delight, AR) to replace him.
Mar *Too Much Tequila* reaches UK #49.

1962

Feb The group adapts its original hit to cash in on the current huge Twist dance craze with *Tequila Twist*, but it stalls at US #99.
July Radio DJs once again flip the A-side *Tequila Twist* and play the catchy B-side Latin dance number *Limbo Rock*, which climbs to US #40. (When revived with added lyrics by Chubby Checker a few months later, it will hit US #1 and spur a hot new Limbo dance craze.)
Oct The band's own *Limbo Dance* makes US #97.

1965

After several more switches in the line-up and further singles releases, Burgess decides to fold the band. (None of the original members will have distinguished hit careers elsewhere, but Glen Campbell becomes a country/pop superstar, and Seals and Crofts form a soft-rock duo which will have a string of US Top 20 hits in the '70s.)

1988

While *Tequila* has made a brief return to the limelight when featured in the 1987 Pee Wee Herman movie "Pee Wee's Big Adventure", Flores trademarks the group's name and forms a new Champs with Alden, to embark on the oldies club circuit. (Curb Records (US) will bring the group's hits to compact disc with the 1994 release of ***Greatest Hits - Tequila***.)

GENE CHANDLER

1961

Nov After two years of US army service in W. Germany, Chandler (b. Eugene Dixon, July 6, 1937, Chicago, IL), who had led the Gaytones vocal group at Englewood High School, rejoined R&B vocal quintet the Dukays (originally formed in 1957) in Chicago in 1959. Signed to Nat Records, they made US #64 with *The Girl's A Devil* in July 1961. Its intended follow-up, the catchy *Duke Of Earl*, is sold by Nat to Vee-Jay Records, which already owns the publishing, where A&R man Calvin Carter is convinced it will be a hit. Vee-Jay signs him as a soloist but he remains a member of the Dukays for Nat. At the suggestion of another A&R executive Carl Davis, he also becomes Gene Chandler, taking the name from his favorite actor, Jeff Chandler.

1962

Feb [17] While *Nite Owl*, the official Dukays follow-up, reaches US #73, *Duke Of Earl*, credited to Gene Chandler, tops the US chart for the first of three weeks, becoming a million-seller. Chandler begins performing as "The Duke Of Earl", appearing on stage in a top hat, cape and monocle. He also has a cameo role in the movie "Don't Knock The Twist".
Apr ***The Duke Of Earl*** and single *Walk On With The Duke*, both credited to "The Duke", peak at US #69 and #91 respectively, but he soon reverts to the name Gene Chandler.
Dec *You Threw A Lucky Punch* (an "answer" disc to Mary Wells' US hit *You Beat Me To The Punch*) reaches US #49.
May *Rainbow*, B-side of *Lucky Punch*, climbs to US #47.
Sept *Man's Temptation* reaches US #71, Chandler's final hit for Vee-Jay.

1964

May Having moved to Ewart Abner's newly-formed Constellation Records, his label debut *Soul Hootenanny (Pt.1)* peaks at US #92, followed by a rush of US chart singles: *Just Be True* makes US #19 in August and, *Bless Our Love* reaches US #39 in November, while 1965 will see *What Now* peak at US #40 in January, *You Can't Hurt Me No More* climb to US #92 in March, *Nothing Can Stop Me* make US #18 in June and *Good Times* rise to US #92 by August.

1966

Jan ***Gene Chandler - Live On Stage In '65*** makes US #124, as the extracted *Rainbow '65* (a live treatment of his 1962 hit) peaks at US #69.
Mar *(I'm Just A) Fool For You* charts at US #88 and Chandler leaves Constellation.

1967

Jan *I Fooled You This Time*, recorded for Checker in Chicago, makes US #45, but Chandler signs a long-term deal with Brunswick Records and three chart singles follow: *Girl Don't Care* (US #66 in April), *To Be A Lover* (US #94 in June) and *There Goes The Lover* (US #98 in September).

1968

June *Nothing Can Stop Me*, reissued in the UK by the Soul City label, gives him a UK chart entry at #41.
Sept *There Was A Time* makes US #82.
Nov A duet with Barbara Acklin, *From The Teacher To The Preacher*, reaches US #57.

1969

Dec Chandler moves into label management with Bamboo Records, signing Mel & Tim, and producing their million-selling US #10 *Backfield In Motion*. He also launches the less prominent Mr. Chand Records, to showcase his own productions.

1970

Sept He recaptures his initial chart form with *Groovy Situation*, for Mercury, which reaches US #12.
Nov *Simply Call It Love* makes US #75, while ***The Gene Chandler Situation*** reaches only US #178.
[11] *Groovy Situation* becomes Chandler's second RIAA-certified gold single.

1971

Jan Chandler teams with Jerry Butler for *You Just Can't Win (By Making The Same Mistake)*, which peaks at US #94, his last chart single for eight years.
Apr The duetted ***Gene & Jerry - One & One*** reaches US #143.

1977

June Chandler is sentenced to one year's imprisonment in Chicago, after being found guilty of selling 400 grams of heroin to an undercover FBI agent. He will serve four months of the sentence.

1979

Jan Now a vice president of Chi-Sound Records, he records ***Get Down*** for the label, with producer Carl Davis. The album will spend nearly six months on the US chart, peaking at #47, while its title track *Get Down* reaches US #53.
Mar *Get Down* becomes a huge UK dance-floor hit, at UK #11.
Oct *When You're #1* stops 98 places short at US #99 and makes UK #43, while parent album ***When You're #1*** reaches US #153.

1980

July *Does She Have A Friend For Me* reaches UK #28.
Aug Eventually spending five months on the survey, ***Gene Chandler '80*** climbs to US #87. (Chandler will continue as an executive of Chi-Sound and does not give up recording, even when the hits cease. Albums such as ***Here's To Love*** (1981), ***I'll Make The Living (If You'll Make The Loving Worthwhile)*** (1982) and ***Live At The Regal*** (1986) will continue to keep his name alive in the US R&B market throughout the decade, during which he will also record for the 20th Century, Salsoul and Fastfire labels.)

THE CHANTAYS

Bob Spickard (guitar); **Brian Carman** (guitar); **Rob Marshall** (piano); **Warren Waters** (bass); **Bob Welch** (drums)

1961

Dec [15] While still at high school in Santa Ana, CA, Spickard and Waters have formed the group in September, inspired by the Rhythm Rockers, the most popular local surf band. While Spickard has learned electric guitar and Waters selected bass, they have recruited classmate Marshall, who plays classical piano, Carman, who tried saxophone but soon abandoned it for guitar, and Welch on drums. Spickard coined their name, based on the French verb "chanter" (to sing), although they planned to be an instrumental group. The combo now performs its first self-promoted live gig, at the Tustin Youth Center, Santa Ana. Playing with borrowed amplifiers, they make a $95 profit.

1962

July They are spotted by DJ Jack Sands while playing at Lake Arrowhead, CA. Impressed by their sound and audience popularity, he becomes their manager and arranges for them to record two Spickard/Carman compositions, *Move It* and *Pipeline*, at Pal Studios in Cucamonga, CA.
Sept Signed to Downey Records on the strength of its

demos, the group re-records *Move It* and *Pipeline* for commercial release.

1963

Jan After limited reaction to *Move It*, California DJs discover the unusual flip-side instrumental *Pipeline*. Originally titled *Liberty's Whip*, the tune has become the surfing term "pipeline", after Spickard and Carman became inspired watching a film about Hawaiian wave-riders.
Mar [2] With the record a big California hit, it has been picked up from Downey by the Dot label, for national distribution, and enters the US chart.
May [4] *Pipeline* hits US #4 and ***Pipeline*** reaches US #26.
June *Tragic Wind* fails to cross from early California sales to national success, while *Pipeline* rides to UK #15. (Beach Boy Bruce Johnston will revive *Pipeline* and make UK #33 in 1977).
Dec *Pipeline* receives the Record Of The Year award in Australia, where it has hit #1.

1964

July The group begins a three-month tour of Hawaii minus Welch, who has left for university in Europe, replaced on drums by Steve Khan. At the tour's end Waters also leaves for college and Carman begins working for Rickenbacker Guitars.

1965

Nov *Fear Of The Rain* is released on Reprise Records, with the group playing under the pseudonym the Ill Winds.
Dec Spickard is invited to take the group to Japan for three-week tour. With guitar-instrumentals hugely popular in Japan, *Pipeline* is revered as a classic. Most original members are unable to take time off from study or day jobs, so Spickard and Marshall invite drummer Tommy Hannigan and ex-the Rhythm Rockers guitarist, John Longstreth, to join the group for the trek, during which their manager Mark Howlett learns and plays bass. The Chantays receive superstar treatment and mass fan adoration, playing one gig to a 24,000 audience.

1966

July As the Ill Winds, the original line-up records *A Letter*, which has no chart success, and the Chantays split up. (The band members move into business careers in California, staying in touch with each other and staging a one-off live Chantays reunion in 1979. In 1980, Spickard will form a part-time group, the California Good Time Band, including Carman and Welch.)

HARRY CHAPIN

1971

June The son of a big band drummer and a member of the Brooklyn Heights Boys Choir, Chapin (b. Dec. 7, 1942, Greenwich Village, New York, NY), who has begun playing the trumpet at the age of seven and performed in a musical act with his brothers before attending college, has studied both architecture and philosophy at Cornell University, Ithaca, NY, following a period at the Air Force Academy. After six years making film documentaries (from 1965 and including the 1969 Oscar-nominated "Legendary Champions", made with Jim Jacobs), he advertises in the **Village Voice** for help in performing narrative songs he has written. He is joined by John Wallace (a Brooklyn, NY choirboy friend) on bass, Ron Palmer on acoustic guitar, and Tim Scott adding an unusual blend on cello.
[29] Having rehearsed for a week, the group debuts at the Village Gate, New York, supporting his brothers, the Chapins, and establishes a live reputation performing Chapin's literate "story songs".
Dec After interest from several record companies, Chapin signs a nine-album deal worth $600,000, plus a $40,000 advance, with Elektra Records and gets free studio time at the label's Los Angeles, CA studios.

1972

June His self-penned debut album ***Heads And Tales***, produced by Jac Holzman, makes US #60 during a six-month chart stay.
[3] Extracted *Taxi*, despite its near seven-minute length, reaches US #24.
Nov [18] *Sunday Morning Sunshine* peaks at US #75, as its parent album ***Sniper And Other Love Songs*** climbs to US #160.

1974

Mar [23] *W-O-L-D*, the story of a radio station DJ, reaches US #36, while Chapin's third album ***Short Stories*** makes US #61.
June [1] *W-O-L-D*, his only UK chart success, makes #34.
Dec Chapin dismantles his band as he starts work on a musical, "The Night That Made America Famous". He retains Wallace and Masters for the show, adding Doug Walker (electric guitar) and Howie Fields (drums), with brothers Tom, Steve and Jim.
[17] Still-climbing ***Verities And Balderdash*** is certified gold by the RIAA.
[21] *Cat's In The Cradle*, based on a poem by his wife about a neglectful father, tops the US chart. (The song will garner Chapin a Grammy nomination for Best Pop Vocal Performance, Male and provide a US #6 and UK #7 cover hit for thrash metal band Ugly Kid Joe in 1993.)
[31] *Cat's In The Cradle* is confirmed gold by the RIAA.

1975

Jan Boosted by its success, its parent album ***Verities And Balderdash*** hits US #4.
Feb [26] Chapin's musical revue, "The Night That Made America Famous", opens at the Ethel Barrymore Theatre on Broadway, New York. (The show will close on April 6th - after 75 performances - and will receive two Tony nominations.)
Mar [29] *I Wanna Learn A Love Song* makes US #44. Chapin wins an Emmy Award for his music for the ABC-TV children's series "Make A Wish", hosted by his brother Tom. He co-founds WHY (World Hunger Year), raising funds to combat international famine. It will receive over $350,000 from benefit concerts in its first year.
Nov [15] ***Portrait Gallery*** reaches US #53.

1976

May [29] Double live ***Greatest Stories - Live***, recorded in San Diego, Santa Monica and Berkeley during a major West Coast tour in 1975, makes US #48.
July [10] *Better Place To Be (Parts 1 & 2)* peaks at US #86. Increasingly active politically, he is a delegate at the Democratic Convention.
Sept CBS-TV airs "Ball Four", for which Chapin has written the theme.
[15] Chapin is honored for Outstanding Public Service at the third Annual Rock Music Awards show, during a year in which he is also honored with Broadcast Excellence from the International Radio Programming Forum for his Hungerthons, a Humanitarian Award from the Music & Performing Arts Lodge of B'nai B'rith, 1977 Man of the Year from both Junior Achievers of New York and the Long Island Advertising Club. He is also named one of the ten most outstanding young men in America by the US Jaycees.
Nov [20] ***On The Road To Kingdom Come*** reaches US #87.

1977

Apr Chapin performs at London's New Victoria Theatre during a brief UK visit.
Oct [8] Double album ***Dance Band On The Titanic***, produced by his brother Steve, reaches US #58.

1978

Feb [3] Chapin briefs President Jimmy Carter at the White House on the need for a Presidential Commission On Hunger.
June [2] Chapin performs at the Fairfield Halls, Croydon, Surrey, during his latest UK tour.
[7] ***Greatest Stories - Live*** is certified gold by the RIAA.
July [29] ***Living Room Suite*** reaches US #133.
Oct [15] He begins a three-date Irish tour in Dublin, also taking in concerts in Belfast and Cork.

1979

Nov The group's cellist Kim Scholes quits in mid-concert in Dallas, TX, replaced by Yvonne Cable, but stays with the group in an administrative capacity, however.
[10] Another double live album ***Legends Of The Lost And Found - New Greatest Stories Live*** reaches US #163.

1980

Oct Chapin is inducted into the Long Island Hall of Fame.
Dec Newly signed to Boardwalk Records, ***Sequel***, his only album for the label, peaks at US #58.
[13] The extracted six-minute title track *Sequel* (a sequel to *Taxi*) reaches US #23.

1981

Jan [9] Chapin plays his 200th performance, at New York's Bottom Line.
July [16] Scheduled to begin a summer tour with a benefit concert at the Lakeside Theater, Eisenhower Park, Long Island, New York, Chapin is killed on the Long Island Expressway near Jericho, New York, when a tractor-trailer runs into the back of his car while he is driving to a business meeting, rupturing the gas tank and causing the car to explode. The exact cause of death is unknown, but the autopsy reveals that Chapin has had a heart attack either before or after the crash. At a memorial service held in Brooklyn, the Harry Chapin Memorial Fund is announced, launched with a $10,000 donation from Elektra Records.
Aug [17] A benefit concert for the fund is held at the Nassau Veterans Memorial Coliseum, Uniondale, NY, headlined by Kenny Rogers. It is estimated that during his career Chapin has raised over $5 million from benefit for the causes to which he was committed.

1987

Dec [7] "The Gold Medal Celebration" memorial concert takes place on what would have been Chapin's 45th birthday, at Carnegie Hall, New York. Senator Patrick Leahy (D-Vermont), one of his strongest supporters, presents the Special Congressional Gold Medal to his widow, Sandy (an honor which has only been bestowed on 114 US citizens in more than 200 years, and given to only four other songwriters, George & Ira Gershwin, George M. Cohan and Irving Berlin). The show, hosted by Harry Belafonte, features contributions from the Hooters (*One Light In A Dark Valley*), Richie Havens (*W-O-L-D*), Judy Collins (*Cat's In The Cradle*), Pat Benatar (*Shooting Star*), Bruce Springsteen (*Remember When The Music*), Graham Nash (*Sandy*) and others. (A subsequent album, ***Tribute***, documenting the event, will emerge in 1990 on the Relativity label, while ***The Last Protest Singer***, an 11-track round-up of songs recorded just prior to his death, will be released by Sequel Records in 1989).

TRACY CHAPMAN

1986

Having started writing songs at the age of eight, Chapman (b. Mar. 30, 1964, Cleveland, OH) has graduated from Wooster School, Danbury, CT, before attending Tufts University, Medford, MA, where she has majored in anthropology and African studies. (During her sophomore year at Wooster, school chaplain the Reverend Robert Tate takes a collection to buy Chapman a new guitar - he will receive a thank-you credit on the liner notes of her debut album.)

1986

Chapman has joined an African drum ensemble at Tufts in 1985, before honing her solo folk guitar playing, performing self-written acoustic songs on the Boston folk circuit. She records demos at the university's campus radio station, WMFO, which leads fellow student Brian Koppelman to recommend her to his father, Charles, president of SBK Publishing, who in turn introduces her to producer David Kershenbaum and also to Elektra Records, where she links up with manager, Elliott Roberts.

1987

Mar Chapman visits London, performing three nights at the Donmar Warehouse, sharing a bill with Natalie Merchant from 10,000 Maniacs.

May She plays two nights at the Bitter End club in New York, NY.

(During the year, she records her debut album for Elektra with Kershenbaum producing, after several other producers turn down the project.)

1988

Apr Her maiden album ***Tracy Chapman*** is released immediately attracting critical favor and rapid commercial success, particularly in the UK, and sets the tone for subsequent releases, namely bare, self-penned folk-tinged songs wrapped in an instantly-recognisable tremoring vocal. Chapman tours the US and plays some selected UK dates supporting labelmates, 10,000 Maniacs.

June [11] She appears at the televised "Nelson Mandela's 70th Birthday Tribute" concert at Wembley Stadium, Wembley, Middx., and is called back after her initial slot, to fill in for Stevie Wonder, who is unable to go on after a computer program of his is stolen. Her appearance results in ***Tracy Chapman*** selling 12,000 copies two days later and introduces her talent to a global audience.

July [2] ***Tracy Chapman*** tops the UK chart, while the extracted *Fast Car*, drives to UK #5.

Aug [27] ***Tracy Chapman*** also tops the US survey, as *Fast Car* hits US #6.

Sept [2] Together with Peter Gabriel, Bruce Springsteen, Sting and Youssou N'Dour, Chapman performs at Wembley Stadium, Wembley, at the start of a six-week "Human Rights Now" world tour for Amnesty International. The superstar trek will end October 15th in Buenos Aires, Argentina.

Oct [10] *Talkin' 'Bout A Revolution* peaks at US #75.

Dec [24] *Baby Can I Hold You* makes US #48.

1989

Jan [30] Chapman wins the Favorite New Artist, Pop/Rock category at the 16th annual American Music Awards, held at the Shrine Auditorium, Los Angeles, CA.

Feb [13] Chapman is named Best International Artist, Female and Best International Newcomer at the eighth annual BRIT Awards at London's Royal Albert Hall.

[22] She wins the Best Pop Vocal Performance, Female for *Fast Car*, Best Contemporary Folk Recording for ***Tracy Chapman*** and Best New Artist categories, at the 31st annual Grammy Awards.

Mar [29] The RIAA certifies three million sales of ***Tracy Chapman***.

Apr [25] Chapman collects the Female Vocalist, Top Song (*Talkin 'Bout A Revolution*) and Rock Album (***Tracy Chapman***) trophies, at the third SKC Boston Music Awards, at the Wang Center, Boston, MA.

May She participates in an AIDS benefit concert at the Oakland-Alameda County Coliseum, Oakland, CA, with the Grateful Dead and John Fogerty.

Sept Previewing her second album, *Crossroads* peaks at UK #61.

Oct [14] Co-produced by Chapman and Kershenbaum and featuring musical guests Marc Cohn and Neil Young among others, her sophomore effort ***Crossroads*** tops the UK chart, but fails to repeat the multiplatinum status of her debut album.

Nov [4] *Crossroads* stalls at US #90, as ***Crossroads*** hits US #9.

[21] ***Crossroads*** is certified platinum by the RIAA.

1990

Mar [30] The three winners of "Crossroads In Black History", a high-school essay contest and education program initiated by Chapman, receive college scholarships.

Apr [16] Chapman performs at the "Nelson Mandela - An International Tribute For A Free South Africa" concert at Wembley Stadium, Wembley.

May [18] Chapman embarks on a major summer tour of the US at the Starplex Amphitheatre, Dallas, TX, set to end on July 7th.

June [21] She sings *Born To Fight* and *Freedom Now* at a rally for Nelson Mandela at New York's Yankee Stadium, before a sellout crowd of 53,000.

Nov [25] Chapman takes part in a CBS-TV "Motown 30 : What's Goin' On!" special.

1991

Jan [16] Chapman inducts the Impressions into the Rock and Roll Hall of Fame at its annual dinner at New York's Waldorf Astoria Hotel.

[21] She plays at a Martin Luther King celebration at the Guthrie Theatre, Minneapolis, MN.

Nov [3] She participates in the Bill Graham "Laughter Love & Music" memorial concert at San Francisco's Golden Gate Park Polo Field, before an estimated crowd of 350,000.

1992

Mar [14] Chapman performs at "Farm Aid V" at the Texas Stadium, Irving, TX, with Living Colour's Vernon Reid supporting her.

May [9] Co-produced by Chapman and Jimmy Iovine and featuring a host of talent including Bobby Womack, Living Colour's Vernon Reid and members of Tom Petty's Heartbreakers, ***Matters Of The Heart*** debuts at its UK #19 peak.

[21] "True Stories : Too White For Me", a behind-the-scenes look at a Chapman concert in Johannesburg, South Africa, airs on C4-TV.

[23] ***Matters Of The Heart*** makes US #53.

June [17] Chapman guests on NBC-TV's "The Tonight Show".

[28] She headlines the African National Congress 80th anniversary celebration, at London's Brixton Academy, during her current European tour.

Aug [7] She is showcased on ABC-TV's "In Concert" series.

Sept [20] Chapman performs at the Greek Theatre, Los Angeles, during her latest round of US dates.

Oct [16] She sings *The Times They Are A-Changin'* at the Bob Dylan 30th anniversary celebration, held at New York's Madison Square Garden.

1995

Mar [4] Following a two-year sabbatical, Chapman opens a three-week US tour in Grinnell, IA.

Nov [27] Chapman begins another short US tour before a sellout crowd at Sanders Theatre, Cambridge, MA.

[29] She guests on CBS-TV's "Late Show With David Letterman".

Dec [2] Her fourth album in eight years, ***New Beginning*** debuts at its initial US #58 peak.

1996

Jan [18] Chapman guests on NBC-TV's "The Tonight Show".

Feb [2] She plays to a sellout crowd at the Music Hall, Austin, TX, during latest US dates.

[16] The Scholastic Network (US) organization announces that Chapman will review its third "Write Lyrics" contest (open to six million US children), held to raise awareness among 6-12th graders of the power of the written word.

Mar [2] ***New Beginning*** makes UK #47.

June [15] *Give Me One Reason* hits US #3 as its critically acclaimed parent album, ***New Beginning***, hits US #4.

THE CHARLATANS UK

Tim Burgess (vocals); **Mark Collins** (guitar); **Rob Collins** (organ); **Martin Blunt** (bass); **Jon Brookes** (drums)

1988

Sept Based in the Manchester, Gtr. Manchester suburb of Northwich, Blunt (b. 1965), who has formed Makin' Time with Fay Hallam, Syd McGounden and Neil Clitheroe in 1984 in Wolverhampton, W. Midlands, which, signed to Stiff Records' Countdown indie imprint, has released ***Rhythm'N'Soul*** in June 1985 but split in September 1986 after its second album ***No Lumps Or Fat Or Gristle Guaranteed***, has recently dissolved the short-lived Gift Horses (formed with Hallam and her boyfriend Graham Day) and, together with singer-songwriter Barry Kettley, has recruited Brookes (b. 1969) and Rob Collins (b. 1967), calling themselves the Charlatans. Managed by local Omega Records shop owner, Steve Harrison, the band now plays its first gig at Northwich's Vic's Club. Harrison subsequently secures five opening slots for the Charlatans with local cult favorites the Stone Roses, played between November and April 1989, following which Kettley quits, replaced by the Electric Canyons' vocalist (and ICI-plant worker) Burgess (b. May 30, 1968, Salford, Gtr. Manchester) in June, while a second guitarist, John Baker (b. 1969, aka John Day) is also added. Recording demos written by Rob Collins and Burgess, their trademark sound underpinned by Rob Collins' authentic Hammond organ playing (which he has bought from a local church), the new lineup's first gig is at the Walsall Overstrand, Gtr. Manchester, followed by club dates around Manchester. The group's second demo set, recorded in November 1989 at Manchester's Strawberry Studio includes *Indian Rope* which will be its debut single release on their own Dead Dead Good label (established by Harrison) in January 1990, and its first UK Independent Singles chart-topper. Firmly identified with the happening "Madchester" scene led by the Stone Roses, Happy Mondays and Inspiral Carpets, but distinguished by its swirling Hammond organ sound, the Charlatans enjoy a rapidly growing fan following in Manchester and London.

1990

Apr Having signed to Beggars Banquet indie imprint Situation Two, the group tapes its first session for BBC Radio 1's "John Peel Show".

June [16] *The Only One I Know* hits UK #9, hailed as the defining single of the "Madchester" summer. During the month, the Charlatans also record a "Mark Goodier" session again broadcast on Radio 1.

Sept [29] *Then* reaches UK #12.

Oct [6-7] The group takes part in "A Gathering Of The Tribes Festival", held at the Shoreline Amphitheatre, Mountain View, CA, and the Pacific Amphitheatre, Costa Mesa, CA, with the Cramps, Ice-T, Indigo Girls, Queen Latifah and others.

[20] The band's debut album, the Chris Nagle-produced ***Some Friendly*** enters at UK #1, eventually earning a gold disc, while the band undertakes its first US tour (where they are known as the Charlatans UK), followed by end-of-year sold out UK dates.

1991

Feb [21] During further US gigs, tonight's performance at Chicago's Metro club, IL, is recorded (and subsequently issued as an official fan-club bootleg, ***Isolation 21.2.91***).

Mar [2] ***Some Friendly*** reaches US #73, while Baker quits after a French festival gig, to be replaced by ex-Candlestick Park and Waltones guitarist Mark Collins (no relation).

[9] *Over Rising* enters at its UK #15 peak.

Aug [17] *Indian Rope* charts for a week at UK #57.

Oct The band tapes a second session for Radio 1's "Mark Goodier" show.

Nov [9] *Me. In Time* enters at its UK #28 high. Released against Blunt's wishes, he suffers a nervous breakdown, taking a hiatus from the band with a recuperative trip to the seaside.

1992

Mar [7] *Weirdo* bows at its UK #19 peak.
Apr [4] Produced by Flood, the Charlatans' sophomore set ***Between 10th And 11th*** stops at UK #21 in its first week, indicating the demise of the Madchester scene.
May [9] ***Between 10th And 11th*** makes US #173 during a three month US tour (followed by dates in Japan).
[23] *Weirdo* tops the US Modern Rock Tracks chart.
July [25] EP *Tremelo Song* makes UK #44.
Dec [3] Rob Collins is arrested for participating in an armed robbery at an off-licence in Cannock, Staffs. (He will be sentenced to an eight-month prison term to begin in September, though only serving four.)

1993

Dec [18] St. Etienne's *I Was Born On Christmas Day*, featuring Burgess on lead vocal, peaks at UK #37.

1994

Feb [5] *Can't Get Out Of Bed*, the band's first release on the main Beggars Banquet label, debuts at its UK #24 peak.
Mar [19] *I Never Want An Easy Life If Me And He Were Ever To Get There* charts for a week at UK #38.
Apr [2] Critically-panned ***Up To Our Hips*** enters at its UK #8 high.
July [2] *Jesus Hairdo* enters at its UK #48 peak.
Nov [7] The group is showcased on Granada-TV's "With The Charlatans".

1995

Jan [7] *Crashin' In* enters at its UK #31 peak.
May [27] *Just Lookin'*, coupled with *Bullet Comes*, comes in at its UK #32 high.
Aug [26] *Just When You're Thinkin' Things Over* debuts at its UK #12 peak.
Sept [9] Having been effectively written off by the UK music media over the past two years, the group's commercial resurgence is confirmed as ***The Charlatans*** enters at UK #1.
Oct [4] A US tour, underway without the backing of potential tour sponsor Ocean Spray (which has reportedly pulled out after learning of Rob Collins' criminal record) includes tonight's gig at the Metro, Chicago, IL, a bill grossing $16,230 from 1,082 fans.
Nov [6] A 20-date UK tour begins at Aberdeen's Beach Ballroom, Scotland, set to close on December 10th at Hull University, Humberside.

1996

Jul [22] Rob Collins dies when his BMW crashes in Gwent, where the band is recording its 5th album.

RAY CHARLES

1945

May Charles (b. Ray Charles Robinson, Sept. 23, 1930, Albany, GA), who has lived in Greenville, FL, where he sang in the Shiloh Baptist Church and the Red Wing Café, where proprietor Wylie Pittman let him play the piano, since age two, and who has been blind since suffering from glaucoma at age seven, after witnessing his younger brother George fall into a washtub and drown in the family's backyard, studied music (classical piano and clarinet) at St. Augustine's School for the Deaf and Blind in Orlando, FL, before moving to Jacksonville, FL, shortly after his mother's death. He begins playing for his living with various groups, including the Florida Playboys, Henry Washington's Big Band and Joe Anderson's band.

1948

Moving to Seattle, WA, with $600 savings, after being orphaned a year earlier, he enters a talent contest on his first night in town, and is immediately offered a job playing at the local Elks club. 17-year-old R.C. Robinson (as he is billed) forms the McSon Trio, with Gosady McGee on guitar and Milton Garred on bass, to play light jazz and blues modelled on the Nat "King" Cole Trio-style at the Rocking Chair. He also plays regularly at the Washington Social Club, the 908 Club and the Black & Tan.

1949

The trio signs to Jack Lauderdale's Downbeat Records and releases Charles' own composition *Confession Blues*. He alters his billing to his two forenames to avoid confusion with boxer/singer Sugar Ray Robinson. Downbeat becomes Swingtime Records and releases a string of singles by Charles, including *See See Rider* and *I Wonder Who's Kissing Her Now?* Soon to quit the trio and relocate to Los Angeles at Lauderdale's insistence, he will spend much of the next two years touring as Lowell Fulson's musical director.

1951

Jan His first US R&B chart entry is *Baby Let Me Hold Your Hand*, followed by *Kiss-A-Me Baby*, recorded with the McSon Trio.

1952

June Atlantic Records buys Charles' contract from Swingtime for $2,500.
Sept [11] Charles begins his first recording session for Atlantic in New York, NY, cutting four tracks under the supervision of Jesse Stone.

1953

May [17] Charles records six more cuts with Stone in New York. The first release from this session is *Mess Around*, later an R&B standard, written for Charles by Atlantic owner Ahmet Ertegun, and it is one of the first uptempo numbers included in his previously jazz-ballad repertoire.
Aug [18] He records new material in New Orleans, LA, with Ertegun and Jerry Wexler producing. He will also play on Guitar Slim's *The Things I Used To Do*, before forming his own band with David "Fathead" Newman, who has been Swingtime labelmate Lloyd Green's saxophonist.

1954

Mar *It Should Have Been Me*, his first major seller for Atlantic, hits US R&B #7. (Over the next three years, R&B chart successes follow: *Don't You Know*, *I Got A Woman* (#2), *This Little Girl Of Mine* (#2), *Drown In My Own Tears* and *Hallelujah I Love Her So*.)

1957

July His debut album ***Ray Charles*** is released.
Nov [25] Charles' first crossover success is *Swanee River Rock (Talkin' 'Bout That River)*, which makes US #34.

1958

July [5] Charles appears at the "Newport Jazz Festival", Newport, RI, his performance recorded by Atlantic for a live album.
Dec [28] *Rockhouse* peaks at US #79. ***Ray Charles At Newport***, from the summer's festival, is released.

1959

Feb [9] *(Night Time Is) The Right Time* reaches US #95. ***Soul Brothers***, recorded with jazz vibist Milt Jackson, is released.
May Charles plays an outdoor festival at the Herndon Stadium in Atlanta, GA, with B.B. King, Ruth Brown, the Drifters, Jimmy Reed and other major R&B names. His performance is again recorded by Atlantic for future album release.
June [26] Charles records *I'm Movin' On*, impressing rival label ABC-Paramount.
Aug [17] Self-penned gospel-style rocker *What'd I Say* tops the US R&B chart for the first of two weeks and hits US #6, his first million-seller. (Jerry Lee Lewis, Bobby Darin and Elvis Presley will all have '60s hits with revivals of the song.)
Nov Charles signs to ABC-Paramount Records on a three-year contract. (Atlantic is unable to match the offer of $50,000 a year in advances, a 5% royalty rate, a further percentage as his own producer and eventual ownership of his ABC master tapes.) He also establishes his own Tangerine publishing company.
Dec [14] *I'm Movin' On* (a cover of Hank Snow's country number), on Atlantic, makes US #40.

1960

Jan [25] *Let The Good Times Roll*, on Atlantic, makes US #78.
Feb [15] B-side *Don't Let The Sun Catch You Cryin'* stalls at US #95.
Mar ***The Genius Of Ray Charles***, on Atlantic, makes US #17, his first US chart album.
Aug [8] ABC debut *Sticks And Stones* reaches US #40, while an Atlantic album, ***Ray Charles In Person***, recorded at the Herndon stadium in May 1959, reaches US #13.
Nov [14] A revival of Hoagy Carmichael's *Georgia On My Mind*, recorded after Charles' chauffeur constantly sang it on trips, tops the US chart and is his second million-seller.
Dec *Georgia On My Mind* is his UK chart debut, at #24.
[5] Similarly-styled *Come Rain Or Come Shine*, a 1959 recording issued by Atlantic, makes US #83. *Hard-Hearted Hannah*, the B-side of the still-climbing *Ruby*, peaks at US #55. Debut ABC album ***The Genius Hits The Road***, from which *Georgia* is taken and which has US place names as the themes of its songs, hits US #9, his first Top 10 album.
[31] *Ruby* reaches US #28.

1961

Feb [6] *Them That Got* peaks at US #58.
Apr [12] Charles wins the Best Vocal Performance Single Record Or Track - Male and Best Performance By A Pop Single Artist for *Georgia On My Mind*, Best Vocal Performance Album, Male for ***The Genius Of Ray Charles*** and Best R&B Performance for *Let The Good Times Roll* categories for 1960 at the third annual Grammy Awards.
Dedicated To You reaches US #11.
May [1] Instrumental *One Mint Julep*, released on ABC's subsidiary jazz label, Impulse, hits US #8, taken from Charles' largely-instrumental big band US #4 album ***Genius + Soul = Jazz***, arranged by Quincy Jones, which includes a guest line-up of top jazzmen.
June [26] *I've Got News For You* peaks at US #66, as B-side *I'm Gonna Move To The Outskirts Of Town* climbs to US #84.
Sept ***What'd I Say***, comprising earlier Atlantic material, makes US #20, while on the same label, relaxed instrumental album ***The Genius After Hours*** reaches US #49.
Oct [9] *Hit The Road Jack*, written by Charles' friend, R&B singer Percy Mayfield, tops the US chart and becomes his third million-seller, while an album of duets, ***Ray Charles And Betty Carter***, climbs to US #52.
Nov *Hit The Road Jack* hits UK #6.
Dec Atlantic album ***The Genius Sings The Blues*** reaches US #73.
[5] Charles is charged with possession of narcotics, after being arrested in a downtown hotel in Indianapolis, IN. (He has been a heroin addict since age 16 and had previously been arrested in Philadelphia in 1958.)

1962

Jan [13] *Unchain My Heart* hits US #9.
[20] B-side *But On The Other Hand, Baby* peaks at US #72. Atlantic issues ***Do The Twist!*** (which has nothing to do with the current dance craze, but is a compilation of early material with tempos to suit twisting). It makes US #11, his highest-placed Atlantic album.
Mar [10] Charles and Carter duet *Baby, It's Cold Outside* peaks at US #91. Charles now launches his own Tangerine Records label.
May [5] *Hide Nor Hair* reaches US #20.
[12] B-side *At The Club* makes US #44.

[29] Charles wins Best R&B Recording for *Hit The Road Jack* at the fourth annual Grammy Awards.
June Charles records outstanding country music songs in his own style for ***Modern Sounds In Country And Western Music***. It tops the US chart for 14 weeks.
[2] An extracted revival of Don Gibson's *I Can't Stop Loving You* begins a five-week stay at US #1, and will go on to sell two million copies, becoming certified as the year's best-selling single.
[30] B-side *Born To Lose* makes US #41.
July Charles is fined by a court in Atlanta, GA, after refusing to perform at a segregated dance where blacks were only spectators.
[14] *I Can't Stop Loving You* tops the UK chart.
[19] *I Can't Stop Loving You* and ***Modern Sounds In Country And Western Music*** are both certified gold by the RIAA.
Aug ***Modern Sounds In Country And Western Music***, his first UK chart album, hits UK #6.
[11] *Careless Love*, the B-side of *You Don't Know Me*, peaks at US #60.
Sept [8] His second single from the country album, *You Don't Know Me* hits US #2 and is another million-seller. Double album ***The Ray Charles Story***, an Atlantic compilation of his '50s work, reaches US #14, while the ABC compilation ***Ray Charles' Greatest Hits***, containing the more recent hits prior to *I Can't Stop Loving You*, hits US #5.
Oct *You Don't Know Me* hits UK #9.
Dec Charles follows up his successful country experiment with the US #2 ***Modern Sounds In Country And Western Music, Vol. 2***.
[22] Excerpted *Your Cheating Heart* reaches US #29.
[29] *Your Cheating Heart*'s A-side *You Are My Sunshine*, written by Jimmie Davis, the racist former Governor of Louisiana, hits US #7, as *Your Cheating Heart* reaches UK #13.

1963

Mar ***Modern Sounds In Country And Western Music Vol. 2*** reaches UK #15, while Charles opens his own studios and offices in Los Angeles, CA.
[16] *The Brightest Smile In Town* makes US #92.
[30] Its A-side *Don't Set Me Free* reaches US #20 and UK #37.
May [12] Charles embarks on his first UK tour - a six-date swing, opening at London's Finsbury Astoria.
[15] Charles wins the Best R&B Recording category for *I Can't Stop Loving You* at the fifth annual Grammy Awards.
[25] *Take These Chains From My Heart*, extracted from the second country album, hits US #8.
June *Take These Chains From My Heart* hits UK #5, his fourth and last UK Top 10 appearance.
July [20] Double A-side *No One/Without Love (There Is Nothing)* makes US #21 and #29.
Aug Compilation album ***Ray Charles' Greatest Hits*** reaches UK #16.
Oct [19] *Busted*, a return to the bluesy big-band style, hits US #4 and is another million-seller. ***Ingredients In A Recipe For Soul*** hits US #2, while *No One* reaches UK #35.
Nov *Busted* makes UK #21.

1964

Jan [18] His revival of *That Lucky Old Sun* reaches US #20. The song is featured (with eight other Charles numbers) in the film "Ballad In Blue", in which he stars with Dawn Addams and Tom Bell.
Mar [21] *Baby Don't You Cry* makes US #39.
Apr [4] Its flip-side *My Heart Cries For You* makes US #38, as ***Sweet And Sour Tears*** is on its way to US #9.
May [12] Charles wins the Best R&B Recording category for *Busted* at the sixth annual Grammy Awards.
[18] Charles begins filming "Light Out Of Darkness" in Madrid, Spain.
June [27] *My Baby Don't Dig Me* peaks at US #51.
July [7] Charles begins his second UK concert tour, for three weeks.
Aug [2] He performs at the legendary Star-Club in Hamburg, Germany.
[22] Double A-side *No One To Cry To/A Tear Fell*, peaks at US #55 and #50 respectively, as Charles begins a 10-day tour of Japan.
Oct *No One To Cry To* makes UK #38. *Smack Dab In The Middle* peaks at US #52, as parent ***Have A Smile With Me*** makes US #36.
[31] Charles is seized by customs agents after landing at Logan Airport, Boston, MA, for a concert at the Back Bay Theater. He is arraigned before US Commissioner Peter J. Nelligad, charged with possession of narcotics. (Agents claim to have found a small quantity of heroin and marijuana, a hypodermic needle and a spoon.)

1965

Jan [16] His update of *Makin' Whoopee* reaches US #46 and UK #42.
Mar [13] Charles' treatment of Johnnie Ray's *Cry*, peaks at US #58. ***Ray Charles Live In Concert*** makes US #80.
May [1] From it, a revival of his own *Gotta Woman* makes US #79.
June [28] Charles guests on CBS-TV's "It's What's Happening Baby".
Aug [7] A version of Joe Barry's *I'm A Fool To Care* peaks at US #84.
Sept ***Country And Western Meets Rhythm And Blues*** reaches US #116.

1966

Feb [12] *Crying Time* stops at UK #50.
[19] After a string of middling charters, *Crying Time* hits US #6.
Apr [2] *You're Just About To Lose Your Crown*, B-side of the still-climbing *Together Again*, climbs to US #91.
[23] Charles' revival of Buck Owens' country ballad *Together Again* makes UK #48.
[30] *Together Again* reaches at US #19, while ***Crying Time*** heads to US #15.
July [16] Bluesy *Let's Go Get Stoned* makes US #31. It is the first single to give a full co-credit to Charles' own Tangerine Records with ABC.
Oct [8] *I Chose To Sing The Blues* makes US #32, while ***Ray's Moods*** climbs to US #52.
Dec [3] Charles is convicted on charges of possessing heroin and marijuana. He is given a five-year suspended prison sentence, a $10,000 fine, and is put on probation for four years. Random drug tests showing that he has refrained from drug use since his original arrest keep him out of jail. (He has gone cold turkey in 92 hours while in the St. Francis Hospital in Lynwood, CA.)
[10] *Please Say You're Fooling* makes US #64.
[17] Curiously-timed B-side *I Don't Need No Doctor* peaks at US #72.

1967

Mar [2] *Crying Time* wins the Best R&B Recording and Best R&B Solo Vocal Performance, Male Or Female Of 1966, at the ninth annual Grammy Awards.
[18] *I Want To Talk About You* makes US #98.
Apr Double compilation ***A Man And His Soul*** reaches US #77 during a 62-week chart tenure, earning a gold disc for half a million sales.
[22] Charles performs at London's Royal Festival Hall during a UK tour.
June [24] He appears at Constitution Hall in Washington, DC.
July [8] *Here We Go Again*, a return to country soul, makes UK #38 and will peak at US #15 one week hence.
Sept [2] ***Ray Charles Invites You To Listen***, the first album to carry the ABC-Tangerine Records dual logo, reaches US #76.
[12-13] Charles headlines at New York's first "Jazz Festival", at the Downing Stadium.
[30] His dramatic deep-soul theme song, written by Quincy Jones, from the Rod Steiger/Sidney Poitier-starring movie "In The Heat Of The Night", makes US #33.
Dec [9] Charles' re-working of the Beatles' *Yesterday* makes US #25.

1968

Jan *Yesterday* makes UK #44.
[27] Atlantic reissue *Come Rain Or Come Shine* rains at US #98.
Mar [30] *That's A Lie* peaks at US #64.
Apr [6] ***Greatest Hits*** and ***Modern Sounds In Country And Western Music Volume 2*** are both certified gold by the RIAA.
June [22] ***A Portrait Of Ray*** reaches US #51.
July [27] Another Lennon/McCartney cover, *Eleanor Rigby*, makes US #35 (and UK #36 in August).
[17] Its B-side *Understanding* peaks at US #46.
Aug [16] ***A Man And His Soul*** is certified gold by the RIAA.
Sept [21] Charles begins his latest UK tour at London's Royal Festival Hall.
Oct ***Ray Charles' Greatest Hits, Vol. 2***, a UK-only compilation, makes #24.
[5] *Sweet Young Thing Like You* climbs to US #83.
[19] B-side *Listen, They're Playing My Song* spins at US #92.

1969

Feb [8] Charles' duet with Jimmy Lewis on *If It Wasn't For Bad Luck* peaks at US #77.
May [10]***I'm All Yours - Baby!*** climbs to US #167.
[24] *Let Me Love You* makes US #94.
June [13] He appears with Aretha Franklin, Sam and Dave, the Staple Singers and many more, at "Soul Bowl '69", held at the Houston Astrodome, Houston, TX, promoted as the biggest-ever soul music festival.
Aug [2] ***Doing His Thing*** peaks at US #172.

1970

Mar [21] *Laughin' And Clownin'* makes US #98.
July Instrumental-filled ***My Kind Of Jazz***, released on Tangerine, reaches US #155.
Aug ***Love Country Style*** peaks at US #192.
Oct [25] Charles performs at London's Hammersmith Odeon during a UK tour, having played the Royal Festival Hall the previous night.

1971

Jan [2] *If You Were Mine* makes US #41, staying charted for 18 weeks.
Apr [24] *Don't Change On Me* peaks at US #36.
May [22] *Booty Butt*, an R&B instrumental credited to the Ray Charles Orchestra (allowing it to be issued on Tangerine), sits at US #36.
July ***Volcanic Action Of My Soul*** makes US #52, his biggest-selling album for over three years.
Oct [9] *Feel So Bad* peaks at US #68.
Dec Double album ***A 25th Anniversary In Show Business Salute To Ray Charles*** is a collaboration between ABC and Atlantic with an album of Charles' hits from each label. It is released on Atlantic worldwide, but on ABC in the US, where it reaches #152.

1972

Jan [29] His revival of Chuck Willis' *What Am I Living For?* makes US #54.
[20] Charles guests on CBS-TV's Emmy-winning "Carol Burnett Show".
June ***A Message From The People*** is heard at US #52.
Aug [5] A cover of Melanie's *Look What They've Done To My Song, Ma* peaks at US #65.
Dec Final ABC set ***Through The Eyes Of Love*** climbs to US #186.

1973

Charles leaves the label, taking with him the Tangerine Records operation and the rights to all his ABC releases. Tangerine becomes Crossover Records, which will release both Charles' new recordings and reissues.
June Atlantic double album ***Ray Charles Live***, comprising the two earlier live sets from Newport in 1958 and Herndon Stadium in 1959, makes US #182.
[16] Charles' last ABC single, *I Can Make It Thru The Days (But Oh Those Lonely Nights)*, climbs to US #81.
Sept [7] He headlines the second "Ann Arbor Jazz and Blues Festival", Ann Arbor, MI.

Dec [15] His first Crossover single *Come Live With Me* makes US #82.

1975

July Following the release of his debut Crossover album ***Come Live With Me*** the previous year, a second effort ***Renaissance*** peaks at US #175.
Sept [27] His cover of Stevie Wonder's *Living For The City*, taken from ***Renaissance***, reaches US #91.

1976

Feb [28] Charles wins the Best R&B Vocal Performance, Male category for *Living For The City* at the 18th annual Grammy Awards.
Dec Charles and UK jazz singer Cleo Laine's double album of Gershwin's ***Porgy And Bess***, released by RCA, makes US #138.

1977

Feb [28] He is attacked, while performing for disadvantaged youth, by an audience member who rushes on stage with a rope and tries to strangle him.
Mar [15] John Ritter-sitcom "Three's Company", for which Charles sings the theme with Julia Rinker, premieres on ABC-TV.
Nov [12] Charles is the musical guest on NBC-TV's "Saturday Night Live".
[19] *True To Life*, a one-off return to Atlantic, climbs to US #78. (He divorces his second wife, Della, after 22 years of marriage.)

1978

Feb [24] Charles guests on ABC-TV's "The Second Barry Manilow Special", singing *One Of These Days* and duetting with Manilow on *It's A Miracle*.
Oct [13] He performs at London's Royal Albert Hall during a current UK tour.

1980

June [20] "The Blues Brothers", in which Charles appears as the streetwise owner of a musical-instrument store, opens at cinemas across the US.
July [26] TV-advertised compilation album of Charles oldies, ***Heart To Heart - 20 Hot Hits***, reaches UK #29.
Oct Charles teams with Clint Eastwood to release *Beers To You*, from the Eastwood-starring film "Any Which Way You Can".

1983

Mar Newly signed to CBS/Columbia's Nashville division, to concentrate on country-based music, his label debut ***Wish You Were Here Tonight***, recorded in Nashville, is a US Country-chart success, but fails to cross over.
June He appears at the 30th annual "Kool Jazz Festival", in New York, co-headlining with Miles Davis and B.B. King.

1985

Jan [19] Charles participates in ABC-TV's "American Presidential Inaugural Gala".
[28] He takes a major role in the recording of USA For Africa's *We Are The World* fundraising single, leading the song's gospel-like climax.
Apr [23] A duet with Willie Nelson, *Seven Spanish Angels*, from his current ***Friendship*** project, tops the US Country chart.
May [4] ***Friendship***, featuring Charles in ten duets with major country-music stars, including Mickey Gilley and Hank Williams Jr., makes US #75, his first US album-chart entry since 1977.
Dec A country soul-styled seasonal album, ***The Spirit Of Christmas*** is released in the US.

1986

Jan [23] He is inducted by Quincy Jones into the Rock and Roll Hall of Fame at the inaugural ceremony, staged at New York's Waldorf Astoria Hotel.
Dec [26] Charles is honored at the ninth annual Kennedy Center Honors ceremony, in Washington, DC.

1987

Apr [25] Charles guests with Billy Joel on his *Baby Grand*, which reaches US #75. (Less active on the recording front, Charles continues to play live throughout the world, often in a big-band environment. His ongoing acting cameo roles include spots in US TV series "Moonlighting", "St. Elsewhere" and "Who's The Boss", in which he sings *Always A Friend*. He also becomes a regular celebrity in TV advertising campaigns, including clips for American Express, Kentucky Fried Chicken and, most notably, Pepsi Cola.)

1988

Mar [2] Charles is honored by NARAS at the 30th annual Grammy awards ceremony with a Lifetime Achievement Award, noting that he is "the father of soul, whose unique and effervescent singing and piano-playing have personified the true essence of soul music in all his recorded and personal performances of basic blues, pop ballads, jazz tunes and even country music".

1989

May [11-12] Charles performs "A Fool For You" with the New York City Ballet, at the Lincoln Center.
June He undertakes a 16-date US tour, including dates in New York (June 28th) and Little Rock, AZ (July 26th).
Oct [3] Another set of US concerts opens in Valdosta, GA, the first of 18 performances, set to end on December 15th in San Francisco, CA.
Nov Charles is named chairman of the Washington, DC-based Rhythm and Blues Foundation.

1990

Jan [27] *I'll Be Good To You*, a track from Quincy Jones' forthcoming ***Back On The Block***, which sees Charles duet with Chaka Khan, reaches US #18, his first US Top 30 hit since 1967.
Feb [3] *I'll Be Good To You* reaches UK #21.
[21] *I've Got A Woman* is inducted into the NARAS Hall of Fame at the 32nd annual Grammy Awards. Charles also contributes to a tribute to Paul McCartney, who is being honored with a Lifetime Achievement Award, singing *Eleanor Rigby* at the ceremony.
Mar [1] Seven-date mini-tour starts at the Morton H. Myerson Symphony Center, Dallas, TX.
[24] Retrospective ***The Ray Charles Collection*** debuts at its UK #36 peak.
May [5] Charles sings *Let It Be* for the "John Lennon Tribute Concert" organized by Yoko Ono, at the Pier Head Arena in Merseyside.
Sept [17-22] Charles performs at the Blue Note in New York.
[29] Ever restless, Charles embarks on a world tour with B.B. King in Taiwan, set to end in New York on November 10th.
Nov [21] He guests on "The Tonight Show".

1991

Feb [20] Charles and Khan win Best R&B Performance By A Duo Or Group With Vocal category for *I'll Be Good To You* at the 33rd annual Grammy Awards. (It is Charles' 11th Grammy.)
[21] Charles is honored with the Rhythm and Blues Foundation's Legend Award at a ceremony at Tatou in New York.
May [16] He becomes one of the first ten enshrinees of the Atlanta Celebrity Walk, with Jimmy Carter, Martin Luther King, Margaret Mitchell, Andrew Young, Hank Aaron and others.
June [15] Charles performs at the "Playboy Jazz Festvial" at the Hollywood Bowl, Hollywood, CA.
Oct [6] Fox-TV airs "Ray Charles 50 Years In Music" (recorded on September 19th), a musical tribute featuring the soul legend in duets with Stevie Wonder (*Living For The City*), Willie Nelson (*Busted*) and Michael Bolton (*Georgia On My Mind*). Contributions also come from Randy Travis (*Your Cheatin' Heart*), James Ingram (*I Can't Stop Loving You*) and Michael McDonald (*I Got A Woman*).
[20] A Stockholm, Sweden concert is cancelled when promoters discover that Charles is on the UN blacklist for performing in South Africa in 1981.
Nov Three CD/cassette boxed set ***The Birth Of Soul - The Complete Atlantic Rhythm & Blues Recordings, 1952-1959*** is released.

1992

Jan [3] A documentary "The Genius Of Ray Charles", featuring Billy Joel, Willie Nelson, Dr. John, Quincy Jones and others, premieres on PBS-TV.
Feb [16] Charles is awarded Los Angeles County's highest honor, the Distinguished Service Medal. (He will also receive Los Angeles' Black History Honoree Award for 1992, during Black History month.)
Apr [16] A long-time regular, Charles guests again on "The Tonight Show".
May [8] He performs with the Utah Symphony at Symphony Hall, Salt Lake City, UT, before a sellout crowd of 2,812.
July [14] Charles appears at the "Capital Radio Jazz Parade" at London's Royal Festival Hall, during current UK dates.
Aug [11] Charles sings *America The Beautiful* at the opening of Mall of America, Bloomington, MN, the largest shopping mall in the US.
Nov [27-29] His current US tour climaxes with three shows at Caesars Palace, Las Vegas, NV.

1993

Jan [17] Charles participates in "A Call for Reunion - A Musical Celebration" at the Lincoln Memorial Hall, Washington, DC, during President-elect Clinton's inaugural celebrations.
Mar [13] ***Ray Charles - The Living Legend*** bows at its UK #48 peak.
May [22] Charles guests on CBS-TV's "Willie Nelson The Big Six-O" birthday celebrations.
June [2] He receives the Hall of Fame Lifetime Achievement award from Billy Joel at the 24th annual Songwriters Hall of Fame dinner and induction ceremonies, at the Sheraton New York Hotel.
[15] Charles sings *What'd I Say* at the first "Apollo Theatre Hall of Fame" concert from the landmark Harlem theatre, subsequently broadcast on NBC-TV on August 4th.
[19] His latest Warner Bros. effort, the Richard Perry-produced ***My World***, including covers of Paul Simon's *Still Crazy After All These Years* and Leon Russell's *A Song For You*, his most critically-praised outing in some years, peaks at US #145 and marks his sixth decade as a US chart-maker.
July [13] Charles performs at the Westfalenhalle 1, Dortmund, Germany, on his current European tour, sharing the bill with Fats Domino. (Charles will contribute to Inxs' new album, duetting with Michael Hutchence on *Please (You Got That...)* by year's end.)
Dec [14] Charles' star is unveiled in an inaugural ceremony with 15 other artists at the "Sidewalk Of The Stars" outside Radio City Music Hall in New York.

1994

Mar [1] He wins the Best Male R&B Performance category for *Song For You* at the 36th annual Grammy Awards (his 12th trophy) at Radio City Music Hall.
Apr [22] Charles performs, by satellite, at the seventh annual Essence Awards from the Paramount, New York.
May [4] Charles is honored with the Lifelong Contribution To The Music Industry at the sixth annual World Music Awards at the Sporting Club, Monte Carlo, Monaco, at which he also performs *Till There Was You*.
[13] He guest stars on NBC-TV's "Ray Alexander : A Taste For Justice".
July [2] Charles takes part in the "Newport Jazz Festival" at the Saratoga Performing Arts Center, Saratoga Springs, NY.

1995

Mar [2] He is honored with the Lifetime Achievement Award at the sixth annual Rhythm and Blues Foundation's Pioneer Awards.
June [16] Charles performs *America The Beautiful* at the 48th annual Horatio Alger awards, airing on CBS-

TV, before heading to Euope for a short concert tour.
Nov [7] Quincy Jones' new album, ***Q's Jook Joint***, featuring Charles as one of many guests, is released in the US.
[19] Charles sings *Old Man River* at the Frank Sinatra's 80th birthday bash at Los Angeles' Shrine Auditorium.

1996

Mar [23] As active as ever, Charles' latest album, ***Strong Love Affair***, co-produced with Jean-Pierre Grosz, is released in the US on Quincy Jones' Qwest label.

CHEAP TRICK

Robin Zander (vocals, guitar); **Rick Nielsen** (vocals, guitar); **Tom Petersson** (vocals, bass); **Bun E. Carlos** (drums)

1968

Dec The veteran of several local Rockford, IL bands (including the Phaetons, Boyz and the Grim Reapers) since 1961, Nielsen (b. Dec. 22, 1946, Rockford), an avid collector of rare and bizarre guitars (which will number over 100 within 20 years) who has been performing in Europe in 1968 with Petersson (b. May 9, 1950, Rockford), has formed a new band, Fuse, recruiting Carlos (b. Brad Carlson, June 12, 1951, Rockford), who has played with Bo Diddley, Del Shannon, Freddy Cannon and the Shirelles, among others, which now releases ***Fuse*** album for Epic Records. Nielsen, Petersson and Carlos subsequently move to Philadelphia, PA, in 1971, where they gig locally as the Sick Man Of Europe, with ex-Nazz members Robert Antoni and Thom Mooney, and tour said continent in 1972 (with vocalist Randy Hogan in the line-up), before returning to Rockford the following year, where they form a new combo, Cheap Trick, with folk vocalist Zander (b. Jan. 23, 1953, Rockford), who has already been in the short-lived outfit, the Toons, with Carlos.

1974

Oct [31] Recently signed to Epic Records, Cheap Trick makes its live debut at Charlotte's Web, Rockford, IL. The rock quartet will gig incessantly over the next three years, completing more than 200 concerts per annum, including support slots for the Kinks, Santana, Kiss, Boston and many others.

1977

Jan Their debut album ***Cheap Trick*** is released by Epic and sells 150,000 copies in the US, but remains uncharted. Its popularity in Japan is immediate, earning a gold disc.
Oct [22] Their second effort ***In Color*** peaks at US #73 on the strength of continued touring. Once again, it goes gold in Japan.

1978

Feb The group's maiden concert visit to Tokyo is greeted with unexpected "Trickmania". Their dates at the Budokan Arena sell out within two hours. A live recording of the gigs is made, capturing both their performing expertise and the fanatical Japanese reaction.
Apr [2] The band performs at London's Roundhouse during a five-date UK tour, which will also include an appearance on BBC2-TV's "The Old Grey Whistle Test".
July [8] Cheap Trick's third album ***Heaven Tonight*** makes US #48 and achieves platinum status in Japan.
Sept [2] Their debut chart single *Surrender* peaks at US #62.

1979

Jan [16] ***Heaven Tonight*** is certified gold by the RIAA.
Feb [24] ***Cheap Trick At Budokan*** begins a one-year US chart stay.
Mar [10] ***Cheap Trick At Budokan*** reaches UK #29, as the group returns for more UK dates.
Apr [7-8] Cheap Trick plays at the "California Music Festival" at the Memorial Coliseum, Los Angeles, CA, with Van Halen, Aerosmith and Ted Nugent.
June [2] From the live album, *I Want You To Want Me* reaches UK #29.
July [14] ***Cheap Trick At Budokan*** finally hits US #4, and becomes the group's first US platinum-selling album.
[21] Nielsen-penned *I Want You To Want Me* hits US #7. In Japan, the album achieves triple-platinum status.
Aug [13] *I Want You To Want Me* and *In Color* are certified gold by the RIAA.
[25] The group performs at the annual "Reading Festival", where it is joined on stage by Dave Edmunds and Mick Ralphs for an encore version of *Day Tripper*.
Sept [29] Follow-up *Ain't That A Shame*, a live cover of the Fats Domino standard, makes US #35.
Oct [13] Studio album ***Dream Police*** reaches UK #41.
[27] Currently at their commercial peak (and visually trademarked by the appearance of Nielsen dressed in a bow-tie, monogrammed sweater and baseball cap), ***Dream Police*** hits US #6.
Nov [24] The extracted title track *Dream Police* reaches US #26.

1980

Feb [2] *Voices* makes US #32, as the UK-only released *Way Of The World* peaks at #73. Nielsen, Zander and Carlos contribute to John Lennon's ***Double Fantasy*** sessions in New York, NY.
[6] ***Dream Police*** is certified platinum by the RIAA.
June *Voices* is featured on the soundtrack to the current Debbie Harry/Meat Loaf movie, "Roadie".
July [5] *Everything Works If You Let It* makes US #44. A 10" mini-LP, ***Found All The Parts***, featuring songs recorded between 1976 and 1979, makes US #39.
Aug [26] Petersson leaves to form a group with his wife, Dagmar. He is initially replaced by Pete Comita and more permanently by Jon Brant (b. Feb. 20, 1954).
Oct [16] The group begins a seven-date UK tour at the Mayfair, Newcastle, Tyne & Wear, set to end on the 24th at London's Hammersmith Odeon.
Dec [6] *Stop This Game* makes US #48.
[13] George Martin-produced ***All Shook Up*** reaches US #24.
[30] ***All Shook Up*** is certified gold by the RIAA.

1981

Epic rejects an entire album, and the band returns to the studio to record further. (The label will also turn down an album from Petersson in 1982.)

1982

May During the month, the group performs at the San Diego Stadium, San Diego, CA, with Chuck Berry and Joan Jett, grossing $455,180.
June [5] ***One On One*** makes UK #95 for one week.
July [24] The extracted *If You Want My Love* makes US #45.
Aug [7] *If You Want My Love* peaks at UK #57. (In Japan, all eight albums have topped the chart.)
Oct [9] ***One On One*** peaks at US #39, yielding the US #65 *She's Tight* two weeks hence.

1983

Oct ***Next Position Please***, produced by Todd Rundgren, makes US #61.

1985

Oct [12] *Tonight It's You* makes US #44, as the band's tenth album ***Standing On The Edge*** leans towards US #35.

1986

Nov With the extracted *Mighty Wings* currently appearing on the film soundtrack to "Top Gun", ***The Doctor*** makes a call at US #115.
[24] The RIAA certifies multi-platinum sales of three million for ***Cheap Trick At Budokan***.

1988

Apr The band travels to Switzerland to play at the "Montreux Rock Festival", Montreux, Switzerland.
June With the group using outside writers and Petersson rejoining the line-up, ***Lap Of Luxury*** is released, a critical and commercial return to form.
July [9] Richie Zito-produced power ballad *The Flame*, penned by UK Mancunian songwriting team Robert Mitchell and Dick Graham, tops the US chart, after a 14-week climb. Cheap Trick is currently on a US tour, begun in Louisville, KY, as Robert Plant's special guests.
Aug The single's success spurs sales of ***Lap Of Luxury***, making US #16.
[28] A 29-date North American tour ends at the Great Western Forum, Inglewood, CA.
Sept [28] ***Lap Of Luxury*** is certified platinum by the RIAA.
Oct [8] Cheap Trick's version of *Don't Be Cruel* hits US #4, becoming the first Elvis Presley cover to hit the US Top 10 since his death.
Dec [24] *Ghost Town* makes US #33.

1989

Mar [4] *Never Had A Lot To Lose* peaks at US #75.

1990

Mar [11] *Surrender To Me*, Zander's duet with Heart's Ann Wilson, from the movie "Tequila Sunrise", hits US #6.
Aug [25] ***Busted*** makes US #48.
Sept [22] *Can't Stop Falling Into Love* reaches US #12.
[26] Video collection "Every Trick In The Book" is certified gold by the RIAA.
Dec [1] *Wherever Would I Be* makes US #50.
[14] Heart and Cheap Trick play before a sellout crowd of 13,000 at the Great Western Forum, Inglewood, CA, during a US trek.
[22] The group performs at the MetroCentre in their home town of Rockford.

1991

Sept Zander takes part in the second annual "Rock'n'Roll Softball Championship of the World" at the Houston Astrodome, Houston, TX.
Oct [26] Retrospective collection ***The Greatest Hits*** peaks at US #174.

1992

Feb [28] Cheap Trick plays before a sellout crowd of 3,400 at the Star Plaza, Merrillville, IN, during a current US tour.
Mar Petersson guests on tracks from Concrete Blonde's ***Walking In London*** album while Zander completes work on a solo album.
Aug [11] ***One On One*** is certified gold by the RIAA.

1993

May [18] Having signed a solo deal with Interscope Records, Zander releases his freshman effort, ***Robin Zander***, co-produced with Jimmy Iovine, featuring songs co-penned with Mike Campbell, J.D. Souther and Dave Stewart, and musical cameos from Dr. John and Cheap Trick colleague, Petersson.
[17] Nielsen performs with hometown Rockford Symphony Orchestra, performing Michael Kamen's "Concerto for Electric Guitar and Orchestra", as well as some Cheap Trick hits, at a benefit for the Rockford Neighborhood Redevelopment.

1994

Apr [4] The group appears on CBS-TV's "Late Show With David Letterman".
[9] Newly signed to Warner Bros. Records, the band's label debut ***Woke Up With A Monster*** bows at its US #123 peak.
Aug [4] Following July dates with REO Speedwagon, Starship and Foghat, Cheap Trick now supports Meat Loaf at the Coca-Cola Starplex Amphitheatre, Dallas, TX.

Oct [8] The group performs *All Shook Up* at "Elvis Aaron Presley : The Tribute", a multi-star music event staged at the Pyramid Arena, Memphis, TN, broadcast live on pay-per-view TV in the US.

1995

Feb [10] The band's 1978 album ***Heaven Tonight*** is certified platinum by the RIAA.
Oct [28] John Lennon tribute album, ***Working Class Hero***, including Cheap Trick's version of *Cold Turkey*, released by Hollywood Records (US), bows at its US #94 peak.
Nov Reflecting a changing of the guard, the group opens for the Smashing Pumpkins at the Riviera Theatre, Chicago, IL.

CHUBBY CHECKER

1958

Dec Checker (b. Ernest Evans, Oct. 3, 1941, Andrews, SC) has been signed under his real name to Cameo-Parkway Records in Philadelphia, PA, after Henry Colt, his boss at a chicken market, impressed by his singing, brought him to the attention of Cameo's Kal Mann. When "American Bandstand"'s Dick Clark and his wife Bobbie, visit Cameo to commission a novelty recording as a Christmas greeting, they are impressed by Checker's ability to imitate other acts' styles. He records *The Class*, written by Mann, and Cameo changes his name after Bobbie Clark notes his resemblance to a teenage Fats Domino (Fats = Chubby; Domino = Checker). The Clarks send the unlikely Checker debut record out as their Christmas card.

1959

June Cameo releases *The Class* on Parkway label and it climbs to US #38. It features Checker imitating Fats Domino, the Coasters, Elvis Presley and the Chipmunks.
July On "American Bandstand", Dick Clark is bombarded with requests for *The Twist*, a Hank Ballard & the Midnighters 18-month-old B-side, because of nationwide teen enthusiasm for the dance. He suggests that Philadelphia act Danny & the Juniors cover it but they decline, so Clark phones Cameo and suggests the song for Checker, who records it with vocal group the Dreamlovers, in a 35-minute session.

1960

Aug [6] Checker debuts *The Twist* on ABC-TV's "The Dick Clark Saturday Night Show". (The first time that Checker performed the song live was before 3,000 teenagers at the Ice House, Haddonfield, NJ.)
Sept [19] Checker's *The Twist* cover has entered the US chart two weeks after Ballard's original, which peaks at US #28, but the exposure given to Checker's cover by "American Bandstand" now takes it to top of the US chart for one week. It will sell over a million copies and also reaches UK #44.
Nov *The Hucklebuck*, reviving a 1949 Tommy Dorsey dance hit, in the new musical idiom, reaches US #14. The B-side, reviving Jerry Lee Lewis' *Whole Lotta Shakin' Goin' On*, makes US #42 in its own right.
Dec ***Twist With Chubby Checker*** hits US #3. He stars in Clay Cole's "Christmas Rock'n'Roll Show" at the Paramount Theater, Brooklyn, New York, NY, with Neil Sedaka, Bobby Vee, the Drifters, Dion, Bo Diddley and others.

1961

Jan The New York State Safety Council announces that, of 54 cases of back trouble reported in a single week, 49 were due to too much "twisting".
Feb [27] *Pony Time* hits US #1 for the first of three weeks and is Checker's second million-seller, setting off a new dance craze for the "pony". The song is a re-write of *Boogie Woogie*, written and recorded by Clarence "Pinetop" Smith in 1928, but the record is a cover of Don Covay & the Goodtimers' original (which peaks at US #60).
Apr *Pony Time* reaches UK #27.
May *Dance The Mess Around* peaks at US #24 and is a minor dance craze. The B-side, *Good Good Lovin'*, makes US #43.
June ***It's Pony Time*** peaks at US #110.
July Checker features in Dick Clark's "Caravan of Stars", a summer rock stage show in Atlantic City, NJ, with Duane Eddy, Fabian, Bobby Rydell and others.
Aug On the first anniversary of *The Twist*, *Let's Twist Again* is released to catch the beginning of a new wave of interest in the dance, spreading from teen hops to adult clubs and from the US to other countries. It hits US #8 and reaches UK #37, earning Checker a third gold disc.
Oct [22] As the Twist reaches fashionable nightspots like New York's Peppermint Lounge, Checker appears on CBS-TV's "The Ed Sullivan Show" singing *The Twist*, and demand for it is re-sparked. *Let's Twist Again* reaches US #11.
Nov *The Fly*, a Twist variation with arm movements to approximate a buzzing fly, hits US #7.
Dec Checker's revival of Bobby Helms' seasonal hit *Jingle Bell Rock*, as a duet with labelmate Bobby Rydell, makes US #21. Checker is featured in the film "Twist Around The Clock", based around New York DJ Clay Cole.
[11] *Twistin' USA* peaks at US #68.

1962

Jan [13] *The Twist*, re-released in the US, tops the Hot 100, again for the first of two weeks - the only single ever to hit US #1 on two separate occasions. ***For Twisters Only*** subsequently hits US #8 while a compilation album (of tracks from his previous four albums) ***Your Twist Party*** hits US #2. (Bishop Burke in Buffalo, NY forbids students from dancing, singing about or listening to *The Twist* in any school or parish or youth event.)
Feb *The Twist* and *Let's Twist Again* are reissued in the UK, as the dance craze hits the country for the first time. Checker makes a UK promotion visit, demonstrating the dance movements on TV. *The Twist* reaches #14, but *Let's Twist Again* becomes the UK's twist anthem, hitting #2. ***Twist With Chubby Checker*** reaches UK #13, while the ***Bobby Rydell/Chubby Checker*** collection of duets hits US #7.
Mar ***For Twisters Only*** makes UK #17.
[17] B-side of *Slow Twistin'*, *La Paloma Twist*, spins to US #72.
Apr *Slow Twistin'*, a duet with (uncredited) labelmate Dee Dee Sharp, hits US #3 and UK #23. Another Rydell duet, *Teach Me To Twist*, makes UK #45.
May ***For Teen Twisters Only***, which includes the hits *The Fly* and *Slow Twistin'*, climbs to US #17.
[29] Checker wins the Best Rock And Roll Recording Of 1961 category for *Let's Twist Again* at the fourth annual Grammy Awards.
June ***Twistin' Round The World*** peaks at US #54. Checker features in the movie "Don't Knock The Twist", singing six songs which appear on the soundtrack album ***Don't Knock The Twist***, which makes US #29.
July *Dancin' Party* reaches US #12. Sounding much like Gary U.S. Bonds' 1961 hit *Quarter To Three*, it prompts Bonds to sue for plagiarism for £100,000. (The case is settled out of court.)
Sept *Dancin' Party* reaches UK #19.
[3] Checker begins a 14-date, twice-nightly UK tour with the Brook Brothers, the Kestrels and others, at Colston Hall, Bristol, Somerset, set to end on the 21st at the Granada Cinema, East Ham, London.
Nov Double A-side *Limbo Rock* and *Popeye (The Hitchhiker)*, each side promoting a different current dance craze, becomes Checker's biggest two-sided US chart success. *Popeye* peaks first, hitting #10.
Dec *Limbo Rock* (a Champs instrumental US chart hit earlier in the year) hits US #2 and reaches UK #32, as the Checker-Rydell duet *Jingle Bell Rock* makes UK #40 and re-charts at US #92. ***All The Hits (For Your Dancin' Party)***, which includes *Limbo Rock*, reaches US #23, and ***Down To Earth***, a selection of duets with Dee Dee Sharp, makes US #117.

1963

Feb ***Limbo Party*** peaks at US #11, and the compilation set ***Chubby Checker's Biggest Hits*** makes US #27.
Mar [2] Checker hosts "The Limbo Party" stage show, at the Cow Palace, San Francisco, CA, with guests including Marvin Gaye, the Crystals, Lou Christie and the Four Seasons.
[16] *Let's Limbo Some More* peaks at US #20.
Apr B-side of *Let's Limbo*, *Twenty Miles*, becomes a bigger US hit than its A-side, at #15. ***Let's Limbo Some More*** makes US #87.
June *Birdland*, plugging yet another dance craze, the "bird", climbs to US #12. B-side *Black Cloud* makes US #98.
Aug Checker moves in on the Beach Boys/Jan & Dean-led surfing fad with *Surf Party*, but it reaches only US #55 and is overtaken by the back-to-1962 *Twist It Up*, which reaches US #25, at a time when twist songs are thought to be all spun out. ***Beach Party*** makes US #90.
Oct Live ***Chubby Checker In Person*** reaches US #104.
Nov *What Do Ya Say*, recorded in London with producer Tony Hatch, reaches UK #37 after Checker's UK promotional visit and TV slots, but it will be his last UK hit for 12 years.
Dec *Loddy Lo* climbs to US #12.

1964

Feb *Hooka Tooka*, the B-side of *Loddy Lo*, is another double-sided US hit for Checker when it replaces its A-side in the Top 20, at #17.
Apr *Hey, Bobba Needle* reaches US #23.
[12] Checker marries Dutch beauty queen Catharina Lodders (Miss World 1962), with whom he will have a long marriage and three children.
[13] He embarks on a US tour at Washington's Casino Royal, set to end on May 31st at the Twin Coaches, Pittsburgh, PA.
July *Lazy Elsie Molly* makes US #40.
Sept *She Wants T'Swim*, following Bobby Freeman's US top five *C'mon And Swim*, floats at US #50, but the "swim" proves to be a short-lived dance craze.

1965

Jan *Lovely, Lovely* peaks at US #70.
May *Let's Do The Freddie*, a cash-in on Freddie & the Dreamers' stage act "dance" which has become a US craze, makes US #40, but is outsold by the group's own (different) song *Do The Freddie*.
Aug [28] Checker begins a UK tour at the Pavilion, Weymouth, Dorset, a day after guesting on ITV's "Ready Steady Go".
Sept [19] He begins a week of cabaret at Newcastle's La Dolce Vita and Doncaster's Fiesta in the North of England.

1966

July *Hey You! Little Boo-Ga-Loo* is his final hit single on Parkway, at US #76.

1969

Apr Signed to Buddah Records, Checker makes a minor US chart comeback with a cover of the Beatles' ***White Album*** track *Back In The U.S.S.R.* (#82).

1970

June [23] Checker is arrested with three others in Niagara Falls, NY, after police discover marijuana and other drugs in their car.

1973

Jan Double compilation album of his chart singles ***Chubby Checker's Greatest Hits*** makes US #152, his first US Album-chart entry since 1963.
Apr [29] An oldies edition of NBC-TV's "Midnight Special", hosted by Jerry Lee Lewis, features Checker among the guest performers.

1975

Dec Capitalizing on an unexpected revival of the twist in UK discos (and an opportunistic UK revival of *Let's Twist Again* by John Asher, which reaches #14), a double A-side reissue of *Let's Twist Again* with *The Twist* hits UK #5.

1982

Mar Signed to MCA Records, Checker returns to the US Hot 100 for the first time in 13 years, at #91, with *Running*, while ***The Change Has Come*** reaches US #186.

1988

May The Fat Boys team with Checker to record a new version of his most famous hit, this time titled *The Twist (Yo' Twist)*.
June [11] Checker and the group perform the song at "Nelson Mandela's 70th Birthday Tribute" at Wembley Stadium, Wembley, Middx.
July [2] *The Twist (Yo' Twist)* hits UK #2.
Aug *The Twist (Yo' Twist)* peaks at US #16.

1989

Never the best of friends, Ballard and Checker nevertheless participate, together with Joey Dee, in filming a segment for a feature-length documentary on the twist, lensed at Lulu's Roadhouse, Kitchener, ON, Canada.
Oct [26] Checker, supported by his band the Wildcats, begins his first UK tour in several years, at the Swansea Leisure Centre, Swansea, Wales.

1991

Dec [16] Still mining the fruits of his most enduring and career-defining hit, Checker files a lawsuit in the Ontario Court General Division against McDonald's in Canada, seeking $14.8 million for its alleged use of an imitation of his voice on *The Twist* in its french fries commercials.

CHER

1964

Cher (b. Cherilyn Sarkasian La Piere, May 20, 1946, El Centro, CA), having moved to Los Angeles, CA, to attend acting classes, has met Sonny Bono (b. Salvatore Bono, Feb. 16, 1935, Detroit, MI), who is working for Phil Spector, in 1963, and through him begins singing back-up vocals for Spector on singles by the Ronettes and others. Having married Bono in Tijuana, Mexico, Cher is used by Spector as the soloist on the novelty single *Ringo I Love You*, released on Spector's minor label, Annette, to cash in on Beatlemania, although it is credited to "Bonnie Jo Mason".

1965

Mar While Sonny & Cher are experimenting with early duo recordings, Sonny has interested Imperial Records in signing Cher as a soloist, which now issues her first solo single, *Dream Baby*, under her full name Cherilyn. (With Sonny & Cher signed to Atco Records as a duo, Imperial will change the billing to Cher on her future solo material.)
Aug [21] Sharing in the publicity generated as the duo's *I Got You Babe* tops the US chart, her cover of Bob Dylan's *All I Really Want To Do* reaches US #15. (The Byrds' version makes US #40.)
Sept The duo's *I Got You Babe* tops the UK chart, while *All I Really Want To Do* hits UK #9. (The Byrds' version hits UK #4.)
Oct Her maiden solo album ***All I Really Want To Do***, produced by Sonny from his experience with Spector, reaches US #16 and hits UK #7.
Nov [13] *Where Do You Go*, written and produced by Sonny, reaches US #25.

1966

Apr [23] *Bang Bang (My Baby Shot Me Down)*, Cher's first solo million-seller, hits US #2. Produced by Sonny, it combines stark melodrama, racing gypsy violins and arresting tempo changes.
[30] *Bang Bang (My Baby Shot Me Down)* hits UK #3.
June ***The Sonny Side Of Cher*** reaches US #26 and UK #11.
Aug Cher covers Cilla Black's movie-title track *Alfie*.
[27] When the film opens in the US, Cher's version is added over the credits and reaches US #32. Cilla Black's makes only US #95 (though it is a Top 10 hit in the UK, where Cher's cover is not released). *I Feel Something In The Air*, a slightly controversial Sonny song about pregnancy out of wedlock, reaches UK #43. (Released in the US as *Magic In The Air*, it failed to chart.)
Oct Cher's cover of Bobby Hebb's (US #2 and UK #12) hit *Sunny* - in her case, with an implied "o" in the word rather than "u" - is released only in the UK and makes #32. (Georgie Fame's cover reaches UK #13.)
Nov ***Cher*** peaks at US #66. *Behind The Door*, penned by Graham Gouldman, charts briefly at US #97. Its B-side, another slightly controversial lyric, *Mama (When My Dollies Have Babies)*, is promoted in the UK, but gains no airplay and fails to chart.

1967

Sept [9] After a recording gap, with Sonny & Cher engaged on the film "Good Times", Cher's *Hey Joe* makes US #94.
Dec [23] *You Better Sit Down Kids*, written by Sonny about family break-up, hits US #9. ***With Love - Cher*** makes US #47. Both fail to hit in the UK, despite good airplay for the single, and mark the end of Cher's Imperial recording contract.

1968

She signs a solo deal with Atco (to which Sonny & Cher are still contracted), which releases ***Backstage***.

1969

Aug ***3614 Jackson Highway*** (named after the Muscle Shoals Sound Studio address, where it is recorded, with producers Jerry Wexler, Tom Dowd and Arif Mardin) makes US #160. Cher has an acting role in the film "Chastity", produced, written and scored by Sonny. She also sings the theme song *Band Of Thieves*. (Chastity is also the name of the Bonos' daughter.)

1971

May Both the duo and Cher as a soloist are signed to a new recording deal with Kapp Records, initially issuing Cher's *Put It On Me*.
Aug [1] Sonny & Cher start "The Sonny And Cher Comedy Hour" on prime-time CBS-TV (which will follow a successful short summer run with three long, high-rating series). The routines, in a variety of characterizations, serve to hone Cher's acting skills for later film work.
Nov [6] *Gypsies, Tramps And Thieves*, produced by Snuff Garrett (the Bonos' next-door neighbor in Bel Air, CA), a dramatic story-song written for Cher by Bob Stone and arranged by Al Capps, hits US #1 for the first of two weeks. The album ***Gypsies, Tramps And Thieves*** reaches US #16.
[19] *Gypsies, Tramps And Thieves* is certified gold by the RIAA, her second million-seller.
Dec *Gypsies, Tramps And Thieves* hits UK #4.

1972

Feb Double Imperial compilation ***Cher Superpak*** makes US #92.
Mar [25] *The Way Of Love*, a ballad taken from ***Gypsies, Tramps And Thieves***, hits US #7.
Apr [13] ***Cher*** is certified gold by the RIAA.
June [24] *Living In A House Divided* reaches US #22. The Bonos' marriage is starting to founder, despite their successful professional relationship.
Sept ***Foxy Lady*** reaches US #43.
Oct [21] *Don't Hide Your Love* makes US #46.

1973

Jan Garrett stops working with the Bonos after selecting *The Night The Lights Went Out In Georgia*, a Bobby Russell story-song of jealousy and murder, for a Cher single, which Sonny vetoes, unbeknownst to Cher at the time. (Vicki Lawrence's version hits US #1 three months later.)
May ***Bittersweet White Light*** reaches US #140.
Oct [6] *Half Breed*, written specifically for Cher by Mary Dean and Al Capps, and produced by Garrett, who knows it to be a smash, is Cher's first release for MCA and now tops the US chart (but makes no chart impression in the UK), while its parent album ***Half Breed*** heads to US #28.
[12] *Half-Breed* is certified gold by the RIAA.

1974

Feb [20] The Bonos separate, with Cher filing for divorce (she has been dating record company executive David Geffen.)
Mar [2] *Dark Lady*, written by the Ventures' keyboards player, Johnny Durrill, makes UK #36 (it will be her last UK chart entry for over a decade).
[4] ***Half Breed*** is certified gold by the RIAA.
[22] Still-climbing *Dark Lady* is also confirmed gold by the RIAA.
[23] *Dark Lady* hits US #1.
June [26] Cher is finally divorced from Bono, at the Santa Monica Supreme Court, Santa Monica, CA.
[29] *Train Of Thought* reaches US #27.
July ***Dark Lady*** peaks at US #69.
Sept [14] *I Saw A Man And He Danced With His Wife* makes US #42.
Dec Compilation album ***Greatest Hits*** reaches US #152, and marks the end of Cher's MCA recording deal. She signs a $2.5 million deal with Warner Bros., negotiated by Geffen, and is reunited with her first producer, Phil Spector.

1975

Feb [16] CBS-TV series "Cher", a weekly hour of music and comedy, airs for first time, with guests Bette Midler, Elton John and Flip Wilson.
Spector produces a highly-rated single, coupling *A Woman's Story* (later revived by Marc Almond) and *Baby I Love You*. The first release on the Warner-Spector label, it fails to chart.
Apr A final Spector-produced duet (with Harry Nilsson), their revival of *A Love Like Yours*, is released.
May ***Stars***, produced by Jimmy Webb, is Cher's only Warner Bros. album to chart, reaching #153.
June [30] Having met him at the Troubadour club with David Geffen, her sister and others, Cher marries Gregg Allman of the Allman Brothers Band, in Los Angeles. (It will be a stormy liaison, with the couple initially filing for divorce on July 10th.)
Nov [8] David Bowie makes his US TV debut on "Cher", singing *Fame* and duetting with the hostess.

1976

Jan [4] The last "Cher" airs on CBS-TV. (It will be replaced for a while by the less successful "Sonny And Cher" series, a purely professional reunion.)
Oct ***I'd Rather Believe In You*** teams her with producers Steve Barri and Michael Omartian (who has been a session player on the duo's TV show), but raises little interest.

1977

Jan [22] *Pirate* makes US #93.
Nov ***Allman And Woman: Two The Hard Way*** is released. (In marketing the album, Allman and Cher reportedly spends $100,000 of their own money for a promotional tour of Europe because Warner Bros. don't believe in the project.)

1979

Jan [16] Cher's divorce from Allman is finalised.
May [3] Still-climbing *Take Me Home* is certified gold by the RIAA.
[12] Signed to the predominantly disco-oriented Casablanca Records, Cher hits US #8 with *Take Me Home*, the title track from ***Take Me Home*** which will make US #25. She embarks on her first solo tour, to

promote the album. (She is now making the gossip columns as "constant companion" of another Casablanca artist, Gene Simmons of Kiss, even guesting as a crazed fan on *Living In Sin* from his self-titled solo album, but the relationship will not be long-lived.)
[17] ***Take Me Home*** is certified gold by the RIAA.
July [7] *Wasn't It Good* makes US #49.
Oct [13] *Hell On Wheels*, her last hit for Casablanca, makes US #59 and is her final US chart entry for nine years.
Dec At year's end Cher roller-skates at Brooklyn's Empire Ballroom wearing a see-through blouse.

1980

Aug [30] She makes an unannounced appearance as vocalist with Black Rose, a band formed with her current boyfriend, Les Dudek, in New York, NY's Central Park.
Nov ***Black Rose*** is released (also on Casablanca), with Cher on vocals, promoted via a US tour under the band name, opening for Hall & Oates.

1982

Feb Cher's (uncredited) duet with Meat Loaf on *Dead Ringer For Love* hits UK #5. She also appears with him in the mini-movie promo video.
[14] She takes part in the "Night Of 100 Stars" at New York's Radio City Music Hall.
[18] Cher opens in her Broadway acting debut in "Come Back To The Five And Dime, Jimmy Dean, Jimmy Dean", directed by Robert Altman, at the Martin Beck Theater, New York, and will subsequently reprise the role in Altman's film version.
June [6] Cher attends the Tony Awards.
Nov Newly signed to CBS/Columbia, Cher releases ***I Paralyze*** including the March issued *Ruby*.

1984

Mar She is nominated for an Oscar for Best Supporting Actress in the movie "Silkwood".

1985

Feb [13] Cher is honored by Harvard University's Hasty Pudding club as "Woman Of The Year".
Mar She gives another critically-rated acting performance, in a leading role in the Peter Bogdanovich-directed film "Mask".

1986

May [22] Cher guests on NBC-TV's "Late Night With David Letterman".
Oct [9] She appears with Elton John and Pee Wee Herman on the premiere edition of Fox-TV's "The Late Show Starring Joan Rivers".

1987

During an active acting period, she co-stars with Jack Nicholson in "The Witches Of Eastwick", appears in the comedy "Moonstruck" and also films the thriller "Suspect".
Oct *I Found Someone*, produced by Michael Bolton, on Geffen Records, hits UK #5 after an almost 14-year chart absence.
Nov [13] Sonny & Cher sing *I Got You Babe* for the first time in ten years, on "Late Night With David Letterman".

1988

Jan [30] Now signed to Geffen Records, ***Cher***, recorded with several producers, including Peter Asher, Michael Bolton, Jon Bon Jovi, Desmond Child and current flame Richie Sambora, makes UK #26.
Mar [5] Power ballad, co-penned by Bolton, *I Found Someone* hits US #10.
Apr [11] Cher wins an Academy Award as Best Actress for her work in "Moonstruck". The second single from ***Cher***, *We All Sleep Alone*, co-written and co-produced by Jon Bon Jovi, reaches UK #47.
May ***Cher*** makes US #32.
[17] ***Cher*** is certified gold by the RIAA.
June [11] *We All Sleep Alone* reaches US #14.
Aug [20] *Skin Deep*, third single from ***Cher***, peaks at US #79.
Sept [7] She performs at the fifth annual MTV Video Music Awards, held at the Universal Amphitheatre, Universal City, CA.

1989

May [13] Ballad *After All*, Cher's duet with Peter Cetera from the film "Chances Are", hits US #6.
June [1] *After All* is certified gold by the RIAA.
July Reprising a similar production and songwriting cast used for ***Cher***, her second Geffen outing ***Heart Of Stone*** hits US #10.
Aug [16-20] To promote Cher's performances at the Sands Casino Hotel in Atlantic City, NJ, 28-year-old Renée Sohile showcases her collection of Cher memorabilia, assembled over the last 21 years in her Rochester, NY, apartment. In return, Sohile receives 30 opening-night tickets and a first-time audience with her idol.
Sept [6] An ever scantily-clad Cher performs at the sixth annual MTV Video Music Awards, staged at the Universal Amphitheatre.
[20] *If I Could Turn Back Time* is certified gold by the RIAA.
[23] Diane Warren-penned *If I Could Turn Back Time* hits US #3, promoted via a risqué US navy battleship-staged video.
Oct *If I Could Turn Back Time* hits UK #6, as Cher continues filming "Mermaids" with co-stars Bob Hoskins and Winona Ryder.
Dec [23] *Just Like Jesse James*, co-written and co-produced by Desmond Child, hits US #8.

1990

Feb [24] *Just Like Jesse James* reaches UK #11, as parent album ***Heart Of Stone*** hits UK #7.
Mar [8] Cher wins Worst Dressed Female Rock Artist in **Rolling Stone**'s 1989 Music Awards, and Worst Video ("If I Could Turn Back Time") in the magazine's 1989 Critics' Awards.
[31] Her "Heart Of Stone" North American tour begins at the Starplex Amphitheatre, Dallas, TX, set to end on August 29th, before a sellout crowd of 14,966 at the Exhibition Stadium, Toronto, ON, Canada.
Apr [14] *Heart Of Stone* (written by Pete Sinfield and Andy Hill - originally for Bucks Fizz) reaches US #20 and will peak at UK #43 the following week.
July [5] ***Heart Of Stone*** is certified multi-platinum by the RIAA.
Aug [18] *You Wouldn't Know Love* makes UK #55.
Oct [19] Cher performs at the Wembley Arena, Wembley, Middx, during a short UK tour.

1991

Jan [19] *The Shoop Shoop Song (It's In His Kiss)*, featured in "Mermaids", makes US #33.
[26] Cher hosts a specially-made two-hour video in her Malibu, CA home, featuring 22 clips including such artists as Janet Jackson, John Fogerty, Van Halen, Bonnie Raitt and Paul Simon, assembled for the troops involved in Operation Desert Storm in the Gulf War, to be broadcast as "Cher's Video Canteen".
Feb [4] CBS-TV airs her first network TV performance in 14 years, "Cher At The Mirage", in Las Vegas, NV.
Apr [11-12] During current US dates, Cher plays before a sellout crowd of 10,024 at the James L. Knight Center, Miami, FL.
May [4] *The Shoop Shoop Song (It's In His Kiss)*, Cher's treatment of Betty Everett's 1964 US #6 hit, tops the UK chart, her first ever UK #1.
June [16] Cher premieres *Love And Understanding* on Fox-TV's "Backstage Pass To Summer".
[17] Cher guests on BBC1-TV's "Wogan".
[29] ***Love Hurts*** debuts at UK #1, her maiden UK chart-topping album.
July [27] *Love And Understanding* hits UK #10.
[30] Cher guests on NBC-TV's "The Tonight Show".
Aug [3] *Love And Understanding* reaches US #17, as ***Love Hurts*** makes US #48.
[27] ***Love Hurts*** becomes Cher's sixth RIAA-certified gold album.
Oct [15] Fashion maven Mr. Blackwell names Cher the worst-dressed woman of the last three decades. "From toes to nose, she's the tacky tattoo'd terror of the 20th century. A Bono-fide fashion fiasco of the legendary kind."
[19] *Save Up All Your Tears* makes UK #37.
Nov [30] Following a month in which Cher guests on the TV shows "Sally Jesse Raphael", "Late Night With David Letterman" and "The Tonight Show", she takes part in NBC-TV's "Dame Edna's Hollywood".
Dec [14] Her second version of the pop standard *Love Hurts* charts for a week at UK #43 (her first appeared on the 1975 album ***Stars***).

1992

Jan [4] *Save Up All Your Tears* makes US #37.
Feb [10] During an appearance on syndicated TV's "Maury Povich Show", she pledges $450,000 to the Children's Craniofacial Association.
Apr [11] Cher participates in the Grand Opening of Euro-Disney in France.
[25] *Could've Been You* makes UK #31.
May [6-7] She performs at the Wembley Arena, during a current European tour.
[27] Cher postpones her performances at the Paramount, New York, set to mark the debut of the US leg of the "Love Hurts" tour following eight weeks in Europe. These shows are set to be her first-ever New York solo concerts, but she is suffering from bronchitis and sinusitis.
July [2] ***Cher*** is certified platinum by the RIAA.
Oct [26] Persistently seen on US TV promoting her own Lonely Hearts costume jewellery and on commercials for Equal sugar substitute, Cher calls into CNN's "Larry King Show" to speak with presidential candidate Ross Perot, confirming that she will be voting for him.
[27-28, 30-**Nov** 1] Cher performs the re-scheduled gigs at the Paramount grossing $1,068,078.
Nov [14] *Oh No Not My Baby* debuts at its UK #33 peak.
[21] ***Cher's Greatest Hits: 1965-1992***, a UK only retrospective, enters the UK chart at #1.

1993

Jan [16] *Many Rivers To Cross* bows at its UK #37 peak.
Feb [16] Cher accepts an award for Prince, who is named the Best International Solo Artist at the 12th annual BRITS, held at London's Alexandra Palace.
Mar [6] *Whenever You're Near* charts for a week at UK #72.
Apr Cher visits Armenia under the auspices of the United Armenian Fund relief organisation.

1994

Jan [22] *I Got You Babe*, a novelty update recorded by Cher with MTV's animated heroes Beavis and Butt-Head, reaches US #35.
Oct [8] She performs at "Elvis Aaron Presley : The Tribute", a multi-star music event staged at the Pyramid Arena, Memphis, TN, broadcast live on pay-per-view TV in the US. (During the year, Cher writes songs for her forthcoming album to be recorded with producer Stephen Lipson in early '95, having only written two songs in her career. She also launches her gothic mail order catalog **Sanctuary**, with items available from 1-800 726 2882.)

1995

Mar [25] A Comic Relief-benefitting charity single, *Love Can Build Bridges*, recorded by Cher, Chrissie Hynde and Neneh Cherry with Eric Clapton, and originally a US Country #5 in 1991 for the Judds, tops the UK chart.
Oct [28] Newly signed to Reprise Records, Cher's interpretation of Marc Cohn's *Walking In Memphis* debuts at its US #11 peak.
Dec [24] "Christmas With Cher" airs on ITV.

1996

Jan [6] Cher performs on BBC1-TV's "National

Lottery Live" program.
[20] *One By One* hits UK #7 in its week of entry.
Feb [10] ***It's A Man's World***, variously produced by Trevor Horn, Stephen Lipson, Chris Neil, Greg Penny and with songs by Paul Brady, Prefab Sprout's Paddy McAloon, Don Henley and Eric Kaz, hits UK #10, prior to the March US premiere of "Faithful" in which Cher co-stars with Ryan O'Neal.
see also: **SONNY & CHER**

NENEH CHERRY

1980

Cherry (b. Neneh Mariann Karlsson, Oct. 10, 1964, Stockholm, Sweden), the daughter of a Swedish artist, Moki, and a West African percussionist, Ahmadu Jah, having been educated in Manhattan and Sweden, and raised by her mother Moki and stepfather, jazz trumpeter Don Cherry, moves to London, having dropped out of school two years earlier, before visiting her real father's family in Africa. With her music career already underway as a backing vocalist for ska combo the Nails, Cherry moves in with the Slits' vocalist, Ari Upp, after Don Cherry has been invited by the UK punkette outfit to tour the UK.

1981

Cherry joins alternative jazz/funk/punk collective Rip, Rig & Panic, which includes Sean Oliver (bass), multi-instrumentalist Gareth Sager, Bruce Smith (drums) and Mark Springer (keyboards). Initially releasing ***God***, the band's only chart success will come in 1982 with the UK #67 ***I Am Gold***. Cherry will marry Smith in 1982, giving birth to her first daughter, Naima, and will also cut two solo tracks *Stop The War* and *Give Sleep A Chance*, a pair of songs about the war in the Falkland Islands, in the same year.

1985

Rip, Rig & Panic dissolves into the trimmed-down and short-lived outfit Float Up C.P. and then into God Mother & Country, before the unit splits permanently, leaving Cherry free to pursue a solo career. Separated from Smith, she soon begins writing and recording demos with her new beau, producer Cameron "Booga Bear" McVey, of the production team Dynamik Duo and subsequent band, Morgan McVey, at his home studio in Notting Hill, London.

1989

Jan [14] Having appeared duetting with Matt Johnson on *Slow Train To Dawn* from The The's 1986 album ***Infected***, and more recently inked a publishing deal with Virgin Music and signed as a solo artist to Circa Records, her part hip-hop dance smash chart debut *Buffalo Stance* hits UK #3.
Mar Her second daughter Tyson Cherry Kwewanda McVey is born.
June [3] *Manchild*, written by Cherry, McVey and Massive Attack's Robert Delnaja, hits UK #5.
[17] ***Raw Like Sushi***, highlighted by Cherry's aggressive urban-themed, dance-stance hip-hop R&B meld, debuts at its UK #2 peak, behind Jason Donovan's ***Ten Good Reasons***.
[24] *Buffalo Stance* hits US #3, as its parent album ***Raw Like Sushi*** enters the US survey, beginning a climb to #40.
Aug [26] *Kisses On The Wind* reaches UK #20.
Sept [6] Cherry collapses in her dressing room during the sixth annual MTV Video Music Awards, at the Universal Amphitheatre, Universal City, CA. Lyme disease is suspected but never fully diagnosed. She pulls out of a major US tour as the support act to the Fine Young Cannibals.
[30] *Kisses On The Wind* hits US #8.

1990

Jan [6] *Heart* peaks at US #73.
[20] *Inna City Mamma* makes UK #31.
Feb [18] Cherry wins the Best International Newcomer and Best International Artist category at the ninth annual BRIT Awards, held at London's Dominion Theatre.
Mar [8] She is named the Best New Female Singer in **Rolling Stone**'s 1989 Critics Awards.
Apr [16] Cherry participates in the "Nelson Mandela - An International Tribute For A Free South Africa" benefit at Wembley Stadium, Wembley, Middx.
Oct [13] *I've Got You Under My Skin*, Cherry's contribution to ***Red Hot + Blue***, an anthology of Cole Porter songs to benefit AIDS education, and originally written for the stage musical "Born To Dance" in 1936, reaches UK #25, and proves to be the most successful single cut from the project.
Dec [7] Cherry marries long-time boyfriend McVey.

1991

June [19] She is featured on BBC2-TV's rap special, "Def II : Rap Rap Rapido".
[20] *Buffalo Stance* is certified gold by the RIAA.
Dec [2] *Buffalo Stance* is honored as one of the Most Performed Pop Songs Of 1990 at the BMI Awards at London's Dorchester Hotel.

1992

Mar After taking a short sabbatical, travelling through Spain and England, she returns with McVey to her childhood home in Hassleholm, Sweden, to set up housekeeping in Moki's converted schoolhouse and begin work on her second album.
[7] Soundtrack album to the Wim Wenders film, "Until The End Of The World", to which Cherry contributes *Move With Me (Dub)*, makes US #114.
Oct [1] Cherry performs her new single *Money Love* on BBC1-TV's "Top Of The Pops".
[3] *Money Love* debuts at its UK #23 peak.
Nov [7] Her sophomore effort ***Homebrew***, featuring Lenny Kravitz, Michael Stipe (on the *Trout* duet), and rappers Gangstarr, and recorded in her native Sweden, debuts at its UK #27 peak.

1993

Feb [4] Cherry makes the front cover of **Rolling Stone** magazine.
Apr [23] She guests on syndicated TV's "The Arsenio Hall Show".
May [1] *Buddy X* makes US #43.
June [19] *Buddy X* bows at its UK #35 peak.

1994

Sept [10] *7 Seconds*, Cherry's duet with Youssou N'Dour, hits UK #3.
Oct [8] *7 Seconds* bows at its US #98 peak.
Nov [24] *7 Seconds* is named Best Song at the inaugural MTV European Music Awards held at the Pariser Platz, Berlin, Germany, against the backdrop of the Brandenburg gate.

1995

Mar [25] Comic Relief charity single, *Love Can Build A Bridge*, recorded by Cherry, Cher and Chrissie Hynde with Eric Clapton, and originally a US Country #5 in 1991 for the Judds, hits UK #1.
May [3] Cherry takes part in the seventh World Music Awards in Monte Carlo.
Oct [17] Tribute album ***Inner City Blues - The Music Of Marvin Gaye***, featuring Cherry's interpretation of *Trouble Man*, is released worldwide by Motown.
[19] Don Cherry dies from liver cancer at age 58 at his step-daughter's home near Malaga, Spain.

THE CHI-LITES

Eugene Record (lead vocals);
Marshall Thompson (drums);
Robert "Squirrel" Lester (vocals);
Creadel Jones (vocals); **Clarence Johnson** (vocals)

1960

The group forms in Chicago, IL, as an R&B quintet, the Hi-Lites, initially led by Thompson (b. April, 1941, Chicago), who backed R&B acts at Chicago's Regal Theater and, with Jones (b. 1939, St. Louis MI), has also been a member of the Desideros; Record (b. Dec. 23, 1940, Chicago), Johnson and Lester are all ex-Chantours performers. A rival band, also called the Hi-Lites, claims the original title use, so they become Marshall & the Chi-Lites. (Marshall is Thompson's forename, and C is added as a location identify of their home town, Chicago.) Initially infused with their respective street-corner harmony and doo-wop influences, they sign to Mercury Records, and release *Pots And Pans*. Subsequently passing through several R&B companies during the mid-'60s, including the Blue Rock, Daran and Ja Wes labels, and gaining local success - not least with the 1964 issue of *You Did That To Me* (their first release credited simply as the Chi-Lites) - the band, now minus Johnson, signs to the Dakar label, through MCA, in 1967.

1969

Apr [12] Newly signed to another MCA subsidiary, Brunswick, by Carl Davis, the Chi-Lites' *Give It Away* climbs to US #88. It is written by Record, who is establishing himself as a successful songwriter, particularly for fellow Brunswick artist, Barbara Acklin (initially the label's receptionist, whom he also marries).
Aug [16] Sentimental ballad *Let Me Be The Man My Daddy Was* peaks at US #94.
Sept ***Give It Away*** makes US #180 during a three-week stay on the chart.

1970

Sept [12] Funky outing *I Like Your Lovin' (Do You Like Mine)* makes US #72, after topping the US R&B chart.

1971

Jan [23] *Are You My Woman? (Tell Me So)* also climbs to US #72.
May [29] With Record now helming the unit as singer/writer/producer, his *(For God's Sake) Give More Power To The People* reaches US #26, while ***(For God's Sake) Give More Power To The People*** heads towards US #12.
Aug [21] *We Are Neighbors* climbs to US #70.
Sept *(For God's Sake) Give More Power To The People* makes UK #32.
Nov [27] *I Want To Pay You Back (For Loving Me)* peaks at US #95.
Dec [11] During a 14-week chart stay, the Record-penned, partly-narrated ballad *Have You Seen Her* hits US #3 (it will be frequently covered, not least by MC Hammer in 1990).

1972

Feb *Have You Seen Her* hits UK #3.
May [27] The group, now at the height of its pop and R&B success, tops the US chart with the harmonica-laden *Oh Girl*, breaking a six-week top-spot residence by Roberta Flack's *The First Time Ever I Saw Your Face*.
June *Oh Girl* reaches UK #14. (It too will re-hit in 1990, as a worldwide cover smash for Paul Young.) ***A Lonely Man*** hits US #5, earning a gold disc.
Sept [2] Sombre *The Coldest Days Of My Life* peaks at US #47.
Oct [21] *A Lonely Man/The Man And The Woman (The Boy And The Girl)* peaks at US #57, as ***The Chi-Lites Greatest Hits*** begins a 24-week US chart stay, set to reach #55.
Dec [30] *We Need Order* peaks at US #61, as the group completes its most successful year.

1973

Apr [14] *A Letter To Myself* climbs to US #33, as ***A Letter To Myself*** makes US #50. Record is made a senior executive at Brunswick.
June [30] *My Heart Just Keeps On Breakin'*, supplied by Fort Knox DJ Stan McKenny, reaches US #92.
Sept [22] *Stoned Out Of My Mind* reaches US #30 and tops the R&B chart, as ***Chi-Lites*** peaks at US #89.
Dec [29] *I Found Sunshine* peaks at US #47.

1974

Mar [23] *Homely Girl* peaks at US #54.
May [4] School-themed love ballad *Homely Girl*, co-written by Record with McKenny, hits UK #5, as the group begins a UK tour.
July [20] *There Will Never Be Any Peace (Until God Is Seated At The Conference Table)*, inspired by a graffiti legend in a Boston nightclub, peaks at US #63.
Aug [3] *I Found Sunshine* makes UK #35. ***Toby*** peaks at US #181 (their lowest album-showing in five years, and their last for six more.)
Sept [7] *You Got To Be The One* peaks at US #83.
Nov [30] Perky, uptempo *Too Good To Be Forgotten* hits UK #10.

1975

Jan [26] The group begins a five-week UK tour with a cabaret engagement at Bailey's in Leicester, Leics.
Apr [12] *Toby/That's How Long* reaches US #78. Rumors persist of Record's dissatisfaction with their current form.
June Re-released double A-side *Have You Seen Her/Oh Girl* hits UK #5.
Oct [18] Another Record pop/soul ballad *It's Time For Love* hits UK #5.
Nov [22] *It's Time For Love* stalls at US #94 (and is the group's final US chart single). Record, increasingly active as a writer and producer for other Brunswick acts, including Acklin, Gene Chandler, Erma Franklin and the Staples Singers, announces his decision to leave the Chi-Lites as ***Half A Love*** fails to sell, to be replaced by Danny Johnson. When Jones also quits, David Scott joins, prior to making way for Stanley "T.C." Anderson.

1976

Sept [11] *You Don't Have To Go* hits UK #3. The remaining members sign a new deal with Mercury, who release the Thompson-produced ***Happy Being Lonely***. Two compilation albums are also issued: ***Very Best Of The Chi-Lites*** (Brunswick) and ***Chilitime*** (London).

1977

Still without Record, the Chi-Lites release ***The Fantastic Chi-Lites*** on Mercury, while Brunswick retails the US-only ***Greatest Hits Volume 2***.

1979

Aug With other Chi-Lites now inactive, Record signs to Warner Bros. as a solo act and releases *Magnetism* and ***Welcome To My Fantasy***, the first of three projects for the label, in between subsequent Chi-Lites recordings.

1980

Nov Record has reunited the Chi-Lites and established the label Chi-Sound which releases the US #179 ***Heavenly Body***, followed by ***Me And You***, which will make US #162 in May 1982.

1983

Aug Now trimmed to the trio of Record, Thompson and Lester, and established on the US label Larc (licensed in the UK through specialist dance label Red Bus), ***Bottom's Up***, led by Record, climbs to US #98.
[20] Taken from it, *Changing For You* peaks at UK #61. (Moving on to the Private I label, they will release ***Steppin' Out*** the following year. The band will remain popular on the soul cabaret circuit during the '80s and '90s, particularly in the UK, where compilation albums will periodically appear (including ***The Chi-Lites Classic*** (1984) and ***20 Golden Pieces Of The Chi-Lites*** (1985)), and will release one new studio set in 1986 (***Hard Act To Follow*** on the Nuance label). As the group's leader, Record continues his production career, helming Gene Chandler's 1991 outing ***Just Push Play***. On September 21st 1995, Thompson will participate in a class action suit filed in an Atlanta, GA federal court in which a number of popular veteran soul acts seek back-dated pension fund remuneration from allegedly unscrupulous record labels.)

CHIC

Nile Rodgers (guitar); **Bernard Edwards** (bass); **Tony Thompson** (drums); **Alfa Anderson** (vocals); **Luci Martin** (vocals)

1972

After playing together in various New York, NY clubs since meeting in 1970, Edwards (b. Oct. 31, 1952, Greenville, NC) and Rodgers (b. Sept. 19, 1952), ex-'60s rock combo New World Rising, team with Thompson (b. Nov. 15, 1954) to form the Big Apple Band, a rock-fusion trio. Following steady club work and tours, backing soul acts New York City and Carol Douglas, and switching to the newly-emerging disco genre, briefly name-changing to Allah & the Knife-Wielding Punks, the trio adds Norma Jean Wright as its female lead voice, in 1976.

1977

June Now supplemented by a second female vocalist, Anderson, the group adopts the name Chic, and self-produces several dance-oriented tracks in an unsuccessful attempt to win a recording deal. Tom Cossie and Mark Kreiner license Chic's masters of the already-recorded tracks, and form M.K. Productions, subsequently handling the band's business affairs.
Sept The group signs to Atlantic Records (which had earlier turned it down), after the personal intervention of company president Jerry Greenberg.
Dec Edwards and Rodgers write and produce an overlooked debut solo disco album for Wright (released the following year by Bearsville Records as ***Norma Jean***).

1978

Jan [14] Chic's debut *Dance Dance Dance (Yowsah Yowsah Yowsah)* hits UK #6.
Feb [16] Still-rising on the US survey *Dance Dance Dance (Yowsah Yowsah Yowsah)* is certified gold by the RIAA.
[25] *Dance Dance Dance (Yowsah Yowsah Yowsah)* also hits US #6, becoming a million-seller.
Mar [4] Written and produced by Edwards and Rodgers, ***Chic***, recorded in just three weeks for $35,000, reaches US #27. By the time it is released, Wright, who contributed to the album, has already left to pursue her solo career, to be replaced by Martin.
[29] ***Chic*** is certified gold by the RIAA.
May [13] *Everybody Dance* hits UK #9.
June [17] *Everybody Dance* makes US #38.
Dec [7] Still-rising *Le Freak* is certified platinum by the RIAA.
[9] Era-defining dance cut *Le Freak* hits US #1 for the first of six weeks. One of the biggest-selling singles of the decade, it will become Atlantic's best-selling single to date.
[16] *Le Freak* hits UK #7.
[23] ***C'Est Chic***, containing *Le Freak*, hits US #4. Later to be regarded as a landmark dance album, and once again written and produced by Edwards and Rodgers, the seminal disc, featuring guest vocalists David Lasley and Luther Vandross, showcases what will become their trademark skills: Rodgers' chopping disco-rhythm guitar sound underpinned by Edward's dextrous bass playing, offset by the twin female vocals and melodic string arrangements by concert master Gene Orloff.
[27] ***C'Est Chic*** is confirmed platinum by the RIAA.

1979

Jan [20] The group performs at London's Hammersmith Odeon.
Mar [1] Still-climbing *I Want Your Love* is certified gold by the RIAA.
Apr [7] Insistent *I Want Your Love* hits UK #4, as ***C'Est Chic*** hits UK #2, kept off the top by German bandleader James Last's ***Last The Whole Night***.
[14] Indistinguishable from Chic, a Rodgers/Edwards production for Sister Sledge, *He's The Greatest Dancer* hits UK #6 (and US #7, another million-seller, on May [12]. (Sister Sledge's album and single ***We Are Family*** will follow, with further hit singles and a second album, ***Love Somebody Today***, all successfully guided by the Chic Organization Ltd.).
May [5] *I Want Your Love* hits US #7 and is another million-seller.
June [26] Still-rising *Good Times* is ratified gold by the RIAA.
July [21] *Good Times* hits UK #5. (Built around a distinctive Edwards bass line, it will become one of the most imitated in popular music in succeeding years, not least for Queen's 1980 US chart-topper *Another One Bites The Dust*. The Sugarhill Gang will will also borrow the arrangement for their *Rapper's Delight*, subsequently required to give joint composer credits to Rodgers and Edwards.)
Aug [18] *Good Times* tops the US chart.
Sept [1] Edwards and Rodgers-helmed ***Risqué*** reaches UK #29.
[22] ***Risqué***, recorded at New York's Power Station complex and once again featuring string arrangements by Orloff, hits US #5.
Nov [3] *My Forbidden Lover* reaches UK #15 and US #43.
Dec [6] ***Risque*** is certified platinum by the RIAA.

1980

Jan [5] *My Feet Keep Dancing* (featuring a unique ensemble tap dance bridge by Eugene Jackson, Faynard Nicholas and Sammy Warren) reaches UK #21, while an early compilation album, ***Les Plus Grands Succés De Chic: Chic's Greatest Hits***, makes US #88.
[19] Same compilation, but retitled ***The Best Of Chic***, reaches UK #30.
Feb [2] Rodgers/Edwards' production of *Spacer* by Sheila B. Devotion makes UK #18.
Aug [9] Diana Ross' *Upside Down*, produced by Rodgers/Edwards, hits UK #2 (and will chart-top in the US on Sept [6]). It is taken from ***Diana***, also produced by the duo, though remixed by Ross - without their cooperation - because she feels her vocals have been sublimated to their production.
[30] Chic's fourth self-contained studio album ***Real People*** reaches US #30.
Sept [20] The extracted *Rebels Are We* peaks at US #61.
Nov [22] Double A-side *Real People/Chip Off The Old Block* reaches US #79.

1981

Aug [15] Increasingly in demand for their hit production and writing skills, the Edwards and Rodgers-helmed ***Koo Koo***, a solo set by Debbie Harry, hits UK #6 and will peak at US #25 on Sept [19].

1982

Jan [23] Chic's ***Take It Off***, featuring the Brecker Brothers, Jocelyn Brown and Fonzi Thornton, makes US #124.
June [26] *Soup For One*, the theme from the film of the same title (with a score by Rodgers and Edwards), is Chic's last US chart single, at #80.
Oct [2] Rodgers/Edwards-created *Why*, from ***Soup For One,*** recorded by Carly Simon, hits UK #10, having peaked at US #74 on Aug [7].
Dec [11] With the disco era now passed, ***Tongue In Chic*** makes US #173.

1983

Mar [12] *Hangin'* peaks at UK #64. (Following the release later in the year of Chic's final album ***Believer***, the group fades from commercial favor, leaving Rodgers and Edwards to concentrate on independent projects. Rodgers, initially releasing his debut solo ***Adventures In The Land Of The Good Groove***, will produce a prodigious body of work throughout the remainder of the decade, including David Bowie's ***Let's Dance***, Madonna's breakthrough album ***Like A Virgin***, and other projects for artists including Duran Duran, Aretha Franklin, Jeff Beck, Mick Jagger, Al Jarreau, Grace

Jones, Johnny Mathis and Spanish-language group, Olé-Olé. He will also briefly join the Honeydrippers, with Robert Plant, Jimmy Page and Beck.)

1985

Rodgers releases his sophomore solo album ***B-Movie Matinee***, while Edwards completes his debut ***Glad To Be Here***. Both Edwards and Thompson join Power Station, with Robert Palmer and members of Duran Duran (releasing ***The Power Station***), which leads Edwards into the successful production of a number of Palmer solo albums, climaxing with the artist's US chart-topper *Addicted To Love*, in 1986.

1987

Sept *Jack Le Freak*, a Stock/Aitken/Waterman updated segued medley, reaches UK #19. (A second segued mish-mash, *Megachic - Chic Medley*, will peak at UK #58 on July [14] 1990.) Rodgers continues promoting the eponymous debut album by his recently-formed (and short-lived) trio, Outloud (with Phillipe Saisse and Felicia Collins), and will end the decade as the co-founder of the Ear Candy label, established with former cohort Tom Cossie, in New York.

Dec [5] ***Freak Out***, a Telstar UK-only compilation comprising Chic and Sister Sledge material, peaks at #72.

1992

Feb [22] Re-formed and signed to Warner Bros. Records, Chic, now featuring Edwards and Rodgers with Sylver Logan Sharp and Jenn Thomas (vocalists from Washington DC group Brown's Creation), makes UK #48 with *Chic Mystique*, taken from their comeback album ***Chic-Ism***. (The comeback will prove short-lived with Edwards and Rodgers returning to still in-demand production work. Rodgers will sign his extensive publishing portfolio to Sony Music Publishing in 1995.)

1996

Apr [18] Having recently completed recording and producing Power Station's second album with Robert Palmer, Andy Taylor and Thompson, and having performed earlier today during the "J.T. Super Producers '96" concert series in Tokyo, Japan, alongside Steve Winwood, Slash, Sister Sledge, Simon Le Bon and Rodgers, Edwards, claiming to be unwell, retires to his hotel room, where he is found dead later in the evening by Rodgers. (The following week the cause of death will be confirmed as pneumonia. Thompson will say of his colleague: "My best friend, my mentor and one of the greatest people I've ever known". Edwards is survived by six children from his first marriage.)

CHICAGO

Peter Cetera (vocals, bass); **Robert Lamm** (vocals, keyboards); **Terry Kath** (guitar); **Danny Seraphine** (drums); **James Pankow** (trombone); **Lee Loughnane** (trumpet); **Walter Parazaider** (saxophone); **Laudir de Oliveira** (percussion)

1966

Parazaider (b. Mar. 14, 1945, Chicago, IL), after studying at DePaul University, Chicago, where he meets fellow students Loughnane (b. Oct. 21, 1946, Chicago), Pankow (b. Aug. 20, 1947, St. Louis, MO), and Seraphine (b. Aug. 28, 1948, Chicago), has been playing in Jimmy & the Gentlemen with Kath (b. Jan. 31, 1946, Chicago), when the two of them begin auditioning for music jobs, one of which is for a group called the Executives, for which Seraphine is also auditioning. The three of them decide to form their own band, the Missing Links, recruiting Loughnane and Lamm (b. Oct. 13, 1944, Brooklyn, New York, NY), who Parazaider and Seraphine find playing in Bobby Charles & the Wanderers at a bar on the South Side, and name-change to the Big Thing.

1967

Feb [15] The newly-formed group congregates in Parazaider's apartment, where they make a gentlemen's agreement to devote themselves to the project. They soon begin rehearsing in his mother's basement in Maywood, IL.

May [22] The band makes its concert debut as the Chicago Transit Authority, with a two-week residency at the Stardust Lounge, Rockford, IL.

Aug [29] They begin a week-long stint at Shula's Supper Club in Niles, MI, during which they are spotted by subsequent manager James William Guercio, who Parazaider had met at DePaul, and who is now producing fellow Chicagoans, the Buckinghams.

Nov [1-5] They make their hometown debut, playing five nights at the Club Laurel in Chicago.

Dec [13-17] The group opens for the Exceptions at Barnaby's, a new club in Chicago. The Exceptions' bass player, Peter Cetera (b. Sept. 13, 1944, Chicago), is so impressed with them that he will leave the group by year's end and join the Big Thing.

1968

June [18] Having been relocated to Los Angeles, CA by Guercio (who has by now finished with the Buckinghams and renamed the Big Thing the Chicago Transit Authority, also paying their rent), the group plays the local Kaleidoscope venue.

Sept [12-14] The band makes its debut at the Fillmore West in San Francisco, CA.

1969

Jan Chicago flies to New York to begin recording its debut album. Having been turned down by CBS/Columbia twice and in spite of Guercio currently producing the label's new signing Blood Sweat & Tears, the band finally signs after producer Mike Curb has recorded a demo which has interested other labels.

Feb [21] The group makes its Fillmore East debut in New York.

May [17] Chicago's debut album ***Chicago Transit Authority*** begins a three-year stay on the US chart. Unusually for a first effort, it is a double album. Containing a popular fusion of jazz/pop ballads and rock (and protest chants from the 1968 Democratic Convention in Chicago), it will reach US #17 and hit UK #9. Touring to promote the project, the group supports Janis Joplin and Jimi Hendrix.

[20] Cetera, watching a baseball game in Dodger Stadium, Los Angeles, is set upon by four marines, who inflict a broken jaw in three places, leaving him in intensive care for two days.

July After legal threats from the city of Chicago transportation department, Guercio shortens the group's name to Chicago.

Aug [1] They take part in the "Atlantic City Pop Festival", Atlantic City, NJ.

[23] First single from the debut album, the Robert Lamm-penned *Questions 67 And 68*, answers at US #71.

[30-31] The group participates in the "Dallas Pop Festival", Dallas, TX.

Sept [13] Chicago performs at the "Toronto Rock'n'Revival Show" in the Varsity Stadium at the University of Toronto, Toronto, ON, Canada, on a bill which includes Chuck Berry, Cat Mother & the All Night Newsboys, Alice Cooper, Bo Diddley, Fats Domino, the Doors, Kim Fowley, Doug Kershaw, Jerry Lee Lewis, Little Richard, Screaming Lord Sutch, Gene Vincent, Tony Joe White and the Plastic Ono Band.

Dec [4] Chicago begins a 14-date European tour at London's Royal Albert Hall, set to end on the 21st in Newcastle, Tyne & Wear.

1970

Jan [8-11] The group plays four dates at the Fillmore West, at the start of an 11-month US tour, supported by the Guess Who.

Feb [14] Their cover of the Spencer Davis Group's *I'm A Man* hits UK #8. Follow-up double album ***Chicago*** begins a 134-week US chart stay, eventually hitting #4 and UK #6.

June [6] *Make Me Smile*, written by Pankow, hits US #9.

July [28] The group performs at the "Expo '70" exhibition in Montreal, PQ, Canada.

Aug [28] Chicago plays at the "Isle Of Wight Festival" at Godshill, Isle of Wight, during a break in its North American tour.

Sept [5] *25 Or 6 To 4*, written by Lamm, becomes a worldwide smash, hitting UK #7.

[12] *25 Or 6 To 4* hits US #4.

Nov [26] The group performs its 162nd, and last, concert of the year, at the Auditorium Theatre, Chicago.

1971

Jan [2] Re-released from their debut album, *Does Anybody Really Know What Time It Is?* hits US #7. Their third double album ***Chicago III*** hits US #2.

[20] The group begins a 72-date North American tour at the Warehouse, New Orleans, LA, set to close on May 23rd at Millett Hall, Miami University, Oxford, OH.

Apr [3] *Free* reaches US #20, as ***Chicago III*** makes UK #31.

[5-10] Chicago becomes the first rock group to play at the Carnegie Hall in New York, with six sellout concerts, recorded for the forthcoming four-album set ***Chicago At Carnegie Hall***.

June [1] The group begins a 15-date world tour at London's Royal Albert Hall. Covering Germany, France, Denmark, Sweden, Italy, Greece, Thailand and Japan, it will end on the 19th at H.I.C. Arena, Honolulu, HI.

[12] *Lowdown* makes US #35.

July [12] Chicago begins another major US tour, at the Santa Clara Fairgrounds, San Jose, CA.

Aug [14] Double A-side *Beginnings/Color My World*, from the first album, hits US #7.

Nov [20] Another reissue, the previously-charted *Questions 67 And 68*, coupled with an earlier UK hit, *I'm A Man*, reaches US #24. An argument between some band members and Guercio precedes the release of ***Chicago At Carnegie Hall***. Guercio insists it should be released, but Chicago feels the recordings are of poor quality. It hits US #3, the highest-charting four-album box set.

1972

Feb Chicago embarks on a world tour, playing in 16 countries, including Japan, Australia, Yugoslavia, Poland and Czechoslovakia, in less than a month.

Aug [19] New studio album, and their first one-disc set, ***Chicago V*** begins a nine-week stay at US #1.

Sept [23] *Saturday In The Park*, from ***Chicago V***, hits US #3, becoming the group's first gold single, while in the UK, the album climbs towards #24. Guercio writes and directs the film "Electra Glide In Blue", which features performances from four Chicago members.

Nov [9] *Saturday In The Park* is certified gold by the RIAA.

Dec [9] *Dialogue (Part I & II)* reaches US #24.

1973

Feb Chicago records at Guercio's newly-built Caribou Studio, with Oliveira on percussion. (He will become a full-time member in 1974.)

July [28] ***Chicago VI*** hits US #1, where it will stay for five weeks.

Aug [18] *Feelin' Stronger Every Day*, written by Cetera and Pankow, hits US #10. Japan-only release ***Chicago Live In Japan*** will sell over one million copies in the Far East.

Dec [8] *Just You'n'Me*, written by Pankow, hits US #4.

1974

Jan [2] *Just You'n'Me* is confirmed gold by the RIAA.

Apr [27] Another double album, ***Chicago VII***, tops the US chart.

May [1] *(I've Been) Searchin' So Long*, from ***Chicago VII***, hits US #9.

Aug [1] The group begins work on new album at the Caribou Ranch.

[10] Second single from ***Chicago VII***, the Loughnane-penned *Call On Me*, hits US #6. Keyboardist Lamm releases solo album ***Skinny Boy***, the title track of

which, with vocals from the Pointer Sisters, is also included on ***Chicago VII***.
Nov [30] Taken from their seventh album, Cetera's *Wishin' You Were Here*, featuring backing vocals from Al Jardine, and Carl and Dennis Wilson of the Beach Boys, whom Guercio is also managing, reaches US #11.

1975

Apr [5] *Harry Truman*, written by Lamm and the first single from the forthcoming ***Chicago VIII***, reaches US #13.
May [3] ***Chicago VIII*** tops the US chart, as the group embarks on 12-city US tour with the Beach Boys in support, with more than 700,000 paying a total of $7.5 million to see the bands.
June [7] *Old Days*, written by Pankow, hits US #5.
Sept [20] *Brand New Love Affair (Part I & II)*, also penned by Pankow, peaks at US #61.
Dec [13] ***Chicago IX - Chicago's Greatest Hits*** begins a five-week stay at US #1.

1976

May Chicago's Mayor Richard Daley awards the group the city's "Medal Of Merit".
Aug [7] *Another Rainy Day In New York City*, written by Lamm, makes US #32, as parent ***Chicago X*** hits US #3, during a 44-week chart stay.
Oct [23] Ballad *If You Leave Me Now*, written by Cetera and featuring a distinctive Jimmie Haskell arrangement, tops the US chart and will add to the band's growing list of radio standards.
Nov [13] *If You Leave Me Now* tops the UK chart, becoming Chicago's biggest worldwide smash.
Dec [4] ***Chicago X*** reaches UK #21.

1977

Jan [31] Chicago wins the Favorite Band, Duo Or Group, Pop/Rock category at the fourth annual American Music Awards, held at the Santa Monica Civic Auditorium, Santa Monica, CA, while undertaking another world tour, beginning with sellout dates in the UK and Europe.
Feb [19] *If You Leave Me Now* wins Best Pop Vocal Performance By A Duo, Group Or Chorus and Best Arrangement Accompanying Vocals, at the 19th annual Grammy Awards.
Apr [30] *You Are On My Mind*, written by Pankow, makes US #49.
June Guercio, increasingly involved in other projects, stops managing Chicago. The band appears at Geraldo Rivera's "One To One" benefit show.
Oct Chicago becomes the first act to be awarded the Gold Ticket, for playing to over 100,000 fans at New York's Madison Square Garden.
[11] Still-climbing ***Chicago XI*** is certified platinum by the RIAA.
Nov [12] ***Chicago XI***, the last album produced by Guercio, hits US #6.
[19] *Baby, What A Big Surprise*, written by Cetera, with a backing vocal from Carl Wilson, makes UK #41.
Dec [3] *Baby, What A Big Surprise* hits US #4.

1978

Jan [23] Kath, an avid gun collector for six years, accidentally shoots himself in the head while playing with what he believes is an unloaded gun at a friend's house in Woodland Hills, CA. Bandleader Doc Severinsen visits the group after Kath's funeral and persuades it to continue as Chicago.
Apr [1] *Little One*, written by Seraphine and David "Hawk" Wolinski, and with a featured lead vocal from Kath, makes US #44.
June [3] *Take Me Back To Chicago*, a Seraphine/Wolinski-penned tune about the late Freddy Page of the Illinois Speed Press, featuring Chaka Khan on backing vocals, peaks at US #63.
Aug Group signs a management deal with Wald-Nanas Associates, and will begin recording its 13th album, with Phil Ramone at Criteria Studios in Miami, FL. Donnie Dacus is recruited from the Stephen Stills Band to replace Kath.
Oct [27] Still-rising ***Hot Streets*** is certified platinum by the RIAA.
Dec [2] *Alive Again*, penned by Pankow, reaches US #14, as parent album ***Hot Streets***, their first not to feature "Chicago" in the title, reaches US #12 and is supported by a "comeback" US tour, highlighted, at some of the big-city concerts, by an orchestra conducted by Bill Conti.

1979

Mar [3] *No Tell Lover* reaches US #14.
Apr [28] *Gone Long Gone*, written by Cetera, peaks at US #73.
Sept [1] *Must Have Been Crazy*, the first (and only charting) single from the new album ***Chicago 13***, recorded with Ramone at Le Studio in Montreal, Canada, written and sung by Dacus, climbs to US #83.
[29] ***Chicago 13***, breaking the sequence of roman numerals album titles (and released in the UK as ***Street Player***), reaches US #21.(The album is their first to sell under a million copies, which is probably of less concern to the band than the 12" version of *Street Player* being ceremoniously burned at the 'death to disco' rally during a Chicago White Sox game at Comiskey Park).
Dec [10] ***Chicago XIII*** is ratified gold by the RIAA.
[21-22] Chicago joins the Eagles and Linda Ronstadt for two benefit concerts at San Diego's Sports Arena and Los Angeles' Aladdin Theater, which raise almost $500,000 for the presidential campaign of California governor Jerry Brown.

1980

Sept [13] Having signed a new multi-million-dollar deal with Columbia, ***Chicago XIV***, produced by Tom Dowd and recorded at the Record Plant in Los Angeles (with guitarist Chris Pinnick filling in for the departed Dacus), makes US #71 and becomes the group's least successful album, going "aluminum, maybe plywood" in Pankow's words.
[20] *Thunder And Lightning*, written by Lamm and Seraphine, makes US #56.

1981

Dec [12] While Columbia has bought Chicago out of the remainder of its contract, its final album on the label, ***Chicago - Greatest Hits, Volume II*** enters the US chart set to make #171.

1982

Jan [23] While Chicago signs to the Full Moon label, and Bill Champlin (ex-Sons of Champlin), a successful solo artist (his album ***Runaway*** makes US #178 in February), joins as an additional vocalist, Cetera's self-written and-produced solo album, ***Peter Cetera***, also released on Full Moon, enters the US survey set to reach #143.
Sept [11] Chicago ballad *Hard To Say I'm Sorry*, written by Cetera with new producer David Foster, and used in the Daryl Hannah-starring movie "Summer Lovers", tops the US chart.
[15] *Hard To Say I'm Sorry* is certified gold by the RIAA.
[18] ***Chicago 16*** hits US #9, their first Top 10 album in five years.
Oct [9] *Hard To Say I'm Sorry* hits UK #4.
[23] Parent album ***Chicago 16*** makes UK #44.
Dec [4] *Love Me Tomorrow* reaches US #22.
[14] ***16*** is confirmed platinum by the RIAA.
[25] UK-only TV-advertised compilation ***Love Songs*** makes UK #42.

1983

Jan [29] A third ***Chicago 16*** extract *What You're Missing* peaks at US #81.

1984

June [23] *Stay The Night* reaches US #16, taken from ***Chicago 17***, released on Full Moon, which will hit US #4. Produced and partly co-written by Foster, it features backing vocals by Cetera's brother Ken, Richard Marx and Donny Osmond.
Oct [20] *Hard Habit To Break*, co-written by Steve Kipner, hits US #3.
Nov [24] *Hard Habit To Break* hits UK #8.
Dec ***Chicago 17*** reaches UK #24.

1985

Jan [19] Cetera/Foster composition *You're The Inspiration* hits US #3.
Feb [23] *You're The Inspiration* reaches UK #14. Amid internal acrimony, Cetera leaves to pursue a solo career. He is replaced by Jason Scheff, son of Jerry Scheff, Elvis Presley's bass player for many years. Recent recruit Pinnick also quits.
Apr [20] *Along Comes A Woman* reaches US #14.

1986

Jan [27] Chicago wins the Favorite Band, Duo Or Group, Pop/Rock category, at the 13th annual American Music Awards, held at the Shrine Auditorium, Los Angeles.
May [13] The RIAA certifies multi-platinum sales of ***17*** (at four million).
Aug [2] Cetera's ballad theme from the film "The Karate Kid II", *The Glory Of Love*, tops the US chart. It will also hit UK #3, while his second solo album ***Solitude/Solitaire*** reaches US #23.
Sept [27] Chicago's new version of its 1970 hit *25 Or 6 To 4* makes US #48, as Cetera's ***Solitude/Solitaire*** peaks at UK #56.
Nov [18] Cetera's ***Solitude/Solitaire*** is confirmed gold by the RIAA.
[21] The RIAA certifies platinum sales of ***Chicago III***, ***Chicago At Carnegie Hall IV***, ***Chicago VII*** and ***Chicago VIII*** and two million sales each for ***Chicago Transit Authority***, ***Chicago V***, ***Chicago VI*** and ***Chicago X***.
Dec [1] ***Chicago 18*** is confirmed gold by the RIAA.
[6] *The Next Time I Fall*, which sees Cetera teamed with Christian singer Amy Grant, tops the Hot 100.

1987

Feb [14] Cetera's *Big Mistake* peaks at US #61.
[21] *Will You Still Love Me?* hits US #3 during a 23-week run, as its parent album ***Chicago 18***, again produced by Foster, reaches US #35. Cetera co-writes and produces former Abba star Agnetha Fältskog's ***I Stand Alone***, duetting with her on the title track.
May [30] Chicago's *If She Would Have Been Faithful* reaches US #17. (Champlin duets with Patti LaBelle on *The Last Unbroken Heart*, featured in NBC-TV's "Miami Vice".)
July [18] *Niagara Falls* stalls at US #91.

1988

Mar [6] "In The Heat Of The Night", which features Champlin giving his best Ray Charles impression, premieres on NBC-TV.
Apr [30] Cetera/Fältskog duet *I Wasn't The One (Who Said Goodbye)* peaks at US #93.
Aug ***Chicago 19***, produced by Ron Nevison, makes US #37.
[27] *I Don't Wanna Live Without Your Love* hits US #3.
Sept Third Cetera album ***One More Story***, produced by Madonna's musical director, Patrick Leonard, makes US #58.
Oct [1] Cetera's *One Good Woman* hits US #4.
Lamm announces a solo project with co-producer Randy Goodrum, as the group reveals plans to take part in Amnesty International's 25th anniversary.
Dec [3] Cetera's *Best Of Times* peaks at US #59.
[10] *Look Away*, written by US hit meistress Diane Warren, tops the US chart.

1989

Jan [18] *Look Away* is certified gold by the RIAA, while ***19*** will be confirmed platinum, on February 1st.
Mar [25] *You're Not Alone* hits US #10.
May [13] Cetera and Cher's duet *After All*, from the Cybil Shepherd/Robert Downey Jr. film "Chances Are", hits US #6.
[27] Chicago begins its first tour with the Beach Boys since 1975 at the Pacific Amphitheatre in Costa Mesa, CA.

June [1] *After All* is certified gold by the RIAA.
[17] *We Can Last Forever* peaks at US #55.
Dec [2] A 15-track UK compilation album ***The Heart Of Chicago*** reaches UK #15.
[23] *Look Away* wins the Top Pop Singles category in **Billboard**'s The Year In Music statistical round-up.

1990

Feb [10] ***Greatest Hits 1982-1989*** makes US #37.
[24] *What Kind Of Man Would I Be?*, produced by Chas Sandford, hits US #5.
Aug [18] *Hearts In Trouble*, from the Tom Cruise-starring vehicle "Days Of Thunder", peaks at US #75.
[21-22] Chicago makes its debut at New York's Radio City Music Hall, during a current US tour, sans Seraphine, who leaves the group a quarter of a century after joining.

1991

Feb [10] Cetera joins nearly 100 celebrities in Burbank, CA, to record *Voices That Care*, co-written by him and David Foster and fiancée Linda Thompson Jenner, to benefit the American Red Cross Gulf Crisis Fund.
Mar [9] *Chasin' The Wind*, written by Diane Warren, makes US #39, as parent album ***Twenty 1***, again helmed by Ron Nevison, peaks at US #66. Still drumless following Seraphine's departure, John Keane fills in, while additional guitarist Dwayne Bailey has become a full-time band recruit.
Apr Seraphine files a lawsuit in Los Angeles US District Court against the other band members, claiming he is owed $1.5 million from his partnership share, in addition to punitive damages.
May [23, 25] Chicago performs at the Fox Theatre, Detroit, MI as it embarks on its annual summer tour.
Aug [9] The RIAA certifies platinum sales of *If You Leave Me Now* and ***Chicago II*** and multi-platinum sales of five million for ***Chicago IX - Chicago's Greatest Hits***.
Sept [19-22] The group, still a major live attraction, plays four sellout concerts at Mexico's National Auditorium, Mexico City, grossing more than $1.3 million.
Nov Columbia's Legacy imprint releases ***Chicago - Group Portrait***, a four CD/cassette boxed set, tracing the band's career up to 1981.

1992

Mar [29] Champlin and Pankow participate in the 12th annual "Musicians for UNICEF" benefit, at the Palamino Club, Los Angeles, raising $8,000.
June [12-13] Chicago and the Moody Blues, on a tour with shared billing, appear at the New Pine Knob Music Theatre, Clarkston, MI.
July [23] The band receives its own star on the Hollywood Walk of Fame in Hollywood, CA.
Sept [12] Cetera's *Restless Heart* reaches US #35.
[26] His album ***World Falling Down***, co-produced with Andy Hill and Foster and featuring musical guests Champlin (who has recently recorded ***Burn Down The Night*** for Japan-only release) and Chaka Khan, peaks at US #163.
Oct [13-14] Augmented by a new full-time drummer, Tris Imboden, Chicago performs at the Westbury Music Fair, Westbury, NY, during a two-week swing of its current US tour.

1993

Jan [30-31] The group begins short tour of South-East Asia in Singapore.
Feb [13] Cetera/Khan duet *Feels Like Heaven* peaks at US #71.
July [24] Cetera's *Even A Fool Can See* makes US #68. (By year's end, Cetera will sign a deal with Chicago-based indie River North Records.)
Aug [31] Chicago concludes its annual summer tour at the Concord Pavilion, Concord, CA.

1994

Mar [19] Re-charted ***The Heart Of Chicago*** hits UK #6.
July [6] ***Greatest Hits 1982-1989*** reaches RIAA-certified sales of two million.
Aug [4] The RIAA certifies multi-platinum sales of five million for ***17***.
Sept [17-18] The group finishes its latest tour at the Greek Theatre, Los Angeles.

1995

Mar Having acquired the masters to its 16 Columbia albums, the band sets up its own Chicago Records to sell its back catalog, which still racks up sales of 600,000 a year.
Apr Lamm contributes *Without Her*, with Gerry Beckley and Carl Wilson, to ***For The Love Of Harry (Everybody Sings Nilsson)*** tribute album.
May [23] Now signed to Giant Records, the band's new album, the Bruce Fairbairn-produced ***Night And Day***, a big band effort with contributions from the Gipsy Kings, Jade and Paul Shaffer is released.
June [17] ***Night And Day*** makes US #90.
July [14] A US summer tour, with Christopher Cross as support act, opens at the Coca-Cola Starplex Amphitheatre, Dallas, TX.
Oct [28] *Forever Tonight*, Cetera's duet with star of NBC-TV's "Wings" Crystal Bernard, peaks at US #86.
Nov [18] The group, now comprising Champlin, Parazaider, Lamm, Loughnane, Scheff, Pankow, Imboden and guitarist Keith Howland, takes part in a "Gala For The President At Ford's Theatre" from Washington, DC, in the presence of President and Mrs. Clinton.

1996

Feb [16] Arcade Records (Europe) having licensed the band's entire back catalog for European release, releases ***The Very Best Of Chicago***, which includes two new cuts including the simultaneously issued *Let's Take A Lifetime*.

THE CHIEFTAINS

Paddy Maloney (uilleann pipes, tin whistle); **Derek Bell** (harp, tiompán, harpsichord); **Martin Fay** (fiddle); **Kevin Conneff** (bodhrán, vocals); **Matt Malloy** (flute); **Sean Keane** (fiddle)

1976

Mar [20] Maloney (b. 1938, Donnycarney, Dublin, Eire) and Fay (b. 1936, Dublin), having first played together in the 1950s in the Irish folk collective Ceolteoiri Chaulann, have formed the Chieftains in 1963 with fellow members, bodhran player Sean Potts (b. 1930) and flautist Michael Tubridy (b. 1935), providing the core of varying lineups which released the first of many traditional Irish music sets, ***Chieftains 1*** in 1964 on the Dublin-based Claddagh label. Performing as a loosely knit ad-hoc unit, with members keeping their day-jobs, during the remainder of the decade it is not until 1969 that they release a second album ***Chieftains 2***, one which brings the group's central figure, Moloney's skillful pipes playing to the fore. Having added Keane (b. 1946, Dublin) and Peadar Mercier (b. 1914, Eire) for ***Chieftains 3*** (in 1971) and augmented by Bell (b. 1935, Belfast, N. Ireland) for ***Chieftains 4*** (in 1973), their status as Ireland's top traditional/Celtic roots band has spread to the UK where they are now a popular live act (selling out London's Royal Albert Hall in 1975, and signing to Island Records), and to the US where a mix of transplanted Irish fans and college students attend their concerts and spur the group's fifth album ***Chieftains 5***, to now make US #187.

1976

With Conneff having replaced Mercier, they release ***Women Of Ireland***, followed by ***Bonaparte's Retreat*** (also this year), ***Chieftains 7*** (1977) ***Chieftains Live*** (also in 1977), ***Chieftains 8*** (in 1978).

1979

With Potts and Tubridy having left and now joined by ex-Planxty member Molloy (b. Ballaghadeereen, County Roscommon, Eire), the Chieftains release ***9 Boil The Breakfast Early***, featuring bodhran player Conneff's vocals for the first time. During the year, the band also performs as the opening act for the Pope before 1.35 million people at an outdoor mass held at Dublin's Phoenix Park.

1981

C&W-inflected ***Chieftains 10*** is released (issued in the US as ***Cotten Eyed Joe***).

1983

The Chieftains undertake an historic tour of China, the first western group to perform with a Chinese folk orchestra and the first band to ever perform on the Great Wall Of China (scenes captured on the subsequent video and album releases ***The Chieftains In China*** released in 1984). Mid-'80s albums that follow are ***Ballad Of The Irish Horse*** (1985) and ***Celtic Wedding*** (1987), the same year that their first collaboration with Irish flautist James Galway, ***In Ireland***, is also released.

1988

Aug Having issued ***Year Of The French*** earlier in the year, ***Irish Heartbeat***, a collaboration with Van Morrison, makes US #102.

1989

A Chieftains Celebration, also the title of a week of sold-out concerts in Dublin performed the previous year featuring Nanci Griffith and Morrison, is released. (During the year the Chieftains are named by the Irish government as Ireland's Musical Ambassador.)

1990

July [21] The Chieftains appear at Roger Waters' "The Wall" at the site of the Berlin Wall in Potzdamer Platz, Berlin, W. Germany. The event is broadcast live throughout the world, and raises money for the Leonard Cheshire-established Memorial Fund For Disaster Relief.
(A second Galway teaming, ***The Celtic Connection*** is released.)

1991

Dec [21] Having issued ***Reel Music/The Filmscores***, a collection of their movie themes work, earlier in the year, ***The Bells Of Dublin***, a multi-artist celebration helmed by the Chieftains and including guests Jackson Browne, Elvis Costello, Marianne Faithfull, Griffith and Rickie Lee Jones, makes US #107.

1992

Apr [4] ***An Irish Evening - Live At The Grand Opera House, Belfast***, with five tracks featuring Roger Daltrey and Griffith, makes US #120. Later in the year ***Another Country***, exploring the influences of traditional Irish music on Country and a collaboration performed with Willie Nelson, Chet Atkins and Emmylou Harris, among others, is released.

1993

Celtic Harp, a tribute to Irish harpist Edward Bunting, is released.

1994

Mar [17] The Chieftains give a St. Patrick's Day concert at New York's Carnegie Hall. (They also perform at a pay-per-view TV music tribute to the Who, organized by Daltrey.)
May They perform at "The Great Music Experience" broadcast live by satellite from the Todaiji Temple, Nara, Japan, performing with Joni Mitchell, Dylan, Ry Cooder, Michael Kamen and the Tokyo Philharmonic Orchestra.

1995

Feb [19] ***The Long Black Veil***, including music guests the Rolling Stones, Sinead O'Connor, Sting, Mark Knopfler and Ry Cooder among many, becomes the group's first UK chart record, debuting at its #17 peak.

Mar [17] Still rising on the US survey, ***The Long Black Veil*** is certified gold by the RIAA.
Apr [1] ***The Long Black Veil*** reaches US #22.
July [4] The group participates in "A Capitol Fourth 1995" concert broadcast live by PBS-TV from the US capitol's West Lawn, hosted by Stacy Keach.
[15] An 11-date US tour opening for Sarah McLachlan begins at Jones Beach Theatre, Wantagh, NY (a bill grossing $223,323 from 6,785 attendees), set to end on August 1st at the Cynthia Woods Mitchell Pavilion, The Woodlands, TX.
Sept [12] The Chieftains perform with host Luciano Pavarotti at his "War Child" benefit concert held at Novi Sad Park, Italy.

1996

Feb [28] *Have I Told You Lately That I Love You*, their duet with Morrison, is named the Best Pop Collaboration at the 38th annual Grammy Awards held at Los Angeles' Shrine Auditorium.
Mar [30] Having started a 20-city US tour in Houston on the 2nd, ***Film Cuts*** makes US #193.

THE CHIFFONS

Judy Craig (lead vocals); **Barbara Lee** (vocals); **Patricia Bennett** (vocals); **Sylvia Peterson** (vocals)

1960

Sept The New York-based vocal group, comprising Bennett (b. Apr. 7, 1947, Bronx, New York, NY), Craig (b. 1946, Bronx), Lee (b. May 16, 1947, Bronx) and Peterson (b. Sept. 30, 1946, Bronx), has come together earlier in the year, while all the girls are still attending high school, singing during lunchbreaks and in the neighborhood after school. Ronnie Mack, a local songwriter and pianist, has drafted them to rehearse and perform some of his songs for a demo tape and has sold *Tonight's The Night*, featuring guitar work by Butch Mann (later of the Drifters), to local label Big Deal, now resulting in a minor US hit at #76. The following year, while making the industry rounds with his demos, Mack interests Brooklyn quintet the Tokens (of *The Lion Sleeps Tonight* 1961 US #1 fame), who are producing under the name Bright Tunes, who subsequently sign Mack and the Chiffons.

1962

Dec *He's So Fine* is recorded (with the Tokens playing back-up instruments) at Mirror Sound Studios, Manhattan, NY, where the session engineer, impressed by the "doo-lang" chant with which the group accompanies the song, suggests that it should form the introduction.

1963

Jan Capitol Records, with which the Tokens have a first-refusal deal, reject *He's So Fine*, but the smaller Laurie label buys it.
Mar [30] *He's So Fine* tops the US chart for the first of four weeks, and will sell over a million copies.
May Mack collapses in the street, and is hospitalized in New York with Hodgkin's Disease. At his hospital bed, he is presented by the Tokens with a gold disc for his #1 hit, but dies shortly afterwards.
[11] *He's So Fine* reaches UK #16.
June ***He's So Fine*** peaks at US #97.
July Follow-up *One Fine Day*, hits US #5. Composers Goffin and King, having originally recorded this song with Little Eva on lead vocal for the Tokens, take it to the Chiffons' producers, who buy the whole production and erase Little Eva's voice track, substituting the Chiffons'. The Tokens also record the Chiffons, under the pseudonym the Four Pennies, on *My Block*. Released on Laurie subsidiary label Rust, it peaks at US #67.
Aug [10] *One Fine Day* makes UK #29.
Oct *A Love So Fine*, the third consecutive Chiffons release with the word "fine" in the title, peaks at US #40.
Nov *When The Boy's Happy (The Girl's Happy Too)*, credited to the Four Pennies, is released. It charts briefly at US #95, but the pseudonym is soon abandoned.

1964

Jan *I Have A Boyfriend* reaches US #36.
June [5] The group begins a nine-date US tour at the Swing Auditorium, San Bernadino, CA, opening for the Rolling Stones on their first US visit.
Aug *Sailor Boy* peaks at US #81. The group sues, to extricate itself from the contract with Bright Tunes - a deal from which they earned little, since the producers financed all their studio time with deductions from the Chiffons' royalties. A court eventually frees them on the grounds of having been minors when they signed the original agreement. With other labels now wary of them, the group returns to Laurie to sign a direct deal.

1965

July [31] *Nobody Knows What's Going On* reaches US #49.

1966

June *Sweet Talkin' Guy*, written by Doug Morris and Elliot Greenburg, restores them to the US Top 10 after three years, hitting #10.
July [2] *Sweet Talkin' Guy* reaches UK #31.
Aug *Out Of This World*, a near-clone of *Sweet Talkin' Guy*, makes US #67.
Oct *Stop, Look and Listen* stalls at US #85, and is the group's last US hit.

1969

Craig quits the group, which, despite barren chart years, is still performing in New York and touring the US on a regular basis.

1972

Apr Reissued in the UK, *Sweet Talkin' Guy* hits #4.

1976

Aug [31] US district court judge Richard Owen finds George Harrison guilty of "subconscious plagiarism" of the Ronnie Mack song *He's So Fine* when writing his 1970 million-seller *My Sweet Lord*. Earnings from the song, frozen since the suit was filed in 1971, go partly to the inheritors of Mack's estate. Taking advantage of the publicity surrounding the trial and verdict, the Chiffons record their own version of *My Sweet Lord*.

1992

May [15] While the group has often reunited to work the US oldies circuit (including the "The Royalty Of Doo-Wop" US tour with the Belmonts, the Diamonds, the Flamingos and the Silhouettes in 1989), and Ace Records (UK) has issued the 33-track CD retrospective ***The Chiffons - Greatest Recordings***, original member Barbara Lee Jones dies of a heart attack at age 48.

CHINA CRISIS

Gary Daly (vocals); **Eddie Lundon** (guitar); **Brian McNeil** (keyboards); **Gazza Johnson** (bass); **Kevin Wilkinson** (drums)

1982

Aug [14] After leaving school at age 17, Daly (b. May 5, 1962, Kirkby, Merseyside) and Lundon (b. June 9, 1962, Kirkby) have joined forces in Kirkby in 1979 to become what will be the long-time core of China Crisis. Gigging locally, they developed a loyal following as an integral part of the early '80s Mersey music scene. Signed to Liverpool independent label, Inevitable, the group's *African And White*, originally released in February, has been picked up by Virgin Records, and now makes UK #45, which leads to a long-term contract with the label.

1983

Feb [19] With new recruits Johnson and Wilkinson, the follow-up *Christian* reaches UK #12, as their self-penned parent album ***Difficult Shapes And Passive Rhythms***, produced by Mike Howlett, climbs to UK #21. The band begins a European tour supporting Simple Minds.
June [11] Wistful *Tragedy And Mystery* makes UK #46.
Oct [22] *Working With Fire And Steel* peaks at UK #48.
Nov ***Working With Fire And Steel - Possible Pop Songs Vol. 2***, again helmed by Howlett, reaches UK #20.

1984

Jan [28] Taken from the album, *Wishful Thinking* hits UK #9.
Mar [17] *Hanna Hanna* makes UK #44.

1985

Jan The group's car turns over on an icy road during an early morning journey home from the recording studio. Daly suffers a broken arm and Johnson a broken upper jaw, but the others escape without serious injury.
Apr [27] Steely Dan-influenced *Black Man Ray*, recorded at sessions with ex-Steely Dan Walter Becker producing, reaches UK #14.
May [11] Becker-produced ***Flaunt The Imperfection*** debuts at UK #9, as the group undertakes a UK tour.
June [29] Extracted from the album, *King In A Catholic Style (Wake Up)* reaches UK #19.
Flaunt The Imperfection peaks at US #171, as the band undertakes a US concert trip.
Sept [14] *You Did Cut Me* peaks at UK #54.

1986

Jan China Crisis becomes the first major rock act to play in Gibraltar.
Apr The group takes part in the "Soundwave For Greenpeace" benefit at London's Royal Albert Hall.
July The group teams with producers Clive Langer and Alan Winstanley to record a new album.
Sept Daly and Lundon play a few UK pub dates under the name Kirk Douglas & the Long Coats From Hell.
Nov [15] *Arizona Sky*, taken from forthcoming album, makes UK #47.
Dec Their fourth self-written album ***What Price Paradise?*** peaks at UK #63.

1987

Jan [31] *Best-Kept Secret*, also from the album, makes UK #36.
Mar ***What Price Paradise?*** peaks at US #114.

1989

May [13] ***Diary Of A Hollow Horse***, recorded at George Benson's studio in Hawaii and costing over £300,000, makes UK #58. Virgin, dissatisfied with the project, decides to release the band but retain Daly and Lundon. The duo remains loyal to the band, which breaks up.

1990

Sept [15] A 14-track ***China Crisis Collection***, chronicling the band's singles career to date, debuts at UK #32. (Daly and Lundon will continue writing together for a period, before reuniting in 1992 to record demos, eventually releasing *Every Day The Same* on the Stardumb label (UK) in August 1994. McNeil joins Glaswegian band Horse, before working as an engineer at ÇaVa Studios in Glasgow. Johnson, after recording with ex-Lucy Show Mark Van Dola, quits the business and takes a computer-programming course. Wilkinson becomes a session drummer, before joining Fish's backing band.)

THE CHORDETTES

Lynn Evans (lead vocals); **Jinny Osborn** (tenor vocals); **Carol Buschman** (baritone vocals); **Janet Ertel** (bass vocals)

1949

Sept The Chordettes, formed by Osborn, daughter of the president of the Society for the Preservation and Encoragement of Barbershop Quartet Singing in America, Inc., with Ertel, Buschman (Ertel's sister-in-law) and Dorothy Hummitszch, in 1946, perfect their harmonies on local engagements around their hometown of Sheboygan, WI. Through Osborn's father's connections as president of the Kingsbury Brewery, they sing *Ballin' The Jack* on "Arthur Godfrey's Talent Scouts" radio show (securing the slot after being seen performing at a party in Rhode Island, at which Henry Ford, Harvey Firestone and the Secretary of the Treasury are present), which, in turn, wins them a regular spot on his new CBS-TV show, "Arthur Godfrey & His Friends".

1950

Feb Having recorded their debut album ***Harmony Time*** for CBS/Columbia in November, their first single *Candy And Cake*, by Arthur Godfrey & the Chordettes, is released.

1952

At a barbershop convention in Youngstown, OH, Evans, a local schoolteacher and housewife currently singing tenor in an all-girl quartet, the Belles of Harmony, fills in for the pregnant Hummitzsch (now Dorothy Schwartz), performing *Drifting And Dreamin'*, *Sentimental Journey*, *Angry*, *Moonlight Bay* and others.

1954

Following the expiration of their Columbia contract, which has yielded seven singles with Godfrey and one with Bill Lawrence (another singer on the show) and the albums ***Harmony Time Volume Two***, ***Harmony Encores*** and ***The Chordettes Sing Your Requests***, and after their departure from the "Arthur Godfrey & His Friends" show, and modifying their music style to meet changing tastes, they sign with Archie Bleyer's fledgling Cadence label. (In addition to being Godfrey's former musical director, Bleyer is dating Chordette Ertel, who will soon become Mrs. Bleyer.)

Apr The quartet's first Cadence single *True Love Goes On And On* is released.

Dec After several other singles, *Mr. Sandman* hits US #1, where it will remain for seven weeks, and sells over a million copies. The song has been written by Pat Ballard, music editor of **College Humor** magazine, for Guy Mitchell, who passed on it. Bleyer had discovered it on the flip of Vaughn Monroe's *Doing The Mambo*. (Osborn, married to the Mariners' Tom Lockard, also regulars on "Arthur Godfrey & His Friends", had been on maternity leave when they cut the track, and Chicago airline stewardess Margie Needham stood in for her. Nancy Overton, who has been in the Heathertones, will take Ertel's place on the road for most of the group's career, before being replaced in turn by former Bon-Bon, Joyce Weston.)

1955

Jan [8] *Mr. Sandman* reaches UK #11, despite Top 20 competition from covers by Max Bygraves (#16 - Jan [22]) and Dickie Valentine (#5 - Feb [5]).

1956

Jan [28] *The Wedding* peaks at US #91.

Mar [31] *Eddie My Love* reaches US #17. Their cover of the Teen Queens' (US #22) R&B original, it shows their continued interest in the growing teen market. (Another cover, by the Fontane Sisters, outsells both, reaching US #12.)

July [21] *Born To Be With You*, written by Don Robertson, who had penned the earlier *Humming Bird* single, hits US #5. (The song will be successfully reprised by Dave Edmunds in 1973.)

Sept [8] *Born To Be With You* hits UK #8, and is their first UK top tenner.

Nov [17] The soldier-boy love anthem *Lay Down Your Arms* reaches US #16. (In the UK, Anne Shelton's original hits #1 and becomes an enduring "forces favorite".)

[24] B-side *Teen Age Goodnight* makes US #45.

1957

Aug [5] The group guests on the first edition of Dick Clark's "American Bandstand" to be nationally aired on ABC-TV.

Oct [19] *Soft Sands*, flipside of the still-climbing *Just Between You And Me*, peaks at US #73.

[26] *Just Between You And Me* reaches US #19.

1958

Apr [5] The group's second million-seller is the teen novelty *Lollipop*, which hits US #2. The original version by Ronald & Ruby (Ruby being a pseudonym for co-writer Beverly Ross) makes US #39.

May [10] *Lollipop* hits UK #6, although a cover by the Mudlarks attracts more airplay and hits #2.

June [21] *Zorro*, the theme from the Walt Disney-produced ABC-TV series "Zorro", reaches US #17.

1959

Apr [4] *No Other Arms, No Other Lips* reaches US #27.

Sept [5] *A Girl's Work Is Never Done* peaks at US #89.

1961

Aug [12] The group's version of Mano Hadjadakis' movie-theme song *Never On Sunday* becomes their last US Top 20 hit, reaching #13.

Sept [30] B-side *Faraway Star* makes US #90 for one week and proves to be their chart swan song. (Their cabaret career will continue for a while, but - following Osborn's decision to quit - the remaining trio decides to do likewise. Compilation albums of their material will remain among Cadence's most consistent sellers, until Bleyer folds the company in September 1964.)

1963

Jan [12] Janet Ertel becomes mother-in-law to half of another former Cadence act, when Phil Everly of the Everly Brothers marries her daughter (and Bleyer's stepdaughter), Jackie Ertel.

1988

June Evans, now retired from teaching and singing with Swing Four, decides to re-form the Chordettes, calling on Nancy Overton, Overton's sister (and fellow Heathertone) Jean Swain and Doris Alberti, who has been singing barbershop for 20 years, to complete the quartet.

Nov [22] Janet Bleyer dies of cancer in Sheboygan. (Archie Bleyer will outlive her by a matter of months.)

1991

June [8] The Chordettes make their venue debut at New York's Radio City Music Hall, as special guests at "The Royal New York Doo-Wop Show".

THE CHRISTIANS

Garry Christian (vocals); **Russell Christian** (vocals); **Henry Priestman** (vocals); **Roger Christian** (vocals)

1984

Having flirted musically with the Yachts in the late '70s and It's Immaterial in the early '80s, Priestman (b. July 21, 1958, Liverpool, Lancs.), who becomes the main songwriting and creative force in the band, meets the three Christian brothers, Garry (b. Feb. 27, 1955, Liverpool), Russell (b. July 8, 1956, Liverpool) and Roger (b. Feb. 13, 1950, Liverpool), part of a family of 11 Christian offspring, in Pete Wylie's Liverpool studio. As a soul a cappella trio, they have previously called themselves Equal Temperament, the Gems and even Natural High - the name used for their appearance in 1974 on the ITV talent show "Opportunity Knocks".

1985

The Christian brothers begin to concentrate on Priestman's material - songs that will become the core of the band's career. They play a live concert, the "Liver Aid Ethiopian Famine" benefit, in Liverpool. Much time is spent in Priestman's eight-track studio, recording a demo tape of what will later become their first three singles.

1986

Mar A day before signing to the independent label Demon, the band is snapped up by Island Records on the strength of its demo. First recording efforts, with Clive Langer producing, prove fruitless, but a subsequent teaming with Laurie Latham suits both the group and the record company.

Sept *Forgotten Town*, *Hooverville* and *When The Fingers Point* are cut with Latham, but - as the group embarks on a UK mini-tour - Roger Christian becomes irritated by the attention being focused on the more photogenic (and head-shaven) Garry, and also strongly objects to touring.

Nov Relations become strained and Priestman himself threatens to leave on three occasions, if the family bickering continues.

1987

Feb The band makes its debut as a trio (i.e. without Roger) on C4-TV's "Saturday Live".

Mar [14] Their debut single *Forgotten Town* reaches UK #22.

Apr The Christians tour the UK and complete work on their first album.

July [18] *Hooverville (They Promised Us The World)* reaches UK #21.

Oct [24] *When The Fingers Point* makes UK #34.

[31] ***The Christians*** debuts at its UK peak, #2, behind Fleetwood Mac's ***Tango In The Night***, becoming Island's best-seller by a debuting group. The largely Priestman-penned set showcases Garry Christian's distinctively smooth soul/rock vocal style.

1988

Jan [30] *Ideal World* reaches UK #14, as the group undertakes an extensive European tour, establishing itself as a major UK act.

Mar ***The Christians*** peaks at US #158.

May [14] Its fifth extract *Born Again* reaches UK #25.

June The group opens for Fleetwood Mac on selected UK dates.

Oct [29] Their cover of the Isley Brothers' classic *Harvest For The World* hits UK #8.

1989

May [20] *Ferry 'Cross The Mersey*, on which the Christians join with fellow-Liverpudlians Paul McCartney, Gerry Marsden, Holly Johnson and Stock/Aitken/Waterman to aid the relatives of those who lost their lives in the recent Hillsborough soccer disaster, enters the UK chart at #1.

Oct [7] Roger Christian makes his solo chart debut, at UK #63, with *Take It From Home* (and will release ***Checkmate*** in August).

Dec [30] The group's *Words* reaches UK #18.

1990

Jan [27] Their sophomore effort ***Colour***, recorded in Guernsey and Liverpool and once again written by Priestman and helmed by Latham, tops the UK chart in its first week of release.

Apr [7] *I Found Out* peaks at UK #56.

May [5] The Christians sing *Revolution* at the "John Lennon Tribute Concert" at the Pier Head Arena in Merseyside, to celebrate the late-Beatle's songs.

Sept [22] *Greenbank Drive* peaks at UK #63.

Oct [7] The group begins an eight-date UK tour at the Liverpool Empire, set to end on the 16th at the Brighton Centre.
Nov [28] They play the first of four concerts of a further mini-tour at Manchester's Apollo Theatre.

1992

May The band works on new tracks with producer Laurie Latham at Helicon Mountain Studios, having already cut material with Martin Phillips and Eden Studios.
Sept [19] *What's In A Word* reaches UK #33.
Oct [10] ***Happy In Hell***, co-produced by Phillips and Latham, debuts at its UK #18 peak.
[13] A nine-date UK tour (their first in two years) begins at the Corn Exchange, Cambridge, Cambs., set to end on the 24th at Newport Centre, Newport, Gwent, Wales.
Nov [14] Extracted from their third album, *Father* makes UK #55.

1993

Mar [6] *The Bottle* bows at its UK #39 peak.
Nov [20] Career retrospective ***The Best Of The Christians***, including two new cuts, the Latham co-produced *The Perfect Moment* and *Small Axe*, debuts at its UK #22 peak.

1994

July [21-24] During occasional UK dates, the band performs during the "Heineken Music Festival", Wollaton Park, Nottingham, Notts. (Garry Christian will also take part in an EMI Music songwriters' week workshop at the Huntsham Court Hotel, Devon in October.)

LOU CHRISTIE

1962

Oct Having won a State Scholarship at Moon Township High School, to study classical music and voice training, and sung on unsuccessful releases by the Classics (1960) and Lugee & the Lions (1961), Christie (b. Lugee Alfredo Giovanni Sacco, Feb. 19, 1943, Glenwillard, PA) records his first solo single, *The Gypsy Cried*, highlighting his trademark falsetto, for CO&CE Records in Pittsburgh, PA. It is his first recorded composition with Twyla Herbert, a clairvoyant 15 years his senior, with whom he has written since 1958.

1963

Mar [16] *The Gypsy Cried*, picked up by the Roulette label, peaks at US #24.
June [1] Four Seasons-esque *Two Faces Have I* is his first US Top 10 hit, at #6.
Aug [10] *How Many Teardrops* makes US #46.
Sept His freshman effort ***Lou Christie*** climbs to US #124.

1964

After touring the US with Dick Clark's "Caravan Of Stars" package, Christie is called up for US army reserve duty and spends six months stationed at Fort Knox, KY.

1965

Out of the army, he signs a management deal with Bob Marcucci (former mentor of Fabian and Frankie Avalon), and a recording deal with MGM. Christie and Herbert write *Lightnin' Strikes*, which MGM hesitantly releases.

1966

Feb [19] *Lightnin' Strikes* tops the US chart for one week.
Mar [3] *Lightnin' Strikes* is certified gold by the RIAA.
[19] *Lightnin' Strikes* is Christie's UK chart debut, reaching #11. In the US its success prompts labels owning his earlier recordings to release them: *Big Time* on Colpix charts at #95, while *Outside The Gates Of Heaven* on CO&CE makes #45.
[26] ***Lightnin' Strikes*** peaks at US #103.
Apr [30] The official follow-up to *Lightnin' Strikes* is the similarly-arranged *Rhapsody In The Rain*, which is banned by many US radio stations for its suggestive lyrics, but nevertheless climbs to US #16.
[16] He returns home to the US during a UK tour, missing five appearances. Promoter Mervyn Conn considers legal action for alleged breach of contract.
May [7] *Rhapsody In The Rain* makes UK #37.
July [1] Christie begins a US tour in Honolulu, HI, with Herman's Hermits, the Animals and Jerry Lee Lewis.
[23] *Painter*, from the parent album ***Painter Of Hits***, peaks at US #81.

1967

May [6] Newly signed to CBS/Columbia, *Shake Hands And Walk Away Cryin'* peaks at US #95.

1969

Oct After two quiet years, Christie has signed to Buddah Records for *I'm Gonna Make You Mine*, which provides a major chart comeback hitting US #10.
Nov [1] *I'm Gonna Make You Mine* hits UK #2, behind the Archies' *Sugar Sugar*.
[30] During a promotional tour of the UK, Christie appears at the London Palladium, the same day he also appears on BBC1-TV's "Top Of The Pops".

1970

Jan [24] *She Sold Me Magic*, his last UK hit, reaches #25, while *Are You Getting Any Sunshine?* peaks at US #74. (He will be resident in the UK for some years during the '70s, having married an English girl, former beauty queen Francesca Winfield. He also runs the highly successful Five Arts company, managing other acts and making TV commercials.)

1974

Mar [9] Christie's final US hit, at #80, is his update of the '30s standard *Beyond The Blue Horizon*, for the independent Three Brothers label.

1992

May [8-9] While Christie recorded with the Midsong International, Lifesong and Elektra labels during the '70s (and also taking part-time employment in a variety of jobs including cattle farming and off-shore oil drilling), Rhino Records (US) has released ***Enlightnin'ment - The Best Of Lou Christie*** in 1988 and Polygram (US) has brought further hits to compact disc the following year with ***Rhapsody In The Rain***. Still relying, as he has for the past two decades, on oldies revival tours and club engagements, he now appears at WCBS-FM Radio's 20th Anniversary Concert (alongside the likes of the Ronnie Spector, Gary US Bonds the Dixie Cups and others), held at New York's Radio City Music Hall.

CLANNAD

Maire Ni Bhraonain (lead vocals, harp); **Pol O. Braonain** (guitar, keyboards, vocals); **Ciaran O. Braonain** (bass, synthesizers, vocals); **Noel O. Dugain** (guitar, vocals); **Padraig O. Dugain** (mandola, guitar, vocals)

1973

The daughter Maire (b. Aug. 4, 1952, Dublin, Eire), and sons of Irish showband leader Lee O. Braonain, and their Dugain uncles, form Clannad (Gaelic for "family") in Gweedore, County Donegal, Eire, with the main intention of entering Irish folk festivals, having initially begun performing together at Leo's Tavern (Lee O. Braonain's local hostelry) in 1970. Signed to the Irish division of Philips Records, releasing this year's ***Clannad*** debut (followed by ***Clannad II*** in 1974, ***Dulaman*** in 1976 (on the Gael-Linn label) and ***Clannad In Concert*** in 1979 (on Ogham Records), their European success will extended to W. Germany, where they perform a tour in 1975, while in 1979 Clannad sells out five nights at New York's Bottom Line, strongly supported by the local Irish community.

1980

Sister Enya Ni Bhraonain (b. May 17, 1961, Eire) joins the band on vocals and keyboards, appearing uncredited on ***Cran Ull*** (released in Eire on Tara Records). (She will play on one further Clannad album, ***Fuain*** before leaving in 1982, to subsequently launch a successful solo career in 1988 as Enya, with the global smash, *Orinoco Flow*.)

1982

Feb After six popular Irish tours and six domestically-released albums, Clannad is commissioned to score the music for "Harry's Game", an ITV drama series about the troubles in N. Ireland.
Nov [20] *Theme From Harry's Game*, released on RCA Records and written by Pol O. Braonain, hits UK #5, its haunting melodic style also attracting significant critical praise.

1983

May [5] The group wins Best Theme From A Television Or Radio Production for *Theme From Harry's Game* at the 28th annual Ivor Novello awards, held at London's Grosvenor House Hotel. Their UK debut album, ***Magical Ring***, reaches UK #26, going gold after a 21-week run.
July [2] *New Grange* peaks at UK #65.
Sept Clannad sets off on a lengthy European tour.

1984

Jan The group begins work composing and recording all the accompanying music for the 26-part "Robin Of Sherwood" ITV series.
May Selected excerpts from the score are released on ***Legend***, which reaches UK #15 during a 40-week chart stay. From it, the main theme, *Robin (The Hooded Man)*, makes UK #42.
June [2] ***Magical Ring*** is reissued and charts for a week at UK #91.

1985

Feb Clannad receives a British Academy Award for Best Soundtrack Of The Year for the "Robin Of Sherwood" project, the first Irish group to do so. Meanwhile, U2 begins using *Theme From Harry's Game* to close every concert, giving Clannad's music worldwide exposure.
Mar The group begins six months recording new non-theme songs in Dublin, London and Switzerland.
Nov The resultant self-penned ***Macalla*** (Gaelic for "echo"), produced by Steve Nye, is heard at UK #33.

1986

Jan [26] The group begins a 23-date UK tour at Manchester's Opera House, set to end on February 23rd at the Glasgow Pavilion, Scotland.
Feb [1] *In A Lifetime*, an uncredited duet from the album, featuring U2's Bono and Maire, reaches UK #20.
Apr With its international reputation as a pioneering gaelic/world music act gaining strength, ***Macalla*** peaks at US #131.

1987

Apr [25] The band begins recording a new album, at Rockfield Studios, Monmouth, Gwent, Wales, aiming for a more commercial style by enlisting production help from Russ Kunkel and Greg Ladanyi, who in turn invite contributions from Bruce Hornsby, Steve Perry and J.D. Souther.
Nov [7] Subsequent fruits, ***Sirius***, makes UK #34.

1988

Feb Following a two-year hiatus, Clannad begins a world tour, which will take in the UK, Europe, Australia and North America with all dates selling out. It includes seven SRO concerts in their native Dublin, to celebrate the city's millennium.
Mar ***Sirius*** peaks at US #183, spurred by a US tour.
July Clannad returns to Ireland to work on music for a new three-part BBC1-TV series, "The Atlantic Realm".

1989

Feb [4] ***Atlantic Realm***, produced by Pol and Ciaran O. Braonain and released by BBC Records, makes UK #41.
May [27] RCA-released 16-track compilation, ***Pastpresent***, the latest and most prominent of a number of retrospectives (including the 1987 K-tel-issued ***Clannad The Collection***), hits UK #5.
July [1] Reissued *In A Lifetime* reaches UK #17.

1990

Oct [20] The band, now minus Pol O. Braonain but still managed by longtime cohort David A. Kavanagh, releases the Ciaran O. Braonain-produced ***Anam***, which debuts at its UK #14 peak.

1991

Mar [29] "Hostage : Tribute To Brian Keenan", a concert recorded at the Point, Dublin, and featuring Clannad, airs on BBC2-TV.
May [10] A six-date UK tour begins at Manchester's Apollo Theatre, set to end on the 15th at London's Hammersmith Odeon.
July [23] "Clannad In Donegal" TV documentary airs on C4.
[28] The group participates in the "Abbot Ale Cambridge Folk Festival" at Cambridge's Cherry Hinton Hall.
Aug [10] *Both Sides Now*, pairing the group with Paul Young, charts for a week at UK #74 (it is also featured on the soundtrack to the movie, "Switch").

1992

May [23] Previewing her maiden album, Maire Ni Braoinain's *Against The Wind* makes UK #64.
[24] The group takes part in the "Scottish Fleadh" festival at Glasgow's The Green.
June [7] Clannad performs at "Fleadh 92" festival in London's Finsbury Park.
[13] Maire Ni Braonain's solo debut, credited to the anglicised Maire Brennan, ***Maire***, makes UK #53 in its week of entry.
July [10] The band begins a week-long UK tour at the Cornwall Coliseum.

1993

Apr [24] With American awareness of *Harry's Game* peaking, following its prominence in 1992 in the movie soundtrack to "Patriot Games" and its current use as the theme to a Volkswagen TV commercial, the Atlantic Records-issued ***Anam***, now augmented in the US by both *Harry's Game* and *In A Lifetime*, reaches US #46.
May [3] Celebrating 20 years in the music arena, Clannad begins a six-date UK tour at Edinburgh's Usher Hall.
[15] ***Banba***, featuring session players Anto Drennan (guitar), Mel Collins (saxaphone), John Donnelly (drums) and Dennis Woods (keyboards) among others, debuts at its UK #5 peak.
June [22] A seven-date UK tour opens at Edinburgh's Usher Hall, set to end on the 29th at London's Royal Albert Hall.
July [29] Clannad guests on NBC-TV's "The Tonight Show".
Aug [21] ***Banba*** peaks at US #110.

1995

Jan Following a recent duet with Shane MacGowan of *You're The One* from the movie "Circle Of Friends", Maire's ***Misty Eyed Adventures***, produced by Calum Malcolm and Donal Lunny, is released by US Atlantic's imprint label, Celtic Heartbeat.

1996

Mar [23] Critically revered as ever, Clannad's ***Lore*** makes US #195.
Apr [6] ***Lore*** enters at its UK #14 peak.
May [3] The group begins a month-long European tour at the Royal Concert Hall, Nottingham, Notts.

ERIC CLAPTON

1962

Educated at Ripley Primary School and St. Bede's Secondary Modern, Clapton (b. Eric Clapp, Mar. 30, 1945, Ripley, Surrey), has been given his first guitar by his grandparents, Rose Clapp and her second husband Jack, who raised him after his parents separated. After two years of mild interest in blues, R&B and rock'n'roll, he learns guitar licks from the records of old blues masters like Blind Lemon Jefferson and Son House. While studying stained-glass design at Kingston College of Art, Kingston, Surrey, he makes his first public performance as a busker and towards the end of the year works on a building site by day, playing with local amateur bands by night.

1963

Jan Clapton joins the Roosters, a London-based R&B band which includes Tom McGuinness (later of Manfred Mann and McGuinness Flint). The pair will leave to join Merseybeat-style combo Casey Jones & the Engineers in August.
Oct Clapton is asked to replace lead guitarist "Top" Topham in R&B group the Yardbirds, who have just taken over the Rolling Stones' residency at the Crawdaddy club in Richmond, Surrey. With his playing ability and his suitably sharp dressing, he becomes the group's focal point and is given the nickname "Slowhand" by the group's manager, Giorgio Gomelsky.
Dec The band records live demos while backing Sonny Boy Williamson on a UK tour.

1964

Feb Gomelsky takes the demos to various labels. Decca turns them down, feeling it already has too many R&B bands, but the group secures a deal with EMI's Columbia label and cuts three songs at its first recording session.
[28] They play the first "Rhythm & Blues Festival", at the Town Hall, Birmingham, Warks.
June Their debut single, a revival of Billy Boy Arnold's *I Wish You Would*, fails to chart but gains exposure on TV and in the pop press.
Oct Despite a BBC ban, their revival of Don & Bob's R&B standard *Good Morning Little Schoolgirl* makes UK #44.
Dec Their debut album ***Five Little Yardbirds***, recorded live at the Marquee club in London, is released.
[24] The band opens "Another Beatles Christmas Show" at London's Hammersmith Odeon.

1965

Mar Opposing the group's shift from R&B to mainstream pop, Clapton leaves. (Two weeks later, the Yardbirds hit UK #3 with *For Your Love*.) John Mayall invites him to join his Bluesbreakers.
Aug After a brief spell with the Bluesbreakers, Clapton sets off in a large American car with a group of musicians known variously as the Glands and the Greek Loon Band. The intention is to play their way around the world, but at Athens some members have to return to the UK. The remaining musicians step in for a Greek club band and the club owner tries to blackmail Clapton into staying. He is forced to flee, minus his clothes and new Marshall amplifier.
Nov While Clapton has rejoined the Bluesbreakers, his first recording with the band, *I'm Your Witchdoctor* (produced by Yardbird Jimmy Page), is issued on the Immediate label. Clapton earns his first session fee, on Champion Jack Dupree's *From New Orleans To Chicago*. Producer Mike Vernon invites Clapton and Mayall to record for his Purdah label, resulting in ***Lonely Years***, an authentic-sounding set of Chicago blues. Vernon is invited to produce the Bluesbreakers' eponymous album, which features Clapton's first recorded lead vocal (on Robert Johnson's *Ramblin' On My Mind*).

1966

As the Powerhouse, Clapton and fellow musicians Jack Bruce, Paul Jones, Peter York and Steve Winwood cut three tracks for Elektra Records, which are included on the compilation ***What's Shakin'***.
June Drummer Ginger Baker sits in on a Bluesbreakers' performance in Oxford and later suggests to Clapton that they form a group. Clapton proposes Bruce as bass player/singer. (Bruce had joined and then left the Bluesbreakers to join Manfred Mann.) The three begin secret rehearsals, but UK music paper **Melody Maker** runs a speculative scoop.
July Clapton plays his last Bluesbreakers gig, at the Marquee, before Mayall fires him in favor of Peter Green, later of Fleetwood Mac. Meanwhile, Clapton's new group, Cream, is already signed to Robert Stigwood's Reaction label. As the group's popularity soars, the "Clapton Is God" graffiti legend appears on buildings in London.
Oct [29] First UK Cream release is the atypical and low-key *Wrapping Paper*, which makes #34.

1967

Jan [28] *I Feel Free*, co-written by Bruce and Pete Brown, reaches UK #11 while their debut album ***Fresh Cream*** hits UK #6 and sets the tone for the group's sound: blues/jazz solos and general instrumental fireworks, with a pop tinge.
Apr Cream tours the US, where the music press has already built a strong following. Live shows feature considerable improvisation by all members, as Clapton's lead guitar playing secures a growing cult following. Clapton guests on the Mothers of Invention's ***We're Only In It For The Money***.
June [25] Clapton is a guest musician on the Beatles' global broadcast of *All You Need Is Love*.
July [15] *Strange Brew* reaches UK #17, and confirms Cream as a mainstream success.
Oct Cream tours the US, while the mainstream press (such as **Time** magazine) becomes interested in the band's spreading reputation.
Dec Cream's ***Disraeli Gears*** hits UK #5.

1968

Feb In spite of triumphant appearances in the UK, US and Europe, rumors are rife that Cream plans to split. *Sunshine Of Your Love*, taken from ***Disraeli Gears***, is Cream's first US chart single, reaching #36.
June [1] *Anyone For Tennis*, an uncharacteristic Cream track used as theme for the film "The Savage Seven", makes US #64.
[15] *Anyone For Tennis* reaches UK #40.
[29] ***Disraeli Gears*** hits US #4.
July [10] Clapton announces that Cream will break up after a US tour and selected UK dates.
Aug [10] Cream double album ***Wheels Of Fire***, combining a studio-recorded set and a live one from the Fillmore West in San Francisco, CA, tops the US chart for four weeks. In the UK, the album is marketed both as a double album, which hits #3, and as a single album with just studio recordings, hitting #7.
[31] In the US, the album's success re-boosts sales of *Sunshine Of Your Love*, which now hits US #5, selling over a million. ***Fresh Cream*** now reaches US #39, 69 weeks into its 92-week chart run.
Sept [6] Clapton plays lead guitar (his Les Paul) on George Harrison's *While My Guitar Gently Weeps* on ***The Beatles***. He also contributes to Harrison's solo album, ***Wonderwall Music***.
Oct [26] *Sunshine Of Your Love* reaches UK #25. The farewell US tour begins.
Nov [9] *White Room* hits US #6.
[25-26] 10,000 ecstatic fans attend the group's last two live shows, at London's Royal Albert Hall (supported by Yes and Taste), but thousands more miss out on

tickets. The members explain that the band's music has gone as far as it can. Cream disbands.
Dec [10-11] Clapton takes part in the Rolling Stones' TV show "Rock And Roll Circus", filmed in a London studio, with the Who, John Lennon and others. (The show is never transmitted.)

1969

Feb Clapton and Baker, with Steve Winwood, form a new group, eventually named Blind Faith. Cream's debut set ***Fresh Cream*** is reissued in the UK and hits #7.
[22] *White Room* reaches UK #28.
Mar [8] *Crossroads* reaches US #28.
[15] Cream's ***Goodbye*** tops the UK chart and hits US #2, behind Glen Campbell's ***Wichita Lineman***.
May Ric Grech, bass player and violinist with Family, joins Blind Faith.
[3] Cream's *Badge* peaks at US #60.
[10] *Badge* reaches UK #18.
June [7] Blind Faith makes its debut in a free concert in London's Hyde Park, before an audience of 36,000. When the group announces its first US tour, advance promotion bills it as "The Ultimate Supergroup".
July [12] Blind Faith's US live debut at New York's Madison Square Garden, is the start of a sellout US stadium tour which earns a fortune, yet convinces members that Blind Faith is musically unsatisfying, and that it will split once the tour is over. Delaney & Bonnie open for Blind Faith on the tour.
Aug The group's only album, ***Blind Faith***, is released amid controversy over the naked 11-year-old girl pictured on its sleeve.
Sept Blind Faith completes the US tour, but Clapton has already lost interest and carries on touring with Delaney & Bonnie.
[13] After rehearsing on the plane trip, Clapton appears with the Plastic Ono Band, at its debut at the "Toronto Rock'n'Roll Revival Show" in the Varsity Stadium at the University of Toronto, Toronto, ON, Canada, which is recorded for Lennon's ***Live Peace In Toronto***.
[20] ***Blind Faith*** tops both the US and UK charts for two weeks. Clapton spends hours jamming with Blind Faith's US support act, Delaney & Bonnie. Cream's ***The Best Of Cream*** hits US #3.
[25] Clapton, Lennon, Yoko Ono, Ringo Starr and Klaus Voorman record the Plastic Ono Band's *Cold Turkey*.
Nov ***The Best Of Cream*** hits UK #6.
Dec [15] Clapton appears as part of the Plastic Ono Supergroup in a UNICEF "Peace For Christmas" benefit concert at London's Lyceum Ballroom.

1970

Jan Blind Faith splits and Clapton joins (and helps finance) the "Delaney & Bonnie And Friends" US trek. As well as the Bramletts, the tour band includes George Harrison, Rita Coolidge, Dave Mason, Bobby Keyes and others. A tour album, ***Delaney And Bonnie On Tour***, will be released on Atlantic.
Mar Clapton records his first solo album, ***Eric Clapton***, in Los Angeles, CA, with members of the touring band and Leon Russell.
June [14] He plays a charity concert for Dr. Benjamin Spock's Civil Liberties Defense Fund at London's Lyceum Ballroom. His band, having fallen out with Delaney Bramlett and available to tour, is Carl Radle (bass), Bobby Whitlock (keyboards), Jim Gordon (drums) with Traffic's Dave Mason on guitar. Mason plays only one concert, but the others stay with Clapton to become Derek & the Dominos. They set out on a summer club tour of the UK and also play on George Harrison's ***All Things Must Pass*** (although Clapton's role will be uncredited). (His own sessions for the year include work on Leon Russell's debut album, Vivian Stanshall and Neil Innes' ***Labio-Dental Fricative*** and as a member of an all-star band for gospel singer Doris Troy's Apple Records album.) Producer Phil Spector also cuts a Derek & the Dominos single, *Tell The Truth*, which is withdrawn soon after its release.
Aug Clapton heads for Miami, FL, to work on a new album.
[26] Derek & the Dominos start recording at Criteria Studios in Miami. Clapton invites Duane Allman to join its recording, after seeing him play nearby with the Allman Brothers. A double album is finished in less than ten days.
[29] ***Eric Clapton*** peaks at US #13.
Sept ***Eric Clapton*** reaches UK #17, while ***Live Cream*** hits UK #4 and US #15.
Oct [23] Derek & the Dominos perform at New York's Fillmore East during its first US tour.
Nov Derek & the Dominos' ***Layla And Other Assorted Love Songs*** is released. Clapton refuses to have his name printed on the sleeve in an attempt to escape his guitar-hero image. It reaches US #16, but does not chart in the UK.
[5] The band tapes its network TV debut, in Nashville on "The Johnny Cash Show".
Dec [12] Clapton's version of J.J. Cale's *After Midnight*, from his first album, makes US #18.

1971

Apr Recordings begin on a second Derek & the Dominos album, in England, but are scrapped when the band's personal problems, mainly with drugs, hinder progress. Clapton retires to his Surrey home, his drug dependency worsening, and will stay a virtual recluse for the year, except when he makes occasional live appearances.
Aug [1] Clapton plays in George Harrison's group for the "Concert For Bangla Desh", at New York's Madison Square Garden, which includes Leon Russell, Billy Preston, Ringo Starr, Klaus Voorman and others. (Later in the year, Clapton performs selected tour dates with the Dominos and works on sessions for Harrison, Dr. John, a reunited Bluesbreakers and as part of the all-star band on Howlin' Wolf's ***The London Sessions***.)
Dec He guests at a Leon Russell concert at London's Rainbow Theatre.

1972

Apr With Clapton inactive, the compilation album ***History Of Eric Clapton*** hits US #6 during a 42-week chart run. It features his work with the Yardbirds, the Bluesbreakers, Cream, Blind Faith, Derek & the Dominos and Delaney & Bonnie.
June Vault-searching Polydor Cream album ***Live Cream Vol. 2*** reaches UK #15 and US #27.
July [14] ***History Of Eric Clapton*** is certified gold by the RIAA.
Aug Derek & the Dominos' *Layla*, written with Jim Gordon about George Harrison's wife, Patti, and inspired by Persian poet Nizami's **The Story Of Layla And Majnun**, hits UK #7, as ***History Of Eric Clapton*** makes UK #20.
Oct Polydor releases ***Eric Clapton At His Best***, a collection of songs from the albums ***Eric Clapton*** and ***Layla***, which reaches US #87.
Nov [11] Reissued *Badge* makes UK #42.
Dec [2] *Let It Rain*, written with Bonnie Bramlett, makes US #48.

1973

Jan [13] The Who's Pete Townshend entices Clapton back on stage after his heroin addiction, organizing an all-star comeback concert for him at London's Rainbow Theatre. Townshend also recruits Ron Wood, Steve Winwood, Jim Capaldi and others. The concert is recorded and released as ***Eric Clapton's Rainbow Concert***. Despite these efforts, Clapton retreats once again.
Feb Polydor's second retrospective album, ***Clapton***, reaches US #67.
Mar RSO Records releases ***Derek & The Dominos In Concert***, which reaches US #20 and UK #36.
[10] *Bell Bottom Blues* makes US #78.
Sept ***Eric Clapton's Rainbow Concert*** enters the UK and US charts, peaking at #19 and #18 respectively.
Nov Clapton begins electro-acupuncture treatment for his drug addiction. He follows two months' treatment with a period of convalescence on a friend's farm in Wales. Cream's ***Heavy Cream*** peaks at US #135.

1974

Apr [10] When Clapton informs label boss Stigwood that he is ready to return, Stigwood throws a party at a Chinese restaurant in London's Soho district and invites producer Tom Dowd to oversee a forthcoming project, which they record in Miami, FL. Clapton has only two songs in mind: Charles Scott Boyer's *Please Be With Me* and his own *Give Me Strength*. The assembled band comprises Radle, Jamie Oldaker (drums), Dick Sims (keyboards), George Terry (guitar) and Yvonne Elliman and Marcy Levy (vocals), a unit which will form the basic line-up for his next four albums. (Levy will resurface years later as Marcella Detroit, one half of Shakespear's Sister.)
Aug [1] Clapton is joined on stage in Atlanta, GA, by Pete Townshend and Keith Moon, during which Townshend hits Clapton over the head with a plastic ukelele.
[8] Still-climbing ***461 Ocean Boulevard*** is certified gold by the RIAA.
[17] The first fruit of his comeback sessions, a rock/reggae version of Bob Marley's *I Shot The Sheriff*, hits UK #9, as ***461 Ocean Boulevard***, named after the Miami studio address, tops the US chart for the first of four weeks and will hit UK #3 on the 31st.
Sept [14] *I Shot The Sheriff* tops the US survey and will be confirmed gold by the RIAA five days later.
Dec [4] Clapton performs at London's Hammersmith Odeon.
[7] *Willie And The Hand Jive* makes US #26, as Clapton tours Japan.

1975

Apr [19] ***There's One In Every Crowd*** reaches UK #15 and US #21.
June [7] His interpretation of the spiritual *Swing Low Sweet Chariot* reaches UK #19. Clapton tours Australia and Hawaii before touring the US.
Aug [30] His cover of Bob Dylan's *Knockin' On Heaven's Door* makes UK #38.
Sept [20] The live album ***E.C. Was Here*** reaches UK #14. With Clapton still the reluctant guitar player, Terry has handled most of the lead guitar work.
Oct [18] ***E.C. Was Here*** reaches US #20.

1976

July Clapton plays at the "Crystal Palace Rock Festival", London, with Freddie King.
Sept [18] ***No Reason To Cry***, with guest appearances from Bob Dylan and the Band, hits UK #8.
Nov [13] ***No Reason To Cry*** reaches US #15.
[25] Clapton performs *Further On Up The Road* at the Band's "The Last Waltz" farewell concert, on Thanksgiving Day at San Francisco's Winterland Ballroom. (Clapton's live band now includes South American percussionist Sergio Pastora. Current session appearances include Joe Cocker's ***Stingray***, Stephen Bishop's ***Careless*** and Ringo Starr's ***Rotogravure***.)
Dec [11] *Hello Old Friend* reaches US #24.

1977

Feb Cream albums ***Disraeli Gears*** and ***Wheels Of Fire***, now reissued by RSO, make US #165 and #195 respectively. Roger Daltrey thanks Clapton for playing on his solo album by giving him a 72-pint barrel of Fullers beer before work gets underway. Later in the day, Clapton is helped home from the studio, having not played a single note.
Apr [30] During a concert at London's Rainbow Theatre, Clapton pauses to take a ten-minute break. When he returns he tells the audience that he is "tired and emotional" at the end of an arduous tour.
June Pastora leaves the group to return to South America.
Aug [5] Clapton and the band perform at the town bullring at the Nuevo Pabellon Club, Barcelona, Spain, having sailed in a chartered yacht from Cannes to Ibiza to attend the gig.
Dec [3] ***Slowhand*** reaches UK #23. (During the year Clapton also contributes to Ronnie Lane and Pete

Townshend's ***Rough Mix*** and Roger Daltrey's ***One Of The Boys***.)

1978

Jan [21] *Lay Down Sally* makes UK #39.
Mar [14] The still-climbing ***Slowhand*** is certified platinum by the RIAA.
Apr [1] *Lay Down Sally* hits US #3, as ***Slowhand*** hits US #2 (behind ***Saturday Night Fever***).
[17] *Lay Down Sally* is confirmed gold by the RIAA.
July [15] Clapton performs at the "Blackbushe Festival", Blackbushe Aerodrome, near Camberley, Surrey, as his ballad *Wonderful Tonight*, a second song written for his girlfriend Patti, reaches US #16.
Sept [27] He sponsors a West Bromwich Albion UEFA soccer cup tie against Galatasaray of Turkey and presents each player with a gold copy of ***Slowhand*** before the kick-off.
Nov Clapton embarks on a two-month European tour with Radle, Oldaker and Sims.
[14] Still-climbing ***Backless*** is certified platinum by the RIAA.
[18] The extracted *Promises* makes UK #37.
Dec [9] ***Backless*** reaches UK #18.

1979

Jan [13] ***Backless*** hits US #8.
[20] *Promises* hits US #9.
Mar Clapton begins a world tour with an all-new UK band, featuring Albert Lee (guitar), Chris Stainton (keyboards), Dave Markee (bass) and Henry Spinetti (drums). In Japan, a live album is recorded at the Budokan, while *Watch Out For Lucy*, the B-side of *Promises*, makes US #40.
[27] Clapton marries Patti Harrison at Temple Bethel, Tucson, AZ.
May [19] Clapton and Harrison celebrate their recent marriage with a reception at their Hurtwood Edge, Ewhurst, home in Surrey, at which ex-husband George Harrison, Paul McCartney and Ringo Starr play an impromptu set. Mick Jagger, David Bowie, Elton John and Lonnie Donegan also attend.

1980

May [2] Clapton begins a 13-date UK tour at the New Theatre, Oxford, Oxon. The tour, featuring Clapton's 1979 band with new recruit Gary Brooker, formerly with Procol Harum, on keyboards and vocals, is set to end on the 18th at the Civic Hall, Guildford, Surrey.
[17] Live Budokan album, ***Just One Night***, hits UK #3.
[30] Radle dies of chronic kidney disease.
June [21] ***Just One Night*** hits US #2, where it will hold for six weeks, behind Billy Joel's ***Glass Houses***.
[23] ***Just One Night*** is certified gold by the RIAA.
Aug [16] *Tulsa Time*, backed with J.J. Cale's *Cocaine*, reaches US #30.
Nov [22] *Blues Power* peaks at US #76.

1981

Mar [7] ***Another Ticket*** reaches UK #18.
[14] Clapton goes into hospital in St. Paul, MN, with bleeding ulcers causing the cancellation of a 60-date US tour.
Apr [22] Clapton is hospitalized with injuries from a car accident.
May [2] *I Can't Stand It* hits US #10, as its parent album ***Another Ticket*** hits US #7. (Clapton contributes to Phil Collins' debut album, beginning a long-running co-operative arrangement between them.)
[12] ***Another Ticket*** is certified gold by the RIAA.
June [20] *Another Ticket* reaches US #78.
Sept Clapton leaves RSO to set up his own WEA-distributed label, Duck Records. He plays a set with Jeff Beck at "The Secret Policeman's Other Ball" in London, in aid of Amnesty International. (The pair will be featured on the concert album.)

1982

Apr [3] Reissued *Layla*, now established as a rock classic, hits UK #4.
May [1] A history of Clapton's solo career, ***Time Pieces - The Best Of Eric Clapton***, reaches UK #20.
June [12] ***Time Pieces - The Best Of Eric Clapton*** makes US #101, as *I Shot The Sheriff* re-enters the UK chart at its #64 peak.

1983

Feb ***Money And Cigarettes***, produced by Tom Dowd and featuring Ry Cooder and Albert Lee among others, makes US #16 and UK #13.
Mar [17] Clapton joins Carmine Appice, Jeff Beck, Andy Fairweather-Low, Ronnie Lane, Jimmy Page and Bill Wyman at the second "Prince's Trust Rock Gala", held at London's Royal Albert Hall, to benefit the ARMS (Action for Research into Multiple Sclerosis) charity.
[26] Clapton's first Duck Records single release, *I've Got A Rock'n'Roll Heart*, reaches US #18.
Apr [23] Self-penned *The Shape You're In* peaks at UK #75.
June [23] Clapton is awarded the Silver Clef by the Nordoff-Robbins Music Therapy Centre.
Sept [20] He participates in a further Ronnie Lane Benefit Concert for the ARMS charity, at the Royal Albert Hall.
Dec [8] Clapton joins Jeff Beck, Jimmy Page, Ry Cooder and others to play at a third ARMS benefit, at Madison Square Garden.

1984

June Compilation album ***Backtrackin'*** reaches UK #29.
July Clapton joins Bob Dylan on stage at Wembley Arena, Wembley, Middx.

1985

Mar [23] ***Behind The Sun***, produced by Phil Collins, Ted Templeman and Russ Titelman, debuts at its UK #8 peak.
[16] Extracted *Forever Man* peaks at UK #51.
Apr [26] *Forever Man* reaches US #26.
May [7] Clapton guests on NBC-TV's "Late Night With David Letterman".
[25] ***Behind The Sun*** makes US #34.
July [6] *See What Love Can Do* peaks at US #89.
Sept During his current world tour, Clapton leaves his wife of six years for a young photographer and TV actress, Lori Del Santo, whom he met at a party in Italy. She will give birth to Clapton's son, Conor.
Oct [21] Clapton, and friends George Harrison, Dave Edmunds and others, join Carl Perkins for a C4-TV special at London's Limehouse Studios.

1986

Jan [4] Having written the score for the BBC1-TV nuclear-age thriller "Edge Of Darkness" with Michael Kamen, its title theme *Edge Of Darkness* peaks at UK #65.
Apr [7] Clapton wins the Best Theme For A TV Or Radio Production for *Edge Of Darkness* at the 31st annual Ivor Novello Awards, held at the Grosvenor House Hotel.
He makes a cameo appearance in the Michael Caine-starring film, "Water".
June [20] Clapton takes part in the fourth annual "Prince's Trust Rock Gala" concert, with Phil Collins, Elton John, Paul McCartney, George Michael, Rod Stewart, Tina Turner and others, at Wembley Arena, Wembley.
Oct [16] Clapton joins Keith Richards, Linda Ronstadt, Etta James, Julian Lennon and others, on stage at the Fox Theatre in St. Louis, MO, for Chuck Berry's 60th birthday concert performance, featured in Taylor Hackford's documentary film, "Hail! Hail! Rock'n'Roll".
Dec ***August***, once again produced by Phil Collins, who also completes its rhythm section with Nathan East (bass) and Greg Phillinganes (keyboards), hits UK #3.

1987

Jan [7] He begins the first series (of what will become an annual event) of six concerts at London's Royal Albert Hall.
Feb [9] Clapton receives the Outstanding Contribution To British Music trophy at the sixth annual BRIT Awards, held at London's Grosvenor House Hotel. *Behind The Mask*, co-written by Michael Jackson, Chris Mosdell and Greg Phillinganes (originally recorded for Phillinganes 1984 album, ***Pulse***), reaches UK #15.
[13] ***Behind The Sun*** is ratified gold by the RIAA.
Mar ***August*** makes US #37. He again teams with Kamen to write the score for the Mel Gibson-starring movie, "Lethal Weapon".
Apr [21] ***August*** is certified gold by the RIAA.
[27] Clapton plays a sellout night at New York's Madison Square Garden, during a month-long US tour.
June [5-6] He takes part in the fifth annual "Prince's Trust Rock Gala" concert, with George Harrison, Elton John, Ben E. King, Ringo Starr and others, at Wembley Arena, Wembley.
[27] Clapton and Tina Turner's *Tearing Us Apart* peaks at UK #56.
Oct [17] ***The Cream Of Eric Clapton***, a Polydor-released 17-track anthology, hits UK #3, during a 105-week UK chart run.
Nov Clapton embarks on a tour of Japan.

1988

Jan [25] He performs the first of nine concert dates at the Royal Albert Hall.
Apr A four-CD/cassette boxed set, ***Crossroads***, a major career retrospective, fails to chart in the UK, but makes US #34.
May [14] ***Crossroads*** tops the US Compact Disc survey.
June Clapton's wife Patti files for divorce, officially ending their nine-year union.
[5-6] He takes part in the sixth annual "Prince's Trust Rock Gala" concert, with the Bee Gees, Leonard Cohen, Peter Gabriel and others, at the Royal Albert Hall, an event which will raise over £3 million. He is backed by Elton John and Mark Knopfler on his performance of *Cocaine*.
[7] Clapton is honored for a career spanning 25 years with an anniversary dinner at London's Savoy Hotel, highlighted by George Harrison's after-dinner speech.
[11] Clapton joins Dire Straits on stage at "Nelson Mandela's 70th Birthday Tribute" concert at Wembley Stadium, Wembley.
July He completes the soundtrack for a new Mickey Rourke movie, "Homeboy".
Sept Enlisting Knopfler again, Clapton embarks on major US dates backed by Buckwheat Zydeco.

1989

Jan [20] Clapton performs the first of his annual dates (12) at the Royal Albert Hall.
Feb He completes work with Michael Kamen on the soundtrack for the Mel Gibson-starring sequel, "Lethal Weapon 2".
May [31] Clapton attends the first "International Rock Awards", held in Lexington Avenue Armory, New York. He is awarded an "Elvis" as Best Guitarist.
Aug [1] He finishes a world tour with a free concert, in front of 70,000 fans, for the King's Trust (established in 1988 by His Majesty King Mswati III), in Mozambique, Africa.
Sept [10] Clapton guests on BBC Radio's "Desert Island Discs". (His choices are: Puccini's *Senza Mamma*, Bizet's *Duet from the Pearl Fishers*, Robert Johnson's *Crossroads Blues*, Muddy Waters' *Feel Like Going Home*, Stevie Wonder's *I Was Made To Love Her*, Ray Charles' *Hard Times*, Freddie King's *I Love The Woman* and Prince's *Purple Rain*.)
Oct He joins the Rolling Stones on stage at Shea Stadium, New York, playing lead guitar on *Little Red Rooster*.
Dec [12] Extracted *Pretending* peaks at US #72.

1990

Jan [18] Having performed six dates at the venue in 1987, nine in 1988 and twelve in 1989, Clapton begins an 18-night stand at the Royal Albert Hall, with four different programs, three different bands, Robert Cray and Buddy Guy and a 60-piece orchestra, set to end on February 18th.

[27] ***Journeyman*** reaches US #16.
Feb [17] *Bad Love*, written with Foreigner's Mick Jones, reaches UK #25, as ***Journeyman*** hits UK #2, behind Phil Collins' ***But Seriously***.
Mar [8] Clapton wins Best Guitarist in **Rolling Stone**'s 1989 Readers' Poll.
[10] *Bad Love* debuts at its US #88 peak.
[24] He performs on NBC-TV's "Saturday Night Live".
[28] Clapton begins the first leg of a 56-date US tour at the Omni, Atlanta, GA (set to end on May 5th at the Shoreline Amphitheatre, Mountain View, CA), before a sellout crowd of 16,757, with a band comprising Phil Palmer (guitar), Steve Ferrone (drums), Alan Clark and Greg Phillinganes (keyboards), Nathan East (bass), Ray Cooper (percussion), Tessa Niles and Katie Kissoon (backing vocals).
Apr [2] Having pleaded guilty by letter to Walton-on-Thames magistrates court, Clapton is fined £300, ordered to pay £10 costs, and banned from driving for three months, after being booked for speeding at 105 mph the previous December.
[21] *No Alibis* peaks at UK #53.
June [6] Clapton is named Living Legend Of The Year at the second "International Rock Awards", in New York. After the ceremonies, he performs *Sweet Home Chicago* as part of an all-star band including Billy Joel and Steven Tyler.
[30] He joins Phil Collins and Genesis, Pink Floyd, Robert Plant, Paul McCartney, Cliff Richard and the Shadows, Status Quo, Elton John, Mark Knopfler and Tears For Fears, all previous Silver Clef winners, on a star-studded bill at Knebworth Park, Knebworth, Herts., in aid of Nordoff-Robbins Music Therapy Centre.
July [23] Clapton begins the second leg of his US tour at the Miami Arena, Miami, set to end at the Mississippi Coast Coliseum, Biloxi, MS, on September 2nd.
Aug [27] Three members of Clapton's entourage (tour manager Colin Smythe, bodyguard Nigel Browne and agent Bobby Brooks) are killed in a helicopter crash near East Troy, WI, following a concert at the Alpine Valley Music Theatre by Clapton, Robert Cray and Stevie Ray Vaughan, who also dies.
Oct [20] ***The Layla Sessions - 20th Anniversary Edition*** makes US #157.
Dec [22] Clapton wins Top Album Rock Tracks Artist in **Billboard**'s The Year In Music statistical round-up.

1991

Feb [5] Now a traditional annual Clapton fest, he begins a 24-date stand at the Royal Albert Hall. With each now divided into five segments, he plays with a four-piece band comprising Phillinganes, East and Phil Collins, a second four-piece band, with Steve Ferrone taking Collins' place, a nine-piece band, a blues band with guitarists Albert Collins, Robert Cray, Buddy Guy and Jimmie Vaughan and a nine-piece band with an orchestra conducted by Michael Kamen. The series will end on March 9th.
[20] Clapton wins the Best Rock Vocal Performance, Male category for *Bad Love* at the 33rd annual Grammy Awards, at New York's Radio City Music Hall. (It is his second Grammy, having won his first as part of ***The Concert For Bangla Desh***, Album of the Year in 1972.)
Mar [19] The RIAA certifies two million sales of ***Journeyman***.
[20] Clapton's four-year-old son Conor climbs out of an open window and plunges 700' to his death from the 53rd floor of the East 57th Street apartment, Manhattan, New York, where his mother, Lori Del Santo, has been staying. Clapton, who has only been in New York for 24 hours, staying in a nearby hotel, is taken to hospital severely traumatised.
[26] He issues a statement asking those who wish to express sympathy over the tragedy to make a donation to the Great Ormond Street Children's Hospital in London.
Apr [3] Clapton begins a US tour at the Meadowlands Arena, East Rutherford, NJ, before a sellout crowd of 20,548.
July [2] He watches his friend John McEnroe compete at the All-England Lawn Tennis Championships at Wimbledon.
Sept [4] Clapton jams with Buddy Guy at the latter's Los Angeles' Roxy showcase. (Along with Jeff Beck and Mark Knopfler, Clapton has recently featured on Buddy Guy's first album in 12 years, ***Damn Right I Got The Blues***.)
[29] He joins the house band on Fox-TV's "The Sunday Comics".
Oct [26] ***24 Nights***, chronicling his Royal Albert Hall residency in February, debuts at its UK #17 peak and reaches US #38.
Nov [30] *Wonderful Tonight (Live)* reaches UK #30.
Dec [18] George Harrison's 13-date Japanese tour, featuring Eric Clapton, ends at the Dome, Tokyo.

1992

Jan [11] Compilation album, ***Two Rooms : Celebrating The Songs Of Elton John And Bernie Taupin***, to which Clapton has contributed *Border Song*, reaches US #18.
[16] Clapton tapes an MTV "Unplugged" show at Bray Studios, Bray, Berks., performing an all-acoustic set on the cable station's eclectic, non-electric series, "Unplugged". Backed by Nathan East (bass), Ray Cooper (percussion), Chuck Leavell (keys) and Andy Fairweather-Low (guitar), he sings new material inspired by Conor's death (not least *The Circus Left Town* and *Tears In Heaven*), together with the old chestnuts, including *Layla*. The show will premiere in the US on March 11th, making European screens on the 27th.
Feb [1] Clapton's mostly instrumental soundtrack ***Rush*** (for the film starring Jason Patric), but including two vocal tracks including *Tears In Heaven*, enters the US chart on its way to #24.
[12-14, 16-18, 22-24, 26-28] Following shows at the Brighton Centre, Birmingham Arena and Sheffield Arena, Clapton plays his annual Royal Albert Hall dates.
[26] Appearing on syndicated TV's "Entertainment Tonight", Clapton describes the scene upon arriving at the New York duplex on the day his son died: "By the time I got to the apartment, it was filled with policemen and paramedics. It didn't seem like it had anything to do with me. I felt it was someone else's life and I still feel that way."
Mar [21] Mournful ballad, *Tears In Heaven*, with lyrics penned Will Jennings, hits UK #5.
[26] ***Rush*** soundtrack is confirmed gold by the RIAA.
[28] *Tears In Heaven* hits US #2 for the first of four weeks.
Apr [15] Clapton receives a Lifetime Achievement Award at the 38th annual Ivor Novello Awards, held at London's Grosvenor House, the same day that *Tears In Heaven* is certified platinum by the RIAA.
[17] ***24 Nights*** is certified gold by the RIAA.
[25] Clapton begins a 25-date US tour before an 18,326 sellout crowd at the Reunion Arena, Dallas, TX, set to end on May 25th at the Miami Arena, Miami.
May While simultaneously working on his new studio album at London's SARM West Studio with producers Kamen and Steve McLaughlin, Clapton once again combines with Kamen and saxophonist David Sanborn to record the soundtrack to "Lethal Weapon 3".
June [26-28] Clapton plays sellout dates at Wembley Stadium, Wembley, on a bill shared with Elton John.
July ***Barcelona Gold***, a various artists Olympics-celebrating album to which he has contributed one track, is released.
[14] The RIAA certifies two million sales of ***Crossroads***.
Aug [8] *Runaway Train*, featuring Elton John, reaches UK #31.
[21-22] Clapton and John perform at Shea Stadium, Flushing, NY, its 120,000 concert tickets worth $4,594,205 having sold out in 90 minutes on June 20th.
[29-30] They repeat their Shea Stadium success at Dodger Stadium, Los Angeles.
Sept [5] Featured in "Lethal Weapon 3", *It's Probably Me*, a duet with Sting, reaches UK #30.
[9] Clapton wins the Best Male Artist category for *Tears In Heaven* (which he also performs) at the ninth annual MTV Video Music Awards, held at the Pauley Pavilion, Los Angeles.
[12] ***Unplugged***, documenting his historic MTV taping in January, intially debuts at UK #6.
[26] ***Unplugged*** initially hits US #2.
Oct [3] The extracted low-key acoustic guitar-led update of *Layla* debuts at its UK #45 peak.
[16] Clapton performs *Love Minus Zero* and *Don't Think Twice It's Alright* at the "Bob Dylan 30th Anniversary Celebration" at New York's Madison Square Garden, and also backs Dylan on *My Back Pages* with George Harrison, Roger McGuinn and Tom Petty.
Nov [28] The re-cut version of *Layla* reaches US #12.
Dec [10] The RIAA certifies three million sales of ***Unplugged***.

1993

Feb [21-23, 25-27, **Mar** 1-3, 5-7] Clapton plays his annual Royal Albert Hall season, with Andy Fairweather Low, Richie Hayward, Duck Dunn, Jerry Portnoy and Chris Stainton in the backing band.
[24] Interrupting his latest string of London concerts, Clapton collects six trophies at the 35th annual Grammy Awards, held at the Shrine Auditorium, Los Angeles: *Tears In Heaven* (which he also performs) wins Record Of The Year, Song Of The Year and Best Pop Vocal, Male; ***Unplugged*** nabs Album Of The Year and Best Rock Album, Male, while extract *Layla* wins Best Rock Song. In accepting his final award for Record Of The Year from Tina Turner, Clapton says: "There are a lot of people I would like to thank, but most of all I want to thank my son, for his love and for this song." In humbly accepting the Song Of The Year trophy earlier in the evening, he said: "I think the other song, the Vanessa Williams song (*Save The Best For Last*) should have got it because it kept us out of the number one slot for a couple of months."
Mar [13] ***Unplugged*** now tops the US chart.
[20] ***Unplugged*** now hits UK #2.
May [12] Clapton is named Best Selling British Artist Of The Year and World's Best Selling Rock Artist Of The Year at the fifth annual World Music Awards, at the Sporting Club, Monte Carlo, Monaco.
[26] *Tears From Heaven* wins the Best Film Theme Or Song category at the 38th annual Ivor Novello Awards, held at London's Grosvenor House Hotel.
June [15] Clapton duets with B.B. King on *Rock Me Baby* at the first "Apollo Theatre Hall of Fame" concert from the landmark New York theatre in Harlem. (The show will air on NBC-TV on August 4th.)
July [17] ***The Best Of Eric Clapton*** reaches UK #25.
Oct [1-2] Clapton performs at the National Exhibition Centre, Birmingham, W. Midlands, during current UK dates.
Nov ***Stone Free : A Tribute To Jimi Hendrix***, featuring Clapton's version of *Stone Free*, is released on Reprise.
[10] The RIAA certifies multi-platinum sales of ***Slowhand*** (three million).
Dec [18] Clapton attends Keith Richards' 50th birthday party in New York.

1994

Jan [19] Clapton inducts the Band into the Rock and Roll Hall of Fame at the ninth annual dinner at New York's Waldorf Astoria Hotel, and plays on *The Weight* at the post-dinner jam.
Feb [7] He wins the Best Male Artist, Pop/Rock category at the 21st annual American Music Awards at Los Angeles' Shrine Auditorium.
[28] During his current annual stint at the Royal Albert Hall, Clapton plays his 100th performance at the venue, in aid of the "Children In Crisis" charity.
May [2] Clapton previews his forthcoming album at the annual T.J. Martell Foundation Humanitarian Award benefit from New York's Lincoln Center.
[4] He is named World's Best-Selling Rock Artist Of The Year and Best-Selling British Recording Artist Of The Year at the sixth annual World Music Awards at the Monte Carlo Sporting Club.
Sept [24] ***From The Cradle***, featuring Clapton's versions of 16 blues classics, enters the UK chart at

#1, as Clapton guests on the season opener of NBC-TV's "Saturday Night Live".
Oct [1] ***From The Cradle*** bows at the US summit.
[3] His "Nothing But The Blues" North American tour opens at the Montreal Forum, Montreal, PQ, Canada, set to end on November 3rd at the Great Western Forum, Inglewood, CA.
[15] *Motherless Child* charts for a week at UK #63.
[23] *Tears In Heaven* is named one of the Most Performed Songs Of The Year at the annual BMI Awards ceremony at London's Dorchester Hotel.
Dec [7] Clapton is honored with an Artistic Excellence Award at the fifth annual Billboard Music Awards.

1995

Jan [1] Clapton is awarded an OBE in H.R.H. Queen Elizabeth II's New Year's Honours List.
Mar [1] Clapton, in the midst of his annual stint at the Royal Albert Hall, wins the Best Traditional Blues Album category for ***From The Cradle*** at the 37th annual Grammy Awards held at the Shrine Auditorium.
[25] Comic Relief charity single, *Love Can Build A Bridge*, a US Country #5 for the Judds in 1991, with Cher, Chrissie Hynde and Neneh Cherry joining Clapton, tops the UK chart.
Apr [5] Clapton, having a week earlier joined Bob Dylan onstage at Brixton Academy on *I Shall Be Released*, embarks on a European tour at the Spektrum, Oslo, Norway.
[29] ***The Cream Of Eric Clapton*** makes US #80.
June [3] Clapton is named Top Classic Rock Artist (Male) at the inaugural Blockbuster Entertainment Awards, held at Hollywood's Pantages Theatre.
Aug [10] The RIAA certifies seven million sales of ***Timepieces - The Best Of Eric Clapton***.
[28] Clapton begins a US tour with a sellout date at the Reunion Arena, Dallas, TX.
Oct [24] ***Crossroads 2 (Live In The Seventies)***, a second four-CD Chronicles boxed-set, this time mostly comprising live material, but including four previously unreleased studio cuts, is released in the US.
Nov [7] Clapton receives his OBE from H.R.H. the Prince of Wales at Buckingham Palace, admitting that he was "mellowing out with age", and then receives the Merit Award from Cher at the **Q** Awards at London's Park Lane Hotel.
[15] He now receives the Silver Clef Award from Steven Seagal at the eighth annual Nordoff-Robbins dinner held at the Roseland Ballroom in New York. (He also pays $17,000 for a Gibson "Lucille" guitar signed by B.B. King at the event's auction.)
[20] ***The Cream Of Clapton*** is certified gold by the RIAA.
Dec [31] Clapton appears on BBC2's "Jools Hootenanny" with Supergrass, Alanis Morissette, Dick Dale and Dr. John.

1996

Feb [18-20, 22-24, 26-28, **Mar** 1-3] Clapton celebrates his tenth anniversary at the Royal Albert Hall with twelve further concerts.
Apr [20] ***Crossroads 2 (Live In The Seventies)*** bows at its US #137 peak.
June [29] Clapton headlines the "MasterCard Masters of Music Concert for the Prince's Trust" in London's Hyde Park, at the culmination of the "National Music Festival". (It is the first rock show to be held in Hyde Park in 20 years.)
see also: **BLIND FAITH, CREAM, THE YARDBIRDS**

THE DAVE CLARK FIVE

Mike Smith (vocals, keyboards); **Dave Clark** (drums); **Lenny Davidson** (vocals, guitar); **Denis Payton** (saxophone); **Rick Huxley** (guitar)

1958

Film stuntman Clark (b. Dec. 15, 1942, Tottenham, London) and bassist Chris Walls advertise in **Melody Maker** for musicians to form a band. They are joined by Huxley (b. Aug. 5, 1942, Dartford, Kent) on rhythm guitar, Stan Saxon as singer and sax player and Mick Ryan on lead guitar. The Dave Clark Five featuring Stan Saxon makes its debut at South Grove Youth Club, Tottenham. After several personnel changes and experience gained on the live circuit, the band, still semi-professional, goes on to sign a long-term contract with the Mecca ballroom chain in 1961, with a line-up comprising Clark on drums, Huxley, a lighting engineer, switched to bass, Davidson (b. May 30, 1944, Enfield, Middx.), a progress clerk, on guitar and backing vocals and Payton (b. Aug. 11, 1943, Walthamstow, London), an electrical engineer, replacing tenor saxophonist Jim Spencer. The new focal point of the group will be Smith (b. Dec. 12, 1943, Edmonton, London), a classically-trained pianist, who has been in the Impalas with Davidson and who will take over vocals permanently when Saxon fails to turn up for a gig, having stood-in previously when Saxon's voice has given way.

1962

Jan The band makes its live debut at the South Grove Youth Club, Tottenham, where the group was formed. Clark, who controls the group's recordings, sells the master of *Chaquita*, an instrumental modelled on the Champs' *Tequila*, to Ember Records.
June Pye Records signs the band to its Piccadilly label and releases their first vocal record, *I Knew It All The Time*, released on the Congress label in the US. *Chaquita*, credited to the Dave Clarke Five, is issued on Ember eight weeks later.
Dec The Piccadilly deal is wound up with the release of *First Love*, another instrumental.

1963

Jan The band is spotted by an EMI Columbia A&R employee while playing its home venue, the Tottenham Royal, leading to a new record deal.
Mar A rock version of nursery rhyme *The Mulberry Bush* is the group's Columbia debut, but fails to chart.
[2] 300 girls march to Tottenham Town Hall with 4,500 signatures petitioning to return the group to the Royal Ballroom, after theater-owners Mecca had switched them to the Basildon venue. Mecca director Eric Morley says that "if there is an opportunity to move the group back, I will give it consideration".
Oct [26] The band's cover of the Contours' *Do You Love Me*, helped by a publicity stunt involving the Duke of Edinburgh's supposed criticism of the lyrics, makes UK #30. Brian Poole & the Tremeloes' simultaneously released version tops the UK chart.
Dec The group wins the Mecca Gold Cup as the ballroom circuit's best band of 1963.

1964

Jan [12] They complete their residency at Basildon's Locarno, Essex, where they have played for the last year, to be followed by a few nights a week at the Tottenham Royal, before going professional in March.
[18] *Glad All Over*, written by Smith and Clark (as most of the group's major hits will be) tops the UK chart, replacing the Beatles' *I Want To Hold Your Hand* and prompting "London Topples Liverpool"-type stories in the UK tabloid press. Its eventual UK sales exceed 870,000.
[25-26] ABC Pathé films them in action at the Tottenham Royal for a seven-minute pictorial.
Feb [9] They top the bill on ITV's "Sunday Night At The London Palladium". Further TV appearances during the month include: "Thank Your Lucky Stars" (15th), "Scene At 6:30" (20th), "Ready Steady Go!" (21st) and "Top Of The Pops" (19th and 26th).
Mar [7] *Bits And Pieces* hits UK #2, eventually selling 590,000 domestic copies. It is banned by many ballroom managers, who fear damage to wooden dancefloors since its "stomping" break encourages dancers to stamp their feet in time with the rhythm.
[7] The band makes its radio debut on the BBC's Light Programme, "Saturday Club", joining the Crystals and Adam Faith.
[14] The group turns professional and signs to the Harold Davidson Organisation in a deal which guarantees it £50,000 a year for live performances. Its first professional engagement is a week at the Empire Theatre, Liverpool, Lancs.
[29] They begin a six-week UK tour, with the Hollies, the Kinks, the Mojos and Mark Wynter, at the Coventry Theatre, set to end at the Granada Theatre, Tooting, London, on May 13th.
Apr [25] *Glad All Over* hits US #6.
[26] The group appears at the annual "**New Musical Express** Poll Winners" concert at the Empire Pool, Wembley, Middx., with the Beatles and others.
May ***A Session With The Dave Clark Five*** hits UK #3.
[2] *Bits And Pieces* hits US #4, and ***Glad All Over*** (the first in a long series of US albums unissued in the UK) hits US #3.
[30] The group performs at New York's Carnegie Hall.
[31] The band appears on CBS-TV's "The Ed Sullivan Show", performing *Can't You See That She's Mine* and *Do You Love Me*. (The group's first US tour is a huge success, despite Huxley suffering facial injuries when the Five are mobbed by fans in Washington, DC. Over the next three years, the Five will visit the US constantly, maintaining a high chart profile by their ready availability for live and TV work.)
June [6] *Do You Love Me* reaches US #11. *I Knew It All The Time* on Congress Records (licensed from UK Piccadilly two years earlier) peaks at US #53.
[15] The group performs at Croydon's Fairfield Hall with the Applejacks and the Mojos.
[20] Dave Clark Five summer season begins at the Blackpool Winter Gardens, Lancs.
[27] *Can't You See That She's Mine* hits UK #10.
July [18] *Can't You See That She's Mine* hits US #4 and ***The Dave Clark Five Return!*** hits US #5.
Aug [22] *Thinking Of You Baby*, featured in the MGM film "Get Yourself A College Girl" (in which they co-star with the Animals), reaches UK #26.
Sept [12] *Because*, the group's first ballad written by Clark and Smith, hits US #3.
Oct ***American Tour*** travels to US #11.
Nov [7] *Any Way You Want It* reaches UK #25, and *Everybody Knows* makes US #15.

1965

Jan [9] *Any Way You Want It* reaches US #14.
[18] The band embarks on an Australian tour.
[21] ***Glad All Over*** is certified gold by the RIAA.
Feb ***Coast To Coast*** hits US #6.
[6] *Everybody Knows* peaks at UK #37.
[8] The group begins filming its first feature film, directed by John Boorman from a Peter Nichols screenplay, on location in London and the West of England.
Mar [20] Ballad *Come Home* makes US #14.
Apr [10] Their revival of Chuck Berry's *Reelin' And Rockin'* peaks at UK #24.
May [22] A second Australasian tour starts, set to end on June 12th. *Reelin' And Rockin'* rolls to US #23, while ***Weekend In London*** rests at US #24.
June [18] The band appears at New York's Academy of Music at the beginning of a six-week US concert trek.
[26] *Come Home* lodges at UK #16.
[28] The group appears in CBS-TV's "It's What's Happening Baby".
July [8] "Catch Us If You Can" premieres at the Rialto Cinema in London's West End.
[17] The group guests on the 200th edition of ITV's "Thank Your Lucky Stars".
Aug [7] Their revival of Chris Kenner's *I Like It Like That* hits US #7.
[13] Smith suffers two broken ribs when he is pulled off stage by fans at a show in Chicago, IL, on the first day of a further US tour.
[14] *Catch Us If You Can* hits UK #5, as the soundtrack album ***Catch Us If You Can*** hits UK #8.
Sept "Catch Us If You Can" movie is released in the US as "Having A Wild Weekend".
[25] *Catch Us If You Can* hits US #4. The soundtrack album ***Having A Wild Weekend*** reaches US #15.

Oct The group appears on ABC-TV's "Shindig!", performing *Having A Wild Weekend*.
Nov [8] The band appears at the Royal Variety Performance in London, in the presence of H.R.H. the Queen and Prince Philip, performing a version of Jim Reeves' *Welcome To My World*.
[27] A remake of Bobby Day's *Over And Over* makes UK #45.
Dec [25] *Over And Over* hits US #1 and will become a million-seller, the group's only US chart-topper.

1966

Jan *I Like It Like That* makes US #32.
Mar [12] *At The Scene*, unreleased in the UK, reaches US #18.
Apr Compilation ***The Dave Clark Five's Greatest Hits*** hits US #9. "The Swingin' Set", in which the Five feature with Nancy Sinatra and the Animals, opens in London's West End as the B-feature to Elvis Presley's "Frankie & Johnny".
May [7] R&B-flavored *Try Too Hard* climbs to US #12.
[16-17] The band films a guest spot for the "Lucy Looks At London" TV special.
[21] *Look Before You Leap* makes UK #50.
June [12] The group makes its 12th appearance on CBS-TV's "The Ed Sullivan Show" - a record for any UK act.
July [9] *Please Tell Me Why* reaches US #28 and ***Try Too Hard*** US #77.
Aug [24] Still-climbing ***The Dave Clark Five's Greatest Hits*** is certified gold by the RIAA.
Sept [3] *Satisfied With You* makes US #50.
Oct ***Satisfied With You*** climbs to US #127.
Nov [19] *Nineteen Days* peaks at US #48 on the 19th day of the month.
Dec Compilation album ***The Dave Clark Five : More Greatest Hits*** peaks at US #103.

1967

Jan The group forms its own film company, Big Five Films, to make "low-budget features and documentaries". (The first documentary, "Hold On - It's The Dave Clark Five", a profile of the group itself, will be sold to US TV.)
Feb [11] *I've Got To Have A Reason* makes US #44.
Apr ***5 By 5*** peaks at US #119.
[15] Their update of Marv Johnson's *You Got What It Takes* makes UK #28.
May [13] *You Got What It Takes* hits US #7.
June [16] The group begins a US tour in Boston, MA, set to end in New Jersey on July 23rd.
July [1] A rocked-up revival of oldie *You Must Have Been A Beautiful Baby* reaches US #35.
Aug [26] *A Little Bit Now* peaks at US #67, and ***You Got What It Takes*** reaches US #149, their last album to chart in the US.
Nov [25] *Red And Blue* reaches US #89.
Dec [2] *Everybody Knows* (not the Five's 1964 hit but a ballad written by Les Reed and Barry Mason, with Lenny Davidson on lead vocal) hits UK #2, behind the Beatles' *Hello Goodbye*.

1968

Jan [20] *Everybody Knows* peaks at US #43, their final US chart entry.
Mar Ballad *No One Can Break A Heart Like You* makes UK #28.
Aug [31] "Hold On - It's The Dave Clark Five" airs on ITV, with guests Richard Chamberlain and Lulu.
Oct Their cover of Raymond Froggatt's *Red Balloon* floats to UK #7.
Dec The football chant-styled *Live In The Sky* peaks at UK #39.

1969

May [11] The group guests on ITV's "This Is Tom Jones".
Nov Now retired from major touring, the group begins a series of successful oldie revival cuts with Jackie DeShannon's *Put A Little Love In Your Heart*, which makes UK #31.

1970

Jan Medley *Good Old Rock'n'Roll*, covering the US hit by Cat Mother & the All-Night Newsboys (and featuring rock oldies like *Long Tall Sally*, *Lucille* and *Blue Suede Shoes*), hits UK #7.
Apr *Everybody Get Together*, a treatment of the Youngbloods' US hit *Get Together*, hits UK #8.
July Another revival, Jerry Keller's *Here Comes Summer*, makes UK #44.
Aug The group announces its break-up: Clark and Smith will continue until 1973, to complete a ten-year contract with EMI, though Clark has already begun an acting course at London's Central School of Speech and Drama.
Nov *More Good Old Rock'n'Roll*, a medley made by Clark and Smith on the lines of the earlier hit, reaches UK #34 and is the group's final UK chart single.

1971

Southern Man and *Won't You Be My Lady* are released, without chart success. (Clark and Smith will release singles, mostly covers of US hits like Tommy James' *Draggin' The Line* and the Stampeders' *Sweet City Woman* under the name Dave Clark & Friends until 1973. Smith will go on to collaborate with ex-Manfred Mann Mike D'Abo, releasing an eponymous album in 1975, which they will promote on tour as support to Sailor, before moving to session work (notably on the original ***Evita*** album), commercial jingle writing and promotion prior to producing Michael Ball in 1993. Clark will concentrate on business activities, including music publishing and showbiz involvement with protégés like John Christie. Davidson will move to antique dealing, Payton to real estate and Huxley to musical equipment retailing.)

1978

Apr [1] ***25 Thumping Great Hits***, compiled by Clark from the original group recordings (all of which have remained his property) and licensed to Polydor Records, hits UK #7.

1985

June Several compilation editions of the '60s program "Ready Steady Go!" are shown on C4-TV, leased by Clark, who purchased the tapes and rights to the series following its demise. The new compilations are by Clark and frequently feature his former group (including some US concert footage).
Aug [24] Smith bubbles under the UK chart (at #82) with *Medley*, featuring a newly-recorded version of snippets of classic group hits, released by Proto.

1986

Apr [9] The musical "Time", devised, co-written and produced by Clark, premieres at London's Dominion Theatre, with Cliff Richard in the leading role. (It will have a long and moderately-successful run, and David Cassidy will later take over the lead.)
May ***Dave Clark's Time - The Album***, an all-star package of songs from the musical, reaches UK #21. It features Richard, Freddie Mercury, Dionne Warwick, Leo Sayer, Ashford and Simpson, and Stevie Wonder. Most of the material is new but *Because*, sung on the album by Julian Lennon, is a revival of the Dave Clark Five's 1964 hit.

1990

Nov Mooncrest releases Smith's ***It's Only Rock'n'Roll***.
Dec [24] Dave Clark, through his company Right Time Production, takes out double-page ads in the world's press, thanking those who helped him win £665,000 damages, interest and court costs in a major court action against Rank Theatres Limited, claiming that Rank "had failed to run an efficient box office at the Dominion Theatre, London, being responsible for the premature closure of the "Time" musical and loss of box-office revenue."

1991

Nov [24] Clark is by Freddie Mercury's bedside when he dies of complications from AIDS in his Holland Park, London home.

1993

Apr Having finally reached agreement on the license of his entirely self-owned back-catalogue with EMI (except in North America where he has negotiated a separate deal with Hollywood Records), Clark begins the long overdue compact-disc release of the Dave Clark Five archive with the issue of ***Glad All Over Again***, a greatest hits collection. (The US version will be released as a double CD by Hollywood, under the title ***The History Of The Dave Clark Five***, and chart for a week at #127 on Aug [21].) Asked by **Ice** magazine about the possibility of an accompanying nostalgic live reunion, Clark responds: "No. I was offered a fortune ten years ago and five years ago. I'm sure we could pack out certain venues, but we've done that. Leave it to all the new exciting bands that are around."
[24] ***Glad All Over Again*** reaches UK #28.
May [1] Reissued *Glad All Over* bows at its UK #37 peak.

PETULA CLARK

1942

Encouraged by her father into a showbiz career (her first "paid" job is for a bag of candy from the management of Bentalls department store in Kingston-upon-Thames, Surrey, when she sings with the resident band in the store's entrance, while shopping), Clark (b. Nov. 15, 1932, Epsom, Surrey) is launched into wartime entertainment in the UK as a child performer, finding radio stardom on "It's All Yours" at the Criterion Theatre, "Variety Band Box" and "The Children's Hour", as well as playing over 150 shows in her first two years on the stage. (Nicknamed "The Forces Girl", she performs 500 shows for the troops.) She will sign with the Rank Organisation in 1943, making "Murder In Reverse", the first of more than two dozen films over the next decade. (Her movies through her teens and into the mid-'50s will include: "Vice Versa", "The Card", "London Town", "I Know Where I'm Going", "White Corridors", "Romantic Age" and "Drawn Daggers".)

1946

July [17] "Cabaret" airs for the first time on BBC-TV. The show will run until November 2nd. (She will also be a regular on BBC radio, appearing in the programs "Cabin In The Cotton", "Calling All Forces" and "Guest Night".)

1949

Her maiden record, *Put Your Shoes On Lucy*, is released on EMI's Columbia label, prior to her signing to the newly-formed Polygon label on the recommendation of its musical director, Alan Freeman, (she will stay with the label until 1971, seeing it change its name to Nixa and then Pye Records in the '50s).

1950

Nov [24] Following the release of *You Are My True Love* earlier in the year, "Pet's Parlour" airs for the first time on BBC-TV. (The show will run until July 24th, 1953, winning Clark the award for Most Outstanding Artist On UK TV.)

1954

July [24] While her version of the seasonal children's novelty *Where Did My Snowman Go?* just missed the published UK Top 12 in December 1952, another children's song, *The Little Shoemaker* (recorded while she is still partly in shock, following a car accident on the way to the studio), now hits UK #7.

1955

Feb [5] *Majorca* reaches UK #12.
Sept [30] "Pet's Parade" airs for the first time on BBC-TV, set to run until February 14th, 1957.

1956

Jan [7] Clark's version of the much-covered ballad *Suddenly There's A Valley*, her first single on Nixa, hits UK #7.

1957

Sept [28] Having ended her management relationship with her father, and moved out of the family home into an apartment in Stratton Court in London's West End earlier in the year, Clark's cover of Jodi Sands' US hit, *With All My Heart*, hits UK #4.
Dec [14] Her treatment of *Alone* hits UK #8, ahead of the Shepherd Sisters' original US version (at UK #14) and the Southlanders' (at UK #17).

1958

Mar [15] *Baby Lover* makes UK #12 (her last UK success for three years).
Nov Clark gives her first French-language show at the Alhambra Theatre, Paris, France, after Leon Cabat, president of the Vogue label, France's Nixa counterpart, unhappy that Clark's UK hits are being covered in France by Dalida, encourages her to sing French-language versions. (The following day she meets Vogue Records promotion man Claude Wolff, and they become romantically attached, with Clark also signing to the label. During the year she also appears on a French radio show, "Musicarama".)

1961

Feb [25] *Sailor*, Norman Newell's English adaptation of Lolita's German hit, *Seeman*, hits UK #1 for a week, besting a competing Top 10 version by Anne Shelton.
Apr [15] *Something Missing* makes UK #44.
June [8] Clark marries Wolff in Paris.
Aug [26] *Romeo*, a remake of the 1925 hit *Salome*, hits UK #3, also becoming a huge hit in Europe with international sales subsequently topping one million.
Dec [23] *My Friend The Sea* hits UK #7.

1962

Feb [10] *I'm Counting On You* reaches UK #41.
July [28] *Ya Ya Twist*, her rocking adaptation of Lee Dorsey's US R&B hit, sung in French and intended for the European market, reaches UK #14. Another period without major UK hits follows, but *Monsieur* and *Chariot*, sung in French, and *Casanova*, in German, are all European million-sellers. (An English version of *Chariot*, *I Will Follow Him*, is a hit for Little Peggy March. *Monsieur* wins the Grand Prix Du Disque, France's equivalent of the Grammy.) Freeman takes an executive role at Pye, leaving Tony Hatch to take over as Clark's producer.
[29] She guests on ITV's "Thank Your Lucky Stars", with Cliff Richard, the Shadows, Helen Shapiro, Frank Ifield, Karl Denver, Craig Douglas, and Ronnie Carroll.

1963

May [18] *Casanova/Chariot*, a UK double A-side featuring the original foreign-language versions, makes UK #39.

1964

Jan [12] Clark returns to the UK to record a segment for ITV's "Big Night Out", followed by a BBC-TV taping of "Language Of Love" with Amanda Barrie and Richard Briers, due to air on February 13th. Further TV appearances during the next few months will include ITV's "Ready Steady Go!" with the Rolling Stones, on April 24th, and BBC-TV's "A Swinging Time" on June 11th.
Dec [19] Tony Hatch, who has been producing French sessions for Clark, has interested her in his song *Downtown*, originally written with the Drifters in mind. Completed in only its second studio take, it hits UK #2, behind the Beatles' *I Feel Fine*. (Warner Bros. A&R executive Joe Smith, on vacation in London, hears the song and signs Clark to the label in the US.)
[14] Clark returns to London, not least to record ITV's "Ready Steady Go!", airing on the 18th, a BBC-TV "Top Of The Pops" appearance and a cameo in a new ITV series, "The Ladybirds", on the 31st.
[27] While in London, Clark guests on ITV's "Sunday Night At The London Palladium".

1965

Jan [23] *I Feel Fine* fails to hold off *Downtown* in the US, where it hits #1 for the first of two weeks, making Clark the first UK female to top the US charts since Vera Lynn in 1952.
Mar [1] *Downtown* becomes Clark's only RIAA-certified record.
[14] On her first visit to the US, Clark sings *Downtown* and *I Know A Place* on CBS-TV's "The Ed Sullivan Show".
[27] *I Know A Place* reaches UK #17.
Apr [13] Clark wins the Best Rock And Roll Recording Of 1964 category for *Downtown*, at the seventh annual Grammy Awards.
May [1] *I Know A Place* hits US #3, and Clark becomes the only female vocalist to chart her first two singles in the US top three. (This achievement will stand until Cyndi Lauper repeats the feat in 1984.) ***Downtown*** reaches US #21.
[16] Clark returns to "The Ed Sullivan Show".
July [3] ***I Know A Place*** peaks at US #42, coinciding with her first North American tour dates.
Aug [21] *You'd Better Come Home* reaches US #22.
[28] *You'd Better Come Home* makes UK #44.
Oct [23] *Round Every Corner* peaks at UK #43, with Clark again guesting on "The Ed Sullivan Show".
Nov [27] Clark co-penned *You're The One* reaches UK #23, but is not released as a single in the US. (The Vogues' cover version hits US #4.) Clark is offered the chance to co-star with Elvis Presley in "Paradise Hawaiian Style", but declines.
[13] *Round Every Corner* reaches US #21.
[15] She begins a season at the Copacabana in Manhattan, New York.
Dec Clark films a segment for the "TNT Award Show", alongside Joan Baez, Bo Diddley, Ray Charles, Lovin' Spoonful, the Ronettes, Ike & Tina Turner, Roger Miller, the Byrds and Donovan, singing *You're The One*, *My Love* and *Downtown*.
[4] ***Petula Clark Sings The World's Greatest International Hits*** makes US #129.

1966

Feb [5] *My Love*, recorded in New York in November, during her engagement at the Copa, a track Clark dislikes and tries not to have released, tops the US chart for the first of two weeks and is her second (though uncertified) US million-seller. (Clark becomes the first UK female singer to have two US #1s.)
Mar [5] *My Love* hits UK #4.
[15] She wins the Best Contemporary (Rock'n'Roll) Vocal Performance, Female category, for *I Know A Place* at the eighth annual Grammy Awards.
Apr [23] *A Sign Of The Times* makes UK #49 and US #11.
June [4] ***My Love*** reaches US #68.
[6] Clark opens in cabaret at London's Savoy Hotel.
[16] A six-week BBC-TV series, "This Is Petula Clark", premieres.
July [30] *I Couldn't Live Without Your Love* (the first co-credited Hatch/Trent song) hits UK #6, as the album ***I Couldn't Live Without Your Love*** makes UK #11.
Aug *I Couldn't Live Without Your Love* hits US #9.
Oct [9] Clark appears live on "The Ed Sullivan Show".
[13] She opens at the Copacabana, New York, for a two-week residency.
Nov Clark makes her Las Vegas, NV, cabaret debut, on a bill including Woody Allen.
[5] ***I Couldn't Live Without Your Love*** makes US #43.
[26] *Who Am I* reaches US #21.

1967

Jan [21] *Color My World* reaches US #16.
Feb [18] Clark's version of the Charlie Chaplin-penned *This Is My Song* (from his movie "Countess From Hong Kong" starring Sophia Loren and Marlon Brando), recorded in Reno, NV, tops the UK chart for the first of two weeks, eventually selling over 500,000 copies, and beating a rival version by Harry Secombe, which hits #2. Clark's recording is produced by Claude Wolff, with Ernie Freeman arranging. She premieres the song before its release, on "The Hollywood Palace". A compilation album, ***Petula Clark's Hit Parade***, reaches UK #18 and *Colour My World* hits UK #16.
Mar [3] Clark appears at the London Palladium in the presence of H.R.H. Princess Margaret.
Apr *This Is My Song* hits US #3.
[8] ***Color My World/Who Am I*** makes US #49.
[28] She performs before President Johnson as a star cabaret guest at the annual White House Press Correspondents' Dinner.
July [1] *Don't Sleep In The Subway*, a song created by Tony Hatch from unfinished segments of three other compositions, reaches UK #12 and will hit US #5.
Sept [30] *The Cat In The Window (The Bird In The Sky)*, written by Gary Bonner and Alan Gordon, reaches US #26.
Oct ***These Are My Songs***, produced by Sonny Burke, makes UK #38 and US #27.
Dec [2] Clark guests on BBC1-TV's "Dee Time".

1968

Jan [13] *The Other Man's Grass (Is Always Greener)* reaches UK #20 and will make US #31.
Mar [6] *Kiss Me Goodbye*, penned by Les Reed and Barry Mason, makes UK #50.
Apr ***The Other Man's Grass Is Always Greener*** reaches UK #37 and US #93.
[6] *Kiss Me Goodbye* reaches US #15.
[8] NBC-TV special "Petula" airs. The show is part-sponsored by Chrysler, for whom Clark has recorded TV ads for the company's Plymouth range to the tune of *The Beat Goes On* the previous year.
Aug [24] *Don't Give Up* makes US #37.
Oct Having turned down two previous straight film roles, she plays the part of Sharon McLonergan in a movie adaptation of E.Y. "Yip" Harburg's 1947 musical, "Finian's Rainbow", at the invitation of Quincy Jones, head of the Warner Bros. music department, with Fred Astaire and Tommy Steele, and directed by Francis Ford Coppola.
[12] ***Petula*** peaks at US #51.
Dec *American Boys* makes US #59.

1969

Jan Clark splits with Hatch and Trent after two unsuccessful single releases.
Feb [15] Compilation ***Petula Clark's Greatest Hits, Vol.1*** makes US #57, as ***Finian's Rainbow*** makes US #90.
Mar *Happy Heart* peaks at US #62.
[31] ***Portrait Of Petula*** reaches US #37.
Aug She co-stars with Peter O'Toole in "Goodbye Mr Chips", a remake of the 1939 Robert Donat/Greer Garson film, while *Look At Mine* peaks at US #89.
Oct Clark's performance at London's Royal Albert Hall is recorded for subsequent album release and also becomes the first show broadcast in color on BBC-TV.
Nov ***Record Retailer*** announces Clark will play a nude bedroom scene in the forthcoming film, "Stanyan Street".
[14] "An Evening With Petula" airs at midnight - the first BBC1 show to be transmitted in color.
[29] *No One Better Than You* spends a week at US #93.
Dec [20] ***Goodbye Mr. Chips*** makes US #164.

1970

Jan ***Just Pet*** peaks at US #176.
Feb Clark records Les Reed songs in London with Tony Hatch.

Aug ***Memphis***, recorded in Memphis with Chips Moman, makes US #198.

1971

Apr While *The Song Of My Life* has reached UK #32 in March, ***Warm And Tender***, produced by Arif Mardin, peaks at US #178 (her last US chart album).

1972

Jan [15] Clark's version of Rice/Lloyd Webber's *I Don't Know How To Love Him* from "Jesus Christ Superstar", recorded in Miami while she was appearing at the Diplomat Hotel, makes UK #47. (Her US chart singles during the year will be: *My Guy* (#70, Aug [26]) and *Wedding Song (There Is Love)* (#61, Dec [2]). She subsequently leaves Pye in the UK and Warner Bros. in the US, signing to Deutsche Grammophon, which releases her on the Polydor label in Britain, and on MGM in the US. (No big sellers will emerge from this deal, though five Polydor albums are released over four years, during which time Clark will tour the UK, open a season at Caesar's Palace in Las Vegas, NV, perform in Australia, Japan, South Africa, and host two variety series for BBC-TV.)

1977

Feb [12] TV-advertised compilation album ***20 All-Time Greatest*** reaches UK #18, coming between a short recording return to Pye (which produces a disco version of *Downtown*) and a signing to CBS, neither being commercially productive. Clark will go on to co-star with Paul Jones in the April 1979-premiering ITV musical drama "Traces Of Love", whilst otherwise living in semi-retirement in her Geneva chateau, where she devotes much time to her husband and three children.

1982

Mar [6] After an initial reluctance to follow in Julie Andrews' footsteps, Clark has starred as Maria in a 1980 stage revival of "The Sound Of Music" at London's Apollo Victoria Theatre, which has run successfully for 14 months. Making an occasional return to recording, *Natural Love*, recorded for the US Scotti Brothers label, now peaks at US #66. (During the remainder of the decade, Clark will make the feature film "Never Never Land", take a non-singing stage role in a short run of George Bernard Shaw's "Candida", perform with the London Philharmonic Orchestra at London's Royal Albert Hall in February 1983, the recording of which is released as a live double album, undertake a residency at Caesar's Palace, Atlantic City, NJ, in July 1987 having performed her first shows in the US for ten years in 1986, before *Downtown '88*, a typically-fashionable '80s update of her '60s classic, hits UK #10 on Dec [24], 1988, an event which sees Clark return to TV appearances, including a performance on BBC1-TV's "Top Of The Pops", and work with Dee Shipman on "Someone Like You", a musical about the US Civil War, which will premiere on October 25th, 1989 at the Arts Theatre, Cambridge, Cambs.)

1996

Jan While longtime fan Michael Jackson has paid for Clark to record three demos for him, with a view to future release in October 1991, Clark's first album of the '90s, ***Treasures Volume 1***, and an extracted single, *Oxygen*, have been released on the Scotti Bros. label in June the following year. Clark has also undertaken her first UK tour in over ten years in October 1992, before joining the New York cast of "Blood Brothers" with David and Sean Cassidy at the Music Box Theater on August 16th in 1993. Having previously deputized for Elaine Paige in the role, Clark now takes over the part of Norma Desmond in the long-running "Sunset Boulevard" musical at London's Adelphi Theatre.

THE CLASH

Joe Strummer (vocals, guitar); **Mick Jones** (guitar); **Paul Simonon** (bass); **Nicky "Topper" Headon** (drums)

1976

June After nine abortive months with seminal punk outfit London SS, Jones (b. June 26, 1953, Brixton, London) forms the Clash in Shepherds Bush, London, with art-school student Simonon (b. Dec. 15, 1955, Brixton), who has never played before, but learns bass guitar. Bernie Rhodes from Malcolm McLaren's London Sex boutique becomes their manager. Guitarist Keith Levene (later of Public Image Ltd.) and drummer Terry Chimes join, and Strummer (b. John Mellors, Aug. 21, 1952, Ankara, Turkey) is persuaded to leave R&B group the 101ers, which he formed in 1974 with Alvaro Pena-Rojas.

Aug [13] The Clash gives its first "official" public performance, in a London rehearsal hall.

[29] Their formal debut (after an unannounced support slot behind the Sex Pistols in Sheffield, S. Yorks.) takes place at Screen On The Green, Islington, London.

Sept [20] The band plays the 100 Club punk festival, London, but club owners are wary of potential punk violence and gigs generally prove hard to find. Levene leaves after only five shows.

Oct [23] They play "A Night Of Pure Energy" at the ICA Theatre, London.

Dec [6] The band embarks on the Sex Pistols' highly-controversial "Anarchy In The UK" tour (all but three gigs will be cancelled).

1977

Jan [1] The Clash plays on the opening night of the Roxy Club in London's Covent Garden. With record companies now showing interest in the punk genre, the Clash signs to CBS Records worldwide (after recording some demos for Polydor in December), a deal negotiated by Rhodes. Their debut album is recorded over three weekends. Chimes leaves and is replaced by "Topper" Headon (b. May 30, 1955, Bromley, Kent).

Mar The group pulls out as the support act to a John Cale tour.

Apr [9] Their typically antagonistic debut single *White Riot* makes UK #38.

[30] The band's 14-cut, rapid-fire filled debut, ***The Clash***, largely written by Strummer and Jones and produced by Mickey Foote, reaches UK #12, immediately showcasing its raw, aggressive, guitar-driven punk angst.

May [1] The "White Riot" UK tour starts at the Roxy, with the Jam and the Buzzcocks as support bands (the Jam will pull out on the 29th). *Remote Control* is released.

[9] London's Rainbow Theatre is vandalized during a Clash gig.

June [10] Strummer and Headon are each fined £5 in London for spray-painting "Clash" on a wall.

[11-12] The duo is detained overnight in prison in Newcastle, Tyne & Wear, having failed to appear at Morpeth magistrates court on May 21st to answer a robbery charge relating to the theft of a Holiday Inn pillowcase. They are fined £100. The latest UK tour, which starts a few days later, is wryly named "Out On Parole".

July [16] The group takes an "Awayday" to Birmingham as consolation for the cancelled "Digbeth Punk Festival", to headline "Britain's Burning - The Last Big Event Before We All Go To Jail" at the Birmingham Rag Market, with the Slits, the Saints, Cherry Vanilla and the Tom Robinson Band.

Aug [5] The Clash performs at the second European punk festival in Mont de Marsan, France.

Oct [8] *Complete Control*, recorded with reggae producer Lee "Scratch" Perry, makes UK #28.

The group spends an afternoon in a German jail after a dispute over a hotel bill which a promoter should have paid.

Dec During a further UK tour, a punk riot ensues at a Winter Gardens, Bournemouth, Dorset gig.

1978

Feb Strummer is hospitalized for 11 days with hepatitis.

Mar [4] *Clash City Rockers* makes UK #35. Their debut album, still not released in the US (where CBS deems it unsuitable for radio play), sells more than 100,000 on import, making it the biggest-selling imported album ever in the US.

[30] Simonon and Headon are arrested in Camden Town, London, for criminal damage, after shooting down racing pigeons with air guns from the roof of Chalk Farm Studios. Four police cars and one helicopter are required to make the arrest. Fines this time total £800.

Apr [30] The band headlines the "Anti-Nazi League Carnival" in London, organized by Rock Against Racism.

July [1] *(White Man) In Hammersmith Palais* makes UK #32, as the group embarks on a ten-date UK tour at Granby Hall, Leicester, Leics., set to end on the 12th at the Top Rank, Birmingham, W. Midlands. With some work already completed for a second album, they meet Blue Öyster Cult producer Sandy Pearlman, and finish the project with him.

[8] Strummer and Simonon are arrested and fined (£25 and £50 respectively) for being "drunk and disorderly" after a show at the Apollo Theatre in Glasgow, Scotland.

Sept [9] The group performs at London's Harlesden Roxy.

Oct [21] Rhodes is fired as manager after both the band and CBS find him increasingly hard to deal with. He is replaced by one of the Clash's early champions, **Melody Maker** journalist Caroline Coon.

Nov [1] Rhodes, who has a contract giving him 20% of the band's income, is granted a court order stating that all Clash earnings are to be paid directly to him.

[25] Their second album ***Give 'Em Enough Rope*** debuts at UK #2, behind the ***Grease*** soundtrack.

Dec [2] The Clash plays two sellout concerts at London's Lyceum Ballroom, as they begin their "Sort It Out" UK tour.

1979

Jan [6] *Tommy Gun* reaches UK #19, their biggest-selling single to date.

[31] The group begins a North American tour in Vancouver, BC, Canada, with Bo Diddley as the unlikely support act.

Feb [17] They perform at New York, NY's Palladium Theater during the US leg of the tour, dubbed "Pearl Harbor '79", opening the show with *I'm So Bored With The USA*.

Mar [24] *English Civil War (Johnny Comes Marching Home)* reaches UK #25.

Apr [7] ***Give 'Em Enough Rope*** makes US #128.

June [23] Four-track EP, *The Cost Of Living*, headed by a revival of Bobby Fuller's *I Fought The Law*, reaches UK #22. Coon is fired as manager.

Aug The group records 12 songs in three days with veteran producer Guy Stevens (he had previously recorded their Polydor demo in December 1976), at Wessex Studios.

Sept Their second US tour, with the Undertones opening, is dubbed "The Clash Take The Fifth" (a reference to temporary fifth member Mickey Gallagher, of Ian Dury's Blockheads, on keyboards). US Support acts include R&B stalwarts Sam & Dave, Screamin' Jay Hawkins and Lee Dorsey, plus country-rocker Joe Ely and psychobilly band the Cramps.

[21] The group performs at the Palladium, New York.

Oct [6] ***The Clash***, belatedly released in the US, makes #126.

Dec [22] Retailed at a single-price album, the double set ***London Calling*** (originally to have been ***The New Testament***, with its sleeve a pastiche of Elvis Presley's debut album) debuts at its UK #9 peak.

[27] The group co-headlines (with Ian Dury) the second of four benefit concerts for the people of Kampuchea, at London's Hammersmith Odeon.

1980

Jan [19] The extracted title track *London Calling* reaches UK #11. In need of management, the band signs to Blackhill, run by Peter Jenner and Andrew King (former Pink Floyd and currently Ian Dury managers).
Mar [15] "Rude Boy", a fictionalized documentary film of a Clash roadie (played by Ray Gange) made by Jack Hazan and David Mingay, opens at the Prince Charles Cinema in London. Much of it has been filmed behind the scenes on the road over the previous 18 months.
[22] ***London Calling*** reaches US #27.
Apr The group begins a string of one-night stands in Europe.
May [24] *Train In Vain (Stand By Me)*, the band's first US chart single, reaches #23.
[21] Strummer is arrested at a much-troubled gig in Hamburg, W. Germany, after smashing his guitar over the head of a violently-demonstrative member of the audience. He is released after an alcohol test proves negative.
June The band tours the US and Europe, with Jamaican DJ Mikey Dread, with whom they record *Bankrobber*, playing on selected European dates.
Aug They begin recordings for a self-produced album at Electric Ladyland Studios, New York, with tensions between Jones and the others affecting some sessions. (During the year Jones also produces ***Spirit Of St. Louis*** by US singer Ellen Foley, his current girlfriend, and will also co-produce Ian Hunter's ***Short Back'n'Sides***, to be released the following year.)
Sept [6] *Bankrobber*, released in the UK by CBS, after a flood of Dutch imports, reaches UK #12.
Nov 10" mini-album ***Black Market Clash***, customized for the US market, makes US #74.
Dec [6] *The Call Up*, an anti-draft song, reaches UK #40.
[20] Triple album set ***Sandinista!***, issued at the band's insistence at a double-album price and with mixed reactions due to its sprawling contents, reaches UK #19. (The band agrees to relinquish royalties on the first 200,000 copies, if CBS releases it at the cheaper price. Jones is quoted: "Listen, the bottom line on ***Sandinista!*** is that you can dance all the way through it. The only thing is that you have to dance a certain way.")

1981

Jan Strummer, dissatisfied with recent temporary management arrangements, meets Bernie Rhodes by chance in London and, within two months, Rhodes is back as the group's manager.
[31] *Hitsville UK* peaks at UK #56.
Mar ***Sandinista!*** reaches US #24.
May [2] The dance-oriented *The Magnificent Seven* makes UK #34.
[26] The group begins a 17-day stint at Bond's Casino, New York, NY, with Grandmaster Flash & the Furious Five as one of the support acts. On their return to Europe they play a series of dates in London and Paris.
Oct [19] They play at London's Lyceum Ballroom.
Dec [5] *This Is Radio Clash* makes UK #47. Work starts on a new album.

1982

Feb [1] The group performs at the Sun Plaza, Tokyo, Japan, during its first tour there, followed by dates in New Zealand, Australia, Hong Kong and Thailand.
Mar The band returns to the UK and finishes recording, with Glyn Johns completing the final mixing.
Apr [26] On the eve of their UK "Know Your Rights" tour, Strummer disappears, and the dates are postponed. (Although thought to be a Rhodes publicity stunt, Strummer will claim that he went to Paris because his girlfriend's mother was in jail.)
May [8] *Know Your Rights* makes UK #43.
[10] Headon plays his last gig with the band, at the "Lochem Festival" in Holland (officially leaving because of "a difference of political direction"). Chimes returns temporarily to play drums on the band's US tour, its most extensive yet, a trip which will lead to record US sales.
[22] ***Combat Rock*** hits UK #2 in its first week, remaining charted for 23 weeks.
[24] Strummer returns to the band.
July [2] Headon is remanded on bail at Horseferry Road Court, London, charged with stealing a bus stop worth £30 from the Fulham Road and receiving stolen property.
Aug [7] *Rock The Casbah* reaches UK #30.
Sept [22] After a US tour, the band accepts an invitation to support the Who on their farewell US stadium tour: eight major shows, including two at Shea Stadium, New York.
[18] *Should I Stay Or Should I Go?/Straight To Hell* makes US #45.
Oct [9] The group performs both sides of the single on NBC-TV's "Saturday Night Live".
[23] *Should I Stay Or Should I Go?/Straight To Hell* reaches UK #17.
Nov [27] Having completed its opening dates for the Who, the band appears at the first "Jamaican World Music Festival", Montego Bay, Jamaica, on a bill with the Beach Boys, the Beat, the Grateful Dead, Gladys Knight & the Pips and others, marking Chimes' final appearance with the band.

1983

Jan ***Combat Rock*** becomes its biggest-selling US album, hitting #7.
[22] *Rock The Casbah* hits US #8.
Mar [26] *Should I Stay Or Should I Go?* is reissued in the US, now reaching #50.
May Pete Howard, from fellow CBS band Cold Fish, joins on drums. He immediately plays five warm-up gigs in Texas and Arizona.
[28] The group appears on the first of the three-day "US '83 Festival" in San Bernardino, CA. They co-headline the day's bill with Men At Work and the Stray Cats.
Sept A CBS "Clash Communiqué" reads: "Joe Strummer and Paul Simonon have decided that Mick Jones should leave the group. It is felt that Jones has drifted apart from the original idea of the Clash." Jones goes (and will re-emerge with his hitmaking band, Big Audio Dynamite).

1984

Jan Guitarists Vince White and ex-Cortinas Nick Sheppard are added, as Strummer declares in interviews that "a whole new Clash era is underway".
[19] The new Clash line-up makes its live debut in Santa Barbara, CA, at the beginning of a Californian tour.
Feb [25] The group performs at the Festhalle, Bern, Switzerland, during a current European tour.
May [17] The Clash plays the Aragon Ballroom, Chicago, IL, during further US dates.
Dec [6-7] The band performs at two miners' benefits shows at London's Brixton Academy.

1985

Mar The group re-surfaces, playing impromptu acoustic sets in Scotland and the North of England.
July [13] Following an appearance at the "Roskilde Festival", Denmark, in June, the group performs at the "Rock Scene Festival", Quehenna, Finland.
Nov ***Cut The Crap*** reaches UK #16 after being savaged by critics, while the extracted *This Is England* makes UK #24. A "Busking Tour" of the UK does not impart the new credibility that Strummer claims for the band, and he and Simonon call it a day.

1986

Jan ***Cut The Crap*** reaches US #88, by which time the band has broken up. (Simonon will fade from view, concentrating on painting, while Strummer will devote most of the next two years to acting in films made by Alex Cox - notably "Straight To Hell". Headon will sign as a soloist to Mercury Records, releasing the album ***Waking Up*** and three singles, but his career will fall apart in November 1987, when he is jailed for 15 months at Maidstone Crown Court, after supplying heroin to an addict who later dies. He will be released from prison in 1990 and find gainful employment as a cabbie for a Chiswick taxi firm.)

1988

Mar Reissued in the UK as a forthcoming-album trailer, *I Fought The Law* climbs to #29.
Apr [2] Retrospective double ***The Story Of The Clash, Volume 1*** hits UK #7 and will go on to make US #142.
May Another spin-off from the compilation, reissued *London Calling*, makes UK #46.
June After scoring two movie soundtracks, ***Walker*** and ***Permanent Record***, Strummer embarks on his solo "Rock Against The Rich" UK tour. (Now based in Los Angeles, CA, Strummer plays on Bob Dylan's ***Down In The Groove*** and records and tours with his own band, the Latino Rockabilly War.)

1989

May [13] "Lost In Space", a three-episode picture written and directed by Jim Jarmusch, in which Strummer appears as Johnny, is shown at the "Cannes Film Festival", Cannes, France.
Oct [14] Strummer's ***Earthquake Weather***, featuring backing members Zander Schloss (guitar), Jack Irons (drums) and others, makes UK #58.
[27] ***London Calling*** tops **Rolling Stone**'s "Top 100 Albums Of The '80s" critics list.

1990

July [21] Remixed Clash cut, *Return To Brixton* peaks at UK #57.
The Clash's *Rock The Casbah* is the first record to be broadcast on the Armed Forces radio in the Persian Gulf.

1991

Mar [2] *Should I Stay Or Should I Go*, reissued through its use in a TV commercial for Levi's 501 jeans, returns at UK #5, hitting the top a week later, the group's first UK #1. Strummer and Jones are reported to disagree over the song's sponsorship of the product. Jones' view clearly predominates, as Columbia Records include the BAD (Big Audio Dynamite) II cut *Rush*, at his insistence, on the B-side.
[30] The single's success will spur sales of a three-year-old retrospective, ***The Story Of The Clash Vol.1***, which debuts at its UK #13 peak.
Apr [20] Re-issued *Rock The Casbah* reaches UK #15.
May [18] Signed to I.R.S. Records, Simonon's new band, Havana 3 A.M., comprising himself, Nigel Dixon (guitar/vocals), Gary Myrick (guitar/vocals) and Travis Williams (drums), makes US #169 with ***Havana 3 A.M.***.
June [15] Re-released *London Calling* peaks at UK #64.
Sept [26-27] Having replaced Shane MacGowan as lead vocalist of the Pogues, the otherwise Irish group performs with Strummer out front at New York's Beacon Theatre (he has also recently recorded the lead vocal for their current single, *A Rainy Night In Soho*).
Nov [12] ***The Clash*** is certified gold by the RIAA.
[16] A second Clash retrospective, ***The Singles Collection***, debuts at its UK #68 peak.
Dec [4] ***London Calling*** is also confirmed gold by the RIAA.

1995

June [6] The RIAA certifies ***Combat Rock*** for two million sales.
Oct Following Sony imprint Columbia Legacy's 1994 release of the three-CD boxed Clash retrospective ***On Broadway***, and, with the Clash having reportedly been offered between $5 million and $7 million to reform for a "Lollapalooza" US tour, Strummer works on dance tracks in London with techno musicians Richard Norris and Gary from UK dance-trance act Azukz.
see also: **BIG AUDIO DYNAMITE**

JIMMY CLIFF

1962

Cliff (b. James Chambers, Apr. 1, 1948, St. Catherine,

Jamaica), having quit college and moved to Kingston, Jamaica, to pursue a musical career, which includes fronting local band Shakedown Sound and releasing his debut single *Daisy Got Me Crazy*, teams up with local Chinese/Jamaican musician and producer, Leslie Kong, who has been impressed by Cliff's *Dearest Beverley*, a song about an ice-cream parlor, and has a #1 local hit in Jamaica with *Hurricane Hattie*, inspired by the storm which swept across the Caribbean. He will go on to cut four further releases with Kong, *Since Lately*, *King Of Kings*, *My Lucky Day* and *Miss Jamaica*.

1965

On a US tour organized by the Jamaican government, with Prince Buster and Byron Lee's Dragonaires, he meets Chris Blackwell of Island Records, who persuades him to move to the UK, where he initially works as a back-up singer, before recording in his own right and performing live (a mixture of ska and R&B) in Britain and Europe.

1967

July Following the release of *Call On Me*, a one-off single for Fontana Records (UK), in Janauary the previous year, *Give And Take*, his label debut for Island, receives radio interest but just fails to chart. It is taken from his first album, the UK-only issued ***Hard Road To Travel***. (In 1968, Cliff will represent Jamaica in an international song festival in Brazil with his own song, *Waterfall*, a prize-winning entry which becomes a popular hit in South America.)

1969

Nov After five non-charting Island singles, *Wonderful World, Beautiful People*, his debut for Trojan Records, hits UK #6, also reflecting the burgeoning popularity of reggae in the UK.

1970

Jan [24] *Wonderful World, Beautiful People* reaches US #25.
Feb *Vietnam*, a self-penned reggae protest song, makes UK #46.
Mar [28] *Come Into My Life* climbs to US #89. All three cuts are taken from his sophomore album ***Jimmy Cliff***, also released on Trojan in the UK (and by A&M Records in the US to whom he is now signed).
Sept Cliff-penned *You Can Get It If You Really Want*, becomes a UK #2 hit for Desmond Dekker while *Wild World*, Cliff's reggae adaptation of a Cat Stevens song from Stevens' ***Tea For The Tillerman***, hits UK #8. (It is not released in the US, where the original version is a Top 20 hit.)

1971

June Re-signed to Island, Cliff releases ***Another Cycle***, recorded at Muscle Shoals Studios, AL, consisting entirely of R&B/soul material.
Sept The Pioneers hit UK #5 with the Cliff-penned *Let Your Yeah Be Yeah*.

1972

He stars in the semi-autobiographical lead role in Perry Henzell's Jamaican-made film, "The Harder They Come", which receives critical acclaim. Cliff also has four self-penned songs on the soundtrack.

1973

Newly signed to EMI in the UK (where he will have no further chart records) and Warner/Reprise in the US, Cliff releases ***Unlimited***. His conversion of faith to Islam, after meeting Black Muslims in Chicago, IL, while on an American visit, has a profound effect on his songwriting and prompts him to visit Africa, a trip which is mostly concerned with his roots and the lifestyle of his ancestors.

1974

His first full US tour premieres at New York's Carnegie Hall, during a year when he releases the critically well-received ***Struggling Man*** and ***House Of Exile***.

1975

Mar Soundtrack album ***The Harder They Come*** makes US #140, following the cult movie's belated US release.
Nov [8] Following the recent issue of ***Brave Warrior***, ***Follow My Mind*** makes US #195, also proving a strong seller in South America, Africa and Europe. Signed worldwide to Warner Bros., it will be followed by ***Give Thankx*** in 1978, which Cliff rates as his best effort yet.

1980

I Am The Living is released (to be followed by 1981's ***Give The People What They Want***). During the year he performs a concert in Soweto, South Africa, to a racially-mixed audience of 75,000 - his condition for performing the show. He is now a much-toured artist around the African continent, having played in Nigeria, Senegal, Cameroon, Zambia and South Africa. He will also feature in the movie "Bongo Man" and perform at the 14th annual "Montreux Jazz Festival" in Montreux, Switzerland.

1982

Aug [14] Newly signed to CBS/Columbia Records, his label debut, ***Special***, produced in Jamaica by Chris Kimsey, peaks at US #186 and is promoted with a six-week US tour, accompanied by his new band Oneness, sharing the bill with Peter Tosh. It closes with two sellout dates at New York's Felt Forum.
Oct Cliff co-headlines the "World Music Festival" at the Bob Marley Center in Montego Bay, Jamaica.

1983

Aug Cliff returns to Africa for a month-long tour, playing concerts in Lesotho and Zimbabwe.
Oct ***The Power And The Glory*** is released, mostly recorded with Oneness in Jamaica, including two tracks cut with Kool & the Gang in their New Jersey studio.

1985

Feb [26] Cliff is nominated in the first Best Reggae Recording category, for *Reggae Night*, one of the tracks recorded the previous year with Kool & the Gang, at the 27th annual Grammy Awards. Black Uhuru's ***Anthem*** wins.
May Cliff's composition *Trapped* is recorded by Bruce Springsteen as his contribution to the USA For Africa album, ***We Are The World***. Springsteen has also been playing it live for several months, having been said to have first heard Cliff's original version over an airport P.A. system in Europe.
Aug ***Cliff Hanger***, much of which is again recorded with Kool & The Gang, is released.
Dec [14] Artists United Against Apartheid, comprising 49 artists including Cliff, makes US #38 and UK #21 with *Sun City*.

1986

Feb [25] Cliff wins the Best Reggae Recording category for ***Cliff Hanger*** at the 28th Grammy Awards.
July He stars in the currently playing movie "Club Paradise", with Robin Williams, Peter O'Toole and a host of US comedy talent. He has also contributed seven tracks to the soundtrack album, including a duet with Elvis Costello, *Seven Day Weekend*, which is released as a single.
Aug He embarks on a worldwide tour with Oneness, as support act to Steve Winwood.

1988

Mar ***Hanging Fire***, produced by Kool & the Gang's Khalis "Ronald Bell" Bayyan and partly recorded in the Congo, is released.

1989

Sept Having formed his own Cliff Records, ***Images*** is released, produced with Ansel Collins.
[22] Bruce Springsteen joins Cliff on stage at the Stone Pony, Asbury, NJ, to sing *Trapped*.

1991

Jan Cliff participates in the "Rock In Rio II" festival at the Maracana soccer stadium, Rio de Janeiro, Brazil.
Aug [24] He performs on the first day of the Gold Coast Concert Bowl, Squaw Valley, CA, before a sellout crowd of more than 11,000.

1992

July [25] His "World Beat Reggae Festival '92" opens at the Roseland Theatre, Portland, OR, set to end in Dallas on September 30th, promoting, not least, his latest release, the 14-track ***Breakout*** (on JRS Records).
Oct [23] A further 26-date Cliff US tour opens at the Memorial Auditorium, Burlington, VT, set to end on November 28th at the Cameo Theatre, Miami, FL.

1993

Apr [22] Cliff performs at London's Brixton Academy during a short UK visit.

1994

Jan [29] *I Can See Clearly Now*, featured in the John Candy-starring movie "Cool Runnings", reaches US #18.
Mar [26] *I Can See Clearly Now* reaches UK #23.
Aug [14] Cliff takes part in "Woodstock II" at Winston Farm, Saugerties, NY, and later joins the Red Hot Chili Peppers at the Academy in New York.

1995

Mar Disney Records releases ***Rhythm Of The Pridelands Featuring Music Inspired By The Lion King***, including *Hakuna Matata*, a duet by Cliff and Lebo M.
Apr [4] Cliff guests on NBC-TV's "The Tonight Show".
July He re-signs to Island (Jamaica) Records.
Aug *Melody Tempo Harmony*, a duet with Bernard Lavilliers, makes the French Top 10.
Dec [31] Cliff appears on C4-TV's "The White Room New Year Special", with Oasis, David Bowie, PM Dawn, Stevie Wonder and Pulp.

PATSY CLINE

1954

Sept [30] Starry-eyed C&W aspirant, Cline (b. Virginia Patterson Hensley, Sept. 8, 1932, Gore, VA) - she has married Gerald Cline in March 1953 - after teaching herself to dance at age four, winning an amateur talent contest in Lexington, VA, duetting with her mother in the Gore Baptist Church Choir, singing on Winchester (to where the family has just relocated) radio station, WINC, with Joltin' Jim & His Melody Playboys at age 14, and serving an apprenticeship in local beerjoints and taverns, particularly the Front Royal, has won the vocalist category in the fourth annual National Championship Country Music Contest in Warrenton, VA, in August. Connie Barriot Gay, the sponsor of the contest, subsequently records her for an appearance on his WARL radio show, "Town And Country Time" (the tape from which finds its way to Bill McCall, the owner of 4 Star Music Sales, a small label in Pasadena, CA). Managed by bandleader Bill Peer, Cline now signs a two-year contract with the company, before visiting New York, NY, for the first time, to cut four demos at Decca's Pythian Temple Studio. (As a child, she had developed a serious throat infection and was placed in an oxygen tent. On her recovery she had "a voice that boomed forth like Kate Smith's".)

1955

June [1] Through a leasing and distribution deal set up by McCall with Decca's A&R country head, Paul Cohen, Cline tapes her first recording session proper at Bradley Studios in Nashville, TN, with Owen Bradley producing. She will soon make her debut on the prestigious Nashville stage/radio show, "Grand Ole Opry", singing her yet-to-be-released debut single, *A Church A Courtroom And Then Goodbye*. It is an appropriate choice, her sexual notoriety soon causing as many ripples in the C&W fraternity as her music, as her marriage to Gerald Cline dissolves.

1956

Jan [5] She cuts four more tracks at Bradley Studios.
Apr [13] Cline meets future husband, Charlie Dick, after a performance with the Kountry Krackers, a band she sang with on occasion, at the Armory, in Berryville, VA. She becomes a regular on Jimmy Dean's weekly "Town And Country Jamboree", appearing in fringed dude-cowboy regalia.
Nov [8] Cline records four songs at Bradleys, including *Walkin' After Midnight*, written for - and rejected by - Kay Starr and now reworked by its writers, Don Hecht and Alan Block, which McCall has foisted upon her, causing Cline to say, "It's nothin' but a little ol' pop song."

1957

Jan [21] In New York for the second time, Cline appears on the nationally-networked CBS-TV show, "Arthur Godfrey's Talent Scouts". She wins with *Walkin' After Midnight*, encoring with her version of Hank Williams' *Your Cheatin' Heart*. Godfrey will later tell Cline, "You are the most innocent, the most nervous, most truthful and honest performer I have ever seen." (She will become a regular on Godfrey's Wednesday-night variety show.)
Feb [16] She makes her second "Grand Ole Opry" appearance, this time as a guest star, and appears on Alan Freed's "Rock'n'Roll Radio Show".
Apr [6] Rush released by Decca, *Walkin' After Midnight* crosses over from the C&W chart to peak at US #12, selling 750,000 copies.
[24-25] She cuts eight tracks at Decca's Pythian Temple Studio in New York, with vocal assistance from the Anita Kerr Singers.
May [25] Cline embarks on her first tour, with Brenda Lee and Porter Wagoner.
Sept [15] She marries Charlie Dick in Winchester.
Nov [15] **Billboard** honors Cline with its Most Promising Country & Western Female Artist of 1957 award, at the annual DJ convention in Nashville.

1958

Aug [25] A daughter, Julia Simadore, is born.

1959

Jan [8-9] Cline records five tracks at Bradley Studios, backed by Hank Garland and Grady Martin (guitar), Floyd Cramer (piano), Harold Bradley (bass), Bob Moore (stand-up bass), Buddy Harman (drums) and the Jordanaires (vocals).
Aug With their one-year-old daughter in tow, Patsy and Charlie Dick, move from Winchester, to Nashville. By year's end, as her 4 Star contract approaches its end, Cline signs on with new manager, Randy Hughes.

1960

Jan [9] Cline becomes a member of the Grand Ole Opry.
[27] She completes her obligation to 4 Star, recording *Lovesick Blues*, *How Can I Face Tomorrow*, *There He Goes* and *Crazy Dreams* at Bradley Studios.
Nov [16] Now signed direct to Decca, she records *Shoes*, *Lovin' In Vain* and the song that will be the turning point of her career, *I Fall To Pieces*, at Bradley Studios.

1961

Jan [21] She performs at the Grand Ole Opry - one day before giving birth to a son, Randy.
June [14] Cline sustains near-fatal head injuries when thrown through the windshield in a head-on car crash outside the Madison High School, in Nashville.
July [22] She is brought onstage at the Grand Ole Opry in a wheelchair, to tell her fans that she will be back singing soon.
Aug [17] Cline cuts her first tracks since November, including Cole Porter's *True Love*, Bob Wills' *San Antonio Rose* and Gogi Grant's 1956 chart-topper, *The Wayward Wind*. (Four days later, at a four-hour evening session, she will also record Willie Nelson's *Crazy*.)
Sept [4] Establishing Bradley's lavish settings and Cline's sophisticated weepie style, both at variance with current Nashville tradition, *I Fall To Pieces*, written by Hank Cochran and Harlan Howard, reaches US #12, eight months after its release.
Oct [23] *Who Can I Count On*, B-side of still-climbing *Crazy*, spends one week at US #99.
Nov [27] Distinctive ballad *Crazy*, recorded with Cline on crutches, becomes her biggest seller, hitting US #9.
[29] She performs on a sellout Grand Ole Opry bill, with Grandpa Jones, the Jordanaires, Bill Monroe, Minnie Pearl, Jim Reeves, Marty Robbins and Faron Young, at Carnegie Hall in New York.

1962

Jan Cline embarks on a two-week package tour of the Midwest and Canada, with Johnny Cash, George Jones, Bill Monroe and Carl Perkins.
Feb [17] *Strange* makes US #97.
Mar [31] A-side *She's Got You* reaches US #14, as ***The Patsy Cline Showcase*** climbs to US #73.
Apr [26] *She's Got You* makes UK #43.
May [19] *Imagine That* climbs to US #90.
June [15] Cline performs on the "Shower Of Stars" bill at the Hollywood Bowl, Hollywood, CA, with Johnny Cash, Don Gibson, George Jones and others.
[16] *When I Get Through With You* peaks at US #53.
Aug [25] *So Wrong*, penned by Carl Perkins, makes US #85.
Nov [17] *Heartaches* climbs to US #73.
[23] Cline begins a $36,500 five-week engagement at the Merri-Mint Theatre in the Mint Casino, Las Vegas, NV, set to end on December 28th.
Dec [15] Cline has her second UK chart success with *Heartaches* reaching #31.

1963

Feb [4-7] She makes her last recordings at Bradley Studios, cutting a dozen tracks, including *Love Letters In The Sand*, *Blue Moon Of Kentucky*, *Sweet Dreams (Of You)*, *Always* and *Crazy Arms*.
[23] An established Grand Ole Opry headliner and America's highest-ranked female Country star, 30-year-old Cline continues to make the transition from the C&W survey to the pop chart, with *Leaving On Your Mind* peaking at US #83.
Mar [3] Cline makes what will be her last public appearance, on a benefit at the Memorial Building, Kansas City, KS, for the family of disc jockey Cactus Jack Call, who died in a road accident.
[5] Returning from Kansas City, the single-engined Piper Commanche, piloted by Randy Hughes, carrying Cline and her fellow stars, Cowboy Copas and Hawkshaw Hawkins, crashes near Camden, TN, killing all on board.
[10] Over 25,000 mourners attend Cline's funeral.
June [15] Cline's version of Don Gibson's *Sweet Dreams* becomes a posthumous hit, making US #44.
Sept [7] Cline's name appears on the pop chart for the last time as *Faded Love* climbs to US #96 and her album, ***The Patsy Cline Story***, makes #74. Regular subsequent releases, including *When You Need A Laugh*, *He Called Me Baby* and *Anytime*, will reach the C&W chart sustaining Cline's following for the rest of the decade.

1973

Oct [15] Cline becomes the first female solo performer to be inducted into the Country Music Hall of Fame.

1981

While Loretta Lynn has released a tribute album to Cline in 1977, and Cline has also been portrayed by Beverly D'Angelo in "Coal Miner's Daughter", the 1980 film biography of Loretta Lynn, starring Sissy Spacek, tapes of Cline and Jim Reeves, re-arranged and mixed to simulate duet performances, are now released as ***Greatest Hits***. Issued as singles, *Have You Ever Been Lonely* and *I Fall To Pieces* become C&W hits (at #5 and #54 respectively).

1985

Nov [16] Riding the current success of "Sweet Dreams", a Hollywood movie based on Ellis Nassour's biography of Cline, with Jessica Lange in the title role, the soundtrack album, featuring Cline's original songs, ***Sweet Dreams - The Life And Times Of Patsy Cline*** enters the US chart on its way to US #29 and a gold disc.

1988

July ***Live At The Opry***, comprising recordings from 1956 to 1962, makes #60 on the US Country chart.
Aug [19] The Amusement & Music Operators Association announces that *I Fall To Pieces* is the second most played jukebox song of all-time.

1989

Sept [16] ***20 Golden Hits***, released on the DeLuxe label, makes #70 on the US Country chart.

1990

Oct [26] Cline is inducted into the Jukebox Legends Hall of Fame at the Amusement & Music Operators Association 1990 Jukebox Awards Show, in New Orleans, LA.

1991

Jan [12] *Crazy* reaches UK #14, reviving UK interest in the country legend.
Feb [2] UK-only collection ***Dreaming ...*** peaks at UK #55, while another simultaneously-released anthology ***Sweet Dreams*** reaches UK #18 one week later.

1992

Jan [4] A US-only, MCA-released 104-track four-CD/cassette boxed set, ***The Patsy Cline Collection***, gathering together her entire recorded output, charts for a week at US #166. It will be certified gold by the RIAA on March 27th 1993.
Feb [25] *Crazy* is inducted into the NARAS Hall of Fame at the 34th Grammy Awards at New York's Radio City Music Hall.
Sept [19] With *Crazy* voted the fourth most popular country song of all time by readers of this month's **Country America** magazine, further confirming the endurance of her seminal recording legacy, yet another compilation, ***The Definitive Patsy Cline 1932-1963***, reaches UK #11.

1995

Apr [24] While "Always ... Patsy Cline", a two-act musical, featuring 20 of her hits, re-opened the legendary Ryman Auditorium in Nashville, home of the original Grand Ole Opry between 1943-1974, in June 1994 (during the same year "The Real Patsy Cline" video was certified platinum by the RIAA on August 18th, followed by gold certification for yet another compilation ***Heartaches*** on October 20th), "Patsy! A World Premiere Tribute To Patsy Cline", with Gail Bliss in the title role, now begins previews at the Grand Palace, Branson, MO, following the February 3rd confirmation by the RIAA that ***Greatest Hits*** has now amassed six million US sales.

GEORGE CLINTON

1955

Clinton (b. July 22, 1940, Kannapolis, NC), the first of nine children, now living in Newark, NJ, forms doo-wop group the Parliaments, as an extension to his gang, the Outlaws, with Audrey Boykins and her brother, Eugene, Glen Carlos, Charles "Butch" Davis and Herbie Jenkins. They play local hops and dances and sing on street corners, working by day at a Newark barbershop, the Uptown Tonsorial Parlor. During 1956, the Parliaments, comprising Clinton, Jenkins, Robert Lambert, Danny Mitchell and Grady Thomas, will record *The Wind* and *A Sunday Kind Of Love* on acetate in a Newark record booth. Clinton, still attending Clinton Place High School, will also begin work as foreman of the New Jersey Wham-o Hula-Hoop factory.

1958

Apr The Parliaments, already in their third incarnation (with Clinton, Lambert, Thomas, Calvin Simon and the returning Davis), record *Poor Willie* and *Party Boys* for the Hull label.

1959

June ABC-Paramount picks up the Hull recordings to release on its Apt subsidiary, as the group, now comprising Clinton, Davis, Simon, Thomas and Johnny Murray, records *Lonely Island* and *Cry* for the Flipp label.

1963

Clinton, after working for a year in New York as a staff writer for Jobete Music, takes the Parliaments, currently including Thomas, Clarence "Fuzzy" Hawkins and Raymond Davis, to Detroit, MI, to audition for Motown. Although not signed, the Parliaments will cut several demos for the label. While working for Motown, Clinton will team with fellow ex-Jobete, writer Sidney Barnes, and Motown sax session man, Mike Terry, to form the Geo-Si-Mik production team, signing with Ed Wingate's recently-founded Golden World and Ric Tic record labels. Clinton commutes to Detroit every week, working at his New Jersey barbershop on weekends.

1966

Clinton continues to write and produce for Geo-Si-Mik, including the Parliaments' *Heart Trouble* and *My Girl*, which is released on Golden World, but - dissatisfied and disillusioned with the record business - he returns to Newark to work full-time at his barbershop.

1967

Sept [2] The Parliaments' *I Wanna Testify*, recorded in late 1966 for the Revilot label, reaches US #20. Clinton reassembles the group, adding a rhythm section comprising Eddie Hazel (guitar), Lucius Ross (guitar), Billy Nelson (bass), Mickey Atkins (organ) and Ramon Fulwood (drums).
Nov [25] *All Your Goodies Are Gone* peaks at US #80.

1969

Clinton temporarily loses the rights to the name the Parliaments, after Motown buys out Golden World, while LeBaron Taylor leases *A New Day Begins* to Atco. To remain active, Clinton, using the Parliaments' rhythm section, assembles Funkadelic, soon adding Bernie Worrell on keyboards. They sign to Armen Boladian's new Westbound label, releasing their debut single *Music For My Mother* and album ***Funkadelic***.
Nov [1] Funkadelic's *I'll Bet You* peaks at US #68.

1970

Mar Clinton relaunches the Parliaments as Parliament, on Invictus, with the debut album, ***Osmium***.
Apr [4] Funkadelic's *I Got A Thing, You Got A Thing, Everybody's Got A Thing* makes US #80, as ***Funkadelic*** climbs to US #126. (Funkadelic continues to record for Westbound. Keyboardist Bernie Worrell joins the Parliament-Funkadelic (P. Funk) family.)
Sept [12] Funkadelic's *I Wanna Know If It's Good To You?* makes US #81. It will be followed by 1971's *You And Your Folks, Me And My Folks* (US #91 in April) and *Can You Get To That* (US #93 in September.)

1972

Bassist Bootsy Collins, ex-James Brown's backing band, the JB's, joins for the Funkadelic album, ***America Eats Its Young*** while guitarist Gary Shider will join the aggregation for the 1973 Funkadelic follow-up, ***Cosmic Slop***.

1974

June Funkadelic's ***Standing On The Verge Of Getting It On*** is released. Following the collapse of Invictus, Clinton signs Parliament to Casablanca, despite interest from Westbound, which releases ***Funkadelic's Greatest Hits***.
Aug Parliament's *Up For The Down Stroke* makes US #63.

1975

May ***Chocolate City*** peaks at US #91, with the extracted *Chocolate City* stalling at US #94 in June. Funkadelic's *Better By The Pound* will weigh in at US #99 in November.

1976

Feb Parliament's ***Mothership Connection*** lands at US #13.
May *Tear The Roof Off The Sucker (Give Up The Funk)* reaches US #15. Collins releases ***Stretchin' Out***, made with Parliament/Funkadelic members. (Other in-house projects released in the next two years include records by the Horny Horns (P. Funk horn section Fred Wesley, Maceo Parker, Rick Gardner and Richard Griffith; Wesley and Parker, like Collins, having come to Clinton via James Brown's JB's), Parlet (P. Funk vocalists Mallia Franklin, Jeanette Washington and Shirley Hayden) and the Brides Of Dr. Funkenstein (P. Funk vocalists Lynn Mabry and Dawn Silva).)
Oct Parliament's ***The Clones Of Dr. Funkenstein*** climbs to US #20.

1977

Jan [19] Parliament/Funkadelic/Bootsy play the Great Western Forum, Inglewood, CA, to an audience of more than 18,000.
May ***Parliament Live/P. Funk Earth Tour*** makes US #29. Bootsy Collins releases ***Ahh ... The Name Is Bootsy Baby*** while the Horny Horns release ***A Blow For Me, A Toot For You***.
Dec Parliament's ***Funkentelechy Vs. The Placebo Syndrome*** reaches US #13, while Clinton tours with some 40 musicians. His umbrella stage show incorporates separate sets from Parliament /Funkadelic, Parlet, Collins' Rubber Band, the Brides Of Dr. Funkenstein and the Horny Horns.

1978

Feb Parliament's *Flash Light* makes US #16, as Parlet releases ***The Pleasure Principle*** and the Brides Of Dr. Funkenstein issue ***Funk Or Walk***.
Apr [15] Collins' ***Player Of The Year***, produced by Clinton, reaches US #16.
July [8] *Bootzilla* makes UK #43.
[21] At a dinner sponsored by the Rod McGrew Scholarship Fund, Inc. - Communicators With A Conscience, Clinton and Collins are challenged to do something more ambitious and less superficial with their music. (Clinton pledges to donate 50 cents from every ticket sold for his upcoming August and September concerts to the United Negro College Fund.)
Nov [18] Now signed to Warner Bros. Records, Funkadelic's *One Nation Under A Groove* reaches US #28 and proves to be a career-defining highlight for its composer, Clinton.
[25] Funk-defining set ***One Nation Under A Groove*** reaches US #16.
Dec P. Funk plays rapturously-received concerts in London, their adventurous stage show including a life-size flying saucer. Funkadelic's *One Nation Under A Groove* hits UK #9, as Parliament's ***Motor Booty Affair*** makes US #23.
[16] ***Brides Of Funkenstein*** reaches US #70.

1979

Feb Parliament's *Aqua Boogie (A Psychoalpha Disco-Betabioaqua-Doloop)* peaks at US #89.
[3] Funkadelic's ***One Nation Under A Groove*** makes UK #56.
Oct Funkadelic's *(Not Just) Knee Deep* climbs to US #77.
Nov [10] ***Underjam*** reaches US #18.
Dec Parliament's ***Gloryhallastoopid (Pin The Tale On The Funky)*** makes US #77.

1980

Clinton's release schedule is halted by protracted legal disputes with a number of record companies, which center around disputed royalty payments and use of the names Parliament and Funkadelic.

1981

Jan A breakaway trio of P. Funk musicians, using the name Funkadelic, releases ***Connections And Disconnections***, which peaks at US #151.
Feb The official Funkadelic releases ***The Electric Spanking Of War Babies***, featuring Sly Stone.

1982

Dec Newly signed as a solo artist to Capitol (he will record for the label with the P. Funk family, but will not use the names Parliament or Funkadelic), his ***Computer Games***, featuring Collins and Worrell, makes US #40, as *Loopzilla* reaches UK #57.

1983

Jan [29] Clinton's *Atomic Dog* tops the US R&B chart at the start of a four-week run, while its accompanying promo clip will win a **Billboard** award for video animation.

1984

Jan Continuing his innovative brand of eclectic funk /R&B, ***You Shouldn't Nuf Bit, Fish!*** peaks at US #102. It will be followed in June the following year by the release of ***Some Of My Best Friends Are Jokes***, including one cut written with Thomas Dolby, with whom Clinton will also collaborate on *May The Cube Be With You*.

1986

Apr [26] *Do Fries Go With That Shake* peaks at UK #57, while Capitol releases his final album for the label, ***R&B Skeletons In The Closet***.
July [24] Clinton, in his traditionally-outrageous and colorful garb, performs on NBC-TV's "Late Night With David Letterman".

1989

Sept After a lengthy hiatus, during which outstanding legal and financial problems have been largely resolved, Clinton, now under the umbrella of Prince's Paisley Park Studios-based artist roster, returns with ***The Cinderella Theory***, released on the Paisley Park label, which makes US #192.

1990

Nov [2] Recently featured on the Stanley Clarke /George Duke Project release, ***Mothership Connection***, Clinton guests once more on "Late Night With David Letterman", as Prince's "Graffitti Bridge", in which Clinton stars as himself, opens throughout the US.

1991

Jan [6] Clinton appears at Prince's Glam Slam club gig in Minneapolis.
July [11] He performs at London's Brixton Academy during a brief UK visit.

1992

Feb [5] Increasingly revered as a seminal R&B/funk influence, Clinton's Bridgeport Music files suit in New York, NY, against Sony Music Entertainment and rapper Terminator X, for the unauthorized sampling of Clinton's *Body Language* on X's recent *Wanna Be Dancing* recording.
Sept [20-21] He performs at New York's Ritz during a current US tour, set to end on October 24th at the Constitution Hall, Washington, DC.
Oct [26] Nine-date European tour begins at the Royal

Court Theatre, Liverpool, and will climax on November 18th at London's Clapham Grand.

1993

Jan [12] Sly & the Family Stone are inducted by Clinton into the Rock and Roll Hall of Fame at the eighth annual awards dinner, held at the Century Plaza Hotel, Los Angeles, CA.
Feb [24] Clinton's P-Funk All-Stars team with the Red Hot Chili Peppers to perform at the 35th annual Grammy Awards, held at the Shrine Auditorium, Los Angeles.
May [18] Mercury Records issues the Parliament anthology, ***Tear Off The Roof***.
June [5] During a round of current US dates, Clinton appears at KISS Radio's anniversary concert at the Great Woods Center for the Performing Arts, Mansfield, MA, as his *Walk The Dinosaur* appears in the "Super Mario Bros." movie and his son, Trey Lewd, signs with Warner Bros.
July [16] Clinton performs at the "Phoenix Festival" in Long Marston, Stratford-upon-Avon, Warks., during a current European tour which encompasses Germany, England, Belgium, Holland and France.
Oct [30] ***Hey Man ... Smell My Finger*** debuts at its US #145 peak.

1994

Mar [2] Clinton attends the annual Rhythm and Blues Foundation's Pioneer Awards at the Roseland Ballroom, New York.
Aug [27] Ice Cube's *Bop Gun (One Nation)*, with Clinton, debuts at its UK #22 peak, as Clinton plays the first of two sellout dates at the Shoreline Amphitheatre, Mountain View, CA, as part of this year's Lollapalooza US caravan tour.

1995

May He signs to Sony's 550 label.
July [16] Clinton takes part in the "Phoenix Festival" in Long Marston.
Sept [2] He performs *Thank You (Falettinme Be Mice Elf Agin)*] with Larry Graham at the Concert for the Rock and Roll Hall of Fame at Cleveland Stadium, Cleveland, OH.
Oct [10] A John Lennon tribute album, ***Working Class Hero***, with Clinton contributing *Mind Games*, is released in the US by Hollywood Records.

1996

May Reuniting with P. Funk alumni Bernie Worrell and Bootsy Collins for the first time in ten years, Clinton's ***The Awesome Power Of A Fully Operational Mothership*** is released in the US by the 550 label.

THE COASTERS

Carl Gardner (lead tenor); **Leon Hughes** (tenor); **Billy Guy** (baritone); **Bobby Nunn** (bass)

1955

Oct Gardner (b. Apr. 29, 1928, Tyler, TX) and Nunn (b. Birmingham, AL) leave the Robins, an R&B vocal group whose most celebrated recording was *Smokey Joe's Café*, recorded under the direction of songwriters/producers Leiber and Stoller, to start the Coasters (the name reflecting their West Coast roots) with Hughes (b. 1938) and Guy (b. June 20, 1936, Attasca, TX).
Nov Leiber and Stoller sign a deal whereby their masters will be released on the Atlantic subsidiary, Atco. As one of their acts, the newly-constituted Coasters, are a seemingly-ideal vehicle for the duo's studio genius.

1956

Jan The group cuts four tracks at Hollywood Recorders in Los Angeles, CA: *Brazil, Down In Mexico, One Kiss Led To Another* and *Turtle Dovin'*.
Mar Their debut release *Down In Mexico* enters the US R&B chart, to hit #9.
Sept *One Kiss Led To Another*, their first pop-chart entry, makes US #73.

1957

Feb Hughes is replaced by Young Jessie, ex-the Flairs.
May Cranky, funky *Searchin'* hits US #5/R&B #1. Their first million-seller, it establishes the Coasters as one of the most amusing, innovative and influential vocal groups of the rock'n'roll era. Particularly revered by British fans, their songs will soon be revived by the Beatles, the Rolling Stones and almost every UK beat group of the early '60s. The B-side *Young Blood* also makes the Top 10, hitting US #8.
Sept [28] *Searchin'* reaches UK #30.
Oct Of six titles recorded, only *Idol With The Golden Head* reaches the chart, peaking at US #64.

1958

Mar The Coasters, and Leiber and Stoller, move to New York, NY. Jessie and Nunn, loath to travel, are replaced by Cornelius Gunter (b. Nov. 14, 1938, Los Angeles, CA), a second tenor, who began his music career at high school, forming a band which evolved into the Platters, and who has also sung with the Ink Spots and the Flairs during the past year, and ex-Cadets Will "Dub" Jones (bass). The legendary "fifth Coaster", King Curtis (b. Curtis Ousley, Feb. 7, 1934, Fort Worth, TX), whose sax playing will add piquancy to their work, also joins.
July [21] Having rocketed up the survey, *Yakety Yak* tops the US chart. It epitomizes Leiber and Stoller's "Coaster style", which takes the form of "a white kid's view (Leiber's) of a black person's conception of white society."
Sept [6] *Yakety Yak* reaches UK #12.
Dec [11] The group records *Charlie Brown* in New York.

1959

Feb While *The Shadow Knows* fails to chart, the uproarious exploits of incorrigible schoolkid *Charlie Brown* hits US #2, becoming a million-seller. It contains speeded-up voices on one line, intended as a sardonic nod to *The Chipmunk Song*, which is heading towards US #1.
Apr [25] *Charlie Brown* hits UK #6.
May Conceived as three-minute comic operas, and scripted like radio plays, Coasters' records are hailed as pop masterpieces. *Along Came Jones*, mocking the clichés of TV westerns, hits US #9.
Aug *Poison Ivy* hits US #7, and is the group's fourth - and last - million-seller. (The Rolling Stones will cut the most famous of some 20 cover versions.) The B-side, *I'm A Hog For You*, reaches US #38.
Dec Double-sided *Run Red Run/What About Us* peaks at US #36/#47.
[15] *Poison Ivy* reaches UK #15.

1960

Apr [27] The group performs at the Lauderdale County Coliseum, Florence, AL, as part of the all-star "The Biggest Show Of Stars For '60" package tour.
May Their revival of *Besame Mucho*, a million-seller for Jimmy Dorsey in the early '40s, reaches only US #70.
June *Wake Me Shake Me*, written by Guy, recounting the miseries of a recalcitrant garbage man, makes US #51.
Oct Adapted from the half-remembered *Clothesline* by Kent Harris, *Shopping For Clothes* stalls at US #83.

1961

Feb Atco attempts to reverse the Coasters' slide with *Wait A Minute*, by Bobby Darin and Don Kirshner. Cut and shelved over three years earlier, it makes US #37.
Apr *Little Egypt*, about a tattooed burlesque dancer who ends up marrying the singer, lifts them to US #23.
Aug *Girls Girls Girls* peaks at US #96. As Leiber and Stoller's Atlantic workload increases (for the Drifters, Ben E. King, Ruth Brown, LaVern Baker and the Isley Brothers), they are able to devote less time to the Coasters.

1964

Mar After a long chart absence, *T'Aint Nothing To Me* makes US #64. The group continues recording for Atco, without chart success, until 1966.
June [26] The group performs at the Allentown Fair Grounds Grandstand, Allentown, PA, as part of the all-star "Dick Clark & His Caravan Of Stars" package tour.

1967

CBS subsidiary, Date, signs the Coasters. Former Cadillacs frontman, Earl Carroll (b. Nov. 2, 1937, New York, NY), replaces Gunter and a reunion with Leiber and Stoller yields *Down Home Girl* (covered by the Stones), *D.W. Washburn* (covered by the Monkees) and a revival of the Clovers' hit *Love Potion Number Nine*, which (when leased to King Records) creeps into the chart four years later, reaching US #76. (Gunter joins Dinah Washington's revue, before forming his own Coasters. He will be sued in 1971 by H.B. Barnum, manager of the legitimate group.)

1971

Aug [13] King Curtis, is stabbed to death in a bar brawl in New York, NY.

1980

Apr Current bass singer Nathaniel "Buster" Wilson is shot, his dismembered body dumped near Hoover Dam and in a canyon near Modesto, CA.

1986

Nov [5] Bobby Nunn dies.

1987

Jan [21] The Coasters are inducted into the Rock and Roll Hall of Fame at the second annual dinner, held at the Waldorf Astoria Hotel, New York, NY.

1988

May [14] The band, comprising Gardner, Guy, Jones, Gunter and relative newcomer Tom Palmer, participates in Atlantic's 40th birthday concert at New York's Madison Square Garden.

1989

Nov [3] The Coasters participate in the 20th anniversary "Rock'n'Roll Revival Concert", with Chuck Berry, the Five Satins, and others.

1990

Feb [27] Gunter, in Las Vegas, NV, to perform with the latest variation of the group at the Lady Luck Hotel, is gunned down in his car.

1991

Aug [9] The Coasters perform the first of two concerts at "The Apollo R&B Reunion", to benefit the financially-distressed theatre in Harlem, New York.

1994

Mar [2] While retrospective specialist label Rhino Records has released the definitive Coasters CD anthology, ***50 Coastin' Classics***, with Atlantic in December 1992 and after Gardner has attended the ground-breaking ceremony of the Rock and Roll Hall of Fame in Cleveland, OH on June 7th the previous year, the Coasters, still performing regularly as an oldies act, are presented with the Pioneer Award at the fifth annual Rhythm and Blues Foundation Awards at the Roseland Ballroom, New York. Tied in with a UK advertising campaign, the Coasters'*Sorry But I'm Gonna Have To Pass* will debut at its UK #41 peak on Apr [9]. (In September the following year, Gardner will participate in a class action suit brought in a federal court in Atlanta, GA, whereby a number of popular '60s soul acts will seek back-dated pension fund remuneration from allegedly unscrupulous labels.)

EDDIE COCHRAN

1955

Jan Having lived in the Bell Gardens suburb of Los

Angeles, CA, since the age of 12 and having become a proficient guitarist in his early teens, forming a country trio with schoolfriend "Connie" Smith, Cochran (b. Ray Edward Cochran, Oct. 3, 1938, Albert Lea, MN), joins the unrelated Hank Cochran as his guitar accompanist, after being introduced to him by Bob Bull, a member of Richard Ray & the Shamrock Valley Boys whom Cochran had joined on stage at an American Legion club gig in Bell Gardens, in October 1954.

Apr Hank and Eddie, now working as the Cochran Brothers, are signed to American Music Corp. agency, which leads to appearances on live TV shows, "Town Hall Party" and "Hometown Jamboree".

May They audition for Ekko Records' Charles Matthews at Sunset Recorders in Hollywood. The duo's first single for the label is *Mr. Fiddle*, backed with *Two Blue Singin' Stars* but, after playing the "Big D Jamboree" in Dallas, TX, a few days after Elvis Presley, and hearing about the singer from stage staff at the event, they decide to change from their hillbilly leanings to a harder rock'n'roll style.

Oct Cochran, buying guitar strings in Bell Gardens music center, meets aspiring songwriter Jerry Capehart.

1956

Jan The Cochran Brothers become regulars on KVOR-TV's "The California Hayride". They relocate to Napa, CA, to be near the Stockton, CA TV station.

May They spend a week in Hawaii, opening for C&W star Lefty Frizzell.

July During a session at Master Recorders in Los Angeles, the Cochrans decide to part company. (Hank will move to Nashville, TN, where he will become a successful songwriter.) Cochran and Capehart, now good friends, cut *Skinny Jim*, a song they have written together as an answer record to *Long Tall Sally*. Capehart places the song through his contacts at American Music's record label, Crest. It does not sell, but Capehart uses it as a demo to circulate to major record companies.

Aug [14] Cochran, spotted by movie producer Boris Petroff while recording some backing music with Capehart for a Petroff low-budget picture, films a role for the Jayne Mansfield-starring "The Girl Can't Help It", in which he sings *Twenty Flight Rock*, at 20th Century Fox Studios.

Sept [8] Cochran signs a one-year deal with Liberty Records.

Dec Cochran films "Untamed Youth" with Mamie Van Doren, in which he performs *You Ain't Gonna Make A Cotton Picker Out Of You*, on location in Bakersfield, CA.

1957

Apr Cochran embarks on a major tour to promote his chart debut, a cover version of Johnny Dee's (actually John D. Loudermilk of later songwriting fame) *Sittin' In The Balcony*, backed by the Johnny Mann Singers. He plays a week at the Mastbaum Theater in Philadelphia, PA, on a package show which also features Gene Vincent.

[27] *Sittin' In The Balcony* reaches US #18, outselling the original version, which makes US #38.

Aug Cochran embarks on a tour of Eastern and Mid-West states.

Sept [23] *Drive-In Show* makes US #82.

Oct Cochran begins a tour of Australia with Gene Vincent and Little Richard. On his return he joins the second stage of "The Biggest Show Of Stars For '57" package tour, with Buddy Holly & the Crickets, Fats Domino, Chuck Berry, the Everly Brothers, Frankie Lymon, Drifters and Clyde McPhatter among others.

Nov [24] The tour ends at the Mosque, Richmond, VA.

Dec After a show at the Paramount Theater, New York, before Christmas, Phil Everly introduces his girlfriend, Sharon Sheeley, to Cochran.

1958

Mar [10] *Jeannie Jeannie Jeannie* charts for a week at US #94, while Cochran helps with backing vocals on Gene Vincent studio sessions.

Sept [29] Youth angst classic, *Summertime Blues*, co-written with Capehart, is his breakthrough hit and only US Top 10 entry, hitting #8 and gaining a gold disc for a million-plus sales.

Nov [29] *Summertime Blues* is Cochran's UK chart debut, reaching #18.

Dec [25] He opens in Alan Freed's ten-day New York "Christmas Rock'n'Roll Spectacular", with the Everly Brothers, Chuck Berry, Jackie Wilson, Dion & the Belmonts and others at Loew's State Theater in Manhattan.

1959

Jan [5] *C'mon Everybody* makes US #35. Cochran begins filming the Hal Roach/Alan Freed-produced "Go, Johnny Go!", in which he sings *Teenage Heaven*. His role forces him to withdraw from the "Winter Dance Party Tour" of northwestern US states, alongside close friend Buddy Holly.

Feb Deeply affected by the deaths of Holly, Valens and the Big Bopper, Cochran records a version of Tommy Dee's tribute song, *Three Stars* (which will not be released until several years after his own death). He tries to avoid all flying but begins a US tour which will last much of the year, punctuated by returns to Los Angeles for recording sessions. The Kelly Four (named after Cochran's Irish ancestry), comprising Gene Ridgio (drums), Jim Stivers (piano), Mike Henderson (sax) and Dave Schreiber (bass), is formed to back him on the road.

Mar [16] *Teenage Heaven* makes US #99 for one week.

Apr [18] *C'mon Everybody*, showcasing his driving guitar playing (performed on his trademark Gretsch instrument), hits UK #6.

Sept [7] *Somethin' Else* peaks at US #58 (his last US hit). Its writer, Sharon Sheeley, becomes Cochran's fiancée soon afterwards.

Oct [24] *Somethin' Else* reaches UK #22.

1960

Jan [8] Cochran makes what will be his final recording, at Goldstar studios in Hollywood. One of the tracks is *Three Steps To Heaven*.

[9] He flies to the UK to co-headline (with Gene Vincent) a ten-week Larry Parnes package tour which also includes Billy Fury, Joe Brown and Georgie Fame. The trek is a huge success, with ecstatic fan fervor, creating newspaper headlines.

[16] Cochran makes his UK TV debut on Jack Good's live rock show, "Boy Meets Girls", the first of four appearances while on tour.

[24] The tour starts at the Gaumont Theatre, Ipswich, Suffolk.

Feb [6] A revival of Ray Charles' *Hallelujah I Love Her So* makes UK #22.

[21] Cochran, backed by the Wildecats, performs at the "**New Musical Express** Poll Winners Concert", at the Empire Pool, Wembley, Middx.

[22] He makes his UK radio debut on BBC's "Parade Of The Pops".

Mar Cochran invites Sheeley to the UK to join him on tour, and to celebrate her forthcoming 20th birthday on April 4th.

[5] He makes the first of two appearances on the BBC radio show "Saturday Club", where he sings *What'd I Say*, *Milk Cow Blues*, his current release, *Hallelujah I Love Her So*, and *C'mon Everybody*.

Apr The tour has proved so successful that Cochran and Vincent are offered an extension from the end of the month. They accept, but return to the US for the intervening two weeks, Cochran specifically to do some recording.

[16] The UK tour comes to end at the Hippodrome, Bristol, Somerset, on Easter Saturday. Arrangements are made to catch a late train to London after the show for their transatlantic flight next morning, but Cochran, Vincent and Sheeley hire a taxi instead.

[17] En route to London on the A4, near Chippenham, Wilts., the Ford Consul in which they are travelling skids into a roadside lamp post. Tour manager Pat Thomkins and the 19-year-old driver, George Martin, both in the front of the car, are uninjured, but Vincent, Sheeley and Cochran, on the back seat all suffer injuries. Vincent breaks his collarbone and ribs and Sheeley breaks her pelvis, but Cochran is thrown head-first through the windshield. Rushed to hospital in Bath, Somerset, he dies 16 hours later, without regaining consciousness, from brain lacerations. One of the local policemen called to the accident is 16-year-old police cadet David Harman (later Dave Dee of Dave Dee, Dozy, Beaky, Mick & Tich). He salvages Cochran's hardly-damaged Gretsch guitar from the road, and will occasionally play it at the police station before it is returned to Cochran's mother two months later.

[25] Cochran is buried at a private ceremony at Forest Lawn Cemetery in Glendale, CA.

June [25] Ironically-titled self-penned *Three Steps To Heaven* tops the UK chart and is his biggest UK seller, but will never chart in the US.

July [30] ***Singing To My Baby***, his first chart album reaches UK #19.

Oct [22] *Sweetie Pie* makes UK #38, while the commemorative ***The Eddie Cochran Memorial Album*** hits UK #9.

Nov [5] *Lonely*, the other side of *Sweetie Pie*, peaks at UK #41.

1961

July [22] *Weekend* reaches UK #15 during a four-month chart run.

Dec [9] *Jeannie Jeannie Jeannie* makes UK #31.

1963

Jan ***Cherished Memories*** reaches UK #15.

May Reissued ***The Eddie Cochran Memorial Album*** makes UK #11, staying charted for 18 weeks.

[18] The previously unissued *My Way* climbs to UK #23.

Sept [14] Heinz's tribute disc, *Just Like Eddie*, hits UK #5.

Oct [19] A reissue of Cochran's first album, ***Singing To My Baby***, reaches UK #20.

1964

Aug ***My Way***, with further previously unissued material, is released in the UK.

1968

May A UK revival fad for '50s rock'n'roll sees a reissue of *Summertime Blues*, alongside re-releases of Buddy Holly's *Peggy Sue* and Bill Haley's *Rock Around The Clock*. It climbs to UK #34.

1970

May Compilation, ***The Very Best Of Eddie Cochran***, makes UK #34.

1979

Sept [15] Further retrospective, ***The Eddie Cochran Singles Album***, reaches UK #39.

1980

Mar The 20th anniversary of his death is marked in Britain by the release of a limited-edition boxed set, ***20th Anniversary Album***.

1987

Jan [21] Mick Jones inducts Eddie Cochran into the Rock and Roll Hall of Fame, at the second annual dinner held at the Waldorf Astoria Hotel, New York.

1988

Mar *C'mon Everybody* is used as the soundtrack to a UK TV commercial for Levi's 501 jeans (the ad theme is based on Sharon Sheeley's story of how she wore her Levi's to the party at which she first met Cochran. Sheeley appears - uncredited - in a party scene in the ad). Reissued and boosted by TV exposure, the song makes UK #14, 29 years after its first success.

Apr [23] Compilation, ***C'mon Everybody***, which brings Cochran's music to compact disc, reaches UK #53 (while an EP anthology, ***The EP Collection***, will be released on CD by See For Miles Records in 1991).

JOE COCKER

1960

Cocker (b. John Robert Cocker, May 20, 1944, Sheffield, Yorks.), re-named Joe as a youngster by his parents Harold and Madge after their window cleaner, having left Sheffield Central Technical School, buys a cheap drumkit and forms a skiffle group with schoolfriends. He takes a day job as a fitter with the Gas Board and plays in his brother Victor's skiffle group, the Cavaliers, at night, making his first public appearance at the Minerva Tavern in Sheffield. (When he was 12, Cocker sang in one of brother's earlier outfits, the Headliners, at a local youth club.)

1963

When the Cavaliers change their name to Vance Arnold & the Avengers, opening for a number of beat boom bands (including the Hollies), Cocker steps out front and sings calling himself Cowboy Joe. He also sits in with local groups like Dave Berry & the Cruisers.

1964

After an audition for producer Mike Leander in Manchester, Lancs., Cocker is offered a contract with Decca Records. He takes leave of absence from the Gas Board and travels to Decca's studios in London. He debuts with a version of Lennon/McCartney's *I'll Cry Instead*. Despite a good performance and session help from guitarist Big Jim Sullivan and the Ivy League on backing vocals, it fails to chart and Cocker reportedly only receives ten shillings in royalties. He joins his first professional band, the Big Blues, on a brief UK tour with Manfred Mann and the Hollies, and then tours US army bases in France. When he returns to the UK he no longer has a recording contract, so resumes his Gas Board job and plays only an occasional local gig. The band splits and Cocker teams with Chris Stainton to write and record *Marjorine* and form the Grease Band.

1965

The Grease Band, with Cocker on vocals, Stainton on bass, Tommy Eyre on keyboards, Kenny Slade on drums and Alan Spenner and Henry McCullough on guitars, plays soul material in clubs and pubs across the North of England. Its first recording, a live version of blues standard *Saved*, is issued on a free flexidisc with the Sheffield University magazine, **Twikker**.

1967

Cocker and Stainton send a demo tape to promotion man Tony Hall, who gives it to producer Denny Cordell, who arranges a recording session in London.

1968

May [22] *Marjorine*, credited to a solo Joe Cocker and issued on EMI's Regal Zonophone label, makes UK #48.

July [10] Cocker begins a Wednesday residency at the Marquee Club in London.

Oct [15] Cocker takes part in a charity concert in aid of Czech students wishing to stay in the UK, at London's Royal Albert Hall, with Julie Felix, Georgie Fame, Alan Price and Spencer Davis.

[18] Following an appearance at the "National Jazz & Blues Festival" in August, Cocker embarks on a ten-date UK tour, starting at the Newcastle Rutherford, Tyne & Wear, and including a December 8th gig with the Who and Arthur Brown, which will end on December 20th at the Redcar Jazz Club, Yorks.

Nov [6] Cocker's distinctive cover of the Beatles' *With A Little Help From My Friends* hits UK #1 for a week. The Beatles are impressed with his version and send him a congratulatory telegram and place music press ads praising the record. Subsequent TV exposure introduces a wider audience to Cocker's flailing, tortured stage movements. Some find his performance distasteful and, when he makes his debut on CBS-TV's "The Ed Sullivan Show", he is obscured by dancers as he sings, though his powerful, throaty white-soul vocal style impresses many.

Dec [14] *With A Little Help From My Friends* peaks at US #68.

1969

Jan [11] Cocker guests on BBC1-TV's "Happening For Lulu".

Feb [8] He begins a 27-date, twice-nightly UK tour, with bill-topper Gene Pitney, the Marmalade, the Iveys and others, at the Lewisham Odeon, London. The tour will end on March 9th at the ABC Cinema, Blackpool, Lancs.

Apr [27] Cocker pays a return visit to CBS-TV's "The Ed Sullivan Show" with the Grease Band, before embarking on two-month US tour.

May His debut album, ***With A Little Help From My Friends***, consisting mainly of cover interpretations, but including a number of Cocker/Stainton originals, reaches US #35.

July [19] *Feeling Alright* peaks at US #69, as Cocker is in the middle of a three-day stint at the Fillmore West, San Francisco, CA.

Aug Stainton moves to keyboards after Eyre and Slade leave the Grease Band. With Alan Spenner on bass and Bruce Rowlands on drums, the group tours the US, including appearances at the "Denver Pop Festival" and the "Newport '69 Festival" and highlighted by its performance at the "Woodstock Music & Art Fair", Bethel, NY, captured on album and in the film "Woodstock". During the trip, Cocker also meets Leon Russell.

[30] He performs at the "Isle Of Wight Festival Of Music", Woodside Bay, near Ryde, Isle Of Wight.

Oct [16-19] Cocker and the Grease Band play San Francisco's Fillmore West, sharing the bill with Little Richard.

[30] He appears at London's Royal Albert Hall, on a bill with Tiny Tim, the Bonzo Dog Doo Dah Band and Peter Sarstedt.

Nov [8] Cocker's recording of Russell's *Delta Lady* hits UK #10 and peaks at US #69. Russell and Cordell set up Shelter Records and supervise the recording of Cocker's next album at A&M's (Cocker's US label) studios in Los Angeles, CA. ***Joe Cocker!***, which reaches US #11, is the last to feature the Grease Band. The group breaks up after Cocker cancels a US tour. (Stainton will stay with Cocker, while the others take up session work.)

1970

Feb [7] Another distinctive cover of a Beatles song, *She Came In Through The Bathroom Window*, reaches US #30 and earns a gold disc. With no band and a commitment to play US dates, Cocker assembles, with the assistance of Cordell and Russell, a disparate collection of 21 musicians who will be known as Mad Dogs And Englishmen. The "Mad Dogs And Englishmen" tour clocks up 65 concerts in 57 days, leaving Cocker so exhausted that he takes a year off to recuperate in California and then in Sheffield.

May [30] Cocker's cover of the Box Tops' hit, *The Letter*, hits US #7.

July [11] *The Letter* makes UK #39.

Oct "Mad Dogs And Englishmen" tour provides the basis for the double set ***Mad Dogs And Englishmen***, which reaches UK #16 and hits US #2, and an accompanying feature film.

Nov [14] *Cry Me A River*, recorded live at the Fillmore East, New York, in March 1970, reaches US #11.

1971

July [17] Double A-side, *High Time We Went/Black-Eyed Blues*, reaches US #22. ***Cocker Happy***, a compilation of his early hits, is released. Cocker walks onstage, heavily stoned, to sing with "Mad Dogs" veteran Rita Coolidge at the Sheffield City Hall as part of a Byrds package tour. (Cocker, struggling with heroin addiction, has not toured in 19 months nor recorded in over a year, when Stainton asks him over to the US to front a live band. When he arrives, his previous management slaps an injunction on him to prevent him from joining the band, resulting in a six figure settlement, mostly out of Cocker's pocket.)

1972

Jan Cocker reunites with Stainton to tour the UK as the 12-piece Joe Cocker & the Chris Stainton Band, followed by rehearsals in Connecticut in preparation of a six-week US trek.

Feb [12] Reissued *Feeling Alright* makes US #33.

May Double-pack album, ***Joe Cocker/With A Little Help From My Friends***, reaches UK #29.

June [3] Cocker co-headlines London's "Crystal Palace Bowl Garden Party" with the Beach Boys, on a bill also including Melanie, Richie Havens, Sha Na Na and David Blue.

Oct [20] He leaves Australia with six band members, to avoid 18 charges including assault, having been fined $1,200 on drugs charges.

[28] *Midnight Rider*, taken from ***Something To Say***, which consists of studio cuts and live recordings from the year's tour, reaches US #27.

Dec ***Joe Cocker*** makes US #30.

1973

Jan [6] *Woman To Woman*, B-side of *Midnight Rider*, peaks at US #56.

Feb Stainton quits the band and will go on to form Tundra. (Cocker will relocate to Los Angeles later in the year.)

Mar [17] *Pardon Me Sir* makes US #51.

1974

June Cocker performs before the press at the Roxy Theatre, Hollywood, CA. After three songs, with Cocker lying in a foetal position on the floor, the curtain comes down on him.

July [27] *Put Out The Light* makes US #46.

Aug ***I Can Stand A Little Rain*** (released in the UK on Cube Records), produced by Jim Price and featuring guests Nicky Hopkins, Jim Horn, Randy Newman, David Paich and Jeff Porcaro among many others, climbs to US #11.

1975

Mar [29] Billy Preston/Jim Price-penned ballad, *You Are So Beautiful*, listed as a double A-side with *It's A Sin When You Love Somebody* during its first five weeks on the chart, hits US #5.

Oct [4] ***Jamaica Say You Will***, produced by Price, reaches US #42.

1976

June [19] ***Stingray***, produced by Rob Fraboni and backed by soul-funk outfit Stuff, makes US #70. With A&M now releasing Cocker's records in the UK as well, Cube cashes in with ***Live In Los Angeles***.

Oct [2] Cocker appears on NBC-TV's "Saturday Night Live", duetting with John Belushi on Traffic's *Feelin' Alright*, with Belushi doing his famous Cocker impersonation.

1977

Jan Cocker is fined £50 and banned from driving for a year after pleading guilty to a drinking and driving offence. He had been arrested at Christmas visiting his parents in Sheffield, for an offence committed in August 1973. By year's end, his new manager, Michael Lang, who had organized Woodstock, takes him off to tour South America.

Dec [24] ***Joe Cocker's Greatest Hits*** reaches US #114.

1978

Nov [4] ***Luxury You Can Afford***, Cocker's first album on the Asylum label, produced by R&B legend Allen Toussaint, makes US #76.

Dec [27] Fun Time makes US #43.

1981

Oct [3] The Crusaders' *I'm So Glad I'm Standing Here Today*, on which Cocker guests on lead vocals, makes US #97 and UK #61. The track and *This Old*

World's Too Funky For Me, which also features Cocker, are from the group's ***Standing Tall***.

1982

Feb [24] Cocker sings *I'm So Glad I'm Still Standing Here Today* with the Crusaders at the 24th annual Grammy Awards. (Cocker signs to Island Records, who fly him to Compass Point Studios in Nassau, Bahamas, to record ***Sheffield Steel*** with label boss Chris Blackwell producing and Sly & Robbie providing the rhythm section.)
Nov [6] Cocker's duet with Jennifer Warnes on the Jack Nitzchse, Buffy Saint-Marie and Will Jennings-penned ballad *Up Where We Belong*, from the soundtrack of Taylor Hackford's film "An Officer And A Gentleman", begins a three-week stay at US #1. Cocker's critically well-received ***Sheffield Steel***, including covers of songs by Steve Winwood, Bob Dylan and Jimmy Webb, makes US #105.

1983

Feb [12] *Up Where We Belong* hits UK #7. Cocker makes an extensive US tour before playing Europe, with a triumphant return to Sheffield on his first major UK concert in more than ten years.
[23] *Up Where We Belong* wins the Best Pop Performance By A Duo Or Group With Vocal category at the 25th annual Grammy Awards.
Apr [11] *Up Where We Belong* wins Best Film Song at the annual Academy Awards.

1984

June [30] Newly signed to Capitol Records, Cocker's ***Civilised Man*** reaches the anchor position on the UK Top 100 and makes US #133.
Nov [17] *Edge Of A Dream*, the theme from the film "Teachers", peaks at US #69.

1986

Mar [15] *Shelter Me* makes US #91. Cocker records Randy Newman's *You Can Leave Your Hat On* for the Adrian Lyne helmed film "9½ Weeks".
May ***Cocker***, recorded in Memphis, TN, and London, and featuring Michael Boddicker, Albert Hammond and Journey's Neal Schon, among others, makes US #50.

1987

Nov Helmed by the production team of Dan Hartman and Charlie Midnight, Cocker releases ***Unchain My Heart***, which reaches US #89, while the extracted title track, *Unchain My Heart*, a cover of Ray Charles' 1961 smash, makes UK #46. He contributes *Love Lives On* to the movie "Harry And The Hendersons" (UK title: "Bigfoot And The Hendersons").

1988

June [5-6] Cocker takes part in the sixth annual "Prince's Trust Rock Gala" concert, with Eric Clapton, Phil Collins, Peter Gabriel, Elton John and others, at London's Royal Albert Hall.
[11] He contributes to a soul supergroup including (Ashford & Simpson and Al Green) performing at "Nelson Mandela's 70th Birthday Tribute", staged at Wembley Stadium, Wembley, Middx.

1989

Jan [17] *Up Where We Belong* is certified platinum by the RIAA.
[21] Cocker takes part in a "Celebration For Young Americans" concert during one of President-Elect George Bush's inauguration parties at the Convention Center in Washington, DC.
Nov [11] Cocker performs a free concert at the Berlin Wall, Germany.

1990

Jan [13] *When The Night Comes*, co-written by Bryan Adams, Jim Vallance and Diane Warren, peaks at UK #65.
[20] *When The Night Comes* reaches US #11.
Feb [2] ***One Night Of Sin***, its title track a remake of a 1956 Smiley Lewis song, makes US #52.
May [5] Cocker sings *Come Together* and *Isolation* at the "John Lennon Tribute Concert" held at the Pier Head Arena in Merseyside to celebrate the songs of Lennon.
June [5] Cocker guests on NBC-TV's "The Tonight Show".
[8] He begins a 28-date North American "The Power And The Passion Tour" with Stevie Ray Vaughan & Double Trouble, at the Shoreline Amphitheatre, Mountain View, CA, set to end July 22nd in Vancouver, BC, Canada. His band includes Phil Grande (guitar), T.M. Stevens (bass), Steve Holley (drums), Deric Dyer (sax), Jeff Levine (keys), long-time cohort Chris Stainton (keyboards) and backing vocalists Maxine Green and Cydney Davis.
[30] *What Are You Doing With A Fool Like Me*, penned by Diane Warren, spends one week on the US Hot 100 at #96.
July [31] Cocker plays a benefit at the County Bowl, Santa Barbara, CA with Pat Benatar for 524 of his Santa Barbara neighbors, whose homes were destroyed by fire.
Aug [4] ***Joe Cocker Live***, recorded at the Memorial Auditorium, Lowell, MA, makes US #95.
Oct [7] Cocker joins Richie Havens and others to play a free rock concert in the Old Town Square in Prague, Czechoslovakia.

1991

Jan [18] Cocker performs at the "Rock In Rio II" festival at Maracana soccer stadium in Rio de Janeiro, Brazil, before an estimated crowd of 60,000.
June [7] He appears at Manchester's Old Trafford stadium, having begun work on a new album at London's Metropolis Studios with David Tickle producing.
July [20] Cocker participates in the "Telluride Midsummer Music Festival" at the Town Park, Telluride, CO.
Aug [19] When manager Lang suggests that Cocker should consider winding down into semi-retirement, he informs him that he no longer requires his services and contacts Roger Davies to take over.
Oct [17] Despite not being a guitarist, Cocker performs on the third night of the "Guitar Legends" concerts in Seville, Spain, with Robert Cray and Steve Cropper in his back-up band.

1992

Jan [11] Compilation album, ***Two Rooms : Celebrating The Songs Of Elton John And Bernie Taupin***, to which Cocker has contributed *Sorry Seems To Be The Hardest Word*, reaches US #18.
Mar [21] *(All I Know) Feels Like Forever*, written by Bryan Adams and Diane Warren and featured in the movie "The Cutting Edge", reaches UK #25.
[26] Former manager Lang files suit in a New York federal court for alleged non-payment of fees.
Apr [11] 15-track ***Night Calls***, a collection of new cuts and recent near-misses, debuts at its UK #25 peak.
[21] A five-date UK tour begins at Newcastle City Hall, set to end on the 26th at London's Town & Country Club.
[27] Cocker guests on BBC1-TV's "Wogan".
May [23] John Miles-written *Now That The Magic Has Gone* reaches UK #28
June [16] Cocker plays a one-off UK date at London's Royal Albert Hall.
[27] Anthology, ***The Legend - The Essential Collection***, debuts at its UK #4 peak.
July [4] Cocker performs with the show's host on ITV's "Tom Jones : The Right Time".
[18] A re-recorded version of *Unchain My Heart* reaches UK #17.
Aug [8] ***Night Calls*** peaks at US #111.
[12] He guests on "The Tonight Show".
[16] Cocker begins a North American tour at the Poplar Creek Music Theatre, Hoffman Estates, IL, supported on most dates by the Neville Brothers.
Sept [11] Cocker performs at the "Blues Music Festival '92" with B.B. King, Buddy Guy, Dr. John and the Fabulous Thunderbirds at Hardee's Walnut Creek Amphitheatre, Raleigh, NC.
Oct [5] His set at the "Montreux Jazz Festival" is recorded for MTV's "Unplugged" series.
Nov [18] Cocker appears on ITV's "Des O'Connor" show. (Having recently contributed to a Star G.A.S. (Stars Against Alcohol Behind The Wheel) promotion effort in Germany, his duet with Sass Jordan, *Trust In Me*, appears on the soundtrack to "The Bodyguard".)
[21] *When The Night Comes* debuts at its UK #61 peak.

1993

Mar [26] Cocker guests on MTV UK's "MTV Unplugged".

1994

Aug [11] Cocker guests on CBS-TV's "Late Show With David Letterman".
[13] *The Simple Things* debuts at its UK #17 peak, as Cocker appears at "Woodstock II" at Winston Farm, Saugerties, NY.
Sept [17] Newly signed to Sony Music's 550 imprint, his label debut ***Have A Little Faith*** debuts at its UK #9 peak.
Oct [29] *Take Me Home*, featuring Bekka Bramlett, makes UK #41.
Dec [31] *Let The Healing Begin* reaches UK #32.

1995

Feb [17] Cocker guests on NBC-TV's "The Tonight Show", before playing the first of two nights at the House of Blues in Los Angeles, in the midst of a two-month long North American tour.
Sept [23] *Have A Little Faith* debuts at its UK #67 peak, during a two-week chart stay.
Nov A career documenting retrospective cross-label boxed set, ***The Long Voyage Home : The Silver Anniversary Collection***, is released by A&M.

1996

July [27] Cocker embarks on 30-city US "Barnburner" caravan tour in Portland, OR.

COCKNEY REBEL

See: **STEVE HARLEY**

COCTEAU TWINS

Elizabeth Fraser (vocals); **Robin Guthrie** (bass, guitar, drum programming, keyboards); **Simon Raymonde** (bass, piano, keyboards)

1981

Nov The original Cocteau Twins, formed by Fraser (b. Aug. 29, 1958, Grangemouth, Stirlingshire, Scotland), who has met ex-oil refinery engineer Guthrie (b. Jan. 4, 1962, Grangemouth,) in a pub and bassist Will Heggie in Grangemouth, travel from their native Falkirk, Scotland, to London, armed with two demo tapes. One is given to BBC Radio 1 DJ John Peel (for whom they will record two radio sessions), the other to Raymonde (b. Apr. 3, 1962, London), a shop assistant (and son of Chucks' *Loo Be Loo* hitmaker, '60s arranger/producer Ivor Raymonde, who also co-wrote Dusty Springfield's *I Only Want To Be With You*) working in an outlet beneath the 4AD record company office. After listening to it, 4AD label manager Ivo Watts-Russell offers to help.

1982

June Their debut album, ***Garlands***, is released, having cost just £900 to record in nine days, and is an instant UK Independent chart hit, at #2. The Twins resist all offers of management as well as overtures from major record labels, electing always to release material in their own time through 4AD. (For the remainder of 1982 and into 1983, they will support OMD on a 50-date European tour.)
Oct 12" EP, *Lullabies*, is released, with another significant Independent chart success.

1983

Oct [22] Following the March release of *Peppermint Pig*, Fraser and Guthrie appear as part of Watts-Russell's occasional 4AD ensemble, This Mortal Coil, on its debut single, a revival of Tim Buckley's *Song To The Siren*, which reaches UK #66 and will remain on the Independent chart for over a year. Heggie leaves (subsequently emerging in Lowlife), replaced by Raymonde.
Nov Self-written and produced, the dreamy ***Head Over Heels*** finally charts, at UK #51, remaining on the survey for 15 weeks.

1984

May [5] *Pearly-Dewdrops' Drops* is their first pop crossover success, reaching UK #29, despite the band turning down an appearance on BBC1-TV's "Top Of The Pops".
Nov Critically-revered ***Treasure***, once again highlighted by Fraser's uniquely ethereal vocal qualities offset by Guthrie's richly textured musical backdrop, reaches UK #29.

1985

Apr [6] EP *Aikea Guinea* makes UK #41.
Nov [23] 12"-only EP *Tiny Dynamine* makes UK #52.
Dec [7] Further 12"-only EP *Echoes In A Shallow Bay* makes UK #65.

1986

Jan Relativity Records release a US CD-only compilation, ***The Pink Opaque***.
Apr Their fourth album, ***Victorialand***, featuring guest saxophonist Richard Thomas, hits UK #10. In common with all of the band's releases, the cover art, designed by the 23 Envelope art studio, does not include any group member photographs.
Oct [25] *Love's Easy Tears* makes UK #53 and is their last single release for almost two years.
Nov 4AD releases ***The Moon And The Melodies*** a Cocteau collaboration with Harold Budd. The band also complete a sell-out UK tour.

1988

Oct [1] After a two-year hiatus, a new studio album, ***Blue Bell Knoll***, reaches UK #15 and will make US #109.

1990

Sept [15] *Iceblink Luck* peaks at UK #38.
[29] Critically praised as ever, ***Heaven Or Las Vegas***, written and produced by the Cocteau Twins and recorded at London's September Sound Studios, hits UK #7.
Nov [3] The group concludes a European tour at London's Brixton Academy, as ***Heaven Or Las Vegas*** makes US #99, subsequently selling 225,000 copies.
[9] Augmented by guitarists Ben Blakeman and Mitsuo Tate, the band embarks on its first-ever North American concert tour at the Music Hall, New Orleans, LA, set to end at Spreckels Theatre, San Diego, CA on December 10th.

1991

Feb [10] Fraser is nominated in the Best Female Singer category at the 1991 BRIT Awards.
Mar [24] They appear on BBC2-TV's "Snub TV". (Raymonde teams up with Miki and Chris from label-mates Lush, and Russell and Kevin from Moose, to record *And David Seaman Will Be Very Disappointed About That...* under the name the Lillies, for a flexdisc to be included in the September edition of Tottenham Hotspur's fanzine, **The Spur**. During the year Guthrie will produce an album for label-mates Lush.)

1992

Mar While Fraser and Guthrie, who now record at their own Habitat riverside studio in Twickenham, Middx., have had their first baby (Lucy), the group inks a new recording deal with Fontana in the UK (and Capitol Records in the US), after a decade with 4AD.

1993

Oct [2] *Evangeline* debuts at its UK #34 peak.
[30] Self-produced and self-penned as ever, ***Four-Calendar Café***, also featuring Blakeman and Tate, bows at its UK #13 peak.
Nov [20] ***Four-Calendar Café*** debuts at its US #78 peak.
Dec [18] Seasonal covers of *Winter Wonderland*, backed with *Frosty The Snowman*, chart for a week at UK #58.

1994

Feb [5] The group makes its first TV appearance in six years, on BBC2-TV's "The Late Show", as they begin a UK tour at the Portsmouth Guildhall, set to end on the 18th at Brixton Academy.
[26] *Bluebeard* debuts at its UK #33 peak.
Mar [22] Currently on tour in North America, the band performs at the Riviera Theatre, Chicago, IL.
Apr [4] The group guests on NBC-TV's "The Tonight Show".

1995

Feb [25] The band appears on BBC2-TV's "Later With Jools Holland".
Oct [7] *Twinlights* charts for a week at UK #59 as will *Otherness*, also for a week on Nov [4], which features two new cuts and two vintage tracks, all remixed by UK ambient act Seefeel's Mark Clifford.

1996

Apr ***Milk And Kisses***, recorded in Brittany, France and at the group's own September Sound Studios in Twickenham, Middx., is released by Fontana (UK) and Capitol (US).
[27] ***Milk And Kisses*** bows at its UK #17 peak.
May [8] The group performs a headlining date at London's Royal Albert Hall, prior to European shows and a 20-city US visit in the summer. During May, *Alice*, a new cut not available on ***Milk And Kisses***, is included on the newly-released soundtrack to the Bernardo Bertolucci film "Stealing Beauty".

LEONARD COHEN

1956

Cohen (b. Sept. 21, 1934, Montreal, PQ, Canada), having already formed C&W square-dance band, the Buckskin Boys, with childhood friend Mike Doddman, while studying English at McGill University in 1951, has attracted attention as a student poet during the early '50s. His first book of poems, **Let Us Compare Mythologies**, is now published and will win the McGill Literary Award. (Cohen will read some of the poems for release on the Folkways album, ***Six Montreal Poets***.) A second collection of poems, **The Spice Box Of Earth**, appears in 1961, followed by his first published novel, **The Favorite Game**, two years later. After a brief spell at Columbia University, New York, NY, in 1964, Cohen issues a controversial poetry collection, **Flowers Of Hitler**, which wins the Quebec Literary Award, while the Canadian National Film Board produces a documentary film, "Ladies & Gentlemen ... Mr. Leonard Cohen", which premieres the following year.

1966

Cohen publishes his second novel, **Beautiful Losers**. On his way to Nashville, TN, with the intention of selling his songs, he stops off in New York, where he takes root instead, and meets fellow Canadian Mary Martin, an assistant to Albert Grossman, who introduces him to Judy Collins and later CBS/ Columbia talent scout, John Hammond. (Collins will become the first artist to cover his material, *Suzanne* and *Dress Rehearsal Rag* appearing on ***In My Life***.) Hammond signs him to the label and they begin work on his debut album, with Hammond producing (replaced during the sessions by John Simon). A further book, **Parasites Of Heaven**, is published by year's end, containing several poems that become Cohen songs, including **Suzanne** and **Avalanche**.

1967

Apr [30] Cohen joins Judy Collins onstage at an anti-Vietnam War benefit at the Town Hall, New York. (During the year he will also appear at the "Newport Folk Festival", "Canada's Expo '67 World's Fair" and the "Big Sur Festival".)
Dec Cohen appears on CBS-TV's "Camera Three", a Sunday-morning cultural affairs program.

1968

Apr [27] His debut album, ***Songs Of Leonard Cohen***, showcasing his flat baritone vocal delivery, reaches US #83 (but is more successful in the UK in the autumn, reaching #13 and remaining charted for 71 weeks). The extracted *Suzanne* does not chart. (Cohen will never have a hit single in US or UK.) He appears in and scores another Canadian NFB film, "The Ernie Game".
June Selected Poems 1956-1968 is published.

1969

May [10] ***Songs From A Room***, his second album, produced by Bob Johnston in Nashville, which has now become Cohen's base, reaches US #63 and will hit UK #2 and further showcases both his highly-literate but often bleak songwriting skill and his low-key, sparcely-accompanied unique vocal style.

1970

May [10] Cohen performs at London's Royal Albert Hall.
June [27] He participates in the "Bath Festival of Blues & Progressive Music" at Shepton Mallet, Somerset.
Aug [30] Cohen takes part in the "Isle of Wight Festival", Godshill, Isle of Wight, with a touring band comprising Bob Johnston (harmonica and guitar), Ron Cornelius (electric guitar), Charlie Daniels (electric bass and fiddle), Elkin Fowler (banjo and guitar) and Aileen Fowler and Corlynn Hanney (backing vocals). (He plays seven European capitals on the tour, culminating with an appearance at the Olympia, Paris, France.)

1971

May Having recently received an honorary degree from Canada's Dalhousie University in Halifax, NS, Canada, ***Songs Of Love And Hate***, also produced by Johnston, reaches US #145 and hits UK #4. Cohen's songs are used as an integral part of Robert Altman's film, "McCabe And Mrs. Miller", starring Warren Beatty.

1972

Cohen embarks on US and European tours, with Johnston and Cornelius (from his previous touring band), Peter Marshal (bass), David O'Connor (guitar) and backing vocalists Donna Washburn and Jennifer Warnes (at this point in her career going by the name of Warren). A new book of poetry, **The Energy Of Slaves**, is published.

1973

Sept [25] "Sisters Of Mercy", an off-Broadway tribute to his work conceived and directed by Gene Lesser, opens at the Theatre de Lys, New York. (The show will run for 15 performances, closing on October 7th.)
June *Live Songs*, recorded on stage in Paris in 1970, reaches US #156.

1974

Sept [20] Cohen performs again at the Royal Albert Hall.
Oct [5] ***New Skin For The Old Ceremony***, with a soft-rock feel produced by John Lissauer, makes UK #24. (He retires to a Greek island, returning to live performance in 1976.)

1976

Feb ***The Best Of Leonard Cohen*** is issued by CBS/Columbia.

1977

Dec [10] ***Death Of A Ladies Man***, in a move away from the folky acoustic feel of earlier albums, with Phil Spector being brought in to produce, though problems allegedly develop when he reportedly takes the tapes home each night with an armed guard, makes UK #35. (An unrelated book of poetry, **Death Of A Lady's Man**, will be published the following year.)

1979

Sept ***Recent Songs***, co-produced by Henry Lewy and with vocal arrangements and duets with Jennifer Warnes, returns to the spirit of earlier albums but includes unusual instrumental flourishes, such as the use of a Mariachi band.

1984

"I Am A Hotel", a half-hour feature film written, scored and directed by Cohen, wins first prize at the Festival International De Télévision De Montreux, Switzerland.

Sept **Book Of Mercy**, his latest book of poems, is published.

1985

Feb ***Various Positions***, produced by John Lissauer, marks a change of direction for Cohen, with its use of modern musical technology and a more upbeat theme. Cohen embarks on a worldwide tour to promote the album which reaches UK #52, while *Dance Me To The End Of Love* is released as a single and complemented by a video. Columbia never releases the album in the US, instead licensing it to Passport Records. (Cohen wins a Canadian Juno Award for Best Movie Score, for his collaboration with Lewis Furey on the rock-opera "Night Magic".)

1987

June While Cohen has made a cameo appearance as the head of Interpol in NBC-TV's "Miami Vice" the previous year, his long-time backing singer, Jennifer Warnes, releases ***Famous Blue Raincoat***, a collection of Cohen's songs, which includes *First, We Take Manhattan*.

1988

Feb [27] ***I'm Your Man***, his best-received outing in years, debuts at its UK #48 peak.

Mar The extracted *First, We Take Manhattan* is released while Cohen performs three nights at London's Royal Albert Hall.

June [5-6] Cohen takes part in the sixth annual "Prince's Trust Rock Gala" concert, with the Bee Gees, Eric Clapton, Peter Gabriel and others, at the Royal Albert Hall, an event which will raise over £3 million.

Aug [6] A BBC-TV documentary broadcast in July focusing on Cohen also renews interest in ***Greatest Hits***, first released in 1975, which charts for a week at UK #99.

1989

Nov [10] ***Leonard Cohen*** is certified gold by the RIAA.

1990

Feb Cohen guests on *Elvis' Rolls Royce* from Was (Not Was)' ***Are You O.K.?***, as he is inducted into the Canadian Juno Hall of Fame.

1991

Nov [26] A tribute album to the much-lauded singer/ songwriter, ***I'm Your Man***, featuring Cohen covers by John Cale, Lloyd Cole, Nick Cave, James, the Pixies, R.E.M. and others, is released.

1992

Nov ***The Future***, Cohen's first album in four years, is released, with Jennifer Warnes once again providing back up vocals.

Dec [5] ***The Future*** charts for a week at UK #36.

1993

Mar [6] Having recently issued **Stranger Music**, his latest collection of poems and song lyrics and still living with actress Rebecca DeMornay (though they will split the following year), Cohen hosts and performs on ABC-TV's "In Concert", introducing co-act, Mick Jagger.

[21] Cohen wins Male Artist Of The Year and "Closing Time" wins Best Video at the 22nd annual Juno Awards at Toronto's O'Keefe Centre.

Apr [16] Cohen makes another rare US TV appearance, on NBC-TV's "The Tonight Show".

May [10] He performs at London's Royal Albert Hall during his latest UK visit.

June [14] Cohen makes a rare US concert appearance at the Paramount, New York, while playing a handful of dates in Seattle, WA, San Francisco, CA, Los Angeles, CA and San Diego, CA.

Nov Elton John's ***Duets*** album, featuring a collaboration with Cohen on *Born To Lose*, is released.

1994

Jan [15] Cohen guests on BBC2-TV's "Later With Jools Holland".

Mar [20] Cohen is named Songwriter Of The Year at the 23rd Juno Awards at the O'Keefe Centre.

Aug [6] ***Cohen Live*** bows at its UK #35 peak.

1995

Sept [26] While he continues to work on his new album in a mountain cabin in Mt. Baldie, CA, A&M releases another all-star tribute ***Tower Of Song : The Songs Of Leonard Cohen***, featuring Cohen-covers by Billy Joel, Willie Nelson, Sting, Elton John, Bono, Tori Amos, Aaron Neville, Peter Gabriel, Suzanne Vega, the Chieftains and others.

LLOYD COLE & THE COMMOTIONS

Lloyd Cole (vocals, guitar); **Neil Clark** (guitar); **Lawrence Donegan** (bass); **Blair Cowan** (keyboards); **Steven Irvine** (drums)

1984

Jan Cole (b. Jan. 31, 1961, Buxton, Derbys.), raised in Glasgow, Scotland, having met Cowan in the local Tennants Bar, and both on their way to a Ramones concert, decided to form a band in July 1983 and initially recruited Clark (b. July 3, 1955), Irvine (b. Dec. 16, 1959), a former Scottish lightweight boxing champ, and ex-Bluebells member Donegan (b. July 13, 1961), to complete the Commotions behind Cole. Local gigging and demo tapes lead to a record deal with Polydor, secured by the band's manager, Derek MacKillop.

July [7] Their first single, *Perfect Skin*, immediately appealing to the UK music media, climbs to UK #26.

Sept [15] *Forest Fire*, extracted from their forthcoming debut album, makes UK #41.

Oct [12] ***Rattlesnakes*** peaks at UK #13 during a 30-week chart stay. Produced by Paul Hardiman (with string arrangements by Anne Dudley), the critically-revered set is largely penned by Cole, and highlights the band's Byrdlike rhythm style and Cole's distinctive brooding vocal style. A sellout European tour follows.

Nov [17] The extracted title track, *Rattlesnakes*, peaks at UK #65.

1985

Oct [5] *Brand New Friend*, from a forthcoming album, is their first Top 20 hit, reaching UK #19.

Nov Their second project, ***Easy Pieces***, produced by the Clive Langer/Alan Winstanley team, hits UK #5. It achieves significant sales worldwide, but an increasingly disillusioned Cole gives his gold and platinum award discs to his local café, where they are used as tea-trays.

[23] *Lost Weekend* reaches UK #17.

1986

Jan [25] *Cut Me Down* makes UK #38.

June Sandie Shaw's cover version of *[14] To Be Heartbroken*, a track written by Cole on ***Rattlesnakes***, charts for a week at UK #68. Sessions for a new album, produced by Chris Thomas, are recorded in between touring but are shelved.

1987

Oct [17] First fruit of a fresh liaison with producer Ian Stanley is *My Bag*, which makes UK #46. Cowan leaves the group. A UK sellout tour commences, including two nights at London's Brixton Academy.

Nov [7] Third album, ***Mainstream***, featuring Tracey Thorn, hits UK #2. (It is the band's first release in the US on Capitol Records - all prior albums have been issued by Geffen Records.)

1988

Jan [23] The group begins an extensive European tour, as *Jennifer She Said* makes UK #31. A 12" version features covers of Bob Dylan's *I Don't Believe You* and Elvis Presley's classic *Mystery Train*.

Apr [17] They play the final tour date, at Wembley Arena, Wembley, Middx.

[23] While preparing for their first visit to Japan, the EP, *From The Hip*, debuts at its UK #59 peak.

1989

Apr [15] Compilation album ***1984-1989*** reaches UK #14, as the band announces its intention to split.

1990

Feb [10] *No Blue Skies*, marking the beginning of a solo career for Cole, now based in New York, makes UK #42.

Mar [3] Still signed to Polydor, his self-penned ***Lloyd Cole***, similar in style and content to his efforts with the Commotions and featuring Cowan, debuts at UK #11 during a six-week chart stay.

Apr [14] Extracted *Don't Look Back* peaks at UK #59.

June [15] Cole begins a 25-date US tour in Atlanta, GA, which will end on July 20th in Los Angeles, CA.

Oct [4] He plays a benefit gig in New York for IMPACT NYC, which develops educational and recreational programs for homeless children.

1991

Apr [12] Cole guests on C4-TV's "Tonight With Jonathan Ross".

Aug [31] *She's A Girl And I'm A Man* makes UK #55 during a two-week chart stay.

Sept [28] His sophomore solo set, ***Don't Get Weird On Me Babe***, debuts at its UK #21 peak.

Oct [18] Having recently contributed his treatment of *Chelsea Hotel* to the Leonard Cohen tribute album, ***I'm Your Fan***, Cole begins a nine-date UK tour at the Edinburgh Playhouse, set to end on the 28th at the Aston Villa Leisure Centre, Birmingham, W. Midlands.

Dec [21] Cole, with former Commotions Blair Cowan and Neil Clark in his band, plays to a sellout crowd at The Academy, New York, during a short US tour.

1992

Feb [24] He guests on syndicated TV's "Dennis Miller" talk show. He will spend the next 18 months recording his next album with producer Adam Peters in New York.

1993

Sept [25] *So You'd Like To Save The World* begins a two-week chart stay at UK #72.

Oct [23] Its parent album ***Bad Vibes***, featuring guest musicians Fred Maher, Ann Vengsgaard, John Micco, Matthew Sweet and Clark among others, debuts at its UK #38 peak.

1994

June [8] Cole plays a sellout date at the Roxy in Los Angeles, during current US dates.

1995

Sept [16] *Like Lovers Do* debuts at its UK #24 peak.
[19] Rykodisc releases ***Bad Vibes*** in the US, following an eight-city promotional tour.
Oct [7] His first album on Fontana (UK), ***Love Story***, variously produced by Cole with Peters and Stephen Streetbows at its UK #27 peak. (Still chart-less in the US, it will be released by Rykodisc.)
Dec [2] The extracted *Sentimental Fool* charts for a week at UK #73.

NATALIE COLE

1965

The second of legendary singer/pianist Nat "King" Cole's five children, who all grow up in the affluent Los Angeles suburb Hancock Park, Cole (b. Feb. 6, 1950, Los Angeles, CA), having appeared on stage for the first time with her father in 1962, has gone on to form the Malibu Music Men jazz group with Daryl Dragon (later the nautical half of the Captain & Tennille) and Nelson Riddle's son, Nelson. Following her father's death in February, Cole becomes one of only 200 black students at the 20,000-student University of Massachusetts, Amherst, MA, where she studies for a BA degree in child psychology. She becomes politically active as a committed pacifist and a member of the Black Panther Party. She also forms the student band Black Magic, which plays gigs off campus.

1973

Feb Having begun singing in clubs in the early '70s, Cole tries to hide her celebrated background from nostalgic promoters keen to hear her perform her father's work. Now playing at the Executive Inn in Buffalo, NY, she meets Canadian promoter Kevin Hunter, who becomes her manager and secures TV appearances and bookings at larger venues.

1974

Dec R&B writer/producers Chuck Jackson Jr. and the Reverend Marvin Yancy invite her to record demos in Curtis Mayfield's Curtom Studio.

1975

June Turned down by a number of labels, she eventually signs to Capitol Records (the same company for which her father recorded).
July At Yancy's behest, Cole is re-baptized before beginning her first major US tour.
Oct [25] *This Will Be*, taken from her maiden album, ***Inseparable***, makes UK #32.
Nov [22] *This Will Be*, written and produced by Jackson and Yancy, hits US #6.
[29] ***Inseparable*** reaches US #18.

1976

Feb [11] ***Inseparable*** is certified gold by the RIAA.
[28] Cole wins the Best New Artist Of The Year and Best R&B Vocal Performance, Female category for *This Will Be* at the 18th annual Grammy Awards.
Mar [27] *Inseparable* makes US #32.
Apr Cole opens for Bill Cosby at the Hilton Hotel, Las Vegas, NV.
July [17] ***Natalie***, also produced by Jackson and Yancy, reaches US #13, having earned Cole her second gold disc on the 1st.
[31] Cole secretly marries Yancy in Chicago, IL.
Aug [7] *Sophisticated Lady (She's A Different Lady)* reaches US #25.
Oct [30] *Mr. Melody* makes US #49.

1977

Feb [14] She announces publicly, on Valentine's Day, that she was married in 1976 and is now pregnant.
[19] Cole wins the Best R&B Vocal Performance, Female category for *Sophisticated Lady* at the 19th annual Grammy Awards.
Apr [21] Cole guests on ABC-TV's "Sinatra And Friends" special, singing *I've Got Love On My Mind* and duetting with Sinatra on *I Get A Kick Out Of You*.
[23] Her third album, ***Unpredictable***, hits US #8.
[30] The extracted *I've Got Love On My Mind* hits US #5, having earned her first gold single on the 13th.
Aug [12] The RIAA certifies ***Unpredictable*** platinum.
[13] *Party Lights* peaks at US #79.
Dec Cole is voted Best Female Vocalist by the National Association for the Advancement of Colored People (NAACP).

1978

Jan [14] She performs on NBC-TV's "Super Bowl" celebration special on the eve of the game between the Denver Broncos and the Dallas Cowboys.
[16] She co-hosts the fifth annual American Music Awards, at the Civic Auditorium, Santa Monica, CA, at which she also collects the Favorite Female Artist, Soul/R&B trophy.
Mar [30] Cole begins four days of concerts at the Westbury Music Fair, Westbury, NY.
Apr [8] ***Thankful*** reaches US #16.
[15] *Our Love* hits US #10, having already topped the US R&B chart, and will be certified gold on the 6th.
June [21] ***Thankful*** is confirmed platinum by the RIAA.
Sept [9] Double album, ***Natalie ... Live!***, recorded in New Jersey and Los Angeles, reaches US #31, having been certified gold on July 19th.

1979

Jan [12] She wins the Favorite Female Artist, Soul/R&B category at the sixth annual American Music Awards, held at the Civic Auditorium, Santa Monica.
Feb [8] Cole makes her cabaret debut at the MGM Grand Hotel in Las Vegas.
Apr [26-27] She performs at London's Theatre Royal, Drury Lane.
May [5] *I Love You So* peaks at US #52, after being certified RIAA gold on April 2nd. (During the month, Cole wins the Grand Prize at the "Tokyo Music Festival".)

1980

Mar [1] ***We're The Best Of Friends***, an album of Cole duets with Peabo Bryson, makes US #44. From it, *Gimme Some Time* (#8) and *What You Won't Do For Love* (#16) are both R&B hits.
July [26] *Don't Look Back*, taken from the forthcoming ***Don't Look Back***, climbs to US #77.
Sept [20] *Someone That I Used To Love* reaches US #21.

1981

Oct ***Happy Love*** peaks at US #132 while ***The Natalie Cole Collection*** will be her final release on Capitol.

1982

Feb With Cole having inked a worldwide deal with Epic Records, ***I'm Ready*** reaches US #182.

1983

Feb Following her divorce from Yancy (who will pass away in 1985) in 1980, Cole has suffered a serious problem from substance abuse and checks into the Hazelden Clinic for six months rehabilitation.
Sept She joins Johnny Mathis on ***Unforgettable - A Tribute To Nat "King" Cole***.

1985

June [8] *Dangerous*, Cole's debut for Modern Records, peaks at US #57.
July [20] ***Dangerous***, largely produced by Gary Skardina and Marti Sharron, peaks at US #140.
Sept [21] *A Little Bit Of Heaven*, penned by UK songwriters Richard Kerr and Graham Lyle, climbs to US #81.

1987

Aug Having signed to EMI Records subsidiary, Manhattan the previous September, her label debut, ***Everlasting***, is released, variously helmed by nine producers and featuring her cover of *When I Fall In Love* (which will coincidentally give her father a posthumous UK #4 hit at Christmas).
Oct [3] *Jump Start*, having already peaked at UK #44, reaches US #13.

1988

Jan *Over You*, a duet with Ray Parker Jr., makes UK #65.
Feb [6] *I Live For Your Love* reaches US #13.
Mar [25] Still climbing the US survey, ***Everlasting*** is certified gold by the RIAA.
[30] Cole wins the Best Single, Female category at the second annual Soul Train Music Awards, held at the Civic Auditorium, Santa Monica.
Apr [23] *Pink Cadillac* also hits UK #5.
May [7] Her R&B/pop re-working of Bruce Springsteen's *Pink Cadillac* (originally the B-side of his *Dancing In The Dark*) hits US #5. Re-sleeved and re-mastered, ***Everlasting*** makes UK #62 (her first UK chart album) and will peak at US #42.
June [11] She makes a rare live appearance, at "Nelson Mandela's 70th Birthday Tribute" at Wembley Stadium, Wembley, Middx., as part of a soul supergroup with Ashford & Simpson, Joe Cocker, Al Green and others.
July [9] Title cut *Everlasting* reaches UK #28.
Aug [27] *When I Fall In Love* climbs to US #95.
Sept [3] *Jump Start*, reissued in the UK, makes #36, as Cole begins a US tour.
Dec Cole performs two shows at London's Hammersmith Odeon during a short UK visit. (She is currently featured on the soundtrack of the Bill Murray-starring film, "Scrooged".)
[10] Cole wins Best Female Artist at NAACP's 21st Image Awards, from Los Angeles' Wiltern Theatre. (The show will air on January 14th.)

1989

Jan [28] *I Live For Your Love* makes UK #23.
May [20] ***Good To Be Back***, combining top-flight R&B sessioneers, producers and songwriters, hits UK #10.
June [3] *Miss You Like Crazy* hits UK #2, behind *Ferry 'Cross The Mersey*, and tops the US R&B survey.
July [8] *Miss You Like Crazy* hits US #7, as ***Good To Be Back*** heads to US #59.
[22] *Best Of The Night* peaks at UK #56.
Sept [17] Cole marries former Rufus drummer Andre Fischer (who has produced two cuts on her recent album).
Dec [23] *Starting Over Again* peaks at UK #56.

1990

Apr [14] Uptempo *Wild Women Do*, featured in the Richard Gere/Julia Roberts smash movie "Pretty Woman", makes US #34.
[16] Cole participates in the "Nelson Mandela - An International Tribute To A Free South Africa" concert at Wembley Stadium, Wembley, singing *Blowin' In The Wind* with Bonnie Raitt, Anita Baker and Mica Paris.
May [5] Cole sings *Lucy In The Sky With Diamonds* and *Ticket To Ride* at the "John Lennon Tribute Concert", held at the Pier Head Arena in Merseyside, to celebrate the songs of Lennon, as *Wild Women Do* reaches UK #16.
Sept [15] Talent show "Big Break", with Cole as its weekly host, airs for the first time on syndicated TV.
Nov [25] She contributes to the "Motown 30 : What's Goin' On!" special which airs on CBS-TV.
Dec Cole provides guest vocals on David Foster's seasonal single, *Grown-Up Christmas List*.
[29] She participates in the annual "Lou Rawls Parade of Stars Telethon" for the United Negro College Fund.

1991

May Cole contributes *Long 'Bout Midnight* to the GRP label Garfield tribute album, ***Am I Cool, Or What!***
June [14] She appears on BBC1-TV's "Wogan" show.
[19] Cole guests on NBC-TV's "The Tonight Show".
July [20] *Unforgettable*, melding Cole's singing with the original vocal from the standard by her late father, reaches UK #19.
[27] ***Unforgettable ... With Love*** tops the US chart, as it bows at its UK #11 peak. Variously produced by

Fischer, David Foster and Tommy LiPuma, the recording is a tribute to, Nat "King" Cole (an idea originally scotched by EMI, which has resulted in her signing a new record deal with Elektra Records).
Aug [24] *Unforgettable* reaches US #14.
Oct She is featured on the cover of this month's **Ebony** magazine.
Dec Cole is honored for distinguished service to the recording community, at the fourth Membership Awards Luncheon of the Los Angeles chapter of NARAS.
[20] In a **USA Weekend** interview, Cole's mother, Maria, says that she can't listen to ***Unforgettable ... With Love*** or attend any of her daughter's concerts, adding: "I just feel that everything belonged to Nat - it evokes such memories for me."
[26] Cole participates in ABC-TV's "Entertainers '91", which salutes the year's Top 20 entertainers.

1992

Jan [11] Cole wins the Best Female Artist, Best Jazz Artist and Best Music Video ("Unforgettable") categories at the 24th annual NAACP Image Awards.
[27] Cole collects the Favorite Album, Adult Contemporary and Favorite Artist, Adult Contemporary trophies at the 19th annual American Music Awards, held at the Shrine Auditorium, Los Angeles.
[30] "Natalie Sings The Songs Of Nat King Cole With Quincy Jones" benefit concert for the Permanent Charities Committee of the Entertainment Industries Fund for Hunger & Homelessness takes place at the Pasadena Civic Auditorium, Pasadena, CA.
Feb [21] Cole donates receipts from her Apollo Theatre, Harlem concert to help save the landmark venue.
[22] She performs at the traditional Grammy-eve "MusiCares Fundraising Dinner".
[25] Cole sweeps the 34th annual Grammy Awards, from New York's Radio City Music Hall, winning Record Of The Year, Song Of The Year, Best Traditional Pop Performance, Album Of The Year and Best Engineered Album (Nonclassical), with Johnny Mandel also receiving Best Instrumental Arrangement Accompanying Vocal and David Foster winning Producer Of The Year.
Mar [12] Cole performs at "An Evening Of Porter, Gershwin & Coward...", the third annual Rainforest Foundation benefit, at New York's Carnegie Hall, unable to attend the sixth annual Soul Train Music Awards, held at the Shrine Auditorium, at which she wins the R&B/Soul Album Of The Year, Female and Best Jazz Album categories.
May [8] Cole guests on BBC1-TV's "Bruce's Guest Night".
[13] A nine-date UK tour, including two dates at London's Royal Albert Hall, opens at the Theatre Royal, Nottingham, Notts., set to end on the 25th at the Bournemouth International Centre, Bournemouth, Dorset.
[16] *The Very Thought Of You* charts for a week at UK #71.
June [15] Cole and Fischer file for divorce in Los Angeles Superior Court, citing irreconcilable differences.
July [6-7] She performs at the Greek Theatre, Los Angeles, CA, during her current North American summer tour.
[18] Cole attends the wedding of Whitney Houston and Bobby Brown in Mendham, NJ.
Aug [6-7] She sings at New York's Radio City Music Hall.
[30] "Great Performances : Unforgettable, With Love : Natalie Cole Sings The Songs Of Nat King Cole" wins the best Directing, Variety Or Music Program and Sound Mixing, Variety Or Music Series category at the annual Emmy Awards in Pasadena.
Nov [18] Cole takes part in the "Commitment To Life VI" benefit for AIDS Project Los Angeles, at the Universal Amphitheatre, Universal Ampitheatre, CA, honoring Barbra Streisand and David Geffen.
[19-22] She performs at Bally's Casino Resort, Las Vegas.

1993

Jan [13] The RIAA certifies sales of five million for ***Unforgettable ... With Love***, commercially her most successful album.
Feb [20] She is named MusiCares Person Of The Year at the Beverly Hilton Hotel, Los Angeles.
[24] Cole performs *The Lady Is A Tramp* with Tony Bennett at the 35th annual Grammy Awards, held at the Shrine Auditorium.
[25] She inducts Carla Thomas into the Rhythm and Blues Foundation at the Palace Theater, Los Angeles.
Mar [9] Cole co-hosts the seventh annual Soul Train Music Awards with Luther Vandross and Patti LaBelle, also held at the Shrine Auditorium.
[29] She performs two songs from "The Bodyguard" at the 65th annual Academy Awards, in Los Angeles.
June [14] Cole guests on BBC1-TV's "Bruce's Guest Night".
[18] She appears on NBC-TV's "The Tonight Show".
[26] Jazz-phrased ***Take A Look***, her second Elektra offering, co-produced by Andre Fischer and Tommy LiPuma, debuts at its UK #16 peak.
July [10] ***Take A Look*** reaches US #26.
[29] ***Take A Look*** is certified gold by the RIAA.
Sept [4] Cole finishes a two-month US tour, which opened in July at Caesars Palace in Las Vegas, at the Garden State Arts Center, Holmdel, NJ.
Oct [30] She takes part in "A Gala For The President" at Washington's Ford Theater.

1994

Jan [30] Cole sings the national anthem at the start of Superbowl XXVIII at the Georgia Dome, Atlanta, GA.
Mar [1] Cole collects the Best Jazz Vocal Performance trophy for ***Take A Look*** and sings *It's Sandman* at the 36th annual Grammy Awards held at New York's Radio City Music Hall.
[23] She takes part in "Rhythm Country And Blues - The Concert", (she has duetted with Reba McEntire on the album ***Rhythm Country And Blues***) a benefit for the Country Music Foundation and the Rhythm and Blues Foundation, at the Universal Amphitheatre.
June [1] She is honored with the Johnny Mercer Award at the Songwriters Hall of Fame Awards at the 25th annual ceremony, held at New York's Sheraton Hotel & Towers.
Aug Ken Burns' acclaimed PBS documentary "Baseball", to which Cole contributes *Did You See Jackie Robinson Hit That Ball*, airs.
Sept [9-10] Cole plays at Los Angeles' Greek Theatre, during current US dates.
Dec [1] Cole guests on NBC-TV's "The Tonight Show".
[24] Seasonal collection, ***Holly & Ivy*** reaches US #36.

1995

Jan [10] Cole performs at a tribute concert for Ella Fitzgerald at the Universal Amphitheatre.
[12] She inducts Al Green into the Rock and Roll Hall of Fame at the tenth annual dinner held at New York's Waldorf Astoria.
Feb [27] Cole performs at the MusiCares benefit with Tony Bennett, Bonnie Raitt and David Crosby.
May [7] Having sung at the school's annual commencement concert, Cole receives an honorary degree from Berklee College of Music, Boston.
[15] She headlines the first annual Musicians Assistance Program benefit concert held at the House of Blues, Los Angeles.
July [16] She performs at the Pine Knob Music Theatre, Clarkston, MI, during a current round of US dates.
Nov [5] Cole takes part in "The Wizard Of Oz" in the role of Glinda the good witch at the Children's Defense Fund benefit at New York's Avery Fisher Hall.
[19] She sings *They Can't Take That Away From Me* at Frank Sinatra's 80th birthday bash at the Shrine Auditorium.

1996

Feb [11] Cole performs at the Pompano Beach Amphitheatre, Pompano Beach, FL, during current US dates.

JUDY COLLINS

1960

Collins (b. May 1, 1939, Seattle, WA), daughter of blind Denver radio personality and musician Chuck Collins, after studying classical piano in Denver, CO, with acclaimed pianist/conductor Dr. Antonia Brico and making her public debut at age 13 with the Denver Businessmen's Symphony Orchestra, has gradually turned to folk singer/songwriting in the mid-'50s. Dropping out of college in Jacksonville, IL, in 1957, she has returned to Denver to marry her teacher boyfriend Peter Taylor, with whom she lives in a cabin in the Rockies and has a son, Clark. Beginning professional singing with early 1959 engagements in Boulder, CO, the couple has moved to Chicago, IL, where Collins now lands a regular engagement at Chicago's Gate of Horn, billed second to poet Lord Buckley.

1961

Mar Collins signs to Elektra Records after label owner Jac Holzman hears her performing on the New York folk circuit.
Oct Her maiden album, ***A Maid Of Constant Sorrow***, is released in the US, featuring her interpretations of traditional folk songs, a well-received set which furthers her growing reputation on the burgeoning folk scene.

1962

July Her sophomore set, ***Golden Apples Of The Sun*** is released, again to wide critical approval.
Sept She debuts at New York's Carnegie Hall.
The pressures of increasing fame and the break-up of her marriage take their toll. By the end of the year she is seriously ill with tuberculosis and spends six months in hospital.

1963

Dec Returning with her third effort, ***Judy Collins #3*** (with arrangements by Jim McGuinn, soon to find fame with the Byrds), the album contains overtly political material, as Collins becomes increasingly active in the growing protest movement.

1964

Apr ***Judy Collins #3***, reaches US #126.
Oct ***Live The Judy Collins Concert***, featuring songs by Bob Dylan, Tom Paxton and Phil Ochs, is released.

1965

Nov [27] Her ***Fifth Album***, produced by Joshua Rifkin, climbs to US #69.

1967

Jan *Hard Lovin' Loser*, taken from ***In My Life***, released the previous December, is her first US single chart entry, reaching #97.
Apr [8] ***In My Life***, recorded in London and including *Suzanne* and *Dress Rehearsal Rag*, the first recordings of songs by Leonard Cohen, and other numbers from Peter Weiss' stage production of "The Marat/Sade", with orchestral backing, peaks at US #46.
July Collins introduces a visibly nervous Cohen on stage during a concert in Central Park, New York.
Dec [9] She performs again at Carnegie Hall.
[31] Collins guests on the New Year's Eve broadcast of CBS-TV's "The Smothers Brothers Show".

1968

Jan [20] She appears with Bob Dylan, the Band and others in a concert at Carnegie Hall, New York, commemorating the recently-deceased folk singer, Woody Guthrie.
Mar [14] Collins arrives in the UK for her first professional visit, which will include her ITV debut on "Whole Scene Going" and dates in London, Nottingham, Norwich and Birmingham.
Dec [21] Her version of Joni Mitchell's *Both Sides Now*, from ***Wildflowers***, is her biggest chart single, hitting US #8.

[28]***Wildflowers***, mixing her own compositions with interpretations of songs by Jacques Brel, Brecht/Weill and newer writers Joni Mitchell and Randy Newman, hits US #5 in its 52nd week on the chart, and becomes her all-time best-seller.

1969

Jan [20] The RIAA certifies gold sales for ***Wildflowers***.
Mar [1] ***Who Knows Where The Time Goes*** reaches US #29. Her backing band for this includes short-term beau Stephen Stills, who is subsequently inspired to write *Suite : Judy Blue Eyes*, recorded by Crosby, Stills & Nash on their debut album.
[8] *Someday Soon* peaks at US #55.
[12] Collins wins the Best Folk Performance Of 1968 category for *Both Sides Now* at the 11th annual Grammy Awards.
July [15] She opens in the New York Shakespeare Festival production of Ibsen's "Peer Gynt" at the Delacorte Theater in New York's Central Park, playing Solveig, in a cast which includes Stacy Keach, Estelle Parsons and Olympia Dukakis. The play will close August 2nd.
Aug [23] *Chelsea Morning*, another Joni Mitchell song, makes US #78.
Oct [8] ***Who Knows Where The Time Goes*** is confirmed gold by the RIAA.
Nov [14] Collins performs at the Royal Albert Hall, London, while ***Recollections***, a compilation of early material, reaches US #29.
Dec [27] Her revival of the Byrds' *Turn! Turn! Turn!* peaks at US #69.

1970

Jan [23] Collins, testifying at the trial of the "Chicago Seven", is denied permission to sing her testimony.
Feb [28] *Both Sides Now* marks her UK chart debut, at #14.
Dec [21] ***In My Life*** is certified gold by the RIAA.

1971

Jan ***Whales And Nightingales*** makes US #17. It includes *Farewell To Tarwathie*, a traditional Scottish whaling song arranged around real recordings of the song of the humpback whale.
Feb [20] An arrangement of the traditional standard *Amazing Grace*, recorded in St. Paul's Chapel at Columbia University and taken from ***Whales And Nightingales***, reaches US #15 and hits UK #5. It is her biggest UK hit and will enjoy one of the longest runs in UK chart history. (Initially on the survey for 32 weeks and continuing via constant re-entries in the lower region, it moves up to #20 in mid-1972 and finally exits in January 1973, after 67 weeks.)
Apr ***Whales And Nightingales***, her first UK chart album, makes #37.
[6] The RIAA confirms ***Whales And Nightingales*** a million-seller.

1972

Jan [29] *Open The Door (Song For Judith)* climbs to US #90, as ***Living*** heads to US #64. Collins takes a year off to write prose and begin work co-directing "Antonia : A Portrait Of The Woman", a film about her former piano teacher, Antonia Brico (which will later be nominated for an Academy Award).
July Compilation album, ***Colors Of The Day/The Best Of Judy Collins***, climbs to US #37.

1973

Mar ***True Stories & Other Dreams***, notable for its original songs, including *Ché* and *Song For Martin*, reaches US #27.
[31] The extracted *Cook With Honey* simmers at US #32.

1974

Jan [22] ***Colors Of The Day/The Best Of Judy Collins*** is certified gold by the RIAA.

1975

June [7] ***Judith***, produced by Arif Mardin and featuring musical guests Steve Gadd, Hugh McCracken and Eric Weissberg among others, hits UK #7 becoming her biggest-selling UK album, and will reach US #17.
May [31] Ballad *Send In The Clowns*, taken from Stephen Sondheim's musical "A Little Night Music", hits UK #6.
Aug [2] *Send In The Clowns* makes US #36.
Nov [19] ***Judith*** is certified gold by the RIAA.

1976

Oct [16] ***Bread And Roses***, produced by Jerry Wexler, reaches US #25.

1977

Oct [22] Compilation, ***So Early In The Spring : The First 15 Years***, peaks at US #42.
Nov [26] *Send In The Clowns* climbs to US #19 during a second chart run, and completes 27 weeks on the Hot 100.

1979

Apr [28] While *Hard Times For Lovers*, her last US hit single, has climbed to #66 on Mar [31], ***Hard Times For Lovers*** peaks at US #54. It is followed by ***Running For My Life***, which stops at US #142 on May [17] the following year, and April 1982's ***The Times Of Our Lives***, which climbs to US #190. ***Home Again***, released in 1984, completes her recording career with Elektra.

1987

While a UK-only TV-advertised compilation, ***Amazing Grace***, has made #34 in December 1985, and, after a lengthy break from recording, Collins returns, on the Gold Castle label (US), with ***Trust Your Heart***, which includes a new recording of *Amazing Grace*. Collins' book, **Trust Your Heart : An Autobiography**, is also published.

1989

Feb While Gold Castle has released the live ***Sanity And Grace*** in 1988, she launches the Judy Collins Harmonics cosmetics line, its first product being Liposome Eye Gel.

1990

June [21] Collins sings *Amazing Grace* at a Nelson Mandela rally at Yankee Stadium, New York. (Now signed to CBS/Columbia, she returns with ***Fires Of Eden***, her best-received work in years. The album, produced by Joel Dorn and Lucy Simon, includes interpretations of *The Air That I Breathe* and her version of the future Grammy-winning song, *From A Distance*.)
Sept *Both Sides Now* is confirmed as one of the BMI's Most Performed Songs Between 1940-1990, with over three million performances.
Dec [4] Collins guests on NBC-TV's "The Tonight Show".

1991

June [20] Collins is honored at the 27th Annual Awards Dinner Dance of the Music & Performing Arts Unit of B'nai B'rith, at New York's Marriott Marquis Hotel.

1992

Jan [15] Her son Clark Taylor is found dead from carbon monoxide poisoning in his estranged wife's garage in St. Paul, MN.
July [1] She takes part in a fundraiser for the Hollywood Women's Political Committee, raising over $350,000, with Barbra Streisand, Chynna Phillips, Patti Austin, Vanessa Williams and Mary-Chapin Carpenter.
Oct [26] Collins teams with Cissy Houston, Lesley Gore, Carly Simon, Lucy Simon, the Roches, Odetta, Maureen McGovern and Bella Abzug as the Clintones, to record *America The Beautiful* and *Michael Row The Boat Ashore* for torchlight parades around the US on the 28th, to promote the Democratic cause called Women Light the Way for Change.

1993

Jan [19] She performs *Amazing Grace* at "An American Reunion : The Fifty-Second Presidential Gala" at the Capital Centre, Landover, MD.
Feb [21] Collins participates in the "First Ladies Of Song" gala at the Alice Tully Hall in New York, celebrating the life and work of Eleanor Roosevelt.
Apr Following a high-profile early morning jog with President Clinton in Washington, DC, on March 24th, a video collection, "The Best Of Judy Collins", featuring the artist in concert, is released, as she completes her first novel, **Shameless**, and inks a new deal with Geffen Records, for whom she is recording her label debut of Bob Dylan covers.
May [30] She performs at the "National Memorial Day Concert" on the Capitol's West Lawn in Washington.
June [3] Collins takes part in a benefit hosted by the Hard Rock Café for the Children's Defense Fund at New York's Roseland Ballroom.

1994

Feb [9] Collins begins a series of US dates at the University of Pennsylvania, Indiana, PA.
Mar ***Judy Sings Dylan...Just Like A Woman*** is released by Geffen.

1995

Apr Collins contributes *Take The Chance* to Peter Paul & Mary's new album ***Lifelines***.
July [9] As her novel, **Shameless**, is published by Pocket Books (US) with a two-song CD sampler to promote her same-named new album, Collins performs at the Filene Center, Wolf Trap Farm Park for the Performing Arts, Vienna, VA.
Sept [3] Collins, visiting the country as a spokeswoman for UNICEF, dances onstage with Vietnamese children at Ho Chi Minh City theater.

1996

Mar Clarkson (US) publishes **Voices**, a package including a book biography, a compact disc of cover material together with relevant sheet music.

PHIL COLLINS

1981

Jan Collins (b. Jan. 31, 1951, Chiswick, London) has entered the world of entertainment as a child actor, appearing in "Humpty Dumpty" at age six, performing as the Artful Dodger in a London stage production of "Oliver" at 14 (leaving after nine months when his voice breaks), touring the UK promoting Smith's Crisps in 1960 (demonstrating the dance Do The Crunch at Locarno and Mecca ballrooms) and as an extra in the Beatles film "A Hard Day's Night", among other roles. As a member of art-rock band Flaming Youth in the early '70s (releasing one album, ***Ark 2***) and later one of part-time jazz-rock outfit Brand X (contributing not least to their early albums, ***Unorthodox Behaviour*** (1976) and ***Livestock*** (1977)), Collins, while already a major international star as drummer and subsequently lead singer of Genesis, following Peter Gabriel's 1975 departure, signs to Virgin Records in the UK and Atlantic in the US for a parallel solo career.
Feb [7] Drum-heavy *In The Air Tonight*, from the forthcoming ***Face Value***, hits UK #2, behind John Lennon's *Woman*.
[21] Self-written and-produced debut solo set, ***Face Value***, which Collins claims has been motivated by his divorce from his wife, enters the UK chart at #1, eventually selling over 900,000 copies in the UK and spending 274 weeks on the chart.
Mar [21] Horn-laden *I Missed Again*, the second single from the album, makes UK #14.
May [23] *I Missed Again*, Collins' first US solo single, reaches US #19, its B-side featuring demo versions of

the first two UK hits.
June [27] Heartbroken ballad, *If Leaving Me Is Easy*, reaches UK #17.
July [11] ***Face Value*** hits US #7, earning a gold disc for half a million sales.
Aug [15] *In The Air Tonight* reaches US #19.

1982

Apr [29] *In The Air Tonight* is named International Hit Of The Year at the 27th annual Ivor Novello Awards, held at London's Grosvenor House Hotel.
July [21] Collins, a formative force in its establishment as an annual event, takes part in the inaugural "Prince's Trust Rock Gala" at the Dominion Theatre, London. He plays drums for Ian Anderson (and is also featured as a guest musician on Robert Plant's current ***Pictures At Eleven***.)
Sept ***Something's Going On***, Abba vocalist Frida's solo album, produced by Collins, makes UK #18 and US #41.
Oct [30] Previewing his second solo effort, *Thru' These Walls* peaks at UK #56, while Collins announces his first solo tour, "Phil Collins In Concert With The Fabulous Jacuzzis And The One Neat Guy" (the One Neat Guy will be a different guest star scheduled to appear for each night of the trek).
Nov [13] His sophomore album, ***Hello, I Must Be Going***, a line taken from the song *Captain Spaulding* (sung by Groucho Marx in the film "Animal Crackers"), hits UK #2 during a 160-week chart tenure.

1983

Jan [15] His revival of the Supremes' 1966 million-seller, *You Can't Hurry Love*, taken from the album, gives Collins his first UK #1 single (for two weeks). It is accompanied by a nostalgic mimicking video.
Feb [5] *You Can't Hurry Love* hits US #10, as its parent album, ***Hello, I Must Be Going***, hits US #8.
Mar [26] *I Don't Care Anymore* makes US #39, while the ballad *Don't Let Him Steal Your Heart Away* makes UK #45.
May [5] Collins, with the other members of Genesis, wins the Outstanding Contribution To British Music Award at the 28th annual Ivor Novello Awards, at the Grosvenor House Hotel.
[28] *I Cannot Believe It's True* peaks at US #79.
Dec [17] Adam & the Ants' *Strip*, an unlikely production credit for Collins, makes UK #41. (Collins also helmed *Puss 'N Boots*, a UK #5 hit for Ant in November).

1984

Apr [21] *Against All Odds (Take A Look At Me Now)* tops the US chart for the first of three weeks, and also hits UK #2. Collins had been asked by director Taylor Hackford to write a song for his movie, "Against All Odds". He uses an out-take from ***Face Value*** titled *How Can You Sit There?*, rewriting it as *Against All Odds*. (It will be nominated for an Oscar at the following year's Academy Awards.)
May [10] *Against All Odds (Take A Look At Me Now)* is certified by the RIAA as his first million-selling single.
June [8] Collins takes part in the third annual "Prince's Trust Rock Gala", at the Royal Albert Hall, London.
Oct *In The Air Tonight* receives further airplay through exposure on the NBC-TV series "Miami Vice", in which Collins guests as game-show host Phil the Shill, and also in the Tom Cruise-starring film "Risky Business".
Nov [25] He drums and sings at the recording session for Band Aid's *Do They Know It's Christmas?*, which will become the UK's all-time best-selling single.

1985

Feb [2] *Easy Lover*, a jointly-credited uptempo dance number with Earth, Wind & Fire's Philip Bailey, hits US #2.
[9] *Sussudio*, a taster from his next album, reaches UK #12.
[26] Collins wins the Best Pop Vocal Performance, Male category for *Against All Odds* at the 27th annual Grammy Awards.
Mar [2] ***No Jacket Required***, with help from Sting, Nathan East, Greg Phillinganes and others, and co-produced with longtime cohort Hugh Padgham, debuts at UK #1, where it will remain for five weeks, staying on the survey for 175 weeks.
[11] *Easy Lover* is certified gold by the RIAA.
[13] *Against All Odds (Take A Look At Me Now)* wins the Best Song Musically And Lyrically category at the 30th annual Ivor Novello Awards, at the Grosvenor House Hotel.
[23] *Easy Lover* hits UK #1 for the first of four weeks (as Eric Clapton's ***Behind The Sun***, co-produced by Collins, enters the UK chart).
[30] Sax-laden ballad, *One More Night*, spends the first of two weeks at US #1 and will sell over a million, as ***No Jacket Required*** begins a seven-week run at the top of the US Album chart.
Apr [27] *One More Night* hits UK #4.
July [6] *Sussudio* tops the US chart for one week, his third consecutive US #1 and another million-seller.
[13] Uniquely, Collins performs on the same day at Wembley Stadium, Wembley, Middx., and JFK Stadium, Philadelphia, PA, alternate "Live Aid" venues, jetting over the Atlantic on Concorde between appearances. Amongst his guest slots at the event, he plays drums behind Jimmy Page and Robert Plant in a Led Zeppelin reunion in Philadelphia.
Aug [24] *Take Me Home* reaches UK #19.
Sept [13] *Easy Lover* wins the Best Overall Performance category at the second annual MTV Video Music Awards, held at Radio City Music Hall, New York, NY.
[28] *Don't Lose My Number* hits US #4.
Oct Collins, at the suggestion of Atlantic president Doug Morris, records *Separate Lives* with Marilyn Martin, written by Stephen Bishop in 1982, to be featured as the love theme in the Mikhail Baryshnikov/Gregory Hines film "White Nights".
Nov [30] *Separate Lives* hits US #1 and is Collins' fifth US million-seller from his last six releases.
Dec [14] *Separate Lives* hits UK #4.

1986

Feb [10] Collins wins Best British Male Artist, and ***No Jacket Required*** wins Best British Album, at the fifth annual BRIT Awards.
[25] Collins wins Best Pop Vocal Performance, Male, Producer Of The Year and Album Of The Year for ***No Jacket Required*** at the 28th annual Grammy Awards.
Mar He produces Howard Jones' *No One Is To Blame* (UK #16, US #4).
Apr [7] *Easy Lover* wins the Most Performed Work category at the 31st annual Ivor Novello Awards.
May [10] *Take Me Home* hits US #7.
June [20] Collins takes part in the fourth annual "Prince's Trust Rock Gala" concert, with Paul McCartney, Elton John, Tina Turner, Dire Straits and others, at the Wembley Arena, Wembley.
[27] Collins is honored with the Silver Clef Award at the 11th annual Nordoff-Robbins charity lunch, held in London.
Nov He joins Greg Phillinganes (keyboards) and Nathan East (bass) in Eric Clapton's studio band for Clapton's new album, ***August***. Collins will also be part of Clapton's lengthy world tour to promote it.
Dec ***August***, also produced by Collins, hits UK #3.

1987

Sept EP *12"ers,* comprising remixes of previous singles, is released only on CD, while in the US it is also released as an album.

1988

Feb [26] The "Phil Collins" video is certified gold by the RIAA.
June [5-6] Collins performs at the sixth annual "Prince's Trust Rock Gala" concert, with Clapton, Joe Cocker, Elton John, Howard Jones and others, at London's Royal Albert Hall.
[11] He drums in an all-star band assembled by Midge Ure for the "Nelson Mandela's 70th Birthday Tribute" concert at Wembley Stadium, Wembley.
July A remixed version of his debut single, *In The Air Tonight*, released due to its exposure on a Mercury Communications TV commercial, re-hits the UK Top 10 at #4.
Sept [10] *Groovy Kind Of Love*, his remake of the Mindbenders' 1966 UK #2 smash and featured in the forthcoming film "Buster", tops the UK chart. (Collins stars in the title role as the former Great Train Robber, now flower-seller, Buster Edwards, and also compiles the film's soundtrack album of '60s songs.)
Oct [22] *Groovy Kind Of Love* also heads the US chart.
Dec [3] Co-written and produced by Lamont Dozier and accompanied by a '60s-era video featuring Collins in the roles of four mock band members, the follow-up, *Two Hearts*, hits UK #6.

1989

Jan [10] *Groovy Kind Of Love* is certified gold by the RIAA.
[21] *Two Hearts* tops the US Hot 100, Collins' seventh US #1.
Feb [13] He wins the Best British Male Artist category and ***Buster*** is named Best Film Soundtrack at the eighth annual BRIT Awards, at the Royal Albert Hall.
[15] Collins describes H.R.H. the Queen as a "pretty good jiver" as she dances at Prince Charles' 40th birthday.
[22] *Two Hearts* wins the Best Song Written Specifically for a Motion Picture Or Television category at the 31st Grammy Awards.
Mar [18] Collins' wife Jill gives birth to their first child, a daughter, Lily Jane.
Apr [4] *Two Hearts* wins Best Film Theme Or Song at the 34th annual Ivor Novello Awards. Dozier accepts the award as Collins has 'flu (the pair will subsequently duet on Dozier's *The Quiet's Too Loud* single from his 1991 album, ***Inside Seduction***). (Collins has also recently been awarded a Golden Bug in Sweden and a Genie in Canada, both acting honors for "Buster".)
May [11] He performs at the Songwriters Hall of Fame 20th anniversary celebration in New York.
Aug [24] Collins plays the part of Uncle Ernie in a benefit performance of Pete Townshend's "Tommy" at Universal Amphitheatre, Universal City, CA, with Elton John as the Pinball Wizard, Steve Winwood as the Hawker, Patti LaBelle as the Acid Queen, and Billy Idol as Cousin Kevin. (The show will be broadcast on the Fox network on September 13th.)
Sept [22] Video set "No Jacket Required" is certified platinum by the RIAA.
Nov [18] *Another Day In Paradise*, a ballad written about the plight of urban homelessness, hits UK #2.
Dec [2] ***... But Seriously*** debuts at UK #1, eventually spending 15 weeks at the top. It is the fastest-selling album in UK chart history and will become one of its biggest.
[20] The RIAA certifies gold sales for the still-rising *Another Day In Paradise* and multi-platinum sales for ***Hello, I Must Be Going*** (two million), ***Face Value*** (three million) and ***No Jacket Required*** (six million).
[23] *Another Day In Paradise* tops the US chart.

1990

Jan [6] Self-penned as ever, ***... But Seriously***, again co-produced with Padgham, and featuring Stephen Bishop, Clapton, David Crosby, Don Myrick and Steve Winwood, tops the US chart.
Feb [10] *I Wish It Would Rain*, featuring Clapton fretwork, hits UK #7.
[18] Collins is named Best British Male Artist at the ninth annual BRIT Awards, held at London's Dominion Theatre.
[26] "The Serious Tour", a world trek, begins in Japan, with a backing band comprising Daryl Steurmer (lead guitar), Leland Sklar (bass), Brad Cole (keyboards), Chester Thompson (drums), the Phenix Horns and Fred White, Arnold McCuller and Bridgette Bryant (backing vocals).
Mar [8] He wins the Best Drummer nod in **Rolling Stone**'s 1989 music awards.
[31] *I Wish It Would Rain* hits US #3.
May [5] *Something Happened (On The Way To*

Heaven) reaches UK #15.
[31] The North American leg of the tour begins at the Nassau Veterans Memorial Coliseum, Uniondale, NY, with three sellout shows, grossing $1,357,200.
June [30] Ballad *Do You Remember?* hits US #4, as Collins joins Genesis, Pink Floyd, Robert Plant, Paul McCartney, Cliff Richard and the Shadows, Status Quo, Eric Clapton, Elton John, Mark Knopfler and Tears For Fears, all previous Silver Clef winners, on a star-studded bill at Knebworth Park, Herts., in aid of the Nordoff-Robbins Music Therapy Centre.
Aug [4] *That's Just The Way It Is* reaches UK #26.
[14] The RIAA certifies gold sales for *One More Night* and *Sussudio* and three million sales for ***... But Seriously***.
[17] Collins receives a certificate of appreciation for permitting the COTS (Coalition for Temporary Shelter) to solicit donations at gigs. $21,440 is raised.
[22-25] Continuing sellout shows during "The Serious Tour", Collins performs before 65,945 at four shows at the Spectrum, Philadelphia, PA.
Sept [6] He appears at the seventh annual MTV Awards, from the Universal Amphitheatre.
[8] CBS-TV special, "Seriously, Phil Collins", airs.
[21] He guests on NBC-TV's "The Tonight Show".
[26] Collins appears on NBC-TV's "Late Night With David Letterman".
[28] He begins a four-night sellout stint at New York's Madison Square Garden, before 70,097 people (with one show airing on pay-per-view cable TV).
Oct [2] His 127-show, 9-month, 16-country, 59-city "The Serious Tour" comes to an end.
[6] *Something Happened On The Way To Heaven* hits US #4.
[13] *Hang In Long Enough* makes UK #34.
Nov [17] ***Serious Hits ... Live!***, a double-set collecting the best recordings from Collins' recent "The Serious Tour", debuts at UK #2, behind ***The Very Best Of Elton John***.
[26] Collins wins the Top Adult Contemporary Artist, Top Worldwide Album and Top Adult Contemporary Single categories at the inaugural **Billboard** Music Awards, held at the Barker Hangar, Santa Monica Airport, CA.
Dec [5] His "Seriously Live" video is certified platinum by the RIAA.
[15] *Do You Remember (Live)* peaks at UK #57.
[17] Still-rising ***Serious Hits ... Live!*** is certified gold, "The Singles Collection" video certified platinum and his debut album ***Face Value*** certified multi-platinum (for four million sales) by the RIAA.

1991

Jan [12] *Hang In Long Enough* reaches US #23.
[28] Collins wins the Favorite Pop/Rock Album for ***... But Seriously*** and Favorite Pop/Rock, Male Artist categories at the 18th annual American Music Awards, at the Shrine Auditorium, Los Angeles. (While in the US, Collins films a minor role in Steven Spielberg's Robin Williams/Dustin Hoffman-starring "Hook", a modern-day adaptation of "Peter Pan".)
Feb [2] ***Serious ... Hits Live!*** reaches US #11.
[5] He plays drums for the opening series of 24 Eric Clapton concerts at the Royal Albert Hall, London.
[16] *Who Said I Would* peaks at US #73.
[20] *Another Day In Paradise* is named Record Of The Year at the 33rd annual Grammy Awards, at Radio City Music Hall, New York. (It is Collins' sixth solo Grammy.)
[26] ***No Jacket Required*** is now certified for seven million sales.
Mar [7] Collins is once again named Best Drummer in the annual **Rolling Stone** Readers' Picks music awards.
May [2] He is hailed Songwriter Of The Year at the 36th annual Ivor Novello Awards, held at the Grosvenor House Hotel.
[4] Collins sings *Another Day In Paradise* with a 13-piece band at the Berklee Performance Center, Boston, MA, and receives an honorary doctorate from Berklee College president, Lee Eliot Berk. ABC-TV premieres "An American Saturday Night", which sees Collins duetting with Sam Moore.
[15] *Another Day In Paradise* takes top honors at the eighth annual ASCAP Pop Awards Dinner, at the Beverly Hilton Hotel, Los Angeles.
June [15] Collins participates in the third annual World Music Awards from the Sporting Club, Monte Carlo, Monaco.
Sept [6] He performs at the "Symphony for the Spire" benefit at Salisbury Cathedral, Salisbury, Wilts., before the Prince and Princess of Wales, trying to raise £6.5 million for the restoration of the cathedral's spire.
Oct [3] Collins is named ASCAP's UK Songwriter Of The Year for the fourth time, at their 11th annual dinner, at Claridges in London.
[15] The RIAA certifies *In The Air Tonight* gold.
[23] Collins wins a legal fight brought against his ex-wife (Andrea), preventing her from taking full ownership of a $1,400,000 Vancouver, BC, Canada, house he had bought in 1987, and placed in trust for their two children, Joely and Simon.
Dec [2] *Do You Remember* is named Most Performed Song Of The Year at the annual BMI-PRS dinner held at London's Dorchester Hotel.

1992

Jan Collins begins filming "Frauds", playing an insurance claims inspector, in Australia.
[11] Various artists tribute album ***Two Rooms : Celebrating The Songs Of Elton John And Bernie Taupin***, to which Collins has contributed *Burn Down The Mission*, reaches US #18.
Mar He buys an $8.5 million Beverly Hills mansion once owned by Cole Porter. In addition to his 14-acre UK residence, this Tudor-style home includes a 60-seat dining room within its 14,000-square feet.
Sept [22] *Another Day In Paradise* and *Something Happened On The Way To Heaven* are honored at the annual ASCAP PRS Awards as two of the most-performed songs in 1991.
Dec [9] Collins hosts the third annual **Billboard** Music Awards, at the Universal Amphitheatre.

1993

May [15] David Crosby's *Hero*, which Collins has co-written, co-sung and co-produced, bows at its UK #56 peak.
[30] Collins guests on ITV's "Aspel & Co.".
July [17] *Hero* makes US #44.
Sept [11] "And The Band Played On", based on Randy Shilts' book about the AIDS epidemic, and in which Collins plays the manager of a San Francisco bath-house, premieres on HBO-TV.
Oct [29] Collins guests on CBS-TV's "Late Show With David Letterman".
[30] *Both Sides Of The Story* debuts at its UK #7 high.
Nov [20] ***Both Sides*** enters the UK chart at #1.
[27] *Both Sides Of The Story* reaches US #25, as ***Both Sides*** debuts at its US #13 peak.
Dec [21] ***Both Sides*** is certified platinum by the RIAA.

1994

Jan [5] Collins guests on ITV's "Des O'Connor Tonight".
[22] *Everyday* reaches UK #15.
Mar [19] Ballad *Everyday* reaches US #24.
Apr [1] Collins embarks on a 25-date European tour in Utrecht, Netherlands, set to end on May 7th in Lisbon, Portugal.
[6] The RIAA certifies two million sales of ***Serious Hits ... Live***.
May [7] *We Wait And We Wonder* debuts at its UK #45 peak, during a two-week chart stay.
[25] Collins begins a North American tour with a sellout date at the Cynthia Woods Mitchell Pavilion, The Woodlands, TX.
June [14] Collins is made a Lieutenant of the Royal Victorian Order, for his work as trustee for the Prince's Trust in H.R.H. Queen Elizabeth II's Birthday Honours list.
Aug [8] The RIAA certifies four million sales of ***... But Seriously***.
[11] His North American tour ends at the Great Western Forum, Inglewood, CA.
Oct [14] *Another Day In Paradise* and *Hold On To My Heart* win awards at the 14th annual ASCAP dinner at London's Park Lane Hotel.

1995

Mar [17] Collins' "Far Side Of The World Tour" opens in Johannesburg, South Africa.
Apr [29] He completes the last part of his Latin American leg of the world trek in San Juan, Puerto Rico, following shows in Argentina, Uruguay, Peru and Brazil.
May [3] Far Eastern segment begins at the Coliseum, Hong Kong.
Aug Jazz quartet Fourplay's ***Elixir*** album, featuring a contribution by Collins, is released by Elektra (US) (and follows the March release of Manhattan Transfer's ***Tonin'*** which also boasted a Collins guest spot).
Oct [27] *Everyday* is named Song Of The Year at the annual PRS/ASCAP Awards in London.
Nov [7] Quincy Jones' ***Q's Jook Joint***, with Collins one of many guest contributors, is released.
Dec [11] **Cliff Dane's Rock Accounts 95**, which shows Collins as the top earner of the year, is published.

1996

Feb [23] With Collins' version of *Somewhere* currently featured on the US released ***The Songs Of West Side Story***, Walt Disney announces that it has commissioned him to write the soundtrack and songs for its planned 1998 animated feature "Tarzan".
Mar In an amicable parting, Collins publicly announces his departure from Genesis, saying: "For me now it will be music for movies, some jazz projects, and of course my solo career. I wish the guys all the very best in the future. We remain the best of friends."
see also: **GENESIS**

COLOR ME BADD

Bryan Abrams (vocals); **Sam Watters** (vocals); **Mark Calderon** (vocals); **Kevin Thornton** (vocals)

1990

Influenced by the doo-wop era popular some ten years prior to their births, the a cappella/pop/hip-hop outfit, whose deft R&B harmony vocals are offset by mild rap interjections and a post-New Kids On The Block street-urchin dance image, formed in Oklahoma City, OK, by Northwest Classen High School friends Adams (b. Nov. 16, 1969, Oklahoma City), Calderon (b. Sept. 27, 1970, Oklahoma City), Thornton (b. June 17, 1969, Oklahoma City) and Watters (b. July 23, 1970, Oklahoma City), secure a recording contract with Irving Azoff's Giant Records, having been spotted by Kool & the Gang's Robert Bell playing a support slot at a local Oklahoma gig, who has subsequently taken the group to New York, NY in search of a recording deal.

1991

June [8] Their debut smash, the teen-teasing *I Wanna Sex You Up*, taken from the movie soundtrack to "New Jack City", tops the UK chart and hits US #2, behind Extreme's *More Than Words*.
[27] The RIAA certifies two million sales of *I Wanna Sex You Up*.
Aug [3-4] Instantly installed as teen favorites, Color Me Badd performs two sellout dates at the KMEL "Summer Jam '91", also featuring C&C Music Factory, Ralph Tresvant, Salt'n'Pepa, Cathy Dennis, Monie Love and others, at the Shoreline Amphitheatre, Mountain View, CA, which grosses $1,026,849.
[24] Radio-friendly, harmony-laced *All 4 Love* hits UK #5.

[31] Their debut album, ***C.M.B.***, hits US #3.
Sept [7] ***C.M.B.*** also hits UK #3.
[21] *I Adore Mi Amor* tops the US chart for the first of two weeks and will be certified gold by the RIAA three days later.
Oct [5] The group guests on NBC-TV's "Saturday Night Live".
[12] *I Adore Mi Amor* debuts at its UK #44 peak.
[27] The band nabs the Best New Group trophy at the UK **Smash Hits** Poll Winners Awards.
Dec [3] They perform *I Wanna Sex You Up* at the second annual **Billboard** Music Awards, held at the Barker Hangar, Santa Monica Airport, CA.
[15] The group appears on ITV's "Disney Club" show.
[31] They end the year performing at the Paseo Stadium, Agana, Guam, before a sellout 4,169 crowd.

1992

Jan [25] *All 4 Love* tops the US chart, having been certified gold on the 16th.
[27] They collect the Favorite Single, Soul/R&B trophy at the 19th annual American Music Awards, held at the Shrine Auditorium, Los Angeles, CA.
[26] Color Me Badd appears on Fox-TV's "In Living Color Super Halftime Party" during Superbowl Sunday.
Feb [12] The group guests on TV-AM's "Good Morning Britain".
[22] *Heartbreaker* charts for a week at UK #58.
[25] They sing *I Adore Mi Amor* at the 34th annual Grammy Awards, held at New York's Radio City Music Hall, and present the Best Rap Duo Or Group trophy with Boyz II Men.
Mar [4] The group performs on syndicated TV's "The Arsenio Hall Show".
[12] They win the Best R&B/Soul Single, Group or Duo and Song Of The Year categories at the sixth annual Soul Train Music Awards, held at the Shrine Auditorium, Los Angeles.
[28] The group is the musical guest on NBC-TV's "Saturday Night Live".
Apr [4] *Thinkin' Back* reaches US #16.
[23] They appear as themselves on an episode of Fox-TV's "Beverly Hills 90210".
[24] Previewing a forthcoming US tour supporting Paula Abdul, the group appears at the Q-106 "Q-Jam", at the Starlight Bowl, San Diego, CA, with Tony Terry, Kym Sims, Kriss Kross, Tracie Spencer and PM Dawn, among others, before a 3,853 crowd.
June [13] *Slow Motion* reaches US #18, three days before they return home to perform at the Myriad Convention Center Arena, Oklahoma City.
July [15] ***C.M.B.*** is RIAA certified for three million US sales.
[27] Currently featured on the soundtrack to "Mo' Money", the band plays at the "Delaware State Fair", Harrington, DE, grossing $71,625.
Oct [2-3] Having completed its US itinerary, the group begins an 11-date tour of the Far East in Jakarta, Indonesia, visiting Singapore and Malayia before closing in Nagoya, Japan, on the 16th.
[17] *Forever Love*, from "Mo' Money", reaches US #15.
Nov [18] Color Me Badd appears at the "Commitment To Life VI" benefit for AIDS Project Los Angeles, at the Universal Amphitheatre, Universal City, CA, honoring Barbra Streisand and David Geffen.

1993

Jan [16] ***Young, Gifted & Badd - The Remixes*** charts for a week at US #189.
Nov [20] *Time And Chance* charts for a week at UK #62.
Dec [4] Its parent album ***Time And Chance***, co-produced by Jimmy Jam and Terry Lewis with Ice Cube (credited as DJ Pooh), debuts at its US #56 peak, hinting at the group's early demise, in contrast to its multi-platinum debut.
[11] Its title cut, *Time And Chance* reaches US #23.

1994

Feb [2] *Time And Chance* is certified gold by the RIAA.
[7] The group presents the Rap/Hip Hop New Artist category at the 21st American Music Awards held at the Shrine Auditorium.
[19] *Choose* reaches US #23.
Apr [16] *Choose* charts for a week at UK #65.
[17] They appear on BBC2-TV's "The O Zone" during short UK promotional visit.
June [26] The group takes part in the "B96 Summer Jam" at the World Music Theatre, Tinley Park, IL.

1996

May [4] Color Me Badd returns with the highest entry on the Hot 100 this week, with *The Earth, The Sun, The Rain* at US #46, previewing the forthcoming ***Now And Forever***.

SHAWN COLVIN

1988

Apr [15] Weaned on folk music by her father, Colvin (b. Shanna Colvin, Jan. 10, 1958, Vermillion, SD) began playing her brother's four-string tenor guitar at age 10 and has been most influenced during her teens by the music of Joni Mitchell while moving with her family from South Dakota to London, ON, Canada and then to Carbondale, IL, where she graduates at the State of Illinois University, while performing local solo folk/rock gigs (her first at a club called the American Tap) and forming the Shawn Colvin Band, a hard-rock combo. Subsequently moving to Texas to join country-swing band the Dixie Diesels in the late '70s, Colvin then relocates to San Francisco, CA, taking up a solo residency at the LaVal's Subterranean club in Berkeley, before joining the Buddy Miller Band in New York, NY, becoming its lead singer and meeting her future sidemen, pedal steel guitarist/violinist Larry Campbell and multi-instrumentalist John Leventhal (who will become her professional and personal partner). Playing around the northeastern club circuit until 1983, she decides to pursue a solo career and following performances on open-mike night at New York's Folk City, she secures a residency at the Other End, performing five nights a week and is also a regular at Manhattan's Cottonwood Cafe. Heard on backing vocals for Suzanne Vega's 1987 transatlantic hit *Luka* (they met while performing on the same bill at New York's Bottom Line club) it is not until Colvin relocates once more to Boston, MA, that she finally breaks through, initially taking up a residency at the Passim club in Cambridge, MA. Tonight's concert at the Somerville Theater, Somerville, MA is recorded and will subsequently be made available by Colvin on a cassette sold at future gigs (together with songs from a March 6th gig opening for Loudon Wainwright III at the Ironhorse, Northampton, MA). These recordings will also be broadcast on WERS-FM, leading to the first headlining concert of her career at Harvard's Paine Hall, Boston in September of this year and to her signing to Columbia Records.

1990

Jan [10] During a US club tour she performs at the Birchmere, Alexandria, VA.
Mar [10] Released the previous year, ***Steady On***, co-penned with Leventhal who also co-produced the album with Steve Addabbo, and featuring guests Vega and Bruce Hornsby, reaches US #111 as Colvin undertakes a European tour opening for Vega.
July [28] With Colvin featured on the track *Stander On The Mountain* and in duet on *Lost Soul*, Hornsby's ***A Night On The Town*** reaches US #20.

1991

Feb [20] Colvin wins the Best Contemporary Folk Recording (for ***Steady On***) at the 33rd annual Grammy Awards.

1992

Nov [14] Her sophomore set, the Larry Klein-produced ***Fat City***, once again supported by US tour dates and continuing to reveal a highly literate songwriter with an engaging soprano voice, featuring guests Booker T. Jones, Hornsby, Mary-Chapin Carpenter (her friend since 1988), Richard Thompson and her idol (and Klein's wife) Joni Mitchell, debuts at its US #142 peak.

1993

Aug [26] Colvin participates in "Voices For Choices", held in Santa Monica, CA, with Melissa Etheridge, Heart and others.
Nov [27] Taken from ***Fat City***, *I Don't Know Why*, which will be nominated for Song Of The Year at the 36th annual Grammy Awards, charts for a week at UK #62.

1994

Feb [12] *Round Of Blues* makes UK #73.
June Having split from Leventhal, Colvin undertakes a solo US summer tour followed by a further two-month itinerary in trio with Campbell and multi-instrumentalist Steuart Smith.
Sept [3] Her version of the Police's 1981 chart-topper *Every Little Thing She Does Is Magic* enters at its UK #65 peak.
[10] Recorded in New York, ***Cover Girl***, Colvin's interpretations of a dozen songs (including those written by Jimmy Webb, Tom Waits, Bob Dylan and Steve Earle) which have inspired her during her career, six recorded in the studio and six performed live at the Bottom Line in 1993, enters at its US #48 high. Guests include Carpenter, drummer Jim Keltner and the Heartbreakers' Benmont Tench.
[17] ***Cover Girl*** charts for a week at UK #67 (with the addition of an additional Waits' cover, *Ol' 55*).
Oct [19] Her current US tour is highlighted by a performance at the Symphony Hall, Boston to an audience of 2,451.
Dec [10] A pre-taped "Later With Jools Holland" featuring Colvin, airs on BBC2-TV the same night she performs at the Austin Music Hall, Austin, TX.

1995

Jan [7] *One Cool Remove*, a duet with Carpenter, debuts at its UK #40 peak.
[21] She participates in a benefit concert for "Voters for Choice" at Constitution Hall, Washington, DC, also featuring Hornsby, Rickie Lee Jones and Bruce Cockburn.
Apr [22] This year's Earth Day concert in Washington, DC includes a performance by Colvin.
July [26] PBS-TV's "In The Spotlight", showcasing Carpenter and featuring Colvin, is broadcast. (Curtis Stigers' current album ***Time Was*** is released by Arista Records featuring a duet on the title cut with Colvin.)
Aug [12] Reissued *I Don't Know Why* charts for a week at UK #52.
[20] On US tour dates opening for Lyle Lovett, Colvin plays at the Greek Theatre, Los Angeles, CA to a crowd of 5,092.
Sept [5] Plump Records (established by her New York-based management company AGF Entertainment) releases ***Live '88*** comprising much of the material found on her 1988 solo live cassette which Colvin originally sold at her concerts, and with liner notes by Jackson Browne.
Oct [7] She participates in the sixth annual Music Festival at Verde Valley School, Sedona, AZ, in support of the school's Native American Scholarship Fund (founded by Browne).

1996

Feb [6] Hollywood Records (US) releases the soundtrack to "Mr. Wrong" which includes a new cut by Colvin. (Having recently moved back to her home base in Austin, TX, Colvin continues work on music for the forthcoming film "Edie And Pen".)

THE COMMODORES

Lionel Richie (vocals, keyboards); **William King** (trumpet); **Thomas McClary** (lead guitar); **Milan Williams** (keyboards, trombone, guitar, drums); **Ronald LaPraed** (bass, trumpet); **Walter "Clyde" Orange** (vocals, drums)

1967

The Mighty Mystics are formed at Tuskegee Institute, Tuskegee, AL, when six students, including McClary (b. Oct. 6, 1950) and Richie (b. June 20, 1949, Tuskegee), combine in the second semester of their freshman year and enter a talent contest to impress girls. The Mystics later link with another campus group, the Jays, which includes King (b. Jan. 30, 1949, Alabama) and Willams (b. Mar. 28, 1948, Mississippi). The Commodores name is decided by the toss of a dictionary and a finger-point from King. Becoming local favorites in Montgomery, AL, the Commodores are sent by the Tuskegee Institute to play a benefit at New York's Town Hall in 1968, with local entrepreneur Benny Ashburn handling the band's publicity.

1969

The band members continue their studies at the Institute, having aroused popular support on New York's club scene. During the summer, they return to New York and contact Ashburn, who secures them an audition at Small's Paradise, Harlem's best-known club.

Sept Orange (b. Dec. 10, 1947, Florida) replaces Andre Callahan as the group's drummer, while bassist Michael Gilbert is drafted and replaced by LaPraed (b. Sept. 4, 1946, Alabama). Ashburn and the band form Commodores Entertainment Corp., harnessing the group's business qualifications.

1970

Ashburn, now their full-time mentor and manager, secures the Commodores dates on the European club circuit. They travel on board the S.S. France, and become local favorites in St. Tropez and other French resorts. While on tour, they also meet a vacationing Ed Sullivan.

1971

Searching for an exciting opening act for Motown Records' biggest stars, the Jackson 5, Motown's creative vice president, Suzanne de Passe, sees the group perform at New York's Turntable and books them for the tour. They sign to the label, having released the Swamp Dogg-produced *Keep On Dancing* on Atlantic earlier in the year. (It will be three years before Motown releases their first album.) During the year, the group also begins its first Far East tour.

1973

July [20] The Commodores embark on 20-date first leg of a tour opening for the Jackson 5 at Civic Arena, Pittsburgh, PA, set to end August 21st at the Municipal Auditorium, New Orleans, LA.

1974

June Instrumental *Machine Gun*, written by Williams, crosses over from the R&B chart to US #22, also making UK #20 (and will be subsequently played after the national anthem at closedown on Nigerian TV and radio stations.)

Aug ***Machine Gun*** peaks at US #138, also achieving gold sales status in Japan and Nigeria, where it becomes the biggest-selling international album to date.

Nov UK follow-up, *The Zoo (Human Zoo)*, reaches #44 while *I Feel Sanctified* peaks at US #75.

1975

Mar Their second album, ***Caught In The Act***, is released, set to peak at US #26 during a 33-week chart stay.

June Taken from the album, *Slippery When Wet* makes US #19 and wins the Bronze Prize at the "Tokyo Music Festival". Following their own headlining tour, the Commodores are invited to support the Rolling Stones on their world trek.

Dec Richie-written and-sung R&B ballad, *Sweet Love*, hits US #5, as ***Movin' On*** heads to US #29. Despite international tours and sales, most band members are still completing degree courses, studying while on the road and returning to university for mid-term and final exams.

1976

July During a tour supporting the O'Jays, ***Hot On The Tracks*** peaks at US #12.

Oct A second Richie ballad, *Just To Be Close To You*, hits US #7.

1977

Feb Follow-up from the album, *Fancy Dancer* peaks at US #39, as the Commodores begin their own headlining world tour.

Apr Their fifth album, ***Commodores***, is released, set to hit US #3 and spend over a year on the chart. (The band's European tour is interrupted after LaPraed's wife dies of cancer and he returns to the US. Darryl Jones stands in for a California Ballroom, Dunstable, Beds. gig, but the group cancels its final date at the New Victoria Theatre, London. The Commodores' next two albums will be dedicated to LaPraed's late wife.)

June The band appears with Donna Summer in the disco movie "Thank God It's Friday", and contributes to its soundtrack.

Aug Ballad *Easy* hits US #4 and UK #9, written by Richie, as are most of the group's biggest hits. (An unexpected cover version of *Easy* by Faith No More peaks at UK #3 and US #58 in 1993.) The group is on a 70-city US tour which will gross $6 million.

Sept Funky *Brickhouse*, a dance anthem, hits US #5.

Oct Released as double A-side with revived *Sweet Love*, *Brickhouse* climbs to UK #32.

Dec *Too Hot Ta Trot* makes US #24. The Commodores complete their most successful year to date with sellout US dates. The live double album, ***Commodores Live!***, hits US #3.

1978

Mar Double A-side *Too Hot Ta Trot/Zoom* makes UK #38.

Apr [14] An eight-date UK leg of a 21-date European concert tour, which opened at the Congressgebouw, the Hague, Holland, bows at the Brighton Dome, E. Sussex, set to end on the 23rd at London's Hammersmith Odeon.

May [13] ***Commodores Live!*** makes UK #60, their UK Album chart debut.

July *Flying High* makes UK #37.

Aug [12] Career-defining Richie soul ballad, *Three Times A Lady*, hits US #1, displacing the Rolling Stones' *Miss You*. Dedicated to his wife, the song was inspired by Richie's parents' 37th wedding anniversary. The disc will later be certified double platinum. (Richie will also receive a Country Songwriter award from ASCAP in Nashville.)

[19] *Three Times A Lady* begins a five-week chart stay at UK #1, becoming Motown's biggest selling single. A worldwide smash, it spurs ***Natural High*** to hit US #3 and UK #8 (on Sept [2]).

[22] ***Natural High*** is certified platinum by the RIAA.

Nov *Flying High* makes US #38, while *Just To Be Close To You* peaks at UK #62, as the group ends a four-month US tour in Louisville, KY.

Dec ***Greatest Hits*** peaks at US #23.

1979

Jan [12] The group wins the Favorite Single, Pop/Rock category at the sixth annual American Music Awards, held at the Civic Auditorium, Santa Monica, CA.

[20] ***Greatest Hits*** reaches UK #19.

Aug The Commodores participate in the "Saarbrucken Festival", Saarbrucken, W. Germany, at the start of a 19-date European tour.

Oct While their new studio album, ***Midnight Magic***, hits US #3 and UK #15 (on Oct [6]), the Richie-composed country/soul ballad *Sail On* hits US #4 and UK #8. It focuses on the failing marriage of his friend, William Smith, and is passed on the chart by another Richie ballad, *Still*.

Nov [17] *Still* hits US #1, replacing the Eagles' *Heartache Tonight*. It also hits UK #4.

1980

Jan [18] The group collects the Favorite Band, Duo Or Group, Soul/R&B trophy, at the seventh annual American Music Awards, held at the ABC-TV Studios, Los Angeles, CA, as *Wonderland* makes US #25 and UK #40.

Apr [25] LaPraed marries Jacqueline Echols in Tuskegee. They will spend their honeymoon on the group's 95-date US tour.

July [12] Spiritually-inspired ***Heroes*** makes UK #50, and will hit US #7. From it, *Old-Fashion Love* makes US #20.

Oct Title cut, *Heroes*, peaks at US #54 while their current tour is also less commercially successful than any in recent years.

1981

Jan The Commodores perform the title theme to the movie "Underground Aces". Richie, thinking of a solo career, duets with Diana Ross on his self-penned *Endless Love*. The group's *Lady (You Bring Me Up)* hits US #8 and makes UK #56.

Feb [3] ***Heroes*** is certified platinum by the RIAA.

July [25] Richie's final album with the group, ***In The Pocket***, makes UK #69 and will climb to US #13.

Nov A final Richie-penned ballad for the group, *Oh No*, hits US #4 and UK #44.

Dec [16] ***In The Pocket*** is certified platinum by the RIAA.

1982

Feb The final group single featuring Richie's vocals, *Why You Wanna Try Me*, peaks at US #66. He leaves to pursue a highly-successful solo career as a writer, performer and producer.

Aug [28] A UK-only K-tel compilation, ***Love Songs***, hits #5, becoming their most successful UK album.

[17] Manager Ashburn dies of a heart attack in New Jersey.

Dec *Painted Picture* peaks at UK #70, as Richie's debut solo, *Truly*, hits US #1. A US compilation album on Motown, ***All The Greatest Hits***, makes US #37.

1983

Apr The Commodores record the theme for the NBC-TV sitcom "Teachers Only", called *Reach High*. McClary quits to record the solo ***Thomas McClary*** and releases the single *Thin Walls*, still with Motown.

May [16] The group performs *Brick House* at the 25th Motown Anniversary held at Los Angeles' Civic Center.

June Another compilation, ***Commodores Anthology***, peaks at US #141.

Sept *Only You* makes US #54.

Nov Their first album since Richie's departure, ***Commodores 13***, reaches US #103. (As live interest also wanes, the group will spend the next year re-assessing with no activity. Urgently needing a new vocalist, they recruit ex-Heatwave UK singer, J.D. Nicholas (b. Apr. 12, 1952, Watford, Herts.), who has recently been a backing vocalist for Diana Ross.)

1985

Jan Composed by Orange as a tribute to Marvin Gaye and Jackie Wilson, *Nightshift* hits US #3. It features co-lead vocals by Orange and Nicholas and is taken from ***Nightshift***, which makes US #12 and UK #13.

Mar [9] *Nightshift* hits UK #3.

[13] ***All The Great Hits*** is certified gold by the RIAA.

May [8] The RIAA certifies gold sales for ***Nightshift***.

[11] *Animal Instinct* peaks at UK #74, and will reach US #43.

Sept *Janet* peaks at US #87.

Nov Another UK TV-advertised compilation, on

Telstar, ***The Very Best Of The Commodores***, makes UK #25. Motown drops the group after 11 years.

1986

Feb [25] *Nightshift* is named the Best R&B Performance By A Duo Or Group With Vocal at the 28th annual Grammy Awards, which helps them win a new recording deal with Polydor Records. The band also signs a management deal with Natalie Cole's manager, Dan Cleary.
Nov [1] Their Polydor debut, *Goin' To The Bank*, makes UK #43 and will reach US #65, as the band begins a tour of Belgium, Holland, Germany and the UK.
Dec ***United*** makes US #101.
[6] *Goin' To The Bank* makes US #65.

1988

Sept Used extensively as the theme to the Halifax Building Society TV commercial, *Easy* re-enters the UK chart, making #15.
Oct ***Rock Solid*** is released together with a single, *Solitaire*.

1991

Oct [10] The band is inducted into the National Association of Brick Distributors' second annual Brick Hall of Fame gala in New York, in recognition of services to the brick industry, for their song *Brickhouse*.

1993

Jan [23] Faith No More's unexpected cover of the Commodores' *Easy* hits UK #3.

1995

May [13] While the group has been trimmed to the trio of Orange, King and Nicholas, releasing ***No Tricks*** on the SRS label in February 1993 (originally issued by the Japanese Pony Canyon label in '92), accompanied by US summer tour dates the same year with their new backing unit, Mean Machine, ***The Very Best Of The Commodores***, still mining their prime hits, reaches UK #26.
see also: **Lionel RICHIE**

RY COODER

1969

Having taken up the guitar at the age of three (a prodigious talent nurtured not least under the traditional instruction of the Reverend Gary Davis) and having started out as a member of Jackie DeShannon's backing group at age 17, Cooder (b. Ryland Peter Cooder, Mar. 15, 1947, Los Angeles, CA), who has grown up with a glass eye since the age of four following an accident with a knife, also played with Taj Mahal in the seminal blues group the Rising Sons in Los Angeles, in 1966, going on to join Captain Beefheart's Magic Band the following year on ***Safe As Milk***, and completed studio-session guitar work throughout the remainder of the decade with the Everly Brothers, Paul Revere & the Raiders, Randy Newman and a host of others. Visiting London with arranger/producer Jack Nitzsche, Cooder now meets the Rolling Stones. Tipped to join the band in Brian Jones' place, he does not do so, but plays mandolin on the Stones' ***Let It Bleed***, works with Nitzsche and Newman on the soundtrack for the Mick Jagger/James Fox film, "Performance", playing dulcimer and bottleneck guitar, and also works on the "Candy" film soundtrack.

1970

Dec Having signed to Reprise Records as a solo artist, Cooder is extensively featured on Little Feat's debut album, ***Little Feat***.
[3-6] He performs at San Francisco's Fillmore West on a bill with Savoy Brown.

1971

Jan His debut album, ***Ry Cooder***, covering material by "Sleepy John Estes, "Blind" Willie Johnson and Leadbelly, among others, is critically praised for its authentic folk-blues approach. During the year, he also plays on the Rolling Stones' ***Sticky Fingers***.

1972

Mar ***Into The Purple Valley***, featuring long-time backing band cohorts Jim Dickinson and Jim Keltner, marks Cooder's US chart debut, reaching #113. It is followed by a third effort, ***Boomer's Story***, released in November.

1974

June ***Paradise And Lunch***, including his reggae-tinged interpretation of *It's All Over Now*, and further showcasing his prodigious talent, not least as a leading slide guitarist, peaks at US #167.

1976

Nov The Tex-Mex flavored ***Chicken Skin Music*** reaches US #177. Cooder tours with "The Chicken Skin Revue", with Hawaiian steel guitarist Gabby Pahinui, Tex-Mex accordionist Flaco Jiminez, and a gospel vocal back-up trio led by Bobby King, who all played on the album.

1977

Jan [29-30] Cooder performs at London's Hammersmith Odeon during a five-date UK tour.
Sept ***Live Show Time***, recorded at the Great American Music Hall, San Francisco, CA, with "The Chicken Skin Revue", peaks at US #158.

1978

June ***Jazz*** is released, reviving late-'40s big band music with sidemen from the era and arrangements by Joseph Byrd. Cooder reunites with Captain Beefheart to work on the "Blue Collar" film soundtrack.

1979

Aug The Lee Herschberg-produced ***Bop Till You Drop*** (the first rock album to be recorded using the digital process), featuring Chaka Khan, Bobby King and David Lindley, among others, reaches US #62 and marks Cooder's UK chart debut, at #36 (Aug [18]). During the month, he performs at the "Cambridge Folk Festival", Cambridge, Cambs.

1980

June He scores Walter Hill's movie "The Long Riders", drawing on US hillbilly-folk styles, and will subsequently provide music for Hill's follow-up film, "Southern Comfort", though the soundtrack release for the latter will remain unissued.
Sept [26] Cooder plays at the Dublin Stadium, Dublin, Eire, at the start of a European tour.
Oct [25] Self-produced ***Borderline*** peaks at UK #35, and will make US #43.

1982

Feb He scores the film "The Border", starring Jack Nicholson, its soundtrack album also featuring Sam the Sham and Freddy Fender.
May [1] Self-produced ***The Slide Area***, once again showcasing his multi-instrument and cross-genre musical chops, reaches UK #18 and will climb to US #105, but Cooder, unhappy with its US sales, backs out of tours and retreats to work at home in Santa Monica, CA, mostly on movie soundtracks.

1983

June Cooder plays club dates in San Francisco, CA, in a small band assembled by Duane Eddy.
Dec [8] He plays with Eric Clapton, Jeff Beck, Jimmy Page and others at a Ronnie Lane benefit concert for Ronnie Lane for ARMS, at New York's Madison Square Garden.

1985

Jan Having contributed to 1984's "Streets Of Fire" soundtrack, he scores Wim Wenders' modern-day western "Paris, Texas".
May Cooder's album soundtrack for Louis Malle's "Alamo Bay", which includes contributions from John Hiatt and Los Lobos, is released by independent Slash Records.

1986

May While Warner Bros. releases the 13-track ***Why Don't You Try Me Tonight? - The Best Of Ry Cooder*** in the UK, his latest film work, the blues-imbued soundtrack to ***Crossroads***, including collaborations with Mississippi musicians Sonny Terry and the Frank Frost Blues Band, makes US #85.

1987

Feb [24] Cooder performs in a blues supergroup, including Willie Dixon, Albert King, B.B. King, Koko Taylor, Robert Cray, Junior Wells, Etta James and Dr. John, at the 29th Grammy Awards at Los Angeles' Shrine Auditorium.
Nov Now primarily an in-demand film-music writer (he has recently scored "Blue City"), Cooder releases his first non-movie album, ***Get Rhythm***, including the title cut revival of a Johnny Cash song, made with his current band (including Van Dyke Parks on keyboards and Keltner on drums), guest vocalists Larry Blackmon (of Cameo) and actor Harry Dean Stanton (who starred in "Paris, Texas"), which peaks at US #177 and UK #75 (Nov [21]).

1988

June ***Pecos Bill***, with Cooder playing music to Robin Williams' narrative, is released in the US on the Windham Hill label.

1989

Feb [22] ***Pecos Bill*** wins the Best Recording For Children category at the 31st annual Grammy Awards. (Later in the year, his latest soundtrack recordings, ***Johnny Handsome*** and ***Steel Magnolias*** will be released.)

1990

July [12-15] Cooder, a consistently-popular live draw, performs four nights at London's Hammersmith Odeon, with David Lindley.
Oct [13] He appears at New York's Beacon Theatre, during the "Benson & Hedges Blues Festival".

1991

Sept He is featured on John Lee Hooker's Charisma debut, ***Mr. Lucky***. By year's end, Cooder has formed Little Village with Nick Lowe, John Hiatt and Jim Keltner (having rejected other possible band names including Moula Banda and 2 Guitars, Bass & Drums). The accomplished grouping first played together on John Hiatt's 1987 ***Bring The Family***.

1992

Jan [30] Cooder participates in the "Friends Of Smitty" benefit for keyboardist William Smith, who has recently suffered a stroke, at the Palace Theatre, Burbank, CA.
Feb [29] ***Little Village***, the group's first (and only) album, released by Reprise, debuts at its UK #23 peak.
Mar [14] ***Little Village*** makes US #66, supported by well-received US and UK concert dates.
Oct [11] Cooder and Lindley take part in the "Healing The Sacred Hoop The Next 500 Years" fundraiser at the Shoreline Amphitheatre, Mountain View, CA.

1993

Feb [25] Cooder's joins Steve Cropper's all-star band at the fourth annual Rhythm and Blues Foundation Awards at the Palace Theater, Los Angeles.
Apr [19] Seasoned session veteran Steve Douglas dies during a Ry Cooder recording session in Los Angeles. (He will take part in a tribute show for Douglas at the Great American Music Hall, San Francisco, with Booker T. Jones, Hal Blaine and Don Randi at month's end.)
Dec Having joined Aerosmith onstage during a Great Western Forum, Inglewood, CA concert during the

summer, Cooder's latest film soundtrack work, ***Geronimo***, is released by Columbia Records.

1994

Mar [1] Cooder and Indian mohan vina musician Vishwa Mohan Bhatt win the Best World Music Album category for ***A Meeting By The River*** (released the previous year, also featuring his 14-year old son Joachim) at the 36th annual Grammy Awards held at New York's Radio City Music Hall.
Apr [9] Following the release of his most recent soundtrack ***Trespass***, the critically revered ***Talking Timbuktu***, which sees Cooder teamed with West African guitarist Ali Farka Toure, debuts at its UK #44 peak (and will also spend a record-setting 25 weeks atop the US World Music survey).

1995

Mar [1] ***Talking Timbuktu*** wins the Best World Music Album category (his second consecutive award) at the 37th annual Grammy Awards at the Shrine Auditorium.

SAM COOKE

1951

Cooke (b. Samuel Cook, Jan. 22, 1931, Clarksdale, MS), one of Reverend Charles S. Cook's eight children, having performed in the local Christ of Holiness Church with two of his sisters and a brother as the Singing Children at age nine, and, moved to adult gospel-singing with R.B. Robertson's Highway QCs and the Pilgrim Travelers, has become the lead tenor with star gospel group the Soul Stirrers in 1950 (joining them in Pine Bluff, AR), replacing Robert "R. H." Harris. As Cooke quickly develops a distinctive vocal style within the innovative gospel unit, they begin recording for the Specialty label (for whom Cooke has already worked as a member of the Pilgrim Travelers in 1948).

1956

Specialty Records' A&R producer Robert "Bumps" Blackwell, sensing pop potential in Cooke's voice, records several non-gospel tracks with him and releases *Lovable*, a reworking of the Soul Stirrers' *Wonderful* with Cooke thinly disguised as "Dale Cooke" so as not offend his gospel fans. The pseudonym is seen through, however, and Art Rupe, safeguarding his label's large stake in the gospel market, refuses to release any more pop records by Cooke.

1957

June Two weeks after Cooke has confirmed a solo deal with Specialty, Rupe assigns his contract and his latest session, comprising eight songs, to Blackwell, in exchange for back royalties. Blackwell and Cooke sign with Bob Keene's Keen Records, where the gospel-styled but purely secular ballads *(I Love You) For Sentimental Reasons* and *Lonely Island* are Cooke's first two releases.
Dec [1] Cooke appears on CBS-TV's "The Ed Sullivan Show" (Buddy Holly & the Crickets also debut), singing *You Send Me*.
[2] *You Send Me*, credited to his brother Charles (Cooke is still signed to Speciality as a writer), tops the US chart for the first of two weeks, eventually selling 1.7 million copies. (Like much of his work during this period, the song is arranged by Rene Hall, who has been Billy Ward & the Dominoes' bandleader for years.)

1958

Jan [17] *You Send Me*, issued in the UK by London Records, charts for a week at #29.
Feb [10] *I'll Come Running Back To You*, a 1956 Speciality pop number, now reaches US #18. *(I Love You) For Sentimental Reasons*, released by Keen in 1957, also makes US #17.
Mar [31] *You Were Made For Me*, released immediately prior to *You Send Me*, makes US #39, while his debut album, ***Sam Cooke***, reaches US #16.
Apr [5] Irving Feld's "Greatest Show Of Stars" begins a 80-day tour in Norfolk, VA, with Cooke headlining, alongside the Everly Brothers, Clyde McPhatter and a host of rock and R&B names.
[14] *Lonely Island*, the flip side of *You Were Made For Me*, reaches US #26.
Sept [15] *Win Your Love For Me* reaches US #22.
Nov [10] Cooke and Lou Rawls, a member of his tour backing group, the Pilgrim Travelers Quartet, suffer minor injuries in a car crash in Marion, AR, in which Cooke's driver, Edward Cunningham, is killed.
Dec [28] *Love You Most Of All* reaches US #26.

1959

Apr [20] *Everybody Likes To Cha Cha Cha*, released to cash in on a novelty dance craze, makes US #31.
July [13] *Only Sixteen*, written by "Barbara Campbell" (a collective pseudonym for Cooke and friends Lou Adler and Herb Alpert, and Cooke's wife's maiden name), reaches US #28.
Aug *Only Sixteen* reaches UK #23 (on the HMV label), but Craig Douglas' cover version tops the UK chart for four weeks.
Nov [9] RCA Records, aware that Cooke's contract with Keen is close to expiry, offers him a $100,000 guarantee.
[23] *There, I've Said It Again* makes US #81. Cooke and his manager, J.W. Alexander (ex-Pilgrim Travelers), who have recently questioned Keen's royalty accounting, form Kags publishing company.

1960

Jan [22] Cooke signs to RCA (through his new manager, Jess Rand), which acquires his Keen back catalog and pairs him with producers Hugo Peretti and Luigi Creatore.
Mar [14] Cooke's first West Indies tour opens in Montego Bay, Jamaica. He is a sellout sensation in the Caribbean. (This visit and two subsequent concert trips are significant because Cooke's style will have a major influence on a generation of Jamaican artists-to-be, including Bob Marley and Jimmy Cliff.)
Apr [4] RCA debut, *Teenage Sonata*, makes US #50.
June [27] Belatedly issued on Keen, *Wonderful World* (a perennial favorite for later cover versions by Herman's Hermits, Art Garfunkel and others) climbs to US #12.
July Self-penned *Wonderful World* reaches UK #27.
Oct [3] Gospel-styled *Chain Gang* hits US #2 and UK #9 and is his second US million-seller.
Dec [19] *Sad Mood* reaches US #29.

1961

Jan Cooke launches his own SAR record label, one of the early artist-owned labels, with J. W. Alexander and his latest manager, Roy Crain, using their initials to form the name. (It will find chart success later in the year with the Simms Twins' *Soothe Me* and between 1962 and 1964 with several singles by the Valentinos, which comprises the Womack brothers.)
Mar [27] *That's It, I Quit, I'm Movin' On* makes US #31.
July [24] Self-written (like the great majority of his hits) *Cupid* reaches US #17. (It will bring US and UK chart success later to Johnny Nash, the (Detroit) Spinners and Tony Orlando & Dawn.)
Sept *Cupid* hits UK #7.
Oct [23] *Feel It* peaks at US #56.

1962

Mar [24] *Twistin' The Night Away*, an infectious tribute to the worldwide dance craze, hits US #9, eventually selling 1.5 million copies.
Apr *Twistin' The Night Away* hits UK #6.
July [14] Another dance-styled release, *Having A Party*, reaches US #17, as ***Twistin' The Night Away***, Cooke's first US chart album in four years, makes #72.
Aug [25] *Bring It On Home To Me*, a mid-tempo ballad gospel-style duet with Lou Rawls, and the other side of *Party*, reaches US #13.
Oct [8] Cooke embarks on his first UK tour, with Little Richard. On his return, he will tour the US with Jackie Wilson.
Nov [17] *Nothing Can Change This Love* reaches US #12.
[24] Its gospel-phrased B-side, *Somebody Have Mercy*, peaks at US #70.
Dec Compilation, ***The Best Of Sam Cooke***, with most of his biggest successes from *You Send Me* to *Bring It On Home To Me*, reaches US #22 and confirms both his remarkable songwriting and vocal talent and his status a leading R&B star.

1963

Feb [23] His revival of Little Richard's *Send Me Some Loving* makes US #13.
Apr ***Mr Soul*** climbs to US #92.
May [25] *Another Saturday Night*, penned on the road during Cooke's UK tour, hits US #10 and reaches UK #23.
July His youngest son, Vincent, drowns in the family swimming pool.
Sept [7] *Frankie And Johnny*, a smooth R&B version of an old folk song, reaches US #14 and UK #30.
Oct ***Night Beat*** makes US #62.
Dec [14] Cooke's version of Willie Dixon's familiar blues standard, *Little Red Rooster*, recorded in an all-star session with Ray Charles on piano and Billy Preston on organ, reaches US #11.

1964

Feb [15] Cooke announces he is to revise his live concert schedule, cutting his previous eight months on the road to two, to devote more time to developing his record label.
[24] After "whupping" Sonny Liston in their World Heavyweight Championship bout in Miami Beach, FL, Cassius Clay announces, among many other things, that "Sam Cooke is the world's greatest rock'n'roll singer - the greatest singer in the world."
Mar [14] *(Ain't That) Good News* reaches US #11.
Apr Cooke shows his appreciation of Clay's endorsement by duetting with him on US TV.
June ***Ain't That Good News*** reaches US #34. It includes Cooke's protest civil rights composition, *A Change Is Gonna Come*, written after he heard Bob Dylan's *Blowin' In The Wind*.
[24] Cooke begins a two-week engagement at Manhattan's Copacabana club, New York, with a 20' x 100' billboard (dreamed up by his current manager, Allen Klein) in Times Square announcing, "Who's The Biggest Cook In Town?", followed days later by another billboard which says, "Sam's The Biggest Cooke In Town". (He had debuted there in 1958 on a date headlined by Jewish dialect comedian Myron Cohen.)
July [4] *Tennessee Waltz*, the B-side of the still-climbing *Good Times*, makes US #35.
[18] *Good Times* reaches US #11.
Sept [16] Cooke stars in the first edition of ABC-TV's Jack Good-produced pop show, "Shindig", with the Righteous Brothers and the Everly Brothers.
Oct Cooke films a screen test for Norman Jewison.
Nov [7] The boisterous *Cousin Of Mine* makes US #31, while the more soulful B-side, *That's Where It's At*, peaks at US #93. A live album, ***Sam Cooke At The Copa***, recorded earlier in the year at the Copacabana club, reaches US #29 (and will stay charted in the US for over a year).
Dec [11] Cooke is shot dead at the $3-a-night Hacienda Motel at 9137 S. Figueroa, Los Angeles, CA, by its manager Bertha Franklin, after spending the previous night at PJs nightclub and checking in with 22-year-old Elisa Boyer. Franklin claims that Cooke had attempted to rape Boyer, and then tried in anger to assault Franklin herself, when his intended victim fled to phone the police. The coroner's office returns a verdict of justifiable homicide.
[18] Cooke's funeral is held in Chicago, where his body is laid in a glass-topped coffin at the A.R. Leak Funeral Home prior to burial. A reported 200,000 fans file past to pay their respects and, as the sheer numbers get out of hand, the glass doors of the establishment are smashed. The service, attended by

many of his musical contemporaries and friends, becomes chaotic, despite Ray Charles singing *Angels Keep Watching Over Me*. Lou Rawls and Bobby "Blue" Bland also perform at the service.

1965

Feb [27] *Shake*, the first posthumous single release, hits US #7. (Rod Stewart will cover it, as will Otis Redding, often dedicating it to Cooke when singing the track in concert.)
Mar [6] B-side, *A Change Is Gonna Come*, makes US #31, as ***Shake!*** reaches US #44. Further chart action during the year sees the extracted *It's Got The Whole World Shakin'* make US #41 (May [8]), *When A Boy Falls In Love* peak at US #52 (June [26]), ***The Best Of Sam Cooke, Volume 2***, a compilation of his later hits, climb to US #128 in August, *Sugar Dumpling* make US #32 (Sept [4]) and ***Try A Little Love*** peak at US #120 in November.

1966

Feb [26] The reissue of a minor 1961 hit, *Feel It*, makes US #95.
Apr [30] *Let's Go Steady Again*, first released in 1959 as the B-side of *Only Sixteen*, is Cooke's final posthumous US chart entry, spending a week at #97.

1985

July [20] ***Live At The Harlem Square Club***, recorded in Miami, FL, on January 12th, 1963, makes US #134. Regarded as a seminal live recording, it effortlessly captures Cooke's enormous vocal prowess and soul sensibilities.

1986

Jan [23] Cooke is inducted into the Rock and Roll Hall of Fame at the inaugural annual dinner held at the Waldorf Astoria Hotel, New York.
Apr *Wonderful World*, once again familiar from its exposure in the Harrison Ford/Kelly McGillis film "Witness" and reissued after a similar cover version use in a UK TV advertising campaign (for Levi's 501 jeans), hits UK #2. ***The Man And His Music*** makes US #175.
May [10] Follow-up, a UK reissue of *Another Saturday Night*, peaks at #75, as the double compilation, 28-track ***The Man And His Music*** hits UK #8, his only UK chart album.

1987

Mar [7] Cooke is posthumously inducted into the Songwriters Hall of Fame at the 18th annual awards dinner, held at the Hotel Plaza Grand Ballroom, New York. (The Soul Stirrers will also be inducted into the Rock and Roll Hall of Fame at the fourth annual dinner, at the Waldorf Astoria Hotel, New York, on Jan [18], 1989, though NARAS will still have failed to acknowledge either Cooke or any of his songs for the annual Grammy Awards.)

1993

June [15] Cooke is posthumously honored with the Chairman's Award by the Apollo Theatre Foundation in New York.

1995

Mar William Morrow publishes **You Send Me : The Life And Times Of Sam Cooke** written by Daniel Wolff.
June [21] Out of print since its original release 32 years ago, the planned June (US) issue of ***Night Beat*** (produced by Hugo & Luigi) by Allen Klein's ABCKO label has been delayed following a June 8th injunction placed on the release by BMG Music which claims to own the rights. The case is now resolved by US District Court judge Loretta Preska who instructs ABCKO's distributor Polygram to include stickers on the CDs stating: "Originally manufactured in 1963 by Tracy Ltd. for the RCA Records label." ABKCO's license to manufacture and distribute the seminal album expires either on August 31st 1997 or 1999, the exact date to be determined by ongoing litigation.

ALICE COOPER

Alice Cooper (vocals); **Glen Buxton** (guitar); **Michael Bruce** (guitar, keyboards); **Dennis Dunaway** (bass); **Neal Smith** (drums)

1965

Cooper (b. Vincent Furnier, Feb. 4, 1948, Detroit, MI), the son of a preacher, and raised in Phoenix, AZ, forms the Earwigs with schoolmates at Cortez High, playing mainly Rolling Stones and Who covers. Name-changing to the Spiders the following year, with Buxton (b. Nov. 10, 1947, Akron, OH), Bruce (b. Mar. 16, 1948), Dunaway (b. Dec. 9, 1948, Cottage Grove, OR), Smith (b. Sept. 23, 1947, Akron, OH), and Cooper on vocals, they have a #1 in Phoenix with *Don't Blow Your Mind*, released on the local Santa Cruz label. Making periodic visits to play in Los Angeles, CA, they permanently relocate to Hollywood in 1968 and begin playing as the Nazz. Discovering that another Nazz exists on the East Coast, with Todd Rundgren a member, they name-change for a final time to Alice Cooper, a moniker which is soon applied to Furnier himself as well as the band. (Legend has it that the name came from a spirit called up at a ouija board session.) The group's first break is in linking with Frank Zappa and his manager, Shep Gordon, recently graduated from University of Buffalo, who has seen them at the Cheetah club in Los Angeles. Zappa and Gordon sign the combo to their Straight label, savior of many an unorthodox artist of the time.

1969

July ***Pretties For You*** captures the sound of a musically-unremarkable garage band, but is a minor US hit, at #193.
Sept [13] The group takes part in the "Toronto Rock'n'Roll Festival" at the Varsity Stadium, University of Toronto, Toronto, ON, Canada, with Bo Diddley, Chicago Transit Authority, Jerry Lee Lewis, Chuck Berry, Gene Vincent, Little Richard, Fats Domino and the Plastic Ono Band.

1970

May ***Easy Action*** differs little from their first album and with a reputation as one of the worst bands in Los Angeles, they eventually pack up and move to Detroit.
June The band makes a group cameo appearance in the movie "Diary Of A Mad Housewife", starring Richard Benjamin.

1971

July Newly signed to Warner Bros. Records, and under the guidance of producer Bob Ezrin, ***Love It To Death*** is released.
Apr [24] The extracted *Eighteen* climbs to US #21, while its parent album follows and peaks at #35. The group's stage sets are now becoming more elaborate and expensive, to match the theatrical nature of the performance, led in dramatic fashion by Cooper. As he begins to incorporate bizarre live props (including an electric chair, a guillotine and large snakes) into their stage performance, Cooper also develops a popular demonic visual appearance, not least through the liberal use of black make-up.

1972

Jan ***Killer*** consolidates their success as a top box-office draw by reaching US #21.
[29] The extracted *Under My Wheels* skids to US #59.
Feb ***Killer*** is the group's UK chart debut, at #27.
Apr [22] *Be My Lover* makes US #49.
July [29] Written by Cooper and Bruce, *School's Out* hits US #7.
Aug [12] *School's Out* tops the UK chart for the first of three weeks, cementing the group's international success and becoming a global rock teen anthem. Its parent album, ***School's Out***, hits US #2 (becoming Warner Bros.' biggest-selling record in their history) and UK #4.
Sept ***Love It To Death***, reissued in the UK, reaches #28.
Nov [6] ***Love It To Death*** is certified gold by the RIAA.
[10] The group plays a one-off UK date at Glasgow's Greens Playhouse.
[11] *Elected* peaks at US #26 and will hit UK #4.

1973

Mar *Hello, Hurray* makes US #35 and hits UK #6.
[24] ***Billion Dollar Babies***, with contributions from Marc Bolan, Donovan and Harry Nilsson, sees the group at its peak of popularity, entering the UK chart at #1 and displaying its nadir of gleeful bad taste with songs like *I Love The Dead*. The highly-theatrical live show based around the album is massively successful, and equally gory.
Apr [21] ***Billion Dollar Babies*** tops the US chart.
June [2] *No More Mr. Nice Guy* reaches US #25 and hits UK #10.
Sept [1] Extracted title cut, *Billion Dollar Babies*, peaks at US #57.
Dec [7] ***Muscle Of Love*** is certified gold by the RIAA.

1974

Jan [19] ***Muscle Of Love*** reaches UK #34 and will hit US #10.
[26] Featured single, *Teenage Lament '74*, makes US #48.
Feb [16] *Teenage Lament '74* reaches UK #12. Following this, Cooper fires his original band and brings in Dick Wagner and Steve Hunter (guitars), Prakash John (bass), Penti Glan (drums) and Joseph Chrowski (keyboards). The first two have played anonymously on previous Cooper album sessions, while all have performed with Lou Reed.
June [2] 13-year-old teenager in Calgary, AB, Canada, hangs himself accidentally at a hanging party inspired by Alice Cooper's mock scaffold scene depicted in a TV show.
Oct Compilation album, ***Alice Cooper's Greatest Hits***, hits US #8.

1975

Mar [22] ***Welcome To My Nightmare***, produced by Ezrin and featuring actor Vincent Price, reaches UK #19 and will hit US #5. The accompanying stage show is more full of props and gore than ever, and is documented on film. Cooper makes a guest appearance on ***Flash Fearless Vs. The Zorg Women Pts. 5 And 6***, a comic concept album.
May [30] ***Welcome To My Nightmare*** is certified gold by the RIAA.
June [21] Uncharacteristically-melodic *Only Women Bleed* ballad, co-written with Wagner and taken from ***Nightmare***, reaches US #12, and will later be covered by other artists (including Julie Covington, who will hit UK #12 with her version, in 1979).
[23] In Vancouver, BC, Canada, with his "Welcome To My Nightmare" tour, Cooper falls from the stage and breaks six ribs.
Oct Cooper raises $200,000 for charity in 30 cities during his Halloween charity drive.
Nov [22] *Welcome To My Nightmare* makes US #45.

1976

Aug [14] ***Alice Cooper Goes To Hell*** reaches UK #23, and will peak at US #27 on Dec [18].
Sept [18] Cooper co-hosts "Don Kirshner Rock Awards" with Diana Ross, and sings *I Never Cry*.
Nov [23] ***Alice Cooper Goes To Hell*** is certified gold by the RIAA.

1977

Jan [8] *I Never Cry* reaches US #12.
Mar Cooper becomes the owner of the Maltese Falcon statuette featured in the classic movie.
Apr [5] The RIAA confirms a million sales of *I Never Cry*.
May He is put under house arrest in Sydney, Australia, after a concert for 40,000 fans, under investigation for the commercial failure of his 1975 Australian tour.

[28] *(No More) Love At Your Convenience* is Cooper's first UK hit single in over three years, peaking at #44, as its parent album, ***Lace And Whiskey*** debuts at its UK #33 high.
June [5] Cooper's boa constrictor, long a co-star of his live act, suffers a mortal bite from the rat it is being fed for breakfast. The distraught artist holds a public audition for a new performing boa, and a snake named Angel gets the gig.
July [2] ***Lace And Whiskey*** makes US #42.
Aug [13] *You And Me*, from the album, hits US #9.

1978

Jan [14] Live set, ***The Alice Cooper Show***, the first to feature Cooper's new band (with Fred Mandel replacing Joseph Chrowski on keyboards) on record, makes US #131, but Cooper is in a psychiatric hospital, receiving treatment for chronic alcoholism. He will, however, be featured in a cameo role in the movie "Sergeant Pepper's Lonely Hearts Club Band".
Dec [23] *How Are You Gonna See Me Now?*, dedicated by Cooper to his wife, reaches US #12 and UK #61. Its parent album ***From The Inside***, based on his hospital experience, with relevant album packaging, and produced by David Foster with lyrics by Bernie Taupin, makes UK #68.

1979

Jan [27] ***From The Inside*** makes US #60, though Cooper is yet to regain full health.
July [27] Cooper's Indian art store in Scottsdale, AZ, is mysteriously fire-bombed, resulting in the destruction of $200,000-worth of stock, including some of his own gold discs.

1980

May [24] ***Flush The Fashion***, produced by Roy Thomas Baker, makes UK #56.
July [5] *Clones (We're All)* makes US #40, as its parent album, ***Flush The Fashion***, climbs to US #44, while Cooper makes an appearance in the movie "Roadie", starring Meat Loaf.

1981

Sept [13] ***Special Forces***, produced by Richard Podolor, makes UK #96 and will peak at US #125.

1982

Feb Cooper begins a UK tour, initially supported by Big Country, at the Brighton Centre, Brighton, E. Sussex.
Mar [13] His live cover of Love's *Seven And Seven Is* makes UK #62.
May [8] UK-only double A-side, *For Britain Only/Under My Wheels*, peaks at #66.
Sept ***Zipper Catches The Skin***, co-produced with Erik Scott, fails to chart (possibly because the title makes potential buyers squirm).

1983

Nov [12] ***Dada***, his final recording for Warner Bros., makes UK #93.

1986

June [26] Reviving *School's Out*, Swiss band Krokus makes US #67.
Oct [13] The RIAA certifies platinum sales for ***Alice Cooper's Greatest Hits***, ***Billion Dollar Babies*** and ***Killer***.
[18] After a time in the musical wilderness, a link-up with the movie "Friday The 13th Part 6" provides *He's Back (The Man In The Mask)*, which makes UK #61 and prompts a new contract, with MCA Records.
[28] Cooper begins "The Nightmare Returns" tour in Lansing, MI.
Nov [1] ***Constrictor*** charts briefly in both the US and UK, reaching #59 and #41 respectively, as the hard rock musical climate revives, with many new glam-shock metal groups citing Cooper as a major influence.

1987

Aug Currently featured in a cameo role in John Carpenter's movie, "Prince Of Darkness", Cooper performs at the annual "Reading Festival", Reading, Berks.
Nov [7] ***Raise Your Fist And Yell*** climbs to UK #48, but stalls at US #73.

1988

Apr Cooper's new controversial live show, highlighted by a particularly sensitive moment when he slashes open the belly of a female dummy and pulls out a baby, is taken to Europe. *Freedom* makes UK #50 during the UK leg.
[7] Cooper accidentally hangs himself in a rehearsal. His safety rope snaps and he dangles for several seconds before a roadie saves him.

1989

Aug [26] Newly signed to Epic Records, *Poison* hits UK #2, behind Jive Bunny & the Mastermixers *Swing The Mood*, as its parent album, the Desmond Child-produced ***Trash***, featuring Jon Bon Jovi, Richie Sambora, Kip Winger and all Aerosmith members except Brad Whitford, hits UK #2.
Oct [21] *Bed Of Nails* reaches UK #38.
Nov [25] *Poison* hits US #7 (his first US chart single in nine years), as the parent album, ***Trash***, reaches US #20.
Dec [2] *House Of Fire* peaks at UK #65.
[4] *Poison* is certified gold by the RIAA.

1990

Feb [5] ***Trash*** is confirmed platinum by the RIAA.
[17] *House Of Fire* makes US #56.
Mar [18-21] Cooper plays sellout shows in his hometown, Detroit, at the Fox Theatre, with his new touring band, Al Pitrelli (guitar), Pete Friezzin (guitar), Tommy "T-Bone" Caradonna (bass), Derick Sherinian (keyboards), Jonathan Mover (drums) and Devon Meade (backing vocals), during a major North American "Trash" tour.
May [5] *Only My Heart Talkin'* makes US #89.
Sept [19] The RIAA belatedly certifies platinum sales for ***School's Out***.

1991

July [6] *Hey Stoopid* reaches UK #21.
[13] ***Hey Stoopid***, featuring Slash, Ozzy Osbourne and Joe Satriani, debuts at its UK #4 peak.
[20] ***Hey Stoopid*** makes US #47.
Aug [3] *Hey Stoopid* reaches US #78.
[25] Cooper is inducted into the Hollywood Rock Walk of Fame.
Sept [13] He sells copies of ***Hey Stoopid*** for 99 cents in New York's Times Square. This is just one unusual location he uses for his 12-city "The Nightmare On Your Street Tour", playing surprise gigs - the first being at a Los Angeles radio-station parking lot. Others include a Miami park, a Los Angeles parking lot and the roof of a St. Louis record store.
[27] An 11-date British tour opens at Belfast's Avoneil, N. Ireland, set to end on October 10th at the National Exhibition Centre, Birmingham, W. Midlands.
Oct [5] *Love's A Loaded Gun* debuts at its UK #38 peak.
Nov [22] Cooper comes to the rescue of Patrick and Dee Ann Kelly of Riverside, CA, whose home is being foreclosed on the 24th. Patrick Kelly had daubed Cooper's face on a psychedelic painting on the house to help sell it. Cooper signs autographs to raise money as 4,000 people turn up for Kelly's yard sale. The event helps the Kellys make their mortgage payments. (During the year Cooper also appears as Freddy Krueger's father in the sixth and final "Nightmare On Elm Street" movie, titled "Freddy's Dead : The Final Nightmare".)

1992

Jan [18] Cooper guests on ITV's "Aspel & Co".
June [6] *Feed My Frankenstein*, featured on the "Wayne's World" soundtrack, reaches UK #27. Cooper also makes a cameo appearance in the movie, greeted by characters Wayne and Garth with the notion "We are not worthy".

1994

May [20] Cooper guests on C4-TV's "The Big Breakfast", during a week-long UK promotional tour.
[28] *Lost In America* debuts at its UK #22 peak.
June [18] ***The Last Temptation Of Alice Cooper***, tied in with a three-part comic book series to be published by **Marvel**, hits UK #6 in its week of entry.
July [23] *It's Me* debuts at its UK #34 peak.
[30] ***The Last Temptation Of Alice Cooper*** bows at its US #68 peak.
Dec [8] A keen golfer, Cooper scores a hole in one at a golf competition at the Arizona Biltmore Country Club, AZ.

1996

Mar [26] Warner Bros. releases ***Songs In The Key Of X***, music from and inspired by Fox-TV's "The X-Files", which includes a duet by Cooper with White Zombie's Rob Zombie.

JULIAN COPE

1984

Mar Having imploded the successful Liverpool, Merseyside band Teardrop Explodes, which he formed, on its fourth anniversary in November 1982, Cope (b. Oct. 21, 1957, Bargoed, Wales), who was raised in Tamworth, Staffs., musically inspired by '60s psychedelic groups including the 13th Floor Elevators, the Standells, Blues Magoos and the Outcasts and vocalist Scott Walker, has been offered a solo deal to remain with Mercury Records, which has already issued his UK #64 debut single, *Sunshine Playroom*, in November 1983, taken from the now-released freshman effort, ***World Shut Your Mouth***, which peaks at UK #40.
Apr [21] The extracted *The Greatness And Perfection Of Love* makes UK #52.
Sept Cope releases the one-off *Competition* on the independent Bam Caruso label, under the pseudonym Rabbi Joseph Grodan.
Nov [24] ***Fried*** makes UK #87 for one week (and includes the single *Sunspots*), while Cope retreats, allegedly with a drug problem. (His third solo effort, ***Skellingtons***, will be rejected by Mercury, which subsequently releases the artist from his contract.)

1986

Oct [25] Newly signed to Island Records, *World Shut Your Mouth* (a re-recorded version of the title cut to his Mercury debut) climbs to UK #19, spurred by an appearance on BBC1-TV's "Top Of The Pops".

1987

Jan [23] His current UK tour is highlighted by an appearance at the Westminster Central Halls, London.
Feb [7] Previewing his Island album debut, *Trampolene* jumps to UK #31.
Mar Mini-album, ***Julian Cope***, opens his US chart account at #109.
[14] The Warne Livesey-produced, self-written ***Saint Julian*** (the title referring to a tobacco brand, with allusions to his own cult status) reaches UK #11 and will make US #105.
Apr [4] *World Shut Your Mouth* peaks at US #84.
[18] *Eve's Volcano (Covered In Sin)* makes UK #41.
June [19-21] Cope participates in the annual "Glastonbury Festival", Glastonbury, Somerset.

1988

Mar Bill Drummond (of KLF), who originally managed and produced the Teardrop Explodes, issues the album ***The Man***, which includes the sardonic tale, *Julian Cope Is Dead*.
Oct [9] Cope embarks on a three-week UK tour to promote ***My Nation Underground***, which reaches UK #42 (Oct [29]) (and will climb to US #155 the following January).
[15]*Charlotte Anne* makes UK #35.

1989

Feb [4] His revival of the Vogues' *5 O'Clock World*

stops at UK #42.
June [24] *China Doll* peaks at UK #53.

1990

Sept Unable to interest Island in its release, Cope releases ***Skellington*** on his own Copeco label. By year's end, he will make an appearance dressed as a space alien at an anti-Poll Tax rally in London.

1991

Feb [23] His solo career resumes with *Beautiful Love*, which, spurred by a dolphin-playing video clip, makes UK #32.
Mar [16] Eco-themed ***Peggy Suicide***, a 73-minute, 19-track project, debuts at its UK #23 peak.
Apr [20] *East Easy Rider* brakes at UK #51.
May [22-23] His current UK tour is highlighted by a pair of dates at London's Brixton Academy.
Aug [3] *Head* debuts at its UK #57 peak.
Sept Cope's first volume of autobiography, **Head On**, assessing the period 1977-82, is published.

1992

Jan [21] Cope guests on C4-TV's "Return To The Dome".
Mar He works on new tracks with producer Donald Ross Skinner at the Fallout Shelter studio.
July [3] He begins a seven-date tour in the Scottish Highlands at Findhorn Foundation Universal Hall, set to end on the 21st at Aberdeen's Lemon Tree.
Aug [8] Reissued *World Shut Your Mouth* debuts at its UK #44 peak.
[15] ***Floored Genius***, a retrospective collection of Cope and Teardrop Explodes highlights from 1979-91, bows at its UK #22 peak.
Oct Cope and Pretenders cohort James Eller work on tracks for Cope's new backing band, Transmission, at Monnow Valley Studios, Wales, with Johnny Marr producing.
[24] EP *Fear Loves This Place* makes UK #42.
[26] A University of Bradford Union gig kicks off ten-date "The Head-On Tour", set to end November 6th at London's Town & Country club. (Several concerts are cancelled due to illness, with Cope honoring those dates in January 1993.)
[31] Having recently passed his driving test, ***Jehovah Kill***, a 16-song set lyrically centered around the ecologically-damaging effects of the motor car, promoted by Cope with UK music press ads railing against the evils of the modern world, debuts at its UK #20 peak, but is shortly followed by a decision by Island to drop him from its roster.

1993

Jan [16] A ten-date UK tour opens at Portsmouth Guildhall (replacing some of the previously postponed gigs), set to close on the 27th at the Town & Country club.
Feb Promoting the US release of ***Jehovah Kills***, and as outspoken as ever, Cope makes the following observations in **Details** magazine: On Madonna: "She is corporate womanhood." On U2: "The only thing that keeps me from killing Bono is the fact that I would go to jail, and it would martyr him. What U2 are doing is evil. U2 are sick fucks."
June Having signed a US-only deal with Def American Records, Cope releases ***Skellington 2***, another fan-club mail order-only set, recorded in 36 hours in April, before embarking on a short UK tour in July.
July [16] Cope takes part in the "Phoenix Festival" at Long Marston, Stratford-upon-Avon, Warks.

1994

July [16] ***Autogeddon***, including the typically-controversial track *Don't Call Me Mark Chapman*, reaches UK #16 in its week of entry.

1995

Jan [29] Cope plays a one-off gig at the Bristol Bierkeller, an acoustic benefit for **The Big Issue** magazine for the homeless.
Aug [12] *Try Try Try* debuts at its UK #24 peak.
Sept [9] ***Julian Cope Presents 20 Mothers***, released on his own Echo label through MCA, bows at its UK #20 peak.

1996

Feb [11] Cope plays a sole gig, supporting Ozric Tentacles, at London's Shepherd's Bush Empire.
see also: TEARDROP EXPLODES

ELVIS COSTELLO & THE ATTRACTIONS

Elvis Costello (vocals, guitars); **Steve Nieve** (keyboards); **Bruce Thomas** (bass); **Pete Thomas** (drums)

1975

Living in Liverpool, Merseyside with his mother (who moved the family there from London in 1968) who has separated from his father, bandleader Ross McManus, Costello (b. Declan Patrick McManus, Aug. 25, 1954, London) has begun writing songs and taken up the guitar at age 15, leaving school the following year and subsequently becoming a computer operator at an Elizabeth Arden cosmetics factory in London in 1973. Inspired by seeing future collaborator Nick Lowe perform at the Cavern, Costello (still called McManus and already married with a son) forms his own band, Flip City, in London, and moonlights on the local club scene, honing his songwriting skills (and will also spend time as a roadie for Brinsley Schwarz, whose bass player is Lowe).

1976

Costello sends Flip City demos, recorded at Pathway Studios, to record companies. One reaches Jake Riviera's newly-formed pioneering Stiff Records and, seeing potential in the patchy demo (which will emerge on the bootleg album ***5,000,000 Costello Fans Can't Be Wrong***), the label head contacts him. With Stiff interested in signing Costello as a solo artist, Flip City disbands as he begins gigging as D.P. Costello (his grandmother's maiden name).

1977

With six of his demos already played on Charlie Gillett's Capital Radio show, "Honky Tonk", McManus, at Riviera's suggestion, renames himself Elvis Costello. While a backing band is assembled, US West Coast group Clover, currently in the UK, is brought in to provide the rhythm section on his debut effort (going by the name Shamrock), under the production guidance of Lowe.
Apr His first single, *Less Than Zero*, written about Fascist leader Oswald Mosley, is released on Stiff.
May Ballad, *Alison*, with a line from its chorus will provide the title for Costello's first album, is released.
[27] He makes his live debut as Elvis Costello at the Nashville in London.
July [9] He quits his day job at Elizabeth Arden.
[14] Costello and his backing band, the Attractions, play their first gig together, as a support act to the still-male Wayne County at the Garden, Penzance, Cornwall. The line-up is bassist Thomas (b. Aug. 9, 1954, Sheffield, Yorks.), ex-Sutherland Brothers & Quiver, keyboardist Nieve (b. Steven Nason), from the Royal College of Music, and drummer Thomas (ex-Chilli Willi & the Red Hot Peppers).
[26] Seeking a US record deal, Costello performs outside the London Hilton Hotel, where there is a CBS sales conference in progress. He is arrested and subsequently fined £5 for obstruction, although it is thought the incident is nothing more than an imaginative Stiff PR ruse.
Aug [20] The self-penned ***My Aim Is True***, produced by Nick Lowe, reaches UK #14, featuring the current single *Red Shoes*. Its quirky new-wave rock-driven style is highlighted by Costello's highly-articulate and literate lyrical bite.
Sept [10] Costello plays at the Crystal Palace Bowl, London, on a bill headed by Santana.
Oct [3] "Stiffs Live" label package tour of the UK, with Costello, Lowe, Ian Dury, Wreckless Eric and Larry Wallis begins.
Nov [5] At the end of the tour, Riviera takes Costello, Lowe and the Yachts with him to the newly-formed Radar Records, leaving Stiff to Dave Robinson.
[15] Costello begins his first US tour at the Old Waldorf, San Francisco, CA, set to end on December 16th in New York, NY.
Dec [17] Deputizing for the Sex Pistols on NBC-TV's "Saturday Night Live", Costello stops in the middle of performing *Less Than Zero* and says, "I'm sorry ladies and gentlemen, there's no reason to do this song", and launches into *Radio Radio*, which he had previously been told not to sing.
[24] Reggae-phrased *Watching The Detectives*, Costello's last recording for Stiff and his first Singles chart entry, reaches UK #15.

1978

Jan Costello returns for a three-month tour of North America, with Mink DeVille and Rockpile, ending with two sellouts at the El Mocambo Club, recorded for a subsequent live album.
Mar [18] ***My Aim Is True*** reaches US #32, after 36 weeks on the survey. Unlike the UK edition, it includes *Watching The Detectives* and is licensed for release to CBS/Columbia for North America.
Apr [1] Self-written and again produced by Lowe, ***This Year's Model***, issued with the Attractions, hits UK #4, as a 14-date UK tour opens at the Bracknell Sports Centre, set to end on the 16th at London's Roundhouse. (Bruce Thomas cuts his hand in the dressing room of Manchester's Rafters club, after demonstrating how to smash a bottle during a bar-room brawl. Nick Lowe fills in for some dates.)
[15] *(I Don't Want To Go To) Chelsea* reaches UK #16.
May [20] ***This Year's Model*** makes US #30, again with a different track listing to the UK version.
June [17] *Pump It Up* reaches UK #24.
Oct [26] Costello & the Attractions appear on BBC1-TV's "Top Of The Pops".
Nov [4] *Radio Radio*, a lament about the state of the nation's airwaves, reaches UK #29.
Dec Costello plays seven sold-out nights at London's Dominion Theatre. He leaves his wife and young son. (They will be reunited a year later.)

1979

Jan [20] ***Armed Forces***, its sleeve designed by Barney Bubbles, hits UK #2.
Feb [15] A Taste Of Honey beats out Costello, among other nominees, to win Best New Artist at the 21st annual Grammy awards.
[23] ***Armed Forces*** is certified gold by the RIAA.
Mar [10] *Oliver's Army* hits UK #2, as its parent album, ***Armed Forces***, hits US #10.
Apr [1] During his "Armed Funk" US tour Costello plays three sets at three clubs - the Great Gildersleeves, the Lone Star Cafe and the Bottom Line, in one night in New York. In a much-publicized subsequent incident in a bar at the Holiday Inn in Columbus, OH, Costello has an argument with Stephen Stills and Bonnie Bramlett, who is so angered by his allegedly racist remarks about Ray Charles and James Brown that she starts punching him, which is explained by Costello as "bringing a silly argument to a quick end ... and it worked, too."
June [16] *Accidents Will Happen* reaches UK #28, its promo clip directed by Annabel Jankel and Rocky Morton. He produces the first Specials album, while Riviera sets up his new label, F-Beat, following the collapse of Radar.
Dec [22] Costello performs at the first of four benefit concerts for the people of Kampuchea, at London's Hammersmith Odeon.

1980

Feb [23] F-Beat is launched with ***Get Happy!***, produced by Lowe, hitting UK #2 in its week of entry behind the compilation ***The Last Dance***. The 21-track quick-fire set (released as a single album), with five cuts coming in at under two minutes, was recorded in Holland.

Mar [8] *I Can't Stand Up For Falling Down*, Costello's cover of an old Sam & Dave song, hits UK #4.

Apr [12] ***Get Happy!*** reaches US #11. (Linda Ronstadt, who has already recorded *Alison* on her 1978 album, ***Living In The USA***, covers three Costello tunes (*Party Girl*, *Girls Talk* and *Talking In The Dark*) on ***Mad Love***.)

[26] *Hi Fidelity* reaches UK #30.

June [14] *New Amsterdam* makes UK #36.

Aug [17] Costello performs at the Playhouse Theatre during the "Edinburgh Rock Festival".

[23] He takes part in the "Heatwave Festival", Mosport Park, Toronto, ON, Canada.

Nov ***Taking Liberties***, a US-only compilation of out-takes, demos and unreleased UK 45s, reaches US #28. (It features *Hoover Factory*, written by Costello to help save the historic Hoover vacuum cleaner-manufacturing site, located on the A40 motorway outside London.) A similar album is released in the UK, with different track-listings in cassette-form only, as ***Ten Bloody Mary's And Ten How's Your Fathers***.

[30] Elvis Costello and Squeeze play a joint benefit concert at the Top Rank club in Swansea, S. Wales, for the family of boxer Johnny Owen, who has died from injuries received during a title bout in the US.

Dec [20] *Clubland* peaks at UK #60.

1981

Jan [31] ***Trust***, produced by Lowe and featuring Glenn Tilbrook from Squeeze, debuts at its UK #9 peak.

Feb ***Trust*** reaches US #28, as Costello tours the US, with Squeeze as his opening act.

May [18-29] Costello & the Attractions record a country album with veteran producer Billy Sherrill, at CBS Studios in Nashville, TN.

June [20] Squeeze's Costello-produced ***East Side Story*** makes UK #19.

Sept [4] The RIAA certifies gold sales of his debut ***My Aim Is True***.

Nov [7] Country outing, ***Almost Blue***, helmed by Sherrill, hits UK #7. The extracted *A Good Year For The Roses* (originally recorded by George Jones, with whom he has recorded *Stranger In The House* on a current Jones album) hits UK #6 and will make US #50.

[8] ITV's "South Bank Show" airs a documentary on Elvis Costello, focusing on the ***Almost Blue*** sessions.

Dec [31] Costello performs at the Palladium, New York, during a US tour to promote ***Almost Blue***, during which he appears at Nashville's legendary Grand Ole Opry.

1982

Jan Costello & the Attractions play at London's Royal Albert Hall with the Royal Philharmonic Orchestra.

[16] His cover of Patsy Cline's *Sweet Dreams*, from ***Almost Blue***, makes UK #42.

Apr [10] *I'm Your Toy*, recorded live with the RPO, peaks at UK #51.

June [26] *You Little Fool* makes UK #52.

July [10] ***Imperial Bedroom***, produced by Geoff Emerick and returning to Costello's bitter-sweet self-penned rock style, debuts at UK #6.

Aug [7] The extracted single, *Man Out Of Time*, peaks at UK #58.

Sept [25] ***Imperial Bedroom*** reaches US #30.

Oct [2] *From Head To Toe* makes UK #43.

Dec *Party Party*, from the teenage film soundtrack album ***Party Party***, makes UK #48.

1983

May While a change of distribution is negotiated for F-Beat, Costello releases a single as The Imposter, creating his own Imp label.

June [18] *Pills And Soap* makes UK #16.

Aug [6] *Everyday I Write The Book* reaches UK #28. ***Punch The Clock***, with backing vocals from Afrodiziak and co-produced by Clive Langer and Alan Winstanley, hits UK #3 and reaches US #24. (The sleeve features Costello with a half-smile, which he later describes as a "welcoming" look.)

Sept [17] *Let Them All Talk* peaks at UK #59.

Oct [22] *Everyday I Write The Book* reaches US #36.

1984

May [5] Another Imposter single, *Peace In Our Time* (the only one released on the Imposter label), makes UK #48.

June [30] *I Wanna Be Loved/Turning The Town Red*, promoted by a Godley & Creme-lensed video, reaches UK #25.

July ***Goodbye Cruel World***, once again helmed by Langer & Winstanley, hits UK #10 and makes US #35.

Aug [25] *The Only Flame In Town*, featuring co-vocalist Daryl Hall, makes UK #71 and US #56. Increasingly independent from his backing band, Costello spends the rest of the year touring mainly college venues in the US with singer-songwriter T-Bone Burnette, while also maintaining a live itinerary with the Attractions.

1985

Apr TV-advertised, Telstar-released ***The Best Of Elvis Costello - The Man*** hits UK #8.

May [18] Early cut (from ***Armed Forces***), *Green Shirt*, peaks at UK #68.

July Costello and Burnette issue *The People's Limousine* as the Coward Brothers, Costello's only new release of the year.

[13] Costello performs at the Wembley Stadium, Wembley, Middx. portion of the "Live Aid" fundraiser.

Dec ***The Best Of Elvis Costello & The Attractions*** makes US #116. (During the year Costello appears in Alan Bleasdale's ITV drama "Scully", for which he has written the theme, *Turning The Town Red*. and also produces ***Rum, Sodomy And The Lash***, the second album by Anglo-Irish band the Pogues.)

1986

Feb [8] Costello's remake of the Animals 1965 UK #3, *Don't Let Me Be Misunderstood*, credited to the Costello Show with backing by a group of US musicians, billed as the Confederates, makes UK #33.

May ***The King Of America***, for which Costello reverts to his given name, reaches UK #11 and US #39. Produced by T-Bone Burnette, it covers a wide musical vista, reflecting Costello's interests in Tex-Mex, country, cajun and Irish music. The players are drawn from Hall & Oates, Tom Waits, Los Lobos and the James Burton/Jerry Scheff/Ron Tutt axis which backed Elvis Presley in the late '60s. The Attractions play on only one track. (Nieve and Thomas are soon to be recruited for the house band on C4-TV's "The Last Resort".)

[16] He marries the Pogues' bassist, Caitlin O'Riordan, in Dublin, Eire.

Aug Costello makes his acting debut as a bungling magician in the film "No Surrender".

[30] *Tokyo Storm Warning*, released on the Imp label, peaks at UK #73.

Oct ***Blood & Chocolate***, a reunion with Nick Lowe (with help from Colin Fairley), reaches UK #16 and US #84. Once again fully backed by the Attractions, Costello is listed under the name Napoleon Dynamite.

1987

June [19-21] Costello participates in the annual "Glastonbury Festival", Glastonbury, Somerset.

Nov With Demon Records (of which he is a director) having recently issued his latest collection of rarities and out-takes as ***Out Of Our Idiot***, Costello signs a worldwide recording deal with Warner Bros. Records. He insists on a clause which states that Warners may not release his product in South Africa while apartheid remains. Paul McCartney elicits Costello's help to write *Back On My Feet*, the B-side of McCartney's *Once Upon A Long Ago*. This will lead to further McCartney/Costello collaborations for respective solo albums, an experience which McCartney will later compare to working with John Lennon.

1988

Aug He finishes work on a new album in Los Angeles, CA, after a month's recording in Dublin. He also records in New Orleans with the Dirty Dozen Brass Band and co-writes two tracks with Ruben Blades on the latter's first English-language album, ***Nothing But The Truth***. By year's end, and still using his real name, he also scores the film soundtrack to "The Courier".

1989

Feb [18] Warner Bros. debut, ***Spike***, co-produced by Costello, Burnette and Kevin Killen, and featuring musical guests Jim Keltner, McCartney, Roger McGuinn and Christy Moore, hits UK #5.

Mar [18] *Veronica*, written with McCartney, makes UK #31.

May [14] Costello plays the first of four concerts titled "A Month Of Sundays" at the London Palladium, in the midst of a UK tour.

[20] EP *Baby Plays Around* peaks at UK #65.

June [24] *Veronica* reaches US #19, as ***Spike*** makes US #32 (while McCartney's ***Flowers In The Dirt***, partly co-written and performed with Costello, is also released).

July Costello embarks on a major US tour, with a band comprising Jerry Scheff, Pete Thomas, Larry Knechtel, Marc Ribot, Michael Blair and Steven Soles. On the West Coast leg of the trip, he will jam with Jerry Garcia and James Burton at the Sweetwater club in San Francisco, CA, at a concert to celebrate the 21st anniversary of the Village Music record store in Mill Valley.

Sept [6] Costello wins the Best Male Video category for "Veronica" at the sixth annual MTV Video Music Awards, held at the Universal Amphitheatre, Universal City, CA.

Oct [28] ***Girls Girls Girls***, a comprehensive retrospective compilation released on Demon, charts for a week at UK #67, as Costello performs at the "Montreux Jazz Festival", Montreux, Switzerland, with Squeeze's Chris Difford and Glen Tilbrook.

1990

Mar [8] Costello is named Best Songwriter in **Rolling Stone**'s 1989 Critics Awards.

Oct [26] He takes part in the fourth annual Bridge School benefit, at the Shoreline Amphitheatre, Mountain View, CA, with Neil Young, Jackson Browne, Steve Miller and Edie Brickell.

1991

May Costello releases ***Mighty Like A Rose,*** featuring drummer Keltner, former sideman James Burton on guitar, keyboardist Larry Knechtel, bassist Rob Wasserman and the ever-present Lowe. It includes *How To Be Dumb*, a thinly-veiled reply to former Attraction Bruce Thomas, who fell out with his bandleader in 1987 and published a book **The Big Wheel** in 1990, about how dreadful he felt life on the road was with the group. The differences between Thomas and Costello made an Attractions reunion for ***Mighty Like A Rose*** impossible. Costello also includes two songs co-penned with McCartney from their earlier liaison, *So Like Candy* and *Playboy To A Man*.

[11] *The Other Side Of Summer* makes UK #43.

[18] Costello guests on "Saturday Night Live".

[25] ***Mighty Like A Rose*** debuts at its UK #5 peak, as a US tour begins at the County Bowl, Santa Barbara, CA. (He also guests on support act Sam Phillips' current album, ***Cruel Inventions***.)

June [8] ***Mighty Like A Rose*** makes US #55.

[22] Costello performs at New York's Madison Square Garden.

July [1-3, 5-7] He appears at London's Hammersmith Odeon during a current UK tour.

[27] Costello is featured on BBC2-TV's "Bringing It All Back Home".

Aug [3] He takes part in the "Feile '91 Festival" at the Semple Stadium, Thurles, Co. Tipperary, Eire.

Sept [5] ***My Aim Is True*** becomes Costello's first RIAA platinum-certified album.

Nov [24] "120 Minutes", with Costello, airs on MTV Europe. (During the year, he has also scored the music for a ten-hour TV drama series "GBH", contributed *Ship Of Fools* to the Grateful Dead tribute covers album, ***Deadicated*** (US #24), and recorded a track for a forthcoming Bob Wasserman album **Trios**.)

1992

Jan [4] The Chieftains' ***The Bells Of Dublin***, to which Costello contributes *St. Stephen's Murders*, makes US#107.
Feb [29] "Elvis Costello - Come In And Hear It", the first of a four-part documentary, airs on Radio 1.
Mar [7] Soundtrack album to the Wim Wenders film, "Until The End Of The World", to which Costello has contributed a cover of the Kinks' *Days*, makes US #114.

1993

Feb [20] Always creatively restless, Costello has teamed with an eclectic music ensemble, the Brodsky Quartet, to release ***The Juliet Letters***, an album based on the true story of a Verona professor who answers letters addressed to Juliet Capulet. Costello states: "This is no more my stab at 'classical music' than it is the Brodsky Quartet's first rock 'n' roll album. It does, however, employ the music which we believe touches whichever part of the being that you care to mention." The album peaks at US #125, having already made UK #18 on Jan [30].
[22] Costello and the Brodsky Quartet perform ***The Juliet Letters*** at London's Theatre Royal, Drury Lane (and will play four similar US dates in the spring).
Mar [20] Wendy James' solo debut, ***Now Ain't The Time For Your Tears***, entirely written (over one weekend) by Costello, makes UK #43, while he continues negotiations to re-license his own back catalogue and works on his next solo album (working title ***Idiophone***).
Apr [8] Costello guests on C4-TV's "Harry Enfield's Guide To Opera".
Oct [19] Rykodisc releases a four-CD/cassette boxed set of three albums plus a live album as part of a new deal, licensing his back-catalog in the US.

1994

Mar [5] *Sulky Girl* debuts at its UK #22 peak.
[19] Marking a return both to his trademark late '70s sound and a reunion with Lowe and the Attractions, ***Brutal Youth*** debuts at its US #34 peak, as ***The Best Of Elvis Costello - The Man*** collection (now re-issued by Demon) makes UK #50.
Apr [1] Costello guests on CBS-TV's "Late Show With David Letterman", performing on TV with the Attractions for the first time in eight years.
[30] *13 Steps Lead Down* charts for a week at UK #59.
May [25] He plays at the Mud Island Amphitheatre, Memphis, TN, during his current US tour.
June [1] Costello duets with Tony Bennett on *They Can't Take That Away From Me* on the latter's MTV "Unplugged" show.
Aug [23] Van Morrison tribute album ***No Prima Donna***, to which Costello contributes *Full Force Gale*, is released, while his treatment of *Sally Sue Brown* appears on the Arthur Alexander tribute album (US) ***Adios Amigos***.
Sept Costello splits from Jake Riviera after a 17-year relationship. He will set up his own By Eleven company.
Oct [4] Rykodisc releases ***The Very Best Of Elvis Costello And The Attractions***, a 22-track compilation personally selected by Costello.
Nov [12] Released in the UK by Demon, ***The Very Best Of Elvis Costello And The Attractions*** makes UK #57.
[26] EP *London's Brilliant Parade* debuts at its UK #48 peak.

1995

Feb [11] He appears on BBC2-TV's "Later With Jools Holland".
Mar [26] Costello embarks on a 13-date UK tour at the Brighton Centre, Brighton, E. Sussex.
Apr ***18 Original Hits By 18 Unoriginal Artists***, to which Costello has contributed his version of Jerome Kern's *They Didn't Believe Me*, is released by Polygram (UK).
May [16] He guests on "Late Show With David Letterman" from London, singing *Bama Lama Bama Loo* with Little Richard and Chuck Berry.
[17] A showcase performance of his new album ***Kojak Variety*** held at London's Shepherd's Bush Empire is broadcast live via satellite to US alternative radio.
[23] Costello wins the Outstanding Contemporary Song Collection category at the 40th annual Ivor Novello Awards held at London's Grosvenor House.
[27] ***Kojak Variety***, a solo collection of cover versions begun by Costello five years ago including his interpretations of Bob Dylan's *I Threw It All Away*, Little Richard's *Bama Lama Bama Loo*, Ray Davies' *Days*, Randy Newman's *I've Been Wrong Before* and Jesse Winchester's *Payday* among others, bows at its UK #21 and US #102 peaks.
June [23 - **July** [1] He performs with Bill Frisell during the "Southbank Meltdown Festival", an event for which he is also artistic director, at London's Royal Festival Hall. (Their set will be recorded for subsequent release as ***Deep Dead Blue - Live At Meltdown***.)
Aug [2] Together with the Attractions, Costello begins a five-night stint at New York's Beacon Theatre. His sets include songs written for others including *Complicated Shadows* and *You Bow Down*, and *God Give Me Strength*, written with Burt Bacharach via fax and phone, as part of material being written for the Martin Scorsese-lensed movie "Grace Of The Heart" about the legendary Brill Building.
[12] Reissued ***King Of America*** makes UK #71.

1996

Mar [26] Warner Bros. releases ***Songs In The Key Of X***, music from and inspired by Fox-TV's "The X-Files", which includes a collaborative cut by Costello and Brian Eno. (Meanwhile, Costello is in Nashville recording with the Fairfield Four.)
May Co-produced by Costello and Geoff Emerick and backed by the Attractions, ***All This Useless Beauty*** is released by Warner Bros.

COUNTING CROWS

Adam Duritz (lead vocals, piano); **David Bryson** (rhythm guitar); **Dan Vickrey** (lead guitar); **Charlie Gillingham** (keyboards); **Matt Malley** (bass); **Steve Bowman** (drums)

1993

Jan [12] Influenced by the music of Van Morrison and the Band among others, college drop-out Duritz (b. Aug. 1, 1964, Baltimore, MD), the son of two Jewish physicians, who has indulged in non-prescription drugs, and Bryson (b. Nov. 5, 1961, San Francisco, CA) have been playing together since early 1990 as a folk/roots duo in the San Francisco Bay area, and have initially formed Sordid Humor, recording one album, 1991's ***Light Music For Dying People*** (which will remain unreleased until its issue in 1994 by Capricorn Records (US).) The pair has subsequently recruited Malley (b. July 4, 1963), Gillingham (b. Jan. 12, 1960, Torrance, CA) and Bowman (Jan. 14, 1967), playing northern California club dates as Counting Crows and recording a demo of Duritz compositions (some of which will appear on its debut album), and which grabs the attention of Geffen Records imprint DGC which signs the group. Filling in for no-show Van Morrison, who is being inducted into the Rock and Roll of Fame at the eighth annual induction dinner held at New York's Waldorf Astoria, the band is introduced tonight by an enthusiastic Robbie Robertson and performs its first big-time engagement.
Nov [27] Having completed its debut album under the direction of T-Bone Burnette, first cut, *Mr. Jones* enters the US Modern Rock Tracks chart set to hit #2. (During the year, the band undertakes US tours with Midnight Oil, the Cranberries and Suede.)

1994

Jan [1] Mostly recorded in a Los Angeles, CA mansion, Counting Crows' debut album, ***August & Everything After***, largely written by Duritz and Bryson, and including a guest appearance by Maria McKee, enters the US chart.
[15] With its line-up now augmented by Vickrey (b. Aug. 26, Walnut Creek, CA), the group is the music guest on NBC-TV's "Saturday Night Live".
[21] Touring with Cracker, the band performs at Lupo's Heartbreak Hotel, Providence, RI, on a bill grossing $7,500 from 1,500 attendees.
Mar [12] ***August & Everything After*** debuts at its UK #16 peak.
[15-16] The group completes two nights at the Whisky, Los Angeles, CA, in front of 1,000 fans before playing another pair of dates at the city's Roxy Club on the 17-18th.
[31] The band appears on CBS-TV's "Late Show With David Letterman".
Apr [16] ***August & Everything After*** finally hits US #4.
[30] *Mr. Jones* bows at its UK #28 peak.
June [11] With Ben Mize (b. Feb. 2, 1971) having replaced Bowman, the group participates in the "KROQ Weenie Roast" at Irvine Meadows Amphitheatre, Irvine, CA, an event grossing $323,750.
July [9] *Round Here*, including the band's live cover of the Psychedelic Furs' *Ghost In You* as an extra CD-single cut, charts for a week at UK #70.
Aug [1], [3] Following its own headlining US tour, and now opening for the Rolling Stones, Counting Crows performs at the Robert F. Kennedy Memorial Stadium, Washington, DC, on a pair of dates which gross a house record $3,990,966 from 108,960 fans.
Sept [8] "Mr. Jones" wins the Best New Artist Video category at the 11th annual MTV Video Music Awards held at New York, NY's Radio City Music Hall.
[25, **Oct** 3-4] The group performs three dates at the Greek Theatre, Los Angeles in front of a crowd of 16,577. (During the intervening week, Duritz is advised by doctors not to sing for seven days after soft nodules are found on his throat.)
[22] *Rain King* makes UK #49.
Nov [15-16] A nine-date UK tour, begun on the 6th at Glasgow Barrowlands, Glasgow, Scotland, climaxes with a pair of dates at London's Shepherd's Bush Empire.

1995

Jan [30] Counting Crows wins the Favorite Artist/ Alternative Music category at the 22nd annual American Music Awards, held at Los Angeles' Shrine Auditorium.
Feb [11] "Later With Jools Holland", featuring an appearance by the band, airs on BBC2-TV.
July [18] Capitol Records (US) releases the film soundtrack to "Clueless" which includes a new recording by the band.

1996

Jan [25] Confirming its status as one of the most successful debut rock albums of all time in the US, the RIAA certifies six million sales of ***August & Everything After***.

COUNTRY JOE & THE FISH

Country Joe McDonald (guitar, vocals); **Bruce Barthol** (bass); **Barry Melton** (guitar, vocals); **David Cohen** (keyboards); **Gary "Chicken" Hirsch** (drums)

1965

Dec After four years' US navy service, McDonald (b. Joseph McDonald, Jan. 1, 1942, El Monte, CA) and Melton (b. 1947, Brooklyn, NY) attend university at Berkeley, CA, in 1964. They become involved in the local folk music scene, forming the Instant Action Jug Band, with McDonald beginning to write the politically-conscious lyrics that will distinguish much of his work. After almost a year as an acoustic band, they decide to go electric and form Country Joe & the Fish, with a line-up comprising McDonald and Melton, with Cohen (b. 1942, Brooklyn) , Barthol (b. 1947, Berkeley) (guitar), John F. Gunning (drums) and Paul Armstrong (bass). The band initially fails to secure a recording deal, but cuts two limited-edition EPs for the **Rag Baby** folk magazine.

1966

Oct [21-22] The group performs at San Francisco, CA's Avalon Ballroom.
Nov Ed Denson, the editor of **Rag Baby** and the band's manager, arranges a recording deal with specialist folk label Vanguard. Gunning and Armstrong have left, Barthol has switched to bass and Hirsch has joined on drums.
[11-13] The band appears at San Francisco's Fillmore Auditorium.
Dec [30-31] They close the year making a return appearance at the Avalon Ballroom, with Moby Grape.

1967

Apr [14-16] Country Joe & the Fish share a bill with Howlin' Wolf at the Fillmore Auditorium.
June [17] The band performs on the second day of the "Monterey Pop International Festival" at the County Fairgrounds, Monterey, CA.
Aug [5] *Not So Sweet Martha Lorraine*, from the group's debut album, makes US #95.
[8-9] The group takes part in the "Hawaiian Pop Rock Festival" at Waikiki Shell, Waikiki, HI.
Sept [23] Their debut album, ***Electric Music For The Mind & Body***, regarded as a definitive psychedelic album, despite a lack of airplay, climbs to US #39.
Dec [28-31] The band performs at the Avalon Ballroom, San Francisco.

1968

Feb [3] ***I Feel Like I'm Fixin' To Die*** peaks at US #67, its title track, a light but barbed Vietnam war commentary, becoming a popular live anthem. (The band plays London's Roundhouse during its first European tour.)
May [16-18] The group performs at Fillmore West.
Aug McDonald pulls the group out of Jerry Rubin's hippie "Festival Of Love", which coincides with the Chicago Democratic Convention.
[24] ***Together*** makes US #23.
Sept Barthol leaves to avoid the draft and is replaced by Mark Ryan.
Oct [4] Country Joe & the Fish embark on an eight-week US tour at the California Western University, San Diego, CA, set to end on November 29th at Queen's College, New York, NY.
Dec [28] The band performs before 100,000 people at the "Miami Pop Festival" in Hallandale, FL.

1969

Jan [9-11] The group plays at the Fillmore West, San Francisco, on a bill with Led Zeppelin. (Shortly thereafter Ryan, Hirsch and Cohen quit the line-up.)
Feb McDonald recruits Mark Kapner (keyboards) and, from Big Brother & the Holding Company, Peter Albin (bass) and David Getz (drums). They begin recording and McDonald invites in a surprising array of session players, including members of Count Basie's band and the Oakland Symphony Orchestra.
Apr The new line-up undertakes a European tour.
July ***Here We Are Again*** is released, but the line-up which recorded it has already broken up, with Albin and Getz re-forming Big Brother & the Holding Company.
Aug [16] McDonald brings in Doug Metzner (bass) and Greg Dewey (drums) to perform at the "Woodstock Music and Art Fair", Bethel, NY.
[31-**Sept** 1] The group takes part in the "New Orleans Pop Festival", New Orleans, LA.
Sept [22] The band appears at the Royal Albert Hall, London, at the start of a European tour.
Dec McDonald releases the solo ***Thinking Of Woody***, a tribute to folk singer Woody Guthrie.

1970

Mar Their sophomore solo effort, ***Tonight I'm Singing Just For You***, is issued.
[18] McDonald is convicted of obscenity and fined $500 for leading an audience in Worcester, MA, in his notoriously popular "gimme an F..." fish cheer.
May ***C. J. Fish***, recorded by the band, peaks at US #111.
[28-31] The group performs once again at the Fillmore West, San Francisco, with Blues Image.
June McDonald disbands the group and continues his solo career.

1971

Apr ***Hold On, It's Coming***, recorded in London with a collection of English musicians, including Spencer Davis, is released. McDonald joins Jane Fonda and Donald Sutherland's "Free The Army" anti-war revue and tours US army bases, but quits after a public row with Fonda.
June [27] The re-assembled group performs at the closing night at the Fillmore East, with the Beach Boys, the Allman Brothers Band, the J. Geils Band, Mountain and Edgar Winter.
Aug ***War War War***, based on Robert W. Service's World War I book of poetry, **Rhymes Of A Red Cross Man**, played, sung and produced by McDonald, reaches US #185.
Nov Double band compilation, ***The Life & Times Of Country Joe & The Fish From Haight-Ashbury To Woodstock*** peaks at US #197.

1972

Feb Live solo ***Incredible! Live! Country Joe!*** reaches US #179.
May [7] McDonald, still a major concert draw, has assembled Country Joe & His All-Star Band, a large (and fluid) group for club and touring work, not least a performance at the rain-soaked "Bickershaw Festival", near Wigan, Lancs. The following September, he will issue the ***Country Joe LP Paris Sessions***, and in 1974, after the the All-Star Band splits following financial collapse. (McDonald will form a duo with his old friend Melton. Based mostly in Paris, they will clock up around 150,000 miles on tour.)

1975

Apr Solo album ***Country Joe*** is released. He returns to Berkeley and joins Energy Crisis, a band formed by Phil Marsh and Bruce Barthol.
June Energy Crisis is now being called Country Joe & His Band and even Country Joe & the Fish. The group tours heavily, as far afield as Australia and Japan.
Nov McDonald, now a solo artist with Fantasy Records, has his last US chart entry, with ***Paradise With An Ocean View***, which makes US #124.

1976

Jan [10] *Breakfast For Two* makes US #92.
Apr Heavily involved in the Save The Whale campaign, McDonald records his own song, *Save The Whales*, a hit single in several countries.
June The original group line-up for the first three albums re-forms for the "Cardiff Castle Festival" in Wales, while Fantasy Records issues a group album, ***Reunion***.
Aug Solo album ***Love Is A Fire*** is released.
Dec McDonald leaves the original Fish, which soon breaks up.

1977

Apr Spending much of the year touring solo, McDonald performs during a three-day rally in Tokyo, Japan, with Jackson Browne, Richie Havens and others, to raise $150,000 for an international effort to save whales and dolphins from industrialized fishing.

1978

May ***Rock'n'Roll Music For The Planet Earth*** is released.
Aug McDonald reunites again with Melton for European gigs, including the third annual "Winterthur MusikFestival", in Switzerland.
Sept McDonald returns to California to join the Barry Melton Band, which has been playing Melton's songs and old Fish material, and the group evolves into yet another Country Joe & the Fish, mainly touring around California and Texas.

1982

May McDonald appears in a benefit concert at the Moscone Center in San Francisco, CA, with the Grateful Dead, Boz Scaggs and Jefferson Starship, in aid of the Vietnam Veterans' Project. He will continue to pop up at miscellaneous events throughout the decade, for example taking part in the 13th annual "Maine Arts Festival", at Deering Oaks Park, Portland, ME in August 1989.

1995

Nov [11] While McDonald has made a 1991 recording return on the Rykodisc label, with ***Superstitious Giants*** (featuring Jerry Garcia) and appeared at an alternative (and free) version of "Woodstock II" on the original site in Bethel, NY on August 13th 1994, Melton, who has performed in the early '90s in the Dinosaurs, a group of Bay Area psychedelic veterans, having failed in his June 3rd 1992 attempt to capture judgeship in California primary elections, has become successfully installed as a Public Defender in Mendocino Country, CA since January 25th 1994. McDonald, in a controversial move, now unveils a memorial to Berkeley's 22 Vietnam War dead in the city's Veterans Memorial Building.

COWBOY JUNKIES

Margo Timmins (vocals); **Michael Timmins** (guitar); **Alan Anton** (bass); **Peter Timmins** (drums)

1979

Toronto, ON, Canada-based Michael Timmins (b. Apr. 21, 1959, Montreal, PQ, Canada) forms Hunger Project with Anton (b. Alan Alizojvodic, June 22, 1959, Montreal), playing music mainly influenced by the Velvet Underground and Siouxsie & the Banshees. They audition for a female vocalist and one of Timmins' three sisters, Margo (b. June 27, 1961, Montreal), offers but is rejected. Subsequently relocating to New York and eventually to London in search of underground sympathy, they regroup as Germinal in 1983, playing improvisational and experimental material. The band fails to impress, however, and Timmins ends up working at the Record & Tape Exchange in Notting Hill, London.

1985

Having returned to Canada, Timmins and Anton are now based at 547 Crawford Street, and put together the Cowboy Junkies with Timmins' younger brother Peter (b. Oct. 29, 1965, Montreal) on drums, older brother John, who soon leaves the line-up, on guitar, and sister Margo, who passes the second audition. They write and perform in a sparse, quiet and natural style and, after three months of Canadian club gigging, decide to record their debut album with the help of engineer friend Peter Moore.

1986

Recorded on one Caltrec Ambiosonic microphone in six hours, the nine-track ***Whites Off Earth Now!!***, is released on Cowboy Junkies' own Latent label and sells 3,000 copies regionally.

1987

Nov [27] Focusing more on a mellow country blues mix, and splashing out $162, Cowboy Junkies record their second album, ***The Trinity Session***, in one day at the Church of the Holy Trinity, Toronto. Dominated by Margo and Michael Timmins' compositions, it is again released initially on Latent, but will ultimately make a reasonable financial return, accumulating over one million worldwide sales.

1988

Aug As the band begins an 18-month solid touring schedule, taking in the US, Europe and Japan, ***The Trinity Session*** attracts considerable record company interest and the group signs to RCA.

Dec In the US, RCA reissues the album, while an understated, slow cover version of Lou Reed's *Sweet Jane*, hits US #5 on **Billboard**'s Modern chart. Reed is quoted as saying that the single is "the best and most authentic version I've heard".

1989

Jan [28] ***The Trinity Session*** enters the US chart, set to reach US #26 during a 29-week residence. Its sales are boosted mainly through the heavy rotation on MTV of the "Sweet Jane" Junkies video clip.

Mar During UK dates, the group performs at the Corn Exchange, Cambridge, Cambs., while ***The Trinity Session***, which UK independent label Cooking Vinyl has licensed prior to the RCA deal, achieves UK #1 Independent Album chart success.

Apr Back in Northern Ontario, Canada, the band records ***Sharon In Quaker Meetinghouse***, which remains unreleased.

Dec They record ***The Caution Horses*** sessions at Eastern Sound, Toronto.

1990

Mar [24] Their third album, recorded by candlelight over three arduous days, ***The Caution Horses***, released worldwide by RCA, debuts at its UK #33 peak. Co-produced by Moore and Michael Timmins, it once again features mainly Michael Timmins compositions, while taking a greater retro country roots direction than its predecessors.

Apr [21] ***The Caution Horses*** peaks at US #47. Clearly an albums-oriented act, extracted singles will merely remain hot alternative and college airplay hits.

[27] They perform on NBC-TV's "Late Night With David Letterman" singing *'Cause Cheap Is How I Feel*.

May [1] Following a five-month tour lay-off, the Cowboy Junkies begin another lengthy North American sojourn in New Haven, CT, set to climax with three dates in their hometown, Toronto, from July 5th-7th.

June [19] The group guests on NBC-TV's "The Tonight Show".

Sept On a major US tour supporting Bruce Hornsby, they have to cancel several gigs, after Margo Timmins contracts pneumonia.

1991

Jan In preparation for their next Toronto recording sessions Margo takes voice control classes as part of a possible move to sing louder.

Feb RCA reissues ***Whites Off Earth Now!!***

May [18] ***Deadicated***, a collection of Grateful Dead covers, including the Cowboy Junkies' *To Lay Me Down*, reaches US #24.

1992

Jan [29] They guest on BBC2-TV's "Rapido".

Feb [11] The group appears on "Late Night With David Letterman".

[15] Their fourth album, ***Black Eyed Man***, featuring two songs by Townes Van Zandt and a duet with John Prine on *If You Were The Woman And I Was The Man*, debuts at its UK #21 peak.

[29] They open a British tour at Belfast's Mandela Hall, N. Ireland, set to end on March 6th at London's Royal Albert Hall, as ***Black Eyed Man*** debuts at its US #76 peak.

Mar [23] The group plays the first of a handful of Canadian dates, at the Grand Theatre, Kingston, ON, Canada.

[31] They open a US tour, co-headlining with John Prine, in Northampton, MA, set to end on May 19th at the Silva Hall, Hult Center for the Performing Arts, Eugene, OR.

1993

Dec [14] The group takes part in the "WEQX Holiday Concert For The Hungry" at Saratoga Winners, Latham, NY, with Paul Weller, Teenage Fanclub, Nick Heyward and Catherine Wheel.

1994

Jan [31] Cowboy Junkies return to "The Tonight Show".

Feb [19] The band's final album for RCA, ***Pale Sun, Crescent Moon***, including the band's treatment of Dinosaur Jr.'s *The Post*, peaks at US #114 (and will sell 263,000 copies in the US).

[22] The group begins a series of North American dates at Toad's Place, New Haven, CT.

June [24] They play a hometown gig before a sellout crowd at the Bathurst Street Theatre, Toronto.

1996

Mar [4] After a period in which Michael Timmins has scored two Canadian films ("House" and "The Boy's Club") and the band has signed to Geffen Records, the group, previewing its forthcoming album, guests on CBS-TV's "Late Show With David Letterman".

Apr [27] Their label debut on Geffen, ***Lay It Down***, recorded at producer John Keane's Athens, GA home studio, makes US #55.

THE COWSILLS

Bill Cowsill (guitar, vocals); **Bob Cowsill** (guitar, vocals); **Barbara Cowsill** (vocals); **Sue Cowsill** (vocals); **Paul Cowsill** (keyboards, vocals); **Barry Cowsill** (bass, vocals); **John Cowsill** (drums)

1965

Bill (b. Jan. 9, 1948, Newport, RI) and Bob Cowsill (b. Aug. 26, 1949, Newport) form a duo, using a guitar brought home by their father, chief petty officer William "Bud" Cowsill, on leave from the navy. With brothers Barry (b. Sept. 14, 1954, Newport) on bass and John (b. Mar. 2, 1956, Newport) on drums, they begin playing local frat parties near their Newport home as the Cowsills. Following his retirement after 20 years in the US navy, Bud Cowsill begins managing the family band, incorporating seven-year-old Susan (b. May 20, 1960, Newport) as a singer and brother Paul (b. Nov. 11, 1952, Newport) on keyboards. Under their father's disciplined management, the group becomes a slick club-entertainment unit and, at talent agents' suggestion, their mother Barbara (b. 1928, Newport) is drafted as a further vocalist. Remaining brother Richard (b. Aug. 26, 1950, Newport) becomes the Cowsills' road manager and sound engineer. Playing regularly at a local club and releasing *All I Really Wanta Be Is Me* and *And The Next Day Too* for Johnny Nash's Joda label, they are seen by a producer of the NBC-TV "Today" morning program and are booked to appear on the show.

1967

Dec While struggling financially with investment, equipment and transport debts, Bud Cowsill has met writer/producer Artie Kornfeld the previous year, who, impressed with the group's stage act, has helped them move to New York. With Kornfeld's further assistance, the Cowsills have been signed to Leonard Stogel's management company and to MGM Records, which releases the family's debut single, *The Rain The Park And Other Things*. Co-written and produced by Kornfeld, it hits US #2 and becomes a million seller. MGM sends the family on a 22-city US West Coast tour at a cost of $250,000, to promote both the hit and ***The Cowsills***, which climbs to US #31.

[28] A major showcase concert at New York's Town Hall is highly rated: the group is billed as "America's First Family Of Music" (and becomes the inspiration for TV's "The Partridge Family").

1968

Feb *We Can Fly* reaches US #21.

Mar [30] ***We Can Fly*** reaches US #89.

Apr *In Need Of A Friend* peaks at US #54.

July *Indian Lake* hits US #10.

Oct *Poor Baby*, taken from the album, reaches US #44.

[12] ***Captain Sad And His Ship Of Fools*** peaks at US #105.

Dec Now relocated to Santa Monica, CA, where they are offered their own TV series, based on their lives (they reject it, however, when it is suggested that Shirley Jones play their mother), the Cowsills appear on NBC-TV in their own special. Susan dedicates *What The World Needs Now Is Love* to brother Richard, currently serving with the armed forces in Vietnam.

1969

Feb [22] Compilation ***The Best Of The Cowsills***, makes US #127.

Mar The American Dairy Association launches a promotion, offering three unreleased Cowsills tracks, *All My Days*, *Nothing To Do* and *The Fun Song*, for 69 cents.

May The group's version of the title song from the rock musical "Hair" hits US #2 and is a second million seller.

[31] Live ***The Cowsills In Concert***, which includes *Hair*, makes US #16.

1971

May [8] With Bill now pursuing a solo career (he was fired by his father for smoking marijuana), the group leaves MGM and signs to London Records for ***On My Side***, which makes US #200 (with no extracted hit singles).

1972

The group disbands after an unsuccessful tour of US bases in Europe, as the family declares bankruptcy. Several of the band will battle drugs, alcohol and depression, before turning the corner and pursuing further education or alternative careers.

1985

Jan [21] Barbara Cowsill dies of emphysema, aged 56, in Tempe, AZ, estranged from her children. (Father Bud will die in a plane crash in 1992.)

1994

July While Bob, Susan (who teamed briefly with ex-Bangle Vicki Peterson in the Psycho Sisters in the early '90s) and Paul have reunited to play occasional US nostalgia dates (including an unannounced set on a Smithereens bill at the Roxy, West Hollywood, for a Pediatrics AIDS Foundation benefit on December 17th 1991), their first CD collection, ***The Cowsills***, is released by Razor Tie Records in the US. (Susan now lives in New Orleans, LA with Peter Holsapple, playing with the Continental Drifters, Bill plays in Blue Shadows in Vancouver, BC, Bob is a computer trainer in Los Angeles, John plays drums for Jan & Dean and lives in California and Barry reportedly lives in New Orleans, having moved there from Monterey, CA.)

THE CRANBERRIES

Dolores O'Riordan (vocals); **Noel Hogan** (guitar); **Mike Hogan** (bass); **Feargal Lawler** (drums)

1989

The band, its members inspired by the music of the Smiths, is formed in Limerick, Eire as Cranberry Saw Us by brothers Noel Hogan (Dec. 25, 1971, Moycross, Limerick), who is currently on the dole, and Mike Hogan (Apr. 29, 1973, Moycross), an apprentice on the Youth Training Scheme (the siblings are descendants from 19th century Irish poet Michael Hogan) who recruit Lawler (Mar. 4, 1971, Parteen, Limerick), currently working as a hairdresser, and Niall Quinn as its lead singer. A year later, Quinn quits the lineup, but recommends a school friend of his girlfriend's sister, 18-year old O'Riordan (b. Dolores Mary Eileen O'Riordan, Sept. 6, 1971, Ballybricken, Limerick), as a possible replacement. Learning of an opening in the group, O'Riordan successfully passes the audition and completes the permanent quartet which makes its live debut as the Cranberries performing six songs in front of 60 people on a Saturday night at Ruby's, a club in the basement of a Limerick Hotel. O'Riordan, the youngest of seven daughters by Terence and Eileen O'Riordan (an older sister accidentally burned down the family home during their childhood), who has been singing in pubs, church choirs and at the annual Slogadh music festivals since the age of five and wrote her first song (*Calling*) at age 12, begins adding lyrics to Noel Hogan's instrumental demos, a songwriting arrangement which will underpin the band's future material. During further gigs around Limerick, Dublin and Cork, local producer Pearse Gilmore becomes the band's manager/producer, recording a three-track demo at his own Xeric Studio, 300 copies of which are released as *Nothing Left At All* to local record stores in 1990. This same demo also begins circulating around the UK record industry, not least through the efforts of the John Best PR agency which arranges for a large number of A&R scouts to attend a gig at the O'Henry's club in Cork, Eire.

1991

June While the band undertakes a UK tour opening for Moose (for whom O'Riordan will guest on its 1992 album ***XYZ***) and following hot rival label bidding, Island Records signs the band (initially via a licensing arrangement with Gilmore's Xeric label) to a six-album deal. (A further UK club tour will follow shortly, opening for Top.)

Oct The Cranberries' debut EP *Uncertain* is released by Island on the Xeric label containing the title track plus *Nothing Left At All*, *Pathetic Senses* and *Them*.

1992

Jan The Cranberries begin recording their first album at the Xeric Studio with Gilmore, but the members' relationship with their producer/manager turns sour and the session is shelved. Subsequently firing Gilmore (litigation between the two parties will only be resolved in 1995), the group will enlist the services of Rough Trade label founder Geoff Travis, and embark on new recording sessions under the wing of producer Stephen Street at the Windmill Studios, Dublin, Eire.

Oct The band's *Dreams* is released in the UK, becoming **Melody Maker**'s Single Of The Week.

1993

Feb [27] Orchestrated, melancholic and acoustic guitar-driven follow-up, *Linger* charts for a week at UK #74 while the band opens for Belly on a UK tour.

Mar [13] Debut album ***Everybody Else Is Doing It, So Why Can't We?***, with ten of its 12 Celtic-tinted cuts co-penned by O'Riordan and Noel Hogan, initially spends a week at UK #64, as the group supports Hothouse Flowers on European dates.

June The Cranberries embark on a six-week US jaunt in Colorado, opening for The The.

Nov [12] The band performs at the Draft House, Cleveland, OH, on a bill which grosses $7,500 from a 750-strong audience. (It is currently opening for Suede, though at some dates, burgeoning interest in the Cranberries will result in reverse billing.)

[20] ***Everybody Else Is Doing It, So Why Can't We?*** reaches US #18.

1994

Jan [14] Following further US dates opening for Duran Duran, the band performs at London's Astoria 2 Theatre.

[26] *Linger*, still climbing the US chart, its video being heavily rotated on MTV, is certified gold by the RIAA.

Feb [12] *Linger* finally hits US #8.

[19] Reissued *Linger* reaches UK #14.

May [14] Reissued *Dreams* makes UK #27 and US #42.

June [11] The Cranberries, fronted by a now blonde-haired O'Riordan, perform on BBC2-TV's "Later With Jools Holland".

[25] 16 months after its release, ***Everybody Else Is Doing It, So Why Can't We?*** tops the UK chart.

July [5] The group appears on ITV's "The Beat".

[18] O'Riordan marries the band's tour manager Don Burton at the Holy Cross Abbey, County Tipperary, Eire.

[30-**Aug** 1] It performs at the "Feile Festival", Thurles, Tipperary, Eire.

[13] During US tour dates, the band is a popular draw at the "Woodstock II" festival, held at the Winston Farm, Saugerties, NY (its performance of *Dreams* will subsequently appear on the event's album).

Oct [1] A&M-released Carpenters tribute album, ***If I Were A Carpenter***, to which the group contributes *Close To You*, bows at its US #70 peak.

[3] An 11-date UK tour opens at the Manchester Academy, Manchester, Gtr. Manchester, set to close on the 16th and 17th at London's Shepherd's Bush Empire. (Previously scheduled for earlier in the year, the tour has been postponed after O'Riordan badly damaged her knee in a skiing accident which requires metal pins to be inserted in her leg.)

[8] *Zombie* reaches UK #14.

[15] The group's sophomore set ***No Need To Argue***, again produced by Street, debuts at its UK #2 peak behind R.E.M.'s ***Monster*** (the Cranberries are scheduled to perform European dates with R.E.M. the following summer).

Nov [10] A further US tour bows at the State Theatre, Detroit, MI, a gig grossing $55,521 from 3,000 fans, set to close with the second of two consecutive nights at New York's Beacon Theatre on December 17th.

[11] The Cranberries appear on CBS-TV's "Late Show with David Letterman".

Dec [10] *Ode To My Family* reaches UK #26. During the month, the band performs on the second night of KROQ's annual "Almost Acoustic Christmas" at the Universal Amphitheatre, Universal City, CA.

1995

Jan [12-13] Further UK dates, begun on the 4th at Nottingham's Rock City, Notts., are highlighted by a pair of concerts at London's Royal Albert Hall.

Feb [4] ***No Need To Argue*** hits US #6. (A new song by the band is featured on the US-released ***Boys On The Side*** film soundtrack, while another, *Pretty*, is included on the Columbia-issued ***Pret A Porter*** soundtrack.)

[25] The group is the music guest on NBC-TV's "Saturday Night Live".

Mar [1] Following the global chart success of its first two albums, a headlining world tour bows with a month of Australian dates beginning at the Metropolis Concert Club, Perth.

[11] A pre-taped "Later With Jools Holland" appearance airs on BBC2-TV.

[18] *I Can't Be With You* reaches UK #23.

[31] The Cranberries are named Best Irish Act at the 10th annual Irish Recorded Music Awards held at Dublin's Burlington Hotel.

Apr [1] The North-American leg of the group's current world trek kicks of at the Arena, Seattle Center, Seattle, WA, on a bill grossing $128,993 from 5,864 attendees.

[18] The Cranberries' acoustic "MTV Unplugged" performance airs from New York's Brooklyn Academy of Music.

May [15] The band's planned free concert in the grounds of the Washington Monument, Washington, DC is aborted after only one song: police stop the gig after 10,000 fans turn up, some 8,000 more than expected.

[30] Further UK dates close with the band's appearance at the Edinburgh Festival Theatre, Edinburgh, Scotland.

July [1] Eurodisco version of *Zombie* by A.D.A.M., featuring Amy, debuts at its UK #16 peak.

[23] A European stadium tour kicks off at the National Ground, the Arms Park, Cardiff, an all-star bill which takes £1,286,890 at the box-office.

[28] The RIAA certifies four million US sales of ***No Need To Argue***.

Aug [8] Their hectic tour schedule sees a return to the US for month-long dates beginning at the Blockbuster-Sony Music Entertainment Center, Camden, NJ.

[12] *Ridiculous Thoughts* bows at its UK #20 peak.

[22] New Cranberries tracks are featured on the soundtrack ***Empire Records***, released in the US.

Sept [12] O'Riordan performs *Ave Maria* with Luciano Pavarotti at the "War Child" benefit concert held at the Novi Sad Park, Italy (which will be included on the March 1996 album ***Pavarotti & Friends Together For The Children Of Bosnia***).

[26] Island/Philips New Media releases the group's multimedia CD-ROM project, ***Doors And Windows***, which includes ten minutes of band interviews, rare photos, a video clip of its performance at "Woodstock II" and five previously unreleased tracks.

Nov [23] *Zombie* is named Best Song at the second annual MTV Europe Music Awards held in Paris, France, at which the band also performs.

Dec The group's first two albums are repackaged in the UK as a double-CD.

1996

Jan [5] The RIAA confirms US sales of four million copies of ***Everybody Else Is Doing It, So Why Can't We?***.

Mar [10] The band wins the Best-Selling Album (Foreign Or Domestic) for ***No Need To Argue*** category at the 25th annual Juno Awards held at the Copps Coliseum, Hamilton, ON, Canada.

May [7] Island releases the group's third album, the 13-track ***To The Faithful Departed*** worldwide.

CRASH TEST DUMMIES

Brad Roberts (vocals, guitar); **Dan Roberts** (bass); **Ellen Reid** (keyboards); **Benjamin Darvill** (harmonica); **Mitch Dorge** (drums)

1990

Having graduated from the University of Winnipeg, MB, Canada with an honors degree in English Literature and Philosophy, frontman and songwriter Brad Roberts (b. Jan. 10, 1964, Winnipeg) and his younger brother Dan (b. May 22, 1967, Winnipeg) initially form a quartet with Darvill (b. Jan. 4, 1967, Winnipeg) and Reid (b. July 14, 1966, Selkirk, MB, Canada) in Winnipeg, without a drummer in the lineup. After rejecting names including the Chemotherapists and Skin Graft, the Crash Test Dummies, managed by Jeff Rogers at Swell Music in Toronto, ON, Canada, secure a recording contract with Arista Records, having impressed the label with its demo tape recordings of original acoustic, folk-rock based material.

1991

Nov [2] *Superman's Song*, hallmarked by Brad Roberts' distinctive deep-baritone vocal, makes US #56. It is taken from the quartet's debut album, ***The Ghosts That Haunt Me***, a ten-track set produced by Steve Berlin, recorded at the Wayne Finucan Studio in Winnipeg with temporary drummer Vince Lambert, and highlighted by Brad's wry, often philosophically bizarre lyrics. The critically-revered set will sell over 400,000 copies in Canada.

1992

Mar [30] The band is named Group Of The Year at the 21st annual Juno Awards held at the O'Keefe Centre for Performing Arts in Toronto.

(Following a year of touring in support of its debut set, the group will return to Winnipeg where Brad Roberts will write material for a follow-up album, before heading to Lake Geneva, WI for recording sessions in late '93.)

1994

Mar [15] The group performs on CBS-TV's "Late Show With David Letterman".

[21-22] A US tour is highlighted by two nights at the Great American Music Hall, San Francisco, CA which take $15,870 at the box-office.

Apr [7] Still climbing both the UK and US charts, the infectious, radio friendly folk-rock confection, *Mmm, Mmm, Mmm, Mmm* is certified gold by the RIAA.
[16] *Mmm Mmm Mmm Mmm* hits US #4.
[30] *Mmm Mmm Mmm Mmm* hits UK #2.
May [7] Mostly recorded at Music Head Recording in Lake Geneva, the band's sophomore set ***God Shuffled His Feet***, produced by ex-Talking Head Jerry Harrison and featuring permanent new drummer Dorge (b. Sept. 15, 1960, Winnipeg), hits US #9.
[11-13] A 17-date US tour opening for Elvis Costello begins with a pair of concerts at the Universal Amphitheatre, Universal City, CA, which gross $275,663.
[14] ***God Shuffled His Feet*** enters at its UK #2 peak.
June [21] Crash Test Dummies appear on NBC-TV's "The Tonight Show."
July [16] The group plays during the four-day "Phoenix Festival", Long Marston, Stratford-upon-Avon, Warks.
[17] It is featured on BBC2-TV's "The O Zone".
[23] *Afternoons And Coffeespoons* reaches UK #23.
[30-31] The band performs at the "Tennents In The Park Festival", Strathclyde Country Park, Lanarkshire.
Aug [2] The band is featured on ITV's "The Beat".
[6] *Afternoons And Coffeespoons* makes US #66.
Oct [1-2] The group participates in the Artists for Shambala benefit at the Shambala Preserve, Canyon County Wildlife Sanctuary in CA.
[23] An eight-date UK tour gets underway at Nottingham's Rock City, Notts, set to end on November 4th at the Wolverhampton Civic Hall.
Nov [24] The band wins the Breakthrough Artist category at MTV's inaugural European Music Awards held at the Pariser Platz, Berlin, Germany, at the site of the Brandenburg Gate.

1995

Jan [25] The group performs *Mmm Mmm Mmm Mmm* at the 22nd annual American Music Awards held at Los Angeles, CA's Shrine Auditorium.
Apr [5] The RIAA certifies US sales of two million for ***God Shuffled His Feet***.
[15] The group's cover version of XTC's *The Ballad Of Peter Pumpkinhead*, specifically credited as featuring longtime member Reid, debuts at its UK #30 peak, and is featured in the current movie soundtrack to "Dumb And Dumber".
[17] The band appears on C4-TV's "The White Room".

RANDY CRAWFORD

1967

Crawford (b. Veronica Crawford, Feb. 18, 1952, Macon, GA), having sung in church and school choirs and worked since the age of 15 in local night clubs in Cincinnati, OH, where she was raised, performs for three months in St. Tropez, France, during her summer break on a trip to Europe. Returning to Cincinnati, she sings on a regular basis in jazz clubs and is signed by an agent. She will make her debut New York performance on the same bill as George Benson at jazz/soul club Nico's, in 1972, the same year her first single *If You Say The Word* is released by Columbia Records (US), which will issue one further Crawford single, *Don't Get Caught* in 1973. Following further club dates around the US, she will perform again with Benson, and also Quincy Jones, at the World Jazz Association tribute concert to the late Cannonball Adderley in Los Angeles, CA in November 1975, with two songs recorded for inclusion on her debut album.

1976

Signed to Warner Bros. Records, her maiden album, the jazz-soul phrased ***Everything Must Change***, is released in the US only. Featuring Crusader Joe Sample and other noted jazz/soul musicians, it garners strong reviews but limited sales. It will be followed by the Bob Montgomery-produced ***Miss Randy Crawford***, again only issued in North America in September 1977, which once again showcases her sweet soul, high-pitched vocal prowess. (During that year, her vocal talent will also appear on ex-Genesis member Steve Hackett's second solo album, ***Please Don't Touch*** and jazz musician Harvey Mason's ***Marching In The Streets***.)

1979

June ***Raw Silk***, a further jazz/R&B meld, produced by Stephen Goldman and including songs written by Allen Toussaint, Ashford & Simpson and Oscar Brown among others, is released in the US.
Sept Jazz combo the Crusaders have invited Crawford to sing the vocal lead on the 11-minute title track for their MCA album, ***Street Life***, which now reaches US #18 (during a 20-week tenure atop the US Jazz chart).
[15] Title cut *Street Life* hits UK #5.
Nov [10] *Street Life* makes US #36.

1980

June [28] ***Now We May Begin***, on which the Crusaders have co-written, played on or produced most of the selections, reaches US #180, as the extracted *Last Night At Danceland* peaks at UK #61.
Sept [20] Ballad co-written by Sample with Will Jennings, *One Day I'll Fly Away*, hits UK #2, as its parent album, ***Now We May Begin***, hits UK #10. (Its success prompts WEA UK to release her first three albums as catalog items.)

1981

Mar Crawford's *Love Theme - The Competition* is released by MCA from the soundtrack to the Richard Dreyfuss-starring movie, "The Competition".
July [18] *You Might Need Somebody*, co-penned by Tom Snow, makes UK #11. ***Secret Combination***, produced by Tommy LiPuma and featuring top-notch sessioneers including Lenny Castro, Jim Horn, Ernie Watts and Toto's Steve Lukather and Jeff Porcaro, hits UK #2 (during a one-year chart stretch) and reaches US #71.
Sept [12] Crawford's cover version of Brook Benton's *Rainy Night In Georgia* climbs to UK #18. She adapts it to *Rainy Night In London* during her sellout stint at the Theatre Royal Drury Lane, London, on a UK tour.
Nov [7] *Secret Combination*, with a live recording of *Street Life* on the flip-side, makes UK #48.

1982

Jan [30] Her cover version of John Lennon's *Imagine* peaks at UK #60.
Feb [24] Crawford wins the Best Female Artist category at the first annual BRIT Awards held at the Grosvenor House Hotel, London.
June [12] Ballad, *One Hello*, written by Carole Bayer Sager and Marvin Hamlisch, makes UK #48.
[19] ***Windsong***, again helmed by Tommy LiPuma, hits #7 in the UK, where she remains more commercially successful.
Aug [7] ***Windsong*** peaks at US #148.

1983

Feb [26] *He Reminds Me* peaks at UK #65.
May Crawford duets with Al Jarreau on five cuts for ***Casino Nights***, recorded live at the 1982 "Montreux Jazz Festival".
Oct ***Nightline*** makes UK #37 and US #164.
[15] Title track *Nightline* reaches UK #51.

1984

Oct UK-only compilation, ***Miss Randy Crawford - The Greatest Hits***, released by TV-advertising label K-tel, hits UK #10, as Crawford completes a successful European tour.
Dec [8] Her duet with Rick Springfield, *Taxi Dancing*, from his album ***Hard To Hold***, peaks at US #59.

1986

June ***Abstract Emotions***, produced and largely written by Reggie Lucas, reaches UK #14 and will make US #178 in August.

1987

Jan Uncharacteristically self-penned ballad, *Almaz*, championed not least by BBC Radio 1 DJ Steve Wright, hits UK #4.
Oct [14] Further 16-track UK compilation album, ***The Love Songs***, TV-advertised by Telstar Records, peaks at UK #27.

1988

Aug Crawford is invited to perform in two concerts with the London Symphony Orchestra, as part of its summer season at London's Barbican Centre. Consistent with her continuing UK popularity, they are both sellouts.

1989

Oct [21] ***Rich And Poor***, mostly produced by Robin Millar and recorded in London, peaks at UK #63 (going on to make US #159 on Jan [6], 1990) and includes Crawford's interpretation of *Knockin' On Heaven's Door*, heard in the Mel Gibson/Danny Glover movie "Lethal Weapon 2", and featuring Eric Clapton on guitar and David Sanborn on saxophone.

1990

Dec [1] Crawford performs at the 23rd Annual NAACP Image Awards, set to air on January 14th.

1991

Oct [1] Still hugely popular in Japan, Crawford begins a seven-date tour at the Shibuya Kokaido, Tokyo, set to end on the 8th at the Kanagawa Kenmin Hall, Yokohama.

1992

Feb [8] Zucchero's *Diamante*, on which Crawford is the featured vocalist, makes UK #44. It is included on Crawford simultaneously released ***Through The Eyes Of Love***, which also boasts her cover version of Journey's *Who's Crying Now.*
Apr [5] Crawford begins an 11-date UK tour at the Sunderland Empire, set to end on the 18th at the Plymouth Pavilions, Plymouth, Devon.

1993

Apr [3] ***The Very Best Of Randy Crawford*** hits UK #8, to be followed by the release of a new studio set ***Don't Say It's Over*** in October, featuring top-drawer session talent including Abe Laboriel, Paul Jackson and Misha Segal among others.

1994

Jan [26] Crawford begins a European tour in Zurich, Switzerland. She will also perform US dates in September.

1995

Nov [27] Following Warner Bros. (US) decision not to renew her contract after 17 years, and after a two-year recording sabbatical by Crawford, ***Naked And True***, produced by Ralf Droesemeyer, and already issued in Europe by WEA Germany (under a new and separate agreement), is released in the US through Mesa Records.

ROBERT CRAY

1975

Living in Tacoma, WA, Cray (b. Aug. 1, 1953, Columbus, GA), the son of a serviceman who has taken his family to Virginia, California and Germany before settling in Tacoma, having been a long-time admirer of blues singer/guitarist Albert Collins, who has performed at a graduation dance at Cray's high school, where he has already formed his own One Way Street blues band, met his bass player Richard Cousins in 1973 and, through him, joined Collins' West Coast touring band. After completing a two-year apprenticeship with Collins, Cray and Cousins strike out independently to form what will become the Robert Cray Band, featuring Cray (guitar and vocals), Cousins (bass), Peter Boe (keyboards) and David Olson (drums).

1978

His debut album, ***Who's Been Talkin'***, is cut during constant touring in US. (It will be shelved for two years and released in the US by the short-lived Tomato label, its license subsequently picked up by Atlantic and by blues/R&B specialist label Charly Records in the UK. (During the year, Cray will also appear as the bassist in Otis Day & the Knights house band in the movie "Animal House".)

1983

After almost a decade of regular live West Coast performances, Cray records ***Bad Influence***, released on Hightone Records in the US and Demon in the UK. (It will take four years to chart, but in the short term garners four prestigious W.C. Handy Awards for the Blues, including Best Contemporary Album.) The Robert Cray Band will make its first UK and European tour the following year, with critics acclaiming the group's skillful contemporary blues style.

1985

Oct [12] ***False Accusations***, his first chart entry, peaks at UK #68 and tops the UK Independent chart. In the US, it wins the Best Blues Album award from the National Association of Independent Record Distributors (NAIRD). Cray collaborates with Albert Collins and guitarist Johnny Copeland on ***Showdown!*** for Alligator Records.

1986

Feb Cray signs to Mercury Records, and begins recording ***Strong Persuader*** with Hightone producers Bruce Bomberg and Dennis Walker. Ceaseless touring will mean the band plays 170 engagements through the year, including its seventh European tour since 1984.
Mar ***Showdown!*** makes US #124.
May ***False Accusations*** peaks at US #141.
Oct [16] Cray joins Keith Richards of the Rolling Stones, along with Eric Clapton and others, on stage in St. Louis, MO, for Chuck Berry's 60th birthday concert performance, featured in the film "Hail! Hail! Rock'n'Roll".
Nov Cray makes his network TV debut on NBC-TV's "Late Night With David Letterman".
[16] He wins a record six Handy Awards at America's seventh National Blues Awards, hosted by B.B. King and Carl Perkins.
Dec Cray tapes a special for UK TV with Tina Turner, to be shown on HBO in the US the following year.

1987

Feb [24] ***Showdown!*** wins the Best Traditional Blues Recording category at the 29th annual Grammy Awards at the Los Angeles, CA's Shrine Auditorium, as well as performing with a blues supergroup comprising Willie Dixon, B.B. King, Albert King, Ry Cooder, Dr. John and others.
Mar Cray begins a US arena tour, supporting Huey Lewis & the News, as ***Bad Influence***, originally released on Hightone in 1983, peaks at US #143.
Apr ***Strong Persuader***, Cray's Mercury debut, reaches US #13, the first blues album to crack the Top 20 since Bobby Bland's ***Call On Me*** in 1972.
[18] *Smoking Gun* is his Singles chart breakthrough, shooting to US #22.
[27] Cray backs Eric Clapton on a sellout night at Madison Square Garden, New York, as part of a one-month US tour together.
May He supports Tina Turner in Europe, including seven sellout performances at the Wembley Arena, Wembley, Middx.
[30] *Right Next Door (Because Of Me)* climbs to US #80.
June *Right Next Door (Because Of Me)* makes UK #50.
[19-21] Cray takes part in the annual "Glastonbury Festival", Glastonbury, Somerset.
July ***Strong Persuader*** reaches UK #34.
Nov Cray begins a tour of Japan, once again supporting Clapton.

1988

Mar [2] Cray nabs the Best Contemporary Blues Recording trophy for ***Strong Persuader*** at the 30th annual Grammy Awards.
June He begins a headlining US tour.
Sept [13] ***Don't Be Afraid Of The Dark***, recorded in Los Angeles, with producers Bromberg and Walker, and featuring David Sanborn guesting on sax, debuts at its UK #13 peak, and will reach US #32.
Oct [8] *Don't Be Afraid Of The Dark* peaks at US #74.

1989

Feb [22] Cray wins his second consecutive Best Contemporary Blues Recording statuette for ***Don't Be Afraid Of The Dark*** at the 31st annual Grammy Awards.

1990

Jan [18] He opens at the Royal Albert Hall, London, on the bill of Eric Clapton's 18-night stand, having recently added fret work to Clapton's current ***Journeyman*** album.
Aug [27] Following a concert at the Alpine Valley Music Theatre, East Troy, WI, featuring Cray, Clapton and Stevie Ray Vaughan, the latter is killed along with three members of Clapton's entourage in a helicopter crash.
Sept [29] Now billed as a solo artist, and having assembled a new backing unit comprising Cousins, Jimmy Pugh (keyboards), Tim Kaihatsu (guitar), and Kevin Hayes (drums), ***Midnight Stroll*** debuts at UK #19.
Oct [25] Cray guests on "Late Night With David Letterman", before playing a sellout concert at New York's Beacon Theatre at the start of a US tour.
[27] ***Midnight Stroll*** makes US #51.

1991

Jan [9] Cray begins a new world concert trek at the Club Quattro, Tokyo, Japan.
[16] Cray inducts Howlin' Wolf into the Rock and Roll Hall of Fame at the sixth annual dinner, with Wolf's widow Lilly Burnett in attendance, staged at New York's Waldorf Astoria Hotel, and performs *In The Mood* with Bonnie Raitt and John Lee Hooker at the after-dinner jam.
[24-27] He plays on Eric Clapton's Hammersmith Odeon, London bill.
Mar [21] Cray guests on NBC-TV's "The Tonight Show".
May [10] He performs at the Pacific Amphitheatre, Costa Mesa, CA, with Steve Winwood.
July [6] During his UK visit, Cray plays at London's Crystal Palace Bowl.
[11-14] He takes part in the 16th "North Sea Jazz Festival" at the Congress Centre, The Hague, Netherlands.
Aug [18] Cray participates in the annual "Newport Jazz Festival" at Jones Beach Theatre, Wantagh, NY, with B.B. King and John Lee Hooker (and is featured on Hooker's forthcoming Charisma debut ***Mr. Lucky***).
Oct [15-19] Cray performs at "Guitar Legends", a five-concert series staged as part of "Expo '92", in Seville, Spain.

1992

Mar [21] Cray joins Boz Scaggs, Johnny Rivers, and a reunited Doobie Brothers and Michael McDonald, to celebrate the 25th anniversary of the Memphis Horns at the Great American Pyramid, Memphis, TN.
Aug [21] He performs at the Wolf Trap Farm Park, Vienna, VA, during current US dates.
[12] Produced by Dennis Walker, ***I Was Warned***, with bassist Karl Sevareid having replaced Cousins, debuts at its UK #29 peak.
Oct [3] ***I Was Warned*** climbs to US #103.
[7] Cray plays at the intimate Toad's Place, New Haven, CT, at the start of a 12-date US tour, set to end on the 24th at the American Theatre, St. Louis, MO.
Nov [5] Cray and B.B. King embark on the 16-date "JVC Super Session '92 Tour" in Wettingen, Switzerland, set to close on the 24th at the Circus, Stockholm, Sweden.

1993

Jan Following a performance at "America's Reunion On The Mall" as part of President Clinton's inauguration celebrations, Cray now takes part in the benefit for the UCLA Environmental Science and Engineering Program at the Universal Amphitheatre, Universal City, CA.
Mar [8] *I Was Warned* wins the Outstanding Blues Album category at the Bay Area Music Awards at San Francisco's Bill Graham Civic Auditorium.
Apr [23] Cray performs a sellout show at the Rialto Square Theatre, Joliet, IL, during current US dates.
Oct [16] ***Shame + Sin*** charts for a week at UK #48, and will debut at its US #143 peak on the 23rd (eventually selling 140,000 copies in the US).
Dec [2] He guests on "The Tonight Show".

1994

Apr [23] Cray takes part in Earth Day celebrations at the Target Centre, Minneapolis, MN, with Melissa Etheridge and Natalie Merchant, among others, at the end of a three-month US tour.
June [4] He supports Santana at the Aladdin, Las Vegas, during his latest tour.
Nov [25] Cray plays before a crowd of 55,935 supporting the Rolling Stones at the Joe Robbie Stadium, Miami, FL.

1995

May [27] Self-produced set ***Some Rainy Morning***, his first album not to feature a horns section, debuts at its US #127 peak, having done likewise the previous week at UK #63.
June [18] In a continuing European tour supporting the Rolling Stones, Cray now performs before a crowd of 72,000 at the Pink Pop Site, Landgraaf, Netherlands.
Oct [15] During selected US dates, Cray performs at the American Theatre, St. Louis, MO.

1996

Jan [24] Following another appearance on "The Tonight Show", Cray takes his latest tour north of the border to the Vogue Theatre, Vancouver, BC, Canada.

CREAM

Eric Clapton (vocals, guitar); **Jack Bruce** (vocals, bass); **Ginger Baker** (drums)

1966

June Having had successful stints in the Yardbirds and John Mayall's Bluesbreakers, Clapton (b. Eric Clapp, Mar. 30, 1945, Ripley, Surrey) has returned from a trip to Greece with holiday combo the Greek Loon Band in November 1965, and rejoined the Bluesbreakers, which includes singing bass player Bruce (b. John Asher, May 14, 1943, Glasgow, Scotland), a former Royal Scottish Academy of Music scholar and veteran of other '60s R&B UK bands, including the Graham Bond Organisation and Alexis Korner's backing group. Clapton is impressed by Bruce, who leaves to join Manfred Mann in search of better money. After attending a Bluesbreakers gig in Oxford, Baker (b. Peter Baker, Aug. 19, 1939, Lewisham, London), ex-member of trad-jazz outfits for the likes of Acker Bilk and Terry Lightfoot, suggests forming a new group with Clapton, who nominates Bruce, with whom Baker has played in Alexis Korner's Blues Incorporated in 1962 and the Graham Bond Organisation in 1963, for bass player.
July [16] After Bruce has agreed to leave Manfred Mann, Cream is born. The players' reputations quickly secure a UK recording contract with Robert Stigwood's Reaction Records and with Atlantic in the US. The original idea is for a purist blues trio, but Cream emerges as a rock-blues band.
[31] Billed under their individual names, the trio plays its first major concert at the sixth annual "Jazz &

Blues Festival" at Windsor, Berks.
Oct [29] Their first UK release, the atypical and low-key Jack Bruce/Pete Brown-penned *Wrapping Paper*, makes #34.

1967

Jan [28] *I Feel Free*, co-written by Bruce and Pete Brown, reaches UK #11. Their debut album ***Fresh Cream*** hits UK #6, and sets the tone for their popular sound: a blues/jazz base showcasing power rock instrumental fireworks.
Feb [5] Cream plays at London's Savile Theatre.
Mar [26] The group begins a week-long stint (using the Lovin' Spoonful's equipment) in Murray the K's "Music In The Fifth Dimension" stage show, at the RKO Theater, Manhattan, New York.
Apr Cream tours the US, where the music press has already guaranteed a strong audience following. Live shows feature much improvisation by all members, as Clapton's lead guitar playing finds a growing cult following.
[16] The band appears at the "**Daily Express** Record Star Show" at the Empire Pool, Wembley, Middx.
June ***Fresh Cream*** debuts the band on the US chart reaching US #39 during a 92-week chart run.
July [2] The trio performs at the Savile Theatre, with the Jeff Beck Group and John Mayall's Bluesbreakers.
[15] *Strange Brew* reaches UK #17, confirming Cream as a mainstream success.
Aug [13] Cream performs on the final day of the seventh annual "National Jazz & Blues Festival" at Balloon Meadow, Royal Windsor Racecourse, Windsor.
[22] A second US tour begins with a two-week stint at the Fillmore West, San Francisco, CA.
Dec ***Disraeli Gears***, with its distinctive cover illustrated by Martin Sharp and photographed by Bob Whitaker, hits UK #5, and is their US breakthrough, at #4, eventually topping one million sales.
[2] The group appears on the late night BBC-TV revue "Twice A Fortnight".

1968

Feb In spite of triumphant appearances in the UK, the US and Europe, rumors are rife that they plan to split. *Sunshine Of Your Love*, taken from the Felix Pappalardi-produced ***Disraeli Gears***, is their first US chart single, making #36.
[27] The band begins a eight-week US tour at the Fillmore Auditorium.
Apr [17-21] The group performs at the Avalon Ballroom, San Francisco, on a bill with the MC5 and the Psychedelic Stooges.
June [1] *Anyone For Tennis*, an uncharacteristic track used as the theme for "The Savage Seven" film, peaks at US #64.
[15] *Anyone For Tennis* makes UK #40.
July [13] **Melody Maker** reveals that Cream is to split, after Clapton says in an interview "The Cream has lost direction".
Aug [10] Double album ***Wheels Of Fire***, combining a studio-recorded set and a live one from the Fillmore West in San Francisco, tops the US chart for the first of four weeks. In the UK the album is marketed both as a double, which hits #3, and as a single studio album, which hits #7.
[31] In the US, the album's success re-boosts sales of *Sunshine Of Your Love*, which now hits US #5, eventually selling over a million copies.
Sept It is announced that Cream will split after a farewell US tour and final UK dates.
Oct [26] *Sunshine Of Your Love* reaches UK #25, as their career closing tour gets underway in the US.
Nov [1] The band plays at Madison Square Garden, New York, at the end of the farewell trek.
[9] *White Room* hits US #6.
[25-26] 10,000 fans attend the group's last two live shows, at London's Royal Albert Hall (supported by Yes and Taste), as 1,000's more miss out on tickets.

1969

Feb Clapton and Baker form Blind Faith, with Ric Grech (ex-Family) on bass and Stevie Winwood (ex-Traffic) on keyboards and vocals. Bruce heads for a solo career which will continue into the '90s and yield ***Songs For A Tailor*** (released by year's end), ***Things We Like*** (1970), ***Harmony Row*** (1971), ***Out Of The Storm*** (1974), ***How's Tricks*** (1977), ***I've Always Wanted To Do This*** (1980), ***Truce*** (1982), ***Automatic*** (1987) and ***A Question Of Time*** (1990). (He will also form West, Bruce & Laing in 1972, releasing ***Why Dontcha***, and move on to collaborate with Robin Trower and Bill Lordan in the short-lived 1981 trio BLT.) The first Cream album ***Fresh Cream*** is reissued in the UK, now hitting #7.
[22] *White Room* reaches UK #28.
Mar Farewell fling ***Goodbye*** tops the UK chart and hits US #2.
[8] *Crossroads* reaches US #28.
May [3] *Badge*, taken from ***Goodbye***, makes US #60 and will reach UK #18 on May [10].
Aug After the group breaks up, re-cycling of material begins in earnest: ***The Best Of Cream*** hits US #3 and will peak at UK #6 in November.

1970

Jan [12] While Clapton undertakes an increasingly successful solo career, Baker's newly-formed outfit Air Force makes its debut at the Birmingham Town Hall, Birmingham, Warks. (Baker will subsequently spend time living in Nigeria, where he forms the short-lived band Salt, before assembling the Baker-Gurvitz Army in 1973, followed by the Nutters and Bakerland, prior to leaving the UK in 1981 to live on an olive farm in Italy. His solo album releases will include ***11 Sides Of Baker*** (1977), ***From Humble Origins*** (1983), ***Horses And Trees*** (1986), ***In Concert*** (1987) and ***Middle Passage*** (1990).)
July ***Live Cream*** hits UK #4 and reaches US #15. A second performance set, ***Live Cream - Volume 2***, reaches UK #15 and US #27 in June 1972, while the compilation album ***Heavy Cream*** makes US #135 in November of 1972, when a reissued *Badge* also makes UK #42. ***Disraeli Gears*** and ***Wheels Of Fire*** will be reissued in the US by RSO Records in February 1977, re-charting at #165 and #197 respectively.

1987

Sept [26] TV-advertised ***The Cream Of Eric Clapton***, chronicling solo Clapton hits with those of Cream, begins an initial 79-week UK chart run during which it will hit #3.

1993

Jan [12] Momentarily reconciling lingering bitterness between Baker and his former colleagues, the trio reunites for the first time in nearly 25 years to perform *Sunshine Of Your Love*, *Born Under A Bad Sign* and *Crossroads* at the eighth annual Rock and Roll Hall of Fame awards dinner held at the Century Plaza Hotel, Los Angeles, CA. The performance celebrates the band's induction by Z.Z. Top. Now living in California, Baker's most recent music collaboration has been with Los Angeles outfit Masters of Reality (though he will re-emerge in June 1994 as one third of BBM, with Bruce and Gary Moore, releasing ***Around The Next Dream***, while Bruce, prior to joining Baker and Moore in BBM, will release his latest solo set ***Somethinels*** (on CMP Records) in March, featuring musical guests Clapton, Clem Clempson and Maggie Reilly among others.
see also: **BLIND FAITH, Eric CLAPTON**

CREEDENCE CLEARWATER REVIVAL

John Fogerty (vocals, guitar); **Tom Fogerty** (rhythm guitar); **Stu Cook** (bass); **Doug "Cosmo" Clifford** (drums)

1959

Raised in Berkeley, CA, John Fogerty (b. May 28, 1945, Berkeley), a singer and guitarist, who is also teaching himself to play piano, tenor sax, drums, dobro, harmonica and a number of other instruments, forms a rock'n'roll band with his Portola Junior High School, El Cerrito, CA, friends: bass player Cook (b. Apr. 25, 1945, Oakland, CA) and drummer Clifford (b. Apr. 24, 1945, Palo Alto, CA). The trio plays local parties before John's brother, Tom (b. Nov. 9, 1941, Berkeley), also a multi-instrumentalist, joins on rhythm guitar and becomes co-lead vocalist, subsequently becoming the band's main focus, billed as Tommy Fogerty & the Blue Velvets. When they leave school, the group begins playing in Bay Area clubs and bars from 1963 while Tom Fogerty also takes a job as a packing and shipping clerk at the Berkeley-based Fantasy Records.

1964

May The group auditions as an instrumental band for Fantasy, which was recently the subject of the TV documentary "Anatomy Of A Hit" (relating the story of the Vince Guaraldi Trio's 1963 US Top 30 success, *Cast Your Fate To The Wind*). Fantasy's Hy Weiss signs them, but encourages their UK-style beat music over their instrumentals flings. They adopt the name the Visions, but Weiss prints labels for their debut single as the Golliwogs, to make them sound British, a name which the band dislikes but accepts.
Nov *Don't Tell Me No Lies*, released on Fantasy, features Tom on lead vocals.

1965

Band continues to record as the Golliwogs with UK-style rockers *Where You Been* and *You Can't Be True*, but with little commercial success.

1966

Jan Fantasy establishes its new Scorpio subsidiary label for teen-oriented releases, and the Golliwogs are moved to it. *Brown-Eyed Girl* becomes a moderate local hit, selling 10,000 copies around northern California. (It is also the group's first UK release, on Vocalion). Hopes of promoting the disc (and its follow-up, *Fight Fire)* nationally are thwarted, when John Fogerty and Clifford are drafted for national service.
Dec *Walking On The Water* is the final Golliwogs release.

1967

July With both draftees back in the band, they spend six months rehearsing a tougher rock blend than their UK-influenced sound, with John now on lead vocals. They also decide on a new name: Creedence comes from Creedence Nuball, a friend of Tom's, Clearwater from a beer commercial and Revival is a statement of intent.
Nov *Porterville* is the first Creedence Clearwater Revival disc on Scorpio.

1968

Apr While building a solid live reputation, the band cuts a demo of its version of Dale Hawkins' *Suzie Q*, which is played by a local radio station. A strong reaction urges Fantasy's new owner, Saul Zaentz, to relaunch the group on the main label as Creedence Clearwater Revival. *Suzie Q* is re-recorded in the studio in a lengthy version which is split into Parts 1 and 2 on both sides of the single.
May [31-**June** 2] The group plays at San Francisco's Avalon Ballroom on a bill with Taj Mahal.
June The band's debut album, ***Creedence Clearwater Revival***, which includes *Porterville*, *Suzie Q*, some soul and R&B revivals and a smattering of John Fogerty originals, is released in the US.
July [2-7] They play at San Francisco's Fillmore West with the Paul Butterfield Blues Band.
Sept [19-21] The group performs three further dates at the Fillmore West.
Oct *Suzie Q (Part 1)* reaches US #11, while ***Creedence Clearwater Revival*** reaches US #52.
Dec From the album, their revival of Screamin' Jay Hawkins' *I Put A Spell On You* makes US #58.

1969

Jan [16-19] The group once again plays the Fillmore West, this time on a bill with Fleetwood Mac.

Mar [8] *Proud Mary*, an exuberant tale of a Mississippi steamboat, written by John Fogerty on the morning he was discharged from the US army, hits US #2 for the first of three weeks (behind Tommy Roe's *Dizzy*). It becomes the group's first million-seller (and will be the most-covered Creedence song, with a 1971 million-selling version by Ike & Tina Turner, and covers by Solomon Burke and Sonny Charles & Checkmates Ltd.; Elvis Presley will also include his version on an album in 1970). ***Bayou Country***, developing their "swamp-rock" idiom and fulfilling Fogerty's musical fantasy/odyssey, hits US #7 and is their first million-selling album.

[13-16] They play the Fillmore West again, sharing a bill with Jethro Tull.

Apr [10] The group signs to appear at the forthcoming "Woodstock Music & Art Fair" for $10,000. (Canned Heat ($13,000), Johnny Winter ($7,500) and Janis Joplin ($15,000) will all sign within the next ten days.)

June [28] Million-selling *Bad Moon Rising* also hits US #2 (behind Henry Mancini's *Love Theme From Romeo And Juliet*), while its B-side, *Lodi*, makes US #52.

[20-22] Creedence Clearwater Revival takes part in the "Newport '69 Pop Festival" at San Fernando Valley State College, Devonshire Downs, Northridge, CA, playing to 150,000 people, sharing a bill with Jimi Hendrix, Jethro Tull, the Byrds and others.

[27] The group appears at the "Denver Pop Festival" in the city's Mile High Stadium, with Jimi Hendrix, Frank Zappa's Mothers of Invention and others.

July *Proud Mary*, the group's UK chart debut, hits #8.

[4] The group performs at the "Atlanta Pop Festival", Atlanta, GA, to 140,000 people, with Led Zeppelin, Canned Heat, Johnny Winter and Joe Cocker, among others.

Aug [1] Creedence plays at the "Atlantic City Pop Festival", Atlantic City, NJ, alongside Jefferson Airplane, the Byrds, Little Richard, Santana and others.

[15] The group performs at the "Woodstock Music & Art Fair", Bethel, NY, but does not consent to its performance being used for the subsequent movie or album.

Sept [20] *Bad Moon Rising* begins a three-week reign at UK #1.

[27] A third million-seller, *Green River*, hits US #2, also their third runner-up of the year (this time behind the Archies' *Sugar Sugar*), while its B-side, *Commotion*, climbs to US #30.

Oct [4] ***Green River***, mostly penned by John Fogerty, and another million-seller, hits US #1, where it will stay for four weeks, deposing ***Blind Faith*** and then yielding to the Beatles' ***Abbey Road***.

Nov [22] *Fortunate Son* reaches #14. (The song will be included in **Rolling Stone** magazine's all-time Top 100 singles, polled in 1988.)

Dec [20] *Down On The Corner*, the other side of *Fortunate Son*, hits US #3.

[27] *Green River* makes UK #19.

1970

Jan ***Willy And The Poorboys*** (its title taken from a phrase in the included *Down On The Corner*) hits US #3 and is another million-seller.

Feb ***Green River*** reaches UK #20.

Mar [7] *Travelin' Band*, a Little Richard pastiche by John Fogerty, backed with *Who'll Stop The Rain*, an allegory about the Vietnam War, hits US #2 (behind Simon & Garfunkel's *Bridge Over Troubled Water*). *Down On The Corner* peaks at UK #31.

Apr ***Willy And The Poor Boys*** hits UK #10.

[14-15] The band performs at London's Royal Albert Hall, on its maiden European tour.

May [2] ***Bayou Country*** has a belated one-week stay at UK #62, aided by the London concert (which is recorded by Fantasy), supported by Booker T. & the MG's.

[9] *Travelin' Band* hits UK #8.

June [6] *Up Around The Bend*, paired with *Run Through The Jungle*, hits US #4 and is a million-seller.

July [18] *Up Around The Bend* hits UK #3.

Aug [22] ***Cosmo's Factory***, named after the warehouse they rehearsed in, tops the US chart for the first of nine weeks, eventually selling over three million copies and confirming the band's current position as the leading US pop/rock outfit.

Sept [12] ***Cosmo's Factory*** is the band's only UK album chart topper, for one week.

[26] *Long As I Can See The Light* reaches #20.

Oct [3] Country-rocker *Lookin' Out My Back Door*, taken from ***Cosmo's Factory*** and backed with *Long As I Can See The Light*, hits US #2 and is their seventh US million-selling single.

1971

Jan The group's ***Pendulum***, which still features an increasingly disgruntled John Fogerty, hits US #5 (the band's last US Top 10 album) and gains a gold disc. It also makes UK #23.

Feb [7] Tom Fogerty leaves the band to spend more time with his family (but will return to record *Goodbye Media Men* and several solo albums released on Fantasy).

Mar [13] *Have You Ever Seen The Rain?*, backed with *Hey Tonight*, hits US #8 and is yet another million-seller.

Apr [3] *Have You Ever Seen The Rain?* makes UK #36.

Aug [21] *Sweet Hitch-Hiker*, the group's last million-selling single, hits US #6 and makes UK #36. The band begins its first US tour as a trio.

Sept The group starts its second European tour at the Concertgebouw, Amsterdam, Holland. Clifford collapses following the show, suffering from scarlet fever.

Oct [14] Arco Industries, which holds the copyright of Little Richard's *Good Golly Miss Molly*, files a suit against John Fogerty and his publishing company, Jondora Music, alleging that *Travelin' Band* partially plagiarises the '50s hit. (The suit is later dropped.)

1972

Feb The band undertakes a tour of Australia and Japan.

May ***Mardi Gras***, highlighted by the previous year's *Sweet Hitch-Hiker*, makes US #12 and earns another gold disc.

June [10] The extracted country-styled *Someday Never Comes* reaches US #25. The album has been produced by all three members, the result of a demand for group democracy after a long period of Fogerty domination, but the band's strength and unerring commercial aim are dimmed. Rock critic Jon Landau calls it "the worst album I have ever heard from a major band". It fails to chart in the UK. Meanwhile, Tom Fogerty's eponymous debut solo album reaches US #180, his only chart success.

Oct [16] The band announces its decision to split. John Fogerty continues recording, adopting a bluegrass/country-rock style which he will market under the name the Blue Ridge Rangers.

1973

Jan ***Creedence Gold***, the first of several Creedence compilation albums, reaches US #15 and earns a gold disc.

Feb [24] The Blue Ridge Rangers' revival of Hank Williams' *Jambalaya (On The Bayou)* reaches US #16.

May [26] *Hearts Of Stone*, also by the Blue Ridge Rangers, makes US #37.

June ***The Blue Ridge Rangers*** peaks at US #47.

Aug A second collection, ***More Creedence Gold***, makes US #61.

Dec Fantasy, with which Fogerty is increasingly at odds, releases the Creedence album ***Live In Europe***, recorded live on the world tour in September 1971. It peaks at US #143.

1975

Oct John Fogerty's debut solo album, ***John Fogerty***, is released on Asylum, with all instruments played by him.

Nov [1] Self-penned extraction, *Rockin' All Over The World*, reaches US #27 (and will be a UK #3 hit when covered by Status Quo in 1977).

Dec [27] *Almost Saturday Night*, also from John Fogerty, peaks at US #78 (and will also be a UK hit for Dave Edmunds).

1976

Mar [20] The group's version of *I Heard It Through The Grapevine*, first heard on ***Cosmo's Factory***, and belatedly released as a single, makes US #43. The 11-minute track receives airplay when circulated as a 12" single.

Mar Creedence double compilation album, ***Chronicle (The 20 Greatest Hits)***, makes US #100, while Clifford and Cook appear in the Don Harrison Band, recording for United Artists.

May [22] John Fogerty's *You Got The Magic* peaks at US #87. His album ***Hoodoo*** is planned, but is withdrawn one week before release. (Disillusioned by the record industry, Fogerty quits the business for many years, and retires with his family to a farm in Oregon. His brother Tom will re-emerge with the band Ruby in 1978, but will later go to Hawaii to work in real estate. Cook becomes a producer, while Clifford forms a trio with Chris Solberg (ex-Santana) and Louis Ortega (ex-Doug Sahm), to little notable success.)

1979

July [14] Compilation, ***Greatest Hits***, reaches UK #35.

1981

Jan ***Live The Concert*** makes US #62. This is originally released as ***The Royal Albert Hall Concert***, until Fantasy realises that the wrong tape has been used and that it contains a show recorded at the Oakland-Alameda County Coliseum, in 1970, rather than at the London venue.

1983

Having re-united briefly in 1980 to play at Tom Fogerty's wedding reception, Creedence re-forms for a school reunion gig in El Cerrito.

1985

Jan [31] John Fogerty makes his first public live appearance in years, playing in an A&M soundstage show with Albert Lee and Booker T. Jones, singing mainly R&B covers.

Mar [23] John Fogerty makes a comeback with the solo ***Centerfield*** on Warner Bros, and, released to much critical praise, it hits US #1, selling over a million copies and earning a platinum disc (also making UK #42). (Fogerty chooses the title after attending the 1984 All-Star Baseball game at Candlestick Park in San Francisco and sitting in centerfield.) He includes *Zaentz Kan't Dance* to vent his feelings about his former label boss, who threatens legal action. The track is retitled *Vance Kan't Dance*.

[2] *The Old Man Down The Road*, extracted from the album, hits US #10, spurred by an acclaimed video.

Apr [27] Also from ***Centerfield***, ***Rock'n'Roll Girls*** reaches US #20.

June [29] Title track, *Centerfield* (which is the B-side of *Rock'n'Roll Girls*), climbs to US #44.

Oct A UK TV-advertised compilation, ***The Creedence Collection***, reaches UK #68.

1986

Aug [27] Fogerty begins his first tour in 14 years.

Sept [20] *Eye Of The Zombie* by Fogerty reaches US #81.

Oct Fogerty's ***Eye Of The Zombie*** climbs to US #26. (He will continue making occasional live appearances in the US.) ***Creedence's Chronicle***, originally charting in 1970, makes US #165.

1987

July [4] Fogerty performs at the "Welcome Home" benefit for Vietnam War veterans in Washington, DC, singing a selection of Creedence classics.

1988

Nov [7] The jury finds in favor of Fogerty (who has to

sing in the courtroom during the case) over a lawsuit brought by Fantasy (encouraged by Clifford) claiming that *Old Man Down The Road* infringed *Run Through The Jungle*'s copyright, but the action costs the artist $400,000 in legal fees.

1989

May He plays at an AIDS benefit concert in Oakland with the Grateful Dead and Tracy Chapman. The backing band is Jerry Garcia, Bob Weir, Randy Jackson and Steve Jordan, joined on encore by Clarence Clemons.

Nov John Fogerty takes part in "Earthquake Relief" with Bonnie Raitt, Neil Young, Aaron Neville, the Chambers Brothers, Los Lobos and Santana in San Francisco.

1990

Feb [24] He participates in the "Roy Orbison All-Star Benefit" concert at the Universal Amphitheatre, Universal City, CA, singing *Ooby Dooby*.

Sept [6] Tom Fogerty dies in Scottsdale, AZ, of respiratory failure after a lengthy battle with tuberculosis.

Dec [13] The RIAA certifies a slew of Creedence singles and albums. *Proud Mary*, *Lodi*, *Down On The Corner*, *Who'll Stop The Rain* and *Lookin' Out My Back Door* are all confirmed platinum, while *Suzie Q*, *Commotion*, *Run Through The Jungle* and *Sweet Hitch-Hiker* are all certified gold. ***Creedence Clearwater Revival*** and ***Creedence Gold*** are certified platinum, while ***Chronicle***, ***Bayou Country*** and ***Willie & The Poor Boys*** are awarded multiplatinum discs for two million sales each, ***Green River*** is certified multiplatinum for three million sales and ***Cosmo's Factory*** is confirmed at the four-million mark.

1991

Jan [16] Fogerty sings *Proud Mary* with Chaka Khan at the traditional jam session after the sixth annual Rock and Roll Hall of Fame dinner, held at New York's Waldorf Astoria Hotel.

July [20] He sings three Creedence numbers at the second annual "Pops Staples Day" festivities in Drew, MS.

Nov [3] Fogerty, backed by the Grateful Dead, sings *Born On The Bayou*, *Green River*, *Bad Moon Rising* and *Proud Mary* at the "Laughter, Love And Music: To Celebrate The Lives Of Bill, Steve and Melissa" memorial concert in San Francisco's Golden Gate Park Polo Field, before an estimated 350,000 people.

1992

Jan [15] Fogerty inducts the late rock promoter Bill Graham at the seventh annual Rock and Roll Hall of Fame dinner, held again at the Waldorf Astoria Hotel.

May [2] Reissued *Bad Moon Rising* charts for a week at UK #71.

1993

Jan [12] Despite the band being inducted by Bruce Springsteen into the Rock and Roll Hall of Fame at the eighth annual awards dinner, held at the Century Plaza Hotel, Los Angeles, John Fogerty refuses to allow Clifford or Cook onstage for his ceremony-ending jam of Creedence hits.

Feb [3] An appeals court sides with Fantasy in overturning a portion of the 1988 verdict concerning delayed royalty payments allegedly owed to John Fogerty, amounting to $1.4 million.

Mar [8] Fogerty performs at the 1993 Bay Area Music Awards at San Francisco's Bill Graham Civic Auditorium.

1995

Sept [2] Fogerty sings *Born On The Bayou* and *Fortunate Son*, backed by Booker T. & the MG's and harmonises with Sam Moore on *Hold On I'm Coming* at the Concert for the Rock and Roll Hall of Fame at Cleveland Stadium, Cleveland, OH.

THE CREW CUTS

John Perkins (lead vocals); **Pat Barrett** (tenor vocals); **Rudi Maugeri** (baritone vocals); **Ray Perkins** (bass vocals)

1954

Apr Inspired by the success of the Four Lads, who came from the same school in Toronto, ON, Canada, the Perkins brothers, John (b. Aug. 28, 1931, Toronto) and Ray (b. Nov. 28, 1932, Toronto), Barrett (b. Sept. 15, 1933, Toronto), and Maugeri (b. Jan. 27, 1931, Toronto) have formed the Canadaires in 1952 at the Cathedral Choir School. After establishing a local reputation, appearing on Gene Carroll's TV talent show and singing on a radio show in Cleveland, OH, where influential disc jockey Bill Randle admired them, suggested a change of name and recommended them to Mercury Records, who signed them sight unseen, the Crew Cuts debut with *Crazy 'Bout You Baby*, written by Barrett and Maugeri, which hits US #8. In the can after 32 takes, it is the Crew Cuts' only self-penned hit.

May *Sh-Boom*, an obscure but ultra-catchy R&B novelty by black vocal quintet the Chords, outsells all national pop hits. Mercury A&R men hustle the Crew Cuts into the studio to rush out a cover.

June White radio stations saturate the airwaves with the Crew Cuts' new release, which becomes a US #1 best-seller and obliterates the original, raising questions about the ethics of white artists duplicating localized black hits and relying on segregated radio to boost sales. Many acts adopt the tactic, but few pursue it as overtly as the Crew Cuts. *Sh-Boom* reaches UK #12 and earns a gold disc. (Some rock historians will cite this as the first rock'n'roll hit.)

Sept A diluted version of *Oop Shoop*, an R&B mover by Shirley Gunter & the Queens, returns the Crew Cuts to the chart, at US #18, but they miss with *Dance Mr. Snowman* and *The Whiffenpoof Song*.

Nov ***The Crew Cuts On Campus*** is their only chart album, at US #14.

1955

Jan The group scores a double-sided Top 10 hit: a cover of the Penguins' *Earth Angel* at US #3 and a cover of Gene & Eunice's *Ko Ko Mo* at US #6. *Earth Angel* also hits UK #4.

Apr Their cover version of Nappy Brown's manic US #25, *Don't Be Angry*, makes US #14. Its B-side covers the Danderliers' *Chop Chop Boom*.

June Rush-released *Two Hearts Two Kisses* (a Charms original) fails, but *A Story Untold* (a Nutmegs original) reaches US #16.

Aug *Gum Drop*, another Charms cover, hits US #10.

Dec *Angels In The Sky*, originally recorded by Tony Martin, makes US #11, as its B-side, *Mostly Martha*, also charts, at US #31.

1956

Feb The Crew Cuts' version of *Seven Days* peaks at US #18, overtaking Clyde McPhatter's original.

June Their cover of Marie Knight's *Tell Me Why* reaches only US #45.

1957

Jan The Crew Cuts' final chart entry - at US #17 - covers the country hit *Young Love* by Sonny James, while the original tops the survey.

1958

The group signs with RCA Records, releasing seven non-charting singles, followed by sides on Vee Jay, Wails, ABC, Chess, Warwick and Firebird.

1963

Following the failure of *Crew Necks And Khakis*, *Electronic Chair*, *Hip Huggers* and ***The Crew Cuts Go Folk***, the group breaks up and, looking back on a decade of rock'n'roll enervation, comments: "If we came out with a cover that was hot, it would certainly squelch the smaller distributor. But that was their (Mercury's) doing and we really didn't even think about it at all."

1982

The group releases an album for First American Records, and will subseqently perform occasionally on the oldies circuit, before finally retiring, with Pat living in New Jersey and working in the auto business, Ray working in real estate in California, John working in newspapers in New Orleans and Rudi, managing director at Radio Arts Syndication in California.

JIM CROCE

1963

Croce (b. Jan. 10, 1943, Philadelphia, PA), while studying at Villanova University, Villanova, PA, begins broadcasting a folk program on campus radio and develops his songwriting skills, having bought his first guitar two years earlier, while working part-time in a Philadelphia toy store. He also auditions for the college glee club and the Spires, which includes in its line-up one Tommy West. Croce heads for New York's Greenwich Village, playing solo and with his girlfriend Ingrid, performing at the 2nd Fret, the Gilded Cage and the Main Point clubs before making regular appearances at the Riddle Paddock venue in Lima, PA.

1966

Having toured Africa and the Middle East as part of a US State Department-sponsored trek the previous year, a newly-married Croce and Ingrid teach at summer camp in Pine Grove, PA. During the year he also composes the score for the Emmy award-winning documentary "Miners' Story".

1968

With Croce having spent much of 1967 still performing at the Riddle Paddock and working as a special education teacher at Pulasky Junior High in Chester, PA, the pair moves to New York at the suggestion of Tommy West, who is now running a production company with Terry Cashman and Gene Pistilli.

1969

Jan Cashman, Pistilli and West have secured a deal for the Croces with Capitol Records, which issues their debut album, ***Approaching Day***, produced by the trio.

1970

Oct The Croces return to Pennsylvania and the small town of Lyndell, where Jim takes various temporary jobs, not least as a truck driver and telephone lineman. While there they meet guitarist Maury Muehleisen.

1971

Feb Croce sends six new songs, including *Time In A Bottle* and *You Don't Mess Around With Jim*, to Tommy West, who invites him back to New York to cut the material.

Oct [11] Two weeks after the birth of his son Adrian, Croce records 11 tracks at the Hit Factory, which will comprise his ***You Don't Mess Around With Jim*** album.

1972

July [1] Newly signed to ABC Records, the self-penned, Cashman-and-West produced ***You Don't Mess Around With Jim*** enters the US chart, eventually hitting #1 and staying on the ranking throughout 1973 and well into 1974.

Sept Title cut, *You Don't Mess Around With Jim*, hits US #8.

Dec *Operator (That's Not The Way It Feels)* peaks at US #17.

1973

Feb [17] ***Life And Times*** enters the US chart (and will stay on the survey throughout 1973, eventually hitting #7.) Once again, the album effortlessly showcases Croce's easy vocal style and songwriting gifts.

Mar *One Less Set Of Footsteps* makes US #37.
July [21] Produced by Cashman and West, *Bad Bad Leroy Brown* (inspired by a character Croce met in Fort Dix, NJ, while working as a lineman) hits US #1 after an 11-week climb.
Sept [12] TV movie "She Lives", starring Desi Arnaz Jr., concerning the death of a woman from cancer, uses a track from ***You Don't Mess Around With Jim*** as its theme: *Time In A Bottle* will gain considerable radio play. The night of the telecast, Croce completes the recording of his third album, ***I Got A Name***.
[13] Croce makes his last recordings at the Hit Factory.
[20] Having performed at Northwestern State University of Louisiana, Natchitoches, LA, Croce is due to perform his second concert that day, 70 miles away in Sherman, TX. His Beechcraft D-18 twin-engine chartered aircraft hits a tree on take-off from Natchitoches Municipal Airport, killing Croce, aged 30, and five others, including his longtime guitarist, Maury Muehleisen.
Nov Posthumously-released *I Got A Name*, featured in the film "The Last American Hero", hits US #10, while *Time In A Bottle* enters the chart the same week.
Dec [15] ***I Got A Name*** bows on the US survey. It will eventually hit #2 and earn a gold disc for million-plus sales.
[29] Recorded over two years earlier, *Time In A Bottle* hits US #1, overtaking Charlie Rich's *The Most Beautiful Girl*.

1974

Jan [12] ***You Don't Mess Around With Jim*** finally tops the US chart after 18 months on the survey. *It Doesn't Have To Be That Way* makes US #64.
Feb [19] Croce posthumously wins the Favorite Male Artist, Pop/Rock category at the inaugural American Music Awards, held at the Aquarius Theater, Hollywood, CA.
Apr *I'll Have To Say I Love You In A Song* hits US #9.
May Frank Sinatra's version of *Bad Bad Leroy Brown* makes US #83.
July *Workin' At The Car Wash Blues* reaches US #32.
Oct [5] Compilation, ***Photographs & Memories - His Greatest Hits***, enters the US chart (and will hit #2, becoming Croce's fourth gold disc).

1975

Nov ***The Faces I've Been***, a double retrospective of recordings made between 1961-71, with side four featuring Croce's storytelling underscored by musical accompaniment, and released on Cashman and West's Lifesong label, reaches US #87. The extracted *Chain Gang Medley* will make US #63 in February the following year, while ***Time In A Bottle - Jim Croce's Greatest Love Songs***, a collection of material already released, will peak at US #170 12 months later.

1990

May [30] Croce is posthumously inducted into the Songwriters Hall of Fame at the 20th annual awards ceremony, held at the New York Hilton Hotel. Accepting the award on his behalf, Croce's son A.J. also performs *Bad Bad Leroy Brown*.

CROSBY, STILLS, NASH & YOUNG

David Crosby (vocals, guitar); **Stephen Stills** (vocals, guitar); **Graham Nash** (vocals, guitar); **Neil Young** (vocals, guitar)

1968

July Following the break-up of Buffalo Springfield, Stills (b. Jan. 3, 1945, Dallas, TX) is working out future plans with Atlantic Records (having recently turned down the lead singer slot in Blood Sweat & Tears, and recently returned from New York, NY where he has been playing on Judy Collins' ***Who Knows Where The Time Goes*** album), when Crosby (b. David Van Cortland, Aug. 14, 1941, Los Angeles, CA), ex-the Byrds, who is working on a solo project, takes Nash (b. Feb. 2, 1941, Blackpool, Lancs.), currently touring the US with the Hollies and to whom he was introduced two years earlier by Mama Cass Elliot, to meet him at his Los Angeles Laurel Canyon home. The trio, all with substantial musical experience and a history of success, embarks on a creative jamming session and decides to form a group.
Aug David Geffen, on behalf of Atlantic Records, begins the legal and contractual process necessary to unite them on the label. Crosby, Stills & Nash travel to the UK, to compose and rehearse in London (and so that Nash can serve the Hollies one month's notice).
Dec [8] Nash leaves the Hollies after a charity concert at the London Palladium.

1969

Jan [15] The new trio, having rehearsed in Moscow Road, London, until the New Year, and in John Sebastian's house in Long Island, NY, signs to Atlantic after the label agrees "to assign to CBS all right, title, etc., to the exclusive services of Richard Furay" in exchange for acquiring the rights to Graham Nash, who is still signed to Epic through the Hollies. (This releases Furay to record for Epic as part of Poco.) They fly to California to begin recording.
June Their debut album, ***Crosby, Stills & Nash***, is released. (It will sell over two million copies in the US in 12 months, but will never hit higher than US #6 during a two-year residence). The trio, about to tour the US for the first time, needs to find musicians to back the vocal/acoustic line-up (on the album, Stills and Clear Light's drummer, Dallas Taylor, have played most instrumental parts). Atlantic boss Ahmet Ertegun suggests Young (b. Nov. 12, 1945, Toronto, ON, Canada), who agrees to join, initially on a casual basis, as lead guitarist and occasional vocalist, provided his separate work with Crazy Horse is unaffected. He brings with him ex-Buffalo Springfield bassist Bruce Palmer, who soon leaves and is replaced by session man Greg Reeves. (Young becomes a full-time member, but his arrival will start a trend of group splits and reunions over the next 20 years, always sparked by the independent spirits of the four personalities).
Aug [16] The group performs its second live gig, at the "Woodstock Music & Art Fair", Bethel, NY, opening as the acoustic Crosby, Stills & Nash, and then being joined by Young and the band for an electric set.
[18] The band plays at the Greek Theatre, Los Angeles, with Buffalo Springfield's Bruce Palmer joining them on stage.
[23] *Marrakesh Express*, a Nash song which the Hollies had failed to finish recording in April 1968, makes US #28. A lengthy US tour begins.
Sept ***Crosby, Stills & Nash*** peaks at UK #25, *Marrakesh Express* at #17.
[19-20] The group performs at New York's Fillmore East. (They had been scheduled to make their debut in late July, but the shows were cancelled.)
[30] While the trio is rehearsing at Crosby's Novato, CA home for an upcoming four-night stint at the Winterland Ballroom, San Francisco, CA, Crosby's girlfriend, Christine Hinton, is killed in a car crash, on the day the album is certified gold in the US.
Nov [29] From the album, *Suite : Judy Blue Eyes* (penned by Stills for his girlfriend, Judy Collins) makes US #21 (the label credit is still to Crosby, Stills & Nash).
Dec [6] Crosby, Stills, Nash & Young guest at the Rolling Stones concert at the Altamont Speedway, Livermere, CA. After their act, the event turns into violent tragedy when a murder occurs during the Stones' set.

1970

Jan They embark on the European leg of their "Carry On" tour, ending at London's Royal Albert Hall, and then split for three months to pursue individual work. Stills buys a house from Ringo Starr and settles in the UK, taking guitar lessons from Jimi Hendrix, and working on his first solo album.
Mar [11] The group wins Best New Artist category at the 12th annual Grammy Awards.
May [9] *Woodstock*, a Joni Mitchell song celebrating the festival, is the first Crosby, Stills, Nash & Young release, and peaks at US #11.
[16] The first CSN&Y album, ***Déjà Vu***, tops the US chart, having been certified gold after its first week on release. Subsequently revered as a classic rock outing, all four members have contributed songs (totalling 800 hours' work in the studio), which are self-produced by the group. The band tours the US again after its three-month sabbatical, replacing Reeves and Taylor with Calvin "Fuzzy" Samuels and John Barbata (ex-Turtles). ***Déjà Vu*** hits UK #5.
[25] ***Déjà Vu*** is certified gold by the RIAA.
[21] The group records *Ohio* at the Record Plant, Los Angeles, a song Young has been urgently inspired to write the previous evening, having seen graphic media reports of the killing of four people during student disturbances at Kent State University.
June [2-7] CSN&Y play a week-long stint at New York's Fillmore East.
July [25] Nash's song *Teach Your Children*, with Jerry Garcia on pedal steel, makes US #16.
Aug [8] *Ohio* reaches US #14. (The week before, *Teach Your Children* and *Ohio* stood at #16 and #17 respectively on the Hot 100.)
[14] While on tour, Stills is arrested on suspected drugs charges at a San Diego, CA motel, after being found crawling along a corridor in an incoherent state. He is freed on $2,500 bail. (At the end of the US tour, after a performance at New York's Carnegie Hall, the group splits for the first time, following internal dissent, mainly between Young and the others.)
Oct [31] *Our House*, another Nash composition from ***Déjà Vu***, peaks at US #30.
Dec Stills' solo album, ***Stephen Stills***, recorded in London in May, with contributions from Crosby and Nash, Eric Clapton, Jimi Hendrix and others, hits US #3 and UK #30, as he embarks on a 52-date North American tour to promote the album. He subsequently begins work on a second album in London, with his new Stephen Stills Band (which includes former CSN&Y sidemen Samuels and Taylor).

1971

Jan [30] *Love The One You're With* from the album, the title suggested to Stills by Billy Preston, reaches US #14 (and UK #37 two months later).
Apr [3] *Sit Yourself Down*, from Stills' album, makes US #37.
May [1] Crosby's *Music Is Love*, with Nash and Young featured, climbs to US #95. It is from his album ***If Only I Could Remember My Name***, recorded with help from Jerry Garcia, Joni Mitchell, Nash, Young and others. The album reaches both US and UK #12.
[12] Stills is a guest at Mick and Bianca Jagger's wedding in St. Tropez, France.
Nash compiles the live double album ***4-Way Street*** from recordings made at the group's Chicago, IL, Los Angeles and New York gigs. Already certified gold on ship-out, it hits US #1 and UK #5, confirming CSN&Y as the most popular ex-band after the Beatles (they are currently voted Best International Group in the **Melody Maker** poll). Young's parallel solo career, with the Top 10 success of ***After The Gold Rush***, makes any group reunion unlikely in the short term.
July [24] Final single from Stills' first album, *Change Partners*, makes US #43, while Nash releases solo album, ***Songs For Beginners***, reaching US #15 and UK #13. His extracted *Chicago*, written about the fate of the Chicago Seven, peaks at US #35.
Aug Solo album, ***Stephen Stills 2*** (recorded with the 1970 line-up of the Stephen Stills Band, before its split after a long US tour) hits US #8 and makes UK #22, as Stills is in the midst of another (52-date) solo tour.
[26] ***Songs For Beginners*** is certified gold by the RIAA.
Sept [25] From his solo set, Stills' *Marianne* makes US #42.
Oct [2] Nash's *Military Madness* peaks at US #73.
[4] Stills joins Crosby and Nash on stage at a Carnegie

Hall concert in New York.
While recording in Miami, Stills, joined by Chris Hillman and Al Perkins from the Flying Burrito Brothers, Taylor, percussionist Joe Lala, bassist Kenny Passarelli and keyboard player Paul Harris, forms the new group Manassas.
Dec [4] Crosby and Nash, on a tour of Europe, perform at London's Royal Albert Hall, then head to Stockholm, Sweden, for a concert on the 6th.

1972

May Stills' double album, ***Manassas***, hits US #4 and UK #30, while Crosby and Nash unite on ***Graham Nash/David Crosby***, which hits US #4 and peaks at UK #13.
[30] ***Graham Nash/David Crosby*** is certified gold by the RIAA.
June [17] Their extracted single, *Immigration Man*, featuring Dave Mason on lead guitar, makes US #36, as Stills' *It Doesn't Matter*, written with Chris Hillman, peaks at US #61. Crosby and Nash begin to play regular gigs together around the US.
July [22] Stills' follow-up (with Manassas), *Rock And Roll Crazies*, reaches US #92.
[29] Young and Nash, backed by Young's new band, the Stray Gators, produces the one-off single *War Song* which makes US #61.
Aug [12] Stills plays alongside Jefferson Airplane and James Brown at the "Festival Of Hope" benefit concert for the Nassau Society of Crippled Children & Adults at Roosevelt Raceway, Garden City, New York, as *Southbound Train* by Crosby and Nash peaks at US #99.
Oct [8] Stills & Manassas perform at London's Edmonton Sundown during a UK tour, having made their live debut in March in Amsterdam, Holland.

1973

Jan Crosby and Nash join Young on some dates of his US tour with the Stray Gators. Stills marries French singer Veronique Sanson.
May Second Manassas album, ***Down The Road***, reaches US #26 and makes UK #33.
June [2] The extracted single, *Isn't It About Time*, peaks at US #56.
Crosby, Stills, Nash & Young come together in Hawaii to play, and then rehearse at Young's Broken Arrow ranch in La Honda, CA. Sessions for the projected album, ***Human Highway***, break up acrimoniously after several tracks have been recorded, but they plan to play an October tour (which will also come to naught when Young pulls out).
Sept Hillman, Perkins and Harris leave Manassas to form the Souther Hillman Furay Band with J.D. Souther and Richie Furay. Stills replaces them with Donnie Dacus (guitar), Jerry Aiello (keyboards) and Russ Kunkel (drums).
Oct [4] Crosby and Nash join Stills and Manassas on stage at the Winterland Ballroom, San Francisco, followed later by Young. It results in a 50-minute CSN&Y set.

1974

Feb Nash's solo album, ***Wild Tales***, reaches US #34.
Mar [15] A CSN&Y reunion is officially confirmed.
May The quartet reunites at Young's ranch to rehearse for live work, while Stills disbands Manassas.
July [9] A CSN&Y US 30-date tour opens in Seattle, WA, where they perform a four-hour set to 15,000 people, backed by Kunkel and Lala from Manassas and bassist Tim Drummond. Personnel conflicts continue as Young elects to travel separately from the other three.
Sept [14] The group returns to the UK, playing (with the Band and Joni Mitchell) at Wembley Stadium, Wembley, Middx., before 80,000 people.
Nov [2] Nash-compiled group anthology album, ***So Far***, comprising the quartet's best-known material, tops the US chart (the third CSN&Y #1 in three releases) having reached UK #25 on Oct [19].
Dec The foursome start recording again, with Russ Kunkel (drums) and Leland Sklar (bass), but once again arguments cut short the sessions. They record *Wind On The Water*, *Human Highway*, *Homeward Through The Haze* and *Through My Sails*.
[14] Crosby and Nash play as a duo at a San Francisco joint benefit concert for the United Farm Workers and for Project Jonah, devoted to whale protection.

1975

Jan The group tries to record again, at the Record Plant in Sausalito, CA, with Russ Kunkel, Lee Sklar and Bill Kreutzmann. A major row between Nash and Stills - over a single harmony note - prompts Young to leave the studio, vowing never to return. Stills signs a new recording deal with CBS/Columbia, and forms a new band with Lala, Dacus, Aiello, George Perry on bass and Ronald Ziegler on drums.
July [26] Stills' Columbia debut, ***Stills***, reaches UK #31.
Aug [9] ***Stills*** makes US #19, as Young joins him onstage at a Greek Theatre, UCLA, Berkeley, CA gig.
[23] The extracted single, *Turn Back The Pages*, makes US #84. Stills plays a six-week US tour with his new band (plus Rick Roberts from Firefall).
Nov [29] Signed to the ABC label, Crosby and Nash's ***Wind On The Water***, with their new band - Danny Kortchmar (guitar), Craig Doerge (keyboards), Leland Sklar (bass) and Russ Kunkel (drums), hits US #6.
Dec [6] Taken from it, *Carry Me*, with James Taylor guesting on acoustic guitar, peaks at US #52.
[31] Stills and Young play a New Year's Eve club gig in San Francisco.

1976

Jan [25] Stills appears with Bob Dylan (and stages a guitar duel with Carlos Santana) on the all-star bill of the "Night Of The Hurricane 2" benefit concert for imprisoned boxer Hurricane Carter, at the Houston Astrodome, Houston, TX.
Feb [14] ***Stephen Stills - Live on Atlantic***, with tracks mainly recorded by Stills and Manassas before it was disbanded, makes US #42.
July [3] Stills' ***Illegal Stills***, on CBS/Columbia, makes US #31 and UK #54. He links again with Young to record an album as the Stills/Young Band, and tours the US (the band is basically Stills' current outfit, with new drummer Joe Vitale, plus Young as co-lead vocalist and guitarist). The Stills/Young Band tour is almost halted when the latter pulls out after the first few dates, with throat problems. Chris Hillman deputizes to allow Stills to complete the tour.
Aug [21] Crosby and Nash's *Out Of The Darkness* makes US #89.
Sept [18] Its parent album, ***Whistling Down The Wire***, reaches US #26.
Oct [16] The Stills/Young Band's ***Long May You Run***, released on Young's current label, Reprise, reaches UK #12.
Nov Stills plays a solo, mainly acoustic, US tour, before talking to Crosby and Nash about another reunion.
[17] ***Long May You Run*** reaches US #26 and is certified gold for 500,000 US sales.
[25] Young and Stills appear with the Band at its "Last Waltz" farewell concert at San Francisco's Winterland.
Dec Crosby and Nash make a brief UK concert visit before meeting up with Stills at Criteria Studios in Miami to record. (Stills had seen Crosby and Nash at the Greek Theatre in Los Angeles, which had led to the reunion. Another attempt at recording CSN&Y in Miami had failed prior to the Stills/Young tour.)

1977

Jan [29] Compilation album, ***Still Stills - The Best Of Stephen Stills***, peaks at US #127.
June [2] CS&N begin a month's tour at the Pine Knob Music Theatre, Clarkston, MI.
July [23] The trio's album, ***CSN***, reaches UK #23.
Aug [13] ***CSN*** hits US #2, and is certified platinum by the RIAA.
[27] From it, *Just A Song Before I Go*, written for a bet in 15 minutes by Nash, hits US #7. A major US tour begins.
Nov [12] *Fair Game*, also taken from ***CSN***, makes US #43.
Dec [17] ***Crosby/Nash Live***, climbs to US #52.

1978

June CS&N, following the recording of yet another album, which doesn't see the light of day, embark on a further US tour, this time playing an acoustic-only set.
Nov [4] Greg Reeves sues CSN&Y, claiming $1 million in back royalties.
[11] Retrospective ***The Best Of Crosby/Nash***, on ABC, reaches US #150.
[18] Stills' solo album, ***Thoroughfare Gap***, peaks at US #83.

1979

Jan Stills plays a lengthy US tour with the California Blues Band, comprising Dallas Taylor, George Perry, Mike Finnigan and Jerry Tolman, with Bonnie Bramlett (ex-Delaney & Bonnie) on back-up vocals, as Nash joins Jackson Browne for a series of California benefits.
Feb Crosby and Nash begin recording a new album for CBS/Columbia.
Mar [2] Stills plays at the "Havana Jam Festival" in Cuba, sharing a bill with Billy Joel and Kris Kristofferson.
June [14] Nash participates in the "Survival Sunday" benefit at the Hollywood Bowl for Musicians United For Safe Energy (MUSE).
Sept [19-23] Crosby, Stills & Nash come together again, to play at New York's Madison Square Garden anti-nuclear benefit concerts organized by MUSE.
Oct Crosby and Nash take part in the "Bread & Roses Festival" at the Greek Theatre, UCLA, Berkeley.

1980

Mar [29] Nash's solo album, ***Earth And Sky***, on Capitol, reaches US #117, while Crosby is attempting to find a label for his solo projects.
June [14] Stills and Nash perform as soloists in a further "No Nukes" benefit concert at the Hollywood Bowl, CA, headlined by Bruce Springsteen.
July [16] Documentary film "No Nukes" premieres in New York, and includes CS&N's set from the September 1979 concert.
Oct Stills and Nash begin work on a new album, while also playing a series of North American dates.

1981

Jan Compilation album, ***Replay***, with tracks from both CS&N and Stills' solo albums, peaks at US #122.
Sept Nash rejoins the Hollies to appear on BBC1-TV's "Top Of The Pops", on which they perform the UK #29 hit *Holliedaze*.

1982

Mar [28] Crosby is arrested in Los Angeles, en route to an anti-nuclear demo, for driving while under the influence of cocaine, possessing quaaludes and "drug paraphernalia", and carrying a concealed .45-calibre pistol.
Apr [13] Crosby is arrested again, when police find him preparing cocaine in his dressing room at Cardi's nightclub in Dallas, with a concealed gun nearby.
June Crosby, Stills & Nash play the "Peace Sunday" anti-nuclear concert at the Rose Bowl in Pasadena, CA, alongside Bob Dylan, Joan Baez, Stevie Wonder and others.
Aug [14] ***Daylight Again***, another CS&N reunion, with most of its songs written by Stills, hits US #8 and collects their second platinum award for million-plus US sales.
[21] From it, the Nash-penned *Wasted On The Way*, with Timothy B. Schmit contributing a vocal part, hits US #9.
Nov [20] *Southern Cross*, also from ***Daylight Again***, reaches US #18.

1983

Feb [12] CS&N's *Too Much Love To Hide* peaks at US #69.
July [30] Their remake of the Supremes' *Stop! In The Name Of Love*, which sees Nash rejoin the Hollies again, reaches US #29, as parent album, ***What Goes***

Around, makes US #90. (This line-up of the Hollies - Nash, Allan Clarke, Tony Hicks and Bobby Elliott - tours the US before disbanding once more.) Live CS&N album, ***Allies***, and, extracted *War Games* both peak at US #43.
Aug [5] After sleeping through most of his trial, Crosby is convicted in Texas on charges of possessing cocaine and carrying a gun into a bar. He is sentenced by Judge Pat McDowell to five years in the Texas State Penitentiary (but remains free while the sentence is appealed).

1984

Sept [15] Back on Atlantic as a solo artist, Stills peaks at US #61 with *Stranger*, as ***Right By You*** makes US #75.
Dec Judge McDowell allows Crosby to enter a drug rehabilitation program in lieu of serving time in jail.

1985

Jan Crosby enters a drug-treatment programme at Fair Oaks Hospital, Summit, NJ.
Mar [7] He is returned to jail in Dallas, after absconding from Fair Oaks.
July [13] Crosby, out on an appeal bond, joins Stills, Nash and Young to perform at the "Live Aid" concert in Philadelphia, PA, as part of a major US CS&N tour.
Dec [12] Crosby, after spending 17 days as a fugitive from justice, turns himself in to the FBI in Florida to face charges.

1986

May [17] Nash's *Innocent Eyes*, on the Atlantic label, makes US #84, as its parent album, ***Innocent Eyes***, looks at US #136. Crosby, now serving time in the Texas State Penitentiary, joins an inmates' rock group. He will be released from jail in August, after which he embarks on a series of solo gigs. (The first CS&N shows after his release are benefits for the Bridge School, organized annually by Young, and Greenpeace.)

1987

Feb CS&N are prevented from taking part in a Greenpeace benefit in Vancouver, BC, Canada, when Crosby is not allowed into the country.
May [15] Crosby marries long-time girlfriend Jan Dance in Los Angeles. Nash and his wife Susan renew their wedding vows at the ceremony. Crosby celebrates by signing a solo deal with A&M.

1988

Jan Young is prevented from rejoining CS&N by label boss David Geffen.
May [14] CS&N open Atlantic Records' 40th anniversary concert in New York's Madison Square Garden.
Sept CSN&Y return to the studio to cut their first tracks together in 14 years.
Dec [11] Nash attends Roy Orbison's memorial service with Don Henley, Tom Petty, and Bonnie Raitt, among others.

1989

Jan CSN&Y's comeback album, ***American Dream***, co-produced by the group with Niko Bolas, reaches US #16 and UK #55.
Feb [25] The extracted single, *Got it Made*, peaks at US #69.
Mar Crosby's solo album, ***Oh Yes I Can***, co-produced by Crosby with Craig Doerge and Stanley Johnston, makes US #104.
Nov [21] With Young once more retreating to his solo career, CS&N give a 20-minute performance of *Teach Your Children*, *Long Time Gone* and *Carried Away* in the Tiergarten Park in front of the Brandenburg Gate, Berlin, Germany.

1990

Mar [31] CSN&Y play a benefit concert for their erstwhile drummer Dallas Taylor, who is in need of a liver transplant, at the Civic Auditorium, Santa Monica, CA. Don Henley and the Desert Rose Band also play on the bill.
Apr [1] The group plays another fundraiser for the California Environmental Protection Initiative.
[7] The trio sings *Suite : Judy Blue Eyes* at "Farm Aid IV".
[16] Crosby guests on the season premiere of NBC-TV's "Shannon's Deal".
[17] Taylor has a liver transplant at Cedars-Sinai Medical Center, Los Angeles.
July [5-7] The group performs at the Mann Music Center, Philadelphia, PA, grossing $528,137 during their current US tour, which is set to end on September 22nd.
[21] CS&N's ***Live It Up***, produced by Joe Vitale, Stanley Johnston and the performing trio, makes US #57.
Oct [12] "The Inside Track", a weekly one-hour one-on-one interview show with music, presented by Nash, premieres on the A&E cable network. Crosby is his first guest.
[12-13] The group performs at the "From Chile - An Embrace Of Hope" Amnesty International benefits at the National Stadium, Santiago, Chile.
[19] Nash and Stills sing with Judy Collins on "The Inside Track."
Nov [17] Though fully recovered from his chemical dependency, Crosby breaks his left leg, ankle and shoulder when he comes off his Harley Davidson motorbike near his home.

1991

Feb [10] Stills joins nearly 100 celebrities in Burbank, CA, to record *Voices That Care*, a David Foster-and fiancée Linda Thompson Jenner-composed and-organized charity record to benefit the American Red Cross Gulf Crisis Fund.
[12] Crosby is honored as MusiCares Man of the Year at the NARAS Musicares lunch at New York's Waldorf Astoria Hotel. (Founded by NARAS, MusiCares provides health and welfare programs for those in the music industry.)
[20] Crosby provides harmony vocal to Phil Collins' *Another Day In Paradise* at the 33rd annual Grammy Awards, at Radio City Music Hall, New York.
May [16-17] The group performs to a sellout crowd of 9,633 at the Mark Etess Arena, Trump Taj Mahal, Atlantic City, NJ, during current US dates.
Oct [1] The trio sings at the ACLU Foundation of Southern California's 1991 Torch of Liberty Awards dinner at the Beverly Hilton Hotel, Los Angeles.
Nov [3] Crosby Stills and Nash sing *Teach Your Children*, *Love The One You're With*, *Long May You Run*, *Long Time Gone*, *Southern Cross*, *Only Love Can Break Your Heart*, *Wooden Ships* and *Ohio* at the "Laughter, Love And Music: To Celebrate The Lives of Bill, Steve and Melissa" memorial concert at San Francisco's Golden Gate Park Polo Field, before an estimated 350,000 crowd.
[20] The group guests on NBC-TV's "Late Night With David Letterman".
Dec [3] Crosby presents the Bill Graham Award to Amnesty International executive director, Jack Healey at the **Billboard** Music Awards.

1992

Jan [4] Four-CD/cassette boxed-set career retrospective, ***Crosby Stills & Nash***, featuring remixes and alternate takes of many of their songs, debuts at its US #109 peak. The compilation is dedicated to Mama Cass, "without whom most of this music may never have been made".
[21] Crosby guest stars on ABC-TV's "Roseanne" playing Bonnie Bramlett's character's husband.
Mar [28-29] The group plays two concerts at London's Hammersmith Odeon.
Apr [11] Crosby joins a host of performers and actors welcoming Democratic presidential candidate Jerry Brown to his "We The People Can...II" awareness and fundraising concert at the Air Center Hangar, Santa Monica.
June [10] The band performs at the Meadowlands Summerfest, East Rutherford, NJ, during a major US summer tour, set to end September 1st at the Deer Creek Music Center, Noblesville, IN.
Sept [26] Crosby Stills & Nash perform at a benefit concert at the Joe Robbie Stadium in Miami, also featuring Jon Secada, Whoopi Goldberg, Paul Simon, Gloria Estefan and Bonnie Raitt, to raise funds for those left homeless by the recent Hurricane Andrew disaster.
Oct [8] The group performs at London's Royal Albert Hall during a five-date leg of their European tour.
Nov [8] They participate in the "Imua Hawaii" benefit at the NBC Arena, Honolulu, HI, to help victims of Hurricane Iniki, with Jackson Browne, Jimmy Buffett and Bonnie Raitt.

1993

Jan [17] Stills performs at "An American Reunion: The People's Inaugural Celebration" during inaugural festivities at the Lincoln Memorial in Washington, DC.
May [6] Crosby guests on Fox-TV's "The Simpsons".
[15] *Hero*, a duet with Phil Collins from Crosby's forthcoming solo album, ***Thousand Roads***, bows at its UK #56 peak.
July [3] ***Thousand Roads,*** featuring songs penned by Stephen Bishop, Paul Brady, Phil Collins, John Hiatt, Joni Mitchell and Jimmy Webb, and variously produced by Collins, Marc Cohn, Phil Ramone and Don Was, peaks at US #133.
[17] *Hero* makes US #44.
[28] Crosby & Nash perform at the Pine Knob Music Theatre, Clarkston, MI, during their current US tour.
Nov [5] Nash takes part in the seventh annual benefit for the Bridge School at the Shoreline Amphitheater, Mountain View, CA.

1994

Feb [9] During current US dates, they perform at the Majestic Performing Arts Center, San Antonio, TX.
June [21] Currently on tour with the Neville Brothers, they play to a sellout crowd of 4,050 at the James L. Knight Center, Miami, FL.
Sept [3] CS&N's ***After The Storm*** makes US #98.
Oct [5] It announced that Crosby Stills & Nash's current 25th anniversary concert tour is to be cancelled, because Crosby is in urgent need of a liver transplant.
Nov [20] Following a three-week wait, Crosby receives a liver transplant at UCLA's Medical Center in a seven-hour operation.
Dec [9] Nash and Stills perform with Jackson Browne at the National Academy of Songwriters' ninth annual Salute To The American Songwriter, as they are honored with the Lifetime Achievement Award. (Crosby will remain in hospital until the 13th.)

1995

Feb [18] Hootie & the Blowfish's breakthrough single, *Hold My Hand*, with Crosby featured on backing vocals, hits US #10.
[27] Crosby performs at the MusiCares benefit, with Tony Bennett, Natalie Cole and Bonnie Raitt.
May [6] Crosby & Nash perform a benefit at Oklahoma City, OK's Zoo Amphitheater, for the parents of the Alfred P. Murrah Federal Building bomb victims after Stills has launched the Human Spirit Fund, a non-profit organization to raise funds for the future educational needs for young survivors of the recent Oklahoma City bombing tragedy.
see also: **BUFFALO SPRINGFIELD, THE BYRDS, THE HOLLIES, Neil YOUNG**

CHRISTOPHER CROSS

1971

The son of an army officer, Cross (b. Christopher Geppert, May 3, 1951, San Antonio, TX) joins Flash, a local hard-rock band (as its singer and guitarist), which establishes a healthy live reputation and opens for many rock acts, including Led Zeppelin, Jefferson Airplane and Deep Purple. After two years with the outfit, Cross quits to concentrate on songwriting while studying as a pre-med student, before joining a Top 40 covers bar band. Sending pop/ballad demos of his solo work to record companies in 1975, he forms a backing band and performs his own material with keyboardist Rob Meurer, bassist Andy Salmon and Tommy Taylor on drums. Having built up a strong live reputation in Texas, Cross and the band are spotted the following year by Tim Neece, a manager, and Michael Brovsky, who encourage him to record a more polished set of demo tapes.

1978

Oct After a showcase performance arranged for Warner Bros. Records A&R chief, Michael Ostin, at the Alamo Roundhouse in Austin, TX, Cross signs to the label, establishes his own publishing company, Pop'n'Roll, and moves to Los Angeles with his backing band.

1979

Producer Michael Omartian is brought in to work on the singer's songs for his debut album. A host of seasoned music veterans, including Michael McDonald, J.D. Souther, Don Henley and Nicolette Larson, participates in the sessions.

1980

Jan Cross contributes guitar parts to Carole King's ***Pearls - Songs Of Goffin And King***, recorded at Pecan Street Studios in Austin.

Feb His freshman album, the entirely self-penned ***Christopher Cross***, is released in the US. Highlighted by his radio-ready, melodic pop/rock composition skills and smooth alto vox, it will spend over two years on chart and peak at US #6.

Apr [26] The extracted *Ride Like The Wind*, featuring McDonald on backing vocals, hits US #2.

Ride Like The Wind makes UK #69 during a one-week chart stay.

Aug [30] Follow-up US single, the ballad *Sailing*, tops the US chart.

Nov [29] *Never Be The Same* peaks at US #15, as Cross embarks on major US dates.

1981

Feb *Sailing* docks at UK #48, while ***Christopher Cross*** begins a 77-week chart run, eventually peaking at UK #14 (May [9]) and earning a gold disc.

[22] Cross sweeps the 23rd annual Grammy Awards, winning in five categories (beating the previous best by Frank Sinatra and Barbra Streisand): Record Of The Year (*Sailing*), Album Of The Year (***Christopher Cross***), Song Of The Year (*Sailing*), Best New Artist and Best Arrangement Accompanying Vocalist (*Sailing*).

May [23] *Say You'll Be Mine* reaches US #20.

Oct [17] *Arthur's Theme (Best That You Can Do)*, co-penned with Bacharach, Carole Bayer Sager and Peter Allen for the Dudley Moore/Liza Minnelli movie "Arthur", tops the US chart for the first of three weeks (and makes UK #56).

1982

Jan *Arthur's Theme*, reissued in the UK after the success of the film, hits UK #7. Cross visits the UK for selected sellout dates.

Apr *Arthur's Theme* wins an Oscar for Best Song From A Film at the 55th Academy Awards.

June Co-produced by Cross, the Alessi brothers' ***Long Time Friends*** is released. The extracted single, *Put Away Your Love*, peaks at US #71.

1983

Feb His sophomore set, ***Another Page***, is released. Produced again by Omartian, and featuring backing vocals by Art Garfunkel, Karla Bonoff and Carl Wilson, it makes US #11 and hits UK #4.

Mar [5] The extracted *All Right* climbs to US #12 and UK #51.

June [11] *No Time To Talk*, also from ***Another Page***, makes US #33 but fails in the UK.

1984

Feb [4] After a slow start, the third single from the album, *Think Of Laura*, hits US #9, benefitting not least from its exposure in ABC-TV's "General Hospital" soap series.

July [7] *A Chance For Heaven*, a Christopher Cross track chosen as the official swimming theme for the 23rd Olympiad, and released on a special celebration album, sinks at US #76.

1985

Nov [9] As a prelude to his third album, *Charm The Snake* reaches US #68. ***Every Turn Of The World***, featuring songs co-written with Bobby Alessi, Will Jennings and producer Omartian, makes US #127.

1986

July Cross contributes *Loving Strangers* to the soundtrack of the Tom Hanks/Jackie Gleason movie "Nothing In Common".

1988

Aug After a long silence, Cross releases his fourth album, ***Back Of My Mind***, via the reactivated Reprise label. Continuing in his melodic pop vein, it is again helmed by Omartian, and features vocal backing from Michael McDonald and Christine McVie. Its limited sales indicate that his style, briefly fashionable, is no longer popular and it fails to chart, despite the release of an extracted duet with Frances Ruffelle, *I Will (Take You Forever)*.

1995

Mar [21] While UK outfit East Side Beat has seen fit to cover *Ride Like The Wind* (resulting in a UK #3 hit in December 1991), and following its initial release via PolyGram in Japan in February 1992, Cross has issued his first album in four years, ***Rendezvous***, on Ariola in September of that year. Co-produced with Rob Meurer, it featured long-time supporter McDonald, keyboardist Robbie Buchanan and the late Jeff Porcaro. Now signed to the Rhythm Safari label in the US, Cross releases ***Window***, mostly co-written and co-produced with keyboardist Rob Meurer. (Cross will perform on piano night at Nashville, TN's Ace of Clubs, during the city's "Tin Pan South" songwriters' week on April 17, 1996.)

SHERYL CROW

1991

The third of four children, Crow (b. Feb. 11, 1962, Kennett, MO), who has grown up in the small farming community of Kennett, the daughter of amateur big band musician parents, began playing piano by ear at the age of six. Having attended her first concert (to see Peter Frampton), Crow began writing songs at the age of 13 also singing in high school bands (including the rock combo Kashmir with her boyfriend) from the age of 16. Subsequently graduating with a classical music degree at the University of Missouri in 1984, she has relocated to St. Louis, MO, to teach music at an elementary school, before moving to Los Angeles, CA in 1986 to pursue her muse as a songwriter and performer, landing her first assignment as a backing singer on Michael Jackson's September 1987-bowing "Bad" 18-month world tour. Returning to Los Angeles, her songwriting efforts, encouraged by her friend Don Henley, secure covers by Eric Clapton and Wynonna Judd, while Crow also performs back-up singing duties on a number of major albums (including Henley's 1989 album ***The End Of The Innocence*** on *If Dirt Were Dollars*) and tours (for the likes of Rod Stewart, Joe Cocker and George Harrison), despite a temporary struggle with depression (which results in therapy and a spell on Prozac). Producer Hugh Padgham, impressed by her ability at a session for Pangaea label artist Vinx, passes her demo tape to A&M Records which now signs her to a solo deal. However recordings with Padgham for her debut album are deemed too slick and are shelved at a reported cost of $250,000, though she remains with the label for another try. While working on new material at the encouragement of labelmate David Baerwald, Crow begins attending informal mid-week songwriting/jamming sessions in Los Angeles begun by songwriter (and boyfriend) Kevin Gilbert and producer Bill Bottrell (at the latter's home studio) known as the "Tuesday Night Music Club", a productive spell which will yield Bottrell-produced tracks for her debut album release.

1993

Oct The resulting ***Tuesday Night Music Club*** is issued along with its lead-off single, the initially non-charting *Run, Baby, Run*. The album, co-written and performed by Crow with its title's members, Bottrell, Gilbert, Baerwald, David Ricketts, Dan Schwartz and Brian MacLeod (plus her trumpet playing father Wendell Crow on *We Do What We Can*), is supported with a couple of tours opening first for Big Head Todd & the Monsters followed by John Hiatt.

1994

Mar [19] ***Tuesday Night Music Club*** enters the US Album chart spurred by increasingly positive reaction from radio.

Apr [4] Crow plays at the Orpheum Theater, Boston, MA, opening for Crowded House.

May [21] Funky-pop leaning *Leaving Las Vegas* makes US #60.

June [18] *Leaving Las Vegas* charts for a week at UK #66.

July [7] A US tour opening for the reunited Eagles (with further dates at the beginning of 1995) begins at the Cleveland Municipal Stadium, OH, a gig grossing $2,313,147 from 46,103 attendees, set to end on September 13th at the Robert F. Kennedy Memorial Stadium, Washington DC.

Oct [1] A&M Records' Carpenters tribute album ***If I Were A Carpenter***, which includes Crow's version of *Solitaire*, debuts at its US #70 peak.

[8] *All I Wanna Do*, recalling Stealers Wheel's 1973 hit *Stuck In The Middle With You*, hits US #2, behind Boyz II Men's *I'll Make Love To You*. Crow performs *Don't Be Cruel* at "Elvis Aaron Presley: The Tribute", a multi-star music event staged at the Pyramid Arena, Memphis, TN (with Don Was as music director) and broadcast live on US pay-per-view TV.

[18-20] Crow opens for Bob Dylan at the Roseland Ballroom, New York, NY.

Nov [5] *All I Wanna Do* hits UK #2.

[22] *All I Wanna Do* is certified gold by the RIAA.

[25] Crow duets with Mick Jagger on *Under My Thumb* at a Rolling Stones concert (at which she is also on the bill) at Joe Robbie Stadium, Miami, FL.

[26] ***Tuesday Night Music Club*** intially makes UK #22, the same day that an MTV-produced breast-health awareness commercial featuring Crow begins airing in the US (also recording a track for the 14-cut various artists album ***Women For Women*** slated for January '95 release for the same cause).

Dec [5] She participates in the "Z-100 Acoustic Christmas" event held at New York's Madison Square Garden with Weezer, Indigo Girls, Hole, Green Day, Melissa Etheridge and others.

[17] On a bill with the Cramps, Jesus & Mary Chain, Radiohead, Fretblanket and Butt Trumpet, she appears at the "Deck The Hall Ball" held at the Exhibition Hall, Seattle, WA.

[31] Crow performs a New Year's Eve gig at the Hard Rock Cafe, Maui, HI.

1995

Jan [19] She appears at "Commitment To Life VIII", an AIDS Project Los Angeles benefit, honoring Elton John, Tom Hanks and Ron Meyer at the Universal Amphitheatre, Universal City, CA.

[24] Arista Records releases the film soundtrack to "Boys On The Side", which includes Stevie Nicks' version of a new Crow composition, *Somebody Stand By Me*, plus Crow's interpretation of Derek & the Dominos' *Keep On Growing*.

[27] Crow is the featured performer on TBS-TV's "Live From The House Of Blues".

Feb [11] *Strong Enough* debuts at its UK #33 peak.

[16] She appears on CBS-TV's "The Late Show With David Letterman".

[20] A headlining US tour gets underway at the Jesse Hall Aud, Columbia, MO.
Mar [1] Crow performs *All I Wanna Do* at the 37th annual Grammy Awards held at Los Angeles' Shrine Auditorium, at which the song nabs Record Of The Year and Best Pop Vocal Performance, Female, while Crow is also voted Best New Artist.
[10] She plays at the opening night gala of the Hard Rock Hotel & Casino in Las Vegas, NV.
[25] *Strong Enough* makes US #5 as ***Tuesday Night Music Club*** finally hits US #3, a year after its debut.
Apr [8] Atlantic Records' ***Encomium: A Tribute To Led Zeppelin***, featuring Crow's cover of *D'yer Maker*, bows at its US #17 peak.
[20] Her "MTV Unplugged" appearance airs from the Brooklyn Academy of Music, NY. (During the month Polygram releases ***18 Original Hits By 18 Unoriginal Artists*** which includes Crow on *All By Myself*.)
May [3] Crow appears at the seventh annual World Music Awards held at the Sporting Club in Monte Carlo, Monaco, airing on ABC-TV on the 30th.
[27] *Can't Cry Anymore* bows at its UK #33 peak.
June [3] Reactivated ***Tuesday Night Music Club*** finally hits UK #8, the same day that Crow is named Top New Artist at the inaugural Blockbuster Entertainment Awards held at Hollywood's Pantages Theatre, CA.
[14-18] Crow performs during the White Nights International Cultural Festival held at Oktybrsky Concert Hall in St Petersburg, Russia.
[19] The RIAA certifies five million sales of ***Tuesday Night Music Club***.
July [29] *Run, Baby, Run* bows at its UK #24 peak.
Aug [26] *Can't Cry Anymore* reaches US #36.
[31] Participating in this year's annual "H.O.R.D.E. Festival" US tour, Crow plays at South Park Meadows, Austin, along with the Black Crowes, Blues Traveler, Ziggy Marley, Ian Moore, G. Love & Special Sauce.
Sept [2] During a second headlining US trek, she performs *The Weight* backing Robbie Robertson, and *Get Off Of My Cloud* and *Let It Bleed* at the Concert for the Rock and Roll Hall of Fame opening ceremony held at the Cleveland Stadium, Cleveland, OH.
Nov [11] Still mining her two-year old debut album, *What I Can Do For You* charts for a week at UK #43.

1996

Mar [12] Philips Media releases the ***All Access: The H.O.R.D.E. Festival*** CD-ROM culled from performances on last year's H.O.R.D.E. tour including one by Crow.
[25] At the invitation of the First Lady, Crow performs a solo set in Baumholder, Germany for families of US troops stationed in Bosnia-Herzegovina who are being visited by Mrs. Clinton on a support mission.
[26] Warner Bros. Records (US) releases ***Songs In The Key Of X***, music from and inspired by the Fox-TV show "The X-Files", including a new cut by Crow.
Aug Salt 'N' Pepa's ***Flavor In Your Ear*** is scheduled for release, including a duet with Crow on *I Can't Breathe*.

CROWDED HOUSE

Neil Finn (guitar, vocals); **Paul Hester** (drums); **Nick Seymour** (bass)

1985

Following the demise of the quirky Australasian outfit Split Enz, Neil Finn (b. May 27, 1956, Te Awamutu, North Island, New Zealand) and recent Split Enz recruits Paul Hester (b. Jan. 8, 1959, Melbourne, Victoria, Australia) and Nick Seymour (b. Dec. 9, 1958, Benalla, Victoria, Australia), form the Mullanes (Neil's middle name), playing around the Melbourne area. With Neil offered a contract with Capitol Records in Los Angeles, the trio, initially augmented by guitarist Craig Hooper, relocates to California, where they play acoustic local club shows billed as the Largest Living Things, before settling on the moniker Crowded House (a reference to the members' cramped living conditions at their rented house off Sunset Blvd.). (Meanwhile, Split Enz founder Tim Finn (b. June 25, 1952,Te Awamutu) completes his second solo album, ***Big Canoe*** (which follows 1984's debut ***Escapade***) before beginning work on a musical in Rome, Italy, where his current belle, actress Greta Scaachi, is filming.)

1986

Aug [30] The group's debut album, ***Crowded House***, produced by Mitchell Froom and showcasing Neil Finn's singer/songwriting skills, enters the US chart on its way to #12 and platinum sales, during a 58-week survey tenure. The band embarks on a US tour augmented by ex-Split Enz keyboardist Eddie Raynor.

1987

Apr [25] Radio-friendly extract, *Don't Dream It's Over*, hits US #2.
June *Don't Dream It's Over* peaks at UK #27, the group's only UK chart appearance of the decade.
July [25] Follow-up, *Something So Strong*, again taken from the debut album, hits US #7.
Sept [11] "Don't Dream It's Over" wins the Best New Artist Video category at the fourth annual MTV Video Music Awards, held at the Universal Amphitheatre, Universal City, CA, at which they also perform.
[12] *World Where You Live* peaks at US #65, while the band records its second album.

1988

June [11] Paul Young sings *Don't Dream It's Over* at "Nelson Mandela's 70th Birthday Tribute" at Wembley Stadium, Wembley, Middx.
Aug Their sophomore effort, ***Temple Of Low Men***, reaches US #40.
[13] The extracted *Better Be Home Soon* peaks at US #42.
Sept [7] Crowded House performs for the second straight year at the annual MTV Video Music Awards, held at the Universal Amphitheatre.

1989

Apr [7] The band is joined by Roger McGuinn on *Mr. Tambourine Man*, *Eight Miles High* and *So You Want To Be A Rock'n'Roll Star* in concert in Los Angeles. The tracks will be released under the name *Byrdhouse* on a CD EP.

1991

Feb [14] After a lengthy hiatus during which the band has split up, re-formed, completed and shelved two albums, recorded a cover of *She's Not There* for the soundtrack to the 1990 Australian movie "The Crossing", and added Tim Finn, who had been working on a project with brother Neil and realized that the songs were perfect for the reunited Crowded House, the group returns to perform on the Los Angeles radio station KIQQ, on board a boat off the Californian coast.
June [12-13] The band plays at The Borderline in London.
[22] *Chocolate Cake* debuts at its UK #69 peak.
July [12] The group guests on NBC-TV's "Late Night With David Letterman", promoting its third album, ***Woodface***, which makes US #83 on the 20th and UK #34 on the 13th. (During the month, they perform a secret gig at Club Lingerie in Los Angeles as the Largest Living Things, with Roxy Music's Phil Manzanera guesting on a cover of Roxy's *Love Is The Drug*.)
Sept [11] They appear on NBC-TV's "The Tonight Show" midway through a US tour, highlighted by a gig at the Universal Amphitheatre, Universal City.
Oct [10] London dates include a performance at the Hammersmith Odeon.
[11] The band is featured on ABC-TV's "In Concert '91".
Nov [5] They appear at Birmingham's Goldwyns venue during a UK tour. Prior to a Glasgow, Scotland gig, Tim Finn announces that he is quitting the band by "mutual consent", leaving them to continue as a three piece. (He will return to his home in Madrid, Spain, before continuing his solo career.)
[23] *Fall At Your Feet* reaches UK #17, having peaked at US #75 the previous week.
Dec [16-17] The group grosses $84,548 at a pair of US tour gigs at the Wiltern Theatre, Los Angeles.

1992

Feb [27] An eight-date UK trek opens at Manchester's Apollo Theatre, set to end on March 7th at the Guildhall, Portsmouth, Hants.
Mar [3] The band is featured on C4-TV's "Return To The Dome" before appearing on BBC1-TV's "Top Of The Pops" on the 5th.
[21] Belated ***Woodface*** extract, *Weather With You*, tied in with a sponsorship deal with Chiltern Radio's weather forecasts, hits UK #7.
[28] The group appears on the INXS-topping bill of "A Concert For Life" at Centennial Park, Sydney, New South Wales, Australia, to benefit the Victor Chang Cardiac Centre and AIDS Patient Services and Research Centre at the St. Vincent Hospital, Sydney, as ***Woodface*** recharts, hitting UK #6.
May Tim Finn works on his Capitol Records debut, with producers Clive Langer and Alan Winstanley at Outside Studios.
June [8] The group performs at the Hanover Music Hall, Germany, during a week-long series of concert and festival dates in Germany.
[24] They play at the Wembley Arena during a week-long UK tour.
[27] *Four Seasons In One Day* reaches UK #26.
July [7] A nine-date British tour begins at the Brighton Centre, Brighton, E. Sussex, set to close on the 17th at Dublin Stadium, Dublin, Eire.
Oct [1] The band returns to the UK to appear on "Top Of The Pops".
[3] Still mining ***Woodface***, *It's Only Natural* reaches UK #24.

1993

Apr The group finishes its new album (with Youth and Bob Clearmountain producing) at Platinum Studios, Melbourne.
June Neil and Tim Finn are recognised in H.R.H. Queen Elizabeth II's Birthday Honours list, receiving the O.B.E. for their service to their native New Zealand.
July [3] Tim Finn's *Persuasion* makes UK #43, as a prelude to ***Before & After***, which debuts the following week at its UK #29 peak.
Sept [4] The group, now augmented by keyboardist Mark Hart (b. July 2, 1953, Fort Scott, KS) embarks on the nine-date North American leg of the "WOMAD" festival, while their fourth album, ***Together Alone***, is set for release by Capitol.
[18] Tim Finn's *Hit The Ground Running* debuts at its UK #50 peak.
Oct [9] The group's *Distant Sun* reaches UK #19.
[23] Critically-revered ***Together Alone*** enters at its UK #4 high.
Nov [27] The extracted *Nails In My Feet* reaches UK #22 (with a live version of *Don't Dream It's Over* available on the CD-single format).

1994

Jan [29] ***Together Alone*** bows at its US #73 peak.
Feb [14] The band wins the Best International Group category at the 13th annual BRIT Awards at London's Alexandra Palace.
[19] *Locked Out* debuts at its UK #12 pinnacle.
Mar [16-17] The group plays sellout dates at Los Angeles' Wiltern Theatre, during extensive North American tour.
Apr Hester quits, citing pressures of touring and lack of motivation and will be replaced by Melbourne native Peter Jones.
May [4] Crowded House is named the World's Best-selling Australian Recording Artist Of The Year at the sixth World Music Awards, held at the Sporting Club, Monte Carlo, Monaco, the same day the band is performing at the Arena, Edmonton Convention Center, Edmonton, AB, Canada.
June [11] *Fingers Of Love* bows at its UK #25 peak,

as the group takes part in the "Fleadh Festival" in London's Finsbury Park.
Sept [24] *Pineapple Head* debuts at its UK #27 high.

1995

Jan [24] The group plays the Entertainment Centre, Sydney, Australia, during a current tour supporting R.E.M. (Meanwhile Dave Dobbyn's ***Twist*** album, produced by Neil Finn, is certified platinum in his native New Zealand.)
Apr Tim, recently teamed with Andy White and Hothouse Flowers' vocalist Liam O'Maonlai as A.L.T., releases the one-off album ***Attitude***.
Oct [14] *Suffer Never*, recorded by Neil and Tim Finn and billed simply as Finn, debuts at its UK #29 peak.
[28] Their first project together as a duo, ***Finn*** reaches UK #15 in its week of entry.
Nov [15] Finn performs at London's Islington Union Chapel.
Dec [9] Finn's *Angel's Heap* debuts at its UK #41 peak during a two week chart stay.

1996

June [4] Following the group's final gig in London at the Hanover Grand the day before, Neil Finn officially announces the band has amicably split after ten years together.
[24] EMI (UK) releases ***Recurring Dream-The Best Of Crowded House***, a retrospective collection which also features three new cuts including the current single *Instinct*.
see also: **SPLIT ENZ**

ARTHUR CRUDUP

1941

Sept Crudup (b. Aug. 24, 1905, Forrest, MI), who has been raised in Mississippi, has sung in his church choir and in a number of gospel groups including the Harmonizing Four with whom he relocated to Chicago, IL in 1934. Influenced by the Chicago blues scene and taught to play the guitar by local musician Papa Harvey in 1937, he has been signed by A&R scout and music publisher Lester Melrose, who spotted him performing on a street corner, to Okeh imprint Bluebird Records in 1939, which now releases Crudup's (nicknamed "Big Boy") debut recordings, the self-penned *If I Get Lucky* and *Black Pony Blues*.

1945

May [5] *Rock Me, Mama* marks Crudup's US R&B chart bow, set to hit #3. Further R&B chart success will follow with *Who's Been Foolin' You* (#5), *Keep Your Arms Around Me* (#3) and *So Glad You're Mine* (#3 the following year). With his songs becoming in-demand cover material, Brownie McGhee will record Crudup's *Mean Old Frisco* in 1946.

1946

Realizing he has been deprived of sizeable royalties owed to him by Melrose, Crudup has returned to Mississippi and signs to RCA's Victor label with whom he will record until the early-'50s, composing and recording blues songs, a number of which (for example, *Dust My Broom*) will become blues standards.

1950

Moonlighting from Victor, Crudup records for the Mississippi-based Trumpet label under the name Elmore Jones (he will also record under the moniker Percy Crudup (his son's name).

1951

Nov [3] Released on the RCA label, his final chart disc, *I'm Gonna Dig Myself A Hole*, hits US R&B #9. Crudup continues touring with the likes of Sonny Boy Williamson and Elmore James.

1954

July [10] Memphis radio station WHBQ plays Elvis Presley's cover version of Crudup's *That's All Right*, which will kick-start the most successful solo career in pop history. (Presley will also go on to record Crudup's *I'm So Glad You're Mine*.) Meanwhile a deeply disillusioned (and broke) Crudup retires from the music industry to begin sweet potato farming in Mississippi.

1959

Presley, who reveres Crudup as a major influence, arranges a comeback recording session for the bluesman for Fire Records, after which Crudup once again retreats from the music arena.

1968

Encouraged by the efforts of Philadelphia, PA-based blues promoter Dick Waterman (who has managed to collect $60,000 in back royalties for Crudup from rights' agencies, ASCAP and BMI), Crudup makes a welcome return, recording initially for Bob Koester's Delmark label which releases ***Look On Yonder's Wall***.

1970

He tours Europe for the first time, promoting his latest release, ***Crudup's Mood***.

1972

Increasingly recognized for his pioneering influence in the evolution of rock'n'roll, ***The Father Of Rock And Roll*** is released.

1973

Crudup opens for Bonnie Raitt on a US tour having signed a new recording deal with Liberty Records which releases the critically-praised ***Roebuck Man***. During the year a film documentary based on Crudup's life and music, "Arthur Crudup: Born In The Blues" premieres in the US.

1974

Mar [28] Crudup dies following a heart attack, in Nassawadox, VA. (Various compilations and reissues will appear over the next two decades (including ***Big Boy Crudup & Lightnin' Hopkins*** (1982), ***I'm In The Mood*** (1983), ***Crudup's Rockin'*** (1985) and ***Give Me A 32-20*** (1988), while the ironically named (though unrelated) Bluebird Records UK label will bring Crudup's best work to compact disc with the release of ***That's All Right Mama*** in 1992.)

THE CRUSADERS

Wilton Felder (tenor saxophone, bass); **Joseph Sample** (keyboards); **Nesbert "Stix" Hooper** (percussion); **Wayne Henderson** (trombone)

1956

After playing together in a high school marching band in their native Houston, TX, Felder (b. Aug. 31, 1940, Houston), Hooper (b. Aug. 15, 1938, Houston) and Sample (b. Feb. 1, 1939, Houston) form a jazz, blues and R&B outfit, naming themselves variously the Chitterling Circuit, the Nite Hawks and the Swingsters. They begin playing covers of material by B.B. King, Lightnin' Hopkins and Dizzy Gillespie, among others, in their own "Gulf Coast" jazz-blend style. The trio moves to Texas Southern University, Houston, and is joined by Henderson (b. Sept. 24, 1939, Houston) and two other students, becoming the Modern Jazz Sextet. The original trio, plus Henderson, will drop out of college in 1958 and move to Los Angeles, CA, playing as an R&B dance-club group, the Nighthawks (and later backing Jackie DeShannon).

1961

Switching back to a jazz-based style and changing their name to the Jazz Crusaders, the quartet signs to World Pacific Jazz Records, their debut album, ***Freedom Sound***, gaining specialist interest. As their session skills improve they will become increasingly in-demand Los Angeles musicians over the next five years (and will remain so throughout their career, contributing to over 200 gold albums, more than any other group).

1966

Apr Having released a popular succession of jazz albums over four years (***Looking Ahead***, ***At The Lighthouse***, ***Tough Talk***, ***Heatwave*** and ***Chile Con Soul***), the Jazz Crusaders' version of Stevie Wonder's *Uptight (Everything's Alright)* crosses over to reach US #95.
June ***Lighthouse '66***, the second live album recorded at the Lighthouse Club in the '60s, fails to cross over, but sells well in the specialist field.

1969

Following more popular jazz albums (***Talk That Talk***, ***Festival Jazz***, ***Lighthouse '68***, ***Uh Hah***), the Jazz Crusaders' ***Powerhouse*** crosses over to US #184 (and is their only chart appearance on Pacific Jazz). Following ***Lighthouse '69***, the label releases the compilation ***Best Of The Jazz Crusaders***.

1970

Nov Having signed a two-year contract with Motown's Chisa jazz label, ***Old Socks, New Shoes ... New Socks, Old Shoes*** is released, peaking at US #90 during a four-month stay.

1971

Jan [2] The extracted *Way Back Home* also makes US #90. (Seeking a wider audience for its innovative jazz-funk fusion, the band drops Jazz from its name and becomes the Crusaders.)
June ***Pass The Plate***, on Chisa, makes US #168. They leave the label and sign to ABC Records subsidiary, Blue Thumb.

1972

Mar Double album, ***Crusaders 1***, on Blue Thumb climbs to US #96, during a six month chart spell, and is their first official UK release, licensed by Island Records.
Sept [2] *Put It Where You Want It*, subsequently covered by the Average White Band, peaks at US #52.

1973

June [2] *Don't Let It Get You Down* makes US #86, while the double album from which it is taken, ***The 2nd Crusade***, climbs to US #45 and tops the US Jazz chart.
Dec Their second album of the year, ***Unsung Heroes***, peaks at US #173.

1974

Apr Follow-up ***Scratch*** begins a 20-week chart stay, peaking at US #73.
May [25] The extracted title track, *Scratch*, climbs to US #81 (and is their last chart single for five years).
Oct Double album, ***Southern Comfort***, tops the Jazz survey upon release and later peaks at US #31 (their first gold disc).

1975

Apr The Rolling Stones invite the Crusaders to open their UK tour dates, becoming the only instrumental act to support the British group.
Oct [4] ***Chain Reaction*** reaches US #26. It features guest guitarist Larry Carlton (b. Mar. 2, 1948, Torrence, CA), who will record seven albums with the group.

1976

July The band begins its first full European tour, with all dates selling out.
[17] ***Those Southern Knights*** reaches US #38. (It is the last Crusaders album for Henderson, who quits to pursue a solo career and to produce. The band will continue as a trio, hiring musicians Billy Preston, Chuck Rainey, Robert "Pops" Popwell and Carlton for future albums and using guest vocalists as required.)

1977

Jan [22] ***The Best Of The Crusaders*** peaks at US #122.
July [9] ***Free As The Wind*** makes US #41.

Sept The Crusaders participate in the three-day tenth annual "Quaker City Jazz Festival", at the Tower Theater, Philadelphia, PA.

1978

Feb While the three remaining members are individually still much in demand as session musicians, Sample's first solo album, ***Rainbow Seeker***, released on ABC, makes US #62.

Sept [9] The group album, ***Images***, reaches US #34. Their seventh consecutive Jazz Album chart topper, remaining at the summit for three months, it is also certified gold. The Crusaders begin a sellout US stadium tour.

[23] A nine-date UK tour opens at the Colston Hall, Bristol, Avon, set to end on October 3th at the Top Rank, Brighton, E. Sussex.

Nov Felder's debut solo album, ***We All Have A Star***, reaches US #174, as the Crusaders begin a major European tour including packed concerts in London, Paris, Berlin and Amsterdam.

1979

Feb Sample's sophomore effort, ***Carmel***, tops the US Jazz chart and makes US #56.

June Following heated record company bidding, MCA signs the Crusaders to a long-term worldwide contract.

Sept [6] An eight-date UK tour, including three dates at London's Hammersmith Odeon, opens at the Queensway Hall, Dunstable, Beds., set to end on the 13th at the Apollo Theatre, Manchester, Gtr. Manchester.

[15] *Street Life*, with a lead vocal by Randy Crawford, hits UK #5, as its parent album, ***Street Life***, hits UK #10 (and is largely responsible for launching Crawford's successful recording career, to which the Crusaders will contribute their individual songwriting and performing talents).

[22] ***Street Life*** reaches US #18 and tops the US Jazz ranking for a record 20 weeks.

Nov [10] *Street Life*, co-penned by Sample with long-time writing collaborator Will Jennings, makes US #36. The Crusaders tour with Crawford at major venue sellouts in the US and UK before undertaking a major Japanese tour, as Hooper's debut album, ***The World Within***, with guest Jerry Butler, on MCA, peaks at US #166.

1980

July [26] ***Rhapsody And Blues*** makes UK #40 with soul veteran Bill Withers contributing guest vocals on the *Soul Shadows* track.

Aug [16] Self-produced as ever, ***Rhapsody And Blues*** reaches US #29.

Nov Felder, now also signed to MCA, releases his second album, ***Inherit The Wind***, its title track becoming a US and UK Dance hit, featuring guest vocalist Bobby Womack.

1981

Jan Sample's ***Voice In The Rain***, his first album for MCA, featuring Flora Purim and Josie James, reaches US #65.

Sept [26] The group's ***Standing Tall*** makes UK #47 as it climbs to its US #59 peak.

Oct [3] The extracted *I'm So Glad I'm Standing Here Today*, featuring Joe Cocker on vocals, makes US #97 and UK #61.

1982

June [4] The group plays at the "Jazz Of The '80s Festival" at the Jack Murphy Stadium, San Diego, CA.

Aug [7] ***Royal Jam***, recorded with B.B. King and the Royal Philharmonic Orchestra, peaks at US #144.

1983

For the first time in 22 years, the Crusaders fail to release an album (although Sample reaches US #125 with ***The Hunter*** in April), mainly due to the departure of founding member and drummer Stix Hooper.

1984

Feb The Crusaders are the featured rhythm section on Tina Turner's UK #40 cover of the Beatles' *Help*.

Apr [7] ***Night Ladies*** peaks at UK #55.

May With new drummer Leon "Ndugu" Chancler replacing Hooper, their dance-based ***Ghetto Blaster*** reaches US #79 and UK #46.

Sept The Crusaders begin a UK tour.

1985

May With increased vocal support from Bobby Womack (which will also help him relaunch his career), a third Felder album, ***Secrets***, becomes his most commercially successful, at US #81. (Sample will also release his solo ***Oasis*** in December).

1986

Aug Sample releases ***Swing Street Café***, featuring session guitarist David T. Walker.

Dec To celebrate the Crusaders' 30th anniversary, Sample and Felder invite top jazz session musicians (including part-time Crusader Larry Carlton) and guest vocalist Nancy Wilson to record ***The Good And Bad Times***, which hits US Jazz chart #4. It is followed by Sample's ***Roles*** in June of the following year, MCA's release of an 11-track compilation of vocalist-featured Crusaders highlights collected as ***The Vocal Album*** in November 1987, the group's ***Life In The Modern World*** in June 1988, and Sample's US #129, ***Spellbound***, in April 1989 (featuring vocalists Michael Franks, Al Jarreau and Take 6).

1991

Jan Sample establishes the United Negro College Fund (UNCF) Rhodes Scholarship to encourage young African-Americans to rebuild their communities. (In turn, Warner Bros. Records, the United Negro College Fund, Rhodes Keyboards and Time Warner Inc. have established a national music scholarship program in the name of Joe Sample.)

Mar Sample's ***Ashes To Ashes*** tops the US Jazz chart.

May [11] ***Healing The Wounds***, reuniting Felder and Sample, and with a new line-up including Marcus Miller, debuts at its US #174 peak.

1992

Oct With the Crusaders now a spent force, MCA releases a comprehensive 32-song, three-CD/cassette boxed-set retrospective, ***The Golden Years***. Sample will remain the most commercially active member releasing the Tommy LiPuma-produced ***Invitation*** (US #194, Apr [10], 1993) followed by ***Did You Feel That?***, issued by his new group Soul Committee in September 1994.

THE CRYSTALS

Barbara Alston (vocals); **Mary Thomas** (vocals); **Dee Dee Kennibrew** (vocals); **Lala Brooks** (vocals); **Pat Wright** (vocals)

1961

May The group has formed earlier in the year while Kennibrew (b. Dolores Henry, 1945, Brooklyn, New York, NY), Wright (b. 1945, Brooklyn), Brooks (b. 1946, Brooklyn) and Thomas (b. 1946, Brooklyn) are at high school in Brooklyn. Initially singing for fun, the girls have met songwriter Leroy Bates (whose daughter Crystal gives the group its name) and worked on demos of his songs for music publisher, Hill and Range Music. After meeting them at the publisher's New York office, producer Phil Spector now signs the Crystals as the first act on his new Philles label and they record *Oh Yeah, Maybe Baby*, backed with *There's No Other (Like My Baby)*, at Mirasound Studios, New York.

Dec US DJs first reject the single, but then begin playing the B-side.

1962

Jan [6] After two months, *There's No Other (Like My Baby)*, a Spector re-working of a Bates original, reaches US #20.

May [26] *Uptown* (intended for Tony Orlando until Spector persuades its writers, Barry Mann and Cynthia Weil, that it should have a female vocal) reaches US #13, with Alston on lead vocal.

Aug *He Hit Me (And It Felt Like A Kiss)* fails to reach the US Top 100, suffering airplay problems because of the apparent allusion to masochism in its lyrics. Spector allows it to die when he hears Gene Pitney's demo of *He's A Rebel* and recognizes it as a potential smash.

Nov [3] The Crystals' version of *He's A Rebel* tops the US chart for the first of two weeks and will become a million-seller. Its lead vocal has actually been recorded by Darlene Love (b. Darlene Wright, July 26, Los Angeles, CA), backed by Fanita James and Jack Nitzsche's wife Gracia (fellow members of the Blossoms). The bona fide Crystals are holed up in New York, while Spector is hurriedly recording in Los Angeles, to beat a rival version of the song by Vikki Carr onto the market. The group reduces to a quartet when Thomas leaves to get married.

1963

Jan *He's A Rebel* reaches UK #19.

Feb [16] *He's Sure The Boy I Love*, featuring Darlene Love and the Blossoms in the real Crystals' absence, reaches US #11.

Mar ***He's A Rebel*** is the quartet's only album chartmaker, at US #131.

[2] The group performs at Chubby Checker's "Limbo Party" show at the Cow Palace, San Francisco, CA, with Marvin Gaye and the Four Seasons, among others.

June [8] *Da Doo Ron Ron*, regarded as the first fully-fledged landmark of the Phil Spector "sound", and featuring Brooks on lead vocal, hits US #3 and is another million-seller.

July *Da Doo Ron Ron* hits UK #5, and is the group's first major international hit.

Sept [14] Further Spector helmed classic, *Then He Kissed Me*, hits US #6. Relations between the group and their producer are, however, progressively more strained: the group feels its creative input to be minimal and not career-enhancing; Spector is concerned about production to the exclusion of the artists' position.

Oct *Then He Kissed Me* hits UK #2.

Nov Philles seasonal compilation, ***A Christmas Gift For You***, on which the group is featured, singing *Santa Claus Is Comin' To Town* and *Rudolph The Red-Nosed Reindeer*, is released.

Dec Frances Collins replaces Wright, who returns to college.

1964

Feb [8] *Little Boy* sells disappointingly (US #92). Spector halts its UK release and puts it on the B-side of a newly-recorded track, *I Wonder*.

[14] The group performs on ITV's "Ready Steady Go!" with the Rolling Stones, Dusty Springfield and others.

[16] They embark on a UK tour, with Manfred Mann (backing the group on the six-week tour), Johnny Kidd, Heinz and Joe Brown, at the Coventry Theatre, Coventry, Warks.

Mar *I Wonder* makes UK #36.

Aug [1] *All Grown Up*, the group's US chart swan song, peaks at #98.

Nov [13] The group embarks on second Dick Clark's "Caravan Of Stars" tour of the year with Johnny Tillotson, the Drifters, the Supremes, Brian Hyland, Bobby Freeman, the Hondels, Dee Dee Sharp, Lou Christie and others, in New Haven, CT, set to end December 6th in Chattanooga, TN.

1965

Oct Dissatisfied, the group has bought itself out of the Philles contract and signed to United Artists. *My Place*, its label debut, suffers from a lack of the group's identifiable sound and fails to chart. Following the release of *Are You Trying To Get Rid Of Me, Baby?* in

February the following year, UA does just that and drops the Crystals, who continue to perform live for a while, before retiring to domestic life.

1971

June The group re-forms to play the now-burgeoning US oldies live circuit, and appears in one of Richard Nader's major "Rock'n'Roll Revival" concerts in New York. A UK re-issue of *Da Doo Ron Ron* in November 1974 will see the enduring hit reach #15. (After raising a family, Love will re-emerge in the late '80s, releasing her CBS/Columbia debut, ***Paint Another Picture***, in 1988 and contributing the Spector-esque cut, *All Alone On Christmas* (US #83/UK #31), to the soundtrack of "Home Alone II" in 1992, performing on the US nostalgia circuit and playing the role of Danny Glover's wife in "Lethal Weapon". Kennibrew will recruit Gretchen Gale and Marilyn Byers to tour as the Crystals on the US nostalgia circuit from the mid-'80s. EMI Records will bring the group's past glories to CD with the November 1992 release of ***The Best Of The Crystals***.)

THE CULT

Ian Astbury (vocals); **Billy Duffy** (lead guitar)

1982

The band, formed out of the post-punk/new-wave era in Bradford, W. Yorks., as Southern Death Cult, fronted by American Indian-costumed and coiffured vocalist Astbury (b. Ian Lindsay, May 14, 1962, Heswall, Lancs.), using his given name Ian Lindsay, plays a non-nihilistic development of punk-rock which endears it to the UK rock press. A strong word-of-mouth buzz precedes the group's shift to London, where its debut gig at the Heaven club attracts more people than the venue can hold.

1983

Jan Signed to an independent label, Situation 2, the band's debut, *Fat Man*, makes UK #50 and tops the UK Independent chart, while the group supports Bauhaus on a UK tour.

Feb [26] Southern Death Cult's final gig is at Manchester Polytechnic, Gtr. Manchester. The band then splits.

Apr Lindsay, deciding to form a group free from the hype that had overwhelmed the first line-up, recruits Duffy (b. William H. Duffy, May 12, 1961, Manchester, Lancs.), ex-Theatre Of Hate, Jamie Stewart (rhythm guitar) and drummer Ray Mondo (both ex-Ritual), and shortens their name to Death Cult.

June ***Southern Death Cult***, anthologizing single, demo, live and radio session tracks by the original band, makes UK #43.

July Remaining with Situation 2, Death Cult debuts with the eponymously-titled 4-track 12" EP *Death Cult*. Lindsay reverts to his real surname of Astbury, as the band makes its live debut in Oslo, Norway, followed by other European dates.

Sept [18] The group plays the "Futurama Festival" in Leeds, S. Yorks, as the climax to its maiden UK tour.

[21] Mondo quits, as Nigel Preston, ex-Sex Gang Children, joins on drums.

Oct *God's Zoo* is released, while the band undertakes another UK tour.

1984

Jan The band amends its name further to the Cult and appears on C4-TV's "The Tube".

May *Spiritwalker*, promoted on a UK tour, tops the UK Independent chart.

Aug The Cult makes its live US debut.

Sept ***Dreamtime***, initially coupled with a live album recorded at London's Lyceum Ballroom on May 20th, reaches UK #21. It is released on Beggars Banquet, the WEA-distributed parent label of Situation 2.

[11] The group begins a UK tour in Sheffield to promote ***Dreamtime***.

Dec Following a further UK tour, an appearance on BBC2-TV's "Whistle Test" and a Wembley Arena, Wembley, Middx., appearance supporting Big Country, the band makes UK #74 with *Resurrection Joe*. The **Zig Zag** magazine poll votes the Cult Best Group and Best Live Act of 1984.

1985

May The band tours Europe, followed by further UK gigs, after which Preston leaves.

July *She Sells Sanctuary* reaches UK #15. On recordings for a new album, Mark Brzezicki of Big Country fills the still-vacant drum seat.

Sept The band tours Japan with Les Warner (b. Feb. 13, 1961) as temporary drummer. He soon joins permanently.

Oct *Rain* makes UK #17 while the group plays another nationwide UK tour.

Nov ***Love***, which completes the band's metamorphosis from its gothic-punk beginnings to a Led Zeppelin-inflected heavy rock group, hits UK #4 and makes US #87.

Dec *Revolution*, remixed from the album, reaches UK #30.

1986

Jan The band plays a European tour, supported by the Sisterhood (soon to become the Mission), beginning a three-month period spent performing in North America and Europe.

June [28] The Cult plays its only London concert of the year at the Brixton Academy. (Other UK gigs are arena concerts at the Ibrox Stadium, Glasgow, Scotland, and the Milton Keynes Bowl, Milton Keynes, Bucks.)

Aug Recording sessions at Manor Studios in Oxfordshire for a new album prove unsatisfactory and are not completed.

Nov Astbury and Duffy remix album tracks at Def Jam's New York Studios, with label chief Rick Rubin, and decide to entirely re-cut the album.

1987

Mar From the New York sessions, *Love Removal Machine* reaches UK #18. The band plays its first UK tour in over a year. Ex-Zodiac Mindwarp bassist Kid Chaos joins, and Stewart switches from bass to rhythm guitar.

Apr [18] ***Electric***, produced by Rubin, hits UK #4 and will make US #38.

May *Lil' Devil*, taken from the album, reaches UK #11.

Aug *Wild Flower*, a double-single package which includes two live tracks recorded at Brixton in March, reaches UK #24. By the year's end, the band will have supported Billy Idol on a UK tour, and toured as headliners, with Guns N' Roses opening.

Sept Astbury is arrested and charged with assault after a concert in Vancouver, BC, Canada.

1988

The group relocates to Los Angeles, CA, splitting with its UK management and firing Warner, who is offered £2,000 and a drum kit as compensation. While the Cult remains inactive for an extended period, the aggrieved Warner Bros. Records plan legal action against the band. Matt Sorum (b. Nov. 19, 1960, Long Beach, CA) is recruited as the new drummer.

1989

Apr [8] *Fire Woman* reaches UK #15.

[22] Full-blown melodic metal outing, ***Sonic Temple*** hits UK #3.

[29] ***Sonic Temple*** enters the US chart as it climbs to hit #10. (The group supports Metallica on 65-date North American "Damaged Justice" tour, following which they will embark on their own "The Prayer Tour").

July [8] *Fire Woman* makes US #46.

[22] *Edie (Ciao Baby)* makes UK #32.

Sept [6] The group performs at the sixth annual MTV Video Music Awards, from the Universal Amphitheatre, Universal City, CA.

[30] *Edie (Ciao Baby)* makes US #93.

Nov [18] *Sun King*, with *Edie (Ciao Baby)* on the B-side, makes UK #39.

1990

Jan [9] Further US tour dates begin at Tempe, AZ, set to finish at the end of March.

Mar [10] *Sweet Soul Sister* makes UK #42.

Apr Stewart, who is quitting to concentrate on writing, producing and spending time with his wife, plays his last gig with band at the Universal Amphitheatre.

Oct [6-7] Astbury organizes "A Gathering Of The Tribes Festival", held at the Shoreline Amphitheatre, Mountain View, CA, and the Pacific Amphitheatre, Costa Mesa, CA, with the Cramps, Ice-T, Indigo Girls, Queen Latifah, the Charlatans UK and others.

1991

July Astbury and Duffy put the finishing touches to the Cult's new ***Ceremony*** album at A&M studios in Los Angeles, co-producing with Richie Zito. The album features help from Charlie Drayton (bass) and Micky Curry (drums).

Sept [14] *Wild Hearted Son* debuts at its UK #40 peak.

Oct [5] ***Ceremony*** hits UK #9 and will reach US #25 a week later.

Nov [22] The group begins a short UK tour with its first domestic date in over two years, at the Birmingham National Exhibition Centre, with Drayton and Curry forming the rhythm section. (For their subsequent European tour, Kynley Wolf (bass) and Michael Lee (drums) are recruited.)

Dec [31] The Cult, supported by Lenny Kravitz, plays a sellout show at the Maple Leaf Gardens, Toronto, ON, Canada, before a crowd of 10,873, during their current North American tour. (After a subsequent Canadian gig, Astbury is arrested for attacking a university baseball team who were hitting fans in the front row.)

1992

Feb [29] *Heart Of Soul* charts for a week at UK #51, as the group makes a surprise appearance at the four-day "Kick Out The Jams" festival in Detroit, MI, raising $34,000 for the education of the children of the recently deceased MC5 leader, Rob Tyner.

May [7] Original drummer Nigel Preston dies in Brixton, London. (After leaving the group in 1985, he had drummed with Theatre of Hate, Sex Gang Children and Baby Snakes, before playing with the Gun Club in Europe prior to his death.)

June [6] The group headlines "The Cult In The Park '92 Festival" in London's Finsbury Park.

[11] The band plays at Bally's Casino Resort, Las Vegas, NV, during its latest US dates.

South Dakotan Oglala Lakota Sioux's Tom and Jennifer Crazy Bear DuBray file a $61-million lawsuit against the group and its record company, claiming that the photo of their 11-year-old son Eternity appeared on the cover of ***Ceremony*** without their permission.

1993

Jan [30] *She Sells Sanctuary (MCMXCIII Remixes)* bows at its UK #15 peak.

Feb [13] With a current line-up of Astbury, Duffy, Lee (drums) and Wolf, ***Pure Cult***, an up-to-date greatest hits collection, enters in pole position on the UK chart.

May [29-30] The group, now comprising Astbury, Duffy, ex-Mission bassist Craig Adams (b. Apr. 4, 1962, Otley, Yorks.) and drummer Scott Garrett (b. Mar. 14, 1966, Washington, DC), supports Guns N' Roses at the National Bowl, Milton Keynes.

1994

Oct [8] *Coming Down* charts for a week at UK #50.

[22] ***The Cult*** reaches UK #21.

[29] ***The Cult*** debuts at its US #69 peak, as the group plays Toad's Place, New Haven, CT, during current US dates.

1995

Jan [7] *Star* charts for a week at UK #65 peak.

[22] The group takes part in the annual "Big Day Out" at the Royal Showgrounds, Melbourne, Victoria, Australia.

Feb [13] They begin North and Latin American tour

at La Luna, Portland, OR. (Following March dates in Rio De Janeiro, Brazil, the band splits cancelling the second leg of its tour, due to Astbury's "nervous exhaustion", although excessive alcohol consumption is rumored to be the cause.)

1996

Feb Astbury plays a first gig with his new band Holy Barbarians in Los Angeles.

CULTURE CLUB

Boy George (vocals); **Jon Moss** (drums); **Roy Hay** (guitar, keyboards); **Mikey Craig** (bass)

1978

George (b. George O'Dowd, June 14, 1961, Eltham, Kent), the third of six children, his brothers boxers and his father a boxing club manager, having spent his early teens idolizing rock stars Marc Bolan and David Bowie, is a regular at Billy's, a club run by Steve Strange (later of Visage) and Rusty Egan which will spark the London club boom of the early '80s. He has a flamboyant style, with his elaborate clothes and make-up, and becomes friends with budding pop media figure Marilyn (aka Peter Robinson), a cross-dresser with a penchant for the blonde bombshell look, and Martin Degville (later of Sigue Sigue Sputnik), with whom he shares a flat in Birmingham, W. Midlands, for a year. When the crowd moves to Blitz and Hell (London club centers for the dressy New Romantic fashion scene), George attracts burgeoning media attention. Malcolm McLaren, ex-manager of the Sex Pistols, working with the group Bow Wow Wow, invites George to appear at the band's London Rainbow concert as Lieutenant Lush. The alliance soon dissolves, but George forms a band after meeting ex-DJ Craig (b. Feb. 15, 1960, Hammersmith, London). They call themselves In Praise Of Lemmings, changing to Sex Gang Children when guitarist John Suede joins. George's friend Kirk Brandon (of Theatre Of Hate) introduces them to Moss (b. Sept. 11, 1957, Wandsworth, London), a professional musician who has had brief associations with the Clash, the Damned and Adam & the Ants.

1981

George renames the band Culture Club. Suede leaves, to be replaced by Hay (b. Aug. 12, 1961, Southend, Essex), from Russian Bouquet and a veteran of other semi-pro Essex bands. The group debuts in an Essex club and approaches young producer Steve Levine to oversee their first demos. They record *White Boy* and *I'm Afraid Of Me* at the EMI studios, but the label turns them down.

1982

May Virgin Records signs them, releasing *White Boy*.
June *I'm Afraid Of Me* again fails to chart. While George's striking image attracts increasing media interest, particularly in the fashion pages (many of his outfits are designed by Sue Clowes), BBC Radio 1 DJ Peter Powell asks the band to record four songs for his show. Only three are ready so they hastily write a fourth, *Do You Really Want To Hurt Me*.
Oct [23] *Do You Really Want To Hurt Me*, produced (as will all future hits) by Levine, tops the UK chart for the first of three weeks.
[30] Their debut album, ***Kissing To Be Clever*** (named after an early song that never made it past the demo), and containing versions of all three singles, hits UK #5.
Dec *Time (Clock Of The Heart)*, not included on their debut album, hits UK #3.

1983

Jan ***Kissing To Be Clever*** makes US #14, remaining charted for 88 weeks.
Mar [26] During a 25-week chart tenure, *Do You Really Want To Hurt Me* hits US #2 having entered the survey in December the previous year. With Virgin yet to establish a full US operation, the record is distributed by Epic.
Apr *Church Of The Poison Mind*, with Helen Terry contributing to the vocals, hits UK #2.
June [18] *Time (Clock Of The Heart)* also hits US #2 for the first of two weeks.
Aug [27] A US-only release, a remix of *I'll Tumble 4 Ya*, hits US #9.
Sept [24] Catchy pop smash, the band-penned *Karma Chameleon*, tops the UK chart at the start of a six-week run and becomes a million-seller, with a striking video filmed on a Mississippi steamboat.
Oct [22] ***Colour By Numbers***, written by the group, tops the UK chart for the first of three weeks (returning to the top spot for a further two on Nov [19]). A global success, the album, produced by Levine, will achieve multiplatinum status in Australia, Canada, Japan, New Zealand and the US.
Dec [3] *Church Of The Poison Mind* hits US #10 while the lush ballad, *Victims*, backed with a grandiose video featuring a full orchestra, hits UK #3.

1984

Feb [4] *Karma Chameleon* tops the US chart for the first of three weeks, while ***Colour By Numbers*** heads to US #2, where it will stay for six weeks, unable to dislodge Michael Jackson's ***Thriller***.
[21] Culture Club wins the Best British Group category and *Karma Chameleon* is named Best British Single at the third annual BRIT Awards, at London's Grosvenor House Hotel.
[28] Culture Club wins the Best New Artist Of 1983 category at the 26th annual Grammy Awards.
Mar *It's A Miracle* hits UK #4.
Apr [21] *Miss Me Blind* hits US #5.
June [16]*It's A Miracle* reaches US #13. George moves away from his braids and baggy clothes and puts on a black wig as the first in a succession of new looks.
July [8] Boy George appears on CBS-TV's "Face The Nation".
Oct Anti-war themed *The War Song* hits UK #2.
Nov ***Waking Up With The House On Fire*** hits UK #2 and US #26. The group tours the US with a million-dollar stage production and an extended band including a horn section and backing singers Ruby Turner and Mo Birch.
[17] *The War Song* reaches US #17.
[25] George and Moss contribute to the Band Aid recording of *Do They Know It's Christmas* in Notting Hill, London, with George taking a lead vocal role.
Dec *The Medal Song* peaks at UK #32.

1985

Feb [2] *Mistake No. 3* peaks at US #33.
After a UK tour the band agrees to take a break. (Craig and Hay head for tax exile, although Hay will shortly return with a new band, This Way Up. Moss plumps for production work, subsequently forming Heartbeat UK and Promised Land following Culture Club's demise, and George for club dancefloors and associated hedonism. By year's end, George and Hay will have co-written *Passing Friend* for inclusion on the Beach Boys' ***Beach Boys***.)

1986

Apr Moving away from stalwart producer Levine, *Move Away* (helmed by Arif Mardin and Lew Hahn) hits UK #7.
May *God Thank You Woman* reaches UK #31. George appears in an episode of the NBC-TV series "The A Team".
[31] *Move Away* reaches US #12. Its parent album, ***From Luxury To Heartache***, produced by Mardin, hits UK #10 and US #32.
July George makes a brief appearance at an anti-apartheid concert on London's Clapham Common. He has lost his familiar chubbiness, arrives inexplicably covered in flour and introduces himself as "your favorite junkie". Within a week, his brother, fearing for George's life, leaks the story of George's heroin addiction to the press. The pop star, who had publicly denounced drugs, is now himself an addict.
[12] The police arrest George, Marilyn and several others. No sooner have the headlines slipped off the front pages than New York keyboardist Michael Rudetski (who played on the last Culture Club album and was signed up for the next) dies of a drug overdose in George's home. (Rudetski's parents later take unsuccessful legal action against George for contributing to their son's death.) George is arrested for possession of cannabis. He tells the court he will undertake Dr. Meg Patterson's electronic "black box" treatment to cure his addiction.

1987

May [2] While George has recently appeared on the BBC1-TV chat show "Wogan", confirming Culture Club's split and his drug rehabilitation and discussing new ambitions for a solo career, the band's career highlights album ***This Time*** hits UK #8 during a ten-week chart stay. (A further compilation ***At Worst ... The Best Of***, combining both Culture Club and Boy George solo material, will make US #169 on Dec [4] 1993.)
see also: **BOY GEORGE**

THE CURE

Robert Smith (guitar, vocals); **Lol Tolhurst** (keyboards); **Simon Gallup** (bass); **Porl Thompson** (guitar); **Boris Williams** (drums)

1977

Apr Having recently left school, Smith (b. Apr. 21, 1959, Crawley, Sussex), Tolhurst (b. Feb. 3, 1959), Michael Dempsey and Thompson (b. Nov. 8, 1957, London) see a classified ad in **Melody Maker** headed "Wanna Be A Recording Star?", stating that the German record giant Hansa is looking for new bands. Now called Easy Cure, after running through Obelisk at the Notre Dame Middle School, and the Goat Band and then Malice while at St. Wilfrid's Middle School, they gather in Smith's parents' dining room with singer Peter O'Toole, where they make a rough tape for Hansa. Within a month the band has auditioned for Hansa and has signed for £1,000, using the money for equipment, enabling them to play at local Crawley venues like the Rocket. O'Toole soon quits to join a kibbutz, leaving Smith to take over lead vocals.
Oct The group makes the first of two visits to London's SAV Studios to record their first demos.

1978

Mar Hansa drops the band after they have refused to comply with the label's request to record cover versions instead of their own material. Thompson soon quits, leaving the band as a trio. While Dempsey finds work as a psychiatric hospital porter and Tolhurst works in a chemical job, and with Smith refusing to find any work, they name-change to the Cure, and raise £50 to record four tracks in the nearby Chestnut Studios.
July After being turned down by a number of labels, Chris Parry, an A&R employee at Polydor Records who soon sets up his own Fiction label, signs them.
Sept The group starts recording at Morgan Studios in North London. They also secure a spot on a Gen X tour, but are dropped when Tolhurst walks in on Billy Idol and a young lady in a compromising position.
Dec Their debut single, *Killing An Arab*, inspired by a passage in Albert Camus' novel **The Stranger**, is released in a one-off deal with UK independent label, Small Wonder, after Polydor has refused to release any product until the New Year.

1979

Jan Despite only one single release, **Sounds** magazine features the band as a cover story.
Feb The National Front causes a riot at a Cure gig at the Nashville, London, over the controversial *Killing An Arab*.
Apr The group begins a one-month residency at

London's Marquee. (Smith sets up his own Dance Fools Dance label, its first release being the Obtainers' *Yeah Yeah Yeah.*)
June [9] Art-punk debut album, ***Three Imaginary Boys*** (subsequently released in the US as ***Boys Don't Cry*** via Elektra Records), makes UK #44, as the group embarks on an extensive UK tour. The extracted single, *Boys Don't Cry*, receives excellent reviews but fails to chart.
Aug [31] The Cure plays at the "Reading Festival", Reading, Berks.
Sept Smith, showing an early penchant for heavy make-up and sporting a post-punk dyed-black hair-do, meets the Banshees' Steve Severin at a Throbbing Gristle gig and is invited to support Siouxsie & the Banshees on a UK tour. Prior to the date in Aberdeen, Scotland, John McKay and Kenny Morris quit the Banshees and Smith is invited to join the band. He agrees, providing he can continue with the Cure on the tour.
[18] The tour resumes at Leicester's De Montfort Hall, with Smith playing both sets.
Nov At the end of the tour, friction with Smith causes Dempsey to leave, joining labelmates the Associates, to be replaced on bass by Simon Gallup (b. June 1, 1960, Surrey), a friend of Smith's from the band Lockjaw. An acquaintance from Crawley, Mathieu Hartley, a part-time hairdresser and also keyboard player in local band the Magpies, also joins on keyboards. The new line-up makes its debut at Eric's, Manchester, playing until the year's end with the Associates and the Passions on the "Future Pastimes" tour. *Jumping Someone Else's Train* is well-reviewed but fails to chart.
Dec Smith and Tolhurst issue *I'm A Cult Hero* under the joke name of the Cult Heroes, with Gallup and Horley, and Sussex postman Frank Bell on vocals. By year's end, the group makes its US live debut.

1980

Mar As the Cult Heroes they support the Passions at the Marquee.
Apr Smith participates in a benefit concert at the Rainbow Theatre, London, for jailed Stranglers' guitarist Hugh Cornwell.
May [10] Having established a significant cult following, the group's second album, ***17 Seconds***, produced by Mike Hedges, reaches UK #20.
[17] The extracted single, *A Forest*, makes UK #31, after the group has made its debut on BBC1-TV's "Top Of The Pops".
July A world tour starts in Holland, and will take in New Zealand, Australia, US, Scandinavia, Germany, Belgium, France, Spain and Italy.
Sept Hartley quits after a gruelling 24-date club tour in Australia and New Zealand, before the recording of the next album, leaving the band to continue as a trio.
Nov [6] The group embarks on a UK tour which will end on the 18th at the Hammersmith Palais, London.

1981

Jan The Cure provides the instrumental soundtrack to a short film, "Carnage Visors", which will prelude the band's own performance on its summer "Faith" tour.
Apr [25] *Primary* makes UK #43, as ***Faith*** debuts at UK #14. (The cassette version of the album contains the soundtrack music for "Carnage Visors".)
Oct *Charlotte Sometimes*, with a singularly-inappropriate Mike Mansfield promo video, makes UK #44.
Nov They begin work on a new album, at the Windmill Studio in Surrey.

1982

Jan The initial sessions are scrapped, with the band going into RAK Studios to record under new producer, Phil Thornalley.
Apr "Fourteen Explicit Moments" tour begins, to promote the forthcoming album, ***Pornography***.
May [15] The band finally breaks the Top 10 barrier when ***Pornography***, produced by Phil Thornalley, debuts at UK #8.
[27] While on tour, a fight breaks out in Strasbourg, France, between Gallup and Smith. (When the trek ends, Gallup is no longer with the band. He leaves for 18 months to form the Cry, but will return for ***The Head On The Door***. Smith goes camping in Wales, while Tolhurst travels to France and Spain.)
July [31] *Hanging Garden* makes UK #34, while the band continues to tour Britain. Steve Goulding joins on bass, with Tolhurst switching to keyboards.
Nov Smith is asked to rejoin the Banshees, replacing John McGeoch, who is suffering from nervous exhaustion. (Tolhurst, meanwhile, produces And Also The Trees.)
Dec *Let's Go To Bed*, which Smith dislikes so much that he tries to release it under the pseudonym the Recur, makes UK #44. Smith steps in to play guitar for Siouxsie & the Banshees again, on a tour of the Far East, following John McGeoch's departure. He will stay with them, between Cure commitments, through most of 1983).

1983

Feb Smith is approached by Nicholas Dixon, a choreographer with the Royal Ballet, to write the music for "Les Enfants Terribles". After experimenting with Siamese Twins and an accompanying dance sequence on the BBC2-TV show "Riverside", he shelves the plan.
Apr The Cure, no longer officially together, are offered a slot on BBC-TV's "The Oxford Roadshow". Smith recruits Tolhurst, Brilliant's Andy Anderson on drums and SPK's Derek Thompson on bass to perform *100 Years* and *Figurehead*, subsequently deciding to re-form the Cure.
May The Cure headlines the "Elephant Fayre Festival" in St. Germain's, Cornwall, with Phil Thornalley, who had played bass for the band on "Top Of The Pops", agreeing to stay, along with Anderson.
July *The Walk*, produced by Steve Nye, reaches UK #12.
Aug Smith has recorded *Like An Animal*, with Steve Severin of the Banshees and vocalist Jeanette Landray, under the name the Glove, which climbs to UK #52.
Sept Low-priced compilation, ***Boys Don't Cry***, featuring early material, charts at UK #93 (re-entering at #77 months later). Mini-album, ***The Walk***, compiled for US release by Sire Records, enters the US chart at #179.
Nov *The Love Cats*, recorded at the Studio Des Dames in Paris, hits UK #7.

1984

Jan Mini-album, ***Japanese Whispers***, compiling recent singles, peaks at UK #26.
Mar ***Japanese Whispers***, an expanded version of the UK release, reaches US #181.
Apr *The Caterpillar* makes UK #14, while the band is again on a UK tour, with the Oxford and London (Hammersmith Odeon) concerts being recorded.
May ***The Top*** hits UK #10 and reaches US #180. (Thompson, invited to play sax on the album, rejoins.)
June Scheduled to tour with Siouxsie & the Banshees, Smith is forced to pull out, suffering from exhaustion after the Cure's own recent stint on the road. (He retreats to Wales and the Lake District, only to re-surface when the Cure plays the "Rock Around The Dock" show at Glasgow Barrowlands.)
Sept On a tour of the Far East, Anderson's increasingly bizarre behavior comes to a head when he attacks the other four band members.
Oct Smith fires Anderson, and the band arrives in the US to tour, without a drummer. Vince Ely, Psychedelic Furs' original drummer, fills in for 11 dates, before Boris Williams (b. Apr. 24, 1957, Versailles, France), who Thornalley knows through his work with the Thompson Twins and Kim Wilde, completes the rest of tour.
Nov ***Concert - The Cure Live*** reaches UK #26.
[19] The group participates in a charity concert for MENCAP at Camden Palace, London, some of which is broadcast live on BBC2-TV's "Whistle Test". Williams takes up Smith's offer of a full-time role in the band.
Dec Thornalley leaves to pursue a solo career.

1985

Jan Smith patches up his differences with Gallup, who is pursuing a less-than-successful career with Cry (and later Fools Dance), and asks him to rejoin.
Aug [17] Smith-penned *In Between Days (Without You)* reaches UK #15.
Sept ***The Head On The Door*** hits UK #7, becoming the band's most successful album to date. It will also make US #59 a few weeks later, spurred not least by their breakthrough "The Head On The Door" US tour.
Oct *Close To Me* makes UK #24, complemented by an acclaimed claustrophobic video by Tim Pope, their regular visual collaborator.

1986

Feb [15] *In Between Days (Without You)*, released the previous summer, makes US #99.
May The band's new, updated version of *Boys Don't Cry* climbs to UK #22. The line-up has stabilized as a quintet based around Smith and Tolhurst, with Gallup back on bass, Porl Thompson on guitar and Boris Williams on drums. They play a benefit concert for Greenpeace at the Royal Albert Hall, London.
[31] Retrospective album of their successes to date, ***Standing On A Beach - The Singles***, achieves their highest-ever chart hit, at UK #4 (it also makes US #48). A similarly-comprehensive video collection is simultaneously released.
June The band plays at the annual "Glastonbury Festival", Glastonbury, Somerset.
July [27] Concert-goer Jon Moreland, having been jilted by his girlfriend, clambers onto the stage at a Cure concert in Los Angeles, CA, and stabs himself repeatedly. The 18,000 crowd cheer enthusiastically, thinking it to be part of the show.
Aug The band tours Spain and France, after which it begins recording at the Miraval Studios, located in a vineyard in Southern France.
Dec The Cure re-signs with Fiction.

1987

Jan They finish recording a new album in Brussels, Belgium, sessions which had begun at the Compass Point complex in the Bahamas.
Mar The band tours South America, playing major dates in Argentina and Brazil.
May *Why Can't I Be You?* reaches UK #21, as they perform at the "Golden Rose Festival" in Montreux, Switzerland.
June [6] Co-produced by Dave Allen and Smith, double album ***Kiss Me, Kiss Me, Kiss Me*** hits UK #6 and will reach US #35.
July *Catch*, taken from the album, reaches UK #27. The Cure embarks on a US tour, with Psychedelic Furs' Roger O'Donnell on keyboards.
Aug [8] *Why Can't I Be You?* peaks at US #54.
Oct *Just Like Heaven* reaches UK #29.
Dec A major European tour ends at the Wembley Arena, Wembley, Middx., as Zomba prepares to publish **10 Imaginary Years**, the Cure's biography.

1988

Jan [9] *Just Like Heaven* makes US #40.
Feb *Hot! Hot! Hot!* rises to UK #45, peaking at US #65 on April 9th.
Aug [13] Smith marries his childhood sweetheart, Mary Poole, at the Benedictine Monastery, Worth Abbey, Sussex, with Gallup as his best man.
Dec The group re-assembles as Smith, Gallup, Thompson, Williams and O'Donnell, now a full-time member, to work on a new album.

1989

Feb Smith fires Tolhurst, feeling that he is no longer making a contribution. (He will go on to form the group Presence.)
Apr *Lullaby* hits UK #5.
May [13] With words by Smith and music composed by the band, and once again helmed by Smith and Allen, ***Disintegration*** debuts at its UK #3 peak (and will reach US #12), as the group embarks on "The

Prayer Tour" of Europe, set to climax with three nights at Wembley Arena, Wembley.
June [17] *Fascination Street*, from the film "The Lost Angels", makes US #46.
Aug With Smith unable to overcome his chronic fear of flying, the band sets sail on the QE2 in preparation for its biggest US tour to date.
Sept *Lovesong* reaches UK #18.
[6] The Cure performs at the sixth annual MTV Video Music Awards, held at the Universal Amphitheatre, Universal City, CA.
Oct [21] The group's biggest US smash, *Love Song*, hits US #2, behind Janet Jackson's *Miss You Much*.
Dec [16] *Lullaby* peaks at US #74.

1990

Feb [18] The group wins the Best Music Video category at the ninth annual BRIT Awards, at London's Dominion Theatre.
Apr [14] *Pictures Of You* reaches UK #24, set to peak at US #71 on May 19th.
June [24] The Cure participates in the "Glastonbury Festival Of Contemporary Performing Arts", Glastonbury, Somerset, closing their set with the forthcoming single *Never Enough*. O'Donnell quits after the gig, and is replaced by one-time roadie Perry Bamonte (b. Sept. 6, 1960, London). After the group's Eastern European tour, they decide to take six months off.
Sept [1] The Cure broadcasts a four-hour pirate radio show from a secret central London location, to premiere their new album of remixes, ***Mixed Up***. The show features interviews, unreleased recordings, news, weather, traffic reports and commercials, all presented in unpredictable Cure style.
Oct [6] *Never Enough* reaches UK #13.
Nov [3] ***Rubáiyát***, Elektra's 40th anniversary compilation, to which the band has contributed a cover of the Doors' *Hello I Love You*, makes US #140.
[10] *Close To Me*, remixed by Paul Oakenfold from the compilation album ***Mixed Up***, and originally released in 1985, reaches UK #13.
[17] *Never Enough* climbs to US #72, as ***Mixed Up*** debuts at its UK #8 peak.
[24] ***Mixed Up*** reaches US #14.

1991

Jan [19] The group plays at the "Great British Music Weekend" at the Wembley Arena, Wembley.
[26] Revised mix of *Close To Me* makes US #97.
Feb [10] The Cure wins the Best British Group category at the 10th annual BRIT Awards, at the Dominion Theatre, and perform live to close the ceremony.
[23] ***Standing On A Beach - The Singles*** re-charts for a week at UK #74.
Apr [6] The Cure's ***Entreat*** hits its UK #10 chart peak.
Aug [19] Back-catalog boxed set, ***Assemblage***, comprising 12 Cure CDs, ***Mixed Up*** and five single picture CDs, is released.
Dec [5] The Cure are seen in concert on US pay-per-view television.

1992

Mar [28] *High* debuts at its UK #8 peak.
Apr [1] *High (Remix)* charts for a week at UK #44.
[10] The first of ten "Cure Party Nights" (to preview the group's new album) gets underway at the Portsmouth Pier, Portsmouth, Hants.
[28] Smith is taken ill with stomach pains during a show at the Corn Exchange, Cambridge, Cambs., in the midst of the group's current UK tour.
May [2] *High* makes US #42, as ***Wish*** debuts at UK #1.
[9] ***Wish*** bows at its US #2 peak, behind Def Leppard's ***Adrenalize***.
[14] The group begins a 39-date US tour at the Providence Civic Center, Providence, RI, set to end before a sellout crowd of 14,688 on July 23rd at the Nassau Veterans Memorial Coliseum, Uniondale, NY.
June [6] Radio-friendly *Friday I'm In Love* hits UK #6.
[16] Smith sustains a black eye after being hit in the face during a show at the Monterrey Stadium, Monterrey, Mexico.
Aug [8] *Friday I'm In Love* reaches US #18.
[17-19] The group performs at the Sydney Entertainment Centre, Sydney, New South Wales, Australia, during a tour of Australia and New Zealand, grossing in excess of a million Australian dollars.
Sept [9] "Friday I'm In Love" wins the European Best International Video category at the ninth annual MTV Video Music Awards, held at the Pauley Pavilion, Los Angeles, CA.
[21] A 33-date European tour begins at the Spektrum, Oslo, Norway, set to close on November 15th in Lille, France.
Oct [17] *A Letter To Elise* debuts at its UK #28 peak.
Nov [18] The nine-date UK leg of the "Wish Tour '92" begins at the Birmingham NEC, set to end with four dates at London's Olympia Grand Hall on the 26th-28th and 30th.

1993

June [13] The group performs at XFM Radio's Finsbury Park concert.
Sept [25] Live album, ***Show***, debuts at its UK #29 peak.
Oct [9] ***Show*** bows at its US #42 peak.
Nov [6] ***Paris*** charts for a week at UK #56.
[13] ***Paris*** debuts at its US #118 peak, as the group contributes *Purple Haze*, to the ***Stone Free: A Tribute To Jimi Hendrix*** album.

1994

Apr [11] The group appears on MTV UK's "Unplugged".
Sept [16] Following a court case which started in February, Justice Chadwick rules against Tolhurst in his suit against Smith and Parry over royalties from the ***Kiss Me Kiss Me*** album, leaving him with an estimated £1,000,000 legal bill. Smith has described him in court as a "tired, shambling shadow of his former self" and that his role in the band was "almost to that of court jester".

1995

June [25] Following a New Year appearance at the "Hollywood Rock Festival" in Brazil, and having contributed *Dredd Song* to the forthcoming "Judge Dredd" soundtrack, the Cure, now comprising Smith, Gallup, Bamonte, a returning O'Donnell and new drummer Jason Cooper, takes part in the annual "Glastonbury Festival" at Glastonbury, Somerset.

1996

May [7] Recorded in a country house near Bath, Avon, and including a brass section, string quartet, an Indian orchestra and a Mexican trumpeter, the Cure's first new studio album in four years, ***Wild Mood Swings*** is released by Elektra, produced by Steve Lyon.
[11] The group makes its very first live US network television debut on NBC-TV's "Saturday Night Live". It will be followed by a ten-date UK tour beginning on the 21st, with a 40-date US trek scheduled to open in July.

CYPRESS HILL

Sen Dog (rap voice); **B-Real** (vocals); **Muggs** (DJ/producer)

1986

Dog (b. Sennen Reyes, Nov. 20, 1965, Havana, Cuba) and his younger brother Ulpiano Sergio Reyes (aka Mellow Man Ace), who have moved with their family from Havana to the Los Angeles suburb of Southgate, CA in 1971, form the rap-quartet DVX with fellow "Spanglish" Latino rappers, Muggs (b. Lawrence Muggerud, Jan. 28, 1968, Queens, NY) and B-Real (b. Louis Freese, June 2, 1970, Los Angeles, CA). When Mellow Man Ace elects on a solo career (which will kick-start with the 1990 release, ***Escape From Havana***), the remaining trio renames itself Cypress Hill in 1988 after a Southgate neighborhood location and continues performing to a mostly Latin youth crowd in Los Angeles, its hardcore rapping style (often with a pro-marijuana message) finding favor with Ruffhouse Records, which signs the act in 1991 and releases its debut set, ***Cypress Hill*** in November of the following year.

1992

Feb [22] *The Phuncky Feel One*, B-side of the still-climbing and controversially-themed *How I Could Just Kill A Man*, peaks at US #94.
Mar [7] *How I Could Just Kill A Man* makes US #77.
Apr [11] Stoned-funk rap debut, ***Cypress Hill***, highlighted by Muggs' slow-beat production and revered by the hip-hop community, reaches US #31.
Aug [15] Currently touring with Cypress Hill, Los Angeles-based rap outfit House Of Pain's ***House Of Pain***, produced by Muggs, enters the US Album chart, set to reach #14.
Dec [9] The band wins the Hot Rap Singles Artist category at the 3rd annual **Billboard** Music Awards held at the Universal Amphitheatre, Universal City, CA.

1993

Jan [5] ***Cypress Hill*** is certified platinum for one million US sales by the RIAA.
July [31] Previewing the group's sophomore album, *Insane In The Brain* peaks at its UK #32 debut.
Aug [7] With its similarly hardcore message and laid-back style, the group's follow-up album ***Black Sunday*** enters the US chart at #1, the same day it also debuts at its UK #13 peak.
[24] Still climbing the US survey, *Insane In The Brain* is certified gold by the RIAA.
Sept [25] *Insane In The Brain* reaches US #19, received as a hardcore hip hop classic.
Oct [2] Sans airplay, *When The Shit Goes Down* debuts at its UK #19 peak.
Dec [11] *I Ain't Goin' Out Like That* debuts at its UK #15 peak.

1994

Jan [15] *We Ain't Goin' Out Like That*, sampling Black Sabbath's *The Wizard*, makes US #65.
[22] The band embarks on a UK tour.
[27] Cypress Hill is voted Best Rap Group in **Rolling Stone**'s 1994 Music Awards Critics' and Readers' Picks polls.
Feb [26] *Insane In The Brain* re-charts, bowing at its UK #21 peak.
May [7] *Lick A Shot* debuts at its UK #20 peak.
July [26] ***Black Sunday*** is certified multi-platinum by the RIAA with sales of two million. The band is now a quartet with the recent addition of part-time Beastie Boy percussionist Eric Bobo.

1995

July [4] The "Lollapalooza '95" touring festival, including Cypress Hill, Hole, Sonic Youth, Pavement, Sinead O'Connor, Beck, Jesus Lizard, Mighty Mighty Bosstones and others kicks off at the Gorge, George, WA.
Sept Capricorn Records (US) releases ***Hempilation*** (to benefit NORML (the National Organization for the Reform of Marijuana Laws), to which Cypress Hill has eagerly contributed *I Wanna Get High*.
Oct [7] *Throw You Set In The Air* bows at its UK #15 peak as the band undertakes UK dates climaxing at London's Brixton Academy.
[21] *Throw Your Set In The Air* makes US #45.
Nov [18] Having entered at its UK #11 high the previous week, ***Cypress Hill III (Temple Of Boom)*** debuts at its US #3 pinnacle.

1996

Feb [17] *Illusions* enters the UK chart at its #23 peak.
July [22] The group embarks on the "Smokin' Groove" summer tour, with Ziggy Marley & the Melody Makers, in Sacramento, CA.

D

DICK DALE

1960

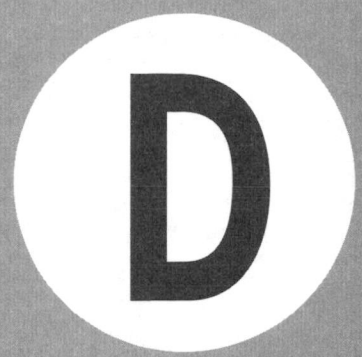

Feb Having grown up in Quincy, MA, but moved with his family to Southern California as a teenager, Dale (b. Richard Anthony Monsour, May 4, 1937, Quincy) forms the Del-Tones in Balboa, CA, where the group takes up a residency at the Rinky Dink Ice Cream Parlor and then the Rendezvous Ballroom, originally playing country and rockabilly, and quickly become one of the most popular live acts in the area. Dale plays lead guitar and begins to develop a fast, heavily-reverberated staccato style to simulate the rhythms of his favorite sport, surfing.
Aug He forms his own locally-distributed Deltone label and, after three undistinguished vocal singles, begins to record the mainly instrumental material which is drawing the strongest reaction from his live audience. His unique sound becomes known as "Surf Guitar", a style which launches a rock sub-genre based in Southern California - Surf Music.

1962

Jan [20] *Let's Go Trippin'* makes US #60. A guitar instrumental, it is regarded by many as the first surf record ever. (Many Californian surf groups, including the Beach Boys, will subsequently record cover versions of the hit, and the lead guitarists in several of these groups are ex-pupils of Dale's).

1963

Feb ***Surfers' Choice***, on Deltone, makes US #59, to the interest of major labels.
Mar Dale signs a seven-year contract to Capitol Records, which also buys up his Deltone label recordings.
June ***King Of The Surf Guitar*** is released along with its 45 rpm title cut. Both are strong sellers in California, where Dale is known mainly for his live act, but fail to impress nationwide.
Oct [26] Guitar instrumental, *The Scavenger*, peaks at US #98.
Dec ***Checkered Flag***, on which the music focus switches from surf to hot rods (a diversification also made by the Beach Boys and other surf-based acts), makes US #106. (By year's end, Dale will have appeared in the movies "Beach Party" and "A Swingin' Affair".)

1964

July ***Summer Surf*** is released. The poorly-received ***Rock Out With Dick Dale: Live At Ciro's***, released the following March, will prove to be his last album for Capitol. (He will also make another movie appearance, in "Muscle Beach Party", during the year.)

1966

Dale falls ill, suffering from intestinal tumors and cysts, and retires from performing. After initially being pronounced incurable, he is successfully operated on to remove the tumors.
(Recuperating in Hawaii the following year, he meets and marries a Tahitian dancer named Jeannie. The couple will return to Riverside, CA, where they will open a nightclub in 1969, the year Dale also forms a new Del-Tones to play there and at other old haunts around Southern California.)

1974

Oct He plays surf-style guitar on *Teenage Idol*, a solo track recorded in Los Angeles by Keith Moon of the Who, and later released on ***Two Sides Of The Moon***.

1990

Over the past 15 years, Dale has played with punk band the Penetrators and has recovered from serious burns (received in 1984, when oil he was heating for making popcorn set on fire). In 1987, *Pipeline*, a duet with Stevie Ray Vaughan, features on the soundtrack to the movie "Back To The Beach" (starring Frankie Avalon and Annette Funicello) for which the duo later received a Grammy nomination. Dale also guests on the surf instrumental *Metal Beach* from Paul Shaffer's ***Coast To Coast***, and his *Mr. Eliminator* is used as the theme for MTV Europe.

1992

Apr After Rhino Records (US) has issued the 18-track CD compilation ***King Of The Surf Guitar: The Best Of Dick Dale & His Del-Tones***, Dale, now living in retirement on his 81-acre ranch in Twentynine Palms, CA, begins recording his first album of original material in 27 years at the urging of **San Francisco Chronicle** rock critic, Joel Selvin. The album, ***Tribal Thunder***, follows his recent guest performance on Psychefunkapus' *Surfing On Jupiter*. (HighTone Records will release the album in 1993, as Dale plays sellout dates at Slim's in San Francisco.) His remergence will continue with an appearance on CBS-TV's "Late Show With David Letterman" November 4th 1994, followed by his first-ever UK gigs at London's Highbury Garage on March 28-29th 1995 and a guest appearance on New Year's Eve's BBC2-TV's "Jools Hootenanny" show.

THE DAMNED

Dave Vanian (vocals); **Brian James** (guitar); **Captain Sensible** (bass); **Rat Scabies** (drums)

1976

May The band forms as a trio from the same burgeoning London punk scene which has given birth to the Sex Pistols, with Sensible (b. Ray Burns, Apr. 23, 1955, UK), who has played in various bands, including Johnny Moped (as guitarist), since 1970, James (b. Brian Robertson, Feb. 18, 1955), ex-Brighton outfit Bastard and proto-punk outfit London SS, and Scabies (b. Chris Miller, July 30, 1957, Kingston-upon-Thames, Surrey), ex-Rot and London SS, who has met James while rehearsing as a drummer for the "Puss In Boots" musical. After two Cardiff, South Glamorgan, Wales gigs in Nick Kent's Subterraneans backing band, the trio recruits Vanian (b. David Letts. Oct. 12, 1956), who is working as a gravedigger in Hemel Hempstead, Herts., to form the Damned. Andy Czezowski becomes the band's manager.

July [6] The group debuts at London's 100 Club, supporting the Sex Pistols.

Aug [21] Its fifth gig is at the "Mont de Marsan" punk festival in the South of France. On the outward bus trip, Scabies has a fight with Nick Lowe, which leads to a working friendship.

Sept The band splits from Czezowski and signs to Stiff Records, with the label's Jake Riviera becoming its new manager (followed by co-label helmer Dave Robinson).

[21] They play at London's 100 Club punk festival, with the Buzzcocks and others.

Oct [22] Their debut single, James' *New Rose*, with Lennon/McCartney's *Help!* on the B-side, is released. Produced by Nick Lowe and regarded as the first-ever "punk" release, it fails to chart but is Stiff's biggest seller to date and helps the label secure a distribution deal with Island.

Dec [6] The band supports the Sex Pistols on their "Anarchy in the UK" tour, but is fired after agreeing to play for Derby councillors in private (to assess their suitability for the youth of the town).

1977

Apr [8] The Damned, the first UK punk group to play US dates, opens at CBGB's, home of the New York punk scene, on a US tour organized by Stiff's Advancedale Management.

[16] Their frenzied debut album, ***Damned, Damned, Damned***, produced by Lowe and recorded and mixed in only eight hours, makes UK #34. *Neat Neat Neat*, another James song, is paired with Scabies' *Stab Your Back* as the first Stiff single through Island.

May A UK tour, supported by the Adverts, follows their return from the US. (The trek's poster announces: "The Damned can play three chords; the Adverts can play one. Hear all four at...")

June [14] A gig at the Lincoln Drill Hall is interrupted by anti-punk gangs.

[30] Vanian suffers a dislocated shoulder during an attack in their dressing room after a West Country gig.

Aug James insists on a second guitarist, and previously unemployed Robert "Lu" Edmunds joins, heightening tensions within the band. Problems arise recording their second album as producer Shel Talmy is dropped and Pink Floyd's Nick Mason is recruited.

Sept *Problem Child*, recorded with Mason, is released.

Oct [1] Scabies leaves during a European tour. Jon Moss (later of Culture Club) temporarily replaces him on drums.

Nov ***Music For Pleasure*** is released, supported by a UK tour with US band the Dead Boys.

Dec The group leaves Stiff after the release of *Don't Cry Wolf*.

1978

Feb [28] The group splits. James forms his own band, Tanz Der Youth (before forming Brian James' Brains & the Hellions and then the Lords of the New Church); Sensible switches to guitar and joins the Softies, before forming the short-lived King. Meanwhile, Vanian joins the Doctors of Madness, Scabies links with the White Cats, and Moss and Edmunds go into the Edge.

Apr [8] The Damned re-forms for a farewell gig at London's Rainbow Theatre, smashing their equipment after the final encore.

Sept [5] Vanian, Scabies and Sensible play another reunion gig, as Les Punks, at London's Electric Ballroom, with Lemmy of Motorhead on bass, and decide to re-form. While acquiring the rights to the Damned name from its legal owner, James, the trio plays for two months as the Doomed, with temporary bass player Henry Badowski.

1979

Jan [7] Having regained the Damned name, a new line-up, with Alistair Ward (ex-Saints) on bass, debuts at the Greyhound pub, Croydon, Surrey. The band is signed to Chiswick Records.

May [26] *Love Song* reaches UK #20.

Oct [27] *Smash It Up* makes UK #35.

Nov [24] ***Machine Gun Etiquette***, produced by the band with Roger Armstrong, reaches UK #31.

Dec [8] *I Just Can't Be Happy Today* makes UK #46. With three consecutive hit singles, the band is a leading live punk attraction.

1980

Feb Ward leaves to join heavy metal band Tank, and is replaced by Paul Gray, ex-Eddie & the Hot Rods, as the group continues to tour exhaustively.

Oct [18] *The History Of The World Part 1* peaks at UK #51.

Nov [29] Double set, ***The Black Album***, reaches UK #29, including the seasonal *There Ain't No Sanity Claus*.

1981

Jan The band leaves Chiswick after differences of opinion, but continues to tour.

Mar Another US trek follows the US release of ***The Black Album***.

June The band tours Europe, while Chiswick issues *Wait For The Blackout*, coupled with *Jet Boy Jet Girl* by Captain Sensible and the Softies.

July Scabies and James, having reunited for a one-off gig at the Clarendon pub, London, as the Damned Dead Sham Band (with Stiv Bators and Dave Treganna), plays a fifth anniversary Damned gig at London's Lyceum Ballroom.

Nov The band signs to NEMS Records.

Dec [5] EP *Friday The 13th*, their only NEMS release, with *Disco Man* and a version of the Rolling Stones' *Citadel*, makes UK #50, as ***The Best Of The Damned***, with live versions of the Stiff singles, on Chiswick's Big Beat label, reaches #43. The band plays at the "Christmas on Earth" festival in Leeds, S. Yorks.

1982

May While Scabies and the Ruts' Paul Fox have recently made a handful of live appearances as Rats & Foxes, the Damned signs to Bronze Records, while Captain Sensible makes a solo deal with A&M.

July [3] Sensible's first solo release, *Happy Talk*, a cover of a song from the musical "South Pacific", tops the UK chart for the first of two weeks, setting the record for the biggest jump (from an entry at #33) to pole position.

[17] The Damned's *Lovely Money* makes UK #42.

Sept [11] *Wot* by Captain Sensible reaches UK #26, as his solo album, ***Women And Captains First***, peaks at #64. Meanwhile, the Damned's *Dozen Girls* is released.

Oct [23] ***Strawberries***, packaged with a strawberry-smelling lyric sheet, reaches UK #15. Roman Jugg joins on keyboards, replacing Tosh, who had joined a year earlier for both the album and subsequent tour.

Dec The **Evening Standard**'s "Win A Pub Crawl With Captain Sensible" competition is cancelled after doctors warned Sensible that his bad liver might not withstand the binge.

1983

Apr Bronze drops the band and Gray leaves. (Scabies' solo single, *The Naughty Gnome Song*, is never released, but he teams with Sensible on *I Hate War* for the various artists ***Wargasm*** compilation, which also includes Sensible's version of *Hey Joe*.)

1984

Apr [14] Sensible's *Glad It's All Over*, backed by a medley of the Damned oldies, titled *Damned On 45*, hits UK #6.

June [16] *Thanks For The Night*, on the Damned label, makes UK #43.

Aug [11] Sensible solo, *There Are More Snakes Than Ladders*, peaks at UK #57. He leaves the band to concentrate on solo work and acting, including a Weetabix TV commercial, and prompts a personnel shuffle: Jugg moves from keyboards to guitar and Bryn Merrick joins on bass. The band contributes *The Last Mile* (a cover of Nico's first single) - as the Sleepeaters - to the Bam Caruso compilation, ***From The House Of Lords***.

Oct The Damned, with the new line-up, signs worldwide to MCA Records.

1985

Apr [6] *Grimly Fiendish*, their MCA debut, reaches UK #21, with a new, mainstream-pop direction evident.

July [6] *The Shadow Of Love* reaches UK #25.

[27] ***Phantasmagoria***, produced by Jon Kelly, enters the UK chart at #11, and is followed by extensive international touring.

Sept [28] *Is It A Dream* makes UK #34.

1986

Feb [22] Their remake of Barry Ryan's 1968 UK #3 hit, *Eloise*, gives the band its biggest seller, hitting UK #3.

Nov [29] *Anything* makes UK #32.

Dec ***Anything*** charts briefly at UK #40.

1987

Feb [14] *Gigolo* reaches UK #29.

May [16] A revival of Love's *Alone Again Or* reaches UK #27.

Nov [28] *In Dulce Decorum* peaks at UK #72.

Dec [12] A definitive best of compilation, ***Light At The End Of The Tunnel***, released through MCA, charts for a week, at UK #87.

1988

June [13] The Damned plays at London's Town & Country club. (By year's end, Vanian, Scabies and Jugg release ***Give Daddy The Knife Cindy*** as Naz & the Nomads, on Chiswick.)

1989

July The group decides to quit again and begins a farewell tour of the UK. (Sensible, now married to a Dolly Mixture, contributes *Sporting Life* to the benefit album ***The Liberator - Artists For Animals*** and will continue to record for a number of UK independent labels.) Vanian will assemble the short-lived Dave Vanian & the Phantom Chords for UK dates the in November the following year.

1992

July [25-26] Having reunited the previous year, not least opening on four UK dates for the Ramones, they play two nights at London's Town & Country club.

1996

Feb [24] Following the 1994 MCA retrospective, ***Eternally Damned - The Very Best Of The Damned*** and Sensible's Dec [10] UK #71 peaking version of *The Hokey Cokey* the same year, the group, now plays at the Forum, Kentish Town, London, an event billed as the 20th Anniversary Special.

DANNY & THE JUNIORS

Danny Rapp (lead vocals);
Dave White (first tenor, backing vocals);
Frank Mattei (second tenor, backing vocals);
Joe Terranova (baritone, backing vocals)

1957

Rapp (b. May 10, 1941, Philadelphia, PA) has formed the Italian-American vocal quartet with friends Terranova (b. Jan. 30, 1941, Philadelphia), White (b. David White Tricker, Sept. 1940, Philadelphia) and Mattei as the Juvenairs, while they are still attending high school in Philadelphia, in 1955. Now out of school, they are introduced by their singer friend, Johnny Medora, to his vocal tutor, Artie Singer, a music entrepreneur who offers to manage them. White, Medora and Singer write *Do The Bop* for the group to record on Singer's new Philadelphia-based label, Singular Records. DJ Dick Clark hears the song and persuades Singer it would be more commercial if revised to *At The Hop*, which is how it is finally recorded.
Nov With 7,000 copies of *At The Hop* sold in Philadelphia on Singular, it is picked up for national distribution by ABC-Paramount Records following an appearance on Clark's "American Bandstand" TV showcase.

1958

Jan [11] Era-defining *At The Hop* tops the US chart for the first of seven weeks, and will sell over a million copies.
Feb *At The Hop* hits UK #3.
Mar [22] *Rock And Roll Is Here To Stay*, written by White, reaches US #19.
July [26] *Dottie* makes US #39.

1960

Oct [15] After a hit-free period, but still a popular live draw, the group (minus White, who has been replaced by Bill Carlucci) has signed to Swan Records, releasing the topical dance song, *Twistin' USA*, which reaches US #37.

1961

Mar [18] *Pony Express* makes US #60.
Oct [21] *Back To The Hop*, an attempted update of their original hit, peaks at US #80.

1962

Jan [25] They have teamed with labelmate Freddy Cannon (and uncredited backing vocals from the Four Seasons) for another Twist cash-in, *Twistin' All Night Long*, which peaks at US #68.
Apr [19] *Doin' The Continental Walk* stops at US #93.

1963

Jan [24] The group switches to another Philadelphia label, Guyden Records, and another dance craze, for its final US hit, *Oo-La-La-Limbo*, which peaks at #99, though shortly after, the band breaks up. (White will have subsequent success, co-writing Len Barry's 1965 US #2, *1-2-3*, and releasing the solo album, ***David White Tricker***, in 1971.)

1976

July While Danny & the Juniors have assisted former Shirelle Shirley Alston on a version of *Sincerely* on her 1975 album ***With A Little Help From My Friends***, the reissued classic *At The Hop* makes UK #39.

1983

Apr [5] Rapp is found dead in Parker, AZ, having apparently shot himself. (Danny & the Juniors, led by Terranova, will re-emerge to play on the oldies circuit and will release *Some Kind Of Wonderful* on the Topaz label in 1987.)

TERENCE TRENT D'ARBY

1980

Apr Son of a Pentecostal preacher, the Reverend James Benjamin Darby, and a teacher, Frances, D'Arby (b. Mar. 15, 1962, New York, NY), having moved during his childhood from New York to Chicago, IL, and Florida and been the regional Golden Gloves boxing champ, quits studying journalism at the University of Central Florida to enlist in the US army. After an initial post at Fort Sill, OK, he is sent to join Elvis Presley's old regiment, the Third Armored Division, near Frankfurt, W. Germany. Attracted by German nightlife, he will join a local nine-piece funk outfit, Touch, as its singer in 1982 (recording a number of tracks which will be released by Polydor Records (UK) in 1989 as ***Touch***). Setting his sights on going AWOL from the army (as he will later claim), he links up with Klaus Pieter Schleinitz, known as K.P., the press officer for European record label, Ariola International. Officially discharged from the army in April 1983 (he will continue to romanticize the episode for many years), D'Arby leaves the disintegrating band in January the following year and heads for London with K.P., becoming his full-time manager.

1987

Apr [11] Having been signed to CBS/Columbia Records the previous June on the strength of his demo tape, and now permanently resident in London, D'Arby's debut single, *If You Let Me Stay*, instantly showcasing his impressive rock/R&B vocal strength, hits UK #7. He begins a deliberately-outspoken relationship with the press (telling the **New Musical Express**, for example: "I think I'm a genius. Point fucking blank"). Often performing cover versions of his favorite soul oldies, he makes an impressive appearance on C4-TV's "The Last Resort" singing *(What A) Wonderful World*, and also participates in an "Artists Against Apartheid" concert at London's Royal Albert Hall, while touring the UK as support to Simply Red.
July [11] *Wishing Well* hits UK #4.
[25] ***Introducing The Hardline According To Terence Trent D'Arby***, produced by Martyn Ware of Heaven 17, tops the UK chart. Following his own short "Hardline Introduction" UK tour (with shows in Glasgow, Birmingham, Bristol and London) to support the album, he supports David Bowie on UK dates.
Sept D'Arby visits the US on a promotional trip, his first visit to his home country (which he frequently denounces in interviews) since joining the US army.
[30] He makes his US live debut at a Roxy, Los Angeles, CA concert.
Oct [31] *Dance Little Sister* reaches UK #20.
Nov [10] D'Arby cancels a concert in Vienna, Austria, in protest over Kurt Waldheim's confirmation as the new President of Austria.
[21] *If You Let Me Stay* peaks at US #68.
Dec He performs two London shows, one at Holloway women's prison and one at Wandsworth prison.

1988

Jan [23] Ballad *Sign Your Name* hits UK #2, behind Belinda Carlisle's *Heaven Is A Place On Earth*.
Feb [8] D'Arby wins Best International Newcomer at the seventh annual BRIT Awards, defeating Los Lobos, L.L. Cool J, Bruce Willis and the Beastie Boys. In his acceptance speech he asks the immigration authorities to give him a UK passport.
Mar ***Introducing The Hardline*** is certified quadruple platinum, having sold 1,200,000 copies in the UK alone, as D'Arby embarks on a major US tour.
Apr At Easter, he causes media alarm by releasing a promotion picture of himself naked and crucified.
[2] *Wishing Well* hits US R&B #1.
[30] ***Introducing The Hardline*** tops the US R&B survey.
May [7] *Wishing Well* tops the US chart for one week and ***Introducing The Hardline*** hits US #4.
June In an article in **Rolling Stone**, D'Arby claims it will definitely be his last-ever interview.
Aug [13] *Sign Your Name* hits US #4. (He is also currently featured singing on Brian Wilson's solo debut album.)
Oct [22] *Dance Little Sister* reaches US #30.
Dec [31] D'Arby becomes a father when his girlfriend, Mary Vango, gives birth to a daughter, Seraphina.

1989

Feb [22] D'Arby wins the Best R&B Vocal Performance, Male category for ***Introducing The Hardline*** at the 31st Grammy Awards.
Nov [4] His critically-slammed second album, ***Neither Fish Nor Flesh***, reaches UK #12 and will make US #61. It will disappear from view with ferocious speed, despite efforts from concerned CBS executives worldwide.

1990

Jan [27] *To Know Someone Deeply Is To Know Someone Softly* peaks at UK #55.
Apr [16] D'Arby participates in the "Nelson Mandela - An International Tribute To A Free South Africa" concert at Wembley Stadium, Wembley, Middx.
May [5] He sings *You've Got To Hide Your Love Away* at the "John Lennon Tribute Concert" at the Pier Head Arena in Merseyside to celebrate the songs of Lennon.
Nov [25] D'Arby performs on CBS-TV's "Motown 30: What's Goin' On!" special.

1991

Feb Asked for a comment by a reporter at the opening of Mick Fleetwood's new Los Angeles club, Fleetwood's, D'Arby is quoted as saying, "Every time I open my mouth, I ruin my career."
Mar D'Arby's former management company sues him for £76,000 in unsettled royalties from his first album.
[9] The Peace Choir, of which he is a part, makes US #54 with a re-working of John Lennon's *Give Peace A Chance*.
Sept [9] The British Electric Foundation's ***Music Of Quality & Distinction Volume 2***, to which the singer has contributed a cover of *It's Alright Ma, I'm Only Bleeding* , is released.

1992

May D'Arby works on new tracks with producer Mark Stent at the Hotnights and Olympic studios.

1993

Apr [24] *Do You Love Me Like You Say?* reaches UK #14.
May [15] Self-produced ***Terence Trent D'Arby's Symphony Or Damn Exploring The Tension Inside The Sweetness***, his first album in three years, a concept set divided into two parts: *Confrontation* and *Reconciliation*, and highly-rated by many reviewers, debuts at its UK #4 peak.
June [5] ***Symphony Or Damn*** peaks at US #119, as

D'Arby performs at the "KISS Radio Anniversary Concert" at the Great Woods Center for the Performing Arts, Mansfield, MA.
July [3] *Delicate*, featuring Des'ree, reaches UK #14.
[8] D'Arby guests on syndicated TV's "The Arsenio Hall Show".
[9] Having joined Bruce Springsteen onstage at a New York Madison Square Garden benefit in June, D'Arby joins Duran Duran's current tour in Monterrey, Mexico, set to end on August 24th at Bally's Casino Resort, Las Vegas, NV.
Sept [11] *She Kissed Me* reaches UK #16.
Oct [9] *Delicate* peaks at US #74.
Nov [19] D'Arby plays a sole London date, at the Brixton Academy.
[27] *Let Her Down Easy* reaches UK #18.

1994

Feb [28] D'Arby guests on NBC-TV's "The Tonight Show".

1995

Jan [19] D'Arby appears at the "Commitment To Life VIII" benefit for AIDS Project Los Angeles, honoring Elton John, Tom Hanks and Ron Meyer at the Universal Amphitheatre, Universal City.
Feb [4] Soundtrack album ***Pret-A-Porter***, including the previously unreleased D'Arby track *Supermodel Sandwich*, reaches US #29.
[7] ***Promised Land*** TV soundtrack album, featuring D'Arby's version of *A Change Is Gonna Come* backed by Booker T. & the MG's, is released.
Apr [22] *Holding On To You* reaches UK #20.
[29] A short-haired, bleached-blond D'Arby returns with his fourth album, ***Terence Trent D'Arby's Vibrator***, which bows at its UK #11 peak. Once again self-written and self-produced it features a host of music guests including Patrice Rushen, ex-Bros twin Matt Goss and Branford Marsalis.
May [8] D'Arby guests on CBS-TV's "Late Show With David Letterman".
[27] Switching labels to Sony's Work Group imprint, ***Terence Trent D'Arby's Vibrator*** charts for a week at US #178.
July [17] The 15-date UK leg of his "Vibrator" world tour begins at Bristol's Colston Hall, Avon set to end at King George's Hall, Blackburns, Lancs.
Aug [5] *Vibrator* charts for a week at UK #57.
[17] D'Arby guests on NBC-TV's "The Tonight Show".
Nov [3] Currently on tour in the US, D'Arby plays a small club date at Toad's Place in New Haven, CT.

BOBBY DARIN

1956

Mar Brought up by his mother Nina whom he believes (until told at the age of 32) is his sister, thinking his grandmother to be his mother, and having won a scholarship to Hunter College, New York, NY, Darin (b. Walden Robert Cassotto, May 14, 1936, Bronx, New York) quits after just one term to pursue acting, recording and songwriting with mentor/manager Don Kirshner (with whom he has doubled as a bus boy/singer on the Borscht Belt), and records a cover of Lonnie Donegan's hit, *Rock Island Line*, for Decca Records. Signing with Atlantic Records subsidiary Atco the following May, he goes on to release three Herb Abramson-produced singles.

1958

June Departing radically from his usual black R&B fare, Atlantic boss Ahmet Ertegun has produced *Splish Splash*, a pop novelty co-written in ten minutes by Darin and disc jockey Murray the K's mother.
Aug [9] *Splish Splash* hits US #3 and reaches #18 in the UK, where Charlie Drake's comedy cover will also hit #7.
[16] Frustrated by his lack of success on Atco, Darin has cut two of his songs, *Early In The Morning/Now We're One*, as the Ding Dongs for Brunswick but Atlantic objects and secures the rights to the single, which now reaches US #24 under a new pseudonym, the Rinky Dinks. Brunswick recruits Buddy Holly to cover both sides and his single scores at #32.
Nov [22] The teen-oriented *Queen Of The Hop* hits US #9, Darin's second million-seller, and UK #24, while Ruth Brown reaches US #24 with the Darin-penned *This Little Girl's Gone Rockin'*.

1959

Feb [28] *Plain Jane*, written by Pomus and Shuman, reaches US #38.
June [13] *Dream Lover*, his own composition, hits US #2, his third million-seller.
July [3] *Dream Lover* tops the UK chart for the first of four weeks.
Oct [10] Darin's cover of the jazzy *Mack The Knife* from Bertholdt Brecht and Kurt Weill's "Threepenny Opera", which is currently playing in New York, hits US #1, where it will remain for nine weeks, earning Darin a fourth gold disc.
[16] *Mack The Knife* also hits UK #1, as ***That's All***, the album from which *Mack The Knife* was taken, climbs to US #7 and UK #15.
Nov [29] Darin wins the Record Of The Year category for *Mack The Knife* and is named Best New Artist Of 1959 at the second annual Grammy Awards.

1960

Mar [5] Brassy, swinging arrangements of standards become his forté, with *Beyond The Sea* (originally a 1945 hit for French composer Charles Trenet) hitting both US #6 and UK #8, earning Darin a fifth US gold disc. He hits the night club/cabaret circuit, starting with the Sahara Hotel in Las Vegas, NV.
Apr [23] Darin's update of the Gold Rush ballad, *Clementine*, reaches US #29 and hits UK #8, while his second album, ***This Is Darin***, hits US #6 and UK #4 (his last UK album hit for 25 years).
July [9] His revival of the jazz standard *Won't You Come Home Bill Bailey* reaches US #19 and UK #34.
[16] Its B-side, *I'll Be There*, a Darin original, peaks at US #79 (and five years later will provide a hit for Gerry & the Pacemakers).
Sept [10] *Beachcomber*, a piano solo, anchors at US #100.
Oct [29] *Somebody To Love*, the other side of the still-climbing *Artificial Flowers*, makes US #45, while his live album, ***Darin At The Copa***, hits US #9.
Nov [5] *Artificial Flowers*, from the musical "Tenderloin", reaches US #45.
Dec [1] Darin marries film star Sandra Dee in the home of a judge in Camden, NJ.
[31] *Child Of God*, the B-side of the still-climbing *Christmas Auld Lang Syne*, charts for a week at US #95. (During the year he appears in movie "Pepe", starring Mexican comedian Cantinflas, and "Heller In Pink Tights", with Sophia Loren and Anthony Quinn.)

1961

Jan [5] *Christmas Auld Lang Syne* makes US #51.
Apr [1] His reworking of Hoagy Carmichael's *Lazy River* reaches US #14 and UK #12.
May Greatest hits compilation, ***The Bobby Darin Story***, reaches US #18.
July [15] Darin's revival of Nat "King" Cole's 1948 hit, *Nature Boy*, makes US #40 and UK #24.
Oct [21] Another update, *You Must Have Been A Beautiful Baby*, hits US #5 and UK #10, as his fifth album, ***Love Swings***, peaks at US #92.
Come September, an instrumental credited to the Bobby Darin Orchestra, makes UK #50. The tune is the title theme from his latest movie (co-starring his wife Sandra and Rock Hudson). Darin features in two other movies during the year: "State Fair" with Pat Boone and "Too Late Blues" with Stella Stevens and Fabian. (During the filming of "State Fair" in Dallas, TX, Hurricane Carla strikes, and Darin, Frankie Laine and Alice Faye later stage a charity concert at the Majestic Theatre, which raises $65,000 to help the victims).

1962

Jan ***Twist With Bobby Darin***, exploiting the latest dance craze, makes US #48.
Feb [10] *Irresistible You* reaches US #15.
[17] *Irresistible You*'s flipside, *Multiplication*, reaches US #30, as *Multiplication* hits UK #5.
Apr [28] *What'd I Say* reaches US #24.
May Its parent album, ***Bobby Darin Sings Ray Charles***, makes US #96.
July Darin begins a month-long season at the Flamingo, Las Vegas, before embarking on an open-air tour with Count Basie and the Tarriers.
Aug [25] His own composition, *Things*, hits US #3 and UK #2, becoming his sixth and last US million-seller.
Sept After five years on Atco, Darin has signed with Capitol Records.
Oct An Atco compilation, ***Things And Other Things***, charts at US #45.
[27] Atco releases his version of the standard *Baby Face*, which makes US #42 and UK #40.
Nov [10] The self-penned *If A Man Answers*, the title song from his latest film (co-starring his wife), reaches US #32 and UK #24. (His first Capitol album, ***Oh! Look At Me Now***, makes US #100.)
Dec [1] Darin cancels a lucrative one-nighter to celebrate his second wedding anniversary
[15] Atco vault recording, *I Found A New Baby*, climbs to US #90.
(During the year Darin also gets star billing in "Pressure Point" with Sidney Poitier and "Hell Is For Heroes" with Steve McQueen.)

1963

Mar [16] *You're The Reason I'm Living* hits US #3, as Darin embraces the C&W and folk idioms. His nightclub guitarist during this period is Jim (Roger) McGuinn, later the instigator of the Byrds.
Mar ***You're The Reason I'm Living*** makes US #43.
May *Heart! (I Hear You Beating)* by Wayne Newton at US #82 is the first hit for Darin's new publishing/recording venture, TM Music Inc.
June [15] *18 Yellow Roses* hits US #10 and returns Darin to the UK chart, at #37.
Oct [5] While his nightclub career thrives, his recording success declines: *Treat My Baby Good* makes US #43 and ***18 Yellow Roses*** peaks at US #98.
Dec [14] *Be Mad Little Girl* makes US #64. (Darin's role in "Captain Newman MD" attracts an Oscar nomination for Best Supporting Actor.)

1964

Feb He is voted National Heart Ambassador for the American Heart Association.
Mar [14] Darin's revival of *I Wonder Who's Kissing Her Now* peaks at US #93.
July [4] His version of the Edith Piaf classic, *Milord*, makes US #45 for Atco.
Oct [17] *The Things In This House* peaks at US #86. Darin feels Capitol is neglecting his interests in favor of their youth-market roster, which includes the Beatles, the Beach Boys and Peter & Gordon.
Dec ***From Hello Dolly To Goodbye Charlie*** peaks at US #107.

1965

Jan Darin sings at President Johnson's Inauguration Gala in Washington, DC.
Feb [20] His last Capitol chart single, the show tune *Hello Dolly*, makes US #79.
July ***Venice Blue*** peaks at US #132.
Aug *That Funny Feeling*, from his latest movie, "That Funny Feeling" (co-starring Sandra Dee), is released.
Sept Darin returns to Atlantic, but his first two singles make no chart impact.

1966

June [4] *Mame*, borrowed from the current Broadway musical, returns Darin to the charts, at US #53.
Nov [5] Encouraged by publishers Charles Koppelman and Don Rubin to investigate contemporary material, their folk-rock production of Tim Hardin's *If I Were A*

Carpenter gives Darin a transatlantic Top 10 comeback, hitting US #8 and UK #9.
Dec [24] *The Girl That Stood Beside Me* peaks at US #66.

1967

Feb [18] *Lovin' You*, written by John Sebastian, reaches US #32. During the year, he stars in two movies, "Gunfight In Abilene" and "Cop Out" (with James Mason). He and Sandra Dee are divorced. His only Atlantic album to chart, ***If I Were A Carpenter***, peaks at US #142.
Apr [29] *The Lady Came From Baltimore*, another Tim Hardin song, makes US #62.
July [29] A cover of the Lovin' Spoonful hit, *Darling Be Home Soon*, climbs to US #93.

1968

After working tirelessly for Robert F. Kennedy's presidential campaign (they sometimes sang together on plane trips), Darin leaves Atlantic to launch his own label, Direction, with his first release, ***Born Walden Robert Cassotto ("written, arranged, produced, designed and photographed by Bobby Darin")***, featuring poetry and protest material.
Aug Darin sells his publishing company for $1 million.

1969

Feb [22] *Long Line Rider* is the only one of five Direction singles to chart, peaking at US #79. "The Happy Ending", with Jean Simmons, is his first film in over a year.
Aug Having denied Tim Hardin a hit with his own *If I Were A Carpenter*, Hardin's only US chart hit (at #50), *Simple Song Of Freedom*, is written by Darin (who will sign to Motown the following year, subsequently issuing five non-charting singles and two albums).

1971

Apr He undergoes nine-hour surgery to insert two artificial valves in his heart which is thought to have been weakened by a childhood attack of pneumatic fever.
June During recuperation, Darin marries Andrea Yeager.

1973

Jan Having hosted an NBC-TV variety series the previous summer, the nationally-syndicated television series, "The Bobby Darin Show", begins weekly transmission, running until April.
Feb [24] *Happy* peaks at US #67.
May His last film is "Happy Mother's Day" with Patricia Neal.
Dec [20] Darin dies in the Cedars of Lebanon Hospital, Hollywood, CA, following surgery to repair a heart valve. At 37, he had outlived his early conviction that he wouldn't reach 30. (In keeping with his wishes, his body is donated, without a funeral, to UCLA's medical school.)

1985

Oct Atlantic compilation, ***The Legend Of Bobby Darin - His Greatest Hits***, makes UK #39.

1990

Jan [17] Darin is inducted into the Rock and Roll Hall of Fame at the fifth annual dinner, at New York's Waldorf Astoria Hotel, as film director Barry Levinson plans to make a biopic about him.

1995

Nov [21] Following his son Dodd's publication of **Dream Lovers**, written about Dee and Darin, the previous year, ***As Long As I'm Singing : The Bobby Darin Collection***, a comprehensive 96-track four-CD boxed set assembled by Jeff Bleil, author of the Darin biography **That's All**, and James Austin, is released by Rhino Records (US).

DAVE DEE, DOZY, BEAKY, MICK & TICH

Dave Dee (lead vocals, tambourine); **Dozy** (bass); **Beaky** (guitar); **Mick** (drums); **Tich** (lead guitar)

1961

The group is formed, semi-professionally at first, in Salisbury, Wilts., as Dave Dee & the Bostons, with Dee (b. David Harman, Dec. 17, 1943, Salisbury), an ex-police cadet (who was among the police called to the scene of Eddie Cochran's fatal car crash), Dozy (b. Trevor Davies, Nov. 27, 1944, Enford, Wilts.), Beaky (b. John Dymond, July 10, 1944, Salisbury) and Tich (b. Ian Amey, May 15, 1944, Salisbury). Several drummers come and go before Mick (b. Michael Wilson, Mar. 4, 1944, Amesbury, Wilts.) completes the quintet at the end of the year. After building a live reputation around the UK West Country, the group turns professional the following year for a residency at the Top Ten club in Hamburg, W. Germany, where an act is developed fusing rock'n' roll and uptempo R&B (in gradually-honed, four-part harmony vocals) with comedy patter and carefully-choreographed "casual" clowning.

1964

Sept Having played as the ballroom rock band at the Butlin's Clacton-on-Sea, Essex holiday camp for the summer season, the group supports the Honeycombs on a one-nighter in Swindon, Wilts., and impresses the Honeycombs' managers, Ken Howard and Alan Blaikley, with its highly-polished act.
Oct Howard and Blaikley sign the group to a management contract, change its name to Dave Dee, Dozy, Beaky, Mick & Tich, and negotiate a recording contract with Fontana.

1965

Jan [29] Their debut single, *No Time*, is released, but fails to chart, despite appearances on UK TV's "Gadzooks! It's All Happening" (their TV premiere) and "Ready Steady Go!". A Continental-styled waltz-time song, it is written by Howard and Blaikley (who will write all of their singles) and produced by Steve Rowland (who will produce most later releases).
July *All I Want*, a ballad, is released.

1966

Jan *You Make It Move*, in a thumping, uptempo style which will be a trademark of the group's early hits, reaches UK #26.
Feb [12] The group begins a 14-date, twice-nightly tour, with Gene Pitney, Len Barry and others, at the Gaumont Cinema, Ipswich, Suffolk, set to end on the 27th at the ABC Cinema, Southampton, Hants.
Apr *Hold Tight*, an audience-raising stomping chant adapted from the Routers' *Let's Go* and subsequently used as a chant by soccer fans at the World Cup during the coming summer tournament, hits UK #4. The group begins to adopt garish but fashionable (and ever-changing) stage attire, building the act from a comedy routine to a blend of color and drama.
May [1] The group takes part in the annual "**New Musical Express** Poll Winners Concert" at the Empire Pool, Wembley, Middx.
July [2] *Hideaway* hits UK #10, as the group's first album, ***Dave Dee, Dozy, Beaky, Mick & Tich***, reaches UK #11.
[23] While travelling by train to Liverpool, the group has breakfast with Prime Minister Harold Wilson and his wife Mary.
Oct [1] The group opens a 33-date UK tour, with the Walker Brothers and the Troggs, at the Granada Cinema, East Ham, London, set to close on November 13th at London's Finsbury Park Astoria.
[8] *Bend It*, a *Zorba's Dance*-styled accelerating-tempo song about a supposed dance, but with lyrics conveying double entendres (helped by Dee's wry vocal delivery), hits UK #2. Its bazouki sound is created on an electrified mandola. The single is widely banned by US radio, prompting a re-recorded US version which takes the emphasis off the apparent salaciousness, though it still fails to chart in the US.
Dec [5] The group begins a tour of W. Germany, with the Spencer Davis Group, at the Circus Krone, Munich.

1967

Jan [7] *Save Me* hits UK #4. ***If Music Be The Food Of Love (Prepare For Indigestion)*** reaches UK #27.
Apr [8] *Touch Me, Touch Me* reaches UK #13.
[11] The group begins a tour of New Zealand, Australia, Singapore and Hong Kong, with Eric Burdon & the Animals and Paul & Barry Ryan, in Christchurch, New Zealand.
July [1] *Okay!*, with Tich playing balalaika, hits UK #4.
Nov [4] *Zabadak*, a highly-experimental song with a gibberish vocal and a percussive mock-Caribbean arrangement, hits UK #3.
Dec [9] Band members are involved in two separate car crashes on their way to a show in Manchester - Dave Dee and Mick escape with shock and bruises when Dave's Humber Super Snipe skids on a patch of ice, while Beaky and Tich receive concussion, cuts and bruises when the E-Type Jaguar they are travelling in crashes on the M6. Tich, who is travelling to the venue by train, is the only one who makes it to the destination, so the gig is cancelled.

1968

Feb [3] *Zabadak* peaks at US #52, the group's only US chart success.
Mar [20] *The Legend Of Xanadu*, a story song with a dramatic Latin arrangement, tops the UK chart for one week and is the group's biggest UK seller. It features a distinctive whipcrack sound (achieved in the studio with two pieces of plywood slapping and an empty bottle sliding on guitar strings), which leads to Dee brandishing a bullwhip on stage - an effective (audience-approved) addition to their flamboyant live act.
Mar [27] The group begins a 26-date UK tour supporting the Bee Gees with Grapefruit at London's Royal Albert Hall, set to end on April 28th at the Granada Cinema, Tooting, London.
Aug [3] *Last Night In Soho* hits UK #8 and is another story song, with a chorus and additional backing musicians.
Sept [29] The group plays a four-day stint at the City Hall, Vienna, Austria, with Ray Charles and Diana Ross & the Supremes.
Nov [2] *The Wreck Of The Antoinette*, the group's third mini-musical drama, reaches UK #14.

1969

Mar [22] *Don Juan*, a dramatic *Xanadu*-style song and arrangement, reaches UK #23.
May [31] *Snake In The Grass*, without the dramatics but with a subtle arrangement far removed from the sledgehammer beat of their early hits, reaches UK #23 - the last in a run of 13 consecutive UK Top 30 hits, all Howard/Blaikley compositions.
Aug Dee leaves the group for a solo vocal career (having already done solo work on TV, both acting and singing), while the others continue as D, B, M & T. (Dee forms the record production company Avenue Artists Production, with agents Bob James and Len Cannon. The first releases from the company are *Do It Yourself* by the Chances and *Daffodillo* by the Nite People.)
Dec Dave Dee breaks box office records at Manchester's Talk Of The North with his new four-piece backing band, David.

1970

Mar Dee's solo ballad *My Woman's Man* reaches UK #42.
Aug D, B, M & T's *Mr. President* makes UK #33. (The group will go on to record ***Fresh Ear***, before breaking up. Finding only minor success as an actor, Dee will move to the backroom of the record industry, becoming head of A&R at WEA's UK division in 1973, though he will reform for *She's My Lady*, a one-off single in October the following year released on the Antic label, under his own auspices through WEA.

Dee will subsequently go on to form his own Double D record label.)

1982

Sept [21] The group has another one-off reunion, in an all-star concert at London's Hammersmith Odeon, organised by Dee as a UK record industry charity committee member. Celebrating 15 years of BBC Radio 1, and featuring acts including Billy Fury, Dave Berry, the Troggs and Herman's Hermits, the show is a benefit for the industry's charity, the Nordoff Robbins Music Therapy Centre. The group's live revival of *The Legend Of Xanadu* appears on the event's souvenir compilation, ***Heroes And Villains***. They stay together long enough to tour Germany, where interest in the group is still strong, and where D, B, M & T have been playing regularly for many years.

1991

Oct [6] While Dee has remained in public view as the UK host of a German-licenced TV rock archive show, "The Beat Club", broadcast on ITV since 1989, D, B, M & T, (with a new "Mick" added in 1988), still playing on the nostalgia circuit and based at their own club in Marbella, Spain, perform at the "Biggest '60s Party In Town" at London's Olympia Hall.

THE SPENCER DAVIS GROUP

Steve Winwood (guitar, keyboards, vocals); **Spencer Davis** (guitar); **Muff Winwood** (bass); **Pete York** (drums)

1963

Aug Former Birmingham University student Davis (b. July 17, 1937, Swansea, West Glamorgan, Wales), the year of his birth is claimed by the artist, contradicting record company legend and subsequent sources which variously place his arrival in the early 1940s, a teacher and part-time blues musician in Birmingham, Warks., and ex-London skiffle group the Saints, forms the group after meeting York (b. Aug. 15, 1942, Redcar, Cleveland) and the Winwood brothers: 15-year old Steve (b. May 12, 1948, Birmingham) and Muff (b. Mervyn Winwood, June 15, 1943, Birmingham), named after the TV puppet Muffin the Mule, at the Golden Eagle, a Birmingham pub. He has been playing there as a folk/blues soloist, and they initially play as the trad Muff-Woody Jazz Band, before evolving as a tough R&B quartet, appropriately called the Rhythm & Blues Quartet.

1964

June [1] The group is spotted and signed by Chris Blackwell, who owns the fledging Island Records. As yet lacking full resources to promote his acts, Blackwell licenses the group's output to Philips Records' Fontana label, their label debut reviving John Lee Hooker's *Dimples*.
Sept [11] The group plays at Birmingham's Town Hall, supporting Alexis Korner's Incorporated.
Nov *I Can't Stand It*, covering the Soul Sisters' 1964 US #46 original, is their UK chart debut, at #47.

1965

Mar Their revival of Brenda Holloway's *Every Little Bit Hurts* makes UK #41.
June *Strong Love* peaks at UK #44.
Aug [8] The group plays on the last day of the fifth annual "National Jazz & Blues Festival" at the Richmond Athletic Ground, Richmond, Surrey.
Sept [24] They begin a 24-date, twice-nightly UK tour, with the Rolling Stones, Unit 4 + 2 and others, at London's Finsbury Park Astoria, set to end on October 17th at the Granada Cinema, Tooting, London.

1966

Jan [20] *Keep On Running*, penned by Blackwell's Jamaican protegé Jackie Edwards and originally a B-side, is their breakthrough hit, topping the UK chart after deposing the Beatles' *Daytripper/We Can Work It Out*.
Feb ***Their First LP*** (originally released in July 1965) and the new set, ***The Second Album***, are simultaneous UK hits, hitting #6 and #3 respectively.
Mar [12] *Keep On Running* peaks at US #76.
Apr [14] The group embarks on a UK tour with the Who, at the Gaumont Cinema, Southampton, Hants.
[16] *Somebody Help Me* hits UK #1 for the first of two weeks.
May [1] The band takes part in the annual "**New Musical Express** Poll Winners Concert", at the Empire Pool, Wembley, Middx.
July [11] They begin shooting "The Ghost Goes Gear" film on location in the Windsor, Berks. area and Chiddingstone Castle, Kent, with Dave Berry.
[29] They play on the first day of the sixth annual "National Jazz & Blues Festival" at Windsor.
Aug [22] The group makes its cabaret debut - a week at the Fiesta, Stockton, Cleveland and the Franchi, Jarrow, Tyne & Wear.
Sept *When I Come Home* reaches UK #12.
Oct *Autumn '66* hits UK #5.
[1-2] The band represents the UK in the annual "Grand Gala Du Disques" in Amsterdam, Holland.
Nov *Gimme Some Lovin'*, written by the Winwoods and Davis, hits UK #2, kept from #1 by the Beach Boys' *Good Vibrations*.
Dec "The Ghost Goes Gear" is released in the UK as the support film to "One Million Years BC".
[5] A German tour with Dave Dee, Dozy, Beaky, Mick & Tich opens at the Circus Krone, Munich.

1967

Feb *I'm A Man*, co-penned by Steve Winwood with producer Jimmy Miller and originally written as background music for a US documentary film on 'Swinging London', hits UK #9.
[25] *Gimme Some Lovin'*, in a remixed form with added instrumentation and a female-vocal backed chorus, now hits US #7, becoming their biggest US success.
Mar [11] They begin a 21-date UK tour with the Hollies, the Tremeloes and Paul Jones, at the Granada Cinema, Mansfield, Notts., set to end on April 2nd at the Empire Theatre, Liverpool, Lancs.
[20] The group wins the Carl Alan Award for the Most Outstanding Group Of 1966.
Apr [2] Having given lengthy notice of their intention, both Winwood brothers leave (Steve to form Traffic, and Muff to become a management executive of Blackwell's West End Promotions, managing Millie, Traffic, Jimmy Cliff, Smoke and others, and eventually scale executive heights in the UK record industry with CBS).
May [6] *I'm A Man* hits US #10 as ***Gimme Some Lovin'*** makes US #54.
[7] The new line-up of Davis, York, organist Eddie Hardin (b. Edward Harding, Feb. 19, 1949) and lead guitarist Phil Sawyer (b. Mar. 8, 1947), debuts at the annual "**New Musical Express** Poll Winners Concert" at the Empire Pool, Wembley. (Sawyer will be replaced by Ray Fenwick.)
July [22] *Somebody Help Me*, belatedly released in the US, reaches #47, while ***I'm A Man*** makes US #83. The group opens a US tour in Lake Geneva, WI.
Sept [16] Psychedelia-tinged *Time Seller*, recorded by the new line-up, reaches UK #30, though the group has lost its distinctive sound, based not least around Winwood's vocals.
Nov The group makes a cameo appearance in a dancehall sequence in the movie "Here We Go Round The Mulberry Bush", for which they also write six songs.

1968

Jan Their final UK hit is *Mr. Second Class*, which reaches #35.
Aug [11] The group takes part in the eighth "National Jazz & Blues Festival" at Kempton Park Racecourse.
Oct Hardin and York leave to work as a duo, recording ***Tomorrow Today*** for Bell Records.
[15] The band performs at a charity concert in aid of Czech students wishing to remain in Britain, at London's Royal Albert Hall.
Nov A North American tour, begins with a new line-up comprising Dee Murray (bass) and Dave Hynes (drums). (Hynes will shortly be replaced by Nigel Olsson.)

1969

Jan [24-25] The group plays at an all-night gig at London's Lyceum Ballroom, with Love Sculpture, Gun and Joe Cocker.
July Davis breaks up the band (Murray and Olsson moving on to accompany Elton John), and moves to California to work as a soloist. (He will continue to play and record, mostly in the US, throughout the '70s.)

1973

Davis, having formed a duo with Peter Jameson in 1971 and having released the solo albums ***It's Been So Long*** and ***Mousetrap***, briefly re-forms the group with Hardin, York, McCracken and Fenwick - for US and UK tours. The reunion does not last and the band finally quits, with Davis eventually assuming an executive post at Island Records, Los Angeles (and also recording ***Crossfire*** in 1984). (York will return to his roots, playing with Chris Barber's jazz band.)

1994

Oct [26] While Davis, having played with York and Zoot Money in Blues Reunion in 1988, and formed a new but short-lived Spencer Davis Group in 1990 with Don Kirkpatrick and Ed Tree (guitars), Rick Seratte (keyboards), Charlie Harrison (bass) and ex-Wang Chung member Bryan Hitt (drums) (after which Hitt accepted an invitation to join REO Speedwagon, while York moved to Germany to host the TV show "Super Drummers"), will tour the US as a member of the Classic Rock All-Stars (with Mike Pinera, Jerry Corbetta and Peter Rivera) in 1995, the Winwood brothers now accept an honor for one million US radio and television plays of *Gimme Some Lovin'* at the annual BMI Awards ceremony in London, acknowledging producer Jimmy Miller who died four days earlier.
see also: **BLIND FAITH, TRAFFIC, Steve WINWOOD**

DAWN

See: **Tony ORLANDO & DAWN**

BOBBY DAY

1957

Sept Day (b. Robert Byrd, July 1, 1930, Fort Worth, TX), having moved to Watts, Los Angeles, CA, as a youngster, and later served an R&B apprenticeship under Johnny Otis at the Barrelhouse Club, is active both as a songwriter and member of vocal group, the Hollywood Flames. Over a period of time the group goes through a variety of name-changes, settling on the Satellites when Day releases *Little Bitty Pretty One* as Bobby Day & the Satellites for songwriter/producer Leon Rene's Class Records.
Dec [7] A cover version of *Little Bitty Pretty One* by Thurston Harris on Aladdin Records, helped by an appearance on Dick Clark's "American Bandstand", hits US #6, while Day's original peaks at #57. Day is also climbing the US chart as one of the Hollywood Flames, with their sole US (#11) pop hit, *Buzz Buzz Buzz*, backed with *Crazy*.

1958

Feb *Buzz Buzz Buzz*, which has Earl Nelson (later half of Bob & Earl of *Harlem Shuffle* fame) on lead vocals, reaches US #11. Despite this group success, Day will subsequently concentrate on his solo career.
Oct [18] *Rockin' Robin*, penned by Jimmie Thomas and featuring a distinctive Plas Johnson flute riff, hits US #2 (including one week at #1 on the R&B chart), becoming a million-seller and staying on the survey for five months. Sales are aided by its B-side, *Over And Over*, which has made US #41 on Aug [30].

Nov *Rockin' Robin* reaches #29 in the UK, where it is Day's only hit.

1959

Jan [31] *The Bluebird, The Buzzard And The Oriole*, continuing the lyrical theme of *Rockin' Robin*, peaks at US #54.
Apr [25] *That's All I Want* spends one week at US #98.
June [27] *Gotta New Girl* makes US #82 for a single week, ending Day's chart career.

1990

July [27] Having continued recording through the '60s for RCA, Rendezvous, Sureshot and other labels, it is his songs which have proved most enduring. The Dave Clark Five hit US #1 with the million-selling *Over And Over* in 1965, while Michael Jackson hit US #2 and UK #3 in 1972 with *Rockin' Robin. Little Bitty Pretty One* had US Top 30 hit revivals by Clyde McPhatter in 1962 and the Jackson 5 in 1972, while Day also found business success through two companies, Byrdland Attractions and Quiline Publishing. (He returned to live work in the nationwide tour "Thirty Years Of Rock'n'Roll", with Donnie Brooks and Tiny Tim, and also worked with Jewel Akens.) Hospitalized since July 15th, Day dies of cancer.

DE LA SOUL

Posdnuos (vocals); **Trugoy the Dove** (vocals); **P.A. Pasemaster Mase** (vocals)

1989

Feb [3] Long Island, NY high school friends and would-be rappers Trugoy (the inverted American spelling of "yogurt") (b. David Jude Jolicoeur, Sept. 21, 1968, Brooklyn, NY), Posdnuos (an inversion of his nickname, "Sound-Sop") (b. Kelvin Mercer, Aug. 17, 1969, Bronx, NY) and Mase (b. Vincent Lamont Mason, Mar. 24, 1970, Brooklyn, NY) have formed De La Soul in Amityville, NY in 1987, their first demo, *Plug Tunin'* coming to the attention of New York-based rap group Stetsasonic's Paul Houston (aka Prince Paul), whose efforts secure the trio a recording contract with seminal hip-hop-pioneering label, Tommy Boy. Following two largely unnoticed singles in 1988, *Plug Tunin'* and *Jenifa (Taught Me)*, De La Soul has prepared its heavily sampled debut album with Prince Paul helping out at the production desk. The trio has also contributed to the Jungle Brothers' ***Done By The Forces Of Nature***, which now enters at its UK #41 peak.
Mar [25] Licensed to Jazz Summers' Big Life label in the UK and co-produced by De La Soul with Prince Paul and featuring rapper Q-Tip, the critically-revered, mellow psychedelic/hip-hop fused ***3 Feet High And Rising***, sampling diverse snippets ranging from television show soundtracks to the music of Steely Dan and Curiosity Killed The Cat, enters the UK chart, the first of 57 weeks on the survey.
Apr [1] With the innovative set already labeled D.A.I.S.Y (Da Inner Sound Y'all) Age Soul, ***3 Feet High And Rising*** begins a 29-week US chart tenure, set to reach #24.
May [6] The extracted *Me Myself And I*, borrowing from Funkadelic's *Knee Deep*, reaches UK #22.
July Their unauthorized sampling of the Turtles' 1969 US #9 hit *You Showed Me* on the album's *Transmitting Live From Mars*, sparks a $1.7 million law-suit by the Turtles' Howard Kayland and Mark Volman, which will eventually be settled out of court.
[22] *Say No Go* peaks at UK #18, the same day *Me Myself And I* makes US #34, having already topped the US Black Singles chart on June [10].
Nov [4] *Eye Know* climbs to UK #14.

1990

Jan [13] *The Magic Number* paired with *Buddy*, hits UK #7.
[27] ***3 Feet High And Rising*** peaks at UK #13, increasingly acknowledged as a landmark rap recording, which establishes a commercial trail for the likes of PM Dawn, A Tribe Called Quest and Digable Planets.
Apr [7] Having formed the hip-hop alliance Native Tongues with Queen Latifah, A Tribe Called Quest, Monie Love, the Jungle Brothers and others, De La Soul's collaboration with Latifah on *Mama Gave Birth To The Soul Children* reaches UK #14.

1991

May [4] Previewing its sophomore set, *Ring Ring Ring (Ha Ha Hey)* hits UK #10.
[25] Discarding its popular ground-breaking DAISY Age freshman outlook, the more muscular and darkly aggressive ***De La Soul Is Dead***, again co-produced by Prince Paul and the trio, debuts at its UK #7 peak.
June [8] ***De La Soul Is Dead*** reaches US #26.
[19] BBC2-TV's "Def II: Rap Rap Rapido" documentary airs, featuring De La Soul.
Aug [2] The trio performs at the Feile Festival, Semple Stadium, Tipperary, Eire, on a bill with Elvis Costello, James and Transvision Vamp among others.
[10] *A Roller Skating Jam Named 'Saturdays'* makes UK #22.
[24] Following a headlining UK tour, De La Soul takes part in the annual Reading Festival, Reading, Berks.
Sept [20-21] The poorly attended "Summer Is Dead" rap festival, including the group on the bill, takes place at Wembley Hall, Wembley, Middx.
Nov [23] *Keepin' The Faith* peaks at UK #50.

1993

Sept [18] With samples from Michael Jackson's *I Can't Help*, the Bar-Kays' *Song And Dance* and Smokey Robinson's *Quiet Storm*, De La Soul's *Breakadawn* enters at its UK #39 high.
Oct [9] Featuring Biz Markie, Maceo Parker and Fred Wesley among its guests, ***Buhloone Mindstate***, once again co-helmed by the group with Prince Paul at New York's Quad Studios, enters at its respective UK #37 and US #40 peaks, the same day *Breakadawn* stops at US #76.

1994

Apr [2] The group's collaboration with Teenage Fanclub on *Fallin'* spends a week at UK #59.

DEACON BLUE

Ricky Ross (vocals); **Lorraine McIntosh** (vocals); **Graeme Kelling** (guitar); **James Prime** (keyboards); **Ewan Vernal** (bass, keyboard bass); **Douglas Vipond** (drums, percussion)

1982

Ross (b. Dec. 22, 1957, Dundee, Tayside, Scotland), a former youth club leader and teacher, joins Woza, a local band in Glasgow, Strathclyde, Scotland, providing keyboards and vocals, while continuing to work part-time as a teacher for children with behavioral difficulties, in the Maryhill district. The outfit will remain together for a year, supporting bands including Friends Again and the Waterboys throughout the region. Concentrating on songwriting, he sends an 11-track solo demo tape to publishers in London the following year and, only to be advised to form a band to showcase his composing talent.

1985

Ross forms Deacon Blue (the name inspired by a Steely Dan song from their ***Aja*** album), initially as a five-piece, featuring Prime (b. Nov. 3, 1960, Kilmarnock, Strathclyde, Scotland) on keyboards, Vipond (b. Oct. 15, 1966, Johnstone, Strathclyde, Scotland) on drums, Kelling (b. Apr. 4, 1957, Paisley, Strathclyde, Scotland) on guitar and fellow ex-Woza, Vernal, (b. Feb. 27, 1964, Glasgow) on bass.

1986

Nov Following sole label interest by Gordon Charlton of CBS London's A&R department, his boss, Muff Winwood, has signed the band earlier in the year after a gig in Glasgow. Deacon Blue now begins two months of recording at AIR Studios, London. Ross' girlfriend, Lorraine McIntosh (b. May 13, 1964, Glasgow), although not yet a member of the band, lends considerable vocal assistance to many tracks, all of which are penned by her beau.

1987

Mar The group's debut release, *Dignity*, is released during constant UK touring.
May ***Raintown*** is issued to critical affection and initially spends two weeks on the UK Album chart at #82, helped considerably by strong regional sales in the Glasgow area.

1988

Feb Re-release of *Dignity*, now remixed by Bob Clearmountain, together with four previously-unissued bonus tracks on the CD single format, sees their UK singles chart debut peak at UK #31.
Apr Reissue of *When Will You Make My Telephone Ring*, featuring the backing vocals of soul veterans Jimmy Helms, Jimmy Chambers and George Chandler (who will form Londonbeat), makes UK #34, but does not make any impression in the US, where it is their debut release.
July Deacon Blue embarks on its first headlining major venue UK tour, including an appearance at the annual "Reading Festival", Reading, Berks., supported by fellow Scottish act Fairground Attraction, while *Chocolate Girl* makes UK #43.
Aug [13] Re-promotion of the album ***Raintown*** activates the eventual UK chart peak at #14. To further spur sales, CBS issues a 10,000 limited edition of ***Raintown***, now twinned with a bonus album collection of B-sides and rarities under the title ***Riches***.
Oct Their first new A-side recording since 1986, *Real Gone Kid* proves their major breakthrough, hitting UK #8. With McIntosh as a full band member, Ross has written the song about ex-Lone Justice vocalist Maria McKee, inspired by an onstage performance by her earlier in the year.

1989

Mar *Wages Day*, which includes a B-side cover version of Julian Cope's *Trampolene*, reaches UK #18.
Apr [15] Their second album, ***When The World Knows Your Name***, produced by Warne Livesey at Glasgow's Cava Studio, and once again featuring words and music by Ross, debuts at UK #1, supplanting Madonna's ***Like A Prayer***.
May [1] The band embarks on an 18-date headlining tour at Dublin Stadium, Dublin, Eire, which will incorporate two nights at the Hammersmith Odeon, London, before closing at the Hippodrome, Bristol, Avon, on the 28th.
June *Fergus Sings The Blues*, packaged as a "souvenir from Scotland" boxed single, reaches UK #14.
Aug [1] A six-date US promotional tour, which will end at the Paradise, Boston, MA, on the 9th, starts at Slim's in San Francisco, CA.
Sept *Love And Regret* reaches UK #28.
Dec [12] An eight-date sellout UK mini-tour begins at the Mean Fiddler, London.

1990

Jan [13] Appropriately-timed *Queen Of The New Year*, the fifth single from ***When The World Knows Your Name***, reaches UK #21.
May [5] The group sings *A Hard Day's Night* at the "John Lennon Tribute Concert" at the Pier Head Arena in Merseyside, to celebrate the songs of Lennon.
June [3] 250,000 attend "The Big Day", Scotland's largest-ever free open-air festival, headlined by the group, from various locations in Glasgow, airing live on C4-TV.
[22-24] They take part in the three-day "Glastonbury

Festival of Contemporary Performing Arts" near Glastonbury, Somerset.

Sept [1] Departing from his own songwriting, Ross has elected to record four Burt Bacharach/Hal David hits from the '60s. Led by the main radio choice, *I'll Never Fall In Love Again*, the *Four Bacharach & David Songs (EP)*, produced by Jon Kelly, becomes Deacon Blue's biggest hit, at UK #2, held from the top spot by Bombalurina's *Itsy Bitsy Teeny Weeny Yellow Polka Dot Bikini*.

[4] Now elevated to the UK's largest venues, Deacon Blue plays the first of eight sellout shows (including three at the Wembley Arena, Wembley, Middx.), at the Aberdeen Exhibition Centre, Aberdeen, Scotland. Further dates will follow in the US, Germany, Spain and Holland.

[22] Billed as a collection of B-sides, film tracks and miscellaneous sessions, ***Ooh Las Vegas***, immediately hits UK #3.

1991

Jan The group begins recording its fourth album, at Guillaume Tell studios in Paris, France, with producer Kelly and engineer Steve Jackson. Ricky Ross masterminds the charity album ***The Tree And The Bird And The Fish And The Bell***, a collection of Glasgow songs by Glaswegian artists including Deacon Blue, Wet Wet Wet and Big Dish.

May [25] *Your Swaying Arms* debuts at its UK #23 peak.

June [15] Jon Kelly-helmed, Ross-penned ***Fellow Hoodlums*** bows at UK #2, behind Seal's ***Seal***.

Aug [10] The extracted Ross original *Twist & Shout* hits UK #10.

Sept [3] The band begins a US national promotion tour in Los Angeles, CA.

Oct [19] *Closing Time* makes UK #42.

Nov [26] The group begins a 22-date British tour in Dublin, set to end on December 28th in Glasgow.

Dec [14] *Cover From The Sky* debuts at its UK #31 peak.

1992

May Deacon Blue begins working on new tracks, with Paul Oakenfold and Steve Osborne producing, at AIR Studios, London.

Nov [28] *Your Town* bows at its UK #14 peak.

1993

Feb [13] *Will We Be Lovers* debuts at its UK #31 peak.

Mar [4-5] Deacon Blue plays two warm-up dates at London's Clapham Grand, in preparation for a major UK tour.

[13] The Osbourne-Oakenfeld produced ***Whatever You Say, Say Nothing*** debuts at its UK #4 peak.

[31] The group embarks on a 17-date "In Your Town" jaunt, at Edinburgh's Ingliston RHS, set to end on Apr [24] at London's Brixton Academy.

Apr [21] BBC2-TV airs the "Deacon Blue : From Raintown To Your Town" documentary.

[24] *Only Tender Love* bows at its UK #22 peak.

July [16] EP *Hang Your Head* bows at its UK #21 peak.

Oct [31] The 13-date second leg of "In Your Town" begins at City Hall, Newcastle, Tyne & Wear, set to end on November 24th at Irvine Magnum Centre, Irvine, Strathclyde, Scotland.

1994

Apr [2] *I Was Right And You Were Wrong* debuts at its UK #32 peak.

[21] Deacon Blue begins a 19-date UK tour also at the Magnum Centre, Irvine set to end on May 18th at Dundee's Caird Hall.

May [14] Collecting six years of hits, ***Our Town - Greatest Hits*** tops the UK chart.

[28] Reissued *Dignity* debuts at its UK #20 peak.

DEAD OR ALIVE

Pete Burns (vocals); **Tim Lever** (keyboards, saxophone); **Mike Percy** (bass); **Steve McCoy** (drums)

1980

Feb Having been involved in the late '70s in a succession of new wave Liverpool, Merseyside, bands (including the Mystery Girls with Pete Wylie and Julian Cope), Burns (b. Aug. 5, 1959, Liverpool) records his first EP *Birth Of A Nation*, as a member of Nightmares In Wax, released on local label, Inevitable Records. Major personnel changes in Nightmares In Wax leave Burns as the only original member, and a new line-up in May becomes Dead Or Alive, with Burns, Martin Healey (keyboards), Sue James (bass), Mitch (b. Mick Read) (guitar) and Joe Musker (drums). *I'm Falling* is released on Inevitable.

1982

Mar EP *It's Been Hours Now*, released on the Black Eyes label, reaches #13 on the UK Independent chart and draws the attention of major labels. Wayne Hussey (b. Jerry Lovelock, May 26, 1958, Bristol, Somerset) (guitar) and Percy (b. Mar. 11, 1961) have now replaced Mitch and James.

Dec The band signs to Epic Records and begins a change of musical approach from rock to a dance-oriented pop style.

1983

June *Misty Circles*, their Epic debut is released (to be followed by *What I Want* and *I'd Do Anything*, all of which receive promising UK club action).

Aug Hussey leaves to join the Sisters Of Mercy (and later the Mission). Healey and Musker also go, replaced by Lever (b. May 21, 1980) and McCoy (b. Mar. 15, 1962).

1984

Apr [21] Dead Or Alive's revival of KC & the Sunshine Band's *That's The Way (I Like It)* is the group's first hit, at UK #22.

May ***Sophisticated Boom Boom***, produced by Zeus B. Held, reaches UK #29, as Burns' physical appearance, a heavily made-up, highly-coiffured, Boy Georgesque image, excites media attention.

1985

Mar [9] Pop-dance aimed *You Spin Me Round (Like A Record)*, their first collaboration with production team Stock/Aitken/Waterman, tops the UK chart for the first of two weeks, after a 15-week climb to the summit.

Apr [27] *Lover Come Back To Me* reaches UK #11.

May [25] ***Youthquake***, produced by SAW, debuts at UK #9 and provides the springboard for their first major tour and international success.

July [13] *In Too Deep* reaches UK #14.

Aug [17] *You Spin Me Round (Like A Record)* is their first US hit, reaching #11.

Sept ***Youthquake*** makes US #31, as the band tours the US with the live line-up of Burns, Lever, Percy, McCoy, Russ Bell (guitar) and Chris Page (keyboards).

Oct [5] *Lover Come Back To Me* peaks at US #75 and *My Heart Goes Bang (Get Me To The Doctor)* reaches UK #23. The band finally moves from Liverpool to set up a permanent base in London.

1987

Jan *Something In My House* reaches UK #12, following *Brand New Lover* which made UK #31 in September the previous year.

Feb [14] SAW-produced ***Mad, Bad And Dangerous To Know*** reaches UK #27 and will make US #52.

Mar [14] *Brand New Lover* reaches US #15.

Apr *Hooked On Love* peaks at UK #69, while the band spends the rest of the year on lengthy stadium tours of Japan and the US.

May [9] *Something In My House* stops at US #85.

Oct *I'll Save You All My Kisses* peaks at UK #78.

1988

July [30] ***Rip It Up***, a compilation of earlier hits remixed, peaks at US #195 during a two-week stay on the chart. (It will be followed by a batch of poorly received material: *Turn Round And Count 2 Ten* spends one week at UK #70 (Sept [3]), *Come Home With Me Baby* peaks at UK #62 and US #69 (July [29], 1989), while its parent album, ***Nude***, makes US #106, after which the band dissolves. (Burns, who will remain popular in Japan, will record ***Nukleopatra***, released there on Epic Records in October 1995, selling some 500,000 copies.)

DEBARGE

Eldra DeBarge (vocals, keyboards); **Mark "Marty" DeBarge** (trumpet, sax); **James DeBarge** (keyboards); **Randy DeBarge** (bass); **Bunny DeBarge** (vocals)

1978

As one-half of ten siblings in a family whose white father left their black mother to raise them alone, the original DeBarge quintet is formed by four boys, Eldra (b. June 4, 1961, Grand Rapids, MI), Mark (b. June 19, 1959, Grand Rapids), James (b. Aug. 22, 1963, Grand Rapids) and Randy (b. Aug. 6, 1958, Grand Rapids) and a sister, Bunny (b. Mar. 10, 1955, Grand Rapids). All of the family members have sung gospel at Bethel Pentecostal Church in Grand Rapids, MI, where their uncles ran the choir. Having achieved little as a gospel quintet in their home town, DeBarge moves to Los Angeles, CA, in the hope of signing to Motown Records, where two older brothers, Bobby and Tommy, are in the band Switch, recording for Motown subsidiary Gordy.

1979

Following an impromptu audition for Jermaine Jackson in Motown's offices, Berry Gordy signs the quintet (currently known as the DeBarges), convinced that positive comparisons between the group and earlier label stars the Jackson 5 will be inevitable.

1982

Sept Having released their debut album ***The DeBarges*** in 1980, and shortened their name to Debarge, ***All This Love***, co-produced by Eldra Debarge and Iris Gordy, reaches US #24, showcasing the group's easy-flowing R&B vocal harmony skills.

1983

Apr [9] Taken from it, *I Like It* makes US #31, as ***All This Love*** is certified gold in the US.

July [9] *All This Love* peaks at US #17.

Oct Their third album, ***In A Special Way***, produced by Eldra for his own Super 3 Production company and including songs written by each member, reaches US #36.

1984

Jan [21] *Time Will Reveal* makes US #18.

May [5] Ballad *Love Me In A Special Way* reaches US #45, while ***In A Special Way*** is RIAA-certified gold.

June DeBarge begins a nationwide tour supporting Luther Vandross, without Bunny, who is pregnant.

Sept DeBarge appears in Berry Gordy's first movie, "The Last Dragon", with ex-Prince cohort Vanity.

[7] Janet Jackson announces that she and James DeBarge have wed. (The marriage will last less than a year.)

1985

Mar ***Rhythm Of The Night*** is released variously produced by Richard Perry, Giorgio Moroder and Jay Graydon and includes three songs written by Eldra, who is assuming an increasingly dominant position within the group (many US fans assume he is DeBarge).

Apr [27] The title track, *Rhythm Of The Night*, written by Diane Warren and also featured in "The Last Dragon", hits US #3.

May [25] ***Rhythm Of The Night*** makes UK #94.
June [1] ***Rhythm Of The Night*** reaches US #19.
June *Rhythm Of The Night*, the group's UK chart debut, hits UK #4.
Aug [10] Ballad *Who's Holding Donna Now* hits US #6.
Oct [12] DeBarge begins a UK visit, as *You Wear It Well* reaches US #46 and peaks at UK #54.

1986

Jan Younger brother, Chico (b. Jonathan Debarge, 1966, Grand Rapids), signs a solo deal with Motown (eight of the ten children have at one point been signed to the label).
[11] Now billed as El DeBarge with DeBarge, *The Heart Is Not So Smart* reaches US #75.
Feb Eldra quits the line-up but is retained by Gordy for a solo deal.
July [5] Shortening his own name to El, *Who's Johnny*, the theme from the Ally Sheedy/Steve Guttenberg-starring movie "Short Circuit", hits US #3 and peaks at UK #60.
[12] *Who's Johnny* tops the US Black chart.
July Album debut by El, ***El DeBarge***, variously produced by Robbie Buchanan, Jay Graydon and Peter Wolf, climbs to US #24, as his solo career now eclipses the group's.
Sept [20] *Love Always*, El's second single, makes US #43.
Dec ***DeBarge Greatest Hits***, the group's last album on Gordy, is released, while Chico's debut album, ***Chico DeBarge***, is issued, set to peak at US #90.

1987

Jan [31] El's *Someone* makes US #70.
Feb [21] Chico's solo, *Talk To Me*, reaches US #12.
Mar Having left the group, Bunny's maiden album, ***In Love***, peaks at US #172.
July With DeBarge disintegrating, Bobby and James DeBarge release ***Bad Boys*** on the independent label Striped Horse, under the family name.

1988

July Chico is dropped from the Los Angeles Sheriff's Department anti-drug telethon after being arraigned in Grand Rapids on narcotics charges. He and his brother Robert are accused, with five others, of bringing quantities of cocaine from California to sell in Michigan.
[11] Robert is released on $5,000 bail in Los Angeles, on condition that he joins a residential drug programme.
Oct As El prepares another solo project, Chico is working with film director Spike Lee on the soundtrack for a forthcoming Lee project.
[27] Chico and Robert are found guilty of cocaine trafficking.

1989

May Having switched to the main Motown label and recently contributed *Goodnight My Love* to the Richard Perry-produced ***Rock, Rhythm & Blues*** compilation, El's self-produced ***Gemini*** (with songs co-penned with Darell DeBarge), is released but the album and extracted singles fail to crossover from R&B success.
Oct [10] Another family member, Thomas DeBarge, asks for drug treatment after being jailed on a cocaine charge in Grand Rapids.

1990

Mar [14] El joins James Ingram, Al B. Sure! and Barry White at the fourth annual Soul Train Music Awards, at the Shrine Auditorium, Los Angeles, singing *The Secret Garden*, a track which features the four soloists, from Quincy Jones' ***Back On The Block***.
[27] Thomas is sentenced to prison on a drugs charge in Grand Rapids.

1991

July El records at Ignited Studios in Los Angeles with producer Maurice White.
Oct *After The Dance* by Fourplay (Bob James, Nathan East, Lee Ritenour, Harvey Mason), featuring El DeBarge on vocals, is released on Warners Bros.
Dec [21] Tone Loc's *All Through The Night*, for which El provides guest vocals, peaks at US #80.

1992

Mar Al Green's ***Love Is Reality***, featuring El on *I Can Feel It*, is released.
June Newly signed to Warner Bros., El issues ***In The Storm***. (During July El will marry for the second time.)

1993

Jan [24] El appears at "Sexual Healing - A Tribute To Marvin Gaye" in support of the fight against AIDS, at "Midem" in Cannes, France, with Ashford & Simpson and a host of top R&B names.
Aug [10] Following Jomanda's minor US chart success with a revival of *I Like It*, El's second Warner Bros. album, ***High Rise***, is released.

1994

June [18] El's ***Heart, Mind & Soul***, produced by Babyface, debuts at its US #137 peak.

1995

Aug [16] Following the recent release of his solo debut ***It's Not Over***, Robert dies of complications from AIDS.

CHRIS DE BURGH

1974

Sept Having graduated from Trinity College, Dublin, Eire, toured Eire with Horslips at the end of 1973 and honed his writing and singing skills entertaining guests at his family's 12th-century castle hotel in Ireland, De Burgh (b. Christopher John Davidson, Oct. 15, 1948, Argentina), the son of a diplomat, signs to A&M Records in the UK after meeting producer/songwriters Doug Flett and Guy Fletcher.
Nov On his first UK gigs, he supports A&M stablemates Supertramp on their "Crime Of The Century" tour.

1975

Feb His self-penned debuts, *Hold On* and ***Far Beyond These Castle Walls***, produced by Robin Geoffrey Cable, attract critical attention.
July The extracted *Flying* receives scant sales in the UK but will go on to top the Brazilian charts for 17 weeks.
Nov The light-rock, once again self-written sophomore effort, ***Spanish Train And Other Stories*** is released.

1976

Apr After *Lonely Sky* is released at the year's outset, *Patricia The Stripper* is issued.
Dec *A Spaceman Came Travelling*, taken from ***Spanish Train And Other Stories***, is released, without chart success, but becomes a UK turntable hit and a perennial festive favorite.

1980

July After successful live work all over the world (notably in South Africa the previous year, and in South America and Europe), and two further self-written albums, ***At The End Of A Perfect Day*** (1977) and ***Crusader*** (1979), ***Eastern Wind*** is issued, De Burgh's first with a backing band (which now accompanies him on stage). Still eluding the UK and US surveys, it is a smash in Norway - selling 125,000 copies and making it the country's second best-selling album after the Beatles' ***Abbey Road***.

1981

Sept [19] Compilation album, ***Best Moves***, released at the suggestion of A&M's Canadian office, with De Burgh's own pick of his earlier songs and one new number, is his UK chart debut, at #65.

1982

Oct [30] *Don't Pay The Ferryman*, remixed from his new album, ***The Getaway***, makes UK #48.
Nov [6] ***The Getaway***, which sees De Burgh teamed with producer Rupert Hine, reaches UK #30.

1983

July [2] *Don't Pay The Ferryman* is his US breakthrough, making #34, spurring ***The Getaway*** to make US #43 during a five-month chart stay.
Sept [10] *Ship To Shore* peaks at US #71.

1984

May [19] ***Man On The Line*** debuts at its UK #11 peak.
[26] *High On Emotion* makes UK #44.
Aug [25] *High On Emotion* also reaches US #44, with ***Man On The Line*** peaking at US #69.

1985

Feb [6] UK only TV-advertised compilation released by Telstar, ***The Very Best Of Chris De Burgh***, introduces him to a wider UK audience, and hits UK #6 during a 70-week chart residence.
Aug [24] His sophomore album ***Spanish Train And Other Stories***, belatedly charts at UK #78.
Dec [19] He takes part in "Carol Aid", a London benefit performance in aid of the Band Aid Appeal, along with Cliff Richard, Lulu and others.

1986

Aug [2] *The Lady In Red*, written for and about his wife, and De Burgh's 24th single release, tops the UK chart for the first of three weeks.
[9] Its parent album, the Paul Hardiman-produced ***Into The Light*** hits UK #2. Having refined his easy-flowing, self-penned easy listening romantic style, both are De Burgh's biggest sellers to date. Press reports state that H.R.H. Prince Andrew and his wife Sarah Ferguson have taken a copy with them on their honeymoon.
Oct *Fatal Hesitation* makes UK #44 and another early album, ***Crusader***, shows briefly at UK #72.

1987

Jan [3] Festive reissue of *A Spaceman Came Travelling*, a double A-side with *The Ballroom Of Romance*, makes UK #40.
May [23] *The Lady In Red* is his biggest US hit, at #3, and takes the global smash's combined UK/US sales well over a million.
June ***Into The Light*** reaches US #25.

1988

Jan [2] Released before Christmas, *The Simple Truth (A Child Is Born)* peaks at UK #55.
July *Love Is My Decision*, the theme to the film "Arthur 2: On The Rocks", sung by De Burgh, is released in the US.
Oct [15] ***Flying Colours*** debuts at UK #1.
Nov *Missing You* hits UK #3.

1989

Jan *Tender Hands* makes UK #43.
Oct *This Waiting Heart* peaks at UK #59.
Nov [25] 16-track retrospective collection, ***From A Spark To A Flame - The Very Best Of Chris De Burgh***, hits UK #4.

1990

Sept [29] Performance set, ***High On Emotion - Live From Dublin***, reaches UK #15.

1991

May [12] De Burgh performs at "The Simple Truth" Kurds benefit at the Wembley Arena, Wembley, Middx.
[25] *The Simple Truth* re-charts, at UK #36.
Sept [7-8] He plays at Alton Towers theme park, Alton, Derbys.
Oct [3] *The Lady In Red* is honored at ASCAP's 11th annual London Awards, at Claridges.

1992

Apr [15] De Burgh guests on BBC1-TV's "This Is Your Life".
[18] *Separate Tables* reaches UK #30.
May [9] ***Power Of Ten*** debuts at its UK #3 peak.
Sept [8] A three-month European tour begins at the Aberdeen Exhibition & Conference Centre, Aberdeen, Scotland, set to end on December 13th at the Wembley Arena.
[22] *Lady In Red* is honored at the annual ASCAP PRS Awards as one of the most-performed songs of 1991.

1993

Jan [11] A 21-date tour of South Africa (where he remains immensely popular) begins, set to close on February 9th, drawing 100,000 people and taking $2 million. (His total S. African sales over the last 15 years amount to some 350,000 units.)
June [6] De Burgh sings *Say Goodbye To It All* and *Up There In Heaven* aboard the QE2 in the D-Day-remembering TV show "We'll Meet Again".

1994

May [21] *Blonde Hair Blue Jeans* charts for a week at UK #51.
[28] Its parent album ***This Way Up***, featuring session players Neil Taylor (guitar), Vic Martin (keyboards), Phil Spalding (bass) and Jimmy Copley (drums), bows at its UK #5 peak.

1995

Nov [18] Following a tumultuous year, which almost saw the break-up of his marriage because of his alleged adultery with his former nanny Maresa Morgan, his latest album ***Beautiful Dreams*** debuts at its UK #33 peak.
Dec [9] The extracted *The Snows Of New York* charts for a week at UK #60.

JOEY DEE & THE STARLITERS

Joey Dee (vocals); **Carlton Latimer** (keyboards); **Willie Davis** (drums); **Larry Vernieri** (back-up vocals); **David Brigati** (back-up vocals)

1961

Sept After playing in clubs and at dances in northern New Jersey for a couple of years and being the resident band at the Riviera Club, Dee (b. Joseph DeNicola, June 11, 1940, Passaic, NJ), who has also sung back-up in Brigati's doo-wop group, the Hi-Fives, in the late '50s) & the Starliters have become the house band at the Peppermint Lounge, a socialite-favored New York club on West 45th Street, in September the previous year. As Chubby Checker's *The Twist* now becomes popular at the venue, the Starliters are noted in the local media as an integral part of the dance craze, attention which leads to a recording contract with Roulette Records.
Oct Dee and Roulette producer, Henry Glover, write *Peppermint Twist*, tying the dance to the venue.

1962

Jan [27] *Peppermint Twist* tops the US chart for the first of three weeks, replacing Checker's *The Twist* after its second spell at US #1. ***Doin' The Twist At The Peppermint Lounge*** hits US #2, equalling Chubby Checker's ***Your Twist Party*** as the highest-placed twist album ever on the US chart.
Feb Dee & the Starliters feature in "Hey Let's Twist", a quickly-made exploitation movie which also stars Jo-Ann Campbell and Teddy Randazzo. *Peppermint Twist* reaches UK #33, outdone by Danny Peppermint & the Jumping Jacks version, which reaches UK #26. (It will be Dee's only UK chart entry.)
Mar [17] Double A-sided *Hey Let's Twist*, from the film, and *Roly Poly* make US #20 and #74 respectively.
Apr Soundtrack album, ***Hey Let's Twist***, climbs to US #18.
May [5] Their revival of the Isley Brothers' *Shout* hits US #6 - the only version of this R&B classic to reach the US Top 40.
July ***Back At The Peppermint Lounge, Twistin'*** reaches US #97.
Oct Dee appears in a second movie, "Two Tickets To Paris", with Gary Crosby and others.
[13] His solo single from the film, *What Kind Of Love Is This?* (written by Johnny Nash), reaches US #18.
Dec [1] *I Lost My Baby* stops at US #61.

1963

Feb [16] *Baby, You're Driving Me Crazy* charts for a week at US #100.
June [1] The group reaches US #36 with *Hot Pastrami And Mashed Potatoes*, a dance-oriented follow-up to the Dartells' US Top 20 hit, *Hot Pastrami*, a month earlier.
Aug [3] *Dance Dance Dance* closes the group's US chart career, peaking at #89.

1964

Dee opens his own New York club, the Starliter, and plays there with a new group line-up which includes Felix Cavaliere, Gene Cornish and Eddie Brigati (younger brother of original Starliter David), who will go on to form the Young Rascals later in the year. (Dee will later sell his club and begin touring, continuing to work regularly - eventually on the US oldies circuit - right through to the '90s, by which time his band will include his son, Joey Dee Jr. The Peppermint Lounge does not fare so well losing its liquor license in 1965 and, by 1971, it has become a topless club.)

1989

While he has established the Starlite Starbrite Foundation For The Love Of Rock'n'Roll in Florida in 1987 to help rock veterans who have fallen on hard times (with an aim to raise $20 million for a retirement community in Clearwater, FL, and health insurance for needy musicians), Dee, Hank Ballard and Chubby Checker play at Lulu's Roadhouse, Kitchener, ON, Canada, for a reunion which will be part of a feature-length documentary on the twist.

DEEP PURPLE

Ian Gillan (vocals); **Ritchie Blackmore** (guitar); **Jon Lord** (keyboards); **Roger Glover** (bass); **Ian Paice** (drums)

1967

Chris Curtis (b. Christopher Crummy, Aug. 26, 1941, Oldham, Lancs.), the former Searchers drummer, approaches London businessman, Tony Edwards, a textile company boss, to manage him. Edwards invites John Coletta, an advertising consultant, to invest in Curtis and the group Edwards wants him to put together, despite the fact that neither of them have any experience in the music business. Curtis recruits his flatmate, Lord (b. June 9, 1941, Leicester, Leics.), ex-Artwoods and currently playing with the Flowerpot Men, who in turn invites Blackmore (b. Apr. 14, 1945, Weston-Super-Mare, Avon), ex-Outlaws, Screaming Lord Sutch and Neil Christian & the Crusaders, and now living in Germany, to form a new band. Musicians are auditioned from a **Melody Maker** ad, in Deeves Hall, a country house in Hertfordshire.

1968

Feb The group initially forms as Roundabout with a line-up of Lord, Blackmore, Curtis (vocals), Dave Curtis (bass) and Bobby Woodman (drums).
Mar After unpromising rehearsals, the line-up is changed. Woodman and both Curtises are replaced by Paice (b. June 29, 1948, Nottingham, Notts.) and singer Rod Evans (b. Jan. 19, 1945, Edinburgh, Lothian, Scotland), both ex-MI5 and ex-Maze, and bassist Nick Simper (b. Nov. 3, 1946, Southall, Middx.), ex-Johnny Kidd & the Pirates (who survived the car crash which killed Kidd).
Apr [20] The group makes its live debut in Tastrup, Denmark, and changes its name to Deep Purple (after rejecting Concrete God - legend has it that *Deep Purple* is Blackmore's grandmother's favorite song), using US group Vanilla Fudge as its model.
May Deep Purple records an album (in an 18-hour session) and is signed to EMI Records in the UK and Bill Cosby's Tetragrammaton label in the US.
Aug [10] The group's first major UK performance is at the "Sunbury Festival", Sunbury, Middx.
Sept [21] Their debut single, a revival of the Joe South-penned Billy Joe Royal hit, *Hush*, hits US #4.
Oct ***Shades Of Deep Purple*** reaches US #24, again without a UK placing. The group begins a North American tour, but Blackmore contracts hepatitis and, after one gig in Quebec with Randy California deputizing, they cancel the remaining dates.
Dec [7] Their revival of Neil Diamond's *Kentucky Woman* reaches US #38.

1969

Feb ***The Book Of Taliesyn*** reaches US #54.
[8] Taken from it, a revival of Ike & Tina Turner's *River Deep, Mountain High* makes US #53.
July ***Deep Purple*** peaks at US #162. Evans and Simper both leave (Evans goes to the US to join Captain Beyond), and the US Tetragrammaton label folds, leaving Deep Purple with no product outlet.
Aug Glover (b. Nov. 30, 1945, Brecon, Powys, Wales) and Gillan (b. Aug. 19, 1945, Hounslow, Middx.), join from the UK group Episode Six, playing their first gig with the band at London's Speakeasy club.
Sept [24] Deep Purple performs ***Concerto For Group And Orchestra***, composed by Lord, with the Royal Philharmonic Orchestra conducted by Malcolm Arnold, at London's Royal Albert Hall, under the auspices of the new Marshall 600-watt mixer P.A. system, featuring H F Horn Speaker Cabinets.

1970

Jan ***Concerto For Group And Orchestra***, originally recorded for the BBC at the Royal Albert Hall concert, reaches UK #26 (the group's UK chart debut) and US #149 (on Warner Bros.).
Feb [7] Deep Purple begins a short UK tour at Leicester University, Leicester, Leics.
June [8] During its European tour, the group has its van and equipment impounded by East German police after mistakenly driving too close to the border, forcing them to miss the next evening's gig.
July [18] Deep Purple plays in London's Hyde Park, supporting Pink Floyd.
Aug ***Deep Purple In Rock*** hits UK #4, during a 68-week stay on the chart, and will make US #143.
Oct [17] *Black Night* (its riff based on Ricky Nelson's *Summertime*, its title from an Arthur Alexander song) is the group's first UK singles hit, at #2, behind Freda Payne's *Band Of Gold*.
[27] Gillan plays the role of Jesus in Tim Rice and Andrew Lloyd Webber's "Jesus Christ Superstar", in a live performance at St. Peter's Lutheran Church, New York, NY.
Nov Studio cast recording of ***Jesus Christ Superstar***, featuring Gillan, is released and eventually hits UK #6 and tops the US chart.
Dec [26] *Black Night* peaks at US #66.

1971

Mar *Strange Kind Of Woman* hits UK #8.
July The group tours the US with the Faces.
Sept [22] Deep Purple plays at Manchester, Gtr. Manchester's Free Trade Hall during a short UK tour.
[25] ***Fireball*** tops the UK chart for a week, and will reach US #32.
Oct The band forms its own Purple label, distributed by EMI.
[25] A concert in Hamilton, ON, Canada, is cancelled after Gillan is admitted to a New York hospital suffering from exhaustion.
Nov The band begins three weeks of rehearsals at Clearwell Castle, Clearwell, Gloucs., before heading

for Montreux, Switzerland, to record.
Dec [3] Deep Purple is recording in Montreux Casino, when the building burns down during a set by Frank Zappa's Mothers of Invention. The group immortalizes the incident in *Smoke On The Water* on its next album.
[18] *Fireball* reaches UK #15.

1972

Apr [22] ***Machine Head*** tops the UK chart for the first of three weeks, aided by a TV advertising campaign (and will later hit US #7.) *Never Before* reaches UK #35 as Lord releases ***Gemini Suite***, with the London Symphony Orchestra.
June [30] The band performs on the first night at the re-opened Rainbow Theatre, London.
Aug The group tours Japan, where concerts are recorded for album release.
Oct ***Purple Passages***, a compilation on Warner Bros. of tracks from the group's three Tetragrammaton albums, reaches US #57. Gillan informs the group that he will leave after existing tour commitments.
Dec The group plays its last gig of the year, having been on the road for 44 out of 52 weeks.

1973

Jan Live album, ***Made In Japan***, recorded during the group's 1972 summer tour, reaches UK #16.
Mar ***Who Do We Think We Are*** hits UK #4 and US #15.
Apr ***Made In Japan*** begins a climb to hit US #6.
June [29] Gillan quits after a show in Osaka at the end of a tour of Japan. (Former Marbles singer Graham Bonnet will briefly replace him.) Glover will also leave the following month, initially to become Purple label's A&R man, and to begin a solo career with the label. (Both reportedly leave over differences with Blackmore.)
July [28] *Smoke On The Water*, from ***Machine Head***, is belatedly released in the US and hits #4, selling a million and earning the group its only gold disc for a single.
Sept Former Government vocalist, David Coverdale (b. Sept. 22, 1949, Saltburn-by-the-Sea, Cleveland), working in a menswear shop called Gentry in Redcar, Yorks., playing semi-pro with the Fabuloser Brothers (who supported Deep Purple at Bradford University in 1972), answers an ad placed by Purple, as does ex-Trapeze bassist Glenn Hughes (b. Aug. 21, 1952, Penkridge, Staffs.). Coverdale, asked to supply a photo of himself, sends the only one in his possession - taken as a boy in scout uniform. He also sends a tape with two Fabuloser Brothers tracks and two acoustic solo numbers, including *Everybody's Talkin'* and *Dancing In The Street*. He and Hughes join as replacements for Gillan and Glover, who both sign solo deals, with Oyster and Island respectively.
Oct [20] *Woman From Tokyo*, issued as a US single, peaks at #60.

1974

Mar [9] ***Burn***, featuring the new line-up, hits UK #3 and US #9.
[30] *Might Just Take Your Life* peaks at US #91.
Apr Lord's sophomore album ***Windows*** is released by Purple Records.
May [22] The band plays at Kilburn State Gaumont, during a UK tour which has started in Scotland and is set to end at Southend, Essex in June.
Nov [13] An impostor posing as Blackmore borrows a Porsche in Iowa City, IA, and wrecks it, having already conned food and shelter out of several Deep Purple fans. (Blackmore is in the US at the time, but in San Francisco, CA, with the band.) The impostor is arrested and charged with misrepresentation.
[30] ***Stormbringer***, recorded in W. Germany, hits UK #6 and reaches US #20.

1975

Apr [7] Blackmore quits to put together his own band, Rainbow, with members of Ronnie James Dio's Elf, and is replaced by ex-James Gang guitarist Tommy Bolin (b. Aug. 1, 1951, Sioux City, IA). (Rainbow will open for Deep Purple on their "Stormbringer" tour.)
Sept [6] Compilation album, ***24 Carat Purple***, reaches UK #14.
Oct [16] Glover's ***The Butterfly Ball***, released late in 1974, is performed at London's Royal Albert Hall, with Gillan as lead vocalist.
Nov [29] ***Come Taste The Band***, featuring Bolin on guitar, reaches UK #19. The group begins a world tour, taking in the Far East, Australasia, the US, Europe and the UK. **The Guinness Book of Records** lists the group as the "world's loudest band".

1976

Jan [10] ***Come Taste The Band*** makes US #43.
July [19] The group splits at the end of the UK tour dates in Liverpool, Merseyside. (Coverdale begins a solo career before forming Whitesnake, Lord and Paice team with Tony Ashton to form Paice, Ashton and Lord, while Hughes rejoins his former band, Trapeze, and Bolin returns to the US to form the Tommy Bolin Band.) Gillan's solo debut ***Child In Time*** makes UK #55.
Nov [27] ***Deep Purple Live*** reaches UK #12.
Dec [4] Bolin dies from a heroin overdose at the Newport Hotel in Miami, FL.
[11] ***Made In Europe***, the US version of ***Deep Purple Live***, makes US #148.

1977

Feb Paice, Ashton and Lord's ***Malice In Wonderland*** is released on Oyster Records.
Apr Gillan's sophomore solo album ***Clean Air Turbulence*** is issued by Island Records (followed in November by ***Scarabus***, also on Island).
May [7] Belated UK release, *Smoke On The Water*, reaches #21.
Oct [22] EP *New Live And Rare*, including an unheard live version of *Black Night*, makes UK #31.

1978

Apr Glover's sophomore album, ***Elements***, is released by Polydor Records.
Oct [14] Compilation EP *New Live And Rare II* makes UK #45.

1979

Apr [28] ***The Mark II Purple Singles***, a compilation of A and B-sides made by the Gillan, Lord, Glover, Blackmore, Paice line-up, reaches UK #24.
Oct [27] Now recording under the band name "Gillan" (with guitarist Steve Byrd, keyboardist Colin Towns, bassist John McCoy and drummer Peter Barnacle), ***Mr. Universe*** reaches UK #11.

1980

June [21] Gillan's *Sleepin' On The Job* peaks at UK #55.
July Rumors spead that Blackmore has bought the house featured in the film "The Amityville Horror".
Aug [2] TV-advertised hits compilation album, ***Deepest Purple***, tops the UK chart for one week.
[16] Gillan's ***Glory Road*** hits UK #3 and will make US #183.
[30] *Black Night*, reissued in the UK to tie in with the album, makes #43.
Oct [11] Gillan's *Trouble* reaches UK #14.
Nov Compilation EP *New Live And Rare III*, including *Smoke On The Water*, makes UK #48. ***Deepest Purple/The Very Best Of Deep Purple*** reaches US #148.
Dec [13] Live album, ***In Concert***, featuring tracks recorded between 1970-72, makes UK #30. (During the year, a bogus Deep Purple, fronted by Rod Evans, plays a US tour. Blackmore and Glover will take legal action to prevent Evans from using the name.)

1981

Feb [14] Gillan's *Mutually Assured Destruction* peaks at UK #32. (Over the next two years only Gillan material will chart from solo projects: ***Future Shock*** (UK #2, Apr [25]), *New Orleans* (UK #17 in May), *No Laughing In Heaven* (UK #31, July), *Nightmare* (UK #36, October), the live ***Double Trouble***, his second album of the year (UK #12, Nov [7]) and 1982's *Restless* (UK #25, January), *Living For The City* (UK #50, September) and ***Magic*** (UK #17, Oct [9]).)

1982

July Lord's third solo set ***Before I Forget*** is issued by Harvest.
Sept [4] ***Deep Purple Live In London***, originally recorded for BBC radio in 1974, reaches UK #23.

1983

Aug Gillan rejoins Black Sabbath, debuting with them at the annual "Reading Festival" and recording ***Born Again*** with them.

1984

Mar [10] Amid rumors that each member is offered $2 million to re-form, Blackmore, Gillan, Glover (who has just finished his third solo album ***Mask***), Lord and Paice sign to Polydor Records (and Mercury in the US).
Nov ***Perfect Strangers*** hits UK #5 and US #17, as the band embarks on a world tour.

1985

Jan [26] The extracted *Knocking At Your Back Door* peaks at US #61.
Feb [2] Title track, *Perfect Strangers*, makes UK #48.
June [15] *Knocking At Your Back Door*, backed with *Perfect Strangers*, peaks at UK #68.
July [6] Double compilation album, ***The Anthology***, makes UK #50.

1987

Jan [24] ***The House Of Blue Light*** hits UK #10 and will go on to reach US #34, as the band tours Europe and causes a storm when Blackmore repeatedly refuses to play *Smoke On The Water*.

1988

June A re-recording of the band's original hit, *Hush*, makes UK #62.
July [16] ***Nobody's Perfect***, recorded live during 1987, reaches UK #38, as the group embarks on a two-month "Nobody's Perfect" US tour beginning in Saratoga, NY.
Aug ***Nobody's Perfect*** makes US #105.

1989

July [29] Gillan, who together with Glover has released ***Accidentally On Purpose*** the previous year, quits Deep Purple again, citing "musical differences".
Dec Gillan's collaboration with Brian May, Bruce Dickinson and Robert Plant as Rock Aid Armenia on a remake of *Smoke On The Water* makes UK #39, with all profits from the record going to the victims of the Armenian earthquake disaster.

1990

July [28] Gillan's first solo album since leaving the group, ***Naked Thunder***, makes UK #63 (and will be followed by ***Toolbox*** released in 1991, the same year Virgin Records (UK) releases (***Trouble - The Best Of Gillan***.)
Oct [20] Deep Purple, now comprising Blackmore, Lord, Glover, Paice and Joe Lynn Turner, and newly signed to RCA Records, releases *King Of Dreams*, which peaks at UK #70.
Nov [3] ***Slaves & Masters*** debuts at UK #45.
[17] ***Slaves & Masters*** makes US #87.
Dec [2] They begin rehearsals for the "Slaves And Masters" tour in Florida.

1991

Jan [22] "Slaves and Masters" trek begins in Ljubljana, Yugoslavia. (They are scheduled to play in Tel Aviv, Israel, the night it is attacked by Iraqi scud missiles.)
Mar [2] *Love Conquers All* debuts at its UK #57 peak.
Apr [10] The North American leg of their tour opens at the Memorial Auditorium, Burlington, VT.
[22] The band cancels its remaining 14 US concerts to re-group, after a gig at the Syria Mosque in Pittsburgh, PA.

1992

Dec Reunited Deep Purple, comprising Blackmore, Lord, Paice, Glover and Gillan (despite his protestation: "I look at Purple as an ex-wife. We got married in '69 and divorced in '73, then we got married again in '84 and divorced again in '89 - I made my mind up I was never gonna marry that (woman) ever again", begin recording at Peter Maffay's studio outside Munich, Germany.

1993

July [11] As a new album, ***The Battle Rages On***, is set for release on Giant, Deep Purple embarks on a 69-date world tour at the New Pine Knob Music Theatre, Clarkston, MI, set to end on December 3rd in Osaka, Japan.
Aug [7] ***The Battle Rages On*** debuts at its UK #21 peak, and will chart for a week at US #192 on the 21st.
Nov [7-8] The group performs two shows at London's Brixton Academy.

1995

June [24] *Black Night (Remix)* charts for a week at UK #66, as EMI issues a digitally remastered ***In Rock*** with 13 out-takes added.

1996

Feb [15] The group, now comprising Gillan, Glover, Lord, Paice and Steve Morse (b. July 28, 1954, Hamilton, OH), formerly of Kansas and Dixie Dregs, begins a 19-date UK tour at Plymouth Pavilions, Plymouth, Devon, set to end on March 8-9th with another pair of dates at the Brixton Academy.
[17] ***Purpendicular*** enters at its UK #58 peak.
see also: **BLACK SABBATH, RAINBOW**

DEF LEPPARD

Joe Elliott (vocals); **Phil Collen** (guitar); **Steve Clark** (guitar); **Rick Savage** (bass); **Rick Allen** (drums)

1977

Nov The group has been formed earlier in the year in Sheffield, S. Yorks., when ex-schoolboys Pete Willis and Elliott (b. Aug. 1, 1959, Sheffield) leave their own fledgling group, Jump, to join heavy metal band Atomic Mass, led by British Rail apprentice Savage (b. Dec. 2, 1960, Sheffield). Elliott abandons his guitar-playing ambitions to take lead vocals and Savage switches to bass, allowing Willis to play guitar. The name is changed to Def Leppard (from Elliott's initial suggestion of Deaf Leopard), while Clark (b. Apr. 23, 1960, Hillsborough, S. Yorks.), an acquaintance of Willis' at Stannington College in Sheffield, joins on second guitar. They now begin rehearsing on the top floor of a Sheffield spoon factory (the first rehearsal starts with *Suffragette City*).

1978

July The group's live debut is at Westfield School, Sheffield, for a £5 fee. Small pub gigs follow, with a series of drummers (none of whom proves suitable).
Nov The group records a three-track EP, with stand-in drummer Frank Noon, in the small Fairview Studios in Kingston-upon-Hull, Humberside, and forms its own Bludgeon Riffola label with a £150 loan from Elliott's father. They recruit Derbyshire drummer Allen (b. Nov. 1, 1963), who played in Smokey Blue at age ten, and who, at 15, is the youngest in an already youthful band (Elliott is the oldest, at 19), when he responds to an article titled "Leppard Loses Skins" in a local music paper in which the band said they wanted a new drummer.

1979

Jan The three-track EP *Getcha Rocks Off* is released in an initial pressing of 1,000. It is picked up first by local Radio Hallam's rock show, for which the band records six songs. A session for BBC Radio 1's prestigious John Peel show follows and the music press identifies the band with the emergent new wave of British heavy metal. The record is picked up and re-pressed by Phonogram Records and sells 24,000 copies. Sheffield record retailer Peter Martin notes the demand for the record and, during the summer, he and promoter Frank Stuart Brown become the group's first managers.
Aug Def Leppard signs to Phonogram's Vertigo label and begins recording with producer Tom Allom. An album is completed in only 18 days.
Nov [17] Its Vertigo debut, *Wasted*, debuts at UK #61.

1980

Mar [8] Follow-up, *Hello America*, makes UK #45.
[29] The band's debut album, ***On Through The Night***, reaches UK #15. The group supports Sammy Hagar and AC/DC on UK tours and meets Peter Mensch, an employee of AC/DC's New York-based Leber/Krebs management, who becomes the group's new manager and directs it towards the US market.
July [5] ***On Through The Night*** reaches US #51.
Aug [22-24] The group participates at "Reading Rock '80" in Reading, Berks., with Gillan, Iron Maiden, Krokus, Magnum, Ozzy Osbourne, UFO and Whitesnake. UK fans react against the band's new US market orientation, showering them with a hail of bottles which forces them to leave the stage. (US audiences will, however, be far more receptive when it embarks on a national tour opening for Ted Nugent.)

1981

Aug [1] ***High'n'Dry***, recorded with a new producer Robert John "Mutt" Lange over three months, a collaboration which has resulted in a smoother sound directly aimed at US FM rock radio, reaches UK #26.
Sept [12] ***High'n'Dry*** makes US #38, with the help of a US tour, co-headlining with Blackfoot. Willis finds himself increasingly out of step with the rest of the band and considers leaving. (By the end of the year the group, exhausted by the demands of non-stop touring, slips into a period of inactivity.)

1982

The group spends several months in the studio working on an album, again with Lange producing. During the sessions, Willis' alcohol problem and incompatability with the rest of the group comes to a head and he is fired. Collen (b. Dec. 8, 1957, Hackney, London), ex-glam-rock band Girl, replaces him.

1983

Feb [5] ***Pyromania*** begins a 92-week US chart run, during which time it will spend two weeks at #2, behind Michael Jackson's ***Thriller***.
[19] The extracted *Photograph*, peaks at UK #66.
Mar ***Pyromania*** reaches UK #18. The group begins a world tour to promote the project, starting in Britain, and going on to the rest of Europe and, by the time it reaches the US, the album is in the Top 10. With strong live support, it continues selling and will eventually shift more than six million copies in the US alone. The US trek is also followed by Japanese and Australian dates.
May [21] *Photograph* reaches US #12.
Aug [13] *Rock Of Ages* peaks at US #16 and will make UK #41 on Sept [3], with another extract, *Foolin'* reaching US #28 on Nov [5].

1984

Jan The group members take an eight-month break before teaming up to record, once again with Lange at the desk. Pre-production in Dublin, Eire, indicates that Lange has been overworked and is too tired to work effectively (he had followed ***Pyromania*** with ***Heartbreak City*** for the Cars and Foreigner's ***4***).
June [30] A remix of *Bringin' On The Heartbreak*, from ***High'n'Dry***, peaks at US #61. ***High'n'Dry*** also including a new track, *Me And My Wine*, re-charts, to make US #72.
Aug Recording begins at Wisseloord in Holland with producer/writer Jim Steinman (of Meatloaf and Bonnie Tyler repute).
Dec Recording is halted for a Christmas break, and the group decides to fire Steinman and produce the album itself.
[31] Racing a fellow driver in an Alfa Romeo down a stretch of the A57 from Sheffield to Derbys., Allen crashes his Corvette Stingray. The impact of the crash tears off his left arm and badly damages his right. Surgeons sew the arm back on, only to be forced to remove it three days later when infection sets in.

1985

Jan [2] The rest of the group returns to Holland to continue recording. Allen affirms by phone that he wants to return to the band.
Apr Allen rejoins the group. Little progress is made in the studio, even with the services of Lange's engineer, Nigel Green. It is decided to scrap the tapes and wait until Lange is ready to work. Meanwhile, Allen learns to play, in spite of his disability, working with a Fairlight computer to create drum sounds, and uses it to record most of the album's drum tracks on his own. He has a sophisticated Simmons electronic drumkit custom-built, with an SD57 computer to store sounds and fills. By the summer, Lange is ready to record.

1986

Aug [17] Allen makes his first UK public appearance since his accident, as Def Leppard plays the first of three "Monsters Of Rock" festivals, including Castle Donington, Derbys., in the UK and Europe. (Prior to this the band has played some low key dates in Ireland with Status Quo, with Jeff Rich as a second drummer.) Receptions are warm, especially for Allen, and the experience gives them fresh motivation in the studio.

1987

Aug *Animal*, the first extract from the forthcoming ***Hysteria***, is released, hitting UK #6.
[29] The band-penned ***Hysteria***, three years in the making and produced by Lange (who also receives a co-writing credit), debuts at UK #1, and will go on to spend 95 weeks on the chart. A highly-successful UK concert-in-the-round tour follows.
Sept [5] *Women* peaks at US #80.
Oct *Pour Some Sugar On Me* reaches UK #18, as the group embarks on a major world tour.
Dec *Hysteria* reaches UK #26.
[26] *Animal* reaches US #19.

1988

Feb [15] The group cancels a show in El Paso, TX, after it receives threats to disrupt the concert, following a September 7th, 1983, gig, when Elliott referred to El Paso as "the place with all those greasy Mexicans".
Mar [26] *Hysteria* hits US #10.
Apr *Armageddon It* reaches UK #20.
July [16] Road crew technician Steve Cayter dies of a brain haemorrhage on stage, before a show at the Alpine Valley Music Theatre, East Troy, WI.
[23] After 49 weeks on the US charts, ***Hysteria*** finally climbs to the top. (Only Fleetwood Mac's and Whitney Houston's eponymous albums have taken longer.) The band also becomes the first to have sold more than five million copies of two consecutive albums in the US. *Pour Some Sugar On Me* hits US #2, as *Love Bites* reaches UK #11.
Oct [8] *Love Bites* tops the US chart, as the band's 14-month worldwide tour ends at the Memorial Arena in Seattle, WA.

1989

Jan [21] *Armageddon It* hits US #3.
[30] The group wins the Favorite Album, Heavy Metal/Hard Rock and Favorite Artist, Heavy Metal/Hard Rock categories at the 16th annual American Music Awards, held at the Shrine Auditorium, Los Angeles, CA.
Feb *Rocket*, the sixth single from ***Hysteria***, reaches UK #15.
[13] The group performs live at the eighth annual BRIT awards, held at London's Royal Albert Hall.
[25] Elliot is hit in the face by a coin thrown by a fan

at a concert in Spain.
Apr [29] *Rocket* reaches US #12.
Sept [6] Def Leppard performs live at the annual MTV Video Music Awards, at the Universal Amphitheatre, Universal City, CA.
Dec Clark is admitted to a psychiatric hospital in Minnesota, after being found lying comatose in a gutter.

1990

May [9] The RIAA certifies ten million sales of ***Hysteria***.

1991

Jan [8] Clark is found dead by his girlfriend in his Chelsea flat in London, after a drinking binge with friend Daniel Van Alphen. Pathologist Dr. Iain West says his death is due to a compression of the brain stem resulting from excessive alcohol mixed with anti-depressants and painkillers.
June [14] Elliott duets with Hothouse Flowers' Liam O'Maonlai on C4-TV's "Friday At The Dome".
Dec Savage and Elliott team with Commitments' Maria Doyle, Van Morrison's sax player on the road and others, to form Glam Slam, an ad-hoc '70s-nostalgia band, at a charity concert in Dublin, performing *Ballroom Blitz, Merry Xmas Everybody, 20th Century Boy* and others.

1992

Apr [4] *Let's Get Rocked* hits UK #2, behind Shakespear's Sister's *Stay*.
[11] ***Adrenalize***, produced by the band with Mike Shipley, enters the UK chart at #1.
[18] ***Adrenalize***, its title chosen by the group's fan club, also bows on the US chart at #1, where it will stay for five weeks.
[20] Former Dio, Trinity, Whitesnake and Rivergroup lead guitarist, Vivian Campbell (b. Aug. 25, 1962, Belfast, N. Ireland), most recently in Shadow King with Lou Gramm, makes his major concert debut with Def Leppard at the "Freddie Mercury Tribute Concert", at Wembley Stadium, Wembley, Middx. (He had auditioned for the group at Mate's Studio in Burbank, CA, and made his debut with the band at a low-key gig in a Dublin, Eire club.)
May [9] *Let's Get Rocked* reaches US #15.
[27] The group performs at the Frankfurt Music Hall during a short tour of Germany.
[29] ***Adrenalize*** reaches the RIAA-certified three million sales plateau.
June [21] A five-date "7 Day Weekend" UK tour, set to end on July 1st at the Birmingham National Exhibition Centre, opens at the Glasgow SECC.
July [4] *Make Love Like A Man* reaches UK #12.
[18] *Make Love Like A Man* makes US #36.
[20-24] Elliott fills in for disc jockey Simon Bates on BBC Radio 1.
Aug Members of Def Leppard team with Hothouse Flowers to form the ad-hoc offshoot group, Acoustic Hippies From Hell.
[19] Allen talks about his accident and returning to the drumkit on BBC1-TV's "Fighting Back".
Sept [13] The group plays to a sellout crowd of 8,000 at the Yakima Valley Sundome, Yakima, WA, during its current North American tour.
[22, 24] They postpone dates in Las Cruces, NM and Tucson, AZ, after their sound-equipment truck is found abandoned, reportedly after Herschel Williams, the group's sound equipment driver, had attempted to rob a used-appliance store. He is later charged with possession of a dangerous drug and causing criminal damage in Las Cruces.
[26] *Have You Ever Needed Someone So Bad* reaches UK #16.
Oct [30] The band grosses $445,005 from a 19,778 sellout crowd at the Palace of Auburn Hills, Auburn Hills, MI.
[31] *Have You Ever Needed Someone So Bad* reaches US #12.
Dec [31] The group plays its final gig of the year, at the America West Arena, Phoenix, AZ.

1993

Jan [30] *Stand Up (Kick Love Into Motion)* reaches US #34.
Feb [6] *Heaven Is* reaches UK #13.
May [1] *Tonight* makes US #62 and debuts at its UK #34 peak.
June [6] They perform at Sheffield's Don Valley Stadium, their only UK date of the year.
July [4] The group begins the US leg of its tour at the Summer Music Theater, George, WA, set to end on September 20th at the State Fairgrounds, Oklahoma City, OK.
Sept [25] *Two Steps Behind* reaches UK #32.
Oct [16] ***Retro=active***, comprising rarities and unreleased material including a new cut by the recently deceased rock veteran Mick Ronson, debuts at its UK #6 peak.
[23] *Two Steps Behind*, taken from the Arnold Schwarzenegger movie "The Last Action Hero", reaches US #12, as ***Retro=active*** debuts at its US #9 peak.

1994

Jan [22] *Action* reaches UK #14, as *Miss You In A Heartbeat* reaches US #39.
May [7] Elliott's duet with Ronson, *Don't Look Down*, charts for a week at UK #55.
June The group is voted Best British Band at the inaugural **Kerrang!** Great British Heavy Metal Awards at the Notre Dame Hall in London's Leicester Square.
Nov [29] The RIAA certifies nine million sales of ***Pyromania***.

1995

July [5] Allen is arrested on charges of spousal abuse at Los Angeles airport, after allegedly grabbing his wife Stacy by the throat, dragging her into a restroom, and slamming her head against a wall.
Aug [31] The group performs a six-song acoustic set at a PolyGram conference for retailers and staff.
Oct [21] *When Love And Hate Collide* hits UK #2, behind Simply Red's *Fairground*.
[23] The group performs three concerts in three continents on the same day: they begin at the Cave Of Hercules in Tangiers at 5:00 a.m.; then perform at midday at London's Shepherd's Bush Bottom Line, before playing at the Commodore in Vancouver, BC, Canada, at 9:00 p.m.
Nov [4] With the band delaying the release of its new album ***Slang*** (written earlier in the year in a house in Spain) until 1996, a compilation ***Vault - Greatest Hits 1980-199***, including the new track *When Love And Hate Collide*, bows at its UK #3 peak.
[18] ***Vault - Greatest Hits 1980-1995*** debuts at its US #15 peak.

1996

Jan [20] *When Love And Hate Collide* makes US #58.
May [14] Having outlasted the great majority of its '80s hard-rock contemporaries, and marking a more experimental musical approach (which even includes funk and soul phrasings), ***Slang***, co-produced by the band with engineer Pete Woodroffe, is released worldwide. It also marks the first time Allen has played an acoustic drum kit since his car accident in 1984. The project will be promoted with a world tour beginning later this month in Bombay, India.

DESMOND DEKKER

1963

Orphaned at an early age and having lived in the St. Thomas township in Jamaica and worked as a welder before joining studio group the Aces, Dekker (b. Desmond Dacres, July 16, 1941, Kingston, Jamaica) records his first Jamaican single, *Honour Your Mother And Father*, for the Yabba label (which Island Records boss Chris Blackwell will pick up for UK release). (With the Aces, he will have hits in Jamaica with *Generosity* (1964), *Get Up Adinah* (1964), *King Of The Ska* (1965), *007 (Shanty Town)* (1966), *Jezebel* (1966), and *Rock Steady* (1966).) After running through a variety of producers, Dekker & the Aces will start recording for Leslie Kong in 1966 (and will continue to be produced exclusively by Kong until his death in 1971).

1967

Aug *007 (Shanty Town)*, a #1 disc in Jamaica (where Dekker has 20 such chart-toppers), a celebration of the Kingston "rude boy" lifestyle, has become an underground club hit in the UK for six months and now reaches #14, released on the Pyramid label.

1969

Apr [16] Dekker becomes the first Jamaican artist to hit UK #1, with the Kong co-penned rock-steady reggae classic, *The Israelites*.
May [4] He appears on ITV's "The Golden Shot", hosted by Bob Monkhouse.
June [28] *The Israelites* hits US #9, a rare Top 10 achievement for a reggae single.
July The self-penned *It Miek* hits UK #7, as ***This Is Desmond Dekker*** reaches UK #27.
Sept *Israelites* peaks at US #153.
[21] Dekker participates in the first "Caribbean Music Festival" at the Empire Pool, Wembley, Middx., with Johnny Nash, Jackie Edwards, Jimmy Cliff, Max Romeo and others.
Dec [6] He performs at London's East Ham Granada with Arthur Conley, Percy Sledge and Max Romeo.

1970

Jan *Pickney Gal* makes UK #42.
Apr [26] Dekker takes part in the second "Caribbean Music Festival" at the Empire Pool, with Bob & Marcia, Boris Gardner and the Pioneers.
Oct *You Can Get It If You Really Want* hits UK #2. Written by Jimmy Cliff for the movie "The Harder They Come", it is the first non-original song Dekker has recorded.

1971

After his producer Kong dies of a heart attack, Dekker, who has visited the UK regularly since the success of *007 (Shanty Town)*, moves to London, as the ska phenomenon is being replaced by reggae, with a new generation of Jamaican artists emerging, spearheaded by Bob Marley & the Wailers.

1975

June *The Israelites* is reissued in the UK by the Cactus reggae label and hits UK #10.
Sept *Sing A Little Song* reaches UK #16. Dekker will remain largely unproductive during the remainder of the decade releasing no new material, while specialist reggae label Trojan will issue the compilations ***Double Dekker*** and ***Dekker's Sweet 16 Hits***.

1980

July With Dekker now occasionally performing around London, ***Black And Dekker***, updating versions of his old hits, backed by UK band the Rumour, is released by Stiff Records (UK). It will be followed by his second and final album of a new decade, ***Compass Point*** in July 1981, produced by Robert Palmer and named after the recording complex in the Caribbean.

1985

Jan [6] Having been declared bankrupt the previous year following problems with his manager, Dekker performs with fellow reggae artists Dennis Brown, Smiley Culture, Lee Perry and others, at the "Ethiopian Benefit Concert" at London's Brixton Academy.

1990

The Israelites is used as the theme song for an award-winning Maxell Tapes TV commercial which misinterprets the lyrics of the original song in a Bob Dylan *Subterranean Homesick Blues* video card-reading style to become "My ears are alight".

1993

Feb [6] Revered as a pioneering figure in reggae history, the rock-steady veteran, still consistently touring in the UK and US, plays at the Grand, Clapham Junction, London, during current UK dates, while Rhino Records releases a retrospective for American fans, ***Rockin' Steady - The Best Of Desmond Dekker***.

DEL AMITRI

Justin Currie (lead vocals, bass); **Iain Harvie** (guitar)

1985

May The band has been formed in Glasgow, Scotland in 1983 by its permanent nucleus of Currie (b. Dec. 11, 1964, Glasgow) and Harvie (b. May 19, 1962, Glasgow), who have recruited guitarist Bryan Tolland and drummer Paul Tyagi, and released its debut recording *Sense Sickness* through the local indie label No Strings in August of that year. Subsequently picked up by Chrysalis Records (though licensed via its own Big Star label), Del Amitri's debut album, the Hugh Jones-produced ***Del Amitri*** is now issued (only in the UK), a folk-rock set written by all four members (which will be re-released on CD in 1993). Despite annual tours through the rest of the decade, it won't be until 1988 that the band begins recording a follow-up, with Michael Slaven replacing Tolland and the group signing a long-term deal with A&M Records.

1989

Aug Bittersweet *Kiss This Thing Goodbye*, co-written by Currie, Harvie and Slaven makes UK #59.

1990

Feb [24] ***Waking Hours*** enters the UK chart set to hit #6 during a 44-week run. Recorded over an 18-month period, its maturing folk-rock/pop material has been variously produced by Jones, Gil Norton and Mark Freeguard.
The extracted *Nothing Ever Happens*, written by Currie, reaches UK #11.
Mar Re-issued *Kiss This Thing Goodbye* makes UK #43.
June [23] ***Waking Hours*** makes US #95 while *Move Away Jimmy Blue* reaches UK #36.
July [7] *Kiss This Thing Goodbye* reaches US #35.
Nov *Spit In The Rain* reaches UK #21.

1992

May [7] A 19-date UK tour, set to end on July 18th at their hometown Glasgow Barrowlands venue, begins at Leeds Polytechnic, Leeds, Yorks.
[16] Previewing the band's third album in seven years, *Always The Last To Know* reaches UK #13.
June [13] With Currie and Harvie now augmented by Brian McDermott (drums), David Cummings (guitar) and Andy Alston (keyboards), the Norton-produced, largely Currie-penned ***Change Everything*** hits UK #2 in its first chart week.
July [18] The extracted *Be My Downfall* reaches UK #30.
Sept [19] *Just Like A Man* reaches UK #25.
[23] An 18-date North American trek gets underway at the First Avenue, Minneapolis, MN (a bill grossing $14,840 from a sellout 1,457 crowd), set to close on October 17th at the 86th Street Music Hall, Vancouver, WA.
[26] ***Change Everything*** peaks at US #178.
Oct [17] *Always The Last To Know* reaches US #30.
Dec [7] A further 13-date UK tour begins.

1993

Jan [23] Still mining the third album, *When You Were Young* debuts at its UK #20 peak.

1994

Mar Four months of recording sessions begin at Haremere Hall, the Chapel, the Funny Farm, Palladium, Park Lane and Helicon Mountain studios.

1995

Feb [18] *Here And Now* enters at its UK #25 peak.
Mar [11] Now trimmed to the quartet of Currie, Harvie, Cummings and Alston, ***Twisted***, produced by Al Clay and built around Currie/Harvie compositions, enters at its UK #3 high.
Apr [29] Ballad *Driving With The Brakes On* (written by Currie who has only recently passed his driving test) debuts at its UK #18 peak.
July [8] Conversely jaunty *Roll To Me* bows at its UK #22 peak.
[23] Del Amitri performs at the Arms Park, Cardiff, Wales on a bill with R.E.M. and the Cranberries which grosses £1,286,890.
Sept [9] ***Twisted*** peaks at US #170.
[15-16] During a US visit, the group plays a pair of dates at the First Avenue, Minneapolis, to 3,229 fans.
Oct [28] *Tell Her This* reaches UK #32 in its week of entry.
Nov [4] *Roll To Me* hits US #10.
Dec [26] Del Amitri appears on CBS-TV's "Late Show With David Letterman".

DELANEY & BONNIE

Delaney Bramlett (guitar, vocals);
Bonnie Bramlett (vocals)

1967

Delaney Bramlett (b. July 1, 1939, Pontotoc Co., MS), who has already cut a number of solo singles including *Liverpool Lou* and *You Never Looked Sweeter* for the Vocalion label in 1965, and Bonnie Lynn (b. Bonnie Lynn O'Farrell, Nov. 8, 1944, Acton, IL) meet in Los Angeles, CA on Jack Good's rock TV show, "Shindig", on which he is a member of the resident band the Shindogs, while she is a session singer (formerly with Ike & Tina Turner's Ikettes and also backing the Doors, Albert King and Little Milton, having made her first live performance at the age of 15). They marry within a week of meeting, at the opening of a bowling alley in Los Angeles, and decide to begin performing as a white rock/soul duo. The following year, they will record ***Home*** with Booker T. & the MG's (produced by Leon Russell) for Stax Records in Memphis (though the set will not be released until 1974).

1969

July Signed to Elektra Records, the duo's ***The Original Delaney And Bonnie - Accept No Substitute*** makes a minor US chart showing at #175.
Sept Delaney & Bonnie & Friends (the latter a frequently-changing aggregation of session men) are hired as the opening act on a US tour by Blind Faith, which leads to an immediate friendship with Eric Clapton, who admires their music and joins in inter-date jam sessions on the tour bus.
Dec [1] Delaney & Bonnie & Friends embark on a seven-date UK tour at London's Royal Albert Hall, set to end on the 7th at the Fairfield Halls, Croydon, Surrey.
[15] Delaney & Bonnie join John Lennon's one-off Plastic Ono Supergroup for the "Peace For Christmas" concert at London's Lyceum Ballroom.

1970

Jan After Blind Faith folds, Clapton joins Delaney & Bonnie's Friends as guitarist on a two-month US tour of their own, which he has agreed to co-finance.
Mar [7] *Comin' Home*, credited jointly to the group and Clapton, but penned by Bonnie and Clapton, by Atco Records, reaches US #84 and #16 in the UK, where it is their only hit. The Bonnie-sung ballad, *Groupie (Superstar)*, penned by Bonnie and Leon Russell, on the B-side, will become a million-selling song when covered and revised to *Superstar* by the Carpenters in 1971.
Apr Clapton departs at tour's end to work on his first solo album, on which the Bramletts will both guest, and many of the Friends (Jim Gordon, Carl Radle, Bobby Keys, Bobby Whitlock, Jim Price and Rita Coolidge) also leave, to become part of the "Mad Dogs and Englishmen" touring group with Joe Cocker.
June ***Delaney & Bonnie & Friends On Tour With Eric Clapton*** reaches US #29 and UK #39.
Sept [19] *Soul Shake*, the B-side of *Free The People*, which peaked at US #75 on June [6], makes US #43.
Nov ***To Bonnie From Delaney*** reaches US #58.
Dec [26-29] They perform at San Francisco's Fillmore West.

1971

May ***Motel Shot***, featuring Dave Mason, Gram Parsons, John Hartford and Leon Russell, peaks at US #65.
July [24] *Never Ending Song Of Love* is their biggest US hit single, reaching #13. It is quickly covered and taken to UK #2 by the New Seekers.
Nov [6] *Only You And I Know* reaches US #20.

1972

Feb [12] *Move 'Em Out* makes US #59.
May [6] *Where There's A Will There's A Way* (US #99) ends their singles chart career, before a label switch to CBS/Columbia Records sees ***D & B Together*** climb to US #133, but the title proves ironic, as the couple divorce and split professionally soon afterwards. (Both will record solo through the later '70s: Bonnie will release ***Sweet Bonnie Bramlett*** (1973), ***It's Time*** (1975), ***Lady's Choice*** (1976) and ***Memories*** (1978), while Delaney will record ***Delaney*** (1972), ***Something's Coming*** (1973), ***Mobius Strip*** (1974), ***Giving Birth To A Song*** (1975) and ***Class Reunion*** (1977).)

1976

Dec While visiting Gregg Allman's Juliette, GA farm, Bonnie goes into a field with a shotgun to commit suicide, but has a change of heart.

1979

Mar [16] Bonnie makes music media headlines when, after singing back-up vocals with Stephen Stills at a gig in Columbus, OH, she gets into a fierce argument with Elvis Costello (who is staying at the same Holiday Inn) about racial matters relating to music, and punches the English rocker in the face.

1988

Aug [8] Bonnie (who has made her acting debut on the syndicated TV series "Fame" the previous year) marries Danny Sheridan, with whom she forms the Bandaloo Doctors with Jonah Koslen, Kevin Valentine and Jimmy Crespo. They make their debut at "Farm Aid III".

1992

Jan [30] Bonnie Sheridan (whose recent acting credits have included Oliver Stone's "The Doors" and ABC-TV's "Roseanne") takes part in the "Friends Of Smitty" benefit for William Smith, who has suffered a stroke, at the Palace Theatre, Burbank, CA.

JOHN DENVER

1965

Singer/songwriter Denver (b. Henry John Deutschendorf, Dec. 31, 1943, Roswell, NM), the son of a US Air Force Colonel, raised in Arizona, Alabama, Oklahoma, Texas and Japan, having studied architecture at Texas Tech. in Lubbock, TX, travels to California to pursue his interest in folk music. (He had been given a vintage Gibson guitar by his grandmother at the age of 12.) While working as a draughtsman in Los Angeles, CA, he plays the folk scene at night, eventually recording demos, and adopting a performing surname after his favorite city. Discovered by the New Christy Minstrels' Randy Sparks, and playing gigs at Ledbetters, Sparks' club near the UCLA campus, he successfully auditions for the Chad Mitchell Trio, joining the folk combo and replacing Mitchell himself, having beaten out 250 other hopefuls.

1968

Having married Ann Martell the previous year (whom he met at a Trio concert in 1966 at her college, Gustavus Adolphus, St. Peter, MN), and after two and a half years in the Trio, during which he has been developing his songwriting skills, Denver signs as a solo artist to RCA Records.

1969

Nov His first solo album, ***Rhymes And Reasons***, produced by the Chad Mitchell Trio's arranger, Milton Okun, peaks at US #148.
Dec [20] It features his composition *Leaving On A Jet Plane*, which, now covered by Peter, Paul and Mary, hits US #1, subsequently confirmed as a million-seller.

1970

May ***Take Me Tomorrow*** peaks at US #197.

1971

Aug [28] Pop/country-fused *Take Me Home, Country Roads*, his debut chart single, hits US #2 and will become his first million-seller as a performer. It is credited to Denver with Fat City (Bill Danoff and Taffy Nivert, the writers of the song) and taken from ***Poems, Prayers And Promises***, which reaches US #15, also becoming his first gold album, selling over half a million copies during an 80-week chart stay.
Dec [18] *Friends With You* makes US #47, as ***Aerie*** peaks at US #75.

1972

Mar [18] His revival of Buddy Holly's *Everyday* reaches US #81.
Aug [19] *Goodbye Again* makes US #88.
Nov ***Rocky Mountain High*** is his first US Top 10 album, at #4, and earns another gold disc. It is dedicated to Denver's favorite environment - the Colorado mountains - where he and his wife have settled in Aspen.

1973

Mar [3] The extracted title track, *Rocky Mountain High*, hits US #9.
Apr [29] Denver begins a weekly live BBC2-TV special, "The John Denver Show", from the BBC's Shepherds Bush Green studios.
June [23] Self-penned ***Rocky Mountain High***, Denver's UK chart debut, peaks at UK #11, and the reactivated ***Poems, Prayers And Promises*** reaches UK #19.
[30] ***Rhymes And Reasons*** climbs to UK #21.
July [21] *I'd Rather Be A Cowboy* peaks at US #62.
Sept ***Farewell Andromeda*** reaches US #16 (earning a gold disc).
[29] The extracted *Farewell Andromeda (Welcome To My Morning)* peaks at US #89.

1974

Jan [12] *Please, Daddy* peaks at US #69.
Mar [30] Compilation album, ***John Denver's Greatest Hits***, begins a three-week stay at US #1, and will sell five million copies during a chart tenure of over three years, as *Sunshine On My Shoulders* (written with Dick Kniss and Mike Taylor) also hits US #1. It will be used as the theme song to the NBC-TV sitcom "Sunshine", starring Cliff DeYoung and Elizabeth Cheshire, which will premiere on March 6th, 1975.
July [27] *Annie's Song*, a loving ode to his wife Ann, inspired by a temporary rift in their marriage, tops the US chart for the first of two weeks and earns a gold disc for million-plus sales. It was written by Denver in ten minutes, while riding on a ski-lift. (At the height of this success, Denver will play seven concerts at the Universal Amphitheatre, Universal City, CA, which sell out in 24 hours.)
Aug [10] ***Back Home Again*** is his second consecutive US Album chart topper, and another million-seller.
Oct [5] ***Back Home Again*** hits UK #3.
[12] *Annie's Song* tops the UK chart for one week. (It will be Denver's only UK solo hit single.)
Nov [9] The extracted title track, *Back Home Again*, hits US #5, becoming Denver's second million-selling single from the album. He is proclaimed as the state's poet laureate, by Governor John Vanderhoof of Colorado, for his promotion of the Rocky Mountains.

1975

Feb [15] *Sweet Surrender*, from the Walt Disney film "The Bears And I", reaches US #13.
[18] He collects the Favorite Male Artist, Pop/Rock trophy at the second annual American Music Awards, held at the Civic Auditorium, Santa Monica, CA.
Apr [12] His live double set, ***An Evening With John Denver***, recorded at the Universal Amphitheatre from 1974's sold-out US concert tour, hits US #2 (another gold disc) having made UK #31 on Mar [29].
May [19] ABC-TV's "An Evening With John Denver" wins Outstanding Special - Comedy/Variety Or Musical at the 27th Emmy awards.
June [7] *Thank God I'm A Country Boy*, written by Denver's long-serving back-up guitarist, John Sommers, and originally on ***Back Home Again***, has been extracted in a new version and hits US #1 (his third US #1 and fifth million-selling single).
Sept [20] Denver guests on the premiere edition of ABC-TV's "Saturday Night Live With Howard Cosell".
[27] *I'm Sorry* is another US chart-topper and million-seller. After it drops to #2, its B-side, *Calypso*, a tribute to marine explorer Jacques Cousteau and titled after his ship, picks up major airplay in its own right, giving it a double A-side credit, which keeps it at #2 for four further weeks from Oct [11].
Oct [18] ***Windsong***, after debuting two weeks earlier behind Pink Floyd's ***Wish You Were Here***, hits US #1 for the first of two weeks. (Denver will shortly launch his own record label, named Windsong after this album. Its most successful act will be the Starland Vocal Band, including former Fat City members and *Take Me Home, Country Roads* writers Bill and Taffy Danoff, whose *Afternoon Delight* will hit US #1 in 1976.)
Dec [27] Seasonal album, ***Rocky Mountain Christmas***, reaches US #14 and earns another gold disc, as *Christmas For Cowboys* peaks at US #58.

1976

Jan [24] *Fly Away*, with vocal back-up from Olivia Newton-John (who had a UK hit with a cover of Denver's *Take Me Home, Country Roads* in 1973), reaches US #13, as the seasonally-packaged double album ***The John Denver Gift Pack*** (comprising both the Christmas album and ***Windsong***), peaks at US #138.
[31] He wins the Favorite Male Artist, Pop/Rock, Favorite Male Artist, Country, and Favorite Album, Country categories, at the third annual American Music Awards, held again at the Civic Auditorium, Santa Monica.
Mar [29] Denver begins a concert week at the London Palladium, which is recorded for future release, with a band comprising John Sommers and Steve Weisberg (guitars), Dick Kniss (bass), Hal Blaine (drums) and Lee Holdridge (arrangements), as ABC-TV airs "John Denver And Friends" special.
Apr [3] *Looking For Space* reaches US #29, as ***The Best Of John Denver*** and ***Windsong*** belatedly reach UK #7 and #14.
May [22] *It Makes Me Giggle* peaks at US #60.
[29] UK-only release album, ***Live In London***, recorded earlier in the year, hits UK #2.
July Denver plays a week of concerts in Los Angeles (donating the proceeds to more than 30 different charities).
Sept [25] ***Spirit*** hits US #7, earning a platinum disc, and UK #9.
Oct [2] Extracted *Like A Sad Song* makes US #36.
Dec Newsweek proclaims Denver "the most popular singer in America".

1977

Jan [29] *Baby, You Look Good To Me Tonight* peaks at US #65.
Mar [22] Johnny Cash, Glen Campbell and Roger Miller join Denver in his ABC-TV special, "Thank God I'm A Country Boy".
Apr [2] A second compilation album, ***John Denver's Greatest Hits, Volume 2***, hits US #6, earning another platinum disc.
[9] ***Best Of John Denver Vol.2*** hits UK #9.
[21] Denver guests on ABC-TV's "Sinatra and Friends" special, singing *My Sweet Lady* and duetting with Sinatra on *September Song*.
May [14] *My Sweet Lady* (originally the B-side of *Thank God I'm A Country Boy*) makes US #32.
Aug Denver plays a ten-day season at Harrah's in Lake Tahoe, NV.
Oct He makes his film debut in comedy "Oh, God", starring alongside George Burns.

1978

Jan [14] *How Can I Leave You Again* makes US #44, as parent album, ***I Want To Live***, reaches US #45.
Feb [18] ***I Want To Live*** reaches UK #25.
[23] Denver emcees the 20th annual Grammy Awards, taking over from Andy Williams.
Mar [8] He plays a week of concerts at South Lake Tahoe, NV, as his annual Pro/Am Ski tournament takes place.
Apr [1] *It Amazes Me* peaks at US #59.
May [13] *I Want To Live* makes US #55.
[15] Denver's two-month US tour ends at the Great Western Forum, Inglewood, CA.
July Irish flautist James Galway hits UK #3 with an instrumental version of *Annie's Song*.

1979

Jan [9] "The Music For UNICEF Concert", to celebrate the International Year Of The Child, takes place in the General Assembly Hall of the United Nations in New York, NY. Denver sings *Rhymes & Reasons*, donating the royalties from the song to UNICEF. (NBC-TV will air "A Gift Of Song - The Music For UNICEF Concert" the following night.) He is increasingly involved in social and environmental causes, including a two-year commitment to the Presidential Commission On World And Domestic Hunger, and supporting the Wilderness Society, Friends Of The Earth and the World Wildlife Fund.
Mar [3] ***John Denver*** reaches US #25.
Apr Denver embarks on his first UK tour in three years, including four sellout dates at the Wembley Arena, Wembley, Middx.
[21] ***John Denver*** makes UK #68.
June [11-21] Denver records ***Autograph*** at Filmways/Heider studios, Hollywood, CA, with his regular studio and live band - James Burton (guitar), Glen D. Hardin (keyboards), Emory Gordy Jr. (bass), Hal Blaine (drums), Jim Horn (horns), Herb Pedersen (banjo), Denny Brooks (acoustic guitar) and Danny Wheetman (mandolin and harmonica).

1980

Jan [5] ***A Christmas Together***, recorded with the Muppets, reaches US #26 and is a million-seller. Denver has also guested on a recent Muppets Christmas special on TV.
Apr [5] *Autograph* peaks at US #52.
[19] ***Autograph*** reaches US #39.
June [28] *Dancing With The Mountains* peaks at US #97. (Denver co-produces the TV special "The Higher We Fly", which wins the coveted Earl Osborn Award from the Aviation/Space Writer's Association, and will be honored at the Houston Film Festival.)

1981

Sept [19] *Some Days Are Diamonds (Some Days Are Stone)* makes US #36, as the parent album, ***Some Days Are Diamonds***, recorded at the Sound Emporium, Nashville, TN, with producer Larry Butler, reaches US #32. Denver's performance in

Tokyo, Japan, is attended by the Crown Prince of Japan (his first pop concert).
Nov [21] *The Cowboy And The Lady* peaks at US #66.
Dec [26] Denver's duet with Placido Domingo on *Perhaps Love* makes UK #46.

1982

Jan [30] Its parent album ***Perhaps Love*** reaches UK #17.
Feb [13] *Perhaps Love* peaks at US #59.
May [2] ***Seasons Of The Heart***, his first self-produced album, with help from Barney Wyckoff, makes US #39, and is his last to earn a gold disc.
[22] The extracted *Shanghai Breezes* reaches US #31.
Aug [21] Title track, *Seasons Of The Heart*, stalls at US #78.

1983

Oct ***It's About Time***, recorded at Criteria Studios, Miami, FL, with help from the Wailers and the I-Threes, makes US #61 and UK #90. Shortly after their 15th anniversary, Denver and his wife Ann separate, and later divorce.

1984

Feb He writes and performs *The Gold And Beyond*, the theme song for the 1984 Winter Olympics, singing it for US TV on the slopes of Mount Sarajevo. He opens an exhibition of his photographs (a 15-year legacy of Rocky Mountain landscape and wildlife) at Manhattan's Hammer Galleries in New York.
Sept Denver travels to Africa on a fact-finding trip for the Hunger Project. He records *Africa Sunrise* in Burkina Fasso and Mozambique, which will be included on ***Dreamland Express***.
Nov [24] He plays an informal concert at the US Embassy in Moscow, and teams with French singer Sylvie Vartan for *Love Again*, which peaks at US #85 (his last US Hot 100 entry of the decade).
Dec ***The John Denver Collection***, a TV-advertised compilation album on Telstar, reaches UK #20.

1985

Sept [7] ***Dreamland Express***, produced by Roger Nichols, reaches US #90.
Denver embarks on a 12-day concert tour of the Soviet Union.

1986

June [10] Denver joins with a host of other singers and groups to celebrate the Nitty Gritty Dirt Band's 20th anniversary, at the Red Rocks Stadium, Denver, CO.
July [30] RCA Records drops Denver from his contract. Industry insiders speculate that RCA's new owner, General Electric, a top military contractor, takes exception to his recording *Let Us Begin (What Are We Making Weapons For?)*, which he had made with top Soviet singer, Alexandre Gradsky, in Moscow's Melodiya studio.
Aug ***One World*** makes UK #91.

1987

Dec Denver ends the year appearing in special Christmas TV shows, with Julie Andrews and the Muppets, and his own "A Rocky Mountain Christmas". During the past 12 months, he has also filmed "Rocky Mountain Reunion", a documentary about endangered species (which will win six awards, including the American Film Festival's New York City Blue Ribbon Award for Best Educational Production), another documentary, "John Denver's Alaska : The America Child", has become a member of the National Space Institute and European Space Agency, and has become further involved in the charity works of the Human/Dolphin Foundation, and the Hunger Project. He has also been presented with the Presidential World Without Hunger Award by Ronald Reagan, funded his own Windstar Foundation and taken part in an annual Celebrity Pro/Am Ski Tournament.

1988

Aug Aviation Week & Space Technology magazine, under the headline "Ural Mountain High", says that Denver has asked the Soviet Union to launch him to the Mir Space Station. The Soviets are reported to be considering it, with a price tag of $10 million.
Oct ***Higher Ground***, his first album in three years, on his new Windstar label, enters the US Country chart.
Dec Denver records *And So It Goes* with the Nitty Gritty Dirt Band, for inclusion of the group's ***Will The Circle Be Unbroken Volume Two***.

1989

July [5] Denver hosts the NBC-TV special "In Performance At The White House", the first of three concerts filmed before President and Barbara Bush.

1990

Oct UK group New Order settles out of court with Denver's publisher, Cherry Lane Music, for their alleged infringement of copyright of *Leaving On A Jet Plane*, on their song *Run*. New Order's Steven Morris says, "It's New Order's contribution to sending John Denver into space."
Nov [24] ***The Flower That Shattered The Stone***, his second Windstar release, dedicated to his year-old daughter, Jesse Belle Denver, climbs to US #185.
Dec [19] NBC-TV airs Denver's "Christmas In Washington" special.

1991

Sept Denver is presented with an ecology award by CD replicator American Helix for his commitment to the planet, during a concert at the Valley Forge Music Fair, Devon, PA.
Dec [10] He files for divorce and asks for a temporary restraining order to bar his wife from entering his Aspen home.
[13] CBS-TV airs "John Denver's Montana Christmas Skies" special.

1992

June Denver attends a press conference with the Dalai Lama at the "Earth Summit" in Rio de Janeiro, Brazil.
[26-27] He performs at the Sydney Entertainment Centre, Sydney, New South Wales, Australia.
July [19] During his current US tour, Denver plays at the Fiddler's Green Amphitheatre, Englewood, CO in his home state.
Dec [27] He performs at a benefit at the Wheeler Opera House, Aspen, CO, to raise money to fight the state's new anti-gay ordinance.

1993

Sept [24] Denver agrees to give a benefit concert for Tipsy Taxi and perform 25 hours of public service in exchange for having the charge of driving under the influence brought against him on August 21st reduced to the lesser charge of driving while his ability was impaired. He also pays a $50 fine.

1994

May [1] As part of a six-week "Heart To Heart" Asian tour, Denver becomes the first US pop star to perform in Vietnam, when he gives a concert at Hanoi's Opera House. After the show he says "This was the least responsive audience that I think I've ever had".
July [10] During a current US tour, Denver plays to a sellout crowd of 4,159 at the Summer Pops Bowl Amphitheatre, San Diego, CA, with the San Diego Symphony Orchestra.
Aug [21] Exactly one year after being charged for driving under the influence, Denver's 1963 Porsche convertible leaves the road near his Aspen home. He is charged with careless driving and for driving under the influence.

1995

June [17] Denver performs at New York's Radio City Music Hall during his current US tour.
July [1] As his career continues its resurgence, Legacy Records' two-CD ***Wildlife Concert***, released in support of the Wildlife Conservation, debuts at its US #104 peak.

1996

May Rhino (US) releases twin-CD anthology ***The Rocky Mountain Collection***.

DEPECHE MODE

Dave Gahan (vocals); **Martin Gore** (synthesizer); **Andy Fletcher** (bass synthesizer); **Alan Wilder** (synthesizer)

1980

May Vince Clarke (b. July 3, 1961, Basildon, Essex), ex-No Romance In China, and one-half of a gospel duo, teams with former St. Nicholas School student friends, bank clerk Gore (b. July 23, 1961, Basildon), ex-the French Look and Norman & the Worms, and insurance clerk Fletcher (b. July 8, 1960, Nottingham, Notts.), to form a trio in Basildon. They call themselves Composition of Sound, after rejecting such colorful suggestions as Peter Bonetti's Boots, the Lemon Peels, the Runny Smiles and the Glow Worms. They play their first gig, as an all-guitar line-up, at Scamps in Southend, Essex, and are then spotted headlining a Saturday-night electronic showcase at Croc's in Rayleigh, Essex, by Some Bizzare Records' supremo Stevo, who includes their track *Photographic* on his compilation album, ***Some Bizzare Album***, but does not sign them. With Clarke unhappy in his singing role, they look for a singer, and spot Gahan (b. May 9, 1962, Epping, Essex), currently studying window design at Southend Technical College, whom they hear performing *Heroes* with another local band when they turn up at a scout hall to rehearse. He joins the group and they make their first appearance as a four-piece at Fletcher and Gore's old St. Nicholas School in Basildon. (It is Gahan, thumbing through a French fashion magazine, who comes up with the name Depeche Mode after seeing the phrase (meaning "fast fashion").)
Oct The group, now with Fletcher playing synthesizer, records a three-song demo, sending the tape to every club and promoter they know of, which leads to a booking at the Bridgehouse in Canning Town, East London, on a regular "Futurist" night.
Dec Demo tapes sent to several labels evoke no response, but the band is approached at the Bridgehouse gig by independent Mute label's owner, ex-Silicon Teen member Daniel Miller, whose act, Fad Gadget, they are supporting. (Apparently Miller had heard their demo, describing it as "bloody awful".) He finances the recording of a first single and album, although they will not sign a proper contract with Mute until 1986, despite overtures from larger companies.

1981

Apr [11] Their debut single, *Dreaming Of Me*, written by Clarke and produced by Miller, peaks at UK #57.
Aug [8] *New Life* reaches UK #11, as the band makes its BBC1-TV "Top of the Pops" debut to promote the disc.
Oct [17] *Just Can't Get Enough* hits UK #8.
Nov [14] The group's debut album, the synth-pop ***Speak And Spell***, hits UK #10, as the band ends its first UK tour at London's Lyceum Ballroom, now hailed as a leading act in the short-lived New Romantic scene.
Dec [1] Clarke, the chief songwriter, but a studio addict who is unwilling to tour, announces that he is leaving the band to form Yazoo with Alison Moyet. (After his departure, virtually all the band's material will be written by Gore, who is much influenced by the German outfit Einsturzende Neubauten.)

1982

Jan Clarke is replaced by vocalist and synth player Alan Wilder (b. June 1, 1959, London), ex-the Dragons, Daphne & the Tenderspots and Hitmen, who responds to a **Melody Maker** ad - "Name band. Synthesizer. Must be under 21", despite being 22. He initially joins for their first US trip, but will remain as a permanent fixture.

Feb ***Speak And Spell*** is the group's US chart debut, at #192.
Mar [13] *See You*, recorded between Clarke's departure and Wilder's arrival, hits UK #6, while the band is making its US debut at the Ritz Club in New York, NY.
Apr [3] The **New Musical Express** prints an April Fool's Day gag announcing that they are planning to release a boxed set of Depeche Mode's and Haircut 100's versions of major hits from the past 25 years.
May [15] *The Meaning Of Love* reaches UK #12.
Sept [25] *Leave In Silence* reaches UK #18.
Oct [16] Gore-penned ***A Broken Frame***, recorded as a trio and co-produced with Miller, hits UK #8, as the group embarks on its biggest UK tour yet.
Dec [18] ***A Broken Frame*** peaks at US #177.

1983

Mar [5] *Get The Balance Right* reaches UK #13, as the band undertakes a major tour of Canada, the US, Japan and Hong Kong.
Aug [20] *Everything Counts* hits UK #6.
Sept ***Construction Time Again***, featuring the assistance of freelance sampling innovator Gareth Jones, hits UK #6.
Oct [22] *Love In Itself.2* reaches UK #21, after seven consecutive Top 20 hits.

1984

Apr [14] *People Are People* hits UK #4.
Aug ***People Are People*** peaks at US #166. (It will, however, re-chart in 1975 and go on to make US #71.)
Sept [22] Sexually-themed, Gore-penned *Master And Servant* hits UK #9.
Oct ***Some Great Reward*** hits UK #5.
Nov [17] Double A-side, *Somebody/Blasphemous Rumours*, reaches UK #16. (Gore moves to West Berlin during the year, to be with his girlfriend, and will reside there until 1986.)

1985

June [8] *Shake The Disease* reaches UK #18.
Aug [3] *People Are People*, their US singles chart debut, reaches #13 after a three-month climb.
[17] ***Some Great Reward*** makes US #51.
Sept [14] *Master And Servant* peaks at US #87.
Oct *It's Called A Heart* reaches UK #18, as the compilation, ***The Singles 1981-85***, the gatefold sleeve of which contains a collage of the group's bad reviews, hits UK #6. Released in the US as ***Catching Up With Depeche Mode***, the album will make #113 in early 1986. (By year's end, Gahan has married Joanne, secretary of the band's fan club. They will have a son, Jack, in 1987, before divorcing in 1991.)

1986

Jan The group starts work on a new album, at the Hansa Studios in Berlin, W. Germany.
Mar Using a guitar for the first time on a single, Depeche Mode reaches UK #15 with *Stripped*.
Apr ***Black Celebration*** debuts at UK #4, and will go on to make US #90.
[17] The band plays at the Wembley Arena, Wembley, Middx., during European dates.
May *A Question Of Lust* reaches UK #28.
Aug The group completes a lengthy tour and begins an eight-month sabbatical, during which they will write material for a new album (and allow Wilder to experiment with his side-band, Recoil, which now releases ***Recoil 1 & 2*** on Mute).
Sept *A Question Of Time* reaches UK #17.

1987

Feb The group begins work on a new album, at Guillaume Tell Studio in Paris, France, with engineer/producer Dave Bascombe.
May *Strangelove* reaches UK #16.
Aug [22] *Strangelove* peaks at US #76.
Sept *Never Let Me Down* stops at UK #22.
Oct [10] ***Music For The Masses*** hits UK #10.
Nov ***Music For The Masses*** makes US #35.

1988

Jan *Behind The Wheel* reaches UK #21.
Feb [13] *Never Let Me Down Again* peaks at US #63.
May [21] *Route 66/Behind The Wheel* climbs to US #61.
[28] Import *Little 15* peaks at UK #60.
June [18] "Music For The Masses" world tour ends before a sellout crowd of 75,000 at the Rose Bowl, Pasadena, CA, as part of a festival of UK bands with Orchestral Manoeuvres In The Dark. (The concert is filmed by famed D.A. Pennebaker and subsequently released on video as "Depeche Mode 101".)
Sept [7] Depeche Mode performs *Strangelove* at the fifth annual MTV Awards, at the Universal Amphitheatre, Universal City, CA, as ***Music For The Masses*** tops two million sales worldwide.
Oct [22] A remixed version of *Strangelove* makes US #50.

1989

Mar [11] *Everything Counts* reaches UK #22.
[25] ***101***, a live recording of the band's 1988 Rose Bowl concert, hits UK #5.
Apr [25] "101" movie premieres in Los Angeles, CA, as its related album, ***101***, makes US #45.
June [24] EP ***Counterfeit***, credited to Martin L. Gore, makes UK #51 in its week of entry in the album chart.
Sept [16] *Personal Jesus* reaches UK #13.

1990

Feb [24] *Enjoy The Silence* hits UK #6, aided by the Anton Corbijn-directed "monarch-with-a-deck-chair" video, starring central character, Gahan.
Mar [3] *Personal Jesus* reaches US #28.
[20] Five fans are treated for minor injuries at the Cedars-Sinai Medical Center, Los Angeles, after thousands of fans seeking autographs at a promotion at Wherehouse Records are crushed. The group is there to sign copies of its new album, ***Violator***. (Wherehouse agree to pay $25,000 to the City of Los Angeles, to compensate for the facilities provided by the Police and Fire Departments.)
[31] ***Violator***, produced by Flood, debuts at UK #2, behind David Bowie's ***Changesonebowie***.
May [5] ***Violator*** hits US #7, and will go on to become the group's first US million-seller.
[26] *Policy Of Truth* reaches UK #16.
[29] The group begins a major 43-date North American leg of the "World Violation Tour" at the Civic Center, Pensacola, FL, set to end with sellout dates on August 4-5th at Dodger Stadium, Los Angeles, grossing $2,408,750.
July [14] *Enjoy The Silence* hits US #8, after worldwide Top 10 success.
Oct [13] *World In My Eyes*, remixed by Francis Kevorkian, reaches UK #17.
[20] *Policy Of Truth*, also reworked by Kevorkian, reaches US #15.
Nov [19-20, 23] Depeche Mode plays at Wembley Arena, Wembley, during the European leg of its "World Violation Tour".
Dec [22] *World In My Eyes* peaks at US #52, as the group wins the Top Modern Rock Tracks Artist category in **Billboard**'s The Year In Music survey.

1991

Feb [10] *Enjoy The Silence* wins the Best British Single category at the tenth annual BRIT Awards, at the Dominion Theatre, London.
July [23] Celebrating his 30th birthday, Gore forms a one-off band with Fletcher and the Mission's Wayne Hussey called the Sexist Boys, performing glam-rock hits in wigs and make-up.
Oct [3] *Enjoy The Silence* and *Policy Of Truth* are honored at ASCAP's 11th annual London Awards, at Claridges.
Nov [11, 25] Mute re-releases all the band's previous UK singles on CD format.

1992

Mar The band begins work on its tenth studio album, in Madrid, Spain, after taking a year off.
Apr ***Bloodline***, a second Wilder solo project still under the name Recoil, is released.
Oct After sessions in Madrid and Hamburg, the group continues working on its new album at the Olympic Studios, Barnes, London, with Flood producing.
Nov Fletcher, now more the group's manager than an active musician, marries his girlfiend Grainne.

1993

Feb [27] *I Feel You*, remixed by Eno, debuts at its UK #8 peak, spurred again by a Corbijn-lensed promo clip.
Mar [13] *I Feel You* reaches US #37.
Apr [3] Flood-produced ***Songs Of Faith And Devotion***, penned by Gore, enters the UK chart at pole position.
[10] ***Songs Of Faith And Devotion*** enters the US chart at #1.
May [15] *Walking In My Shoes* reaches UK #14.
July [3] *Walking In My Shoes* peaks at US #69.
[31] The group plays its first UK concert in 2½ years at the Crystal Palace National Sports Centre, London, its only UK date of a European tour.
Sept [10] Depeche Mode embarks on the US leg of its world tour at the Centrum in Worcester, MA, set to end on October 29th at the Omni, Atlanta, GA.
[25] EP *Condemnation* debuts at its UK #9 peak.
Nov [4] Gore is arrested in the early morning at Denver's Westin Hotel, CO, after refusing to lower the volume in his room.
Dec [20] The group performs at the Wembley Arena, at the end of a short UK tour.
[25] ***Songs Of Faith And Devotion - Live*** charts for a week at US #193.

1994

Jan [29] *In Your Room* hits UK #8, as the group continues the 11-date leg of "The Devotional Tour" in South Africa, before moving on to Singapore, Hong Kong, the Philippines and Thailand. (Daryl Bamonte fills in for Fletcher, who is now handling business matters offstage.)
May [12] The US leg of the tour opens in Sacramento, CA.

1995

June After 13 years with the band, Wilder leaves, citing "increasing dissatisfaction with the internal relations and working practices of the group".
Aug [17] Police find Gahan in his Los Angeles home with a two-inch laceration on his wrist, after an apparent suicide attempt with a razor blade. He is taken to Cedars-Sinai Medical Center.
Oct [14] A Leonard Cohen tribute album, ***Tower Of Song : The Songs Of Leonard Cohen***, to which Gore has contributed *Coming Back To You*, charts for a week at US #198.
Dec With Gahan fully recovered, the band begins work on its next album, co-producing with Tim Simenon.
see also: **ERASURE, YAZOO**

DES'REE

1991

Aug [31] Weaned on R&B music (particularly influenced by the recordings of Billie Holiday. Stevie Wonder, Bob Marley and Joan Armatrading), Des'ree (b. Des'ree Weeks, 1968, London), the daughter of London-based West Indian parents who lived in Barbados, W. Indies between 1978-1980, has written her first song, *Love Is Here*, at the age of 13 having returned to London with her family (it will subsequently appear on her second album). Realizing that her muse lies in writing and performing a soulful brand of R&B, Des'ree sends her first demo tape to Sony Music, is signed by the label's Lincoln Elias and has recorded her first release all within the space of 12 weeks. The resulting *Feel So High*, her maiden single issued by Sony's Soho Square imprint (via the Dusted Sound label) now enters the UK chart, initially set to make #51.

1992

Jan [25] The re-released *Feel So High* reaches UK #13.
Feb [29] The largely self-penned ***Mind Adventures***, co-produced by Ashley Ingram and Phil Legg and showcasing her already mature songwriting and soulful soprano, bows at its UK #26 high.
Mar [21] *Mind Adventures* debuts at its UK #43 peak.
July [4] Ballad *Why Should I Love You?* makes UK #44.
Nov [21-23] Des'ree opens for Simply Red at a sold-out engagement at the Wembley Arena, Wembley, Middx.

1993

June [19] While recording for her follow-up album, *Delicate*, released by Terence Trent D'Arby featuring Des'ree, enters the UK chart set to reach #14.

1994

Apr [16] The lead-off track from her sophomore set, the instantly infectious *You Gotta Be* initially reaches UK #20.
May [21] ***I Ain't Movin'***, co-produced by Des'ree with Ingram and the Family Stand production team of V. Jeffrey Smith and Peter Lord Moreland, enters at its UK #13 peak.
June [25] *I Ain't Movin'* makes UK #44.
Sept [3] *Little Child* charts for a week at UK #69.
Dec [7-9] Her first US tour opening for Seal ends with three sold-out nights at the Wiltern Theatre, Los Angeles, CA.
[14] Des'ree guests on NBC-TV's "The Tonight Show".

1995

Feb [11] She is the music guest on NBC-TV's "Saturday Night Live".
Mar [3] Des'ree appears at the seventh annual World Music Awards in Monte Carlo, which will air on ABC-TV on May 30th.
[11] Licensed in the US to Sony imprint 550 Music, *You Gotta Be* hits US #5 after six months on the chart, having become the most played video clip on VH-1 (US) (and set for further exposure at the trailer-theme to ABC's "Good Morning America" daily broadcast).
[18] Reissued *You Gotta Be* reaches UK #14.
Apr [1] ***I Ain't Movin'***, released in the US to include cuts from her maiden album, reaches #27.
[29] *Feel So High*, now re-promoted in the US with a new video clip filmed in California's Joshua Tree National Forest, makes US #67.
May [13] Following her first headlining US tour in March, further North American dates, again supporting Seal, begin in Miami, FL.
[23] *You Gotta Be* is named Best Contemporary Song at the 40th annual Ivor Novello Awards held at London's Grosvenor House hotel.
[23] ***I Ain't Movin'*** is certified platinum by the RIAA.
June [13] She performs at eighth annual Essence Awards.
[30] Des'ree makes her second appearance on "The Tonight Show".
July [22] She guests on BBC1-TV's "Steve Wright's People Show".
Sept MCA Soundtracks (US) releases ***Clockers***, including *Silent Hero* by Des'ree.
Dec [14] She appears at "The Greatest Music Party In The World" held at Birmingham, W. Midland's National Exhibition Centre, W. Midlands.

THE DETROIT SPINNERS

See: THE SPINNERS

DEVO

Bob Mothersbaugh (guitar, vocals); **Bob Casale** (guitar); **Mark Mothersbaugh** (synthesizers); **Jerry Casale** (bass); **Alan Myers** (drums)

1974

After taking an early '70s experimental approach to music while studying art at Kent State University, OH, Bob Casale and Mark Mothersbaugh form a deliberately anonymous four-piece version of the band in Akron, OH, with Bob Mothersbaugh and a third sibling, Jim, on drums. The latter leaves, replaced by Myers, while Casale brings in his own brother, Jerry, on bass and Mark goes on to briefly play in Jackrabbit (alongside Chrissie Hynde, later of the Pretenders). (With the pairs of brothers regrouping with Myers to form the De-Evolution Band, based on a self-invented musical philosophy ("the sound of things falling apart") in September 1975, they produce a ten-minute short film "The Truth About De-Evolution" which wins a prize at the annual "Ann Arbor Film Festival". Subsequently shortening the name to Devo, the group's first release, the double A-side *Jocko Homo/Mongoloid*, recorded in a garage, is issued in the US in December 1976 on their own Booji Boy label, named after their supposed "mascot".)

1977

July *(I Can't Get Me No) Satisfaction*, their fractured version of the 1965 Rolling Stones' classic, is the second US release on Booji Boy. They make a New York live debut shortly after, introduced on stage by David Bowie, and are befriended and championed by him and Iggy Pop. This arouses interest from Stiff Records in the UK.
Sept [23] The group appears at the "Punk Rock Fashion Show" in Los Angeles, CA, alongside Blondie and others. (Their early live performances are each prefaced by the showing of their own 16mm movie, "In The Beginning Was The End", expounding their mock philosophy of De-Evolution.)

1978

Mar Having licensed Devo's Booji Boy material for the UK, Stiff releases *Jocko Homo/Mongoloid*, which peaks at UK #51, helped by an appearance on BBC-TV's "The Old Grey Whistle Test".
May *(I Can't Get Me No) Satisfaction* makes UK #41, while they make a UK live debut. Their highly non-conformist style of anonymous, robotic presentation, dressed in matching one-piece industrial suits, is quickly embraced by the new-wave music media in the UK.
June [24] They perform at the "Knebworth Festival", Knebworth, Herts, with Genesis, Jefferson Starship, Tom Petty, the Atlanta Rhythm Section and Roy Harper.
Aug Their final Stiff hit, *Be Stiff*, peaks at UK #71, by which time the band is signed to Virgin Records in the UK and Warner Bros. in the US.
Sept Virgin debut *Come Back Jonee* peaks at UK #60.
[23] Its parent album ***Are We Not Men? We Are Devo!***, produced in Germany by Brian Eno, reaches UK #12.
Dec The group performs at London's Hammersmith Odeon.

1979

Jan Mini-album, ***Be Stiff***, a compilation of the Booji Boy singles, is released in the UK.
June [30] ***Duty Now For The Future***, produced by Ken Scott, makes UK #49. They appear in Neil Young's movie, "Rust Never Sleeps", the title of which is an ad slogan given to Young by Devo.

1980

May [31] ***Freedom Of Choice***, co-produced by Robert Margouleff, reaches UK #47.
June [8] The group performs at London's Rainbow Theatre.
Nov [15] *Whip It* (taken from ***Freedom Of Choice***, which climbs to US #22 in its wake), is their first US chart entry and their best-selling single, reaching US #14. It earns a gold disc for million-plus US sales, and also peaks at UK #51.

1981

May Mini-album, ***Devo Live***, reaches US #49 and will chart-top in Australia, where the group will undertake a sellout tour the following year.
Sept [12] ***New Traditionalists***, a self-produced set, hosts no hit singles, but makes UK #50 and US #24.
Oct [24] Their typically quirky update of Lee Dorsey's *Working In The Coal Mine*, recorded for the National Lampoon movie "Heavy Metal", makes US #43.

1982

Jan Devo appears in another Neil Young-premiering film, "Human Highway".
Feb [12] MTV flies the winner of a competition to Hawaii to party with Devo.
Nov [18] The group guests on NBC-TV's "Late Night With David Letterman".
Dec ***Oh No, It's Devo!***, produced by Roy Thomas Baker, makes US #47.

1983

June [11] *Doctor Detroit*, their theme to the Dan Aykroyd-starring movie climbs to US #59. ("Are We Not Men?", a collection of typically wacky Devo promo clips, mostly conceived by Jerry Casale, from 1977-82, will be released in 1984).

1985

Oct ***Shout***, their first album to be released by Warner Bros. in the UK, is issued and includes Devo's version of the Jimi Hendrix song *Are U Experienced*.

1986

Dec Virgin Video (UK) simultaneously releases two Devo titles, "We're All Devo" and the semi-spoof documentary home video "The Men Who Make The Music".

1987

Aug ***E-Z Listening Disk***, a US-only CD on Rykodisc featuring muzak versions of their hits, is a stop-gap release, while they prepare a new album. Meanwhile, Mark Mothersbaugh mounts an exhibition of postcards in Los Angeles, and works with a band called the Visiting Kids.

1988

Aug After two years' work in the Marina Del Rey Studio (during which time David Kendrick has replaced Myers), Devo releases ***Total Devo*** on Enigma Records.

1990

July [14] *Post Post-Modern Man (If I Had A Hammer)*, from their forthcoming album, ***Smooth Noodle Maps***, is released in the US on Enigma.
Oct [15-16] The group performs at London's Town & Country club, during a brief UK visit, but will call it a day by year's end. (***Hot Potatoes : The Best Of Devo***, a hits collection, will be released in 1993 by Virgin UK, while US label Rykodisc will issue rarer material on ***Hardcore Volume 1*** and **2** and ***Live : The Mongoloid Years*** over the next three years.)

1995

Sept Of its members, Jerry Casale continues to complete a documentary of Neil Young while Bob Mothersbaugh, Bob Casale and Kendrick still work together, at Mark Mothersbaugh's composing corporation, Mutato Muzika, in the Hollywood Hills, CA, turning out successful commercials jingles and TV themes (including those for "Davis Rules", "Pee Wee's Playhouse", Nickelodeon TV's "Rugrats", MTV's "Liquid Television", "Great Scott" and Disney's "Adventures In Wonderland", for which he was nominated for a daytime Emmy Award in 1992). In a 1992 interview in **Variety**, Mark Mothersbaugh claimed that Devo were ripped off financially, saying of the music industry: "I don't like the lifestyle anymore. There are so many diseases out there that all the good reasons for going on the road have gone away. But it was fun at the time." Since then, Devo has been increasingly regarded as retro-hip, with Nirvana cutting a version of the band's *Turnaround* prior to its demise and Soundgarden covering *Girl U Want*. With a new Devo recording recently featured on the film soundtrack to "Mighty Morphin Power Rangers", Inscape now releases the CD-ROM game "Devo Presents The Adventures Of The Smart Patrol", conceived by Mark Mothersbaugh and Jerry Casale.

DEXY'S MIDNIGHT RUNNERS

Kevin Rowland (vocals, guitar); **Al Archer** (guitar); **Pete Williams** (bass); **Pete Saunders** (organ); **Andy Growcott** (drums); **"Big" Jimmy Patterson** (trombone); **Steve "Babyface" Spooner** (alto sax); **Jeff "J.B." Blythe** (tenor sax)

1978

July Rowland (b. Aug. 17, 1953, Wolverhampton, Warks, of Irish parents), having made his debut in Lucy & the Lovers, has gone on to become the guitarist in the Birmingham, W. Midlands-based punk band, the Killjoys, on its only single, *Johnny Won't Get To Heaven*, on Raw Records in 1977. Rowland and the band's rhythm guitarist, Al Archer, have left the combo in November the same year to form their own band in the '60s-soul mould and now form Dexy's Midnight Runners (named after dexedrine, a widely-used pep pill, though the band itself abides by a strict "no drink or drugs" code), with Rowland, Archer, Saunders, Spooner, Patterson, Williams, J.B., and Bobby Junior on drums. Adopting a visual image taken from characters in the Robert De Niro-starring movie "Mean Streets", the group will be teamed with ex-Clash manager Bernie Rhodes the following year, who negotiates a recording deal with EMI, after the band has completed a nationwide tour with the Specials.

1980

Feb [9] Their debut release, *Dance Stance*, a Rowland comment on anti-Irish prejudice, makes UK #40.
May [3] Horn-laden *Geno*, a tribute to '60s UK soul singer Geno Washington, featuring Mick Talbot on keyboards, tops the UK chart.
July [20] Their "Intense Emotion Revue" tour ends at the Metro Marquee, Ashington, Northumberland.
[26] The band's debut album, ***Searching For The Young Soul Rebels***, hits UK #6. It is only released after Rowland had seized the master tapes from its producer, Pete Wingfield, and refused to return them until more favorable contract terms were agreed.
Aug [2] *There There My Dear* hits UK #7. (Rowland will be given a suspended prison sentence after a fight with members of another band during the filming of the single's promo video.)
Sept [25] The group begins an extensive tour of Europe.
Oct *Keep It Part Two*, released as a single at Rowland's insistence but against the wishes of the rest of the band and EMI, who protest about its uncommerciality, fails to chart and acrimony breaks out in the band's ranks.
Nov [7] The band splits into two: Rowland and Patterson remain as the nucleus of Dexy's Midnight Runners and recruit Micky Billingham (keyboards), Steve Wynne (bass), Billy Adams (guitar), Paul Spears (tenor sax), Brian Maurice (alto sax) and ex-Secret Affair Seb Shelton (drums) while the others leave to form the Bureau.

1981

Mar [28] *Plan B*, recorded by the new lineup, but released unwillingly by EMI during rock-bottom relations between the uncompromising Rowland and the label, peaks at UK #58. The band will leave EMI shortly afterwards.
Aug [8] Now signed to Phonogram's Mercury label, the Tony Visconti-produced *Show Me* reaches UK #16.
Oct Bass player Wynne leaves and is replaced by Giorgio Kilkenny. *Liars A To E*, an eccentric single with a string accompaniment, is released.
Nov The band appears at the Old Vic Theatre, London, in "The Projected Passion Review" and gains positive reviews from a press previously alienated by Rowland.

1982

Mar The group takes a new direction with a fusion of its traditional soul style with Irish folk, and adds a three-piece fiddle section comprising Helen O'Hara (b. Nov. 5, 1956), Steve Brennan and Roger MacDuff, which shares billing on records as the Emerald Express. The visual image also changes: the original "Mean Streets" look and the more recent anoraks, balaclavas and sports gear are discarded for dungarees and gypsy-like accoutrements.
[27] *The Celtic Soul Brothers*, resulting from the new collaboration, makes UK #45.
June Surviving original group member Patterson leaves, followed by the two sax players, who feel their role in the new music is too insignificant.
Aug [7] *Come On Eileen* hits UK #1, where it will remain for four weeks, and sells over a million copies in the UK, as its parent album, ***Too-Rye-Ay***, hits UK #2.
Oct [9] Their revival of Van Morrison's *Jackie Wilson Said* hits UK #5, credited to Kevin Rowland & Dexy's Midnight Runners which, Rowland explains, is a basic nucleus of himself, Adams and Shelton, augmented by hired musicians in various combinations, where necessary. When the band plays the hit on BBC1-TV's "Top Of The Pops", an apparent misunderstanding on the part of the TV production staff leads to the display of a large photo of darts player Jocky Wilson as a studio backdrop, instead of the intended Jackie Wilson picture.
Dec [25] *Let's Get This Straight (From The Start)/Old* reaches UK #17.

1983

Feb [8] *Come On Eileen* wins the Best British Single category at the second annual BRIT Awards, at London's Grosvenor House Hotel.
Mar [26] ***Geno***, an EMI compilation, makes UK #79.
Apr [16] A new version of *The Celtic Soul Brothers*, giving Rowland lead billing, reaches UK #20. A tour by the augmented band follows, after which the group splits up, as the nucleus musicians take a hiatus.
[23] *Come On Eileen* tops the US chart for one week, replacing Michael Jackson's *Billie Jean*, and is itself replaced by Jackson's *Beat It*, as the parent album, ***Too-Rye-Ay***, reaches US #14.
May [5] *Come On Eileen* wins the Best Selling A-side category at the 28th annual Ivor Novello Awards luncheon, at London's Grosvenor House Hotel.
June [11] US follow-up, *The Celtic Soul Brothers*, peaks at US #86.

1985

Sept After a long silence, ***Don't Stand Me Down*** reaches UK #22, though, at Rowland's insistence, no single is extracted.
Nov [1] The group begins a ten-date "Park Street South" UK tour at the Playhouse, Edinburgh, Scotland, after a six-night warm-up at the Paris Olympia, Paris, France. The tour, which will end at the Dominion Theatre, London, is not well received and the band splits again afterwards.

1986

Dec After three years out of the UK Singles chart, the band (now basically a solo Rowland) returns with *Because Of You*, the theme tune to BBC1-TV's "Brush Strokes" comedy series, which reaches UK #13.

1988

May Rowland returns as a soloist (though still signed to Mercury and billed as Kevin Rowland of Dexy's Midnight Runners) with *Walk Away* and ***The Wanderer***.

1991

Apr Rowland declares bankruptcy, with debts of over £100,000. A building society reclaims his £250,000 home in West Hampstead. (He will engineer a comeback with Patterson, having met up with him again after time apart. They begin work on a new album, ***Manhood***, and will make their first TV appearance since 1985, on C4-TV's "Saturday Zoo" on March 27th, 1993.)
June [22] ***The Very Best Of Dexy's Midnight Runners***, comprising hit highlights from the band's association with both Mercury and EMI, reaches UK #12.

1994

Nov [20] The **News Of The World** runs a story that Rowland is on the dole and has been checked in to Thurston House, a drug rehab clinic run by the Chemical Dependency Centre charity.

NEIL DIAMOND

1962

At New York University as a pre-med major and on a fencing scholarship, Diamond (b. Jan. 24, 1941, Brooklyn, New York, NY), drops out six months before graduation to become an apprentice songwriter at a small publishing company, Sunbeam Music, earning $50 a week. He has become interested in songwriting as a teenager while at Erasmus High School (where Barbra Streisand is a fellow student and singer in the school's choral society), when folk singer Pete Seeger visits his winter holiday group at Surprise Lake camp. He has subsequently graduated from the Abraham Lincoln High School two years after Neil Sedaka, and teamed with friend Jack Parker as an Everly Brothers-style duo, Neil & Jack, cut two non-charting singles, *What Will I Do* (1960) and *I'm Afraid* (1961) for the small New York label Duel Records.

1965

After several "production line" songwriting jobs, he sets up on his own in a tiny Manhattan office above a jazz club, releasing the one-off solo single, *Clown Town*, for CBS/Columbia Records. He continues to perform as well as write, mainly in Greenwich Village coffee houses, where he is seen by songwriters Jeff Barry and Ellie Greenwich, who, impressed by his style and material, sign him to their writing and publishing organization.

1966

Feb With Diamond's songs starting to earn royalties with hitmaking acts - Jay & the Americans reach US #18 with *Sunday And Me*; Cliff Richard records *Just Another Guy* (the B-side of his UK #1 hit, *The Minute You're Gone*) - and further songs cut by Jimmy Clanton, Bobby Vinton and the Angels among others, Barry and Greenwich arrange an audition with Atlantic Records which recommends Diamond to Bert Berns at the Atlantic-distributed New York label Bang Records, to whom he signs with Barry and Greenwich as his producers.
July [2] His Bang debut, the introspective *Solitary Man*, peaks at US #55.
Oct [15] *Cherry Cherry* is his first major hit, at US #6.
Nov Its parent album, ***The Feel Of Neil Diamond***, peaks at US #137.
Dec [17] *I Got The Feelin' (Oh No No)* makes US #16.
[31] The Monkees' follow-up to their US chart-topping debut, the Diamond-penned *I'm A Believer* (placed with them by Jeff Barry), with advance orders of 1,051,280 on the day of release, tops the US chart for the first of seven weeks and heads the UK chart for four, selling an additional 750,000 copies in Britain to add to total US sales of over three million.

1967

Mar [4] *You Got To Me* reaches US #18.
Apr [29] The Monkees hit US #2 and UK #3 with

another Diamond song, *A Little Bit Me, A Little Bit You*, another multi-million seller.
May [27] *Girl, You'll Be A Woman Soon* hits US #10. Although Diamond's records are not yet charting in the UK, his songs are: Lulu's cover of one of his B-sides, *The Boat That I Row*, hits UK #6, while Cliff Richard's double A-side, *I'll Come Running* and *I Got The Feelin' (Oh No No)* reaches UK #26.
Aug [26] The gospel-influenced *Thank The Lord For The Night Time* reaches US #13.
Oct ***Just For You*** makes US #80.
Nov [18] *Kentucky Woman* reaches US #22.

1968

Feb [3] His revival of Gary "U.S." Bonds' *New Orleans*, his first non-original single, peaks at US #51.
Apr [20] *Red Red Wine*, revived later as an international hit by UB40, peaks at US #62. Diamond leaves Bang, partly through frustration over its refusal to issue *Shilo* as a single, which he considers his best song to date, and signs to MCA Records' new Uni label, moving from New York to Los Angeles, CA, in the process.
June [1] His first Uni release, the autobiographical *Brooklyn Roads*, taken from ***Velvet Gloves And Spit*** and produced by Chip Taylor, makes US #58. One of the other songs on the album, the anti-drug but naive *Pot Smoker's Song*, alienates him from the drug-tolerant rock mainstream of the late '60s (and Uni removes the cut from re-pressings of the album).
Aug [3] *Two-Bit Manchild* peaks at US #66. Diamond makes a guest appearance in the CBS-TV detective series "Mannix".
Sept Bang label compilation album, ***Greatest Hits***, reaches US #100.
Nov [23] *Sunday Sun* peaks at US #68.
Dec Diamond records at American Sound Studios in Memphis, TN, immediately prior to Elvis Presley using the complex.

1969

Apr [26] *Brother Love's Traveling Salvation Show* reaches US #22, while ***Brother Love's Traveling Salvation Show***, on Uni, makes US #82.
Aug [16] *Sweet Caroline* hits US #4 and is Diamond's first million-plus seller.
Dec [27] *Holly Holy*, his second million-seller, hits US #6.

1970

Jan ***Touching You, Touching Me*** reaches US #30.
Mar [7] His cover of Buffy Saint-Marie's *Until It's Time For You To Go*, extracted from the album, makes US #53.
Apr [25] Bang Records issues the disputed *Shilo* to rival Diamond's current material, peaking at US #24.
May [30] Percussive, African-styled *Soolaimon*, a foretaste of Diamond's *African Trilogy* suite, makes US #30.
Sept [12] *Solitary Man*, reissued by Bang, reaches US #21.
Oct [10] *Cracklin' Rosie* is Diamond's first US chart-topper (for one week), and his third million-seller. ***Gold***, his first live album, recorded at the Troubadour in Hollywood, CA, hits US #10, while ***Shilo***, a Bang assemblage of early tracks, makes US #52.
Dec *Cracklin' Rosie* hits UK #3. ***Tap Root Manuscript***, which includes the experimental *African Trilogy*, reaches US #13.
[19] Diamond's early revival of the Hollies' *He Ain't Heavy He's My Brother* reaches US #20, and another Bang reissue, *Do It*, originally the B-side of *Solitary Man*, makes US #36.

1971

Mar *Sweet Caroline*, reissued in Britain as the follow-up to *Cracklin' Rosie*, hits UK #8, as ***Do It***, another Bang compilation, makes US #100.
Apr ***Tap Root Manuscript*** and ***Gold*** chart simultaneously in the UK, making #19 and #23 respectively.
May [8] The autobiographical *I Am ... I Said* (which Diamond will later claim was his hardest major song to write) hits US and UK #4 and is another domestic million-seller.
June [19] Its B-side, *Done Too Soon*, concerning prominent names who died young, peaks at US #65.
July [31] Diamond's own version of *I'm A Believer*, reissued by Bang, makes US #51.
Dec [18] *Stones* reaches US #14, as its parent album, ***Stones***, climbs to US #11.

1972

Jan ***Stones*** reaches UK #18.
Mar [16] Diamond performs at London's Royal Albert Hall, during a UK tour.
July [1] *Song Sung Blue* tops the US chart for one week and is another million-seller (also climbing to UK #14).
Aug ***Moods*** hits US #5 and UK #7.
[24] A concert at Los Angeles' Greek Theatre is recorded for the live album, ***Hot August Night***. (The ten-show sellout grosses $278,923, setting a new house record.)
Oct [5] Having just played two performances at the Grand Ole Opry in Nashville, TN, Diamond begins a 20-night series of sellout concerts, grossing $266,698, at New York's Winter Garden Theater, after which he announces he will take a break from live work to spend time with his family and friends. (This sabbatical will last for more than three years.)
[7] *Play Me* reaches US #11.
Dec [30] *Walk On Water*, taken from ***Moods***, reaches US #17, his last release on Uni, which is absorbed by its parent MCA label.

1973

Jan Live double album, ***Hot August Night***, hits US #5 during a 78-week run, and reaches UK #32.
Mar Double compilation album, ***Double Gold***, another Bang anthology, makes US #36.
May [5] A live version of *Cherry Cherry*, taken from ***Hot August Night***, reaches US #31.
June His MCA contract having expired, Diamond signs to CBS/Columbia Records in a ten-album deal negotiated with label boss Clive Davis, guaranteeing the star $5 million.
[20] Diamond sings *Cherry Cherry* on ABC-TV's "American Bandstand 20th Anniversary".
Aug [25] *The Long Way Home*, originally the B-side of *I Thank The Lord For The Night Time*, peaks at US #91.
Sept ***Rainbow*** makes US #35.
[22] *The Last Thing On My Mind* peaks at US #56.
Dec [1] *Be*, his first CBS/Columbia single, and taken from his soundtrack for the movie "Jonathan Livingston Seagull", makes US #34.
Dec Soundtrack album, ***Jonathan Livingston Seagull***, hits US #2.

1974

Jan [12] ***Hot August Night*** makes UK #32.
Feb [16] ***Jonathan Livingston Seagull*** reaches UK #35.
Mar [2] Diamond wins the Album Of Best Original Score Written For A Motion Picture category for ***Jonathan Livingston Seagull*** at the 16th annual Grammy Awards. (His score will also snare a Golden Globe trophy.)
[9] ***Rainbow*** makes UK #39.
[30] *Skybird*, from the film soundtrack, peaks at US #75.
July [13] Compilation album, ***His 12 Greatest Hits***, on MCA, reaches US #29 and will make UK #13 on the 27th.
Nov [16] ***Serenade***, produced by Tom Catalano, reaches UK #11 and will hit US #3.
[23] Extracted *Longfellow Serenade*, Diamond's first US Top 10 single for over two years, hits #5.

1975

Mar [1] *I've Been This Way Before* makes US #34.

1976

Jan Diamond makes his first concert appearance since October 1972, when he begins a tour of Australia and New Zealand.
June [30] Diamond has a minor drug bust when police, entering his California home on a search warrant (ostensibly checking a report of intruders), find less than one ounce of marijuana. (He gives the attendant police copies of his new album ***Beautiful Noise***.)
July [4] He gives his first US live performance after his lay-off, at the new Aladdin Theater For The Performing Arts in Las Vegas, NV.
[17] ***Beautiful Noise***, produced by friend and near neighbor, the Band's Robbie Robertson, hits UK #10.
Aug [7] *If You Know What I Mean*, the lead-off single from the new album, reaches US #11.
[14] ***Beautiful Noise*** hits US #4, Diamond's first million-selling album.
[21] *If You Know What I Mean* makes UK #35.
Oct [2] *Don't Think ... Feel*, with Dr. John adding Hammond organ, makes US #43.
[30] MCA compilation, ***And The Singer Sings His Song***, peaks at US #102.
Nov [13] The extracted title song, *Beautiful Noise*, reaches UK #13.
[25] Diamond appears in an all-star guest line-up in the Band's "Last Waltz" farewell concert at the Winterland Ballroom, San Francisco, CA, which is filmed (for later cinema release as "The Last Waltz") by Martin Scorsese. Diamond sings *Dry Your Eyes*, written with Robertson, and joins an all-star cast in *I Shall Be Released*.

1977

Feb [21] Diamond stars in an NBC-TV special, taped at a Greek Theatre concert in front of a celebrity-filled audience in September 1976.
Apr [9] A second live double album, ***Love At The Greek***, again recorded at the Greek Theatre and produced by Robertson, hits US #8, another million-seller.
June Diamond performs at the London Palladium during current UK dates.
Aug [6] ***Love At The Greek*** hits UK #3.
Dec [24] *Desiree* makes UK #39.

1978

Jan [28] ***I'm Glad You're Here With Me Tonight***, produced by Bob Gaudio, reaches UK #16.
Feb [11] *Desiree* reaches US #16.
[18] ***I'm Glad You're Here With Me Tonight*** hits US #6, selling over a million.
Dec [2] His ballad duet with Barbra Streisand, *You Don't Bring Me Flowers*, tops the US chart, returning to the pinnacle after dropping to #3 after its first week at #1, and sells over a million. (Written for a Norman Lear TV show "All That Glitters", it was recorded by the duo and produced by Gaudio after CBS/Columbia heard of the spliced "duet" of their individual versions, in the same key, played by Gary Guthrie, a DJ at WAKY in Louisville, KY, which had a huge listener response.)
[9] Compilation album, ***20 Golden Greats***, a UK-originated anthology of Uni/MCA material, hits UK #2 and stays charted for six months.
[23] *You Don't Bring Me Flowers* hits UK #5.

1979

Jan [20] ***You Don't Bring Me Flowers***, which includes the duet, reaches UK #15.
[27] ***You Don't Bring Me Flowers***, produced by Gaudio, hits US #4, and sells over a million.
Mar [24] *Forever In Blue Jeans* reaches US #20.
Apr [21] *Forever In Blue Jeans* reaches UK #16.
June [16] *Say Maybe* peaks at US #55. Diamond begins work on a remake of the 1927 Al Jolson movie "The Jazz Singer", taking the lead role opposite Sir Laurence Olivier and providing the soundtrack songs. His performance will guarantee Diamond a place in movie history, as he receives the largest salary ever paid for a debut film role.

1980

Feb [9] ***September Morn***, again produced by Gaudio, reaches UK #14.
[16] ***September Morn***, another million-seller, hits US #10.

[27] Diamond and Streisand perform *You Don't Bring Me Flowers*, which collected two nominations, live at the 22nd annual Grammy Awards ceremony.
Mar [1] The extracted title track, *September Morn*, written with Gilbert Becaud, reaches US #17.
Apr [26] *The Good Lord Loves You* peaks at US #67.
Dec [27] *Love On The Rocks*, from ***The Jazz Singer***, reaches UK #17.

1981

Jan [10] *Love On The Rocks* hits US #2, and again secures a gold disc.
Feb [7] Soundtrack album, ***The Jazz Singer***, released (like its spin-off singles, for contractual reasons) on Capitol Records, hits US #3 and is a million-seller. (The film is successful, though not a blockbuster, much of its popularity a result of the hit songs and album.)
[21] *Hello Again*, taken from the movie soundtrack, peaks at UK #51.
Mar [7] MCA compilation, ***Love Songs***, makes US #43.
[21] ***The Jazz Singer*** hits UK #3 during a two year-plus chart tenure.
[28] *Hello Again*, taken from the movie soundtrack, hits US #6.
June [13] *America*, the third and last extract from ***The Jazz Singer***, hits US #8. With its patriotic immigrant theme, it becomes Diamond's most played and requested song in the US.
Dec [19] ***On The Way To The Sky*** makes UK #39.
[26] ***The Jazz Singer*** wins the Top Soundtrack Album category in **Billboard**'s The Year In Music.

1982

Jan [9] *Yesterday's Songs* reaches US #11.
[16] ***On The Way To The Sky*** reaches US #17, and is another million-seller.
Mar [27] Its extracted title track, *On The Way To The Sky*, reaches US #27.
June [26] Compilation album, ***12 Greatest Hits, Volume II***, a collection of both CBS/Columbia and Capitol material, reaches UK #32.
July [3] *Be Mine Tonight* makes US #35.
[10] ***His Twelve Greatest Hits, Volume II*** makes US #48.
Nov [13] *Heartlight*, inspired by the movie "E.T." and written with Burt Bacharach and Carole Bayer Sager, hits US #5.
[20] ***Heartlight***, mostly written and produced by Bacharach and Sager, makes UK #43.
[27] *Heartlight* makes UK #47 as its parent album, ***Heartlight***, hits US #9, yet another million-seller.

1983

Feb [19] *I'm Alive*, penned with David Foster, makes US #35.
May [21] *Front Page Story*, another collaboration with Bacharach and Sager, peaks at US #65, as Diamond plays five sellout dates at the Joe Louis Arena, Detroit, MI, grossing $1,394,152 during his current US tour.
July ***Classics - The Early Years***, a compilation of Bang material released on Columbia, makes US #171.
Dec ***The Very Best Of Neil Diamond***, a K-tel TV-advertised compilation, makes UK #33.

1984

Mar Diamond is inducted into the Songwriters Hall of Fame at the annual ceremony held in New York.
Aug ***Primitive***, variously produced by Diamond, Denny Diante and Richard Perry, hits UK #7.
Sept [8] *Turn Around* peaks at US #62, as its parent album, ***Primitive***, makes US #35.

1986

May ***Headed For The Future***, variously helmed and written by Bacharach and Sager, Diamond, David Foster, Maurice White and Stevie Wonder, makes UK #36.
June [28] Its title cut, *Headed For The Future*, stops at US #53 as ***Headed For The Future*** reaches US #20, and is another million-seller.
July Diamond is awarded the Gold Ticket for playing to over 100,000 fans at New York's Madison Square Garden.

1987

Jan [25] Diamond sings the American National Anthem for "Super Bowl XXI", between the New York Giants and the Denver Broncos, at the Rose Bowl, Pasadena, CA.
Nov [28] His third live double album, ***Hot August II***, recorded again at the Greek Theatre, peaks at UK #74, and will go on to make US #59.
Dec [18-20] Diamond finishes a US tour at the Miami Arena, Miami, FL.

1989

Nov [18] ***The Best Years Of Our Lives***, produced by David Foster, makes UK #42, having already made US #46 and been awarded platinum status.
June [28] Diamond begins ten sellout concerts at the Great Western Forum, Inglewood, CA, grossing $3,498,000.
Oct [13] He begins a European tour in Dublin, Eire, set to end at the Wembley Stadium, Wembley, Middx., on November 22nd. (H.R.H. Princess Diana is scheduled to attend the November 15th concert at Wembley.)

1990

Jan [22] Diamond is honored with the Award Of Merit at the 17th American Music Awards, at Los Angeles' Shrine Auditorium.

1991

Sept [20] He guests on NBC-TV's "The Tonight Show".
Oct [12] ***Lovescape***, variously produced by Peter Asher, Diamond, Val Garay, Humberto Gatica, Albert Hammond and Don Was, makes US #44.
Nov [16] ***Lovescape*** reaches UK #36.
Dec [17-18] His "Love In The Round" tour opens with two sellout shows at the Fort Worth/Tarrant County Convention Center Arena, Fort Worth, TX.

1992

Mar [11-16, 22-23] Diamond performs before a total audience of 142,570 during eight sellout shows at the Great Western Forum, Inglewood. (At the show on the 16th, he donates $25,000 to the Magic Johnson Foundation from sales of souvenir books at the concerts.)
Apr [13] He begins a 23-date sellout tour of Australia, where he is making his first visit in 16 years, at the Sydney Entertainment Centre, Sydney.
July [16-19, 21-22, 24-25] Diamond plays eight sellout shows at the Wembley Arena, Wembley, grossing £2,114,971.
[25] ***The Greatest Hits 1966-1992***, a deceptively part-live hits collection, tops the UK chart, where it will stay for three weeks.
Aug [13-16, 20-21] He plays six sellout shows at New York's Madison Square Garden. (Diamond will be the second-highest grossing act of the year in the US, being seen by more than 1.5 million people, paying a total in excess of $40 million.)
Nov [21] *Morning Has Broken* debuts at its UK #36 peak.
[28] "Neil Diamond's Christmas Special" airs on HBO-TV, as ***The Christmas Album*** bows at its UK #50 peak.
Dec [19] NBC-TV airs Diamond's "Christmas In Washington" special, as ***The Christmas Album***, helmed by Peter Asher, hits US #8.
[26] ***The Greatest Hits 1966-1992*** makes US #90.

1993

Jan Having spent twenty years with Columbia Records, Diamond signs a new long-term recording (six albums) and publishing contract with the label's parent corporation, Sony Music Entertainment.
Feb [16] His "Love In The Round" tour continues, at the Charlotte Coliseum, Charlotte, NC. The record-breaking tour will end on June 19th at the Carrier Dome, Syracuse, NY.
Sept [27] Diamond guests on CBS-TV's "Late Show With David Letterman".
Oct [9] ***Up On The Roof - Songs Of The Brill Building*** debuts at its UK #28 peak, and will do the same on the 16th in the US.
Dec [20] Diamond guests on NBC-TV's "The Tonight Show".
[21] He finishes his US tour at the Great Western Forum, a bill grossing $2,462,488.

1994

July [23] Performance album ***Live In America*** makes US #93.
Oct [26] His wife, Marcia, files for divorce in Los Angeles Superior Court, citing irreconcilable differences.
Nov [26] Frank Sinatra's ***Duets II***, which sees Ol' Blue Eyes duet with Diamond on *The House I Love In*, reaches US #29.
Dec [2] Diamond guests on "The Tonight Show".
[22] He takes part in CBS-TV's "Opryland's Country Christmas".
[24] ***The Christmas Album Volume II*** makes US #51.

1995

June Diamond performs at graduation ceremonies at New York University. (During the year, he also works with Sager on music for Steven Spielberg's forthcoming animated feature, "Balto".)

1996

Feb [12] Diamond tapes "Under A Tennessee Moon", previewing his new country-oriented album, at Nashville's Ryman Auditorium, TN, set for broadcast on the 24th on ABC-TV.
[14] He appears on CBS-TV's "Late Show With David Letterman".
[17] ***Tennessee Moon***, its songs co-written with the likes of Harlan Howard, Gary Burr and Hal Ketchum, and featuring a duet with Waylon Jennings, reaches UK #12 in its week of entry.
Mar [16] ***Tennessee Moon*** reaches US #14.
[29] Diamond begins a nine-date Australian tour at the Entertainment Centre, Sydney, New South Wales, set to end on April 19th at the Burswood Dome, Perth, Western Australia.
May [11-12] He now embarks on the UK leg of his tour at Manchester's Nynex Arena, set to end June 4th at Sheffield Arena.
June [20] Diamond performs at the FleetCenter, Boston at the start of a US tour through the summer.

THE DIAMONDS

Dave Somerville (lead vocals); **Mike Douglas** (baritone vocal); **Evan Fisher** (tenor vocal); **John Felton** (bass vocal)

1954

Stan Fisher (lead), Ted Kowalski (tenor), Phil Levitt (baritone) and Bill Reed (bass) form the original Diamonds while students at the University of Toronto in Toronto, ON, Canada. Auditioning for the TV show "Now Is Your Choice", they meet radio technician Somerville, who joins immediately when hearing them harmonize in an empty studio room. After weeks of rehearsal, they make their first live appearance at St. Aquinas Church, sans Fisher who is unable to make the gig.

1955

Aug Having crossed the border with manager Nat Goodman, who has secured them an audition with Coral Records in New York, the group, with Douglas having replaced Levitt, now makes its first recordings. After two misses, *Black Denim Trousers* and *Smooch Me*, they return to Canada, before heading for Cleveland, OH., where they audition a cappella, for Bill Randle, who sets up a new contract with Mercury Records. After their first single, *The Stroll*, Kowalski and Reed leave, to be replaced by Californians Evan Fisher and Felton.

1956

Apr [26] The Diamonds' cover of Frankie Lymon & the Teenagers' *Why Do Fools Fall In Love?* reaches US #16, the third most successful of three US Top 20 versions (Lymon hits #7, while a treatment by Gale Storm makes #15).
May [31] Their version of the Willows' *Church Bells May Ring* this time eclipses the original (at #62), reaching US #20.
Aug [2] The Diamonds' treatment of the Clovers' *Love Love Love* climbs to the same US chart peak as the original (#30) almost simultaneously.
Oct [4] *Ka-Ding-Dong/Soft Summer Breeze*, a double-sided release, reaches US #35 and #34 respectively (the B-side on Oct [11]). Another cover of *Ka-Ding-Dong*, by the Hilltoppers, makes US #38, while the original by the G-Clefs peaks at #53. (There is also a bigger US hit version of *Soft Summer Breeze*, by Eddie Heywood (#12).)

1957

Apr [11] *Little Darlin'* is their biggest and most enduring hit, selling over a million and hitting US #2 for eight weeks, during a six-month chart spell. The original version by the Gladiolas makes US #41.
July *Little Darlin'* hits UK #3, and proves to be their only UK hit.
Oct [5] *Zip Zip* reaches US #45.
Nov [16] *Silhouettes* hits US #10, while losing out on the Rays' original, which hits #3.

1958

Feb [8] *The Stroll* is their second-biggest seller and hits US #5, popularizing the dance of the same name.
May [24] *High Sign*, a rare Diamonds original, stops at US #38.
Aug [2] Another non-cover, *Kathy-0*, makes US #45.
Nov [29] *Walking Along* reaches US #29.

1959

Mar [21] *She Say (Oom Dooby Doom)* is their last US Top 20 hit, peaking at #18. As imitators of the '50s black doo-wop vocal tradition, their records fall from chart success as the vocal-group sound rapidly loses commercial favor at the close of the decade.

1961

Aug [26] Following several personnel changes, and after two years of playing in nightclubs and lounges, the group returns with a revival of the Danleers' 1958 hit ballad, *One Summer Night*, which reaches US #22, after which the Diamonds will split.

1969

Somerville joins the Four Preps, and will form a duo in 1971 with the group's founder Bruce Belland. Subsequently teaming with Danny Cox, to sing on Allen Ludden's "Gallery" TV show, Somerville then joins Keith Barber and Gail Jensen as W.W. Fancy.

1989

Following an April 27th, 1973 reunion to appear on NBC-TV in a "Midnight Special" show devoted to oldie hitmakers, alongside Little Richard, Little Anthony & the Imperials and Jerry Lee Lewis, and still performing on the nostalgia circuit, the latest Diamonds cast embarks on "The Royalty Of Doo-Wop" US tour with the Belmonts, the Chiffons, the Flamingos and the Silhouettes. (Original member Felton died on May 18th, 1982.)

BO DIDDLEY

1951

Diddley (b. Otha Ellas Bates, Dec. 30, 1928, McComb, MS, but given the surname McDaniel in infancy, on adoption by his mother's first cousin, sharecropper Gussie McDaniel), who has learnt to play the violin before taking up the guitar in his teens (first bought for him by his sister Lucille), begins playing regularly as an electric blues/R&B act (inspired to play the blues after hearing John Lee Hooker's *Boogie Chillen*) at the 708 club on the south side of Chicago, IL, where he has lived since the age of eight. He has already been a street-corner performer since his schooldays, as part of the Hipsters with Roosevelt Jackson, Samuel Daniel and Jerome Green, who have name-changed to the Langley Avenue Jive Cats (Diddley lives on Langley Avenue as does Jackson), with the addition of Clifton James and harmonica player Billy Boy Arnold. (Diddley gained his professional moniker from the nickname given to him in his teens whilst training as a Golden Gloves boxer.)

1955

Mar [2] Diddley, with Green on maracas, Frank Kirkland on drums, Lester Davenport on harmonica and Otis Spann on piano, demos *Bo Diddley*, *I'm A Man* and *You Don't Love Me*.
June Diddley is signed to Chess Records' subsidiary label, Checker, and debuts with the demo which had secured them their deal, the double A-sided *Bo Diddley/I'm A Man*, which hits #2 on the US R&B chart but fails to cross over to the pop market. (*Bo Diddley* is borrowed from the 1953 R&B hit, *Hambone*, by the Hambone Kids.)
Aug [20] He appears at the Apollo Theater, Harlem, New York, NY, with a band which will play with him regularly throughout the '50s: Spann on piano, Arnold on harmonica, Kirkland on drums and Green on bass, maracas and general onstage banter with Diddley.
Nov [20] He appears on CBS-TV's "The Ed Sullivan Show" in a 15-minute segment with other R&B artists, and plays *Bo Diddley*, despite having rehearsed *16 Tons*.

1956

June His first UK release is the EP *Rhythm & Blues With Bo Diddley*, which arouses little interest outside esoteric R&B circles.
July *Who Do You Love*, subsequently another of his most-covered numbers, is released in the US.

1958

Dec [25] Alan Freed's "Christmas Rock & Roll Spectacular", in which Diddley is one of the featured artists, opens a ten-day run at Loew's Theater, Manhattan, New York. (During the year, Diddley moves to Washington, DC, and designs his rectangular-shaped guitar which will become his trademark instrument of choice.)

1959

Aug [1] *Crackin' Up* is his first US pop-chart entry, peaking at #62.
Oct [31] *Say Man*, a semi-comic jive talk repartée between Diddley and Jerome Green over an archetypal Diddley rhythm track, is his biggest US hit, reaching #20.

1960

Mar [26] *Road Runner*, another much-covered original, peaks at US #75.

1962

Sept [29] *You Can't Judge A Book By The Cover* makes US #48.
Dec ***Bo Diddley*** peaks at US #117 - the only US album entry of his career.

1963

Sept [22] Diddley arrives in London for a UK tour and immediately records a spot for ITV's "Thank Your Lucky Stars".
[29] He begins his first UK tour (with "The Duchess", a guitarist by the name of Norma Jean Wofford, whom he heard play in a support act on a bill in Pittsburgh, PA, on guitar and back-up vocals, and Green), jointly supporting the Everly Brothers with the Rolling Stones, who are also on their first UK tour, and drop all of Diddley's songs from their own act out of respect, at the New Victoria Theatre, London. The tour will end at the Hammersmith Odeon, London, on November 3rd. While in London, Diddley will also play the capital's only R&B club, the Scene, three times.
Oct *Pretty Thing* makes UK #34, while ***Bo Diddley*** reaches #11, both on the strength of his tour success.
[9] ***Bo Diddley Is A Gunslinger*** reaches UK #20.
[23-24] Mid-tour, Diddley tapes radio and TV appearances for BBC's "Saturday Club" and ITV's "Scene At 6.30".
Nov [30] ***Bo Diddley Rides Again*** reaches UK #19.

1964

Feb ***Bo Diddley's Beach Party*** reaches UK #13.
June *Mona (I Need You Baby)* makes UK #42.
Sept He releases the album ***Two Great Guitars***, on which he duets with Chuck Berry on two lengthy guitar jams.

1965

Mar *Hey Good Lookin'* makes UK #39.
Sept [25] Diddley begins a 21-date UK tour at the Imperial Theatre, Nelson, Lancs.
Oct [2] He fails to show for a gig at the Birdcage, Portsmouth, Hants., after his car breaks down. 2,000 fans have their money returned.
Dec Diddley films a segment for the TNT Award Show, performing *Bo Diddley* and *Who Do You Love*, alongside Joan Baez, the Byrds, Ray Charles, Lovin' Spoonful, the Ronettes, Ike & Tina Turner, Roger Miller, Petula Clark and Donovan.

1967

Feb [11] *Ooh Baby* peaks at US #88 - his first US hit single for five years, but also his final one.
Apr [16] Diddley, on a UK tour, plays the Saville Theatre, London, supported by Ben E. King.
July [4-9] He performs at the Fillmore West, San Francisco, CA, sharing the bill with Big Brother & the Holding Company.
Nov [17-19] Diddley plays at the Avalon Ballroom, San Francisco. (The following year, Diddley will record the critically-acclaimed album ***Super Blues Band*** with Muddy Waters and Little Walter.)

1969

Sept [13] He performs at the "Rock'n'Roll Revival" concert, alongside Chuck Berry, Jerry Lee Lewis, Little Richard and John Lennon and the Plastic Ono Band, among others, at the Varsity Stadium, University of Toronto, Toronto, ON, Canada. (He will also be seen in D.A. Pennebaker's movie of the event, released in 1970 as "Sweet Toronto" and in revised form, in 1972, as "Keep On Rockin'".)

1970

June [6] Diddley tops the bill at "Hampden Scene '70" in Glasgow, Scotland, with Chuck Berry, Blue Mink, Radha Krishna Temple, Atomic Rooster, Taste, the Pretty Things, Beggars Opera and Spiggy Topes.
Oct [22-25] He performs at San Francisco's Fillmore West with Lightnin' Hopkins.

1971

June [11] Diddley appears in the sixth "1950s Rock & Roll Revival Concert" with a host of '50s and '60s rock legends, at New York's Madison Square Garden. (He will appear in a further half-dozen of these regular concerts over the next ten years.)
Oct ***Another Dimension*** attempts to set Diddley within the prevailing politically-aware lyrical trend, but his old fans are unimpressed.

1972

Aug [5] Diddley takes part in the first-ever "London Rock'n'Roll Revival Festival" at Wembley Stadium, Wembley, Middx., on a bill with Bill Haley, Little Richard, Jerry Lee Lewis, Gary Glitter, Wizzard, MC5, Billy Fury, Emile Ford and Heinz.

1973

July ***The London Bo Diddley Sessions*** is released, including six tracks recorded with UK musicians in

London (including Roy Wood of the Move and Wizzard). (Later in the year, Diddley is featured in the film "Let The Good Times Roll", along with contemporaries Fats Domino, Bill Haley, Little Richard and others.)

1976

Apr With the demise of the Checker label, and newly signed to RCA Records, Diddley releases ***The 20th Anniversary Of Rock'n'Roll***, featuring Joe Cocker, Alvin Lee, Leslie West, Elvin Bishop, Keith Moon, Billy Joel, Roger McGuinn and Carmine Appice. His career as rock'n'roll/R&B elder statesman continues, and he maintains a busy live performance schedule, both as a headliner and as a support artist.

1979

Jan [20] Never shying away from working with younger, emergent acts, he opens for the Clash on their first US tour.

1986

Having appeared in the 1980 Dan Aykroyd/Eddie Murphy movie "Trading Places", Diddley records the album ***Hey Bo Diddley*** live in concert, with Dick Heckstall-Smith's Mainsqueeze as his backing band, during a European tour.

1987

Jan [21] Diddley is inducted into the Rock and Roll Hall of Fame at the second annual induction dinner, at New York's Waldorf Astoria Hotel.
Sept [12] ***La Bamba*** movie soundtrack, featuring Diddley's *Who Do You Love?*, tops the US chart.
Nov [4] Diddley and Ron Wood, collectively known as the Gunslingers, open a North American tour at the Newport Music Hall, Columbus, OH, set to end on the 25th with a show at The Ritz, New York, which is recorded and will be released as ***Live At The Ritz*** on the JVC label, in August 1988. (The pair will also undertake a two-week tour of Japan the following March.)

1989

Jan [21] Diddley performs at the "Celebration for Young Americans" at President Bush's inauguration at the Washington Center, Washington, DC, with Dr. John, Willie Dixon and others.
Apr [27] He has his handprints and name set in stone at Sunset Boulevard's Rock Walk, Los Angeles, CA, with Willie Dixon.
July [11] A Bo Jackson Nike TV commercial, with Diddley saying "Bo, you don't know diddley", airs for the first time during Major League Baseball's All-Star game in the US. (The following year, Diddley will state: "You work your buns off all these years - going up and down the highway, riding those raggedly airplanes and stuff like that. Then I make a commercial with Bo Jackson and all I say is 'Bo, you don't know Diddley'. All of a sudden I'm back up at the top again. I ain't figured it out yet.")
Diddley releases ***Breakin' Through The B.S.*** on the Triple X label, through his own Bad Dad Productions, his first US studio album in 15 years.

1990

May [4] A US tour begins at the 21st annual "New Orleans Jazz & Heritage Festival", at the Fair Grounds Race Track, New Orleans, LA, set to end with five nights at Anton's club, Washington, on November 4th.

1991

Jan Diddley combines with Ben E. King and Doug Lazy to remake the Monotones' *Book Of Love*, featured in the movie of the same name.
Feb [14] Diddley headlines the opening of Fleetwood's, a blues club owned by Mick Fleetwood, on Santa Monica Boulevard, Santa Monica, CA.
Apr [27] He takes part in a blues festival at the St. Denis Theatre, Montreal, PQ, Canada.
June [4] Diddley participates in the "Celebrate The Soul Of American Music" at the Pantages Theatre, Los Angeles, to benefit the Thurgood Marshall Scholarship Fund.
[19] He plays at the Astoria Theatre, London, during a current UK tour.
Oct [15] Diddley performs on the opening night of "Guitar Legends", a five-concert series, as part of Expo '92, in Seville, Spain.

1992

Sept [1] He teams with Kentucky Fried Chicken to launch the "KFC Musical Feast" contest.
Oct [27] He files a lawsuit seeking $75,000 from the estate of his ex-manager, Martin Otelsberg whom he claims diddled him out of earnings for unauthorized personal expenses.
Nov [19] Diddley appears at the annual "Hopefest" blues concert at the Park West Theatre, Chicago, hosted by the Chicago Coalition For The Homeless.

1994

June A Los Angeles judge rules that Diddley was indeed cheated by his late manager Otelsberg, and orders his widow to pay Diddley $400,000. (Diddley will spend the summer touring the US with Chuck Berry.)
Nov [25] Diddley supports the Rolling Stones at Joe Robbie Stadium, Miami, FL, before a crowd of 55,935.

1996

Feb [29] 41 years after he recorded his first music, Diddley is honored with the Lifetime Achievement Award at the seventh annual Rhythm and Blues Foundation Pioneer Awards held at Los Angeles' Hollywood Palladium at which he also performs *Bo Diddley*. In his acceptance speech, the music veteran who has never been awarded a Grammy says: "It's about time I won something".
Apr Following his last two albums, 1993's ***This Should Not Be*** and ***The Mighty Bo Diddley*** in 1995, Diddley's latest set, the Mike Vernon-produced ***A Man Among Men***, is released by Atlantic Records (US), and features a host of talent who contribute in recognition of his influence, not least Keith Richards, Richie Sambora, Ron Wood, Jimmie Vaughan, Johnny "Guitar" Watson and Diddley's grandson, Philosopher G, rapping on *Kids Don't Do It*.

DIGABLE PLANETS

Butterfly (vocals); **Ladybug** (vocals); **Doodlebug** (DJ)

1989

The first version of hip-hop trio Digable Planets is formed by Butterfly (b. Ishmael Butler, July 3, 1969, Seattle, WA), who is musically influenced by '60s rap-poetry pioneers the Last Poets and his father's collection of Blue Note jazz records, with fellow students at New York, NY's City College, recruiting the first Ladybug (b. Katrina Lust) and DJ, Squibble the Termite (b. Michael Gabredikan). Naming the group after the notion that every individual is a separate planet, and fusing a hybrid sound of jazz samples with smooth hip-hop vocals, Butterfly subsequently enlists replacement performers Doodlebug (b. Craig Irving, Feb. 20, 1967, Philadelphia, PA) from the New York-based rap-poetry collective Dread Poets Society and his friend and second Ladybug, aka Mecca (b. Mary Ann Vieira, July 25, 1973, Washington, DC) in 1991, and signs the group to Elektra Records (via the Pendulum label) the following year.

1993

Feb [20] *Rebirth Of Slick (Cool Like Dat)*, sampling music by Art Blakey and already a US R&B #6 hit, makes UK #67.
[27] ***Reachin' (A New Refutation Of Time And Space)***, including further jazz samples from the likes of the Crusaders, Eddie Harris, the Last Poets and Sonny Rollins, debuts at its US #15 peak.
Mar [6] *Rebirth Of Slick (Cool Like Dat)* also reaches US #15.
[16] *Rebirth Of Slick (Cool Like Dat)* is certified gold by the RIAA.
[24] ***Reachin' (A New Refutation Of Time And Space)*** is certified gold by the RIAA.

1994

Mar [1] Digable Planets perform the nominated *Rebirth Of Slick* at the 36th annual Grammy Awards held at New York's Radio City Music Hall.
Oct [29] *9th Wonder (Blackitolism)* peaks at US #80.
Nov [5] ***Blow Out Comb*** debuts at its US #32 peak.

DINOSAUR JR.

J. Mascis (lead vocals, guitar); **Lou Barlow** (bass); **Murph** (drums)

1985

July Growing up in college town Amherst, MA, dentist's son and golf enthusiast Mascis (b. Donald Joseph Mascis, Dec. 10, 1965, Amherst) played in the Amherst Youth Orchestra before forming the hardcore punk outfit Deep Wound, for which he was drummer, in 1981 with guitarist Barlow (b. July 17, 1966, Northampton, MA), singer Charlie Nakajima and bassist Scott Helland (releasing one (US only) EP *I Saw It* on Radiobeat Records in 1983). With Mascis switching to guitar and Barlow to bass, Deep Wound has transformed into the short-lived Mogo's Flute before settling into the trio, initially just called Dinosaur, with Mascis' friend and ex-All White Jury drummer Murph (b. Emmett Murphy, Dec. 21, 1964). Recorded for $500 and released by local indie Homestead Records (where the band's manager Gerard is working), the group's debut album ***Dinosaur*** is now released, showcasing Mascis' Neil Young-recalling vocal style and rapid-fire waves of guitar. During the following year, with Mascis still attending college, the band will play a four-week US tour opening for Sonic Youth, before signing to hardcore US label SST Records for its follow-up set ***You're Living All Over Me*** (released in July 1987, with later copies emerging to credit Dinosaur Jr., to avoid confusion with another US band, the potentially litigious Dinosaurs).

1988

Oct Its demo having impressed UK indie Blast First Records boss Paul Smith, the label releases ***Bug*** which receives much praise from the alternative music press, not least for the extracted *Freak Scene* which tops the UK Independent singles chart and is hailed as an underground classic in the US. Squabbles between Mascis and Barlow come to head, however, with the latter leaving the band (and going on to form Sebadoh the following year which will sign to Sub Pop Records after two albums, in 1992).

1989

Feb While the band struggles to find a permanent new bassist (with the Screaming Trees' Donna Biddell standing in on an Australian tour), Dinosaur's Jr.'s raucous cover of the Cure's *Just Like Heaven* is released, becoming another Indie chart hit.
June Caroline Records releases the Neil Young tribute album ***The Bridge*** which includes the band's cover of *Lotta Love*. (With the group's line-up still uncertain, Mascis spends much of the following year producing the debut album for Buffalo Tom and contributing to Sonic Youth's ***Goo***, before signing with Warner Bros. imprint, blanco y negro.)

1991

Feb *The Wagon*, the only Dinosaur Jr. release to feature temporary members Don Fleming and Jay Spiegel, makes UK #49, its first release on blanco y negro.
Mar [30] Largely the solo work of Mascis with Murph only featured on three of its tracks, ***Green Mind*** debuts at its US #168 peak. (While Mascis will contribute

material to, and appear in, the forthcoming movie "Gas Food Lodging" during the summer, the group will perform at this year's "Reading Festival", Reading, Berks., before ending the year with a European tour having recruited permanent new bassist Mike Johnson (b. Michael Allen Johnson, Aug. 27, 1965).)

1992

Nov [14] Having spent much of the year recording a fifth album, its preview track, *Get Me* charts for a week at UK #44, its promo clip featuring an appearance by actor Matt Dillon.

1993

Jan [30] *Start Choppin'* bows at its UK #20 peak.
Feb [20] ***Where You Been*** enters at its UK #10 high, debuting at its US #50 peak a week later.
June [12] The extracted *Out There* bows at its UK #44 peak.

1994

Aug [27] *Feel The Pain*, written by Mascis while sitting in a chiropractor's waiting room, enters at its UK #25 high.
Sept [17] With Murph having departed the band (leaving Mascis to also play the drums), ***Without A Sound*** bows at its US #44 peak having already entered at its UK #24 pinnacle the previous week.

1995

Feb [11] *I Don't Think So* charts for a week at US #67.
May As the group's founder and mainstay, Mascis, who has recently bought a house in his hometown of Amherst, performs a series of solo acoustic dates in the UK. (Johnson will release his second solo album ***Year Of Mondays*** on TAG Recordings (US), the following February.)

1996

May Reprise releases ***Martin And Me***, by Mascis, an acoustic solo live set of the performer with his Martin guitar, including two covers, Carly Simon's *Anticipation* and Lynyrd Skynyrd's *Every Mother's Son*.

CELINE DION

1988

Apr [30] The youngest of 14 children who has grown up in a musical family, Dion (b. Mar. 30, 1968, Charlemagne, Quebec, PQ, Canada) has given her first public performance at the age of 5, and at 12 has recorded a demo which finds its way to Quebec-based music entrepreneur Rene Angelil. Taking her under his wing, Angelil will steer the young singer's career, initially remortgaging his house to finance the recording of her maiden album. Possessed with a powerful singing voice, Dion's international recognition begins with her winning the Gold Medal at the 1982 Yamaha World Song Festival in Tokyo, Japan, followed by her becoming the first Canadian to receive a gold disc in France in 1983 (for the 700,000-selling *D'Amour Ou D'Amite*). Recruited to perform for Switzerland, Dion now wins the 33rd annual Eurovision Song Contest held at the Royal Dublin Society, Dublin, Eire with *Ne Partez Pas Sans Moi*. Recording four French-speaking platinum-selling albums in Canada during the decade, the last of these, ***Des Mots Qui Sonnent*** will be recorded in France in 1990, to be released there and in Canada the following year, an album comprising her interpretations of the lyrics of French-Canadian pop writer Luc Plamondon.

1991

Mar [2] Having signed a major label deal with Epic Records in the US, her English-speaking debut, *Where Does My Heart Beat Now* hits US #4.
[3] Dion is named Female Vocalist Of The Year and ***Unison*** is acclaimed Album Of The Year at the 20th annual Juno Awards held in Toronto, ON, Canada, the first time that a French Canadian has won these categories.
[23] ***Unison***, her first English-speaking album variously produced by Chris Neil, David Foster and Andy Goldmark, makes US #74.
Aug [25] During a Canadian tour opening for Michael Bolton, Dion performs at the CNE, Toronto, on a bill grossing $396,063.
June [1] *(If There Was) Any Other Way*, written by Paul Bliss, reaches US #35.

1992

Mar [30] Still climbing the US chart, *Beauty And The Beast*, recorded with Peabo Bryson for the Disney movie of the same name, wins the Best Song Written For A Motion Picture Or Television category at the 65th annual Academy Awards held in Los Angeles, CA, while on the same night, Dion is once again named Female Vocalist Of The Year at the 21st annual Juno Awards.
Apr [18] *Beauty And The Beast*, hits US #9.
May [23] *Beauty And The Beast* also hits UK #9.
July [2] Her first US tour, again opening for Bolton, and set to close on August 13th at the Coca-Cola Star Lake Amphitheatre, Burgettstown, PA, bows at the Coca-Cola Starplex Amphitheatre, Dallas, TX, taking $292,174 at the box-office.
[11] *If You Asked Me To*, Dion's cover of Patti LaBelle's 1989 US #79 original, hits US #4.
[27] ***Celine Dion***, once again partly produced by Foster, reaches US #34.
Sept [29] Dion performs on US-TV's syndicated "Arsenio Hall Show".
Oct [3] *Nothing Broken But My Heart* reaches US #29.
Nov [14] *Love Can Move Mountains*, written by Diane Warren, debuts at its UK #46 peak.
Dec [8] Dion appears on NBC-TV's "The Tonight Show".

1993

Jan [2] *If You Asked Me To* makes UK #57.
[30] *Love Can Move Mountains* reaches US #36.
Feb [25] *Beauty And The Beast* is named Best Pop Performance, Duo Or Group With Vocal at the 35th annual Grammy Awards held at the Shrine Auditorium, Los Angeles.
Mar [12] ***Celine Dion*** is certified platinum by the RIAA.
[21] Dion hosts the 22nd annual Juno Awards held at the O'Keefe Centre for the Performing Arts, Toronto at which she also nabs four trophies including Female Vocalist Of The Year and Single Of The Year.
Apr [3] *Where Does My Heart Beat Now* charts for a week at UK #72.
Sept [25] *When I Fall In Love*, a duet remake of the Nat King Cole standard, recorded with British singer Clive Griffin and featured in the movie "Sleepless In Seattle", reaches US #23.

1994

Feb [6] The Disney Channel (US) broadcasts an hour-long "Celine Dion" special featuring live performances of her most popular work.
[12] *The Power Of Love*, Dion's cover of Jennifer Rush's 1985 UK #1, tops the US chart and hits UK #4.
[19] Dion participates in the "Jacksons Family Honors" held at the MGM Grand Hotel in Las Vegas, NV.
Mar [5] Marking a switch in labels to Epic's 550 Music imprint, ***The Colour Of My Love*** hits UK #10, in its week of entry.
[19] ***The Colour Of My Love*** hits US #4.
[20] Dion is named the Female Vocalist Of The Year for the fourth consecutive year at the 23rd annual Juno Awards held again at the O'Keefe Centre for the Performing Arts in Toronto.
[25-28, 31-**Apr** 1] She headlines a sold-out five-night concert series at the Theatre du Forum, Montreal, PQ.
[26] ***Dion Chante Plamondon***, the newly-named title of her 1990 recording, ***Des Mots Qui Sonnent***, is released in the US by 550 Music.
Apr [8] *The Power Of Love* is certified platinum by the RIAA.
[30] *Misled* initially makes UK #40.
June [18] *Misled* reaches US #23.
Aug [8] Dion appears on CBS-TV's "The Late Show With David Letterman".
[20] Her third US concert tour opening for Bolton ends at the Coca-Cola Star Lake Amphitheatre, Burgettstown, PA, in front of 22,683 fans, before swinging north for final Canadian dates.
[27] *Think Twice* peaks at US #95.
Dec [5] ***Unison*** is certified gold by the RIAA.
[7] "Gala For The President", including a performance by Dion, taped before President Clinton at Ford's Theatre, Washington on October 30th, airs on ABC-TV.
[17] Dion marries her 52-year old longtime manager Rene Angelil at the Notre Dame Basilica, Montreal, Canada.

1995

Jan [26] Ten months after originally charting, ***The Colour Of My Love*** now tops the UK chart.
[28] *Only One Road* peaks at US #93.
[30] She performs *The Power Of Love* at the 22nd annual American Music Awards held at the Shrine Auditorium.
Feb [2] The RIAA certifies three million sales of ***The Colour My Love***. (By year's end, the album will have sold over two million copies in the UK, over one million in Japan, 1.4 million in Canada and be certified eight-times platinum in Australia.)
[4] *Think Twice*, written by Pete Sinfield and Andy Hill, tops the UK chart.
Mar [1] Dion presents (with Andy Williams) the Best Pop Vocal Collaboration statuette to Al Green (and an absent Lyle Lovett) at the 37th annual Grammy Awards also held at the Shrine Auditorium.
[4] With *Think Twice* in its fifth week at UK #1 and with ***The Colour Of My Love*** now in its sixth week atop the UK albums survey, Dion becomes the first artist since the Beatles (with *I Feel Fine* and ***Beatles For Sale*** in January 1965) to simultaneously hold pole position on both UK charts for five consecutive weeks.
[30] ***The Colour Of My Love*** is named Album Of The Year and Best Selling Album (Foreign or Domestic) at the 24th annual Juno Awards held again at Toronto's O'Keefe Centre for the Performing Arts.
May [3] Dion collects the World's Best-Selling French-Canadian and Canadian Female Artist of the Year trophies at the seventh annual World Music Awards held at the Sporting Club in Monte Carlo, Monaco, airing on ABC-TV on May [30].
[23] *Think Twice* wins the Best Song Musically And Lyrically category at the 40th annual Ivor Novello Awards held at the Grosvenor House Hotel, London.
[27] *Only One Road* hits UK #8.
June [17] Dion appears on ITV's "The Brian Conley Show".
Sept [16] Already a chart-topper in France in June, *Pour Que Tu M'Aimes Encore (To Love Me Again)* hits UK #7 the same day that her 1991 album ***Unison*** charts for the first time in the UK peaking at #56.
Oct [7] ***D'Eux***, already on its way to three-million plus sales in France, and featuring 12 songs written and produced by French music star Jean-Jacques Goldman, debuts at its UK #7 peak. (It has already been released by 550 Music in the US in May as ***The French Album***.) (During the month, Dion reportedly abandons sessions with legendary producer Phil Spector having stayed in the studio until 4:00 a.m. working on one song.)
Nov [4] Her 11-country European tour climaxes with five UK arena dates, ending with tonight's performance at Birmingham's National Exhibition Centre, W. Midlands.
Dec [2] Reissued *Misled*, now remixed by E-Smoove, debuts at its UK #15 peak.
[4] *To Love You More*, a power ballad produced by Foster and recorded by Dion with Japanese instrumental trio Kryzler & Company, becomes the first non-Japanese language song to hit #1 on the Japanese Oricon chart since Irene Cara's *Flashdance* in 1983.

1996

Mar [10] ***D'Eux*** is named Best-Selling Francophone Album at the 25th annual Juno Awards held the Copps Coliseum, Hamilton, ON.

[23] Diane Warren-penned, Foster-produced *Because You Loved Me*, taken from the "Up Close And Personal" film soundtrack, tops the US chart (having already hit UK #10 on the 2nd), as ***Falling Into You***, a 14-track album from which the single is taken and which also includes her version of Eric Carmen's 1975 hit *All By Myself* and three cuts written and produced by Meat Loaf collaborator Jim Steinman, enters the UK chart at #1.

[30] ***Falling Into You*** enters at its US #2 peak.

DION & THE BELMONTS

Dion DiMucci (lead vocals); **Fred Milano** (tenor vocals); **Carlo Mastrangelo** (bass vocals); **Angelo D'Aleo** (tenor vocals)

1957

Sept Having made his first public appearance six years earlier, on "Paul Whiteman's Teen Club", and after recording four songs for his mother as a St. Valentine's Day gift, DiMucci (b. July 18, 1939, Bronx, New York, NY) records *The Chosen Few*, credited as Dion & the Timberlanes, for Mohawk Records, and it is subsequently picked up by the larger Jubilee label. Backed by a group of singers he has never met before, Dion feels he can find better singers from his own neighborhood and rounds up the best street-corner crooners he knows in the Bronx, including Milano (b. Aug. 22, 1939, Bronx), Mastrangelo (b. Oct. 5, 1938, Bronx) and D'Aleo (b. Feb. 3, 1940, Bronx). The new group rehearses on the 6th Avenue 'D' train to Manhattan.

1958

June [30] Earlier in the year, the group's name has changed to Dion & the Belmonts, taken from Belmont Avenue, which cuts through their corner of the Bronx. *We Went Away* on Mohawk has followed and a third single, *Tag Along*, has also failed to impress, though its writer, Gene Schwartz, has set up his own Laurie label to record Dion. His Laurie debut, *I Wonder Why*, a doo-wopping upbeat number, now reaches US #22.

Oct [3] Dion begins a 19-date "The Biggest Show Of Stars For 1958 - Autumn Edition" tour with Frankie Avalon, Bobby Darin, Bobby Freeman, Buddy Holly & the Crickets, Clyde McPhatter, the Coasters and others, at the Auditorium, Worcester, MA, set to end on the 19th at the Mosque, Richmond, VA.

[13] *No One Knows* reaches US #19, written by Ernie Maresca, whose name will appear under several Dion hits.

1959

Jan [5] *Don't Pity Me* makes US #40.

[23] Dion begins a 24-date "Winter Dance Party" tour, with Buddy Holly, the Big Bopper, Ritchie Valens and Frankie Sardo, at George Devine's Million Dollar Ballroom, Milwaukee, WI, set to close on February 15th at the Illinois State Armoury, Springfield, IL. (Midway through the tour, Holly, Valens and the Big Bopper all perish in a plane crash near Mason City, IA.)

May [18] New York songwriters Doc Pomus and Mort Shuman provide *A Teenager In Love*, which hits US #5 and is a million-seller.

June *A Teenager In Love* makes UK #28, despite covers by Marty Wilde (#2) and Craig Douglas (#13), which scoop the major UK sales. The group become fan-mag pin-ups, discussing in print their penchant for clothes (collegiate sweaters mostly) and revealing such unlikely interests as skin diving. D'Aleo is conscripted into the US Navy on national service, and the group continues as a trio.

Oct [5] *Every Little Thing I Do* makes US #48.

[19] Maresca-penned B-side, *A Lover's Prayer*, peaks at US #73.

1960

Feb [8] A richly-harmonized, saxophone-propelled reworking of a 1937 Rodgers and Hart number, *Where Or When*, hits US #3 and is their second million-seller.

May [23] The group revives a song first heard in the 1940 Walt Disney movie "Pinocchio", *When You Wish Upon A Star*, which makes US #30.

Aug [15] Their version of Cole Porter's *In The Still Of The Night* makes US #38.

Oct [17] The group splits. Dion stays with Laurie as a soloist and the Belmonts sign to the Sabina label.

Dec [19] Returning to teen-oriented material, Dion's solo debut, *Lonely Teenager*, reaches US #12, with its B-side, *Little Miss Blue*, peaking at US #96.

1961

Mar [6] After *Lonely Teenager* has made UK #47 in January, *Havin' Fun* peaks at US #42.

May [15] Dion's *Kissin' Game* peaks at US #82.

July [10] The Belmonts, minus Dion, reach US #18 with *Tell Me Why*.

Sept [18] The group's revival of *Don't Get Around Much Anymore* peaks at US #57.

Oct [23] Dion hits US #1 for the first of two weeks with the million-selling *Runaround Sue*, a whooping rocker with an exuberance which belies its tale of woe, with uncredited vocal backing from the Del Satins. Co-written with Maresca (about his girlfriend Sue, who will subsequently marry Dion), it is musically derived from Gary "U.S." Bonds' recent US chart-topper, *Quarter To Three*. (Some 20 years later, the song will become a US hit for Leif Garrett and a UK success for Racey.)

Nov *Runaround Sue* takes Dion to UK #11.

1962

Jan [14] Movie "Teenage Millionaire", in which Dion appears with Jimmy Clanton and which features songs by Chubby Checker and Jackie Wilson, goes on general release in the UK. (Dion also appears in "Don't Knock The Twist" and "Ten Girls Ago", with Buster Keaton, Bert Lahr and Eddie Foy Jr., in which he sings three songs.)

[20] The Belmonts peak at US #75 with *I Need Someone*. Dion's ***Runaround Sue*** makes US #11.

Feb [24] Dion's *The Wanderer* hits US #2 and is a million-seller, while its B-side, *The Majestic*, makes US #36. He sings both songs in the movie "Twist Around The Clock".

Mar *The Wanderer* hits UK #10. (It will be his last UK hit until it returns to #16 in 1976. Status Quo will also revive it for a UK #7 hit in 1984).

May [19] Maresca has left the demo studio to write a smash of his own: the *Runaround Sue*-inflected *Shout Shout (Knock Yourself Out)*, which hits US #6.

[26] Dion's *(I Was) Born To Cry* makes US #42.

June [9] Its B-side, *Lovers Who Wander*, hits US #3.

Aug [18] A Dion original, *Little Diane* (with a prominent kazoo in the backing), hits US #8, spurring his album, ***Lovers Who Wander***, to reach US #12.

Sept [15] The Belmonts climb to US #28 with *Come On Little Angel* (co-written by Maresca).

[16] Dion begins his first UK tour, with Del Shannon, Buzz Clifford, Joe Brown and the Angels.

Dec [15] The Belmonts' *Diddle-Dee-Dum (What Happens When Your Love Is Gone)* peaks at US #53.

[22] *Love Came To Me*, self-penned by Dion, hits US #10. He leaves Laurie to sign a major contract with CBS/Columbia.

1963

Jan ***Dion Sings His Greatest Hits***, which has only two solo cuts and ten with the Belmonts, reaches US #29. After years of gruelling package tours, Dion graduates to the live supper-club circuit.

Feb [23] Dion's Columbia debut, a revival of Leiber and Stoller's *Ruby Baby* (originally a hit for the Drifters in 1955), hits US #2 and sells over a million.

Apr His first Columbia album, also titled ***Ruby Baby***, reaches US #20.

[20] Laurie joins the lucky streak with girls' names and issues *Sandy*, which climbs to US #21.

May [4] The Belmonts' own girl-name single, *Ann-Marie*, peaks at US #86.

[18] Dion's *This Little Girl* reaches US #21.

July [13] Dion's revival of the Del Vikings' *Come Go With Me*, his last on Laurie, and originally on one of his albums, makes US #48. A Laurie compilation, ***Dion Sings To Sandy (And All His Other Girls!)***, peaks at US #115.

Aug [3] On Columbia, the offbeat and downbeat *Be Careful Of Stones That You Throw*, a moral tale about not taking people at face value, reaches US #31.

Oct [19] Dion begins the UK "Greatest Record Show Of 1963" tour with Brook Benton, Lesley Gore, Trini Lopez and Timi Yuro, at London's Finsbury Park Astoria.

[26] Yet another girl song (and yet another by Maresca), Dion's *Donna The Prima Donna* hits US #6.

Nov [2] During the tour, Dion appears live on ITV's "Ready Steady Go", singing *Donna The Prima Donna*, but becomes irritated by the audience dancing around him and walks out, despite being scheduled to perform another song.

Dec [28] Dion hits US #6 with *Drip Drop* (another Leiber/Stoller Drifters oldie, from 1958), completing a run of 18 Hot 100 hits in three years.

1965

Apart from a minor hit with Chuck Berry's *Johnny B. Goode* (US #71), the British Invasion and a developing narcotic problem combine to move Dion out of the public eye and he becomes involved in blues. His other singles are pure blues: Muddy Waters' *I'm Your Hoochie Coochie Man* and Willie Dixon's *Spoonful* but, with little US airplay, they fail to chart. Dion experiments with folk and blues material but Columbia refuses to make much of it public.

1966

With folk-rock hitting the charts, Columbia issues three folk-oriented singles credited to Dion & the Wanderers, but they receive little promotion. By the end of the year, the artist buys himself out of his label contract.

1967

May Released on ABC-Paramount in the US (and HMV Records in the UK), ***Together Again***, is a surprise reunion of Dion with the Belmonts on a collection of material which owes much to their R&B vocal-group roots. Two singles, *Berimbau* and *Movin' Man* are extracted, but only collectors show interest.

June [1] The Beatles' ***Sgt. Pepper's Lonely Hearts Club Band*** hits US #1 with Dion one of only two singers (the other is Bob Dylan) featured on its sleeve.

1968

Nov [17] Dion guests on CBS-TV's "The Smothers Brothers Comedy Hour".

Dec [14] He hits US #4 with Dick Holler's later much-covered martyr memorial song, *Abraham Martin And John*, and earns another gold disc. (Schwartz has invited Dion, now living in Miami, FL, to once again record for Laurie, which he has done in the folky style he has been honing since the passing of his blues passion. It completes what Dion will later describe as a watershed year in his life and career, having finally kicked his heroin habit in the spring.)

1969

Jan After an absence of five years on the US Album chart, ***Dion***, featuring *Abraham Martin And John* and several unexpected selections, peaks at #128.

Feb [8] His folk-styled reworking of Jimi Hendrix's *Purple Haze* peaks at US #63.

Apr [26] Only months after Judy Collins' version leaves the Top 10, Dion's cover of Joni Mitchell's *Both Sides Now* makes US #91.

1970

June As a singer/songwriter bent over his acoustic guitar, Dion enters another phase of his career and signs to Warner Bros. Records.

July [4] A candid allusion to his heroin addiction, *Your*

Own Back Yard peaks at US #75 (to become his last chart single). Two albums, ***Sit Down Old Friend***, featuring just Dion and his guitar, and ***You're Not Alone***, with a small group accompaniment, will be released.

1972

Jan [1] ***Sanctuary*** (which contains live versions of *The Wanderer* and *Ruby Baby* recorded at New York's Bitter End club, with newer acoustic material) anchors at US #200 for the first of two weeks.
June [2] Dion & the Belmonts reunite again for a one-off show at the ninth "Rock'n'Roll Spectacular" at New York's Madison Square Garden.
Dec ***Suite For Late Summer***, a concept album with orchestral accompaniment, produced by Russ Titelman, peaks at US #197.

1973

Mar The Dion & the Belmonts' performance from Madison Square Garden is released as ***Reunion***, which makes US #144.
Apr ***Dion's Greatest Hits***, collating ten of his hits, peaks at US #194.
Oct Dion's ***Born To Be With You***, on which Phil Spector oversaw production (Phil Gernhard and Cashman & West shared the actual producing) is released on the Phil Spector International label, in the UK only. Meanwhile, the Belmonts assist former Shirelle, Shirley Alston, on her version of *Where Or When* from her album, ***With A Little Help From My Friends***.

1976

June [26] *The Wanderer*, reissued in the UK, reaches #16.
Aug The production team of Steve Barri and Michael Omartian fails to bring commercial success for Dion with ***Streetheart***, and he leaves Warner Bros.

1978

Return Of The Wanderer, produced by Terry Cashman and Terry West on their own Lifesong Records, with Dion returning to his Bronx roots, is released.

1980

May [17] ***Dion And The Belmonts' 20 Golden Greats***, a K-tel TV-advertised compilation, reaches UK #31. (Dion will begin a long-term association with the Christian Dayspring label, releasing a handful of inspirational albums through the '80s, as part of his commitment as a born-again Christian, which has re-directed his life.)

1983

Mar [4] Having recorded ***Inside Job*** for Dayspring Records the previous year, Dion participates in the 22nd "Rock'n'Roll Revival Spectacular" at Madison Square Garden. He will spend much of the remainder of the decade making occasional nostalgia-related appearances, also recording his second and final album for Dayspring, ***I Put Away My Idols*** released in 1984.

1989

Jan [17] Arista Records hosts a tribute for Dion, recently signed to the label, at the Hard Rock Café in New York.
[18] Lou Reed inducts Dion into the Rock and Roll Hall of Fame at the fourth annual dinner, at New York's Waldorf Astoria Hotel.
Aug [26] Now credited once more as Dion DiMucci, *And The Night Stood Still*, written by Diane Warren, peaks at US #75, as *King Of The New York Streets* makes UK #74. Its parent album, ***Yo Frankie***, produced by Dave Edmunds and with guest appearances from Bryan Adams, k.d. lang, Lou Reed and Paul Simon, makes US #130, as the Belmonts prepare to go on "The Royalty Of Doo-Wop" tour with the Chiffons, the Diamonds, the Flamingos and the Silhouettes.

1990

Jan [17] Dion joins Frankie Valli onstage at the fifth annual Rock and Roll Hall of Fame after-dinner jam, held at the Waldorf Astoria Hotel, to sing *Goodnight Sweetheart*.
Feb Dion contributes *Mean Woman Blues* to a benefit album of Elvis Presley covers, ***The Last Temptation Of Elvis***.
Dec [5] Dion joins Frankie Valli, Graham Nash, Ben E. King, Keith Sweat, Johnny Gill, Eddie Kendricks and Dennis Edwards in a rendition of *The Longest Time*, to honor its writer, Billy Joel, who is being inducted as a NARAS Grammy Living Legend, at the Royale Theatre, New York. (Dion remains in the limelight, his theme to the CBS-TV sitcom "Lenny" being heard on TV every week.)

1993

Jan Columbia's Legacy label has released ***Bronx Blues : The Columbia Recordings (1962-1965)***, a Dion career retrospective, in 1991, while Dion has continued to appear at rock'n'roll reunion events (notably the "Royalty Of Rock - The Ultimate Reunion" at Madison Square Garden, with Ben E. King & the Drifters, Ronnie Spector & the Ronettes, and Little Anthony & the Imperials on January 10th 1992. As Dion now inducts Dick Clark into the Rock and Roll Hall of Fame at the eighth annual dinner, held at the Waldorf Astoria, he comments: "I met Dick when I was 17 and at that time I looked up to him like a father. In the '70s, I started regarding him as a brother. These days, I look at him as a son." Dion will continue to undertake regular US tours (opening for the Everly Brothers this year and with Gene Pitney the following summer).

DIRE STRAITS

Mark Knopfler (guitar, vocals); **John Illsley** (bass); **Terry Williams** (drums); **Alan Clark** (keyboards)

1977

July English graduate and former **Yorkshire Evening Post** journalist Knopfler (b. Aug. 12, 1949, Glasgow, Strathclyde, Scotland), a part-time teacher and pub-rock player and songwriter, having spent two months with northern UK band Brewer's Droop before forming Café Racers, is sharing a flat with fellow group members in Deptford, London. His cohorts are social worker and guitarist brother David (b. Dec. 27, 1952, Glasgow), and sociology undergraduate and bank manager's son Illsley (b. June 24, 1949, Leicester, Leics), and they frequently jam and rehearse Knopfler's own material. They are joined by session drummer Withers (b. Apr. 4, 1948), and given their name by a friend of his who notes their financial plight, dubbing them Dire Straits. The band scrapes together £120 to record a five-song demo tape at London's Pathway studios.
Aug A copy is given to DJ Charlie Gillett, who features the songs on his weekly BBC Radio London show, "Honky Tonk".
Oct Phonogram Records' A&R man John Stainze, one of many impressed by the broadcast demos, tracks the band down and, after strong competition, signs it to Phonogram's Vertigo label.
Nov Billed as Dire Straights, the band plays London's Hope & Anchor pub.
Dec NEMS agent Ed Bicknell hears the band's tape when Stainze enquires about an agency deal for it and, after seeing the group perform at Dingwalls club in London, he offers to manage them and an informal agreement is reached.

1978

Jan [20] The group begins a 16-date UK tour opening for Talking Heads.
Feb [14] Dire Straits begins recording its first album, at Basing Street Studios, London, with producer Muff Winwood. (The project will cost £12,500 to complete.)
Mar The band secures a short residency at the Marquee, London, and gains strong reviews.
May They support the Climax Blues Band on a UK tour, and Styx in Europe (Paris, Hamburg and the Hague), while their debut single, *Sultans Of Swing* (originally included on the demo), is released in the UK to strong reviews.
June [9] The band embarks on its first headlining UK tour, set to end on July 8th at St. Albans' Civic Hall, as Bicknell secures a US deal with Warner Bros. Records.
Sept [2] Dire Straits' debut album, the Mark Knopfler-penned ***Dire Straits***, released in May, makes UK #38, showcasing his distinctive and skillfully fluid guitar work and blues-tinged vocal style, both reminiscent of J.J. Cale. Knopfler visits the Muscle Shoals Studios, AL, meeting producer Jerry Wexler and playing on a Mavis Staples' session. A deal is struck with Wexler and Barry Beckett for them to produce Dire Straits' second album.
Oct ***Dire Straits*** is released in the US and gains heavy airplay, as the band plays sellout tours in Holland, Belgium and W. Germany. The album tops the charts in Australia and New Zealand.
Nov The group flies to the Bahamas to record a follow-up at Compass Point Studios, Nassau, before returning to the UK for Christmas.

1979

Feb [23] Dire Straits begins its first North American tour, comprising 51 sold-out shows over 38 days, at the Paradise Club, Boston, MA.
Mar Bob Dylan attends a Los Angeles, CA, concert and invites Knopfler and Withers to play on his next album.
Apr [7] *Sultans Of Swing* hits UK #8 and US #4.
[14] ***Dire Straits*** hits US #2 during a 41-week chart tenure.
[21] Boosted by the success of *Sultans Of Swing*, ***Dire Straits*** hits UK #5. (The album will eventually be a million-seller in both the UK and US, and will spend 104 weeks on the UK survey.)
May [1-12] Mark Knopfler and Withers work with Bob Dylan in Muscle Shoals, on his forthcoming ***Slow Train Coming***.
June [20-21] The group ends a sellout UK tour at London's Hammersmith Odeon.
[30] ***Communique***, once again entirely written by Mark Knopfler, and released to coincide with another sellout UK and European tour, hits UK #5.
Aug [4] ***Communique*** makes US #11.
[11] The extracted *Lady Writer* peaks at UK #51.
[25] *Lady Writer* makes US #45.
Sept The band begins its second US tour.
Dec After major Dublin, Eire and Belfast, N. Ireland dates, and four London concerts (following a November tour of Scandinavia), the band calls a six-month work break to recover.

1980

Apr Phil Lynott's ***Solo In Soho***, featuring Mark Knopfler's distinctive fret-work, makes UK #28.
July [25] After a month's recording sessions with new producer Jimmy Iovine, David Knopfler quits the band to pursue a solo career, which will yield ***Release*** (UK #82, 1983), ***Behind The Lines*** (1985), ***Cut The Wire*** (1987) and ***Lips Against The Steel*** (1988). New York session man Sid McGinnis replaces him temporarily.
Sept Following auditions, Lindes (b. June 30, 1953, Monterey, CA), ex-Darling, and Clark (b. Mar. 5, 1952, Durham, Durham) are recruited on guitar and keyboards respectively.
Oct [20] The band begins a two-week North American tour, as ***Making Movies*** is released.
Dec [6] Steely Dan's ***Gaucho***, featuring Mark Knopfler on guest guitar, enters the US chart.
[19-20] A one-month UK tour is punctuated by two dates in Dortmund, W. Germany, with Roxy Music and Talking Heads, which are televised across Europe to a multi-million audience.

1981

Jan ***Making Movies***, with assistance from E Street Band keyboardist Roy Bittan, reaches US #19.
[31] *Skateaway*, taken from it, peaks at US #58.
Feb [14] ***Making Movies***, assisted by the still-climbing *Romeo And Juliet*, hits a belated UK chart

peak of #4.
[21] *Romeo And Juliet* hits UK #8.
Mar [18] Recently returned from a successful appearance at the San Remo Song Festival in Italy, Dire Straits embarks on its first tour of Australia and New Zealand. (The concert in Auckland will be the highest-grossing in the band's career to date.)
Apr [11] *Skateaway* makes UK #37.
May [3] The group begins a sellout concert tour of W. Germany, Sweden, Denmark, Norway, Finland, Holland, France, Switzerland, Italy, Belgium and Luxembourg, which will end on July 6th.
Oct [17] *Tunnel Of Love* peaks at UK #54.

1982

Feb Knopfler is invited by film producer David Puttnam to compose and perform the soundtrack score to Bill Forsyth's "Local Hero" movie. (He is also currently featured on Van Morrison's latest release, ***Beautiful Vision***.)
Mar [1] The band begins recording its fourth album.
Apr Phil Lynott's ***The Phil Lynott Album***, including Knopfler's lead guitar on *Ode To Liberty* (which he also co-produced), is released.
July "Local Hero" soundtrack music is recorded, after Knopfler visits location shooting in Scotland.
Sept [18] Despite its seven-minute length, *Private Investigations* hits UK #2, behind Survivor's *Eye Of The Tiger*.
Oct [2] Knopfler written-and-produced ***Love Over Gold***, featuring the 14-minute opus *Telegraph Road*, hits UK #1, where it will stay for four weeks.
Nov [13] ***Love Over Gold*** reaches US #19. Withers leaves and is replaced on drums by Terry Williams, ex-Man and Dave Edmunds' band Rockpile.

1983

Jan [22] *Industrial Disease* peaks at US #75.
Feb [5] EP *Twisting By The Pool* reaches UK #14.
[8] Dire Straits wins Best British Group at the second annual BRIT Awards, at London's Grosvenor House Hotel.
Mar [12] Knopfler's solo single, *Going Home*, the theme from "Local Hero", debuts at its UK #56 peak.
Apr Marketed in the US as a mini-album, ***Twisting By The Pool*** makes US #53.
May Knopfler's ***Local Hero*** soundtrack album reaches UK #14.
[5] *Private Investigations* wins the Outstanding British Lyric category at the 28th annual Ivor Novello Awards, at London's Grosvenor House Hotel.
July [22-23] A pair of concerts at London's Hammersmith Odeon are recorded for future release.
Nov Knopfler produces Bob Dylan's ***Infidels***, and marries Lourdes Salomon at Kensington Register Office, London.

1984

Feb [25] Double A-side, *Love Over Gold/Solid Rock* (both live versions), makes UK #50.
Mar Double performance set recorded in July the previous year, ***Alchemy - Dire Straits Live***, hits UK #3.
Apr [19] *Going Home* wins the Best Film Theme Or Song category at the 29th annual Ivor Novello Awards, again held at London's Grosvenor House Hotel.
May ***Alchemy - Dire Straits Live*** makes US #46.
June Illsley releases the solo album ***Never Told A Soul*** on Vertigo.
Oct ***Cal***, Knopfler's soundtrack score to the movie of the same name, reaches UK #65, while Aztec Camera's ***Knife***, produced by Knopfler, reaches UK #14 and US #175. Knopfler also writes the music for "Comfort And Joy", his second score for director Bill Forsyth.
Nov Five months of recording begin at the Air Studios, Montserrat, W. Indies.

1985

Mar [23] Tina Turner hits US #7 with the Knopfler-penned *Private Dancer* (a leftover from material written for ***Love Over Gold***).
May [4] Ballad *So Far Away* reaches UK #20.
[25] Recorded with the line-up of Knopfler, Illsey, Clark, Williams and Guy Fletcher (keyboards), ***Brothers In Arms***, written by Knopfler and co-produced with Neil Dorfsman, debuts at UK #1 and holds the top slot for three weeks.
June [15] Bryan Ferry's ***Boys And Girls***, featuring session fret-work by the much in-demand Knopfler, hits UK #1.
[27] Dire Straits is awarded the 1985 Silver Clef for Outstanding Services To British Music by the Nordoff-Robbins Music Therapy Centre.
July [13] After ten consecutive concerts at Wembley Arena, Wembley, Middx., the band plays at the "Live Aid" benefit at Wembley Stadium. (This will be followed by the 12-month "Brothers in Arms" world sojourn, ending in Australia in mid-1986. Clark leaves, and Guy Fletcher joins on keyboards, for the tour.)
Aug [10] *Money For Nothing*, featuring co-writer Sting on lead-in vocals (the immortal "I want my MTV"), and taken from ***Brothers In Arms***, hits UK #4.
[31] ***Brothers In Arms*** begins a nine-week tenure at US #1. (It will top charts in 25 countries and eventually sell over 20 million albums worldwide.)
Sept [21] Aided by an innovative animated Steve Barron-directed promo video which gets heavy MTV and other US TV exposure, *Money For Nothing* tops the US chart for the first of three weeks, the band's biggest US hit and its first million-selling single.
Dec The extracted title track, the peace-themed anthem *Brothers In Arms* reaches UK #16. (It is notable as the first-ever commercially issued CD-single in the UK, a limited pressing of 400 copies.)

1986

Jan [25] Uptempo *Walk Of Life* hits US #7.
Feb *Walk Of Life* hits UK #2.
[10] Dire Straits is named Best British Group, for the second time, at the fifth annual BRIT Awards, at London's Grosvenor House Hotel.
[25] They win the Best Rock Performance By A Duo Or Group With Vocal category for *Money For Nothing*, while ***Brothers In Arms*** is named Best Engineered Recording (Non-Classical) and Knopfler snares the Best Country Instrumental Performance category with one of his original guitar heroes, Chet Atkins, for *Cosmic Square Dance* from ***Stay Tuned***, at the 28th annual Grammy Awards.
Apr [26] *So Far Away* reaches US #19.
May *Your Latest Trick* reaches UK #26.
May Knopfler, his acoustic guitar-maker Steve Phillips and Brendan Croker play at the Grove, a small Leeds folk club, as a prelude to a more formal forthcoming collaboration.
June [20] Knopfler and Illsley take part in the fourth annual "Prince's Trust Rock Gala" concert, with Eric Clapton, Phil Collins, Paul McCartney, Elton John, Tina Turner and others, at the Wembley Arena.
Sept [15] "Money For Nothing" wins the Best Video and Best Group Video categories at the third annual MTV Video Music Awards, broadcast simultaneously from the Universal Amphitheatre, Universal City, CA, and the Palladium, New York. (The song lyric "I want my MTV" has become the cable station's catchphrase.)
Oct [24] The group's sound engineer, Peter Grange, is killed in a road accident in Gloucestershire.
[25] In a celebrity car race before the Australian Grand Prix, Knopfler breaks his collarbone in an accident.

1987

Jan Knopfler guests at one of Eric Clapton's annual concert marathons at London's Royal Albert Hall.
Feb [9] ***Brothers In Arms*** is named Best British Album at the sixth annual BRIT Awards, held at London's Grosvenor House Hotel.
[24] "Dire Straits Brothers In Arms" wins the Best Music Video, Long Form category at the 29th annual Grammy Awards.
Mar Knopfler duets with Chet Atkins at "The Secret Policeman's Third Ball", at the London Palladium, in aid of Amnesty International.
Aug [1] "Money For Nothing" is the first music video broadcast on MTV Europe.
Nov Benefitting from the advent of compact disc, ***Brothers In Arms*** sells its three-millionth copy in the UK, becoming Britain's all-time bestselling album and its second-biggest-selling recording of any kind. (Only Band Aid's *Do They Know It's Christmas?* has a higher UK sales total.)
Dec Knopfler writes and performs the soundtrack music for the Rob Reiner-directed film "The Princess Bride".

1988

Jan Knopfler's wife, Lourdes, gives birth to twin sons, who will inspire their daddy's composition, *I Love You Too Much* (which is subsequently recorded by Jeff Healey).
Feb Willy De Ville's ***Miracles***, produced by Knopfler, is released by Polydor Records.
Apr Knopfler works with Dylan on the latter's ***Down In The Groove***.
May Illsey releases his sophomore effort, ***Glass***, on Vertigo.
June [11] The band headlines the "Nelson Mandela 70th Birthday Tribute" concert at Wembley Stadium, televised worldwide, with Eric Clapton guesting as second guitarist. The show helps ***Brothers In Arms*** back into the UK Top 20 after 162 weeks on chart.
July Knopfler guests on Joan Armatrading's ***The Shouting Stage***.
Sept Knopfler contributes and part-produces Randy Newman's ***Land Of Dreams*** and accompanies Eric Clapton on his US tour as guitarist and vocalist.
[15] After much speculation, Knopfler announces the official end of Dire Straits.
Oct [29] Greatest hits compilation, ***Money For Nothing***, including live versions of *Twisting By The Pool* and *Telegraph Road*, debuts at UK #1. A multiplatinum success in the UK, in the US it peaks at #62, although its track listing is criticized.
Nov [5] The extracted reissue, *Sultans Of Swing*, peaks at UK #62.

1989

Mar Dire Straits are featured on the Greenpeace-supporting album ***Rainbow Warriors***, initially launched in Russia. (US country act Highway 101 hits US Country #2 with *Setting Me Up*, originally written by Knopfler for Waylon Jennings in 1984, while the Judds' ***River Of Time***, featuring their version of Knopfler's *Water Of Love*, with the artist on guest guitar, is released the following month.)
Apr [4] Knopfler and Illsley (as Dire Straits) are honored with the Outstanding Contribution To British Music at the 34th annual Ivor Novello Awards lunch, at the Grosvenor House Hotel.
Sept [11] Jim Henson's "The Ghost Of Faffner Hall", on which Knopfler is one of many guests, airs on HBO-TV.

1990

Mar [17] The Notting Hillbillies' ***Missing ... Presumed Having ...*** debuts at UK #2. Knopfler has formed the band in a deliberate attempt to return to a more low-key performing act, with old friends Phillips (whom he met in 1965 and formed the Doulian String Pickers), Croker, who teamed with Phillips in 1976 in Nev & Norris, and Guy Fletcher, with whom Knopfler has been producing Croker and Phillips at his Notting Hill, London, home studio.
Apr [2] They embark on a UK tour.
[19] Knopfler appears alongside David Gilmour, Mark King, Lemmy and Gary Moore, as witnesses in a comedy drama courthouse sketch on BBC-TV's "French and Saunders", and they end the sketch jamming together.
[21] ***Missing ... Presumed Having ...*** makes US #52.
May [19] A modest venue Notting Hillbillies UK tour ends. They then appear on NBC-TV's "Saturday Night Live" with the live line-up augmented by Nashville-based Paul Franklin on pedal steel and Marcus Cliff (of Croker's Five O'Clock Shadows) on bass.
June [30] Knopfler joins Phil Collins and Genesis, Pink Floyd, Robert Plant, Paul McCartney, Cliff Richard and the Shadows, Status Quo, Elton John, Eric Clapton and Tears For Fears, all previous Silver Clef winners, on a star-studded bill at Knebworth Park, Knebworth, Herts., in aid of the Nordoff-

Robbins Music Therapy Centre.
July [1] Knopfler, Illsey and the band's manager, Ed Bicknell, decide, over lunch at the Halcyon Hotel, Holland Park, to reconvene Dire Straits to record their sixth studio album and plan a parallel world tour.
Nov [24] ***Neck And Neck***, a Mark Knopfler/Chet Atkins guitar-laden duet album, debuts at its UK #41 peak.
Dec [1] ***Neck And Neck*** peaks at US #127. (During the year, Knopfler has also released his soundtrack score to "Last Exit To Brooklyn".)

1991

Feb While recording for a new Dire Straits album project at London's Air Studios, Knopfler contributes a guitar solo to *Voices That Care*, a David Foster and Linda Thompson Jenner-composed and organized charity record to benefit the American Red Cross Gulf Crisis Fund.
[20] Knopfler and Atkins win the Best Country Vocal Collaboration category for *Poor Boy Blues* and Best Country Instrumental Performance for *So Soft, Your Goodbye* at the 33rd annual Grammy Awards, at New York's Radio City Music Hall.
Aug [23] The first date of a two-year, 300-gig world tour begins in Dublin, with the line-up comprising Knopfler, Illsley, Fletcher, Clark, Phil Palmer (guitar), Chris White (sax), Chris Whitten (drums) and Danny Cummings (percussion). They will play to some 7.1 million paying fans.
[31] *Calling Elvis* debuts at its UK #21 peak.
Sept [21] Dire Straits' first new album in over six years, ***On Every Street***, enters at UK #1.
Oct [5] ***On Every Street*** reaches US #12.
[29] The band plays five sellout shows at the Sydney Entertainment Centre, Sydney, New South Wales, Australia, grossing AUS $2,078,830 from a combined audience of 45,573.
Nov [2] *Heavy Fuel* bows at its UK #55 peak.

1992

Feb [26] The group plays to a sellout crowd of 16,000 at New York's Madison Square Garden, during the North American leg of its tour.
[29] *On Every Street* debuts at its UK #42 peak.
June [3-8] Dire Straits performs at London's Earls Court, during a UK trek which includes stadium dates at Cardiff Arms Park, Gateshead Athletic Stadium, Maine Road Manchester and Woburn Abbey.
[27] *The Bug* charts for a week at UK #67.
[30] German leg of the tour opens at the Schleyerhalle, Stuttgart.
Sept [29] "Dire Straits Live : Rendezvous With The Sultans Of Swing" pay-per-view broadcast airs from Arenes De Nîmes, Provence, France.
Oct [6-7] Their world tour now reaches the Plaza De Toros De Las Ventas in Madrid, Spain.

1993

May [8] Knopfler receives an honorary music doctorate from the University of Newcastle-upon-Tyne, Tyne & Wear.
[22] EP *Encores* and ***On The Night***, a 76-minute live album recorded at Les Arenes, Nîmes, and the Feyenoord Stadium, Rotterdam, Netherlands, debut at their respective UK #31 and #4 peaks.
June [5] ***On The Night*** makes US #116.

1994

Sept A tribute album to Arthur Alexander, ***Adios Amigo***, including Knopfler's pairing with Chuck Jackson on *You Better Move On*, is released in the US.
Oct [14] Knopfler's *The Bug* is honored at the 14th ASCAP dinner at London's Park Lane Hotel.

1995

July [8] ***Live At The BBC***, released by Windsong Records, featuring six tracks from the group's debut album, and *What's The Matter Baby* recorded at the Paris Theatre in July 1978 and *Tunnel Of Love* from a 1981 edition of "The Old Grey Whistle Test", peaks at UK #71.

1996

Jan [2] A tribute album ***notfadeaway: remembering buddy holly***, including Knopfler's version of *Learning The Game* with Waylon Jennings, is released in the US.
Mar [16] Knopfler's *Darling Pretty* reaches UK #33 in its week of entry. It is a taster for his solo album ***Golden Heart***, set for release by Waner Bros. on the 26th. Recorded over the past two years in Dublin, Eire and Nashville, TN, it includes guest appearances by former Dire Straits colleague Fletcher, Vince Gill, Paul Brady and the Chieftains, and precedes a European tour set to begin in April backed by a five-piece band.

THE DIXIE CUPS

Barbara Ann Hawkins (vocals); **Rosa Lee Hawkins** (vocals); **Joan Johnson** (vocals)

1963

Oct Having sung together since grade school in New Orleans, LA, the vocal trio of sisters Barbara Ann Hawkins (b. Oct. 23, 1943, New Orleans) and Rosa Lee Hawkins (b. Sept. 24, 1944, New Orleans) and their cousin Johnson (b. Jan. 15, 1945, New Orleans), appearing as the Meltones are spotted in a local talent contest by Joe Jones (the New Orleans singer/pianist who had a 1960 #3 US hit with *You Talk Too Much*), who becomes their manager and takes them to New York, NY, to audition for Red Bird Records.

1964

Jan Signed to Red Bird, and provisionally named Little Miss & the Muffets, the girls are placed with producers Jeff Barry and Ellie Greenwich, who try them out on *Chapel Of Love*, a song the duo have written with Phil Spector, and which has been recorded unsatisfactorily with both the Ronettes and the Crystals.
June [6] *Chapel Of Love* tops the US chart for the first of three weeks becoming a million seller. It is credited to the Dixie Cups after a last-minute name change just before the record's release.
July *Chapel Of Love* reaches UK #22.
Aug Follow-up, *People Say*, climbs to US #12.
Sept ***Chapel Of Love*** peaks at US #112. (In a practice peculiar to Red Bird, this same album will reappear twice, with the same contents, in the next nine months, the title being changed first to ***People Say*** and then to ***Iko Iko*** - to tag the album after the current hit.)
Nov *You Should Have Seen The Way He Looked At Me* peaks at US #39.

1965

Feb *Little Bell* makes US #51.
May *Iko Iko*, a sparse, percussive arrangement of a traditional New Orleans chant, recorded spontaneously at the end of a session, reaches US #20, the group's final US chart entry.
June *Iko Iko* is their second and also final UK hit, peaking at #23. (It will be revived, and make UK #35, by all-girl outfit the Belle Stars, in 1982. Their version will feature prominently in the 1988 hit movie "Rain Man".)
July *Gee, The Moon Is Shining Bright* fails to chart in the US, and Jones, deciding to move his group to a larger label, signs a new deal with ABC-Paramount Records. (The Dixie Cups will have several singles and ***Ridin' High*** released on RCA during the next 12 months, without success, mainly due to the lack of a hit-sensitive team (like Red Bird's Barry and Greenwich) behind them. Without moving on further, the group splits with the Hawkins returning to New Orleans where they will take up careeers in modeling).

1992

May [8-9] With the Hawkins sisters joined by a third female vocalist Dale Mickle (who has replaced Johnson), the reunited Dixie Cups continue to perform on the US nostalgia circuit, taking part, for example, in WCBS-FM's 20th anniversary concert at New York's Radio City Music Hall.

DR. DRE

1991

June [15] Having grown up in Los Angeles, CA's South Central ghetto, a neigborhood where daily themes of violence and drug use fuel much of his subsequent work, Dre (b. Andre Young, Feb. 18, 1965, Compton, CA), already a member of the World Class Wreckin' Cru, has graduated to become a founding member of N.W.A. (Niggaz With Attitude) with Ice Cube (b. O'Shea Jackson, June 15, 1969, Los Angeles), the pair having initially formed a rap-writing partnership for group member and ex-drug dealer Eazy-E (b. Eric Wright, Sept. 7, 1973, Los Angeles). Joined by M.C. Ren (b. Lorenzo Patterson, June 16) and DJ Yella (b. Antoine Carraby, Dec. 11), also ex-World Class Wreckin' Cru and produced by Dre, N.W.A. has gone on to pioneer and define the burgeoning gangsta rap genre, explicitly depicting and glamorizing the anti-police brutality and sexism of inner-city gang life, with the best-selling albums, the double-platinum ***Straight Outta Compton*** (US #37 and UK #41 in 1989), the platinum ***100 Miles And Runnin'*** (US #27, 1990) and their final effort, ***Efil4zaggin*** which now enters the US chart at #1 (also set to make UK #25), all released on Eazy-E's Ruthless Records. Following an acrimonious split and with each of its members going on to solo ventures (and Eazy-E dying from AIDS in 1995), Dre will establish his own niche as a highly successful solo performer, writer and producer (who should not be confused with "Yo! MTV Raps" show-host and WQHT Hot 97 DJ, Doctor Dre).

1992

May [9] Dre's first solo recording, *Deep Cover*, the title theme from the film of the same name, credited as Dr. Dre Introducing Snoop Doggy Dogg, and released by Solar Records, enters the US R&B chart set to reach #46. Meanwhile Dre has founded his own Death Row Records which he aims to be "the Motown of the '90s", licensed to Interscope Records and Warner Bros.

1993

Feb [13] Dre's first album ***The Chronic***, its title being slang for marijuana, heavily sampling Parliament/ Funkladelic material, hits US #3, hailed as redefining the rap genre and featuring his rapping protégé and current murder suspect Snoop Doggy Dogg on most tracks.
Mar [20] *Nuthin' But A 'G' Thang*, sampling Leon Haywood's 1975 R&B smash, *I Want'a Do Something Freaky To You*, hits US #2.
[24] *Nuthin' But A 'G' Thang* is certified platinum by the RIAA.
July [3] *Dre Day*, co-written by Dre, Dogg and Colin Wolfe, hits US #8.
Aug [10] *Dre Day* is certified gold by the RIAA.
Oct [16] *Let Me Ride*, sampling Parliament's *Mothership Connection (Star Child)* and appropriately featuring George Clinton, reaches US #34.
Nov [3] The RIAA certifies three million US sales of ***The Chronic***.
Dec [11] Snoop Doggy Dogg's ***Doggy Style***, produced by and featuring Dre, enters at US #1, the first time a debut artist has reached pole position in the US in its first week. The album will eventually sell over four million copies in the US and 140,000 in the UK.

1994

Jan [22] *Nuthin' But A 'G' Thang*, backed with *Let Me Ride*, bows at its UK #31 peak.
Feb [7] Dre wins the Best Artist, Rap/Hip-Hop and Best New Artist, Rap/Hip-Hop categories at the 21st annual American Music Awards held at Los Angeles' Shrine Auditorium.
Mar [1] Dre wins the Best Rap Solo Performance (for *Let Me Ride*) at the 36th annual Grammy Awards, held at New York City's Radio City Music Hall.
Apr [9] The Dre-produced soundtrack ***Above The Rim***, released by Death Row, enters the US chart at its

#2 peak.
Aug [30] He is sentenced to five months in jail when Los Angeles' Municipal Court Judge determines that no contest pleas to charges of drunk driving violated terms of his probation for the 1992 incident when he broke TV show host Dee Barnes' jaw in a brawl. He is also ordered to pay a $1,053 fine and attend a 90-day alcoholism education program.
Sept [3] *Dre Day* makes UK #59 in its week of entry.
Oct [8] ***Concrete Roots - Anthology***, released in the US on the Hitman label and comprising a collection of rap efforts either written, performed or produced by Dre, including those by N.W.A., the Wreckin' Cru, Michel'le and Cli-N-Tel, bows at its US #43 peak.

1995

Apr [15] Reunited with ex-N.W.A. member Ice Cube, *Natural Born Killaz* bows at its UK #45 peak, taken from the Dogg-starring film short, "Murder Was The Case". The Dre-produced soundtrack to the film (which is also directed by Dre) has already debuted at US #1 on Nov [5] the previous year.
[22] *Keep Their Heads Ringin'*, featured in the movie "Friday", hits US #10.
May [10] *Keep Their Heads Ringin'* is certified gold.
June [10] *Keep Their Heads Ringin'* bows at its UK #25 peak. (Bowing to criticism in the US over its distribution agreement with the always controversial Death Row stable, Warner Bros., severs ties with Death Row licensee Interscope, which will sign up with MCA Records by year's end.)
Aug [13] Rap documentary "The Show" featuring Dre, premiers in the US.
Sept [7] Dre collects the trophy for Best Rap Video (for "Keep Their Heads Ringin'") at the 12th annual MTV Video Music Awards held at New York's Radio City Music Hall.
Oct [10] Dre's latest production, ***Dogg Food*** by Tha Dogg Pound is released in the US headed for double-platinum sales status.

1996

Jan [8] Dre is named as a co-defendant (with other Death Row/Interscope executives) in a suit brought in Los Angeles by Solar Records' chairman Dick Griffey and rapper D.O.C. (Tracy L. Curry) alleging the illegal dissolution of a 1991 partnership which subsequently become Death Row Records.
Apr Amid rumors of an N.W.A. reunion, Dre sells his stake in Death Row to co-founder Suge Knight.
[13] *California*, by 2Pac featuring Dr. Dre, debuts at its UK #6 peak.

DR. FEELGOOD

Lee Brilleaux (vocals, guitar);
Wilko Johnson (guitar); **John B. Sparks** (bass);
The Big Figure (drums)

1971

The band is formed on Canvey Island, Essex, to play hard, traditional rock and R&B and electric blues, taking its name from the 1962 US hit *Doctor Feel-Good* by bluesman Piano Red (recorded under the name Dr. Feelgood & the Interns). Childhood friends Johnson (b. John Wilkinson, 1947) and the Big Figure (b. Johnny Martin) are both ex-the Roamers, and the others have played in groups in the Essex area. During a break from university, Johnson returns home to find that Sparks (b. 1953) and Brilleaux (b. Lee Green, 1953, Durban, South Africa) have put together a jug band. Some time later, with Brilleaux now working in a solicitor's office, Sparks goes to Johnson's house and asks if he wants to start another group. Initially they have no drummer (Will Birch plays at some gigs) and Figure is recruited. While establishing its own reputation as a hard-working pub-rock act, the band backs '60s star Heinz, as new material, mostly written by Johnson, is introduced into the stage act during three years of heavy club work.

1974

July [8] Signed to United Artists Records, the band makes its first recording, a medley of rock oldies, *Bony Moronie/Tequila*, live at Dingwall's club in London.
Aug [26] Recording sessions for its first album begin, with producer Vic Maile, at Rockfield Studios, Monmouth, Gwent, Wales.
Nov Johnson-penned *Roxette* is released.

1975

Jan Their debut album, ***Down By The Jetty***, is released, recorded in mono to reflect the band's raw, basic R&B sound.
[28] The group embarks on the "Naughty Rhythms Tour", with Chilli Willi & the Red Hot Peppers and Kokomo, in Watford, Herts.
May [23] A live show at City Hall, Sheffield, S. Yorks. is recorded for an album.
Nov [1] Self-produced ***Malpractice*** reaches UK #17. The band tours widely in the UK, finding huge support from the music press, which champions its hard-edged sound and dynamic live presence as a major rock trend.
[8] A second gig at the Kursaal Ballroom in Southend, Essex (just eight miles from the band's Canvey Island base), is recorded for a live album.

1976

Oct [9] Live ***Stupidity***, compiled from the Sheffield and Southend recordings, tops the UK chart for a week, a rare live chart-topper. (During the year, the band makes its first tour of the US, a 10-city trek of the South supporting Kiss. Because Kiss cannot be seen without makeup, the Feelgood are not allowed backstage. Johnson objects and refuses to go on, so the band is dropped from the tour.)

1977

Mar Johnson leaves for a solo career after disagreements over the band's material. Henry McCulloch plays as temporary guitarist on one UK tour and is subsequently replaced by John "Gypie" Mayo.
June [11] ***Sneakin' Suspicion***, produced by Bert DeCoteaux at Rockfield Studios (recorded before Johnson's departure), hits UK #10. The title track *Sneakin' Suspicion*, written by Johnson, is the band's first hit single, reaching UK #47.
Oct [8] *She's A Wind Up* makes UK #34. Produced by Nick Lowe, it is taken from ***Be Seeing You*** (its sleeve reflecting a current craze within the band for Patrick McGoohan's "The Prisoner" TV series) which peaks at UK #55.

1978

June [22] The group tops the bill of the fifth anniversary concert at Dingwall's club in London.
Sept [28] Dr. Feelgood plays at the Odeon Cinema, Chelmsford, Essex, during a current UK tour.
Oct *Down At The Doctor's* makes UK #48.
[7] Its parent album, the Richard Gottehrer-produced ***Private Practice***, makes UK #41.
[28-29] The group ends a major UK tour at London's Hammersmith Odeon.

1979

Feb The Mayo/Lowe-penned *Milk And Alcohol*, also from ***Private Practice***, is the band's biggest-selling single, hitting UK #9, helped by its availability on white (milk) and brown (alcohol) colored vinyl.
May *As Long As The Price Is Right*, a Larry Wallis song, reaches UK #40.
June [9] Live ***As It Happens***, recorded at UK gigs at the Pavilion, Hemel Hempstead, Herts., and Crocs in Rayleigh, Essex, makes UK #42.
Dec *Put Him Out Of Your Mind* peaks at UK #73, and is the band's last UK chart single. It is taken from ***Let It Roll***, produced by Mike Verson.

1980

Sept ***A Case Of The Shakes*** is released and, amid some disillusionment within the band, Mayo considers leaving.
[12] The group embarks on the UK leg of a world tour at the Pavilion, Hemel Hempstead.

1981

Jan Mayo quits, to be replaced by Johnny Guitar, ex-the Count Bishops.
Aug ***On The Job***, the band's third live album, recorded at Manchester University, Manchester, Gtr. Manchester (and featuring Mayo), is released.
Nov Compilation, ***Dr. Feelgood's Casebook***, is the band's final release on Liberty/UA.

1982

Oct After Sparks and Figure have left Buzz Barwell (drums, ex-Lew Lewis Band) and Pat McMullen (bass, ex-Count Bishops) having replaced them, Brilleaux remains as the only original member. Following another European tour, ***Fast Women And Slow Horses*** is released on the independent UK label Chiswick Records.

1983

Phil Mitchell (bass) replaces McMullen and Gordon Russell replaces Guitar, as Brilleaux continues to lead the band through its timeless hard R&B act. (They will work regularly in the small, sweaty club environment which suits them best and release ***Doctor's Orders*** in June 1986, the same year Brilleaux will also release the solo ***Brilleaux***.)

1989

Having issued ***Mad Man Blues*** the previous year and after forming their own Grand label (on which they will release another stage set, ***Live In London***, in May 1990), the group resumes touring, with Brilleaux, Mitchell, Kevin Morris (drums) and, from Steve Marriott's group, Steve Walwyn (guitar), while United Artists brings the early career highlights to CD with ***Singles (The UA Years)***.

1994

Apr [7] Having toured the UK each year up until February 1993 (promoting its final two albums ***Primo*** (1991) and ***The Feelgood Factor*** (1993), when Brilleaux has had to disband the unit because of ill health, and shortly after re-forming a new Dr. Feelgood with Walwyn, Morris, Dave Bronze (bass) and Ian Gibson (piano), Brilleaux dies of throat cancer in Canvey Island.

DR. HOOK

Ray Sawyer (lead vocals, guitar);
Dennis Locorriere (guitar); **Jance Garfat** (bass, vocals); **George Cummings** (steel and lead guitar); **Bill Francis** (keyboards, vocals);
Rik Elswit (guitar, vocals); **John Wolters** (drums, vocals)

1968

The group forms in Union City, NJ, when Locorriere (b. June 13, 1949, Union City) joins Sawyer (b. Feb. 1, 1937, Chickasaw, AL), Cummings and Francis, who have been playing together for some years under various short-lived names. They subsequently recruit Garfat (b. Mar. 3, 1944, CA), Elswit (b. July 6, 1945, NY) and Wolters (b. Apr. 28, 1945), and play local bars, billed as the Chocolate Papers. The group will have no fixed name until a club owner demands one for his advertising poster for a gig in February the following year, when Cummings coins the moniker Dr. Hook & the Medicine Show. (The name Dr. Hook becomes associated with frontman Sawyer, who wears an eye patch, having lost his right eye in an auto accident, which gives him a piratical appearance.)

1970

Producer Ron Haffkine hears a Dr. Hook demo tape and asks the group to perform humorist/songwriter Shel

Silverstein-penned *Last Morning* in the Dustin Hoffman-starring movie "Who Is Harry Kellerman And Why Is He Saying Those Terrible Things About Me?".

1971

June Haffkine signs the band to a recording deal with CBS/Columbia Records before the movie opens, realising it will be a success, and the band moves to Haffkine's home in Connecticut, to spend several months in rehearsal before cutting a debut album in San Francisco.

1972

June [3] The plaintive and offbeat *Sylvia's Mother*, also written by Silverstein, hits US #5, and will earn a gold disc for a million-plus sales. Their debut album, ***Dr. Hook & The Medicine Show***, which includes the hit, reaches US #45.
Aug *Sylvia's Mother* hits UK #2.
Sept [30] *Carry Me, Carrie* peaks at US #71.
Nov The group's second show at the "Greater Baton Rouge State Fair", Baton Rouge, LA, is cut short when the band fails to keep its act clean, following a warning after the first show.

1973

Jan ***Sloppy Seconds*** makes US #41.
Mar [17] *The Cover Of "Rolling Stone"* hits US #6 and is the group's second million seller. In the UK, the BBC refuses to play it because of the mention of the magazine, a commercial enterprise, prompting the band to re-record the song as *The Cover Of "Radio Times"* (the BBC's own weekly magazine), though the single still fails to chart.
[29] The group fulfills the ambition implicit in the song by appearing on the cover of **Rolling Stone** magazine.
July [21] *Roland The Roadie And Gertrude The Groupie* peaks at US #83.
Nov [3] *Life Ain't Easy* reaches US #68, as ***Belly Up!*** makes US #141. (It will be followed by the non-charting ***Fried Face*** in 1974 and their final CBS offering, ***Ballad Of Lucy Jordan***.)

1975

Feb Having been dropped by CBS the previous year, facing financial difficulties and shortening its name to Dr. Hook, the group signs a one-year option deal with Capitol Records.
July Their label debut ***Bankrupt*** reaches US #141.
Sept [6] *The Millionaire* reaches US #95.
Nov [20] "Dr. Hook's Christmas Show" UK tour starts at Oxford Polytechnic, Oxford, Oxon.

1976

Apr *Only Sixteen*, a revival of Sam Cooke's 1959 hit, taken from ***Bankrupt***, is halfway up the US Hot 100 when Capitol's option runs out. The label continues promoting both the single and the band, and it climbs to hit US #6 (Apr [17]), selling over one million copies.
Aug *A Little Bit More*, written by Bobby Gosh and recorded in Nashville, TN, reaches US #11 and UK #2 (held from the top for four weeks by Elton John & Kiki Dee's *Don't Go Breaking My Heart*). The album ***A Little Bit More*** makes US #62 and hits UK #5 (Aug [14]), as the band appears on Nashville's "Grand Ole Opry" broadcast and, soon after, relocates to the Country capital.
Dec Locorriere-penned ballad, *If Not You*, reaches US #55 and hits UK #5.

1977

Jan Sawyer cuts an eponymous solo album of country songs, backed by Nashville session men.
Aug [6] *Walk Right In*, the group's remake of the Rooftop Singers' 1963 smash, makes US #46. ***Revisited***, compiled of material cut during the band's Columbia days, is released.
Nov [5] ***Making Love And Music*** reaches UK #39.

1978

Apr *More Like The Movies*, another Silverstein composition, reaches UK #14.

1979

Jan ***Pleasure And Pain*** makes US #66, eventually selling over half a million copies. The extracted radio-friendly *Sharing The Night Together*, after a four-month chart climb, hits US #6 and will also earn a gold disc for million-plus sales.
Mar [3] *All The Time In The World* peaks at US #54.
Aug [11] *When You're In Love With A Beautiful Woman*, written by Even Stevens, hits US #6, another US million seller.
Nov [3] ***Pleasure And Pain*** makes UK #47.
[17] The extracted *When You're In Love With A Beautiful Woman* tops the UK chart for the first of three weeks.

1980

Jan *Better Love Next Time* makes US #12 and UK #8.
Apr *Sexy Eyes* hits US #5 (another million seller) and UK #4.
May [10] ***Sometimes You Win***, from which it is extracted, reaches UK #14 and will make US #71.
Aug *Years From Now* peaks at US #51 and UK #47.
Nov *Sharing The Night Together* makes UK #43, almost two years after its US success. Capitol releases the cut after the band has left the label and signed a new deal with Casablanca Records (which releases the group's product through Mercury in Britain).
Dec [6] ***Rising*** on Casablanca/Mercury makes UK #44 and will climb to US #175, while the extracted *Girls Can Get It* reaches US #34 and UK #40.
[13] Compilation album, ***Dr. Hook's Greatest Hits***, hits UK #2, behind Abba's ***Super Trouper***, and will peak at US #142.

1981

Apr [25] *That Didn't Hurt Too Bad* peaks at US #69.
Nov [14] Performance set ***Dr. Hook Live In London*** makes UK #90.

1982

Apr [17] *Baby Makes Her Blue Jeans Talk* reaches US #25, as its parent album, ***Players In The Dark***, reaches US #118.
July [24] *Loveline* reaches US #60. (The band will continue to play and tour, despite the lack of further recording success, into the mid-'80s, eventually splitting when both vocal frontmen, Sawyer and Locorriere, move to solo careers (the latter also becoming a session singer in Nashville, TN), before a new version of Dr. Hook, led by Sawyer, but featuring no other former members, tours Britain in September 1988.)

1992

Feb [1] *When You're In Love With A Beautiful Woman*, re-released as part of EMI's Classic Tracks promotion, debuts at its UK #44 peak.
June [6] *A Little Bit More* debuts at its UK #47 peak.
[20] A 20-track retrospective, ***Completely Hooked - The Best Of Dr. Hook***, hits UK #3 (and will re-chart at UK #68 in May 1994).

DR. JOHN

1957

Sept The son of a modeling mother and record store-owner father, Dr. John (b. Malcolm John Rebennack, Nov. 21, 1940, New Orleans, LA), who, as a baby, was featured on Ivory Soap packets, and was weaned on blues club music during his teens, having played on countless sessions for New Orleans' Ace, Ebb and Ric R&B labels for the likes of Joe Tex and Professor Longhair, begins to establish himself as one of a handful of white musicians working on the New Orleans black music scene and now records his first release, *Storm Warning*, for Rex Records, under his real name, Mac Rebennack, set for release in November.

1958

He tours with Frankie Ford and Jerry Byrne (for whom he co-writes the rock'n'roll standard *Lights Out*), and releases his first album for Ace, followed by others for Rex and the black musicians' co-operative, AFO (founded by New Orleans' producer and arranger Harold Battiste).

1960

Mar Lloyd Price's *Lady Luck*, penned by Rebennack, reaches US #14.

1962

Leaving New Orleans for Los Angeles, CA, and by now playing piano (his left ring finger was shot while he was breaking up a fight in 1961, leaving him unable to play guitar), he is an in-demand session player, working on numerous records for Sonny Bono, Phil Spector, H.B. Barnum and Battiste (who has moved with him).

1964

Forming various bands, such as the Drits and Dray and Zu Zu, he develops a new identity as Dr. John Creux the Night Tripper, fusing New Orleans R&B with the emergent psychedelia of West Coast rock. He also sets up Pulsar, a subsidiary of Mercury Records, recording King Floyd and Alvin Robinson. The following year, the release of *Zu Zu Man*, recorded for A&M Records (US), will foreshadow the sound and structures of the first Dr. John album.

1968

His critically-revered debut (as Dr. John the Night Tripper), the Creole-brewed ***Gris Gris*** featuring Jesse Hill and Battiste, is released on Atco Records and includes the much-covered *I Walk On Gilded Splinters* (which will also be sampled by both PM Dawn (in 1992) and Beck (on its 1994 US #10 hit, *Loser*).

1969

Apr The seven-track follow-up, ***Babylon***, is released.
Dec [7] Dr. John performs at London's Lyceum Ballroom.

1970

June [27] Dr. John takes part in the "Bath Festival of Blues & Progressive Music" at Shepton Mallet, Somerset, promoting his latest album ***Remedies***, again released to excellent reviews.

1971

Sept Aretha Franklin's *Spanish Harlem*, featuring Dr. John on organ, hits US #2 and UK #14.
Oct His fourth Atco album, ***Dr. John, The Night Tripper (The Sun, Moon And Herbs)***, recorded in London and including contributions from recent converts Mick Jagger and Eric Clapton, peaks at US #184.

1972

Apr [29] His revival of the Dixie Cups' *Iko Iko* is his first US chart entry, peaking at US #71.
May [5] Dr. John takes part in the three-day "Bickershaw Festival", near Wigan, Lancs., on a bill with the Grateful Dead, Country Joe, Donovan and Pacific Gas & Electric.
July ***Dr. John's Gumbo***, produced by Jerry Wexler, peaks at US #112.
Sept [9] Dr. John participates in the annual "Ann Arbor Jazz & Blues Festival" in Ann Arbor, MI.

1973

June Allen Toussaint-produced ***In The Right Place***, his biggest-selling album, reaches US #24.
[30] The extracted *Right Place Wrong Time* hits US #9, and is Dr. John's only major hit single. He tours Europe, accompanied by highly-rated New Orleans band, the Meters.
July ***Triumvirate***, recorded with Mike Bloomfield and John Paul Hammond, peaks at US #105.
Oct [27] The extracted *Such A Night* makes US #42.

1974

Feb [13] Dr. John jams with Johnny Winter and Stevie Wonder at New York's Bottom Line.
May [25] *(Everybody Wanna Get Rich) Rite Away*

peaks at US #92 and ***Desitively Bonnaroo*** makes US #105. (Increasingly beset by personal and health problems, these will be his last Atco releases and his last US chart entries, with subsequent albums mostly recorded via one-off label deals.)

1975

Nov ***Hollywood Be Thy Name***, produced by Bob Ezrin, on United Artists, and credited to Rizzum & the Blues Revue, is released.

1976

Nov ***Cut Me While I'm Hot*** is released on DJM.
[25] Dr. John takes part in the Band's "The Last Waltz" Thanksgiving Day farewell concert at San Francisco's Winterland Ballroom, singing *Such A Night*, performing a duet with Joni Mitchell on the latter's *Coyote*, and joining with Bobby Charles and members of the Band on *Down South In New Orleans*. His performance is recorded on both the album and feature film of the event.

1977

Dr. John joins the short-lived RCO All Stars, the group formed by ex-Band drummer Levon Helm, and featuring Paul Butterfield and former MG's Steve Cropper and Donald "Duck" Dunn.

1981

Having moved to New York and recorded three albums for A&M's Horizon imprint (***City Lights***, ***Tango Palace*** and ***Love Potion***), and unable to secure an attractive US recording contract, Dr. John concentrates on touring Europe as a solo artist. He does, however, record the piano instrumental album ***Dr. John Plays Mac Rebennack*** for the Clean Cuts label.

1982

He releases the acclaimed ***The Brightest Smile In Town*** for Demon Records. He also records ***Take Me Back To New Orleans*** with Chris Barber, released on the Black Lion label.

1984

Feb Showing that - despite his health problems - he is still capable of pulling innovatory surprises, he releases the hip-hop-infused *Jet Set*, produced by Ed "The Message" Fletcher on Arthur Baker's New York Streetwise label, which is optioned in the UK by Beggars Banquet.

1987

Feb [24] Having co-produced Jimmy Witherspoon's ***Midnight Lady Calls The Blues*** with songwriting legend Doc Pomus the previous year, Dr. John performs as part of a blues supergroup, comprising Willie Dixon, Albert King, B.B. King, Koko Taylor, Robert Cray, Junior Wells, Etta James and Ry Cooder, at the 29th annual Grammy Awards at Los Angeles' Shrine Auditorium.

1989

Jan [21] Dr. John takes part in an R&B evening at the Washington Center, Washington, DC, during President Bush's inaugural celebrations, with Bo Diddley, Percy Sledge, Etta James, Willie Dixon, Albert Collins and Sam Moore.
July [23] He opens a 28-date, 27-city US "Tour For All Generations", as part of Ringo Starr's His All-Starr Band, at the Park Central Amphitheatre, Dallas, TX.
Aug [5] Newly signed to Warner Bros. Records, Dr. John's ***In A Sentimental Mood***, comprising cover versions of blues songs and romantic standards, tops **Billboard**'s Traditional Jazz Albums chart for the first of four weeks, having already peaked at US #142.

1990

Feb [21] *Makin' Whoopee* (from ***In A Sentimental Mood***) wins the Best Jazz Vocal Performance, Duo Or Group category at the 32nd annual Grammy Awards, at the Shrine Auditorium.
May [6] He performs at the 21st annual "Jazz & Heritage Festival", at the Fair Grounds Race Track, New Orleans.
June [2] His performance at the Trump Regency Hotel, Atlantic City, NJ, is filmed for the "SRO" TV series.
Dec [4] ***The Simpsons Sing The Blues*** album, to which Dr. John has contributed piano on *I Love To See You Smile*, is released.
[28] Having recently released ***Bluesiana Triangle*** (a jazz set recorded with David "Fathead" Newman and Art Blakey), Dr. John guests on NBC-TV's "Late Night With David Letterman".

1991

Jan Great Southern label releases ***On A Mardi Gras Day***, a live album cut with Chris Barber at the Marquee club, London, in April 1983, as Dr. John prepares for a lengthy US tour.
Apr [24] Dr. John performs at the tenth anniversary of "The Arts At St. Ann's" series at St. Ann's Church, Brooklyn Heights, New York, with Aaron Neville and John Cale.
May [18] ***Deadicated***, a collection of Grateful Dead covers to which he has contributed *Deal*, reaches US #24.
July [10] Dr. John guests at Taj Mahal's Bottom Line, New York gig.

1992

Apr Following a Japanese tour, he headlines the "JazzFest" annual music jamboree, in New Orleans, previewing cuts from his forthcoming jazz history-chronicling album for Warner Bros., ***Goin' Back To New Orleans***, featuring music from the 1850s to the 1950s.
June [18] Dr. John guests on NBC-TV's "The Tonight Show".
Aug [8] He embarks on a 25-date "Blues Music Festival '92" tour in Oregon, with B.B. King, Ray Charles, Buddy Guy and Joe Cocker sharing gigs with him. (He has also contributed *Blue Skies* to the just-released movie soundtrack of "Glengarry Glen Ross".)

1993

Feb [24] ***Goin' Back To New Orleans*** wins the Best Traditional Blues Album category at the 35th annual Grammy Awards, held at the Shrine Auditorium.
Apr [6] Sony Kids' ***Put On Your Green Shoes*** album, to benefit Songwriters and Artists for the Earth, the Earth Island Institute and Save the Children, featuring Dr. John, is released in the US.
May [5] Dr. John is featured on PBS-TV's "A Beatles Songbook".
July [10] During his latest UK visit, he plays a one-off London show at the Kentish Town Forum.

1994

Jan [29] Her performs at the opening of the House of Blues club and eatery in New Orleans.
Apr [24] Dr. John, currently promoting his latest album ***Television*** (released by G.R.P. Records), takes part in the 25th annual "New Orleans Jazz & Heritage Festival".
July [2] He plays at the "Newport Jazz Festival", Saratoga Performing Arts Center, Saratoga Springs, NY.
Aug [23] Dr. John joins B.B. King and Little Feat at the Blossom Music Center, Cuyahoga Falls, OH, during the current "Blues Music Festival" tour. (By year's end, Dr. John's autobiography **Under A Hoodoo Moon**, written with Jack Rummell, is published.)

1995

Mar [28] ***Till The Night Is Gone : A Tribute To Doc Pomus***, including a cut from Dr. John, is released by Rhino Records (US).
May [11] Along with Eric Clapton, Robert Cray, Jimmie Vaughan and Buddy Guy, Dr. John performs at a tribute to Stevie Ray Vaughan at PBS station KLRU in Austin, TX, for the program "Austin City Limits".
July Following the Rhino release of ***The Very Best Of Dr. John*** (the retro-label issued a more definitive collection ***Mos' Scocious : The Dr. John Anthology*** in 1993) his new album ***Afterglow***, a collection of jazz vocal music from the '40s and '50s recorded in big band style, is issued by Blue Thumb.
Sept [2] He performs *Blueberry Hill* and *What'd I Say* and backs Robbie Robertson on *The Weight* at the Concert for the Rock and Roll Hall of Fame at Cleveland Stadium, Cleveland, OH.
Dec [3] Dr. John performs a medley of B.B. King's hits with Etta James at the 18th annual Kennedy Center Honors.
[31] He takes part in BBC2-TV's "Jools Hootenanny" with Eric Clapton, Supergrass, Alanis Morissette and Dick Dale.

THOMAS DOLBY

1979

Jan Keyboardist/songwriter/performer/producer Dolby (b. Thomas Morgan Robertson, Oct. 14, 1958, Cairo, Egypt), who has begun building his own synthesizers after studying projectionism and meteorology at college in London, has played keyboards with a variety of groups and is a sound mixer at live gigs for groups including the Members, the Passions, U.K. Subs and the Fall during the late '70s. He now joins Bruce Woolley & the Camera Club for a few months, continuing his varied musical apprenticeship on a US tour with Lene Lovich, writing and producing her 1980 mini-hit *New Toy* (UK #53).

1981

Mar He releases *Urges/Leipzig* on his own independent label, Armageddon, which brings him to the attention of Foreigner, who enlist his keyboard wizardry on ***4***, and that of Def Leppard, who employ him for the ***Pyromania*** project. (He will remain a much in-demand session player, also contributing to albums by Joan Armatrading and M.)
July He forms his own Venice In Peril label and signs a worldwide license-and-distribution deal with EMI Records.
Oct [10] His first single through EMI, *Europa And The Pirate Twins*, makes UK #48.

1982

Sept [11] *Windpower* makes UK #31, as Dolby promotes the album, touring the UK as a one-man show with computers, keyboards, videos, slides and tape machines, and confirms his position as a leading exponent of new techno-rock.
[18] Self-produced ***The Golden Age Of Wireless***, having first charted in May, now peaks at UK #65, but will be a major US success climbing to US #13 (in June the following year).
Nov [13] *She Blinded Me With Science* makes UK #49.

1983

Mar [14] *She Blinded Me With Science* hits US #5, boosted by an ingenious "mad scientist" video featuring eccentric UK TV scientist Magnus Pyke.
Mar US-only titled album ***Blinded By Science*** reaches US #20.
July [2] *Europa And The Pirate Twins* peaks at US #67.

1984

Feb [18] *Hyperactive* reaches UK #17, as its parent album, the self-produced and largely self-penned ***The Flat Earth***, including guests Woolley and Robyn Hitchcock, becomes his biggest UK seller, reaching #14.
Mar [24] *Hyperactive* peaks at US #62, as ***The Flat Earth*** makes US #35.
Apr [21] His acoustic version of Dan Hicks' *I Scare Myself* makes UK #46. (In the previous 12 months Dolby has also completed session and mixing work with acts including Whodini, Adele Bertei and Malcolm McLaren on his album, ***Duck Rock***.)

1985

Mar [25] He joins Stevie Wonder and Herbie Hancock in a keyboard medley trio on stage at the 27th annual Grammy Awards.

July [13] He plays keyboards for David Bowie's "Live Aid" performance at Wembley Stadium, Wembley, Middx. (During the next 18 months, Dolby will be involved in many projects, including co-productions of Joni Mitchell's ***Dog Eat Dog*** and Prefab Sprout's ***Steve McQueen*** (US title: ***Two Wheels Burning***), single collaborations with George Clinton and Ryiuchi Sakamoto, and his own Dolby's Cube, an ensemble including Clinton, Lene Lovich and members of Earth Wind & Fire. He will also score the soundtracks for Ken Russell's film "Gothic" and George Lucas' "Howard The Duck".)

1987

Jan Dolby settles in Los Angeles, CA, where he recruits members for his backing band, which he names the Lost Toy People, to record his first album in three years. During the year he will contribute to Belinda Carlisle's ***Heaven On Earth*** and produce four new songs for Prefab Sprout's ***From Langley Park To Memphis***.

1988

Apr Having recently completed production work for South African artist Johnny Clegg and the soundtrack to the movie "Ferngully ... The Last Rainforest", *Airhead*, his first single in four years, peaks at UK #53.
May [7] ***Aliens Ate My Buick***, co-produced with Bill Bottrell, makes UK #30. In typical quirky Dolby fashion, the album includes contributions from George Clinton, Ed Asner and TV personality Robin Leach.
July Dolby marries "Dynasty" TV star Kathleen Beller. ***Aliens Ate My Buick*** peaks at US #70.

1990

July [21] Dolby plays the role of the teacher in Roger Waters' re-creation of ***The Wall*** at the Potsdamer Platz, Berlin, W. Germany.
Sept [8] Prefab Sprout's ***Jordan The Comeback***, produced by Dolby, hits UK #7.
(During the year, Dolby will also co-produce Ofra Haza's ***Desert Winds***.)

1992

May [23] *Close But No Cigar* reaches UK #22.
June [3] Dolby performs as part of "The Original Songwriters" series at the Orange Pub in London.
July [18] *I Love You Goodbye* makes UK #36.
[31] Dolby plays his first UK gig in four years, at London's Mean Fiddler.
Aug [8] ***Astronauts & Heretics***, dedicated to his bass player Terry Nelson Jackson, who has perished in the plane crash which has taken the lives of Reba McEntire's band, and featuring guests Jerry Garcia, Bob Weir (the first time they have guested together on someone else's album) and Eddie Van Halen, debuts at its UK #35 peak.
Oct [3] Further extract, *Silk Pyjamas*, stops at UK #62.
Dec Dolby is featured on the soundtrack to the Robin Williams-starring movie, "Toys".

1993

Jan [25] His daughter, Talia Claire Robertson, is born in Los Angeles.
Oct [23-24] Dolby participates in a five-part exhibition on virtual reality programs at the Guggenheim Museum, New York, experiencing his "Virtual String Quartet". (By year's end he will form Headspace to undertake an increasing demand for multimedia projects, including the video game ***Mind's Eye*** and his projected 1994 release, ***Cyberia***. Capitol will release ***The Best Of Thomas Dolby*** in April 1995.)

FATS DOMINO

1949

One of a family of nine, Domino (b. Antoine Domino, Feb. 26, 1928, New Orleans, LA), who was taught to play boogie-woogie based piano in his early teens by his brother-in-law, New Orleans musician Harrison Verrett, almost lost his fingers in an accident in the bedmaking factory where he worked at the age of 14 but regained their use and his playing ability. Having married his childhood sweetheart, Rose Marie, a year earlier, he is now playing piano in the honky-tonks in New Orleans for $3 a week, when bandleader/producer Dave Bartholomew, scouting on behalf of Imperial Records, hears him performing with Billy Diamond's combo at the Hideaway club, and decides to sign and record him.
Dec [10] Bartholomew helps him rewrite *Junker's Blues* (the first song he heard Domino play) as *The Fat Man*, which is recorded in New Orleans at Domino's first session in Cosimo Matassa's J&M studio.

1950

Apr *The Fat Man*, a useful tie-in with Domino's own "Fats" nickname (and now professional moniker) from his 5ft 5in, 224lb stature, with Herb Hardesty on sax, hits US R&B #6, the first of 61 R&B survey hits he will score between now and 1964. (By 1953, the song will have sold a million, earning Domino his first gold disc.)
Oct After three less successful releases, *Every Night About This Time*, recorded again with Bartholomew's band, hits R&B #5.

1951

Dec Having formed his own, Domino hits US R&B #9 with *Rockin' Chair*. Bartholomew continues to help with arranging and writing (until 1955), but finds Domino's innovative playing (a "creative" approach to keeping time) difficult to work with.

1952

June [21] *Goin' Home* tops the US R&B chart and becomes a million seller.

1953

June *Goin' To The River* hits US R&B #2 and earns a third gold disc.
Aug *Please Don't Leave Me* hits US R&B #5.

1954

Mar *You Done Me Wrong* hits US R&B #10. Domino fails to make the R&B chart again this year, but concentrates on touring the US, with visits to New York in the spring, the West Coast and the North-West in the summer, and the Mid-West and Chicago in December, his popularity growing steadily out of the secular market.

1955

Jan [28] In New York, Domino begins a 42-date US tour on the "Top Ten R&B Show", with the Clovers, Joe Turner, the Moonglows, Faye Adams and other major R&B acts.
May [22] A show to be headlined by Domino at the Ritz ballroom in Bridgeport, CT, is cancelled by local police, who justify the action by pointing to a "recent near-riot" at New Haven Arena, during a rock'n'roll dance.
June [11] *Ain't That A Shame* tops the R&B chart for the first of 11 weeks, and is his first single to cross over and hit US #10. It is a million seller, but is outsold by Pat Boone's version, which hits US #2 and UK #7.
Nov [12] In **Billboard**'s annual US DJ poll, Domino is named the country's Favorite R&B artist.

1956

Apr *Bo Weevil* makes US #35 (his second single to cross over).
June *I'm In Love Again* hits US #3 and tops the R&B chart for seven weeks, becoming another million seller, while its B-side, *My Blue Heaven*, reaches US #21.
Aug [28] Domino begins a co-headlining (with Frankie Lymon & the Teenagers) ten-day series of performances in Alan Freed's annual rock'n'roll show at the Paramount Theater, Brooklyn, New York.
Sept *When My Dreamboat Comes Home* reaches US #14, with its B-side, *So Long*, peaking at #44. *I'm In Love Again* marks his UK chart debut, reaching UK #12.
Nov ***Fats Domino - Rock And Rollin'*** is his first chart album, reaching US #18.
[10] In the annual **Billboard** DJ poll, Domino is again voted Favorite R&B Artist, as well as being the ninth most-played male vocalist (Elvis Presley being the most-played).
[18] Domino appears on CBS-TV's "The Ed Sullivan Show" singing his revival of the standard *Blueberry Hill*. (The song had originally been written for Gene Autry to sing in the movie "The Singing Hill", before being popularized by Glenn Miller.)
Dec *Blueberry Hill* hits US #3, tops the US R&B chart for eight weeks and sells over a million. He appears in the film "Shake, Rattle and Roll", with R&B singer Joe Turner, performing *I'm In Love Again*, *Honey Chile* and *Ain't That A Shame*.

1957

Jan *Ain't That A Shame* reaches UK #23, as Domino appears in the Jayne Mansfield-starring movie "The Girl Can't Help It", singing *Blue Monday*.
Feb *Honey Chile* reaches UK #29, while *Blueberry Hill*, after a lengthy climb, hits UK #6.
Blue Monday hits US #9 (another million seller), and replaces *Blueberry Hill* at US R&B #1, remaining there for eight weeks. Its B-side, *What's The Reason I'm Not Pleasing You* (originally a pre-war hit for Guy Lombardo), makes US #50.
[2] Domino appears on NBC-TV's "The Perry Como Show" singing *Blueberry Hill* and *Blue Monday*.
[15] Domino begins a US tour (lasting until May 5th) as part of "The Greatest Show of 1957", a rock'n'roll caravan which also includes Chuck Berry, Clyde McPhatter, LaVern Baker and others.
Mar ***This Is Fats Domino!***, which includes both *Blueberry Hill* and *Blue Monday*, reaches US #19. *Blue Monday* reaches UK #23.
Apr ***Rock And Rollin' With Fats Domino*** (his belatedly-charting debut album, including *Ain't That A Shame*) reaches US #17. *I'm Walkin'* hits US #5, and spends six weeks at R&B #1, replacing *Blue Monday*. (By the time *I'm Walking* drops from R&B #1 in April, Domino will have been at the top of the chart for 22 consecutive weeks with three different singles.)
May *I'm Walking* reaches UK #19.
July *Valley Of Tears* hits US #6 and its B-side, *It's You I Love*, stops at US #22, while *Valley Of Tears* makes UK #25.
Aug *When I See You* reaches US #29 with the B-side, *What Will I Tell My Heart*, making US #64.
Oct *Wait And See* reaches US #23, its flip-side, *I Still Love You*, peaking at US #79.
Nov [12] The rock'n'roll movie "Jamboree" (released in the UK as "Disc Jockey Jamboree"), featuring Domino singing *Wait And See* with a host of rock acts, premieres in Hollywood, CA.
[14] Five audience members are arrested at the all-star "Biggest Show Of Stars" package, which includes Domino, at the Boston Garden, Boston, MA.
Dec *The Big Beat* reaches US #26, the title track to movie of the same name, in which Domino performs *I'm Walking*. Its B-side, *I Want You To Know*, makes US #48.

1958

Apr *The Big Beat* stops at UK #20.
May *Sick And Tired* reaches US #22, while the flip, *No No*, peaks at US #55.
July *Little Mary* makes US #48, while *Sick And Tired* reaches UK #26.
Sept *Young School Girl* peaks at US #92.

1959

Jan *Whole Lotta Loving* hits US #6 and is another million seller.
Mar Both sides of the double-A *Telling Lies* and *When The Saints Go Marching In* reach US #50.
June *I'm Ready* reaches US #16, its flip-side, *Margie*, making #51 and UK #19.
Sept *I Want To Walk You Home*, yet another million seller, hits US #8, with the B-side, *I'm Gonna Be A Wheel Some Day*, reaching US #17.
Oct *I Want To Walk You Home* makes UK #14.
Dec *Be My Guest* hits US #8 and is another million seller, while its flipside, *I've Been Around*, peaks at US #33.

1960

Jan *Be My Guest*, Domino's biggest UK hit single since *Blueberry Hill*, reaches UK #11.
Mar *Country Boy* reaches US #25 and UK #19.
May *Tell Me That You Love Me/Before I Grow Too Old* make US #51 and #84 respectively.
Aug Strings-backed *Walking To New Orleans* hits US #6 and reaches UK #19, with the B-side, *Don't Come Knockin'*, making US #21, Domino's last million-selling single.
Oct *Three Nights A Week* reaches US #15, its B-side, *Put Your Arms Around Me Honey*, peaking at US #58.
Nov *Three Nights A Week* makes UK #45.
Dec *My Girl Josephine* reaches US #14, while the B-side, *Natural Born Lover*, climbs to US #38.

1961

Jan *My Girl Josephine* makes UK #32.
Feb *What A Price* reaches US #22 and its B-side, *Ain't That Just Like A Woman*, peaks at US #33.
Apr [2] Domino begins a wide-ranging tour of North America as part of "The Biggest Show of Stars 1961", with Chubby Checker, Bo Diddley, and others.
Apr Both sides of *Shu Rah/Fell In Love On Monday* peak separately at US #32.
July *It Keeps Rainin'* reaches US #23 and UK #49.
[8] Domino completes a 19-day tour of southwestern US states, grossing $83,000.
Sept *Let The Four Winds Blow* reaches US #15.
Dec *What A Party* reaches US #22 and UK #43, with its B-side, *Rockin' Bicycle*, charting briefly at US #83.

1962

Feb His revival of Hank Williams' 1952 country hit, *Jambalaya (On The Bayou)*, reaches US #30 while its B-side *I Hear You Knocking* (originally recorded by Domino's New Orleans contemporary, Smiley Lewis) makes US #67.
Mar *Jambalaya (On The Bayou)* reaches UK #41.
Apr He records what will be his last session for Imperial in New Orleans. Meanwhile, another Hank Williams revival, *You Win Again*, reaches US #22 as its B-side, *Ida Jane*, peaks at US #90.
June His last few Imperial A-sides will fail to make the US Top 40, as Domino's never-changing sound begins to seem passé alongside the rapidly-developing R&B styles of the early '60s, and the dance discs by Chubby Checker, Dee Dee Sharp and others. *My Real Name* reaches US #59.
July *Nothing New (Same Old Thing)* and the B-side, *Dance With Mr. Domino*, peak at US #77 and #98 respectively. Domino takes part in the "Antibes Jazz Festival" in Juan Les Pins, South of France.
Aug 1960-62 hits compilation, ***Million Sellers By Fats***, peaks at US #113.
Oct *Did You Ever See A Dream Walking?*, reviving a pre-war hit by Eddy Duchin, makes US #79, his last hit single on Imperial.

1963

Apr [6] Domino's Imperial contract expires and he signs to ABC-Paramount Records, to record in Nashville, TN.
June *There Goes (My Heart Again)*, on ABC, an unmistakably familiar Domino sound (despite the substitution of a Nashville recording session for New Orleans), reaches US #59.
Oct ***Here Comes Fats Domino***, on ABC, makes US #130 and includes his revival of the standard *Red Sails In The Sunset*, styled towards Ray Charles' R&B/country arrangement of *I Can't Stop Loving You*, which makes US #35 and UK #34.

1964

Jan *Who Cares* peaks at US #63, taken from ***Fats On Fire***.
Mar *Lazy Lady* stops at US #86.
Sept *Sally Was A Good Old Girl* reaches US #99.
Nov *Heartbreak Hill* is Domino's last ABC hit, also making US #99.

1965

He signs a two-year deal with Mercury Records. However, only a few records are produced (two singles, including a version of *I Left My Heart In San Francisco*, ***Fats Domino '65***, recorded live in Las Vegas, and the live album ***Southland USA***, which is never released).

1966

Aug Domino plays two four-day stints at the Village Gate in New York.

1967

Mar [27] He makes his first-ever UK visit, playing the first of six nights, supported by Gerry & the Pacemakers and the Bee Gees, to a rapturous audience at London's Saville Theatre.
Dec The Mercury contract has expired, and Domino records *The Lady In Black* and a follow-up single on his own Broadmoor label, co-owned with Dave Bartholomew.

1968

Sept Domino signs to Reprise Records and his last US chart single, at #100, is a cover of the Beatles' *Lady Madonna*, written in reverential Domino style by Paul McCartney. (Two similar Beatles' covers, *Lovely Rita* and *Everybody's Got Something To Hide Except Me And My Monkey*, are issued as follow-ups.)
Oct ***Fats Is Back***, on the Reprise label and produced by Richard Perry, peaks at US #189, Domino's final US chart album.

1970

May Compilation, ***Very Best Of Fats Domino***, reaches UK #56 (his only UK chart album). (A reissued *Blueberry Hill*, will also make UK #41 in May 1976.)

1979

May At the end of a relatively quiet decade for Domino, during which he recorded a live set for Atlantic Records, in Montreux, Switzerland in 1973, and also appeared in the movie "Let The Good Times Roll", his first album in many years, ***Sleeping On The Job***, recorded at Sea-Saint Studios in New Orleans, is released by Sonet Records. (Into the '90s, Domino will spend much time living at home in New Orleans with his wife and family. He will play regularly in Las Vegas and other venues where his nostalgic style, which is still basically the same as in 1949, will draw an appreciative audience, but he will not undertake lengthy tours.)

1986

Jan [23] Domino is inducted into the Rock and Roll Hall of Fame at the inaugural dinner, at New York's Waldorf Astoria Hotel.

1987

Feb [24] *Blueberry Hill* is inducted into the NARAS Hall of Fame at the 29th annual Grammy Awards. (Domino is further honored by the NARAS at the 30th annual Grammy Awards, with a Lifetime Achievement Award, noting that he is "one of the most important links between rhythm and blues and rock and roll, a most influential performer whose style of piano-playing and 'down home' singing have led the way for generations of other performers").

1990

Domino records his first album in five years, a double live package recorded in New Orleans on the Tomato label, and also guests on the Dirty Dozen Brass Band's eponymously-titled album. His earlier work comes back into public view with ***My Blue Heaven - The Best Of Fats Domino (Volume One)*** which is released to tie in with the Steve Martin/Rick Moranis comedy movie, "My Blue Heaven".

1991

Oct EMI issues a definitive four-CD/cassette, 100-song Domino boxed-set retrospective, ***They Call Me The Fat Man***. Usually reclusive, Domino embarks on a round of promotion for the definitive collection.
[24] New Orleans mayor Sidney Barthelemy proclaims "Fats Domino Day".
Nov [5] In town for a show at New York's Bottom Line, Domino guests on NBC-TV's "Late Night With David Letterman".

1992

Oct [28] Domino makes a return visit to the UK, playing at London's Hammersmith Odeon.

1993

July [13] He shares a bill with Ray Charles at the Westfalenhalle 1, Dortmund, Germany, during current European dates.

1994

Oct [8] Domino performs *Jailhouse Rock*, with Michael Bolton singing, at "Elvis Aaron Presley : The Tribute", an all-star music event at the Pyramid Arena, Memphis, TN, broadcast live in the US on pay-per-view TV.

1995

Feb Domino plays his first club gig in 15 years at the first anniversary celebrations of the House of Blues in New Orleans.
Mar [2] He receives the Rhythm and Blues Foundation's Ray Charles Lifetime Achievement Award at the sixth annual Pioneer Awards at Los Angeles' Hollywood Palladium.

LONNIE DONEGAN

1952

Donegan (b. Anthony James Donegan, Apr. 29, 1931, Glasgow, Strathclyde, Scotland), his father a violinist with the National Scottish Orchestra, having played professionally in jazz bands since his army service in 1949 and allegedly gaining his stage name when, on the same London bill as US blues guitarist Lonnie Johnson, he is inadvertently introduced as "Lonnie" Donegan by a confused MC, joins Ken Colyer's Jazzmen as guitar and banjo player. With Colyer, in which he is reunited with an army buddy, trombonist Chris Barber, Donegan's blues and folk influences earn him a solo spot in the band's act, leading a small group (Colyer on guitar, Barber on bass, and Bill Colyer on washboard) on US blues and work songs, generically dubbed "skiffle". A number of Donegan recordings will be taped on his first studio session the following year with Colyer's band, though the tracks are not used. Barber subsequently splits from Colyer in January 1954 along with many of his musicians, including Donegan, and forms Chris Barber's Jazz Band, signing to Decca Records.

1955

The band records a 10" album, ***New Orleans Joy***, which contains two tracks, *Rock Island Line* and *John Henry*, credited to the Lonnie Donegan Skiffle Group.

1956

Feb [4] *Rock Island Line*, learned from a Leadbelly song and credited to Donegan, hits UK #8 during 25 charted weeks. (Donegan never receives any royalties from it, having been paid a £50 session fee when it was recorded.) He signs to Pye-Nixa in the UK as a soloist.
Apr [21] *Rock Island Line* hits US #8 and takes the cumulative sales over a million.
May Donegan, accompanied by a trio comprising stand-up bass, drums and Denny Wright on electric guitar, tours the US for a month, billed as "The Irish Hillbilly".
[19] He makes his US TV debut on NBC-TV's "The Perry Como Show", alongside Ronald Reagan, who is appearing in some comedy sketches.
June *Lost John*, his first Pye solo release, hits UK #2 and US #58. Its B-side, *Stewball*, charts briefly at UK #29.
July [7] *Skiffle Session* reaches UK #20 and is the first

EP by a UK artist to chart.
Sept [29] *Bring A Little Water Sylvie/Dead Or Alive* hits UK #7. Back from the US, Donegan and the group begin a lengthy UK tour, which will hardly cease over the next two years, prompting would-be musicians all over the UK to form easy-to-play-in skiffle groups, many of them the roots of rock'n'roll and British beat careers of the late '50s and the '60s.

1957

Jan [5] 10" album, ***Lonnie Donegan Showcase***, reaches UK #27 on the Singles chart. It is the first album by a UK artist to chart (UK Album charts do not exist at this time).
Feb [16] *Don't You Rock Me Daddy-O* hits UK #4, beating off a cover from the Vipers Skiffle Group, which hits #10.
Mar [27] Donegan performs at New York's Madison Square Garden, as part of a US tour arranged as an exchange with Bill Haley & the Comets, who are on a UK visit.
Apr [13] *Cumberland Gap* tops the UK chart, while *Daddy-O* is still in the Top 10, and holds pole position for five weeks, again defeating a Vipers cover version, which hits UK #10.
June [28] Donegan is currently starring in the "Skiffle Sensation of 1957" at London's Royal Albert Hall, as the double A-side, *Puttin' On The Style/Gamblin' Man*, hits UK #1 for the first of two weeks. It is taken from the live ***Putting On The Style***, Donegan's first excursion from folk/blues-based material into novelty/comedy.
Nov [9] *My Dixie Darling* hits UK #10, while Donegan is filming appearances in a movie version of the UK TV pop music show, "6.5 Special".
Dec [28] *Jack O' Diamonds* reaches UK #14.

1958

May [31] An adaptation of Woody Guthrie's *Grand Coolie Dam* hits UK #6.
July [19] Double A-side, *Sally Don't You Grieve/Betty Betty Betty*, hits UK #11.
Sept [27] *Lonesome Traveller* makes UK #28.
Nov [29] *Lonnie's Skiffle Party* reaches UK #23.
Dec [6] *Tom Dooley*, adapting the Kingston Trio's smooth original US #1 to Donegan's more frenetic style, hits UK #3 and stays there for six weeks, while the original shadows its way to #4.

1959

Feb [28] *Does Your Chewing Gum Lose Its Flavour (On The Bedpost Overnight?)*, originally a hit in 1924 for Ernest Hare & Billy Jones, hits UK #3.
May [16] *Fort Worth Jail* reaches UK #14.
July [25] His cover of Johnny Horton's US chart-topper, *Battle Of New Orleans*, spends the first of four weeks at UK #2. Donegan is forced to change the lyric and substitute "bloomin'" for "ruddy", which is banned by BBC radio. (This is not his first brush with the BBC censor: in 1956 *Diggin' My Potatoes* was banned for "obscenity" and it remained BBC-blacklisted through the '50s.)
Sept [12] *Sal's Got A Sugar Lip* reaches UK #13.
Dec [6] *San Miguel* peaks at UK #19.

1960

Jan He records in the US with writer/producers Leiber and Stoller. (The tracks will appear in the UK as the EP *Yankee Doodle Donegan*.)
Mar [26] *My Old Man's A Dustman*, recorded live on stage in Doncaster, Yorks., is the first single by a British act to enter the UK chart at #1 (only Elvis Presley achieved this previously), where it stays for four weeks.
May [16] Donegan takes part in the Royal Variety Performance in London.
June *I Wanna Go Home*, a version of the traditional *Wreck Of The John B*, hits UK #5. (It will be revived later by the Beach Boys as *Sloop John B*.)
Sept *Lorelei* reaches UK #12.
Nov Donegan appears with Cliff Richard and Adam Faith in the pop music segment of the "Royal Variety Show" in London.
Dec *Lively*, a music hall-styled novelty in Donegan's "Dustman" mode, makes UK #14, while the seasonal and simultaneously-issued *Virgin Mary* reaches UK #27.

1961

June *Have A Drink On Me* hits UK #8. (This is another diplomatically-changed lyric: Huddie Ledbetter's original was titled *Have A Whiff On Me*.)
Sept *Michael Row The Boat*, an uptempo contrast to the Highwaymen's (US and UK #1) gentle version, hits UK #6.
[25] A belated US release of *Does Your Chewing Gum Lose Its Flavor (On The Bedpost Overnight?)* is his third and last chart entry, hitting US #5, and combined UK and US sales now top one million.

1962

Feb *The Comancheros*, inspired by the John Wayne movie, reaches UK #14.
May An uncharacteristic revival of the standard ballad *The Party's Over* hits UK #9. It was recorded after he sang it in a coffee bar in Timaroo, New Zealand, on an Australasian tour, just before Christmas. (It was the only song that both Donegan and the pianist knew.)
July Another ballad, the self-composed *I'll Never Fall In Love Again* is only his second UK single not to chart (though the song will be a million seller for Tom Jones in the late '60s). The "Putting On The Donegan" TV series airs.
Sept *Pick A Bale Of Cotton* reaches UK #11 and is his last hit single. The compilation ***A Golden Age Of Donegan*** is his first entry in the UK Album chart, hitting UK #3 during a 23-week survey tenure.
Oct [9] Donegan begins a month-long engagement at New York's Village Gate.
Dec [7] He releases *The Market Song*, a duet with Max Miller, as he prepares to play Buttons in "Cinderella" at the Grand Theatre, Leeds, Yorks.

1963

Feb Compilation, ***A Golden Age Of Donegan Vol. 2***, reaches UK #15.
Apr [5] Donegan's new ITV series debuts.
May [20] He embarks on a summer season at the Queen's Theatre, Blackpool, Lancs.

1964

July [27] Donegan begins a six-week cabaret season in Australia.

1965

Dec Having released ***The Folk Album*** earlier in the year, he records the official 1966 Soccer World Cup song, *World Cup Willie*, but it fails to chart (even when the England team wins the competition the following summer). By now, much of his live work is in cabaret and he spends half of each year in the US, much of it in Las Vegas, NV.

1966

His publishing company, Tyler Music (Tyler being his wife's maiden name), the owner of the copyright of most of his hit adaptations of traditional material and well-covered songs like *I'll Never Fall In Love Again*, signs young songwriter Justin Hayward. (Hayward will later join the Moody Blues, and his songs for the group, notably *Nights In White Satin*, will prove to be huge long-term royalty earners for the company.)
Apr [1] Donegan flies to Cyprus to begin a three-week tour entertaining the troops in the Far East.
Nov *Auntie Maggie's Remedy* is the last release on Pye. (He will issue only one album, ***Lonniepops*** in 1970 and eight singles over the next 11 years. Most are his own independent Tyler Records productions, licensed variously to Decca, RCA, Black Lion and Pye for UK release.) He also appears as a regular on "The Saturday Crowd" in 1969 and as a panelist on the mid-'70s ITV talent show, "New Faces".

1976

Donegan suffers a heart attack and is warned to stop working. He moves to California in semi-retirement, to recuperate.

1978

Feb [25] ***Putting On The Style***, produced by Adam Faith on Chrysalis Records, makes UK #51, Donegan's first chart entry for 15 years. Playing on it are Ringo Starr, Elton John, Brian May of Queen, and many others who acknowledge Donegan's influence in prompting them to play music in the first place.

1979

May ***Sundown***, again for Chrysalis, eschews the superstars and offers more country-flavored material, recorded with the help of friend and guitarist Albert Lee. Donegan also makes an country album with fiddle player Doug Kershaw.

1981

Feb [23] He takes part in the "25 Years Of British Pop" segment at the Royal Variety Performance.
Nov ***Jubilee Concert***, a live set of oldies, is released to mark his 25th anniversary in music. He also records a skiffle EP with Scots group the Shakin' Pyramids.

1985

Donegan undergoes surgery after recurrent heart attacks, from which he recovers sufficiently to work again at a reasonable pace.

1986

Dec He forms a new band, Donegan's Dancing Sunshine Band, with clarinettist Monty Sunshine, a former colleague from the Chris Barber Band 30 years earlier. Maintaining his musical popularity worldwide via live work with the new band, Donegan, still living in California but spending three months each year in the UK, will also attempt acting in dramas, not least, in BBC1-TV's police drama, "Rockliffe's Babies" (1987). He will also perform at the 1989 "**Country Music Magazine** Festival" in Lincolnshire, despite the event's low attendance.

1995

May [23] While a number of compilations have brought his past glories to compact disc over the past ten years (including ***The Hit Singles Collection*** in 1987 and ***Golden Hour Of Lonnie Donegan*** (on Knight Records in 1991), Donegan has continued to perform the occasional nostalgia date and is now honored with the Outstanding Contribution To British Music award at the 40th annual Ivor Novello Awards, held at London's Grosvenor House.

RAL DONNER

1961

May After a single for Scottie Records has failed to score, Donner (b. Ralph Donner, Feb. 10, 1943, Chicago, IL), a church-choir graduate who fronted his first band at 13 and worked clubs between Chicago and New York, NY, at 15, seeing chart potential in a track from Presley's ***Elvis Is Back***, has gone to an egg-box studio in Florida and made a creditable duplication of *The Girl Of My Best Friend*, which now reaches US #19. Local studio musicians, the Starfires, become his permanent backing band. The results are leased to George Goldner's Gone label.
Sept Risking a permanent reputation as a Presley clone, Donner records an original song, *You Don't Know What You've Got (Until You Lose It)*, with similar smouldering intensity. It hits US #4 and UK #25 (his first and last time on the UK chart).
Nov Assisted by ABC-TV's "American Bandstand", on which he appears four times, Donner's third single, *Please Don't Go*, reaches US #39.

1962

Feb *She's Everything (I Wanted You To Be)* makes US #18.
Apr *(What A Sad Way) To Love Someone* peaks at US

#74, making five hit singles in a row for Donner, but it is his last chart entry.
Donner leaves Gone Records after royalty disputes and, for the next two decades, continues to record, with only modest sales, for a wide range of labels, including Reprise, Tau, Fontana, Red Bird, Mid-Eagle, Rising Sons, MJ, Sunlight, Chicago-Fire, Starfire, Thunder and Inferno.

1981

Donner is asked to contribute his celebrated Presley impersonation to the soundtrack of the Warner Bros. film "This Is Elvis".

1984

Apr [6] After a long hospitalization in Chicago, Donner dies of lung cancer, aged 41.

DONOVAN

1964

Donovan (b. Donovan Philip Leitch, May 10, 1946, Maryhill, Glasgow, Scotland), after moving to Hatfield, Herts., at age ten, having left college after a year and making his first public appearance at the Cock pub in St. Albans, Herts., is living in a seaside art studio in St. Ives, Cornwall, writing songs between waiting tables in cafés, and frequently travelling around Britain to perform in folk clubs with kazoo player Gypsy Dave. (While in Manchester, Lancs., he is arrested on a charge of stealing 5,000 cigarettes and some chocolates from a cinema, and spends two weeks on remand in Strangeways Prison.) Performing at another seaside town, Southend, Essex, he is spotted by Geoff Stephens and Peter Eden, who offer to manage him.

1965

Jan Demo recordings of some of his own songs, recorded at Stephens and Eden's instigation at a Denmark Street studio in London, interest both Pye Records and Bob Bickford, a production staff member of the ITV show "Ready Steady Go".
Feb Donovan appears on "Ready Steady Go" for three consecutive weeks (the first act ever to have a mini-"residency" on the show), and is signed by Pye Records amid widespread media comments about his apparent similarity in style and appearance (denim cap, racked harmonica, guitar inscribed "this guitar kills", etc.) to folk star Bob Dylan.
Mar Donovan and Dylan meet during Dylan's UK tour (documented in D.A. Pennebaker's fly-on-the wall film "Don't Look Back"). Donovan's debut, *Catch The Wind*, enters the UK chart simultaneously with Dylan's first UK hit single *The Times They Are A-Changin'*.
Apr *Catch The Wind* hits UK #4 (while Dylan's single peaks at UK #9).
[11] Donovan appears at the "**New Musical Express** Poll Winners Concert" at the Empire Pool, Wembley, Middx., with the Beatles, the Rolling Stones, Tom Jones and others.
May [28] Donovan and Joan Baez lead a Vietnam War protest march to Trafalgar Square in London.
June ***What's Bin Did And What's Bin Hid***, including six of his own songs, hits UK #3.
[3] Donovan stars on the first folk and C&W "Folk Room" series on BBC Radio.
July [3] *Colours* hits UK #4, as *Catch The Wind*, released in the US by country/folk label Hickory Records, reaches US #23.
[7] Donovan flies to the US for a four-day visit to promote the single, appearing on the TV shows "Shindig" and "The Hollywood Palace". While there, he appears at the "Newport Folk Festival", Newport, RI, ironically on the same bill as Bob Dylan, who is booed for playing an electric set backed by the Paul Butterfield Blues Band.
Aug He records friend and one-time road manager Gypsy Dave.
Sept *Universal Soldier*, written by Buffy Saint-Marie, heads a four-track EP of the same title devoted to anti-war protest songs (the other three tracks are penned by Mick Softley, Bert Jansch and Donovan), which reaches UK #13.
[7] Donovan films a promo clip of *Universal Soldier* for BBC-TV's "Top Of The Pops" on the D-Day landing beaches in Normandy, France.
[18] *Colours* peaks at US #61 and ***Catch The Wind*** makes US #30.
[25] He begins a 28-day UK tour.
[30] Donovan's ABC-TV "Shindig" debut airs.
Oct His solicitors announce that he has ended his management contract with Stephens and Eden and signed with Ashley Kozak as his business manager and his father as his personal manager, remaining with Allen Klein in the US. They also announce that the Vic Lewis Organisation will act as his agents. Stephens and Eden immediately serve a high court writ on the solicitors, to prevent Donovan working with anyone else but them.
[15] He takes part in a "Ban The Bomb" concert at the Fairfield Halls, Croydon, Surrey.
[30] *Universal Soldier* peaks at US #53. (Glen Campbell's cover makes US #45.)
Nov *Turquoise* reaches UK #30, while the largely self-penned ***Fairy Tale*** climbs to UK #20.
[19] Donovan takes part in the "Glad Rag Ball" at the Empire Pool, Wembley, on a bill with the Hollies, the Kinks, the Who, the Merseybeats, Georgie Fame, Wilson Pickett and the Barron Knights.
Dec His first recording with producer Mickie Most, a move away from Donovan's folk context to more experimental pop fields, is initially titled *For John And Paul*, amended to *Sunshine Superman*.
[6] Donovan begins a two-week Scandinavian tour at the Tivoli Gardens, Copenhagen, Denmark.

1966

Jan ***Fairy Tale*** peaks at US #85.
[19] "A Boy Called Donovan" special airs on ITV.
Feb Pye pulls *Sunshine Superman* from its release schedule, while Donovan is in dispute with his original management, and issues the earlier recording, *Josie*, as a UK single, which fails to chart.
Mar [14] Donovan begins a 28-day European tour of Germany, Austria, Switzerland, France, Belgium and Holland.
July As the Donovan/Most production deal is cleared, he signs to Epic Records for US releases, continuing to lease productions to Pye in Britain.
Sept [3] Released first in the US, *Sunshine Superman* hits #1 for a week and earns Donovan his first gold disc for a million-plus sales.
Oct ***Sunshine Superman*** reaches US #11 and ***The Real Donovan***, a compilation of earlier tracks on Hickory, makes US #96.
Dec [10] *Mellow Yellow*, arranged by John Paul Jones and with "whispering" vocal assistance from Paul McCartney, hits US #2 and is a second million seller, despite being banned in Boston, MA, for allegedly being abortion-themed. (Donovan has supplied somewhat louder than "whispering" vocal assistance on the Beatles' *Yellow Submarine*.)

1967

Jan *Sunshine Superman* hits UK #2. Donovan is commissioned by the National Theatre to compose incidental music for a new production of Shakespeare's "As You Like It", starring Laurence Olivier, at the Old Vic.
[15] Donovan gives a one-man concert at London's Royal Albert Hall, including the 12-minute ballet "Golden Apples".
Feb [2-3] He takes part in the "International Film Festival" in Cannes, France.
Mar *Mellow Yellow* hits UK #8.
[11] *Epistle To Dippy*, never released as a UK single, reaches US #19. ***Mellow Yellow*** (also not issued in Britain) makes US #14.
Apr [24] He begins a six-night engagement at London's Saville Theatre.
June [25] Donovan joins an all-star chorus at a live TV broadcast, at EMI's London studios, of the recording of the Beatles' *All You Need Is Love*.
July UK version of ***Sunshine Superman*** (a compilation of tracks from the US albums ***Sunshine Superman*** and ***Mellow Yellow***) reaches UK #25.
Aug [13] Donovan plays on the final day of the seventh "National Blues Festival" at the Royal Windsor Racecourse, Windsor, Berks.
Sept [16] *There Is A Mountain*, with lyrics from a 16th-century Japanese haiku poem, and featuring striking flute work by Harold McNair, reaches US #11.
Nov Budget album, ***Universal Soldier***, compiled from earlier EP and single tracks, hits UK #5, while *There Is A Mountain* hits UK #8.
[23-25] Donovan plays at the Fillmore West, San Francisco, CA.
Dec [30] *Wear Your Love Like Heaven* reaches US #23.
[31] Donovan guests on BBC1-TV's "Hogmanay Show".

1968

Jan Boxed double album, ***A Gift From A Flower To A Garden***, with one disk of commercial material (including the recent hit single) and another of children's songs, reaches US #19. The material is also released as two separate albums, ***Wear Your Love Like Heaven*** and ***For Little Ones***, which climb to US #60 and #185 respectively.
Feb [19] Donovan flies to India (in the wake of the Beatles' visit) to attend a Transcendental Meditation course under Maharishi Mahesh Yogi, and becomes his disciple for a while.
Mar *Jennifer Juniper*, written about Jenny Boyd, hits UK #5. The B-side, *Poor Cow*, is from the film of the same name, to which Donovan contributes several soundtrack songs.
Apr [20] *Jennifer Juniper* reaches US #26. ***Like It Is, Was And Evermore Shall Be***, a compilation on Hickory, peaks at US #177.
May ***A Gift From A Flower To A Garden*** makes UK #13.
[22] He guests on ITV's "It Must Be Dusty".
June [2] Donovan plays at the "Barn Barbecue Concert & Barn Dance" at Whittlesey near Peterborough, Northants., with John Mayall's Bluesbreakers, Fairport Convention, Blossom Toes, Fleetwood Mac, the Move, James & Bobby Purify, Amen Corner and others.
July *Hurdy Gurdy Man* hits UK #4.
[7] He performs on the second day of the "Woburn Music Festival" in Woburn, Beds., with Fleetwood Mac, John Mayall's Bluesbreakers, Champion Jack Dupree, Tim Rose, Taste and Duster Bennett.
Aug [3] *Hurdy Gurdy Man* hits US #5.
Sept Live ***Donovan In Concert*** album, recorded in the US at the Anaheim Convention Center Arena, Anaheim, CA, earlier in the year, while he was on tour, reaches US #18.
Oct [25] Donovan performs at New York's Carnegie Hall.
Nov [2] *Lalena*, unreleased in the UK as a single, reaches US #33.
[17] Donovan guests on CBS-TV's "The Smothers Brothers Comedy Hour".
Dec *Atlantis* stops at UK #23, while the US-only ***The Hurdy Gurdy Man*** makes US #20.

1969

Mar [1] *To Susan On The West Coast Waiting*, again unissued in Britain, makes US #35.
Apr Compilation, ***Donovan's Greatest Hits***, hits US #4, and gains another gold disc.
May [24] *Atlantis*, originally the US B-side of *To Susan On The West Coast Waiting*, out-performs its A-side and hits US #7.
Aug *Barabajagal (Love Is Hot)*, recorded with the Jeff Beck Group, with Lesley Duncan and Madeleine Bell on backing vocals, reaches UK #12, Donovan's last UK hit single.
Sept [6] *Barabajagal (Love Is Hot)* makes US #36.
Oct ***Barabajagal***, including several former hit singles, reaches US #23, but is not issued in the UK.
Nov Hickory compilation, ***The Best Of Donovan***,

makes US #144. (By year's end, Donovan contributes songs to the movie "If It's Tuesday, This Must Be Belgium", starring Suzanne Pleshette and Ian McShane.)

1970

June [28] Having split from Mickie Most and forming his own band, Open Road, for live and studio work, Donovan appears at the Bath Festival Of Progressive Music at Shepton Mallet, Somerset, with Led Zeppelin, Pink Floyd and others.

Aug [30] Donovan plays on the final day of the "Isle Of Wight Festival", at Godshill, Isle of Wight.

Sept ***Open Road***, described by Donovan as an experiment in "Celtic rock" and featuring pianist Mike O'Neill, bassist Mike Thompson and drummer John Carr, reaches US #16 and UK #30.

[26] *Riki Tiki Tavi* peaks at US #55.

Oct Donovan marries Linda Lawrence, the former girlfriend of Rolling Stone Brian Jones.

Dec Double album, ***Donovan P. Leitch***, a compilation of material originally released in the US by Hickory, appears on Janus Records, peaking at US #128, as Open Road breaks up.

1971

Mar [13] *Celia Of The Seals* (on which Open Road bassist Danny Thompson has dual billing) peaks at US #84. (Donovan spends some months writing songs and music for, and acting the title role in, the David Puttnam-produced Jacques Demy film fantasy "The Pied Piper", after which he moves to Ireland for an extended period, for tax reasons.)

July Double album ***HMS Donovan***, including a selection of children's songs with music set to the words of Lewis Carroll, Edward Lear and W.B. Yeats, is his last recording for Pye in the UK.

Oct [21] Donovan becomes a father when his daughter Astrella is born.

1972

Jan He writes the score for Franco Zefferelli's film "Brother Sun, Sister Moon". While still living in Ireland, he also tours with the folk group Planxty.

May [6] Donovan takes part in the "Bickershaw Festival", near Wigan, Lancs.

Sept He reunites with Mickie Most, and a new UK deal is signed with Epic Records. (The reunion only lasts through the recording of one album.)

1973

Mar ***Cosmic Wheels***, produced by Most and recorded with a star session band including Chris Spedding (guitar), Jim Horn (sax) and Cozy Powell (drums), reaches UK #15 and US #25. (It is Donovan's last album to make the UK chart.)

June [2] The extracted *I Like You* is his final US hit single, peaking at #66.

1974

Feb ***Essence To Essence***, produced by Andrew Oldham and with Carole King and Peter Frampton guesting, peaks at US #174. After its release, Donovan moves to California.

Dec ***7-Tease***, a studio concept album based on the theatrical show with the same title (with dancers, costumes, lighting and visual effects) which Donovan has staged in California during the year and produced in Nashville by Norbert Putnam, reaches US #135.

1976

June [19] Having spent part of the previous year touring in Australia and New Zealand, the self-produced, US-recorded ***Slow Down World*** peaks at US #174 and is his final US chart entry. Another reunion with Most, and a label move to Most's RAK label, will produce ***Donovan***, released in October the following year.

1980

Aug He performs at the "Edinburgh Festival" in Edinburgh, Scotland, and records ***Neutronica*** (followed by ***Love Is The Only Feeling***), to be released in W. Germany.

Dec He appears with Billy Connolly and Ralph McTell on a Christmas benefit show for children's charities, at the London Palladium.

1981

Nov He forms a new stage band, with Danny Thompson (bass), Tony Roberts (saxophone and woodwinds) and John Stephens (drums), who play on *Lay Down Lassie* and ***Love Is Only Feeling***. (Following the release of a comeback album with producer Jerry Wexler, re-working his earlier hits *Sunshine Superman* and *Season Of the Witch* for the Allegiance label album, ***Lady Of The Stars*** in 1983, his career will remains quiet through the rest of the decade, with occasional low-key tours and little in the way of recordings.)

1990

Nov [26] While his celebrity took a backseat to two of his children, Donovan Leitch and Iona Skye (who are emerging as film actors in Hollywood) in the late '80s, he is becoming increasingly hip once more, and now supports the Happy Mondays (who have recorded the tribute song *Donovan*) at the Wembley Arena, Wembley, as his first album of the '90s, ***Rising*** is released by Permanent Records.

Dec [1] In a further show of renewed interest, Trevor and Simon, the comedy duo from BBC1-TV's "Going Live", record - under the guise of the Singing Corner - with Donovan. The result is a version of *Jennifer Juniper*, which makes UK #68.

1992

Apr [4] Donovan embarks on a 39-date UK tour at the Victoria Rooms, Bristol, Avon, set to end on May 22nd at the Town Hall, Middlesbrough, Cleveland.

1993

Jan Legacy/Epic Records releases ***Troubadour: The Definitive Collection 1964-1976***, a 44-song retrospective boxed set including Donovan's major hits, rare demos and previously unreleased material.

1994

Apr Having played four consecutive Thursday showcases at West Hollywood's Luna Park, to mark his signing to American Records, ***Count On Me*** is released.

JASON DONOVAN

1979

Oct Donovan (b. June 1, 1968, Malvern, Melbourne, Victoria, Australia), his UK-born father, Terry, one of Australia's best-known actors and his mother TV presenter Sue McIntosh, auditions for an upcoming TV soap opera, "Skyways", and gets the role, opposite actress Kylie Minogue. After a string of Australian TV roles in "I Can Jump Puddles", "Golden And Pennies", "Home" and "Marshland", he lands the part of Scott Robinson in the new daily soap opera "Neighbours" in 1986 (once again playing opposite Minogue, who now stars as his girlfriend Charlene - the couple will have a TV wedding, though their much-rumored private union will never be confirmed), having just passed his Higher School Certificate at De La Salle College in Malvern.

1988

Having won the Logie award for Best New Talent and been awarded a commendation as Best Actor from the Australian Television Society the previous year, Donovan also nabs a silver Logie award as Most Popular Actor, and is approached by Mushroom Records to consider a career in music. Australian band Noiseworks give him a song, and as a result he visits London to record two cuts with Pete Hammond at PWL Studios. PWL supremo Pete Waterman, who has already successfully manoeuvred Minogue's singing career, suggests that he record a Stock/Aitken/Waterman track. While still a regular on "Neighbours", he also plays "Happy" Huston in a World War II TV mini-series.

Sept PWL debut, *Nothing Can Divide Us*, hits UK #5.

1989

Jan [7] SAW-written and produced duet with Kylie Minogue, *Especially For You*, tops the UK chart, selling more than 950,000 copies, helped by a kiss'n'cuddle performance on BBC1-TV's "Top Of The Pops".

Mar Donovan receives Logie nominations for Most Popular Personality, Most Popular Actor and Most Popular Music Video.

[11] *Too Many Broken Hearts* tops the UK chart, selling over 500,000 copies, and establishes Donovan as major teen pin-up in Britain.

Apr He embarks on the Pete Waterman-hosted UK "Hit Man Roadshow" tour, singing four songs to backing tracks. He also films his last appearance for "Neighbours", convinced that a music career based in the UK is the best way forward.

May [20] ***Ten Good Reasons*** tops the UK chart, will be awarded multiplatinum status and become one of the bestsellers of the year.

June [10] *Sealed With A Kiss*, a cover of Brian Hyland's 1962 US and UK #3, tops the UK chart.

Sept *Every Day (I Love You More)* hits UK #2.

Dec *When You Come Back To Me*, including seasonal Christmas lyrics, hits UK #2 behind Band Aid II's re-recording of *Do They Know Its Christmas?*, which was instigated by SAW and features Donovan and Minogue, among others.

1990

Apr [14] *Hang On To Your Love*, yet another SAW composition, hits UK #8.

June [9] His second album, ***Between The Lines***, debuts at UK #2, behind Soul II Soul's ***Soul II Soul (1990 A New Decade)***.

July [7] *Another Night* reaches UK #18, breaking Donovan's run of six straight Top 10 UK hits.

Sept [8] A remake of the Cascades' 1963 US #3, *Rhythm Of The Rain*, hits UK #9.

[10] Donovan begins a ten-date UK tour in Southampton, Hants, set to end on the 23rd with the last of three nights at London's Hammersmith Odeon.

Oct [23] He performs at Wembley Arena, Wembley, Middx.

Nov [10] *I'm Doing Fine*, possibly hindered by a Beatles-mimicking promo video, reaches UK #22, as teen interest in Donovan shows signs of waning.

[11] Donovan wins Best Male Solo Singer and Worst Male Solo Singer at the **Smash Hits** Poll Winners Party at the London Arena, Docklands.

1991

Mar [15] "Blood Oath", a movie featuring Donovan in the cameo role of Private Talbot, premieres in London.

May [6] BBC1-TV airs the "Children's Royal Variety Performance", which features a contribution by Donovan.

[25] *R.S.V.P.* reaches UK #17.

June [10] Donovan guests on BBC1-TV's "Wogan" show.

[12] He makes his UK stage debut, starring in a revival of Andrew Lloyd Webber and Tim Rice's "Joseph And The Amazing Technicolor Dreamcoat" at the London Palladium.

[29] *Any Dream Will Do*, from the stage show, tops the UK chart.

July [14] He guests on ITV's "The Dame Edna Experience".

Aug Donovan's solicitors Sheridans issue a libel writ against **The Face** for printing a poster showing Donovan wearing a T-shirt with a slogan which casts doubt on his heterosexuality.

[19] He hosts disc jockey Simon Bates' Radio 1 show, "Bates' Mates", for the week.

[31] *Happy Together*, reviving the Turtles' 1967 US #1/UK #12 smash, hits UK #10, his final outing for the PWL hit factory, as ***Joseph And The Amazing Technicolor Dreamcoat***, the cast album featuring Donovan, enters at UK #1.

Sept [28] PWL-issued ***Greatest Hits*** debuts at its UK #9 peak.
Oct [27] Donovan wins Best Male Solo Singer at the **Smash Hits** Poll Winners Awards.
Dec [28] ITV airs "Amnesty International's Big 30" concert, which features Donovan among others.

1992

Jan [4] *Joseph Mega-Remix*, re-hashed from the show, reaches UK 13.
Apr [3] Donovan wins a reported £200,000 in libel damages against **The Face**, subsequently offering to reduce the amount so that the magazine will not go out of business.
May Having completed an 11-month run in "Joseph" (replaced for five weeks by BBC TV/Radio personality Philip Schofield), he continues working on new tracks at RAK and Maison Rouge Studios, London, with Phil Thornalley (RAK) and Nigel Wright (Maison Rouge) producing. Having opened the store's 1990 January sale, Donovan is refused entry to Harrods for being improperly dressed, after arriving wearing shorts and a vest.
[16] Donovan is voted Number One Man at the SOS Number One awards at BBC Television Centre.
July [3] He guests on the last-ever broadcast of BBC1-TV's "Wogan".
[12] BBC1-TV airs the first part of the two-part Australian mini-series "Shadows Of The Heart", with Donovan portraying a farmer.
[18] *Mission Of Love* debuts at its UK #26 peak.
Nov [18] Donovan appears on ITV's "Des O'Connor" show.
[22] He embarks on a 17-date UK tour which will include two dates at Wembley Arena, on Dec [13-14], at the Brighton Centre, Brighton, E. Sussex.
[28] Donovan's revival of the standard ballad *As Time Goes By* bows at its UK #26 peak.

1993

Apr [10] While the world awaits his next album, Donovan guests on BBC1-TV's "Going Live!"
Aug [7] *All Around The World*, the first single from his forthcoming album, debuts at its UK #41 peak.
Sept [11] ***All Around The World*** enters at its UK #27 high, during a two-week chart stay.
Oct [4] Donovan returns to "Joseph And The Amazing Tehnicolor Dreamcoat", until January 15th the following year.

1994

Sept [7] Donovan participates in "Best For The Bush" benefit for Queensland farmers at Melbourne's Sports & Entertainment Centre.

1995

Nov Donovan collapses while waiting to be served lunch at Gusto's Deli in Sydney, New South Wales, Australia, near the singer's Bondi Beach home. Ambulancemen use oxygen to revive him. He had previously collapsed at the Viper Room in Los Angeles, CA while in the US to celebrate Kate Moss' birthday.

THE DOOBIE BROTHERS

Patrick Simmons (guitar, vocals); **Michael McDonald** (keyboards, synthesizers, vocals); **Tom Johnston** (guitar, vocals); **Jeff "Skunk" Baxter** (guitars); **Tiran Porter** (bass); **John Hartman** (drums); **Keith Knudsen** (drums, vocals); **Cornelius Bumpus** (saxophone)

1970

Mar The group is formed in San Jose, CA, initially under the name Pud, playing free Sunday concerts in a local park. It comprises Johnston (b. Visalia, CA), who studied graphic design at San Jose State and was introduced by Moby Grape's Skip Spence to Hartman (b. Mar. 18, 1950, Falls Church, VA), recently arrived from West Virginia with the intention of re-forming his favorite band Moby Grape, and bassist Greg Murph (who is soon replaced by Dave Shogren (b. San Francisco, CA). They begin jamming in a house, on Twelfth Street, frequented by members of San Jose's Hells Angels chapter.
Sept Simmons (b. Jan. 23, 1950, San Jose, CA), a folk/bluegrass guitarist, joins, and the group becomes the Doobie Brothers ("Doobie" being California slang for a marijuana joint), at the suggestion of room-mate Keith Rosen. They become the house band at the Chateau Liberté, a saloon in the Santa Cruz, CA mountains. A six-track demo is sent by Pacific Recording Studios owner Paul Curcio to Lenny Waronker at Warner Bros. Records, which signs them.

1971

Apr ***The Doobie Brothers***, produced by Ted Templeman (ex-Harpers Bizarre), fails to chart, despite the extensive Warner Bros.' sponsored "Mother Brothers" US tour to promote it.
Oct Porter, previously with Simmons in a folk trio, replaces Shogren on bass, and Mike Hossack (b. Sept. 18, 1950, Patterson, NJ), a second drummer/percussionist, is added to boost the live sound.

1972

Oct ***Toulouse Street***, the group's US chart debut, reaches #21 and earns a gold disc (eventually going platinum) during a 119-week stay on the chart.
Nov [4] Johnston-penned *Listen To The Music*, taken from it, makes US #11, and will remain one of their most enduring and popular numbers.

1973

Feb [24] *Jesus Is Just Alright*, previously recorded by the Byrds, reaches US #35.
June ***The Captain And Me*** hits US #7 and is another gold disc (eventually going on to two-million-plus sales).
[30] Extracted from it, *Long Train Runnin'* hits US #8.
Sept Hossack quits, to form his own band, Bonaroo, and is replaced on percussion by Knudsen (b. Oct. 18, 1952, Ames, IA), ex-drummer with Lee Michaels' band.
Oct [6] *China Grove* reaches US #15, the third hit single penned by Johnston.
Dec [24] Johnston is arrested in Visalia, for marijuana possession.

1974

Jan [26] The group plays at the Rainbow Theatre, London, the first of four UK dates on its first European tour.
Apr [6] *Listen To The Music* makes UK #29.
May [11] ***What Were Once Vices Are Now Habits*** reaches UK #19, and will hit US #4, earning another platinum disc. It includes session guitar contributions from Baxter (b. Dec. 13, 1948, Washington, DC), who is with Steely Dan, but plays live with the Doobie Brothers between Steely Dan commitments.
June [8] *Another Park, Another Sunday* reaches US #32, with the group consistently touring the US.
July With the demise of Steely Dan as a live band, Baxter joins the Doobie Brothers full-time, completing their ambition to field a three-guitar line-up on stage.
[20] They return to the UK to appear at the "Knebworth Festival", Knebworth, Herts., with the Allman Brothers and Van Morrison.
Aug [31] *Eyes Of Silver* makes US #52.
Nov [16] *Nobody* peaks at US #58.

1975

Jan [12] The group opens an 18-show, nine-city tour of Europe as part of Warner's "Looney Tunes" package, with Little Feat, Graham Central Station, Bonaroo, Montrose, and Tower of Power.
Mar [15] Simmons' composition, *Black Water*, originally the B-side of *Another Park, Another Sunday*, hits US #1 for one week, becoming their first million-selling single.
[23] They take part in a benefit for SNACK (Students Needs Athletics Culture & Kicks), which is looking to raise funds to make up a shortfall in the San Francisco school system budget, at San Francisco's Kezar Stadium.
Apr While on a seven-week US trek, Johnston becomes ill with a stomach disorder and has to drop out. Ex-Steely Dan vocalist/keyboards player, Michael McDonald (b. Dec. 2, 1952, St. Louis, MO), is recruited at Baxter's suggestion and, after rehearsing for 48 hours in New Orleans, LA, he joins the tour as a full-time member.
May Baxter makes a guest appearance on guitar at an Elton John concert in London. ***Stampede***, recorded prior to McDonald's arrival, hits US #4 (the group's fourth gold album).
[24] ***Stampede*** reaches UK #14.
June [21] From it, a revival of Holland/Dozier/Holland's *Take Me In Your Arms (Rock Me)* (a US hit for Kim Weston) reaches US #11 and UK #29.
[29] At a concert in Oakland, CA, Elton John returns Baxter's favor, duetting on *Listen To The Music*.
Aug [30] *Sweet Maxine* makes US #40.
Sept The band plays at the "Great American Music Fair" in Syracuse, NY, an event marred by violent conflict between would-be free festival demonstrators and state troopers.
Oct Playing a concert in Nashville, TN, the band discovers that its chaffeur, provided by local Limos Unlimited, is an undercover narcotics agent. Returning to their hired plane after the concert, they find it surrounded by police. A search at 3:00 a.m. reveals only a bottle of vitamins.

1976

Jan [17] *I Cheat The Hangman* peaks at US #60, as Johnston rejoins after his illness.
Apr [17] ***Takin' It To The Streets***, again produced by Templeman (and the first to feature the distinctive vocals of McDonald), makes UK #42.
May [22] ***Takin' It To The Streets*** hits US #8, and will eventually earn another platinum sales award. The extracted title track *Takin' It To The Streets*, penned by McDonald, reaches US #13.
July [17] The band backs Carly Simon on her US #46 hit of McDonald's *It Keeps You Runnin'*.
Sept [4] *Wheels Of Fortune* peaks at US #87.

1977

Jan [22] ***Best Of The Doobies***, a compilation of hit singles, hits US #5. A consistent catalog seller, it will eventually shift over six million domestic units.
[29] *It Keeps You Runnin'*, included on the compilation album, makes US #37.
May [7] The Doobie Brothers participate in Bill Graham's "Day on the Green #1" at Oakland-Alameda County Stadium, Oakland, CA, in front of 57,500 fans.
July [1] The band opens a month-long US tour at the Rushmore Civic Plaza, Rapid City, SD.
Aug [27] A second Motown revival, a cover of Marvin Gaye's 1966 hit, *Little Darling (I Need You)*, makes US #48.
[28] The group performs at the "Reading Festival", Reading, Berks., as part of a four-date UK tour, now presenting a tighter, funkier sound (the pervasive influence of McDonald) than their earlier guitar boogie.
Sept [17] ***Livin' On The Fault Line***, produced by Templeman, with horn and string arrangements by David Paich, reaches UK #25.
[27] The band plays at the "Rock'n'Bowl" at South Bay Bowl, Redondo Beach, CA, a benefit concert for the US Special Olympics.
Oct [15] ***Living On The Fault Line*** hits US #10 (earning another gold disc).
Nov [12] The extracted *Echoes Of Love* peaks at US #66.

1978

Jan [28] The group, now minus Johnston, who has departed for a solo career, guests on the ABC-TV sitcom "What's Happening!!"
July [1] The Doobie Brothers play at the Catalyst, Santa Cruz, in a benefit show for veteran actor Will Geer.
Aug [26] The band performs at the first "Canada Jam Festival", in Ontario, CA, before 80,000 people, sharing the bill with the Commodores, Kansas, the Village

People, Dave Mason, and Atlanta Rhythm Section.

1979

Mar With the band's new single and album climbing up the US chart and showing signs of being their all-time best sellers, both Baxter and Hartman decide to leave, the former to return to session work and production, the latter to quit music and return to his horse ranch in Sonoma County.

[10] *What A Fool Believes* makes UK #31.

Apr [7] ***Minute By Minute***, the result of their move into funky soul, tops the US chart for five weeks and is their third US million-selling album (with sales eventually topping three million).

[14] Taken from it, *What A Fool Believes*, written by McDonald and Kenny Loggins, is the band's second US #1 (for one week) and second million-selling single.

May After extensive auditions, ex-Moby Grape keyboards and sax player Cornelius Bumpus (b. Jan. 13, 1952), experienced session drummer Chet McCracken (b. July 17, 1952, Seattle, WA), and ex-Clover guitarist John McFee (b. Nov. 18, 1953, Santa Cruz) replace the departed members in time for a summer US tour.

June [23] Extracted title track, *Minute By Minute*, co-penned by McDonald and Lester Abrams, reaches US #14.

July [1] The Doobie Brothers celebrate their tenth anniversary at Los Angeles' Friars Club, with Eddie Floyd, the Jacksons, Kenny Loggins and Sam & Dave joining the band in an all-star jam of *Soul Man*.

[21] *Minute By Minute* makes UK #47.

Sept [19-23] The band plays in the "Musicians United For Safe Energy" (MUSE) anti-nuclear concerts at New York's Madison Square Garden, alongside Bruce Springsteen, Jackson Browne, Carly Simon, Bonnie Raitt, James Taylor and others.

Oct [13] *Dependin' On You* reaches US #25.

Dec Johnston, signed to Warner's. as a soloist, makes US #100 with ***Everything You've Heard Is True***.

1980

Jan [12] Johnston's *Savannah Nights* reaches US #34.

Feb [27] The Doobie Brothers win the Record Of The Year and Song Of The Year categories for *What A Fool Believes*, Best Pop Vocal Performance By A Duo Or Group Or Chorus for *Minute By Minute*, and McDonald nabs Best Arrangement Accompanying Vocalist(s) for *What A Fool Believes*, at the 22nd annual Grammy Awards.

July [16] Movie "No Nukes", documenting the previous year's Madison Square Garden anti-nuclear concerts, including a set by the Doobie Brothers, premieres in New York.

Oct [25] *Real Love*, co-written by McDonald and Patrick Henderson, hits US #5, taken from ***One Step Closer***, yet another Templeman-produced set, featuring constant Doobie's sideman, percussionist Bobby LaKind, which hits US #3 (their final platinum album) and has made UK #53 the previous week.

Nov Porter leaves both the group and the music scene, and session bassist Willie Weeks takes his place for live work.

1981

Jan [10] Its extracted title track, *One Step Closer*, reaches US #24.

Feb [7] *Wynken, Blynken And Nod* (taken from the various artists album, ***In Harmony***, on Sesame Street Records, which makes US #156 at the same time), climbs to US #76.

Mar [7] *Keep This Train A-Rollin'* peaks at US #62.

June Johnston's solo album, ***Still Feels Good***, makes US #158.

Oct After a concert in Hawaii to complete touring for the year, the band decides to split. Simmons and McDonald are both working on solo albums, and it is felt there is too much conflict of interest within the group to continue.

Dec Compilation album, ***Best Of The Doobies, Volume II***, reaches US #39, and earns the group another gold disc.

1982

Feb [20] *Here To Love You* peaks at US #65.

Mar [31] The official break-up of the group is announced, with news of a forthcoming temporary re-formation for a farewell US tour.

July Their goodbye tour begins at the King's Dominion, Doswell, VA, with Warners recording performances for a final live album.

Aug McDonald begins his successful solo career with *I Keep Forgettin' (Every Time You're Near)* and ***If That's What It Takes***.

1983

May [7] *So Wrong*, Simmons' first solo, reaches US #30.

June Simmons' ***Arcade***, on Elektra, peaks at US #52.

July [2] Simmons' *Don't Make Me Do It* (written by Huey Lewis & the News) climbs to US #75.

Aug Live double album, ***The Doobie Brothers Farewell Tour***, reaches US #79.

[6] *You Belong To Me* (previously a hit for Carly Simon, and a song co-written by McDonald and Simon via mail), also peaks at US #79.

1986

Dec [17] Even after the band splits, they reunite to play the first annual benefit show for Stanford Children's Hospital, Palo Alto, CA, where a wing will be named after them.

1987

Jan *What A Fool Believes*, reissued as a featured track from McDonald's ***Sweet Freedom : Best Of Michael McDonald***, peaks at UK #57.

May [23] The group reunites for a one-off show at the Hollywood Bowl, Hollywood, CA, which will lead to a reunion tour.

June [21] A new line-up of the Doobie Brothers, with Johnston back (but without McDonald), plays the last of ten reunion concerts, at the "Mountain Aire Festival", CA.

July [4] The band participates in "The July Fourth Disarmament Festival" in the Soviet Union, with James Taylor, Santana, Bonnie Raitt and several Russian groups.

1989

June Having signed to Capitol Records the previous year, the group, with original members Johnston, Simmons, Hartman, Porter and Hossack, the group embarks on a major US "Cycles" tour to promote its comeback album, ***Cycles***. They are joined by Dale Ockerman (keyboards), Jimmy Fox (percussion) and Richard Bryant (vocals), with Bumpus taking lead vocals on the Michael McDonald-written Doobie songs.

July [12] Their "Caygua County Fair", Weedsport, NY gig is cancelled when Johnston comes down with laryngitis, also causing further dates to be axed.

[15] *The Doctor* hits US #9 as its parent album, ***Cycles***, reaches US #17 and gains them their 11th gold disc.

[29] *The Doctor* peaks at UK #73.

Sept [16] *Need A Little Taste Of Love* makes US #45.

1990

Jan [18-19] The band plays sellout shows at the Portland Center for the Performing Arts, Portland, OR, during the current leg of its "Cycles" tour.

July The group makes a brief visit to Japan, with Daryl Hall & John Oates and Boz Scaggs.

1991

May [18] ***Brotherhood*** makes US #82.

June [17] The group guests on NBC-TV's "The Tonight Show".

July [5] Still touring, they perform at the Jones Beach Theatre, Wantagh, NY, supported by Joe Walsh.

Aug [8] The band plays at the 51st annual "Sturgis Bike Rally" in Sturgis, SD, before a crowd of 200,000.

1992

Mar [21] McDonald joins the band for a one-off gig to celebrate the Memphis Horns' 25th Anniversary, at the Pyramid, Memphis, TN.

Oct [18] 12 Doobie Brothers alumni play a benefit at the Greek Theatre, Los Angeles, for the children of sometime Doobies' percussionist Bobby LaKind, who is suffering from inoperable brain cancer. (They will play a second benefit the following night, at the Concord Pavilion, Concord, CA.)

Dec [24] LaKind loses his battle with cancer at the age of 47.

1993

Aug [7] The group embarks on a 22-date US tour at the Oakdale Music Theatre, Wallingford, CT, set to end on September 6th at Nebraska State Fair, Lincoln, NE. (Simmons is now also part of country/rock band, Four Wheel Drive, with Poco's Rusty Young, while Knudsen and McFee play in Japan each year, with that country's superstar, Yazawa. Hartman, who has become a fireman in Petaluma in 1979 and part-time reserve policeman from 1988 to 1991, is now turned down for his application to become a police officer on the grounds he lied about the full extent of his drug use.)

Dec [4] The "Sure Is Pure" remix of *Long Train Runnin'* hits UK #7.

1994

May [14] *Listen To The Music*, with various remixes by Motiv8, Ramp and Jon of the Pleased Wimmin and the Development Corporation, debuts at its UK #37 peak.

July [2] The group, now comprising Johnston, Simmons, McFee and ex-New Grass Revival John Cowan, embarks on a US tour with Foreigner at the Cynthia Woods Mitchell Pavilion, The Woodlands, TX.

1995

Mar [8] The band begins a seven-date UK leg of a European tour, again with Foreigner, at the Bournemouth Inernational Centre.

July [14] A further 34-date US tour with the Steve Miller Band opens at the Deer Creek Music Center, Noblesville, IN, before a crowd of 12,473. (McDonald joins them for the tour - the first time Simmons, Johnston and McDonald have been in the group together since 1978.)

see also: **Michael McDONALD, STEELY DAN**

THE DOORS

Jim Morrison (vocals); **Ray Manzarek** (keyboards); **Robbie Krieger** (guitar); **John Densmore** (drums)

1964

Feb Morrison (b. Dec. 8, 1943, Melbourne, FL), the son of a US Navy recruit, after dropping out of Florida State University, enrolls in the Theater Art Department of UCLA. Two months after graduating, he meets Manzarek (b. Feb. 12, 1935, Chicago, IL), a prodigal classical pianist who plays in blues band Rick & the Ravens, with his brothers Rick and Jim on weekends at a Santa Monica, CA bar, and who is already recording for the local Aura label, on a Venice, Los Angeles, CA beach.

1965

July Morrison, who has already begun substantial abuse of drugs and alcohol, experimentation which will always remain close to his heart, and Manzarek decide to form a group after Morrison sings his song, *Moonlight Drive*, to Manzarek, who recruits Densmore (b. Dec. 1, 1944, Los Angeles), a physics and psychology major, having met him at a Transcendental Meditation course at Los Angeles' Third Street Meditation Center.

Sept Morrison, Manzarek and Densmore record a demo of Morrison's songs, *Moonlight Drive*, *Summer's Almost Gone*, *Break On Through* and *End Of The Night* at World Pacific Studios. They are helped by the other two Manzareks and a female bass player, who all leave immediately afterwards because they dislike the material. CBS/Columbia's Billy James signs the group, while former jug band/bottleneck guitarist Krieger (b. Jan. 8, 1946, Los Angeles), who variously spells his forename Robbie and Robby and who has earlier played with Densmore in the Psychedelic Rangers band, is recruited on guitar.

1966

Morrison names the group the Doors, inspired not by William Blake's quote, "There are things that are known and things that are unknown: in between are doors", from his poem "The Doors : Open And Closed", which he reads in Aldous Huxley's document of a mescaline experience, **The Doors Of Perception**, but by another quote within the Huxley text, "all the other chemical Doors in the Wall are labelled Dope..." After rehearsing for five months, they play at the London Fog club on Sunset Boulevard, Los Angeles, and on the last night of their tenure are seen by the booker from the Whisky A-Go-Go, who hires them to a residency as the house band. During a six-month stint at the Whisky, they obtain a release from Columbia and are then seen by Love's Arthur Lee, who recommends them to his label boss, Jac Holzman, who sees them and then signs them to Elektra Records, before they are fired for performing Morrison's *The End*.

1967

Jan Their debut album, ***The Doors*** (on which Krieger is credited as Robby Krieger), establishes a powerful, theatrical, rock-blues style, and will hit US #2 during a 121-week stay on the chart. It yields the extracted *Break On Through*, as well as featuring the 11-minute opus, *The End*.
Feb The Doors perform at a concert sponsored by CAFF (Community Action For Facts & Freedom), with Buffalo Springfield and Peter, Paul & Mary at the Valley Center, CA.
June [9-10] The group plays at the Fillmore West, San Francisco, CA.
July [29] *Light My Fire*, extracted from the album in a much-abridged version (the original, at 6 minutes 50 seconds, is considered too long), tops the US chart for the first of three weeks, sells over a million and gives Elektra its first #1. (The band will turn down a $50,000 offer to use the song in Buick car TV ad.)
Aug [16] The band-penned *Light My Fire* makes UK #49.
Sept [17] The group appears on CBS-TV's "The Ed Sullivan Show", on which they are requested to omit the line "Girl, we couldn't get much higher" from *Light My Fire*. They agree, then Morrison sings it anyway.
[29-30] The Doors perform at the Avalon Ballroom, San Francisco, sharing the bill with Captain Beefheart.
Oct [28] *People Are Strange*, from the forthcoming album, reaches US #12.
Nov Their sophomore album, ***Strange Days***, including the subsequently popular live number *When The Music's Over*, hits US #3.
Dec [9] Morrison is arrested after a concert in New Haven, CT, during which he has badmouthed the police. He is charged with a breach of the peace and resisting arrest.
[26-31] The group appears again at the Fillmore West, sharing the bill with Chuck Berry.

1968

Jan [13] *Love Me Two Times*, extracted from ***Strange Days***, reaches US #25.
Feb Univeral Pictures offers the band $500,000 to star in a feature film which is never made.
May [4] *The Unknown Soldier* makes US #39. The band makes its own promo film for it, which includes Morrison being "shot".
[10] Morrison, although not arrested, upsets law enforcers again when he incites a crowd to riot, during a concert in Chicago, IL.
[18] The band appears at the "Northern California Folk-Rock Festival" with the Grateful Dead, the Steve Miller Band, the Animals, Jefferson Airplane and others.
July [5] The Doors play at the Hollywood Bowl, Hollywood, CA, with Steppenwolf and the Chambers Brothers. The show, which is filmed, will subsequently be released on video as "The Doors Live At The Hollywood Bowl".
Aug [3] *Hello I Love You*, an atypical commercial pop song, is the Doors' second US #1 (at the peak for the first of two weeks) and second million seller.
Sept [7] ***Waiting For the Sun***, containing *Hello I Love You*, is the band's only US chart-topping album, spending the first of four weeks at #1. (The sleeve contains the full libretto of Morrison's theatrical poem "Celebration Of The Lizard", which will not appear on record until the 1970 album, ***Absolutely Live***.) The Doors are filling major US rock venues, but Morrison's hard-drinking, drug-infused lifestyle and overtly sexual deportment make the band a controversial success. *Hello I Love You* reaches UK #15, as the group visits Britain for promotion and concerts, making its BBC1-TV "Top of the Pops" debut. (The Kinks' Ray Davies will initiate legal action against the group, alleging copyright infringement of his *All Day And All Of The Night* on their *Hello I Love You*).
Oct [6] A film documentary, "The Doors Are Open", lensed at their Roundhouse, Chalk Farm, London gig, is broadcast on UK TV. ***Waiting For The Sun*** reaches UK #16, the group's first album success in Britain.

1969

Feb [15] *Touch Me* hits US #3 and is another million seller.
Mar [1] After a concert at the Dinner Key Auditorium in Miami, FL, Morrison is charged with "lewd and lascivious behavior in public by exposing his private parts and by simulating masturbation and oral copulation", in addition to profanity, drunkenness and other minor offences. The prospect of court appearances makes tour booking impossible for the next five months.
Apr [3] Morrison is arrested in Los Angeles by the FBI and is charged with interstate flight to avoid prosecution on his Miami charges.
[19] *Wishful Sinful* makes US #44.
June [5] The band premieres its documentary film, "Feast Of Friends" at Cinemathique 16 in Los Angeles. Local politicians in St. Louis, MO, and Hawaii force cancellations of scheduled Doors appearances.
Aug [2] *Tell All The People* peaks at US #57.
Sept *Runnin' Blue* peaks at US #64, as the horn-laden ***The Soft Parade*** hits US #6.
[13] The band plays at the "Toronto Rock'n'Roll Revival Show", with John Lennon's Plastic Ono Band, Chuck Berry and others, in the Varsity Stadium at the University of Toronto, Toronto, ON, Canada.
Nov [11] Morrison is arrested again after trying to interfere with an air hostess on a plane from Los Angeles to Phoenix, AZ. The charge is the potentially very serious one of interfering with the flight of an aircraft, as well as public drunkenness. (The charge is later dropped, when the hostess withdraws her evidence.)

1970

Jan [17-18] The Doors play two nights at New York, NY's Felt Forum, recorded (as are several later concerts) for a live album.
Apr R&B/rock-fused ***Morrison Hotel*** hits US #4 and UK #12, including *Queen Of The Highway*, dedicated to Morrison's new bride, Pamela.
[10] At a Doors concert in Boston, MA, Morrison, once again uncomfortable at keeping his clothes on, asks the crowd if they want to see his genitals.
May [2] *You Make Me Real/Roadhouse Blues*, taken from the album, makes US #50.
Aug [4] Morrison is charged with public drunkenness when discovered unconscious on an elderly woman's doorstep in Los Angeles.
[29] The Doors perform alongside Joni Mitchell, the Who, Sly & the Family Stone and others on the second day of the "Isle of Wight Festival" at Godshill, Isle of Wight.
Sept Double album, ***Absolutely Live***, recorded in January in New York, containing a full version of *Celebration Of The Lizard*, hits US #8 at a time when live performances by the group are sporadic.
[20] In a Miami court, Morrison is found guilty of indecent exposure and profanity, though he is acquitted on the charge of "lewd and lascivious behavior".
[26] ***Absolutely Live*** peaks at UK #69.
Oct [30] Morrison is sentenced for the offences of which he was found guilty in September, and receives eight months' hard labor, followed by 28 months probation and a $500 fine from Judge Murray Goodman. He will remain free while the sentence is appealed.
Nov [8] On his 27th birthday, Morrison makes the recordings of his poetry (which will later form the basis of ***An American Prayer***).
[12] The Doors play their last concert with Morrison, in New Orleans, LA. (They will complete the recording of another album, which will be released as ***L.A. Woman*** six months later.)

1971

Jan Compilation album, ***Doors 13***, reaches US #25.
Mar Morrison moves to Paris, France, to concentrate on writing poetry. His first book, **The Lords And The New Creatures**, goes into paperback after selling an initial 15,000 in hardback. The rest of the band continues to rehearse weekly, in the hope that its focal figure will to return to music.
May [15] *Love Her Madly* is the band's biggest single for over two years, reaching US #11.
June ***L.A. Woman***, recorded in the last sessions with Morrison, with Jerry Scheff (bass) and Marc Benno (rhythm guitar) helping out, hits US #9.
July [3] Morrison is found dead in a bathtub in Paris. The cause of death is given as a "heart attack induced by respiratory problems", the suddenness of the death leading to much speculation.
[9] His family having disowned him, Morrison is buried in the Père Lachaise cemetery in Paris (where his grave will become a graffiti-covered shrine). (His headstone reads "Kata ton daimona eay toy" - Greek for "True to his own spirit".) The cemetery also contains the remains of Oscar Wilde, Edith Piaf, Frédèric Chopin and Honoré de Balzac.
Sept [4] Haunting *Riders On The Storm* reaches US #14, extracted from ***L.A. Woman***, which climbs to UK #28, having just received a gold disc for half a million sales in the US.
Nov [25] Manzarek, Krieger and Densmore announce that they will continue as the Doors.
Dec [4] *Riders On The Storm* reaches UK #22. The remaining Doors trio releases ***Other Voices***, which reaches US #31.
[25] *Tightrope Ride*, a track without Morrison, peaks at US #71.

1972

Apr Double compilation album, ***Weird Scenes Inside The Gold Mine***, climbs to US #55 and UK #50.
Sept The trio releases ***Full Circle***, which reaches US #68.
Oct [21] *The Mosquito* peaks at US #85.
Dec With inspiration lacking, and deprived of its single most important element, the band breaks up. (Manzarek will record two solo albums and produce many other acts. Krieger and Densmore will form the Butts Band with Jess Roden, Phillip Chen and Roy Davies, before moving on to session and solo work. Krieger will also form Robbie Krieger & Friends and Versions.)

1973

Oct Another Doors compilation album, ***Best Of The Doors***, peaks at US #158, after the group has announced its break-up.

1974

Apr [25] Pamela Morrison dies from a suspected heroin overdose.
May [1] Manzarek and Iggy Pop begin rehearsing a new band in Los Angeles. (Manzarek will release two solo albums, ***The Golden Scarab*** and ***The Whole Thing Started With R'n'R*** over the next two years, while *Riders On The Storm*, re-released in the UK,

will reach #33 on Apr [10], 1976.)

1979

Jan When the 1970 tapes of Morrison reciting his poetry are unearthed, the other three former Doors reunite to provide a musical backing for the words and, along with snippets of original live performances, the results are released as ***An American Prayer - Jim Morrison***, which makes US #54, rekindling interest in the group.
Feb [10] Picture-disc reissue of *Hello I Love You* peaks at UK #71.
Aug Morrison's most controversial song from the Doors' first album, *The End*, is prominently featured on the soundtrack of Francis Ford Coppola's film, "Apocalypse Now".

1980

Nov While Manzarek has recently produced the first of four albums (over the next three years) for the Los Angeles band X, a fresh retrospective, ***The Doors' Greatest Hits***, reaches US #17.

1981

July On the tenth anniversary of Morrison's death, Manzarek, Krieger and Densmore lead fans in a graveside tribute ceremony in Paris.
Sept [18] The compilation album ***The Doors' Greatest Hits*** is awarded a platinum disc for US sales of over a million.

1983

Nov ***Alive, She Cried***, an album compiled from live tapes lost for over a decade but discovered in a Los Angeles warehouse (after the former band members have initiated a search for them), reaches US #23 and UK #36 (and yields *Gloria* (recorded at a soundcheck in 1969) which will peak at US #71 on Jan [7] the following year).

1987

July [4] While the compilation album ***Classics*** has made US #124 in June 1985, ***Live At The Hollywood Bowl***, the soundtrack of a Doors gig filmed and taped at the venue in the late '60s (and simultaneously released on home video), now reaches UK #51 and will peak at US #154. The interest generated also brings the digitally-remastered compilation album, ***Best Of The Doors***, back into the US chart - to #127.

1990

Krieger, now signed to Café Records, continues to remain active, having released last year's I.R.S. solo ***No Habla***, writing the score for a Discovery TV channel documentary, "Who Are They", and performing annually at the "Love Ride", benefitting Muscular Dystrophy.

1991

Mar [1] Public interest in Morrison and the band, which has remained at cult level since his death, is substantially revived by Oliver Stone's film, "The Doors", with Val Kilmer playing Morrison, Kyle MacLachlan as Manzarek, Kevin Dillon as Densmore and Frank Whalley as Krieger, which opens to generally positive reviews. Doors-related books and merchandise are also launched.
Apr [6] Soundtrack album ***The Doors*** debuts at its UK #11 peak.
[13] ***The Doors*** (soundtrack) hits US #8, while ***The Best Of The Doors***, re-released on CD with a bonus track and repromoted to tie in with the film, reaches US #32. ***Greatest Hits***, re-issued on cassette only, also reaches US #17.
[20] ***L.A. Woman*** bows at its UK #73 peak.
[27] *Break On Through* reaches UK #64.
May [5] ***The Doors***, the group's debut album from 1967, makes UK #43.
[25] ***The Best Of The Doors*** reaches UK #17.
June [1] ***In Concert*** debuts at its UK #24 peak, the group's fifth UK chart album in three months.
[15] Reissued *Light My Fire* hits UK #7, as ***In Concert***, collecting performance cuts from the band's three live albums, makes US #50.
July [25] A portion of *The End* highlights the closing credits for the final broadcast of syndicated TV's "The Dennis Miller Show".
Aug [10] *Riders On The Storm* debuts at its UK #68 peak.

1993

Jan [12] In celebrating their induction into the Rock and Roll Hall of Fame at the eighth annual dinner at the Century Plaza Hotel, Los Angeles, CA, the remaining Doors members, aided by Pearl Jam lead vocalist Eddie Vedder, reunite to perform two songs at the post-dinner jam.
July [1-7] The "Doors Break On Through Tour", a travel trek to Paris to visit points of interest relevant to Morrison, takes place, with a vigil held on the 3rd at Père Lachaise on the 22nd anniversary of his death.

1995

May [23] ***An American Prayer*** is reissued on CD with three bonus cuts, re-worked by Densmore, Krieger and Manzarek.

LEE DORSEY

1961

Oct After mixed fortunes in the boxing ring (as Kid Chocolate) and the US Navy, Dorsey (b. Irving Lee Dorsey, Dec. 24, 1924, New Orleans, LA, although some sources claim Portland, OR), returning to his home town, having already released *Lottie Mo* on Joe Banashak's Instant label, records the nonsensical but catchy *Ya Ya*, supervised by studio gang boss Harold Battiste, on Bobby Robinson's Fury label. A million seller, it hits US #7 and enables him to quit his day job in an auto wrecking yard and go on tour, playing prestigious R&B venues in California and Texas. (Among several covers of *Ya Ya* will be those by Petula Clark and John Lennon.)

1962

Feb *Do Re Mi*, equally jaunty and written by local R&B hero Earl King, reaches US #27, but the Fury label has problems and Dorsey soon slips from public view. (Later, both Dusty Springfield and Georgie Fame cut versions of the song.)

1965

Aug Marshall Sehorn and Allen Toussaint have teamed up to plan a Lee Dorsey revival. *Ride Your Pony*, written by Toussaint and retailed through a lease deal with Bell/Amy Records, restores him to the US chart, at #28, as he makes a triumphant stage return at New York's Apollo Theatre, after a three-year hiatus.

1966

Feb *Get Out Of My Life Woman* makes US #44 and launches him in the UK, reaching #22. Like all of his most notable material, it is written and produced by Toussaint.
May *Confusion* makes UK #38.
Sept *Working In The Coal Mine*, ostensibly a song of hapless resignation, is one of the year's hottest international soul/dance hits, making #8 in both the US and UK. (The song will spark cover versions by such unlikely performers as Devo and the Judds in the '80s.) The laid-back Dorsey, described as "Mr. TNT" by some hyperbolic promoters, tours Europe.
Nov *Holy Cow* hits UK #6, becoming his biggest UK hit but also, paradoxically, his last. (The Band will revive the song on their 1973 ***Moondog Matinee*** album, while the Shadows and Chas & Dave will also cut UK versions.)
Dec *Holy Cow* reaches US #23 as his only chart album, ***The New Lee Dorsey***, peaks at US #129 and UK #34.

1967

May *My Old Car* reaches only US #97.
Oct *Go-Go Girl* makes US #62.

1968

Sept [9] Dorsey performs at the Purley Orchid and London Cromwellian clubs during a UK visit.

1969

June *Everything I Do Gohn Be Funky (From Now On)* proves to be his chart swan song, at US #95.

1970

Concept album, ***Yes We Can***, is released. (*Occapella* and *Sneaking Sally Through The Alley*, both taken from it, will subsequently be covered by Ringo Starr and Robert Palmer.) Dorsey will continue to work on and off with Toussaint, but with only regional success, and will devote more time to managing his auto repair shop.

1986

Dec [1] Having guested on Southside Johnny & the Asbury Jukes 1976 debut album, and having released his own ***Night People***, in 1976, as well as being persuaded by the Clash to come out of his semi-retirement and support them on a 1980 US tour, Dorsey dies of emphysema in New Orleans.

THE DRIFTERS

Clyde McPhatter (lead tenor);
Gerhart Thrasher (tenor); **Andrew Thrasher** (baritone); **Bill Pinckney** (bass)

1953

May Atlantic boss Ahmet Ertegun, having gone to see the Dominoes at Manhattan's Royal Roost and finding that their lead singer McPhatter (b. Nov. 15, 1931, Durham, NC), ex-Mount Lebanon Singers, has been fired, tracks him down to a room in Harlem, New York, NY, and signs him to the label, suggesting that McPhatter form a new group. The singer rounds up some vocalist friends (David Baldwin, William Anderson, James Johnson and David Baughan) but the first recording session, co-produced by Ertegun and Jerry Wexler (his first time in the studio), is a disaster and the friends leave McPhatter to find a new group.
June McPhatter rehearses with other friends, who form the Thrasher Wonders gospel group, and then cuts the first Drifters' song, *Gone*, with Gerhart Thrasher (b. Wetumpka, AL), his brother Andrew (b. Wetumpka, AL) and Willie Ferbee.
Aug Pinckney (b. Aug. 15, 1925, Sumter, NC), from the Jerusalem Stars, replaces Ferbee on the second session and as the initial Drifters line-up is settled. They cut *Money Honey*, written by Jesse Stone and featuring him on piano. McPhatter asks George Treadwell to manage the group.
Nov [21] *Money Honey*, credited to Clyde McPhatter & the Drifters, later covered by Elvis Presley and others, tops the US R&B chart for the first of 11 weeks and becomes a million-seller. (The band secures a ten-year contract which provides twice-yearly seasons at the Apollo Theatre in Harlem).

1954

Apr McPhatter's unorthodox, free-ranging tenor voice becomes one of the most popular sounds in US R&B: *Such A Night* (covered by Johnnie Ray in a version banned by some US radio stations and by the BBC, though it tops the UK pop chart) hits #5 and *Lucille* hits #7. McPhatter is drafted, becoming a forces entertainer in the Special Services (though he will record occasionally with the group when on leave). The similarly-voiced David Baughan returns to take lead vocal on stage.
July [10] *Honey Love* (written by McPhatter with Atlantic's Wexler) is another US R&B #1, although banned by Memphis radio station WDIA because of perceived offensive lyrics.
Nov Baughan leaves and Johnny Moore (b. 1934, Selma, AL) joins from the Hornets, becoming lead

singer.
Dec *Bip Bam* (also recorded by B.B. King) hits US R&B #7, while a revolutionary arrangement of *White Christmas* (later copied by Presley) hits #2 on the same survey.

1955

June *Whatcha Gonna Do* hits US R&B #8. McPhatter cuts his first solo sides while on Service leave.
Aug Andrew Thrasher is fired by Treadwell and replaced by Charlie Hughes.
Sept The Moore-fronted Drifters record in Los Angeles with producer Nesuhi Ertegun. Among the songs cut is Leiber and Stoller's *Ruby Baby* (which will make US R&B #13 and become a million seller for Dion).
Dec The Drifters hit the US pop chart for the first time as *White Christmas* reaches US #80.

1956

Apr [19] McPhatter is discharged from the armed forces. (He does not rejoin the group but begins a successful solo US chart career with *Seven Days*.)

1957

Feb The Drifters reach US #69 with *Fools Fall In Love*, another Leiber/Stoller song.
June After the group reaches US #79 with *Hypnotized*, Moore is drafted and Bobby Hendricks (b. Feb. 22, 1938, Columbus, OH) from the Flyers comes in as lead tenor. (The next two years will see constant short-term personnel changes.)
Sept [6] "The Biggest Show Of Stars For 1957" package tour, with Chuck Berry, Buddy Holly & the Crickets, Paul Anka, Frankie Lymon & the Teenagers, the Everly Brothers, Clyde McPhatter and others, opens at the Syria Mosque, Pittsburgh, PA, set to close on November 24th at the Mosque, Richmond, VA. (The white artists on the bill are unable to play on several dates because of segregation laws which forbid black and white acts to perform on the same stage.)

1958

June The latest Drifters line-up (Hendricks, Thrasher, Jimmy Millender and Tommy Evans (b. Sept. 1, 1927)) has a double-sided hit with an oldie, *Moonlight Bay* (US #72), and Leiber and Stoller's *Drip Drop* (US #58), but they rile manager Treadwell and he fires them.
July Treadwell, who owns the Drifters name and nominates those who trade under it, hires another vocal group, the Crowns (comprising Charles Thomas (b. Apr. 7, 1937), Doc Green (b. Oct. 8, 1934), Rudy Lewis and lead singer Ellsbury Hobbs), to become the Drifters. Hobbs will soon go into the army and be replaced by Ben E. King (b. Benjamin Earl Nelson, Sept. 28, 1938, Henderson, NC).

1959

June Now freelancing for Atlantic, Leiber and Stoller have supervised the new group's first session, and their elaborate string-backed production transforms *There Goes My Baby* into an eerie, ethereal R&B classic. Co-written by lead singer King, it hits US #2 and earns the group a second gold disc.
Oct *Dance With Me* reaches US #15 and UK #17, while its B-side, *True Love True Love*, featuring Johnny Lee Williams on lead vocal, makes US #33.

1960

Feb Using their own compositions for the Coasters, Leiber and Stoller have asked Brill Building tunesmiths Pomus and Shuman to write material for the Drifters. After *True Love True Love*, they create *This Magic Moment*, which makes US #16 with King as lead singer again (as on the group's next three hits).
May From the same team, *Lonely Winds* reaches US #54. Despite colossal record sales and packed houses, the Drifters receive only modest wages. King complains and, when manager Treadwell invites him to resign, he does so.
Oct [17] Pomus, Shuman, Leiber and Stoller writing en masse provide the Drifters with *Save The Last Dance For Me*, which tops the US chart for the first of three weeks, hits UK #2 and is a million seller.
Dec Pomus/Shuman-penned *I Count The Tears*, King's last with the Drifters, reaches US #17 and UK #28.

1961

Mar With Rudy Lewis (b. May 27, 1935, Chicago, IL), ex-Clara Ward Singers, taking the lead, and new recruit Tommy Evans with Bill Thomas on guitar, the Drifters have cut a Goffin/King song, *Some Kind Of Wonderful*, which makes US #32.
June Co-written by Burt Bacharach, *Please Stay* reaches US #14.
Sept Pomus and Shuman's *Sweets For My Sweet* makes US #16. (The repertoire of every group on Merseyside will include Drifters' material, but only the Searchers hit UK #1 (in August 1963), with a revival of *Sweets For My Sweet*.)
Dec Pomus and Shuman's *Room Full Of Tears* peaks at US #72.

1962

Mar Goffin and King's *When My Little Girl Is Smiling* reaches US #28 and UK #31.
May Vocal rendering of Acker Bilk's chart-topper, *Stranger On The Shore*, peaks at US #73.
Nov The Drifters hit US #5 with their fourth million seller, *Up On The Roof*, written by Goffin and King.

1963

Mar Leiber and Stoller have modified a Barry Mann and Cynthia Weil composition, *On Broadway*, and have allowed Phil Spector to add the attractive guitar frills. It hits US #9.
June They also produce *Rat Race*, co-written with Van McCoy, which makes US #71. ***Up On The Roof***, a compilation of singles, peaks at US #110.
Sept Written by Mann and Weil, *I'll Take You Home* reaches US #25 and UK #37. Leiber and Stoller withdraw from their involvement with the group, to concentrate on the launch of their Red Bird label.

1964

Feb New Atlantic staff producer, Bert Berns, takes over and the Drifters' cover of *Vaya Con Dios*, a huge seller for Les Paul and Mary Ford in 1953, reaches US #43.
May Berns' own song, *One Way Love*, takes the Drifters to US #56 (but provides UK soul man Cliff Bennett with his Top 10 breakthrough at home).
June After Rudy Lewis has died unexpectedly (from asphyxiation on the morning of the recording of *Under The Boardwalk*), Johnny Moore returns to take over lead vocals, and the group's transition from R&B to smooth soul-pop is apparent in *Under The Boardwalk*, which hits US #4 and makes UK #45.
Sept A *Boardwalk* sequel, *I've Got Sand In My Shoes*, reaches US #33.
Nov Mann and Weil's *Saturday Night At The Movies* makes US #18. ***Under The Boardwalk*** (again, a singles compilation) makes US #40.
Dec The group participates in Murray The K's "Big Holiday Show" in New York.

1965

Jan Goffin and King's *At The Club* makes US #43 and UK #35.
Feb ***The Good Life*** peaks at US #103.
[23] They sing *At The Club* on NBC-TV's "Hullabaloo".
Mar [22] The group arrives in Britain for a three-week round of TV and radio shows and concerts.
Apr *Come On Over To My Place*, a double-sider by Mann and Weil, reaches US #60 and UK #40, while the Atlantic standard, *Chains Of Love*, reaches US #90.
July *Follow Me* makes US #91.
Aug Written by Jeff Barry and Ellie Greenwich, *I'll Take You Where The Music's Playing* reaches US #51.

1966

Mar While Moore has recruited bass singer Bill Brent formerly of early '50s harmony group the Hornets (from which Moore had also come), their cover of a 1955 million seller for Dean Martin, *Memories Are Made Of This*, makes US #48. The record marks the departure of producer Bert Berns, now running his own Bang and Shout records and at legal loggerheads with Atlantic.
Dec Produced by Bob Gallo and Atlantic engineer Tom Dowd, *Baby What I Mean* peaks at US #62 and UK #49.

1968

While Bill Fredericks has joined in 1967, the latest Drifters singles collection, ***Golden Hits***, reaches US #122 and UK #27.
Aug [16-18] The Drifters perform at San Francisco's Avalon Ballroom, sharing the bill with Bill Haley & the Comets and the Flamin' Groovies.

1971

With Johnny Moore leading the latest line-up of Fredericks, Butch Leake (who joined in 1970) and Gant Kitchings, the Drifters remain on the club circuit. Following the death of George Treadwell, his wife Faye assumes managerial control.

1972

Mar Reissued back to back, *At The Club/Saturday Night At The Movies* begins climbing the UK chart, eventually hitting #3.
June Reactivated ***Golden Hits*** reaches UK #26.
[13] Clyde McPhatter dies of heart, kidney and liver disease in Teaneck, NJ, following his serious alcohol and drug addiction.
Aug A minor hit seven years earlier, *Come On Over To My Place*, hits UK #9.
Sept [15] The group embarks on a UK tour, set to end on October 22nd.

1973

Aug Still led by Moore, the Drifters have signed a deal with the UK office of Bell Records and start a run of hits - all written and produced by permutations of Roger Cook, Roger Greenaway, Geoff Stephens, Barry Mason, Les Reed and Tony Macaulay. The first of these, *Like Sister And Brother*, hits UK #7, followed by *Kissin' In The Back Row Of The Movies* (UK #2, July, 1974) and *Down On The Beach Tonight* (UK #7, November).

1975

Feb *Love Games* reaches UK #33.
Oct The Drifters, now well-known on the UK club/cabaret/television show circuit, hit UK #3 with *There Goes My First Love*.
[12] The group performs at London's Hammersmith Odeon during a current UK tour.
Dec *Can I Take You Home Little Girl* hits UK #10.

1976

Jan [24] With Atlantic taking advantage of their renewed popularity, the repackaged ***24 Original Hits*** hits UK #2, behind Queen's ***A Night At The Opera***, during a 34 week-chart tenure. Overshadowed by the reissue, the latest Bell album, ***Love Games***, charts briefly at UK #51. (During the year, *Hello Happiness* makes UK #12 (April), *Every Nite's A Saturday Night With You* reaches UK #29 (September) and *You're More Than A Number In My Little Red Book* hits UK #5 (December), though none of the group's Bell output makes the US chart.)

1979

Mar The group performs a two-week season at London's Talk of the Town.
Apr *Save The Last Dance For Me/When My Little Girl Is Smiling* returns to the UK chart, at #69. (During the mid-'80s Ben E. King sings alongside Moore in the still-performing group - but only until the reissued *Stand By Me* returns him to the limelight, in 1987.)

1986

Oct ***The Very Best Of The Drifters*** reaches UK #24.

1987

Jan [21] McPhatter is posthumously inducted into the Rock and Roll Hall of Fame at the second annual dinner, held at New York's Waldorf Astoria Hotel.

1988

Jan [20] The Drifters are inducted into the Rock and Roll Hall of Fame at the third annual ceremony, staged at the Waldorf Astoria. (At least 40 people can legitimately claim to have been bona fide Drifters over the group's 35-year history and most of them have also masqueraded in several bogus groups of touring "Drifters". One time member Doc Green will die from cancer on March 10th the following year.)

1992

Feb [8] While a TV-advertised compilation, ***The Best Of Ben E. King & The Drifters***, has reached UK #15 on Nov [10], 1990 (moving the group's transatlantic chart career into a fifth decade), and regardless of lineup changes, the Drifters will remain popular act on the nostalgia circuit, (taking part, for example, in the "Royalty Of Doo Wopp" show at the Somerville Theater, Boston, MA, with the Belmonts, the Fleetwoods and Shirley Reeves of the Shirelles on February 8th 1992). Pinkney will attend the groundbreaking ceremony of the Rock and Roll Hall of Fame in Cleveland, OH on June 7th he following year.
see also: **Ben E. KING**

DURAN DURAN

Simon Le Bon (vocals); **Andy Taylor** (guitar); **Nick Rhodes** (keyboards); **John Taylor** (bass); **Roger Taylor** (drums)

1978

The group is formed in Birmingham, W. Midlands, by schoolmates club DJ Rhodes (b. Nicholas Bates, June 8, 1962, Moseley, Warks.) and John Taylor (b. Nigel John Taylor, June 20, 1960, Birmingham) on guitar, with bass player and clarinettist Simon Colley, vocalist Stephen Duffy (b. May 30, 1960, Birmingham) and a drum machine. The group's name is taken from the character played by Milo O'Shea in the Jane Fonda-starring science-fiction movie "Barbarella", and the band plays many early gigs at Barbarella's club in Birmingham.

1979

Colley and Duffy leave and are replaced by vocalist Andy Wickett, ex-TV Eye, and drummer Roger Taylor (b. Apr. 26, 1960, Castle Bromwich, Warks.), formerly of local punk groups the Crucified Toads and the Sex Organs. The group cuts a demo tape with local producer Bob Lamb. John Taylor switches to playing bass, guitarist John Curtis comes and goes, and the band puts an ad in **Melody Maker** for a "live wire guitarist", subsequently recruiting Andy Taylor (b. Feb. 16, 1961, Tynemouth, Tyne & Wear). Wickett leaves and the band gains temporary vocalists Alan Curtis and Jeff Thomas.

1980

Jan Brothers Paul and Michael Berrow, owners of Birmingham's newly-opened Rum Runner club, sign the band to a management contract and give it a residency at the club.
Apr Le Bon (b. Oct. 27, 1958, Bushey, Herts.), who, as a child, appeared in a Persil TV commercial and is a drama student (already a veteran of punk band Dog Days) at Birmingham University, is recruited after one rehearsal, having been suggested by ex-girlfriend Fiona Kemp, who is a barmaid at the Rum Runner. (He will become the band's principal lyricist and lead vocalist.)
July After Le Bon completes his final term at university, he joins full time and the group plays to a strong reaction at the Edinburgh Festival in Edinburgh, Scotland.
Nov Duran Duran plays its first major UK tour dates, supporting Hazel O'Connor, while the Berrow brothers negotiate a worldwide recording deal with EMI Records, whose A&R director Dave Ambrose, has been scouting them on the tour.

1981

Mar [28] Their first release, *Planet Earth*, produced by Colin Thurston, reaches UK #12. The band's musical and visual style fits neatly into the flamboyant New Romantic music movement in the UK which is rapidly spreading as a backlash against punk-originated new wave, with similar contemporaries, like Spandau Ballet, Ultravox and Visage, also hitting the chart. (Media coverage is wide, and the photogenic line-up, showcased in several promotional videos directed by Russell Mulcahy, will raise Duran Duran to UK teen-sensation status by the end of the year.)
Apr The group begins a world tour which will keep them on the road until Christmas.
May [23] *Careless Memories* makes UK #37.
June The band begins its first headlining UK tour at the Dome, Brighton, E. Sussex.
Aug [22] *Girls On Film*, with a risqué promo video directed by Godley & Creme (banned by the BBC in the UK and MTV in the US), hits UK #5.
Sept [5] ***Duran Duran*** hits UK #3 during a 118-week stay on the chart.
Dec [19] *My Own Way* reaches UK #14.

1982

Apr The band begins a world tour which will last until year's end.
May [29] Synthesizer-heavy ***Rio*** hits UK #2 (and will stay charted for the rest of the year).
June [26] *Hungry Like The Wolf*, taken from the album, with a high-class promo video directed by Mulcahy in Sri Lanka, hits UK #5.
July [29] Andy Taylor marries the group's hairdresser, Tracey Wilson, at the Chateau Marmont, in Los Angeles, CA, during US tour dates supporting Blondie.
Sept [11] Radio-friendly ballad, *Save A Prayer*, hits UK #2.
Nov [13] ***Carnival***, a US-only mini-album release, featuring earlier tracks remixed by the band and David Kershenbaum, makes US #98.
Dec [11] *Rio*, with Andy Hamilton guesting on saxophone, hits UK #9.

1983

Feb [19] Teen band Kajagoogoo tops the UK chart with the Nick Rhodes/Colin Thurston-produced *Too Shy*.
[26] Aided by US cable music station MTV's heavy rotation of its promo video, *Hungry Like The Wolf* climbs to US #3. It hits the charts in all major territories around the world and is a million seller. ***Rio***, which has been slowly climbing the US chart since June 1982, hits US #6 and will also become a million seller during its 129-week chart stay.
Mar [26] *Is There Something I Should Know* debuts at UK #1, with Duran Duran joining a small number of acts, including Elvis Presley, Cliff Richard and the Beatles, who have achieved this feat (which, up until the late '80s remains a rare achievement). The band attracts 5,000 fans while making an appearance at a video shop in New York and mounted police are deployed to control the crowd. This is the first noted US manifestation of Duran-fever, though such incidents are common for the band in Britain.
May [14] *Rio* reaches US #14.
July [20] The band headlines a charity concert for MENCAP at the Dominion Theatre, London, attended by H.R.H. the Prince and Princess of Wales.
Aug [6] *Is There Something I Should Know* hits US #4, becoming another million seller. It is added to the US version of the group's first album ***Duran Duran***, which climbs to US #10, another million seller.
Nov The band begins a five-month, 51-concert world tour, which will travel to the UK, Japan, Australia, Canada and the US.
[5] *Union Of The Snake*, previewing a forthcoming album, hits UK #3.
Dec [3] ***Seven And The Ragged Tiger***, co-produced by Alex Sadkin, Ian Little and the band, tops the UK chart for one week.
[24] *Union Of The Snake* hits US #3.
The band's second world tour ends at New York's Madison Square Garden, as they are voted Best Group in the **Daily Mirror**/BBC-TV "Nationwide"/Radio 1 Rock & Pop Awards.

1984

Feb ***Seven And The Ragged Tiger*** hits US #8.
[11] *New Moon On Monday*, taken from the album, hits UK #9.
[28] The group wins the Best Video Short Form for "Girls On Film/Hungry Like The Wolf" and Best Video Album for "Duran Duran" categories at the 26th annual Grammy Awards.
Mar [17] *New Moon On Monday* hits US #10.
Apr The band completes its world tour, having played to over 750,000 people and been recorded and filmed at many venues for subsequent live album and TV/video release.
May [5] *The Reflex*, remixed as a single by Nile Rodgers (ex-Chic), tops the UK chart for the first of four weeks.
June [23] *The Reflex* begins a two-week stay atop the US survey, another worldwide million seller.
July [27] Roger Taylor marries Giovanna Cantonne in Naples, Italy.
Aug [18] Nick Rhodes weds American model Julie Anne in London (they will divorce in 1993).
Nov [17] *The Wild Boys*, produced in London by Rodgers and the band, hits UK #2, behind Chaka Khan's *I Feel For You*.
[25] The band takes part in the all-star recording session for Band Aid's *Do They Know It's Christmas?* at Sarm Studios in London, with Le Bon taking one of the lead vocal lines.
Dec [15] *The Wild Boys* hits US #2 and is included on the otherwise live album, ***Arena*** (recorded on stage during the world tour), which hits UK #6 and US #4 and is the band's fourth million-selling album. Its release ties in with the TV showing of "Sing Blue Silver", a documentary filmed both on stage and behind the scenes during the world tour, directed by Michael Collins and Russell Mulcahy.

1985

Jan While Duran Duran is temporarily inactive, Andy and John Taylor form a recording-only spare-time group with Robert Palmer, producer Bernard Edwards and fellow ex-Chic drummer Tony Thompson, named Power Station after the New York studio where they are recording.
Feb Power Station makes its performing debut on NBC-TV's "Saturday Night Live".
[11] "Wild Boys" wins the Best British Music Video category at the fourth annual BRIT Awards, at London's Grosvenor House Hotel.
Mar [13] *The Reflex* is named International Hit Of The Year at the 30th annual Ivor Novello Awards, also held at the Grosvenor House Hotel.
[16] Duran Duran's *Save A Prayer* reaches US #16.
[30] Power Station's *Some Like It Hot*, penned by the Taylors with Robert Palmer, reaches UK #14.
Apr [6] Its parent album, ***The Power Station***, debuts at UK #12.
May [11] *Some Like It Hot* hits US #6.
[25] *A View To A Kill*, the theme from the forthcoming James Bond film, co-written by Duran Duran and composer John Barry, who scored the film, hits UK #2.
June [1] Power Station's revival of Marc Bolan's *Get It On*, taken from ***The Power Station***, reaches UK #22.
July [13] Duran Duran plays at the "Live Aid" benefit concert in Philadelphia, PA., as does Power Station, though with Michael Des Barres filling in for an absent Palmer. On the same day, Duran Duran's *A View To A Kill* begins a two-week tenure atop the US chart and is the band's sixth million-selling single (and the first James Bond film theme to hit US #1). (In retrospect, John Taylor will reflect: "From Live Aid on, you had to have a social conscience and we

represented '80s decadence. After Live Aid it was like: U2 in, Duran out.")
[27] ***The Power Station*** hits US #6.
Aug [3] Power Station's *Get It On* hits US #9, one place higher than the original 1972 T. Rex version, then titled *Bang A Gong*. Palmer is replaced in Power Station by ex-Silverhead and Chequered Past singer Des Barres, since the other members are still keen to work live. The new line-up makes a brief guest appearance in an episode of NBC-TV's "Miami Vice". Meanwhile, Le Bon, Rhodes and Roger Taylor form their own sideline recording band, Arcadia, and record an album.
[10] Sailing fanatic Le Bon is airlifted from his boat Drum after it overturns while racing.
Oct [12] Power Station's *Communication* makes US #34.
Nov [9] *Communication* peaks at UK #75, after which the group disbands. Arcadia's first single, *Election Day* (featuring narration by Grace Jones), hits UK #7, as its parent album, ***So Red The Rose***, makes UK #30.
Dec [4] Arcadia's *Election Day* hits US #6.
[27] Le Bon marries model Yasmin Parvanah.

1986

Jan ***So Red The Rose*** reaches US #23.
[22] ***So Red The Rose*** is certified platinum by the RIAA.
Feb Arcadia's *The Promise* peaks at UK #37.
Mar [8] Arcadia's *Goodbye Is Forever* is the US follow-up from the album and reaches #33.
Apr Between Power Station winding down and Duran Duran regrouping for album recordings, John Taylor's solo *I Do What I Do*, the theme from the movie "9½ Weeks", makes UK #42.
[26] *I Do What I Do* reaches US #23. Roger Taylor announces that he is to take a year's sabbatical from Duran Duran and retreats to his country home in Gloucestershire. (He will not return to the group.)
May Le Bon races Drum in Australia.
June Beginning album sessions as a quartet, Duran Duran completes them as a trio when Andy Taylor also leaves, to pursue a solo career in Los Angeles, having already recorded *Take It Easy* for the soundtrack of film "American Anthem". (He moves to the US, signs to MCA Records and begins work on a solo album with ex-Sex Pistol Steve Jones.)
July Arcadia's *The Flame*, remixed from the album as a third UK single, peaks at #58. Taylor rejoins Le Bon and Rhodes for a live TV appearance on a Pan-European six-hour version of C4-TV's "The Tube", but this marks the end of Arcadia's activity.
Aug [2] Andy Taylor's solo single, *Take It Easy*, reaches US #24.
[31] Le Bon is best man at the wedding of Bob Geldof and Paula Yates.
Nov Duran Duran's *Notorious*, the title track from a forthcoming album, hits UK #7.
[15] Andy Taylor's first solo release for MCA, *When The Rain Comes Down* (featured in the NBC-TV series "Miami Vice"), makes US #73.
Dec ***Notorious***, co-produced by Nile Rodgers and the band, showcasing the new Duran Duran trio (Andy Taylor is heard on only four tracks, recorded before his departure), with es-Missing Persons Warren Cuccurullo (b. Dec. 8, 1956, Brooklyn, NY) guitar, and session man Steve Ferrone (b. Apr. 25, 1950, Brighton, E. Sussex) (ex-Average White Band) on drums, reaches UK #16.

1987

Jan [10] *Notorious* hits US #2, as the parent album, ***Notorious***, reaches US #12.
Mar *Skin Trade*, extracted from the album, makes UK #22.
[14] *Skin Trade* reaches US #39.
Apr Duran Duran appears live at "The Secret Policeman's Third Ball" at the London Palladium, amid rumors that this might be its last concert.
May Their "Strange Behaviour" tour ends with three nights at the Wembley Arena, Wembley, Middx. *Meet El Presidente*, a further excerpt from ***Notorious***, reaches UK #24, while Andy Taylor's debut solo album, ***Thunder***, makes UK #61 (May [30]) and US #46.
[16] *Meet El Presidente* peaks at US #70. (The group ends its world tour with a benefit for homeless children, at New York's Beacon Theatre, with Lou Reed and Nile Rodgers helping out onstage.)

1988

Jan Le Bon, Rhodes and John Taylor recruit Cuccurullo as a full-time Duran member and also drummer Sterling Campbell to work on a new album recorded in Paris with producers Jonathan Elias and Daniel Abraham.
June Duran Duran signs a new management deal with Peter Rudge.
Oct *I Don't Want Your Love* reaches UK #14.
[21] They give a free concert in the parking lot of Capitol Records, on the corner of Sunset and Vine in Hollywood, CA, drawing an estimated crowd of 5,000.
[29] ***Big Thing***, reaches UK #15.
Dec [3] *I Don't Want Your Love* hits US #4, as ***Big Thing***, co-produced by the band with Elias and Abraham, reaches US #24. (For reasons best known to themselves, the group is now going under the moniker Duranduran, an aberration which only lasts for this album.)

1989

Jan *All She Wants Is* hits UK #9.
Feb [18] *All She Wants Is* reaches US #22.
Apr *Do You Believe In Shame*, from ***Big Thing***, reaches UK #30.
[8] *Do You Believe In Shame*, featured in the Mel Gibson/Michelle Pfeiffer film "Tequila Sunrise", peaks at US #72.
Aug [25] Le Bon becomes a father to daughter Amber Rose. (John Taylor will parent a girl, Atlanta, in 1992 with TV presenter girlfriend, Amanda de Cadenet.)
Nov [25] Compilation hits album, ***Decade***, hits UK #5.
Dec [23] *Burning The Ground* makes UK #31.

1990

Jan [20] ***Decade*** makes US #67.
Aug [11] *Violence Of Summer (Love's Taking Over)* reaches UK #20.
Sept [1] ***Liberty*** debuts at its UK #8 peak.
[15] ***Liberty*** makes US #46.
[29] *Violence Of Summer (Love's Taking Over)* peaks at US #64.
Oct [27] Andy Taylor's remake of the Kinks' *Lola* peaks at UK #60.
Nov [24] Duran Duran's *Serious* makes UK #48.

1992

Mar They continue working on a new album, begun the previous year, at the Maison Rouge Studio with co-producer J. J. (John Jones).
July Album plans are delayed after Le Bon breaks his wrist and collarbone in a motorcycle accident, while riding in "Supersport 400" in Wales.
Dec [13] The band performs at a KROQ radio station show at the Universal Amphitheatre, Universal City, CA.

1993

Feb [6] Regarded as something of a comeback, *Ordinary World* hits UK #6.
[15] The group is the musical guest on NBC-TV's "The Tonight Show".
[20] *Ordinary World* hits US #3, the group's first US Top 10 success in five years.
[27] Lush, funk-oriented ***Duran Duran (The Wedding Album)***, recorded at guitarist Cuccurullo's home studio and released after a change of management from Peter Rudge to Left Bank Management, debuts at its UK #4 peak. Including a cover of Velvet Underground's *Femme Fatale*, the album is seen as a major return to form.
Mar [13] ***Duran Duran*** debuts at its US #7 peak.
[19] The group performs "An Acoustic Evening With Duran Duran" at Birmingham Symphony Hall, followed the next night by a similar show at the Dominion Theatre, London.
Apr During its current world tour, the band performs ten dates in South Africa.
[17] *Come Undone*, helped by CD format which also includes *Rio*, *Is There Something I Should Know* and *A View To A Kill*, reaches UK #13.
May [13] The group is featured on the 1,000th "The Arsenio Hall Show", recorded at the Hollywood Bowl, Los Angeles.
[14] Duran Duran broadcast live from Tower Records, Los Angeles, to fans in London, Sydney and Tokyo. The sole concert is known as the "No Ordinary World Tour".
June [5] The band takes part in KISS Radio's all-star anniversary concert at the Great Woods Center for the Performing Arts, Mansfield, MA.
[19] *Come Undone* hits US #7.
July [14] 29-date first leg of a North American tour opens at the Sun Dome, Tampa, FL, set to end on August 24th at Bally's Casino Resort, Las Vegas, NV.
Aug [23] The group receives its star on the Hollywood Walk of Fame in Hollywood, CA.
Sept [7] The UK leg of the world tour opens at the Sheffield Arena, Sheffield, S. Yorks.
[11] *Too Much Information* reaches UK #35.
Oct [16] *Too Much Information* makes US #45, as the group's comeback tour is postponed indefinitely, when LeBon is incapacitated with a torn vocal chord.

1994

Jan [11-13] With LeBon fully recovered, the group plays at New York's Radio City Music Hall.
[22] They begin a six-date UK tour at Manchester's G-Mex Centre, set to end on the 31st at Bournemouth International Centre.
May [25] *Ordinary World* is named the Most Performed Work at the 39th annual Ivor Novello Awards still held at Grosvenor House.
Sept [24] Earlier compilation ***Decade*** re-charts at UK #66.
Oct [14] *Come Undone* and *Ordinary World* are honored at the 14th ASCAP dinner at London's Park Lane Hotel.

1995

Mar [10] The band performs at the opening night gala of the Hard Rock Hotel & Casino in Las Vegas, NV.
[25] *Perfect Day* debuts at its UK #28 peak.
Apr [8] ***Thank You***, a covers album including *Lay Lady Lay*, *Crystal Ship*, *White Lines*, *Ball Of Confusion*, *Watching The Detectives*, *Success* and *911 Is A Joke*, reaches UK #12 in its week of entry.
[22] ***Thank You*** debuts at its US #19 peak.
May [29] The group takes part in an all-star "New Rock 102.1 Fest" at the Marcus Amphitheatre, Milwaukee, WI, with Bush, Faith No More, Ramones, Violent Femmes and others.
July [1] *White Lines (Don't Do It)* reaches UK #17.
Sept [12] Le Bon performs with Luciano Pavarotti at the latter's annual "Pavarotti And Friends Together" at his War Child charity benefit at Novi Sad Park, Modena in northern Italy.

IAN DURY & THE BLOCKHEADS

Ian Dury (vocals); **Chaz Jankel** (keyboards, guitar); **Davey Payne** (saxophone); **John Turnbull** (guitar); **Norman Watt-Roy** (bass); **Mickey Gallagher** (keyboards); **Charley Charles** (drums)

1970

Nov Dury (b. May 12, 1942, Upminster, Essex), partially crippled since contracting polio at the age of seven (which has left him with a stricken leg and hand), forms the initially part-time Kilburn & the High Roads, while still a lecturer at Canterbury College of Art, Kent, with pianist Russell Hardy. Playing for the first three years with a line-up augmented by Ted Speight (guitar), Terry Day (drums), George Khan (sax) and Charlie Hart (bass), the band is introduced to regular work on London's pub circuit in January 1973, by future Stiff Records founder Dave Robinson, where they are spotted by writer and broadcaster Charlie Gillett, who becomes their manager, later to be replaced by Robinson.

1973

May [3] When the band's battered transit van almost falls to pieces, three other pub circuit bands, Ducks Deluxe, Brinsley Schwarz and Bees Make Honey, play a benefit show at Camden Town Hall, London, to raise money for repair bills.
Oct The group, now comprising Dury, always its central creative force, Russell, Keith Lucas (guitar), Davey Payne (sax), David Newton-Rohoman (drums) and Humphrey Ocean (bass), tours the UK as support to the Who.

1974

Jan Signed to WEA's Raft label, the band records an album, produced by Tony Ashton (ex-Ashton, Gardner & Dyke), which is not issued because the label closes down. WEA lets Kilburn & the High Roads go (but will release the album in the UK in 1978, after Dury's subsequent success).
July Tommy Roberts becomes the group's new manager securing a deal with Pye Records' Dawn imprint.
Nov Their debut release is the single *Rough Kids*, followed by *Crippled With Nerves* in February.

1975

June ***Handsome*** is no more commercially successful than the singles, but will be reissued in Dury's later successful days. The disillusioned group breaks up, forcing the cancellation of some projected European live dates. Dury and Rod Melvin will spend the rest of the year writing and planning a new Kilburns.
Nov Six-piece group, Ian Dury & the Kilburns, is formed, with Robinson as manager, organizing a regular gig at the Hope & Anchor in Islington, London.

1976

Mar Ex-Byzantium Jankel joins the band on keyboards, replacing Russell Hardy, and begins to write with Dury.
June [17] The group splits after a last gig at Walthamstow Town Hall, London, mainly because Dury's doctor orders him off the road for health reasons. (Dury and Jankel stay together and spend a year writing songs for what will become the first Ian Dury solo album.)

1977

Aug Dury signs to Robinson's Stiff Records. *Sex And Drugs And Rock And Roll*, connecting the pub-rock scene to the exploding punk movement, is released.
Sept Ian Dury & the Blockheads is formed for the "Stiff Live Stiffs" UK promotional tour (with Elvis Costello, Nick Lowe and others), for which Dury and Jankel recruit several of the session men they have used in recent recordings, including Charles (drums), Gallagher (keyboards), Turnbull (guitars), Watt Roy (bass) and Payne (saxophone).
Nov Dury's second solo single, the reverential *Sweet Gene Vincent*, is released.

1978

Mar The band tours the US, supporting Lou Reed.
May *What A Waste*, written by Dury, Jankel and current Blockheads, becomes Dury's first hit single, at UK #9. ***New Boots And Panties!*** chart peaks at US #168, as Dury & the Blockheads tour the UK, with legendary comedian Max Wall as the support act. (Wall records *England's Glory*, written for him by Dury, and it is released on Stiff.)
June Humphrey Ocean, a former art-school friend and Kilburns' alumnus, covers Dury's *Whoops A Daisy*, also on Stiff.
[1] The group embarks on a 12-date UK tour at the Odeon, Edinburgh, Scotland, set to end on the 14th at the Odeon, Ilford, Essex.
Oct ***Wotabunch***, the Kilburn & the High Roads' album left on the shelf at WEA in 1974, is released.

1979

Jan [27] *Hit Me With Your Rhythm Stick*, penned by Dury and Jankel, tops the UK chart for one week, with over 900,000 sales over the 1978 Christmas period in the UK alone.
Feb [10] ***New Boots And Panties!***, highlighting Dury's trademark lyrical wit, hits UK #5 more than 15 months after it debut.
June [2] ***Do It Yourself***, marketed in a variety of "wallpaper pattern" sleeve designs, hits UK #2, behind Abba's ***Voulez-Vous***.
[5-6] The group begins a major 39-date UK tour, including a week-long stint at London's Hammersmith Odeon, at the Colston Hall, Bristol, Avon, set to end on August 1st at the New Theatre, Oxford, Oxon.
Aug R&B/disco-flavored *Reasons To Be Cheerful (Part 3)*, recorded in Rome, hits UK #3, as ***Do It Yourself*** makes US #126.
Dec Dury appears at the "People Of Kampuchea" benefit concert at London's Hammersmith Odeon, along with Paul McCartney, the Who, Robert Plant and many others.

1980

Chaz Jankel leaves for a solo career, signing to A&M (most notably penning *Ai No Corrida*, a subsequent hit for Quincy Jones), while Mickey Gallagher rejoins, having earlier left to join the Clash on tour.
July [5] Wilko Johnson (ex-Dr. Feelgood and the Solid Senders) joins on guitar.
Sept *I Want To Be Straight*, Dury's first recording to feature Johnson on guitar, reaches UK #22.
Nov *Sueperman's Big Sister* (the incorrect spelling is deliberate, to avoid copyright problems) reaches UK #51.
Dec [13] ***Laughter*** makes UK #48, while Dury & the Blockheads play their "Soft As A Baby's Bottom" UK tour.

1981

Feb ***Laughter*** peaks at US #159.
Aug Having signed a new worldwide deal with Polydor Records, Dury releases *Spasticus Autisticus* in time for the Year Of The Disabled, but most UK radio stations refuse to play it. It fails to chart (as will all his Polydor singles) and is deleted the following month, with a Polydor statement: "Just as nobody bans handicapped people - just makes it difficult for them to function as normal people - so *Spasticus Autisticus* was not banned, it was made impossible to function." The United Nations rejects the song as a contribution to the Year Of The Disabled.
Oct [17] ***Lord Upminster***, recorded at Compass Point Studios in Nassau, Bahamas, with the legendary rhythm section of Sly & Robbie replacing the Blockheads on all but one track, and also marking a Jankel return, peaks at UK #53.
Nov ***Juke Box Duries***, compiled from earlier Stiff singles, is released. (The Blockheads, sans Dury, will release a revival of *Twist And Shout*, recorded on stage in London, the following December.)

1984

Jan [2] Dury takes part in a peace benefit, "The Big One" at London's Apollo Theatre, Victoria.
Feb ***4,000 Weeks Holiday***, credited to Ian Dury & the Music Students, makes UK #54. Originally scheduled for the previous year, it was withheld by Polydor until *Fuck Off Noddy* and a song about holiday tycoon Billy Butlin were removed. The extracted *Very Personal* ends Dury's unproductive spell with Polydor.

1985

June Paul Hardcastle's re-mix of *Hit Me With Your Rhythm Stick*, recorded for Stiff with Dury's approval, peaks at UK #55. Dury begins to be heard (if not seen) regularly on UK TV, doing voice-overs for holiday and electrical goods advertisements.
Nov *Profoundly In Love With Pandora*, his theme to ITV's "The Secret Diary Of Adrian Mole, Aged 13¾", makes UK #45. (During the year, Dury reunites with the Blockheads for live work, and appears with Bob Geldof in the movie "Number One". He will take further acting roles the following year in Roman Polanski's movie "Pirates" and in the BBC-TV series "King Of The Ghetto".)

1987

Another Dury theme for a second "Adrian Mole" series is aired on ITV. Dury appears in the ill-received Bob Dylan movie "Hearts Of Fire" and scores the music for "Night Moves", a UK TV play about truckers. He will successfully leave behind his flagging recording career and switch his attention to acting, writing music and his first love, painting. (During the year, Demon Records issues the 16-track CD retrospective, ***Sex & Drugs & Rock & Roll***.)

1989

Nov Dury-written and conceived musical, "Apples", opens at the Royal Court Theatre, London, while its cast recording, ***Apples*** is issued on WEA Records.

1990

Sept [5] Ex-Blockhead Charley Charles dies in London's Park Royal Hospital from complications relating to cancer.
[25-27] The Blockheads re-form for a one-off gig at London's Town & Country Club.

1991

July [27] *Hit Me With Your Rhythm Stick*, a remix of Dury's 1978 UK chart-topper, charts for a week, at UK #73.

1992

Mar Recently featured in the Rutger Hauer-starring movie "Split Second", Dury begins a host slot on ITV's "Metro" series.
May Carter USM's ***1992 - The Love Album***, featuring Dury's voice, is released in the UK.
Aug [8-9] Dury performs on the bill of the Madness reunion concerts at London's Finsbury Park, shortly before the release of his latest solo album, ***The Bus Driver's Prayer & Other Short Stories*** on Demon Records. (Becoming a host on ITV's "Metro", Dury will continue to tour the UK and Eire, not least appearing on August 6th, 1994 at "Madstock" also held at Finsbury Park.)

BOB DYLAN

1959

June [5] Dylan (b. Robert Allen Zimmerman, May 24, 1941, Duluth, MN) who ran away to Chicago, IL at the age of ten, began learning to play the guitar and harmonica at age 12, before travelling for a while with a Texas carnival at age 13. Having had his bar-mitzvah on May 22nd 1954, he now leaves Hibbing High School, having played regularly and formed several groups including rock'n'roll band the Golden Chords, noting in the yearbook that he is leaving "to follow Little Richard". Initially, however, he starts a course at the University of Minnesota. Leaving the campus in 1960, to concentrate on playing and singing, he is briefly employed as a pianist with Bobby Vee's backing group, the Shadows. Adopting a new stage name, courtesy of poet Dylan Thomas, he then travels to New York, NY down Highway 61, to visit Woody Guthrie, chief precursor of the current folk boom (and a particular influence on Dylan), but who has been paralysed with a rare hereditary disease known as Huntington's Chorea for the past eight years.

1961

Feb [3] In New York, Dylan makes his first recordings, on some friends' home equipment, playing the standard *San Francisco Bay Blues* among similar numbers.
Apr [11] His first New York live gig is at Gerde's Folk City in Greenwich Village, opening for bluesman

John Lee Hooker, where he first meets Joan Baez.
[24] Dylan earns a $50 session fee playing harmonica on recordings for Harry Belafonte's *Midnight Special*.
Sept [30] He joins folk singer Carolyn Hester on an album session for CBS/Columbia Records, again on harmonica. He impresses producer John Hammond Sr., who has noted a glowing **New York Times** review of his performance at Gerde's Folk City and offers Dylan a recording contract.
Oct [4] As a showcase, he plays at New York's Carnegie Chapter Hall - to 53 people.
[20] Dylan records his debut album, ***Bob Dylan***, which includes raw, authentic versions of traditional songs.

1962

Mar ***Bob Dylan*** is released in the US including the extracted rockabilly-styled *Mixed Up Confusion/ Corrina Corrina*. Both fail to chart, but cause a major stir on the folk scene. (By year's end, his composition *Blowin' In The Wind* is published in **Broadside** magazine.)
Aug Robert Zimmerman legally changes his name to Bob Dylan.
Dec [21] He makes his first UK appearance at the King & Queen pub in Foley Street, London. (The following night he will appear at the Singers' Club Christmas Party at the Pindar of Wakefield pub in Grays Inn Road, London.)

1963

Jan [12] During his brief visit to London, Dylan is given a part as a folk singer in a UK BBC radio play, "The Madhouse On Castle Street", singing *Blowin' In The Wind* and *Swan On The River*.
Apr [12] A solo concert at New York's Town Hall draws positive reviews, and is recorded by CBS for a live album (which does not materialize).
May ***The Freewheelin' Bob Dylan*** is released, featuring major compositions of his own, including *A Hard Rain's Gonna Fall*, *Blowin' In The Wind* and *Masters Of War*, and establishes him as a leader in the burgeoning folk singer-songwriter and youth protest movements. (Its cover also features his current girlfriend, Suze Rotolo.)
[12] Dylan is invited to appear on CBS-TV's "The Ed Sullivan Show", but - having been forbidden to sing *Talking John Birch Society Blues* - he declines.
[17] He meets Joan Baez again, at the "Monterey Folk Festival", Monterey, CA. (The two will become the stars of the year's "Newport Folk Festival", Newport, RI, at which Baez will introduce Dylan, and will develop a long-term personal and creative union.)
Aug Folk trio Peter, Paul & Mary's version of Dylan's *Blowin' In The Wind* hits US #2 and UK #13, and is a million seller. (They will follow it with another hit cover from ***The Freewheelin' Bob Dylan***, *Don't Think Twice, It's Alright*).
Sept Following Peter, Paul and Mary's success, interest in *Blowin' In The Wind* and its writer spurs ***The Freewheelin' Bob Dylan*** to US #22 and a gold disc.
Oct [26] Dylan performs at New York's Carnegie Hall.

1964

Apr ***The Times They Are A-Changin'***, much of its content on a strong protest theme, reaches US #20.
May With Dylan's name constantly promoted in the UK by the Beatles and others, ***The Freewheelin' Bob Dylan*** makes UK #16. (It will return later in the year to top the chart.)
[17] Dylan performs at London's Royal Festival Hall.
July ***The Times They Are A-Changin'*** reaches UK #20. (This will also later return with bigger sales.)
Oct ***Another Side Of Bob Dylan***, revealing more personal themes, makes US #43.
Dec ***Another Side Of Bob Dylan*** hits UK #8.

1965

Jan [14-15] Dylan records his new album, ***Bringing It All Back Home***, at Columbia Studio A in New York.
Apr [17]***The Freewheelin' Bob Dylan*** finally tops the UK chart, for the first of two non-consecutive weeks, after a year on sale.
[30] Received as a major celebrity, an eight-date UK "Don't Look Back" tour opens at Sheffield City Hall, Sheffield, Yorks. The visit is documented on film in fly-on-the-wall fashion by D.A. Pennebaker, and later released as "Don't Look Back". The movie reveals that pressure on the young star is growing steadily more intense as his popularity grows. *The Times They Are A-Changin'*, released as Dylan's first UK single (to tie in with the tour), hits UK #9 following sellout London concerts. ***The Times They Are A-Changin'*** hits UK #4.
May [9] The tour ends with a gig at London's Royal Albert Hall which is recorded for a never-released live album, though bootlegs will be prolific.
[15] Rock guitar-driven *Subterranean Homesick Blues* makes US #39 (his first US hit single) and hits UK #9.
[26] Dylan is admitted to St. Mary's Hospital, Paddington, London, with a viral infection.
[29] ***Freewheelin' Bob Dylan***, having returned to the UK top spot the previous week, is swept aside by Dylan's new album, ***Bringing It All Back Home***, which hits UK #1 (for one week) and US #6, earning his second gold disc. The album includes *Subterranean Homesick Blues* on a complete side of electric, rock-oriented material, on which Dylan is backed by a group including Al Kooper and Paul Butterfield. The other side maintains his acoustic folk roots and includes *Mr. Tambourine Man*. His first album, ***Bob Dylan***, makes UK #13, giving him five simultaneous UK Top 20 album placings.
June [25] Dylan appears at the "Newport Folk Festival" and plays a controversial full-electric set backed by Al Kooper, Barry Goldberg and members of the Paul Butterfield Blues Band. The diehard folk "purists" in the audience try to boo him off the stage.
[26] The Byrds hit US #1 with their folk-rock cover of *Mr. Tambourine Man* (which hits UK #1 a few weeks later). It is the first chart-topping Dylan composition and sparks several pop and folk-rock hit covers of his material by major acts like the Turtles (*It Ain't Me Babe*), Cher (*All I Really Want To Do*), Joan Baez (*It's All Over Now, Baby Blue* and *Farewell Angelina*) and Manfred Mann (*If You Gotta Go, Go Now*).
July [3] *Maggie's Farm*, taken from ***Bringing It All Back Home***, reaches UK #22.
Aug [28] He takes part in the "Forest Hills Music Festival", Forest Hills, New York.
Sept [3] Dylan plays at the Hollywood Bowl, Hollywood, CA, backed by Al Kooper, Harvey Brooks, Robbie Robertson and Levon Helm.
[4] *Like A Rolling Stone*, noted for its revolutionary length (six minutes) as well as its rock backing (notably Al Kooper's rolling organ), hits US #2 and UK #4, becoming Dylan's first million-selling single. It is susequently regarded as a landmark recording.
Oct The critically-revered ***Highway 61 Revisited***, mixing Dylan's intricate (and much studied) lyrics with mainstream rock, hits US #3 and UK #4.
Nov [6] *Positively 4th Street*, in a similar style to *Like A Rolling Stone*, hits US #7 and UK #8.
[22] Dylan marries Sara Lowndes.
Dec [4] He plays at the Berkeley Community Theater, Berkeley, CA. (The concert will be released as the live ***Long Distance Operator*** in 1992.)

1966

Jan [29] *Can You Please Crawl Out Your Window* peaks at US #58.
Feb [5] *Can You Please Crawl Out Your Window* reaches UK #17.
[14-17] Dylan begins recording at Columbia Music Row Studios in Nashville, TN, for what will be the album ***Blonde On Blonde***.
Apr *One Of Us Must Know (Sooner Or Later)* makes UK #33.
May [5] A 14-date British tour opens at the Adelphi Theatre, Dublin, Eire.
[21] Boisterous *Rainy Day Women #12 & 35* hits US #2, behind the Mamas & the Papas' *Monday Monday*, and will become Dylan's second million-selling single.
[26-27] Dylan plays at London's Royal Albert Hall at the end of another UK tour, this time backed by an electric band largely consisting of the Hawks (later to become the Band). Purists in the audience conclude that the folk singer has "sold out" and again make their feelings vocal.
June *Rainy Day Women #12 & 35* hits UK #7.
July [25] Dylan suffers injuries (never fully detailed, but apparently involving a broken neck vertebrae) when he crashes his Triumph 55 motorcycle near his home in Woodstock, NY. His recuperation, purportedly on Cape Cod, MA, leads to a period of reclusive inactivity, interpreted by many as an attempt to escape into family life, away from the extreme pressures of two years' success.
Aug Double album, the critically-worshipped ***Blonde On Blonde***, including an entire side devoted to *Sad Eyed Lady Of The Lowlands*, hits US #9, his fourth gold album in US, with sales over half a million. *I Want You*, a lightweight pop number taken from the album, reaches US #20 and UK #16.
Oct [8] Ballad *Just Like A Woman*, also from the album, reaches US #33 (but is not issued in the UK, where Manfred Mann's cover hits #10). It is announced that Dylan is spending his recuperative period writing a novel. ***Blonde On Blonde*** hits UK #3.

1967

Feb UK compilation, ***Greatest Hits***, hits UK #6.
May [17] The "Don't Look Back" documentary premieres.
June US-compiled ***Greatest Hits*** (with a different track listing from the UK version), hits US #10 and earns another gold disc.
[3] *Leopard Skin Pillbox Hat* peaks at US #81. (During almost 18 months of "retirement", Dylan stays in Woodstock, apparently inactive. Tapes of sessions at Big Pink, a large old house in Woodstock, recorded with the Band, later begin to circulate. Several acts, including Manfred Mann (*The Mighty Quinn*), Peter, Paul and Mary (*Too Much Of Nothing*) and Julie Driscoll & Brian Auger (*This Wheel's On Fire*), will have hits with songs originating from these sessions, which will form the basis of ***Great White Wonder***, the first big-selling bootleg rock album.)
Oct Dylan returns to the studio (without the Band) to record an album of new material.

1968

Jan [20] Dylan plays with the Band at a memorial concert for Woody Guthrie (who died, aged 55, on September 3rd, 1967) at Carnegie Hall - his first public appearance since his motorcycle crash.
Feb [29] Still without a Grammy as a performer, ***Bob Dylan's Greatest Hits*** wins the Best Album Cover - Photography category at the tenth annual Grammy Awards.
Mar ***John Wesley Harding***, simpler and more country-influenced than his pre-accident recordings, recorded in Nashville with Charlie McCoy, Kenny Buttrey and Pete Drake, hits US #2.
[9] ***John Wesley Harding*** tops the UK chart for the first of ten consecutive weeks. (No Dylan single is taken from this album, but Jimi Hendrix will have a hit with a hard-rock cover of *All Along The Watchtower*.)
May [25] ***John Wesley Harding*** returns to the top of the UK chart for another three-week run.

1969

May Country-influenced ***Nashville Skyline***, recorded in Nashville, TN, with assistance from Johnny Cash (they duet on *Girl From The North Country*), hits US #3. Cash and Dylan also record a TV special at the legendary Grand Ole Opry, which will air on ABC-TV on June 7th.
[24] ***Nashville Skyline*** begins a four-week stretch at UK #1.
June [7] *I Threw It All Away*, taken from the album, peaks at US #85 and UK #30.
Aug [31] Having snubbed Woodstock (held near his home base), Dylan and the Band headline the "Isle Of Wight Festival", Godshill, Isle of Wight, with part of the set being recorded (for eventual release on ***Self-Portrait***). He earns £35,000 for his hour-long set.
Sept [6] Ballad *Lay Lady Lay*, taken from ***Nashville***

Skyline (but originally written, by request, for the film "Midnight Cowboy" and rejected), hits US #7 and UK #5. Dylan's first Top 10 single for three years, it will also be his last.

Nov [29] *Tonight I'll Be Staying Here With You*, also from ***Nashville Skyline***, makes US #50.

1970

Mar [11] Johnny Cash's annotation for ***Nashville Skyline*** wins Best Album Notes Of 1969 at the 12th annual Grammy Awards.

June [9] Dylan is awarded an honorary Doctorate in Music from Princeton University, Princeton, NJ.

July [11] Double album, ***Self-Portrait***, a scrapbook collection of new songs, live cuts and familiar covers (including songs by Paul Simon, Gordon Lightfoot and the Everly Brothers), pasted by critics as a waste of talent, nevertheless provides Dylan's third successive UK #1 (for one week) and hits US #4.

Aug [15] Largely instrumental *Wigwam*, from ***Self-Portrait***, makes US #41.

Sept [12] Dylan takes part in the "Woody Guthrie Memorial Concert" at the Hollywood Bowl, Los Angeles, CA, with Pete Seeger and Arlo Guthrie.

Nov [11] His long-awaited novel, the surreal **Tarantula**, is published, to wide press attention.

[28] ***New Morning*** tops the UK survey for one week.

Dec ***New Morning*** hits US #7, critically greeted as a return to form. (By year's end Dylan has invested in the fraudulent tax shelter Home-Stake Oil Production Company in Tulsa, OK, and is swindled out of more than $120,000.)

1971

Jan [10] He makes a rare TV appearance, on Earl Scruggs' "Fanfare Show".

Feb [8] Dylan documentary film, "Eat The Document", featuring mostly his 1966 UK tour with the Band, is premiered at New York's Academy of Music, to benefit the effort to end strip-mining in Pike County. The movie is only ever shown commercially twice more.

Mar [16] He records *Watching The River Flow* and *When I Paint My Masterpiece* in a session with Leon Russell guesting on piano.

July [31] Dylan appears in George Harrison's "Concert for Bangla Desh" at New York's Madison Square Garden (and performs one side of the triple album of the event, which hits US #2). This is Dylan's only major live appearance of the year.

Aug [7] *Watching The River Flow* reaches US #41 and UK #24.

Dec [31] Dylan joins the Band onstage at the Academy of Music, New York.

1972

Jan Double compilation album, ***Bob Dylan's Greatest Hits, Vol. II*** (***More Bob Dylan Greatest Hits*** in UK), reaches US #14 and UK #12.

[8] Specially-recorded protest single, *George Jackson*, about the black militant shot dead in a prison fracas, makes US #33.

Dec [18] He arrives on location in Mexico to start filming his role as the outlaw Alias in Sam Peckinpah's "Pat Garrett And Billy The Kid".

1973

Sept Following the film's release, Dylan's soundtrack album, ***Pat Garrett And Billy The Kid***, which includes three tracks with his vocals, is released by CBS/Columbia and reaches US #16 and UK #29. His contract with the label expires and he does not renew it.

Oct [27] The movie soundtrack's highlight, Dylan singing *Knockin' On Heaven's Door*, is released, and becomes his biggest-selling single since *Lay Lady Lay*, reaching US #12 and UK #14. (It will be much covered, not least in hit versions by Eric Clapton and Guns N' Roses.)

Nov It becomes clear that Dylan is not re-signing to CBS, and it is announced that he will move to David Geffen's Asylum label and is recording an album with the Band. Columbia releases ***Dylan***, a collection of out-takes and rejected covers from ***Self-Portrait***.

1974

Jan Almost universally decried, ***Dylan*** reaches US #17, while its extracted revival of Elvis Presley's *A Fool Such As I* makes US #55.

[3] Dylan and the Band open a 39-date US tour (the first in nearly eight years) at the Amphitheatre in Chicago, IL, to support their first Asylum album together, cut the previous November. (Several dates will be recorded for a live album.) There are more than five million ticket applications for the 660,000 tickets available.

Feb [16] Asylum debut, ***Planet Waves***, is, ironically, Dylan's first US chart-topper (occupying pole position for the first of four weeks).

Mar [9] ***Planet Waves*** hits #7 in the UK, where it is released by Island Records.

[23] *On A Night Like This*, taken from ***Planet Waves***, makes US #44.

July Live double album, ***Before The Flood***, a compilation of performances from the US tour, produced by Phil Ramone, with the Band getting one side to itself, features reworked versions of some of Dylan's '60s hits and climbs to US #3 and UK #8 (July [20]).

Aug [2] Dylan settles his differences with CBS chief executive Clive Davis and re-signs to the label for five years.

[31] Live single from the album, *Most Likely You Go Your Way (And I'll Go Mine)*, peaks at US #66.

Sept Songs are recorded for a new CBS/Columbia album, ***Blood On The Tracks***, but after it is scheduled for release, Dylan is dissatisfied with some of the recordings, and the album is delayed.

1975

Mar [1] After five numbers have been reworked, ***Blood On The Tracks***, inspired by the break-up of his marriage, tops the US chart for the first of two weeks and hits UK #4.

[23] Dylan participates in the Bill Graham-organized SNACK (Students Need Athletics Culture & Kicks) benefit at San Francisco's Kezar Stadium, to raise funds to make up for a shortfall in the San Francisco school system budget. The 60,000 crowd also sees performances by Neil Young, Joan Baez, the Doobie Brothers, Jefferson Starship, the Grateful Dead, Santana, and the Band.

Apr [5] *Tangled Up In Blue*, from the album, makes US #31.

July Dylan sanctions the official release of the double album ***The Basement Tapes***, after years of bootlegs of these 1967 recordings with the Band. Compiled and remixed by the Band's Robbie Robertson, the album hits US #7 and UK #8 (Aug [2]).

Oct [23] Dylan previews his forthcoming "Rolling Thunder Revue Tour" by playing an early morning set at Folk City in Greenwich Village as a surprise for the club's owner, Mike Porco. Joan Baez, Ronee Blakley, Ramblin' Jack Elliott, Bob Neuwirth, Mick Ronson and Allen Ginsberg join him.

[30] The initially low-key and spontaneous North American tour, starts in Plymouth, MA, with an ensemble of music guests, including Joni Mitchell, Joan Baez, Mick Ronson and Roger McGuinn, joining in along the way.

Nov [2] Dylan and Alan Ginsberg visit Jack Kerouac's grave in Lowell, MA.

Dec [8] "The Rolling Thunder Revue" ends its first run at Madison Square Garden with "Night of the Hurricane", a benefit for boxer and convicted murderer Rubin "Hurricane" Carter. Muhammad Ali acts as compere and Roberta Flack guests. (Carter will be released from jail on bail, pending an appeal on March 21st, 1976.)

1976

Feb [7] ***Desire***, including much of the new material sung on the tour, with lyrics by Jacques Levy, vocals by Emmylou Harris and violin by Scarlet Rivera, begins a five-week run at US #1, earning Dylan's first US platinum disc for million-plus album sales, and hits UK #3. The extracted track *Hurricane*, which pleads the case for Carter, reaches US #33 and UK #43.

Apr [10] *Mozambique*, also from ***Desire***, makes US #54, as "The Rolling Thunder Revue" begins another US sojourn.

[22] His show at Clearwater, FL, is taped by NBC for a projected special.

Sept [14] NBC-TV airs the "Hard Rain" special, sponsored by Craig Powerplay Car Stereo & Craig Series 5000 Audio Components.

Oct [16] ***Hard Rain***, recorded live from shows at Fort Worth, TX, and Fort Collins, CO, hits UK #3 and will reach US #17.

Nov [25] Dylan joins the Band at its "The Last Waltz" farewell concert at the Winterland Ballroom, San Francisco, CA, with a host of other guests. He sings *Baby Let Me Follow You Down*, *I Don't Believe You (She Acts Like We Never Have Met)*, *Forever Young* and *I Shall Be Released*, on which he is joined by an all-star cast.

1977

Feb Asked to choose the most overrated and underrated books of the previous 75 years by the **Times Literary Supplement**, Dylan chooses the Bible on both counts. After seeing Shomo Haviv, billed as the "Israeli Bob Dylan", in concert in New York, Dylan says that if he ever tours Israel he will bill himself as "the American Shomo Haviv".

[10] On his re-trial, Ruben Carter is sentenced to three life terms.

Mar [1] Dylan's wife Sara files for divorce. Dylan spends most of the year preoccupied with domestic matters and completes the largely autobiographical film "Renaldo and Clara".

1978

Feb [1] The four-hour "Renaldo and Clara" premieres in Los Angeles.

Mar [1] During the Japanese leg of a world tour, Dylan performs (recorded for a future album) at Tokyo's Budokan concert hall.

May [5] Dylan tracks are included on the triple album of the Band's final concert, ***The Last Waltz***, and he appears in Martin Scorsese's same-titled documentary film of the event.

[7] 90,000 tickets for Dylan's UK concerts at Earls Court, London, are sold out in eight hours.

June [15-21] Dylan opens his European tour at Earls Court before a combined audience of 94,000, his first UK appearance since 1969.

[24] ***Street Legal*** hits UK #2.

July [15] Dylan plays at an open-air festival at Blackbushe Aerodrome, near Camberley, Surrey, with Eric Clapton, Joan Armatrading and Graham Parker.

Aug [12] ***Street Legal*** reaches US #11.

[19] *Baby Stop Crying*, taken from ***Street Legal***, and Dylan's biggest UK hit single for five years, interest being spurred by his Wembley concerts, reaches UK #13.

Sept Dylan is awarded the Gold Ticket for playing to over 100,000 fans at Madison Square Garden.

Nov [4] *Is Your Love In Vain* peaks at UK #56 (and is Dylan's last UK chart single).

Dec [16] His three-month, 62-date, final US leg of the "Street Legal" world tour closes in Miami, FL.

1979

Jan Dylan launches his own label, Accomplice Records, though little will come of it.

June [2] Live double album, ***Bob Dylan At The Budokan***, recorded in Japan as part of a ten-country world tour and originally intended only for the Japanese market, but released to combat the sale of bootlegs of 1978 tour recordings, hits UK #4.

[16] ***Bob Dylan At The Budokan*** reaches US #13.

Sept [8] Jerry Wexler/Barry Beckett-produced ***Slow Train Coming***, with its evangelistic lyrical approach confirming rumors of Dylan's conversion to born-again Christianity, hits UK #2. Mark Knopfler of Dire Straits contributes to some tracks.

[22] ***Slow Train Coming*** hits US #3, his second platinum album.

Nov [1] "Slow Train Coming" US tour opens at the Warfield Theatre, San Francisco, where the new religious material is booed.
[3] *Gotta Serve Somebody* reaches US #24.

1980

Feb [27] Dylan wins Best Rock Vocal Performance, Male, for *Gotta Serve Somebody* at the 22nd annual Grammy Awards.
July [5] ***Saved***, continuing the Christian theme and featuring a sleeve painted by Dylan himself, hits UK #3 and will make US #24 (his first since ***Another Side Of Bob Dylan*** not to enter US Top 20).
Nov Another US tour reintroduces earlier songs into his stage set, plus some oldies unrecorded by Dylan, like *Fever* and *Abraham, Martin And John*.

1981

June A European tour to preface Dylan's forthcoming album again features a repertoire which balances the newer evangelistic material with familiar oldies.
[11] He performs at "Open Air '84" in Offenbach, W. Germany, with Joan Baez and Santana.
Aug [29] Religion-inspired ***Shot Of Love***, though also including a tribute to the comedian Lenny Bruce, hits UK #6, and will reach US #33.
Oct [16] Dylan begins his "Shot Of Love" US tour at the Milwaukee Auditorium, Milwaukee, WI.

1982

Mar [15] Dylan is inducted into the Songwriters Hall of Fame at the 13th annual awards dinner held at the New York's Hilton Hotel. Accepting his award, Dylan says: "I think this is pretty amazing because I can't read or write a note of music. Thank you."
June [6] He appears at the anti-nuclear rally "Peace Sunday - We Have A Dream", before 85,000 people at the Rose Bowl, Pasadena, CA, with Joan Baez (duetting with her on *Blowin' In The Wind* and *With God On Our Side*), Dan Fogelberg, Jackson Browne, Stevie Wonder and others.

1983

Dec Dylan, after a period when he is reported to be recording but unhappy with the results, releases ***Infidels***, co-produced by Mark Knopfler. Recorded after a trip to the Middle East, it becomes his best-selling (gold in the US) album for four years, reaching US #20 and hitting UK #9.

1984

Jan [28] *Sweetheart Like You*, taken from ***Infidels***, reaches US #55 (and is Dylan's last US chart single of the decade).
Mar [22] Dylan appears live on NBC-TV's "Late Night With David Letterman" (on the same show as Liberace), playing three songs backed by rock band the Plugz.
Dec Performance set, ***Real Live***, recorded in London, Dublin and Newcastle during Dylan's European tour in the summer, reaches US #115 and UK #54.

1985

Jan [28] Dylan takes part, with more than 30 other major US acts, in the Los Angeles session which produces USA For Africa's *We Are The World*, to benefit the starving in Africa and elsewhere. The single will top the US and UK charts, selling over seven million copies worldwide.
July ***Empire Burlesque*** reaches US #33 and UK #11, with Dylan backed by members of Tom Petty's band, the Heartbreakers.
[13] Dylan closes "Live Aid" at the JFK Stadium in Philadelphia, PA, backed by the Rolling Stones' Keith Richards and Ron Wood on guitars.
Sept Backed by Tom Petty & the Heartbreakers, he performs at the inaugural "Farm Aid" benefit, at the University of Illinois, Champaign, IL.
Dec [14] Artists United Against Apartheid, comprising 49 artists including Dylan, makes US #38 and UK #21 with *Sun City*.

1986

Jan Retrospective five-album boxed-set, ***Biograph***, a 53-song compilation of Dylan's recording career from 1962 to 1981, including 18 unreleased tracks, climbs to US #33.
[20] Dylan performs at the concert, organized by Stevie Wonder, to celebrate the first Martin Luther King Day in the US.
Feb He tours Australasia and Japan, backed by Tom Petty & the Heartbreakers.
Aug ***Knocked Out Loaded***, produced in London by Dave Stewart of Eurythmics, reaches UK #35. Dylan returns to London to film the movie "Hearts Of Fire", in which he plays opposite Rupert Everett and Fiona Flanagan as a jaded, middle-aged rock star.

1987

June Dylan tours the US with the Grateful Dead, who back his set as well as playing their own (inevitably) longer one.
Oct For a European tour (which opens in Israel), he is backed by Petty's band, with former Byrd Roger McGuinn supporting. George Harrison joins Dylan on stage on the final date, at Wembley, Middx. (After one of the Wembley shows, he is presented with a platinum disc to celebrate five million UK record sales.)
Dec Movie "Hearts Of Fire" is released in the UK after an almost six-month transatlantic delay. Critically panned, it is generally ignored by the public and considered to be one of Dylan's most ill-advised career moves.

1988

June [25] ***Down In The Groove*** reaches UK #32 and will make US #61. Much of the material is non-original (the album was first intended to comprise only cover versions, like ***Self-Portrait***, but its format is twice changed by Dylan during a six-month delay from original release date). The list of contributing musicians includes Eric Clapton, hip-hoppers Full Force, Knopfler, Ron Wood, ex-Sex Pistol Steve Jones and ex-Clash bassist Paul Simonon. Jerry Garcia, Bob Weir and Brent Mydland of the Grateful Dead also play on the album, and two of the new songs, *The Ugliest Girl In The World* and *Silvio*, are co-written with their lyricist, Robert Hunter. The six covers range from Wilbert Harrison's *Let's Stick Together* to the traditional *Shenandoah*. Dylan arrives in the UK for live dates in Birmingham and London.
Sept He contributes *Pretty Boy Floyd* to the Woody Guthrie/Leadbelly tribute album, ***Folkways: A Vision Shared***.
Oct "Lucky" Dylan joins George "Nelson" Harrison, Jeff "Otis" Lynne, Roy "Lefty" Orbison and Tom "Charlie T. Jnr." Petty in the Traveling Wilburys. Their debut, ***Traveling Wilburys Volume One***, and single, *Handle With Care*, are released to great success.
Nov Dylan and his brother David Zimmerman sell the Orpheum Theater in Minneapolis, MN, for $1.4 million.
Dec [4] Dylan is part of the line-up (including Crosby, Stills, Nash & Young, Tracy Chapman, and the Grateful Dead) at the sellout "Oakland Coliseum Music Festival", Oakland, CA.

1989

Jan [18] Bruce Springsteen inducts Dylan into the Rock and Roll Hall of Fame at the fourth annual induction dinner, at New York's Waldorf Astoria Hotel, and joins the traditional post-dinner jam session.
Feb [18] ***Dylan And The Dead***, a live souvenir of their 1987 double-header tour, makes UK #38 and will reach US #37.
June Dylan plays sold-out dates in Birmingham and London before returning to New Orleans, LA, to complete recording a new album with U2 producer Daniel Lanois.
July [1] A US tour dates begin in Peoria, IL.
Sept [24] Dylan participates in the "L'Chai - To Life!" telethon with his son-in-law Peter Himmelman (married to his daughter Maria), Harry Dean Stanton and others.
Oct [14] ***Oh Mercy***, helmed by Lanois and with backing from the Neville Brothers, hits UK #6 and will make US #30.

1990

Jan [12] Dylan opens an international tour with four-hour long warm-up concerts at Toad's Place, New Haven, CT.
[18] He opens a six-day, two-city rock festival in São Paulo, Brazil, on a bill with Bon Jovi, Terence Trent D'Arby, Eurythmics, Marillion and Tears For Fears.
[30] Dylan is awarded France's highest cultural honor, the Commandeur dans l'Ordre des Arts et des Lettres by Minister Jack Lang in a ceremony at the Palais Royal, Paris.
Feb [24] Dylan takes part in the "Roy Orbison Concert Tribute" to benefit the homeless, at the Universal Amphitheatre, Universal City, CA, on a bill with Bruce Hornsby, Bonnie Raitt, B.B. King and others.
Mar [1] He joins Bruce Springsteen onstage at a Tom Petty show at the Great Western Forum, Inglewood, CA, duetting on versions of Creedence Clearwater Revival's *Travellin Band* and the Animals' *I'm Crying*.
June [4] On a European tour, Dylan is joined by U2's Bono at a concert in Dublin, and will subsequently receive Van Morrison on stage in Athens and Nina Simone in Amsterdam.
Aug Gregg and Donna French buy Dylan's childhood home at 2425 W. Seventh St., Hibbing, for $57,000.
Oct [6] ***Under The Red Sky***, largely produced by Don and David Was and featuring David Crosby, Bruce Hornsby, George Harrison, Elton John, Al Kooper, Slash and the Vaughan Brothers, again produced by Lanois, makes US #38 after peaking at UK #13 on Sept [29].
[13] Dylan performs for 4,000 cadets in the Dwight D. Eisenhower Hall at the US Military Academy, West Point, NY, with hundreds of cadets joining him on *Blowin' In The Wind*.
[15-19] He plays sellout dates at New York's Beacon Theatre, grossing $399,240.

1991

Feb [20] Dylan is awarded a Lifetime Achievement Award at the 33rd annual Grammy Awards.
Mar [1-2] He performs before two sellout crowds at the Sports Palace, Mexico City, Mexico.
Apr [13] ***The Bootleg Series Volumes 1-3 (Rare & Unreleased 1961-1991)*** debuts at its UK #32 peak.
[20] ***The Bootleg Series Volumes 1-3 (Rare & Unreleased 1961-1991)*** makes US #49.
June [22] ***For Our Children***, to which Dylan has contributed *This Old Man*, reaches US #31.
Oct [17] He performs *Shake Rattle'n' Roll* with Keith Richards at the "Guitar Legends" series in Seville, Spain.

1992

Jan [18] Dylan performs live at NBC-TV's "Late Night With David Letterman" tenth anniversary show from Radio City Music Hall.
Feb Sony Music International acquires Dylan's back catalog in the US (previously administered by Warner Chappell).
Apr [11] Richard Dickinson, who killed his mother while listening to *One More Cup Of Coffee For The Road*, is allowed by correction officials to see Dylan in concert in Hobart, Tasmania, Australia, as part of his treatment for schizophrenia.
May [13-14, 16-17, 19-21] Dylan plays a week of sellout shows at the Pantages Theatre, Hollywood, during his current North American tour.
Oct [16] Dylan is honored at Madison Square Garden with the all-star "The Bob Dylan 30th Anniversary Celebration" concert, to celebrate being signed to CBS/Columbia for more than three decades. He sings *It's Alright Ma, I'm Only Bleeding*, is joined by Roger McGuinn, Eric Clapton, Tom Petty, George Harrison and Neil Young for *My Back Pages* and sings with the ensemble on *Knockin' On Heaven's Door*.
Nov [14] ***Good As I Been To You*** bows at its UK #18 peak.
[21] ***Good As I Been To You*** debuts at its US #51 peak.

1993

Jan [17] Dylan sings *Chimes Of Freedom* at "A Call For Reunion: A Musical Celebration" during the presidential inaugural festivities at the Lincoln Memorial. (He also joins the Band and Stephen Stills for *I Shall Be Released* at the "Unofficial Bluejeans Bash" later in the week.)
Feb [6] CMA's 35th anniversary show "A Country Celebration", in which Dylan duets with Willie Nelson, airs on CBS-TV.
[7-9, 11-13] He performs a week-long season at London's Hammersmith Apollo.
Mar [23] Dylan is featured on Willie Nelson's latest release, ***Across The Borderline***, co-writing and singing *Heartland*.
Apr [23] He makes his debut at the 24th annual "New Orleans Jazz & Heritage Festival", New Orleans. (The Allman Brothers Band's Dickey Betts plays guitar on *Cat's In The Well* and *Everything Is Broken*.)
May [8] *Highway 61 Revisited* is featured on BBC2-TV's "Tales Of Rock'n'Roll".
[18] Dylan and Michael Bolton's *Steel Bars* wins a citation at BMI's 41st annual pop awards dinner, at the Regency Beverly Wilshire Hotel, Los Angeles.
[22] He guests on CBS-TV's "Willie Nelson The Big Six-O" birthday celebrations.
July [16] Due to ill-health, Dylan cancels a concert in Lyon, France - his first no-show in 32 years.
Aug [20] He embarks on a 31-date US tour at the Memorial Coliseum, Portland, OR, set to end on October 9th at the Shoreline Amphitheatre, Mountain View, CA.
Sept [11] ***Bob Dylan - A 30th Anniversary Celebration Concert***, a double live set from last October's Dylan tribute fest, debuts at its US #40 peak.
Nov [13] His latest studio set, ***World Gone Wrong***, bows at its US #70 peak.
[20] ***World Gone Wrong*** bows at its UK #35 high.

1994

Jan [1] An ad for Coopers & Lybrand, featuring Richie Havens singing *The Times They Are A-Changin'* airs during the Orange Bowl, the first time a Dylan song has been used in advertising. (Later in the month Dylan will purchase Sha'arei Am, a Santa Monica, CA synagogue.)
Apr [9] Currently on a US tour, supported by Arrested Development, Dylan plays to a sellout crowd of 2,020 at the Lied Center, University of Kansas, Lawrence, KS.
Aug [14] Having shunned the original, Dylan performs at "Woodstock II" at Winston Farm, Saugerties, NY.
[24] He files suit in Los Angeles federal court against Apple Computer Inc., claiming they planned to steal his name for a forthcoming CD-ROM project.
Oct [17] Prior to sellout dates at the Roseland Ballroom, New York from the 18th to the 20th, Dylan joins Grateful Dead onstage at Madison Square Garden, singing *Rainy Day Women #12 And #35*.
Nov [2] Ruth Tyrangiel files a $5 million palimony lawsuit in Los Angeles, alleging she co-wrote songs and helped manage his career during a 20-year relationship, which he broke off in 1993.
[18] Dylan tapes an hour-long MTV "Unplugged" program set to air on December 15th at Sony's New York studios, with Pearl Jam's producer Brendan O'Brien on keyboards.
Dec [3] ***Greatest Hits Volume 3***, including one new cut - *Destiny*, debuts at its US #126 peak.

1995

Feb [21] Graphix Zone releases "Highway 61 Interactive", a multimedia CD-ROM trip through selected Dylan historical, audio and visual archives from the 1960s.
Mar [1] ***World Gone Wrong*** wins the Best Traditional Folk Album category at the 37th annual Grammy Awards held at Los Angeles' Shrine Auditorium.
Apr [11] Dylan ends a European tour at the Point, Dublin, Eire.
[29] ***Unplugged*** hits UK #10 in its week of entry.
May [20] *Dignity* bows at its UK #33 peak as ***Unplugged*** debuts at its US #23 peak.
June [18-19] Dylan plays at the Giants Stadium, East Rutherford, NJ, before crowds totalling 101,697, supporting the Grateful Dead.
July [27] He sings *Like A Rolling Stone* with the Rolling Stones at their Grammont, Montpelier, France.
Aug [11] Dylan attends Jerry Garcia's funeral at St. Stephen's Episcopal Church, Belvedere, CA. On the day of his death, Dylan has said "There's no way to measure his greatness or magnitude. I don't think eulogizing him will do him justice. There's no way to convey the loss. It just digs down really deep".
Sept [2] Dylan performs *All Along The Watchtower* and, with Bruce Springsteen, *Forever Young*, at the Concert for the Rock and Roll Hall of Fame at Cleveland Stadium, Cleveland, OH.
[23] ***Greatest Hits*** re-charts at UK #47.
Oct [24] He performs at KQRS' 27th Birthday Concert at the Target Center, Minneapolis, during his current tour.
Nov [19] Dylan sings *Restless Farewell* at Frank Sinatra's 80th birthday tribute at the Shrine Auditorium. (Two days earlier, he joined Sinatra, Bruce Springsteen and Steve & Eydie around a piano for an impromptu sing-song.)
Dec [11, 14] In a never-ending itinerary and currently on tour with Patti Smith, Dylan plays sellout dates at New York's Beacon Theatre.

E

THE EAGLES

Glenn Frey (guitar, vocals); **Bernie Leadon** (guitar, vocals); **Randy Meisner** (bass, vocals); **Don Henley** (drums, vocals)

1971

Apr The four founding members, Frey (b. Nov. 6, 1948, Detroit, MI), Henley (b. July 22, 1947, Gilmer, TX), Leadon (b. July 19, 1947, Minneapolis, MN) and Meisner (b. Mar. 8, 1946, Scottsbluff, NE) are recruited by Linda Ronstadt in Los Angeles, CA (her search has centered mainly around the local Troubadour club), to play in her backing band for a forthcoming three-month road trip. Frey and Henley are employed on a full-time basis (along with Richard and Mike Bowden, brothers who have already played with Henley in Shiloh), while Leadon and Meisner, still members, respectively, of the Flying Burrito Brothers and Rick Nelson's Stone Canyon Band, are only available part time. During the summer months, local musician and friend John Boylan will suggest that the four artists form their own group, not least because of their individual talents and extensive musical apprenticeships in both the country and rock fields. Frey is a three-year veteran of Longbranch Pennywhistle, a duo formed with J.D. Souther, whom he met the day he arrived in Los Angeles in 1968. The pair, who released an eponymous debut album on the Amos label in September 1969, also share a Los Angeles home in Echo Park with singer/songwriter Jackson Browne. Henley, who initially joined Texan band the Four Speeds in the summer of 1963, moved to Los Angeles in May 1970 to record an album as a member of Shiloh (formerly Felicity), another Texas-based group, who were discovered and brought to the Golden State by Kenny Rogers. Their debut recording, ***Shiloh***, produced by Rogers, was also released on the Amos label, where Henley first met Frey. Leadon, who played banjo in the Scottsville Squirrel Barkers in 1962 with future Byrd, Chris Hillman, was in several local Florida groups before moving to Los Angeles in 1967, to replace Rick Cunha in Hearts & Flowers for the recording of their second Capitol album, ***Of Horses Kids And Forgotten Women***. In August of that year, he joined Dillard & Clark, playing on their debut A&M release, ***Fantastic Voyage***, but left them in May 1969 to replace Jeff Hanna in the Corvettes, which became an earlier backing unit for Ronstadt during her summer '69 tour. He then reunited with Hillman in the Flying Burrito Brothers between September of that year and July '71. Meisner, having spent the early '60s with Nebraska outfit the Dynamics, subsequently moved to Denver, CO to join the Soul Survivors, before arriving in Los Angeles in 1966, the band by that time named the Poor. In August 1968 he became a founding member of Poco but quit following personality clashes in April 1969. The following month, Rick Nelson, having previously seen Poco playing at the Troubadour, asks him to form his backing group, the Stone Canyon Band, for which Meisner recruits two ex-Poor members. He will stay with Nelson until June '71.

Aug Urged by his secretary to visit Jackson Browne at the singer/songwriter's Echo Park home, Asylum Records label boss David Geffen also meets Frey and the other band members for the first time. Impressed by their ability and intentions, Geffen signs the Eagles, immediately booking them into a month-long residency performing at the Gallery Club in Aspen, CO, where they will play four sets a night, honing their act and rehearsing mostly self-written compositions.

1972

Mar The group travels to the UK to record its maiden album, overseen by its engineer and producer, Glyn Johns, at the Olympic Studios, Barnes, London.

July [22] *Take It Easy*, penned by Frey and Browne (who has also recorded the track and secured a recording deal with Asylum), is their chart debut, reaching US #12.

Oct ***The Eagles***, including the hit single, climbs to US #22. It establishes an easy-flowing, guitar-led, harmonious style, subsequently hailed "country rock" (much to the lasting annoyance of Henley and Frey), which will trademark all subsequent recordings and prove irresistible to American radio.

Nov [18] The extracted Henley/Leadon composition, *Witchy Woman*, hits US #9.

[24] Following a second short (seven-date) tour in the UK, the Eagles appear as part of a star-billed, KROQ radio station-sponsored "Woodstock Of The West" festival.

1973

Mar [10] Jack Tempchin-penned *Peaceful Easy Feeling*, also from the debut album, reaches US #22.

[16] While working on their second project in the UK, the band performs at the Royal Festival Hall.

June Cowboy-themed ***Desperado***, again recorded in London with producer Johns (now at Island Studios), reaches US #41. (Its title track ballad, although never a single, will be much covered by the likes of Ronstadt, Bonnie Raitt and the Carpenters.) Movie director Sam Peckinpah's plans to turn the album into a cowboy film never materialize. The album, with tracks penned by all four members of the band (with the help of long-term Eagles annex, Souther), further develops their rich, harmonic-country rock sound, again belying its recording roots in London.

July [21] The extracted *Tequila Sunrise*, written by emerging songwriting tandem Henley and Frey, peaks at US #64.

Oct [27] *Outlaw Man*, also from ***Desperado***, makes US #59.

Nov [3] The group begins a seven-date UK tour at the Palace Theatre, Manchester, Gtr. Manchester, supporting Neil Young with Crazy Horse, set to end on the 10th at the Royal Festival Hall.

1974

Jan Don Felder (b. Sept. 21, 1947, Topanga, CA) contributes slide guitar on *Good Day In Hell* during sessions for the band's third album, at the Record Plant in Los Angeles. Having played in a number of bands in Gainesville, FL (including the Continentals with Stephen Stills in 1960, when Felder was only 13), he spent three years (1968-71) with Flow, cutting one album for CTI in 1970. Following session work in Boston, MA, he moved to Los Angeles (where his only contact was Leadon), eventually joining Asylum artist David Blue's backing band. His Eagles session work impresses to the point of an invitation to permanently join the line-up. Producer Bill Szymczyk takes over from Johns in midstream, at the recommendation of Joe Walsh (who has recently toured with the band), to give them a more rock-oriented polish.

Apr [6] The group performs at the "California Jam" rock festival before an estimated audience of 200,000.

May ***On The Border*** reaches US #17 (later going gold). Mostly recorded at The Record Plant, the harder set includes three songs co-written with Souther and one (*Ol' 55*) by Tom Waits.

[4] ***On The Border*** reaches UK #28.

June [29] *Already Gone* makes US #32.

Oct [12] Frey/Henley/Souther/Browne concoction, *James Dean*, peaks at US #77.

1975

Mar [1] Acoustic guitar-based ballad, *The Best Of My Love*, tops the US chart for a week, and will become their first million-selling single.

June [21] The Eagles perform at Elton John's headlining concert at London's Wembley Stadium, Wembley, Middx., to an audience of 100,000.

July [12] ***Desperado*** belatedly makes UK #39.

[19] ***One Of These Nights*** hits UK #8.

[26] ***One Of These Nights*** tops the US chart for five weeks. Helmed again by Szymczyk, all nine tracks are penned by current band members, except *I Wish You Peace*, credited to Leadon and future US President's daughter, Patti Reagan Davis.

Aug [2] Title track, *One Of These Nights*, featuring

Henley's lead vocal, tops the US chart.
Sept [6] *One Of These Nights*, their first UK chart single, reaches #23.
Nov [8] Easy-tempoed, cheating love-themed *Lyin' Eyes*, with a lead vocal by co-writer Frey, hits US #2 for two weeks, behind Elton John's *Island Girl*.
[15] *Lyin' Eyes* reaches UK #23.

1976

Jan [15] Following a press announcement confirming that Leadon has left the band over musical differences, successful rock solo guitarist and ex-James Gang and Barnstorm member Joe Walsh (b. Nov. 20, 1947, Wichita, KS), who has already made a few one-off appearances onstage with the Eagles, and shares their manager (Irving Azoff), makes his live debut as a permanent member of the band at the beginning of a series of dates in Australia, New Zealand and Japan, set to end on February 10th. (Leadon will stay with the Asylum label, re-emerging with the Bernie Leadon/Michael Georgiades Band in mid-1977 with the US #91, ***Natural Progressions***, before playing with the Nitty Gritty Dirt Band in the '80s.)
Feb [24] ***Greatest Hits*** is certified platinum by the RIAA, the first such ratification.
[28] The Eagles win the Best Pop Vocal Performance By A Duo, Group Or Chorus category for *Lyin' Eyes* at 18th annual Grammy Awards.
Mar [13] String-laden (arranged by Jim Ed Norman, who has been in Shiloh with Henley) *Take It To The Limit*, with lead vocals by co-writer Meisner, hits US #4 and UK #12, as compilation album ***Their Greatest Hits, 1971-1975*** tops the US chart, set for a five-week stay and platinum certification. By month's end, the group begins further recording sessions (which will end in October) at Criteria Studios in Miami, FL.
[20] ***Their Greatest Hits, 1971-1975*** hits UK #2.

1977

Jan [15] Szymczyk-produced ***Hotel California*** tops the US chart for a week and is certified platinum. (It will return to US #1 for a further week in February, and in March, then for five consecutive weeks in April/May, and will prove to be the group's commercial apex, eventually selling over nine million copies in the US alone.)
Jan [31] The band wins the Favorite Album, Pop/Rock category at the fourth annual American Music Awards, held at the Civic Auditorium, Santa Monica, CA.
Feb [5] The extracted easy-paced *New Kid In Town*, written by Henley/Frey/Souther, reaches UK #20.
[26] *New Kid In Town* top the US chart on its way to million-plus sales.
Mar [5] ***Their Greatest Hits, 1971-1975*** is voted Album Of The Year by National Association of Record Merchandisers (NARM).
[14] The group begins a month's US tour at Civic Center, Springfield, MA.
[18] The band is joined on stage by the Rolling Stones' Ron Wood for an encore at its Madison Square Garden, New York concert, Mick Jagger and Bill Wyman, also at the concert, remain in the audience.
Apr [25] The Eagles' European tour begins at the Empire Pool, Wembley, Middx. On the final night, Elton John will sit in on piano for an encore of Chuck Berry's *Carol*. (It will end on May 18th at the Scandinavium, Gothenberg, Sweden.)
May [7] Title track, *Hotel California*, another million seller, tops the US chart. The six-and-a-half minute single, highlighted by the twin guitar solos of Walsh and Felder, is destined to become a classic radio oldie and, epitomizing their career, will also become the song most associated with them.
[14] *Hotel California* hits UK #8 and parent album ***Hotel California*** hits UK #2 behind ***The Carpenters 1969-1973***, while the group is on an eight-date UK tour, performing sold-out concerts in Glasgow, Scotland, Bingley Hall, Stafford, Staffs., and four nights at the Empire Pool, Wembley.
[28, 30] The Eagles join Foreigner, Heart and the Steve Miller Band, playing two concerts at the Oakland-Alameda County Coliseum Stadium, Oakland, CA, before a crowd of 100,000.
June [18] A US summer tour begins at the Civic Center, Roanoke, VA. At the height of its success, the band is also at the zenith of excess, as Frey will later recall: "Led Zeppelin might argue with us, but I think we had the greatest traveling party of the '70s. It was called the Third Encore. Don Henley had a birthday in Cincinnati, and they flew in cases of Chateau Lafite Rothschild. I seem to remember the wine was the best, the drugs were good and the women were beautiful."
[25] *Life In The Fast Lane*, written by Henley/Frey/Walsh, reaches US #11.
Sept Following a European tour, Meisner leaves, exhausted from life on the road. He will retreat to Oregon, thereafter pursuing a solo career. (The title track of his 1980 debut ***One More Song***, (US #50), with Frey and Henley on backing vocals, eulogizes his last days with the Eagles. He will release further solo albums, but only 1982's ***Randy Meisner*** will chart (US #94). Rejoining a re-formed Poco in 1989, Meisner will then link with Billy Swan and Bread's James Griffin to form Black Tie in 1990.) He is replaced by Timothy B. Schmit (b. Oct. 30, 1947, Sacramento, CA), who also succeeded him in Poco.

1978

Feb [23] The group wins the Record Of The Year category for ***Hotel California*** and Best Arrangement For Voices for *New Kid In Town* at the 20th annual Grammy Awards.
May [7] The Eagles beat **Rolling Stone** magazine 15-8 in a softball game.
The band is featured on the soundtrack album to the rock film "FM".
July [23] A four-week Canadian tour begins in Edmonton.
Dec [23] Their revival of Charles Brown's blues standard, *Please Come Home For Christmas*, backed with their own *Funky New Year*, reaches US #18 and UK #30.

1979

Sept [3] ***The Long Run*** begins an eight-week run at the top of the US chart and will eventually sell over four million domestic copies. The Szymczyk-produced album, featuring Jimmy Buffett and saxophonist David Sanborn, has been released after a substantial and increasingly frustrating period of recording which will prompt the band's eventual split. (As Henley will later recount: "We spent too much time working on the album, when all one need do was listen to early Stones records to realize that all this striving for perfection is totally unnecessary.")
Oct [13] ***The Long Run*** hits UK #4.
Nov [10] *Heartache Tonight*, written by Frey and Henley with Bob Seger and J.D. Souther, hits US #1, selling over one million copies, but only makes UK #40.
Dec The extracted title track, *The Long Run*, charts briefly at UK #66 (and will be the Eagles' last UK singles chart entry).
[21] They appear with Chicago and Linda Ronstadt at a benefit show for Democratic presidential candidate Jerry Brown.

1980

Feb [2] Henley-sung *The Long Run* hits US #8.
[27] *Heartache Tonight* wins Best Rock Vocal Performance By A Duo Or Group at the 22nd annual Grammy Awards.
Mar [20] 28-year-old Joseph Riviera holds up the Asylum Records office in New York, demanding to see either Jackson Browne or the Eagles, wanting them to finance his trucking operation. He surrenders when told that neither act is in the office, not least since they live in California.
Apr [19] Schmit's co-written ballad, *I Can't Tell You Why*, on which he also takes the lead vocal, hits US #8.
Nov [22] Double album, ***Live***, reaches UK #24 and will hit US #6. Compiled from onstage recordings, it is released after a year of minimal group activity, confirming rumors that the band has effectively ceased to exist.

1981

Jan ***Live*** is certified platinum by the RIAA for one million sales.
[30] They nevertheless win the Favorite Band, Duo Or Group, Pop/Rock and Favorite Album, Pop/Rock categories at the eighth annual American Music Awards, held at the ABC-TV Studios, Hollywood, CA.
Feb [7] The extracted *Seven Bridges Road* reaches US #21, the group's swan song. All ex-Eagles members will pursue solo projects, with varying degrees of success: Felder's career will quickly fade following his 1983 US #178 album, ***Airborne***, while Schmit will release two chart albums, ***Playin' It Cool*** (US #160 in 1984) and ***Timothy B.*** (US #106, 1987). In the short term, Walsh resumes his solo album career with ***There Goes The Neighborhood***, the first of six commercially unsuccessful albums he will release up to 1991's ***Ordinary Average Guy*** (US #112 - June [29]). He will also nominate himself for Vice President of the US in two presidential campaigns. Henley and Frey, the only two members to appear on every Eagles recording, will achieve the greatest solo commercial success, with Frey, often collaborating with Jack Tempchin, releasing ***No Fun Aloud*** (US #31 in 1982) and ***The Allnighter*** (his US #37 and UK #31 label debut for MCA in 1984). In 1985, he scores his biggest solo successes with *The Heat Is On* (US #2 and UK #12) from the "Beverly Hills Cop" movie, achieving a second US #2 later that year with *You Belong To The City*. Continuing his solo success, Frey will make US #37 in 1988 with ***Soul Searchin'***, returning once more to the album survey in 1992 with ***Strange Weather***, followed by ***Live*** in August 1993.

1982

Dec Rounding up the band's later singles, ***Eagles' Greatest Hits, Vol. 2*** reaches US #52.

1985

May [18] UK-only retrospective, ***The Best Of The Eagles***, enters chart, set to hit UK #8 on Aug [27], 1988 (it will re-chart, making UK #57 in August 1989 and UK #48 in May 1993). Increasingly revered, the Eagles back catalog will remain popular throughout the decade, particularly outside the US, while at home, their hit singles become staple oldies on radio.

1989

Sept [29] While the prospect of a fully-fledged Eagles reunion remains unfulfilled despite reported studio try-outs, Frey finally joins Henley onstage for the first time since the group broke up, at a concert in Los Angeles. The pair will subsequently perform with Schmit the following year, during Henley's April 24th-25th Walden Woods benefit festival in Worcester, MA.

1993

Nov [13] ***Common Thread : The Songs Of The Eagles***, a charity album to benefit Walden Woods, featuring various country artists' (Clint Black, Suzy Bogguss, Alan Jackson, Travis Tritt, Tanya Tucker) cover versions of Eagles songs, and released on Irving Azoff's Giant Records, hits US #3.
Dec [7] Fueling industry rumors of a reunited comeback, a quasi-Eagles reunion takes place on the Hollywood set of the filming of Travis Tritt's video for *Take It Easy*, with Henley, Frey, Felder, Walsh and Schmit.

1994

Feb [13] Henley, Frey and Walsh play before a packed crowd at the Double Diamond Club in Aspen, CO, to benefit the Grassroots-Aspen Experience.
Apr [25-26] The group performs two identical shows for future MTV "Unplugged" broadcast.
May [3] The Eagles file suit in Los Angeles Superior Court to prevent Elektra Entertainment from releasing a 29-track greatest hits package in North America.
[7] Henley and Frey are honored with ASCAP's Founders Award at its 11th Pop Music Awards and the ninth Film & Television Music Awards at Los Angeles' Beverly Hilton Hotel.

[27-29, 31-**June** 1] The "Hell Freezes Over" US tour (a reference to a previous Henley quote about the prospects of an Eagles reunion) opens with sellout dates at Irvine Meadows Amphitheatre, Irvine, CA. (By year's end the tour will have grossed more than $70 million, with 49 sellout dates on the 50-date tour.)
July [4] New compilation ***The Very Best Of The Eagles*** hits UK #4.
Oct [6] Frey undergoes abdominal surgery to relive pain from diverticulitis at Los Angeles' Cedars-Sinai Medical Center. His hospitalization has forced postponement of the "Hell Freezes Over" tour.
Nov [12] *Get Over It* reaches US #31.
[19] ***Hell Freezes Over*** reaches UK #28 in its week of entry.
[26] ***Hell Freezes Over***, comprising eerily impeccable live versions of past glories as performed for their MTV taping in April, with the addition of four new cuts including the current single *Get Over It*, debuts at US #1.

1995

Jan [9-10] The tour resumes at Tacoma Dome, Tacoma, WA, breaking the house record.
[28] Taken from the album, the ballad *Love Will Keep Us Alive* (in classic easy-flowing Eagles style, though actually written by UK songwriters Peter Vale, Jim Capaldi and Paul Carrack) tops the US Adult Contemporary ranking.
Mar [11] The group performs at the second night gala of the Hard Rock Hotel & Casino in Las Vegas, NV.
Apr [5] The RIAA certifies five million sales of ***Hell Freezes Over***.
May [16] One of the most successful performance comebacks in rock history, the Eagles' "Hell Freezes Over" US tour finishes, having been seen by more than two million people and grossing in excess of $135 million.
[20] Henley marries Sharon Summerall at his Vista Ranch, with Sting, Billy Joel, Bruce Springsteen, Jackson Browne, Bob Seger, Sheryl Crow and the Eagles in attendance.
[25] Henley and Frey and their publishing companies Cass Country Music and Red Cloud Music file suit against US cable network TNN and its parent company Gaylord Entertainment, charging "deliberate and willful" use of their material without permission.
June [3] The group is named Top Classic Rock Artist at the inaugural Blockbuster Entertainment Awards at Hollywood's Pantages Theatre.
[6] The RIAA certifies multi-platinum sales of ***Hotel California*** (14 million) and ***Their Greatest Hits, 1971-1975*** (22 million).
July [24] Two eight-week old eaglets named Desperado and Best Of My Love die of hydration in their nests at Dolly Parton's Dollywood theme park in Pigeon Forge, TN, home to the National Foundation to Protect America's Eagles.
Oct [14] Walsh sets up an Eagles Web-site (http://www.joewalsh.avnet.co.uk/eagles).
Nov [11-12, 20-21] The Eagles embark on its "Hell Freezes Over" world tour with sellout dates at the Yokohama Arena, Yokohama, Japan.
[29] Following sellout dates in New Zealand, the world trek now reaches Flinders Park, Melbourne, Victoria, Australia, with Melissa Etheridge opening for the Eagles. (By year's end the tour will have grossed in excess of another $30 million.)

1996

Jan [30] The Eagles are named Favorite Pop/Rock Band, Duo or Group and ***Hell Freezes Over*** is named Favorite Rock/Pop Album at the 23rd annual American Music Awards held at the Shrine Auditorium.
July [5-6] The European leg of the tour opens at the Royal Dublin Society Concert Hall, Dublin, Eire.
see also: **Don HENLEY, Joe WALSH**

STEVE EARLE

1982

After seven years of songwriting for others as a staff writer for a succession of country music publishers in Nashville, TN (where he relocated in 1975), Earle (b. Jan. 17, 1955, Fort Monroe, TX), who grew up in Schertz, near San Antonio, TX, ran away from home several times, dropped out of high school in ninth grade and began a five-year period of songwriting (notably with Townes Van Zandt) and playing in Texas clubs, coffee houses and honky tonks in 1969, decides to kick-start his own performing career once more, initially playing a rockabilly/country mix. He signs with local Nashville label LS1, which releases his debut recordings on the four-track EP *Pink And Black*. This attracts Epic Records' Nashville division, for whom he records ***Cadillac***. Two weeks prior to its scheduled release, however, and with cover artwork completed, Epic cans the project. (It would have included the Earle-penned *My Baby Worships Me*, a subsequent country hit for Waylon Jennings.) Following four chart-less Epic singles, *Nothing But You*, *Squeeze Me In*, *What'll You Do About Me* and *A Little Bit In Love*, the label drops Earle in 1984.

1986

Oct [25] Newly signed to MCA Records at the instigation of notable Nashville shaker Emory Gordy Jr. (now a staff producer at the label who has worked with him on the Epic album), Earle's label debut, the rocking, outlaw-country styled ***Guitar Town***, co-produced by Gordy Jr. and Tony Brown, is released, set to make US #89 and hit #1 on the US Country chart during a 66-week stay. Following its success and sellout dates throughout the US, Earle will be voted Top Country Artist in **Rolling Stone** magazine and heralded as a pioneer of "new country" alongside Randy Travis and Dwight Yoakam at future country music award shows. (Epic finally releases ***Cadillac*** now - as ***Steve Earle : Early Tracks***.)

1987

Feb [24] Earle performs at the 29th annual Grammy Awards, at Los Angeles, CA's Shrine Auditorium.
July [4] Now billed with his backing band as Steve Earle & the Dukes (Zip Gibson (lead guitar), Kelly Looney (bass), Craig Wright (drums), Ken Moore (keyboards) and Bucky Baxter (steel guitar)), his second MCA album, ***Exit O***, peaks at UK #77 and will make US #90, as further US tour dates are undertaken.

1988

Jan One-off country cut, *Six Days On The Road*, featured in the Steve Martin/John Candy-starring hit comedy "Planes, Trains And Automobiles", reaches US Country #29.
Nov [11] Moving further towards the rock mainstream and signed to the MCA subsidiary, Uni Records, ***Copperhead Road*** makes country and rock breakthroughs, reaching US #56.
Dec [31] *Johnny Come Lately* spends a week at UK #75.

1989

Jan [14] ***Copperhead Road*** makes UK #44, helped by a UK concert tour. The title cut *Copperhead Road* makes UK #45. In between recording projects, Earle and the Dukes continue to tour, not least opening for Bob Dylan on his US summer trek.

1990

July [7] Co-produced with Joe Hardy, ***The Hard Way*** reaches UK #22, once again fusing rock and country.
Aug [18] ***The Hard Way*** peaks at US #100.
Sept [5] An 11-date UK tour opens at the Civic Hall, Wolverhampton, W. Midlands, set to end at the Belfast Superdrome, Belfast, N. Ireland.
Dec [1] Earle and the Dukes, still touring incessantly, perform in St. Louis, MO, on their latest US dates, while Earle has also found time to produce an album for the Immigrants in Los Angeles, CA.

1991

May [23] Earle takes part in the 20th annual "Kerriville Folk Festival", at the Quiet Valley Ranch near Austin, TX, set to end June 9th.
July [26] During a UK concert visit, Earle performs at the annual "Cambridge Folk Festival", Cambridge, Cambs.
Sept [7] He is featured in the country cable station TNN's "The Texas Connection".
Oct [19] ***Shut Up And Die Like An Aviator*** makes UK #62.

1992

Sept [30] Earle is released on $1,000 bail following his arrest in Nashville for failing to report for jury duty.

1993

Mar [2] MCA retrospective, ***Essential Steve Earle***, is released.
Aug Following a year of seclusion, Earle emerges with a low-key gig at Jack's Guitar Bar, in Nashville.

1994

Sept [14] Earle begins a year-long jail sentence, having plead guilty to the charge of drug possession after crack cocaine, a glass pipe and ten syringes were found in his Mercury coupe car when he was stopped on July 25th but failed to turn up for his September 2nd sentencing by a Davidson County court judge.
Dec Released from prison after serving two months, Earle signs a new record deal with Nashville indie label, Winter Harvest.

1995

Mar [14] Independent Nashville label Winter Harvest releases ***Train A Comin'***, Earle's first studio effort, an acoustic set, in five years. (During the month he also records a duet version of Buddy Holly's *Crying Waiting Hoping* with Marty Stuart at the Nashville's Treasure Isle Studio for inclusion on the January 1996 tribute album ***notfadeaway : remembering buddy holly***.)
Apr [18] Earle makes his first public appearance since being released from jail, at the 328 Performance Hall, Nashville.
Oct With Earle covers currently featrured on Emmylou Harris' ***Wrecking Ball***, Earle announces the formation of his own label, Mutiny Records/E-Squared with partners Jack Emerson and Dub Cornet.
Nov [25] Earle appears on BBC2-TV's "Later With Jools Holland".

1996

Jan [17] With a new Earle cut, *Ellis Unit One*, featured on the "Dead Man Walking" movie soundtrack, Earle plays a sellout gig at the Great American Music Hall, San Francisco, CA.
Apr [20] Earle begins a 13-date European tour at the Paradiso in Amsterdam, Holland, set to end on May [11] at the Corn Exchange, Cambridge, Cambs.
Mar [23] ***I Feel Alright*** debuts at its US #106 and UK #44 peaks. (Meanwhile Earle is producing ***Nowhere Road For The Outlaws : 20th Anniversary***, Willie Nelson and Waylon Jennings' follow-up to their groundbreaking 1976 album ***Wanted : The Outlaws***.)

EARTH, WIND & FIRE

Maurice White (vocals, drums, percussion, kalimba); **Verdine White** (vocals, bass); **Philip Bailey** (vocals, conga, percussion); **Larry Dunn** (piano, synthesizers); **Al McKay** (guitars); **Fred White** (drums); **Ralph Johnson** (drums); **Johnny Graham** (guitar); **Andrew Woolfolk** (tenor saxophone)

1970

Maurice White (b. Dec. 19, 1941, Memphis, TN), who has formed the Salty Peppers with vocalist Wade

Flemons (b. Sept. 25, 1940, Coffeyville, KS) and pianist Don Whitehead the previous year, brings the band to Los Angeles, CA, and changes its name to Earth, Wind & Fire. Having sung solo in his local church at age six, prior to becoming a member of the Rosehill Jubilettes quartet, he has played drums with Porter Junior High School, Memphis, schoolfriend Booker T. Jones (later of Booker T. & the MG's) and performed locally with the Mad Lads, while still a student. After a brief period at Roosevelt University in Chicago, IL, White attended the Chicago Conservatory of Music in 1960, studying composition and percussion with James Mack, majoring in music, with a view to becoming a teacher. Beginning as a session drummer in 1962, White played on Betty Everett's *You're No Good*, before working regularly at Vee-Jay Records and then becoming the resident drummer at Chess Records, where he worked with Billy Stewart, Chuck Berry, Howlin' Wolf, Willie Dixon, Sonny Boy Williamson, Jackie Wilson, the Impressions, the Dells and Etta James. In 1966 he joined the Ramsey Lewis Trio, subsequently playing on ten Lewis albums. While recording with them, he introduced the kalimba, a small finger piano from Africa (he made frequent trips to Africa and the Middle East during the '60s, becoming fascinated with Egyptology, cultural influences which will affect much of his subsequent EW&F work, not least their album covers). During his tenure with the jazz combo, White also formed Hummit Productions with Flemons (writer of the hits *Here I Stand* and *Easy Lovin'*) and Whitehead, a member of local Afro Arts Ensemble. In completing the Earth, Wind & Fire line-up, White recruits singer Sherry Scott and percussionist Phillard Williams (who will go by the name Yackov Ben Israel), and calls on his brother Verdine (b. July 25, 1951) to play bass. Michael Beal (guitar and harmonica) will join, as will Chet Washington (tenor sax), Leslie Drayton (trumpet) and Alex Thomas (trombone). With Flemons on vibes and electric piano, and Whitehead on piano and vocals, the ten-strong band signs to Warner Bros.

1971

Apr Their debut album, ***Earth, Wind And Fire***, produced by Joe Wissert, reaches US #172 during a 13-week chart stay.

July [17] The extracted *Love Is Life* is their first US singles chart entry, at #93.

1972

Jan ***The Need Of Love*** is released, climbing to US #89. (Retaining brother Verdine, White dismantles the first line-up and recruits Philip Bailey (b. May 8, 1951, Denver, CO) (vocals, percussion), who had moved to Los Angeles to work as musical director for the Stovall Sisters gospel group, Larry Dunn (b. June 19, 1953, CO), (piano, organ, clavinet), who was with Bailey, a member of Friends & Love, who opened for EW&F when they played Denver in 1971), Jessica Cleaves (vocals) of the Friends of Distinction, Roland Bautista (guitar), Ronnie Laws (tenor sax, flute) and Ralph Johnson (b. July 4, 1951, CA) (drums, percussion). The group signs with the Cavallo & Ruffalo management team, who secure them an opening slot on tour with another of their acts, John Sebastian. CBS/Columbia Records label boss, Clive Davis, sees the band at the Rockefeller Center, New York, NY, and signs them to the label, buying their contract from Warner Bros.

Apr The new line-up begins work on its Columbia debut, with producer Wissert, at Sunset Sound Studios, Hollywood, CA.

Nov Their Columbia debut album, ***Last Days And Time***, including selections by Pete Seeger (*Where Have All The Flowers Gone*) and Bread (*Make It With You*), makes US #87.

1973

June ***Head To The Sky***, again produced by Wissert, is released, set to reach US #27 on its way to gold certification. Al McKay (b. Feb. 2, 1948, LA), ex-Watts 103rd St. Rhythm Band, replaces Bautista, Andrew Woolfolk (b. Oct. 11, 1950, TX) (also a member of Friends & Love with Bailey and Dunn) replaces Laws, and New Birth member Johnny Graham (b. Aug. 3, 1951, KY) is added on guitar.

Sept [15] *Evil* makes US #50.

Nov The group records the ***Open Our Eyes*** project, with White's mentor, Charles Stepney, working as associate producer and co-arranger, at the Caribou Ranch, Nederland, CO. (Cleaves has now left the band, quitting after a show in Boston, MA.) Each EW&F project will always revolve around Maurice White, its innovator, principal songwriter and central creative force.

1974

Jan [5] *Keep Your Head To The Sky* peaks at US #52.

Mar ***Open Our Eyes*** reaches US #15 on its way to two million-plus sales. White produces Ramsey Lewis' ***Sun Goddess*** (which reaches US #12 at year's end). Earth, Wind & Fire opens for Sly & the Family Stone at New York's Madison Square Garden.

May [18] *Mighty Mighty* reaches US #29.

Aug [17] *Kalimba Story* peaks at US #55.

Sept ***Another Time***, a reissue of their first two albums, reaches US #97.

Oct [19] *Devotion* makes US #33.

Dec The group begins recording ***That's The Way Of The World*** album at Caribou and Wally Heider Recording, Hollywood, CA.

1975

Feb [15] *Hot Dawgit*, with Ramsey Lewis, makes US #50 prior to a second collaboration, *Sun Goddess*, making US #44 on Apr [19].

May ***That's The Way Of The World***, billed as ***Original Soundtrack From The Sig Shore Production "That's The Way Of The World"***, tops the US chart for three weeks, eventually selling over two million. Earth, Wind & Fire is featured as a rock band in the movie "Shining Star".

[24] Film theme, *Shining Star*, hits US #1, gaining a gold disc for a million sales. White's brother, Fred (b. Jan. 13, 1955, Chicago, IL), joins on drums and percussion.

Sept [20] *That's The Way Of The World* reaches US #12, as the band embarks on its first European tour, supporting Santana.

1976

Jan Double album, ***Gratitude***, tops the US chart for three weeks, and again achieves double-platinum status.

Feb [7] *Sing A Song* hits US #5, another million seller.

[28] Earth, Wind & Fire wins Best R&B Vocal Performance By A Duo, Group Or Chorus for *Shining Star* at the 18th annual Grammy Awards.

Apr [24] *Can't Hide Love* makes US #39, as the group works on a new album at Wally Heider's.

Oct [9] *Getaway* reaches US #12. ***Spirit***, dedicated to Charles Stepney, who had succumbed to a heart attack in the midst of recording the album, hits US #2. Held off the top by Stevie Wonder's ***Songs In The Key Of Life***, it is still a double-platinum seller. The current line-up is Maurice, Verdine and Fred White, Bailey, Dunn and Johnson, now augmented by McKay (guitars, percussion), Graham (guitars), and Woolfolk (saxophones, percussion).

1977

Jan [31] The group wins the Favorite Band, Duo Or Group, Soul/R&B category at the fourth annual American Music Awards, held at the Civic Auditorium, Santa Monica, CA.

Mar [19] Having already made US #21 on Jan [29], *Saturday Nite* is the group's UK chart debut, reaching #17.

Aug [20] Backing group girl trio, the Emotions, recently on tour with Earth, Wind & Fire, hits US #1 with the White written-and-produced *Best Of My Love*.

1978

Jan [7] Recorded at Hollywood Sound, Sunset Sound and Burbank Studios, Los Angeles, CA, the previous summer and featuring ace percussionist Paulinho DaCosta, ***All'N'All*** hits US #3, again reaching double-platinum status. With the band at its commercial peak, the album effectively showcases more than ever the various jazz, r&b, funk, ballad and disco elements which have percolated in previous releases.

[16] The group again wins the Favorite Band, Duo Or Group, Soul/R&B category at the fifth annual American Music Awards, held at the Civic Auditorium, Santa Monica.

Feb [11] *Serpentine Fire* reaches US #13.

[18] ***All'N'All***, the group's first UK Album chart entry, reaches #13.

Mar [18] Brassy, uptempo *Fantasy* reaches UK #14.

Apr [22] *Fantasy* makes US #32.

May [27] *Jupiter* makes UK #41.

Aug [26] *Magic Mind* peaks at UK #54, as the group records tracks for the forthcoming ***I Am*** album.

Sept [16] Jazz-inflected cover of *Got To Get You Into My Life*, the Lennon/McCartney song which the band performs in film "Sergeant Pepper's Lonely Hearts Club Band", hits US #9 and is a US million seller.

Oct [22] Earth, Wind & Fire begins a 75-date sold-out US tour in Louisville, KY. (Their live show, now featuring stunning magic effects designed by Doug Henning, has become a major reason for the success.)

[28] *Got To Get You Into My Life* makes UK #33.

1979

Jan [9] The "Music For UNICEF Concert", to celebrate the International Year Of The Child, takes place in the United Nations General Assembly Hall in New York, featuring Earth Wind & Fire performing a medley of *September* and *That's The Way Of The World*, with royalties going to UNICEF. (NBC-TV will air "A Gift Of Song - The Music For UNICEF Concert" the following day.)

[12] The group once again snares the Favorite Band, Duo Or Group, Soul/R&B category at the sixth annual American Music Awards, held at the Civic Auditorium, Santa Monica.

[27] *September* hits UK #3, as the compilation ***The Best Of Earth, Wind & Fire Vol.1*** hits US #6, the group's fourth consecutive US double-platinum seller.

Feb [10] *September* hits US #8, as ***The Best Of Earth, Wind & Fire Vol. 1*** hits UK #6. Maurice White establishes the American Recording Company (ARC) in Los Angeles, with an artist roster including the Emotions, Deniece Williams, Weather Report and D.J. Rogers. His production skills are much in demand and he will oversee albums by other artists over the next decade, including those by Barbra Streisand, Jennifer Holliday, Neil Diamond, Ramsey Lewis and Valerie Carter.

[15] ***All'N'All*** wins Best R&B Vocal Performance By A Duo, Group Or Chorus, and *Runnin'* wins Best R&B Instrumental Performance, at the 21st annual Grammy Awards.

Mar Group performs five sellout nights at the Wembley Arena, Wembley, Middx.

July [7] ***I Am*** hits UK #5.

[14] Uptempo, jazz dance-based *Boogie Wonderland*, featuring the Emotions on guest vocals, hits UK #4 and US #6 and is another gold disc, while ***I Am*** hits US #3.

Sept [15] David Foster, Bill Champlin and Jay Graydon-penned R&B ballad, *After The Love Has Gone*, hits US #2 (another million-seller) and UK #4.

Oct [18] During another sellout US tour, 15 youths are arrested at the group's Madison Square Garden concert, charged with mugging audience members. The band is presented with the Gold Ticket Award for performing to over 100,000 fans at the venue.

Nov [3] *Star* reaches UK #16.

[10] *In The Stone* peaks at US #58.

Dec *Can't Let Go* and *In The Stone* reach UK #46 and #53 respectively. By year's end, Earth, Wind & Fire will have toured the US, Europe and Asia.

1980

Jan [19] *Star* breaks their run of major US hit singles, stalling at US #64, as the group prepares for a South American concert visit.

Feb [27] *After The Love Has Gone* wins Best R&B Vocal Performance By A Duo, Group Or Chorus, and

Boogie Wonderland wins Best R&B Instrumental Performance, at the 22nd annual Grammy awards.
Oct [18] *Let Me Talk* climbs to UK #29 and US #44.
Nov [1] Double album, ***Faces***, including songwriting contributions from Foster, Brenda Russell, James Newton Howard and Valerie Carter among others, hits UK #10, and will reach US #10.
Dec [20] *You* makes US #48.
[27] *Back On The Road* peaks at UK #63.

1981

Jan [30] The band wins the Favorite Band, Duo Or Group, Soul/R&B category at the eighth annual American Music Awards, held at the ABC-TV Studios, Hollywood, CA, their fourth such triumph in five years.
Feb [28] *And Love Goes On* peaks at US #59, as Earth, Wind & Fire undertakes another US tour.
May The group records tracks for ***Raise!*** at the band's own studio, the Complex, Los Angeles.
Nov ***Raise!***, with string arrangements by Foster and Billy Meyers, and horn arrangements by Jerry Hey, is released, set to hit US #5. Bautista rejoins, replacing McKay, who left in 1980 to concentrate on record production. Johnson switches to percussion and vocals.
[28] Funked-up *Let's Groove* hits UK #3.
Dec [19] Catchy dance anthem, *Let's Groove*, hits US #3. Once again heading for million-plus sales, it will also spend a record-breaking 11 weeks at the top of the US R&B chart.

1982

Jan [9] ***Raise!*** reaches UK #14, as the group embarks on a major US tour.
Feb [13] *Wanna Be With You* peaks at US #51.
[20] *I've Had Enough* reaches UK #29.
Dec ***Raise!*** wins the Top Black Album category in **Billboard**'s year-end chart round-up awards.

1983

Feb [23] The group wins Best R&B Performance By A Duo, Group Or Chorus for *Wanna Be With You*, at the 25th annual Grammy awards.
Mar [19] *Fall In Love With Me* reaches US #17 and UK #47. ***Powerlight*** makes US #12 and UK #22.
May [21] *Side By Side* stalls at US #76.
Sept Bailey's debut solo album, ***Continuation***, produced by George Duke, makes US #71.
Dec [3] *Magnetic* peaks at US #57. ***Electric Universe***, repeating the usual Earth, Wind & Fire formula, stalls at US #40. (Bautista and Johnson both leave the band during the year.)

1984

Mar When *Touch* fails to chart, White disbands the group, concentrating for the next two years on his Kalimba production company.
Oct Bailey records a solo album, ***Chinese Wall***, at Townhouse Studios in London, with Phil Collins producing.
Nov Bailey also records a spiritual solo album, ***The Wonders Of His Love***, for US religious label Myrrh, which will sell over 250,000 copies in the US. (Having become a born-again Christian in 1975, he will continue parallel recording careers in both the pop and Christian markets.) Subsequent Myrrh albums will include: ***Triumph*** (1986), ***Wonders Of Love*** (1988) and ***Family Affair*** (1990).

1985

Feb [2] *Easy Lover*, a Bailey duet with Phil Collins written by them with Nathan East, hits US #2 and will top the UK survey on Mar [23] while Bailey's R&B/pop album, ***Chinese Wall***, will reach US #22 and UK #29 and a second extract, *Walking On The Chinese Wall*, will make US #46 on May [11] also reaching UK #34 by month's end. Both single and album will be RIAA certified gold on Mar [11]. (He will continue his solo outings but also rejoin Earth, Wind & Fire when it returns to recording during 1987.)
Sept [13] *Easy Lover* wins the Best Overall Performance category at the second annual MTV Video Music Awards, held at Radio City Music Hall, New York.
Oct [26] White's solo revival of *Stand By Me* makes US #50. His debut solo album ***Maurice White*** reaches US #61.

1986

Feb [8] White's *I Need You* makes US #95.
Apr [7] *Easy Lover* is honored as the Most Performed Work at the annual Ivor Novello Awards, at London's Grosvenor House Hotel.
May Third pop/soul album by Bailey, ***Inside Out***, peaks at US #84.
[10] K-tel-issued Earth, Wind & Fire career retrospective, ***The Collection***, hits UK #5.
Oct White and Bailey meet to discuss re-forming Earth, Wind & Fire.

1987

Feb [24] Bailey wins the Best Gospel Performance, Male category for ***Triumph*** at the 29th annual Grammy Awards.
Nov Having achieved six double-platinum and two platinum albums, and with numerous gold awards, Earth, Wind & Fire reunites with White, Bailey, Verdine White, Andrew Woolfolk and Sheldon Reynolds, who has been playing guitar for the Commodores. ***Touch The World***, with session musicians backing White and Bailey's vocals, fails to chart in the UK, but climbs to US #33 where a nine-month world tour will help the record sell more than two million copies.
Dec [12] *System Of Survival*, produced by White and Preston Glass, tops the US R&B survey, making US #60 the following week (it has already reached UK #54).

1990

Mar [3] With Earth, Wind & Fire now comprising the White brothers, Bailey, Woolfolk, Reynolds with Ralph Johnson re-joining and new recruit Sonny Emory, who has been playing drums for the Crusaders, ***Heritage*** makes US #70, but again fails to score in UK. The set features current hot American acts M.C. Hammer, on extracted *Wanna Be The Man* and Motown teen unit the Boys, guesting on the title cut.
Sept [13] The group begins a 24-date European tour at Ahoy in Rotterdam, Holland, set to end on October 17th at the Bercy, Paris, France.

1992

Mar After a year in which, following nearly two decades with CBS, Earth, Wind & Fire has returned to Warner Bros., and renewed its management alliance with Bob Cavallo, the Maurice White-produced El DeBarge album, ***In The Storm***, is released (White also oversaw a solo project by Barbara Weathers, in 1990).
June [6] The group performs at the "Earth Pledge Concert" on the Great Lawn of New York's Central Park.
Oct [16] The band participates in a tribute to the late Temptations singer, Eddie Kendricks, at a concert in Redondo Beach, CA.
Dec [12] ***The Very Best Of Earth, Wind And Fire*** makes UK #40, while the recently-issued three CD/cassette boxed set, ***The Eternal Dance***, is a more comprehensive, if not definitive, appraisal of the band's substantial musical and commercial achievements.

1993

Sept [25] *Sunday Morning* makes US #53.
Oct [2] ***Millenium***, the group's newest Warner Bros. album, debuts at its US #39 peak.

1994

Jan [5] The group is enshrined into the Image Hall of Fame at the NAACP 26th annual Image Awards in Pasadena, CA.
Dec [5-6] "An Intimate Evening With Earth, Wind & Fire", the group's first tour in six years, ends with two sellout shows at Hollywood's Pantages Theatre.

1995

June [1] Following a recent tour of Japan, where they have signed to the Avex label (and where Maurice White has written the music to the Japanese animated series "Gatchaman" in 1994), Earth, Wind & Fire begins "The Legend Continues : Earth, Wind And Fire 1995 Summer Tour" at the Festival Hall, Tampa Bay Performing Arts Center, Tampa, FL.
Sept [14] The group unveils its star on the Hollywood Walk of Fame.

EAST 17

Tony Mortimer (vocals, keyboards); **Brian Harvey** (lead vocals); **John Hendy** (keyboards, bass, vocals); **Terry Coldwell** (vocals)

1990

Dec Mortimer (b. Oct. 21, 1970, London), having met Hendy (b. Mar. 26, 1971, London) at St. George Monoux Secondary School, Walthamstow, London in 1982 (Harvey and Coldwell have also attended the school although the four future band members won't socialize together until the late '80s when they begin hanging out in Walthamstow's shopping precinct and a disused Bosch tool factory nearby), has left school in 1985 and signed on to the dole, also borrowing money from his parents, to record demo tapes of his own compositions at home during much of the rest of the decade. (Hendy has left school to find work as builder, Harvey has become a plumber's mate while spinning discs on his pirate radio station MF, while Coldwell has worked as a roofer.) At a party in Walthamstow earlier this year, Mortimer has met an associate of Pet Shop Boys (and ex-Bros) manager Tom Watkins, who, after hearing Mortimer's latest demo (which he is not overly impressed by), auditions him as a dancer for his girl-trio act, Faith Hope & Charity. Mortimer beats more than 50 other hopefuls and makes his debut with the trio in October at the **Smash Hits**' Awards show, as the warm-up act. Having made further demos for Watkins (and at the urging of the manager's colleague Richard Stannard who is particularly impressed by the song *Deep*), Mortimer is offered a management deal on the condition that he forms a band. Recruiting his three ex-school friends, Mortimer and the group now signs a management deal with Watkins.

1992

Apr [1] The quartet signs with London Records (also on the strength of *Deep*) initially calling itself E17 - Walthamstow's postal code - but later expands the moniker to East 17.
Sept [19] Its debut single *House Of Love*, featuring Pedigree, Son Of A Bitch, Glossy Coat and Wet Nose mixes, hits UK #10 (and will top the charts in Finland, Israel and Sweden) promoted via PAs around the country, the first being at a Bristol, Avon fair. (Late in the month, Mortimer is diagnosed with Hepatitis B prior to a routine appendectomy operation, though it is subsequently discovered that there has been a mix-up in his medical records.)
Oct Following a UK schools tour, the group is the runner-up in the **Smash Hits**' Awards Best New Dance Act category, behind the Shamen.
Nov [21] *Gold*, with Collar Size, the Dark Bark, Paws On The Floor, Rabid, Techno Bonio remixes available, hits UK #28.

1993

Feb [6] Mortimer-penned ballad *Deep* hits UK #5.
[27] Following the launch of the teen-pop based debut album ***Walthamstow*** (reviewed by **Vox** as "lad-pop") at Walthamstow Town Hall attended by Mayoress of Waltham Forest and 3,000 screaming girl fans, the album enters at UK #1. Followed by an overseas promotional tour, the album will be certified platinum in the UK (300,000 sales) and sell over two million worldwide.
Apr [17] *Slow It Down*, featuring the Perpetual, Perpetual Motion, Speed It Up and On & On mixes, hits UK #15.
May [22] The group performs in Hawaii, although its

North American commercial success will prove elusive.
July [3] The band's cover of the Pet Shop Boys' 1985 UK chart-topper *West End Girls*, featuring Faces On Posters and Kicking In Chairs mixes, reaches UK #11.
Nov During a month when Harvey is arrested for possession of cannabis after being stopped at 5:30 a.m. on his way home from a party at Hendy's home, East 17's "Pie & Mash" video is released in the UK.

1994

Jan [15] *It's Alright*, aided by the Guvnor Mix, hits UK #3.
Mar The group's world tour opens in Australia (where it is particularly popular), before concerts in Europe (which are sell-outs except for two German dates).
May [21] Infectious pop-rap nugget, *Around The World*, also released in Other World and Overworld Vocal mixes, hits UK #3 accompanied by a 20-date, month-long sold-out UK tour.
June At the end of the month, three of the members take vacations: Harvey goes to St. Lucia, Coldwell and Hendy visit Majorca, while Mortimer stays behind to work on a second album at the CHAPS and Strongroom Studios.
Sept During the month, Harvey and Mortimer host BBC1-TV's "Top Of The Pops".
Oct [1] *Steam*, released with Vapoureyes and Carter USM remixes, hits UK #7.
Nov The group begins its 13th promotional tour of Europe during a month when its second video set, "Letting Off Steam" is issued.
Dec [4] The band performs at the 1994 "**Smash Hits** Poll Winners' Party".
[6] East 17 appears at BT's 10th anniversary concert held at the London Arena, a bill also featuring Kylie Minogue, Dave Stewart, Belinda Carlisle, Mary-Chapin Carpenter and the Kinks.
[10] Ballad *Stay Another Day*, written by Mortimer (with Rob Kean and Dominic Hawken) for his brother, tops the UK chart on its way to million-plus UK sales.
[12] The group guests on ITV's "The Zig & Zag Show".
[31] ***Steam***, co-produced by Phil Harding, Ian Curnow, Stannard and Rob Kean, hits UK #3 on its way to double-platinum UK sales. (During the month the band fails to appear at the annual "Prince's Trust Concert" after Harvey's bout of tonsilitis deteriorates.)

1995

Feb [27] East 17 performs its forthcoming single *Let It Rain* at the 13th annual BRIT Awards, held at London's Alexandra Palace.
Mar The group embarks on a tour of the Far East.
Apr [1] *Let It Rain*, co-written by Mortimer, Kean, Harding and Curnow, hits UK #10.
[20] The quartet begins an eight-date UK/Eire tour at the Sheffield Arena, set to end on May 1st at Dublin's Point Depot, Eire.
May [23] Mortimer is named Songwriter Of The Year at the 40th annual Ivor Novello Awards, held at London's Grosvenor House hotel.
June [17] *Hold My Body Tonight* debuts at its UK #12 peak.
Oct [23] The band is featured on BBC2-TV's "The O Zone".
Nov [4] *Thunder* debuts at its UK #4 peak the same day the group appears on ITV's "Scratchy & Co.".
[11] East 17 is featured on BBC1-TV's "Live And Kicking".
[23] The group performs at the second annual MTV Europe Awards held at Le Zenith, Paris, France, at which it is also named Best Dance Act.
[25] ***Up All Night*** debuts at its UK #7 peak.
Dec [15] The band performs during the five-day "Greatest Music Party In The World" at Birmingham's National Exhibition Centre, on a bill with David Bowie, Rod Stewart, Eternal, Michelle Gayle and others.

1996

Jan [13] East 17 plays a sell-out show at Moscow's Olympiiski Arena, Russia.
Feb [10] *Do U Still?* hits UK #7 in its week of entry.

SHEENA EASTON

1979

June Easton (b. Sheena Orr, Apr. 27, 1959, Bellshill, Glasgow, Scotland), the youngest of six children, graduates as a teacher of speech and drama from the Royal Scottish Academy of Music and Drama, a month after successfully auditioning as a singer for EMI Records in London, having served a less formal musical apprenticeship, spending evenings performing on the local club and pub circuit in Glasgow, during her student days.

1980

Apr Her debut release, the Dominic Bugatti/Frank Musker-written *Modern Girl* peaks at UK #56.
July [2] She is featured in an edition of the Esther Rantzen-hosted BBC1-TV series "The Big Time", which gives everyday people an opportunity to sample their ambitions. Easton is seen at her audition, recording her first single and undergoing the grooming and marketing process which EMI traditionally undertakes when launching a new act.
Aug [30] Boosted by this national TV exposure, a well-timed second single, the jaunty commuter-themed pop ditty *9 To 5*, written by Florrie Palmer, shoots to UK #3.
Sept [20] TV has also re-activated demand for *Modern Girl*, which re-charts to hit UK #8, giving Easton the rare achievement for a British female singer of two simultaneous UK Top 10 hits.
Nov [8] Leeson and Vale-penned *One Man Woman* reaches UK #14.
[17] She appears in the "Royal Variety Show", London, in the presence of H.R.H. the Queen Mother.

1981

Feb [14] Her Christopher Neil-produced maiden album, ***Take My Time***, reaches UK #17.
[21] Title track *Take My Time* makes UK #44.
May [2] *Morning Train (9 To 5)* hits US #1 for the first of two weeks, eventually selling over a million copies. (Its title has been amended for the US market, to avoid confusion with Dolly Parton's film-theme song, *9 To 5*, which hit US #1 in March.)
Her renamed debut album, ***Sheena Easton***, reaches US #24.
[23] Bugatti/Palmer-composed *When He Shines* makes UK #12.
July [18] *Modern Girl* reaches US #18.
Aug [8] *For Your Eyes Only* hits UK #8. It is the theme song for the current James Bond movie of the same name, and Easton becomes the only Bond-theme singer to be seen on screen (singing the song during the credits).
Oct Her sellout UK tour ends with two dates at the Dominion Theatre, London.
[10] ***You Could Have Been With Me***, again produced by Neil, and recorded at the Caribou Ranch in Nederland, CO, reaches UK #33.
[17] *For Your Eyes Only* hits US #4, as the uptempo *Just Another Broken Heart* makes UK #33.
Nov She undertakes a 12-date tour of Japan.
Dec [12] The extracted title track, *You Could Have Been With Me*, peaks at UK #54, as Easton wins the **Daily Mirror**/"Nationwide" Rock & Pop Awards Best Female Singer category and the **TV Times** Readers' Female Personality Of The Year award in the UK, and **Billboard**'s Top New Artist category in the US.

1982

Feb [20] *You Could Have Been With Me* reaches #15 in the US, where her ballad releases are more warmly received, particularly by American radio.
[24] Easton wins the Best New Artist category at the 24th annual Grammy Awards.
Apr [3] ***You Could Have Been With Me*** makes US #47.
May Easton performs her first US dates.
June [5] *When He Shines* reaches US #30.
Aug She returns to the US for a major 30-date tour, followed by further performances in the Far East.
[7] Uptempo *Machinery* makes UK #38 and will be her last solo UK hit single for nearly nine years.
Sept [25] *Machinery* peaks at US #57 as ***Madness, Money And Music*** makes UK #44.
Oct [30] ***Madness, Money And Music*** makes US #85.
Nov [13] The extracted ballad, *I Wouldn't Beg For Water*, peaks at US #64.

1983

Mar [26] Easton's duet with Kenny Rogers on the David Foster-produced revival of Bob Seger's ballad, *We've Got Tonight*, hits US #6. It also tops the US Country survey, and will reach UK #28.
Sept [25] NBC-TV special, "Sheena Easton ... Act 1", wins an Emmy for Oustanding Directing In A Variety Or Musical Program.
Oct [29] Synthesized pop confection, *Telefone (Long Distance Love Affair)*, hits US #9. ***Best Kept Secret***, co-produced by Jay Graydon and Greg Mathieson and recorded with top flight US session musicians, makes US #33 and UK #99.

1984

Mar [10] Mournful ballad, *Almost Over You*, reaches US #25 and will be followed by the contrasting *Devil In A Fast Car*, which stalls at US #79 on Apr [21] and *Strut*, pointing Easton in a funkier direction, which will hit US #7 on Nov [24].

1985

Jan [15] Easton marries record executive Rob Light.
Feb ***A Private Heaven*** makes US #15, becoming her most successful US album.
[26] Easton wins the Best Mexican/American Performance category with Luis Miguel for *Me Gustas Tal Como Eres* at the 27th annual Grammy Awards.
Mar [2] *Sugar Walls*, written by Prince, hits US #9. The mildly erotic symbolism in its lyrics arouses some controversy, but does not deprive it of airplay. Easton becomes the first artist in history to achieve top five hits on the US Pop, R&B, Country, Dance, and Adult Contemporary charts.
Apr [6] *Sweat* stalls at US #80.
Nov She records the title theme, *Christmas All Over The World*, for the Dudley Moore-starring film "Santa Claus - The Movie".
Dec [14] *Do It For Love* reaches US #29. ***Do You***, produced and partly written by Nile Rodgers, makes US #40, continuing her foray into the dance market.

1986

Mar [1] Her revival of Martha & the Vandellas' 1967 US #10, *Jimmy Mack*, peaks at US #65.
July She teams with producer Narada Michael Walden for a two-song contribution to the Rob Lowe movie "About Last Night".
Sept [27] *So Far So Good*, from "About Last Night", makes US #43.

1987

Sept [5] *U Got The Look*, a duet with Prince, makes UK #11. Press rumors of a romantic liaison are fuelled by provocative antics on the promotional video clip.
Oct [17] *U Got The Look*, taken from Prince's album ***Sign O' The Times***, hits US #2, behind Lisa Lisa & Cult Jam's *Lost In Emotion*.
[28] Easton makes her acting debut as Caitlin Davies, Crockett's girlfriend on NBC-TV's "Miami Vice".

1989

Feb [11] The title track from the forthcoming album, *The Lover In Me*, makes UK #15.
Mar ***The Lover In Me***, completing Easton's successful transition from light-pop performer to strutting dance siren, produced and co-written with current dance hit-making duo L.A. Reid and Babyface, makes US #44.
[4] ***The Lover In Me*** reaches UK #30.
[25] *Days Like This* makes UK #43. Similar EMI career retrospectives are released, titled ***For Your Eyes Only - The Best Of Sheena Easton*** (UK) and ***The Collection*** (US).
[4] *The Lover In Me* hits US #2, behind Debbie

Gibson's *Lost In Your Eyes*.
July [22] *101* peaks at UK #54.
Oct [26] Easton guest stars as an avid whale watcher on Showtime TV's "It's Garry Shandling's Show".
Dec [16] *The Arms Of Orion*, a further Prince/Easton collaboration, makes US #36 (on Paisley Park) and reaches UK #27.

1990

June [3] Easton takes part in "The Big Day", an open air festival from various locations in Glasgow, aired live on C4-TV.

1991

Feb [10] Easton joins nearly 100 celebrities in Burbank, CA, to record *Voices That Care*, a David Foster and fiancée Linda Thompson Jenner-composed and organized charity record to benefit the American Red Cross Gulf Crisis Fund.
Mar [28] Promoting her first release in two years, Easton is interviewed on syndicated TV's "The Arsenio Hall Show", having recently made regular TV appearances promoting nationwide fitness centers (she will also make the cover of **Shape** magazine in October).
May [4] ***What Comes Naturally*** makes US #90.
[25] *What Comes Naturally* reaches US #19, four days prior to her appearance C4-TV's "Tonight With Jonathan Ross".
July [4] She appears on CBS TV's "Disney's Great American Celebration".
Nov [7] Easton debuts (portraying Aldonza) in a stage production of "Man Of La Mancha" in Chicago, IL co-starring with Raul Julia.

1992

Mar [31] "Man Of La Mancha" premieres at the Marquis Theater on Broadway, NY.
Apr Easton contributes *A Dream Worth Keeping*, penned by Jimmy Webb and Alan Silvestri, to the cartoon soundtrack from "Ferngully ... The Last Rainforest".
[29] Easton collapses during a matinee performance of "Man Of The Mancha", and is helped offstage by co-star Julia. She spends the night in hospital suffering from an intestinal disorder.
Dec Recently listed as one of Britain's wealthiest women, having amassed an eight-figure fortune, and preparing a recording return to her earlier adult contemporary-ballad style with producer Don Grierson, she also launches her own "Seven Minute Flat Stomach" fitness video.

1995

Apr Following the August 1993 MCA release of Easton's ***No Strings***, an album of standards produced by Patrice Rushen, and her recent appearance during December and January of this year as a participant in "The Colors Of Christmas" festive tour, also featuring Roberta Flack, James Ingram and Peabo Bryson, Easton's latest effort, ***My Cherie***, returning to her early AC ballad style style, is released in the US.

THE EASYBEATS

"Little" Stevie Wright (vocals); **Harry Vanda** (guitar); **George Young** (guitar); **Dick Diamonde** (bass); **Gordon "Snowy" Fleet** (drums)

1964

Forming in Sydney, New South Wales, Australia, in 1963, three of the group's members - Wright (b. Stephen Wright, Dec. 20, 1948, Leeds, Yorks.), Young (b. Nov. 6, 1947, Glasgow, Strathclyde, Scotland) and Fleet (b. Aug. 16, 1946, Bootle, Lancs.) - are UK-born, while Vanda (b. Harry Vandenberg, Mar. 22, 1947, the Hague, Holland) and Diamonde (b. Dingeman Van Der Sluys, Dec. 28, 1947, Hilversum, Holland) are Dutch. All are in Australia due to family emigration, and meet while living at the Villawood Migrant youth hostel. With its name coined by Fleet (supposedly taking it from the BBC Light Programme pop show "Easybeat", hosted by Brian Matthew), the group secures a resident slot performing at Sydney's Beatle Village club, where they meet producer Ted Albert, who secures a recording deal for the band with Australian Parlophone.

1965

Mar After making their radio debut at the 2UW Theatre and their TV debut on "Sing Sing Sing", *For My Woman* is released.
July *She's So Fine* hits #1 in Australia, the first of five hits (including the chart-toppers *Easy As Can Be*, *Woman* and *Come And See Her*), which rapidly establish them as a major Antipodean teen draw.

1966

June Signed internationally to United Artists, they move to the UK to work with producer Shel Talmy. The group's first UK single, *Come And See Her*, is released.
Nov [13] The band supports the Four Tops at London's Saville Theatre.
Dec [17] *Friday On My Mind*, written by Vanda and Young, hits UK #6 and tops the chart down under, though its March '67 follow-up, *Who'll Be The One?*, fails to score.

1967

Apr [1] The band performs at the Drill Hall, Scunthorpe, Lincs., during a UK tour. (Wright is hit in the left eye by a piece of candy thrown by fan at a Bristol, Somerset gig, and will see a Harley Street eye specialist.)
May [13] The group returns to Australia for a three-week concert visit, which will include a civic reception in Sydney. Fleet decides against further touring and, upon returning to the UK, they are minus a drummer. Tony Cahill is subsequently recruited.
[20] *Friday On My Mind* reaches US #16, while ***Friday On My Mind*** makes US #180.
Aug [4] The group begins a US tour, with Gene Pitney, the Buckinghams, the Happenings, the Fifth Estate and the Music Explosion, in Hartford, CT.
Nov The band forms its own independent recording company, Staeb Productions.

1968

Mar [24] Having appeared on UK TV's "Dee Time" the previous day, the Easybeats appear at a charity benefit concert at the Wembley Empire Pool, Wembley, Middx., on a bill with the Move, Cliff Richard, Amen Corner and Cat Stevens among many others.
Apr [27] Ballad, *Hello, How Are You?*, reaches UK #20 - and proves to be their UK chart swan song.
Sept Their final United Artists' release, *Good Times*, fails to score. A new recording deal is inked with Polydor in the UK and a Motown subsidiary, Rare Earth, in the US, but it will only yield a career-closing US #100 single *St. Louis* on [Nov] 15, the following year.

1974

Vanda and Young, having moved back to Australia, open a studio complex in Sydney, and soon have success with John Paul Young. They will go on to produce AC/DC in the mid-'70s - Young's two brothers, Angus and Malcolm, are group members.

1978

Oct Vanda and Young have varied success as Flash & the Pan, Paintbox and the Marcus Hook Roll Band - as electro-pop combo Flash & the Pan they make a UK chart debut (#54) with *And The Band Played On (Down Among The Dead Men)*. (Further chart success will come with *Hey St. Peter* (US #76 in August 1979) and *Waiting For A Train*, which hits UK #7 in June 1983.)

1993

July A 45-track compilation, ***Their Music Goes 'Round Our Heads***, featuring the songs of Vanda and Young, including many of those written for the Easybeats, is released in Australia on the Sony label.

ECHO & THE BUNNYMEN

Ian McCulloch (vocals); **Will Sergeant** (guitar); **Les Pattinson** (bass); **Pete de Freitas** (drums)

1978

Nov [11] As a trio comprising McCulloch (b. May 5, 1959, Liverpool, Lancs.), Sergeant (b. Apr. 12, 1958, Liverpool) and Pattinson (b. Apr. 18, 1958, Ormskirk, Lancs.), the band makes its live debut at Eric's club in Liverpool. McCulloch originally formed the Crucial Three with future Wah! leader Pete Wylie (b. Mar. 22, 1958, Liverpool) and Julian Cope (b. Oct. 21, 1957, Bargoed, Mid Glamorgan, Wales) in May 1977, but rehearsals in Liverpool proved fruitless. A second attempt with Cope, under the banner A Shallow Madness, also stalled, in the summer of 1978, and - in September of that year - McCulloch and restaurant chef Sergeant recorded demos with the aid of a drum machine which they christened "Echo". Sergeant's previous musical experience has been in bedroom band Industrial Device with schoolfriend Paul Simpson, while Pattinson (previously Jeff Lovestone in the Jeffs, a band whose members were all called Jeff and which evolved into the psychedelic combo, Love Pastel), another fellow student friend of Sergeant's at Days Lane school, who has recently been working at the Douglas boatyard in Preston, Lancs., joins on bass four days prior to the band making its first performance.

1979

Mar The trio signs to local independent Zoo label and releases *Pictures On My Wall*. Its B-side *Read It In Books*, is an old Crucial Three song, written by McCulloch and Cope, who has gone on to form the Teardrop Explodes.
Sept With heightened record label interest, the group signs to the small WEA-distributed Korova label, but will leave their publishing interests with Zoo Music.
[8-9] The group appears at the "Futurama Festival" at the Queen's Hall, Leeds, S. Yorks. (By year's end, "Echo" is made redundant and is replaced by Pete de Freitas (b. Aug. 2, 1961, Port of Spain, Trinidad, West Indies).)

1980

May The band's second single, the raw, guitar-jangling Ian Broudie (future Lightning Seeds founder)-produced *Rescue*, reaches UK #62.
Aug [2] Their debut album, ***Crocodiles***, showcasing an alternative, moody (sometimes Doors-recalling) rock approach, highlighted by McCulloch's histrionic vocal style, reaches UK #17, spurred by an accompanying UK tour.

1981

Apr [18] Five-track 12"-only EP *Shine So Hard*, with its featured track *Crocodiles*, makes UK #37.
June [6] Written by the band, ***Heaven Up Here*** hits UK #10 and peaks at US #184.
July [25] *A Promise*, recorded in Wales and produced by Hugh Jones, makes UK #49.
Sept [27] The group headlines the "Daze Of Future Past" festival at the Queen's Hall, Leeds.

1982

June [19] Broudie-produced *The Back Of Love* reaches UK #19.
July [16-18] The band takes part in the first Peter Gabriel-inaugurated "WOMAD Festival" at the Royal Bath & West Showground, Shepton Mallet, Somerset.

1983

Feb [5] *The Cutter* hits UK #8, again produced by Broudie. ***Porcupine*** hits UK #2 and peaks at US #137.
July [23] *Never Stop* reaches UK #15. (Sergeant releases a solo album, ***Themes For Grind***.)
Dec "Porcupine", a video collection based around the album, is released by Virgin Video.

1984

Feb [4] Self-written and produced and haunting *The*

Killing Moon hits UK #9, while a live US-only mini-album, ***Echo & The Bunnymen***, reaches #188.

Apr [28] *Silver* reaches UK #30. It is taken from ***Ocean Rain***, self-produced and recorded by the band in France, which hits UK #4 and makes US #87. Accompanying publicity describes it as the "greatest album ever made". Coinciding with its release, the group organizes "Echo & The Bunnymen Present A Crystal Day", an event in which the band takes its most fervent fans on a day trip around Liverpool, culminating in a live show.

July [28] Anthemic *Seven Seas* reaches UK #16.

Sept [22] The group performs at the first "York Rock Festival" at York Racecourse, York, Yorks., with the Sisters of Mercy, Spear of Destiny, the Chameleons and the Redskins.

Nov McCulloch's solo revival of Kurt Weill's standard, *September Song*, makes UK #51.

1985

Nov Following an 18-month sabbatical, *Bring On The Dancing Horses*, the band's most radio-friendly release (due, not least to its Laurie Latham harp-featuring production) reaches UK #21, and ***Songs To Learn And Sing***, collecting their most popular cuts to date, hits UK #6.

1986

Jan ***Songs To Learn And Sing*** peaks at US #158.

Feb De Freitas leaves, and is temporarily replaced by Mark Fox (b. Feb. 13, 1958), only to rejoin in September.

Dec Retrospective Bunnymen video collection, "Picture", is issued by WEA Video.

1987

June [13] After another long musical silence, *The Game* debuts at its UK #28 peak.

July [18] ***Echo & The Bunnymen***, produced by Latham with musical guests Henry Priestman (of the Christians) and the Doors' keyboardist Ray Manzarek, hits UK #4 and will make US #51, its most successful American release.

Aug [15] *Lips Like Sugar* makes UK #36.

Oct The group is forced to cancel its US tour after McCulloch is thrown 12' from the stage into the orchestra pit by an over-zealous fan at the Arlington Theatre, Santa Barbara, CA.

1988

Mar [5] *People Are Strange*, a Manzarek-produced revival of the Doors' 1967 US #12 hit and taken from the movie soundtrack "The Lost Boys", reaches UK #29. (It will also feature on WEA compilation ***Under The Covers***.)

Aug Press reports state that the band has split, despite a denial. McCulloch quits for a solo career while the others elect to continue as before.

1989

June [14] De Freitas is killed when his motorbike collides with a car.

Oct [7] Now signed as a solo act to WEA, McCulloch's debut album, ***Candleland***, peaks at UK #18 (and will peak at US #179 on Nov [25]), while the previewing *Proud To Fall* has made UK #51 in Sept.

1990

Feb McCulloch contributes a version of *Return To Sender* to the compilation ***The Last Temptation Of Elvis***, released to benefit the Nordoff-Robbins Music Therapy charity, and will subsequently return with his new band, the Prodigal Sons.

Mar McCulloch's *Faith And Healing*, produced by Ray Shulman, is released on Sire in the US, following its UK issue in October '89.

[16] McCulloch begins a US tour in Dallas, TX.

May [12] McCulloch's *Candleland (The Second Coming)*, featuring the Cocteau Twins' Elizabeth Fraser on vocals, peaks at UK #75.

Nov Still signed to Korova, the remaining members of Echo & the Bunnymen (with Damon Reece having replaced De Freitas) fail to chart with ***Reverberation***, while undertaking a two-month UK tour which will climax at the ICA, the Mall, London, on December 8th.

1991

Mar [16] Reissued, following the popular UK TV showing of "The Lost Boys", *People Are Strange* makes UK #34.

Aug [10] Towards the end of a UK tour, the band performs at the "Cheltenham Summer Festival", held at Cox's Meadow, Cheltenham, Gloucs.

Sept The group announces the formation of its own Euphoric label.

Dec [20-21] They play at London's Borderline club.

1992

Jan [28-30] McCulloch launches his new band, McCulloch's Mysterio Show, at Covent Garden's Africa Centre, after a two-year absence.

Feb [13] Echo & the Bunnymen play their first gig of the year, at Liverpool 051, opening a short UK tour, set to end March 7th at The Underworld, Camden Town, London.

Mar [7] McCulloch's *Lover, Lover, Lover* makes UK #47.

[21] Its parent album ***Mysterio***, with Roddy Frame and the Cocteau Twins' Robin Guthrie and Elizabeth Fraser guesting, released on East West, debuts at its UK #46 peak.

May [29] Echo & the Bunnymen play a benefit concert for the Third World In Need Charity, at Chester College, Chester.

June [19] They perform at the Marquee, New York, during a short US tour and will return for a second US club jaunt in the autumn. By year's end, McCulloch begins work on new material at Eden Studios, with Ian Richardson and Ian Kolla producing.

1994

Nov Electrafixion, which sees McCulloch and Sergeant back together having recruited Leon De Sylva (bass) and Tony McGuigan (drums), releases its debut EP *Zephyr*, signed to WEA (UK) and Sire Records (US).

1995

Oct Opening for the Boo Radleys, Electrafixion embarks on a UK tour promoting its debut album ***Burned***, with two songs co-penned by McCulloch and ex-Smith guitarist Johnny Marr (an album's worth of material had been recorded, but the tapes were stolen).

1996

Mar [16] Electrafixion's *Sister Pain* enters at its UK #27 peak.

see also: **Julian COPE, TEARDROP EXPLODES**

DUANE EDDY

1958

Mar [24] Eddy (b Apr. 26 1938, Corning, NY), having moved to Tucson, AZ, then Coolidge, AZ, in his teens, is a guitarist leading a band called the Rebels, when he meets DJ Lee Hazlewood and Lester Sill, who raises the finance to cut four sides by the band, which are leased to Jamie, a fledgling Philadelphia label. The throbbing and reverberating *Moovin' N' Groovin'* makes US #72 and introduces the "twangy guitar" trademark sound of Duane Eddy.

July [28] With guitar instrumentals like Bill Justis' *Raunchy* and Link Wray's *Rumble* in the charts, Eddy concocts *Rebel Rouser*, with whooping, handclaps, tremelo effects and abundant echo. It hits US #6 after promotion on Dick Clark's "American Bandstand", where Eddy is revealed to be young, shy and handsome. It is his first million seller, and fans are also roused in the UK, where the single reaches #19.

Sept [15] *Ramrod* reaches US #27. Always cut at Audio Recorders in Phoenix, using producer Hazlewood's novel drainpipe echo chamber, Eddy's hits follow the same pattern of catchy tune and rhythm, played on the bass strings of his Gretsch, and composer credits are usually shared by producer and artist.

Nov [24] With a title (like most of his hits) suggestive of its mood, *Cannonball* reaches US #15 and UK #22. Eddy's studio Rebels comprise Al Casey (guitar, piano), Buddy Wheeler (bass), Donnie Owens and Corky Casey (guitar) and Mike Bermani (drums). Tracks are often taken to Gold Star Studios in Hollywood, where a sax part is added by Plas Johnson or (later) Steve Douglas.

1959

Feb [16] *The Lonely One* reaches US #23. Eddy's debut album, ***Have Twangy Guitar Will Travel***, hits US #5. (It will remain his biggest seller.)

Apr [20] *Yep!* peaks at US #30 and UK #17. Its B-side, Eddy's pulsating version of Henry Mancini's *Peter Gunn* (recently a US-only smash for Ray Anthony & His Orchestra), hits UK #6.

July [27] *Forty Miles Of Bad Road* hits US #9 and UK #11, with its B-side, *The Quiet Three*, set to make US #46.

Aug His second album, ***Especially For You***, is released, set to make US #24.

Sept [12] ***Have Twangy Guitar Will Travel*** hits UK #6.

Oct [19] The extracted *First Love First Tears* reaches US #59.

[26] Its A-side, the fast and furious *Some Kinda Earthquake*, makes US #37 and UK #12.

[31] ***Especially For You*** hits UK #6 in its week of entry.

1960

Jan ***The Twang's The Thang*** peaks at US #18. It contains none of his hits and is another mixture of new and old. The ubiquitous "rebel yells" are credited to Ben Demotto.

[18] *Bonnie Came Back* (based on *My Bonnie Lies Over The Ocean*) makes US #26 and UK #12.

Apr In a package with Bobby Darin, Clyde McPhatter and Emile Ford, Eddy storms the UK with his current Rebels, comprising Larry Knechtel (piano), Jim Horn (sax), Al Casey (bass) and Jimmy Troxel (drums). *Shazam!* (a **Marvel** comics exclamation) reaches US #45 and hits UK #4. ***The Twang's The Thang*** hits UK #2.

July [4] *Because They're Young* movie title theme, Eddy's biggest international disc, hits US #4 and UK #2, becoming his second million seller. With James Darren and Tuesday Weld, he also acts in the movie, which stars Dick Clark as a high-school teacher.

Aug [29] *Kommotion* reaches US #78 and UK #13.

Nov [14] *Peter Gunn* makes a belated US chart entry, reaching #27.

Dec Folksy ***Songs Of Our Heritage*** makes UK #13, but fails to score in the US. Eddy wins the Top World Musical Personality category in the annual **New Musical Express** Readers' Poll.

1961

Feb Collection of hits, ***A Million Dollars' Worth Of Twang***, reaches US #11 but marks the end of Eddy's relationship with the Sill/Hazlewood team.

[6] Movie theme, *Pepe*, reaches US #18 and hits UK #2.

Apr ***A Million Dollars' Worth Of Twang*** hits UK #5. Eddy makes his second movie appearance in "A Thunder Of Drums". Jamie releases four more Eddy hits: the familiar *Theme From Dixie* (US #39 on Apr [17], and UK #7), film theme *Ring Of Fire* (US #84 on June [5], and UK #17), the Knechtel/Eddy collaboration *Drivin' Home* (US #87 on July [24], and UK #30) and an old album track, *My Blue Heaven* (US #50 on Sept [18]).

Aug ***Girls Girls Girls*** reaches US #93. Eddy marries Miriam Johnson, with whom he will shortly record a gospel album.

Oct A one-off single for Parlophone, his version of Duke Ellington's *Caravan*, makes UK #30.

1962

May [19] Now signed to RCA Victor, Eddy's debut single for the label, a revival of the perennial *Deep In The Heart Of Texas*, reaches US #78 and UK #19. His first

RCA album, ***Twistin' N' Twangin'***, reaches US #82.
June ***A Million Dollar's Worth Of Twang Vol. 2*** makes UK #18.
Aug [25] *The Ballad Of Paladin*, the theme from Richard Boone's popular CBS-TV western series "Have Gun Will Travel", reaches US #33 and hits UK #10. ***Twistin' N' Twangin'*** hits UK #8.
Nov ***Twangy Guitar - Silky Strings*** reaches US #72.
Dec [8] Reunited with Hazlewood, Eddy shuns rock'n'roll for novelty pop, complete with singalong chorus, and releases *Dance With The Guitar Man*, which makes US #12 and hits UK #4 to become his third million seller. ***Twangy Guitar - Silky Strings*** reaches UK #13.

1963

Jan His third RCA album, ***Dance With The Guitar Man***, reaches US #47, opening another year of chart action: *Boss Guitar* reaches UK #27 on Mar [9] and US #28 the following week, while ***Dance With The Guitar Man*** reaches UK #14 on Mar [16]; *Lonely Boy Lonely Guitar* stalls at US #82 on June [8] (and will make UK #35), with *Your Baby's Gone Surfin'* reaching US #93 (Sept [14]) and UK #49. ***Twangin' Up A Storm*** climbs to US #93 during October. In 1964, *The Son Of Rebel Rouser* will make US #97 on Jan [11], while ***Lonely Guitar*** will prove to be Eddy's final US charting album, at US #144, in May.

1967

Oct [6] After appearing in the movies "The Savage Seven" and "Kona Coast", which necessitates little on the recording scene, Eddy returns to the UK to begin a tour. (He will also take part in the "1968 First Rock'n'Roll Show" at the Royal, Tottenham, London on May 3rd the following year.)

1973

Having made a cameo appearance on B.J. Thomas' US #15 hit, *Rock And Roll Lullaby*, in April '72, Eddy produces Phil Everly's solo album ***Star Spangled Springer***, adding his twangy trademark to its closing moments.

1975

Apr [5] *Play Me Like You Play Your Guitar*, produced by English writer/producer Tony Macaulay, returns Eddy to the UK chart, hitting #9.

1983

May [22] Having made commercially unsuccessful recordings for Elektra Records in 1978 (including *You Are My Sunshine*), Eddy makes his live comeback in the US (after a 15-year absence) at the Baked Potato, Los Angeles, CA, with a band comprising Ry Cooder (guitar), Don Randi (keyboards), Hal Blaine (drums), Steve Douglas (sax) and John Garnache (bass), which will subsequently embark on a US tour.

1986

Mar The Art of Noise has enlisted Eddy's aid on its revival of *Peter Gunn* which now hits UK #8, as Eddy twangs his guitar on BBC1-TV's "Top Of The Pops" and C4-TV's "The Tube". It will also make US #50 on July [5] and collect the Best Rock Instrumental Performance (Orchestra, Group Or Soloist) trophy at the 29th annual Grammy Awards on February 24th, 1987.

1994

Jan [19] While Capitol Records has released a new Eddy album, ***Duane Eddy***, produced by Jeff Lynne, with help from friends Ry Cooder, John Fogerty, George Harrison and Paul McCartney in September 1987, and Rhino Records (US) has issued a twin-CD career anthology, ***Twang Twang***, in 1993, Eddy is now inducted by John Fogerty into the Rock and Roll Hall of Fame at the ninth annual dinner at New York's Waldorf Astoria Hotel.

DAVE EDMUNDS

1968

Feb Having learnt to play guitar while still at school, where he formed his first band, the 99ers, Edmunds (b. Apr. 15, 1944, Cardiff, Wales) is now a member, as a guitarist and co-vocalist, of Love Sculpture, whose debut, *River To Another Day*, is released on the Parlophone label. Having also played with Welsh group the Raiders in the mid-'60s, Edmunds subsequently moved to London to become a member of the Image. Together with the band's drummer, Tommy Riley, they then formed a trio with bassist John Williams and were given the name the Human Beans by EMI Records, for whom the Image recorded on its Parlophone subsidiary in 1967. The Human Beans debut, a cover of the Tim Rose composition *Morning Dew*, was issued by another EMI imprint, Columbia, in July of that year, prior to the band changing its moniker to Love Sculpture, by which time Bob Jones had replaced Riley.
July EMI, requiring a blues album to capitalize on the current UK boom in the genre, put Love Sculpture to the task. The resulting ***Blues Helping*** is recorded in 15 hours, with no editing, and is produced by Kingsley Ward and Malcolm Jones at London's Abbey Road Studios.
Nov Following the release of *Wang Dang Doodle* (a Willie Dixon song) and *Blues Helping*, neither of which sells, the positive response to a frenetic seven-minute instrumental adaptation of Khachaturian's "Sabre Dance", recorded for BBC Radio 1 DJ John Peel's "Top Gear" UK show, results in Parlophone releasing a new five-minute version.
Dec [28] *Sabre Dance* hits UK #5.

1969

Jan ***Forms And Feeling*** is released, as the group begins a six-week US tour. Upon its return, the band splits and, by year's end, Edmunds will sign a solo management and recording deal with Gordon Mills' MAM agency and will return to Wales, where he will build his own Rockfield Recording Studios in Monmouth, Gwent, with producer Ward. Becoming a permanent success over the next 20 years, one of Edmunds' first production projects at the complex will be for Shakin' Stevens & the Sunsets.

1970

Nov [28] Edmunds' cover of Smiley Lewis' *I Hear You Knocking*, the first release on Mills' new MAM label, tops the UK chart (and will sell three million copies worldwide).

1971

Feb [13] *I Hear You Knocking* hits US #4.
May [15] EMI-released *I'm Coming Home*, on its Regal Zonophone label, fails to chart domestically but makes US #75.

1972

June ***Rockpile***, featuring Williams and Andy Fairweather-Low, is released but also fails to chart, as Edmunds and EMI part company.

1973

Feb His debut release on the Rockfield label, which is run by Ward, is a cover of the Ronettes standard, *Baby I Love You*. Attempting to recreate the Wall of Sound style as a tribute to its producer, Phil Spector, it hits UK #8.
July Similar effort, *Born To Be With You*, originally recorded by the Chordettes, hits UK #5, while Edmunds performs dates with Welsh group, Man.

1974

Feb Edmunds appears in the David Puttnam-produced film "Stardust" and is involved with much of the original soundtrack collection. The material is recorded under the name the Stray Cats (a fictitious band including David Essex and Keith Moon). Brinsley Schwarz asks Edmunds to produce its next album, ***New Favourites***, and in so doing Edmunds strikes up a significant working relationship with the group's bass player, Nick Lowe. (Edmunds' second album, the RCA-issued ***Subtle As A Flying Mallet*** will be issued the following April.)

1976

Sept He signs to Led Zeppelin's Swan Song label, where the first two releases, *Here Comes The Weekend* and *Where Or When*, also fail to score. The Flamin' Groovies' ***Shake Some Action***, produced by Edmunds, makes US #142.

1977

Feb He launches his new band, Rockpile, with a short UK and European tour. The group, comprising Edmunds, Lowe, Terry Williams and guitarist Billy Bremner has been formed with the intention, says Lowe, "to play smelly rock'n'roll in bars and clubs".
Apr *Get It* is released as a Dave Edmunds solo, but fails to chart. Rockpile begins a US tour opening for Bad Company.
July [30] Edmunds' *I Knew The Bride* (written by Lowe) reaches UK #26.
Oct Rockpile undertakes an extensive UK tour.
Nov Edmunds plays on Nick Lowe's first Stiff Records tour package, "Last Chicken In The Shop".

1978

Sept ***Tracks On Wax*** is released, with much of its material co-written with Lowe. The album and three subsequent extracts fail to chart.
[9] Rockpile performs at the "Knebworth Festival", Knebworth, Herts., the day before setting out on a UK trek with Nick Lowe and the Smirks, set to end October 8th at the Locarno, Bristol, Avon. During the tour, Edmunds will take the stage with Emmylou Harris & the Hot Band at London's Hammersmith Odeon, and he and Tommy Riley will back Carl Perkins for ITV's "South Bank Show".
Oct Edmunds tours the US on a package with Elvis Costello and Mink De Ville.

1979

June [8] Rockpile begins a 19-date UK tour at the Birmingham Odeon, set to end on the 29th at the Edinburgh Odeon.
July His recording of a Costello composition, *Girls Talk*, hits UK #4.
Aug [11] ***Repeat When Necessary***, showcasing Edmunds long-held preference for straight-ahead rock'n'roll, reaches UK #39.
Sept [29] *Girls Talk* peaks at US #65, as its parent album, ***Repeat When Necessary***, makes US #54.
Oct *Queen Of Hearts* makes UK #11.
Dec [29] While *Crawling From The Wreckage* (written by Graham Parker) reaches UK #59, Rockpile performs with Wings and Elvis Costello at the "Concert For The People Of Kampuchea" benefit at London's Hammersmith Odeon.

1980

Jan Rockpile tours the UK, supported by US band the Fabulous Thunderbirds (for whom Edmunds will produce two successful albums).
Feb Edmunds' version of *Singin' The Blues* (a '50s hit for both Guy Mitchell and Tommy Steele) makes UK #28.
Sept Rockpile's *Wrong Way*, written by Squeeze's Difford and Tilbrook, is released on the F-Beat label.
Oct Rockpile's album, ***Seconds Of Pleasure***, is also released by F-Beat and makes UK #34 and US #27.
Nov The extracted *Teacher Teacher* makes US #51.

1981

Feb Rockpile breaks up.
Apr [4] Edmunds' revival of John Fogerty's *Almost Saturday Night* peaks at UK #58.
[18] Edmunds' album, ***Twangin'***, reaches UK #37 and US #48.
June [6] *Almost Saturday Night* peaks at US #54.
[27] *The Race Is On* reaches UK #34. It features the

Stray Cats (not those from the "Stardust" film but a US rockabilly band, whose debut album Edmunds has produced - to great success).

1982

Jan [30] ***The Best Of Dave Edmunds*** peaks at US #163. Tracing his career from *Sabre Dance* to the present, it proves to be his swan song for Swan Song.
Apr [10] With Edmunds having signed to Arista, ***D.E.7*** makes UK #60 and includes a Bruce Springsteen song, *From Small Things Big Things Come.*
June [12] ***D.E.7*** makes US #46 during a North American tour by Edmunds.
July He is hospitalized with internal haemorrhaging during his US visit.
Aug Fully recovered, Edmunds performs at the "Reading Festival", Reading, Berks.
Sept [3-5] Edmunds takes part in the three-day "US Festival" in San Bernardino, CA, in front of an estimated 400,000 people.

1983

Apr Co-produced with Jeff Lynne, ***Information*** reaches UK #92 and US #51 while the ELO-esque extract *Slipping Away* peaks at UK #60.
June Edmunds produces *On The Wings Of A Nightingale*, the Paul McCartney-penned comeback for the Everly Brothers.
July [30] *Slipping Away* makes US #39.

1984

Oct ***Riff Raff***, including six tracks produced by Lynne, peaks at US #140.

1985

Apr [20] *High School Nights* reaches US #91.
July Soundtrack album for "Porky's Revenge" is released, including five Edmunds cuts.
Oct [21] Edmunds co-ordinates Carl Perkins' C4-TV special, "Blue Suede Shoes", recorded at Limehouse Studios in London, enlisting guitarist friends Eric Clapton and George Harrison. (The program will air on December 24th and, is subsequently released on video.)

1987

Feb ***I Hear You Rockin'***, an Arista collection of live hits recorded in New York, NY and Passaic, NJ, makes US #106.
June [5-6] Edmunds participates in the fifth annual "Prince's Trust Rock Gala", at the Wembley Arena, Wembley, Middx., with Elton John, Bryan Adams, George Harrison, Ringo Starr, Alison Moyet and others, before embarking on a tour of Holland and Germany.

1988

Sept Having spent much of the last two years producing (the Everly Brothers, Mason Ruffner, Status Quo and k.d. lang) and contributing songs to the Steve Martin/John Candy movie "Planes, Trains And Automobiles", Edmunds signs to Capitol and records a new album in Los Angeles, CA. (He is also slated to produce Nick Lowe's first album for Warner Bros., Dion's debut for Arista and a comeback album by the Stray Cats.)

1989

Nov Edmunds appears at Jerry Lee Lewis' Hammersmith Odeon concert, with Brian May, Van Morrison, John Lodge, Stuart Adamson and others.

1990

Mar [7] Dave Edmunds' Rock'n'Roll Revue, a touring troupe put together by Edmunds, including Dion, Graham Parker, the Fabulous Thunderbirds' Kim Wilson and others, opens in Kingston, NY, and - after 26 dates - will wind up on April 6th at the Universal Amphitheatre, Universal City, CA.
Apr [7] Capitol-released *King Of Love* makes UK #68, while its parent album, ***Closer To The Flame***, peaks at US #146.
May [5] Edmunds takes part in the "John Lennon Tribute Concert" at the Pier Head Arena in Merseyside, to celebrate the songs of Lennon, with proceeds from the event going to the Lennon and Ono-established Spirit Foundation. He performs *A Day In The Life*, *Strawberry Fields Forever* and *Working Class Hero*. (Edmunds will also participate in a second tribute show in Japan, held on Dec [21-22], by which time he will also have guested on Carlene Carter's latest album, ***I Fell In Love***.). His hit catalog will not be released on compact disc until March 1993 (the Rhino Records US-only issued ***Anthology (1968-1990)***).

1994

July ***Plugged In***, a new album with covers of *I Got The Will*, *Halfway Down* and a new song, *One Step Back*, written with Z.Z. Top's Billy Gibbons, is released in the US by Pyramid/Rhino.

1995

June [21] Now living in Los Angeles, Edmunds records *It Doesn't Matter Anymore* wth Suzy Bogguss at Sound Stage Studios in Nashville, TN, for inclusion on the tribute album ***notfadeaway : remembering buddy holly***, set for US release in February the following year.

ELASTICA

Justine Frischman (lead vocals, guitar); **Donna Matthews** (guitar); **Annie Holland** (bass); **Justin Welch** (drums)

1993

May [7] Having played her last gig as its rhythm guitarist with UK indie act Suede in January 1992 at the ULU Bar in London's Malet Street (alongside then-boyfriend and lead singer Brett Anderson), Frischman (b. 1968, Twickenham, Middx.), the daughter of a singer mother and Nat West Bank building architect father, who attended St. Paul's School, Twickenham with future Senseless Things drummer Cass Browne, has begun writing songs and playing the guitar in her mid-teens and is band-hungry by the time she attends the London University to study architecture (where she has met Anderson to first perform with Suede on March 10th 1990). Subsequently meeting Spitfire drummer Welch (b. 1972, Nuneaton, W. Midlands) at the June 1992 "Glastonbury Festival" (having first met him when he has unsuccessfully auditioned for Suede) the pair decides to form a new band and is offered free studio time by EMI Publishing's Mike Smith, who has recently signed her new boyfriend Damon Albarn's band Blur) at London's Rathbone Place studio. Recruiting Holland (b. Brighton, E. Sussex), whose previous jobs have included painting Royal Mail post-boxes red, and Matthews (b. Newport, Wales), the latter from a want-ad in **Melody Maker**, and having recorded four songs (including *Vaseline)* at a second Rathbone Place session in February of this year, the lineup plays its first gig tonight, a 15-minute set performed under a pseudonym, opening for Truman's Water at the Old Trout pub outside London, followed by further gigs around the South-east including its debut as Elastica at the capital's Camden Falcon.
Sept [18] The band's first session for the "John Peel Show" airs on BBC's 1-FM radio station.
Nov Following a handshake deal with Deceptive Records boss Steve Lamacq at a gig at the Spice of Life pub, in Charing Cross, London, 1500 copies of the band's debut single *Stutter* are released by the label to rave reviews in the UK music media (including Single Of The Week nods in both **Melody Maker** and the **New Musical Express**, hailing Frischman's chic Riot Grrrl post-punk style.

1994

Feb [12] Wire-inspired *Line Up* bows at its UK #20 peak, helped by a headlining gig at Camden's Electric Ballroom.
Apr [18] 1-FM radio airs a three-song Elastica "Evening Session".
July [9] The band performs another set on the "John Peel Show".
Oct [22] Already hailed as one of the leaders of Britain's "New Wave of the New Wave" movement (and signed to Geffen Records in the US) *Connection* bows at its UK #17 peak.
Nov [2-6] The band performs at the "Festival FNAC Inrockuptibles" in Lille, France
[19] Elastica appears on BBC2-TV's "Later With Jools Holland".

1995

Feb [25] *Waking Up* debuts at its UK #13 peak.
Mar During its maiden US tour, the band performs two sellout gigs in Los Angeles, CA followed by a showcase at the "South By South West Convention" in Austin, TX the next day.
[25] ***Elastica***, the group's debut album recorded at Konk Studios, debuts at UK #1.
Apr [8] The group performs on BBC2-TV's "Later With Jools Holland".
May [26] Elastica appears on NBC-TV's "Late Show With David Letterman".
[27] Once again reminiscent of Wire, *Connection* makes US #53 on the same day the band plays at the Theatre of Living Arts, Philadelphia, PA, grossing $6,930 from 810 fans.
June [10] ***Elastica*** makes US #66.
July [6] Together with Gene, S*M*A*S*H, Boo Radleys and Lush, Elastica raise £15,000 for the Shelter charity at a Kentish Town Forum benefit in London.
[23] Invited to stand-in for remaining dates following the mid-tour departure of Sinead O'Connor, the band plays its first "Lollapalooza" gig in Toronto, ON, Canada. (Holland will quit the lineup after a few dates, allegedly tired of touring, to be temporarily replaced by Beck bassist Abbey Travis.)
Aug [26] *Stutter* makes US #67.
Nov [26] With a new cut featured on the film soundtrack to "Trainspotting", the band's current US swing stops at the Roxy Theatre, Atlanta, GA, a bill with Soul Asylum and Loud Lucy, which attracts 1500 fans.

ELECTRIC LIGHT ORCHESTRA

Jeff Lynne (vocals, guitars); **Richard Tandy** (keyboards, vocals); **Kelly Groucutt** (bass, vocals); **Bev Bevan** (drums); **Mik Kaminski** (violin); **Hugh McDowell** (cello); **Melvyn Gale** (cello)

1971

Oct After much manœuvering on the local band scene, the first line-up of the Electric Light Orchestra is formed in Birmingham, W. Midlands, comprising Lynne (b. Dec. 30, 1947, Birmingham), Roy Wood (b. Nov. 8, 1947, Birmingham), Bevan (b. Beverley Bevan, Nov. 24, 1946, Birmingham), McDowell (b. July 31, 1953), Andy Craig, Wilf Gibson, Bill Hunt (b. May 23, 1947) and Tandy (b. Mar. 26, 1948, Birmingham). Wood, a veteran of local '60s bands Gerry Levene & the Avengers and Mike Sheridan & the Nightriders, has recently dissolved Birmingham's most successful beat group, the Move (who formed in 1966 and whose line-up also included Carl Wayne and Bevan, previously an ex-Viking and member of Denny Laine's 1962 backing band, the Diplomats). Wood has asked local musician and friend Lynne (who had been a guitarist/vocalist for Idle Race since 1966) to replace Wayne as lead singer in the Move in January 1970. Lynne has accepted, on the condition that he can also be involved in Wood's splinter project, a band devoted to playing "jazz and classically-influenced free-form music" with instrumentation aligned more to an orchestra than a rock band. This novel idea, financed by manager Don Arden, who secures them a contract with EMI subsidiary Harvest, materializes as the Electric Light Orchestra, while remnant Move recordings and live commitments continue into the following year.

1972

Apr [16] ELO makes its live debut at the Greyhound pub in Croydon, Surrey, but its innovative style is not well received.

July [15] Having planned ELO for several years, Wood surprisingly quits the project to immediately form his own, more pop-oriented, group, Wizzard. He takes Hunt and McDowell with him, while Craig leaves altogether. Lynne recruits cellists Mike Edwards and Colin Walker and bassist Mike D'Albuquerque.

Aug ELO's first single, the Lynne-composed *10538 Overture*, hits UK #9, while its album debut, ***Electric Light Orchestra***, featuring Lynne and Wood, is released by Harvest, set to reach UK #32. United Artists in the US, to whom the band is signed, having rung Arden to confirm the album title and having been left the message "No answer" by a secretary who could not reach him, release it as ***No Answer***. It will make US #196.

[12] The new line-up debuts at the "Reading Festival", Reading, Berks.

1973

Feb First post-Wood release, a highly-orchestrated version of Chuck Berry's *Roll Over Beethoven*, with a quasi-classical intro, hits UK #6.

Mar Their sophomore effort, ***ELO II***, is released, making UK #35 and US #62, venturing further into a rock/classical fusion.

June [2] The group begins a 40-date US tour in San Diego, CA.

July [28] *Roll Over Beethoven* makes US #42.

Sept McDowell rejoins from Wizzard. Gibson and Walker leave, and Mik Kaminski (b. Sept. 2, 1951, Harrogate, Yorks.) joins as principal violinist.

Nov *Showdown*, later an R&B hit for Candi Staton, reaches UK #12.

Dec Lushly-orchestrated concept album, ***On The Third Day***, is released through Warner Bros. in the UK but fails to chart. United Artists releases the album in the US, where it will make #52.

1974

Feb [2] *Showdown* peaks at US #53.

Apr [6] *Ma-Ma-Ma-Belle* reaches UK #22.

May [25] *Daybreaker* stalls at US #87.

Oct ***Eldorado***, billed as "A Symphony By The Electric Light Orchestra", is released, set to make US #16, selling over one million copies.

Nov Live ***The Night The Light Went On In Long Beach***, is released worldwide, excluding the UK and US, while Harvest issues ***Showdown***, a compilation of singles and tracks from the first two albums. Edwards and D'Albuquerque leave and are replaced by bassist Kelly Groucutt (b. Sept. 8, 1945, Coseley), ex-Barefoot, and cellist Melvyn Gale (b. Jan. 15, 1952, London), ex-London Palladium orchestra. This new line-up will remain together for the next five years and will be responsible for ELO's most productive and commercially successful period.

1975

Mar [15] With ELO using a 30-piece string section for the first time, the ballad *Can't Get It Out Of My Head*, from ***Eldorado***, becomes the group's first US Top 10 album, hitting #9. (The band will spend most of the year touring the US.)

Oct ***Face The Music*** is released, much of it recorded at Musicland Studios in Munich, W. Germany (where the group will record most of its future work), and will hit US #8. Having firmly established their multi-layered, heavily-textured classical-rock style, it is clear that the Beatles-influenced Lynne has become the central creative force in the group, writing, arranging and producing all ELO material, giving the band a distinctive and immediately recognizable generic sound, which will barely alter with each subsequent release.

1976

Feb [14] Having already hit UK #10 on Jan [31], *Evil Woman* hits US #10, as a successful North American tour gets underway.

May [22] *Strange Magic* reaches US #14.

July *Strange Magic* makes UK #38.

Aug [28] Reissued *Showdown* peaks at US #59.

Sept ELO, now signed to Arden's Jet label, releases a US-only greatest hits collection, ***Olé ELO***, which will reach US #32.

Dec [4] ***A New World Record*** is released and attracts immediate radio interest. It will go on to sell five million copies worldwide.

[18] *Livin' Thing* hits UK #4.

1977

Jan [8] *Livin' Thing* reaches US #13, as its parent album, ***A New World Record***, will hit US #5.

[17] ELO begins a major North American tour at the Veterans' Memorial Auditorium, Phoenix, AZ. (It will end three months later on April 6th at Place de Nationale, Montreal, PQ, Canada.)

Mar [1] Dramatic *Rockaria!* hits UK #9.

Apr [2] ELO's version of the Move's only US hit, the Lynne-penned *Do Ya*, reaches US #24, after Todd Rundgren has performed the song as part of his live show. Harvest releases the compilation ***The Light Shines On***, as Lynne, locked away in a chalet in Bassins, Switzerland, writes songs for a new album.

June [18] *Telephone Line*, from ***A New World Record***, hits UK #8.

[25] ***A New World Record*** peaks at UK #6, eight months after its release. An extensive world tour begins, which, with the year's record sales, will gross the band more than $10 million.

Sept [24] *Telephone Line* hits US #7.

Nov [26] With worldwide advance orders of four million, the double album ***Out Of The Blue***, again written and produced by Lynne, hits UK #4.

Dec [10] *Turn To Stone* reaches UK #18.

1978

Jan [8] ***Out Of The Blue*** hits US #4. (During its chart run, US distribution for Jet switches to CBS/Columbia and the band sues United Artists for allegedly allowing millions of defective copies to reach the market.)

Feb [4] *Turn To Stone* reaches US #13.

[25] *Mr. Blue Sky*, highlighting Lynne's long-term lyrical fascination with the weather, hits UK #6.

Mar Lynne receives the Album Of The Year trophy for ***Out Of The Blue*** from Lord George Brown at the Capital Music Awards, held at the Grosvenor House Hotel, London.

Apr [29] *Sweet Talkin' Woman* reaches US #17.

June [9] During a major venue UK tour (including seven dates at the Empire Pool, Wembley, Middx.), the band is featured on the pre-taped UK TV "Kenny Everett Show" and will be the subject of a one-hour documentary in July, on the more highbrow "South Bank Show" on ITV.

Aug [12] While *Wild West Hero* has already hit UK #6 on the 5th, *Mr. Blue Sky* makes US #35. Group begins a world tour, with an elaborate set featuring lasers and a huge illuminated ELO spaceship emblazened with the band's familiar gold logo.

Oct [21] *Sweet Talkin' Woman* hits UK #6, becoming the fourth UK hit from ***Out Of The Blue***.

Nov [18] *It's Over* peaks at US #75.

Dec [16] EP *ELO* makes UK #34. (Tracks are *Can't Get It Out Of My Head*, *Strange Magic*, *Ma-Ma-Ma-Belle* and *Evil Woman*.) Lynne's first solo, *Doin' That Crazy Thing*, is released but, like Bevan's solo, *Let There Be Drums*, it fails to chart.

1979

Jan [20] Jet-release vinyl boxed-set, ***Three Light Years***, comprising ***On The Third Day***, ***Eldorado*** and ***Face The Music***, makes UK #38. Kaminski's offshoot project, Violinski, reaches UK #17 with *Clog Dance*, while Harvest will issue ***The Light Shines On Vol. 2*** in March.

May [4] ELO is honored with the Outstanding Contribution To British Music award at the 24th annual Ivor Novello Awards lunch, at the Grosvenor House Hotel, London.

June [9] *Shine A Little Love* hits UK #6.

[16] ***Discovery*** hits UK #1, the group's first UK chart-topping album.

July [5] ***Discovery*** hits US #5.

[21] *Shine A Little Love* hits US #8.

Aug [11] *The Diary Of Horace Wimp* hits UK #8.

Sept [8] *Don't Bring Me Down* hits US #4. Dedicated to the Skylab space project, it is the band's biggest US single success, selling over one million copies.

[22] *Don't Bring Me Down*, hits UK #3.

Nov [17] *Confusion* makes US #37.

Dec [1] *Confusion*, backed with *Last Train To London*, hits UK #8.

[8] Jet-issued ***ELO's Greatest Hits*** hits UK #7 and will make US #30 on the 22nd. Increasingly concentrating on recording (the band has toured annually since 1972), Lynne scales down the full-time band to Bevan, Tandy and Groucutt, calling on Gale when required.

1980

Feb [2] *Last Train To London* makes US #39.

May Having been commissioned to write songs for the Olivia Newton-John starring movie, "Xanadu", the soundtrack's debut release, *I'm Alive*, makes UK #20.

June Title track *Xanadu*, teaming ELO with Newton-John, is released and will hit UK #1 (the band's first chart-topping single).

July Soundtrack album, ***Xanadu***, with one side featuring songs by ELO, the other by the film's star, hits UK #2 and US #4, becoming the only successful element of an otherwise commercially disastrous project. Its subsequent singles are: *I'm Alive*, which reaches US #16 on July [12], *All Over The World*, US #13 on Oct [4] (having already made UK #11 in September), *Xanadu*, which hits US #8 on Oct [11] and *Don't Walk Away*, which reaches UK #21 on Dec [6].

1981

May [19] *Xanadu* wins Best Film Song, Theme Or Score at the 26th annual Ivor Novello Awards lunch, held at the Grosvenor House Hotel.

Aug [29] ***Time*** tops the UK chart and reaches US #16.

Sept [5] *Hold On* Tight hits UK #4. (It is the first disc credited to the ELO acronym. They will revert to their full name in 1986, when signed to CBS/Epic.)

Oct [3] *Hold On Tight* hits US #10, as the group begins a major tour, the first since the early '70s, playing to less than capacity audiences, however.

Nov [7] *Twilight* makes UK #30 before peaking at US #38 on the 28th.

1982

Jan [30] *Ticket To The Moon/Here Is The News* reaches UK #24.

Mar For the first time since *Nightrider* six years earlier, an ELO single (*The Way Life's Meant To Be*) fails to chart in the UK and US. In an unrelated incident, Bevan has to be flown back to the UK hours before a concert in Bremen, suffering from a severe stomach complaint. After The Fire's drummer Pete King deputizes without rehearsal.

1983

July [16] ELO's *Rock'n'Roll Is King* makes UK #13. Recorded in Holland, ***Secret Messages***, with Kaminski guesting, and featuring string arranger Louis Clark, is released, set to hit UK #4 and US #36.

Aug [20] *Rock'n'Roll Is King* reaches US #19.

Sept *Secret Messages* makes UK #48.

Oct [8] *Four Little Diamonds* stalls at US #86. It will be the group's last hit for two years, as Lynne begins a parallel production career (which will eventually result in the band's demise), having already helmed Dave Edmunds' 1983 ***Information***. Bevan leaves to join Black Sabbath (but will rejoin in time for the next ELO album).

1986

Mar Signed to CBS/Epic, ELO, now reduced to a three-

piece of Lynne, Bevan and Tandy, returns to the US charts with *Calling America*, which reaches UK #28.
[15] The group makes its first concert appearance in four years, in its home town Birmingham, joined onstage by George Harrison.
Apr [5] *Calling America* reaches US #18. The band appears at the "Heartbeat '86" charity benefit in Birmingham (its last live appearance). The band's final album under Lynne's authority, ***Balance Of Power***, is released, set to hit UK #9 and US #49, but the extracted *So Serious* and *Getting To The Point* fail to chart.

1987

June [5-6] Lynne takes part in the fifth annual "Prince's Trust Rock Gala" at London's Wembley Arena, having recently produced material on ***Duane Eddy***, Eddy's comeback album for Capitol. Increasingly in demand as both a producer and songwriter, Lynne will work with and for a number of rock legends well into the '90s, collaborating most successfully with George Harrison on his November-released album, ***Cloud Nine*** (featuring the Lynne-produced US #1 and UK #2, *Got My Mind Set On You*).

1988

Oct Having co-written and co-produced *Let It Shine* for Brian Wilson's July release, ***Brian Wilson***, Lynne teams with Randy Newman for tracks on ***Land Of Dreams*** and helps successfully relaunch Roy Orbison's recording career with what proves to be his final album, ***Mystery Girl***, and worldwide hit, *You Got It*, before combining with Orbison as part of the Traveling Wilburys along with Bob "Lucky" Dylan, George "Nelson" Harrison and Tom "Charlie T. Jnr." Petty. Their debut single, *Handle With Care*, is released from future Grammy-winning ***Traveling Wilburys Volume 1***, co-produced by "Nelson" and "Otis", to be issued in November.

1989

Dec [23] TV-advertised ELO's ***The Greatest Hits***, on Telstar Records, reaches UK #23. (Relaunched in October 1990 as ***The Very Best Of The Electric Light Orchestra***, it makes UK #28 - Oct [27].) Lynne's writing and production credits for the year include Tom Petty's ***Full Moon Fever*** and tracks for Del Shannon's final album, ***Rock On*** (to be released in 1991).

1990

July Having successfully written and produced for a number of colleagues over the past decade, Lynne turns the spotlight on himself via a solo deal with Reprise. The first fruit, *Every Little Thing*, makes UK #59.
[7] His solo album, ***Armchair Theatre***, makes US #83 and will reach UK #24 (Aug [4]) prior to the release of the ELO boxed-set retrospective ***Afterglow***. By year's end, Lynne will have also contributed to the November-released ***The Traveling Wilburys Volume 3***.

1991

Mar Without Lynne's involvement, Bevan convenes an ELO II comprising Groucutt, Kaminski, Eric Troyer (keyboards), guitarists Pete Haycock and Neil Lockwood and longtime ELO collaborator, Louis Clark. The ensemble will release the June [1] UK #34-peaking Jeff Glixman-produced ***Electric Light Orchestra 2*** album on Telstar (previewed by the UK #60 *Honest Men*, on May [11]), touring into 1992, notably at the Hammersmith Odeon on October 10th, the album having surfaced in the US on the Scotti Brothers label. (The first date of ELO II's spring 1993 European tour in Ballymena, N. Ireland, will be cancelled following objections from Ian Paisley's Democratic Unionist Party, which claims that the band plays "devil music".)

1994

July [9] ***The Very Best Of The Electric Light Orchestra*** hits UK #4. (A life-long fan Lynne will be asked by the remaining Beatles to co-construct and co-produce *Free As A Bird* and *Real Love*, the first two new Beatles singles issued as part of ***Anthology 1*** and ***Anthology 2*** in 1995/96.)
see also: **BLACK SABBATH, MOVE, WIZZARD**

THE ELECTRIC PRUNES

James Lowe (guitar, autoharp, vocals);
Ken Williams (lead guitar);
Weasel Spagnola (rhythm guitar);
Mark Tulin (bass); **Preston Ritter** (drums)

1967

Feb [11] Having spent 1964 playing in a bluegrass band in Hawaii, Lowe has returned to Los Angeles in 1965 and formed the southern California quintet Electric Prunes with Spagnola, subsequently securing a recording contract with Reprise, which has issued the band's non-charting debut, *Ain't It Hard* in May the previous year. Major success now comes with the psychedelia-laden *I Had Too Much To Dream (Last Night)* (written by female duo Annette Tucker/Nancie Mantz), which reaches US #11. It will also make UK #49.
Apr [16] The group guests on CBS-TV's "The Smothers Brothers Comedy Hour".
May [6] 12-track debut album, ***The Electric Prunes***, makes US #113.
[13] The extracted *Get Me To The World On Time*, from the same writers, taken from the album, reaches US #27 and will make UK #42.
July *The Great Banana Hoax*, written by Lowe and Tulin, fails to chart.
Sept [2] ***Underground*** debuts at its US #172 peak.
Dec The group makes a brief concert trip to Europe.

1968

Jan The original quintet is augmented by many other musicians on the innovative ***Mass In F Minor***, an electronic rock transposition of a Catholic mass, written and arranged by David Axelrod. It is a minor seller in the US, reaching #135 (Feb [17]), but will remain a popular cult album from the era. Following its release, the original group members depart, but Axelrod keeps the name alive by drawing from the additional musicians who played on the album. He will record a similar "god-rock" opus, ***Release Of An Oath***, with the revised line-up of Mark Kinkaid (guitar, vocals), Ron Morgan (guitar), Brett Wade (bass, flute, vocals), John Herren (keyboards), and Richard Whetstone (drums, guitar, vocals), but it will fail to chart. The band's final disc, ***Just Good Old Rock'n'Roll***, released in May 1969 and recorded following the departure of Herren and Axelrod, will close the group's brief musical career.

EMERSON, LAKE AND PALMER

Keith Emerson (keyboards); **Greg Lake** (bass, vocals); **Carl Palmer** (drums)

1970

Aug [25] The trio makes its live debut at the Guildhall, Plymouth, Devon. Keyboard wizard Emerson (b. Nov. 2, 1944, Todmorden, Yorks.) has served his musical apprenticeship with the T-Bones, prior to joining the quasi-classical, jazz, rock and blues quartet the Nice (with Brian Davison, Lee Jackson and David O'List) in 1967. Their dramatic stage shows were highlighted by a shirtless Emerson, knife-stabbing his instruments and ritually burning flags, theatrics which he will extend and expand upon during ELP's heyday. Lake (b. Nov. 10, 1948, Bournemouth, Dorset) has cut his guitar and vocal teeth with the Gods, prior to joining King Crimson in 1969 and, having linked with Emerson in April 1970, has embarked on auditions for a drummer to complete their planned progressive rock outfit. Ex-Crazy World of Arthur Brown and the recently-disbanded heavy-rock combo Atomic Rooster member, Palmer (b. Mar. 20, 1947, Birmingham, W. Midlands), gets the gig (he was the 16-year-old drummer for Chris Farlowe's Thunderbirds in 1963).
[29] Dedicated to musical finesse and showmanship from its earliest days, ELP performs at the "Isle Of Wight Festival", Godshill, Isle of Wight on the penultimate day, alongside the Doors, the Who and Joni Mitchell.
Dec With the band signed to Island in the UK and Atlantic (via the Cotillion label) in the US, its debut album, ***Emerson Lake & Palmer***, produced (as with all subsequent projects) by Lake, is released, set to hit UK #4. It immediately establishes their consistent musical approach: technically, accomplished instrumental virtuosity performing a rock/classical fusion, accompanied by grandiose lyrical concepts. (Pete Sinfield of King Crimson becomes the trio's main wordsmith).

1971

Mar ***Emerson Lake & Palmer*** reaches US #18.
[26] The group is recorded live at City Hall, Newcastle, Tyne & Wear, playing its own arrangement of Mussorgsky's "Pictures At An Exhibition".
May [1] Unreleased as a UK single, *Lucky Man* (from the debut album) reaches US #48.
June [26] ***Tarkus***, a concept album which apparently pits Tarkus, a mechanised armadillo, in a battle against mythical beast the Manticore, hits UK #1 for a week and will hit US #9 in August.
Dec UK budget-priced (£1.49) live classical adaptation, ***Pictures At An Exhibition***, hits UK #3 and will hit US #10 in February 1972.

1972

Apr The band performs at the "Mar-Y-Sol Festival" in Puerto Rico, where its *Take A Pebble/Lucky Man* is recorded for a live album of the event.
[15] Their revival of B. Bumble & the Stingers' *Nut Rocker*, showcasing Emerson's frantic keyboard antics and included on ***Pictures At An Exhibition***, peaks at US #70.
July Their fourth album, ***Trilogy***, hits UK #2 and will hit US #5 in September, while the extracted *From The Beginning* will make US #39 on Oct [28].

1973

Feb [2] Emerson's hands are injured on stage in San Francisco, CA, during a currrent US tour. His piano, rigged to explode as a stunt during the set, detonates prematurely.
[3] *Lucky Man*, re-promoted in the US to coincide with tour, peaks at #51.
Mar The film "Pictures At An Exhibition", featuring the band in a concert performance of the work, premieres in Los Angeles, CA.
Dec The group's UK debut single, *Jerusalem*, taken from a forthcoming project, ***Brain Salad Surgery***, fails to chart, confirming their principal status as an album-selling band. Both are released on the group's recently formed Manticore label (which will include on its roster, lyricist Sinfield, Italian progressive rock-band P.F.M. and, curiously, Little Richard).
[29] ***Brain Salad Surgery***, with its striking "skull" cover by H.R. Giger, hits UK #2 and will reach US #11.

1974

Aug [31] Live triple album, ***Welcome Back My Friends To The Show That Never Ends; Ladies And Gentlemen ... Emerson, Lake And Palmer***, typical, in both its length and title, of the band's increasingly excessive style, hits UK #5, and will hit US #4 the following month.

1975

Dec [27] Lake's seasonal solo departure, *I Believe In Father Christmas* hits UK #2 and will become a re-charting seasonal favorite both in the UK and US, where it will, however, only make #95. (Emerson's solo *Honky Tonk Train Blues*, his revival of a Meade Lux Lewis classic, will reaches UK #21 the following year on May [1].)

1977

Apr [16] Dysfunctional double album, ***Works***, hits UK #9, set to make US #12 in May. Largely a showcase for the trio's solo works, they combine as a band only for the fourth side.
July [16] A racing-keyboards/guitar interpretation of Aaron Copland's *Fanfare For The Common Man*, hits UK #2, behind Hot Chocolate's *So You Win Again*.
Sept [10] Lake's *C'est La Vie*, also from ***Works***, makes US #91.
Oct The group demands an apology from **Gay News** after the paper publishes an ad for the Gayway Dating Service, featuring an illustration of the group copied from ***Trilogy***.
[25] The band performs at the Coliseum, Jackson, MS, during an extensive US tour accompanied by a symphony orchestra.
Nov ELP are awarded the Gold Ticket for playing to over 100,000 fans at Madison Square Garden, New York, NY.
Dec [10] Compilation, ***Works, Volume Two***, rounding up singles (including *Honky Tonk Train Blues* and *I Believe In Father Christmas*) and previously-unissued out-takes, makes UK #20 and will reach US #37. As the contradictory raw and basic style of the punk movement explodes in the UK, the grand excesses displayed by bands such as ELP have turned them, particularly in the eyes of the music press, into musical dinosaurs whose era has ended.

1978

Dec [9] ***Love Beach***, their final studio album, reaches UK #48 and will make US #55.
[30] Having performed a farewell world tour during the latter half of the year, the band announces its official break-up.

1979

Dec Live ***Emerson, Lake & Palmer In Concert*** is released to fulfill contractual obligations. Recorded during the band's 1978 US tour, it reaches US #73, while ***The Best Of Emerson, Lake & Palmer*** will make US #108 in December 1980. Each member has already initiated new projects: Palmer forms P.M. (with four US musicians, releasing ***One P.M.*** on Ariola in 1980) before joining John Wetton, Steve Howe and Geoff Downes in Asia the following year. Following an eponymous solo album released by Chrysalis in 1981 (which makes both UK and US #62) and a 1983 sophomore effort, ***Manoeuvres***, Lake joins Palmer in Asia (temporarily replacing Wetton) later that year, leaving the band the following year and reuniting with Emerson in 1985. Emerson releases a 1980 album, ***Inferno***, the first of a number of film soundtracks he will complete throughout the decade, including the US #183 peaking ***Nighthawks***, ***Best Revenge*** and ***Muderock***.

1985

Emerson and Lake agree to record together, aiming for a comeback similar to that achieved by their contemporaries, Yes, a year earlier. The duo cannot interest Palmer in the project, so ex-Rainbow rock drummer veteran, Cozy Powell (b. Dec. 29, 1947, Cirencester, Gloucs.), is recruited instead (maintaining the ELP abbreviation).

1986

June Signed to Polydor, the new trio debuts with ***Emerson, Lake & Powell***, which will make UK #35 and US #23.
July [19] The extracted *Touch And Go* peaks at US #60. The band tours the US. (The union will not last long and Powell will leave to pursue other projects.)

1987

May Emerson performs a specially-composed lament at a thanksgiving service for record executive Tony Stratton-Smith, at St. Martin's-in-the-Fields in Trafalgar Square, London.

1988

Feb Having rehearsed with Palmer in 1987, in an unsuccessful effort to reform the original group, Emerson and Lake have enlisted ex-Hush drummer Robert Berry (b. San Jose, CA) in his place, to form 3, releasing ***To The Power Of Three*** on Geffen, which makes US #97. Again, this proves to be a short-lived combination.
Nov Priority Records releases Emerson's seasonal collection, ***The Christmas Album.***

1992

June [27] After a number of false starts, a legitimate reunion album, ***Black Moon***, released on Victory Records by the original trio, debuts at its US #78 peak. Brought together after film producer Phil Carson asked them to write a soundtrack for a movie (which is subsequently not made), the album typically includes an arrangement of Prokofiev's "Romeo And Juliet". Former label, Atlantic, simultaneously issues the double retrospective, ***The Atlantic Years***.
July [25] The group performs to a sellout crowd of 10,700 at the Jones Beach Theatre, Wantagh, NY, during a North American tour (their first in 15 years), set to end on September 6th at the Orpheum Theatre, Vancouver, BC, Canada (the second US leg will commence on January 13th, 1993).
Sept [12] Japanese dates begin at the Shi Kikaido, Nagoya.
Oct [2-3] The band plays consecutive nights at the Royal Albert Hall, London, during the European leg of their world tour, set to end November 28th at the Colston Hall, Bristol, Avon. The Royal Albert Hall performances are taped for the January 26th, 1993 release, ***Live At The Royal Albert Hall***.

1993

Feb [3-4] The group performs at New York's Radio City Music Hall, during the North American leg of its world tour, set to end on March 17th at Los Angeles' Wiltern Theatre, with a live broadcast on the Entertainment Radio networks.
Nov [16] Four-CD/cassette boxed set career anthology, ***Return Of The Manticore***, is released in the US.

1994

Oct [25] A month after ELP has released its latest work, ***In The Hot Seat*** (released on Victory in the US and London Records in the UK), Lake gives a $5,000 check to the Sara Anne Wood Rescue Center in Litchfield, NY. (Wood is a young girl believed to have been murdered by an alleged Massachusetts serial killer, Lewis Lent.) They also earmark royalties to their song *Daddy* to the center. (ELP's publishing catalog will be assigned to Music Sales on July 1st the following year.)
see also: **ASIA, KING CRIMSON, RAINBOW**

EMF

James Atkin (vocals); **Ian Dench** (guitar); **Zak Foley** (bass); **Derry Brownson** (keyboards, percussion); **Mark Decloedt** (drums)

1989

Dec [29] Having formed in a Cinderford, Forest of Dean, Gloucs., sports shop, the group makes its debut, booked into the venue by Foley (b. Zachary Foley, Dec. 9, 1970, Gloucester, Gloucs.), at the Bilson pub in Cinderford, with Foley, Dench (b. Aug. 7, 1964, Cheltenham, Gloucs.), previously a student at the Ruskin College of Art in Oxford, Oxon., and guitarist in the recently-disbanded Apple Mosaic on Virgin subsidiary MDM, Brownson (b. Derry Brownstone, Nov. 10, 1970, Gloucester), who has failed an audition for Apple Mosaic while still a member of the Light Aircraft Company (formerly Faces of Glory) and that band's remaining members, Atkin (b. Mar. 28, 1969, Cinderford) and Decloedt (b. June 26, 1969, Gloucs.). While Foley, Brownson, Atkin and Decloedt all attended Heywood School, Cinderford, Dench first met lead singer Atkin while working as a graphic artist at the Centre for Environmental Education, hanging out in lunch breaks at a nearby music shop where Atkin worked. Legend surrounding the meaning of the group's initials alternates between Epson Mad Funkers and Ecstasy Mother Fuckers.

1990

Nov Signed to EMI Records imprint Parlophone by Nick Mander, and currently touring the UK as support act to Adamski (having completed an earlier slot behind Boo Yaa Tribe), EMF's debut single, *Unbelievable*, recently introduced to the nation's youth at the annual televised "Smash Hits Party", hits UK #3. Its irresistible anthemic-pop hook will spur the group-written smash to global success throughout 1991.
Dec [16] The group performs at London's Marquee, having recently played a gig in an underground cave in Gloucestershire.

1991

Jan [9] The band embarks on a 17-date UK tour at the Cambridge Junction, Cambridge, Cambs., set to end on the 30th at London's Town & Country Club.
Feb [9] Follow-up, *I Believe*, hits UK #6.
[14] EMF makes an unscheduled 20-minute appearance at a Carter The Unstoppable Sex Machine gig at London's ULU, in aid of Cancer Research, and is greeted with "You're shit, you're shit", chanted by the crowd.
Apr [7] EMF is voted Best UK Newcomer at the DMC "World DJ Awards" in London.
May [4] *Children* reaches UK #19.
[7] The group embarks on its first major UK tour, a 15-date trek, at Exeter University, Exeter, Devon, set to climax on the 25th at Leicester Polytechnic, Leics.
[18] Their debut album, ***Schubert Dip***, enters at its UK #3 peak. (The album will not be without controversy. EMI will be censured in the House of Commons for its refusal to use parental advisory stickers on the album, and the band has to recut the track *Lies*, after objections from Yoko Ono about the group's sampled use of Mark Chapman's voice.)
June [22] ***Schubert Dip*** reaches US #12.
July [3] The group guests on C4-TV's "The Best Of The Word".
[8] North American tour opens at Le Spectrum, Montreal, PQ, Canada.
[12] EMF appears at the New Music Seminar in New York, NY.
[20] *Unbelievable* tops the US chart, earning a gold sales disc.
Aug [31] *Lies* debuts at its UK #28 peak.
Sept [5] The band performs *Unbelievable* live via satellite from London's Town & Country, for the annual MTV Awards ceremony being held at the Universal Amphitheatre, Universal City, CA.
[10] ***Schubert Dip*** is certified platinum by the RIAA.
Oct [27] EMF is named Best British Group at the **Smash Hits** Poll Winners Awards.
Nov [21] The group guests on NBC-TV's "Late Night With David Letterman".
[23] *Lies* reaches US #18.
Dec [3] During a US tour, the band grosses $13,239 at the Spreckels Theater, San Diego, CA, supported by Carter USM.
[28] The group appears on ITV's "Amnesty International's Big 30 Concert".

1992

Jan [9] The band performs a charity gig at Cinderford Dean Snooker & Bowls Centre, for the blind.
Feb [11] The group interrupts the Ralph Jezzard co-produced sessions at Wessex Sound Studios to appear on C4-TV's "Return To The Dome".
Apr [21] EMF embarks on a nine-date UK tour at London's Camden Underworld, set to end on May 2nd at Coventry's Polytechnic.
May [2] EP *Unexplained* bows at its UK #18 peak.
[11] EMF appears on BBC2-TV's "Dance Energy

House Party".
June [6] They guest on ITV's "Tom Jones : The Right Time", duetting with the show's star on *Unbelievable*.
July The group makes a promotional tour of the US.
Aug [1] They take part in the "Thurles Feile Festival".
[29] EMF participates in the second day of the 20th annual "Reading Festival", Reading, Berks.
Sept [1] The band embarks on 28-date UK tour at the Norwich UEA, set to end on October 15th at the Guildhall, Portsmouth, Hants. (During the tour they are thrown out of a Britannia Hotel at 5:00 a.m. during an EMI sales conference.)
[19] *They're Here*, available as a Cenobite remix by Jezzard and a Mosh mix by Joey Beltram, with the CD format containing a cover of Traffic's *Low Spark Of High Heeled Boys*, debuts at its UK #29 peak.
Oct [10] Their sophomore album, ***Stigma***, debuts at UK #19 peak.
Nov [28] The extracted *It's You* reaches UK #23.
Dec [9] The group plays at the Bank, New York, during a short North American tour.
[16] They guest on NBC-TV's "The Tonight Show".

1993

June [4] The band plays a charity gig at Cinderford Dean Centre, their local snooker hall.

1995

Feb [25] *Perfect Day*, with Holger Czukay and Johnny Dollar remixes, debuts at its UK #27 peak.
Mar [18] ***Cha Cha Cha*** reaches UK #30 in its week of entry.
[23] A UK and Irish tour begins at the Tivoli Theatre, Dublin, set to end on April 17th at Bristol University's Anson Rooms, Avon, as part of the "Sound City Fest".
July [1] The group guests on BBC1-TV's "Steve Wright's People Show".
[8] *I'm A Believer*, with comedians Vic Reeves and Bob Mortimer, debuts at its UK #3 peak.
Oct [28] *Afro King* charts for a week at UK #51.

EN VOGUE

Terry Ellis (vocals); **Cindy Herron** (vocals); **Maxine Jones** (vocals); **Dawn Robinson** (vocals)

1990

July [21] The all-female quartet, formed in the San Francisco, CA Bay area in 1988 by beauty queen Herron (b. Sept. 26, 1965, San Francisco), Jones (b. Jan. 16, 1966, Paterson, NJ), the pair first meeting in 1986 while performing in a San Francisco stage production, Ellis (b. Sept. 5, 1966, Houston, TX), who met Herron at an audition in Houston, and Robinson (b. Nov. 28, 1968, New London, CT), who became friends with Jones at their local hairdresser's, has auditioned and signed to the production team of Thomas McElroy and Denzil Foster (fresh from their success with Timex Social Club and Tony!, Toni!, Tone!), who create a latter-day Supremes-like, synchronized funky-diva image and sound around the performers' powerful four octave-range R&B vocals. Securing them a deal with Atlantic Records, En Vogue's debut single, *Hold On*, hits US #2, earning a platinum disc for million-plus sales, having already hit #5 in the UK in May, where the follow-up, *Lies*, is currently peaking at #44, while the group's maiden album, ***Born To Sing***, including six cuts co-written by the group with producers McElroy and Foster, reaches US #21 and UK #23 (June [2]).
Oct [13] *Lies*, already a US R&B chart-topper, reaches US #38.
Nov [21] The group sings at the Summit, Houston, during a current US tour supporting M.C. Hammer.

1991

Jan Herron makes her movie debut in "Juice".
Feb [9] The third extract from their debut album, *You Don't Have To Worry*, tops the US R&B survey.
Mar [12] They nab the Best R&B/Urban Contemporary Single, Group Or Duo trophy at the fifth annual Soul Train Music Awards, held at the Shrine Auditorium, Los Angeles, CA.
Apr [12] En Vogue embarks on a 35-date, supporting Freddie Jackson, at the Music Hall, Cincinnati, OH.
June [10] The group participates in the live pay-per-view TV special "James Brown - Living In America".
Oct [19] Having wound up their "Born To Sing" roadwork, ***Simply Mad About The Mouse***, to which En Vogue has contributed a track, debuts at its US #160 peak. (Atlantic, meanwhile, issues ***Remix To Sing***, a six-cut remix album of existing songs augmented by their new treatment of the seasonal *Silent Nite*.)
Dec En Vogue, currently seen in Spike Lee-directed Diet Coke US TV commercials, graces the cover of **Essence**.

1992

Mar [21] The group guests on NBC-TV's "Saturday Night Live".
Apr [11] Their sophomore effort, the sassy ***Funky Divas***, once again largely written and produced by McElroy and Foster, debuts at its US #8 peak.
May [13] En Vogue appears on syndicated TV's "The Arsenio Hall Show".
[16] Dominating the US Top 40 and Urban radio, *My Lovin' (You're Never Gonna Get It)* hits US #2, behind Kris Kross' *Jump*.
[23] *My Lovin' (You're Never Gonna Get It)* hits UK #4.
June [6] ***Funky Divas*** initially reaches UK #26.
July [8] The group guests on NBC-TV's "The Tonight Show".
Aug [15] *Giving Him Something He Can Feel*, featured in the movie "Sparkle", debuts at its UK #44 peak.
Sept [9] En Vogue performs *Free Your Mind* at the ninth annual MTV Video Music Awards, held at the Pauley Pavilion, Los Angeles, also winning the Best Choreography category for "My Lovin' (Never Gonna Get It)".
[12] Their version of Curtis Mayfield's *Giving Him Something He Can Feel* hits US #6.
Oct [31] *Free Your Mind* hits US #8.
Nov [28] *Free Your Mind*, paired with a reissued *Giving Him Something He Can Feel*, reaches UK #16.

1993

Jan [16] *Give It Up, Turn It Loose* debuts at its UK #22 peak.
[20] En Vogue performs the *Star Spangled Banner* and two of its own songs at MTV's "1993 Rock & Roll Inaugural Ball" in Washington, DC.
[21] The group guest stars as schoolgirls on NBC-TV's "A Different World". (They will follow this next month, with appearances in Fox-TV's "In Living Color" and "Roc".)
[25] They collect the Favorite Album, Soul/R&B trophy at the 20th annual American Music Awards, held at the Shrine Auditorium.
[30] *Give It Up, Turn It Loose* reaches US #15.
Feb [13] ***Funky Divas***, charting for a second time, hits UK #4.
[15] A press statement confirms that En Vogue has been selected to appear in forthcoming Nike TV commercials in the US.
[24] They perform *Never Gonna Get It* at the 35th annual Grammy Awards from the Shrine Auditorium.
Mar [4] They are voted Best R&B Group in **Rolling Stone**'s 1993 Music Awards Critics' Picks
[8] ***Funky Divas*** wins the Outstanding Urban/ Contemporary Album Or EP and Outstanding Female Vocalist categories at the 1993 Bay Area Music Awards, at the Bill Graham Civic Auditorium, San Francisco.
[9] En Vogue wins Best R&B/Soul Album (***Funky Divas***) and the Sammy Davis Jr. Award as Entertainer(s) Of The Year at the seventh annual Soul Train Music Awards, held at the Shrine Auditorium.
Apr [10] *Love Don't Love You* charts for a week at UK #64.
May [10] En Vogue performs at Wembley Arena, Wembley, Middx., at the end of a nine-date European tour of Germany, Holland, Belgium, France and England.
[22] *Love Don't Love You* reaches US #36.
Sept [2] En Vogue wins the Best R&B Video, Best Choreography and Best Dance Video categories for "Free Your Mind" at the 10th annual MTV Video Music Awards, held at the Universal Amphitheatre, Universal City, CA, as the group embarks on a Luther Vandross-supporting tour at the Target Center, Minneapolis, MN.
Oct [16] *Runaway Love*, featuring F Mob, debuts at its US #51 peak, having done the same in the UK at #36 on the 9th.
[30] ***Runaway Love*** makes US #49.
Nov [29-30] The group performs at Wembley Arena, during the UK leg of its current tour. (They will subsequently quit the tour, citing Herron's pregnancy, but the rumor mill has the stress of working with Vandross as the reason.)

1994

Jan [5] They are named Outstanding Duo Or Group at the NAACP's 26th annual Image Awards in Pasadena, CA.
Feb [7] The group wins Soul/R&B Band, Duo Or Group at the 21st annual American Music Awards at the Shrine Auditorium.
[26] *Whatta Man*, an R&B/hip-hop meeting with Salt-n-Pepa, hits US #3.
Apr [2] *Whatta Man* hits UK #7.
Sept [8] *Whatta Man* wins the Best Dance Video, Best R&B Video and Best Choreography categories at the 11th annual MTV Video Music Awards.

1995

Nov [14] While the band is hiatus, Ellis releases her maiden solo effort ***Southern Gal***, produced by Foster and McElroy. (Robinson is also working on her solo debut, with a new En Vogue project not due until 1997.)

BRIAN ENO

1971

Jan Electronics whizz Eno (b. Brian Peter George St. John le Baptiste de la Salle Eno, May 15, 1948, Suffolk), having studied at Winchester School of Art between 1966 and 1969, where he becomes president of the Students' Union and meets saxophonist Andy Mackay, has made his first experimental recording in 1965, a slowed-down tape of a metal lampstand being struck, over-dubbed with a friend's rendition of a poem. A self-proclaimed "non-musician", he is nevertheless an accomplished synthesizer player by the time Mackay, who has joined Roxy Music, invites him to join the band, initially as soundman and technical adviser, but then to play Mackay's keyboards. He is responsible for much of the groundbreaking style of Roxy's sound and, bizarre and androgynous in appearance, is an eye-catching contribution to its colorful image.

1973

July After two albums, ***Roxy Music*** and ***For Your Pleasure***, ten months of touring and hospitalization after being knocked down by a car, personality clashes (notably with the band's frontman, Ferry) result in Eno leaving for a solo career.
Nov A collaboration with King Crimson's Robert Fripp produces ***No Pussyfooting***, released by Island Records.

1974

Mar [9] His heavily- improvised solo debut, ***Here Come The Warm Jets***, reaches UK #26 and will make US #151, featuring Fripp and Roxy Music guitarist Manzanera.
June [1] Eno takes part in a concert at London's Rainbow Theatre with Kevin Ayers, ex-Velvet Underground members John Cale and Nico and others, which is recorded for subsequent release as ***June 1st 1974***.
Nov Equally-inventive and experimental second solo effort, ***Taking Tiger Mountain By Strategy***, is

released, based on the rustic versus technological contradiction inherent in its title, which is taken from a Chinese revolutionary opera.

1975

Apr He works with John Cale on the latter's ***Slow Dazzle***. (This partnership will continue with ***Helen Of Troy***, to be released in November. During the year he will also work on Phil Manzanera's ***Diamond Head*** and Robert Wyatt's ***Ruth Is Stranger Than Richard***; produce Robert Calvert's ***Lucky Lief And The Longships***; issue a boxed set of writings, ***Oblique Strategy***; make a lecture tour of UK universities and undertake a concert trek with pub-rock band the Winkies.)
Nov Further Fripp collaboration, ***Evening Star***, is released by E.G. Records.
Dec Completing a busy year, he launches his own Island-licensed record label, Obscure, to release ***Discreet Music***, which marks a major departure from his earlier, more vocal work that will lead to his increasingly avant-garde "ambient" projects. He has also released the 14-track (of which only five feature vocals) improvisational ***Another Green World***, a less manic follow-up to ***Tiger Mountain***.

1976

Aug Taking advantage of a Roxy Music hiatus, Manzanera puts together the group 801, with Eno, Bill McCormick (bass, vocals), Francis Monkman (piano, clarinet), Lloyd Watson (guitar, vocals) and Simon Phillips (drums). The group plays three times, with the final gig, at London's Queen Elizabeth Hall, recorded for ***801 Live***, which will be released by year's end. Eno spends the latter part of the year working with David Bowie on his album, ***Low***, contributing vocals, synthesizer and guitar segments and co-writing the track *Warzawa*. His collaborations with Bowie will prove long-term, and he subsequently co-writes the hit single *Heroes*, in 1977, and produces 1979's ***The Lodger***.

1977

May Emerging US band, Talking Heads, performs at London's Rock Garden club after supporting the Ramones on a UK tour. Eno is present on one of the two nights, meets the band and invites them to his house, thus beginning a significant musical alliance.

1978

June Talking Heads' ***More Songs About Buildings And Food*** marks the advent of Eno's production collaboration with the band.
[17] Eno's first album in two years, and his last "rock" release, ***Before And After Science***, climbs to US #171, and features his most melodic and formally-structured song to date, *Here She Comes*. Unhappy with the album's vocal focus, Eno will resolve to record only instrumental music hereafter (for his own releases).
Aug Devo's debut album, ***Are We Not Men?***, is produced by Eno (he will also oversee maiden recordings by Ultravox).
Oct [21] ***Music For Films***, Eno's first true "ambient" album is released, charting briefly at UK #55, as he continues to promote the discovery of "a totally new way of listening to music". Critical reactions are mixed, but the album, and its successors, all featuring gentle, contemplative instrumental sounds, develop a faithful cult audience. (By year's end, Eno also records two albums with German avant-garde group Cluster: ***Cluster And Eno*** and ***Eno, Moebius And Roedelius - After The Heat***.)

1979

Mar ***Music For Airports*** is the first album released on Eno's Ambient label. It will gradually gather over 200,000 worldwide sales in 10 years.

1980

Eno's ambient vision progresses with the release of ***Fourth World Volume 1 Possible Musics*** (recorded with Jon Hassell) and ***The Plateaux Of Mirror*** (recorded with Harold Budd). Both are issued on the Editions E.G. label, which has been established by and for avante-garde artists including Eno and, later, Daniel Lanois, Roger Eno and Laraaji. (Roxy Music will join the main E.G. label in December 1981.)

1981

Mar [7] Having successfully produced two further Talking Heads albums, ***Fear Of Music*** and ***Remain In Light***, ***My Life In The Bush Of Ghosts***, a collaboration with the band's founder David Byrne, reaches UK #29 and will make US #44.

1982

May [8] Eno's ***Ambient 4 - On Land*** peaks at UK #93.

1984

U2 vocalist Bono phones Eno, at the suggestion of the band's Larry Mullen, to ask him to produce their forthcoming album, explaining the band's desire to progress creatively. The sessions, recorded in an old Irish castle and co-produced by sometime Eno engineer Daniel Lanois, result in much Eno-inspired experimentation, with spontaneous composition and the introduction of non-traditional sound recordings.
Oct When the U2 album ***The Unforgettable Fire*** is issued, much of the experimental material is absent, though Eno's influence remains. It will become a major international success and confirm Eno as an influential and innovative backroom figure and a highly sought-after collaborator.

1987

U2, Eno and Lanois (the producers largely credited with its triumphs) reunite for the subsequent Album Of The Year Grammy Award-winning ***The Joshua Tree***, which becomes the band's most successful album to date. With Eno's entire back catalog now based at E.G., the label reissues his earlier releases on compact disc, as well as his most recent ambient recordings, 1985's ***Thursday Afternoon***, ***The Pearl*** (recorded with Budd in 1986) and ***Apollo*** (a 1984 collaboration with his brother, Roger, and Lanois). An 11-track compilation, ***Desert Island Selection***, rounds up highlights from his 1973-78 rock period.

1992

July [20] Eno presents an illustrated lecture, "Perfume, Defence And David Bowie's Wedding", at the Sadler's Wells Theatre, London.
Sept [14] With Land Records having released his first vocal album in 14 years, ***Wrong Way Up*** in November 1990, a reunion project with John Cale, recorded at Eno's 24-track home studio in Suffolk, where he has also been developing an aphrodisiac male scent ("it works for me anyway"), and continuing his parallel career at the forefront of the ambient movement and as a highly successful rock producer, including an album for Carmel in 1991, Eno's latest release, ***Nerve Net***, with guests Fripp, Tench, John Paul Jones and Markus Draws, makes UK #70. (It is closely followed by the issue of ***The Shutov Assemble***, a collection of his ambient highlights since 1985, principally compiled for the Russian painter, Sergei Shutov, who, having met Eno, has bemoaned the lack of availability of the musician's work in Russia.)

1993

Nov [16] ***Brian Eno II***, the first of two three-CD boxed sets, is released by Virgin.

1994

Feb [14] Eno wins Best British Producer category (for James' ***Laid*** and U2's ***Zooropa***) at the 13th annual BRIT Awards held at London's Alexandra Palace.
Mar [15] He wins the 13th Frankfurt Music Prize in Frankfurt, Germany.
Sept [24] ***Wah Wah***, a collaboration with the group James, reaches UK #1 in its week of entry.

1995

May [23] Eno is honored with the Radio 1 Award for Continuing Innovation In Music at the 40th annual Ivor Novello Award, held at London's Grosvenor House.
Sept [16] ***Help***, a various artists album, featuring Paul McCartney, Paul Weller, Blur, Suede, Radiohead, Sinead O'Connor and Stone Roses among others, in aid of the War Child charity with Eno serving as executive producer, tops the UK Compilation chart.
Oct [14] ***Spinner***, an ambient collaboration with Jah Wobble, peaks at UK #71.
Nov [7] Eno wins the Inspiration Award, with David Bowie (with whom he has recently reunited to produce Bowie's ***Outside*** project), at the annual **Q** Awards at London's Park Lane Hotel.

1996

Feb [19] Eno is once again named Best Producer at the 1996 BRIT Awards held at London's Earl's Court Exhibition Centre. He also shares the Freddie Mercury Award (with Radiohead's Tom Yorke) for their work on ***Help***.
Mar [26] Warner Bros. Records releases ***Songs In The Key Of X***, music from and inspired by the Fox-TV show "X-Files" including a collaboration by Eno with Elvis Costello.
see also: **ROXY MUSIC**

ENYA

1982

Educated from age 11-17 at a convent in Millford, Eire, and having joined her relatives as a keyboardist and vocalist in the Irish band Clannad in 1980, appearing uncredited on ***Cran Ull***, released in Eire on Tara Records and this year's ***Fuain***, Enya (b. Eithne Ni Bhraonain, May 17, 1961, Gweedore, County Donegal, Eire), a classically trained pianist daughter of showband leader Lee O. Braonain and mother Maira, a music teacher at Gweedore Comprehensive School, has elected to pursue a solo career and forms a musical partnership with producer (and Clannad manager) Nicky Ryan and lyricist Roma Ryan, both of whom encourage the artiste to write her own music. With Roma sending Enya's tapes to a number of film producers, David Puttnam will be first to use her, for the score to his 1985 feature "The Frog Prince".

1987

Feb BBC Records releases ***The Celts***, the 70-minute soundtrack to the BBC-TV series "The Celts". The producers, impressed by Enya's first piece, *The March Of The Celts*, commissioned her to compose the entire soundtrack.
June [27] ***The Celts***, now renamed and re-promoted as ***Enya***, spends four weeks on the UK chart, peaking at #69. (The album will revert to its original title when successfully reissued in 1992.)

1988

Oct [29] Having been signed to WEA Records by label boss Rob Dickins, her first single, the unique *Orinoco Flow* (named after Venezuela's Orinoco River and including a lyrical reference to Dickins) hits UK #1 and showcases Enya's ethereal vocal style and meticulously-built oceanic synthesized sound. It is taken from the equally innovative album ***Watermark***, which hits UK #5 the following week during a 63-week chart tenure. Produced by Nicky Ryan (with lyrics by Roma), the part-English part-Gaelic set, composed by its performer, is the result of hundreds of hours in the Ryans' home studio, overdubbing scores of vocal tracks to produce a multi-layered cathedral of sound.
Dec The extracted follow-up, *Evening Falls*, peaks at UK #20.

1989

Feb [4] ***Watermark*** enters the US chart, eventually reaching #25 and multi-platinum status (its global tally will eventually top eight million).
Apr [15] Released in the US by Geffen Records as *Orinoco Flow (Sail Away)*, the single peaks at #24.
June *Storms In Africa (Part II)* makes UK #41. (During

the following year while Enya prepares her third album, music from ***Watermark*** will be featured in the film soundtracks to both "L.A. Story" and "Green Card".)

1991

Nov [2] Previewing her second WEA album, *Caribbean Blue* reaches UK #13.
[16] ***Shepherd Moons***, recorded at her home in Eire with the Ryans, debuts at UK #1.
Dec [14] Emotionally-stirring excerpt, *How Can I Keep From Singing*, reaches UK #32.

1992

Mar [28] ***Shepherd Moons*** reaches US #17, while *Caribbean Blue* peaks at US #79. The album, once again certified double platinum in the US, will remain in pole position on the Top Adult Alternative/New Age album chart for over one year, ahead of the also still-charting ***Watermark*** and ***Enya*** (which has been released in North America by Atlantic Records).
May [26] The soundtrack film to the Tom Cruise-starring movie "Far And Away" is released including Enya's *Book Of Days*.
Aug [8] *Book Of Days* hits UK #10.
Nov [21] Title cut from her 1987 album, *The Celts*, reaches UK #29.
[28] Reissued ***The Celts*** debuts at its UK #10 peak.

1993

Feb [24] ***Shepherd's Moon*** wins the Best New Age Album category at the 35th annual Grammy Awards held at the Shrine Auditorium, Los Angeles, CA.
Apr [14] Enya is named Top Irish Female Artist at the annual IRMA (Irish Recorded Music Industry) Awards, held at the National Concert Hall, Dublin, Eire.

1995

Nov [25] Taken from her forthcoming new album, *Anywhere Is* hits UK #7.
Dec [9] With her global record sales to date put at 18,961,754, Enya's new album ***The Memory Of Trees*** hits UK #5. Continuing in a similar vein to its predecessors, it has once again been co-written with producer Nicky Ryan, at Aigle Studio, and includes a note of thanks, in Gaelic, to executive producer Rob Dickins.
[30] ***The Memory Of Trees*** reaches US #18 and immediately heads to the top of the US New Age survey, displacing ***Shepherd's Moon***.

ERASURE

Vince Clarke (keyboards); **Andy Bell** (vocals)

1985

Songwriter and expert keyboardist Clarke (b. July 3, 1961, Basildon, Essex), who has already found success with Depeche Mode, Yazoo (paired with Alison Moyet) and ad-hoc project the Assembly, all for Daniel Miller's independent Mute label, plans, together with producer Eric "E.C." Radcliffe, to record a ten-track album with ten different guest vocalists. The project proves impractical and, instead, Clarke invites Bell (b. Apr. 25, 1964, Peterborough, Cambs.), an ex-choirboy who has been with the band the Void, to join him in his latest venture, Erasure. Clarke has discovered his new partner after auditioning 42 hopefuls who have answered a "vocalist wanted" ad in the UK magazine **Melody Maker**.
Oct Debut single, *Who Needs Love Like That*, on Mute, climbs to UK #55.
Nov *Heavenly Action* bubbles under the UK chart, at #100, and a tour is cancelled.
Dec After a short promotional visit to Germany, the duo makes its UK live debut at London's Heaven club.

1986

Jan [23] They perform at the Hacienda, Manchester, Gtr. Manchester, during their first UK tour, which includes backing singers Jim Burkman and Derek Ian.
Apr *Oh L'Amour* makes UK #85. (It will be successfully covered by Dollar in 1988.)
June [14] Their debut album, ***Wonderland***, produced by Flood and featuring guitarist Maurice Michael, bassist Dave Foster and saxophonist Gary Barnacle, reaches UK #71. It sets the style for all subsequent Erasure releases: Mute-released, synthesizer-led, electro-dance pop - usually uptempo - recordings, mostly co-written by the duo (though musically steered by Clarke) and highlighted by Bell's dramatic vocal style, heavily reminiscent of Moyet.
Dec [13] *Sometimes*, an earlier club hit throughout Europe, hits UK #2.

1987

Mar [28] Similarly synthesizer-driven *It Doesn't Have To Be* reaches UK #12.
Apr [11] Their sophomore album, ***The Circus***, hits UK #6, as the duo takes "The Circus" tour to Europe and the US.
June Erasure is the opening act on ITV's first "The Roxy" Network Chart show, performing *Victim Of Love*, which hits UK #7, while the live performance video "Erasure : Live At The Seaside" is released by Virgin Video.
July ***The Circus*** peaks at US #190.
Aug Erasure supports Duran Duran on their US tour.
Oct [31] *Two Ring Circus*, featuring six remixes and three re-recordings of the original album ***The Circus***, hits UK #6 on the singles chart (and will also make US #186 on the albums chart).

1988

Mar [19] Ballad, *Ship Of Fools*, hits UK #6.
Apr [14] The duo embarks on a sellout "The Innocents" UK tour.
[30] Stephen Hague-produced ***The Innocents*** debuts at UK #1. Including 12 Clarke/Bell compositions and a cover of the Ike & Tina Turner hit, *River Deep, Mountain High*, it will peak at US #49.
June [18] *Chains Of Love* reaches UK #11 and will make US #12.
July [13] The band begins an extensive US tour.
Oct [22] Acoustic guitar-driven *A Little Respect* hits UK #4.

1989

Jan [7] Released in December 1988, the seasonal *Crackers International E.P.*, including the hot airplay cuts *Stop* and *The Hardest Part*, hits UK #2, selling over 500,000 domestic copies.
Feb [13] Erasure wins the Best British Group category at the eighth annual BRIT Awards, at the Royal Albert Hall, London.
Mar [4] *A Little Respect* reaches US #14, as Virgin Video's "The Innocents" package tops the UK Video chart.
May Released as a mini-album in the US, ***Crackers International*** makes #73.
July [18-19] Bell participates in the seventh "Prince's Trust Rock Gala", at the National Exhibiton Centre, Birmingham, W. Midlands, with Joan Baez, Van Morrison, Alexander O'Neal, Level 42 and others.
[22] *Stop!* makes US #97.
Oct [28] ***Wild!*** enters the UK chart at #1, where it will stay for two weeks (also reaching US #57). The extracted *Drama!* hits UK #4, with *You Surround Me* making UK #15 in December.

1990

Mar [11-12] The duo plays sellout dates at the Great Western Forum, Inglewood, CA, during current US tour.
[24] Extracted from ***Wild!***, *Blue Savannah* hits UK #3, the duo's seventh Top 10 UK hit.
June [9] *Star* peaks at UK #11. During the year, ***Wild!***, ***The Circus*** and ***The Innocents*** will all re-chart in their home territory.
July BMG Video releases "Wild!", which becomes another best seller in the UK.
Aug [8] A major US tour ends at the Jones Beach Theatre, Wantagh, NY.
Oct Erasure contributes *Too Darn Hot* (from the 1948 "Kiss Me Kate" musical) to ***Red Hot + Blue***, an anthology of Cole Porter songs to benefit AIDS education, and will also be featured duetting with Lene Lovich on the February 1991 animal rights-supporting release, ***Tame Yourself***, performing *Animal Rage*.

1991

May [2] *Blue Savannah* is named the Most Performed Work Of 1990 at the 36th annual Ivor Novello Awards lunch, at the Grosvenor House Hotel, London.
June [15] The band appears on BBC1-TV's "Paramount City".
[29] *Chorus* debuts at its UK #3 peak, set to make US #83 on Aug [17].
Sept [28] *Love To Hate You* hits UK #4.
Oct [26] Continuing a familiar musical and chart pattern, ***Chorus***, recorded at the Chateau du Pape Studios in Germany, debuts at UK #1. Meanwhile, ***The Innocents*** becomes the band's first RIAA-certified platinum disc in the US.
Nov [2] ***Chorus*** bows at its US #29 peak.
Dec [7] Having performed at the Red Hot & Dance Aids benefit concert on December 1st, the EP *Am I Right?* bows at its UK #15 peak.

1992

Jan [11] *Am I Right?* remix debuts at its UK #22 peak.
Mar [3] The duo is featured on C4-TV's "Return To The Dome".
Apr [4] *Breath Of Life* hits UK #8.
June [6] The band is featured duetting with the host on *The Ballad Of Lucy Jordan* on ITV's "Tom Jones : The Right Time".
[7] The duo embarks on a UK tour with 13 dates at the Apollo Theatre, Manchester, Gtr. Manchester.
July [13] Heralding a substantial revival of '70s Swedish pop act Abba, Erasure's EP *Abba-esque*, produced by Dave Bascombe, enters the UK chart at #1, where it will lodge for five weeks. (Its success will prompt the UK #1 reissue of an Abba's greatest hits collection and will spawn the novelty rise of Abba/Erasure-mimicking act, Bjorn Again.)
[25] ***Abba-esque***, categorized as an album in the US, makes #85.
[27-29] The band performs three final nights of a 15-date residence at the Hammersmith Odeon, London, during a summer UK tour. Prior to performing around the rest of Europe, they will have played 51 sellout UK dates.
Sept [21] Erasure plays at Spodek Sporthall, Katowice, Poland, during the European leg of the tour.
Oct [27] The duo begins a sold-out residency at the Beacon Theatre, New York, NY, to November 8th (excluding the 29th) during a North American concert visit which will also include eight dates at the Wiltern Theatre in Los Angeles, CA, beginning on the 17th. Billed as the "Phantasmagorical Entertainment Tour", the performances feature eight dancers and two backing vocalists.
Nov [7] *Who Needs Love (Like That)*, a remix of the duo's 1985 debut, enters UK chart at its #10 peak.
[28] After an unbroken six-year run of 18 Top 30 UK singles successes, the appropriate collection, ***Pop! - The First 20 Hits***, enters the UK chart at #1, remaining charted for four months, as the duo plays the first of two dates at San Francisco's Warfield Theatre.

1993

Jan [16] ***Pop! - The First 20 Hits*** makes US #112.
Feb [16] Bell duets with k.d. lang, performing *No More Tears (Enough Is Enough)* at the 12th annual BRIT Awards, held at the Alexandra Palace, London. (The song will be featured in the forthcoming "Coneheads" motion picture.)
Dec [23] "Erasure : The Tank, The Swan And The Balloon Live!" airs on BBC1-TV.
[24] Bell guests on C4-TV's "Camp Christmas".

1994

Apr [23] *Always* debuts at its UK #4 peak.
[24] "The O Zone Erasure Special" airs on BBC2-TV.
May [21] The band appears on BBC2-TV's "Later

With Jools Holland".
[28] ***I Say, I Say, I Say*** enters the UK chart at #1.
June [4] ***I Say, I Say, I Say*** debuts at its US #18 peak.
July [30] The extracted *Run To The Sun* bows at its UK #6 high.
Aug [3] Erasure guests on ITV's "Michael Ball Show".
[6] *Always* reaches US #20.
Dec [4] The duo performs at the annual **Smash Hits** Poll Winners' Party.
[10] *I Love Saturday* debuts at its UK #20 peak.

1995

Feb [2] BBC1-TV's "Top Of The Pops", using Clarke's new theme for the first time, airs.
[18] The duo guests on BBC2-TV's "Later With Jools Holland".
Aug Soundtrack album ***Clive Barker's Lord Of Illusions***, including the new Erasure cut *Magic Moments*, is released.
Sept [23] *Stay With Me* debuts at its UK #15 peak.
Oct Erasure performs its first ever acoustic show at Spy in New York, with guest Nick Johnston.
Nov [4] ***Erasure***, co-produced by the duo with Gareth Jones and Thomas Fehlmann, reaches UK #14 in its week of entry.
[11] ***Erasure*** debuts at its US #82 peak.
Dec [9] *Fingers And Thumbs (Cold Summer's Day)* bows at its UK #20 high.
see also: **DEPECHE MODE, YAZOO**

DAVID ESSEX

1964

Son of an East End docker, Essex (b. David Albert Cook, July 23, 1947, Plaistow, London), having left school in 1963, is the drummer in semi-professional East London group the Everons when **Daily Express** critic Derek Bowman, his subsequent manager, sees the group play at a pub in Walthamstow, London. Essex's debut recording, *And The Tears Come Tumbling Down*, released in April 1965, will be the first of seven non-charting Fontana label-released singles over a subsequent two-year period. Always maintaining dual acting and music careers, he will initially appear as a beatnik in the Lynn Redgrave/Rita Tushingham-starring 1967 film "Smashing Time".

1971

Oct Having failed to score with further releases in 1968, with one-off singles for Uni (*Love Story*) and Pye (*Just For Tonight*), and in 1969, the Decca-issued *That Takes Me Back* and *Day The Earth Stood Still*, Essex finally secures a major break, landing the lead role as Jesus to Jeremy Irons' Judas Iscariot in Jean Michael Tebelak's religious-rock musical "Godspell", on London's West End stage, first at the Roundhouse, then at Wyndham's Theatre. (After a year of success, he is contacted by UK film producer David Puttnam, who offers him a major movie role.)

1972

Oct [23] Essex begins a seven-week break from "Godspell" to film "That'll Be The Day" with Ringo Starr, Keith Moon, Billy Fury, Dave Edmunds and others on the Isle of Wight. He plays aspiring rock star Jim MacLaine in Ray Connolly's drama, set in the UK of the late '50s.

1973

Apr [12] "That'll Be The Day" premieres in London, becoming a critical and box-office success.
May Essex receives the Variety Club of Great Britain's Most Promising Newcomer Award.
Sept With Essex signed to CBS Records on the strength of his stage and screen popularity, his label debut, the self-penned *Rock On*, which evokes the nostalgia of his recent movie, hits UK #3, also launching him as a UK teen-idol pin-up.
Oct [18] A two-week media tour of Europe begins with an appearance on "Top Pop" in Holland.
Dec [8] *Lamplight* hits UK #7, while his maiden album, the self-written ***Rock On***, produced by Jeff Wayne, who will become an integral part of Essex's success, also peaks at UK #7.

1974

Feb [18] Essex begins filming "Stardust", the sequel to "That'll Be The Day". Chronicling MacLaine's rise and fall as a pop star, it co-stars Adam Faith and Larry Hagman.
Mar [9] *Rock On* hits US #5, eventually selling over one million copies in the US, as its parent album ***Rock On*** is set to make US #22.
May [18] *America* reaches UK #32.
June [22] *Lamplight* peaks at US #71, his final US chart disc.
Oct [24] "Stardust" premieres in London.
Nov [16] Self-penned pop ditty, *Gonna Make You A Star*, tops the UK chart for the first of three weeks, while ***David Essex*** will hit UK #2 on Dec [14], the combination proving to be his commercial apex.

1975

Jan [18] *Stardust*, the title song from the recent movie, hits UK #7.
July [26] *Rollin' Stone* hits UK #5.
Oct [4] *Hold Me Close* tops the UK chart for the first of three weeks.
[11] Third Wayne-produced, Essex-written collaboration, ***All The Fun Of The Fair***, hits UK #3. With UK soul outfit the Real Thing guesting as backing vocalists, the album features noted session musicians Chris Spedding (guitar), Mike Thorn (bass) and Barry de Souza (drums). (As his world tour comes to a close, Essex has been a sellout success in France, Germany, Australia, Spain, Japan and the US.)

1977

Jan [8] Following a year of declining UK chart success which has seen the lush ballad *If I Could* make #13 in January, the grandiose *City Lights* reach #24 in April, the live album ***On Tour*** stall at #51 in June, fourth studio set, ***Out On The Street***, peak at #31 on Nov [6], with the extracted *Coming Home* making #24 the following month, Essex tops the bill at the **Daily Mirror** Pop Club Awards, held at Bingley Hall, Stafford, Staffs.
Oct [8] *Cool Out Tonight*, his first self-produced effort, reaches UK #23, as ***Gold And Ivory***, his final recording for CBS, makes #29.

1978

Mar [25] Testing revival of Lorraine Ellison's soul classic, *Stay With Me Baby*, makes UK #45 during a month in which Essex produces five tracks (three of them written by him) for a forthcoming album by fellow cockney, Twiggy.
May He is named the Variety Club of Great Britain's Show Business Personality Of The Year.
June Essex signs a worldwide (except North America) recording deal with Phonogram.
July [1] Wayne's collaborative musical opus, ***The War Of The Worlds***, featuring Essex, enters the UK chart.
Sept Essex opens in the role of Ché Guevara in Tim Rice and Andrew Lloyd Webber's musical "Evita", on the London West End stage.
[23] His featured song, *Oh What A Circus*, his first release for Phonogram's Mercury label, hits UK #3.
Nov [4] *Brave New World* peaks at UK #55, as the CBS-issued 16-track greatest hits collection, ***The David Essex Album***, reaches UK #29.
Dec [2] His current UK tour is highlighted by a performance at the Empire Pool, Wembley, Middx.

1979

Mar [24] *Imperial Wizard*, the title track from Essex's forthcoming Mercury label debut, reaches UK #32.
Apr [14] ***Imperial Wizard*** (including *Oh What A Circus*) peaks at UK #12.

1980

May Essex stars in the critically-panned motorbike racing-themed movie, "Silver Dream Racer", opposite Beau Bridges, and is also responsible for writing and recording the film's soundtrack, from which *Silver Dream Machine*, aided by the movie's publicity, hits UK #4. While his next acting project the following year will see him return to the stage, portraying Lord Byron in a Young Vic production of "Childe Byron", he will release three albums by the end of 1982: ***Hot Love*** reaches UK #75, while its title track peaks at UK #57, both in June 1980; ***Be-Bop The Future*** fails to score in September 1981, while ***Stage-Struck*** makes UK #31 on Aug [7] 1982, spurred by its hit single, the UK #13, Aug [7]-peaking *Me And My Girl (Night Clubbing)*.

1983

Jan [1] With Essex having hosted a talent show for BBC1-TV during the summer of 1982, the TV-advertised album ***The Very Best Of David Essex***, a compilation of CBS and Mercury hits, makes UK #37.
[15] Ballad, *A Winter's Tale*, co-written by Tim Rice and its producer, Mike Batt, hits UK #2, behind Phil Collins' *You Can't Hurry Love*.
Oct Essex, as chief mutineer Fletcher Christian, co-stars with Frank Finlay in "Mutiny" (whose cast also includes Essex's current girlfriend, Sinitta), a musical version of "Mutiny On The Bounty", written by Essex. Initially released as a studio production on record only, with backing by the Royal Philharmonic Orchestra, the Batt-produced ***Mutiny*** reaches UK #39. Extracted *Tahiti* hits UK #8.
Dec Continuing Essex's association with Batt, ***The Whisper*** makes UK #67, while *You're In My Heart* peaks at UK #59. It will be followed by 1984's non-charting ***This One's For You*** and a one-off March 1985 single, *Falling Angels Riding*, which reaches UK #29.

1986

Dec K-tel TV-advertised album, ***Centre Stage***, containing Essex's versions of hit songs from stage and screen, makes UK #82. His remaining chart item of the decade will be *Myfanwy*, which makes UK #41 in May 1987 (taken from the musical "Betjeman", which consists of works by the late UK Poet Laureate, Sir John Betjeman, set to music by UK DJ Mike Read). Starring as a lecherous lock-keeper in the October 1988-premiering BBC1-TV sitcom "The River", Essex will release ***Touching The Ghost*** on his own Lamplight label the following year, while his debut hit composition, *Rock On*, will be revived by US actor Michael Damian and will hit US #1 on June [3] 1989.

1990

Sept [26] Essex embarks on a 37-date UK tour at the Huddersfield Town Hall, set to end on November 27th at the Mayflower, Southampton, Hants.

1991

June [9] Essex plays a sole London date at the Hammersmith Odeon.
Nov [2] With Castle Communications having released the CD retrospective ***The Collection*** in July 1990, a second, equally-comprehensive compilation, the Mercury-released, TV-advertised ***His Greatest Hits***, reaches UK #13. Currently completing a UK tour, Essex has set music to and produced the winning words from the Child To Child Lyric contest during October. (The winning song will be performed by Knowsley School, Liverpool on December 23rd in the National Youth Choir's Christmas Concert at the Royal Albert Hall.)

1992

Sept [29] Essex announces a plan for a student production of "Godspell" near Kampala, Uganda, as he begins a month-long post teaching drama and music at teacher's training college.

1993

Feb Essex completes recording sessions for his

forthcoming album on Lamplight, with producer Batt, at the Abbey Road Studios in London.
Apr [24] ***Cover Shot***, a collection of Essex's interpretations of 12 various pop classics, hits UK #3.
May [11] Having completed a two-year stint as president of Voluntary Service Overseas begun on September 29th 1990, and approaching a 30-year music, stage and screen career, he now completes a 39-date UK tour at St. David's Hall, Cardiff, Wales.
Oct [27] Essex opens as Tony Lumpkin, at the Queen's Theatre, Shaftesbury Avenue, London, in a new production of Oliver Goldsmith's "She Stoops To Conquer".

1994

Oct [22] TV-advertised ***Back To Back***, a further mix of covers and new self-written material, makes UK #33 in its week of entry.
Nov [26] His revival of Buddy Holly's *True Love Ways* with Catherine Zeta Jones bows at its UK #38 peak, his first chart single in over seven years.

1996

Mar [23] Following the release in the US of ***Living In England*** on the reactivated Cleveland International label in August the previous year, Essex' latest album, ***Missing You*** reaches UK #26.

GLORIA ESTEFAN

1973

Emilio Estefan (b. Mar. 4, 1953, Havana, Cuba), having left his native Cuba at 13 for Madrid, Spain, before settling in Miami, FL at 14, plays accordian in restaurants, when away from his day job in the marketing department at the rum beverage corporation Bacardi. His boss there has seen him performing at an Italian eaterie on Biscayne Boulevard and asks Estefan if he could hire him to play at a private party. Estefan invites bass player Juan Avila (b. 1956, Cuba) and drummer Enrique E. Garcia (b. 1958, Cuba), both Miami-raised, to help him provide dance music for the engagement, following which the trio begins a successful round of restaurant, wedding and party gigs as the Miami Latin Boys, later augmented by guitar, keyboards, horns and percussion.

1974

The daughter of a Cuban soldier and bodyguard to President Fulgencio Batista, Gloria (b. Gloria Fajardo, Sept. 1, 1957, Havana), who has moved to Miami at age two, meets Estefan when he comes to offer advice to music students at her high school. He cajoles Gloria, who has been working as a Spanish and French interpreter at Miami airport, into singing with his Miami Latin Boys at a wedding reception that she is attending with her mother. He subsequently offers Gloria a permanent slot as vocalist (insisting that there is no Miami club band currently fronted by a female singer), but she initially turns him down, being more concerned with studying for a psychology degree at the University of Miami, Coral Gables, FL. Gloria's mother persuades her to compromise, singing with the band at weekends and studying during the week. In addition to forming a romantic liaison with Estefan, Gloria spends enough musical time with him to warrant a group name-change - to Miami Sound Machine.

1976

Following the band's first single, *Renacer*, local Hispanic label Audio Latino releases the debut album ***Renacer***, a collection of Spanish-language ballads and pop-dance numbers.

1978

Sept [1] After a two-year romance, Emilio and Gloria are married. By year's end, Gloria earns a BA degree in psychology from university.

1984

Sept Having released five Spanish-language albums between 1979 and 1983 for Discos CBS International, the Miami-based Hispanic division of CBS, and with keyboardist Raul Murciano (Gloria's cousin) gone from the line-up, the Garcia-penned *Dr. Beat*, the band's first single in English (and only its second track recorded in the language), is released as the B-side to a Spanish-language song in the US, but becomes popular in UK clubs and crosses over to hit UK #6. The group visits the UK for BBC1-TV's "Top Of The Pops". This success pre-dates any outside the Latin market in the US, and, by year's end, Columbia issues the non-charting ***Eyes Of Innocence***.

1985

During the year the group appears in Japan at the 15th annual "Tokyo Music Festival", where its performance wins the Grand Prize. In Miami, the city renames the street on which the Estefans live Miami Sound Machine Boulevard, in honor of the group's local success and the good PR it brings to Miami.

1986

Feb [8] *Conga*, based on a traditional Cuban street dance and again penned by Garcia, hits #10, the group's first US chart entry.
Apr Sylvester Stallone asks them to write and perform the theme for a movie he is working on, and they also contribute *Hot Summer Nights* to the Tom Cruise-starring film "Top Gun".
May [10] *Bad Boy*, penned by Lawrence Dermer, Joe Galdo and Rafael Vigil, hits US #8. With the Miami Sound Machine currently touring as a ten-piece brass-heavy outfit, the group's first all-English album, ***Primitive Love***, which contains both *Conga* and *Bad Boy*, reaches US #23 (going on to be certified double platinum for two million US sales, in March 1990).
June [28] *Bad Boy* reaches UK #16.
Sept [20] *Words Get In The Way*, their first ballad in English, hits US #5 and begins a long-term release pattern of uptempo Latin-flavored pop-dance singles, interspersed with Gloria-penned love songs.
Dec Billboard lists the band as Top Pop Singles Act, Best New Pop Act and Performance Pop Act in its annual sales round-up.

1987

Jan [17] *Falling In Love (Uh-Oh)* makes US #25.
Aug [1] In deference to Gloria's obvious star status at the front of the group, its billing changes to Gloria Estefan & the Miami Sound Machine on the Latin-swaying *Rhythm Is Gonna Get You*, which hits US #5, and ***Let It Loose***, produced by Emilio & the Jerks (namely Dermer, Galdo and Vigil), which makes US #16. Recorded at the Criteria Studios in Miami, it also features guest saxophonist, Clarence Clemons.
Oct [24] *Betcha Say That* makes US #36.

1988

Mar [5] Ballad, *Can't Stay Away From You*, hits US #6.
May [14] Further love song, *Anything For You*, once again written by Gloria, is the band's biggest hit to date, topping the US chart for a week. It is taken from ***Let It Loose***, which re-climbs the US chart, to hit #6, and will eventually sell over three million US copies.
Sept [17] *Anything For You*, eventually recorded in English, Spanish and "Spanglish" versions, makes UK #10.
Nov ***Let It Loose*** extract *1-2-3* hits UK #9, following a promotional visit by the band which includes an appearance on ITV's "Live From The Palladium".
Dec The band wins the Top Adult Contemporary Singles, Top Pop Singles, Top Adult Contemporary Artist, Top Pop Album Artist (Duo Or Group), Top Pop Artist, Top Pop Singles Producer and Top Hot Crossover Artist categories in **Billboard** magazine's annual chart survey roundup.

1989

Jan [14] *Rhythm Is Gonna Get You* reaches UK #16, as Epic Records UK makes a hasty effort to catch up with the band's US success, reissuing several singles throughout the year.
[30] Estefan & the Miami Sound Machine win the Favorite Band, Duo Or Group, Pop/Rock category at the 16th annual American Music Awards, held at the Shrine Auditorium, Los Angeles, CA.
Mar [18] *Can't Stay Away From You* hits UK #7.
[25] UK-only released collection, ***Anything For You***, tops the survey.
July The act's billing is shortened once more. Now hailing simply Gloria Estefan (though her professional and marital union with Emilio continues), the solo album ***Cuts Both Ways*** is released, set to hit US #8 (and will sell over two million US copies), with the Miami Sound Machine, still listed in the album's liner notes, currently comprising: Jorgé Casas (bass), Clay Ostwald (keyboards), John De Faria (guitars), Rafael Padilla (percussion) and Randy Barlow (trumpet).
Aug [5] ***Cuts Both Ways*** tops the UK chart, as the extracted *Don't Wanna Lose You* hits UK #6.
Sept [16] Gloria-penned ballad, *Don't Wanna Lose You*, tops the US chart.
[20] The group files a $1-million lawsuit against its former managers, Stan Moress and Herb Nanas, after being dropped from the Amnesty International bill, following claims that Bruce Springsteen wanted to increase the length of his sets. (Judge Robert M. Takasugi will dismiss the suit in May 1992.)
[25-27] Gloria Estefan performs three nights at Wembley Arena, Wembley, Middx., during an eight-date UK tour (which will be followed by dates in Holland and Belgium).
Oct [7] *Oye Mi Canto (Hear My Voice)*, written by Gloria with Casas and Ostwald, reaches UK #16.
Nov [25] Self-explanatory *Get On Your Feet* reaches US #11 and will make UK #23 in December.

1990

Jan [22] Gloria co-hosts and performs at the 17th annual American Music Awards, staged at the Shrine Auditorium.
Mar [3] Ballad, *Here We Are*, hits US #6 and will shortly reach UK #23.
[6] Estefan and the group are awarded the Crystal Globe Award at the 21 Club in New York, in recognition of selling more than five million albums outside their country of origin.
[20] The group's tour bus is rammed by a tractor-trailer near Tobyhanna, Scranton, PA, on a snowy highway in the Pocono Mountains, on its way to a concert in Syracuse, NY. Emilio Estefan cuts his hand and, their son Nayib fractures a shoulder, but Gloria suffers serious injury, fracturing and dislocating vertebrae in her spine. After treatment by Dr. William Pfeifer at a nearby community medical center in Scranton, she is flown to Manhattan's Orthopedic Institute Hospital for Joint Diseases, where Dr. Michael Neuwirth carries out a four-hour operation on the 22nd.
May Columbia Video issues a greatest hits "Evolution" clip collection.
[5] Uptempo *Oye Mi Canto (Hear My Voice)* makes US #48.
[20] Estefan wins the Crossover Artist Of The Year category at the second annual Latin Music Awards.
Aug [18] Acoustic guitar-led Estefan-penned love song, *Cuts Both Ways*, makes US #44, having peaked at UK #49.
Oct Still the most popular Latin-American act worldwide, Spanish-language versions of recent hits, mainly ballads, are successfully released as ***Exitos De Gloria Estefan***.

1991

Jan [29] Estefan makes her live comeback, performing her new single, *Coming Out Of The Dark*, at the 18th annual American Music Awards, at the Shrine Auditorium.
Feb [9] *Coming Out Of The Dark*, a gospel-tinged ballad from ***Into The Light***, whose songs partly deal with Gloria's rejuvenation and recovery from last year's accident, reaches UK #25.

[16] ***Into The Light***, debuts at peak UK #2, behind Queen's ***Innuendo***.
[28] Estefan is profiled on NBC-TV's "First Person With Maria Shriver".
Mar [1] Estefan begins an eight-month world tour at the Miami Arena, before a crowd of 12,000, set to end October 15th, complete with a five-piece backing-vocal corps including Jon Secada and soul veteran Betty Wright.
[9] ***Into The Light***, produced by Emilio with Casas and Ostwald at the Crescent Moon Studios in Miami, hits US #5.
[30] *Coming Out Of The Dark* hits US #1. (It is co-written by Gloria with Emilio and Secada, whose smash debut album, ***Jon Secada***, Gloria will co-produce in 1992, also contributing songs and vocals.)
May [4] Second extract, *Seal Our Fate*, reaches UK #24 and will stall at US #53 the following week.
[12] Estefan appears live by satellite from Holland in "The Simple Truth" concert for Kurdish refugees, at Wembley Arena.
June [6] New York lawyer Peter Parcher issues a statement saying that Gloria Estefan, his client, will fight a $10-million copyright infringement lawsuit filed by her former pianist, Eddie Palmieri, who alleges that she "borrowed" his 1981 song, *Paginas de Mujer*, in composing her recent hit, *Oye Mi Canto*.
[15] *Remember Me With Love* reaches UK #22.
[18] Gloria performs at a White House state dinner for the Brazilian President, Fernando Collor de Mello, in Washington, DC.
July [6] Further US leg of "Into The Light" tour begins in San Antonio, TX.
Aug [3] *Can't Forget You* peaks at US #43.
[13] The Estefans donate $5,000 to the Ronald McDonald House in Scranton, to show their appreciation for the care their son received following the tour bus accident.
Sept [28] On the closing date of her US tour at Madison Square Garden, New York, NY, Estefan invites audience member George Septien to propose marriage to his sweetheart, Angela Orozco, who accepts in front of the 14,500 capacity crowd.
Oct [5] *Live For Loving You* makes UK #33, set to reach US #22 on Dec [14].
Nov [11] During the Australasian leg of her world sojourn, Estefan performs the first of four concerts at the Entertainment Centre, Sydney, New South Wales, Australia, which will collectively gross $1,135,267.

1992

Jan [26] She sings during the half-time show at Superbowl XXVI, between the Washington Redskins and the Buffalo Bills, at the Metrodome, Minneapolis, MN.
Feb [7-8] She performs a pair of dates at the Palacio De Los Deportes, Mexico City, Mexico, grossing $1,057,739, at the start of a sellout trek which takes her to Colombia, Aruba, Puerto Rico and Venezuela.
Apr [11] Estefan attends the opening day ceremonies of Euro Disney near Paris, France.
May [14] Following an appearance the previous night on NBC-TV's "The Tonight Show", Gloria receives the 1992 Lo Nuestro Lifetime Achievment Award at the 14th annual Premio Lo Nuestro A La Musica Latina Awards (Latin Music Awards).
June [17] Currently featured on the Columbia-released ***Til Their Eyes Shine (The Lullaby Album)*** benefitting the "Voices Victims" project of the Institute for Intercultural Understanding, Estefan receives the Humanitarian Award at 28th annual Music & Performing Arts Unit of B'nai B'rith Dinner Dance, at the Imperial Ballroom in the Sheraton Hotel, New York.
July [11] ABC-TV airs "A Call To Action In The War Against AIDS", featuring Estefan singing *Coming Out Of The Dark*.
[18] Estefan attends Whitney Houston and Bobby Brown's nuptials in Mendham, NJ.
Aug [17] With the Estefans having recently bought Miami Beach's famous art deco Cardozo Hotel from Island label boss Chris Blackwell for $5 million, Gloria wins the Performer Of The Year and Song Of The Year categories at the fourth annual Desi Entertainment Awards, held at the Wiltern Theatre, Los Angeles.
Sept [2] Following the devastation caused by Hurricane Andrew in Florida, the Estefans begin a relief effort, converting their Miami offices into a distribution centre for donated diapers, food and water.
[7] Gloria makes a surprise visit to the Florida Relief Center after touring the disaster area in a US army helicopter.
[26] She headlines an all-star benefit she has co-organized for Hurricane Andrew victims at Joe Robbie Stadium, Miami, which raises $1,468,000 towards the relief effort. The benefit also features Jon Secada, Whoopi Goldberg, Paul Simon, Crosby Stills & Nash and Bonnie Raitt.
Oct [31] Gloria-penned familiar-sounding ballad, *Always Tomorrow*, reaches UK #24.
Nov [21] *Always Tomorrow* peaks at US #81.
Dec [7] She performs at the "Royal Variety Performance" at the Dominion Theatre, London, in the presence of their Royal Highnesses the Prince and Princess of Wales (to be broadcast on the 12th), having performed at the "**Smash Hits** Poll Winners Party" the previous afternoon.
[26] Remix medley, *Miami Hit Mix,* coupled with the seasonal *Christmas Through Your Eyes* (co-written by Gloria and Diane Warren), hits UK #8, as ***Greatest Hits*** hits US #15 and UK #2. The retrospective album, which curiously omits *Cuts Both Ways*, includes four new tracks.

1993

Jan [24] The Estefans receive the National Music Foundation's 1993 Humanitarian Award for their work in helping victims of Hurricane Andrew, at a dinner hosted by Dick Clark at the Hilton Hotel, Universal City, CA.
[25] Having never received a Grammy, not even in the Latin categories, Estefan once again co-hosts (with Wynonna Judd and Bobby Brown) the American Music Awards, the 20th annual event, held at the familiar Shrine Auditorium venue.
Feb [13] *I See Your Smile* debuts at its UK #48 peak.
Mar [27] Estefan guests on BBC1-TV's Saturday morning show "Going Live".
Apr [3] *I See Your Smile* makes US #48, as *Go Away* debuts at its UK #13 peak.
[27] Estefan guests on "Aretha Franklin : Duets", the soul legend's first TV special, from New York's Nederlander Theatre. She sings *Natural Woman* with Franklin and Bonnie Raitt, and *Coming Out Of The Dark.* (The show, to benefit the Gay Men's Health Crisis, will air on Fox-TV on May 9th.)
June [21] She guests on NBC-TV's "The Tonight Show".
July [3] *Mi Tierra* debuts at its UK #36 peak, the day after her appearance on BBC2-TV's "Later With Jools Holland" airs.
[10] ***Mi Tierra***, Estefan latest Spanish collection of Latin American music, also featuring Sheila E., Cacaho, Luis Enriqué and Tito Puente, bows at its UK #11 peak.
[24] ***Mi Tierra*** reaches US #27.
Aug [14] *If We Were Lovers*, backed with *Con Los Anos Que Me Quedin*, debuts at its UK #40 peak.
Sept [13] Estefan is honored with the Hispanic Heritage Award by Housing Secretary Henry Cisneros at a Washington reception.
Oct [13] Estefan guests on CBS-TV's "Late Show With David Letterman".
Dec [18] *Montuno* debuts at its UK #55 peak.
[25] Her seasonal collection, ***Christmas Through Your Eyes*** climbs to US #43.

1994

Mar [1] She wins the Best Tropical Latin Album category for ***Mi Tierra*** (her first) at the 36th annual Grammy Awards from New York's Radio City Music Hall.
[10] Estefan also wins the Best Artist, Best Album (***Mi Tierra***) and Best Song (*Mi Tierra*) categories at the fifth Uno Ano De Rock Awards at the indoor sports pavilion in Real Madrid, Spain.
[22] ***Mi Tierra*** is named Best-selling Latin Recording at NARM's Best Seller Awards in San Francisco.
May [4] Estefan is named the World's Best-selling Recording Artist Of The Year at the sixth annual World Music Awards at Monte Carlo's Sporting Club.
[18] She wins the Tropical/Salsa Album Of The Year (***Mi Tierra***), Female Artist and Song Of The Year (*Mi Tierra*) at the inaugural Billboard Latin Awards at Miami's Intercontinental Hotel.
July [9] The third annual AIDS special, "In A New Light '94", in which she sings *Always Tomorrow*, airs in ABC-TV.
Aug [16] Estefan attends Madonna's 36th birthday party at the latter's Coconut Grove, FL mansion.
Oct [22] *Turn The Beat Around*, reviving Vicki Sue Robinson's 1976 hit, reaches UK #21.
[29] An album comprised of cover versions of some of her favorite songs, ***Hold Me, Thrill Me, Kiss Me*** hits UK #5 in its week of entry.
Nov [12] ***Hold Me, Thrill Me, Kiss Me*** hits US #9.
[19] *Turn The Beat Around*, from "The Specialist", reaches US #13.
Dec [5] Estefan gives birth to Emily Marie in Miami.
[10] *Hold Me, Thrill Me, Kiss Me*, originally recorded by Noble & King in 1953 and perhaps best known by Mel Carter's 1965 hit version, reaches UK #11.

1995

Feb [18] *Everlasting Love*, her treatment of Robert Knight's 1967 hit, debuts at its UK #19 peak.
Mar [11] *Everlasting Love* reaches US #27.
[13] Estefan guests on CBS-TV's "Late Show With David Letterman".
[20] She appears on syndicated TV show "Oprah Winfrey Show", singing some of her hits.
June [5] Palmieri's $10 million 1991 lawsuit against Estefan is dropped because the New York judge rules his evidence was legally insufficent and could not be used.
Aug [31] Estefan performs before a crowd of 16,000 Cuban refugees at the Guantanamo naval base in Cuba.
Sept [24] 29-year-old jet-ski rider Howard Clark, wave-running off South Beach Miami, is killed when his personal watercraft slams into the Estefans' 30' powerboat. (The Estefans will be absolved of any blame.)
Oct [14] Spanish-language Christmas album ***Abriendo Puertas***, written and arranged by Kike Santander, debuts at its US #67 peak.
[21] ***Abriendo Puertas*** makes UK #70.
[27] Estefan sings in a live television show at the Vatican's Paul VI Audience Hall, Rome, Italy to honor veteran Second Vatican Council priests.
Dec [9] Estefan performs at the National Council of La Raza Awards in Los Angeles, set to air on the Fox network on the 28th.
[10] She takes part in the NBC-TV special "Christmas In Washington" at the National Building Museum in Washington. (The show will air on the 13th.)

1996

Feb [28] ***Abriendo Puertas*** is named the Best Tropical Latin Performance at the 38th annual Grammy Awards held at the Shrine Auditorium.
Mar [25] Estefan performs the nominated *Moonlight*, featured in last year's Harrison Ford-starring movie "Sabrina", at the 68th annual Academy Awards held at Los Angeles' Dorothy Chandler Pavilion.
Apr [28] She takes part in "Witness : A Concert For Human Rights", also featuring Bryan Adams, Peter Gabriel and Don Henley, and broadcast live on VH-1 from the Universal Amphitheatre, Universal City, CA.
May [4] *Reach*, co-written by Estefan and Diane Warren to celebrate the forthcoming centennial 1996 Olympic Games and the lead-off single to ***Destiny***, her first English-language speaking album in five years, makes US #58, and continues to climb. (She is also working on an English-speaking album of Afro-Antillean music due for release in July.)

MELISSA ETHERIDGE

1986

Etheridge (b. May 29, 1961, Leavenworth, KS), having been given a Stella Harmony guitar by her father at age eight, writing her first song *Don't Let It Fly Away It's Love* soon after, and performing *Lonely As A Child* at a talent contest at the Leavenworth Plaza Tower mall at age 11, has joined local covers bands performing around Kansas during her teens. Subsequently attending the Berklee College of Music, Boston, MA, at age 18, she has headed to Los Angeles, CA on her 21st birthday seeking a career in music. Making a demo of her blues-rock based self-penned material in 1983 (which finds its way to Bill Leopold, who becomes her manager) and performing at local events (including the "West Coast Women's Festival" in Santa Barbara, CA on September 1st 1984), Etheridge has secured a residency playing five nights a week at the Executive Suite in Long Beach, CA, where she is spotted by Island Records founder Chris Blackwell, who now signs her to the label beating out competition from A&M, Capitol, EMI and Warner Bros. (though her first recorded release will be a contribution to the 1988 film soundtrack to the Nick Nolte-starring movie "Weeds").

1988

June [18] Her maiden album ***Melissa Etheridge***, showcasing her blues-rock strumming guitar style and raspy vocal chops, enters the US chart set to reach #22 during a 65-week tenure. It features drummer Craig Kampf, Waddy Wachtel on guitar, Wally Badarou on keyboards and longterm side man and co-producer Kevin McCormick (bass).

July [1] During a year in which she plays concerts in Canada, England, Germany, Holland, Italy, Holland and the US, opening for both Bruce Hornsby & the Range and Huey Lewis & the News, Etheridge takes part in the "Montreux Jazz Festival", Montreux, Switzerland.

Sept [14] Etheridge participates in WBCN Radio's "Back To School Party" at the Nightstage, Boston, MA, during a month in which she also performs in New York, NY, San Francisco, CA and Los Angeles.

Dec [12] Etheridge performs at New York's Bottom Line.

[13] She makes her network TV debut on NBC's "Late Night With Letterman".

1989

Feb [22] Etheridge performs *Bring Me Some Water* at the 31st Grammy Awards at the Shrine Auditorium, Los Angeles.

Apr [8] *Similar Features* peaks at US #94.

June [24] Etheridge takes part in the "Mariposa Folk Festival" in Barrie, ON, during a seven-date tour of Canada.

July [15] Don Henley's ***The End Of The Innocence***, including Etheridge on backing vocals with Edie Brickell on *Gimme What You Got*, enters the US chart.

[17] She opens for Little Feat at the Garden State Arts Center, Holmdel, NJ, during a short East Coast swing.

Sept [30] Largely self-written ***Brave And Crazy***, with Fritz Lewak now on drums (who will become an integral part of her backing band), and including Bono on backing vocals, charts for a week at UK #63.

Oct [7] ***Brave And Crazy*** enters the US chart set to reach #22 during a 58-week ride.

Nov [4] The extracted *No Souvenirs* peaks at US #95.

Dec [13] Etheridge finishes a 17-date European tour at the National Exhibition Centre, Birmingham, W. Midlands.

1990

Mar [17-18] Etheridge makes her Australian debut during a brief visit at the Concert Hall, Perth, Western Australia.

June [4] She takes part in the annual "Pink Pop Festival", Landsgraaf, Holland.

[7-9] Etheridge plays three nights at New York's Beacon Theatre.

July [4] She performs a one-off England date at London's Town & Country Club.

Nov [18] She plays her last concert for several months at the Northwestern University's McGaw Hall, Evanston, IL.

1991

Sept [1] She takes part in "Rhythmfest" held in Atlanta, GA.

1992

Jan [21] Etheridge participates in a Voters For Choice concert in Washington, DC.

Apr [4] ***Never Enough***, featuring guitarists Steuart Smith and Mark Goldenberg, debuts at its US #21 peak.

May [9] ***Never Enough*** charts for a week at UK #56, where her US commercial success will prove consistently difficult to replicate.

[16] A 57-date North American leg of the "Never Enough" tour opens at the Memorial Auditorium, Burlington, VT, set to end at the Thunder Bay Community Auditorium, Thunder Bay, ON, Canada on September 24th.

[22] ***Never Enough*** is certified gold by the RIAA.

June [11] Etheridge guests on CBS-TV's "Late Show With David Letterman".

July [3] She performs *2001* and *Dance Without Sleeping* on NBC-TV's "The Tonight Show".

Oct [10] Etheridge performs at Ahoy, Rotterdam, Holland, during a brief four-date trip to Europe.

Dec [17] She plays her last concert of the year at WNEW-FM Radio's "Christmas Concert" at New York's Beacon Theatre.

1993

Jan [1] Following a performance at a Voters For Choice benefit, Etheridge takes part in the Triangle Ball, a gay and lesbian fete, as part of President Clinton's inaugural celebrations, where she publicly reveals that she is gay.

Feb [24] Etheridge's *Ain't It Heavy* wins the Best Rock Vocal Performance, Female at the 35th annual Grammy Awards, held at the Shrine Auditorium.

Apr [1] Etheridge performs at the "March On Washington" event in Washington, DC.

June [20] Following an appearance at the annual "Rock Am Ring Festival", in Germany, Etheridge performs at the "Halfway Festival", Amsterdam, Holland.

Aug [26] She joins with Heart and Shawn Colvin to participate in a "Voices For Choices" benefit in Santa Monica, CA.

Sept [6] Etheridge takes part in the Walden Woods Benefit at Foxboro Stadium, Foxborough, MA with Don Henley, Elton John and Sting.

Oct [9] ***Yes I Am***, produced by Hugh Padgham, enters the US chart at #16, but will stay on the survey for over two years.

Dec [24] Etheridge closes out the year co-hosting C4-TV's "Camp Christmas" with Erasure's Andy Bell, during which she also sings an acoustic version of *Santa Claus Is Coming To Town*.

1994

Jan [25] A world tour to promote ***Yes I Am*** opens at the UNO Lakefront Arena, New Orleans, LA. The year-long dates will see her open for Sting, the Eagles and Jimmy Buffett.

Apr [23] Etheridge joins with Robert Cray, Natalie Merchant and others at an Earth Day concert at the Target Centre, Minneapolis, MN.

May [23] ***Melissa Etheridge*** is certified platinum by the RIAA.

June [20] She participates in another Walden Woods benefit, in Nashville, TN with Henley and Vince Gill.

[24] Etheridge performs at a "LifeBeat" benefit, with k.d. lang, Jon Secada, Sarah McLachlan and others, at New York's Beacon Theatre.

Aug [13] Self-penned *Come To My Window* reaches US #25, during a 44-week stay on the chart, as Etheridge takes part in "Woodstock II" at Winston Farm, in Saugerties, NY.

[8] Etheridge performs *Hound Dog* at "Elvis Aaron Presley : The Tribute", an all-star music event staged at the Pyramid Arena, Memphis, TN (with Don Was as music director), and broadcast live on US pay-per-view TV.

[28] ***Yes I Am*** is certified multi-platinum by the RIAA for two million sales (though still uncharted in the UK).

Oct [23] She participates in the "Stonewall Equality Show" benefit concert at London's Royal Albert Hall, with Sting, Elton John, Alison Moyet and others.

Nov [12] She enjoys Melissa Etheridge Day as she gives a benefit concert at her old high school in Leavenworth, KS to raise money for a ball field to be named for her late father John Etheridge, a teacher, counselor and athletic director at the school.

[14] ***Brave And Crazy*** is certified platinum by the RIAA.

[30] Prior to an Atlanta Omni gig with Hootie & the Blowfish, Etheridge meets with 14 students to discuss her career as a musician and songwriter as part of the Grammy In The Schools "Soundcheck" program.

Dec [5] She takes part in Z-100 Radio's "Acoustic Christmas" at New York's Madison Square Garden, sharing the bill with, among others, Bon Jovi, Sheryl Crow, Toad The Wet Sprocket, Green Day, Indigo Girls, Hole and Weezer.

[7] Etheridge performs *I'm The Only One* at the fifth annual **Billboard** Music Awards held at the Universal Amphitheatre, Universal City, CA.

[20] Etheridge performs *Happy Christmas (War Is Over)* on "The Tonight Show".

1995

Jan [12] Following her induction of the late Janis Joplin into the Rock and Roll Hall of Fame, Etheridge performs *Piece Of My Heart* at the event's tenth annual traditional induction dinner jam held at New York's Waldorf Astoria.

[19] She performs at the "Commitment To Life VIII" benefit for AIDS Project Los Angeles, honoring Elton John, Tom Hanks and Ron Meyer at the Universal Amphitheatre.

[21] *I'm The Only One* hits US #8 having entered the survey on August 6th the previous year.

[24] Arista releases the soundtrack to "Boys On The Side", which includes a new Etheridge cut *I Take You With Me*. (During the month, Trisha Yearwood's country album ***Thinkin' About You*** is released by MCA (US) including her treatment of Etheridge's *You Can Sleep While I Drive*.)

Feb [28] Etheridge backs Carly Simon on *You're So Vain* at Arista boss Clive Davis' pre-Grammy bash at the Los Angeles House of Blues, with Annie Lennox and Sarah McLachlan.

Mar [1] She collects the trophy for Best Female Rock Vocal Performance and performs the winning song, *Come To My Window*, at the 37th annual Grammy Awards held at the Shrine Auditorium.

[4] *Come To My Window*, breaking Rod Stewart's 44-week record (for *Have I Told You Lately*) on the US AC chart, makes its 45th weekly appearance on the survey.

[10] She performs at the opening night gala of Hard Rock Hotel & Casino in Las Vegas, NV.

[11] *If I Wanted To*, backed with *Like The Way I Do*, reaches US #16.

[21] Her "Unplugged" set premieres on MTV (US), a solo performance save one duet, *Thunder Road* with Bruce Springsteen, taped at the Brooklyn Academy of Music, New York.

[25] 18 months after its chart bow ***Yes I Am*** reaches US #15 (just one place higher than its original entry position).

Apr [4] The current issue of **The Advocate** includes a PETA ad featuring Etheridge strategically posing nude with companion Julie Cypher.

June [27] During current extended live dates, Etheridge falls offstage while performing at the Jones Beach Theatre, Wantagh, NY.

Aug [16] ***Yes I Am*** reaches the RIAA-certified five million US sales plateau.

Sept [2] Etheridge performs *Leader Of The Pack* and duets with Jackson Browne on *Wake Up Little Susie* at the Concert for the Rock and Roll Hall of Fame at

Cleveland Stadium, Cleveland, OH.
Oct [16] She performs at Dingwalls in London, during a brief European visit.
Nov [25] In Auckland, North Island, New Zealand, Etheridge begins an Antipodean tour down under, opening for the Eagles.
Dec [2] ***Your Little Secret***, again produced by Padgham, debuts at its US #6 peak (though again it will not chart in the UK).
[20] She performs once again on the "Late Show With David Letterman".

1996

Jan [16] ***Your Little Secret*** is certified platinum by the RIAA.
[17] Etheridge begins a European trek at the Tower Ballroom, Hull, Humberside.
Mar [15] The Canadian-leg of a world tour begins at Lakehead University, Thunder Bay, Ontario.
[30] *I Want To Come Over*, promoted via a video clip starring Gwyneth Paltrow, reaches US #22.

EURYTHMICS

Annie Lennox (vocals);
Dave Stewart (keyboards, guitar)

1971

The daughter of a shipyard worker Lennox (b. Dec. 25, 1954, Aberdeen, Grampian, Scotland), who has learned to play the flute and piano while growing up, but who withdrew from a scholarship course at London's Royal Academy of Music, is working in Pippins, a restaurant in Hampstead, London, where she meets Stewart (b. Sept. 9, 1952, Sunderland, Tyne & Wear), who stowed away - aged 15 - in the back of a van belonging to folk outfit Amazing Blondel, after a gig in his hometown of Newcastle, Tyne & Wear. Having made his first recording with Brian Harrison as Harrison & Stewart, releasing *Deep December* on the local Multicord label in Sunderland, he joins Longdancer, helping to record two albums for Elton John's Rocket label in the early '70s, and develops a major drug dependency. Stewart subsequently proposes to Lennox. (They do not get married, but will live together for four years.) The first time the duo will appear on disc together will be as two-thirds of Catch (with Stewart's best friend Peet Coombes on guitar), on the November 1977 release of the group's only single *Borderline/Black Blood*, which becomes a minor hit in Holland.

1979

June Signed to Logo Records (who had issued the Catch release), the trio has expanded to include bassist Eddy Chin and drummer Jim Toomey, changed its name to the Tourists, and now peaks at UK #52 with *Blind Among The Flowers*.
July [8] The Tourists perform at London's Lyceum Ballroom at the beginning of a short UK tour supported by US act, the B-52's. Their subsequent UK chart career will comprise: *The Loneliest Man In The World*, which makes #32 in August, a remake of Dusty Springfield's *I Only Want To Be With You*, the band's biggest hit, at #4, in October, *So Good To Be Back Home*, which hits UK #8 in January 1980 and their label debut for RCA in September, *Don't Say I Told You So*, which makes #40, the Tourists' final single. They also score three UK charting albums during this period: ***The Tourists*** (#72), ***Reality Affect*** (#23) and ***Luminous Basement*** (#75).

1980

Oct While on tour in Australia, the Tourists disband.
Dec After the band splits, Stewart and Lennox visit Conny Plank's studio in Cologne, W. Germany, to record demos. With the help of former Can members, Holger Czukay and Jaki Liebezeit, and DAF members, Robert Gorl and Gabi, they cut *Never Gonna Cry Again*. A week after their affair ends, Lennox and Stewart form Eurythmics. (The new name comes from a 1900s dance and mime form by Emil Jacques-Dalcrose, based on Greek formats of teaching children music by movement.)

1981

July [4] Signed worldwide to RCA Records, the duo debuts with *Never Gonna Cry Again*, which peaks at UK #63. (They will have ongoing legal problems with their previous label, Logo, until a court-case settlement in 1987.)
Nov Eurythmics' maiden UK tour includes dates at the Newcastle Polytechnic, Newcastle, and the Nelson College, Burnley, Lancs.

1982

Apr The duo performs at the Heaven club, London, during a UK club trek.
Dec [4] After successive non-charting singles (*Belinda*, *This Is The House* and *The Walk*) and an album (***In The Garden***), the synthesizer-based *Love Is A Stranger*, with Kiki Dee guesting on back-up vocals, peaks at UK #54.

1983

Feb ***Sweet Dreams (Are Made Of This)*** hits UK #3 and makes US #15 and includes Blondie's Clem Burke on drums. It firmly establishes what will become a highly successful musical union: lyrics and vocals supplied by Lennox, accompanied by Stewart's initially synthesizer-heavy, radio-friendly melodies. An accomplished multi-instrument-playing musician, Stewart will also produce all Eurythmics output.
Mar *Sweet Dreams (Are Made Of This)* hits UK #2, behind Bonnie Tyler's *Total Eclipse Of The Heart*. It is supported by an innovative video, scripted and controlled (as are all their early visuals) by the duo.
Apr *Love Is A Stranger*, now re-issued, hits UK #6.
July *Who's That Girl?* hits UK #3. The accompanying video features Bananarama (whose Siobhan Fahey will later marry Stewart).
Sept [3] *Sweet Dreams (Are Made Of This)* hits US #1 for a week, eventually becoming a million seller.
Nov Bright, uptempo, whistle-introed cut, *Right By Your Side*, hits UK #10.
[12] *Love Is A Stranger*, belatedly released in the US, reaches #23.
Dec [8] Lennox flies to Vienna, Austria, to see a throat specialist about a recurring vocal problem.

1984

Jan [27] The duo begins a 175-date world tour in Australia.
Feb [4] *Here Comes The Rain Again* hits UK #8. With string arrangements by Michael Kamen and guest horn-playing by Dick Cuthell, ***Touch***, recorded at a disused church in Crouch End, London, which has become the duo's home base (subsequently known as the Church), tops the UK chart and will hit US #7.
[21] Lennox wins Best British Female Artist at the third annual BRIT Awards, at London's Grosvenor House Hotel.
Mar Lennox marries German Hare Krishna devotee, Rahda Raman. (The union will last for six months.)
[31] *Here Comes The Rain Again* hits US #4.
Apr [19] Lennox and Stewart are named Songwriters Of The Year at the 29th annual Ivor Novello Awards luncheon, at the Grosvenor House Hotel.
June [23] *Who's That Girl?*, another belated US release, peaks at #21.
July Mini-album, ***Touch Dance***, containing four dance remixes from ***Touch***, reaches UK #31 and US #115.
Sept [8] *Right By Your Side* makes US #29. Already used as the backing track on the UK TV commercial for "Kelly Girl", it is reported that *Sweet Dreams* will be used as the theme for the forthcoming US TV soap opera "Paper Dolls".
[18] Eurythmics win the Best New Artist Video category for "Sweet Dreams" at the inaugural MTV Video Music Awards, held at Radio City Music Hall, New York, NY, hosted by Dan Aykroyd and Bette Midler.
Dec [1] *Sex Crime (1984)*, from Virgin Films' movie adaptation of George Orwell's "1984", peaks at US #81.
[8] *Sex Crime (1984)* hits UK #4. The Eurythmics' soundtrack, ***1984 (For The Love Of Big Brother)***, recorded at Compass Point, Nassau, reaches UK #23.

1985

Jan Haunting ballad, *Julia*, from ***1984***, makes UK #44.
May [11] *Would I Lie To You?* reaches UK #17.
[18] ***Be Yourself Tonight*** hits UK #3 and and will reach US #9. With the duo firmly established on the international rock circuit, the album includes guest appearances from Kamen, Elvis Costello, Stevie Wonder, Aretha Franklin and Tom Petty's backing band, the Heartbreakers.
July [13] *Would I Lie To You?* hits US #5. Scheduled to play at the "Live Aid" concert, Eurythmics cancel when Lennox's voice problems recur.
[27] *There Must Be An Angel (Playing With My Heart)*, featuring Wonder's harmonica break, tops the UK chart and will reach US #22 on Sept [21].
Nov [23] *Sisters Are Doing It For Themselves*, a Lennox vocal duet with Franklin, hits UK #9.
Dec [7] *Sisters Are Doing It For Themselves* reaches US #18. (Lennox makes her acting debut in Hugh Hudson's film "Revolution", starring Al Pacino and Donald Sutherland.)

1986

Jan [25] Airplay favorite, *It's Alright (Baby's Coming Back)*, reaches UK #12.
Feb [10] Lennox is named the Best British Female Artist, for the second time, and Stewart wins the Best British Producer category at the fifth annual BRIT Awards at the Grosvenor House Hotel.
Mar [8] *It's Alright (Baby's Coming Back)* makes US #78.
June [21] *When Tomorrow Comes* reaches UK #30.
July [12] ***Revenge***, once again featuring drummer Burke and further orchestration by Kamen, seeing Stewart concentrate solely on guitar work for the first time and enlisting Patrick Seymour to assume keyboard duties, hits UK #3, staying charted for 52 weeks.
Oct [4] *Thorn In My Side* hits UK #5.
[11] *Missionary Man* reaches US #14, as ***Revenge*** makes US #12.
Dec [2] While performing *Missionary Man* in Birmingham, W. Midlands, Lennox rips off her bra before the assembled multitude.
[6] *Thorn In My Side* makes US #68. (By this time Stewart, credited as David A. Stewart to avoid confusion with a namesake, is a much in-demand producer and session man working with major stars, including Bob Dylan, the Ramones, Bob Geldof, Daryl Hall, Tom Petty, Mick Jagger and Feargal Sharkey.)

1987

Jan [3] Ballad, *The Miracle Of Love*, reaches UK #23.
Feb [9] Stewart is named Best British Producer, for the second year running, at the sixth annual BRIT Awards, at the Grosvenor House Hotel.
[24] Eurythmics win the Best Rock Performance By A Duo Or Group With Vocal category for *Missionary Man* at the 29th annual Grammy Awards.
[28] *Missionary Man* makes UK #31.
Apr [15] Lennox and Stewart are announced Songwriter(s) Of The Year and *It's Alright (Baby's Coming Back)* wins the Best Contemporary Song category at the 32nd annual Ivor Novello Awards, at the Grosvenor House Hotel. Stewart and Lennox have been responsible for writing all Eurythmics hits to date.
June [4] While the duo is performing in Berlin, over 1,000 East Berlin fans gather at the Berlin Wall chanting "the wall must go". Police arrive to remove the rioters.
Aug [1] Stewart marries Siobhan Fahey (now one-half of Shakespear's Sister) at Château Dangu, Normandy, France.
Oct [31] *Beethoven (I Love To Listen To)* reaches UK #25.
Nov [21] ***Savage*** hits UK #7.

1988

Jan *Shame* makes UK #41.

[30] *I Need A Man* makes US #46.
Feb ***Savage*** peaks at US #41.
Apr [16] *I Need A Man* reaches UK #26. All three singles from the album have failed to make the Top 20 in both the UK and US. Dave Stewart launches his own AnXious Records (his first success coming with Londonbeat's *9AM*).
June [11] Eurythmics perform at "Nelson Mandela's 70th Birthday Tribute" at Wembley Stadium, Wembley, Middx.
[24] Virgin Video releases "Savage", adding to previous best-selling Eurythmics video packages, which include "Eurythmics Live" and the early clips retrospective "Sweet Dreams".
[25] *You Have Placed A Chill In My Heart* peaks at US #64.
July [2] *You Have Placed A Chill In My Heart* reaches UK #16.
Dec [31] Lennox's first project without Stewart, *Put A Little Love In Your Heart*, a duet with Al Green, reviving Jackie DeShannon's 1969 US #4, reaches UK #28. It is taken from the soundtrack to the seasonal movie "Scrooged", starring Bill Murray.

1989

Jan [14] Lennox and Green's *Put A Little Love In Your Heart* hits US #9.
Feb [13] Lennox is named Best British Female Artist, for the third time, at the eighth annual BRIT Awards, at the Royal Albert Hall, London.
Mar [6] She attends the launch of ***Rainbow Warriors*** in Moscow and films a TV clip to promote Greenpeace.
May Following his production of Russian rocker Boris Grebenshikov's new album, ***Radio Silence***, Stewart joins Lennox in Paris, to pen songs for the forthcoming ***We Too Are One***, to be released on Arista, to which Eurythmics are newly signed.
Sept [9] *Revival*, previewing a new album, reaches UK #26.
[23] ***We Too Are One*** tops the UK chart. Featuring regular Eurythmics session support, Seymour and drummer Ollo Romo, the album also includes guest performances by Nathan East, Larry Klein, Mike Campbell and Dutch saxophonist, Candy Dulfer.
Nov [4] The extracted *Don't Ask Me Why* makes US #40.
[18] *Don't Ask Me Why* reaches UK #25.
Dec ***We Too Are One*** reaches US #34.

1990

Feb Lennox announces that she is taking a two-year sabbatical while Stewart forms a new band, the Spiritual Cowboys, with Izzy Mae Doorite (guitars), Wild Mondo (keyboards), Christopher D. James (bass), Zac Bartel (drums), Martin O'Dale (drum warp) and John Texas Turnbull (guitars).
[10] Eurythmics *King And Queen Of America* reaches UK #29.
[18] Lennox wins the Best British Female Artist category, for a fourth time, as Stewart collects his third Best British Producer trophy at the ninth annual BRIT Awards, held at the Dominion Theatre, London.
Apr Stewart, listed as David A. Stewart featuring Candy Dulfer, links with the saxophonist on the UK hit #6 *Lily Was Here*, the instrumental theme from the film "De Kassiere", while its parent album, the full soundtrack work, peaks at UK #35 (Apr [7]), both released on Stewart's own AnXious label.
[16] Stewart takes part in the "Nelson Mandela - An International Tribute To A Free South Africa" concert at Wembley Stadium, with Bonnie Raitt, Neil Young, Simple Minds, the Neville Brothers, Peter Gabriel, Tracy Chapman, Anita Baker and many others.
May ***We Too Are One*** remnant, ballad *Angel*, reaches UK #23.
June [6] Stewart debuts the Spiritual Cowboys at the second International Music Awards in New York.
Sept [15] ***Dave Stewart & the Spiritual Cowboys*** peaks at UK #38, while a single, *Jack Talking*, stalls at UK #69.
Oct Lennox contributes *Ev'rytime We Say Goodbye* to ***Red Hot + Blue***, an anthology of Cole Porter songs to benefit AIDS education.
[17] Spiritual Cowboys, with ex-Pretender Martin Chambers on drums, begin a US tour at the Citi, Boston, MA.
Nov [13] ***Rock The World***, a benefit album with a Eurythmics contribution, is released to raise money for the London-based rehabilitation centre, the Phoenix House.

1991

Jan The Peace Choir, an all-star line-up of singers and musicians, including Stewart, records a new version of John Lennon's peace anthem *Give Peace A Chance*, adapted by Sean Lennon and Lenny Kravitz.
Mar [16] Reissued *Love Is A Stranger* makes UK #46.
[30] Comprehensive ***Eurythmics Greatest Hits*** debuts at UK #1, remaining charted throughout 1993. Its release is confirmation that Lennox and Stewart have gone their separate ways.
July [27] ***Greatest Hits*** makes US #72.
Nov [16] Reissued *Sweet Dreams (Are Made Of This)* bows at its UK #48 peak.
Dec [28] Stewart participates in Amnesty International's Big 30 concert, which airs on ITV. He has also recently begun co-writing "Motorcycle Mystics", a movie he is developing with Timothy Leary.

1992

Apr Stewart buys Lennox's share in the Church studio, having recently sold 50% of his AnXious label to the East West label. He will team with ex-Specials, Fun Boy Three and Colour Field vocalist, Terry Hall, to form Vegas (with Romo and Manu Guiot) in July. The group will release ***Vegas*** (which includes a cover version of Charles Aznavour's 1974 UK chart-topper, *She* (UK #43) and other UK chart hits *Possessed* (#32) and *Walk Into The Wind* (#65) on RCA in September. By year's end, Stewart will also collaborate with "Thunderbirds" creator Gerry Anderson on the music for a 13-part children's animated series, "GFI" (having already penned the theme for the October 27th, 1991-premiering BBC1-TV thriller, "Jute City").
Nov [27] Performance highlights album ***Eurythmics Live 1983-1989*** debuts at its UK #22 peak.

1995

Jan Having completed a contractual obligation to BMG with one Vegas album, the creatively restless Stewart, who is continuing to develop a Jack Nicholson-starring movie "Golf" having contributed to the soundtrack album of the 1993 film "The Ref", and recently formed the Art Directors Collective with Anthony Fawcett Stewart, now signed to East West Records, releases his first solo album ***Greetings From The Gutter***, which includes *Heart Of Stone* which peaked at UK #36 on Sept [3] the previous year.
see also: **Annie LENNOX**

THE EVERLY BROTHERS

Don Everly (vocals, guitar);
Phil Everly (vocals, guitar)

1955

Don (b. Isaac Donald Everly, Feb. 1, 1937, Brownie, KY) and Phil (b. Jan. 19, 1939, Chicago, IL), who, aged six and eight, appeared on the Earl May Seed Company radio show, becoming known as Little Donnie & Baby Boy Phil, are the sons of radio performers Ike & Margaret Everly, and have appeared on their parents' shows on stations in Iowa (notably the weekly "Little Donnie" showcase, broadcast by the family when they lived in Shenandoah, IA) and in Knoxville, TN, where they now live. In the hope of either selling some of their compositions or making their own demo to secure a recording deal, the brothers go to Nashville, TN. With the help of his father's friend, Chet Atkins, Don places *Thou Shalt Not Steal* with a publisher for $600 (to be recorded by Kitty Wells) and the duo is offered a session with CBS/Columbia Records. (The first recording by either brother was actually made by Don in the early '50s in Chicago, where the family lived temporarily, his version of the Mills Brothers' *Paper Doll* hit, recorded into a message machine.)
Nov [9] The Everly Brothers make their first studio recordings, four tracks cut in 22 minutes, with country singer Carl Smith's backing band, at Nashville's Old Tulane Hotel studios.

1956

Feb Columbia releases two original Everlys' country songs, *Keep A-Lovin' Me* and *The Sun Keeps Shining*, as a double A-side, but they fail to sell. Further tracks from the session, *If Her Love Isn't True* and *That's The Life I Have To Lead*, are shelved. Columbia passes on its option, and the brothers again make the rounds of Nashville labels, eventually, and again through Atkins, sign as staff writers by Roy Acuff and Wesley Rose's publishing company, while Rose also becomes their manager.

1957

Mar [1] Rose has interested Archie Bleyer at New York, NY-based Cadence Records in the duo. Bleyer is looking to add another country act to Gordon Terry, the only genre performer currently on his roster, and asks the Everlys to record a song by Felice and Boudleaux Bryant, *Bye Bye Love* (which some 30 acts, including Terry, have rejected). In a session supervised by Atkins, it is recorded at RCA's Nashville studio, but not in a traditional country fashion. The style - close Appalachian harmonies over acoustic guitars and a rock'n'roll beat - will become the Everly Brothers' trademark sound.
Apr They tour around Mississippi tent shows, as the single is released.
May [11] They make their debut on Nashville's "Grand Ole Opry".
June [17] *Bye Bye Love* hits US #2 for four weeks (behind Pat Boone's *Love Letters In The Sand*) and becomes a million seller. It also hits US C&W #1 and R&B #5.
July [12] The Everly Brothers appear on DJ Alan Freed's premiere ABC-TV show "The Big Beat", singing *Bye Bye Love*. Also appearing on the first show are Frankie Lymon, Buddy Knox, Connie Francis and others.
Aug *Bye Bye Love*, released in the UK on London label, hits #6 during a 16-week Top 30 run.
[4] Duo guests on CBS-TV's "The Ed Sullivan Show", singing *Bye Bye Love* and *Wake Up Little Susie*. (By the end of the year, they will have been seen on most of US TV's top-rated variety shows, including those of Patti Page, Arthur Murray and Perry Como - the latter, also shown in the UK, offers potential British fans their first view of the Everly Brothers.)
Sept [6] "The Biggest Show Of Stars For 1957" package tour, with the Everly Brothers, Chuck Berry, Buddy Holly & the Crickets, Paul Anka, Frankie Lymon & the Teenagers, the Drifters, Clyde McPhatter and others, opens at the Syria Mosque, Pittsburgh, PA, set to close on November 24th at the Mosque, Richmond, VA. (The white artists on the bill are unable to play on several dates because of segregation laws which forbid black and white acts to perform on the same stage.)
Oct [14] *Wake Up Little Susie*, another Bryants' song with a classic teen-calamity lyric (and, although hardly risqué, banned from airplay in Boston), tops the US chart for the first of two weeks and is a second million seller. It also hits C&W #1 and R&B #2.
Dec *Wake Up Little Susie* hits UK #2, behind Harry Belafonte's *Mary's Boy Child*.

1958

Feb [24] *This Little Girl Of Mine* (a US R&B #9 for its composer, Ray Charles, in 1955), effectively combining country and rhythm and blues, reaches US #26. Their debut album, ***The Everly Brothers - They're Off And Running!***, makes US #16.
Apr [5] They begin an 80-day North American tour in Norfolk, VA, co-starring in Irving Feld's "Greatest

Show Of Stars" with Sam Cooke, Paul Anka, Frankie Avalon and others.
May [12] *All I Have To Do Is Dream*, a ballad written by the Bryants in some 15 minutes, hits US #1 for the first of four weeks, another million seller, and will prove to be their best selling Cadence single. The contrasting B-side *Claudette*, written by Roy Orbison about his wife and featuring frenetic strumming by the brothers on their Gibson guitars, reaches US #30.
July [5] *All I Have To Do Is Dream/Claudette* hits UK #1, where it will stay for seven weeks (their first UK chart-topper).
Aug [25] Rocking *Bird Dog*, which they struggled through 15 studio takes to perfect, becomes their fourth million seller and tops the US chart for a week. (Bleyer had originally wanted to use the voice behind the Nestlé commercials puppet dog, Farfel, to replace the "he's a bird - he's a dog" refrain, although ultimately, common sense prevailed).
Sept The brothers enter the studio with bassist Floyd Chance to record country/folk songs, released as ***Songs Our Daddy Taught Us***.
[22] *Bird Dog* flip-side, the Boudleaux Bryant-composed ballad *Devoted To You*, once again featuring Chet Atkins on guitar, hits US #10.
Nov [15] *Bird Dog* hits UK #2, behind Tommy Edwards' *It's All In The Game*.
Dec [15] *Problems*, another archetypal teen-dilemma song written by both Bryants, hits US #2 and will be the Everlys' fifth million seller. Its B-side, *Love Of My Life*, will also peak at US #40.
[25] The Everly Brothers headline Alan Freed's "Christmas Rock'n'Roll Spectacular" at Loew's State Theater, Manhattan, New York, alongside Chuck Berry, Bo Diddley, Jackie Wilson and others.

1959

Jan [16] They make a brief debut UK visit to appear on the TV show "Cool For Cats", receive a **New Musical Express** award as World #1 Vocal Group and attend a Savoy Hotel reception in their honor - all within 24 hours, before flying on to Europe.
Feb [7] *Problems* hits UK #6.
Mar [2] The brothers return to the RCA Nashville Studio to record their next two singles, taped, for the first time, in stereo, and produced, as ever, by Bleyer.
May [9] Resulting *Poor Jenny* (another teen soap opera) reaches US #22.
[23] A-side, the folky ballad *Take A Message To Mary*, reaches US #16 and UK #20.
July [11] *Poor Jenny* makes UK #14.
Sept [26] Written by Don, *('Til) I Kissed You* hits US #4, and is another million seller. Recorded with backing by the Crickets (Sonny Curtis playing lead guitar), it is the first Nashville-recorded rock'n'roll/country record to employ a full drumkit (with tom-toms) in the studio. (Before this, drummers have used a snare drum and brushes.)
Oct [24] *('Til) I Kissed You* hits UK #2, behind Bobby Darin's *Mack The Knife*.
[25] The Everly Brothers announce that they are considering parting from Cadence, and are talking with both RCA and the newly-formed Warner Bros. Records.
Dec [15] They record their first session outside Nashville. *Let It Be Me*, an English translation of Gilbert Becaud's French *J'Appartiens* (a US hit for Jill Corey in 1957), is cut in Bell Sound Studios in New York, and is their first session with an orchestral backing - eight violins and a cello conducted by Bleyer.

1960

Feb [17] The Everly Brothers sign a ten-year contract worth $1 million with Warner Bros.
[22] *Let It Be Me* hits US #7.
Mar *Let It Be Me* makes UK #13. Meanwhile, the duo records eight songs in Nashville for Warners, but none of them is felt strong enough to be a single. Don writes *Cathy's Clown* at home, and it is finely tuned by Phil. They cut it two days later, for rush release as a single.
Apr [6] They begin their first UK tour with a concert at London's New Victoria Theatre, backed by the Crickets.
May [23] *Cathy's Clown*, the Everly Brothers' all-time biggest seller (selling three million copies worldwide), tops the US chart for five weeks and UK chart for eight (with the catalog number WB 1, it gives Warner Bros. a UK #1 with its first release). Its B-side, *Always It's You*, makes US #56.
June The remaining tracks from the first Warners sessions are released on ***It's Everly Time!***, which hits US #9 and UK #2 - their most successful chart album.
July [18] Cadence releases the Phil-penned *When Will I Be Loved*, which hits US #8 and UK #4. Its B-side, a revival of Gene Vincent's *Be-Bop-A-Lula*, makes US #74.
Sept Cadence album, ***The Fabulous Style Of The Everly Brothers***, a compilation of hit singles, reaches US #23.
Oct [10] *So Sad (To Watch Good Love Go Bad)*, a country-styled ballad written by Don and extracted from the first Warner album after strong radio play, hits US #7 and UK #5. The B-side revives Little Richard's *Lucille*, in a new arrangement which features eight top Nashville session guitarists strumming acoustically in unison, and it makes US #21 and UK #14.
Nov UK version of ***The Fabulous Style***, a compilation with only four songs in common with the US version, hits UK #4.
[28] Final Cadence remnant, the Boudleaux Bryant-ballad *Like Strangers*, reaches US #22.

1961

Jan *Like Strangers* reaches UK #11, while the second Warner album, ***A Date With The Everly Brothers***, hits US #9. The brothers move from Nashville to Hollywood and, at Rose's suggestion, take acting lessons.
Mar [27] Their most successful double A-side is *Walk Right Back* (written by Sonny Curtis of the Crickets), at UK #1 for four weeks and US #7, and *Ebony Eyes* (a John D. Loudermilk ballad with a poignant love-and-death theme) at US #8 and UK #17. ***A Date With The Everly Brothers*** hits UK #3.
May [19] The brothers launch their own record label, Calliope, designed as a showcase for new acts.
June [19] *Stick With Me Baby* makes US #41.
[26] A revolutionary arrangement of the 1934 Bing Crosby oldie *Temptation*, making prominent use of a female chorus, reaches US #27. It was recorded against their manager Rose's advice and, amid some other disagreements, the brothers and he part company (the most serious effect will be the denial of Acuff/Rose-signed Bryants' songs). Jack Rael, Patti Page's manager for 15 years, is appointed as their new manager.
July *Temptation* hits UK #1 for two weeks. Amid a minor spurt of oldie-mania on US radio, the original Cadence single, *All I Have To Do Is Dream*, re-charts at US #96. Also on the US chart, at #34, is the brothers' rock instrumental version of Elgar's *Pomp And Circumstance*, their only Calliope-label success. Credited to Adrian Kimberly, it is actually arranged and performed by Don, with help from Neal Hefti. (The Calliope label will soon become inactive.)
Oct [9] Uptempo *Muskrat* makes US #82 and UK #20.
[16] A-side *Don't Blame Me*, a ballad first recorded by Ethel Walters in 1933, reaches US #20.
Nov [25] The brothers are inducted into the US Marine Corps Reserves, initially for six months' active service. They report to Camp Pendleton, San Diego, CA, for duty in the 8th Battalion working as artillerymen handling 105mm howitzers.

1962

Feb Don marries Venetia Stevenson, the former wife of actor Russ Tamblyn.
[18] On weekend leave from marine training, the brothers appear, in full uniform and with regulation cropped haircuts, on CBS-TV's "The Ed Sullivan Show", to sing their new single, *Crying In The Rain*.
Mar *Crying In The Rain*, written for them by Carole King and Howard Greenfield, hits #6 in both the US and UK.
May [24] Don and Phil end their six-month service.
June [16] *How Can I Meet Her?* peaks at US #75.
[23] A-side, *That's Old Fashioned (That's The Way Love Should Be)*, hits US #9 and UK #12. It is announced that the Everly Brothers' record sales top 35 million.
July ***Instant Party*** makes UK #20 (their last UK chart album for eight years).
Sept ***The Golden Hits Of The Everly Brothers***, a compilation of singles since *Cathy's Clown*, reaches US #35, but fails in the UK. (This album will still be on Warner's catalog 26 years later, when it is released on CD.)
Oct [13] Prior to the opening of a 22-date, twice-nightly UK tour, Don Everly collapses on stage at London's Prince of Wales Theatre, during rehearsal. He is hospitalized briefly, then flown back to the US for medical treatment. Phil continues solo, with the Everlys' guitarist, Joey Page, substituting on harmony vocals. The tour, with Frank Ifield, Ketty Lester and others, will end November 11th at the Empire Theatre, Liverpool, Lancs.
Nov [3] *I'm Here To Get My Baby Out Of Jail*, from the Cadence album ***Songs Our Daddy Taught Us***, stalls at US #76.
[24] *Don't Ask Me To Be Friends*, on Warner, peaks at US #48. In the UK, it is the B-side to the Gerry Goffin/Jack Keller song *No One Can Make My Sunshine Smile*, which reaches UK #11.
Dec Duo's only seasonal album, ***Christmas With The Everly Brothers And The Boys Town Choir***, mostly of traditional carols, is released.

1963

Jan With top Nashville session men, the brothers record ***The Everly Brothers Sing Great Country Hits***, which includes versions of *I Walk The Line*, *I'm So Lonesome I Could Cry*, *Oh Lonesome Me*, *Release Me*, and other C&W classics.
Apr *So It Always Will Be* makes UK #23. Like all the duo's releases this year, it does not make the US Hot 100.
June *It's Been Nice* makes UK #26.
Sept [29] The duo opens a UK tour, supported by Bo Diddley and the Rolling Stones, and later joined by Little Richard.
Nov Written by Barry Mann and Cynthia Weil, *The Girl Sang The Blues* and *Love Her* (which the Walker Brothers will later revive as their first hit) climbs to UK #25.

1964

July *The Ferris Wheel* stops at UK #22.
[25] *The Ferris Wheel* peaks at US #72. Also released is ***The Very Best Of The Everly Brothers***, a compilation of new recordings of their biggest hits, including six originally released on Cadence. (Warner has tried to buy the Everly Brothers' early material from Bleyer, but he has already sold it to his ex-artist Andy Williams - who wants to keep his own early tracks from being reissued outside his control.) The album fails to chart, but will stay on Warner's catalog into the '80s.
Sept [16] The Everly Brothers appear on the first edition of ABC-TV's "Shindig" singing *Gone Gone Gone*.
Dec [12] Co-written by the Everlys, and in a frantic Bo Diddley-like arrangement, *Gone Gone Gone* reaches US #31 and UK #36.

1965

Jan ***Gone Gone Gone*** is released, featuring two songs penned by Loudermilk. The rift with Rose has been resolved and half the album's songs are written by the Bryants.
Mar ***Rock'n'Soul*** contains versions of '50s rock'n'roll hits, including *That'll Be The Day*, *Hound Dog* and *Kansas City*.
May Their revival of the Crickets' *That'll Be The Day*, taken from the album, reaches UK #30.
June Another Everly co-written R&B/rocker, *The Price Of Love*, recorded in Nashville on April 4th, is rush-released to tie in with a UK and rest-of-Europe tour. It hits UK #2, but fails to chart in the US.
July A West to East Coast US tour follows the

European trek.
Sept Uptempo country-styled *I'll Never Get Over You* peaks at UK #35. ***Beat Soul*** develops the ***Rock'n'Soul*** theme but concentrates on R&B oldies. It shows a tougher edge to the duo than any earlier recordings, and features session players Jim Gordon and Billy Preston, and songs like *Hi-Heel Sneakers*, *People Get Ready* and *Walking The Dog*. It reaches US #141, but fails to chart in the UK, despite the current R&B fixation.
[16] The Everly Brothers appear on ABC-TV's second season premiere of "Shindig", singing a revival of Mickey & Sylvia's *Love Is Strange*. (Phil is scheduled for two weeks' Marines service, followed by two more in November - both brothers are still US marines reservists.)
Oct [2] The Everlys represent the US at Holland's annual Grand Gala Du Disque, at the Congresscentrum, Amsterdam.
[8] They embark on an 18-date, twice-nightly UK "Star Scene '65" tour with Cilla Black, Billy J. Kramer and Paddy, Klaus & Gibson at the Granada Theatre, Bedford, Beds., set to end on the 28th at the ABC Theatre, Wigan, Lancs.
Nov *Love Is Strange*, boosted by appearances on ITV's "Ready Steady Go!" and BBC-TV's "Top Of The Pops", reaches UK #11.

1966

Mar ***In Our Image***, with their more customary sound, is released. It includes Don's ballad, *It's All Over* (a non-selling US single which will be a UK Top 10 hit for Cliff Richard in 1967).
May They work on ***Two Yanks In England***, their first London-recorded album, which is issued two months later. The session musicians include guitarist Jimmy Page and bassist John Paul Jones (both later in Led Zeppelin). The Hollies also participate, with the group's Graham Nash, Tony Hicks and Allan Clarke writing eight of the 12 songs under their pseudonym L. Ransford. The brothers also record separate solo albums.
June The duo returns to the US, following a record-breaking Far East tour.

1967

Feb ***The Hit Sound Of The Everly Brothers***, consisting mainly of covers and revivals (including *Blueberry Hill* and *Let's Go Get Stoned*), fails to chart.
July [8] *Bowling Green*, a hymn to the Everlys' Kentucky roots, despite being written by Englishman Terry Slater, reaches US #40, after a two-year chart absence by the duo. (Slater, the duo's bass player, has been a friend ever since his group, the Flintstones, opened the Everlys' 1963 UK tour. He moves to Los Angeles, CA and becomes a long-time co-writer with Phil, as the brothers' music moves to the country-rock field, though they will fail to become part of its commercial success.) ***The Everly Brothers Sing***, featuring five Slater songs, is released.

1968

May Loudermilk-penned *It's My Time* makes UK #39 (the Everly Brothers' last UK hit single for 16 years).
Oct [27] The duo guests on CBS-TV's "The Smothers Brothers Comedy Hour".
Nov ***Roots***, with country songs and excerpts from the old Everly family radio show recorded in 1952, as well as new material, including *Living Too Close To The Ground* and *Ventura Boulevard*, features a re-recording of the 12-year-old *I Wonder If I Care As Much*, a Don and Phil co-composition which was the B-side of *Bye Bye Love*.

1969

Despite their lack of recording success they continue to tour and are a popular guest act on US network TV shows, including those of the Smothers Brothers, Johnny Cash and Glen Campbell, not only singing, but introducing comedy into their act.
Apr *I'm On My Way Home Again/The Cuckoo Bird*, recorded in Los Angeles with Clarence White and Gene Parsons of the Byrds, is issued only in the US but fails to chart.
Aug [1-3] The duo performs at the Fillmore West, San Francisco, CA, supported by the Sons of Champlin.

1970

Feb [6] The Everly Brothers record a live album at the Grand Hotel, Anaheim, CA. The resulting double album, ***The Everly Brothers Show***, is their last recording for Warner Bros. *Yves* (written by Scott McKenzie) is the Warner swan-song single.
July [8] They host "The Everly Brothers Show" on ABC-TV. It is an 11-week prime-time summer replacement for "The Johnny Cash Show", and is country-music oriented, with regular comedy relief from Joe Higgins and Ruth McDevitt. (The show will end on September 10th.)
Aug The Barnaby label, owned by Andy Williams, finally makes use of the early Everly tracks purchased from Bleyer in the '60s. After years off the market, 20 are packaged on a double album, ***The Everly Brothers' Original Greatest Hits***, with a nostalgic sleeve complete with a '50s rock'n'roll quiz. It reaches US #180.
Oct CBS issues the double ***Original Greatest Hits***, which hits UK #7.

1971

Don Everly is the first of the duo to release a solo album, ***Don Everly***, issued on Lou Adler's Ode label. It attracts little attention (the apparently brooding, angst-ridden nature of much of its material is widely thought to reflect the turmoil in his personal life).

1972

June Newly signed to RCA Records, the brothers release ***Stories We Could Tell***, recorded at Lovin' Spoonful John Sebastian's house, with guest players including Ry Cooder, Delaney & Bonnie, Graham Nash and David Crosby. Songs include Rod Stewart's *Mandolin Wind*, Jesse Winchester's *The Brand New Tennessee Waltz* and the title track by Sebastian.

1973

Feb ***Pass The Chicken And Listen***, also on RCA, marks a return to Nashville and a reunion with producer Atkins.
July [14] The personal conflict which has been building up between the brothers finally comes to a head at the John Wayne Theater at Knott's Berry Farm in Hollywood, CA. Entertainment manager Bill Hollinghead stops the show midway through the second of three scheduled sets, unhappy with Don's performance, and Phil smashes his guitar and storms off. Don performs the third set solo and announces their break-up to the audience ("The Everly Brothers died ten years ago").
Sept Phil signs a solo deal with RCA. ***Star Spangled Springer***, produced by Duane Eddy and with musical assistance from Warren Zevon, Jim Horn, Earl Palmer and James Burton, recorded just before the split, is released. The critically-acclaimed album includes the original version of *The Air That I Breathe* (later a worldwide hit for the Hollies).

1974

June [8] ***The Very Best Of The Everly Brothers*** makes UK #43.
Oct Don releases another solo album on Ode, ***Sunset Towers***, backed by the UK group Heads, Hands & Feet.

1975

Jan Phil signs to the UK Pye label, releasing ***There's Nothing Too Good For My Baby*** (US title: ***Phil's Diner***) to be followed in November by ***Mystic Line***.

1976

Apr [3] UK TV-advertised 20-track compilation album, ***Walk Right Back With The Everlys***, sparks a major revival of interest, hitting UK #10. This inspires BBC Radio to produce a multi-part "Everly Brothers Story" documentary series, which is syndicated around the world.

1977

Feb [10] Don starts work on a solo album ***Brother Juke Box***, at Acuff-Rose Sound Studios, Nashville, with Rose producing. It will be released on Hickory Records in the US and DJM Records in the UK.
May [7] ***Living Legends***, a collection of Cadence material on the TV-advertised label Warwick Records, reaches UK #12.
Sept Warner Bros. issues ***The New Album***, which contains (with a couple of exceptions) previously-unreleased Everly Brothers tracks from the '60s. By year's end, Phil will record a duet, *Don't Say You Don't Love Me No More* (with Clint Eastwood's co-star Sandra Locke), to be included in next year's "Any Which Way But Loose".

1982

Nov Via a one-off US-only deal, Elektra Records has issued Phil's Snuff Garrett-produced ***Living Alone*** in 1979, while his 1981 recordings for Curb Records have also failed to chart. Now signed to Capitol, and produced in London by Shakin' Stevens' producer, Stuart Colman, Phil makes UK #47 with his label debut, *Louise*.

1983

Jan In the UK, K-tel's Christmas TV-advertised Everly Brothers compilation, ***Love Hurts***, with a sleeve message from Phil, peaks at #31 and has a 22-week chart run.
Mar Phil's duet with Cliff Richard, *She Means Nothing To Me*, hits UK #9 and features Mark Knopfler on guitar.
May Capitol album, ***Phil Everly***, produced by Stuart Colman at London's Eden Studios, charts at UK #61 for a week.
June [30] After ten years of estrangement, differences are finally settled, and the Everly Brothers announce plans for a reunion concert in September. Phil is quoted as saying, "We settled it in a family kind of way - a big hug did it!"
Sept [23] The Everly Brothers Reunion Concert is a sellout affair at the Royal Albert Hall, London, as the duo slips effortlessly back together to perform their repertoire in classic style. The event is filmed for TV and, later, home video release, and recorded. (More concerts will follow in the US and elsewhere.)

1984

Jan Live double album, ***The Everly Brothers Reunion Concert***, on Impression Records, is the duo's first non-compilation album to chart in UK for 22 years, reaching #47.
Mar Double album, ***Reunion Concert***, on Passport Records in the US, peaks at #162, after a 14-year US Album chart absence.
Oct [13] Signed to Mercury, the brothers reach US #50 and hit UK #4 with *On The Wings Of A Nightingale*, written for them by Paul McCartney. It is taken from their first studio album since re-forming, the Dave Edmunds-produced ***The Everly Brothers***, which reaches UK #36.
Nov The album, retitled ***EB 84***, climbs to US #38, their best US Album-chart placing since 1962.

1986

Jan [23] The duo is inducted into the Rock and Roll Hall of Fame at the inaugural annual dinner, held at the Waldorf Astoria Hotel, New York.
Born Yesterday, again produced by Edmunds, makes US #83.
Oct [2] The Everlys are honored with their own star on the Hollywood Walk of Fame, at 7000 Hollywood Boulevard, Hollywood, CA.

1987

Feb [1] Phil gives Don a custom-built guitar, made from mother-of-pearl inlaid African blackwood and a pound of gold, on his 50th birthday.

1988

Aug A granite statue of the Everly Brothers is

unveiled in the duo's home state, at City Hall, Everly Brothers Boulevard, Central City, KY.

1989

May *Don't Worry Baby*, featured in the Mel Gibson/Michelle Pfeiffer-starring movie "Tequila Sunrise" (with the Beach Boys guesting on this revival of their 1964 hit), and ***Some Hearts***, from which it is taken, are released.
Aug Phil duets with Nanci Griffith on *You Made This Love A Teardrop* on the latter's ***Storms***, as the brothers are featured on Johnny Cash's *Ballad Of A Teenage Queen* with Rosanne Cash.

1990

Apr [27] Don's daughter, Erin, marries Guns N' Roses' lead singer, Axl Rose, at Cupid's Wedding Chapel in Las Vegas, NV.
Oct [26] The Everly Brothers are inducted into the Jukebox Legends Hall of Fame at the Amusement and Music Operators annual awards show in New Orleans, LA.

1991

July [13] The non-profit-making Everly Brothers Foundation buys 80 acres of land in the brothers' home-town of Central City for $40,000, with plans to build a theme park and museum honoring the pair (who recently completed a UK tour, supported by guitar legend Duane Eddy).

1996

Mar [21] With the Everly Brothers now well into their fifth decade of performing and still a popular live draw in the US where they undertake popular annual summer tours with the likes of Dion (1992) and Kris Kristofferson (1994) (and occasionally play in Europe as evidenced by a May 10th, 1993 concert at London's Royal Albert Hall (19 days before another retrospective ***Golden Years Of The Everly Brothers - Their 24 Greatest Hits*** reached UK #26), US cable network TNN airs "The Life And Times Of The Everly Brothers" documentary.

EVERYTHING BUT THE GIRL

Tracey Thorn (vocals);
Ben Watt (guitars, keyboards, vocals)

1982

Jan Although both Thorn (b. Sept. 26, 1962, Brookmans Park, Herts.) and Watt (b. Dec. 6, 1962, Barnes, London) have already been separately signed to Ian McNay's London-based indie label Cherry Red by A&R head, Mike Alway, they have never met, but are coincidentally both attending Hull University, Humberside, when Watt, eager to finally meet his labelmate, puts out an announcement over the university's paging system asking to meet her in reception. A lasting romantic and professional partnership is immediately formed. Thorn (who is studying literature), whose first band as a teenager was in a suburban punk outfit Stern Bops, has already made her recording debut on the label as one third of the Marine Girls (on 1981's ***Beach Party***, to be followed by 1983's ***Lazy Ways***) and is completing her maiden solo effort, ***A Distant Shore***, which has cost £120 to record but which will become a long-term UK Independent chart fixture with sales over 60,000). Watt, the son of an actress mother Romany and successful Parlophone-signed Scottish bandleader father Tommy (who rejected an offer from George Martin to help with orchestral arrangements on early Beatles recordings), has already released the Kevin Coyne-produced 1981 solo single, *Can't*, and will complete his debut album, ***North Marine Drive***, to be released by Cherry Red at the end of the year.

1983

Jan [5] The duo performs for the first time as Everything But The Girl (a name taken from a second-hand furniture store in Hull), at London's ICA Theatre. Paul Weller of the Style Council guests on their version of *The Girl From Ipanema*.
July *Night And Day*, their revival of the Cole Porter standard, is their only release as a duo for Cherry Red.

1984

Mar Thorn guests on the Style Council's ***Café Bleu***.
May After leaving Cherry Red for a new label, blanco y negro (formed by Alway and Rough Trade's Geoff Travis), their first hit, *Each And Everyone* reaches UK #28.
June [9] Working Week's *Venceremos - We Will Win*, on which Thorn is featured, peaks at UK #64.
July Their debut album, ***Eden***, reaches UK #14, while *Mine* makes UK #58. Produced by Robin Millar and recorded at the Powerplant Studios in London, the album sets the tone for much of their subsequent work: self-written (often independently from each other), thoughtful compositions sung principally by Thorn with soft, often jazz-phrased acoustic accompaniment by Watt.
Sept The duo embarks on a 24-date UK tour.
Oct [6] *Native Land* stalls at UK #73.

1985

May Their sophomore effort, ***Love Not Money***, again produced by Millar, and featuring the studio band of Neil Scott (electric guitar), Phil Moxham (bass) and June Miles Kingston (drums), hits UK #10 also becoming popular in Europe, particularly Italy and Holland.

1986

Aug Lush, orchestrally-arranged, duo-penned *Come On Home* makes UK #44.
Sept Heavily orchestrated (by Watt), ***Baby The Stars Shine Bright*** reaches UK #22. Produced by Mike Hedges, it features noted UK jazz musician Peter King in the horn section, beginning a long-term liaison between him and the group.
Oct [11] *Don't Leave Me Behind* stalls at UK #72.

1987

June While Thorn contributes vocals to a forthcoming album by Lloyd Cole, Cherry Red brings her ***A Distant Shore*** and Watt's ***North Marine Drive*** to compact disc. The latter includes five tracks included on an April 1982-released 12" single, *Summer Into Winter*, which he recorded with ex-Soft Machine vocalist Robert Wyatt.

1988

Mar [10] They embark on a UK tour at Loughborough University, Leics., set to end on the 25th at the Dome, Brighton, E. Sussex.
[12] ***Idlewild***, recorded at Livingston Studios, London, reaches UK #13, as the extracted *These Early Days* spends a week at UK #75.
July [23] Their faithful revival of Rod Stewart's *I Don't Want To Talk About It*, hits UK #3, their biggest success to date.
Aug Reissued ***Idlewild*** reaches UK #21.
Sept The duo opens for Joan Armatrading during her US tour.

1990

Feb [17] ***The Language Of Life***, recorded in Los Angeles, CA, with producer Tommy LiPuma and an uncharacteristically large complement of top-notch session musicians including Joe Sample, Michael Brecker, Jerry Hey and Stan Getz, hits UK #1.
Apr [21] ***The Language Of Life*** makes US #77.
Oct [8] They perform the last of five Japanese dates at the Kosei Shinjuku Hall, Osaka, Japan.
[16-17] On the UK leg of its current world tour, the duo performs two nights at the Hammersmith Odeon, London.

1991

Oct [5] ***Worldwide***, their first self-produced effort, recorded at the Livingston Studios, enters at its UK #29 peak. The following day, the duo performs the first of two concerts at the Bloomsbury Theatre, London.
Dec [1] They appear at the "Red Hot & Dance" AIDS benefit concert.

1992

Feb [13-15] A short UK trek is highlighted by a trio of concerts at the Queens Theatre, London.
Mar [7] EP *Covers* (featuring their acoustic versions of Mickey & Sylvia's *Love Is Strange*, Cyndi Lauper's *Time After Time*, Bruce Springsteen's *Tougher Than The Rest* and Elvis Costello's *Alison*), reaches UK #13.
June [26] Suffering chronic abdominal and chest pains, Watt is admited to a London hospital and diagnosed with the rare (and potentially life-threatening) Churg-Strauss Syndrome. Following surgery to remove part of his intestines and stomach muscles, the duo is understandably forced to cancel the final three dates on its second UK tour of the year, with Watt required to slowly recuperate. (By year's end Atlantic Records (US) will release ***Acoustic***, a full-length album extension of their earlier *Covers* EP which also includes EBTG's version of Tom Waits' *Downtown Train*, among others. A Japanese-only CD, ***Essence & Rare '82-'92*** will also be released during the year.)

1993

May [8] EP *The Only Living Boy In New York*, reviving the Simon & Garfunkel song on its title cut, makes UK #42.
[17] A nine-date tour opens at the Glasgow Pavilion, set to end on the 27th-28th at London's Queens Theatre.
[22] UK-only compilation ***Home Movies - The Best Of Everything But The Girl*** debuts at its UK #5 peak.
June [19] EP *I Didn't Know I Was Looking For Love* charts for a week at UK #72.
July [9] The duo embarks on a further UK tour at Derby Assembly Rooms, running until the 20th at the Town Hall, Cheltenham, Gloucs.

1994

June [4] EP *Rollercoaster*, written by Watt, charts for a week at UK #65.
[25] Self-penned and produced ***Amplified Heart***, including guests Richard Thompson, Dave Mattacks and Kate St. John among others, reaches UK #20 in its week of entry.
Aug [20] Co-penned *Missing* initially charts for a week at UK #69 in its original version.
Nov [16] The duo begins the second leg of its US acoustic tour in Atlanta, GA.

1995

Jan [21] Massive Attack's *Protection*, featuring an uncredited Thorn on lead vocal (she has also co-written the deep-beat track), bows at its UK #14 peak.
June [24] They appear at the annual "Glastonbury Festival" at Worthy Farm, Glastonbury, Somerset.
Sept US label Knitting Factory Works' ***Outloud***, a benefit compilation for the Gay Human Rights Commission with a new cut by Everything But The Girl, is released.
Nov [14] The duo plays at the Red River Opry in Tempe, AZ, during its latest four-week, 15-show, nine-state US tour, set to end on November 30th in New York.
[25] *Missing*, radically remixed by Todd Terry as a dance record, now hits UK #3.

1996

Feb [17] Their US breakthrough is finally forthcoming as *Missing* (in its revised version) hits US #2, behind Mariah Carey & Boyz II Men's *One Sweet Day*.
Mar [13] The duo begins an eight-date UK tour at Bristol University's Anson Rooms, set to end on the 22nd at London's Shepherd's Bush Empire.
[16] Reactivated ***Amplified Heart***, now including both versions of the global hit *Misssing*, makes US #46, earning a gold disc.
May [21] While their last (1994-released) album has only just peaked in the US, blanco y negro (UK) and Atlantic (US) release the duo's new album, ***Walking***

Wounded, including guests Howie B and Spring Heel Jack, fusing elements of jazz, jungle, ambient and pop, and led by its title track as the first single.

EXTREME

Gary Cherone (lead vocal); **Nuno Bettencourt** (guitar); **Pat Badger** (bass); **Paul Geary** (drums)

1988

Calling itself Extreme, the metal/funk quartet has played a year of club dates and performed a series of "Heavy Metal Wednesdays" at the Channel Club, Boston during the summer of 1987, before winning an MTV video contest, which is seen by an A&M Records A&R scout, who signs the group to the label. The band has been formed in 1986 out of two Boston rock combos - Dream, featuring Cherone (b. July 24, 1961, Malden, MA) and Geary (b. July 2, 1961, Medford, MA) who released the 1985 album ***The Dream*** on the Toppe indie label (US), and Sinful, whose members included Bettencourt (b. Sept. 20, 1966 Azores, Portugal). The following year, Badger (b. July 22, 1967, Boston, MA) was recruited, having been discovered by Bettencourt in Dorchester, MA, where he was making custom guitars in a music shop, following one semester at the Berklee College of Music.

1989

Apr [8] Their debut album, ***Extreme***, enters the US chart on its way to #80, its release accompanied by a North American tour.

1990

Dec [1] During a second US concert trek, Extreme grosses $35,521 at The Ritz, New York, NY.

1991

May [2] The group plays at London's Marquee during a UK visit which will end with a show at London's Astoria Theatre on the 30th.
June [8] Harmony-laced acoustic ballad, *More Than Words*, written by Cherone and Bettencourt on the former's mother's porch, tops the US chart for one week, as ***Extreme II Pornograffitti***, mixing elements of heavy metal, funk, blues and pop, hits US #10.
[22] *Get The Funk Out* reaches UK #19.
Aug [3] *More Than Words* hits UK #2, behind labelmate Bryan Adams' record-breaking *(Everything I Do) I Do It For You.*
[17] ***Extreme II Pornograffitti*** reaches UK #12.
Sept The group's manager, Arma Andon, insures Bettencourt's fingers for $5 million with Lloyd's of London, after he jams his digits playing basketball.
Oct [6] The band begins a 13-date British tour at the Point, Dublin, Eire, set to end on the 22nd at London's Hammersmith Odeon.
[12] *Decadence Dance* debuts at its UK #36 peak.
[19] *Hole Hearted* hits US #4.
[27] The group appears at the "**Smash Hits** Poll Winners Party".
Nov [18-19] Extreme plays at London's Hammersmith Odeon during a four-date UK visit.
[30] *Hole Hearted* reaches UK #12.

1992

Jan [30] The group performs at London's Astoria Theatre, as part of the "American Dream" concert series.
Feb [12] They perform live at the 11th annual BRIT Awards, at London's Hammersmith Odeon.
Apr [16] Extreme wins the Act Of The Year, Outstanding Rock Single (*Hole Hearted*), Outstanding Pop Single and Outstanding Song/Songwriter (*More Than Words*) and Outstanding Instrumentalist (Bettencourt) categories at the Boston Music Awards, at the Wang Center, Boston.
[20] Extreme participates in "A Concert For Life" in front of 70,000 at Wembley Stadium, as a tribute to Queen's lead singer, Freddie Mercury, and as a fundraiser for AIDS Awareness.
May [16] *Song For Love* reaches UK #12.
[30] The band performs at KISS Radio's 13th anniversary concert at the Great Woods Center for the Performing Arts, Mansfield, MA, to benefit the Genesis Fund.
July [7] The group embarks on a European stadium tour as the support act on Bryan Adams' "Waking Up The Neighbours" trek.
Aug [2] They participate in the "Thurles Feile Festival" in Thurles, Tipperary, Eire.
[26] The group plays before an 18,950 sellout crowd at the Lansdowne Park Grandstand, Central Canada Exhibition, Ottawa, ON, during a tour of Canada.
Sept [12] *Rest In Peace* reaches UK #13.
[26] ***III Sides To Every Story*** debuts at its UK #2 peak, behind ***The Best Of Belinda Carlisle***.
Oct [10] ***III Sides To Every Story*** bows at its US #10 peak.
[13] A breach of contract lawsuit brought by ex-manager Joanne Codi is heard in Brockton Superior Court, Brockton, MA.
[28] The group performs seven songs in front of 1,500 fans at the Avalon, Boston, courtesy of ticket giveaways from WAAF Radio, as a warm-up for their European tour.
[31] *Rest In Peace* rests at US #96.
Nov [6] The band begins a 32-date European tour at the Pavilhao Cascais, Cascais, near Lisbon, Portugal, set to climax on December 22-23rd at the Wembley Arena, Wembley, Middx.
[14] *Stop The World* debuts at its UK #22 peak.
Dec [31] Extreme participates in "MTV Drops The Ball '93" from New York's Roseland Ballroom.

1993

Jan [29] During selected US dates, the group sells out New York's Beacon Theatre.
Feb [6] *Tragi Comic* debuts at its UK #15 peak.
[11] Bettencourt sits in with the "world's most dangerous band" on NBC-TV's "Late Night With Letterman".
[20] *Stop The World* peaks at US #95.
Apr [7] ***III Sides To Every Story*** wins Album Of The Year, *Stop The World* Outstanding Song/Songwriter and Outstanding Video, Outstanding Instrumentalist (Bettencourt) at the Boston Music Awards at the Wang Center.
June [24] The group begins another US tour - supporting Bon Jovi - at the Open Air Theatre, San Diego, CA, set to end on August 8th at the Merriweather Post Pavilion, Columbia, MD.

1994

Apr [2] Cherone opens in the title role of Boston Rock Opera's production "Jesus Christ Superstar" at the Middle East Downstairs in Cambridge, MA.
[6] Geary announces on WAAF that he was leaving the group as an active member, to be replaced by Michael Mangini, of local Boston band Rick Berlin The Movie.
May [12] Mangini debuts with the band at Local 186 club in Allston, MA.
June The group contributes *Strutter* to the US-released Kiss tribute album, ***Kiss My Ass***.
Dec Bettencourt forms the A&M-backed Colorblind Records with Arma Andon. The first signing is rap act Top Choice Clique.

1995

Feb [11] ***Waiting For The Punchline*** hits UK #10 in its week of entry, as the group receives a star on Tower Records' Walk of Fame in Boston.
[17] The band guests on CBS-TV's "Late Show With David Letterman".
[25] ***Waiting For The Punchline*** debuts at its US #40 peak.
Mar [11] *Hip Today* charts for a week at UK #44.
[18] Currently on a US tour, Extreme plays a hometown gig at the Orpheum Theatre, Boston. (During another spell of anonymity, Cherone will reprise his role in "Jesus Christ Superstar".)

F

FABIAN

1959

Jan After being spotted on a doorstep at the age of 15 by Frankie Avalon's manager, Bob Marcucci, and signed up for his looks (Marcucci thinks he resembles Ricky Nelson), Fabian (b. Fabiano Bonaparte, Feb. 6, 1943, Philadelphia, PA) comes to national prominence with *I'm A Man* reaching US #31. Fabian is transformed into, and marketed as, a pop idol who will be quickly worshipped by teenagers. (After the first two singles had failed to score, Marcucci and his Chancellor Records partner, Peter de Angelis, enlisted hot Brill Building writers Doc Pomus and Mort Shuman, who assessed the situation and provided the hit.)

Apr The same team provides *Turn Me Loose*, which hits US #9. The close proximity of Dick Clark's "American Bandstand" studio proves beneficial to Fabian, who now provokes hysteria in his audiences.

May His debut album, ***Hold That Tiger!***, rises to hit US #5, during a five-month chart stay.

June Chancellor quickly releases the tailor-made *Tiger*, Fabian's only million-seller, which hits US #3. Publicity has increased and teen magazines, previously preoccupied with "The Fabulous Fabian", now allude to him as "Tiger".

Sept Double-sided *Come On And Get Me/Got The Feeling* reaches US #29 and #54 respectively.

Nov For his big-screen debut, Fabian co-stars with Stuart Whitman in the Don Siegel movie "Hound Dog Man". The film's title song (by Pomus and Shuman) reinstates Fabian to the Top 10, at US #9, and becomes his only UK hit, charting for one week at #46. Also from the film, the B-side, *This Friendly World*, makes US #12.

Dec His sophomore set, ***Fabulous Fabian***, hits US #3, giving him a total of seven hit singles and two hit albums in 12 months.

1960

Feb Record sales fall but Fabian's Hollywood appeal increases, and during the year he plays alongside Bing Crosby in "High Time" and John Wayne in "North To Alaska". Meanwhile, the double-sider *String Along/About This Thing Called Love* reaches US #31 and #39.

Nov *Kissin' And Twistin'*, a Don Kirshner/Al Nevins song, peaks at US #91 and is his last hit (less than two years after his chart debut).

1961

With his chart success fading, Fabian concentrates on his burgeoning acting career. (Over the next 25 years he will appear in some two dozen films, including "Love In A Goldfish Bowl" with Tommy Sands, "Ride The Wild Surf" with Barbara Eden, Shelley Fabares and Tab Hunter, and "Dr. Goldfoot And The Girl Bombs" with Vincent Price. He will also make the occasional revival show/cabaret tour as the Tiger Of Yore. During the late '80s he will set out on "Fabian's Good Time Rock'n'Roll Revue" US tour, with Lesley Gore and the Marvelettes, and will even resurface in the '90s as the composer of the Jasmine Multimedia released CD-ROM "Wild West" soundtrack issued in October 1995.)

THE FACES

Rod Stewart (vocals); **Ron Wood** (guitar); **Ian McLagan** (keyboards); **Ronnie Lane** (bass); **Kenney Jones** (drums)

1969

June The band, formed in Britain from ex-members of the Small Faces and the Jeff Beck Group, signs to Warner Bros. Records, while the lead singer, Stewart (b. Roderick Stewart, Jan. 10, 1945, Highgate, London), signs a separate deal for £1,000 to Mercury Records as a solo artist. The group, also featuring Lane (b. Apr. 1, 1946, Plaistow, London), Jones (b.

Sept. 16, 1948, Stepney, London), Wood (b. June 1, 1947, Hillingdon, Middx.), who has been in the Jeff Beck Group with Stewart, and McLagan (b. May 12, 1945, Hounslow, Middx.), debuts at Cambridge University, Cambs., as Quiet Melon, supplemented by Art Wood (Ron's elder brother), Long John Baldry and Jimmy Horowitz.

1970

Apr ***First Step***, including the extracted *Flying*, reaches UK #45 and #119 in the US (where the group is still billed as the Small Faces), and the band tours to promote it, building a solid live following on both sides of the Atlantic with its "lads-night-out" brand of rock and shambolic stage presence.

1971

Mar ***Long Player***, credited to the Faces, reaches US #29.
May ***Long Player***, including the single *Had Me A Real Good Time*, makes UK #31.
Aug [28-29] The Faces perform at the "Weeley Festival", Weeley, near Clacton, Essex.
Oct Stewart's solo career explodes with the worldwide chart topper *Maggie May*. The group backs him on his many TV appearances leading to a regular billing of Rod Stewart & the Faces, which causes rancor within the band.
Dec ***A Nod's As Good As A Wink ... To A Blind Horse***, produced by Glyn Johns, hits UK #2 and US #6. Their revival of the Temptations' hit, *(I Know) I'm Losing You*, more in keeping with Stewart's solo style, reaches US #24.

1972

Feb Blues-rocking *Stay With Me* hits UK #6.
Mar *Stay With Me* reaches US #17, as the group embarks on UK and US tours at large venues (with Stewart's solo success still overshadowing the band's reputation as a unit).
May [26-29] The Faces take part in the "Great Western Express Festival", sharing a bill with the Beach Boys and Monty Python.
Aug [12] The group tops the bill on the second day of the annual "Reading Jazz, Blues and Rock Festival", Reading, Berks.
Dec [8] They begin a nine-date UK tour in Newcastle, Tyne & Wear.

1973

Mar *Cindy Incidentally* hits UK #2 and makes US #48.
Apr ***Ooh La La*** hits UK #1 and reaches US #21, but is publicly disowned by Stewart, who has shown little interest in the project.
May Lane leaves and is replaced by Japanese bassist Tetsu Yamauchi (b. Oct. 21, 1947, Fukuoka, Japan), formerly of Free. (Lane will invest his earnings from the group in a mobile studio and forms his own group, Slim Chance.)
Nov Lane adopts a gypsy lifestyle, travelling in a caravan across the UK. Slim Chance makes its debut in Romany style at Chipperfield's Circus on London's Clapham Common.

1974

Jan Double A-side, *Pool Hall Richard/I Wish It Would Rain*, hits UK #8.
Feb Live album, ***Coast To Coast Overture And Beginners***, issued on Mercury rather than Warner Bros., with the band credited as Rod Stewart & the Faces, hits UK #3 and US #63, while Lane's *How Come* reaches UK #11.
June *The Poacher*, Lane's second hit, makes UK #36.
July [6] The group plays at the "Buxton Festival", Buxton, Derbys.
Aug Lane's ***Anymore For Anymore*** climbs to UK #48.
Dec *You Can Make Me Dance Sing Or Anything* reaches UK #12, as the band hits the road again in the UK.

1975

Apr Stewart quits the UK for tax reasons.
June Wood tours the US, playing guitar with the Rolling Stones.
July [26] Jones claims that Stewart's flight to the US to play solo has cost him £80,000 in lost earnings.
Sept Remnants of the group back Stewart on a US tour to promote his solo album, ***Atlantic Crossing***, augmented by guitarist Jesse Ed Davis and a string section.
Oct [12] Stewart plays what will be his last gig with the band.
Dec [27] The Faces' split becomes official, while the Small Faces' *Itchycoo Park* is enjoying renewed chart success, at UK #9. Stewart says that he has severed all connections with the group, complaining that Ron Wood is on "permanent loan to the Stones".

1976

June Jones and McLagan re-form the Small Faces - unsuccessfully - with Steve Marriott. (Jones will replace Keith Moon in the Who in 1979, McLagan will release the solo albums ***Troublemaker*** (1979) and ***Bump In The Night*** (1980), before touring as a backing-band member for the Stones - for whom Wood remains a permanent front-stage fixture into the '90s.)

1977

May [28] ***The Best Of The Faces*** reaches UK #24.
June EP *The Faces*, reprising earlier hits, makes UK #41.
Oct Lane joins Pete Townshend for ***Rough Mix***, which makes UK #44 and US #45. (Lane will later contract multiple sclerosis and become involved, with his rock contemporaries, in raising funds for research, not least at the two "ARMS" concerts on September 20-21st, 1983, at London's Royal Albert Hall and on December 8th at New York's Madison Square Garden.)

1993

Feb [16] While ***The Best Of Rod Stewart***, including a number of Faces' hits, has charted for one week, at UK #58 the previous Nov [7], the Faces, minus Lane, whom Stewart fails to thank in his acceptance speech, and with Bill Wyman on bass, reunite for a one-off performance behind the Lifetime Achievement Award recipient, Stewart, at the 12th annual BRIT Awards, held at London's Alexandra Palace.
see also: **Jeff BECK, FREE, THE ROLLING STONES, THE SMALL FACES, Rod STEWART, THE WHO**

FAIRPORT CONVENTION

Sandy Denny (vocals); **Ian Matthews** (vocals); **Richard Thompson** (guitar); **Simon Nicol** (guitar); **Ashley Hutchings** (bass); **Dave Mattacks** (drums)

1967

June At Fairport Convention's first gig, at a Golders Green, London church hall, audience member Martin Lamble (b. Aug. 28, 1949, St. John's Wood, London) declares himself a better drummer than Shaun Frater and, when a rehearsal proves this to be true, Frater is replaced. The other group members, ex-Ethnic Shuffle Orchestra members Hutchings (b. Jan. 26, 1945, Muswell Hill, London) and Nicol (b. Oct. 13, 1950, Muswell Hill), with Thompson (b. Apr. 3, 1949, London), soon recruit local librarian Judy Dyble (b. Feb. 13, 1949, London) and ex-Pyramid harmony group Matthews (b. Ian Matthew McDonald, 1946, Lincs.), a Bradford Football Club apprentice, as vocalists. The group plays mainly cover versions at various "underground" venues in London, notably at the UFO Club. At one gig they meet American producer Joe Boyd, who is establishing his own production and management company, Witchseason.
Nov In a deal arranged by Boyd, the group's first single, *If I Had A Ribbon Bow* (originally recorded by Maxine Sullivan in 1936), is released on Track Records.

1968

Jan Fairport Convention plays its first major gig at London's Saville Theatre, supporting Procol Harum.
Apr [15] The group takes part in the "Barn Barbecue Dance" at Thurmaston, Leics., with John Mayall's Bluesbreakers, Peter Green's Fleetwood Mac, the Equals, the Alan Bown, Jimmy James & the Vagabonds and Soft Machine.
June The group's debut album, ***Fairport Convention***, is released on Polydor. As well as original songs, it contains material by Joni Mitchell (for whom Boyd has obtained a UK publishing deal earlier in the year) and a musical arrangement of George Painter's poem "The Lobster".
[2] The band performs at another "Barn Barbecue Concert & Dance" at Whittlesey, near Peterborough, Cambs., with Donovan, John Mayall's Bluesbreakers and others.
July Dyble leaves (and has a brief spell with Giles, Giles & Fripp before joining Trader Horne and then Penguin Dust). Sandy Denny (b. Alexandra Denny, Jan. 6, 1947, Wimbledon, London), who has briefly sung with the Strawbs and is becoming a noted folk singer in her own right, joins, and Fairport Convention begins to incorporate more traditional English folk influences.

1969

Jan Newly signed to Island Records, their label debut, ***What We Did On Our Holidays***, includes, through Denny's influence, traditional songs including *Nottamun Town* and *She Moved Through The Fair*. Matthews leaves after contributing to only one track, unhappy with the traditional drift, and will go on to form Matthews Southern Comfort prior to a successful solo career. The band is also currently featured on Al Stewart's ***Love Chronicles***.
Mar [24] The group takes part in a "Folk Meets Pop" concert with Al Stewart, Sallyangie and Pat Sky at London's Royal Festival Hall.
May [14] Returning from a gig in Birmingham, Warks., the band's van crashes, killing Lamble, and Thompson's girlfriend, Jeannie Franklyn. (An appearance at the "Newport Folk Festival" in Newport, RI, is cancelled because of the crash.) Following the tragedy and initially reluctant to tour, Joe Boyd rents a house near Winchester, Hants., for the band to rehearse in.
July [2] The band plays at London's Royal Albert Hall, with Family and the Incredible String Band.
Aug ***Unhalfbricking*** is their first chart album, reaching UK #12, while the extracted *Si Tu Dois Partir*, a French version of Dylan's *If You Gotta Go, Go Now*, is the group's only UK hit single, at #21.
Sept Dave Mattacks (b. Mar. 1948, Edgware, Middx.) replaces Lamble, while Dave Swarbrick (b. Apr. 5, 1947, London), a trad-folk violinist from the Ian Campbell Folk Group who played on the last album, becomes a full-time member.
[20] The group premieres its forthcoming album, ***Liege And Lief***, in concert in Plymouth, Devon, at the start of a UK tour, which includes a performance at London's Royal Festival Hall, where they are supported by Joni Mitchell.

1970

Feb ***Liege And Lief***, promoted as "the first British folk/rock album ever", reaches UK #17. Six of the eight tracks are traditional tunes played in a contemporary electric style. A new-versus-old folk dispute begins to split the band, with Denny eager to be more contemporary, while Hutchings wants to play only traditional music: the result is that they both leave. (Hutchings will form Steeleye Span and then the Albion Band, while Denny forms Fotheringay with her husband, Trevor Lucas, and Jerry Donahue). The band decides not to replace Denny, but recruits bassist Dave Pegg (b. Nov. 2, 1947, Birmingham, W, Midlands), ex-rock bands like the Uglies, the Exception and the Way of Life (he was in the latter two with future Led Zeppelin members Robert Plant and John Bonham), who was recently in Ian Campbell's Folk Group with Swarbrick.
Mar [15] Fairport Convention plays at London's Lyceum Ballroom.
[30] Fotheringay makes its London concert debut at the Royal Festival Hall.
June [26] The Fairports perform at the "Bath Festival Of Blues & Progressive Music", Shepton Mallet, Somerset.

July ***Full House*** makes UK #13.
[26] Fairport plays at the London Palladium with the Incredible String Band, before embarking on a US tour.
Oct *Now Be Thankful* is released with the B-side, *Sir B. McKenzie's Daughter's Lament For The 77th Mounted Lancers' Retreat From The Straits Of Loch Knombe In The Year Of Our Lord 1727, On The Occasion Of The Announcement Of Her Marriage To The Laird Of Kinleakie*, which makes **The Guinness Book Of Records** as the longest-ever song title.

1971

Jan The group is reduced to a four-piece when Thompson leaves to go solo.
July ***Angel Delight*** hits UK #8 and spends one week at US #200.
Oct [8] Denny undertakes solo dates, beginning at the Waltham Forest North East London Polytechnic.
Nov ***Babbacombe Lee***, a concept album based on Victorian-era condemned prisoner John Lee ("the man they couldn't hang"), peaks at US #195. Thompson and Denny join the band on stage during a show at London's Rainbow Theatre. Nicol leaves at the end of a US tour (and will found the Albion Country Band).

1972

Jan Denny embarks on a four-week solo tour of the US.
Mar The Rainbow concert prompts Trevor Lucas to bring Denny, Hutchings, Thompson and Mattacks together as the Bunch, to record ***Rock On***, an album of rock'n'roll covers. Mattacks leaves to drum with the Albion Country Band, and temporary members Roger Hill (guitar), David Rea (guitar) and Tom Farnell (drums) are recruited.
Aug Mattacks rejoins the group and brings with him guitarists Trevor Lucas (b. Dec. 25, 1943, Bungaree, Australia) and Jerry Donahue (b. Sept. 24, 1946, New York City, NY) (both ex-Fotheringay).
Nov Double compilation set, ***The History Of Fairport Convention***, is released.

1973

Mar ***Rosie***, recorded chiefly under Swarbrick's direction and aiming at the pop market, fails to chart - as does its title track.
June [29] Band performs at a charity concert at the Dome, Brighton, E. Sussex.
Oct ***Nine*** is released.
Nov Fairport Convention sets out on a world tour, as Denny rejoins the band, having played with them on stage in Auckland, North Island, New Zealand, in January.
[30] They cancel a concert at London's Rainbow Theatre, as Donahue flies to US to be with his critically-ill father, Sam.
Dec [16] Tour ends at the Fairfield Halls, Croydon, Surrey.

1974

Oct ***Live Convention (A Moveable Feast)***, featuring recordings from performances at the Sydney Opera House, Sydney, New South Wales, Australia, the Rainbow Theatre and the Fairfield Halls, is released.

1975

Jan Mattacks leaves again and is replaced by Bruce Rowlands, after Paul Warren drums temporarily on a European jaunt.
July ***Rising For The Moon*** reaches UK #52 and US #143.

1976

Jan Denny, Lucas and Donahue leave at the end of a US tour.
Mar Ex-Wizzard keyboard player Bob Brady, Dan Ars Bras (guitar) and Rodger Burridge (mandolin/fiddle) are recruited for two months, to play UK and European tours, after which they leave again. (The band is currently playing under the abbreviated Fairport name.)
May ***Gottle O'Geer***, intended as a Swarbrick solo album, is recorded as a group set to fulfill the band's Island contract.

1977

Jan Island releases the 1971 live performance album ***Live At The LA Troubadour***.
Feb Band's first album for Vertigo Records, ***A Bonny Bunch Of Roses***, is released. Nicol returns to complete a four-man line-up with Pegg, Swarbrick and Rowland.
May Denny releases the solo album ***Rendezvous***.

1978

Apr Swarbrick plays Thomas Hardy's father in ITV's "Thomas Hardy - A Man Who Noticed Things". (He had made his movie debut as a fiddle player in "Far From The Madding Crowd".)
[21] Denny dies of a brain haemorrhage, after falling downstairs at a friend's house in London.
May ***Tipplers Tales*** is released.
[3] The band embarks on a 14-date UK tour at the Winter Gardens, Bournemouth, Dorset, set to end on the 28th at the Village Bowl, Banbury, Oxon.

1979

Although the Vertigo albums have been well received, the band announces its intention to split after playing a farewell tour, having gone through 15 different line-ups and 20 members.
Apr [28] The group performs at London's Theatre Royal, Drury Lane, billing the show as "the last major London performance ever".
Aug [4] An opening breakfast spot for Led Zeppelin (prior to her death, Denny had sung backing vocals on a Zeppelin track, *Battle Of Evermore*) at the "Knebworth Festival", Knebworth, Herts., is followed the same night by a gig at Cropredy, Oxon. (The band will re-form annually, to play either at Cropredy, where Swarbrick lives, or in the grounds of nearby Broughton Castle.)
Dec ***Farewell, Farewell*** is released in an initial pressing of 3,000, to be sold from Pegg's home but, when the pressing runs out, it is reissued on Simons Records.

1980

Aug Their first annual reunion concert features Richard and Linda Thompson, who have made successful solo and duo album careers.

1981

Aug Dyble returns for the group's second reunion concert. (A recording of the show will be released in 1982 as Fairport's fourth live album, ***Moat On The Ledge***. In between reunions, the members all find moderate success elsewhere in the folk arena.)

1986

Jan [5] The group begins a 12-date UK tour at the Wimbledon Theatre, London, set to end on the 18th at the Octagon Theatre, Sheffield, S. Yorks., before embarking on a concert series in Australia.

1987

Aug Matthews joins the line-up for the band's latest reunion, which has by now reached folk-festival size and is a 48-hour shindig, to celebrate its 20th anniversary.
Oct ***Heyday***, consisting of tracks from BBC Radio sessions, is released on Hannibal Records, which is owned by the band's ex-manager, Boyd.

1988

Apr Island issues ***The Best Of Fairport Convention***, having recently brought a number of catalog items to CD.

1989

Jan [28] ***Red And Gold*** reaches UK #74. The group, now comprising Nicol (the only member left from the original 1967 line-up), Pegg, Mattacks and Allcock and violinist Ric Sanders (who has joined in 1985), who also perform lucratively with Jethro Tull, embarks on a UK tour at Wimbledon Theatre.
Feb [4] Lucas dies.
Mar Mattacks, Nicol and Pegg guest on UK singer Sally Barker's debut album, ***The Rhythm Is Mine***, released on Hannibal.

1990

Feb Still considered commercially viable, a '90s incarnation of Fairport Convention signs to Polydor and releases ***Fairport Convention***.
Aug [18-19] The group headlines its annual "Cropredy Folk Festival", before a crowd of 14,000 at which Procol Harum's Gary Brooker sings *A Whiter Shade Of Pale*, backed by Fairport. The following year, a North American tour will open on April 16th at Barrymoores, Ottawa, ON, Canada, promoting the release of ***The Five Seasons***.

1992

Feb [20] The group performs at the Winding Wheel, Chesterfield, Derbys., on its 25th-anniversary tour.
July [29] They play a rare London date at Harlesden's Mean Fiddler.
Aug [14-15] The group's annual "Cropredy Festival" takes place.

1994

Jan [9] They begin 27-date UK tour at Leamington's Royal Spa Centre, set to end on February 8th at the Marlowe Theatre, Canterbury, Kent. (Sanders rejoins the band having severed four extensor tendons after putting his arm through a plate glass window in 1992. Following five months in plaster, he is allowed to play again in December 1993.)
Aug [12-13] Lindisfarne, Roy Harper and Blodwyn Pig join Fairport Convention at the annual "Cropredy Festival".

1995

Feb [12] During its annual early year UK jaunt, the group plays at London's Shepherd's Bush Empire, promoting ***Jewel In The Crown***, its first new studio album in four years.
see also: **MATTHEWS SOUTHERN COMFORT, RICHARD THOMPSON**

ADAM FAITH

1955

July Faith (b. Terence Nelhams, June 23, 1940, Acton, London) leaves school wanting to enter the film world, a desire which leads him to Rank Screen Services, where he is employed as a messenger boy (and will eventually progress to assistant film editor). When the Lonnie Donegan-led skiffle craze strikes Britain the following year, Faith starts to play with some fellow workers in the Worried Men, a skiffle group which secures a residency at the 2I's coffee bar in Soho, London, in 1957, from where an edition of BBC-TV's "6.5 Special" is broadcast live. The show's director, Jack Good, notes Nelhams in the group and suggests he could succeed as a soloist, with a change of name. A more likely one is picked out of a book of boys' (Adam) and girls' (Faith) names. After a second "6.5 Special" appearance, towards the end of the year, he is signed to EMI Records.

1958

Jan His debut single *(Got A) Heartsick Feeling*, on EMI's HMV label, is released.
Nov After his follow-up, the Bacharach/David song *Country Music Holiday*, also fails to score, HMV drops him. Disillusioned, Faith involves himself in his film-editing job at Rank, temporarily abandoning his musical career.

1959

Apr Recommended by John Barry (with whom he worked on "6.5 Special") for BBC-TV's new "Drumbeat", Faith is offered a residency on the weekly show. (He will stay with the series through its 22-week run, performing mainly covers of US rock hits like *C'mon Everybody* and *Believe What You Say*.

Ah! Poor Little Baby, is also released on the Top Rank label, as Faith gains a dynamic manager, Eve Taylor.
Oct Songwriter Johnny Worth who, while performing as a member of the Raindrops, met Faith on "Drumbeat", believes the singer to be the ideal interpreter for his song *What Do You Want*, which he and arranger Barry conceived in the mode of Buddy Holly's recent chart-topper, *It Doesn't Matter Any More*. They interest EMI/Parlophone producer John Burgess, who agrees to record Faith.
Dec [4] *What Do You Want* hits UK #1 in only its third charted week, topping the survey for a further two weeks. It is Parlophone's first #1 hit, selling 50,000 copies a day at its peak, and a total of over 620,000 in Britain alone. Establishing Faith's vocal trademarks (his hiccupping Hollyish phrasing and exaggerated pronunciation of "buy-bee" (baby)), it marks the start of a long partnership between songwriter Worth (under his pen-name of Les Vandyke), Barry (whose pizzicato string arrangement is the record's other notable feature) and Faith.

1960

Mar [10] *Poor Me*, a clone of the first hit, also tops the UK chart. (Faith later borrows this title for his early autobiography.) Sellout tours follow, teen-mag coverage proliferates and Faith quickly becomes the UK's second-biggest teenage idol, behind Cliff Richard.
Apr He appears in his first movie, the slightly controversial (and X-rated) "Beat Girl", which also stars Shirley Ann Field, in a story of teenage rebellion. Music for the movie is written by Barry, with Faith singing three songs.
May [16] Faith performs at the "Royal Variety Performance" in London.
[21] *Someone Else's Baby* hits UK #2, behind the Everly Brothers' *Cathy's Clown*.
June He appears in a second film, "Never Let Go", a crime thriller starring Richard Todd and Peter Sellers.
July *Made You*, from "Beat Girl", hits UK #5, despite a BBC Radio ban due to explicit lyrics. Its B-side, a revival of the traditional *When Johnny Comes Marching Home*, sung over the credits in "Never Let Go", gets airplay instead and makes UK #11.
Oct *How About That* hits UK #4.
Dec Faith appears on BBC-TV's "Face To Face", a penetrating interview program featuring the incisive John Freeman, and acquits himself intelligently. Meanwhile, Faith's debut album, ***Adam***, hits UK #6 and stays in the UK Top 20 for 36 weeks. The seasonal *Lonely Pup (In A Christmas Shop)* hits UK #4.

1961

Feb *Who Am I* hits UK #5, while the soundtrack album from "Beat Girl" belatedly charts at UK #11.
May Lionel Bart-penned *Easy Going Me* reaches UK #12.
Aug *Don't You Know It* also makes UK #12.
Oct Faith stars in the film "What A Whopper!", a low-budget UK comedy concerning a Loch Ness Monster hoax.
Nov *The Time Has Come*, from "What A Whopper!", hits UK #4.

1962

Jan [28] Faith appears on the BBC-TV discussion program "Meeting Point", with the Archbishop of York, Dr. Donald Coggan.
Feb *Lonesome*, Faith's first ballad A-side, reaches UK #12.
Mar ***Adam Faith*** reaches UK #20.
May *As You Like It*, Faith's last single backed by Barry (now heavily committed to film work), hits UK #5.
Sept Faith stars with Anne Baxter and Donald Sinden in the film "Mix Me A Person", in which he plays a man wrongly imprisoned for murder.
Oct *Don't That Beat All*, arranged by Johnny Keating, and a notable break from the familiar sound, hits UK #8.
Dec After 13 consecutive UK Top 20 singles, *Baby Take A Bow* reaches UK #22. Faith opens in pantomime in the title role of "Aladdin" at the Pavilion, Bournemouth, Dorset.

1963

Feb *What Now* makes UK #31, as Faith, like most of his pre-Beatles contemporaries, reels under the chart onslaught of Merseybeat sounds.
July *Walkin' Tall* steps to UK #23. Faith decides to recruit the Roulettes - Russ Ballard (lead guitar), Pete Salt (rhythm guitar), John Rodgers (bass) and Bob Henrit (drums) - as his backing group, to add a hard, beat-group edge to his vocal sound, which becomes less mannered and more aggressive.
Oct He commissions singer/songwriter Chris Andrews to write new material, and *The First Time*, with the Roulettes backing and a new contemporary sound, hits UK #5.

1964

Jan *We Are In Love*, from the same team, reaches UK #11, spurred by Faith's appearance on the second edition of BBC-TV's "Top Of The Pops".
Apr Andrews-penned *If He Tells You* reaches UK #25.
[16] Faith embarks on a three-week UK package tour, his first in 18 months, with Dave Berry, Eden Kane and others, at the Colston Hall, Bristol, Somerset.
June *I Love Being In Love With You* makes UK #33.
Sept Andrews-written *Only One Such As You*, an atypical chest-thumping ballad, fails to chart. Meanwhile, Faith has discovered vocalist Sandie Shaw and persuades Taylor to sign her. (Shaw will cover Lou Johnson's US Bacharach/David hit, *(There's) Always Something There To Remind Me*, which tops the UK chart.)
Dec Faith's cover of Johnson's *A Message To Martha (Kentucky Bluebird)*, also written by Bacharach and David, reaches UK #12.
[26] Faith embarks on a tour of South Africa, though the Roulettes are banned from accompanying him by the Musicians' Union.

1965

Feb *Stop Feeling Sorry For Yourself* reaches UK #23, while the Andrews-penned, Roulettes-backed *It's Alright* (originally the UK B-side of *I Love Being In Love With You*) belatedly reaches US #31, a beneficiary of the "British Invasion" of the US charts.
Apr *Talk About Love* peaks at US #97 (his last US chart entry). In Britain, the reflective *Hand Me Down Things* is his second non-charting single on Parlophone.
June *Someone's Taken Maria Away*, a pastiche of the Bacharach/David style by Andrews (influenced by *Concrete And Clay*), makes UK #34.
July ABC-TV sues Faith for appearing on "Ready Steady, Go!" on April 16th, one day before a scheduled "Thank Your Lucky Stars" appearance, which it states is contrary to the terms of his contract.
Sept ***Faith Alive***, recorded on stage with the Roulettes before 100 fan club members at Abbey Road Studios, makes UK #19. (Shortly after, he splits with the Roulettes.)

1966

Feb Faith issues a writ against EMI, claiming its breach of contract by not releasing a minimum of two records a year in Europe.
June [13] Faith makes his small-screen acting debut as a blackmailer on ITV's Play Of The Week thriller, "(Cat) In The Night".
Oct Following three more non-charting singles (including a revival of Perry Como's *Idle Gossip* and the later P.J. Proby/Tom Jones-flavored *To Make A Big Man Cry*), a cover of Bob Lind's *Cheryl's Goin' Home* makes UK #46 and is Faith's final UK singles chart entry.

1967

May [9] Faith guests in the first edition of the new ITV pop show, "As You Like It".
Aug [19] He marries dancer Jackie Irving, one-time girlfriend of Cliff Richard.
Nov *To Hell With Love* is Faith's final Parlophone release. (He has already given up cabaret appearances and will cease recording, determined to take up acting full time. Over the next three years, he will work from the bottom up in repertory theatre around the UK, progressing to the lead in a touring revival of "Billy Liar", the part of Feste in "Twelfth Night", and a role as the murderer (opposite Dame Sybil Thorndike) in Emlyn Williams' "Night Must Fall".)

1971

He takes the title role in ITV's drama series "Budgie", playing a constantly-stymied, working-class, small-time opportunist. The series is both a critical and ratings success.

1973

Apr Having discovered singer/songwriter Leo Sayer, and become his manager the previous year, Faith produces ***Daltrey***, the first solo album by the Who's Roger Daltrey, which includes several compositions by Sayer. (Shortly afterwards, Faith has a serious car accident. He will later describe the near-fatal crash as a major turning point in his life.)

1974

Feb [18] Having recovered from his accident (apart from a slight limp), Faith begins filming with David Essex on "Stardust", the sequel to Essex's previous success, "That'll Be The Day", taking the rock-star-manager role played by Ringo Starr in the earlier movie.
July After seven years without recording, Faith releases ***I Survive***, co-produced with David Courtney, with contributions from Paul McCartney. Although rated by the critics, both it and two extracted singles fail to revive his chart career and he retires, to concentrate on acting, management and production.
Oct "Stardust" premieres in London, and Faith's performance gains critical plaudits.

1976

Mar [4] Faith opens at London's Comedy Theatre in Stephen Poliakoff's play, "City Sugar". Over the next five years ***Scouse The Mouse***, an album featuring Faith, Ringo Starr, Barbara Dickson and actor Donald Pleasence, will be released (December 1978), while Faith will produce Lonnie Donegan's ***Puttin' On The Style***, a star-studded nostalgia/comeback set issued in February 1978, while his acting pursuits will include starring as a team manager alongside Ian McShane in the 1979 soccer movie "Yesterday's Hero".

1980

Apr [30] Movie "McVicar", the true story of prison escapee John McVicar, in which Faith stars with Roger Daltrey, premieres in London. (The following year a TV-advertised compilation, ***20 Golden Greats***, reaches UK #61 (Dec [26].)

1988

Oct Faith opens on the London West End stage in a musical version of "Budgie" in which he reprises his old TV role, while also refurbishing his singing talent for live stage work.

1991

Feb [3] Faith has become an increasingly successful financial adviser and shares pundit (through his own Faith Corporation), initially basing his office in the tea-room of the Fortnum & Mason department store, London, when **The Sunday Times** reports that he may have to resign from the board of Savoy Management Ltd., because of his close links with the recently-failed Levitt Group. His weekly investment advice column, "Faith In The City", continues to appear in the **The Mail On Sunday** UK newspaper.
Nov [27] Now starring in the TV series, "Love Hurts", Faith returns to the recording scene with ***Midnight Postcards***, which debuts at its UK #43 peak.

FAITH NO MORE

Mike Patton (lead vocals); **Jim Martin** (guitar); **Billy Gould** (bass); **Roddy Bottum** (keyboards); **Mike "Puffy" Bordin** (drums)

1980

Having both served apprenticeships in Los Angeles, CA punk outfits in the late '70s, and now based in the Bay Area of San Francisco, CA, Gould (b. Apr. 24, 1963, Los Angeles) and his old school friend, classically-trained pianist Bottum (b. July 1, 1963, Los Angeles), have decided to form a new band. Adding drummer Bordin (b. Nov. 27, 1962, San Francisco), who is studying at Berkeley University, CA, and who specializes in ferocious African drum-beat rhythms in 1981, the group is still seeking a permanent guitarist when Bordin's friend, Cliff Burton of Metallica, insists that they audition his friend Jim Martin (b. July 21, 1961, Oakland, CA), who is playing with Vicious Hatred. Martin eventually joins the fledgling Faith No More (who profess that they got their name from a greyhound on which they placed a bet).

1983

Unable to find a suitable singer, the band play clubs and invites an audience member to supply vocals each night. Chuck Mosely, a friend of Gould's, regularly turns up to monopolize the microphone, until he eventually joins the band full time.

1985

Signed to Mordam, a small San Francisco indie label, which advanced money for the recording of their eponymous debut album the previous year, the resultant set, ***Faith No More***, fusing funk with metal, proves popular on US college radio stations and grabs the attention of Slash Records, a Warner Bros.-licensed label, which offers the band a more substantial contract with major company backing the following year.

1987

Oct Their second album, ***Introduce Yourself***, mixing rap and heavy rock, is released. Despite constant US tour promotion (mainly with the Red Hot Chili Peppers) to support the album, hits will not not forthcoming, although the video for the extracted *We Care A Lot* will be heavily rotated on US MTV into the new year.

1988

Feb The group makes debut European performances, including a sellout night at London's Marquee club.
May Faith No More returns for a second UK visit, on which Mosely's bizarre stage performances increasingly concern the rest of the band. ***Introduce Yourself*** attracts little sales interest in either the US or UK.
June The group fires Mosely and issues press statements which include the words "ego" and "undependable".
Nov During a search for a replacement lead singer, a demo tape from San Francisco band Mr. Bungle arrives, featuring the vocals of Mike Patton (b. Jan. 27, 1968, Eureka, CA) on the track *The Raging Wrath Of The Easter Bunny*. He is immediately hired and, invited to pen lyrics for the rhythm tracks the band has already recorded for the next album. (Patton had seen Faith No More at Centerarts, Humboldt State University, Arcata, CA.)
Dec *We Care A Lot* makes UK #53, as the new line-up makes its live debut in the Bay Area.

1989

Feb Work on their third album, produced by Matt Wallace, is completed at a studio in Sausalito.
June The group plays a showcase gig at the Roxy in Los Angeles, to preview the forthcoming album. They are joined on stage by Slash and Duff from Guns N' Roses, for a version of *War Pigs*.
July *The Real Thing* is released, to great critical and, ultimately, commercial success. The CD release contains two tracks not otherwise available.
[4] The group embarks on its third UK tour, including a slot at the Marquee club.
Oct Currently more popular in Britain, they return for a full 15-date tour.
Dec The band returns to the US circuit, now supporting Metallica on a full arena tour.

1990

Jan [12] Continuing to tour in North America, the band performs in Toronto, ON, Canada with Soundgarden and Voivod.
[27] *Epic* makes UK #37, as another sellout UK tour begins.
Feb [21] The group receives a Grammy nomination for Best Heavy Metal/Hard Rock performance.
Apr [22] They begin a six-date UK tour at the Barrowlands, Glasgow, Scotland, set to end on the 27th at London's Hammersmith Odeon.
[28] With their new US single, *Epic*, receiving heavy play on MTV, the UK-reissued *From Out Of Nowhere* reaches #23, supported by further live dates, as the previously slow-selling ***The Real Thing*** begins a steady sales surge in both territories.
May [5] ***The Real Thing*** finally reaches UK #34.
July [14] *Falling To Pieces* makes UK #41.
Aug Performance video, "Live At Brixton", is released.
[24] The group performs at the annual "Reading Festival", Reading, Berks.
[30] They play at the "Monsters Of Rock" festival in Bologna, Italy.
Sept [8] *Epic* proves their major breakthrough, hitting US #9, and is reissued in the UK, peaking at #25. The RIAA certifies ***The Real Thing*** a million seller, the group's first. Peaking at US #13, it re-charts to reach UK #30, eventually spending a total of 33 weeks on the UK survey during the year. Following another "Monsters Of Rock" appearance in Paris, France on September 3rd, Faith No More returns to the US for a 37-date tour supporting Billy Idol, which will end November 5th.
Oct [13] ***The Real Thing*** reaches US #11.
Nov [9] The group headlines the bill of **Rip** magazine's fourth anniversary celebrations, at the Hollywood Palladium, New York.
[10] *Falling To Pieces* peaks at US #92.
[15] Faith No More plays at the Convention Center Auditorium, Sioux City, IA, during a handful of dates supporting Robert Plant.
Dec [1] The group guests on NBC-TV's "Saturday Night Live".

1991

Jan Faith No More plays at the "Rock In Rio II Festival" at the Maracana soccer stadium in Rio de Janeiro, Brazil.
Feb [16] UK-only live album ***Live At The Brixton Academy*** on Slash, reaches UK #20.
Mar [2] Faith No More wins Outstanding Group, Male Vocalist, Drummer, Keyboardist/Synthesist and *Epic* wins Outstanding Song at the 14th annual local Bammy Awards, at the Civic Auditorium, San Francisco, as guitarist Jim Martin lands the role as "the world's greatest guitar player" in "Bill And Ted Go To Mars", with the band also contributing *Perfect Crime* to the movie's soundtrack.
Sept [5] "Falling To Pieces" wins the Best Special Effects category at the eighth annual MTV Video Music Awards, held at the Universal Amphitheatre, Universal City, CA.
[21] While the band begins working on a new album at San Francisco Coast Recorders Studio, Patton has found time to record with his still-active side outfit, Mr. Bungle whose debut album ***Mr. Bungle*** makes UK #57.
Oct The group performs at the "Day On The Green" concert in San Francisco, with Metallica, Queensryche and Soundgarden. (Commenting on the ongoing recordings of Faith No More's new album Patton says, "It sounds cynical and bitter, but it would make a lot of people's jobs, including ours, a lot easier if we just made the last album again.")

1992

May [14] The band, in Britain to promote the new set, plays an announced date at London's Marquee as Haircutz That Kill.
June [6] *Midlife Crisis* debuts at its UK #10 peak.
[20] ***Angel Dust*** bows at UK #2, behind Lionel Richie's ***Back To Front***.
July [4] ***Angel Dust*** debuts at its US #10 pinnacle.
[29] The group, currently in the midst of a major US tour with Guns N' Roses and Metallica, plays Giants Stadium, East Rutherford, NJ.
Aug [22] *A Small Victory* reaches UK #29.
Sept [12] *A Small Victory (Remixes)* charts for a week, at UK #55.
Oct [30] They begin the 40-date European leg of the world trek at the Lisebergshallen, Gothenburg, Sweden, set to close on December 19th in Zurich, Switzerland.
Nov [28] *Everything's Ruined* reaches UK #28.

1993

Jan [13] The group guests on NBC-TV's "The Tonight Show".
[22] During their latest tour leg, they play to a sellout crowd of 3,500 at the Hollywood Palladium.
[23] *I'm Easy*, reviving the Commodores' 1977 US #4/UK #9 hit, *Easy*, and backed with *Be Aggressive*, hits UK #3.
Mar [8] Bottum is named Outstanding Keyboardist/ Synthesist at the 1993 Bay Area Music Awards at the Bill Graham Civic Auditorium, San Francisco.
Apr [3] *Easy* makes US #58.
July [3-4] The group performs at the Torhout and Wechter festivals in Belgium on successive days.
[17] They appear at "The Phoenix 1993 Festival" at Long Marston, Stratford-upon-Avon, Warks.
Nov [6] *Another Body Murdered*, with Boo Yaa Tribe, debuts at its UK #26 peak.

1994

June Kiss tribute album ***Kiss My Ass***, to which band members have contributed *Calling Doctor Love* as Shandi's Addiction with members of Rage Against The Machine and Tool, is released in the US.

1995

Mar [11] *Digging The Grave* debuts at its UK #16 peak, as the group plays at Manchester University, Gtr. Manchester during latest UK dates.
[25] ***King For A Day, Fool For A Lifetime*** hits UK #5 in its week of entry. (During the making of the album, Gould has come down with pneumonia, Martin has left and his replacement, Mr. Bungle's Trey Spruance, will only last until the end of the recording. Dean Menta will, in turn, replace him.)
Apr [15] ***King For A Day, Fool For A Lifetime*** debuts at its US #31 peak.
May [27] *Ricochet* enters at its UK #27 high, as the group performs at the Q101 Jamboree show at the World Music Theatre, Tinley Park, IL.
Aug [5] *Evidence* reaches UK #32.
Sept With its latest album falling off the Top 200 Album survey after just eight weeks, the band cancels a US tour set to begin on the 19th.
Oct [28] Mr. Bungle's ***Disco Volante*** charts for a week at US #113.
Nov [15-16] Faith No More begins a six-date UK and Irish tour at London's Brixton Academy.

1996

May [7] Bottum's parallel side combo, Imperial Teen's debut album ***Seasick*** is released on Slash.

MARIANNE FAITHFULL

1964

June Faithfull (b. Dec. 29, 1946, Hampstead, London), daughter of a British university lecturer and an Austrian baroness, and an ex-pupil of St. Joseph's

Convent School in Reading, Berks., is taken to a party in London by her boyfriend, artist John Dunbar, where she is introduced to the Rolling Stones' manager, Andrew Loog Oldham. Impressed by her looks and, learning that she has aspirations to be a folk singer, he offers to sign and record her.

Sept With Faithfull signed by Oldham to Decca Records, her cover of the Jagger/Richard ballad, *As Tears Go By*, hits UK #9.

[19] She makes her live debut at the Adelphi Cinema, Slough, Bucks.

Oct [31] Faithfull appears on BBC-TV's "Juke Box Jury", commenting on one record, "I'd like it at a party if I was stoned".

Nov Her version of Bob Dylan's *Blowin' In The Wind*, more obviously folky than her debut, is released.

[4] She collapses and is confined to bed, pulling out of a scheduled 26-date UK tour with Gerry & the Pacemakers, Gene Pitney, the Kinks and others. US singer Jackie DeShannon takes her place.

Dec [14] Faithfull flies to the US for TV and radio dates.

1965

Jan *As Tears Go By* reaches US #22.

Feb [16] She begins a 30-date, twice-nightly UK package tour, headlined by Roy Orbison, at the Adelphi Cinema, Slough, set to end on March 21st at the Empire Theatre, Liverpool, Lancs.

Mar *Come And Stay With Me*, written by Jackie DeShannon, is her biggest hit, at UK #4.

Apr *Come And Stay With Me* reaches US #26.

[16] Faithfull begins a US tour with Gene Pitney (with whom she is rumored to be having a romance.)

May [6] Faithfull marries Dunbar at Cambridge Register Office, Cambs. She parts from Oldham after disagreements and releases *This Little Bird*, which hits UK #6. A simultaneous cover (also on Decca), by the Oldham-produced Nashville Teens, makes UK #38.

[24] She participates in the one-off "Brighton Song Festival" at the Dome, Brighton, E. Sussex, with Lulu, Manfred Mann, Dave Berry and others, singing *Go Away From My World*.

[31] Faithfull becomes a resident guest on the new-look BBC2-TV series "Gadzooks! It's The In Crowd".

June J.D. Loudermilk-penned *This Little Bird* makes US #32. Two albums are issued simultaneously in the UK: the folk package ***Come My Way***, which charts at UK #12, and ***Marianne Faithfull*** (including her first two hit singles), which makes UK #15.

[19] She appears at the "Uxbridge Blues And Folk Festival" in Uxbridge, Middx., with several R&B bands, including the Who, Solomon Burke, Zoot Money and Cliff Bennett & the Rebel Rousers.

July ***Marianne Faithfull*** reaches US #12.

Aug [1] Faithfull collapses during a concert at Morecambe, Lancs., and cancels all forthcoming engagements, including a US tour set for the end of the month.

[14] *Summer Nights* hits UK #10.

Oct *Summer Nights* reaches US #24.

Nov Her cover of the Beatles' *Yesterday* loses out on the UK chart to Matt Monro's version, which reaches #36. Faithfull gives birth to a son, Nicholas.

Dec *Go Away From My World* (released on an EP in the UK) peaks at US #89.

[16] Faithfull is featured on the ITV broadcast of a tribute to "The Music Of Lennon & McCartney".

1966

Feb ***Go Away From My World*** makes US #81. (Its title seems prophetic, as Faithfull and Dunbar shortly separate and she becomes Mick Jagger's constant companion, remaining with the Stone for almost four years.)

Mar [24] Faithfull begins a four-week engagement at the Paris Olympia, France, before appearing at the "Golden Rose Festival" in Montreux, Switzerland.

Nov ***Faithfull Forever*** peaks at US #147.

1967

Feb [12] She is with Jagger at Keith Richard's house in West Wittering, W. Sussex, when police raid the premises, but, unlike Jagger and Richard, she is not charged with drug possession.

Mar Following the April 1966 release of *North Country Maid* and the February release of *Love In A Mist*, her treatment of the Ronettes' *Is This What I Get For Loving You*, with Oldham producing, makes UK #43.

Apr Faithfull begins her acting career, opening at London's Royal Court Theatre in Chekhov's "The Three Sisters".

June [25] She sings in the chorus of the Beatles' *All You Need Is Love*, recorded live during the "Our World" global TV broadcast. (By year's end, Faithfull appears in "I'll Never Forget Whatsisname" with Oliver Reed and Orson Welles.)

1968

May She co-stars with Alain Delon in the film "Girl On A Motorcycle" (US title: "Naked Under Leather"), which is savaged by the critics.

Nov [22] Faithfull miscarries Jagger's baby.

Dec [12] She participates in the filming of the Rolling Stones' "Rock And Roll Circus" musical extravaganza, planned as a TV film, though never shown.

1969

Feb *Something Better* is Faithfull's last single for Decca. Its B-side, *Sister Morphine*, a drug-weary song written with Jagger and Richard, is later regarded as one of her most notable releases. This is her last recording for several years, as she continues to pursue acting.

Apr Compilation, ***Marianne Faithfull's Greatest Hits***, peaks at US #171.

May Faithfull and Jagger are arrested at their shared London home on charges of marijuana possession.

July [8] On the Australian set of the film "Ned Kelly", in which she is to co-star with Mick Jagger, Faithfull is discovered in a coma, suffering from a self-inflicted overdose. She is dropped from the movie and goes to hospital for treatment of heroin addiction.

1970

Faithfull and John Dunbar are divorced after several years of separation. She stars as Ophelia alongside Nicol Williamson in a film version of Shakespeare's "Hamlet".

1973

Oct [18] She appears - dressed as a nun - on the NBC-TV David Bowie-headlining "The Midnight Special" (titled "The 1980 Floor Show" in the UK) from London's Marquee club, performing *I Got You Babe*.

1975

Nov Her recording return is a version of Waylon Jennings' *Dreaming My Dreams* (taken from the Grease Band-backed parent set, ***Dreaming My Dreams***) for the independent NEMS label. It charts in Eire but not in the UK. (A second set with the group, the country-based ***Faithless***, will be released in March 1978.)

1979

Nov [23] Recently married to Ben Brierly, bassist with punk band the Vibrators, she is arrested at Oslo Airport, Norway, for possession of marijuana.

Dec [1] Now signed to Island Records, Faithfull's ***Broken English*** makes UK #57, despite a boycott by Island's distributor, EMI, due to objections to its lyrical content. Extracted from the album, her cover of Shel Silverstein's *The Ballad Of Lucy Jordan* is her first UK hit single for over 12 years, reaching #48. The album will also climb to US #82 the following March.

1981

Oct [17] ***Dangerous Acquaintances***, co-produced by Steve Winwood, makes UK #45 and will peak at US #104. It will be followed by her third Island set, ***A Child's Adventure***, produced by Wally Badarou, Harvey Goldberg and Barry Reynolds, which peaks at UK #99 and US #107 in March 1983.

1985

Having contributed a track the previous year to ***Lost In The Stars : The Music Of Kurt Weill*** at the invitation of producer Hal Willner, and still battling a constant drug problem, Faithfull falls down a flight of stairs (apparently while stoned) and breaks her jaw.

1987

Aug [15] ***Strange Weather***, a covers album (including a remake of *As Tears Go By)* produced by Willner and featuring songs by Jagger/Richards, Dr. John and Tom Waits, makes UK #78.

1988

Apr Now living in Cambridge, MA, and married to writer Giorgio Della Terza, Faithfull has a deportation order served on her by the US immigration authorities. (She will move to Eire.)

1989

Sept [2-4] She teaches "Love, Fear And The Ridiculous : Songwriting And Performing" at the Omega Institute in Rhinebeck, NY.

Dec [9-10] Faithfull performs Kurt Weill and Bertholdt Brecht's "Seven Deadly Sins" at St. Ann's Cathedral, Brooklyn, NY.

1990

July [20] Faithfull participates in a live performance of Roger Waters' "The Wall" in Berlin, Germany.

Aug [18] ***Blazing Away***, featuring live performances at St. Ann's Cathedral and studio tracks with Dr. John, Garth Hudson, Marc Ribot, Barry Reynolds and Lew Soloff guesting, makes US #160, while Faithfull tours the US, accompanied by Reynolds.

Sept [27] She plays a rare UK date at London's Borderline.

1992

Jan [4] Having performed with them at the London Palladium, as part of the "Chieftains Music Festival 1991" the previous July 7th, the Chieftains' ***The Bells Of Dublin***, to which Faithfull has contributed *I Saw Three Ships A Sailing*, peaks at US #107. (During the year she also completes acting work in two movies "Turn Of The Screw" and "Shopping", the latter will premiere the following year.

1994

Aug [23] ***No Prima Donna***, a various artists compilation tribute to Van Morrison to which Faithfull has contributed *Madame George*, is released.

[29] Her autobiography **Faithfull** is published to tie in with the September release of the Island album ***Faithfull : A Collection Of Her Best Recordings***.

Oct [8] She performs *Crayfish* at "Elvis Aaron Presley : The Tribute", an all-star tribute staged at the Pyramid Arena, Memphis, TN, broadcast on US pay-per-view TV.

1995

Jan [19] Faithfull participates in the "Commitment To Life VII" benefit AIDS Project Los Angeles, honoring Elton John, Tom Hanks and Ron Meyer, at the Universal Amphitheatre, Universal City, CA.

Apr Island releases her latest album, the Angelo Badalamenti-produced ***A Secret Life***.

GEORGIE FAME & THE BLUE FLAMES

Georgie Fame (vocals, keyboards);
Colin Green (guitar); **Peter Coe** (saxes, flute);
Tony Makins (bass); **Bill Eyden** (drums);
Speedy Acquaye (congas)

1959

Aug On holiday at Butlins in Pwllheli, Gwynedd, Wales, Fame (b. Clive Powell, Sept. 26, 1943, Leigh, Lancs.) stands in for an injured pianist in the resident group Rory Blackwell & the Blackjacks. Blackwell convinces the 16-year-old to quit his cotton factory job and move to London as a full-time Blackjack, but

within a month the band folds, leaving him stranded. Rather than returning home ingloriously, he lands a gig playing piano in an East End London pub.
Oct Songwriter Lionel Bart spots him and recommends an audition for top UK rock'n'roll manager Larry Parnes. With pianists at a premium, Powell is hired and is given his new name. (Renaming his acts is a penchant of Parnes, creator of Tommy Steele, Marty Wilde, Vince Eager, Duffy Power and others.)

1960

Feb In addition to backing Parnes' stars, Fame is allowed to develop his own vocal talents by opening the second half of the current Gene Vincent/Eddie Cochran UK tour.
Apr Fame makes his disc debut, playing piano on Gene Vincent's *Pistol Packin' Mama.*

1961

June Fame joins Parnes' billtopper Billy Fury's permanent backing group, the Blue Flames.
Dec Fury replaces the Blue Flames with the Tornados. Georgie Fame & the Blue Flames secure a residency at the Flamingo, a jazz cellar in London's Soho, initially playing the regular "Twist Sessions" but, before long, they amass a following for their heady jazz/rock/blues beat melange.

1962

July As R&B rivals to Alexis Korner's Blues Incorporated at the nearby Marquee club, the Blue Flames expand from four to seven members, playing brassy jazz-rock.
Nov Inspired by Booker T. and Jimmy McGriff, Fame now plays a Hammond B3 organ - one of the first in London.

1963

Aug The group begins a Friday-night residency at the Scene, Great Windmill Street, London.
Sept Signed to EMI's Columbia label, the Blue Flames debut live album, ***Rhythm And Blues At The Flamingo***, cut at the Flamingo and produced by ex-Cliff Richard sidekick Ian Samwell, spreads the reputation, already building with their 40-gigs-per-month schedule.

1964

Oct His second set, ***Fame At Last***, reaches UK #15.

1965

Jan [14] For his fourth single, Fame has re-worked *Yeh Yeh*, an Afro-Cuban song by Lambert, Hendricks & Ross, which hits UK #1 and reaches US #21, making it a million seller. With John Mayall, the Rolling Stones, the Animals and the Yardbirds, Fame now leads the R&B boom and, in common with John Mayall's Bluesbreakers, the Blue Flames becomes an academy for aspiring musicians, with John McLaughlin, Mickey Waller and Mitch Mitchell among those passing through.
Mar Written by jazzman Johnny Burch, *In The Meantime* takes Fame to UK #22 and US #97. Appearances on US TV shows are taped in Britain because his band contains two blacks - a prime reason why they never tour the US.
[20] They begin a 21-date, twice-nightly UK tour as special British guests on the "Tamla Motown Package Show", featuring the Supremes, Stevie Wonder, Martha & the Vandellas and others, at the Finsbury Park Astoria, London, ending April 12th at the Guildhall, Portsmouth, Hants.
July Currently topping numerous jazz, pop and vocal polls, Fame makes UK #33 with *Like We Used To Do.*
Aug [7] They perform at the fifth annual "National Jazz & Blues Festival", at the Athletic Ground, Richmond, Surrey.
Sept [21] The group participates in the "Pop From Britain" concert at London's Royal Albert Hall, with Cliff Bennett & the Rebel Rousers, the Fourmost and the Moody Blues.
Nov [20] *Something* reaches UK #23.

1966

May ***Sweet Things*** hits UK #6.
July [21] Fame's own composition, *Get Away*, tops the UK chart for a week.
[31] The group plays at the sixth annual "National Jazz & Blues Festival", at Windsor, Berks.
Sept [10] *Get Away* peaks at US #70.
Oct ***Sound Venture*** hits UK #9.
[1-2] Fame plays his last gigs with the Blue Flames, representing the UK in the annual "Grand Gala Du Disque" in Amsterdam, Holland. (Fame disbands his Blue Flames to pursue a more flexible career. Over the years, he will front many combos and orchestras of varying composition and size.)
[9] He plays a jazz-oriented concert with the Harry South Orchestra at London's Royal Festival Hall.
[15] His cover of Bobby Hebb's hit, *Sunny*, makes UK #13, one place behind the original.
[20] With the new Georgie Fame Band, he begins a 16-date, twice-nightly UK tour at London's Finsbury Park Astoria, with Chris Farlowe, Eric Burdon & the Animals and others, set to end on November 6th at the Odeon Cinema, Leicester, Leics.
Dec [26] His "Fame In '67" show opens at the Saville Theatre, London, and will run until January 17th.

1967

Jan [21] Fame reaches UK #12 with his version of Billy Stewart's *Sitting In The Park.*
Feb [2] He performs at the Cannes Musical Trade Fair, Cannes, France.
Mar ***Hall Of Fame*** reaches UK #12, while his own composition *Because I Love You*, also his debut on CBS/Columbia Records, makes UK #15.
May [25] Fame performs at the Royal Albert Hall, backed by the Count Basie Orchestra.
July ***Two Faces Of Fame*** reaches UK #22.
Sept *Try My World* makes UK #37.
Oct Fame takes part in the "International Popular Music Festival" in Rio de Janeiro, Brazil.

1968

Jan [24] Inspired by the movie "Bonnie And Clyde", Mitch Murray and Peter Callender have written *The Ballad Of Bonnie And Clyde*, which becomes Fame's third UK chart topper. It also hits US #7, to become his biggest (but last) US hit, earning him another gold disc. (Fame spends most of the year touring, not least to promote ***The Third Face Of Fame***.)

1969

Jan [17] Fame performs at the Royal Albert Hall with Ten Years After and Family.
July His cover of Kenny Rankin's *Peaceful* reaches UK #16.
Dec *Seventh Son* makes UK #25, taken from ***Seventh Son***. (He will undertake a tour of Australia the following April.)

1971

Teamed with ex-Animal Alan Price, *Rosetta* makes UK #11, taken from the collaborative ***Fame And Price, Price And Fame Together***, both promoted with a short-lived BBC-TV series. (After his heyday, Fame moves increasingly towards adult-oriented material. He plays several concerts backed by big bands or orchestras, performs a tribute to songwriter Hoagy Carmichael, appears on numerous television variety shows, makes TV commercials, notably for Esso, fronts various versions of the Blue Flames and continues to record, releasing ***All Me Own Work*** (1972), ***Georgie Fame*** (1974), ***That's What Friends Are For*** (1978), ***Georgie Fame Right Now*** (1979), ***Closing The Gap*** (1980), ***Hoagland*** (a tribute to Carmichael, recorded with Annie Ross, 1981), ***In Goodman's Land*** (1983), ***Rhythm & Blues At The Flamingo*** (1984), ***My Favourite Songs*** (1984) and ***No Worries*** (1988).)

1989

June Fame returns to a higher profile when he is the featured keyboard player on Van Morrison's tour, also appearing on his album, ***Avalon Sunset***.
Nov UK retrospective label Connoisseur releases an authoritative collection, ***Georgie Fame : The First 30 Years***.

1991

Dec [9] Still in demand on the jazz circuit, Fame performs at Ronnie Scott's club, London, promoting his first album of the '90s, ***Cool Cat Blues***, which features guest musicians Steve Gadd, Jon Hendricks, Robben Ford, Boz Scaggs and Richard Tee, and a duet version of *Moondance* with its writer, Van Morrison.

1992

July [21] He appears at the "First International Jazz Festival", Winter Gardens Empress Ballroom, Blackpool, Lancs., with Alan Price.
Sept [11] The soundtrack to the Jack Lemmon-starring "Glengarry Glen Ross", featuring Fame singing *Easy Street*, is released in the US.

1996

Jan Having become increasingly collaborative with Van Morrison, the pair serves up ***How Long Has This Been Going On***, Morrison's first jazz outing for which Fame, still playing his trademark Hammond B-3 organ, has recruited top-flight jazz musicians including Pee Wee Ellis.

FAMILY

Roger Chapman (vocals); **Charlie Whitney** (guitar); **John "Poli" Palmer** (keyboards); **John Weider** (bass); **Rob Townsend** (drums)

1967

The roots of the band lie in the Farinas (earlier known as the Roaring Sixties), a group formed by Whitney (b. June 24, 1944, Skipton, N. Yorks.) in 1962, while attending art college in Leicester, Leics., with Chapman (b. Apr. 8, 1942, Leicester), who was previously working for a building contractor, sax player Jim King (b. 1947, Northants.), Harry Ovenall on drums and bassist Ric Grech (b. Nov. 1, 1946, Bordeaux, France), who had previously played in a band with Chapman. As the Farinas, they released *You'd Better Stop* on Fontana Records in August 1964, and played extensive UK club and college dates. Now relocating to London from Leicester, they move into a Chelsea house, making contact with a friend, film producer John Gilbert, who gives financial help and eventually becomes their manager. They name-change to Family at the suggestion of US producer Kim Fowley.
Sept Another one-off deal, with Liberty Records, results in the first Family single, *Scene Through The Eye Of A Lens*.

1968

July A new recording deal, with Reprise Records, results in ***Music In A Doll's House***, showcasing Chapman's powerful vocal presence and featuring new drummer Rob Townsend (b. July 7, 1947, Leicester), a veteran of several Leicester bands. Produced by Traffic's Dave Mason, it makes UK #35. They make their London debut at the Royal Albert Hall, supporting US folk singer Tim Hardin.

1969

Mar ***Family Entertainment*** hits UK #6.
Apr John Weider (b. Apr. 21, 1947), formerly with Teddy & the Cannons and Eric Burdon & the Animals, joins on bass, when Grech quits to join Blind Faith on the eve of Family's first US tour (cancelled after a few dates when Chapman's visa is revoked).
July [5] They support the Rolling Stones at their free concert in Hyde Park, London.
Oct Jim King leaves to join Ring Of Truth and is replaced by ex-Eclection, Deep Feeling and Blossom Toes keyboardist, John "Poli" Palmer (b. May 25, 1943).

Nov *No Mule's Fool* is their first UK hit single, reaching UK #29.

1970

Jan ***A Song For Me***, the first album to be produced by the band, hits UK #4.
Mar While on a North American tour, Chapman's passport is stolen in New York, so the rest of the band has to perform without him in Canada.
Sept EP *Strange Band*, featuring the stage favorite *The Weaver's Answer*, reaches UK #11.
Nov ***Anyway***, a part-live and part-studio-recorded set, hits UK #7. Jenny Fabian's cult novel **Groupie** is published, allegedly based on Family's touring exploits.
[19] The group embarks on a ten-date UK tour at Sophia Gardens, Cardiff, Wales, set to end on December 1st in its hometown, at the De Montfort Hall, Leicester.

1971

Mar ***Old Songs, New Songs***, featuring updated versions of old Family material, is released.
June Weider leaves to form Stud and is replaced by John Wetton (b. July 12, 1949, Derby, Derbys.) from Mogul Thrash.
Aug *In My Own Time*, Family's most successful single, hits UK #4.
Oct ***Fearless*** returns the group to the UK Album chart, at #14 - and is Family's best US showing, at #177.

1972

May [7] The group takes part in the "Bickershaw Festival" near Wigan, Lancs.
Sept ***Bandstand*** yields the UK #13 hit *Burlesque* and makes UK #15 itself, but Palmer and Wetton both quit; Palmer to do session work and Wetton to join King Crimson. Replacements are Tony Ashton (b. Mar. 1, 1946, Blackburn, Lancs.) and Jim Cregan (b. Mar. 9, 1946), ex-Stud and Blossom Toes.

1973

Sept *It's Only A Movie*, released on the band's own new Raft label, proves to be its last hit, at UK #30.
Oct [13] Family plays the final concert of its farewell tour in Leicester, before disbanding.

1990

Mar [17] Grech dies in Leicester General Hospital of kidney and liver failure following a brain haemorrhage. (Chapman and Whitney, Family's songwriters, stayed together to form the Streetwalkers, releasing five albums between 1974-1977, before Chapman pursued an active solo career, beginning with ***Chapman*** in 1979, the first of ten albums up to ***Walking The Cat*** in 1989. Cregan moved to Cockney Rebel, before joining Rod Stewart's band and marrying Linda Lewis, while Ashton and Townsend joined '70s outfit Medicine Head.)
see also: **THE ANIMALS, ASIA, BLIND FAITH, Steve HARLEY, KING CRIMSON**

CHRIS FARLOWE

1959

Farlowe (b. John Henry Deighton, Oct. 13, 1940, Berkhamstead, Herts.), a winner at age nine in a talent contest at Islington Town Hall, London, and an ex-member of the John Henry Skiffle Group, who won the All-England Skiffle Championship at the Mecca ballroom, Tottenham, London, in 1957, widens his musical horizons to R&B and rock'n'roll and forms the Thunderbirds, though it will be November 1962 before the semi-professional group releases its debut single, *Air Travel*, a one-off cut for Decca Records, which coincides with regular appearances at London's Flamingo Club.

1963

Aug Farlowe, who has taken his stage name from US jazz guitarist Tal Farlowe, having made his first professional solo appearance at the Astoria Bar, Frankfurt, W. Germany, earlier in the year, has formed the Chris Farlowe Four, which now begins a residency at the Scene, Great Windmill Street, London.
Sept *I Remember*, penned by Farlowe, is released on EMI's Columbia imprint.
Oct Farlowe and the Thunderbirds, comprising Albert Lee (guitar), Dave Greenslade (keyboards), Bruce Waddell (bass) and Ian Mague (drums), begin a further Thursday and Sunday residency at the Scene, London.

1965

June Mod-aimed *Buzz With The Fuzz* (the final Columbia single) is withdrawn when EMI objects to the mod slang of the lyrics.
Aug Farlowe releases *Stormy Monday Blues* under the name Little Joe Cook, on Guy Stevens' Sue label. The authenticity of the performance fools most into believing that it has been recorded by an obscure black US blues singer.
Oct Farlowe and the Thunderbirds sign to Immediate Records releasing *The Fool*, produced by Eric Burdon of the Animals.

1966

Feb The Mick Jagger-produced Farlowe solo *Think* (a Jagger/Richard song due to be included on the Rolling Stones' ***Aftermath***) makes UK #37.
Apr ***14 Things To Think About*** reaches UK #19.
[17] Farlowe is treated in hospital for cuts and bruises after his car skids and overturns on the M1 motorway between Birmingham, Warks, and London.
July [28] *Out Of Time*, another Jagger/Richard song, already featured by the Stones on ***Aftermath*** in a sparser arrangement than the orchestral swirl Jagger created for Farlowe, tops the UK chart.
Oct [20] Farlowe begins a 16-date, twice-nightly tour at London's Finsbury Park Astoria, with Georgie Fame, Geno Washington, the Paul Butterfield Blues Band and special guests the Animals, set to end on November 6th at the Odeon Cinema, Leicester, Leics.
Nov Farlowe's treatment of a third Jagger/Richard composition, *Ride On Baby*, makes UK #31. (The Stones' version had been rejected from ***Aftermath***.)
Dec ***The Art Of Chris Farlowe***, more soul/R&B-oriented than its predecessor, reaches UK #37.

1967

Feb *My Way Of Giving* makes UK #48.
Apr [16] Farlowe appears at the "Daily Express Record Star Show" at Wembley's Empire Pool, Wembley, Middx.
June His revival of the jazz standard *Moanin'* makes UK #46.
Dec *Handbags And Gladrags*, penned by Manfred Mann's Mike D'Abo, makes UK #33.

1968

May Farlowe disbands the Thunderbirds, whose line-up has recently included Pete Solley (keyboards) and Carl Palmer (drums), deciding to take a rest from the music scene (though their final album ***The Last Goodbye*** will appear the following year). (He will concentrate on his small London antiques business, specializing in World War II Nazi memorabilia.)
Oct [12] Jack Good-produced TV show "Innocence, Anarchy And Soul", with Farlowe, Lulu, Lonnie Donegan, Lance LeGault, the Alan Bown Set and others, airs on ITV.

1970

Sept Farlowe returns from semi-retirement to lead the band the Hill (which releases one album on Polydor (UK), ***From Here To Mama Rosa***), before handling vocals in Jon Hiseman's jazz-rock band, Colosseum. When the group folds in November 1971, Farlowe will join Atomic Rooster as vocalist.

1975

Oct *Out Of Time*, reissued on the revived Immediate label, makes UK #44.
Nov His comeback album, ***Chris Farlowe And His Band Live***, is released, again by Polydor UK. (His only other solo recording this decade will as lead vocalist on the Dave Greenslade-penned theme song to BBC1-TV's crime series "Gangsters", released on the BBC label in January 1978.)

1982

Feb He contributes the tracks *Who's To Blame* and *Hypnotising Ways* to Jimmy Page's score for "Death Wish II".
Sept [21] Farlowe, along with a host of '60s hitmakers, appears in the "Heroes And Villains" concert at London's Hammersmith Odeon, benefitting the Nordoff-Robbins' Music Therapy charity.
Oct Following his success at the "Heroes And Villains" concert, Farlowe releases *Let The Heartaches Begin*.

1988

July Having made occasional recordings, including his own ***Out Of The Blue*** (1985) and 1986's ***Born Again***, both made with a new Thunderbirds lineup comprising Tim Hinkley, "Big" George Webley, Mo Witham, John Martin and Steve Gregory, Farlowe now guests as a featured vocalist on Jimmy Page's ***Outrider***. (Farlowe will mostly retire from the music scene, occasionally making rare live appearances including one with Maggie Bell at Covent Garden's Roadhouse, London in March 1993. The reactived Immediate label will bring the singer's career highlights to compact disc with the December 1993 release of ***The Best Of Chris Farlowe - Out Of Time***.)

THE FARM

Peter Hooton (lead vocals); **Steve Grimes** (guitar); **Roy Boulter** (drums); **Carl Hunter** (bass); **Ben Leach** (keyboards); **Keith Mullen** (guitar)

1983

Hooton (b. Sept. 28, 1962, Liverpool, Lancs.), currently printing his own Liverpool F.C. fanzine **The End**, and Grimes (b. June 4, 1962, Liverpool) form the Excitements in Liverpool, name-changing to the Farm in 1984, having recruited Phillip Strongman (bass), Andy McVann (drums) and a brass section comprising Anthony Evans, Steve Levy, George Maher and John Melvin. Going on to secure minor UK indie hits with *Hearts And Minds, Some People* and *Body And Soul* (for which the band sells the rights for £800 in 1986) in the mid-'80s, the line-up changes in 1986, following the death of McVann in a police-car accident. He is replaced by Boulter (b. July 2, 1964, Liverpool). With the band always revolving around Hooton and Grimes, earlier members leave as Hunter (b. Apr. 14, 1965, Bootle, Lancs.), Leach (b. May 2, 1969, Liverpool) and Mullen complete the sextet.

1989

Managed by Keith Sampson (ex-host of an alternative music show on Radio City in Liverpool) and linked with Madness vocalist Suggs (Graham McPherson), the band forms its own Produce label, set up with £20,000 from Littlewoods pools heir Barney Moore, and also buys back the publishing rights to earlier songs, while Hooton and Grimes sign a songwriting deal with Virgin Music.

1990

May The Farm's cover of the Monkees' *Stepping Stone*, paired with *Family Of Man*, peaks at UK #58.
Sept [29] Hooton/Grimes-penned *Groovy Train*, an era-defining indie/dance/pop chugger, hits UK #6.
Oct [4] The group begins an eight-date UK tour at Goldwyns, Birmingham, W. Midlands, set to end on the 15th at Cambridge University, Cambridge, Cambs.
Dec [19-20] The band closes another short UK tour with performances at London's Astoria Theatre, as *All Together Now* (musically based around Pachelbel's

classical piece, *Canon And Gigue In D Major*) hits UK #4.

1991

Jan [18] The group plays on the first day of the "Great British Music Weekend" at Wembley Arena, Wembley, Middx, sharing the bill with equally alternative hipsters, Happy Mondays, James, Northside, 808 State and Beats International.
Mar [4] The group guests on C4-TV's soap opera "Brookside".
[16] Hooton/Grimes-written ***Spartacus*** enters at UK #1, featuring nine cuts produced by McPherson, two by Terry Farley and Peter Heller and one by the Beautiful South's Paul Heaton and Stan Cullimore.
Apr [20] Pete Wylie and the Farm's *Sinful!* reaches UK #28.
May [4] *Don't Let Me Down* debuts at its UK #36 peak.
June [22] The Farm plays a show at London's Finsbury Park.
Aug [31] *Mind* reaches UK #31.
Sept The band embarks on six-week US tour, supporting Big Audio Dynamite II. (Mullen later receives 82 stitches to his head and a hand when he intervenes in a mugging of Farm fans outside the Warfield Theatre, San Francisco, CA.)
Nov [16] *Groovy Train* makes US #41.
[28] The band begins a 16-date British tour at the Dublin Stadium, Dublin, Eire, set to end on December 20-21st at Liverpool's Royal Court Theatre.

1992

Jan [4] *Love See No Colour*, the first release on its own End Product label, peaks at UK #58, as the group works on its sophomore album at Mayfair Mews Studios, once again helmed by McPherson.
Feb [3] The group guests on ITV's "Stage One".
Mar The Farm lends *Altogether Now* to the Labour Party for use in the General Election campaign.
Apr [26] They take part in the "Norwich Sound City '92" festival at the Waterfront, Norwich, Norfolk.
May [20] The group headlines a benefit for the Russian Orphans Appeal at the Ministry Of Sound, South London.
June The band signs a recording deal - reportedly worth over £1 million - licensing its End Product label to Sony (except in the US, where they are signed to Sire).
July [4] *Rising Sun* sets at its UK #48 peak.
Aug The Farm is dropped from the bill of two Madness gigs at Finsbury Park. (Hooton will speculate that Morrissey, having the right to veto support acts, wanted them off the show.)
[29] The group performs at the annual "Reading Festival", Reading, Berks.
Oct [1] The Farm joins Arthur Scargill at a mass demonstration march from Hyde Park to Trafalgar Square, organized by the Lesbian & Gay Rights Coalition.
[17] They appear on BBC1-TV's "Going Live!" to promote their new single, *Don't You Want Me*.
[23] The group begins a 20-date UK tour at Liverpool's Irish Centre, set to close on November 18th at the University of East Anglia, Norwich.
[31] *Don't You Want Me*, covering the Human League's 1981 chart-topper reaches UK #18.
Dec [14] The band plays a one-off London date at the Astoria.

1993

Jan [9] The reissued *Love See No Colour* now reaches UK #35, but marks the premature end of its relationship with Sony.

1994

Aug Newly signed to Sire/Reprise Records worldwide, the band issues its first album in three years, ***Hullabaloo***, produced by Gary Wilkinson in London and Liverpool.

JOSE FELICIANO

1964

Blind since birth, Feliciano (b. Sept. 10, 1945, Lares, Puerto Rico), who has lived in Harlem, New York, NY, since age five, mastering acoustic and 12-string guitar in his teens, has left home in 1963 to become a regular on the Greenwich Village coffee-house circuit, singing and playing guitar in a style which encompasses Latin-American, folk and R&B influences. Now signed to RCA Records, after being spotted playing at Gerde's Folk City by an A&R executive visiting the club to check out another act, Feliciano releases his debut single, *Everybody Do The Click*, and album, ***The Voice And Guitar Of José Feliciano***.

1965

While releasing ***A Bag Full Of Soul***, he also begins a series of Latin-American recordings, sung in Spanish, which are a major success in Central and South America, as well as among the US Hispanic community.

1968

Aug Feliciano's early revival of the Doors' 1967 million seller, *Light My Fire*, is his first chartmaker, hitting US #3 and selling a million. Its slowed-down, sparse acoustic-with-woodwind arrangement and soul-inflected vocal defines Feliciano's style. It is taken from ***Feliciano!***, on which familiar songs by Lennon/McCartney, Tom Paxton, Bacharach/David, Bobby Hebb and Gerry & the Pacemakers are similarly customized. His first chart album and also his biggest seller, it hits US #2, earns a gold disc and stays on the survey for 59 weeks.
Nov *Light My Fire* hits UK #6 (the Doors' original peaked at UK #49), as ***Feliciano!*** hits UK #6. Its US follow-up, customizing Tommy Tucker's *Hi-Heel Sneakers*, reaches US #25, while its B-side, *Hitchcock Railway*, makes US #77. Rush-released *The Star-Spangled Banner*, recorded live at the fifth game of the Baseball World Series (Detroit Tigers vs. St. Louis Cardinals) in Detroit, MI, also makes US #50.
Dec [28] He appears at the "Miami Pop Festival" in Hallandale, FL, before 100,000 people, with Chuck Berry, Marvin Gaye, Joni Mitchell and others.

1969

Jan ***Souled*** reaches US #24.
Feb Taken from the album, revivals of Bruce Channel's *Hey! Baby* and the Supremes' *My World Is Empty Without You* are a minor double-sided US hit at #71 and #87.
Mar [12] Feliciano wins the Best Contemporary Pop Vocal Performance, Male category for *Light My Fire* and is named Best New Artist of 1968, at the 11th annual Grammy Awards.
Apr [27] Feliciano stars in his own US TV special with guests Andy Williams, Glen Campbell, Dionne Warwick and Burt Bacharach.
May His cover of the Bee Gees' *Marley Purt Drive* peaks at US #70.
Aug ***Feliciano/10 To 23*** (the title arising from the inclusion of a recording taped when he was ten) reaches US #16, marking his second gold disc.
Sept The self-composed *Rain* climbs to US #76.
Nov ***Feliciano/10 To 23*** makes UK #29, while the extracted *And The Sun Will Shine* (another Bee Gees-cover) is his second and last UK hit single, at #25.

1970

Jan Double album, ***Alive Alive-O!***, recorded in concert at the London Palladium, reaches US #29, earning Feliciano a third gold disc. (He had a tussle with UK authorities before performing at the venue, due to Britain's six-month quarantine rule for animals entering the country, which meant that his guide dog could not accompany him.)
June ***Fireworks*** goes off at US #57.
July Double A-side, *Destiny/Susie-Q*, peaks at US #83.
Aug ***Fireworks*** makes UK #65, Feliciano's final UK chart album.

1971

May Compilation, ***Encore! José Feliciano's Finest Performances***, reaches US #92.
Nov ***That The Spirit Needs*** peaks at US #173.

1973

June Having played five shows at New York's Palace Theater the previous September, ***Compartments***, recorded with Steve Cropper (ex-Booker T. & the MG's), peaks at US #156.

1975

Jan *Chico And The Man*, the theme from the Freddie Prinze/Jack Albertson NBC-TV comedy series (sung by Feliciano over the credits), stops at US #96, while ***And The Feeling's Good*** makes US #136.
Sept ***Just Wanna Rock'n'Roll*** reaches US #165.

1976

Sept Having left RCA, he records *Angela* for the Private Stock label. It will be followed by ***Sweet Soul Music***, co-produced by Jerry Wexler and marking a return to Feliciano's early R&B/soul fire, released in February 1977.

1981

He signs to Motown Latino (the R&B label's Hispanic imprint) to concentrate on Spanish-language recordings, while the English-language ***José Feliciano*** is also released ny the same label. An April 1993 released Motown Latino album, ***Escenas De Amor***, creates interest in the Hispanic market, but a second Motown English-language album, ***Romance In The Night***, will fare no better than the first and Feliciano will leave the label.

1984

Feb [28] Feliciano wins Best Latin Pop Performance for ***Me Enamore*** at the 26th annual Grammy Awards. (He will continue regular US live and TV work in the '80s, always a popular club draw with his interpretations of familiar material, but will have no further chart success.)

1987

Feb [24] He nabs Best Latin Pop Performance for ***Lelolai*** at the 29th annual Grammy Awards. (Now signed to EMI, he will release ***Tu Immenso Amor*** later in the year and ***I'm Never Gonna Change*** in 1989.)

1990

Feb [21] Feliciano wins Best Latin Pop Performance for the third time, for ***Cielito Lindo***, at the 32nd Grammy Awards, held at the Shrine Auditorium, Los Angeles, CA. (He issues the jazz-inflected ***Steppin' Out*** on the Optimism label by year's end).

1994

Dec Feliciano performs for Pope John Paul II for the "Christmas At The Vatican" TV special, and then is granted a private audience with the Pontiff.

1996

May [1] Having signed with Cherry Lane publishing in July 1991, part of the deal being that he make instructional videos for Cherry Lane Video and instrumental recordings for the company's Guitar Recordings, Inc., and released ***Street Life '92*** in October 1992, and still touring including an Australian and Far Eastern trek in March '94, Feliciano has recently released the double CD ***Feliciano - The Big Three-O*** on Brian Lane's Fragile label, featuring new recordings in English and Spanish to celebrate his 30th anniversary in the music business. He now receives the El Premio lifetime achievement honor at **Billboard**'s seventh annual International Latin Music Conference held in Miami, FL.
July Newly signed to PolyGram Latino worldwide, Feliciano's latest album, ***El Americano***, is released in the US.

BRYAN FERRY

1964

June Ferry (b. Sept. 26, 1945, Washington, Durham), having won tickets from Radio Luxembourg to see Bill Haley & His Comets at the Empire Theatre, Sunderland, Tyne & Wear, in his teens, forms his first band, the Banshees, in Sunderland. Moving to Newcastle, Tyne & Wear, in September, to study fine arts at university, he becomes the vocalist with the Gas Board, a soul/R&B band, and works as a DJ. Leaving university with a degree in July 1968, Ferry moves to London to work variously as a van driver, antiques restorer and a ceramics teacher at a Hammersmith girls' school, teaching himself piano and writing songs, and occasionally dabbling in the visual arts.

1971

Nov Having lost his teaching job the previous year after school authorities have objected to his turning classes into music sessions, Ferry has decided to form a band to play the songs he has been writing and Roxy Music is born (its name inspired by a cinema, with Music added because there is an existing US group called Roxy). The first regular line-up of Roxy Music will begin playing the following year, and Ferry, the inspiration behind the unit, will remain its central creative force, steering the group's successful career as its main writer and lead vocalist.

1973

Oct Ferry's first solo album, ***These Foolish Things***, co-produced by Ferry, John Porter and John Punter and backed by a session group which includes Roxy drummer Paul Thompson, is a collection of covers of his favorite oldies. (Ferry was exposed from an early age to standards, by his aunt Ethel.) Aided by the concurrent success of Roxy Music, the album hits UK #5, while the extracted single, reviving Bob Dylan's *A Hard Rain's Gonna Fall*, hits UK #10.

1974

June [8] His update of Dobie Gray's *The "In" Crowd* reaches UK #13.

Aug [10] ***Another Time, Another Place***, comprising, aside from the Ferry-composed title track, more pop and R&B covers of songs by Willie Nelson, Joe South, Bob Dylan, Ike Turner and others, hits UK #4.

Sept [28] Ferry's version of the Platters' *Smoke Gets In Your Eyes*, taken from the album, reaches UK #17.

Dec After spending most of the year on a Roxy Music world tour, Ferry performs three solo dates, including one at London's Royal Albert Hall, with backing by the group (in evening dress) and an orchestra. The suave dinner-jacket look has become Ferry's trademark, even though his current image with Roxy Music is military chic.

1975

July [12] *You Go To My Head* makes UK #33.

1976

June [26] As a Roxy Music sabbatical is announced, *Let's Stick Together*, a Wilbert Harrison R&B number extracted from his forthcoming ***Let's Stick Together***, hits UK #4.

Aug EP *Extended Play* comprises four assorted revivals from the recent album: *Heart On My Sleeve*, written specially for him by Gallagher & Lyle, *The Price Of Love*, *Shame Shame Shame* and *It's Only Love*. The second track (originally a 1965 UK hit for the Everly Brothers) gains most airplay and hits UK #7 - the first EP to make the UK Top 10 since the Beatles' *Magical Mystery Tour* nine years earlier. With Roxy Music drummer Paul Thompson and the group's ex-bassist, John Wetton, plus session guitarist Chris Spedding, the Bryan Ferry Band is formed for live work.

Oct [9] ***Let's Stick Together***, a more even mix of oldies and his own material, reaches UK #19.

Nov [6] ***Let's Stick Together*** is Ferry's first US chart entry, at #160.

Dec *Heart On My Sleeve*, issued as a US single on Atlantic, makes #86. Ferry is romantically linked to US model Jerry Hall (who features on the sleeve of Roxy Music's ***Siren*** and on the video vocals of *Let's Stick Together*. She later leaves him for Mick Jagger).

1977

Jan Ferry announces the full touring line-up of his new band, which includes Roxy Music's Phil Manzanera on second guitar, Ann Odell on keyboards, a brass section and three backing singers.

Feb [1] The new group embarks on a UK tour as the prelude to a world trek, helping *This Is Tomorrow* to hit UK #9.

Mar [12] As the tour moves on through Europe, ***In Your Mind***, solely comprising Ferry compositions, hits UK #5.

Apr Ferry contributes *She's Leaving Home* to the soundtrack album of Lou Reizner's film "All This And World War II".

May After a short break, the second half of his world tour begins, taking in Australia, Japan and the US. ***In Your Mind*** reaches US #126. After the tour, the band disperses and Ferry bases himself in Los Angeles, CA, where he writes songs for a new album.

June *Tokyo Joe*, taken from ***In Your Mind***, reaches UK #15.

Dec Ferry moves to a hotel in Montreux, Switzerland, and, over the next three months records ***The Bride Stripped Bare*** at the Montreux Casino Studio, with a session crew including Waddy Wachtel and Neil Hubbard (guitars), Rick Marotta (drums) and Alan Spenner (bass).

1978

May [20] *What Goes On*, penned by Lou Reed, peaks at UK #67.

Aug [26] *Sign Of The Times* makes UK #37, but a projected summer UK tour to preface the new album is cancelled because of poor ticket sales.

Oct [7] ***The Bride Stripped Bare***, taking its title from the work of Marcel Duchamp, and containing a mixture of new songs and R&B oldies, including Sam & Dave's *You Don't Know Like I Know* and Al Green's *Take Me To The River*, reaches UK #13.

Nov [25] ***The Bride Stripped Bare*** peaks at US #159, as Ferry reassembles Roxy Music to record ***Manifesto***.

1982

June [26] Ferry marries Lucy Helmore at a society wedding in Sussex (their son will be named after Otis Redding).

1985

June [15] After two chart-topping Roxy Music albums (***Flesh And Blood*** and ***Avalon***), a live mini-album (***The High Road***) and now signed to E.G. Records, Ferry re-emerges as a solo artist with ***Boys And Girls***, which heads the UK chart. It features guest musicians, including Mark Knopfler, David Sanborn, Nile Rodgers and David Gilmour. During its recording, Ferry tells writer/producer Keith Forsey that he is too busy to record a new song, *Don't You (Forget About Me)*. (It is later a US #1 for Simple Minds.) *Slave To Love* hits UK #10.

July [13] Ferry and the band play in the "Live Aid" benefit concert at Wembley Stadium, Wembley, Middx.

Aug ***Boys And Girls***, released on Warner Bros., makes US #65.

Sept *Don't Stop The Dance* reaches UK #21.

Dec *Windswept* makes UK #46.

1986

Apr *Is Your Love Strong Enough?*, featured in Ridley Scott's film "Legend", reaches UK #22.

[26] TV-advertised compilation, ***Street Life - 20 Greatest Hits***, with both Roxy Music and Ferry solo successes, tops the UK chart for the first of five weeks, becoming one of the best-selling albums of the year. (Ferry has also contributed vocals to Tangerine Dream's US #96, ***Legend***.)

1987

Oct After another lengthy spell in the studio, Ferry's first new recording in two years is *The Right Stuff*, co-written with Smiths guitarist Johnny Marr, which reaches UK #37.

Nov [14] ***Bête Noire***, co-produced by Pat Leonard and also featuring Marr, hits UK #9. Released in the US on Reprise, it peaks at #63.

Dec [5] Ferry performs on NBC-TV's "Saturday Night Live".

1988

Feb Ferry-penned *Kiss And Tell* reaches UK #41.

Apr Featured in the Michael J. Fox movie "Bright Lights Big City", *Kiss And Tell* moves to US #31.

Oct A remixed *Let's Stick Together* makes UK #12, a prelude to the greatest hits album ***The Ultimate Collection***.

Nov [19] ***The Ultimate Collection*** hits UK #6 in its week of entry.

1989

Jan [16] Ferry plays first of four nights at the Wembley Arena.

Feb Reissued and remixed, *The Price Of Love* makes UK #49.

Apr [22] *He'll Have To Go* stops at UK #63.

Aug ***Street Life - 20 Great Hits*** makes US #100. (A Ferry performance video, "New Town - Bryan Ferry In Europe" will be released in the US the following March.)

1992

June [6] Ferry takes part in the "Earth Pledge Concert" on the Great Lawn of New York, NY's Central Park.

Aug [11] "Honeymoon In Vegas" soundtrack, to which Ferry has contributed a cover of *Are You Lonesome Tonight?*, is released.

1993

Mar [13] *I Put A Spell On You*, from the forthcoming ***Taxi*** album, reaches UK #18.

Apr [3] Co-produced with Robin Trower, Ferry's third collection of cover versions, the soul-inflected ***Taxi***, which includes his interpretations of *Will You Love Me Tomorrow*, *Just One Look* and *Amazing Grace*, while the title cut is a version of J. Blackfoot's 1983 R&B hit, debuts at its UK #2 peak, behind Depeche Mode's ***Songs Of Faith And Devotion***.

[30] Ferry guests on NBC-TV's "The Tonight Show".

May [1] ***Taxi*** bows at its US #79 peak.

[24] Ferry appears on ITV's "The Beat".

June [5] *Will You Love Me Tomorrow* reaches UK #23.

Sept [11] *Girl Of My Best Friend* makes UK #57.

1994

Sept [17] ***Mamouna***, reuniting Ferry with Eno, sparking rumors of a Roxy Music reunion, reaches UK #11 in its week of entry.

Oct [8] ***Mamouna*** debuts at its US #94 peak.

[29] *Your Painted Smile* charts for a week at UK #52.

Nov [21-23] Ferry plays three dates at New York's Beacon Theatre, during a US tour.

[24] He guests on CBS-TV's "Late Show With David Letterman".

1995

Feb [11] Title cut *Mamouna* charts for a week at UK #57, as Ferry plays the Plymouth Pavilion, Plymouth, Devon, during his European tour.

Mar [12] Following concerts in Australia, the Japanese leg of a world tour tour opens at the NHK Hall, Tokyo, Japan, followed by shows in Brazil before continuing with more US dates.

Nov [4] ***More Than This - The Best Of Bryan Ferry And Roxy Music*** reaches UK #15 in its week of entry.

see also: **ROXY MUSIC**

THE 5TH DIMENSION

Marilyn McCoo (vocals); **Florence LaRue** (vocals); **Lamonte McLemore** (vocals); **Billy Davis, Jr.** (vocals); **Ron Townson** (vocals)

1966

The vocal quintet forms initially as the Versatiles in Los Angeles, CA, with McLemore (b. Sept. 17, 1939, St. Louis, MO) and McCoo (b. Sept. 30, 1943, Jersey City, NJ), who has made her TV debut at 15 in "Spotlight On Young" and, at 19, won the Miss Bronze Grand Talent Award and Miss Congeniality honor in California. Both are ex-members of the Hi-Fis (along with Floyd Butler and Harry Elston, later in Friends of Distinction), who released one Ray Charles-backed and-produced single, *Lonesome Mood*, the previous year. They are joined by Davis (b. June 26, 1940, St. Louis), formerly of the Emeralds and the Saint Gospel Singers, then a member of El Toros, and Townson (b. Jan. 20, 1933, St. Louis), placed third in the Metropolitan Opera auditions in St. Louis, before joining the Wings Over Jordan choir and touring with Dorothy Dandridge and Nat "King" Cole and who appeared in the movie "Porgy And Bess", before moving to Los Angeles, and forming the a cappella combo the Celestial Choir of Thirty Five Voices. Both have known McLemore in hometown vocal groups. LaRue (b. Feb. 4, 1944, Philadelphia, PA), a California State University graduate and ex-teacher, has been discovered by McLemore, who photographed her being crowned Miss Bronze California Pageant by the previous year's winner, McCoo. Now assembled, they tour the US with the Ray Charles Revue for six months and Marc Gordon becomes their manager. He takes them back to Los Angeles and introduces them to Johnny Rivers, who has started his own Soul City label through Liberty Records.

1967

Feb Signed by Rivers, the group becomes the 5th Dimension, the name suggested by Townson and his wife Babette because Rivers says the Versatiles is dated. Their version of a Mamas & the Papas' album track, *Go Where You Wanna Go*, produced by Rivers, reaches US #16.

May *Another Day, Another Heartache*, a P.F. Sloan/Steve Barri song, makes US #45. Producer Rivers has to re-schedule sessions for a first album in order to take part in the "San Remo Song Festival". During the break, rehearsal pianist Jim Webb spends a weekend at a fair, where he sees a hot air balloon in action and is inspired to write *Up, Up And Away*. Back at the studio, he plays it to the others, who insist on recording it and ask to hear other Webb songs, from which they choose four more to complete the album.

July *Up, Up And Away* is the group's first Top 10 hit, at US #7.

Aug Their debut album, ***Up, Up And Away***, hits US #8, earning a gold disc during an 83-week chart stay.

Dec *Paper Cup*, also written by Webb, makes US #34.

1968

Jan ***The Magic Garden***, produced by Bones Howe and with all but one song (Lennon/McCartney's *Ticket To Ride*) penned by Webb, is a polished, harmony-rich concept album, but with poor marketing, it makes only US #105 (though sales are consistent and it stays on the survey for 31 weeks).

Feb [29] *Up, Up And Away* sweeps the 10th annual Grammy Awards, winning the Record Of The Year, Song Of The Year, Best Performance By A Vocal Group (Two To Six Persons), Best Contemporary Single and Best Contemporary Group Performance Vocal Or Instrumental categories. (The Johnny Mann Singers' version also wins a Grammy, for Best Performance By A Chorus (Seven Or More Persons).)

Mar *Carpet Man*, from ***The Magic Garden***, reaches US #29.

July 5th Dimension's cover of Laura Nyro's laid-back summer song, *Stoned Soul Picnic*, hits US #3, selling over a million to become group's first gold single.

Sept ***Stoned Soul Picnic*** reaches US #21.

Nov *Sweet Blindness*, another Nyro song from the album, makes US #13.

1969

Feb *California Soul* reaches US #25.

Apr [12] *Aquarius/Let The Sunshine In* is the group's biggest hit, topping the US chart for the first of six weeks and selling two million copies in three months. The medley from the Broadway rock musical "Hair", was cut after the group saw Ronnie Dyson sing *Aquarius* in the show. Producer Howe linked the two instrumental tracks in the Los Angeles studio and the group overdubbed the final vocals in Las Vegas, NV (where they were appearing at Caesar's Palace with Frank Sinatra).

May *Aquarius/Let The Sunshine In* reaches UK #11, the group's first UK hit. (Due to a misunderstanding, an abridged version intended for US AM radio, which omits much of *Aquarius*, is released in Britain, but it does not affect sales and remains uncorrected.)

July ***The Age Of Aquarius*** hits US #2 during a 72-week chart run, earning another gold disc.

Aug *Workin' On A Groovy Thing*, a Neil Sedaka co-composition taken from the album, reaches US #20.

Sept [21] The group appears on CBS-TV's "Woody Allen Special".

Nov [8] *Wedding Bell Blues*, another Nyro song and also from ***Aquarius***, is the group's second #1 and third million-selling single, topping the US chart for the first of three weeks. (During their most successful year, McCoo has married Davis, while LaRue and manager Gordon have also tied the knot.)

1970

Feb *Wedding Bell Blues* makes UK #16 (the group's second and final UK hit), while the last extract from the album, Nyro's song *Blowing Away*, reaches US #21.

Mar Newly signed to Bell Records, their label debut, *A Change Is Gonna Come/People Gotta Be Free*, a medley of Sam Cooke's 1965 hit and the Young Rascals' 1968 #1, reaches US #60, dually credited with its B-side, *The Declaration*.

[11] *Aquarius/Let The Sunshine In* is named Record Of The Year and Best Contemporary Vocal Performance By A Group Of 1969, at the 12th annual Grammy Awards.

May *The Girls' Song*, the final Soul City release, reaches US #43, while the Bell single *Puppet Man* (another Sedaka song) makes US #24.

June ***Portrait***, on Bell, climbs to US #20, while the Soul City compilation, ***The 5th Dimension/Greatest Hits***, hits US #5, both albums gaining gold discs.

July *Save The Country* (again by Nyro) reaches US #27.

Sept Another Soul City compilation, ***The July 5th Album***, reaches US #63, while *On The Beach (In The Summertime)*, from ***Portrait***, makes US #54. (Davis sets up his own management company, his first signing being Roy Gaines.)

Oct The group represents the US at the "October Festival", Warsaw, Poland.

Dec A Bacharach/David ballad, *One Less Bell To Answer*, hits US #2 for two weeks (behind George Harrison's *My Sweet Lord*), and is another million seller.

1971

Apr ***Love's Lines, Angles And Rhymes*** reaches US #17, while the extracted title cut, *Love's Lines, Angles And Rhymes*, reaches US #19.

June *Light Sings*, from the Broadway musical "The Me Nobody Knows", makes US #44.

Nov Live double album, ***The 5th Dimension Live!!***, reaches US #32, while a revival of the Association's *Never My Love*, taken from it, climbs to US #12. A further compilation, ***Reflections***, peaks at US #112.

1972

Jan [28-30] The group plays its only UK career concerts at London's Royal Albert Hall, the Odeon Cinema, Birmingham, W. Midlands, and the Empire Theatre, Liverpool, Merseyside.

Feb *Together Let's Find Love* makes US #37.

Apr ***Individually And Collectively***, featuring group and solo performances, makes US #58.

June *Last Night I Didn't Get To Sleep At All*, penned by UK writer Tony Macaulay, is the group's fifth and last million-selling single, at US #8.

Nov *If I Could Reach You* hits US #10, while the compilation ***Greatest Hits On Earth*** (containing the hits from both Soul City and Bell catalogs), reaches US #14, the group's last gold disc. The Fifth Dimension also performs at the White House, at the invitation of President Nixon.

1973

Feb *Living Together, Growing Together*, from the movie "Lost Horizon", makes US #32.

Apr ***Living Together, Growing Together*** peaks at US #108, while *Everything's Been Changed* stops at US #70.

Sept *Ashes To Ashes* makes US #52. Their last Bell release, *Flashback* will peaks at US #82 in January the following year.

1975

Sept Signed to ABC Records, the group is reunited with Jim Webb for ***Earthbound***, a concept-packaged set of his songs, which makes US #136.

Nov McCoo and Davis leave the group for solo careers (though they remain with ABC Records).

1976

Apr *Love Hangover* is the last 5th Dimension chart single, at US #80; the Diana Ross version on Motown hits #1. (The group will retreat to the supper-club circuit, where it retains a solid following.)

May McCoo and Davis peak at US #91 with their first duet, *I Hope We Get To Love In Time*.

1977

Jan [8] McCoo and Davis hit US #1 with *You Don't Have To Be A Star (To Be In My Show)*, selling over one million copies, while their ***I Hope We Get To Love In Time*** reaches US #30 and earns a gold disc.

Feb [19] *You Don't Have To Be A Star (To Be In My Show)* wins a Grammy Award as Best R&B Vocal Performance By A Duo at the 19th annual ceremony.

Apr The duo scores its only UK success as *You Don't Have To Be A Star (To Be In My Show)* hits UK #7.

May *Your Love* by McCoo and Davis reaches US #15.

June [15] The duo co-hosts a CBS-TV summer variety series of six programs, "The Marilyn McCoo And Billy Davis Jr. Show".

Sept *Look What You've Done To My Heart* is McCoo and Davis' last hit, peaking at US #51, while their second (and final) ABC album, ***The Two Of Us***, makes US #57.

1978

Mar The 5th Dimension signs to Motown, but ***Star Dancing*** arouses little interest.

Oct McCoo and Davis sign to CBS/Columbia Records for ***Marilyn And Billy***, which peaks at US #146. A second 5th Dimension Motown album, ***High On Sunshine***, will fail to chart when released the following April and the group is dropped from the label.

1980

McCoo and Davis split professionally. She moves to RCA to record solo material (plus the occasional duet with Davis), but will fare better on TV, hosting the show "Solid Gold", before playing Tamara Price on the US soap series "Days Of Our Lives" and appearing onstage in both "Man Of La Mancha" and "Anything Goes".

1990

Sept *Up Up And Away* is honored as one of BMI's Most Performed Songs Of 1940-1990, as it surpasses its three-millionth performance.

1991

Aug [9] As McCoo, who has just released her first solo gospel album, ***The Me Nobody Knows***, Davis,

Gordon, McLemore and Townson prepare to begin a reunion tour on the 10th, the group receives a star on Hollywood's Walk of Fame.

1995

May [16] While McCoo regularly co-hosts the annual gospel Dove Awards, all former members of the 5th Dimension have continued touring in various combinations into the '90s, mainly on the nightclub nostalgia circuit, where its hit repertoire has adapted neatly to the MOR atmosphere. A new album ***Fifth Dimension In The House*** is now released on Dick Clark Productions' Click Records (US).

FINE YOUNG CANNIBALS

Roland Gift (vocals); **Andy Cox** (guitars); **David Steele** (keyboards, bass)

1984

Cox (b. Jan. 25, 1960, Birmingham, Warks.) and Steele (b. Sept. 8, 1960, Isle of Wight) are already rhythm veterans of hit UK act the Beat (known in the US as the English Beat), formed in 1978 with Everette Morton (b. Apr. 5, 1951, St. Kitts, West Indies), Dave Wakeling (b. Feb. 19, 1956, Birmingham) and reggae toaster Ranking Roger (b. Roger Charlery, Feb. 21, 1961, Birmingham), playing ska-influenced rock from its Birmingham base. Releasing records on the 2-Tone and subsequently its own Go-Feet labels, the group's Top 10 hits were *Hands Off, She's Mine* (#9, February 1980), *Mirror In The Bathroom* (#4, May 1980), *Too Nice To Talk To* (#7, December 1980) and swan song *Can't Get Used To Losing You* (#3, May 1983). Its chart albums were ***Just Can't Stop It*** (#3, May 1980) and ***Wha'ppen*** (#3, May 1981). With the Beat having split in 1983, Wakeling has gone on to form General Public with Ranking Roger, while Cox and Steele invite Gift (b. May 28, 1962, Birmingham), ex-sax player with the Kingston-upon-Hull, Humberside band Acrylic Victims and an actor with the Hull Community Theatre Workshop (where he has made his singing debut on an Al Jolson number), recently playing in a blues band in Finsbury Park, London, near where he is also working on a Camden market stall, to be the vocalist to their rhythm section.

Dec Calling themselves the Fine Young Cannibals, after a 1960 Natalie Wood/Robert Wagner-starring movie, "All The Fine Young Cannibals", the group signs to London Records, which has spotted them performing on a home video of their song *Johnny Come Home* on C4-TV's "The Tube", and begins recording debut sessions (with Martin Parry on percussion) aimed at a soul/dance/rock blend which will be dominated by Gift's distinctive soul falsetto vocal quality.

1985

June Their debut single, *Johnny Come Home*, featuring trumpet player Graeme Hamilton, is released and, boosted by another showing of their original home video on "The Tube", it will hit UK #8.

Nov The follow-up, *Blue*, lyrically attacking the current Conservative Government policies, makes UK #41.

Dec [21] Mainly self-composed, ***Fine Young Cannibals*** enters the UK chart, set to reach UK #11.

1986

Feb Their cover version of Elvis Presley's 1969 US #1 hit, *Suspicious Minds*, featuring Jimmy Somerville on backing vocals, hits UK #8.

[22] On their first American visit, a concert in Boston, MA is delayed by two hours due to an tear gas incident in the audience.

Mar [5] A UK tour opens at Goldiggers in Cheltenham, Gloucs.

Apr Fourth extraction, *Funny How Love Is*, makes UK #58.

[26] *Johnny Come Home* peaks at US #76. With the band signed in the US to I.R.S. Records, the parent album ***Fine Young Cannibals*** is currently on a 28-week chart ride and will reach US #49 during their first North American tour. While in the US they meet film director Barry Levinson, who commissions the trio to provide four songs for his forthcoming Richard Dreyfus/Danny DeVito picture "Tin Men", also inviting them to feature prominently in the movie as the house band in the main restaurant scenes, performing several numbers, including the future hit *Good Thing*.

Aug Film director Jonathan Demme asks the band to contribute a new song for his currently-filming project "Something Wild".

1987

Mar Steele suffers a broken arm and concussion after being hit by a car in London.

Apr Fine Young Cannibals' cover version of Buzzcocks' *Ever Fallen in Love*, chosen for the "Something Wild" soundtrack, hits UK #9. It will be their only release in the three-year period between their first and second albums. On BBC1-TV's "Tom O'Connor Roadshow" in Wales, the group appears in the female Welsh national costume with Gift in miner's overalls and helmet.

July "Tin Men", featuring the group as a '60s soul band in its movie debut, premieres in the US. Gift will increasingly follow a parallel acting career, appearing in major roles over the next two years, including those in the Stephen Frears-directed "Sammy And Rosie Get Laid" (1987) and the John Hurt-starring "Scandal" (1989). These film commitments will put Fine Young Cannibals on hold for a period of two years.

Oct While Gift is away, Cox and Steele contribute material to the forthcoming John Hughes movie, "Planes, Trains And Automobiles", and, while experimenting in the studio, they knock up an authentic-sounding house cut, *I'm Tired Of Getting Pushed Around*.

1988

Feb Having received an excellent club reaction to a white-label promo pressing under the deliberately non-informative act name, Two Men, A Drum Machine and A Trumpet, London Records has issued *I'm Tired Of Being Pushed Around*, which reaches UK #18. Its success will encourage other UK dance acts to commission remixes and production from the duo.

June Cox/Steele-produced *Heat It Up* reaches UK #21 for the Wee Papa Girl Rappers. They will also complete production of forthcoming recordings for Birmingham-based Pop Will Eat Itself, before returning to full Fine Young Cannibals sessions with Gift, which will be recorded both in London and with Prince cohort David Z at the Paisley Park Studios in Minneapolis, MN.

1989

Jan [7] First fruits of new recordings, *She Drives Me Crazy*, fusing heavy-rock guitar with a dance-rhythm track penned by Steele and Gift, enters the UK chart, set to hit #5, and begins a worldwide chart visit.

Feb [18] The group's sophomore set, ***The Raw And The Cooked***, a cunning mix of pop, dance and soul, still largely self-written and produced, tops the UK chart at the beginning of a 66-week chart tenure.

Apr [8] *She Drives Me Crazy* is the first song to be featured on the USA Network's TV broadcast of "American Bandstand" with new host David Hirsh.

[15] *She Drives Me Crazy* hits US #1 for a week, spurred by its Phillipe De Couffle video, his first since New Order's "True Faith".

May *Good Thing* hits UK #7.

June [3] ***The Raw And The Cooked*** tops the US chart (displacing Madonna's ***Like A Virgin***), where it will stay for seven weeks.

July [8] *Good Thing* becomes Fine Young Cannibals' second US #1, again topping for a week.

Aug Third extract, *Don't Look Back*, makes UK #34, as the band prepares for a major US tour.

Oct [7] *Don't Look Back* reaches US #11.

[14] Fine Young Cannibals play the first of four sellout dates at the Shoreline Amphitheatre, Mountain View, CA, during a US tour with De La Soul as support.

Nov The band returns to Britain to perform a short series of shows, climaxing in three sellout gigs at London's Brixton Academy.

Dec [2] *I'm Not The Man I Used To Be* peaks at US #54, having already reached UK #20. ("The Raw And The Cooked" video collection, comprising five clips, including the promo for the Two Men, A Drum Machine and A Trumpet hit, is released. Gift spends Christmas and the New Year in New Zealand, where he will buy some land.)

1990

Feb [18] Fine Young Cannibals win the Best British Group category and ***The Raw And The Cooked*** is named Best Album By A British Artist at the ninth annual BRIT Awards, at London's Dominion Theatre, but will return their trophies, stating that "it is wrong and inappropriate for us to be associated with what amounts to a photo opportunity for Margaret Thatcher and the Conservative Party" and adding that this action is taken "with regret".

[24] Fifth extract from the second album, *I'm Not Satisfied*, remixed by Cox/Steele, makes UK #46.

Mar [3] *I'm Not Satisfied* peaks at US #90.

Apr [3] Returning once again to acting, Gift opens as Romeo in "Romeo And Juliet" in the Hull Truck Company Production at the Spring Street Theatre at the start of a UK repertory tour.

Oct [20] Cox/Steele-produced Monie Love Featuring True Image single, *It's A Shame (My Sister)*, reaches UK #12.

Nov [3] ***Red Hot + Blue***, a various artists compilation of Cole Porter songs to benefit AIDS education, including the Fine Young Cannibals' cover of *Love For Sale*, written for the 1930 stage musical "The New Yorkers", hits UK #6 on the Compilation Album chart.

Dec [15] Cox/Steele-remixed mini-album, ***The Raw And The Remixed***, reworking cuts from their second album, spends one week at UK #61.

1992

Sept [22] After Gift and Steele have been honored at last year's ASCAP PRS Awards on October 3rd, *She Drives Me Crazy* is now named one of the Most Performed Songs Of 1991 at the annual ASCAP PRS Awards.

1993

Mar Fine Young Cannibals continue working on their third self-produced album, at RAK Studios, London.

Sept Al Green's ***Don't Look Back***, co-produced and co-written with Steele and Cox, is released by BMG Records.

1995

Oct [26] 28-year old John Paul Vagg charged with impersonating Steele at Horseferry Road Magistrates' Court, having been arrested on August 16th in the Bermondsey area of London. Charges will be dismissed. (At six years and counting, the world still awaits the group's recording return.)

THE FIVE SATINS

Fred Parris (vocals); **Bill Baker** (vocals); **Al Denby** (vocals); **Jim Freeman** (vocals); **Ed Martin** (vocals); **Jessie Murphy** (piano)

1956

With its roots in the Scarlets, a high-school combo formed in 1953 in New Haven, CT, which included Parris (b. Mar. 26, 1936, CT), Denby, Sylvester Hopkins (b. 1958), Nate Mosely and Bill Powers, and after making four ballad singles for Red Robin Records, none of which were chart hits, Parris, now with the US Army in the Far East, has written *In The Still Of The Night* during a long night of military guard duty. When he returns to the US on leave, the group records it with other songs on a two-track machine in a New Haven church basement. Renamed the Five Satins, and lining up as Parris, Denby, Freeman (b. Dec. 3, 1940), Martin and Murphy, they are signed to local label Standord Records.

July Their first Standord single, *All Mine*, fails to score, but *In The Still Of The Night* begins to sell in the New York, NY area, prompting Ember Records to buy the rights and reissue it.

Nov *In The Still Of The Night* reaches US #24 during a 19-week chart stay, and makes #1 in New York, where it will remain a perennial radio favorite as a classic example of era-defining doo-wop.

1957

Feb [15] The group begins a US tour on Irving Feld's "Greatest Show Of 1957" rock package, with Chuck Berry, Fats Domino, LaVern Baker and many others, ending on May 5th.

Aug Following the release of *Wonderful Girl* and *Oh Happy Day*, they return to the US chart with *To The Aisle*, which reaches #25 in a 17-week run. Baker has joined as lead singer for the discs, with Parris having returned to Japan and army duty soon after the release of *In The Still Of The Night*.

1958

Parris returns to the US, having been discharged, and reassembles the Five Satins with West Forbes, Freeman, ex-Scarlet colleague Hopkins and Lou Peeples.

1960

Jan While *Shadows* peaked at US #87 the previous December, *In The Still Of The Night*, still being played by East Coast US DJs, returns to the US chart, reaching #81.

May *I'll Be Seeing You* makes at US #79.

1961

Jan *In The Still Of The Night* makes another fleeting return to the US chart, at #99, during a short-lived doo-wop revival, but newer singles on Ember have failed to score, and the group will move through the '60s with releases on Cub, Chancellor, Red Bird and United Artists labels claiming no chart success. (Parris will then try a solo career on Checker, Atco and RCA.)

1973

After re-forming (with original member Freeman and newcomers Jimmy Curtis and Nate Marshall) as Fred Parris & the Five Satins, and finding success on the now-burgeoning US oldies circuit, the group appears with other '50s hitmakers in the movie "Let The Good Times Roll", partly filmed at the Madison Square Garden Rock Revival Show, New York, performing *In The Still Of The Night* and an a cappella *I'll Be Seeing You*, among others.

1975

Oct Having briefly signed to Kirshner Records the previous year, recently assisted former-Shirelle Shirley Alston on her version of *In The Still Of The Night* for her album ***With A Little Help From My Friends***, and now recording in contemporary style as Black Satin, they make US R&B #49 with *Everybody Stand Up And Clap Your Hands* on Buddah Records.

1982

Mar Restored as a nostalgia act, Fred Parris & the Five Satins, they have their first US Hot 100 entry for 21 years with the nostalgic *Memories Of Days Gone By*, which reaches #71.

FIVE STAR

Deniece Pearson (lead vocals); **Doris Pearson** (vocals); **Stedman Pearson** (vocals); **Lorraine Pearson** (vocals); **Delroy Pearson** (vocals)

1983

The group forms as a teen-trio in Romford, Essex, when the three daughters of Buster (Stedman) and Dolores Pearson, Doris (b. June 8, 1966, Romford), Lorraine (b. Aug. 10, 1967, Romford) and Deniece (b. June 13, 1968, Romford) beg their father to let them record his newly-demoed song, *Problematic*. (Pearson, originally from Jamaica, is an ex-professional guitarist, who played during the '60s in tour bands behind many overseas acts working in Britain, including soulsters Wilson Pickett and Lee Dorsey, and reggae singers Desmond Dekker and Jimmy Cliff. Having produced and written songs and then run independent reggae label K&B, he launched Tent Records to focus on commercial dance music.) Impressed by his daughters' recording, he realises they have potential as a professional act and records a second demo of Lorraine's song, *Say Goodbye*. Dolores prompts the idea of sons Stedman (b. June 29, 1964, Romford) and Delroy (b. Apr. 11, 1970, Romford) also joining, though they are still attending college and school respectively. Stedman agrees readily and, through his design and choreographic skills, the group begins to fashion its own costumes, dance steps and visual image. Delroy is in line for a place in West Ham's junior soccer team when he leaves school, but elects instead to join the group, which is managed by Pearson.

Sept Five Star makes its UK TV debut on BBC1's "Pebble Mill At One", singing *Say Goodbye*. RCA Records takes an interest and Pearson begins to negotiate with them, stressing that Five Star is already contracted, but that Tent Records as a whole is a negotiable deal.

Oct *Problematic* is released to strong club reaction by Tent, independently distributed through PRT.

1984

Apr Pearson signs Tent Records to RCA, which releases *Hide And Seek* and October's *Crazy*.

1985

June *All Fall Down*, produced by Nick Martinelli and co-written by '70s UK hitmaker Barry Blue, reaches UK #15, promoted via a hectic schedule of lip-synch personal appearances in UK clubs and discos. (Its B-side, *First Avenue*, written by Deniece, will receive a Grammy nomination as Best R&B Instrumental Of The Year.)

Aug Second Martinelli production, *Let Me Be The One*, reaches UK #18, as the group's debut album, the pop/dance-fused ***Luxury Of Life***, the fruits of six producers and nine different studios, reaches UK #12. (It will climb further up the chart to accompany each succeeding single, eventually peaking at #12 on Feb [22] 1986. By 1987, it will have sold over 300,000 copies in UK, earning a platinum disc.)

Oct *Love Take Over*, extracted from the album but remixed by *19* hitmaker Paul Hardcastle, makes UK #25, while *All Fall Down* peaks at US #65.

Nov *R.S.V.P.*, also from the album, reaches UK #45, as the group visits the US for the first time on a promotional trip. The Walt Disney organization, noting Five Star's youth appeal, offers them a TV show of their own, but Pearson declines on the grounds that the group is not yet well-enough established. ***Luxury Of Life*** makes US #57.

Dec The group appears in the "Celebration Of Youth" concert in London, attended by H.R.H. Queen Elizabeth II.

1986

Jan They spend six weeks in Los Angeles, CA, recording a second album and completing club, TV and radio promotional work.

Feb [15] *System Addict*, the seventh single from the debut album, is the group's first UK Top 10 hit, at #3.

Mar [1] *Let Me Be The One* makes US #59 (having hit #2 on the R&B survey).

May [3] *Can't Wait Another Minute*, recorded in Los Angeles, hits UK #7.

June The group accepts an invitation to write the theme for the UK youth TV series "How Dare You", but declines George Michael's invitation to support Wham! at its farewell concert at Wembley Stadium, Wembley, Middx.

Aug [9] *Find The Time* hits UK #7.

Sept [14] Their "Children Of The Night" UK tour (sponsored by Crunchie Bars), with an eight-piece accompanying band, opens at the Arts Centre, Poole, Dorset, set to end at London's Hammersmith Odeon.

[27] ***Silk And Steel***, which includes the two previous hits, tops the UK chart. (It will be a long-term seller, eventually passing the triple-platinum mark and selling over a million in the UK alone.)

Oct [4] The extracted *Rain Or Shine*, written by Pete Sinfield and its producer, Billy Livsey, proves to be Five Star's commercial peak, hitting UK #2, behind the Communards' *Don't Leave Me This Way*, and earning a gold disc for half-a-million-plus sales.

Nov [1] *Can't Wait Another Minute*, produced by Richard James Burgess, makes US #41 and hits US R&B #7.

[29] *If I Say Yes*, from ***Silk And Steel***, reaches UK #15, while the group makes a short US tour, spurring ***Silk And Steel*** to make US #80.

1987

Jan The Pearson family moves from Romford to a larger house in Sunningdale, Berks., where electronic gates and security cameras safeguard their privacy and new home recording studio.

[31] *If I Say Yes* peaks at US #67.

Feb [9] Five Star is named Best British Group at the sixth annual BRIT Awards, at London's Grosvenor House Hotel.

[21] *Stay Out Of My Life*, the fifth single from their second album and written by Deniece, hits UK #9.

May [2] *The Slightest Touch*, the last extract from ***Silk And Steel***, hits UK #4.

Aug [29] *Whenever You're Ready* reaches UK #11.

Sept [26] ***Between The Lines***, recorded in London and the US, hits UK #7.

Oct [17] *Strong As Steel*, from the album, makes UK #16.

[26-27] Major dates on the "Children Of The Night, 1987" tour (this time sponsored by Ultrabrite toothpaste), at Wembley Arena, are filmed for UK home-video release.

Nov [23] The group performs at the "Royal Variety Performance" in London.

Dec [12] *Somewhere, Somebody*, produced by Dennis Lambert and included on the third album, makes UK #23.

1988

June [11] *Another Weekend* reaches UK #18.

Aug [27] ***Rock The World***, the work of several producers, including Leon Sylvers III from the US and Delroy Pearson, climbs to UK #17, while the extracted *Rock My World* reaches UK #28.

1989

Apr *With Every Heartbeat* makes UK #49.

Oct [21] ***Greatest Hits*** peaks at UK #53.

1990

May [31] The group reportedly moves out of its Sunningdale mansion just days before the bailiffs were expected to evict them for non-payment of the mortgage.

July Newly signed to Epic Records, *Treat Me Like A Lady* is released in the US, while *Hot Love* peaks at UK #68, marking a dramatic decline in their fortunes.

Oct [8] Stedman admits public indecency and agrees to pay a £100 fine and be bound over for a year, at Kingston court, after an incident at a public lavatory in New Malden, Surrey.

1992

Aug The group's BRIT award trophy, stage outfits and silver discs are auctioned for a total of £1,593. (Five Star's next album will be made available for licensing from its own Tent label in March 1994.)

ROBERTA FLACK

1968

A member of her local church choir since an early age (where her father is the organist), Flack (b. Feb. 10, 1937, Black Mountain, near Asheville, NC), a high-school classmate of Donny Hathaway, having graduated in music from Howard University in Washington, DC, before working as a high-school music teacher in North Carolina, returns to Washington to teach and also begins singing in local clubs during the evenings. Atlantic Records recording artist Les McCann sees her performing (as a pianist and singer) and arranges an audition with label boss Ahmet Ertegun and producer Joel Dorn, which results in her signing to the label.

1970

Jan Her maiden album, ***First Take***, produced by Dorn and, as its title suggests, recorded in less than a day, is released and will enter and exit the chart several times prior to its US #1 peak in 1972.
Oct Her sophomore effort, ***Chapter Two*** reaches US #33.

1971

Aug *You've Got A Friend*, a cover duet with Donny Hathaway of a Carole King song (simultaneously a US #1 hit for James Taylor), reaches US #29.
Nov Another duet with Hathaway, reviving *You've Lost That Lovin' Feelin'*, peaks at US #71.

1972

Jan ***Quiet Fire*** reaches US #18.
Feb Her revival of the Shirelles' 1961 hit, *Will You Still Love Me Tomorrow*, peaks at US #76.
Apr [15] Through its exposure in the Clint Eastwood movie "Play Misty For Me", a track from Flack's debut album, reviving Ewan MacColl's folk ballad *The First Time Ever I Saw Your Face*, begins a six-week run atop the US chart, selling over two million copies. It is the longest-running #1 hit by a solo female artist since Gogi Grant's *The Wayward Wind* in 1956.
[29] ***First Take*** (released in 1970) finally tops the US chart for the first of five weeks and earns a gold disc.
June Duet soul-filled album, ***Roberta Flack And Donny Hathaway***, hits US #3 and earns another gold disc.
July *The First Time Ever I Saw Your Face* reaches UK #14, as ***First Take*** makes UK #47.
Aug Third duet with Hathaway, *Where Is The Love*, hits US #5 (selling over a million) and makes UK #29.
Dec [10] Flack and two members of her backing group, bassist Jerry Jemmott and guitarist Cornell Dupree, are injured when Jemmott crashes Flack's new Citröen sedan car driving into Manhattan, New York, NY. The men both have fractured and broken bones, while Flack needs surgery to her lip.

1973

Feb [24] Ballad, *Killing Me Softly With His Song*, which Flack heard sung by Lori Lieberman (for whom it was written - about singer Don McLean) while on a TWA flight from Los Angeles, CA to New York, hits US #1 for the first of five weeks and is another million seller. (Flack has spent three months perfecting it in the studio prior to its release.)
Mar [3] Flack wins trophies for *The First Time Ever I Saw Your Face*, which is voted both Song Of The Year and Record Of The Year, and for *Where Is The Love*, which is named Best Pop Vocal Performance By A Duo, at the 15th annual Grammy Awards.
[24] *Killing Me Softly With His Song* hits UK #6.
June [19] "Roberta Flack ... The First Time Ever", her first TV special, featuring guests Seals & Crofts, airs on ABC-TV.
Oct ***Killing Me Softly*** hits US #3 (earning another gold disc) and makes UK #40, while *Jesse*, written by Janis Ian, reaches US #30.

1974

Feb [19] She wins the Favorite Female Artist, Soul/R&B category, at the inaugural American Music Awards held at the Aquarius Theater, Hollywood, CA.
Mar [2] *Killing Me Softly With His Song* wins Record Of The Year and Song Of The Year and Flack wins the Best Pop Vocal, Female category at the 16th annual Grammy Awards. (Dorn leaves Atlantic Records during the recording of Flack's new album, ***Feel Like Makin' Love***. Flack takes over production herself but, due to her inexperience and artistic perfectionism, it will take eight months to complete. Upon its release, Flack will use the production pseudonym Rubina Flake.)
Aug *Feel Like Makin' Love* tops the US chart for one week, selling over a million, and reaches UK #34.

1975

May ***Feel Like Makin' Love*** reaches US #24.
June *Feelin' That Glow* peaks at US #76.
Dec [8] Flack guests on Bob Dylan's "The Rolling Thunder Revue" at the end of its first run at New York's Madison Square Garden with "Night Of The Hurricane", a benefit for boxer and convicted murderer Rubin "Hurricane" Carter.

1978

Feb After a lengthy chart absence (during which she has cut down on live performances to pursue other concerns, including her work in various educational programs for disadvantaged US youth), Flack's ***Blue Lights In The Basement*** hits US #8 and earns another gold disc.
May Taken from the album, *The Closer I Get To You*, a ballad duet with Hathaway (written by James Mtume and Reggie Lucas), hits US #2 and UK #42.
July *If Ever I See You Again*, the title song from the Joe Brooks film, reaches US #24.
Oct ***Roberta Flack*** reaches US #74.

1979

Jan [13] Hathaway dies, after falling from a New York hotel-room window. (He had been working on more duet material with Flack, which will eventually emerge in 1980. Grief-stricken, Flack will remain out of the public eye for much of the year.)

1980

Mar *You Are My Heaven*, a duet with Hathaway, makes US #47.
June Uptempo *Back Together Again*, another Flack/Hathaway pairing, penned by Mtume and Lucas, peaks at US #56 and hits UK #3. ***Roberta Flack Featuring Donny Hathaway***, co-produced by Flack and Eric Mercury, makes US #25 and UK #31 (June [21]).
Sept *Don't Make Me Wait Too Long* makes UK #44.

1981

Jan Performance double-set, ***Live And More***, recorded with Memphis soul singer Peabo Bryson, reaches US #52.
July ***Bustin' Loose***, the MCA-released, Flack-performed soundtrack from the film of the same title, peaks at US #161. Flack also records a popular US TV commercial for Kentucky Fried Chicken.

1982

June *Making Love*, the title song from the Kate Jackson/Harry Hamlin film, reaches US #13.
Aug ***I'm The One*** makes US #59, with the extracted title cut *I'm The One* peaking at US #42.

1983

Jan Flack announces a tour which will take her and Bryson through Europe, the Middle East, the Far East, Australasia, South America and the US. She also moves from Atlantic to Capitol Records.
Sept Flack and Bryson's ballad duet, *Tonight I Celebrate My Love*, reaches US #16 and hits UK #2 - Flack's biggest-selling UK single. ***Born To Love***, with Bryson, makes US #25 and UK #15. She moves into a New York apartment in the Dakota building - the block in which John Lennon lived at the time of his death.

1984

Jan *You're Looking Like Love To Me*, another duet with Bryson, taken from the album, peaks at US #58.
Feb [8] ***Born To Love*** is certified gold by the RIAA.
Mar Flack is honored with an hour-long musical tribute on the steps of New York's City Hall. (Washington will also give her a public honor, declaring April 22nd, Roberta Flack Day.)
Apr TV-advertised compilation album, ***Roberta Flack's Greatest Hits***, reaches UK #35.

1988

May [14] Having re-signed to the label, she participates in Atlantic Records' 40th anniversary concert at Madison Square Garden.
Aug [20] Flack plays a benefit concert in Nantucket, MA, for the island's only health-care facility, the Nantucket cottage hospital.

1989

Jan [7] *Oasis* tops the US R&B chart, as its parent album, ***Oasis***, her first in six years and variously produced by Marcus Miller, Quincy Jones, Andy Goldmark, Jerry Hey and Michael Omartian, peaks at US #159.

1990

June [30] Flack tapes a show at the Trump Regency Hotel, Atlantic City, NJ, for the forthcoming "SRO" US TV series.
Aug She produces and is a featured vocalist on Nino Tempo's ***Tenor Saxophone*** album.
Sept *Killing Me Softly With His Song* is honored as one of the BMI's Most Performed Songs Of 1940-1990, as it surpasses its fourth-millionth performance.

1991

Feb [7] Flack takes part in a benefit concert for Howard King at New York's Bottom Line.
Oct [11] She appears on BBC1-TV's "Wogan" with Maxi Priest.
Nov [10] Flack performs at Symphony Hall, Boston, MA, at a benefit for Cohen Hillel Academy in Marblehead, MA, and Halcyon Place, to help families of critically ill children.
[13] She duets with Aaron Neville on *The First Time Ever I Saw Your Face* at the Wang Center, Boston, MA, as part of local DJ Matt Siegel's tenth anniversary.
[16] Diane Warren-penned *Set The Night To Music*, with Maxi Priest, hits US #6.
Dec [7] Flack's first album in nearly three years, ***Set The Night To Music***, produced by Arif Mardin and featuring Patti Austin, Quincy Jones and Greg Phillinganes, among others, peaks at US #110.

1992

Mar [8] She performs at "Free To Laugh : Comedy & Music For Amnesty International" at the Wiltern Theatre, Los Angeles.
Apr Flack is featured on "The Legend Of Paul Bunyan" Golden Book Video Classic singing *John Henry*. She also records an album of songs by Eikichi Yazawa for the Japanese market.
June [25] She plays at the Filene Center, Wolf Trap Farm Park for the Performing Arts, Vienna, VA, with Grover Washington, during current US dates.
Sept [25] Flack takes part in the "Caring In Concert" AIDS benefit pay-per-view special, from the Mann Music Center, Philadelphia, PA, with Dionne Warwick, Burt Bacharach and comedienne Elayne Boosler.
Oct [6-11] She performs a week of concerts in New York.
Nov [26] Flack embarks on a 19-date tour of the Far East in Singapore, set to end on December 27th at the Hotel Lotte Crystal Ballroom, Seoul, Korea.

1993

Apr [2] Flack makes a guest appearance on ABC-

TV's soap opera "Loving", singing *Amazing Grace* during the funeral of character Trisha Alden McKenzie.
Dec [14-19] "The Colors Of Christmas" tour, with Flack, Peabo Bryson, Patti Austin and Jeffrey Osborne, plays at New York's Radio City Music Hall.

1994

Feb [19] ***Softly With These Songs - The Best Of Roberta Flack***, an Atlantic hits anthology, hits UK #7 in its week of entry.
Aug [6-7] Flack performs at Los Angeles' Greek Theatre with Al Jarreau.
Oct ***Roberta***, a set of updated jazz, blues and soul classics, is released.
Dec [21-23] Annual "The Colors Of Christmas" tour, with Flack, Bryson, Sheena Easton and James Ingram, performs at the Center for the Performing Arts, Cerritos, CA.

1995

Jan [30] Flack co-presents, with Michael Bolton, the Pop/Rock New Artist trophy at the 22nd annual American Music Awards held at Los Angeles' Shrine Auditorium.
Mar [3] A New York cab driver, who has already been jailed several times for stalking Flack over a ten-year period, is arrested trying to force his way into her New York apartment, screaming "I'll kill her if I see her".
[20] Flack guests on syndicated TV's "Oprah Winfrey Show", singing a selection of hits.
Dec [3] Flack, Bryson, Ingram and Melissa Manchester sellout the Westbury Music Fair, Westbury, NY as part of the annual "Colors Of Christmas" tour.

FLEETWOOD MAC

Mick Fleetwood (drums); **John McVie** (bass); **Christine McVie** (keyboards, vocals); **Lindsey Buckingham** (guitars, vocals); **Stevie Nicks** (vocals)

1967

Apr Fleetwood (b. June 24, 1942, London), ex-the Cheynes (who backed the Ronettes on the Rolling Stones 1964 UK tour), the Bo Street Runners, Peter B's Looners and Shotgun Express (the latter with Rod Stewart), joins John Mayall's Bluesbreakers. The group comprises Mayall, Fleetwood, John McVie (b. Nov. 26, 1945, London) and Green (b. Peter Greenbaum, Oct. 29, 1946, London), who has played with Fleetwood as a member of both the Looners and Shotgun Express and replaced Eric Clapton in the Bluesbreakers in July 1966. In spare studio time offered by Mayall, Green, Fleetwood and John McVie cut early versions of *Fleetwood Mac*, *Double Trouble* and *It Hurts Me Too*, and form a close alliance, though within a month, Fleetwood and Green are fired.
July Without Mayall, the Bluesbreakers have recently worked for Blue Horizon label owner Mike Vernon as a backing band for US bluesman Eddie Boyd, who is keen to sign a domestic blues outfit for his label. After auditioning (and rejecting) Midlands-based band the Levi Set, he introduces their guitarist, Jeremy Spencer (b. July 4, 1948, West Hartlepool, Lancs.), to Green and Fleetwood. Fleetwood Mac is formed, comprising Green, Fleetwood, Spencer and bassist Bob Brunning, with early warm-up gigs at the Black Bull pub in Fulham, London.
Aug [12-13] The band makes its major debut at the "Windsor Jazz & Blues Festival", Windsor, Berks.
Sept [17] Following its London bow at the Marquee club and an appearance at an open-air festival in the Midlands, the group plays at the Saville Theatre, London. McVie, fired from the Bluesbreakers, joins to replace Brunning, who leaves to form the Sunflower Brunning Blues Band.
Nov [3] The group releases its debut single, *I Believe My Time Ain't Long*, billed as Peter Green's Fleetwood Mac. It becomes the resident house band for the Blue Horizon label, backing Otis Spann, Duster Bennett and others on a variety of albums.
Dec The group embarks on a UK college and club tour.

1968

Mar A new blues boom hits Britain and the band's debut album, ***Fleetwood Mac***, mixing originals with blues classics by Robert Johnson and Howlin' Wolf, hits UK #4 and makes US #198.
Apr *Black Magic Woman*, written by Green, reaches UK #37. (Santana's version will hit US #4 in January 1971.)
May Fleetwood Mac embarks on a short tour of Scandinavia.
July Their cover of Little Willie John's blues *Need Your Love So Bad*, highlighted by Mickey Baker's (of Mickey & Sylvia) string arrangement, reaches UK #31, as the group begins its first US tour, debuting at Detroit, MI's Grande Ballroom, before going on to San Francisco, CA, and the Shrine Auditorium, Los Angeles, CA.
[13] Fleetwood Mac guests on CBS-TV's "The Ed Sullivan Show".
Aug [25] The group begins a two-month UK tour at the Nag's Head Pub, Battersea, London, with new addition Danny Kirwan (b. Mar. 13, 1950, London), who had been spotted by Green playing in the trio Boilerhouse. (The **Melody Maker** ad placed for a new guitarist received 300 replies, with no applicant proving good enough.)
Sept *Mr. Wonderful* hits UK #10, featuring Christine Perfect (b. July 12, 1943, Birmingham, Warks.) on piano, although she is still a member of the group Chicken Shack.
Dec [4] They begin a 30-date US tour, including shows at the Fillmore East, Boston Tea Party, and Chicago's Electric Factory. (After the Chicago gig, they record at the Chess Ter-Mar Studios with Willie Dixon, Otis Spann, J.T. Brown, S.P. Leary and Honeyboy Edwards.)
[23] Fleetwood Mac takes part in the "Miami Pop Festival" in Hallandale, FL, with Marvin Gaye, Steppenwolf, Three Dog Night and the Grateful Dead, among others.

1969

Jan [29] *Albatross*, written by Green, tops the UK chart. A haunting guitar instrumental, it lifts the group out of the blues bracket and establishes its name throughout Europe.
Feb ***English Rose*** peaks at US #184.
Mar The group embarks on a European tour, including an eight-date UK segment, with B.B. King, Sonny Terry & Brownie McGhee and Duster Bennett.
May Green-penned *Man Of The World* hits UK #2, behind the Beatles' *Get Back*. The group's contract with Blue Horizon ends amid financial acrimony and it signs a one-off deal with Rolling Stones' manager Andrew Loog Oldham's Immediate label, not least because interest is also currently being expressed by the Beatles' Apple label (although nothing comes of this).
July [16] The band begins a six-week US tour.
Aug *Need Your Love So Bad* is reissued, this time making UK #32.
[5-10] They play at the Fillmore West, San Francisco, sharing the bill with Jr. Walker.
Sept ***Pious Bird Of Good Omen*** reaches UK #18. While the group negotiates a new contract, Blue Horizon releases a collection of old material, and re-promotes *Need Your Love So Bad*, which charts for a third time, at UK #42.
Oct ***Then Play On*** hits UK #6 and peaks at US #109, marking their debut on the Reprise label.
Nov *Oh Well* hits UK #2. The song's religious overtones reflect Green's renouncement of his Jewish faith and his embracing of Christianity (he begins to appear on stage in a long white robe, underlining a new messianic image).
Dec ***Blues Jam At Chess*** is released, featuring the group and a selection of blues greats recorded in 1968.

1970

Jan Spencer releases the solo ***Jeremy Spencer***, on which he is backed by the group.
Feb [27] Topping his increasingly erratic behaviour, Green tells the **New Musical Express** that he is going to give his all of his earnings away.
Mar *Oh Well* reaches US #55.
Apr [11] Green quits the band in Munich, W. Germany, during a European tour, the pressures of stardom now proving intolerable. To avoid breach of contract, he agrees to finish the tour and then leave.
[25] The group takes part in a music festival at Reading Football Club's ground in Reading, Berks., with Christine Perfect, Colosseum, Viv Stanshall's Big Grunt, Mike Raven, Mike Cooper, Chicken Shack and the Liverpool Scene.
May [24] Green plays his last gig with the group at the "Bath Festival", Bath, Somerset.
June *The Green Manalishi (With The Two-Prong Crown)* hits UK #10. In his last single for the group, Green gives a heart-rending graphic description of the mental terrors that are haunting him.
Aug [8] Having released her maiden solo album ***Christine Perfect*** on Blue Horizon/Sire Records in June, Perfect flies to the US to join Fleetwood Mac, after announcing that she is quitting the music business for good. (She was voted **Melody Maker**'s Female Vocalist Of The Year in 1969 and will subsequently go under the surname McVie, having married John.)
Oct ***Kiln House***, the name of the rented house in Alton, Hants., where Fleetwood Mac recorded the album, reaches UK #39 and US #69. Spencer becomes the creative lead on their first album release without Green (but it will be six years before they have another major hit album).
Nov Green's solo album, ***The End Of The Game***, is released.
Dec The group embarks on a series of UK dates and buys Benifolds mansion near Haslemere, Surrey, where they will live and work together.

1971

Feb Spencer leaves during a US tour, after telling the group, at the Hollywood Hawaiian Hotel, Los Angeles, he is "just popping out for a bit to buy newspapers" at Pickwick's book store on Sunset Boulevard. (It is the last they see of him for two years. It later transpires that he has suffered from similar pressures to those that afflicted Green, and, relinquishing his pop career, he joins the religious cult the Children of God.) The band cancels the scheduled Whisky A Go Go dates before Green flies to the US to help the group complete the tour, but returns to his self-imposed retirement at its end. (Spencer will record the albums ***Jeremy Spencer And The Children Of God*** in 1973, for CBS, and ***Flee*** for Atlantic in 1979.)
Apr At the end of the troubled trek, the group is in disarray, having lost its two main songwriters and guitarists. Judy Wong, wife of Jethro Tull's Glenn Cornick introduces the group to Los Angeles musician Bob Welch (b. July 31, 1946, Los Angeles), who replaces Spencer. They begin recording a new album of Welch, Kirwan and Christine McVie compositions. (Welch has been playing in soul show-band the Seven Souls in Las Vegas, NV, backing James Brown, Aretha Franklin and others, which breaks up in Hawaii in 1969, when Welch and two other group members head for Paris, forming the R&B trio Head West. That splits, when Welch, set to take up an offer with Stax in Memphis, TN, heads back to Los Angeles.)
July ***Fleetwood Mac In Chicago***, recorded in January 1969, makes US #190.
Oct ***Black Magic Woman*** peaks at US #143.
Nov ***Future Games*** makes US #91. They continue to tour the US extensively.

1972

Feb ***Greatest Hits*** reaches UK #36.
May ***Bare Trees*** makes US #70.
Aug Kirwan leaves the band. (After refusing to

appear on stage, he becomes the first member of the group to be fired. In the mid '70s, he will record for DJM, before being admitted to a psychiatric hospital.) He is replaced by Long John Baldry sideman Bob Weston, while vocalist Dave Walker also joins, recruited from Savoy Brown, as the group returns to Britain to record its next album.
Sept The band performs at the North Carolina Motor Speedway, Rockingham, NC, with Three Dog Night, Alice Cooper, Poco, Black Oak Arkansas, the James Gang and others.

1973

May ***Penguin***, cut at the Rolling Stones' mobile studio, reaches US #49. It features a guest appearance from Green, but fails to chart in the UK. The Fleetwood Mac penguin association is John McVie's idea. (He is a member of the London Zoological Society and has become a keen student of the species.)
June Reissued *Albatross* hits UK #2. Walker's departure leaves the group as a five-piece once more.
Sept The band begins a tour to promote the forthcoming ***Mystery To Me*** album, and Weston begins an affair with Fleetwood's wife, Jenny. Romantic entanglements wreck the tour and the group pulls out of all further engagements, while Weston is sacked.
Nov [1] The group's manager, Clifford Davis, angered at the group's decision to cut short the tour, sends a letter to Welch informing him that he intends to take a new Fleetwood Mac to the US in January and asking whether he might be interested in being a part of its line-up. Welch phones the band at Benifolds, their UK base, to inform them of their manager's plan. Davis goes ahead and assembles a bogus Fleetwood Mac to fulfill the dates, resulting in a bitter legal battle. (The impostors later form Stretch and have a 1975 hit with *Why Did You Do It*.)
Dec ***Mystery To Me*** makes US #67.

1974

Jan The bogus Fleetwood Mac gives up its tour after two weeks, having met with a poor response.
At the suggestion of Welch, the real band relocates to Los Angeles, closer to its record company (Reprise) and attorney (Mickey Shapiro) and with a better chance of securing the rights to their name, still owned by Davis.
Sept The group embarks on a 43-date US tour to promote the new ***Heroes Are Hard To Find***, earning a reduced fee to placate promoters hurt by the bogus Mac episode.
Nov ***Heroes Are Hard To Find*** reaches US #34. As legalities are resolved, the band decides to settle permanently in California.
Dec Welch leaves. (He will form the band Paris and enjoy later solo success with ***French Kiss***, ***Three Hearts*** and ***Sentimental Lady***.) Fleetwood visits Sound City Studios in Van Nuys, CA, to preview it as a potential recording venue. As a demonstration, producer Keith Olsen plays Fleetwood a track from an album by the singing/songwriting duo Buckingham & Nicks. By chance, Lindsey Buckingham (b. Oct. 3, 1947, Palo Alto, CA) is in another part of the studio and strikes up a rapport with Fleetwood, who later meets his partner and girlfriend, vocalist Stevie Nicks (b. Stephanie Nicks, May 26, 1948, Phoenix, AZ).
[31] The duo is invited to join Fleetwood Mac, completing the tenth line-up since 1967. (Buckingham and Nicks were members of Bay Area group Fritz. Two years after the group's split in 1971, the duo moved to Los Angeles and recorded their debut album, ***Buckingham Nicks***, on Polydor. Following its commercial failure, and in order to finance further songwriting efforts, Buckingham worked as a session-man and toured with Don Everly, while Nicks worked as a waitress in Hollywood.)

1975

Mar ***Vintage Years***, collecting recordings from 1967-1969, peaks at US #138.
Aug ***Fleetwood Mac***, co-produced by the band with Olsen, enters the US chart. The songwriting talents of Christine McVie and Buckingham/Nicks begin to flower, as airplay and sales increase over the next year.
Dec Reissued ***Fleetwood Mac In Chicago*** reaches US #118.

1976

Jan *Over My Head* reaches US #20.
June Nicks-penned *Rhiannon (Will You Ever Win)*, also from the eponymous album, peaks at US #11.
July [4] The group plays at Tampa Stadium, Tampa, FL, on its current US tour with the Eagles.
Sept *Say You Love Me* reaches US #11.
[4] 15 months after the record enters the US chart, ***Fleetwood Mac*** hits #1, going platinum, and will reach UK #23 on Nov [13], aided by a white-vinyl format. *Say You Love Me* makes UK #40.

1977

Jan [26] Peter Green is committed to a mental hospital by Sir Ivor Rigby after his case is heard at Marylebone Court, following an incident the previous month when he threatened accountant Clifford Adams, who was trying to deliver a £30,000 royalty cheque, with an air rifle at his Westbourne Park, London home. Green insists that he wants no royalty cheques. (Having been committed to a home in 1973 by his father, Green has been working as a gravedigger and hospital porter.)
Feb Affected by personal problems within the group (the McVies are separating, the Buckingham and Nicks relationship is unsteady and the Fleetwoods' divorce proceedings are beginning), ***Rumours***, co-produced by Fleetwood Mac with Richard Dashut and Ken Caillat, is finally released. Creatively reflecting much of this turmoil, it will connect with radio and public alike, eventually topping both the UK and US charts, with worldwide sales in excess of 15 million, spending more than 130 weeks on the US survey and more than 400 on the UK listing.
[28] The group begins a seven-month US tour at the University of California, Berkeley, CA, set to end at the Hollywood Bowl, Los Angeles on October 4th.
Mar *Go Your Own Way* hits US #10 and UK #38.
Apr [2] ***Rumours*** tops the US chart.
May *Don't Stop* reaches UK #32.
June [29-30] The group plays at New York's Madison Square Garden during its current tour.
Aug Nicks-written and vocalized *Dreams* tops the US chart and makes UK #24.
Sept Christine McVie-penned *Don't Stop* hits US #3.
Oct Another McVie composition, *You Make Loving Fun* peaks at UK #45.
Dec *You Make Loving Fun* hits US #9.

1978

Jan [16] The band wins the Favorite Band, Duo Or Group, Pop/Rock and Favorite Album, Pop/Rock categories at the fifth annual American Music Awards, held at the Civic Auditorium, Santa Monica, CA.
[28] ***Rumours*** finally tops the UK chart.
Feb [23] ***Rumours*** is named Album Of The Year at the 20th annual Grammy Awards, the group's only NARAS honor.
Mar [11] Reissued *Rhiannon* makes UK #46.
July [17] The group begins a summer US tour at the Alpine Valley Music Theatre, East Troy, WI.
Sept Kenny Loggins' *Whenever I Call You Friend*, featuring Nicks, hits US #5.

1979

July [28] Green's comeback, an instrumental album, ***In The Skies***, on Creole Records, makes UK #32.
Oct [10] The group is awarded its star on the Hollywood Walk of Fame, Hollywood, CA.
Nov *Tusk*, recorded (and filmed) with the U.S.C. Trojan Marching Band at Los Angeles' Dodger Stadium, hits US #8 and UK #6, creating a record for the number of musicians playing on a single.
[10] Double album, ***Tusk***, on which the group has reportedly spent $1 million, produced by the same team (but with Buckingham's influence clearly enhancing the creativity), tops the UK chart.
[15-16] The group performs at Madison Square Garden, as it prepares to embark on its latest US tour.
[17] ***Tusk*** hits US #4.
[26] The band begins a lengthy US trek at the Mini-Dome, Idaho State University, in Pocatello, ID.

1980

Jan Nicks-penned *Sara* reaches UK #37.
Feb *Sara* hits US #7.
May *Think About Me* reaches US #20.
[24] Green's ***Little Dreamer***, on PVK Records, peaks at UK #34 (after which he will again fade into obscurity and live as a recluse).
June *Sisters Of The Moon* peaks at US #86.
Sept [1] The group finishes a tour at Los Angeles' Hollywood Bowl. (A long period of solo activity begins before Fleetwood Mac records together again.)
Oct [4] Buckingham, Nicks and Fleetwood present the U.S.C. Trojan Marching Band with a platinum disc, for its contribution to *Tusk*, at half-time during a game at Dodger Stadium.
Dec [20] ***Fleetwood Mac Live*** makes UK #31 and will reach US #14.

1981

Feb The extracted *Fireflies* peaks at US #60.
May The band reconvenes at the Honky Chateau Studios in Heronville, France.
July Mick Fleetwood's ***The Visitor***, recorded at great cost in Ghana, West Africa, makes US #43. (It recoups little in sales and the losses incurred will, together with real estate ventures, contribute to Fleetwood's eventual bankruptcy.)
Sept [5] Nicks' *Stop Draggin' My Heart Around*, with help from Tom Petty & the Heartbreakers, hits US #3 and UK #50 in the same week that her debut solo album, ***Bella Donna***, produced by Jimmy Iovine, tops the US chart, having made UK #11 on Aug [15].
Nov Buckingham's solo album, ***Law And Order***, co-produced with Dashut and featuring Fleetwood and Christine McVie, reaches US #32.

1982

Jan Buckingham's *Trouble* hits US #9 and UK #31, while Nicks' ballad duet with Don Henley, *Leather And Lace*, written for Waylon Jennings and Jessi Colter by Nicks, hits US #6.
Apr Nicks' *Edge Of Seventeen (Just Like The White Winged Dove)* reaches US #11.
July Nicks' *After The Glitter Fades* reaches US #32.
Aug [7] After a three-year studio gap, the group album ***Mirage***, produced by Buckingham with help from Dashut and Caillat, tops the US chart for the first of five weeks (having hit UK #5 on July [10]).
[24] Fleetwood Mac's *Hold Me* hits US #4.
Sept [3-5] The group takes part in the three-day "US Festival", financed by Apple Computers' founder Steven Wozniak, in San Bernardino, CA, along with Jackson Browne, the Cars, the Grateful Dead, Eddie Money, Police, Santana, Talking Heads and many others.
Oct *Gypsy*, written by Nicks, reaches US #12 and UK #46, as the band concludes an 18-date stadium tour of the US, with John Cougar and John Waite in support.

1983

Jan *Love In Store* reaches US #22.
[29] Nicks marries Kim Anderson, the widowed husband of her best friend Robin Anderson, who died of leukemia in 1982, outside her Los Angeles home. (The marriage will not last and their divorce will be finalized in April 1984.)
Feb UK-only release, *Oh Diane*, penned by Buckingham, hits #9.
May Nicks' distinctive vocals can be heard on Robbie Patton's US #52, *Smiling Islands*.
July Nicks' solo album, ***The Wild Heart***, again produced by Iovine, and featuring guests Don Felder, Fleetwood, Henley and Petty among others, hits US #5 and UK #28.
Aug From it, *Stand Back* hits US #5, while Buckingham's jaunty solo, *Holiday Road*, from the movie "National Lampoon's Vacation", peaks at US #82.
Nov Nicks' *If Anyone Falls* reaches US #14.

1984

Jan Nicks' *Nightbird* makes US #33.
Feb ***Christine McVie***, her solo set co-written with Todd Sharp, produced by Russ Titelman and featuring Buckingham, Eric Clapton, Ray Cooper, Fleetwood and Steve Winwood, reaches US #26.
Mar Taken from it, *Got A Hold On Me* hits US #10.
May [1] Mick Fleetwood files for bankruptcy.
June *Love Will Show Us How* climbs to US #30 for Christine McVie.
Sept ***Go Insane***, Buckingham's sophomore solo effort, co-produced with Gordon Fordyce, makes US #45.
Oct *Go Insane* reaches US #23.

1985

Oct The group reunites, when Christine McVie, working on the soundtrack to the Blake Edwards' film "A Fine Mess" and trying to record a version of Presley's *Can't Help Falling In Love*, enlists the help of Buckingham and John McVie, which leads to new Fleetwood Mac recordings. With the group having led a nomadic studio existence in the past, the new album will be overdubbed and mixed in Buckingham's own studio at his Bel Air home.
Dec Nicks' third solo album, ***Rock A Little***, again largely overseen by Iovine, makes US #12 (receiving RIAA platinum certification on January 21st 1986) and UK #30.

1986

Nicks has a succession of hit singles from the album: *Talk To Me* (US #4/UK #68), *I Can't Wait* (US #16/UK #54), *Needles And Pins*, with Tom Petty & the Heartbreakers (US #37), and the ballad *Has Anyone Ever Written Anything For You* (US #60). (Nicks will play two gigs on Tom Petty's Australian tour, until immigration authorities intervene.)
Oct [18] Christine McVie marries Portuguese composer Eduardo Quintela de Mendonca in London.

1987

Apr ***Tango In The Night*** is released, set to become the band's biggest seller since ***Rumours***.
May [30] *Big Love* hits US #5 and UK #9, its B-side being part one of the album cut *You And I Part 2*. ***Tango In The Night*** hits US #7.
Aug [7] Buckingham, unhappy with the prospect of touring with the band to promote ***Tango In The Night***, tells his colleagues that he is quitting the group.
[15] *Seven Wonders* reaches US #19 and peaks at UK #56.
Sept Secret rehearsals begin in Venice, CA, with new members Billy Burnette (b. May 8, 1953, Memphis, TN), son of rockabilly star Johnny Burnette and who has released the solo album ***Billy Burnette***, on Polydor in 1980, and Rick Vito (b. Oct. 13, 1949, Darby, PA), but Buckingham changes his mind and commits himself to a final tour, before embarking on a solo career.
Oct [31] ***Tango In The Night*** tops the UK chart for the first of two weeks.
Nov [7] *Little Lies* hits US #4 and UK #5.

1988

Jan *Family Man* peaks at UK #54.
Feb [6] *Everywhere* reaches US #14 and will hit UK #4.
Apr *Family Man* peaks at US #90.
May [7] ***Tango In The Night*** returns to the UK summit for the first of two more weeks.
June *Isn't It Midnight* stops at UK #60.
Aug The group's "Shake The Cage" tour of Europe and Australia, with Burnette and Vito, begins.
[12] "Stevie Nicks Live At Red Rocks" video is certified gold by the RIAA.
Dec [31] Warner Bros.-released 17-track ***Greatest Hits*** hits UK #3.

1989

Jan [21] *As Long As You Follow* makes US #43.
May Christine McVie (and Friends) contribute *Roll With Me Henry* to the Richard Perry-produced ***Rock, Rhythm & Blues*** compilation.
June [10] Nicks' ***The Other Side Of The Mirror*** hits UK #3 and will reach US #10.
July [1] Her *Rooms On Fire* reaches US #16.
[11] ***The Other Side Of The Mirror*** is certified gold by the RIAA.

1990

Jan [23] The RIAA certifies four million sales of ***Bella Donna***.
Mar [24] The group begins "The Mask" world tour in Australia.
Apr [21] ***Behind The Mask***, co-produced by the band with Greg Ladanyi, enters the UK chart at #1.
May [19] *Save Me* makes US #33, as its parent album, ***Behind The Mask***, reaches US #18.
[26-27] The group embarks on the US leg of "The Mask" tour at the Champs de Brionne Amphitheatre, George, WA, set to end at Jones Beach, Wantagh, NY, on August 2nd.
Aug [21] European leg of "The Mask" tour begins in Ghent, Belgium.
Sept [1] Fleetwood Mac plays at Wembley Stadium, Wembley, Middx., with Jethro Tull and Hall & Oates.
[12] Nicks and Christine McVie announce their intention to leave the band at the end of its current tour.
Nov [1] The group receives the commemorative Gold Ticket award for 100,000 ticket sales at Madison Square Garden, after a sellout show there.
Dec [7] Nicks and Christine McVie make their (first) final appearance with Fleetwood Mac at the Great Western Forum, Inglewood, CA, before a sellout crowd of 16,314. Buckingham joins them on stage to sing an acoustic rendition of *Landslide* with Nicks, before joining the band on *Go Your Own Way*.

1991

Feb Buckingham, Christine McVie, John Lee Hooker and others attend the opening of Mick Fleetwood's blues club, Fleetwood's, in Los Angeles.
Aug [31] Nicks' *Sometimes It's A Bitch*, written by Jon Bon Jovi and Billy Falcon, makes UK #40.
Sept [14] Nicks' ***TimeSpace - The Best Of Stevie Nicks*** debuts at its UK #15 peak.
[21] Nicks' ***TimeSpace - The Best Of Stevie Nicks*** reaches US #30.
Oct [12] Nicks' *Sometimes It's A Bitch* peaks at US #56.
[25] Nicks performs *Jane's Song*, written for environmentalist Jane Goodall, at the "International Tribute To Jane Goodall" in Dallas, TX.
Nov Vito quits Fleetwood Mac, signing a solo deal with Modern.
[9] Nicks' *I Can't Wait* bows at its UK #47 peak.

1992

Feb Mick Fleetwood's new band, Zoo (originally called the Cholos), featuring Bekka Bramlett (daughter of Delaney & Bonnie), Billy Thorpe, Gregg Wright, Tom Lilly and Brett Tuggle, signs to Capricorn Records and will release its only album ***Shakin' The Cage*** in July.
[12] ***TimeSpace - The Best Of Stevie Nicks*** is certified gold by the RIAA.
[25] Vito's ***King Of Hearts***, with Nicks duetting on *Desiree*, is released.
June John McVie's solo debut, ***John McVie's "Gotta Band" With Lola Thomas*** is released by Warner Bros.
Aug [8] Buckingham's ***Out Of The Cradle***, co-produced with longtime cohort Dashut (and taking its title from a Walt Whitman poem), charts for one week at UK #51.
[8] ***Out Of The Cradle*** peaks at US #128.
[11] Nicks and Roseanne and Tom Arnold join Ringo Starr on stage to sing *With A Little Help From My Friends* at his Greek Theatre, Los Angeles show.
Dec [10-11] Buckingham plays his first-ever solo shows at the Coach House, San Juan Capistrano, CA.

1993

Jan [19] In a much-ballyhooed return, Fleetwood Mac re-forms its most popular line-up, of mainstay Fleetwood, Buckingham, the McVies and Nicks for a one-off performance of *Don't Stop*, which incoming President Bill Clinton had used as his theme tune during campaigning, at the Presidential Inaugural concert from the Capital Centre, Landover, MD. (Following the performance, Nicks will nix all rumors suggesting a full-time Mac reunion. She is planning a September release for her next solo album.)
Feb [22] Buckingham makes his live hometown solo debut at the Wiltern Theatre, Los Angeles.
Mar [8] Buckingham embarks on his first solo US tour in Solana Beach, CA.
Nov [10] The RIAA certifies two million sales of ***The Wild Heart***.

1994

May [14] ***Greatest Hits*** re-charts at UK #38.
June [4] ***Street Angel***, Nicks' sixth album, variously produced by Glyn Johns, Roy Bittan and Thom Punुnzio, reaches UK #16 in its week of entry.
[25] ***Street Angel*** , following a label switch to Atlantic, debuts at its US #45 peak.
July [9] Nicks' *Maybe Love Will Change Your Mind* makes UK #42.
[16] *Maybe Love Will Change Your Mind* makes US #57.
[21] The group, now including Dave Mason (b. May 10, 1946, Worcester, Worcs.) Fleetwood's ex-Zoo cool colleague Bekka Bramlett (Apr. 19, 1968, Westwood, CA), the daughter of Delaney & Bonnie) in the line-up, performs a surprise 25-minute set at the opening of Mick Fleetwood's Fleetwood's Restaurant & Blues Club in Alexandria, VA.
Aug [12] The band plays New York's Beacon Theatre with Bad Company, in the midst of a US summer tour opening for Crosby Stills & Nash.
Sept [4] They take part in the "Field Of Dreams Festival" at the Farley Speedway track in Dyersville, IA.
Oct [11] Fleetwood Mac appears at the Wang Dang Doodle benefit for the Willie Dixon-created Blues Heaven Foundation at Los Angeles' House of Blues club.

1995

July [28] The "Can't Stop Rockin'" US summer tour, with Fleetwood Mac, REO Speedwagon, Pat Benatar an Orleans, plays a sellout date at Jones Beach Theatre, Wantagh, NY.
Sept [23] Archive set ***Live At The BBC*** makes UK #48 in its week of entry.
Oct [21] ***Time***, produced by the band with Richard Dashut, bows at its UK #47 peak.

1996

Feb [18] Fleetwood/Castle Records releases the double-CD ***Peter Green's Fleetwood Mac : Live At The BBC***, a seminal archive recording, co-executive produced by Mick Fleetwood.
May Buckingham and Nicks team up for the single *Twister*, the title song to the newly-premiering movie.

EDDIE FLOYD

1962

May Having moved to Detroit, MI, in his teens, Floyd (b. June 25, 1935, Montgomery, AL) helped to form the R&B/doo-wop Falcons in 1956, which reached US #17 in July 1959 with *You're So Fine*. Wilson Pickett replaced Joe Stubbs as the Falcons' lead singer in 1960, as the group began developing a more soulful, gospel style. With the Falcons' *I Found A Love* now peaking at US #75, Pickett leaves and the group breaks up, with Floyd settling in Washington, DC, where he starts Safice Records with local DJ Al Bell and former Moonglow Chester Simmons, though the venture is not immediately successful. He also writes songs, and *Comfort Me*, penned for Carla Thomas (who is attending university in Washington), is his introduction to the Stax label.

1965

Oct After Bell moves to Memphis, TN, to become national sales director for Stax, Floyd is signed as a staff songwriter. *634-5789*, a smash for ex-colleague

Pickett (later covered by James Brown, Ry Cooder and Tina Turner among others), is his first collaboration with MG's guitarist Steve Cropper, followed by another Pickett hit, *Ninety Nine And A Half*, and Otis Redding's classic rendition of *Don't Mess With Cupid*.

1966

Sept Floyd's demo of his own *Knock On Wood*, originally written with Cropper for Redding, is polished up and issued as a single. The archetypal Stax record and the acme of '60s soul, it shoots to #1 on the R&B chart, crosses to US #28 and reaches UK #19.

1967

Mar *Raise Your Hand*, with Floyd formally contracted as an artist as well as writer, peaks at US #79 and UK #42. (It will become a Springsteen stage staple and will be included on his 1987 boxed set. Janis Joplin and the J. Geils Band cut interim covers.)
Apr Floyd tours Europe with the warmly-received Stax package, which includes Otis Redding, Booker T. & the MG's, Sam & Dave, Arthur Conley and the Mar-Keys.
May ***Knock On Wood*** makes UK #36.
July *Don't Rock The Boat* peaks at #98.
Aug *Love Is A Doggone Good Thing* peaks at US #97 and *Things Get Better* becomes his final UK hit, at #31.
Oct *On A Saturday Night* peaks at US #92.

1968

Sept *I've Never Found A Girl* makes US #40.
Dec *Bring It On Home To Me*, a Sam Cooke song and Floyd's first non-original chart entry, reaches US #17. (It will be followed in 1969 by *Don't Tell Your Mama (Where You've Been)* (US #73, August) and *Why Is The Wine Sweeter* (US #98, November.)

1970

Apr *California Girl* makes US #45, his last chart entry. During his recording and singing career he will continue to write songs for other Stax acts, including Sam & Dave, Rufus Thomas and the Mad Lads and record a comeback album ***Experience*** for Malaco Records in 1977.

1996

Feb [29] Having performed at President George Bush's inaugural ball in January 1989, and now into his fourth decade on the road, Floyd's enduring popularity, especially in Europe, allows no question of retirement. His hobby is collecting cover versions of *Knock On Wood*, which has so far attracted over 60, by acts as diverse as David Bowie, Cher, Count Basie, Eric Clapton, and Amii Stewart, who had the biggest hit version. He now becomes a recipient of a Pioneer Award at the eighth annual Rhythm and Blues Foundation ceremony held in Los Angeles.

THE FLYING BURRITO BROTHERS

Gram Parsons (guitar, vocals); **Chris Hillman** (guitar, mandolin, vocals); **Chris Ethridge** (bass); **Sneaky Pete Kleinow** (pedal steel); **Michael Clarke** (drums)

1968

Oct Singer-songwriter/guitarist Parsons (b. Cecil Connor, Nov. 5, 1946, Winter Haven, FL) quits the Byrds before their South African tour because of his anti-apartheid views. They split shortly after (to be re-formed by Roger McGuinn with new personnel) and Parsons recruits other ex-Byrds, Hillman (b. Dec. 4, 1942, Los Angeles, CA) and Kleinow (b. 1934, South Bend, IN), plus Ethridge and temporary drummer Jon Corneal, to form the Flying Burrito Brothers in Los Angeles.

1969

Feb Following regular gigging as residents at the Palomino on Monday nights and the Whisky on Tuesday nights, they sign to A&M Records and record ***The Gilded Palace Of Sin***. Corneal leaves during the sessions to join Dillard & Clark and is replaced by Clarke (b. June 3, 1944, New York, NY), another ex-Byrd.
May ***The Gilded Palace Of Sin*** peaks at US #164, as the band begins a US tour with Three Dog Night.
Sept With Ethridge leaving just before sessions begin for their next album, ***Burrito Deluxe***, Hillman switches to bass and Bernie Leadon (b. July 19, 1947, Minneapolis, MN), ex-Hearts & Flowers and Dillard & Clark, joins on guitar and dobro. Parsons begins to drift apart from the others (who are becoming frustrated by the apparent lack of commercial progress of their country-rock style), spending much time with old friends, the temporarily Los Angeles-based Rolling Stones. He will leave amid much bad feeling, following the April 1970 release of ***Burrito Deluxe***, to be replaced by Rick Roberts.

1971

June ***Flying Burrito Brothers*** returns them to the US chart, at #176. (Parsons, meanwhile, has moved to London, where, for two years, he spends much time with the Stones and even more time drinking, but does not record or perform until 1973's ***GP***.)
July Leadon leaves, joining with members of Linda Ronstadt's backing group to form the Eagles, while Kleinow returns to session work and is replaced by Al Perkins on pedal steel. Byron Berline (fiddle), Kenny Wertz (guitar), who has played in Hillman's early group, the Scottsville Squirrel Barkers, and Roger Bush (bass) all join, though the morale of remaining original members is low.
Oct After recording the live album ***Last Of The Red-Hot Burritos***, this line-up disintegrates. Clarke joins Los Angeles group the Dependales before going to Hawaii again, while Hillman and Perkins leave for Stephen Stills' band, Manassas. Roberts reorganizes the band by bringing in ex-Dillard & Clark Don Beck (pedal steel), Nashville session man Alan Munde (banjo, guitar) and ex-Southwind Erik Dalton (drums), and they play a tour of Europe from which another performance set, ***Live In Amsterdam***, will eventually emerge in 1975.

1972

Feb [20-22] The band supports Mountain at London's Rainbow Theatre.
June ***Last Of The Red Hot Burritos*** peaks at US #171, by which time the group is no more, though Roberts stays with A&M as a solo artist.

1973

Sept [19] Parsons is found dead in a room at the Joshua Tree Inn, Joshua Tree, CA. His death is ascribed to heart failure following a drug overdose. In a bizarre epilogue, his body in its coffin is stolen by his road managers, Phil Kaufman and Michael Martin, taken out into the desert and burned. They are apparently carrying out Parsons' own wishes.

1974

July A&M releases a Burritos double compilation album, ***Close Up The Honky Tonks***, which includes 11 previously unissued songs.

1975

Oct Original group members Chris Ethridge and Sneaky Pete Kleinow revive the Flying Burrito Brothers' name, signing to CBS/Columbia Records and releasing ***Flying Again***, with a line-up completed by former Canned Heat member Joel Scott Hill (bass), Floyd "Gib" Guilbeau (fiddle) and ex-Byrds Gene Parsons (drums). This, ironically, is their highest-placed album on the US chart, reaching #138.

1976

June Their second Columbia album, ***Airborne***, is released, minus Ethridge, but with the addition of Skip Battin (b. Feb. 2, 1934, Gallipolis, OH) (bass) from the New Riders of the Purple Sage.

1979

May With the band currently comprising Kleinow, Guilbeau, Battin, Greg Harris (guitar) and Ed Ponder (drums), they perform in Tokyo, Japan, which results in the live album ***Live In Tokyo*** (issued as ***Close Encounters To The West Coast*** in Japan).

1981

Following the release of ***Flying High*** the previous year, ***Hearts On The Line***, credited to the Burrito Brothers ("Flying" having been dropped from the name), which currently consists of Battin, Guilbeau and Kleinow, plus John Beland on guitar and vocals, is released.

1985

Oct Following the issue of ***Sunset Sundown*** on Curb Records (US) in January 1982 (which featured only Beland and Guilbeau as the Burrito Brothers), a tour yields two US albums on Relix Records, ***Cabin Fever*** and ***Live From Europe***, both now credited to the Flying Brothers. This line-up includes original member Kleinow, plus Skip Battin, Greg Harris and Jim Goodall, the team that also produces ***Back To The Sweethhearts Of The Radio***, in 1988.
see also: **THE BYRDS, CANNED HEAT, THE EAGLES, Gram PARSONS**

DAN FOGELBERG

1973

Fogelberg (b. Aug. 13, 1951, Peoria, IL), a songwriter/guitarist/pianist since age 14, has dropped out of studying art at Illinois University, Champaign, IL, in 1971, to work on the folk circuit, before touring the US as support to Van Morrison the following year and moving to Los Angeles, CA, to work as a session guitarist. Now signed to CBS/Columbia, his debut album, ***Home Free***, recorded in Nashville, TN, with producer Norbert Putnam, is released, featuring a wish list of guest musicians, including Jackson Browne, Roger McGuinn, Buffy Saint-Marie and Joe Walsh.

1974

He signs a management deal with Irving Azoff, whom he first met in Illinois when Azoff was handling R.E.O. Speedwagon. Azoff persuades another of his acts, Joe Walsh, to produce Fogelberg's second album, ***Souvenirs***, for which Fogelberg switches to Epic via his deal with the Full Moon label and through which all of his future output will be released. Uneasy with the Los Angeles lifestyle, he leaves, eventually settling in Boulder, CO.

1975

Feb The self-penned ***Souvenirs***, featuring producer Walsh, Graham Nash and Eagles Don Henley, Glenn Frey and Randy Meisner, reaches US #17, eventually selling over two million copies.
Mar *Part Of The Plan* reaches US #31, as Fogelberg undertakes a major US tour opening for the Eagles. He also contributes two songs, *Old Tennessee* and *Love Me Through And Through*, to his backing band Fools Gold's eponymous debut album (the band lines up as Denny Henson (guitar), Doug Livingston (guitar, keyboards) and bassist Tom Kelly).
Nov Self-produced ***Captured Angel***, featuring eight self-penned tracks, climbs to US #23, eventually earning a platinum disc.

1977

July [23] ***Nether Lands***, co-produced with Putnam, and featuring guests Henley, J.D. Souther, jazz flautist Tim Weisberg and Kenny Buttrey, and recorded at the Caribou Ranch, Nederland, CO, reaches US #13 and becomes his third million seller.

1978

May [6] The film soundtrack album ***FM*** to which Fogelberg has contributed *There's A Place In The World For A Gambler*, enters the US chart set to hit #5.
Oct [14] ***Twin Sons Of Different Mothers***, recorded with Tim Weisberg, hits US #8 and is another million seller.
Dec The extracted *The Power Of Gold* reaches US #24.

1980

Mar His biggest commercial success comes with the ballad *Longer*, at US #2, and its parent album, ***Phoenix***, at US #3. Both are million-sellers, while in the UK *Longer* peaks at #59 and ***Phoenix*** makes #42 (Apr [5]), his only UK chart action. Fogelberg donates the royalties from *Face The Fire* to the Campaign for Economic Democracy Education Fund, which promotes the use of solar energy in place of nuclear fuel.
May *Heart Hotels* reaches US #21 and is featured on the soundtrack to the John Travolta-starring movie "Urban Cowboy".

1981

Feb Sentimental New Year's Eve ballad, *Same Old Lang Syne*, hits US #9.
Oct ***The Innocent Age***, a 17-part song cycle, featuring his previous chart single and *Only The Heart May Know*, a duet with Emmylou Harris, hits US #6 and is his sixth consecutive million-selling album. It also includes *Hard To Say*, which hits US #7.

1982

Mar [6] *Leader Of The Band*, the third US Top 10 single from ***The Innocent Age***, hits #9.
May [29] *Run For The Roses*, written about the Kentucky Derby race classic, reaches US #18.
June [6] Fogelberg appears at the anti-nuclear rally "Peace Sunday - We Have A Dream", before 85,000 people at the Rose Bowl, Pasadena, CA, with Bob Dylan, Jackson Browne, Joan Baez, Stevie Wonder and others.
Dec [4] *Missing You* reaches US #23.
[18] Compilation album, ***Dan Fogelberg/Greatest Hits***, reaches US #15.

1983

Mar *Make Love Stay* reaches US #29. Fogelberg produces the debut solo album, ***Beauty Lies***, for Michael Brewer (ex-Brewer & Shipley).

1984

Mar ***Windows And Walls***, featuring Timothy B. Schmit, Russ Kunkel and Tom Scott, co-produced with Marty Lewis, peaks at US #15, while *The Language Of Love*, taken from it, reaches #13.
May *Believe In Me*, also from the album, makes US #48.

1985

Apr *Go Down Easy* peaks at US #85.
June Gaining inspiration from a visit to the "Telluride Bluegrass Festival", Telluride, CO, in 1983, Fogelberg has recorded a traditional country music album, ***High Country Snows***, enlisting help from genre acts including Ricky Skaggs, Charlie McCoy, Emory Gordy Jr. and the Desert Rose Band, which reaches US #30.

1987

June Clean-shaven for the first time since ***Souvenirs***, Fogelberg returns to more familiar territory with ***Exiles***, written about his recent divorce. Recorded in Los Angeles and co-produced with Russ Kunkel, it makes US #48 and includes the title theme from the Warren Miller movie "Beyond The Edge".
[13] *She Don't Look Back* peaks at US #84.

1990

Oct [6] Having invited Schmit, David Crosby and Bruce Cockburn, who co-wrote one of the tracks, to contribute, Fogelberg makes US #103 with the self-produced ***The Wild Places***, recorded at his Mountain Bird Studio in Colorado. It includes his extracted cover of the Cascades' 1963 US #3, *Rhythm Of The Rain*.

1991

Oct [11] Fogelberg takes part in "Ban The Dam Jam" benefit at the Beacon Theatre, New York, NY.

1992

Aug [1] He plays at the Coca-Cola Starplex Amphitheatre, Dallas, TX, during his current US tour.
[16] Currently lobbying Congress to help pass the Endangered Species Act, Fogelberg is honored by State Senator Jeremy Weinstein in New York for his ongoing environmental efforts.

1993

Oct [16] With string arrangements by David Campbell, the self-written and produced as ever, ***River Of Souls***, which includes the acerbic *All There Is*, dedicated to Donald Trump, debuts at its US #164 peak, as Fogelberg plays at Atlanta, GA's Chastain Park Amphitheatre.

1994

Apr [17] During a current string of US dates, Fogelberg plays to a sellout crowd of 1,989 at Sangamon State University, Springfield, IL.
Sept [14] Fogelberg performs at the Cynthia Woods Mitchell Pavilion, the Woodlands, TX.

1995

May [30] Newly signed to Giant Records, Fogelberg plays at Festival Hall, Tampa Bay Performing Arts Center, Tampa, FL.
Sept [29] Fogelberg begins a series of US shows at the Majestic Theatre, San Antonio, TX, as his new album ***No Resemblance Whatsoever***, a follow-up to his 1978 collaboration with flautist Tim Weisberg, written and produced by the pair, is released by Giant.

WAYNE FONTANA & THE MINDBENDERS

Wayne Fontana (vocals); **Eric Stewart** (guitar); **Bob Lang** (bass); **Ric Rothwell** (drums)

1963

While working as an apprentice telephone engineer in 1961, Fontana (b. Glynn Geooffrey Ellis, Oct. 28, 1945, Manchester, Lancs.) formed the Jets, a semi-professional outfit playing the Manchester club circuit. The group now gets its first break performing a showcase gig at the Oasis for Fontana Records producer Jack Baverstock. Only Fontana and Lang (b. Jan. 10, 1946, Manchester) show up, so substitute locals Stewart (b. Jan. 20, 1945, Manchester) and Rothwell (b. Eric Rothwell, Mar. 11, 1944, Stockport, Lancs.), who holds a London College of Music Diploma, are recruited at the last minute. Despite a disastrous performance, Baverstock sees enough potential to sign them. Fontana christens his new group the Mindbenders, taken from the title of a UK psychological horror film starring Dirk Bogarde, which is playing at his local cinema.
June The group debuts with revivals of Bo Diddley's *Road Runner* and Fats Domino's *Hello Josephine*.
July *Hello Josephine* makes UK #46.

1964

June Following the release of *For You, For You*, backed with current beat favorite *Love Potion No. 9*, in October and *Little Darlin'* in February, their cover of Ben E. King's *Stop Look And Listen* makes UK #37.
Nov The group's treatment of Major Lance's US hit *Um Um Um Um Um Um*, written by Curtis Mayfield, is its first major UK chart success, hitting #5, as the band joins Brenda Lee's UK tour.

1965

Feb *The Game Of Love*, a song by Clint Ballard Jr., which will bring continent-hopping success, hits UK #2, while ***Wayne Fontana And The Mindbenders*** reaches UK #18.
[27] The group begins a 21-date, twice-nightly UK tour supporting Del Shannon, with Herman's Hermits and others, at the City Hall, Sheffield, Yorks, set to end on March 22nd at the Odeon Cinema, Glasgow, Scotland.
Mar [9] Fontana is taken ill with nervous exhaustion and pulls out of the tour. The Mindbenders continue without him.
Apr [24] Their US chart debut is spectacular, as *The Game Of Love* climbs to hit #1, becoming a million seller. The group visits the US for promotion, but is refused performance visas by US officials concerned about the flood of UK groups entering and working where US bands might play instead. Before being allowed in, the Mindbenders has to obtain proof from **Billboard** and **Cash Box** magazines that its single is the top-selling US record and that the visit is justifiable on popularity grounds.
May US album, ***The Game Of Love***, a variation of the UK release, makes US #58.
[25] The group participates in the "British Song Festival" at the Dome, Brighton, E. Sussex, coming third with 99 points.
July Ballard composition, *Just A Little Bit Too Late*, reaches UK #20 and US #45.
Oct *She Needs Love* makes UK #32, the last single released by Fontana with the group.
[2] The group represents Britain in the annual "Grand Gala Du Disque" at the Congresscentrum, Amsterdam, Holland.
[6] An announcement is made that Fontana and the Mindbenders will split on October 31st by mutual consent, a move prompted by the label, for whom both parties will continue to record.
[30] The band makes its last appearance together at the Pavilion, Buxton Gardens, Derbys.
Nov [3] Fontana begins an 18-date, twice-nightly tour with Herman's Hermits, the Fortunes, Billy Fury & the Gamblers, and others, at the Gaumont Cinema, Wolverhampton, Warks., set to end on the 22nd at the Odeon Cinema, Manchester.
Dec Fontana's first solo success, *It Was Easier To Hurt Her*, a US hit for Garnett Mimms, makes UK #36.
[11] He makes his solo TV debut on "Thank Your Lucky Stars".

1966

Jan ***Eric, Rick, Wayne And Bob***, recorded immediately prior to the split, is released.
Mar The Mindbenders rapidly outsells its former "tambourine player" (as Fontana is referred to after the split) with *A Groovy Kind Of Love*, which hits UK #2.
May *A Groovy Kind Of Love* also hits US #2, while the Mindbenders' UK follow-up, *Can't Live With You, Can't Live Without You*, reaches #28, as Fontana's *Come On Home* also charts, at UK #16.
July ***The Mindbenders*** reaches UK #28.
Aug The Mindbenders' US album, ***A Groovy Kind Of Love***, peaks at US #92, while Fontana's single, *Goodbye Bluebird*, makes UK #49.
[12] Fontana begins Radio England's "Swingin' '66" UK tour, with the Small Faces, Crispian St. Peters, Neil Christian and Genevieve, at the Odeon Cinema, Lewisham, London.
Sept The Mindbenders' *Ashes To Ashes* peaks at UK #14 and US #55, its final US hit.
[27] The group begins a week-long UK tour as Dusty Springfield's opening act at London's Finsbury Park Astoria , set to close on October 3rd at the Odeon Cinema, Manchester.
Nov Fontana's *Pamela Pamela* reaches UK #11, his biggest solo hit, but also his last. (It is written by Graham Gouldman (b. May 10, 1946, Manchester, Lancs.), who will later team up with Stewart in 10cc.)

1967

Aug [5] The Mindbenders advertise in the **New Musical Express** for a "top class drummer/vocalist".
Sept The Mindbenders appears as a beat group at a

school dance in the UK-made Sidney Poitier-starring film "To Sir With Love". The band's cover of the Box Tops' *The Letter*, far outsold by the original, is its last UK chart single, reaching only #42. (During the year, Fontana has released *24 Sycamore* (April), *Impossible Years* (September) and *Gina* (November).)

1968

Lang leaves the group and is replaced for the final weeks of the band's life by Graham Gouldman, a successful songwriter for artists including the Yardbirds, Herman's Hermits, Jeff Beck and the Hollies. Rothwell also departs and the Mindbenders finally dissolves. (Fontana will release six more singles during the next 18 months, before his recording career ends. Stewart will play sessions for two years before joining Lol Creme and Kevin Godley in Hotlegs, to have a hit with *Neanderthal Man* at #2 in 1970, and will re-recruit Gouldman for 10cc. Lang will drop out of music, re-emerge in Racing Cars in 1976, who will score with *They Shoot Horses Don't They* at UK #14 in 1977, and quit again, to run a stereo equipment company. Rothwell will establish an antiques business.)

1970

Fontana gives up his singing career and works for Chappell music publishers as a resident songwriter. (The "English Invasion Revival" tour of the US will bring him back to the live arena in 1973, before he resumes a recording career in 1976, releasing *The Last Bus Home* for Polydor. A further rock'n'roll revival tour in 1979 encourages him to put together a new Mindbenders group to perform his old '60s hits, performing at the "Festival Of The Tenth Summer", Manchester, in July 1986. Recognition briefly returns in the late '80s, when *The Game Of Love* is featured in the Robin Williams movie "Good Morning Vietnam" and Phil Collins revives *A Groovy Kind Of Love* as a chart-topping single from the film "Buster".)

see also: **10CC**

FRANKIE FORD

1959

After forming his own band, the Syncopators, at high school in New Orleans, LA, winning local talent contests and appearing at local venues with Carmen Miranda, Ted Lewis and Sophie Tucker, and singing *Botch-A-Me*, a current Rosemary Clooney hit, on Ted Mack's "Original Amateur Hour" on NBC-TV in 1952, Ford (b. Frank Guzzo, Aug. 4, 1940, Gretna, LA) records for Johnny Vincent's Ace label, which has already scored major US hits with New Orleans acts, notably Huey "Piano" Smith & the Clowns, based in Jackson, MS, at the suggestion of manager Joe Caronna, who has seen him performing with the Syncopators. Ford cuts *Cheatin' Woman* and *Last One To Know* at Cosimo Matassa's studio, with Huey Smith, Red Tyler, Frank Fields, Charlie Williams and Robert Parker backing him.

Apr Ford reaches US #14 with *Sea Cruise*. (The song will become a minor rock classic, with later versions including another US chart entry by Johnny Rivers in 1971.)

Aug *Alimony*, again recorded with Huey Smith & the Clowns, peaks at US #97. (Both this and *Sea Cruise* have been recorded by dubbing new vocals by Ford on to existing backing tracks by the Clowns - after erasing the original vocals by band's own singer Bobby Marchan.)

1960

Jan An American tour begins in New York City, ending on June 6th in Mexico. With the Syncopators unable to support him, Ford assembles a road band, called the Skyliners, including his distant cousin Mac Rebennack, who later finds fame as Dr. John.

Feb *Time After Time* peaks at US #75. (After releasing five singles on Ace, Ford and his manager leave the label following disagreements over royalty statements, and form Spinett Records. Ford records *Morgus The Magnificent* as Morgus & the Three Ghouls (who are Huey Smith, Robert Parker and Mac Rebennack.)

Oct Signed to Imperial Records, he makes US #87 with a cover version of fellow New Orleans artist Joe Jones' *You Talk Too Much*, eclipsed by Jones' original, which hits US #3. His revival of the Boyd Bennett/ Fontane Sisters 1955 hit, *Seventeen*, will reach US #72 the following April.

1962

Ford begins a three-year stint in the US army, which takes him to Korea, Vietnam, Guam and Thailand as part of a special entertainment unit where he writes, directs stage shows and casts musical talent. Following his tour of duty he will have a local New Orleans hit in 1966 with *I Can't Face Tomorrow*.

1971

Jan Ford buys a New Orleans club which will henceforth be the base for his activities, and starts to record again, for the Paula label in Shreveport, LA.

1994

Apr [22] Having recorded for the White Cliffs, Doubloon, Paula, Cinnamon, ABC, Briarmeade, SYC and Stardust labels during the '70s, and continued regular performing on the New Orleans live circuit into the '90s, having appeared on US and UK TV in a live Mardi Gras concert transmitted from New Orleans in the late '80s, Ford now takes part in the 25th annual "New Orleans Jazz & Heritage Festival".

FOREIGNER

Lou Gramm (vocals); **Mick Jones** (guitar); **Rick Wills** (bass); **Dennis Elliott** (drums)

1976

Feb The band is formed by Jones (b. Dec. 27, 1944, London), who has begun his career in Nero & the Gladiators and played on the same Paris Olympia bill as the Beatles in 1964 during six years living in Paris, France working with Johnny Hallyday, also spending two years with Spooky Tooth (which evolved out of Wonderwheel, a band he formed with Gary Wright), before emigrating to the US to work as an A&R scout and then joining the Leslie West Band, after he meets ex-King Crimson multi-instrumentalist Ian McDonald (b. June 25, 1946, London) in New York, NY, at a studio session for singer Ian Lloyd. Jones recruits Elliott (b. Aug. 18, 1950, London), whom he had met at an Ian Hunter session, and three Americans: Ed Gagliardi (b. Feb. 13, 1952, New York) on bass, Al Greenwood on keyboards, and Black Sheep singer Lou Gramm (b. Lou Grammatico, May 2, 1950, Rochester, NY) on lead vocals. The bi-nationality of the personnel leads to the band's name.

1977

Feb After a year in rehearsals, during which the group has signed to Atlantic Records, its hard-rock debut, ***Foreigner***, co-produced by John Sinclair and Gary Lyons with Jones and McDonald, is released.

May [13] Jones-written *Feels Like The First Time*, from the album, makes UK #39.

June *Feels Like The First Time* hits US #4.

Aug [26] The album's second extract, *Cold As Ice*, written by Gramm and Jones, reaches UK #24.

Oct *Cold As Ice* hits US #6.

[22] ***Foreigner*** hits US #4, eventually going quadruple platinum.

1978

Feb *Long Long Way From Home* reaches US #20.

Mar [18] Foreigner plays at the "California Jam II" festival in Ontario, CA, during a six-week world tour set to end at London's Rainbow Theatre.

Aug [27] The group plays the final day of the annual "Reading Festival", Reading, Berks.

Sept *Hot Blooded*, from their sophomore set, ***Double Vision***, again written by Jones and Gramm, hits US #3 and is a million seller.

[9] ***Double Vision***, co-produced by Jones, McDonald and Keith Olsen, hits US #3 on its way to five-million US sales.

[16] ***Double Vision***, makes UK #32.

Nov Its title track, *Double Vision*, is another million-seller, hitting US #2.

[4] *Hot Blooded* makes UK #42.

1979

Mar *Blue Morning, Blue Day* reaches US #15 and UK #45.

Aug [27] The group headlines the annual "Reading Festival". (Prior to recording the group's third album, Jones replaces Gagliardi with ex-Roxy Music, Small Faces and Peter Frampton backing band bass player Rick Wills, who nabs the job when travelling to the US to collect debts owed to him by Peter Frampton's management, subsequently auditioning for Foreigner).

Oct Jones/Gramm-penned *Dirty White Boy* reaches US #12.

[27] ***Head Games***, co-produced by Jones, MacDonald and Roy Thomas Baker, hits US #5, garnering two further platinum discs.

Dec *Head Games*, the title track, reaches US #14.

1980

Mar *Women* reaches US #41.

Sept Greenwood and McDonald leave and the band stabilizes as a four-piece.

1981

Aug [22] After a lengthy gap, ***4***, the epitome of adult-oriented rock, tops the US chart for the first of ten weeks. Co-helmed by Jones and magic-touch rock producer Robert John "Mutt" Lange, it will become the group's most successful project, eventually selling over six million US units.

Sept Jones-penned *Urgent*, featuring Motown sax man Jr. Walker, hits US #4.

[5] *Urgent* peaks at UK #54.

Oct [17] *Juke Box Hero* makes UK #48.

Nov [28] Uncharacteristic ballad, *Waiting For A Girl Like You*, written by Jones and Gramm, becomes a US million seller. It fails to make US #1, but spends an unprecedented ten weeks at #2, mostly behind Olivia Newton-John's *Physical*.

1982

Jan [23] *Waiting For A Girl Like You*, the group's first UK Top 10 record, hits UK #8.

Feb [5] ***4***, featuring keyboardist Thomas Dolby, finally hits its UK #5 peak in a 62-week chart run. During its current North American tour, the band plays sellout dates at the Cow Palace, San Francisco, CA, and the Great Western Forum, Inglewood, CA.

Apr [3] *Juke Box Hero* reaches US #26.

May [5] The group begins a five-date UK mini-visit at the Playhouse, Edinburgh, Scotland, with further dates at the National Exhibition Centre, Birmingham, W. Midlands, and Wembley Arena, Wembley, Middx.

[15] *Urgent* re-charts in the UK, climbing to #45.

June [26] *Break It Up* reaches US #26.

Aug [14] *Luanne* peaks at US #75.

1983

Jan Greatest hits collection, ***Records***, makes UK #58 and includes a live version of *Hot Blooded*, recorded on a US tour in 1982.

Feb ***Records*** hits US #10 on its way to triple-platinum status.

1985

Jan [19] After a lengthy recording hiatus, the gospel-tinged, choir-accompanied rock ballad, *I Want To Know What Love Is*, created by Jones, hits UK #1. It features guest contributions from the Thompson Twins' Tom Bailey, Jennifer Holliday and the New Jersey Mass Choir.

[26] ***Agent Provocateur***, co-produced by Alex Sadkin and Jones, also tops the UK chart.
Feb [2] *I Want To Know What Love Is* heads the US survey, another million-seller, as ***Agent Provocateur*** hits US #5, eventually nabbing two platinum US sales awards.
May Jones/Gramm-penned *That Was Yesterday* reaches US #12 and UK #28.
June A remixed version of *Cold As Ice* peaks at UK #64, while *Reaction To Action* and *Down On Love* both reach US #54.

1987

Feb Gramm solo album, ***Ready Or Not*** (US #27), and solo US Top 10 hit, *Midnight Blue*, hint at his departure.
Apr [18] *Midnight Blue* hits US #5.
June [13] Gramm's *Ready Or Not* makes US #54.
July *Say You Will*, from the forthcoming Foreigner album ***Inside Information***, peaks at UK #71.
Dec [19] ***Inside Information***, co-produced by Jones with Frank Filipetti and featuring Bailey and Hugh McCracken among others, makes UK #64 and will reach US #15 (its final US platinum disc of the decade).

1988

Feb [20] *Say You Will* hits US #6.
May Jones-written ballad, *I Don't Want To Live Without You*, from the album, hits US #5.

1989

Sept ***Mick Jones***, including songs originally written for the London stage musical "Metropolis", peaks at US #184. The first single from the album is *Just Wanna Hold*, co-written with Ian Hunter and Mick Jagger under the pseudonym "M. Phillips".
Nov As Gramm releases a further solo album, ***Long Hard Look*** (US #85 - Feb [17] 1990), Jones concentrates more on production projects, which include Billy Joel's ***Stormfront***, and songwriting, not least co-penning Eric Clapton's Grammy-winning *Bad Love* hit.

1990

Jan [27] Gramm's *Just Between You And Me* hits US #6.
Mar [31] His follow-up, *True Blue Love*, makes US #40.
May [25] Gramm quits the group, set to embark on a solo summer tour supporting Steve Miller.
Dec Gramm and former Whitesnake guitarist Vivian Campbell team with Kevin Valentine (drums) and Bruce Tirgon (bass) to form Shadowking.

1991

July [6] Foreigner's first album in three years, ***Unusual Heat***, featuring its new lead vocalist Johnny Edwards, a bar-band veteran from Louisville, KY, spends a week at UK #56.
[15] The band plays a one-off London date at the Marquee club.
Aug [3] ***Unusual Heat*** peaks at US #117, a dramatic reversal of fortune for the Gramm-less band.
[9] They play on the second night of a Billy Joel benefit at Indian Field Ranch, Montauk, Long Island, NY.
Sept [16] The group plays before a sellout crowd of 5,670 at the Mexico National Auditorium, during its current American tour.
Nov [22] The band shares a bill with the Smithereens, Ray and Dave Davies, the Raindogs and RTZ at WBCN's "Rock Of Boston" concert at Boston Garden.

1992

May [16] ***The Very Best Of Foreigner*** reaches UK #16.
June Gramm rejoins Foreigner, having re-teamed with Jones, writing together again while under martial law in a hotel during the Los Angeles riots. (The departing Edwards will team with former Ratt axeman Warren DeMartini.)
Oct [31] With returned lead singer Gramm and new member, drummer Mark Schulman, the band's ***The Very Best ... Beyond***, featuring 13 hits plus three new tunes, including new single *With Heaven On Our Side*, peaks at US #123.
Nov [17] The group performs at the Roxy, Atlanta, GA, during a current North American tour.

1993

May [7] Five-month US tour opens at St. Lucie County Civic Center, Fort Pierce, FL.
Nov [2] ***Classic Hits Live*** is released in the US.

1994

Jan [19] Jones inducts Duane Eddy into the Rock and Roll Hall of Fame at the ninth annual dinner at New York's Waldorf Astoria Hotel.
July [2] The group, now comprising Jones, Gramm, Schulman, Bruce Turgon (bass), Jeff Jacobs (keyboards) and Scott Gilman (saxophone), begins a US summer tour, sharing the bill with the Doobie Brothers, at the Cynthia Woods Mitchell Pavilion, the Woodlands, TX
Oct [22] *White Lie* charts for a week at UK #58.
Nov [12] Arista-issued ***Mr. Moonlight***, recorded by the central quartet of Jones, Gramm, Turgon and Jacobs and produced by Jones, Gramm and Mike Stone, debuts at its UK #59 peak. (The album will not be released Stateside until February 1995, when it appears on the Rhythm Safari label.)

1995

Mar [8] The group begins a UK tour with the Doobie Brothers at the Bournemouth International Centre, set to end on the 16th at Wembley Arena, before embarking on a tour of Germany.
May [6] *Until The End Of Time*, featuring guitar veteran Duane Eddy, makes US #42.
June [23-24] Currently on tour with Cheap Trick and Loverboy, Foreigner plays two dates at the Universal Amphitheatre, Universal City, CA.
Aug [12] The band performs at the first American Association For Nude Recreation's "MusicFest '95", held at a 160-acre nudist park in Turtle Lake Resort, Union City, MI, in front of a totally naked audience.

1996

July [3] Foreigner embarks on veteran rockers US package tour, with Peter Frampton and REO Speedwagon, in Darien Lake, NY.
see also: **KING CRIMSON**

THE FORTUNES

Glen Dale (guitar, vocals); **Barry Pritchard** (guitar, vocals); **David Carr** (keyboards); **Rod Allen** (bass, vocals); **Andy Brown** (drums)

1963

Mar Allen (b. Rodney Bainbridge, Mar. 31, 1944, Leicester, Leics.), Pritchard (b. Apr. 3, 1944, Birmingham, Warks.) and Dale (b. Richard Garforth, Apr. 2, 1943, Deal, Kent), living in manager Reg Calvert's house (Allen and Pritchard are working as backing singers, having made their debut at age 13 on ITV's "Carroll Levis Show" before forming a skiffle group, while Dale is a solo singer in the "Danny Storm Beat Package Show"), form the Cliftones. Brown (b. Jan. 7, 1946, Birmingham) and Carr (b. Aug. 4, 1943, Leyton, London), recommended by Brian Poole, soon augment the trio.
Sept Renamed the Fortunes, they sign to Decca Records, becoming one of the first provincial beat groups to do so, which releases the group's debut, a revival of the Jamies' *Summertime, Summertime*.

1964

Jan *Caroline* becomes a familiar radio sound in the UK for some years, being adopted by UK pirate station Radio Caroline as its theme tune and given daily spins.

1965

Jan [16] The group makes its UK TV debut on "Ready Steady Go!"
Aug [21] Following two further singles, *You've Got Your Troubles*, penned by Roger Greenaway and Roger Cook (currently members of the Kestrels), hits UK #2, behind the Beatles' *Help!*
Oct [9] *You've Got Your Troubles* hits US #7.
Nov [3] The group begins an 18-date, twice-nightly UK tour, with Herman's Hermits, Wayne Fontana, Billy Fury & the Gamblers and others, at the Gaumont Cinema, Wolverhampton, Warks., set to end on the 22nd at the Odeon Cinema, Manchester, Lancs.
[6] *Here It Comes Again* hits UK #4.
Dec [18] *Here It Comes Again* reaches US #27, as ***The Fortunes***, containing the hits, is released in Britain.
[24] The group takes part in Murray The K's nine-day Christmas show in New York, NY.

1966

Feb [4] They play the first of six concerts over a weekend, as a rehearsal for the Who's first bill-topping UK tour, starting March 25th, with the Merseys and Screaming Lord Sutch.
Mar [12] *This Golden Ring* reaches UK #15, but has stopped at US #82 a week earlier despite their recent US tour with Peter & Gordon and the Moody Blues. (It is the group's last hit in either country for more than five years.)
June [3] Dale leaves to go solo, and is replaced by Shel MacRae (b. Andrew Semple, Mar. 8, 1943, Burbank, Scotland) from the Kimbos. *Is It Really Worth Your While?* is the first single released by the new line-up.
[21] Manager Reg Calvert is shot dead by business rival Major William Smedley. (Calvert had gone to Smedley's Duck Street, Wendens Ambo home and, during a confrontation, was shot once in the chest, dying of lacerations of the lung and liver. Smedley, a former Liberal Party executive, will be cleared of murder.)
July [9] Allen is taken to hospital after fans pull him off stage at a Starlite Rooms gig in Lincoln, Lincs.
[24] The group makes its cabaret debut with a week-long engagement at the Greaseborough Social Club, Rotherham, Yorks.
Aug Dale releases his first solo single, a cover of Lennon/McCartney's *Good Day Sunshine*.

1967

Apr [19] The group turns down an invitation to perform at Queen Juliana of the Netherlands' birthday party because they are playing cabaret in Newcastle, Tyne & Wear, that week.
Aug The band moves from Decca to United Artists Records. Several UA singles between now and late 1970 are released, though the group makes considerably more money recording ad jingles, including *It's The Real Thing* for Coca-Cola, and playing northern club dates in the UK. Carr will leave the group as a four-piece in August 1968.

1970

June [20] Their cover of Pickettywitch's (US #67) *That Same Old Feeling* is released in World Pacific Records - in competition with the original - and peaks at US #62.

1971

May Having signed a new deal with Capitol Records, the Fortunes re-team with writer/producers Roger Cook and Roger Greenaway for *Here Comes That Rainy Day Feeling Again*.
July [31] *Here Comes That Rainy Day Feeling Again* reaches US #15.
Sept Scotsman George McAllister joins, returning the band to a quintet.
Oct [23] *Freedom Come Freedom Go* hits UK #6 and peaks at US #72. In hitting UK #7 (Feb [26], 1972), *Storm In A Teacup* will close the Fortunes' chart account (though a number of non-charting singles on Capitol will follow).

1991

Oct [6] Having released one-off singles on the Mooncrest and Target labels during the '70s and having employed their harmony vocal strengths and back-catalog of familiar hits to continue as a supper-club act in the UK, without ever finding their way back into the rock/pop mainstream, the group now takes part in "The Biggest '60s Party In Town" at London's Olympia Hall.

THE FOUR SEASONS

Frankie Valli (lead vocals); **Bob Gaudio** (vocals, organ); **Nick Massi** (vocals, bass); **Tommy DeVito** (vocals, guitar)

1953

Valli (b. Francis Castelluccio, May 3, 1937, Newark, NJ), having been taken under the wing of country singer Texas Jean Valley, who had heard him sing *White Christmas* in a school play, passing him off as his kid brother Frankie Valley and taken him to auditions, cuts his first record, a version of George Jessel's *My Mother's Eyes* for Mercury Records' subsidiary Corona, via a connection made by fellow Newark Central High student, Paul Kapp. It is credited to Frank Valley & the Travelers and is followed by *Somebody Else Took Her Home*. The following year, Valli joins the Variety Trio, a vocal group comprising Hank Majewski and brothers Nick and Tommy DeVito (b. June 19, 1936, Montclair, NJ), working at the Bellbrook Tavern and El Morocco Club. The group changes its name to the Variatones and works solidly on the New Jersey club circuit (including dates at the Broadway Lounge in Passaic, NJ, and Newark's Silhouette club).

1956

June Signed to RCA Records, the Variatones are renamed the Four Lovers and record Otis Blackwell's *(You're The) Apple Of My Eye*, which peaks at US #62. Despite an appearance on CBS-TV's "The Ed Sullivan Show" and several follow-ups, the Four Lovers' career goes no further.

1959

Under the name Frank Tyler, Valli releases the solo *I Go Ape* (written by Bob Crewe and Frank Slay) on Okeh, and the group name-changes again, to Frank Valle & the Romans, for *Come Si Bella* on the Cindy label.

1960

Massi (b. Nicholas Macioci, Sept. 19, 1935, Newark), ex-local group Hugh Garrity & the Hollywood Playboys, replaces Majewski, as the band teams with independent New York producer Bob Crewe, acting as his session vocal group for two years on productions released under such names as the Village Voices (*Redlips*) and Billy Dixon & the Topics (*I Am All Alone*) on Crewe's Topix label.

1961

Nick DeVito quits and is briefly replaced by Charlie Calello, who will become the group's musical arranger, before Gaudio (b. Nov. 17, 1942, Bronx), formerly with *Short Shorts* hitmakers the Royal Teens, joins. Gaudio's developing talent as a songwriter is giving the group a solid (if, as yet, hit-less) repertoire of original material. (He also plays a stand-up electronic organ on stage with the group, having recorded the keyboard instrumental *10 Million Tears*, as Turner Di Centri.)

1962

Jan The band guests on back-up vocals on Danny & the Juniors' collaboration with Freddy Cannon, *Twistin' All Night Long*, which peaks at US #68.

Feb Crewe leases the group's recording of a Bell Sisters' oldie, *Bermuda*, to George Goldner's Gone label, which releases it credited to the Four Seasons (the name of a bowling alley on Chesnut Street in Union, NJ, where the Four Lovers had played in the Branch Room cocktail lounge of the alley).

July The band spends the summer performing at Martell's Sea Breeze in Point Pleasant Beach, NJ. Crewe and arranger Calello, meanwhile, analyze the gimmicks behind major recent hits and decide to incorporate as many as possible into the next Four Seasons' recording. Gaudio offers his recently-penned ballad, *Sherry* (written in 15 minutes), a song originally penned as *Terry*, then *Jackie*, either as a tribute to the First Lady or New York DJ Jack Spector's daughter.

Aug Gimmick-laden *Sherry* is released, highlighted by the prominent piercing falsetto end of Valli's three-octave tenor range (the group is billed as the Four Seasons, featuring the "sound" of Frankie Valli on most albums). Crewe almost issues the disc on Perry, a label in which he has an interest, but instead leases it to Vee-Jay in Chicago, IL, when Randy Wood shows interest. The day after the group appears singing *Sherry* on Dick Clark's "American Bandstand" on ABC-TV, Vee-Jay gets orders for 180,000 copies.

Sept [15] *Sherry* hits US #1 in just four weeks and will stay on top for five. It will sell two million domestic copies and also top the R&B chart for a week.

Nov [17] *Big Girls Don't Cry*, a similar commercial blend jointly penned by Crewe and Gaudio, who had seen a movie in which John Payne smacks a woman across the face and responds with that line, also tops US chart for the first of five weeks (and the R&B survey for four) and is a second million-plus seller. *Sherry*, meanwhile, hits UK #8.

Dec Their debut album, ***Sherry And 11 Others***, including the two chart-toppers, plus an update of the Four Lovers' *Apple Of My Eyes* and several oldies, like *Peanuts*, *La Dee Dah*, *Teardrops* and *Oh Carol*, hits US #6. A seasonal collection of carols and secular Christmas songs, ***The Four Seasons Greetings***, is also released and, extracted from it, a *Sherry*-styled revival of *Santa Claus Is Coming To Town* reaches US #23.

[9] The band appears on CBS-TV's "The Ed Sullivan Show".

1963

Feb *Big Girls Don't Cry* reaches UK #13.

Mar [2] The band guests on Chubby Checker's "Limbo Party" show at the Cow Palace, San Francisco, CA, as *Walk Like A Man* begins a three-week run at US #1, and will become the group's third million seller. (The Four Seasons will have been in pole position for 13 of the preceding 27 weeks and has become the first group to score three consecutive US #1s.)

Apr *Walk Like A Man* reaches UK #12, while ***Big Girls Don't Cry And Twelve Others***, a collection of mainly vocal group oldies, like *Sincerely*, *Silhouettes* and *Goodnight My Love*, hits US #8.

May Their revival of Fats Domino's *Ain't That A Shame* reaches US #22, though much of its airplay is nabbed by the Crewe/Gaudio-penned ballad B-side, *Soon (I'll Be Home Again)*, which peaks at US #77.

July *Ain't That A Shame* makes UK #38, while ***Sherry And 11 Others*** reaches UK #20.

Aug ***Ain't That A Shame And 11 Others***, a mixture of new songs and more vocal-group revivals, makes US #47. Taken from it, *Candy Girl*, written by Larry Santos, hits US #3, while its B-side, Gaudio's *Sherry*-like *Marlena*, reaches US #36.

Oct Compilation, ***Golden Hits Of The Four Seasons***, climbs to US #15. From the previous album, the Latin-styled Gaudio/Calello-penned *New Mexican Rose* makes US #36 and the B-side, *That's The Only Way*, peaks at US #88.

Dec Crewe and the group are at loggerheads with Vee-Jay, mainly over alleged non-payment of royalties, and the band threatens to withhold future material. (Vee-Jay is a victim of its successful marketing of the group, selling millions of records with the costs this incurs, then suffering cashflow problems waiting for distributors' payments.)

1964

Feb Crewe and the group have signed a new deal with another Chicago-based label, Mercury, for release on Philips' subsidiary. Their label debut, *Dawn (Go Away)*, written by Gaudio with Sandy Linzer, hits US #3 (kept from the top by the Beatles' *I Want To Hold Your Hand* and *She Loves You*) and is another million seller.

Mar ***Born To Wander***, the group's first album on Philips, is a collection of quieter, mainly folk-influenced harmony songs (mostly Gaudio originals) following the current US folk "hootenanny" craze, and makes US #84. (It includes the West Coast-styled death ballad *No Surfin' Today*, which moves them into the territory of their chief US competitors, the Beach Boys, and Crewe/Gaudio's *Silence Is Golden*, later a worldwide hit for the Tremeloes.)

Apr Vee-Jay, retaining rights to earlier group recordings, issues a revival of Maurice Williams & the Zodiacs' *Stay* (from ***Ain't That A Shame*** and also a current UK hit for the Hollies), which makes US #16. The Four Seasons' current and former labels match each other with single and album releases, as ***Dawn (Go Away) And 11 Other Great Songs*** reaches US #25.

May *Ronnie*, a new Crewe/Gaudio song, hits US #6.

June ***Stay And Other Great Hits***, a compilation of earlier tracks on Vee-Jay, makes US #100.

July [18] *Rag Doll*, recorded in a rushed Sunday session in a Broadway basement studio the day before a US tour, tops the US chart for the first of two weeks and is another million seller. On Vee-Jay, their update of the Shepherd Sisters' oldie, *Alone* (taken from ***Big Girls Don't Cry***), makes US #28.

Sept *Rag Doll* hits UK #2, while in the US ***Rag Doll*** hits #7, as a Vee-Jay compilation, ***More Golden Hits By The Four Seasons***, reaches US #105.

[5] It is reported that President Lyndon Johnson has invited the group to perform at the upcoming Democratic Party national convention.

Oct *Save It For Me*, a Crewe/Gaudio song from ***Rag Doll***, hits US #10, while *Sincerely*, another Vee-Jay reissue, makes US #75. Vee-Jay double set ***The Beatles Vs. The Four Seasons***, repackages ***Introducing The Beatles*** and ***Golden Hits Of The 4 Seasons*** and makes US #142.

Nov *Big Man In Town* reaches US #20.

1965

Feb *Bye Bye Baby (Baby Goodbye)* reaches US #12 (it will be a UK #1 in 1975 for the Bay City Rollers).

Apr *Toy Soldier* makes US #64, the fourth Four Seasons single in a row not to be a UK hit, despite the success of *Rag Doll*.

May ***The 4 Seasons Entertain You***, including the recent hits, reaches US #77.

Aug *Girl Come Running* reaches US #30. Massi leaves the group, tired of touring, replaced temporarily by Calello, before Joe Long (b. Sept. 5, 1941) joins. (Massi will concentrate on his studio and talent office at 48 Washington St., Bloomfield, NJ, called Vitomass Productions, with partner Tommy DeVito.)

Dec An adaptation of the group's sound, to incorporate a brassy, Motown-like dance beat, on the ultra-commercial Sandy Linzer/Denny Randell/Crewe song *Let's Hang On* sees the disc hit US #3, and is the group's first million seller since *Rag Doll*. A novelty falsetto version of Bob Dylan's *Don't Think Twice, It's Alright*, credited to the Wonder Who, reaches US #12. It soon transpires that this is the Four Seasons under a pseudonym. (Valli clowned with a "Rose Murphy" voice during recordings of some Dylan songs for album use, with a result so outrageous and commercial it was felt worthy of release - though not at the expense of *Let's Hang On*, hence the pseudonym.)

1966

Jan *Let's Hang On* hits UK #4, while back home *Little Boy (In Grown Up Clothes)* peaks at US #60. This new track is on Vee-Jay, along with ***On Stage With The Four Seasons***, as part of the legal settlement between Crewe and the group and Vee-Jay, which has concluded that the former is free to continue releasing records on Philips, but owes a Vee-Jay an album in lieu. (Vee-Jay will be bankrupt within months and all recorded masters will revert to the producer and group.) Philips' first compilation, ***The Four Seasons' Gold Vault Of Hits***, hits US #10 and earns a gold disc. ***Big Hits By Burt Bacharach, Hal David And Bob***

Dylan, a set of mainly straight covers of familiar songs, plus the Wonder Who hit *Don't Think Twice*, makes US #106.
Feb Valli's first solo, *(You're Gonna) Hurt Yourself*, makes US #39. When this charts, the group has three simultaneous hits on the US Singles chart, under three different names.
Mar *Working My Way Back To You* (later revived by the Spinners) hits US #9 and makes UK #50, while the album ***Working My Way Back To You*** makes US #50.
June Classical adaptation, *Opus 17 (Don't You Worry 'Bout Me)*, reaches US #13 and UK #20.
July The Wonder Who's double A-side gimmick, *On The Good Ship Lollipop/You're Nobody Till Somebody Loves You*, stops at US #87 and #96.
Oct Their arrangement of the Cole Porter standard *I've Got You Under My Skin* reaches UK #12.
Nov Valli's second solo, *The Proud One*, later revived by the Osmonds, peaks at US #68.

1967

Jan Crewe and the Four Seasons have acquired the early tracks from Vee-Jay and have had them repackaged into the compilations ***2nd Vault Of Golden Hits*** (which also features the recent Philips successes) and ***Lookin' Back***, which reach US #22 and #107 respectively.
Feb *Tell It To The Rain*, by the new Petrillo/Cifelli writing team, hits US #10 and makes UK #37.
May *Beggin'* reaches US #16. (It fails to chart in Britain, but will later be a minor UK hit for Timebox).
July Compilation, ***New Gold Hits***, reaches US #37. Included on it is *C'mon Marianne*, which hits US #9 (later revived by Donny Osmond) and the Wonder Who's *Lonesome Road*, which stops at US #89. In another triple chart representation, Valli enjoys his biggest solo hit so far, the million seller *Can't Take My Eyes Off You*, which hits US #2. (Andy Williams' cover will take the UK honors.)
Sept Valli's *I Make A Fool Of Myself* reaches US #18.
Nov Mildly psychedelic *Watch The Flowers Grow* blossoms at US #30.

1968

Feb Valli's *To Give (The Reason I Live)* reaches US #29.
Mar His revival of the Shirelles' *Will You Love Me Tomorrow* makes US #24.

1969

Jan After a lengthy period with no Four Seasons discs on the US chart (their *Saturday's Father* in mid-1968 having stalled), *Electric Stories* peaks at US #61.
Feb Double compilation album, ***Edizione D'Oro (The Four Seasons Gold Edition - 29 Gold Hits)***, reaches US #37 and earns a gold disc.
Mar The group's concept album, ***The Genuine Imitation Life Gazette***, a lyrically serious work on sociological themes, written by Gaudio and Jake Holmes, makes US #85. Both sides of the single from it, *Something's On Her Mind/Idaho* chart briefly at US #98/#95. Gaudio signs a contract with CBS/Columbia Records for his own Gazette label, its first release being Lock Stock & Barrel's *Happy People*.
July Valli's *The Girl I'll Never Know (Angels Never Fly This Low)* peaks at US #52.
Oct The group's *And That Reminds Me (My Heart Reminds Me)*, a revival of an old Della Reese number, makes US #45 on the Crewe label, while contract renegotiations are proceeding with Philips.

1970

Apr Gaudio and Jake Holmes write and produce the concept album ***Watertown*** for Frank Sinatra.
May *Patch Of Blue* peaks at US #94. It is the first chart single to bear the credit Frankie Valli & the Four Seasons (and will be their last to make the US survey for five years).
June ***Half And Half***, ten tracks split evenly between Valli solos and the Four Seasons songs, peaks at US #190 and marks the end of the group's period with Philips.

1971

Jan DeVito retires because of hearing difficulties, and is temporarily replaced by Bob Grimm, while drummer Gary Wolfe also joins (the group has never, until now, used a full-time drummer on stage), as the new line-up begins the group's first UK tour for seven years.
Feb *You're Ready Now*, a 1966 track by Valli which failed to score, is reissued in the UK after northern dancefloor success and reaches #11.
Apr Double compilation album, ***Edizione D'Oro***, reaches UK #11.
Sept *Whatever You Say*, a Gaudio song recorded in London in a one-off deal with UK Warner Bros., is released.
Nov UK compilation, ***The Big Ones***, reaches UK #37. Grimm and Wolfe leave and are replaced by bassist/vocalist Demetri Callas and drummer Paul Wilson, while keyboards player Al Ruzicka also joins.

1972

Jan The Four Seasons sign to Motown Records subsidiary Mowest, but only ***Chameleon*** and a handful of singles are released, none of which charts. Gaudio gives up performing to concentrate on writing and production, first replaced by Clay Jordan, a Motown session man, and then by Billy De Loash.
Dec The group takes part in "An Evening Of Solid Gold" before a sellout crowd at New York's Madison Square Garden, with Jay & the Americans, the Four Tops and Martha Reeves. (Moving to the main Motown label the following year, the Four Seasons will release two singles from movies: *How Come* (from "Tom Sawyer") and *Scalawag Song* (from "Scalawag"), before their contract ends.)

1975

Mar [22] Following Long's decision to quit (continuing to work in the music business until becoming an insurance man in New Jersey), Valli and Gaudio have leased Valli's solo of the Bob Crewe/Kenny Nolan-penned ballad *My Eyes Adore You*, which was recorded for Motown but has since been bought from the label, to Private Stock Records. It now tops the US chart for a week, becoming a million seller, and will hit UK #5.
May Motown (UK)-reissued *The Night*, which failed to chart in 1972 but has since become in demand in discos, hits UK #7, as Valli's disco-flavored *Swearin' To God* hits US #6. Gaudio recruits a new Four Seasons around Valli: John Paiva (guitar), a former member of the Classaires, Lee Shapiro (keyboards), from the Manhattan School of Music, ex-Critters lead singer Don Ciccone (b. Feb. 28, 1946, New York) (bass) and Gerry Polci (b. 1954, Passiac, NJ) (drums and vocals), who has studied with Dave Brubeck Quartet's Joe Morello. Gaudio starts writing new material with girlfriend Judy Parker and also secures the group a new deal with Warner-Curb Records.
July Valli's *Swearin' To God* makes UK #31.
Oct Gaudio/Parker-penned, disco-tinged *Who Loves You* hits UK #6.
Nov *Who Loves You* hits US #3. Valli's revival of Ruby & the Romantics' *Our Day Will Come*, produced by Hank Medress and Dave Appell, reaches US #11.
Dec ***Who Loves You*** reaches US #38.

1976

Jan Double album, ***The Four Seasons Story***, a best-of compilation on Private Stock, makes US #51.
Feb [21] From ***Who Loves You***, Gaudio and Parker's *December '63 (Oh, What A Night)* (originally written about prohibition, as *December '33*), featuring Valli and Polci sharing lead vocals, tops the UK chart.
Mar [13] *December '63 (Oh, What A Night)* tops the US chart for the first of three weeks and becomes another million-seller, while ***The Four Seasons Story***, on Private Stock, reaches UK #20.
Apr [3] The group embarks on an 11-date UK tour at the Winter Gardens, Bournemouth, Dorset, ending at Batley Variety Club, W. Yorks.
May Polci-sung *Silver Star* hits UK #3 and US #38, while Valli's *Fallen Angel* makes US #36 and UK #ll.
[29] ***Who Loves You*** reaches UK #12.
Aug Valli's *We're All Alone*, written by Boz Scaggs, peaks at US #78.
Nov UK TV-advertised compilation, ***Greatest Hits***, on K-tel, hits #4.
Dec *We Can Work It Out*, from Lou Reizner's ***All This And World War II*** album (and the film documentary of the same name), makes UK #34.

1977

Apr [25] The group begins its latest UK tour with a week-long stint at the London Palladium.
May ***Helicon*** peaks at US #168.
June *Rhapsody* makes UK #37.
Aug *Down The Hall* climbs to US #65 and UK #34.
Sept Valli announces he is leaving the Four Seasons to pursue a wholly MOR-oriented solo career. (During their years together, the Four Seasons have sold more than 85 million records and have had more chart discs than any other US group.)

1978

Aug [26] Valli spends the first of two weeks atop the US chart with *Grease*, Barry Gibb's title song from the movie "Grease". It is his all-time biggest solo record, earning a platinum disc for two million US sales, and it also hits UK #3. (His follow-up, *Fancy Dancer*, produced by Gaudio, will peak at US #77 the following February.)

1980

May A Four Seasons reunion tour begins (without Valli, who, during the year, has the last of three ear operations to cure a problem brought on by otosclerosis, a rare disease which had rendered him deaf), with a new line up featuring Polci, Ciccone, Larry Lingle (b. Apr. 4, 1949, Kansas, MO) (guitar) and Jerry Corbetta (b. Sept. 23, 1947, Denver, CO) (keyboards). Gaudio and Massi both guest during the trek.
Aug Valli's *Where Did We Do Wrong*, a duet with Chris Forde, peaks at US #90.
Dec Four Seasons' *Spend The Night In Love* stops at US #91.

1985

Sept While Valli and the Four Seasons have teamed with the Beach Boys on the appropriately titled, Crewe/Gaudio-penned *East Meets West*, released by FBI Records the previous year, Valli and the Four Seasons are fully reunited on the Curb/MCA album ***Streetfighter***, which involves many old collaborators, including Calello, Linzer and Gaudio, who produces the set.

1988

June [25] ***The 20 Greatest Hits***, a collection of Valli and Four Seasons hit highlights released by Telstar Records, makes UK #38. (Rhino Records releases the comprehensive ***25th Anniversary Collection*** three-CD set in the US.)
Oct After a successful US summer tour, Valli & the Four Seasons return to the UK Singles chart with a Ben Leibrand re-mix of *December '63 (Oh, What A Night)* and *Big Girls Don't Cry* featured on the soundtrack of "Dirty Dancing II". (Valli will continue to tour the US with a variety of Four Seasons backing him and will also pursue a movie career, appearing in "Dirty Laundry" (1987), "Eternity" and "Modern Love".)

1990

Jan The Four Seasons are inducted into Rock and Roll Hall of Fame by Bob Crewe at the fifth annual dinner, at New York's Waldorf Astoria Hotel.
Dec [5] The group sings *Uptown Girl* at the NARAS "Living Legends" award ceremony, honoring Billy Joel.

1991

Jan [12] John Travolta and Olivia Newton-John's *Grease Megamix*, featuring Valli, hits UK #3.

1992

Feb [12] The group begins a 25-date British tour, which includes a date at the London Palladium on March 1st, at Symphony Hall, Birmingham, W. Midlands.
[21] ***The Very Best Of Frankie Valli And The Four Seasons*** hits UK #7. (The band's new album, ***Hope + Glory***, featuring mainly Gaudio and Valli, with help from session musicians, is released on Curb in the US.)

1993

Mar Valli receives a gold disc for the UK sales of ***The Very Best Of Frankie Valli & The Four Seasons***, presented to him outside 10 Downing Street by Members of Parliament Peter Brooke, the National Heritage Secretary, and Greg Knight.

1994

Oct [15] Remixed *December, 1963 (Oh, What A Night)* reaches US #14. (With an eventual combined chart run of 54 weeks (over two releases), it will become the longest staying single in US chart history.)

1995

Jan [30] Valli and the Manhattan Transfer (he has recently duetted with them on an update of *Let's Hang On* for the vocal group's ***Tonin'*** album) present the Top Pop/Rock Female trophy at the 22nd annual American Music Awards, held at the Los Angeles' Shrine Auditorium.
May [31] Gaudio and Crewe are inducted into the Songwriters' Hall of Fame at the 26th annual ceremonies, held at New York's Sheraton Hotel.

THE FOUR TOPS

Levi Stubbs (lead vocals); **Renaldo "Obie" Benson** (vocals); **Abdul "Duke" Fakir** (vocals); **Lawrence Payton** (vocals)

1953

Pershing High School classmates Stubbs (b. Levi Stubbles, June 6, 1936, Detroit, IL) and Fakir (b. Dec. 26, 1935, Detroit) have already sung together in an R&B quartet with two other friends before teaming with Benson (b. 1937, Detroit, MI) and Payton (b. 1938, Detroit), when they are asked to sing together at a friend's birthday party in Detroit. The combination works so well that they meet for a repeat session at Fakir's house the next day and form the Four Aims. They begin singing at high-school graduation parties, church and school functions, and local one-nighters and, after several auditions, are accepted by a talent agency which books them first into small clubs in Detroit in 1954, then into venues further afield, beginning with a week at the Ebony Lounge, Cleveland, OH, which earns the R&B quartet $300, having made their first professional public appearance in Flint, MI.

1956

May As the Four Aims, the group has already made its first recordings backing Chateau label artistes Caroline Hayes and Delores Carroll and sung back-up or opened for such acts as Brook Benton, Count Basie, Della Reese and Billy Eckstine. (The name has been changed to the Four Tops, at the suggestion of their musical conductor, to avoid confusion with the Ames Brothers, while Stubbles shortens his name to Stubbs.) After Payton's cousin Roquel "Billy" Davis has sent a demo of the group's *All My Life, Could It Be You* and *Kiss Me Baby* to Chicago, IL-based Chess Records boss Leonard Chess, he has agreed to sign the quartet on the condition that Davis become a staff writer for the company's existing acts. The Four Tops now record *Kiss Me Baby/Could It Be You*, though the single fails to attract attention and they decide to concentrate on their club act, polishing dance routines and vocal arrangements.

1960

Sept Having toured the US with the Larry Stelle Revue during 1958-1959, and released another one-off record, this time for the Red Top label, and now signed by John Hammond to CBS/Columbia Records, the group stays only long enough to release *Ain't That Love*, another poor seller.

1961

The group tours with Billy Eckstine's revue (he has first seen them perform at the Thunderbird in Las Vegas, NV), frequently working with him in Vegas. They release a version of the standard *Where Are You?*, which is also a current hit for Dinah Washington, on Riverside Records and will record further sides for the Singular label the following year.

1963

Mar The band meets Berry Gordy Jr., head of the fast-growing Tamla-Motown Records in Detroit, and signs to his label for a $400 advance. The first recordings are jazz-oriented and Gordy plans to put the group on the specialist Workshop label. They spend the rest of the year singing back-up on other Motown artists' records, including the Supremes' first Top 30 success, *When The Lovelight Starts Shining Through His Eyes*.

1964

The Four Tops are singing at Detroit's 20 Grand Club when Motown producers Holland, Dozier and Holland call them to the studio after their performance. Eddie Holland sings them a song he thinks will suit them and, through the small hours, the group records *Baby I Need Your Loving*.
Oct *Baby I Need Your Loving* reaches US #11. (Mersey group the Fourmost also makes UK #24 with their cover.)
Dec *Without The One You Love* peaks at US #43.

1965

Feb Ballad, *Ask The Lonely*, reaches US #24.
Apr Their debut album, ***Four Tops***, climbs to #63.
May [21] During a UK promotion trip, the band appears on ITV's "Ready Steady Goes Live!"
June [19] Holland/Dozier/Holland's *I Can't Help Myself* tops the US chart for the first of two weeks (and the R&B chart for nine), deposing on both surveys another Motown/H/D/H production, the Supremes' *Back In My Arms Again*, and is the group's first million seller.
[28] The group is featured on CBS-TV's "It's What's Happening Baby" special.
July *I Can't Help Myself* is the first UK Four Tops hit (reaching #23) and the group begins a sellout club tour of Europe, with the UK leg arranged by Beatles manager Brian Epstein.
Aug Speedy Motown follow-up, *It's The Same Old Song*, is recorded on a Thursday and is in shops by the following Monday, set to hit US #5. Columbia reissues *Ain't The Love*, which peaks at US #93.
Sept *It's The Same Old Song* reaches UK #34.
Dec ***The Four Tops' Second Album*** climbs to US #20, while *Something About You* reaches US #19.

1966

Apr *Shake Me, Wake Me (When It's Over)* makes US #18.
June Slower-paced *Loving You Is Sweeter Than Ever* peaks at US #45.
Sept ***Four Tops On Top*** reaches US #32, while in the UK *Loving You Is Sweeter Than Ever* makes #21.
Oct Revolutionary *Reach Out I'll Be There*, with an unorthodox instrumental blend of flutes, oboes and arab drums, begins a two-week stay atop the US survey and is the group's second million seller. Within two weeks it is also at UK #1 (for the first of three weeks) and seals the group's worldwide success.
Nov [13] The quartet makes its only UK appearance of the year, at London's Saville Theatre.
Dec ***Four Tops On Top*** is their first UK album success, hitting #9.

1967

Jan Performance set, ***Four Tops Live!***, recorded at the Roostertail club in Detroit, a more MOR-directed effort containing versions of *If I Had A Hammer* and *Climb Every Mountain*, reaches US #17, while *Standing In The Shadows Of Love*, a highly-commercial near-clone of *Reach Out*, hits #6 in both the US and UK.
[28] The group embarks on a nine-date, twice-nightly UK tour, with the Merseys, the Dakotas, Madeleine Bell, the Remo Four and the Johnny Watson Band, at London's Royal Albert Hall, set to end on February 5th at the De Montfort Hall, Leicester, Leics., after which the band will visit Italy, France, Germany and Spain for TV appearances.
Mar ***Four Tops Live!*** hits UK #4 (and will be a consistent seller, remaining on the chart for 72 weeks).
[9] A Four Tops special airs on BBC2-TV.
Apr *Bernadette* hits US #4 and UK #8, becoming another million seller.
May Another cabaret-styled album, ***Four Tops On Broadway***, containing mainly show tunes, climbs to US #79.
June *Seven Rooms Of Gloom* reaches US #14 and UK #12, while its B-side, *I'll Turn To Stone*, stops at US #76.
Sept ***Four Tops Reach Out*** makes US #11.
Oct *You Keep Running Away* reaches US #19 and UK #26. (Holland, Dozier and Holland leave Motown over royalty disputes and the group will be supervised by other Motown house producers, such as Frank Wilson, Smokey Robinson, Ivy Hunter and Johnny Bristol.)
Nov ***The Four Tops Greatest Hits***, a compilation of hit singles to date, hits US #4.

1968

Jan Their revival of the Left Banke's 1966 hit, *Walk Away Renée*, taken from ***The Four Tops Reach Out***, hits UK #3, while the album hits UK #4.
Feb [10] Compilation album, ***Greatest Hits***, tops the UK chart for a week. The Tops are the first black act to achieve this distinction (though stablemates the Supremes will repeat it a week later).
Mar Following its UK success, *Walk Away Renée* reaches US #14.
Apr Another album extract, the group's version of Tim Hardin's *If I Were A Carpenter* (a 1966 hit for Bobby Darin), hits UK #7.
June *If I Were A Carpenter* makes US #20.
Sept *Yesterday's Dreams* climbs to US #49 and UK #23.
Oct *Yesterday's Dreams* reaches US #93, while *I'm In A Different World* (a belatedly-released Holland/Dozier/Holland song/production) makes US #51.
Dec *I'm In A Different World* climbs to UK #27.

1969

Feb The year's chart action begins with ***Yesterday's Dreams*** which reaches UK #37. It is followed by *What Is A Man* (US #53 and UK #16 in June), ***Four Tops Now!*** (US #74 in July), the Jim Webb-penned *Do What You Gotta Do* (UK #11, October) and *Don't Let Him Take Your Love From Me* (US #54, December), the same month ***Soul Spin*** reaches US #163.

1970

Apr *I Can't Help Myself* is reissued in the UK and hits #10.
May [24] Currently on a British tour, they perform at the Fairfield Halls, Croydon, Surrey.
June Their treatment of the much-recorded *It's All In The Game* makes US #24 and hits UK #5, as ***Still Waters Run Deep*** ebbs to US #21 and UK #29.
Oct Taken from the album, the mellow-grooving *Still Water (Love)*, produced by Frank Wilson, reaches US #11 and hits UK #10.
Nov ***Changing Times*** makes US #109, while a collaboration with the Supremes for ***The Magnificent 7*** makes US #113.
[8] The group appears on CBS-TV's "The Ed Sullivan Show".

1971

Jan The Four Tops and the Supremes' duetted version of *River Deep, Mountain High* peaks at US #14.
Feb *Just Seven Numbers (Can Straighten Out My Life)* makes US #40.
Apr Benson's collaboration with Al Cleveland and Marvin Gaye, *What's Going On*, hits US #2 for Gaye.
May *Just Seven Numbers* makes UK #36.
[29] ***The Magnificent 7*** enters the British chart, set to hit UK #6.
July [3] Another teaming with the Supremes, on *You Gotta Have Love In Your Heart*, makes US #55.
[17] *In These Changing Times* peaks at US #70, and a further collaboration with the Supremes, on ***The Return Of The Magnificent Seven***, reaches US #154.
[24] Their version of *River Deep, Mountain High* reaches UK #11.
Oct The group's revival of Jimmy Webb's *MacArthur Park* makes US #38.
[22] The Four Tops embark on a UK tour at Regal Theatre, Edmonton, London, followed later by a week-long residency at the Fiesta Club, Sheffield, S. Yorks.
Nov The Four Tops have recorded a dynamic version of a Moody Blues B-side, *A Simple Game*, with Moody Blues producer Tony Clarke (and uncredited Moody members), who interested the group in the song when he gave them a demo during their recent British visit. (Another Moody Blues song, *So Deep Within You*, is cut at the same time.) It becomes the biggest UK Four Tops hit (at #3) since *Walk Away Renée*. A compilation album, ***Greatest Hits Vol. 2***, reaches US #106 and UK #25, with the extracted duet with the Supremes, *You Gotta Have Love In Your Heart*, reaching UK #25.

1972

Jan A third Four Tops/Supremes collaboration album, ***Dynamite***, climbs to US #160.
Feb *A Simple Game* peaks at US #90.
Apr UK-reissued *Bernadette* reaches #23.
June ***Nature Planned*** makes US #50. Gordy moves Motown's base from Detroit to Hollywood, but the Four Tops decide not to move with the company. They are negotiating with Dunhill, when the label's writer/producers Dennis Lambert and Brian Potter walk in with demos of two songs they composed with the Four Tops in mind, *Keeper Of The Castle* and *Ain't No Woman (Like The One I've Got)*, the quality of which prompts the group to sign to Dunhill.
July *In These Changing Times* peaks at US #70.
Aug *Walk With Me Talk With Me Darling* makes UK #32.
Oct *(It's The Way) Nature Planned It*, also still on Motown, reaches US #53.
Dec Their debut Dunhill album, ***Keeper Of The Castle***, climbs to US #33, as the group performs before a sellout crowd at "An Evening Of Solid Gold" at New York's Madison Square Garden, with the Four Seasons, Jay & the Americans, and Martha Reeves.

1973

Jan *Keeper Of The Castle*, the group's first single for Dunhill, hits US #10 and makes UK #18 (on Probe).
Apr *Ain't No Woman (Like The One I've Got)* hits US #4 and earns a gold disc for millon-plus sales.
May Motown album, ***The Best Of The Four Tops***, peaks at US #103.
Aug *Are You Man Enough*, taken from the film soundtrack to "Shaft In Africa", hits US #15.
Oct Their second Dunhill album, ***Main Street People***, makes US #66.
Nov *Sweet Understanding Love* peaks at US #33 and UK #29, while Motown's UK double compilation, ***The Four Tops Story, 1964-72***, makes UK #35 (their last UK chart entry in the '70s).

1974

Feb *I Just Can't Get You Out Of My Mind*, taken from ***Main Street People***, reaches US #62. It is followed by the 10-track album ***Meeting Of The Minds*** (US #118 in May), the extracted *One Chain Don't Make No Prison* (US #41, June), *Midnight Flower* (US #55, September) and the performance set, ***Live And In Concert***, which peaks at US #92 in November. (The following year, *Seven Lonely Nights*, the first release on ABC (which absorbed its Dunhill subsidiary), peaks at US #71 in May, with ***Night Lights Harmony*** climbing to US #148 (June) and *We All Gotta Stick Together* charting for one week at US #97 on Dec [6]. Their last charting discs of the decade will see *Catfish* peak at US #71 and the ***Catfish*** album reach US #124, both in November 1976.)

1978

Apr Following the November 1977 release of ***The Show Must Go On***, the Four Tops perform Stevie Wonder's *Isn't She Lovely* at Aretha Franklin's wedding to Glynn Turman.
Oct [1-7] The group plays a week of cabaret at Baileys, Watford, Herts., before embarking on a UK tour of one-nighters, which will end on November 3rd at London's Hammersmith Odeon, promoting its final ABC outing ***At The Top***.

1981

Nov [7] Newly signed (for its fourth decade of recording) to the disco-oriented Casablanca Records, the band's label debut, *When She Was My Girl*, reaches US #11.
[14] *When She Was My Girl* hits UK #3.
Dec Its parent album***Tonight!***, produced by David Wolfert on Casablanca and critically regarded as a return to form, reaches US #37.

1982

Jan [30] Storming soul-chugger, *Don't Walk Away*, taken from the album, reaches UK #16.
Mar [13] Ballad, *Tonight I'm Gonna Love You All Over*, the third single from ***Tonight!***, reaches UK #43.
[27] UK TV-advertised K-tel compilation album, ***The Best Of The Four Tops***, reaches UK #13.
June [5] *Back To School Again*, from the movie soundtrack to "Grease 2", peaks at US #71.
[26] *Back To School Again* makes UK #62.
Aug *One More Mountain*, on Casablanca, is released to coincide with the group's first UK tour for some time.
Sept [4] *Sad Hearts*, taken from their final Casablanca album ***One More Mountain***, peaks at US #84.

1983

Mar [25] The Four Tops return to Motown for the company's 25th anniversary NBC-TV special, re-signing with Berry Gordy shortly after. The "Battle Of The Bands" between the Four Tops and the Temptations, during the special, leads the two veteran soul groups to tour together, initially in the US and then internationally.
Nov *I Just Can't Walk Away*, on Motown, makes US #71, taken from ***Back Where I Belong.***

1985

July ***Magic***, variously produced by Reggie Lucas, Willie Hutch, Johnny Bristol, Hal Davis and Kerry Ashby, reaches US #140.

1986

July Stubbs who has recently provided the voice for the man-eating plant Audrey II in the film version of musical "The Little Shop Of Horrors" is immortalized by UK singer Billy Bragg in *Levi Stubbs' Tears*, which reaches UK #29.
Oct ***Hot Nights*** is the group's final release of its second spell with Motown.

1987

July [29] Michigan State Governor James Blanchard declares an annual state-wide "Four Tops Day", honoring the group for its contribution to American music and its civic activities in Detroit. (Arkansas Governor, and future US President, Bill Clinton plays sax for them at a Traverse City, MI governors' meeting performance.)

1988

Aug *Reach Out I'll Be There (remix)* reaches UK #11.
Sept Newly signed to Arista Records, ***Indestructible*** makes US #149. It includes contributions from Phil Collins, Aretha Franklin, Kenny G, Huey Lewis and Narada Michael Walden. Its title track *Indestructible* also makes US #35 and UK #55, while the band contributes *Loco In Acapulco* to the soundtrack of the Phil Collins movie "Buster".

1989

Jan *Loco In Acapulco* hits UK #7.
Feb [10] The group plays a warm-up gig at London's Town & Country club, before embarking on 12-date UK tour at Manchester's Apollo Theatre, set to end on the 25th at the Colston Hall, Bristol, Avon.
Mar [3] The Four Tops return to the US to perform at the 24th "Rock'n'Roll Revival Spectacular" with Sha Na Na, Jay Black & the Americans, and Tommy James & the Shondells at Madison Square Garden.
May [20] Aretha Franklin's ***Through The Storm***, to which the Four Tops has contributed, enters the US chart (set to reach #55) while the reissued *Indestructible* peaks at UK #30.

1990

Jan [12-14] The group begins a US tour with three dates in Atlantic City, NJ.
[17] Stevie Wonder inducts the Four Tops into the Rock and Roll Hall of Fame at the fifth annual dinner, at New York's Waldorf Astoria Hotel. At the traditional after-dinner jam, the group sings *I Can't Help Myself.*
Nov [25] The Four Tops take part in CBS-TV's "Motown 30 : What's Goin' On!" special.

1991

Jan [12] ***Their Greatest Hits***, a UK-only Telstar TV-advertised collection, peaks at UK #47.
Nov [4-7] The group plays at Butlin's Southcoast World, Bognor Regis, W. Sussex, with the Stylistics, Edwin Starr, Jimmy Ruffin, Jr. Walker and Ben E. King.

1992

Jan [11] The Four Tops are inducted into the Image Hall of Fame at the 24th NAACP Image Awards, at Los Angeles' Wiltern Theatre.
Mar [1] The group participates in ABC-TV's "Muhammad Ali's 50th Birthday".
Apr [5] They perform on the "Giants Of Motown Show", with the Temptations, Martha Reeves, the Supremes and the Marvelettes, at Wembley Arena, Wembley, Middx.
[11] The group takes part in the Grand Opening of Euro-Disney near Paris, France.
Sept [26] ***The Singles Collection*** reaches UK #11, as the group wraps up a 17-date UK tour.
Dec [26-28] Still touring constantly, the Four Tops bow out of 1992 at Bally's Casino Resort, Las Vegas, NV.

1993

July [4] Now celebrating their 40th anniversary, the Four Tops, in the midst of another US tour, play an Independence Day show at the "Meadow Brook Music Festival", Rochester, MI.

1994

Sept [3-4] The group plays at the Westbury Music Fair, Westbury, NY, on its current US tour with the Four Seasons.
Dec [28] CBS-TV airs the 17th annual Kennedy Center Honors at which the Four Tops perform a tribute to Franklin with Patti LaBelle and the choir of Detroit's New Bethel Baptist Church.

1995

June [23] The quartet appears on the "Legend Of Motown" tour with the Temptations, the Spinners, the Supremes, Jr. Walker, at the Pine Knob Music Theatre, Clarkston, MI.
Dec Releasing the seasonal album ***Christmas Here***

With You (including two cuts with Franklin) in the US, and currently featured on a US-TV Velveeta Cheese commercial singing *It's The Same Old Song* with appropriate lyrics, they continue touring, without a personnel change in 43 years.

THE FOURMOST

Brian O'Hara (guitar, vocals); **Mike Millward** (guitar, vocals); **Billy Hatton** (bass); **Dave Lovelady** (drums)

1961

Mar [1] O'Hara (b. Mar. 12, 1942, Liverpool, Lancs.) and Hatton (b. June 9, 1941, Liverpool) have formed a group with two friends, while attending Bluecoat Grammar School in Liverpool, in 1958. For three years, the quartet, calling itself the Four Jays, plays gigs on a part-time basis around Liverpool. Still amateurs, they now make their debut at Liverpool's Cavern club, three weeks before the Beatles' first performance there. Millward (b. May 9, 1942, Bromborough, Cheshire), an old friend of O'Hara and Hatton, moves to Liverpool to join the group in November when a guitarist slot falls vacant. Lovelady (b. Oct. 16, 1942, Liverpool) replaces an earlier drummer the following September, joining from another semi-professional band in Crosby, Liverpool. All four still have day jobs: O'Hara is an accountant's clerk; Millward, a solicitor's clerk; Hatton, an apprentice engineer and Lovelady, a student architect. Turning professional in November 1962, the group changes its name to the Four Mosts.

1963

June Brian Epstein takes over the band's management, amends the name to the Fourmost and signs the group to EMI's Parlophone label.
July [3] Their debut single, *Hello Little Girl*, is recorded at Abbey Road Studios. It is an early Lennon/McCartney song which the Beatles have chosen not to record commercially. As with his launch of Billy J. Kramer, Epstein encourages full exploitation of this Beatles connection.
Oct [19] *Hello Little Girl* hits UK #9.
Dec [24] "The Beatles Christmas Show", in which the group appears with the Beatles, Rolf Harris, the Barron Knights, Tommy Quickly, Billy J. Kramer & the Dakotas and Cilla Black, mixing music and pantomime, opens at London's Finsbury Park Astoria, running until January 11th.

1964

Jan [25] A second Lennon/McCartney song, the soft-rock ballad *I'm In Love*, reaches UK #17.
Apr [26] The group plays at the "**New Musical Express** Poll Winners Concert" at the Empire Pool, Wembley, Middx., with the Beatles, the Hollies, the Rolling Stones and a host of other major names.
May [13] The band starts an eight-month residency, with Frankie Vaughan, Tommy Cooper and stablemate Cilla Black, in the "Startime" variety show at the London Palladium. (Their career suffers from their being locked into this contract, unable to tour Britain throughout the year.)
[23] *A Little Loving*, written by Russ Alquist, hits UK #6.
[24] A Pathé Pictorial film, in which they are featured singing *A Little Loving* in Dougie Millings' Soho tailor shop, goes on general release.
Aug [15] *How Can I Tell Her*, an upbeat Carter/Lewis song in unusual march time, makes UK #33.
Dec [12] "Startime" variety show at the London Palladium, ends.

1965

Jan [23] *Baby I Need Your Lovin'*, their cover of the Four Tops' first US hit, reaches UK #24 (causing some dissension between Motown and EMI, since it inadvertently breaks the agreement that EMI, as Motown's UK distributor, will not release cover versions of the former's singles). The group makes a cameo appearance in Gerry & the Pacemakers' film "Ferry Cross The Mersey", performing *I Love You Too*.
[29] The band begins a 22-date, twice-nightly UK tour, with Cilla Black, P.J. Proby, Tommy Roe, Tommy Quickly and Sounds Incorporated, at the ABC Cinema, Croydon, Surrey, ending February 21st at the Liverpool Empire.
Mar [1] The group begins a further 15-date, twice-nightly UK trek of independent theatres in "The P.J. Proby Show" with Proby and Brian Poole & the Tremeloes, at London's Finsbury Park Astoria, set to end on the 16th at the Usher Hall, Edinburgh, Scotland.
July *Everything In The Garden* fails to chart, as the appeal of the Merseybeat sound rapidly fades.
Sept The group's only album, ***First And Fourmost***, with 14 tracks (which are mostly covers of US rock and pop originals), is released.
[21] The Fourmost participate in the "Pop From Britain" concert at London's Royal Albert Hall, with Cliff Bennett & the Rebel Rousers, Georgie Fame & the Blue Flames and the Moody Blues.
Dec Millward is admitted to Clatterbridge Hospital, Babbington, Cheshire, suffering from leukaemia.
[13] Freddie Self, who has deputized before, fills in for Millward at a gig at London's Savoy Hotel.
[27] George Peckham becomes Millward's permanent replacement. (Bill Parkinson (b. Morecambe, Lancs.), will take his place for a time, before Peckham rejoins full-time.)

1966

Jan [15] *Girls Girls Girls*, a Leiber/Stoller song previously recorded by the Coasters, makes UK #33 - their final chart success.
Mar [7] Millward dies, aged 23, in Bromborough Hospital.
May [1] The group plays on a bill topped by the Beatles and the Rolling Stones at the "**New Musical Express** Poll Winners Concert" at the Empire Pool.
Nov Following the August release of *Here, There And Everywhere*, a cover of a track from the Beatles' album ***Revolver***, the group's last Parlophone single is a revival of George Formby's *Auntie Maggie's Remedy*.

1967

July Now signed to CBS Records, the Fourmost release a cover of Jay & the Techniques' US hit, *Apples, Peaches, Pumpkin Pie*. (Two further CBS singles, including *Rosetta*, produced by Paul McCartney, will follow. The group will move into musical/comedy cabaret in UK northern clubs during the remainder of the '60s, before eventually disbanding.)

PETER FRAMPTON

1972

May Frampton (b. Apr. 22, 1950, Beckenham, Kent), who first played guitar in public as a boy scout at the age of eight, performing Cliff Richard's *A Girl Like You* and Adam Faith's *Poor Me* at a variety show, went on to join UK pop outfit the Herd in 1966 at age 16. He was voted "The Face Of 1968" as a magazine pop pin-up and left Humble Pie, the rock group he formed in 1969 with Steve Marriott in October 1971, convinced that he could pursue a solo career, having been invited by George Harrison to contribute his guitar talents to Harrison's ***All Things Must Pass*** opus. Now signed as a solo artist to A&M Records, he releases his debut set, ***Wind Of Change***, which features Ringo Starr, Billy Preston and a host of top session men.
Sept [16] Frampton makes his solo stage debut in New York, NY, supporting the J. Geils Band, with his own new backing band, Frampton's Camel: Mike Kellie (ex-Spooky Tooth) on drums, Mickey Gallagher (ex-Bell & Arc) on keyboards and Rick Wills (ex-Cochise) on bass, all three having just left Parrish & Gurvitz.
Oct Self-penned and produced ***Wind Of Change*** peaks at US #177.

1973

May ***Frampton's Camel***, with Kellie replaced by US drummer John Siomos, formerly with Mitch Ryder, makes US #110.

1974

June ***Somethin's Happening*** (on which the "Camel" appendix is dropped), makes US #25. Gallagher leaves to join Glencoe and is replaced by former Herd member Andy Bown, who also doubles on bass when Wills leaves to play with Roxy Music.

1975

May [17] ***Frampton***, recorded with Siomos and Bown, reaches US #32, as Frampton continues a punishing tour schedule of some 200 dates a year (mainly in North America).

1976

Apr [10] After four average-selling studio albums, ***Frampton Comes Alive!***, a double set recorded on stage at the Winterland Ballroom, San Francisco, CA, tops the US chart at the beginning of a broken ten-week run which will climax with a straight five-week stay in October. With blanket US rock radio support it will become the most successful live album in rock history, eventually selling over 15 million copies.
May [8] *Show Me The Way*, taken from the album, hits US #6 and features a Frampton trademark sound: the "voicebox" guitar technique of forming words by channelling the sound through a mouthpiece.
June *Show Me The Way* hits UK #10.
[26] ***Frampton Comes Alive!*** hits UK #6.
Aug [28] *Baby, I Love Your Way*, also from the live album, reaches US #12.
Sept *Baby, I Love Your Way* makes UK #43.
[8] Frampton spends the day at the White House, Washington, DC, at the invitation of President Ford, passing the time watching TV with Stephen Ford.
[18] He performs *Baby I Love Your Way* on CBS-TV's "Don Kirshner's Second Annual Rock Music Awards" from the Hollywood Palladium, Hollywood, CA.
Nov [13] *Do You Feel Like We Do* hits US #10 and will make UK #39.

1977

Apr He establishes the Peter Frampton Musical Endowment Fund at San Francisco State University, to honor the fact that ***Frampton Comes Alive!*** was recorded in the city.
July [2] A new studio recording, the self-penned ***I'm In You*** reaches UK #19.
[16] ***I'm In You*** hits #2 in the US, where it will go double platinum.
[30] Grandiose title cut ballad *I'm In You*, hits US #2 for the first of three weeks and makes #41 in the UK, where it is his final chart single.
Oct His revival of Stevie Wonder's *Signed, Sealed, Delivered (I'm Yours)*, with Wonder guesting on harmonica, reaches US #18.

1978

Jan *Tried To Love* makes US #41.
Apr [1] The Philadelphia Furies, a soccer team co-owned by Frampton, Mick Jagger, Paul Simon and Rick Wakeman, loses its first match of the North America Soccer League 3-0 to the Washington Diplomats.
June [29] Frampton suffers a broken arm and cracked ribs in a car crash in the Bahamas, which will put him out of action for months.
July [24] Robert Stigwood's critically-panned film "Sgt. Pepper's Lonely Hearts Club Band" is released, co-starring Frampton (as Billy Shears) and the Bee Gees.
Aug Its soundtrack album, ***Sgt. Pepper's Lonely Hearts Club Band***, featuring Frampton, hits US #5 and UK #38.

1979

July [21] ***Where I Should Be*** reaches US #19, as the extracted *I Can't Stand It No More* heads to US #14.

Aug Frampton is awarded the Gold Ticket for playing to over 100,000 fans at New York's Madison Square Garden.

1981

July Self-penned and-produced as ever, ***Breaking All The Rules***, reaches US #47. When its follow-up ***The Art Of Control*** peaks at US #174 on Sept [18] the following year, its poor sales prompts A&M and Frampton to split after more than a decade.

1986

Feb [8] With Frampton newly signed to Virgin Records in the UK and Atlantic in the US, the synthesizer-based ***Premonition*** enters the US survey set to make US #80.
Mar [1] The extracted *Lying* peaks at US #74.

1987

Apr He joins one-time schoolfriend David Bowie as guitarist for the latter's worldwide "Glass Spider" live trek. (He will also support Stevie Nicks on her solo tour. Later in the year, A&M will release the 13-track label retrospective, ***Peter Frampton Classics***.)

1988

July Increasingly inclined to session work, Frampton features on the newly released Karla Bonoff album, ***New World***.
Dec [3] Will To Power tops the US chart with a medley reviving Frampton's *Baby, I Love Your Way* and Lynyrd Skynyrd's *Freebird*.

1989

Oct ***When All The Pieces Fit***, co-produced by Frampton with Chris Lord-Alge, makes US #152, after which Frampton will once again return to a period of inactivity.

1991

Aug After playing a few UK dates with his new backing band Escape Committee the previous December, *The Bigger They Come*, teaming Frampton with former Humble Pie colleague Steve Marriott, is featured in the Don Johnson/Mickey Rourke movie, "Harley Davidson & the Marlboro Man".
Nov Frampton sits in with Lynyrd Skynyrd at their Universal Amphitheatre, Universal City, CA show, performing J.J. Cale's *The Breeze*.

1992

Feb [14] While planning to release a new album featuring five tracks he co-wrote and recorded with Marriott prior to his death last year, Frampton embarks on a series of low-key two-hour US gigs with his new band, comprising Bob Mayo (keyboards/guitar), John Regan (bass) and Michael Braun (drums), at Hammerjacks Concert Hall, Baltimore MD.
July [10] Frampton and Kansas headline the "KSHE Klassic Koncert" at the Riverport Amphitheatre, Maryland Heights, MO.
Oct [20] A 30-song, two-CD retrospective set, ***Shine On - A Collection***, drawn from his 11 solo albums and including two previously unreleased cuts from a 1991 reunion with Marriott, is released.
[30] Frampton sits in with the World's Most Dangerous Band on NBC-TV's "Late Night With David Letterman".

1993

Feb [19] Frampton takes part in the 20th anniversary "Lynyrd Skynyrd & Friends LYVE (Pronounced Live)" pay-per-view performance from the Fox Theatre, Atlanta, GA.

1994

May [14] Giving the song its third US chart appearance, Big Mountain hits US #6 with a reggae version of *Baby I Love Your Way*, taken from the movie "Reality Bites".
July [19] Promoting his latest album, ***Peter Frampton*** (released in April by Relativity Records), Frampton performs at New York's Beacon Theatre, during his "Frampton Comes Alive ... Again" summer tour, with Robin Trower.

1995

Oct [10] Having sold over 15 million copies in the US of the best-selling live album ever, ***Frampton Comes Alive II*** is released on the El Dorado label.

1996

July [3] Frampton embarks on veteran rockers US package tour, with Foreigner and REO Speedwagon, in Darien Lake, NY.
see also: **HUMBLE PIE**

CONNIE FRANCIS

1955

Francis (b. Concetta Maria Franconero, Dec. 12, 1938, Newark, NJ), a child accordianist and a star turn at family gatherings and neighborhood shows, who has made her her live debut at Palisades Park, Irvington, NJ, graduating to local television at age ten, having appeared on Arthur Godfrey's networked talent show (he suggests her name-change), divides her time between schooling and singing (including four years as a regular on NBC-TV's "Star Time"). She signs, at age 16, to MGM Records and makes demos, singing soundalikes of Kay Starr and Jo Stafford, and dubs Tuesday Weld's singing voice for Alan Freed's film "Rock Rock Rock". Her first nine singles fail to chart and she is about to enroll at New York University when her fortunes change.

1957

Nov She makes her chart debut, supporting country singer Marvin Rainwater on *The Majesty Of Love* - a one-week hit at US #93 which nevertheless becomes an accredited million seller.

1958

Mar To please her father, Francis has used the last 20 minutes of a session to record one of his favorite songs, *Who's Sorry Now*. Featured on the first broadcast of Dick Clark's "American Bandstand" and plugged on the program, it hits US #4, becoming a million seller.
May [16] *Who's Sorry Now* begins a six-week run at UK #1, displacing Rainwater's *Whole Lotta Woman*.
June Her cover of the 1918 oldie, *I'm Sorry I Made You Cry*, makes US #36 and UK #11.
July *Heartaches/I Miss You So* misses the Top 100. (No other Connie Francis single will miss the US Top 50 until 1965.)
Sept *Stupid Cupid*, written by Neil Sedaka (before his own hits) and Howard Greenfield, and originally given to the Shepherd Sisters, reaches US #17.
[26] Coupled with the 30-year-old Guy Lombardo standard *Carolina Moon, Stupid Cupid* tops the UK chart for the first of six weeks.
Nov Another Sedaka/Greenfield composition, *Fallin'*, reaches US #30 and UK #20 while the oldie B-side *I'll Get By* reaches UK #19.

1959

Jan *My Happiness*, a 1933 weeper by Jon & Sandra Steele found by Francis in the **Musicians Handbook**, hits US #2 and UK #4 to become another million seller. Unreleased in the US, *You Always Hurt The One You Love* (a 1944 smash for the Mills Brothers) reaches UK #13.
Apr *If I Didn't Care*, a Jack Lawrence '30s standard, reaches US #22.
May Francis asks Sedaka and Greenfield to write a song called *Bobby* to celebrate her romance with Bobby Darin. Instead they give her a paean to Frankie Avalon, *Frankie*, which hits US #9. Its B-side, *Lipstick On Your Collar*, becomes one of her most memorable hits, at US #5 and UK #3, and her third gold disc.
Sept *You're Gonna Miss Me* makes US #34, paired with her own composition, *Plenty Good Lovin'*, which stops at US #69 and UK #18.
Dec Francis personalizes a gloomy 1927 ballad, *Among My Souvenirs*, which hits US #7 and UK #11, while the patriotic B-side, *God Bless America*, stirring only American hearts, reaches US #36 and is another million seller.

1960

Mar ***Rock'n'Roll Million Sellers*** makes UK #12 and *Valentino*, unreleased in the US, reaches UK #27.
Apr [2] Francis wins the Best Selling Female Artist category at first annual NARM awards. (She will also win the award in 1961 and 1962.)
Recorded in Britain, *Mama*, a sentimental ballad learned from her grandmother and sung in Italian, hits US #8 and UK #2 to become her fifth gold disc. It features on her first US chart album, ***Italian Favorites***, which hits #4, while ***Connie's Greatest Hits*** makes US #17. *Mama*'s B-side, *Teddy*, written by Paul Anka, reaches US #17.
June [27] Written by Greenfield and his new partner, Jack Keller, the country-styled *Everybody's Somebody's Fool* hits US #1 and UK #5, while its B-side, another Italian song, *Jealous Of You*, hits US #19, becoming gold disc number six. *Mama/Robot Man*, a UK-only release, hits #2.
Sept [26] Greenfield and Keller have also provided *My Heart Has A Mind Of Its Own*, which hits US #1, displacing Chubby Checker. (Francis becomes the first female singer ever to have consecutive #1s.) It also hits UK #3 and earns another gold disc, while the B-side, *Malaguena*, reaches US #42.
Dec Hitting US #7 and UK #12, Winfield Scott's bouncy *Many Tears Ago* brings her fourth million seller of the year, while the B-side, *Senza Mamma (With No One)*, charts for a week at US #87 and ***More Italian Favorites*** hits US #9. Francis opens a season at the Copa in New York.

1961

Feb ***Connie's Greatest Hits*** climbs to UK #16, her last UK chart album for 16 years.
Mar Francis hits US #4 and UK #5 with another Sedaka/Greenfield-penned million seller, *Where The Boys Are*, also the title of her first MGM movie, co-starring George Hamilton. The B-side, *No-One*, reaches US #34.
May Greenfield/Keller's country-flavored *Breakin' In A Brand New Broken Heart* hits US #7 and UK #12, while Francis' live album, ***Connie At The Copa***, reaches US #65. ***Jewish Favorites*** makes US #69 for the convent-educated girl.
Aug Reverting to oldies, her treatment of a 1928 song, *Together*, hits #6 in both the US and UK, and will become her tenth gold disc. The B-side, *Too Many Rules*, also charts, at US #72, while ***More Greatest Hits*** climbs to US #39.
Oct Double-sided *(He's My) Dreamboat/Hollywood* (both written by John D. Loudermilk) reaches US #14/#42. ***Never On Sunday***, a collection of movie themes, her fourth hit album of the year, reaches US #11.
Dec Double-sided *When The Boy In Your Arms (Is The Boy In Your Heart)/Baby's First Christmas* hits US #10 and #26, as only *Baby's First Christmas* charts in the UK at #30. (Cliff Richard has already hit UK #3 with his version of the A-side.)

1962

Mar [31] *Don't Break The Heart That Loves You* is Francis' third US #1 and makes UK #39.
Apr *Do The Twist* reaches US #47.
June *Second Hand Love* (co-written by Phil Spector) hits US #7.
[30] She records four tracks for the movie "Follow The Boys" in London, with Norman Newell, Geoff Love and Ron Goodwin.
Aug Containing five of her recent Top ten hits, ***Connie Francis Sings*** stops at US #111.
Sept Co-written by Francis, *Vacation* hits US #9 and UK #10, her last significant UK hit. Francis' book,

For Every Young Heart, is published in the US by Prentice Hall.
Oct *I Was Such A Fool (To Fall In Love With You)/He Still Thinks I Care* reaches US #24 and #57. The B-side, taken from her US #22 album, ***Country Music Connie Style***, was originally a George Jones C&W item.

1963

Jan *I'm Gonna Be Warm This Winter* reaches US #18 but only UK #48, while the flip-side, *Al Di La*, stops at US #90. (During the year Francis maintains her US chart presence, reaching the Top 50 with five singles: *Follow The Boys* (the title song from her second movie - #17), *If My Pillow Could Talk* (#23), *Drownin' My Sorrows* (#36), *Your Other Love* (#28) and the President Kennedy tribute *In The Summer Of His Years* (#46). The latter is first sung by Millicent Martin on BBC-TV's "That Was The Week That Was" the night after his assassination. Francis' chart albums during the year include: ***Modern Italian Hits*** (#103), ***Follow The Boys*** (#66), ***Award Winning Motion Picture Hits*** (#108), ***Great American Waltzes*** (#94), ***Big Hits From Italy*** (#70) and ***The Very Best Of Connie Francis*** (#68).)

1964

During the year, Francis scores four further hit singles: *Blue Winter* (#24), *Be Anything (But Be Mine)* (#25), *Looking For Love* (the theme song from her third movie - #45) and *Don't Ever Leave* (#42), while the year's charting albums are: ***In The Summer Of His Years*** (#126), ***Looking For Love*** (#122) and ***A New Kind Of Connie*** (#149).
Apr Francis begins a round-the-world tour in Hawaii.

1965

Feb *Whose Heart Are You Breaking Tonight* peaks at US #43.
Mar *For Mama (La Mama)* reaches US #48.
May She makes her 25th appearance (believed to be a record) on CBS-TV's "The Ed Sullivan Show" while *Wishing It Was You* makes US #57.
[20] She arrives in Britain for TV and radio dates, including "Ready Steady Goes Live!", "The Eamonn Andrews Show" and "Thank Your Lucky Stars".
[21] Francis begins work on a new album at Pye's London studios, with musical director Johnny Gregory and recording manager, MGM's A&R chief, Danny Davis.
June *My Child* reaches UK #26 while *Forget Domani* peaks at US #79, taken from the Rex Harrison-starring movie "The Yellow Rolls Royce" and ***Connie Francis Sings For Mama*** reaches US #78.
Dec Her revival of Al Morgan's 1949 *Jealous Heart* makes US #47.

1966

Jan *Jealous Heart* reaches UK #44. ***When The Boys Meets The Girls***, a soundtrack album (for her fourth and last movie in which she co-stars with Harve Presnell), credited to Francis but also featuring cuts by Herman's Hermits, Liberace and Louis Armstrong among others, makes US #61.

1969

Mar [29] *The Wedding Cake* is her US chart swan song, at #91, but Francis continues to headline on the nightclub/cabaret circuit, taking time out for charity shows and entertaining US troops in Vietnam.

1972

Sept She sings for President Lyndon Johnson at the White House, Washington, DC.

1974

Nov [8] After an appearance at the Westbury Music Fair in Westbury, NY, Francis is attacked at knifepoint and raped in a second floor room at Howard Johnson's Motel. Emotionally shattered, she retreats from public view. (She will be awarded $3,055,000 in damages.)

1977

Aug [27] ***20 All Time Greats*** hits UK #1 for the first of two weeks and earns a platinum disc.

1993

Mar [21] Over the past 15 years, Francis has recovered from botched nasal surgery in 1978, her brother George's gangland-style killing in 1981, written an autobiography (1984's **Who's Sorry Now**), spent time in a rest home before returning to live work in Hollywood and Las Vegas in 1988, recorded *Something Stupid* with Boy George, and now returns to the town of her 1974 attack to perform to a sellout crowd. Her latest UK hits compilation, released 26 years after her last UK chart hit, ***The Singles Collection***, will reach UK #12 on May 1st.

FRANKIE GOES TO HOLLYWOOD

"Holly" Johnson (vocals); **Paul Rutherford** (vocals); **Brian "Nasher" Nash** (guitar); **Mark O'Toole** (bass); **Peter "Ged" Gill** (drums)

1980

Aug Based in Liverpool, Lancs., and inspired to name the band after a headline about Frankie Vaughan's attempt to begin a Hollywood career, the five members of Frankie Goes To Hollywood play their first gig, as support act to Hambi & the Dance. Johnson (b. William Johnson, Feb. 19, 1960, Khartoum, Sudan) has been with Big In Japan, appearing on their eponymous single and subsequent EP, *From Y To Z And Never Again*, leaving to go solo and releasing the singles *Yankee Rose* on Eric's Records and *Hobo Joe*, before forming the band Hollycaust. Rutherford (b. Dec. 8, 1959, Liverpool, Lancs.) has been with the Spitfire Boys, singing on their only single, *Mein Kampf*, and briefly with the Opium Eaters, before moving to live temporarily in the US. O'Toole (b. Jan. 6, 1964, Liverpool) has been performing in local groups, while his cousin Nash (b. May 20, 1963, Liverpool) has played with Dancing Girl and then Sons of Egypt with Gill (b. Mar. 8, 1964, Liverpool).

1982

Nov They make their national debut on UK radio with a live session for DJ David "Kid" Jensen. Their TV debut is an appearance on C4-TV's "The Tube", including a rough video version of their self-penned track *Relax*. Their performance attracts record company interest, particularly from "The Tube"-theme composer and noted producer Trevor Horn.

1983

Nov The sexually explicit *Relax* is released as the first single on the Zang Tumb Tumm label, produced by company co-owner Horn. The B-side is a cover of fellow Merseysiders Gerry & the Pacemakers' *Ferry Cross The Mersey*. "Relax" and "Frankie Says ..." T-shirts, the idea of journalist and Zang Tumb Tumm executive Paul Morley, start to appear. The initial risqué promotion video is banned by UK TV and a second version is filmed.

1984

Jan [13] BBC Radio 1 announces a ban on *Relax*, after a one-man campaign against the record by DJ Mike Read, who calls it "obscene". A ban by BBC-TV follows.
[28] *Relax* tops the UK chart for the first of five weeks, after a ten-week climb. BBC1-TV's "Top Of The Pops" is unable to feature the disc while it is still banned.
Mar Sales of *Relax* reach one million in the UK, spurred by the ban and the myriad releases and seven remixes of the single on 7", 12", picture disc and "cassingle". The single also hits US #10 (and will be featured on the soundtrack to the US movie "Police Academy").
June [16] With much media and public anticipation, the Horn-produced follow-up, *Two Tribes*, enters at UK #1. It goes silver in two days and gold in seven, and Frankie Goes To Hollywood becomes the first band to achieve this with its second release. BBC Radio 1 receives the airplay premiere of the single. The record's intro includes an impersonation of Ronald Reagan by UK mimic Chris Barrie, while its accompanying video, directed by Godley & Creme, features Reagan and Chernenko lookalikes wrestling. The single stays at #1 for nine weeks and sells over one million copies in the UK alone. (The group is the only act to have platinum singles with its first two releases.) *Relax* returns to the chart, where it eventually re-hits at UK #2, with *Two Tribes* still in pole position.
Nov [10] Double album, ***Welcome To The Pleasure Dome***, enters the UK chart at #1, with the country's biggest album ship-out to date.
Dec [8] Festive ballad, *The Power Of Love*, hits UK #1, with the help of a Godley & Creme nativity video, and Frankie Goes To Hollywood becomes the first band since Gerry & the Pacemakers to have a UK #1 with its first three singles. In typical ZTT promotion, the pre-release posters for the single have proclaimed: "The Power Of Love - Frankie Goes To Hollywood's third number one".
Welcome To The Pleasure Dome reaches US #33.

1985

Feb [11] The group wins the Best British Newcomer category, *Relax* is named Best British Single and Trevor Horn is named Best British Producer at the fourth annual BRIT Awards, at London's Grosvenor House Hotel.
Mar [12] The band begins a three-week British tour, at the Royal Dublin Society Hall, Dublin, Eire.
[13] *Two Tribes* wins the Best Contemporary Song category at the 30th annual Ivor Novello Awards, at the Grosvenor House Hotel.
Apr [6] Title cut, *Welcome To The Pleasure Dome*, hits UK #2.
[9] A major European tour opens in Copenhagen, Denmark, and the group has to spend the rest of 1985 tax-exiled from Britain.
Nov Recording begins in Amsterdam on a new album.

1986

May The band appears at the "Montreux Rock Festival", Montreux, Switzerland, and destroys its equipment. This is later seen by a TV audience of 20 million.
Sept [13] *Rage Hard*, from the forthcoming album, hits UK #4.
Nov ***Liverpool***, costing over twice as much to record as the double set ***Welcome To The Pleasure Dome***, partly due to Horn's costly tinkering, which is said to cost £500,000, hits UK #5 and stops at US #88.
[28] *Warriors Of The Wasteland* reaches UK #19.

1987

Jan [11] The group begins what will be a final tour at Manchester's Grand Metropolitan Centre.
Mar [21] *Watching The Wildlife* reaches UK #28, with condoms given away free as a promotional gimmick. The group's last public appearance is on C4-TV's "Saturday Live", after which ZTT announces that the band will split for nine months to concentrate on solo projects, though the move will prove permanent. (After Johnson and Rutherford quit, the remaining three re-form Frankie with ex-Promise singer Grant Boult. On the verge of signing with Circa Records, Johnson stops them from using the band name and Circa pulls out of any deal.)
Apr Johnson appears solo at an AIDS benefit concert in London, as the break-up is finally made official.
July Johnson signs a solo deal with MCA Records, which supports him during forthcoming litigation.
Aug ZTT serves an injunction against Johnson, which the artist counters. The rest of Frankie Goes To Hollywood form a new outfit, called the Lads (which fails to release any material), despite rumors that the Smiths' Morrissey was set to replace Johnson.
Oct *The Power Of Love* is used as a backing track to first UK TV condom commercial.

1988

Jan The ZTT and Perfect Songs case against Johnson in London's High Court attracts much media attention.
Feb In the outcome of the case Johnson, who is awarded substantial costs, wins an important victory for British recording artists relating to contracts and royalty payments.
Aug Rutherford signs a solo deal with the 4th & Broadway label. Newspaper reports state that the remainder of the band (with new lead singer Dee Harris), desperate to make a comeback, have indulged in an orgy of alcohol, drugs and vandalism during recording sessions at the Music Works Studio, Highbury, North London.
Oct Rutherford's debut single, the house-based *Get Real*, makes UK #47.

1989

Feb [11] Holly Johnson's self-penned debut solo, *Love Train*, hits UK #4.
May [6] Johnson's ***Blast*** debuts at UK #1.
[22] The extracted *Americanos* also hits UK #4.
July [1] Third extract, *Atomic City*, reaches UK #18.
[8] *Love Train* peaks at US #65.
Sept While Rutherford's single *Oh World* has recently made UK #61, Johnson's *Heaven's Here* stops at UK #62.

1990

Feb Johnson contributes a cover of *Love Me Tender* to the compilation album ***The Last Temptation Of Elvis***, to benefit the Nordoff-Robbins Music Therapy charity.
Dec Previewing his second solo project, Johnson's *Where Has Love Gone* peaks at UK #73.

1991

While Rutherford forms Pressure Zone with Tommy Payne, Marco Perry and Dave Clayton (and will go on to demo with Public Image Ltd.'s Bruce Smith the following year), Johnson's self-penned *Across The Universe* fails to chart, as will its parent album ***Dreams That Money Can't Buy***. Nash, who sold his North London home and returned to work as an electrician in 1990, records demos with Grant Boult, together forming Low and signing to Swanyard Records which releases its debut single, *Tearing My Soul Apart*. Gill is now working for the Love Station production company, while O'Toole has moved to Los Angeles, CA, working on some demos, but will return to Liverpool in early 1992.

1993

Apr While Nash is quoted in last October's **Q** magazine as saying that Frankie will not re-form "... while John Lennon's dead", Johnson, in an interview with **The Times**, reveals that he is HIV positive, subsequently writing an AIDS awareness piece for **Details** magazine's July issue. (He will also release a one-off single *Legendary Children (All Of Them Queer)* on the Club Tool (UK) label in September 1994.)
Oct [9] Reissued *Relax*, now with a house mix by Ollie J. and a hi-nrg mix by Jam & Spoon, hits UK #5.
[30] ***Bang! - Greatest Hits Of Frankie Goes To Hollywood*** debuts at its UK #4 peak.
Nov [20] Re-released *Welcome To The Pleasuredome* reaches UK #18 in itsweek of entry.
Dec [25] Reissued *The Power Of Love* hits UK #10. Rounding out the revamping of its principal work, *Two Tribes*, remixed by Fluke and Ollie Dagois, will debut at its UK #16 peak on Feb [26] 1994, while the reissue of ***Welcome To The Pleasuredome*** will reach UK #24 on Mar [1] the following year.

ARETHA FRANKLIN

1952

Franklin (b. Mar. 25, 1942, Memphis, TN), is the fourth of six children who have been raised by her father, the Reverend C.L. Franklin, pastor of the 4,500-member New Bethel Church, Detroit, MI and the most famous gospel preacher of the '50s - commanding $4,000 a sermon, and dubbed the "Million Dollar Voice", after her mother Barbara left in 1948 (and dies this year). Having learnt to play the piano by listening to Eddie Heywood records, but rejecting the offer of professional lessons from her father, Franklin has been taught to sing by family friends Mahalia Jackson and the Ward Sisters, Frances Steadman and Marion Williams. Gospel star James Cleveland now comes to live with the Franklin family and encourages her musical ambitions, though her biggest influence is her father's friend, hymn writer and gospel singer Clara Ward. Having heard Ward sing *Peace In The Valley* at a relative's funeral, she decides on a singing career.

1956

At the age of 14, Franklin's first recordings, for Chicago's Checker label, are live versions of Ward hymns, sung at her father's church and released as ***The Gospel Sound Of Aretha Franklin***. (It includes *The Day Is Past And Gone*, which she will perform 17 years later at the funeral of Clara Ward in Philadelphia, PA.) Taking lessons with voice teacher Leora Carter, Franklin's first club date will be at Chicago's Trade Winds on a bill headlined by Buddy Hackett.

1960

After leaving school, Franklin tours as a gospel vocalist. Then, encouraged by Sam Cooke, she tailors her style to the secular field. Leaving the family home in Detroit, she moves to New York, NY, taking dance and vocal lessons.
Aug [1] She makes her first secular recordings in a New York demo studio, cutting four tracks: *Right Now*, *Over The Rainbow*, *Love Is The Only Thing* and *Today I Sing The Blues*. Curtis Lewis, the writer of *Today I Sing The Blues*, trying to sell his song, brings the demo to the attention of CBS/Columbia Records veteran A&R man John Hammond. Jo King, owner of the studio where Franklin is rehearsing, hears of Hammond's interest and invites him to studio. He signs Franklin to a five-year deal following an audition arranged by Major "Mule" Holly, bassist with jazz pianist Teddy Wilson.
Oct Her first Columbia album, ***The Great Aretha Franklin***, is released. Produced by Hammond, it is a mixture of jazz, R&B and standards. *Today I Sing The Blues* is issued as a single and hits US R&B #10.
Dec [11] Franklin makes her New York stage debut at the Village Vanguard, with a program of standards.

1961

Mar [13] Her US pop chart debut, at #76, is *Won't Be Long*, recorded with the Ray Bryant Combo.
Nov Her revival of *Rock-A-Bye Your Baby With A Dixie Melody* reaches US #37 (and will be Franklin's only sizeable US hit on Columbia).

1962

Feb *I Surrender, Dear* reaches US #87, while its B-side, *Rough Lover*, makes US #94. ***The Electrifying Aretha Franklin*** is released and the singer marries Ted White, now her manager. *Don't Cry, Baby* will peak at US #92 in July, with her version of *Try A Little Tenderness* making US #100 in September, both featured on ***The Tender, The Moving, The Swinging Aretha Franklin*** which climbs to US #69 in December. The following year only *Trouble In Mind*, which peaks at US #86 in January, will chart, while ***Laughing On The Outside*** will be released.

1964

Oct *Runnin' Out Of Fools* reaches US #57 and the critically-revered ***Unforgettable: A Tribute To Dinah Washington*** is issued. It will be followed by two Columbia charting albums in 1965, ***Runnin' Out Of Fools*** (at US #84 in January), extracted *Can't You Just See Me* peaks at US #96, and ***Yeah!!!***, which will make US #101 in July.

1966

Aug ***Soul Sister***, her last album for Columbia, climbs to US #132.
Sept Dissatisfied with the artistic direction and lack of commercial success (Columbia has lost $90,000 on Franklin over six years), Franklin is unwilling to re-sign to the label. Atlantic Records outbids Columbia for her talent (paying the singer $25,000), with producer Jerry Wexler believing her Mitch Miller-guided recording path has been wrong and that she needs a tough R&B frame to recapture her gospel vocal fire. (This leads to a long and fruitful working relationship between Franklin and Wexler, who is later assisted by Arif Mardin and Tom Dowd.)

1967

Jan [27] For her first Atlantic sessions, Wexler takes Franklin to Rick Hall's Florence Alabama Music Emporium (FAME) studios in Muscle Shoals, AL, using the rhythm section he paired with Wilson Pickett. A week's sessions to cut an album are planned, but after one day's recording, which produces just *I Never Loved A Man (The Way I Love You)*, a song Franklin discovered herself and told Wexler she wanted to record, and a backing track for *Do Right Woman, Do Right Man*, a heated exchange between her husband and one of the horn players results in a quick return to New York.
Feb [8] With Wexler-distributed acetates of *I Never Loved A Man* already getting airplay on top US R&B stations, Franklin, with the help of sisters Erma and Carolyn, completes *Do Right Woman, Do Right Man* in New York, so that the single has a B-side and can be released.
[24] Detroit declares "Aretha Franklin Day" and Martin Luther King Jr. presents her with the Southern Christian Leadership Award at the Cobo Hall.
Mar [25] *I Never Loved A Man (The Way I Loved You)* tops the US R&B chart for the first of seven weeks, also crossing over to hit US #9. It earns Franklin's first gold disc for million-plus sales, as the album ***I Never Loved A Man (The Way I Loved You)*** hits US #2 (also earning a gold disc) and the media and music business dub her "Lady Soul".
June [3] A new arrangement of Otis Redding's R&B hit, *Respect*, begins a two-week stay at US #1 (and tops the R&B chart for eight weeks), her second million seller.
July *Respect* hits UK #10. In the US, Columbia has released a compilation album of earlier material, ***Aretha Franklin's Greatest Hits***, which makes #94.
Aug [12] ***I Never Loved A Man*** reaches UK #36, as she headlines New York's first "Jazz Festival" at the Downing Stadium.
Sept *Baby I Love You* is Franklin's third million-selling single, hitting US #4 (and topping the R&B survey for six weeks) and UK #39.
Oct ***Aretha Arrives***, recorded in New York in June, hits US #5, while another Columbia collection, ***Take A Look***, peaks at US #173, with the extracted title track *Take A Look* making US #56.
Nov *(You Make Me Feel Like A) Natural Woman*, written by Carole King, hits US #8.
Dec Two more Columbia singles chart briefly in the US: *Mockingbird* (#94) and *Soulville* (#83), as Franklin is named **Billboard** magazine's Top Female Vocalist Of The Year.

1968

Feb Featuring Joe South on blues guitar, *Chain Of Fools*, her revival of an R&B hit by Don Covay, hits US #2 and earns another gold disc, paired with her revival of the Rolling Stones' *(I Can't Get No) Satisfaction*, which makes UK #43. ***Aretha: Lady Soul***, mostly recorded just before Christmas, also hits US #2. (Eric Clapton guests on the track *Good To Me As I Am To You*.)
[29] Franklin wins her first Grammys as *Respect* in named Best R&B Recording and Best R&B Solo Vocal Performance, Female Of 1967, at the 10th annual Grammy Awards.

Apr *(Sweet Sweet Baby) Since You've Been Gone* hits US #5 (and is another million seller), while its B-side, *Ain't No Way*, written by her sister Carolyn, reaches #16. The A-side also makes UK #47, while ***Lady Soul*** reaches UK #25.
May [7] On her first tour of Europe, Franklin's performance at the Olympia Theatre, Paris, France is recorded for future album release.
June She headlines the "Soul Together" concert at New York's Madison Square Garden, to raise money for the Martin Luther King Jr. Memorial Fund.
July *Think* hits US #7 (Franklin's first self-penned million seller) and reaches UK #26. Its B-side, reviving Sam Cooke's *You Send Me*, makes US #56. Franklin opens the Democratic Party's national convention in Chicago, IL, singing *The Star Spangled Banner*.
Aug ***Aretha Now*** hits US #3, as ***Lady Soul*** is certified gold.
Sept While Franklin spends time in the studio working on her next album, her revival of Dionne Warwick's *I Say A Little Prayer* hits UK #4. In the US, where it is a double A-side with *The House That Jack Built*, it hits #10 and #6 respectively, another million seller. ***Aretha Now*** hits UK #6.
Nov ***Aretha In Paris***, recorded at May's concert, reaches US #13.
Dec Another Covay revival, *See Saw*, peaks at US #14 and the flip-side, *My Song*, makes US #31, another US million seller.

1969

Feb [15] Vickie Jones is arrested on fraud charges for impersonating Franklin in concert at Fort Myers, FL. No-one in the audience asks for their money back.
Mar ***Soul '69***, from the September sessions, including some pop-jazz fusions, reaches US #15. Franklin tours the US, but some performances are described as patchy (attributed to her collapsing marriage, which is heading for divorce).
[12] Franklin wins Best R&B Vocal Performance, Female, for *Chain Of Fools* at the 11th annual Grammy Awards.
Apr Her treatment of the Band's *The Weight* reaches US #19 and its B-side, reviving the Miracles' *Tracks Of My Tears*, stops at #71.
May She works on another album in the studio, with slide guitarist Duane Allman joining the regular session musicians.
June *I Can't See Myself Leaving You* reaches US #28, while its flip-side, John Hartford's much-covered *Gentle On My Mind*, makes US #76.
[13] She headlines a major R&B music spectacular, "Soul Bowl '69", at the Houston Astrodome, Houston, TX, with Ray Charles, the Staple Singers, Sam & Dave, Percy Sledge, Jimmy Witherspoon, Johnny "Guitar" Watson, Clara Ward and many others - including Franklin's long-time friend, gospel singer James Cleveland.
July [22] Franklin is arrested for causing a disturbance in a Detroit parking lot, a symptom of the personal difficulties she is facing as her seven-year marriage to White fragments.
Aug Compilation album, ***Aretha's Gold***, reaches US #18.
Oct *Share Your Love With Me* reaches US #13, while Franklin records for the first time at Criteria Studios in Miami, FL, cutting nine tracks (again with Allman in attendance), including a revival of the Beatles' *Eleanor Rigby* and her own composition, *Call Me*.
Dec *Eleanor Rigby* reaches US #17.

1970

Mar ***This Girl's In Love With You***, a mixture of the year's New York and Miami recordings, reaches US #17. It includes a version of the Beatles' *Let It Be*, recorded in December 1969, before the release of the Beatles' own version. Franklin returns to Miami for further sessions at Criteria, mostly to cut strong R&B and blues oldies with the Dixie Flyers.
[11] Franklin wins the Best R&B Vocal Performance, Female category for *Share Your Love With Me* at the 12th annual Grammy awards.
May *Call Me*, coupled with a revival of Dusty Springfield's *Son Of A Preacher Man*, also recorded in Miami, makes US #13.
July *Spirit In The Dark* reaches US #23.
Aug Returning to New York to record, she cuts a version of *Bridge Over Troubled Water*, with Billy Preston among the session musicians. (It will be released in 1971.)
Sept Her version of Ben E. King's *Don't Play That Song* reaches US #11 and UK #13 and is her first million-selling single since *See Saw* in 1968. Remarried, and with a new backing band, led by saxman King Curtis (comprising Cornell Dupree on guitar, Richard Tee on piano, Jerry Jemmott on bass and Bernard Purdie on drums), Franklin begins a series of well-received US concerts.
Oct ***Spirit In The Dark*** reaches US #25.
Dec A cover of Elton John's *Border Song (Holy Moses)* reaches US #37.

1971

Mar [5-7] Franklin performs three nights at the Fillmore West in San Francisco, CA, with Ray Charles (they perform an encore duet on the third night), King Curtis and Tower Of Power.
[16] Franklin wins Best R&B Vocal Performance, Female, for *Don't Play That Song* at the 13th annual Grammy Awards.
Apr Her revival of Marvin Gaye and Tammi Terrell's *You're All I Need To Get By* reaches US #19.
June Franklin's interpretation of Paul Simon's *Bridge Over Troubled Water* (he had already claimed to have had her in mind when writing the song, prior to Simon & Garfunkel's own version in 1970) hits US #6. Coupled with *A Brand New Me*, it is another million seller.
July ***Aretha Live At Fillmore West***, recorded in March, hits US #7.
Aug [17] Franklin sings at the funeral of King Curtis (who was fatally stabbed on a street four days earlier) in New York, with Stevie Wonder, Cissy Houston and others, as the Rev. Jesse Jackson preaches the sermon.
Oct ***Aretha's Greatest Hits*** reaches US #19. Her revival of Ben E. King's *Spanish Harlem*, featuring Dr. John on keyboards, hits US #2 and UK #14, another million seller.
Dec *Rock Steady*, a further million seller, hits US #9.

1972

Feb [1] Franklin sings *Take My Hand, Precious Lord* at the funeral of her old friend and one-time mentor Mahalia Jackson, in Chicago, IL.
Mar *Young, Gifted And Black* reaches US #11, and will be certified gold.
[14] Franklin nabs the Best R&B Vocal Performance, Female category for *Bridge Over Troubled Water* at the 14th annual Grammy Awards.
June *Day Dreaming*, her fourth consecutive million seller, hits US #5.
July Double gospel album, ***Amazing Grace***, a collaborative effort with James Cleveland and the Southern California Community Choir, and recorded at the New Temple Missionary Baptist Church on South Broadway, in the Watts district of Los Angeles, CA, in January, hits US #7. Her last Wexler-produced album, it earns a gold disc for half a million sales. The Columbia compilation album, ***In The Beginning/The World Of Aretha Franklin***, 1960-1967 reaches US #160.
Aug *All The King's Horses* makes US #26.
Sept *Wholy Holy*, recorded with James Cleveland and co-penned by Marvin Gaye, peaks at US #81.

1973

Mar *Master Of Eyes (The Deepness Of Your Eyes)* climbs to US #33.
[3] Franklin once again wins the Best R&B Vocal Performance, Female category for ***Young, Gifted And Black*** and also the Best Soul Gospel Performance for ***Amazing Grace*** at the 15th annual Grammy Awards.
Apr She begins a major US stadium tour.
Aug Jazz-tinged album, ***Hey Now Hey (The Other Side Of The Sky)***, recorded in Los Angeles with producer Quincy Jones, makes US #30.
Sept Her revival of Jimi Hendrix's *Angel* reaches US #20 and UK #37.

1974

Mar Her update of Stevie Wonder's *Until You Come Back To Me (That's What I'm Gonna Do)* hits US #3 (selling over a million) and UK #26.
[2] *Master Of Eyes (The Deepness Of Your Eyes)* is named Best R&B Vocal Performance, Female at the 16th annual Grammy Awards.
Apr With Wexler, Mardin and Dowd producing again, ***Let Me In Your Life*** reaches US #14. Franklin is made an Honorary Doctor of Law at Bethune-Cookman College, Daytona Beach, FL.
June *I'm In Love* reaches US #19.
Sept *Ain't Nothing Like The Real Thing*, another Gaye/Terrell revival, climbs to US #47.
Dec *Without Love* reaches US #45.

1975

Jan ***With Everything I Feel In Me*** makes US #57.
Mar [1] Franklin collects her tenth statuette for Best R&B Vocal Performance, Female (for *Ain't Nothing Like The Real Thing*) at the 17th annual Grammy Awards, her eighth successive win in the category.
Oct *Mr. D.J. (5 For The D.J.)* makes US #53.
Dec [27]***You*** peaks at US #83.

1976

Jan [31] She is named Favorite Female Artist, Soul/ R&B, at the third annual American Music Awards, held at the Civic Auditorium, Santa Monica, CA.
Aug [7] ***Sparkle***, the Curtis Mayfield-produced soundtrack album to the blaxploitation movie "Sparkle", reaches US #18. (Extracted *Something He Can Feel* reaches US #28.)
Oct *Jump*, also from the soundtrack, peaks at US #72.

1977

Jan [19] Franklin performs an a cappella *God Bless America*, at Jimmy Carter's Inaugural Eve Gala in Washington, DC.
[31] She nabs the Favorite Female Artist, Soul/R&B category, at the fourth annual American Music Awards, held at the Santa Monica Civic Auditorium. Compilation album ***Ten Years Of Gold*** reaches US #135.
Feb *Look Into Your Heart* stops at US #82.
June *Break It To Me Gently* peaks at US #85, and tops the US R&B chart for a week.
July Lamont Dozier-produced ***Sweet Passion*** reaches US #49.
Nov Franklin fails to turn up for three shows at the London Palladium. Her non-appearance is reportedly due to contractual problems regarding transport and accomodation costs for her entourage.

1978

Apr Franklin marries actor Glynn Turman (having divorced her second husband, musician Ken Cunningham). At the ceremony, conducted by her father, the Four Tops sing *Isn't She Lovely*.
June ***Almighty Fire*** makes US #63.
[21] She begins a five-date appearance at Las Vegas, her first engagement there in eight years.
July [9] Franklin performs at the Rev. Gibson's 18th annual "Youth On Parade Program" at Los Angeles' Good Shepherd Baptist Church.

1979

Feb [13] She opens a cabaret season at Harrah's restaurant in Lake Tahoe, NV.
Nov [10] ***La Diva*** peaks at US #146.

1980

June [20] "The Blues Brothers", featuring Franklin as a waitress singing *Think*, opens throughout the US. Shortly afterwards, she ends her 15-year association with Atlantic and signs to Arista Records, under the executive production of label boss, Clive Davis.
Nov ***Aretha***, produced by Mardin, is her Arista debut, making US #47.

[17] Franklin performs in the Royal Variety Performance in London.
Dec [13] Her version of the Doobie Brothers' *What A Fool Believes* makes UK #46.

1981

Jan *United Together* makes US #56.
June *Come To Me* peaks at US #84.
Sept *Love All The Hurt Away*, a duet with George Benson, makes US #46.
[26] *Love All The Hurt Away* makes UK #49, as its parent album, ***Love All The Hurt Away***, to US #36.

1982

Feb [24] Franklin wins the Best R&B Vocal Performance, Female category for *Hold On, I'm Comin'* at the 24th annual Grammy Awards.
Aug She takes part in the "Budweiser Superfest" at the Rose Bowl, Pasadena, CA, on a bill with Stevie Wonder, Patti Austin, James Ingram, Ashford & Simpson, Luther Vandross and others.
Sept [25] Percolating *Jump To It* makes UK #42.
Oct [9] Luther Vandross-produced third Arista album, ***Jump To It***, reaches US #23 and earns a gold disc. The title track, *Jump To It*, makes US #24, and tops the R&B chart for four weeks.
Nov [25] She performs at the "Jamaica World Music Festival", to an audience of 45,000 at the Bob Marley Performing Center in Montego Bay, Jamaica, with the Clash, the Grateful Dead, Gladys Knight and others.

1983

Jan [17] Franklin wins the Favorite Album, Soul/R&B category, at the tenth annual American Music Awards, held at the Shrine Auditorium, Los Angeles.
July *Get It Right* peaks at US #61 and UK #74.
Aug ***Get It Right***, again produced by Vandross, reaches US #36.

1984

Jan [16] She wins the Favorite Female Artist, Soul/R&B category, at the 11th annual American Music Awards, held again at the Shrine Auditorium. (During the year Franklin is also honored with US **Ebony** magazine's annual award for American Black Achievement, but her year is marred when she is successfully sued for breach of contract, when she is unable, mainly through her continuing fear of flying, to open in the Broadway musical "Sing, Mahalia, Sing". Producer Ashton Springer is awarded $234,364.)

1985

May Franklin's voice is proclaimed "one of Michigan's natural resources" by the State Government.
July ***Who's Zoomin' Who?***, produced by Narada Michael Walden, is issued, set to make US #13, becoming her first certified million-selling album and gaining a platinum disc. The Rev. C.L. Franklin is shot during a civil rights campaign. (He survives, but lapses into a coma.)
Oct The extracted *Freeway Of Love* hits US #3 and peaks at UK #68.
Nov Further uptempo dance smash, *Who's Zoomin' Who*, hits US #7 and reaches UK #11.
Dec Franklin's duet with Annie Lennox of the Eurythmics on *Sisters Are Doin' It For Themselves* makes US #18 and hits UK #9.

1986

Jan ***Who's Zoomin' Who?*** reaches UK #49.
[27] She wins the Favorite Female Video Artist, Soul/R&B, and Favorite Female Artist, Soul/R&B categories at the 13th annual American Music Awards, held at the Shrine Auditorium.
Feb [25] Yet again, Franklin wins the Best R&B Vocal Performance, Female category for *Freeway Of Love* at the 28th annual Grammy Awards.
Mar *Another Night* reaches US #22 and makes UK #54.
May Reissued *Freeway Of Love* peaks at UK #51.
[24] TV-advertised compilation, ***The First Lady Of Soul***, makes UK #89.
Nov [11] *Jumpin' Jack Flash*, the title song from the Whoopi Goldberg movie, produced by its co-writer Keith Richards, reaches US #21 and UK #58.

1987

Jan [21] Keith Richards inducts Franklin into the Rock and Roll Hall of Fame at the second annual dinner, at New York's Waldorf Astoria Hotel.
Feb [7] Her duet with George Michael, *I Knew You Were Waiting (For Me)*, written by Climie Fisher and Dennis Morgan, tops the UK chart, as *Jimmy Lee* reaches US #28.
Mar ***Aretha***, produced by Walden, makes US #32 and UK #51.
Apr [18] *I Knew You Were Waiting (For Me)* tops the US survey, only her second US chart-topper, coming 20 years after her first.
July [4] *Rock-A-Lott* peaks at US #82.
[27] Over a three-day period, Franklin records gospel songs at the New Bethel Baptist Church on C.L. Franklin Boulevard, Detroit, with guests the Rev. Jesse Jackson, the Franklin Sisters and Mavis Staples. Meanwhile, her father dies, having never come out of his coma.

1988

Feb Double album, ***One Lord, One Faith, One Baptism***, from the sessions commemorating Rev. Franklin, peaks at US #106.
Mar [2] Franklin wins the catagories of Best R&B Vocal Performance, Female, for ***Aretha*** and Best R&B Performance By A Duo Or Group With Vocal, with George Michael, for *I Knew You Were Waiting (For Me)* at the 30th annual Grammy Awards.
Aug [22] PBS-TV airs "Aretha Franklin: The Queen Of Soul", a one-hour documentary with contributions from Ray Charles, Eric Clapton, Whitney Houston and Smokey Robinson.
Sept Franklin joins George Michael on stage in Detroit to sing *I Knew You Were Waiting (For Me)*.

1989

Feb [22] Franklin nabs the Best Soul Gospel Performance, Female category for ***One Lord, One Faith, One Baptism*** at the 31st annual Grammy Awards.
May [27] *Through The Storm*, a duet with Elton John, reaches US #16 and makes UK #41.
June [3] Star-filled album, ***Through The Storm***, makes UK #46 and includes duets with James Brown (recorded just prior to his recent incarceration), and labelmates the Four Tops and Whitney Houston.
July [29] *It Isn't, It Wasn't, It Ain't Never Gonna Be*, with Whitney Houston, makes US #41 spurring ***Through The Storm*** to US #55.
Sept *It Isn't It Wasn't, It Ain't Never Gonna Be* reaches UK #29.

1990

Apr [26] New York US District Judge Whitman Knapp orders Franklin to pay $209,364.07 with interest, based on her failure to appear in "Sing, Mahalia, Sing".
Aug [9-10] Franklin performs at New York's Radio City Music Hall.
Dec [5] She is honored by the NARAS as a Living Legend.

1991

Mar [23] Franklin sings at the funeral of Army Specialist Anthony Riggs at the Little Rock Baptist Church, Detroit. Riggs had been back in the US for a day, after returning from the Gulf War where he was part of a Patriot missile battery group. At first, he was thought to be the victim of a random act of violence, but his wife and brother-in-law will subsequently be arrested for his murder.
July [27] *Everyday People* charts for one week at UK #69.
Aug [15-18] Franklin makes her debut at Caesar's Palace, Las Vegas, NV.
[17] ***What You See Is What You Sweat***, produced by Walden, Elliot Wolff, Vandross and Burt Bacharach and Carole Bayer Sager, among others, peaks at US #153.
Sept [13-14] Franklin returns for more dates at Radio City Music Hall.
Oct [20] Leading union workers at Detroit's Westin Hotel in song, she sings a belated *Happy Birthday* to the Rev. Jesse Jackson.
Nov [11] Franklin guests on CBS-TV's "Murphy Brown".

1992

Feb [25] She sings *Ever Changing Times* with Michael McDonald at the 34th annual Grammy Awards, at Radio City Music Hall.
[26] Franklin is honored with the Lifetime Achievement Award at the Rhythm and Blues Foundation's Third Annual Pioneer Awards, at New York's Rainbow Room.
Apr Movie soundtrack to "White Men Can't Jump", featuring Franklin's *If I Lose*, makes US #92.
June [12] She sings *Everyday People* and *Bridge Over Troubled Water* at the "Man Of The Year" tribute honoring Clive Davis at New York's Friars Club at the Waldorf Astoria Hotel.
July [14] She opens the second night of the Democratic Convention singing *The Star Spangled Banner*.
[18] Franklin attends the nuptials of Whitney Houston and Bobby Brown in Mendham, NJ.

1993

Jan [17] Franklin performs at "A Call For Reunion: A Musical Celebration" during the Inaugural festivities at the Lincoln Memorial in Washington, DC.
[19] She sings *I Have A Dream* at "An American Reunion: The Fifty-second Presidential Gala" from the Capital Center, Landover, MD.
Feb [24] ***Queen Of Soul - The Atlantic Recordings*** retrospective wins the Best Album Notes category (for Dave Marsh, Jerry Wexler, David Ritz, Thulani Davis, Ahmet Ertegun, Tom Dowd and Arif Mardin) at the 35th annual Grammy Awards, held at the Shrine Auditorium.
Apr [27] "Aretha Franklin: Duets", the diva's first TV special, featuring paired performances with Gloria Estefan, Elton John, George Michael, Bonnie Raitt, Smokey Robinson and Rod Stewart, is taped at New York's Nederlander Theatre. The show will air on May 9th, on Fox-TV.
[30] Franklin is one of the eight honorees at the sixth annual **Essence** Awards, at the Paramount, New York.
Oct [16] She sings the US national anthem before Game 1 of the World Series between the Toronto Blue Jays and the Philadelphia Phillies at the SkyDome, Toronto, Canada.
Dec [29] Franklin appears on CBS-TV's 16th annual Kennedy Center Honors to honor Marion Williams.

1994

Feb [12] *A Deeper Love*, featured in the movie "Sister Act ", debuts at its UK #5 peak.
Mar [1] Franklin performs *Natural Woman* and receives a Lifetime Achievement Award at the 36th annual Grammy Awards from New York's Radio City Music Hall.
[5] *A Deeper Love* makes US #63.
[12] Franklin guests on NBC-TV's "Saturday Night Live".
[19] Arista-issued ***Greatest Hits 1980-1994***, including four new cuts, not least *Honey*, written and produced by L.A. Reid & Babyface, debuts at its UK #27 peak and makes US #85.
Apr [22] Franklin takes part in the seventh annual Essence Awards at New York's Paramount.
May [1] She participates in the 25th annual "New Orleans Jazz & Heritage Festival".
June [20] Franklin performs at the White House in Washington, DC.
July [2] *Willing To Forgive* reaches UK #17.
[16] *Willing To Forgive* reaches US #26, her first US Top 30 hit in seven years.
Oct [8] She plays to a sellout crowd of 3,400 at the Star Plaza Theatre, Merrillville, IN, during current North American dates.

Nov [3] Franklin performs at New York's Carnegie Hall to benefit the New York chapter of the National Academy of Arts and Sciences.
[5] Atlantic-era compilation ***Queen Of Soul - The Very Best Of Aretha Franklin***, reaches UK #20.
[25] She hosts the third annual "Franklin Scholarship Awards Dinner And Dance" at Cobo Exhibition Hall, Detroit. Chaka Khan and Tevin Campbell also perform.
Dec [4] Franklin is honored at the 17th annual Kennedy Center Honors for her cultural contributions. At 52, she becomes the youngest-ever recipient.

1995

Jan [10] She performs at a tribute concert to Ella Fitzgerald at the Universal Amphitheatre, Universal City, CA.
June [30] Franklin sings at Mud Island Amphitheatre, Memphis, TN, while Saks Fifth Avenue files a suit in Michigan's Oakland County Circuit Court against her, alleging $262,851.15 owed on a line of credit.
Sept [2] She performs *I Can't Turn You Loose*, *Natural Woman* and, with Al Green, *Freeway Of Love* at the Concert for the Rock and Roll Hall of Fame at Cleveland Stadium, Cleveland, OH.
[29] She takes part in the "KISS-FM Classic Soul" concert at New York's Madison Square Garden with Gladys Knight, the Isley Brothers and Kool & the Gang, before a sellout crowd of 15,174.
Nov [14] The film soundtrack ***Waiting To Exhale***, featuring the Babyface-helmed *It Hurts Like Hell* by Franklin, is released.

FREDDIE & THE DREAMERS

Freddie Garrity (vocals); **Derek Quinn** (lead guitar); **Roy Crewsdon** (rhythm guitar); **Pete Birrell** (bass); **Bernie Dwyer** (drums)

1961

Oct The group is formed by Garrity (b. Nov. 14, 1936, Manchester, Lancs.), a former engineer, brush salesman, shoe salesman and milkman, who has previously sung in local skiffle group the Red Sox, which makes its first public appearance at the British Legion Hall in Chorlton, Lancs., followed by stints in the John Norman Four and then the Kingfishers, which he joins after selling his amplifier, at his girlfriend's request, to the group's rhythm guitarist, Crewsdon (b. May 29, 1941, Manchester). Quinn (b. May 24, 1942, Manchester), Birrell (b. May 9, 1941, Manchester) and Dwyer (b. Sept. 11, 1940) all join, as the new group evolves from the Kingfishers, before name-changing to the Dreamers, losing guitarist Ernie Molloy, who quits to become a milkman. They now make their first UK TV and radio appearances, on BBC's "Let's Go" and "Beat Show" respectively.

1962

Sept [12] The group plays at the Cavern Club, Liverpool, Lancs., on a bill with the Beatles.

1963

Mar After a year of growing popularity in northern England, followed by seaside dates at Dreamland, Margate, Kent, and then a stint in Hamburg, W. Germany, they are spotted by John Barry and signed to EMI's Columbia label, following intense talent-scouting by the company in both Manchester and Liverpool following the rapid success of the Beatles.
May [31] The group performs at London's Royal Albert Hall, on a bill with Billy Fury, Mark Wynter, the Tornados, Shane Fenton & the Fentones, Heinz and others.
June [22] Their debut recording, reviving James Ray's *If You Gotta Make A Fool Of Somebody*, which they had heard the previous year during a summer season with the Barron Knights, hits UK #3. They quickly become popular UK TV favorites, thanks to a zany, low-comedy stage act focused on Garrity's kicks, jumps and giggles while performing.
Aug [31] A Mitch Murray (writer of the first two Gerry & the Pacemakers chart-toppers) song, *I'm Telling You Now*, co-written with Garrity, hits UK #2, behind Billy J. Kramer & the Dakotas' *Bad To Me*.
Dec [7] *You Were Made For Me*, another Murray composition, makes a UK top three hat-trick, at #3, while their first album, ***Freddie And The Dreamers***, hits UK #5. (The group makes its film debut in "What A Crazy World", starring Joe Brown, Marty Wilde and Susan Maughan, and its pantomime bow in "Cinderella" at the Royalty Theatre, Chester, Cheshire.)

1964

Mar [7] *Over You* hits UK #13.
[22] The group performs on ITV's "Sunday Night At The London Palladium".
Apr [18] They embark on a UK tour, with Roy Orbison, at the Adelphi Cinema, Slough, Bucks., ending May 16th at the City Hall, Newcastle, Tyne & Wear.
June [13] Their treatment of Paul Anka's *I Love You Baby*, with a trademark Big Jim Sullivan guitar solo, reaches UK #16.
July [18] *Just For You*, another Mitch Murray tune, and featured in the pop movie "Just For You", debuts at its UK #41 peak.
Dec [24] The group opens in "Another Beatles' Christmas Show" at London's Hammersmith Odeon, set to end on January 16th.
[26] Their revival of the G-Clefs' 1961 hit, *I Understand*, returns them to UK Top 10, hitting #5, taken from their second album, ***You Were Made For Me***, which includes covers of the Applejacks' *Tell Me When* and the Merseybeats' *I Think Of You*. The group appears in the low-budget UK musical film "Every Day's A Holiday" (US title: "Seaside Swingers") as a bunch of singing holiday camp chefs, with fellow singers Mike Sarne and John Leyton. The film premieres at the Warner Cinema in London's Leicester Square.

1965

Feb During a world tour, a timely US visit places them on national TV shows "Shindig" and "Hullaballoo", where their stage antics and catchy songs are an immediate success, prompting Tower Records to reissue *I'm Telling You Now* and Mercury Records (to which their latest material is signed) to release *I Understand*.
Mar [8] The group embarks on a tour of Australia and New Zealand.
Apr A US bubblegum manufacturer distributes gum with Freddie & the Dreamers cards. A full set of 66 makes a 3' square group picture.
[10] *I'm Telling You Now* tops the US chart for the first of two weeks, taking its total sales to over a million.
May [1] *I Understand* makes US #36.
[8] *A Little You*, penned by Gordon Mills, and the first to feature orchestral backing, reaches UK #26.
June [5] The band begins an 18-week season at Queen's Theatre, Blackpool, Lancs., with comedians Tommy Cooper and Jewel & Warriss, as *Do The Freddie*, made specifically for the US market, with Garrity adding his vocals to an already-cut backing track recorded by American session musicians, creating a teen dance based on his stage movements, reaches #18 and *You Were Made For Me*, on Tower, peaks at #21.
[19] ***Freddie And The Dreamers*** reaches US #19.
July [24] ***Do The Freddie*** makes US #85.
Aug [28] *A Little You* stops at US #48, their final Stateside hit.
Oct The group begins a US tour of concert and college dates.
Nov [20] Their final UK hit, reviving Dick & Deedee's *Thou Shalt Not Steal*, peaks at #44. (They will then move into club and cabaret work, including regular winter pantomime and summer seaside residencies, where family audiences will replace the pop fans. The original line-up will split in 1968, with Garrity continuing on the oldies and cabaret circuit, backed by a new group of Dreamers. Garrity and Birrell will also find success on ITV's weekly children's show "Little Big Time" in October 1968.)

1992

The Best Of Freddie & the Dreamers - The Definitive Collection is released on compact disc, as Freddie (who made his "legitimate" stage debut in a UK production of "The Tempest" in 1988) continues to perform on the nostalgia circuit with a new set of Dreamers (not least appearing at October 1991's "The Biggest '60s Party In Town" at London's Olympia Hall). The original Dreamers have now all left the music business, with Quinn working for a soft drinks company, Birrell a taxi driver, Crewsdon owning a bar in the Canary Islands and Dwyer's whereabouts unknown.

FREE

Paul Rodgers (vocals); **Paul Kossoff** (guitar); **Andy Fraser** (bass); **Simon Kirke** (drums)

1968

May Two ex-members of R&B band Black Cat Bones, Kossoff (b. Sept. 14, 1950, London), son of actor David Kossoff, and Kirke (b. July 28, 1949, Shrewsbury, Shrops.) form the band. They recruit Rodgers (b. Dec. 12, 1949, Middlesbrough, Cleveland), ex-Roadrunners and Brown Sugar, after hearing him at the Fickle Pickle, an R&B club in Finsbury Park, London. Fraser (b. Aug. 7, 1952, London) joins, after being fired from John Mayall's Bluesbreakers. Alexis Korner watches their first gig and names them Free, after his own '60s trio, Free At Last.
June [21] The group supports Albert King at London's Marquee Club.
Nov Island Records, which has signed the band and wants it to be called the Heavy Metal Kids, releases the blues/rock band debut ***Tons Of Sobs***, which fails to chart in Britain, but will make US #197 almost a year on.

1969

July Their debut single, *Broad Daylight*, is issued, as the group builds a strong live reputation through constant UK touring.
Sept The band tours the US, supporting Blind Faith.
Nov Their sophomore album, ***Free***, is their UK chart debut at #22.

1970

May [24] The group takes part in the "Hollywood Music Festival" near Newcastle-under-Lyme, Staffs.
July *All Right Now*, a highly commercial riff-based rocker written by Fraser and Rodgers, hits UK #2 for three weeks, unable to dislodge Mungo Jerry's *In The Summertime*, and establishes Free as a major act.
Aug ***Fire And Water***, including the hit, climbs to UK #2, after the group makes a major impact at the "Isle Of Wight Festival", Godshill, Isle Of Wight.
Oct *All Right Now* hits US #4 as ***Fire And Water*** makes US #17, where the group is signed to A&M Records.

1971

Jan Follow-up single, *Stealer*, peaks at US #49.
[14-17, 21-24] The group performs at the Fillmore West, San Francisco, CA, on a bill with the Spencer Davis Group, Bloodrock and Taj Mahal.
Feb ***Highway*** makes UK #41 and peaks at US #190.
May [9] At the end of a Pacific tour, the band dissolves, to pursue individual projects, frustrated by intra-group friction and disappointed by its lack of sales consistency.
[21] The group formally announces that it has split, though it will re-form before year's end.
June Penned by Fraser and Rodgers, *My Brother Jake*, released two weeks before the split, hits UK #4.
July Performance set, ***Free Live!***, also hits UK #4.
Oct ***Free Live!*** makes US #89.
Nov Kossoff and Kirke release ***Kossoff, Kirke, Tetsu And Rabbit***, with bassist Tetsu Yamauchi (b. Oct. 21, 1947, Fukuoka, Japan) and keyboardist John "Rabbit"

Bundrick, while Rodgers forms Peace with Stewart McDonald (bass) and Mick Underwood (drums), which tours Britain supporting Mott The Hoople. Andy Fraser forms the short-lived trio Toby, with Adrian Fisher on guitar and Stan Speake on drums.

1972

Jan Re-formed after Peace and Toby have dissolved, Free tours Britain and recommences recording.
June ***Free At Last*** hits UK #9 and US #69, while the extracted *Little Bit Of Love* makes UK #13. The group tours the US, but Kossoff suffers drug abuse-associated health problems, which cause him to miss several dates.
July [22] Fraser leaves - to form Sharks - on the eve of Free's tour of Japan. Kossoff's drug problems render him unavailable, so Tetsu and Rabbit are recruited for the trip, on which Rodgers plays guitar.
Sept Eight days of a UK tour are cancelled after Kossoff is knocked out on stage, during rehearsals at the Mayfair, Newcastle, Tyne & Wear. He is rushed to hospital for X-rays and is found to have concussion.
Oct Kossoff, fit again, rejoins for the UK trek and the recording of another Free album, but officially leaves the group to make his solo debut, ***Back Street Crawler***. (He will form a band of that name in 1974, signing to Atlantic Records and releasing ***The Band Plays On*** and ***Second Street***.)

1973

Jan Wendell Richardson of Osibisa is temporarily added on guitar for UK dates.
Feb *Wishing Well* hits UK #7, as ***Heartbreaker*** makes UK #9 and US #47.
July Free announces its final split. Rodgers, after turning down an offer to join Deep Purple, stays with Kirke to form Bad Company, while Tetsu replaces Ronnie Lane in the Faces. (Rabbit will join the Who as sideman.)
Aug Reissued *All Right Now* reaches UK #15.

1974

Mar [23] Compilation, ***The Free Story***, hits UK #2.

1975

May ***The Best Of Free*** makes US #120.
Aug [30] Physically deteriorating, Kossoff "dies" for 35 minutes in hospital.
Nov [23] Kossoff returns to the stage, opening a tour with Back Street Crawler at the Empire Theatre, Liverpool, Merseyside.

1976

Mar [19] Kossoff dies of heart failure on a flight from Los Angeles, CA to New York, NY, after a history of drug abuse.

1978

Mar *The Free EP*, compiling *All Right Now*, *My Brother Jake* and *Wishing Well*, reaches UK #11. (It will remain a steady seller in Island Records' UK catalog and will re-chart at #57 in October 1982.)

1982

Mar Fraser has a minor US hit with *Do You Love Me*, peaking at #82, having worked with Robert Palmer on ***Clues*** and Brian Eno on ***Before And After Science***. (Rodgers joins Jimmy Page in the Firm in 1985, releasing ***The Firm*** and ***Mean Business*** in 1986, before forming the Law with Kenney Jones in 1990.)

1991

Mar [2] *All Right Now*, a remix of the group's 1970 UK #2 hit reissued to coincide with its use in a Wrigleys Chewing Gum ad, hits UK #8.
[9] ***The Best Of Free - All Right Now*** hits UK #2, behind Chris Rea's ***Auberge***.

1992

Oct Having released one album as founder and lead singer of the Law (the UK #61 and US #126-peaking ***The Law***) in the spring of 1991, Rodgers fronts Steve Vai, Nuno Bettencourt and Joe Walsh on Bad Company's *Can't Get Enough Of Your Love*, *Feel Like Making Love* and Free's *All Right Now* at "Guitar Legends" held at Expo '92 in Seville, Spain.

1993

Oct [19] ***Molten Gold: The Anthology***, a two-CD/cassette set, is released on PolyGram's Chronicles series.
see also: **BAD COMPANY, THE FACES, JOHN MAYALL**

BOBBY FREEMAN

1958

Apr Freeman (b. June 13, 1940, San Francisco, CA), having first recorded in 1955 as a singer and pianist with vocal group the Romancers, who were briefly signed to Dootone Records, while attending high school in San Francisco, is still a student when he is spotted playing in a club. He is signed to Josie Records, recording his own composition, *Do You Wanna Dance*.
June *Do You Wanna Dance* hits US #5 and becomes a much-revived rock standard: there will be later hit versions in the US/UK by Cliff Richard (1962), Del Shannon (1964), the Beach Boys (1965), the Mamas & The Papas (1968), Bette Midler (1973) and the Ramones (1978).
Aug *Betty Lou Got A New Pair Of Shoes* makes US #37, taken from his debut album ***Do You Wanna Dance***.
Dec *Need Your Love* peaks at US #54.

1959

Feb Freeman graduates from high school, turning professional (with three US hits already under his belt), but two Josie singles during this year will be less successful: *Mary Ann Thomas* making US #90 in June, and *Ebb Tide* #93 in December (both featured on ***Get In The Swim***).

1960

Oct He re-surges with the dance-craze song, *(I Do The) Shimmy Shimmy*, on the King label, which makes US #37 during a three-month chart tenure. (During the year his third album ***Loveable Style Of Bobby Freeman*** will also be released by King.)

1964

Jan After a lengthy recording silence and while resident at a club in North Beach, San Francisco, Freeman becomes the first act to work with local DJs Tom Donahue and Bob Mitchell, when they set up Autumn Records, cutting the label's debut single, *Let's Surf Again*.
Aug Freeman's *C'mon And Swim*, Autumn's second release, hits US #5. The single is produced by another local DJ, Sylvester Stewart (later to find fame as Sly Stone of Sly & the Family Stone).
Nov *S-W-I-M*, another Stewart production, peaks at US #56, Freeman's last US chart hit. (Following this year's release of ***C'mon And Swim***, he will continue working, mostly around the San Francisco area, not least at the annual Bammy Awards shows. In the late '60s and early '70s he will record intermittently, in a less rock-oriented soul style, for labels such as Double Shot and Touch.)

THE FUGEES

Lauryn 'L' Hill (vocals); **Clef Jean** (rap vocal, guitar, producer); **Pras Michel** (rapper/producer)

1994

July [2] Son of a preacher man, Jean (b. Whyclef Jean, Oct. 17, 1972, Haiti), who emigrated from Haiti at the age of nine to live in the Marlboro housing project in Brooklyn, NY, weened on the music of Bob Marley, Thelonius Monk and Jimi Hendrix, has originally formed the hip-hop unit Tranzlator Crew with his cousin, Michel (b. Prakazrel Michel, Oct. 19, 1972, Haiti), the son of a church deacon and equally influenced by Marley and Tuff Gong label reggae. Based in New Jersey, the pair has enlisted Michel's high school friend Hill and teen-actress (b. May 25, 1975, East Orange, NJ) to complete its rap trinity but has had to choose a new band name when threatened with litigation by the already installed new wave combo, Translator. Settling on the Fugees moniker (an edit of "refugees") and recording at their own Jean-assembled Booga Basement studio in East Orange, the posse has been signed to the Columbia-associated Ruffhouse label, and recorded its diverse hip-hop debut album, ***Blunted On Reality*** in 1993, co-produced by Jean and Michel, which now enters the US R&B survey, set to make #62. The same day, the extracted *Nappy Heads*, sampling Kool & The Gang's *Heaven At Once* and Earth Wind & Fire's *I Think About Lovin' You*, also enters the Hot 100, set to reach #49 on Aug [13]. The Fugees subsequently earn a strong live reputation over the next 18 months, not least for their ability to swap instruments, including lead, rhythm and bass guitars and an accordion, throughout their set.

1996

Jan [31] After an extended pause between albums, partly due to Hill's burgeoning acting career (which has included a role in "Sister Act II") and her ongoing studies at New York's Columbia University, the trio's sophomore album, ***The Score***, recorded at the Booga Basement, executive produced by Michel, co-produced by Jean and Hill, featuring DJ Red Alert and including a bonus remix of the current single *Fu-Gee-La* by Sly & Robbie and a cover of Marley's *No Woman, No Cry*, is released in the US.
Mar [4] *Fu-Gee-La* is confirmed gold by the RIAA.
[30] Borrowing from Teena Marie's 1988 US #85 hit *Ooh La La La*, the Fugees' *Fu-Gee-La* reaches US #29.
Apr [1] The trio plays to a packed and enthralled crowd at a rap-extravanganza held at Los Angeles' House Of Blues, CA.
[6] *Fu-Gee-La* reaches UK #21 in its week of entry.
May [17] Exploding at retail not least due to the current unavailability of the hot radio choice *Kiilling Me Softy*, and still climbing the US chart,***The Score*** is already certified triple platinum by the RIAA.
[25] In its 13th week on the survey, ***The Score*** tops the US chart.
June [8] Their smooth, hip-hop phrased version of Roberta Flack's 1973 soul standard US #1, *Killing Me Softly With His Song*, now titled *Killing Me Softly* enters the UK chart at #1 with ***The Score*** still climbing at UK #3. The group's idea behind the cover is to "bring musicality back to hip-hop".
[16] The Fugees perform at the Tibetan Freedom Concert in San Francisco, CA.
July [22] The trio sets out on the 33-date, multi-artist "Smokin' Grooves" North American caravan tour beginning at the Cal Expo Amphitheatre in Sacramento, CA, set to end on September 2nd at the Blockbuster Pavilion, Devore, CA.

THE FUGS

Ed Sanders (guitar, vocals); **Ken Weaver** (drums, vocals); **Tuli Kupferberg** (vocals)

1965

After a string of performances at a tiny theater in Greenwich Village, New York, NY, focusing on poetry, with beat bards Allen Ginsberg and Gregory Corso joining in, the Fugs becomes a rock group, with Sanders (b. Aug. 17, 1939, Kansas City, MO) and Kupferberg (b. Naphtali Kupferberg, Sept. 28, 1928, New York), writer of much of their material and the author of the book **1001 Ways To Beat The Draft**, on vocals, accompanied by Peter Stampfield and Steve Weber (ex-Holy Modal Rounders), and Weaver (b. Galveston, TX) (drums, vocals), Vinnie Leary (guitar),

Lee Crabtree (piano), Pete Kearney (guitar) and John Anderson (bass). The band signs to the avant-garde jazz label ESP and releases ***The Fugs' First Album***. With offensive lyrics (*Kill For Peace* and *Coca Cola Douche* being prime examples), the group becomes known for the taboo-breaking severity of its gigs, sometimes offending audiences, who exit en masse, but it also performs versions of William Blake poems.

1966

Aug ***The Fugs*** gives the band its first chart appearance, at US #95.

Nov Its success boosts sales of the earlier ***The Fugs' First Album***, which charts at US #142.

1967

Although it is acknowledged that the group's "appeal" lies mainly in its live performance, the Fugs sign to Reprise Records and go on tour, with Stefan Grossman (b. Apr. 16, 1945, New York) on guitar and Charlie Larkey on bass.

1968

Jan Their first Reprise album, ***Tenderness Junction***, is released. *Out Demons Out*, taken from it, becomes something of an anthem and will later be adopted in the UK by the Edgar Broughton Band. The Fugs' abrasive lyrical approach, referencing sex, drugs and Vietnam, again unnerves audiences.

Feb [2-4] The group performs at the Avalon Ballroom, San Francisco, CA, sharing the bill with Electric Flag.

Apr [12-14] The Fugs play again at the Avalon Ballroom, on a bill with the Ace of Cups.

Sept [20-21] The band performs at London's Camden Town Roundhouse, at the start of a European tour.

Oct With the line-up of Sanders, Kupferberg, Weaver, Larkey and Bob Mason (as second drummer), ***It Crawled Into My Hand, Honest*** peaks at US #167, the band's last chart album. It contains a pastiche of a highly-commercial psychedelic pop single, *Crystal Liaison*, which gains some unaccustomed airplay.

1969

Nov ***The Belle Of Avenue A*** is released, and the group splits. (Sanders will remain visible into the '70s as a writer, reporting for the underground press and writing a book, **The Family**, on the Charles Manson case and trial, and will record the solo albums ***Sanders' Truck-Stop*** and ***Beer Cans On The Moon***. Reprise will release the Fugs' live album, ***Golden Filth***, which was recorded on stage at the Fillmore East in New York, in 1970. Sanders and Kupferberg will re-form the Fugs in 1980, cutting ***Refuse To Be Burnt Out***, followed by ***No More Slavery*** (1986) and ***Star Peace*** (1987).)

THE BOBBY FULLER FOUR

Bobby Fuller (vocals, guitar); **Randy Fuller** (bass); **Jim Reese** (rhythm guitar); **Dwayne Quirico** (drums)

1964

Fuller (b. Oct. 22, 1942, Goose Creek, TX), having built a studio in his parents' home in El Paso, TX in 1960, recording a number of tracks and placing them with local labels including Yucca and Todd, has also run a local teen nightclub, the Rendezvous, playing there in the early '60s with a group called the Embers, who will later become the Fanatics and eventually, after many personnel changes, the Bobby Fuller Four. He now closes the Rendezvous in the summer, forms his own label, Exeter Records and releases a new single on it every few weeks, including surf music and an early version of *I Fought The Law* by Bobby Fuller & the Fanatics.

Nov The group leaves Texas for Hollywood, CA, and hoped-for stardom, taking tapes of Fuller's songs. The name is changed to Bobby Fuller & the Cavemen for a gig at La Cave Pigalle, then to the Bobby Fuller Four, when they acquire a residency at PJ's, breaking all attendance records at their first gig.

Dec They sign with Bob Keene, owner of a group of small Los Angeles, CA record labels, who decides to try them in different guises on several of his outlets. The first release is *Those Memories Of You*, as Bobby Fuller & the Fanatics, on Donna Records.

1965

Feb *Take My Word*, with the group billed as the Bobby Fuller Four, is released on another of Keene's labels, Mustang Records.

Mar They sign for an appearance as a surf band in the movie "Ghost In The Invisible Bikini". Its producer, Phil Spector, sits in with the group on piano at gigs and attempts, unsuccessfully, to sign them to his Philles label.

July They have a Los Angeles-area hit with *Let Her Dance*, its riff a re-working of *La Bamba*, leased to Liberty Records for national distribution, though it fails to sell outside California, and appear on several US TV shows, including "Shindig", "Shebang" and "Hollywood A Go-Go". Their debut album, ***KRLA King Of Wheels***, is also released, with co-operation from a Los Angeles radio station.

Sept *Never To Be Forgotten* also sells well in Los Angeles, but fails to chart nationally.

Oct Fuller revamps *I Fought The Law*, a revival of a Crickets' song which he has attempted before. This time it is a powerful guitar-driven version which will prove to be his breakthrough success.

1966

Mar *I Fought The Law* hits US #9.

Apr *I Fought The Law* makes UK #33, while their second album, ***The Bobby Fuller Four: I Fought The Law***, peaks at US #144.

May Another revived Crickets song in similar style, *Love's Made A Fool Of You*, reaches US #26, as the band embarks on its first national tour.

June As *The Magic Touch* is issued, Fuller falls out with Keene over the A-side choice, plus Keene's decisions not to record a live album at PJ's, a project close to Fuller's heart and to cancel a projected UK visit. He decides to quit the tour and go solo, while the single fails to score.

July [18] Fuller is found dead in his car, outside the apartment he shares with his mother at 1776 Sycamore, West Hollywood, Los Angeles, his body badly beaten and reeking of gasoline. The circumstances of his death are never uncovered, and Keene releases a statement dismissing police reports which call it accidental death or suicide. The question of foul play never arises, despite the odd mode of death. The group continues for a while, under Bobby's brother, as the Randy Fuller Four, but with no chart success they will split in 1968. Rhythm guitarist Reese will die on October 26th, 1991.

BILLY FURY

1958

Oct Former schoolmate of Beatle Ringo Starr at St. Silas Church of England, Dingle, Liverpool, Lancs., Ronald Wycherley (b. Apr. 17, 1940, Liverpool), following a childhood fraught with illness (including rheumatic fever, which has left him with a weak heart), is a deckhand on River Mersey tug boats and writing songs with his guitar as a hobby, when Larry Parnes' "Rock Extravaganza", headlined by Marty Wilde, comes to the Essoldo Cinema, Birkenhead, Lancs., across the Mersey from his home. Wycherley talks his way into Wilde's dressing room, hoping to interest him in some songs. Parnes, impressed by the teenager's obvious vocal talent and the strength of his on-the-spot demos, offers to sign him if Wycherley will go on stage and sing a couple of his songs as a "local addition" to the bill. Although petrified, Wycherley complies, and the audience reaction makes Parnes realize his hunch is right. He signs the singer to a management contract and christens him Billy Fury, quickly getting him on tour and on UK TV, in Jack Good's "Oh Boy!"

Nov [26] Fury, now signed by Parnes to Decca Records, records his first session at the company's studio in West Hampstead, London.

1959

Feb Self-penned *Maybe Tomorrow*, featured in the TV play "Strictly For Sparrows", reaches UK #18, aided by Fury's success in his nationwide tour.

May [23] Fury takes part in an "Oh Boy" party at the Strand Ballroom, Islington, London.

June *Margo Don't Go* makes UK #28.

Oct The curtain is dropped during Fury's act at the Theatre Royal, Dublin, Eire, his wild, Presley-like stage movements being deemed "offensive" by the management.

1960

Apr *Colette*, dual-tracked in an Everly Brothers' style atypical of Fury, is nevertheless his first UK Top 10 success, hitting #9.

June *That's Love*, another Fury original, reaches UK #19. By now, he is also a huge TV success in Britain, starring weekly on the rock music shows "Boy Meets Girls" (with Marty Wilde) and "Wham!" (which he headlines). 10" album, ***The Sound Of Fury***, reaches UK #18, featuring self-penned (under the name Wilbur Wilberforce) Elvis-style rockabilly tracks produced by Jack Good and backed by Joe Brown and other top session players. Later, it will later be regarded by critics as the great early UK rockabilly album, but Decca does not see Fury's recording career moving in this direction, sensing the commercial potential of strong rock ballads and carefully-chosen US cover versions.

Oct *Wondrous Place* reaches UK #25.

1961

Feb *A Thousand Stars*, his cover of US hit by Kathy Young & the Innocents, peaks at UK #14.

Apr His version of Marty Robbins' *Don't Worry* makes UK #40.

Aug Fury's treatment of the Goffin/King ballad *Halfway To Paradise* (a US hit for Tony Orlando), is his biggest UK disc yet, hitting #3 during a five-month chart stay. With big orchestral backing, this confirms him as a teen heart-throb rather than a rockabilly hero.

Sept Fury takes part in the "Great Pop Prom" at London's Royal Albert Hall, with Adam Faith, Helen Shapiro, Cliff Richard & the Shadows and the John Barry Seven.

Oct Dramatically-backed revival of the oldie *Jealousy* also hits UK #3, while ***Halfway To Paradise*** hits UK #5.

1962

Jan *I'd Never Find Another You* (another Goffin/King/Orlando cover) hits UK #2, also winning a Carl-Alan award in Britain as Favorite Dancefloor Record.

Mar Eager to record R&B material, Fury has recorded Gladys Knight & the Pips' *Letter Full Of Tears*, which reaches UK #17. He collapses during a UK tour.

June Big production ballad, *Last Night Was Made For Love*, hits UK #5.

July Promised an Elvis-like career in films, Fury stars in Michael Winner's "Play It Cool", essentially playing himself. The movie is lightweight but popular. *Once Upon A Dream*, from the film, hits UK #7, while the other movie songs are gathered on the EP *Play It Cool*, which sits at #2 on the UK EP chart for many weeks.

Sept Just before embarking on a 50-date UK tour, Fury comes down with suspected measles and misses the first 11 dates.

Nov *Because Of Love*, Fury's version of a number sung by Elvis Presley in the movie "Girls! Girls! Girls!", reaches UK #18.

1963

Feb [23] Fury appears on ITV's "Thank Your Lucky Stars".
Mar *Like I've Never Been Gone* takes him back into the UK top five, at #3.
May [31] Fury stars at London's Royal Albert Hall, topping a bill featuring Mark Wynter, the Tornados, Freddie & the Dreamers, Shane Fenton & the Fentones, Heinz and others.
June *When Will You Say I Love You* hits UK #3. By now Fury is flanked in UK Top 10 by a whole new wave of UK hitmakers from his native Liverpool - Billy J. Kramer (at #1), the Beatles (#2), and Gerry & the Pacemakers (#6). ***Billy*** hits UK #6.
Aug Atypically lightweight *In Summer* is the last of a trio of consecutive UK top five hits, at #5. With the beat boom on the ascendant, Fury is now associated with the old school of balladeers (even though he performs rock in a similar style to most beat groups on stage, backed by the Tornados) and will henceforth have a tougher time commercially. (He survives, however, as a major chart name longer than any of his pre-beat contemporaries, apart from Cliff Richard.)
[9] He tops the bill on the first edition of ITV's major pop show, "Ready Steady Go!"
Oct *Somebody Else's Girl* reaches UK #20.
[3] Fury embarks on a UK tour of with Joe Brown and Karl Denver.
Nov Live album, ***We Want Billy***, reaches UK #14.
Dec [7] The Beatles, appearing on BBC-TV's "Juke Box Jury", vote Fury's new single *Do You Really Love Me Too (Fool's Errand)*, a hit.

1964

Jan Uptempo *Do You Really Love Me Too (Fool's Errand)* makes UK #13.
[3] The Tornados undertake their final engagement with Fury, in Amsterdam, Holland.
Mar [21] Fury makes his radio debut with his new backing band, the Gamblers, on BBC Radio's "Saturday Club".
May Ballad, *I Will*, his cover of a US hit by Vic Dana, reaches UK #13.
Aug Fury revives Conway Twitty's former #1, *It's Only Make Believe*, hitting UK #10.
Nov [4] "The Billy Fury Show" debuts on UK TV.
Dec [31] Fury enters the London Clinic with a mystery illness. Taken sick over Christmas, he is expected to stay in the clinic for two weeks.

1965

Jan [6] He leaves the clinic, after tests prove negative.
Feb [6] *I'm Lost Without You*, a Teddy Randazzo ballad which is the most startlingly melodramatic of all Fury's recordings, reaches UK #16.
Mar [1] Fury makes his US TV debut on ABC-TV's "Shindig".
Apr [18] Film "I Gotta Horse", starring Fury and his racehorse, Anselmo, opens in London's West End. (Anselmo had finished fifth in the 1964 Derby.)
July [17] Fury guests on the 200th edition of "Thank Your Lucky Stars".
Aug [14] *In Thoughts Of You* hits UK #9, his final UK Top 10 hit.
Oct [2] Fury begins a ballroom and cabaret tour at the Gliderdrome, Boston, Lincs.
[9] *Run To My Lovin' Arms*, covered from Jay & the Americans, reaches UK #25.
Nov [3] Fury and the Gamblers embark on an 18-date, twice-nightly UK tour with Herman's Hermits, Wayne Fontana, the Fortunes and others, at the Gaumont Cinema, Wolverhampton, W. Midlands, set to end on the 22nd at the Odeon Cinema, Manchester, Lancs.

1966

Feb *I'll Never Quite Get Over You* reaches UK #35, Fury's poorest UK chart showing for five years. He also records the title song, *How's The World Treating You?*, from a play at the Wyndhams Theatre, where it is featured each night.
Aug Fury's revival of Tennessee Ernie Ford's *Give Me Your Word* reaches UK #27, bringing to an end his hit run and his contract with Decca. His remarkable total of 20 UK Top 20 entries is surpassed in the '60s only by the Beatles, Elvis Presley and Cliff Richard.

1967

Jan He signs a new recording contract with EMI's Parlophone label, which will produce 11 non-charting singles before the end of 1970. Fury, wary of his recurring heart problems (which have occasionally hospitalized him and caused tour date cancellations), takes a back seat from live performances (apart from an occasional appearance) and spends much time on his farm, devoting his efforts to horse breeding and pursuing his animal-conservation interests.

1972

May He releases a one-off single, *Will The Real Man Please Stand Up*, on his own label, Fury Records.
Aug [5] Fury participates in the "London Rock'n'Roll Festival" at Wembley Stadium, Wembley, Middx., sharing an unlikely bill with Little Richard, Gary Glitter, Wizzard, Jerry Lee Lewis, Bill Haley, the MC5, Bo Diddley, Emile Ford and Heinz.

1973

Apr [12] Movie "That'll Be The Day", starring David Essex, premieres in London's West End. The film includes Fury in a cameo role as Stormy Tempest, a clone of his younger self, singing several songs including *Long Live Rock*, written for him by Pete Townshend.

1981

Oct After many years in retirement, much of it enforced by his poor health, Fury decides to regenerate his recording career, signing to Polydor Records and working with Shakin' Stevens' producer, Stuart Colman, a partnership which initially yields *Be Mine Tonight*.

1982

Sept *Love Or Money* returns him to the UK Singles chart after 16-year gap, peaking at #57.
Nov His revival of Bobby Vee's *Devil Or Angel* makes UK #58.

1983

Jan [28] Fury dies from heart failure. His *I'm Lost Without You* will be played at his funeral. (A lectern inscribed in his honor will be consecrated in Liverpool Cathedral in November 1993 and a garden bench near his grave at Mill Hill Cemetery will be a lasting memorial to him. His death also brings about a short burst of UK chart activity with the compilation, ***The Billy Fury Hit Parade***, making UK #44 in February, ***The One And Only***, completed with Colman just before his death, peaking at UK #54 in March, while *Forget Him* provides an inappropriately-titled posthumous UK chart swan song, climbing to #59 in June.)

G

KENNY G

1981

Having taken up the saxophone as a child, G (b. Kenneth Gorelick, June 6, 1956, Seattle, WA), is already an accomplished player in his Franklin High School Band, which has toured Europe when he was 15, by the time he joins Barry White's Love Unlimited Orchestra at age 17, having graduated from alto, through tenor to soprano sax (though he will continue to play all three). Subsequently attending the University of Washington where he studies accounting while also performing with the Seattle-based funk outfit Cold, Bold & Together, he has gone on to join Jeff Lorber's Fusion band which records for Arista Records which now signs G as a solo artist and which will release his first album, the Lorber/Meco Monardo-produced ***Kenny G*** the following year, introducing his brand of light-pop jazz-sax fusion, on which he plays all three sax variations and the flute.

1984

Mar [24] His sophomore set ***G-Force*** (also the name of his band) begins his chart career on its way to US #62. Co-produced by G with Wayne Braithwaite, it features guest musicians Kashif, Lillo Thomas, B.J. Nelson and singer Freddie Jackson, among others.
Apr *Hi! How Ya Doin?*, already a US R&B #23 success, makes UK #70 with ***G-Force*** climbing to UK #56.

1985

June [1] His follow-up set ***Gravity***, credited as Kenny G & G Force and featuring co-producer Kashif on *Love On The Rise*, and on which G also plays the flute and synthesizer, enters the US survey set to reach #97.

1986

Sept [6] ***Duotones***, produced by Narada Michael Walden and Preston Glass, begins a 102-week US chart ride during which it will hit #6. During the month, George Benson's ***While The City Sleeps...***, including G guesting on sax, reaches UK #13 and US #77.
Aug *What Does It Take (To Win Your Love)*, with a guest vocal by Ellis Hall, makes UK #64.
Nov [22] Steve Miller Band's *I Want To Turn The World Around*, featuring G's sax-playing, makes US #97.

1987

Mar Aretha Franklin's ***Aretha***, featuring G on sax, makes US #32 and UK #51.
July [11] The extracted sax-ballad *Songbird* becomes a rare instrumental crossover smash, hitting US #4, and is climbing to reach UK #22.
Aug [8] ***Duotones*** reaches UK #28.
Sept Lee Ritenour's ***Portraits***, featuring G, is released in the US.
Nov [7] *Don't Make Me Wait For Love*, with Lenny Williams on vocal, reaches US #15.

1988

Oct [22] ***Silhouette***, featuring vocal guest Smokey Robinson on *We've Saved The Best For Last*, enters the US survey set to hit #8.

1989

Jan [7] *Silhouette* reaches US #13.
Mar [4] *We've Saved The Best For Last* with Robinson makes US #47.
May Natalie Cole's ***Everlasting***, featuring G, makes US #42 and UK #62.
July While Stevie Nicks' ***The Other Side Of The Mirror***, with G guesting on *Two Kinds Of Love*, has hit US #10 the previous month, G is also featured on Michael Bolton's newly-released ***Soul Provider***.
Aug [26-27] A pair of dates in his hometown of Seattle are recorded for release in December as ***Live***.

1990

Jan [27] The extracted *Going Home* makes US #56.
Mar [24] ***Live*** reaches US #16.
Apr [14] UK-only titled ***Montage*** makes UK #32.
May [19] The Winans' ***Return***, with G as one of its music guests, enters the US chart, set to make #90.
July [19] His "Kenny G Live In Concert" video is certified platinum by the RIAA.
Sept [30] Towards the end of an autumn US tour opening for Michael Bolton, G performs at the Hearst Greek Theatre at the University of California-Berkeley, Berkeley, CA., a sellout event grossing $187,670 from 8,500 attendees.
Dec [8] Whitney Houston's ***I'm Your Baby Tonight***, numbering G among its guests, hits US #3.

1991

May [31] ***Gravity*** is certified gold by the RIAA.
July [20] The ***Dying Young*** film soundtrack, for which G has performed four cuts including the title theme, enters the US survey set to make #50. (During the year, G guests on Dudley Moore's ***Songs Without Words*** and Richard Smith's ***Bella Firenze***.)

1992

Mar [14] *Missing You Now*, recorded with Bolton, reaches US #12.
Apr [18] Celine Dion's ***Celine Dion***, featuring G as one of its music guests, enters the US chart set to reach #34.
May *Missing You Now* reaches UK #28.
Dec [9] His debut album ***Kenny G***, which never charted, is confirmed gold by the RIAA.

1993

Jan [30] Released the previous December and variously produced by G with David Foster, Walter Afanasieff and Dan Shea, ***Breathless***, featuring vocal guests Aaron Neville and Peabo Bryson and reflecting an increasingly melodic direction which captivates both jazz and AC radio formats, hits US #2.
Mar [20] *Forever In Love* reaches US #18.
Apr Heads Up Records (US) releases ***Tony Gable & 206***, produced by G and on which he plays throughout.
May [1] *Forever In Love* makes UK #47.
[29] Its parent album ***Breathless*** hits UK #4.
July [17] *By The Time This Night Is Over*, with Peabo Bryson, reaches US #25.
[24] *By The Time This Night Is Over* makes UK #56.
Nov [20] Frank Sinatra's ***Duets***, to which G contributes *All The Way/One For My Baby (And One More For The Road)*, debuts at its US #2 peak.
Dec [25] *Sentimental* makes US #72.

1994

Feb [7] G wins the Best Artist, Adult Contemporary category at the 21st annual American Music Awards held at Los Angeles, CA's Shrine Auditorium.
Mar [1] He performs *Forever In Love* at the 36th annual Grammy Awards held at New York's Radio City Music Hall, the tune also winning the Best Instrumental Composition category.
[15] G receives the best R&B Jazz Album trophy (for ***Breathless***) at the eighth annual Soul Train Awards also held at the Shrine Auditorium.
[22] ***Breathless*** is named the best-selling Jazz Recording at NARM's 1993-4 Best Seller Awards held in San Francisco, CA.
May [4] G performs at and is named the World's Best-selling Jazz Artist of the Year at the sixth annual World Music Awards held at the Sporting Club, Monte Carlo, Monaco (due to air on the 31st on ABC-TV).
Aug [19] A five-month headlining US tour opens at the Freedom Hall Coliseum, Kentucky State Fair, Louisville, a gig grossing $114,993.
[30] ***G-Force*** is certified platinum by the RIAA.
Nov [29] Having performed earlier in the month at a Carousel of Hope benefit for the Children's Diabetes Foundation at the Beverly Hilton Hotel (with Neil Diamond, Natalie Cole and Phil Collins), the RIAA certifies multi-platinum sales for ***Breathless*** (seven million) and ***Kenny G Live*** (three million).
Dec [7] G is named Artist Of The Year in the contemporary Jazz category at the fifth annual **Billboard** Music Awards held at the Universal

Amphitheatre, Universal City on the same evening that his participation in "Gala For The President" airs on ABC-TV, an event taped before President Clinton at Ford's Theater, Washington on October 30th.
[10] Self-produced ***Miracles - The Holiday Album***, with string arrangements by William Ross, tops the US chart becoming the first Christmas-themed album to hit US #1 since Mitch Miller's ***Holiday Sing A Long With Mitch*** in January 1962.
[17] "Christmas At Home With The Stars", including an appearance by G, is broadcast on ABC-TV.
[28] He performs his last concert of the year at the Arlene Schnitzer Concert Hall, Portland Center for the Performing Arts, Portland, OR. (During the year, G has performed 36 shows to 206,607 fans on bills grossing $5,823,873.)
[30] G appears on NBC-TV's "The Tonight Show".

1995

Mar [14] G attends a committee hearing on Capitol Hill, Washington, DC to protest potential congressional cuts in federal funding for the arts.
Apr [5] The RIAA certifies multi-platinum sales for ***Silhouette*** (four million) and ***Breathless*** (eight million).
June [3] G is named Top Pop Artist (Male) at the inaugural Blockbuster Entertainment Awards in Los Angeles, set to air on the 6th on CBS-TV.
Sept [14] He participates in the T.J. Martell Foundation 20th anniversary dinner, honoring his label boss Clive Davis with its annual Humanitarian Award.
Oct [26] ***Miracles*** reaches the five million sales plateau in the US.
Nov [29] The RIAA certifies five million sales of ***Duotones***.
Dec [1] G guests on "The Tonight Show".
[6] He is named Top Contemporary Jazz Artist at the sixth annual **Billboard** Music Awards broadcast live on Fox-TV from New York's Coliseum.
[18] G, his wife, two-year old son Max and their two dogs escape injury after fire causes $275,000 in damages to their Benedict Canyon home in Los Angeles, where his studio is also based.

PETER GABRIEL

1975

May Lead vocalist of Genesis, Gabriel (b. May 13, 1950, Cobham, Surrey), who has attended Charterhouse School in Godalming, Surrey with his erstwhile bandmates, leaves the group at the close of its "Lamb Lies Down" tour after a concert in St. Etienne, France. He remains with Charisma Records as a solo artist, though it will be nearly two years before he releases a debut album. Curiously, his first production project following his departure from the group is for UK comic actor Charlie Drake's *You'll Never Know*, also released on Charisma and co-written with Martin Hall.
Aug [16] He makes a belated press announcement confirming his decision to split from Genesis, for personal reasons.
Nov Various artists compilation album, ***All This And World War II***, featuring Gabriel's version of the Beatles' *Strawberry Fields Forever*, makes UK #23. The following July, Gabriel will begin recording sessions at Nimbus Studios, Toronto, Canada.

1977

Mar [12] Extending the artist's complex and literate musical style, a process begun as the principal creative force in Genesis, the self-penned ***Peter Gabriel***, produced by Bob Ezrin and, confusingly, the first of four eponymously-titled albums, hits UK #7, as Gabriel begins his first solo tour in North America.
Apr Prior to a short European tour, he makes his London solo stage debut at the Hammersmith Odeon, backed by, among others, Robert Fripp of King Crimson on guitar. Genesis' new vocalist and longtime drummer Phil Collins sits in on drums during Gabriel's encore number, *Here Comes The Flood*.
May ***Peter Gabriel*** reaches US #38.
[21] Acoustic guitar-led *Solsbury Hill* reaches UK #13 and peaks at US #68.
Dec Gabriel is arrested in West Germany on suspicion of being a member of the Baader-Meinhof gang.

1978

June [24] His sophomore album, ***Peter Gabriel***, featuring Roy Bittan (keyboards), Sid McGinniss (guitar) and Jerry Marotta on drums, produced by Fripp and containing the recently issued *DIY*, hits UK #10.
Aug ***Peter Gabriel*** reaches US #45.
[9] Gabriel performs at the "Knebworth II" outdoor music festival, Knebworth, Herts., on a bill including the Tubes and Frank Zappa.

1979

Mar The Tom Robinson Band's *Bully For You*, co-written by Gabriel, peaks at UK #68.
May [12] Gabriel joins Kate Bush and Steve Harley in a benefit concert at the Hammersmith Odeon, for the family of Bush's lighting engineer Billy Duffy, who died in an accident. (During the month, Gabriel also sings guest vocals on Robert Fripp's album ***Exposure***.)
Aug [26] He is joined onstage by Collins at the "Reading Festival", Reading, Berks., for an encore of *The Lamb Lies Down On Broadway*. (Gabriel spends part of the year working with writer Atejanmdo Jodorowsky on the screenplay for a movie version of Genesis' concept album/stage show "The Lamb Lies Down On Broadway", due to be financed by Charisma, but the movie never materializes.)

1980

Mar [15] *Games Without Frontiers*, his first solo Top 10 single, hits UK #4. With Bush on backing vocals, the notable whistling is provided by producers Steve Lillywhite, Hugh Padgham, and Gabriel.
May [31] *No Self Control* makes UK #33.
June [14] His third album, ***Peter Gabriel***, produced by Lillywhite and including guest appearances by Bush, Collins, Fripp and Paul Weller of the Jam, tops the UK chart. Charisma has licensed the album to Mercury Records in the US, after Atlantic, the US licensee of the two previous Gabriel albums, has turned it down. Noting the UK chart success of (the included) *Games Without Frontiers*, Atlantic tries to buy the album back, but to no avail. (Gabriel also records the album in German for a separate release.)
July Jimmy Pursey (ex-Sham 69) releases *Animals Have More Fun* in the UK, co-written and co-produced by Gabriel.
Aug The third album, ***Peter Gabriel***, peaks at US #22.
[23] Tribal-tinged *Biko*, a protest song concerning the death in South Africa of black activist Steve Biko, reaches UK #38.
Sept [20] *Games Without Frontiers* makes US #48.

1982

July [16-18] Gabriel inaugurates the "World Of Music Arts And Dance" (WOMAD) Festival at the Royal Bath & West Showground, Shepton Mallet, Somerset. Becoming a regular (and personally costly) annual event, it meshes culture and music from around the globe, predating the late '80s "World Music" genre.
Sept [18] His fourth album, ***Peter Gabriel***, co-produced with keyboardist David Lord and the last to use this title, hits UK #6. (Once again, the German market is treated to its own lingual version.)
Oct [2] A one-off reunion with Genesis at Milton Keynes Bowl, Milton Keynes, Bucks., for a WOMAD benefit concert, helps offset some of the losses of the recent Shepton Mallet Festival.
[16] *Shock The Monkey*, taken from the latest album and featuring Peter Hammill as backing vocalist, makes UK #58.
Nov The fourth eponymous effort, ***Peter Gabriel***, reaches US #28. Geffen, to whom Gabriel is newly signed in the US, stickers the sleeve with the title "Security" to give the album a separate identity from the earlier three. (A documentary feature on Gabriel is broadcast on ITV's "The South Bank Show".)

1983

Jan [29] *Shock The Monkey* reaches US #29, his first single to chart higher in the US than the UK.
May [5] Gabriel and Genesis are honored for their Outstanding Contribution To British Music at the 29th annual Ivor Novello Awards lunch, at the Grosvenor House Hotel, London.
June Double album, ***Peter Gabriel Plays Live***, instigated by US Geffen, to satisfy fans in the absence of new studio material, though in fact Gabriel adds new studio overdubbing to the tracks, hits UK #8.
July The extracted *I Don't Remember* reaches UK #62.
Aug ***Peter Gabriel Plays Live*** makes US #44.
Sept [10] A live version of his debut hit, *Solsbury Hill*, peaks at US #84.
Nov Tom Robinson reaches UK #39 with the Gabriel co-written *Listen To The Radio: Atmospherics*.

1984

June *Walk Through The Fire*, taken from film soundtrack to "Against All Odds" (and an out-take from his third album), makes UK #69.

1985

Apr ***Birdy***, the soundtrack album for the film of the same name, composed and performed by Gabriel and co-produced with Daniel Lanois, makes UK #51.
Dec [14] Artists United Against Apartheid, comprising 49 artists including Gabriel featured on the album track *No More Apartheid*, makes US #38, and UK #21 with the extracted single *Sun City*.

1986

May [24] *Sledgehammer*, accompanied by an acclaimed and innovative claymation promo video by Steve Johnson, using stop-motion techniques with revolutionary flair, hits UK #4.
[31] Richly diverse ***So***, co-produced by Gabriel and Lanois and featuring musical guests Laurie Anderson, P.P. Arnold, Bush, Stewart Copeland, Simple Minds' Jim Kerr, Nile Rodgers and pianist Richard Tee, enters the UK chart at #1 and will become his biggest-selling album of the '80s.
June [4] Amnesty International's "A Conspiracy Of Hope" two-week US tour begins at the Cow Palace, San Francisco, CA, featuring Gabriel, U2, Sting, Bryan Adams and Lou Reed.
[28] Gabriel takes part in an anti-apartheid concert on London's Clapham Common, with Elvis Costello, Boy George, Sade, Sting, Billy Bragg and Hugh Masekela among others, before an estimated half-million crowd.
July [26] *Sledgehammer* tops the US chart for a week, becoming a million seller internationally, while ***So*** will hit US #2.
Oct [25] *In Your Eyes*, taken from the album and with backing vocals by Youssou N'Dour, reaches US #26.
Nov Gabriel's ballad duet with Kate Bush, *Don't Give Up*, taken from ***So***, hits UK #9 and is promoted by two different videos. ***Biko*** is included on the all-star compilation album, ***Conspiracy Of Hope***, released in aid of Amnesty International.

1987

Feb [9] Gabriel wins the Best British Male Artist and Best British Music Video (for "Sledgehammer") categories, at the sixth annual BRIT Awards, at the Grosvenor House Hotel.
Mar [7] *Big Time* hits US #8, accompanied by another eye-catching video and featuring Copeland on drums. During the month Gabriel performs live in Japan for the "Hurricane Irene" benefit.
[28] Continuing his long-term support for Amnesty International, Gabriel appears at their benefit, the "Secret Policeman's Third Ball" in London.
Apr [4] *Big Time* reaches UK #13.
[15] *Don't Give Up* is named Best Song Musically And Lyrically at the 32nd annual Ivor Novello Awards, at the Grosvenor House Hotel.
[25] *Don't Give Up* peaks at US #72.
July The fourth extract from ***So***, *Red Rain*, makes UK #46.

Sept [11] "Sledgehammer" sweeps the fourth annual MTV Video Music Awards, held at the Universal Amphitheatre, Universal City, CA, winning the Best Video, Best Male Video, Best Concept Video, Best Overall Performance, Best Special Effects, Best Art Direction, Best Editing, Best Direction and Most Experimental categories. Gabriel also collects the prestigious Video Vanguard trophy.
Nov A new live version of *Biko*, taken from the soundtrack album of the film "Cry Freedom", makes UK #49. Gabriel contributes to ex-Band member Robbie Robertson's eponymous first album, notably on the cut *Fallen Angel*.

1988

June [5-6] He participates in the sixth annual "Prince's Trust Rock Gala", at London's Royal Albert Hall.
[11] Gabriel performs his anti-apartheid anthem *Biko*, at "Nelson Mandela's 70th Birthday Tribute" at Wembley Stadium, Wembley, Middx.
July Gabriel's impressive show reel of video hits, collectively released as "CV", tops the UK Music Video chart.
Aug The controversial Martin Scorsese-directed film "The Last Temptation Of Christ", with a Gabriel score, premieres in the UK and US.
Sept [2] A second six-week Amnesty International "Human Rights Now" world tour, with Gabriel, Tracy Chapman, Bruce Springsteen, Sting and others, opens at Wembley Stadium.

1989

Mar [6] Gabriel attends the launch of the ***Greenpeace - Rainbow Warriors*** album (which is released on the Melodiya label) in Moscow, USSR, with Annie Lennox, the Thompson Twins and U2.
June Following their Amnesty performances together, Gabriel has contributed to Youssou N'Dour's latest album, ***Set***, while the extracted duet, the UK #61 single *Shaking The Tree*, will later provide the title for a Gabriel greatest hits compilation.
[17] ***Passion*** reaches UK #29 and US #60, featuring instrumental highlights from his film score to "The Last Temptation Of Christ", augmented by additional music composed by Gabriel and performed with Asian and African musicians.
July [8] *In Your Eyes*, the final ***So*** extract, makes US #41.

1990

Feb [21] Gabriel wins the Best New Age Performance category for ***Passion - Music For The Last Temptation Of Christ*** at the 32nd annual Grammy Awards, at the Shrine Auditorium, Los Angeles, CA.
Apr [16] Gabriel participates in "Nelson Mandela - An International Tribute To A Free South Africa" concert at Wembley Stadium, with Bonnie Raitt, Neil Young, Simple Minds, the Neville Brothers, Aswad and Tracy Chapman among others.
Sept [24] Geoffrey Oryema's album, ***Exile***, with Gabriel guesting and production by Brian Eno, is released in the UK.

1991

Jan [5] Gabriel's first greatest hits collection, ***Shaking The Tree: Sixteen Golden Greats***, peaks at UK #11, featuring a sleeve shot by controversial artist Robert Mapplethorpe. The extracted and reissued pairing *Solsbury Hill/Shaking The Tree*, with N'Dour, makes UK #57.
Feb [9] ***Shaking The Tree: Sixteen Golden Greats*** makes US #48.
Mar [9] The Peace Choir's *Give Peace A Chance*, featuring Gabriel in an all-star cast, makes US #54.
Apr Gabriel performs before a 70,000 crowd at the Stade de l'Amitie, Dakar, Senegal, with N'Dour.
May [12] He appears by satellite from the Hague, Holland, singing *Games Without Frontiers* with Sting's band, as part of "The Simple Truth" concert for Kurdish refugees, from Wembley Arena, Wembley.
Aug [15-21] Gabriel-organized "Real World Week of Recording", with Sinead O'Connor and Van Morrison among the many who participate, takes place at his Real World Studio in Box, Wilts.
Sept [10] The soundtrack to Wim Wenders' new film, "Until The End Of the World", featuring Gabriel, is released.
Dec The RIAA certifies three million US sales of ***So***.

1992

Apr [27] Manu Katche's album, ***It's About Time***, to which Gabriel has contributed vocals on *Warm Doorway* and a duet with Sting on *Silence*, is released.
Sept [26] His first new solo vocal recording in six years, *Digging In The Dirt*, reaches UK #24.
Oct [7] Gabriel guests on BBC1-TV's "What's That Noise".
[10] ***Us*** enters at its UK #2 peak, behind R.E.M.'s ***Automatic For The People***. Released via Gabriel's newly created Real World label, formed in association with the still-running WOMAD organisation, and recorded at his Real World Studio in Box, Wilts., the self-analytical, soul-searching set, focusing not least on his separation from ex-girlfriend, actress Rosanna Arquette, features a truly global array of musicians from as far afield as Armenia, Egypt, Kenya, Russia and Senegal, in addition to more familiar guests, including Eno, Katche, Sinead O'Connor and co-producer Lanois.
[17] ***Us*** debuts at its US #2 peak.
Nov [21] *Digging In The Dirt* makes US #52, accompanied by a traditionally intricate special-effects video clip.
Dec Gabriel attends the annual Reebok Human Rights Awards in Boston, MA, with Joan Baez, Richie Havens and Michael Stipe.

1993

Jan [21-24] ART 93 exhibition at the Business Design Centre, Islington, London, displays the work of 11 artists from around the world, who were commissioned by Gabriel to interpret one track each from his latest album.
[23] *Steam* rises to hit UK #10 and will reach US #32 the following week.
Feb [16] Gabriel collects the Best Producer trophy at the 12th annual BRIT Awards, held at London's Alexandra Palace, at which he also performs *Steam*.
[24] Gabriel opens the 35th annual Grammy Awards, held at the Shrine Auditorium, with a Cirque du Soleil-featured performance of *Steam*, and takes home the Best Short Form Video trophy for "Digging In The Dirt".
Apr [8] Gabriel plays a sellout date at the Academy, New York.
[10] *Blood Of Eden* makes UK #43.
May [18] ***Plus From Us***, a various artists collection of music, including contributions from Eno, Lanois, Bill Laswell, the Meters, William Orbit and David Rhodes, compiled by Gabriel (as a record of the inspiration behind the songs on ***Us***) is released on the Real World label.
[24] The five-date UK leg of a European tour, set to end on June 1st at London's Earls Court, opens at the Sheffield Arena, Sheffield, S. Yorks.
June [18] Gabriel opens a North American tour at the Community War Memorial, Rochester, NY, with a sellout performance before a 7,996 crowd. The tour will end on August 4th at the Miami Arena, Miami, FL.
Sept [4] A nine-date "WOMAD Festival" opens in US, running until the 19th.
Oct [2] *Kiss That Frog* makes UK #46.

1994

Mar [1] Gabriel wins the Best Music Video Short Form category (his third) for "Steam" at the 36th annual Grammy Awards, staged at New York's Radio City Music Hall.
[5] *Because Of You* reaches UK #24.
June [15] He arrives in Israel for Middle East dates.
[25] *Lovetown* bows at its UK #49 peak.
July [16] Gabriel plays at the Jones Beach Theatre, Wantagh, NY, during the "WOMAD" tour.
[24] He joins Angelique Kidjo onstage during Africa Fete's performance at New York's Central Park Summerstage.
Aug [9] Gabriel is the featured musical guest on CBS-TV's "Late Show With David Letterman".
[11] Gabriel sells out New York's Beacon Theatre, sharing the bill with Lou Reed.
[28] "The Secret World Of Peter Gabriel" documentary airs on ITV.
Sept [3] *SW Live* EP, including *Red Rain*, debuts at its UK #39 peak.
[8] "Kiss That Frog" wins the Best Special Effects category at the 11th annual MTV Video Music Awards, held at Radio City Music Hall.
[10] Performance set ***Secret World Live*** hits UK #10 in its week of entry.
Oct [1] ***Secret World Live*** debut at its US #23 peak.
Nov [5] Gabriel's multimedia-pioneering "Xplora 1 : Peter Gabriel's Secret World" CD-ROM nabs Best Musical category at the inaugural "Cybermania : The Ultimate Gamer Awards" in Los Angeles.
Dec [7] Gabriel attends the annual Reebok Human Rights Youth In Action ceremony at Boston's Northeastern University.

1995

July [24-29] Following previous recording weeks in 1991 and 1992, Gabriel reprises his "Real World Recording Week" at his Box studios, inviting some 80 musicians from around the world for a free-form village recording marathon. Artists include Deep Forest from France, Karl Wallinger from Wales and Tim Finn from New Zealand.
Sept [26] Leonard Cohen-tribute album ***Tower Of Song : The Songs Of Leonard Cohen***, including Gabriel's version of *Suzanne*, is released in the US.
Dec [5] Gabriel and Michael Stipe co-host a cocktail party in Los Angeles, to provide an update on Witness, a program initiated by Gabriel in 1992 to provide video equipment to human rights activists around the world.
[6] Gabriel presents the prestigious Century Award to Joni Mitchell at the 1995 **Billboard** Music Awards from New York's Coliseum, broadcast live on Fox-TV.

1996

Feb [28] Gabriel takes home the Best Music Video Longform trophy (for "Secret World Live") at the 38th annual Grammy Awards held at the Shrine Auditorium.
Apr [28] He takes part in "Witness : A Concert For Human Rights", also featuring Bryan Adams, Gloria Estefan and Don Henley, and broadcast live on VH1 from the Universal Amphitheatre.
see also: **GENESIS**

GALLAGHER & LYLE

Benny Gallagher (vocals, guitar);
Graham Lyle (vocals, guitar)

1970

Apr The singing/songwriting duo from Largs (near Glasgow), Scotland, have relocated to London in 1966, secured a publishing deal and released their debut effort ***Trees***, via Polydor Records, in June the following year. Concentrating mainly on composition towards the end of the decade, they have been signed by Terry Doran to the Beatles-owned Apple Music Publishing in 1969 where two songs, *Sparrow* and *International*, are covered by Mary Hopkin and Noel Harrison respectively. Their contract with Apple now expired, the duo meets Tom McGuinness (ex-Manfred Mann), who invites them to join his recently-formed band McGuinness Flint (with drummer Hughie Flint), as vocalist/guitarists and resident songwriters.
Dec McGuinness Flint's *When I'm Dead And Gone*, written by the duo about blues legend Robert Johnson, hits UK #2 and will make US #47 in February. Gallagher and Lyle will remain with the band for two years, also penning the May 1971 UK #5 smash *Malt And Barley Blues* and the majority of the songs on two Capitol Records albums, ***McGuinness Flint*** and ***Happy Birthday Ruthie Bab***, before signing an independent deal with the label in January 1972.

Bowie/Tom Conti movie "Merry Christmas Mr. Lawrence" (in which Sakamoto also stars) climbs to UK #16.

1984

Jan Sylvian solo, *Red Guitar*, reaches UK #17.
June He exhibits his Polaroid photo montages at London's Hamilton's Gallery.
July His debut solo album, ***Brilliant Trees***, hits UK #4. It yields *The Ink In The Well* (UK #36 in August) and *Pulling Punches* (UK #56 in November).
Nov Karn teams with former Bauhaus lead singer, Peter Murphy, as Dali's Car. Signed to Paradox Records, their debut is ***The Judgement Is The Mirror***, peaking at UK #66.
Dec Double album, ***Exorcising Ghosts***, a compilation of Japan's Virgin material, peaks at UK #45. Dali's Car's *The Waking Hour* makes UK #84.

1985

Dec Sylvian solo ***Words With The Shaman*** makes UK #72, while ***His Alchemy - An Index Of Possibilities*** is released on cassette only. The following year, Sylvian will reach UK #53 with *Taking The Veil* (August), from the UK #24 double set, ***Gone To Earth*** (September).

1987

Jan Karn's *Buoy*, featuring Sylvian on guest vocals, floats to UK #63, followed by the former's ***Dreams Of Reason Produce Monsters***, which peaks at UK #89 on Feb [28].
July Jansen and Barbieri resurface as the Dolphin Brothers, releasing ***Catch The Fall*** on Virgin.
Nov [7] Sylvian's third album, ***Secrets Of The Beehive***, makes UK #37 and includes the October UK #66, *Let The Happiness In*. He will team with Holger Czukay for ***Plight And Premonition***, which will peak at UK #71 on Apr [2] the following year, while his solo album, ***Orpheus***, fails to chart. Virgin will press 30,000 CDs of all Sylvian's solo work, released as ***The Weather Box*** compilation in December 1989.

1991

Apr [20] Reunited, Sylvian, Karn, Jansen and Barbieri, now calling themselves Rain Tree Crow, have recorded ***Rain Tree Crow*** for Virgin, which debuts at its UK #24 peak, and includes the March UK #62, *Blackwater*. The reunion will only sustain this one album, however, as Karn, Barbieri and Jansen go on to form the rhythm section backing No-Man on a 1992 UK tour, before staying together for Karn's 1993 solo effort ***Bestial Cluster*** and the trio-credited 1994 set ***Beginning To Melt***. Sylvian will make UK #58 on June [20], 1992 with *Heartbeat (Tainai Kaiki II)* and then go on to team with Robert Fripp for ***The First Day***, which will reach UK #21 on July [17] 1993, and the extracted single, *Jean The Birdman* (UK #68 - Aug [28] 1993, preceding their live collaboration ***Damage***, issued in September 1994.

JEAN-MICHEL JARRE

1967

Abandoning his studies at the Conservatoire de Paris under Jeanine Reuff to work in his self-created studio experimenting with synthesizers, having also briefly joined Pierre Schaeffer's Music Research ensemble, Jarre (b. Aug. 24, 1948, Lyons, France), the son of composer Maurice Jarre, and a child prodigy playing piano and guitar from the age of five, makes his first professional recording, the soundtrack to the film "Des Garçons Et Des Filles". Signing to the EMI Pathe label the following year, his premiere disque, ***Cage - Erosmachine***, will be released in France in 1969. Two years later Jarre will make his solo public debut at the Paris Opera, and will become the youngest composer to appear at Palais Garnier. Over the subsequent five years Jarre will write jingles in addition to his film and ballet scores, which will include ***Deserted Palace***, released in France in 1972, and the soundtrack to the Jean Capot film "Les Granges Brûlées" in 1973.

1977

Jan Recently married to actress Charlotte Rampling and newly signed to Francis Dreyfus' label Disques Dreyfus, Jarre begins working on a new album.
Sept *Oxygène Part IV* hits UK #4 and becomes familiar as a popular instrumental for TV programs. ***Oxygène***, with multi-layered synthesizers and sound effects, is released through a Dreyfus license to Polydor Records. It hits UK #2 (Sept [3]) and US #78, ultimately selling over ten million copies worldwide, bringing Jarre's unique orchestral electronic tapestry to a global audience for the first time. The following year, he will compose the score for the Peter Fleischmann film "La Maladie De Hambourg".

1979

Jan *Equinoxe Part 5* makes UK #45.
Feb [10] Antarctic-themed ***Equinoxe***, following a similar musical path to the previous album, reaches UK #11 and will make US #126, going on to sell seven million copies worldwide, confirming Jarre's status as Europe's most popular solo instrumentalist.
July [14] One million spectators attend Jarre's Bastille Day concert at Place de la Concorde, Paris (the first in a decade of mega-concerts Jarre will perform around the globe). It features a complex weave of lasers, synthesizers and fireworks, all controlled by computers, a spectacular event which will hallmark all his future live work.
Sept He begins work on the soundtrack to the Peter Weir movie "Gallipoli".

1981

June [20] Self-composed and produced (as ever), ***Magnetic Fields*** hits UK #6 and will peak at US #98.
Oct Jarre becomes the first western rock artist to perform in China, with five major concerts in Beijing, backed by 35 Chinese musicians. The event, in front of 400,000 spectators, is filmed by Andrew Piddington for a TV special, and is recorded for album release to offset the phenomenal costs involved. Some 15 tons of equipment packed in 30 army trucks, have been shipped to China for the five gigs. The subsequent double album, ***The Concerts In China***, will hit UK #6 on May [15] the following year.

1983

July Jarre has recorded ***Music For Supermarkets***, made expressly to voice his distaste and disregard for the music business, with only one copy of the album being pressed. The album is now auctioned at the Hôtel Drouot, Paris, though the successful bidder is unknown. Jarre destroys the master tapes, but the project is given a public airing on Radio Luxembourg.
Nov ***The Essential Jean-Michel Jarre***, a compilation of his most celebrated works, reaches UK #14, and will be certified platinum in France, Germany, Italy and the UK.

1984

Nov Ethnic opera, ***Zoolook***, with Jarre's familiar instrumentation augmented by foreign-language vocal inserts, and featuring guests Laurie Anderson, Adrian Belew and Marcus Miller, makes UK #47. The following April, the album will win the Grand Prix at the French Acadamie Du Disque.

1986

Apr [5] The latest in his increasingly grand live spectaculars is held in Houston, TX, for the city's 150th anniversary and NASA's 25th anniversary. Jarre plays to an estimated 1.3 million people, while the largest-ever light, laser and firework show plays around him, illuminating Houston's glass skyscrapers. It is the biggest event of its kind, despite his modest star status in the US. "Rendez-Vous Houston" is filmed by video director Bob Giraldi, for worldwide TV showing. The set is inspired by the Challenger space shuttle disaster. Included is *Ron's Song*, which shuttle crew member Ron McNair had intended to play on his saxophone while in space.
Rendez-Vous hits UK #9 and US #52.
Aug *Fourth Rendez-Vous* peaks at UK #65.
Oct [6] With 450 projectors on a 20' podium, Jarre stages another grand event, "Rendez-Vous Lyons - A Concert For The Pope" in his hometown, to honor the visit of Pope John Paul II.

1987

July [18] ***In Concert Lyons/Houston*** reaches UK #18, as "Rendez-Vous Lyons", directed by François Gauthier, receives its premiere.

1988

Sept Jarre plans another stage spectacular, this time in London's Docklands, to coincide with the release of his new album. The local Newham council authority objects - on public safety grounds - and refuses to grant a license to allow the concert to go ahead.
Oct [8-9] His "Destination Docklands" extravaganza proceeds, despite wind, rain, traffic and Newham council, but as two smaller shows instead of one large event. Jarre arranges for Hank Marvin of the Shadows to fly in from Australia to perform.
[15] ***Revolutions***, concerning itself with the conflict between Islam and computers, hits UK #2, behind Chris DeBurgh's ***Flying Colours***, and includes guest guitarist Marvin on the track *London Kid*.
Nov *Revolutions* peaks at UK #52.

1989

Jan *London Kid* also peaks at UK #52.
Oct Reissued *Oxygène IV* makes UK #65.
[14] ***Jarre Live*** reaches UK #16.
Dec The "Concert D'Images" exhibition, chronicling ten years of Jarre's career, opens at the Espace Photographiques des Halles in Paris.

1990

June [23] ***Waiting For Cousteau*** docks at UK #14, inspired by, and dedicated to, fellow Frenchman, sea-faring biologist Jacques Cousteau.
July [14] Jarre performs to another record crowd (estimated at 2.5 million) for a Bastille Day concert in the La Défense area of Paris. Themed "Paris, La Defense: A Town In Concert", the event, based around a specially built pyramid, is documented on film by Mike Mansfield, for subsequent transmission.

1992

Jan [19-21] After a one-hour, 17-track retrospective, ***Images - The Best Of Jean-Michel Jarre***, has debuted at its UK #14 peak on Oct [26] the previous year, Jarre is included on the jury for the first International Visual Music Awards, held during Midem in France.
Dec [1-3] He performs his latest live spectacle at the Lost City in Sun City, Johannesburg, SA.

1995

July [14] Following the 1993 succcess of his latest work ***Chronologie*** (at UK #11, June [5], with *Chronologie Part 4* debuting at its UK #55 peak on June [26]), Jarre performs his latest extravaganza in Paris.

AL JARREAU

1968

Jarreau (b. Mar. 12, 1940, Milwaukee, WI) having sung since the age of four, influenced by his older brothers' interest in jazz and singing, begins improvising vocals, singing along to radio songs. Choosing music over a career in sports (he is a gifted basketball and baseball player) and having received his Master's Degree in Psychology, he works with guitarist Julio Martinez in a Sausalito, CA club. He will spend the next five years developing his

Revival for the duo's recent album ***We Two Are One***).
Dec Now signed to Capitol Records, the Gap Band's last album of the decade, ***Round Trip*** makes US #189.

1996

Feb [3] Following Charlie Wilson's first solo album ***You Turn My Life Around***, released on the Bon Ami label, via MCA in August 1992 and two further, and still incomprehensive collections, ***Best Of The Gap Band*** on Mercury in 1994 and Rhino Records' (US) ***Testimony*** in 1995, the group's first studio set of the '90s, ***Ain't Nothin' But A Party*** has also been issued in '95. Now mostly reduced to performing on US R&B package tours, the latest, teaming the Gap Band with the S.O.S. Band and Kool & the Gang, reaches Atlanta's Civic Center, GA. Intersound Records (US) is set to release Charlie Wilson's sophomore effort, partly produced by Dr. Dre and featuring Brian McKnight, in June.

ART GARFUNKEL

1970

Garfunkel (b. Nov. 5, 1941, Forest Hills, New York, NY) and long-time musical partner Paul Simon, whom he met at school in Queens, New York, at age 11, have established the most successful recording duo since the Everly Brothers. Following the 800-hour recording sessions for the multiplatinum ***Bridge Over Troubled Water***, they split, for professional reasons, but remain friends. While both artists are retained with independent recording contracts for CBS/Columbia Records, Garfunkel's first solo projects are within the film world, initially playing the character of Negley in Mike Nichols' black comedy war movie "Catch 22", which has been filmed in Italy in May 1969. He will follow-up co-starring with Jack Nicholson, opposite Ann-Margret and Candice Bergen, in "Carnal Knowledge" in 1971.

1973

Oct Having spent a characteristically long period of time crafting his music, Garfunkel emerges with his debut solo single, the Jimmy Webb-penned ballad *All I Know*, and ***Angel Clare***, co-produced with ex-Simon & Garfunkel producer Roy Halee and featuring guest musicians J.J. Cale, Jerry Garcia and former colleague Simon, in addition to a studio band comprising Hal Blaine (drums), Larry Knechtel (keyboards), Joe Osborn (bass) and Dean Parks (guitar). The album hits US #5 and reaches UK #14 with its title the name of the romantic hero of Thomas Hardy's novel, **Tess Of The D'Urbervilles**.
Nov [10] *All I Know* hits US #9.

1974

Feb [9] His cover of Van Morrison's *I Shall Sing* makes US #38.
Oct [26] Garfunkel's version of Tim Moore's lost love-themed *Second Avenue* makes US #34.

1975

Oct [19] Garfunkel publicly reunites with Simon for the first time, on NBC-TV's "Saturday Night Live". The pair will continue to team up on an ad-hoc basis for special events (and even tours) over the years, but always as a sideline to their solo careers.
[25] His revival of the Flamingos' 1959 hit, *I Only Have Eyes For You*, enhanced by a Del Newman string arrangement, tops the UK chart.
Nov [8] ***Breakaway***, produced by Richard Perry and enriched with a familiar line-up of top-notch session players, including Stephen Bishop, Andrew Gold, Nicky Hopkins, John Jarvis, Russ Kunkel and Knechtel, hits UK #7. Blessed with an instantly recognisable pure, angelic singing voice, Garfunkel is, however, reliant throughout his career on songs written by others, his selections here including compositions by Bishop, Hal David and Albert Hammond, Bruce Johnston, Stevie Wonder and others.
[29] *I Only Have Eyes For You* reaches US #18, as its parent album ***Breakaway*** hits US #7.
Dec *My Little Town*, a reunion cut written and co-performed by Simon and included on ***Breakaway***, hits US #9.

1976

Jan [31] Title cut, *Breakaway*, written by Scottish songwriters Gallagher & Lyle, makes US #39.
Dec [7] Garfunkel begins recording his third album, at the Muscle Shoals Sound Studios, Muscle Shoals, AL. With the singer self-producing for the first time, the sessions will move on to New York, California, and Dublin, Eire, and last until December the following year.

1978

Mar [18] A cover version of the Sam Cooke standard *(What A) Wonderful World*, recorded in a trio with James Taylor and Paul Simon, reaches US #17.
[24-25] During a 50-city US tour, his first since Simon & Garfunkel days, he performs a pair of sellout dates at Carnegie Hall, New York, one in collaboration with Webb.
Apr [1] ***Watermark***, including the first excerpt *Crying In My Sleep* (released in August 1977), reaches UK #25 and will make US #19. With Garfunkel backed by another stellar list of guest musicians (including Irish folk band the Chieftains, David Crosby, Steve Gadd and Ralph MacDonald), ten of the 12 cuts have been written by songwriting veteran Jimmy Webb (who also played keyboards on the album), with whom Garfunkel is developing a lasting professional relationship.

1979

Feb Garfunkel hosts NBC-TV's "Saturday Night Live", in which Paul Simon also appears.
Apr [14] *Bright Eyes*, written and produced by UK composer Mike Batt and heavily featured in the animated film version of Richard Adams' allegorical novel, **Watership Down**, tops the UK chart for the first of six weeks. Enjoying a 19-week tenure on the UK chart, it becomes a rare UK million seller but will disappear without trace in the US.
May [26] Produced by Louie Shelton, ***Fate For Breakfast***, featuring backing vocals from the Alessi brothers, Bishop, James Gilstrap and Leah Kunkel, among others, hits UK #2 and will make US #67.
July [14] His update of the Skyliners' 1959 hit, *Since I Don't Have You*, makes US #53 and will reach UK #38 on the 28th.
Sept Garfunkel's acting career flourishes with a lead role in the Nicholas Roeg-directed "Bad Timing". While filming the movie in Europe, his girlfriend commits suicide in New York. By year's end he will appear in another film project, "Illusions".

1981

Sept [19] Simon & Garfunkel unite for a concert in New York's Central Park attended by some 400,000 people. Following its success (documented on film, television and video), the duo will undertake a 12-month world tour beginning in the spring of 1982 (although press reports will indicate growing personal friction as the sojourn progresses). The Gallagher & Lyle-penned *A Heart In New York* peaks at US #66.
[26] ***Scissors Cut***, reuniting Garfunkel with Roy Halee (its engineer), Jimmy Webb, who provides three new compositions, including the title cut, and Paul Simon, who provides vocal assistance on *In Cars*, makes UK #51 and will peak at US #113.

1984

Nov A UK-only TV-advertised compilation, ***The Art Garfunkel Album***, climbs to #12, but will remain unreleased in the US.

1986

July Garfunkel is featured in the role of a teacher in the go-go rap movie, "Good To Go".
Dec Having performed a Jimmy Webb seasonal cantata work, "The Animals Christmas", in London and New York, CBS releases ***The Animals Christmas***, a collaboration between Garfunkel, Webb, gospel singer Amy Grant, the London Symphony Orchestra and the King's College School Choir.

1988

Feb *So In Love*, his reworking of the Tymes' 1963 US chart-topper, is released (from a forthcoming album). While promoting it in the UK, Garfunkel is visibly upset by the host's probing questioning of personal issues on the BBC1-TV show "Wogan" and refuses to perform the song.
Mar Variously produced by Garfunkel, Geoff Emerick, Jay Graydon and Steve Gadd, and featuring guest work from Bishop, David Foster, Nicky Hopkins, Kunkel, Hugh McCracken and Kenny Rankin, among a typically top-flight musical aggregation, ***Lefty*** peaks at US #134.
May His cover version of the Percy Sledge standard, *When A Man Loves A Woman*, is released.
Sept Plans are announced by his manager, Ken Greengrass, for Garfunkel to return to live European work, including a scheduled appearance at the Prince's Trust charity concert in London, with James Taylor.

1989

July [12] Disney announces its forthcoming cable TV channel's Shelley Duvall-produced "Mother Goose Rock'n'Rhyme", with a host of music celebrities, including Garfunkel as the Rhymeland bartender.

1990

Jan [17] He sings *Bridge Over Troubled Water* and *The Boxer* with Paul Simon at the musical jam after the fifth annual Rock and Roll Hall of Fame dinner, at which Simon & Garfunkel are inducted, at New York's Waldorf Astoria Hotel.
June Garfunkel performs in Sofia, Bulgaria, at the request of the US State Department, at an outdoor rally for democracy attended by an audience estimated at 1.4 million.

1991

June CBS releases an incomplete 12-track retrospective, ***Garfunkel***.

1992

May While the singer is heard each week as the vocal on the Marvin Hamlisch-penned theme to CBS-TV's "Brooklyn Bridge", his version of the Hoagy Carmichael standard, *Two Sleepy People*, is included on the soundtrack album to the Penny Marshall-directed movie, "A League Of Their Own".

1993

Oct [1] Having reunited with Simon earlier in the year, for a benefit performance in Los Angeles, CA, Garfunkel now begins ten-date residence with his former partner at the Paramount, New York.
[26] ***Up 'Til Now***, a mix of new material, alternate takes and unreleased tracks, is released. (Garfunkel will undertake spring, summer and fall US tour dates the following year.)
see also: SIMON & GARFUNKEL

MARVIN GAYE

1957

Gaye (b. Marvin Pentz Gay Jr., Apr. 2, 1939, Washington, DC), the son of an apostolic minister who has sung and played organ in his father's church, returns to Washington with an honorable disharge from the US air force and joins doo-wop group the Marquees, who record, via an introduction from friend and adviser Bo Diddley, *Hey Little School Girl* (produced by Diddley) and *Baby You're My Only Love* for Okeh. The following year the Marquees are absorbed into the seminal doo-wop group the Moonglows by Harvey Fuqua in Washington, and relocate, as Harvey & the Moonglows, to Chicago, IL

- in 1959 - where they record *Almost Grown* for Chess Records. Fuqua and Gaye leave the Moonglows in 1960 and move to Detroit, MI, where Fuqua sets up the Tri-Phi and Harvey labels. He signs as an artist to Gwen Gordy's Anna label, a subsidiary of her brother Berry Gordy's Motown Records, into which his own labels are then absorbed. Through this connection, Gaye finds work as a session drummer (for the Miracles) and back-up vocalist (for the Marvelettes) at both Anna and Motown.

1961

May Having signed to Motown imprint Tamla as a solo artist and married Berry Gordy's younger sister Anna, who at 37, is 17 years his senior, Gaye records his first solo, *Let Your Conscience Be Your Guide*, and ***The Soulful Moods Of Marvin Gaye***, a collection of ballads and only the second album released by the label.

1962

Oct With "The Motown Revue" (including the Miracles, Mary Wells, the Supremes and Little Stevie Wonder), Gaye begins a two-month US tour.
Dec [1] In a change of pace with new producer William "Mickey" Stevenson, *Stubborn Kind Of Fellow*, with backing vocals by Martha & the Vandellas, is Gaye's US chart debut, at #46 (also making US R&B #8), taken from ***Stubborn Kind Of Fellow***.
[19] Gaye begins a ten-day run at the Apollo Theatre in Harlem, New York, NY, with "The Motown Revue".

1963

Mar [2] Gaye performs at Chubby Checker's "Limbo Party" show at the Cow Palace, San Francisco, CA, with the Four Seasons and the Crystals, among others.
[16] *Hitch Hike*, covered two years later by the Rolling Stones, reaches US #30.
July [20] *Pride And Joy* hits US #10, while the performance set ***Live On Stage*** is released.
Nov [2] *I'm Crazy 'Bout My Baby, the* B-side of the still-climbing *Can I Get A Witness*, peaks at US #77.
Dec [28] *Can I Get A Witness*, again covered by the Rolling Stones at a later date, reaches US #22.

1964

Apr Under Gordy's direction, Gaye is teamed with Mary Wells to record ***Together***.
[18] *You're A Wonderful One* reaches US #15.
June [6] *Once Upon A Time*, a duet with Wells released on the main Motown label, makes US #19, taken from ***Together***, which climbs to US #42.
July *Once Upon A Time* is Gaye's UK chart debut, at #50 for a week.
[4] Its B-side, *What's The Matter With You Baby*, reaches US #17. ***Greatest Hits***, a compilation of Gaye's singles to date, makes US #72.
[25] *Try It Baby* reaches US #15.
Sept Gaye performs on Murray The K's "Rock'n'Roll Extravaganza" at the Brooklyn Fox Theater, New York, with labelmates the Temptations, the Supremes, the Miracles, the Contours and Martha & the Vandellas, plus UK group the Searchers and others.
Oct [17] Martha & the Vandellas' *Dancing In The Street*, co-written by Gaye and Wiiliam Stevenson, hits US #2, behind Manfred Mann's *Do Wah Diddy Diddy*. Gaye is also currently doubling as a session drummer on a number of Motown hits, notably early scores by Little Stevie Wonder.
[28] Gaye participates in US TV's "TAMI Show", with an all-star cast.
Nov [7] *Baby Don't You Do It* (later revived by the Who) reaches US #27.
[17] Gaye arrives in the UK for TV appearances, meeting up with Dionne Warwick after hearing that she has been in a car crash. He appears on "Scene At 6.30" (18th), "Ready Steady, Go!" (20th), "Thank Your Lucky Stars" (28th) and "Saturday Club" (December 5th).
[28] *What Good Am I Without You*, on which Gaye sings with another Motown act, Kim Weston, peaks at US #61.
Dec *How Sweet It Is (To Be Loved By You)* makes UK #49.

1965

Jan [30] *How Sweet It Is (To Be Loved By You)* hits US #6.
Mar ***How Sweet It Is To Be Loved By You*** peaks at US #128.
May [15] *I'll Be Doggone* hits US #8, also becoming Gaye's first US R&B #1 and million seller.
June [28] Gaye takes part in CBS-TV's "It's What's Happening Baby".
July [29] He sings *His Eye Is On The Sparrow* at the funeral of his sister-in-law, Loucye Gordy Wakefield, in Detroit.
Aug [14] *Pretty Little Baby* reaches US #25.
Nov [20] *Ain't That Peculiar* hits US #8, also topping the R&B ranking, and is another million seller. Gaye releases two albums which reveal different sides of his style: ***A Tribute To The Great Nat "King" Cole*** and ***Hello Broadway*** (a collection of show tunes).

1966

Mar Gaye reportedly screen tests for the title role in the film "The Nat King Cole Story".
[26] *One More Heartache* reaches US #29.
July [2] *Take This Heart Of Mine* makes US #44.
Aug ***Moods Of Marvin Gaye***, mostly a singles compilation, climbs to US #118.
Sept [10] *Little Darlin' (I Need You)* makes US #47 and UK #50.
Oct Another compilation album, ***Marvin Gaye Greatest Hits, Vol. 2***, peaks at US #178.

1967

Mar Gaye and Weston's ***Take Two*** collaboration is released.
[4] The extracted *It Takes Two* reaches US #14 and UK #16.
July [15] Gaye's duet with Philadelphia, PA singer Tammi Terrell on *Ain't No Mountain High Enough* reaches US #19. This will be Gaye's most enduring pairing, and he records with Terrell until her tragic death. In the summer, she will collapse into his arms at a Hampden-Sydney College, VA concert, after which doctors diagnose that she has a brain tumor.
Aug [5] *Your Unchanging Love* makes US #33.
Nov [4] Gaye and Terrell's *Your Precious Love* hits US #5, while their further duet album, ***United***, reaches US #69.

1968

Jan [20] The duo enjoys its second US Top 10 success with *If I Could Build My Whole World Around You* which hits US #10 and makes UK #41.
Feb [17] Gaye's solo, *You*, makes US #34.
Mar ***Greatest Hits*** makes UK #40.
[30] *If I Could Build My Whole World Around You*'s B-side, *If This World Were Mine*, peaks at US #68.
May [25] Another Gaye/Terrell duet, *Ain't Nothing Like The Real Thing*, hits US #8 and UK #34.
Sept [14] *You're All I Need To Get By*, with Terrell, hits US #7.
Oct ***You're All I Need*** makes US #60. Gaye sings the national anthem before a game during the World Series between the Detroit Tigers and the St. Louis Cardinals.
Nov [2] Gaye's solo *Chained* reaches US #32, while *You're All I Need To Get By* climbs to UK #19.
[9] Another duet with Terrell, *Keep On Lovin' Me Honey*, makes US #24.
Dec [14] Gaye's first US #1, for the first of seven weeks, and also Motown's longest-running #1, is *I Heard It Through The Grapevine*, a Norman Whitfield/Barrett Strong song, already a million seller for Gladys Knight & the Pips on Motown in 1967. After lying unused for some months after he recorded it, Gaye's dramatically different version becomes the biggest-selling single of Motown's 20-year history and is taken from ***In The Groove***, which reaches US #63.
[28] Gaye performs at the "Miami Pop Festival" in Hallandale, FL, with Chuck Berry, Junior Walker, Fleetwood Mac and others.

1969

Feb *You Ain't Livin' Till You're Lovin'*, a duet with Terrell, climbs to UK #21.
Mar [26] *I Heard It Through The Grapevine* begins a three-week run at UK #1, as it becomes a global smash.
[8] Gaye and Terrell's duet, *Good Lovin' Ain't Easy To Come By*, makes US #30.
June [28] *Too Busy Thinking About My Baby* hits US #4 and is another million seller. (Its B-side, *Wherever I Lay My Hat*, will be a UK #1 hit in 1983 for Paul Young.)
[20] Gaye performs at the "Newport '69" festival at San Fernando Valley State College, Devonshire Downs, CA.
July *Good Lovin' Ain't Easy To Come By* reaches UK #26, while ***M.P.G.*** is Gaye's first US album Top 50 placing, at #33. At the same time, the compilation ***Marvin Gaye And His Girls***, featuring duets with Terrell, Wells and Weston, peaks at US #183.
Sept *Too Busy Thinking About My Baby* hits UK #5.
Oct Another duetted album with Terrell, ***Easy***, makes US #184.
[18] Solo *That's The Way Love Is* hits US #7, taken from ***That's The Way Love Is***, which stops at US #189.
Dec [27] *What You Gave Me*, with Terrell, reaches US #49. Another duet with Terrell, *The Onion Song* hits UK #9, the last chart disc for the duo. It will reach US #50 in May 1970. (Years later it will be confirmed that Valerie Simpson deputized for Terrell on this song, and several others.)

1970

Feb [7] *How Can I Forget* reaches US #41.
Mar [16] Terrell dies, aged 24, in Graduate Hospital, Philadelphia, having undergone eight brain operations in 18 months. Grief-stricken, Gaye retires from the public eye.
[21] *Gonna Give Her All The Love I've Got*, the B-side of *How Can I Forget*, peaks at US #67.
May [16] *California Soul*, penned by Ashford & Simpson, makes US #56.
[23] Top-side *The Onion Song*, also penned by Ashford & Simpson, makes US #50.
June *Abraham, Martin And John*, written by Dick Holler (a US hit for Dion and a Motown release for the Miracles), hits UK #9, as ***Marvin Gaye And Tammi Terrell's Greatest Hits*** reaches US #171 and UK #60.
July [11] *The End Of Our Road* makes US #40.
Dec Compilation ***Marvin Gaye Super Hits*** climbs to US #117.

1971

Jan [17] He sings the American national anthem before Super Bowl V, between the Baltimore Colts and the Miami Dolphins, at the Orange Bowl, Miami, FL.
Apr [10] Gaye, having had fruitless tryouts for the Detroit Lions football team, returns to the spotlight with a creative tour-de-force in a new, more subtle style, the result of his own writing and production, voicing concern about poverty, pollution and the Vietnam War: the peace-themed *What's Going On* hits US #2 for the first of three weeks (behind Three Dog Night's *Joy To The World*) and becomes a million seller.
July ***What's Going On*** hits US #6.
Aug [21] Environment-themed *Mercy Mercy Mercy (The Ecology)*, from the album, hits US #4 and is another million seller.
Nov [6] Third US single from the album, *Inner City Blues (Make Me Wanna Holler)*, hits US #9. In Britain, where his new style has not met with the same positive reaction, both the album and single of ***What's Going On*** fail to chart, although both will be viewed historically by the critics as landmark recordings. *Save The Children* is extracted from the album and reaches UK #41. (A one-off single unconnected to any album, *You're The Man* will make US #50 on June [3] the following year.)

1973

Jan Gaye plays a benefit concert for the Boys Club in Trenchtown, Kingston, Jamaica, sharing the bill with home town hero - Bob Marley.

Feb [3] Following the success of Isaac Hayes and Curtis Mayfield in similar ventures, Gaye has written and performed the soundtrack for a detective movie, "Trouble Man", its title track, *Trouble Man*, hitting US #7, while ***Trouble Man*** (with three vocals and ten instrumental tracks) reaches US #14.

May [1] With Washington, DC proclaimimg "Marvin Gaye Day", he sings *What's Going On* at the city's Cardoza High School auditorium, before performing at the Kennedy Center in the evening.

Sept [8] Sexually-charged *Let's Get It On*, again self-produced (with Ed Townsend), but this time in an earthier R&B style than the ethereal *What's Going On*, tops the US chart for the first of two weeks, is another million seller and makes UK #31.

Oct ***Let's Get It On***, a celebration of sexuality, performed in an appropriately muscular, steamy style, hits US #2.

Nov *Let's Get It On* makes UK #39. Motown has teamed Gaye with his fourth female singing partner, Diana Ross, and their ***Diana & Marvin***, climbs to US #26.

[17] Their duet single, *You're A Special Part Of Me*, reaches US #12.

Dec [15] Gaye's solo, *Come To Get This*, from ***Let's Get It On***, makes US #21.

1974

Jan [4] Gaye makes his first concert appearance in five years, at the Oakland-Alameda County Coliseum, Oakland, CA.

Feb [16] *You Sure Love To Ball*, also from the album, reaches US #50.

Apr *You Are Everything*, a Gaye/Ross revival of the Stylistics' US #9 smash, hits UK #5.

May [4] Another Ross/Gaye duet, *My Mistake (Was To Love You)*, reaches US #19, while the triple-set compilation ***Marvin Gaye Anthology***, containing most of his hit singles to date, reaches US #61.

Aug [17] Gaye/Ross duet, *Don't Knock My Love* makes US #46, while their *Stop Look Listen (To Your Heart)* peaks at UK #25. ***Marvin Gaye Live!***, recorded in concert at Oakland, Gaye's return to the stage after a six-year absence, hits US #8, as ***Diana & Marvin*** hits UK #6 during a 43-week chart tenure.

Nov [2] Gaye's solo, *Distant Lover*, later a favorite stage number, reaches US #28.

1975

Oct [12] He performs at a UNESCO benefit at New York's Radio City Music Hall. (The following day he will be commended at the United Nations by the US Ambassador to Ghana, Shirley Temple Black, and UN Secretary General, Kurt Waldheim.)

Nov [29] Gaye performs a benefit concert for the Reverend Cecil Williams Glide Church in San Francisco, CA.

1976

May [15] Continuing in a similar vein to ***Let's Get It On***, ***I Want You***, co-produced with Leon Ware and T-Boy Ross, reaches UK #4.

June [5] ***I Want You*** hits US #4.

[26] The extracted title track, *I Want You*, reaches US #15.

Aug [18] **Variety** reports that Gaye faces two consecutive five-day prison terms in Los Angeles, CA's County Jail for contempt of court, after failing to pay alimony and child support.

[28] *After The Dance*, also from the album, peaks at US #74.

Sept [26-27] Gaye plays sold-out concerts in London, to rave reviews, at the Royal Albert Hall and the Palladium, both recorded for subsequent album release.

Oct [30] Compilation ***Marvin Gaye's Greatest Hits*** reaches US #44, retitled ***The Best Of Marvin Gaye*** in the UK, where it climbs to #56.

1977

Apr Though they have not lived together for years, Gaye and Anna Gordy are only now divorced.

May [30] Gaye beats Muhammad Ali, Tony Orlando and Angel Cordero at the Muhammad Ali invitational track meet at Cerritos College, CA, aired by CBS-TV.

June [25] Dance-oriented *Got To Give It Up*, another million seller, tops the US chart and hits UK #7. The double live album, ***Marvin Gaye Live At The London Palladium***, which includes *Got To Give It Up* as its only studio track, hits US #3.

Sept He embarks on a US tour in New York, supported by the Average White Band and Luther Vandross.

Oct Gaye marries Janis Hunter in New Orleans, LA.

1978

Jan Marshals break into the Marvin Gaye Recording Studio, closing the building down because of $175,000 in unpaid franchise taxes. (Berry Gordy will pay the bill and save the studio.)

Sept [20] Gaye signs a new seven-year deal with Motown, worth $600,000 for his next two albums and $1 million for each subsequent project.

Oct [7] **Billboard** reports that Gaye has twice filed bankruptcy papers earlier in the year, with unsecured debts of $7 million.

Nov Gaye collapses on stage in Chattanooga, TN, during a current US tour.

1979

Feb Double album, ***Here, My Dear***, a tortured reflection on the break-up of Gaye's marriage to Anna Gordy, with profits from the album going to pay the divorce settlement, hence its title, reaches US #26.

[10] Gaye teams with Stevie Wonder, Diana Ross and Smokey Robinson for *Pops We Love You*, a tribute to Berry Gordy's father on his 90th birthday. It reaches US #59. (Gaye, beset by problems, including an addiction to hard drugs, especially free-base cocaine, and pursued by the US Internal Revenue Service (IRS), for an unpaid tax bill over $2 million, moves to self-imposed exile and seclusion in Maui, HI, where he reportedly tries to commit suicide with a cocaine overdose, and lives in a trailer.)

Apr [2] Gaye duets with Stevie Wonder at the former's 40th birthday party in Hollywood, CA.

Sept [28] He sings the national anthem before a championship fight between Larry Holmes and Ernie Shavers, which is shown on ABC-TV. Earlier, his own fighter, Andy Price, has lost to Sugar Ray Leonard, two minutes and 45 seconds into the first round.

1980

June [13] The UK leg of a European tour begins at Royal Albert Hall.

July [4] He performs during US Independence Day celebrations at the Venue, London.

[7] Gaye takes part in the 14th annual "Montreux Jazz Festival" in Montreux, Switzerland.

[8] His UK tour ends in shambles when, set to perform at a Royal Gala Charity Show at the Lakeside Country Club in Surrey, he finally comes on stage just before midnight, minutes after H.R.H. Princess Margaret has exited, tired of waiting. He will also miss his flight home to the US the following day.

1981

Feb [28] ***In Our Lifetime***, Gaye's last new album for Motown, issued without his approval, makes UK #48 and will reach US #32. He will swear never to record again, stating his intentions in an interview with **Blues & Soul** : "If (Gordy) refuses to release me, then you'll never hear any more music from Marvin Gaye ... I'll never record again". Now increasingly erratic as a performer and suffering from paranoid delusions brought on by years of drug abuse, Gaye divides his time between London and Ostend, Belgium. He severs his contract with Motown, while CBS/Columbia pays Motown $1.5 million for his contract.

June [13] "Heavy Love Affair" UK tour begins, set to end on July 1st.

Aug Reissued ***Diana & Marvin*** climbs to UK #78.

1982

Nov [20] Signed, after lengthy negotiations (involving the IRS, which is due most of Gaye's royalties), to CBS/Columbia, Gaye's *(Sexual) Healing*, a sensual progression from *Let's Get It On*, hits UK #4. He returns to California, where his mother is awaiting an operation for a kidney ailment. (*(Sexual) Healing* has begun a ten-week tenure atop the US R&B chart on the 6th, the first disc to do so since Ray Charles' *I Can't Stop Loving You* in 1962.)

[27] ***Midnight Love***, recorded at Studio Katy, Ohaine, Belgium, with old friend Fuqua and brother-in-law Gordon Banks, hits UK #10 and will reach US #7, achieving million-plus sales. Gaye returns to the US, living in Hollywood and then Palm Springs, CA, and sells his $1 million home to pay off a tax bill.

1983

Jan [17] He wins the Favorite Single, Soul/R&B category at the tenth annual American Music Awards, held at the Shrine Auditorium, Los Angeles.

[29] *(Sexual) Healing* hits US #3 (also selling a million), while *My Love Is Waiting* reaches UK #34.

Feb [13] Gaye sings *The Star Spangled Banner* at the NBA (National Basketball Association) All-Star Game at the Great Western Forum, Inglewood, CA.

[23] He wins his first Grammy for *(Sexual) Healing*, named Best Male Vocal Performance and Best Instrumental Performance at the 25th annual awards, at the Shrine Auditorium. (Gaye also performs the number live.)

Mar [25] Gaye participates in the taping of Motown's 25th anniversary concert at the Civic Auditorium, Pasadena, CA, set to air on NBC-TV on May 16th.

Apr [18] He embarks on his final US tour in San Diego, CA, set to end on August 14th. Despite eight sellout shows at New York's Radio City Music Hall, the series is not a financial success, and an ever-increasing consumption of drugs, along with several death threats over the course of the tour, further accelerate Gaye's decline.

Sept Gaye's version of *I Heard It Through The Grapevine* is used over the credits of the movie "The Big Chill".

Nov ***Every Great Motown Hit Of Marvin Gaye*** reaches US #80. Gaye moves into his parents' house (which he bought for them in the '60s) in Crenshaw, Los Angeles.

Dec TV-advertised compilation, ***Greatest Hits***, reaches UK #13.

1984

Mar Gaye announces more than once to relatives that he intends to take his own life – once having a gun forcibly removed from his grasp.

Apr [1] Gaye, still living at his parents' home at 2101 South Grammercy in Los Angeles and with family and friends concerned over his mental state, is shot by his father during a violent argument. He is pronounced dead at 1:01 p.m. at the California Hospital Medical Center.

[5] Gaye's funeral takes place at the Forest Lawn Cemetery in Los Angeles. The service is attended by Smokey Robinson, Stevie Wonder, Berry Gordy, Harvey Fuqua, Quincy Jones, Ray Parker Jr., and producers Norman Whitfield and Eddie and Brian Holland. Robinson reads the 23rd Psalm and Wonder sings *Lighting Up The Candle*. (The following day he is cremated and his ashes thrown overboard into the sea by Anna and his three children.)

Nov [2] Gaye's father is sentenced to five years for voluntary manslaughter.

1985

Jan [1] Gaye's rendition of *The Star Spangled Banner* on video is the first clip to air on new US AC cable station VH1.

Apr *Missing You* by Diana Ross, a Lionel Richie-penned tribute to the late soul legend, hits US #10.

May *Sanctified Lady* reaches UK #51.

June ***Dream Of A Lifetime***, a compilation of tracks recorded shortly before Gaye's death and unreleased material from his time at Motown, reaches UK #46.

Dec ***Romantically Yours***, drawn from unissued 1979 jazz-oriented big-band sessions, is released.

1986

May ***Motown Remembers Marvin Gaye***, a compilation of previously unreleased 1963-72 material, peaks at US #193. *I Heard It Through The Grapevine* is reissued in the UK after being used in a TV commercial for Levi's jeans, and hits UK #8.

1987

Jan [21] Gaye is posthumously inducted into the Rock and Roll Hall of Fame at the annual dinner at New York's Waldorf Astoria Hotel. (As Gaye's back catalog continues to be re-promoted, ***Love Songs***, combining individual ballad hits of Gaye and Smokey Robinson, a UK-only release, will peak at #69 on Nov [19] the following year, re-charting at UK #39 in November 1990, the same year Gaye receives a star (the 1,920th) on the Hollywood Walk of Fame at 1500 Vine Street (on September 27th).)

1991

May [10] "Through The Grapevine - The Life Of Marvin Gaye" play opens at the Shaw Theatre, Euston, London.
Dec ***Greatest Hits*** will become his second RIAA-certified gold album in December. The following April, his son, Marvin Gaye Jr., begins recording sessions with Lou Rawls' son, Lou Jr., as the duo Nu Breed: The Next Generation, while Gaye's daughter Nona will also make her debut later in the year.

1994

Mar [26] While Motown, in conjunction with Rhino Records, has issued ***Seek And You Shall Find: More Of The Best*** in the US the previous May, a collection of Gaye's rarities, B-sides and lesser-known material, BBC2-TV now airs a special on Gaye in its "Arena" series.
Apr [30] ***The Very Best Of Marvin Gaye*** hits UK #3.
May [14] *Lucky Lucky Me* charts for a week at UK #67.

1995

Apr Beginning a 12-month period of renewed interest in the R&B legend, Motown releases a four-CD boxed set anthology ***The Master (1961-1984)*** , including 13 previously unreleased cuts.
Oct [17] Tribute album ***Inner City Blues : The Music Of Marvin Gaye***, with Gaye covers by Madonna with Massive Attack, Neneh Cherry, Boyz II Men, Stevie Wonder, Lisa Stansfield, Digable Planets, Sounds Of Blackness and Speech, among others, and including a technology-enhanced synchronized duet on *Save The Children* by Bono and Gaye, is released.
[19] MTV-US airs the tie-in documentary "Inner City Blues : The Music Of Marvin Gaye".
Nov [2] Gaye is posthumously inducted into the Soul Train Hall of Fame at the 25th annual Soul Train Awards from the Shrine Auditorium.

1996

Feb [28] He is posthumously honored with the Lifetime Achievement Award during a salute to his work, including a duet of *What's Going On* by Seal and Annie Lennox, at the 38th annual Grammy Awards also held at the Shrine Auditorium.

THE J. GEILS BAND

Peter Wolf (vocals); **J. Geils** (guitar); **Danny Klein** (bass); **Seth Justman** (keyboards and vocals); **Magic Dick** (harmonica); **Stephen Jo Bladd** (drums and vocals)

1967

Geils (b. Jerome Geils, Feb. 20, 1946, New York, NY) and Klein (b. May 13, 1946, New York), having performed in a jug band at Worcester Technical College, Worcester, MA, and having dropped out to go professional, moving to Boston, MA, and switching from jug band music to blues playing in local band the Hallucinations, with Dick (b. Richard Salwitz, May 13, 1945, New London, CT), Wolf (b. Peter Blankfield, Mar. 7, 1946, New York), a part-time art painter and ex-DJ calling himself Woofuh Goofuh on Boston's WBCN with an encyclopaedic knowledge of R&B music, and Bladd (b. July 13, 1942, Boston) now form the J. Geils Blues Band. (Geils, Dick, Klein, Wolf and Bladd will provide the band's nucleus for 16 years.)

1969

Boston University student and organ-player Justman (b. Jan. 27, 1951, Washington, DC) joins and "Blues" is dropped from their name. The group's reputation builds, with the band performing at local club the Catacombs, followed by much success at the Boston Tea Party. Atlantic promotion man Mario Medious sees the band performing on a bill with Dr. John in Boston.
Aug They are asked to take part in the "Woodstock Music & Art Fair", Bethel, NY, but decline, Geils later explaining, "three days in the mud - who needs it?"

1971

Jan The group's debut album on Atlantic, ***J. Geils Band***, an R&B-based affair produced by Dave Crawford and Brad Shapiro and including covers of John Lee Hooker and Otis Rush songs, makes US #195, and garners the Most Promising New Band award from **Rolling Stone** magazine (it will be issued by Edsel Records on compact disc in the UK, in 1989). Critics praise the group as "the best white blues/R&B act since Paul Butterfield".
June [27] The band plays on the final night of the Fillmore East, New York, with headliners the Allman Brothers, the Beach Boys and Mountain.
Dec Their sophomore album, ***The Morning After***, beginning a five-album relationship with producer Bill Szymczyk, reaches US #64.

1972

Jan [15] Their cover of Bobby Womack's *Looking For A Love*, the group's first Hot 100 chart entry, makes US #39.
Apr [1] Four people die, including a 16-year-old hacked to death in his sleeping bag, during the "Mar Y Sol Festival", Puerto Rico, at which the J. Geils Band are appearing.
Nov Critically-revered performance set, ***Live - Full House***, makes US #54, with some reviewers prepared to hail the group as the best live band in America.

1973

Apr The group appears on ABC-TV's "In Concert", but is censored due to the offensive lyrics of a song.
May ***Bloodshot***, again helmed by Szymczyk, hits US #10 and becomes their first gold album, marking $1 million worth of US sales. The extracted reggae-tinged *Give It To Me* will peak at US #30 on June [23], while a second extract, *Make Up Your Mind*, makes US #98 on Sept [8].

1974

Jan Departing from the band's traditional R&B base and moving towards straight rock, ***Ladies Invited*** makes US #51.
Aug [7] Wolf marries actress Faye Dunaway in Beverly Hills, Los Angeles, CA. (The marriage will end in divorce in 1979.)
Oct [19] ***Nightmares ... And Other Tales From The Vinyl Jungle*** enters the US chart, set to reach US #26 during a 22-week run.

1975

Jan [4] Justman and Wolf-penned *Must Of Got Lost* reaches US #12.
Oct With the band now on a familiar release-and-tour pattern of one project per year, ***Hotline***, co-produced by Szymczyk and Allan Blazek, makes US #36.
Nov The group records gigs in Boston and at the Cobo Arena, Detroit, MI, for a second live (double) album, ***Blow Your Face Out***, which will climb to US #40 on June [26], 1976 (the previewing *Where Did Our Love Go* having already reached US #68 on May [1]).

1977

July Having simplified its name to Geils, their self-produced label debut ***Monkey Island*** reaches US #51, their final album for Atlantic.
Aug [20] The extracted *You're The Only One* climbs to US #83.

1979

Feb Reverting to their full moniker and newly signed to EMI America, ***Sanctuary*** reaches US #49 and earns the group its second gold disc, also yielding the US #35 *One Last Kiss* and *Take It Back*, which peaks at US #67 on Apr [7].
May The band performs at London's Hammersmith Odeon, during a UK tour.
June [9] *One Last Kiss* makes UK #74, opening the band's UK chart account.
July Atlantic-issued ***Best Of The J. Geils Band*** peaks at US #129.

1980

Feb ***Love Stinks***, fusing their now familiar brand of rock and pop, reaches US #18 and earns a third gold disc. Taken from it, *Come Back* makes US #32 on Mar [22], while the title cut, *Love Stinks*, peaks at US #38 on May [31].
June [1] The band performs at London's Lyceum Ballroom, as part of an extensive European tour. (During the UK segment, Wolf is injured in a pub fight in London, after being attacked by six thugs. He requires stitches for facial cuts and, when the group appears five days later at the "Pink Pop Festival" in Holland, Wolf performs on crutches.)
July [19] *Just Can't Wait* reaches US #78.

1981

Dec [25] The group gives a Christmas Day concert for a captive audience, at the Norfolk Correctional Center near Boston.

1982

Feb [6] Million-plus-selling jaunty pop-rock hit, *Centerfold*, written by Justman, tops the US chart for the first of six weeks, while its parent album, the Justman-produced ***Freeze Frame*** also hits US #1. With the group now at its commercial zenith, the album will become its only RIAA platinum-certified album.
[27] *Centerfold* becomes the group's biggest UK hit at #3.
Mar During a US tour, the band plays three sellout shows for 46,000 fans, grossing $518,000, at the Boston Garden, Boston.
[13] ***Freeze Frame*** reaches UK #12.
Apr [10] Title track, *Freeze Frame*, co-penned by Justman and Wolf with appropriate shutter-clicking sound effects, hits US #4 and becomes their second million-selling single.
[24] *Freeze Frame* makes UK #27.
May [26] The group begins a major UK tour, supporting the Rolling Stones, at the Capitol Theatre, Aberdeen, Scotland.
July [3] Third extract, *Angel In Blue*, makes US #40 and UK #55.
[25] UK tour ends at Roundhay Park, Leeds, W. Yorks.

1983

Jan Live ***Showtime!***, recorded at the New Pine Knob Theatre, Clarkston, MI, in September 1982, reaches US #23, earning the group a sixth gold disc.
[8] *I Do* climbs to US #24. Amid much acrimony, Wolf leaves for a solo career, with press reports indicating that he has been sacked, although his departure will coincide with a marked decline in future commercial success for the J. Geils Band.
Mar [19] *Land Of A Thousand Dances* reaches US #60.

1984

Aug Wolf's solo ***Lights Out***, co-written and co-produced by Michael Jonzun, reaches US #24, while its title cut, *Lights Out*, reaches US #12 on Sept [8], followed by the US #36 *I Need You Tonight* (Nov

[24]) and a third extract, *Oo-Ee-Diddley-Bop!*, which makes US #61 in May 1985. (Wolf will remain with EMI-America until 1987, when he releases the US #53 ***Come As You Are***, which includes the US #15 title track, *Come As You Are*, and the US #75 *Can't Get Started*, before signing to MCA in 1989.)

Dec [1] The group's *Concealed Weapons* peaks at US #63. Its first post-Wolf album, ***You're Getting Even While I'm Getting Odd*** with Justman handling lead vocals, makes US #80. (*Fright Night*, from the film of the same name, reaching US #91 on Aug [17] the following year, the J. Geils Band's chart career is over.)

1987

June With group members having dissolved into solo projects and session work (Justman has recently guested on Deborah Harry's 1986 release, ***Rockbird***), EMI-America issues a ten-track retrospective, ***Flashback***.

1989

Wolf moves to Nashville, TN, where he lives for six months, working with songwriters Taylor Rhodes and Robert White Johnson to prepare his debut album for MCA, ***Up To No Good***, which will make US #111 on Apr [7] the following year.

1992

May [30] Wolf, still a popular figure in the Boston area, performs at KISS Radio's 13th anniversary concert at the Great Woods Center for the Performing Arts, Mansfield, MA, to benefit the Genesis Fund. He will also surface at a Bruce Springsteen gig on December 14th, joining the Boss for an encore of *In The Midnight Hour* at the Boston Garden.

Oct [23] Geils, now running a shop in Ayer, MA, where he works on vintage race and sports cars, reunites with Dick, premiering their "Magic Dick/J. Geils Blue Time" concert at the Paradise club, Boston, with backing assistance from Jerry Miller (guitar), Rory McLeod (stand-up bass) and Steve Ramsay (drums). The pair are also developing a new harp designed to make the instrument more versatile.

1994

Jan [10] Following the release by Rhino Records (US) in April the previous year of the 38-track double-CD ***The J. Geils Band Anthology : A Houseparty***, the J. Geils Band is inducted into the Boston Garden Hall of Fame during the Boston Bruins/Toronto Maple Leafs hockey game. Geils and Dick, together with Miller, Ramsay and bassist Michael Ward have formed Bluestime, set to issue ***Bluestime*** on the Rounder label (US) in May. Dick will also join B.B. King's backing band for a 52-city US tour beginning in October 1995 while Wolf, having spent considerable time and energy parting ways with MCA, will sign a new solo deal with Reprise Records in 1995, which will release ***Long Line***, his first album in seven years on May 14th 1996.

GENESIS

Phil Collins (vocals, drums); **Tony Banks** (keyboards); **Mike Rutherford** (guitars)

1966

Sept As students at Charterhouse School in Godalming, Surrey, aspiring vocalist Peter Gabriel (b. May 13, 1950, Cobham, Surrey) and Banks (b. Mar. 27, 1950, East Heathly, Sussex) have formed the Garden Wall, with Chris Stewart on drums, in 1965, while fellow pupils Rutherford (b. Oct. 2, 1950, Guildford, Surrey) and guitarist Anthony Phillips (b. Dec. 14, 1951, Putney, London) are members of the Anon, with Rivers Job (bass), Richard MacPhail (vocals) and Rob Tyrell (drums). With the Garden Wall having performed an end-of-term concert in July, and with both bands afflicted by the natural attrition of older members leaving school, the remaining enthusiasts from both combos (Phillips, Rutherford, Gabriel, Banks and Stewart) join forces as the (New) Anon and record a six-track demo tape of songs mostly written by Phillips and Rutherford.

1967

Jan They send the tape to ex-Charterhouse pupil and would-be music impresario Jonathan King at Decca Records, whom they have initially approached when he recently attended Old Boys' Day at Charterhouse. Suitably impressed, King finances further demo sessions and renames the group Genesis.

Dec Still at school, the band inks a one-year contract with Decca Records, and King produces its first label sessions at London's Regent Sound Studio.

1968

May Stewart departs, replaced on drums by John Silver, while *A Winter's Tale* is issued by Decca, following the February release of their debut single, *The Silent Sun*.

Aug King books studio time in the school summer holiday to produce and record a complete Genesis album.

1969

Mar ***From Genesis To Revelation*** is released, with an orchestral track having been added after the sessions, in an attempt to make the group sound more like the Moody Blues. It sells just 650 copies. The band will temporarily go by the name Revelation so as not to be confused with an American band called Genesis. When the US band splits, however, they revert back to their favored moniker.

June *Where The Sour Turns To Sweet* is their last Decca release.

July At the end of their final term at school (though Banks will shortly begin a physics course at Essex University), the group decides to pursue a professional career. Silver leaves and is replaced on drums by John Mayhew, recruited through a classified ad in **Melody Maker**.

Sept Following rehearsals in August, Genesis plays its first paid gig at a cottage in Surrey, owned by Mrs. Balm, Gabriel's former Sunday school teacher, and for which they receive a princely £25 for four sets. (By the end of the year they will have played a series of youth club, social club and college bookings, including a "First Year Apprentice Dance" at Worley Social Club and further gigs at the Cheadle Hulme Youth Club and Twickenham Technical College, where they are paid £50.)

Oct For five months the group lives together in a cottage near Dorking, Surrey, rehearsing its stage act and writing songs for a second album.

1970

Mar Charisma Records owner, Tony Stratton-Smith, having seen the band in concert, signs them to his fledgling label and also becomes its manager.

July After completing the new album, Phillips, reportedly suffering from stage fright, and Mayhew leave. (Phillips will record several guitar-based solo albums in the late '70s.)

Sept Collins (b. Jan. 31, 1951, Chiswick, London), a former child actor (who was in a crowd scene in the Beatles' "A Hard Day's Night", and who has been a member of Hickory, backing singer John Walker on a tour of the North of England, and has been part of Flaming Youth), joins on drums, after auditioning with 14 others in response to a **Melody Maker** ad looking for drummer "sensitive to acoustic music".

Oct The group's sophomore effort, the self-written ***Trespass***, is released in the UK, further developing the band's progressive-rock inclinations.

Dec Mick Barnard, a temporary replacement for Phillips, is in turn replaced by ex-Quiet World member Steve Hackett (b. Feb. 12, 1950, London) on guitar.

1971

Jan Two-part single, *The Knife*, taken from ***Trespass***, is issued, as Genesis begins to build a solid live following in the UK.

June Gabriel breaks his ankle, temporarily halting live work and prompting an early return to studio recording.

Aug Genesis makes its first appearance at the annual "Reading Festival", Reading, Berks.

Nov ***Nursery Cryme***, on which Collins sings his first lead vocal on one track, again fails to chart. Gabriel's growing fondness for using theatrical props and masks attracts the attention of the music press, though these and his between-songs stories are initially included to cover up the band's tuning and to settle Gabriel's own nerves.

1972

Jan The group's first non-UK gig is performed in Brussels, Belgium.

May *Happy The Man* is released.

Aug They make their second appearance at the "Reading Festival".

Oct With the band having steadily built a loyal fan base, principally through its dramatic live work, ***Foxtrot*** dances to UK #12. Its 24-minute track, *Supper's Ready*, becomes a popular live anthem during the group's initial career phase, a period which sees Genesis evolve from its early art-rock roots to a maturing progressive-rock act.

Dec [11] The band makes its US debut at Brandeis University, Waltham, MA.

1973

Feb [4] Now a major-league draw, Genesis begins its maiden headlining tour of the UK at the Hippodrome, Bristol, Avon, to be followed by its first complete US concert trek.

Aug ***Genesis Live***, recorded on stage in Leicester, Leics., and Manchester, Gtr. Manchester, and originally taped for a US radio broadcast, hits UK #9, while the group makes its third consecutive appearance at the "Reading Festival".

Oct ***Selling England By The Pound***, co-produced by Genesis and John Burns and again featuring a Collins lead-vocal track (*More Fool Me*), hits UK #3. Promoter Tony Smith takes over from Tony Stratton-Smith as the band's manager.

Nov Another major UK tour is followed by a second extensive US trek.

1974

Jan Genesis performs five sellout nights at London's Theatre Royal, Drury Lane.

Feb ***Selling England By The Pound*** becomes their first US chart entry, making #70.

Apr [20] *I Know What I Like (In Your Wardrobe)*, an edited extract from the recent album, reaches UK #21.

May [11] Three-year-old ***Nursery Cryme*** steals a belated UK chart showing, at #39.

June ***Genesis Live*** reaches US #105.

Oct London Records in the US releases the 1969 ***From Genesis To Revelation***, which now peaks at #170.

Nov While *Counting Out Time* is released, the group begins its "The Lamb Lies Down" world tour, with an elaborate stage show led by Gabriel's theatrical antics and based around its new double album, ***The Lamb Lies Down On Broadway***. The group will perform the show 102 times.

Dec [7] ***The Lamb Lies Down On Broadway***, the band's most ambitious project to date, recorded on the Island Studios mobile, hits UK #10.

1975

Jan ***The Lamb Lies Down On Broadway*** reaches US #41.

May At the end of the highly successful "Lamb Lies Down" sojourn in St. Etienne, France, Gabriel plays his last show with the band, before leaving the line-up for personal reasons (eventually embarking on a successful solo career, initially remaining on the Charisma label). Exhaustive auditions to find a suitable replacement reveal that the remaining members have most confidence in Collins, who will hereafter fulfill a dual role as drummer and lead vocalist.

Oct The quartet begins recording sessions at the Trident Studios, London.

Nov [1] Hackett's maiden trip, ***Voyage Of The Acolyte***, reaches UK #26.

1976

Mar [13] ***A Trick Of The Tail***, co-produced with David Hentschel, hits UK #3, confounding critics who had written the band off following the departure of its central figure. (During the '80s, Princess Diana will reveal that ***A Trick Of The Tail*** is her favorite rock album.)
[28] Ex-Yes and King Crimson drummer, Bill Bruford, joins for a US tour, freeing Collins to make his debut as lead singer.
May [8] ***Voyage Of The Acolyte*** makes US #191.
[15] ***A Trick Of The Tail*** makes US #31 (this being the first Genesis album to identify individual songwriting credits).
Dec After a series of UK gigs, Bruford returns to session work and is replaced by American session drummer Chester Thompson.

1977

Jan [1] The group begins a three-day stint at the newly re-opened Rainbow Theatre, Finsbury Park, London, where 80,000 ticket applications were received.
[29] ***Wind And Wuthering***, once again co-produced by Hentschel and Genesis and recorded in Holland the previous November hits UK #7.
Feb [1] The London film premiere of "Genesis In Concert" is attended by H.R.H. Princess Anne, while the band prepares for a three-month, 45-city US tour.
Mar [5] Rutherford-penned ballad, *Your Own Special Way*, makes UK #43.
Apr [2] *Your Own Special Way*, their first US chart single, peaks at #62, as ***Wind And Wuthering*** makes its way to US #26.
June [4] Three-track EP, *Spot The Pigeon* (including *Match Of The Day*, *Pigeons* and *Inside Out*), perches at UK #14.
[23] Genesis plays three sold-out nights at London's Earls Court Exhibition Centre.
Oct [7] Hackett announces his intention to leave. (He will release five more UK chart albums for Charisma: ***Please Don't Touch*** (#38 - May [20] 1978), ***Spectral Mornings*** (#22 - June [2] 1979), ***Defector*** (#9 - June [28] 1980), ***Cured*** (#15 - Sept [5] 1981) and ***Highly Strung*** (#16 - Apr 1983), over the next six years, before signing with Lamborghini Records in 1983, which issues ***Bay Of Kings*** and ***Till We Have Faces***, closing his solo chart account in 1984. He will go on to form GTR with Steve Howe (ex-Yes) and Max Bacon in 1986, when the Arista-released ***GTR*** reaches UK #41 and US #11, before to returning to a solo career with ***Momentum*** (1988 on Start), ***Guitar Noir*** (1993 on Permanent) and ***Blues With A Feeling*** (1994 on Virgin, released on Herald Records in the US in 1995.)
Nov [5] Live double album, ***Seconds Out*** (including Hackett), hits UK #4. The remaining members work on a new album as a trio, recording in Holland with Hentschel.

1978

Jan ***Seconds Out*** reaches US #47.
Feb American guitarist Daryl Steurmer replaces Hackett, as a guest for stage-work only.
Mar [29] The band arrives in the US for a 20-date tour, the first leg of the "World Tour 78", which will keep it on the road for most of the year.
Apr [15] The first trio-penned release, *Follow You, Follow Me*, hits UK #7
[22] ***And Then There Were Three***, referencing its dwindling line-up total, appropriately hits UK #3.
May ***And Then There Were Three*** reaches US #14, earning the band its first US gold disc.
[15] The group begins the European leg of its world tour.
June [24] The band shares top billing with Jefferson Starship at the "Knebworth Festival", Knebworth, Herts., with Devo, Tom Petty, the Atlanta Rhythm Section and Roy Harper also on the bill, as *Follow You, Follow Me* makes US #23.
[29] The group is honored with the Silver Clef Award at the annual Nordoff-Robbins Music Therapy lunch, in London.
July Banks-penned *Many Too Many* peaks at UK #43.
Aug [21] BBC1-TV's "Nationwide" airs "Three Dates With Genesis", a behind-the-scenes look at their current tour.
Sept [22] Increasingly active with extra-curricular activities, Collins' jazz/rock fusion offshoot, Brand X, begins a six-date tour at the Bristol Hippodrome, set to end on the 29th at the Hippodrome, Birmingham.
Nov Promotional picture disc, *Pleasure Signal*, by Wildings & Bonus, which features Collins and other Brand X members, is released.

1979

Jan After months of arduous live work, Genesis is still on hold, as Banks and Rutherford record solo albums and Collins tries to resolve his marital difficulties.
Nov Banks' solo debut ***A Curious Feeling***, featuring Chester Thompson and singer Kim Beacon and released by Charisma, charts at UK #21 and US #171.

1980

Mar [29] The band begins a six-month world tour in Vancouver, BC, Canada.
Rutherford's debut solo, ***Smallcreep's Day***, reaches UK #13 and US #163.
Apr [5] ***Duke***, recorded at Abba's Polar Studios in Stockholm, Sweden, and featuring "Albert" on a front-cover drawing by Lionel Koechlin, tops the UK chart, their first #1, as the trio-penned *Turn It On Again* hits UK #8.
May [24] Collins, Banks and Rutherford amuse Los Angeles, CA fans by turning up at the Roxy club box office to personally sell tickets for their forthcoming performance at the venue.
June *Duchess* climbs to UK #46. ***Duke*** reaches US #11 and will earn the band's second US gold disc.
Aug [16] Taken from the album, *Misunderstanding* reaches US #14.
Sept Collins-written *Misunderstanding* makes UK #42.
Oct [4] *Turn It On Again* peaks at US #58.

1981

Feb With Collins' parallel solo career now underway, Genesis launches its own Duke Records label, distributed by Atlantic Records in the US. John Martyn, Leo Kosmin and the band Nine Ways To Win are all signed, but the project is short-lived.
Sept [5] *Abacab* hits UK #9.
[26] Radio-ready ***Abacab***, Genesis' most accessible outing to date, featuring the horn section from Earth, Wind & Fire (and a far cry from the group's ***Trespass/Nursery Cryme*** days), hits UK #1 for the first of two weeks.
Nov ***Abacab*** hits US #7. Their first US Top 10 success, it will also earn the group a platinum disc.
[7] *Keep It Dark* makes UK #33.
[28] Trio-penned *No Reply At All* reaches US #29.

1982

Feb [20] Title track *Abacab*, written by Banks and Collins, reaches US #26.
Mar [20] *Man On The Corner* makes UK #41, set to reach US #40 on May [8].
June [12] Double album, ***Three Sides Live*** (its fourth side comprising unreleased studio cuts from 1979-81), hits UK #2.
[26] Three-track EP, *3 x 3*, featuring *Paperlate*, hits UK #10.
Aug [7] *Paperlate*, featuring Earth, Wind & Fire, makes US #32, as ***Three Sides Live*** hits US #10, earning a gold disc.
Oct [2] The "Six Of The Best" WOMAD benefit concert at Milton Keynes Bowl, Milton Keynes, Bucks., sees the present Genesis line-up reunited - as a one-off - with the festival's founder Gabriel, while Hackett also joins for the encore, *I Know What I Like*. Rutherford's second solo album, ***Acting Very Strange***, climbs to UK #23 and US #145.

1983

May [5] The members of Genesis (including Gabriel and Hackett) are honored with the Outstanding Contribution To British Music award at the 28th annual Ivor Novello Awards lunch, held at the London's Grosvenor House Hotel.
June Banks releases two further solo projects, his soundtrack for Michael Winner's "The Wicked Lady" film (on Atlantic) and his own ***The Fugitive***, which reaches UK #50.
Sept [17] Drum-heavy opus, *Mama*, hits UK #4.
Oct [15] ***Genesis***, co-produced with Hugh Padgham, tops the UK chart. Recorded at the Farm in Surrey, it is an entirely self-contained effort and marks the group's final transition from its grand, overtly theatrical progressive-rock stance of the '70s to an even more popular, relaxed, stripped-down, melody-based contemporary-rock style, not entirely dissimilar to Collins' increasingly successful solo work.
[29] *Mama* peaks at US #73.
Nov ***Genesis*** hits US #9 and is the group's second US million seller.
Dec [17] Piano led *That's All!* reaches UK #16.

1984

Feb *Illegal Alien* lands at UK #46.
[11] Pop ditty *That's All!* hits US #6.
Mar ***Nursery Cryme*** and ***Trespass*** are reissued in the UK, and will chart briefly at #68 (Mar [31]) and #98 (Apr [21]) respectively.
Apr [21] *Illegal Alien* finds a home at US #44.
July [28] Ballad *Taking It All Too Hard* reaches US #50.

1986

Feb Following a one-off Banks EP *Tony Banks* issued the previous September, recorded with Toyah and Jim Diamond (Banks will also release *Short Cut To Nowhere* a collaboration with Fish in October this year), Rutherford's side-band, Mike & the Mechanics, featuring Paul Carrack (ex-Ace, Squeeze and Nick Lowe, among others), Paul Young (ex-Sad Café), Peter Van Hooke and Adrian Lee, now hits US #6 and UK #21 with *Silent Running*, the theme from the film "On Dangerous Ground".
Mar ***Mike & the Mechanics*** reaches UK #78 and will peak at US #26, earning a gold disc.
June [7] A second Mike & the Mechanics single and an airplay favorite, *All I Need Is A Miracle*, hits US #5 and will make UK #53.
[14] Genesis' unabashed pop outing, *Invisible Touch*, reaches UK #15.
[21] ***Invisible Touch***, once again co-produced with Padgham at the Farm studio, enters UK chart at #1.
[28] With solo group projects littering the US chart, ex-Genesis or Genesis-related singles currently account for seven positions on this week's Hot 100.
[19] *Invisible Touch* becomes the band's first US chart-topper, while ***Invisible Touch*** will hit US #3, eventually garnering five platinum discs.
Aug [9] Mike & the Mechanics' *Taken In* reaches US #32.
Sept [15] Genesis performs live at the third annual MTV Video Music Awards, broadcast simultaneously from the Universal Amphitheatre, Universal City, CA, and the Palladium, New York, NY.
[24-27] During its current world tour, the group sells out the Spectrum, Philadelphia, PA, grossing over $1.2 million. (During a stint at New York's Madison Square Garden in October, they are awarded the venue's Gold Ticket for playing to over 100,000 fans.)
Oct [4] Ballad, *In Too Deep*, featured in the movie "Mona Lisa", reaches UK #19.
[11] Further love song, *Throwing It All Away*, hits US #4.
Nov Collection of recent video promos released as "Visible Touch" tops the UK Music Video chart.

1987

Jan [3] *Land Of Confusion*, benefitting from a popular video created by ITV puppet masters Fluck and Law (from the "Spitting Image" series), reaches UK #14.
[31] *Land Of Confusion* hits US #4.
Mar [28] The fourth UK single taken from ***Invisible Touch***, *Tonight, Tonight, Tonight*, reaches UK #18.
Apr [4] *Tonight, Tonight, Tonight*, through its exposure in a TV beer commercial, hits US #3.
June [11] *Throwing It All Away* reaches UK #22.
[27] Ballad *In Too Deep* hits US #3, as the group

completes its lengthy "Invisible Touch" tour, which, together with the album, has proved to be the band's most commercially successful project to date (the US leg of the live sojourn will gross $15,500,000 alone).
July A round-up of Banks' solo highlights, ***Soundtracks*** is released by Charisma.

1988

Mar [2] "Land Of Confusion" wins the Best Concept Music Video at the 30th annual Grammy Awards.
May [14] As longtime label residents, Genesis participates in Atlantic Records' 40th anniversary bash at Madison Square Garden, New York, although each band member is currently occupied with solo projects during what has now become a ritual hiatus period in between Genesis recordings.
Dec Virgin Video releases the comprehensive Genesis visual sets, "Genesis 1" and "Genesis 2", also twinned as a boxed set, while the "Invisible Touch Tour" will be issued the following May.

1989

Jan [28] Mike & the Mechanics' *The Living Years*, with a poignant father/son relationship lyric co-authored by Rutherford and B.A. Robertson, hits UK #2 and will top the US chart on Mar [25].
Feb [4] Mike & the Mechanics' ***The Living Years*** hits UK #2.
July [18-19] Mike & the Mechanics take part in the seventh annual "Prince's Trust Rock Gala" at the National Exhibition Centre, Birmingham, W. Midlands.
[28] Mike & the Mechanics' 23-date US tour begins at Lake Compounce, Bristol, CT, set to end August 27th at Pacific Amphitheatre, Costa Mesa, CA.
Aug Banks' new side project Bankstatement releases its only album ***Bankstatement*** on Virgin.

1990

Apr The RIAA certifies ***The Lamb Lies Down On Broadway***, ***A Trick Of The Tail***, ***Wind And Wuthering*** and ***Selling England By The Pound*** gold, finally acknowledging sales in excess of 500,000 each in the US.
June [30] Phil Collins and Genesis perform on a UK-only bill, with Pink Floyd, Robert Plant, Paul McCartney, Cliff Richard and the Shadows, Status Quo, Eric Clapton, Elton John, Mark Knopfler and Tears For Fears, all previous Silver Clef winners, at Knebworth Park, in aid of the Nordoff-Robbins Music Therapy Centre.

1991

Mar The third Mike & the Mechanics album, ***Word Of Mouth*** (UK #11 and US #107 - Apr [27]), and the extracted title track (UK #13, US #78), emerge. *A Time And Place*, from the album, will also make UK #58 in June.
[31] BBC2-TV airs the "Genesis - The Story So Far" documentary.
June [10] Banks' solo album, ***Still***, featuring ex-Marillion vocalist Fish on *Angel Face* and *Another Murder Of A Day*, and contributions from Nik Kershaw and Duran Duran's Andy Taylor, is released by Virgin, as Genesis regroups to begin recording a new album at their own Fisher Lane Farm Studios.
Sept [7] Rutherford takes part in a polo benefit for the Rhino Wildlife Trust, at the Guards Polo Club Autumn Festival, Smith's Lawn, Windsor, Berks.
Nov [9] Parental conflict-themed *No Son Of Mine* hits UK #6.
[23] Its parent album, ***We Can't Dance***, the group's first release in five years, co-produced with Nick Davis (who collaborated on both Rutherford and Banks' recent solo projects), debuts at UK #1.
[30] ***We Can't Dance*** debuts at its US #4 peak.
Dec [3] Genesis performs at the second annual Billboard Music Awards, held at the Barker Hangar, Santa Monica Airport, Santa Monica, CA.

1992

Jan [18] *No Son Of Mine* reaches US #12.
[25] *I Can't Dance*, spurred by a fittingly satirical video clip, hits UK #7.
Feb [22] Mike & the Mechanics' *Everybody Gets A Second Chance* makes UK #56.
Apr RIAA certifies sales of five million for ***Invisible Touch*** in the US.
[25] Airy ballad, *Hold On My Heart*, reaches UK #16.
May [8] 50-city "We Can't Dance" world tour bows in Dallas, TX, a high-tech, state-of-the-art, video-enhanced spectacle also featuring a 200' long stage, three Sony jumbotron video screens and twin 80' sound towers. The 26-date North American leg of the tour will gross $30,368,945 and will be seen by 1,115,238 people.
June [13] ABC-TV airs the "Genesis Opening Night" rockumentary special.
[27] *Hold On My Heart* reaches US #12.
July [1] The European leg of the tour, sponsored by Volkswagen, begins in Paris, France. (Concerts in Gothenburg and Copenhagen have to be cancelled, when the group's equipment trucks are caught up in the current French farmers' dispute.)
[10-11, 13] Their three sellout performances at the Niedersachsenstadion, Hannover, Germany, prove to be the highest-grossing concerts worldwide in 1992, with 174,984 people paying $6,515,992 to see the band.
Aug [2] The European leg of the tour, ends at the "Knebworth Festival", with Lisa Stansfield and Runrig supporting the bill-topping Genesis.
[8] Televangelist-satirizing *Jesus He Knows Me* reaches UK #20.
[22] ***We Can't Dance*** waltzes back to re-hit UK #1.
Sept [12] *Jesus He Knows Me* reaches US #23.
Nov [2-8] Genesis ends a further 13-date UK concert trek with a week-long stint at London's Earls Court.
[16] The group takes part in the annual "Prince's Trust" concert at London's Royal Albert Hall.
[21] *Invisible Touch (Live)* debuts at its UK #7 peak.
[28] The first half a double live set recorded on their recent world tour, ***The Way We Walk Volume One: The Shorts***, enters at UK #3 peak.
Dec [9] Genesis collects the Number One Boxscore Concert trophy at the third annual **Billboard** Music Awards, held at the Universal Amphitheatre, an event hosted by Collins, who works double duty as the band also opens the show with a live performance of *I Can't Dance* (which includes the front man's visual impersonation of Michael Jackson's crotch-grabbing dance style).
[26] ***The Way We Walk Volume One: The Shorts*** halts at US #35.

1993

Jan [23] *Never A Time* reaches US #21, as ***The Way We Walk Volume Two: The Longs*** debuts at UK #1.
[25] Genesis wins the Favorite Band, Pop Rock category at the 20th annual American Music Awards, held at the Shrine Auditorium.
Feb [20] *Tell Me Why* bows at its UK #40 peak.
[27] ***The Way We Walk Volume Two: The Longs*** debuts at its US #20 peak.

1994

Oct [14] *Hold On My Heart* is honored at the 14th ASCAP dinner at London's Park Lane Hotel.
[23] *Never A Time* is named one of the Most Performed Songs Of The Year at the annual BMI Awards ceremony at London's Dorchester Hotel.
[26] *In Too Deep* and *The Living Years* are both cited for two million US broadcast performances.

1995

Mar [18] Mike & the Mechanics' ***Beggar On A Beach Of Gold***, continuing his association with writer B.A. Robertson and vocalists Young and Carrack, hits UK #9 in its week of entry, and includes the extracted singles - *Over My Shoulder* (Mar [11], UK #12), *A Beggar On A Beach Of Gold* (June [24, UK #33) and *Another Cup Of Coffee* (Sept [2], UK #65).

1996

Jan Interested in its potential use for stage lighting, Rutherford and Banks invest in Cambridge Technology Display, a company established to market "flat-tube" technology developed by Cambridge University scientists to create light-emitting polymers.
Mar [16] Mike & the Mechanics' ***Hits*** debuts at its UK #3 peak.
[28] And then there were two: in an amicable parting, Collins publicly announces his departure from the band saying "For me now it will be music for movies, some jazz projects, and of course my solo career. I wish the guys all the very best in the future. We remain the best of friends." Rutherford and Banks are left with the unenviable task of finding his replacement before beginning work on the group's 20th album.
see also: **Phil COLLINS, Peter GABRIEL**

GERRY & THE PACEMAKERS

Gerry Marsden (vocals, lead guitar);
Les Chadwick (bass); **Les Maguire** (piano, saxophone); **Freddie Marsden** (drums)

1959

The group is formed by Gerry Marsden (b. Gerard Marsden, Sept. 24, 1942, Liverpool, Lancs.), who has joined his first band, skiffle group the Red Mountain Boys, at the age of 14, with his brother Freddie Marsden (b. Nov. 23, 1940, Liverpool) and Chadwick (b. John Leslie Chadwick, May 11, 1943, Liverpool), and pianist Arthur McMahon, initially as a part-time skiffle and rock outfit. Their original name is the Mars Bars (a naive ploy to seek sponsorship from the Mars confectionery maker, an idea which backfires when the company insists it change its name). The Pacemakers is agreed upon as an alternative, and the group makes its first public appearance at Holyoak Hall, Liverpool.

1960

May [3] The band plays at the Liverpool Stadium, on a bill topped by Gene Vincent, who, only two weeks earlier, was seriously injured in the car crash, which took Eddie Cochran's life.
June [6] They appear with the (Silver) Beatles, on the first of many engagements, at the Grosvenor Ballroom, Liscard, Lancs.
Dec Offered a four-month contract to play in Hamburg, W. Germany, the members give up their day jobs (Gerry is a tea-chest maker) to become full-time musicians.

1961

May McMahon leaves, and Chadwick switches from lead to bass guitar. Maguire (b. Dec. 27, 1941, Wallasey, Lancs.), ex-the Undertakers, joins on piano and occasional saxophone, rounding off the group's line-up, which (with a repertoire of 300 songs acquired, prior to and, during the German trip) is now wholly rock/R&B based.
Oct [19] The band links with the Beatles for a one-off performance as the combined "The Beatmakers", performing at Litherland Town Hall, Liverpool. (The two groups will constantly play alongside each other on a string of engagements at the Cavern club and other Liverpool venues throughout 1961 and 1962.)

1962

Jan [4] **Mersey Beat** publishes its first group popularity poll. Gerry & the Pacemakers come second to the clear winners, the Beatles.
Feb [20] Gerry & the Pacemakers participate in a "Rock'n'Trad Spectacular" with the Beatles, and Rory Storm & the Hurricanes, at the Floral Hall, Southport, Lancs.
June Brian Epstein, already overseeing the Beatles, signs Gerry & the Pacemakers to a management contract.
Dec EMI's George Martin is invited to see the group playing at the Majestic Ballroom, Birkenhead, Lancs. and, noticeably impressed by their inclusion of *How Do You Do It?*, a song intended for Adam Faith and subsequently recorded by the Beatles under Martin's supervision, signs them to the Columbia label.

1963

Jan [22] The first recording session in London produces Gerry and Chadwick's own *Away From You*, and versions of the standard *Pretend* (saved for an album), and Mitch Murray's *How Do You Do It*.
Mar [7] The group participates in the "Mersey Beat Showcase" concert, with the Beatles, Billy J. Kramer & the Dakotas and the Big Three at the Co-operative House, Nottingham, Notts.
[14] Gerry is fined £60 at Uxbridge Magistrates Court, for attempting to evade customs duty on a guitar bought in Hamburg when arriving at Heathrow Airport on December 1st, 1962.
[16] The group appears on ITV's "Thank Your Lucky Stars".
Apr [13] *How Do You Do It* hits UK #1 where it will stay for three weeks, selling half a million copies, as Gerry & the Pacemakers become the first Liverpool group to top the **Record Retailer** charts.
May [8] The group embarks on 21-date package tour with the Beatles, David Macbeth, Louise Cordet and special guest star Roy Orbison, at the Adelphi Cinema, Slough, Bucks., set to end on June 9th at the King George's Hall, Blackburn, Lancs.
June [16] They perform a one-off date at the Odeon Cinema, Romford, Essex, with the Beatles and Billy J. Kramer & the Dakotas, who are currently #1 and #3 in the UK chart with *From Me To You* and *Do You Want To Know A Secret*, with the Pacemakers at #2.
[22] *I Like It*, this time custom-written for the group by Murray, begins a four-week stay at UK #1.
[29] ITV airs "Lucky Stars (Summer Spin)", a Mersey Beat special, with Gerry & the Pacemakers, the Beatles, Billy J. Kramer & the Dakotas, the Fourmost, the Searchers and others.
Oct [30] The group appears on ITV's "They've Sold A Million".
Nov [2] Having recorded the custom-penned Lennon/McCartney composition *Hello Little Girl* (subsequently a hit for the Fourmost) but rejected as a single by Gerry, an anthemic revival of Rodgers and Hammerstein's *You'll Never Walk Alone* (from the musical "Carousel") hits UK #1, remaining at the top for four weeks, and proves to be their biggest UK seller (776,000 copies). (The record will become synonmous with both the city of Liverpool and its football team, whose fans subsequently adopt the song as its defining tribal chant.) It also gives the group the distinction of having hit UK #1 with their first three singles. (This record will stand for 21 years, until equalled in 1984 by another Liverpool combo, Frankie Goes To Hollywood. The B-side of Frankie's first chart-topper *Relax* will, coincidentally, be a revival of Gerry's *Ferry 'Cross The Mersey*.)
How Do You Like It?, featuring *You'll Never Walk Alone*, hits UK #2.
Dec [13] The group tops the bill on ITV's "Sunday Night At The London Palladium" (although this particular show comes from the Prince of Wales Theatre).
[23] The band opens in "Babes In The Wood" pantomime at the Gaumont Cinema, Hanley, Staffs.

1964

Feb [8] Written by Gerry, *I'm The One* hits UK #2, held from the top for two weeks by the Searchers' *Needles And Pins*, as they begin a 21-date twice-nightly package tour, with the Fourmost, Ben E. King, Jimmy Tarbuck, Tommy Quickly and others, at the Odeon Cinema, Nottingham, set to close on March 1st at the De Montfort Hall, Leicester, Leics.
Mar [7] The premiere issue of the **Gerry & The Pacemakers Monthly**, published from the same source as the **Beatles Monthly**, goes on sale.
Apr [4] The group begins a tour of Australia and New Zealand, with Brian Poole & the Tremeloes.
May [3] They make their US TV debut on CBS-TV's "The Ed Sullivan Show", singing *Don't Let The Sun Catch You Crying*.
[6] Gerry & the Pacemakers make their North American concert debut at the Eaton Auditorium, Toronto, ON, Canada.
[9] *Don't Let The Sun Catch You Crying*, a ballad written by Gerry, hits UK #6, the group's first single not to make UK top five. (Marsden will be successfully sued for breach of copyright, related to an earlier song with the same title by Ray Charles.)
June [2] The band begins work on its own feature film, with Gerry writing a batch of new songs for the soundtrack.
July [4] *Don't Let The Sun Catch You Crying*, released on the Laurie label, hits US #4, their first and biggest US hit.
[18] *I'm The One*, having failed earlier in the US, now makes US #82.
Sept [5] *How Do You Do It*, issued in the US to follow up the Top 10 success, hits #9. US ***Don't Let The Sun Catch You Crying*** (compiled from UK singles and album tracks) reaches US #29.
[19] *It's Gonna Be Alright*, an uptempo trailer of music from their movie, makes UK #24 - a chart disaster by the group's previous standards, but also a sign that pop music in the UK is rapidly developing away from the Pacemakers' pure Merseybeat style.
Oct [28-29] The band takes part in the "TAMI Show", also featuring the Beach Boys, Chuck Berry, the Rolling Stones and others at the Civic Auditorium, Santa Monica, CA.
Nov [7] *I Like It*, a late issue in US, reaches #17, as the group embarks on a 26-date, twice-nightly UK tour, with Gene Pitney, the Kinks, Marianne Faithfull and others, at the Granada Cinema, Walthamstow, London. The tour will end on December 6th at the Futurist, Scarborough, N. Yorks.
Dec [6] "Ferry 'Cross The Mersey", written by Tony Warren, creator of ITV's "Coronation Street", premieres at the New Victoria Cinema, London. The movie stars Gerry & the Pacemakers as a facsimile of themselves, rising to success in a beat contest. Cilla Black, the Fourmost and some lesser-known Liverpool acts make cameo appearances in the largely location-shot movie.
[26] The group opens in Brian Epstein's presentation "Gerry's Christmas Cracker" at the Odeon Cinema, Liverpool, with the Hollies, Tommy Quickly, the Fourmost and Cliff Bennett & the Rebel Rousers.
Gerry And The Pacemakers' Second Album, another compilation of UK singles and album tracks, peaks at US #129.

1965

Jan [23] Ballad title song, *Ferry 'Cross The Mersey*, written by Gerry, returns the group to the UK Top 10, at #8.
[24] "Ferry 'Cross The Mersey" is screened at the Liverpool Odeon, in aid of the Variety Club of Great Britain.
[30] *I'll Be There*, the group's revival of the Bobby Darin ballad, reaches US #14.
Feb Soundtrack album ***Ferry 'Cross The Mersey***, also featuring material from other Merseyside acts Cilla Black and the Fourmost, makes UK #19.
Mar [20] As the movie is released 'cross the Atlantic, *Ferry 'Cross The Mersey* gives the group its final US Top 10 success (as it already has in the UK), hitting #6. The soundtrack album reaches US #13, while the simultaneously-released US-only ***I'll Be There*** (pairing the ballad hit with revived '50s rock numbers) makes US #120.
Apr [17] The band begins a ten-day stint in Murray The K's show at the Brooklyn Fox Theater, New York, at the start of a major US tour. *I'll Be There* reaches UK #15.
May [8] *It's Gonna Be Alright* peaks at US #23.
July [3] *You'll Never Walk Alone*, finally released as a US single, stops at #48. Compilation selection ***Gerry And The Pacemakers' Greatest Hits***, not released in their home country, makes US #44.
Sept [11] *Give All Your Love To Me*, a ballad recorded at Capitol Records' New York studios while the group is touring and again unreleased in the UK, peaks at US #68.
[21] The band participates in the "Pop From Britain" concert at London's Royal Festival Hall.
Oct [2] The group appears on ABC-TV's "Shindig", singing *Ferry 'Cross The Mersey*.
[11] Gerry marries former fan club secretary Pauline Behan at St. Mary's Church, Woolton, Lancs. (The Pacemakers, whose members are already married, all attend the wedding.)
Nov [1] The group begins a week-long cabaret stint at Stockton Fiesta, followed by a further seven-day engagement at Mr. Smith's in Manchester.
Dec [3] Band plays the first of three days at the Star-Club, Hamburg, their first appearance at the venue since 1961.
[4] Their treatment of the '50s ballad *Walk Hand In Hand*, an attempt to recapture the spirit of *You'll Never Walk Alone*, reaches UK #29 and is the group's final UK chart entry.

1966

Apr [16] *La La La*, an *I Like It*-styled beater and the group's first non-charting UK single, peaks at US #90.
June [10] The band opens in "The Big Star Show Of 1966" summer season at the Royal Aquarium, Great Yarmouth, Norfolk.
Aug [7] TAMI show movie "Gather No Moss", in which the group features, has its UK premiere at Birmingham's Futurist Cinema.
Oct [22] *Girl On A Swing*, originally an album track by the Happenings, reaches US #28.

1967

Mar [27] The group is the guest attraction on a bill, with Fats Domino (making his UK debut) and the Bee Gees, for one week at London's Saville Theatre.
May [8] Gerry & the Pacemakers announce their intention to split in the next few months, recognizing they can no longer keep pace with the rapidly changing UK rock scene. Gerry will continue as a solo vocalist.
June [2] Marsden's first solo single, *Please Let Them Be*, is released on CBS, but fails to chart, a fate which will be shared by further solo releases on CBS, NEMS, Decca, Phoenix, DJM and Pentagon over the next ten years, despite his success in other areas of showbusiness.
July [7-13] Marsden heads a UK team, also featuring Dodie West, Roger Whittaker, Lois Lane and Oscar, at the annual "Knokke-Le-Zoute Song Contest" in Belgium. They beat Holland to win for the second year running.

1968

Feb [19] Gerry takes over the leading role from Joe Brown in the musical "Charlie Girl" on London's West End stage. (He will stay with the show for 3½ years, and have further stage success in "Pull Both Ends", also securing a regular slot on UK children's TV on the "Sooty And Sweep Show" in 1970.)

1973

June [28] Gerry assembles a new Pacemakers line-up (ex-Merseybeat Billy Kinsley on bass, Chris Foley on piano and Pete Block on drums) for the "British Re-Invasion Show", at New York, NY's Madison Square Garden, playing with the similarly re-united Searchers, Herman's Hermits and Wayne Fontana & the Mindbenders.

1975

Nov With a further version of the Pacemakers (Baz Coleman on keyboards, Billy Wheeler on bass and ex-Pickettywitch Keith Hall on drums), Gerry undertakes a successful eight-week nostalgia tour of Australia. (He will subsequently divide his time between solo live and TV work, and nostalgia tours and hit re-recordings with variable Pacemaker line-ups. ***20 Year Anniversary***, containing re-recorded versions of old group favorites, will appear in UK on the DEB label in 1983.)

1985

June [15] With *You'll Never Walk Alone* having been adopted as a crowd anthem by Gerry's own favorite soccer team, Liverpool FC, soon after his 1963 hit, he has been asked to perform the song on several special occasions such as the memorial service in Liverpool Cathedral following the death of Bill Shankly,

Liverpool's legendary former manager. When a fire at the ground of Bradford City Football Club, W. Yorks., kills over 50 spectators, a multi-artist recording of the song, credited as the Crowd, is arranged by 10cc's Graham Gouldman, with money from its sales contributing to a fund for the victims' families. Gerry takes the lead vocal in the hymnal style of his original recording, and the record now tops the UK chart - making him the first-ever act to hit #1 with two different versions of the same song.

1989

May [20] A collaboration, teaming Marsden, Paul McCartney, the Christians, Holly Johnson and Stock Aitken & Waterman, enters the UK chart at #1 with *Ferry 'Cross The Mersey*, released to raise money for the Hillsborough Football ground disaster fund, after 95 fans have died at the start of a Liverpool semi-final F.A. Cup game.

1990

July [13] While See For Miles Records have released ***The EP Collection*** in 1987, UK retrospective specialist label, Connoisseur, issues the comprehensive archive album, ***The Collection***. (A US compilation, ***The Best Of Gerry & The Pacemakers - The Definitive Collection*** will emerge as part of EMI's Legend Of Rock'n'Roll series in 1991.)

1991

Dec [2] With Gerry and his latest set of Pacemakers still a significant draw on the nostalgia circuit, *Ferry 'Cross The Mersey* is now honored for achieving one million broadcast performances, at the annual BMI Awards, held at London's Dorchester Hotel.

ANDY GIBB

1975

The youngest of four boys (his brothers Barry, Maurice and Robin are already a show business fixture as the Bee Gees), Gibb (b. Mar. 5, 1958, Chorlton-Cum-Hardy, Lancs.) has returned to Australia, to where his family initially emigrated six months after his birth in 1958, subsequently relocating to Ibiza in 1973 and then to the Isle of Man the following year, where he now secures a major hit with *Words And Music* on the ATA label. Having begun his singing apprenticeship at local clubs while living in Ibiza, he will support the Bay City Rollers on an Australian tour and open for the Sweet in Sydney, New South Wales, by year's end.

1977

Mar Gibb signs to Robert Stigwood's RSO label, the recording home of the Bee Gees, who are currently completing sessions for the soundtrack to "Saturday Night Fever".
July [9] *I Just Want To Be Your Everything*, written by brother Barry during an intensive two-day session at Stigwood's Bermuda estate, reaches UK #26.
[30] His label debut, *I Just Want To Be Your Everything*, tops the US chart, after a 14-week climb.
Flowing Rivers makes US #19. Highlighted by Gibb's distinctive vocal, a minor variation on the Gibb brothers' unique falsetto style, the predominantly self-written pop project has been produced by Barry, together with regular Bee Gees' cohorts, Albhy Galuten and Karl Richardson.

1978

Mar [3] *(Love Is) Thicker Than Water*, co-written with Barry and featuring Joe Walsh on guitar, replaces the Bee Gees' *Stayin' Alive* at US #1, but is itself replaced - a week later - by his older brothers' *Night Fever*.
June [17] Gibb becomes the first artist to hit US #1 with his first three releases, when *Shadow Dancing*, penned by all four Gibbs, tops the chart.
Shadow Dancing peaks at UK #42, and ***Shadow Dancing***, recorded at the Bee Gees' creative nerve centre, Criteria Studios, Miami, FL, and featuring Eagles guitarist Don Felder with the Gibbs' regular rhythm section of George Bitzer (keyboards), Harold Cowart (bass), Joey Murcia and Tim Renwick (guitars) and Ron "Tubby" Ziegler (drums), hits US #7 and UK #15.
July Gibb is joined on stage by the Bee Gees at a concert in Miami, the first time all four brothers have appeared live together.
Sept [23] Featuring a, by now, trademark Barry Gibb and Galuten light, pop string arrangement, *An Everlasting Love* hits UK #10 and US #5.
Dec [16] Ballad, *(Our Love) Don't Throw It All Away*, co-written by Barry and Bee Gees' sideman Blue Weaver, hits US #9, and will peak at UK #32 the following February.

1980

Mar [8] *Desire* hits US #4, while its parent album, ***After Dark***, begins climbing to US #21 and includes a pair of duets with Olivia Newton-John. With Gibb settled into a familiar recording routine, the album has been co-produced by the ever-present Barry (who also wrote much of the material) with Galuten and Richardson, and features the usual crew of Criteria Studio musicians, now fully augmented by ex-Amen Corner members, Weaver (keyboards) and Dennis Bryon (drums).
May [24] Airy ballad, *I Can't Help It*, with Newton-John, reaches US #12.
Dec ***Andy Gibb's Greatest Hits***, with three new cuts, including a duet with Pat Arnold, makes US #46.

1981

Jan [24] *Time Is Time*, co-penned by Andy and Barry, clocks in at US #15.
Apr [11] *Me (Without You)* makes US #40.
June [10] Gibb opens as Frederic in Gilbert and Sullivan's "The Pirates Of Penzance" at Los Angeles, CA's Ahmanson Theater.
Sept [12] *All I Have To Do Is Dream*, a duet by Gibb and his current flame, "Dallas" TV star Victoria Principal, makes US #51.

1982

Gibb is fired as TV host on the US show "Solid Gold", for missing several tapings. He will be replaced by Rex Smith, who originally played the role of Frederic in the New York production of "The Pirates Of Penzance". He is also dismissed from the Broadway production of "Joseph And The Amazing Technicolor Dreamcoat", having already starred in the Los Angeles and Canadian productions, for skipping 12 performances in a month.

1985

Gibb is treated for drug dependency at the Betty Ford Clinic in California, following a well-publicized addiction to cocaine, which he allegedly blames on the break-up of his relationship with Ms. Principal.

1988

Jan Having filed for bankruptcy in Miami the previous year claiming less than $50,000 in assets and debts of more than of $1 million, Gibb signs to Island Records to record a new album in the UK.
Mar [7] While working on the project, Gibb is admitted to the John Radcliffe Hospital, Oxford, Oxon., with severe stomach pains.
[10] Gibb dies of heart failure, five days after his 30th birthday. (A 12-song retrospective released by Polydor, ***Andy Gibb***, will bring his hits to compact disc in 1991, including one previously unreleased cut, *Man On Fire*, whose vocal was recorded just prior to Gibb's death, its rhythm track added by his brothers three years later.)

DEBBIE GIBSON

1983

Gibson (b. Aug. 31, 1970, Long Island, NY) has been writing songs since childhood (including *Make Sure You Know Your Classroom* at age six) and learning piano (with Morton Estrin, who taught Billy Joel) from age five, when she plays the littlest elf in a production of "The Elves And The Shoemaker" near her Merrick, NY home. Her parents, recognizing her skills (she has already won $1,000 in a songwriting contest with *I Come From America* at age 12) and her perfect-pitch singing voice, invite Doug Breithart to become her manager. Under his guidance, she learns to play, write, arrange, engineer and produce songs and will demo-record over 100 of her own compositions in a multi-track home studio.

1985

Gibson, having made TV ads for Oxydol detergent and Wendys burger restaurants, is offered the lead role in a US production of "Les Miserables", but is dropped when producers discover she is only 15. (She has already been an extra in the movies "Ghostbusters" and "Sweet Liberty".)

1986

Sept [2] Still attending school, she signs worldwide to Atlantic Records and begins recording her maiden album, with producer Fred Zarr.

1987

Sept [5] Her self-penned chart debut, the bubbly *Only In My Dreams*, hits US #4 and will head the Dance Top 12" Singles category in **Billboard**'s Year End In Music.
Oct *Only In My Dreams* peaks at UK #54.
Dec [19] *Shake Your Love* hits US #4.

1988

Feb *Shake Your Love* hits UK #7, while Gibson's debut album, ***Out Of The Blue***, featuring ten of her self-written, light and catchy pop songs (four of which are also produced by her), hits US #7. US critics hail her as the most versatile and talented of a sudden crop of successful teenage female singers.
Mar *Only In My Dreams*, reissued in the UK to tie in with Gibson's short promotional mini-concert tour, makes UK #11.
Apr [9] The extracted title track, *Out Of The Blue*, hits US #3.
May *Out Of The Blue*, also released on an early UK 3" CD single format, reaches UK #1.
June [11] Its parent album ***Out Of The Blue*** reaches UK #28.
[25] *Foolish Beat* tops the US chart, making Gibson the youngest artist ever to write, produce and perform a US #1 single.
[26] Gibson graduates, with honors, from Calhoun High School, Merrick.
July *Foolish Beat* hits UK #9.
[1] She begins her first headlining major US concert tour, supported by labelmates Times Two, in Boston, MA.
Sept [16] A performance in Pittsburgh, PA, is filmed for the future video release, "Live In Concert - The Out Of The Blue Tour".
[24] *Staying Together* reaches US #22 and will peak at UK #53 on Oct [15].
Oct [31] Gibson reportedly holds a seance at a Halloween party, in an attempt to contact Liberace and Sid Vicious.
Dec [6] ***Out Of The Blue*** is RIAA certified for three million US sales.

1989

Feb Ballad, *Lost In Your Eyes*, makes UK #34.
[11] Sophomore effort, the similarly self-written ***Electric Youth***, hits UK #8.
Mar [4] *Lost In Your Eyes* becomes her second US chart-topper.
[11] ***Electric Youth***, again co-produced with Zarr, and recorded at the Z Studio in Brooklyn, New York,

begins a five-week stay at US #1.
Apr [19] Gibson participates in the "Prince's Trust Rock Gala" at the London Palladium, on a bill with Paula Abdul, Erasure, T'Pau, Wet Wet Wet and others.
May [13] *Electric Youth*, written "about treating young people like people and helping to develop their ideas and creativity", reaches US #11 and UK #14.
June [25] Gibson deputizes for Shadoe Stevens on his US syndicated radio show, "American Top 40".
Aug [12] *No More Rhyme* reaches US #17, as *We Could Be Together* makes UK #22.
Sept [30] *We Could Be Together* peaks at US #71.

1990

Mar Gibson attends New York's LaGuardia High School for "Grammys In The School", a program of afternoon workshops.
Nov [17] She acts as musical honorary chairperson for the seventh annual Music Industry Tennis Party for the T.J. Martell Foundation, at the National Tennis Center, Flushing Meadow, New York.
Dec [15] Gibson's third album, ***Anything Is Possible***, peaks at US #41. In addition to her usual studio band, she has completed the 16-track album with assistance from Jocelyn Brown, Lamont Dozier, Paul Buckmaster and Freddie Jackson, among others, much of its early preparation having been written and recorded at Gibson's home studio.

1991

Jan [12] Its extracted title cut, *Anything Is Possible*, written and produced with Dozier, reaches US #26.
Gibson participates in the "Rock In Rio II" festival at the Maracana soccer stadium in Rio de Janeiro, Brazil.
Feb Among a number of side projects, Chris Cuevas, managed by Gibson's mother, releases his debut single, *Hip Hop*, co-written with Gibson, while her clothing boutique in the Harajunkin district of Tokyo, Japan, continues trading.
[10] Gibson joins nearly 100 celebrities in Burbank, CA, to record *Voices That Care*, a David Foster and fiancée Linda Thompson Jenner-composed and-organized charity record to benefit the American Red Cross Gulf Crisis Fund.
[14] Gibson makes a cameo guest appearance on Fox-TV's "Beverly Hills 90210".
Mar [9] *Anything Is Possible* debuts at its UK #51 peak, while ***Anything Is Possible*** will make UK #69 on the 30th.
July [23] Gibson previews her upcoming late summer tour (set to open in Latham, NY) with a private performance in the backyard of her Long Island home.
[30] She performs at New York radio station WHTZ's eighth birthday party, with Jon Bon Jovi, Mariah Carey and the Black Crowes.
Aug [15] She sings *Lost In Your Eyes* on ABC-TV's "The International Special Olympics All-Star Gala".
Dec Gibson testifies before a Senate Subcommittee on Patents, Copyrights & Trademarks in support of S 1623, the Audio Home Recording Act of 1991 in Washington, DC.

1992

Jan [7] Now managed by her mother Diane (under Gibson Management Inc.), Debbie opens on Broadway in the role of Eponine in "Les Miserables" (until March 29th).
Nov [12] She gives $5,000 to the family of Gail Shollar, murdered on November 3rd during a car-jacking.

1993

Feb [6] ***Body And Soul***, presenting a significantly matured artist, both in terms of subject matter and musical range, debuts at its US #109 peak. With collaborations with other songwriters, notably Carole Bayer Sager, Evan Rogers, Carl Sturken and Narada Michael Walden, the varied set also features a number of co-producers, including Phil Ramone and Elliot Wolff.
[13] *Losin' Myself*, accompanied by a steamy, "all-grown-up" video promo clip, peaks at US #86.
Apr [3] *Shock Your Mama* charts for a week at UK #74.
June [9] A Japanese tour, where she still remains a major attraction, opens at Nakano Sun Plaza Hall, Tokyo.
July [15] Gibson opens in the role of Sandy in the 20th-anniversary production of "Grease" at London's Dominion Theatre.
[31] *You're The One That I Want*, Gibson's duet with fellow "Grease" star Craig McLachlan updating the John Travolta/Olivia Newton-John original, reaches UK #13.

1995

Mar During the month Gibson joins the Circle Jerks onstage at CBGB's in New York performing *I Wanna Destroy You*.
July [4] Newly signed to SBK Records, her label debut, the self-produced ***Think With Your Heart***, featuring a 44-piece orchestra, is released.

GIN BLOSSOMS

Robin Wilson (lead vocals, guitar); **Jesse Valenzuela** (guitar, vocals); **Scott Johnson** (lead guitar); **Bill Leen** (bass); **Philip Rhodes** (drums)

1992

Apr The Byrds influenced country-rock/roots quintet has been formed in Tempe, AZ in 1989, and within 12 months, the Gin Blossoms has released its self-financed debut album ***Dusted*** on its own local indie label, a melodic set which has caught the ear of A&M Records who signs the group in 1991, releasing their second set, the 5-track EP ***Up And Crumbling*** comprising *Allison Road, Angels Tonight*, *Just South Of Nowhere*, *Keli Richards* and *Mrs. Rita*. Now completing its first album for the label, the band, at odds with its principal songwriter and lead guitarist Doug Hopkins, who suffers from alcohol abuse and depression, fires him, which leads to an unpleasant and protracted dispute over the publishing division and contracts for songs to be included on the forthcoming project.

1993

Feb Produced by ex-Replacements member John Hampton in Memphis, TN, ***New Miserable Experience***, a melodic, guitar-based country-rock outing highlighted by the departed Hopkins' thoughtful if mournful lyrics on five cuts, and an antidote to the recent grunge/punk explosion compared by music critics to the Byrds and R.E.M., is released by A&M.
Oct [16] The extracted *Hey Jealousy*, written by Hopkins, reaches US #25.
Dec [4] Having left a detoxification center in Phoenix a day earlier, Hopkins is found dead at his home in Tempe having committed suicide by gun. He will be replaced by Scott Johnson.

1994

Feb [5] *Found Out About You*, also written by Hopkins, reaches US #25 as ***New Miserable Experience*** reaches US #30.
[7] The group performs at the 21st annual American Music Awards held at the Shrine Auditorium, Los Angeles, CA.
[12] With UK releases licensed to Fontana Records, *Hey Jealousy* reaches UK #24.
Mar [5] ***New Miserable Experience*** makes UK #53.
Apr [16] *Found Out About You* bows at its UK #40 peak.
July [9] ***Kiss My Ass***, a Kiss-tribute album including the band's version of *Christine Sixteen*, debuts at its US #19 peak.
Aug [18] The RIAA certifies sales of two million copies of ***New Miserable Experience***.
Sept [16] A fall tour opening for the Spin Doctors begins at South Park Meadows, Austin, TX, a bill grossing $76,412. Two days later the group will appear at "Farm Aid VII" at the Louisiana Superdrome, New Orleans, LA.

1995

July [27] Gin Blossoms perform on CBS-TV's "Late Show With David Letterman".
Aug [22] The soundtrack album to "Empire Records" is released in the US including a new cut *Til I Hear It From You* by the Gin Blossoms.
Sept [2] The band performs *Wait* and *Feel A Whole Lot Better* at the Concert for the Hall of Fame at Cleveland Stadium, Cleveland, OH.
Nov [3] The group plays at the Glen Helen Blockbuster Pavilion, Devore, CA on a bill with R.E.M. which grosses $526,204 from 14,781 fans.

1996

Feb [10] *Til I Hear It From You*, featured on the soundtrack album ***Empire Records***, makes UK #39 in its week of entry.
Mar [2] Their sophomore set, the 12-track, group-penned ***Congratulations I'm Sorry***, again helmed by Hampton during seven-week sessions at the Ardent Studio, Memphis, TN, hits US #10 in its week of entry, having made UK #42 the week before. It confounds music critics who assumed the band's success thus far was largely due to Hopkins' songwriting prior to his death.
[30] *Til I Hear It From You*, released as a double A-side with *Follow You Down*, hits US # 9.
Apr [2] During a UK visit and following last night's gig at Manchester University, Gtr. Manchester, the Gin Blossoms perform at London's Shepherd's Bush Empire.
May [4] *Til I Hear It From You*, now coupled with *Follow You Down*, returns to the US Top 10 at #10.

GARY GLITTER

1960

Jan Having taken his stepfather's surname to front Paul Russell & His Rebels, Glitter (b. Paul Gadd, May 8, 1940, Banbury, Oxon.) has met film producer Robert Hartford Davis while playing a residency at the Safari club in Trafalgar Square, London, in 1958 and who has become his manager and secured a contract with Decca Records, which now issues his recording debut, *Alone In The Night*, a ballad released under the name Paul Raven. It fails to chart, despite an airing on UK TV's "Cool For Cats" and a bottom-of-the-bill support slot, still backed by the Rebels, on a UK package tour including Anthony Newley, Mike Preston and Mike & Bernie Winters, undertaken in February.

1961

Aug Now a solo act, recently returned from a tour of Scandanavia, and having played a small part in a Davis film, "Stranger In The City", Paul Raven, as he is still known, releases a second single, *Walk On Boy*, on the Parlophone label, which becomes successful in the Middle East.
Nov *Tower Of Strength*, his treatment of a Bacharach/Hilliard song, is overshadowed by Frankie Vaughan's UK #1 hit version, and Parlophone drops him. Initially shelving his recording career, becoming, not least, a warm-up man for ITV's "Ready Steady Go!", he subsequently links with the Mike Leander Orchestra, making a short UK tour as its vocalist, before the unit splits and he goes on to form Paul Raven & Boston International, later the Bostons. (The group becomes a popular live act in W. Germany, where it will spend much of the next five years.)

1968

June With the singer recently signed to MCA by Leander (who has become head of the label's UK division), the company releases *Musical Man* (written by Leander) under the name Paul Monday, though he will revert to Paul Raven for his next single, *Soul Thing*, released in August.

1969

Oct Issued under the moniker Rubber Bucket, *We Are*

All Living In One Place, featuring a chanting chorus of 3,000 people (assembled in front of the MCA offices to watch police evict squatters next door), is released. Despite heavy publicity, this single also fails to ignite a chart career, as will a version of George Harrison's *Here Comes The Sun* (released as Paul Monday), which emerges by year's end.

1970

July A cover of Sly Stone's *Stand*, released as Paul Raven, is his final MCA single.

Oct He appears on the original cast-recording album ***Jesus Christ Superstar***.

1971

With a switch of image and musical direction he records a 15-minute dance-chant stomp, *Rock'n'Roll*, under the new name Gary Glitter (chosen after considering Terry Tinsel, Stanley Sparkle and Vicky Vomit).

1972

Mar Bell UK releases *Rock'n'Roll*, split between both sides of a single (with *Rock'n'Roll Part 2* as the featured song). Initially popular on UK dancefloors, the unique cut is picked up by Radio Luxembourg, before becoming an airplay favorite on BBC Radio 1.

June Glitter/Leander-penned *Rock'n'Roll* hits UK #2, where it stays for three weeks.

Aug [5] Glitter participates in the "London Rock'n'Roll Festival" at Wembley Stadium, Wembley, Middx., sharing an unlikely bill with Little Richard, Jerry Lee Lewis, Bill Haley, the MC5, Billy Fury, Bo Diddley, Emile Ford, and Heinz.

Sept [9] *Rock'n'Roll* hits US #7 (and will remain an enduring crowd-pleasing chant anthem at US sporting events well into the '90s).

Oct The similarly dance-rock, drum-heavy follow-up, *I Didn't Know I Loved You (Till I Saw You Rock'n' Roll)*, hits UK #4.

Nov The debut album in his most popular incarnation, ***Glitter***, hits UK #8 and peaks at US #186.

Dec [16] *I Didn't Know I Loved You (Till I Saw You Rock'n'Roll)* reaches US #35. (Bell will release five more Glitter singles in the US, but this will prove to be his US chart swan song.)

1973

Jan Glitter buries his Paul Raven persona when he ceremoniously places old records and photos of his former self in a coffin which he sinks in the River Thames.

Feb *Do You Wanna Touch Me (Oh Yeah)*, in the already established glam-pop Glitter style, hits UK #2.

Apr *Hello Hello I'm Back Again* also hits UK #2. In common with all of Glitter's early (and biggest) hits, it has been co-written with its producer, Leander.

July *I'm The Leader Of The Gang (I Am)* begins a four-week stay at UK #1, while his second album, ***Touch Me***, hits UK #2.

Nov Slow-chanting *I Love You Love Me Love* enters the UK chart at #1, where it will stay for four weeks, eventually selling more than a million copies in the UK alone. Currently at his commercial peak, Glitter's concert shows at London's Rainbow Theatre, highlighted by his pomp-rock glitter costumes and platform shoes, are filmed for the documentary "Remember Me This Way".

1974

Mar His backing combo, the similarly-dressed Glitter Band, begins a short parallel career, also via Bell, hitting UK #4 with *Angel Face*. (Their remaining UK hits will be: *Just For You* (#10), *Let's Get Together Again* (#8), *Goodbye My Love* (#2), *The Tears I Cried* (#8), *Love In The Sun* (#15) and *People Like You And People Like Me* (#5), their final chart disc in March 1976.) In addition to touring and recording on their own, they continue to work with Glitter, whose ballad *Remember Me This Way* hits UK #3.

June *Always Yours* replaces Ray Stevens' *The Streak* at UK #1.

July [6] ***Remember Me This Way*** hits UK #5.

Nov [29-30] Glitter performs at London's Hammersmith Odeon during a UK tour.

Dec Again co-written with Leander, *Oh Yes! You're Beautiful* hits UK #2.

1975

May *Love Like You And Me* hits UK #10, while *Doin' Alright With The Boys*, which hits UK #6 in June will be his last Top 10 hit of the decade. His remake of the Rivingtons' *Papa Oom Mow Mow* peaks at UK #38 in November, as the glitter begins to fade.

1976

Jan [28] He announces his retirement with a televised "farewell" show.

Mar [4] Glitter begins an eight-date farewell tour at City Hall, Sheffield, S. Yorks, set to end on the 14th at London's New Victoria Theatre.

[27] *You Belong To Me* makes UK #40.

May [1] Compilation album ***Greatest Hits*** reaches UK #33.

Dec [19] After the briefest of retirements, Glitter makes his live comeback with an appearance at a Royal Charity concert broadcast on ITV, from London's Theatre Royal, Drury Lane.

1977

Feb *It Takes All Night Long* reaches UK #25, as he begins a UK tour including dates at Batley Variety Club, Manchester Golden Garter and Baileys, Watford, Herts.

May The Glitter Band splits.

July *A Little Boogie Woogie In The Back Of My Mind* reaches UK #31. Glitter will spend much of the next few years touring outside the UK on the strength of his '70s fame. He has a stint as a very portly Frank-n-Furter in an Antipodean production of "The Rocky Horror Show" and, unable to curb his legendary and profligate spending habits, he will be declared bankrupt, incurring substantial tax debts which he will spend much of the next decade diligently working to repay.

1980

Sept GTO releases a four-track EP, *Gary Glitter*, which makes UK #57.

Nov [13] Having released *What Your Momma Don't See (Your Momma Don't Know)*, Glitter launches a comeback tour at Cromwell's club, Norwich, Norfolk.

1981

Oct His cover version of *And Then She Kissed Me*, released on Bell, reaches UK #39. With a reunited Glitter Band he completes a UK tour (which is not a financial success), following which he signs to Arista Records.

Dec *All That Glitters*, a segued mix of his biggest hits, makes UK #48.

1982

Apr Heaven 17's ambitious British Electric Foundation project, ***Music Of Quality And Distinction***, including a collaboration with Glitter on *Suspicious Minds*, is released in the UK.

July Joan Jett & the Blackhearts' version of *Do You Wanna Touch Me* reaches US #20. Back home, Glitter is increasingly regarded as a novelty nostalgia figure who, by his own admission, will never go away.

Aug [14] Glitter guests on Bernard Falk's BBC1-TV show "Covetousness" with former Member of Parliament John Stonehouse.

1984

July *Dance Me Up*, an updated version of his '70s style, reaches UK #25, and Glitter even returns to appear on BBC1-TV's "Top Of The Pops".

Dec Festive *Another Rock'n'Roll Christmas* hits UK #7, but closes Glitter's UK Singles-chart account for the decade, it is included on the simultaneously-released Arista album, ***Boys Will Be Boys***. (Glitter will be admitted to hospital, suffering from an accidental overdose of sleeping pills on March 1st 1986.)

1988

June [18] Following the November 1987 release of the 16-track original-hits Glitter compilation, ***C'mon C'mon The Gary Glitter Party***, also featuring his version of Marc Bolan's *Get It On*, KLF incarnation, the Timelords' *Doctorin' The Tardis*, which borrows from Glitter's *Rock'n'Roll*, hits UK #1, with Glitter teaming with the group to record a remix. Peversely hip as an aged, bewigged but affable pop star, he appears on the cover of UK music paper **New Musical Express** and secures his own chat segment on ITV's late-night show, "Night Network".

1990

Dec [13-14] Always larger-than-life, he continues to provide popular cult entertainment (not least for the UK advertising industry), notably including a now annual Christmas tour - dubbed "The Gary Glitter Gang Show" - which climaxes at the Wembley Arena, Wembley.

1995

Dec [16] Having released ***Leader*** on his own Attitude label in 1991, an album which has been produced by his son, Paul Gadd Jr., at the Greenhouse Studios, Glitter's third decade of chart action began with the nostalgic *And The Leader Rocks On (Megamix/Medley)* at UK #58 on Oct [10], 1992, followed by *Through The Years* (UK #49, Nov [21]) and the latest in a series of compilations, ***Many Happy Returns - The Hits*** (UK #35 in the same month). Continuing to undertake annual "Gary Glitter's Really Famous Gangshow" UK tours each December, Glitter, long thought to be a toupee wearer, has his bald pate exposed by a former teenage love to the **News Of The World** on October 3rd 1993. Not even this event prevents Glitter from experiencing more nostalgic success, with *Hello, Hello, I'm Back Again (Again!)* now debuting at its UK #50 peak, the day before the irrepressible 56-year old performs at the Sheffield Arena, Sheffield, S. Yorks., on a bill with Suzi Quatro.

THE GO GO'S

Belinda Carlisle (vocals); **Jane Wiedlin** (guitar); **Charlotte Caffey** (guitar); **Kathy Valentine** (bass); **Gina Schock** (drums)

1978

Ex-high school cheerleader Carlisle (b. Aug. 16, 1958, Hollywood, CA) and Wiedlin (b. May 20, 1958, Oconomowac, WI), who has moved to Los Angeles, CA at the age of six and studied fashion after leaving college, form the inexperienced all-female new-wave outfit the Misfits with Caffey (b. Oct. 21, 1953, Santa Monica, CA), bassist Margo Olaverra, and drummer Elissa Bello, who is replaced by Schock (b. Aug. 31, 1957, Baltimore, MD) the following year when the group name-changes to the Go-Go's, having learned its trade gigging earnestly around the Los Angeles punk club scene.

1980

May Having performed in the UK for the first time earlier in the year opening for Stiff Records-signed act Madness, the Go-Go's first single, the new-wave/pop blend *We Got The Beat*, is released as a one-off single by Stiff in the UK. During subsequent US dates ex-Textone Valentine (b. Jan. 7, 1959, Austin, TX), joins after a four-day crash course after Olaverra is taken ill, a replacement which proves to be permanent.

1981

Oct Signed to Miles Copeland's I.R.S. label, *Our Lips Are Sealed*, co-penned by Fun Boy Three vocalist Terry Hall and Wiedlin, reaches US #20, during a 30-week stay on the Hot 100.

1982

Mar [6] Their maiden album, ***Beauty And The Beat***,

produced by Richard Gottehrer, tops the US chart for the first of six weeks.
Apr [10] Extracted *We Got The Beat* hits US #2.
Aug [14] Their sophomore effort ***Vacation*** enters the US chart on its way to #8 and gold sales status and will peak at UK #75.
Oct *Get Up And Go* makes US #50.
Dec The group is named the Top Artist in **Billboard**'s Year End In Music statistical round-up.

1984

May *Head Over Heels* reaches UK #11 as the group's final album in its first incarnation, ***Talk Show***, peaks at US #18.
Aug *Turn To You* makes US #32.
Oct *Yes Or No* peaks at US #84. (Wiedlin quits the band unhappy with Carlisle and Valentine's ongoing drug problems. A replacement guitarist, Paula Jean Brown briefly joins the group.)
Nov [10] Extracted *We Got The Beat* hits US #2.

1985

May [10] At a press conference, the Go-Go's announce that they they are formally splitting up. (Carlisle will remain signed to I.R.S. as a soloist, set to embark on her debut album with help from Caffey, before moving to MCA and Virgin Records in the UK. Wiedlin will release ***Jane Wiedlin*** (US #127 in October) and will sign with EMI USA Records in 1987, issuing ***Fur*** (US #105 and UK #48 in 1988), ***Tangled*** in 1990 and ***World On Fire : The Best Of Jane Wiedlin*** in 1993 also pursuing a parallel acting career appearing in "Clue", "Sleeping Beauty", "Bill And Ted's Excellent Adventure" and "Star Trek IV" among other films, while Caffey will re-emerge with Meredith Brooks and Gia Ciambotti in the Graces in 1989, making US #56 with *Lay Down Your Arms* and US #147 with ***Perfect View*** on A&M.)

1990

Oct [8] Briefly reforming for a forthcoming reunion tour, the Go-Go's shoot a benefit poster for PETA (People for the Ethical Treatment of Animals), posing nude with the byline "We'd rather go naked than wear fur".
Nov [10] Following an appearance on NBC-TV's "Late Night With David Letterman", the Go-Go's begin a one-off 20-city reunion tour at the University of Delaware, Newark, DE, set to end on December 15th at the Kaiser Arena, Oakland, CA, and tied in with the I.R.S.-released ***Greatest***, a hits collection which peaks at US #127.
Dec [13] They guest on NBC-TV's "The Tonight Show".

1991

Jan [26] Included on ***Greatest***, *Cool Jerk* charts for one week at UK #60.
Sept The group plays at a benefit for AIDS sufferer Craig Lee, a writer for the **L.A. Weekly**, at The Palace, Hollywood, with X member Exene Cervenka deputizing for Belinda Carlisle.

1994

Sept [27] A more comprehensive two-CD, 36-track retrospective ***Return To The Valley Of The Go-Go's*** is released by I.R.S., including three newly-recorded cuts and once again coinciding with a reunion US tour which will include ex-Bangle Vicki Peterson deputizing for a pregnant Caffey. (The tour will close on December 8th at the Globe Theatre, Norwalk, CT, having included a November 21st date at Los Angeles' Troubadour club and an October 25th appearance on CBS-TV's "Late Show With David Letterman".)

1995

Jan [26] The band appears on NBC-TV's "Tonight Show".
[30] The Go-Go's perform *Tutti Frutti* with Little Richard to open the 22nd American Music Awards held at Los Angeles' Shrine Auditorium.
Feb [21] Caffey gives birth to a girl, Astrid Charlotte (her husband being Red Kross guitarist Jeff McDonald).
[23-24] The tour reaches London's Shepherd's Bush Empire for a pair of concerts.
Mar With Carlisle signing a new solo deal with I.R.S., the group disbands once more. Wiedlin's new outfit froSTed will embark on its maiden US tour opening for the newly named Big Audio on October 26th, while Caffey, together with Wiedlin and ex-Bangle Susannah Hoffs will provide the title cut to the September-premiering movie "Now And Then".
see also: **Belinda CARLISLE**

LESLEY GORE

1962

While still studying at the Dwight Preparatory School for Girls, Englewood, NJ, Gore (b. May 2, 1946, New York, NY) sings with a seven-piece jazz group at the Prince George Hotel, Manhattan, New York. The group sends demos via its booking agent, Joe Glaser, to Mercury's Irving Green. Unimpressed by the group, he sees soloist potential in Gore, initially signing her to a singles-only contract.

1963

Feb Armed with more than 250 demos, Mercury staff producer Quincy Jones visits Gore at her home in Tenafly, NJ, to choose material for her maiden 45.
Mar [30] Having selected *It's My Party*, Jones produces the cut with Gore at Bell Sound Studios, New York. It is rush-released after Jones encounters Phil Spector that same evening on the steps of Carnegie Hall (where Charles Aznavour is performing) and learns that Spector is intending to cut the song with the Crystals.
Apr [6] Gore hears *It's My Party* on WINS radio while driving home from school.
June [1] *It's My Party* tops the US chart and is a million seller. Written by John Gluck Jr., Wally Gold and Herb Weiner, the song will receive a Grammy nomination for Best Rock'n'Roll Record the following year, and will become a pop standard on US radio.
July [13] *It's My Party* hits UK #9. (Among several cover versions over the years, Dave Stewart and Barbara Gaskin's treatment of the pop classic will top the UK chart and make US #72 in October 1981.)
Aug [17] Its follow-up, *Judy's Turn To Cry*, continuing the storyline of the first single, hits US #5. ***I'll Cry If I Want To*** reaches US #24.
Oct [19] Gore begins the "Greatest Record Show Of 1963" UK tour, with Dion, Brook Benton, Trini Lopez and Timi Yuro, at London's Finsbury Park Astoria.
Dec [7] *She's A Fool* hits US #5. (By year's end, she has received several awards: The National Association Of Record Merchants (NARM) votes her the Most Promising Female Vocalist Of 1963; she wins the Most Promising Female Vocalist Popularity Poll Of 1963 (the American disc Jockeys award), and **16** magazine votes her Best Female Vocalist at their Third Annual Gee-Gee Awards.)

1964

Feb [1] A John Madara and David White-penned ballad, *You Don't Own Me*, Gore's second million seller, hits US #2, held off the top spot for three weeks by the Beatles' *I Want To Hold Your Hand*. ***Lesley Gore Sings Of Mixed-Up Hearts*** peaks at US #125.
Apr [25] *That's The Way The Boys Are* reaches US #12.
June [20] *I Don't Wanna Be A Loser* makes US #37, during a month when Gore graduates from high school.
Aug Her sophomore album, ***Boys, Boys, Boys***, reaches US #127, while she makes a cameo appearance in the teen film "Girls On The Beach".
Sept Gore enrolls at Sarah Lawrence College, Bronxville, NY.
[12] The Jeff Barry and Ellie Greenwich-penned *Maybe I Know* reaches US #14.
Oct [28-29] While *Maybe I Know* peaks at UK #20, Gore participates in the "TAMI Show" (Teenage Awards Music International) at the Civic Auditorium, Santa Monica, CA, also featuring the Beach Boys, Chuck Berry and the Rolling Stones, among others.
Nov [14] *Hey Now* makes US #76 with its B-side, *Sometimes I Wish I Were A Boy*, peaking at US #86 the following week.
Dec ***Girl Talk*** reaches US #146. US trade magazines **Cashbox**, **Music Business** and **Record World** name Gore the year's Best Female Vocalist.

1965

Feb [13] Another Barry and Greenwich song, *Look Of Love*, makes US #27.
Apr [24] *All Of My Life* reaches US #71.
Aug [7] *Sunshine, Lollipops And Rainbows*, co-written by Marvin Hamlisch, from the Frankie Avalon movie "Ski Party", in which Gore has a cameo role, reaches US #13. ***The Golden Hits Of Lesley Gore*** makes US #95. TAMI show movie, "Gather No Moss", in which she features, has its UK premiere at Birmingham's Futurist cinema.
Oct [9] *My Town, My Guy And Me*, her first co-written hit, reaches US #32.
Dec [18] ***My Town, My Guy And Me*** peaks at US #120, as the extracted single, *I Won't Love You Anymore (Sorry)*, written by Gore and her brother Michael, makes US #80.

1966

Feb [12] *We Know We're In Love* peaks at US #76.
Apr [11] Gore guests on NBC-TV's "Hullabaloo", singing *Young Love*.
[23] *Young Love* makes US #50.
July During her summer vacation, Gore makes her TV-acting debut in "The Donna Reed Show".
Aug [29] Gore appears on the final broadcast of "Hullabaloo", with Paul Anka, the Cyrkle and Peter & Gordon.

1967

Jan [19] Gore appears on "Batman" as Catwoman's assistant Pussycat, singing *California Nights*, which reaches US #16 on Mar [18], its parent album, ***California Nights***, peaking at US #169 in May. (Making her theatrical debut in "Half A Sixpence" in June, Gore will score two further hits during the year: *Summer And Sandy* (US #65 on July [8]) and *Brink Of Disaster* (US #82 on Oct [28]).)

1968

May Having received a B.A. degree in English and American literature, Gore will leave Mercury in 1969, following her final single for the label, a cover of Laura Nyro's *Wedding Bell Blues*.

1970

Gore signs to ex-Four Seasons producer Bob Crewe's label (he produced her 1967 album, ***California Nights***), cutting four singles, none of which charts, and recording a duet with Oliver, under the name Billy & Sue.

1972

She signs to Mowest Records, cutting ***Someplace Else Now***, and continues to perform on the nightclub circuit, where she has made her living over the past few years. She also returns to stage work, appearing in summer stock productions of "Finian's Rainbow" and "Funny Girl".

1975

Gore appears on the bill of "Richard Nader's Rock'n'Roll Revival" at New York's Madison Square Garden. She reunites with Quincy Jones, who signs her to A&M to record ***Love Me By Name***. Produced by him, the album includes musical guests the Brothers Johnson, Dave Grusin, Herbie Hancock and Tom Scott.

1980

Nov She contributes lyrics (for *Out Here On My Own*, a US #19 hit for Irene Cara) to her brother Michael's Academy Award-winning score for "Fame".

1993

Mar [20] While Mercury has expanded ***The Golden Hits Of Lesley Gore*** to an 18-track compilation for its 1987 compact-disc release, Gore, an occasional performer on the nostalgia circuit during the '80s, takes part in an oldies concert at the Fox Theatre, Detroit, MI, with Gary Puckett, Gary Lewis and the Buckinghams.

GRAND FUNK RAILROAD

Mark Farner (vocals, guitar);
Craig Frost (keyboards); **Mel Schacher** (bass);
Donald Brewer (drums)

1968

On leaving Terry Knight & the Pack (who made US #46 with *I (Who Have Nothing)* on the local Flint, MI label Lucky Eleven, in January 1967), Farner (b. Sept. 29, 1948, Flint), whose promising football career ended as a teenager from knee injuries after which he took up playing the guitar, joins local band the Bossmen, with Dick Wagner (who will go on to play in Alice Cooper's backing band), before linking with the Fabulous Pack (the Pack minus Knight), in which Brewer (b. Sept. 3, 1948, Flint), ex-leader of the Jazz Masters, is the drummer. Farner and Brewer recruit bassist Schacher (b. Apr. 3, 1951, Owosso, MI), ex-? & the Mysterians and a one-time schoolfriend of Farner's, and within a week begin rehearsing material at the Flint Federation Musicians Hall, before recording at the Cleveland Recording Studio. Knight becomes the group's manager and, inspired by the Grand Trunk Railroad, the band changes its name, with a variation on the middle word.

1969

July Capitol Records signs the band after seeing it play the "Atlanta Pop Festival" at the International Raceway, Hampton, GA, in front of 125,000 people.
Aug The group participates in the three-day "Texas International Pop Festival" in Dallas, TX. A reported 120,000 see Grand Funk Railroad perform with Chicago, Led Zeppelin, Janis Joplin and many others.
Nov [8] *Time Machine* makes US #48, while the Knight-produced debut, ***On Time***, climbs to US #27 (Knight will serve as the band's manager, producer, spokesman and musical mentor).
Dec [27] *Limousine Driver* brakes at US #97.

1970

Mar [14] *Heartbreaker*, written by Farner during his time in the Bossmen, peaks at US #72, while their sophomore effort, ***Grand Funk***, rumbles to its US #11 peak.
June The band spends $100,000 on a block-long billboard in New York's Times Square, to promote its forthcoming ***Closer To Home***.
[13] The group performs at the "Cincinnati Pop Festival", Cincinnati, OH.
Aug With the group's often poorly-reviewed, grinding, hard-rock style now firmly established, ***Closer To Home*** hits US #6, with its title cut *Closer To Home* reaching US #22 on Oct [24].

1971

Jan [16] *Mean Mistreater* makes US #47. ***Live Album*** hits US #5.
Feb [6] *Inside Looking Out*, penned by Eric Burdon and Jackie Lomax, makes UK #40, the group's sole UK-chart appearance.
May [3] 150 reporters are invited to New York's Gotham Hotel to meet the critically-loathed band: only six show.
[29] *Feelin' Alright*, written by Dave Mason, makes US #54.
June [5] Breaking the Beatles' box-office record, Grand Funk sells out an appearance at New York's Shea Stadium in 72 hours.
Survival, their fifth album in just two years, hits US #6.
July [4] Grand Funk Railroad performs a sole London date in Hyde Park.
Sept [11] *Gimme Shelter*, a cover of the Rolling Stones' anthem, reaches US #61.

1972

Jan ***E Pluribus Funk*** hits US #5, with the extracted *Footstompin' Music* peaking at US #29 on Feb [26].
Mar [27] The group fires manager Knight, setting off an acrimonious series of multi-million dollar lawsuits between the two parties. John Eastman, Paul McCartney's brother-in-law, takes over the band's business affairs.
May [20] *Upsetter* peaks at US #73.
June Compilation album, ***Mark, Don & Mel 1969-71***, climbs to US #17.
Nov [25] *Rock'n'Roll Soul* reaches US #29. Their self-produced ***Phoenix***, featuring local Flint session musician Craig Frost (b. Apr. 20, 1948, Flint) on organ, hits US #7. ***Mark, Don And Terry 1966-67***, harking back to their earlier roots, charts briefly at US #192.
Dec [23] Knight, his attorney and two deputy sheriffs, turn up at Madison Square Garden with a court order giving him the right to seize $1 million in money or assets (pending the settlement of several outstanding lawsuits) and a 20' moving van, in the middle of rehearsals for an "In Concert" taping. They confiscate the band's equipment after the show.

1973

Sept With Frost now a permanent member of the group, which has trimmed its name to Grand Funk, ***We're An American Band***, produced by Todd Rundgren, hits US #2.
[29] *We're An American Band*, the group's first single to feature Brewer's lead vocal, and solely penned by him, hits US #1.

1974

May [4] Their cover of Little Eva's *The Locomotion* hits US #1 in just eight weeks. For only the second time in rock history a cover version tops the chart after the original has hit #1. (The first was *Go Away Little Girl*. A third instance occurs when the Carpenters hit US #1 with *Please Mr. Postman*, after the Marvelettes before them.) Its parent album, ***Shinin' On***, hits US #5.
Aug [24] *Shinin' On*, written by Brewer and Farner, reaches US #11.

1975

Jan The Jimmy Ienner-produced ***All The Girls In The World Beware!!!*** hits US #10, with the extracted *Some Kind Of Wonderful* hitting US #3 on Feb [22].
[2] A 44-date world tour opens in Mobile, AL, set to end on May 28th in Hawaii, including stops in Denmark, Sweden, Germany, Switzerland, Holland, England, Canada and Japan.
June [7] Farner-penned *Bad Time* hits US #4.
Oct The group reverts to its original name, Grand Funk Railroad, as ***Caught In The Act*** makes US #21.

1976

Feb [7] *Take Me* makes US #53, with *Sally* peaking at US #69 on Apr [3].
Mar [6] ***Born To Die***, featuring coffins on its cover, and intended to be the band's final album following a decision to split, reaches US #47.
Sept [18] With the group reassembled following Frank Zappa's offer to produce a new album, and now signed to MCA, the resultant ***Good Singin' Good Playin'*** reaches US #52.
[18] *Can You Do It* makes US #45.
Dec [11] Capitol-released retrospective, ***Grand Funk Hits***, climbs to US #126.

1977

At Brewer's suggestion, the band dissolves once more. He forms Flint with Schacher and guitarist Billy Elworthy, recording an eponymously-titled album for Capitol, while Farner releases ***Mark Farner***, produced by Dick Wagner, followed by ***No Frills*** in 1978.

1981

Jan Grand Funk has re-formed, with Farner, Brewer and bassist Dennis Bellinger (Frost is with Bob Seger's Silver Bullet Band, while Schacher does not rejoin because of a fear of flying - he will become a collector and restorer of vintage Jaguar cars), releasing ***Grand Funk Lives*** on the Full Moon label, which peaks at US #149. During the year, Farner launches Singing Spruce Enterprises, a health-food store. He becomes a born-again Christian after his wife and two children leave him, though the family will later reconcile, a third child being born in 1988.

1983

Having recently contributed to the "Heavy Metal" film soundtrack, the re-formed group's second and final album, ***What's Funk?***, is released. After a career during which they have sold over 20 million records, the band splits permanently, with Brewer going on to join Frost in Bob Seger's backing unit. Farner, increasingly devoted to his religious beliefs, forms the Christian combo Vision in 1985, with Lynyrd Skynyrd's keyboardist Billy Powell, having also formed Mark Farner's Common Ground Ministry mid-decade.

1991

Dec While Farner continues to deliver a regular number of albums for the Christian Frontline label - (***Just Another Injustice*** (1988), ***Wake Up*** (1990) and this year's ***Some Kind Of Wonderful***), also becoming a familiar name on the Inspirational Charts and at the annual Dove Awards, ***We're An American Band***, ***E Pluribus Funk***, ***Survival***, ***Live Album*** and ***Grand Funk***, are all certified platinum (for one million US sales) by the RIAA.

GRANDMASTER FLASH, MELLE MEL & THE FURIOUS FIVE

Joseph Saddler (Grandmaster Flash);
Melvin Glover (Melle Mel)

1976

Sept [2] Flash (b. Joseph Saddler, Jan. 1, 1958, Barbados, W. Indies), having worked as a mobile DJ in the Bronx, New York, NY, to where his parents emigrated in the early '60s, begins developing the hip-hop scratch-mixing technique originated by Bronx DJ, Jamaican Kool Herc. Adding rappers Cowboy (b. Keith Wiggins, Sept. 20, 1960), Kidd Creole (b. Nathaniel Glover) and Melle Mel (b. Melvin Glover) to his roadshow, he forms Grandmaster Flash & the 3 MCs. He adds two more rappers, Duke Bootee (b. Ed Fletcher) and Kurtis Blow, later replaced by Raheim (b. Guy Todd Williams), as the dance/rap ensemble evolves into Grandmaster Flash & the Furious Five. They now play their first major gig at Harlem's Audubon Ballroom, New York.

1979

Following the success of the Sugarhill Gang's *Rapper's Delight*, New York record companies begin signing other rap outfits, allowing Flash to make his recording debut on the Enjoy label with *Superrappin'*, whose rapid-fire rap exchanges by the Furious Five galvanize the urban street scene. Disappointed by its lack of chart success, Flash seeks an alternative label deal, releasing *We Rap More Mellow* on Brass Records (as the Younger Generation) and *Flash To The Beat* for Bozo Meko (as Flash & the Five), before signing to Sylvia Robinson's innovative rap stable, Sugarhill.

1980

Sept Their debut on Sugarhill, the party-themed, 8-minute 11-second rap *Freedom*, despite not making the Hot 100, becomes a popular urban track in their native New York and reaches US R&B #19, followed by *The Birthday Party*, which is released in December.

1981

May *The Adventures Of Grandmaster Flash On The Wheels Of Steel* is released, subsequently hailed as a definitive disc in the progression of the hip-hop/rap genre. It features harshly-mixed samples of Blondie's *Rapture*, Chic's *Good Times*, the Furious Five's own *Birthday Party*, Spoonie Gee's *Monster Jam*, Queen's *Another One Bites The Dust* and the Sugarhill Gang's *8th Wonder*, a medley selected by Robinson, who is also its producer. Its follow-up, *Flash To The Beat*, fails to attract the same attention.

1982

Aug New York-club interest in *The Message* (which has taken it to US R&B #4), a further era-defining rap anthem written by Creole, Mel and Robinson, spreads to the UK, where it hits #8.
Oct [30] Its parent album, the Robinson-helmed ***The Message***, makes UK #77 and will reach US #53.
Nov [6] *The Message*, having gone gold in 25 days, climbs to US #62, failing to substantially cross over from its specialist market.

1983

June Discord within the group sees Melle Mel, the dominant voice within the rap roster, emerge in his own right, taking the Furious Five with him and releasing *The Message II (Survival)*, while Sugarhill issues Flash's final effort for the label, *New York, New York*.
Nov Earlier-recorded *White Lines (Don't Don't Do It)*, a combination of Grandmaster Flash & Melle Mel and an anti-cocaine rap anthem, becomes another US dance and urban-radio success. Flash leaves the group and begins a lengthy $5-million courtcase against Sugarhill to use the full group name (a contest which he will lose). Mel, still on Sugarhill, is with rapping buddies Scorpio and Cowboy, but Raheim and Kid side with Flash.

1984

Feb *White Lines (Don't Don't Do It)* re-enters the UK chart to hit #7.
June Sugarhill compilation, ***Greatest Messages***, climbs to UK #41. Now established as Grandmaster Melle Mel & the Furious Five, their contribution to the breakdance movie "Beat Street", titled *Beat Street Breakdown Part 1*, on Atlantic, makes UK #42.
Aug [11] *Beat Street Breakdown Part 1* peaks at US #86.
Sept Mel's *We Don't Work For Free* reaches UK #45.
Oct Mel is featured as the intro rapper on the global Chaka Khan dance smash, *I Feel For You*, which hits US #3 and UK #1. *Sugarhill Work Party*, released credited to Grandmaster Melle Mel, climbs to UK #45.

1985

Jan Mel hits UK #8 with *Step Off (Part 1)*.
Feb Now signed to Elektra Records, Grandmaster Flash returns with his first solo release, *Sign Of The Times*, which charts briefly at UK #72, as its parent album, ***They Said It Couldn't Be Done***, makes a one-week appearance at UK #95.
Mar Still on Sugarhill, Grandmaster Melle Mel's *Pump Me Up* is his final UK or US chart appearance, at #45. In November, Mel's *Vice* is included on the US #1 soundtrack album for NBC-TV's "Miami Vice".

1986

May Flash's sophomore album for Elektra, ***The Source***, makes US #145.
July [19] He performs at "UK Fresh", at the Capital Music Festival, Wembley Arena, Wembley, Middx.

1987

Apr [25] ***Ba Dop Boom Bang*** peaks at US #197, featuring *U Know What Time It Is?* (A lack of commercial success encourages all parties involved to reunite as Grandmaster Flash, Melle Mel & the Furious Five, to perform at a charity concert hosted by Paul Simon at New York's Madison Square Garden.)

1988

Feb Still contracted as a solo artist to Elektra, Grandmaster Flash releases ***On The Strength***, his recordings now overshadowed by a new generation of popular rap stars who owe much to the innovative recordings made at Sugarhill at the beginning of the decade. (The album's final track is *Back In The Old Days Of Hip-Hop*). Cowboy dies the following year on September 8th.

1992

May While *White Lines (Don't Don't Do It)* continues to be reissued and remixed (not least by mixmaster Ben Liebrand in 1990), the equally influential *The Message* has been updated with new Melle Mel lyrics, for a new version by Nikolaj Steen. Its release coincides with ***Greatest Hits***, a 14-track CD retrospective of the various Grandmaster Flash/Melle Mel/Furious Five combination highlights (except the omitted *The Adventures Of Grandmaster Flash On The Wheels Of Steel*), issued in the UK by Sequel Records.

1993

Dec [31] Flash performs a New Year's Eve gig at the Apollo Theatre, followed by two nights at Madison Square Garden, with Kurtis Blow, Kool Moe Dee, Melle Mel, Whodini, Biz Markie and Doug E. Fresh.

1994

Jan [15] *White Lines (D & S Remixes)* makes UK #59, as the group - now comprising Melle Mel, Raheim, Creole and Scorpio - embarks on "Old School Reunion Tour" with Kurtis Blow, Whodini, Sugarhill Gang and Kool Moe Dee. (The following year, Duran Duran's cover of *White Lines* will reach UK #25 on June 17th.)

AMY GRANT

1976

Raised in Nashville, TN, Grant (b. Nov. 25, 1960, Augusta, GA), who has taken up the guitar at summer camp as a teenager and become a committed Christian after attending Bible classes at the encouragement of her sister's boyfriend, is still attending high school when she is signed, at age 15, to the Contemporary Christian, Waco, TX-based Word label which now releases her first album, ***Amy Grant***. It will be followed by a run of Inspirational chart-topping albums, ***My Father's Eyes***, released in 1979 while she is still studying at Nashville's Vanderbilt University, ***Never Alone*** in 1980, ***Amy Grant In Concert*** volumes ***I*** and ***II***, both issued in 1981, and ***Age To Age*** and ***A Christmas Album*** both released in 1982, all produced by her longtime collaborator Brown Bannister.

1985

May Now signed to A&M Records, and during a one-year plus stay atop the Inspirational survey, the still religious-themed ***Straight Ahead*** (released the previous year) crosses over to make US #133, having already been certified gold by the RIAA on the 2nd.
June [15] Its follow-up set, ***Unguarded*** enters the US chart on its way to #35, yielding the pop/inspirational hits *Find A Way* (US #29 - July [27]) and *Wise Up* which will climb to US #66 on Sept [14].
[24] ***Age To Age*** is certified platinum by the RIAA.
Nov [25] The RIAA certifies gold sales of ***A Christmas Album***.

1986

Feb [25] Grant wins the Best Gospel Performance, Female category (for the fourth consecutive year) for ***Unguarded*** at the 28th annual Grammy Awards.
June [16] ***Unguarded*** is confirmed platinum by the RIAA.
Nov The Jimmy Webb-written ***The Animals Christmas***, performed by Grant with Art Garfunkel, is released by Columbia Records (US).
Dec [6] *The Next Time I Fall*, a pop ballad duet with Peter Cetera, tops the US chart, as the 17-track ***Amy Grant - The Collection***, comprising the bulk of her Inspirational hits, makes US #66.

1987

Apr [21] The RIAA confirms gold sales of her 1979 release ***My Father's Eyes***.

1988

Aug [6] *Lead Me On*, penned by Grant with longtime co-writer Michael W. Smith (and Wayne Kirkpatrick), peaks at US #96 as its parent album, the Bannister-produced ***Lead Me On***, a further foray into the pop field, makes US #71.
Dec [22] ***Lead Me On*** is certified gold by the RIAA.

1989

Feb [22] Despite its pop leanings, ***Lead Me On*** wins the Best Gospel Performance, Female category at the 31st annual Grammy Awards.
Aug [23] ***Amy Grant - The Collection*** is certified platinum by the RIAA.
Nov [17] The RIAA also confirms platinum status for ***A Christmas Album***.
Dec [18] Married to singer-songwriter Gary Chapman, Grant gives birth to a daughter, Gloria.

1990

May [26] Confirming her status at the leading lady of Contemporary Christian music, **Billboard**'s Music Of The '80s Poll roundup names Grant, Gospel Artist of the Decade and ***Age To Age*** Gospel Album of the Decade.

1991

Apr [17] She appears on US-TV's syndicated "The Arsenio Hall Show".
[20] Her second pop outing ***Heart In Motion***, variously produced by Bannister, Michael Omartian and Keith Thomas, heads the renamed Top Contemporary Christian Albums chart.
[27] The bouncy pop-aimed extract, *Baby Baby*, co-written by Grant (for her baby daughter Millie) with Thomas, hits US #1.
May [14] Grant guests on NBC-TV's "The Tonight Show".
June [15] *Baby Baby* hits UK #2.
July [4] A US tour opens at the Civic Arena, Pensacola, FL.
Aug [17] *Every Heartbeat* hits US #2 behind Bryan Adams' *(Everything I Do) I Do It For You*, and also reaches UK #25.
[31] ***Heart In Motion*** hits US #10.
Sept [7] ***Heart In Motion*** makes UK #25.
Oct [25] CBS-TV airs "Disney World's 20th Anniversary" including an appearance by Grant.
Nov [9] Ballad *That's What Love Is For*, produced and co-written by Michael Omartian, peaks at UK #60.
[23] *That's What Love Is For* hits US #7.

1992

Feb [15] *Good For Me* charts for a week at UK #60.
[25] Grant sings the Record Of The Year-nominated *Baby Baby* at the 34th annual Grammy Awards, held at New York's Radio City Music Hall.
Mar [21] *Good For Me*, a fourth extract from ***Heart In Motion***, hits US #8.
[31] Grant ends a short UK tour at the Apollo Theatre, Manchester, Gtr. Manchester.
Apr [25] Having already been named Artist Of The Year at the 23rd annual (Christian) Dove Awards earlier in the month, Grant appears at an all-star concert at the Irvine Meadows Amphitheatre, Laguna Hills, CA, held to benefit the Pediatric AIDS Foundation.
June [20] Ballad *I Will Remember You* reaches US #20.
Aug [11] The soundtrack to "Honeymoon In Vegas", including Grant's version of *Love Me Tender*, is released in the US.
Oct [11] Grant gives birth to her third child, Sarah Cannon Chapman (named after the given name of her friend, Country legend Minnie Pearl) in Tennessee.
Dec [18] She guests on NBC-TV's "The Tonight Show".
[26] Her second seasonal collection, ***Home For The Holidays*** again produced by Brown Bannister, hits US #2, unable to dislodge ***The Bodyguard*** soundtrack.

1993

Feb [1] The RIAA certifies sales of four million of ***Heart In Motion***.

1994

Aug [13] *Lucky One* charts for a week at UK #60.
Sept [10] Once again co-produced by Bannister, Thomas and Omartian, ***House Of Love*** reaches US #13 in its week of entry.
Oct [8] The extracted, familiarly bouncy *Lucky One*, co-written with Thomas, reaches US #18.
[22] *Say You'll Be Mine* makes UK #41 in its week of entry.

1995

Feb [18] *House Of Love*, a duet with Vince Gill, reaches US #37.
Mar [23] ***House Of Love*** is certified multi-platinum by the RIAA for sales of two million.
Apr [11] The RIAA also certifies two million sales of ***Home For Christmas***.
June [15] Grant undergoes eye surgery to correct a detached cornea in a Nashville hospital.
July [22] Her treatment of Joni Mitchell's *Big Yellow Taxi* reaches UK #20.
[29] *Big Yellow Taxi* makes US #67.
Sept [10] A US tour, originally scheduled to end on August 27th but interrupted by her summer surgery, finally ends.
Oct [14] *House Of Love* makes UK #46 in its week of entry.

1996

Feb [6] Hollywood Records (US) releases the soundtrack to the movie "Mr. Wrong", which includes Grant's version of 10cc's 1976 UK #6 hit, *The Things We Do For Love*.

EDDY GRANT

1966

Grant (b. Edmond Montague Grant, Mar. 5, 1948, Plaisance, Guyana), having moved with his parents to London in 1960, where his first musical experience was as a trumpeter in the Camden Schools' Orchestra (though he later learns to play both the piano and guitar), forms a group with two friends from Acland Burghley School in Hornsey Rise, London, Pat Lloyd (b. Mar. 17, 1948, Holloway, London) and John Hall (b. Oct. 25, 1947, Holloway), in 1965. Joined by twin brothers Derv and Lincoln Gordon (b. June 29, 1948, Jamaica), they rehearse for almost a year, now emerging as the Equals (with Derv Gordon on lead vocals, Grant on lead guitar, Lincoln Gordon on rhythm guitar, Lloyd on bass and Hall on drums), playing a repertoire of ska-influenced R&B songs mostly written by Grant. UK independent label President Records signs the band and releases its debut single, *I Won't Be There*, which attracts UK pirate-radio airplay. As a sideline from the group, Grant also records one of the first English ska albums, ***Club Ska***, under a string of pseudonyms (to give the impression of a various-artists compilation album).
Dec *Hold Me Closer* is released, though several DJs instead pick up on the riff-driven Grant-penned B-side, *Baby Come Back*.

1967

Mar The Equals spend the first of six months working in Europe, based mostly in Holland and Germany, where Ariola Records releases *Baby Come Back*. It becomes a major hit, bringing the group extensive TV work, and goes on to sales success in Holland and Belgium.
Dec The low-priced ***Unequalled Equals***, promoted on pirate station Radio Caroline as an ideal party album, hits UK #10 and puts the group in the unusual position of having a UK chart album before a single.

1968

Feb Supported by pirate stations, Caroline in the UK and Radio Veronica from Holland, much heard in the UK, *I Get So Excited* makes UK #44.
Mar ***Equals Explosion*** reaches UK #32. (It includes Grant's *Police On My Back*, which will be revived by the Clash on their 1980 album, ***Sandinista***.)
July [3] *Baby Come Back*, reissued as an A-side, tops the UK chart for the first of three weeks, deposing the Rolling Stones' *Jumpin' Jack Flash*. UK sales will top 250,000 and the Equals receive a gold disc for combined European sales of over one million.
Sept *Laurel And Hardy* makes UK #35. It will also be the group's only US hit, at #32 on Oct [26]. (Further Equals UK hits will follow: *Softly Softly* (#48, December 1968), *Michael And The Slipper Tree* (#24, April 1969), *Viva Bobby Joe* (which will be taken up by soccer crowds who sing the adaptation *Viva Bobby Moore* at appearances by the England captain) (#6, August 1969), *Rub-A-Dub-Dub* (#34, January 1970) and *Black Skin Blue Eyed Boys* (#9, January 1971).)

1969

Sept [22] During a visit to W. Germany, Grant's car veers off an autobahn and he is hospitalized.

1972

Following an illness which prevents live work, Grant leaves the Equals to set up his own production company, the first step towards his own complete recording operation. (He will continue, for a while, to produce the Equals, in which he is replaced by Jimmy Haynes. Haynes will leave in mid-1973, to be replaced by Dave Martin, while Hall will quit early in 1975 and Neil McBain will take over on drums. Though failing to return to the charts, the Equals will remain a popular UK and Continental live attraction until the mid-'70s.)

1973

For the next three years, Grant will work as a producer (for the Pioneers and others), using the songwriting and performing royalties from his Equals days to set up his own Ice Records label (initially based in Guyana) and the Coach House recording studio in London.

1977

Grant's debut solo album is ***Message Man***, on which he has overdubbed every voice and instrument himself, establishing a self-sufficient pattern which will highlight later recordings.

1979

July Via a deal between Ice and UK label Ensign, the self-performed and-produced ***Walking On Sunshine*** is released, while the extracted *Living On The Front Line*, a hard-edged reggae/funk blend, is a major disco hit and reaches UK #11. (The album's title cut, *Walking On Sunshine,* makes US R&B #86 in November and will hit UK #4 when covered by Rocker's Revenge in 1982.)

1981

May Following the jaunty, reggae/pop fusion UK #8 hit, *Do You Feel My Love*, taken from ***Love In Exile***, in December the previous year, *Can't Get Enough Of You* reaches UK #13.
June [20] ***Can't Get Enough*** becomes Grant's first UK chart album, making #39. A second excerpt, *I Love You, Yes I Love You*, peaks at UK #37 in August. (Grant subsequently relocates his home and the Ice recording studio to the Caribbean, basing himself in St. Phillip, Barbados.)

1982

Nov [13] With Ice Records signed to a new marketing and distribution deal with RCA, *I Don't Wanna Dance* tops the UK chart for the first of three weeks, becoming one of the UK's biggest-selling singles of the year.

1983

Feb Self-written and-produced ***Killer On The Rampage*** becomes Grant's biggest-selling UK album, hitting #7. The extracted *Electric Avenue* hits UK #2.
Mar Double A-side reissue, *Living On The Frontline/Do You Feel My Love*, on Mercury (which still holds the rights originally leased to Ensign), reaches UK #47.
Apr *War Party* peaks at UK #42.
July [2] Via a deal with Portrait Records, *Electric Avenue* hits US #2 and earns a gold disc for over one US million sales. ***Killer On The Rampage*** hits US #10, also earning gold status.
Sept [17] *I Don't Wanna Dance* peaks at US #53.
Nov *Till I Can't Take Love No More* makes UK #42.

1984

May *Romancing The Stone*, written by Grant for the Michael Douglas/Kathleen Turner-starring film "Romancing The Stone" (though not featured in the movie), peaks at UK #52.
July [21] *Romancing The Stone* reaches US #26.
Nov TV-advertised K-tel compilation, ***All The Hits : The Killer At His Best***, reaches UK #23.

1988

Mar Grant returns to the UK chart after a four-year absence, with *Gimme Hope Jo'anna*, an anti-apartheid song dressed as reggae-funk, aimed at South Africa. It hits UK #7.
Apr Now licensing his releases via EMI's Parlophone label, Grant issues ***File Under Rock***.
Oct [16] Grant appears alongside U2, Aztec Camera, Joan Armatrading, Keith Richards and others in the televised "Smile Jamaica" benefit concert at London's Dominion Theatre, to raise money to aid Jamaica's recovery after Hurricane Gilbert. *Put A Hold On It* is released.

1989

May [27] Reissued *Walking On Sunshine* peaks at UK #63.
July [15] Further compilation, ***Walking On Sunshine (The Best Of Eddy Grant)***, reaches UK #20. ***Restless World***, a second album for Parlophone, will be released the following October.

1991

Mar [14] Grant hosts the first Caribbean Music Awards at Harlem's Apollo Theatre, New York.
July He enters an increasingly bitter contest to wrest control of the late Bob Marley's recording and publishing legacy by bidding $13.5 million for rights which have also attracted a $16-million bid by MCA Records and a joint offer of $12 million by Marley's widow, Rita, and Island Records supremo, Chris Blackwell. Rita Marley issues the statement: "We are completely incensed as a family at the idea of Eddy Grant trying to take our heritage away." (The Jamaican Supreme Court will give control to Marley and Blackwell.)

1995

Oct [18] Having signed Ice to a distribution deal with Pinnacle in the UK, releasing ***Paintings Of The Soul*** and the extracted *Paco And Ramone* in January 1992, and issued ***Soca Baptism***, an album of calypso covers, in January 1994, Grant successfully fights off a hostile take-over bid for his publishing company Ice Music Ltd. by his former business manager Michael Dolan, with a court ruling in Grant's favor in Antigua's High Court.

THE GRASS ROOTS

Warren Entner (vocals, rhythm guitar, keyboards); **Creed Bratton** (lead guitar); **Rob Grill** (bass, vocals); **Rick Coonce** (drums)

1966

Songwriters/producers P.F. Sloan and Steve Barri initiate the Grass Roots name as a label of convenience for a studio project as a Byrds/Turtles-type folk/rock duo, at the request of Lou Adler's Dunhill label. Their first release is a cover of Bob Dylan's *Mr. Jones (Ballad Of A Thin Man)*. When its follow-up receives airplay on a local Los Angeles, CA radio station, Sloan recruits San Francisco, CA band the Bedouins, with its lead singer, Bill Fulton, recording a new vocal for the song. After cutting more tracks, the band returns to San Francisco, following disagreements over creative input.

July [30] Sloan and Barri's own song, *Where Were You When I Needed You*, in a strident folk-rock arrangement, gives the Grass Roots its US chart debut, reaching #28. An album ***Where Were You When I Needed You***, played, sung and mostly written by the duo, is released, without charting.

Sept [17] *Only When You're Lonely*, again performed by Sloan and Barri as the Grass Roots, reaches US #96.

1967

July [1] The duo has recruited Entner (b. July 7, 1944, Boston, MA), Bratton (b. Feb. 8, 1943, Sacramento, CA), Grill (b. Nov. 30, 1944, Los Angeles) and Coonce (b. Aug. 1, 1947, Los Angeles), who already playing together as a Los Angeles bar band, the 13th Floor, to become the Grass Roots, while Sloan and Barri continue to produce and write for the group. *Let's Live For Today*, a cover of an Italian hit by Italy-based UK group the Rokes, now hits US #8.

Sept ***Let's Live For Today***, with Sloan and Barri singing and playing alongside the new members (and featuring seven of their compositions), peaks at US #75. [16] Taken from it, *Things I Should Have Said*, reaches US #23. Sloan severs his ties with the group, leaving Barri to continue as its sole producer.

Nov [25] *Wake Up, Wake Up* reaches US #68.

Dec *Feelings*, the group's first self-penned single, fails to chart.

1968

Nov [2] *Midnight Confessions*, the group's treatment of a minor regional hit in the Northwest for the Evergreen Blues Band (written by their manager, Lou Josie), hits US #5 and earns a gold disc for million-plus US sales. (Like their entire output, it fails to chart in the UK.)

Dec Compilation album, ***Golden Grass***, reaches US #25, earning a gold disc for 500,000 US sales.

1969

Jan [18] *Bella Linda* makes US #28.

Mar [8] Their cover of Marmalade's 1968 UK hit, *Lovin' Things*, reaches US #49.

Apr ***Lovin' Things*** climbs to US #73. Bratton leaves and is replaced by Denny Provisor (keyboards), who has recorded as a soloist for Valiant Records, and Terry Furlong (lead guitar).

May [31] *The River Is Wide*, a revival of the Forum's US #45 hit of only two years earlier, reaches US #31. *I'd Wait A Million Years* makes US #15 on Sept [13], while *Heaven Knows* peaks at US #24 on Dec [13].

1970

Jan ***Leaving It All Behind*** climbs to US #36. The year's remaining chart action sees the Provisor-penned *Walking Through The Country* reach US #44 on Mar [21], *Baby Hold On* make US #35 (June [27]) and *Come On And Say It* peak at US #61 on Oct [17], while ***More Golden Grass***, a collection of hit singles amassed since the original volume, climbs to US #152 in December.

1971

Apr [3] *Temptation Eyes* reaches US #15, followed by the US #9 *Sooner Or Later* (July [31]).

Nov A further compilation, ***Their 16 Greatest Hits***, reaches US #58 and earns a gold disc for half a million US sales. Coonce and Provisor quit, and are replaced by Reed Kailing (lead guitar), Virgil Webber (keyboards) and Joel Larson (drums).

Nov [27] *Two Divided By Love*, written by Dennis Lambert and Brian Potter, reaches US #16.

(The following year *Glory Bound*, their fourth Michael Price/Dan Walsh-penned hit, will make US #34 (Mar [25]), *The Runway* will reach US #39 (July [22]), while ***Move Along*** peaks at US #86 the same month. In 1973, *Love Is What You Make It* will reach US #55 on Mar [24], the group's last single for Dunhill.)

1975

Sept [20] With the Grass Roots now signed to the Haven label, *Mamacita*, written by Barry Mann and Cynthia Weil, reaches US #71 (the group's final chart record), taken from the band's final album, ***Grass Roots***.

1980

Grill's solo album, ***Uprooted***, recorded at the suggestion of his friend John McVie, and with Mick Fleetwood and Lindsey Buckingham guesting, is released. (Grill will be Fleetwood Mac's opening act on their "Tusk" tour.)

1983

Apr [5] With Grill having assembled a new Grass Roots the previous year, US Interior Secretary James Watt announces that the Beach Boys and the Grass Roots are being banned from performing at the annual "Fourth Of July" celebration in Washington, DC, citing that the acts attract "the wrong element of people". Fortunately permitted to play elsewhere, the Grass Roots becomes a popular act on the nostalgia circuit joining, for example, the Buckinghams, Gary Lewis, and the Turtles for the "Happy Together Tour" across the US.

1992

Apr [4] Still active on the US oldies circuit (they participated in the June 1987 VH1-sponsored "Classic Superfest" reunion concert series, with the Byrds, Herman's Hermits, Paul Revere & the Raiders and the Turtles), the Grass Roots appear on a "Rockin' Back To The '60s" bill also featuring the Chiffons, Micky Dolenz, Gary Puckett, the Turtles, the Buckinghams and Cannibal & the Headhunters, at the SkyDome, Toronto, Canada. (Meanwhile, Entner has become a successful manager, whose clients include Faith No More. Bratton has continued as a songwriter and occasional actor, while Coonce works as a social worker in Vancouver, BC, Canada.)

THE GRATEFUL DEAD

Jerry Garcia (lead guitar); **Bob Weir** (rhythm guitar); **Ron "Pigpen" McKernan** (organ, harmonica); **Phil Lesh** (bass); **Bill Kreutzmann** (drums)

1963

Garcia (b. Jerome John Garcia, Aug. 1, 1942, San Francisco, CA), who has spent nine months on a tour of duty for the US army in 1959, the son of a 1930s big-band leader, previously a founding member of a Bay Area bohemian troupe, the Thunder Mountain Tub Thumpers, and half of the Jerry & Sarah Garcia duo, who record two demos which will miraculously appear on a 1982 Italian bootleg, ***California Easter***, McKernan (b. Sept. 8, 1945, San Bruno, CA), who has recently been in a short-lived group with Garcia, named the Zodiacs which has also included future Dead drummer Kreutzmann (b. Apr. 7, 1946, Palo Alto, CA), Weir (b. Robert Hall, Oct. 6, 1947, San Francisco), Tom Stone, Robert Hunter (who first met Garcia in 1960 when the latter moved to Palo Alto), Marshall Leicester, David Parker and Bob Matthews, all veterans of varied Northern California folk, bluegrass and blues outfits, including the Wildwood Boys, the Black Mountain Boys and the Hart Valley Drifters, come together in Palo Alto as Mother McCree's Uptown Jug Champions. Matthews and Parker will remain part of the later Grateful Dead "family", as soundman and accountant respectively.

1965

Apr As the jug-band formula hardens into a rock/R&B mix, the personnel fluctuates until the group re-emerges as the Warlocks (its name taken from an Egyptian prayer that Garcia discovers in a dictionary), with Garcia, McKernan and Weir, joined by Kreutzmann and bassist Dana Morgan Jr., playing Rolling Stones and Chess Records R&B numbers around the Bay Area bars, making its local debut in Menlow Park.

May [3] The Warlocks record mainly instrumental demos at a Los Angeles, CA studio, later to emerge, like so much Dead material, as a bootleg.

June [7] Lesh (b. Philip Chapman, Mar. 15, 1940, Berkeley, CA) replaces Morgan on bass.

Nov [6] The group, renamed the Grateful Dead (having considered the tag the Emergency Crew), after Garcia finds the name in the **Oxford Dictionary** while at a pot party at Lesh's house, plays alongside Jefferson Airplane and the Mothers of Invention on the opening night bill at Bill Graham's Fillmore Auditorium in San Francisco.

Dec [4] Involved with Ken Kesey's (author of **One Flew Over The Cuckoo's Nest**) Merry Pranksters commune in La Honda, band members begin a number of Kesey-led "Acid Tests", a series of public experimentations with the still-legal hallucinogenic LSD. The experience profoundly changes both the group's music, moving it towards high amplification and intensity, and their audience, from R&B fans to members of the new drug culture. They also acquire a financial benefactor in chemist Owsley Stanley, a wholesale manufacturer of LSD, who designs them a customized hi-tech PA system. Designer Rick Griffin also links up with the band, which continues to develop an original and highly improvisatory style.

1966

June The group moves to the Haight-Ashbury neighborhood of San Francisco, centre of the new hippy culture, to live communally at 710, Ashbury Street. It becomes the base for an exhaustive series of free concerts, played in addition to their paid performances. A one-off debut single, *Don't Ease Me In*, backed with *Stealin'*, is recorded for the Scorpio label, a subsidiary of Berkeley-based Fantasy Records.

July [1] *Don't Ease Me In*, the group's first 45, is released. They will shortly sign with MGM Records, but the label's failure to come to terms with how the band should be recorded ends the agreement.

Aug [19-20] They perform at the Avalon Ballroom, San Francisco.

Oct The band plays at the "LSD Made Illegal" meeting in San Francisco. (By year's end, the group will have returned to the Avalon Ballroom, San Francisco, on a bill with Jefferson Airplane, Quicksilver Messenger Service and others, though plans to release a ten-album set from the live sessions are shelved.)

Dec [20] The group plays at the Fillmore Auditorium, sharing the bill with soul legend Otis Redding.

1967

Jan [14] They appear at the first "Human Be-In", at Golden Gate Park, San Francisco, along with Jefferson Airplane, Dizzy Gillespie's band and Quicksilver Messenger Service and, by month's end, are signed to the Warner Bros. label.

Feb [24-26] The band plays further dates at the Fillmore Auditorium.

Mar [17] Their debut album, ***Grateful Dead***, recorded in just three days, is released by Warner Bros, as the group begins a three-day stint at the Fillmore West.

May Having gained muted critical response, since it clearly fails to capture the group's live essence in the studio, ***Grateful Dead*** reaches US #73. (It will sell consistently over some years, and, eventually earn a gold disc.)

June [18] The band is the sixth act to play (in between Jimi Hendrix and the Who) on the third and final evening of the "Monterey International Pop Festival" at the County Fairgrounds, Monterey, CA, though disagreements with music industry executives will mean they are left out of the film documentary of the event, despite being one of the Festival's main attractions.

Sept [29] During this time, the Haight-Ashbury scene begins to dissolve, while the band acquires a second drummer, Mickey Hart (b. 1950, Long Island, NY), a fan who became friendly with Kreutzmann, jammed with the group and was recruited.

Oct [2] Lesh, McKernan and Weir are charged with possession of cannabis, following a police raid on their house at 710, Ashbury Street, charges which are subsequently dropped, on a technicality).

1968

Feb Recordings begin for a second album, which, in sharp contrast to the debut will take six months to complete, augmented by keyboardist Tom Constanten, Lesh's room-mate, whose use of prepared tapes arouses the group's interest. Hart's father Lenny becomes their manager.

May [18] The band appears at the "Northern California Rock Festival" on a bill featuring the Doors, the Steve Miller Band and others.

June [22] They headline at the Fillmore East, on a bill which sees the Jeff Beck Group make its US debut.

Aug [4] The group performs at the "Newport Pop Festival" in Costa Mesa, CA, alongside the Byrds, Steppenwolf, Sonny and Cher, Canned Heat, Jefferson Airplane and others.

[23-24] Following another three-day stand at the Fillmore West, they play the Shrine Auditorium, Los Angeles.

Sept ***Anthem Of The Sun***, featuring eight live and four studio recordings, and also heralding the return to the Dead fold of Hunter as lyricist, sells moderately, reaching US #87, but not well enough to cover the considerable recording costs (halfway through, they fired producer Dave Hassinger and took over the recording themselves), which will leave the band in debt to Warner Bros. until the early '70s.

[2] The group appears at the three-day "Sky River Rock Festival and Lighter-Than-Air Fair", in Sultan, WA, with Santana, Muddy Waters, Country Joe & the Fish, the Youngbloods and others.

Dec [6] The group performs at the "Quaker City Rock Festival" at the Spectrum, Philadelphia, PA, with Iron Butterfly and Steppenwolf.

[28] The band plays at the "Miami Pop Festival" in Hallandale, FL, with acts including Chuck Berry, Joni Mitchell, the Box Tops, Fleetwood Mac, Marvin Gaye, Steppenwolf and Country Joe & the Fish.

1969

Continuing financial problems lead the Grateful Dead to accept Bill Graham's long-standing offer to handle their bookings. They continue to play free gigs, but Graham books them into packed clubs around the nation.

July [10] Hugh Hefner-hosted "Playboy After Dark" TV broadcast features the Grateful Dead.

Aug ***Aoxomoxa*** reaches US #73, but they still owe Warner Bros. $100,000 and one more album.

[15] The Grateful Dead perform at the era-defining "Woodstock Music & Art Fair", Bethel, NY, to more than 400,000 people.

[31] They appear at the "New Orleans Pop Festival" in Prairieville, LA, with Country Joe & the Fish and Jefferson Airplane.

Dec [6] They play at the ill-fated Rolling Stones concert at Altamont Speedway, Livermere, CA, where a murder occurs during the Stones' act. (The event is later recalled by the group in *New Speedway Boogie* on ***Workingman's Dead***.)

1970

Jan [31] The entire line-up (minus McKernan) is busted for possession of marijuana in New Orleans.

Feb [13] The band performs once again at the Fillmore East. (The group at last releases a full live recording, the double ***Live/Dead***, recorded "live" in the studio before an audience of friends, which reaches US #64. It includes a four-page lyric booklet and a 25-minute version of the stage favorite, *Dark Star*. Constanten leaves to concentrate on Scientology studies.)

Mar It is discovered that the group's manager, Lenny Hart, has embezzled approximately $150,000 from the band.

May [23] Grateful Dead plays its first gig outside the US, a four-hour set at the "Hollywood Rock Music Festival" in Newcastle-under-Lyme, Staffs.

Aug On ***Workingman's Dead***, the complexity of earlier albums is dropped in favor of Garcia's country-rock roots and harmony vocals, though a psychedelic sensibility remains. The album includes contributions from two new members of Dead's constantly expanding "family", John Dawson and David Nelson. It reaches US #27 (earning a gold disc) and UK #69.

Sept [19] The extracted *Uncle John's Band* makes US #69.

Nov Released on the Sunflower label, ***Vintage Dead***, with live recordings from the Avalon Ballroom, San Francisco, in 1966, peaks at US #127.

[4] Garcia, Lesh and Kreutzmann begin recording sessions at Wally Heider's Studio C in Los Angeles with David Crosby, Paul Kantner, Grace Slick, Jorma Kaukonen, Jack Casady and David Freiberg as the Planet Earth Rock And Roll Orchestra. The sessions will remain unreleased.

Dec Recorded in a similar vein to ***Workingman's Dead***, ***American Beauty*** reaches US #30 and earns another gold disc. The album's guests include the New Riders of the Purple Sage, which in reality is a Garcia-led spin-off country outfit, featuring him on pedal steel, Dawson, Nelson, Hart and Dave Torbert. The combo will become a permanent aggregation, opening for the Grateful Dead and even signing to CBS/ Columbia in 1971. Unable to cope with his dual role, Garcia will, however, quit the New Riders after their debut album release.

1971

Feb [18] Hart temporarily quits the band to pursue a solo career.

May [31] 36 fans are medically treated after unknowingly drinking LSD-laced cider at a Grateful Dead Winterland Ballroom concert.

July ***Historic Dead***, a compilation of early 1966 recordings on Sunflower, reaches US #154. Garcia cuts his debut solo album, ***Hooteroll*** with Howard Wales, released on the Douglas label.

Oct Keith Godchaux (b. July 19, 1948, San Francisco) joins as an additional keyboardist.

Dec Double live album, ***Grateful Dead***, reaches US #25.

[25] The extracted *Truckin'* brakes at US #64.

1972

Members begin to splinter off into other projects, Garcia in particular playing on several other projects. His second solo album, ***Garcia***, is released by Warner Bros. with a cover shot showing his right hand, which has its third finger missing, the result of a childhood accident in 1946, when his brother Tiff chopped it in half with an axe.

Mar [25] Godchaux's wife, Donna (b. Aug. 22, 1947, San Francisco), is added as a supplemental vocalist.

Apr [7-8] The band performs at the Empire Pool, Wembley, Middx., during a two-month European tour.

[22] The extracted *Sugaree* peaks at US #94. Weir cuts ***Ace*** (the track *One More Saturday Night* will become a staple of the Grateful Dead's concerts), while Hart releases ***Rolling Thunder***. (Meanwhile, McKernan has sustained serious liver damage and is forced to rest and stop drinking. He is to be temporarily replaced by Merle Saunders.)

May [7] The band performs in a mud bath at the "Bickershaw Festival" near Wigan, Lancs., with Captain Beefheart, the Kinks and Country Joe & the Fish.

June [17] McKernan plays his final gig with the Dead at the Hollywood Bowl, Los Angeles.

1973

Jan Triple live album, ***Europe '72***, a celebration of the group's European trek, reaches US #24, and introduces the latest group annex, husband/wife Keith and Donna Godchaux on keyboards and vocals.

Feb [10] *Sugar Magnolia* peaks at US #91.

Mar [8] McKernan dies from a stomach haemorrhage and liver failure brought on by alcohol poisoning, in the yard of a Corte Madera, CA apartment.

With the Warner Bros. contract fulfilled, the group sets up Grateful Dead Records for the band's work, and Round Records for more esoteric releases from members of the "family". In the next two years, the latter will issue further Garcia solo album, ***Reflections***, a Lesh/Ned Lagin set, ***Seastones***, a Weir/Torbert offshoot, ***Kingfish***, and solo albums by chief lyricist Hunter, namely ***Tales Of The Great Rum Runners*** (1973) and ***Tiger Rose*** (1975). (These initiatives will eventually lead to the band's own studio, publishing company, booking agency and travel agency, though the labels will subsequently fail.)

[27] Garcia is once again busted for drugs, this time on Interstate 295 near Philadelphia, PA.

July [28] With the Band and the Allman Brothers Band, the group co-headlines the "Watkins Glen Festival" in upstate New York, drawing an all time-record festival audience of 600,000 people.

Aug [1] On his 31st birthday, Garcia is greeted by a naked dancer bursting out of a gigantic birthday cake during a Dead concert.

Sept Live ***History Of The Grateful Dead Volume 1 (Bear's Choice)***, recorded at the Fillmore East, New York, in February 1970, reaches US #60.

Dec Jazz-inflected but still improvisational, ***Wake Of The Flood***, the first album on the Grateful Dead's own label, reaches US #18.

1974

Apr Compilation album, ***The Best Of/Skeletons From The Closet***, on Warner Bros., makes US #75. An album of fresh material, ***Grateful Dead From The Mars Hotel*** makes UK #47 on Aug [3] and will peak at US #16 in August.

Oct [16-20] The group performs five consecutive nights at the Winterland, San Francisco, with Hart having rejoined the line-up.

1975

Mar [23] The group takes part in an all-star benefit at San Francisco's Kezar Stadium to raise funds to make up a shortfall in the San Francisco school system budget. (During the month, Garcia's next solo project, ***Old And In The Way*** is released by Round.)

Aug [13] After a lengthy sabbatical from live work, during which the Godchauxs have recently released ***Keith And Donna Godchaux***, the Grateful Dead performs at the Great American Music Hall, San Francisco.

Sept [28] The group plays a free concert in Lindley Park, San Francisco.

Oct ***Blues For Allah***, marking a new licensing deal with United Artists, reaches US #12.

Nov [1] ***Blues For Allah*** makes UK #45. Hart returns to the band.

[15] *The Music Never Stopped* makes US #81.

1976

Feb Garcia's ***Reflections*** is issued by Round in the US and UA in the UK.

Apr In the latest side project, Weir and Dave Torbert have combined as Kingfish releasing ***Kingfish*** on the Grateful Dead label (which will also issue Hart's ad-hoc outfit, Diga Rhythm Band's album ***Diga*** later in the year).

June [3] Following another long lay-off from live work, the band embarks on a US tour, beginning in

Portland, OR.

July [31] Double live album, ***Steal Your Face***, recorded at the Winterland in September 1974, makes US #56. It is released chiefly to recoup losses made on a disastrous group film project.

Aug [7] The group appears at Wembley Stadium, Wembley, on a bill with Santana and the New Riders of the Purple Sage.

Sept [4] ***Steal Your Face*** makes UK #42.

Oct [9] The group performs at the Oakland-Alameda County Stadium, Oakland, on a bill with the Who.

1977

May [8] They appear at Cornell University, Ithaca, NY.

June Documentary film, "The Grateful Dead", premieres.

July With its own label now folded, the band signs directly to Arista (which will also issue Dead solo material, including Garcia's current ***Cats Under The Stars*** album and his 1982 ***Run For The Roses***, and Weir's ***Heaven Help The Fool*** (1979) and ***Bobby And The Midnights*** (1981).

Aug [20] The group's first Arista release, the Keith Olsen-produced ***Terrapin Station***, reaches UK #30 and will make US #28.

Sept The group headlines an 11-hour concert at Old Bridge, NJ, with the New Riders of the Purple Sage and the Marshall Tucker Band.

Dec Warner double retrospective, ***What A Long Strange Trip It's Been: The Best Of The Grateful Dead***, reaches US #121. (The first half of the title will be borrowed, nine years later, by **Rolling Stone** magazine, for a book of its own finest moments.)

1978

Sept [14-16] The band performs three dates at the Sound & Light Amphitheatre in the shadow of the Great Pyramid in Cairo, Egypt, the last of which is timed to coincide with a lunar eclipse. Proceeds from the concerts go to the Egyptian Department of Antiquities and the Faith & Hope Society for the Handicapped.

Dec [31] The Grateful Dead play their 48th, and last, gig at the Winterland Ballroom, San Francisco, before Bill Graham closes the venue. Sharing the bill are the Blues Brothers and the New Riders of the Purple Sage. (During the year, Round Records and two publishers will sue United Artists for $5 million punitive damages, $290,000 in record royalties, $180,000 in publishing royalties, $407,000 in net profits and $50,000 in unreimbursed advertising costs.)

1979

Jan ***Shakedown Street***, produced by Little Feat's Lowell George, reaches US #41.

[2-4] The band plays the Fillmore West, on a bill with Blood Sweat & Tears.

Feb [17] The Godchauxs leave the group over musical and personal differences.

Apr [22] Brent Mydland (b. Oct. 21, 1952, Munich, W. Germany), ex-Silver and now with Weir's side band, Bobby & the Midnights, joins on keyboards and vocals. Billed as the Rhythm Devils, Kreutzmann, Hart and Lesh contribute the percussion soundtrack to Francis Ford Coppola's Vietnam epic, "Apocalypse Now".

1980

Jan [13] The Grateful Dead co-headlines a benefit concert for the people of Kampuchea, with the Beach Boys and Jefferson Starship, at Oakland-Alameda County Coliseum.

Apr [5] The group appears as the musical guest on NBC-TV's "Saturday Night Live".

June ***Go To Heaven***, notable in being their first album cover to feature a group photo, reaches US #23.

[5] The band celebrates its 15th anniversary with a commemorative concert at Compton Terrace in Phoenix, AZ.

July [2] Weir, Hart and manager Danny Rifkin are arrested on suspicion of inciting a riot, after they intervene in an attempted drug arrest during a Grateful Dead concert at the Sports Arena, San Diego, CA.

[19] *Alabama Getaway* makes US #68.

[21] Former keyboardist Keith Godchaux is seriously injured when his car is in collision with a flat-bed truck near Marin County, CA. He dies two days later.

Sept Hart, Lesh and Kreutzmann have combined as the ad-hoc outfit the Rhythm Devils to release ***Rhythm Devils Play River Music***, issued on the Passport label (US).

1981

Mar The group plays its first UK gig for five years, at London's Rainbow Theatre.

May Double live album, ***Reckoning***, recorded in New York in 1980, and featuring a totally acoustic set, reaches US #43.

Sept [30] The band undertakes a European tour, set to end on October 17th.

Oct Further double live, ***Dead Set***, from a San Francisco concert, makes US #29.

1982

The group abandons recording, and tours periodically. Their concert treks are, by now, communal experiences for "Deadheads" (the fans who follow their heroes around the US on tours arranged by the "family" business), who are encouraged by the band to plug tape recorders into the mixing desk at concerts to make instant bootlegs, a unique and popular advantage of attending a Grateful Dead gig. Fans also begin to write to the group, expressing concern about Garcia. He has become addicted to heroin, and both his health and standard of his contribution to the band have deteriorated.

May [28] The group plays at a benefit concert for the Vietnam Veterans Project, at San Francisco's Moscone Center, also attended by Country Joe & the Fish and Jefferson Starship.

Sept [5] The group performs at the "US Festival", financed by Apple Computers founder Steven Wozniak, in Devore, San Bernardino, CA, to 400,000 people, along with Jackson Browne, the Cars, Fleetwood Mac, Eddie Money, Police, Santana, Talking Heads and many others.

Nov [25] The band appears at the "Jamaica World Music Festival" at the Bob Marley Performing Centre near Montego Bay, Jamaica.

1983

Apr [16-17] Stephen Stills joins the band on stage to perform a version of his *Love The One You're With*, at a pair of gigs at the Meadowlands Arena, East Rutherford, NJ. (During the year, Hart's ***Yamantaka*** will emerge on the Celestial label.)

1984

Oct [27] At a concert in Berkeley, the band allocates a specific recording area for its fans to bootleg the show.

Dec Weir's latest solo effort, ***Where The Beat Meets The Street*** is released by CBS/Columbia Records.

1985

Jan [18] Garcia's drug problem comes to a head, when he is busted for substance possession in Golden Gate Park, and is subsequently sentenced to community service, having pleaded guilty. The others tell him the band cannot go on if he continues his addiction, so he agrees to seek help.

1986

June [26] With Garcia seemingly fit, the band resumes full-time touring, on a US package trek with Bob Dylan, and Tom Petty & the Heartbreakers.

[10] Garcia lapses into a five-day diabetic coma, resulting in the band's withdrawl from the tour. When recovered, he begins a musical collaboration with R&B keyboardist Merle Saunders.

Dec [15] Concert touring resumes at the Oakland-Alameda County Coliseum.

1987

The Grateful Dead complete a video and record a long-overdue studio album. The initial plan is to retread old songs, but Hunter becomes involved and the album takes on a theme of aging and redirection.

June The Grateful Dead tour again, supporting Bob Dylan. At his insistence, the traditional encouragement of tape-recording by the audience is suspended.

July [29] Garcia reaches an agreement with the Ben & Jerry ice-cream organization over the introduction of a "Cherry Garcia" flavor. 50% of royalties go to Garcia's Rex Foundation.

Aug Comeback project (still for Arista Records), ***In The Dark***, hits US #6.

[23] An escapee from a drug treatment center shoots a policeman and is then shot dead himself at a Grateful Dead "Summer Of Love" 20th-anniversary celebration concert.

Sept [15] The Grateful Dead receive a platinum disc - their first - for US sales of ***In The Dark***.

[19] ***In The Dark*** makes UK #57.

[26] *Touch Of Grey* hits US #9 (the band's first major hit single).

Dec [31] The band spends New Year's Eve performing at the Oakland-Alameda County Coliseum.

1988

June Dylan's latest album, ***Down In The Groove*** is released, featuring Garcia, Weir and Mydland, while *The Ugliest Girl In The World* and *Silvio* are co-written by Dylan and Hunter.

Sept [24] The group closes a nine-concert series at New York's Madison Square Garden with an extra benefit show for Cultural Survival, Greenpeace and Rainforest Action Network. They are joined on stage by Bruce Hornsby & the Range, Daryl Hall & John Oates, Suzanne Vega, former Rolling Stone Mick Taylor and ex-Hot Tuna, Jack Casady. The ten concerts gross $3,768,244.

Dec [4] The group performs at the sellout "Oakland-Alameda County Coliseum Music Festival", with Crosby, Stills, Nash & Young, Tracy Chapman and Bob Dylan.

1989

Feb [18] Live album, from the 1987 Bob Dylan/ Grateful Dead tour, ***Dylan And Dead***, released by CBS, makes UK #38 and peaks at US #37.

Apr Hart solo album, ***Music To Be Born***, featuring an in-the-womb recording of his son Taro's heartbeart, is released while Garcia's ***Almost Acoustic*** album will emerge later in the year.

May [18] The Grateful Dead plays an AIDS benefit in Oakland with Tracy Chapman, Huey Lewis & the News and John Fogerty, among others. (Garcia also jams with Elvis Costello and James Burton at the Sweetwater club in San Francisco to celebrate the 21st anniversary of the Village Music record store in Mill Valley.)

July [9-10] The group plays two sellout gigs, with Little Feat, at Giants Stadium, East Rutherford, NJ.

[12] Garcia, Weir and Hart appear before a Congressional caucus to draw attention to the destruction of the Malaysian rain forests. Rhode Island's Republican representative, Claudine Schneider, urges the band to encourage Deadheads to vote.

Aug In an interview in this month's **Musician** magazine, Garcia says of Deadheads : "They're acting out their version of how much freedom there is in America to go for a wild ride. What's left is, well, you can follow the Grateful Dead on the road. You can't be locked up for that, yet. So it's an adventure. And an adventure, as part of the American experience, is essential."

Nov ***Built To Last*** peaks at US #27.

Dec [6] The group plays an Earthquake Benefit at the Oakland-Alameda County Coliseum, raising $310,280 from the sellout crowd.

[10] Patrick Shanahan dies following a Grateful Dead concert at the Great Western Forum, Inglewood, CA, after being taken into police custody and being restrained by a chokehold.

[27-28, 30-31] As the group plays its final dates of 1989 at the Oakland-Alameda County Coliseum, with support act Bonnie Raitt, **Forbes**' annual year-end list of the 40 highest paid entertainers in the world ranks the Grateful Dead at #29, with an estimated annual income of $12.5 million.

1990

Feb [23-24] Hart plays two sellout shows with the Paul Winter Consort and Oscar Castro Neves at the Cathedral of St. John the Divine, New York.

[25-27] A never-ending live sojourn continues, as the band begins another major US tour with sellout dates at the Oakland-Alameda County Coliseum, grossing $905,520.

May [5-6] They break the house record at California State University, Dominguez Hills, Carson, CA, taking in some $1,230,000 from two sellout crowds of 30,000 each.

July [16] During the latest series of dates with various supporting acts, including Edie Brickell, Crosby Stills & Nash and Bruce Hornsby, the group plays a sellout concert at the Rich Stadium, Buffalo, NY.

[26] Mydland dies from overdose of an intravenous injection of morphine and cocaine, outside his Lafayette, CA home.

Aug Oakland police issue an arrest warrant for Randall Delpiano, who has been jailed in the past for impersonating Weir. He violates his parole on a 15-month jail sentence for fraud and theft charges. (Weir takes part in a 200-mile cycle trip across Montana's Flathead National Forest, to draw attention to the threat of clear-cuttings on forests.)

[16] RCA Records announces that Bruce Hornsby "has responded affirmatively to a request from his longtime friends (the Grateful Dead) to help them through this difficult period", with reference to Hornsby playing dates with them after the death of their keyboard player, Brent Mydland. (Garcia is featured on *Across The River*, the first single from Hornsby's latest album. Garcia and Hornsby also collaborate with Branford Marsalis and Bob Wasserman to record the music for Spike Lee-directed commercials for Levi jeans.)

[31] The tour kicks off at the Shoreline Amphitheatre, Mountain View, CA.

Sept Hart signs a deal with Harper & Row Books to write two non-fiction works, the first to be called **Drumming At The Edge Of Magic**, with the proviso that two trees must be planted for every tree cut down to produce his books. He also releases ***At The Edge***, a solo album, on Rykodisc.

[7] Ex-Tubes keyboardist Vince Welnick is recruited as a permanent replacement for Mydland and makes his Dead debut at the Richfield Coliseum, Richfield, OH.

[14-16, 18-20] The Dead play six sellout dates at New York's Madison Square Garden, before a total audience of 110,945 paying $2,368,825. (These six dates bring the group's total performances at the Garden to 31, breaking Elton John's record of 30.)

Oct [20] Their first official live album in nine years, ***Without A Net***, makes US #43.

[27] The group performs in Paris, France, as part of its first European tour in nine years.

Dec [27-28, 30-31] The Dead play their 21st New Year's Eve concert in the Bay Area, at the Oakland-Alameda County Coliseum, at the end of four sellout dates. (During the year, the band will have grossed over $30 million and have been seen by more than 1.5 million people in the US alone.)

1991

Mar [17-18, 20-21] The band plays four sellout dates before a combined crowd of 70,000 at the Capital Center, Landover, MD.

[27] Garcia's one-man exhibition opens at the Ambassador Gallery in Soho, New York, while the band is playing at the Nassau Veterans Memorial Coliseum, Uniondale, NY.

Apr [3-5] 57 people are arrested during a three-day set of Grateful Dead concerts in Atlanta, GA. The total drug haul from the arrests is 4,856 "tabs" of LSD, 29 bags of "mushrooms", 24 "lids" of marijuana, one vial of crack cocaine and 18 cylinders of nitrous oxide.

[20] The Dead and Damn Yankees play before an estimated gathering of 30,000 military personnel and their relatives at the Norfolk Naval Air Station, Norfolk, VA.

[23] ***Deadicated***, a collection of Grateful Dead songs recorded by various artists, is released, featuring: Burning Spear (*Estimated Prophet*), Elvis Costello (*Ship Of Fools*), Cowboy Junkies (*To Lay Me Down*), Dr. John (*Deal*), the Harshed Mellows (*U.S. Blues*), Bruce Hornsby & the Range (*Jack Straw*), Indigo Girls (*Uncle John's Band*), Jane's Addiction (*Ripple*), Los Lobos (*Bertha*), Lyle Lovett (*Friend Of The Devil*), Midnight Oil (*Wharf Rat*), Suzanne Vega (*China Doll*), Dwight Yoakam (*Truckin'*) and Warren Zevon and David Lindley (*Casey Jones*), with a portion of the proceeds going to the Rainforest Action Network and Cultural Survival.

[30] Weir testifies to help Senate Bill 712, an anti ticket-scalping law, pass in the California legislature.

May [3-5] After breaking house records at the Orlando Arena and the Sam Boyd Silver Bowl, the band plays three sellout dates at the Cal Expo Amphitheatre, Sacramento, CA.

[18] ***One From The Vault***, recorded in concert at the Great American Music Hall, San Francisco, in August 1975, peaks at US #106.

June [1] The group plays to a sellout crowd of 40,000 at the Los Angeles Coliseum.

[22] The band performs at Soldier Field, Chicago, IL, to a capacity crowd of 58,416, with support act Roger McGuinn. (Johnny Clegg, Little Feat, Santana and Dwight Yoakam will also open for the Dead during their current dates.)

July Kitchen Sink Press publishes the first issue of **Grateful Dead Comix**, scheduled quarterly.

Aug [1] Appearing in a business suit to testify in front of a Senate Special Commission on Aging, Hart suggests that music is spiritually uplifting for the elderly, saying that: "rhythm is there in the cycles of the seasons, in the migration of the birds and animals, in the fruiting and withering of plants and in the birth, maturation and death of ourselves."

Sept [14] Garcia's ***The Jerry Garcia Band***, comprising John Kahn (bass), Melvin Seals (keyboards), David Kemper (drums) and Jackie LaBranch and Gloria Jones (vocals), debuts at its US #97 peak. (Garcia also releases ***Jerry Garcia/David Grisman*** recorded with Grisman, on the Acoustic disc label, which the pair will follow-up in 1993 with ***Not For Kids Only***.)

[20-22, 24-26] Following nine sellout concerts at Madison Square Garden, the band plays six capacity shows at the Boston Garden. (The 15 shows are seen by more than 250,000 people, paying $5,787,178.)

Oct Bob and Wendy Weir's **Panther Dream**, a children's book about the Rainforest, is published, while the former also launches two new breakfast cereals, "Rainforest Crisp" and "Rainforest Granola".

[15] Garcia, questioned about the Dead's teenage fans in **Rolling Stone** magazine, replies: "What do they find fascinating about these middle-aged bastards playing basically the same thing we've always played?"

Nov [3] The band takes part in the Bill Graham memorial concert at San Francisco's Golden Gate Park Polo Field, before an estimated crowd of 300,000.

[16] The Jerry Garcia Band plays a sellout performance at the Knickerbocker Arena, Albany, NY, during a series of East Coast dates.

[27] Mickey Hart & Planet Drum performs at New York's Carnegie Hall.

Dec [16] Ace Records in the UK releases ***Infrared Roses***, a collection of live Dead tracks produced by Bob Bralove.

[27-28, 30-31] The group rounds out another active year with four more sellout shows at the Oakland-Alameda County Coliseum.

1992

Feb [22] A new 46-concert, 21-city tour begins at the Oakland-Alameda County Coliseum.

[25] Hart wins the Best World Music Album category for ***Planet Drum***, released the previous year by Rykodisc, at the 34th annual Grammy Awards, held at New York's Radio City Music Hall.

Mar [9] Weir visits congressmen and conservation leaders during a two-concert stop in Landover, lobbying against a bill which would leave millions of acres of Montana wilderness open to logging and mining.

Apr [15] Weir performs on CBS-TV's "What About Me? I'm Only Three", an environmental awareness program aimed at youngsters.

May [30] ***Two From The Vault***, featuring a pair of August 1968 Dead shows from the Fillmore West and Shrine Auditorium, debuts at its US #119 peak.

July [1] The tour ends at the Buckeye Lake Music Center, Hebron, OH. (Of the 46 shows performed, 44 have been sellouts, with 1,143,146 devotees paying $27,394,833.)

[11] A range of eight Garcia-designed $28.50 ties go on sale in Bloomingdales, New York, though the Dead designer maintains he will not be wearing any himself, unlike President-elect Bill Clinton, whose wife Hillary will buy him some for Christmas. (The collection will gross $10 million in US sales by year's end.)

[14] Weir and Wasserman embark on a handful of dates at the Orpheum Theatre, Minneapolis, MN.

Aug [1] The Jerry Garcia Band plays at the Irvine Meadows Amphitheatre, Laguna Hills, CA.

[4] Garcia is taken sick at his home in Marin County, CA., suffering not least from exhaustion and an enlarged heart.

[6] The Lithuanian Olympic basketball team (to whom the band has donated $5,000 earlier in the year) is brought no luck by their Grateful Dead-designed outfit, losing 127-76 to the USA Dream Team in Barcelona, Spain. (The group's other extra-curricular activities include a merchandising division which offers downhill skis, dolls, backpacks, ties, books, videos, comic books and golf equipment.)

[14] The Grateful Dead organization cancels a forthcoming 18-date tour of New York, Boston, Philadelphia and Washington, scheduled to start September 9th as well as earlier dates in Oregon and California, because of Garcia's illness. A spokesman says, "Thirty years of Camel Straights will leave their mark."

Oct [10] Mickey Hart & Friends take part in the "All Our Colors - The Good Road Concert" at the Shoreline Amphitheatre, with Santana, Jackson Browne, Steve Miller, John Lee Hooker, White Boy & the Wagonburners, and Red Thunder.

[31] A slimmer and more health-conscious Garcia returns to live work with a Jerry Garcia Band Halloween gig in Oakland.

Dec [9] Hart wins the Top World Music Artist and Top World Music Album (***Planet Drum***) categories at the third annual **Billboard** Music Awards, held at the Universal Amphitheatre, Universal City, CA.

[11-13, 16-17] The group finishes a short series of dates, which started out at the McNichols Arena, Denver, CO, at the Oakland-Alameda County Coliseum.

1993

Jan [24-26] The band performs its first dates of the year with further sellout shows at Oakland-Alameda County Coliseum.

Mar [31] The group begins a five-date sellout stint at the Nassau Veterans Memorial Coliseum.

Apr [21] Kreutzmann saves 17-year-old John Paid from drowning off the coast in Mendocino, CA.

Sept [16-18, 20-22] Following the usual round of summer stadium dates, some of them with Sting as its support act, the Grateful Dead plays a six-date series at Madison Square Garden.

Dec The group's own Grateful Dead Records releases ***Dick's Picks #1***, the first in a planned series of live albums, culled from the band's extensive tape vault and compiled by long-time Dead taper, Dick Latvala.

1994

Jan [19] Bruce Hornsby inducts the Grateful Dead into the Rock and Roll Hall of Fame at the ninth annual dinner from New York's Waldorf Astoria Hotel. Absentee Garcia is represented in the shape of a lifesize cardboard cutout.

Feb [25-27] The group plays further sellout dates at the Oakland Coliseum.

Mar [23-25, 27-28] They perform before sellout crowds totalling 82,674 at Nassau Veterans Memorial Coliseum, Uniondale, NY.

June [17-19] The group breaks the house and the highest grosser records at Autzen Stadium, University of Oregon, Eugene, OR.
Sept [27-29, **Oct** 1-3] They break another house record at Boston Garden, when 86,079 see them during a six-night stint.
Nov [23] Denver Federal Judge Zita Weinshienk grants a temporary restraining order to Grateful Dead Productions Inc. and the Grateful Dead Merchandising Inc. to prohibit the sale of bootleg merchandise. The lawsuit names "Does 1-500" as defendants.
Dec [15-16, 18-19] The band sells out the Los Angeles Sports Arena, as the band grosses a further $50,000,000 during the year.

1995

Jan [26] The Beverly Prescott Hotel in San Francisco renames Room 807, which includes several Garcia pieces of artwork and fabrics, as the Jerry Garcia Suite.
[31] *The Best Of Skeletons From The Closet* reaches the RIAA-certified three million sales plateau.
July [9] At the end of a jinxed tour, which sees three fans struck by lightning outside the RFK Stadium in Washington (one of them suffering cardiac arrest), more than 100 fans injured when a wooden deck collapses at a campground lodge in Wentzville, MO, and 3,000 fans rioting at the Deer Creek Music Center, Noblesville, IN show, the Grateful Dead play what will be its last-ever show at Soldier Field, Chicago, IL
Aug [9] Garcia is found dead in his sleep at the Serenity Knolls drug treatment center in Forest Knolls, CA. He is pronounced dead at 4.23 a.m. after a staff nurse and a Marin County paramedic fail to revive him with CPR. The coroner's report will indicate that Garcia probably used heroin the day before he died, though the official cause of death is officially a heart attack caused by hardening of the arteries. San Francisco Mayor Frank Jordan orders city flags lowered to half mast and a tie-dyed Dead flag temporarily place on the City Hall flagpole. Bob Dylan is quoted as saying : "There's no way to convey the loss. It just digs down really deep." Between 1990 and his death, the band has grossed $226.4 million in gross ticket sales, and the band's corporation tops $50 million in annual revenue.
[10] ***In The Dark*** is certified platinum.
[11] Garcia's funeral takes place at St. Stephen's Episcopal Church, Belvedere, CA.
Sept [2] **Entertainment Weekly** devotes this week's magazine as a tribute to Garcia.
[22] Fan-focusing documentary film "Tie-Died : Rock 'n'Roll's Most Deadicated Fans", having already been premiered at several film festivals earlier in the year, opens nationwide on 50 screens in the US.
Oct Arista announces that 15 albums, previously only available by mail order from Grateful Dead Records, will be re-released.
[14] ***Hundred Year Hall*** debuts at its US #26 peak.
[17] ***The Music Never Stopped : Roots Of The Grateful Dead***, a project overseen by Garcia and Weir and featuring the original versions of songs the Dead covered, is released in the US by Shanachie.
Nov [7] The International Astronomical Union confirms an asteroid named Garcia. Deadheads Simon Radford at the Radio Astronomy Observatory in Tucson, AZ and Ed Olszewski at the University of Arizona's Stewart Observatory are responsible.
Dec [6] The Grateful Dead issues a statement: "After four months of heartfelt consideration, the remaining members of the band met yesterday and came to the conclusion that the 'long strange trip' of the uniquely wonderful beast known as the Grateful Dead is over".

1996

Mar [14] The group's legendary gig on February 13th 1970 at the Fillmore East is finally released as a three-CD set by the band's Dick's Picks mail-order company.
Apr [4] Garcia's widow Deborah and Weir wade into the Ganges River near Rishikesh and sprinkle a portion of Garcia's ashes. The rest will be strewn on waters near the Golden Gate Bridge in San Francisco on the 15th.
June Billed as "Deadapalooza", Hart's new band Mystery Box and Weir's new outfit Ratdog perform together on a US summer tour with Bruce Hornsby and Los Lobos.

AL GREEN

1967

After moving to Grand Rapids, MI, at age nine, Green (b. Al Greene, Apr. 13, 1946, Forrest City, AR), is the youngest member of his father Robert's Greene Brothers gospel quartet with brothers Walter and William, but has gradually moved towards secular R&B in the late '50s, a similar musical transition made by Sam Cooke. "Fired" by his father from the family group after being caught listening to the "profane" music of Jackie Wilson, he forms the Creations in 1964 with high-school friends Palmer James, Curtis Rogers and Gene Mason. The group begins playing the "chitlin' circuit" and enjoys local success with recordings on the Zodiac label during the mid-'60s. Now performing as Al Greene & the Soul Mates, they form their own record company, Hot Line Music Journal, to release their debut single, *Back Up Train.*

1968

Feb [3] Distributed nationally by Bell, *Back Up Train* climbs to US #41 and wins the group a spot at New York's prestigious Apollo Theatre. The follow-up, *Don't Hurt Me No More*, fails to chart along with its parent album ***Back Up Train***, and, unable to maintain momentum, the group breaks up leaving Green to go solo. He drops the last letter of his surname and returns to club singing.

1969

In Midland, TX, Green meets bandleader Willie Mitchell, also chief producer and vice president of Hi Records in Memphis, TN, who, after hearing Green sing, signs him to the label. He takes him to Memphis to record with the Hi label house band, comprising Al Jackson (drums), Leroy Hodges (bass), Mabon Hodges (guitar), Charles Hodges (organ), Wayne Jackson (trumpet), James Mitchell (baritone sax), Andrew Love (tenor sax), Ed Logan (tenor sax) and Jack Hale (trombone). (With minor variations, the line-up will play on all Al Green records until 1978.) The first two releases are versions of the Beatles' *I Want To Hold Your Hand* and *You Say It*, the latter being a minor R&B hit.

1971

Jan [2] Green's slowed-down version of the Temptations' hit, *Can't Get Next To You*, makes US #60.
Nov [6] *Tired Of Being Alone* reaches US #11 and hits UK #4. ***Al Green Gets Next To You*** makes US #58, immediately showcasing the singer's distinctive, high-pitched, sweet-soul vocal style.
Dec [3] Green begins a short UK tour at the New Century Hall, Manchester, Lancs.

1972

Feb [12] *Let's Stay Together*, written by Green, Al Jackson and Mitchell, tops the US chart at the beginning of a nine-week stay and hits UK #7. (Tina Turner's 1983 revival will hit UK #6 and US #26, her first solo success.)
May [27] *Look What You Done For Me* hits US #4 and will reach UK #44.
Let's Stay Together hits US #8, earning a gold disc, having topped the US R&B survey for ten weeks.
Sept [2] *I'm Still In Love With You* hits US #3, Green's third consecutive US million seller, and reaches UK #35. ***Al Green***, recorded during Green's Soul Mates days, reaches US #162 for the Bell label.
Nov [4] *Guilty* peaks at US #69.
Dec [23] *You Ought To Be With Me* hits US #3 and is a fourth million seller (each one has been penned by the Green/Jackson/Mitchell combination). ***I'm Still In Love With You*** hits US #4 during a 67-week chart stay.

1973

Feb [17] *Hot Wire*, another Soul Mates track, makes US #71. ***Green Is Blues*** reaches US #19.
Apr [14] *Call Me (Come Back Home)* hits US #10.
July [12] Its parent album, ***Call Me***, is certified gold by the RIAA, having made US #10, yielding yet another hit, *Here I Am (Come And Take Me)* which hits US #10 on Sept [8].

1974

Jan [19] *Livin' For You* makes US #19, while ***Livin' For You*** heads to US #24, and *Let's Get Married* reaches US #32 on May [25].
[22] *Livin' For You* is certified gold by the RIAA.
Feb [19] Green wins the Favorite Album, Soul/R&B category at the inaugural American Music Awards, held at the Aquarius Theater, Hollywood, CA.
Oct [25] While Green is taking a shower at his Memphis home, ex-girlfriend Mary Woodson bursts in, pours boiling hot grits over him and then fatally shoots herself with his gun. Green is hospitalized with second-degree burns. (Rumors persist that the incident prompts Green to become a born-again Christian, but Green claims his spiritual rebirth had already taken place in 1973. His Christianity becomes more prominent from this point, as he joins the ministry and becomes an ordained pastor of the Full Gospel Tabernacle in Memphis.)
Dec [21] *Sha-La-La (Make Me Happy)* hits US #7 and UK #20.

1975

Jan ***Al Green Explores Your Mind*** reaches US #15, becoming his 12th gold disc. (Included is *Take Me To the River*, which will become Talking Heads' first hit, in 1978.)
Apr [19] *L-O-V-E (Love)* reaches US #13 and UK #24. ***Al Green's Greatest Hits*** makes US #17 and UK #18 (May [17]), his first UK chart album.
July [26] *Oh Me, Oh My (Dreams In My Arms)* climbs to US #48.
Oct [1] Al Jackson, instrumental in the composition and performance of Green's biggest hits, is shot dead by an intruder at his Memphis home.
Nov [15] ***Al Green Is Love*** reaches US #28.
Dec [27] *Full Of Fire* makes US #28.

1976

May [1]***Full Of Fire*** peaks at US #59. Green buys the Church of Full Gospel Tabernacle in Memphis and becomes its minister. (He will continue his pop career and, when not touring, will preach at the church.)
June [3-6] Green performs a seven-show stint at the Uris Theatre, New York, with Ashford & Simpson.

1977

Jan [8] *Keep Me Cryin'* reaches US #37 (his final collaboration with producer Mitchell).
[8] ***Have A Good Time*** climbs to US #93.
July [13] ***Al Green's Greatest Hits, Volume II*** reaches US #134. Green breaks from Mitchell and forms a band to record at his own American Music Studio in Memphis. The line-up is Reuben Fairfax (bass), James Bass (guitar), Johnny Toney (drums), Buddy Jarrett (alto sax), Fred Jordan (trumpet) and Ron Echols (tenor and alto sax).

1978

Jan Following the non-charting ***Truth 'n' Time***, the self-produced ***The Belle Album*** reaches US #103, its tracks co-written by Green, Fairfax and Jordan.
[21] *Belle* peaks at US #83, its lyric confirming Green's inner conflict between a sexual and spiritual life.
Feb [13] Los Angeles, CA declares "Al Green Day", as the artist performs at the city's Dorothy Chandler Pavilion.
June [17] Green wins the Grand Prize and $14,000, for his performance of *Belle* at the seventh "Tokyo Music Festival" in Japan.

1979

After a bad fall from a stage in Cincinnati, OH, which results in a 15-day stay in hospital, Green decides to make a full commitment to his church: "I realized that I was being disobedient to my calling. I was moving towards God, but I wasn't moving fast enough. That was God's way of saying I had to hurry up."

1980

While an R&B retrospective, ***Cream Of Al Green***, is released, Green issues ***The Lord Will Make A Way***, the first in a string of pure gospel releases, which find success in the specialist inspirational field throughout the decade.

1982

Feb [24] ***The Lord Will Make A Way*** wins the Best Traditional Soul Gospel Performance category, Green's first such trophy, at the 24th annual Grammy Awards.
Higher Plane, including versions of *Amazing Grace* and *Battle Hymn Of The Republic*, is released.
Sept [9] Green opens on Broadway with Patti LaBelle in a production of Vinnette Carroll's gospel musical, "Your Arm's Too Short To Box With God". (The show will run until November.)
Nov ***Precious Lord***, a mix of standard hymns and songs written by Green with Moses Dillard, begins a new series of gospel albums.

1983

Feb [23] ***Higher Plane*** wins the Best Contemporary Soul Gospel Performance category, while ***Precious Lord*** is named Best Traditional Soul Gospel Performance, at the 25th annual Grammy Awards. Green will continue to collect gospel Grammys throughout the decade, ***I'll Rise Again*** winning Best Male Soul Gospel Performance in 1984, and his duet with Shirley Caesar, *Sailin' On The Sea Of Your Love* securing Best Soul Gospel Performance By A Duo Or Group at the 27th annual ceremony, in 1985.
Dec Green releases the plain white-cover, white-vinyl, seasonal ***White Christmas***, produced by Moses C. Dillard Jr. The strictly spiritual set, ***Trust In God*** will be released in February 1995.

1986

Jan [25] He guests on NBC-TV's "Saturday Night Live".
Feb Newly signed to A&M Records his label debut ***Going Away***, mixing gospel and R&B releases and marking a reunion with producer Mitchell, is released.

1987

Feb [24] Green wins his only non-gospel Grammy, collecting the Best Soul Performance, Male trophy for the *Going Away* single at the 29th annual Grammy Awards.
Mar [23] He also collects the Best Gospel Recording, Solo trophy at the inaugural Soul Train Music Awards, held at the Civic Center, Santa Monica, CA.
May Spiritual ***Soul Survivor*** makes US #131, again released on A&M.

1988

Mar [2] The extracted *Everything's Gonna Be Alright* wins the Best Soul Gospel Performance, Male category at the 30th annual Grammy Awards.
June [11] Green appears at "Nelson Mandela's 70th Birthday Tribute" concert at Wembley Stadium, Wembley, Middx., and reaches new fans.
Oct Following a biographical interview on the C4-TV show "Wired", Green, making a more mainstream commercial comeback, links with Eurythmics' Annie Lennox for the duet *Put A Little Love In Your Heart* (which will make UK #28), from the Bill Murray-starring movie "Scrooged".
[15] UK compilation ***Hi-Life - The Best Of Al Green***, climbs to #34, while *Let's Stay Together*, used on a UK TV aftershave ad, is reissued.

1989

Jan [14] *Put A Little Love In Your Heart* hits US #9.
June A second newly-recorded A&M soul gospel studio set, ***I Get Joy***, is issued, including *As Long As We're Together*.
Oct Arthur Baker & the Backbeat Disciples' *The Message Is Love*, with Green the featured vocalist, makes UK #38.
Green christens four-month-old Walker Louis Baron, son of A&M's West Coast publicity director Diana Baron, and sings *You Are My Everything* at the ceremony.

1990

Feb [21] *As Long As We're Together* wins the Best Soul Gospel Vocal Performance, Female Or Male category at the 32nd annual Grammy Awards, held at the Shrine Auditorium, Los Angeles.
May [18] Green guests on NBC-TV's "The Tonight Show".

1991

Jan [10] CBS-TV sitcom "Good Times", starring Farrah Fawcett and Ryan O'Neal, with the Andy Goldmark-penned theme sung by Green, premieres.
May [3] Green returns to "The Tonight Show".
Oct He is featured on Arthur Baker's *Leave the Guns At Home* single and attends a New York press conference to promote handgun control, with political advocate James Brady.
Dec ***Greatest Hits*** becomes his sixth RIAA-certified gold album.

1992

Mar [4] Green makes his annual NBC-TV's "The Tonight Show" appearance.
Sept [11-13] Following an April performance at the 23rd annual "New Orleans Jazz & Heritage Festival", New Orleans, LA, Green participates in the "Ann Arbor Blues & Jazz Festival", Ann Arbor, MI.
[17] He jams with Curtis Stigers at the Music & Entertainment Industry Chapter of the City of Hope benefit at Century Plaza Hotel, Los Angeles.
Oct [8] During a month-long US tour, Green performs at the Greek Theatre, Los Angeles.
[16] He participates in a tribute to the late Temptations singer, Eddie Kendricks, at a concert in Redondo Beach, CA.
[31] UK-retrospective ***Al*** makes UK #41, released by Beechwood Music.

1993

Jan [17] He participates at Freedom Hall, Washington, DC, as part of the "Reunion On The Mall" during Inauguration festivities.
June [15] Green sings at the "Apollo Theatre Hall Of Fame" concert, set to air on NBC-TV on August 4th.
Oct [2] *Love Is A Beautiful Thing* debuts at its UK #56 peak (and will be featured on the soundtrack to the 1996 film "The Pallbearer"). It is taken from the September-released, UK-only ***Don't Look Back***, his first for RCA/BMG Records, co-produced and co-written with Fine Young Canibals' David Steele and Andy Cox at London's RAK Studio.

1994

Feb [18] He plays to a sellout crowd of 4,444 at the Masonic Auditorium, Detroit, MI.
Apr [19] Green guests on CBS-TV's "Late Show With David Letterman", duetting with Lyle Lovett on *Funny How Time Slips Away*, featured on the compilation ***Rhythm Country & Blues***.
May [13-15] Green takes part in "Music Midtown", a three-day festival at 10th and Peachtree Street in Atlanta, GA.
July [28] During current US dates, Green performs at the Westbury Music Fair, Westbury, NY.

1995

Jan [12] Natalie Cole inducts Green into the Rock and Roll Hall of Fame at the tenth annual dinner. At the after-dinner jam session, Green sings *Funny How Time Slips Away* with Willie Nelson.
Mar [1] Green shares the Best Pop Vocal Collaboration trophy with Lyle Lovett, for *Funny How Time Slips Away*, and presents (with B.B. King) the Best Metal Performance statuette to Soundgarden at the 37th annual Grammy Awards, held at the Shrine Auditorium.
[10] He performs at the opening night gala of the Hard Rock Hotel & Casino in Las Vegas.
Apr [19] Green makes his first club appearance in some 20 years at Willie Mitchell's Rhythm and Blues club in Beale Street, Memphis.
May [19] The Minister of Soul, as he is now affectionately known, performs at New York's Beacon Theatre.
Sept [2] He sings *Tired Of Being Alone* and *A Change Is Gonna Come* and duets with Aretha Franklin on *Freeway Of Love* at the Concert for the Rock and Roll Hall of Fame at Cleveland Stadium, Cleveland, OH.
Nov [2] Green is inducted into the Soul Train Hall of Fame at the 25th annual awards ceremony from the Shrine Auditorium. He also performs *Love And Happiness* and *Your Heart's In Good Hands*. (The show will air on CBS-TV on the 22nd.)
[7] MCA releases the US-only ***Your Heart's In Good Hands*** comprising eight songs from the his 1993 UK set ***Don't Look Back***, augmented by new cuts produced by Narada Michael Walden.
[16] He appears on "The Tonight Show".
Dec [6] Green performs a gospel version of Hootie & the Blowfish's *Hold My Hand* with the band at the 1995 **Billboard** Music Awards, broadcast live on Fox-TV from New York's Coliseum.
[10] He takes part in "Christmas In Washington" TV special at the National Building Museum in Washington, set to air on NBC-TV on the 13th.
[11] Green guests on "Late Show With David Letterman".
[31] He plays a New Year's Eve gig at the Fox Theatre, Detroit, MI.

1996

Feb [3] ***Greatest Hits*** makes US #169.
Mar [8] Green receives the Pioneer In Music Award at the National Association of Black Owned Broadcasters ceremony held in Washington, DC.

GREEN DAY

Billie Joe (vocals/guitar); **Mike Dirnt** (bass); **Tré Cool** (drums)

1990

Nov Dirnt (b. Michael Pritchard, May 4, 1972, CA), born to a heroin-addicted mother, but adopted by a Native American mother and a white father, who divorced when he was seven, leaving him to live briefly with his father before returning to his birthmother, has become boyhood friends with Billie Joe (b. Billie Joe Armstrong, Feb. 17, 1972, San Pablo, CA) in their Rodeo neighborhood, a suburb of Berkeley, CA, becoming inseparable around the time of Billie Joe's father's death when he was 10. Dirnt has subsequently left home at 15 living in a truck, before renting a room in Armstrongs' parent's house and finally residing in an Oakland, CA squat (which will be the inspiration for future track *Welcome To Paradise*), soon to be joined by Billie Joe. The pair spends weekends at the Gilman Street Project club, and, having toyed with guitars since the age of 11, form Sweet Children in 1987 with Al Sobrante on drums. Changing their name to Green Day (inspired by their song of the same name, written about hanging out and smoking pot) in 1989, they recruit replacement drummer John Kiftmeyer and tour the country travelling in an old van performing punk covers and self-penned material. Returning to California, Kiftmeyer quits and they recruit Cool (b. Frank Edwin Wright III, Dec. 9, 1972, Germany), also a Gilman Street regular who has been playing drums in the Lookouts, a band formed by his neighbor Lawrence Livermore who has also founded the small indie label, Lookout Records. With its final lineup settled, the trio has recorded its first 7" EP, *1,000 Hours* released earlier in the year by Lookout which has signed the band following a showcase gig in Mendocino, CA to an audience of 12 people, and which is now followed by the raw, punk-inspired, 20-cut, angst-ridden album debut, ***1039/Smoothed Out Slappy Hours***.

1993

Apr Gaining momentum after constant club gigging and the release of the its second Lookout album ***Kerplunk*** the previous May, a major label bidding war ends with Green Day signing to Reprise Records.
Nov The band opens for Bad Religion on a US tour.

1994

Feb [19] Third album, ***Dookie*** enters the US albums survey at the beginning of a two-year-plus chart tenure. Produced by Rob Cavallo their rapid fire, hard-core punk delivery is styled after the UK punk pioneers of the mid-'70s (particularly the Buzzcocks and the Sex Pistols), an influence which will also dictate the band's anti-establishment behavior.
June [5] During a European promo visit, the band performs a concert in Barcelona, Spain.
[9] They take part in the "MTV 120 Minutes" Music Festival, at London's Astoria Two.
Aug [14] Happily swathed in mud, Green Day performs at "Woodstock II", held at Winston Farm, Saugerties, NY.
[20] *Basket Case* bows at its UK #55 peak.
[24] With Green Day one of its major attractions, the "Lollapalooza" annual US package tour reaches the Blockbuster Desert Sky Pavilion, Phoenix, AZ, a concert grossing $518,554 from 18,206 attendees.
Sept [8] The band performs *Basket Case* (which the cable network has heavily rotated) at the 11th annual MTV Video Music Awards, emceed by Roseanne Barr at New York's Radio City Music Hall.
[11] Green Day appears at the Hate-Free America fundraiser "The Concert To End Hate", at the Arena, Seattle Center, WA.
Oct [29] *Welcome To Paradise* enters at its UK #20 peak.
Dec [3] Green Day is the music guest on NBC-TV's "Saturday Night Live".
[5] Midway through its own headlining US tour, the band performs at Z-100's "Acoustic Christmas", an event held at New York's Madison Square for 17,719 fans, on a bill with Weezer, Indigo Girls, Hole, Melissa Etheridge, Bon Jovi, Sheryl Crow, Toad The Wet Sprocket and others.

1995

Jan [26] Green Day is named Best New Band, Best New Male Singer (Billie Joe Armstrong), Best Album (***Dookie***) and Best Album Cover in **Rolling Stone**'s 1995 Music Awards (Readers' Picks) and Best New Band (in the Critics' Picks section).
[28] Reissued *Basket Case* hits UK #7 as ***Dookie*** finally hits US #2.
Feb [11] ***Dookie*** reaches UK #13.
Mar [1] ***Dookie*** wins Best Alternative Music Performance at the 37th annual Grammy Awards held at Los Angeles' Shrine Auditorium.
[18] *Longview* debuts at its UK #30 peak. (During the month, the band's managers, Elliot Cahn and Jeff Saltzman pact with MCA Records to form the alternative-music-based (510) Records.)
May [20] *When I Come Around* bows at its UK #27 peak.
[27] The group plays the first of two consecutive benefit gigs on its current US tour for the Berkley Free Clinic, Haight-Ashbury Clinic, Food Not Bombs and San Francisco Coalition on Homelessness charities at the Henry J. Kaiser Auditorium, Oakland.
[31] The RIAA certifies sales of eight million copies of ***Dookie***, now the biggest-selling punk album of all-time in the US.
June [3] Green Day is named Top Modern Rock Band at the inaugural Blockbuster Entertainment Awards held at Hollywood's Pantages Theatre.
[20] The band appears at the **Kerrang!** Awards held at London's Cumberland Hotel.
[27] Early Lookout recordings, ***1039/Smoothed Out Slappy Hours*** and ***Kerplunk*** are certified gold by the RIAA.
Aug [25] Green Day performs at the "Reading Festival", Reading, Berks.
Sept [20] Further UK dates include tonight's gig at London's Brixton Academy. The film soundtrack to "Angus" is released in the US including Green Day's *J.A.R.*
Oct [7] *Geek Stink Breath* reaches UK #16 in its week of entry.
[17] Green Day kicks off another US tour at the Arena, Seattle Center, WA for 5,982 fans.
[21] ***Insomniac***, a 33-minute set co-produced with Rob Cavallo, hits UK #8 in its entry week.
[28] ***Insomniac*** debuts at its US #2 peak, unable to dislodge Mariah Carey's ***Daydream***.
Nov [8] The trio performs on CBS-TV's "Late Show With David Letterman".
[21] Towards the end of its US trek, Billie Joe is arrested after mooning the audience during a show at the Milwaukee Arena, WI, and will pay a $141.85 fine for indecent exposure.

1996

Jan [6] *Stuck With Me* bows at its UK #24 peak.
Feb [27] ***Insomniac*** is certified double-platinum by the RIAA.
Mar [9] The band wins the Outstanding Hard Music Album and Outstanding Drummer categories at the 19th annual Bammie Awards held at the Warfield Theater, San Francisco.

NANCI GRIFFITH

1978

Daughter of a barbershop quartet-singing father and thespian mother, raised in Louisiana and Dallas, TX, and inspired by the folk singing of Carolyn Hester and Bob Dylan, Griffith (b. Nanci Caroline Griffith, July 6, 1953, Seguin, TX) began performing at the age of 14, before majoring in Education at the University of Texas. Married to Eric Taylor and determined on a musical career, the folk singer/songwriter has earned her musical spurs performing in Austin and Houston, TX nightspots (including the seminal Anderson Fair Retail Restaurant), before signing a one-off deal with the local Austin BF Deal label, which issues her maiden album, ***There's A Light Beyond These Woods***, a largely self-penned live set.

1982

Following three years of continued low-key club work, Griffith is signed to another Texas label, Featherbed, and releases her sophomore effort, the self-written and co-produced (with John and Laurie Hill) ***Poet In My Window***, which again showcases the artist's thoughtful lyrics and distinctive soft vocal style.

1984

June [26] Griffith begins recording her third album at Jack Clement's Cowboy Arms Hotel, Nashville, TN. Co-produced with Jim Rooney, the resulting ***Once In A Very Blue Moon***, released later in the year, includes a guest appearance by Lyle Lovett on a cover of his *If I Were The Woman You Wanted*.

1985

Oct Having signed to Rounder Records, which has also licensed and released her first two albums on compact disc, Griffith releases ***Last Of The True Believers*** (issued in the UK by Demon Records), a mostly self-written folk/country meld which includes *Love At The Five And Dime*, set to be a country hit for Kathy Mattea in April 1986, and *The Wing And The Wheel*, a title she will also use for her own publishing company.

1986

June With critical praise growing with each release, Griffith finally secures a major-label contract - with MCA - and begins recording sessions with co-producer Tony Brown (who was responsible for signing her) at the Soundstage and Back Stage Studios in Nashville, TN.

1987

Apr Her MCA debut, ***Lone Star State Of Mind***, is released, its title cut co-written by longtime cohort Pat Alger, and featuring her mainstay backing band (the Blue Moon Orchestra). Warmly received by a burgeoning cult following, it also includes an early cover of Julie Gold's *From A Distance*.

1988

Mar [26] Spurred by a UK tour, ***Little Love Affairs***, a similarly sensitive set of Griffith originals and carefully chosen folk/country covers, once again helmed by Griffith and Brown, reaches UK #78.
Aug [19-20] Her two-date engagement at the Anderson Fair club in Houston is recorded for subsequent release, in November, as ***One Fair Summer Evening***.

1989

Sept [23] ***Storms***, produced by Glyn Johns and featuring musical guests Bernie Leadon, Albert Lee and Phil Everly, reaches UK #38 and will mark Griffith's US chart debut, at #99, after 11 years of recording. The following year, Griffith will take part in "The Big Day", an open-air festival from various locations in Glasgow, Scotland, airing live on C4-TV on June 3rd.

1991

Sept [28] ***Late Night Grande Hotel***, produced by Rod Argent and Peter Van Hooke, and featuring Tanita Tikaram and a duet with Everly, debuts at its UK #40 peak.
Oct [12] ***Late Night Grande Hotel*** charts for one week at US #185. Its poor commercial showing in the US, where the genre-defying Griffith has been caught between the rock, folk and country fields, results in this being her final MCA outing.

1992

Jan [4] The Chieftains' ***The Bells Of Dublin***, to which Griffith, who is immensely popular in Eire, has contributed *The Wexford Carol*, peaks at US #107.
Mar [14] A further Chieftains album, ***An Irish Evening Live At The Grand Opera House, Belfast, With Roger Daltrey and Nanci Griffith***, recorded in 1991, climbs to US #120 (and will win a Grammy Award the following year for Best Traditional Folk Album).
Oct [16] Griffith takes part in "The Bob Dylan 30th Anniversary Celebration", singing *Boots Of Spanish Leather*, with Carolyn Hester.

1993

Mar [16] Griffith begins a US tour at the Robert W. Woodruff Arts Center Symphony Hall, Atlanta, GA.
[20] Newly signed to Elektra Records, Griffith's label debut, reuniting her with earlier producer Jim Rooney, ***Other Voices, Other Rooms*** (named after a 1948 Truman Capote book) debuts at its US #54 and UK #18 peaks. An ambitious collection of Griffith covers of her favorite songs, guest dignitaries include Chet Atkins, Bob Dylan, Carolyn Hester, Indigo Girls, Emmylou Harris, Leo Kottke, John Prine, Guy Clark and Arlo Guthrie.
Apr [15] She appears on NBC-TV's "The Tonight Show".
June [18] Griffith embarks on a seven-date UK tour at the Dome, Brighton, E. Sussex, set to end on the 29th at the Empire Theatre, Sunderland, Tyne & Wear and including an appearance on the Pyramid Stage at the "Glastonbury Festival", Worthy Farm, Pilton, Somerset.

July [31] She begins a 17-date US summer tour at the Mann Music Center, Philadelphia, PA, set to end on August 29th at Estes Park, CO.
Nov [13] ***The Best Of Nanci Griffith*** reaches UK #27 in its week of entry.

1994

Mar [1] Griffith wins the Best Contemporary Folk Album category for ***Other Voices, Other Rooms*** at the 36th annual Grammy Awards from New York's Radio City Music Hall.
Aug [19] During current US dates, Griffith performs at the Filene Center, Wolf Trap Farm Park for the Performing Arts, Vienna, VA.
Sept [14] Griffith guests on CBS-TV's "Late Show With David Letterman".
Oct [1] ***Flyer***, produced by Peter Collins and two cuts helmed by R.E.M.'s Peter Buck, debuts at its US #48 and UK #20 peaks.
[10-11] She performs at London's Royal Albert Hall with the Blue Moon Orchestra.
Nov [2-5] Griffith plays four dates at the Richard Rodgers Theatre in New York.

1995

Jan [13-14] Griffith begins a US tour at the Andrew Jackson Hall in Nashville, set to end at New York's Beacon Theatre on April 18th.

1996

Jan [2] ***notfadeaway : remembering buddy holly***, to which Griffith contributes *Well All Right* with the Crickets, is released. She reveals she wanted to be a Cricket as a young girl.
[29] Griffith returns to the "Late Show With David Letterman".
Apr [23] Hootie & The Blowfish's new album ***Fairweather Johnson*** is released, including Griffith guesting on *Earth Stopped Cold*.

GUESS WHO

Burton Cummings (vocals, keyboards); **Randy Bachman** (guitar); **Jim Kale** (bass); **Garry Peterson** (drums)

1962

The group forms in Winnipeg, MB, Canada, as Chad Allan & the Reflections, comprising members of two local teenage bands - Allan Kobel (guitar, vocals), who changes his name to Chad Allan, Bob Ashley (piano) and Kale (b. Michael James Kale, Aug. 11, 1943, Canada), all ex-Allan & the Silvertones, and Bachman (b. Sept. 27, 1943, Winnipeg, Canada) and Peterson (b. May 26, 1945, Canada), ex-the Velvetones. The band's first release is a cover of Mike Berry's UK hit, *Tribute To Buddy Holly*, recorded in Minneapolis, MN, for Canadian-American Records. Much of the group's early repertoire is Cliff Richard songs and Shadows instrumentals, learned from imported UK singles, material which makes them unique in southern Canada.

1963

Mar *Tribute To Buddy Holly* makes Winnipeg radio station CKY's Top 10 and attracts the attention of Canada's largest label, Quality Records, which signs the group.
Dec *Shy Guy*, on Quality, is another local CKY hit, at #20.

1964

Jan Through Allan's UK friends, the group has obtained and learned the Beatles' first UK album, and adopted the Merseybeat style. Allan and Bachman trade in their old Gretsch and Jazzmaster guitars for more appropriate Rickenbackers.
May When Detroit, MI group the Reflections has a US and Canadian Top 10 hit with *(Just Like) Romeo And Juliet*, the band changes its name to Chad Allan & the Original Reflections, releasing *A Shot Of Rhythm And Blues* in an arrangement similar to Gerry & the Pacemakers' version. To avoid confusion as both Reflections groups are on Quality, the name is finalized as Chad Allan & the Expressions.

1965

May The group's revival of Johnny Kidd's *Shakin' All Over* (learned from an old UK single) becomes a Canadian chart-topper. With the "British Invasion" in full swing, and the group's style a close approximation to the UK sound, Quality credits *Shakin' All Over* to "Guess Who?" and the publicity hints at a major UK group moonlighting. US licensee Scepter Records follows suit, and this ploy seems to work.
July [3] *Shakin' All Over* reaches US #22 and the band tours the US with the Turtles and the Crystals. The pressure of constantly appearing on stage causes Ashley to suffer increasing nervous problems. One night, when the Crystals mischievously pull him on stage during their act, he cracks and quits the group. Cummings (b. Dec. 31, 1947, Winnipeg), ex-Winnipeg group the Deverons, replaces Ashley and becomes joint lead vocalist with Allan. *Tossin' And Turnin'*, under the group's real name, tops the Canadian chart.
Shakin' All Over is released with a sleeve credit to "Guess Who? - Chad Allan & the Expressions". The name sticks, not only because of their recent hit but also at the request of Scepter Records, which takes them to New York, NY, to cut follow-up material for the US market. *Hey Ho, What You Do To Me* is released, followed by the ballad *Hurting Each Other* (later revived by the Carpenters).

1966

Allan leaves, after suffering voice problems which are aggravated whenever he forces his vocals during live gigs. He is briefly replaced by Bruce Dekker, an ex-Deverons colleague of Cummings, though the group shrinks to a quartet in the longer term, with Cummings handling all vocals.

1967

Feb [16] After wide pirate-radio airplay, *His Girl*, leased from Quality by the UK independent King label, enters the UK chart for a week, at #45. The group visits the UK for promotion but falls out with King, which wants a direct UK signing before organizing a tour. The band refuses and returns to Canada, $25,000 in debt. One recording session is held in the UK, with the band cutting songs by UK writers Jimmy Stewart and Jerry Langley.

1968

The Quality contract has lapsed and the group takes a regular slot on CBC-TV show "Where It's At" (with Allan rejoining). Through this, they meet producer Jack Richardson, who is working for an ad agency. Impressed by the band, he has them record a promotional album for Coca-Cola, then mortgages his house to pay for the recording of an album (which will become ***Wheatfield Soul***) and sets up the Nimbus 9 label for its release.

1969

Jan Third Guess Who single on Nimbus 9, the Cummings/Bachman composition *These Eyes*, is a hit in Canada and gains the group and the label a US deal with RCA.
May [31] Having topped the Canadian chart, *These Eyes* hits US #6.
June ***Wheatfield Soul*** makes US #45. The band is urged to move to Los Angeles, CA (but will remain based in Winnipeg, setting an example to Canadian rock talent which has always felt the need to move to the US to succeed).
[25] *These Eyes* wins a gold disc for one million-plus US sales.
Aug [23] *Laughing*, another Cummings/Bachman ballad, hits US #10.
Oct [28] *Laughing* is certified gold by the RIAA.
Nov ***Canned Wheat Packed By The Guess Who*** reaches US #91.
[19] *Undun*, B-side of *Laughing*, climbs to US #22.

1970

Jan [8-11] The group performs at San Francisco's Fillmore West, CA, on a bill with Chicago.
Feb [28] *No Time* hits US #5, the third consecutive million seller.
Apr [16] The group flies to the UK to appear on BBC1-TV's "Top Of The Pops", staying in the country for one day.
May [9] Double A-side, *American Woman/No Sugar Tonight*, begins a three-week stay atop the US chart - the fourth gold disc and the band's biggest US seller. (Because the song's lyric is a put-down of less desirable US attitudes, from a Canadian point of view, when the group is invited to play at the White House, it is specifically asked not to play *American Woman*.) The album of the same title, also a gold-disc winner, hits US #9.
July *American Woman* reaches UK #19, Guess Who's second and final UK chart single. Bachman leaves, his Mormon religion proving impossible to reconcile with the high-living band style which accompanies success. (He will reunite with Allan, plus two other Bachman brothers, to form Brave Belt, emerging later - minus Allan - as Bachman-Turner Overdrive.) A new Guess Who album, featuring Bachman, is shelved. Cummings takes control of the band and recruits two guitarists - Kurt Winter (ex-Brother, another Nimbus 9 act) and Greg Leskiw (ex-Wild Rice).
Sept [5] *Hand Me Down World* reaches US #17.
Dec [5] *Share The Land* hits US #10, while ***Share The Land*** reaches US #14 (earning another gold disc).

1971

Feb [27] *Hang On To Your Life* peaks at US #43.
May [8] *Broken*, B-side of the still-climbing *Albert Flasher*, makes US #55.
June Compilation album, ***The Best Of The Guess Who***, reaches US #12.
[15] ***The Best Of The Guess Who*** is certified gold by the RIAA.
[26] *Albert Flasher* climaxes at US #29.
Sept ***So Long, Bannatyne***, lacking Cummings' lyrics and Bachman's music, makes US #52.
Oct [2] The extracted *Rain Dance* reaches US #19.

1972

Jan [15] *Sour Suite* peaks at US #50.
Apr [8] *Heartbroken Bopper* makes US #47. ***Rockin'*** reaches US #79. Leskiw leaves the group (to form Mood Jga Jga and record for Warner Bros.), and is replaced on guitar by Don McDougall. The group embarks on 22-city North American tour.
June [10] *Guns, Guns, Guns* shoots to US #70.
Oct [28] *Runnin' Back To Saskatoon* reaches US #96. ***Live At The Paramount***, recorded at a Seattle, WA, concert, reaches US #39. Bassist and founder member Kale leaves (to record with Scrubaloe Caine and later front his own Jim Kale Band, in Winnipeg). He is replaced by Bill Wallace, an ex-colleague of Winter's in Brother.

1973

Feb ***Artificial Paradise*** peaks at US #112.
Mar [10] *Follow Your Daughter Home*, from the album, makes US #61.
Aug ***#10*** reaches US #155. The title is not strictly accurate: this is the tenth album since ***Wheatfield Soul***.

1974

Jan ***The Best Of The Guess Who, Volume II*** makes US #186.
Apr [20] *Star Baby* reaches US #39. Winter and McDougall are fired by Cummings. They are replaced by Toronto, ON, Canada-born Domenic Troiano, who has been playing guitar with the James Gang. He is the first (and last) member of Guess Who not to hail from Winnipeg.
June ***Road Food***, recorded before Winter and

McDougal's departure, reaches US #60.
Sept [5] *Clap For The Wolfman*, from ***Road Food***, including snatches of dialogue from renowned US radio DJ Wolfman Jack, hits US #6.
Dec [4] *Dancin' Fool* reaches US #28.

1975

Feb ***Flavors*** reaches US #48.
Aug ***Power In The Music*** makes US #87. (Cummings disbands the group, signs to Portrait as a soloist and moves to Los Angeles. Troiano returns to Toronto and forms his own band; Peterson founds the short-lived Delphia, while Wallace plays with various local groups around Winnipeg.)
Dec Cummings' self-penned solo debut on Portrait, *Stand Tall*, hits US #10 and is a million seller while ***Burton Cummings***, produced by Richard Perry, makes #30. (He will have three minor hits, all failing to crack the Top 60, during 1977 and 1978, and will subsequently release ***My Own Way To Rock*** (US #51 in 1978), the Canada-only ***Woman Love*** on Epic (1980) and ***You Saved My Soul***, on the Alfa label, which makes US #37 the following year.)

1977

May Compilation album, ***The Greatest Of The Guess Who***, reaches US #173.

1979

Kale and McDougall, along with Allan McDougall (vocals), David Inglis (guitar), Vince Masters (drums) and David Parasz (horns), regroup as Guess Who, recording ***All This For A Song***. The album, a single, *Sweet Young Thing*, and a reunion achieve little commercially (as will other attempted reunions).

1985

Apr Cummings is featured with fellow Canadians Neil Young, Bryan Adams, Joni Mitchell, Anne Murray, Gordon Lightfoot and others, on the Band Aid-prompted *Tears Are Not Enough*, a charity disc recorded by Canadian artists under the name Northern Lights, in aid of African famine relief.

1989

May [12] Guess Who embarks on a Dick Clark's "American Bandstand" tour at the RPI Fieldhouse, Troy, NY, with a current line-up of Kale, Ken Carter (vocals), Dale Russell (vocals, guitar), Peterson and Mike Hanford (keyboards), and will continue touring as a nostalgia act well into the '90s, changing its line-up to replace Hanford with Leonard Shaw and lead vocalist Carter with Terry Hatty by 1995.
see also: **BACHMAN-TURNER OVERDRIVE**

GUNS N' ROSES

Axl Rose (lead vocals); **Slash** (guitar); **Izzy Stradlin** (guitar); **Duff McKagan** (bass); **Steven Adler** (drums)

1985

Rose (b. William Bailey, Feb. 6, 1962, Lafayette, IN), who discovers his real surname is Rose when he is 17, his biological father having left home when he was a baby (his mother Sharon subsequently marrying his step-father, L. Stephen Bailey), calling himself Axl after one of the local bands he has played with in Indiana, where his first musical experience was singing in a church choir at age five, hitch-hikes to Los Angeles, CA, to meet up with old friend Stradlin (b. Jeffrey Isbell, Apr. 8, 1962, Lafayette), who has been playing for years on the Los Angeles club circuit without success. Earning $8 an hour smoking cigarettes as part of a science experiment at UCLA, Los Angeles, they hook up with Tracii Guns and Rob Gardener to form Rose, which blossoms into Hollywood Rose and finally L.A. Guns. Adler (b. Jan. 22, 1965, Cleveland, OH) and Slash (b. Saul Hudson, July 23, 1965, Stoke-on-Trent, Staffs.), whose father, Anthony, designed album covers, including Joni Mitchell's ***Court And Spark***, while his clothes-designing mother, Ola, seamed David Bowie's suits for the film "The Man Who Fell To Earth", schoolfriends from Bancroft Junior High, are playing in the Road Crew, when Slash sees Rose and Stradlin at a Los Angeles club, Gazzari's. (Adler has already lost out to C.C. DeVille to play in Poison.) McKagan (b. Michael McKagan, Feb. 5, 1964, Seattle, WA), playing in Seattle bands Fartz, 10 Minute Warning, Fastbacks, Veins and On The Rocks, is the last to join, after he replies to a classified ad for a bassist for Road Crew. The band, now settled as Adler, McKagan, Rose, Slash and Stradlin (Guns and Gardener have split from Rose and Stradlin in May, following a disagreement over a West Coast club tour), united by a desire to play earthy, gutsy rock'n'roll, chooses the name Guns N' Roses after rejecting Heads of Amazon and AIDS. Two people show up for their first official Los Angeles gig, though they quickly become local cult favorites (not least at the Troubadour club), uniquely matching their vision of punk nihilism with traditional heavy metal.
June The group heads off on "The Hell Tour '85" a series of dates in the Pacific Northwest, immediately running into difficulties when its van breaks down on the way. They hitch to their first gig, only to find the rest of the tour has apparently been cancelled.

1986

Feb Guns N' Roses release 10,000 copies of a four-track EP, *Live ?!*@ Like A Suicide*, on the Uzi/Suicide label.
Mar [25] Following intensive live work in California and record label competition, the band is signed worldwide to Geffen Records by A&R heads Tom Zutaut and Teresa Ensenat. Prior to signing, Rose has his birth-name legally changed to W. Axl Rose.
Aug Having fired early manager Vicky Hamilton, the group signs with Alan Niven and Doug Goldstein of Stravinsky Brothers Management, after Aerosmith's manager, Tim Collins, has turned them down, and begins recording at Daryl Dragon's Rumbo Recorders in Canoga Park, Los Angeles, with producer Mike Clink.

1987

Jan Geffen releases the 1986 Uzi/Suicide EP, *Live ?!*@ Like A Suicide*.
Apr The group opens for Iron Maiden on its US tour, but pulls out halfway through when Rose loses his voice. At the same time, Slash is sent to Hawaii to recuperate from ongoing chemical abuse. Most band members openly acknowledge and celebrate drug and drink problems.
May Rose is admitted to intensive care at a Los Angeles hospital after a fight with police, and is allegedly given electro-shock treatment.
June [19] Guns N' Roses make their UK debut at London's Marquee.
July They begin a US tour, this time behind headliners Motley Crue.
Aug [1] Their debut album, ***Appetite For Destruction***, produced by Mike Clink and written, arranged and performed by Guns N' Roses, begins a slow rise up both the US and UK surveys.
Oct [3] Los Angeles-themed *Welcome To The Jungle* initially peaks at UK #67, as the band supports the Cult on another US concert trek.
Nov Guns N' Roses visit the UK for its first major-venue tour, inviting heavy-metal group Faster Pussycat to open. (During the five-date trip, which includes a sellout performance at London's Hammersmith Odeon, Adler breaks his hand in a bar-room brawl and is temporarily replaced by Cinderella drummer, Fred Coury.)

1988

Feb Always a turbulent and volatile group, they fire Rose after he has missed a performance in Phoenix, AZ, reinstating him three days later.
July [15] In the middle of an unbroken 14-month touring period, Guns N' Roses begin a major-venue US tour behind Aerosmith, but soon become the main attraction. A rider in the latter's contract insists that Guns N' Roses confine chemical abuse to the dressing room, so as not to tempt Aerosmith members.
[28] Mid-tour, McKagan gets married, with former Cult bassist Haggis filling in for one gig.
Aug [6] Their debut album finally hits US #1, after 57 weeks on the chart, having sold more than five million copies. It will also hit UK #5 over one year later.
[20] The band interrupts a US tour to play the ninth annual "Monsters Of Rock" Festival, with Iron Maiden, Kiss, David Lee Roth, Megadeth and Helloween, at Castle Donington, Leics., before an estimated crowd of 92,000. Their third major festival appearance is marred as "slam-dancing" crowd antics result in two deaths during their performance of *It's So Easy*. Not knowing this until after their set has finished, Rose allegedly tells the crowd upon leaving the stage: "Have a good fuckin' day and don't kill yourselves". The group had already stopped playing three times, in an attempt to calm the situation. (The band joins Iron Maiden's "Summer '88" tour, but has to cancel some California dates when Rose loses his voice.)
Sept [7] "Welcome To The Jungle" clip wins the Best New Artist Video category at the fifth annual MTV Video Music Awards, held at the Universal Amphitheatre, Universal City, CA, where the group also performs.
[10] *Sweet Child O' Mine*, written about Axl's girlfriend Erin Everly, tops the US chart, despite Axl's concern that Geffen has edited the track from six to four minutes, and will also reach UK #24.
Oct *Welcome To The Jungle*, used in the latest Clint Eastwood Dirty Harry movie, "Dead Pool", in which the group has a cameo spot (also used by the Cincinnati Bengals football team as its theme), enters the US chart at #57 and #31 in the UK, where it is released as a double A-side with *Night Train*. Rose guests at recordings of Don Henley's third solo album.
Nov Finishing a US tour with Aerosmith, on which Rose was arrested in Atlanta, GA, Chicago, IL and Philadelphia, PA, the band cancels plans for a follow-on UK visit with Metallica in favor of a long rest. Reissued *Welcome To The Jungle*, doubled with *Nightrain*, peaks at UK #24.
Dec Eight-cut mini-album, ***G N' R Lies***, including four tracks from earlier EP, *Live ?!*@ Like A Suicide* added to four new cuts, is released, as the group visits Japan and Australia for live dates. The group flees Australia for New Zealand, when a warrant for Rose's arrest is issued (for making statements apparently condoning drug use during a concert).
[6] ***Appetite For Destruction*** earns multi-platinum status for six million sales, while the group wins Top Pop New Artist category in **Billboard**'s Year End In Music chart round-up.
[24] *Welcome To The Jungle* finally hits US #7.

1989

Jan ***G N' R Lies*** hits US #2.
[30] *Sweet Child O' Mine* is named the Favorite Single, Heavy Metal/Hard Rock at the 16th annual American Music Awards, held at the Shrine Auditorium, Los Angeles. Don Henley fills in on drums (for a flu-stricken Adler) for the group's performance of *Patience*.
Feb [11] With ***Appetite For Destruction*** at #2 and ***G N' R Lies*** at #5, Guns N' Roses becomes the first group in 15 years to simultaneously lodge two albums in the US top five.
Mar [11] *Paradise City* hits US #5, as Guns N' Roses are pulled from a planned AIDS benefit, "Rock And A Hard Place", at New York, NY's Radio City Music Hall, after gay activists object to the homophobic lyrics of the album track *One In A Million*, which has already been accused of being racist by the Simon Wiesenthal Center. (The benefit will not take place.)
Apr [1] *Paradise City* hits UK #6,
June [3] *Patience* hits US #4. During the month the band makes a failed attempt to begin pre-production work on a new album in Chicago, IL.
[17] *Sweet Child O' Mine*, remixed and reissued, hits UK #6.

July [8] *Patience* pays off at UK #10.
[22] ***Appetite For Destruction*** hits UK #5 during 131 weeks on the chart and ***G N' R*** Lies reaches UK #22, seven months after originally charting.
Aug [5] *Nightrain* runs out of steam at US #93.
[30] Stradlin is arrested for making a public disturbance, having urinated on the floor, verbally abused a stewardess and smoked in the non-smoking section, on a US Air flight.
Sept [6] The group collects the Best Heavy Metal Video trophy for "Sweet Child O' Mine", at the sixth annual MTV Video Music Awards, held at the Universal Amphitheatre, at which Rose sings *Free Fallin'* with Tom Petty. Motley Crue's Vince Neil reportedly throws a punch at Stradlin backstage during the proceedings.
[9] *Nightrain*, now reissued for the third time in the UK, reaches UK #17.
Oct Stradlin pleads guilty to his public-disturbance charge. A Phoenix court sentences him to a six-month probation, during which he must get counseling, and orders him to pay a $2,000 fine and $1,000 for cleaning costs.
[18] At a Los Angeles Coliseum support gig for the Rolling Stones, for whom the Roses are opening on a limited number of US dates, Rose accuses Slash of "dancing with Mr. Brownstone", a thinly-veiled drug reference, also announcing that this might be "his last gig" with the band.
[19] Rose, back on stage, delivers a five-minute anti-drug oration and apologizes for saying he would quit.
Dec [23] The group wins the Top Pop Album Artists and Top Pop Album Artists - Duo/Group categories in **Billboard**'s The Year In Music annual chart survey.

1990

Jan [22] Slash and McKagan, obviously inebriated, utter obscenities on live TV during the 17th American Music Awards, while collecting trophies for Favorite Heavy Metal/Hard Rock Artist and Favorite Metal/Hard Rock Album (***Appetite For Destruction***), at the Shrine Auditorium.
Mar [8] Rose is voted Worst Male Singer and Worst Dressed Male Rock Artist in **Rolling Stone** magazine's 1989 awards, though the group is conversely acknowledged as Best Heavy Metal Band.
[28] Adler signs an agreement which will result in his leaving the band the following month.
Apr [7] The band performs *Welcome To The Jungle*, *Civil War* and *Down On The Farm* (a UK Subs cut) at "Farm Aid IV" at the Hoosier Dome, Indianapolis, IN. (They will contribute *Civil War* to the Romanian Angel Appeal charity album, ***Nobody's Child***, while, by month's end, band members will also have guested on comedian Sam Kinison's ***Leader Of The Banned*** album.)
[28] Rose marries Erin Invicta Everly, daughter of singer Don Everly, at Cupid's Wedding Chapel in Las Vegas, NV.
May [24] Rose files for divorce, citing irreconcilable differences, in Los Angeles. (They will subsequently reconcile and then split again.)
June Guns N' Roses' version of Bob Dylan's *Knockin' On Heaven's Door* is featured in the Tom Cruise vehicle "Days Of Thunder" and, like all of its videos to date, becomes a heavily rotated clip on MTV.
July Slash, Duff and Sorum play a five-song set at a listening party for Iggy Pop's new ***Brick By Brick*** album in Los Angeles.
[31] 13 deputies arrive at Rose's West Hollywood apartment with batons drawn. He files a complaint against the sheriff's department.
Sept Adler is sacked, initially linking up with former Hanoi Rocks guitarist, Andy McCoy.
Oct Following try-outs by former Pretender Martin Chambers and Sea Hag's Adam Maples, the Cult's Matt Sorum (b. Nov. 19, 1960, Mission Viejo, CA) replaces Adler, after Slash has been impressed by his performance at a Cult gig at the Universal Amphitheatre. (Sorum has been in Australian new-wave band I.Q., and toured with guitarist Gregg Wright, and Gladys Knight, before joining the Cult.) Guns N' Roses sue the K-Mart chain for $2 million, for allegedly using their name and picture in ads for a toy drum kit. The suit somehow claims that the group has "suffered damage to their reputation, loss of goodwill and mental anguish".
[30] Rose is released on $5,000 bail, having been arrested for allegedly hitting a neighbor, Gabriela Kantor, over the head with a bottle after she rang the police to complain about loud music. (He will later say: "Frankly, if I was going to hit her with a wine bottle, she wouldn't have gotten up.")
Nov [19] Rose files documents prohibiting Kantor from having any further contact with him or his wife.

1991

Jan Rose is granted an annulment after nine months of marriage.
[20-23] With Sorum making his group debut, Guns N' Roses, also augmented by ex-Wild keyboardist Dizzy Reed (b. Darren Reed, June 18, 1963, Hinsdale, NY), recruited from Los Angeles band the Wild, perform in front of a 120,000 audience during the four-day "Rock In Rio II" festival at the Maracana soccer stadium in Rio de Janeiro, Brazil.
Apr Now the band's sole manager, Alan Niven announces that at all future interviews given by the group, journalists must sign a restrictive contract giving the band's management final approval on all material.
May [9] The band previews its upcoming tour with a three-date "Here Now And Going To Hell" warm-up at the Warfield Theatre, San Francisco, followed by dates at the Pantages Theatre, Los Angeles (11th) and the Ritz, Manhattan, New York (16th).
[24-25] Their "Get In The Ring tour", backed by Skid Row, opens at Alpine Valley Music Theatre, East Troy, WI, before a combined crowd of 75,593, grossing $2,050,560. Before the concert, Rose visits the Milwaukee County Medical Complex having torn ligaments in the bottom of his left foot when he jumped off a speaker at the Ritz gig. (Following the performance, doctors from the Green Bay Packers and Milwaukee Brewers tend to him.)
[28] The band is fined for performing past Indianapolis' Hamilton County's curfew at Noblesville, IN.
June [17] The group goes on stage two hours after its scheduled time, at the Nassau Veterans Memorial Coliseum, Uniondale, NY concert.
July [2] Rose sparks a riot at the Riverport Amphitheatre, Maryland Heights, MO concert, having yelled at security guards to remove a camera from a fan, before leaping into the crowd to enact his own style of security. More than 50 people, including 15 police officers, are injured in the ensuing brouhaha. The newly-opened theater sustains $200,000 in damages during the hour-long riot by 3,000 of the 15,400 audience. 13 adults and two juveniles are arrested on charges of assaulting an officer, resisting arrest, destruction of property and failure to disperse. The damage is so severe that a July 4th concert at the venue has to be cancelled, while Guns N' Roses gigs in Chicago and Bonner Springs are also axed.
[8] Jerome Harrison of St. Louis, MO, files suit in the St. Louis County Circuit Court seeking damages against Rose, other unidentified members of the band and its entourage, security staff and concert promoters, claiming he was assaulted during the riot that erupted at the previous week's concert. Four third-degree assault charges and a property-damage charge are filed against Rose. The Riverport owners will also file suit, seeking damages equal to any judgements that may be awarded to injured concertgoers.
[11] During a concert at Fiddler's Green Amphitheatre, Englewood, CO, Rose halts the show during the fifth song, demanding that security remove a heckling spectator.
[13] *You Could Be Mine*, featured on the soundtrack of "Terminator 2", debuts at its UK #3 peak.
[19] Adler files suit in Los Angeles County Superior Court, alleging that he was fraudulently removed from the group and stripped of his partnership interest in the band, also claiming that the band introduced him to hard drugs. The lawsuit also asks the judge to annul the March 28th, 1990 agreement. (He will form a new band Road Crew, the name of the group he had started with Duff and Slash in 1983, with Davy Vain (vocals) James Scott (guitar) Ashley Mitchell (bass), all ex-Vain from Santa Rosa, and Shawn Rorie (guitar), ex-Sister Strange from the Bay Area, though he will manage to get fired from this band too.)
[30] During a four-day stint at the Great Western Forum, Inglewood, CA, police tear up a traffic ticket over a citation for Rose's limousine, which has made an illegal left turn outside the venue. Police captain James Seymour says it was done to avoid a riot, after Rose threatens not to play if it is issued. Seymour says, "We don't need 19,000 people at the Forum rioting over a traffic ticket."
Aug [7] St. Louis County prosecutor Robert McCulloch files five misdemeanor charges against Rose.
[10] *You Could Be Mine* peaks at US #29.
Sept [5] The group performs their version of Paul McCartney's *Live And Let Die* live at the eighth annual MTV Video Music Awards ceremony, at the Universal Amphitheatre.
[17] At 12:01 a.m., 4.2 million copies (the largest shipping in pop history) of ***Use Your Illusion I*** and ***Use Your Illusion II*** are simultaneously released for retail sale in the US.
[21] *Don't Cry* debuts at its UK #8 peak.
[23] Stradlin announces that he will no longer tour with the band.
[28] ***Use Your Illusion II*** and ***Use Your Illusion I***, featuring guest vocalist Alice Cooper and covers of *Live And Let Die* and the Damned's *New Rose*, debut at UK #1 and #2 respectively and will remain charted throughout 1993.
Oct [5] ***Use Your Illusion II*** and ***Use Your Illusion I*** debut at US #1 and #2, the first time an act has held down the top two slots since Jim Croce (in January 1974) with ***You Don't Mess Around With Jim*** and ***I Got A Name***.
Nov [16] *Don't Cry* hits US #10, becoming the band's fourth RIAA certified gold single.
[25] Rose confirms on MTV's "Rockline" that Stradlin will be leaving, apparently tired of touring and making videos.
[27] Slash plays guitar on Michael Jackson's *Black And White* performance on ABC-TV's "MTV 10" special, one of two tracks the recent friends have collaborated on for Jackson's forthcoming ***Dangerous***.
[28] An official announcement is made that Stradlin and the band are going their separate ways, and that Kill For Thrills' Gilby Clarke (b. Aug. 17, 1962, Cleveland, OH) will take his place.
Dec [9-10, 13] The group performs three SRO shows at New York's Madison Square Garden, before a combined audience of 54,491, grossing $1,339,860.
[21] *Live And Let Die* debuts at its UK #5 peak. ***Use Your Illusion I*** and ***II*** both reach the three-million plateau in the US.
[31] The band celebrates New Year's Eve with a sold-out concert at the Joe Robbie Stadium, Miami, FL.

1992

Jan [13] The group walks onstage at 12:25 a.m., finishing at 3:05 a.m. at the Ervin J. Nutter Center, Wright State University, Dayton, OH sellout date.
[27] Guns N' Roses win the Favorite Artist, Heavy Metal/Hard Rock category at the 19th annual American Music Awards, held at the Shrine Auditorium.
Feb [8] *Live And Let Die* reaches US #33.
Mar [7] Rose-penned *November Rain* debuts at its UK #4 peak.
[14] A New York newspaper reports that Slash has signed a multi million-dollar deal to promote Black Death vodka.
[25] US Surgeon-General Antonia Novello slams Slash's Black Death vodka pact on NBC-TV's "Today".
Apr [1-2] The group performs to 39,291 capacity crowds at the Palacio De Los Deportes, Mexico City, Mexico.
[3] According to its owner, Stephen Trimboli, Slash

has sex with porn star Savannah at the bar of New York City's Scrap Bar.
[10] The group cancels a second Rosemont Horizon, Rosemont, IL concert when officers from Cook County Sheriff's Department threaten to arrest Rose on misdemeanor assault charges stemming from the 1991 Riverport Amphitheatre riot.
[20] The band takes part in "A Concert For Life", the Freddie Mercury tribute staged at Wembley Stadium, Wembley, Middx. After the show, Rose is left stranded at Heathrow Airport, after arriving minutes before a scheduled Air Canada flight to Vancouver, BC, Canada was due to leave. He argues with Customs over his homeopathic medicines going through the X-Ray machine and undergoes a body search.
May [16] The European leg of the group's extensive world tour, supported by Faith No More and Soundgarden, bows in Dublin, Eire.
[23] *Knockin' On Heaven's Door* debuts at its UK #2 peak, behind KWS' *Please Don't Go*.
June [6] Aerosmith's Steve Tyler and Joe Perry, Soundgarden, Lenny Kravitz and guitar hero Jeff Beck guest on the band's US TV-cable pay-per-view extravanganza, "Guns N' Roses Invade Paris!" broadcast live from France.
[13] The group performs at Wembley Stadium at the start of a brief UK tour.
July [12] Rose is arrested by U.S. Customs agents at Kennedy International Airport on misdemeanor charges. Port Authority spokesman Allen Morrison later says he was "co-operative".
Aug [8] Rose walks off stage at the Olympic Stadium, Montreal, PQ, Canada, approximately 15 minutes into the group's set, citing vocal problems. 2,000 fans begin throwing missiles, breaking windows and looting a souvenir shop. (Support act Metallica also cut their set short, when James Hetfield receives second-degree burns when a pyrotechnic effect goes awry.)
[25] Their US tour resumes in Phoenix, AZ.
[29] From ***Use Your Illusion I***, the sweeping, lengthy rock-ballad, *November Rain*, hits US #3.
RPM Records, the group's South African record label, wins an appeal against the ban on ***Use Your Illusion I*** and ***II*** in South Africa, after the country's chief censor, the Committee of Publications, has received a complaint from a "concerned citizen".
Sept [9] "November Rain" wins the Best Cinematography category at the ninth annual MTV Video Music Awards, held at the Pauley Pavilion, Los Angeles, while the band also collects the Michael Jackson Video Vanguard trophy. The band also performs the song as the show's finale, assisted by Elton John on piano.
[10] Slash marries actress/model Renee Suran in Marina Del Rey, CA.
Oct [9] Following three weeks of rehearsal in the Chicago Music Complex's Showcase Room, Izzy Stradlin & the Ju Ju Hounds, comprising Rick Richards (ex-Georgia Satellites) (guitar), Jimmy Ashurst (ex-Broken Homes) (bass), Charlie "Chalo" Quintana (ex-Cruzados and Dylan road band) (drums), make their UK debut at London's Mean Fiddler.
[31] ***Izzy Stradlin & The Ju Ju Hounds***, featuring Ron Wood, Mikey Dread, Ian McLagan and Nicky Hopkins, debuts at its US #102 peak, having made UK #52 a week earlier, with *Pressure Drop* debuting at its UK #45 peak on Sept [26].
Nov [10] Rose is found guilty of property damage and assault during the notorious 1991 St. Louis concert. St. Louis County associate circuit judge Ellis Gregory gives the singer two years probation and orders him to pay $50,000 in donations to five local social-service organizations.
[25] A Latin American tour segment begins in Venezuela.
[28] *Yesterdays* makes US #72, while *Yesterdays/ November Rain* hits UK #8.
Dec [3] The group is ordered to stay in Chile until a probe as to why traces of cocaine have reportedly been found in one of the band member's clothing is resolved. (In a separate incident on their South American trek, a riot ensues after a gig in Columbia, leaving 10 injured and 178 arrested.)
[9] The band wins the Billboard Top 200 Albums Group category at the third annual **Billboard** Music Awards, held at the Universal Amphitheatre, during which they perform live by satellite from Buenos Aires. During a busy day, Rose is charged with "endangering human lives" by Brazilian police, having thrown a chair off the mezzanine level into a crowd of people at the hotel where they are staying.

1993

Mar [30] The group grosses more than $500,000 at the British Columbia Place Stadium, Vancouver, during Canadian dates in Hamilton, ON, Winnipeg, MB, Saskatoon, SK and Edmonton, AB.
Apr [30] Clarke breaks his wrist while taking a test run on a motorcross course in Castiac Lake, CA, in preparation for the T.J. Martell Foundation celebrity race on May 8th. Four gigs are cancelled.
May [12] The group is named World's Best Selling Hard-Rock Artist Of The Year at the fifth annual World Music Awards, at the Sporting Club in Monte Carlo, Monaco.
[22] Stradlin deputizes for Clarke at the start of a 25-city tour in Tel Aviv, Israel.
[29] The group plays the first of two "Get In The Ring Motherf**ker Round 11" concerts at the National Bowl, Milton Keynes, Bucks., as EP, *The Civil War*, debuts at its UK #11 peak.
July [3] Paul Rodgers-assembled ***Tribute To Muddy Waters*** album, released on Victory Music and featuring guest fret work from Slash, debuts at its UK #9 peak, having made US #91 in May. (The soundtrack album to the Dan Aykroyd-starring "Coneheads" movie, including Slash and Michael Monroe's cover of Steppenwolf's *Magic Carpet Ride*, is released in the US.)
Oct [16] McKagan's solo album, ***Believe In Me***, featuring Slash, Reed, Sorum, Jeff Beck and Lenny Kravitz, having debuted at its UK #27 peak the previous week, now bows at its US #137 peak.
[21] Rose's legal case in St. Louis is settled out of court. (The band has recently settled out of court with Adler for a reported $2.5 million.)
Nov [20] *Ain't It Fun* debuts at its UK #9 peak.
Dec [4] ***The Spaghetti Incident***, an album of covers, including material recorded by the Damned, the New York Dolls, Iggy & the Stooges, the UK Subs, and most controversially, a song written by Charles Manson, debuts at its UK #2 peak, behind Meat Loaf's ***Bat Out Of Hell II - Back Into Hell***.
[11] ***The Spaghetti Incident*** debuts at its US #4 peak.

1994

Jan [19] Rose inducts Elton John into the Rock and Roll Hall of Fame at the ninth annual dinner at New York's Waldorf Astoria, and jams with Bruce Springsteen on *Come Together* at the after-dinner jam.
Mar [19] Taken from ***The Spaghetti Incident***, *Since I Don't Have You*, reviving the Skyliners' 1959 US #12, peaks at US #69.
June [11] *Since I Don't Have You* hits UK #10.
July [18] Erin Everly reveals in **People** that she was constantly abused by Rose. With press reports earlier in the year indicating that Clarke has been fired (and replaced by Paul Huge), his debut solo album, ***Pawnshop Guitars***, released by Virgin America, reaches UK #39.

1995

Jan [7] Their version of the Rolling Stones' *Sympathy For The Devil*, also included on the movie soundtrack to "Interview With The Vampire", reaches US #55.
[14] *Sympathy For The Devil* debuts at its UK #9 peak.
Feb [25] Having assembled an ad-hoc side band in the absence of a new Guns N' Roses project, Slash's Snakepit's ***It's Five O'Clock Somewhere*** reaches UK #15 in its week of entry, featuring Clarke, Sorum and Alice In Chain's Mike Inez.
Mar [4] ***It's Five O'Clock Somewhere*** debuts at its US #70 peak.
May [12] Rose files a restraining order against 34-year old fan in Karen McNeil in Los Angeles Superior Court. She is charged with trespassing at his Malibu home on April 27th.
Sept [2] Slash performs *Red House* with Boz Scaggs at the Concert for the Rock and Roll Hall of Fame at Cleveland Stadium, Cleveland, OH.
Nov [30] With Guns N' Roses seemingly in disarray, ex-member Clarke files a suit in California Superior Court, Los Angeles, against the band for commercial misappropriation of his name, likeness, photograph, voice and performance and seeking a share of profits and punitive damages.

H

HAIRCUT 100

Nick Heyward (guitar, vocals); **Graham Jones** (guitar); **Les Nemes** (bass); **Phil Smith** (saxophone); **Mark Fox** (percussion, congas); **Blair Cunningham** (drums)

1981

Sept With the band formed in Beckenham, Kent, by poster-boy frontman Heyward (b. May 20, 1961, Beckenham), Nemes (b. Dec. 5, 1960, Croydon, Surrey) and Jones (b. July 8, 1961, Bridlington, North Humberside) in 1980, temporary drummer Patrick Hunt, recruited for early gigs around South London, has been replaced by session player Cunningham (b. Oct. 11, 1957, Memphis, TN), one of nine drum-playing brothers, in March 1981, principally to record a studio demo tape under the guidance of engineer Karl Adams, who subsequently becomes their manager. Smith (b. May 1, 1959, Redbridge, Surrey) is also asked to join permanently, after helping out on the demo sessions. Adams hawks the band's songs around UK record companies in search of a deal, finding increasing interest as the group plays higher-profile gigs and begins to attract positive music press attention with its perky, clean-cut pop sound and similarly ingenuous visual image, with some observers even hailing them as the new Monkees. Heated competition by the UK labels ends as Haircut 100 signs to Arista Records.

Nov [21] Their debut single, the Heyward-penned *Favourite Shirts (Boy Meets Girl)*, hits UK #4.

Dec Fox (b. Feb. 13, 1958), after sitting in on studio rehearsals, becomes a full-time member.

1982

Mar [13] *Love Plus One* hits UK #3, as their album debut, ***Pelican West***, confirming them as UK teen idols of the moment, hits UK #2, behind Barbra Streisand's ***Love Songs***, selling over 300,000 in its first week. Produced by Bob Sargeant, it will remain charted for 34 weeks, its sleeve handsomely depicting the band members' preference for cable-knit Arran sweaters.

May [1] Further showcasing the band's deft pop harmonies, the Heyward-written *Fantastic Day* hits UK #9.

Aug [7] *Love Plus One* makes US #37, though it is to be their only US hit single, while ***Pelican West*** climbs to US #31.

Sept [4] *Nobody's Fool* hits UK #9.

Nov The group's second album release is postponed, as Heyward leaves amid general acrimony and Fox, who had quit because of a personality clash with Heyward, returns to take up lead vocals.

1983

Jan Heyward is retained as a solo act by Arista, allowing Haircut 100 to move to Polydor Records, who re-target the group towards a more mature market.

Apr Heyward appears at the Albany Empire, Deptford, London, with Glenn Tilbrook in Morris & the Jazz Reesons.

[16] Heyward scores his first UK solo hit with *Whistle Down The Wind*, at #13.

July [9] *Take That Situation*, originally written by Heyward for the sophomore Haircut 100 project, peaks at UK #11.

Aug Haircut 100's *Prime Time* clocks in at UK #46, but subsequent singles, including the follow-up, *Two Up Two Down*, fail to chart.

Oct [22] Heyward's solo *Blue Hat For A Blue Day* reaches UK #14. His debut solo album, ***North Of A Miracle***, co-produced with Geoff Emerick, using noted session players (including Dave Mattacks (drums), Steve Nieve (keyboards) and Tim Renwick (Quiver)), is acclaimed for its maturity of performance and songwriting, and hits UK #10.

Dec The extracted *On A Sunday* peaks at UK #52.

1984

Jan ***North Of A Miracle*** stalls at US #178.

June [16] *Love All Day* reaches UK #31 for Heyward.
July Haircut 100 album, ***Paint On Paint***, long delayed in the hope of a boost from a hit single, is released, but its chart failure results in the dissolution of the group. (Nemes and Smith will both re-emerge in Rick Astley's backing band in the late '80s; Cunningham will return to work as an in-demand session musician, eventually joining the Pretenders, before becoming a regular member of Paul McCartney's backing band in the early '90s; and Jones becomes a vocalist for Boys Wonder, while Fox, initially playing on records for Matt Bianco, Halo James and the Beat, eventually becomes A&R head for the East West label in London, responsible, not least, for signing the Beloved.)
Dec [1] Heyward's *Warning Sign*, a one-off funk try-out, reaches UK #25, followed by *Laura*, which climbs to UK #45 in June 1985.

1986

May Heyward's *Over The Weekend*, featured on the soundtrack to the Tom Hanks-starring film "Nothing In Common", peaks at UK #43.
June [28] Heyward supports Wham! at the duo's farewell concert, "The Final", at Wembley Stadium, Wembley, Middx.
Oct Heyward's sophomore effort, the harmony-drenched, self-written ***Postcards From Home***, is released. Co-produced with his manager, Graham Sacher, it features ex-Haircut colleague Nemes on bass. Its chart failure leads to Heyward leaving Arista to sign a worldwide deal with Warner Bros. Records in 1988, when - in September - *You're My World* peaks at UK #67.

1992

Dec While BMG has issued the Arista-chronicling ***Best Of Nick Heyward And Haircut 100***, in December 1989, Heyward's contract with Warner Bros. has only yielded one album, ***I Love You Avenue***, released in the same year. Now signed to CBS/Columbia, the ever-youthful Heyward begins working on new material at the Marcus Studios, with producer Julian-Gordon Hastings.

1993

Aug [21] Newly signed to Epic Records, Heyward's *Kite* debuts at its UK #44 peak, as he makes a rare live appearance, at London's Borderline club, with former Haircut 100 pal Nemes prominent in his four-piece band.
Oct [16] *He Doesn't Love You Like I Do* debuts at its UK #58 peak, taken from the newly released ***from monday to sunday***, a 12-track self-penned, self-produced set.
Dec [14] Heyward takes part in the "WEQX Holiday Concert" at Saratoga Winners, Latham, NY, with Paul Weller, Cowboy Junkies, Teenage Fanclub and Catherine Wheel.

1994

Feb [10] With *Kite* having picked up heavy airplay on US college and alternative stations and hitting #4 on th US Modern Rock chart, Heyward pays a sellout gig at the Roxy in Los Angeles, CA, during current US dates.

1996

Jan [13] While *The World* has debuted at its UK #47 high on Sept [30] the previous year, *Rollerblade*, also due to be included on a forthcoming album, enters at its UK #37 peak.

BILL HALEY & HIS COMETS

Bill Haley (vocals, guitar); **Frank Beecher** (lead guitar); **Billy Williamson** (steel guitar); **Johnny Grande** (piano, piano accordian); **Rudy Pompilli** (sax); **Al Rex** (bass); **Ralph Jones** (drums)

1944

After leaving school in Boothwyn, PA, Haley (b. July 6, 1925, Highland Park, Detroit, MI), who has shown musical aptitude since his early youth, making his first paid appearance at the Booth Corners Friday-night auction mart and finding work at the nearby Sunset and Rainbow amusement parks, before forming his own C&W band on leaving high school, and has joined Wilmington, DE radio station WDEL DJ Cousin Lee's band, singing (yodelling is his speciality) and playing guitar. He answers an ad in **Billboard** to replace the recently drafted 18-year old yodeller Kenny Roberts in the Shorty Cook-led Downhomers, with whom he records *We're Recruiting* for the Vogue label. (Haley is exempt from the draft because a botched mastoid operation in infancy has made him blind in his left eye.) The band is based at radio station WOWO in Fort Wayne, IN, where they perform a daily show and host the Saturday-night Hoosier Hop barn dance.

1946

Disillusioned, Haley leaves the band and returns to his parents' home near Philadelphia, PA. Shortly thereafter he marries Dorothy Crowe, whom he met at a parish church show in Salem, NJ, while touring with Cousin Lee, and moves to Keane, NH, and Lebanon, PA, before settling in Chester, PA.

1948

Forming the Four Aces of Western Swing with Al Constantine (accordian), Tex King (guitar) and Barney Barnard (bass), Haley records *Four Leaf Clover Blues* and a cover of Hank Williams' *Too Many Parties, Too Many Pals*, for the local Cowboy Records in Philadelphia, the city's first record label. (Two further Cowboy singles are released, *Candy Kisses*, backed with Red Foley's *Tennessee Border*, and Reno Browne & Her Buckaroos' *My Sweet Little Girl From Nevada*, on which Haley is the featured vocalist.)

1949

Apr [16] Having joined radio station WPWA in Chester (near Boothwyn) as a DJ, also playing live on air with the Four Aces, Haley gains his first national press exposure on the "First Hillbilly And Western Marathon", a benefit for cancer research, which raises $16,000, with Rusty Keefer replacing Tex King. By year's end, the Four Aces release a one-off single for the Center label, *Stand Up And Be Counted*, backed with *Loveless Blues*.

1950

Haley disbands the Four Aces and recruits guitarist Billy Williamson, pianist Johnny Grande and bassist Al Rex (b. Al Piccarelli), who introduces the slap bass style and, to avoid conflict with another local group also called the Four Aces, Haley names his new outfit Bill Haley & the Saddlemen, subsequently billed as the Cowboy Jive Band. They record two singles for the Keystone label, *Deal Me A Hand (I Play The Game Anyway)* and *Susan Van Dusen*, and cut *Why Do I Cry Over You* for Atlantic Records the following year.

1951

Haley is asked by Holiday Records boss Dave Miller to record *Rocket 88*, an R&B chart-topper for Jackie Brenston on the Chess label. Haley's version sells about 10,000 copies. The similar *Green Tree Boogie*, a Haley original, fares no better, and is followed by versions of Memphis Slim's *I'm Crying* and the seasonal *A Year Ago This Christmas*, which do not bring success.

1952

Juke Box Cannonball, re-working Roy Acuff's *Wabash Cannonball*, is Haley's final single on Holiday, before Miller founds Essex Records, which releases the country-styled *Icy Heart*, replying to Hank Williams' 1951 Country hit *Cold, Cold Heart*. It is coupled with *Rock The Joint*, another R&B cover of a 1949 Jimmy Preston record which is being used as the theme to Jim Reeves' WPWA show "Judge's Rhythm Court", which precedes Haley's live country show. It sells 75,000 copies. The Saddlemen release their final single, *Rocking Chair On The Moon*, following which Al Rex quits, soon taking over Haley's radio show. "Lord Jim" Ferguson becomes Haley's new manager and books the group into a summer residency at the Stone Harbor Café in Stone Harbor, NJ. At the suggestion of WPWA DJ Bix Reichner, the band name-changes to the Comets, releasing *Stop Beatin' Around The Mulberry Bush*.

1953

June Haley has dropped the cowboy image, renaming his group Bill Haley & His Comets and adding a drummer, Dick Richards. The combo's debut release is Haley's own *Crazy Man Crazy*, which is promptly covered by the Ralph Marterie Orchestra, which receives considerable airplay, although Haley's version benefits in sales, reaching US #12.
Oct Like its predecessor, *Fractured*, *Live It Up* bubbles under the US Top 20. The Comets record two final singles for Essex, *I'll Be True*, coupled with *Ten Little Indians*, and *Straight Jacket*, coupled with *Chattanooga Choo-Choo*, and a one-off for Transworld, *Yes Indeed*, coupled with *Real Rock Drive*. *(We're Gonna) Rock Around The Clock*, written by Jimmy Myers, who, working under the professional name of Jimmy DeKnight, shares office space with Jack Howard, and songwriter Max Freedman and recorded the previous year by Sunny Dae & His Knights, becomes a live favorite during the Comets' six-month residency at the Broomall Café in Chester and during their summer residency in Wildwood, NJ. However, Miller will not let Haley record the song, because of his dislike of Myers. When Haley leaves Essex, Myers initiates a deal with Decca's Head of Artist Acquisitions and the company's main producer, Milt Gabler, who has had major success with Louis Armstrong, Ella Fitzgerald, Louis Jordan and the Inkspots.

1954

Apr [12] Haley and the Comets make their first recordings for Decca at the company's Pythian Temple Studios, New York, NY. With the help of guitarist Danny Cedrone, who has played on previous Saddlemen sessions, and studio drummer Billy Guesack, the Comets record *(We're Gonna) Rock Around The Clock* and *Thirteen Women*, an R&B tune by Dickie Thompson.
June [3] *(We're Gonna) Rock Around The Clock* initially charts for a week at US #23. With a current sales tally of 75,000, Decca picks up the group's option.
[7] *See You Later Alligator*, *Shake Rattle And Roll* and *ABC Boogie* are recorded at Pythian Temple in four hours.
Nov [11] *Shake, Rattle And Roll*, Haley's second Decca single and a cover of the Charles Calhoun-penned R&B version by Big Joe Turner, hits US #7. (The American Hockey League Springfield Indians will adopt Haley's version, playing the disc before and after every home game and after each goal scored by the team.)

1955

Jan [8] *(We're Gonna) Rock Around The Clock* charts briefly, peaking at UK #17.
[22] *Dim, Dim The Lights (I Want Some Atmosphere)* reaches US #11, as *Shake, Rattle And Roll*, released on Brunswick in the UK, hits #4.
Mar [26] *Birth Of The Boogie* makes US #26.
Apr [16] *Mambo Rock* peaks at UK #14.
[30] *Mambo Rock*, the flipside of *Birth Of The Boogie*, reaches US #18.
May [14] *(We're Gonna) Rock Around The Clock*, now benefitting from its inclusion in the film "The Blackboard Jungle", starring Glenn Ford, re-enters the US chart.
July [9] Having climbed steadily, *(We're Gonna) Rock Around The Clock* begins the first of eight weeks at US #1. It will become one of the biggest-selling singles in chart history, also spending a total of 24 weeks in the US Top 40 - 19 of which are in the Top 10. Although it is not the first rock'n'roll record, it is certainly the most successful in a bursting genre and will be regarded as a landmark recording in rock history.
Sept [23] *Razzle Dazzle*, coupled with *Two Hound*

Dogs, reaches US #15.
Oct [15] *(We're Gonna) Rock Around The Clock* re-enters the UK chart.
[20] Haley performs on the same bill as Elvis Presley at Brooklyn High School Auditorium, Cleveland, OH.
Nov [14] Haley and the Comets perform in Lubbock, TX, on a show booked by local radio station KDAV, which also features two local newcomers, Buddy (Holly) & Bob (Montgomery).
[26] *(We're Gonna) Rock Around The Clock* begins the first of two spells (interrupted by Dickie Valentine's festive *Christmas Alphabet*), five weeks in total, at UK #1. While "The Blackboard Jungle" is on UK release, youths rip up cinema seats and dance in the aisles, in the nation's first experience of post-war hooliganism.
[26] *Rock-A-Beatin' Boogie*, B-side of the still-climbing *Burn That Candle*, peaks at US #41.
Dec [31] Haley and the Comets end their phenomenal year at the Michigan State Fair Coliseum, Detroit, MI, as *Burn That Candle* makes US #20. (By year's end, salaried members Dick Richards, Marshall Lytle and Joey Di'Ambrosia leave to form the Jodimars, signing a deal with Capitol Records. Williamson and Grande, who are partners with Haley, continue in the band. For live commitments they hire a new group, featuring Frank Beecher, who had joined Buddy Greco's band in 1948 before playing in Philadelphia lounge act the Larry Wayne Trio and who has played guitar on the group's records since *Happy Baby*, following Danny Cedrone's death from a heart attack in 1954, Al Rex, who re-joins, and newcomers Rudy Pompilli, a former member of the Ralph Marterie Orchestra who was voted **Downbeat**'s Best New Sax player of 1953 in the magazine's Jazz Poll, and Don Raymond (drums). (Raymond's tenure with the Comets is a short one, and he is replaced by Dean Tinker, who in turn is replaced by Ralph Jones, a fellow ex-member of Pompilli's in Little Arnie's Four Horsemen and the Merry Men. Both Jones and Tinker met Haley on their own WPWA jazz show.))

1956

Jan [14] *Rock-A-Beatin' Boogie*, a Haley original given to the Treniers at the time of *Rocket 88*, hits UK #4.
Feb [11] *See You Later, Alligator*, originally recorded by Bobby Charles, hits US #6. Selling over one million copies in a month, it will nevertheless be Haley's last US Top 10 hit.
Rock Around The Clock reaches US #12, the first rock album to make the US Album chart.
Mar [17] *See You Later, Alligator* hits UK #7.
[23] Haley and the Comets record *Rudy's Rock*, *Goofin' Around*, *Hey Then, There Now*, *Tonight's The Night* and *Hook, Line And Sinker* in a single session.
Apr [21] *R-O-C-K*, featured in the movie "Rock Around The Clock", reaches US #29, as *The Saints Rock'n'Roll*, a rock version of the traditional *When The Saints Go Marching In* and the B-side of *R-O-C-K*, makes US #42. (Haley stars, with Alan Freed and Little Richard, in the first rock'n'roll exploitation movie "Rock Around The Clock". The film and its hasty follow-up, "Don't Knock The Rock", are hugely popular worldwide (although banned in some countries), causing unprecedented scenes in movie theaters. "Don't Knock The Rock" takes $4 million gross in the US. The enterprising management of the Center Theater in Charlotte, NC runs a 36-hour rock'n'roll marathon, during which the film runs continuously. The films are a major boost to Haley's stardom, but also serve to undermine it - revealing a chubby family man sharing the screen with the outrageous Little Richard. Featured in the film are *Happy Baby*, *Rock-A-Beatin' Boogie*, *Razzle Dazzle*, *ABC Boogie*, *Mambo Rock*, *Rudy's Rock*, *R-O-C-K*, *See You Later, Alligator* and *Rock Around The Clock*.)
June A teenager is cut on the arm before a Haley performance at the National Grand Armory in Washington, DC. 17-year old William Warfield also suffers a cut over his eye and is rushed to hospital, where he is diagnosed as having concussion.
[30] In the latest in a series of unprecedented growing-pain incidents for the rock'n'roll genre, a further 25 fans are hospitalized following disturbances at a concert at the Convention Hall in Asbury Park, NJ.
July [7] *The Saints Rock'n'Roll* hits UK #5, as *Hot Dog Buddy Buddy*, featured in "Don't Knock The Rock", peaks at US #60.
[21] B-side, *Rockin' Through The Rye*, an update of an 18th-century Scottish folk tune, *Comin' Thro' The Rye*, makes US #78.
Aug [25] *Teenager's Mother (Are You Right?)*, the flip of Haley's still-climbing cover of Little Richard's *Rip It Up*, peaks at US #68.
Sept [15] *Rip It Up*, featured in "Don't Knock The Rock", reaches US #30. (Scheduled to watch "The Caine Mutiny" at Balmoral Castle, H.R.H. Queen Elizabeth II requests a viewing of "Rock Around The Clock". She is more fortunate than most of her loyal subjects: the Rank cinema chain cancels Sunday-night showings of the film in several major UK cities, since the Sabbath has been chosen as the favored night out for the rock'n'roll-inspired Teddy Boy gangs.)
[22] *Rockin' Through The Rye*, Haley's fifth consecutive UK Top 10 single, hits #3, as the first Comets session with Haley, Beecher, Williamson, Grande, Pompilli, Rex and Jones takes place.
[22] The first Comets session with Haley, Beecher, Williamson, Grande, Pompilli, Rex and Jones takes place.
[29] Haley equals a record established in 1955 by Ruby Murray, when he has five songs simultaneously in the UK Top 30: *Rockin' Through The Rye* (#4), *The Saints Rock'n'Roll* (#11), *Rock Around The Clock* (#13), *Razzle Dazzle* (#17) and *See You Later, Alligator* (#19).
Oct [6] *Razzle Dazzle* reaches UK #13.
[20] Given impetus by the release of the movie "Rock Around The Clock", *See You Later, Alligator* reaches UK #12 while *(We're Gonna) Rock Around The Clock* will hit UK #5 on Nov [3].
Rock'n'Roll Stage Show reaches US #18.
Nov [10] ***Rock'n'Roll Stage Show*** makes UK #30 (there will be no separate album chart until 1958.)
[24] *Rudy's Rock*, featured in "Rock Around The Clock", makes US #34.
Dec [8] *Rip It Up* hits UK #4.
[15] Title track, *Don't Knock The Rock*, backed with *Choo Choo Ch'Boogie*, makes US #45.
[22] *Rudy's Rock* and *Rock Around The Clock* re-enter the UK survey, at #26 and #24 respectively. (By year's end, Haley will headline the first rock'n'roll package tour of North America. The Irving Feld-promoted "Galaxy Of The Stars" also features the Platters and Frankie Lymon & the Teenagers.)

1957

Jan [5] Both *Rockin' Through The Rye* and *Rock Around The Clock* re-enter the UK chart, at #19 and #25 respectively, the latter dropping out for a week, before making its fifth and final re-entry (of this decade), at #22.
[8] The group begins a world tour in Sydney, New South Wales, Australia, before two sellout crowds of 7,000 fans, breaking the previous Australian attendance figure. This first-ever rock'n'roll tour of the country continues with two nights at the Brisbane Stadium, Brisbane, Queensland and, dates on the 11th and 12th at the Tivoli Theatre, Adelaide, South Australia, followed by gigs in Melbourne, Victoria and Sydney, before returning to Melbourne on the 23rd and finishing the three-week stay in Sydney. During the group's visit, they perform before more than 300,000 fans.
[31] Decca Records, UK distributor of the Brunswick label, announces that *(We're Gonna) Rock Around The Clock* has now sold over a million copies (mostly 10" 78s) in the UK alone - the first time this feat has been achieved (although Harry Belafonte and Paul Anka will do the same 12 months later).
Feb [2] 1952-recorded *Rock The Joint*, licensed from Essex by the UK London label, reaches UK #20.
[5] Haley arrives from New York on the liner "Queen Elizabeth" at Southampton, Hants., for his long-awaited UK concert debut. He is greeted at the dock by an estimated crowd of between 3,000 and 5,000. The first US rock artist to tour the UK, he is mobbed for 20 minutes by fans when his train reaches London.
[6-9] His 18-date UK tour, highlighted by continued fan mania, begins at the Dominion Theatre, London, set to end on the 23rd at the Gaumont Cinema, Southampton, Hants.
[16] *Don't Knock The Rock* hits UK #7.
Apr [13] *Forty Cups Of Coffee/Hook, Line And Sinker*, the B-side of *Don't Knock The Rock*, peaks at US #70. Pompilli is taken ill and Frankie Scott cuts sessions in his place.
June [10] *(You Hit The Wrong Note) Billy Goat* makes US #60.
Nov The band records some of its more familiar hits in the styles and languages of some non-English speaking countries.

1958

Feb [6-7] The group returns to the recording studio to cut forthcoming singles.
[20] A 12-date, six-day "The Big Gold Record Stars" package tour of Florida, with Haley, the Everly Brothers, Buddy Holly & the Crickets, Jerry Lee Lewis and Jimmie Rodgers, opens at the Kellog Auditorium, Orlando, FL, set to end on the 25th at the War Memorial Auditorium, Fort Lauderdale, FL.
May [12] *Skinny Minnie* reaches US #22.
June [18] Al Rex plays his last gig with the band on a tour of the UK, and is later replaced by Rudy Pompilli's brother, Al.
Aug [11] *Lean Jean* peaks at US #67.
Sept [22] The Comets, minus Haley, make US #35 with *Week End*, under the name the Kingsmen.
Oct [26] Haley & His Comets play the first rock'n'roll concert in Germany at the West Berlin Sportspalast, during a European tour, which opened at the Paris Olympia. There is a major riot among the 7,000 fans. (On the day Haley and the band arrive in W. Germany, Bundeswehr Federal Minister of Defence, Strauss, announces that jazz concerts are to be encouraged in the country, causing E. Germany's Minister of Defence, Willi Stoph, to declare that Haley is promoting nuclear war by engendering fanatical, hysterical enthusiasm among the German youth which would lead it to a mass rock'n'roll grave.)
[29] On the final date of the German leg of their tour, they perform at the Kellesberg Hall, Stuttgart, where they are visited backstage by Elvis Presley. Also during the German segment of the tour, they make the movie "Hier Bin Ich, Hier Bliebe Ich" ("Here I Am, Here I Stay") with Caterina Valente.

1959

Jan [7] The band records at the Pythian Temple and will record final sessions for Decca in November.
Nov [9] *Joey's Song* makes US #46.

1960

Jan [18] *Skokiaan (South African Song)* is Haley's last US hit for Decca, at #70. He signs to the new Warner Bros. label and releases a re-recording of his 1948 song *Candy Kisses*, but both it and subsequent singles for the label fail to chart, despite heavy promotion. (After Warner drops him he will record for a series of smaller labels.)
Apr Jones quits the Comets after a tour of Mexico. Following the success of *Florida Twist* in Mexico, where it has become the country's biggest-selling single ever, Haley begins recording what will become a series of Spanish-language tracks for the territory.

1962

Following the release of a live album the previous year, ***Twistin' Knights At The Round Table*** on the Roulette label, and after another tour of Mexico, Beecher quits the Comets, reportedly over money owed to him. Grande soon follows, after which the Comets will split. Haley subsequently loses his money, the band (with the exception of Pompilli), his wife and his house.

1964

June Haley, having briefly returned to Decca for

Green Door/Yeah, She's Evil and still enjoying Latin dance hits in South America (recording for the Mexican Orfeon label) and continuing to regularly tour Europe, performs before a crowd of 30,000 in Berlin.

1968

Apr [13] *Rock Around The Clock*, reissued by MCA, reaches UK #20.
May [2] Haley performs at London's Royal Albert Hall during a three-week UK tour, which also includes Duane Eddy, during a current rock'n'roll revival. (He will continue his career on the increasingly successful rock'n'roll revival circuit in both the US and UK.)
June [8] ***Rock Around The Clock***, on the Ace of Hearts label, makes UK #34.
Aug During a tour of Sweden, Haley, whose band currently includes Nick Nastos (guitar) and Al Rappa (bass), signs a recording contract with Sonet Grammophon boss, Dag Heckses, in Stockholm.
[16-18] The group appears at the Avalon Ballroom, San Francisco, CA, on a bill with the Drifters and the Flamin' Groovies.

1969

Oct [18] Haley is given an eight-minute ovation at Richard Nader's first "Rock'n'Roll Revival" concert with Chuck Berry, the Platters, the Coasters, the Shirelles, Jimmy Clanton and Sha Na Na, at the Felt Forum, Madison Square Garden, New York. (In years to come, however, it will be UK and German fans who remain most faithful).
Nov [29] Haley takes part in a second "Rock'n'Roll Revival" concert, with Jackie Wilson, Shep & the Limelites, the Five Satins, the Penguins, Gary U.S. Bonds and others, at Madison Square Garden.

1970

A previously taped concert at New York's Bitter End is released as ***Bill Haley's Scrapbook***, on Kama Sutra. During the year he also cuts a country album in Nashville, TN, produced by Sam Charters, and opens a mango farm in Mexico. The following year, ***Rock Around The Country***, with versions of Creedence Clearwater Revival's *Who'll Stop The Rain*, Joe South's *Games People Play* and Kris Kristofferson's *Me And Bobby McGee*, will be released on Sonet.

1972

Aug [5] Haley headlines the first-ever UK Rock'n'Roll Revival Show at Wembley Stadium, Wembley, Middx. It also features Chuck Berry, Little Richard, Jerry Lee Lewis and Bo Diddley. (Over the next 12 months, Haley stars in "Let The Good Times Roll", a film compiled from Nader's nostalgia concerts over the past four years and records ***Rock And Roll Music***, produced by Sam Charters in Nashville.)

1974

Apr [20] Coinciding with a UK visit by Haley, *Rock Around The Clock* re-enters the UK chart yet again, reaching #12.
May [25] *Rock Around The Clock* also re-enters the US survey, peaking at #39.

1976

Feb [5] Rudy Pompilli dies of lung cancer in Chester.
Dec [3] During a Haley performance at the Victoria Theatre, London, a fight breaks out between Teddy Boys and bouncers, resulting in the cancellation of a second scheduled show. Shortly after, Haley will retire from performing for three years, not least because of the death of Pompilli. He will be subsequently quoted as saying: "We had a pact. If he died first, I would stop playing, and if I died first, he would not play."

1979

Mar Haley performs at London's Rainbow Theatre, before recording what will be his final album, ***Everyone Can Rock'n'Roll***, at the Fame Studios, Muscle Shoals, AL, with producer Kenny Denton, during the summer.
Nov [26] Despite having been ill for much of the decade, Haley gives a spirited performance on the "Royal Variety Show" at the London Palladium, his last UK appearance.

1980

May Haley, who is suffering from a brain tumor, nevertheless embarks on a tour of South Africa, playing what will be his last concerts, having been forced to postpone a European tour earlier in the year, due to his deteriorating health.

1981

Feb [9] Haley is found dead, fully clothed, on his bed at his home in Harlingen, TX. Justice of the Peace Tommy Thompson rules that his death is from natural causes and assumes that he had suffered a heart attack some six hours before he was found. (He has sold an estimated 60 million records during a seminal and pioneering rock'n'roll career.)
May [9] *Haley's Golden Medley*, featuring snippets from his classic hits, makes UK #50.

1987

Jan [21] While *Rock Around The Clock* has been inducted into the NARAS Hall of Fame at the 24th annual Grammy awards on February 24th, 1982, Haley is posthumously inducted into the Rock and Roll Hall of Fame at the second annual dinner at the Waldorf Astoria Hotel, New York. Among several Haley career compilations issued posthumously during the '80s, the most complete is ***Rock & Rollin' Bill Haley***, a five-album boxed set of Decca tracks issued on the German Bear Family label in 1984.

1992

Oct [31] While Haley's son Scott has joined his father (who is entered for record sales feats) in **The Guinness Book Of Records** by running up and down the stairs of the 72-floor Westin Peachtree Plaza Hotel Atlanta, GA, eight times on his 32nd birthday (January 26th), the rock'n'roll legend's old backing group, now introduced as Bill Haley's Comets, continues to perform on the nostalgia circuit, playing at Dick Fox's Halloween Night Doo-Wop at the Westbury Music Fair, Westbury, NY, with Earl "Speedo" Carroll & the Cadillacs, Don & Juan, the Tokens, Yesterday's News, the Eternals and many others.

DARYL HALL & JOHN OATES

Daryl Hall (vocals, guitar);
John Oates (vocals, guitar)

1967

Students at Temple University, Hall (b. Daryl Hohl, Oct. 11, 1949, Pottstown, PA) and Oates (b. Apr. 7, 1949, New York, NY) meet while fleeing in the same freight elevator from a gang fight at a dance in Philadelphia, PA's Adelphi Ballroom, where Hall has been leading his own band, the Temptones and Oates his outfit, the Masters. (Hall has had piano and vocal training as a child, while Oates has been playing guitar since the age of eight and begun his music career with a Motown covers band in the sixth grade. Both have been raised in the suburbs of Philadelphia, but have frequented the ghetto areas, absorbing musical influences and later joining R&B/doo-wop groups. Hall has recorded a single as part of Kenny Gamble & the Romeos, with Gamble, Leon Huff and Thom Bell, who will all become successful soul producers, and has done regular session work for Gamble and Huff at Sigma Sound Studios.) Discovering shared interests, Hall & Oates team up to sing in various R&B and doo-wop outfits, before going their separate ways - Oates to a new college, and Hall to his first serious band, Gulliver.

1969

Oates also joins Gulliver (which has recorded one album for Elektra), just before it disbands. He makes a trip to Europe, while Hall finds studio work in Philadelphia, singing back-up for the Stylistics, the Delfonics and the Intruders, among others. The duo will record a number of demos, produced by John Madara and Tom Sellers over the next two years. (These eventually emerge, augmented by two Gulliver cuts, in the US in 1976, as ***Past Times Behind***).

1972

Nov Signed to Atlantic as Hall & Oates, their freshman effort, the Arif Mardin-produced ***Whole Oats***, is released during a year largely spent building a solid live reputation in the Philadelphia area, under the guidance of their manager (and latter-day Sony Records chief), Tommy Mottola.

1974

Jan While the duo has relocated to Greenwich Village, New York, NY, their R&B-styled ***Abandoned Luncheonette***, also produced by Mardin (and subsequently described by Hall as "our first real album"), is released, its cover depicting "The Diner Graveyard" eaterie.
Mar [23] The extracted pop and soul-fused *She's Gone* makes US #60. (The song will be a US R&B #1 six months later, for Tavares.)
June The duo begins work on a new album, with Todd Rundgren producing, at the Secret Sound Studios, New York.
Nov ***War Babies*** climbs to US #86. Overtly rock-oriented, it is a departure from previous work and results in Atlantic terminating the duo's recording contract.

1975

Sept The duo signs to RCA, where ***Daryl Hall And John Oates*** (sometimes known as the ***Silver Album*** because of the silver make-up sleeve shot of the duo, created by Mick Jagger's make-up man, Pierre LaRoche) is a slow US chart mover, until the extracted *Sara Smile*, written by Hall for girlfriend Sara Allen, takes off.

1976

May [19] Hall & Oates embark on an eight-date UK tour at the Colston Hall, Bristol, Avon, set to end on the 28th at the Town Hall, Leeds, W. Yorks.
June [26] R&B-tinged ballad, *Sara Smile*, hits US #4 after five months on the chart, becoming a million seller, as ***Daryl Hall And John Oates*** reaches US #17, earning a gold disc for a half million sales.
July [3] ***Daryl Hall And John Oates*** spends a week at UK #56.
Oct [2] ***Bigger Than Both Of Us***, recorded at Cherokee Studios and Sound Labs in Los Angeles, CA with producer Chris Bond, reaches UK #25.
[30] The duo-penned *She's Gone*, reissued by Atlantic, hits US #7 and makes UK #42.
Nov [6] ***Bigger Than Both Of Us*** climbs to US #13, also becoming Hall & Oates' first platinum album.
[20] ***Abandoned Luncheonette*** reaches US #33, more than 2½ years after its chart debut.
Dec [25] *Do What You Want, Be What You Are* makes US #39.

1977

Jan [23-24] The duo performs at London's Hammersmith Odeon at the end of a European tour.
Mar [26] Further excerpt, *Rich Girl*, written by Hall about a friend of Sara Allen's whose father is a fast-food king, becomes the duo's first #1 hit, topping the US chart for the first of two weeks. (The notorious serial killer David Berkowitz, known as "Son of Sam", will later claim that the song motivated his crimes.)
Apr [16] ***No Goodbyes***, collecting their early Atlantic tracks, peaks at US #92.
June [11] Oates-inked *Back Together Again* reaches US #28.
Aug [13] *It's Uncanny*, on Atlantic, reaches US #80. (Hall records tracks for a solo album produced by Robert Fripp at the Hit Factory, New York, although it will not emerge until 1980).
Oct [15] Bond-produced ***Beauty On A Back Street***,

which Oates will later claim is the duo's only recording he dislikes, makes UK #40.

[22] ***Beauty On A Back Street*** reaches US #30.

Nov [12] *Why Do Lovers (Break Each Other's Heart?)* reaches US #73.

1978

June ***Livetime***, recorded on the road with the duo's regular band - Caleb Quaye (lead guitar), Kenny Passarelli (bass), Roger Pope (drums), David Kent (keyboards, backing vocals) and Charles DeChant (sax, keyboards, percussion) - makes US #42. They spend much of year playing live, including a Care-Free chewing gum-sponsored tour of US high schools which have sent Care-Free the most gum wrappers.

Sept David Foster-produced ***Along The Red Ledge*** reaches US #27 and features musical guests George Harrison, Cheap Trick's Rick Nielsen, Todd Rundgren and Toto's Steve Lukather and Steve Porcaro.

Nov [4] *It's A Laugh*, taken from the album, reaches US #20.

1979

Jan [27] *I Don't Wanna Lose You* makes US #42.

Nov ***X-Static***, once again helmed by Foster, reaches US #33. The duo has spent much of the year touring, while Oates has also written the soundtrack for the Peter Fonda/Susan Saint James film "Outlaw Blues".

1980

Jan [26] Hall-written extract, *Wait For Me*, reaches US #18.

Mar Hall & Oates hire Studio C at New York's Electric Lady Studios and begin their first self-produced sessions, backed by their road band: G.E. Smith (lead guitar), Tom "T-Bone" Wolk (bass, synthesizers, guitar), Mickey Curry (drums) and Charles DeChant (sax).

May Hall's debut solo album, ***Sacred Songs***, recorded in 1977 with Fripp, reaches US #58.

June *Running From Paradise* (from ***X-Static***, and not released as a US single) makes UK #41 (the duo's first UK hit single in almost four years).

Sept Self-produced ***Voices***, from the New York sessions, peaks at US #17 in a 100-week chart run, during which it will earn a platinum disc for million-plus sales. It includes *Every Time You Go Away* and *Diddy Doo Wop (I Hear The Voices)*, which is Hall's reaction to the "Son of Sam" revelations.

[11] An 11-date UK tour begins at the Hippodrome, Bristol, set to end on the 24th at the Odeon Theatre, Birmingham, W. Midlands.

[13] The extracted *How Does It Feel To Be Back* peaks at US #30, while their revival of the Righteous Brothers' *You've Lost That Lovin' Feelin'* makes UK #55.

Nov [29] *You've Lost That Lovin' Feelin'* reaches US #12.

Dec *Kiss On My List*, also from ***Voices***, makes UK #33.

1981

Apr [11] Perky *Kiss On My List*, written by Hall with Sara Allen's younger sister, Janna, who - reputedly - has never written a song before, tops the US chart for three weeks, selling over one million copies.

July [4] Equally pop-aimed *You Make My Dreams* hits US #5.

Sept ***Private Eyes***, self-produced in four more months of sessions at the Electric Lady Studios, is Hall and Oates' first US Top 10 album, hitting #5 and earning a platinum disc.

Nov [7] Its extracted title track, *Private Eyes*, becomes the pair's third US chart-topper and their fourth million-selling single.

1982

Jan [30] *I Can't Go For That (No Can Do)* also tops the US survey, deposing Olivia Newton John's *Physical* (which had toppled *Private Eyes* ten weeks earlier). Their third million-seller in four releases, it also spends a week at US R&B #1, an extremely rare feat for a white act - only the fourth instance since 1965. In addition, they are listed under "Black Music" in the **World Book Encyclopaedia**.

Feb *I Can't Go For That (No Can Do)*, written by the duo with Sara Allen in the studio, and recorded on the spot, is its biggest UK Singles chart success to date, hitting #8.

[27] ***Private Eyes*** hits UK #8.

Apr *Private Eyes*, reissued as a UK follow-up, makes #32.

May [22] Written by Hall with both Allen sisters, *Did It In A Minute*, their third Top 10 US single from ***Private Eyes***, hits #9.

Aug [14] *Your Imagination* reaches US #33, as the duo works on a new album, once again at the Electric Lady Studios, with the sessions filmed by MTV for a documentary.

Dec [18] *Maneater*, the duo's fifth US #1 (and sixth million seller), begins a four-week gorge atop the Hot 100, while in the UK it hits #6 - their highest UK chart placing. Self-produced, it is taken from their tenth album, ***H_2O***, which hits US #3 (also a million seller), having already reached UK #24 on Oct [30].

1983

Jan Also from ***H_2O***, the Hall-penned ballad, *One On One*, reaches UK #63.

[17] Hall & Oates win the Favorite Band, Duo Or Group, Pop Rock category, at the tenth annual American Music Awards, held at the Shrine Auditorium, Los Angeles.

Apr [9] *One On One* hits US #7.

May *Family Man*, the fourth single from the album, and a cover of a 1982 UK #45 hit by Mike Oldfield, reaches UK #15.

June [25] *Family Man* hits US #6. Taking a rest from the road, prior to the next round of recording, Hall will spend much of the year collaborating with other acts, while Oates hones his skiing and race-driving skills.

Nov *Say It Isn't So* peaks at UK #69. RCA releases ***Rock'n'Soul (Part 1)***, a compilation of 11 US Top 10 hits including the current single and the forthcoming release, *Adult Education*, which will hit US #7 and UK #16 and will earn another platinum disc.

Dec [17] *Say It Isn't So* hits US #2, where it spends four weeks behind Paul McCartney and Michael Jackson's *Say Say Say*.

1984

Jan [16] Hall & Oates win the Favorite Band, Duo Or Group, Pop Rock category, at the 11th annual American Music Awards, held at the Shrine Auditorium.

Mar *Adult Education* reaches UK #63.

Apr [7] *Adult Education* hits US #8. (The RIAA confirms suggestions in **Billboard** and **Newsweek** that Hall & Oates are now the most successful duo in US recording history, having amassed a total of 19 US gold and platinum awards.)

Aug Hall duets on Elvis Costello's second US chart success, *The Only Flame In Town*, which peaks at #56.

Oct Diana Ross' *Swept Away*, written and produced by Hall, reaches US #19. ***Big Bam Boom*** is released, Hall & Oates first new album in two years, co-produced with Bob Clearmountain (with the help of New York electro dance-remixer Arthur Baker).

Dec [8] The duo-penned *Out Of Touch* tops the US chart for the first of two weeks (Hall & Oates' sixth US #1 single) and makes UK #48. ***Big Bam Boom*** hits US #5 (their fifth consecutive platinum album) and reaches UK #28.

1985

Jan [28] Following the 12th annual American Music Awards, at the Shrine Auditorium, at which the duo has collected the Favorite Band, Duo Or Group, Pop/Rock trophy, Hall & Oates take part in the all-star recording session in Los Angeles for the USA For Africa charity single, *We Are The World*.

Feb [16] *Method Of Modern Love* hits US #5 and reaches UK #21.

May Hall & Oates, paying tribute to the soul music that inspired them in their youth, perform at the re-opening of the legendary Apollo Theatre in Harlem, joined, at the duo's invitation, by David Ruffin and Eddie Kendricks of the Temptations. The event benefits the United Negro College Fund.

[4] *Some Things Are Better Left Unsaid*, the third single from the 1984 album, reaches US #18.

June RCA-UK releases a remixed version of *Out Of Touch*, which peaks at UK #62.

July [6] *Possession Obsession*, also from ***Big Bam Boom***, reaches US #30.

[13] Mick Jagger performs at "Live Aid" at the JFK Stadium, Philadelphia, backed by Hall & Oates.

[27] Paul Young's cover of *Everytime You Go Away* tops the US chart, which will also be featured in the closing scenes of John Hughes hit movie "Planes, Trains And Automobiles".

Oct [12] Live single, *A Night At The Apollo Live!*, a medley of two of the Temptations' '60s hits, *The Way You Do The Things You Do* and *My Girl*, recorded at the Apollo benefit concert, reaches US #20 and makes UK #58, while its parent album, ***Live At The Apollo With David Ruffin And Eddie Kendricks***, reaches US #21 and UK #32.

Dec [14] Artists United Against Apartheid, comprising 49 artists including Hall & Oates, makes US #38 and UK #21 with *Sun City*.

1986

Aug Hall has teamed with Jagger and Eurythmics' Dave Stewart to write the US #51 *Ruthless People*, which Jagger performs for the Bette Midler/Danny DeVito-starring movie "Ruthless People".

Sept During an amicable sabbatical, Hall's sophomore album, ***Three Hearts In The Happy Ending Machine***, produced by Stewart and featuring Bob Geldof and Joni Mitchell among its musical guests, is released, set to reach US #29 and UK #26, while the extracted *Dreamtime* reaches UK #28 and will hit US #5 on Oct [4].

Dec [6] Hall's solo *Foolish Pride* makes US #33. Oates' musical collaborations during the year have included producing an album for the Parachute Club and co-writing *Electric Blue* (a US #7 hit for Australian band Icehouse in 1988).

1987

Jan [21] Hall & Oates induct Smokey Robinson into the Rock and Roll Hall of Fame at its second annual dinner, at the Waldorf Astoria Hotel, New York.

Feb [21] Hall's *Someone Like You* peaks at US #57.

1988

June Still managed by Tommy Mottola, Hall & Oates are reunited and signed to Clive Davis' Arista Records, which releases ***Ooh Yeah!***, co-produced with T-Bone Wolk, the only remaining member of the previous backing band. It will reach US #24 and UK #52 (June [18]).

[11] The extracted Hall-penned *Everything Your Heart Desires* hits US #3.

Aug [27] *Missed Opportunity*, also from the album, reaches US #29.

Sept [24] Hall & Oates, together with Suzanne Vega and Bruce Hornsby & the Range, join the Grateful Dead for the end of their series of nine concerts at New York's Madison Square Garden, in a benefit show to help save the world's tropical rain forests. The duo performs *Every Time You Go Away* and Marvin Gaye's *What's Going On* with the Grateful Dead.

Nov [5] *Downtown Life* reaches US #31.

1989

Jan [18] Hall & Oates induct the Temptations into the Rock and Roll Hall of Fame at the fourth annual dinner, at the Waldorf Astoria Hotel.

Nov Eric Clapton's ***Journeyman***, featuring Hall as a guest, is released.

1990

Feb ***The Last Temptation Of Elvis***, a UK compilation to benefit the Nordoff-Robbins Music Therapy charity, including Hall & Oates' treatment of *Can't*

Help Falling In Love, is released in the UK.
Mar [17] Hall & Oates join their labelmates to celebrate Arista Records' 15th anniversary "That's What Friends Are For" concert at Radio City Music Hall, raising more than $2 million. The proceeds go to the Gay Men's Health Crisis and other AIDS organizations. (The show will air on CBS-TV on April 17th.)
Apr [22] The duo participates in the "Earth Day" festivities in Central Park, New York, with the B-52's and others.
Aug Oates takes part in 200-mile cycle trip across Montana's Flathead National Forest to draw attention to clear-cuttings which are threatening US forests.
Sept [1] Hall & Oates support Fleetwood Mac at Wembley Stadium, Wembley, Middx.
Oct [27] Their second Arista album, ***Change Of Season***, marking a return to a simpler and more acoustic musical style, variously co-produced with Wolk. Jon Bon Jovi, Ric Wake, David A. Stewart, Dave Tyson and Danny Kortchmar, debuts at its UK #44 peak.
Nov [17] ***Change Of Season*** peaks at US #61.
[26-27] A 12-date UK tour is highlighted by performances at London's Hammersmith Odeon.
Dec [1] Ballad, *So Close*, co-produced by Jon Bon Jovi and Kortchmar, reaches US #11, having stalled at UK #69.

1991

Jan [25-26] Hall & Oates perform at the Mark Etess Arena, Trump Taj Mahal, Atlantic City, NJ.
[26] *Everywhere I Look* charts for a week at UK #74.
Feb [10] The duo begins the "Change Of Season" tour, an all-acoustic affair, with DeChant (saxophone/percussion), Wolk (guitar), Kasim Sultan (upright bass), Bobby Mayo (piano/guitar), Mike Braun (drums/percussion) and two classic instrumentalists, Eileen Ivers and Lisa Haney, which has already premiered in Europe at smaller-than-usual venues, including London's Town & Country club, at the Mid-Hudson Civic Center, Poughkeepsie, NY.
[16] *Don't Hold Back Your Love* makes US #41.
Mar [5] The tour is interrupted after Hall is taken ill.
May [3] The duo performs at the USA Harvest National Hunger Relief "food-raising" concert at Louisville Gardens, KY, during "Kentucky Derby Festival" Week.
[12] Hall & Oates appear via satellite from Fort Lauderdale, FL, in "The Simple Truth" concert for Kurdish refugees, at Wembley Arena, Wembley, Middx.
Sept [11] The duo performs before a sellout crowd at the Mexico National Auditorium, Mexico City, Mexico.
Oct [19] UK-only retrospective, ***The Best Of Hall & Oates - Looking Back***, debuts at its UK #9 peak.

1992

Jan [11] ***Two Rooms: Celebrating The Songs Of Elton John And Bernie Taupin***, to which Hall & Oates have contributed their version of *Philadelphia Freedom*, reaches US #18.
June [20] Hall guests on ITV's "Tom Jones: The Right Time" show.
Oct [16] The duo participates in a tribute to their friend, the late Eddie Kendricks, at a concert in Redondo Beach, CA.
Nov Hall, still recording the next Hall & Oates album with Arif Mardin at London's Hit Factory, also works on tracks for a third solo outing at the Battery Studios, London, with producer Mike Peden.

1993

Feb [8] Oates appears on syndicated TV's "The Arsenio Hall Show", while Hall, now resident in London and newly signed to Epic Records, completes work on his label debut, ***Soul Alone***, variously by Hall with V. Jeffrey Smith, Peter Lord Moreland and former Chime, Michael Peden.
Sept [25] Recorded in New York, ***Soul Alone*** debuts at its US #177 peak, as the extracted soul-era inspired *I'm In A Philly Mood* bows at its UK #59 peak.
Oct [2] *I'm In A Philly Mood* debuts at its US #82 peak.
[23] ***Soul Alone*** charts for a week at UK #57.
Dec [15] Hall guests on NBC-TV's "The Tonight Show".

1994

Jan [22] Hall's *Stop Loving Me, Stop Loving You* , with various remixes by Bob Jones, Daniel Abraham and Tosh, reaches UK #30.
Apr [2] *I'm In A Philly Mood* re-charts at UK #52.
May [14] Hall's *Help Me Find A Way To Your Heart* charts for a week at UK #70.
July [2] Hall's *Gloryland*, with the assistance of the gospel group Sounds Of Blackness, debuts at its UK #36 peak.

1995

June [17] Hall and Dusty Springfield's duet *Wherever Would I Be*, featured on her comeback album ***A Very Fine Love*** and in the Sandra Bullock movie "While You Were Sleeping", makes UK #44.

1996

Jan [21, 23, 25, 27] Having toured the US the previous summer with Carly Simon, the duo now plays at the Fox Arena, Foxwoods Resort Casino in Ledyard, CT with the singer, in support of the American Indian College Fund. (The following month Rhino Records (US) releases ***The Atlantic Collection***, rounding up Hall & Oates' Atlantic career highlights including the seminal *She's Gone*, while RCA continues to prepare a definitive Hall & Oates boxed-set scheduled for release in August.)

M.C. HAMMER

1987

Hammer (b. Stanley Kirk Burrell, Mar. 30, 1962, Oakland, CA) begins his career in music with a $40,000 investment from Oakland A's baseball players Mike Davis and Dwayne Murphy. The youngest of seven siblings and the son of a poker club-managing father, he was nicknamed "Little Hammer" when working as a batboy for the A's, allegedly due to his likeness to home-run king Henry "Hammerin' Hank" Aaron. After high school, Hammer pursued a college degree in communications and a career as a professional baseball player, but failed on both counts. He then joined the navy and was stationed in California for most of his three-year service, apart from spending six months in Japan. On leaving the military he became a regular churchgoer and avid Bible reader, forming a religious rap duo, the Holy Ghost Boys. He now forms Bustin' Records, selling his debut single, *Ring 'Em*, from the trunk of his car. He also agrees to give the investing baseball stars 10% of all his earnings. Hammer forms a band with two DJs and the backing group Oaktown's 3-5-7, featuring Tabatha "Terrible T." King, Djuana "Sweet L.D." Johnican and Phyllis "Little P" Charles, and cuts ***Feel My Power*** with producer Felton Pilate, once of Con Funk Shun, which sells 60,000 copies.

1988

May Hammer has secured a multi-album deal and a $750,000 advance, after Capitol Records A&R executive Joy Bailey has seen the rapper perform at Oakland's Oak Tree cabaret club, and the label reissues ***Feel My Power*** as ***Let's Get It Started***, adding four new songs.

1989

Apr [8] ***Let's Get It Started*** tops the US R&B chart and goes on to reach US #30, eventually selling more than 1.5 million copies.

1990

Jan [22] Hammer wins the Favorite Artist, Rap Music, and Favorite Album, Rap Music, categories at the 17th annual American Music Awards, held at the Shrine Auditorium, Los Angeles, CA.
Feb Hammer guests on Earth, Wind & Fire's ***Heritage***, on the cut *Wanna Be The Man*. Two of Hammer's growing entourage, Kent Wilson (Lone Mixer) and Kevin Wilson (2 Bigg), leave.
Mar [10] His second album, ***Please Hammer Don't Hurt 'Em***, released on Capitol, enters the US Album chart at #69.
Apr [28] *U Can't Touch This* enters the Hot 100 at #27, the highest rap entry to date.
June Hammer contributes to a West Coast Rap All-Stars single, *We're All The Same*, which is featured on an eponymously-titled various-artists rap collection on Warner Bros., also including Tonë Loc and Young MC. Increasingly in demand for commercial opportunities, Hammer signs a one-year sponsorship deal with British Knights athletic footwear which will include "U Can't Touch This" video-style ads. He will also parade for Pepsi-Cola in a multi-package tour/commercials/sponsorship agreement into 1991.
[9] ***Let's Get Started*** leaves the US Top 200 Album chart after an 80-week residence and remains unavailable, until a Capitol re-promotion in both the US and UK in six months time. In the same week, ***Please Hammer Don't Hurt 'Em*** hits US #1 at the start of a debut record setting 21 chart-topping weeks. (By December, the rap album recorded for $10,000, will have logged the longest uninterrupted residence in either the #1 or #2 positions since separate mono/stereo albums listings began in 1963. Hammer is presented with a Ferrari Testarossa by Capitol, after betting the label that ***Please Hammer*** would be the biggest-selling rap album ever.)
[15] A 60-city "Please Hammer Don't Hurt 'Em" US tour, with After 7, Michelle, Oaktown's 3-5-7 and Troop supporting, begins in Louisville, KY.
[16] *U Can't Touch This* hits US #8, sampling Rick James' *Super Freak*, for which James will ultimately be remunerated. The dance smash will become Hammer's signature tune, while its accompanying video, featuring hot dance routines by Hammer in ultra-baggy bright trousers, will become the most heavily rotated video on MTV during the year.
July Hammer's Bustin' Records and Capitol enter into agreement to provide albums by new acts like Oaktown's 3-5-7, One Cause One Effect and Special Generation.
[28] His US success begins translating on a worldwide basis as *U Can't Touch This* hits UK #3 during a rare four-month chart stay.
Aug [11] ***Please Hammer Don't Hurt 'Em*** hits UK #8.
Sept [7] "U Can't Touch This" wins the Best Rap Video and Best Dance Video categories at the seventh annual MTV Video Music Awards, held at the Universal Amphitheatre, Universal City, CA, at which Hammer also performs.
[15] Follow-up single, recalling the Chi-Lites 1973 US and UK #3 hit, *Have You Seen Her?*, hits US #4 and becomes his first RIAA gold-certified single.
[18] He takes part in ABC-TV's "All-Star Tribute To Oprah Winfrey".
Oct [8] Hammer throws the first ball out at an Oakland A's play-off game. Catcher Terry Steinbach fails to snag his errant pitch and it goes to the backstop.
[13] *Have You Seen Her?* hits UK #8.
[21] The Hammer phenomenon is featured on an NBC-TV "News Special".
[22] Now touring with Vanilla Ice and En Vogue, Hammer performs before a sellout crowd of 10,250 at the Dean County Memorial Coliseum, Madison, WI.
Nov Still a hot seller, at US #2, behind white rapper Vanilla Ice's #1, ***To The Extreme***, with whom Hammer is conducting a mutually promotion-seeking ongoing rap duel, the RIAA confirms seven million unit sales of ***Please Hammer Don't Hurt 'Em***.
[2] Criticism that Hammer is incapable of creating his own material fails to impress consumers, as *Pray*, heavily sampling Prince's *When Doves Cry*, hits US #2.
[29] Hammer participates in the annual "Lou Rawls Parade of Stars Telethon", raising funds for the United Negro College Fund.

1991

Jan [12] *Pray* hits UK #8.

[22] Fremont, CA declares "M.C. Hammer Day" to honor Hammer's contributions as a role model and for his charity work, as settlement between Hammer and Murphy and Davis - over monies due to them for their original investment - is reached.
[28] Hammer collects five trophies: Soul/R&B Album and Rap Album for ***Please Hammer Don't Hurt 'Em***, Soul/R&B Single for ***U Can't Touch This***, Soul/R&B, and Rap Male Artist, at the 18th annual American Music Awards, at the Shrine Auditorium.
Feb While in New York for the launch of Mattel's Hammer doll, he visits Wadleigh Junior High School in Harlem as part of NARAS' Grammy-in-the-Schools program.
[9] In a dramatic and unexpected fall from favor, *Here Comes The Hammer* stalls at US #54, despite a $1 million promotional mini-film video clip. It is the first chart single Hammer has penned alone and features no sampling. It is featured in the movie "Rocky V".
[10] Hammer is named Best International Newcomer at the tenth annual BRIT Awards, held at London's Dominion Theatre.
[20] He wins the Best R&B Song and Best Rap Solo Performance categories for *U Can't Touch This*, and Best Music Video, Longform, for "Please Don't Hurt 'Em The Movie" at the 33rd annual Grammy Awards, at Radio City Music Hall, New York.
[23] Hammer guests on the NBC-TV comedy show "Amen", playing a dual role as himself and the Reverend Pressure.
Mar [2] Hammer is named Musician Of The Year (despite not actually being one) and ***Please Hammer Don't Hurt 'Em*** wins Outstanding Album at the 14th Bammy Awards, at the Brooks Hall Civic Auditorium, San Francisco, as *Here Comes The Hammer* reaches UK #15.
[3] ***Please Hammer Don't Hurt 'Em*** wins International Album Of The Year at the 20th annual Juno Awards, at the Queen Elizabeth Theater, Vancouver, Canada.
[7] Hammer is named Best Male Rapper, Best Dressed Male Artist and Worst Male Singer in the annual **Rolling Stone** Readers' Picks.
[9] Hammer-produced single, also from "Rocky V", *Go For It! (Heart And Fire)*, by Joey B. Ellis and Tynetta Hare, reaches UK #20. (It has already made US #70 in December 1990.) The Peace Choir, featuring Hammer among its number, makes US #54 with a remake of *Give Peace A Chance*.
[12] Hammer wins the Best Rap Album with ***Please Hammer Don't Hurt 'Em***, Best R&B/Urban Contemporary Song Of The Year with *U Can't Touch This*, and the Sammy Davis Jr. Award (to recognize outstanding achievements in music and entertainment in 1990) at the fifth annual Soul Train Awards, at the Shrine Auditorium.
[18] Hammer and Pepsi-Cola, the sponsor of his world tour, donate $7,700 to the Open Family Foundation in Melbourne, Victoria, Australia, a charity which helps homeless youngsters.
[25] Hammer wins four more trophies for Best Selling Album Of The Year, Best Selling Album Male/Female, Best Selling Black Music Album/Male, and Best Selling Rap Album at the annual National Association of Recording Merchandisers' 1990 Best Seller Awards, held during its annual convention in San Francisco.
[26] An upcoming show at the 43,000-seater Tokyo Dome, Tokyo, Japan, sells out in six hours, a feat only previously achieved by Michael Jackson and the Rolling Stones.
Apr [13] ***Let's Get It Started*** makes UK #46, as ***Please Hammer Don't Hurt 'Em*** is now certified for sales of ten million by the RIAA.
May [1] Hammer guests on BBC1-TV chat show "Wogan", before embarking on an 11-date UK tour at the Birmingham National Exhibition Centre the following day. (During his London dates, he will make a surprise appearance at Stockwell Park School in South London, warning the pupils of the dangers of drugs.)
[3] Lite Light, co-owned with his father Lewis and brother Louis, wins the Kentucky Oaks, for three-year old fillies, at Churchill Downs, Louisville, by ten lengths. (Hammer's horse will also win $250,000 at the Coaching Club American Oaks in July.)
[12] Hammer appears live at "The Simple Truth" concert for Kurdish refugees, at Wembley Arena, Wembley, Middx.
Hammer pays Sinead O'Connor's $2,624 air fare to fly her from Los Angeles to her home in Eire.
June [5] Hammer files a $30-million libel suit against the **Globe** magazine, following the magazine's printed allegations that he stood by and watched two of his brothers and several employees gang rape a woman.
[8] *Yo!! Sweetness* reaches UK #16.
[20] He is honored at the 27th Annual Awards Dinner Dance of the Music & Performing Arts Unit of B'nai B'rith, at the Marriott Marquis Hotel, New York.
July [8] Hammer is honored as Oakland's "Booster Of The Year".
[20] *(Hammer Hammer) They Put Me In The Mix* medley debuts at its UK #20 peak.
[28] An estimated 2,000 youths riot after a Hammer concert in Penticton, BC, Canada. About 90 of them are jailed in connection with the incident.
Aug Hammer begins recording a new album at the Plant, Sausalito, CA.
Sept [7] ABC-TV premieres the "Hammerman" cartoon series.
Oct [3] Hammer offers a $50,000 reward for the return of Michael Jackson's white glove, which was stolen from the Motown Museum, as part of a promotional gimmick for a dance-off challenge between the Hammer and the "King Of Pop".
[6] Fox-TV airs the "Ray Charles : 50 Years In Music, Uh-Huh!" special, which features many artists, including Hammer, paying tribute to the legend.
[15] Hammer premieres his ***Too Legit To Quit*** project for EMI Music's top executives in Los Angeles.
[26] The extracted cut, *2 Legit 2 Quit*, bows at UK peak, #60.
Nov [2] ***Too Legit To Quit*** debuts at its UK #41 high.
[7] Hammer is the musical guest on NBC-TV's "Saturday Night Live".
[23] ***Too Legit To Quit*** hits US #2.

1992

Jan [11] While *Addams Groove*, written for, and featured in, "The Addams Family" movie, hits US #7 and UK#4, and *2 Legit 2 Quit* finally hits US #5, Hammer participates in the third annual MTV "Rock'n'Jock" softball game, held to benefit the T.J. Martell Foundation For Leukemia.
[27] Hammer co-hosts the 19th annual American Music Awards, held at the Shrine Auditorium, also collecting the Favorite Artist, Rap Music, trophy.
Feb He takes part in the NBA's "Stay In School" rally at his alma mater, McClymonds High School, West Oakland. Also performing at the event are John Fogerty, Chris Isaak, Mickey Thomas and Dennis De Young.
Mar [1] Hammer participates in ABC-TV's "Muhammad Ali's 50th Birthday" tribute special.
[12] He wins the Best R&B/Soul Music Video category at the sixth annual Soul Train Music Awards, held at the Shrine Auditorium.
[21] *Do Not Pass Me By*, featuring gospel vocalists Tremaine Hawkins and Trina Johnson, makes US #62.
[30] "Hammer's MTV Birthday Bash" airs on MTV (US). (Claiming that the rapper owes him 2.7% of all his earnings in remuneration for a 1987 $5,000 loan, a former navy friend of Hammer's, Vincent Williams, files a fraud suit against him in a District Court in San Francisco.)
Apr [1] His "Too Legit To Quit" tour, with Boyz II Men the support act on many of the gigs, opens at Hampton Coliseum, Hampton, VA.
[3] CBS-TV airs the "Hammer From The Heart" prime-time special, as ABC-TV prepares to announce that the hammer will fall on his cartoon series.
[4] *Do Not Pass Me By* reaches UK #14. (Hammer signs a worldwide promotional deal with Kentucky Fried Chicken.)
May [1] At Hammer's second annual "USA Harvest Hunger Relief Concert" in Louisville, he asks concertgoers to each bring a can of food.
[23] *This Is The Way We Roll* peaks at its US debut, #86.
June [22] Three members of his tour crew are wounded in a drive-by shooting at an Albuquerue, NM, park, while at a barbecue.
[25] Joseph Mack, a dancer in Hammer's entourage, is shot on stage during the rap star's concert at the University of Nevada, Reno, NV.
July [24] Before an evening concert at the Hulman Center, Terre Haute, IN, Hammer visits the inmates of the United States Penitentiary in the town.
Aug [1-2] Hammer takes part in the "KMEL Summer Jam '92", the largest rap festival ever staged, at the Shoreline Amphitheatre, Mountain View, CA.
[16] He joins other volunteers at a kitchen in the Atlanta Union Mission, Atlanta, GA shelter for the homeless, to help launch another USA Harvest hunger-relief drive. He delivers 500,000 lbs of food collected from corporations and concert fans.
Sept [17] International leg of his "Too Legit To Quit Tour" opens at Palacio De Los Deportes, Mexico City, Mexico.
Oct Another lawsuit, filed by James Earley, seeks $5.7 million. Earley claims that Hammer had promised him 40% of the income from ***Please Hammer Don't Hurt 'Em***, but that he only received $100,000.
[31] NBC-TV sitcom "Out All Night", in which Hammer sings *Gaining Momentum*, airs.
Nov [20] "Too Legit" tour reaches the Rainbow Hall, Nagoya, Japan, after stops in Indonesia, Singapore, the Philippines, Thailand and Korea.
Dec [4] At a press conference at his Fremont home, Hammer announces the formation of Roll-Wit-It Entertainment, his new artist/sports management, production and video company.
[18] Hammer's "USA Harvest Hunger Relief" food drive ends with a donation of 42,000 lb of food to the city of Oakland.

1993

Jan Muhammad Bilal Abdullah sues Hammer for more than $16 million, claiming he stole his *Oh, Oh You Got The Shing* composition, renaming it *Here Comes The Hammer*.
June [9] As Hammer keeps the lowest profile of his career, he makes a US TV appearance, on "The Arsenio Hall Show".

1994

Mar [12] *It's All Good* makes US #46.
[19] Following a label switch to Giant, Hammer's ***The Funky Headhunter*** debuts at its US #12 peak. (**Rolling Stone** had reported that Hammer was trying to make a three-album deal for $25 million.) *It's All Good* makes UK #52.
May [21] *Pumps And A Bump* reaches US #26.
Aug [13] *Don't Stop* charts for a week at UK #72.

1995

June [3] Now reverting to his original M.C. Hammer moniker, *Straight To My Feet*, featuring baseball/football star Deion Sanders, charts for a week at UK #57.
Sept [30] ***Inside Out*** debuts at its US #119 peak.
Nov [2] Hammer is inducted into the Soul Train Hall of Fame at the 25th annual Awards ceremony held at the Shrine Auditorium.

1996

Apr [3] Having appeared at #19 on **Forbes** magazine's 1991 list of highest-paid entertainers, Hammer now files for bankruptcy in Oakland, listing debts exceeding $10 million, including an outstanding American Express bill of $28,650.64

HAPPY MONDAYS

Shaun Ryder (vocals); **Mark "Cow" Day** (guitar); **Paul Davis** (keyboards); **Paul Ryder** (bass); **Gary "Gaz" Whelan** (drums); **Mark "Bez" Berry** (percussion)

1984

Nov Hailing from Salford, near Manchester, Gtr. Manchester, Shaun Ryder (b. Aug. 23, 1962, Little Hulton, Lancs.), who has left his parents home in Connison Avenue at 14, spent time in youth custody for theft and worked for the Post Office for three years before being fired, his brother Paul (b. Apr. 24, 1964, Manchester), their stand-up pub comic father once beaten by a nine-year old Lisa Stansfield in a talent contest, Whelan (b. Feb. 12, 1966, Manchester) and Day (b. Dec. 29, 1961, Manchester) have formed a loose outfit based around music and alcohol in 1980, initially practising in a local school room in Swinton, Gtr. Manchester. Davis (b. Mar. 7, 1966, Manchester) has been recruited the following year, as the un-named band plays mainly cover versions at local Manchester youth clubs. Eventually settling on the Happy Mondays moniker (proposed by Day who is inspired by the New Order hit *Blue Monday*), the group has built a small local following in Manchester, but is still beaten into last place at a "Battle Of The Bands" contest at the Factory Records-owned Hacienda Club, Manchester.

1985

Feb Davis and the Ryder brothers meet clothes shop owner Phil Sachs while clubbing at the Hacienda, impressed by their demo tape, Sachs offers to manage the band, securing them a spot on the venue's "Opportunity Knocks" talent night and subsequent one-off support dates for New Order.
Oct Their debut single, *Delightful*, a three-track EP produced by Mike Pickering, is released on Factory.
Nov Berry (b. Apr. 18, 1964, Manchester) completes the line-up, recruited as a percussionist and dancer.

1986

Aug New Order's Barney Sumner produces their second single, *Freaky Dancin'*.
Dec Factory boss Tony Wilson links Happy Mondays with former Velvet Underground member John Cale, for a ten-day recording session.

1987

Mar *Tart Tart* makes an impression on the UK Independent chart, while the band embarks on a UK tour.
May Succinctly titled debut album, the Cale-produced ***Squirrel & G-Man Twenty Four Hour Party People Plastic Face Carnt Smile (White Out)***, again scores on the Independent survey, but its bleak, industrial Northwest song themes find few mainstream fans.
June The group supports New Order at major London dates, followed by live appearances at the New Music Seminar trade showcase in New York, NY.
Nov *Twenty Four Hour Party People* is released, again to indie appeal.

1988

June At the instigation of Factory labelmeister Tony Wilson, the band is launched in the US via a series of showcase performances.
Sept The group, now managed by Nathan McGough, crosses the Pennines to a Yorkshire recording studio, to work on new songs.
Nov Their sophomore album, ***Bummed***, produced by Factory's Martin Hannett, is warmly received by the UK music press. Its hallucinatory dance rhythms beckon the growing UK dance craze of rave/acid house, for which the Happy Mondays will be much revered. The album's inner sleeve, depicting a naked woman, results in isolated retail resistence.

1989

Jan The group headlines Panic Station's birthday celebration at the Kilburn National Ballroom, London, but ends the month with two drug busts. Berry is fined £700 for possession of cannabis, while Ryder is detained in Jersey, having been found with cocaine in his pockets.
Feb They record a session for BBC Radio 1's "John Peel Show" and head to New York for a second promotional visit.
Mar The group embarks on sellout nationwide UK tour.
May Shaun Ryder teams with '60s singer Karl Denver to re-record the vocals on the Happy Mondays album cut *Lazyitis (One Armed Boxer)*. An additional hot UK remix, by mix-master Paul Oakenfold, adds samples from David Essex's *Rock On* and Sly & the Family Stone's *Family Affair*.
June The group begins its first full-length US tour, which includes sellout dates in Los Angeles, CA, attended by the Beastie Boys, Guns N' Roses and David Bowie.
Sept *W.F.L.* (a remix, by Erasure's Vince Clarke, of their fourth single, *Wrote For Luck*) becomes their chart debut, peaking at UK #68. Happy Mondays are now hailed as the leaders of the current Manchester "baggy" craze sweeping the UK's acid-house dance rave scene.
Nov [30] The band makes its BBC1-TV "Top Of The Pops" debut, on the same show as fellow Mancunian new-wave first-timers, the Stone Roses, with Kirsty MacColl as a guest vocalist.
Dec [2] *Madchester Rave On* EP peaks at UK #19. Recorded at Richard Branson's Oxfordshire studios, it features *Hallelujah*, *Holy Ghost* and *Clap Your Hands*, its sales boosted, not least, by a sellout major-venue UK tour.

1990

Jan The band tops several UK music magazines' "Best Newcomer" polls and sets off on a European tour, together with an army of fanatical Happy Mondays followers.
Feb They attend a "house" weekend in Iceland, organized by London's Brain club.
[3] ***Bummed*** finally charts, peaking at UK #59.
Mar The group appears alongside Karl Denver in a Bailey Brothers' movie, "Mad Fuckers".
[24-25] The band performs two sellout dates at Manchester's G-Mex Centre, as the band is featured on the front cover of the **New Musical Express**.
Apr [7] They sell-out the Wembley Arena, Wembley, Middx., for a one-off concert which continues well beyond the venue's 11 o'clock curfew time.
[14] Their shuffling cover version of John Kongos' 1971 UK #4 hit, *He's Gonna Step On You Again*, simply issued as *Step On*, hits UK #5 and reactivates ***Bummed*** to UK #60. The single has been recorded at the instigation of the band's US label, Elektra Records, which has requested cover versions by a number of their acts for their 40th anniversary album, ***Rubáiyát***. (The track which will appear on the album will, however, be a cover of Kongos' other hit, *Tokoloshe Man*.)
May Happy Mondays are featured in an ITV documentary about the rise of the Manchester music scene, "Madchester: Sound Of The North". Strange Fruit Records issues *The Peel Sessions*, featuring three tracks from those recordings.
June While the re-issued *Lazyitis (One Armed Boxer)* makes UK #46, the group begins a six-city US tour under the banner "Hacienda Trance American Tour". A second New York Seminar appearance becomes the hottest ticket at this year's event.
[22-24] The group participates in the "Glastonbury Festival of Contemporary Performing Arts", Glastonbury, Somerset.
July Happy Mondays begin recording a new album in Los Angeles. During the sessions, Shaun Ryder cuts a version of Donovan's *Colours* (with the help of fellow Mancunians, Barney Sumner and Johnny Marr) for future solo release. Live footage video titled "Party G-Mex" is released, adding to the 1989 release of "Rave On - The Video".
Oct [27] The band-penned *Kinky Afro* hits UK #5, as UK press stories circulate, claiming that notorious substance abuser Shaun Ryder has checked into a rehabilitation clinic.
Nov [3] ***Rubáiyát***, Elektra's 40th anniversary compilation, including the *Tokoloshe Man* contribution, makes US #140.
[17] Oakenfold co-produced ***Pills'n'Thrills And Bellyaches***, debuts at its UK #4 peak.
[23] A six-date British tour, supported by Donovan, begins at the Whitley Bay Ice Rink, set to end on December 4th at the Point, Dublin, Eire.
Dec [6] **The Sun** newspaper confirms that Ryder has booked himself into the Priory Clinic rehabilitation detox facility in Hale, Gtr. Manchester.

1991

Jan In this month's UK issue of **Penthouse**, Shaun Ryder and Berry appear in a nude spread with similarly disrobed models. (Ryder will also guest-edit the publication's September edition).
[18] The group participates in the "Great British Music Weekend" at Wembley Arena.
Feb [16] Shaun and girlfriend Trisha McNamara become parents to a daughter, Jael Otis Ann Ryder.
Mar [23] *Loose Fit* reaches UK #17.
Apr [7] The group wins the Best UK Indie Act category at the DMC World DJ Awards.
[20] ***Pills'n'Thrills And Bellyaches*** makes US #89.
[24] During a US tour, the band performs at New York's Madison Square Garden, opening for Jane's Addiction.
[27] *Step On* belatedly makes US #57.
May The group cancels its last seven US dates, citing "tiredness and not feeling very well".
June [1] A bill comprising Happy Mondays, the Farm and the La's performs to a half-full Elland Road, Leeds, soccer ground. Happy Mondays are later booed off stage at the "Centro Festival" in Paris, France.
July [10] 30 minutes prior to a concert at Valencia's Bullring, Spain, an overhead lighting rig crashes to the stage, destroying all of the group's musical instruments.
Aug [2] Happy Mondays take part in the "Feile Festival", Semple Stadium, Tipperary, Eire, with the Farm, That Petrol Emotion, Mock Turtles and others.
[4] They headline the "Cities In The Park Festival", Heaton Park, Prestwich, Gtr. Manchester.
Oct [12] Concert set, ***Live***, debuts at its UK #21 peak.
Nov [30] *Judge Fudge* debuts at its UK #24 peak, as rumors that the band is making the movie "Baby Big Head" abound.
Dec [25] Malcolm McLaren-directed "The Ghost Of Oxford Street", in which they play robbers, singing *Stayin' Alive* and co-starring with Tom Jones and the Pogues, airs on C4-TV.

1992

Mar The group returns from recording sessions in the West Indies (with Tom Tom Club's Chris Frantz and Tina Weymouth producing), having completed only one track for a scheduled album. Shaun Ryder is admitted to a London clinic for urgent drug-abuse treatment. Bez breaks his arm twice, while band members are sacked and replaced at regular intervals. Frantz will say later about the sessions: "They just didn't know how much trouble they were getting themselves into. In the end, we were lucky that nobody died."
May They continue working on the new album at Comfort Place Studios, still helmed by Frantz and Weymouth.
Sept [26] *Stinkin Thinkin* reaches UK #31.
Oct [10] ***... Yes Please!*** debuts at its UK #14 peak, as the group embarks on a 13-date UK tour at Leicester's De Montfort Hall, set to end on the 26th at the Guildhall, Portsmouth, Hants.
Nov [21] *Sunshine And Love* charts for a week at UK #62.
Dec [4] Following the demise of the Factory label, manager Nathan McGough meets London Records executive Roger Ames to discuss the possible signing of the band.

1993

Feb [15] During a month in which Ryder, escorted by Donovan's daughter Oriole Leitch (having reportedly left his wife Trish), is fined £650 and banned from driving for 18 months over drink-driving charges stemming from a crash the previous July involving a Lada-driving vicar, he now walks out of a meeting with EMI A&R director Clive Black. He tries to resurrect the deal with EMI, but the rest of the band is not interested. An anonymous source says, "We had a band meeting and there was only one man who wanted the band to stay together - Shaun. He apologized for his behavior. But certain band members said 'No! We've had enough'." Ryder initially sets up a new short-lived band, called the Mondays, with Paul Ryder, Bez, Craig Gannon (ex-Smiths) and Gavan Whelan (ex-James), and also records material with Intastella's Stella Grundy including *Can You Fly Like You Mean It, Gungadin?*. Meanwhile, Day, Davis and Whelan will form a new band with ex-Smith Andy Rourke.

1995

Aug [19] Apparently now clean from drugs, Ryder has assembled his new group Black Grape with ex-Ruthless Rap Assassin Paul "Kermit" Leveridge and ex-Monday Bez. Signed to MCA/Relativity Records, and in a storming return to favor, the band's critically-revered funk-rock debut, ***It's Great When You're Straight ... Yeah*** enters the UK chart at #1.
Nov [18] ***Loads - The Best Of Happy Mondays*** makes UK #41 in its week of entry.

TIM HARDIN

1965

Dec The son of a violinist mother who was also the concert mistress for the Portland Symphony Orchestra and a father who played the double-bass in Navy jazz bands, Hardin (b. Dec. 23, 1941, Eugene, OR), who has traced his ancestry back to famed 19th century outlaw John Wesley Hardin, joined the US Marines for two years, serving in Indochina (although all three of these experiences are more than likely made up by Hardin, an inveterate story-teller), after leaving high school in 1959, following which he briefly stopped in New York, NY, spending one week attending acting classes at the American Academy of Dramatic Art. Relocating to Cambridge, MA in late 1961 where he performed folk and country songs at local coffee houses, he recorded his first album of mainly blues covers in 1962 (though it will remain unreleased until appearing as ***This Is Tim Hardin*** in September 1967 on Atco/Atlantic Records). Returning to New York in late '63 and uniquely for the folk scene, playing electric guitar, he has recruited a backing band playing a mostly self-written folk/jazz/blues mix as an increasingly popular draw in the burgeoning Greenwich Village folk scene, which now leads to his being signed to Verve Records via his managers, Charles Koppelman and Don Rubin.

1966

Dec Currently hailed by Bob Dylan as one of the country's greatest living songwriters and having recently performed a critically-acclaimed set at this year's "Newport Jazz & Blues Festival", his debut set, ***Tim Hardin I***, is released by Verve, including future folk standards *Misty Roses* (which will be covered by a multitude of artists), *Reason To Believe* (currently issued as a non-charting single and subsequently made famous by Rod Stewart) and *Hang On To A Dream* (which Nice will work into its future live work). With Hardin also playing guitar and piano, the Erik Jacobsen-produced set includes backing harmonicist John Sebastian.
Nov [5] Bobby Darin's version of Hardin's *If I Were A Carpenter* hits US #8. (A perennial cover in the years to come it will also chart for the Four Tops (1968), Johnny Cash & June Carter (1970), Bob Seger (1972), and Leon Russell (1974).)

1967

Jan [5] *Hang On To A Dream*, his sole UK chart record, makes #50 for one week.
Sept ***Tim Hardin II***, another largely self-penned set once again showcasing his dreamy, jazz-phrased vocal style, including his original of *If I Were A Carpenter*, is released.

1968

June Popular as a performer on the US college circuit and at European folk venues, ***Tim Hardin III - Live In Concert*** is released as Hardin relocates to live in Woodstock, NY.

1969

Apr [26] Now signed to CBS/Columbia Records, ***Suite For Susan Moore And Damion-We Are-One, One, All In One***, dedicated to his wife and son, enters the US chart set to make #129.
May Verve releases ***Tim Hardin IV*** (and will issue ***The Best Of Tim Hardin*** the following year).
Aug [30] His only US chart single, ironically a cover version of a Bobby Darin song, *Simple Song Of Freedom* reaches US #50.

1971

July [31] ***Bird On A Wire***, mostly a covers album featuring backing support from future members of Weather Report, charts for a week at US #189 (while Hardin continues to nurture a drug and alcohol problem).
Aug [14] Rod Stewart's version of Hardin's *Reason To Believe* makes US #62 (though a second Stewart version from his "Unplugged" performance will reach US #19 in 1993).

1974

Jan Following the release of his final album for Columbia, ***Painted Head*** the previous January, the 11-track, Jimmy Horowitz-produced ***Nine*** is released by Antilles Records in the US. (Largely content to live off royalties, Hardin relocates to London and teams up with Tim Rose as a short-lived folk duo, but will return to the States and to live semi-retirement in Los Angeles, CA by year's end. He will tour sporadically, mostly in Europe, over the next six years but will not record again.)

1980

Dec [29] In the same month as John Lennon's murder, Hardin dies from a heroin overdose in his apartment in Los Angeles. CBS will release its ***Shock Of Grace*** retrospective the following year, while Polygram issues ***The Tim Hardin Memorial Album*** the same year. In 1992, German reissues specialist label Line Records will bring much of Hardin's archive to compact disc while Polydor's Chronicles label will release a double-CD set of 47 Verve recordings made between 1964-1966, ***Hang On To A Dream - The Verve Recordings*** in February 1994.

STEVE HARLEY & COCKNEY REBEL

Steve Harley (vocals); **Duncan Mackay** (keyboards); **Jim Cregan** (guitar); **George Ford** (bass); **Stuart Elliott** (drums)

1973

Nov Harley (b. Steven Nice, Feb. 27, 1951, London), an ex-local newspaper journalist for the **Colchester Gazette**, and folk singer, having advertised in the UK music press for musicians to form a band, in January, has selected Milton Reame James (keyboards), Jean Paul Crocker (electric violin, guitars), Paul Jeffreys (bass) and Elliott (drums) from the subsequent auditions. With Harley on lead vocals, they become Cockney Rebel, performing early gigs at the Beckenham Arts Lab, Beckenham, Kent, a venue which Harley has helped run and make their London debut at the Speakeasy Club in April, prior to signing with EMI Records in the summer. Their first album ***Human Menagerie***, lushly orchestrated by Andrew Powell, is now released and includes the Harley-penned *Sebastian*, the band's debut single, which will become a long-term live favorite and a popular career-breaking hit in the rest of Europe.

1974

June [22] *Judy Teen*, again written by Harley and highlighted by his distinctive vocal style, is the group's breakthrough single, hitting UK #5.
July Co-produced by Harley with Alan Parsons, ***The Psychomodo*** hits UK #8, while Harley disbands the initial Cockney Rebel line-up.
Aug [31] *Mr. Soft* hits UK #8.
Oct For a concert at London's Rainbow Theatre (and an earlier performance at the "Reading Festival", Reading, Berks. in August), Harley has assembled a new backing group: Elliott from the original Cockney Rebel, plus ex-Family guitarist Cregan (b. Mar. 9, 1946), keyboardist MacKay (b. July 26, 1950) and ex-Medicine Head bassist Ford (bass).
Nov The new line-up begins work on an album at EMI's Abbey Road Studios and AIR Studios in London.

1975

Feb [22] With the artist credit of Steve Harley & Cockney Rebel, *Make Me Smile (Come Up And See Me)*, highlighted by Cregan's acoustic guitarwork, tops the UK chart for the first of two weeks and becomes Harley's biggest seller.
Mar [13] *Make Me Smile (Come Up And See Me)* is the band's only US chart appearance, reaching #96, and coincides with its first US concert trip.
[22] Once again co-produced by Harley and Parsons, ***The Best Years Of Our Lives*** hits UK #4, while the band's current gigs include a date at London's Hammersmith Odeon.
June [28] *Mr. Raffles (Man It Was Mean)* reaches UK #13, while *Black Or White* will fail to chart in October.
Dec The group supports the Kinks on a US tour.

1976

Feb [9] The band embarks on a ten-date UK tour at the Apollo Centre, Glasgow, Scotland, set to end on the 22nd at Colston Hall, Bristol, Avon, to promote ***Timeless Flight***.
[28] ***Timeless Flight*** lands at UK #18, and includes the extracted *White White Dove*.
Aug [21] Their revival of George Harrison's *Here Comes The Sun* hits UK #10.
Nov *Love's A Prima Donna* makes UK #41.
Dec [4] Its parent album, ***Love's A Prima Donna***, reaches UK #28.

1977

Feb [12] Cockney Rebel plays a benefit concert for Ireland's homeless, at London's Rainbow Theatre.
July With Cregan now playing in Rod Stewart's backing group, Harley permanently disbands Cockney Rebel and moves to the US, still signed to EMI and having recently contributed vocals to Alan Parsons' ***I Robot*** album.
[30] Concert double album, ***Face To Face - A Live Recording***, performed by the second Cockney Rebel line-up, reaches UK #40. Harley's first solo effort, ***Hobo With A Grin***, recorded in the US, will be released the following August.

1979

May [12] Harley performs with Peter Gabriel and Kate Bush at a benefit concert at London's Hammersmith Odeon for the widowed family of Bush's lighting director, Billy Duffield.
Oct Having released a sucession of non-charting singles, Harley has returned to the UK and releases ***The Candidate*** (which includes the UK #58, *Freedom's Prisoner*). Co-produced with Jimmy Horowitz, its commercial failure results in Harley being dropped by EMI, which will issue the ***The Best Of Steve Harley & Cockney Rebel*** compilation the following year.

1983

Aug With Harley having released *I Can't Even Touch You*, a one-off disc (featuring Midge Ure) for Chrysalis in March 1981, *Ballerina (Prima Donna)*, released on the Stiletto label, makes UK #51, as he appears at the what is billed "The Last Reading Rock Festival", near Reading, Berks.

1986

Feb After a period of apparent inactivity, Harley has teamed with Sarah Brightman on a specially-recorded duet of the title song from Andrew Lloyd Webber's forthcoming musical, "The Phantom Of The Opera". *The Phantom Of The Opera* hits UK #7. Harley is subsequently astonished to be overlooked by the project's producers (in favor of Michael Crawford) for the lead role in the subsequently long-running hit stage show.
Apr Newly signed to RAK Records as a solo artist, Harley releases *Heartbeat Like Thunder* and *Irresistible*, without chart success.
Oct Video "Live From London", featuring many of Cockney Rebel's hits from a 1984 performance, is released.

1988

Mar Use of *Mr. Soft* in a UK TV commercial leads to its reissue by EMI and a second retrospective, the 15-track compact disc ***Greatest Hits***.
Nov [18] Harley contributes to a UK TV telethon charity single, *Whatever You Believe*, credited to Jon Anderson, Steve Harley and Mike Batt.
Dec [21] Early band member Jeffreys is killed aboard Pan Am flight 103 over Lockerbie, Scotland.

1989

Dec [22] Having recently released *When I'm With You* on the Vital Vinyl label, Harley performs at London's Hammersmith Odeon at the end of an intermittent ten-month "All Is Forgiven" reunion tour of the UK, with original member Elliott in the line-up, and Harley's younger brother, Ian Nice, on keyboards.

1990

Apr Ad-hoc outfit Raffles United, comprising Harley and several Cockney Rebel members, plays four consecutive Sunday gigs as a house band in Sudbury, Suffolk.
Nov [29] Continuing an active live schedule, Harley and Cockney Rebel perform at Manchester International 2, Manchester, Gtr. Manchester. They will undertake a 19-date UK tour on May 1st 1992 beginning at the Queens Hall, Bradford, S. Yorks.

1995

Dec [30] Having re-charted at UK #46 on Apr [25], 1992, previewing a third EMI hits collection, the 16-track ***The Best Of Steve Harley And Cockney Rebel***, Harley's career highlight *Make Me Smile (Come Up And See Me)*, currently used in a Carlsberg TV commercial, re-charts again for a week at UK #33.

HARPERS BIZARRE

Ted Templeman (guitar, lead vocals);
Eddie James (guitar, vocals); **Dick Scoppettone** (guitar, vocals); **Dick Yount** (bass, vocals);
John Peterson (drums, vocals)

1966

Nov The group has been formed in Santa Cruz, CA, by Templeman (b. Oct. 24, 1944), Scoppettone (b. July 5, 1945), James (b. Santa Cruz) and Yount (b. Jan. 9, 1943, Santa Cruz) as the Tikis, and has recorded for Autumn and Warner Bros. Records for three years without chart success. Joined by Peterson (b. Jan. 8, 1945, San Francisco, CA), formerly with the Beau Brummels, they re-sign to Warner Bros. under the new name Harpers Bizarre and will have access to many of Los Angeles, CA's best writers, session players, arrangers and producers.

1967

Apr [1] *The 59th Street Bridge Song (Feelin' Groovy)*, their cover of the Paul Simon song, reaches US #13 and UK #34.
May Their debut album, ***Feelin' Groovy***, arranged by Leon Russell and leaning heavily on the writing and arranging talents of Randy Newman, is a moderate US seller, reaching #108. It highlights their close five-part harmonic vocal style, echoing other contemporary groups.
June [17] *Come To The Sunshine*, covering a 1966 Van Dyke Parks' single, makes US #37.
Sept [23] Parks himself plays piano with the group on a revival of Cole Porter's *Anything Goes*, which peaks at US #43 and UK #33.
Dec ***Anything Goes***, including updates of standards like *Three Babes In The Wood*, augmented by new material by Parks and Newman, reaches US #76.
[16] Another revival, Glenn Miller's *Chattanooga Choo-Choo*, makes US #45.

1968

Sept [21] ***The Secret Life Of Harpers Bizarre*** is released, featuring *Battle Of New Orleans*, which is their final chart record, at US #95. The band continues as a quartet, following James' departure.

1969

June The final album from the original line-up, ***Harpers Bizarre 4***, features Ry Cooder guesting on guitar, but its chart failure results in the group's demise. Templeman will stay with Warner Bros. as a producer (notably for the Doobie Brothers and Van Halen), eventually becoming one of the label's top executives. He will also oversee the recording of 1974's ***Beau Brummels*** by the reformed band, whose line-up once again includes Peterson. Scoppettone, James and Yount will reunite as Harpers Bizarre for the one-off album ***As Time Goes By***, released on the Forest Bay label in the US in 1976.

EMMYLOU HARRIS

1974

Having served her musical apprenticeship as a sax player in her high school marching band, as a guitarist and singer while attending the University of North Carolina on a drama scholarship (she will subsequently drop out of further studies at Boston University), and as folk singer in the late '60s on New York's celebrated Greenwich Village club circuit, Harris (b. Apr. 2, 1947, Birmingham, AL), the daughter of a US Marine father who was a POW in Korea for 18 months, already married to her first husband, songwriter Tom Slocum, has released her maiden album, ***Gliding Bird***, for Jubilee Records in 1970. Moving to Washington, DC the following year with her recently born daughter and performing at local clubs including the Red Fox and Cellar Door, she is recommended to country-rock pioneer Gram Parsons, who is looking for a female vocalist partner, by mutual friend Rick Roberts. Meeting for the first time in a bar called Clyde's, they form a personal and professional union, living together for two years in a large ground floor room at the Chateau Marmont in Los Angeles, CA, and collaborating on two Parsons albums, ***G.P.*** (1973) and ***Grievous Angel***, released the following year. Devastated by his death in 1973, she nevertheless embarks earnestly on a solo career.

1975

Mar [15] Parsons' manager, Ed Tickner, now overseeing Harris, has secured the artiste a deal with Reprise Records and ***Pieces Of The Sky*** enters the US chart, set to make US #45. Persuaded by Tickner to record her label debut with Parsons' ex-band members, Harris names them the Hot Band. (This ever-changing backing unit will survive until 1990, and will include James Burton (guitar), Rodney Crowell (guitar), Hank DeVito (steel guitar), Emory Gordy Jr. (bass), Glen D. Hardin (piano), Albert Lee (guitar), Ricky Skaggs (guitar) and John Ware (drums).)
Sept [13] The extracted *If I Could Only Win Your Love* reaches US #58.

1976

Jan [3] A duet with Linda Ronstadt on *The Sweetest Gift*, from Ronstadt's ***Prisoner In Disguise***, enters the US Country chart set to hit #12.
Mar [6] ***Elite Hotel*** reaches UK #17, spurred by Harris' UK #30 cover of Lennon and McCartney's *Here There And Everywhere*, her only UK hit single.
[20] ***Elite Hotel*** lodges at US #25, earning a gold disc and confirming her as an innovative contemporary country/rock artist.
Apr [10] Extracted *Here There And Everywhere* climbs to US #65. She is also currently featured on Bob Dylan's US #1, ***Desire***.
Nov [26] Harris performs at the Band's farewell "The Last Waltz" extravaganza, at San Francisco's Winterland Ballroom, singing *Evangeline*.

1977

Feb [5] Newly signed to the Warner Bros. label, ***Luxury Liner***, produced by Harris' second husband Brian Ahern, and covering songs by Parsons, Townes Van Zandt and Chuck Berry, among others, reaches UK #17.
[19] Harris wins Best Country Vocal Performance for ***Elite Hotel*** at the 19th annual Grammy Awards.
Mar [5] ***Luxury Liner*** reaches US #21.

1978

Mar [18] ***Quarter Moon In A Ten Cent Town*** reaches US #29, having peaked at UK #40 on Feb [4], when it benefitted from her performing at London's Royal Albert Hall.
Sept [18] Harris performs at London's Hammersmith Odeon during another brief UK visit.

1979

Jan [13] Early retrospective, ***Profile/Best Of Emmylou Harris***, makes US #81.
June [16] ***Blue Kentucky Girl***, her first pure-country outing, reaches US #43.

1980

Feb [27] Harris nabs her second Best Country Vocal Performance, Female trophy, for ***Blue Kentucky Girl***, at the 22nd annual Grammy Awards.
Apr [5] UK-only compilation, ***Her Best Songs***, makes #36.
July [12] Bluegrass-tinged ***Roses In The Snow*** reaches US #26, her seventh straight gold disc.
[26] *That Lovin' You Feelin' Again*, a duet with Roy Orbison also featured on the "Roadie" soundtrack, peaks at US #55.
Dec Seasonal collection, ***Light Of The Stable***, with guests Willie Nelson, Dolly Parton, Ronstadt and Neil Young, peaks at US #102. Harris is also currently featured on UK songwriter and future husband Paul Kennerley's concept album, ***The Legend Of Jesse James***.

1981

Feb [14] ***Evangeline***, produced by Ahern and featuring Ricky Skaggs, Waylon Jennings, Albert Lee, Dr. John, and Rodney Crowell among many others, makes UK #53.
[25] *That Lovin' You Feelin' Again* wins the Best Country Performance By A Duo Or Group, at the 23rd annual Grammy Awards.
Apr ***Evangeline*** reaches US #22.
[25] Harris' extracted cover of Pat Ballard's *Mister Sandman*, featuring Ronstadt and Parton on harmony vocals, reaches US #37, her final Hot 100 placing of the decade.

1982

Jan [30] ***Cimarron***, helmed by Ahern and named after

the title-cut cover of Poco's *Rose Of Cimarron*, makes US #46.
Nov [20] Live performance set, ***Last Date***, stops at US #65.

1983

Dec Having moved to Nashville, TN, ***White Shoes***, her last album produced by Ahern (the pair are now separated), makes US #116. A second US compilation, ***Profile II - The Best Of Emmylou Harris*** will peak at US #176 the following October.

1985

Feb [26] Her single, *In My Dreams*, wins the Best Country Vocal Performance, Female category, at the 27th annual Grammy Awards.
June [8] Critically-revered ***The Ballad Of Sally Rose***, co-written and co-produced with Kennerley, with whom Harris is now living in Nashville, and once again featuring Ronstadt and Parton, peaks at US #171. (***Thirteen***, once again co-helmed with new husband Kennerley, and including her treatment of Bruce Springsteen's *My Father's House*, will climb to US #157 the following March.)

1987

Mar [28] ***Trio***, fully teaming Harris with Parton and Ronstadt, hits US #6, earning a platinum sales disc for million-plus sales, having peaked at UK #60 a week earlier.
Aug Acoustic set, ***Angel Band***, co-produced with Emory Gordy Jr., peaks at US #166.
Dec The soundtrack album to "Planes, Trains And Automobiles", including Harris' treatment of *Back In Baby's Arms*, is released.

1988

Mar [2] Harris, Parton and Ronstadt win the Best Country Performance By A Duo Or Group for ***Trio***, at the 30th annual Grammy Awards, her fifth Grammy.
[23] ***Quarter Moon In A Ten Cent Town*** is certified gold by the RIAA.

1989

July [30] Having re-signed with Reprise which has recently issued ***Bluebird***, Harris performs at the 30th annual "Newport Folk Festival", Fort Adams State Park, Newport, RI, on a bill featuring John Lee Hooker, Pete Seeger, John Prine, Leon Redbone, the Clancy Brothers and Theodore Bikel.

1990

June ***Brand New Dance***, produced by Richard Bennett and Allen Reynolds, and including a typically sensitive rendition of Springsteen's *Tougher Than The Rest*, is released. Reprise will also release ***Duets***, rounding up her collaborative career highlights with the likes of John Denver, Gram Parsons, Don Williams and Neil Young, by year's end.

1991

Dec [14] Harris headlines the second annual "Gift Of The Heart" concert at the First Church Unity, Nashville.
[21] ***Roy Rogers Tribute***, on which Harris is featured, peaks at US #113.
[26] Harris participates in CBS-TV's "Kennedy Center Honors" special.

1992

Jan [15] "Emmylou Harris & The Nash Ramblers At The Ryman", filmed at Nashville Ryman's Auditorium, the Grand Ole Opry's original home, on April 3rd, 1991 with her new acoustic backing band featuring Sam Bush (mandolin, fiddle) and Al Perkins (banjo), airs on the TNN cable network. Harris is described in a **USA Today** article by Country Music Foundation director Bill Ivey as having "an authentic intellectual grasp of the history of country music".
Feb [1] Subsequent album, ***Emmylou Harris & The Nash Ramblers At The Ryman***, debuts at its US #174 peak.
[14] Harris guests on PBS-TV's "Garrison Keillor's Hello Love".
Mar She is featured on *She's Leaving Me Because She Really Wants To* from Lyle Lovett's ***Joshua Judges Ruth***.
Apr [1] Harris participates in the silver anniversary of the Country Music Hall of Fame from the Grand Ole Opry, Nashville, set to air on CBS-TV on May 2nd.)
May [16] She performs at the Gene Autry Western Heritage Museum in Los Angeles, as part of a tribute to singing cowboys and cowgirls, hosted by Dennis Weaver.
June Harris contributes *Child Of Mine* to ***Til Their Eyes Shine (The Lullaby Album)***, benefitting the "Voices Victims" project of the Institute For Intercultural Understanding.
July [5] She shares the bill with Little Village at the BBC-Radio One FM "American Music Festival" at London's Crystal Palace Bowl.
[31] During current dates, Harris plays to a sellout crowd of 2,932 at the Valley Forge Music Fair, Devon, PA.
Sept Much in demand as a first lady of country, Harris is featured on Trisha Yearwood's ***Hearts In Armor*** and the Chieftains' ***Another Country***.
Oct [26] She participates in cable network TNN's "Hats Off To Minnie - America Honors Minnie Pearl" special.
Nov [20] Harris performs at the Knickerbocker Arena, Albany, NY, during her latest US tour.
Dec [6] She serves as grand marshal of the 40th annual Nashville Christmas parade.
[11] Harris headlines the third annual "Gift Of The Heart" concert at the First Church Unity, with proceeds going to the Nashville Family Shelter for the homeless.

1993

Jan [19] She participates in the "Salute To Children" concert as part of the Presidential Inauguration celebrations, from the Kennedy Center for the Performing Arts, which airs on the Disney TV channel later in the day.
Feb [17] Harris wins the Female Vocalist award at first German American Country Music Federation awards, in Nashville.
[24] She nabs the Best Country Performance By A Duo Or Group trophy (for ***Emmylou Harris & The Nash Ramblers At The Ryman***) at the 35th annual Grammy Awards, held at Los Angeles' Shrine Auditorium.
May [22] Harris guests on CBS-TV's "Willie Nelson The Big Six-O" birthday celebrations, as she continues work on her Asylum Records debut.
Oct [19] She guests on CBS-TV's "Late Show With David Letterman".
Nov [6] One of the first signings on Reprise's reactivated imprint Asylum Records, Harris' ***Cowgirl's Prayer*** peaks at US #152.

1994

Feb [10] Harris guests on NBC-TV's "The Tonight Show".
June [1] She participates in "The Roots Of Country", to celebrate the re-opening of the famed Ryman Auditorium, set to air on CBS-TV on the 25th.
[3] Harris sings for the staff of Grapevine Distribution, and when Mary Black joins her on *Sunny* the BBC-TV cameras begin rolling. The ad-hoc performance will air on BBC1-TV's "We'll Meet Again" on the 6th.
July [8] She performs with the San Diego Symphony Orchestra at the Summer Pops Bowl Amphitheatre, San Diego, CA having recently released ***Songs Of The West***.
Dec [22] Harris guests on CBS-TV's "Opryland's Country Christmas".

1995

Apr [16] She performs at London's Royal Albert Hall as part of the "New American Music Tour '95" package with Trisha Yearwood and Marty Stuart.
Oct [7] Daniel Lanois-produced ***Wrecking Ball***, a multi-genre set covering material by Bob Dylan, Steve Earle, Jimi Hendrix and Neil Young, makes UK #46 in its week of entry.
[14] ***Wrecking Ball*** debuts at its US #94 peak, having attracted some of the strongest reviews in her already highly-acclaimed career.
[28] Harris takes part, with Lanois, in the annual Bridge School benefit at the Shoreline Amphitheatre, Mountain View, CA, with Neil Young, Bruce Springsteen, Hootie & the Blowfish, the Pretenders, Beck and Blind Melon.
Nov [10] Harris performs at New York's Beacon Theatre.

1996

Jan [4] She guests on CBS-TV's "The Grand Ole Opry 70th Anniversary".
Feb [27] Harris is awarded the 1996 Orville H. Gibson Lifetime Achievement Award at the Gibson Guitar Awards at Los Angeles' Hard Rock Café.
[28] ***Wrecking Ball*** is named Best Contemporary Folk Album at the 38th annual Grammy Awards held at the Shrine Auditorium.
Mar [20] She embarks on her latest North American tour at Bogart's in Cincinnati, OH, set to end on April 11th at the Ventura Theater, Ventura, CA.
June A much-delayed three-CD boxed-set retrospective, ***Portraits*** is released by Reprise Nashville (US).

GEORGE HARRISON

1968

Nov [1] Having co-written *Hurdy Gurdy Man* (though he will remain uncredited), a UK #4 hit for Donovan in June, Harrison (b. Feb. 24, 1943, Wavertree, Liverpool, Lancs. - only in his 40s did Harrison discover that he was born at 11:42 p.m. on the 24th and not, as legend dictated, in the early hours of the 25th) becomes the second Beatle to issue material independently of the group (under his solo name, Paul McCartney has previously scored the music for the December 1966 movie "The Family Way"), with the eastern-flavored album ***Wonderwall Music***, the soundtrack to the film "Wonderwall", which will reach US #49. It is notable as the first long-player to be released on the Beatles' own Apple label and coincides with Harrison's current seven-week production stint in Los Angeles, CA, helming Jackie's Lomax's Apple debut, ***Is That What You Want?***

1969

Mar [12] Harrison and his wife Patti are arrested and charged with possession of 120 joints of marijuana, on the day that Paul McCartney marries Linda Eastman.
May [9] ***Electronic Sounds***, Harrison's experimental collection of electronic noises performed, not least, with his recent acquisition, the Moog synthesizer (introduced to him by keyboard whiz Bernie Krause, who, with Paul Beaver, is an innovative pioneer of instrumental mood music), and released on the short-lived avant-garde Zapple imprint, is released set to make US #191.
Oct With Harrison having produced various artists signed to Apple, *Hare Krishna Mantra*, produced by Harrison for the London Radha Krishna Temple, reaches UK #12 and is an early indication of what will prove to be Harrison's lasting involvement with the Hare Krishna movement, a committed interest which will become his spiritual base and continue to influence his music output.
Nov Established as a second writing force, behind Lennon and McCartney, within the Beatles, Harrison's first composition, *Something*, is released by the group. It hits UK #4 and US #1. (The ballad, originally given to, and recorded by, Joe Cocker), will become a standard, with hundreds of cover versions recorded in the coming years.)
Dec [12] Harrison plays his final gig with Delaney & Bonnie & Friends at the Falkonertheater, Copenhagen, Denmark, having performed a number of dates with the ensemble at the invitation of one of its members, Eric Clapton, a series which began on the 2nd at Bristol's Colston Hall.

1970

Mar [12] Harrison moves to Friar Park, Henley-on-Thames, Berks.
May [26] He begins recording ***All Things Must Pass***.
Dec ***All Things Must Pass*** is released and hits UK #4 (failing to hit #1, not least because of a postal strike which prevents the chart from being published, although it will top the NME Album survey) and US #1, as Harrison becomes the first ex-Beatle to secure a chart-topping album, and eventually logs worldwide sales of three million copies. The triple-album box set is a dense showcase of his talent: co-produced with Phil Spector, Harrison is backed by an all-star band including Ringo Starr, Ginger Baker, Billy Preston, Badfinger and Eric Clapton's Derek & the Dominos making their debut. Bob Dylan contributes two songs: *I'd Have You Anytime*, co-written with Harrison and *If Not For You*, later covered by Olivia Newton-John (a 1971 UK #7, US #25). The third record in the set is a loose collage entitled *Apple Jam*, during which the musicians break into Cliff Richard's 1968 chart-topper, *Congratulations*: its UK songwriters, Bill Martin and Phil Coulter, successfully claim a royalty entitlement from Harrison.
[26] Acoustic guitar-strummed *My Sweet Lord* hits US #1, giving Harrison a second accolade as the first ex-Beatle with a chart-topping single. Originally given away by Harrison to Billy Preston for his Apple album, ***Encouraging Word***, and even scheduled as a Preston single release, it becomes a worldwide #1, selling over five million copies.

1971

Jan [30] *My Sweet Lord* also tops the UK chart at the start of a five-week tenure.
Feb [23] Harrison is fined and banned from driving for a year.
Mar Bright Tunes, which owns the copyright of the late Ronnie Mack's song *He's So Fine*, a hit for the Chiffons (a 1963 UK #16, US #1), makes a legal claim that *My Sweet Lord* plagiarizes its former client's hit, and all royalty payments are frozen. Harrison claims that his song is inspired by the Edwin Hawkins Singers' hit, *Oh Happy Day* (a 1969 UK #2, US #4). (On September 7th, 1976 in the US, district court judge Richard Owens will rule in favor of the plaintiff, but will allow that Harrison perhaps subconsciously adapted the song. Bright Tunes is paid $587,000 and is taken over by ex-Beatles' manager Allen Klein, who continues a damages suit.) The Chiffons will later release a cover version of *My Sweet Lord*.
[27] Harrison-penned *What Is Life* hits US #10.
July [5] *Something* gives Harrison his first independent Ivor Novello Award, winning the Best Song Musically And Lyrically category at the 16th annual luncheon, held at the Connaught Rooms, London.
Aug [1] After a personal plea for help from his friend Ravi Shankar, and 14 years prior to "Live Aid", Harrison organizes "The Concert For Bangla Desh" to aid victims of famine and war in Bangla Desh. Held at New York, NY's Madison Square Garden, the line-up of artists includes Eric Clapton, Bob Dylan, Billy Preston, Leon Russell, Ringo Starr and Ravi Shankar, with musical backing from Badfinger, Jesse Ed Davis, Jim Horn, Jim Keltner, Don Nix and Carl Radle. Due to legal problems, proceeds are frozen and Harrison writes his own cheque to maintain the fund.
Sept [11] *Bangla Desh* hits UK #10 and makes US #23.
Dec [4] The Bangla Desh concert airs on CBS-TV.

1972

Jan Triple live set, ***The Concert For Bangla Desh***, co-produced by Harrison and Phil Spector, tops the UK chart and hits US #2, making Harrison the only artist in chart history to make both the UK and US top five with back-to-back triple albums.
Feb [28] On their way home from a Rick Nelson concert in London, George and Patti are both injured in a car crash. George receives a bruised shoulder and a minor concussion, and requires eight stitches to his scalp. Patti, more seriously injured, breaks several ribs and will remain unconscious for several days.
Mar [23] "The Concert For Bangla Desh" film premieres in New York.
June [5] Harrison and Shankar are honored with the "Child Is Father To The Man" award by UNICEF, because of their efforts to aid famine relief in Bangla Desh.
[28] *My Sweet Lord* wins the Most Performed Work Of The Year trophy at the 16th annual Ivor Novello Awards, once again held at the Connaught Rooms.

1973

Mar [3] ***The Concert For Bangla Desh*** wins the Album Of The Year category, at the 15th annual Grammy Awards.
Apr [26] Harrison forms the Material World Charitable Foundation Trust.
June Following his recent contributions to albums by Ringo Starr and Harry Nilsson, Harrison's self-produced ***Living In The Material World*** hits UK #2 and tops the US chart.
[30] Typically spiritual and self-explanatory, *Give Me Love (Give Me Peace On Earth)* hits UK #8 and tops the US chart. Harrison returns full-time to his own career.
July [25] Making known his displeasure, Harrison pays £1,000,000 in taxes, due from monies collected from the concert for Bangla Desh, to the ever gracious and charitable Inland Revenue.

1974

May [23] Harrison announces the formation of his own record label, Dark Horse. Its first signing is Ravi Shankar, but Splinter is the only success for the label, other than Harrison himself, with *Costafine Town*, which will reach UK #17 and US #77 in November. (Harrison will also contribute to a pair of Splinter albums, listed as Harri Georgeson.)
Nov [2] Harrison becomes the first Beatle to undertake a solo world tour, when he begins a 30-date North American tour, as part of his "George Harrison and Friends" global trek (which also features Shankar and Preston), at the Pacific Coliseum, Vancouver, BC, Canada, set to end on December 20th at Madison Square Garden.
Dec ***Dark Horse*** hits US #4, but fails to chart in the UK. An introspective set, it includes a version of the Everly Brothers' *Bye Bye Love*, a farewell to his former wife, Patti Boyd, who has recently left him for Eric Clapton. (Patti provides backing vocals on the track.)
[13] While in Washington, DC, for a concert, Harrison visits President Gerald Ford at the White House.
[19-20] Harrison performs at Madison Square Garden.

1975

Jan [11] Lyrically unchallenging, *Ding Dong* makes UK #38. (Its B-side, *I Don't Care Anymore*, reflects his mood of the time. The title cut from the recent album, *Dark Horse*, reaches US #15.)
Feb [8] *Ding Dong* makes US #36.
Oct [25] ***Extra Texture (Read All About It)*** peaks at UK #16 and will hit US #8. It proves to be his last Apple album and its vinyl label features a partly eaten apple core.
Nov [1] *You* makes UK #38 and US #20.
Dec [26] Harrison guests on BBC2-TV's "Rutland Weekend Television".

1976

Apr [20] He joins the chorus of "The Lumberjack Song" at a Monty Python's Flying Circus performance at the City Center, New York.
Sept [7] Harrison is found guilty of plagiarising *He's So Fine* for *My Sweet Lord*.
[28] A&M sues Harrison for $6 million, over non-delivery of a new album (via Dark Horse). He has missed the deadline by two months, in part due to his being diagnosed with serum hepatitis earlier in the year. He contacts Warner Bros. and offers the label his new album, on the condition that they buy out his A&M contract.
Nov [20] Harrison guests on NBC-TV's "Saturday Night Live", turning down producer Lorne Michaels' offer of the union minimum payment for the Beatles to reunite on the show. Ironically, McCartney is apparently staying with Lennon in New York and both see the show, the highlight of which is their ex-colleague's duet with Paul Simon on *Here Comes The Sun*.
[30] Back in the UK, he appears on BBC2-TV's "The Old Grey Whistle Test".
Dec [18] Self-written and-produced ***Thirty-Three And A Third***, Harrison's first album released on his own Dark Horse imprint (its title Harrison's age), reaches UK #35.
[25] EMI/Capitol retrospective album, ***The Best Of George Harrison***, comprising his solo Apple highlights and including six Harrison-penned Beatles cuts, makes US #31.

1977

Jan [8] *This Song* makes US #25. Commenting wryly on the *My Sweet Lord* court case, it makes lyrical reference to the publishers of *He's So Fine*.
[15] ***Thirty-Three And A Third*** reaches a third of its title, US #11.
Mar [26] *Crackerbox Palace* makes US #19.
June [9] George and Patti Harrison are officially divorced.
Dec [17] Harrison plays an unannounced live set at his local pub in Henley-on-Thames.

1978

Jan [25] On ITV's "This Is Your Life", Harrison offers his congratulations to its subject, motorcycle racer Barry Sheene.
Mar [27] Eric Idle's pastiche of the Beatles, "All You Need Is Cash", in which Harrison has a cameo role, airs on BBC-TV.
Apr [26] He guests on Starr's US TV special, "Ringo".
Aug [1] Harrison and his girlfriend Olivia Arias, who was an assistant in the merchandising department at A&M before becoming a secretary at Dark Horse, have a son, Dhani, at Princess Christian Nursing Home, Windsor, Berks.
Sept [2] Harrison and Arias marry at the Henley-on-Thames Register Office.

1979

Mar [17] ***George Harrison*** makes UK #39 and will reach US #14. His major new interest in Formula 1 motor racing is highlighted by the track *Faster*, which was inspired by racing driver Jackie Stewart's book of the same name and Niki Lauda's fight to overcome his crash injuries. (Harrison will donate the royalties from the song to the Gunnar Nilsson Cancer Fund. Nilsson was a Formula 1 driver from Sweden who had succumbed to the illness.) Harrison will also take part in a charity race for the Fund at Brands Hatch, driving a 1960 Lotus against Stewart, in his 1973 World Championship Tyrell, James Hunt in his McLaren and Phil Hill in his Ferrari.
[27] Patti Harrison marries Eric Clapton at Temple Bethel, Tucson, AZ.
May [5] *Blow Away* reaches UK #51 and US #16.
[19] Harrison, McCartney and Starr play an impromptu set at a belated reception for Harrison's ex-wife Patti and Eric Clapton, in Clapton's home in Ewhurst, Surrey, a celebration also attended by Mick Jagger, David Bowie, Elton John and Lonnie Donegan.
Aug [22] Harrison's autobiography, **I Me Mine**, is published in a limited edition of 2,000 copies, priced at £148 each. (Harrison's film company, Handmade Films, launched with US businessman Denis O'Brien, scores an unexpected hit during the year: EMI drops out of backing the Monty Python film "The Life Of Brian". Harrison, friendly with the Pythons after appearing on NBC-TV's "Saturday Night Live" with Eric Idle in 1977, raises money with O'Brien to continue the project, and it becomes one of the biggest grossers in the US that year. Harrison appears in the film in a very brief cameo role. EMI also lands Handmade another success, when it sells on the rights to "The Long Good Friday", which is deemed too violent. Further Handmade Films, during the '80s, will

include "Time Bandits", "The Missionary", "Mona Lisa" and "A Private Function", among many hits.)

1981

June [13] Co-produced with Ray Cooper, ***Somewhere In England*** reaches UK #13, and will climb to US #11.
July [4] Harrison returns to chart success with his tribute to John Lennon, *All Those Years Ago*, which reaches UK #13 and hits US #2, behind Kim Carnes' *Bette Davis Eyes*, and also features the two other surviving ex-Beatles.

1982

Nov ***Gone Troppo*** makes US #108, unaided by either artist or label promotion, while the extracted *Wake Up My Love* peaks at US #53 on Dec [4].

1984

Dec [14] Harrison, now spending much of his time at his Australian home, joins Deep Purple on stage in Sydney, New South Wales, Australia.

1985

Jan [18] Handmade Films' "Water", in which Harrison appears with Clapton and Starr in a scene set at the United Nations in New York, premieres in London. Harrison also contributes the song *Focus Of Attention* to the soundtrack.
July Harrison contributes an unreleased Bob Dylan song, *I Don't Want To Do It*, to the soundtrack of the film "Porky's Revenge".
Oct [21] Harrison takes part in the Carl Perkins' C4-TV special, "Blue Suede Shoes", with Eric Clapton, Dave Edmunds, Ringo Starr and others, recorded at Limehouse studios in London. (The program is broadcast at Christmas and is subsequently released on video.)

1986

Mar [15] He performs at the "Heartbeat 86" charity concert at the National Exhibition Centre, Birmingham, W. Midlands, sharing vocals on *Johnny B. Goode* with Robert Plant and Denny Laine.
Sept Harrison guests on two tracks for Duane Eddy's comeback album, ***Duane Eddy***, while Handmade Films' "Shanghai Surprise" is critically mauled. Harrison has spent much time publicly attempting to play down the prima donna antics of its two leading stars, Madonna and Sean Penn. (He also has recorded tracks for the soundtrack and makes a cameo appearance in the film.)

1987

Jan [5] Harrison begins recording his first album in five years at his home studio.
Feb [19] He joins a jam session at Hollywood's Palamino club, with Bob Dylan, Taj Mahal, and John Fogerty.
June [5-6] Harrison participates in the fifth annual "Prince's Trust Rock Gala" at the Wembley Arena, Wembley, Middx., with Elton John, Bryan Adams, Dave Edmunds, Alison Moyet and Ringo Starr, with whom he performs *While My Guitar Gently Weeps* and *Here Comes The Sun*.
Oct [17] Harrison joins Dylan on stage at the latter's Wembley Arena concert, guesting on *Rainy Day Women #12 & 35*.
Nov [14] ***Cloud Nine*** hits UK #10. On it, Harrison has collaborated with Beatles' aficionado, ELO's Jeff Lynne, and together they have created a highly commercial confection of songs far removed from Harrison's '70s persona. Featuring musical guests Clapton, Ray Cooper, Jim Horn, Elton John, Jim Keltner and Gary Wright among others, the album wins over a new generation of fans, many of whom were born after the Beatles' demise.
[14] *Got My Mind Set On You*, reviving James Ray's 1962 original, hits UK #2.

1988

Jan [16] In one of the more significant comebacks in rock history, Harrison hits US #1 with *Got My Mind Set On You*. It is nearly 24 years since he first topped the chart with the Beatles' *I Want To Hold Your Hand*. ***Cloud Nine*** climbs to US #8.
[18] He attends the third annual Rock and Roll Hall of Fame induction dinner, at the Waldorf Astoria, New York, with Ringo Starr and Yoko Ono, to receive entry as a member of the Beatles. In his speech Harrison claims: 'I don't have much to say 'cause I'm the quiet Beatle.'
Mar [5] Harrison and Starr guest on ITV's "Aspel & Co" chat show.
[26] Co-penned with Lynne, *When We Was Fab* reaches UK #25 and US #23. Harrison gives a tongue-in-cheek nod to the Beatles sound and style with a Godley & Creme-produced promotional video clip that includes Ringo Starr.
June [7] Harrison makes an after-dinner speech at Eric Clapton's 25th anniversary dinner, at the Savoy Hotel, London.
Aug **USA Today** reports that a pseudonymic group of musical characters, the Traveling Wilburys, will release its debut album in October and that the group comprises Harrison with Roy Orbison, Tom Petty, Bob Dylan and Jeff Lynne.
Nov ***Traveling Wilburys : Volume One***, featuring Harrison as "Nelson Wilbury", is released (making UK #16 and #3 in the US (where it will sell over a million copies) and includes the hit singles *Handle With Care* and *End Of The Line*.

1989

Jan [8] The documentary movie "Life Of George" airs on ITV.
Mar Harrison is featured on Petty's ***Full Moon Fever*** and Clapton's ***Journeyman***, and also contributes *Cheer Down* to the film soundtrack for "Lethal Weapon 2".
Nov Comprising Harrison highlights from his own label, ***Best Of Dark Horse 1976-1989*** makes US #132.

1990

Mar Session veteran Jim Horn's ***Work It Out*** album, featuring Harrison, Lynne, Petty, Steve Cropper, "Duck" Dunn and members of Toto is released in the US.
Apr [1] Gary Moore's ***Still Got The Blues*** is issued, featuring *That Kind Of Woman*, written by Harrison, a song which Eric Clapton will also record for the forthcoming various-artists charity album, ***Nobody's Child***.
[16] A video filmed with Jim Capaldi of Capaldi's *Oh Lord Why Lord* is screened at the start of the Nelson Mandela tribute concert at Wembley Stadium.
[20] Harrison appears on Simon Bates' BBC Radio 1 program backing his wife Olivia's "Romania Aid" charity, Angel. Harrison contributes a Traveling Wilburys track, *Nobody's Child* (originally recorded by Lonnie Donegan), and a duet with Paul Simon from NBC-TV's "Saturday Night Live", to the ***Nobody's Child*** fundraising album.
Nov [5] After two decades of litigation, final judgement is handed down in a New York federal court by Judge Owen with regard to *My Sweet Lord*. It is decided that Allen Klein's ABKCO will own the world rights to *He's So Fine* (except in the UK and North America, where rights are retained by Harrison). In return for obtaining the rights to *He's So Fine*, Harrison will pay ABKCO $270,020. (In 1981, the court said Harrison could buy *He's So Fine* for $587,000, the price Klein originally paid to buy the composition).
[10] ***Traveling Wilburys Vol. 3***, a second collaboration, reaches UK #14.
Dec [1] ***Traveling Wilburys Vol. 3*** reaches US #11.

1991

Dec [2] *My Sweet Lord* is honored for three million broadcast performances, at the annual BMI awards at London's Dorchester Hotel.
[9] Harrison files a $200-million lawsuit in Los Angeles Superior Court against **The Globe** tabloid, which has intimated that he is a Nazi sympathizer, specifically claiming that he 'parades around his little English village in a storm trooper's uniform'.
[18] Harrison's 13-date Japanese tour, featuring the backing line-up of Eric Clapton, Steve Ferrone, Chuck Leavell, Andy Fairweather-Low, Greg Phillinganes, Nathan East, Ray Cooper, Katie Kissoon and Tessa Niles, ends at The Dome, Tokyo. He has opened his show with *I Want To Tell You* from the Beatles' ***Revolver*** album.

1992

Apr [6] He headlines a benefit concert at London's Royal Albert Hall for the Maharishi's Natural Law party, his first non-Beatles London show. Starr joins him on stage, while Joe Walsh and Gary Moore are the support acts.
July Harrison is featured on *Real Love* from Jimmy Nail's ***Growing Up In Public*** album. He also joins Carl Perkins on stage at the Hard Rock Cafe's 21st anniversary party in London, singing *Everybody's Tryin' To Be My Baby*.
Aug [1] Tour-taped ***Live In Japan*** debuts at its US #126 peak.
Oct [16] Harrison performs *If Not For You* and *Absolutely Sweet Marie* at the "Bob Dylan 30th Anniversary Celebration" at Madison Square Garden. He also backs Dylan, with Clapton, Roger McGuinn and Petty, on *My Back Pages*.
Dec [9] Harrison is presented with **Billboard** magazine's first Century Award (by Petty) at the third annual **Billboard** Music Awards, held at the Universal Amphitheatre, Universal City, CA proclaiming that 'being a Beatle was no hindrance on my career'. Backstage, Harrison, commentating on the UK press says: 'They are like animals. They should have their heads chopped off.'
[14] He participates in a Universal Amphitheatre benefit to establish a trust fund for the recently deceased Toto drummer Jeff Porcaro's children, with Boz Scaggs, Eddie Van Halen, Michael McDonald, Donald Fagen and Don Henley, among others.

1993

Sept [30] Harrison guests on the season premiere of Fox-TV's "The Simpsons".

1994

May HandMade Films is sold to Toronto, ON, Canada-based production company Paragon Entertainment Corp. for $8.5 million.
Oct [23] Harrison's principal songwriting contributions to the Beatles' output, *Something* and *Here Comes The Sun*, are respectively honored for five million and three million broadcast plays at BMI's annual awards ceremony at London's Dorchester Hotel.
Dec [21] His tribute to outgoing Warner Bros. CEO Mo Ostin, titled *Mo*, written specifically to honor his departure, leads a six-CD in-house only hits package presented to Ostin at his leaving ceremony.

1995

Jan [20] While still assembling archive material and recording new songs with McCartney and Starr for the Beatles' forthcoming release of three retrospective double albums and an accompanying documentary, Harrison files suit for $25 million against his former business partner Denis O'Brien in Los Angeles Superior Court, alleging fraudulence and negligence in financial management, which will find in Harrison's favor.
see also: **THE BEATLES**

WILBERT HARRISON

1958

Dec After serving in the US Navy, Harrison (b. Jan. 6, 1929, Charlotte, NC), said to have been born into a family of 23, becomes a nomadic, idiosyncratic R&B singer, already recording one-off singles for the Rockin' (*This Woman Of Mine*) and Duluxe (*Gin And Coconut Milk*) labels in the early '50s, before signing to Glades Records in 1952 and having a regional R&B hit in Miami, FL, with *Don't Drop It*, cut for Savoy Records in 1954. Now in New York, NY, and during studio time paid for by Fury Records' owner Bobby Robinson, with the agreement of Savoy's Herman Lubinsky, to whom Harrison is still officially contracted, he records, from memory, *K.C. Lovin'*, with guitarist Jimmy Spruill and other session players. Harrison recalls the song, written by Jerry Leiber and Mike Stoller, from the original version by Little Willie Littlefield, an R&B chart hit in 1952. Since he knows it as *Kansas City*, that becomes the title used on his single.

1959

May *Kansas City*, released on Fury, tops the US chart for two weeks and the R&B chart for seven weeks, selling over one million copies. Other minor US chart versions of the song are by Rocky Olson (#60), Hank Ballard (#72) and Little Richard (#95). Littlefield's *K.C. Lovin'* is reissued, now retitled *Kansas City*, but, ironically, fails to chart.

July *C.C. Rider*, his Fury follow-up, is released.

1960

Harrison begins a decade on the road on small club and roadhouse tours, developing a one-man-band act, playing drum and harmonica with his guitar, and occasionally piano, since he cannot afford to maintain a travelling band. He records a number of non-charting one-off releases for a variety of labels, including Seahorn, Neptune, Doc, Port and Vest.

1970

Jan Long written off as a one-hit wonder, Harrison resurfaces in New York on Juggy Murray's also believed-dormant Sue label, with *Let's Work Together*, which reaches US #32. It is a revised version of his composition *Let's Stick Together*, originally recorded - without success - for Fury in the early '60s. (This earlier version will be revived by Bryan Ferry in 1976, hitting UK #4.) ***Let's Work Together*** makes US #190.

Feb Canned Heat's cover version of *Let's Work Together* hits UK #2 (and will make US #26 in November), bringing Harrison financial reward through songwriting royalties.

1971

Mar *My Heart Is Yours* makes US #98 and is his final chart entry. Released on Nashville, TN, label SSS International, it is produced in New Orleans, LA, by Allen Toussaint and Marshall Sehorn and is, once again, a song cut years before, without success, for Fury. (Creedence Clearwater Revival will take Harrison on tour to open its shows with his novel act, but this raised profile fails to bring him further chart success. Assorted '70s releases on Buddah, Hotline and Brunswick Records will fail to sell. He will die following a stroke on October 26th 1994.)

P.J. HARVEY

1988

July Raised in sheep-farming country in the small village of Corscombe, Dorset, by her stonemason father Ray and sculptor mother Eva, both friends of the Rolling Stones' Charlie Watts (and sideman Ian Stewart), Harvey (b. Polly Jean Harvey, Oct. 9, 1969, Yeovil, Dorset) has been a saxophone-playing member of her local Plenistow school instrumental combo, Boulogne. Having taken up the guitar and writing her own songs, and graduating from school with nine O-lvels and two A-levels to attend Yeovil Art College, she has formed the short-lived Polekats trio before now joining local guitarist John Parish's band Automatic Dlamini (replacing ex-Headless Horseman, a group also featuring Parish and PJ Harvey's future manager Mark Vernon on keyboards, and future PJ Harvey drummer Rob Ellis (b. Feb. 13, 1962, Bristol, Somerset), having met the group's other guitarist Jeremy Hogg at a party. With Harvey playing guitar, sax and contributing backing vocals, the band, with a fluid line-up, will undertake two European tours and record two albums, the first of which, 1989's ***Here Catch Shouted His Father*** will remain unreleased, while the follow-up ***From A Diva To A Diver***, with Harvey taking a more prominent vocal role, will only emerge in August 1992 on the independent Big International label.

1991

June Automatic Dlamini tapes its only radio session for broadcast on Radio Orchard (having already made its sole television appearance on TSW-TV's "Tongue'n'Groove"). However, with Parish moving on to produce Wall Of Voodoo and Harvey, who has completed a foundation course at Yeovil Art College, eager to find a more productive outlet for her songwriting, she has teamed with Ellis and bassist Ian Olliver (who has also played in Automatic Dlamini) to form the trio PJ Harvey, which will make its live debut at a Charmouth bowling alley in July, and begin sending out demo tapes, one of which reaches Too Pure label co-head Paul Cox who secures the band its first London gig at the Moonlight Club, Hampstead, London in August and funds the recording of its first sessions.

Sept Family Cat's *Color Me Grey*, featuring Harvey on backing vocals, is released by Bad Girl Records (UK). (She will also feature on the group's forthcoming album ***Furthest From The Sun*** and can be heard on Grape Featuring Polly Harvey's *Baby In A Plastic Bag*, to be released in January the following year.)

Nov [3] Following the October release of PJ Harvey's *Dress* (to ecstatic reviews in the alternative UK music press including a Single Of The Week nod in **Melody Maker**), the trio's first session for the "John Peel Show" airs on BBC Radio 1FM.

Dec With Olliver already departing to re-join the still-going Automatic Dlamini, five-string fretless bassist Stephen Vaughan (b. June 22, 1962, Wolverhampton, W. Midlands) joins PJ Harvey for a UK tour highlighted by a show at London's Camden Falcon.

1992

Feb [29] Although officially now signed to Island Records after considerable major label interest, *Sheela-Na-Gig*, released by Too Pure, charts for a week at UK #69.

Apr [11] The band's only album for Too Pure, recorded for £5,000, ***Dry*** enters at its UK #11 peak, critically revered by alternative music critics, impressed not least with its lead singer's frank, overtly sexual, ultra-feminist lyrical direction (a label she publicly rejects). Depicted as a "Riot Grrrl" and fast becoming the darling of the UK music media, Harvey will appear topless in an April edition of the **New Musical Express**.

Aug Having rejected an offer to participate in this year's US Lollapalooza tour and following an appearance at the "Reading Festival", Berks., Harvey, reportedly suffering from exhaustion and having also scrapped album sessions at the Manor, Oxford, Oxon, recorded in June, retreats to Dorset to rest and write new material.

Dec [5] Following its first US dates in November, the band begins recording its second album with producer Steve Albini at Pacyderm Studios in Minneapolis, MN.

1993

Mar During the month, the trio completes another session for 1FM's "John Peel Show".

May [1] PJ Harvey's first Island release, *50 Ft Queenie* debuts at its UK #27 peak.

[8] Produced by Albini, whose hardcore, heavy production work will be criticized by some ("harrowing, uneasy listening", **New Musical Express**) for burying Harvey's vocals, ***Rid Of Me*** enters at its UK #3 high.

[22] ***Rid Of Me*** charts for a week at US #158.

[23] Its UK tour ends at London's Kilburn National Theatre.

July [17] *Man-Size* debuts at its UK #42 peak while the trio plays its first concerts in Japan.

Aug Friction between Harvey and her two band-mates climaxes with the departure of Ellis and Vaughan, leaving her as a solo artist. (During the month while the band opens for U2 on European stadium dates, U2's manager Paul McGuinness also becomes her new manager.)

Sept [24] Harvey guests on NBC-TV's "The Tonight Show".

Oct [30] ***4-Track Demos***, featuring pre-Albini demos of songs from ***Rid Of Me*** and six additional newly-released cuts, enters at its UK #19 high.

1994

Feb [14] Harvey performs the Rolling Stones' *Satisfaction* with Björk at the 13th annual BRIT Awards held at London's Alexandra Palace.

Sept Harvey begins recording her first strictly solo set in London (to where she has also relocated), to be mixed in Dublin, Eire in November.

1995

Feb [16] Billed under the same (but now solo) name P.J. Harvey, her new touring lineup of Eric Drew Feldman (keyboards), Joe Gore (guitar), John Parish (guitar, her ex-bandmate in Automatic Dlamini), Nick Bagnoll (bass) and Jean Marcbutty (drums) performs for the first time together at the Gavin Seminar in New Orleans, LA, to be followed by a gig at the NARM convention in San Diego, CA on the 22nd.

[18] *Down By The Water* bows at its UK #38 peak.

Mar [18] Co-produced by Harvey, Flood and Parish and featuring Gore and ex-Birthday Party bassist Mick Harvey, her first solo album ***To Bring You My Love*** debuts at its US #40 peak having entered at its UK #12 high the previous week.

June [2] A US tour includes tonight's gig at the Trocadero, Philadelphia, PA, a $16,200-grossing bill from 1,274 fans.

[24] She performs at the 25th "Glastonbury Festival" at Worthy Farm, Pilton, Somerset.

July [22] *C'mon Billy* reaches UK #29 peak in its week of entry.

Aug [9] Her second US trek of the year gets underway at the Universal Amphitheatre, Universal City, CA, on a bill with Live and Big Audio Dynamite which grosses $139,543 from 6,353 attendees, set to end on October 11th at the Beacon Theatre, New York, NY.

Sept [11] Harvey appears on CBS-TV's "Late Show With David Letterman".

Oct [28] *Send His Love To Me* enters at its UK #34 peak.

Dec End-of-year accolades include Artist Of The Year nods in **Rolling Stone**, **Spin** and **Village Voice** polls. She is also nominated in the Best Female Rock Performance and Best Alternative Music Performance categories for the forthcoming 38th annual Grammy Awards (though she will lose out to Alanis Morissette and Nirvana respectively).

1996

Feb [12] Nick Cave's ***Murder*** is released including *Henry Lee*, a collaboration with Harvey. (She continues working on her next album with Parish while also writing music for a Mark Bruce Dance Company show scheduled to be staged in London later in the year.)

DONNY HATHAWAY

1968

Hathaway (b. Oct. 1, 1945, Chicago, IL), having been raised in St. Louis, MO by his well-known gospel singer grandmother Martha Pitts and been a gospel singer throughout his childhood and teens, has majored in music theory on a fine arts scholarship at Howard University, Washington, DC, where he meets singer Roberta Flack, in 1964, while playing keyboards with the Ric Powell Jazz Trio in Washington clubs. Now back in Chicago, he meets Curtis Mayfield, who invites him to become a producer for the fledgling Curtom label, where he subsequently works with singer June Conquest, with whom he records a number of duets. He then moves on to work at Chess Records with Woody Herman, before freelancing on production work for Stax with Carla Thomas and the Staple Singers.

1969

Feb While his latest duet with Conquest (billed as June & Donnie), *I Thank You Baby*, gives Hathaway his first chart presence (making US R&B #45), noted session saxophonist King Curtis recommends him to the Atlantic stable, which signs him as a producer, writer and recording artist.

1970

Feb [7] Hathaway's label debut, *The Ghetto (Part 1)*, co-written with Leroy Hutson and produced by Arif Mardin, makes US #87. (Hathaway records his debut album, the mostly self-penned ***Everything Is Everything*** on which he also plays keyboards, which initially fails to chart.)

1971

June The soul-drenched ***Donny Hathaway*** reaches US #89 and is followed by ***Everything Is Everything***, which now peaks at US #73.
Aug [14] His first duet with Flack, their cover of Carole King's *You've Got A Friend*, reaches US #29, two weeks after James Taylor has taken his version to US #1.
Nov [6] Also duetted with Flack, their revival of the Righteous Brothers' 1965 chart-topper, *You've Lost That Lovin' Feelin'* peaks at US #71.

1972

May Concert performance, ***Donny Hathaway Live***, is his first Top 20 entry, peaking at US #18, and will earn a gold disc for half a million US sales.
June [10] *Giving Up*, written by Van McCoy, peaks at US #81, while a reissued duet with June Conquest, on Curtom, reviving Sam & Dave's *I Thank You*, makes US #94 the following week.
Aug [12] Lilting soul duet, *Where Is The Love*, a duet with Flack written by Ralph McDonald and William Salter, hits US #5 and sells over one million copies, earning a gold disc. It also reaches UK #29 - Hathaway's first UK hit. Their joint album, ***Roberta Flack And Donny Hathaway***, hits US #3 and is also certified gold.
Sept Hathaway's ***Come Back Charleston Blue***, composed and performed as the music for the Godfrey Cambridge film of the same name, makes US #198.
[2] He records the theme song for the CBS-TV comedy series "Maude" (a spin-off from "All In The Family" which will run until 1978).
Nov [11] *I Love You More Than You'll Ever Know* peaks at US #60.

1973

Mar [3] Hathaway and Flack win the Best Pop Vocal Performance By A Duo, Group Or Chorus category for *Where Is The Love* at the 15th annual Grammy Awards.
Aug [18] *Love, Love, Love* makes US #44, while its parent album, the semi-autobiographical ***Extension Of A Man***, makes US #69.

1974

Hathaway forms his own freelance production company, helming projects for the likes of Jerry Butler, Aretha Franklin and the Staple Singers. His production work will keep him out of the studio as a solo artist for some time (as will recurrent personal problems).

1978

May [13] Five years after his last chart appearance, Hathaway's fourth duet with Flack, *The Closer I Get You*, a James Mtume/Reggie Lucas song from her album ***Blue Lights In The Basement***, hits US #2 for the first of two weeks, behind Yvonne Elliman's *If I Can't Have You*, having topped the US R&B survey for two weeks and also set to make UK #42.
Sept Hathaway's solo, *You Were Meant For Me*, reaches US R&B #17 but does not cross over to the Hot 100 (and will be his last chart record during his lifetime).

1979

Jan [13] Hathaway dies, aged 33, after falling from the 15th floor of the Essex House Hotel, New York, NY. The death is officially registered as suicide, though some close friends remain sceptical as to the real cause.

1980

Apr [12] A further pairing with Flack, *You Are My Heaven*, written by its co-producer, Eric Mercury, with Stevie Wonder, makes US #47.
May ***Roberta Flack Featuring Donny Hathaway***, which Hathaway was completing at the time of his death, climbs to US #25 and earns a gold disc. On its sleeve notes, Flack writes: "My life is beginning to reveal to me that - Donny Hathaway lives."
June [14] A second Mtume/Lucas song, the mid-tempo *Back Together Again* (featuring backing vocals by Luther Vandross), taken from the album with Flack, reaches US #56 and hits UK #3, resulting in ***Roberta Flack Featuring Donny Hathaway*** reaching UK #31, Hathaway's final chart appearance. While his enthusiasts have to remain content with the incomplete nine-track ***Best Of Donny Hathaway*** as his only Atlantic retrospective prior to Rhino Records (US) bringing ***Everything Is Everything***, ***Donny Hathaway*** and ***Extension Of A Man*** to compact disc in the '90s, Hathaway's daughter Lalah begins her soul career in 1990 with ***Lalah Hathaway***.

RICHIE HAVENS

1966

Havens (b. Jan. 21, 1941, Brooklyn, New York, NY), a former street-corner singer and teenage member of the McCrea Gospel Singers in the Bedford-Stuyvesant section of Brooklyn, has started to sing and play guitar around the burgeoning Greenwich Village folk scene in 1962, having first come to the area as a painter. He hones his music in local clubs and cafés, and his unique guitar style uses an open E-chord tuning and a rapid strumming method which makes the instrument almost percussive in sound. While his 1965 debut album for the local Douglas Record label, ***A Richie Havens Record***, sells only to his Greenwich Village underground following, his newly released ***Electric Havens*** becomes not only a cult favorite, but leads to a contract with MGM Records' new, progressive Verve Forecast label.

1967

His well-received Verve Forecast debut, ***Mixed Bag***, sets the pattern for most subsequent releases: an open strumming-guitar style mixed with an intense vocal treatment of a personalized selection of traditional songs and covers, including *Just Like A Woman* (Bob Dylan) and *Eleanor Rigby* (Lennon/McCartney).

1968

Jan [20] Havens appears with other folk dignitaries, Dylan, Judy Collins, Arlo Guthrie, Pete Seeger and others, in a tribute concert to Woody Guthrie at New York's Carnegie Hall.
Mar ***Something Else Again*** is his US chart debut, peaking at #184, and revives interest in ***Mixed Bag***, which finally reaches US #182 in July.
Dec His growing popularity also sees his second Douglas album, ***Electric Havens***, make US #192.
[28] He performs at the "Miami Pop Festival" at the Gulfstream Racing Park, Hallandale, FL, to 100,000 people, along with Chuck Berry, Three Dog Night, Fleetwood Mac, Marvin Gaye and many others.

1969

Feb Double album, ***Richard P. Havens, 1983***, once again highlighted by Beatles and Dylan adaptations, reaches US #80.
June [7] Havens performs at an open-air concert at London's Hyde Park, supporting Blind Faith.
Aug [16] Havens appears at the "Woodstock Music & Art Fair", Bethel, NY, where his late-night impassioned set is rapturously received. His song *Freedom* becomes one of the anthems of the festival and is included in the movie "Woodstock".
[31] Havens performs at the "Isle Of Wight Festival", Woodside Bay near Ryde, Isle of Wight, with Dylan, the Band, the Who, the Moody Blues, the Nice, Joe Cocker and others.

1970

Jan [28] He takes part in a seven-hour benefit concert at New York's Madison Square Garden, with Jimi Hendrix, Judy Collins, the Young Rascals and others, to raise funds for the Vietnam Moratorium Committee.
Feb With Havens having formed his own Stormy Forest label, its first release is ***Stonehenge***, which includes his offbeat version of the Bee Gees' *I Started A Joke*. It reaches US #155.
May [23-24] He participates in a "Bank Holiday Festival" at Plumpton Race Course, Plumpton, E. Sussex, with Ginger Baker's Air Force, Judas Jump, Chicken Shack, Black Sabbath and Christine Perfect.
Aug [30] He appears at the second "Isle Of Wight Festival", Godshill, Isle of Wight, on a bill featuring Free, Donovan, Jethro Tull, Joan Baez, Jimi Hendrix and others.
Nov An MGM reissue of ***Mixed Bag*** puts it back on the US chart, at #190.

1971

Feb ***Alarm Clock*** reaches US #29.
May [22] Taken from it, a revival of the George Harrison-penned *Here Comes The Sun* is Havens' only single to gain widespread US airplay and his only US Top 20 entry, making US #16.
Oct [19] On a UK visit, Havens is recorded live at the BBC Television Theatre, London, for subsequent broadcast.
Dec ***The Great Blind Degree*** peaks at US #126.

1972

June [3] Havens performs at the Crystal Palace Garden Party, Crystal Palace, London, on a bill with the Beach Boys, Joe Cocker and others.
[4] He begins a six-date UK tour at London's Hammersmith Odeon, set to end on the 18th at Croydon's Fairfield Halls.
Oct Double live album, ***Richie Havens On Stage***, becomes his second-biggest seller, reaching US #55. It includes three stage performances from London's BBC-TV Theatre, the Civic Center, Santa Monica, CA, and the Westbury Music Fair, Westbury, NY, and reprises much material from earlier albums, including his Woodstock highlight, *Freedom*.
Dec [9] Havens takes part in the stage debut of Pete Townshend's rock opera, "Tommy", at London's Rainbow Theatre, with Steve Winwood, Merry Clayton, Keith Moon, Rod Stewart, Peter Sellers and Roger Daltrey.

1974

Following the June 1973 US #182 peaking ***Portfolio***, featuring guitarists Eric Weissberg and Jerry Friedman, Havens appears as Othello in the Patrick McGoohan-directed movie of Jack Good's musical "Catch My Soul", based on Shakespeare's "Othello". Co-starring with Tony Joe White, Lance LeGault and Delaney & Bonnie, he performs six songs.

1976

Oct Having peaked at US #186 with ***Mixed Bag II*** in October 1975, Havens, newly signed to A&M Records, logs his last chart album for 11 years with ***The End Of The Beginning*** at US #157.

1977

Apr [5] Havens appears with Jackson Browne, John Sebastian, Country Joe McDonald and others at a three-day rally in Los Angeles, CA, which raises $150,000 to help protect whales and dolphins from the international fishing industry.
July Havens interrupts a current UK tour (supporting Genesis) to play to an audience of 200 devoted folkies at

the "Stonehenge Free Festival", near Amesbury, Wilts.
Nov [22] He appears in NBC-TV's "Special Treat: How The Beatles Changed The World" special.
(Following the release of ***Mirage***, Havens is dropped from A&M, spending the rest of the year working on the soundtrack for, and appearing in, the Richard Pryor-starring movie "Greased Lightning". He will continue touring over the next ten years, also recording a one-off album ***Connections*** for Elektra Records, released in March 1980 and ***Common Ground***, issued in June 1983.)

1987

Oct Now signed to RBI Records, Havens briefly returns to the US chart with ***Simple Things***, which peaks at #173, released in the UK by Start Records. (During the year, he also makes a cameo appearance in the Dylan-led movie "Hearts Of Fire".)
Dec [7] Havens performs Harry Chapin's *W.O.L.D* at "The Gold Medal Celebration" memorial concert at New York's Carnegie Hall, on what would have been Chapin's 45th birthday.

1990

Nov [9] Still an active participant for social and political causes (he has recently formed the Natural Guard environmental group in California), Havens participates in the "Freedom Festival '90" benefit, simultaneously held in Los Angeles, Hong Kong and Berlin, W. Germany.

1991

Aug [17] ***Songs Of The Civil War***, featuring a cut by Havens, is released.
Oct [2] Havens performs at "Bountiful Boston : A Fall Harvest" at Boston's Prudential Center.

1992

Oct [16] Having been featured on PBS-TV's "Songs Of The Civil War" broadcast in 1991, and still a popular folk veteran at annual genre festivals, Havens, who spent much of his early career covering Dylan songs, performs *Just Like A Woman* at the star-filled "Bob Dylan 30th Anniversary Celebration" tribute to the music legend, at New York's Madison Square Garden.
Dec Havens attends the annual Reebok Human Rights Awards in Boston, with Joan Baez, Peter Gabriel and Michael Stipe.

1993

Mar Rhino releases a Havens retrospective ***Resumé***.
Apr Sony Kids' ***Put On Your Green Shoes***, featuring Havens, is released.
June [5-6] Havens takes part in the "Troubadours Of Folk Festival" at UCLA's Drake Stadium, Los Angeles.

1994

Jan [1] An ad for Coopers & Lybrand, featuring Havens singing *The Times They Are A-Changin'* airs during the Orange Bowl, the first time a Bob Dylan song has been used in advertising.
Feb [10] He performs at the Tibet House benefit concert at Carnegie Hall.
June [2] Havens plays at the Pine Knob Music Theatre, Clarkston, MI, during a series of dates with Jefferson Starship and Mountain.
July [12] He embarks on a one-day tour of rail stations to promote his new album, ***Cuts To The Chase***, travelling on Amtrak (his song *Something About A Train* is their ad theme) from Washington, DC to New York by way of Philadelphia, PA.
Aug [13] Havens appears at the alternative "Woodstock '94" free concert at the original site in Bethel, NY.

1995

Feb [16] He plays at London's Harlesden Mean Fiddler during a brief UK visit.
Apr Havens contributes *The Great Mandala* with the Simon Sisters to Peter Paul & Mary's ***Lifelines*** album.
Oct [16] CD-ROM "GeoSafari", to which Havens lends his voice, is released by Educational Insights.

1996

Feb [3] Havens performs at the Electric Factory in Philadelphia with the Band.

RONNIE HAWKINS

1958

Hawkins (b. Jan. 10, 1935, Huntsville, AR) assembled his first backing group, the Hawks (a name he will retain despite constant personnel changes), at the University of Arkansas in 1952, playing local hillbilly gigs. As musical trends changed, he has turned (by the mid-'50s) into a journeyman rock'n'roller, relying on covers of Chuck Berry and Bo Diddley songs. Unable to arouse much interest in US, he has moved from Fayetteville, AR, to Hamilton, ON, Canada, on the advice of country singer Conway Twitty, and become a successful fixture on the Canadian scene, making his recording debut for the Quality label. Currently (and temporarily) touted as the Black Hawks, and comprising Hawkins, Levon Helm, Sun session player Jimmy Ray Paulman and Willard "Pop" Jones, the band's agent Harold Kudlets books them into a residency at The Golden Rail in Hamilton.

1959

July [4] Signed to the Roulette label, Hawkins' workmanlike revision of Berry's *Thirty Days*, now called *Forty Days*, makes US #45.
Oct [3] A 1955 R&B hit for Young Jessie, *Mary Lou*, becomes Hawkins' biggest seller, peaking at US #26. (17 years later, Bob Seger will revive it on his platinum album, ***Night Moves***.) Roulette's sobriquet for Hawkins, "Mr. Dynamo", proves an overstatement, when Hawkins fails with his next three singles: *Southern Love*, *Lonely Hours* and *The Ballad Of Caryl Chessman*.

1960

16-year-old Robbie Robertson becomes the Hawks' roadie, subsequently joining on bass. When Fred Carter goes to Nashville, Robertson switches to lead guitar.

1963

Mar Featuring Robertson's incandescent guitar, Hawkins' version of Bo Diddley's *Who Do You Love* is widely regarded as his recording zenith, though it remains commercially successful. Later in the year, his current Hawks members - Helm, Robertson, Rick Danko, Richard Manuel and Garth Hudson, desert him and move to the US. They later record as Levon & the Hawks, backing John Hammond and then Bob Dylan, and will ultimately surface as the Band in 1968.
(Hawkins will spend the next five years on the Canadian club circuit, reminiscing about his sexual excesses and sitting out his ten-year Roulette contract.)

1969

Media interest arising from the ascent of the Band and public recommendation from John Lennon, who stays with Hawkins in December while in Canada on his peace trip, reflate Hawkins' reputation. Jerry Wexler signs him to Atlantic subsidiary Cotillion, and he records with Duane Allman and other Muscle Shoals acts in Muscle Shoals, AL.

1970

Jan Cotillion releases a 90-second promotional single, on which Lennon exhorts the virtues of Hawkins' upcoming album.
Feb [28] Hawkins' comeback single, *Down In The Alley*, reaches US #75, from its parent album, ***Ronnie Hawkins***. A second Cotillion album, ***The Hawk*** will follow before he moves to Monument for the 1971 release of *Rock And Roll Resurrection* and *Ain't That A Shame*.

1976

Nov [25] Hawkins sings *Who Do You Love* at the Band's farewell concert ball, "The Last Waltz" at the Winterland Ballroom, San Francisco, CA. He also appears in Bob Dylan's film "Renaldo And Clara", but will fade into relative obscurity thereafter. Winning a (Canadian) Juno Award as Best Country Male Vocalist in 1982, for ***Legend In His Own Spare Time***, his career highlights will reach compact disc in 1990 with the Roulette issue (via EMI) of ***The Best Of Ronnie Hawkins And The Hawks*** in the UK and, in 1991, when Silver Eagles Records releases ***Ronnie Hawkins Greatest Hits And Rock'n'Roll Favorites*** in the US.

HAWKWIND

Dave Brock (guitar, vocals);
Nick Turner (sax, flute, vocals);
Mick Slattery (guitar); **John Harrison** (bass);
Terry Ollis (drums); **Dik Mik** (electronics)

1969

Oct Brock and Slattery have been playing with rock outfit Famous Cure, while Turner is in Mobile Freakout when, having met by chance on tour in Holland, they meet again, having all returned to the UK. Subsequently debuting as Group X at a ten-minute gig at the All Saint's Hall, Notting Hill, London, in July, and based in the local Ladbroke Grove area, they soon name-change to Hawkwind Zoo. Finally settling on Hawkwind, their manager Doug Smith secures the band a deal with United Artists/Liberty Records. Huw Lloyd Langton replaces Slattery, while the line-up is occasionally augmented by Hell's Angels member and ex-Pretty Things drummer Viv Prince. Dick Taylor (also ex-Pretty Things) is brought in to produce the group and ends up playing on their debut recording sessions.

1970

July Hawkwind's first release is *Hurry On Sundown/Mirror Of Illusion*. Harrison leaves and is replaced on bass by Thomas Crimble.
Aug [28-30] While their debut album, ***Hawkwind***, co-produced by the band with Taylor, is released, and true to their "people's band" tag, the group plays at Canvas City, performing a series of free gigs performed on the perimeter of the "Isle Of Wight Festival", Godshill, Isle of Wight.
Sept Langton leaves (he will return nine years later), as does Crimble.

1971

May Dave Anderson (ex-Amon Duul) is recruited, while soundman Del Dettmar becomes the synthesizer player, replacing Dik Mik (who will rejoin three months later).
June With poet Robert Clavert making his debut as lead vocalist, and rock dancer Stacia also making her first performance with the band, Hawkwind appears at the "Glastonbury Fayre", Pilton, Somerset, and attracts the attention of subsequent band cohort, science-fiction writer Michael Moorcock.
Aug Lemmy (b. Ian Kilmister, Dec. 24, 1945, Stoke-on-Trent, Staffs.), ex-Rockin' Vicars and Sam Gopal and once a roadie for Jimi Hendrix, joins on bass after Anderson leaves. (Initially on six-months' trial, he stays nearly four years.)
Oct ***In Search Of Space***, co-produced by the group with George Chkiantz, reaches UK #18. Its "space-rock" image is partially inspired by Calvert and further reflects the band's improvizational, loud-rock and notoriously drug-influenced music style.

1972

Jan Simon King replaces Ollis on drums.
Feb [13] The group plays the "Greasy Truckers Party" at London's Roundhouse. The performance is recorded, with excerpts subsequently appearing on the albums ***Greasy Truckers Party*** and ***Glastonbury Fayre***. Calvert joins the band fulltime and sings many of the lead vocals.
May [5] The band performs at the "Bickershaw

Festival" near Wigan, Lancs.
Aug [19] Cosmic-rock anthem, *Silver Machine*, one of Calvert's songs taken from the "Greasy Truckers" recordings, remixed with Calvert's original vocal re-recorded by Lemmy, hits UK #3 and will remain the band's most enduring musical highlight.
[13] The group plays a six-hour party at London's Rainbow Theatre.
Nov [9] Hawkwind begins a 24-date UK tour at the Civic Hall, Dunstable, Beds., set to end on December 23rd at Liverpool Stadium, Liverpool, Merseyside.
Dec Their self-produced third album, ***Doremi Fasol Latido***, with Lemmy credited as Lemmy the Lurch, reaches UK #14. The success of *Silver Machine* enables Hawkwind to create a lavish 30-date touring show entitled "The Space Ritual".

1973

Feb [7] Hawkwind gives a concert for the inmates of Wandsworth Prison, London.
June Double album ***Space Ritual Alive***, recorded at shows in Liverpool, Lancs., and Brixton, London earlier in the year, hits UK #9.
Aug *Urban Guerilla* makes UK #39, but is withdrawn over concerns about associations with current IRA terrorist activity.
Nov Group, now minus Dik Mik, makes its US debut at Howard Stein's Academy of Music in New York.
Dec ***Space Ritual Alive*** makes US #179 during the band's first US trek.
[15] Upon its return, Hawkwind begins a seven-date UK tour at the Bracknell Sports Centre, Bracknell, Berks., set to end on the 22nd at the Empire Theatre, Edinburgh, Scotland.

1974

Feb Hawkwind begins a second US tour and plays a benefit for acid guru Timothy Leary, who is back in jail after escaping and being recaptured in Switzerland.
Apr Simon House, who played on their recent US tour, joins on keyboards, synthesizer and violin. Dettmar leaves the stage line-up to operate his synthesizer from the mixing desk, though he will quit the group in June, emigrating to Canada.
May Calvert's solo album, ***Captain Lockheed & The Starfighters***, is released on United Artists.
July Simon King breaks his ribs playing soccer, and is replaced by Alan Powell (ex-Chicken Shack, Stackridge, Vinegar Joe), who will remain when King recovers, giving the group two drummers.
Sept [28] Fifth album, ***Hall Of The Mountain Grill***, reaches UK #16 and will peak at US #110. The band plays at the "Harrow Free Festival", Harrow, Middx., and begins a US tour, which is halted in Indiana when state police impound their gear under a new tax law.
Oct The group returns to the US to play 21 re-scheduled dates.
Dec Another UK tour commences and will run through to February.

1975

June [13] ***Warrior On The Edge Of Time*** reaches UK #13 and will peak at US #150. The group tours the US again and also plays dates in Canada. At the border, Canadian customs mistakenly identify amphetamine pills Lemmy has in his luggage for cocaine. The offence is elevated from a misdemeanor to a felony and he spends five days in a police cell, only to discover upon release that he has been fired by the band. Paul Rudolph (ex-Deviants, Pink Fairies, Uncle Dog) is flown out to complete the tour (and will join fulltime). Back in the UK, Lemmy announces the formation of his new group, Motorhead, while Hawkwind tours France.
Aug The band tops the bill at the "Reading Festival", Reading, Berks. Calvert, re-joining for a one-off appearance, decides to stay, while his second solo album, ***Lucky Leif And The Longships***, produced by Brian Eno, fails to chart. Stacia leaves to get married. As the group enters an uncharacteristic period of line-up stability, it will end the year with a UK tour.

1976

Jan Hawkwind signs to Charisma Records.
Apr [24] United Artists compilation, ***Road Hawks***, makes UK #34.
June The Time Of The Hawklords, a sci-fi novel by Michael Butterworth featuring the band as fantasy heroes, is published.
July *Kerb Crawler/Honky Dorky*, on Charisma, is released.
[24] The group performs at Cardiff Castle, Cardiff, Wales, on a bill with Status Quo, the Strawbs, Curved Air and Budgie.
Sept [25] ***Astounding Sounds, Amazing Music*** makes UK #33, as the group embarks on the "Astonishing Sounds" tour.

1977

Jan Turner, encouraged by Rudolph and Powell, leaves the band and will form Sphynx the following year (and Inner City Unit in 1979).
Feb Rudolph and Powell are themselves purged by Calvert and Brock, resulting in a new Hawkwind line-up (with Adrian Shaw on bass) which debuts at the Roundhouse, London. United Artists release a further compilation, ***Masters Of The Universe***.
July [16] ***Quark Strangeness And Charm*** reaches UK #30, as the group tours the UK, including a reprise appearance at this year's "Reading Festival" in August.
Oct During a US concert trek, House leaves, to join David Bowie's world tour, and is replaced by Paul Hayles.

1978

Feb At the end of further US dates, the band is in disarray: Calvert sells his guitar minutes after the final concert finishes and, upon returning to the UK, Shaw forms a new group with House.
June Calvert forms the Hawklords (the name changed for legal reasons) with Smith, who has returned as manager. Shelving the already-taped ***PXR-5***, the new group records ***25 Years On*** with a line-up of Calvert, Brock, Martin Griffiths (drums), Steve Swindell (keyboards), ex-Pilot and String Driven Thing, and Harvey Bainbridge (bass).
[18] Turner's new band Sphynx plays the Camden Town Roundhouse.
Oct [21] ***25 Years On*** makes UK #48, supported by a UK tour. United Artists re-releases *Silver Machine*, which makes UK #34.
Dec Drummer Griffiths quits the Hawklords.

1979

Jan Calvert leaves to go solo. King rejoins on drums, as the four-piece band reassumes the name Hawkwind and begins new recordings in Wales.
May The group performs at the "Leeds Science Fiction Festival", Leeds, S. Yorks.
July [7] ***PXR-5***, released by Charisma, makes UK #59. In yet further personnel changes, Tim Blake (ex-Gong) replaces an exiting Swindell and Langton rejoins.
Sept [8-9] The group takes part in the "Futurama" festival at the Queens Hall, Leeds.

1980

July *Shot Down In The Night* reaches UK #59.
Aug [9] Manager Smith arranges a recording deal, which includes Hawkwind, Motorhead and all-girl heavy-metal outfit Girlschool, with Bronze Records, which allows ***Live 1979***, recorded in St. Albans, Herts., in November, to now make UK #15. The group begins a European tour which will last for the rest of the year.
Sept Ginger Baker (ex-Cream and Blind Faith) joins, replacing King, who was fired in July.
Oct [10] A 22-date UK segment begins at the Apollo Theatre, Manchester, Gtr. Manchester, set to end November 5th at the City Hall, St. Albans.
Nov [8] Currently lining up as Brock, Bainbridge, a returned Lloyd-Langton, Baker and keyboardist Tim Blake, their second Bronze release, ***Levitation*** co-produced by the band with Ashley Howe, debuts at its UK #21 peak.

1981

Mar Baker is sacked, before a scheduled Italian tour, which is cancelled. Griffiths rejoins, Keith Hale replaces Blake and the group appears at the Stonehenge and Glastonbury Festivals.
Oct [31] Newly signed to RCA, their label debut, ***Sonic Attack***, reaches UK #19.

1982

Aug [21] While ***Church Of Hawkwind*** has peaked at UK #26 on May [22] and the group has firmly established itself in the increasingly popular heavy-metal community, it takes part in the third annual "Monsters Of Rock" Festival at Castle Donington, Leics.
Oct [23] With Turner now back in the fold and Hale already gone, their second album within six months, ***Choose Your Masques***, bows at its UK #29 peak.

1983

Jan [15] Now revered as a rock classic, *Silver Machine* enters the UK chart for the third time, at its #67 peak.
Nov [5] Live album ***Zones***, released via a new deal with the UK independent Flicknife Records label, makes UK #57.

1984

Feb [25] United Artists/Liberty retrospective, ***Hawkwind***, anchors at UK #75 for a week.
Mar Continuing its long-held tradition of playing eclectic venues, the band performs at the last-ever "Stonehenge Free Festival", near Amesbury, Wilts., on Solstice Eve, with new bassist Alan Davis and Danny Thompson guesting on drums (both of whom will join permanently). Harvey Bainbridge switches to keyboards.
Nov Flicknife releases ***This Is Hawkwind ... Do Not Panic***.

1985

Feb Brock, Turner, Lloyd Langton, Dave Anderson, Crimble, Bainbridge and Slattery attend the first Hawkwind Convention, in Manchester. (Turner quits shortly thereafter, leaving a line-up of Brock, Bainbridge, Lloyd Langton, Davis and Thompson, which will somehow stay together for next three years.)
Nov Produced by Dave Charles, Brock and Bainbridge, ***Chronicle Of The Black Sword*** strikes, at UK #65. (At a Hammersmith Odeon, London, gig during Hawkwind's current "Black Sword" tour, which includes mime artist Tony Crerar appearing as Elric, and Kris Tait as Elric's wife, Zarozinia, longtime band associate and writer Michael Moorcock joins the group on stage to recite four poems.)

1986

June With numerous Hawkwind compilations bringing parts of its back-catalog to CD for the first time (including three volumes under the ***Anthologies*** series from Samurai Records and ***Hawkwind Collection Parts 1*** and ***2*** from Castle Communications), the group headlines the Bristol Custom Bike Show, before making a customary appearance at the 24th annual "Reading Festival", Reading, Berks., in August.

1987

May While RCA has recently issued a collection of tracks from its early-'80s association with the band as ***Angels Of Death***, it undertakes a short tour of W. Germany, followed by selected dates in the UK.

1988

Apr In support of a forthcoming album celebrating a new deal with the GWR label, Hawkwind begins an extensive UK tour with the current line-up of Brock, Lloyd Langton, Bainbridge, Davis (bass) and Thompson (drums).
May [14] ***The Xenon Codex*** makes UK #79.
Aug [14] Having recently performed with his new band, the Starfighters, Calvert dies after a heart attack at his home in Kent.

Dec Hawkwind embarks on a UK tour with ex-Smart Pils Richard Chadwick replacing Mick Kirton, who has been sitting in for a departed Thompson. The following September, with Lloyd Langton now fully committed to his self-named group (having left Hawkwind in May), and House back in the line-up, the group will set out on its first US tour in 11 years.

1990

Jan They film a contribution to ITV's "Bedrock" series, which will be broadcast in May.
Oct [6] Celebrating their 20th anniversary and refusing to quit, ***Space Bandits***, released via GWR, makes UK #70, coincidentally the band's 20th UK Album-chart entry.
[13] The group begins an eight-date UK tour at Leeds University, set to end on the 22nd at the Apollo Theatre, Manchester, Gtr. Manchester.

1991

Mar Hawkwind embarks on a tour of Europe with Smart Pils' Steve Bemand having temporarily replaced stalwart Brock. They will go on to play two months of dates in the US, promoting their latest offering, ***Palace Springs***.
July [6] The group headlines the "12 Hour Technicolor Dream All Nighter" at London's Brixton Academy.
Dec Retrospective specialists Castle Communications release a three-CD/cassette boxed set, ***Anthology***, as the band plays a handful of UK dates, including York, Cardiff and Wolverhampton.

1992

Apr [23] The group begins a 25-date UK concert sojourn at Leas Cliff Hall, Folkestone, Kent, set to end on May 21st at the Town Hall, Cheltenham, Glos.
May [23] ***Electric Tepee***, released on the Essential label (UK), charts for a week at UK #53.
June [11-12] The group performs at the annual Isle Of Man TT Races.
Aug ***California Brainstorm***, recorded live in Oakland, CA, at the end of 1990, is released in the US on Iloki label.
[15] The band headlines a further "12 Hours of Psychedelic Madness" bill at the Brixton Academy.
Dec [10] Seasonal five-date "Seven Daze Of Hawkmas" tour opens at the Queens Hall, Bradford, S. Yorks, set to end at the Bournemouth Academy, Bournemouth, Dorset, on the 15th.

1993

Apr [5] The group is featured with Samantha Fox on the *Gimme Shelter* benefit single for the Putting Our House In Order charity with 11 other versions of the song by other artists.
Nov [6] ***It Is The Business Of The Future ...*** charts for a week at UK #75 and will be issued in the US on the Griffin label.

1995

Apr [19] Having undertaken a previous US road trip in February 1994 and released its latest album ***The Business Trip***, co-produced by the band with Paul Cobbold for the UK-based Emergency Broadcast Systems label, Hawkwind performs at the Park West, Chicago, IL, on a fresh US outing, with Brock its only original member.

ISAAC HAYES

1964

Hayes (b. Aug. 20, 1942, Covington, TN), orphaned at an early age by an absentee father Isaac and the death of his mother Eula Hayes when he was one, has been brought up by his sharecropper grandparents in rural Tennessee, where he has sung in the church choir from the age of three, and moved with them to Memphis, TN, at age seven where he attended the Manassas High School. Subsequently playing in the high-school band and, as a saxophonist and keyboard player, with various local amateur groups, including the Teen Tones, Sir Isaac & the Do-Dads and Sir Calvin Valentine & His Swinging Cats in the early '60s, Hayes has released his first single *Laura We're On Our Last Go Round* on the Youngstown label in 1962, and has gone on to perform with Gene "Bowlegs" Miller and members from Stax Records group the Mar-Keys, which leads to an invitation from label head Jim Stewart to work as a session musician at the Stax studios, where his first assignment is on an Otis Redding recording.

1965

Now a regular member of the Stax house band, but holding down a day job in a Memphis meat-packing plant, Hayes links with David Porter, an insurance salesman with songwriting aspirations. (They had been rivals in high-school bands, competing at Wednesday Amateur Night contests at the local Palace club, at which Rufus Thomas had been emcee.) Forming an exclusive writing-and-production partnership for Stax, their first collaboration is *Can't See You When I Want To*, which Porter himself records.

1966

Hayes plays on many of the label's most successful mid-'60s releases, by acts including Otis Redding, Carla Thomas, William Bell and Eddie Floyd. Hayes and Porter will also co-write and produce a string of Sam & Dave hits, including *You Don't Know Like I Know*, *Hold On I'm Coming*, *Soul Man* and *When Something Is Wrong With My Baby*.

1968

His debut album, ***Presenting Isaac Hayes***, is the result of a post-party late-night session by Hayes with MG's bassist "Duck" Dunn and drummer Al Jackson, Jr. Sales are unspectacular.

1969

Oct Stax simultaneously releases 27 albums to tie in with a publicity campaign following its new link with Paramount and Gulf & Western. It introduces its subsidiary Enterprise label, on which ***Hot Buttered Soul*** is initially marketed as a makeweight, alongside more obviously commercial items by Booker T. & the MG's, Eddie Floyd, Johnnie Taylor and others. DJs are hooked by the unique formula which Hayes introduces on the four-song album - familiar songs in extended, personalized versions, an intimate "rap" monologue and arrangements with wah-wah guitars and muscular funk rhythm sections in symphonic layers of strings. The album, with its distinctive sleeve design of Hayes' bald head by Christopher Whorf, is by far the biggest success of the 27, hitting US #8 and earning a gold disc.
[25] *Walk On By* reaches US #30, following its B-side pairing *By The Time I Get To Phoenix*'s US #37 peak the previous week.

1970

May ***The Isaac Hayes Movement***, in similar style to the first album (musical features which will define much of his recording career), also hits US #8, a second gold-rated outing. Its sleeve once again promotes Hayes' striking visual image: shaven headed, shaded and bearded, stripped to the waist and garlanded with gold chains. He maintains this appearance on his tours (undertaken with a 40-piece orchestra).
Oct [3] From ***Movement***, his reworking of Jerry Butler's *I Stand Accused* climbs to US #42.

1971

Jan ***To Be Continued*** makes US #11.
Mar [13] His revival of *The Look Of Love*, from the third album, makes US #79.
July [13] Hayes' personalized cover of the Jackson 5's *Never Can Say Goodbye* reaches US #22, only weeks after the original has hit #2.
Sept MGM's film "Shaft", starring Richard Roundtree as a black New York private eye, opens in the US, with a soundtrack composed and performed by Hayes.
Nov [6] Spurred by the success of the still-rising title theme, the double soundtrack album, ***Shaft***, hits US #1 and earns a gold disc.
[20] Featuring instantly memorable wah-wah guitar and staccato brass hooks, *Theme From Shaft* also tops the US chart for the first of two weeks, becoming Hayes' only million-selling single.

1972

Jan Double album, ***Black Moses***, packaged in a sleeve which folds out to form a large cross and illustrates a biblically-attired Hayes by a riverbank, hits US #10 and earns another gold disc. *Theme From Shaft* hits UK #4, while ***Shaft*** makes UK #17. The music from the film is the chief factor in spreading the commercial success of Hayes' music outside the US.
[15] Hayes plays the first of five German dates, during a European tour which will be highlighted by his being banned from playing a scheduled date at London's Royal Albert Hall on the 24th.
Feb [12] *Black Moses* makes UK #38.
Mar [14] *Theme From Shaft* wins the Best Instrumental Arrangement and Best Engineered Recording categories, while ***Shaft*** is named Best Original Score Written For A Motion Picture at the 14th annual Grammy Awards. The theme also wins an Oscar for Best Film Song, and a similar honor at the Golden Globe Awards. Meanwhile, his 1968 debut album, reissued by Atlantic Records as ***In The Beginning***, makes US #102.
Apr [8] *Do Your Thing*, an edited version from ***Shaft***, climbs to US #30.
[29] Hayes' instrumental cover of Al Green's *Let's Stay Together* reaches US #48.
May [27] Hayes and Porter's duet *Ain't That Loving You (For More Reasons Than One)* peaks at US #86.
Aug Hayes plays at "Wattstax '72", a benefit concert given by Stax artists (others include the Staple Singers, Carla Thomas, Luther Ingram and Albert King) for the seventh annual "Watts Festival" in Los Angeles.
Dec [9] *Theme From The Men*, written by Hayes for the ABC-TV anthology series of spy and police thrillers "The Men", reaches US #38.

1973

Jan Hayes makes his first live appearance in the UK.
Mar [3] *Black Moses* is named Best Pop Instrumental Performance By An Arranger, Composer, Orchestra And/Or Choral Leader, at the 15th annual Grammy Awards.
July Double concert set ***Live At The Sahara Tahoe***, which features his full, orchestra-backed cabaret act, makes US #14, earning another gold disc.
Sept Hayes sues Stax after his quarterly cheque for $270,000 bounces at the Union Planters Bank.
Nov [28] Yet-to-peak ***Joy*** is certified gold by the RIAA.
Dec ***Joy*** reaches US #16.

1974

Jan Hayes completes work on two more movie soundtrack projects for release later in the year.
Feb [2] A truncated version of the lengthy title track to his recent album, *Joy, Part 1*, makes US #30.
June [15] *Wonderful* peaks at US #71, while Hayes' ***Tough Guys*** soundtrack, from the film of the same name, peaks at US #146.
Aug Double soundtrack album, ***Truck Turner***, a movie in which Hayes also has a star acting role as a pro footballer, reaches US #156.

1975

Aug Following the altercation with Stax over royalty payments, Hayes has moved from Enterprise to set up his own Hot Buttered Soul label, licensed to ABC Records. With Hayes tailoring his output more closely to the prevailing disco trend, ***Chocolate Chip*** reaches US #18 (and earns a further gold disc).
[30] Extracted title track, *Chocolate Chip*, peaks at US #92. Enterprise releases a compilation album, ***The Best Of Isaac Hayes***, which makes US #165.

1976

Jan [25] Hayes plays alongside Stevie Wonder and Bob Dylan in the latter's "The Rolling Thunder Revue" at "Night Of The Hurricane 2", in front of 40,000 people at Houston Astrodome, Houston, TX, a benefit concert for imprisoned boxer "Hurricane" Carter.
Mar [20] ***Disco Connection***, billed as by the Isaac Hayes Movement, reaches US #85.
Apr [3] ***Groove-A-Thon*** peaks at US #45.
May [1] Instrumental title track, *Disco Connection*, hits UK #10, becoming Hayes' only UK hit single beyond *Shaft*.
Aug [28] ***Juicy Fruit (Disco Freak)*** reaches US #124.
Dec [23] Hayes files for bankruptcy, listing debts of $6 to $9 million.

1977

Mar Double album ***A Man And A Woman***, recorded live at the Fox Theatre, Atlanta, GA, with Dionne Warwick, makes US #49, his last release on Hot Buttered Soul and the end of his association with ABC. He and Warwick also make a joint guest appearance on an episode of NBC-TV's "The Rockford Files".
June Declared a bankrupt with $6 million debts (his $30,000 Eldorado is auctioned for $13,500), Hayes moves from Memphis to Atlanta (where he will work regularly at Master Sounds Studios) and signs a new recording deal with Polydor Records.

1978

Jan His Polydor label debut, ***New Horizon***, makes US #78.
Oct [31] The Isaac Hayes Movement begins an eight-date UK tour, with Edwin Starr and the Hot Buttered Soul Singers, at the Free Trade Hall, Manchester, Gtr. Manchester, set to end on November 10th at London's Rainbow Theatre.
Dec ***For The Sake Of Love*** reaches US #75, while the extracted *Zeke The Freak* becomes a popular disco floor-filler.

1979

Jan [12] Hayes wins the Favorite Male Artist, Disco category, at the sixth annual American Music Awards, held at the Civic Auditorium, Santa Monica, CA.
Nov ***Don't Let Go*** reaches US #39, during a 30-week chart tenure, and will be his final gold disc, with half a million US sales.
Dec Hayes' duet with Millie Jackson, *Royal Rappin's*, makes US #80.

1980

Feb [2] Title track *Don't Let Go*, an updated hustling disco-style revival of Jesse Stone's R&B standard, peaks at US #18.
June ***And Once Again*** reaches US #59. The following year, Hayes appears as the villain in John Carpenter's film "Escape From New York", and will become an increasingly active actor during the decade.

1985

Feb Two dancefloor-aimed revivals of *Theme From Shaft*, by Eddy & the Soul Band and Van Twist, return the Hayes composition to the UK chart, reaching #13 and #57 respectively.

1986

Aug While US R&B group the Fabulous Thunderbirds revive his early composition, *Wrap It Up* (US #50), Hayes' latest acting roles include cameos in "The A-Team" and "Hunter" (in his archetypal black tough guy role). He also co-stars, with Paul Sorvino and Barry Bostwick, in the TV movie "Betrayed By Innocence".
Dec Hayes, having leased a three-bedroom, 2,500 sq.ft. penthouse at Le Parc apartments, Windy Hill Road, Atlanta, turning the bedroom space into a home recording studio and having recently signed to CBS/Columbia, releases a revival of Freddie Scott's 1963 hit, *Hey Girl*, which incorporates a topically-relevant anti-crack rap, *Ike's Rap*, on the flip. It hits US R&B #9, while the parent album, ***U-Turn***, makes US R&B #37.

1987

Feb Hayes begins a US promotional tour for ***U-Turn***, which was co-produced with the members of Surface. Hayes plays all instruments, replacing the symphony orchestras with synth-created "orchestral" arrangements. (By year's end, he will appear in the movie "Counter Force", with George Kennedy and Andrew Stevens, and will also complete "I'm Gonna Git You Sucka" and "Dead Aim", with Corbin Bernsen and Ed Marinaro.)

1989

Feb [23] Hayes is jailed by an Atlanta judge for owing $346,300 in child support and alimony, and is subsequently unable to promote his recent Columbia release, ***Love Attack***.

1992

Nov [27] Having signed an agreement (together with Dionne Warwick) with the cultural minister of Ghana, to help renovate the country's Cape Coast and Elmina slave castles during the summer (he also shot a video for his single, *Dark And Lovely*, on the Ivory Coast the previous year), Hayes is performing live once more, appearing at a concert in New Orleans, LA. His acting career is set to continue, as he is selected for the role of Asneeze in Mel Brooks' forthcoming movie, "Robin Hood - Men In Tights".

1994

June Hayes signs with Virgin imprint Pointblank Records.
July In return for introducing investors to the area of Ada, Hayes is crowned a King in Ghana, with new name "Nene Katey Ocansey", and given an area of land on which he can build his own house.
Aug [21] Hayes performs at the "For The Children Of The World" Scientology fund-raiser at Saint Hill Manor in East Grinstead, E. Sussex.
Dec [27] Watoto de Afrika children's choir, who Hayes has seen at a Christmas event at the Peabody Hotel in Memphis, for which he was guest of honor, back him on a version of Sting's *Fragile*.

1995

Feb Hayes attends the 14th annual BRIT Awards and appears on BBC1-TV's "Danny Baker Show", during a visit to the UK.
May [23] Pointblank simultaneously releases his first new efforts in seven years, the well-received instrumental set ***Raw And Refined*** and the vocal album ***Branded***, the latter recorded with help from Andrew Love, Michael Toles and Lester Snell.
June [30] He guests on CBS-TV's "Late Show With David Letterman".
July [13] He performs at LIFEbeat's second "The Beat Goes On" benefit at New York's Beacon Theatre.
Oct Hayes participates in the Million Man March Afro-American march in Washington, DC.

HEART

Ann Wilson (lead vocals);
Nancy Wilson (guitar, vocals); **Roger Fisher** (guitar); **Howard Leese** (keyboards, guitar); **Steve Fossen** (bass); **Michael Derosier** (drums)

1974

Ann Wilson (b. June 19, 1951, San Diego, CA), living in Seattle, WA, and having already played in local bands Ann Wilson & the Daybreaks and Bordersong, has joined Seattle-based group the Army, formed in 1963 by Fossen (b. Nov. 15, 1949) and brothers Mike and Roger Fisher (b. Feb. 14, 1950), in 1970. Having embarked on a romantic relationship with Roger Fisher, Ann takes over lead vocals, as the band performs hard-rock covers of material by Led Zeppelin and others at small venues on the Pacific Northwest club circuit. Renaming itself White Heart in 1972, and now trimmed to Heart, the band is joined by Ann's sister Nancy (b. Mar. 16, 1954, San Francisco, CA), who had played alongside Ann as a part-time member of Bordersong, and who has completed college and a short spell as a solo folk singer. She replaces Mike Fisher in the line-up, who takes on the triple-play as her boyfriend, and the band's manager and sound engineer.

1975

The group relocates to Vancouver, BC, Canada, primarily to avoid Mike Fisher being drafted. After establishing a renewed live reputation in Canada, and now joined by Derosier (b. Aug. 24, 1951, Canada), Heart signs to Shelly Siegal's Vancouver-based independent Mushroom label and records ***Dreamboat Annie***, a mixture of folkish ballads and hard rock. It sells 30,000 copies in Canada.

1976

June With independent distribution, Mushroom releases the Mike Flicker-produced ***Dreamboat Annie*** in the US.
[5] The extracted *Crazy On You*, which is the group's US chart debut, reaches #35.
Oct [30] After a slow chart climb, ***Dreamboat Annie*** hits US #7 (eventually spending 100 weeks on the chart and selling over two million copies).
Nov [6] Extracted *Magic Man*, written by the Wilson sisters, hits US #9.
Dec The group returns to Seattle, signing a new US deal with CBS/Portrait Records. Mushroom sues for breach of contract and the group countersues to prevent the release of a second Mushroom album made up of allegedly unfinished demos. (By year's end, the band makes its UK debut in London, also appearing on the TV shows "The Old Grey Whistle Test" and "Supersonic".)

1977

Feb [5] Title song, *Dreamboat Annie*, written at the Wilsons' parents' house on a coffee table in the lounge, reaches US #42.
[12] ***Dreamboat Annie***, released by Arista in the UK, makes #36.
May [28, 30] Heart plays two concerts at Oakland-Alameda County Stadium, Oakland, CA, in front of 100,000-strong audience, on a bill also featuring the Eagles, Foreigner and Steve Miller.
July [16] Their debut Portrait album, ***Little Queen*** again helmed by Flicker, hits US #9 (a second million seller).
[30] ***Little Queen*** reaches UK #34.
Sept [3] *Barracuda*, taken from the album and written by the sisters with Roger Fisher and Derosier, reaches US #11.
Oct [8] The title cut, *Little Queen*, makes US #62.
Dec [3] A third extract, *Kick It Out*, peaks at US #79.

1978

Feb [4] Reissued Mushroom single, *Crazy On You*, peaks at US #62.
Mar [18] The band plays at the "California Jam 2" festival in Ontario, CA, to 250,000 people, with Aerosmith, Santana, Ted Nugent and others.
June ***Magazine***, the second Mushroom project again produced by Flicker, reaches US #17. It has finally been issued after a Seattle judge decides that Mushroom may release the album, but that Heart first had the right to remix and re-record the material. With the sleeve bearing a disclaimer, and despite the group's reluctance to acknowledge its existence, it becomes a million-selling platinum album.
[17] Extracted *Heartless* reaches US #24.
Dec [16] *Straight On* peaks at US #15, taken from the second Portrait album, ***Dog And Butterfly***, which reaches US #17, their fourth million-seller. Co-produced by the band with Flicker, the title track *Dog And Butterfly* will make US #34 the following Mar [31].

1980

Jan While the band is completing the recording of its next album, the Wilson sisters/Fisher brothers relationships sour. Roger Fisher leaves, and later forms his own band in Seattle.
Mar With the Portrait label now absorbed into Epic, ***Bebe Le Strange*** hits US #5, a further platinum success, during a 77-date US tour, with Leese (b. June 13, 1951, Canada) and Nancy Wilson jointly covering Fisher's guitar role.
[29] The extracted *Even It Up* makes US #34.
Dec Double album ***Greatest Hits/Live***, a compilation of hit singles, with six tracks recorded during their recent concert trek, makes US #13.

1981

Jan [10] *Tell It Like It Is*, Heart's revision of Aaron Neville's 1967 million seller, hits US #8 - Heart's first US Top 10 hit since *Magic Man* in 1976.
Apr [4] The group's treatment of *Unchained Melody* becomes the eighth version of the song to make the US Hot 100, at US #83.
May The band begins an extensive six-month US tour, following which Fossen will quit the group.
Oct [2] Ann and Nancy Wilson perform, alongside Paul Simon, Joan Baez and others, in the "Bread & Roses Festival" at the Greek Theatre, Berkeley, CA, to benefit a prisoners' aid group operated by Baez's sister, Mimi Farina.

1982

June Nancy Wilson appears in film "Fast Times At Ridgemount High" (and will also act in the later movie "The Wild Life").
July [3] *This Man Is Mine*, taken from the forthcoming ***Private Audition*** album, reaches US #33.
[19] ***Private Audition*** peaks at UK #77 and will reach US #25 and marks the debut of newcomer Mark Andes (b. Feb. 19, 1948, Philadelphia, PA), ex-Spirit, Jo Jo Gunne and Firefall, who has replaced Fossen on bass. (By year's end, Heart will have also toured the UK as the opening act for Queen.)

1983

Sept [17] *How Can I Refuse*, from the forthcoming album, reaches US #44.
Oct Produced by Keith Olsen, ***Passionworks***, their last album for Epic, reaches US #39 and features ex-Montrose and Gemma drummer Denny Carmassi, who has replaced Derosier.
Nov [12] Their final Epic single, *Allies*, peaks at US #83.

1984

July Ann Wilson's duet with Loverboy's Mike Reno on *Almost Paradise*, the love theme from the movie "Footloose", hits US #7. (Reno has replaced the film's producers' original male choice, Foreigner's Lou Gramm, who rejected the project.)

1985

Jan Now signed to Capitol Records, the band starts work on a new album.
Aug [24] Lead-off single, the power ballad *What About Love?*, hits US #10.
Nov [11] The group opens a UK tour at the Apollo Theatre, Manchester, Gtr. Machester, supporting Tears For Fears.
Dec [7] *Never*, written by Ann with Walter Bloch and Holly Knight, hits US #4.
[21] Ron Nevison-produced, melodic rock-based ***Heart***, their first album for Capitol tops the US chart for one week, eventually earning a platinum disc.

1986

Mar [22] After being rejected by Stevie Nicks, Heart's *These Dreams*, a ballad co-written by Martin Page and Bernie Taupin and dedicated to 21-year-old cancer victim Sharon Hess, who has spent two weeks with the band prior to her death, tops the US chart for a week, displacing Starship's *Sara*.
Apr *These Dreams* reaches UK #62, Heart's first UK chart single. *Nothin' At All*, will hit US #10 on June [21], and *If Looks Could Kill* will make US #54 on Aug [9].

1987

Jan [24] Ann Wilson's solo, *The Best Man In The World*, featured in the Eddie Murphy movie "The Golden Child", makes US #61.
July [11] Power ballad, *Alone*, becomes the group's biggest hit single, topping the US chart, for the first of three weeks. Penned by hit-writers Billy Steinberg and Tom Kelly, it gives the songwriting duo their third US #1, following Madonna's *Like A Virgin* and Cyndi Lauper's *True Colors*.
Aug *Alone* hits UK #3, their first UK Top 10 single, and prompts a UK promotional visit and major tour dates. The Nevison-produced ***Bad Animals***, recorded at the group's own Seattle-based studio of the same name, and which includes *Alone*, hits US #2 (another platinum disc) and UK #7 (Aug [8]).
Oct [3] Diane Warren-written *Who Will You Run To*, also taken from the album, hits US #7 and reaches UK #30.
Dec *There's The Girl* makes UK #34.

1988

Jan [23] *There's The Girl* reaches US #12.
Mar *These Dreams/Never* hits UK #8, a double A-side reissue of two tracks from their 1985 album, ***Heart***, which also now charts, at UK #19.
[26] *I Want You So Bad* reaches US #49. (A Heart video compilation, "If Looks Could Kill", mainly focusing on the Wilson sisters, is released.)
May Heart embarks on a two-month US tour, supported by Michael Bolton.
June Further mining the group's back catalog, *What About Love* climbs to UK #14.
Oct Reissued *Nothin' At All* makes UK #38.
Nov Capitol releases a UK-only Heart collection, ***With Love From Heart***.

1989

Mar [11] Ann Wilson's duet with Cheap Trick's Robin Zander on *Surrender To Me*, from the Mel Gibson/Kurt Russell film "Tequila Sunrise", hits US #6.

1990

Apr [14] Richard Zito-produced ***Brigade*** hits UK #3.
May [19] ***Brigade*** also hits US #3, on its way to RIAA multiplatinum certification.
[26] Robert John "Mutt" Lange-written *All I Wanna Do Is Make Love To You*, according to the Wilson sisters originally offered to Don Henley, hits US #2, having already hit UK #8. The song becomes the group's first RIAA-certified gold single.
June [8] Heart begins an extensive six-month North American "Brigade" tour, supported on selected dates by the Black Crowes.
July [28] *I Didn't Want To Need You* reaches UK #47, set to make US #23 on Aug [18].
Oct Early members, Fossen, Derosier and Roger Fisher, re-emerge in a new hard rock act, Alias, linking with ex-Sheriff members, Fred Curci (vocals) and Steve De Marchi (guitar), which hits US #2 with the power ballad *More Than Words Can Say* from their debut album, ***Alias***.
Nov [18] During its current tour, and with Cheap Trick in support, Heart plays at the Palace of Auburn Hills, Auburn Hills, MI.
Dec [1] Third ***Brigade*** extract, *Stranded*, reaches US #13, having peaked at UK #60 on Nov [17].
[8] Heart performs a benefit concert for the Seattle Aquarium, Nature Conservancy, Washington Environmental Council and Washington Wildlife & Recreation Coalition at the Seattle Coliseum.

1991

Feb Ann Wilson adopts Marie Lamoureaux Wilson, born February 3rd.
Mar [2] *Secret* peaks at US #64.
June [22] Disney album ***For Our Children***, to which Ann and Nancy contribute *Autumn To May*, reaches US #31.
Sept [14] *You're The Voice*, from a new live album, debuts at its UK #56 peak. The single does not chart in the US, amid complaints that MTV has refused to show its video clip on the grounds that it is too political.
[28] ***Rock The House Live!***, co-produced by the group with Richard Erwin and recorded at the Centrum, Worcester, MA, on November 28th, 1990, debuts at its UK peak, #45.
Oct [12] ***Rock The House Live!*** enters at its US #107 high.

1992

Jan As Seattle becomes a hip rock city some 20 years after the emergence of Heart, Ann Wilson, currently featured on the *Brother* track from an Alice In Chains acoustic EP *Sap*, participates in a benefit for a Seattle centre for victims of child abuse.
June [6] The Lovemongers, an extra-curricular acoustic quartet which teams the Wilson sisters with Sue Ennis and Frank Cox, plays a benefit at the Fifth Avenue Theatre, Seattle.
July Ann Wilson performs with Alice In Chains at a Los Angeles acoustic benefit for an animal rights organisation.
Nov [23] The Lovemongers release a four-song acoustic EP, *Battle Of Evermore*, on Capitol. The title track, a Led Zeppelin cover, is featured in director Cameron Crowe's (Nancy's husband) current Seattle-based film, "Singles".

1993

Apr [6] Ann and Nancy Wilson sing the national anthem at the Seattle Mariners' season-opener against the Toronto Blue Jays at the Kingdome, Seattle.
Aug [26] Heart takes part in the "Voices For Choices" benefit at the Civic Center in Santa Monica, CA, with Shawn Colvin and Melissa Etheridge.
Nov [5] They take part in the seventh annual Bridge School benefit at the Shoreline Amphitheatre, Mountain View, CA.
[27] *Will You Be There (In The Morning)*, from the group's forthcoming album, reaches UK #19.
Dec [4] Following the departure of Carmassi and Andes, Heart's ***Desire Walks On***, produced by Duane Barron and John Purdell, debuts at its US #48 peak.
[9] They perform to a sellout crowd at Los Angeles' Wiltern Theatre during current US dates.
[11] ***Desire Walks On*** bows at its UK #32 peak. During the year, Capitol also issues one of the earliest rock-related CD-ROM's, Heart's ***Twenty Years Of Rock & Roll***, a multimedia archive biography.
[16] Heart, featuring replacement drummer Denny Fongheiser (b. Apr. 21, 1959, Alameda, CA) and bassist Fernando Saunders (b. Jan. 17, 1954, Detroit, MI) guests on CBS-TV's "Late Show With David Letterman".

1994

Jan [20] They appear on NBC-TV's "The Tonight Show".
Feb [7] Ann and Nancy Wilson present the Favorite Heavy Metal/Hard Rock Artist trophy at the 21st annual American Music Awards.
[12] *Will You Be There (In The Morning)* reaches US #39.
[23] They perform to a sellout crowd at the National Auditorium, Mexico City, Mexico.
Aug [12] Heart begins a five-night stint at Seattle's 500-seat Backstage Club, not least to record cuts for an all-acoustic album.
Oct [8] Ann Wilson performs *I Want You, I Need You, I Love You* at "Elvis Aaron Presley : The Tribute", an all-star tribute staged at the Pyramid Arena, Memphis, TN, broadcast live on US pay-per-view TV.

1995

Sept [2] Heart performs *Battle Of Evermore* and *Love Hurts* at the Concert for the Rock and Roll Hall of Fame at Cleveland Stadium, Cleveland, OH.
[30] Recorded in August 1994, and comprising live acoustic reworkings of familiar Heart material and new covers including Elton John's *Seasons* and Joni

Mitchell's *River*, produced by ex-Led Zeppelin bassist John Paul Jones, ***The Road Home*** makes US #87.

HEATWAVE

Johnnie Wilder Jr. (vocals); **Keith Wilder** (vocals); **Rod Temperton** (keyboards); **Eric Johns** (guitars); **Mario Mantese** (bass); **Ernest "Bilbo" Berger** (drums, percussion)

1973

Johnnie Wilder (b. July 3, 1949, Dayton, OH), an American G.I. originally stationed in W. Germany in 1969, has played in a number of short-lived army bands touring the weekend service-club circuit, the most durable proving to be the Noblemen, which he fronted until being discharged in 1972. Returning to Kaiserslautern, W. Germany, following a few months back in the US, he now forms Heatwave, a more permanent R&B/pop-based outfit with his brother Keith (b. Dayton, OH) and Tommy Harris, who is soon replaced by Czechoslovakian refugee Berger. Over the next two years, the line-up will be augmented by the UK-born Temperton, who has also served a musical apprenticeship in W. Germany, and Johns (b. Los Angeles, CA) who both answer a classified ad placed in a music magazine by the Wilder brothers. In Switzerland, in 1975, Johnnie Wilder also recruits Spanish-born Mantese, while guitarist Jessie Whitten (b. Chicago, IL) completes the Heatwave personnel. In 1976, the band will tour the UK club circuit and European USAF bases, where its strong reputation attracts the GTO label, to whom the group signs a recording deal, subsequently teamed with producer and successful hitmaker, Barry Blue.

1977

Mar Disco-aimed *Boogie Nights*, produced by Blue and written by Temperton, hits UK #2.
June Double A-side, *Too Hot To Handle/Slip Your Disc To This*, reaches UK #15.
[11] The band's debut album, ***Too Hot To Handle***, makes UK #46.
Nov [12] *Boogie Nights* hits US #2, behind Debby Boone's *You Light Up My Life*, and becomes one of the year's four biggest-selling singles in the US, earning a platinum disc for sales of over two million. ***Too Hot To Handle*** peaks at US #11 and is also certified platinum. While on a visit home to Chicago, Whitten is fatally stabbed. Roy Carter, ex-UK group the Foundations, replaces him on guitar and keyboards.

1978

Temperton retires from live work to concentrate on his songwriting for Heatwave and others (ultimately proving to be one of the UK's most successful writers, penning hits for George Benson, the Brothers Johnson, Aretha Franklin, Herbie Hancock and Manhattan Transfer among many others. His most notable composition will be the title cut to the best-selling album of all-time, Michael Jackson's ***Thriller*** (1982), for which Temperton will win a slew of awards).
Feb [4] *The Groove Line* reaches UK #12.
Apr [18] A change of pace from the group's previously solid funk releases, the soul ballad *Always And Forever*, highlighting Johnnie Wilder's distinctive falsetto vocal style, reaches US #18, later becoming a US million seller.
June [1] A 17-date UK tour begins at the Nottingham Palais, Nottingham, Notts., set to end on July 3rd at the Plymouth Fiesta, Plymouth, Devon.
[24] ***Central Heating*** reaches UK #26 and will hit US #10, again certified platinum.
July *Mind Blowing Decisions*, another soul ballad, but written by Johnnie Wilder, reaches UK #12.
[15] *The Groove Line* hits US #7. It is the band's third US million seller but also its final US hit single. Mantese is involved in a car accident which partially paralyses him, forcing him to leave. Carter and Johns also quit. In a major reshuffle, ex-Fatback band member Calvin Duke (organ, keyboards), Derek Bramble (bass), Keith Harrison (guitar, vocals) and the Wilders' cousin, William L. Jones (guitar), are all recruited as replacements, in time for a major US tour.
Dec Double A-side, *Always And Forever* (a US hit not previously released in the UK), and a new version of *Mind Blowing Decisions*, which includes an extended reggae remix, hits UK #9.

1979

Feb [24] In an accident-prone band history, Johnnie Wilder is paralysed from the neck down in a car accident during recording sessions in New York, but, after initial hospitalization, he fights back to an active life with the help of a specially-designed, multi-function wheelchair with facial movement controls. This allows him to continue work with the band, producing and singing in the studio. J.D. Nicholas (b. Apr. 12, 1952, Watford, Herts.) joins, to take over Wilder's vocal role on stage.
June *Razzle Dazzle* reaches UK #43 while its parent, ***Hot Property***, recorded in New York with producer Phil Ramone, and with arrangements by Dave Grusin, makes US #38, earning a gold disc.

1981

Feb After a two-year chart absence by Heatwave, the Temperton-penned *Gangsters Of The Groove* reaches UK #19.
[21] Its parent album ***Candles***, produced by James Guthrie and Johnnie Wilder and recorded in Los Angeles, reaches UK #29 and will climb to US #71.
Apr *Jitterbuggin'*, from ***Candles***, makes UK #34.

1982

July Berger and Nicholas leave (the latter joining the Commodores as lead vocalist). ***Current***, produced in Los Angeles, by Blue and Wilder, makes US #156, as Heatwave's commercial appeal wanes and they retreat to occasional club tours and isolated single releases (mainly for the Soul City and Brothers Organisation labels in the late '80s).

1990

Sept [9] Heatwave performs at KISS-FM's launch party in London. It is the band's first UK appearance in five years.

1991

Feb [23] While a new version of *Mind Blowing Decisions*, recorded by a re-formed unit of Johnnie Wilder with Billy Jones and Tim Houpe and produced by Aswad's Drummie Zeb and Tony Gad, has peaked at UK #65 on Sept [1] the previous year (eight days before the grouped played its first UK gig in five years at the KISS-FM launch party) a UK TV-advertised retro retread, ***Gangsters Of The Groove - The '90s Mix***, released by Telstar, charts for a week at UK #56. A more comprehensive and less expensive UK collection of the original versions, ***Dance Hits***, is issued by Sony Collector's Choice in April 1992. Temperton will receive a Special Award For International Achievement at the 38th annual Ivor Novello Awards, at London's Grosvenor House Hotel on May 26th 1993.

HEAVEN 17

Glenn Gregory (vocals); **Ian Craig Marsh** (synthesizer); **Martyn Ware** (synthesizer)

1980

Oct One-time computer operators, Marsh (b. Nov. 11, 1956, Sheffield, Yorks.) and Ware (b. May 19, 1956, Sheffield), quit the Human League and establish the British Electric Foundation (soon abbreviated to B.E.F.), a production umbrella for several projects. (The synthesizer-based duo sell the rights to the Human League name to Phil Oakey when they leave the band, in exchange for 1% of future royalties: the success of *Don't You Want Me* will reportedly earn them almost £100,000.) The first such project is Heaven 17, named after a group in Anthony Burgess' book, **A Clockwork Orange**, an electronic dance-styled outfit, with ex-photographer Gregory (b. May 16, 1958, Sheffield), whom they met at Sheffield's Meatwhistle drama centre, recruited as a vocalist.

1981

Apr ***Music For Stowaways***, an entirely instrumental limited edition cassette, is the first B.E.F. UK release, on Virgin Records, while Heaven 17 debuts on the same label with *(We Don't Need This) Fascist Groove Thang*, which overcomes a BBC radio ban (because of the title) and climbs to UK #45.
Oct [3] Heaven 17's debut album, ***Penthouse And Pavement***, including a follow-up, *I'm Your Money*, climbs to UK #14, while a third extract, *Play To Win*, makes UK #46. B.E.F.'s ***Music For Listening To*** is also released.
Nov Title track, *Penthouse And Pavement*, featuring Josie Jones as guest vocalist, peaks at UK #57. John Wilson joins the group on bass.
Dec Ware and Marsh produce, and write several songs for, Hot Gossip's Geisha Boys And Temple Girls.

1982

Feb *Height Of The Fighting (He-La-Ho)*, a re-recording (from ***Penthouse And Pavement***) featuring jazz-funk band Beggar & Co.'s horn section, is released.
Apr B.E.F.'s ***Music Of Quality And Distinction, Vol. 1***, with a different guest singer for most tracks, including Gary Glitter, Paul Jones, Billy MacKenzie, Sandie Shaw and Tina Turner, and largely comprising classic-pop cover versions, makes UK #25, but the project will lose £10,000. Gregory sings on two tracks: *Perfect Day* and a revival of Glen Campbell's *Wichita Lineman*. It is B.E.F.'s last project of the decade, as Marsh and Ware devote their energies to Heaven 17.
Nov Heaven 17's *Let Me Go* makes UK #41.

1983

Mar [19] Having peaked at UK #41 in November, *Let Me Go*, released in the US by Arista, climbs to #74 (Heaven 17's singular US chart 45), while ***Heaven 17*** reaches US #68.
May Trio-penned *Temptation*, an electronic/soul fusion on which Gregory duets with vocalist Carol Kenyon, is their biggest UK hit, at #2, while its parent album, the self-written and produced ***The Luxury Gap*** hits UK #4.
July *Come Live With Me* hits UK #5, as ***The Luxury Gap*** makes US #72.
Sept *Crushed By The Wheels Of Industry* reaches UK #17.
Dec Tina Turner's first solo hit, *Let's Stay Together*, co-produced by Ware, with Gregory on backing vocals, hits UK #6 and will peak three months later, at US #26.

1984

Sept *Sunset Now* reaches UK #24, while ***How Men Are*** makes UK #12 in October, followed by a second excerpt, the UK #23 *This Is Mine*, in November.
[25] Gregory and Ware take part in the all-star recording for Band Aid's *Do They Know It's Christmas?* at SARM Studios in London.

1986

July Following the January UK #52 peaking ... *(And That's No Lie)* the previous year, ***Endless***, a compilation of hit singles and earlier album tracks, is released only on cassette and CD, and peaks at UK #70.
Nov ***Pleasure One***, the group's first new recording for two years, makes a brief UK chart showing at #78. It yields the January 1987 UK #51, *Trouble*, and will peak at US #177 in April 1987.

1988

Sept Their final Virgin album, ***Teddy Bear, Duke & Psycho***, is released, including the recent single, *The Ballad Of Go Go Brown*. Ware and Marsh continue to focus on production projects (the former has recently produced the multiplatinum ***Introducing The Hardline According To Terence Trent D'Arby***).

1991

Sept With the current UK proliferation of hit cover versions, Ware and Marsh resurrect the B.E.F. project, which in many ways foreshadowed the current trend. In releasing the second collection, ***Music Of Quality And Distinction Vol. 2***, issued in the US as ***A History Of Modern Soul Vol. 2***, they have approached a number of artists (including D'Arby, Scritti Politti's Green, R&B novice Lalah Hathaway, Chaka Khan, Billy MacKenzie, Mavis Staples and Tina Turner among others, requesting versions of their favorite songs.

1992

Nov [28] A retread of Heaven 17's biggest hit, now released as *Temptation (Brothers In Rhythm Remix)*, hits UK #4.

1993

Feb [27] Equally revised *(We Don't Need This) Fascist Groove Thang* makes UK #40 in its week of entry.
Mar [20] Virgin-issued second career retrospective, ***Higher And Higher - The Best Of Heaven 17***, bows at its UK #31 peak.
Apr [5] The group is featured on the *Gimme Shelter* benefit single for the Putting Our House In Order charity with 11 versions of the song by other artists.
[10] *Penthouse And Pavement* charts for a week at UK #54, as Ware pens *If It's Wednesday It Must Be Wembley* for his hometown soccer team Sheffield Wednesday.
see also: **HUMAN LEAGUE**

JIMI HENDRIX

1954

Hendrix (b. Johnny Allen Hendrix as registered by his mother Lucille, a full-blooded Cherokee Indian, - but renamed James Marshall Hendrix four years later by his father - Nov. 27, 1942, Seattle, WA), having survived a bout of pneumonia in July 1945, buys an acoustic guitar for $5 from a friend of his father Al. Being left-handed, he turns his guitar upside down and teaches himself to play it by listening to the records of bluesmen Muddy Waters, Elmore James and B.B. King and rockers Chuck Berry and Eddie Cochran, devoting more attention to this than his school studies.

1960

Feb [20] Hendrix, now a member of the Rocking Kings, having played gigs in 1959 at the Polish Hall in Seattle and at their first appearance at the National Guard Armory, performs at Washington Hall with the band.

1961

May [31] Hendrix enlists in the army for three years at Fort Ord, CA, and is posted to the 101st Airborne Paratroopers, stationed at Fort Campbell, KY, as a member of the elite Screaming Eagles squad, attaining the rank of private first class during his service.

1962

July [2] He is honorably discharged because of "medical unsuitability", after breaking his ankle during his 26th and final parachute jump. With Hendrix going on to team up with former band members in Bob Fisher & the Barnevilles, they tour the US backing the Marvelettes and Curtis Mayfield & the Impressions, before Hendrix moves to Vancouver, Canada, where he gets a gig with Bobbie Taylor & the Vancouvers, playing regularly at Dantes Inferno club.

1963

Returning to Tennessee, Hendrix meets "Gorgeous" George Odell and, through him, hooks up with a package tour headed by Sam Cooke and Jackie Wilson. A succession of tours will follow, playing with Little Richard, Hank Ballard, the Supremes, Tommy Tucker and others. During the year, Hendrix also makes his vinyl debut on two Lonnie Youngblood singles.

1964

Hendrix relocates to New York, where he plays the club circuit with the Isley Brothers, also playing guitar on all of their 1964 recordings, not least *Testify*, King Curtis and John Paul Hammond. He strikes up a relationship with soul singer Curtis Knight and they write and record together. (One of the songs they will record is the prophetic *Ballad Of Jimi*, written by Knight in 1965, after Hendrix tells him he will die in exactly five years time.)

1965

Apr [17-18] Now a member of Little Richard's backing band, Hendrix performs at the Paramount Theater, New York.
Oct [15] He signs a three-year recording contract with Ed Chalpin, head of PPX Productions, receiving $1 and a guarantee of a 1% royalty on records he is currently recording with Curtis Knight. (Chalpin will enforce this agreement on post-fame Hendrix collaborations with Knight recorded in 1967, and will also cause continued litigation problems for Hendrix and major record labels for many years.)

1966

June Hendrix forms his own group, Jimmy James & the Blue Flames, which plays a mix of R&B standards and original material. They will eventually head to Greenwich Village in New York.
July [5] The Animals' Chas Chandler, on the recommendation of Keith Richard's girlfriend, Linda Keith, sees Hendrix play at the Café Wha? in New York's Greenwich Village and suggests that Hendrix should come to London.
Sept [24] Hendrix and Chandler arrive in London (legend has it that on the flight Hendrix decides to change the spelling of his name from Jimmy to Jimi) and soon recruit drummer Mitch Mitchell (b. John Mitchell, July 9, 1947, Ealing, London), who has been playing in ITV's "Ready Steady Go!" session band and with Georgie Fame's Blue Flames, and Noel Redding (b. David Redding, Dec. 25, 1945, Folkestone, Kent), to form the three-piece Jimi Hendrix Experience. (Mitchell has a background in the arts, having worked as a child actor in TV commercials, appearing in the BBC-TV series "Jennings At School" and "Whacko", and the ITV series "Emergency Ward 10" and "Redcap", as well as compering ITV's "In Search Of Adventure", before moving on to music in his teens. Redding, having been to art school and played with the Modern Jazz Group and Loving Kind, with whom he will still occasionally gig, joins on bass, despite having been auditioned for the Animals on guitar.)
Oct [18] The Jimi Hendrix Experience's first major gig is as support for French pop star Johnny Hallyday at the Paris Olympia. Chandler spends much of his own money publicizing the new group.
[23] The Experience records for the first time, at De Lane Lea Studios in London, cutting *Hey Joe* and *Stonefree*.
Nov [8-11] They play four nights at the Big Apple club, Munich, W. Germany, for which they are paid £300.
[25] The press meets Hendrix for the first time, when the trio performs at a reception in their honor at the Bag O' Nails club, London.
Dec [1] Hendrix signs an exclusive four-year management deal with Mike Jeffrey, Kit Lambert and Chris Stamp's Yameta Company.
[16] The first Jimi Hendrix Experience single, a cover of the Leaves hit (although Hendrix prefers Tim Rose's version) *Hey Joe*, is released on Polydor Records after being rejected by Decca.
[29] The trio makes its TV debut, performing *Hey Joe* on BBC1-TV's "Top Of The Pops".

1967

Jan [29] After several London and provincial club gigs during the month, they perform at London's Saville Theatre on a bill with the Koobas, Thoughts and headliners, the Who.
Feb [4] *Hey Joe* hits UK #6 and Hendrix's "wild man" image is promulgated in the press, while album recordings are completed, at the Olympic Studios, Barnes, London.
[22] The Experience supports Soft Machine at London's Roundhouse.
Mar [5] They play the Twenty Club in Mouscron, Belgium, and the Twenty Club, Lille, France, during a 48-hour weekend jaunt to the Continent.
[17-19] The trio performs at the legendary Star-Club, Hamburg, W. Germany.
[21] Mike Jeffrey signs a five-year, $1-million recording deal with Reprise Records in the US.
[30] During an appearance on BBC1-TV's "Top Of The Pops", a technician inadvertently puts on the backing track of Alan Price's *Simon Smith And His Amazing Dancing Bear* instead of *Purple Haze*, to which Hendrix responds, "I don't know the words to that one, man."
[31] The group begins its first UK tour, a 24-date, twice-nightly package with Cat Stevens, the Walker Brothers and Engelbert Humperdinck, at the Astoria Theatre, Finsbury Park, London, set to end April 30th at the Granada Theatre, Tooting, London. On this first date Hendrix is taken to hospital after setting his guitar alight and suffering minor burns to his hands. (In addition to his guitar distortion and feedback stage devices, Hendrix will make a nightly habit of playing the instrument with his teeth, before setting fire to it. Rank Theatres warn Hendrix to tone down his act during the tour, prompting the response: "I am bemused by the whole thing. All I want to do is sing and play guitar.")
Apr [4] The Experience guests on the first broadcast of BBC1-TV's "Dee Time", with Kiki Dee, Lance Percival and Cat Stevens.
[17] Hendrix jams with Georgie Fame and Ben E. King at London's Speakeasy club.
May [4] *Purple Haze*, released on the new Track label after the Yameta deal, hits UK #3. (With its allusions to mind-expanding drugs, it is taken up as an anthem for the new "love generation".)
[9] Hendrix is a guest of honor at the Variety Club of Great Britain's "Tribute To The Recording Industry" luncheon at London's Dorchester Hotel.
[12] Their debut album, ***Are You Experienced?***, is released, with Hendrix using a Stratocaster guitar. It hits UK #2 during a 33-week chart stay, held off the top by the Beatles' ***Sgt. Pepper***.
[15] The Jimi Hendrix Experience embarks on its first European tour at the Neue Welt, Berlin, W. Germany, set to close at the Jaguar Club, Scala, Herford, W. Germany, on the 28th, following shows in Sweden, Denmark and Finland.
[29] They top the bill at "Barbecue '67" at Tulip Bulb Auction Hall, Spalding, Lincs., with the Move, Cream, Geno Washington, Zoot Money and, bottom of the bill, Pink Floyd.
June [3] *The Wind Cries Mary*, Hendrix's third successive Top 10 hit, peaks at UK #6 after plans for a live EP are shelved in favor of the ballad.
[4] The band plays at the Saville Theatre, with Procol Harum, the Chiffons and Denny Laine's Electric String Band. With Paul McCartney and George Harrison in attendance, they open with *Sgt. Pepper's Lonely Hearts Club Band*.
[18] The Jimi Hendrix Experience makes its US debut on the final evening of the "Monterey International Pop Festival" at the County Fairgrounds, Monterey, CA, having been booked at the urging of Paul McCartney. They only play four original songs, but Hendrix's versions of *Wild Thing* and *Like A Rolling Stone* get a tumultuous reception, especially when he sets fire to, and smashes, his guitar for the familiar finalé (though the next time the group performs on a bill with the Mamas & The Papas at the Hollywood Bowl, CA, they are booed).
[20-25] They play six nights at the Fillmore West, San Francisco, CA.

July [3-4] In an unlikely billing, the Experience performs at the Scene, New York, with the Seeds and Tiny Tim.

[8] A US tour with the Monkees opens at the Coliseum, Jacksonville, FL. As in Britain, Hendrix quickly gains notoriety through the media. The group's music and Hendrix's outrageous showmanship are entirely inappropriate for the Monkees' teenybop audience and they are dropped after only eight gigs. (Chandler claims that protests from the right-wing Daughters of the American Revolution have brought this about, but in reality Chandler planned the support spot as a publicity stunt, knowing the outrage Hendrix's act would cause.)

[20] The group records *Burning Of The Midnight Lamp* at the Mayfair Recording Studio in New York, with Hendrix on harpsichord and Aretha Franklin's backing group, the Sweet Inspirations, on backing vocals.

Aug [19] After playing several dates at the Café A Go Go and Salvation clubs in New York, and the Ambassador Theater in Washington, DC, they play a final US date at the Earl Warren Showgrounds, Santa Barbara, CA, with Moby Grape, Tim Buckley and Captain Speed.

[27] They make their fourth appearance at the Saville Theatre, with the Crazy World of Arthur Brown and Tomorrow, but the second show is cancelled when news of Brian Epstein's death is announced.

Sept *Burning Of The Midnight Lamp* reaches UK #18.

[25] The Experience performs at "Guitar-In", a concert at London's Royal Festival Hall, in aid of the Liberal Party, with Bert Jansch, Paco Pena and Sebastian Jorgensen & Tim Walker.

Oct [9] The band plays at the Paris Olympia, France.

[14] Hendrix achieves his first US chart entries, on Reprise, when *Purple Haze* peaks at #65 and ***Are You Experienced?*** hits #5, during a 101-week run.

Nov [14] The group begins a 15-date, twice-nightly UK package tour, with the Move, Pink Floyd, Amen Corner, the Nice and others, at the Royal Albert Hall, set to end December 5th at Green's Playhouse, Glasgow, Scotland. (The Experience will have played a total of 180 dates in 1967 alone.)

Dec [1] Their second album, ***Axis: Bold As Love***, enters the UK chart, set to hit #5.

[22] The trio participates in the "Christmas On Earth Continued" concert at London's Olympia, with the Who, the Move, Traffic, Eric Burdon & the Animals and Pink Floyd, among others.

Capitol Records releases ***Get That Feeling***, which makes UK #39 and US #75, featuring Hendrix with Curtis Knight. It was recorded in the summer in the US, to appease ex-manager Chalpin, who claimed Hendrix had broken his contract.

1968

Jan [4] The group begins a four-date Scandinavian tour at Lorensberg Cirkus, Gothenburg, Sweden, but tensions develop, both within the group and with the management. Hendrix is incarcerated overnight in a Swedish jail, after wrecking a hotel room during a fight with Redding.

[13] *Foxy Lady* peaks at US #67.

[30] Hendrix attends "The British Are Coming" press reception at the Copter Club in the Pan Am Building, New York.

Feb ***Axis : Bold As Love*** hits US #3 during a year-long chart stay.

[1] The group begins a three-month US tour at the Fillmore West, during which Hendrix will cut out his stage antics and concentrate on the music.

Mar [30] *Up From The Skies* peaks at US #82.

Apr Compilation album, ***Smash Hits***, comprising both sides of the first four singles and four tracks from the first album, hits UK #4 and, with a different US track listing (including *All Along The Watchtower*), US #6.

[4] Hendrix plays an all-night blues session with B.B. King and Buddy Guy in Virginia Beach, VA, on the night of Martin Luther King's assassination.

May [10] Their US tour comes to a close at the Fillmore East, New York.

[20] Hendrix formally signs to Reprise Records in the US.

[30-31] Following three dates in Italy, the Experience takes part in two "Monster-Konzerts" at the Hallenstadion, Zurich, Switzerland, with Eric Burdon & the Animals, John Mayall's Bluesbreakers, the Move, the Small Faces, Traffic and others.

June [10] After completing the tour, the trio begins sessions, which will stretch to six months, for a new album at New York's Record Plant. Hendrix brings in other musicians, with Steve Winwood (keyboards) and Jefferson Airplane's Jack Casady playing on *Voodoo Chile*.

[12] Hendrix guests on ITV's "It Must Be Dusty", duetting with Dusty Springfield on *Mockingbird*.

July [6] The band performs at the "Woburn Music Festival", Woburn Abbey, Beds.

[15] They play at the opening of Chandler and Jeffrey's Sergeant Pepper club in Palma, Majorca.

[30] The group embarks on 47-date North American tour at Independence Hall, Lakeshore Auditorium, Baton Rouge, LA.

Aug [23] They participate in the "New York Rock Festival", at the Singer Bowl, Flushing Meadow, Queens, New York, with Big Brother & the Holding Company, the Chambers Brothers and Soft Machine.

Sept Hendrix's revival of Dylan's *All Along The Watchtower* hits UK #5.

[14] Hendrix performs at the Hollywood Bowl, supported by Soft Machine, Eire Apparent and Vanilla Fudge.

Oct Double album ***Electric Ladyland***, with a controversial sleeve picturing Hendrix surrounded by naked women, is released. Some shops refuse to display it, though it hits UK #6 regardless.

[19] *All Along The Watchtower* reaches US #20.

Nov [16] ***Electric Ladyland***, including guest performances by Al Kooper, Buddy Miles and Winwood among others, tops the US chart for the first of two weeks. The US sleeve features a psychedelic design incorporating the Experience, in place of the naked women.

Dec [1] The four-month North American tour comes to a close at the Coliseum, Chicago, IL. Pressures on Hendrix increase, with disagreements between his management team, Chandler and the more commercially-minded Jeffrey, resulting in Chandler selling his share in the band to Jeffrey. The group temporarily splits, with Mitchell and Redding returning to Britain without Hendrix.

[21] *Crosstown Traffic* peaks at US #52.

1969

Jan [4] The Jimi Hendrix Experience performs live on BBC1-TV's "Happening For Lulu" and plays an impromptu *Sunshine Of Your Love* as a tribute to the recently-split Cream, much to the annoyance of the progam's producers.

[8] The group begins another brief European sojourn at Lorensburg Cirkus, Gothenburg, set to end on the 23rd at Sportpalast, Berlin, W. Germany.

Feb [18, 24] The Experience plays two concerts at London's Royal Albert Hall.

Apr [11] A 23-date North American tour begins at the J.S. Dorton Arena, Raleigh, NC, set to end on June 1st with the last of three consecutive shows at the Waikiki Shell, Honolulu, HI.

[19] *Crosstown Traffic* makes UK #37.

May [3] Hendrix is arrested when he arrives at Toronto International Airport, Toronto, ON, Canada, for a concert at the Maple Leaf Gardens, and is charged with possession of heroin. He is released on $10,000 bail, denying hard-drug use (but a cloud will hang over him until his acquittal in December).

June [29] The band plays its final concert together on the last day of the three-day "Denver Pop Festival" at the Mile High Stadium, Denver, CO. (Redding, fearing being fired, elects to quit, having already formed his own band, Fat Mattress, which opened for the Experience during the recent tour. Hendrix will spend the summer recording in New York with Electric Flag drummer/drummer/vocalist Buddy Miles and bassist Billy Cox, a friend from his army days.)

July [2] Mitchell and Redding announce that their split from Hendrix is permanent (though Mitchell is back with him the same month, for a performance at the "Newport Jazz Festival", Newport, RI).

[10] Hendrix, bassist Cox and percussionists Jerry Velez (b. Aug. 15, 1947, Puerto Rico) and Juma Sultan (b. Apr. 13, 1942, Monrovia, CA) perform *Lover Man* on NBC-TV's "The Tonight Show".

Aug [18] For $125,000, the highest fee of any attending performer, Hendrix plays at the "Woodstock Music & Art Fair" in Bethel, NY, backed by the Gypsy Sons & Rainbows, drawn from musicians he has played with during the year, including Mitchell, Cox, Sultan, Velez and Larry Leeds (rhythm guitar). The set is highlighted by *The Star Spangled Banner*, a seminal performance captured on the "Woodstock" film and album. (His second set ends the festival.)

Nov [27] Hendrix, following three weeks of recording at the Record Plant in New York, celebrates his 27th birthday by attending the Rolling Stones' Madison Square Garden concert.

Dec Chalpin wins a suit against Hendrix in ongoing litigation over their 1965 agreement, and Hendrix will have to hand over a new album of live material for release by Chalpin.

[10] After eight hours of deliberation, the jury at Toronto Court House finds Hendrix not guilty on charges of possession of heroin and marijuana. Hendrix testifies at his trial that he has experimented with drugs but has since "outgrown" the experience.

[31] Hendrix's Band of Gypsys, comprising Hendrix, Miles and Cox, debuts at the Fillmore East, New York, one of the two sets being recorded for the live album ***Band Of Gypsys***.

1970

Jan [28] Their performance, in front of 19,000 people at the "Winter Festival For Peace" benefit in aid of the Vietnam Moratorium Committee at Madison Square Garden, ends abruptly when Hendrix says, "I'm sorry we just can't get it together" and walks off stage in the middle of the second number, *Earth Blues*. The group splits shortly afterwards.

Apr [25] Hendrix begins "The Cry Of Love" tour at the Great Western Forum, Inglewood, CA. (Illegal recordings of this gig will appear as the first Hendrix bootleg, ***Enjoy***, on the Rubber Dubber label, though a plethora of earlier recordings will also emerge.)

May ***Band Of Gypsys*** hits US #5, during a 61-week chart stay, and is given to Capitol in a one-off deal, to compensate Chalpin, who also receives a $1 million payment and a percentage of future Hendrix earnings.

June [15] Hendrix records his first session at Electric Ladyland Studios in New York. (A great deal of money and effort has been spent in creating a state-of-the-art "dream" studio.)

July [4] Hendrix plays on the second day of the three-day "Second Atlanta International Pop Festival" at the Middle Georgia Raceway in Byron, GA, before an estimated 200,000 people, with Jethro Tull, the Chambers Brothers, Rare Earth and others.

[26] He plays his last gig in his hometown of Seattle at Sicks Stadium, during which he is abusive to the audience. While there, he is awarded an honorarium by Garfield High School, the school which he attended but never graduated from.

Aug [1] Following participation at the Rainbow Bridge Vibratory Color-Sound Experiment occult organization at Rainbow Bridge, Maui, HI, as part of a film project, recordings of which will emerge on six subsequent bootlegs, "The Cry Of Love" tour closes at the Honolulu International Center Arena, Honolulu.

[26] A party is held to celebrate the official opening of the Electric Ladyland Studios.

[30] In only his second UK appearance in three years, Hendrix comes on stage at 3:00 a.m. to play what will be his last UK performance, at the "Isle Of Wight Festival", East Afton Farm, Godshill, Isle of Wight, as ***Band Of Gypsys*** hits UK #6.

Sept [6] After bad experiences in Denmark (he leaves the stage with the words "I've been dead for a long time") and Germany (the audience boos his late appearance), Hendrix makes what will be his final concert appearance at the "Love And Peace Festival" on the Isle of Fehmarn, Germany, cutting short a European tour after Cox is flown back to the US, suffering from a bad drug experience, Hendrix returns to London.

[16] Hendrix jams with Eric Burdon and War on stage at Ronnie Scott's in London, his final public appearance.

[18] After leaving the tragic message, "I need help bad, man", on Chandler's answering machine, a call made from his girlfriend Monika Dannemann's London flat, Hendrix is pronounced dead on arrival at St. Mary Abbot's Hospital, London, close to midnight.

[21] Eric Burdon appears on TV claiming that Hendrix has left a suicide note.

[23] An inquest is adjourned by Dr. Gavin Thurston, who is awaiting the pathologist's report.

[28] Pathologist Professor Donald Teale reports that Hendrix's death was the result of inhalation of vomit due to barbiturate intoxication. An open verdict is recorded. (***Monterey Pop Festival***, a shared album with Hendrix on one side and Otis Redding on the other, has already entered the US chart and reaches #16, but will not be released in Britain.)

Oct [1] Following a funeral service at the Dunlap Baptist Church, Renton, WA, where his aunt played organ during his childhood, Hendrix is buried in the Greenwood Cemetery in Renton.

Nov [21] *Voodoo Chile* tops the UK chart, as the film documentary "Experience" shows at the ICA, The Mall, London.

1971

Mar ***The Cry Of Love***, the last album sanctioned and recorded by Hendrix, is released and hits US #3 and UK #2. It contains songs he had been working on for his planned concept album, ***The First Rays Of The New Rising Sun***. The US chart also sees the first cash-in album, ***Two Great Experiences Together!***, on Maple Records, featuring Hendrix and sax player Lonnie Youngblood. It peaks at #127. (Due to Hendrix's complicated contractual affairs the market will be flooded, throughout the early '70s, by albums bearing his name, the majority being jam sessions never intended for release.)

[8] WPAX Hanoi, a radio station put together by Yippies in New York to be broadcast to MUS troops, opens its first broadcast with Hendrix's version of *The Star Spangled Banner*.

May [8] *Freedom* peaks at US #59.

Sept Ember label album, ***Experience***, drawn from Royal Albert Hall performances in February 1969, hits UK #9.

Oct ***Rainbow Bridge***, not containing any recordings made during Hendrix's visit to Hawaii in July 1970, but rather a random collection of 1968-70 performances, reaches US #15.

Nov [27] The extracted *Dolly Dagger* makes US #74. ***Gypsy Eyes/Remember*** climbs to UK #35, as ***Jimi Hendrix At The Isle Of Wight*** reaches UK #17.

Dec ***Rainbow Bridge*** peaks at UK #16.

1972

Feb Assembled by producer Alan Douglas, ***Hendrix In The West***, a collection of live performances recorded at the Berkeley Community Center, San Diego Sports Arena and the "Isle Of Wight Festival" (and highlighted by his version of Chuck Berry's *Johnny B. Goode*, which makes UK #35), hits UK #7 and US #12.

Dec ***War Heroes***, a curious mixture of unfinished studio material including a version of Henry Mancini's *Peter Gunn Theme*, makes UK #23 and US #48.

1973

Mar [5] Former manager Jeffrey is killed in a plane crash over France.

July ***Soundtrack Recordings From The Film Jimi Hendrix***, a vinyl documentary of Hendrix's life, makes UK #37 and US #89. The following year, jazz arranger Gil Evans, with whom Hendrix was due to record the week he died, will release ***The Gil Evans Orchestra Plays The Music Of Jimi Hendrix***.

1975

Apr [19] ***Jimi Hendrix*** makes UK #35.

Aug ***Crash Landing*** is the second in a number of further posthumous albums produced by Douglas, who was given stewardship of the 600 hours of tapes that were part of Hendrix's estate. (On some cuts Douglas has used session musicians to overdub existing parts so that only the original guitar and vocal remain.) The album hits US #5 and UK #35 on Sept [13].

Nov [29] Douglas-helmed release ***Midnight Lightning***, makes UK #46.

Dec Redding releases his first album in five years, ***Clonakilty Cowboys***.

[20] ***Midnight Lightning*** reaches US #43.

1979

Aug While ***The Essential Jimi Hendrix*** has made US #114 the previous August (and features a one-sided bonus single containing Hendrix's previously unissued version of Van Morrison's *Gloria*), ***The Essential Jimi Hendrix Volume 2*** peaks at US #156. Both volumes will be issued by Reprise as a 32-track twin-CD set in 1989, again under the supervision of Douglas.

1980

Apr The final Douglas release, ***Nine To The Universe***, featuring Hendrix's jamming on sessions during the recording of his final album in 1969, climbs to US #127.

May [22] Four Hendrix gold albums are stolen from the Electric Ladyland Studios.

1982

Aug [21] ***The Jimi Hendrix Concerts***, another selection of live recordings 1968-70, reaches UK #16 and will make US #79. The following February, ***The Singles Album*** will peak at UK #77, while ***Kiss The Sky***, compiling further miscellaneous recordings 1967-69,will make US #148 in November 1984. The performance set ***Jimi Plays Monterey*** will stop at US #192 in March 1986.

1988

Oct U2's newly-released album of their 1987 US tour, ***Rattle And Hum***, samples Hendrix's version of *The Star Spangled Banner* from Woodstock as the intro to *Bullet The Blue Sky*. (The fortunes of ex-Hendrix sidemen vary: Redding is living in Eire, playing in the Secret Freaks band, Mitchell sells Hendrix's white Fender Stratocaster for $340,000 at a Sothebys auction, while Buddy Miles is most prominently featured as one of the voices of the California Raisins TV-advertising raisin combo.)

1989

Mar [11] ***Radio One***, comprising previously unavailable BBC-recorded radio sessions, issued by Castle Collectors in Britain, makes UK #30.

1990

Apr [21] Neatly combining promotion efforts to prepare consumers for "Hendrix Year" releases and the current use of the song for a Wrangler Jeans TV commercial, *Crosstown Traffic* peaks at UK #61. Respected UK journalist Charles Shaar Murray's universally well-reviewed Hendrix appraisal, **Crosstown Traffic** is also published this month.

Aug ***If 6 Was 9 - A Tribute To Jimi Hendrix*** is released, featuring cover versions of Hendrix material by acts including Thin White Rope, Monks Of Doom, Thee Hypnotics, Giant Sand and an alleged pseudonymous XTC.

Sept [18] During the 20th-anniversary reminders of Hendrix's death, the "Live At The Isle Of Wight" video is released. Redding, being interviewed on BBC Radio 1, claims that he has been defrauded of £8 million in royalties since Hendrix's death.

Oct [20] EP *All Along The Watchtower* peaks at UK #52.

Nov [3] Having generally repromoted Hendrix products all year long in a 20th anniversary of his death jamboree, Polydor Records hits UK #5 with ***Cornerstones 1967-1970***, another Hendrix retrospective collection. (During his lifetime, Hendrix only released five albums. In the 20 years *since* his death over 300 different titles have emerged, not including bootlegs.)

1991

Jan [26] ***Lifelines/The Jimi Hendrix Story***, comprising home demos, rare live recordings, alternate takes and a 1969 Inglewood Forum concert, peaks at US #174.

June [22] Actor Eddie Murphy splashes out $30,800 on Hendrix memorabilia at a Sotheby's rock auction, including $7,150 for a green velvet waistcoat, $19,800 for a black suede headband and a paltry $3,850 for a tie-dyed silk scarf.

Nov [21] Hendrix is inducted into the Hollywood Walk of Fame on Hollywood Boulevard, between Art Carney and Fred Zinneman.

1992

Jan [15] He is inducted into the Rock and Roll Hall of Fame at the seventh annual dinner, at New York's Waldorf Astoria Hotel.

Feb [25] Hendrix is posthumously honored with NARAS' 1992 Lifetime Achievement Award at the 34th Grammy Awards, in New York.

Nov [21] While Mitchell has recently teamed with ex-Rolling Stone Mick Taylor to play US dates and Redding is still gigging with a band near his home town in West Cork, Eire, also performing with Hendrix impersonator Randy Hansen, the guitar legend's back catalog is estimated to generate worldwide annual album sales of up to three million units per year, as the latest Hendrix retrospective, ***The Ultimate Experience***, reaches UK #25.

1993

Apr [16] Al Hendrix, the legend's father, files suit in US district court in Seattle for fraud and malpractice, against his former attorney and various foreign investment companies.

June [19] ***The Ultimate Experience***, marking a new acquisition of the Hendrix catalog by MCA Records in the US, makes US #72 (and will re-chart at UK #28 on July [31]).

Dec [10] Following an anonymous request (possibly by ex-flame Kathy Etchingham), Scotland Yard re-opens the investigation into the circumstances of Hendrix's death. Yard spokeswoman, Carol Bewick, says: "Scotland Yard so far has been requested by the Crown Prosecution Service to conduct inquiries into the circumstances of the death of Jimi Hendrix".

1994

Apr [30] Rounding up a selection of his blues covers, ***Blues*** hits UK #10 in its week of entry.

May [14] ***Blues*** debuts at its US #45 peak. (24 years after his death, his catalog is estimated to generate three million unit sales per year.)

Aug [13] ***Woodstock***, including cuts from the historic performance never previously issued, bows at its UK #32 peak and will reach US #37 on the 27th.

1995

Apr [29] ***Voodoo Soup***, the studio album he was recording at the time of his death, tentatively titled ***First Ray Of The New Rising Sun***, augmented by the additional instrumental *New Rising Sun*, debuts at its US #66 peak.

July [28] Al Hendrix finally wins, after a two-year legal battle, the rights to all of his son's music in a settlement worth an estimated $70 million. With the help of Microsoft co-founder Paul Allen, who is planning a Hendrix museum in Seattle, he had sued attorney Leo Branton Jr. for mismanaging his son's copyrights and masters.

Aug 19-year-old Englishman from Cambridge, Danny Waldmann, becomes the first recipient of the $5,000 Jimi Hendrix Scholarship at Berklee College of Music in Boston, MA.

Sept 4] The "Jimi Hendrix Tribute Concert" takes place in Seattle with performances by Buddy Miles, Redding and Billy Cox among others.
Oct [24] RCA Victor (US) releases the latest Hendrix tribute album, ***In From The Storm***, including interpretations of the artist's material by the likes of Santana, Corey Glover, Brian May, Redding, Sting, Miles, Steve Vai and others.

DON HENLEY

1980

Following the release of their final US chart-topping studio album ***The Long Run***, the Eagles, which Henley (b. July 22, 1947, Gilmer, TX) has formed with Glenn Frey in 1971, splits permanently, with all members pursuing solo projects. Henley, the son of NAPA auto parts dealer Con Junell Henley and his wife Hughlene (née McWhorter), raised in the Texas Cass County hamlet of Linden, had originally been in Texan band the Four Speeds during the mid-'60s and moved to Los Angeles, CA in May 1970, to record an album as a member of Shiloh (formerly Felicity), another Texas-based group, who were discovered and brought to the Golden State by Kenny Rogers, to record ***Shiloh*** for the Amos label, where Henley first met Frey. Subsequently playing together as members of Linda Ronstadt's backing group in the summer of '71, the pair went on to become the founders and only constant members of the multiplatinum-achieving Eagles, for whom they also undertook much of the songwriting and lead vocal tasks. Following the band's demise, Henley, a drummer/vocalist by trade, signs a solo recording contract with Asylum Records, which also issued all the Eagles material.
Nov [21] Henley is arrested when a naked 16-year-old girl is found in his Los Angeles home, suffering from a drug overdose. He will be fined $2,000, given two years' probation and ordered to attend a drug-counselling scheme.

1981

As remnant Eagles releases wind up an enormously successful chart career, Henley enters the Record One Studio in Sherman Oaks, CA, with co-producers Danny Kortchmar and Greg Ladanyi, to record his debut album.

1982

Jan [23] Henley duets with Fleetwood Mac's Stevie Nicks on her *Leather And Lace* ballad, which peaks at US #6.
Oct [2] His first solo single, the illiteracy-themed *Johnny Can't Read*, makes US #42 as its parent album, ***I Can't Stand Still***, edges towards US #24, boasting musical guests Bob Seger, J.D. Souther, ex-Eagles Timothy B. Schmit and Joe Walsh, Toto's Steve Lukather and Jeff Porcaro, Andrew Gold, Russ Kunkel, Louise Goffin, Max Gronenthal and Warren Zevon.

1983

Jan [8] Gutter press-attacking *Dirty Laundry* hits US #3, becoming a million-seller, and peaks at UK #59.
Feb [26] Title cut, *I Can't Stand Still*, makes US #48.

1984

Dec Newly signed by former Asylum chief David Geffen to his new Geffen Records, Henley's sophomore album, ***Building The Perfect Beast***, is released, set to make US #13. With the same production team, it features contributions from Lindsey Buckingham, Sam Moore, Randy Newman, David Paich, Souther and others.

1985

Feb [9] Its first excerpt, *The Boys Of Summer*, aided by an award-winning black-and-white video directed by Jean Baptiste Mondino, and co-written with Mike Campbell, hits US #5 and reaches UK #12.
Mar ***Building The Perfect Beast*** reaches UK #14.
May [4] Danny Kortchmar-penned *All She Wants To Do Is Dance* hits US #9, while a third extract, *Not Enough Love In The World*, will make US #34 on July [27].
Sept [13] "Boys Of Summer" wins the Best Video, Best Art Direction, Best Cinematography and Best Direction categories at the second annual MTV Video Music Awards, held at Radio City Music Hall, New York, NY.
Oct [19] *Sunset Grill*, the fourth cut from the album, reaches US #22.
Dec [31] At Henley's New Year's Eve party at his ranch in Aspen, CO, presidential candidate Gary Hart meets his alleged mistress-to-be Donna Rice, for the first time.

1986

Feb [25] Henley wins the Best Rock Vocal Performance, Male category for *The Boys Of Summer* at the 28th annual Grammy Awards.

1989

Jan [30] He drums with Guns N' Roses at the 16th annual American Music Awards, held at Los Angeles' Shrine Auditorium.
Aug [8] Henley begins a major US tour in St. Louis, MO.
[12] Following a five-year recording absence for Henley, ***The End Of The Innocence***, featuring Edie Brickell, Bruce Hornsby, Ivan Neville, Axl Rose, Souther and Take 6, among others, and mostly co-produced with Kortchmar, reaches UK #17 and begins its rise to US #8.
[26] *The End Of The Innocence*, the title track from the album, with his lyrics added to a Hornsby melody, who also plays its distinctive piano accompaniment and co-produces, hits US #8 and UK #48.
Dec [9] Second extracted single, *The Last Worthless Evening*, reaches US #21.

1990

Feb [12] Henley jams with Sting, Bruce Springsteen and Paul Simon at a benefit for the Rainforest Foundation, at the China club, Hollywood, raising $1 million.
[21] Henley wins the Best Rock Vocal Performance, Male category for *The End Of The Innocence* at the 32nd annual Grammy Awards, held at the Shrine Auditorium.
Apr [24-25] During a major US tour, Henley plays two sellout benefit concerts, as part of an ongoing personal cause to preserve the historic Walden Woods, at the Centrum, Worcester, MA. He is joined over the two nights by Glenn Frey, Jimmy Buffett, Bonnie Raitt, Timothy B. Schmit and actors Ed Begley Jr., Carrie Fisher, Don Johnson and Dana Delany. (Henley's tour band comprises Scott Plunkett (synthesizer), John Corey (guitar, synthesizer), Timothy Drury (piano, synthesizer), Frank Simes (guitar), Jennifer Condos (bass) and Ian Wallace (drums).)
May [5] Further ballad, *The Heart Of The Matter*, reaches US #21.
Aug [13] Henley, Raitt, Arlo Guthrie, Aimee Mann and members of the group Boston announce that they have purchased 25 acres of Walden.
[25] *How Bad Do You Want It?* makes US #48, as Henley and Kortchmar produce the title track to Timothy B. Schmit's new album, ***Tell Me The Truth***.
Sept [7] "The End Of The Innocence", directed by David Fincher, is named Best Male Video category at the seventh annual MTV Video Music Awards, held at the Universal Amphitheatre, Universal City, CA.
Oct [29] Henley is honored with the People for the American Way's Spirit of Liberty Award at Los Angeles' Beverly Wilshire Hotel, being cited for his anti-censorship and pro-environment efforts.
Dec [22] The final extract from his third album, *New York Minute*, makes US #48.

1991

Jan [16] Henley inducts the Byrds into the Rock and Roll Hall of Fame at the sixth annual dinner held at the Waldorf Astoria Hotel, New York, and then performs *Turn! Turn! Turn!*, *Mr. Tambourine Man* and *Feel A Whole Lot Better* with the Byrds and Jackson Browne at the after-dinner jam.
Feb [9] Henley joins Arlo Guthrie at a day-long environmental benefit, the "Indian River Festival", near Vero Beach, FL, as ***The End Of The Innocence*** is certified multiplatinum by the RIAA for three million sales.
June [29] During a current US tour, he performs at the Miami Arena, Miami, FL.
July [31] Henley plays a sellout date at the Sandstone Amphitheatre, Bonner Springs, KS, with Bonnie Raitt and Chris Isaak.
Aug [9] He performs at a Billy Joel-produced benefit concert at Indian Field Ranch, Montauk, Long Island.
[31] Henley makes his Las Vegas, NV debut at the Grand Ballroom.
Sept [5] He sings *The Heart Of The Matter* at an otherwise rap and metal-crowded eighth annual MTV Video Music Awards, at the Universal Amphitheatre.
Oct [21-22, 24] Henley participates in three sellout concerts for the Walden Woods Benefit at New York's Madison Square Garden. He has donated 50 cents on every ticket sold during his summer tour to the Walden Woods Project.
Dec Henley embarks on a short US book-signing itinerary, promoting the fund-raising collection of essays **Heaven Is Under Our Feet**, a compendium edited with Dave Marsh, with proceeds also going towards his Walden Woods environmental crusade.

1992

Mar [12] Henley appears at the third annual Rainforest Foundation "An Evening Of Porter, Gershwin & Coward..." benefit, at New York's Carnegie Hall.
Apr [16] He receives a special recognition award for his efforts with regard to the Walden Woods project, at the Boston Music Awards, held at the Wang Center, Boston, MA.
July Patty Smyth's rock ballad, *Sometimes Love (Just Ain't Enough)*, featuring Henley's unmistakable co-vocal, hits US #2. Henley joins Mojo Nixon on stage for a version of the latter's *Don Henley Must Die* at a Nixon gig at the Hole In The Wall, Austin, TX, prompting Nixon to confirm that: "Henley had balls the size of church bells."
Sept Henley duets with Trisha Yearwood on *Walkaway Joe*, from her ***Hearts In Armor*** album, at the Country Music Week in Nashville, TN. Among his current recording cameos, Henley is featured as the vocal on *Watching TV* from the new Roger Waters album, ***Amused To Death***.
Oct [11] Henley participates in the "Healing The Sacred Hoop The Next 500 Years" benefit at the Shoreline Amphitheatre, Mountain View, CA, with Bonnie Raitt, Little Feat, Todd Rundgren, Ry Cooder & David Lindley, Chris Williamson and Floyd "Red Crow" Westerman.
[17] *Sometimes Love Just Ain't Enough* reaches UK #22.
Nov [4] Henley is interviewed on syndicated TV's "Whoopi Goldberg" show.
Dec [14] He performs at a star-filled Universal Amphitheatre benefit to establish a trust fund for Toto's late drummer Jeff Porcaro's children, while the ***Leap Of Faith*** soundtrack to the current Steve Martin movie, featuring a Henley cut, is released.

1993

Jan [20] He performs at the Bill Clinton-attended "MTV Presidential Inaugural Ball" in Washington, DC.
[28] Geffen Records files a breach-of-contract suit against Henley in the Los Angeles Superior Court, seeking at least $30 million in damages and an injunction barring him from recording for another label, claiming that he has failed to deliver an agreed number of albums under the terms of his 1988 renegotiated contract with them.
Apr [30] An announcement is made that the Walden Woods Project has purchased the pertinent 18.6 acre site.
May [23] Henley takes part in a 6.2 mile celebrity walk in Concord, MA, for the Walden Woods Project.
June [27] He performs at Milwaukee's Summerfest at

the Marcus Amphitheatre, Michigan, WI.
Sept [6] Henley, Sting, Elton John, Melissa Etheridge and special guests Aerosmith, perform a Walden Woods benefit at Foxboro Stadium, Foxborough, MA.
Oct [20] Henley guests on CBS-TV's "Late Show With David Letterman". (Elton John's ***Duets*** album, to which Henley has collaborated on *Shakey Ground*, will be released in November while Henley will return to live in Texas by year's end.)

1994

Feb [13] Having already taken part in an Eagles quasi-reunion the previous December 7th on the set of Travis Tritt's video for *Take It Easy*, Henley (together with former colleagues Frey and Joe Walsh) plays before a packed crowd at the Double Diamond Club in Aspen, CO, to benefit the Grassroots-Aspen Experience, a collaboration which will lead to a full-blown and highly lucrative Eagles reunion which will occupy much of Henley's time over the next two years.
June [20] He heads another Walden Woods benefit, this time in Nashville, TN with Melissa Etheridge and Vince Gill.
Sept [27] ***Kermit Unpigged***, which sees Henley duetting with the Muppets, is released on Jim Henson Records in the US.

1995

Jan [19] Henley appears at the "Commitment To Life VIII" benefit for AIDS Project Los Angeles, honoring Elton John, Tom Hanks and Ron Meyer at the Universal Amphitheatre.
Mar [9] He testifies before a Senate Judiciary Committee hearing in support of the new Digital Performance Right in Sound Recordings Act of 1995.
May [20] Henley marries model Sharon Summerall at his Malibu ranch, attended by Glenn Frey, Joe Walsh, Tim Schmit, David Crosby, Randy Newman, Jimmy Buffett, Sting, Billy Joel, Jackson Browne, Bruce Springsteen and Sheryl Crow.
Aug Henley's attorneys file a complaint with the FCC alleging that Cincinnati radio station ZWEBN aired an early morning telephone conversation with the singer against his express wishes. The station denies airing the conversation.
Dec [9] A solo anthology assembled to fulfill his Geffen contract, ***Actual Miles : Henley's Greatest Hits***, including three new cuts, the seven-minute *The Garden Of Allah*, featuring Crow and Kortchmar (and Kirk Douglas in a cameo role in its video clip), his cover of Leonard Cohen's *Everybody Knows* (which also appears on the recently released tribute album ***Tower Of Song : The Songs Of Leonard Cohen***) and *You Don't Know Me At All*, debuts at its US #48 peak.

1996

Feb [23] Henley makes his first ever appearance on CBS-TV's "Late Show With David Letterman".
Apr [28] With confirmation that Henley, now freed from his Geffen contract, has signed a new three-album deal with Warner Bros. Records, he takes part in "Witness : A Concert For Human Rights", with Bryan Adams, Gloria Estefan and Peter Gabriel, and broadcast live on VH-1 from the Universal Amphitheatre.
see also: **THE EAGLES**

HERMAN'S HERMITS

Peter Noone (vocals); **Derek "Lek" Leckenby** (lead guitar); **Keith Hopwood** (rhythm guitar); **Karl Green** (bass);
Barry "Bean" Whitwam (drums)

1963

Noone (b. Nov. 5, 1947, Davyhulme, Manchester, Lancs.), who sold programs as a schoolboy at Manchester United soccer matches, has studied at the Manchester School of Music and Drama and has appeared in the ITV soap "Coronation Street", before being offered a part in a film starring Judy Garland in 1961, an opportunity scotched, however, by his parents. Now in a group with Green (b. July 31, 1947, Salford, Lancs.) and Hopwood (b. Oct. 26, 1946, Manchester), Noone meets Leckenby (b. May 14, 1946, Leeds, Yorks.), who is playing in the Wailers with Whitwam (b. July 21, 1946, Manchester), in the Cavern, Manchester. They team up as the Heartbeats, with Noone using the name Peter Novak, and play at youth clubs and teen dancehalls, eventually signing with managers Harvey Lisberg and Charlie Silverman. The group's name is changed after Green notes a likeness between Noone and the character Sherman in the TV cartoon "The Rocky And Bullwinkle Show". "Sherman" becomes "Herman" and the band's name develops to Herman & His Hermits, later shortened to Herman's Hermits.

1964

Lisberg and Silverman send producer Mickie Most a plane ticket and book him into Manchester's Midland Hotel, before taking him to see the group on stage in Bolton, Lancs. Most sees a facial likeness between Noone and a young John F. Kennedy and decides that the singer's "little-boy-lost" look would make him the ideal frontman for a pop act aimed as much at mums and dads as teenagers.
Sept [26] Signed to Most and via him to EMI's Columbia label, the group tops the UK chart with its debut single, *I'm Into Something Good*, a cover of Earl-Jean's US #38 hit. (Like most of the records which follow, it includes little of the Hermits themselves; Noone's vocals are backed by sessionmen, such as guitarists Jimmy Page and Big Jim Sullivan, with John Paul Jones (who later forms Led Zeppelin with Page) taking care of the bass and most of the arrangements.)
Dec [5] *Show Me Girl*, submitted by *Something Good* writers Goffin and King, who are impressed by the Hermits' cover version, reaches UK #19.
[12] *I'm Into Something Good* climbs to US #13. A million seller, it earns the group's first gold disc.

1965

Jan On its first US visit, the group makes a cameo appearance in the teen movie "When The Boys Meet The Girls", starring Connie Francis and Harve Presnell.
Feb [27] The group begins a 21-date, twice-nightly UK package tour headed by Del Shannon, at the City Hall, Sheffield, Yorks, set to end March 22nd at the Odeon Cinema, Glasgow, Scotland.
Mar [13] Their revival of the Rays' 1957 million seller, *Silhouettes*, hits UK #3.
[27] The John Carter/Ken Lewis (Ivy League) composition, *Can't You Hear My Heartbeat*, hits US #2, behind the Supremes' *Stop! In The Name Of Love* and will become Herman's Hermits' second million seller.
Apr [11] The band appears at the annual "**New Musical Express** Poll Winners Concert" at the Empire Pool, Wembley, Middx., with the Beatles, the Rolling Stones, the Kinks and many others.
[30] The group begins its first full US tour, a 34-day trek on Dick Clark's "Caravan Of Stars", set to end on June 2nd.
May [1] Trevor Peacock-penned *Mrs. Brown You've Got A Lovely Daughter* begins a three-week reign atop the US chart, having entered at #12, the highest first-week placing for a single in seven years, due to unprecedented airplay. It is extracted from the US-only released album, ***Introducing Herman's Hermits***, which hits US #2. *Mrs Brown You've Got A Lovely Daughter* earns a gold disc for a million-plus US sales, but is not released as a single in the UK; the group is not enamored of it and thinks the arrangement too corny for the British market.
[15] *Silhouettes* hits US #5 and is a million seller on combined US/UK sales.
[22] Their update of Sam Cooke's *Wonderful World* hits UK #7.
June [6] The group appears on CBS-TV's "The Ed Sullivan Show" and will also perform on the network's "It's What's Happening Baby" on the 28th.
July Noone is voted one of the ten best-dressed men in the UK. The group's second US album ***Herman's Hermits On Tour***, hits US #2, while the first is still in the Top 10.
[10] *Wonderful World* hits US #4.
[14] The group performs at a dance for Doncaster Rovers soccer club at the Doncaster Top Rank Ballroom, before leaving for a US concert visit.
[22] A Dick Clark package tour begins in the US, set to end on August 8th. (After a Bridgeport, CT gig, a local police chief states "I can assure any organization planning to sponsor entertainment of this type in the future that no permit will be issued by the police department", citing unruly behavior by teenagers.)
Aug [7] *I'm Henry VIII, I Am*, their revision of a 1911 music-hall song, extracted as a US-only single from ***Herman's Hermits On Tour***, again after strong pre-release airplay, hits #1 and becomes another US million seller. On holiday in Hawaii, Noone meets, and "interviews" for the **New Musical Express**, Elvis Presley, who is working on location for the film "Paradise, Hawaiian Style".
Sept [25] *Just A Little Bit Better* reaches UK #15. ***Herman's Hermits***, a belatedly-released UK compilation of the two US albums, makes #16.
Oct [16] *Just A Little Bit Better* hits US #7.
[25] Herman hosts NBC-TV's "Hullabaloo".
Nov [3] The group begins an 18-date, twice-nightly UK tour, with Billy Fury, Wayne Fontana, the Fortunes and others, at the Gaumont Cinema, Wolverhampton, Warks., set to climax on the 22nd at the Odeon Cinema, Manchester.
Dec Compilation album ***The Best Of Herman's Hermits***, hits US #5.

1966

Jan [21] The group begins its first tour of Australasia and Japan.
[29] *A Must To Avoid*, often referred to by Noone as *A Muscular Boy*, a dig at his own indistinct phrasing of the lyrics, hits UK #6 and US #8 (a week earlier), and is another million seller.
Mar [12] US-only *Listen People*, the group's first A-side ballad, hits US #3 and earns yet another gold disc.
Apr [7] The band begins a 12-date, twice-nightly UK tour, with Dave Berry, the Mindbenders, David and Jonathan, and Pinkerton's Assorted Colours, at the ABC Cinema, Dover, Kent, ending on the 20th at the ABC Cinema, Edinburgh, Scotland.
[16] UK-only released *You Won't Be Leaving*, with *Listen People* on the B-side, reaches UK #20. The teen-movie soundtrack album, ***Hold On!***, climbs to US #14, featuring 11 Herman's Hermits' songs.
[21] Movie "Hold On!" premieres in Los Angeles, CA.
May [1] They play at their second annual "**New Musical Express** Poll Winners Concert" at the Empire Pool, on a bill topped by the Beatles and the Rolling Stones.
[7] Extracted from ***Hold On!***, *Leaning On A Lamp Post*, their revival of the George Formby oldie, hits US #9.
June [25] The group guests on the last edition of ITV's "Thank Your Lucky Stars".
July [1] They begin another US tour, with the Animals, Jerry Lee Lewis and Lou Christie, in Honolulu, HI, set to end on August 10th.
[9] *This Door Swings Both Ways* reaches UK #18 and will stop at US #12 on Aug [13].
Sept ***Both Sides Of Herman's Hermits*** peaks at US #48.
Nov [2] "The Canterville Ghost", featuring Noone, Sir Michael Redgrave and Douglas Fairbanks Jr., airs on US TV.
[5] *No Milk Today*, written by Graham Gouldman (later of 10cc), hits UK #7, as *Dandy*, written by Ray Davies of the Kinks, hits US #5.
Dec [24] *East West*, also by Gouldman, reaches UK #37, and US #27 the following week.

1967

Jan ***The Best Of Herman's Hermits, Volume II*** peaks at US #20.
Mar [18] *There's A Kind Of Hush (All Over The World)* hits UK #7, and the following week in the US,

where it is a million seller.
Apr Noone visits Roscommon in Eire, to trace the roots of his grandfather Tommy Noone, who emigrated to England 50 years earlier.
[8] *Kind Of Hush* US B-side, the former UK hit *No Milk Today*, makes #35.
[25] The group is featured in CBS-TV's Leonard Bernstein-hosted "Inside Pop - The Rock Revolution".
May ***There's A Kind Of Hush All Over The World*** reaches US #13.
July [13] The band opens a North American tour with the Who, on their first US tour, as its support act, and the Blues Magoos in Calgary, ab, Canada, set to end September 9th in Honolulu.
[22] *Don't Go Out Into The Rain (You're Going To Melt)* reaches US #18.
Sept [16] *Museum*, written and also recorded by Donovan (Mickie Most later admits he used the same backing track for both versions), reaches US #39. It is released in UK but is the group's first chart failure.
[24] The group guests on CBS-TV's "The Smothers Brothers Comedy Hour".
Oct US-only issued ***Blaze*** peaks at US #75.

1968

Jan ***The Best Of Herman's Hermits, Volume III*** reaches US #102.
Feb [10] *I Can Take Or Leave Your Loving* climbs to UK #11 and US #22.
May [10] The band begins a ten-date, twice-nightly UK tour, with Amen Corner, Dave Berry, the Paper Dolls, John Rowles and the Echoes, at the Town Hall, Birmingham, W. Midlands, ending on the 19th at Nottingham's Theatre Royal.
[25] *Sleepy Joe* reaches UK #12.
June [8] *Sleepy Joe* peak at US #61, as a new generation of US bands eclipses Herman's Hermits, who have nevertheless lasted longer than many of their UK contemporaries.
Aug [17] John Carter and Geoff Stephens-written *Sunshine Girl* hits UK #8.
Sept The group, with Noone as the romantic lead opposite Sheila White, stars in the film "Mrs. Brown You've Got A Lovely Daughter", inspired by the hit single. The ***Mrs. Brown You've Got A Lovely Daughter*** soundtrack album makes US #182.
Nov [5] Noone marries Mireille Strasser in London, on his 21st birthday. (He enters into a business partnership with Graham Gouldman, which includes studio production work and the opening of a New York boutique named Zoo.)
Dec [25] "Pinocchio", with Herman in the title role and Burl Ives as Geppetto, airs on US TV.
[28] The group guests on BBC1-TV's "Val Doonican Show".

1969

Jan [18] *Something's Happening*, a rewrite of a European song, hits UK #6.
May [4] The band appears on ITV's "This Is Tom Jones".
[17] Carter/Stephens-inked *My Sentimental Friend* hits UK #2, the group's second-biggest UK success.
Dec [6] *Here Comes The Star*, their cover of an Australian hit noted during a tour there, peaks at UK #33.

1970

Mar [21] *Years May Come, Years May Go* hits UK #7, the group's final release on UK Columbia.
June [13] *Bet Yer Life I Do*, written by members of Hot Chocolate and released on Most's newly-formed RAK label, makes UK #22.
Nov [9] The group participates in the Royal Variety Performance in London.

1971

Jan [9] *Lady Barbara*, another Hot Chocolate song, reaches UK #13, and is the group's final UK hit single. It is credited to Peter Noone & Herman's Hermits, leading to accurate speculation of an impending split. The Hermits base themselves in the US, to work the nostalgia circuit, while Noone remains in the UK, recording for Most's RAK label.
June [12] Noone's only solo hit, at UK #12, is his treatment of David Bowie's *Oh You Pretty Thing*, featuring its composer on piano. (The follow-up, another Bowie song, *Right On Mother*, will fail to chart, as will later '70s solo projects on RAK, Philips, Casablanca and Bus Stop.)
Oct Compilation, ***The Most Of Herman's Hermits***, reaches UK #14. The Hermits, with new lead singer Peter Cowap, sign to RCA Records and release *She's A Lady*. (Occasional later UK singles without Noone for the Buddah and Roulette labels will also fail to chart, though the group will continue to perform as a live act for several years (and assist former Shirelle Shirley Alston on her version of *Silhouettes* from her album, ***With A Little Help From My Friends*** in 1975), with another new "Herman", singer/guitarist Garth Elliott .Green will also move on, running his own business and writing songs, not least with his neighbor, Ten Years After's Ric Lee. A UK TV-advertised compilation album, ***Greatest Hits***, will make #37 on Oct [15] 1977.)

1973

June [28] Noone briefly reunites with the Hermits, to top the bill of the "British Invasion" nostalgia concert at New York's Madison Square Garden, before 13,000 people. Also playing are the Searchers, Gerry & the Pacemakers and Wayne Fontana & the Mindbenders. Noone and the group will permanently part company later in the year, with the former continuing in cabaret and in theatrical stage roles.

1980

Living in Los Angeles, Noone forms the short-lived Tremblers in 1980, with Gregg Inhofer and Gee Connor on guitars, Mark Browne on bass and Robert Williams on drums, and records the album ***Twice Nightly***. He will go on to enjoy his biggest stage success in the starring role (as Frederic) of the 1983 London version of Gilbert and Sullivan's "The Pirates Of Penzance", having taken over the part from Rex Smith on Broadway in 1982. His re-recording of *I'm Into Something Good* will be featured in the 1988 comedy caper "The Naked Gun : From The Files Of Police Squad".

1994

June [4] While both the Hermits, lining up as Leckenby, Whitwam, Geoff Foote and Rod Gerrard, and Noone have continued to perform separately on the nostalgia circuit, Noone, now living in Montecito, CA, is still highly visible in the '90s as an ever-youthful VJ on the US cable TV channel VH-1 and as interviewer for the station's music magazine, "My Generation". Leckenby now dies of non-Hodgkin's lymphoma in Manchester, after playing his final gig with Herman's Hermits in Moses Lake, WA on May 29th.

JOHN HIATT

1974

Jan Singer/songwriter/guitarist Hiatt (b. Aug. 20, 1952, Indianapolis, IN) has earned his musical spurs in '60s bands including Four Fifths, the White Ducks and Joe Lynch & the Hangmen, before moving to Nashville, TN, in the early '70s, where he signed as a songwriter to Tree Publishing earning $25 a week. His weekly salary rising to $50, he now begins gigging at the Exit Inn, while his first song placement is *Thinking Of You*, which Tracy Nelson records with Mother Earth, followed by Three Dog Night's US #16 cover of his *As Sure As I'm Sitting Here*. Nelson's manager, Travis Rivers, takes him to see Don Ellis at Epic Records, where Hiatt cuts *We Make Spirit (Dancing In The Moonlight)*, produced by Glen Spreen and Chips Moman, and releases his debut album, ***Hangin' Around The Observatory***, which sells 15,000 copies.
Apr Hiatt performs two sellout gigs at a University coffee house in Minneapolis, MN, to be followed by a two-week summer tour around Wisconsin. Subsequently returning to Nashville, he records his sophomore effort, ***Overcoats***, during which he contracts hepatitis.

1975

Dropped by both Epic and Tree, Hiatt heads back to Indianapolis, where he hears from booking agent Mike Kappis, who sends him out on the road as a soloist, opening for the likes of Sonny Terry & Brownie McGhee, Leon Redbone and Tom Waits over the next three years.

1978

May Hiatt, now living in San Francisco, CA, moves to Los Angeles, CA.
Nov With Hiatt having recently opened for Leo Kottke, the guitarist urges his manager, Denny Bruce, to see Hiatt perform at the Caves in Santa Monica, CA. Impressed, Bruce pays for him to assemble a backing band and secures a recording deal, initially with Bug Records, though subsequently with MCA. The following year, and opening for Southside & the Asbury Jukes, Hiatt undertakes a UK tour with his live backing band, White Limbo, including Howard Epstein (bass) and Don Schmidt (drums), to promote his MCA debut, ***Slug Line***, produced by Bruce.

1981

Jan Having released his own ***Two Bit Monsters***, again helmed by Bruce, the previous year, Hiatt has been recruited to Ry Cooder's backing band and is featured on Cooder's current US #43, ***Borderline***.

1987

July By now a recovering alcoholic, Hiatt has recorded three critically acclaimed albums between 1982-1985: ***All Of A Sudden*** (produced by Nick Lowe, 1982), ***Riding With The King*** (co-produced by Lowe with Ron Nagel and Scott Matthews, 1983) and ***Warming Up To The Ice Age*** (helmed by Tony Visconti,1985). Newly signed to A&M Records, Hiatt finally achieves a chart breakthrough, as ***Bring The Family***, produced by John Chelew, peaks at US #107 and features the backing band of Cooder (guitar), Lowe (bass) and Jim Keltner (drums), with whom he will form Little Village in 1992.
Sept [30] Hiatt takes part in "A Black And White Night", starring Roy Orbison, at the Coconut Grove in the Ambassador Hotel, Los Angeles.

1988

Aug Hiatt performs at the annual "Reading Festival", Reading, Berks.
Oct Produced by Glyn Johns, ***Slow Turning***, featuring musical guests Bernie Leadon and Dr. Hook's Dennis Locorriere, makes US #98. The following September, Geffen will release the appropriately titled Hiatt compilation ***Y'All Got Caught? The Ones That Got Away 1979-85***.

1990

Feb [24] He takes part in the "Roy Orbison Concert Tribute" to benefit the homeless, at the Universal Amphitheatre, Universal City, CA.
June [22] Hiatt guests on NBC-TV's "Late Night With David Letterman".
July [7] ***Stolen Moments***, produced again by Johns and featuring singer Ashley Cleveland, charts for a week at UK #72.
[28] ***Stolen Moments*** makes US #61.
Dec [12-13] Hiatt, supported by Edie Brickell & New Bohemians, plays two sellout shows at New York's Beacon Theatre.

1991

Oct Hiatt wins the BMI's 1991 Country Music Award for *Bring Back Your Love To Me*, recorded by Earl Thomas Conley. He also features on the recently-released Bonnie Raitt set ***Luck Of The Draw***.

1992

Feb [29] Having formed Little Village with Cooder, Keltner and Lowe, ***Little Village*** debuts at its UK

#23 peak.
Mar [14] ***Little Village*** makes US #66.
Apr [22] Little Village performs at New York's Beacon Theatre, before a sellout crowd of 2,711.
July [5] The group takes part in the "Radio 1 FM American Music Festival" at the Crystal Palace Bowl, London, on a bill with Emmylou Harris.
[25] Hiatt guests on the TNN cable network's "American Music Shop".

1993

June [12] Hiatt takes part in the 20th anniversary Los Lobos concert at the Greek Theatre in Griffith Park, Los Angeles.
July ***Love Gets Strange***, containing 18 previously released Hiatt covers by various artists, ten of which Hiatt never recorded, is released in the US.
Sept [16] Following an appearance on CBS-TV's "Late Show With David Letterman", Hiatt performs at the Irving Plaza, New York City.
[25] Recorded in a two-week period, ***Perfectly Good Guitar***, featuring guest musicians Michael Ward and Wire Train's drummer Brian MacLeod among others, debuts at its US #47 peak, having charted for a week at UK #67 on the 11th. In a promotional giveaway, Hiatt offers a "perfectly good guitar" to anyone who in 25 words or less can write about a "perfectly good guitar". Answers to "John Hiatt Is Cool", 1426 N. La Brea Ave., Hollywood, CA 90028.

1994

Jan [15] Hiatt plays at the Boathouse, Norfolk, VA at the start of selected US dates.
Feb [23] He opens the "Incredible Shrinking Tour", a four-day tour of Chicago, IL, also taking in the Park West, the Lounge Ax and Schuba's Tavern venues.
Mar [15] Hiatt guests on NBC-TV's "The Tonight Show".
Apr [1] He plays a sellout show at Los Angeles' Wiltern Theatre.
June [20] Set to become one of the biggest-selling debut albums of all-time in the US, Hootie & the Blowfish's ***Cracked Rear View***, its title taken from a Hiatt song, is released by Atlantic Records (US).
Aug [30] Hiatt ends his US tour, supporting Jackson Browne, at the Summer Pops Bowl Amphitheatre, San Diego, CA.
Dec His final A&M outing, the live set, ***Hiatt Comes Alive At Budokan*** is released.

1995

Mar [28] Rhino Records releases ***Till The Night Is Gone : A Tribute To Doc Pomus***, including a cut by Hiatt.
Oct [26] Hiatt returns to the "Late Show With David Letterman".
Nov [11] After two decades recording with Epic, MCA, Geffen and A&M, Hiatt's Capitol debut, ***Walk On***, recorded during his 13-month "Perfectly Good Guitar Tour" and featuring Raitt and the Jayhawks, bows at its US #48 and UK #74 peaks, as he plays a sellout date at First Avenue, Minneapolis, MN, during current US dates.
Dec [11] Hiatt guests on "The Tonight Show".

1996

Feb [2] He plays to a sellout crowd at the Michigan Theatre, Ann Arbor, MI, during his latest US tour.

HOLE

Courtney Love (vocals, guitar); **Eric Erlandson** (guitar); **Melissa Auf Der Maur** (bass); **Patty Schemel** (drums)

1987

Love (b. Love Michelle Harrison, July 9, 1965, San Francisco, CA), daughter of sometime Grateful Dead associate and biographer Hank Harrison (the band's Phil Lesh is Love's godfather) and wealthy hippie therapist mother Linda Carroll, has experienced a turbulent childhood after her parents separated when she was one, with custody granted to her mother (who will remarry twice) who renames her daughter, Courtney Michelle Harrison. Commuting with her mother from 1972 between New Zealand and Eugene OR, her unsettled upbringing has contributed to Love's rebellious nature, and, after stealing a Kiss T-shirt from Woolworths, she attends the first of a number of reform schools. Set on a music career after hearing the Sex Pistols' ***Never Mind The Bollocks*** in the late '70s, Love moves into her own apartment in Portland, OR, where her first attempt to form a band quickly dissolves. Supported by money from a trust fund and her part-time vocation as a stripper, Love spends much of 1981-1982 travelling around the world, a trip which includes a stay in Liverpool, Merseyside, England where she mixes with the local music fraternity including Julian Cope and Pete Burns. Returning to Portland, she successfully auditions for Faith No More (though departs the lineup after only four shows), before now forming Sugar Babylon with future L7 member Jennifer Finch and future Babe In Toyland Kat Bjelland. Subsequently sacked from the band, she will work her way around several US cities, often working as a stripper, in search of a break in either an acting career (she gained a cameo role in the Alex Cox's 1986 punk bio-flick, "Sid And Nancy" and the director's follow-up film, "Straight To Hell") or in music.

1989

Nov Relocated to Los Angeles, CA, Love places an ad in the local **Recycler** newspaper reading: "I want to start a band. My influences are Big Black, Sonic Youth and Fleetwood Mac." She holds auditions and recruits guitarist Erlandson (b. Jan. 9, 1963, Los Angeles), Caroline Rue (drums) and Jill Emery (bass), to complete the first lineup of the controversially-named Hole (actually taken from the Euripides play **Medea**), which earnestly begins demo recordings. (During the year Love also gets married for the first time to L.A. punk band Leaving Trains' transvestite lead singer James Moreland in Las Vegas, NV, though the union is short-lived.)

1991

Oct [12] Already a favorite with the rebellion-seeking UK music media, and following Hole's grunge-based earlier releases, the debut E.P. *Rat Bastard* (led by the song, *Retard Girl*) in July the previous year, and *Dicknail* (issued by the Seattle-based alternative label Sub Pop in March of this year), Caroline Records (US) has released the band's first album, the stark Kim Gordon (of Sonic Youth) and Don Fleming-produced ***Pretty On The Inside*** which now spends one week at UK #59 (issued via the Germany-based City Slang label) and which includes the recent single, *Teenage Whore*.
Nov During a month when Hole undertakes a mini-European tour, Love's new boyfriend, Nirvana's frontman Kurt Cobain informs viewers of C4-TV's "The Word" that "Courtney Love's the best fuck in the world".

1992

Feb [24] Much to the delight of the alternative music press, Love marries Cobain in Hawaii and will give birth to their daughter, Frances Bean Cobain (amid speculation that she has abused drugs during the pregnancy) on August 19th.
[28] After a Hole gig in Los Angeles, Emery quits the band.
Apr [24] On her 25th birthday, ex-Dumbhead drummer Patty Schemel (b. Apr. 24, 1967, Marysville, Seattle, WA) successfully auditions for Hole's vacant drum seat (following Rue's departure) while Love and Erlandson have recently signed a recording deal for Hole with Geffen Records imprint DGC (to whom Nirvana is coincidentally contracted) having rejected an overture from Madonna's Maverick label. Kristen Pfaff will also join the band by year's end replacing Emery's stand-in, Leslie Hardy.

1993

Apr [17] *Beautiful Son* charts for a week at UK #54.

1994

Apr [8] With Hole's DGC label debut scheduled for release the following week, Love's husband is found dead at the couple's Seattle home having committed suicide with a self-inflicted gunshot. Love is immediately thrust into the spotlight with the media following her every move (she reportedly carries Cobain's ashes with her wherever she travels).
[9] *Ms World* charts for a week at UK #64.
[23] ***Live Through This*** debuts at its UK #13 peak during a two-week chart stay.
[30] ***Live Through This*** enters the US album chart.
June [16] 27-year old Pfaff is found dead in her bathtub from a heroin overdose. She will be replaced by Melissa Auf Der Maur (b. Mar. 17, 1972, Montreal, PQ, Canada) who will make her band debut at this summer's "Reading Festival", Reading, Berks.
Sept [7] During a US trek opening for Nine Inch Nails, Hole performs at the Riverside Theatre, Milwaukee, WI, on a bill grossing $79,688 from 3,391 fans.
Dec [5] Hole participates in Z100's "Acoustic Christmas" held at New York's Madison Square Garden on a bill with Weezer, Melissa Etheridge, Indigo Girls, Bon Jovi, Sheryl Crow, Toad The Wet Sprocket and others.
[17] Hole is the music guest on NBC-TV's "Saturday Night Live".
With Love's notoriety and celebrity as the anti-establishment, drug-abusing, confrontational, single-parent widow of Kurt Cobain secure, Hole's ***Live Through This*** tops several end-of-year magazine critics' polls including those in the **Village Voice**, **Rolling Stone**, **Spin**, the **Los Angeles Times** and **Option**.

1995

Jan [14] *Doll Parts* makes US #58.
[21] During Hole dates in Australia, Love, currently hailed as the queen of the media-invented Riot Grrrl movement, is arrested for offensive behavior on-board a Qantas Airways plane flying between Brisbane, Queensland and Melbourne, Victoria.
[23] Love pleads guilty at Melbourne's Broadmeadows Magistrates' Court, to abusing a flight attendant. Freed on a $300 bond, she is required to be on "good behavior" for one month and is fined $500.
[28] ***Live Through This*** peaks at US #52, nine months after its chart debut.
Mar [18] Teenagers Ryan O'Donnell and Robert Lukas file misdemeanor assault complaints against Love for allegedly punching them during a concert on March 14th. A court date will be set for November 2nd.
Apr [15] *Doll Parts* bows at its UK #16 peak.
[17] Hole's "MTV Unplugged" performance, recorded on February 14th at the Brooklyn Academy of Music, NY, is broadcast in the US.
[25] During a European tour and 30 minutes into an Amsterdam, Holland gig, Love walks offstage after an audience member throws a cup of liquid at her.
[26] ***Live Through This*** is certified platinum by the RIAA.
May [4] UK dates end with an appearance at London's Brixton Academy.
June [11] Love is hospitalized and released from Harborview Medical Center in Seattle after apparently taking too much prescription medicine.
July [4] The "Lollapalooza '95" touring festival, including Hole, Sonic Youth, Cypress Hill, Pavement, Sinead O'Connor, Beck, Jesus Lizard, Mighty Mighty Bosstones and others kicks off at the Gorge, George, WA. Love celebrates the occasion by indulging in a backstage brawl with Bikini Kill singer Kathleen Hanna who will file assault charges.
[29] *Violet* bows at its UK #17 peak.
[31] Love walks out of a Lollapalooza, Burgettstown, PA show after a fan throws a shotgun shell on to the stage.
Aug [9] Celebrating the closure of the Lollapalooza trek, Love is carried offstage by a security guard during the final concert after swearing at fans and

twice jumping into crowd to attack them.
Sept [7] Hole performs at the 12th annual MTV Video Music Awards held at Radio City's Music Hall. Across town, the off-Broadway, Courtney Love-themed play, "Love In The Void" opens at Here, with actress Carolyn Baemler playing the controversial lead role.
[28] Love pleads guilty to a charge of fourth degree assault regarding her attack on Hannah during the July 4th Lollapalooza gig, and is given a one-year suspended sentence on condition that she refrain from violence for two years and enroll in anger-management classes.
Oct [15] Jonathan James Hogan files a complaint in a Santa Clara County, CA court claiming that Love punched and kicked him in the groin when he climbed onstage at the Edge nightclub in Palo Alto, CA, in an attempt to dance with her.
Nov [6] Charges against Love brought by Lukas and O'Donnell in March are dismissed by Orange County, CA judge Janis Halker after a three-day trial.
[9] Hole performs at the Hollywood Palladium, Hollywood, CA.

1996

Apr Movie "Feeling Minnesota", starring Keanu Reeves and Love, opens in US theatres.

THE HOLLIES

Allan Clarke (vocals); **Graham Nash** (guitar); **Tony Hicks** (guitar); **Eric Haydock** (bass); **Bobby Elliott** (drums)

1963

Jan Based in Manchester, Lancs., the group has been formed in 1961 by former schoolfriends Clarke (b. Harold Allan Clarke, Apr. 5, 1942, Salford, Lancs.) and Nash (b. Feb. 2, 1942, Blackpool, Lancs.), who were previously teamed as the Two Teens duo, joined by Haydock (b. Feb. 3, 1943, Stockport, Lancs.) and Don Rathbone (drums). Initially named the Fourtones, then, with the addition of another guitarist, evolving into the Deltas, before finally settling on the Hollies in 1962, they are seen by EMI producer Ron Richards, who is checking out the UK beat scene in the wake of the Beatles' initial success, performing at the Cavern club in Liverpool, and he invites them to a label audition in London. The second guitarist does not want to turn professional, so group manager Allan Cheetham invites Hicks (b. Dec. 16, 1943, Nelson, Lancs.), from local group the Dolphins, to audition instead. When EMI signs the band, Hicks joins full time.
Apr [4] The first Hollies recording session produces the debut single, a revival of the Coasters' *(Ain't That) Just Like Me*.
June [29] *(Ain't That) Just Like Me* reaches UK #25.
July Rathbone moves from drums to the group's management and is replaced by Elliott (b. Dec. 8, 1942, Burnley, Lancs.), an ex-colleague of Hicks in the Dolphins who has been playing with Shane Fenton & the Fentones. The new line-up tours widely throughout the UK.
Sept [13] Nash, driving down from Scotland in the group's van, checks to see if the door is locked. It isn't, and he falls out as it travels at 40 m.p.h. The band continues on to London to deputize for Gene Vincent on "Go Man Go".
Oct *Searchin'*, a revival of another Coasters oldie, reaches UK #12 (despite a unanimous thumbs-down review from BBC-TV's "Juke Box Jury", on which panellist Pat Boone advises viewers to go out and buy the original version).
[29] The group begins sessions for its first album and, by year's end, will have made its UK TV debut on "Scene At 6.30".

1964

Jan [1] The Hollies perform *Stay*, their new single, on the premiere edition of BBC-TV show "Top Of The Pops".
[18] *Stay*, their revival of Maurice Williams & the Zodiacs' 1960 US chart-topper, a copy of which Elliott and Hicks had found in a junk shop while on tour of Scotland, hits UK #8.
Feb [29] The Hollies are featured on ITV's "Thank Your Lucky Stars".
Mar Their debut album, ***Stay With The Hollies***, hits UK #2.
Apr The band's treatment of Doris Troy's *Just One Look* hits UK #2, as the group begins recording its second album.
[26] The group takes part in the annual "**New Musical Express** Poll Winners Concert" at the Empire Pool, Wembley, Middx., with the Beatles, the Dave Clark Five, Gerry & the Pacemakers and many others.
May [16] *Just One Look* is the group's first US chart entry, at #98.
June *Here I Go Again* hits UK #4.
Oct *We're Through*, the Hollies' first self-penned A-side, by Clarke, Hicks and Nash under the name L. Ransford, hits UK #7.
[24] Clarke has his tonsils removed in Manchester Hospital, and all tour dates are cancelled until November 15th.
Nov ***In The Hollies Style*** is released in the UK, but does not chart.
Dec [26] The group opens as guests on the Brian Epstein presentation "Gerry's Christmas Cracker", headlined by Gerry & the Pacemakers, with Cliff Bennett & the Rebel Rousers and Tommy Quickly, at the Liverpool Odeon, Lancs.

1965

Mar Gerry Goffin/Russ Titelman song, *Yes I Will* (later recorded by the Monkees as *I'll Be True To You*), hits UK #9.
[5] The band begins a 14-date, twice-nightly UK package tour headlined by the Rolling Stones with Dave Berry & the Cruisers, Goldie & the Gingerbreads, the Checkmates and others, at the Regal Theatre, Edmonton, London, set to end on the 18th at the ABC Theatre, Romford, Essex.
Apr [16-23] The group makes its first visit to the US, playing a week-long engagement at the Paramount Theater, Brooklyn, New York, with Little Richard and others. They also record an appearance on NBC-TV's "Hullabaloo".
May [5] On returning from the US, the band records *I'm Alive* at Abbey Road Studios.
June Nash, Clarke and Hicks form the Gralto Music publishing company.
July *I'm Alive*, written by Clint Ballard Jr., tops the UK chart, deposing Elvis Presley's *Crying In The Chapel*, before yielding to the Byrds' *Mr. Tambourine Man*.
Sept [18] The group begins a ten-day US tour at McCormack's Place, Chicago, IL, alongside the Yardbirds.
Oct *Look Through Any Window*, a Graham Gouldman song, hits UK #4, while ***The Hollies*** hits UK #8.
[18] On their return from a US tour, they begin a week's cabaret at Mr. Smith's in Manchester.
Nov [19] The Hollies take part in the Glad Rag Ball at the Empire Pool, Wembley, with Donovan, the Kinks, the Who, the Merseybeats, Georgie Fame, Wilson Pickett and the Barron Knights.

1966

Jan *If I Needed Someone*, a cover of the George Harrison-penned track from the Beatles' ***Rubber Soul*** album, and cut by the Hollies at the suggestion of George Martin, reaches UK #20. Harrison publicly denounces their interpretation as "soul-less".
[22] *Look Through Any Window* reaches US #32.
Feb ***Hear! Here!*** makes US #145.
Mar *I Can't Let Go*, a Chip Taylor composition selected by Hicks from two demos at Dick James Music (the other is John Phillips' *California Dreamin'*), hits UK #2.
[8] The group begins a 12-day tour of Poland, with Lulu, in Warsaw.
Apr Haydock is asked to leave the band, after missing several gigs.
May [7] *I Can't Let Go* reaches US #42.
[10] The band records the theme for the Peter Sellers-starring film "After The Fox" at Abbey Road Studios, with Sellers contributing a spoken part. Between bass players, they hire Jack Bruce for the session, while the track's composer, Burt Bacharach, plays piano.
[18] Bernie Calvert (b. Sept. 16, 1942, Brierfield, Lancs.), previously with Hicks in the Dolphins, joins the group on bass, playing on another Gouldman song, *Bus Stop*, on his first day.
June Clarke, Hicks and Nash are invited by the Everly Brothers to submit songs for an album to be recorded in the UK. After a day sifting through material at London's Mayfair Hotel, the Hollies join the Everlys in the studio for recording, along with sessioneers Jimmy Page and John Paul Jones.
July *Bus Stop* hits UK #5, while ***Would You Believe*** reaches UK #16.
Sept [2] Calvert makes his TV debut with group, on "Five O'Clock Club".
[17] *Bus Stop*, the group's US breakthrough, hits US #5.
Oct [15] The band begins a 20-date, twice-nightly UK tour, with the Small Faces, Paul Jones, Paul & Barry Ryan and others, at the ABC Cinema, Aldershot, Hants., set to close on November 6th at City Hall, Newcastle, Tyne & Wear.
Nov *Stop Stop Stop*, written by the group and powered by an unusual six-string banjo riff, hits UK #2.
Dec ***For Certain Because*** reaches UK #23.
[10] *Stop Stop Stop* hits US #7.
[17] ***Bus Stop*** makes US #75.

1967

Jan [11] The group begins sessions for a new album at Abbey Road.
Feb [9] They begin a short tour of Germany and Yugoslavia. While in Hamburg, Elliott is taken to hospital, where it is reported that he is "very ill with an inflamed appendix, but responding to treatment". He is hospitalized for several weeks and, when the group returns to London to complete the album, session drummers Clem Cattini and Dougie Wright deputize.
Mar [11] The band begins a 21-date, twice-nightly UK tour with the Spencer Davis Group, the Tremeloes, Paul Jones and others, at the Granada Theatre, Mansfield, Notts., set to end on April 2nd at the Empire Theatre, Liverpool. Elliott will defy doctors' orders and join the tour on the 25th, but after two shows, he goes straight back to bed (former Sounds Incorporated drummer Tony Newman deputizes for him). The group will cancel £30,000 worth of concert work because of Elliott's illness.
[18] *On A Carousel*, taken from the album sessions, hits UK #4, as ***Stop! Stop! Stop!*** (the US equivalent of ***For Certain Because***) reaches US #91.
May [27] *On A Carousel* reaches US #11.
June [13] Hicks enters St. George's Hospital, London, for a minor operation to cure a sinus condition.
[24] *Carrie-Anne*, another Clarke/Hicks/Nash song, almost two years in the writing (and finished during rehearsals at a TV studio), hits UK #3.
[25] Nash joins a select few, to sing on the Beatles' live TV recording of *All You Need Is Love*.
July ***Evolution*** reaches UK #13 and US #43 while their US distribution switches from Imperial Records to Epic.
[8] As Imperial exercises its sell-off period (with additional releases), product from the two labels overlaps. *Pay You Back With Interest*, on Imperial, reaches US #28.
Aug [12] *Carrie-Anne*, on Epic, hits US #9. Imperial compilation album, ***The Hollies' Greatest Hits***, reaches US #11.
[28] The group begins a three-week US tour with the Turtles.
Sept They begin recording ***Butterfly***, an admittedly ***Sgt. Pepper***-inspired set.
Oct [14] *King Midas In Reverse*, chiefly written by Nash and released as a single against the advice of producer Richards, who feels its more experimental structure and lyric will alienate traditional Hollies fans, reaches UK #18.
[28] *King Midas In Reverse* makes US #51.

Nov [4] *Just One Look*, released on Imperial, makes US #44.
Dec [30] *Dear Eloise*, extracted from ***Butterfly*** as a US-only single to tie in with the group's US tour, reaches #50. In Los Angeles, Nash meets former Byrd David Crosby, while attending a recording session by the Mamas & The Papas.

1968

Jan The group records the Clarke/Nash song *Wings* for inclusion on World Wildlife Fund charity album, ***No One's Gonna Change My World***.
Mar Work starts in the studio for a new album, but most of the material will either remain unissued or unfinished (including Nash's *Marrakesh Express*, later a hit for Crosby, Stills & Nash).
Apr *Jennifer Eccles*, written by Clarke and Nash as a deliberate contrast to the complexity of *King Midas* (Jennifer is Clarke's wife's forename and Eccles is Nash's wife's maiden name), hits UK #7.
[28] The band guests on CBS-TV's "The Smothers Brothers Comedy Hour".
May [17] The group begins a 12-date, twice-nightly "Spring Tour '68", with the Scaffold, Paul Jones and the Mike Vickers Orchestra, at the Granada Theatre, Shrewsbury, Salop, set to end on the 29th at the Odeon Theatre, Derby, Derbys. The Lewisham Odeon concert is recorded by EMI for a live album (but is never released).
[18] *Jennifer Eccles* makes US #40.
July The Hollies' management announces that Nash and Bernie Calvert are planning solo albums. Nash has grown unhappy with the group's musical direction since *King Midas* and speculation is already rife that he will leave.
Aug The group plays a UK cabaret season, wearing matching suits and widening the stage repertoire to include songs like *Puff (The Magic Dragon)* and Roger Miller's *Dang Me*.
Sept [7] The Hollies appear on BBC2-TV's "Colour Me Pop".
[14] *Do The Best You Can* stalls at US #93.
Oct In disagreement with a Hicks-proposed plan to record an album entirely comprising Bob Dylan songs, Nash announces that he will leave in December.
[12] Compilation album, ***The Hollies' Greatest***, tops the UK chart at start of six-week run.
[26] Tony Hazzard-penned *Listen To Me* reaches UK #11.
Dec [8] Nash leaves at the end of a charity concert at the London Palladium, and goes into rehearsals in London with David Crosby and Stephen Stills, for their new self-named trio project.

1969

Jan The group auditions for a new singer/guitarist and Terry Sylvester (b. Jan. 8, 1945, Liverpool, Lancs.), ex-the Escorts and the Swingin' Blue Jeans, is recruited and will make his live debut with them at Cardiff University.
Feb Sylvester's first studio session with the group is for *Sorry Suzanne*, after which the group proceeds with ***Hollies Sing Dylan***.
[24] Sylvester makes his Hollies' TV premiere on BBC1-TV's "Dee Time".
Apr *Sorry Suzanne*, penned by Tony Macaulay and Geoff Stephens, hits UK #3.
May [3] "Hollies In Concert" performance airs on BBC2-TV.
[31] *Sorry Suzanne* makes US #56.
June ***Hollies Sing Dylan*** hits UK #3.
[25] The group records a Bobby Russell/Bobby Scott composition, *He Ain't Heavy, He's My Brother*, with Elton John playing piano. Sessions continue for ***Hollies Sing Hollies***, a set entirely comprised of compositions by group members.
Oct The band appears on "The Bobbie Gentry Show" on UK TV, singing several atypical country-style songs.
Nov Epic ballad, *He Ain't Heavy, He's My Brother*, hits UK #3, while ***Hollies Sing Hollies*** is released without charting.

1970

Mar [10] Elton John joins them again at Abbey Road, this time on *I Can't Tell The Bottom From The Top*.
[21] *He Ain't Heavy, He's My Brother* hits US #7 and total world sales top a million.
May *I Can't Tell The Bottom From The Top* hits UK #7. "Oh Flux", a musical co-written by Clarke with his brother-in-law, opens at the Gulbenkian Theatre, Canterbury, Kent.
June [13] *I Can't Tell The Bottom From The Top* peaks at US #82, while ***He Ain't Heavy, He's My Brother*** reaches US #32.
Oct *Gasoline Alley Bred*, penned by Tony Macaulay with Roger Greenaway and Roger Cook, reaches UK #14.
Dec ***Confessions Of The Mind*** makes UK #30.

1971

Feb ***Moving Finger***, the US equivalent of ***Confessions Of The Mind***, reaches US #183, while the group undertakes a tour of the Far East.
Mar [16] The Hollies' first session at AIR Studios in London produces *Hey Willy*.
June *Hey Willy* reaches UK #22, while ***Distant Light*** is released.
Oct [25] Their manager Robin Britten announces that Clarke is leaving the band. He will sign to RCA and shortly record ***My Real Name Is 'Arold***. Swedish singer Mikael Rickfors, ex-Bamboo (who have recently toured with the Hollies), is recruited on lead vocals.
Dec [13] A week-long stint at Batley Variety club, Batley, W. Yorks., will seemingly be Clarke's last concert dates with the Hollies.

1972

Mar *The Baby*, written by Chip Taylor, the first (and only) hit to feature Rickfors' lead vocal, reaches UK #26. It is also the group's first release for Polydor.
Sept ***Distant Light*** makes US #21.
[2] The extracted *Long Cool Woman In A Black Dress*, a Creedence Clearwater Revival-styled near-solo track penned by Clarke, belatedly hits US #2, earning the group a gold disc for million-plus sales and, re-promoted by EMI, also reaches UK #32.
Nov *Magic Woman Touch* is the first Hollies UK single not to chart.
Dec [16] Also from ***Distant Light***, *Long Dark Road* reaches US #26.

1973

Mar [17] *Magic Woman Touch* reaches US #60 and ***Romany*** makes US #84.
July Clarke is invited back into the group, having cut two solo albums (with little commercial success), and Rickfors returns to Sweden. Clarke's new agreement with his colleagues allows him to concurrently make solo albums.
Oct Clarke's song, *The Day That Curly Billy Shot Crazy Sam McGhee*, in similar style to *Long Cool Woman*, reaches UK #24.
Nov [15] The group records *The Air That I Breathe*, after being introduced to Phil Everly's version of the song. Meanwhile, ***The Hollies' Greatest Hits*** compilation reaches US #157.

1974

Mar *The Air That I Breathe*, written by Albert Hammond and Mike Hazlewood, hits UK #2.
Apr [6] Its parent album ***The Hollies*** reaches UK #38 though it it will fail to yield a successful follow-up.
June ***The Hollies*** makes US #28.
Aug [3] *The Air That I Breathe* hits US #6 and is a million seller, collecting another gold disc.

1975

Apr [19] *Sandy*, a Bruce Springsteen song discovered by Clarke, who is an early champion of the US artist in the UK, recording several of his songs on later solo albums, stalls at US #85. (Months later, when the band is playing the Bottom Line in New York, Springsteen comes backstage to voice his approval of its version.)
Another Night climbs to US #123.
July [5] Title track, *Another Night*, makes US #71.

1976

Mar [5] The group embarks on a 14-date UK tour at London's Royal Albert Hall, promoting ***Boulder To Birmingham***, set to end on the 28th at Norwich Theatre, Norwich, Norfolk. (By year's end, two more albums, ***Write On*** and ***Russian Roulette***, are also released, while the group splits from producer Richards.)

1977

Apr [9] Live album, ***The Hollies Live Hits***, recorded on stage in Christchurch, New Zealand, in February 1976, hits UK #4. (The following March ***A Crazy Steal*** will be released, while Clarke issues his solo effort ***I Wasn't Born Yesterday***. A TV-advertised EMI compilation, ***20 Golden Greats*** will hit UK #2, behind ***Saturday Night Fever*** on July [29] 1978, a month before Clarke returns to the fold, enabling the group to begin its first studio sessions in over a year. With the group reunited with producer Richards, ***Five Three One - Double Seven O Four*** will emerge in March 1979 - its title the digits of its Polydor catalog number, promoted with a concert at the Wembley Conference Centre, Wembley in the same month.)

1980

June *Soldier's Song*, teaming the band with writer/producer Mike Batt and the London Symphony Orchestra, makes UK #58, the group's first UK chart single since *The Air That I Breathe*.
Oct ***Buddy Holly***, a return to the ***Hollies Sing Dylan***-concept, now entirely reviving Buddy Holly songs, is released.

1981

May Sylvester leaves, after an acrimonious argument. Within days, Calvert follows him, leaving Clarke, Hicks and Elliott as a trio.
June Attempts to work with other musicians and vocalists include the never-released *I Don't Understand You*, with Labi Siffre, and *Carrie*, with its writer, John Miles. (*Carrie* will be released in 1988 as the B-side of the hit reissue, *He Ain't Heavy, He's My Brother*.)
July [30] At EMI's invitation, Hicks and Elliott put together the segued tracks *Holliedaze* and *Holliepops*, a variation on the currently huge "Stars On 45" craze.
Sept *Holliedaze (A Medley)* reaches UK #28. Hicks, Clarke and Elliott reunite with Graham Nash (who flies in from Hawaii) and Eric Haydock, to perform it on BBC1-TV's "Top Of The Pops".

1982

Nash decides he would like to record with the group again, and he and Clarke strike a deal with Atlantic Records in the US, for a Nash-Hollies reunion album. Instrumental backing tracks are laid down in London and Los Angeles in March, May and June.

1983

Feb Nash, Clarke, Hicks and Elliott record the vocals and final tracks for ***What Goes Around***, at Nash's Rudy Records Studios in Los Angeles.
July [30] A revival of the Supremes' *Stop! In The Name Of Love* reaches US #29, taken from ***What Goes Around***, which makes US #90. The group's "What Goes Around" US tour follows, mixing Hollies classics with later Nash material, before the reunion ends, with Nash returning to his solo career and work with David Crosby.

1984

Nov The Hollies re-sign to EMI, this time to record for the Columbia label. The line-up comprises the Clarke/Hicks/Elliott core, plus keyboard player Denis Haines, Alan Coates on harmony vocals and ex-Mud bassist Ray Stiles. A series of singles, including *Too Many Hearts Get Broken*, *This Is It* and *Reunion Of The Heart*, will be released by the label over the next three years. On tour in W. Germany in October 1987, the group is approached to record *Stand By Me* (not the Ben E. King song), which makes the German chart but is not issued in the UK.

1988

Sept [24] *He Ain't Heavy, He's My Brother*, reissued following exposure in a UK Miller Lite Beer TV ad, tops the UK chart for the first of two weeks, finally giving the group its second UK #1 single. It holds off a challenge from Bill Medley's version, from the film soundtrack to "Rambo III".

Oct [8] The group begins a major UK tour as ***All The Hits And More - The Definitive Collection***, an EMI-released double-album rounding up all Hollies hit singles and live favorites, makes UK #51. The re-promoted, ***20 Golden Greats*** climbs to UK #64.

Dec [31] The reissued *The Air That I Breathe* peaks at UK #60.

1993

Apr [10] ***The Air That I Breathe - The Best Of The Hollies*** reaches UK #15.

May EMI issues a retrospective three-CD boxed set, ***Treasured Hits And Hidden Treasures***, which also includes new songs by Hicks, Elliott and Clarke, not least a Richard Marx composition, *Nothing Else But Love*, and the Nik Kershaw-penned *The Woman I Love*, which has already peaked at UK #42 on Mar [20] (its B-side is the Hollies' treatment of Prince's *Purple Rain*).

[26] The Hollies are honored with the Outstanding Contribution To British Music at the 38th Ivor Novello Awards, held at London's Grosvenor House Hotel.

1995

Sept [14-15] Still constantly touring, the Hollies reunite with Nash at Abbey Road Studios to record *Peggy Sue Got Married*, adding to the Buddy Holly original vocal and guitar tracks recorded by him in his New York apartment in 1958, for inclusion of the the tribute album ***notfadeaway : remembering buddy holly*** to be released the following February.

see also: **CROSBY STILLS NASH & YOUNG**

BUDDY HOLLY & THE CRICKETS

Buddy Holly (vocals, guitar); **Sonny Curtis** (guitar); **Joe B. Mauldin** (bass); **Jerry Allison** (drums)

1953

Sept Holly (b. Charles Hardin Holley, Sept. 7, 1936, Lubbock, TX; his name will be inadvertently changed from Holley to Holly, when it is misspelt on his first recording contract), having entered the J.T. Hutchinson Junior High School, Lubbock, in the seventh grade in 1949, has met Bob Montgomery, with whom he forms the duo Buddy & Bob. Playing mainly country and bluegrass, but also influenced by major R&B/doo-wop vocal groups, they have become a popular attraction around Lubbock and now perform on radio for the first time, on local country station KDAV's "Sunday Party", a show open to anyone who wishes to perform. (DJs Dave Stone and "Hipockets" Duncan had hosted Saturday night "KSEL Jamboree" in Lubbock and, when they moved from KSEL to KDAV, they introduced the idea there.) Adding Larry Welborn on bass, the group earns a regular Sunday-afternoon slot, their segment becoming known as "The Buddy And Bob Show". While at KDAV, they will record several demos the following year (which will eventually appear as ***Holly In The Hills*** after Holly's death).

1955

Oct [14] The growth of rockabilly in the wake of tumultuously-received tours by Elvis Presley, has encouraged Holly to move his music from its pure-country base, as Buddy & Bob appear, supporting Bill Haley & His Comets, on a show, booked by KDAV, where the group is spotted by Nashville, TN-based agent Eddie Crandall, who is travelling with the tour.

[15] Buddy & Bob open for Presley on the "Big D Jamboree" at Lubbock's Cotton Club.

Dec [3] Crandall wires Dave Stone from Nashville, his telegram reading, "Have Buddy Holly Cut 4 Original Songs On Ascetate Don't Change His Style At All. Get These To Me As Soon As Possible."

[7] Holly records the four songs at Nesman Recording Studio in Wichita Falls, TX.

1956

Jan Talent scout Jim Denny, having been contracted by Crandall, is rejected by Columbia, but interests Decca Records' Nashville office in signing Holly, but as a soloist. The trio splits, with Montgomery insisting that Holly grabs the opportunity. (Montgomery will stay in music, on the production and publishing side, while Welborn will join local rock'n'roll outfit the Four Teens as its lead guitarist.) Holly recruits guitarist Curtis (b. May 9, 1937, Meadow, TX), whom he had met on the "Sunday Party" when Curtis was a member of KDAV announcer Ben Hall's country band, and bassist Don Guess, whom he has known since his junior high days and who has been playing with Holly and Montgomery as the Rhythm Playboys since the previous summer.

[9] Billed as Buddy Holly & the Two-Tunes, they begin a 14-date US tour, headlined by Hank Thompson, in Little Rock, AR, set to end on the 23rd in Memphis, TN.

[26] They cut their first sessions for Decca at Bradley's Barn Studio, Nashville, with producer Owen Bradley, and Grady Martin (rhythm guitar) and Doug Kirkham (percussion), recording *Blue Days, Black Nights*, *Don't Come Back Knockin'*, *Love Me* and *Midnight Shift*.

Apr [16] Holly's first single, *Blue Days, Black Nights*, written by Ben Hall, is released.

May The group embarks on a one-month US tour behind bill-topper Sonny James, opening the show and providing a rhythm section for acts who lack their own sidemen.

July [22] The band cuts a second Nashville session. (Decca will sit on these recordings and release them after Holly's success with the Crickets, as ***That'll Be The Day***, credited to Buddy Holly & the Three Tunes. The third "Tune" is newly joined drummer Allison (b. Aug. 31, 1939, Hillsboro, TX), who is still at Lubbock High.)

Sept The group embarks on a three-week tour with Hank Thompson. Guess leaves shortly thereafter, followed by Curtis, who will go on to play with Slim Whitman and then the Phillip Morris Country Show, in Nashville.

Nov [15] Holly, in Nashville to appear at the "Disk Jockey Festival", makes his final Decca recording at Bradley's Barn. (The label decides that it does not wish to pick up the annual option on his five-year contract.) He and Allison drive to New Mexico to see independent producer Norman Petty, who has a studio in Clovis and has recently produced Buddy Knox.

1957

Feb [24-25] The group, comprising Holly, Allison, Welborn, Lubbock native Niki Sullivan (rhythm guitar) and Gary and Ramona Tollet (backing vocals), records a new version of Holly's composition *That'll Be The Day*, its title taken from an oft-used phrase by John Wayne in the film "The Searchers", at Petty's studio. Shortly thereafter, Holly forms a new band with Allison, Sullivan and Mauldin (bass), who, at 16, is still at Lubbock High and, currently in the Four Teens with Welborn, who is asked to play with Holly at a dance in Carlsbad, NM. On the way back from the gig, Holly asks if Mauldin would like to join full time. They tape several demos for Petty, naming themselves the Crickets in the process. Two of the cuts, *Last Night* and *Maybe Baby*, are sent to Roulette. While they await a reply, they fail an audition for "Arthur Godfrey's Talent Scouts". After Roulette turns them down, Petty contacts Murray Deutch of Peer-Southern, who had 50% publishing with Nor Va Jak on Petty's hit *Almost Paradise*, giving him the demos with the proposal that, if he can get the Crickets a recording deal, he could have 50% publishing on *That'll Be The Day*. After being rejected by Atlantic, Columbia and RCA, Deutch finally persuades Coral (ironically a Decca subsidiary) A&R chief, Bob Thiele, to sign the band as a favor to him.

May [27] *That'll Be The Day* is released on the Brunswick label, another Decca subsidiary, used by Thiele as an imprint on which he issues records in which other Coral staffers are not interested. Shortly thereafter, Holly is signed to Coral as a solo artist, with all Crickets records remaining on Brunswick.

July Petty becomes the group's manager.

Aug [2] The Crickets open a month's US tour to promote the new single, with Clyde McPhatter, the Cadillacs, Otis Rush and others, at the Washington, DC's Howard Theater, set to end on the 22nd at the Apollo Theatre in Harlem, New York, NY (which has booked the band on the assumption that it is the Dean Barlow-led Crickets).

[30] The group plays on the opening day of Alan Freed's ten-day "Great Holiday Rock'n'Roll Show" at the Paramount Theater, Brooklyn, New York, on a bill with Little Richard, the Del Vikings, the Diamonds, Mickey & Sylvia, the Moonglows, the Five Keys, Larry Williams, Jo-Ann Campbell, Shaye Cogan, Ocie Smith, the Cleftones and Jimmie Rodgers. After the Apollo gigs, they appear on ABC-TV's "American Bandstand", performing *That'll Be The Day*.

Sept [6] "The Biggest Show Of Stars For 1957" package tour, with Holly & the Crickets, Chuck Berry, Paul Anka, the Drifters, Frankie Lymon & the Teenagers, the Everly Brothers, Clyde McPhatter and others, opens at the Syria Mosque, Pittsburgh, PA, set to close on November 24th at the Mosque, Richmond, VA. (The white artists on the bill are unable to play on several dates because of segregation laws which forbid black and white acts to perform on the same stage.)

[21] *That'll Be The Day* hits US #3, selling over a million. At the end of the month, a second single is released on Brunswick's sister label Coral, credited only to Buddy Holly (a dual release ploy which will continue for the next year). The song is *Peggy Sue*, originally written by Holly as *Cindy Lou*, but renamed after Allison's Lubbock High School girlfriend, Peggy Sue Gerron.

Nov [1] *That'll Be The Day* begins a three-week stay at UK #1, as ***The Chirping Crickets*** is released in the US. (The success of the song will extend into the '70s, when it is revived as the title theme to the David Essex-starring UK rock'n'roll era movie, "That'll Be The Day".)

Dec [1] The band appears on CBS-TV's "The Ed Sullivan Show", performing *That'll Be The Day* and *Peggy Sue*, with Sullivan also interviewing Holly.

[30] The group, now a trio (Sullivan quits and will sign a solo deal with Dot Records, before moving to Los Angeles, CA, where he will front the group Soul Incorporated), begins a 12-day stint on an Alan Freed package at the Brooklyn Paramount Theater, on a bill with Fats Domino, Jerry Lee Lewis, the Everly Brothers, the Rays, Danny & the Juniors, Paul Anka and others.

1958

Jan [4] *Peggy Sue* hits US #3, becoming a million seller. Holly's distinctive vocal style, coupled with his dextrous playing of the little-known Fender Stratocaster guitar, combines with his unique horn-rimmed glasses look to provide an instantly recognisable trademark.

[11] *That'll Be The Day* re-charts for a week at UK #29.

[18] *Peggy Sue* hits UK #6.

[25] The Crickets' *Oh Boy!* hits US #10, as Holly records tracks at the Bell Sound Studios in New York with producer Milton De Lugg.

[26] The group makes a second appearance on "The Ed Sullivan Show", performing *Oh Boy!*

[30] They begin a 12-date, week-long "Lee Gordon's World Hit Parade" tour of Australia, playing in Sydney, Newcastle, Brisbane and Melbourne, with Jerry Lee Lewis, Jodie Sands, Australian singer Johnny O'Keefe and bill-topper Paul Anka.

Feb [1] *Oh Boy!* hits UK #3.

[20] A 12-date, six-day "The Big Gold Record Stars" package tour of Florida, with the Everly Brothers, Bill Haley & His Comets, Jerry Lee Lewis and Jimmie Rodgers, begins at the Kellog Auditorium, Orlando,

FL, set to end on the 25th at the War Memorial Auditorium, Fort Lauderdale, FL.

Mar [1] The group begins its only UK tour, a 25-date, twice-nightly package, with Gary Miller, the Tanner Sisters, Des O'Connor and Ronnie Keene & His Orchestra, at the Trocadero, Elephant & Castle, London. It will climax on the 25th at the Gaumont Theatre, Hammersmith, London.

[2] Holly & the Crickets appear on ITV's peak-time live variety show, "Sunday Night At The London Palladium".

[15] *Listen To Me* reaches UK #16, giving them four simultaneous UK Top 20 hits.

[27] They are also seen on the last broadcast of Jack Payne's BBC-TV show, "Off The Record".

[28] Back in the US, the group begins a further 61-date "Alan Freed's Big Beat Show" package trek, with Jerry Lee Lewis, Chuck Berry, Frankie Lymon, the Diamonds, Danny & the Juniors, Screamin' Jay Hawkins and others, at Brooklyn's Paramount Theater, set to end on May 9th at the Arena, Hershey, PA.

Apr [5] The Crickets' *Maybe Baby*, recorded at the Tinker US air force base in Oklahoma City, OK, during a break in the "Biggest Show Of Stars For 1957" tour the previous September, reaches US #18. A Holly solo, ***Buddy Holly***, is issued in US.

[19] *Maybe Baby* hits UK #4.

May [3] 19-year old Albert Reggiani suffers multiple wounds to the chest, when he is stabbed during a riot at the end of a Holly & the Crickets-featuring "Alan Freed Big Beat Show" at the Boston Arena, Boston, MA, a venue which subsequently bans all future concerts. Several others are injured among the estimated 5,000-plus fans.

June [19] Holly records his first sessions without the Crickets, with producer Dick Jacobs at Coral Records Studios at the Pythian Temple, New York, covering two Bobby Darin songs, *Early In The Morning* and *Now We're One*, backed by a small group (including saxophonist Sam "The Man" Taylor). (The two tracks had been scheduled to be released by Darin - under the name the Ding Dongs, on Brunswick, after his Atco option lapses, but, because of the success of *Splish Splash*, Atco picks up his option and releases the songs as by the Rinky Dinks, all of which precedes Holly's versions.) While in New York, Holly meets his future wife, Puerto Rican Maria Elena Santiago, when visiting Murray Deutch at Peer-Southern.

[14] Holly's *Rave On*, recorded at the Bell Sound session in January, makes US #37. Holly fails an initial medical, which might have led to his military call-up, because of a stomach ulcer.

July [4] The group embarks on an 11-date "Summer Dance Party" tour, with Tommy Allsup's Western Swing Band, in Angola, IN.

Aug [2] *Rave On*, written by Norman Petty, Bill Tilghman and Sunny West, hits UK #5. By now, Holly has successfully and uniquely bridged the gap between the raw energy of the early rock'n'roll pioneers and the oncoming softer sound of the teen-beat trend.

[9] The Crickets' *Think It Over* and *Fool's Paradise* reach US #27 and #58 respectively.

[15] Holly and Santiago are secretly married at Holly's parents' home in Lubbock, by pastor Ben Johnson.

[25] A Holly solo, ***Early In The Morning***, reaches US #32 and UK #17.

[23] *Think It Over* reaches UK #11.

Sept [10] In Clovis, while recording *Reminiscing* and *Come Back Baby*, Holly produces *Jolé Blon*, the first single by his friend Waylon Jennings, a DJ at KLLL.

[30] Holly and Phil Everly produce Lou Giordano's *Stay Close To Me*, recorded at Beltone Studios in New York.

Oct [2] Holly guests on Alan Freed's "The Big Beat" on the WNEW-TV show, where he is interviewed by the host and mimes to *It's So Easy*.

[3] The group begins the 19-date "The Biggest Show Of Stars For 1958 - Autumn Edition" tour, with Frankie Avalon, Bobby Darin, Dion & the Belmonts, Bobby Freeman, Clyde McPhatter, the Coasters and others, at the Auditorium, Worcester, MA, set to end on the 19th at the Mosque, Richmond.

Following a decision by Holly to end his association with Norman Petty (with whom relations have soured) and to set up a base in New York with his wife, Holly and the Crickets decide to go their separate ways. Allison (also recently married, to Peggy Sue) and Mauldin will return to Texas, with Holly giving them full rights to the Crickets' name so that they can continue recording. Earl Sinks will replace Holly on vocals, while Tommy Allsup joins on guitar. (Sinks and Allsup will both leave shortly, leaving the Crickets as a duo, before Curtis returns.) Allison, meanwhile, will have a solo US hit (#68), under the pseudonym Ivan (his middle name), with a cover of Johnny O'Keefe's *Real Wild Child*, a song he heard on the tour of Australia. (Holly plays guitar and sings backing vocals on the track.)

[21] Holly records four tracks, *It Doesn't Matter Anymore*, *Moondreams*, *Raining In My Heart* and *True Love Ways*, at Pythian Temple, accompanied by a 12-piece string section from the Dick Jacobs Orchestra.

[28] The Crickets make their final TV appearance on "American Bandstand", miming to *Heartbeat* and *It's So Easy*.

Dec [27] Holly makes his first live appearance in Lubbock, since gaining fame, at a KLLL live remote from the Morris Fruit & Vegetable Store.

[31] He flies back to New York.

1959

Jan [17] *Heartbeat*, a Holly solo (with the original version of the much-revived *Well All Right* on B-side), reaches UK #30.

[22] He makes his last-ever recordings, in the Brevoort, his 8th Street, Greenwich Village, New York apartment.

[23] Holly begins a 24-date "Winter Dance Party" tour, with a back-up band comprising Tommy Allsup (guitar), Carl Bunch (drums) and Waylon Jennings (bass), on a bill also featuring the Big Bopper, Ritchie Valens, Frankie Sardo and Dion & the Belmonts, at George Devine's Million Dollar Ballroom, Milwaukee, WI, set to end on February 15th at the Illinois State Armoury, Springfield, IL.

[24] *Heartbeat* peaks at US #82.

Feb [2] Holly plays the 11th date of the tour at the Surf Ballroom in Clear Lake, IA, before an estimated crowd of between 1,000 and 1,500. During the concert, Holly sits in on drums for several other acts, while the Belmonts' bass singer, Carlo Mastrangelo plays drums on Holly's set, standing in for an ailing Bunch, who is suffering from foot frostbite.

[3] At approximately 1:00 a.m., Holly, Valens (who has won a coin toss with Allsup for a seat) and the Big Bopper (who has been given Jennings' seat), tired of bus travel (en route from Duluth to Green Bay on the 1st, the bus broke down, resulting in a concert in Appleton, WI, being cancelled), hire a Beechcraft Bonanza light plane from Dwyer's Flying Service, paying $36 each for their tickets, to take them to the city airport in Fargo, ND, for the next date at Moorhead, MN. In bad weather, the plane crashes in a field approximately eight miles north west of the airfield, only minutes after take-off near Mason City, IA. Holly, Valens, the Big Bopper and pilot Roger Peterson are all killed. Owner Jim Dwyer spots the wreckage at around 9:35 a.m. (The two Moorhead shows are combined into one later in the day. Promoters audition for local talent to fill the bill, following an appeal on KVOX radio station. The Central High School, Fargo band gets the gig, with Bobby Velline (subsequently famous as Bobby Vee) singing, as he knows more lyrics than anyone else in the band.)

[4] Jimmy Clanton and Frankie Avalon headline in Sioux City, IA, dropping other commitments to finish the tour. (Ronnie Smith joins Allsup, Jennings and Bunch. Smith fronts Odessa, TX-band Ronnie Smith & the Poor Boys, from which Bunch was initially recruited.)

[7] Holly's funeral is held at the Tabernacle Baptist Church in Lubbock, with over 1,000 people attending. The pallbearers are Montgomery, Allison, Mauldin, Sullivan, Curtis and Phil Everly. He is buried in Lubbock City Cemetery.

Apr [4] The ironically-titled *It Doesn't Matter Anymore*, a song written for Holly by Paul Anka, and recorded at his final New York sessions, with an innovatory pizzicato string arrangement, reaches US #13.

[11] B-side, *Raining In My Heart*, makes US #88.

[25] *It Doesn't Matter Anymore* begins a three-week run at UK #1, while the Crickets, on their first track without Holly, make UK #26 with *Love's Made A Fool Of You* (a Holly composition, first cut by him as a demo for the Everly Brothers, with Bob Montgomery).

May While Tommy Dee's *Three Stars*, an early tribute to Holly, Valens and the Big Bopper makes US #11, a memorial album, ***The Buddy Holly Story***, compiling most of his hits both solo and with the Crickets, reaches US #11 and hits UK #2 (May [16]). (It will stay charted in both countries for over three years, and will become Coral's biggest-ever seller.)

Aug Holly will have no more hit singles in US, but a long series of posthumous UK chart successes - with either reissued or discovered material - begins with ***Midnight Shift***, which reaches UK #26.

Oct [3] *Peggy Sue Got Married*, a lyrical sequel to Holly's first solo hit, and taken from one of his demos (with extra over-dubbing by the Jack Hansen Combo), makes UK #13.

1960

Jan [16] The (post-Holly) Crickets, rejoined by Sonny Curtis, reach UK #27 with *When You Ask About Love*.

May [7] *Heartbeat*, promoted in competition with a new cover version by the England Sisters, re-enters the UK chart, at #30.

[14] The Crickets' *Baby My Heart* makes UK #33.

June [18] *True Love Ways*, one of Holly's final New York studio recordings (and later one of his most-covered ballads), reaches UK #25.

Nov [5] *Learning The Game*, another overdubbed home demo, recorded on December 17th, 1958, makes UK #36, while a second posthumous compilation ***The Buddy Holly Story Vol. 2*** hits UK #7.

1961

Feb [11] *What To Do*, recorded in Holly's apartment on December 3rd, 1958, makes UK #34.

Apr ***In Style With The Crickets*** reaches UK #13.

Aug [12] A cover of Elvis Presley's *Baby I Don't Care*, originally on Holly's 1958 solo album, backed with *Valley Of Tears*, reaches UK #12.

Sept Bobby Vee enters United Recording Studios, Hollywood, with the Crickets, to record a number of Holly hits (including *Peggy Sue* and *Well All Right*), which will be released as ***Bobby Vee Meets The Crickets*** the following year.

Oct UK vocalist Mike Berry's *Tribute To Buddy Holly* peaks at UK #24

Nov ***That'll Be The Day*** (a compilation of 1956 Decca recordings, reissued at a low price) hits UK #5.

1962

Norman Petty, after agreements with Coral Records and Holly's parents, acquires control of Holly's released and unreleased recordings. Taking the large number of solo home demos, he works in the studio with the Fireballs (already hitmakers with instrumentals *Torquay* and *Bulldog*, and later bigger still with *Sugar Shack* and *Bottle Of Wine*), replacing the early over-dubbings with backing more sympathetic to Holly's style and intentions.

Mar [17] *Listen To Me* re-enters the UK chart, at #48.

Aug [4] The Crickets, now comprising Allison, Curtis, pianist Glen D. Hardin (b. May 18, 1939, Wellington, TX), and new vocalist Jerry Naylor (b. Mar. 6, 1939, Chalk Mountain, TX), have their biggest post-Holly hit with the Goffin & King song *Don't Ever Change*, which hits UK #5.

Oct [13] *Reminiscing*, an unreleased track written by King Curtis (who also plays sax on the disc), from Holly's final sessions, reaches UK #17.

Nov [2] The Crickets embark on a 21-day UK tour, their first since 1958, with Bobby Vee.

1963

Jan [12] ***Bobby Vee Meets The Crickets*** hits UK #2.

Feb ***Reminiscing***, compiled by Petty from unissued material with Fireballs backing tracks, is released, after many rumours of its release and several apparent delays. Reviews, four years after Holly's death, are excellent.
[16] The Crickets reach UK #17 with the Holly-like Sonny Curtis song *My Little Girl*, featured by them in the UK pop movie "Just For Fun".
Apr [13] ***Reminiscing*** hits UK #2 (behind Cliff Richard and the Shadows' ***Summer Holiday***).
[20] A racing version of Chuck Berry's *Brown-Eyed Handsome Man* hits UK #3. It is taken from ***Reminiscing***, which reaches US #40.
June [15] The Crickets' country-styled *Don't Try To Change Me* makes UK #37.
July [13] *Bo Diddley*, another rocking cover from the album, hits UK #4.
Oct [12] *Wishing*, a newly-dubbed version of another demo (cut by Holly for the Everly Brothers), hits UK #10, while ***I Remember Buddy Holly***, a tribute album by Bobby Vee, is also released.

1964

Jan [11] *What To Do*, this time with the Fireballs backing, re-enters the UK chart, making #27.
May [30] *You've Got Love* makes UK #40.
June [27] ***Buddy Holly Showcase***, another of Petty's compilations of previously unissued tracks, hits UK #3.
Aug [1] The Crickets' final hit single, at UK #21, is a re-write of Ritchie Valens' *La Bamba*, titled *(They Call Her) La Bamba*. (The Crickets will continue to re-form into the '90s, although line-up changes will be extensive and continuous, but always revolving around Jerry Allison, who owns the name, and usually Sonny Curtis.)
Sept [19] *Love's Made A Fool Of You*, Holly's original demo for the Everly Brothers, makes UK #39.

1965

July [3] ***Holly In The Hills***, resurrecting the early Holly and Montgomery radio-station recordings from 1954/5, reaches UK #13. During a short-lived rock'n'roll revival, a reissue of *Peggy Sue/Rave On* will make UK #32 on Apr [13], 1968 with a subsequent compilation ***Buddy Holly's Greatest Hits***, hitting UK #9 on June [22].

1969

Apr [12] ***Giant***, made up of Holly's home recordings, reaches UK #13.
Dec [24] ***The Buddy Holly Story***, which is Coral's biggest selling album, is finally certified gold for half a million US sales.
[30] *That'll Be The Day* is also confirmed gold by the RIAA.

1972

Jan [15] Inspired by Holly's legacy, and crystallizing an increasingly held view which reveres the bespectacled singer as a seminal figure in the development of rock'n'roll, Don McLean's *American Pie Parts I &II* hits US #1.

1975

July [26] Reissued again ***Buddy Holly's Greatest Hits***, (which re-charted at UK #32, in September 1971) now makes UK #42.
Sept Shooting begins in Mississippi on 20th Century Fox, "Not Fade Away", a story about the Crickets' first tour, in 1957, with Steve Davies as Holly, Gary Busey as Allison and Bruce Kirby as Mauldin. Three weeks into filming, production is stopped, ostensibly due to "artistic differences" between the studio and director Jerry Friedman.

1976

Sept [7] Paul McCartney commemorates Holly's 40th birthday with the inauguration of "Buddy Holly Week" in the UK. (McCartney, a lifetime Holly fan who has long acknowledged his influence on the Beatles, has purchased the publishing rights to his song catalog from Nor Va Jak.) At the same time, the Buddy Holly Memorial Society is formed in the US by Bill Griggs. (Allison, Mauldin and Curtis will perform at the second annual "Buddy Holly Week" celebration held between September 7-14th the following year, while filming will begin on "The Buddy Holly Story", with Gary Busey as Holly, and Don Stroud and Charles Martin Smith playing the Crickets, in November the same year.)

1978

Mar [25] Further retrospective, ***20 Golden Greats***, tops the UK chart and will make US #55 in August.
May [18] "The Buddy Holly Story" has its world premiere at the Medallion Theater in Dallas, TX.
Aug The Buddy Holly Memorial Society holds its first Buddy Holly Convention, at the Ramada Inn, Wethersfield, CT. Allison, Sullivan and Mauldin play together for the first time in 20 years, joining Curtis.

1979

Feb [3] A concert, hosted by Wolfman Jack, at the Surf Ballroom in Clear Lake, commemorates the final performances of Buddy Holly, the Big Bopper and Ritchie Valens exactly 20 years ago. Acts appearing include Jimmy Clanton, Del Shannon and the Drifters.
Mar Six-album boxed set, ***The Complete Buddy Holly***, containing every one of Holly's recordings, is released in the UK.

1980

Feb [27] Jerry Allen, Sheriff of Mason City, unearths a manila envelope marked "Charles Hardin Holley", containing Holly's glasses, the Big Bopper's watch and several other items.
Mar A statue of Holly is erected in front of Lubbock Civic Center. ***For The First Time Anywhere***, containing original recordings without additional dubbing or subsequent backing tracks, will be released in 1983. The following year ***Greatest Hits*** will anchor at UK #100 on Sept [8].

1986

Jan [23] Holly is posthumously inducted into the Rock and Roll Hall of Fame at the inaugural dinner, held at the Waldorf Astoria Hotel, New York.
Mar [3] He is also inducted into the Songwriters Hall of Fame at the 17th annual awards ceremony, held at the Hotel Plaza Grand Ballroom, New York. Revered as one of the most influential rock'n'roll composers, Holly's songs have been much covered, not least providing hits for the Beach Boys (*Peggy Sue*), John Denver (*Everyday*), the Bobby Fuller Four (*Love's Made A Fool Of You*), Cliff Richard and Peter & Gordon (*True Love Ways*), the Rolling Stones (*Not Fade Away*), Linda Ronstadt (*It's So Easy*), Santana (*Well All Right*) and James Taylor (*Everyday*), while the likes of the Beatles, Blind Faith, Elvis Costello, Grateful Dead, Waylon Jennings, the Nitty Gritty Dirt Band and Bruce Springsteen are among the dozens of acts to include Holly songs on their albums over the years.

1988

Apr The Crickets release ***Three Piece*** on Allison's Rollercoaster label, their first album in over a decade.
Sept The Crickets sign to CBS and will record *Got The T-Shirt*, winner of the 1987 "Buddy Holly Week" Song Contest.
[7] McCartney joins the Crickets on stage at the annual "Buddy Holly Week" festival in London.
Dec *True Love Ways*, re-released by MCA, after exposure on a TV ad for Terry's All Gold chocolates, makes UK #65.

1989

Feb [3] Southeast Texas Musical Heritage Society unveils statues of Holly, Valens and the Big Bopper in Port Arthur, TX.
Mar [11] UK TV-advertised compilation, ***True Love Ways***, hits UK #8.
Sept New Rose Records in France releases the various artists compilation ***Everyday Is A Holly Day***.

1990

Gary Busey pays $242,000 for an acoustic guitar owned by Holly, at a US auction.
Sept [4] For his annual tribute, McCartney performs at the Lone Star Roadhouse, New York, to celebrate Holly's birthday, a gig also attended by Allison, Mauldin and Maria Elena Holly.
Oct [23] Following its West End stage premiere in London, the musical "Buddy", bows at the Shubert Theatre, New York.

1992

July [12] Allison, Mauldin and Payne attend a ceremony at which Busey unveils bronze memorials of Holly, Blind Lemon Jefferson and Bob Wills, at the "Texas Music Alley" exhibit in Dallas, following which the attending Crickets join Busey in a musical tribute to Holly.

1993

Feb [20] Confirming Holly's timeless appeal, all the more extraordinary given the two-year time span of his original hit chapter back in the late '50s, yet another UK retrospective collection, ***Words Of Love***, bows at UK #1. Holly has now hit the Top 10 of the UK Album chart in each decade, from the '50s to the '90s.

1995

Sept [7] While Lubbock City Council voted to purchase $175,000 worth of Holly memorabilia the previous July 28th from a local corporation who bought it from Sothebys, "Buddy Holly - The Influence", an exhibit displaying Holly photgraphs, letters and the journal in which he inscribed the lyrics to *That'll Be The Day*, now opens on the 59th anniversary of his birth, at the Museum of Texas Tech University in Lubbock.

1996

Jan [2] Decca Records releases ***notfadeaway : remembering buddy holly***, a new tribute collection to celebrate the 60th anniversary of Holly's birth, including covers by the Mavericks, Nanci Griffith and the Crickets, Los Lobos, the Band, the Tractors, Mary-Chapin Carpenter, Joe Ely and Todd Snider, Marty Stuart and Steve Earle, Suzy Bogguss and Dave Edmunds, the Nitty Gritty Dirt Band, Waylon Jennings and Mark Knopfler, and *Peggy Sue Married*, pairing Holly's demo cut in his New York apartment in 1958 with a new Hollies version recorded in September 1995.

THE HONEYCOMBS

Denis D'Ell (vocals, harmonica);
Martin Murray (lead guitar);
Alan Ward (rhythm guitar, keyboards);
John Lantree (bass); **Honey Lantree** (drums)

1963

The group is formed by Murray (b. Oct. 7, 1941, London), a former guitarist in various skiffle and rock groups and a hairdresser by day, who recruits Ward (b. Dec. 12, 1945, Nottingham, Notts.) and persuades fellow hairdressing colleague Honey Lantree (b. Ann Lantree, Aug. 28, 1943, Hayes, Middx.), whose hobby is playing drums, to join. Honey's brother John Lantree (b. Aug. 20, 1940, Newbury, Berks.) eventually fills in on bass, while D'Ell (b. Denis Dalziel, Oct. 10, 1943, Whitechapel, London) is recommended by a friend of Murray's as a vocalist. Initial gigs around North London are undertaken as the Sherabons, before the catchier Honeycombs, derived from Honey's nickname and the group's hair-stylist background, sticks as a permanent moniker.

1964

Playing the local club and dancehall circuit, the group is spotted at the Mildmay Tavern by songwriters Ken Howard and Alan Blaikley, who become its managers.

They sign the group to Pye Records and team it with independent producer Joe Meek.
Aug [29] Their first release, the Howard/Blaikley composition *Have I The Right?*, tops the UK chart.
Oct Murray suffers a fall during a ballroom gig and breaks bones in his leg and right hand. With both in plaster, he is unable to play and is temporarily replaced on guitar by Peter Pye (b. July 12, 1946, Walthamstow, London). The group plays its first major UK tour, packaged with Lulu, Millie Small and the Applejacks.
Oct [31] *Is It Because?* makes UK #38.
Nov [14] *Have I The Right?* hits US #5 and becomes a million seller. UK DJ Jimmy Savile presents the group with a gold disc on BBC-TV's "Top Beat" show, staged at London's Royal Albert Hall.
Dec [26] The group appears on the Christmas edition of ITV's "Thank Your Lucky Stars", performing *Eyes*, which fails to chart. By year's end, Murray has permanently left the line-up.

1965

Jan The group leaves for a four-week tour of Australia and New Zealand.
[23] *I Can't Stop*, not released in UK, is a US follow-up, at #48 (and the group's only other US hit single), while ***Here Are The Honeycombs*** peaks at US #147.
Apr [23] Murray's new group, the Lemmings, debuts with *My Little Girl* on Pye.
May [1] *Don't Love You No More* is cancelled as a single release, after the group records Ray Davies' (of the Kinks) song, *Something Better Beginning*, which reaches UK #39.
Aug [7] The Honeycombs embark on a 24-date tour of Japan.
Sept [25] *That's The Way*, with Honey duetting with D'Ell on vocals, strongly supported by UK pirate radio ships which give it blanket airplay, sails to UK #12.

1966

Jan ***All Systems Go*** yields a belated UK release of *I Can't Stop*, its opening track, but receives scant attention, as will the follow-up, *Who Is Sylvia?*
Apr D'Ell, Ward and Pye leave the group. Colin Boyd (vocals), Rod Butler (lead guitar) and Eddie Spence (organ) replace them, as the band evolves into the New Honeycombs.

1967

Mar Honey Lantree leaves, to pursue a solo career.
[24] D'Ell releases his first solo single, *It Breaks My Heart*, on CBS.
May Lantree rejoins, as the group, now badly adrift of changing pop-music fashions, drifts into club and variety work, before breaking up.

1991

June [7] While D'Ell attempted a comeback as a solo singer during the '70s, appearing on ITV's "Opportunity Knocks", the Honeycombs, who reunite for occasional nostalgia performances, participate in a tribute to Joe Meek held in Lewisham, London, also featuring Cliff Bennett, Mike Berry, Heinz, Moontrekkers, Danny Rivers, Screaming Lord Sutch and the Tornados.

JOHN LEE HOOKER

1943

Hooker (b. Aug. 22, 1919, Clarksdale, MS, his birth-year is disputed anywhere between 1917 and 1921, though a clue is given by the Tanzanian postal service in 1994), having learned guitar from his musician stepfather Will Moore as a teenager, joined the army at age 14 but booted out three months later, has drifted through Memphis, TN, in the early '30s, working as a theater usher in a Beale Street locale for a few months, before Moore takes him back to Mississippi. He now relocates to Detroit, MI, from Cincinnati, OH, where he stayed for several years working in a factory during the Depression, his musical experience developing as both a gospel singer, with the Fairfield Four, and blues performer sitting in with local musicians like Robert Nighthawk. In Detroit he works as a janitor at the Chrysler car plant by day and plays at night in clubs like the Forest Inn and Club Basin (having actually made his first public appearance at the City Auditorium, Atlanta, GA) with a three or four-piece blues band, typically, Bob Thurman on piano, Otis Finch on sax, and Tom Whitehead on drums, making a name as a popular blues act.

1948

Oct Hooker is spotted in Detroit night spot the Monte Carlo by Elmer Barbee, who introduces him to Bernie Bessman, a local distributor and record-store owner, who owns the Sensation label.
Nov [3] A debut recording session is held in a local studio with just Hooker and his guitar. The self-penned *Boogie Chillun* sets the pattern for his primitive, intense blues style and is a huge US hit nationally in the burgeoning "race" (later R&B) market, causing Bessman to lease the master to Modern (over the next five years it will sell a million copies). When the record breaks, Hooker is still working as a janitor at Chrysler.
Dec His second session is for independent producer and another Detroit record store owner, Joe Von Battle, who circumvents the Modern contract by selling *Black Man Blues* to King Records for release by "Texas Slim". (Hooker will record for anyone who shows interest, avoiding contractual complications by using a new name. Between 1949 and 1954 he will issue about 70 singles on 21 different labels including Acorn, Regal, Chess, Gotham, Staff and Chart Records, under ten different pseudonyms, including Delta John, Johnny Lee, Johnny Williams, the Boogie Man, Little Pork Chops, Birmingham Sam & His Magic Guitar and John Lee Booker.) *Crawlin' King Snake*, released on on Modern the following year, sells well and will be much covered by late-'60s electric blues bands, while *I'm In The Mood* becomes Hooker's second major R&B hit in 1951, and will sell an estimated million copies over a period of some years. (It will also appear on the movie soundtrack to "The Hot Spot" in 1990.)

1955

Oct Having made his debut as a radio DJ in Detroit in 1952, Hooker signs a recording contract with Vee-Jay Records in Chicago, IL, which recognizes his potentially wider appeal and moulds him into a tighter, more commercial performer on disc, backing him with disciplined R&B session men, including guitarist Eddie Taylor and drummer Tom Whitehead. During a decade in which he records dozens of 78s, his first album, ***The Folk Blues Of John Lee Hooker*** will be released by Riverside Records in 1959.

1960

June [24] He is one of the few purely blues artists at the second annual "Newport Folk Festival", Newport, RI. The performance is recorded by Vee-Jay, for later release as ***Concert At Newport***. By the end of the year, his second Riverside studio set, ***That's My Story*** will be released.

1961

Apr [11] Bob Dylan makes his first New York, NY appearance, opening for Hooker at Gerde's Folk City in New York. (By year's end, Vee Jay will release Hooker's ***Folklore Of John Lee Hooker***.)

1962

July [21] Self-composed *Boom Boom* is Hooker's only US crossover success, reaching #60 (and will also be a hit for the Animals, in 1964). (During the year, Hooker tours Europe with the "American Blues Folk Festival 1962" concert package.)

1964

June [1] Releasing ***I Want To Shout The Blues***, Hooker arrives in the UK for a 28-day tour.
July With the UK R&B boom in full swing and many of Hooker's songs revived by UK bands, familiar oldies by his contemporaries, like Howlin' Wolf and Jimmy Reed, are making the UK Singles chart. Hooker's *Dimples* (also covered by the Animals), recorded on May 27th, 1956, climbs to UK #23. He plays it on ITV's "Ready Steady Go!".

1965

May [10] Hooker embarks on his fourth UK tour.
Nov [24-27] He plays at the "Blues Bag" at the Café Au Go Go, Greenwich Village, New York, on a bill with Muddy Waters, Otis Spann and Blues Project.

1967

Feb ***House Of The Blues***, a budget-priced reissue of tracks recorded for Chess in the early '50s, is a rare Hooker UK chart album, reaching #34.
June [8] He returns to the UK, to tour until July 2nd. Newly signed to ABC Records, recording albums for its Impulse (jazz) and Bluesway (blues) subsidiary labels, as well as ABC itself, over the next eight years, the first is ***It Serves You Right To Suffer*** followed by ***Live At The Cafe Au Go-Go*** and ***Urban Blues***, both released in 1968.

1970

Aug [11] Having released ***If You Miss 'Im...I Get 'Im*** the previous year on Bluesway, Hooker headlines the "Ann Arbor Blues & Jazz Festival", Ann Arbor, MI, with Buddy Guy, Johnny Winter and others. (By year's end, and after a messy divorce, Hooker leaves Detroit to take up residence in San Francisco, CA.)

1971

Apr Double album ***Hooker'n'Heat***, recorded with Canned Heat for Liberty Records, reaches US #73, his first US Album chart appearance.
May ***Endless Boogie***, on ABC, makes US #126.
Nov [25] Hooker embarks on his first-ever European tour, set to end on December 8th. ***Never Get Out Of These Blues Alive***, featuring musical guest Van Morrison together with Robert Hooker (organ), Elvin Bishop (piano), Charlie Musselwhite (harmonica) and Luther Tucker (guitar), will reach US #130 the following April.

1974

With his ABC contract finished, and on the verge of quitting the business altogether (to open a motel), Hooker inks a new deal with Atlantic Records, cutting albums ***Detroit Special*** and ***Don't Turn Me From Your Door***. A double album, ***The Cream***, a selection of classic songs recorded live at the Keynote club in Palo Alto, CA, will be released by the US independent blues label, Tomato Records in 1978, before Hooker, together with Lightnin' Hopkins, Big Mama Thornton and others, appears at "The Boogie'n'Blues Concert" at New York's Carnegie Hall in April the following year.

1980

June [20] "The Blues Brothers", in which Hooker has a cameo role alongside several other blues and R&B legends, including Ray Charles, James Brown and Aretha Franklin, opens. (While his music will also be featured in the 1986 Steven Spielberg directed movie "The Color Purple", Hooker will continue to tour, both solo and as part of blues-bill packages, throughout the decade.)

1988

Aged 69, and now signed to Mike Kappus' Rosebud Agency, Hooker continues to tour the US and overseas. His style, and some of his repertoire, have remained virtually unchanged over more than 30 years: the stark, fierce vocal/guitar combination still making him a unique and rare survivor among his late-'40s blues contemporaries. In mid-year, he records an album with a cast of long-time admirers, including Robert Cray, Carlos Santana, Bonnie Raitt, Los Lobos, George Thorogood and others which will emerge as ***The Healer***.

1989

July [30] Hooker performs at the 30th "Newport Folk Festival", Fort Adams State Park, Newport, on a bill featuring Emmylou Harris, Pete Seeger, John Prine, Leon Redbone, the Clancy Brothers and Theodore Bikel.

Aug [22] Hooker celebrates his 72nd birthday at the Bay Area club, Sweetwater, with Albert Collins, Robert Cray, Ry Cooder and Carlos Santana.

Sept Pete Townshend's concept album, ***The Iron Man***, featuring Hooker in a prominent character vocal role, is released.

1990

Feb [21] *I'm In The Mood*, a duet with Bonnie Raitt, wins Best Traditional Blues Recording at the 32nd annual Grammy Awards, at the Shrine Auditorium, Los Angeles, CA.

Mar [31] Having briefly entered the UK chart in 1989, the critically-revered ***The Healer***, released on the Silvertone label, now peaks at UK #63 and makes US #62, during a 38-week stay on the survey.

July [7] During a UK visit, Hooker performs at London's Hammersmith Odeon.

Oct [14] Hooker wins Best Contemporary Male Blues Artist, Blues Vocalist Of The Year, Contemporary Blues Album Of The Year for ***The Healer*** and the W.C. Handy Blues Award at the 11th annual National Blues Awards in Memphis. (He will also receive the Blues Artist Of The Year award at the Soul Beat Awards in Oakland, CA.)

[16] "A Tribute To John Lee Hooker" at Madison Square Garden, New York, is part of the nine-day Benson & Hedges Blues '90 season, with guests Gregg Allman, Joe Cocker, Albert Collins, Ry Cooder, James Cotton, Bo Diddley, Willie Dixon, Mick Fleetwood, John Hammond, Al Kooper, Huey Lewis, Charlie Musselwhite, Johnny Winter and members of Little Feat.

1991

Jan [16] Hooker is inducted into the Rock and Roll Hall of Fame at the sixth annual dinner held at the Waldorf Astoria Hotel in New York, performing *I'm In The Mood* with Bonnie Raitt and Robert Cray at the traditional event-ending jam.

Feb [2-3] He plays two sellout concerts at the Great American Music Hall, San Francisco.

Apr [22] Hooker begins the fourth annual Benson & Hedges Blues touring showcase, which will include dates in Houston, TX, Dallas, TX and Atlanta, GA., ending on June 29th, at the China Club, Los Angeles.

Sept [21] ***Mr. Lucky***, his Charisma debut, featuring Cooder, Cray, Van Morrison, Keith Richards, Carlos Santana, Johnny Winter and others, debuts at its UK #3 peak, as yet another generation of critics and audiences get hooked.

Oct [5] ***Mr. Lucky*** peaks at US #101.

1992

Mar ***Mr. Lucky*** wins the Outstanding Blues Album category at the annual Bay Area Music Awards.

Apr [12] During a current US tour, Hooker performs before a sellout crowd of 2,347 at the Adler Theatre, the River Center, Davenport, IA.

May [5] He guests on *Driftin' Blues* from John Hammond's newly released ***Got Love If You Want It*** album.

Oct [10] Hooker participates in the "All Our Colors - The Good Road Concert" benefit at the Shoreline Amphitheatre, Mountain View, CA, with Santana, Jackson Browne, Steve Miller and others.

[14] He appears on NBC-TV's "The Tonight Show".

[31] *Boom Boom* reaches UK #16, an achievement which will see Hooker incongruously guest on BBC1-TV's "Top Of The Pops".

Sept Branford Marsalis' album ***I Heard You Twice The First Time***, featuring Hooker, is released in the US.

Nov [7] At age 73, Hooker is enjoying his most commercially successful period in the UK, as ***Boom Boom***, again featuring guests Morrison and other guests including Albert Collins and Jimmie Vaughan, debuts at its UK #15 peak.

1993

Jan [16] The extracted *Boogie At Russian Hall* debuts at its UK #53 peak.

May [15] *Gloria*, teaming Hooker with Morrison, bows at its UK #31 peak.

June [12] Hooker takes part in the 20th anniversary Los Lobos concert at the Greek Theatre in Griffith Park, Los Angeles.

Oct [17] ITV's "South Bank Show" devotes today's program to Hooker.

1994

Aug Virgin releases the archive collection, ***The Legendary Modern Recordings***.

[22] In celebration of what is claimed to be his 75th birthday, Tanzania issues a limited edition stamp of Hooker, available in the US for $4.

Oct [11] As One Way Records releases ***Simply The Truth***, Hooker performs at the Wang Dang Doodle benefit for the Willie Dixon-created Blues Heaven Foundation at Los Angeles' House Of Blues club.

Nov [21-22] Hooker plays to a sellout crowd at the Arlington Theatre, Santa Barbara, CA, with Bonnie and John Raitt.

1995

Feb [11] *Chill Out (Things Gonna Change)* debuts at its UK #54 peak, during a two week chart stay.

[24] Hooker imprints his hands in cement at Hollywood's Rock Walk.

Mar [4] ***Chill Out***, featuring Carlos Santana (who co-produced), Morrison, Charles Brown and Booker T. Jones, reaches UK #23 in its week of entry.

[18] ***Chill Out*** makes US #136.

Sept [26] Capitol issues the three-CD boxed set retrospective ***Alternative Boogie***.

Oct [7] Hooker performs at the Universal Amphitheatre, Universal City, CA, sharing the bill with Robert Cray, John Mayall and Buckwheat Zydeco.

1996

Feb [28] ***Chill Out*** is named Best Traditional Blues Album at the 38th annual Grammy Awards held at the Shrine Auditorium.

THE HOOTERS

Rob Hyman (vocals, keyboards); **Eric Bazilian** (vocals, lead guitar); **John Lilley** (rhythm guitar); **Andy King** (bass); **David Uosikkinen** (drums)

1984

June Hyman and Bazilian, based in Philadelphia, PA, having already released two albums under the name Baby Grand with lead vocalist David Kagan and producer Rick Chertoff, have formed the nucleus of the Hooters in 1978 (the name taken from the nickname they gave to their keyboard harmonica), recruiting other local musicians. Releasing their debut single, the ska-tinged *Fighting On The Same Side*, and album, ***Amore***, on the local independent label in 1980, Hyman and Bazilian contributed vocals, rhythm backing and arrangement to Cyndi Lauper's 1983 maiden album, ***She's So Unusual***. They feature most notably on the current US chart-topper, *Time After Time*, which Hyman has also co-written and which coincides with the Hooters signing a major recording contract with CBS/Columbia.

1985

June [29] Their debut for Columbia, *All You Zombies*, peaks at US #58.

July [13] Due to the group's local status, it is given the privilege of opening the US segment of "Live Aid" in its native Philadelphia.

Sept Spurred by significant regional sales, label-debut album, ***Nervous Night***, climbs to US #12.

Oct [26] Second extract, *And We Danced*, waltzes to US #21 and coincides with the group's first major-venue nationwide US tour. (They will make subsequent US concert treks, supporting the likes of Don Henley, Loverboy and Squeeze.)

1986

Feb [22] *Day By Day* reaches US #18.

May [24] *Where Do The Children Go*, featuring Patty Smyth on vocals, makes US #38.

Sept [15] The Hooters perform live at the third annual MTV Video Music Awards, broadcast simultaneously from the Universal Amphitheatre, Universal City, CA, and the Palladium, New York, NY. By month's end, Bazilian and Hyman retreat to a cabin in Virginia to write songs for a follow-up album, which will be recorded in New York during the coming winter months.

1987

May Bryan Adams invites the Hooters to support him on his forthcoming tour.

Aug [29] *Johnny B* peaks at US #61.

Sept Their second Columbia album, ***One Way Home***, with Fran Smith Jr. having replaced King on bass, reaches US #27.

Oct [31] From the recent album, *Satellite*, a criticism of tele-evangelists, peaks at US #61.

1988

Jan *Satellite* reaches UK #22 but fails to lift the album into the UK chart. The follow-ups, *Karla With A K* and *Johnny B*, also fall short.

1989

Dec [16] Traditional American folk tune, *500 Miles*, with Peter, Paul & Mary guesting on vocals, makes US #97.

1990

Feb [10] Its parent album, ***Zig Zag***, peaks at US #115.

June [16] The group tapes a show at the Trump Regency Hotel, Atlantic City, NJ, for the syndicated TV series "SRO".

[26] The Hooters win the Public Choice Award and an industry award for ***Zig Zag*** at the third annual Philadelphia Music Awards, at the Academy of Music, Philadelphia.

July [21] The group takes part in Roger Waters' performance of "The Wall" at the site of the Berlin Wall in Potzdamer Platz, Berlin, Germany. The event is broadcast live throughout the world, and raises money for the Memorial Fund for Disaster Relief.

1991

Aug Hyman and Bazilian are featured on Taj Mahal's ***Like Never Before*** album.

1993

May [11] Having recently contributed to an album for the Sony Kids/Epic label to benefit Songwriters and Artists for the Earth, the Earth Island Institute and Save the Children, with fellow artists Dr. John, Lauper and Kenny Loggins, the Hooters (now comprising Bazilian, Hyman, Uosikkinen, Lilley, Smith and newcomer Mindy Jostyn) release ***Out Of Body*** on MCA, their first album of the decade, recorded at Ardent Studios in Memphis, TN. (While Sony Music will issue ***Greatest Hits 1*** he following year, Bazilian will link with Joan Osborne for her maiden album in 1995, not least writing and performing on the Grammy-nominated cut *One Of Us*.)

HOOTIE & THE BLOWFISH

Darius Rucker (lead vocals; guitar); **Mark Bryan** (guitar); **Dean Felber** (bass); **Jim "Soni" Sonefeld** (drums)

1986

Influenced not least by the music of Al Green and Kiss, Rucker (b. May 13, 1966, Charleston SC), who has sung in choirs in high school (and is currently in his university's Carolina Alive choir which performs for President Reagan) is majoring in journalism at the University of South Carolina in Columbia, SC, and now forms the Wolf Brothers with fellow student Bryan (b. May 6, 1967, Gaithersburg, MD), performing one-off shows at the local USC campus beer joint hangout, Pappy's. The pair recruits Felber (b. June 9, 1967, Bethesda, MD) the following year (a hometown childhood friend of Bryan's - they have played together in the high school band Missing In Action) who is also studying (Finance and Marketing) at USC, forming Hootie & the Blowfish (a compound of nicknames - "Hootie" (Ervin Harris) and "Blowfish" (Donald Feaster) of two friends in Rucker's university show choir) with early drummer Brantley Smith. With the band slowly building a loyal local following, Sonefeld (b. Oct. 20, 1964, Grand Rapids, MI), is recruited from the Columbia-based band Tootie & the Jones (he is also attending USC on a soccer scholarship), replacing Smith in 1989, when they also team with future manager Rusty Harmon with whom they will establish their Fishco Inc. business partnership the following year. Touring extensively around the South-eastern states (some 250 gigs a year) between 1990-1993, with early dates in Myrtle Beach, SC, Raleigh, NC, and Greensboro, SC, the group will cut two short demo tapes with producer Dick Hodgin, the debut set, the five-cut *Hootie & The Blowfish* (1990) followed by the four-track *Time* (1991) which they sell on cassette only at shows and local record stores. (In between these releases, California indie label J.R.S. Records signs the band but has to release it from a contract after eight months when it fails to bear fruit). Subsequently issuing the self-financed, six-song EP ***Kootchypop*** in July 1993, recorded at Reflections Studio, Charlotte, NC with the help of R.E.M. producer Don Dixon, which will sell some 50,000 copies through a licensing deal with Florida-based wholesaler Rock Bottom, record company interest peaks when Atlantic A&R scout Tim Sommer, attending consecutive gigs in Charleston and Columbia and impressed by ***Kootchypop*** signs the band on October 31st 1993.

1994

July [5] Their self-penned 11-track Atlantic debut, ***Cracked Rear View***, produced in Los Angeles, CA by Don Gehman, an exuberant, no-nonsense melodic rock set highlighted by Rucker's powerful rock/soul vocal style, is released in the US, its title taken from a John Hiatt song, *Learning How To Love You*.

Sept [2] Personally picked by the host after he heard the band on New York radio station WNEW-FM, the band performs on CBS-TV's "Late Show With David Letterman".

Oct [25] Hootie & the Blowfish begins a US tour opening for Big Head Todd & the Monsters at the Morris Civic Auditorium, South Bend, IN, a bill grossing $17,623 from 1,007 attendees (less than half-full capacity).

Dec [27] The band appears on NBC-TV's "Tonight Show".

[31] The group is featured on ABC-TV's "New Year's Rockin' Eve '95" performing from the Convention Center, Winston-Salem, NC.

1995

Jan [4] The group's first gig of the year is at the National Guard Armory, Chattanooga, TN grossing $17,445 from 1,163 fans.

[27] TBS-TV broadcasts "Live From The House Of Blues", featuring Hootie & the Blowfish.

Feb [18] *Hold My Hand*, featuring David Crosby on backing vocals, hits US #10, its video currently heavily rotated on both MTV and VH-1 (US).

Mar [4] *Hold My Hand* makes UK #50.

[18] Becoming a mainstay on the US survey, ***Cracked Rear View*** makes a conversely fleeting appearance on the UK chart, debuting at its #12 peak.

Apr [8] Atlantic-released ***Encomium: A Tribute To Led Zeppelin***, including Hootie's version of *Hey Hey What Can I Do*, debuts at its US #17 peak. (***18 Original Hits By 18 Unoriginal Artists***, including the band's previously unreleased *Fine Line* will be issued by Polygram the following month.)

[9] The group ends a current US tour opening for Toad The Wet Sprocket with a concert in Washington, DC.

May [5] The band makes another appearance on the "Late Show With David Letterman".

[27] ***Cracked Rear View*** tops the US chart after a ten-month chart climb, the same day *Let Her Cry* charts for a week at UK #75.

June [14] With the quartet augmented by veteran multi-instrumentalist Peter Holsapple, a further North American tour, its first as headliners, named "Summer Camp With Trucks" (also the title of a tour documentary to be released by WarnerVision in November), opens at the Salem Civic Center, VA, set to end on September 13th at the Capital City Stadium, Columbia (to be followed by small-venue European dates).

July [8] *Let Her Cry* hits US #9.

[15-16] The band performs at the "American Music Festival" on a bill with Widespread Panic, Freddy Jones Band, Brian Setzer, Todd Snider, Peter Murphy, Steve Forbert and Sonia Dada at the Winter Park Ski Area, CO, attended by 16,726 fans.

[21] Before performing tonight's gig at the Hearst Greek Theatre, University of California-Berkeley, the group appears on the "Tonight Show".

Aug [15] Currently opening for the band, singer-songwriter Ed McCain's debut album ***Honor Among Thieves***, featuring guest work from Rucker and Bryan on *Solitude*, is released in the US.

Sept [7] The group collects the trophy for Best New Artist Video ("Hold My Hand") at the 12th annual MTV Video Music Awards held at New York's Radio City Music Hall.

(During the month Reprise Records (US) releases the various artists ***Friends - The Album***, including a previously unissued Hootie cut *I Go Blind* .)

Oct [1] Hootie participates in "Farm Aid VIII", from the Cardinal Stadium, Kentucky Fair & Expo Center, Louisville, KY (which grosses $1,273,975 from a 47,044 crowd), also featuring its founder Willie Nelson, John Mellencamp, Neil Young, John Conlee, and the Dave Matthews Band among others.

[21] *Only Wanna Be With You*, its promo video including a cameo by Miami Dolphins' quarterback Dan Marino, hits US #6, the same day Rucker sings the National Anthem at Game 1 of the World Series between the Atlanta Braves and the Cleveland Indians.

[28] The band performs at the Neil Young-organized Bridge School Benefit, held at the Shoreline Amphitheatre, Mountain View, CA on a bill with Bruce Springsteen, the Pretenders, Beck, Blind Melon and Emmylou Harris.

Nov [9] The group plays at the "Boomer Esiason Heroes Foundation Concert" (a benefit to boost awareness of cystic fibrosis), at the Manhattan Center Studios, New York, NY.

[13] The RIAA certifies that ***Cracked Rear View*** has reached the 11 million sales plateau, becoming the third biggest-selling album in Atlantic Records' history.

[19] Rucker sings *The Lady Is A Tramp* at Frank Sinatra's 80th birthday bash accompanied by the band at Los Angeles' Shrine Auditorium.

[21] Rucker appears on the "Late Show With David Letterman" alongside McCain.

Dec [6] Hootie & the Blowfish perform a gospel version of *Hold My Hand* with Al Green at the 1995 **Billboard** Music Awards broadcast live on Fox-TV from New York's Coliseum, at which ***Cracked Rear View*** is named Album Of The Year.

1996

Jan [22] ***Cracked Rear View*** is now certified for 12 million US sales by the RIAA, tieing it as the third biggest-selling debut album of all-time with ***Whitney Houston*** and Meat Loaf's ***Bat Out Of Hell***.

[26] The band announces the formation of Breaking Records (with Atlantic) to feature new signings, a label to be headed by Harmon.

[27] *Time* reaches US #14.

[30] Manager Harmon and band members file suit in US District Court in Los Angeles against Haim Mizrahi claiming infringement of copyright and seeking an injunction against the marketing and reproduction of its masters. At issue are the 15 recordings originally included on the pre-Atlantic cassette releases *Hootie & The Blowfish* and *Time* and the 1993 EP ***Kootchypop***. (Mizrahi's case will prove to be without merit.) Later in the day, Hootie wins the Favorite New Artist category at the 23rd annual American Music Awards held at Los Angeles' Shrine Auditorium. (Garth Brooks, having been named Favorite Artist Of The Year leaves his trophy on the podium saying: "With all due respect to the people who voted, I'm gonna leave this right here." Explaining his actions backstage, Brooks insists that Hootie should have won instead.)

Feb [28] Hootie performs *Old Man & Me* at the 38th annual Grammy Awards held at Los Angeles' Shrine Auditorium, at which they also collect the Best New Artist and Best Pop Vocal Performance by a Duo or Group (*Let Her Cry*) trophies.

Apr [20] The group's own online web-site premieres on "http://www.atlantic.records.com/hootie".

[22] MTV (US) premieres the band's "Unplugged" performance, taped on the 19th at its former campus, the University of South Carolina.

[23] On a day when the group once again performs on the "Late Show With David Letterman" and having renegotiated its deal with the label, Atlantic Records releases ***Fairweather Johnson*** which includes guest Nanci Griffith on *Earth Stopped Cold At Dawn* and *She Crawls Away*, a song written about Rucker's baby daughter. With shared songwriting credits, the 14 cuts have been chosen from 21 tracks recorded once again with producer Don Gehman.

[27] The album's first single, *Old Man & Me*, a reworking of a song which appeared on ***Kootchypop***, debuts on the Hot 100 at US #28. It is also available as the band's first enchanced multi-media E-CD at $3.49, and includes a full video clip of the single plus the previously unissued *Before The Heartache Rolls In*. (Following its release, the band heads to Europe for a six-week tour beginning in May, not least due to the fact that their previous album only sold one million copies outside the States, followed by scheduled US dates beginning in July.)

MARY HOPKIN

1968

May After singing in her local Congregational Tabernacle choir since the age of four, before performing as a teenager at folk clubs and on regular spots on Welsh TV, Hopkin (b. May 3, 1950, Pontardawe, Wales), has made her first recording, *Llais Swynol Mary Hopkin*, a Welsh language EP, for the regional Cambrian label in 1967. Now winning the ITV talent show "Opportunity Knocks", Hopkin is spotted by model Twiggy, who recommends her to Paul McCartney, and he signs her to the Beatles' newly-formed Apple label.

Aug [27] The McCartney-produced *Those Were The Days*, written by Gene Raskin, and based on the melody of the traditional Russian folk song *Darogoi Dlimmoyo*, first recorded in the 1920s by Alexander Wertinsky, launches Apple in the UK alongside the Beatles' own *Hey Jude*.

Sept [25] *Those Were The Days* replaces *Hey Jude* at UK #1, topping the chart for the first of six weeks (the first female to do so this year) and eventually selling over 750,000 copies.

Oct During the month Hopkin makes her debut on CBS-TV's "The Ed Sullivan Show", singing *Those Were The Days*.

Nov [2] *Those Were The Days* hits US #2, where it will stay for three weeks, behind the Beatles' *Hey Jude*, and becomes a million seller. (Hopkin also records the song in Spanish, French, German, Italian and Hebrew and, by early 1969, the cumulative worldwide sales will exceed eight million.)

1969

Mar ***Post Card***, produced by McCartney and including covers of songs written by Harry Nilsson and Donovan among others, hits UK #3.

[21] Hopkin begins her maiden UK tour, with headliner Engelbert Humperdinck, at the Gaumont Cinema, Worcester, Worcs., set to end on April 12th at the Odeon Cinema, Manchester, Lancs.

Apr [19] *Goodbye*, written and produced by McCartney, hits UK #2. Hopkin meets her future husband, record producer Tony Visconti, while recording more foreign-language versions of her songs. During he month she also records the movie theme to "Where's Jack?" for Paramount Pictures.

May [31] *Goodbye* reaches US #13, while ***Post Card*** makes US #28.

Dec Hopkin stars in the pantomime "Dick Whittington" at the London Palladium, with Tommy Steele.

1970

Feb [21] *Temma Harbour*, produced by Mickie Most, hits UK #6. Hopkin appears on Cilla Black's BBC1-TV show, singing six songs, from which the UK's entry for the 1970 Eurovision Song Contest will be selected.

Mar [28] *Temma Harbour* makes US #39.

Apr [4] *Knock Knock Who's There*, having been selected as the UK Eurovision entry, hits UK #2. (The contest is won by Eire's entry, Dana's *All Kinds Of Everything*.)

Aug [1] Her McCartney-produced revival of Doris Day's *Que Sera, Sera (Whatever Will Be, Will Be)* climbs to US #77.

Nov [14] *Think About Your Children*, penned by Hot Chocolate's Errol Brown, reaches UK #19 and will make US #87 on Dec [12].

1971

July *Let My Name Be Sorrow* makes UK #46.

Oct Hopkin's own favorite recording, ***Earth Song - Ocean Song***, produced by Visconti and including contributions from Ralph McTell and Dave Cousins of the Strawbs, is released.

Dec *Water, Paper And Clay* is her last release on Apple and fails to chart. Hopkin marries Visconti, and will work with him through the '70s, often singing back-up vocals on his productions for David Bowie and others.

1972

Aug A UK single recorded for Bell Records with Visconti, under the name Hobby Horse, reviving the Jamies' 1958 US hit, *Summertime Summertime*, is released.

Nov Compilation, ***Those Were The Days***, collecting the Apple singles, is released.

Dec The seasonal *Mary Had A Baby* is released in the UK on Regal Zonophone. (Hopkin is herself pregnant at the time, and a son, Morgan, is born shortly afterwards.)

[23] *Knock Knock Who's There* makes US #92.

1977

May After *If You Love Me*, recorded for Visconti's Good Earth label, has made UK #32 on Apr [3] the previous year, *Wrap Me In Your Arms*, also on Good Earth, is released. Hopkin features - with various artists - on a Chrysalis fantasy concept album, ***The King Of Elfland's Daughter***, and takes lead vocal on the extracted *Lirazell* and *Beyond The Fields We Know*.

1981

Oct After devoting time to her family, Hopkin has teamed with Mike Hurst (ex-Springfields) and Mike D'Albuquerque (ex-ELO) as Sundance, a harmony trio, which has signed to Bronze Records the previous year and now releases *What's Love*. The group supports Dr. Hook on a UK tour, after which Hopkin and Sundance part company (she is replaced by former beauty queen Mary Stavin). Her marriage to Visconti ends, and a relationship with Dr. Hook vocalist Dennis Locorriere develops.

1984

May She returns to the UK chart as lead vocalist with Oasis, a group which includes Peter Skellern on piano and vocals and Julian Lloyd Webber on cello. Their debut album for WEA, ***Oasis***, reaches UK #23, although the unit will not continue on a permanent basis partly because Hopkin becomes ill and leaves in advance of a planned tour. In 1984 she will participate with other artists in an EMI recording of Dylan Thomas' **Under Milk Wood**, produced by George Martin.

1991

July [14] Having released a comeback album, ***Spirit***, on the Filmtrax label in 1989, Hopkin now makes her return to the stage, as part of "The Chieftains Music Festival 1991" at the London Palladium. The following year sees the reissue of her original albums, recorded for Apple at the beginning of her career, bringing her most successful work to compact disc.

BRUCE HORNSBY

1978

Having excelled at basketball and piano in high school, practised his keyboard skills at home on the family's Steinway grand, been a member, as a teenager, of a Grateful Dead-covers band, Bobby Hightest & the Octave Kids, with his brother, and studied music at the University of Miami, Coral Gables, FL, and the Berklee School of Music, Boston, MA, Hornsby (b. Bruce Randall Hornsby, Nov. 23, 1954, Williamsburg, VA), whose father played saxophone in his uncle's band, Sherwood Hornsby & the Rhythm Boys, forms a home-town group, the Bruce Hornsby Band, with his older brother Bobby and a drummer friend, John Molo, and begins playing endless bars and lounges around the Southern states. He also begins seven years of recording demo tapes of his newly-written material, sending them regularly to record companies.

1980

At the invitation of Michael McDonald, who has been impressed by a performance he has seen at a Steak & Ale Bar, Hornsby moves to Los Angeles, CA, with his brother John, where both work for three years at 20th Century Fox Publishing, writing production-line pop songs. They have been directed there with the help of McDonald and his fellow Doobie Brother Jeff Baxter, who has set up a showcase for the Hornsby siblings attended by 20th Century Fox executive, Ronnie Vance.

1982

In Hollywood, Hornsby has met Huey Lewis, who is impressed by his writing and playing abilities, and has made demos with producer David Foster. He becomes friends with Lewis but, hoping his own success will come shortly, Hornsby turns down Lewis' request to include a Hornsby composition, *Let The Girls Rock*, on his forthcoming album, ***Sports***. The following year, Hornsby, recommended as a keyboardist by friend and bass player Joe Puerta, is invited to join the backing band being formed for a lengthy US tour by Sheena Easton.

1985

Years of writing, recording and submitting dozens of demo tapes to over 70 record companies finally pay off when Hornsby and his newly-formed band, the Range - David Mansfield (violin, mandolin, guitar); George Marinelli (guitar, vocals); Joe Puerta (bass, vocals); John Molo (drums), managed by Tim Neece, are signed worldwide to RCA Records, having recently turned down an offer from new-age label, Windham Hill.

1986

Aug [23] His chart debut with the Range, *Every Little Kiss*, peaks at US #72. (The group begins its first full US tour and when ***The Way It Is*** is released, with radio instantly attracted to its title cut, dates begin selling out.)

Sept [6] *The Way It Is* also receives immediate UK radio attention and reaches UK #15. ***The Way It Is***, which includes three tracks produced by Lewis, climbs to UK #16.

Oct Hornsby & the Range tour the UK opening for Huey Lewis & the News, and make a strong impact on BBC1-TV's primetime show "Wogan".

Dec [13] *The Way It Is*, a self-written song addressing the race issue, and led by Hornsby's distinctive piano style, hits #1 for a week, after a steady climb on the US chart since September. It remains charted for 22 weeks.

1987

Jan [31] Hornsby & the Range are the musical guests on NBC-TV's "Saturday Night Live".

Feb [24] They win Best New Artist at the 29th annual Grammy Awards.

Mar [14] Huey Lewis & the News top the US chart with the tele-evangelist-criticizing *Jacob's Ladder*, written by Bruce and John Hornsby in the summer of 1985. The track is relegated to a B-side in the UK.

[21] *Mandolin Rain* hits US #4, while ***The Way It Is***, after a six-month US chart climb, hits #3. Mostly co-produced by Horsnby with Elliot Scheiner, its self-written (often with brother John) melodic rock tracks showcase the already seasoned skills of the Range, whose line-up comprises Mansfield, Marinelli, Molo and Puerta.

Apr *The Way It Is* receives an ASCAP Award as the Most Played Song Of The Year, while *Mandolin Rain* charts briefly, at UK #70.

July [11] A remixed *Every Little Kiss* reaches US #14. With his distinctive keyboard style increasingly in demand, Hornsby guests on Clannad's ***Sirius***, and on country performer Tom Wopat's latest recording.

Oct The band begins work on its sophomore album, with Neil Dorfsman sharing production credits with Hornsby. Peter Harris replaces Mansfield in the Range.

1988

May [28] ***Scenes From The Southside***, a musical biography of the Hornsby brothers' adolescence in the South, and including their own version of *Jacob's Ladder*, reaches UK #18.

June ***Scenes From The Southside***, hits US #5.

July [2] *The Valley Road* hits US #5, having made UK #44.

Sept [3] *Look Out Any Window*, extracted from ***Scenes From The Southside***, reaches US #35. Also an accomplished accordian player, Hornsby contributes to albums by Patti Austin (***The Real Me***), Kim Carnes (***View From The House***) and Huey Lewis (***Small World***) during the year.

1989

Aug [26] *The End Of The Innocence*, a collaborative songwriting and production effort by Hornsby for Don Henley, a recording also underpinned by his hallmark piano playing, hits US #8.

Dec Hornsby guests on new Columbia signing Shawn Colvin's debut effort, ***Steady On*** (US #112), a favor she will return for Hornsby's third album. Hornsby will also appear on her second album, ***Fat City***, in 1993.

1990

Feb [21] *The Valley Road*, a collaboration with the Nitty Gritty Dirt Band on the latter's ***Will The Circle Be Unbroken, Vol. 2***, wins the Best Bluegrass Recording category at the 32nd annual Grammy Awards, at the Shrine Auditorium, Los Angeles.

[23] Herbie Hancock recruits Bruce Hornsby and others for a taping of Showtime-TV's "Coast To Coast" show at Los Angeles' China club.

Apr [7] Hornsby performs *The End Of Innocence* with Henley at "Farm Aid IV".

[21] The band appears at an Earth Day eve "A Performance For The Planet" concert at the Merriweather Post Pavilion, Columbia, MD, on a bill with Indigo Girls, Michael Stipe, Natalie Merchant, Billy Bragg and others.

July [28] Currently touring the US with the Cowboy Junkies in support, ***A Night On The Town***, co-

produced with Don Gehman and featuring Colvin, Bela Fleck, Jerry Garcia and David Lasley as music guests, reaches US #20, becoming the band's third RIAA-certified gold album, having already made UK #27 on June [30]. It showcases a harder guitar-based style, relying less on Hornsby's distinctive piano treats.
Aug [16] RCA announces that Hornsby "has responded affirmatively to a request from his longtime friends (the Grateful Dead) to help them through this difficult period", with reference to Hornsby playing dates with the band following the death of their keyboard player, Brent Mydland. He will perform with the band at Madison Square Garden (September 15th-20th) and at subsequent venues.
[18] First single from the current album, *Across The River*, featuring the Grateful Dead's Jerry Garcia, reaches US #18.
Sept [11] Hornsby guests on NBC-TV's "Late Night With David Letterman".
Oct [1] A four-concert UK tour begins at the Hippodrome, Birmingham, W. Midlands, with further dates at London's Town & Country Club and Hammersmith Odeon, and Manchester's Apollo Theatre.
Nov [3] Ballad, *Lost Soul*, with Hornsby and Shawn Colvin duetting, peaks at US #84.
[17] Hornsby & the Range play a sellout show at William & Mary Hall, William & Mary College in Williamsburg, Hornsby's hometown. (As Hornsby continues to contribute to other projects, guesting on albums for the Cowboy Junkies, Tommy Conwell, Marti Jones and Jimmy Barnes, among the others, the group's song *Set Me In Motion* is featured in the movie "Backdraft".)

1991

Feb [10] Hornsby performs an instrumental rendition of the American national anthem, with Branford Marsalis, at the NBA All-Star game in Charlotte, NC.
Mar ***The Way It Is*** is certified multi platinum by the RIAA for three million sales.
[9] The Peace Choir, with Hornsby one of its many luminaries, makes US #54 with its Lenny Kravitz-engineered *Give Peace A Chance*.
Apr [20] Hornsby takes part in the "Earth Day 1991 Concert" at Foxboro Stadium, Foxborough, MA, with Billy Bragg, Jackson Browne, Rosanne Cash, Bruce Cockburn, Indigo Girls, Queen Latifah, Ziggy Marley, Willie Nelson and 10,000 Maniacs. 18-year old cancer sufferer Gregg Wolfson of Salem, MA, plays keyboards with the band as part of a dream-come-true arrangement organized by the Starlight Foundation of Boston. He will succumb to his illness on July 3rd.
May [11] Hornsby adds his autograph to a $12,000 Young Chang grand piano being auctioned at the Peabody Hotel, Orlando, FL, to raise money for the "Give Kids The World" charity foundation.
June [12] Hornsby is named Keyboard Player Of The Year at the third annual International Rock Awards at London's Docklands Arena.
July Bonnie Raitt's ***Luck Of The Draw***, featuring Hornsby's distinctive ivory playing on the extracted single *I Can't Make You Love Me*, is released.
Sept [19] Berklee School Of Music alumnus Hornsby is honored at the Spasso Café & Bar in Boston for his work with the Starlight Foundation.
[20] Hornsby contributes to NBC-TV's "A Comedy Salute To Michael Jordan" special.
Oct [18] He performs on keyboards at the "Guitar Legends Festival" in Seville, Spain.
Nov [13] Hornsby plays at KISS Radio DJ Matt Siegel's tenth anniversary party at the Avalon, Boston, appearing with Aaron Neville and Roberta Flack. (His guest appearances during the year include contributions to Robbie Robertson's ***Storyville***, Bob Seger's ***The Fire Inside*** and Squeeze's ***Play***.)

1992

Jan [11] ***Two Rooms : Celebrating The Songs Of Elton John And Bernie Taupin***, including Hornsby's reading of *Madman Across The Water*, reaches US #18.
[30] Twin sons, Russell Ives Hornsby and Keith Randall Hornsby, are born in Richmond, VA.
Aug [7] Recorded with Branford Marsalis specifically for the 1992 Olympics TV coverage, Hornsby's *Twenty Nine-Five* airs over the long-jump competition segment of NBC's night-time broadcast of the 1992 Olympic Games. (The title refers to the distance needed to break Bob Beamon's existing record.)
Oct [11] Hornsby performs at an Elizabeth Taylor AIDS Foundation benefit at New York, NY's Madison Square Garden, with Elton John, George Michael and Lionel Richie.
[22] He co-headlines a free concert with Linda Ronstadt, held for presidential candidate Bill Clinton, at the Pacific Amphitheatre, Costa Mesa, CA.
Nov Leon Russell's recording return ***Anything Can Happen***, co-produced and co-written with Hornsby, is released by Virgin. (It is one of some 50 albums that Hornsby, as a top collaborator, has contributed to in the past three years. Others include sets by Bob Dylan, Liquid Jesus, Willie Nelson, Phil Collins, Stevie Nicks, Sting and Crosby, Stills & Nash.)

1993

Jan His Olympics-contributed song, *Twenty Nine-Five*, is made ineligible for consideration as Best Pop Instrumental by NARAS at the forthcoming Grammy Awards, since the organization claims that the track was only made available on a free promotional compact disc as part of Coca-Cola's Olympics advertising campaign and was never commercially issued, thus invalidating its nomination status.
[20] Hornsby participates in the Arkansas Ball at the Presidential inaugural celebrations.
May [1] Recorded at his home studio in Williamsburg, Hornsby's fourth outing, ***Harbor Lights***, reaches US #46, minus the Range for the first time. The jazz-inflected set includes musical guests Phil Collins, Jerry Garcia, Branford Marsalis, Pat Metheny, and Bonnie Raitt, who duets on *Rainbow Cadillac*. The album's cover artwork is a 1951 painting by Hornsby's grandfather's cousin, 20th century expressionist painter Edward Hopper.
[3] Hornsby guests on NBC-TV's "The Tonight Show".
[8] ***Harbor Lights*** bows at its UK #32 peak.
[21] He appears on NBC-TV's "Late Night With David Letterman".
June [8] Hornsby is showcased on VH-1-TV's "Center Stage".
[21] During a brief UK visit, Hornsby performs at the Camden Jazz Café, London.
Nov [27] *Fields Of Gray* peaks at US #69.
Dec [2] Hornsby guests on CBS-TV's "Late Show With David Letterman".
[3] He plays a sellout date at the Orpheum Theatre, Boston.

1994

Jan [19] Hornsby inducts the Grateful Dead into the Rock and Roll Hall of Fame at the ninth annual dinner at New York's Waldorf Astoria, and backs Etta James on *Wang Dang Doodle* at the perfunctory after-dinner jam.
Feb [4] He guests on "The Tonight Show".
[19] Hornsby takes part in the Jackson Family Honors at the MGM Grand Hotel, Las Vegas, NV.
Mar [1] Hornsby wins the Best Pop Instrumental category with Branford Marsalis for *Barcelona Mona* at the 36th annual Grammy Awards at New York's Radio City Music Hall.
[31] He participates in a benefit concert for the University of Miami School at the Dade County Auditorium, Miami, FL.
Aug [3-4] On a current US tour supporting Raitt, Hornsby plays at Radio City Music Hall.
[13] Hornsby joins the Band onstage at "Woodstock II" on Winston Farm, Saugerties, NY.
Nov [9] His US tour with Raitt ends at the Coliseum, North Charleston, SC.

1995

Jan [21] He takes part in a benefit for Voters For Choice at Constitution Hall, Washington, with Rickie Lee Jones, Shawn Colvin and Bruce Cockburn.
Apr [1] Hornsby performs the national anthem prior to the Boston Celtics vs. Miami Heat basketball game at Boston Garden.
[22] He participates in an Earth Day benefit in Washington.
May [4] Hornsby performs a benefit solo performance at the Carpenter Center, Richmond, VA for the Virginia Special Olympics.
[6] He plays another benefit, this time at the Harrison Opera House in Norfolk, VA, in aid of the Chesapeake Bay Foundation.
June [7] Hornsby performs the national anthem at the first game of the NBA Championships in Orlando, FL, between the Orlando Magic and the Houston Rockets.
Aug [5] Further showcasing his jazz leanings and again released as a solo set, ***Hot House***, including contributions from Jerry Garcia, Bela Fleck, Pat Metheny and Chaka Khan and promoted via 14 venue in-store performances at US multi-media stores, debuts at its US #68 peak.
[11] He attends Jerry Garcia's funeral at St. Stephen's Episcopal Church in Belvedere, CA.
Sept [2] As Hornsby co-writes and plays on Chaka Khan's new single *Love Me Still*, from the movie "Clockers", he leads a jam session of Grateful Dead's *Scarlet Begonias* and *Northbound Train* at the Concert for the Rock and Roll Hall of Fame at Cleveland Stadium, Cleveland, OH.
[6] Hornsby and Branford Marsalis perform the national anthem before the Baltimore Orioles game at Camden Yards, as Orioles shortstop Cal Ripken Jr. passes Lou Gehrig's consecutive games-played record of 2,130 games.
[16] Taken from ***Hot House***, *Walk In The Sun* makes US #54.
[29] Hornsby guests on NBC-TV's "The Tonight Show".
Dec [3] "Bruce Hornsby And Friends" TV special, including duets with Henley, Raitt, Metheny and Bob Weir, airs on PBS-TV's "In The Spotlight" series.
[8] He takes part in the KISS FM's Christmas Party at Boston's Hard Rock Café.

1996

Jan [3] Hornsby guests again on the "Late Show With David Letterman". (***West Side Story***, an all-star update of the famous musical to which he has contributed *Cool*, with Patti Austin, Mervyn Warren, will be released in the US the following month.)
June Hornsby embarks on a US summer tour billed as "Deadapalooza", with Mickey Hart's new band Mystery Box and Bob Weir's new outfit Ratdog, also with Los Lobos.

HOT CHOCOLATE

Errol Brown (vocals); **Tony Wilson** (bass, vocals); **Harvey Hinsley** (guitar); **Larry Ferguson** (keyboards); **Patrick Olive** (percussion); **Tony Connor** (drums)

1970

Aug The group has been formed in Brixton, London, by songwriters Brown (b. Nov. 12, 1948, Kingston, Jamaica) and Wilson (b. Oct. 8, 1947, Trinidad), their first recording - in 1969 - being a reggae-styled adaptation (with his agreement) of John Lennon's *Give Peace A Chance*, a one-off release on the Beatles' Apple label. Given the name the Hot Chocolate Band by the label's Mavis Smith, the line-up is rounded out with session musicians, including Olive (b. Mar. 22, 1947, Grenada), Ferguson (b. Apr. 14, 1948, Nassau, Bahamas), drummer Ian King and guitarist Franklyn De Allie. The group signs to Mickie Most's RAK Records, after Brown and Wilson have approached the label head with three of their songs. Most agrees that *Bet Yer Life I Do* is ideal for Herman's Hermits, takes *Think About Your Children* for Mary Hopkin and suggests that Hot Chocolate (to which the name is now shortened) record the remaining cut, *Love Is Life*. The band, which will remain on RAK, under Most's production guidance, well into the '80s, now makes its live debut at the Nevada Ballroom, Bolton, Lancs.

Sept *Love Is Life* hits UK #6 and introduces the group's trademark sound, characterized by Brown's distinctive pop/soul voice and his attention-grabbing image, in the form of his shaved head.

Oct Hinsley (b. Jan. 19, 1948, Northampton, Northants.), ex-Cliff Bennett's Rebel Rousers, whose session work on Herman's Hermits' *Bet Your Life I Do* leads to an invitation to join Hot Chocolate on guitar, replaces the departed De Allie.

1971

Apr Follow-up, *You Could Have Been a Lady*, reaches UK #22, while *I Believe (In Love)* hits UK #8 in September and *You'll Always Be A Friend* peaks at UK #23 in November concluding a successful singles-chart year for the band.

1973

Mar Connor (b. Apr. 6, 1947, Romford, Essex), ex-Madisons, Audience and Jackson Heights (and currently a window cleaner), replaces King on drums.

May A further Brown/Wilson composition, *Brother Louie*, lyrically themed on inter-racial love and racism, hits UK #7.

Aug *Rumours* makes UK #44, while the Stories' cover version of *Brother Louie* tops the US chart. Hot Chocolate signs to the MAM agency for live work (and will play a UK tour approximately every 18 months).

1974

Apr *Emma* hits UK #3 and is featured on the band's forthcoming Most produced debut album, ***Cicero Park***, released in June. A further extract, *Cheri Babe*, makes UK #31 in December.

1975

Apr [26] Released in the US by Big Tree Records, *Emma* hits US #8 and spurs ***Cicero Park*** to make US #55.

July [19] Having already peaked at UK #11 in June, the horn-heavy *Disco Queen* reaches US #28.

Sept *A Child's Prayer* hits UK #7.

Nov Wilson leaves to sign a solo deal with Bearsville Records, while percussionist Olive takes over on bass. [29] Funk/pop outing *You Sexy Thing* hits UK #2.

Dec [6] ***Hot Chocolate*** becomes their first UK chart album, making #34.

1976

Feb [7] *You Sexy Thing* hits US #3 and will remain the group's biggest US hit, selling over one million copies.

[14] It also heats up ***Hot Chocolate***, which peaks at UK #41.

Apr [17] *Don't Stop It Now* reaches UK #11 and will make US #42 on May [15], followed by the UK #14 peaking *Man To Man* on July [30]. Its parent album ***Man To Man*** will reach UK #32 on Aug [7], climbing to US #172 on Oct [2].

Dec [4] While *Heaven Is The Back Seat Of My Cadillac* has stopped at UK #25 in September, the first of many successful compilations, ***Hot Chocolate 14 Greatest Hits***, hits UK #6, selling 500,000 copies in the UK alone.

1977

July [2] *So You Win Again*, a rare outside composition for the group written by Russ Ballard, proves to be its biggest UK hit, topping the chart.

Sept [10] *So You Win Again* makes US #31, while *Put Your Love In Me* hits UK #10 in December.

1978

Apr Brown-inked *Every 1's A Winner* reaches UK #12.

[29] Its parent album, ***Every 1's A Winner***, makes UK #30.

Dec Piano-led ballad, *I'll Put You Together Again*, written by Don Black and Geoff Stephens for the musical "Dear Anyone", reaches UK #13.

1979

Feb [10] *Every 1's A Winner*, released via a new deal with Infinity Records in the US, hits #6 and earns the group a second gold disc for one million-plus sales, while its parent album reaches US #31.

June *Mindless Boogie*, the group's first UK 12" single, dances to UK #46.

July The group undertakes its first headlining US tour, comprising 12 auditorium dates, followed by a 45-date UK trek.

Aug [11] *Going Through The Motions* peaks at UK and US #53, with ***Going Through The Motions*** making US #112. The group follows its UK tour with a lengthy concert trek of Europe, including a string of dates in Germany, where they are particularly popular.

1980

Jan [5] A second TV-advertised compilation, ***20 Hottest Hits***, hits UK #3 and is another half-million seller.

June *No Doubt About It*, written for the group by Steve Glen, Mike Burns and Mickie Most's brother Dave, about a real-life UFO sighting by Glen and Burns, hits UK #2.

Aug *Are You Getting Enough Of What Makes You Happy* reaches UK #17. It is taken from ***Class*** which also yields *Love Me To Sleep*, which drops off at UK #50. *You'll Never Be So Wrong* will peak at UK #52 the following June.

1982

May Again produced by Mickie Most, and restoring Hot Chocolate to the UK Top 10 (for the tenth time), *Girl Crazy* hits #7 and is followed by the equally radio-ready, young-love themed *It Started With A Kiss*, which hits UK #5 in August. Both are Brown compositions.

Oct [9] *Chances* makes UK #32, a week after its parent album, ***Mystery***, reaches UK #24.

1983

Jan [15] *Are You Getting Enough Happiness*, released in the US after the group signs to EMI America, peaks at US #65, but closes the band's US chart career.

June *What Kinda Boy You Looking For (Girl)* hits UK #10, while yet another Brown composition, *Tears On The Telephone*, makes UK #37 in October.

Nov [1] The band embarks on a major UK tour.

1984

Mar *I Gave You My Heart (Didn't I)* reaches UK #13, and is the last new recording by Hot Chocolate to chart. It marks the end of a 14-year association with Most and the RAK label, a combination which has yielded an impressive tally of 30 UK chart singles.

1987

Feb Dutch disco DJ and mix-master, Ben Liebrand, has created a new dance remix of the group's *You Sexy Thing*, adding '80s percussion and rhythm tracks to the original recording which hits UK #10.

Mar [14] 16-track, TV-advertised compilation, ***The Very Best Of Hot Chocolate***, tops the UK chart with sales of half a million. As a third retrospective, it continues the chart tradition that the group's only commercially successful albums are hit collections.

Apr A "Groove Mix" retread of *Every 1's A Winner*, again created by Liebrand, peaks at UK #69.

May After a lengthy silence and confirmation that Hot Chocolate has split, Brown signs to WEA Records as a solo artist, initially working with producers Tony Swain and Steve Jolley.

Aug His *Personal Touch* reaches UK #25 while the follow-up *Body Rockin'*, produced by Richard James Burgess, will peak at UK #51 in December.

1990

Dec Having released his debut solo album ***That's How Love Is*** in February the previous year, and now tipped by producer Pete Waterman as the UK Christmas chart-topper, Brown's *Send A Prayer*, produced by the Stock/Aitken/Waterman hit-machine, fails to chart. (A reissued *It Started With A Kiss* will reaches UK #31 on Mar [20] 1993, one week before a fourth Hot Chocolate hits collection, ***Their Greatest Hits***, tops the UK chart.)

THE HOUSEMARTINS

Norman Cook (vocals); **Paul Heaton** (vocals, guitar); **Stan Cullimore** (bass); **Hugh Whitaker** (drums)

1984

Based around Heaton (b. May 9, 1962, Birkenhead, Lancs.), who has arrived in the town after a year of travelling around Europe, the band comes together in its permanent home of Hull, Humberside. In typically low-key fashion, Heaton places a postcard in his front-room window, requesting young musicians to get in touch with him. Cullimore (b. Apr. 6, 1962, Hull), who lives in the same street, responds, while drumme Whitaker and vocalist Ted Key are recruited from Hull band the Gargoyles. The group gains local live experience, then tours widely for seven months, playing small gigs throughout the UK, many of which support left-wing political causes including miners' support groups and CND, eventually coming to the attention of record labels.

1985

July [21] The band performs *Drop Down Dead*, among other tracks, on BBC Radio 1's the "John Peel Show".

Oct The Housemartins sign to Andy McDonald's Go! Discs label in London, who are impressed with their demo tape songs, *Flag Day* and *Sitting On The Fence*, and, in typically dry and self-effacing comic fashion, an enduring band trait, the Housemartins are promoted as "the fourth best band in Hull". Their debut single, *Flag Day*, produced by Jeffrey Wood and recorded at the end of June, is released (and will amass total sales in New Zealand of 60 copies).

Nov Cook (b. Quentin Cook, July 31, 1963, Brighton, E. Sussex), an ex-club DJ from Brighton, E. Sussex, replaces Key, who departs to open a vegetarian restaurant in Hull.

1986

Feb During early touring on "The Twisted Roadshow", the band, claiming poverty, helps pay for National Travel bus passes by collecting Mars bar wrappers with promotion coupons, and introduces "Adopt-A-Housemartin": wherever the band is playing, members of the audience are requested to invite band members to stay at their home for the night, thus saving the band hotel bills.

Mar Originally recorded as a B-side but let out of the pen as a single, *Sheep* is the band's chart debut, making UK #54.

June [20-22] The Housemartins appear at the annual three-day "Glastonbury Festival", Somerset, alongside the Cure, the Pogues, Lloyd Cole and others.

[28] Originally titled *French England*, but finally released as *Happy Hour*, and helped by strong airplay and an inventive semi-animated promotional video showing the band in a similar light to early Madness promos, the Heaton/Cullimore composition hits UK #3 (and will prove to be the group's finest hour in New Zealand, with some 600 copies sold).

July [5] Debut album, the self-penned ***London 0 Hull 4***, a soccer score title play on the band's continual promotion of its home town and provincial working-class pride, hits UK #3. (The album will climb to US #124 in a year's time.)

Sept [30] The group begins a UK tour in Birmingham, W. Midlands.

Nov [1] Further showcasing Heaton and Cullimore's lyrical ingenuity, their *Think For A Minute* ballad, also showcasing the band's penchant for melodic harmony, reaches UK #18.

Dec [20] With two well-timed UK TV specials heavily plugging their new single, the group tops the UK chart at Christmas with its biggest seller, an a cappella version of Isley Jasper Isley's *Caravan Of Love* (the original reached US #51 and UK #52 the previous December). An a cappella vocal set supporting the Housemartins on their UK tour is merely the band's alter-ego unit.
[27] Boxed-set, ***The Housemartins' Christmas Singles Box***, spends a week at UK #84.

1987

Feb [9] The group wins the Best British Newcomer category at the sixth annual BRIT Awards, at London's Grosvenor House Hotel.
Mar The popular UK tabloid press reveals that some members of the band are both gay and affluent and not the cheeky, affable, working-class lads from Hull they pertain to be. The most "scandalous" claim is that Cook's real name is Quentin and that he is from the relatively wealthy South instead of the North, as his image suggests.
June *Five Get Over Excited*, reaching UK #11, is the first release featuring drummer Dave Hemmingway (b. Sept. 20, 1960, Hull), who was recruited from local Hull band the Velvetones to replace Whitaker, who quit due to ideological differences with his colleagues. The group appears at a number of "Red Wedge" concerts, a music collective devoted to encouraging the young left-wing vote in the run-up to the UK General Election.
Sept [12] *Me And The Farmer* reaches UK #15.
Oct [3] ***The People Who Grinned Themselves To Death***, co-produced by the group with John Williams, and featuring musical guests Pete Wingfield and trumpet player Guy Barker, hits UK #9.
Dec [5] *Build* reaches UK #15.

1988

Jan Announcing that the group intends to split, and claiming that the Housemartins was only planned as a three-year project, its management releases this statement: "In an age of Rick Astley, Shakin' Stevens and the Pet Shop Boys, quite simply they weren't good enough."
May [7] *There Is Always Something There To Remind Me* (not a cover of Sandie Shaw's 1964 hit but a new song by Heaton and Cullimore, taken from a BBC Radio 1 session) is their swan-song chart single, reaching UK #35.
[21] Double album, ***Now That's What I Call Quite Good***, a 24-track compilation of hits, rarities and out-takes, is the band's farewell score, at UK #8.

1989

May Heaton launches his new outfit, the Beautiful South, named with typical sarcasm, with fellow ex-Housemartin Hemmingway, bassist Sean Welch, singer and co-writer David Rotheray, vocalist Briana Corrigan, ex-Anthill Runaways, and drummer, former Housemartin roadie, David Stead. Cook, already finding parallel success as a dance-record remixer, using his club DJ background to retread releases by James Brown, Nitro Deluxe and Eric B. & Rakim among others, will score two hits by year's end (*Won't Talk About It/Blame It On The Bassline*, UK #29, and *For Spacious Lies*, UK #48), eventually going on to form the floating dance troupe Beats International, whose April 1990 UK #17 album debut, ***Let Them Eat Bingo***, contains the earlier UK #1, *Dub Be Good To Me* (a cover of the S.O.S. Band's *Just Be Good To Me*) and the subsequent UK #9, *Won't Talk About It*, and UK #51, *Burundi Blues*, before forming Freak Power in 1993.

1992

Aug The band's original drummer, Hugh Whitaker, is remanded in custody for allegedly assaulting James Hewitt with an axe and setting fire to his house on three occasions between August 1990 and August 1991. (He will be found guilty in May, 1993, and sentenced to six years in prison.)
see also: **THE BEAUTIFUL SOUTH**

WHITNEY HOUSTON

1983

Clive Davis, founding head of Arista Records, sees and hears potential in Houston (b. Aug. 9, 1963, Newark, NJ) at a Manhattan, New York, NY showcase arranged by Arista A&R executive Gerry Griffith, and signs her to a worldwide contract. Houston, who like her singing mother Cissy and her cousin Dionne Warwick, has begun her vocal career, at age eight, singing *Guide Me, O Thou Great Jehovah* in a gospel setting - the New Hope Baptist Junior Choir, has already inked a management deal with Seymour Flics and Gene Harvey in 1981 and is sought as a backing vocalist for such recording artists as Chaka Khan and Lou Rawls by the time she joins Arista. Houston has also sung with her mother at nightclub and concert engagements as a teenager, developing her own solo numbers and has sung lead vocals on the Michael Zager Band's second album title cut, *Life's A Party*. Zager offered to sign Houston to a recording contract, but her mother declined on her behalf. Houston has also pursued a career as a model, featuring in US magazine **Glamour** and on the front cover of **Seventeen**, and, as an actress, appearing in TV shows including "Silver Spoons" and "Gimme A Break".

1984

June Although an early commercial glimpse is witnessed on the US #46-peaking *Hold Me* duet with Teddy Pendergrass, Davis continues to mould, teach and nurture his prodigy in a quest to record the perfect debut album, not least enlisting the help of a number of talented songwriters including Michael Masser, Peter McCann, Linda Creed and Gerry Goffin and producers, Masser, Narada Michael Walden and Kashif.

1985

Mar Her maiden album, the pop/R&B-filled ***Whitney Houston***, is finally released in the US, though its early sales progress is moderate (it will take 12 months to top the US chart).
July [27] After a slow chart rise, her debut single, *You Give Good Love*, produced by Kashif, hits US #3. Its release in the UK sparks some club/dance interest, but it fails to make the chart.
Oct [26] Released in August, the Masser-produced (and co-written with Gerry Goffin) ballad, *Saving All My Love For You*, her cover of a 1978 Marilyn McCoo & Billy Davis Jr. album cut, hits US #1.
Dec [14] Becoming an international smash *Saving All My Love For You* also hits UK #1. ***Whitney Houston***, destined to spend over 100 consecutive weeks on the UK chart, peaks at #2, behind the various artists compilation ***Now! That's What I Call Music 6***.

1986

Jan [27] Houston wins the Favorite Video Single, Soul/R&B, and Favorite Single, Soul/R&B categories for *Saving All My Love For* at the 13th annual American Music Awards, held at the Shrine Auditorium, Los Angeles, CA.
Feb [15] Walden-produced *How Will I Know* tops the US Hot 100 and R&B charts and hits UK #5.
[25] Houston collects the trophy for Best Pop Vocal Performance, Female, for *Saving All My Love For You* at the 28th annual Grammy Awards.
Mar [8] ***Whitney Houston*** finally tops the US chart.
May [17] *The Greatest Love Of All* (originally the B-side of *You Give Good Love*), a cover version of the 1977 hit by George Benson, becomes her third consecutive US #1 and hits UK #8.
Aug She wins an Emmy award for Outstanding Individual Performance In A Variety Program and announces her first major live US dates.
Sept [15] Also performing on the show, Houston wins the Best Female Video category for "How Will I Know?" at the third annual MTV Video Music Awards, broadcast simultaneously from the Universal Amphitheatre, Universal City, CA, and the Palladium, New York, NY.
Nov Houston arrives in the UK for her first European live dates, which are all sellouts.

1987

Jan [26] Houston collects another batch of trophies, namely for Favorite Female Artist, Soul/R&B, Favorite Video Single, Soul/R&B, Favorite Album, Soul/R&B, Favorite Female Artist, Pop/Rock, and Favorite Album, Pop/Rock, at the 14th annual American Music Awards, held at the Shrine Auditorium.
Feb With Davis once again in the role of executive producer, a similar grouping of writers and producers completes work with Houston on her sophomore effort, in an attempt to repeat the formula which led to the multi-platinum success of her debut album.
[24] Houston sings *The Greatest Love Of All* at the 29th Grammy Awards held at the Shrine Auditorium.
Apr She completes early promotion work for the lead-off single with a live appearance at the "Montreux Rock Festival", Montreux, Switzerland.
June [6] George Merrill/Shannon Rubicam (who later find success as the Boy Meets Girls duo)-penned, Walden-produced *I Wanna Dance With Somebody (Who Loves Me)* tops the UK chart.
[13] Her sophomore album, ***Whitney***, enters the UK survey at #1.
[27] *I Wanna Dance With Somebody (Who Loves Me)* tops the US chart. ***Whitney*** becomes the first album by a female singer to debut on the **Billboard** chart at #1, where it will remain for 11 weeks. It continues a familiar mix of sassy dance-pop numbers and ballads, including a duet version, with her mother Cissy, of the standard "Chess" piece, *I Know Him So Well*.
July Arista signs a two-year development deal with Tri-Star Pictures to find a film vehicle for its leading female vocalist.
Sept [11] Houston performs at the fourth annual MTV Video Music Awards, held at the Universal Amphitheatre.
[26] Ballad, *Didn't We Almost Have It All*, co-written by producer Michael Masser and Will Jennings, continues her unbroken run as another US chart-topper, and reaches UK #14. A world tour to further promote sales of her second album is announced.
Nov [28] Tom Kelly/Billy Steinberg-penned *So Emotional* hits UK #5.

1988

Jan [9] *So Emotional* tops the US chart, her sixth consecutive US #1.
[25] Houston wins the Favorite Female Artist, Pop/Rock, and Favorite Single, Pop/Rock categories, at the 15th annual American Music Awards, held at the Shrine Auditorium.
Mar [2] She collects her second Best Pop Vocal Performance, Female trophy (this time for *I Wanna Dance With Somebody (Who Loves Me)*)at the 30th annual Grammy Awards.
[30] She also wins the Album Of The Year, Female category, at the second annual Soul Train Music Awards, held at the Civic Center, Santa Monica, CA.
Apr [23] Houston breaks a chart record as *Where Do Broken Hearts Go* hits US #1, pipping Billy Ocean's *Get Outta My Dreams (Get Into My Car)*, to become her seventh consecutive US chart-topper, overtaking the previous record of six achieved by both the Beatles and the Bee Gees. In the UK, the single makes #14.
June [4] The fifth single from ***Whitney***, *Love Will Save The Day*, is released to tie-in with her UK visit and hits UK #10.
[11] Already in the middle of a sellout world tour, Houston headlines the "Nelson Mandela's 70th Birthday Tribute" celebration at Wembley Stadium, Wembley, Middx.
Aug [27] *Love Will Save The Day* breaks the chart-topping run, hitting US #9.
Oct [15] *One Moment In Time*, a ballad headlining Davis' current project - a special various artists 1988 Olympics musical tribute, ***One Moment In Time***, tops the UK survey for the first of two weeks.
Nov [12] *One Moment In Time*, written by John Bettis and Albert Hammond, hits US #5.

1989

Jan [30] Houston wins the Favorite Female Artist, Soul/R&B, and Favorite Female Artist, Pop/Rock, categories at the 16th annual American Music Awards, held at the Shrine Auditorium.
Feb [22] She sings *One Moment In Time* at the 31st Grammy Awards, staged at the Shrine Auditorium.
July [29] Houston's duet with labelmate and longtime friend Aretha Franklin *It Isn't, It Wasn't, It Ain't Ever Gonna Be* makes US #41, set to reach UK #29 on Sept [23]. While Houston prepares her third album with new producers, she is increasingly showered with Hollywood scripts and is alternately most rumored to be considering movies starring opposite Robert De Niro and her friend Eddie Murphy.

1990

May [30] She receives this year's Hitmaker Award at the 20th annual Songwriters Hall of Fame ceremony, held at the New York Hilton, also on hand to induct Smokey Robinson into the Hall.
Oct [3] Houston attends a celebration at the White House, Washington, DC, for National Children's Day.
[19] At its fourth annual ceremony at New York's Radio City Music Hall, **Essence** magazine honors Houston.
[20] First single from her third album, the dance swinging *I'm Your Baby Tonight*, begins a global chart rise, first hitting UK #5.
Nov [17] ***I'm Your Baby Tonight*** hits UK #6 in its week of entry. It is mostly co-written and produced by the R&B hit making production duo L.A. Reid and Babyface, but also features composition and production by Masser, Rickey Minor, Luther Vandross, Stevie Wonder and Walden.
Dec [1] *I'm Your Baby Tonight*, written and produced by L.A. Reid and Babyface, tops the US chart for one week.
[8] Blocked out by hot rap albums by Vanilla Ice and M.C. Hammer, ***I'm Your Baby Tonight*** hits US #3.

1991

Jan [12] Yet to appear in a motion picture, Houston receives an award for Distinguished Achievement from the American Cinema Award Foundation in Los Angeles, CA, in a ceremony which also recognizes James Stewart and Lauren Bacall.
[19] *All The Man That I Need* reaches UK #13.
[27] Houston captures America's heart, performing *The Star Spangled Banner* at Super Bowl XXV at Joe Robbie Stadium, Miami, FL. Even though her vocal segment is pre-recorded, she synthesizes current American patriotism, related to the Gulf War crisis. Demand for the performance results in a rush-released single and video.
Feb [23] Houston achieves her ninth US #1 in just over five years, as *All The Man That I Need*, a 1982 Sister Sledge US R&B #45, hits US #1 for the first of two weeks, and ***I'm Your Baby Tonight*** approaches triple-platinum US sales. She appears as the musical guest on NBC-TV's "Saturday Night Live".
[30] *The Star Spangled Banner*, having sold 750,000 copies in just eight days, with its proceeds going to the Gulf Crisis Fund, reaches US #20.
[31] HBO-TV's "Welcome Home Heroes" special airs, with a live Houston concert from the Norfolk Naval Air Station, at which she welcomes home US troops from the Persian Gulf with a repeat performance of *The Star Spangled Banner*.
Apr [18] Following cancellation of a European tour because of the Gulf War, a North American concert trek bows at the Thompson Boling Assembly Center Arena, Knoxville, TN.
[23] A criminal complaint is filed against Houston by Ransom Brotherton of Lexington, KY, who alleges that she punched him in the eye and threatened to have him killed as he tried to break up a fight between Houston's brother Michael and Kevin Owens in the Radisson Plaza Hotel, Lexington, on the 19th. She is also accused of "terroristic threatening". Michael Houston's injuries required 12 stitches around his eye.
May [7] Judge Lewis Paisley dismisses the assault charges against Houston on the recommendation of Fayette County DA, Norrie Wake.
[12] Houston sings *Miracle*, transmitted by satellite for "The Simple Truth - A Concert For Kurdish Refugees" concert, as ***I'm Your Baby Tonight*** achieves RIAA multi-platinum status for sales of three million.
June [8] Third cut from her recent album, the L.A. Reid and Babyface ballad *Miracle*, hits US #9.
July [13] *My Name Is Not Susan* reaches UK #29.
[23] After a performance at New York's Madison Square Garden, Houston is presented with a plaque commemorating seven million worldwide sales of her ***I'm Your Baby Tonight*** album, at New York's Grolier Club. Soon after, she will cancel the rest of her US tour, citing throat problems.
Sept [3-14] Houston plays a lengthy series of concerts at Wembley Arena, Wembley.
[7] *My Name Is Not Susan* reaches US #20.
[15] During her UK visit, Houston speaks at the "Reach Out & Touch People With HIV And AIDS Rally" in London's Hyde Park.
[28] *I Belong To You* debuts at its UK #54 peak.
Dec [3] Houston wins the Top R&B Artist, Top R&B Singles Artist, Top R&B Album and Top R&B Album Artist categories, for ***I'm Your Baby Tonight***, at the second annual Billboard Music Awards.
[22] The Whitney Houston Foundation sponsors a Christmas party at Symphony Hall, Newark, NJ for 150 children from Parents Anonymous.

1992

Mar [1] Houston participates in ABC-TV's "Muhammad Ali's 50th Birthday" special.
May [6] Her first network TV special, "Whitney Houston - This Is My Life", airs on ABC-TV. Produced by Houston's Nippy Inc. (Nippy is her childhood nickname), the show features live clips, interviews and the first official confirmation of her engagement to singer Bobby Brown, who proposed to her in August 1991.
June [12] Houston sings *That's What Friends Are For* with Dionne Warwick, honoring Clive Davis as "Man Of The Year" at a tribute held at the New York Friars Club, Waldorf Astoria Hotel.
[27] Guests Dionne Warwick, CeCe Winans, Jasmine Guy and others, celebrate with Houston at her bridal shower at the Rihga Royal Hotel, Manhattan, NY.
July [18] Houston marries Brown in a ceremony at her Mendham, NJ mansion. Stevie Wonder sings at the nuptials.
Oct [3] She attends a biannual "Children's Diabetes Foundation" benefit at the Beverly Hilton, Los Angeles.
[21] Pregnant with her first child, Houston cancels her scheduled European tour on the advice of doctors.
Nov [25] "The Bodyguard", in which Houston makes her major motion-picture debut opposite Kevin Costner, in a movie written some 20 years previously by Lawrence Kasdan with Ryan O'Neal and Diana Ross in mind, opens nationwide to poor reviews but ecstatic box-office returns.
[28] *I Will Always Love You*, taken from the soundtrack to "The Bodyguard", hits US #1. Written by Dolly Parton (who made US #53 with the ballad in 1982), Houston's stirring version, recorded at the suggestion of Costner and produced by David Foster, begins a record-breaking 14-week stay atop the US chart.
Dec [9] Houston guests on ITV's "Des O'Connor Tonight", promoting "The Bodyguard".
[12] ***The Bodyguard***, featuring six Houston tracks, and single cuts from Kenny G, Aaron Neville, Joe Cocker and Sass Jordan and others, hits US #1, and will inhabit the top-spot well into 1993.
[17] Lodged at UK #1, *I Will Always Love You* passes the one million-sales plateau in the UK (the biggest selling record of the year) on its way to becoming one of the most successful singles, worldwide, of all-time.
[19] US chart-sales collators Soundscan reveal that last week's US sales for *I Will Always Love You* hit 399,000, topping the previous record of 392,000 held by Bryan Adams' *(Everything I Do) I Do It For You* from 1991.

1993

Feb [20] With *I Will Always Love You* still in pole position, *I'm Every Woman*, Houston's update of Chaka Khan's 1978 US #21 solo chart debut, hits US #4.
[27] In its 14th straight week at US #1, *I Will Always Love You* becomes the longest-ever US chart-topper, taking over from Boyz II Men's 1992 hit, *End Of The Road* (which, incidentally, falls off the survey after a 32-week run this very day). Already certified quadruple platinum with four million US sales, the disc is also the second-biggest selling US single of all time, behind USA For Africa's *We Are The World*. In addition to its staggering domestic achievements, *I Will Always Love You* is still #1 in Austria, Australia, Belgium, Canada, Denmark, Germany, Holland, Norway, Sweden, Switzerland and has spent ten weeks atop the UK survey. Meanwhile, *I'm Every Woman* hits UK #4 and ***The Bodyguard*** original soundtrack continues its stranglehold at US #1 for the 12th straight week (also topping the UK Compilation Album chart), having sold over seven million copies and climbing in the US alone. The phenomenon has also hit #1 in: Australia, Austria, Belgium, Canada, Denmark, Eire, Finland, France, Germany, Greece, Holland, Italy, Japan, New Zealand, Norway, Portugal, Spain, Sweden and Switzerland, with a current global tally of 15 million sales. Arista president, Clive Davis, expects the final figure to approach 30 million.
Mar [4] Houston gives birth, at home, to a 6lb 12oz girl, Bobbi Kristina Houston Brown.
[9] She wins Best R&B/Soul Female Song for *I Will Always Love You*, which also nabs the People's Choice category at the seventh annual Soul Train Music Awards, held at the Shrine Auditorium, the first of many trophies she will collect for the record-breaking hit.
Apr [3] *I Have Nothing*, co-penned by producer Foster and his wife Linda Thompson, hits US #4.
May [1] *I Have Nothing* hits UK #3.
June [3] Houston makes her first public appearance since the birth of her daughter, at a fundraiser for the St. Jude's Children Research Hospital, Memphis, TN, at Los Angeles' Century Plaza Hotel.
[28] The **New York Post** prints a story that Houston has been hospitalized after overdosing on diet pills. She sues the tabloid for $10 million in compensatory damages and $50 million in punitive damages. (Two days later, the paper will print a correction.)
July [17] *Run To You* reaches US #31.
Aug [7] *Run To You* reaches UK #15.
Sept [30] Houston, and husband Brown, are stopped in their limousine at Kennedy International Airport, New York, by nine police officers, looking for drug dealers.
Nov [6] A final ***The Bodyguard*** extract *Queen Of The Night* debuts at its UK #14 peak.

1994

Jan [5] Houston receives the Entertainer Of The Year, Outstanding Female Artist and Outstanding Music Video (*I'm Every Woman*) awards at the 26th annual NAACP Image Awards, staged at Pasadena Civic Auditorium.
Feb [7] She wins the Favorite Pop/Rock Female Artist, Pop/Rock Single (*I Will Always Love You*), Pop/Rock Album (***The Bodyguard***), Soul/R&B Female Artist, Soul/R&B Single (*I Will Always Love You*) and Adult Contemporary Album (***The Bodyguard***) categories at the 21st annual American Music Awards, held at the Shrine Auditorium.
[14] ***The Bodyguard*** is named Best Soundtrack at the 13th annual BRIT Awards, held at London's Alexandra Palace.
Mar [1] Houston performs *I Will Always Love You* at the 36th Grammy Awards at New York's Radio City Music Hall, as she picks up three more Grammys - Record Of The Year and Best Pop Vocal Performance, Female for *I Will Always Love You* and Album Of The Year for ***The Bodyguard***.
[15] *I Will Always Love You* is named R&B Song Of The Year at the eighth annual Soul Train Music Awards, at the Shrine Auditorium. Houston also wins the 1994 Sammy Davis Jr. Award and sings with Bobby Brown.
[20] ***The Bodyguard*** is confirmed Best Selling Album Of The Year at the 23rd annual Juno Awards at the

O'Keefe Centre in Toronto, ON, Canada.
[22] ***The Bodyguard*** is also named Best-selling Chartmaker Recording and Best-selling Soundtrack at the NARM 1993/4 Best Seller Awards in San Francisco, CA.
Apr [9] Houston performs at the fifth annual RainForest benefit concert at New York's Carnegie Hall, with Elton John, Sting, James Taylor, Aaron Neville, Tammy Wynette, Branford Marsalis and Luciano Pavarotti.
[14] She embarks on a South American tour at San Carlos De Apoqundo Stadium, Santiago, Chile.
May [4] Houston is named World's Best-selling Pop Artist Of The Year, R&B Artist, American Recording Artist, Overall Recording Artist and Female Recording Artist Of The Year at the sixth annual World Music Awards at the Sporting Club in Monte Carlo, Monaco, set to air on the 31st on ABC-TV.
June [3] Following an announcment that Houston is slated to play the title role in a new TV version of Rodgers and Hammerstein's "Cinderella", she files suit against Pro Rok, promoters of her April 24th San Juan concert, claiming they had defrauded her out of a percentage of the receipts.
[14] At a news conference in New York, it is announced that Houston has signed a one-year $1 million contract with AT&T to perform ads promoting the company's new voice enhancement service, "AT&T TrueVoice".
July [17] Houston headlines the pre-show at the World Cup Final between Brazil and Italy at the Rose Bowl, Pasadena.
Aug [21] At Arrowhead Pond of Anaheim, Anaheim, CA concert during her current US tour, Houston asks for a spotlight to be turned on Sydney and Justin Simpson, whose father O.J. Simpson is currently on trial for the murder of their mother Nicole Brown.
Sept [2] A second restraining order is served on Charles Gilberg in Morristown, NJ, who claims to be the father of Houston's daughter. (He had disrupted a church service in Newark in 1991.)
[16-30] Houston plays seven sellout shows at New York's Radio City Music Hall, grossing $2,668,940.
Oct [4] Houston performs in the Rose Garden of the White House after a state dinner for Nelson Mandela.
Nov [12] HBO broadcasts live from Ellis Park, Johannesburg, South Africa "Whitney - Concert For A New South Africa", as part of Houston's concert tour of the nation to celebrate the country's recent unification.

1995

Mar [2] Houston presents her mother Cissy with the Pioneer Award at the Rhythm and Blues Foundation's sixth annual awards at the Palladium, Los Angeles.
June [15] She obtains a restraining order against 38-year old New Yorker, Steven J. Marriott of Lloyd Harbor, NY, who claims he is her brother.
[22] Houston is honored at the second annual "VH-1 Honors" ceremony at the Shrine Auditorium.
Sept [21] A press release confirms that Houston and Brown have separated.
Nov [2] Houston is inducted into the Soul Train Hall of Fame at the 25th annual awards, from the Shrine Auditorium.
[17] Houston and Brown publicly reconcile at Bar None in Miami, FL.
[18] Houston's *Exhale (Shoop Shoop)*, penned by the soundtrack's writer and producer Babyface for the movie "Waiting To Exhale" in which Houston stars, debuts at its UK #11 peak.
[25] *Exhale (Shoop Shoop)* bows at US #1, making Houston only the third artist and the second female (Mariah Carey is the first) to enter in pole position. It is also her 11th chart-topper, tying her with Madonna in joint fifth place with most #1s in the US.

1996

Jan [20] ***Waiting To Exhale***, including three cuts by Houston, tops the US chart.
Feb [24] *Count On Me*, a duet with CeCe Winans, also featured on the ***Waiting To Exhale*** soundtrack, enters at its UK #12 peak.
May [4] Having performed the song with Winans at the 38th annual Grammy Awards at the Shrine Auditorium on February 28th, *Count On Me* hits #8. (Meanwhile Houston begins filming the Penny Marshall-directed "The Preacher's Wife" opposite co-star Denzel Washington.)

HOWLIN' WOLF

1949

Following some years of farm labor, followed by service in the US Army in World War II, the physically imposing Wolf (b. Chester Arthur Burnett, June 10, 1910, West Point, MS), who has grown up on a Mississippi cotton plantation and learnt to play blues guitar and harmonica from early blues pioneers Charlie Patton and Willie Brown among others, having made his first public performance in 1928, has moved to West Memphis, AR, to try to earn a living as a musician, and formed the House Rockers in 1948, who have built a local reputation as a hot, electric blues band. With his name now established as Howlin' Wolf (it refers to his early singing style, a personal adaptation of Jimmie Rodgers' "blue yodel", while legend also suggests that he was called "The Wolf", from **Little Red Riding Hood**, by his family, when he misbehaved as a child), having previously used the pseudonyms Bigfoot and Bullcow, the House Rockers secure a daily half-hour live-music spot on local West Memphis radio station, KWEM.

1951

Mar Via his radio slot, Wolf comes to the attention of Ike Turner, who is working in the area as a field A&R man for Los Angeles, CA-based Modern Records, and Memphis, TN-based producer Sam Phillips, a regular supplier of local recordings to Modern and to Chess Records in Chicago, IL.
May [14] Phillips records Wolf at his Sun Studio, leasing the results to Chess, and subsequently upsetting Modern, which claims rights to Wolf and arranges for Turner to record him independently at KWEM.
Nov Different recordings of the same Wolf composition, *Moanin' At Midnight*, are concurrently released on Modern's subsidiary RPM, and on Chess. The song is incorrectly labelled *Mornin' At Midnight* on RPM, while Chess avoids split sales by promoting the other side, *How Many More Years*. The RPM release is the first to reach the US R&B Top 20, but is quickly replaced by the Chess single.

1952

Feb Modern relinquishes its claims to Wolf when Phillips produces a contract signed the previous August, although two more Turner-produced records will appear on RPM.
July [10] Phillips records the last of five Howlin' Wolf sessions. Wolf signs directly to Chess, persuaded by a cash advance, and takes his guitarists, Hubert Sumlin and Willie Johnson, with him.

1953

Now based in Chicago, where he will remain, Wolf secures his first club dates in the city with the help of Muddy Waters, and starts to record at Chess studios, with house musicians Willie Dixon (bass), Otis Spann (piano) and Earl Phillips (drums) augmenting the band. Over the next ten years he will record most of his classic repertoire for the label, including his own compositions *Smokestack Lightnin'*, *No Place To Go*, *Sitting On Top Of The World*, *Evil*, *Killin' Floor*, *I Ain't Superstitious* and *Who's Been Talking*, and Willie Dixon's *Spoonful*, *Down In The Bottom*, *Back Door Man*, *The Red Rooster* and *Wang Dang Doodle*, while his first album, ***Howlin' Wolf*** will be issued by the label in 1958.

1961

Nov [24] Wolf arrives in the UK for his first tour, while *Little Baby* is released by Pye Records as his first UK single. The following year, Secretary of State Dean Rusk, in his capacity as co-chairman of the "Washington Jazz Festival", Washington, DC, asks Chess if Wolf is available to appear, which he does.

1964

June Following the release earlier in the year of ***Folk Festival Of The Blues***, recorded live the previous July with Spann, Buddy Guy and Muddy Waters, at Chicago's Copa Cabana club, his first (and only) pop hit is *Smokestack Lightnin'*, which belatedly strikes UK #42 (it was recorded in 1956). (Wolf's songs are now staple repertoire for emerging UK R&B groups. Among them, *Smokestack Lightnin'* will be covered by the Yardbirds and Manfred Mann, *Spoonful* by Cream and Ten Years After, *The Red Rooster* (as *Little Red Rooster*) by the Rolling Stones, and *I Ain't Superstitious* by Jeff Beck, Rod Stewart and Savoy Brown. In the US, *Back Door Man* is revived by the Doors, *Killin' Floor* by Electric Flag and *How Many More Years* by Little Feat.)
Oct [19] Wolf begins the five-day "American Negro Blues Festival", with Willie Dixon, Lightnin' Hopkins, Sonny Boy Williamson and others, at Fairfield Halls, Croydon, Surrey.
Nov [26] A UK club tour kicks off at London's Marquee club.

1965

May [26] Three months after Chess has issued the '50s Wolf compilation ***Moanin' In The Moonlight***, and at the group's invitation, he appears with the Rolling Stones on an ABC-TV "Shindig" slot, performing *How Many More Years*. The following month Chess will also issue the newly-recorded ***Poor Boy***, with another set, ***Real Folk Blues*** released in 1966.

1967

Apr [14-16] He performs at the Fillmore West, San Francisco, CA, on a bill with Country Joe & the Fish.
Sept Wolf records the ***Super Super Blues Band*** with Bo Diddley and Muddy Waters, including new versions of several familiar songs, which will be released by Chess the following May.

1968

July [26-28] He plays at San Francisco's Avalon Ballroom, with the Quicksilver Messenger Service. (The following April, impressed by Waters' "psychedelic" ***Electric Mud*** release, Wolf records the similarly-conceived ***The Howlin' Wolf Album***, which, in private, he calls "birdshit").

1971

Sept Having recovered from a 1970 car accident, Wolf, in London with guitarist Sumlin to record an album with a stellar UK line-up including Eric Clapton, Ringo Starr, Steve Winwood and Bill Wyman and Charlie Watts of the Rolling Stones, has recorded ***The London Howlin' Wolf Sessions***, which now becomes his only US chart album, making #79.

1972

Sept [8] Wolf appears at the "Ann Arbor Jazz & Blues Festival", Ann Arbor, MI (organized in memory of blues pianist Otis Spann), with Muddy Waters, Dr. John, Bobby Bland and many others. During the year, Chess releases the live album ***Live & Cookin' At Alice's Revisited***.

1973

Shortly after suffering two heart attacks, Wolf is badly injured in a car crash and is hospitalized for weeks with kidney damage. He continues to gig and record sporadically, and releases ***The Back Door Wolf***.

1975

Nov He performs live at the Chicago Amphitheatre, Chicago, with B.B. King, Bobby "Blue" Bland and Little Milton and, the following night, plays what will be his last-ever gig, at the 1815 Club on Chicago's West Side, as he returns to hospital with kidney complications soon after.

1976

Jan [10] After years of deteriorating health, Wolf dies of complications from kidney disease in the Veterans Administration Hospital in Hines, IL.

1991

Jan [16] Howlin' Wolf is inducted into the Rock and Roll Hall of Fame at the sixth annual ceremony, held at New York's Waldorf Astoria Hotel. (Chess (US) and Charly (UK) will continue to bring his seminal and influential music to compact disc via the ***Chess Masters*** volume series, while specialist retrospective German label Bear has recently issued the comprehensive ***Memphis Days Volume 1*** and ***2***.)

HUMAN LEAGUE

Philip Oakey (vocals, synthesizer); **Adrian Wright** (onstage slides, films); **Ian Burden** (bass, synthesizer); **Joanne Catherall** (vocals); **Susanne Sulley** (vocals); **Jo Callis** (synthesizer)

1977

Sept Having already performed together as part of theatre group Meat Whistle, Martin Ware (b. May 19, 1956, Sheffield, Yorks.) and Ian Craig Marsh (b. Nov. 11, 1956, Sheffield), both computer operators, have formed a synthesizer duo, the Dead Daughters, in Sheffield earlier in the year, its name taken from a sci-fi computer game, "Star Force". As a synthesizer and tape-oriented band, influenced not least by the experimental electronic German unit Kraftwerk, and significantly out of step with the prevailing UK punk movement, they recruit Addy Newton and Ware's friend Oakey (b. Oct. 2, 1955, Sheffield), a hospital porter, who comes in as a lead vocalist. Known for a few months as the Future, the band now settles on Human League (taken from another computer game), as short-term member Newton leaves to form Clock DVA, and Wright (b. Philip Adrian Wright, June 30, 1956, Sheffield) joins, to handle "stage visuals".

1978

Mar On the strength of a demo tape comprising *Being Boiled*, *Circus Of Death* and *Toyota City*, recorded in Sheffield in January, the group signs to the Edinburgh, Scotland-based independent Fast Product Records, while label owner Bob Last also becomes its manager.

June Their debut release for Fast is *Being Boiled*, written by Oakey, Ware and Marsh. On hearing the cut, ex-Sex Pistol Johnny Rotten dubs the group "trendy hippies".

1979

Mar The band tours the UK as support act to Siouxsie & the Banshees.

Apr Following negotiations with Fast, which has just released the instrumental EP *Dignity Of Labour*, Virgin Records announces a long-term deal with the band.

May Human League opens for Iggy Pop on a European tour.

July Their Virgin debut, the 12"-only *I Don't Depend On You*, is released, credited to the Men.

Oct The group's first album, ***Reproduction***, containing a new recording of *Circus Of Death*, and the extracted *Empire State Human* are released, as the band sets up its own Monumental Pictures Recording Studios in Sheffield.

Dec The band is dropped from the supporting slot on a Talking Heads UK tour.

1980

May Dual-single package, *Holiday '80*, with a new recording of *Being Boiled*, peaks at UK #56.

[15] The group begins a 12-date UK tour at the Mayfair, Newcastle, Tyne & Wear, set to end on the 29th at Unity Hall, Wakefield, W. Yorks. Wright, previously the slide projectionist and light-show operator, now appears on stage as a full band member.

[31] Their sophomore effort ***Travelogue***, leading the way for a growing number of UK synthesizer-based acts, reaches UK #16.

June *Empire State Human* is reissued, peaking at UK #62, while the band appears in the new-wave rock showcase movie "Urgh! A Music War".

Oct After internal disagreements, Ware and Marsh quit to form British Electric Foundation (and later Heaven 17). In leaving, they sell the rights to the Human League name to Oakey in exchange for 1% of the group's future royalties (and will subsequently receive an estimated £100,000 from the royalties of *Don't You Want Me*). Bassist Burden (b. Dec. 24, 1957, Sheffield) is drafted from local band Graph, and Oakey, now left as the band's central force, also recruits two teenage girls, Catherall (b. Sept. 18, 1962, Sheffield) and Sulley (b. Mar. 22, 1963, Sheffield), whom he spotted dancing at the Crazy Daisy disco in Sheffield High Street, where they are working as cocktail waitresses. The new line-up sets off for a month-long tour of Europe.

1981

Mar Under the production guidance of Martin Rushent, the fresh line-up develops a more mainstream commercial sound, as *Boys & Girls*, featuring the new female vocalists, peaks at UK #48.

May *The Sound Of The Crowd* reaches UK #12. Callis (b. May 2, 1955, Glasgow, Scotland), ex-guitarist for Scottish pop-punk band the Rezillos, is added to the line-up on synthesizer.

Aug [22] Pop-aimed and synth-based *Love Action (I Believe In Love)*, written by Oakey and Burden and credited to Human League Red, hits UK #3.

Oct The group announces a forthcoming headlining UK tour, set to begin in November.

[24] *Open Your Heart* (credited to Human League Blue) hits UK #6.

[31] Its parent project, ***Dare!***, co-produced by the band with Rushent, tops the UK chart and will remain on the survey for 71 weeks. Containing a batch of hit singles, the album will eventually sell over five million copies worldwide.

Dec [12] Oakey/Callis/Wright-penned pop synthesizer classic, *Don't You Want Me*, taken from the album, and featuring traded vocals between Oakey and Catherall, hits UK #1 for the first of five weeks, aided by a film-within-a-film video clip. It is the biggest-selling UK single of 1981, topping a million sales, and is also Virgin's first UK #1 single. (Virgin will buy Oakey a BMW motorbike as a token of its appreciation.)

1982

Jan [23] Their debut album ***Reproduction*** now makes UK #34.

[30] Capitalizing on the group's success, the original *Being Boiled* reissued through EMI and despite its dissimilarity to current League material, hits UK #6.

Feb Reissued *Holiday '80* double-pack makes UK #46, as Oakey announces his engagement to Catherall.

[24] The group wins the Best British Newcomer category at the inaugural BRIT Awards, held at the Grosvenor House Hotel, London.

July [3] *Don't You Want Me* hits US #1 for the first of three weeks, and will become a million-plus seller.

[10] ***Dare!***, climbing the US chart since February, hits #3. UK mini-album, ***Love And Dancing***, comprising dance-oriented re-mixes from ***Dare!***, hits UK #3.

Sept ***Love And Dancing*** makes US #135.

Nov [27] *Mirror Man*, written by Oakey, Callis and Burden, hits UK #2.

1983

May [14] *(Keep Feeling) Fascination* also hits UK #2. (It will be the group's last recording for a year, as members spend much studio time working on a new album, during which disputes with Rushent will result in his quitting the project.)

Aug [20] *(Keep Feeling) Fascination* hits US #8, while a US-only released mini-album, ***Fascination!***, is on its way to #22.

Nov *Mirror Man*, belatedly released in US, reaches #30.

1984

May [12] Uncharacteristically guitar-led *The Lebanon* reaches UK #11, while ***Hysteria***, co-produced by the group with both Hugh Padgham and Chris Thomas, hits UK #3 but stays charted for just 18 weeks, partly because the group refuses to tour or do any promotion for the project (but later admits this was a mistake: "We thought we were so popular we didn't have to").

June *The Lebanon* peaks at US #64.

July [7] Oakey/Callis/Wright-inked ballad, *Life On Your Own*, reaches UK #16.

Aug ***Hysteria*** makes US #62.

Oct [27] Oakey's collaboration with disco producer Giorgio Moroder on *Together In Electric Dreams*, the theme from the movie "Electric Dreams", hits UK #3 and features a Peter Frampton guitar solo.

Dec [8] *Louise* reaches UK #13.

1985

Jan The group retires to Oakey's 24-track home studio and begins recording with producer Colin Thurston. Callis departs, to work with Feargal Sharkey, while session guests include Associates drummer Jim Russell and members of the Comsat Angels.

July A second Oakey/Moroder collaboration, *Goodbye Bad Times*, makes UK #44.

Aug ***Philip Oakey And Giorgio Moroder*** peaks at UK #52.

Sept On the assigned release date, the new Human League album fails to appear, the sessions with Thurston having been ditched.

1986

Feb The group travels to Minneapolis, MN, to work with R&B hit production team Jimmy Jam and Terry Lewis, the men behind Janet Jackson's multi-platinum album, ***Control***, and the hottest producers of the moment. Four months are spent recording a new album.

Sept [6] *Human*, the first release from the Jam & Lewis sessions, hits UK #8. ***Crash*** hits UK #7. It emerges that the producers have brought in session singers and players as was seen fit during the recordings. Oakey admits that the sessions had ended in acrimony, but the album re-establishes the group in the international marketplace.

Nov [22] Infidelity-themed ballad, *Human*, written by Jam & Lewis, tops the US chart, while ***Crash*** lands at US #24. Following its successful chart return, the group plans its first live performances in four years. *I Need Your Loving* spends a week at UK #72 and will peak at US #44 on Jan [24].

1988

Oct *Love Is All That Matters*, remixed from the two-year-old album ***Crash***, makes UK #41.

Nov [12] 13-track, TV-advertised compilation, ***Greatest Hits***, hits UK #3.

1990

Sept [29] Reuniting the band, which now comprises Oakley, Sulley and Catherall with Russell Dennett (guitar) and Neil Sutton (keyboards), both of whom played on the 1986 "Crash" tour, with producer Rushent, and after a traditionally lengthy period, Human League's sixth album, ***Romantic?***, immediately peaks at UK #24, but disappears from the survey after only two weeks.

Nov [10] The extracted *Heart Like A Wheel*, which has already stopped at UK #29 in September, makes US #32. (On Oct [31], 1992, the Farm's update of *Don't You Want Me*, will reach UK #18.)

1995

Jan [21] Newly signed to East West Records, for both the UK and US, as a trio comprising Oakey, Sulley and Catherall, the group's label debut, *Tell Me When*, with mixes by the Utah Saints, the Development Corporation and Red Jerry, hits UK #6.

Feb [4] Returning to its familiar synth-based sound, ***Octopus***, produced by Ian Stanley, hits UK #6 in its week of entry.

Mar [25] *One Man In My Heart* reaches UK #13.

Apr [3] The group begins a four-day promotional visit of the US, followed by selected dates in June.
[15] *Tell Me When* reaches US #31, the group's first US chart success in eight years.
May [15] The group performs at Z-100's Mayday concert at New York's Roseland Ballroom.
June [17] *Filling Up With Heaven* bows at its UK #36 peak.
Oct [28] Revised career highlight, *Don't You Want Me (Remix)* debuts at its UK #16 peak.

1996

Jan [20] *Stay With Me Tonight* makes UK #40 in its week of entry.
see also: **HEAVEN 17**

HUMBLE PIE

Peter Frampton (guitar, vocals);
Steve Marriott (guitar, vocals);
Greg Ridley (bass); **Jerry Shirley** (drums)

1969

Sept The hard-rock combo has been formed in London in April, by guitarists/vocalists Frampton (b. Apr. 22, 1950, Beckenham, Kent) and Marriott (b. Jan. 30, 1947, Bow, London), who have just left the Herd and the Small Faces respectively. Having met for the first time in Paris, doing session work for French singer Johnny Hallyday, the pair has recruited Ridley (b. Oct. 23, 1947, Carlisle), from Spooky Tooth, and Shirley (b. Feb. 4, 1952), from Apostolic Intervention and Little Women, in July, and, following rehearsals at Marriott's country cottage, they have signed to Immediate Records, which has issued their now charting UK #32 debut, ***As Safe As Yesterday Is***, which includes *Natural Born Bugie*, at UK #4, the group's only UK smash.
Oct [8] The group embarks on a nine-city UK tour at the Coventry Theatre, Coventry, Warks.
Dec Hastily assembled follow-up album, the acoustic-flavored ***Town And Country***, fails to chart.

1971

Mar Signed to A&M Records in 1970, and following that year's label debut, ***Humble Pie***, the band releases ***Rock On***, which climbs to US #118, supported not least by continuous US touring.
May [13-16] Humble Pie plays at the Fillmore West, San Francisco, CA, on a bill with Swamp Dogg.
Oct While *I Don't Need No Doctor* peaks at US #73 and, amid much rancor, Frampton quits, to pursue a solo career, and will achieve significant success in the mid-'70s. He is replaced by Dave "Clem" Clempson (b. Sept. 5, 1949) from Colosseum.

1972

Jan Live album, ***Performance - Rockin' The Fillmore***, recorded in the US and featuring Frampton, restores them to the UK chart, at #32, and marks their major US breakthrough, reaching #21.
Mar [11] The band appears at London's Rainbow Theatre, Finsbury Park.
May ***Smokin'*** becomes their most successful UK release, rising to UK #28 and hitting US #6, while the extracted *Hot'n'Nasty* peaks at US #52.
Sept They play before a sellout crowd of 14,000 at Long Beach Arena, Los Angeles, CA.
Nov The two early Immediate albums are repackaged together in the US by A&M as ***Lost And Found***, which emerges at #37.

1973

Apr R&B/rock-fused double album, ***Eat It***, featuring vocal trio the Blackberries, reaches US #13 and UK #34.

1974

Apr ***Thunderbox*** reaches US #52.
May [18] Humble Pie supports the Who at Charlton Athletic Football Club, Charlton, London, with Lou Reed and Bad Company also on the bill.
July [6] They co-headline the "Buxton Festival" with the Faces and Mott The Hoople.

1975

Mar Tired of touring, the group splits, as its final album of the decade, ***Street Rats***, makes US #100.
July Marriott records the solo album, ***Marriott***, then forms the Steve Marriott All-Stars (which includes Clempson and Ridley) for a year, before coming full circle in 1976, rejoining a reunited Small Faces.

1980

Apr After a second attempt at a solo career, Marriott re-forms Humble Pie with Shirley, adding Bobby Tench (formerly with Jeff Beck) on guitar and vocals, and Anthony Jones on bass. Signed to Atco in the US and Jet Records in the UK, they release ***On To Victory***, which battles to US #60, with the extracted *Fool For A Pretty Face (Hurt By Love)* peaking at US #52.

1981

Apr While the group is in Chicago, IL, on a US tour, Marriott crushes his fingers in a hotel door. Dates are cancelled, while his hand heals sufficiently for him to return to guitar playing.
June His hand recovered, Marriott is now hospitalized with an ulcer when the tour reaches Dallas, TX, and more shows are cancelled. The new line-up's second album, ***Go For The Throat***, stalls at US #154 and the group disbands permanently. (Shirley will subsequently become a DJ at WNCX, Cleveland, OH.)

1991

Apr [20] Having made a fleeting return to his rockin' roots with UK pub band Packet of Three in the mid-'80s, releasing ***Packet Of Three*** in April 1986, and currently re-teamed with erstwhile co-founder Frampton for recording sessions, Marriott dies in a fire in his 16th-century cottage in Arkesden, Essex.
see also: **Peter FRAMPTON, THE SMALL FACES**

BRIAN HYLAND

1960

Aug [8] Hyland (b. Nov. 12, 1943, Queens, New York, NY), who has formed his first group, the Delphis, at age 12, is still a sophomore student attending Franklin K. Lane High School in Brooklyn, New York, when Kapp Records head Dave Kapp has signed him, initially to his Leader subsidiary, and released *Itsy Bitsy Teenie Weenie Yellow Polka Dot Bikini* and *Rosemary*. Now reissued on the main Kapp label, *Itsy Bitsy Teenie Weenie Yellow Polka Dot Bikini* hits US #1 for a week, will become a million seller and makes an overnight star of its 16-year-old singer.
Oct From the same songwriters, Lee Pockriss and Paul Vance, the follow-up, *Four Little Heels*, peaks at US #73 and UK #29, while its B-side, *That's How Much*, makes US #74.
Dec *Lop-Sided Overloaded And It Wiggled When We Rode It* - about a donkey - somehow fails to chart.

1961

Sept Having left Kapp, and newly signed to ABC-Paramount, *Let Me Belong To You* reaches US #20 (and is the first of many specifically-tailored adolescent love songs written by Peter Udell and Gary Geld which will maintain Hyland's chart presence).
Nov [27] *I'll Never Stop Wanting You* peaks at US #83.

1962

Apr The first of three Udell/Gold teen-romance classics, *Ginny Come Lately* reaches US #21 and hits UK #5.
July *Sealed With A Kiss* hits US and UK #3, winning Hyland his second gold disc.
Aug [25-26] Hyland performs two shows at the Steel Pier, Atlantic City, NJ, on a bill with Jerry Lee Lewis, Joey Dee and Dee Dee Sharp, during a State Fairs US summer tour.
Nov *Warmed Over Kisses (Left Over Love)* reaches US #25 and UK #28.

1963

Jan [5] *I May Never Live To See Tomorrow* peaks at US #69.
Feb [4] Hyland begins his first UK tour.
Mar [9] *If Mary's Not There* stalls at US #88.
Oct [10] *I'm Afraid To Go Home* peaks at US #63 (and will be his final Paramount hit).
Nov [22] Hyland is in Dallas, TX, as part of Dick Clark's "Caravan Of Stars" package tour, on the day President John F. Kennedy is assassinated.

1966

Apr [16] Newly signed to Phillips Records and recorded in London with the label's A&R executive Johnny Franz the previous September, *3000 Miles* spends one week at US #99.
Aug Entered under the name Steve O'Brien, Hyland wins a talent contest at the Palamino in Los Angeles, CA, singing a Beatles song.
Sept [3] Produced by Snuff Garrett and arranged by Leon Russell, *The Joker Went Wild* reaches US #20.
Oct [28] Hyland embarks on another Dick Clark US package tour, with Sam the Sham & the Pharoahs, the Yardbirds and others.
Dec [10] *Run Run Look And See* reaches US #25.

1967

During the year, Hyland has three final US hits with the Philips label: *Hung Up In Your Eyes* (#58, February), *Holiday For Clowns* (#94, June) and *Get The Message* (#91, August).

1969

Mar Hyland resurfaces on Dot Records with *Tragedy*. A prior Top 10 hit for both Thomas Wayne and the Fleetwoods, it peaks at US #56.
Apr [12] His cover of Jimmy Charles' 1960 US top five hit, *A Million To One*, makes US #90. Dot links ***Tragedy/A Million To One*** as an album package which charts at US #160.
July [19] *Stay And Love Me All Summer* leaves at US #82.

1970

Dec Hyland hits US #3 and UK #41 with a third million seller, his version of Curtis Mayfield's classic *Gypsy Woman*, a 1961 US #20 hit for the Impressions. Released on Uni (Hyland's sixth label), it is produced by early-'60s contemporary Del Shannon, with whom he has also formed a production company.

1971

Jan Uni album, ***Brian Hyland***, peaks at US #171.
Mar [27] His update of Jackie Wilson's *Lonely Teardrops* becomes Hyland's US chart swan song, at #54. (He has scored 22 Hot 100 hits over 11 years.)

1975

July Reissued in the UK, *Sealed With A Kiss* hits #7. (With his label ABC unable to locate Hyland to promote the single, rumors suggest that the company has been contacted by a dozen doppelganging Hylands in response to its appeal to locate him.)

1991

Nov Hyland is currently featured on ***The Christmas Album ... A Gift Of Hope*** produced by San Diego Children's Hospital. He re-emerged in the mid-'70s and has spent much of the past decade recording as a country artist and performing on the nostalgia circuit. His past hits have endured as airplay favorites and have increasingly succeeded as cover versions, not least in the UK, where Jason Donovan hit #1 in June 1989 with *Sealed With A Kiss*, and Bombalurina achieved the same feat in August 1990, with their unique version of *Itsy Bitsy Teenie Weenie Yellow Polka Dot Bikini*).

I

JANIS IAN

1965

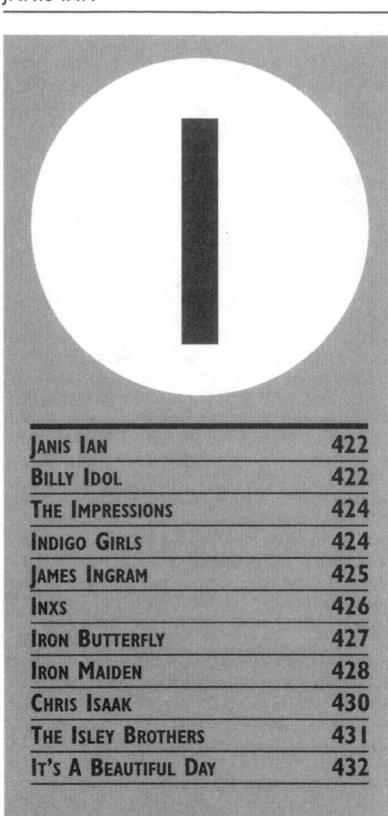

July Ian (b. Janis Eddy Fink, May. 7, 1951, New York, NY), already a competent guitarist and pianist studying at the High School of Music And Art in Manhattan, New York, NY, has begun her folk-styled, observational songwriting while still in junior high school, with one particular composition, *Hair Of Spun Gold*, already published in 1963 in the folk music magazine **Broadside**, to which she has regularly been sending her work. Now beginning regular live work at various New York folk haunts like the Village Gate, where she is spotted by Elektra Records, which wants to sign her as a singer, but passes on her as a songwriter, and the Gaslight club, Ian, who has adopted her brother's first name as her last, writes *Society's Child (Baby I've Been Thinking)*, a song dealing with older-generation hypocrisy and discrimination about teenage inter-racial love, and meets with producer Shadow Morton, who cuts the track. Atlantic Records pays for the session, but refuses to release it. 22 other companies subsequently turn it down.

1966

Jerry Schoenbaum signs her to Verve Folkways Records, which releases *Society's Child* as her debut single. Initial progress is slow, with many US radio stations finding its lyrical content too controversial.

1967

Apr [25] Leonard Bernstein features *Society's Child* in a CBS-TV special, "Inside Pop - The Rock Revolution", after **New York Times** critic Robert Shelton had given Bernstein's TV producer a copy. Its airing results in renewed radio interest and a US Hot 100 chart debut.

July [15] *Society's Child (Baby I've Been Thinking)* reaches US #14, while her maiden album, ***Janis Ian***, makes US #29.

1968

Jan Self-penned ***For All The Seasons Of The Mind***, produced by Morton and again issued on the progressive Verve-Forecast label, climbs to US #179.

Nov ***The Secret Life Of J. Eddy Fink*** is released, featuring musical guest Richie Havens on drums. Extensive US club and college touring and the demands of the pop marketplace leave her disillusioned, so she retires to live in Philadelphia, PA, where she also marries.

1974

Jan Having returned to live performance in 1971 after being signed to Capitol Records and issuing her label debut ***Present Company*** the same year, and following Roberta Flack's successful US #30 treatment of her *Jesse* in 1973, Ian signs to CBS/Columbia Records, where her work will develop an introspective, sensitive style incorporating her folk roots with acquired jazz and blues influences.

July Her first Columbia album, ***Stars***, which includes her own version of *Jesse*, makes US #83. Its title track will be covered by Cher and Glen Campbell, among others.

1975

Sept [13] *At Seventeen*, highlighting Ian's sensitive lyrical and vocal style, hits US #3, her first million seller, while its parent album, the self-written Brooks Arthur-produced ***Between The Lines***, is on its way to US #1, earning a gold disc for half a million sales.

Oct [11] Ian and Billy Preston guest on the first-ever NBC-TV show "Saturday Night Live".

1976

Feb [28] Ian wins the Best Pop Vocal Performance, Female category at the 18th annual Grammy Awards, while ***Between The Lines*** also nabs the Best Engineered Recording (Non-Classical) trophy.

Mar Once again produced by Arthur, ***Aftertones*** reaches US #12.

June Ian makes her live UK debut at London's New Victoria Theatre.

1977

Feb [14] Ian receives 461 Valentine's Day cards, after indicating that she had never received any in the lyrics of *At Seventeen*.

Mar ***Miracle Row***, co-produced with Ron Frangipane, makes US #45. It will be followed by the Joe Wissert-produced ***Janis Ian*** which will peak at US #120 in October 1978.

1979

Dec *Fly Too High*, which makes UK #44, is her first UK success. The song was written and recorded by Ian and producer Giorgio Moroder for the movie "Foxes", starring Jodie Foster, with a rhythm section comprising Keith Forsey and Harold Faltermeyer. It is taken from ***Night Rains***, featuring Chick Corea, Ron Carter and Bruce Springsteen's E. Street Band saxophonist Clarence Clemons, which also yields the UK #44 July 1980 hit, *The Other Side Of The Sun*.

1981

July [18] *Under The Covers* peaks at US #71, while ***Restless Eyes***, recorded in Los Angeles, CA, with producer Gary Klein, climbs to US #156, Ian's final chart appearance of the decade.

1992

Nov [2] Having remained a popular live performer in the singer-songwriter field throughout the '80s, during which she moved to Nashville, TN, Ian has had to sell her publishing rights in 1991 to pay off an IRS debt, and following a July visit to the Cambridge Folk Festival, Cambridge, Cambs., returns to the UK to perform at London's Dominion Theatre. While a new cut, *Days Like These*, was included in the soundtrack album to John Mellencamp's "Falling From Grace" movie in February, her back catalog begins to emerge on CD with the release of ***Up Til Now*** (Columbia) and ***Present Company*** (Capitol), both of which augment the 1990 issue of the 10-track retrospective, ***At Seventeen***.

1993

May [4] Newly signed to the Morgan Creek label, Ian releases her first album in over a decade, ***Breaking Silence***, its title alluding to her lesbianism, which she now talks openly about in interviews.

June [10] Ian guests on NBC-TV's "The Tonight Show".

Nov [7] She makes a rare UK visit, performing at the Cambridge Theatre, London.

Dec [31] Participating in shock-jock Howard Stern's "The Miss Howard Stern New Year's Eve Pageant" pay-per-view US TV special Ian says of the event: "It was absolutely the most disgusting thing I've ever been a part of, and I hope they ask me back next year."

1995

May [16] While Ian has signed a global publishing agreement with Bug Music in March, Beacon Records now releases new album, ***Revenge***, following a two-week promotional tour of Europe.

Sept PolyGram Chronicles releases the 42-song CD compilation, ***Society's Child : The Anthology***. Ian continues to write a column for the bi-monthly **Performing Songwriter** magazine and has established her own subscriber service for all things Ian at P.O. Box 121797, Nashville, TN 37212-1797.

BILLY IDOL

1976

Oct [18] Already seen on UK television as a devoted Sex Pistols follower on the group's notorious Bill Grundy-hosted ITV "Today"-appearance shocker, and a member of the band's dedicated Bromley, Kent-contingent fan annex, Idol (b. William Michael Albert Broad, Nov. 30, 1955, Stanmore, Middx.) has teamed with bassist Tony James, ex-London S.S. and future Sigue Sigue Sputnik, who is equally keen on the burgeoning UK punk movement. Within two weeks of their August meeting, the pair joins Gene October's hardcore punk combo Chelsea, with Idol now making his first formal live appearance with the band, playing guitar at an ICA, London gig. Within two months, however, both he and James will quit the band, taking drummer John Towe with them.

Dec [10] Also recruiting guitarist Bob Andrews, allowing Idol to assume a full lead vocal role, new punk outfit Generation X makes its live debut at the Central College of Art and Design, London.

[21] Generation X baptises the Roxy Club, Covent Garden, London.

1977

Feb The band reveals in a **New Musical Express** interview that it doesn't drink or take drugs. "The revolution can't happen if you're knackered tomorrow" says Idol.

July Having grabbed attention via a four-song "John Peel Show" Radio 1 session, the group signs to Chrysalis Records.

Sept Its first release, *Your Generation*, a sound of the times, makes UK #36. (Before the end of the decade, Generation X, billed as Gen X from late 1979, will nab four more UK chart singles: *Ready Steady Go* (#47, Mar 1978), *King Rocker* (#11, Jan 1979), *Valley Of The Dolls* (#23, Apr 1979) and *Friday's Angels* (#62, June 1979), and the albums ***Generation X*** (#29, Apr [29] 1978) and ***Valley Of The Dolls***, produced by Ian Hunter (#51, Mar [3] 1979). Towe will leave in December 1977 to join the Adverts, and will be replaced by Mark Laff.)

1980

Oct *Dancing With Myself*, a masturbation-themed Idol-penned single, which he will retain in his solo repertoire, stalls at UK #62.

Nov Andrews and Laff quit, but Idol and James are determined to continue, and recruit ex-Clash drummer Terry Chimes and Chelsea's James Stephenson on guitar.

1981

Feb The final Gen X album, ***Kiss Me Deadly***, fails to score, and the reissued *Dancing With Myself* stalls at UK #60. Dissatisfied, Idol quits the band and heads for New York, where he links with Kiss manager Bill Aucoin and producer Keith Forsey, both of whom will help steer his solo career. Idol forms a new band around himself, with New York guitarist Steve Stevens a key element. Aucoin secures Idol an ongoing Chrysalis solo contract with a $250-a-week retainer.

Nov His debut solo the E.P. ***Don't Stop***, produced by Forsey and already directing Idol away from the rawness of punk towards a more mainstream new-wave rock, reaches US #71, remaining charted for over a year, and includes a solo version of *Dancing With Myself.*

1982

Sept Summer-rock anthem, *Hot In The City*, makes a US radio breakthrough to reach US #23 (and UK #58) and spurs its parent album, ***Billy Idol***, again Forsey-helmed, to US #45 during a two-year chart residence, as Idol prepares to make his solo UK live debut.

1983

July [2] Rock-driven *White Wedding* makes US #36.

Dec ***Rebel Yell*** is released, set to hit US #6. Idol's most accessible rock outing to date, with eight of its nine cuts co-written with Stephens, it will eventually reach double-platinum status with two million US sales.

1984

Mar [24] *Rebel Yell* makes US #46 and UK #62.

July Idol finally makes a UK chart impression, with the melodic *Eyes Without A Face* reaching #18 and also hits US #4.

Sept Always eager to explore sexual themes, *Flesh For Fantasy* presses at UK #54 and US #29.

Dec [8] *Catch My Fall* makes US #50.

1985

Jan [31] Idol is controversially featured on the cover of **Rolling Stone** magazine, wearing even less of his rock bondage gear than usual and showing a considerable amount of cheek.

June Chrysalis UK releases the compilation album ***Vital Idol***. It initially spends six months on the chart, hitting UK #7.

July *White Wedding* is re-released in the UK, for the third time, and hits #6.

Oct [12] Reissued *Rebel Yell* now hits UK #6, while its parent album, ***Rebel Yell***, makes UK #36, three years after its original US success.

1986

Oct *To Be A Lover* reaches UK #22.

Nov His fourth solo album, ***Whiplash Smile***, retaining the successful working trio of Idol, Forsey and Stevens and also featuring varied musical guests, including Jocelyn Brown, Harold Faltermeyer and Richard Tee, hits UK #8.

Dec [20] *To Be A Lover* hits US #6, as its parent album, ***Whiplash Smile***, hits US #6.

1987

Feb [24] Idol sings *To Be A Lover* at the 29th Grammy Awards at Los Angeles, CA's Shrine Auditorium.

Mar [7] Second extract, *Don't Need A Gun*, reaches UK #26 and US #37.

June [27] Idol-penned, acoustic guitar-led ballad, *Sweet Sixteen*, reaches US #20.

July *Sweet Sixteen* makes sweet #17 in the UK.

Oct His revival of Tommy James & the Shondells' *Mony Mony* hits UK #7.

Nov [21] *Mony Mony "Live"* tops the US chart, as ***Vital Idol*** hits US #10.

1988

Jan The "exterminator" mix of *Hot In The City* returns it to the UK survey at #13, and also recharts in the US, at #48.

June Idol and girlfriend Perri Lister become parents to a son, Willem Wolf Broad.

July [9] Second compilation album, ***Idol Songs - 11 Of The Best***, hits UK #2, behind Tracy Chapman's eponymous album, as Idol takes a lengthy recording hiatus.

Aug A belated release of *Catch My Fall* makes UK #63.

1989

Aug [24] Idol takes part in a benefit production of Pete Townshend's "Tommy" at Universal Amphitheatre, Universal City, CA, playing the role of Kevin, alongside Elton John as the Pinball Wizard, Steve Winwood as the Hawker, Patti LaBelle as the Acid Queen and Phil Collins as Uncle Ernie.

1990

Feb [6] Idol is hospitalized at Cedars-Sinai Medical Center, Los Angeles, after fracturing his right leg and left wrist in a motorcycle accident after apparently running a stop sign and smashing into a car.

Apr [18] He has a further operation, to place a steel rod in his injured leg.

May [12] With Stevens departed to solo projects, ***Charmed Life***, showing Idol's sneer to be intact despite his accident and featuring new axeman, Texas guitarist Mark Younger-Smith, reaches UK #15, and will make US #11.

July [9] Idol performs impromptu duets at Los Angeles nightclub Spice with Tom Jones, singing *Got To Be Your Lover*, *Great Balls Of Fire* and *Babaloo*, following a press conference.

Aug [4] *Cradle Of Love*, aided by a teen-babe featuring, MTV heavily-rotated video clip, rocks at US #2, having already stopped at UK #34. It will also be featured in the Andrew Dice Clay movie, "The Adventures Of Ford Fairlane".

[25] "Charmed Life" tour, with a backing band comprising Younger-Smith (lead guitar), Larry Seymour (bass), Bonnie Hayes (keyboards), Tal Bergman (drums) and Carla Day and Donna McDaniels (backing vocals), and support act Faith No More, begins in Montreal, PQ, Canada, with Idol happily brandishing his still-needed walking stick.

Sept [7] "Cradle Of Love" wins the Best Video From A Film category at the seventh annual MTV Video Music Awards, held at the Universal Amphitheatre.

Oct [6] His revival of the Doors' *L.A. Woman* makes US #52 and UK #70, as Idol plays at the Omni in Atlanta, GA.

[31] During a show in Seattle, WA, Idol dumps 600 dead fish in Faith No More's dressing room. They respond by walking on stage naked during his set.

Nov At the end of the month, Idol has to cancel four European dates on his "Charmed Life" tour, after his corneas are lacerated by grit, following an outdoor gig in Norway.

Dec [13] A four-date British tour opens at the Royal Dublin Society Hall, Dublin, Eire, as *Prodigal Blues* makes UK #47.

1991

Jan [20] Idol performs at the marathon "Rock In Rio II" festival at the Maracana soccer stadium in Rio de Janeiro, Brazil.

June [27-30] Idol takes part in the annual "Roskilde Festival", Roskilde, Denmark.

Oct [3] *Cradle Of Love* is honored for broadcasting achievements at ASCAP's 11th annual London Awards, at Claridges Hotel.

[11] Idol allegedly punches dinner companion Amber Nevel in the face outside a West Hollywood restaurant.

Nov [20] He surrenders to the authorities, and is booked on assault and battery charges and ordered to appear on December 18th at the Beverly Hills Municipal Court, Beverly Hills, CA.

1992

Jan [21] Idol pleads guilty to assault and battery charges. Sentencing on the two misdemeanor assault and battery counts is set for April 1st, with Idol facing six months in prison. At the initial hearing deputy District Attorney Mark Vezzani claims that the musician's large silver rings cut Ms. Nevel's mouth, bruised her and caused slight concussion.

Apr [1] On April Fool's Day, Idol is ordered to pay $2,700 in fines and appear in a series of anti-drug commercials, following his "no contest" plea in the case brought by Nevel.

June [19] The lawyer for Cherlanne Thompson drops the court case she is bringing against Idol, claiming the singer burned her with a cigarette and attempted to rape her. Idol denies ever meeting Thompson, who had formerly claimed, incorrectly, in 1988, that she had a "very close relationship" with one-time Kiss drummer Peter Criss.

Sept [24] Idol catwalks at a "Jean Paul Gaultier In LA" fashion benefit for AMFAR AIDS research, at the Shrine Auditorium.

Oct As Idol continues to work on a new album, co-producing with Robin Hancock, he takes his son Willem to Sea World in San Diego to visit Clyde, a 520lb sea lion, and Shamu the Killer Whale. **Sea World News** sends out a press release to inform the world of this event.

1993

July [3] *Shock To The System*, previewing his new album, ***Cyberpunk***, reaches UK #30.

[10] After a lengthy recording layoff, ***Cyberpunk***, a rock/techno fusion departure which includes a cover version of Velvet Underground's *Heroin*, debuts at its UK #20 peak. It also includes the world's first interactive computer biography in a limited-edition digipak format.

[17] ***Cyberpunk*** bows at its US #48 peak but will fall off the survey after only seven weeks.

Aug [12] He guests on NBC-TV's "The Tonight Show".

Sept [18] Idol plays a sole UK date at the National Bowl, Milton Keynes, Bucks., supporting Bon Jovi.

1994

Aug [5] Following a similar incident in January when he collapsed outside Tatou, a Beverly Hills restaurant and nightclub, Idol is admitted to Los Angeles' St. Joseph Medical Center, following an apparent drug overdose at his Hollywood Hills home.
Sept [10] His theme song for the currently-playing hit movie of the same name, *Speed* debuts at its UK #47 peak, during a two week chart stay.

1995

Mar [10] Idol performs at the opening night gala of the Hard Rock Hotel & Casino in Las Vegas, NV.
Dec [15] He appears at LIVE 105's Acoustic Christmas at the Community Theatre, Berkeley, CA, on a bill with Oasis, Sonic Youth, Garbage, Love & Rockets, No Doubt, Toadies and Radiohead among others.

THE IMPRESSIONS

Jerry Butler (vocals); **Curtis Mayfield** (vocals); **Arthur Brooks** (vocals); **Richard Brooks** (vocals); **Sam Gooden** (vocals); **Fred Cash** (vocals)

1958

Three members of Tennessee vocal quintet the Roosters, Brooks brothers Arthur (b. Chattanooga, TN) and Richard (b. Chattanooga) with Gooden (b. Sept. 2, 1939, Chattanooga), relocate to Chicago, IL, in 1957, leaving behind Fred Cash (b. Oct. 8, 1940, Chattanooga) and Emanuel Thomas. Songwriter/producer Butler (b. Dec. 8, 1939, Sunflower, MS) joins as a temporary replacement and recruits his friend Curtis Mayfield (b. June 3, 1942, Chicago), with whom he had sung in the Traveling Soul Spiritualists Church and then formed the Modern Jubilaires and Northern Jubilee Singers, to make the line-up a quintet which releases early recordings on small Chicago labels, Bandera (*Listen To Me*) and Swirl (*Don't Leave Me*). Practising in a field park in Seward Park in the Cabrini-Green projects on the North Side of Chicago, the group then demos *Pretty Baby* and *My Baby Loves Me* for the Vee-Jay label. Vi Muszynski hopes to make them the first act on her new label, which she is trying to link up with Vee-Jay, but negotiations break down and the group signs directly to Vee-Jay.
Apr Now under the supervision of Vee-Jay A&R man Calvin Carter, and rechristened the Impressions, the group records four songs, two written by Butler and the Brooks brothers.
May One of these, the R&B ballad *For Your Precious Love*, is the group's first single release, credited to Jerry Butler & the Impressions.
Aug *For Your Precious Love* peaks at US #11. Its success prompts Butler to go solo and he is replaced by original Rooster Cash, but, without Butler's name, the group fades into obscurity and two further Vee-Jay singles fail to follow-up. The Impressions temporarily split, and Mayfield earns a living playing guitar on Butler's records and writing songs for him (and also taking a job selling cigars for the Alfred Dunhill company), including the hits *Let It Be Me* and *He Will Break Your Heart*.

1961

Dec Mayfield has re-formed the group, clearly now its creative leader and songwriter, moving to New York in 1959 and securing a contract with ABC-Paramount the following year. More than a year after signing with the label, *Gypsy Woman* reaches US #20. The next year, two further ABC singles will chart in the US, *Grow Closer Together* which spends a week at US #99 in February and *Little Young Lover* which reaches US #96 in July.

1963

Feb *I'm The One Who Loves You* peaks at US #73. Mayfield returns to Chicago, taking Cash and Gooden with him, while the Brooks brothers stay in New York having quit the line-up.
May Their first single as a trio, *Sad, Sad Girl And Boy*, peaks at US #84.
Sept Their debut album, ***The Impressions***, featuring Johnny Pate's arrangement of a strong horn section and gospel-style vocal interplay, reaches US #43.
Nov The Impressions' biggest commercial success is *It's All Right*, conceived backstage at a Nashville, TN gig, which hits US #4 having already topped the US R&B survey. With the group becoming an influential force on both US and UK R&B acts, Major Lance and Gene Chandler, among others, record Mayfield's songs (chiefly through his role as staff producer at Okeh Records).

1964

Feb *Talking About My Baby* reaches US #12.
May *I'm So Proud* makes US #14, while ***The Never-Ending Impressions*** climbs to US #52.
July Gospel-flavored *Keep On Pushing* hits US #10.
Oct *You Must Believe Me* reaches US #15, while the group's biggest-selling album, ***Keep On Pushing***, hits US #8.

1965

Jan Taken from the album, the gospel song *Amen*, written by Jester Hairston and featured in the film "Lilies Of The Field", hits US #7.
Mar *People Get Ready*, reflecting Mayfield's increasing social awareness, makes US #14. (It will also be a hit for both Aretha Franklin and Rod Stewart, among dozens of cover versions.)
Apr ***People Get Ready*** makes US #23 and ***The Impressions' Greatest Hits*** reaches US #83.
May Upbeat R&B *Woman's Got Soul* reaches US #29.
June *Meeting Over Yonder* makes US #48. Mayfield forms his own Mayfield Records label, distributed by New York's Calla Records and signs the Fascinations.
Sept *I Need You* peaks at US #64.
Oct *Just One Kiss From You* stops at US #76, while ***One By One*** makes US #104.

1966

Jan *You've Been Cheatin'* makes US #33, as Mayfield sets up another label, Windy C. (He signs the Five Stairsteps and June Conquest but, after only seven releases, the label folds.)
Feb *Since I Lost The One I Love* peaks at US #90, followed by *Ridin' High* which reaches US #79 in March, *Too Slow* which peaks at US #91 in April and *Can't Satisfy* which makes US #65 in September. In 1967, *You Always Hurt Me* will reach US #96 in March, ***The Fabulous Impressions*** will make US #184 in July with *I Can't Stay Away From You* peaking at US #80 in September.

1968

Feb With the US R&B chart-topper *We're A Winner*, Mayfield explicitly confronts black politics and the disc is partly banned by US radio, but still reaches US #14, the group's last single for ABC. When the contract expires, Mayfield and Emanuel Thomas establish their own Curtom label in March with the company motto "We're A Winner", signing the Impressions to the label.
Apr ABC continues to release existing Impressions material: ***We're A Winner*** makes US #35, the group's best placing in three years.
May *We're Rolling On (Part 1)* reaches US #59.
Aug *I Loved And I Lost* climbs to US #61.
Oct *Fool For You*, their first Curtom single, reaches US #22, while the ABC compilation album, ***The Best Of The Impressions***, peaks at US #172.
Dec On Curtom, *This Is My Country* reaches US #25, while ABC's *Don't Cry My Love* makes US #71.

1969

May *Seven Years* climbs to US #84.
June ***The Young Mods' Forgotten Story*** reaches US #104.
[20-22] The group performs at San Francisco, CA's Fillmore West, with Santana and Ike & Tina Turner.
Aug *Choice Of Colors*, from the album, makes US #21 and also tops the US R&B ranking.
Nov Also from the album, *Say You Love Me* stops at US #58.

1970

June Mayfield has quit the Impressions to pursue a solo career, but continues to oversee all aspects of the group's career, writing and producing some of their Curtom releases and recruiting his replacement, Leroy Hutson. *Check Out Your Mind* reaches US #28.
Sept *(Baby) Turn On To Me* peaks at US #56. In March 1971 *Ain't Got Time* makes US #53, as another ABC compilation album, ***16 Greatest Hits***, peaks at US #180, with *Love Me*, the last Mayfield-penned Impressions song to chart, reaching US #94 in August. The following year, ***Times Have Changed*** will spends two weeks at US #192 in April.

1973

Mar ***Curtis Mayfield/His Early Years With The Impressions*** charts at US #180. (During the year, Hutson leaves for a solo career. Cash and Gooden recruit Reggie Torian and Ralph Johnson, and this line-up records the soundtrack for the movie "Three The Hard Way". Chicago TV station WTTW reassembles most of the original Impressions, the '60s line-up and the current group for the TV special "Curtis". Most of the sound recordings will later be released on ***Curtis In Chicago***.)

1974

July Still with Curtom, the Impressions reach US #17, and top the US R&B survey for the fourth time, with *Finally Got Myself Together*, written and produced by Ed Townsend. ***Finally Got Myself Together*** makes US #176. The following year *Sooner Or Later* peaks at US #68 in July, ***First Impressions*** makes US #115 in August, *Same Thing* stops at US #75 in November while the title cut *First Impressions*, becomes the group's only UK chart entry, reaching #16 in December. With Johnson leaving to form his own group, Mystique, replaced by Nate Evans, ***Loving Power*** will make US #195 in March 1976.

1977

Feb ***The Vintage Years***, featuring 13 hits by the Impressions and 13 by Jerry Butler, stops at US #199. (With their commercial impact clearly lessened, the group will record for a number of labels over the next five years, including Cotillion, Chi-Sound, on which they release an updated version of *For Your Precious Love* in 1981, and MCA, issuing ***Come To My Party*** (1979), ***Fan The Fire*** (1981) and ***In The Heat Of The Night*** (1982), before reuniting with both Butler and Mayfield for a US reunion tour in 1983.)

1991

Jan [16] Tracy Chapman inducts the Impressions into the Rock and Roll Hall of Fame at the sixth annual ceremony, at New York's Waldorf Astoria Hotel.

1993

Mar [26] With MCA having released a twin-CD/cassette anthology, ***Curtis Mayfield & the Impressions - The Anthology 1961-1977***, in 1992, the Impressions, now lining up as Gooden, Johnson, Cash and Smokey Hampton, and continuing to perform regularly, play at the Valley Forge Music Fair, Devon, PA, in a show titled "An Evening Of Love Songs With The Dells And Jerry Butler".
see also: **Jerry BUTLER, Curtis MAYFIELD**

INDIGO GIRLS

Amy Ray (vocals, guitar); **Emily Saliers** (vocals, guitar)

1987

Ray (b. Apr. 12, 1964, Decatur, GA) and Saliers (b.

July 22, 1963, New Haven, CT), having met while attending high school in Decatur, have initially performed as the folk duo Saliers & Ray from 1980, only becoming Indigo Girls while attending Atlanta, GA's Emory University in 1983. Building a loyal following from gigs around Atlanta and the South-east during the mid-'80s, the acoustic-driven, folk harmony duo, musically inspired by the likes of Joni Mitchell, Neil Young, Bob Dylan and the Sex Pistols, have released their debut recording *Crazy Game* on their own Indigo label in 1985, with an EP issued the following year. Their maiden album, the ten-track, self-penned set ***Strange Fire*** is now released, again on Indigo, bringing them to the attention of Epic Records which will sign the duo in 1988.

1989

Apr [15] ***Indigo Girls***, produced by Scott Litt and featuring members of Hothouse Flowers and fellow-Georgians R.E.M., enters the US chart set to reach #22 during a 35-week run. A promotion tour will include opening slots for R.E.M. and Neil Young in the US and 10,000 Maniacs in Europe.
Aug [26] Saliers-written *Closer To Fine*, with Hothouse Flowers' Peter O'Toole assisting on vocals and mandolin, makes US #52.

1990

Jan [13] Reissued via Epic, their maiden effort ***Strange Fire*** now makes US #159.
Feb [21] They win the Best Contemporary Folk Recording category (for ***Indigo Girls***) at the 32nd annual Grammy Awards.
Nov [3] ***Nomads-Indians-Saints***, again produced by Litt, makes US #43, and features Mary-Chapin Carpenter on backing vocals on the extracted Saliers-penned, Grammy-nominated *Hammer And A Nail*.
Dec [13] A US tour includes tonight's gig at the Exposition Building, Portland, ME.

1991

Feb ***Tame Yourself***, a various artists compilation benefitting People for the Ethical Treatment of Animals (PETA), and including Indigo Girls' *I'll Give You My Skin* with Michael Stipe, is released in the US.
July [19] The pair performs on NBC-TV's "Late Night With David Letterman", promoting its US-only live EP release, ***Back On The Bus Y'All***. (During the year, the ever-touring duo will open for the likes of Joan Baez, Jackson Browne and Carpenter.)

1992

Apr [16] ***Indigo Girls*** is certified platinum and ***Nomads-Indians-Saints*** gold by the RIAA.
May [30] ***Rites Of Passage***, a more rock-framed set produced by Peter Collins and featuring the Roches and Siouxsie & the Banshees drummer Budgie among other guests, debuts at its US #21 peak.
Aug [8] The extracted Saliers-penned *Galileo*, with Jackson Browne and David Crosby on backing vocals, peaks at US #89.
Oct [3] A co-headlining European tour with the Neville Brothers is highlighted by a gig at London's Hammersmith Odeon.

1994

Jan [22] Soundtrack album ***Philadelphia***, including the Indigo Girls cut *I Don't Wanna Talk About It*, enters the US chart set to hit #12.
May [28] ***Swamp Ophelia***, once again helmed by Collins and featuring their regular bassist, ex-Gang Of Four's Sara Lee, and violinist Lisa Germano among others, debuts at its US #9 peak.
June [11] ***Swamp Ophelia*** charts for a week at UK #66.
[28-29] Indigo Girls play to 11,683 fans over two nights at Radio City Music Hall, New York, NY.
[30] The duo performs on CBS-TV's "Late Show With David Letterman".
July [5] ***Swamp Ophelia*** is certified gold by the RIAA.
Nov [18] ***Rites Of Passage*** is certified platinum by the RIAA.
Dec [5] During a US trek, the pair performs at the "Z100 Acoustic Christmas" event held at New York's Madison Square Garden alongside Weezer, Melissa Etheridge, Bon Jovi, Sheryl Crow, Toad The Wet Sprocket and Hole.
[19-21] Their current US tour ends with three nights at the Robert W. Woodruff Arts Center Symphony Hall, Atlanta, dates grossing $117,224 from 4,869 fans.

1995

Jan The ***Boys On The Side*** soundtrack, they have also made cameo appearances in the film, including *Joking* and *Power Of Two* by Indigo Girls, is released in the US.
Mar [21] The pair performs on NBC-TV's "The Tonight Show".
June [24] Having recently played their first ever dates in Australia and New Zealand, the Indigo Girls participate in the this year's "Glastonbury Festival", their only European gig this year, promoting not least the newly-released retrospective collection, the 15-track ***4.5*** (issued in the UK only on July 4th).
Sept Knitting Factory Works (US) releases ***Outloud***, a benefit compilation album for the Gay Human Rights Commission, including a new cut by the Indigo Girls.
Oct [28] ***1200 Curfews***, a two-CD 26-song collection of live highlights and six previously-unreleased songs, debuts at its US #40 peak.

JAMES INGRAM

1980

Apr Having moved, in the mid-'70s, to Los Angeles, CA, from Akron, OH, as a member of Revelation Funk, and begun solo performances around the Los Angeles R&B club circuit, Ingram (b. Feb. 17, 1952, Akron) has spent two years touring and recording with Ray Charles, introduced to each other by mutual musician friend Joel Webster, playing keyboards and singing background vocals (he is the pianist on Charles' 1978 US R&B hit version of *I Can See Clearly Now*), and has also performed in the rhythm section for the Coasters on Dick Clark's oldies package tours. Subsequently working for the ATV publishing company singing on demos for $50 per song, he has become musical director for Leon Haywood, who has secured Ingram his first recording contract for RCA Records, which only lasted for three unreleased songs, playing not least on Haywood's current hit single, *Don't Push It Don't Force It*. Meanwhile, Warner Bros. Records producer Russ Titelman has sent Quincy Jones a demo of a Barry Mann and Cynthia Weil composition, *Just Once*, with Ingram on vocals. Jones, already introduced to Ingram via mutual friend, Shalamar singer Howard Hewett, invites him to be one of the featured vocalists on his forthcoming album, ***The Dude***.
Aug Ingram is heard on backing vocals on Carl Carlton's US #22 hit, *She's A Bad Mama Jama*.
Nov Soul ballad, *Just Once*, from ***The Dude***, credited to Quincy Jones, but sung by Ingram, reaches US #17.

1981

Feb [25] Ingram performs *Just Once* at the 23rd annual Grammy Awards, at which he has been nominated for Best New Artist, Best Pop Male Vocal and Best R&B Vocal.
June Invited by Jones to tour Japan, he performs in front of 20,000 people, backed by Jones' 50-piece orchestra.

1982

Feb Ingram's song *Hold On* is covered by sax man Ernie Watts on his album ***Chariots Of Fire***.
[24] Ingram wins Best R&B Vocal Performance, Male for the still-climbing *One Hundred Ways* at the 24th annual Grammy Awards, the only artist to win the award without having released an album.
Mar R&B ballad, *One Hundred Ways*, credited as Quincy Jones featuring James Ingram and another extraction from Jones' ***The Dude***, reaches US #14.
May With Ingram now signed as a solo artist to Jones' Qwest imprint, *Baby Come To Me*, a duet with labelmate Patti Austin, peaks at US #73.
Aug Ingram performs at the "Budweiser Superfest" at the Rose Bowl, Pasadena, CA, with Stevie Wonder, Aretha Franklin, Quincy Jones, Patti Austin, Ashford & Simpson, Luther Vandross, Third World and Frankie Beverly & Maze.
Dec Donna Summer's *State Of Independence*, featuring Ingram in a stellar backing-vocal cast, makes UK #14 (and US #41).

1983

Feb [19] Rod Temperton-penned *Baby Come To Me*, revived and used as the love theme for ABC-TV soap "General Hospital", tops the US chart for the first of two weeks, prior to Michael Jackson's *Billie Jean* (both hits produced by Jones).
Apr Ingram joins Austin on stage at the 55th Academy Awards to perform the Oscar-nominated *How Do You Keep The Music Playing?*
May Producer Jones assembles an all-star cast of musicians and writers for Ingram's debut album, including Larry Carlton (guitar), David Paich, Michael McDonald, David Foster, Greg Phillinganes, Jimmy Smith (keyboards, synthesizers), Louis Johnson and Nathan East (bass), Harvey Mason (drums), and Ernie Watts and Tom Scott (reeds). Work begins on the album at Westlake Audio Studios, Los Angeles.
Aug Austin/Ingram duet, *How Do You Keep The Music Playing?*, the theme to the Goldie Hawn/Burt Reynolds movie "Best Friends", makes US #45.
Nov His debut album, showcasing Ingram's top-drawer R&B vocal skills, ***It's Your Night***, is released, and will earn a gold disc, despite peaking at US #46. In addition to its other stellar musical guests, it features veteran keyboardist Jimmy Smith, idolized by Ingram as a youngster as "the world's greatest organist".
Dec Michael Jackson's *P.Y.T. (Pretty Young Thing)*, written by Ingram, hits US #10 and will make UK #11 in April the following year.

1984

Jan Ingram guests on a two-hour Quincy Jones US TV special.
Mar *Yah Mo B There*, an inspirational duet with Michael McDonald, reaches US #19.
Apr Mann-penned ballad, *There's No Easy Way*, peaks at US #58, while ***It's Your Night*** reaches UK #25.
Dec *What About Me?*, sung in trio with Kenny Rogers and Kim Carnes, and produced by David Foster, reaches US #15.

1985

Feb Remixed *Yah Mo B There* reaches UK #12, after two false starts the previous year (#44, February, and #69, April).
[26] Ingram and McDonald win the Best R&B Performance By A Duo Or Group With Vocal category for *Yah Mo Be There* at the 27th annual Grammy Awards.

1986

Aug His sophomore set, ***Never Felt So Good***, is released. Produced by Keith Diamond, it makes US #123 and UK #72, but yields no UK or US chart singles action.

1987

Mar [14] Ballad, *Somewhere Out There*, duetted with Linda Ronstadt, and taken from the Steven Spielberg-produced animated movie "An American Tail", hits US #2 and will hit UK #8 in August. During the summer, Ingram's *Better Way* will be featured on the soundtrack to the hit sequel movie "Beverly Hills Cop II".

1988

Mar [2] *Somewhere Out There* is name Song Of The Year at the 30th annual Grammy Awards.
July Patti Austin's ***The Real Me***, featuring Ingram, is released. By year's end he signs a new recording deal with Warner Bros. at the instigation of label boss, Mo Ostin.

1989

Nov [15] Previously reluctant to tour (spending time with his five children is his priority), Ingram embarks on his first major US tour as the support act for R&B diva Patti LaBelle, not least to promote his third album, ***It's Real***, which has been variously produced by Thom Bell, Gene Griffin, Gerald Levert, Dennis Matkosky, Michael Powell, Teddy Riley, Monty Seward, Bernard Taylor and Ingram.

1990

Mar [14] Ingram sings at the fourth annual Soul Train Awards, at the Shrine Auditorium, Los Angeles.
Aug [14] He guests on NBC-TV's "The Tonight Show".
Oct [20] *I Don't Have The Heart*, co-produced with Thom Bell, who was introduced to the vocalist by Quincy Jones, tops the US chart. (After seven previous Top 40 hits, either uncredited or a part of a duo, this is Ingram's first solo hit.)
Nov [10] ***It's Real***, originally released last year, finally climbs to US #117.
Dec [11] He performs on CBS-TV's "1990 Grammy Legends Show".

1991

Sept [19] Ingram sings *I Can't Stop Loving You* for the "Ray Charles : 50 Years In Music" special held in Pasadena, CA, to benefit the Starlight & Starlight Pavilion Foundations, set to air on Fox-TV on October 6th.
Oct [19] ***The Power Of Great Music***, a greatest hits set augmented by three new cuts, debuts at it US #168 peak.
Nov [2] **Billboard** trade magazine includes a tenth anniversary James Ingram tribute supplement.

1992

Jan [7] *The Heart Of A Hero*, written by Jeffrey Osborne, is recorded in Los Angeles by an all-star cast which includes Ingram, to raise money for AIDS research.
Sept [13] PBS-TV's "Evening At The Pops" series showcases Ingram in performance with Patti Austin and the Boston Pops Orchestra, conducted by John Williams.
[29] The soundtrack to "Sarafina!", including Ingram's *One More Time*, is released in the US.

1993

June [8] Ingram guests on syndicated TV's "The Arsenio Hall Show", to promote the release of his first studio album of the decade, ***Always You***, variously produced by Bell, Keith Thomas and Maurice White.

1994

Jan [17] Ingram returns to "The Tonight Show".
[29] He begins a Far East tour in Kuala Lumpur, Malaya.
Mar [21] Ingram and Dolly Parton sing their current duet, *The Day I Fall In Love*, from the movie "Beethoven's 2nd", at the 66th annual Academy Awards from the Shrine Auditorium.
Apr [16] *The Day I Fall In Love* debuts at its UK #64 peak.
Oct [15] Ingram appears at the Celebrity Tribute To Medicine, a Washington, DC event honoring 28 African-Americans who have excelled in science and medicine.
Nov [26] "The Colors Of Christmas", a festive package tour with Ingram, Roberta Flack, Sheena Easton and Peabo Bryson, begins a two month-long US trek at the Palace of Auburn Hills, Auburn Hills, MI. (After the tour, Ingram will continue working on a project with Jeffrey Osborne, having been dropped by Qwest.)

1995

June [1] Ingram and Anita Baker perform *When You Love Someone*, featured on the film soundtrack to the Billy Crystal movie "Forget Paris", on NBC-TV's "Tonight Show".
Aug [22] Songwriter Bruce Roberts' album ***Intimacy***, featuring Ingram, is released in the US.
Dec [3] The annual "Colors Of Christmas" tour, now with Ingram, Flack, Bryson and Melissa Manchester, sells out the Westbury Music Fair, Westbury, NY. Recently featured on the Disney-released ***The Music Of Cinderella*** album, Ingram will also appear on the the all-star update of the musical ***West Side Story***, singing *Maria* with Michael McDonald and David Pack, released in the US the following February.

INXS

Michael Hutchence (vocals); **Tim Farriss** (guitar); **Kirk Pengilly** (guitar, saxophone, vocals); **Andrew Farriss** (keyboards); **Garry Beers** (bass, vocals); **Jon Farriss** (drums, vocals)

1979

Sept [1] Having originally formed as the Farris Brothers in Sydney, New South Wales, Australia, in August 1977, to play their debut at member Tim Farriss' (b. Aug. 16, 1957, Perth, Western Australia, Australia) 20th birthday party, and spending 1978 writing and performing in Perth, Australia, the newly named INXS, a moniker suggested by Midnight Oil manager Garry Morris, with its original six-member line-up of Hutchence (b. Jan. 22, 1962, Lain Cove, Sydney, Australia), the Farriss brothers (Andrew (b. Mar. 27, 1959, Perth), Jon (b. Aug. 10, 1961, Perth), and Tim), Andrew and Jon having been schoolfriends of Hutchence's at Davidson High School, Pengilly (b. July 4, 1958, Sydney) and Beers (b. June 22, 1957, Sydney), who, with Tim Farriss, have been to Forest High School, is back in its native Sydney and performs its first concert under the name INXS, at the Oceanview Hotel, Toukley, Australia. The band, whose line-up will remain unchanged throughout its history, will spend the next four years playing over 250 pub and club gigs a year, building a large and dedicated Australian rock-fan base.

1980

May Their first single, *Simple Simon/We Are The Vegetables*, is released in Australia, on the Deluxe label.
Oct Their debut album ***INXS*** is issued, featuring the group's first Australian hit, *Just Keep Walking*.

1981

Mar *The Loved One* (which will be re-recorded in 1987 for the album ***Kick***) is released. During the year, INXS will play some 300 dates in Australia during the "Fear And Loathing Tour", "The Campus Tour", "Stay Young Tour" and "The Tour With No Name".
Oct The group signs to RCA Records, releasing its second Australia-only album, ***Underneath The Colours***, which includes the native hits *Stay Young* and *Loved One*, while lead singer Hutchence also appears on two songs with Cold Chisel (*Speed Kills* and *Forest Theme*) on the soundtrack of the Australian movie "Freedom".

1982

Jan The band tours New Zealand and, upon its return, records *The One Thing*.
Apr Hutchence, Pengilly, who is concurrently involved in a one-off EP release by the Igniters, and Andrew Farriss travel to the UK and US to negotiate the next stage in the group's career.
July WEA signs INXS for Australasia, releasing its third album, ***Shabooh Shoobah***.

1983

Jan INXS, inked to Atlantic Records in the US, embarks on a North American tour as guests of the Kinks and Adam & the Ants.
Mar The group makes its US debut with *The One Thing*, which, with a heavy rotation promo video on MTV, reaches #30. ***Shabooh Shoobah*** makes US #46, while *Don't Change* is the group's freshman release in the UK.
May The band's first headlining date in New York, NY is at The Ritz.
July *Don't Change* reaches US #80.
Sept *Original Sin* is recorded at New York's Power Station Studio, with Nile Rodgers producing and Daryl Hall and Dave Stewart guesting on vocals.
Oct Mini-album, ***Dekadence***, with remixes of four tracks from ***Shabooh Shoobah***, reaches US #148.

1984

Jan The group plays a sellout Australian tour, as *Original Sin* tops the domestic chart.
May INXS' UK live debut is at London's Astoria Theatre, and reflects the beginning of a determined effort to introduce the band to a worldwide audience. *Original Sin* reaches US #58.
June Its parent album, ***The Swing***, makes US #52.
July The band's early albums, ***INXS*** and ***Underneath The Colours***, are belatedly released in the US.
Aug *I Send A Message* peaks at US #77, while ***INXS*** reaches US #164.
Sept The group completes a three-month US tour, its third, with a sellout show at the Hollywood Palladium. A video collection, "The Swing And Other Stories", documenting the band's Australian history, is prominently featured on MTV and is instrumental in breaking them in the American market.
Nov Returning home, INXS stops off at Guam in the Pacific, becoming the first international group to play there.

1985

Mar INXS starts work on its fifth album, ***Listen Like Thieves***, at Sydney's Rhinoceros Studios, with Chris Thomas producing. ***The Swing*** achieves double-platinum status in Australia.
July [13] The group appears in the Australian segment of the historic "Live Aid" benefit concert, from the Sydney Entertainment Centre, beamed worldwide by satellite.
Aug Work finishes at London's AIR Studios on ***Listen Like Thieves***. (Meanwhile Hutchence co-produces and sings on Fame & Fortune's *Sex Symbol*, while Jon Farriss produces Kam Sha's *Work Until You Drop*.)
[28] "The 1985 INXS World Tour" commences in Australia.
Nov In mid-tour, the group briefly returns home to perform at the "Rockin' The Royals" charity concert in the presence of H.R.H. the Prince and Princess of Wales, in Melbourne, Victoria, Australia.
Dec *This Time* peaks at US #81. The video "The Swing And Other Stories" is issued in the US by Atlantic Video, and in the UK by Channel 5. By year's end INXS will have collected seven trophies at the Australian Countdown Awards, and will bring their concert tally to some 1,500 live shows in just six years.

1986

Feb [2] Following appearances at London's Marquee club and on C4-TV's "The Tube", INXS performs at London's Hammersmith Odeon, supporting ***Listen Like Thieves***, which, licensed to Mercury Records in the UK, makes #48.
Apr [12] The extracted *What You Need* hits US #5, and will peak at UK #51. (Hutchence makes his acting debut in the movie "Dogs In Space", and has a solo Top 10 hit in Australia with *Rooms For The Memory*, from the film.)
May The group embarks on the "If You Got It, Shake It!" world tour, highlighted by two sellout shows supporting Queen at Wembley Stadium, Wembley, Middx.
June [14] *Listen Like Thieves* peaks at US #54, and will make UK #46, while ***Listen Like Thieves*** is on its way to steal US #11, eventually selling some 3.5 million copies worldwide.
Sept *Kiss The Dirt (Falling Down The Mountain)* makes UK #54. The group returns home for its "Si Lo Tienes Muevelo" tour while, in the States the band are voted "Best Live Act Of The Year" by **US** magazine.

1987

Jan INXS heads a major Australian tour with eight other bands, under the banner "Australian Made".
Aug [1] *Good Times*, featured in the movie "The Lost Boys", and teaming the group with rock vocal

compatriot Jimmy Barnes, makes US #47. (Jon Farriss will also produce Richard Clapton's **Glory Road** album during the year, while his brother Andy, having produced the Dropbears' 1984 single, *Shall We Go*, now helms projects for other Australian acts, including the Flaming Hands (*The Edge/Sacrifice*), and Jenny Morris' current album, ***Body And Soul***; he will also produce her 1989 follow-up, ***Shiver***.)
Oct *Need You Tonight* peaks at UK #58.
[16] INXS' 1987-88 "Kick" world tour opens in East Lansing, MI.
Dec [2-14] The tour reaches the UK.

1988

Jan [30] Guitar-stuttered *Need You Tonight* becomes the group's first US #1 hit, aided not least by round-the-clock MTV video exposure.
Feb [6] ***Kick*** hits UK #9, where it will log 103 weeks on the survey, and will go on to hit US #3, becoming the band's biggest worldwide seller with eight million copies sold. The extracted *New Sensation* makes UK #25.
Mar *Devil Inside* reaches UK #47.
Apr [16] Rock radio favorite *Devil Inside*, written, as is much of the band's material, by Hutchence and Andrew Farris, hits US #2, spurred by a Joel Schumacher-directed video clip.
June [24] INXS sells out the Wembley Arena, during its European tour which began in February and during which Jon Farriss is subsequently injured in a skateboard accident, causing dates in Germany, Italy and Switzerland to be cancelled.
July *Never Tear Us Apart* reaches UK #24 and hits US #7, during further US concert appearances.
Aug Video compilation, "Kick Flicks", is released, while *New Sensation*, the fourth cut from ***Kick***, which is on its way to four RIAA-certified platinum discs, heads toward US #3.
Sept [7] "Need You Tonight" wins the Best Video, Best Group Video, Best Editing, Viewers Choice and Breakthrough Video categories at the fifth annual MTV Video Music Awards, held at the Universal Amphitheatre, Universal City, CA.
Oct INXS embarks on the Australian leg of the "Kick" world tour, after which members will take a sabbatical.
Dec Reissued *Need You Tonight* hits UK #2.

1989

Apr Further ***Kick*** extract, *Mystify*, reaches UK #14.
Nov Max Q, an extra curricular project by Hutchence with Ollie Olsen from Australian band No, releases its debut album, ***Max Q***, which makes UK #65 (for Mercury Records) and US #182 (on Atlantic), both INXS' respective territory labels.

1990

Feb Max Q's dance-remixed *Sometimes* makes UK #53.
May [4] Roger Corman's "Frankenstein Unbound", in which Hutchence plays Percy Shelley, opens in cinemas across the US.
Sept From the forthcoming album, *Suicide Blonde* reaches UK #11.
Oct [20] Largely written by Andrew Farriss and Hutchence as always, ***X***, recorded at the Rhinoceros Studio 2, Sydney, their third consecutive album produced by Chris Thomas, featuring harmonica great Charlie Musselwhite, marks the spot at US #5, having already hit UK #2 (Oct [6]).
[27] *Suicide Blonde* hits US #9.
Nov [25] During the "X" world concert trek, the band begins a five-date UK leg at London's Docklands Arena, set to end on December 15th at Bournemouth International Centre, Bournemouth, Dorset, as ***X*** becomes the group's third RIAA-certified platinum album.
Dec [22] *Disappear* reaches UK #21.

1991

Jan [12-14] INXS opens its American tour with two sellout dates at the Palacio de los Deportes, Mexico City, grossing $979,000.
[19] The band performs at "Rock In Rio II" on the festival's second day, at the Maracana soccer stadium in Rio de Janeiro, Brazil, opening its set with *It's Not Unusual*, before an estimated 100,000 fans.
[28] The group plays at the 18th annual American Music Awards held at Los Angeles, CA's Shrine Auditorium.
Feb [3] INXS is the musical guest on NBC-TV's "Saturday Night Live".
[10] The band wins the Best International Group and Hutchence wins Best International Artist, Male categories at the tenth annual BRIT Awards, at London's Dominion Theatre.
[16] *Disappear* hits US #8, as the group, on its current North American tour, supported by the Soup Dragons, plays to a sellout crowd at New York's Madison Square Garden.
Mar A 24 video-clip collection, including five MTV Award-winners, "INXS Video - Greatest Hits 1980-1990", is released.
[6] *By My Side* makes UK #42.
May [11] *Bitter Tears* climbs to US #46.
[12] INXS appears by satellite from Melbourne, in "The Simple Truth" concert for Kurdish refugees, at Wembley Arena, performing *By My Side*.
July [13] INXS headlines the Wembley Stadium "Summer XS" bill, with Hothouse Flowers, Deborah Harry, Jesus Jones, Roachford and Jellyfish, before a sellout crowd of 73,791, grossing £1,426,617, as *Bitter Tears* debuts at its UK #30 peak.
[14] The band records *Shining Star* at London's Metropolis Studios.
[15-16] The UK leg of the tour ends at Glasgow's SE&CC, before the group sets off for a further month-long US trek.
Nov [9] EP *Shining Star* reaches UK #27.
[16] Performance set ***Live Baby Live***, the band's second album release in four months, bows at its UK #8 peak.
[23] ***Live Baby Live*** debuts at its US #72 peak.

1992

Jan The band returns to its favored recording location at Rhinoceros Studios, Sydney, Australia.
Feb [14] Jon Farriss and actress Leslie Bega, star of ABC-TV's "Head Of The Class", marry in Sydney.
Mar [28] Billed as the largest single community event in Australian history, the AIDS-and-heart-research benefit "Concert For Life", headlined by INXS and also starring Crowded House, in Centennial Park, Sydney, to benefit the Victor Chang Cardiac Research Centre and the AIDS Patient Services and Research Centre at St. Vincent Hospital, Sydney, is attended by over 100,000 people, raising over $1.5 million. It will be the group's only domestic appearance of the year.
June [26] INXS wins the HMV International Award at the annual Nordoff-Robbins Music Therapy lunch, at London's Inter-Continental Hotel.
July [25] *Heaven Sent* reaches UK #31, as the group's *Not Enough Time* is featured on the summer Olympics-celebrating ***Barcelona Gold*** collection, released today.
Aug [15] ***Welcome To Wherever You Are***, reuniting the group with producer Mark Opitz for the first time since 1983's ***Shabooh Shoobah***, debuts at UK #1 and will debut at its US #16 peak the following week.
Sept [12] The extracted *Baby Don't Cry* reaches UK #20.
Oct [10] *Not Enough Time* reaches US #28.
[19] Current promo video for their forthcoming single, *Taste It*, featuring foot fetish and voyeurism fantasies, is banned by US-MTV.
Nov [21] *Taste It* reaches UK #21, as the band begins a ten-day rehearsal at Hutchence's chateau in France, in preparation for its 1993 world tour.

1993

Feb [20] *Beautiful Girl* reaches UK #23.
Apr [10] *Beautiful Girl* makes US #46.
May [7] A low-key, 11-city North American club tour begins at the Warfield Theatre, San Francisco, CA, set to end at the Masquerade, Atlanta, GA, on the 22nd. Dubbed the "Get Out Of The House" tour, it is a small-venue follow-up to last year's popular Australian pub tour (which was recently described by Hutchence in **USA Today** as "raw, aggressive and up-front. There was lots of sweat and not enough oxygen)".
[12] The group is named Best-selling Australian Artist Of The Year at the fifth annual World Music Awards, at the Sporting Club in Monte Carlo, Monaco, attended by Hutchence with current model flame (who has replaced Australian starlet Kylie Minogue), Helena Christensen.
Oct [23] *The Gift* debuts at its UK #11 peak.
Nov [20] ***Full Moon, Dirty Hearts***, having bowed at its UK #3 peak on the 13th, debuts at its US #53 high.
Dec [11] *Please (You Got That ...)* enters at its UK #50 peak.

1994

Mar [24] The group plays at the Ervin J. Nutter Center, Wright State University, Dayton, OH, at the start of the US leg of another world tour.
Oct [8] Hutchence sings *Baby Let's Play House* at "Elvis Aaron Presley : The Tribute". an all-star event held at the Pyramid Arena, Memphis, TN, broadcast live on US pay-per-view TV.
[29] *The Strangest Party (These Are The Times)* reaches UK #15.
Nov [12] ***The Greatest Hits***, including two new songs *The Strangest Party* and *Deliver Me*, hits UK #3 in its week of entry.
[19] ***The Greatest Hits*** debuts at its US #112 peak.

1995

July The "Batman Forever" soundtrack, including a solo cut by Hutchence who is preparing his debut solo album with Tim Simenon, is released.
Sept [12] Hutchence pleads guilty to punching photographer Jim Bennett outside a hotel in London on March 20th. He is fined £400 and ordered to pay £1,875 in court costs and other expenses. (Hutchence and latest belle, Paula Yates, are the paparazzi's current, favorite targets.)

1996

Feb Paul Craig of Sound Management Associates becomes worldwide manager of the group (which is also now signed globally to Polygram), taking over from Chris Murphy with whom the band has split.

IRON BUTTERFLY

Doug Ingle (vocals, keyboards);
Erik Braunn (guitar, vocals); **Lee Dorman** (bass);
Ronald Bushy (drums)

1967

Formed the previous year in San Diego, CA, by Ingle (b. Sept. 9, 1946, Omaha, NE), the son of a church organist, Bushy (b. Sept. 23, 1945, Washington, DC), bassist Jerry Penrod (b. San Diego), guitarist Danny Weis (b. San Diego) and vocalist Darryl DeLoach (b. San Diego), the hard-rock combo Iron Butterfly has relocated to Los Angeles, CA, initially working the rock-club circuit, including gigs at Bido Lito's, the Galaxy and the Whisky A-Go-Go, before signing to Atlantic Records' subsidiary, Atco.

1968

Mar ***Heavy*** climbs to US #78 during a 49-week stay on the chart, sustained by the group touring as the opening act for the Doors and Jefferson Airplane. DeLoach quits, and Penrod and Weis leave to form Rhinoceros. Dorman (b. Sept. 19, 1945, St. Louis, MO) and Braunn (b. Aug. 11, 1950, Boston, MA) replace them.
May Iron Butterfly's *Possession* and *Unconscious Power* are featured, with material from Cream, in the film soundtrack to "Savage Seven".
June [7-9] The band performs at the Avalon Ballroom, San Francisco, CA, on a bill with the Velvet Underground.
July Ingle-penned ***In-A-Gadda-Da-Vida***, originally

named ***In The Garden Of Eden*** but apparently transformed due to band-member intoxication, enters the US chart and will hit #4.
Aug Iron Butterfly appears at the "Newport Pop Festival" at Costa Mesa, CA.
Oct [17-19] The group plays at the Fillmore West, San Francisco, with Quicksilver Messenger Service.
[26] *In-A-Gadda-Da-Vida*, edited from the 17-minute album version, reaches US #30.
Dec [6] They take part in the "Quaker City Rock Festival" at the Spectrum, Philadelphia, PA, on a bill with Grateful Dead and Steppenwolf. (At month's end, the group also joins a star bill for the three-day "Miami Pop Festival" at the Gulfstream Racing Park, Hallandale, FL.)

1969

Jan [23-26] The band performs at the Fillmore West, San Francisco.
Feb Their third album, ***Ball***, enters the US chart and will hit #3.
Mar [15] The extracted *Soul Experience* peaks at US #75.
June The group joins Joe Cocker, Creedence Clearwater Revival, Jimi Hendrix and many others on the bill of the "Denver Pop Festival", held at the Mile High Stadium, Denver, CO.
July [4-5] The band plays New York's Fillmore East, with Blues Image.
[19] *In The Time Of Our Lives* makes US #96.
Aug Iron Butterfly performs at the three-day "Atlantic City Pop Festival" in Atlantic City, NJ.
Sept Braunn quits, later forming Flintwhistle with DeLoach and Penrod. Guitarists Larry Rheinhardt (b. July 7, 1948, FL) and ex-Blues Image Mike Pinera (b. Sept. 29, 1948) replace him.

1970

May ***Iron Butterfly Live*** reaches US #20.
Aug ***Metamorphosis***, featuring recent recruits Pinera and Reinhardt, makes US #16. Pinera proclaims: "You gotta change, you better get hip."
Nov [21] *Easy Rider (Let The Wind Pay The Way)*, the title cut taken from the soundtrack to the cult movie success "Easy Rider", makes US #66.

1971

Apr ***In-A-Gadda-Da-Vida*** drops off the US survey after 140 weeks, having sold over three million copies, and is Atlantic Records' biggest album success. (It will remain so until the advent of Led Zeppelin.)
May [23] The group splits, following its farewell live appearance.

1975

Feb Following the release of the compilations ***The Best Of Iron Butterfly/Evolution*** (US #137 - Jan 1972) and ***Star Collection*** (1973), Braunn and Bushy regroup with Phil Kramer (b. July 12, 1952, Youngtown, OH) and Howard Reitzes (b. Mar. 22, 1951, Southgate, CA) to sign with MCA Records, releasing the albums ***Scorching Beauty*** (US #138) and ***Sun And Steel***, before dissolving once more, although, like so many bands of their era, they will reform and will still be playing in the '90s.

1995

Feb [22] While Rhino Records (US) released ***Light And Heavy: The Best Of Iron Butterfly*** in May 1993, the group, comprising Ingle, Bushy, Dorman and newcomer Derek Hilland, began recording a new album in 1994. The 6' 5"-tall Kramer, now a 42-year old executive with Total Multimedia, is reported missing by his wife who last saw him leaving home on the 12th to pick up a friend at Los Angeles Airport in his green 1993 Ford Aerostar van, license-plate # 3EBU O24. NBC-TV's "Unsolved Mysteries" will file a report on the story on November 17th.

IRON MAIDEN

Bruce Dickinson (vocals); **Dave Murray** (lead, rhythm guitar); **Adrian Smith** (guitar); **Dennis Stratton** (guitar); **Steve Harris** (bass); **Nicko McBrain** (drums); **Eddie** (mascot)

1976

May Harris (b. Mar. 12, 1957, Leytonstone, London), after earlier ambitions to be a professional soccer player, and having already led pub band Smiler, meets Murray (b. Dec. 23, 1958, London) and forms a new rock combo, Iron Maiden, named after the medieval instrument of torture, determined to keep the heavy-metal cause alive in the face of the new punk-music movement. The initial personnel features Harris (the only original member to remain in future line-ups), Murray, vocalist Paul Di'anno (b. May 17, 1959, Chingford, London) and drummer Doug Sampson. Based in Leytonstone, Iron Maiden's live debut is at the Cart & Horses Pub, Stratford, in the capital's East End, and the group will continue to play local gigs for the next two years, honing its self-written, uncompromising, loud, intense, power-driven rock style.

1978

The group undertakes regular stints at London pubs the Bridgehouse, Canning Town, and Ruskin Arms, East Ham, though, despite constant gigging, it is unable to illicit record company interest. Having established a strong cult following, Iron Maiden releases an EP of demos, recorded on December 30th, featuring *Iron Maiden*, *Prowler* and *Strange World*, on its own label. DJ Neal Kay, of the Bandwaggon Soundhouse in London, is sent a copy and the tape becomes a massive heavy-metal club hit, with the group subsequently performing regularly at the Soundhouse over the next 12 months.

1979

Feb The band has £12,000-worth of equipment stolen from its van. Ilkay Bayram from London is later convicted of the theft, and most of the equipment is returned.
May DJ Kay organizes his "Heavy Metal Crusade" at London's Music Machine. Iron Maiden appears in what is recognized as the first concert of the "New Wave Of British Heavy Metal" (NWBHM), a phrase coined by **Sounds** journalist (and future **Kerrang!** editor) Geoff Barton.
June During a month when Di'anno is arrested for carrying a knife, Roderick Smallwood from the MAM Agency hears the band's demo and invites them to play at the Windsor Castle and the Swan pubs, subsequently finding nationwide UK gigs.
Oct A showcase at London's Marquee is ignored by every major label.
Nov EP *The Soundhouse Tapes* is released through mail order, having been recorded a year earlier in Cambridge. New guitarist Tony Parsons joins and they record two tracks for the compilation album ***Metal For Muthas***, released through EMI.
[28] The group finally signs with EMI Records.

1980

Jan Parsons is replaced by Stratton (b. Nov. 9, 1954, London), ex-Remus Down Boulevard. Sampson leaves for health reasons and is replaced by Clive Burr (b. Mar. 8, 1958).
Feb Their label debut, *Running Free*, reaches UK #34. The band refuses to mime on BBC1-TV's "Top Of The Pops", becoming the first act to play live on the show since the Who in 1973.
Apr [26] The band's first album, ***Iron Maiden***, bow at its UK #4 peak, spurred by a UK tour with Judas Priest.
June *Sanctuary* reaches UK #29. On its sleeve, Derek Riggs, the group's artistic designer, depicts Iron Maiden's psychotic mechanical mascot, Eddie, knife-slashing PM Margaret Thatcher. After legal action is threatened, her eyes are blacked out. EMI holds a special Iron Maiden party at Madame Tussaud's Chamber of Horrors.
[20] The band plays at the Rainbow Theatre, Finsbury Park, London.
Aug Iron Maiden is featured on ITV's "20th Century Box" special on the NWBHM, as it begins a European tour supporting Kiss.
[23] The group appears at the "Reading Festival", Reading, Berks.
Oct Stratton is fired, and is replaced by ex-Urchin guitarist Smith (b. Feb. 27, 1957, London).
Nov *Women In Uniform*, with picture sleeve featuring PM Thatcher holding a machine gun, waiting for revenge on Eddie, climbs to UK #35, while Eddie is introduced as a permanent feature of the band's live act (and will grow in physical and popular stature over the coming years).

1981

Feb [28] Half-live, half-studio album, ***Killers***, containing four new tracks, reaches UK #12 and will make US #78.
Mar *Twilight Zone/Wrath Child* makes UK #31.
May Iron Maiden begins a sold-out Japanese tour, as part of its "The Killer World Tour", set to play in 15 countries (including Yugoslavia where it becomes the first-ever rock band to perform in the country), during which the band will make its US debut, again opening for Judas Priest.
June *Purgatory* makes UK #52.
Sept At the end of the tour, Di'anno leaves, continuing his music career with Lone Wolf and Battlezone. (He will eventually form rock outfit Killers in May 1992).
Oct He is replaced by ex-Samson vocalist and private school-educated Dickinson (b. Paul Bruce Dickinson, Aug. 7, 1958, Worksop, Notts.), raised from the age of four in Sheffield, Yorks., who has spent a short time in the infantry before going to Queen Mary College, London University, to study history. After playing with the group Speed, he then joined Shots, with Tony Lee and Doug and Tony Siviter, and has been seen by two members of Samson, singing in the Prince Of Wales pub in Gravesend, Kent. He was invited to join and, after finishing his history degree examinations in the summer of 1979, became the group's lead singer. A live EP *Maiden Japan* peaks at UK #43 and US #89.
Nov [15] Dickinson makes his live debut with Iron Maiden.
Dec The group plays a pub gig as Genghis Khan.

1982

Feb [25] "Beast On The Road" tour begins in Dunstable, Beds., set to end 11 months later in Niggata, Japan. During the 179-date, 16-country sojourn, they will play to over one million fans.
Mar *Run To The Hills* hits UK #7, while its video is the band's first to be shown on US MTV.
Apr [10] Iron Maiden knocks Barbra Streisand off the top spot, as ***The Number Of The Beast***, produced by Martin Birch, hits UK #1. It will reach #33 in the US where it will have a 65-week chart run. The group relocates to the Bahamas for tax purposes.
May *The Number Of The Beast* reaches UK #18.
[11] The group begins a six-month US leg of the "Beast On The Road" tour in Flint, MI, set to end on October 23rd in Rochester, NY, including a sold out date at the Palladium, New York, NY, on June 29th, where a now larger-than-life (12') Eddie holds aloft the bitten-off "head" of Ozzy Osbourne. Dickinson will have to wear a surgical collar for some of the gigs, the result of too much head-banging.
July A soccer match with the Scorpions ends in 0-0 tie.
Aug In between US tour dates in El Paso, TX, and Los Angeles, CA, the band flies to London, to make a one-off performance at the annual "Reading Rock Festival".

1983

Jan Drummer Burr quits the line-up amicably, to be replaced by McBrain (b. June 5, 1954), ex-Streetwalkers and Trust, a French band which supported Iron Maiden on a 1981 UK tour.
May *Flight Of Icarus* peaks at UK #11. ***Piece Of***

Mind, recorded in Nassau, hits UK #3 and #14 in the US (where it will earn a platinum disc).
[2] A four-month "World Piece" universal tour, including the group's first headlining US dates, begins at the City Hall, Hull, Humberside.
July *The Trooper* reaches UK #12.
Dec Readers of UK heavy-metal magazine **Kerrang** vote ***Piece Of Mind*** and ***The Number Of The Beast*** the top two heavy-metal albums of all time. Iron Maiden wins a soccer match against Def Leppard in Germany 4-2.

1984

Aug *2 Minutes To Midnight* reaches UK #11. The "World Slavery" tour begins in Poland, running through to a July 1985 finalé in Southern California after 200 shows.
Sept [11] The UK leg of the "World Slavery" tour begins at the Apollo Theatre, Glasgow, Scotland.
Oct [8] The group plays the first of four sellout dates at London's Hammersmith Odeon, at the end of the 24-date UK leg.
Nov *Aces High* peaks at UK #20 while its parent album, ***Powerslave***, recorded at Le Chalet, France, hits UK #2 and reaches US #21.

1985

Mar [14-17] Iron Maiden plays sellout dates at the Long Beach Arena, CA, during the US segment of its tour.
Apr The "World Slavery" tour continues throughout South-East Asia.
June ***Iron Maiden*** is reissued, reaching UK #71.
July [5] The "World Slavery" trek ends in California with a "British Independence Day Celebration" concert.
Oct Live *Running Free* makes UK #19. Their recent 11-month, 26-country tour is documented by the double album ***Live After Death***, which will hit UK #2 and US #19.
Dec Further performance excerpt, *Run To The Hills*, makes UK #26. The group plays a gig at London's Marquee club as the Entire Population Of Hackney.

1986

Sept *Wasted Years* peaks at UK #18, while ***Somewhere In Time*** hits UK #3 and US #11, and marks the beginning of yet another tour.
Nov *Stranger In A Strange Land* reaches UK #22. The band performs a charity benefit gig at London's Hammersmith Odeon with special guests, the heavy metal-pastiche combo, Bad News.

1987

Jan Dickinson is belatedly arrested in Lubbock, TX, for allegedly hitting someone with a microphone and then attempting to strangle him with its cord, back in March 1985.
May Iron Maiden finishes a seven-month world tour and begins work on a new studio project.

1988

Apr [23] ***Seventh Son Of A Seventh Son*** debuts at UK #1 and peaks at US #12, while *Can I Play With Madness* hits UK #3, both achievements confirming Iron Maiden's position as the UK's top metal act.
Aug [20] *Evil That Men Do* hits UK #5, as the band, in the midst of its "Seventh Tour Of A Seventh Tour" world trek, makes its only UK appearance of the year at the "Monsters Of Rock" festival held annually at Castle Donington, Leics.
Sept [4] The group plays a further "Monsters of Rock" concert with Kiss, Anthrax, Great White, David Lee Roth and Helloween at the Willem II Stadion, Tilburg, West Germany.
Oct Not surprisingly, a tape by Iron Maiden wakes fan Gary Dobson from a coma, eight weeks after he was crushed at Castle Donington.
Nov [19] *The Clairvoyant* hits UK #6.

1989

Apr Keen fencer and swordsman, Dickinson is ranked seventh in Great Britain in the domestic rankings for Men's Foil. His team, the Hemel Hempstead Fencing Club, are national champions and go to Paris to represent Great Britain in the European Cup. (Dickinson's song *Bring Your Daughter To The Slaughter*, featured in the film "A Nightmare On Elm Street 5: The Dream Child", receives a Golden Raspberry award for Worst Original Song.)
Nov [18] *Infinite Dreams* hits UK #6.
Dec [30] Dickinson has collaborated with Ian Gillan, Brian May and Robert Plant as Rock Aid Armenia for a remake of *Smoke On The Water*, which makes UK #39, with all profits from the record going to the victims of the recent Armenian earthquake disaster.

1990

Feb [12] EMI releases two 12" singles as a double-package mini-album, the first of a limited-edition collection of ten such releases, to celebrate ten years of Iron Maiden's recording career with the label. The mini-albums will be released consecutively, every week for ten weeks, and will chart on the UK Album survey in the following chronological order: ***Running Free/Sanctuary*** #10 (Feb [24]); ***Women In Uniform/Twilight Zone*** #10 (Mar [3]), ***Purgatory/ Maiden Japan*** #5 (Mar [10]), ***Run To The Hills/The Number Of The Beast*** #3 (Mar [17]), ***Flight Of Icarus/The Trooper*** #7 (Mar [24]), ***2 Minutes To Midnight/Aces High*** #11 (Mar [31]), ***Running Free (Live)/Run To The Hills (Live)*** #9 (Apr [7]), ***Wasted Years/Stranger In A Strange Land*** #9 (Apr [14]), ***Can I Play With Madness/Evil That Men Do*** #10 (Apr [21]) and ***The Clairvoyant/Infinite Dreams (Live)*** #11 (Apr [28]).
Apr [28] Dickinson's solo debut, *Tattooed Millionaire*, reaches UK #18.
May [8] Its parent album, ***Tattooed Millionaire***, is released, co-written with new Iron Maiden recruit, ex-White Spirit guitarist Janick Gers (b. Hartlepool, Lancs.). He replaces Adrian Smith, who leaves to form A.S.A.P., with Zak Starkey (drums), Dave Colwell and Andy Barnett (guitars), Robin Clayton (bass) and Richard Young (keyboards). Jagged Edge drummer Fabio Del Rio also features on the album.
[17] Sidgwick & Jackson publish Dickinson's first novel, **The Adventures Of Lord Iffy Boatrace**.
[19] Dickinson's ***Tattooed Millionaire*** reaches UK #14.
June [19] Dickinson's seven-date UK solo tour begins at the Mayfair, Newcastle, Tyne & Wear, ending at London's Astoria Theatre on May 28th.
[23] His cover version of Mott The Hoople's *All The Young Dudes* reaches UK #23.
July [7] ***Tattooed Millionaire*** climbs to US #100.
[15] Dickinson begins the US leg of his tour in Norfolk, VA. The 25-date trek is set to end on August 15th at the Whisky in Los Angeles.
Aug [25] His *Dive! Dive! Dive!*, recorded at the first Astoria gig on June 27th, makes UK #45.
Sept [20] Iron Maiden embarks on the first leg of its latest world tour at the Mayflower, Southampton, Hants. The 21-date trek is set to end on October 18th at London's Hammersmith Odeon.
[22] *Holy Smoke*, from the forthcoming studio album, hits UK #3.
Oct [13] ***No Prayer For The Dying*** debuts at its UK #2 peak behind Luciano Pavarotti, Placido Domingo and Jose Carreras' ***In Concert***.
[21] Their 55-date "No Prayer On The Road" tour begins in Barcelona, Spain.
Nov [3] ***No Prayer For The Dying*** reaches US #17.
Dec [17-18] Iron Maiden plays at the Wembley Arena, Wembley, during its brief "No Prayer For Christmas Tour".

1991

Jan [5] *Bring Your Daughter To The Slaughter* debuts at UK #1, Iron Maiden's first chart-topping single. EMI is criticized by the media for the cynical ploy of marketing several formats of the release which they know die-hard Maiden fans will immediately buy in quantity, thus boosting the sales performance of the record during a traditionally weak sales period.
[26] The group begins the 33-date US leg of the "No Prayer On The Road" trek in New Haven, CT, set to end on March 14th in San Francisco, CA.
[28] The Japanese leg of the "No Prayer On The Road" begins.
June [21] The band is featured in a Department Of Transportation And Advertising Council ad, with crash-test dummies, Vince and Larry.
July [13] *Rock And Roll*, a rock/tennis world collision featuring Harris, McBrain, Roger Daltrey (vocals), John McEnroe and Pat Cash (guitars), and Andy Barnett (slide guitar), peaks at UK #66.

1992

Jan The group works on its new album at Harris' home studio.
Apr [11] Dickinson and UK comic actor Rowan Atkinson, in the guise of Mr. Bean, hit UK #9 with a re-working of Alice Cooper's *I Want To Be Elected*.
[25] *Be Quick Or Be Dead* debuts at its UK #2 peak, behind Right Said Fred's *Deeply Dippy*, as Dickinson begins work on a second solo album, at London's Battery Studios, with producer Chris Tsangaries.
May [23] ***Fear Of The Dark*** debuts at UK #1, the group's 20th UK chart album and third chart-topper. It will also debut at its US #12 peak the following week.
June [4] The group plays before 400 fans at the Oval pub, Norwich, Norfolk, as the Nodding Donkeys, as a thank you to the watering hole's landlord, Chris Hiles.
[5] The band's traditional album release-accompanying world tour kicks off in Iceland.
[8] The North American leg begins, before a sellout crowd at the Ritz, New York.
July The group is banned from playing in Santiago, Chile, after the Catholic Church pronounces them "devils" and "Satanists".
[18] *From Here To Eternity* reaches UK #21.
Aug [1] Iron Maiden and EMI labelmates Thunder perform at the Pacaeumbu Stadium, São Paulo, Brazil. (During the South American leg of the tour, a combined group team loses a soccer match 6-5 to EMI Music executives, at EMI's Latin American Conference '92 in Buenos Aires, Argentina.)
[15] Iron Maiden participates in "Super Rock '92", with Black Sabbath, Slayer, Helloween and W.A.S.P., at Mannheim Maimarktgelande, West Germany.
[22] The group headlines a bill featuring Almighty, Skid Row, Slayer, Thunder, and W.A.S.P., at the annual "Monsters Of Rock" festival at Castle Donington, before a 62,000 crowd, also broadcast live by Radio 1 as part of its 25th anniversary.
Sept [5] Iron Maiden, Slayer and W.A.S.P. play a further "Monsters Of Rock Festival", at the Hippodrome De Vincennes, Paris, France.

1993

Mar [13] *Fear Of The Dark (Live)* debuts at its UK #8 peak.
Apr [3] ***A Real Live One***, featuring tracks recorded on last year's world concert trek, bows at its UK #3 peak.
[10] ***A Real Live One*** debuts at its US #106 peak.
[13] The seven-date German leg of the European tour opens at the Carl Diem Halle, Wurzburg, set to end on the 21st at the Schwabenhalle, Augsburg.
May [16] A short British tour opens at the Sheffield Arena, Sheffield, set to close on the 24th at the King's Hall, Belfast, N. Ireland, as Dickinson announces that he will be permanently leaving the band at the end of its forthcoming live commitments. (The band invites anyone to send a tape, biography and photo to Maiden Vocalist, Sanctuary Music (Overseas) Ltd., The Colonnades, 82 Bishops Bridge Road, London W2 6BB.)
Oct [16] EP *Hallowed Be Thy Name* debuts at its UK #9 peak.
[30] Performance set ***A Real Dead One*** bows at its UK #12 peak.
Nov [20] Their second live album release in three weeks, ***Live At Donington*** charts for a week at UK #23 (and ends the group's association with EMI), as ***A Real Dead One*** charts for a week at US #140.

1994

Jan Former Wolfsbane singer Blaze Bayley is named as Dickinson's replacement.
June [18] Dickinson's ***Balls To Picasso***, released on Mercury Records, reaches UK #21 in its week of entry.
Aug [13] His ***Balls To Picasso*** charts for a week at US #185. (Solo singles also chart - *Tears Of The Dragon* (May [28] UK #28) and *Shoot All The Clowns* (Oct [8] UK #37).
Dec Dickinson plays a gig in war-torn Bosnia at the Bosnian Cultural Centre in Sarajevo.

1995

Oct [7] Iron Maiden's *Man On The Edge* debuts at its UK #10 peak.
[14] Produced by Harris and Nigel Green, its parent album, ***The X Factor*** hits UK #8 in its week of entry.
Nov [4] ***X Factor***, released in the US by the indie label CMC International, makes US #147.

1996

Feb [8] The group begins a month-long North American tour, set to end on April 4th at the Hollywood Palace, at the Pavilion de la Jeuness, Quebec City, PQ, Canada.
Mar [9] Dickinson's solo effort ***Skunkworks*** makes UK #41.

CHRIS ISAAK

1984

Isaak (b. June 26, 1956, Stockton, CA), the youngest of three sons of a forklift-driver father and housewife mother, Dorothy (who worked part-time in a potato-chip factory), both of whom are enthusiastic rockabilly and country-music lovers, has been musically inspired by Dean Martin, Bing Crosby and band leader Louis Prima, but most particularly by a reissue of the "Sun Sessions" collection of Elvis Presley recordings from 1954-55, which he hears for the first time while studying in Japan, participating in the University of the Pacific exchange program, where he also practices amateur boxing (responsible for his broken nose) and acts as a tour guide for a film studio. He has returned to Stockton, where he graduates with a degree in English and Communication Arts and, with the help of his first manager, Mark Plummer, now forms a rockabilly trio called Silvertone (after a Sears-Roebuck six string guitar model), consisting of guitarist James Calvin Wilsey, bassist Rowland Salley and drummer Kenney Dale Johnson, who will all remain as his permanent backing band. With Isaak as frontman, the band performs on the San Francisco, CA club circuit, most regularly at the Mabuhay Gardens new-wave venue.

1985

Spotted by subsequent manager Erik Jacobsen, who produced a number of fine late-'60s folk/pop acts, Isaak and the band sign to Warner Bros. Records and tour extensively along the US West Coast, to promote their Jacobsen-produced freshman disc, ***Silvertone***. Highlighted by Isaak's stark countrybilly songs and his Roy Orbison-influenced vocal style, the album fails to chart, despite critical acclaim.

1987

Apr [11] Following extensive US and European touring, Isaak's sophomore album, ***Chris Isaak***, again produced by Jacobsen and backed by Silvertone, peaks at US #194. Ten of the album's 11 cuts are self-penned (while *Heart Full Of Soul* is written by Graham Gouldman).
Oct Isaak appears on C4-TV's Jonathan Ross-hosted "The Last Resort", performing *Blue Hotel*, which fails to score anywhere, except in France, where it is a major hit.
Dec ***Chris Isaak*** is included in **USA Today** newspaper's Top 10 recommended albums of the year. US and European touring the following year will be interrupted only by Isaak's acting role in the Jonathan Demme-directed movie "Married To The Mob" (having made his celluloid debut in Bruce Weber's Chet Baker tribute, "Let's Get Lost").

1989

Aug Third album, ***Heart Shaped World***, reaches US #149, but is largely unpromoted by Warner Bros., which considers the self-penned, dark, brooding, '50s-style country love-song set to be uncommercial, following its initial playback to company executives in San Francisco. One cut, however, *Wicked Game*, interests movie maker David Lynch, who has already used Isaak material for "Blue Velvet" and who requires an instrumental version of the song for his forthcoming Nicolas Cage-starring "Wild At Heart". (Isaak's music is increasingly in demand for visual projects, including the US soap "Days Of Our Lives", Sunday-Night movie "The Preppie Murder" and the "Private Eyes" series.)

1990

Oct Lee Chestnut, music director at Power 99, an Atlanta, GA rock station, having seen "Wild At Heart" three times, tracks down the Isaak instrumental and starts playing the vocal version from the 1989 album. Other rock and Top 40 stations follow, as listener response explodes.
Dec [15] *Wicked Game*, made prominent through the more successful European release of "Wild At Heart", hits UK #10. Becoming an overnight media hit after five years, Isaak's hip good looks propel him to fashion spreads in **Esquire** and **Elle** magazines, and cause **People** magazine to list him as one of the most beautiful people in the world. He will also shortly be seen in the Jodie Foster/Anthony Hopkins movie "The Silence Of The Lambs", playing a S.W.A.T. leader.

1991

Feb [16] Repackaged ***Heart Shaped World***, now released as ***Wicked Game*** for the UK market, hits UK #3.
[23] During a hectic UK promo visit, during which the affable and witty Isaak endears himself to audiences and interviewers alike, the 1987 track, *Blue Hotel*, reaches UK #17.
Mar [2] Aided by a steamier second promo video lensed by Herb Ritts in Hawaii and co-starring model Helena Christensen, and after 14 weeks of climbing, *Wicked Game* finally hits US #6, as its hastily rediscovered and repromoted parent album, ***Heart Shaped World***, begins a US chart rise into the Top 10.
Apr [6] ***Heart Shaped World*** hits US #7, having already topped one million world sales.
[9] Isaak guests on NBC-TV's "The Tonight Show".
[24] He sings the national anthem before the Minnesota Twins-Oakland Athletics baseball game at the Metrodome, Minneapolis, MN, also joining the commentators in their broadcast booth for a couple of innings.
May [11] Isaak is the musical guest on NBC-TV's "Saturday Night Live".
June [12] He wins the Lead Male Vocalist Of The Year category at the third International Rock Awards, held at London's Docklands Arena.
[16] He appears on Fox-TV's "Coca-Cola Pop Music Backstage Pass To Summer" special.
July [31] Isaak plays a sellout gig at the Sandstone Amphitheatre, Maryland Heights, MO, on his summer tour supporting Don Henley and Bonnie Raitt.
Sept [5] "Wicked Game" wins the Best Male Video, Best Cinematography and Best Video From A Film categories at the eighth annual MTV Video Music Awards held, at the Universal Amphitheatre, Universal City, CA.
Dec Isaak performs at the KFOG-FM sixth annual "Toys For Tots" concert at the Hard Rock Café in San Francisco.

1992

Mar [7] He takes part in the 15th Bay Area Music Awards, at San Francisco's Civic Auditorium with Steve Miller, Damn Yankees, Sammy Hagar, Huey Lewis, Carlos Santana and Jefferson Starship - The Next Generation.
Dec He participates in a concert to celebrate the 20th anniversary of San Francisco music critic Joel Selvin, on a bill with Todd Rundgren, Van Morrison and Bonnie Raitt.

1993

Mar [15] Having played a major role in David Lynch's "Twin Peaks: Fire Walk With Me", and returned - in January - to California from Nepal, India, where he has completed filming the Bertolucci-directed "Little Buddha" movie, playing the role of an architect, Isaak releases his first album in over three years, ***San Francisco Days***. A bare-bones, stripped-down affair, once again highlighted by his Orbison/Holly-recalling rockabilly vocal twang, it includes his treatment of Neil Diamond's *Solitary Man*.
Apr [3] Lead-off single, *Can't Do A Thing (To Stop Me)*, bows at its UK #36 peak.
[5] Isaak ends a short European tour in Paris, France.
[24] ***San Francisco Days*** debuts at its UK #12 peak.
May [8] ***San Francisco Days*** reaches US 35.
[18] Isaak returns to "The Tonight Show".
June [5] He takes part in KISS Radio's anniversary concert at the Great Woods Center for the Performing Arts, Mansfield, MA.
[29-30] Isaak plays two dates at London's Hammersmith Apollo, during a European tour set to end on July 11th at the "Turku Festival", Turku, Finland.
July [10] Title track, *San Francisco Days*, charts for a week at UK #62.
[14] He embarks on a major US tour, supporting Tina Turner at New York, NY's Radio City Music Hall, set to end on September 24th at the Western Washington Fair, Puyallup, WA.
Sept [8] Isaak guests on CBS-TV's "Late Show With David Letterman".

1994

Feb [19] He plays a benefit concert for the Artists Rights Foundation at Los Angeles, CA's Shrine Auditorium, with Lou Reed and Los Lobos.
Mar *San Francisco Days* wins Outstanding Album at the 17th annual Bammies in San Francisco.
May [25] Isaak returns to "Late Show With David Letterman".
Oct [8] He performs *Blue Moon* at the "Elvis Aaron Presley : The Tribute", an all-star event held at the Pyramid Arena, Memphis, TN.
Dec [29] Isaak plays his last date of 1994 at the Konocti Harbor & Resort & Spa, Kelseyville, CA.

1995

May [27] He guests on BBC2-TV's "Later With Jools Holland".
June [3] ***Forever Blue***, written as ever by Isaak and produced by Jacobsen, reaches UK #27 in its week of entry, as Isaak takes part in the 16th annual KISS concert at the Great Woods Center for the Performing Arts.
[10] ***Forever Blue*** debuts at its US #31 peak.
July [11] Isaak guests on "The Tonight Show".
[13] He performs at LIFEbeat's second "The Beat Goes On" benefit at New York's Beacon Theatre.
Aug [5] *Somebody's Crying* makes US #45.
Oct [23] Isaak embarks on a US tour with a sellout show at the State Theatre, Detroit, MI.
Dec [28] He guests on "Late Show With David Letterman".
[30] Isaak performs at the State Theatre, Minneapolis, MN.

1996

Jan [22] Isaak files suit in Los Angeles' District Court against food manufacturer Hunt-Wesson Inc. and its ad agency Ketchum Communications seeking more than $1 million in compensatory and punitive damages for their alleged *Wicked Game* sound-a-like music used for a Reden Budders popcorn commercial which aired in the US last year.

[28] Currently featured on the soundtrack to the movie "Mr. Wrong", he makes a cameo appearance on NBC-TV's sitcom "Friends", airing after the Superbowl.
Mar [9] Isaak collects five Bammie trophies, including Outstanding Male Vocalist and Musician Of The Year at the Bay Area Music Awards held at San Francisco's Warfield Theatre.

THE ISLEY BROTHERS

Ronald Isley (lead vocals);
Rudolph Isley (vocals); **O'Kelly Isley** (vocals)

1958

Four Isley brothers, Rudolph (b. Apr. 1, 1939, Cincinnati, OH), Ronald (b. May 21, 1941, Cincinnati), O'Kelly (b. Dec. 25, 1937, Cincinnati) and Vernon have left the church choir in their native Cincinnati to form a vocal quartet in 1955. They begin church touring but have quit when Vernon is killed in a bicycle accident. Following a year's break, their parents, Kelly and Sallye Bernice Isley, have persuaded the three brothers to re-form. Travelling to New York, NY in search of a record deal, their first single, the doo-wop styled *The Cow Jumped Over The Moon*, is released on the Teenage label in 1957, but fails to chart, as do subsequent releases on the Mark-X, Gone and Cindy labels. Yet to succeed as commercially successful recording artists, their polished live work now secures them a contract with the influential General Artists' Corporation management agency.

1959

June During a summer appearance at the Howard Theater in Washington, DC, they are seen by RCA Record's Howard Bloom, who signs them to the label. Bloom enlists the skills of production duo Hugo and Luigi to supervise initial Isley Brothers recordings, the first release being *Turn To Me*.
July [29] The Isleys record their second RCA single, *Shout*. An adaptation of the stage favorite *Lonely Teardrops*, with the intro line "You know you make me want to shout", it features their church organist, Professor Herman Stephens.
Sept *Shout* makes US #47 and is a huge R&B hit, selling over one million copies and ultimately becoming a much-covered standard. Its success allows the brothers to move the rest of the family from Cincinnati to New Jersey.

1960

Following the October release of ***Shout*** and the follow-up extract, *Respectable*, the Isleys leave RCA for Atlantic Records, where they are teamed with Jerry Leiber and Mike Stoller (fresh from their success with the Coasters), but the songwriting/production duo are unable to turn the Isleys' gospel energy to commercial advantage, resulting in four non-charting singles.

1962

July Having moved to Wand Records, where the Brothers work with producer Bert Berns, and following the release of the blues ballad *Right Now*, Berns has suggested they record his own song, *Twist And Shout*, originally released by the Top Notes in 1961. *Twist And Shout* tops the R&B chart, peaks at US #17 and becomes a classic radio and dancehall standard (reaching a wider audience, not least through the Beatles' 1964 hit version).
Oct With the current "Twist" dance craze, Wand has the Isleys record *Twistin' With Linda*, which makes US #54, while ***Twist And Shout*** makes US #61.

1963

After the release of *Hold On Baby*, essentially a rewrite of *Twist And Shout*, the Isleys leave Wand for United Artists, but continue to work with Berns. Their UA debut, *Tango*, fails to score and the label instructs the group to record *Surf And Shout*.
July *Twist And Shout* makes UK #42.

1964

Hardened by record company demands, the brothers set up their own label, T-Neck (named after Teaneck, NJ, where the family now lives), initially releasing *Testify*, which features Jimi Hendrix, a member of the Isleys' touring band, on guitar. During the year, the group re-signs to Atlantic, making its first UK tour, supporting Dionne Warwick, followed by a US concert-package trek headlined by Frankie Avalon, and also featuring UK singer Cliff Richard, who is making his first American visit.

1965

Dec Dropped by Atlantic in September, the Isleys are signed by Berry Gordy's Tamla-Motown label which teams them with writers and producers Holland, Dozier and Holland.

1966

Apr The group's first Tamla single, *This Old Heart Of Mine*, makes US #12 and UK #47. It is followed by *Take Some Time Out For Love*, which reaches US #66 in June, when ***This Old Heart Of Mine*** also peaks, at US #140. A third album extract, *I Guess I'll Always Love You*, makes US #61 and UK #45 in August. The group's final mainstream pop hit with the label, *Got To Have You Back*, will spend two weeks at US #93 the following May, before the group parts ways with Motown.

1968

Nov Spurred not least by a UK promotional visit, the reissued *This Old Heart Of Mine* hits UK #3, advancing ***This Old Heart Of Mine*** to UK #23 in December. (During the year, they turn down the opportunity to appear in the Rolling Stones "Rock'n'Roll Circus" movie.)

1969

Jan Encouraged by their UK success, the Brothers return to the US and revive T-Neck, with Ronald as president, Rudolph vice president and O'Kelly as secretary/treasurer. They begin writing and producing their own material and will produce other artists on the label, including the Brothers Three, Dave Cortez, Privilege and Judy White.
Feb *I Guess I'll Always Love You* reaches UK #11.
Apr *Behind A Painted Smile*, another old Tamla cut, hits UK #5.
June Their debut single on the T-Neck label, the self-penned *It's Your Thing*, hits US #2 (held off the top spot by the Beatles' *Get Back*) and makes UK #30.
July ***It's Our Thing*** enters the US chart, set to make #22, eventually shifting over two million copies.
Aug *I Turned You On* makes US #23, while *It's Your Thing* peaks at UK #30.
Sept *Black Berries* climbs to US #79. (From the Tamla vaults, *Put Yourself In My Place* reaches UK #13. Ronnie, Rudolph and Kelly, he has dropped the "O", invite their brothers Ernie (b. Mar. 7, 1952) (guitar, drums) and Marvin (b. Aug. 18, 1953) (bass, percussion) and cousin Chris Jasper (keyboards) to form an extended Isley Brothers, continuing to use brass sections live and in the studio. They later recruit (non-related) drummer Everett Collins.)
Oct *Was It Good To You* peaks at US #83. ***The Brothers : Isley*** reaches US #180, while the group is featured on one side of the double album ***Live At Yankee Stadium*** (US #169), with the Edwin Hawkins Singers and Brooklyn Bridge contributing the other sides.

1970

Mar [11] *It's Your Thing* wins the Best R&B Vocal Performance By A Group Or Duo Of 1969 category at the 12th annual Grammy Awards.
Oct *Get Into Something* peaks at US #89, after two previous singles, *Keep On Doin'* (February) and *Girls Will Be Girls, Boys Will Be Boys* (August), have climbed no higher than US #75.

1971

Feb *Freedom* peaks at US #72.
Aug The Isleys' cover of Stephen Stills' *Love The One You're With* is their biggest hit in two years, reaching US #18.
Oct *Spill The Wine* makes a mark at US #49. ***Givin' It Back***, comprising only cover versions, including treatments of James Taylor's *Fire And Rain*, two Stephen Stills songs, and a medley of Neil Young's *Ohio* and Jimi Hendrix's *Machine Gun*, makes US #67.

1972

Jan Their version of Dylan's *Lay Lady Lay* peaks at US #71, while *Lay-Away* climbs to US #54 in April. The August-released ***Brother, Brother, Brother*** begins a 33-week US chart run, peaking at #29, yielding the US #24, *Pop That Thang*, in September, and the US #51, *Work To Do*, in November.

1973

Apr ***The Isleys Live*** climbs to US #139.
July *That Lady*, with T-Neck switching distribution from Buddah to CBS/Columbia, begins a 20-week chart run, hitting US #6 and ultimately selling over one million copies.
Sept *That Lady* makes UK #14, while its rock/soul fused parent project, ***3+3***, recorded at Record Plant West, Hollywood, enters the US chart, set to hit #8.
Dec ***The Isleys' Greatest Hits*** makes US #195.

1974

Jan *What It Comes Down To* reaches US #55, followed by the self-written *Highway Of My Life*, which makes UK #25 in February. Their revival of Seals & Crofts' smash, *Summer Breeze*, peaks at US #60 in April and reaches UK #16 in June. *Live It Up* makes US #52, as the live album, ***Live It Up***, rounds up the year's chart achievements in September - reaching US #14 - and goes on to earn a platinum sales award.

1975

Jan *Midnight Sky* peaks at US #73.
July *Fight The Power* hits US #4. The Isleys Brothers perform at the Bay area "Kool Jazz Festival", held in San Francisco, CA.
Sept [13] With the brothers currently at their commercial zenith, ***The Heat Is On*** hits US #1 during a 40-week US chart run, giving the group its second platinum album.

1976

Jan Ballad *For The Love Of You (Part 1 & 2)* reaches US #22.
May ***Harvest For The World*** sells half a million copies in its first three days of release, hits US #9, becoming their third consecutive platinum album.
July With *Who Loves You Better* reaching US #47 in June, the title track, *Harvest For The World*, an anti-hunger peace song co-written by the brothers with Jasper, makes US #63 but hits UK #10.
Aug [28] ***Harvest For The World*** debuts at its UK #50 peak.

1977

Apr ***Go For Your Guns*** begins a 34-week US chart run, during which it will hit #6 and earn another platinum disc.
May [14] ***Go For Your Guns*** makes UK #46, as the extracted *The Pride* peaks at US #63, while *Livin' In The Life* climbs to US #40 the following month. A second T-Neck compilation, ***Forever Gold***, reaches US #58 in September.

1978

Apr ***Showdown*** is released, set to hit US #4 (and UK #50 on June [24]), the group's fifth consecutive platinum album, while the disco excerpt *Take Me To The Next Phase* peaks at UK #50 in May. Continuing to release at least one album in each of the next five years, the Isley Brothers will add the following to their extensive chart career: ***Winner Takes All***, recorded at Bearsville Studio, Woodstock, NY, makes #14 (June 1979); the hard-funk *It's A Disco Night (Rock Don't Stop)* stalls at US #90 but rises to UK #14

(December). The platinum-selling ***Go All The Way*** hits US #8 (April 1980), when *Don't Say Goodnight (It's Time For Love)* makes US #39 (the same year that the group is awarded the prestigious Gold Ticket for playing to over 100,000 fans at New York's Madison Square Garden); ***Grand Slam*** peaks at US #28 (March 1981), with the extracted *Hurry Up And Wait* reaching US #58 in May, the group's final US chart single of the decade. Their second album of that year, ***Inside You***, peaks at US #45 in October, the first Isley Brothers album not be gold or platinum certified after nine such releases. ***The Real Deal*** stalls at US #87 in August 1982, while ***Between The Sheets*** returns them to gold status, reaching US #19 in June 1983, its title cut making UK #52 the following month.

1984

After 15 years together, the two younger Isley brothers and Chris Jasper split from the group to form Isley, Jasper, Isley, and negotiate a separate deal with Epic. (The split is apparently acrimonious and the two groups will have little to do with each other.)

1985

Feb Isley, Jasper, Isley's debut album, ***Broadway's Closer To Sunset Boulevard***, reaches US #135. They almost exclusively reflect the rock side of the Isley Brothers and soul fans largely reject the album, which yields the US #63, *Kiss And Tell.*

Nov Isley, Jasper, Isley's gospel-styled *Caravan Of Love* peaks at UK #52, while ***Caravan Of Love*** makes US #77, with the trio having returned to their soul roots. In their current promotion the group claims to have been responsible for all of the Isley Brothers' hits of the past ten years.

Dec ***Masterpiece***, with the Isley Brothers now signed to Warner Bros., peaks at US #140, but *Colder Are My Nights* fails to chart.

1986

Jan [25] *Caravan Of Love* makes US #51.

Mar [31] Kelly Isley dies of a heart attack induced by occlusive coronary artery disease, aged 48, at his home in Alpine, NJ.

Dec [20] UK group the Housemartins tops the UK chart with an a cappella version of *Caravan Of Love.*

1987

July While a third Isley, Jasper, Isley album, ***Different Drummer***, has been issued one month earlier, the Isley Brothers, now reduced to just Ronald and Rudolph, release ***Smooth Sailin'***, written and produced with US soul singer Angela Winbush, which makes US #64.

1988

Feb Chris Jasper solo album, ***Superbad***, peaks at US #182.

Apr [9] ***The Isley Brothers Greatest Hits***, including cuts by Isley, Jasper, Isley, a UK-only compilation, makes #41.

Sept The Christians' revival of *Harvest For The World* hits UK #8.

1989

Sept Now listed as the Isley Brothers featuring Ronald Isley, the group makes US #89 with ***Spend The Night***, while the extracted title cut *Spend The Night* hits US R&B #3.

1990

Apr [14] Released on Elektra, Ernie Isley's solo album, ***High Wire***, peaks at US #174. (He will also contribute a cover of *Let's Go* to the label's 40th anniversary compilation, ***Rubáiyát***, to be released in November.)

May [26] Rod Stewart's second revival of *This Old Heart of Mine*, now featuring Ronald Isley, hits US #10, produced by Bernard Edwards and Trevor Horn.

1992

Jan [15] The Isley Brothers are inducted into the Rock and Roll Hall of Fame at the seventh annual dinner, held at New York's Waldorf Astoria Hotel. Ernie leads the band in a rendition of *Purple Haze* during the traditional post-dinner jam.

Feb [25] Together with co-writer Andy Goldmark and Sony Music Entertainment, Michael Bolton is named in a lawsuit filed on behalf of the Isley Brothers by Three Boys Music Corp., charging them with copying their 1966 song, titled *Love Is A Wonderful Thing*, for Bolton's same-titled 1991 hit single.

June [8] While the court case against Bolton continues, Ronald Isley issues a statement insisting: "There is no doubt in my mind that Michael used my song. It's humiliating that he is being honored while the original writers are ignored." (Bolton has received two awards for *Love Is A Wonderful Thing* in the past three weeks.) "We want him to give back the awards he won. The song he claims is his has the same hook, the same chorus, the same everything as ours. It's not fair." Isley also says he is insulted by a "settlement offer" proposed by a third party, suggesting that the group could write and record a new song with Bolton.

[13] Reunion effort, ***Tracks Of Life***, debuts at its US #140 peak and is notable as the first album to be recorded by Ernie, Marvin and Ronald since 1983's ***Between The Sheets***.

1993

Oct [4] The group guests on syndicated TV's "The Arsenio Hall Show", following the September release of their Elektra Records ***Live*** set.

Dec [31] The group plays a New Year's Eve show at the Fox Theatre, Atlanta, GA.

1994

Aug [13] The Isley Brothers, on tour with Bobby Womack, perform a sellout date at the Greek Theatre, Los Angeles, CA.

1995

Sept [29] As Elektra announces it has dropped the band from its roster, the Isleys take part in the "KISS-FM Classic Soul" show at Madison Square Garden, on a bill with Aretha Franklin, Gladys Knight and Kool & the Gang.

Oct [24] Quincy Jones new album, ***Q's Jook Joint***, featuring Ronald, is released.

1996

Feb [29] *It's Your Thing* and *Shout* are honored at the Pioneer at the eighth annual Rhythm and Blues Foundation Awards held at the Hollywood Palladium, Hollywood, CA.

Mar [2] Already a US R&B chart-topper, *Down Low (Nobody Has To Know)*, R. Kelly's slow-jam featuring erstwhile influence Ronald Isley, reaches UK #23, and will hit US #4 on the 30th, having topped the R&B survey on the 9th.

Apr Newly signed to Island Records the Isley Brothers' label debut ***Please*** is released including the lead-off cut *Let's Lay Together*, one of four songs written and produced by R. Kelly.

IT'S A BEAUTIFUL DAY

David LaFlamme (electric violin);
Pattie Santos (vocals); **Hal Wagenet** (guitar);
Mitchell Holman (bass); **Val Fuentes** (drums)

1968

July [4] Following a brief stint in the US Army, LaFlamme (b. Apr. 5, 1941, Salt Lake City, UT), who has been playing the violin since the age of five, not least in the Utah Symphony Orchestra, has moved to California where he has played with the John Handy Concert Ensemble and been an early member of Dan Hicks & His Hot Licks. Forming It's A Beautiful Day in 1967, their name inspired by the weather condition on their inaugural day, with Holman (b. Denver, CO), Wagenet (b. Willits, CA), Santos (b. Nov. 16, 1949, San Francisco) and Fuentes (b. Nov. 25, 1947, Chicago, IL), the group has signed to local label Sound Records which is run by Matthew Katz (who also becomes their manager), after becoming a popular live attraction, mainly through LaFlamme's distinctive efforts on a unique five-string violin, and the appeal of the song *White Bird*, written by LaFlamme and his wife, Linda, who is also an early lineup member. The group now plays at the last-ever Fillmore Auditorium gig, with Creedence Clearwater Revival and Steppenwolf.

Sept [26-28] The band performs at the newly-named Fillmore West, San Francisco.

1969

May [8-11] The group, now augmented by keyboardist Fred Webb (b. Santa Rosa, CA), plays at the Fillmore West as ***It's A Beautiful Day***, originally released on Sound, is picked up for national distribution by CBS/Columbia Records, together with the group's recording contract.

July [4-6] They play at the Fillmore West with Eric Burdon and his band.

Aug [31-1] The band participates in the "New Orleans Pop Festival", New Orleans, LA.

Nov [15] ***It's A Beautiful Day***, with its distinctive sleeve designed by the Charlatans lead singer, George Hunter, reaches US #47.

1970

Mar [19-22] It's A Beautiful Day once again appears at the Fillmore West.

Apr [18] The group performs at London's Royal Albert Hall on a bill with Santana and Taj Mahal, during a short UK visit.

May ***It's A Beautiful Day*** climbs to UK #28, boosted by the tour.

June [26] The group performs at the three-day "Bath Festival Of Blues & Progressive Music", Shepton Mallet, Somerset, on a bill featuring Led Zeppelin, Pink Floyd, Santana, Donovan and others. The weekend's entertainment costs £2 10s.

July Their sophomore effort, ***Marrying Maiden***, named for the 54th hexigram in the I Ching, makes US #28 and UK #45.

1972

Jan After personnel changes which have seen Tom Fowler and Bill Gregory replace Wagnet and Holman, ***Choice Quality Stuff/Anytime*** reaches US #130, while the performance set ***Live At Carnegie Hall*** peaks at US #144 in December. ***It's A Beautiful Day ... Today***, with LaFlamme replaced by violinist Graig Block after the band has complained that his profit share is too high, and Bud Cockrell also joining, will make US #114 in April the following year, with the group finally disbanding in 1974, after its final album, ***1001 Nights***. Santos subsequently forms Pharoes Whistle, Cockrell forms Pablo Cruise (though the two of them will recorded ***New Beginnings*** for A&M in 1978), while Linda LaFlamme will form Titus Mother before joining A Thought In Passing.

1977

Jan LaFlamme re-emerges as a soloist on Amherst Records, releasing ***White Bird***, which reaches US #159, while the extracted title track *White Bird*, an updated version of the original It's A Beautiful Day favorite, makes the US Hot 100 where the original failed, peaking at #89. His second album, ***Inside Out*** will be released by Amherst the following year.

1995

Jan [21] While Santos has died in an auto accident on December 14th, 1989 in Healdsburg, CA, and Fuentes has gone on to join New Riders of the Purple Sage, LaFlamme, who cropped up on Tracy Chapman's smash 1988 debut album ***Tracy Chapman***, now plays with Jefferson Airplane and Starship members at a tribute to Papa John Creach at the House of Blues in Los Angeles.

J

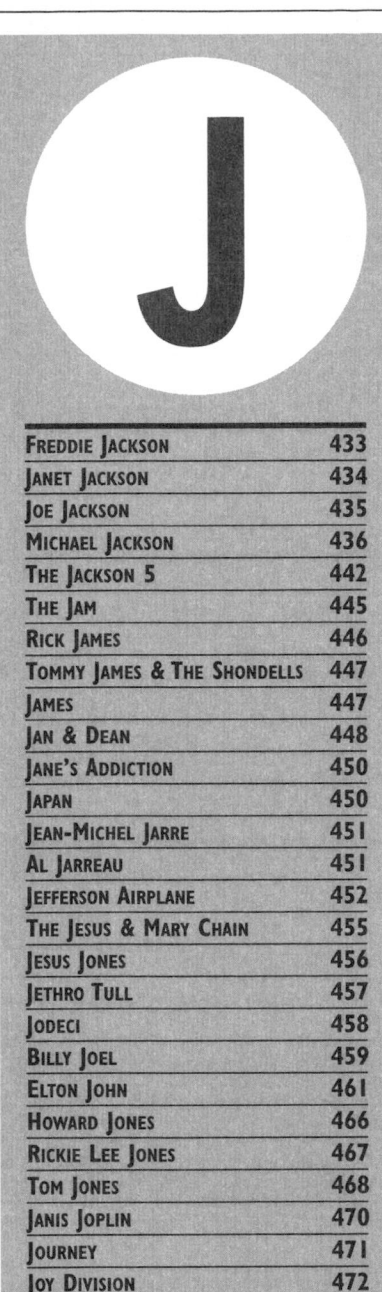

FREDDIE JACKSON

1983

Jackson (b. Frederick Anthony Jackson, Oct. 2, 1956, Harlem, New York, NY), the third of five children raised by his mother in Harlem, having sung in his local White Rock Baptist Church, where he met Ashford & Simpson and earned dollar bills from old ladies, who thought he was cute, left high school and worked in a bank as a computer operator until he had saved enough to pursue an artistic career, has already teamed up with Paul Laurence to form a band, called LJE, playing Top 40-covers music in New York nightclubs. Now relocating to the West Coast, Jackson joins R&B outfit Mystic Merlin.

1984

On his return to New York, Jackson begins vocal backing on tours for Harry Belafonte, Angela Bofill, Evelyn King, Melba Moore, Lillo Thomas and others. Moore signs him to her Hush Productions management company and secures him a worldwide deal with Capitol Records.

Oct [2] On his 28th birthday, Jackson begins recording his debut album.

1985

May Soul-drenched smooching debut, ***Rock Me Tonight***, is released. Variously produced by Robert Aries, Barry Eastmond and Laurence, it will hit US #10, top the US R&B Album chart for 16 consecutive weeks, and reach UK #27. Jackson sets out on an 89-date US tour with Moore.

Aug Laurence-penned soul ballad, *Rock Me Tonight (For Old Times Sake)*, reaches US #18, and tops the US R&B chart for six weeks.

Nov *You Are My Lady* reaches US #12 and UK #49, while its parent album goes platinum.

1986

Feb [22] *He'll Never Love You (Like I Do)* peaks at US #25.

Mar [22] *Rock Me Tonight (For Old Times Sake)* reaches UK #18.

Sept Jackson and Joe Cocker guest on syndicated TV's "Melba And Friends" one-hour special.

[23] Jackson, Moore and James Brown headline an anti-crack rally at New York's Plaza Hotel.

Oct *Tasty Love* peaks at UK #73.

[30] Jackson begins a 55-city tour at the Civic Center, Saginaw, MI, on the US leg of his worldwide "Tasty" tour, with Levert and Meli'sa Morgan.

Nov [8] Jackson and Moore top the US R&B chart with *A Little Bit More*. The following week Jackson replaces himself at #1 with *Tasty Love*. He becomes the first artist to achieve this feat since Dinah Washington's *This Bitter Earth* replaced her Brook Benton-duet, *A Rockin' Good Way*.

Dec [6] His sophomore effort, ***Just Like The First Time***, begins a 26-week tenure atop the US R&B chart, confirming Jackson as a leading vocalist of his genre.

[20] *Tasty Love* makes US #41, as ***Just Like The First Time*** reaches US #23 and UK #30.

[31] Jackson joins Air Supply, Gladys Knight & the Pips and Melba Moore for CBS-TV's "Happy New Year America".

1987

Feb ***Just Like The First Time*** reaches US #23, and will become Jackson's second RIAA-certified platinum album.

[21] *Have You Ever Loved Somebody* tops the US R&B chart.

Mar [14] *Have You Ever Loved Somebody* makes US #69.

Aug [15] *Jam Tonight* tops the US R&B survey and Jackson becomes the only artist in the '80s to have six R&B #1s. It will also peak at US #32 on the 29th.

1988

July *Nice 'n' Slow*, featuring Najée on sax, makes UK #56.

[30] ***Don't Let Love Slip Away***, again produced by Paul Laurence, reaches UK #24 and will make US #48, as Jackson begins a world "Up Close And Personal" tour in the US, as part of the "Budweiser Music Festival", including a brief stint at the Lunt Fontanne Theater, Broadway, New York.

Sept Jackson visits the UK to play four sellout concerts at London's Hammersmith Odeon, before embarking on a tour of Japan. *Crazy (For Me)*, extracted from ***Don't Let Love Slip Away***, makes UK #41.

[27] *Nice 'n' Slow* tops the US R&B chart and moves to US #61.

Oct [15] *Don't Let Love Slip Away* also hits US R&B #1, as will *Hey Lover* on Dec [2].

1989

Jan [30] Jackson wins the Favorite Single, Soul/R&B category for *Nice 'n' Slow* at the 16th annual American Music Awards, held at the Shrine Auditorium, Los Angeles, CA.

His only released recording for the remainder of the year will be *All Over You*, featured in the movie "Def By Temptation", in which Jackson will also make a cameo appearance.

1990

Mar [31] Jackson is inducted into the New York Music Awards Hall of Fame at the Beacon Theatre.

Nov [17] Following a two-year hiatus, Jackson's ***Do Me Again***, co-produced and co-written with Barry Eastmond and Paul Laurence, makes UK #48.

Dec [8] ***Do Me Again***, peaks at US #59, becoming his fourth RIAA-certified gold album as his string of US R&B chart-toppers continues.

1991

Mar [5] Jackson's UK tour bows at London's Hammersmith Odeon.

Apr [12] Jackson embarks on 35-date US trek, with En Vogue opening, at the Music Hall, Cincinnati, OH.

[27-28] He studies with a jazz vocal teacher, as he makes plans to record a jazz album with Anita Baker.

May [7] Jackson appears on NBC-TV's "The Tonight Show".

Aug [30] He is presented with a citation for his work in support of the "Right To Vote" movement by State Senator Bill Owens, during a visit to Boston, MA.

Dec [5] Jackson participates in the **Blues & Soul** 25th anniversary show "Soul Celebration", at London's Royal Albert Hall.

1992

June [4] He takes part in Capitol Records' 50th anniversary all-star gala at the Capitol Tower on the corner of Sunset and Vine, and is currently featured on *All I Ever Ask* from Najee's ***Just An Illusion*** album.

July [18] Jackson attends the wedding of Whitney Houston and Bobby Brown at Houston's Mendham, NJ estate.

Aug [29] ***Time For Love*** debuts at its US #83 peak. Jackson forms his own production company and moves into a new house in New Jersey.

Sept [19] Covering Billy Paul's 1972 US chart-topper, *Me And Mrs. Jones* reaches UK #32.

Oct Jackson is among 50 acts, including Regina Belle and Grover Washington Jr., currently performing in 12 US cities as part of the 1992 "Benson & Hedges Blues" concert series.

Dec [31] Following selected dates throughout November and December, Jackson closes out the year with a performance at the Circle Star Theatre, San Carlos, CA, prior to signing a new recording deal - in early '93 - with RCA Records.

1994

Jan [15] *Make Love Easy* charts for a week at UK #70, as Jackson serves as grand marshal, with actress Joan Van Ark, at the Martin Luther King Jr. National Parade of Celebration, televised live from Atlanta, GA.

Feb [5] ***Here It Is*** debuts at its US #66 peak.

May [7] Jackson performs at the Xanadu Taj Mahal, Atlantic City, NJ, during latest US dates.

Oct [11] Following Capitol's release of ***Greatest Hits***, his first yuletide collection, ***This Christmas***, is released on the Orpheus label.

1995

Mar [18] Now signed to Scotti Bros.' imprint Street Life, following two albums released on RCA, Jackson's variously-produced ***Private Party*** bows at its US #188 peak.
July [12] Jacksons performs at the "Let's Stamp Out AIDS" benefit at the Universal Amphitheatre, Universal City, CA.
Sept [9-10] Currently touring with Gladys Knight, Jackson sings at the Star Plaza Theatre, Merrillville, IN.

JANET JACKSON

1974

Apr [9] Having moved with her family to live in Los Angeles, CA, at age four, Janet (b. Janet Damita Jackson, May 16, 1966, Gary, IN), the youngest in a brood of nine, and the sister of the Jackson 5, appears in her brothers' stage show for the first time at age seven, at the beginning of a season at the MGM Grand Hotel, Las Vegas, NV. (Making her US TV debut on "The Jacksons", a four-week summer variety show, which begins broadcasting on June 16th, 1976, on CBS-TV, the show will feature the group plus sisters LaToya and Rebbie, guest entertainers and a regular comedy-sketch team. Going on to appear as Penny Gordon Woods on CBS-TV's sitcom "Good Times" in September the following year, Jackson will subsequently secure further acting roles in "Different Strokes", "Fame" and "A New Kind Of Family".)

1982

Nov Signed to A&M Records and managed by her father Joseph, she promotes her debut album ***Janet Jackson*** (variously produced by Rene Moore, Foster Sylvers, Jerry Weaver, Bobby Watson and Angela Winbush), by touring high schools and encouraging kids to stay in school. The album reaches US #63 (and will yield two 1983 chart successes, *Young Love* at US #64 in January and *Come Give Your Love To Me* at US #58 in March). By the end of this year, Jackson will have attended a concert in Chicago, IL, with her mother, where they see R&B outfit the Time, whose line-up includes her future producers Jimmy Jam and Terry Lewis.

1984

Sept [7] Having eloped to Michigan Falls, IL, Jackson announces that she and James DeBarge, from Jacksons-styled '80s outfit DeBarge, have wed. (The marriage will be annulled seven months later, and she will return to the Jackson family home, shared with Michael, Tito, and mother Katherine, in Encino, CA.)
Nov ***Dream Street***, with help from Jesse Johnson and Giorgio Moroder, and including a duet with Cliff Richard, climbs to US #147.

1986

Jan ***Control***, produced and co-written by Jimmy Jam and Terry Lewis after A&M's urban music director John McClain has teamed them with Jackson, is released. The collaboration, which will prove long-term, will transform both Jackson's image and celebrity status.
[7] She petitions for divorce from DeBarge.
Mar Jackson begins a 13-city US promotional tour.
[22] Crisp, funk-dance number, *What Have You Done For Me Lately*, tops the US R&B chart.
Apr [5] ***Control***, produced and largely written by Jam & Lewis, enters the UK chart, set to hit #8 during a 72-week chart tenure.
May [3] *What Have You Done For Me Lately* hits UK #3.
[17] *What Have You Done For Me Lately* hits US #4.
June [21] *Nasty* reaches UK #19.
July [5] ***Control*** tops the US chart, achieving platinum status. Jackson, just turned 20, becomes the youngest artist, since 13-year-old Little Stevie Wonder, to top the Album survey.
[19] *Nasty* hits US #3, having already topped the R&B chart.
Sept [6] *When I Think Of You*, helped by a Julien Temple-directed video, hits UK #10.
Oct [11] *When I Think Of You* tops the US chart. 14 years after brother Michael topped the chart with *Ben*, they become the first siblings in the rock era to have solo #1s.
Nov *Control* peaks at UK #42. "Control - The Videos", featuring the Paula Abdul-choreographed dance pieces which have dominated MTV all year, is released.
Dec Jackson begins a US tour. She tops **Billboard**'s year-end survey in six categories: Top R&B Artist, Top Pop Singles Artist, Top Pop Singles Artist Female, Top Dance Sales Artist, Top Dance Club Play Artist and Top R&B Singles Artist.

1987

Jan [24] Title cut, *Control*, hits US #5.
[26] Jackson is nominated in nine categories at the 14th annual American Music Awards, at the Shrine Auditorium, Los Angeles, CA, winning in two: Best R&B Single (*Nasty*) and Best Female R&B Video Artist.
Feb [1] She guests on the first "Hitline USA" TV show.
[21] Currently the #1 R&B single, soul ballad *Let's Wait Awhile* hits US #2, making Jackson the first artist to have five Top 10 hits from one album, all in different positions in the top five.
[24] Jackson makes an impressive live appearance at the 29th annual Grammy Awards, singing *What Have You Done For Me Lately* with help from producers Jam and Lewis, but fails to win any awards.
Mar [23] She collects the Best New Video and Album Of The Year, Female trophies at the inaugural Soul Train Music Awards, held at the Civic Center, Santa Monica, CA.
Apr [4] A remix of *Let's Wait Awhile* re-launches A&M's dance-oriented Breakout label in UK, and hits #3.
June Jackson guest-vocals on A&M co-owner Herb Alpert's Jam and Lewis-produced *Diamonds* which hits US #5 and tops the R&B ranking. *The Pleasure Principle* reaches UK #24.
Aug [8] A remixed sixth extract, *The Pleasure Principle*, reaches US #14 and again tops the US R&B chart.
"Control - The Videos Part II" is released.
Sept [11] "Nasty" video wins an award for its choreographer, Paula Abdul, at the fourth annual MTV Video Music Awards, held at the Universal Amphitheatre, Universal City, CA.
Nov [14] An eight-track remix collection of five hits, *Control*, *What Have You Done For Me Lately*, *Nasty*, *Let's Wait Awhile* and *When I Think Of You*, released as ***Control - The Remixes***, reaches UK #20.

1988

Jan [25] Jackson wins the Favorite Video, Pop/Rock/Soul/R&B combined category at the 15th annual American Music Awards, held at the Shrine Auditorium.
Mar [30] She nabs the Best New Video trophy at the second annual Soul Train Music Awards, held at the Santa Monica Civic Center.
June Jackson spends the latter part of the year re-teamed with Jam and Lewis at their Flyte Time Production studios in Minneapolis, MN, dedicated to repeating the groundbreaking success of ***Control***.
Sept [7] "The Pleasure Principle" wins the Best Choreography category at the fifth annual MTV Video Music Awards, held at the Universal Amphitheatre.

1989

Oct [7] First fruits of their second collaboration, the Jam and Lewis-penned and produced *Miss You Much* hits US #1, having already made UK #25.
[28] In its fourth week of release, ***Janet Jackson's Rhythm Nation 1814*** (the 1814 refers to the year that the US national anthem was composed by Francis Scott Key) hits US #1 for the first of four weeks. (It will remain on the survey well into 1991, on its way to at least six RIAA platinum sales awards. Its UK performance will be less dramatic - it has already peaked at UK #4 in its release week (Sept [30]) and will leave the survey after only 12 weeks, returning regularly, however, during 1990, for a further 29 weeks.) The album is once again produced by Jam and Lewis, while they have also written or co-written all of the songs, except the Jackson-penned *Black Cat*.
Nov [18] Title cut, *Rhythm Nation*, reaches UK #23.

1990

Jan [6] *Rhythm Nation* hits US #2, behind Phil Collins' Christmas chart-topper, *Another Day In Paradise*. Its video clip once again features Jackson's dance army, mostly clad in black, performing synchronized set pieces to great effect for MTV and VH-1 audiences.
[22] Jackson wins Favorite Dance Single and Favorite Soul/R&B Single categories for *Miss You Much* at the 17th American Music Awards, at the Shrine Auditorium.
Feb [17] Ballad *Come Back To Me* reaches UK #20.
[21] "Rhythm Nation 1814" is named Best Music Video, Long Form at the 32nd annual Grammy Awards, at the Shrine Auditorium, though none of the hit singles, the album or Jackson herself will win any Grammys for the current project.
Mar [1] "The Rhythm Nation World Tour 1990", Jackson's first ever, begins at the Miami Arena, Miami, FL, with opening act Chuckii Booker acting as musical director.
[3] *Escapade* tops the US chart.
[14] Jackson wins R&B/Urban Contemporary Album Of The Year, Female for ***Rhythm Nation 1814***, Best R&B/Urban Contemporary Single, Female for *Miss You Much* and Best R&B/Urban Contemporary Music Video for "Rhythm Nation" at the fourth annual Soul Train Awards, at the Shrine Auditorium.
Apr During the month she meets President George Bush at the Ritz Carlton Hotel in Dearborn, MI. She is in town for a concert, he is at a fundraiser in the hotel.
[20] Jackson is bestowed with a star on the Hollywood Walk of Fame, at the start of "Janet Jackson Week" in Los Angeles. (She will also play four sellout dates at the Great Western Forum, Inglewood, CA.)
[21] *Escapade* reaches UK #17.
May [16] Jackson celebrates her 24th birthday at Tokyo's Disneyland, while in Japan for a five-date tour. (She has already made a TV commercial for Japan Airlines, to tie in with this leg of the tour.)
June [2] *Alright* hits US #4.
Aug [4] Jackson collapses three songs into a performance in St. Louis, MO, because of an inner ear infection. She is treated at the Barnes Hospital. Her second concert in St. Louis is cancelled, as are subsequent dates in Auburn Hills, MI.
[18] Ballad *Come Back To Me* hits US #2.
Sept [7] "Rhythm Nation" wins the Best Choreography category at the seventh annual MTV Video Music Awards, held at the Universal Amphitheatre, while Jackson also collects the prestigious Michael Jackson Video Vanguard honor.
[15] *Black Cat* reaches UK #15.
[16] Jackson ends the North American leg of her tour at New York, NY's Madison Square Garden, handing over a cheque for $450,000 to the "Rhythm Nation Scholarship" for the United Negro College Fund, at New York's 21 club. (Jackson has also donated 25 cents on each ticket sold to the non-profit education organisation Cities In Schools, raising $184,000.)
Oct [21] Jackson plays the first of a number of sellout concerts at Wembley Arena, Wembley, Middx., during her European tour.
[27] Sixth extract, the Jackson and Jellybean Johnson-produced rocking *Black Cat*, hits US #1.
Nov [3] *Love Will Never Do (Without You)*, with the 12" and CD versions remixed by Shep Pettibone and C.J. Mackintosh, makes UK #34.
[26] Jackson wins the Hot 100 Singles Artist, Top Pop Album, Hot R&B Singles Artist, Top R&B Albums

Artist, Top R&B Album, Top R&B Artist, Top Dance Club Play Artist and Top Dance 12" Singles Sales Artist categories at the inaugural **Billboard** Music Awards Show, in Santa Monica, CA. (The show will air on Fox-TV on December 10th.)

1991

Jan [19] Jam and Lewis-penned *Love Will Never Do (Without You)* gives Jackson her fifth US #1, making her the first artist to achieve seven top five hits from the same album.
[28] Jackson nabs the Favorite Pop/Rock Female Artist, Soul/R&B Female Artist and Dance/Music Artist categories at the 18th annual American Music Awards, at the Shrine Auditorium.
Mar [11] Stocking up on superstar names prior to a much-rumored sale of the company, Virgin Records inks a $50-million deal with Jackson, reportedly for a mere two albums. The deal has been personally supervised by high-flying label supremo Richard Branson. It is the most lucrative contract in recording history (her brother Michael is simultaneously negotiating an even higher remunerative package with Sony, which he will ink, thus superceding Janet within a week). Richard Branson says, "A Rembrandt rarely becomes available. When it does, there are many people determined to get it. I was determined." Details concerning any guarantees of Jam and Lewis being involved in future recordings are undisclosed.
[12] Jackson wins the Best R&B/Urban Contemporary Music Video category at the fifth annual Soul Train Music Awards, held at the Shrine Auditorium.
[16] She receives the Starlight Foundation of Southern California's Humanitarian Of The Year Award for 1990 at the gala event "The Child In All Of Us", at the Century Plaza Hotel, Los Angeles.
Apr [2-3] During a handful of dates, Jackson performs to sellout crowds of 35,645 at the Joe Louis Arena, Detroit, MI. (When it winds up, the "Rhythm Nation World Tour" will have played 96 sellout dates in North America, 20 in Europe and 15 in Japan and Hong Kong.)
May [21] Jackson and Babyface share Songwriters Of The Year at BMI's 39th annual Pop Performance Awards in Los Angeles.
Sept [5] "Love Will Never Do Without You" wins the Best Female Video category at the eighth annual MTV Video Music Awards, held at the Universal Amphitheatre.

1992

Jan [11] Jackson receives the special Chairman's Award at the 24th annual NAACP Image Awards, held at the Wiltern Theatre, Los Angeles, not least for her charitable contributions.
June [13] Her duet with Luther Vandross, *The Best Things In Life Are Free*, featured on the soundtrack to the Damon Wayans-starring movie, "Mo' Money", hits US #10.
[22] New Yorker Frank Paul Jones, 33, who believes he is Jackson's husband, is arrested in the driveway of the Jackson family compound in Encino, CA, at 10:00 a.m., charged with stalking, making terroristic threats (to Jermaine) and trespassing. (He will be committed to a mental hospital for treatment on October 13th.)
Aug [29] *The Best Things In Life Are Free* hits UK #2, behind Snap's *Rhythm Is A Dancer*.

1993

Feb [24] After a lengthy eulogy, Janet presents brother Michael with the Grammy Legend Award at the 35th annual ceremony, held at the Shrine Auditorium.
May [8] *That's The Way Love Goes* debuts at its UK #2 peak.
[15] *That's The Way Love Goes* tops the US chart, where it will reside for eight weeks, in its third week of release, having become the seventh-highest charting single in survey history.
[29] Her Virgin debut, ***janet.***, once again helmed by Jam & Lewis and co-written with them, and featuring Sounds of Blackness, Public Enemy's Chuck D and opera singer Kathleen Battle, enters the UK chart at #1.
June [5] ***janet.*** debuts at US #1, where it will remain for six weeks.
Aug [7] *If* reaches UK #14.
Sept [2] Jackson sings *That's The Way Love Goes* at the tenth annual MTV Video Music Awards at the Universal Amphitheatre.
[11] *If* hits US #4, as Jackson makes her movie debut in John Singleton's "Poetic Justice".
Nov [27] Ballad featured in "Poetic Justice", *Again* hits UK #6.
Dec [11] *Again* tops the US chart.
[17-18] Jackson plays two sellout dates at New York's Madison Square Garden, grossing $1,097,805.

1994

Jan [27] She is named Best Female Singer and Female Sex Symbol in **Rolling Stone**'s 1994 Music Awards Readers' Picks.
Feb [26] Jackson stops her Delta Center, Salt Lake City, UT concert in the middle of *Throb*, and is treated for flu-like symptoms and dehydration at a nearby hospital. (She is diagnosed with an upper respiratory infection and told to take a two-week rest.)
Mar [1] She wins the Best R&B Song, with Jam and Lewis, for *That's The Way Love Goes* at the 36th annual Grammy Awards held at New York's Radio City Music Hall.
[12] *Because Of Love* debuts at its UK #19 peak.
[15] *If* is named Best R&B Music Video at the eighth Soul Train Awards held at the Shrine Auditorium.
[19] *Because Of Love* hits US #10.
[21] Jackson performs a distinctly off-key rendition of *Again* at the 66th annual Academy Awards ceremony from Los Angeles' Dorothy Chandler Pavilion.
[22] ***janet.*** is named Best-selling Recording, Best-selling R&B Recording and Best-selling Pop Recording of the Year at NARM's Best Seller Awards in San Francisco, CA.
May [14] She is the featured musical guest on NBC-TV's "Saturday Night Live".
June [23] Jackson continues her US tour at the Coca-Cola Star Lake Amphitheatre, Burgettstown, PA.
[25] *Any Time, Any Place*, coupled with *And On And On*, hits US #2, behind All-4-One's *I Swear*, and reaches UK #13.
Sept [8] She wins the Best Female Video category for "If" at the 11th annual MTV Video Music Awards from Radio City Music Hall.
Oct [8] Jackson, alongside her brother Michael and sister-in-law Lisa Marie, attends the all-star "Elvis Aaron Presley : The Tribute" concert at the Pyramid Arena, Memphis, TN.
Nov [26] *You Want This*, with remixes by Jam and Lewis, featuring M.C. Lyte, Mile, Mafia & Fluxy, E-Smoove and Dewey B, debuts at its UK #14 peak.
Dec [24] *You Want This*, coupled with *70's Love Groove*, the latter featured in Robert Altman's "Ready To Wear (Pret-A-Porter)" movie, hits US #8.

1995

Jan [22] Jackson is honored with awards for Achievments in Dance Music at the International Dance Awards from London's Piccadilly Theatre.
Feb [6] She begins a tour of Australia at the Entertainment Centre in Brisbane.
Mar [25] *Whoops Now*, coupled with *What'll I Do*, hits UK #9, as ***janet./janet. remixed***
reaches UK #15 in its week of entry.
Apr [19-20] Jackson's European tour closes out with two dates at Wembley Arena, Wembley, Middx.
June [10] *Scream*, a duet with brother Michael, enters at its UK #3 high.
[17] *Scream* bows at its US #5 peak, becoming the highest debuting single in US chart history, besting the Beatles' #6 *Let It Be*.
[24] *Scream (4th And 5th Formats)* debuts at its UK #43 high, during a two-week chart stay.
Sept [7] Janet and Michael Jackson collect their Best Dance Video, Best Choreography and Best Art Direction trophies for "Scream" at the 12th annual MTV Video Music Awards, from Radio City Music Hall.
[23] *Runaway* debuts at its UK #6 peak.
Oct [14] A&M-released compilation ***Design Of A Decade 1986/1996*** , including all her hits and two new cuts, hits UK #2 in its week of entry, behind Oasis' ***(What's The Story) Morning Glory?***
[21] One of the new cuts, *Runaway* hits US #3.
Nov [4] ***Design Of A Decade 1986/1996*** hits US #3.
Dec [6] Visiting her sick brother Michael at Beth Israel Medical Center North in New York, Jackson is unable to accept the Artist Achievement Award announced at the sixth annual **Billboard** Music Awards broadcast live on Fox-TV from New York's Coliseum.
[16] *The Best Things In Life Are Free*, a remix of her 1992 duet with Vandross, debuts at its UK #7 peak.

1996

Jan [12] Jackson signs a four-album deal with Virgin worth an estimated $80 million - a $35 million advance, $5 million per album and a 24% royalty.
Feb [28] "Scream" is named Best Video, Short Form at the 38th annual Grammy Awards held at the Shrine Auditorium.
Apr [6] *Twenty Foreplay*, with a Todd Terry remix of *Alright* and a Danny Tenaglia remix of *The Pleasure Principle*, debuts at its UK #22 peak.

JOE JACKSON

1973

Jackson (b. Aug. 11, 1954, Burton-upon-Trent, Staffs.), having grown up in Portsmouth, Hants., from the age of one, learns music at an early age, going to violin classes at school and then taking up piano to write classical pieces. Leaving school with an "S Level" examination pass in music, he has already played pub gigs next to a glue factory, when he enrolls at the Royal College of Music, London. While studying on a three-year scholarship for composition, orchestration, piano and percussion, he has also played in a jazz big band led by Johnny Dankworth, and in the National Youth Jazz Orchestra. Leaving the college, he now joins pub band Arms & Legs, playing covers, eventually recording six self-penned non-charting singles for UK label MAM. (Mark Andrews is the outfit's lead singer, later to emerge on A&M as Mark Andrews & the Gents.)

1977

Jackson leaves Arms & Legs to return to Portsmouth, and becomes a featured performer at the local Playboy club, and then musical director for TV show "Opportunity Knocks" winners, Coffee & Cream, who are popular on the cabaret circuit.

1978

Feb Having relocated to London and recorded a demo album of his own songs, he nearly signs to United Artists and Albion Music, when David Kershenbaum of A&M Records hears the demo and now signs him, after Virgin and Stiff Records have both passed.
Oct Aggressive ballad, *Is She Really Going Out With Him?*, is released. Jackson forms a regular band, with himself on vocals and keyboards, Gary Sandford on guitar, Graham Maby (ex-Arms & Legs) on bass and Dave Houghton on drums.
[2] Jackson begins a month-long Monday-night residency at the Nashville Rooms, London, before setting out on a 20-date UK tour, set to end on the 31st at London's Hope & Anchor.

1979

Jan [19] Jackson performs at London's Nashville Rooms.
Mar [24] ***Look Sharp!***, produced by Kershenbaum, makes UK #40 and will reach US #20. *Sunday Papers* and *One More Time* are both extracted releases.
May Jackson tours the US, where *Is She Really Going Out With Him?* reaches US #21.
Aug [25] Reissued in the UK, *Is She Really Going Out With Him?* reaches #13.

1980

Feb *It's Different For Girls* hits UK #5 and will be followed by *Kinda Kute* and *The Harder They Come*, which will both fail to chart.
[16] Self-written ***I'm The Man***, Kershenbaum-produced, reaches UK #12 and will make US #22.
June [7] Jackson takes part in "The Summer Of '80 Garden Party" at the Concert Bowl, Crystal Palace, London, on a bill with the Average White Band, Q-Tips and headliner, Bob Marley.
July Jackson produces UK reggae act the Rasses' album, ***Natural Wild***.
Oct [5] He begins an 18-date UK tour at the Top Rank Ballroom, Cardiff, Wales, set to end at King George's Hall, Blackburn, Lancs. on November 5th.
[25] Now showing a jazz-swing bent, ***Beat Crazy***, credited to the Joe Jackson Band, reaches UK #42 and will make US #41. It is the last album with his regular rock line-up, as all extracted singles fail to score.
Dec The initial Joe Jackson Band splits.

1981

July [25] ***Joe Jackson's Jumpin' Jive***, featuring '40s and '50s bop and jive music, reaches UK #14 and will make US #42, while the extracted title track, *Jumpin' Jive*, makes UK #43. Jackson tours with the band featured on the album, which includes an extensive horn section. He also produces an album by Portsmouth-based band the Keys.

1982

July [10] Having relocated to New York, NY, following the break-up of his marriage, Jackson returns to a more mainstream sound: his most radio-friendly album to date, ***Night And Day***, becomes his biggest UK hit, at #3, after beginning as a poor seller, and will hit US #4.
Oct Piano-based, self-written *Steppin' Out* hits US #6.

1983

Jan Again following US success, *Steppin' Out* finally hits UK #6.
Feb Ballad *Breaking Us In Two* reaches UK #59 and US #18.
Sept Soundtrack album, ***Mike's Murder***, his first attempt at movie scoring, reaches US #64. He was originally commissioned to write one song but completed the entire project (though much of the music is excised from the film itself). The extracted *Memphis* peaks at US #85.

1984

Mar ***Body And Soul***, another Jackson and Kershenbaum production, the last to feature Maby on bass, peaks at UK #14 and US #20.
Apr *Happy Ending*, with vocals from Elaine Caswell, makes UK #58.
June Ballad *Be My Number Two* reaches UK #70, and *You Can't Get What You Want (Till You Know What You Want)* climbs to US #15.
Aug *Happy Ending* peaks at US #57.

1985

Jan [23] Jackson begins the first of five live recording sessions/concerts at the Roundabout Theater in New York. (During the year he composes a 20-minute music score for the Japanese movie "Shijin No Ie" (House Of The Poet), recorded with the Tokyo Symphony Orchestra.)

1986

Apr Three-sided live album, ***Big World***, recorded direct to two-track in New York, reaches US #34 and UK #41.

1987

Apr With Jackson never one to repeat a particular style, his latest project, ***Will Power***, mainly instrumental, with orchestra and jazz session players including Ed Roynesdal, Gary Burke, Vinnie Zumo and Tony Aiello, peaks at US #131.

1988

May [7] Double album, ***Live 1980/86***, featuring 22 live songs from four world tours and four different line-ups, makes UK #66 and will peak at US #91. Jackson produces an album for reggae outfit the Toasters. (He also completes a future Grammy-nominated movie score for the Jeff Bridges-starring Francis Ford Coppola vehicle "Tucker", overseeing and performing its recording.)
Nov Jackson begins sessions for the forthcoming ***Blaze Of Glory*** at Bearsville Studios in Woodstock, NY.

1989

Apr [29] His tenth and final album for A&M, ***Blaze Of Glory***, makes UK #36.
May ***Blaze Of Glory*** begins a 21-week chart rise to US #61, though the extracted *Nineteen Forever* fails to score, despite a typically innovative aging-themed video, a marketing necessity Jackson publicly despises.
June [8] He guests on NBC-TV's "Late Night With David Letterman".
Aug [8-9] Current US dates include two nights at the Beacon Theatre, New York.

1990

Sept [15] A&M issued ***Steppin' Out : The Very Best Of Joe Jackson*** hits UK #7 in its week of entry. (During the year he completes the film score for "Queen's Logic".)

1991

May [10] Jackson guests on NBC-TV's "The Tonight Show".
[11] His debut for Virgin Records, ***Laughter And Lust***, with a heavy metal-pastiche video lensed for its first single *Obvious Song*, bows at its UK #41 peak.
[18] ***Laughter And Lust*** climbs to at US #116.
[22] A six-date UK mini-tour starts at the Nottingham Royal Concert Hall, Nottingham, Notts., set to climax on the 28th at London's Hammersmith Odeon.
July [15-16] He performs at New York's Radio City Music Hall, during the US leg of his world tour, which will end at the State Theatre, Sydney, New South Wales, Australia, on September 21st. (During the following year, Jackson will complete his next film score for "Three Of Hearts".)

1994

Oct [4] Virgin releases his first album in three years, the quasi-classical ***Night Music***, including four instrumental nocturnes and a contribution from Clannad's Maire Ni Bhraonain.
Nov [28-29] Jackson performs two sellout dates at New York's Beacon Theatre.

1995

Jan [14] He begins a major European tour at the Civic Hall, Guildford, Surrey, set to end on March 24th at London Royal Festival Hall.
Apr [19] Jackson performs at Massey Hall, Toronto, ON, Canada, at the start of a series of North American dates.

MICHAEL JACKSON

1963

Weaned on the music and stage presentation of Jackie Wilson and James Brown, Jackson (b. Michael Joseph Jackson, Aug. 29, 1958, Gary, IN) is seen by his mother Katharine practising dance steps in front of the mirror having already seen him perform *Climb Every Mountain* for his kindergarten class the previous year. She and her husband Joe are keen to nurture and promote their offspring's musical ability. With Joe as manager, Michael will join four of his brothers, Jackie, Tito, Jermaine and Marlon, to form the Jackson 5, also sometimes performing as the Ripples & Waves Plus Michael. With Michael as their lead vocalist, they win a succession of talent shows, their first "non-contest" performance being at the opening of a Big Top supermarket. A local fixture by 1965, they enter - and win - a local talent contest at Roosevelt High School in Gary, performing the Temptations' *My Girl*.

1969

As Berry Gordy has signed the group to his Motown label, the Jackson family moves to Los Angeles, CA, the label's new headquarters. At a Sammy Davis Jr. showbiz gathering, Quincy Jones meets 10-year-old Jackson for the first time (although Jackson will not recall the event).

1971

Dec [11] Having established the family base the previous year in Encino, CA, and two years after the first Jackson 5 hit, Jackson, signed as a soloist to Tamla-Motown, hits US #4 with his ballad debut, *Got To Be There*. He also appears on labelmate (and life-time friend) Diana Ross' US TV special, "Diana".

1972

Mar *Got To Be There* hits UK #5, while the parent album ***Got To Be There*** reaches US #14. Jackson spends much time with Ross on the set of her current movie, "Lady Sings The Blues". (Prevented from enjoying a "normal" childhood, both by his phenomenal star status and by the demands of the strict career-only upbringing insisted upon by his father, Jackson will subsequently recall his adolescence as being extremely "lonely", an experience which contributes significantly to his adult penchant for spending much of his time with other former child stars (notably Brooke Shields and Elizabeth Taylor), latter-day youth stars and animals.)
Apr [22] *Rockin' Robin*, once again highlighting Jackson's distinctive treble vocal, and reviving Bobby Day's 1958 US #2, also hits US #2, kept off the top by Roberta Flack's *The First Time Ever I Saw Your Face*.
June With parallel group and solo careers in full swing, Jackson's *Rockin' Robin* hits UK #3, as the UK release of ***Got To Be There*** makes #37.
July [15] *I Wanna Be Where You Are* reaches US #16.
Sept With the Bill Withers original missing out in the UK, Motown releases Jackson's version of *Ain't No Sunshine* only in the UK, where it hits #8. Meanwhile, his second solo album, ***Ben***, hits US #5.
Oct [14] The extracted title track, *Ben*, hits US #1. Penned by American composer Walter Scharf and UK lyricist Don Black, the ballad was written for the movie "Ben" (a follow-up to "Willard"), and originally intended for Donny Osmond. Black is responsible for suggesting that Jackson vocalizes the song.
Dec *Ben* hits UK #7, its parent album ***Ben*** reaches UK #17.

1973

May Tamla releases ***Music And Me***, which peaks at US #92, while *With A Child's Heart* makes US #50.

1975

Apr [5] *We're Almost There*, written by Brian and Eddie Holland, peaks at US #54, but Jackson's final official solo Motown album release, ***Forever, Michael***, makes only US #101. (He will not release another solo album for four years.)
May Although Jermaine will stay at the label, the remaining group quits Motown and re-starts as the Jacksons on Epic Records. Still in the family line-up, Michael also signs a solo deal with Epic, which allows creative freedom and a considerable rise in the Jackson 5's former 2.7% Motown royalty.
Aug [9] Motown-issued *Just A Little Bit Of You* reaches US #23.
Oct The first of many Motown/Jackson compilation albums, ***The Best Of Michael Jackson***, climbs to US #156.

1977

May Jackson escapes on to the roof of a Woolco store in Memphis, TN, after 10,000 fans show up for an

album-signing session.
Oct [3] Rehearsals begin in New York, NY for a movie version of the musical "The Wiz", already a stage success (adapted from "The Wizard Of Oz"). Jackson is chosen to play the Scarecrow, opposite Diana Ross' Dorothy and Richard Pryor's Wiz. While filming, Jackson stays at his sister LaToya's Manhattan apartment. The project links Michael professionally with producer Quincy Jones, responsible for its soundtrack.

1978

Oct Soundtrack album, ***The Wiz***, is released by MCA Records. It contains the Ross/Jackson duet on *Ease On Down The Road*, which makes US #41 and UK #45. Jackson spends six months recording his debut solo album for Epic.

1979

Mar [3] His Epic label debut, *You Can't Win*, peaks at US #81, during a three-week stay on the Hot 100.
Oct [13] Released on July 28th, the Jackson-penned hot dance number, *Don't Stop 'Til You Get Enough*, originally demoed at his 24-track home studio with brother Randy, tops the US chart, his first solo #1 for seven years. It also hits UK #3 and propels its parent album, ***Off The Wall*** (released in August and produced by Jones, who has assembled a top-notch crew of session musicians, guest vocalists and hit-potential material for the project), to hit US #3 and UK #5 (Oct [20]). (It will eventually sell over ten million copies worldwide.)
Dec Title cut, *Off The Wall*, hits UK #7.

1980

Jan [18] Jackson wins the Favorite Male Artist, Soul/R&B, Favorite Album, Soul/R&B and Favorite Single, Soul/R&B categories at the seventh annual American Music Awards, held at the ABC-TV Studios, Hollywood, CA.
[19] Dreamy *Rock With You*, the first of many ex-Heatwave member Rod Temperton songs which will be recorded by Jackson (including three on the current album), also hits US #1, toppling KC & the Sunshine Band's *Please Don't Go*.
Feb [27] Jackson wins Best R&B Vocal Performance, Male category for *Don't Stop 'Til You Get Enough* at the 22nd annual Grammy Awards.
Mar *Rock With You* hits UK #7.
Apr [12] *Off The Wall* hits US #10.
May Ballad *She's Out Of My Life*, featuring an emotional Jackson vocal, hits UK #3 and peaks at US #10 within a month. Jackson becomes the first solo artist to enjoy four hits from one album (a record he himself will break).
Aug *Girlfriend*, penned by Paul McCartney, reaches UK #41, as Michael rejoins the Jacksons, to promote their new album, ***Triumph***.
Sept [6] The Minnie Riperton tribute album, ***Love Lives Forever***, to which Jackson has contributed *I'm In Love Again*, enters the US chart, set to make #35.
Dec Jackson tops **Billboard**'s Black Top Artists and Top Albums (for ***Off The Wall***) categories in the magazine's Year In Music round-up survey.

1981

Jan [30] He wins the Favorite Male Artist, Soul/R&B and Favorite Album, Soul/R&B categories at the eighth annual American Music Awards, held at the ABC-TV Studios.
Mar Carole Bayer Sager's ***Sometimes Late At Night***, including *Just Friends* which is co-produced by Jackson with Burt Bacharach, is released in the US.
May Motown's issue of previously unreleased Jackson tracks, compiled as ***One Day In Your Life***, peaks at US #144. During the Jacksons' "Triumph" tour, Michael collapses from exhaustion in New Orleans, LA.
June [27] Becoming an instant airplay favorite, the Motown-released *One Day In Your Life* tops the UK chart, his first such achievement.
Aug [1] Repromoted album, ***Best Of Michael Jackson***, reaches UK #11, as ***One Day In Your Life*** makes UK #29.
[8] Motown follow-up, *We're Almost There*, makes UK #46, six years after charting in the US.
Dec [25] Jackson calls McCartney and suggests they write and record together, prompting the ex-Beatle to fly to Los Angeles to cut *The Girl Is Mine*.

1982

June Jackson and Jones work on a storytelling record book of Steven Spielberg's hit movie "E.T."
Aug They begin work on a new album, to be called ***Thriller***, at Westlake Studios, Los Angeles. In addition to a formidable session-musician line-up, including Michael Boddicker, Paulinho da Costa, David Foster, Jerry Hey, James Ingram, Paul Jackson, Louis Johnson, Steve Lukather, David Paich, Greg Phillinganes and Jeff and Steve Porcaro, Jones again invites song contributions from, amongst others, Rod Temperton, who offers the title track.
Oct Diana Ross releases the Jackson-written *Muscles* (recorded earlier in the year), which will hit US #10 and UK #15. (The title is also the name of Jackson's pet snake, one of an increasing number of unusual animal companions with whom Jackson will choose to share his Encino mansion.)
Nov [6] Donna Summer's *State Of Independence*, on which Jackson joined the Quincy Jones-created all-star chorus, makes US #41.
[20] First extract from the forthcoming album, the McCartney duet *The Girl Is Mine*, hits UK #8.
Dec [1] ***Thriller*** is released. With demos originally recorded at Jackson's 24-track Encino home, some with Temperton present, the album, produced by Jones and engineered by Bruce Swedien, will break all sales records and become the most celebrated and successful chart album of all time. It will sell over 40 million copies worldwide and hit #1 in every Western country, including the UK and the US, spending a record 37 weeks at #1 in the latter. From it will come an unprecedented seven Top 10 US hit singles. It will sell over one million copies in Los Angeles alone and will receive a record 12 Grammy nominations.

1983

Jan Playfully feuding Jackson/McCartney duet, *The Girl Is Mine*, hits US #2. Jackson makes a quick visit to London to link with McCartney to completing further songs for release on the latter's forthcoming album.
Feb ***E.T. - The Extra-Terrestrial***, released on MCA, peaks at UK #82. It includes a previously unreleased Jackson track and a souvenir booklet featuring pictures of Jackson cuddling E.T.
Mar [5] Jackson-penned *Billie Jean* hits US #1. It will stay there for seven weeks, and will coincide for one week with its UK #1 position. Having entered the US chart in January, it transforms the fortunes of ***Thriller***, Jackson's career, the financial status of Epic Records and the fabric of modern music itself. Only when it hits US #1 does MTV, previously reluctant to air "black videos", begin showing the *Billie Jean* clip (relenting only after a threatened service boycott by CBS). Featuring self-choreographed dancesteps, the visuals combine with audio innovation to provide what many critics regard as the perfect modern-single project. In contrast to future recording, Jackson's vocals for *Billie Jean* were made in one take, and feature an uncredited lyricon solo by Tom Scott.)
[25] Jackson performs both solo and with his brothers for the "25 Years Of Motown" anniversary spectacular at the Civic Center, Los Angeles. It includes a specially-choreographed performance of *Billie Jean*, which will be nominated for an Emmy TV award, and features his celebrated "Moonwalking" dance style. The show will air on NBC-TV on May 16th.
Apr [23] The equally dance-and radio-friendly *Beat It* hits UK #3, behind David Bowie's *Let's Dance* and Culture Club's *Church Of The Poison Mind*. The song features Jones-invited Eddie Van Halen on lead guitar, a service for which Van Halen makes no charge. The accompanying video, directed by Bob Giraldi at a cost of $160,000, also boosts the disc's success, featuring group dance routines led by Jackson, co-created with "Dreamgirls" choreographer Michael Peters.
[30] In an unprecedented chart feat, and separated only by Dexy's Midnight Runners' *Come On Eileen*, Jackson hits US #1 with *Beat It*, failing to replace himself at the top spot by only one week, the shortest gap registered since the Beatles' achievement in 1964.
June [25] Feet-aimed, self-written *Wanna Be Startin' Somethin'* hits UK #8.
July [16] *Wanna Be Startin' Somethin'* hits US #5.
[30] Motown-released *Happy*, the love theme from "Lady Sings The Blues", peaks at UK #52.
Sept Ballad *Human Nature*, penned by lyricist John Bettis and Toto's Steve Porcaro, and also from ***Thriller***, hits US #7. Meanwhile, opportunist singer Lydia Murdock has recorded an "answer" disc to the accusatory *Billie Jean*. Her *Superstar* fails in the US but reaches UK #14, borrowing heavily from the *Billie Jean* riff.
Nov [19] *Say Say Say*, another Jackson/McCartney duet, but from the ex-Beatle's current album, hits UK #2 for two weeks, behind Billy Joel's *Uptown Girl*. (Jackson also sings on *The Man* from McCartney's ***Pipes Of Peace***.)
[26] Title track, *Thriller*, featuring a ghostly rap from horror-movie veteran Vincent Price (who does not appear in the Jon Landis-directed mini-epic video, the peak of Jackson's current video triumphs), hits UK #10, six months ahead of its US release. Meanwhile, *P.Y.T. (Pretty Young Thing)*, written by Jones and James Ingram, hits US #10.
Dec [2] US MTV airs the seminal full-length 14-minute "Thriller" video for the first time. (Jackson's disclaimer at the beginning of the film, "Due to my strong personal convictions, I wish to stress that this film in no way endorses a belief in the occult", is added when church elders of the Encino Kingdom Hall threaten him with expulsion because of its subject matter.)
[10] *Say Say Say* begins a five-week stay atop the Hot 100, knocking Lionel Richie's *All Night Long (All Night)* off its perch.
[26] UK-released ***Michael Jackson 9 Single Pack***, eligible only for the album chart, makes UK #66. (At the end of his most successful year to date, Jackson announces a $5-million sponsorship deal with Pepsi Cola. A rider in the contract ensures that Jackson will not have to hold or drink a can of Pepsi in any promotion.)

1984

Jan [16] He collects seven trophies at the 11th annual American Music Awards, held at the Shrine Auditorium, Los Angeles : Special Award Of Merit, Favorite Male Artist, Pop/Rock, Favorite Single, Pop/Rock, Favorite Album, Pop/Rock, Favorite Video, Pop/Rock, Favorite Male Artist, Soul/R&B, and Favorite Video, Soul/R&B - an unprecedented achievement.
[27] Jackson is hospitalized at the Cedars-Sinai Medical Center with "second-degree burns on his skull", following an accidental flare explosion on the set of the second day of filming a Pepsi commercial at the Shrine Auditorium. A spark ignites his hair on the sixth take of the Giraldi-directed ad and Marlon Brando's son Miko, working as a bodyguard for the Jacksons, is the first to douse the flames. The singed star will receive a letter from President Reagan, written February 1st, stating, "I was pleased to learn that you were not seriously hurt in your recent accident. I know from experience that these things can happen on the set, no matter how much caution is exercised." (Pepsi will pay Jackson $1.5 million in compensation, which he will donate to the Brotman Memorial Hospital, Culver City, CA, where he is treated. The Michael Jackson Burns Center will be opened at the hospital, but will be closed in October 1987 due to financial difficulties.)
Doubleday Publishers announce that it be producing a Jacqueline Onassis-edited Jackson autobiography, to be written with the help of author Stephen Davis.
Mar [3] An uncredited and unmistakable Jackson is heard on Rockwell (Berry Gordy Jr.'s son Kennedy)'s hit single, *Somebody's Watching Me* which hits UK

#6, and will hit US #2 on the 24th.
[7] Jackson is inducted into **The Guinness Book Of Records**, at the American Museum of Natural History in New York, as sales of ***Thriller*** shoot past 25 million, for which President Reagan sends a telegram: "Your deep faith in God and adherence to traditional values are an inspiration to all of us. You've gained quite a number of fans along the road since *I Want You Back* and Nancy and I are among them. Keep up the good work Michael. We're very happy for you."
[21] Jackson is unable to attend the third annual BRIT Awards, at London's Grosvenor House Hotel, to collect trophies for Best British Album (***Thriller***) and Best International Solo Artist.
[27] The Pepsi commercial premieres on MTV.
[28] Jackson wins Record Of The Year and Best Rock Vocal Performance, Male for *Beat It*, Album Of The Year and Best Pop Vocal Performance, Male for ***Thriller***, Best R&B Vocal Performance, Male and Best New R&B Song for *Billie Jean*, Best Recording For Children for ***E.T. The Extra-Terrestrial*** and Producer Of The Year (Non-Classical), shared with Quincy Jones, at the 26th annual Grammy Awards.
Mar [3] *Thriller*, the unprecedented seventh (and final) single from the album, hits US #4.
Apr [5] Jackson wins the latest in a string of best video awards at the second annual American Video Awards. Appropriately, "The Making Of Michael Jackson's Thriller" video is released in the UK and US, and becomes the best-selling music video to date. In addition to featuring the full length Landis-directed "Thriller" film, it also includes *Beat It*, *Billie Jean* and previously unseen rehearsal clips.
[7] *P.Y.T.* reaches UK #11.
[14] Song-parody specialist "Weird Al" Yankovic reaches US #12 with his novelty, *Eat It*, with Rick Derringer assuming Eddie Van Halen's solo.
[27] Philadelphia radio station WWSH broadcasts a "No Michael Jackson" weekend in protest to his airwave saturation of the past year. (Jackson returns to hospital for further scalp and facial laser surgery.)
May During a New York stay, Jackson expresses interest in a jacket worn by elevator operator Hector Cormana, who gives him a spare.
Jackson sings *For The Good Times* with Floyd Cramer, who is accompanying him on piano at his mother Katharine's birthday party at the Bistro Garden restaurant in Beverly Hills.
[5] Yankovic's *Eat It* makes UK #36.
[14] Jackson dons Cormana's jacket on a visit to the White House to receive a Presidential Humanitarian Award from President and Mrs. Reagan.
June [30] Motown vault issues *Farewell My Summer Love*, which reaches US #38 and UK #7. ***Farewell My Summer Love*** makes US #46 and hits UK #9. A compilation ***Michael Jackson & The Jackson 5 - 14 Greatest Hits***, also released by his former label, reaches US #168. Jackson, meanwhile, rejoins the Jacksons for their newly-announced album, ***Victory***, project and subsequent tour. (Completed by Jackson as a favor to his brothers, the tour will be dogged by financial and organizational problems from the moment boxing promoter Don King offers $3 million in upfront advances. Michael's dissatisfaction with the reunion, and the subsequent money squabbles, lead him to donate his portion to children's charities.) He duets with Mick Jagger on the album's lead-off single, *State Of Shock* (a US #3 and UK #14).
July The official Michael Jackson doll, complete with white glove, is launched.
Aug Jackson receives death threats during the "Victory" tour, and his personal security is doubled.
Sept [8] *Girl You're So Together* reaches UK #33 on Motown. He appears as duet vocalist on *Tell Me I'm Not Dreaming*, from brother Jermaine's new album.
[18] He wins the Best Overall Performance Video, Best Choreography and Viewers Choice categories, all for "Thriller", at the inaugural MTV Video Music Awards, held at Radio City Music Hall, New York, hosted by Dan Aykroyd and Bette Midler.
Nov Jackson unveils his Hollywood Star on the Walk of Fame, 6856, Hollywood, Los Angeles.

1985

Jan Following the UK success of Band Aid's single, Jackson and Lionel Richie write the US version, *We Are The World*, for the all-star ensemble USA For Africa, in two hours.
Feb [26] "Making Michael Jackson's Thriller" wins Best Video Album at the 27th annual Grammy Awards. (To further emphasize Jackson's influence on the current music scene, Weird Al Yankovic wins Best Comedy Recording for *Eat It*.)
Mar [3] Jackson visits the UK to attend Madame Tussaud's Waxworks in London, which is inaugurating his waxwork lookalike. Traffic comes to a standstill, as Jackson jumps on to his car to wave to crowds. He also visits the legendary Abbey Road recording studios.
May Jackson receives a $58 million royalty check from Epic Records.
July During a year which will see no new singles or album releases, Jackson's 15-minute 3D space-fantasy film, produced with George Lucas, begins shooting in California. "Captain Eo", starring Jackson and featuring new material, will take over a year to complete, during which time exclusive distributor Disneyland/World will build a movie theatre on both sites specifically to accomodate the project.
Aug [14] Competing with both Paul McCartney and Yoko Ono, Jackson outbids everyone to secure the ATV music-publishing catalog. At $47.5 million, he gains the rights to more than 250 songs written by Lennon/McCartney. Reports indicate that it severely and irreparably sours relations between McCartney and Jackson. (Jackson has also bought the rights to all Sly Stone's songs.)
Oct [12] Diana Ross' *Eaten Alive*, co-written, co-produced and co-vocalized by Jackson with Barry Gibb, peaks at US #77 (having already made UK #71).

1986

Feb 14-year-old heart transplant patient Donna Ashlock, a devoted Jackson fan, receives a surprise phone call from the star, who invites her to his home for lunch and movies the following month.
[25] *We Are The World* wins Song Of The Year at the 28th annual Grammy Awards.
May [6] Jackson's manager Frank DiLeo, business affairs adviser John Branca and Pepsi president Roger Enrico complete Jackson's second contract for the soft drinks giant. This time for $15 million, it will include two further commercials and sponsorship of a solo world tour.
Aug [4] Jackson and co-producer Jones move into studio D at Westlake Studios to record a follow-up to ***Thriller***. Jackson has already written 62 songs for consideration, and Jones invites outsiders to offer more. (The Beatles' *Come Together* is recorded, but rejected.) Jackson insists that his 300lb snake, Crusher, and constant chimp companion, Bubbles, are present at recording sessions. (Bubbles will enjoy studio rides on the back of engineer Bruce Swedien's Great Dane.)
Sept [21] The **National Enquirer** magazine features on its front cover a picture of Jackson in what it purports to be an oxygen chamber, with the accompanying headline: "Michael Jacksons's Bizarre Plan To Live To 150". (During a 1993 TV chat with Oprah Winfrey, Jackson will strongly refute this story, among many others which hint at his bizarre lifestyle, claiming that it was merely a picture of him lying in a burn victims' machine he paid for and donated to the Michael Jackson Burns Center at the Brotman Memorial Hospital.)
[18] After more than a year's preparation, Jackson's "Captain Eo", produced by sci-fi film-maker George Lucas, premieres at Disneyland in Anaheim, CA, and the Epcot Center in Orlando, FL. It includes the never-released dance number *We Are Just Here To Save The World*, written and performed by Jackson.
Nov Shooting begins in New York on the video for the title cut from Jackson's forthcoming album, ***Bad***. A 17-minute mini-film, directed by Martin Scorsese, its locations include the Bronx subway and the Dobbs Ferry School, and it is based on the true story of Edmund Perry, a Harlem student who was shot by a plainclothes policeman, who claimed Perry had tried to mug him.

1987

Feb As the recording of ***Bad*** enters the final stage, Jackson tapes video clips for two planned singles, *The Way You Make Me Feel* and *Smooth Criminal* (at a reported cost of over $5 million).
Co-written by Jackson with Ryuichi Sakamoto and Chris Mosdell, originally for a Greg Phillinganes' 1984 album, ***Pulse***, *Behind The Mask* makes UK #15 for Eric Clapton.
[24] During the US-televised Grammy Awards, Pepsi airs the new Michael Jackson teaser commercial: "This Spring ... The Magic Returns".
May [18] The Jehovah's Witness headquarters in Brooklyn, New York, issues a statement which says that the organization "no longer considers Michael Jackson to be one of Jehovah's Witnesses", by mutual agreement.
[29] Jackson allegedy offers $50,000 to buy the remains of the "Elephant Man", John Merrick. Although he eventually doubles his offer, it is rejected by the London Hospital. (Despite denying the entire story during his 1993 "Oprah" interview, other sources subsequently claim that this original episode was leaked by Jackson's own publicity company.)
June Cabaret artist Valentino Johnson spends $40,000 on plastic surgery, in an attempt to look like Jackson, and subsequently mimics his act. DiLeo considers legal action.
July [13] 50 of America's biggest record retail heads are invited to Jackson's Encino home to preview ***Bad***. Hosted mainly by LaToya and Joe Jackson, dinner and a tour of the mansion are included, with the notoriously shy Michael appearing only briefly to pose for photos.
Aug [8] First single from the album, a ballad duet with Siedah Garrett, *I Just Can't Stop Loving You*, debuts on the US and UK charts. It will top both surveys, initally hitting UK #1 in its second week of release. (The duet was initially rejected by Whitney Houston and Barbra Streisand. A Spanish-language version of the hit, *Todo Mi Amor Eres Tu*, translated and co-produced by Ruben Blades, will also be released.)
[27] Jackson's ***Bad*** is previewed - four days ahead of release - on a Los Angeles radio station.
[31] On a CBS-TV special, "Michael Jackson - The Magic Returns", the 17-minute "Bad" video is aired for the first time. It is clear that, with the tour and promotion efforts surrounding ***Bad***, Jackson intends to outsell ***Thriller***, aiming for the first 50-million-selling album. ***Bad*** is released and is the biggest-shipped album ever worldwide, entering the US and UK charts at #1. Extensive sleeve notes include thanks to Cary Grant and Marlon Brando.
Sept [12] As the familarly Jones-produced ***Bad***, which ships multi-platinum, debuts at UK #1, Jackson, having promised a solo world tour to both Pepsi and his fans, chooses the 38,000-capacity Korakuen stadium, Toyko, Japan, to begin dates that will take over one year to complete. (The biggest-grossing tour of all time, it will take in Japan, Australia, where some concerts will be cancelled through poor ticket sales, North America, the UK and rest of Europe. Jackson's personal entourage will be more than 250-strong, including a chef, hairdresser and manager DiLeo, who will handle all interviews. Also included are two recent business managers, Jimmy Osmond and Miko Brando.)
[19] *I Just Can't Stop Loving You* tops the US Hot 100 and R&B charts.
[26] ***Bad*** tops the US chart, staying at #1 for six weeks, and will begin an 18-week stay at the R&B summit.
Oct [24] Title cut, *Bad*, written and co-produced by Jackson, hits US #1, tops the R&B chart and reaches UK #3, boosted by its Scorsese-lensed, gang-dancing video clip, which extends Jackson's current "Bad" image of belts, buckles, straps and custom-designed

black streetwear.
Dec Dance-chugging *The Way You Make Me Feel* hits UK #3.

1988

Jan [2] A UK TV compilation, credited to Michael Jackson and Diana Ross, ***Love Songs***, climbs to UK #15.
[9] A UK-only mix album of old Jackson and Jackson 5 hits, ***The Michael Jackson Mix***, reaches UK #27.
[23] *The Way You Make Me Feel* hits US #1, having already topped the R&B chart. (It gives producer Jones the unique achievement of the longest span between chart-topping single productions in US chart history; his first US #1 being Lesley Gore's *It's My Party* in June 1963.)
[25] Jackson wins the Favorite Single, Soul/R&B category at the 15th annual American Music Awards, held at the Shrine Auditorium.
Feb Siedah Garrett/Glen Ballard-penned social-conscience song, *Man In The Mirror*, with backing vocals by the Winans, the Andrae Crouch Choir and Garrett herself, reaches UK #21.
[8] Jackson does not attend the seventh annual BRIT Awards, at the Royal Albert Hall, London, to collect his Best International Solo Artist award.
[23] His "Bad" US concert leg opens at the Kemper Arena, Kansas, MO.
Mar [2] Jackson performs *The Way You Make Me Feel* and *Man In The Mirror* at the 30th annual Grammy Awards, held at New York's Radio City Music Hall.
[3] He donates the box-office receipts of $600,000 from his Madison Square Garden, New York, concert to the United Negro College Fund.
[19] He pays a reported $28 million for the Sycamore Ranch in Santa Ynez Valley, CA, where he will live in grand style, surrounded by his own zoo and theme park.
[26] *Man In The Mirror* tops the US Hot 100 and hits R&B #1.
[30] Jackson wins the Best Single, Male and Album Of The Year, Male categories at the second annual Soul Train Music Awards, held at the Civic Center, Santa Monica, CA.
Apr A UK-remix by Stock/Aitken/Waterman studio PWL of the Motown hit *I Want You Back '88* hits UK #8 for a surprised Michael Jackson & the Jackson 5.
May From the recent Stevie Wonder album ***Characters***, the Jackson/Wonder duet *Get It* peaks at US #80 and UK #37.
[5] Jackson becomes the first non-Soviet to be featured advertising a product on Russian television.
[15] With press silence still maintained, Jackson's autobiography, **Moonwalk**, debuts at #1 on the **New York Times** best-seller list. An immediate global best-seller, the book divulges that the millionaire himself regards himself as one of the loneliest people in the world.
June Video compilation, "The Legend Continues", immediately becomes the best-selling UK music video of all time, out-shipping "The Making Of Michael Jackson's Thriller". As all of Jackson's Epic albums re-enter the UK chart, an old Motown compilation, ***18 Greatest Hits***, peaks at UK #85.
July The Jackson entourage arrives in London for a series of dates, including a record seven sellout Wembley Stadium, Wembley, Middx. (72,000-capacity) performances. (Prior to one of them, Jackson presents audience members H.R.H. the Prince and Princess of Wales with a six-figure cheque for the Prince's Trust Charity.) His chimp, Bubbles, is refused entry to the UK under strict quarantine laws, but tour companion, US TV actor Jimmy Safechuck, is allowed in. He has appeared with Jackson in a recent Pepsi commercial and will also perform on stage. During the trip, Jackson visits London toy store, Hamleys (where he buys a doll of himself), and record store HMV, when both agree to open for him after hours.
[2] *Dirty Diana*, featuring Billy Idol's guitarist Steve Stevens, hits US #1. In doing so Jackson becomes the only artist ever to pull five chart-topping singles off one album.
[23] *Dirty Diana* hits UK #4.
[30] Meanwhile, a limited UK-only, five-singles souvenir pack, ***Bad***, charts for a week at #91.
Sept [7] Jackson collects the prestigious Video Vanguard trophy at the fifth annual MTV Video Music Awards, held at the Universal Amphitheatre, Universal City, CA, an honor subsequently presented as the Michael Jackson Video Vanguard Award. (Jackson returns to the UK for more dates, including a concert at Liverpool's Aintree racecourse, Merseyside. The UK press subsequently overreacts to serious crowd problems caused by the sheer number of fans. *Another Part Of Me* reaches US #11 and UK #15.)
[17] *Another Part Of Me* tops the US R&B chart.
Oct [23] Jackson tours the house where Berry Gordy Jr. launched Motown Records in 1959. Jackson donates $125,000 to the Motown Museum, as he prepares for two Detroit concerts in November.
Nov *Smooth Criminal*, the seventh single from ***Bad***, hits US #7 and UK #8.
[13] Los Angeles' Mayor, Tom Bradley, proclaims "Michael Jackson Month", as the singer performs at the Sports Arena.
Dec "Moonwalker", starring Jackson and featuring Sean Lennon, among others, opens in movie theatres throughout the US and UK.
[10] Jackson wins Best Male Artist and Best Album Of The Year (for ***Bad***), at the NAACP 21st Image Awards. (The show will be broadcast on NBC-TV on January 14th.)

1989

Jan [16-18, 26-27] He plays five sellout dates at the Los Angeles Memorial Coliseum & Sports Arena, grossing more than $2 million.
[30] He is presented with the Special Award Of Achievement by Eddie Murphy at the 16th annual American Music Awards, held at the Shrine Auditorium.
Feb [1] Lavon A. Muhammad is sentenced to a maximum of 2½ years for violating a court order to stay away from Jackson. The 41-year-old former legal secretary, claims that Jackson is the father of her 6-year-old twins. She loses a £100-million paternity suit.
[7] Jackson visits Cleveland School, Stockton, CA, the scene of the January 17th schoolyard massacre in which five children were fatally shot.
[13] Jackson fires his manager DiLeo, who reportedly seeks a $60-million settlement to prevent him revealing Jackson's lifestyle secrets to the media. Jackson sends a taped message to the eighth annual BRIT Awards held at London's Royal Albert Hall, where he wins Best Music Video, ("Smooth Criminal"), Best International Solo Artist and Best International Artist, Male.
[18] "Moonwalker" replaces "E.T." at the top of Billboard's Video Sales chart.
Mar *Leave Me Alone*, originally only available as a bonus track on the CD version of ***Bad*** (which has now hit #1 in 24 countries), hits UK #2 but remains unreleased as a single in the US. Its video is extracted from the movie "Moonwalker", which has also proved more popular in Britain.
Apr [12] He wins the Best R&B/Urban Contemporary Single, Male and Best R&B/Urban Contemporary Music Video categories at the third annual Soul Train Music Awards, held at the Shrine Auditorium.
May [2] Jackson, wearing a wig, fake moustache and false teeth, enters Zales jewellers in Simi Valley, CA. Shopping center security guard H.N. Edwards, thinking him to be a robber, alerts police, who quickly arrive with three squad cars and make Jackson strip off his disguise.
[16] Sister Janet, on the VIP tour at Universal Studios, is hounded by fans mistaking her for her more famous brother. Michael, who, not least through ongoing plastic surgery, actually resembles the equally worked-over LaToya, meanwhile takes the tour in disguise (and peace and quiet).
June He begins shooting the video for the ballad *Liberian Girl*, an unprecedented eighth (UK-only) single release from ***Bad***.
July [22] *Liberian Girl* reaches UK #13. (LaToya Jackson's manager, Jack Gordon, alleges Jackson has offered LaToya $5 million to stop publication of her autobiography **La Toya: Growing Up In The Jackson Family**.)
Sept [6] "Leave Me Alone" wins the Best Special Effects category at the sixth annual MTV Video Music Awards, held at the Universal Amphitheatre.
[13] Jackson signs a $28-million deal with L.A. Gear Sportswear to be its spokesperson. The campaign will be unsuccessful and will be dropped after one commercial.
[18] California Raisins commercial featuring a "claymation" version of Jackson airs on US TV. Jackson donates his $25,000 royalty to charity.
Oct [11] Jackson attends a ceremony at his former Gardner Street Elementary School, where the Michael Jackson Auditorium is inaugurated. Jackson's typically succinct speech is, "This is the happiest day of my life. I love you all."
Nov [16] He presents Eddie Murphy with an MTV award on syndicated TV's "The Arsenio Hall Show".

1990

Jan [27] The American Cinema Awards Foundation crowns Jackson Entertainer Of The Decade with Sophia Loren presenting his award.
Feb [21] "Leave Me Alone" wins Best Music Video - Short Form at the 32nd annual Grammy Awards, at the Shrine Auditorium.
Mar [14] Jackson wins the Silver Award as the 1980s Artist Of The Decade at the fourth annual Soul Train Music Awards, at the Shrine Auditorium.
Apr [5] Jackson is invited to the White House by President Bush and will attend the opening ceremonies for Donald Trump's Taj Mahal Hotel in Atlantic City, NJ, later in the month.
May [8] To celebrate its 50th anniversary, the BMI presents its first Michael Jackson award to the singer himself at the Regent Beverly Wilshire Hotel, Beverly Hills, CA. Attendees at the luncheon include Little Richard, Brian Wilson, Herbie Hancock, Gerry Goffin, Jeff Barry and Holland, Dozier and Holland.
[26] **Billboard**'s Music Of The '80s Poll honors Jackson with Pop Album Of The Decade (***Thriller***), Black Artist Of The Decade, Black Album Of The Decade (***Thriller***), Black Single Of The Decade (*Billie Jean*), as ***Thriller*** passes the 21-million mark (US only), according to the RIAA.
June [3] Jackson is admitted to the St. John's Hospital & Health Center, Santa Monica, CA, to undergo tests, after experiencing chest pains. He is diagnosed as having costochondritis, meaning that the cartilage at the front of his rib cage is inflamed. (Lawyer Thomas Wampold files a class-action lawsuit alleging Jackson was not sick, as he said, when he cancelled three Tacoma, WA concerts, therefore committing a breach of contract and disappointing 72,000 fans.)
Aug [18] Jackson invites 130 YMCA children to his ranch to visit his zoo, video arcade and movie theater.
[21] An announcement is made confirming Sandy Gallin as Jackson's new manager.
Sept [14] Los Angeles Area Council of the Boys Scouts of America honors Jackson with the "Michael Jackson Good Scout Humanitarian Award", presented by Disney CEO Michael Eisner.

1991

Mar [20] One week after Janet Jackson has announced the most lucrative record deal in pop history, Michael's new contract with Sony makes his sister's agreement look trivial: with an $18-million cash advance for his forthcoming ***Dangerous*** album release alone, Jackson is made CEO of his own newly formed Nation Records (which will change its name to to MJJ), itself a subsidiary of the Jackson Entertainment Complex, which will also include TV, video and film divisions. His record royalty rate is negotiated at an unprecedented $2 and 8 cents per unit (album) with guarantees for post-***Dangerous*** album advances of $5 million per project. Heralded as the first billion-dollar entertainer contract, it is also announced that movie directors David Lynch, Tim Burton, Christopher Columbus and Sir Richard Attenborough are already lined up to lense forthcoming promo film clips to accompany the ***Dangerous*** singles.

May Jackson, who owns the publishing rights to Dion's classic *The Wanderer*, denies the use of the song by UK soccer F.A. Cup Trophy finalists Wycombe Wanderers, because they wish to change the lyrics.

June [23] Jackson ends a four-day trip in Bermuda, where he has stayed with Texas tycoon H. Ross Perot, and played with child star Macaulay Culkin.

Sept [19] Fox-TV's "The Simpsons", with a reported Jackson voiceover credited to John Jay Smith, airs.

Oct [1] Jackson's crystal-beaded glove is stolen from the Motown Museum in Detroit. Police recover the item two days later in Grand Blanc, MI, and arrest 23-year old Flint, MI, man Bruce Hays on a charge of larceny.

[6] His close friend Elizabeth Taylor marries Larry Fortensky at Jackson's Santa Ynez Valley ranch. (A longtime fan of veteran UK singer Petula Clark, Jackson commissions her to record three demos with a view to future release.)

Nov [14] The video for *Black And White* premieres simultaneously on Fox, BET and MTV, and also BBC1-TV's "Top Of The Pops", which draws a 10.7 million audience for the show. The video will be withdrawn and re-edited after its first showing, amid controversy over its violent content.

[20] On the official release date of his new album ***Dangerous***, 30,000 copies, valued at $400,000, are stolen from a terminal at Los Angeles Airport by three men brandishing shotguns.

[23] Self-penned *Black Or White* debuts at UK #1.

[27] Jackson performs two songs for ABC-TV's "MTV 10" special, including a pre-taped version of *Black And White* featuring Guns N' Roses' Slash, who has contributed guitar to the original single.

[30] The co-self-produced, with Bill Bottrell, Teddy Riley and Bruce Swedien, ***Dangerous***, featuring guest musicians Heavy D, Rene Moore, David Paich, Jeff Porcaro and Slash, among others, debuts at UK #1, topping the chart on a record-breaking three-days' sales. (The European shipment of the album has been 4.1 million copies.)

Dec [7] *Black Or White* hits US #1 in only its third week on the Hot 100, spurred by a fashionable morphing device-using video clip.

[14] ***Dangerous***, its sleeve designed by illustrator Mark Ryden, tops the US chart. Jackson becomes the first artist since Elton John in 1975 to top **Billboard**'s album chart with back-to-back releases.

[26] Jackson is featured on ABC-TV's "Entertainers '91" special, saluting the year's Top 20 entertainers.

1992

Jan [17] "Michael Jackson ... The Legend Continues", with contributions from Quincy Jones, Smokey Robinson, Yoko Ono and Dick Clark, airs on CBS-TV.

[18] Clivilles and Cole remix of *Black And White* debuts at its UK #14 peak, as ***Dangerous*** is initially certified multi-platinum by the RIAA for four million sales. (During the year, ***Off The Wall*** will be confirmed with global sales of 12 million; ***Thriller*** currently stands at 48 million, with ***Bad*** having sold a mere 25 million.)

Feb [2] Jackson holds a New York press conference from Radio City Music Hall to announce a forthcoming world tour to be sponsored by Pepsi, in the largest promotion deal ever. Proceeds will to go to his recently formed Heal The World foundation, devoted to helping children the world over. Video clip of the second cut from ***Dangerous***, the jack-swing *Remember The Time*, featuring Eddie Murphy, model Iman (with whom Jackson shares his first screen kiss) and Earvin "Magic" Johnson in an Egyptian tale directed by John Singleton, premieres on multiple US cable channels at 8:25 p.m. EST.)

[11] Jackson begins a trip to Africa in Gaob, set to include visits to the Ivory Coast and Tanzania.

[15] During the tour, Jackson is crowned "King Of The Sanwis" in the Ivory Coast village of Krinjabo.

[19] He arrives at UK's Stansted Airport, after cutting short his African tour, amid stories that he is concerned about his health. **Abidjian**, an Ivory Coast newspaper describes his visit: "The American sacred beast took it upon himself to remind us we are underdeveloped impure. Our air is polluted, infested with germs. And it's not this mutant genius, this voluntary mutant, this re-created being, bleached, neither white nor black, neither man nor woman, so delicate, so frail, who will inhale it."

[22] *Remember The Time*, paired with the now-issued cover of *Come Together*, hits UK #3.

[27] While in England with his ten-year-old cousin Brett, Jackson visits ailing UK comedian Benny Hill, who is recovering from a heart attack.

[29] Jackson's ***Motown's Greatest Hits*** debuts at its UK #53 peak.

Mar [5] Jackson is awarded a lifetime achievement award in Washington, DC, by the National Association of Black Owned Broadcasters.

[7] *Remember The Time* hits US #3.

[29] MTV airs a "My Dinner With Michael" contest, which will entail 100 winners being flown to Los Angeles to have supper with the singer. They will receive more than four million entries.

Apr [23] At 8:54 p.m., Fox-TV premieres the Herb Ritts-directed video clip accompanying the third ***Dangerous*** extract, *In The Closet*, featuring a ponytailed Jackson performing a courtship dance with model, Naomi Campbell.

May [2] *In The Closet*, also crediting Mystery Girl (rumored to be Princess Stephanie of Monaco), debuts at its UK #8 peak.

Jackson pays for the funeral of nine-year-old Ramon Sanchez Jr., who was shot by a stray bullet on May 6th while drinking a glass of milk in the kitchen of his family's apartment, upon hearing that his parents cannot afford to bury him.

[30] *In The Closet* hits US #6. (In his first interview since 1984, Jackson tells **Ebony** magazine's Robert Johnson that "I haven't scratched the surface yet of what my real purpose is for being here".)

June Concerned-environmentalist Jackson hires a Russian An-124 cargo jet, the world's largest airplane, to haul the set, equipment and personal effects necessary to stage the forthcoming European leg of his "Dangerous" world tour from Los Angeles to Stansted Airport.

[3] Crystal Cartier files a $40-million federal lawsuit against Jackson, Sony Music Entertainment, MJJ Productions and Epic Records, alleging that she originally wrote and recorded *Dangerous*.

[27] His "Dangerous" world tour opens in Munich, West Germany, at the Olympic Stadium. Radio Vision International produces a European-only 45-minute program to be aired direct, climaxing in two songs live from the concert.

(500,000 cassette copies of the single *Someone Put Your Hand Out*, previously unavailable anywhere, are released in Europe through a Pepsi-Cola deal, made possible by returning tokens printed on Pepsi packaging.)

July Jackson issues his second book, **Dancing The Dream**, a collection of his poems and reflections including one hundred photographs, paintings and drawings. Meanwhile, the South African government has seen fit to ban his "In The Closet" video from TV broadcast, saying that it is "of a very sensual nature, which could offend viewers".

[21] Police officer Anne-Margrethe Skov's foot is crushed when a car from Jackson's motorcade runs over it, as fans rush to get a glimpse of the star at Tivoli Gardens amusement park in Denmark.

[25] British and Irish leg of the tour bows at Lansdowne Road, Dublin, Eire.

[27] Jackson sues the **Daily Mirror** for libel and breach of contract, after it prints a less-than-flattering color photo of him on the front page.

Aug [1] *Who Is It*, with IHS remix by Brothers In Rhythm (Steve Anderson and Dave Seaman) and a Most Patience mix by Moby, hits UK #10, as the last of Jackson's Wembley Stadium concerts is postponed when he falls ill with a viral infection.

[8] *Jam* reaches US #26.

[15] ***Tour Souvenir Pack*** debuts at UK #32 peak.

Sept [2] Jackson's taped poem is broadcast on syndicated-TV's "Maury Povich Show" featuring AIDS victim Ryan White's mother Jeanne, and her continuing efforts for AIDS education: "I miss you Ryan White, you showed us how to stand and fight, in the rain. You were a cloudburst of joy, the sparkle of hope in every girl and boy. Ryan White, I love you."

[9] His live performance of *Black And White* is broadcast via satellite from Wembley Stadium, to the ninth annual MTV Video Music Awards held at the Pauley Pavilion, Los Angeles.

[11] L.A. Gear files suit in Los Angeles Superior Court alleging breach of contract and fraud over Jackson's prior endorsement deal. Jackson countersues for $44 million, alleging fraud and breach of contract.

[13] Jackson plays at the Hippodrome, Paris, France, during the European leg of his "Dangerous" tour.

[19] *Jam* reaches UK #13, as Jackson performs in concert from Bucharest, Romania. (HBO-TV, reportedly paying $20 million for the privilege, will air "From Bucharest: The Dangerous Tour" on October 10th.)

Oct [5] Jackson visits a Harley Street doctor, concerned about his throat problems, before flying home to Los Angeles, cancelling the last six dates of his European tour.

Nov [24] His Heal The World Foundation airlifts medical supplies to Sarajevo - in conjunction with AmeriCares - from New York's JFK Airport.

Dec [8] A settlement with the Cleveland Orchestra over Jackson's alleged unauthorized use of the orchestra's Beethoven's Ninth recording for ***Dangerous*** is reached.

[9] Jackson wins the Hot 100 Singles Artists - Male, Hot R&B Singles Artists, Hot Dance Music Club Play Artists and the Hot Dance Music Maxi-Single Sales Artists categories at 1992 **Billboard** Music Awards.

[12] Anthemic ballad, *Heal The World*, hits UK #2, where it will stay for five weeks (behind Whitney Houston's *I Will Always Love You*).

[31] Jackson plays the last of eight sellout concerts at the Tokyo Dome, Tokyo, Japan. (By year's end, he will have launched his perfume line: "Mystique de Michael Jackson" for women and "Legend de Michael Jackson" for men.)

1993

Jan [16] Jackson receives the Silver Anniversary Entertainer Of The Year award and "Black Or White" wins the Music Video Award at the 25th annual NAACP Image Awards, at the Pasadena Civic Auditorium. (The show will air on NBC-TV on the 23rd.)

[19] He performs *Gone Too Soon*, a tribute to Ryan White, and *Heal The World* at President-elect Bill Clinton's "An American Reunion: The 52nd Presidential Gala" inaugural concert from the Capital Centre, Landover, MD, broadcast on ABC-TV.

[25] In addition to opening the show with a performance of *Dangerous*, Jackson nabs the Favorite Album, Pop/Rock, and Favorite Single, Soul/R&B trophies at the 20th Annual American Music Awards. He is also the recipient of the first-ever Michael Jackson International Artist Award, presented to him by longtime confidant, Elizabeth Taylor.

[31] Jackson performs at half-time of "Superbowl XXVII", between the Dallas Cowboys and the Buffalo Bills, at the Rose Bowl, Pasadena, CA. (The show will be seen by a record-setting estimated 133.4 million people, according to Nielsen Media Research.)

Feb [10] Jackson conducts his first TV interview in 14 years on a special edition of "Oprah Winfrey", broadcast live from his Neverland Valley Ranch, Santa Ynez Valley. During the candid coversation, Jackson admits to "cry(ing) through loneliness at age eight. I didn't have any friends growing up. I'd wash my face in the dark and my father would tease me. He was very strict." Concerning a list which Oprah details about persistent press rumors, Jackson claims that he didn't buy or want the Elephant Man bones (despite an original press release being issued by his own cohorts when the story first emerged). On the subject of his much-changed skin color he states: "I have a skin disorder which destroys the pigment of my skin. It's in my family. We're trying to control it. I am a black American." Asked about his notorious crotch-grabbing he responds: "I'm slave to the rhythm." Contradicting another widely-held belief that he insists on being referred to as the "King Of Pop", he again claims that the tag was first mentioned by Elizabeth Taylor at the 1989 Heritage Awards. On his personal life Jackson says that he is dating Brooke Shields and that "I have been in love two times." When probed on the question of virginity, he quietly responds: "I'm a gentleman. Call me old-fashioned." At the interview's end, which has taken place in his house and while walking through his funfair and private cinema (in which he has erected beds in private booths so that terminally sick kids can watch films), he introduces the world premiere of *Give In To Me*, a concert video clip featuring Slash.

[24] As ***Dangerous*** continues its climb back up the US chart (hitting #10 on Mar [6]), following Jackson's current unexpected rush of participatory media promotion, he receives the Grammy Legend Award from his sister Janet at the 35th annual Grammy Awards, held at the Shrine Auditorium. In beginning his longest-ever acceptance speech, he says: "In the last few weeks I've gone from 'where is he?' to 'here he is again'."

Mar [2] Jackson sends condolences to the parents of two-year-old toddler James Bulger, who was recently murdered in Liverpool, Merseyside.

[6] *Give In To Me* hits UK #2.

[9] He collects the Best R&B/Soul Album (***Dangerous***) and Best R&B/Soul Male Single (*Remember The Time*) trophies at the seventh annual Soul Train Music Awards, held at the Shrine Auditorium. He also performs *Remember The Time* in a wheelchair (the first time he has ever done this) because "I was dancing and I went into a spin and I twisted my ankle very badly."

[11] Jackson attends the American Film Institute's dinner at the Beverly Hilton Hotel, Los Angeles, to bestow upon Elizabeth Taylor its Life Achievement Award.

[12] He announces - by satellite - that he will be teaming up with former President Carter to help immunize thousands of pre-school children in Atlanta, as part of the Atlanta Project.

[20] *Heal The World* reaches US #27.

May [12] He is named Best Selling US Artist Of The Year, World's Best Selling Pop and Overall Artist Of The Year, and World's Best Selling Artist Of The Era at the fifth annual World Music Awards, at the Sporting Club, Monte Carlo, Monaco.

[15] *Who Is It* reaches US #14.

[19] Jackson receives a Lifetime Achievement Award from the Hollywood Guinness World of Records Museum.

July [17] *Will You Be There*, from the film "Free Willy", hits UK #9.

Aug [15] The second leg of his world tour kicks off in Hong Kong.

[17] The Los Angeles Police Department begins an investigation into charges brought by the father of a 13-year old boy that Jackson allegedly abused the child at his Encino home earlier in the year.

[21] The LAPD raids Jackson's ranch, seizing evidence including video tapes, which the department later confirms contains no incriminating evidence.

[23] The LAPD formally announces that Jackson is under criminal investigation.

[24] Confidential documents from the Los Angeles County Department Of Children's Services are leaked to reporters, revealing that Dr. Evan Chandler, a Beverly Hills dentist, has claimed that his 13-year-old son has been sexually abused by Jackson. The boy had met Jackson the previous year, when Jackson's limousine broke down in Los Angeles, leading him to the nearest Rent-A-Wreck, where he met June Chandler, the mother of the boy. Jackson had then escorted the boy to Disney World and the World Music Awards in Monaco. As accusations fly back and forth during saturated media coverage, Jackson's private investigator, Anthony Pellicano, will publicly state that Chandler has been trying to extort $20 million from the singer and, having failed to do so, has made the accusation.

[31] Jackson's doctor pronounces the singer fit, following a brain scan. Tito and Jermaine Jackson walk off the set of NBC-TV's "Today" show, when a crew from NBC affiliate KNBC show up to interview the pair about Michael Jackson's troubles.

Sept [11] *Will You Be There*, the first release on Jackson's own MJJ label, hits US #7.

[15] The day after two former Jackson employees claim they saw Jackson "doing what honeymooners do" with young boys, the alleged 13-year old victim formally files a civil suit againt the star, for seduction and sexual abuse. (Amid this controversy, Jackson will decide not to contribute the theme to the "Addams Family Values" movie.)

Nov [12] After a much-troubled tour, which has included cancelled dates in Thailand and Singapore, Jackson nixes remaining dates, citing that pressure from the molestation charges have left him addicted to painkillers.

[14] Rumored to be undergoing addiction treatment at London's Charter Nightingale clinic, Jackson's $10 million sponsorship deal with Pepsi-Cola comes to an end.

[22] Five ex-security guards at Jackson's Neverland ranch file suit alleging that they were fired for knowing too much about Jackson's alleged fondness for young boys.

[23] Santa Monica Superior Court orders Jackson to make a deposition in reference to the civil suit, before January 31st, 1994, also setting a trial date of March 21st, 1994.

[24] EMI Music signs a five-year deal to administer Jackson's ATV Music publishing company for a reported $70 million.

Dec [2] Norwalk, CT newspaper, **The Hour**, reports that Jackson checked into Silver Hill psychiatric hospital, New Canaan, CT on November 29th.

[8] At a press conference in Tel Aviv, Israel, estranged Jackson family member, LaToya, says of the current child-molestation allegations surrounding her brother: "I can't remain silent. I love him but I cannot and will not be a silent collaborator (in) his crimes against small innocent children. You tell me what 35-year old man is going to take a little boy ... and stay with him for five days in his room?"

[10] Jackson returns to the US aboard a private jet, amid heightened security and secrecy to face the music.

[22] Responding publicly for the first time to the current child-sex abuse allegations, Jackson holds a four-minute live satellite broadcast from Neverland Valley, denying everything: "I ask all of you to wait to hear the truth before you label or condemn me. Don't treat me like a criminal because I am innocent." Commenting on a body search, undertaken by the Santa Barbara and Los Angeles police departments earlier in the week, Jackson states: "They served a search warrant on me which allowed them to view and photograph my body, including my penis, my buttocks, my lower torso, thighs and any other areas that they wanted … It was the most humiliating ordeal of my life … I am totally innocent of any wrong-doing."

[25] *Gone Too Soon* reaches UK #23.

1994

Jan [1] Jackson makes his first public appearance since his December 10th return at Barbra Streisand's MGM Grand Hotel concert in Las Vegas.

[5] Jackson presents Debbie Allen with the Outstanding Choreography In Film Or TV Award at the NAACP 26th annual Image Awards in Pasadena, CA, declaring "Not only am I presumed innocent, I am innocent".

[25] Jackson settles his civil suit with a multi-million dollar payment to the boy accusing him of molestation, though Jackson's lawyer Johnnie Cochran insists that the decision to head off a court case was "in no way an admission of guilt".

Feb [15] A four man, four woman US District Court jury in Denver, CO, rule that Jackson did not steal *Dangerous* from Crystal Cartier. (A cappella passages of Jackson singing *Billie Jean* and *Dangerous* on the witness stand the previous day will become available via mail order through the court at $15 a copy.)

[19] The Jackson Family Honors NBC-TV special, postponed from December and set for broadcast on the 22nd, is staged at the MGM Grand Garden, with an all-star cast. (Many of the 12,000 audience demand their money back when Michael appears but does not perform.)

Apr [28] Jackson receives the Caring For Kids' Kids Award from Body Sculpt, an organization that uses body building to persuade children to avoid drugs and remain in school, at the Children's Choice Awards at New York's City Center.

May [13] Photographer Alex Oliveira files $1 million suit against Jackson in Manhattan Federal Court, saying he took no action when his bodyguards beat him up and took his film in New York's Central Park.

[26] Jackson and Lisa Marie Presley are married in La Vega, Dominican Republic, by civil judge Hugh Francisco Alvarez Pérez, an event they will deny took place for more than two months.

June [17] Steeltown Records releases *Big Boy*, Jackson' first-ever recording, cut some 26 years earlier. Available by mail order, label boss Ben Brown discovered the original tape in his pantry and owns the copyright.

July [11] Jackson's spokesman Lee Solters denies that Jackson and Presley are married, despite being seen together at sister Janet's Radio City Music Hall show and a **New York Post** report that they have rented an apartment in Trump Tower.

Aug [1] Presley announces that she and Jackson were indeed married on May 26th.

[6] Jackson shoots Communist-themed video in Budapest, accompanied by his wife.

Sept [8] Jackson opens the 11th annual MTV Video Music Awards from Radio City Music Hall, with Lisa Marie by his side.

[21] Los Angeles and Santa Barbara's District Attorney's offices announce that they will not file child molestation charges.

[27] Marcio Alberto de Paolo and his sister Renata file a $20 million negligence lawsuit in Manhattan Federal Court, claiming they were victims of a hit-and-run accident involving Jackson's van in Sao Paolo.

Oct [5] A DNA test submitted in a Modesto, CA court confirms that Jackson is not the father of James Hall, the 10-year-old son of Michelle Flowers, conceived when Jackson allegedly raped her on New Year's Eve.

[8] Jackson attends the all-star "Elvis Aaron Presley : The Tribute" with Lisa Marie and sister Janet at the Pyramid Arena, Memphis.

(The Boy Scouts Of America express their displeasure at a 1995 Michael Jackson calendar, which shows him wearing a scoutmaster's uniform surround by uniformed scouts. "Michael Jackson is not and has not been a registered leader or member of the Boy Scouts Of America. Our approval for publication was not sought, and the publisher has not returned our phone calls." Quoted in **Ebony**, Jackson reveals that when he asked Lisa Marie to marry him over the phone, he responded "Excuse me, I have to go to the bathroom".)

Dec [30] Judge Domenico Bonaccorsi, at a Rome civic tribunal, rules in favor of singer/songwriter Al Bano Carrisi, who claimed Jackson's *Will You Be There* was based on his *I Cigni Di Balaka*.

1995

Jan [12] Jackson files a $100 million lawsuit against a Los Angeles radio station and two producers of TV tabloid show "Hard Copy", alleging they slandered him when they stated there was a renewed police investigation into new allegations of child molestation.

Feb [23] He appears at the Sony Music Distribution product presentation to herald the forthcoming release of ***HIStory : Past, Present And Future Book 1*** at the annual NARM meeting in San Diego. He also receives the Harry Chapin Memorial Humanitarian Award.

Apr [18] 46 children from 17 countries, as members of the World Children's Congress, visit the Neverland ranch.

June [10] *Scream*, a duet with sister Janet, coupled with *Childhood*, from the film "Free Willy 2", debuts at its UK #3 peak.
[14] Jackson, with Lisa Marie by his side, is interviewed by Diane Sawyer on ABC-TV's "Primetime Live". The show posts a 60 million audience, 30 million less than viewed his Oprah Winfrey appearance.
[15] A 10 metre high, 2,100 kilo statue of Jackson sails under Tower Bridge, as the worldwide hype over the double-set ***HIStory : Past, Present And Future Book 1*** increases to fever pitch. The album - part hits and part new material - features new productions by Jam & Lewis, David Foster, R. Kelly and Dallas Austin.
[16] Jackson releases a statement apologizing for the seemingly anti-semitic lyrics of *They Don't Care About Us*. Steven Spielberg, who has contributed glowing liner notes to ***HIStory : Past, Present And Future Book 1*** distances himself from the controversy.
[17] *Scream* bows at its US #5 peak, re-writing chart history - becoming the highest debuting US single, besting the Beatles #6 *Let It Be*. (The record will be equalled the following week when Notorious B.I.G.'s *One More Chance* debuts at #5, as *Scream* drops a place.)
[22] Jackson is honored for his Heal The World Foundation at the second annual VH-1 Honors.
[24] ***HIStory : Past, Present And Future Book 1*** debuts at UK #1, as *Scream (4th And 5th Formats)* debuts at its UK #43 peak, during a two-week chart stay.
July [8] ***HIStory : Past, Present And Future Book 1*** debuts at US #1.
[21] A Los Angeles Superior Court judge dismisses a suit against Jackson filed by five former security guards, citing that they signed releases barring them from talking to the press, which they have repeatedly done.
[28] In exchange for airing ten free commercial spots, ABC-TV broadcasts "Michael Jackson Changes HIStory", a half-hour special of music videos including the premiere of his new single, *You Are Not Alone*.
Aug [17] With US sales of ***HIStory : Past, Present And Future Book 1*** stalling, Jackson engages in a live online simulchat on America OnLine, CompuServe and Prodigy.
Sept [2] The R. Kelly-penned and produced ballad *You Are Not Alone* becomes the first ever single to debut at US #1.
[7] Jackson lip-synchs his way through a medley of past hits and *You Are Not Alone* at the 12th annual MTV Video Music Awards from Radio City Music Hall at which "Scream" nabs Best Dance Video, Best Choreography and Best Art Direction honors.
[9] *You Are Not Alone* tops the UK chart.
[22] Jackson is the principal inductee at Black Entertainment Television's Walk of Fame in Washington, naming his contribution the most significant in the music video industry. He performs *You Are Not Alone* with the Union Temple Baptist Choir.
Nov [2] Jackson is inducted into the Soul Train Hall Of Fame at the 25th annual ceremonies from the Shrine Auditorium.
[7] Sony releases a statement that the company has entered into a joint agreement with Jackson under which he will merge his ATV publishing copyrights with theirs. Jackson receives an upfront payment reported to be between $90 and $110 million. His own MIJAC Music stays with Warner Chappell.
[23] Jackson wins Best Male Performer category at the second annual MTV European Music Awards, held at Le Zenith in Paris, France.
Dec [6] Jackson collapses onstage while rehearsing for the upcoming HBO special "Michael Jackson : One Night Only" at New York's Beacon Theatre. Emergency workers find him semi-conscious lying on the side of the stage at about 5:00 p.m. EMS technician Kevin Barwick reveals "He was lethargic. He was speaking slowly, mumbling". EMS spokesman John Hanchar says Jackson's blood pressure was measured at 70 over 40 in the ambulance on the way to the Beth Israel Medical Center North. He undergoes tests and is treated for apparent dehydration.
[7] Doctors Allan Metzger and William Alleyne say that "Mr. Jackson will require several days of critical-care monitoring and treatment". He is being treated for inflammation of the stomach, dehydration and kidney and liver irregularities, caused by an electrolyte imbalance.
[8] With Jackson in intensive care on the second floor of the hospital, surrounded by framed posters of Shirley Temple, Mickey Mouse and Topo Gigio, Dr. Alleyne reveals that Jackson is suffering from a viral infection and had been ill for at least a week before collapsing.
[9] Anthemic *Earth Song* debuts at UK #1.
[10] Instead of performing live on HBO as planned, Jackson is instead informed by Lisa Marie that their 18-month marriage is over, although the split will not be made public until the following month.
[12] Jackson leaves hospital in a white van.

1996

Jan [18] Lisa Marie files for divorce from Jackson in a Los Angeles court citing "irreconcilable differences". The world is aghast.
[25] Jackson is named Hype Of The Year in **Rolling Stone**'s Critics Poll.
[30] He is named Favorite Pop/Rock Male Artist at the 23rd annual American Music Awards held at the Shrine Auditorium.
Feb [19] Jackson's performance of *Earth Song* at the 1996 BRIT Awards at London's Earl's Court Exhibition Centre, at which he also picks up the Artist of a Generation award, is interrupted when Pulp's Jarvis Cocker walks on-stage, causing a melée during which it is claimed some of the children sharing the stage with Jackson, are injured. Cocker claims that his behavior, for which he will be arrested but not charged, was "a form of protest at the way Michael Jackson sees himself as some Christ-like figure with the power of healing. Jackson states afterwards that he was "immensely proud that the show went on despite (Cocker's) disgusting and cowardly behavior", a comment for which Cocker momentarily considers suing Jackson for defamation of character.
[28] "Scream" is named Best Music Video, Short Form at the 38th annual Grammy Awards held at the Shrine Auditorium.
Mar [8] "Sisterella", a musical in which co-executive director Jackson has invested, premieres at the Pasadena Playhouse, Pasadena, CA.
[20] In Paris, France, Jackson and Saudi Prince Alwaleed bin Talal bin Abdulaziz announce their partnership in founding the Kingdom Entertainment group with the vague aim to participate in "the global multimedia explosion".
see also: **THE JACKSON 5**

THE JACKSON 5

Jackie Jackson (vocals); **Tito Jackson** (vocals); **Jermaine Jackson** (vocals); **Marlon Jackson** (vocals); **Michael Jackson** (vocals)

1963

The family group is initially formed as a trio in Gary, IN, by Jackie (b. Sigmund Esco Jackson, May 4, 1951, Gary), Tito (b. Toriano Adaryll Jackson, Oct. 15, 1953, Gary) and Jermaine (b. Jermaine La Juane Jackson, Dec. 11, 1954, Gary), the three eldest sons of steelworks crane driver Joe Jackson (an ex-guitarist for the Falcons) and his wife, Katharine (née Scruse). Initially known as the Jackson Family, and at the urging of their parents, the youngsters begin playing dates around Gary. Younger brothers Marlon (b. Marlon David Jackson, Mar. 12, 1957, Gary) and Michael (b. Michael Joseph Jackson, Aug. 29, 1958, Gary) soon join, and they become the Jackson Five (also performing as the Ripples & Waves Plus Michael). They win a succession of talent shows, their first "non-contest" performance being at the opening of a Big Top supermarket. A local fixture by 1965, they enter and win a local talent contest at Roosevelt High School in Gary, performing the Temptations' *My Girl*.

1966

After making their venue debut at Mr. Lucky's, a nightclub in Gary (and now augmented by Johnny Jackson and Ronnie Rancifer as drummer and pianist), the Jackson Five begin to play further afield, with their father as manager, driving them to other cities (most frequently Chicago, IL) in a Volkswagen van. On a trip to New York, NY, they compete in another talent contest, at the Apollo Theatre, Harlem, and win. They also open for such acts as the Emotions, the O'Jays, Sam & Dave, the Temptations and Jackie Wilson.

1967

They support Gladys Knight & the Pips at an Indiana gig, and Knight, recently signed to Motown herself, notes to label boss Berry Gordy Jr. that the act is worth considering.
Aug They appear at an Apollo Theatre talent contest in the most prestigious category for "Superdog".

1968

Feb *Big Boy*, produced by Gordon Keith, is released on Ben Brown's Gary-based Steeltown label and will be followed by one more Steeltown release, *Some Girls Want Me For Their Love*.
May They perform at the Apollo Theatre with the Five Stairsteps, Etta James and Joe Simon.
July The Jackson Five opens for Bobby Taylor & the Vancouvers at the High Chaparral Club, Chicago. Taylor calls Ralph Seltzer, the head of Motown's creative department, to arrange an audition for the group (although subsequent sources claim that the group's introduction to Gordy is made at the instigation of label staffer Suzanne De Passe).
[26] The Jackson Five signs a one-year contract with Motown, receiving 6% of 90% of the wholesale price of each record, which will be split five ways, with each member receiving less than half a penny per single and two cents per album. In addition they will be paid $12.50 for each song recorded, but only if it is released. There is also a clause in the contract preventing them from recording for another label until five years after the expiration of the agreement.
Sept [27] The band performs on an all-Motown bill alongside Gladys Knight & the Pips, Shorty Long and Bobby Taylor & the Vancouvers at a campaign benefit for Gary Mayor Richard Hatcher, at the Gilroy Stadium, Gary.

1969

Mar [11] Motown buys the brothers out of their Steeltown contract.
Aug Gordy relocates the Jackson Five to Hollywood, CA, for grooming and rehearsals. The entire Jackson family moves with them.
[11] Diana Ross introduces the group to 350 invited guests at the Daisy club, Beverly Hills, CA. (The Motown press release removes two years from the ages of each member, and claims that Ross discovered the act.)
[16] The Jackson Five makes its formal debut as a Motown act at the Great Western Forum, Inglewood, CA, with Diana Ross and the Supremes.
Oct [18] The Jackson 5 (Gordy has decided on a switch from "Five" to "5") make their national TV debut on ABC-TV's "Hollywood Palace".
Dec [14] The group debuts on CBS-TV's "The Ed Sullivan Show".

1970

Jan [31] *I Want You Back*, written by Freddie Perren, Fonce Mizell and Deke Richards (collectively, with Gordy, under the name the Corporation), originally intended for Gladys Knight & the Pips (Gordy suggests it should be re-written with the new, young group in mind), with Michael on lead vocal, tops the US chart and becomes a million seller.
Feb Their debut album, ***Diana Ross Presents The Jackson 5***, a Berry Gordy PR exercise perpetuating the impression that it was Ross who discovered the brothers, hits US #5, as *I Want You Back* hits UK #2.

Apr [25] *ABC*, written by the same team in a similar style to *I Want You Back*, affirming the popularity of the group's R&B/pop sound, unlike anything else heard on Motown, tops the US chart, deposing the Beatles' *Let It Be*. The debut album, meanwhile, reaches UK #16.
May [2] The group makes its first headlining appearance, at the Convention Center, Philadelphia, PA.
June [27] The group becomes the first act to top the Hot 100 with its first three chart entries, as *The Love You Save*, a third million seller, hits #1. Meanwhile, *ABC* hits UK #8.
July They break attendance records at the Great Western Forum.
Aug *The Love You Save* hits UK #7. The brothers' second album, ***ABC***, hits US #4 and UK #22.
Sept [26] Motown announces that the Jackson 5 have sold a million discs in nine months.
Oct [9] The group embarks on five-city East Coast tour at the Boston Garden, Boston, MA.
[17] *Mama's Pearl*, written by the Corporation in a similar uptempo style to the three previous chart-toppers, intended as the fourth single, is passed over by Gordy in favor of a complete contrast, the ballad *I'll Be There*, written by Bob West and re-worked by Willie Hutch. It tops the US chart for the first of five weeks, and is Motown's biggest-selling single to date, shifting in excess of four million copies. ***Third Album***, which includes the single, hits US #4.
Nov Gordy cancels three dates in Texas which have been blacklisted by the Southern Christian Leadership Council's Operation Breadbasket because Dick Clark is promoting the tour. Gordy claims, "The Jackson 5 are bigger than any race issue."
Dec ***The Jackson 5 Christmas Album***, combining traditional and contemporary seasonal songs, is 1970's top-selling Christmas disc. (#1 on **Billboard**'s annual Christmas albums chart, it will re-chart during the festive seasons of the next three years.)

1971

Jan [23] *I'll Be There* hits UK #4 (and will be revived by Mariah Carey to UK and US chart success in 1992).
[31] The Jackson 5 play a benefit at Westside High School, Gary, for Mayor Hatcher's re-election campaign. Jackson Street is renamed Jackson 5 Boulevard for the day, as the group is given the keys to the city.
Feb [27] *Mama's Pearl*, now issued as *I'll Be There*'s follow-up, hits US #2, behind the Osmonds' *One Bad Apple*, a song rejected for the Jackson 5 by Gordy, who thought it juvenile. It becomes another million seller.
Apr [18] The group guests on Diana Ross TV special, "Diana!".
[24] *Mama's Pearl* reaches UK #25.
May [8] *Never Can Say Goodbye*, another slower-paced song written by Clifton Davis, is the brothers' sixth consecutive million seller, hitting US #2, behind Three Dog Night's *Joy To The World*, and making UK #33. Their third album, ***Maybe Tomorrow***, reaches US #11.
July [9-10] The group tapes its first TV special, "Goin' Back To Indiana", set to air September 19th.
[20] They embark on a US tour at the Coliseum, Charlotte, NC, with newly signed Motown act the Commodores as support, set to end at the International Convention Center, Honolulu, HI, on September 12th.
Aug [21] Title track, *Maybe Tomorrow*, written by Deke Richards for Sammy Davis Jr., reaches US #20.
Sept [11] Animated "Jackson 5" series premieres on ABC-TV.
Nov ***Goin' Back To Indiana***, the soundtrack of their TV special, reaches US #16, as Michael's parallel solo career begins in earnest with the US #4 smash ballad *Got To Be There*.
Dec Having earlier in the month played a concert for the Los Angeles Chapter of Junior Blind, the group collectively becomes Santa Claus at a party for 700 under-privileged children.

1972

Jan [22] *Sugar Daddy* hits US #10, while ***Jackson 5 Greatest Hits***, a compilation of the singles to date, reaches US #12. (Jackie suffers minor injuries in a car crash.)
May [27] Their revival of Thurston Harris' *Little Bitty Pretty One* (a close musical relative of Michael's solo US #13 revival of *Rockin' Robin*) reaches US #13.
Aug ***Lookin' Through The Windows*** hits US #7.
[26] The title track *Lookin' Through The Windows* reaches US #16.
Oct Compilation ***Jackson 5 Greatest Hits*** reaches UK #26.
[30] The group participates in the "Royal Variety Performance" in London.
Nov Following Michael's solo successes for Motown, the label releases Jermaine's first solo single, *That's How Love Goes*, which reaches US #46, with ***Jermaine*** peaking at US #27.
Dec *Corner Of The Sky*, from the Broadway musical "Pippin", reaches US #18. In the UK, ***Lookin' Through The Window*** reaches #16, as the extracted title track hits #9, their first UK hit single for almost 18 months. At the same time, the brothers' version of the seasonal *Santa Claus Is Coming To Town* is released in the UK, and makes #43.

1973

Mar The group's version of Jackson Browne's *Doctor My Eyes*, recorded as an album track, is released as a UK single after the writer's own US hit version has failed to score in the UK, and hits #9. In the US, Jermaine follows his hit debut with a revival of Shep & the Limelites' 1961 doo-wop ballad, *Daddy's Home*, taken from his debut album after strong radio play. It hits US #9 and earns him a solo gold disc.
Apr [17] Tito and John Jackson are arrested for buying a stolen television and stereo equipment. (Charges against Tito will be dismissed in February 1974, after John pleads guilty.)
May ***Skywriter*** makes US #44, while *Hallelujah Day*, taken from it, reaches US #28.
July The Jacksons are the first-ever major US black group to tour Australia. Meanwhile, *Hallelujah Day* reaches UK #20, and Jermaine's solo album, ***Come Into My Life***, makes US #152.
[20] The group embarks on a 28-date US tour at the Civic Arena, Pittsburgh, PA, set to end on September 2nd at the International Convention Center, Honolulu.
Sept Title track, *Skywriter*, unreleased in the US, reaches UK #25.
Oct *Get It Together*, the title track from the brothers' forthcoming album, reaches US #28.
Nov ***Get It Together*** climbs to US #100, while Jermaine's single, *You're In Good Hands*, peaks at US #79. (It will be his last solo success for three years.) Motown tries out another brother, Jackie, as a soloist, but his album, ***Jackie Jackson***, does not chart and the experiment is not repeated.
Dec [15] Jermaine marries Berry Gordy's daughter Hazel, at the Beverly Hills Hotel in Los Angeles. (This will have important ramifications when the group eventually decides to leave Motown.)

1974

Feb A ten-day tour of Senegal, Africa, is abbreviated to one week, when the brothers are unable to adjust to the food and water.
Apr [9] The group begins a season at the MGM Grand Hotel, Las Vegas, NV, co-headlining with impressionist Frank Gorshin. Janet (b. May 16, 1966, Gary) and LaToya (b. May 29, 1956, Gary) make their first stage appearances with their brothers.
May *Dancing Machine*, taken from ***Get It Together***, hits US #2, behind Ray Stevens' *The Streak*, and is the group's biggest-selling US single since *Never Can Say Goodbye*.
[13] 43 arrests are made at a concert by the group at Robert F. Kennedy Stadium, Washington, DC, after bottles are hurled by youths outside the venue, injuring over 50 people.
June [9] A UK tour is cancelled by Gordy, worried over security problems and the recent death of a fan at a David Cassidy concert in London, after Joe Jackson divulges details of the group's arrival time at Heathrow Airport to a national newspaper.
Nov ***Dancing Machine*** reaches US #16. Meanwhile, the group sings backing vocals on Stevie Wonder's *You Haven't Done Nothin'*, which tops the US chart.
Dec Taken from the album, *Whatever You Got, I Want* makes US #38.

1975

Jan Currently parallel teen stars, Michael Jackson and Donny Osmond co-present the first American Music Awards.
Mar Two-part single, *I Am Love* (7 minutes 56 seconds in total), reaches US #15.
June [30] A press conference is convened to announce the group's new recording deal with Epic Records, effective from March 10th, 1976, which signifies the end of their Motown deal. It is revealed that the group recorded 469 songs for the label, from which only 174 were released, and received only 2.7% royalties on Motown sales and were not allowed to write their own material. Gordy will file a $5-million lawsuit for breach of contract and, in turn, will be countersued because the group were liable to pay full costs of $500,000 on tracks not released. The Jacksons will refuse to record any more material for Motown and Gordy will receive $600,000 in the final, compromised, settlement. The group will also discover that Gordy had registered a patent on the name the Jackson 5 on March 30th, 1972, which will result in the group name-changing to the Jacksons for Epic releases. (Michael will also sign a solo deal with the label. Jermaine, married into the Gordy family, remains at Motown as a soloist and leaves the group, after a summer gig at the Westbury Music Fair, Westbury, NY). Younger brother Randy (b. Stephen Randall Jackson, Oct. 29, 1962, Gary) replaces him, and sisters LaToya and Rebbie (b. Maureen Jackson, May 29, 1950, Gary) join the line-up temporarily.
July [5] Atlanta Mayor Joseph Bradway refuses a permit for the group to perform with James Brown in the city, following the riots in Washington, in May of 1974.
Moving Violation, the group's last Motown recording, makes US #36, while *Forever Came Today*, reviving former Motown stablemates the Supremes' 1968 hit, makes US #60.

1976

June [16] "The Jacksons", a four-week summer variety show, premieres on CBS-TV. The shows feature the group, plus sisters LaToya, Rebbie and Janet, guest entertainers and a regular comedy-sketch team.
Aug Motown triple compilation album, ***Jackson Five Anthology*** (which also includes Michael's and Jermaine's solo hits on the label), reaches US #84.
Nov [6] Jermaine's solo album, ***My Name Is Jermaine***, on Motown, makes US #164.
Dec [11] The extracted *Let's Be Young Tonight* peaks at US #55.

1977

Jan Second CBS-TV series "The Jacksons" airs, but ends March 9th, when it hits the bottom of the ratings.
Feb [5] Their debut Epic album, ***The Jackons***, reaches US #36.
[19] The extracted *Enjoy Yourself*, the group's first Epic single as the Jacksons and their biggest seller since *Dancing Machine* three years earlier, hits US #6, earning a gold disc. Their debut Epic album, ***The Jacksons***, makes US #36.
Apr *Enjoy Yourself* peaks at UK #42.
May On tour in the UK for the first time in five years, the Jacksons participate in the celebrations for H.R.H. Queen Elizabeth II's Silver Jubilee, at the King's Theatre, Glasgow, Scotland.
[21] *Show You The Way To Go*, written by and recorded with producers Kenny Gamble and Leon Huff at Philadelphia International Records, reaches US #28.
June Boosted by the group's just-completed UK concert tour, *Show You The Way To Go* tops the UK chart for a week, their first and only UK #1 hit.
July [16] ***The Jacksons*** makes UK #54.

Sept *Dreamer*, taken from the album, makes UK #22, while Jermaine's solo album, ***Feel The Fire***, peaks at US #174.
Nov *Goin' Places*, the title track from the group's forthcoming album, makes US #52 and UK #26.
Dec [3] ***Goin' Places*** makes UK #45 and will peak at US #63.

1978

Feb *Even Though You've Gone* reaches UK #31.
Nov *Blame It On The Boogie* makes US #54 and hits UK #8, outselling a competing version on Atco by its writer, the unrelated Mick Jackson.

1979

Feb ***Destiny***, the first self-produced brothers album, reaches US #11 and is a million seller. The title track, *Destiny*, makes UK #39.
May *Shake Your Body (Down To The Ground)*, taken from ***Destiny***, hits US #7 and sells over two million copies in the US, earning a platinum disc. It also hits UK #4.
[19] ***Destiny*** reaches UK #33.

1980

The 1975 Motown suit is finally settled, with the Jacksons making a payment of $600,000 (Motown having claimed $20 million), and the label retaining all rights to the use of the name the Jackson 5.
Mar [4] Randy is seriously injured in a car crash, breaking both legs. He nearly dies in the emergency room, when a nurse inadvertently injects him with methadone.
July [12] Jermaine returns, after a three-year chart absence, with the Stevie Wonder-written and-produced *Let's Get Serious*, which hits US #9, also his first solo UK success, hitting #8. Simultaneously, ***Let's Get Serious*** hits US #6, earning a gold disc, having reached UK #22 (June [14]).
Aug *Burnin' Hot*, extracted from Jermaine's solo album, makes UK #32.
Sept *You're Supposed To Keep Your Love For Me*, also Wonder-penned, is Jermaine's solo follow-up and makes US #34.
Oct [18] The Jacksons' self-produced ***Triumph*** reaches UK #13.
Nov *Lovely One* makes US #12 and UK #29, taken from ***Triumph***, which hits US #10 and is their second consecutive platinum album.
Dec LaToya Jackson, the fifth oldest in the family (and the second daughter), signed as a solo artist to Polydor, reaches US #116 with her debut album, ***LaToya Jackson***.

1981

Jan The group's ballad, *Heartbreak Hotel*, also from ***Triumph***, reaches US #22 and UK #44. Meanwhile, Jermaine's solo album, ***Jermaine***, his second for Motown by this title, makes US #44.
Apr The group's *Can You Feel It* hits UK #6, but stalls at US #77.
May Jermaine's *You Like Me, Don't You?*, makes US #50 and UK #41.
July [9] Their 36-city "Triumph" tour, during which live recordings are made for ***Jacksons Live***, opens in Memphis. (The album will be released at the end of the year, and the tour will gross $5.5 million, $100,000 being donated to the Atlanta Children's Foundation after a gig at the Omni in Atlanta, GA.)
Aug *Walk Right Now* makes only US #73, but is their second consecutive UK Top 10 hit, at #7.
Sept LaToya's ***My Special Love*** peaks at US #175.
Nov Jermaine's ***I Like Your Style*** makes US #86, while the extracted *I'm Just Too Shy* peaks at US #60.

1982

Jan Double performance album, ***Jacksons Live***, makes US #30.
Sept Jermaine's *Let Me Tickle Your Fancy*, with backing vocals by Devo, reaches US #18, while ***Let Me Tickle Your Fancy*** (his last album for Motown) makes US #46.

1983

Mar [25] Michael and Jermaine reunite with the brothers to perform at the "25 Years Of Motown" anniversary spectacular at the Civic Center, Los Angeles. The show will air on NBC-TV on May 16th.
Aug [20] UK TV-advertised compilation album, ***18 Greatest Hits***, on the Telstar label, tops the UK chart for the first of three weeks.
Nov [30] A press conference called by boxing promoter Don King at the Tavern On The Green in New York, announces an 18-city, 40-date US tour by the Jacksons (six-strong, with Jermaine rejoining his brothers after leaving Motown), to commence the following summer.

1984

Feb Jermaine signs a solo deal with Arista Records.
[27] The Jacksons' Pepsi commercial premieres on US MTV.
May Following a promotional UK visit, during which Jermaine performs tracks from his forthcoming Arista debut to delegates at the World DJ Convention in London, his UK-only single release, *Sweetest, Sweetest*, makes #52.
June ***Jermaine Jackson***, his Arista debut, reaches US #19 (and UK #57, where it is retitled ***Dynamite***), while sister LaToya signs to the Private I label. Her only solo hit single is *Heart Don't Lie*, at US #56, as ***Heart Don't Lie*** climbs to US #149.
[13] *State Of Shock*, taken from the group's new album, and featuring Mick Jagger duetting on lead vocals with Michael, is released. Los Angeles radio station KIQQ plays it for 22 hours continuously.
July [5] At a press conference on the eve of the "Victory" tour, Michael refutes claims of greed (with regard to the exorbitant ticket prices), and announces that his entire earnings for the tour will go to charity.
[6] The 40-date "Victory" tour opens at Arrowhead Stadium, Kansas City, MO (and will gross $5.5 million). It marks the first time in eight years that all six Jackson brothers have performed together, live on stage. (Don King announces that "anybody who sees this show will be a better person for years to come." Presumably, the tour's main financial backer Chuck Sullivan did not see the show. The losses he takes on the tour will be directly responsible for his family losing control of the New England Patriots national football team and its home stadium in Foxborough, MA some years later.) Meanwhile, Motown capitalizes on the renewed interest and releases the compilation ***Michael Jackson & The Jackson 5 - 14 Greatest Hits*** (on a picture disc), which makes US #168.
Aug *State Of Shock* hits US #3, earning a gold disc, and reaches UK #14. It is taken from ***Victory***, which hits UK #3.
Sept *Torture*, also from the album, reaches US #17 and UK #26. ***Victory*** hits US #4, and earns the group's third platinum disc for an album. Meanwhile, Jermaine's first US single for Arista, *Dynamite*, reaches US #15, as Marlon launches a solo career.
Nov *Body*, a third single from the album, makes US #47.
Dec Michael has written and produced *Centipede*, the only hit single for older sister Rebbie, who is signed to CBS/Columbia, which now makes US #24, while ***Centipede*** makes US #63.
[9] The Jacksons play their last show of the decade together at Los Angeles' Dodger Stadium.

1985

Jan Jermaine's *Do What You Do*, reaches US #13.
[28] Michael, Jackie, Marlon, Randy, Tito and LaToya Jackson all participate in the recording of USA For Africa's *We Are The World*, in aid of African famine relief, which will be a worldwide #1 and a multi-million seller.
Mar Jermaine's duet with actress/singer Pia Zadora on *When The Rain Begins To Fall*, taken from the film "Voyage Of The Rock Aliens" makes US #54 and UK #68, while *Do What You Do* becomes Jermaine's biggest-selling UK single, hitting #6.
July Jermaine's *(Closest Thing To) Perfect*, from the Jamie Lee Curtis movie "Perfect", peaks at US #67. (By year's end, he will have produced three cuts for Whitney Houston's debut abum. The following year, his *I Think It's Love* peaks at US #16 (Apr [26]), *Do You Remember Me?* makes US #71 (July [19]), and ***Precious Moments*** reaches US #46.)

1987

Oct Marlon's debut album, ***Baby Tonight*** makes US #175. Rebbie teams with Cheap Trick's Robin Zander to release *You Send The Rain Away*, as the Jacksons' *Time Out For The Burglar*, from the movie "Burglar", is also issued. The following year, the Motown-reissued *I Want You Back* hits UK #8 in April.

1989

July The Jacksons' ***2300 Jackson Street*** (with Jackie, Jermaine, Tito and Randy) is the group's first album without Michael (although he sings briefly on the title track, which is sung by the entire clan, including Marlon, Janet, Rebbie, LaToya and 16 nieces and nephews). Produced by L.A. Reid & Babyface and Michael Omartian, its title referring to the street in Gary where the family lived, the album makes US #59 and UK #39 (July [1]). The extracted *Nothin' (That Compares 2 U)* peaks at US #77 and UK #33.
Sept [20] Los Angeles Superior Court Judge Francis Rothchild awards Alejandra Oaiza $3,000 a month child support, after Randy Jackson fails to show up for a case which seeks to prove him the father of the child Oaiza is due to give birth to in November.
Oct [21] Jermaine's *Don't Take It Personal* peaks at UK #69.

1990

Jan [6] *Don't Take It Personal* makes US #64 (having made UK #69 the previous October), as its parent album ***Don't Take It Personal*** makes US #115.

1991

Apr [24] Newspaper reports indicate that a Jacksons 48-acre entertainment center is to be built in Asbury Park, NJ.
Nov [20] Randy is sentenced to one month in jail for beating his wife, Eliza Shaffy Jackson, and their daughter, and placed on two years' probation. He will also be ordered to enroll in a Canoga Park hospital for domestic violence counselling.
[30] Allegedly written about brother Michael (and including biting lyrical observations about his brother's skin shading), Jermaine's *Word To The Badd!!* debuts at its US #78 peak.

1992

Jan Randy is committed to a psychiatric ward for 30 days.
Nov [15] The first part of a five-hour TV mini-series, "The Jacksons : An American Dream", produced by Jermaine, airs on ABC-TV. Chronicling the group's rise to fame, the cast includes: Angel Vargas (Tito), Jacen Wilkerson (Marlon), Terrence DaShon Howard (Jackie), Jermaine Jackson II (playing his father) and Jason Weaver as Michael, with Vanessa Williams playing Motown's Suzanne De Passe. Janet, LaToya and Rebbie are portrayed only as young girls. The series has total Jackson family-member approval, with the exception of LaToya. With a soundtrack album, ***The American Dream***, to be released by Polydor in December (US #137), the docu-drama begins with the courtship of Katherine and Joseph Jackson and ends with the Jacksons' 1984 "Victory" tour.

1993

Jan The group's parent company, Jacksons Communications, issues a statement, together with the Kenyan government, announcing plans to build a film-production facility in Nairobi, where they will make four films per year.
Aug [31] Jermaine and Tito walk out of an interview on NBC-TV's "Today" program, when NBC affiliate KNBC show up to interview them. They later hold a press conference, stating their support for their brother.

1994

Feb [19] Heavily-hyped "The Jackson Family Honors" NBC-TV special, postponed from December and set for broadcast on the 22nd, is staged at the MGM Grand Garden, Las Vegas, NV, with an all-star cast. (Many of the 12,000 audience demand their money back when Michael Jackson appears but does not perform.)
Mar [31] Producers Smith-Hemion Productions files suit in Los Angeles Superior Court against the Jacksons alleging they misrepresented their ability to attract a crowd and therefore breached their contract.
June [1] The Jackson Five's first ever recording, *Big Boy*, is released, as Motown issues the four-CD retrospective set ***Soulsation! 25th Anniversary Collection***.
Aug [21] The Jacksons, minus Randy, perform at a UK Scientology fund-raiser "For The Children Of The World" at Saint Hill Manor in East Grinstead, E. Sussex.

1996

Mar [2] Beginning the next generation of the family's musical history, and signed to brother Michael's MJJ Records, Tito's three sons (all called Tito) known as 3T reach US #15 with their debut single *Anything*, having already hit UK #2 on Feb [10].
see also: **Michael JACKSON**

THE JAM

Paul Weller (vocals, guitar);
Bruce Foxton (bass); **Rick Buckler** (drums)

1976

Oct [21] Weller (b. John Weller, May 25, 1958, Woking, Surrey) has met Buckler (b. Paul Richard Buckler, Dec. 6, 1955, Woking) at Sheerwater Secondary Modern school in Woking, where they began jamming together, in 1975, during lunch hours in the music room. Using the session as their group-name inspiration, they have linked with Foxton (b. Sept. 1, 1955, Woking) and Steve Brookes to initially peform '60s R&B/rock covers at local social and working-men's clubs. Brookes soon leaves, with Foxton moving to bass and Weller established on lead guitar and vocals. Concentrating on live work in London, the Jam has played gigs at the Marquee and 100 Club, and regular jaunts at the Red Cow pub, where the group has auditioned for and been dismissed by EMI Records. After an impromptu gig in a Soho market sponsored by Rock On Records on a Saturday morning, the band now opens for the Sex Pistols at the Queensway Hall, Dunstable, Beds.

1977

Feb [25] Following a month's Red Cow residency in Hammersmith and a frenzied gig at the Marquee, the Jam, managed by Weller's father, John, who is currently making his business calls from a building site in Ash Vale, where he is working, signs to Polydor Records for the £6,000 advance offered by A&R man Chris Parry. A four-year deal, it will be re-negotiated after 90 days. The UK music press links the band with the burgeoning punk movement, but the Jam establishes its own niche and a later spotlight in a UK mod revival. They currently sport mohair suits and use Rickenbacker guitars.
May [1] The Jam, following further showcase gigs at London's Hope & Anchor and Nashville Room venues, embarks on the Clash's "White Riot" UK tour at London's Roxy, but pulls out after a show at the Rainbow Theatre, London, on the 29th, following an argument with the headlining punksters.
June [4] Their debut single, *In The City*, produced by Parry, makes UK #40.
[11] Having taken 11 days to record, and with all songs penned by the group's leader, 19-year-old Weller, ***In The City*** reaches UK #20. The Jam begins a 42-date UK headlining debut tour, including a sellout date at London's Hammersmith Odeon. Their mode of transport is a red Ford Cortina. (They only complete 38 of the gigs, due to exhaustion.)
[12] The group is forced to cancel a gig at London's Stamford Bridge by the GLC. Police who are called in to control the disappointed crowd.
Aug [20] Aided by their first appearance on BBC1-TV's "Top Of The Pops", *All Around The World* reaches UK #13.
Nov [19] *The Modern World* makes UK #36. The group visits the US for a 16-date club tour, which is less than well received, before embarking on 23-date UK tour.
Dec [3] Its parent album, ***This Is The Modern World***, despite lukewarm reviews by the UK music press, reaches UK #22. A major UK tour starts, highlighted by a brawl between the band and rugby players at a hotel in Leeds, W. Yorks. Leeds Crown Court subsequently acquits Weller, who moves to London with his first love, Gill.

1978

Mar [25] While the band supports Blue Öyster Cult on an ill-billed US tour, *News Of The World* makes UK #27.
June [18] The group closes out a short UK tour at London's Lyceum Ballroom.
Aug [25] The Jam headlines the first day of the "Reading Festival", Reading, Berks., as the "small-venue" punk ideal fades.
Sept [23] *David Watts*, the band's cover of a Kinks track, backed with *"A" Bomb In Wardour Street*, peaks at UK #25.
Nov [4] Anti-racist-themed *Down In The Tube Station At Midnight* climbs to UK #15.
[18] ***All Mod Cons***, produced by Vic Coppersmith-Heaven and featuring 11 Weller compositions, hits UK #6, once again showcasing the group's rapid-fire, post-punk angst, driven by Weller's distinctive guitar chops and vocal style.
[29] 20-date "Apocalypse" UK tour ends, headlining the first day of the "Great British Music Festival" at the Wembley Arena, Wembley, Middx.

1979

Apr [14] *Strange Town* peaks at UK #15. The Jam begins its first world tour, visiting the US, Canada and Europe.
May [4] The 15-date "The Jam 'Em In" UK leg begins.
Sept [8] *When You're Young* makes UK #17.
Nov [18-19] The group embarks on a 21-date UK tour at the Apollo Theatre, Manchester, Gtr. Manchester, set to end with three nights at London's Rainbow Theatre.
[24] With the Jam firmly established as a "quick" singles band, *The Eton Rifles* shoots to UK #3, as its parent album, ***Setting Sons***, hits UK #4.

1980

Mar Their first US chart appearance, ***Setting Sons***, peaks at US #137 (although major US success will always elude this quintessentially British band).
[22] *Going Underground/The Dreams Of Children* becomes the first UK single of the '80s to debut at #1, where it will stay for three weeks. The band is in Los Angeles, CA, when the news breaks.
Apr [26] Polydor Records reissues the group's early singles, which all re-chart - *In The City* (#40), *All Around The World* (#43), *This Is The Modern World* (#52), *News Of The World* (#53), *David Watts* (#54) and *Strange Town* (#44).
May [26] The Jam participates in the "Pink Pop Festival" at Galeen, Holland.
June [2] The group performs at the "Loch Lomond Festival" in Scotland.
Aug [9] Following a tour of Japan, they take part in the "Turku Rock Festival", Turku, Finland.
Sept [6] *Start* tops the UK chart in its third week of release.
Oct The band begins a major UK and European tour ending in sellout dates at its favored venue, London's Rainbow Theatre.
Dec [6] ***Sound Affects*** hits UK #2. (Weller is currently using his royalties to set up a publishing company, Riot Stories, for political works.)

1981

Jan UK magazine **Melody Maker** arranges for Weller to meet his former hero, the Who's Pete Townshend. During the interview, both artists confirm that they do not like the other's band.
Feb [28] Acoustic guitar-driven *That's Entertainment*, available only as a German import, reaches UK #21. ***Sound Affects*** reaches US #72, as the Jam sets off on another world tour taking in Japan.
Apr [27] The group takes part in an "Unemployment Benefit Concert" at Liverpool's Royal Court Theatre.
June [6] *Funeral Pyre* hits UK #4.
[20] The band embarks on the 11-date "Fun Tour", including dates in selected UK coastal resorts.
Aug Weller makes a program on class awareness for the BBC-TV series "Something Else".
Oct [31] *Absolute Beginners* hits UK #4, as Weller finances two new enterprises: **Jamming** magazine, to be run by Jam devotée Tony Fletcher, and his own Respond record label.
Dec The Jam sweeps the annual **New Musical Express** Readers' Poll, as it plays four standing-room-only Christmas dates in London.

1982

Jan ***The Jam***, a mini-collection of five UK hits, peaks at US #176. During new recording sessions, Weller has a breakdown and decides to quit drinking.
Feb [13] *Town Called Malice/Precious*, released as a 12" single, hits UK #1. The Jam becomes the first band since the Beatles to play two numbers on the same edition of BBC1-TV's "Top Of The Pops", when it performs both sides.
Mar [20] ***The Gift***, revealing a new soul slant, tops the UK chart and reaches US #82. As the group sets off on another tour, called "Trans Global Unity Express" (the four-month trek takes in the UK, Europe, Canada, the US and Japan), an early gig at Bingley Hall, Stafford, Staffs. is filmed for video release.
July [10] Import single, *Just Who Is The Five O'Clock Hero*, hits UK #8. Weller takes two weeks' vacation in Italy with Gill. Disillusioned with the Jam formula and keen to seek new soul direction, he decides to disband the group.
Sept [25] With the public still unaware of Weller's intentions, and the group recently committed to the CND anti-nuclear cause, the Jam's *The Bitterest Pill (I Ever Had To Swallow)*, featuring Belle Star Jenny McKeowen duetting with Weller, hits UK #2.
Oct [28] The Jam announces its split, but will honor a last UK tour.
Nov [5] The group appears on the premiere edition of C4-TV's "The Tube".
[25] Their final UK tour begins at the Apollo Theatre, Glasgow, Scotland, set to end on December 11th at the Brighton Conference Centre, Brighton, E. Sussex, including six sellout performances at the Wembley Arena.
Dec [4] *Beat Surrender* enters at UK #1. Not played by US radio, it fails, like every Jam single release before it, to make the Hot 100.
[18] ***Dig The New Breed***, a 14-track live compilation from 1977 to 1982, hits UK #2, behind ***The John Lennon Collection***, while a UK-hits compilation album, released in only in North America, ***The Bitterest Pill (I Ever Had To Swallow)***, reaches US #135.

1983

Jan While Weller folds **Jamming** magazine, Polydor re-issues all of the Jam's 16 singles, which establishes the precedent of re-charting simultaneously in the UK.
[29] *That's Entertainment*, officially released for the first time in the UK, peaks at #60.
Feb ***Dig The New Breed*** peaks at US #131.
Apr US-only EP, ***Beat Surrender***, reaches US #171.
July [30] *Freak*, Foxton's solo debut on Arista, reaches UK #23.

Aug [27] Reissued ***In The City*** makes UK #100.
Sept The Jam's 29-track double hits compilation, ***Snap!***, initially released with a four-track, limited-edition live EP, hits UK #2. A similar video collection tops the UK music video survey.
Oct While Weller has formed the Style Council with ex-Merton Parka Mick Talbot, his Respond label signs the Questions and Tracie. Buckler joins new group Time UK and Foxton (who has teamed up with keyboardist/producer Stan Shaw) releases his debut solo album, ***Touch Sensitive***, on Arista (which yields the simultaneously released *This Is The Way* (UK #56) and *It Makes Me Wonder* (UK # 74, April, 1984), with Pete Glenister (guitar), Anthony Thistlethwaite (saxophone) and Roddy Lorimer (trumpet). (Weller, always politically active, will also join the Labour Party-promoting "Red Wedge Tour" in time for the next UK General Election.)

1991

June [29] While Foxton has played for the Rhythm Sisters, before joining Jake Burns in a re-formed Stiff Little Fingers, Strange Fruit Records has released the *Jam EP* from an April 1977, BBC Radio 1 "John Peel" show session in 1990. The reissued *That's Entertainment*, from the forthcoming ***Greatest Hits***, now re-charts, at UK #57.
July [13] ***Greatest Hits***, a 19-track compilation containing all 18 UK chart hits, debuts at its UK #2 peak, behind Cher's ***Love Hurts***.

1993

Jan After the double album, ***Extras***, a 26-track collection compiled by Weller and ex-Jam A&R cohort Dennis Munday featuring B-sides, cover versions, original demos and unreleased material, has reached UK #15 on Apr [18] the previous year, Buckler and Foxton now file suit against Weller over the contents of the Jam's joint bank account, claiming they are owed as much as £200,000 in merchandising and royalties accrued since the band's break-up. On Nov [6] the performance album ***Live Jam*** will debut at its UK #28 peak.
see also: **THE STYLE COUNCIL, PAUL WELLER**

RICK JAMES

1965

Nephew of the Tempations' singer Melvin Franklin, James (b. James Johnson, Feb. 1, 1948, Buffalo, NY), having gone AWOL from the US Navy, settles in Toronto, ON, Canada, and forms a rock/soul band, the Mynah Birds, with his room-mate, local singer Neil Young and Goldie McJohn and Bruce Palmer. The group records one album, before relocating to Detroit, MI, where it signs to Motown Records and where James completes production work for Bobby Taylor, the Spinners and the Marvelettes. (The Mynah Birds fail to release any of their own product, not least due to James' arrest for draft evasion, and eventually splits, with Young and Palmer joining Buffalo Springfield in March 1966.) Moving to London in 1970, James forms the blues outfit, the Main Line, commuting for the next seven years between London and North America.

1977

James returns to the US, where he assembles a backing combo, the Stone City Band (Kenny Hawkins, Nat Hughes, Daniel LeMelle, Jerry Livingston, Jerry Rainer and Levi Ruffin Jr.). Inspired by George Clinton and Sly Stone, he develops a rock /funk style he dubs "funk'n'roll". Impressed by his demo tapes, Motown signs him to a worldwide deal with its publishing division, Jobete, picking up his songwriting contract.

1978

July *You And I* reaches UK #46, while his Motown debut album, ***Come Get It!***, co-produced with Art Stewart, begins a climb to US #13.
Sept *You And I* reaches US #13, and is awarded a gold disc.
Oct *Mary Jane*, a barely-disguised hymn to marijuana, hits US R&B #3, but initially fails to cross over. His sophomore album, ***Bustin' Out Of L Seven***, is released. James, with the Stone City Band and vocal trio the Mary Jane Girls (Candice Ghant, Joanne McDuffie, Yvette Marina and Kim Wuletich) in tow, embarks on his first US tour. His wildly extrovert show attracts wide media attention and enthusiastic audiences.
Nov He is out of action for several months with hepatitis. Official sources give "exhaustion" as the cause of the illness, though rumors of his drug abuse persist.

1979

Jan *Mary Jane* finally makes US #41.
Mar ***Bustin' Out Of L Seven*** reaches US #16, yielding *High On Your Love Suite* (US #72 in April) and *Bustin' Out* (US #71 in May).
July James has produced new Motown artist Teena Marie's debut album, ***Wild And Peaceful*** and its single, *I'm A Sucker For Your Love* (with James featured as co-vocalist), which makes US #43. (James and Marie will continue to contribute to each other's recordings.)
Dec His third album, ***Fire It Up***, reaches US #34.

1980

Apr James-produced debut album by the Stone City Band, ***In'n'Out***, reaches US #122.
Sept James' *Big Time* peaks at UK #41, while his fourth album, ***Garden Of Love***, is released. An uncharacteristic ballad set, it reaches US #83.

1981

Apr James-produced second Stone City Band album, ***The Boys Are Back***, is released.
June His fifth album, ***Street Songs***, is released. An extrovert return to funk'n'roll, it hits US #3 and achieves double-platinum status. (It will stay in the Top 100 Album chart for 54 weeks, hit US R&B #1 for 20 weeks and be nominated for a Grammy Award.)
June [13] *Give It To Me Baby*, taken from ***Street Songs***, tops the US R&B chart for the first of five weeks, and makes US #40 and UK #47.
Sept *Super Freak (Pt 1)*, also from the album, reaches US #16. James embarks on a successful US tour with Teena Marie, Cameo and the Sugarhill Gang.
Dec James tops **Billboard**'s Year End In Music Black Top Artists and Black Top Albums (***Street Songs***) categories.

1982

Jan [25] He wins the Favorite Album, Soul/R&B category at the ninth annual American Music Awards, held at the Shrine Auditorium, Los Angeles, CA.
June The Temptations' *Standing On The Top*, featuring James, climbs to US #53.
July *Dance Wit' Me* reaches US #64 and UK #53.
[31] ***Throwin' Down*** peaks at UK #93 and will reach US #13.
Nov [25-27] James joins Aretha Franklin, Gladys Knight, the Clash and others, performing to 45,000 at the "Jamaica World Music Festival" staged near Montego Bay, Jamaica.
Dec James visits the UK for promotion-only work.

1983

May James-produced Mary Jane Girls album, ***Mary Jane Girls***, is released, set to peak at US #56.
Aug *Cold Blooded*, on Motown, hits US R&B #1 but, like all James singles, it is cold-shouldered by MTV and stalls at US #40.
Sept James-produced Stone City Band album, ***Out From The Shadow***, is released.
Oct Written, arranged and produced by James, and featuring Grandmaster Flash, ***Cold Blooded*** reaches US #16.

1984

Jan *Ebony Eyes*, a soul duet with Smokey Robinson, makes US #43.
Aug *17* reaches US #36.
Oct ***Reflections***, a 10-track retrospective compilation with three new recordings added (and dedicated to Marvin Gaye), peaks at US #41.

1985

Apr *Can't Stop* halts at US #50.
June [8] James penned-and-produced *In My House*, for the Mary Jane Girls, hits US #7 (taken from the James-helmed US #18 MJG album, ***Only Four You***).
Sept James' contract with Motown ends in acrimony and he retreats to work in his Le Joint recording studios at home in Buffalo.
Dec His first project since the split with Motown has been writing, arranging and producing US comedian Eddie Murphy's debut album: ***Party All The Time*** hits US #2, while the extracted *How Could It Be* will reach US #26. ***The Flag***, released on Motown's Gordy offshoot the following July, his last recording for the label, will make US #95.

1988

Aug [20] Newly signed to Reprise Records, his first label release, *Loosey's Rap*, featuring rapper Roxanne Shanté, tops the US R&B chart, but fails to cross over, as the parent album, ***Wonderful***, featuring his trademark sexual overtones, peaks at US #148. *This Magic Moment/Dance With Me*, his medley of Drifters hits from the Richard Perry-produced ***Rock, Rhythm & Blues*** various-artists project, will be released the following May.

1990

June [16] M.C. Hammer's *U Can't Touch This*, using *Super Freak* as its rhythm bed, hits US #8. James will successfully negotiate appropriate royalties from the Hammer camp, as the song's central riff becomes a Hammer trademark. (Jay Warner of National League Music, James' publisher, claims that he is the most sampled writer of 1990.)

1991

Aug [2] James and his 21-year-old girlfriend, Tanya Hijazi, are arrested at his Hollywood Hills, Hollywood, CA estate at 7:30 p.m., and charged with assault with a deadly weapon, aggravated mayhem, torture, false imprisonment and forcible oral copulation at the house in July. James is released on $1 million bail.
Sept [21] In the midst of James' arraignment following his arrest, his mother dies of stomach cancer in their hometown, Buffalo.

1992

May James and Hijazi become parents to a son, Tazman.
Dec [14] James and Hijazi surrender to police in Los Angeles to face charges that they assaulted another woman, Mary Sauger, on November 2nd. (Hijazi will plead guilty and will be sentenced to a four-year prison term in August 1993, while one day during James' trial, he will fall asleep and begin snoring in court.)

1994

Jan [20] A plea agreement is finalized which will see James released from jail in September if he successfully completes a live-in drug rehabilitation program in Norco, CA.
July [18] A judge rejects James' appeal to re-enter drug rehab and orders him to begin serving a four month jail term.
[19] After months of legal debate, James is finally sentenced to five years and four months for cocaine use and assaulting two women.
Dec [13] Los Angeles Superior Court Jury awards $225,000 in punitive damages to Sauger, who had been beaten and held hostage by James and Hijazi in a Hollywood hotel room.

1995

Dec Still incarcerated at Folsom Prison, CA, James is nevertheless now able to communicate with his fans via his own online web-site at "http://www. weblive. com/stars/rickjames".

TOMMY JAMES & THE SHONDELLS

Tommy James (vocals); **Eddie Gray** (guitar); **Mike Vale** (bass); **Peter Lucia** (drums); **Ronnie Rosman** (organ)

1963

Having formed his first group at school in Niles, MI, at age 12, James (b. Thomas Gregory Jackson, Apr. 29, 1947, Dayton, OH), backed by Larry Coverdale (guitar), Craig Villeneuve (keyboards), Larry Wright (bass) and Jim Payne (drums), has cut *Long Pony Tail* for a local label in 1962, while he is working for Spin-It Records. Some months after the disc first appears, WNIL DJ Jack Douglas hears it, contacts the singer and asks if he has any other material. James has heard *Hanky Panky* performed in a nightclub in South Bend, IN. (It is the B-side of a single by the Raindrops, who are actually its writers, Jeff Barry and Ellie Greenwich.) When he records the song for Douglas' Snap label, with producer Bob Mack, James ad-libs most of the lyrics. It sells well in Michigan, Illinois and Indiana.

1965

Dec Out of work following his high-school graduation, James receives a phone call from a DJ in Pittsburgh, PA, who has been playing the two-year-old *Hanky Panky*. James flies there for local TV and radio promotion. He forms a new Shondells, after the original group refuses to move from Indiana, by hiring local band, the Raconteurs. The line-up is Rosman (b. Feb. 28, 1945), Vale (b. Michael Vacush, July 17, 1949), Vince Pietropaoli (drums), and George Magura (sax). The latter two soon leave, to be replaced by Gray (b. Feb. 27, 1948) and Lucia (b. Feb. 2, 1947).

1966

July [16] Picked up for national release by Roulette Records in New York, although a Pittsburgh distributor bootlegs 80,000 copies of the original, releasing it on his own Red Fox label, *Hanky Panky* hits US #1, will sell a million copies, and also make UK #38.

Sept With the group having signed direct to Roulette, ***Hanky Panky*** reaches US #46. The R&B-styled *Say I Am (What I Am)*, originally recorded by Jimmy Gilmer & the Fireballs as *What I Am*, reaches US #21. The label teams the group with songwriters/producers Bo Gentry and Richie Cordell, in a partnership which will produce a melodic, exhilarating and commercial style.

Dec *It's Only Love* makes US #31.

1967

Apr *I Think We're Alone Now*, a distinctive bubbling arrangement, hits US #4, the first of five James & the Shondells smashes during the year: *Mirage* (US #10 in June, when ***I Think We're Alone Now*** makes US #74), *I Like The Way* (US #25, July), *Gettin' Together* (US #18, September - originally written with Gene Pitney in mind) and *Out Of The Blue* (US #43, November).

1968

Feb *Get Out Now* makes US #48, marking the end of the group's lightweight-pop period.

Mar Compilation album, ***Something Special! The Best Of Tommy James And The Shondells***, reaches US #174.

June *Mony Mony*, written by Gentry and Cordell with Bobby Bloom (later of *Montego Bay* fame) and James himself, with the group's sound hardened into a rock-solid dance beat, hits US #3. (The writers get the title of the song from a Mutual Of New York sign outside James' apartment in New York. As James later says, "If I'd been looking in the other direction, it would've been called Hotel Taft.")

July [31] A lack of UK chart success ends, as *Mony Mony* hits #1 for the first of two weeks, becoming the country's most popular dancefloor disc of the summer. (It will return to pole position for an additional week on Aug [21].) ***Mony Mony*** makes US #193.

Aug US follow-up, *Somebody Cares*, peaks at #53. After completing a couple of rallies for Bobby Kennedy, the group will perform at several campaign stops for Democratic presidential nominee Hubert Humphrey in his fight against Republican nominee Richard Nixon, until election day.

Nov *Mony Mony*-like *Do Something To Me* makes US #38. Issued as the UK follow-up, it fails to chart. The group, with a growing sense of its own direction, persuades Roulette to allow the next album to be self-produced.

1969

Feb [1] *Crimson and Clover*, a shortened version of the five-minute album-title track, launches the new self-helmed Shondells sound: a complex weave of vocal and instrumental sounds with an ethereal, layered melody, hints of psychedelia and a solid commercial hook. It now tops the US chart and will earn a gold disc, becoming the group's biggest US seller.

May *Sweet Cherry Wine*, a similar production with innovative tempo and rhythm changes, hits US #7. ***Crimson And Clover***, with sleeve notes written by presidential candidate Hubert Humphrey, hits US #8.

July [26] *Crystal Blue Persuasion*, a laid-back summer sound which is James' favorite of his own recordings, hits US #2, behind Zager & Evans' *In The Year 2525*, and is another million-seller.

Aug The group turns down the opportunity to play at the "Woodstock Music & Art Fair" in Bethel, NY because of commitments in Hawaii.

Nov *Ball Of Fire*, for which James teams with new writer and producer partner Bob King, makes US #19, as ***Cellophane Symphony*** peaks at US #141.

1970

Jan *She* reaches US #23.

Feb Compilation album, ***The Best Of Tommy James And The Shondells***, climbs to US #21.

Mar *Gotta Get Back To You*, a shift back to an R&B style, makes US #45.

May *Travelin'* rests at US #91.

June *Come To Me* makes US #47. James collapses on stage in Alabama. The Shondells quit to become Hog Heaven, while James recuperates on his farm in upstate New York. (He will subsequently claim his collapse was blown out of proportion and is not the reason he retired.)

Aug James produces the US #7 hit, *Tighter And Tighter*, for Brooklyn group Alive & Kicking a song he intended to cut as his first solo outing, but did not complete due to remaining nervousness about his vocal performance. His own version will appear on the 1976 album, ***In Touch***.

Sept Encouraged by the group's success, James records the solo *Ball And Chain*, which peaks at US #57.

1971

Jan *Church Street Soul Revival*, originally written and produced for the Exiles in 1969, makes US #62 followed by the US #93 peaking *Adrienne* in May and James' biggest solo success, *Draggin' The Line*, which hits US #4 in August becoming another million seller.

Sept ***Christian Of The World*** reaches US #131, yielding the US #40 *I'm Comin' Home*, in October and the US #41, *Nothing To Hide*, in December.

1972

Feb *Tell 'Em Willie Boy's A'Comin'* peaks at US #89. (*Cat's Eye In The Window* climbs to US #90 in June, *Love Song* makes US #67 in September and *Celebration* reaches US #95 in November).

1973

Mar *Boo, Boo, Don't 'Cha Be Blue* makes US #70, as James turns to the club circuit after 18 months of minor US chart placings.

May [12] James plays two gigs in New Jersey backed by a Shondells, comprising Vale and Lucia. In 1976 James will release ***In Touch***, featuring his versions of *Devil Gate Drive*, Gary Glitter's *Do You Wanna Touch*, *I Love You Love Me Love* and *Tighter And Tighter*. Signing to Fantasy Records the following year, he also issues the Jeff Barry-produced album, ***Midnight Rider***.

1980

Mar James, now signed to Millennium Records, makes US #19 with *Three Times In Love*, after a seven-year chart absence.

Apr ***Three Times In Love***, with guests Luther Vandross, Michael Brecker, and former-Critter Don Ciccone, peaks at US #134. *You're So Easy To Love* will make US #58 the following May.

1987

Nov [21] Joan Jett's version of *Crimson And Clover* has hit US #7 in May 1982, beginning an era in which a number of James hits will be successfully resurrected by several acts: Billy Idol's cover of *Mony Mony* now knocks Tiffany's version of *I Think We're Alone Now* off the top of the US chart. (Tiffany will hit UK #1, while Idol will hit UK #7 with their respective treatments of the James songs.)

1991

Aug [10] Having released ***Hi-Fi*** in July 1989 on Aegis Records, and still performing on the nostalgia circuit, James joins fellow '60s stars the Turtles, Johnny Rivers, Lou Christie and the Marvelettes for the "The Ultimate Summer Concert" at the Pacific Amphitheatre, Costa Mesa, CA. (The group's career overview has been released as ***Anthology*** on Rhino in 1989.)

JAMES

Tim Booth (vocals); **Jim Glennie** (guitar); **Dave Baynton-Power** (drums)

1983

Oct Initially comprising Booth (b. Feb. 4, 1960), who, having studied drama at Manchester University, has joined as a dancer, but soon replaced original vocalist Danny Ryan, Glennie (b. Oct. 10, 1963), James Gott (guitar) and Gavin Whelan (drums), the Manchester-based James, earning £34 per week as part of the British government's Enterprise Scheme, is signed to local independent label Factory, which releases the group's debut single, *Jimone* (pronounced "Jim 1"), which will be followed by *Folklore* and *Hymn For A Village*. Invited to appear on the front cover of the January 1985 issue of the **New Musical Express** as the year's brightest prospect, they decline, but, championed by Morrissey, go on to accept a support slot on a forthcoming Smiths UK tour. Signed to a three-year deal with Sire Records, the group's debut album, ***Stutter***, produced by Lenny Kaye, will be released in August 1986.

1988

Oct [8] Their much-delayed sophomore effort, ***Strip Mine***, charts for a week at UK #90.

The group is featured on the UK TV show "Out Of Order", which investigates its problems with the Sire label, which have accounted for the lengthy delay. Subsequently parting ways with Sire, James will release the live album ***One Man Clapping***, recorded in Bath, Avon, on its own One Man label through Rough Trade in March the following year, a set which includes the future hits *Sit Down* (June) and *Come Home* (November).

1990

May [19] With Baynton-Power (b. Jan. 29, 1961) having replaced Whelan, and bolstered by the arrival of Saul Davies (b. June 28, 1965) (guitar/violin), Andy Diagram (trumpet) and keyboardist Mark Hunter (b. Nov. 5, 1968), the enlarged James, now

signed to Polygram imprint Fontana Records, reaches UK #32 with *How Was It For You*.
June [16] Their debut label album, the band-written ***Gold Mother***, hits UK #2 during an initial 29-week chart run.
July [7] The extracted and re-recorded, *Come Home* reaches UK #32.
Nov [24] The group takes part in the "Rocknight Festival" in Düsseldorf, Germany.
[29] James joins Billy Bragg and others to play at London's Brixton Academy to benefit the Terrence Higgins Trust.
Dec [7-8] They play two dates at Manchester's G-Mex at the end of a UK tour.
[8] *Lose Control* reaches UK #38.

1991

Jan [18] The group participates in the "Great British Music Weekend" at Wembley Arena, Wembley, Middx.
[30] They play a five-song set on the roof of Manchester's Piccadilly radio station, 22 years to the day that the Beatles played atop their Savile Row offices.
Mar [30] The band guests on BBC1-TV's "Going Live!", and will appear on the station's "Eggs 'N' Baker" the following day.
Apr [6] *Sit Down* hits UK #2, behind Chesney Hawkes' *The One And Only*.
May [4] Re-promoted ***Gold Mother***, with a slightly altered track listing, debuts at its UK peak, #2, behind Eurythmics' ***Greatest Hits***.
June [14] The group appears on C4-TV's "Friday At The Dome".
[28] They receive the first Levi's Original Talent Award at the annual Nordoff-Robbins Music Therapy lunch at London's Dorchester Hotel.
Aug [2] The group takes part in the "Feile Festival" at Semple Stadium, Tipperary, Eire, with Elvis Costello, De La Soul, Transvision Vamp and others.
[24] They perform at the annual "Reading Festival", Reading, Berks.
Sept [23] BBC2-TV airs "James In Concert".
[30] 31-date UK tour opens at the Sands Centre, Carlisle, Cumbria, set to end on November 12th at Liverpool's Royal Court.
Oct Leonard Cohen-tribute album, ***I'm Your Fan***, featuring James' version of *So Long Marianne*, is released.
Nov [22] The group appears on C4-TV's "The Word".
Dec [7] *Sound*, previewing the new album, hits UK #9.

1992

Jan [29] The group is featured on BBC2-TV's "Rapido".
Feb [8] *Born Of Frustration* reaches UK #13, as James makes a low-key appearance at Manchester Polytechnic (as a dress rehearsal for an upcoming North American tour).
[15] The group performs at a KITS radio station-sponsored Union Square gig in San Francisco, CA.
[29] Co-produced by the band with Youth and Steve Chase, ***Seven*** enters at its UK #2 peak, behind Simply Red's ***Stars***, confirming James as a leading guitar-based, alternative UK act.
Mar [24] The group plays to a sellout crowd at the Roxy, Los Angeles, CA, during its current North American trek.
Apr [4] *Ring The Bells* bows at its UK #37 peak.
June [26] The group appears at the "Glastonbury Festival", Worthy Farm, Pilton, Somerset, replacing Morrissey, who has pulled out to play at a Madness gig at London's Finsbury Park.
July [4] James headlines a concert at Alton Towers Leisure Park, Alton, Staffs., broadcast live by Radio 1 as part of its 25th anniversary, and featuring support act, Public Image Ltd.
[12] During the group's appearance at "Le Festival Les Heros Sont Immortels", Calais, France, a member of their road crew is set upon in the local 555 club, suffering a fractured skull. Other crew members are also injured.
[18] EP *Seven* debuts at its UK #46 peak.
Sept [25] The band begins its second Stateside tour, sharing a bill with the Tom Tom Club and the Soup Dragons, at the Pacific Amphitheatre, Costa Mesa, CA. (Group member Larry Gott (b. July 24, 1957) is mugged outside a Los Angeles hotel on the first day of their visit. He flies home, leaving the group's tour manager to fill in for him.)
Nov [28] The tour ends at the Roxy Showcase Club, Washington, DC.
Dec [13] The group begins a series of five one-hour acoustic shows, at Glasgow's Royal Concert Hall, set to end on the 17th at Manchester's Free Trade Hall.

1993

Feb [15] James is featured on ITV's "The Beat".
Mar [21] The band plays a secret gig for 175 fans at Bath Moles club, to showcase the forthcoming album, provisionally titled ***Carousel***, produced by Brian Eno at Peter Gabriel's Real World Studios in Box, Wilts.
Sept [4] They embark on the nine-date US "WOMAD" festival, set to end on the 19th.
[11] *Sometimes* debuts at its UK #18 peak.
Oct [9] Helmed by magic-touch producer Brian Eno, ***Laid*** bows at its UK #3 peak.
[29] James guest on NBC-TV's "The Tonight Show".
Nov [20] Title cut *Laid* reaches UK #25.

1994

Jan [11-13] The group plays three dates at New York, NY's Radio City Music Hall, during a North American tour supporting Duran Duran.
Feb [15] The band guests on CBS-TV's "Late Show With David Letterman".
Mar [12] ***Laid*** makes US #72.
Apr [2] *Jam J*, coupled with the melodic *Say Something*, debuts at its UK #24 peak.
[9] *Laid* peaks at US #61.
May [22] During its latest North American tour, James plays a sellout date at the Riviera Theatre, Chicago, IL.
June [11] Following an appearance at Live 105 BFD's Shoreline Amphitheatre show the day before, James now takes part in "KROQ's Weenie Roast" at the Irvine Meadows Amphitheatre, Irvine, CA.
Aug [13] The group takes part in "Woodstock '94" at Winston Farm, Saugerties, NY.
Sept [24] ***Wah Wah***, a further collaboration with Eno recorded as an alternative companion during the original ***Laid*** sessions, reaches UK #11 in its week of entry.
Nov [19] **Music Week** reports that Booth is slated to collaborate on a solo project with Angelo Badalamenti.

JAN & DEAN

Jan Berry (vocals); **Dean Torrence** (vocals)

1957

Berry (b. Apr. 3, 1941, Los Angeles, CA) and Torrence (b. Mar. 10, 1940, Los Angeles) meet while members of Los Angeles' Emerson Junior High School football team where, discovering that the showers are a great place to sing, they form a vocal group, named the Barons, with four friends. When this moves outside school, neighbors Bruce Johnston and Sandy Nelson join on piano and drums. The group splits the following year, leaving only Berry, Torrence and Arnie Ginsburg. Ginsburg becomes infatuated with a stripper at the nearby Follies Burlesque, and the trio, with Torrence on lead vocals, records *Jennie Lee*, inspired by her, in Berry's garage. While Torrence is away for six months, following call-up to the Army reserves, this tape comes to the attention of Joe Lubin at Arwin Records, a small Los Angeles label owned by Doris Day's husband, Marty Melcher, who offers to release it. Berry and Ginsburg sign and the disc is issued, credited to Jan & Arnie.

1958

Aug *Jennie Lee* hits US #8.
Oct Torrence returns from service shortly after Jan & Arnie's follow-up, *Gas Money*, peaks at US #81. Arwin releases one more Jan & Arnie single, *I Love Linda*, but it fails to score, and Ginsburg drops out. The remaining duo starts recording again in Berry's garage.

1959

They meet Lou Adler and Herb Alpert, two youthful veterans of the Los Angeles music business who work frequently with Sam Cooke, and also manage the small Dore label, which has just had a million seller with *To Know Him Is To Love Him* by the Teddy Bears. Adler and Alpert become Jan & Dean's managers and work with them on recordings, taking the basic garage-cut tracks and overdubbing fuller arrangements (written by Alpert) in a professional two-track studio.
Sept [7] The duo performs, with Frankie Avalon, Duane Eddy, the Coasters and many others, in Dick Clark's stage show at the Michigan State Fair, to an audience of 15,000 over four performances.
Oct *Baby Talk*, their cover of an obscure Californian-group original (and the first single under their new work arrangement with Alpert and Adler), hits US #10. Early copies are marketed as by Jan & Arnie, to capitalize on the earlier success, though once it sells, the credit becomes Jan & Dean. The duo appears on Dick Clark's "American Bandstand" for the first time.
Nov *There's A Girl*, an Alpert and Adler-penned follow-up, peaks at US #97.

1960

Mar Their revival of the traditional *Clementine* (credited as a Berry/Torrence composition) peaks at US #65, losing out to Bobby Darin's coincidental swing-style revival, which reaches US #21.
Sept After *White Tennis Sneakers* has failed, their treatment of the Moonglows' oldie, *We Go Together*, makes US #53.
Dec Another cover, of the Crows' *Gee*, peaks at US #81. (Two further Dore singles over the next seven months, *Baggy Pants* and *Let's Fly Away*, plus an album which includes 12 singles tracks, will all fail to chart.)

1961

May Determined to sign to a major label and benefit from fuller promotion, the duo cuts a revival of Hoagy Carmichael and Frank Loesser's *Heart And Soul*, with a gimmicky uptempo vocal treatment. With Adler, they try to gain a deal with Liberty Records. (Trumpet-playing Alpert despises the track, and drops out of the team and business partnership with Adler to develop his ideas for instrumental music. He will co-found A&M Records in 1962.) Liberty is interested in Jan & Dean, but agrees with Alpert about *Heart And Soul*. Adler and the duo signs an interim two-record deal with the independent Challenge label, owned by Gene Autry.
July *Heart And Soul*, released on Challenge, hits US #25, their biggest success in two years.
Sept *Heart And Soul* is the first of only two UK Jan & Dean hits, at #24. In the US, the quickly released follow-up, *Wanted One Girl*, fails to chart, as the duo signs to Liberty and publishing company Aldon Music.

1962

Jan Their Liberty debut, a revival of *A Sunday Kind Of Love*, peaks at US #95.
May Staff producer Snuff Garrett has been brought in to work on *Tennessee*, written by Leon Russell and Buzz Cason, which makes US #69.
Aug The duo meets the Beach Boys for the first time, when both groups play at a teen hop. (The Beach Boys will occasionally back Jan & Dean live during the fall of 1962, as each group becomes familiar with the other's repertoire.)

1963

Feb *Linda*, their revival of Jack Lawrence's 1944 song written about his lawyer's daughter, Linda Eastman (the future Mrs. Paul McCartney), borrows some of the beat and falsetto vocalizing of the recent Four Seasons hits, and reaches US #28. Adler recommends that the duo should get involved in the burgeoning California surf-music scene (until now mainly instrumental) since both are keen surfers. For ***Jan And Dean Take Linda Surfin'***, an album comprising mainly cover versions, they record two surfing songs they know from singing them live - Brian Wilson's *Surfin'* and *Surfin' Safari*, enlisting the help of Wilson and the other Beach Boys to back them in the studio.

July [20] Constant musical and social fraternization with Brian Wilson and the Beach Boys has led to Wilson giving the duo *Surf City* to complete and record. With the Beach Boys' voices as back-up, it tops the US chart for the first of two weeks (a year before the Beach Boys' own first #1, *I Get Around*), and shifts over a million copies, the duo's biggest-selling single. ***Jan And Dean Take Linda Surfin'*** reaches US #71.

Sept *Surf City* is the second and last Jan & Dean UK hit, at #26.

Oct *Honolulu Lulu*, written by Berry with Los Angeles DJ Roger Christian, reaches US #11, while ***Surf City And Other Swingin' Cities*** reaches US #32. Featuring mostly Jan & Dean versions of oldies with US city names in their titles, the album is (like *Honolulu Lulu*) arranged and produced by Berry, and features what will become the duo's staple studio backing crew: the Phil Spector school of with-it session musicians, including drummer Hal Blaine, guitarists Tommy Tedesco, Glen Campbell and Billy Strange, keyboardists Leon Russell and Larry Knechtel, and sax player Steve Douglas.

1964

Jan Like the Beach Boys, Jan & Dean expand their lyrical concerns to include cars and the hot-rod craze: the Berry/Wilson/Christian-penned *Drag City* hits US #10.

Mar ***Drag City***, featuring mostly original material, plus the Routers' *Sting Ray* and the Beach Boys' *Little Deuce Coupe*, reaches US #22.

May *Dead Man's Curve*, a car-race melodrama in pounding arrangement with car horns and crash effects, hits US #8. Its B-side, *The New Girl In School*, originally a Brian Wilson song titled *Gonna Hustle You*, with new lyrics by Berry written at Liberty's request, reaches US #37.

[16] Jan & Dean promote *Dead Man's Curve* on ABC-TV's "American Bandstand".

June ***Dead Man's Curve/The New Girl In School*** peaks at US #80. It eschews surfing concerns in favor of car and girl songs, and features P.F. Sloan and Steve Barri (aka the Fantastic Baggys) as back-up vocalists, together with Berry's girlfriend Jill Gibson (who will later replace Michelle Phillips in the Mamas & the Papas).

Aug *The Little Old Lady (From Pasadena)* hits US #3. It is penned by Roger Christian with Don Altfield, a student with Berry at California College of Medicine (both Berry and Torrence continue their education throughout these hitmaking years; the latter initially in medicine, then switching to architecture and graphic design at USC).

Sept [4] The duo appears with the Animals, Chuck Berry and Del Shannon in a 10-day stand at the Paramount Theater, Brooklyn, New York.

Oct *Ride The Wild Surf*, the title theme from the current Fabian movie, another Berry/Christian/Wilson collaboration, reaches US #16.

B-side, the near-nonsensical *The Anaheim, Azusa And Cucamonga Sewing Circle, Book Review And Timing Association*, climbs to US #77.

Nov ***The Little Old Lady From Pasadena*** and the movie soundtrack album, ***Ride The Wild Surf***, are released within a week of each other, and peak at US #40 and #66 respectively. Both feature Sloan and Barri as backing vocalists and as writers. Both contain *Sidewalk Surfin'*, also extracted as a single. A reworking of the Beach Boys' *Catch A Wave*, with new lyrics about skateboarding, makes US #25 (and promotes sales of the Jan & Dean "Little Old Lady" skateboard, merchandised at the same time).

1965

Mar *(Here They Come) From All Over The World*, a Sloan/Barri song, reaches US #56. It is the theme from "The TAMI Show", a videotaped TV spectacular (later released as the movie "Gather No Moss" in the UK) hosted by the duo, and includes performances from the Rolling Stones, Chuck Berry, the Beach Boys, Marvin Gaye, James Brown and many others. Jan & Dean's own slot on the show is captured on ***Command Performance/Live In Person***, which makes US #33.

June [28] The duo appears on CBS-TV's "It's What's Happening Baby".

July Ballad *You Really Know How To Hurt A Guy*, written by Berry and Christian with Jill Gibson, reaches US #27. Torrence hates the song, and Berry ejects him during recording, so he is not heard on it.

Oct At another Jan & Dean session, brought to a halt by a technical hitch, Torrence relieves his boredom by walking to a nearby studio where the Beach Boys are holding "live-in-studio" sessions with friends, for an off-the-cuff-style album, ***Beach Boys Party***. Asked if he wants to sing something, he suggests the old Regents hit, *Barbara Ann*. After a few minutes' rehearsal, the song is recorded with Torrence on lead vocal. (The track appears on the album, and will be the next Beach Boys hit, at US #2 and UK #3 but, for contractual and inter-label political reasons, Torrence will remain uncredited.)

Nov *I Found A Girl*, a near-psychedelic arrangement of a Sloan/Barri song, reaches US #30, as ***Jan And Dean Golden Hits, Volume 2***, a compilation of singles from *Linda* onwards, peaks at US #107.

Dec *The Universal Coward*, a patriotic and apparently right-wing song borrowed from Buffy Saint-Marie's *The Universal Soldier*, is released as a Jan Berry solo, after Torrence disowns it. It fails to chart, as does Jan & Dean's opportunistic *Folk City*, which follows close behind.

1966

Jan ***Folk'n'Roll***, including the recent unsuccessful singles, several covers of hits, and some Sloan/Barri items, including *Eve Of Destruction*, peaks at US #145.

Feb Familiar in concert, and partially present on most albums, Jan & Dean's surreal comedy bent is given full rein on ***Jan And Dean Meet Batman***, a cash-in on the new cult-appeal TV series. While the album fails to chart, the extracted *Batman* makes US #66.

Mar The duo prepares to film "Easy Come, Easy Go" with Elvis Presley, and signs to undertake a weekly ABC-TV show. The contract with Liberty expires and, although label wants them to re-sign, the duo plans its own Jan & Dean Records as a subsidiary of Lou Adler's Dunhill label.

Apr [12] Berry, preoccupied with his just-received draft notice and an imminent medical-school exam, crashes his Corvette Stingray into a parked truck on Whittier Boulevard in Los Angeles, and is almost killed. (He will be initially in a coma and then totally paralyzed for several months, suffering partial paralysis long after, and suffering brain damage, which will necessitate re-learning processes. Recovery will take many years.)

June ***Filet Of Soul***, consisting of out-takes from the duo's "TAMI Show" performance and unused studio rejects, is released, to Torrence's displeasure, and peaks at US #127. Unhappy with Liberty's plunder-the-vaults policy, but with Berry out of action for the forseeable future (if not for good), Torrence decides to keep the duo's name active on his own terms, while also helping to pay Berry's hospital bills. Setting up the independent J&D Records and Magic Lamp Productions, he puts a new lyric over *The Little Old Lady*'s instrumental track, titling it *Tijuana*, but it fails to chart.

July *Popsicle*, originally on ***Drag City***, reaches US #21. An album of the same title, compiled entirely from old tracks, fails to sell.

Aug Their second J&D release, a revival of the Jamies' oldie, *Summertime, Summertime*, coupled with *California Lullaby*, produced by Torrence, with poor promotion fails to sell.

Sept Previously unissued *Fiddle Around*, now released by Liberty, reaches US #93, and is Jan & Dean's last chart entry.

1967

Mar Torrence concludes a one-year deal with CBS/Columbia to take Jan & Dean releases from Magic Lamp Productions. *Yellow Balloon* is released, but is defeated by Yellow Balloon's own version.

Apr Torrence cuts ***Save For A Rainy Day*** with Jan & Dean's old studio-session musicians. A collection of new and old songs around a general theme of rain, it is released in Los Angeles on J&D, and scheduled for national distribution by Columbia. Berry, who is slowly recovering, refuses to be a sleeping party to it, and CBS cancels, uninterested in only half of the team promoting it.

June Torrence puts his graphic design degree to use, and launches Kittyhawk Graphics, getting an assignment from White Whale Records to design ***The Turtles' Golden Hits*** sleeve, and later White Whale's display advertising and other corporate artwork.

Oct After collaborating with Brian Wilson on tracks for the Beach Boys' ***Smiley Smile***, Torrence has been given the song *Vegetables*, and records a version with help from session men Joe Osborn and Larry Knechtel, released on White Whale under the name the Laughing Gravy.

Nov Berry signs a deal with Warner Bros. Records, supposedly as a therapeutic measure after pressure from his father and doctors. Torrence declines to take part, feeling Berry is ill-served by not having full-time professional help, but does not object to use of his name. (The label releases three unsuccessful singles as by Jan & Dean. Berry later states that vocals on them were actually by session singers, mainly Ron Hicklin.)

1971

Aug With United Artists Records (inheritors of Liberty) as a client of Kittyhawk Graphics, Torrence works closely with the company on the double ***Jan & Dean Anthology Album***, which includes all the hits (and a live performance side), from *Jennie Lee* in 1958 to the Laughing Gravy's *Vegetables* in 1967.

1972

Jan Berry signs a solo deal with Lou Adler's Ode label, releasing the self-penned *Mother Earth*.

Mar In a short-term deal with United Artists, Torrence forms the Legendary Masked Surfers with Bruce Johnston and Terry Melcher (once both in the Rip Chords and Bruce & Terry, as well as being Beach Boys sidemen), using old Jan & Dean backing tracks for *Gonna Hustle You (The New Girl In School)* with the original, raunchier lyrics.

May Berry revives Huey "Piano" Smith & the Clowns' *Don't You Just Know It* on Ode.

July The second Legendary Masked Surfers release updates Bruce & Terry's 1964 hit, *Summer Means Fun*, written by Sloan and Barri. (After this, the group becomes California, and later California Music, involving varied personnel, including Curt Becher, Gloria Grinel, Kenny Hinkle and Chad Stuart. Torrence's involvement ends here.)

1973

Jan & Dean re-form for the "California Surfer's Stomp Festival" and a projected US tour, miming to backing tracks because of Berry's uncertainty about performing, but the trek turns out to be a disaster. The following year, Berry releases the solo *Tinsel Town*, co-written with Roger Christian and Joan Jacobs. In June 1975, the duo will perform on stage again, at a rock revival show put together by DJ Jim Pewter, this time with no embarrassing moments, while in August Jan & Dean reunite on Ode to record *Fun City*, written by Berry with Alan Wolfson and Jim Pewter.

1978

Feb [3] "Dead Man's Curve" biopic, starring Bruce Davison and Richard Hatch as Jan & Dean, airs on ABC-TV. Interest in the duo is rekindled and, with

Berry's health improved, they embark on a lengthy coast-to-coast US tour.

1980

July [19] ***The Jan And Dean Story*** collection reaches UK #67. (Torrence joins the Beach Boys' Mike Love to record several tracks for a cassette-only release of '60s hits. Rhino Records (US) will release a live Jan & Dean album, ***One Summer Night - Live*** in 1982 and the duo will continue to make live performances throughout the rest of the decade.)

1995

Sept While EMI has released ***Surf City - The Best Of Jan And Dean*** in its Legendary Masters Series in 1990, Dean, speaking on August 19th 1991 for a group of business and tourism boosters in Huntington Beach, asked the council to copyright the phrase "Surf City" for $2,500, to market Huntington Beach. The same month, on the 31st, Jan married Gertie Filip, between concerts at the Stardust Convention Center, Las Vegas, NV, with Dean as his best man. With Jan & Dean still touring as a popular nostalgia act, performing around 50 dates a year, usually during the summer months, Varese Sarabende now releases ***Teen Suite 1958-1962***, a collection of the duo's (and their precursor Jan & Annie) early garage doo-wop efforts.

JANE'S ADDICTION

Perry Farrell (vocals); **Eric Avery** (bass); **Stephen Perkins** (drums); **Dave Navarro** (guitar)

1988

Oct The band has been formed in Los Angeles, CA in the summer of 1986 after mutual friend Jane introduced Farrell (b. Perry Bernstein, Mar. 29, 1959, Queens, NY), the son of a New York diamond dealer and already the veteran of early '80s combo Psi Com, to Avery (b. Apr. 25, 1965, Los Angeles). Adding school chums Perkins (b. Sept. 13, 1967, Los Angeles) and Navarro (b. June 7, 1967, Santa Monica, CA), Jane's Addiction has played the local club scene and already released its debut effort, the live performance set ***Jane's Addiction*** on the Triple-X indie label the following year. Now signed to Warner Bros. Records, their first label album ***Nothing's Shocking***, melding thrash metal, punk, funk and rock, peaks at US #103 as the group, fronted by the flamboyant Farrell, begins a US tour supporting Iggy Pop.

Dec The video for the extracted *Mountain Song* is banned by US MTV due to nudity.

1989

Feb [14] "Soul Kiss" a videomentary of the band is released.

May [7-8] Jane's Addiction performs at San Francisco's Fillmore Auditorium.

1990

Aug [24] They play at the annual "Reading Festival", Reading, Berks.

Sept [26] The group begins a seven-date UK tour at the Birmingham Institute, Birmingham, W. Midlands, set to end on October 5th at London's Astoria Theatre.

Oct ***Ritual De Lo Habitual*** reaches US #19 having made UK #37 on Sept [8].

Nov [20-21] They sellout two dates at the Ritz, New York during a US tour.

1991

Jan [31] The group opens a four-date stint at the Universal Amphitheatre, Universal City, CA, before four capacity crowds totalling 25,004.

Mar [23] *Been Caught Stealing* debuts at its UK #34 peak during a sell-out European tour.

Apr [24] They play a sellout show, supported by Happy Mondays, at New York's Madison Square Garden, before a crowd of 14,314.

May [18] ***Deadicated***, a collection of Grateful Dead covers to which Jane's Addiction has contributed *Ripple*, reaches US #24.

June [1] *Classic Girl* bows at its UK #60.

[7] ***Nothing's Shocking*** is certified gold by the RIAA.

July [18] The Farrell-conceived alternative acts "Lollapalooza" package tour, including Jane's Addiction, Living Colour and Siouxsie & the Banshees, among others, opens at Compton Terrace, Phoenix, AZ, set to become one of the hottest tickets on the US summer tour circuit, subsequently growing to become the most successful annual caravan trek.

Sept [5] "Been Caught Stealing" wins the Best Alternative Music Video category at the eighth annual MTV Video Music Awards, held at the Universal Amphitheatre.

[24] ***Ritual De Lo Habitual*** becomes the group's first RIAA platinum certified album, despite lacking a US hit single.

[27] Farrell performs nude during the second half of what will prove to be the band's final concert at Aloha Tower, Honolulu, HI.

Oct [16] Farrell is arrested and charged with being under the influence of a controlled substance after a maid who is cleaning his Santa Monica Holiday Inn room finds syringes, white powder and crack pipes.

1992

Surprising critics and fans, Farrell has decided to disband Jane's Addiction. While he works on a video documentary of the original "Lollapalooza" tour, Perkins temporarily joins thrash/funk band Infectious Grooves while Navarro and Avery begin working on Navarro's solo debut, before forming Deconstruction with Michael Murphy for one album, and finally joining Red Hot Chili Peppers in 1994. By year's end, Farrell introduces his new outfit, Porno For Pyros, retaining Perkins, and recruiting ex-Thelonius Monster bassist Martyn Le Noble (b. Apr. 14, 1969, Vlaardingen, Holland) and guitarist Pete DiStefano (b. July 10, 1965, Los Angeles), formerly with K-38.

1993

May [15] Porno For Pyros' Warner Bros. debut ***Porno For Pyros***, co-produced by Farrell with Matt Hyde, debuts at its US #3 peak, having done likewise a week earlier at UK #13.

June [5] The extracted *Pets* debuts at its UK #53 peak.

July [24] *Pets* peaks at US #67. (During the month, the group makes its UK debut at the "Glastonbury Festival", Glastonbury, Somerset. Farrell will continue to oversee his annual "Lollapalooza" US summer tours until backing out of the organization prior to its 1996 start, claiming that it has now become too mainstream.)

JAPAN

David Sylvian (vocals, guitar); **Rob Dean** (guitar); **Richard Barbieri** (keyboards); **Steve Jansen** (drums); **Mick Karn** (saxophone)

1977

The band, having formed in Lewisham, London, with Sylvian (b. David Batt, Feb. 23, 1958, Lewisham), his brother Jansen (b. Stephen Batt, Dec. 1, 1959, London), and school friends Barbieri (b. Nov. 30, 1957) and Karn (b. Anthony Michaelides, July 24, 1958, London), and having played Roxy Music-influenced music at local gigs, recruits Dean from a music paper ad for a second guitarist. With the Batt brothers and Michaelides having adopted their stage names, Japan wins a talent contest sponsored by German record company Ariola-Hansa (which has just opened London offices), and is signed to the label.

1978

Mar The group's debut, *Don't Rain On My Parade*, an oldie from the musical "Funny Girl", is released.

Apr [27] As the band's first album, ***Adolescent Sex***, is issued, a UK tour, supporting Blue Öyster Cult, begins at the Colston Hall, Bristol, Avon, set to end on May 4th with the last of two consecutive nights at London's Hammersmith Odeon.

Aug [14, 31] The group plays two dates at London's Music Machine.

Sept [29] They perform at Birmingham's Barbarella's club.

Nov Two further singles, *The Unconventional* and *Sometimes I Feel So Low*, and a second album, ***Obscure Alternatives***, are released in the UK - to little commercial success, followed by ***Life In Tokyo***, produced by Giorgio Moroder, which is issued the following May, only finding interest, unsurprisingly, in Japan.

1980

Mar Their cover of Smokey Robinson's *I Second That Emotion* is released, the band's last recording on Ariola-Hansa.

Oct Newly signed to Virgin Records, their label debut *Gentlemen Take Polaroids*, makes UK #60. The growing popularity of the fashion and music of the New Romantic movement, which Japan's style has anticipated, is a key element in the group's increased UK airplay, press coverage and subsequent chart success.

Nov [22] The synthesizer-dominated, John Punter-produced ***Gentlemen Take Polaroids*** reaches UK #45.

1981

May Dean leaves, moving to Los Angeles, CA. *The Art Of Parties*, makes UK #48.

Sept Karn exhibits his sculpture work in Japan.

Oct *Quiet Life*, the title track from the earlier album, released on Hansa after the group's departure, reaches UK #19.

Nov Newly recorded on Virgin, *Visions Of China* makes UK #32.

[28] Its parent album ***Tin Drum***, like the single revealing oriental influences, reaches UK #12.

1982

Feb Hansa's reissue of *European Son* (the B-side of *Life In Tokyo*) climbs to UK #31.

[13] ***Quiet Life***, the group's 1980 UK chart debut, now peaks at #53.

Apr Ballad *Ghosts* gains widespread UK airplay and hits UK #5.

June *Cantonese Boy* makes UK #24, amid reports of constant disagreements between Sylvian and Karn, and rumors concerning the band's break-up. These are further fuelled by news of solo projects. Karn is the first to release a solo album for Virgin, ***Sensitive***.

July Hansa reissue of *I Second That Emotion* hits UK #9.

Aug Karn and Jansen contribute to an album by Japanese act Akiko Yano, and Barbieri produces Swedish band Lustans Lakejer. Meanwhile Sylvian has teamed with Japanese musician Ryuichi Sakamoto (of the Yellow Magic Orchestra), on ***Bamboo Houses***. Released under the name Sylvian Sakamoto, it reaches UK #30.

[21] A compilation of early Japan material, ***Assemblage***, reaches UK #26, having originally charted the previous September.

Oct *Life In Tokyo*, reissued by Hansa, makes UK #28, as Japan tours the UK.

Nov [22] Japan officially announces its break-up, following a final concert at London's Hammersmith Odeon.

[27] Karn's solo, ***Titles***, peaks at UK #74.

Dec *Night Porter*, a late Virgin release, reaches UK #29.

1983

Mar Hansa's final Japan release, reviving the Velvet Underground's *All Tomorrow's Parties* (originally on ***Quiet Life***), reaches UK #38.

May Live version of *Canton* is Japan's final UK singles hit, at #42.

June Double live album, ***Oil On Canvas***, recorded during the group's final tour, hits UK #5.

July Sylvian and Ryuichi Sakamoto's *Forbidden Colours*, the collaborative theme to the David

Bowie/Tom Conti movie "Merry Christmas Mr. Lawrence" (in which Sakamoto also stars) climbs to UK #16.

1984

Jan Sylvian solo, *Red Guitar*, reaches UK #17.
June He exhibits his Polaroid photo montages at London's Hamilton's Gallery.
July His debut solo album, ***Brilliant Trees***, hits UK #4. It yields *The Ink In The Well* (UK #36 in August) and *Pulling Punches* (UK #56 in November).
Nov Karn teams with former Bauhaus lead singer, Peter Murphy, as Dali's Car. Signed to Paradox Records, their debut is ***The Judgement Is The Mirror***, peaking at UK #66.
Dec Double album, ***Exorcising Ghosts***, a compilation of Japan's Virgin material, peaks at UK #45. Dali's Car's *The Waking Hour* makes UK #84.

1985

Dec Sylvian solo ***Words With The Shaman*** makes UK #72, while ***His Alchemy - An Index Of Possibilities*** is released on cassette only. The following year, Sylvian will reach UK #53 with *Taking The Veil* (August), from the UK #24 double set, ***Gone To Earth*** (September).

1987

Jan Karn's *Buoy*, featuring Sylvian on guest vocals, floats to UK #63, followed by the former's ***Dreams Of Reason Produce Monsters***, which peaks at UK #89 on Feb [28].
July Jansen and Barbieri resurface as the Dolphin Brothers, releasing ***Catch The Fall*** on Virgin.
Nov [7] Sylvian's third album, ***Secrets Of The Beehive***, makes UK #37 and includes the October UK #66, *Let The Happiness In*. He will team with Holger Czukay for ***Plight And Premonition***, which will peak at UK #71 on Apr [2] the following year, while his solo album, ***Orpheus***, fails to chart. Virgin will press 30,000 CDs of all Sylvian's solo work, released as ***The Weather Box*** compilation in December 1989.

1991

Apr [20] Reunited, Sylvian, Karn, Jansen and Barbieri, now calling themselves Rain Tree Crow, have recorded ***Rain Tree Crow*** for Virgin, which debuts at its UK #24 peak, and includes the March UK #62, *Blackwater*. The reunion will only sustain this one album, however, as Karn, Barbieri and Jansen go on to form the rhythm section backing No-Man on a 1992 UK tour, before staying together for Karn's 1993 solo effort ***Bestial Cluster*** and the trio-credited 1994 set ***Beginning To Melt***. Sylvian will make UK #58 on June [20], 1992 with *Heartbeat (Tainai Kaiki II)* and then go on to team with Robert Fripp for ***The First Day***, which will reach UK #21 on July [17] 1993, and the extracted single, *Jean The Birdman* (UK #68 - Aug [28] 1993, preceding their live collaboration ***Damage***, issued in September 1994.

JEAN-MICHEL JARRE

1967

Abandoning his studies at the Conservatoire de Paris under Jeanine Reuff to work in his self-created studio experimenting with synthesizers, having also briefly joined Pierre Schaeffer's Music Research ensemble, Jarre (b. Aug. 24, 1948, Lyons, France), the son of composer Maurice Jarre, and a child prodigy playing piano and guitar from the age of five, makes his first professional recording, the soundtrack to the film "Des Garçons Et Des Filles". Signing to the EMI Pathe label the following year, his premiere disque, ***Cage - Erosmachine***, will be released in France in 1969. Two years later Jarre will make his solo public debut at the Paris Opera, and will become the youngest composer to appear at Palais Garnier. Over the subsequent five years Jarre will write jingles in addition to his film and ballet scores, which will include ***Deserted Palace***, released in France in 1972, and the soundtrack to the Jean Capot film "Les Granges Brûlées" in 1973.

1977

Jan Recently married to actress Charlotte Rampling and newly signed to Francis Dreyfus' label Disques Dreyfus, Jarre begins working on a new album.
Sept *Oxygène Part IV* hits UK #4 and becomes familiar as a popular instrumental for TV programs. ***Oxygène***, with multi-layered synthesizers and sound effects, is released through a Dreyfus license to Polydor Records. It hits UK #2 (Sept [3]) and US #78, ultimately selling over ten million copies worldwide, bringing Jarre's unique orchestral electronic tapestry to a global audience for the first time. The following year, he will compose the score for the Peter Fleischmann film "La Maladie De Hambourg".

1979

Jan *Equinoxe Part 5* makes UK #45.
Feb [10] Antarctic-themed ***Equinoxe***, following a similar musical path to the previous album, reaches UK #11 and will make US #126, going on to sell seven million copies worldwide, confirming Jarre's status as Europe's most popular solo instrumentalist.
July [14] One million spectators attend Jarre's Bastille Day concert at Place de la Concorde, Paris (the first in a decade of mega-concerts Jarre will perform around the globe). It features a complex weave of lasers, synthesizers and fireworks, all controlled by computers, a spectacular event which will hallmark all his future live work.
Sept He begins work on the soundtrack to the Peter Weir movie "Gallipoli".

1981

June [20] Self-composed and produced (as ever), ***Magnetic Fields*** hits UK #6 and will peak at US #98.
Oct Jarre becomes the first western rock artist to perform in China, with five major concerts in Beijing, backed by 35 Chinese musicians. The event, in front of 400,000 spectators, is filmed by Andrew Piddington for a TV special, and is recorded for album release to offset the phenomenal costs involved. Some 15 tons of equipment packed in 30 army trucks, have been shipped to China for the five gigs. The subsequent double album, ***The Concerts In China***, will hit UK #6 on May [15] the following year.

1983

July Jarre has recorded ***Music For Supermarkets***, made expressly to voice his distaste and disregard for the music business, with only one copy of the album being pressed. The album is now auctioned at the Hôtel Drouot, Paris, though the successful bidder is unknown. Jarre destroys the master tapes, but the project is given a public airing on Radio Luxembourg.
Nov ***The Essential Jean-Michel Jarre***, a compilation of his most celebrated works, reaches UK #14, and will be certified platinum in France, Germany, Italy and the UK.

1984

Nov Ethnic opera, ***Zoolook***, with Jarre's familiar instrumentation augmented by foreign-language vocal inserts, and featuring guests Laurie Anderson, Adrian Belew and Marcus Miller, makes UK #47. The following April, the album will win the Grand Prix at the French Acadamie Du Disque.

1986

Apr [5] The latest in his increasingly grand live spectaculars is held in Houston, TX, for the city's 150th anniversary and NASA's 25th anniversary. Jarre plays to an estimated 1.3 million people, while the largest-ever light, laser and firework show plays around him, illuminating Houston's glass skyscrapers. It is the biggest event of its kind, despite his modest star status in the US. "Rendez-Vous Houston" is filmed by video director Bob Giraldi, for worldwide TV showing. The set is inspired by the Challenger space shuttle disaster. Included is *Ron's Song*, which shuttle crew member Ron McNair had intended to play on his saxophone while in space.
Rendez-Vous hits UK #9 and US #52.
Aug *Fourth Rendez-Vous* peaks at UK #65.
Oct [6] With 450 projectors on a 20' podium, Jarre stages another grand event, "Rendez-Vous Lyons - A Concert For The Pope" in his hometown, to honor the visit of Pope John Paul II.

1987

July [18] ***In Concert Lyons/Houston*** reaches UK #18, as "Rendez-Vous Lyons", directed by François Gauthier, receives its premiere.

1988

Sept Jarre plans another stage spectacular, this time in London's Docklands, to coincide with the release of his new album. The local Newham council authority objects - on public safety grounds - and refuses to grant a license to allow the concert to go ahead.
Oct [15] ***Revolutions***, concerning itself with the conflict between Islam and computers, hits UK #2, behind Chris DeBurgh's ***Flying Colours***, and includes guest guitarist Hank Marvin of the Shadows on the track *London Kid*.
[8-9] His "Destination Docklands" extravaganza proceeds, despite wind, rain, traffic and Newham council, but as two smaller shows instead of one large event. Jarre arranges for Marvin to fly in from Australia to perform.
Nov *Revolutions* peaks at UK #52.

1989

Jan *London Kid* also peaks at UK #52.
Oct Reissued *Oxygène IV* makes UK #65.
[14] ***Jarre Live*** reaches UK #16.
Dec The "Concert D'Images" exhibition, chronicling ten years of Jarre's career, opens at the Espace Photographiques des Halles in Paris.

1990

June [23] ***Waiting For Cousteau*** docks at UK #14, inspired by, and dedicated to, fellow Frenchman, seafaring biologist Jacques Cousteau.
July [14] Jarre performs to another record crowd (estimated at 2.5 million) for a Bastille Day concert in the La Défense area of Paris. Themed "Paris, La Defense: A Town In Concert", the event, based around a specially built pyramid, is documented on film by Mike Mansfield, for subsequent transmission.

1992

Jan [19-21] After a one-hour, 17-track retrospective, ***Images - The Best Of Jean-Michel Jarre***, has debuted at its UK #14 peak on Oct [26] the previous year, Jarre is included on the jury for the first International Visual Music Awards, held during Midem in France.
Dec [1-3] He performs his latest live spectacle at the Lost City in Sun City, Johannesburg, SA.

1995

July [14] Following the 1993 succcess of his latest work ***Chronologie*** (at UK #11, June [5], with *Chronologie Part 4* debuting at its UK #55 peak on June [26]), Jarre performs his latest extravaganza in Paris.

AL JARREAU

1968

Jarreau (b. Mar. 12, 1940, Milwaukee, WI) having sung since the age of four, influenced by his older brothers' interest in jazz and singing, begins improvising vocals, singing along to radio songs. Choosing music over a career in sports (he is a gifted basketball and baseball player) and having received his Master's Degree in Psychology, he works with guitarist Julio Martinez in a Sausalito, CA club. He will spend the next five years developing his improvising vocal style in Los Angeles, CA, clubs including Dino's, the Troubadour and the Bitter End. During 1972 he will secure an engagement at New York's Improvization venue where he meets other artists, including Quincy Jones, Bette Midler and comedian Richard Pryor. The following year, Jarreau will play a residence (lasting into 1974) at Los Angeles coffee house, the Bla Bla Café, where he develops his writing and performs his own material.

1975

Mar Spotted by Warner Bros. Records staffers playing at the Troubadour, he has been signed to the label and releases the critically-acclaimed debut album ***We Got By***.
Dec During a European promotional tour, he wins a German Echo Award for Best International Soloist (reflecting his early popularity in Europe).

1976

July Jarreau performs at the tenth annual "Montreux Jazz Festival", Montreux, Switzerland.
Sept His sophomore effort ***Glow***, once again showcasing his sophisticated, jazz-tinged vocal prowess, reaches US #132. He will begin his first world tour the following January, prior to a double live album ***Look To The Rainbow - Live Recorded In Europe***, recorded on his world trek, making US #49 on September 17th.

1978

Feb [23] Jarreau wins the Best Jazz Vocal Performance category for *Look To The Rainbow* at the 20th annual Grammy awards.
Nov ***All Fly Home*** peaks at US #78. On February 15th the following year, the album will be named Best Jazz Vocal Performance at the 21st annual Grammy awards. In March 1980, he will also win the Silver Award at the Tokyo Music Festival, Tokyo, Japan before ***This Time*** reaches US #27 in August.

1981

Feb [24] Jarreau nabs the Best Pop Vocal Performance, Male for *Breakin' Away* and Best Jazz Vocal Performance, Male (for *Blue Rondo A La Turk*) trophies at the 23rd annual Grammy awards.
Mar Jarreau begins another world tour including Brazil, the Philippines and Japan.
Sept [26] ***Breakin' Away***, produced by Jay Graydon and marking a significant commercial move towards soul, makes UK #60 and will hit US #9.
Oct [3] *We're In This Love Together* peaks at UK #55.
[31] *We're In This Love Together*, his US radio breakthrough, reaches US #15.

1982

Jan *Breakin' Away* makes US #43. He plays standing-room-only dates in UK and Scandinavia.
Feb [24] Jarreau is named Best Pop Vocalist, Male at the 24th annual Grammy awards.
Apr *Teach Me Tonight* peaks at US #70.

1983

May *Mornin'*, written with David Foster and Graydon, reaches US #21. ***Jarreau***, a jazz/soul/pop meld, once again helmed by Graydon, reaches US #13 and UK #39.
June *Mornin'* dawns at UK #28.
July *Boogie Down* peaks at US #77 (and UK #63 in October) as ***Trouble In Paradise*** makes UK #36 (set to reach US #63 in November).

1984

Nov *After All* peaks at US #69. ***High Crime***, featuring producer Graydon and hot session players including Robbie Buchanan, Nathan East, Jerry Hey and Greg Phillinganes, pays off at US #49 and UK #81, as Jarreau plays sold-out US and UK dates. The resulting ***Al Jarreau In London***, recorded on this year's visit, will make US #125 the following October.

1986

Apr Jarreau teams with Melissa Manchester to sing *The Music Of Goodbye*, the love theme from the movie "Out Of Africa".
June Guesting on Bob James and David Sanborn's ***Double Vision***, Jarreau revives Lenny Welch's 1963 hit *Since I Fell For You*. Featured in the ABC-TV series "Moonlighting", it will be included (with an additional Jarreau cut) on the soundtrack album.
July Jarreau performs at the 20th annual "Montreux Jazz Festival".
Sept ***L Is For Lover***, his tenth album for Warner Bros., produced by Nile Rodgers, makes US #81 and UK #45.

1987

Mar Jarreau's title theme from "Moonlighting" hits UK #8.
July [18] *Moonlighting* reaches US #23.

1989

Jan [21] Variously produced by Duke, Graydon and Philippe Saisse, ***Heart's Horizon*** tops the US Contemporary Jazz chart and also makes US #75.
Apr Joe Sample's ***Spellbound***, including guest work by Jarreau, is released.
July [12] Jarreau performs at the 23rd annual "Montreux Jazz Festival", at the start of a tour with a backing band comprising Joe Sample, Steve Gadd, Lenny Castro, Freddy Washington, Buzzy Feiten and Saisse.
[28] His "Select Live Under The Sky '90" tour kicks off in Tokyo, set to end on August 9th at the Queen Elizabeth Stadium, Hong Kong.

1991

Feb [10] Jarreau joins with nearly 100 celebrities in Burbank, CA, to record *Voices That Care*, a David Foster and fiancée Linda Thompson Jenner-composed and organized charity record to benefit the American Red Cross Gulf Crisis Fund.
Mar [9] The Peace Choir, an all-star aggregation featuring Jarreau, makes US #54 with its remake of *Give Peace A Chance*.
May [4] Jarreau receives a honorary doctor of music degree at Commencement Ceremonies at the Berklee College of Music, Boston, MA.
Oct [31] He guests on NBC-TV's "The Tonight Show".
Dec [13-14] During a current US tour, Jarreau performs at the Celebrity Theatre, Anaheim, CA, as ***Heart's Horizon*** becomes his fifth RIAA-certified gold album.

1992

Apr [28] Jarreau participates in the recording of Quincy Jones' ***Hallelujah!***, a contemporary version of "The Messiah" at A&M Studios, Hollywood, CA.
June [13] He guests on ITV's "Tom Jones The Right Time".
[28] During his current US tour, Jarreau plays to a sellout 6,612 crowd at Chastain Park Amphitheatre, Atlanta, GA.
July [11] Having already junked an album recorded with Joe Sample, Marcus Miller and Steve Gadd, Jarreau releases his first album in three years, the R&B-returning Narada Michael Walden-produced ***Heaven And Earth*** which peaks at US #105.
Sept [11] Soundtrack to "Glengarry Glen Ross", featuring Jarreau singing *Blue Skies*, is released.
[26] Jarreau begins a 21-date European tour at the Philharmonie, Koln, Germany, set to end on November 1st at London's Royal Albert Hall.
Nov [4] He guests on "The Tonight Show".
Dec [18-19] His US tour ends at the Universal Amphitheatre.

1993

Jan [24] Jarreau participates in "Sexual Healing - A Tribute To Marvin Gaye" in support of the fight against AIDS at MIDEM with Ashford & Simpson, El Debarge with Chante Moore, George Duke, Nona Gaye, Stanley Jordan, Chaka Khan, Hamish Stuart, Pointer Sisters, Randy Crawford and others.
Feb [24] He collects the Best R&B Male Vocal trophy for ***Heaven And Earth*** at the 35th annual Grammy Awards held at the Shrine Auditorium, Los Angeles, and also performs a segment of Handel's "The Messiah" in duet with Chaka Khan.

1994

Sept Produced by Marcus Miller, ***Tenderness*** is released, largely a covers album featuring the usual top-drawer talent pool including jazz veterans Sample, Steve Gadd, David Sanborn, Michael Brecker, Paulinho Da Costa.

JEFFERSON AIRPLANE

Grace Slick (vocals); **Marty Balin** (vocals); **Paul Kantner** (guitar); **Jorma Kaukonen** (guitar); **Jack Casady** (bass guitar); **Spencer Dryden** (drums)

1965

July [6] Balin (b. Martyn Jerel Buchwald, Jan. 30, 1942, although he will subsequently claim 1943, Cincinnati, OH), performing in a professional production of "West Side Story", having cut the solo singles *I Specialize In Love* and *Nobody But You* for the Challenge label, and having spent some time with folk group the Town Criers while living in Los Angeles, CA, begins the process of recruiting players for a band he intends to assemble to play at a club he has acquired at 3138 Fillmore Street, near the marina district of San Francisco, CA. He has persuaded three investors to contribute $3,000 each, with his newly-formed group to retain a 25% interest, to purchase and renovate the now-closed Honeybucket club. His first recruit is guitarist Kantner (b. Mar. 12, 1941, San Francisco), who has failed in his attempt to form a folk duo with David Freiberg and whom Balin meets at local club the Drinking Gourd. Kantner, in turn, recommends guitarist/vocalist Kaukonen (b. Dec. 23, 1940, Washington, DC), whom he has met at Santa Clara University, Santa Clara, CA, and who is about to head for Europe when he is approached. Upright bass player Bob Harvey and drummer Jerry Peloquin round out the new band's rhythm section. Signe Anderson (b. Signe Toly, Sept. 15, 1941, Seattle, WA), who had sung in Portland, WA, as the girl of Two Guys & A Girl, is heard by Balin at the Drinking Gourd, where her brother is tending bar, and completes the line-up. They adopt their moniker after local blues musician Steve Talbot gives Kaukonen the name of a fictitious blues singer, Blind Thomas Jefferson Airplane, a parody of Blind Lemon Jefferson.
Aug [13] The group makes its debut on the opening night of the Matrix club, a gig reviewed by the **San Francisco Chronicle**'s Ralph Gleason, which leads to Airplane receiving contract offers from several major companies. Peloquin is soon replaced by Skip Spence (b. Alexander Spence, Apr. 18 1944, Windsor, ON, Canada), who Balin thinks looks right for the part, despite the fact that he has never played drums. He soon learns.
Oct [16] Jefferson Airplane headlines the first Family Dog commune, "A Tribute To Dr. Strange" dance, at Longshoreman's Hall, San Francisco. Kantner is much taken with Grace Slick (b. Grace Barnett Wing, Oct. 30, 1939, Chicago, IL), who is singing with another band on the bill, the Great Society.
Nov Harvey is replaced by Casady (b. John Casady, Apr. 13, 1944, Washington), with whom Kaukonen played in Washington rock'n'roll band, the Triumphs, in the late '50s. He is about to start a new term at Montgomery Junior College in Maryland when he receives the call from Kaukonen to join.
[6] The band participates in the first San Francisco Mime Troupe benefit, organized by Bill Graham, also featuring Lawrence Ferlinghetti, Allen Ginsberg and John Handy.
Dec [10] Jefferson Airplane performs at the inaugural concert held at Bill Graham's Fillmore Auditorium,

with the Great Society, the John Handy Quintet, the Mystery Trend and Sam Thomas & the Gelemen's band.
[16-18] With a $25,000 deal signed by newly-appointed manager Matthew Katz and RCA's West Coast A&R man Neely Plumb, the group cuts its first tracks (*It's No Secret, Runnin' Round The World, High Flyin' Bird, It's Alright* and *Run Around*) for the label in Los Angeles, with Tommy Oliver producing.

1966

Feb [26] Following the release of its debut single, *It's No Secret*, in January, the band plays at the Fillmore West on a bill with Big Brother & the Holding Company, Quicksilver Messenger Service, the Grass Roots and the Great Society. (During the year they will perform at the venue more than ten times, sharing the bill on most of those occasions with either the Grateful Dead or Paul Butterfield.)
May Spence leaves, and heads to Mexico, before returning to the Bay Area to form Moby Grape. His replacement is jazz-schooled drummer Dryden (b. Apr. 7, 1938, New York, NY), currently drumming with the Ashes (which will evolve into Peanut Butter Conspiracy.)
June [24] The group takes part in the "KFRC Presents The Beach Boys Summer Spectacular" at the Cow Palace, San Francisco, sharing a bill with the headliners, Lovin' Spoonful, Chad & Jeremy, Percy Sledge, the Byrds and Sir Douglas Quintet, among others.
July [4] They participate in the "Berkeley Folk Festival", Berkeley, CA.
Aug Just prior to the release of its debut album, the group fires manager Katz, replacing him with the interim Bill Thompson.
Sept The band appears at the "Monterey Jazz Festival", Monterey, CA, the first rock group to do so.
Oct [15] Anderson, unable to cope with the demands of being a new mother and playing in a band, makes her final appearance with the Airplane in the middle of a three-day stint at the Fillmore Auditorium.
[16] Slick makes her debut with the group, bringing with her two songs she has performed with the Great Society, the bolero-like *White Rabbit* and *Somebody To Love*. (The Great Society has recorded two live albums but Columbia will not release them until Slick finds fame with Jefferson Airplane.)
Nov Their debut album, ***Jefferson Airplane Takes Off***, recorded in December 1965, is released in the US by RCA, and makes #128 (it will not be released in Britain until 1971).

1967

Jan [8] Now managed by Bill Graham, the band appears at an RCA promotional party at Webster Hall, Greenwich Village, New York.
[14] They play at the first "Human Be-In", in Golden Gate Park, San Francisco, before embarking on their first East Coast tour.
Feb [3-5] They perform at the Fillmore Auditorium with Quicksilver Messenger Service.
May [7] The group guests on CBS-TV's "The Smothers Brothers Comedy Hour".
June ***Surrealistic Pillow***, the first album to feature Slick's vocals, and produced by Rick Jarrard, with the Grateful Dead's Jerry Garcia as musical adviser, hits US #3, earning a gold disc.
[17] The band is the sixth act to appear on the second evening of the "Monterey International Pop Festival" at the County Fairgrounds, Monterey, CA. *Somebody To Love*, written by Darby Slick, Grace's brother-in-law, hits US #5.
[20-25] The group plays at the Fillmore with the Jimi Hendrix Experience.
July [29] *White Rabbit*, a surreal interpretation of **Alice In Wonderland** written by Slick, hits US #8, also becoming a million seller.
Sept ***Surrealistic Pillow*** is released in the UK, in an edited form which excludes major tracks, such as *White Rabbit* and *Plastic Fantastic Lover*, and substitutes tracks from the unissued-in-the-UK first album.
[15] The group plays with the Grateful Dead at the Hollywood Bowl, Hollywood, CA.
[23] *The Ballad Of You And Me And Pooneil* makes US #42.
Dec [23] *Watch Her Ride* reaches US #61.
[31] The band performs a New Year's Eve concert, with Big Brother & the Holding Company, at the Fillmore West.

1968

Feb Now once again managed by Bill Thompson (due to Graham's dismissal), the group's ***After Bathing At Baxter's***, marking the beginning of a working relationship with producer Pat Ieraci, reaches US #17. (Casady is also currently featured on Jimi Hendrix's album, ***Electric Ladyland***, and Country Joe & the Fish's ***Together***.)
[14] Airplane and the Grateful Dead each take a 10% interest in a partnership to administer the Carousel Ballroom in San Francisco.
Apr [20] *Greasy Heart* stops at US #98.
[30] The band opens the Kaleidoscope club on Sunset Strip in Los Angeles with Canned Heat.
June [28] The group appears on the cover of **Life** magazine, which features articles on Cream, the Doors, Jimi Hendrix, Janis Joplin, the Mothers of Invention and the Who, under the caption "Jefferson Airplane, Top Rock Group, With Music That's Hooked The Whole Vibrating World".
July [5] Bill Graham takes over the running of the Carousel Ballroom, renaming it the Fillmore West, while the band buys a house at 2400 Fulton in San Francisco (for $65,000, selling it in 1985 for $650,000), which will become its headquarters.
Aug [4-5] The group performs at the "Newport Pop Festival" in Costa Mesa, CA, alongside the Byrds, Canned Heat, the Grateful Dead, Sonny & Cher, Steppenwolf and others.
[29] Jefferson Airplane makes its first UK live appearance at a party at the Revolution club in London, at the start of its first European tour, which includes a well-received appearance at the "Isle Of Wight Festival" and a free gig at Parliament Hill Fields in London.
Sept [6-7] The group plays two nights at London's Roundhouse, on a bill with the Doors.
Oct [24-26] Returned home, they perform at the Fillmore West.
Nov ***Crown Of Creation*** hits US #6.
[10] The group makes its third appearance on CBS-TV's "The Smothers Brothers Comedy Hour".
Dec [7] The extracted title track, *Crown Of Creation*, makes US #64. French movie director Jean-Luc Godard films the band playing on a rooftop, for his projected "An American Movie" film. After Godard drops his plans, the footage is picked up by documentary film-maker D.A. Pennebaker, and is used in "One P.M." Kaukonen and Casady form a splinter group, initially called Hot Shit, then renamed Hot Tuna.

1969

Jan Slick is hospitalized with a suspected throat growth, undergoing a second operation for nodes on her vocal chords.
Apr Live album, ***Bless Its Pointed Little Head***, recorded at the Fillmore West on October 24-26th, 1968, and the Fillmore East, November 28-30th, 1968, makes US #17.
May [16] Casady is arrested for possession of marijuana, in New Orleans, and will receive a 2½ year suspended sentence.
June [28] ***Bless Its Pointed Little Head*** becomes the group's first UK chart entry, spending a week at #38.
Aug [1] The band performs at the "Atlantic City Pop Festival", Atlantic City, NJ, before an audience of 110,000.
[12] The group headlines a concert at Tanglewood, Lenox, MA, with B.B. King and special guest stars, the Who.
[17] Jefferson Airplane closes the second day, by now early Sunday morning, of the "Woodstock Music & Art Fair", Bethel, NY.
Oct [17] Kantner is busted for marijuana possession in Honolulu, HI, found guilty of a misdemeanor and fined $350.
Nov [26] The group plays at the Fillmore East, with Slick dressed as Hitler and Rip Torn making an appearance as Richard Nixon.
Dec ***Volunteers***, the band's most overtly political work, reaches US #13.
[6] The band takes part in the Rolling Stones' ill-fated concert at Altamont Speedway, CA. Balin is attacked halfway through a song, by one of the Hells Angels "handling" security.
[20] The extracted title track, *Volunteers*, makes US #65.
[31] The group plays New Year's Eve show at the Winterland Ballroom in San Francisco.

1970

Feb Dryden, long disillusioned, quits, set to join New Riders of the Purple Sage in 1971. He is replaced by Joey Covington, who has been drumming with Hot Tuna.
[27] The group is fined $1,000 for obscenity in Oklahoma City, OK.
Mar ***Volunteers*** reaches UK #34.
May [16] Balin is arrested for drug possession in a Bloomington, MN hotel room. He will be sentenced to one year's hard labor and a $100 fine, reduced on appeal to just the fine.
June [27] The group co-headlines the "Bath Festival of Blues & Progressive Music" at the Royal County Fairgrounds, Shepton Mallet, Somerset, with Led Zeppelin. Tickets for the all-weekend festival are £2 10s.
Oct Slick, now pregnant by Kantner, is unable to make live appearances. Casady and Kaukonen, who have, for some time, been playing occasional support gigs to Jefferson Airplane as Hot Tuna, either with other musicians or as an acoustic duo, formalize the offshoot group. They recruit violinist Papa John Creach (b. May 28, 1917, Beaver Falls, PA), who also becomes a member of Jefferson Airplane, making his debut with the band at Winterland on the 5th (Balin will refuse to perform in a tribute to Janis Joplin, who had died the previous day). Kaukonen switches to electric guitar and Covington plays drums. A Hot Tuna gig at the New Orleans House, Berkeley, is recorded and given a low-key album release.
Nov Kantner and Slick have invited Jerry Garcia, David Crosby and Graham Nash to contribute to ***Blows Against The Empire***, billed as by Paul Kantner & Jefferson Starship (the first use of this name), which reaches US #20 and is the first album to be nominated for the sci-fi writers' Hugo Awards.
Dec Hot Tuna plays US dates with Covington as drummer and Papa John Creach on violin.

1971

Jan [25] Slick gives birth to a daughter, modestly named God, at a San Francisco hospital, subsequently reducing the child's name to China.
Feb Compilation album, ***The Worst Of Jefferson Airplane***, reaches US #12.
Apr Balin leaves the group, taking a year off before returning to produce the band Grootna for Columbia Records in 1972, before becoming lead vocalist for Bodacious D.F. the following year.
May [13] Slick crashes her Mercedes into a wall near the Golden Gate Bridge in San Francisco. She is hospitalized briefly, causing Jefferson Airplane recording sessions to be cancelled.
July Hot Tuna's second album, ***First Pull Up Then Pull Down***, makes US #43.
Aug [2] Jefferson Airplane launches its own RCA-distributed label, Grunt Records.
Oct The first Grunt release, Jefferson Airplane's ***Bark***, climbs to US #11, eventually earning a gold disc.
[2] ***Bark*** makes UK #42.

1972

Jan [1] *Pretty As You Feel*, an edit from a 30-minute studio jam, featuring Jerry Garcia, Carlos Santana and Creach, makes US #60.
Kantner and Slick's ***Sunfighter***, which features baby China on the cover, makes US #89. Creach also releases his first solo album on Grunt, featuring guest spots from

Airplane members, while Hot Tuna appears on David Crosby's ***If Only I Could Remember My Name***.
Apr Jefferson Airplane members regroup for fresh recording sessions, during which Covington leaves to join Black Kangaroo, and is replaced by ex-Turtles drummer, John Barbata (b. Apr. 1, 1946, NJ).
May Hot Tuna's ***Burgers*** makes US #68.
Aug [12] Airplane plays at the Roosevelt Raceway, Long Island, NY, as part of the "Festival of Hope" benefit for the Nassau Society For Crippled Children And Adults.
[21] Slick is maced and Kantner slightly injured when a scuffle ensues, after the group's equipment manager calls police "pigs" during a show at the Rubber Bowl, Akron, OH. Police arrest Casady and drag him offstage.
Sept ***Long John Silver*** reaches US #20.
[2] ***Long John Silver*** charts for one week at UK #30.
[22] US tour, which has included guitarist David Frieberg (b. Aug. 24, 1938, Boston, MA), fresh from Quicksilver Messenger Service, ends at Winterland, with Balin guesting. It will prove to be the last Jefferson Airplane gig for 17 years. The Hot Tuna members make a final break and resist any attempts to woo them back. (The band will make six more albums before breaking up in 1978.)

1973

Apr ***30 Seconds Over Winterland***, a live album recorded during the last US tour, is released.
July Kantner, Slick and Frieberg's ***Baron Von Tollbooth And The Chrome Nun*** reaches US #52.
Oct Balin's new group with Vic Smith, Bodacious D.F., releases its self-titled debut album.

1974

Feb Slick's maiden solo album, ***Manhole***, makes US #127, while Hot Tuna's ***The Phosphorescent Rat*** reaches US #148. Slick, Kantner, Creach, Barbata, 19-year-old ex-Steelwind guitarist Craig Chaquico (b. Sept. 26, 1954, Sacramento, CA), ex-Steelwind and the Kantner-Slick solo efforts, and Kaukonen's bass-playing younger brother, Peter (under the name Peter Kangaroo), begin rehearsing under the name Jefferson Starship.
Mar [19] Jefferson Airplane officially becomes Jefferson Starship.
Apr Jefferson Starship begins its first US tour. Peter Kaukonen will leave at its conclusion, to be replaced by UK session player Pete Sears, who worked on ***Manhole***.
June ***Early Flight***, an album of unreleased and rare Jefferson Airplane material, peaks at US #110.
July The new group goes into the studio for the first time.
Nov [21] Balin, having vowed he would never perform with them again, joins the band on stage at the Winterland Ballroom in San Francisco.
[23] *Ride The Tiger* peaks at US #84.
Dec ***Dragonfly*** lands at US #11, and earns a gold disc.

1975

Jan With earlier differences now resolved, Balin rejoins permanently.
May Hot Tuna's ***America's Choice*** reaches US #75.
[23] Jefferson Starship takes part in an all-star benefit to raise funds to make up a shortfall in the San Francisco school budget at the city's Kezar Stadium.
Aug Creach leaves, to settle in Los Angeles and front his own band.
Sept [6] ***Red Octopus*** begins a four-week tenure at US #1, and will sell over two million copies.
[30] Jefferson Starship joins the Grateful Dead for a free concert at San Francisco's Lindley Park.
Oct [18] Balin-penned *Miracles* hits US #3, becomes a million seller and will become a staple cut on US radio.
Dec Hot Tuna's ***Yellow Fever*** makes US #97.
[29] Slick and Kantner break up, after living together for seven years. (Slick will marry the group's 24-year-old lighting engineer, Skip Johnson, in November the following year.)

1976

Jan [10] *Play On Love* reaches US #49.
July [31] ***Spitfire*** charts for a week at UK #30.
Aug [14] ***Spitfire*** hits US #3.
Sept [18] *With Your Love*, from ***Spitfire***, reaches US #12, as the group performs *Miracles* at the Don Kirshner Rock Awards.
[28] ***Spitfire*** is certified platinum by the RIAA.
Dec [25] *St. Charles* peaks at US #64, as Hot Tuna's ***Hoppkorv*** makes US #116.

1977

Mar [5] ***Flight Log (1966-1976)***, an anthology of Airplane, Starship, Hot Tuna, Slick and Kantner material, lands at US #37.

1978

May [6] ***Earth*** hits US #5, having been certified platinum by the RIAA on the 4th.
[13] The extracted *Count On Me* hits US #8.
[20] Hot Tuna's ***Double Dose*** reaches US #92.
June [17] Slick's alcohol problem prevents her from taking the stage at the "Lorelei Festival" in Hamburg, West Germany. As a result, fans riot, stealing or destroying much of the band's equipment, and causing the cancellation of their final German date.
[24] The group appears at the "Knebworth Festival", Knebworth, Herts., without Slick, who has effectively quit the band.
July [29] *Runaway* reaches US #12.
Oct [7] *Crazy Feelin'* makes US #54. Balin quits the band, leaving Kantner as the only original member.

1979

Mar [10] Second collection of hits, ***Jefferson Starship Gold***, reaches US #20.
Apr [12] The vocal gap is filled by Mickey Thomas (b. Dec. 3, 1949, Cairo, GA), who sang lead vocal on Elvin Bishop's *Fooled Around And Fell In Love*. Barbata leaves, and is replaced by Aynsley Dunbar (b. Jan. 10, 1946, Liverpool, Lancs.).
May [12] The new line-up debuts live at a free concert in Golden Gate Park, San Francisco.
Nov [12] Balin presents a rock opera, "Rock Justice", in a four-day run at the Old Waldorf club, San Francisco.
Dec [31] Jefferson Starship's New Year's Eve concert at X6s club, San Francisco, is widely broadcast live on US radio.

1980

Jan [19] *Jane* reaches US #14. (The group plays a benefit concert at Oakland-Almeda County Coliseum, Oakland, CA, in aid of the people of Kampuchea, with the Grateful Dead and the Beach Boys.)
Feb [2] ***Freedom At Point Zero*** hits US #10.
Mar [1] The extracted *Jane* reaches UK #21.
[15] ***Freedom At Point Zero*** reaches UK #22.
[22] *Girl With The Hungry Eyes* makes US #55.
May [3] Slick's solo album, ***Dreams***, reaches US #32.
June [14] ***Dreams*** reaches UK #28.
Oct [25] Kantner suffers a stroke, from which he will fully recover.

1981

Mar Slick rejoins Jefferson Starship, just as her solo album, ***Welcome To The Wreckers' Ball***, peaks at US #48.
May [23] The group's *Find Your Way Back* reaches US #29.
June The band's album, ***Modern Times***, reaches US #26, as Balin's first solo set, ***Balin***, peaks at US #35.
Aug [8] The group's *Stranger* reaches US #48, with Balin's solo ballad, *Hearts*, hitting US #8.
Oct [24] *Atlanta Lady (Something About Your Love)*, the second single from Balin's album, reaches US #27.

1982

May [28] The group takes part in a benefit concert for the Vietnam Veterans' Project, at the Moscone Center in San Francisco, with Boz Scaggs, Country Joe McDonald and the Grateful Dead.
Oct Drummer Don Baldwin (ex-Elvin Bishop Band) joins, Dunbar having left after album sessions have been completed.
Dec [11] *Be My Lady* reaches US #28.

1983

Mar [5] Balin's *What Love Is*, makes US #63, as his second solo album, ***Lucky***, peaks at US #165.
[19] The group's *Winds Of Change* makes US #38, as its parent album ***Winds Of Change*** reaches US #26.
Aug Kantner's solo effort ***The Planet Earth Rock And Roll Orchestra*** is released in the US.

1984

June The group begins an extensive North American tour to promote the Ron Nevison-produced ***Nuclear Furniture***, which enters the US chart, on its way to #28.
July [21] Power ballad, *No Way Out*, written by Peter and Ina Wolf, reaches US #23.
Sept [29] *Layin' It On The Line* peaks at US #66.
Oct Kantner appears on stage with Balin's band at Golden Gate Park, to perform an old Jefferson Airplane song, *It's No Secret*.

1985

Mar After much legal wrangling, Kantner has departed from the band with a lump sum of $250,000 and the provision that Jefferson is dropped from the band's name. Frieberg has followed him, their departure confirmed by Thomas as a sacking during an interview on MTV. The group initially plays as Starship Jefferson but soon settles on the abbreviated Starship. (Meanwhile, the Kantner, Balin and Casaday Band debuts at the eighth Annual Bay Area Music Awards. After club appearances and a free gig in Golden Gate Park, Balin leaves his own group to join the KBC Band full time.)
Nov [16] First Starship single, *We Built This City*, tops the US chart. Written by Martin Page, Bernie Taupin, Dennis Lambert and Peter Wolf, it achieves a chart peak not attained by either Jefferson Airplane or Jefferson Starship. With Freiberg departing during its recording, the parent album, ***Knee Deep In The Hoopla***, hits US #7.
Dec The KBC Band makes its official debut at the re-opening of the Fillmore. Signe Anderson takes the stage for *It's No Secret*.
[21] *We Built This City* reaches UK #12.

1986

Feb Ballad *Sara* peaks at UK #66.
Mar [15] *Sara* tops the US chart for a week. (Though written by co-producer Peter Wolf with his wife Ina, the song is named after Thomas' wife.)
Apr [23] Starship cancels a tour of Europe.
May [24] *Tomorrow Doesn't Matter Tonight* reaches US #26.
July China Kantner makes a guest appearance on US MTV. The band becomes the first national spokesgroup for the National Network of Runaway Youth Services.
[26] Starship's *Before I Go* peaks at US #68.
Dec [13] The KBC Band, comprising Kantner, Balin and Casady, makes US #89 with *It's Not You, It's Not Me*, while the parent (debut) album, ***KBC Band***, reaches US #75.

1987

Apr [4] Starship's power ballad, *Nothing's Gonna Stop Us Now*, used as the theme for the film "Mannequin", tops the US chart.
May [9] Starship's first UK chart-topper finally comes, more than two decades after the original formation of Jefferson Airplane: *Nothing's Gonna Stop Us Now* hits UK #1, where it will stay for four weeks, and is the second-biggest selling single of the year in Britain. Meanwhile, in the US, a double compilation album, ***2400 Fulton Street***, credited to Jefferson Airplane, and including re-mastered versions of songs from the group's first six studio albums, reaches US #138.
June [20] Starship participates in the 20th-anniversary "Summer Of Love" concert in San Francisco.
July [18] ***No Protection*** reaches UK #26.
Aug [29] *It's Not Over ('Til It's Over)* hits US #9.
Sept ***No Protection***, including both recent Top 10 hits, reaches US #12.

Nov [7] *Beat Patrol*, taken from the album, stops at US #46.

1988

Aug Starship performs at the annual "Reading Festival", Reading, Berks.
Nov Slick, Kantner, Kaukonen and Casady begin writing and rehearsing for a forthcoming album and tour.

1989

Jan [14] *Wild Again*, Starship's contribution to the Tom Cruise-starring movie "Cocktail", peaks at US #73.
Apr The group wins its lawsuit, first filed in 1966, against former manager Matthew Katz.
June [22] Slick, commenting on Jefferson Airplane's forthcoming reunion album (which will reunite her with Kantner, Kaukonen, Casaday and Balin for a permanent new Jefferson Airplane), says, "We're your parents' worst nightmare because now we are your parents."
Aug Starship's ***Love Among The Cannibals***, recorded by the remaining members with new additons, Brett Bloomfield (bass) and Mark Morgan (keyboards), makes US #64.
[29] During a US reunion tour, Jefferson Airplane, augmented by Kenny Aronoff (drums), Peter Kaukonen (guitar), Zebra's Randy Jackson (guitar) and Tim Gorman (keyboards), plays at the New York State Fair, Syracuse, NY.
Sept [23] Jefferson Airplane's comeback album, ***Jefferson Airplane***, released on Epic Records, and featuring the current line-up of Balin, Slick, Kantner, Kaukonen and Casady now joined by Kenny Aronoff, who has effectively replaced Dryden, enters the US chart, set to make #85. (Much of the album has been recorded individually by each group member. Balin cut his tracks with Toto.)
Oct [7] Jefferson Airplane gives a free concert in Golden Gate Park for a 65,000 crowd. Each fan is asked to bring a can of food to donate to the San Francisco Food Bank. Starship's *It's Not Enough* reaches US #12.
Nov Starship, now comprising Thomas (vocals), Baldwin (drums), Chaquico (guitar), Morgan (keyboards) and Bloomfield (bass), have to postpone a planned tour, after Thomas suffers facial injuries in a bar-room brawl. He is hospitalized with a broken cheek-bone, which requires reconstructive plastic surgery.
Dec [16] Starship's *I Didn't Mean To Stay All Night* peaks at US #75.

1990

Mar [8] Jefferson Airplane is named Most Unwelcome Comeback in **Rolling Stone** magazine's 1989 Critics Awards.

1992

As various off-shoot combinations continue to work - Jefferson Starship The Next Generation, comprising Kantner, Casady, Creach, Gorman, Slick Aguilar, Prairie Prince and Darby Gould; Hot Tuna with Casady, Kaukonen and Michael Falzarano; Kantner fronting his own Wooden Ships band and Balin releasing the ***Better Generation*** solo album (including the Airplane tracks *It's No Secret* and *Volunteers*) on GWE Records, RCA releases a 51-track three, CD/cassette boxed-set career retrospective, ***Jefferson Airplane Loves You***, comprising live numbers, alternative takes and previously unreleased material.

1993

Jan [25] Slick presents a eulogy to the late rock promoter and former Airplane manager, Bill Graham, in honoring him with the Award Of Merit at the 20th annual American Music Awards, held at the Shrine Auditorium, Los Angeles.
Apr [30] Jefferson Starship's "Deep Space 1993" tour begins. (Balin now joins the Next Generation line-up.)

1994

Feb [22] Papa John Creach dies of heart and respiratory problems in Los Angeles at the age of 76.
June [7] Slick is sentenced to 200 hours of community service and four A.A. meetings a week for three months after pointing a loaded gun at a police officer, called to her Tiburon, CA home to investigate a domestic dispute on March 5th.

1995

Jan [21] Slick, Kantner, Balin, Casady, Gould, Aguilar, Prince, Gorman, Merl Saunders and David LaFlamme play at the House of Blues tribute to Papa John Creach in Los Angeles.
June [27] Starship, now comprising Kantner, Balin, Casady, Gorman, Prince, Aguilar and Gould, releases a new album ***Deep Space/Virgin Sky*** on the Intersound label, as they continue a current US tour which will include an August 12th performance in front of a totally nude crowd at the 160-acre Turtle Lake Resort, Union City, MI nudist park for the American Association for Nude Recreation.

1996

Jan With Slick as a no-show, reportedly suffering from a foot ailment, the Grateful Dead's Phil Lesh inducts Jefferson Airplane into the Rock and Roll Hall of Fame at the 11th annual dinner from New York's Waldorf Astoria Hotel. The group sings *Volunteers* at the perfunctory after dinner jam.

THE JESUS & MARY CHAIN

William Reid (guitar, vocals); **Jim Reid** (guitar, vocals); **Douglas Hart** (bass); **Bobby Gillespie** (drums)

1984

May William Reid (b. Oct. 28, 1958, East Kilbride, Scotland) and his younger brother Jim (b. Dec. 29, 1961, East Kilbride) have formed a band in 1983 with Hart, after writing and recording songs at home on a portastudio, bought by their father with his severance pay, and sending out their bedroom demos as the Poppy Seeds. William has already worked in a cheese-packing plant at age 16, while Jim, also leaving school at 16, has been employed by Rolls-Royce Aerospace. Having recruited an interim drummer, Murray Dalglish, by way of a classified ad, to play their first gig at Glasgow's Nightmovers club, the Reid brothers and Hart now move to London, where they meet Alan McGee, owner of the small independent Creation label, who signs them and becomes their manager.
June [9] Having moved into a bedsit in Fulham, London, the Jesus & Mary Chain play at McGee's Living Room club, above the Roebuck pub in Tottenham Court Road, London.
Oct [11] Gillespie (b. June 22, 1964, Scotland) makes his debut with the band at Glasgow's Venue, also appearing as a member of his own Primal Scream outfit, as the group embarks on a Creation package tour of Europe.
Nov *Upside Down* (with a B-side revival of Syd Barrett's *Vegetable Man*), produced by McGee's friend "Slaughter" Joe Foster, is released. Recorded at a cost of £174, it will eventually sell over 35,000 copies. McGee's expert promotion of the band brings media attention, as the group plays live sets, sometimes consisting of only two songs, predictably interesting the UK music press.
Dec The group is arrested in West Germany and charged with possession of amphetamine sulphate, after playing at the UK ICA Rock Week.

1985

Feb *Upside Down* tops the UK Independent chart. McGee signs the band to the WEA-marketed label, blanco y negro.
Mar *Never Understand*, produced by the Reid brothers, spends four weeks on the UK chart, peaking at #47. A riot follows a particularly short, and over-booked, gig at North London Polytechnic, increasing their post-punk notoriety, during a UK tour, with many cancelled dates.
May WEA's record plant staff refuse to press the group's third single, considering the proposed B-side, *Jesus Sucks*, to be obscene and blasphemous.
June *You Trip Me Up* peaks at UK #55.
Oct Atypical ballad, *Just Like Honey*, makes UK #45.
Nov Their debut album, the guitar-heavy ***Psychocandy***, heralded as a post-punk masterpiece by the UK music press, makes UK #31. (During the year, the band also contributes *Inside Me* to ***Tapeworm***, a **New Musical Express** cassette-only compilation.) Gillespie will leave the lineup the following year to concentrate solely on Primal Scream.

1986

Feb ***Psychocandy*** makes US #188.
Aug *Some Candy Talking* reaches UK #13, helped by a ban by BBC Radio 1 DJ Mike Smith, who refuses to play it because of its apparent references to drugs. Live UK performances follow, with John Moore joining on drums.
Dec The band performs at Kilburn's National Ballroom during an eight-date UK tour, with Moore switching to rhythm guitar and ex-SPK's James Pinker joining on drums.

1987

May Follow-up, *April Skies*, hits UK #8.
Aug *Happy When It Rains* peaks at UK #25.
Sept [12] ***Darklands***, with William Reid writing and singing lead vocal for the first time, hits UK #5 in its week of entry. The album features only the Reid brothers, with no guest musicians. The group, now split from McGee, tours without a drummer, employing a roadie to play a drum-tracks cassette through the PA. The gigs are poorly received.
Oct ***Darklands*** peaks at US #161, as sometime band member John Moore quits the group permanently to set up John Moore's Expressway. (The group's roadie and soundman, Dave Evans, who also plays in Acid Angels in his spare time, joins on rhythm guitar.)
Nov Their North American "Darklands" tour is dogged by gig violence, including an incident at the RPM club in Toronto, ON, Canada, when Reid is arrested after allegedly hitting troublesome fans with a mike stand. Charged with assault, he is later acquitted. The extracted *Darklands* reaches UK #33. The band is thrown off ITV's "The Roxy" for not bothering to mime or pretend to play their instruments for a rehearsal of *Darklands*.
Dec The group is banned from appearing on the short-lived US TV version of "Top Of The Pops" because its name is considered blasphemous.

1988

Apr Jim Reid is given an absolute discharge after agreeing to pay £500 to the Salvation Army, the judge's nominated charity, for the November 1987 Toronto offence.
[16] *Sidewalking* peaks at UK #30, as new drummer, ex-Dif Juz member Richard Thomas, joins.
[30] ***Barbed Wire Kisses***, a compilation of B-sides, out-takes and unreleased material, issued in the absence of a newly-recorded album, hits UK #9 and will peak at US #192. (By year's end, the group will have contributed *Surfin' USA* to the WEA covers album, ***Under The Covers***.)

1989

Sept *Blues From A Gun*, written and produced by the Reids, charts at UK #32.
Oct [21] Fourth album, and again self-produced, ***Automatic*** reaches UK #11, as the band recruits bassist Ben Lurie for a UK tour to promote the release.
Nov Second extract, *Head On*, peaks at UK #57. (The group will contribute *Who Do You Love?* to the "Earthgirls Are Easy" film soundtrack).

1990

Jan [6] *Blues From A Gun* hits #1 on the US Modern Rock survey for the first of two weeks.
[28] They begin a major US tour in Portland, OR, set

to end on March 25th in Pittsburgh, PA.
Feb Various artists collection ***The Last Temptation Of Elvis***, released to benefit the Nordoff-Robbins Music Therapy charity, and including the group's cover of *Guitar Man*, is released in the UK.
Mar [24] ***Automatic*** makes US #105.
Sept [8] A six-date UK mini-tour begins at the Town & Country club, London, as the four-track EP, *Rollercoaster*, makes UK #46.

1992

Jan With Hart and Thomas having quit in April 1991, the Reid brothers work on new material at their own Drugstore Studios, with a new line-up of Lurie (bass), Mathew Parkin (guitar) and Barry Blacker (drums).
Feb [15] *Reverence* debuts at its UK #10 peak. BBC-TV bans the single's new video clip, citing the unacceptable lyrics, "I wanna die just like Jesus, I wanna die just like JFK".
Mar [21] *Far Gone And Out* reaches UK #23.
[24] A nine-date "The Rollercoaster Tour", with Dinosaur Jr., My Bloody Valentine and Blur, opens at Manchester's Apollo Theatre, set to end at London's Brixton Academy on the April 7th.
Apr [4] ***Honey's Dead***, reaches UK #14 in its week of entry.
May [2] Newly signed (in the US only) to Def American at the instigation of A&R executive Marc Geiger, ***Honey's Dead*** debuts at its US #158 peak.
June [24] The group guests on NBC-TV's "Late Night With David Letterman".
July [4] *Almost Gold* debuts at its UK #41 peak.
[13] The "Lollapalooza II" alternative-bands package tour, including the Jesus & Mary Chain, opens at the Shoreline Amphitheatre, Mountain View, CA.
Aug [28] William Reid joins Pearl Jam on stage at the Irvine Meadows, CA "Lollapalooza" finale with seven other guitarists, for a cover of Neil Young's *Rockin In The Free World*, before joining the entire "Lollapalooza" cast for Funkadelic's *Standing On The Verge* at the end of the Red Hot Chili Peppers' set.
Oct [21] Their own North American tour begins at the Duke Ellington Ballroom, DeKalb, IL, set to close on November 22nd at the Universal Amphitheatre, Universal City, CA.
Dec [5] The group, now comprising the Reids, Lurie and new drummer Steve Monti, plays a one-off UK date at London's Brixton Academy.

1993

July [10] EP *The Sound Of Speed EP*, which includes *Snakedriver*, a cut featured on the movie soundtrack to "The Crow", bows at its UK #30 peak.
[24] Its parent album, ***The Sound Of Speed***, reaches UK #15.

1994

July [30] *Sometimes Always*, featuring William Reid's current belle Mazzy Star's Hope Sandoval on vocals, debuts at its UK #22 peak.
Aug [16] The group, together with its publishers Honey Songs and Careers-BMG Publishing Inc., files suit in Manhattan Federal Court seeking unspecified damages and a court order, blocking the use of music in a Reebok commercial, claiming it was stolen from *Reverence*.
[27] Mostly acoustic ***Stoned And Dethroned***, which the band hoped Lee Hazelwood would have produced but is actually helmed by the Reids and features Sandoval on *Sometimes Always* and ex-Pogue Shane MacGowan on *God Help Me*, reaches UK #13 in its week of entry.
Sept [10] ***Stoned And Dethroned*** debuts at its US #98 peak, released on the renamed American Recordings label.
Oct [15] *Sometimes Always* debuts at its US #96 peak, as the group embarks on latest North American tour.
[22] *Come On* debuts at its UK #52 peak.
Nov [2] The band guests on CBS-TV's "Late Show With David Letterman".
Dec [17] The group takes part in the "Deck The Hall Ball" before a sellout crowd at Seattle's Exhibition Hall with Sheryl Crow, Radiohead, the Cramps, Fretblanket and Butt Trumpet.

1995

June [17] *I Hate Rock 'N' Roll* charts for a week at UK #61.
Oct [27] ***Stoned And Dethroned*** is given the College Award at the annual PRS/ASCAP Awards held in London.

JESUS JONES

Mike Edwards (vocals, guitar); **Jerry De Borg** (guitar, vocals); **Iain Baker** (keyboards, samples); **Al Jaworski** (bass, vocals); **Gen** (drums)

1988

Nov Edwards (June 22, 1964, London), inspired from an early age to pursue a career in music, not least by his purchase - in 1973 - of the Sweet's *Hellraiser*, having travelled the world with his parents during adolescence, has moved from the West Country to London in 1986, with schoolfriends Gen (b. Simon Matthews, Apr. 23, 1964, Devizes, Wilts.) and Jaworski (b. Jan. 31, 1966, Plymouth, Devon), initially forming Big Colour, which has evolved into Camouflage and finally Jesus Jones by the beginning of 1988. Always the central force in the band, Edwards has recruited De Borg (b. Oct. 30, 1963, Kentish Town, London), and Baker (b. Sept. 29, 1965, Carshalton, Surrey), who will go by the name Barry D until 1992, and has sent a demo to ex-Teardrop Explodes keyboardist Dave Balfe, who is now running his own Food label and immediately signs the band.

1989

Feb Their single debut, *Info-Freako*, made as a demo for £125, makes UK #42.
July *Never Enough* reaches UK #42, as the group embarks on its first UK tour.
Aug [27] Jesus Jones performs on the last day of the annual "Reading Festival", Reading, Berks.
Sept *Bring It On Down* makes UK #46.
Oct [14] Their debut album, ***Liquidizer***, reaches UK #32, showcasing the band's anti-retro, sample-heavy, dance-rock techno-fusion musical mix, directed by Edwards.
Nov The group plays the final gig of its first headlining UK tour at London's Town & Country club, before a sellout crowd of 2,200.
Dec [9] *I Don't Want That Kind Of Love*, from the various-artists Food EP, *Food Christmas*, also featuring Crazyhead and Diesel Park West, charts for a week at UK #63. Its promotional video has been taped at Star Trax in Piccadilly Circus, London, for a total cost of £24.95.

1990

Feb The group becomes one of the first UK acts to perform in Romania, playing four dates.
Mar They embark on a European tour supporting the Cramps, followed by further gigging in Australia and Japan in April.
May [5] Their breakthrough hit, the Edwards-penned *Real Real Real*, reaches UK #19.
[10] The group begins a six-date UK tour at the Bierkeller, Bristol, Avon, set to end on the 17th at Kilburn's National Ballroom.
June The band plays at the annual "Glastonbury Festival", Glastonbury, Somerset.
Aug [26] The group makes its second final-day appearance at the "Reading Festival", Reading, Berks.
Sept [17] They begin a month-long US club tour in San Diego, CA.
Oct [13] *Right Here Right Now* makes UK #31, partly themed on the historic events currently dismantling communism in eastern Europe.
[21] They embark on an eight-date UK tour at the Ritz, Manchester, Gtr. Manchester, set to end with two nights at London's Town & Country club on the 29th and 30th.

1991

Jan [19] The group takes part in the "Great British Music Weekend" at Wembley Arena, Wembley, Middx., as *International Bright Young Thing*, remixed by Phil Harding and Ian Curnow, hits UK #7.
Feb [8] They begin a 16-date UK tour at the Queen's University, Belfast, N. Ireland, set to end on the 27th at London's Town & Country club.
[9] ***Doubt*** debuts at UK #1. The 12-track set is largely written and produced by Edwards, and will eventually sell over two million copies worldwide.
Mar [23] *Who? Where? When?* peaks at UK #21, the fourth extract from ***Doubt***.
Apr [20] The group takes part in "Earth Day Concert 1991" at Foxboro Stadium, Foxborough, MA.
June Still-rising ***Doubt*** is certified gold by the RIAA.
[12] They win the Top Newcomer category at the third International Rock Awards, at London's Docklands Arena.
[22] ***Doubt*** reaches US #25.
[29-30] The band appears at the "Bizarre" Festival in Germany, on a bill with the Alarm, New Model Army and Iggy Pop.
July [13] The group takes part in "Summer XS" at Wembley Stadium, on a bill with INXS, Hothouse Flowers, Deborah Harry, Roachford and Jellyfish, before a sellout crowd of 73,791.
[27] Radio favorite, *Right Here, Right Now*, hits US #2, behind Bryan Adams' *(Everything I Do) I Do It For You*, and re-charts at UK #31.
Aug [22] The band begins a US tour in Miami, FL, which will include three dates at New York, NY's Academy Theatre in October.
Sept [5] "Right Here, Right Now" wins the Best New Artist Video category at the eighth annual MTV Video Music Awards, held at the Universal Amphitheatre, Universal City, CA.
[10] The group appears on syndicated TV's "The Arsenio Hall Show".
Oct [8] They are the musical guest on NBC-TV's "The Tonight Show".
[11-12, 18] The group performs at New York's Academy Theatre.
Nov [9] *Real Real Real* hits US #4, as ***Doubt*** now earns a US platinum disc.
Dec [21] The group appears with other Food acts, Blur, Diesel Park West, Sensitize and Whirlpool, at the "Food Xmas Party" at London's Brixton Academy, with proceeds going to the Great Ormond Street Hospital.

1992

Jan The band performs during the "Rock In Rio II" festival in Brazil.
May [5] The group plays to a sellout crowd of 1,500 at the Academy, New York, during a short US visit. Upon their return to the UK, they will begin work on new tracks with producer Warne Livesey, at Food Records' Think Studios, Camden Town, London.
July [25] They take part in the "Slough Festival '92", Upton Court Park, Slough, Bucks.

1993

Jan [16] *The Devil You Know*, spurred by appearances on "Top Of The Pops", "Going Live!" and "The O-Zone", hits UK #10.
Feb [6] Their third album, once again dominated by Edwards' techno-rock vision, ***Perverse***, produced by Livesey, debuts at its UK #6 peak, and will make US #59 the following week.
Mar [16] The group begins a 14-date UK tour at the Corn Exchange, Cambridge, Cambs., set to end on April 1st at London's Astoria Theatre.
Apr [10] *The Right Decision* makes UK #36 in its week of entry.
[16] A US tour opens at the Palace of Auburn Hills, Auburn Hills, MI.
June [6] The group embarks on Japanese dates at Factory Hall, Sapporo.
[22] They perform at New York's Roseland Ballroom, supported by Stereo MC's, during a second North

American swing.
July [17] *Zeroes & Ones* reaches UK #30.

1996

May [4] Still working on its next abum for EMI, the band undertakes a small-venue UK tour, including tonight's gig at the Joiner's Arms, Southampton, Hants.

JETHRO TULL

Ian Anderson (vocals, flute);
Mick Abrahams (guitar); **Glenn Cornick** (bass);
Clive Bunker (drums)

1963

Anderson (b. Aug. 10, 1947, Edinburgh, Lothian, Scotland), who has moved to Blackpool, Lancs., at the age of 12, where his father is owner of the RSA Boiler Fluid Company Ltd., forms the Blades, named after James Bond's club, in Blackpool, with ex-Atlantics Michael Stephens on guitar and fellow blues-minded schoolfriends, Jeffrey Hammond-Hammond (b. July 30, 1946) on bass and drummer John Evans (b. Mar. 28, 1948). Their first gig, at the Holy Family youth club, nets £2. They go on to play jazz/blues and danceable soul music for northern club audiences and, in 1965, name-change - first to the John Evan Band (Hammond thinks Evan sounds better than Evans) and then the John Evan Smash, apparently to please Evans' mother, who paid for the group's van.

1967

Nov With Cornick (b. Apr. 24, 1947, Barrow-in-Furness, Cumbria) having replaced Hammond-Hammond on bass, the group moves to Luton, Beds., to be near London and the heart of the UK blues boom. Within days, the road-weary crew has left, but Anderson and Cornick remain in the capital.
Dec The duo forms a new band with guitarist Abrahams (b. Apr. 7, 1943, Luton) and drummer Bunker (b. Dec. 12, 1946, Blackpool), both members of McGregor's Engine, and signs to Terry Ellis and Chris Wright's booking agency, playing two gigs a week under a variety of names, including Navy Blue and Bag of Blues. Jethro Tull, named after the 18th-century agriculturalist, receives the most audience enthusiasm, and sticks.

1968

Feb MGM Records releases Abrahams' *Sunshine Day*, taken from a Derek Lawrence-produced demo, with an earlier Lawrence recording of the John Evan Band on the B-side, its first pressing mistakenly crediting the band as Jethro Toe.
June The group gains a residency at London's Marquee club. Ellis and Wright suggest that Anderson should abandon his flute playing, giving the focus to lead guitarist Abrahams, but the idea is resisted.
[29] The band supports Pink Floyd at the first free rock festival in London's Hyde Park.
Aug [11] Jethro Tull becomes the sensation of the "Sunbury Jazz & Blues Festival", Sunbury-on-Thames, Surrey, gaining rapturous music-press notices. On the strength of this, Island Records offers a recording contract.
[23] The group performs again at London's Marquee.
Nov Their debut album, the blues-tinged ***This Was***, released on Island, hits UK #10 and includes the extracted *A Song For Jeffrey*, dedicated to ex-member Hammond-Hammond.
[2] Jethro Tull performs at London's Roundhouse, as Anderson's unique stage presence, including the wearing of long ragged overcoats and standing on one leg while playing the flute, grabs the limelight.
Dec A personality clash develops between Anderson and Abrahams, who leaves to form Blodwyn Pig.
[12] The band takes part in the Rolling Stones' "Rock'n'Roll Circus" (filmed as a TV spectacular, but never screened).

1969

Jan ***Love Story***, the last album featuring Abrahams, reaches UK #29. Tony Iommi (later of Black Sabbath), and Davy O'List of the Nice are interim members, before Martin Barre (b. Nov. 17, 1946) joins permanently.
[24] Jethro Tull makes its US debut, sharing the bill with Led Zeppelin, at the Fillmore East, New York, NY, at the start of a two-month tour.
Mar [13-16] The group plays further dates at the Fillmore East, on a bill with Creedence Clearwater Revival and Santana.
Apr [12] Reprise issues ***This Was*** in the US, set to peak at #62.
May *Living In The Past*, the first single featuring Barre, hits UK #3. The group performs what will prove to be its most successful UK single on BBC1-TV's "Top Of The Pops" for the first time.
[6] Jethro Tull embarks on a six-date UK tour, with Ten Years After and Clouds, at the Free Trade Hall, Manchester, Lancs., set to end on the 15th at the Town Hall, Birmingham, Warks.
June [20-22] Jethro Tull participates in the three-day "Newport '69 Pop Festival" at Devonshire Downs, Northridge, CA.
July [3-6] The band performs at the four-day "Newport Jazz Festival", Newport, RI.
Aug [9] ***Stand Up***, in a gatefold sleeve from which card figures of the band actually "stand up" when opened, tops the UK chart. All its songs are written by Anderson, apart from his arrangement of Bach's *Bouree*.
[12-14] The group performs at San Francisco's Fillmore West, sharing a bill with Chuck Berry.
Nov [15] ***Stand Up*** climbs to US #20, while *Sweet Dream* hits UK #7. It is the band's first release on Ellis and Wright's formative Chrysalis label (Island will handle the next two albums).

1970

Jan Double A-side, *The Witch's Promise/Teacher*, hits UK #4.
Feb [7] Anderson marries record company secretary Jennie Franks at Watford Register Office. She will contribute lyrics to ***Aqualung***, but the marriage will not last.
May ***Benefit***, Tull's last blues-oriented affair, and featuring early cohort John Evan (now reverting back to John Evans) as a keyboardist (joining initially on a temporary basis, he will stay for ten years), hits UK #3 and US #11, and features the remaining line-up of Anderson, Barre, Bunker and Cornick.
July [3-5] The group plays at the three-day "Atlanta Pop Festival" at the Middle Georgia Raceway in Byron, GA, before an estimated 200,000 people, on a bill with Jimi Hendrix, B.B. King, Johnny Winter and others.
Oct The band, including Hammond-Hammond and drummer Barrie Barlow (b. Sept. 10, 1949), returns to the US for a 31-date tour.
Nov [4] In the midst of the tour, the band plays a benefit concert at Carnegie Hall in New York, in the presence of the Duke and Duchess of Bedford. $10,000 is raised to benefit the Phoenix House Drug Rehabilitation Centre.
Dec [6] Cornick leaves to form his own band, Wild Turkey, and Hammond-Hammond rejoins full time.

1971

Apr Their fourth album, ***Aqualung***, an Anderson-penned concept album loosely based on organized religion, co-produced by Anderson and Terry Ellis, hits UK #4.
June ***Aqualung*** hits US #7, the group's first US Top 10 success.
[10] The band plays in a cloud of tear gas at the Red Rock Amphitheatre, Denver, CO, after police fire canisters into the audience. 28 people are hospitalized. On their return to the UK, Bunker leaves to get married (going on to form Jude with Robin Trower, Frankie Miller and Jim Dewar), and is replaced by Barlow, from Requiem.
Aug From ***Aqualung***, *Hymn 43* is the group's first US chart single, at #91. It receives heavy FM airplay, as do the album cuts *Locomotive Breath* and *Crosseyed Mary*.
Sept Five-song EP, headed by *Life Is A Long Song*, reaches UK #11.
Oct [18] Jethro Tull makes its Madison Square Garden, New York, debut during a US tour.
Nov [14] The group makes the first of what will be a record-setting 14 appearances at the Boston Garden, MA.

1972

Feb The band makes its first tour of Europe, with gigs in Amsterdam, Rotterdam and Brussels.
Mar [2] Tull begins a UK tour at Portsmouth Guildhall, including dates at London's Royal Albert Hall on the 21st and 22nd.
Apr ***Thick As A Brick*** hits UK #5.
June [3] ***Thick As A Brick*** hits US #1 for the first of two weeks.
July Double compilation album, ***Living In The Past***, featuring mostly unreleased or singles-only material, plus a live side recorded at New York's Carnegie Hall, hits UK #8.
Nov [11] ***Living In The Past*** enters the US survey set to hit #3, and will subsequently be revered as a career peak.

1973

Jan [13] *Living In The Past*, extracted for the first time as a US single, reaches #11.
June [22-23] Band previews material from its forthcoming album, ***A Passion Play***, at concerts in Wembley, Middx.
Aug [18] ***A Passion Play*** is poorly received by many critics, labelled pretentious. Regardless, and having already made UK #13 in July, it hits US #1 for one week (a single edit of title track having already peaked at US #80). (During the month the group announce that they are retiring from live performances because of "critical abuse". Anderson will admit later that this statement was a silly mistake.)

1974

Nov [9] Largely orchestral (but song-based) album, ***War Child***, reaches UK #14 and will hit US #2. The album had been developed in conjunction with a planned film which never surfaces. The lengthy world tour to promote the album includes a string quartet augmenting the band.

1975

Jan The extracted *Bungle In The Jungle* makes US #11.
Oct [4] Recorded in the band's new mobile studio, ***Minstrel In The Gallery*** reaches UK #20 and will hit US #7.
Nov [1] Title track, *Minstrel In The Gallery*, peaks at US #79.

1976

Jan Hammond-Hammond leaves, to concentrate on art, and is replaced by John Glascock (b. 1953, London), from Carmen.
Feb [7] ***M.U. - The Best Of Jethro Tull Vol. 1***, containing a previously unreleased track, *Rainbow Blues*, makes UK #44 and will reach US #13.
Mar *Locomotive Breath*, issued as a US single, reaches #62.
May [29] ***Too Old To Rock'n'Roll, Too Young To Die*** reaches UK #25. It contains material taken from a play planned by Anderson and David Palmer and never staged, but forms the basis of the band's ITV special.
July [3] ***Too Old To Rock'n'Roll, Too Young To Die*** reaches US #14.
Dec Seasonal EP, *Ring Out Solstice Bells*, reaches UK #28, as Jethro Tull appears again on BBC1-TV's "Top Of The Pops" as a last-minute replacement for Rod Stewart.

1977

Feb [1] The group embarks on its first UK tour in three years in Aberdeen, Scotland. (Anderson acknowledges, in a newspaper article, that he paid a

£500,000 lump-sum tax bill, but says that when he first came to London he cleaned toilets for a living, and has kept one of the urinals as a souvenir in his house.)

Mar [12] ***Songs From The Wood*** reaches UK #13 and will hit US #8. The album explores Anderson's interest in folk music (he has recently produced an album for Steeleye Span).

May *The Whistler* peaks at US #59, as keyboard player David Palmer joins the band.

Aug The Scotsman newspaper reports that Anderson is planning to buy Strathaird on the Isle of Skye for £250,000, including 15,000 acres with a mansion and coastal township. (His management of the Strathaird salmon processing plant will prove highly profitable, and he will also become a founding member of the Environmental Committee of the Scottish Salmon Growers' Association.)

Oct ***Repeat : The Best Of Jethro Tull Vol. 2*** is released. With only one new track, it stalls at US #94 and fails to make UK Top 50.

Dec The group is awarded the Gold Ticket for playing to over 100,000 fans at Madison Square Garden.

1978

May [1] A nine-date "Heavy Horses" UK tour opens at Edinburgh's Usher Hall, set to end on the 9th and 10th with sellout shows at London's Hammersmith Odeon.

[13] Pastoral-themed ***Heavy Horses*** reaches UK #20 and will make US #19.

Oct [9] The band's US tour is highlighted by a concert at Madison Square Garden, broadcast live to a 400-million worldwide TV audience.

[28] ***Live : Bursting Out*** performance set reaches UK #17 and will make US #21.

1979

Oct [12] Anderson, unlucky not to catch the missile in his lengthy trademark beard, is pierced in the eye by a thorn from a rose thrown by an over-zealous fan at a concert in New York's Madison Square Garden, during the "Stormwatch" tour.

[13] ***Stormwatch*** reaches UK #27 and US #22. Glascock, who has never played live with the band, has become too ill to record, leaving Anderson to play the bass.

Nov [17] Glascock dies after open-heart surgery, aged 26. Ex-Fairport Convention's Dave Pegg (b. Nov. 2, 1947, Birmingham) joins the band.

1980

June Anderson records a solo album. As well as Barre and Pegg from Jethro Tull, he brings in Eddie Jobson (b. Apr. 28, 1955, Billingham) (ex-Roxy Music) on keyboards and violin, and Mark Craney on drums. The group leader will release it as a Jethro Tull album, but discards Barlow, Evan and Palmer in favor of the new line-up. (Evan and Palmer will form Tallis, and subsequently Barlow, Tandoori Cassette with Zal Cleminson, Charlie Tumahai and Ronnie Leahy.)

Sept [13] The resultant album, ***A***, with Jobson's influence evident, reaches UK #25 and will climb to US #30. Jobson stays only for the subsequent tour, before leaving to go solo. (He will feature on the 1981 full-length video "Slipstream".)

1982

Apr [24] ***Broadsword And The Beast***, featuring new drummer Gerry Conway (b. Sept. 11, 1947, Norfolk) and keyboard player Peter-John Vettesse, who had been spotted playing in the band Rich and Famous, reaches UK #27, after a group tour. Paul Burgess takes over from Conway on the US leg of the trek.

May ***Broadsword And The Beast*** makes US #19.

Aug [5] The group takes part in the "5th Golden Summernight Concert" in Nurnberg, West Germany, with Neil Young.

1984

Sept After Anderson's solo debut, the synthesizer-oriented ***Walk Into Light***, with help only from Vettesse, has made UK #78 the previous November, Tull's ***Under Wraps*** reaches UK #18 and US #76, and features new drummer Doane Perry, with Vettesse making another important contribution. Tull tours the UK and Europe but, during Northern American dates, Anderson develops a throat infection serious enough to cause the postponement of later shows. *Lap Of Luxury* peaks at UK #70.

1985

Mar The group performs a special for German TV, with Jobson temporarily returning on keyboards, and features in a London Symphony Orchestra presentation of Jethro Tull's music, which plays in Europe and the US. (Anderson's throat becomes problematic again and he decides to take a sabbatical for a year.)

Oct ***Original Masters***, a compilation of the band's best work up to 1977, stops at UK #63.

1986

Jan *Said She Was A Dancer* peaks at UK #55.

A Classic Case - The London Symphony Orchestra Plays The Music Of Jethro Tull, from the earlier German TV special, makes US #93.

1987

Sept [26] ***Crest Of A Knave*** reaches UK #19 and climbs to US #32.

Oct [4] The group begins a world a tour in Edinburgh, Scotland.

1988

June Jethro Tull, now comprising Anderson, Barre, Pegg, Perry and Martin Allcock (keyboards), embarks on a four-week US tour as part of its 20th-anniversary celebration.

July [9] ***20 Years Of Jethro Tull***, a 65-track retrospective collection documenting the band's history and available in five-album, three-cassette, or three-CD format, charts for a week at UK #78 and will make US #97, as the band plays a major anniversary concert at Wembley Arena, Wembley.

1989

Feb [22] Through no fault of its own, the group incongruously, and controversially, wins the Best Hard Rock/Metal Performance nod for ***Crest Of A Knave*** at the 31st annual Grammy Awards, the category's inaugural year.

Sept [2] ***Rock Island*** reaches UK #18 and will make US #56.

Oct [23] The group embarks on the "Rock Island Tour" at RPI Fieldhouse, Troy, NY, set to end December 10th with a sellout show at the Civic Auditorium, San Francisco, CA. The following April 5th, Tull will begin a 24-date UK concert trek.

1990

Sept [1] Jethro Tull supports Fleetwood Mac at Wembley Stadium, Wembley, Middx.

1991

July The group celebrates the forthcoming release of the ***Catfish Rising*** album with a country ceilidh in a barn near Anderson's Home Counties residence, with Fairport Convention providing the music.

Sept [14] ***Catfish Rising*** debuts at its UK #27 peak.

[28] ***Catfish Rising*** bows at its US #88 peak.

Oct [3-4] The group begins a six-date UK tour with two shows at Manchester's Apollo Theatre, set to end on the 9th at London's Hammersmith Odeon.

[10] The band is inducted into the National Association of Brick Distributors' second annual Brick Hall of Fame gala in New York, in recognition of services to the brick industry, for the title of their album, ***Thick As A Brick***.

Nov [6] The group plays a three-song set at a press conference at the New Campus Club, Providence, RI.

[7] A US tour opens at the Civic Center, Providence, set to close at the Civic Center, San Francisco, on December 17th.

1992

Mar [13] A ten-date UK tour bows at the Plymouth Pavilions, Plymouth, Devon, set to end on the 24th at the Guildhall, Portsmouth, Hants.

[21] *Rocks On The Road* debuts at its UK #47 peak.

May [1] The European leg of their latest tour starts.

Sept [26] ***A Little Light Music***, a live acoustic album recorded on their spring European trek, including non-electric versions of past hits and obscure cuts and the traditional folk song, *John Flow*, debuts at its UK #34 peak, as Tull plays its "A Little Light Music" acoustic-set European tour.

Oct [2-3] The group begins a North American tour at the Orpheum Theatre, Boston, MA, set to end on November 10th at the Tower Theatre, Upper Darby, PA.

[10] ***A Little Light Music*** peaks at US #150 in its week of entry.

1993

Apr Celebrating a quarter-century in the music arena, the band releases ***25th Anniversary Box Set*** (four CDs issued in a fancy cigar box with a 48-page booklet), largely - and unusually - comprising remixed, live, previously unreleased and newly recorded material.

[28] Jethro Tull appears on NBC-TV's "The Tonight Show".

May [26] The group performs at the Fairfield Halls, Croydon, Surrey, following a performance on the 25th at the Corn Exchange, Cambridge, Cambs.

[29] The extracted *Living In The Past* reaches UK #32.

Oct [2] Continuing its 25th anniversary celebrations, the band begins a 13-date UK tour at the Arts Centre, Poole, Dorset, set to end on the 21st at the Ulster Hall, Belfast, Northern Ireland.

Nov The band issues ***The Other Box Set***, another hefty career volume, collecting rarities, including the previously unreleased ***Shadow Disaster*** album originally shelved in the '70s.

1994

Mar [18] The group begins a North American tour at Warners Theatre, Fresno, CA. (On occasions when Pegg can't play with the band, his son Matthew takes over.)

Aug [11] The band takes part in a Friends of the Earth benefit at London's Clapham Grand.

1995

May [2] Anderson's solo instrumental album, ***Divinities : Twelve Dances With God***, is released in the US on Angel Records.

Sept [16] Tull's ***Roots To Branches*** reaches UK #20 in its week of entry.

[30] ***Roots To Branches*** charts for a week at US #114.

Nov [14-15] The group, now comprising Anderson, Barre, Perry, Andrew Giddings (keyboards) and Jonathan Noyce (bass), filling in for the on-leave Pegg, plays two sellout dates at New York's Beacon Theatre.

JOAN JETT

See: **THE RUNAWAYS**

JODECI

JoJo (vocals); **K-Ci** (vocals); **Mr. Dalvin** (vocals); **DeVante Swing** (vocals)

1990

The vocal quartet is formed in Tiny Grove, NC by two pairs of singing brothers, the Haileys, JoJo (b. Joel Hailey, June 10, 1971, Charlotte, NC) and K-Ci (b. Cedric Hailey, Sept 2, 1969, Charlotte) and the DeGrates, Devante Swing (b. Donald DeGrate Jr., Sept 29, 1969, Newport News, VA) and Mr. Dalvin (b. Dalvin DeGrate Jr., July 23, 1971, Newport News) who first met while singing in different church choirs in Charlotte. Honing a brand of close harmony, romance-themed soul, which will become part of a new R&B direction in the US headed by the likes of Boyz II Men, the quartet is signed to MCA's Uptown imprint after a live audition at the label.

1991

Dec [14] *Forever My Lady*, co-written and co-produced by Al B. Sure!, reaches US #25.

1992

Feb [22] ***Forever My Lady***, largely helmed by Sure!, a popular mix of doo-wop R&B harmony and new jack swing, reaches US #18.
[29] *Stay* makes US #41.
May [15] Jodeci performs at New York, NY's Madison Square Garden, on a bill with Hammer and Boyz II Men.
Aug [15] *Come And Talk To Me*, already the group's third consecutive US R&B chart-topper, reaches US #11.
Nov [7] *I'm Still Waiting* peaks at US #85.
Dec [9] Jodeci collects the Top R&B Artist, Top R&B Albums Artist, Top R&B Single (*Come Talk To Me*) and Top R&B Album (***Forever My Lady***) trophies at the 3rd annual **Billboard** Music Awards broadcast live by Fox-TV from the Universal Amphitheatre, Universal City, CA.

1993

Jan [16] *Cherish* bows at its UK #56 peak.
Apr During the month, K-Ci and DeVante swing are arraigned on weapons possession and aggravated sexual assault charges in Teaneck, NJ.
May [8] *Let's Go Through The Motions*, featured in the movie "Who's The Man?", makes US #65.
Aug [28] *Lately*, the quartet's US R&B #1 update of Stevie Wonder's 1981 ballad, taken from the group's performance earlier in the year on MTV's "Uptown Unplugged", hits US #4.
Dec [11] Ballad *Cry For You* charts for a week at UK #56.

1994

Feb [5] Their sophomore set, ***Diary Of A Mad Band*** hits US #3.
[19] Already a four-week US R&B chart-topper from January 15th, *Cry For You* reaches US #15.
Mar [15] The group wins the Best R&B Single (*Lately*) and Best Group, Band Or Duo categories at the eighth annual Soul Train Music Awards held at the Shrine Auditorium, Los Angeles, CA.
Apr [16] *Feenin'* reaches US #25.
July [16] *Feenin'* enters at its UK #18 peak.

1995

Jan [28] *Cry For You* bows at its UK #20 pinnacle
June [24] *Freek 'N You* peaks at UK #17 in its week of entry.
July [22] *Freek'N You* reaches US #14.
Aug [5] Having already debuted at its UK #4 high a week earlier, ***The Show, The After Party, The Hotel*** debuts at its US #2 peak.
Nov [12] Having appeared at the UrbanAID 4 LIFEbeat benefit concert in New York the previous month, and towards the end of a US tour with Mary J. Blige, Naughty By Nature, Notorious BIG, Luniz and Adina Howard, Jodeci performs at the Thomas & Mack Center, University of Nevada, Las Vegas, NV, a bill which grosses $137,040 from 4,568 attendees.
Dec [9] *Love U 4 Life* reaches UK #23.

1996

Jan [6] *Love U 4 Life* reaches US #31.

BILLY JOEL

1964

Feb [9] The son of a German immigrant, electrical engineer father Howard Joel and Brooklyn native mother Rosalind (née Hyman), Joel (b. William Martin Joel, May 9, 1949, Hicksville, Long Island, NY), whose major preoccupations while growing up in Hicksville attending the Fork Lane School have been studying the piano and boxing (he has broken his nose as a local young welterweight champ), is inspired by seeing the Beatles on CBS-TV's "The Ed Sullivan Show", and looks for a band to join, finding the Echoes, who become a popular local live attraction with a repertoire built around UK-group hits. The following year he finds work playing piano on sessions at a studio at Levittown, notably for Artie Ripp's Kama Sutra Productions, and producer George "Shadow" Morton. He also continues to play with the Echoes, who become the Emeralds, and then the Lost Souls.

1967

He joins Long Island group the Hassles as keyboard player. Signed to United Artists, their first single is a cover of Sam & Dave's *You Got Me Hummin'* (their only UK release, which Joel will continue to perform live during the '80s). The Hassles release four singles and two albums in the US, ***The Hassles*** and ***Hour Of The Wolf***, over an 18-month period. (A retrospective will be released on CD by EMI in 1991.)

1969

When the Hassles split, Joel and drummer Jon Small form an organ/drums hard-rock duo, called Attila. Joel also briefly becomes a rock critic for the arts magazine **Changes** and plays on sessions for TV ads, including a Chubby Checker ad for Bachman Pretzels.

1970

Attila is released by Epic Records in the US, with a sleeve picture of Joel and Small dressed as barbarians. It bombs and the band splits immediately. Joel enters a period of acute depression (aggravated by the ending of a serious romance), checking himself into Meadowbrook Hospital, where he is placed under psychiatric observation.

1971

Apr Joel signs as a soloist to Family Productions, owned by Ripp. The deal involves a lifetime agreement (Ripp will receive royalties from Joel's hit career for the next two decades).
Nov ***Cold Spring Harbor***, recorded in California, is released on Family Productions, through Paramount. Due to mixing/mastering incompetence the album is pressed sounding too fast (an error not corrected until it is re-mixed in 1984). Joel assembles a band to begin a promotional tour.

1972

Jan Embarrassed by the album, despite good live reviews, he leaves for Los Angeles, CA, with girlfriend Elizabeth Weber (ex-wife of Jon Small), where he spends most of the next six months at the Executive Room on Wilshire Boulevard, playing bar piano in a lounge, using the name Bill Martin (his middle name) - the experience inspires his subsequent composition, *Piano Man*.
Apr [1] Still an unknown, he plays the "Mar Y Sol Festival" in Vega Baja, Puerto Rico, where he comes to the attention of CBS/Columbia Records.

1973

Joel and Weber marry, while she attends UCLA's Graduate School Of Management. He is sought by several major labels after *Captain Jack* is played constantly on station WMMR, having been taken from a Philadelphia, PA show broadcast live by the station in 1972. Columbia's chief executive Clive Davis goes to see Joel in the piano bar in Los Angeles. The label signs him but, to pacify Ripp, has to retain the Family Products Romulus and Remus logo on future Joel releases (for which Ripp will receive 25 cents from each album sold).

1974

Apr His debut Columbia album, the self-penned ***Piano Man***, makes US #27 (earning a gold disc for half a million sales some two years later). The autobiographical extracted title track, *Piano Man*, reaches US #25.
July *Worse Comes To Worst*, also from the album, makes US #80.
Aug *Travelin' Prayer* peaks at US #77. Joel puts together a stage band comprising guitarist Don Evans, bass player Pat McDonald, steel guitar and banjo player Tom Whitehorse and drummer Rhys Clark, and plays dates supporting the Beach Boys, the J. Geils Band and the Doobie Brothers. His first major live success is in Philadelphia, where he headlines.

1975

Jan *The Entertainer* makes US #34, as ***Streetlife Serenade*** makes US #35. Joel joins James William Guercio and Larry Fitzgerald's Caribou management company. He and his wife move back from California to New York, where Joel finds renewed songwriting creativity (he claims to have written *New York State Of Mind* within 20 minutes of entering his New York home).

1976

July ***Turnstiles*** peaks at US #122 and includes *Say Goodbye To Hollywood*, a celebration of the Joels' move and a Phil Spector tribute, which will later be covered by Ronnie Spector, as well as the E. Street Band. Produced by Joel and recorded in New York with Elton John's sidemen, Nigel Olsson and Dee Murray, the sessions have not, in Joel's opinion, been entirely successful. Having fired producer Guercio early in the recording, Joel also leaves Guercio's Caribou management, appointing his wife Elizabeth as manager. She renegotiates his contract with Columbia, fixing a new and more favorable royalty rate of $1 per album.

1977

Apr CBS holds a reception at London's Grosvenor House Hotel for Joel, who is carried around the room in boxer's garb by British boxers, Terry Downes, Alan Minter, Colin Powes and John H. Stracey.
Sept He appears on NBC-TV's "Saturday Night Live", playing a new song, *Just The Way You Are*, to a viewing audience of 20 million.
Dec Also recorded in New York, the Phil Ramone-produced ***The Stranger*** hits US #2 and will earn a platinum disc. (Firmly establishing Joel as one of America's leading singer-songwriters, it will become Columbia Records' second-biggest selling album of all time, after Simon & Garfunkel's ***Bridge Over Troubled Water***.)

1978

Feb Radio-bound ballad, *Just The Way You Are*, from the album, hits US #3 (selling over a million copies) and makes Joel's UK chart debut, at #19. After recording the song, Joel himself did not want it included on the album, but was persuaded to do so by Linda Ronstadt and Phoebe Snow who heard it in the studio shortly after it was recorded. Becoming a standard, the song will attract over 200 cover versions, including a UK #12-peaking treatment by Barry White in December.
Mar [19] Joel makes his UK debut performing at London's Theatre Royal, Drury Lane. While in Britain, he also appears on a BBC2-TV "The Old Grey Whistle Test" special.
May [27] *Movin' Out (Anthony's Song)*, also taken from ***The Stranger***, makes US #17 (and UK #35 a month later).
July [8] *Only The Good Die Young* makes US #24, but results in Joel being banned by Catholic radio stations due to its apparent anti-Catholic views - which he denies.
[22] ***The Stranger*** reaches UK #25.
Oct Ballad *She's Always A Woman*, the fourth excerpt from ***The Stranger***, reaches US #17.
Nov [18] ***52nd Street*** begins an eight-week stretch at the top of the US chart, selling over two million copies in its first month of release alone.

1979

Jan The extracted up-tempo *My Life*, Joel's second million-selling single, hits US #3 and UK #12.
Feb [15] Joel wins Record Of The Year and Song Of The Year for *Just The Way You Are* at the 21st annual Grammy Awards.

Mar *Big Shot*, also from ***52nd Street***, reaches US #14.
[17] ***52nd Street*** now hits its UK #10 peak during a 43-week chart run.
May *Until The Night*, a track from ***52nd Street*** written as a tribute to the Righteous Brothers, makes UK #50. *Honesty* reaches US #24.

1980

Feb [27] Joel wins Best Pop Vocal Performance, Male, and Album Of The Year for ***52nd Street*** at the 22nd annual Grammy Awards.
May *You May Be Right* hits US #7, as *All For Leyna* makes UK #40.
June [14] Ramone-produced ***Glass Houses***, featuring studio regulars David Brown (guitars), Richie Cannata (organ), Liberty DeVito (drums), Russell Javors (guitars) and Doug Stegmeyer (bass), begins a six-week reign at US #1 (another platinum disc) having hit UK #9 on Mar [29].
(Joel is awarded the Gold Ticket for playing to over 100,000 fans at New York, NY's Madison Square Garden.)
July [19] *It's Still Rock'n'Roll To Me* tops the US chart, eventually selling over a million.
Sept *It's Still Rock'n'Roll To Me* makes UK #14. *Don't Ask Me Why*, also from the album, reaches US #19.
Nov *Sometimes A Fantasy*, the last extract from ***Glass Houses***, peaks at US #36.

1981

Jan [30] Joel nabs the Favorite Album, Pop/Rock category at the eighth annual American Music Awards, held at the ABC-TV Studios, Hollywood, CA.
Feb [25] He wins the Best Rock Vocal Performance, Male category for ***Glass Houses*** at the 23rd annual Grammy Awards.
Oct [10] Live album, ***Songs In The Attic***, consisting mostly of earlier, pre-***Stranger*** songs, makes UK #57, and will hit US #8, and is notable as the first digitally-recorded live album.
Nov [7] Extracted from it, a new version of *Say Goodbye To Hollywood* reaches US #17.

1982

Jan Ballad *She's Got A Way* reaches US #23.
Apr [15] Joel breaks his left wrist when a car hits his motorcycle in Long Island. He will remain in hospital more than a month for surgery on his hand.
July Joel and his wife Elizabeth are divorced.
Nov ***The Nylon Curtain*** hits US #7, becoming a further million seller, having made UK #27 on Oct [9]. Taken from it, *Pressure* reaches US #20. Meanwhile, on vacation in St. Barthlemy in the Caribbean, Joel, playing piano in the bar of a hotel, meets model Christie Brinkley.
Dec [27] Joel plays a benefit concert in Allentown, PA, as *Allentown* climbs the US chart.
[29] Another benefit concert, at Nassau Veterans Memorial Coliseum, Uniondale, NY, raises $125,000 for Joel's own Charity Begins At Home organization, which will distribute the sum between over 60 different causes.

1983

Feb Blue collar-themed *Allentown* reaches US #17.
Apr *Goodnight Saigon* makes US #56.
Sept [24] *Tell Her About It*, from a forthcoming album, tops the US chart for a week, another million-seller.
Oct ***An Innocent Man***, again produced by Phil Ramone, with tracks performed as individual tributes to the musical styles and stars which influenced Joel's formative years, hits US #4 (selling over two million copies) and UK #2.
Nov *Uptown Girl*, a track from ***An Innocent Man*** in the mould of the early Four Seasons hits, sells over one million copies and hits US #3.
[5] *Uptown Girl* tops the UK chart for the first of five weeks, and is by far his biggest UK seller with sales topping 900,000. The accompanying promo video clip features Brinkley, now Joel's fiancée.

1984

Feb Title track, *An Innocent Man*, hits US #10 and UK #8. ***Cold Spring Harbor*** is reissued in remixed form by Columbia, and reaches US #158 and UK #95.
May Fourth single from ***An Innocent Man***, *The Longest Time*, reaches US #14 and UK #25.
Aug *Leave A Tender Moment Alone*, featuring a Toots Thielemans harmonica solo, reaches US #27 and UK #29. As Joel arrives in Britain for a concert tour, he has five albums in the UK Top 100.

1985

Jan [28] Joel takes part in the recording of USA For Africa's *We Are The World* in Los Angeles, with all proceeds going to African famine relief. (The single will be a multi-million seller and worldwide chart-topper.)
Mar *Keeping The Faith* reaches US #18.
[23] Joel and Brinkley marry on board a yacht in New York Harbor.
Aug *You're Only Human (Second Wind)* hits US #9. It is one of two new recordings included on the double compilation album, ***Greatest Hits Volumes 1 & 2***, which hits US #6 and UK #7.
Nov *The Night Is Still Young* makes US #34.

1986

Jan [1] A daughter, Alexa Ray, is born.
Feb Double A-side reissue of *She's Always A Woman/Just The Way You Are* reaches UK #53.
July [26] *Modern Woman*, taken from the soundtrack of the film "Ruthless People", hits US #10.
Aug ***The Bridge***, with ***Nylon Curtain***-style songs, including a guest appearance by Ray Charles on *Baby Grand*, and contributions from Michael Brecker, Cyndi Lauper and Steve Winwood, hits US #7 and UK #38. (Another cut, *Big Man On Mulberry Street*, later becomes the central theme of an episode of the ABC-TV series "Moonlighting".)
Sept [29] "The Bridge" tour begins at the Civic Center, Glens Fall, NY.
Oct [18] *A Matter Of Trust* hits US #10 and makes UK #52.

1987

Jan [31] *This Is The Time* clocks in at US #18.
Apr [25] *Baby Grand*, the duet with Ray Charles, peaks at US #75. (Joel plays a series of concerts in the USSR, including a date in Leningrad which is recorded for album release.)
Nov [28] Live double album, ***Kohyept***, taken from his recent shows in Leningrad, USSR, charts for a week at UK #92 and will reach US #38.

1988

May [1] A Nevada judge clears Joel of defamation charges after he called musician John Powers a "creep" in a **Playboy** interview.
Nov Joel is featured on the various artists' album ***Oliver And Company***, singing *Why Should I Worry?* from the forthcoming Disney movie of the same name.

1989

Jan [22] Joel sings the American national anthem at "Super Bowl XXIII" between the San Francisco 49ers and the Cincinnati Bengals, at Joe Robbie Stadium, Miami, FL.
Aug [30] He fires his manager and former brother-in-law, Frank Weber, after an audit reveals discrepancies. Joel will subsequently sue him for $90 million in an acrimonious and protracted series of court battles.
Sept [24] On his way to London, Joel is taken sick at New York's Kennedy Airport and is hospitalized with severe abdominal pain caused by kidney stones.
[25] Joel files suit in New York, charging Weber with fraud and breach of fiduciary duty.
[26] He has an operation to remove the offending kidney stones at the New York University Medical Center.
Oct Rock-era chronicling *We Didn't Start The Fire*, lyrically comprising a list of celebrated names and events, hits UK #7.
Nov Joel begins month-long rehearsals at the Suffolk County Police Academy, West Hampton, Long Island, for his upcoming tour. His new band comprises Liberty DeVito (drums), David Brown (guitar), Mark Rivera (sax), Crystal Taliefero (vocals/percussion), Mindy Jostyn (rhythm guitar/violin/harp), Jeff Jacobs (synthesizers) and Schuyler Deale (bass).
[4] ***Stormfront***, featuring guest Richard Marx, hits UK #5.
Dec *Leningrad* peaks at UK #53.
[6] "Stormfront" world tour begins at the Centrum in Worcester, MA, and will include 174 shows in 16 countries, seen by 4.3 million people, before ending in Mexico City, Mexico.
[9] *We Didn't Start The Fire* hits US #1.
[16] Its parent album, ***Stormfront***, co-produced with Foreigner's Mick Jones, also hits US #1.

1990

Jan [26] CBS Records issues cassettes of *We Didn't Start The Fire* with a 10-minute talk by Joel with the **Junior Scholastic** and **Update** magazines for 40,000 students, after the fifth grade class at the Banta Elementary School in Menasha, WI, used the song's lyrics to select topics for history reports.
[22] A New York Supreme Court judge awards Joel $2 million in a partial summary judgement against Frank Weber.
Feb ***The Stranger*** is certified multiplatinum by the RIAA for seven million sales.
Mar *I Go To Extremes* peaks at UK #70.
[8-9, 12-13, 16-17] Joel breaks the house record at the Miami Arena, Miami, FL, selling out six shows before crowds of 96,044 paying $2,184,091.
[17] *I Go To Extremes* hits US #6.
Apr [11] A Richmond, VA judge dismisses a $30-million countersuit filed by Weber.
May [21] Joel plays at Wembley Arena, Wembley, Middx., during his current European tour.
June [2] *The Downeaster Alexa* peaks at US #57. (Joel donates part of the royalties to the Coast Alliance and the East Hampton Baymen's Association charities.)
[22-23] He becomes the first rock act to perform at New York's Yankee Stadium, playing before two sellout crowds of 103,367.
July [3, 5] Joel grosses a further $716,670 from two sellout concerts at the Omni, Atlanta, GA.
Aug [18] *That's Not Her Style* stalls at US #77.
[30] Joel sings *Sea Cruise* with Paul Simon, at Simon's benefit concert at Deep Hollow Ranch, Montauk, NY, for the preservation of the Montauk Point Lighthouse, near his Long Island home. A week later, Joel and Simon will reprise their performance at Joel's benefit for the East Hampton Baymen's Association. (During the week, Joel will also duet with Van Morrison at Amagansett's Stephen Talkhouse, singing *What'd I Say* and *Bring It On Home To Me*.)
Nov [13, 15-16, 19] Joel breaks a house record with four sellouts at the Target Center, Minneapolis, MN, before 72,332 people paying $1,677,284 at the box office.
Dec [1] *And So It Goes* makes US #37.
[5] Joel is honored by NARAS as a Grammy Living Legend, with Johnny Cash, Aretha Franklin and Quincy Jones.
[9, 16-18] Joel breaks the house record at the Knickerbocker Arena, Albany, NY before crowds of 66,733. On the final day of his performance, the Albany county executive declares "Billy Joel Day".

1991

Jan [22] Joel begins the Australian leg of his "Stormfront" tour, after sellout shows in Japan, at the Entertainment Centre, Sydney, followed by concerts in Melbourne, Brisbane, Adelaide and Perth. During his stay, Joel is presented with a crystal award by Sony Music Australia, for being the biggest-selling artist in the company's history.
Mar [7] Joel is named Best Keyboard Player in the annual **Rolling Stone** Readers' Picks music awards.
[19-20, 23-24] His "Stormfront" world tour ends at the Palacio De Los Deportes, Mexico City, Mexico, with four sellout shows seen by record-breaking audiences of 80,832.

Apr The RIAA certifies six million sales of ***52nd Street***, and four million of ***Greatest Hits Vol I & II***.
May [11] Joel adds his autograph to a $12,000 Young Chang grand piano being auctioned at the Peabody Hotel, Orlando, FL, to raise money for the "Give Kids The World" charity foundation.
[15] The New York Appeals Court reinstates Joel's $90-million lawsuit against his former accountants.
[19] Joel receives an honorary doctorate of humane letters from Fairfield University, Fairfield, CT. Philosophy Professor the Reverend Thomas Regan criticizes the honor, stating Joel is "not someone with a lifetime commitment of serving humanity".
July [17] The Billy Joel Park is dedicated in Huntington, Long Island.
Aug [8-9] Joel headlines two benefits for the South Fork/Shelter Island chapter of the Nature Conservancy at the Indian Field Ranch, Montauk, helped by Paul Simon and Don Henley.
Sept [27] CD/video compilation, ***Simply Mad About The Mouse***, a collection of new interpretations of Disney classics, with Joel contributing *When You Wish Upon A Star*, is released.
Oct [17] Joel sends a telegram of support to music manager Jonathan Phelps at the closure-threatened classical Atlanta, GA, station WABE "I support you in your efforts to remain a classical station." Thanking Joel, Phelps admits: "I have a terrible confession to make: 'I never heard the name before'."
Nov [16] Garth Brooks' treatment of Joel's *Shameless* tops the US Country chart for the first of two weeks.

1992

Jan [15] Joel inducts Sam & Dave into the Rock and Roll Hall of Fame at the annual dinner, at New York's Waldorf Astoria Hotel.
Apr [3] He holds a music clinic at the Berklee School of Music in Boston, MA.
May [27] Joel is inducted into the Songwriters Hall of Fame in New York by Paul Simon.
[30] Joel loses his wallet during recording in Boston over Memorial Day weekend. Malden postal clerk Phil Sica spots it when mail is unloaded at the post office. Included is a card declaring Joel an honorary member of the Easthampton police force. (Sica will return the wallet intact.)
June [24] He is awarded his diploma from Hicksville High. He promises his mother that he'll "get out of this dead-end job and start working on a career with a real future".
July [28] Joel is ticketed (for $250) in Amagansett, NY, for taking striped bass from the waters off eastern Long Island to protest state regulations.
Aug [29] *All Shook Up*, from the "Honeymoon In Vegas" soundtrack, peaks at US #92. (He has also recently contributed a version of *In A Sentimental Mood* to the "A League Of Their Own" film album.)
Sept [5] *All Shook Up* reaches UK #27.
[23] Joel files a second $90-million lawsuit in New York Supreme Court, this time against former attorney Allen Grubman, Grubman's law firm and his partners Arthur Indursky and Paul Schindler, alleging they committed a breach of fiduciary duty, malpractice, fraud and conflict of interest.
Nov [18] He performs at the AIDS Project Los Angeles' "Commitment To Life VI" cocktail and dinner party to honor Barbra Streisand and David Geffen, at the Universal Amphitheatre, Universal City, CA.

1993

Feb [25] Joel wins another summary judgement of $675,670.68 plus interest in his ongoing lawsuit against Frank Weber, made by the New York State Supreme Court Judge Edward Lehner.
Mar He donates his 9' Baldwin concert grand piano to the University of New York at Stony Brook on Long Island, to replace one of three destroyed in February when the University's Staller Center for the Arts was flooded by a burst main.
May [8] Joel receives an honorary degree and delivers the commencement address at Berklee College Of Music.
June [5] He attends the wedding of Mariah Carey and Tommy Mottola at the St. Thomas Episcopal Church on 5th Avenue, New York.
[7] Joel is one of many rock celebrities present at the ground-breaking ceremony of the Rock and Roll Hall of Fame in Cleveland, OH.
Aug [10] A $10 million lawsuit is filed in Manhattan Federal Court on behalf of Gary Zimmerman, who claims *River Of Dreams*, *No Man's Land* and *We Didn't Start The Fire* are based on his song *Nowhere Land*. Joel's attorney Leonard Marks says "Billy thinks the suit is utter horseshit".
[21 ***River Of Dreams***, produced by Danny Kortchmar and featuring Color Me Badd and Leslie West among its guests, hits UK #3.
[28] ***River Of Dreams*** enters the US chart at #1.
[30] Joel is the musical guest on the first CBS-TV "Late Show With David Letterman" program.
Sept [4] Title cut *The River Of Dreams* hits UK #3.
Oct [13] "Billy Joel : Shades Of Grey", a documentary on the making of the ***River Of Dreams*** album, airs on PBS-TV.
[16] *The River Of Dreams* hits US #3.
[23] Joel guests on "Saturday Night Live".
[30] Anthemic *All About Soul* reaches UK #32.
Dec [18] *All About Soul* reaches US #29.
[29, 31, **Jan** 2, 6, 8] Joel plays five sellout dates at Nassau Veterans Memorial Coliseum, grossing $2,874,480.

1994

Jan [27] He is named Best Keyboardist in **Rolling Stone**'s 1994 Music Awards Readers' Picks. ***River Of Dreams*** album sleeve designed by his wife is named Worst Album Cover in the magazine's 1994 Music Awards Critics' Picks.
Mar [1] Joel performs *River Of Dreams* at the 36th annual Grammy Awards from Radio City Music Hall.
[5] *No Man's Land* makes UK #50.
[17] Joel gets a ride a fire department emergency vehicle after his van is hit by a truck on the way to Richfield Coliseum, Richfield, OH. (The crew will be reprimanded for violating department policy.)
Apr [13] CNN's "Showbiz Today" reports that the Joels have split after nine years of marriage.
[23] *Lullabye (Goodnight, My Angel)* peaks at US #77.
May [7, 9, 11] Joel plays at Earls Court Exhibition Centre, London, during the European leg of the "River Of Dreams" tour.
July [22, 24, 26, 28-29] Joel, now on a summer tour of the US with Elton John, plays five sellout dates at Giants Stadium, East Rutherford, NJ, grossing $14,889,127.
Aug [25] The Joels are divorced.
Sept [7] Joel sings with James and Hughie Taylor at David's Island House on Martha's Vineyard, MA.
Oct [3] As Joel prepares to set out on the next leg of the "River Of Dreams" tour, he performs "An Evening Of Questions And Answers And Perhaps A Few Songs" at Harvard University's Sanders Theatre, Cambridge, MA.
[17] Joel plays the inaugural concert at the Gateway Arena (later renamed the Gund Arena), Cleveland, OH before a sellout crowd of 19,687.
Nov [14] The day after the "River Of Dreams" tour reaches Australia, Joel announces that his current world tour will be his last.
Dec [7] Joel, via satellite from Sydney, Australia, receives the Century Award from Tori Amos at the fifth annual **Billboard** Music Awards, from the Universal Amphitheatre, broadcast live on Fox-TV.

1995

Jan [23-24] The Japanese leg of the "River Of Dreams" tour ends at the Budokan, Tokyo.
Apr [13-14] During current North American dates, Joel and Elton John (who will also write new songs together during the year) break the house and highest gross record at the Joe Robbie Stadium, Miami, FL, as 103,694 pay $4,385,725 to see the two artists.
July [30] Joel sings *New York State Of Mind* at the "Newport Rhythm and Blues Festival" from the Fort Adams State Park, Newport, RI.
Aug [24] Doug Stegmeyer, Joel's former bass player, dies of a self-inflicted gunshot wound in Syosset, NY.
Oct [14] A&M-released ***Tower Of Song : The Songs Of Leonard Cohen***, to which Joel has contributed *Light Of Breeze*, charts for a week at US #198.

ELTON JOHN

1961

John (b. Reginald Kenneth Dwight, Mar. 25, 1947, Pinner, Middx.), son of ex-Royal Air Force trumpeter, Stanley Dwight and his wife, Sheila, having started piano lessons at age four and played at a local music festival at age 12 (his early piano idols are Winifred Atwell and Charlie Kunz), has already attended the Royal Academy of Music, London, to which he won a part-time scholarship in 1958, when he joins locally performing R&B outfit Bluesology (its name taken from a Django Reinhardt disc), playing piano with existing members Stuart Brown (guitar), Rex Bishop (bass) and Mike Inkpen (drums). Their first paying gig is at the Northwood Hills hotel, Northwood, London, where John has already performed as a resident soloist on Thursday, Friday and Saturday nights, playing pub songs. (Progressing to Jim Reeves covers, he would typically earn £1 a night, plus tips, which he saved to buy his first amp.)

1963

Still a teenager, he attends Pinner County Grammar school, but quits three weeks before his exams. Through his cousin Roy (a professional soccer player who scored a goal and broke his leg in the 1959 FA Cup final between Nottingham Forest and Luton Town), he hears of a job as a "junior" at London's Mills Music Publishers, where he will earn £4 10s a week.

1965

July John writes Bluesology's first release, *Come Back Baby*, produced by Jack Baverstock and issued by Fontana. During the year, Bluesology turns professional - with the help of talent agent Roy Tempest - and, for 18 months, will back major US R&B artists playing UK club dates, including Major Lance, who recommends them to other US acts, including Patti LaBelle & the Blue Belles, the Inkspots, Doris Troy and Billy Stewart, among others, for tours throughout Europe.

1966

Dec Long John Baldry becomes frontman for Bluesology. He expands the group into a nine-piece, adding American guitarist Caleb Quaye and Elton Dean on sax, plus Pete Gavin, Mark Charig and Neil Hubbard. The group becomes known as the John Baldry Show, and moves to the cabaret circuit.

1967

June Disillusioned with the music he is playing for Baldry, John auditions for Liberty Records (currently establishing an independent London office, and advertising in music paper **New Musical Express** for artists and writers) at the Regent Sound Studios in London, where he sings the Jim Reeves' songs *I Love You Because* and *He'll Have To Go*, among others, too nervous to perform his own. He fails the audition, but Liberty's Ray Williams gives him lyrics sent to the label by writer Bernie Taupin (b. May 22, 1950, Sleaford, Lincolnshire), whose mother has rescued his letter, intended for Liberty but discarded in a wastepaper basket. They begin to write by correspondence and do not meet until some 20 songs have been completed. Finally meeting in the reception area of Dick James House, when John calls out, "Is there a lyricist here?", the pair signs to Gralto, the Hollies' publishing company, and temporarily live together in John's parents' house, where it will often take the pianist only 20 minutes to set Taupin's lyrics to music.
Nov [22] Baldry's *Let The Heartaches Begin*, with

the B-side *Lord You Made The Night Too Long*, penned by John and Taupin, the first disc to bear this credit, tops the UK chart. (He has changed his name from Dwight, borrowing Elton Dean and John Baldry's forenames.)

1968

Jan Baldry Show-member Quaye finds work as an engineer at Dick James Music's newly-opened two-track studio in London's West End. John and Taupin sign to Dick James Music Publishing (DJM) as staff writers, for £10 a week each. (They will write together, with one break, for over 25 years.)
Mar [1] The first Elton John solo single, *I've Been Loving You Too Long*, produced by Quaye, is released on Philips. Meanwhile, Roger Cook records John and Taupin's *Skyline Pigeon* for his first solo single, on UK Columbia.

1969

Jan [17] *Lady Samantha*, John's second and final Philips single (produced by EMI plugger Steve Brown) is released, does not chart (selling close to 10,000 copies), but finds significant UK airplay, and will be included on the next album by top US act Three Dog Night. Meanwhile, John unsuccessfully auditions for the position of lead singer with Robert Fripp's new group, King Crimson.
Feb Lulu performs John and Taupin's *I Can't Go On Living Without You* on her BBC1-TV show, as one of the final six British entries for the Eurovision Song Contest. (It comes last in the heats. Peter Warne and Alan Moorhouse's *Boom Bang A Bang* is the chosen song.)
May *It's Me That You Need* is John's first release on DJM Records.
June His DJM debut album, ***Empty Sky***, comprising all the John and Taupin songs, is released.
[25] John plays piano on the Hollies' session for *He Ain't Heavy He's My Brother*, at Abbey Road Studios, London. (He contributes *From Denver To L.A.* to the movie "The Games". It will be released as a US single on Viking in 1970. He begins to do work on sessions for budget cover-version UK labels, including Music For Pleasure and Pickwick, as well as playing on other artists' demos and sessions.)

1970

Mar *Border Song*, featuring the Barbara Moore Choir, is released but, despite strong UK airplay, fails to chart.
May [9] John again plays piano on an Abbey Road Studio session for the Hollies, on *I Can't Tell The Bottom From The Top* (and is guest organist on their *Perfect Lady Housewife*, for inclusion on ***Confessions Of The Mind***).
Aug [22] At the invitation of label boss Russ Regan, John signs to MCA Records' Uni subsidiary in the US, and *Border Song*, from ***Elton John***, marks his US Singles chart debut, at #92.
[25] John makes his live Stateside debut, accompanied by regular sidemen, bassist Dee Murray (b. David Murray Oates, Apr. 3, 1946, Southgate, London) and Nigel Olsson (b. Feb. 10, 1949, Wallasey, Lancs.) on drums, performing at the 20th-anniversary celebrations for Doug Weston's Troubadour in Los Angeles, CA, opening for singer/songwriter David Ackles. With Leon Russell and Quincy Jones in the audience, John will later claim that the "awesome" reviews of this performance changed his life.
Oct ***Elton John*** enters the US chart, set to hit #4. It is produced by Gus Dudgeon, and features the first Elton John Band, with John on vocals and keyboards, Dee, Olsson, and Quaye on guitar.
[31] John begins his freshman US tour at the Boston Tea Party, Boston, MA.
Nov [12-15] He plays the Fillmore West, supporting the Kinks.
[17] A concert in New York, NY forms a live radio broadcast for station WPLJ (and is recorded for album release in 1971).
[20-21] John plays at the Fillmore East, New York, with Leon Russell headlining.

1971

Jan ***Elton John*** reaches UK #11.
[23] Ballad *Your Song* hits UK #7 and US #8.
Feb ***Tumbleweed Connection***, featuring Dusty Springfield as a backing vocalist, hits UK #6 and US #5. Dick James enlists Motown label manager John Reid as John's personal manager. He will remain with the singer for over 20 years.
Apr [24] John's title song from the film "Friends" makes US #34, as he embarks on a major US tour, set to end in June.
May Soundtrack album, ***Friends***, reaches US #36, while ***17-11-70*** (US title: ***11-17-70***), from the November concert in New York, reaches UK #20 and US #11.
Nov John embarks on a major UK tour.

1972

Feb Ex-Magna Carta guitarist, Davey Johnstone (b. May 6, 1951, Edinburgh, Scotland), joins John's backing band.
[5] *Levon* reaches US #24.
Apr Arriving at Los Angeles airport for the start of a US tour, John's stage boots, with 8" lifts, are checked for drugs.
[8] Ballad *Tiny Dancer* makes US #41.
May [7] He formally changes his name by deed poll to Elton Hercules John.
June [3] *Rocket Man* hits UK #2. The lushly-orchestrated (by Paul Buckmaster) ***Madman Across The Water***, featuring Lesley Duncan, Herbie Flowers and Rick Wakeman, among others, makes UK #41 and hits US #8.
Honky Chateau, a reference to its recording location, Strawberry Studios in Chateau d'Herouville, 30 miles from Paris, France, hits UK #2, his sixth consecutive album produced by Gus Dudgeon.
July [15] *Rocket Man* hits US #6, as ***Honky Chateau*** begins a five-week run at US #1.
Sept Uptempo honky-tonk *Honky Cat* makes UK #31.
[23] *Honky Cat* hits US #8, as John begins a US tour.
Oct He makes a guest appearance in Marc Bolan's movie, "Born To Boogie".
[30] John appears in the Royal Variety Show in London.
Nov Full throttle pop'n'roll *Crocodile Rock* hits UK #5.

1973

Feb [3] *Crocodile Rock* begins a three-week run at US #1, earning a gold disc, while *Daniel* hits UK #4.
[10] Its parent album, ***Don't Shoot Me, I'm Only The Piano Player***, hits UK #1, where it will remain for six weeks.
[17] John reveals plans to launch his own Rocket Records label.
Mar [3] ***Don't Shoot Me, I'm Only The Piano Player*** tops the US chart.
May John launches Rocket Records at a village railway station in the English countryside.
June [2] Plane-leaving ballad, *Daniel*, hits US #2, and is another gold single.
July [21] Aggressive rocker, *Saturday Night's Alright For Fighting*, hits UK #7.
Aug [15] A 42-date US tour opens in Mobile, AL, set to end on October 21st.
Sept [7] John plays before a crowd of 25,000 at the Hollywood Bowl, Hollywood, CA, where porn-movie star Linda Lovelace acts as hostess for the evening.
[15] *Saturday Night's Alright For Fighting* reaches US #12.
Oct [27] *Goodbye Yellow Brick Road* hits UK #6.
Nov John becomes vice president of Watford Football Club.
[8] Taupin/John-penned double album, ***Goodbye Yellow Brick Road***, produced by Dudgeon with string arrangements by Del Newman, hits US #1, where it will remain for eight weeks and earn a US gold disc.
Dec [4] "Elton John And Bernie Taupin Say Goodbye Norma Jean And Other Things" airs on UK TV. (ABC-TV will show an extended version in the US in 1974.)
[8] Extracted title track, *Goodbye Yellow Brick Road*, hits US #2 for three weeks, again going gold.
[22] ***Goodbye Yellow Brick Road*** tops the UK chart (his second successive #1), confirming John's status as the leading British singer-songwriter of the '70s.

1974

Jan [5] Seasonal *Step Into Christmas* makes UK #24.
Mar [23] Marilyn Monroe-revering ballad *Candle In The Wind* reaches UK #11.
Apr [13] UK B-side to *Candle In The Wind*, *Bennie And The Jets* is issued as a US A-side and hits #1, again a million seller. It also becomes John's first US R&B chart hit, at #15.
May [5] Despite cancelling a 17-date UK tour, suffering from exhaustion, John performs a benefit for Watford Football Club with Rod Stewart, and will also play for the Invalid Children's Society.
[16] *Daniel* wins the Best Song Musically And Lyrically category at the 19th annual Ivor Novello Awards, held at London's Grosvenor House Hotel.
June [15] Ballad *Don't Let The Sun Go Down On Me*, featuring the Beach Boys' Carl Wilson and Bruce Johnston on backing vocals, reaches UK #16 and hits US #2 (another million seller).
July [13] ***Caribou***, recorded at James William Guercio's studio, the Caribou Ranch in Nederland, CO, with help from the Beach Boys, tops both UK and US charts. John re-signs with MCA Records in North America, for an $8-million, five-album deal, the most lucrative in recording history.
Aug He forms his own publishing company, Big Pig Music.
[5] His overwhelming popularity in the US is reaffirmed as tickets for three October concerts in Los Angeles sell out in minutes, causing a fourth show to be added.
Sept John duets with John Lennon on the former Beatle's *Whatever Gets You Through The Night* (which climbs to UK #36 and hits US #1).
Oct [5] *The Bitch Is Back* reaches UK #15.
John embarks on a 44-date North American tour, highlighted by his increasingly flamboyant stage outfits (including going onstage at a Stooges gig in Atlanta, GA wearing a gorilla suit), which will be seen by approximately 750,000 people.
Nov [2] *The Bitch Is Back* hits US #4.
[23] Compilation album, ***Elton John's Greatest Hits***, tops the UK chart.
[28] John and Lennon sing *I Saw Her Standing There* at a Thanksgiving concert at New York's Madison Square Garden.
[30] ***Elton John's Greatest Hits*** peaks at US #1, remaining at the summit for 10 weeks.
Dec [14] His revival of the Beatles' *Lucy In The Sky With Diamonds*, with a guest appearance by Lennon, hits UK #10.

1975

Jan [4] *Lucy In The Sky With Diamonds* tops the US chart, becoming another million seller.
Feb [2] Neil Sedaka's *Laughter In The Rain*, released on John's Rocket Records, tops the US chart.
[16] John guests with Bette Midler on the CBS-TV premiere of the "Cher" show.
Apr [12] *Philadelphia Freedom*, penned for John's friend Billie Jean King and her Philadelphia Freedom World Team Tennis players, credited to the Elton John Band with an arrangement by Thom Bell, reaches UK #12 and tops the US chart (also becoming his second R&B hit, at #32), as Ringo Starr hits US #3 with a double A-side single, including John/Taupin's *Snookeroo*. John's first album, ***Empty Sky***, is reissued in the US and hits #6. He appears in Ken Russell's movie version of the Who's "Tommy".
[19] John fires band members Murray and Olsson on the eve of the release of an autobiographical album, ***Captain Fantastic And The Brown Dirt Cowboy***.
May [3] John makes his debut on the syndicated TV show "Soul Train", performing *Philadelphia Freedom* and *Bennie And The Jets*.
June [7] ***Captain Fantastic And The Brown Dirt Cowboy***, with a distinctive cartoon cover design by Alan Aldridge and Harry Willcock, hits UK #2, held

off the top by ***The Best Of The Stylistics***, and becomes the first album ever to go straight to US #1, where it stays for seven weeks. (The songs were written on a cruise liner.)
[21] John tops the bill at a sellout open-air concert at Wembley Stadium, Wembley, Middx.
[29] At an Oakland-Alameda County Coliseum, Oakland, CA concert by the Doobie Brothers and the Eagles, John jams on stage with both bands on *Listen To The Music* and Chuck Berry's *Carol*.
July [19] Ballad *Someone Saved My Life Tonight*, a partly autobiographical account of John's recent suicide attempt on the eve of his planned wedding to Linda Woodrow, heiress to the Epicure pickled onion empire, reaches UK #22.
Aug [16] *Someone Saved My Life Tonight* hits US #4.
[25] He plays two benefit shows at Los Angeles' Troubadour, the scene of his US live debut five years earlier, for UCLA's Jules Stein Eye Institute, raising over $150,000.
Oct [21] John receives a star on Hollywood's Walk of Fame during "Elton John Week". (While staying at David Selznick's old mansion, he reportedly takes 60 Valium tablets and jumps into the pool in front of his mother and grandmother. Despite his enormous success and wealth, John has become increasingly depressed and chemically dependent.)
[26] He concludes his US "West Of The Rockies" tour at Los Angeles' Dodger Stadium, the first artist to play there since the Beatles in 1966, dressed in a sequined Dodgers uniform.
Nov [1] Caribbean-tinged *Island Girl* reaches UK #14 and begins a three-week stay atop the US chart, selling a million (and deposing Neil Sedaka's Rocket single, *Bad Blood*, with John on backing vocals).
[8] The poorly received ***Rock Of The Westies*** hits UK #5 and US #1, as John becomes godfather to John and Yoko Lennon's son Sean.

1976

Jan In an interview with **Playboy** magazine, John says, "My real ambition in life is to make enough money to retire and become chairman of my favorite soccer team, the Watford Football Club."
Feb [28] Double A-side, *Grow Some Funk Of Your Own/I Feel Like A Bullet (In The Gun Of Robert Ford)*, reaches US #14.
Mar [7] John is immortalized in wax at Madame Tussaud's in London (the first rock star since the Beatles to be so honored).
Apr [3] *Pinball Wizard*, from the film "Tommy", released in re-recorded form, hits UK #7.
[29] John begins a 29-date UK tour at the Grand Theatre, Leeds, W. Yorks., set to end at the Capitol Theatre, Cardiff, Wales, on June 4th.
May [22] ***Here And There***, recorded live in London and New York, becomes his final DJM album and hits UK #6.
June [12] ***Here And There*** hits US #4.
July [18] John embarks on a 15-date US tour at the Capitol Centre, Landover, MD, set to end on August 21st at the Seattle Coliseum, Seattle, WA.
[24] John's first UK Singles chart-topper (a duet with Kiki Dee, recorded in Toronto, ON, Canada) is *Don't Go Breaking My Heart*, which stays at #1 for six weeks.
Aug [7] Pseudonymously credited to Ann Orson and Carte Blanche, *Don't Go Breaking My Heart* also tops the US survey, for the first of four weeks, and earns a gold disc. (John will perform the song on ITV's "The Muppet Show" with Miss Piggy.)
[10] John begins a seven-date series of sellout shows at Madison Square Garden taking $1.25 million in ticket receipts and breaking the house record set a year earlier by the Rolling Stones.
Oct [9] *Bennie And The Jets*, reissued on DJM as a UK A-side, makes #37.
Nov [13] Double album, ***Blue Moves***, with backing-vocal assistance from David Crosby, Bruce Johnston, Toni Tennille and Graham Nash, hits both UK and US #3, its success unaffected by John's admission in this month's issue of **Rolling Stone** that he is bisexual. (It will be the last album for the time being produced by Dudgeon and written totally with Taupin.)
Dec [4] The extracted haunting ballad, *Sorry Seems To Be The Hardest Word*, reaches UK #11.
[25] *Sorry Seems To Be The Hardest Word* hits US #6.

1977

Jan [31] John wins the Favorite Male Artist, Pop/Rock and Favorite Single, Pop Rock (with Kiki Dee) categories at the fourth annual American Music Awards, held at the Civic Auditorium, Santa Monica, CA.
Feb John comes second in a **Ladies Home Journal** poll in which US school children voted for their hero.
Mar [5] *Bite Your Lip (Get Up And Dance)* reaches US #28.
[19] *Crazy Water*, recorded with help from the Captain & Tennille, reaches UK #27.
May [12] *Don't Go Breaking My Heart* nabs the Best Pop Song category at the 22nd annual Ivor Novello Awards, at the Grosvenor House Hotel.
June [17] John performs for students at Shoreditch College in Egham, Surrey after Jimmy Helms, who had been booked for the Valedictory Ball, drops out. Some students go to his house nearby and buzz his intercom to ask whether he will fill in, John says yes, providing there is no press coverage.
[25] *Bite Your Lip (Get Up And Dance)*, backed with *Chicago*, another duet with Kiki Dee, reaches UK #28. John achieves a lifetime ambition when he becomes chairman of Watford Football Club.
Oct [1] He becomes the first rock artist to be honored in Madison Square Garden's Hall of Fame.
Nov [3] Having recently collapsed during two concert performances, John announces his retirement from live work, during a concert at the Empire Pool, Wembley. (He will return to the live arena 15 months later in Sweden.)
Dec [3] Compilation album, ***Elton John's Greatest Hits Volume Two***, reaches US #21. He records several tracks with US producer Thom Bell, at the Kay Smith Studio in Seattle, WA, and Sigma Sound Studios, Philadelphia, PA.
[15] John hosts BBC1-TV's "Top Of The Pops".

1978

Jan [21] ***Elton John's Greatest Hits Volume Two*** hits UK #6.
Mar [26] He visits DJ Kenny Everett at Capital Radio's Help-A-London Child charity appeal.
Apr [4] John sees Watford clinch promotion as they beat Bournemouth 2-1, before flying to Los Angeles and then returning to the UK to see them beat Scunthorpe 1-0 to win the Fourth Division championship on the 8th.
[15] Rock-pomped *Ego*, his last collaboration with Taupin for three years, makes UK #34.
May [6] *Ego* makes US #34.
June [7] John is featured on NBC-TV's "Headliners With David Frost".
Oct [31] John guests on BBC2-TV's "The Old Grey Whistle Test".
Nov [1] He jams with the alternative "Be Stiff" tour in Hemel Hempstead, Herts.
[2] John appears as a special guest star at the Record Industry dinner and ball at the Hilton Hotel, London.
Dec [9] John's first album without Taupin lyrics (provided instead by Gary Osbourne), ***A Single Man***, produced by John with Clive Franks, ***A Single Man*** reaches US #15. (The album is dedicated to Watford's manager, Graham Taylor, and two tracks feature the soccer team as backing vocalists.)
[16] Extracted *Part Time Love* reaches UK #15 and US #22.

1979

Jan [13] *Song For Guy*, an instrumental dedicated to Guy Burchett, Rocket's motorcycle messenger boy, who died in an accident at age 17, hits UK #4.
[20] Its parent album, ***A Single Man***, hits UK #8.
Feb [3] He makes his first live appearance, since "retiring", in Sweden.
Mar [17-18] Accompanied only by percussionist Ray Cooper, John continues his comeback tour, his first UK trek since 1976, at the Apollo Theatre, Glasgow, Scotland. The 30-date tour, which includes six dates at London's Theatre Royal, Drury Lane, is set to end on April 26th at the Apollo Theatre, Manchester, Gtr. Manchester.
May [4] *Song For Guy* wins the Best Instrumental Or Popular Orchestral Work category at the 24th annual Ivor Novello Awards, at the Grosvenor House Hotel.
[21] John begins an eight-concert run in Leningrad, the first Western solo pop star to tour the USSR. (The trip is filmed for a subsequent documentary, "To Russia With Elton".)
[26] The Thom Bell sessions are released as the EP *Are You Ready For Love*, which makes UK #42. In the US, regarded as a mini-album, it will make #51 on the Album chart (Sept [1]). John performs concerts in Israel, the first Western rock star to do so, as part of the country's independence celebrations.
June [28] John receives the Nordoff-Robbins Silver Clef Award at the fourth annual lunch in London.
Aug [25] *Mama Can't Buy You Love*, from the mini-album, hits US #9.
Sept [27] He collapses on stage at the Universal Amphitheatre, Universal City, CA, suffering from exhaustion due to a bout of 'flu. After resting for ten minutes, he resumes for the three-hour show.
Oct [27] Dance-oriented ***Victim Of Love***, produced by Pete Bellotte and with vocal support from the Doobie Brothers' Michael McDonald and Patrick Simmons, peaks at UK #41 and will make US #35 (Nov [24]).
Nov [17] The extracted title track, *Victim Of Love*, makes US #31 (the only single from the album to chart).

1980

Mar [8] Compilation album, ***Lady Samantha***, containing DJM-label rarities, peaks at UK #56.
June [7] *Little Jeannie* makes UK #33 and hits US #3.
[14] ***21 At 33***, referring to his 21st album in his 33rd year, reaches UK #12. Co-writers include Judie Tzuke, Tom Robinson, Osbourne and Taupin, with backing vocals from Bruce Johnston, Toni Tennille, Glenn Frey, Timothy Schmit and Peter Noone.
July [19] *Little Jeannie* hits US #3, as its parent album, ***21 At 33***, makes US #13.
Sept [6] *(Sartorial Eloquence) Don't You Wanna Play This Game No More* makes UK #44.
[21] John signs to Geffen Records for North America.
[27] *(Sartorial Eloquence) Don't You Wanna Play This Game* reaches US #39. John co-writes Tom Robinson's *Never Gonna Fall In Love Again*, while his own *Dear God* fails to chart.
Nov [8] K-tel TV-advertised ***The Very Best Of Elton John*** peaks at UK #24.

1981

Mar [28] *I Saw Her Standing There Live*, a live track recorded with John Lennon in 1974 and released as a tribute to him, makes UK #40.
June [6] *Nobody Wins*, a re-write of a French song by Jean-Paul Dreau, makes UK #42, as its parent album, ***The Fox***, produced by Chris Thomas, reaches UK #12.
[20] *Nobody Wins* reaches US #21.
[27] ***The Fox*** reaches US #21. *Just Like Belgium*, the UK follow-up single, will fail to score.
Sept [19] *Chloe* makes US #34.

1982

Mar [8] John's first tour for two years opens in New Zealand.
Apr [24] The ballad *Blue Eyes*, co-penned with Osbourne, hits UK #8.
[30] A 25-date European tour opens in Stockholm, Sweden, set to end May 30th in Lille, France.
May [1] ***Jump Up!***, produced by Chris Thomas and featuring Pete Townshend, drummer Jeff Porcaro and keyboardist James Newton-Howard, reaches UK #13.
[29] *Empty Garden (Hey Hey Johnny)*, a tribute to John Lennon, reaches US #13.
June [12] ***Jump Up!*** reaches US #17.

[26] *Empty Garden (Hey Hey Johnny)* peaks at UK #51.
Oct [2] *Blue Eyes* reaches US #12.
Nov [2] A 42-date UK tour begins at the City Hall, Newcastle, Tyne & Wear, set to end on Christmas Eve at the Hammersmith Odeon, London, the last of 14 consecutive shows at the venue.
[13] Compilation album, ***Love Songs***, climbs to UK #39. (Singles *Princess* and *All Quiet On The Western Front* are released, but neither charts.)

1983

June ***Too Low For Zero***, John's first album written entirely with Taupin since ***Blue Moves*** in 1976, hits UK #7 and US #25.
July [2] *I Guess That's Why They Call It The Blues* hits UK #5.
[9] *I'm Still Standing*, spurred by an innovative video, reaches US #12, and will hit UK #4 the following month.
Nov [5] *Kiss The Bride* reaches UK #20 and US #25.
Dec [24] Seasonal *Cold As Christmas* makes UK #33.

1984

Jan [28] *I Guess That's Why They Call It The Blues* hits US #4.
Feb [14] John marries studio engineer Renate Blauer in Darling Point, Sydney, Australia.
Apr [17] He begins a 44-date European tour in Sarajevo, Yugoslavia, set to end at Wembley Stadium, on June 30th.
May [19] John flies from Copenhagen, Denmark, to see Watford Football Club play in their first-ever FA Cup final at Wembley. They lose to Everton, 2-0.
June [23] *Sad Songs (Say So Much)* hits UK #7. ***Breaking Hearts***, reinstating longtime cohorts Johnstone, Murray and Olsson and again produced by Thomas, hits UK #2 and makes US #20.
Aug [11] *Sad Songs (Say So Much)* hits US #5.
Sept [8] Anti-apartheid-themed *Passengers*, John's 50th UK single, hits UK #5.
Oct [26] He performs at Madison Square Garden.
Nov *Who Wears These Shoes* peaks at UK #50 and US #16.

1985

Jan [12] *In Neon* reaches US #38.
Feb *Breaking Hearts (Ain't What It Used To Be)*, released for Valentine's Day and John's own first wedding anniversary, makes UK #59.
Mar [13] John presents George Michael with the Best Songwriter award at the annual Ivor Novello ceremony at the Grosvenor House Hotel, proclaiming Michael to be a "major songwriter in the tradition of Paul McCartney and Barry Gibb".
June [22] *Act Of War*, a duet with Millie Jackson, reaches UK #32. (Tina Turner was offered the song but turned it down.)
[28] John duets with George Michael on *Candle In The Wind* at Wham!'s farewell concert at Wembley Stadium.
July [13] John participates in "Live Aid", with Michael, duetting (for the first time) on *Don't Let The Sun Go Down On Me*, also at Wembley Stadium.
Sept [13] "Sad Songs" wins the Best Choreography category at the second annual MTV Video Music Awards, held at Radio City Music Hall, New York.
Nov [9] Ballad *Nikita*, with vocal help from Michael, hits UK #3. ***Ice On Fire***, helmed by earlier producer Gus Dudgeon and featuring backing vocalists Kiki Dee, Sister Sledge and Pete Wingfield, hits UK #3 and US #48.
[15] A five-month, non-stop European tour begins in Dublin, Eire, set to end April 26th, 1986, in Brussels, Belgium.
Dec [28] *Wrap Her Up*, again featuring Michael on vocals (and in the video clip), reaches UK #12 and US #20.

1986

Jan [18] Dionne Warwick & Friends' AIDS fundraising single, *That's What Friends Are For*, featuring co-vocalists John, Gladys Knight and Stevie Wonder, hits US #1 (and will make UK #16).
[29] John and Taupin are awarded £5 million in back royalties from Dick James Music, after a lengthy and bitter court case.
Feb [10] John is honored for his Outstanding Contribution To British Music at the fifth annual BRIT Awards, held at the Grosvenor House Hotel.
Mar [22] *Nikita* hits US #7, as *Cry To Heaven* makes UK #47.
Apr [7] *Nikita* nabs the Best Song Musically And Lyrically, and John collects the award for Outstanding Contribution To British Music at the 31st annual Ivor Novello Awards, at the Grosvenor House Hotel.
June [20] John participates in the fourth annual "Prince's Trust" concert in London, with Bryan Adams, Eric Clapton and Tina Turner.
Aug [15] He begins a US tour in Detroit, MI.
Oct *Heartache All Over The World* makes UK #45, as its parent album, the Dudgeon-produced ***Leather Jackets***, with guests Queen's John Deacon and Roger Taylor, and Cliff Richard, makes UK #24 and US #91.
[9] John guests on Fox-TV's "The Late Show Starring Joan Rivers" premiere, with Cher and Pee Wee Herman.
Nov [22] *Heartache All Over The World* makes US #55.
Dec [9] John collapses on stage during a concert in Sydney, Australia.
[14] A further Sydney concert is recorded for future release.
[27] John's duet with Cliff Richard, *Slow Rivers*, makes UK #44.

1987

Jan [5] He enters a Sydney hospital for throat surgery, planning to cancel all concerts for the coming year.
Feb [24] John wins Best Pop Performance By A Duo Or Group With Vocal category with Dionne Warwick, Gladys Knight and Stevie Wonder, for *That's What Friends Are For* at the 29th annual Grammy Awards (his only Grammy honor).
Mar **The Sun** newspaper prints a series of front-page stories alleging that John has engaged in lurid homosexual sex-and-drug orgies, reports strenuously denied by the star, who immediately begins libel proceedings against the daily rag.
[25] Neighbors complain about the noise at John's 40th birthday party.
Apr Having re-signed to MCA in the US, John appears at an AIDS benefit show at Wembley Arena, his first live show since his throat operation.
June *Flames Of Paradise*, a duet with Jennifer Rush, makes UK #59.
July [11] *Flames Of Paradise* burns out at US #36.
Sept [11] John and Taupin are presented with the Special Recognition trophy at the fourth annual MTV Video Music Awards, held at the Universal Amphitheatre.
The boxed double album, ***Live In Australia***, chronicling his 1986 tour, reaches UK #70 and US #24, while ***Greatest Hits Volume Three***, on Geffen, peaks at US #84.
Dec John tries, unsuccessfully, to sell his beloved soccer club, Watford.

1988

Jan [23] A live version of his celebrated ballad, *Candle In The Wind*, recorded with the Melbourne Symphony Orchestra, hits US #6.
[28] John inducts the Beach Boys into the Rock and Roll Hall of Fame at the third annual dinner, held at the Waldorf Astoria Hotel, New York.
Feb [13] *Candle In The Wind* hits UK #5, confirming the song's enduring popularity.
Mar [5] Re-promoted double album, ***Live In Australia***, now without its original boxed packaging, peaks at UK #43.
June [5] John appears at the sixth annual "Prince's Trust Rock Gala", at London's Royal Albert Hall, as *I Don't Want To Go On With You Like That* makes UK #30.
July [16] ***Reg Strikes Back*** reaches UK #18 and will make US #16. *Town Of Plenty* peaks at UK #74.
Aug [27] Uptempo *I Don't Want To Go On With You Like That* hits US #2, behind George Michael's *Monkey*.
Sept [8] 2,000 items of John's personal memorabilia are auctioned at Sotheby's in London. His giant "Pinball Wizard" boots, from the film "Tommy", sell for $11,000, as dozens of other items, from gold discs to personalized spectacles, contribute to a seven-figure sale.
[9] US tour begins at the Miami Arena, Miami, FL.
[23] John concludes five sellout performances, supported by Wet Wet Wet, at Madison Square Garden. His final concert breaks the Grateful Dead's career record of 25 sellout Madison Square Garden concerts.
Oct **The Sun** newspaper settles the libel action suit out of court with John for £1 million, and prints an apology admitting that their recent rent-boy sex-scandal story was false. John writes and produces for Olivia Newton-John's album ***The Rumour***.
Nov [12] *A Word In Spanish* reaches US #19, as Elton and Renate John announce an "amicable" divorce.

1989

Mar [20] John embarks on a 50-date European trek, with Nik Kershaw as a support act, in Lyons, France, which will end June 2nd in Edinburgh, Scotland.
[27] He celebrates his 42nd birthday in Paris with a party, reportedly costing £200,000.
May [11] John performs at the Songwriters Hall of Fame 20th-anniversary dinner and wins the National Academy of Popular Music's Hitmaker Award at Radio City Music Hall.
[27] John begins the UK leg of the tour with sold-out dates, while the *Through The Storm* duet with Aretha Franklin makes US #16 and UK #41. He also contributes *I'm Ready* to the Richard Perry-produced ***Rock, Rhythm & Blues*** compilation.
June [3] John takes part in "Our Common Future", a five-hour ecological-awareness world-telecast concert.
Aug Ballad *Healing Hands* makes UK #45.
[24] He recreates his role as the Pinball Wizard at a benefit performance of "Tommy" at the Universal Amphitheatre, with Steve Winwood as the Hawker, Patti LaBelle as the Acid Queen, Phil Collins as Uncle Ernie and Billy Idol as Cousin Kevin.
Sept ***Sleeping With The Past*** initially hits UK #6 and US #23. (Recording of the title cut had begun at 4:15 p.m. with John seeing Taupin's lyrics for the first time: by 6:30 p.m., a finished composition and recording was in the can.)
[6] John plays the first of eight concerts at Madison Square Garden, during a three-month US tour.
Oct [20] *Healing Hands* reaches US #13.
Nov Taupin/John-penned ballad, *Sacrifice*, initially peaks at UK #55.
Dec No longer with a financial interest in the club, John is given the honorary position of Life President of Watford Football Club.

1990

Mar [31] *Sacrifice* reaches US #18.
Apr [7] John makes a surprise appearance at "Farm Aid IV" in the Hoosier Dome, Indianapolis, IN, at which he dedicates *Candle In The Wind* to AIDS victim Ryan White, for whom John has been maintaining a bedside vigil. White will die hours later.
[11] John sings *Skyline Pigeon* and acts as pall bearer at White's funeral in the Second Presbyterian Church in Indianapolis.
May [18-19] He plays at the inaugural concert for the 5,200-seat Mark Etess Arena, Trump Taj Mahal Casino Resort, Atlantic City, NJ.
June [23] Reissued after continuous airplay, *Sacrifice* (now a double A-side with the also-reissued *Healing Hands*) hits UK #1, John's first-ever solo UK chart-topper and his 66th single release. John announces on the BBC1-TV chat show "Wogan" that the royalties from this and all his future UK singles will go to various AIDS charities.
July [7] *Club At The End Of The Street* reaches US #28.
[28] Revived ***Sleeping With The Past*** hits UK #1.
[29] Following years of self-abuse, a close friend urges John to get help and avoid self-destruction. He duly embarks on six weeks of "recovery" in Parkside Lutheran Hospital, Chicago, IL rehabilitation clinic to cure bulimia,

and addiction to drink and drugs. Following his stay, he takes a year off from recording and touring.
Aug *Club At The End Of The Street/Whispers* makes UK #47.
Oct [27] Ballad *You Gotta Love Someone*, produced by Don Was and extracted from the forthcoming boxed-set, makes UK #33.
Nov [10] Double album, ***The Very Best Of Elton John***, his latest collection, hits UK #1.
Dec [15] Boxed-set CD/cassette retrospective compilation, ***To Be Continued ...***, chronicling John's career to date, makes US #82.
[29] *Easier To Walk Away* peaks at UK #63.

1991

Jan [5] *You Gotta Love Someone* reaches US #43.
Feb [10] John is named Best British Male Artist at the tenth annual BRIT Awards, held at London's Dominion Theatre.
Mar [10] He performs at the second annual Rainforest Foundation benefit show held at Carnegie Hall, New York, singing *Come Down In Time* with Sting.
[22] He makes a surprise appearance at George Michael's opening night performance at the Wembley Arena.
Apr [1] John crashes longtime sparring partner Rod Stewart's Wembley concert, dressed to look like Stewart's new bride, Rachel Hunter, and duets on *You're In My Heart.* (The new Mrs. Stewart has helped John with his make-up.)
[21] **The Sunday Times,** in its annual list of the richest Britons, states that John is currently worth £100 million.
May [2] *Sacrifice* wins Best Selling A-Side and Best Song Musically And Lyrically categories at the 36th Ivor Novello Awards, at the Grosvenor House Hotel.
[11] John adds his autograph to a $12,000 Young Chang grand piano being auctioned at the Peabody Hotel, Orlando, FL, to raise money for the "Give Kids The World" charity foundation.
June [22] ***For Our Children***, to which John contributes *The Pacifier*, reaches US #31.
Sept [7] He takes part in a 3.2 mile "From All Walks of Life" walk (to raise awareness of, and funds for, AIDS) in Atlanta, a city he now calls home. (Meanwhile, Johnstone and Olsson team with recent John backing-group recruit Guy Babylon to form ad-hoc outfit the Warpipes, set to perform during John's sabbaticals.)
Oct [3] *Club At The End Of The Street*, *You Gotta Love Someone* and *Sacrifice* are honored at the ASCAP's 11th annual awards at Claridge's in London.
[16] John attends the launch of ***Two Rooms - Celebrating The Songs Of Elton John & Bernie Taupin*** at the Four Seasons restaurant in New York.
Nov [5] He attends a celebrity luncheon to benefit the AIDS Crisis Trust in London with Michael Caine, Elizabeth Taylor and attended by Princess Margaret.
[11] John begins a campaign outside 10 Downing Street organized by the Lions Club International and sponsored by Lenscrafters to collect glasses for near-sighted needy folks in Latin America.
[22] John reviews his career and personal life in a lucid conversation with David Frost on PBS-TV, during which he reveals that between 1976 and 1990 his addiction to drugs and alcohol, his emotional swings and bouts of bulimia left him looking like "a bookmaker at Plumpton Racecourse". Following his rehabilitation in 1990 (during which his admitted greatest fear was the prospect of having to do his own laundry), John decides to live on his own for the first time, in a house in Holland Park, London, his only companion being his dog, Thomas, which he has adopted from the Battersea Dogs Home. During the interview, John says that the nearest to perfection he feels he has come professionally is *Candle In The Wind.*
[24] Coca-Cola begins a global advertising campaign for Diet Coke, with John as the central character in a musical number also controversially featuring technological "cameos" by Louis Armstrong and Humphrey Bogart.
[27] He mourns at a private funeral for Freddie Mercury, who succumbed to AIDS on the 24th.
Dec [7] George Michael and John's live *Don't Let The Sun Go Down On Me* debuts at UK #1.

1992

Jan [4] John matches Elvis Presley's record as the act with the most consecutive years (22) with a Top 40 hit on the US Hot 100.
[11] Tribute album ***Two Rooms - Celebrating The Songs Of Elton John & Bernie Taupin*** reaches US #18. The featured artists and songs are: Oleta Adams (*Don't Let The Sun Go Down On Me*), the Beach Boys (*Crocodile Rock*), Jon Bon Jovi (*Levon*), Kate Bush (*Rocket Man*), Eric Clapton (*Border Song*), Joe Cocker (*Sorry Seems To Be The Hardest Word*), Phil Collins (*Burn Down The Mission*), Hall & Oates (*Philadelphia Freedom*), Bruce Hornsby (*Madman Across The Water*), George Michael (*Tonight*), Sinead O'Connor (*Sacrifice*), Rod Stewart (*Your Song*), Sting (*Come Down In Time*), Tina Turner (*The Bitch Is Back*), the Who (*Saturday Night's Alright For Fighting*) and Wilson Phillips (*Daniel*).
Feb [1] Michael and John's *Don't Let The Sun Go Down On Me* tops the US chart for a week.
[25] James Galway's version of John's *Basque* wins Best Instrumental Composition at the 34th annual Grammy Awards, from Radio City Music Hall.
Mar Two days after announcing their separation H.R.H. Prince Andrew and his wife Sarah attend a party at John's home.
[12] John appears at "An Evening Of Porter, Gershwin & Coward...", the third annual Rainforest Foundation benefit, at Carnegie Hall.
[15] He gives two concerts at the Grand Ole Opry House to benefit the Dee Murray Family Memorial Fund, after his former bassist died on January 14th of a massive stroke, following treatment for malignant melanoma. (John then begins work on new tracks at the Studio Guillaume Tell, Paris, France, as he signs a new recording deal with PolyGram for up to six albums.)
May [27] John and Taupin are inducted into the Songwriters Hall of Fame in New York.
June [1-2] He performs at the Westfalenhalle, Dortmund, West Germany, at the start of the European leg of his current tour.
[20] *The One* hits UK #10.
[26] He presents Def Leppard with the Silver Clef award at the annual Nordoff-Robbins Music Therapy lunch, at London's Inter-Continental Hotel.
[26-28] John plays sellout dates at Wembley Stadium with Eric Clapton.
[27] ***The One***, his 31st UK chart album in 22 years, enters at its #2 peak, behind Lionel Richie's ***Back To Front***.
July [21] John's concert at Barcelona Stadium in Spain is broadcast live by Radio 1, as part of its 25th anniversary.
Aug [8] *Runaway Train*, featuring Eric Clapton, reaches UK #31.
[11] North American tour opens at the Lakewood Amphitheatre, Atlanta.
[21-22] John and Clapton gross $4,594,205 at two sellout shows at the Shea Stadium, Flushing, NY.
Sept [5] He announces at a press conference in New York that he will donate all future royalties from sales of his US singles to AIDS research. Royalties from *The Last Song* will go to six different charities. ***The One*** hits US #8.
[9] He guests on piano for Guns N' Roses' performance of *November Rain* at the ninth annual MTV Video Music Awards held at the Pauley Pavilion, Los Angeles, having already performed *The One*.
[18] John is sued by Los Angeles songwriters George Saadi and Ray Pickens, who allege that he knowingly or subconsciously based the ***Sleeping With The Past*** instrumental *Whispers* on their *Only Memories* tune. Saadi claims he gave a cassette copy of the song to John at a 1984 backstage meeting.
[19] Title cut, *The One*, hits US #9.
[22] *Don't Let The Sun Go Down On Me* and *You Gotta Love Someone* are honored at the annual ASCAP PRS Awards as two of the most performed songs in 1991.
Oct [2-3, 5, 7, 9-10] John plays six sellout dates at Madison Square Garden, before a total audience of 113,406.
[9] He is inducted into Madison Square Garden's Walk of Fame, the first non-athlete to be so honored. During the show, however, John allegedly hits security guard Robert Simms on the back of the head. Simms, who is hospitalized at St. Vincent's for a couple days after, will file a harassment complaint.
[11] John appears at an Elizabeth Taylor AIDS Foundation benefit at Madison Square Garden, with Bruce Hornsby, George Michael and Lionel Richie.
[21] He files a lawsuit in Fulton County Superior Court, Atlanta against the syndicated TV show "Hard Copy" and Paramount Pictures Corp. for extortion, slander, invasion of privacy and reckless endangerment, for reporting that he had moved to Atlanta to be near an AIDS treatment center. John's attorneys contend that reporter Deborah Scranton used a helicopter to spy on him at home and threatened to run a negative story on the star if he declined an interview.
Nov [1] He takes part in Neil Young's annual "Bridge School Benefit", with Sammy Hagar, Pearl Jam and James Taylor, before a sellout crowd of 20,000 at the Shoreline Amphitheatre, Mountain View, CA, as PolyGram begins the reissue of John's early work on CD, including ***Rare Masters***, a new 37-song collection of rare B-sides, out-takes and the complete soundtrack John recorded for the film "Friends".
[4] John and Taupin sign a record $39-million publishing deal with Warner-Chappell, for the rights to both back-catalog (post-1974) and future compositions.
[13-14] He breaks the house record at the Azteca Stadium, Mexico City, Mexico, when two crowds totalling 180,000 see his show. (He will subsequently cancel three concerts in Brazil and Chile, citing tiredness.)
[14] *The Last Song* reaches UK #21.
[18] John takes part in the AIDS Project Los Angeles' "Commitment To Life VI" cocktail-and-dinner party benefit to honor Barbra Streisand and David Geffen.
Dec [19] *The Last Song* reaches US #23.
[31] John, who during the year allegedly received $750,000 to perform on the Sultan of Brunei's yacht for his 46th birthday, appears on Fox-TV's "New Year's Eve Live".

1993

Jan [18] "Elton John Unplugged" airs on MTV Europe, as he resigns his directorship of Watford Football Club.
[28] During a speech at the Marriott Hotel for the annual NATPE convention in San Francisco, CA, John, accepting a cheque for $250,000 from Michael and Roger King (Kingworld) for his newly formed Elton John AIDS Foundation says: "I've had my ups and my downs, and now that I'm up I'm grateful that I escaped being HIV positive when I was down - and I want to give back. I realized how precious life is and that we must educate everyone."
Feb [19] He cuts short an encore in Melbourne, Victoria, during his current Australian tour, after the stage is overcome by crickets.
Mar [4-6, 8-9, 11-12] John grosses AUS $2,958,506 at the Sydney Entertainment Centre, Sydney.
Apr [17] *Simple Life* reaches US #30, making John the first artist to have a Top 40 hit for 24 consecutive years, breaking Elvis Presley's record of 23. He celebrates by playing the second of two sellout shows at the Boston Garden, Boston.
[27] He participates in "Aretha Franklin: Duets", the diva's first TV special (to benefit the Gay Men's Health Crisis), taped at New York's Nederlander Theatre, singing *Spirit In The Dark* and duetting with the Queen of Soul on *Border Song*. (The show will air on Fox-TV on May 9th.)
May [15] He begins the German leg of his world tour at the Westfallenhalle, Dortmund.
[22] *Simple Life* bows at its UK #44 peak.
June [1] John becomes an Officer of Arts and Letters at the Culture Ministry in Paris, an honor bestowed upon him by Culture Minister, Jacques Toubon.

[17] Having flown into Tel Aviv on the 15th for a concert and then flown back out again when he is not afforded VIP treatment at the airport, John opens his rescheduled concert with *The Bitch Is Back*, playing to an appreciative 35,000 crowd.
Sept [4] "A Beacon In The War Against AIDS", in which John performs *The Last Song*, airs on ABC-TV.
[6] John joins Don Henley, Sting, Melissa Etheridge and special guests Aerosmith in a Walden Woods benefit concert at Foxboro Stadium, Foxborough, MA.
[20] John guests on NBC-TV's "The Tonight Show".
[22-23] He performs at the "Slam'n'Jam" tennis tournament/concert and dinner at the Great Western Forum, Inglewood, CA and the Regent Beverly Wilshire, Los Angeles, with Billie Jean King. (John and King beat Martina Navratilova and Bobby Riggs 4-2.)
Nov [1] John tells a high court jury that he spent 16 years fighting bulimia and an addiction to drugs and alcohol during a trial at which he is suing the **Sunday Mirror** for false reporting.
[4] He is awarded £350,000 libel damages after the **Sunday Mirror** is found guilty.
[27] *True Love*, a duet with Kiki Dee, from John's new album ***Duets***, hits UK #2.
Dec [4] ***Duets***, comprising newly recorded collaborations with guest artists including drag queen RuPaul, debuts at its UK #5 peak.
[6] John plays the first of four concert at Sun City in South Africa.
[11] ***Duets*** bows at its US #25 peak.
[21] John guests on C4-TV's "Xmas In New York : RuPaul's Christmas In New York".
[25] *True Love* climbs to US #56.

1994

Jan [19] John is inducted into the Rock and Roll Hall of Fame by Axl Rose at the ninth annual dinner at New York's Waldorf Astoria Hotel. In his induction speech, Rose reveals "For myself, no one has been more of an inspiration than Elton John. When I first heard *Bennie And The Jets*, I knew I had to be a performer".
Feb [14] He co-hosts, with RuPaul, the 13th annual BRIT Awards at London's Alexandra Palace, opening the evening with a performance of *Don't Go Breaking My Heart*.
[18] John is interviewed in "Paula's Boudoir" on C4-TV's "The Big Breakfast".
[26] He performs at the "San Remo Song Festival".
Mar [5] Revised version of his prior UK chart-topper, *Don't Go Breaking My Heart*, duetted with RuPaul, hits UK #7.
[21] John is interviewed on ABC-TV's annual Oscar night "Barbara Walters Special", before hosting his second Academy Awards Viewing Party at Maple Drive, Beverly Hills, to benefit the Elton John AIDS Foundation.
Apr [9] He takes part in the fifth annual RainForest benefit concert at Carnegie Hall, with Sting, Branford Marsalis, James Taylor, Aaron Neville, Tammy Wynette, Luciano Pavarotti and special guest Whitney Houston.
May [21] *Ain't Nothing Like The Real Thing*, a duet with Marcella Detroit, also from ***Duets***, reaches UK #24.
[25] He presents Take That's Gary Barlow with the Best Contemporary Song Award at the 39th annual Ivor Novello awards from Grosvenor House Hotel.
[28] *Don't Go Breaking My Heart* debuts at its US #92 peak.
July [8-9, 12] John and Billy Joel begin a US summer tour with three sellout shows at Veterans Stadium in Philadelphia, grossing $7,315,495. (During the year, the piano men will also begin composing songs together.)
[23] Ballad *Can You Feel The Love Tonight*, featured in the Disney movie "The Lion King" for which John and UK lyricist Sir Tim Rice have contributed most of the songs, reaches UK #14.
Aug [6] *Can You Feel The Love Tonight*, featuring backing vocals from Kiki Dee, Rick Astley and Take That's Gary Barlow, hits US #4.
[25] John takes part in a pro-celebrity tennis tournament at Longwood Cricket Club in Boston, MA, to benefit the Elton John AIDS Foundation.
Sept [19-22] John finishes his US tour with four sellout dates at the Greek Theatre, Los Angeles. (His 1994 US dates have grossed in excess of $56 million and been seen by more than 1.2 million people.)
Oct [8] *Circle Of Life*, also from "The Lion King", debuts at its UK #11 peak.
[10] Tammy Wynette's new duets album, ***Without Walls***, featuring a collaboration with John on *What A Woman Needs*, is released in the US. (After completing the John/Taupin composition, Wynette asks John to sign the lyric sheet, prompting the self-effacing scribble : "To the queen of country music from the queen of England".)
[14] *Simple Life*, *The Last Song* and *The One* are honored at the 14th annual ASCAP dinner at London's Park Lane Hotel.
[15] *Circle Of Life* reaches US #18.
[23] John takes part in the "Stonewall Equality Show" at the Royal Albert Hall, with Sting, Melissa Etheridge and Alison Moyet among others.
[26] *Your Song* and *Candle In The Wind* receive awards at BMI's annual awards ceremony at London's Dorchester Hotel for reaching their respective four millionth and second millionth performance in the US.
Nov Celebrating his work in the UK between 1969-1970 as an uncredited cover song artist for non-original artist compilations, RPM Records releases ***Reg Dwight's Piano Goes Pop***, subsequently re-titled ***Elton John : Chartbusters - The Sessions Years***.
[8] **The Star** magazine reports that John is having a romance with Atlanta bodybuilder Dean Steib. John will subsequently file a lawsuit against the tabloid, saying he had met Steib twice and didn't have "even the remote version of a friendship, not to mention anything else".
[27] John begins an 11-date stint, through to December 12th at London's Royal Albert Hall, accompanied by his longtime percussionist Cooper.

1995

Jan John reactivates the Rocket label. Run by his longtime manager John Reid in New York, the first signing is singer/songwriter Ryan Douglas. (During the month he performs at a private concert with Sting at the Waldorf Astoria Hotel to benefit the Elton John AIDS Foundation.)
Feb [20] He receives the Outstanding Contribution to the British Music Industry award from Sting at the 14th annual BRIT Awards, from London's Alexandra Palace, and performs his current single *Believe*.
[25] John gives an in depth interview to the **New Musical Express** - his first face-to-face in four years. He also appears on BBC1-TV's "Live And Kicking".
Mar [11] Anthemic *Believe* reaches UK #15.
[20-21] John signs copies of his new album with Taupin from midnight at Tower Records' West Hollywood store.
[22] He begins his 1995 North American tour with Billy Joel at the Jack Murphy Stadium in San Diego, CA, before a sellout crowd of 52,665.
[27] John performs *Can You Feel The Love Tonight* and picks up the Oscar for Best Original Song, with lyricist Rice at the 67th annual Academy Awards from the Shrine Auditorium.
Apr [1] ***Made In England***, released on the relaunched Rocket label, hits UK #3 in its week of entry.
[3] VH-1-TV launches a week-long "Elton John-A-Thon", a week of programming intermittently devoted to the star, including interviews, old documentaries and concert performances.
[8] ***Made In England*** debuts at its US #13 peak.
[12] John performs at the sixth annual RainForest benefit concert at Carnegie Hall.
May [9] John is presented with the prestigious Polar Music Prize by the King of Sweden at a ceremony in Stockholm. This year's other recipient is Russian cellist Mstislav Rostropovich.
[13] *Believe* reaches US #13.
[15] John guests on CBS-TV's "Late Show With David Letterman".
[23] *Circle Of Life* is named Best Song Included In A Film at the 40th annual Ivor Novello Awards from the Grosvenor House Hotel.
[27] Title cut *Made In England* reaches UK #18.
June [6] John plays the first of two concerts at the Kremlin Palace of Congresses in Moscow, Russia - 16 years after his first historic Russian concert tour.
[23-25] He performs at the three-day "Rock Over Germany" festival with Rod Stewart and Joe Cocker.
Aug [12] *Made In England* makes US #52, as John plays the second of a brace of sellout dates at the Blockbuster-Sony Music Entertainment Center in Camden, NJ.
Oct [12-14, 17, 19-20] With John featured on Randy Newman's newly released all-star ***Faust*** concept album, he concludes his latest tour at Madison Square Garden, with 91,134 people paying $3,530,399 to see him in concert.
[27] John is named Songwriter Of The Year at the annual PRS/ASCAP Awards held in London.
Nov [9] John and Rice win the Robert Musel Award for the most played song (*Can You Feel The Love Tonight*) on US radio and television in 1994, at the annual BMI/PRS Awards dinner in London.
[15] John guests on the "Late Show With David Letterman".
[16] He visits New York's Hard Rock Café to launch pins to be sold at $5 each to raise money for the Elton John AIDS Foundation for a two-week period up to Worlds AIDS Day on December 1st.
Dec [16] Ballad *Blessed* reaches US #34, as a new compilation ***Love Songs*** hits UK #4.

1996

Jan [1] John is awarded the CBE in H.R.H. Queen Elizabeth II's New Years Honours List.
Feb [3] *Please* makes UK #33 in its week of entry.
Apr [12] He performs at the seventh annual RainForest Benefit concert held at Carnegie Hall.

HOWARD JONES

1973

Jones (b. John Howard Jones, Feb. 23, 1955, Southampton, Hants.), already an accomplished pianist who began playing at the age of seven, has begun to write songs and joined his first group Warrior in 1970, while living temporarily with his parents in Canada, where his father's lecturing job has kept the family on the move. He now studies at the Royal Northern School of Music in Manchester, Gtr. Manchester, but will leave to work in a factory, and later becomes a full-time piano teacher (one of his pupils being his future wife, Jan) and, also playing in amateur bands. In 1979 Jones buys a synthesizer with damages received after a road accident and begins to sing, with his own synth accompaniment, in pubs and clubs around his home in High Wycombe, Bucks. He also meets Jed Hoile, a mime artist who will later become his partner on stage.

1983

May As the result of a 24-track demo tape of *New Song* and *What Is Love*, Jones is signed to WEA Records in the UK and Elektra Records in the US.
Oct His debut single, *New Song*, produced by Colin Thurston, hits UK #3, as Jones makes his UK TV debut with pre-programmed synthesizer backing.

1984

Jan Its equally catchy pop follow-up *What Is Love* hits UK #2.
Mar *Hide And Seek* reaches UK #12.
[17] Jones' freshman album, the self-penned ***Human's Lib***, produced by Rupert Hine and featuring Hine's own drummer, Trevor Morais, and Jones' brother, Martin, playing bass, enters the UK chart at #1, selling 100,000 copies in its first week.
[31] *New Song* reaches US #27, an immediate radio favorite.

June *Pearl In The Shell* hits UK #7.
[9] *What Is Love* makes US #33, as ***Human's Lib*** climbs to US #59.
July Jones tours the US as support act to Eurythmics.
Aug *Like To Get To Know You Well* hits UK #4. The same title is given to a long-form performance video.
Dec Low-priced ***The Twelve Inch Album*** reaches UK #15, a compilation mini-set of re-mixes and extended versions of earlier singles, with two previously unreleased tracks. Jones tours the UK, supported by Strawberry Switchblade, culminating in a performance at London's Royal Albert Hall on Christmas Eve.

1985

Feb *Things Can Only Get Better*, with the help of the TKO Horns and Afrodiziak, hits UK #6. Jones appears on UK TV for the first time with a group calling itself the Howard Jones Big Band.
Mar ***Dream Into Action***, again helmed by Hine, hits UK #2.
Apr [16] He plays a major London concert date at the Wembley Arena, Wembley, Middx.
May *Look Mama* hits UK #10.
June [15] *Things Can Only Get Better* hits US #5, as ***Dream Into Action*** hits US #10.
July *Life In One Day* reaches UK #14.
[13] He participates in the "Live Aid" concert at Wembley Stadium, Wembley.
Sept [7] *Life In One Day* reaches US #19.
Nov [2] *Like To Get To Know You Well*, belatedly released in the US, makes #49.

1986

Mar Re-recorded version of the ballad *No One Is To Blame* (the original appeared on ***Dream Into Action***), produced by Phil Collins, reaches UK #16.
July [5] Revamped *No One Is To Blame* proves a bigger success in the US, where it hits #4, Jones' highest-placed US record, as the six-track mini-album, ***Action Replay***, including the hit, climbs to US #34.
Oct *All I Want* reaches UK #35. ***One To One***, recorded with US producer Arif Mardin, hits UK #10.
Nov He contributes *Little Bit Of Snow* to the Anti-Heroin Project charity album, ***Live-In World***, with proceeds going to the Phoenix House rehabilitation centre for drug and alcohol addicts. ***One To One*** peaks at US #56. The "Last World Dream" and "Howard Jones Live" videos are released.
[29] *You Know I Love You ... Don't You?* makes UK #43.
Dec [20] *You Know I Love You ... Don't You?* reaches US #17.

1987

Feb [14] *All I Want* climbs to US #76.
Mar Ballad *A Little Bit Of Snow* peaks at UK #70. Jones, a lacto-vegetarian (eating dairy products but no fish or meat), opens a vegetarian restaurant in New York, NY, which burns down within 12 months. He will continue to support various causes with performances during the year, including more anti-drug projects, an appearance at the Hurricane Irene benefit and a performance at New York's Madison Square Garden during his "One To One" US trek.

1989

Mar *Everlasting Love* peaks at UK #62.
Apr [1] ***Cross That Line***, produced, composed and arranged by Jones, and featuring Alan Hewitt on chainsaw, charts for a week at UK #64 and will make US #65.
June [3] *Everlasting Love* reaches US #12, as Jones embarks on a US tour.
Aug [26] *The Prisoner* reaches US #30.

1990

Nov [3] ***Rubáiyát***, Elektra's 40th-anniversary compilation, to which Jones has contributed a cover of David Ackles' 1968 original *Road To Cairo*, makes US #140.
[13] Jones contributes to the ***Rock The World*** benefit album, to raise money for the Phoenix House, a London-based rehab center.

1991

May [4] ***Tame Yourself***, a benefit album for the People for the Ethical Treatment of Animals (PETA) and to which Jones has contributed a track, peaks at US #165.

1992

Apr [18] *Lift Me Up* makes UK #52, taken from the East West-released album ***In The Running***.
[28] During a short tour of North America, Jones sells out the Variety Arts Center, Los Angeles, CA.
May [6-7] Jones plays two shows at the Shaw Theatre, Euston, London.
June [13] *Lift Me Up* reaches US #32.

1993

June [5] Ending his association with WEA/East West/Elektra, ***The Best Of Howard Jones*** debuts at its UK #36 peak, during a two-week chart stay and includes his version of Donald Fagen's *D.I.Y.*
Dec [15] Jones performs a sole London date at the Mean Fiddler, Harlesden.

1996

Feb [12] After a two year sabbatical, Jones has returned to live work with last year's unplugged club tour across the States, followed by UK dates including a performance at the Jazz Café in London on November 30th. Plump Records (US) now releases the performance set, ***Live Acoustic America***, recorded during last year's tour.

RICKIE LEE JONES

1973

One of four children, Jones (b. Nov. 8, 1954, Chicago, IL), who has written her first song, *I Wish*, at age seven, has run away from home for the first time in 1969, fleeing with a girlfriend from Phoenix, AZ, to San Diego, CA. They steal a car, but the adventure only lasts three days. Having moved to Olympia, WA, the following year, she has been asked to leave three schools in succession, including Timberline High School in Olympia, where she is removed for insubordination. Now arriving in Los Angeles, CA, Jones begins waitressing in an Echo Park-area Italian restaurant and starts playing her own songs, some in spoken-word monologues, at local clubs, including the Troubadour.

1977

Aug Having written *Easy Money* while working, and singing part-time, at Venice coffee house, Suzanne's, the previous year, she composes *The Last Chance Texaco* and *Chuck E.'s In Love*, the latter about fabled Los Angeles figure Chuck E. Weiss, whom Jones has met in the kitchen at the Tropicana Motel, Los Angeles. They then meet Tom Waits, a Tropicana resident who becomes Jones' sometime beau.

1978

Mar Linking with manager Nick Mathe, they send Warner Bros. Records a four-song EP, *Company*, *Young Blood*, *The Last Chance Texaco* and *Easy Money*, recorded as a demo (originally for A&M). Warner's A&R producer Lenny Waronker also sees Jones at a Troubadour showcase. Little Feat's Lowell George tips the scales when he chooses to record *Easy Money* on his solo album, ***Thanks, I'll Eat Here***, having heard it sung down the phone. Warner Bros. signs Jones to a worldwide contract, on her stipulation that Waronker co-produces her debut.
Nov She appears as the blonde on the sleeve of Tom Waits' newly released ***Blue Valentine***.

1979

Apr Self-written maiden album, ***Rickie Lee Jones***, highlighted by her literate-hobo composition skills and distinctive vocal style, is released simultaneously with *Chuck E.'s In Love*. (The single will hit US #4 (July [7]) and UK #18.) The album hits US #3, earning a platinum disc, and makes UK #18 (July [14]).
May Following a limited showcase US tour of small clubs, Jones appears on NBC-TV's "Saturday Night Live", despite arguing with the producers over her choice of song. She wins out, performing *Coolsville*.
June Jones takes part in a three-hour jam with Bruce Springsteen and Boz Scaggs at Los Angeles' Whisky A Go-Go club.
Sept [1] As follow-up, *Young Blood*, makes US #40, Jones begins her first major tour, including sellout dates at New York, NY's Carnegie Hall.

1980

Feb [27] Jones wins Best New Artist Of 1979 at the 22nd annual Grammy Awards.

1981

Aug After a two-year hiatus, Jones returns with her second album, ***Pirates***, co-produced by Waronker and Russ Titelman and re-utilizing a number of top sessioneers, including Chuck Rainey, Steve Gadd, Steve Lukather, Lenny Castro and Donald Fagen. It will hit US #5, achieving gold status, and UK #37 (Aug [15]).
Oct [24] *A Lucky Guy* peaks at US #64. The following year, Jones will move from Los Angeles to New York, then to Paris, France, in an attempt to cope with the pressures of fame.

1983

July After another two-year retreat, a 10" seven-track mini-album, ***Girl At Her Volcano***, is released, making US #39 and UK #51. With two live cuts, it features revivals of *On Broadway* and *Walk Away Renée*, and a new Tom Waits number, *Angel Wings*. Another Jones-performed Waits ballad will also feature in Martin Scorsese's movie "King Of Comedy".

1984

Feb She returns to live in Los Angeles, with a new boyfriend and cat.
Oct [6] *The Real End* peaks at US #83, while its parent album, ***The Magazine***, is released. Co-produced with James Newton Howard, it makes US #44 and UK #40 and features musical assistance from Toto band members, among others.
Nov "The Magazine" tour begins in the US Midwest.

1985

Jan Jones plays her first Australian dates, followed by a European visit including sellout UK concerts and Eastern bloc gigs, after which she goes to Tahiti, where she meets husband-to-be, French musician Pascal Nebet-Meyer. They live in France for a year, before moving to Ojai, CA.

1989

Apr She gives birth to a daughter, Charlotte.
Aug Jones is a featured artist on Rob Wasserman's ***Duets*** album.
Oct [7] She is the musical guest on "Saturday Night Live". (***Flying Cowboys***, produced by Steely Dan's Walter Becker at the Studio 55, the Village and Cherokee studios, makes UK #50 and will reach US #39.)

1990

Jan [17] Jones sings with Ray Davies at the fifth annual Rock and Roll Hall of Fame after-dinner jam held at New York's Waldorf Astoria hotel.
Feb [21] *Makin' Whoopee* wins the Best Jazz Vocal Performance, Duo Or Group category at the 32nd annual Grammy Awards, at the Shrine Auditorium, Los Angeles.
Mar Jones' low-key two-week "Flying Cowboys Saloon Tour" plays at such venues as Toads and Slim's in San Francisco, CA.
May [30] Jones begins a major US tour, with Lyle Lovett in support, in Atlanta, GA, set to end in Los Angeles on July 11-12th.

1991

Apr She takes part in a "Bread & Roses" benefit, with Huey Lewis and others, at Boz Scaggs' part-owned Slim's in San Francisco.

Oct [12] Torch set, ***Pop Pop***, an acoustic collection which eschews the use of drums and synthesizers, co-produced with Don Was, bows at its US #121 peak.

Sept Apart since May, Jones is officially separated from her husband.

Nov [22] During a brief US tour, Jones performs before a sellout crowd of 1,279 at the Keswick Theatre, Glenside, PA.

1992

Jan [1-3] Jones files divorce papers, requesting custody of her three-year old daughter Charlotte, and does not want to pay spousal support.

[4] The Chieftains' ***The Bells Of Dublin***, to which Jones contributes *O Holy Night*, peaks at US #107.

Feb [8] She performs at the Wiltern Theatre, Los Angeles, before a sellout crowd of 2,200, as part of a handful of dates in California.

Mar Jones is featured on *North Dakota* from Lyle Lovett's newly-released ***Joshua Judges Ruth*** album.

[20] She plays at London's Dominion Theatre, during a brief UK tour - her first since 1983.

July [12] Jones appears at London's Royal Festival Hall during the "Capital Radio Jazz Festival".

Sept [15] She plays to a sellout crowd at the Roxy in Atlanta, during current US dates.

Nov [18] Jones participates in "Commitment To Life VI" at the Universal Amphitheatre, Universal City, CA, honoring Barbra Streisand and David Geffen, and benefitting AIDS Project Los Angeles. (By year's end, she and Becker have written *The Horses*, a single for Daryl Braithwaite, before Jones begins production and vocal work - the following year - on an album for Leo Kottke.)

1993

Sept [22] Jones guests on NBC-TV's "The Tonight Show".

Oct [9] Self-penned and produced ***Traffic From Paradise***, featuring music guests Kottke, Dean Parks, Brian Setzer, Jim Keltner and Lovett, peaks at US #111.

1994

Mar [28-29] Jones plays two sellout dates at New York's Town Hall.

1995

Jan [21] She performs at a benefit for Voters For Choice at Washington, DC's Constitution Hall, with Bruce Hornsby, Shawn Colvin and Bruce Cockburn.

Oct [7] Having departed Geffen Records after three albums and much disatisfaction, and newly signed to Reprise Records, ***Naked Songs***, comprising 15 live solo acoustic recordings of her 1994 concert sweep with acoustic bassist Rob Wasserman, debuts at its US #121 peak.

[21] Jones pulls out of an Irish TV show in Dublin, Eire, when the producers refuse to allow her to sing *The Altar Boy*, because in their view it could offend some religious sensibilities. (She is in Europe to perform other dates in London, Paris and Amsterdam, before returning to the US to complete an autobiographical film with director Ethan Russell.)

TOM JONES

1964

Aug Raised in working-class coal-mining country in Wales, Jones (b. Thomas Jones Woodward, June 7, 1940, Pontypridd, Mid Glamorgan, Wales), having already married his first wife in 1956 and made his professional debut at the Treforest Non-Political Working Men's Club, Glamorgan, in 1957, and his TV premiere appearance on "Donald Peers Presents", has formed his first band, Tommy Scott & the Senators, in 1963, which recorded a number of tracks for EMI, under producer Joe Meek. Having been spotted supporting Mandy Rice-Davies in Pontypridd, by Gordon Mills, an ex-member of UK vocal group the Viscounts, the singer signs a management deal with Mills, who changes his name to Tom Jones (after the film of the same name) and now secures a deal with Decca Records, where his first release revives Ronnie Love's 1961 US hit, *Chills And Fever*.

Dec [3] Jones makes his radio debut on the BBC Radio's "Top Gear".

1965

Mar [11] The follow-up single, *It's Not Unusual*, written by Mills and Les Reed (originally with Sandie Shaw in mind) tops the UK chart for a week, instantly establishing Jones, who displays a powerful and distinctive vocal style, as a leading male solo singer in a scene currently dominated by group acts.

[13] He makes his first major UK TV appearance on BBC-TV's "Billy Cotton Band Show".

Apr [11] Jones appears at the annual "**New Musical Express** Poll Winners" concert at the Empire Pool, Wembley, Middx., backed by new stage group the Squires (who will play with him live throughout the mid-'60s), on a bill which includes the Beatles, the Rolling Stones, the Animals and many others. Later in the day he makes his debut on ITV's "Sunday Night At The London Palladium"

[26] He records *What's New Pussycat* in London with Burt Bacharach.

May *Once Upon A Time* makes UK #32.

[29] *It's Not Unusual* hits US #10. It also makes the R&B chart, with many programmers on black radio stations hearing it "blind", assuming Jones is both American and black.

[2] He makes his US TV debut on CBS-TV's "The Ed Sullivan Show", on a bill also featuring the Rolling Stones.

[10] Jones opens in a four-week UK variety tour at the New Theatre, Cardiff, Wales, followed by further weeks at the Theatre Royal, Nottingham, Notts., the Hippodrome Theatre, Birmingham, Warks., and the Hippodrome Theatre, Bristol, Somerset.

June His debut album, ***Along Came Jones***, reaches UK #11.

[13] Jones makes his second appearance on the "The Ed Sullivan Show".

[18] He begins a one-week stint at New York's Paramount Theatre.

[28] Jones guests on CBS-TV's "It's What's Happening Baby".

July [14] Jones heads the bill on a week-long Murray The K's Brooklyn Fox stage show, with Ben E. King, Gary Lewis & the Playboys and others.

[17] *Little Lonely One*, a pre-Decca track recorded with Meek, released in the US by Tower Records (a subsidiary of Capitol/EMI) to cash in on the success of *It's Not Unusual*, makes US #42.

[31] *What's New Pussycat*, a Bacharach/David song which is the theme to movie of the same title, hits US #3.

Aug [1] Jones embarks on a coast-to-coast US Dick Clark package tour with the Drifters, set to end on September 6th.

[7] His revival of Billy Eckstine's *With These Hands* reaches UK #13.

[28] ***It's Not Unusual*** (a re-titling of ***Along Came Jones***), peaks at US #54.

Sept [4] *What's New Pussycat* reaches UK #11.

Oct [2] *With These Hands* reaches US #27.

[4] Jones returns to the UK after spending almost three months in the US. He says in an interview that, having spent most of the year in the States, he faces the prospect that, "my long-term career will be in Britain".

[9] ***What's New Pussycat?***, compiled specifically for the US market, makes US #114. (Jones records Burt Bacharach's *Promise Her Anything* for the Leslie Caron film of the same name, and duets with Joan Baez on *If You Need Me* on her US TV special.)

Nov [17] Jones stars in his first TV special, "Call In On Tom", on ITV.

Dec [2] He takes part in a charity show at Carnegie Hall, New York, with Sammy Davis Jr. and Louis Armstrong.

[12] Jones guests on CBS-TV's The Ed Sullivan Show".

[29] He attends the premiere of "Thunderball" at the London Pavilion.

1966

Jan [22] *Thunderball*, the Jones-sung theme from the fourth James Bond film and written in a similar style to the highly successful *Goldfinger* from the previous Bond movie, reaches UK #35 and US #25.

Mar [12] *Promise Her Anything* peaks at US #74.

[15] Jones wins Best New Artist Of 1965 at the eighth annual Grammy Awards.

[18] He embarks on an Australian tour with Herman's Hermits.

Apr [12] Jones goes into hospital, ostensibly to have his tonsils removed, although there is speculation that his real intention is to have cosmetic surgery to diminish the size of his nose.

May [6] Jones makes his first TV appearance since leaving hospital, on ITV's "Ready Steady Go!".

June [11] *Not Responsible*, in Jones' ***It's Not Unusual*** style, reaches UK #18.

[21] He receives 14 stitches in his forehead after his Jaguar crashes into a barrier at Marble Arch, London.

July *Not Responsible* makes US #58.

Aug *This And That* peaks at UK #44.

[14] Jones guests in the premiere of ITV's "Bruce Forsyth Show".

Oct ***From The Heart*** reaches UK #23.

Dec [1] Sentimental ballad, *Green Green Grass Of Home*, tops the UK chart for the first of seven weeks, eventually shifting over 1,220,000 copies in Britain. Based on Jerry Lee Lewis' original, it becomes Jones' all-time biggest-selling single and gives Decca its first UK million-selling single by a British artist.

1967

Jan [7] Jones guests on the first edition of ITV's "Doddy's Music Box".

[23] He leaves for a six-day tour of South America, which will include four TV shows in Venezuela.

Feb [18] *Green Green Grass Of Home* reaches US #11.

[12] He headlines ITV's "Sunday Night At The London Palladium".

Mar Jones stays with country music on a revival of Bobby Bare's *Detroit City*, which hits UK #8 and reaches US #27.

[1] He begins a month-long stand at the Talk Of The Town, London.

[18] Jones opens a youth club in Harpenden, Herts.

Apr ***Green Green Grass Of Home*** hits UK #3 and reaches US #65.

[7] Jones' new ITV series premieres.

[13] He flies to Scandinavia for four days of concerts.

May [8] Jones opens a three-week season at the London Palladium.

[20] *Funny Familiar Forgotten Feelings* hits UK #7.

June [17] *Funny Familiar Forgotten Feelings* makes US #49.

July Live album, ***Live At The Talk Of The Town***, recorded at the London club, hits UK #6.

[4] Jones appears on the first telecast of the CBS-TV show "Spotlight", recorded at Elstree Studios in London as a summer replacement for "The Red Skelton Show". (He will regularly star on the show during its two-month run.)

Aug [26] *I'll Never Fall In Love Again*, reviving a ballad written and originally recorded by Lonnie Donegan, though never a hit, reaches UK #2, as a rock revival of Tennessee Ernie Ford's *Sixteen Tons* weighs in at US #68.

Oct *I'll Never Fall In Love Again* makes US #49.

Nov [2] Jones begins his first UK tour in almost three years, at the Astoria Theatre, Finsbury Park, London, set to end on the 26th at Coventry Theatre, Coventry, Warks.

[13] He takes part in the "Royal Variety Show" in London.

Dec [23] *I'm Coming Home* hits UK #2.

1968

Jan ***13 Smash Hits***, not a compilation, but rather a selection of covers of familiar songs by other artists, plus *I'll Never Fall In Love Again*), hits UK #5.
[20] *I'm Coming Home* reaches US #57.
[28] Jones guests on ITV's "Sunday Night At The London Palladium", on a bill with the Supremes and Des O'Connor.
[30] He sings on the premiere of Cilla Black's new BBC1-TV series.
Feb [15] Jones begins a two-week season at New York's Copacabana night spot.
Mar *Delilah*, a dramatic song of passion and revenge, which becomes the archetypical spoof number for Jones impressionists, hits UK #2.
[13] Jones beings a month-long cabaret season at Las Vegas, NV's Flamingo Hotel (which will become one his favored venues over the next two decades), set to end on April 13th.
Apr [17] Jones performs at the Hollywood Bowl, Hollywood, CA during a US tour.
[21] He leaves for Australia, for first leg of a six-month world tour.
May *Delilah* reaches US #15.
June [6] Jones begins a season at Bournemouth Winter Gardens, Dorset.
July ***The Tom Jones Fever Zone*** makes US #14.
Aug [24] *Help Yourself* hits UK #5.
Sept [21] ***Delilah*** tops the UK chart for a week.
Oct [10] Jones begins a 19-date UK tour at the New Victoria Theatre, London, set to close on December 3rd at the Odeon Theatre, Birmingham, Warks.
[12] *Help Yourself* makes US #35.
Dec *A Minute Of Your Time* reaches UK #14.
[4] Movie producer William Jugo offers Jones a role in the movie "Lie To Me", set to begin filming in the Bahamas in June.

1969

Jan ***Help Yourself*** hits UK #4 and US #5.
Feb [7] The weekly musical variety show, "This Is Tom Jones", airs for the first time on ABC-TV. Originated variously in London and Hollywood and with guest stars who usually duet with Jones on at least one song, the series, at the Friday-evening peak time, will bring in high ratings and cement Jones' stature as an "all-round entertainer" in the US. This, in turn, will lead him to settle in the United States and play in Las Vegas during the '70s and much of the '80s. The TV show will run for two years.
[15] *A Minute Of Your Time* reaches US #48.
Apr [21] Jones leaves for Australia for the first leg of a six-month world tour.
May *Love Me Tonight* hits UK #9, as ***Tom Jones Live!*** reaches US #13.
June Jones is invited to sing at the investiture of H.R.H. the Prince Of Wales.
July *Love Me Tonight* makes US #13, while ***This Is Tom Jones*** hits UK #2 and US #4.
[5] Jones performs in San Francisco, CA during California's British Week.
Sept Following a good response to it on the TV show, *I'll Never Fall In Love Again* is reissued in the US and hits #6, earning a gold disc.
[22] Jones appears with the Beatles, James Brown, Crosby, Stills, Nash & Young, Three Dog Night and others on the first telecast of ABC-TV's "The Music Scene".
Nov Performance album, ***Tom Jones Live In Las Vegas***, hits both UK and US #3.

1970

Jan His treatment of the Clyde McPhatter oldie, *Without Love (There Is Nothing)*, hits UK #10.
Feb *Without Love (There Is Nothing)* hits US #5.
Mar [17] Jones begins the first of four shows at London's Hammersmith Odeon.
May *Daughter Of Darkness* hits UK #5 and US #13, as ***Tom*** heads to UK #4 and US #6.
June [12-13] Jones breaks the Madison Square Garden, New York, box-office record with takings of $364,743.
July He breaks the box-office record at Holmdel, NJ, taking $250,000 for six nights. (By 1971, Jones has become the highest-paid singer in the world.)
Sept His revival of the Ben E. King/Shirley Bassey chestnut, *I (Who Have Nothing)*, reaches UK #16 and US #14.
Nov Its parent album, ***I (Who Have Nothing)***, hits UK #10 and reaches US #23.
Dec *Can't Stop Loving You*, unreleased in Britain, reaches US #25.

1971

Jan [15] The weekly TV series, "This Is Tom Jones", airs for the last time.
Feb *She's A Lady* reaches UK #13.
Apr *She's A Lady* hits US #2 and becomes a US million seller.
June *Puppet Man*, written by Neil Sedaka, reaches UK #49 and US #26, while ***She's A Lady*** hits UK #9 and US #17.
Nov *'Til*, a 1962 Top 20 hit for the Angels, hits UK #2 and US #41.
Dec Stage album, ***Live At Caesar's Palace***, recorded at the Las Vegas landmark, reaches UK #27 and US #43.

1972

May *The Young New Mexican Puppeteer* hits UK #6 and reaches US #80. ***Close Up*** will make UK #17 and US #64 the following month, as Jones then achieves a hit single and album for the next two years: *Letter To Lucille*, UK #31 and US #60 (May 1973), ***The Body And Soul Of Tom Jones***, UK #31 and US #93 (June 1973), the compilation album ***Greatest Hits***, UK #15 (Feb [16], 1974) and US #185 (January 1974), and *Something 'Bout You Baby I Like*, UK #36 (September 1974).

1975

Mar [22] Double album, ***20 Greatest Hits***, tops the UK chart for the first of four weeks. (By year's end, Jones will leave his Weybridge home to settle in Beverly Hills, CA.)

1977

Apr *Say You'll Stay Until Tomorrow* makes UK #40 and US #15, while ***Say You'll Stay Until Tomorrow*** reaches US #76. ***Tom Jones Greatest Hits*** climbs to US #191.
Aug Jones acts as a pallbearer at the funeral of musician Johnnie Spence, with Gilbert O'Sullivan and Gordon Mills. ***I'm Coming Home*** will reach UK #12 on Nov [4] the following year, while in 1979 Jones will appear in the TV movie "Pleasure Cove", with Joan Hackett, Shelley Fabares and Harry Guardino.

1983

With his only chart appearance of the decade thus far being ***Darlin'*** which peaked at US #179 in May 1981 and his style now out of mainstream vogue, Jones concentrates on recording country music, signing a new deal with Mercury Records in Nashville. *Touch Me (I'll Be Your Fool Once More)* hits US Country #4. (For the next three years, Jones' US singles success will be restricted to the Country chart: September 1983 - *It'll Be Me* (#34), February 1984 - *I've Been Rained On Too* (#13), June 1984 - *This Time* (#30), January 1985 - *I'm An Old Rock'n'Roller (Dancin' To A Different Beat)* (#67) and 1986's *It's Four In The Morning* (#36), while ***Don't Let Our Dreams Die Young*** makes US #9 (December 1983), ***Love Is On The Radio*** makes US #40 (1984) and ***Tender Loving Care*** makes US #54 (1986).)

1987

Apr Jones returns to the UK for the first extended period since settling in California in the early '70s. The main reason is to promote his role in the album version of the new musical by Mike Leander, "Matador", released by Epic. Based on the true story of a star of the Spanish bullring who rose from poverty in Andalucia, the work is mooted for a London stage production, and Jones is keen to take the lead role should it materialize.
May *A Boy From Nowhere*, a ballad in the traditionally powerful Jones' vocal style, from ***Matador***, hits UK #2, his first UK Top 10 success in 15 years, held off by Starship's *Nothing's Gonna Stop Us Now*. (Jones also makes his first appearance in ten years on BBC1-TV's "Top Of The Pops".)
June To capitalize on his chart success, Decca reissues Jones' original chart-topper, *It's Not Unusual* (which is already getting plays in some UK dance clubs because its distinctive rhythm matches a current Euro-beat dance trend), and it re-charts at UK #17.
[20] The studio cast-recorded album, ***Matador***, makes UK #26.
[27] Also cashing in on his resurrection, a TV-promoted compilation album, ***Tom Jones - The Greatest Hits***, on Telstar Records, makes UK #16. Jones performs at London's Royal Albert Hall, singing a diverse range of material, including *You Can Call Me Al*, *To Be A Lover* and *Kiss*.

1988

Jan A second cut from ***Matador***, *I Was Born To Be Me*, makes UK #61.
Oct Following his performance of Prince's number *Kiss* on the Jonathan Ross late-night C4-TV show, "The Last Resort", Jones has been contacted by Anne Dudley of UK instrumental group the Art of Noise, suggesting that he records the song as guest vocalist on a version by the group. Vocal and instrumental tracks are eventually recorded on opposite sides of the Atlantic, and then meshed into the finished production by Dudley. (She and the rest of the group do not actually meet Jones until the disc is in the shops.) Released on China Records (to which the Art of Noise is contracted), it is an instant UK smash, hitting #5, promoted by an appearance by Jones on the ITV variety show, "Live From The London Palladium".
Nov Jones appears with other Welsh entertainers on the George Martin-produced musical version of Dylan Thomas' **Under Milk Wood**, which is released on disc by EMI. Meanwhile, as a soloist, Jones signs a new recording contract with Jive Records.

1989

Jan [6] Jones guests on NBC-TV's "Late Night With David Letterman".
[14] *Kiss* reaches US #31.
May [20] ***At This Moment*** makes UK #34, as his extracted cover of Phyllis Nelson's hit, *Move Closer*, finds UK #49.
June [3] Jones takes part in "Our Common Future", a satellite broadcast seen in over 100 countries, featuring live performances by Sting in Rio de Janeiro, Brazil, Stevie Wonder in Warsaw, Poland, and others, with Jones singing from Oslo, Norway.
[27] Jones receives a star on the Hollywood Walk of Fame.
July [16] 27-year-old Katherine Berkery files a paternity suit against Jones. Manhattan Family Court Judge Judith B. Sheindlin finds in her favor and orders Jones to pay $200 a week in child support.
[22] ***After Dark***, recorded for TV-advertised label Stylus, sets at UK #46.
Sept [22] Jones and Berkery agree further terms for her child's support.

1991

Jan [26] After a one-year hiatus, during which Jones and his wife have spent time at their two-knocked-into-one council house in Wales, and he has signed a new recording deal with Chrysalis subsidiary Dover Records in the UK, he makes UK #51 with *Couldn't Say Goodbye*, a ballad penned by Diane Warren and Albert Hammond.
Feb [2] The soundtrack to Tim Burton's "Edward Scissorhands" movie, featuring Jones' *With These Hands*, makes US #174.
Mar Jones beats Theophilus P. Wildebeest, portrayed by comedian Lenny Henry, in a TV vote for the sexiest hunk in a live and overtly sexual act, as part of a UK Comic Relief telethon.

[21] Jones kicks off a hip-swirling major 25-date UK tour at the Apollo Theatre, Oxford, Oxon, set to end on April 20th at London's Hammersmith Odeon.
[23] Van Morrison-penned and-produced *Carrying A Torch* peaks at UK #57. It is one of four live tracks on which the Celtic icons have collaborated for Jones' forthcoming album, also titled ***Carrying A Torch***, and recorded at the Townhouse Studios, London.
[29] Increasingly revered as a seminal act, Jones is featured on BBC1-TV's "Omnibus" special "Tom Jones : The Voice Made Flesh", as he plays four nights at the Fox Theatre, Detroit, MI.
Apr [13] ***Carrying A Torch*** makes UK #44.
May [12] Jones appears live at "The Simple Truth" benefit concert for Kurdish refugees at Wembley Arena.
July [21] Jones guests on ITV's "The Dame Edna Experience".
Dec [25] "The Ghost Of Oxford Street", directed by Malcolm McLaren and with Jones playing Gordon Selfridge, singing *Money* and *Nobody Loves You When You're Down And Out*, airs on C4-TV.

1992

Jan [15] Jones guests on ITV's "Des O'Connor Tonight".
June [6] With the singer as host, and performing with a different weekly guest artist in a loose appraisal of rock'n'roll history, "Tom Jones : The Right Time" premieres on ITV (to be broadcast on US cable web VH-1 in '93).
[22] Jones plays a sole London date, at the Town & Country club.
[28] He sings on the final day of the annual "Glastonbury Festival", Glastonbury, Somerset.
July [3-5] Jones performs at the Westbury Music Fair, Westbury, NY.
[4] Reissued *Delilah* debuts at its UK #68 peak, as ***The Complete Tom Jones*** hits UK #8.
Oct [16-17] 31-date UK tour begins at Manchester's Apollo Theatre, set to close on November 22nd at the Fairfield Halls, Croydon, Surrey.
Nov [5] "The Simpsons", in which Jones serenades Margo, airs on Fox-TV.
Dec [1] While Jones is finishing a two-number set for C4-TV's "Jack Dee Christmas Special" at the New Empire Club in London's Tottenham Court Road, a bomb warning is given outside. The audience, subsequently locked in, is treated to an hour of Jones singing.
[6] He performs at London's Town & Country club in aid of Capital Radio's Christmas Appeal. (During the year, he rehearses for the "World Choir Festival" in Cardiff, guests on Dread Zeppelin's ***It's Not Unusual*** album and is featured in the Michael Berger/Tim Rice musical, "Tycoon".)

1993

Jan [24] Jones appears on BBC2-TV's "The O Zone".
Feb [6] *All You Need Is Love*, recorded with Dave Stewart and released to benefit ChildLine, debuts at its UK #19 peak.
[8] Jones guests on NBC-TV's "The Fresh Prince Of Bel Air", playing a guardian angel. (He will also appear on NBC-TV's "The Tonight Show" and "Late Night With David Letterman" before month's end, while "The Right Time With Tom Jones" premieres on VH-1.)
Mar [2] He takes part in the fourth annual RainForest Foundation benefit at New York's Carnegie Hall, with Bryan Adams, Herb Alpert, George Michael, Sting, James Taylor, Tina Turner and Dustin Hoffman.
Apr [5] Jones is featured singing with New Model Army on the *Gimme Shelter* benefit single for the Putting Our House In Order charity, with eleven other versions of the song by other artists. He now signs a new recording deal with Interscope.
Dec [10] "David Foster's Christmas Album", which sees Jones featured on *Mary's Boy Child*, airs on NBC-TV.

1994

May [27] Jones guests on C4-TV's "Viva Cabaret".
July [14] During a current North American tour, Jones performs at the Garden State Arts Center, Holmdel, NJ.
Oct [13] Jones guests on CBS-TV's "Late Show With David Letterman".
Nov [12] *If I Only Knew*, remixed by Inner City and T-Empo, reaches UK #11.
[24] Jones hosts MTV Europe's first annual European Music Awards in Berlin.
[26] Now signed to Interscope Records in the US, Jones' new album (his first in six years), ***The Lead And How To Swing It***, variously produced Teddy Riley, Jeff Lynne, Trevor Horn and Flood, makes UK #55 in its week of entry. (During the year, Jones will be awarded the Fellowship of Welsh College of Music and Drama in Cardiff.)

1995

Jan [14] Jones plays to a sellout crowd of 2,530 at the Massey Hall in Toronto, ON, Canada, during his current North American tour.
Feb [10] He returns to "The Tonight Show".
Mar [8] Jones tapes a performance for TBS-TV's "Live From The House Of Blues", including a duet with Dwight Yoakam on *The Last Time*.
[10-12] He begins a short North American tour at Trump's Castle, Atlantic City, NJ.
Apr [8-9] Jones sings at Bruce Willis' 40th birthday party at the Dynomite Lounge, Ketchum, near Willis' home in Sun Valley.
[13-26] In a more natural habitat, Jones performs at the MGM Grand Garden, Las Vegas.
June [3] Jones takes part in the 16th annual KISS concert at Great Woods Center for the Performing Arts, Mansfield, MA, singing *You're So Vain* with Carly Simon.
Aug [11] He performs before a crowd of 5,171 at the Universal Amphitheatre, Universal City, CA.

JANIS JOPLIN

1963

Jan Saving money to make a trip to California, Joplin (b. Jan. 19, 1943, Port Arthur, TX) has begun earning a living in 1960, singing in clubs in Austin, TX, and Houston, TX, including a residency at the Purple Onion venue, and has become part of the Waller Creek Boys trio, together with R. Powell St. John, later a member of Mother Earth, a songwriter for the 13th Floor Elevators. Joplin now hitchhikes to San Francisco, CA, where she sings in North Beach clubs including the Coffee Gallery, either solo or with Jorma Kaukonen, later of Jefferson Airplane, or Roger Perkins. Her three-octave vocal range impresses those close to her, but she does not progress beyond sporadic singing jobs. In 1964, Joplin returns to Texas in an attempt to straighten out from her increasingly drug-filled (mostly amphetamines), hippy California lifestyle, enrolls at college, makes marriage plans and gives up singing.

1965

June With marriage plans abandoned, Joplin is about to join the 13th Floor Elevators, but returns to San Francisco as lead singer with improvisational blues outfit Big Brother & the Holding Company, the house band at the Avalon Ballroom.
[11] She performs with Big Brother for the first time.
Aug During a visit to Chicago, IL, Big Brother signs to Mainstream Records.

1966

Feb [19] Big Brother plays at San Francisco's Avalon Ballroom with Jefferson Airplane. (During the year, they will perform at the Avalon more than half a dozen times, sharing the bill with such acts as Country Joe & the Fish, Quicksilver Messenger Service, Bo Diddley, the Grass Roots, Sir Douglas Quintet and Love.)

1967

June [17] The group plays a show-stopping performance on the second day of the "Monterey International Pop Festival" at the County Fairgrounds, Monterey, CA. As a brash and powerful lead singer, Joplin is clearly the central focus, and Bob Dylan's manager, Albert Grossman, signs the group.
Aug Mainstream releases the band's debut album, ***Big Brothers & The Holding Company***, which reaches US #60.

1968

Feb Big Brother & the Holding Company, now a major draw on the West Coast, makes its New York, NY debut at the Anderson Theater on Second Avenue.
Mar [8] Big Brother plays on the opening night of the Fillmore East, a converted movie theater on New York's Second Avenue and Sixth Street. (CBS/ Columbia Records buys the group's Mainstream contract and books the band into Studio E in New York to record its label debut.)
Aug Producer John Simon, unhappy with the quality of the recordings, is overruled by Columbia, which releases ***Cheap Thrills***, its title shortened, at the label's insistence, from ***Dope, Sex And Cheap Thrills***).
Sept [28] Grossman announces that Joplin is to split from the group at the end of the year.
Oct [12] ***Cheap Thrills***, after seven weeks on the chart, hits US #1, where it will stay for eight weeks, while the extracted *Down On Me* makes US #43.
Nov *Piece Of My Heart* reaches US #12, as the Mainstream-issued *Coo Coo* climbs to US #84.
Dec [6-7] Joplin makes her last official appearance with Big Brother & the Holding Company at the end of a tour in Hawaii.
[21] Backed by the Kozmic Blues Band, she appears at the "Stax-Volt Yuletide Thing" for the record company's annual convention in Memphis, TN.

1969

Feb [11-14] Joplin plays four nights at New York's Fillmore East. Ex-Big Brother guitarist Sam Andrews (b. Dec. 18, 1941, Taft, CA) joins her new group, initially called Janis & the Joplinaires. Other members include Brad Campbell (bass), Terry Clements (sax) and Marcus Doubleday (trumpet). The line-up changes throughout the year, and Andrews leaves.
Mar [20-23] The singer, increasingly reliant on drugs and alcohol, and her band perform at the Fillmore West, San Francisco.
Apr [21] Joplin and the Kozmic Blues Band perform at London's Royal Albert Hall.
June Joplin appears at the "Newport '69 Pop Festival" at San Fernando Valley State College, Devonshire Downs, CA, on a bill with Joe Cocker, Jimi Hendrix, Buddy Miles and Edwin Hawkins.
Aug [31] Having recently sung at the "Texas International Festival" and the "Atlanta Pop Festival", Joplin sings at the two-day "New Orleans Pop Festival" in Prairieville, LA.
Oct ***I Got Dem Ol' Kozmic Blues Again Mama!*** hits US #5.
Nov [15] Joplin is arrested at a gig at Curtis Hixon Hall in Tampa, FL, and released on $500 bond, after allegedly badmouthing a policeman, though charges are eventually dropped.
Dec The soul-based Kozmic Blues Band has been unsuccessful with live appearances since ***I Got Dem Ol' Kozmic Blues Again Mama!*** and disbands, while *Kozmic Blues* makes US #41.

1970

Feb Bassist Peter Albin (b. June 6, 1944, San Francisco) and drummer David Getz (b. Jan. 24, 1940, Brooklyn, New York), who played with Country Joe & the Fish, recruit guitarist James Gurley (b. Dec. 22, 1939, Detroit, MI), Andrews and guitarist Dave Shallock to re-form Big Brother & the Holding Company.
Apr Joplin appears with Big Brother at the Fillmore West and Winterland Ballroom, San Francisco.
May Joplin's new group, the Full-Tilt Boogie Band, makes its debut at a Hells Angels benefit in San Rafael, CA, with a line-up featuring Campbell, John Till (guitar), Richard Bell (piano), Ken Pearson (organ) and Clark Pearson (drums), which will tour constantly in the coming months.

Aug [6] Joplin participates in a 12-hour anti-war rock festival at New York's Shea Stadium on the 25th anniversary of the dropping of the first atom bomb on Hiroshima.
[8] Joplin buys a headstone for the grave of her greatest influence, Bessie Smith, at the Mount Lawn cemetery in Philadelphia, PA. (Smith died in 1937, after being refused admission to a whites-only hospital.)
Sept Joplin begins recording a new album, which will remain unfinished, at Columbia's West Coast studios in Hollywood.
Oct [4] After partying at Barney's Beanery at 8447 Santa Monica Blvd., Joplin is found dead at the Landmark Hotel, 7047 Franklin Ave., Hollywood, with fresh needle marks in her arm. An inquest rules that death is due to an accidental heroin overdose. (She had been scheduled to record the vocal for *Buried Alive In The Blues* the following day.)
Nov Big Brother & the Holding Company's ***Be A Brother***, featuring uncredited contributions from Joplin, reaches US #134.

1971

Feb [27] ***Pearl***, drawn from the unfinished sessions, hits US #1, where it will stay for nine weeks.
Mar [20] Joplin's much-praised version of Kris Kristofferson's *Me And Bobby McGee* tops the US chart.
Apr ***Pearl*** makes UK #50.
June *Cry Baby* (one of several Jerry Ragavoy songs on ***Pearl***) reaches UK #42 (its B-side is her better-known *Mercedes Benz*). The re-packaged Columbia debut album peaks at US #185.
Sept *Get It While You Can*, again penned by Ragavoy, climbs to US #78, while a Big Brother album, ***How Hard It Is***, featuring occasional vocals from new singer Kathi McDonald, makes US #157.

1972

July Having already hit UK #4 in May, ***Janis Joplin In Concert*** reaches UK #30, while the extracted *Down On Me* makes US #91.
Sept [2] *In The Quiet Morning* dawns at US #69, a tribute to Joplin sung by Joan Baez and written by the folk legend's sister, Mimi Farina.

1975

May While ***Janis Joplin's Greatest Hits*** has reached US #37 in August 1973, ***Janis***, the soundtrack from a Joplin documentary of the same name featuring her 1963-65 work, now makes US #54. It contains live and TV recordings with her two post-Big Brother bands and folk-blues material laid down in Texas before she joined Big Brother. "The Rose", starring Bette Midler, a film supposedly based on Joplin's life, will premiere in Los Angeles on October 10th 1979.
Jun [12] ***Greatest Hits*** is certified gold by the RIAA.

1982

Feb ***Farewell Song*** reaches US #104. It contains a song with the Kozmic Blues Band, one with Full-Tilt, one recorded live in Los Angeles with the Paul Butterfield Blues Band and six from Big Brother & the Holding Company. The Big Brother tracks feature added instrumentation from '80s session musicians.

1988

Jan [19] A memorial in Joplin's honor at the Southeast Texas Musical Heritage Exhibit in Port Arthur is unveiled. 5,000 people attend the ceremony.

1991

Sept [5] Subsequent to the forced closure of a biographical play, "Janis", in August, due to a lawsuit brought by her heirs (sister Laura, brother Michael and her mother Dorothy), who claim exclusive rights to Joplin's "performing style, voice, delivery, mannerisms, appearance and dress, and the actions accompanying her performances", the director-playwright, Susan Ross, files a $3-million counter-claim, alleging anti-trust violations, malicious prosecution and unfair competition.

1995

Jan [12] Following Sony's Legacy label release of the three-CD/cassette boxed set retrospective, ***Janis*** in November 1993, Melissa Etheridge now inducts Joplin into the Rock and Roll Hall of Fame at the tenth annual dinner held at New York's Waldorf Astoria Hotel.

JOURNEY

Steve Perry (vocals); **Neal Schon** (guitar); **Ross Valory** (bass); **Jonathan Cain** (keyboards); **Steve Smith** (drums)

1973

Feb The group is assembled in San Francisco, CA, by former Santana road manager Walter "Herbie" Herbert, who joins together Schon (b. Feb. 27, 1954, San Mateo, CA), having sat in with Derek & the Dominos at a Berkeley Community Theatre gig in 1970, before taking up Carlos Santana's offer to join Santana, ex-Frumious Bandersnatch and Steve Miller Band member Valory (b. Feb. 2, 1949, San Francisco), Tubes drummer Prairie Prince (b. May 7, 1950, Charlotte, NC) and George Tickner, also from Frumious Bandersnatch, on guitar. Herbert becomes the band's manager.
June Keyboards player and vocalist Gregg Rolie (b. June 17, 1947), former William Penn & His Pals and also ex-Santana, currently living in Seattle, WA, where he has been running a restaurant with his father, joins the line-up, as the band, still going by the name the Golden Gate Rhythm Section, begins to play large-venue support to bigger groups, as well as local club work. Demos recorded at Wally Heider's are broadcast on San Francisco's leading rock station KSAN, with listeners invited to enter a "name the band" contest. John Villaneuva, an associate of Herbert's, coins Journey.
Dec [31] Journey makes its live debut at San Francisco's Winterland Ballroom. The following day they will fly to Hawaii to take part in the "Crater Festival".

1974

Feb [5] Following Prince's decision to return to the Tubes, and after 30 drummers have been tried, ex-Jeff Beck, Frank Zappa and John Mayall sideman Aynsley Dunbar (b. Jan. 10, 1946, Liverpool, Lancs.), makes his debut with the band, at the Great American Music Hall, San Francisco.
Nov After constant gigging throughout the year, the band signs to CBS/Columbia Records and begins work on its debut album at CBS Studio A in San Francisco, under veteran producer Roy Halee.

1975

Apr Tickner leaves for medical school after completion of the first album. He is not replaced and the band continues with a single guitarist.
May The group's debut album, ***Journey***, travels to US #138, as the band continues constant live work. Its follow-up set, ***Look Into The Future*** will makes US #100 the following April, six months before Journey undertakes a UK tour supporting Santana.

1977

Mar ***Next*** peaks at US #85. Realizing that they need a strong frontman vocalist (Rolie handles most vocals from behind his keyboards), a search begins.
June Robert Fleischmann, spotted by a Columbia employee at a showcase in Denver, CO, is recruited as lead singer and joins the band for its summer tour supporting Emerson Lake & Palmer, but, when Herbert hears a tape sent to him of Alien Project and contacts its lead singer, he fires Fleischmann after a show in Fresno, CA. He makes his final appearance the following night, at tour's end in Oakland, CA.
Oct [10] Perry (b. Jan. 22, 1953, Hanford, CA), lead singer of the now-defunct Alien Project, joins, making his live debut with the band for an encore at the final performance of a three-night stint at San Francisco's Old Waldorf on the 28th.

1978

Apr ***Infinity***, with Perry on lead vocals and Roy Thomas Baker producing, reaches US #21, eventually staying charted for 123 weeks and earning a platinum disc for million-plus sales, mostly due to the seemingly never-ending "Infinity" tour, their first as a headliner, which, after beginning at the Riviera Theater in Chicago, goes on to encompass dates in a further 171 cities in North America and Europe.
May From the album, *Wheel In The Sky* is the band's first US chart single, reaching #57.
July *Anytime*, also from ***Infinity***, and with Rolie on lead vocals, makes US #83.
Sept Third single from the album, *Lights*, reaches US #68.
Oct Dunbar leaves, by mutual consent (his drumming style now incompatible with the direction in which Perry is taking the band), to join Jefferson Starship, and is replaced on drums by Smith (b. Aug. 21, 1954, Los Angeles), whom the band has been watching nightly on the "Infinity" tour, drumming for support act Montrose. Smith joins the group for a King Biscuit Flower Hour session recorded at San Francisco's the Automatt.

1979

Feb Journey signs an advertising deal with Budweiser beer.
Mar The group embarks on a major tour of the US, Europe and Japan to promote its new album, ***Evolution***.
May ***Evolution***, again helmed by Roy Thomas Baker, reaches US #20 and becomes a second million-seller, while the extracted *Just The Same Way* peaks at US #58.
July [28] Journey takes part in the "World Series Of Rock" at Cleveland Stadium, Cleveland, OH. Also on the bill are Aerosmith, Ted Nugent and Thin Lizzy.
Oct Their first Top 20 hit single is *Lovin', Touchin', Squeezin'*, making US #16.

1980

Jan *Too Late* reaches US #70, while a retrospective album of tracks from the first three albums, ***In The Beginning***, peaks at US #152.
Apr *Any Way You Want It* reaches US #23, while ***Departure***, produced by Kevin Elson, their live sound engineer, and Geoff Workman, Baker's Assistant, hits US #8, their third million seller.
July *Walks Like A Lady* makes US #32.
Sept Double A-side, *Good Morning Girl/Stay Awhile*, stalls at US #55.
[22] The band plays a one-off UK concert at the Rainbow Theatre, London.

1981

Mar Live double album, ***Captured***, hits US #9, and earns the band's fourth platinum disc.
Apr *The Party's Over (Hopelessly In Love)*, from ***Captured***, makes US #34. Rolie, tired of touring, leaves the band and is replaced on keyboards by Cain (b. Feb. 26, 1950, Chicago, IL), ex-the Babys, who opened for Journey on the "Departure" tour.
June [13] Cain makes his debut with the band at the "Mountain Aire Festival", at the Calaveras County Fairgrounds, Angel's Camp, CA, the opening date of its "Escape" tour.
Sept [12] Mike Stone-produced ***Escape***, their most successful project to date and showcasing Journey's now-hallmark adult-oriented rock style led by Perry's powerfully distinctive vocal, hits US #1, staying charted for a total of 146 weeks (and remaining more than a year in the Top 20), and eventually selling over two million copies.
[25] Journey opens for the Rolling Stones at the start of their US tour, at JFK Stadium, Philadelphia, PA, before a crowd of 90,000.
Oct [3] Taken from ***Escape***, the Perry/Cain-penned ballad, *Who's Crying Now*, hits US #4.
Nov Schon's ***Untold Passion***, recorded in collaboration with keyboards player Jan Hammer,

peaks at US #115.
Dec *Don't Stop Believin'*, from ***Escape***, hits US #9.

1982

Feb *Open Arms*, the melody written by Cain while a Baby and rejected by John Waite, who claims it is "too syrupy", hits US #2 for six weeks, behind Joan Jett's *I Love Rock'n'Roll*, and is the band's first million-selling single.
Mar A minor UK breakthrough comes as *Don't Stop Believin'* peaks at UK #62.
[20] ***Escape*** makes a belated first entry into the UK chart.
June [26] During a major-stadium summer tour, Journey tops the bill at an eight-hour concert with Santana, the Tubes, Toto and Gamma, at the Oakland-Alameda County Coliseum, the home of the Oakland Athletics' baseball team, before an assembled crowd of 57,000, grossing $957,000. (Sellout concerts at the Rose Bowl, Pasadena, CA, Cotton Bowl, Dallas, TX, and Astrodome, Houston, TX, will gross over $1 million each.)
July *Still They Ride* reaches US #19.
Sept [4] ***Escape*** finally makes UK #32.
Reissued *Who's Crying Now* peaks at UK #46.
Oct Perry's duet with Kenny Loggins, on his single *Don't Fight It*, reaches US #17.

1983

Feb A second Schon/Hammer collaboration, ***Here To Stay***, climbs to US #122.
Mar Journey's *Separate Ways (Worlds Apart)* hits US #8.
Frontiers, again produced by Stone, hits US #2 for 9 weeks behind Michael Jackson's ***Thriller***, and is a further platinum disc, eventually spending 85 weeks on the chart.
It also hits UK #6, the band's most successful album in Britain. Meanwhile, a video game is marketed in the US, inspired by Journey's ***Escape***.
May During the current US tour, supported by Bryan Adams, Journey grosses $721,527 from three shows at the Meadowlands Arena, East Rutherford, NJ.
June Cain-written *Faithfully*, from ***Frontiers***, reaches US #12.
Aug *After The Fall* reaches US #23, while in the UK the 1979 album, ***Evolution***, charts briefly at #100.
Nov *Send Her My Love* reaches US #23.

1984

Apr Schon's live ***Through The Fire***, in collaboration with Sammy Hagar, Kenny Aaronson and Santana's Mike Shrieve, makes US #42.
June ***Street Talk***, Steve Perry's solo debut, which he started in Hollywood, CA, at the end of the "Frontiers" tour, reaches US #12 and UK #59. It will yield the US #3 hit, *Oh Sherrie*, *She's Mine* (US #21, August), *Strung Out* (US #40, October) and *Foolish Heart* (US #18 in February, 1985).
Nov The group re-assembles to begin work on its ***Raised On Radio*** project at the Plant Studios, Sausalito, CA. With Perry's mother terminally ill, the sessions grind to a halt and, months into the recordings, Smith and Valory are fired, leaving Journey as a trio comprising Perry, Schon and Cain.

1985

Jan [28] Perry joins a host of major US rock acts in Los Angeles, at the recording session for USA For Africa's *We Are The World*, on which he contributes a distinctive lead vocal line.
Mar *Only The Young*, from the soundtrack of the movie "Vision Quest", hits US #9. This is the first Journey release for two years, the band having relaxed its earlier formidable touring and recording schedule for an extended rest, while members have pursued solo projects.

1986

May Regrouped as its three-man core of Perry, Schon and Cain, with musical help from Randy Jackson on bass and Larrie Londin on drums, Journey finally releases the concept album ***Raised On Radio***, produced by Perry, which hits US #4 and also reaches UK #22.
[31] *Be Good To Yourself*, taken from the album, hits US #9.
Aug [16] *Suzanne*, also from the set, reaches US #17.
[23] A US tour begins, with Mike Baird and Randy Jackson recruited on drums and bass respectively, at the "Mountain Aire Festival", at the Calaveras County Fairgrounds, Angel's Camp, CA. The tour, and Journey, will end in Anchorage, AK.
Nov [1] Third album extract, *Girl Can't Help It*, also reaches US #17.

1987

Feb [28] A fourth single from the album, *I'll Be Alright Without You*, reaches US #14.
Mar Journey collects the Best Group, Best Vocalist, Best Guitarist and Best Keyboardist trophies at the annual Bay Area Music Awards. (After this, the group members will go their separate ways - Cain and Schon linking up with former Baby John Waite to create Bad English who will score the 1989 US chart-topper *When I See You Smile* and record two albums before splitting; Smith fronting his fusion band, Vital Information, before teaming up with Rolie and Valory again in 1991 to form Storm, signing with Interscope Records, and releasing ***Storm***. Perry will continue to work on his long overdue sophomore solo project.)
May [23] *Why Can't This Night Go On Forever* peaks at US #60.

1991

Apr ***Evolution*** and the 15-track ***Greatest Hits***, which has hit US #10 in January 1989, are each RIAA certified for three million US sales. (The latter has been issued in the UK as ***The Best Of Journey***.)
Nov [3] Perry, Schon and Cain reunite to participate in the Bill Graham "Laughter Love & Music" memorial concert, at San Francisco's Golden Gate Park Polo Field, before an estimated crowd of 350,000.

1993

Jan [9] Three CD/cassette boxed-set career appraisal, ***Time₃***, makes US #90.
[30] The extracted *Lights* peaks at US #74.
Mar [23] Schon, who has signed the previous year to MCA as a member of Hardline, with ex-Bad English Deen Castronovo, brothers Joey and Johnny Gioeli, from Los Angeles band Brunette, and Todd Jensen to release ***Double Eclipse***, contributes fret work to the Paul Rodgers-assembled ***Tribute To Muddy Waters*** album released on Victory Music.

1994

Aug [6] Perry's *You Better Wait* reaches US #29, as its parent album (only his second solo set) ***For The Love Of Strange Medicine***, featuring his new band - Lincoln Brewster (guitar), Paul Taylor (keyboards), Moyes Lucas Jr. (drums) and Mike Porcaro and Larry Kimpel (bass), debuts at its US #15 peak.
[27] ***For The Love Of Strange Medicine*** bows at its UK #64 peak.
Dec [15-16, 18] Perry finishes the first leg of a solo tour, and his first time on the road since Journey's 1987 tour, with three sellout dates at Pantages Theatre, Hollywood.
[17] Perry's *Missing You* makes US #74.

1995

Apr Higher Octave Records release Schon's new age solo album, ***Beyond The Thunder***, featuring guests spots by fellow Journeymen, Smith and Cain, whose own solo debut ***Back To The Innocence*** has been released the previous month. (By year's end Perry, Schon, Cain, Valory and Smith will be writing new material together, hinting at a possible Journey reunion in 1996.)

JOY DIVISION

Ian Curtis (vocals); **Bernard Albrecht** (guitar); **Peter Hook** (bass); **Stephen Morris** (drums)

1977

May [29] Having come together in Manchester, Gtr. Manchester, as the Stiff Kittens some six months earlier, but without any live exposure, the post-punk band, comprising Curtis (b. July 15, 1956, Macclesfield), Albrecht (b. Bernard Dicken, Jan. 4, 1956, Salford, Lancs.), Hook (b. Feb. 13, 1956, Salford) and Steve Brotherdale, renames itself Warsaw (from a track on David Bowie's ***Low***) for its live debut at Manchester's Electric Circus, bottom of the bill to the Buzzcocks and Penetration.
July [18] Warsaw records a demo of four songs (*Inside The Line*, *Gutz*, *At A Later Date* and *The Kill*) at Pennine Sound studios.
Aug Drummer Brotherdale quits the group and is replaced by Morris (b. Oct. 28, 1957, Macclesfield, Cheshire).
Dec The band becomes Joy Division (a name taken from the Nazi concentration-camp novel, **House Of Dolls**) to avoid confusion with London punk band Warsaw Pakt, which has just released its first album.

1978

Jan [25] Joy Division makes its live debut in Manchester.
Apr [14] The band plays at the "Stiff Test/Chiswick Challenge", an audition night organised by the two UK independent labels at Manchester's Rafters club. It performs last, at 2:00 a.m., but impresses the club DJ, and future manager, Rob Gretton. Journalist Tony Wilson, boss of the new Factory Records label (known for his Manchester-based TV music show, "What Goes On") is also taken with the band's performance.
May [3-4] The group records an album, after attracting the attention of RCA Northwest promotion manager, Derek Branwood. Gretton and Wilson will subsequently buy out their RCA contract for £1,000.
May [27] Joy Division records a Radio Manchester interview, "An Ideal For Living And Chat".
June The 1977 demos are released as the EP *An Ideal For Living*, on the band's own Enigma label - the fold-out sleeve is inscribed "This is not a record - it is an enigma".
July [27] Virgin Records issues a 10" various-artists album, ***Short Circuit : Live At The Electric Circus***, which features Joy Division's *At A Later Date*.
Dec [24] Factory Records double-compilation EP, *A Factory Sample*, including Joy Division's *Digital* and *Glass*, both produced by Martin "Zero" Hannett, with tracks by Cabaret Voltaire, John Dowie and Durutti Column, is released.

1979

Jan [31] The group tapes *Exercise One*, *Insight*, *Transmission* and *She's Lost Control* for BBC Radio 1's "John Peel Show".
May Gretton and Joy Division, with an offer to release the band's first album, ***Unknown Pleasures***, on Radar, through major distributor WEA, choose instead to sign with the independent Factory.
June Joy Division contributes *From Safety To Where* and *Autosuggestion* to the Fast Product compilation EP, *Earcom 2 : Contradiction*.
July Their debut album, ***Unknown Pleasures***, is released, after Wilson uses his life savings of £8,500 to press 10,000 copies. Highlighted by bringing Hook's distinctive bass sound and Morris' drum rhythm to the front of the mix, the critically-revered set begins a lengthy residence on the UK Independent chart. Live performances are increased, which mounts increasing pressure on Curtis, who suffers from epilepsy.
Aug Joy Division plays all-day open-air concert in Leigh, Gtr. Manchester, with A Certain Ratio, Echo & the Bunnymen, Orchestral Manœuvres In The Dark and Teardrop Explodes. An estimated 300 people witness the event.

Sept [8-9] The group participates in the "Futurama" festival at the Queens Hall, Leeds, S. Yorks.
[15] The band is interviewed and performs on BBC-TV's "Something Else".
Oct *Atmosphere/Dead Souls*, under the title *Licht Und Blindheit*, and *Transmission/Novelty* are released.
Nov [26] The group records a second "John Peel Show" session for BBC Radio 1.

1980

Jan The band embarks on a European tour, though several gigs will have to be cancelled due to Curtis' deteriorating health.
Apr The haunting *Love Will Tear Us Apart* is released, to overwhelming critical praise, but initially it reaches only the UK Independent chart. Factory takes the innovative step of providing record shops with a flexi-disc containing the tracks *Komakino*, *Incubation* and *As You Said*; not to be sold, but to be given away to fans. The group completes a new album with Hannett and plays a series of impromptu live UK dates, several of which have to be cancelled as Curtis falls ill.
May [2] Joy Division plays its final gig, during which Curtis has to be helped offstage.
[18] In the early hours of the morning, with Iggy Pop's ***The Idiot*** on his turntable and Werner Herzog's "Strojek" on video, Curtis hangs himself, four days before the group is due to fly to the US to begin its first-ever Stateside tour. (Joy Division's greatest commercial success will come after the singer's death, as their legend influences many a UK alternative act during the '80s).
July [26] *Love Will Tear Us Apart* reaches UK #13.
Aug [2] The group's second album, ***Closer***, hits UK #6, during an eight-week chart stay.
[30] ***Unknown Pleasures*** also belatedly charts, spending a week at UK #71.

1981

Jan Joy Division re-emerges as New Order, with Albrecht, now calling himself Barney Sumner, on vocals.
Oct [24] Joy Division's double album, ***Still***, a collection of live and studio material, hits UK #5. The following August, Factory's video division, Ikon, will issue "Here Are The Young Men", a 60-minute live Joy Division video while on Nov [19], 1983 the reissued *Love Will Tear Us Apart* re-enters the UK chart, peaking at #19.

1988

July After ***The Peel Sessions*** have been collected for release in 1986, a reissue of Joy Division's *Atmosphere*, a consistent Independent seller, now makes UK #34. (New York group the Swans release a version of *Love Will Tear Us Apart*, a song also covered by Paul Young and P.J. Proby, with assistance from Hook.)
[23] Factory-released double compilation, ***1977-1980 Substance***, hits UK #7.

1995

June Faber & Faber publishes **Touching From A Distance**, written by Curtis' widow, a new biography on her late husband.
[17] *Love Will Tear Us Apart (Remix)* debuts at its UK #19 peak.
July [1] ***Permanent : Joy Division 1995*** reaches UK #16 in its week of entry.
see also: NEW ORDER

JUDAS PRIEST

Rob Halford (vocals); **K.K. Downing** (guitar); **Glenn Tipton** (guitar); **Ian Hill** (bass); **Dave Holland** (drums)

1971

The original Judas Priest, its name is taken from Bob Dylan's *The Ballad Of Frankie Lee And Judas Priest* on his album ***John Wesley Harding***, has been formed in 1969 in Birmingham, Warks., as a pop/rock-covers band playing around the Midlands clubs, though only Downing (b. Oct. 27, 1951, Birmingham) and Hill (b. Jan. 20, 1952, Birmingham) will survive from the initial line-up to the group's recording days. The band now gains a strong vocalist and frontman in ex-theatrical lighting engineer Halford (b. Aug. 25, 1951, Birmingham), the brother of Hill's girlfriend. Drummer John Hinch also joins, and the quartet's music toughens into the hard-rock mode currently successful for Deep Purple and fellow Brummie group, Black Sabbath.

1974

Tipton (b. Oct. 25, 1948, Birmingham) comes in as a second guitarist and after more than four years of playing clubs, the band signs to Gull Records, which releases its debut album, ***Rocka Rolla***, produced by Rodger Bain, with the title track also released as a single. Hinch is replaced on drums by Alan Moore.

1976

Mar *The Ripper* is released, trailering the band's second Gull album.
Apr ***Sad Wings Of Destiny*** is also a modest seller, but marks the band's US debut release, via Janus Records.
[6] The group begins an 11-date UK tour at the Plaza, Truro, Cornwall, set to end on the 17th at the City Hall, St. Albans, Herts.
Aug Judas Priest makes its first appearance at the "Reading Festival", Reading, Berks.

1977

Jan With the attraction of Halford's flamboyant stage act, the band is developing a strong grass-roots following with consistent UK touring, and secures a major new contract with CBS/Columbia (and also recruits a new drummer, session-man Simon Phillips.)
May [21] ***Sin After Sin***, the first album for CBS, produced by ex-Deep Purple bassist Roger Glover, provides the group's first chart entry, at UK #23, and includes their rock version of Joan Baez's *Diamonds And Rust*, which is released as a single. Tours of the UK and Europe follow, in support of the album, and new drummer Les Binks joins in place of Phillips.
July [23] On a maiden US tour, Judas Priest supports Led Zeppelin at Oakland-Alameda County Coliseum, Oakland, CA.

1978

Mar [4] ***Stained Class***, including the January-issued revival of Spooky Tooth's *Better By You, Better By Me*, and produced by Dennis Mackay, reaches UK #27, while Gull releases ***Best Of Judas Priest***, compiled from the two earlier albums.
Apr ***Stained Class*** makes US #173, the band's US chart debut.
Oct [24] A seven-date UK tour opens at King George's Hall, Blackburn, Lancs., set to end on the 31st at the Dome, Brighton, E. Sussex.
Nov [18] ***Killing Machine***, produced by James Guthrie, reaches UK #32.
Dec The group cancels a tour of West Germany, after the promoter bans Halford from using his trademark whip.

1979

Feb Judas Priest's first hit single is *Take On The World*, extracted from ***Killing Machine***, which reaches UK #14.
Apr The album is retitled ***Hell Bent For Leather*** (a nod to the group's leather-clad image) in the US, where it makes #128, and includes an additional track, reviving Fleetwood Mac's *The Green Manalishi (With The Two-Prong Crown)*.
May *Evening Star* peaks at UK #53. The band tours abroad again, finding substantial success in the Far East.
Sept The group supports Kiss on a major US tour.
Oct [13] Live album, ***Unleashed In The East***, recorded at the Koseinenkin and Nakano Sunplaza Halls in Tokyo, Japan, proves to be a chart breakthrough, hitting UK #10 and going on to make US #70. It is produced by Tom Allom - a partnership which will endure. Drummer Binks has left, physically and mentally exhausted by the band's gruelling tour schedule, his place taken by Dave Holland.

1980

Mar [9] The band starts a 17-date UK tour at the Colston Hall, Bristol, Avon.
Apr *Living After Midnight* makes UK #12.
[19] Its parent album ***British Steel*** (the first album to feature Holland on drums), is the group's biggest UK success, hitting #4.
June *Breaking The Law*, also from ***British Steel***, peaks at UK #12.
July ***British Steel*** reaches US #34, earning the band a gold disc for half a million sales.
Aug [16] Judas Priest appears at the first "Monsters Of Rock" festival at Castle Donington, Leics., second to Rainbow on the bill, which also includes the Scorpions, April Wine, Saxon and Riot.
Sept *United*, the third single from ***British Steel***, makes UK #26.

1981

Feb *Don't Go*, from a forthcoming album, peaks at UK #51.
Mar [7] Tom Allom-produced ***Point Of Entry*** climbs to UK #14.
May *Hot Rockin'* peaks at UK #60, while ***Point Of Entry*** makes US #30.

1982

July [24] ***Screaming For Vengeance*** reaches UK #11.
Aug The extracted *You've Got Another Thing Comin'* peaks at UK #66.
Oct ***Screaming For Vengeance*** makes US #17 and becomes a million seller, earning the group's first platinum disc. The nine-year-old album, ***Rocka Rolla***, also finally gets a US release, on the Visa label. The group continues to tour intensively, its live show often highlighted by Halford roaring across the stage on a Harley Davidson motorbike.
Nov *You've Got Another Thing Comin'* is the group's only US Singles chart entry, at #67.

1983

May [29] The huge demand for Judas Priest in the US in the wake of its last album sees the group touring North America for much of the year, including today's performance on "Heavy Metal Sunday" during the second "US Festival", alongside Triumph, the Scorpions, Van Halen and others, in San Bernardino, CA.

1984

Feb ***Defenders Of The Faith***, recorded in Ibiza and mixed by Allom in Miami, FL, peaks at UK #19, as the extracted *Freewheel Burnin'* makes UK #42.
Apr ***Defenders Of The Faith***, another US gold album, peaks at #18. After some live promotion dates, the band members take a break for much of this year and 1985, settling into their new home city, Phoenix, AZ.

1985

July [13] Judas Priest emerges from its lengthy lay-off to play at the "Live Aid" concert in Philadelphia, PA.
Dec [23] Teenage Reno, NV Judas Priest fans Raymond Belknap and James Vance shoot themselves, reportedly after listening to ***Stained Class***. Vance survives, but Belknap, who holds a sawn-off shotgun to his chin and fires, dies.

1986

Apr ***Turbo***, with the sound broadened with synth guitars and electronic effects, makes UK #33 and US #17.
May Halford takes part in the Hear'n'Aid heavy-metal charity single, *Stars*, released to benefit famine relief in Ethiopia, which reaches UK #26.
[2] The group's "Turbo - Fuel For Life" world tour begins in Albuquerque, NM, before moving on to Japan and Europe.
Dec [3] James Vance and the family of Raymond

Belknap sue Judas Priest and CBS Records, alleging that they were responsible for the teenagers forming a suicide pact and shooting themselves in the head after listening to the band's records for six hours.

1988

Apr Following the 1987 June [13]-peaking UK #47 (and US #38) ***Priest Live***, recorded on the 1986 tour, the band's revival of Chuck Berry's *Johnny B. Goode*, from the Anthony Michael Hall film of the same title, reaches UK #64.
May [28] ***Ram It Down***, Priest's first studio set for two years, reaches UK #24 and will make US #31.
July [20] The group's North American tour opens.
Nov [29] Vance, now aged 20, having lived three more years after shooting himself, and having gone into a methadone overdose-induced coma on Thanksgiving, dies.

1990

July [16] The Vance/Belknap $6.2-million suit against Judas Priest and CBS Records begins in Reno, before Washoe County district judge Jerry Whitehead.
Aug [24] Whitehead rejects the suit, but does, however, award $40,000 sanctions against CBS Records on the grounds that it attempted to withhold the original master recordings for the album ***Stained Class***, even though much of the prosecution's case was based on supposed subliminal messages contained in the record. Downing says, "It will be another ten years before I can even spell subliminal."
Sept [15] *Painkiller* stalls at UK #74.
[29] Its parent album, ***Painkiller***, debuts at its UK #26 during a two-week chart stay.
Oct [21] The group embarks on a major North American "Painkiller" tour, with new drummer Scott Travis, ex-Racer X, in Montreal, Canada, the first leg set to end December 23rd in Orlando, FL.
Nov [3] The band donates the proceeds from its Lawlor Events Center, Reno gig to the Community Runaway Youth Services organization, in the same week that ***Painkiller*** peaks at US #26.

1991

Mar [23] ***A Touch Of Evil*** charts for a week at UK #58.
July [9] Priest embarks on a headlining "Operation Rock'n'Roll" US tour with Alice Cooper and Motorhead in Salt Lake City, UT, which will prove to be Halford's final trek with the band.

1992

May [13] At a West Hollywood press conference, Halford denies rumors that he is HIV positive or has AIDS.
July Having recently formed Entertainment Management Advisory Services to handle his new career as a solo artist, Halford joins with Pantera on *Light Comes Out Of Black*, featured on the "Buffy The Vampire Slayer" soundtrack.
Aug Halford announces the formation of his new band, Fight, with Russ Parrish (guitar) and Scott Travis (drums), set to make its debut in October at the Foundations Forum Convention, Los Angeles.
Oct Halford sues Sony/CBS on the grounds that his 1984 contract amounts to restraint of trade.
Nov [14] Halford makes a one-off appearance fronting Black Sabbath at the Pacific Amphitheatre, Costa Mesa, CA, standing in for Ronnie James Dio, who has refused to perform at tonight and tomorrow night's gigs because Ozzy Osbourne is re-forming the original Sabbath line-up as part of his farewell solo-concert extravaganza.

1993

Mar Following a year of legal wrangles with Sony, Halford signs a solo deal with its imprint Epic Records, while the rest of the band remains with Sony.
Apr [24] *Night Crawler* charts for a week at UK #63.
May [8] ***Metal Works '73-'93***, a two-CD Judas Priest anthology, charts for a week at UK #37.
June [5] ***Metal Works '73-'93*** peaks at US #155, during a two-week chart stay.
Dec [20] Halford sues EMI April Music in US District Court, Southern District of New York, claiming Judas Priest's contract with the publisher does not apply to Halford's music with Fight.

1995

May Transluxe Records releases ***The Best Of Judas Priest*** in the US, including an interview with original drummer John Hinch and the original versions of *Diamonds And Rust* and *Victim Of Changes*.

K

KANSAS

Steve Walsh (vocals, keyboards); **Kerry Livgren** (guitar); **Rich Williams** (guitar); **Dave Hope** (bass); **Phil Ehart** (drums); **Robby Steinhardt** (violin)

1970

Livgren (b. Sept. 18, 1949, Kansas), Hope (b. Oct. 7, 1949, Kansas) and Ehart (b. Feb. 4, 1950, Kansas), all friends from West Topeka High School, Topeka, KS, form the Gimlets, a Frank Zappa-inspired band, with other local musicians. They play mainly local dance and club dates but, with frequent personnel changes, the original trio remains the only constant. The following year, they recruit classically-trained violinist Steinhardt (b. May 25, 1950, Mississippi), son of a senior Kansas University music lecturer, and relaunch as White Clover, playing around Kansas until the end of the year, when Ehart leaves and the band splits.

1972

Ehart visits the UK in search of musical inspiration but returns home four months later. Back in Topeka, he re-forms White Clover, with Hope, Walsh (b. June 15, 1951, St. Joseph, MO), Williams (b. Feb. 1, 1950, Kansas) and Steinhardt. Livgren also rejoins, while the name is changed to Kansas, and the group begins live work, developing a style which blends UK progressive influences with a refined form of early US heavy metal.

1974

July Kansas has recorded a $300 demo in a Liberal, KS studio the previous year, which Ehart mailed to an East Coast friend with record industry contacts. Months later, while the band is gigging in Dodge City, KS, Kirshner Records' Wally Gold calls from New York, requesting a live showcase, which results in the group being signed. Their debut album, ***Kansas*** now makes US #174 and, supported by constant touring, eventually sells over 100,000 copies.

1975

May ***Songs For America*** reaches US #57, earning a gold disc for half a million sales, as the band continues non-stop US touring. Its follow-up set, ***Masque*** will reach US #70 the following February, earning another gold disc during a 20-week chart run.

1977

Apr ***Leftoverture***, produced by Jeff Glixman, is the band's major commercial breakthrough, hitting US #5, and earning a platinum disc. The extracted *Carry On Wayward Son*, penned by Livgren, who is now their chief songwriter, is Kansas' US Singles chart debut, at #11, it will become a mainstay on American rock radio.

1978

Jan ***Point Of Know Return*** hits US #4 and is a second platinum seller, while its title cut *Point Of Know Return* reaches US #28.

Mar Epic rock ballad, *Dust In The Wind*, also from ***Point Of Know Return***, hits US #6. Kansas' only Top 10 single, it earns a gold disc for million-plus sales, and will become the group's most revered recording and most enduring radio cut.

[25] The group plays at London's Hammersmith Odeon during a UK visit.

May Walsh is the guest vocalist on ex-Genesis guitarist Steve Hackett's second solo album, ***Please Don't Touch***.

June [27] In a ceremony at New York's Madison Square Garden, Kansas is the first group to be chosen by UNICEF as its Deputy Ambassadors Of Goodwill.

July *Carry On Wayward Son* makes UK #51, more than a year after its US success, and is the band's only UK chart appearance. Meanwhile, *Portrait (He Knew)* peaks at US #64.

Aug [26] The group appears at the first "Canada Jam" festival in Ontario, Canada, before an 80,000 crowd, with the Commodores, Earth, Wind & Fire, Village People, Dave Mason, and the Atlanta Rhythm Section.

1979

Jan Double live album, ***Two For The Show***, recorded on tour, makes US #32 and is the group's third consecutive platinum album.

Feb *Lonely Wind* peaks at US #60.

July ***Monolith***, their first self-produced effort, hits US #10 and goes gold. Kansas plays an 80-city US tour to support the album, opening at Von Braun Civic Center, Huntsville, AL.

Aug *People Of The South Wind* reaches US #23.

Oct Further extract, *Reason To Be*, makes US #52.

1980

Mar Walsh's solo, ***Schemer Dreamer***, featuring his band colleagues, reaches US #124. Livgren becomes a born-again Christian (reflected on his solo ***Seeds Of Change***), as will Hope.

Oct *Hold On*, from the forthcoming Kansas album, peaks at US #40.

Nov ***Audio-Visions*** reaches US #26. *Got To Rock On* will roll to US #76 the following January, when Walsh quits the line-up, to be replaced by John Elefante (b. Levittown, NY).

1982

July ***Vinyl Confessions***, with Elefante on lead vocals, makes US #16, while the extracted *Play The Game Tonight* reaches US #17.

Sept Second single from the recent album, *Right Away*, peaks at US #73.

1983

Sept With the group having moved from Kirshner to the CBS Associated label, ***Drastic Measures*** makes US #41. The lower chart placing is a reflection of the year's tour results: like most US stadium-filling bands of the previous two or three years, Kansas has experienced a sharp downturn in audience attendance.

Oct The excerpted *Fight Fire With Fire* peaks at US #58, as Kansas comes off the road and decides to temporarily dissolve. A compilation album, ***The Best Of Kansas*** will make US #154 the following September.

1987

Jan Walsh, Ehart and Williams have resurrected Kansas the previous October and, recruiting Steve Morse (b. July 28, 1954, Hamilton, OH) (ex-Dixie Dregs) on guitar and Billy Greer on bass, has signed to MCA Records for its comeback album, now released as Kansas' reunion album ***Power***, and making US #35.

[17] *All I Wanted*, extracted from ***Power***, reaches US #19.

Feb [28] Title cut *Power* peaks at US #84. A follow-up album ***In The Spirit Of Things*** will climb to US #114 in November 1988.

1990

Oct While Ehart and Walsh produce tracks for the Blondz, ***Best Of Kansas*** is finally certified by the RIAA as the band's fourth platinum disc.

Nov [19] Still a popular draw in the South, Kansas plays a sellout date at the Center Stage, Atlanta, GA, grossing $12,250.

1992

Apr [5] With a current line-up of Walsh, Ehart, Williams, Roberts, Greer and David Ragsdale (violin/guitar), Kansas plays at the Whisky A-Go-Go club in Los Angeles, a recording of which will be released as ***Live At The Whisky*** in July, on the Intersound label (US).

1993

May [12] The group embarks on a US summer tour at the Sting, New Britain, CT, set to end on September 11th at the Auditorium, West Palm Beach, FL.

1995

Sept [22] Still touring the US each year and following Sony Legacy's 1994 issue of the imaginatively titled retrospective ***The Kansas Box***

Set, and the May release earlier this year by Intersound of the group's first studio album in seven years, ***Freaks Of Nature***, Walsh is now charged with DUI, possession of cocaine and driving with a suspended license after crashing his car at 4:00 p.m. on Peachtree Industrial Boulevard in Atlanta.

KC & THE SUNSHINE BAND

Harry Wayne Casey (vocals, keyboards);
Richard Finch (bass); **Jerome Smith** (guitar);
Robert Johnson (drums);
Fermin Goytisolo (congas, percussion)

1973

Casey (b. Harold Wayne Casey, Jan. 31, 1951, Hialeah, FL), working as a record-store assistant in Florida, collects records, as part of his job, from Tone Distributors, who also give him free time in their studios, where he begins to learn production skills, and also meets bass player and TK Records' engineer, Finch (b. Jan. 25, 1954, Indianapolis, IN). Together they form KC (from Casey's nickname) & the Sunshine Junkanoo Band ("junkanoo" being a percussive, beat-driven Caribbean style of local dance music). Playing locally, with a variable line-up comprising between nine and 11 performers, they sign to Henry Stone's Miami-based TK label and release their debut single, *Blow Your Whistle* (recorded by Casey, Finch and session musicians, inspired by the whistle-flute sound which the duo first heard at a wedding reception for local R&B artist, Clarence Reid), which garners strong regional sales and will become a club hit in Europe. The session crew will usually include Smith (b. June 8, 1953, Miami, FL), Goytisolo (b. Dec. 31, 1951, Havana, Cuba), and Johnson (b. Mar. 21, 1953, Miami, FL) and trombonist Charlie Williams (b. Nov. 18, 1954, Rockingham NC), all of whom will become members of the renamed Sunshine Band behind KC.

1974

July [13] For TK, Casey and Finch have written and produced George McCrae's million-selling R&B swayer, *Rock Your Baby*, which now tops the US chart, set to also hit UK #1 two weeks later.

Sept The band makes its UK chart debut with *Queen Of Clubs* (released earlier in the US, to little notice), which hits UK #7, licensed from TK by President Records and released on the disco-oriented Jay Boy label.

Dec *Sound Your Funky Horn* reaches UK #17, while Casey and Finch have written and produced McCrae's third UK hit, *You Can Have It All*, which peaks at #23.

1975

Apr *Get Down Tonight*, recorded by a now-permanent group line-up which has added the horn section of Ronnie Smith, James Weaver and Denvil Liptrot and includes female backing singers Beverley Champion and Jeanette Williams, which also goes on tour, reaches UK #21.

Aug [30] The Casey/Finch-penned *Get Down Tonight* is the band's US chart debut. After climbing for several weeks while they are on a European tour, it hits #1 for a week as they return home. Simultaneously, the Casey/Finch-written and-produced *That's The Way (I Like It)* hits UK #4. (As resident house band at TK Studios, they also back Betty Wright on her UK #25 hit, *Where Is The Love*, and George McCrae on his UK #23, *It's Been So Long*.)

Sept [20] Their debut album, ***KC And The Sunshine Band***, reaches UK #26, while the instrumental single *Shotgun Shuffle*, credited only to the Sunshine Band, charts briefly at US #88.

Nov [22] Infectious pop/dance hit *That's The Way (I Like It)*, according to Casey, a toned-down re-cut of an original, more lascivious version on which the repeated "a-has" were sensual moans, tops the US chart for the first of two weeks and becomes a million-seller. Meanwhile, *I'm So Crazy* reaches UK #34. The group is now a major live attraction in the US, drawing critical praise for its melding of R&B, gospel and Carribean flavors with a white rock sound.

Dec ***KC And The Sunshine Band*** hits US #4, while the instrumental collection, ***The Sound Of Sunshine***, credited to the Sunshine Band, makes US #131.

1976

Jan [31] KC & the Sunshine Band wins the Favorite Single, Soul/R&B category at the third annual American Music Awards, held at the Civic Auditorium, Santa Monica, CA.

Apr *Queen Of Clubs* is re-promoted in the US, and this time is dealt the #66 position.

Aug After an eight-month hiatus between UK releases, *(Shake Shake Shake) Shake Your Booty* reaches UK #22.

Sept [11] In the US, *(Shake Shake Shake) Shake Your Booty* becomes KC's third chart-topper (deposing the Bee Gees' *You Should Be Dancing* and becoming another million seller.)

Dec ***Part 3*** peaks at US #13.

1977

Jan *Keep It Comin' Love* reaches UK #31, while in the US *I Like To Do It* makes #37.

May Taken from ***Part 3***, *I'm Your Boogie Man* makes UK #41.

June [11] *I'm Your Boogie Man* tops the US chart for a week, making the Sunshine Band only the second group (after the Jackson 5) to achieve four US #1 singles in the '70s.

Sept Released months after its UK chart run, *Keep It Comin' Love* (also from ***Part 3***, on which it was segued with *I'm Your Boogie Man*) hits US #2 and tops the R&B ranking.

1978

Jan *Wrap Your Arms Around Me*, the B-side of the six-month-old *I'm Your Boogie Man*, picks up US airplay, and is elevated to A-side status, making US #48.

Mar The flipped *Boogie Shoes*, originally released as the B-side of *Shake Your Booty*, shuffles to US #35, and is included on the soundtrack album to "Saturday Night Fever", which spends 25 consecutive weeks at US #1 between January and July, and 18 weeks at UK #1. This means that, with total sales of ***Saturday Night Fever*** exceeding 25 million, *Boogie Shoes* sells to more people than the combined total of everything else released by KC & the Sunshine Band.

May *Boogie Shoes* makes UK #34.

June Their revival of the Four Tops' *It's The Same Old Song* makes US #35.

Aug *It's The Same Old Song* climbs to UK #49.

Sept Casey-produced, as ever, ***Who Do Ya (Love)*** reaches US #36.

Oct *Do You Feel All Right* peaks at US #63.

1979

Jan *Who Do Ya Love*, the title track from the recent album, makes US #68.

July *Do You Wanna Go Party*, a deliberate effort to move back from the prevailing disco sound to a more basic funk mixture, peaks at US #50, followed by ***Do You Wanna Go Party***, which also climbs to US #50.

1980

Jan [5] Atypical ballad, *Please Don't Go*, a Casey/Finch song written in the studio during recordings for the previous album, on which it was included, is extracted to provide the group with its final US chart-topper and million seller. It is the first US #1 of the '80s (for a week, after 19 weeks of climbing the Hot 100), and will also hit UK #3.

Feb Casey's duet with Casablanca Records' female vocalist Teri DeSario, on a revival of Barbara Mason's 1965 hit, *Yes, I'm Ready*, credited to Teri DeSario with KC, hits US #2 only weeks after *Please Don't Go* has left the top slot, and earns the duo a gold disc for a million-plus sales.

Mar ***Greatest Hits*** compilation reaches US #132.

[8] Alternative track-listing UK-released ***Greatest Hits*** hits UK #10.

July DeSario/KC follow-up duet, *Dancin' In The Streets*, slides to US #66.

1981

TK Records goes bankrupt and the group disbands. Casey signs to Epic, where he records ***The Painter*** (under the group name) and ***Space Cadet*** (as a solo outing).

1982

Jan [15] Casey is seriously injured in a head-on collision near his home in Hialeah. He loses all feeling on the right side of his body as the result of injury to a nerve, and is confined to a wheelchair, until he learns to walk again, following almost a year's recuperation. When he is fit enough to re-enter the studio, he cuts ***All In A Night's Work***, again released by Epic.

1983

Aug [13] *Give It Up* is extracted from ***All In A Night's Work*** in the UK and becomes KC's first hit in over three years and biggest-ever success in Britain. After ten years of UK chart entries, it is his first UK #1, staying on top for three weeks. US Epic declines to issue the single, leading Casey to negotiate his release from the label along with the rights to the track. He launches his own independent US label, Meca Records (Musical Enterprise Corporation Of America), which finally releases *Give It Up*.

Sept ***All In A Night's Work*** reaches UK #46.

Oct The extracted *(You Said) You'd Gimme Some More* makes UK #41.

1984

Mar *Give It Up* reaches US #18, while ***KC Ten***, co-produced by Casey, Robert Walker and Ron Taylor, and also released on Meca, peaks at US #93. (Despite having no further domestic chart entries, KC will continue to tour the US, playing the party-type R&B music in which the Sunshine Band specialized.)

1991

May [11] With Rhino Records (US) having issued ***The Best Of KC & The Sunshine Band*** on CD the previous year, *That's The Way (I Like It)*, re-recording the group's 1975 UK #4, debuts at its UK #59 peak, on the Music Factory Dance label. The following year, KWS' cover of *Please Don't Go* hits UK #1 on May [9].

1995

July Following the ZYX label's release of KC & the Sunshine Band's ***Oh Yeah!***, produced by Robyx and including a new version of *Please Don't Go*, plus a megamix of *That's The Way I Like It* and *I'm Your Boogie Man*, among others, in May 1993, Georgia-based label Intersound Records now issues ***Get Down Live!***, a 16 track live collection plus the all-new club mix *KC In The House*.

R. KELLY

1991

Nov [16] Growing up in the housing projects on Chicago, IL's South Side, Kelly (b. Robert Kelly, Jan. 8, 1969, Chicago, IL) has eschewed the traps of gang life, and, influenced, not least, by the soul offerings of the late Donny Hathaway, has set his sights on a career in music, having taken to playing the piano by ear as a young boy and buying a portable keyboard in his teens, with which he has successfully performed on local street corners as a busker. Subsequently forming the locally popular R&B combo MGM in the late '80s, the group brings Kelly to prominence winning the nationally televised "Big Break" talent contest (hosted by Natalie Cole). Electing to pursue a solo career, he begins honing a self-written, self-produced blend of old-school soul, spiked with erotically-charged, but laid-back '90s dance grooves. Surrounding himself with a collective of dancers and backing singers (which he names Public

Announcement), the multi-instrumentalist singer, managed by Barry Hankerson, is picked by Jive Records, which releases *She's Got That Vibe*, which now becomes his first chart disc, entering the US R&B survey on its way to hit #7.

1992

Feb [29] Kelly's debut album (and the only one to credit Public Announcement), the soul/hip-hop fused ***Born Into The '90s*** charts for a week at UK #67.
Apr [25] *She's Got That Vibe* makes US #59 and will peak at UK #57 on May [16].
June [20] ***Born Into The '90's*** makes US #42.
July [18] Already a two-week US R&B chart-topper, *Honey Love* reaches US #39.
Oct [17] *Slow Dance (Hey Mr. DJ)* makes US #43 having also hit #1 on the US R&B survey.

1993

Jan [26] ***Born Into The '90's*** is certified platinum by the RIAA.
May [29] The final extract from his first album, *Dedicated* reaches US #31.
Dec [4] *Sex Me (Parts I & II)* reaches US #20 having charted for a week at UK #75 on November 20th.
[21] *Sex Me (Parts I & II)* is certified gold by the RIAA.

1994

Mar [12] Now credited simply as R. Kelly, his self-written and produced, overtly sex-themed sophomore set ***12 Play*** hits US #2.
[29] Still rising on the US survey, *Bump N' Grind* is certified platinum by the RIAA.
Apr [9] *Bump N' Grind* tops the US chart.
[26] A three month US tour with Salt 'N' Pepa gets underway at the James L. Knight Center, Miami, FL, a bill grossing $104,859 from 4,236 fans, set to end on June 12th at the Centrum, Worcester, MA.
May [14] *Your Body's Callin'* debuts at its UK #19 peak.
June [11] *Your Body's Callin'* reaches US #13.
July [2] *Back & Forth*, written and produced by Kelly for his protégé and girlfriend, Aaliyah, hits US #5, taken from her debut album, the Kelly-directed ***Age Ain't Nothing But A Number***. (Among several current Kelly production and writing successes, including those for Toni Braxton, Lisa Stansfield, Janet Jackson, Ex-Girlfriend, Gladys Knight, David Peaston and the Winans, N-Phase's *Spend The Night* enters the US R&B chart set to reach #23.)
[6] *Your Body's Callin'* is certified gold by the RIAA.
Aug [31] Kelly weds Detroit-born Aaliyah (née Aaliyah Haughton) in Rosemont, IL amid rumors that his bride is only 15 years old, one year under the state's legal age.
Sept [3] While currently appearing on the bill of this year's Budweiser Superfest Tour, *Summer Bunnies*, sampling the Gap Band's *Outstanding*, makes US #55 and bows at its UK #23 peak.
Sept [17] With Aaliyah's Kelly-produced follow-up *At Your Best (You Are Love)* on the rise to US #6, Changing Faces' *Stroke You Up*, again penned and helmed by him (as is their hot R&B album ***Changing Faces***), hits US #3.
Nov [12] Reissued in the UK, *She's Got That Vibe* now hits #3.
[26] Reactivated ***12 Play*** (which originally made UK #69 in November the previous year), reaches UK #39, its fifth chart appearance of the year, having now been certified UK platinum for 300,000 sales.
Dec [7] He collects the trophy for Top R&B Artist at the fifth annual **Billboard** Music Awards held at the Universal Amphitheatre, Universal City, CA, also performing a steamy version of *Bump N' Grind*.
[30] He performs his final date of the year at the Barton Coliseum, Little Rock, AR, to 3,270 fans.

1995

Jan [28] *Bump N' Grind* hits UK #8, the same day that ***12 Play*** finally peaks at UK #20.
Feb [26-27] Kelly's four-date UK concert visit climaxes with two nights at the Wembley Arena, Wembley, Middx.
Mar [13] He nabs the Best R&B/Soul Single, Male (for *Bump 'N Grind*) at the ninth annual Soul Train Music Awards held at Los Angeles' Shrine Auditorium.
May [6] *The 4 Plays EPs* bows at its UK #23 peak.
Sept [2] Michael Jackson's *You Are Not Alone*, written and produced by Kelly, becomes the first single to ever enter the US Hot 100 chart at #1.
[6] The RIAA certifies US sales of four million for ***12 Play***.
Oct [21] *An Angel* charts for a week at UK #69.
[24] Qwest Records releases Quincy Jones' ***Q's Jook Joint***, including Kelly as a featured guest.
Nov [11] *You Remind Me Of Something* bows at its UK #24 peak.
[18] Inspired by riding in a Jeep, *You Remind Me Of Something* hits US #4.
[25] ***R. Kelly***, written and produced as ever by him and lyrically moving away from blatant sexualism towards themes of romance, enters at its UK #18 high.
Dec [2] ***R. Kelly*** debuts on the US chart in pole position.

1996

Jan [17] ***R. Kelly*** is certified double platinum by the RIAA.
[26] *You Remind Me Of Something* is certified for one million US sales by the RIAA.
Mar [2] Already a US R&B chart-topper, *Down Low (Nobody Has To Know)*, a slow-jam featuring erstwhile influence Ronald Isley, reaches UK #23 in its week of entry and will hit US #4 on the 30th, (he has also recently co-written and produced four cuts for a forthcoming Isley Brothers album including the lead-off single *Let's Lay Together*), and contributed four songs to Toni Braxton's upcoming sophomore set).

CHAKA KHAN

1969

Khan (b. Yvette Marie Stevens, Mar. 23, 1953, Great Lakes, IL), having performed since the age of 12, when she joined school girlfriends in the Crystalettes and entered local talent shows, going on to become a member of the Afro-Arts Theater in Chicago, IL, adopting her show name while working for the Black Panther movement's Breakfast Program ("Chaka" meaning fire), joins the group Shades of Black, having recently run away from home at age 16, following a row with her mother. The following year, Khan marries for the first time and sings in the group Lock & Chain, before joining soul/dance combo Lyfe. Meeting Chicago-based funk/jazz group Ask Rufus, formed out of the remnants of pop band the American Breed (former million sellers with *Bend Me, Shape Me*), in 1971, Khan is subsequently invited to replace departing lead vocalist, Paulette McWilliams.

1973

Aug Signed to ABC Records, the group, featuring Tony Maiden (guitar), Kevin Murphy (keyboards), Nate Morgan (keyboards), Bobby Watson (bass) and André Fischer (drums), shortening its name to Rufus, makes US #175 with its debut album, ***Rufus***.

1974

Aug Rufus' singles chart debut covers Stevie Wonder's *Tell Me Something Good*, which hits US #3 and earns a gold disc for one million sales. ***Rags To Rufus*** hits US #4, and also goes gold.
Dec *You Got The Love* reaches US #11.

1975

Apr *Once You Get Started* hits US #10, while its parent album, ***Rufusized***, hits US #7, the band's second gold album. It also makes UK #48, Rufus' first UK chart entry.
May [22] The band joins Joe Cocker, Pure Prairie League and Earl Scruggs in the "Music - You're My Mother" concert at Fort Campbell, KY, playing to 17,000 US army troops and their families.
June *Please Pardon Me (You Remind Me Of A Friend)* makes US #48.
[21] On a UK tour, Rufus supports Elton John at Wembley Stadium, Wembley Middx., along with the Beach Boys, the Eagles and Joe Walsh.
Dec Curtis Mayfield, who claims Khan is signed to his Curtom label by way of her one-time membership of the Babysitters, sues her for $800,000.

1976

Apr Rufus' second million seller, *Sweet Thing*, hits US #5, taken from ***Rufus Featuring Chaka Khan***, which hits US #7 and is a third gold disc.
June *Dance With Me* makes US #39.

1977

Apr *At Midnight (My Love Will Lift You Up)* reaches US #30, while ***Ask Rufus*** is the band's biggest-selling album to date, reaching US #12 and topping a million sales, earning the band a platinum disc.
June *Hollywood* makes US #32.
Sept [27] Khan participates in the "Rock'n'Bowl" benefit for the US Special Olympics at the South Bay Bowl, Redondo Beach, CA.

1978

Jan Joni Mitchell's ***Don Juan's Restless Daughter*** is released, featuring Khan duetting on *Dreamland*.
Apr ***Street Player*** reaches US #14, earning another gold disc.
June With group billing changed to Rufus & Chaka Khan, *Stay* makes US #38.
July She is heard singing lead vocals on Quincy Jones' US #21, *Stuff Like That*.
Dec Khan has signed a solo deal with Warner Bros. Records, which releases her maiden solo album, ***Chaka***, which reaches US #12 and earns a gold disc for half a million sales. Produced by Arif Mardin, it features the Average White Band, George Benson and members of Rufus.

1979

Jan Taken from the album, the dance diva-showcasing *I'm Every Woman*, written by Ashford and Simpson, reaches US #21, having already topped the R&B chart for three weeks), and reaches UK #11.
Mar Rufus' ***Numbers*** makes US #81.
Aug Now split from Rufus (though she is contracted to make two further albums with the group for ABC), Khan guests on Ry Cooder's newly released ***Bop Till You Drop***. Rufus, meanwhile, recruits David Wolinski for lead vocals, alongside Tony Maiden.

1980

Feb Fulfilling her contract, Rufus & Chaka Khan's *Do You Love What You Feel* reaches US #30, taken from the band album ***Masterjam***, which climbs to US #14 and earns another gold disc.
Aug Her solo album, ***Naughty***, makes US #43.

1981

May Rufus' ***Party 'Til You're Broke*** peaks at US #73.
June Khan's solo album, ***What Cha' Gonna Do For Me***, including an update of Dizzy Gillespie's *Night In Tunisia* featuring Herbie Hancock, David Foster and Gillespie himself, reaches US #17 and earns a gold disc, while the title track, *What Cha' Gonna Do For Me*, peaks at US #53.
Dec Rufus & Chaka Khan's *Sharing The Love* climbs to US #91, from ***Camouflage***, which makes US #98.

1982

Feb Khan and Rufus perform together at New York, NY's Savoy Theater, the show being recorded for a subsequent live album. Meanwhile, Khan contributes vocals to Lenny White's ***Echoes Of An Era***, recording new versions of jazz classics alongside Chick Corea, Stanley Clarke and Freddie Hubbard.

1983

Feb Her revival of Michael Jackson's 1971 hit, *Got*

To Be There, peaks at US #67, taken from the Mardin-produced ***Chaka Khan***, which makes US #52.

Nov Double album, ***Live - Stompin' At The Savoy***, a recording of the February 1982 Khan/Rufus reunion concert, released by Khan's label Warner Bros., makes US #50.

Dec *Ain't Nobody*, taken from the live album, reaches US #22.

1984

Feb [28] Khan wins the Best R&B Vocal Performance, Female, for ***Chaka Khan***, Best R&B Performance By A Duo Or Group With Vocal with Rufus for *Ain't Nobody*, and Best Vocal Arrangement For Two Or More Voices with Arif Mardin for *Be Bop Medley* categories at the 26th annual Grammy Awards.

May *Ain't Nobody* hits UK #8, Rufus' only UK hit single), while ***Live - Stompin' At The Savoy*** makes UK #64.

Nov [10] Khan's revival of *I Feel For You*, written by Prince and originally on his second album, ***Prince***, in 1979, featuring a rap intro by Grandmaster Melle Mel and harmonica fills by Stevie Wonder, tops the UK chart for the first of three weeks, and will hit US #3, selling over a million to earn a gold disc. The Mardin-helmed album, ***I Feel For You***, reaches US #14 and UK #15, and is a US million seller, earning a platinum disc.

1985

Feb *This Is My Night*, exemplifying the electro-funk feel of the album, reaches UK #14, and makes US #60. Khan's UK tour which follows is plagued by her ongoing throat problems.

[26] Khan wins the Best R&B Vocal Performance, Female category, for *I Feel For You* at the 27th annual Grammy Awards (while the song wins Prince the Grammy for Best New R&B Song).

May *Eye To Eye* reaches UK #14, while the ballad *Through The Fire* makes US #60.

Oct Khan's *Can't Stop The Street* is featured in the break-dance/rap movie, "Krush Groove".

1986

Jan [25] *Own The Night*, featured in an episode of NBC-TV's "Miami Vice", peaks at US #57.

May [3] Robert Palmer's *Addicted To Love*, for which Khan has arranged the vocals, hits US #1.

July Written and produced by Scritti Politti, *Love Of A Lifetime* peaks at UK #52. Khan is also currently featured duetting with David Bowie on *Underground*, from the soundtrack of "Labyrinth".

Aug [9] *Love Of A Lifetime* peaks at US #53, while its parent album, ***Destiny***, climbs to US #67 and UK #77, once again produced by Mardin (assisted by his son Joe), and including a song written by Genesis' Mike Rutherford.

[30] Steve Winwood's *Higher Love*, featuring Khan both on the song and in the video clip, hits US #1.

1989

Jan Having begun a European tour in Hamburg, West Germany the previous November 5th, *It's My Party*, co-penned by Cecil and Linda Womack and produced by Russ Titelman, peaks at UK #71, as its parent album, ***C. K.***, variously produced by Khan, Titelman, David Frank, Chris Jasper and Prince, makes US #125.

May Remixed issue of 1979's *I'm Every Woman* hits UK #8. Khan contributes *Fever* to the newly-released Richard Perry-produced ***Rock Rhythm & Blues*** compilation.

June [3] ***Life Is A Dance - The Remix Project***, a UK-only cash-in of remixed Khan/Rufus hits, reaches UK #14.

Oct The extracted remixed version of *I Feel For You* makes UK #45.

1990

Jan [27] Quincy Jones' *I'll Be Good To You*, with Khan and Ray Charles the featured vocalists, reaches US #18.

Dec [11] Khan performs on CBS-TV's "1990 Grammy Legends Show".

1991

Jan [16] She sings *Proud Mary* with John Fogerty at the Rock and Roll Hall of Fame after-dinner jam from New York's Waldorf Astoria Hotel.

June [29] Khan takes part in syndicated TV's "Celebrate The Soul Of American Music", with Oleta Adams, En Vogue, Lalah Hathaway, Levert, Dianne Reeves and co-host, Dionne Warwick.

Sept [9] BEF's ***Music Of Quality & Distinction Volume 2***, to which Khan has contributed *Someday We'll All Be Free*, is released.

[28] R&B outfit Pretty In Pink, featuring Khan's 17-year-old daughter, Milini, peak at US #96 with *All About You*.

1992

Apr [4] *Love You All My Lifetime* makes UK #49.

[28] Khan participates in the recording of Quincy Jones' ***Hallelujah!***, a contemporary version of Handel's "The Messiah" at A&M Studios, Hollywood, CA.

May [2] Returning to her solo career, having spent three years living in Germany and London, Khan's self-produced ***The Woman I Am*** debuts at its US #92 peak.

[23] *Love You All My Lifetime* climbs to US #68.

June She becomes a grandmother, as Milini gives birth to Raven Alexis.

July [9] Khan plays a one-off London gig at the Subterania.

[16] She appears on BBC1-TV's "Summer Scene".

Aug When asked in this month's issue of **Tafrija** magazine how she would most like to be remembered, Khan replies: "As a good old broad that maintained integrity."

[18] Khan plays a sellout show with El DeBarge at New York's Beacon Theatre.

Sept [27] Following a show in San Carlos, CA, Khan undergoes an appendectomy at Anaheim Memorial Hospital, causing her world tour, which opened July 24th in Cincinnati, OH, to be rescheduled.

Nov [25] A Japanese tour opens at the Kosei Nankin Kaikan Hall, Tokyo.

Dec [15] Khan appears on NBC-TV's "Tonight" show duetting on *Feels Like Heaven* with Peter Cetera, which will peak at US #71 on Feb [13].

1993

Jan [24] Khan sings *Ain't That Peculiar* and *How Sweet It Is* at "Sexual Healing", a tribute to Marvin Gaye in support of the fight against AIDS, at Midem, France.

Feb [24] She collects the Best R&B Vocal Performance, Female trophy for ***The Woman I Am*** at the 35th annual Grammy Awards, held at Los Angeles, CA's Shrine Auditorium.

Mar [19] A 26-date "A Night On The Town" concert tour with Philip Bailey, Gerald Albright, Bobby Lyle and Hugh Masekela, opens in Sacramento, CA, set to end on April 25th in San Luis Obispo, CA.

Apr [13] ***Sweet Things : Greatest Hits***, a Rufus and Khan retrospective, is released in the US by MCA Records.

June [4-6] Khan performs at New York's Blue Note club.

July [10] She takes part in the annual "Montreux Jazz Festival", Montreux, Switzerland, during European dates which also see her participate in the "North Sea Jazz Festival" in the Hague, Holland, and the "JVC Jazz Festival" in Nice, France.

[17] *Don't Look At Me That Way* charts for a week at UK #73.

Nov [9-14] Khan plays a week-long stint at New York's Blue Note club.

1994

Apr [22] Khan sings *Bridge Over Troubled Water* with Brian McKnight at the seventh annual Essence Awards at the Paramount, New York.

July [9] ABC-TV's third annual "In A New Light" AIDS special, in which Khan sings *Here I Am*, airs.

[10] Khan takes part in the "JVC Jazz Festival" at the Hollywood Bowl, Hollywood, CA.

Nov [25] Khan performs at the third annual Franklin Scholarship Awards Dinner and Dance at Cobo Exhibition Hall, Detroit, MI.

1995

Jan [10] Khan performs at a tribute concert for Ella Fitzgerald at the Universal Amphitheater, Universal City.

May Having appeared in the West End production of "Mama, I Want To Sing" at the Cambridge Theatre, Khan now begins pre-production on new US TV sitcom, "That's My Baby".

Sept Khan's new single, *Love Me Still*, co-written by Bruce Hornsby and featured in the movie "Clockers", is released, amidst rumors of a Rufus reunion.

Oct [24] Having had new cuts featured on RainForest Alliance benefit album ***Earthrise***, Manhattan Transfer's ***Tonin'***, Guru's ***Jazzmatazz Volume II : The New Reality***, United Nations celebration album ***People*** and ***To Wong Foo, Thanks For Everything, Julie Newmar*** soundtrack, Khan is now one of the featured artists on Quincy Jones' new project ***Q's Jook Joint***, and set to be featured on the #1 soundtrack album ***Waiting To Exhale***.

Dec [31] Khan plays a New Year's Eve show at New York's Beacon Theatre.

JOHNNY KIDD & THE PIRATES

Johnny Kidd (vocals); **Alan Caddy** (guitar); **Brian Gregg** (bass); **Clem Cattini** (drums)

1959

Apr [18] The group is formed in London by Kidd (b. Frederick Heath, Dec. 23, 1939, Willesden, London), former leader of skiffle group the Five Nutters, whose membership included Brian Donelon (washboard), Johnny Gordon (bass), Clive Lazell (snare drum) and Caddy (b. Feb. 2, 1940, London). With the Five Nutters performing in 1958 as the Freddie Heath combo, Kidd and Gordon have formed a third outfit, briefly led by Mike West. Going on to found the Pirates without West, a booking on BBC radio's "Saturday Club" show leads to a recording contract with EMI's HMV imprint. Now booked into the Abbey Road Studios to cut its debut single, the line-up is Kidd, Caddy, Gordon and session men Tony Docherty (guitar) and Ken McKay (drums).

June *Please Don't Touch*, written by Kidd and manager Guy Robinson, reaches UK #25, while Docherty, Gordon and McKay leave, to be replaced by Gregg and Cattini, both ex-Beat Boys.

Dec Revival of the music-hall standard, *If You Were The Only Girl In The World*, is the follow-up.

1960

Jan Gregg and Cattini, former session men in the Larry Parnes' tour back-up band the Beat Boys, join to complete a powerful live group. They all play in pirate gear in front of a galleon backdrop, and Kidd wears an eye-patch which, he later admits, temporarily upsets his eyesight after every show.

Feb Their cover of Marv Johnson's US hit, *You Got What It Takes*, reaches UK #25.

Aug *Shakin' All Over*, almost issued as a B-side, hits UK #2, behind Cliff Richard and the Shadows' *Please Don't Tease*. Driven by a powerful guitar riff from session player Joe Moretti, it becomes a UK standard.

Oct *Restless*, in similar style to *Shakin'*, reaches UK #19.

1961

Apr Their version of Ray Sharpe's US hit, *Linda Lu*, makes UK #47.

July The Pirates leave Kidd to back Tommy Steele's brother, Colin Hicks, as the Cabin Boys, before becoming the basis of producer Joe Meek's studio house band the Tornados. They are replaced by Frank Farley (drums), Johnny Spence (bass) and Johnny

Patto (guitar), previously Cuddly Dudley's backing group, the Redcaps.

1962

Mar Guitarist Mick Green, also formerly with the Redcaps (his ability to play simultaneous lead and rhythm mark him as the UK's answer to James Burton), replaces Patto.

July The group begins a three-week residency at Hamburg's Star-Club, West Germany.

1963

Jan Their treatment of Arthur Alexander's *A Shot Of Rhythm And Blues*, set firmly in an R&B mould, creeps into the UK survey at #48 after two non-charters.

Sept Merseybeat-flavored *I'll Never Get Over You* is Kidd's second-biggest UK single, hitting #4.

Dec *Hungry For Love*, a stage favorite with many UK beat groups, reaches UK #20.

1964

Jan The Pirates, minus Kidd, release an R&B single, a revival of Little Walter's *My Babe*, with Spence vocalizing, and guests on a handful of dates on the Rolling Stones' "Group Scene 64" package tour.

Apr Kidd recruits organist Vic Cooper, while *Always And Ever*, an unlikely rock adaptation of the Latin standard *La Paloma*, is his last UK chart entry, making #46.

July Green leaves to join Billy J. Kramer & the Dakotas, replaced by John Weider (ex-Tony Meehan Combo and a future member of Family).

Oct Their revival of Marvin Rainwater's *Whole Lotta Woman* is released.

Nov [30] The group joins the Brenda Lee tour at the Town Hall, Birmingham, Warks.

1966

Apr Acknowledging his depression about declining interest in his music, now seen as outdated, Kidd splits from the Pirates. Spence and Farley keep the name and, with guitarist Jon Morshead, record *Casting My Spell* for Polydor, before disbanding after a final gig at Walton Hall, Bletchley, Bucks.

May Kidd recruits Nick Simper (bass) and Roger Truth (b. Roger Pinner) (drums) from the Regents, former backing group of Buddy Britten, as the New Pirates and resumes live work.

Aug [18-23] Kidd and the band cut tracks for a new single.

Oct [7] While on tour, Kidd dies in a car crash in Radcliffe, near Manchester, Lancs. Nick Simper, a member of the New Pirates, survives the crash (and will go on to become a founding member of Deep Purple). The group carries on for a while as the Pirates, but bookings dry up without Kidd's name and they split in May 1967.

1976

Dec Former Kidd sidemen Mick Green, Johnny Spence and Frank Farley re-form as the Pirates, and become one of the most highly-rated UK live acts of the late '70s in pubs, clubs and larger venues. Their debut album for Warner Bros., ***Out Of Their Skulls***, charts in the UK at #57, but the follow-up album, 1978's ***Skull Wars*** and a plethora of singles will sell less well despite continuing on stage success, which continues until a final split in 1982. A revised lineup will emerge in the late '80s responsible for the little-noticed ***Live In Japan*** and ***Don't Munchen It! - The Pirates Live In Europe***.

THE GREG KIHN BAND

Greg Kihn (vocals, guitar); **Greg Douglas** (guitar); **Gary Phillips** (keyboards, vocals); **Steven Wright** (bass, vocals); **Larry Lynch** (drums, percussion)

1975

Abandoning his earlier folk singer/songwriter leanings, Kihn (b. Baltimore, MD) having moved to Berkeley, CA the previous year and signing to the new, independent Beserkley record company, initially sings with labelmates Earth Quake and Jonathan Richman (including backing vocals on Richman's hit single *Roadrunner*) and cuts two tracks for the compilation ***Beserkley Chartbusters, Vol. 1***, before forming the first version of the rock combo, the Greg Kihn Band, with Wright and Lynch. The trio hones its material on club gigs in the San Francisco, CA area, with a Sunday night residency at the San Pablo Avenue music hall, usually with Earth Quake's Robbie Dunbar as guest guitarist. His self-penned debut album ***Greg Kihn***, produced, as with its follow-ups, by Matthew King Kaufman, is released.

1976

Mar Dave Carpenter joins the band on guitar, filling the slot which Dunbar has been caretaking. This line-up records ***Greg Kihn, Again***, which features a critically-rated version of Bruce Springsteen's *For You* in a folk/rockish arrangement which the writer admires and later adopts, crediting Kihn.

1978

Aug [26] On tour in the UK, the band plays at the "Reading Festival", Reading, Berks., alongside Status Quo, Spirit and others.

Oct His third album ***Next Of Kihn***, consisting wholly of Kihn originals, reaches US #145. The following September, ***With The Naked Eye***, which includes another highly-rated Springsteen cover, *Rendezvous*, will make US #114 with ***Glass House Rock*** peaking at US #167 in May 1980, the same year the group becomes a quintet augmented by Gary Phillips (ex-Copperhead and Earth Quake) on keyboards and backing vocals.

1981

Sept The band's breakthrough single is *The Breakup Song (They Don't Write 'Em)*, which reaches US #15, staying charted for over five months. It is taken from ***Rockihnroll***, which is Kihn's best-selling album to date, reaching US #32 during a 32-week tenure.

1982

May ***Kihntinued*** reaches US #33.

June *Happy Man*, extracted from the album, peaks at US #62.

July *Every Love Song*, also from ***Kihntinued***, climbs to US #82.

1983

Apr *Jeopardy* becomes Kihn's only UK chart success, peaking at #63.

May [7] Airplay-ready *Jeopardy*, co-penned by Kihn and Wright, becomes a US smash, hitting #2 behind Michael Jackson's *Beat It*, and giving Kihn his first million-seller. ***Kihnspiracy***, from which the hit is taken, and which also includes an unlikely revival of Patsy Cline's country ballad *I Fall To Pieces*, reaches US #15.

1984

June With Greg Douglas having replaced Carpenter, *Love Never Fails* peaks at US #59 while its parent album ***Kihntagious*** makes US #121. It is Kihn's final Beserkley release before signing to major label EMI America.

1985

Apr ***Citizen Kihn*** reaches US #51. It credits Kihn as a soloist, though Wright is still on hand on play several instruments, as well as co-arranging the tracks and co-writing all 11 songs with Kihn. The extracted *Lucky* climbs to US #30.

1986

Apr [5] His final outing for EMI, ***Love And Rock And Roll***, featuring guitarist Joe Satriani, peaks at US #92, also marking the end of Kihn's '80s chart career. A comprehensive Rhino Records retrospective collection, ***Kihnsolidation : The Best Of Greg Kihn*** will bring the artist's career highlights to compact disc in 1989.

1994

Sept Having released two original sets for Rhino, 1990's ***Kihn Of Hearts*** and ***Unkihntrollable*** in 1993, and in between novel and screenplay projects, he finally loses kihnship with his album titles, issuing the acoustic-framed covers album, the well-received ***Mutiny*** on Clean Cut Records, licensed in the UK by Demon, before taking up residency as a DJ in California.

B.B. KING

1949

Influenced by the music of the early blues and jazz guitar pioneers and having sung in his local church choir as a boy, King (b. Riley B. King, Sept. 16, 1925, Itta Bena, MS), the son of a Mississippi sharecropper and a cousin of bluesman Bukka White, who has performed with the Elkhorn Singers in his teens, has been playing self-taught blues guitar semi-professionally since his US army service, also working on farms around Indianola, MS. While leading a trio in Memphis, TN, to where he relocated in 1946 to link up with Sonny Boy Williamson, and initially playing a residency at the 16th Avenue Grill, his local popularity is noted by radio station WDIA and he secures his own regular broadcast slot, "The Sepia Swing Show", also playing music to advertise the alcohol-based medicine Pepticon. The station's publicity man dubs King "The Beale Street Blues Boy", which is shortened to Blues Boy and eventually B.B. Towards the end of the year, King signs to Bullet Records, debuting with *Miss Martha King*, one of four sides he will cut for the label. The following year, he is signed to the Kent/Modern/RPM group of labels by talent scout Ike Turner and will remain with the company until 1962, also forming his own short-lived Blue Boy label imprint during the '50s. (King has developed his own unique blues sound on his Gibson guitar, nicknamed "Lucille". The nickname came about after a gig in Twist, AR: a fight ensued and a kerosene stove was knocked over, forcing an evacuation from the club. King forgot his guitar and dashed back in to rescue it, later discovering that the fight had broken out over a girl named Lucille.)

1952

Feb [2] King hits US R&B #1 with *Three O'Clock Blues*, his eighth single. Ike Turner is featured on piano, Willie Mitchell on trumpet and Hank Crawford on alto sax.

Nov [8] *You Didn't Want Me* also hits US R&B #1. (King, recently divorced, will continue to enjoy regular R&B chart success for the next five years, including two further chart-toppers, *Please Love Me* (1953) and *You Upset Me Baby* (1954).)

1954

Oct [1] King and his band perform at the Meadow Acres Ballroom, Topeka, KS.

Aug [19] King and his band play at the Savoy Ballroom in Hollywood, CA, with Johnny Otis and the Platters, to a capacity audience of 2,400. (He is now averaging some 300 gigs a year with his 13-piece band, a relentless schedule he will maintain until the '90s.)

1957

May [29] King plays with Ray Charles, the Drifters, Ruth Brown, Jimmy Reed and others at an outdoor

R&B festival at Herndon Stadium in Atlanta, GA.
July *Be Careful With A Fool* is King's first crossover success, at US #95.
Nov *I Need You So Bad* makes US #85.

1961

June [25] Having scored with the US R&B #2 hit *Sweet Sixteen* in February the previous year, King takes part in the "Alan Freed Spectacular" at the Hollywood Bowl, Hollywood, CA, with Brenda Lee, Bobby Vee, Jerry Lee Lewis, the Shirelles and the Fleetwoods, among others. (The following year he will move from Kent to the larger ABC label, with which he will record until it is absorbed into MCA in 1979.)

1964

Mar *How Blue Can You Get It*, his first ABC success, peaks at US #97.
May *Rock Me Baby*, recorded for Kent before the label move, is King's first sizeable pop hit, reaching US #34. (It will be much covered and adapted by the UK R&B fraternity.)
June *Help The Poor*, on ABC, peaks at US #98.
Nov *Beautician Blues* stops at US #82, as *Never Trust A Woman* makes US #90.
[21] King plays a concert at the Regal Theater, Chicago, IL, which will be released as the critically-revered seminal live blues recording ***Live At The Regal*** in 1965.

1965

July Achieving one US chart single a year for the next three, *Blue Shadows* peaks at US #97, with *Don't Answer The Door* making US #72 in October 1966, and *The Jungle*, another stockpiled oldie from Kent, reaching US #94 in April the following year.

1968

Apr *Paying The Cost To Be The Boss*, on ABC's Bluesway label, is his second US Top 40 hit, at #39. King is in dispute with his manager, Lou Zito, over financial affairs, a situation mediated by King's accountant, Sidney Seidenberg, who is appointed as his new manager.
[4] On the night Martin Luther King is assassinated, King, Buddy Guy and Jimi Hendrix gather in a club to play an all-night blues session and pass a hat around to collect money for King's Southern Christian Leadership fund.
July *I'm Gonna Do What They Do To Me* climbs to US #74.
Aug *The Woman I Love* peaks at US #94.
Oct Double A-side, *The B.B. Jones/Put It On Me*, featured on the soundtrack to the movie "For The Love Of Ivy", makes US #98/#82. King's first album-chart success is with ***Lucille*** on Bluesway, which peaks at US #192.

1969

Apr [29] King plays at the Free Trade Hall, Manchester, Lancs., during a short UK visit.
May *Why I Sing The Blues* makes US #61.
July ***Live And Well***, produced by Bill Szymczyck, with one studio side and the other recorded at New York's Village Gate club, makes US #56.
[3-6] King plays at the "Newport Jazz Festival", Newport, RI, jamming with Johnny Winter.
Aug [1] He performs at the "Atlantic City Pop Festival", Atlantic City, NJ, before a crowd of 110,000 people, alongside Creedence Clearwater Revival, Jefferson Airplane, the Byrds and others.
[30] He plays at the "International Pop Festival" at the Dallas Speedway in Lewisville, TX, along with Janis Joplin, Canned Heat, Santana, Led Zeppelin and many more.
Oct [11] *Get Off My Back Woman* peaks at US #74.
Nov [7] King is the opening act for the Rolling Stones' sixth US tour, which begins at the State University, Fort Collins, CO, set to end on the 29th at the Boston Garden, Boston, MA.
[22] *Just A Little Love* makes US #76. Under Seidenberg's encouragement, King starts to widen his following from the traditional (and declining) black audience towards a young, international white one, booking rock-oriented venues like the Fillmores East and West, and aiming at audiences already weaned on blues-derived rock bands.
Dec King's revival of Roy Hawkins' *The Thrill Is Gone*, using an imaginative string arrangement, is King's biggest hit single, reaching US #15.

1970

Feb ***Completely Well***, which includes *The Thrill Is Gone*, makes US #38.
Apr *So Excited* peaks at US #54, while ***The Incredible Soul Of B.B. King*** stops at US #193. King begins work on a new album and, in an attempt to repeat the pop-chart success of ***Completely Well***, features leading white rock musicians, including Carole King, Leon Russell and Joe Walsh.
May [21-24] King performs four nights at the Fillmore West with Albert King.
July *Hummingbird* makes US #48.
[3-5] He plays at the three-day "Atlanta Pop Festival" at the Middle Georgia Raceway in Byron, GA, before an estimated crowd of 200,000, with Jimi Hendrix, Jethro Tull, Johnny Winter and others.
Nov ***Indianola Mississippi Seeds***, recorded with King's star sidemen, reaches US #26, as *Chains And Things* climbs to US #45.

1971

Feb *Ask Me No Questions* peaks at US #40.
Mar [16] King wins the Best R&B Vocal Performance, Male category for *The Thrill Is Gone* at the 13th annual Grammy Awards.
Apr ***Live In Cook County Jail*** reaches US #25, as *That Evil Child* peaks at US #97. King is taking an active interest in prisoner welfare, not least participating in a "Donahue Live" TV show from Ohio State Prison - and will become co-chairman of FAIRR - Foundation for the Advancement of Inmate Rehabilitation and Recreation.
June *Help The Poor*, an instrumental version of his 1964 release, makes US #90.
Sept *Ghetto Woman* climbs to US #68.
Oct Reissued ***Live At The Regal*** reaches US #78.
Nov ***B.B. King In London***, featuring sidemen Peter Green, Alexis Korner, Steve Marriott and Ringo Starr, reaches US #57, as *Ain't Nobody Home* makes US #46.
[19] King marks his 25th anniversary in the music business by opening a European tour in London.

1972

Mar ***L.A. Midnight*** reaches US #53. From it, a new version of *Sweet Sixteen* makes US #93.
Apr [1] King plays at the "Mar Y Sol Festival" in Vega Baja, Puerto Rica, with Black Sabbath, the Allman Brothers Band and Emerson, Lake & Palmer, among others.
May *I Got Some Help I Don't Need It* peaks at US #92.
Aug ***Guess Who*** reaches US #65, while the extracted *Guess Who* makes US #62.

1973

Mar Compilation album, ***The Best Of B.B. King***, makes US #101.
Aug *To Know You Is To Love You* peaks at #38, as ***To Know You Is To Love You*** climbs to US #71, also spawning the US #28, *I Like To Live The Love*, in December.

1974

Mar King embarks on his first tour of Australia.
June *Who Are You* peaks at US #78, featured on the US #153 (August) album, ***Friends***.
Sept [8] King takes part in the "Ann Arbor Blues & Jazz Festival" at the Griffin Hollow Amphitheater, St. Clair College, Windsor, ON, Canada.
Nov *Philadelphia* reaches US #64.
Dec ***Together For The First Time ... Live***, a collaboration with King's old friend and associate Bobby Bland (who was also King's personal valet back in 1949), reaches US #43. (***Lucille Talks Back*** will climb to US #140 the following November, while a second set with Bland, ***Together Again ... Live*** will reach US #73 in August 1976. ***King Size*** will make US #154 in February 1977.)

1978

Apr King joins top defence lawyer F. Lee Bailey, his fellow co-chairman of FAIRR, for a joint rap session and concert for the inmates of Norfolk Prison near Boston, sections of which are filmed by ABC-TV for broadcast on "Good Morning America".
May ***Midnight Believer*** peaks at US #124. King switches labels as ABC is absorbed into its parent company, MCA.
Oct [14-15] During his current UK tour, King performs a pair of dates at London's Hammersmith Odeon (having also performed at the venue back in 1977 on October 9th).

1979

Apr He plays a month-long, 30-date USSR tour.
Aug ***Take It Home*** makes US #112.
[24] King celebrates his 30th anniversary of performing by playing at Los Angeles, CA's Roxy.
Sept [22] ***Take It Home*** gives King his first UK album-chart success, peaking at #60.

1980

May Live album, ***Now Appearing At Ole Miss***, climbs to US #162, followed by ***There Must Be A Better World Somewhere*** which peaks at US #131 next March. (A workaholic, King always includes dates in Mississippi during his annual itineraries.)

1982

Jan [21] King donates his entire record collection (some 20,000 discs, including 7,000 rare blues 78s) to Mississippi University's Center for the Study of Southern Culture.
Feb [24] King wins the Best Ethnic Or Traditional Recording category for ***There Must Be A Better World Somewhere*** at the 24th annual Grammy Awards.
May ***Love Me Tender*** makes US #179.
Sept [16] He records ***Blues 'N' Jazz*** on his 57th birthday.

1983

June [23] He plays at the "Kool Jazz Festival" in New York, NY, with Ray Charles, Miles Davis and others.
July ***Blues 'N' Jazz*** reaches US #172.

1984

Feb [28] ***Blues 'N' Jazz*** is named Best Traditional Blues Recording at the 26th annual Grammy Awards.

1985

Feb [28] King, currently featured as himself in a cameo role in the John Landis movie "Into The Night", appears on NBC-TV's "Late Night With David Letterman".
July [13] He participates in "Live Aid" at the J.F.K. Stadium, Philadelphia, PA.

1986

Feb [25] King nabs Best Traditional Blues Recording category for *My Guitar Sings The Blues*, from ***Six Silver Strings***, at the 28th annual Grammy Awards.
Nov [16] He co-hosts America's seventh National Blues Awards with Carl Perkins.

1987

Jan [21] King is inducted into the Rock and Roll Hall of Fame at the second annual dinner, held at New York's Waldorf Astoria Hotel.
Feb [24] He performs with a blues supergroup, featuring Willie Dixon, Albert King, Robert Cray, Etta James, Ry Cooder, Dr. John, Koko Taylor and Junior Wells, at the 29th Grammy Awards held at Los Angeles' Shrine Auditorium.

1988

Mar [2] King is honored by the NARAS at the 30th

annual Grammy Awards with a Lifetime Achievement Award, noting that he is "one of the most original and soulful of all blues guitarists and singers, whose compelling style and devotion to musical truth have inspired so many budding performers, both here and abroad, to celebrate the blues".

1989

Apr [29] U2's *When Love Comes To Town*, on which he is a prominent guest, hits UK #6.
[29] *When Love Comes To Town* peaks at US #68.
June [21-25] King performs at the "Benson & Hedges Blues Festival" in Dallas, TX, the proceeds going to the National Coalition for the Homeless and the Dallas-based group for the homeless, Common Ground.
[29] He plays at the 30th "Newport Folk Festival" at Fort Adams State Park, Newport, RI, with Randy Newman, John Hiatt and Buckwheat Zydeco, among others.
July [13] King performs at the "Montreux Jazz Festival", Montreux, Switzerland.
Aug [1] He guests on "Late Night With David Letterman".
Sept [6] King and U2 win the Best Video From Film award at the sixth annual MTV Video Music Awards ceremony, at the Universal Amphitheatre, Universal City, CA, for "When Love Comes To Town" from U2's movie, "Rattle And Hum".
[12] He joins U2 on their tour of Australia.
Dec [23] King contributes *Joe Cool* to the ***Happy Anniversary, Charlie Brown!*** homage (US #65), commemorating the 40th year of the "Peanuts" comic strip.

1990

Jan [1] He is aboard the Mississippi Tournament of Roses Association float at the 1990 "Rosebowl Parade" in Pasadena, CA.
[23] Herbie Hancock recruits King and others, including Rickie Lee Jones, Lou Reed, Bonnie Raitt, Bruce Hornsby and Sting, for a taping of Showtime TV's "Coast To Coast" from the China club in Los Angeles.
Feb [24] He participates in the "Roy Orbison All-Star Benefit Tribute" held at the Universal Amphitheatre, an event raising $500,000 for the Shelter Partnership and the National Coalition for the Homeless.
Apr [27] King is hospitalized in Las Vegas, NV, after cancelling two dates at the 21st annual "New Orleans Jazz & Heritage Festival" because of health problems related to his diabetes.
May [27] He plays at the 5,864 sellout Valley Forge Music Fair, Devon, PA.
[30] King receives a Lifetime Achievement award at the Songwriters Hall of Fame 21st annual induction dinner, at New York's Hilton Hotel.
June [9] King plays to a sellout crowd at the Pacific Amphitheatre, Los Angeles, as part of the "Benson & Hedges Blues '90" tour, with Joe Cocker, Stevie Ray Vaughan, Dr. John and John Lee Hooker.
Aug [17] He takes part in the annual "JVC Jazz Festival" at Fort Adams State Park, Newport, with Miles Davis, George Benson and others.
Sept ***Live At San Quentin***, recorded 20 years earlier, is released. He also duets with Randy Travis on *Waiting On The Light To Change*, on the latter's album, ***Heroes And Friends***.
[7] King becomes the 1,917th performer to have a star on the Hollywood Walk of Fame.
[29] He begins a world tour with Ray Charles in Taipei, Taiwan.
Dec [4] The Simpsons ***Sings The Blues*** album is released, with King playing guitar on *Born Under A Bad Sign*.
[31] He ends the year as a guest on NBC-TV's "The Tonight Show".

1991

Feb King leads the Zulu Social Aid & Pleasure Club float during the Mardi Gras parade in New Orleans.
[19] The Gibson guitar company honors King ("Lucille" is a Gibson) with the Orville H. Gibson Lifetime Achievement award at New York's Hard Rock Café.
[20] He wins the Best Traditional Blues Recording category for ***Live At San Quentin*** at the 33rd Grammy Awards, held at New York's Radio City Music Hall.
Mar [14] King returns to guest on "The Tonight Show".
Apr [22] He launches the fourth annual "Benson & Hedges Blues" tour at the China Club, Los Angeles.
[29] King and Gibson Guitars celebrate the 40th anniversary of *Lucille* by beginning a tour of Hard Rock Cafés at the Dallas, TX branch.
May [2] The legend opens his own 350-seater restaurant and nightclub, B.B. King's Memphis Blues Club, on Beale Street, Memphis.
[3] He takes part in the annual "Memphis In May Beale Street Music Festival".
[4] King plays at "Volunteer Jam XIV" at the Starwood Amphitheatre, Nashville, TN, with Steppenwolf, Ted Nugent and Jim Dandy.
[14] GRP Records releases ***Am I Cool, Or What?***, a homage to cartoon feline Garfield, featuring King's *Monday Morning Blues*.
July [6] During a European trek, King performs in Zagreb, Yugoslavia, with James Brown.
[12] He appears at the "Montreux Jazz Festival", with Bonnie Raitt.
[18] King plays at London's Royal Festival Hall.
Sept [15] He celebrates his 66th birthday at the 19th annual "San Francisco Blues Festival" with backing-band guests Robert Cray, Boz Scaggs and Bobby McFerrin. The city's mayor, Art Agnos, also presents King with keys to the city.
Oct [2] King's "Super Band" world tour opens in Istanbul, Turkey, set to end in Washington, DC on November 21st.
[11] King guests on "The Tonight Show".
[15-19] He performs at "Guitar Legends", a five-concert series staged as part of "Expo '92", in Seville, Spain.
[29] Memphis City Council names Interstate 55 through Jackson, MS, B.B. King Freeway.

1992

Jan [15] King inducts Bobby Bland into the Rock and Roll Hall of Fame at the seventh annual dinner, held in New York's Waldorf Astoria Hotel.
Feb [4] He performs at his own B.B. King's Blues Club in Memphis.
[25] He wins the Best Traditional Blues Album category for ***Live At The Apollo*** at the 34th annual Grammy Awards, from Radio City Music Hall, New York
Apr [24] King, now regularly touring with Bobby Bland, performs at the Valley Forge Music Fair, Devon, PA.
July [14] Kings plays at the "First International Jazz Festival", Winter Gardens Empress Ballroom, Blackpool, Lancs., before appearing at the "Capital Radio Jazz Parade" at the Royal Festival Hall the following day.
[25] *Since I Met You Baby*, recorded with Gary Moore, peaks at UK #59.
Aug [8] King begins a 25-date "Blues Music Festival '92" tour in Oregon, sharing the bill on selected dates with Ray Charles, Joe Cocker, Robert Cray, Dr. John, the Fabulous Thunderbirds, Buddy Guy and Santana.
[13] He jams with Buddy Guy, Dr. John and the Fabulous Thunderbirds on "The Tonight Show".
Oct [22-24] King begins an eight-date South American tour in Caracas, Venezuela, before embarking on a European trek, with Robert Cray.
Dec [7] Following dates in Indonesia, Singapore, Malayia and Thailand, King opens the Japanese leg of his tour in Osaka, set to end on the 17th in Yokohama.
[29] He performs at the Gainesville Drug Treatment Center, Gainesville, FL, before 300 prison inmates, including his daughter Patty, who is serving three years for drug trafficking.

1993

Mar [26] King headlines a benefit concert at the Memorial Auditorium, Chattanooga, TN, raising $90,000 for the Bessie Smith Hall, set to open in September.
Apr [18] He performs at the Westbury Music Fair, Westbury, NY, at the start of his current US tour with Bobby Bland and Millie Jackson, set to end on May 16th at the Cajundome, Lafayette, LA.
May [22] King guests on CBS-TV's "Willie Nelson The Big Six-O" birthday celebrations.
June [15] He performs *Rock Me Baby* with Eric Clapton at the "Apollo Theatre Hall Of Fame" concert from the landmark New York theater. (The show will air on NBC-TV on August 4th.)
[16] King jams at New York's Hard Rock Café at a launch promoting the 45-date "Blues Music Festival '93", due to start August 2nd at the Starlake Amphitheater, Burgettstown, PA.
Sept [11] King's latest album, ***Blues Summit***, variously produced by Trade Martin, Stewart Levine, Jon Tiven and Vernon Reid, with Robert Cray, Albert Collins, Etta James, John Lee Hooker, Buddy Guy and Irma Thomas among its featured guests, charts for a week at US #182.

1994

Jan King is named Outstanding World Music Artist at the 26th NAACP Image Awards.
Feb [10] While on a current North American tour, King plays at the Frank Erwin Center, University of Texas, Austin, TX, as a duet with George Jones on *Patches* is included in the newly released ***Rhythm Country & Blues*** compilation.
Mar [1] ***Blues Summit*** is named Best Traditional Blues Album at the 36th annual Grammy Awards held at New York's Radio City Music Hall, and performs a Curtis Mayfield medley with Steve Winwood, Bruce Springsteen, Bonnie Raitt, Steve Cropper, Tony! Toni! Tone and Don Was, among others.
May [14] King opens the inaugural Chinese Hard Rock Café in Beijing, and visits the Great Wall during his tour.
Aug [30] King, Little Feat and Dr. John perform at the Pine Knob Music Theatre, Clarkston, MI, as part of the "Blues Music Festival".

1995

Mar [1] King and Al Green present the Best Metal Performance to Soundgarden at the 37th annual Grammy Awards, held at the Shrine Auditorium.
[10] King performs at the opening night gala of Hard Rock Hotel & Casino in Las Vegas.
[11] Manhattan Transfer's ***Tonin'***, to which King and Ruth Brown have contributed *The Thrill Is Gone*, makes US #123.
[22] He begins another round of touring with Bobby Bland at the Morris Civic Auditorium in South Bend, IN.
May [11] King takes part in "Austin City Limits", a PBS station KLRU tribute to Stevie Ray Vaughan, with Eric Clapton, Robert Cray, Jimmie Vaughan and Buddy Guy.
Aug [22] He performs at the Filene Center, Wolf Trap Farm Park for the Performing Arts, Vienna, VA, as part of the "Blues Festival" tour.
Sept [9] The Gibson Guitar company hosts a 70th birthday concert for King at Nashville's Riverfront Stadium.
[28] A&E cable web broadcasts "Blues Summit Concert", a King special pairing him with 11 other artists.
Dec [3] King is honored at the 18th annual Kennedy Center Honors at the Kennedy Center, Washington, set to air on CBS-TV on the 27th.

1996

Jan [22] King guests on CBS-TV's "Late Show With David Letterman".
Feb [3] He appears on CBS-TV's "Touched By An Angel".
[17] King cybertalks with fans on America OnLine, as his first CD-ROM is published. Scheduled to open two new B.B. King Blues Clubs in Orlando, FL and Nashville, TN later in the year, King also announces that he will be slowing down his annual tour itinerary from 250-plus (which he has maintained since the '50s), to a mere 200.

BEN E. KING

1958

May King (b. Benjamin Earl Nelson, Sept. 28, 1938, Henderson, NC), after moving to Harlem, NY as a boy, has graduated from church choir to street corner doo-wop during his years at the James Fenimore Cooper Junior High School, singing with the Four Bs and the Moonglows, before joining the Crowns and taking part in amateur night at Harlem's Apollo Theatre. *Kiss And Make Up* has been issued to minor R&B success in 1957, with the band now sharing a bill with the Drifters at the Apollo. Owning the trademark to the Drifters' name, its manager, George Treadwell, fires the group's members in June and hires the Crowns as the new Drifters the folowing month. King subsequently becomes the featured vocalist on *There Goes My Baby* (which he has co-written), *Dance With Me*, *This Magic Moment*, *Save The Last Dance For Me* and *I Count The Tears* - smash hits which make the Drifters the hottest vocal group of the era.

1960

May [2] Treadwell fires King after he complains about low wages.

Oct [27] Signing a solo deal with Atlantic subsidiary Atco, King, with producers Leiber and Stoller, cuts four sides in three hours: *Spanish Harlem*, *First Taste Of Love*, *Young Boy Blues* and *Stand By Me*, recordings which will become the cornerstone of a lifelong career.

1961

Mar King's double-sided *Spanish Harlem*, a rare collaboration between Jerry Leiber and his apprentice, Phil Spector, hits UK #10. *First Taste Of Love*, written by Spector and Doc Pomus, reaches US #53, but its B-side reaches UK #27. (Aretha Franklin's revival of *Spanish Harlem* will hit US #2 ten years later.)

June *Stand By Me*, polished up by Leiber and Stoller in the Drifters' Latin style, hits US #4 and UK #27, and will become an enduring soul standard, having also topped the US R&B survey for four weeks. (John Lennon will revive it for a US Top 20 hit in 1975.)

Aug *Spanish Harlem* climbs to US #57.

Sept King's version of the standard *Amor* makes US #18 and UK #38, his last UK chart appearance for 25 years.

Oct Pomus/Spector-written *Young Boy Blues* is finally released, rising to US #66. Its B-side, *Here Comes The Night*, charts at US #81. (The cut will be revived in 1984 by the Honeydrippers on their debut album.)

Nov His debut album ***Spanish Harlem*** is released by Atco, licensed in the UK to London Records.

1962

Mar Another Pomus/Spector composition, *Ecstasy*, peaks at US #56.

June Co-written by King (under his wife's name) and Atlantic boss Ahmet Ertegun, *Don't Play That Song* climbs to US #11, taken from his sophomore effort, ***Don't Play That Song***. (Aretha Franklin's version of the title cut will be a million seller in 1970.)

Aug *Too Bad* charts for only two weeks, at US #88.

1963

Apr *How Can I Forget*, a King original, peaks at US #85.

Aug King's version of Leiber and Stoller's (later much-recorded) *I (Who Have Nothing)* reaches US #29 (and will be his last US Top 40 hit for 12 years).

Nov A cover of a song from the musical "My Fair Lady", *I Could Have Danced All Night*, makes US #72.

1964

Feb [3] Having issued ***Songs For Soulful Lovers*** in January, King arrives in the UK for his first visit, having just taken part in the "San Remo Song Festival" in Italy.

[7] He makes his UK TV debut on "Ready Steady Go!" (As soul becomes more synonymous with the modern sounds of Motown and Stax, King's pioneering brand loses impetus; he only has two modest US chart hits during the year: *That's When It Hurts* (#63, April) and *It's All Over* (#72, September).)

1965

Jan *Seven Letters*, taken from the album ***Seven Letters***, makes US #45.

Apr [17] *The Record (Baby I Love You)* spins to US #84.

July King takes part in Murray the K's stage show at the Brooklyn Fox Theater, with Tom Jones, Gary Lewis & the Playboys, and others.

Oct [15] King guests on ITV's "Ready Steady Go" during a UK visit. *Goodnight My Love* will peak at US #91 the following January with *So Much Love* stopping at US #96 in May.

1967

Apr [16] Having released ***What Is Soul?*** two months earlier, he performs at London's Saville Theatre, sharing the bill with Bo Diddley, as *Tears Tears Tears* peaks at US #93.

Sept [29] Following recording sessions at Muscle Shoals Studio in Alabama in June, King embarks on a UK tour, while *Spanish Harlem* spends three weeks on the UK chart, climbing to #30.

1968

Feb King joins forces with Arthur Conley, Solomon Burke and Joe Tex to record together in Memphis and Nashville, TN, but the resultant session will never be released. Over the next five years King will work the cabaret, club and supper circuits - mixing his own hits with those of current stars.

Aug [16] King embarks on a UK tour at the White Lion in Edgware, Middx., set to end with a week-long cabaret stint at the Top Hat Club in Spennymoor, Durham in the first week of September.

1974

Dec Having released his first album in five years, ***Rough Edges*** in 1970 on Crewe Records (the first project for the label founded by Bob Crewe) and ***The Beginning Of It All*** for Mandala Records two years later, King makes a cameo appearance on the Genesis album ***The Lamb Lies Down On Broadway*** - singing the phrase "on Broadway" (even though his was not the voice on the Drifters' recording!)

1975

Apr Ahmet Ertegun, having recently seen King perform in a Miami nightclub, has convinced him to sign with Atlantic, yielding Bert DeCoteaux-produced *Supernatural Thing* which hits US #5, also topping the US R&B survey for a week.

June Its parent album, ***Supernatural***, makes US #39.

1977

July Having released his second Atlantic set, ***I Had A Love*** the previous year, King has joined and is co-credited with the Average White Band for ***Benny And Us***, which makes US #33.

1978

Between now and 1986, King will experience more lean years as his popularity dwindles. After an unsuccessful union with Don Covay, Joe Tex, Wilson Pickett and Solomon Burke as the Soul Clan, King will rejoin the Drifters for European tours in the early '80s. Following this year's ***Let Me Live In Your Life***, he will release ***Music Trance*** in 1980 and ***Street Tough***, for Atlantic, in May 1981.

1986

Dec [20] Featured as the title of a film based on a Stephen King novella, King's *Stand By Me* hits US #9 after a 27-year gap. Its undated sound and production values testify to Leiber and Stoller's studio innovation and King's vocal prowess. (He will donate the sheet music of *Stand By Me* to the Hard Rock Café.)

1987

Jan [21] King inducts Clyde McPhatter into the Rock and Roll Hall of Fame at the second annual dinner, at New York's Waldorf Astoria Hotel.

Feb [21] Before "Stand By Me" premieres in the UK, an advertising agency uses part of the song in a TV commercial promoting Levi 501 jeans. Its nightly exposure takes *Stand By Me* to UK #1, while Percy Sledge's *When A Man Loves A Woman*, featured in the same ad series, hits UK #2.

Mar [21] ***Stand By Me (The Ultimate Collection)***, featuring both King solos and Drifters tracks, including *Spanish Harlem*, makes UK #14.

June [19-21] King performs at the three-day "Glastonbury Festival", Worthy Farm, Pilton, Somerset.

July On the strength of his revived fortunes, EMI Manhattan Records has signed King and an updated version of *Save The Last Dance For Me*, peaks at UK #69.

[5-6] King takes part in the fifth annual "Prince's Trust Rock Gala" at the Wembley Arena, Wembley, Middx., on a bill with Elton John, George Harrison, Ringo Starr and Alison Moyet.

1988

Feb King joins stars including Billy Joel, Joe Walsh, Duane Eddy, Warren Zevon, Robert Cray, Roberta Flack, Cyndi Lauper, Carole King and Ashford & Simpson for NBC-TV's "David Letterman's Sixth Anniversary Special", at New York's Radio City Music Hall.

Apr EMI Manhattan releases the all-new Ben E. King album, ***Save The Last Dance For Me***, recorded with producers Mick Jones, John Paul Jones, Preston Glass and Lamont Dozier, and featuring Mark Knopfler on guitar, Tom Bailey and Ruby Turner.

1989

Aug King guest vocals with Wilson Pickett, Bobby Womack, Don Covay, Darlene Love, Mavis Staples and Ellie Greenwich on *What Is Soul?* from Paul Shaffer's newly released ***Coast To Coast*** album, as he records material for Atlantic with producer Bert D'Coteaux.

1990

Jan [17] King inducts songwriters Gerry Goffin and Carole King into the Rock and Roll Hall of Fame at the fifth annual dinner, held at New York's Waldorf Astoria Hotel. At the perfunctory after-dinner jam, he joins with them on a rendition of *Will You Love Me Tomorrow*.

Sept *Stand By Me* is named one of the BMI's Most Performed Songs Of 1940-1990, as it surpasses the three-millionth performance plateau.

1993

Apr [20] Having combined with Bo Diddley and Doug Lazy to remake the Monotones' *Book Of Love* on Atlantic, featured in the 1991 movie "The Book Of Love" and signed to Ichiban Records the same year, Rhino Records now releases ***Anthology,*** a two CD/cassette retrospective set in the US.

June [15] King sings *Save The Last Dance For Me* at the Apollo Theatre Hall of Fame concert, set to air on NBC-TV on August 4th.

1994

Mar [2] King is presented with the Pioneer Award at the fifth annual Rhythm and Blues Foundation ceremonies at New York's Roseland Ballroom, and then appears with Jerry Butler and Bonnie Raitt on CBS-TV's "Late Show With David Letterman".

[23] He participates in "Rhythm Country And Blues - The Concert", benefitting the Country Music Foundation and the Rhythm and Blues Foundation, at the Universal Amphitheatre, Universal City, CA. His duet with Manhattan Transfer on *Save The Last Dance For Me* will be included on their January 1995 released ***Tonin'*** album.

see also: **THE DRIFTERS**

CAROLE KING

1958

While a student at Queen's College, New York, NY, King (b. Carole Klein, Feb. 9, 1942, Brooklyn, New York), a Brooklyn neighbor and sometime girlfriend of Neil Sedaka, having received singing and piano lessons from her mother from the age of six, and having formed a high-school vocal quartet, the Co-Sines, meets Paul Simon, and begins writing songs professionally. She also starts a songwriting and personal relationship with lyricist and future husband Gerry Goffin, who is working in a local pharmacy, and the two write together for Don Kirshner and Al Nevin's Aldon Music, based in New York's Brill Building. In March 1959, her maiden single, *Baby Sittin'*, will be released on ABC/Paramount, followed by *Short-Mort* on RCA-Victor and *Oh! Neil*, her Alpine Records-released riposte to Neil Sedaka's affectionate pop ode to King, *Oh! Carol*.

1961

Jan [30] The Goffin and King-penned *Will You Love Me Tomorrow*, sung by the Shirelles, tops the US chart. (During the next six years, Goffin and King will write dozens of US Hot 100 hits.)

Sept [18] Goffin/King-written *Take Good Care Of My Baby*, by Bobby Vee, hits US #1 shortly before the US #9 success of their *Up On The Roof*, by the Drifters.

1962

Aug Kirshner hears a demo of *It Might As Well Rain Until September*, which King has made for Bobby Vee, and persuades her to release her own version. After an initial pressing on Companion Records, Aldon Music establishes its own Dimension label specifically to release Goffin/King compositions and issues the track. Meanwhile, Goffin and King's pop confection, *The Locomotion*, tops the US chart, sung by their babysitter, Little Eva.

Oct King-sung *It Might As Well Rain Until September* reaches US #22 and hits UK #3.

1967

Jan [12] With King still accumulating songwriting hits with Goffin, their *Go Away Little Girl* hits US #1 for Steve Lawrence. (Goffin and King separate and will later divorce. King forms Tomorrow Records with journalist Al Aronowitz and releases her own version of *Some Of Your Lovin'*, previously a hit for Dusty Springfield, and an album by the Myddle Class, which includes bass player Charles Larkey, who will become King's second husband.)

1968

Relocated to Los Angeles, CA, King forms the City with Larkey and guitarist Danny "Kootch" Kortchmar. Their album, ***Now That Everything's Been Said***, is released on Lou Adler's Ode label. Due to King's performance nerves, the band does not tour and will soon break up.

1970

Mar Featured as a pianist on James Taylor's US chart debut album, ***Sweet Baby James***, King records her debut album, ***Writer: Carole King***, at Crystal Sound Studio in Los Angeles, produced by Adler.

Oct With the A&M Recording Studio sessions once again helmed by Adler, King records ***Tapestry*** with Larkey, Kortchmar and drummer Russ Kunkel, who will become her regular band, with James Taylor playing guitar and singing backing vocals.

1971

June [19] The same day the double A-sided *It's Too Late/I Feel The Earth* hits US #1 at the beginning of a five-week run, its parent album, the landmark set ***Tapestry*** also tops the US chart. King's commercial performance breakthrough, the self-penned set, produced by Adler, will stay in pole position for 15 weeks during a 302-week chart tenure, eventually selling over 15 million copies worldwide. The re-promoted ***Writer : Carole King*** reaches US #84.

July [24] ***Tapestry*** enters the UK chart, on its way to #4 (Sept [4]) during a 90-week chart stay, as it goes gold in the US. King becomes the first pop artist to perform at New York's traditionally-classical Philharmonic Hall venue at the Lincoln Center.

[31] James Taylor's version of King's *You've Got A Friend* tops the US chart.

Aug *So Far Away/Smackwater Jack* makes US #14.

Sept *It's Too Late*, co-written with Toni Stern, hits UK #6.

1972

Jan [1] *Sweet Seasons* hits US #9, as the Adler-helmed ***Music***, with lyrics by Stern, tops the US chart and reaches UK #18. Overcoming her fear of playing live, King tours both countries.

Mar [9] She performs with James Taylor and Barbra Streisand at a benefit for Presidential candidate George McGovern at the Great Western Forum, Inglewood, CA.

[14] King collects the Record Of The Year for *It's Too Late*, Album Of The Year and Best Pop Vocal Performance, Female for ***Tapestry*** and Song Of The Year for *You've Got A Friend* trophies at the 14th annual Grammy Awards.

Nov *Been To Canaan* reaches US #24. *It Might As Well Rain Until September* is reissued and makes UK #43.

Dec ***Rhymes And Reasons***, featuring David Campbell, Kortchmar, Larkey, Harvey Mason and Ernie Watts, among others, hits US #2 and climbs to UK #40.

1973

May [25] Following a 12-show, three-week tour in April, King performs a free concert in New York's Central Park to an audience of 100,000. (Soundman Chip Monck ensures that everyone can hear the performance.)

July *Believe In Humanity/You Light Up My Life*, from a forthcoming album, reaches US #28, as King performs at the seventh annual "Montreux Jazz Festival", Montreux, Switzerland.

Aug The Adler-helmed, entirely self-written ***Fantasy*** hits US #6.

Oct The extracted *Corazon* peaks at US #37.

1974

Feb [14] King joins Bob Dylan on the last gig of his 39-date US tour in Los Angeles.

Aug *Jazzman*, with Tom Scott guesting on sax, hits US #2.

Nov [9] ***Wrap Around Joy***, with lyrics by David Palmer and string arrangements by David Campbell, tops the US chart.

1975

Jan The extracted *Nightingale*, featuring backing vocals by King's daughters Louise and Sherry Goffin, hits US #9.

Apr King-written and-performed TV soundtrack album ***Really Rosie***, reaches US #20.

1976

Feb *Only Love Is Real* makes US #28.

Mar King has teamed with ex-husband Goffin to work on songs for ***Thoroughbred***, which has vocal support from David Crosby, Graham Nash, James Taylor and J.D. Souther and hits US #3.

1977

Apr King, newly-signed to Capitol Records, where she forms her own Avatar label, starts work on ***Simple Things***, co-produced with Norm Kinney, in Los Angeles. King uses recently Capitol-signed band Navarro, which includes Rick Evers (who becomes her third husband), to back her on the album.

July *Hard Rock Café* makes US #30.

Sept ***Simple Things*** reaches US #17.

1978

Jan Again using Navarro, King records ***Welcome Home*** at the Sound Labs, Hollywood.

Mar Evers dies from an apparent drug overdose.

Apr ***Her Greatest Hits*** collection, released by Ode/Epic, reaches US #47.

June ***Welcome Home***, issued on the Avatar label, reaches US #104.

1979

Mar King records ***Touch The Sky*** at Pecan Street Studios, Austin, TX, with a group of musicians whom she heard on Jerry Jeff Walker's ***Jerry Jeff***.

July ***Touch The Sky*** peaks at US #104.

1980

Jan King records ten of her most famous early songs for ***Pearls - Songs Of Goffin And King***, using the studios at Pecan Street. Her ex-husband Larkey plays bass, and recent Warner Bros. signing Christopher Cross plays rhythm guitar on *The Locomotion*, *Chains* and *Hi De Ho*.

July ***Pearls - Songs Of Goffin And King*** makes US #44.

1982

Apr Now signed to Atlantic Records, King releases ***One To One***, which peaks at US #119. Despite her brief promotional visit, it fails to chart in Britain.

Nov [25] A reclusive live performer, King makes her second appearance of the year on NBC-TV's "Late Night With David Letterman".

1983

Apr ***Speeding Time*** is released, reuniting King with producer Adler, musicians Kortchmar and Kunkel, and lyricist Goffin. It includes, for the first time, her own version of the Everly Brothers 1961 hit, *Crying In The Rain*, which she wrote with Howard Greenfield, and features a sax solo from Plas Johnson. "The Care Bears" movie, with soundtrack songs by King and John Sebastian, will premiere in March 1985.

1987

Mar [7] Goffin and King are inducted into the 18th annual Songwriters Hall of Fame at the awards ceremony at New York's Plaza Hotel.

Apr [23] King sues Lou Adler for breach of contract. She claims that over $400,000 in royalties is owed to her, and requests the return of rights to all of her old recordings.

1988

Feb In a rare live appearance, King joins an all-star group of musicians, including Billy Joel, Joe Walsh, Duane Eddy, Warren Zevon, Robert Cray, Roberta Flack, Cyndi Lauper, Ben E. King and Ashford & Simpson, to make up the house band for "David Letterman's Sixth Anniversary Special" at New York's Radio City Music Hall.

July A celebration of King's music, "Tapestry", opens a two-month run at the Cincinnati Playhouse, OH.

Dec [3] Goffin and King receive the National Academy of Songwriters Lifetime Achievment award.

1989

May King's first album in six years, ***City Streets***, released on Capitol Records, makes US #111. Produced by King with Rudy Guess, guest performers include Eric Clapton, Michael Brecker, Branford Marsalis and Sherry Goffin.

1990

Jan [17] Goffin and King are inducted into the Rock and Roll Hall of Fame at the fifth annual dinner, at New York's Waldorf Astoria Hotel.

1991

Jan [28] She guests stars in CBS-TV's "The Trials Of Rosie O'Neill".

Mar [21] King is featured on ABC-TV's "Afterschool Special - It's Only Rock'n'Roll".

June [22] Kiddie compilation, ***For Our Children***, to which King has contributed *Child Of Mine*, reaches US #31.

1992

Apr King takes part in the 23rd annual "New Orleans Jazz & Heritage Festival", where she is joined on stage by Slash from Guns N' Roses, and Aaron Neville.
June She contributes *If I Didn't Have You To Wake Up To* to ***Til Their Eyes Shine (The Lullaby Album)***, benefitting the "Voices Victims" project of the Institute For Intercultural Understanding.
July "A League Of Their Own" movie, with King's *Now And Forever* as its title theme, premieres in the US.
King goes to Capitol Hill in Washington to help prevent the passing of the Baucus-Burns congressional bill, which would allow timber companies to raise forests at will.

1993

Jan [20] King participates in the "Arkansas Ball" on the day of President Clinton's inauguration in Washington, DC.
Feb [18] "Tapestry", an off-Broadway revue of King's songs, opens in New York.
Apr [9] King guests on "Late Night With David Letterman", promoting her first album in four years, ***Color Of Your Dreams***, which, co-produced with Rudy Guess, is released on the King's X label and includes two songs co-penned with Goffin.
June [2] She embarks on short US tour at the Civic Opera House, Chicago, IL, set to end on July 18th at the Universal Amphitheatre, Universal City, CA.

1994

Apr [2] Performance album ***In Concert***, released on the Priority label, debuts at its US #160 peak.
June King takes over from Petula Clark in "Blood Brothers" on Broadway, staying with the show until January.

1995

Apr [11] King breaks her arm when Bob Dylan hugs her and she falls into the photographers' pit at his Point Depot, Dublin gig during an encore of *Real Real Gone* with Van Morrison and Elvis Costello.
July [17] The RIAA finally certifies ***Tapestry*** at ten million copies sold, becoming the second highest-selling album by a female artist, behind Whitney's Houston debut.
Nov [11] *Up On The Roof* becomes Goffin and King's second UK chart-topper (their first was Herman's Hermits' *I'm Into Something Good* in 1964) as acting duo Robson & Jerome hit the top with their treatment.
[25] ***Tapestry Revisited : A Tribute To Carole King***, featuring various artists' interpretations of the songs from ***Tapestry***, including those by Rod Stewart, Celine Dion, Aretha Franklin, Amy Grant, the Bee Gees, Richard Marx, Eternal and Faith Hill, among others, makes US #88.

1996

Jan [31] King's co-penned standard *Will You Still Love Me Tomorrow* ends a three-month run as the first legally licensed commercial music jingle in Russia, used for McVitie's Hob Nobs cookies.

KING CRIMSON

Robert Fripp (guitar); **Greg Lake** (bass, vocals); **Ian McDonald** (saxophone); **Mike Giles** (drums); **Pete Sinfield** (lyricist)

1969

Jan [13] After the demise of Giles, Giles & Fripp, who released *Kick The Donkey* under the name Brain, in 1966, on Parlophone Records (UK), and following the release of the single *One In A Million* last June, with former Fairport Convention vocalist Judy Dyble and Ian McDonald augmenting the trio to a quintet, the subsequent Wayne Bickerton-produced album for Deram - ***The Cheerful Insanity Of Giles, Giles And Fripp*** - in September, with a sole radio appearance backing Al Stewart on BBC's "My Kind Of Folk", and subsequent TV dates on ITV's "Eamonn Andrews Show" and BBC2-TV's "Colour Me Pop", King Crimson, now comprising Mike Giles (b. 1942, Bournemouth, Dorset), Fripp (b. Apr. 11, 1945, Wimborne, Dorset), McDonald (b. June 25, 1946, London) and Fripp's schoolfriend Greg Lake (b. Nov. 10, 1948, Bournemouth), newly recruited from the Gods, conducts its first rehearsal in the basement of the Fulham Palace Café in Fulham Palace Road, London. (Peter Giles does not join the new line-up, preferring to find gainful employment as a computer operator and solicitor's clerk.) Peter Sinfield, who has been in Infinity with McDonald and will be the group's main lyricist and the originator of its name, a synonym for "Beelzebub", initially becomes the band's road manager. The group is soon signed to E.G., David Enthoven and John Gaydon's fledgling management company.
Apr [9] After a week's residency at the Change in Newcastle, Tyne & Wear (still as Giles, Giles & Fripp), the group makes its London debut at the Speakeasy, followed by a 12-week residency at the Marquee club.
May [11] The band's performance of *In The Court Of The Crimson King*, *21st Century Schizoid Man* and *I Talk To The Wind* airs on BBC Radio 1's "Top Gear".
July [5] The band supports the Rolling Stones at London's Hyde Park concert, before an estimated 650,000 crowd.
[7] After an initial false start at Morgan Studios the previous month, the group begins recording with producer Tony Clark at Wessex Studios. After less than a week, this arrangement will prove to be unproductive, and the group begins self-producing.
Oct [29] King Crimson begins a 20-date US tour at Goddard College, Plainfield, VT, set to end on December 16th at the Fillmore West, San Francisco, CA, to support the album's US release (on Atlantic).
Nov [8] Their self-produced debut album, ***In The Court Of The Crimson King***, released on Island Records, hits UK #5.
Dec The group returns to Britain with the news that McDonald and Giles have decided to quit. (They will record ***McDonald And Giles*** in 1970, and McDonald will help form Foreigner in 1978.)

1970

Feb [14] *In The Court Of The Crimson King* peaks at US #80, as its parent album, the progressive rock-aimed ***In The Court Of The Crimson King*** reaches US #28.
Mar [25] The group appears on BBC1-TV's "Top Of The Pops" performing *Cat Food*, with help from the Giles brothers and jazzman Keith Tippett.
[26] Following Lake's decision to quit to form Emerson, Lake & Palmer, Fripp turns down both the offer of replacing Peter Banks in Yes and joining Aynsley Dunbar's new band, Blue Whale.
May [30] ***In The Wake Of Poseidon*** debuts at its UK #4 peak.
Aug King Crimson begins rehearsals at the Fulham Palace Café with Fripp, Sinfield, vocalist/bassist Gordon Haskell (ex-Fleur De Lys, Cupid's Inspiration and the Flowerpot Men) and saxophonist Mel Collins (ex-Circus), who have both played on the previous album, and drummer Andy McCullough. (Haskell and Fripp were in the Ravens and the League Of Gentlemen during the mid-'60s.)
Oct ***In The Wake Of Poseidon*** reaches US #31.
[26] Haskell quits two days after the band's new album has been completed. McCullough will leave soon after.
Dec Ian Wallace, formerly with the World, joins on drums, and Boz Burrell (b. Aug. 1, 1946, Lincoln, Lincs.), formerly of Boz People, beats out fellow auditioner Bryan Ferry, among others, to be recruited as a singer.

1971

Jan [16] ***Lizard***, with Tippett guesting again and Jon Anderson of Yes singing on one track, reaches UK #30.
Feb [13] Burrell, who has never played the instrument, becomes the group's bass player, after new recruit Rick Kemp threw in the towel after two rehearsals.
Apr ***Lizard*** peaks at US #113.
[12-15] The group plays a four-date engagement at the Zoom Club, Frankfurt, West Germany.
May [11] They embark on a 15-date tour at the Guildhall, Plymouth, Devon, set to close on June 2nd at the Winter Gardens, Bournemouth, Dorset.
Sept [4] They perform a free concert in London's Hyde Park.
Oct [8] The group begins an 18-date UK tour at Lancaster University, Lancaster, Lancs., set to end on the 30th at the Free Trade Hall, Manchester, Gtr. Manchester.
Nov [10] An 18-gig trek of Canada and the American North East bows at the Centennial Hall, London, ON, Canada, set to close on December 11th at the Spectrum, Philadelphia, PA.
Dec After a second North American tour Fripp tells Sinfield, "I can't work with you", and asks him to leave. (Sinfield will produce the first Roxy Music album, write for Emerson Lake & Palmer and go on to a highly successful songwriting career, not least with co-writer Andy Hill.)

1972

Jan [8] ***Islands*** reaches UK #30, as the group begins three weeks of rehearsals for an upcoming US tour. The band will break up for a couple of days, following an argument during rehearsals in Bournemouth.
Feb ***Islands*** makes US #76.
[11] A 32-date US tour opens at the Armoury, Wilmington, DE, set to end on April 1st at the Municipal Auditorium, Birmingham, AL.
Apr Back in the UK, Fripp and the other three members split. They will join Alexis Korner and Peter Thorup in Alexis in May. Burrell will go on to greater success as a co-founder of Bad Company.
June Live album, ***Earthbound,*** recorded during the band's recent US tour, is released. In the US, Atlantic refuses to release it, citing poor sound quality.
July Fripp puts together a new band with ex-Yes member Bill Bruford (b. May 17, 1948, London) (drums), ex-Family John Wetton (b. July 12, 1949, Derby, Derbys.) (bass, vocals), ex-Boris Jamie Muir (percussion) and ex-Round David Cross (b. Plymouth, Devon) (flute, violin).
Sept [4] The new line-up begins rehearsals.
Oct [13-15] They make their live debut at the Zoom Club in Frankfurt.
Nov [10] A 27-date UK tour starts at the Technical College, Hull, Humberside, which will close on December 15th at the Guildhall, Portsmouth, Hants.

1973

Feb [10] Muir injures himself during a show at London's Marquee club, and fails to play the following night. He never plays with the band again and leaves, supposedly to enter a Tibetan monastery. The group remains a quartet.
Mar [18] The band performs at London's Rainbow Theatre, during a nine-date tour of major UK cities.
Apr [9] A further nine-date European tour, which opened at the Niedersachsen Halle, Hanover, West Germany, comes to end at the Olympia, Paris, France.
[14] ***Larks' Tongues In Aspic***, with lyrics written by Richard Palmer-James, reaches UK #20.
[18] The group begins its fourth North American tour at the Packard Music Hall, Warren, OH. The trek, which will include a performance in New York's Central Park, will close at Kent State University, Canton, OH, on July 2nd.
June ***Larks' Tongues In Aspic*** makes US #61.
Sept [19] The group's fifth North American excursion begins at the Capitol Theatre, Quebec, PQ, Canada, winding up at the Civic Auditorium, Santa Monica, CA, on October 15th.
Oct [29] Six-date UK tour ends at the Colston Hall, Bristol, Somerset. This is the last King Crimson performance on home turf until 1981.
Nov [2] An 18-date European concert series begins at the Audimax, Hamburg, West Germany, set to close on the 29th at the Cine Alcala, Madrid, Spain. (Fripp releases ***No Pussyfootin'***, his first collaboration with ex-Roxy Music keyboardist Brian Eno.)

1974

Jan The group records new material at AIR Studios, London.
Mar [19] They begin an 11-date European tour at the Palazsport Delo Sports, Udine, Italy.
Apr [11] A 17-date North American visit opens at the Paintersmill, Owings Mill, MD, set to end on May 5th at the Ford Auditorium, Detroit, MI.
[13] ***Starless And Bible Black*** bows at its UK #28 peak, during a two-week chart stay.
July [1] The current line-up plays live for the last time, in New York's Central Park, at the end of a a 21-date North American tour which opened on June 4th at the Municipal Auditorium, San Antonio, TX.
[8] Now a trio, with Cross having left at the end of the North American tour, King Crimson begins fresh recording work.
Sept [25] After completing album sessions with help from ex-members Collins, Cross and McDonald, Fripp disbands King Crimson. (Wetton moves to Uriah Heep, later forming UK with Bruford and eventually joining Asia. Bruford gigs with Pavlov's Dog, following his departure.)
Oct [26] ***Red*** charts for a week at UK #45.

1975

June Live album, ***USA***, recorded on a 1974 US tour, peaks at US #125.
Nov Fripp and Eno's second collaboration, ***Evening Star***, is released.

1976

Feb Fripp compiles a double-album retrospective of the band's career, ***A Young Person's Guide To King Crimson***, issued with a companion booklet and including two previously unreleased tracks.
May [12] Fripp solo, ***Exposure***, charts at UK #71 (on E.G.) and US #79 (on Polydor).

1980

May Fripp's ***God Save The Queen/Heavy Manners*** makes US #110, an entirely instrumental set featuring an electronic style dubbed "Frippertronics".
Nov Fripp forms one-off band the League of Gentlemen, with Barry Andrews (keyboards), Sarah Lee (bass) and Johnny Toobad (drums). *Heptaparaparshinokh* is released, notable for its B-side solo by Fripp, *Marriagemuzic*, which is intended to play at 33rpm and last 11 minutes 45 seconds.

1981

Apr The League Of Gentlemen's all instrumental album, ***The League Of Gentlemen***, makes US #90.
[2] Discipline, Fripp's new venture, which sees him reunite with Bruford, joined by top New York sessioneer Tony Levin (who has played on John Lennon's ***Double Fantasy*** and Peter Gabriel's solo albums) on bass and Adrian Belew (who has worked with Frank Zappa and Talking Heads) on vocals and guitar, begins rehearsals in London and Holdenhurst Church Hall near Guildford, Surrey.
[30] Discipline plays its first gig at Moles, a vegetarian restaurant and wine bar in Bath, Avon, at the start of a 15-date European tour, set to end on May 16th at the University of Brussels, Brussels, Belgium, combining the traditional Crimson repertoire with new material.
Oct [5] With Discipline having made an easy transition back into King Crimson, the band begins a 45-date world trek of Europe, North America and Japan in the familiar confines of Moles in Bath. The tour will climax on December 17th at the Kenmin Hall, Niigata, Japan.
[10] By the time its first album is released, Discipline's name has formally changed to King Crimson and the album title becomes ***Discipline***, making UK #41.
Nov *Matte Kudasai* is released as a UK single, as ***Discipline*** makes US #45.

1982

Feb [20] The group embarks on an 11-date US tour at the Columbus Agora, Columbus, OH, set to end on March 6th in the Alexander Hall at Princeton University, Princeton, NJ.
Mar [14] Fripp returns home as King Crimson performs at the Wessex Hall, Bournemouth.
July [3] ***Beat***, which includes song lyrics by Belew based on US beat poet Jack Kerouac's work, reaches UK #39 and US #52.
[26] A North American and European sojourn begins at Toad's Place, New Haven, CT, set to end on September 12th at London's Hammersmith Palais. Nine dates of the European leg are supporting Roxy Music.
Dec Fripp's instrumental, ***I Advance Masked,*** with Andy Summers of the Police, makes US #60.

1984

Mar *Sleepless*, extracted from the forthcoming album, is released in a remixed, seven-minute-plus 12" dance version.
Apr The final King Crimson album, ***Three Of A Perfect Pair***, reaches UK #30 and US #58.
[28] The group embarks on what will be its last tour of the decade at the Kani Hoken Hall, Tokyo, Japan. The 35-date trek of Japan and North America will end at Le Spectrum, Montreal, PQ, Canada, on July 10-11th. (The band members will go their separate ways at the tour's conclusion: Fripp will continue a production relationship with the Roches, three sisters recording for Warner Bros. Belew will record two solo albums for Island and form the Bears on IRS. Bruford will record solo, with Patrick Moraz of the Moody Blues and with the band Earthworks, while Levin will return to session work.)
Nov A second collaboration between Fripp and Summers, ***Bewitched***, peaks at US #155. (Fripp will go on to make ***God Save The King*** with the League of Gentlemen in 1985, an eponymous album called ***The League Of Crafty Guitarists*** in 1986 (he has opened Guitar Craft, a guitar school, in '85), and ***The Lady Or The Tiger*** in 1987, in collaboration with Toyah.)

1986

May [16] Fripp marries one-time punk singer Toyah on his 40th birthday. They will form Fripp, Fripp with Trey Gunn (guitar) and Paul Beavis (drums), before renaming themselves Sunday All Over The World, releasing ***Kneeling At The Shrine*** in June 1991. E.G. will release ***Box Set***, a CD collection comprising the more popular albums from the King Crimson archive in December 1989.

1991

Apr [8] Fripp informs E.G. that he wishes to end his relationship with the company, after more than 20 years, having been told the previous year that "we don't make money from you". Nevertheless, E.G. releases a further four-CD/cassette boxed-set, ***The Essential King Crimson - Frame By Frame***.

1993

King Crimson re-forms again, with Fripp, Levin, Belew, Jerry Marotta, Trey Gunn and Stick (a guitar/bass machine), scheduled to release an EP in August, followed by album and tour in 1994. (***The First Day***, a collaborative effort between Fripp and David Sylvian debuts at its UK #21 peak on July [17], and the extracted *Jean The Birdman* makes UK #68 on Aug [28].)

1994

Sept [28] King Crimson begins a 16-date stint in Buenos Aires, Argentina, before heading to Real World Studios in Bath to record a new album.

1995

Jan While Discipline Records releases two Fripp albums, ***The Bridge Between***, by the Robert Fripp String Quintet, and ***Soundscapes Live In Argentina***, the label also releases the group's *Vroom*, a teaser EP for Crimson's forthcoming album.
Apr [15] ***Thrak*** debuts at its UK #58 peak.
May [13] ***Thrak*** bows at its US #83 high, during a two-week chart stay, as the band performs at the Zenith in Paris, France, during its 10-date European tour, set to end at London's Royal Albert Hall on the 18th.
June [3-4] King Crimson performs two sellout shows at New York's Town Hall, during a month-long US tour.
Oct [20] As the double CD bootleg ***B'Boom*** is released, the band plays a sellout show at the Zellerbach Hall, University of California-Berkeley, Berkeley, CA.
see also: **ASIA, BAD COMPANY, EMERSON LAKE & PALMER, FAMILY, FOREIGNER, YES**

THE KINGSMEN

Lynn Easton (saxophone, vocals); **Jack Ely** (guitar, vocals); **Mike Mitchell** (lead guitar); **Bob Nordby** (bass); **Don Gallucci** (organ); **Gary Abbott** (drums)

1958

Sept Easton and Ely have met as teenagers when playing in a group while attending the David Douglas School in Portland, OR. Ely joins Easton's band, the Journal Juniors, when their guitarist fails to show for a gig. The two eventually form a duo to play locally, soon adding Mitchell on guitar and Nordby on bass. Another local band breaks up and Easton's parents arrange for the acquisition of their name, the Kingsmen. Having built a live reputation playing R&B songs and rock instrumentals, and joined by Don Gallucci on keyboards from rival group Gentleman Jim & the Horsemen in 1962, they become firmly established on the US Northwest touring scene, which also includes Paul Revere & the Raiders. A revival of Richard Berry's 1956 R&B song, *Louie Louie*, based on Ricky Rivera & the Rhythm Rockers' *El Loco Cha Cha Cha,* learned from a popular local version by Seattle, WA group, the Wailers, is added to their repertoire and becomes their most in-demand live item, sometimes leading to outrageous 45-minute stage versions.

1963

May *Louie Louie* is recorded for $50 ($10 from Ely and $40 from Easton's mother, Betty) in the small Northwestern Recording Studio in Portland at the suggestion of Ken Chase, programme director of KISN, who has booked the band into his club, the Chase, with Ely on lead vocals. The following day, Paul Revere & the Raiders reportedly record their version in the same studio. The Kingsmen's version is placed with Jerry Dennon's newly-formed local Jerden label, while Revere's is picked up, also from Jerden, by major label CBS/Columbia Records, along with the group's recording contract. Both become good sellers in the Northwest, with the better-distributed Revere's gaining the airplay edge.
Aug [16] Friction occurs in the band when Easton announces that he owns the name, because his parents had arranged the paperwork that way, and wants to assume frontman vocal duties, moving Ely to drums. Instead, Ely and Nordby leave, to be replaced by Gary Abbott (drums) and Norm Sundholm (bass). At the same time the Kingsmen's version of *Louie Louie* becomes a big hit in Boston, MA, after a local DJ declares it the worst record he's ever heard, prompting Wand Records to acquire it from Jerden for national distribution.
Dec [14] *Louie Louie* hits US #2 for the first of six non-consecutive weeks, eventually selling over one million copies. The group appears on TV with Easton miming to Ely's vocals, before embarking on a US tour, minus Gallucci, whose parents say he cannot tour while still a sophomore at high school. He is replaced by Barry Curtis on organ, as Abbott soon quits to join the National Guard. A further personnel change will occur when Nordby quits to pursue a career in country and western, replaced by Mike Peterson.

1964

Feb [1] Widespread controversy over whether Ely's indistinct vocal on *Louie Louie* is masking off-colour lyrics comes to a head when Matthew Welsh, Governor of Indiana, delares the song "pornographic" and asks the State's radio stations to ban it. Berry and

Ely are called in to testify and confirm what they wrote and sung respectively. An FCC investigation concludes "the record to be unintelligible at any speed we played it".
[15] *Louie Louie* reaches UK #26, and is their sole UK hit. It is a huge underground success with London's mod dancers, whose reaction to it in clubs spurs most British sales, since BBC Radio shuns the record.
Mar ***Louie Louie : The Kingsmen In Person***, recorded (apart from the hit single) live at the Chase, reaches US #20. It will stay on chart for 131 weeks. Ely is contacted by a promoter in Oregon who asks if he is the singer on *Louie Louie*, subsequently signing a deal and going out on the road as Jack Ely & the Kingsmen, which will lead the other Kingsmen to offer him $150,000 to desist. (He will release *Love That Louie* on RCA, followed by *Louie Louie '66*, *Louie Go Home* and *Ride Ride Baby*, the latter two with Neil Diamond on backing vocals, on Bang Records.)
Apr [12] The Kingsmen play their first major show on a Murray The K package at the Brooklyn Fox Theater, New York, with Dionne Warwick, Bobby Goldsboro, Ben E. King and others. This will be followed by a 40-day summer tour with the Beach Boys, opening in Hawaii.
May Their revival of Barrett Strong's *Money* reaches US #16.
July [3-4] The group appears at "A Million Dollar Party", presented by KPOI, at the International Center Arena, Honolulu, HI, an event headlined by the Beach Boys.
Aug *Little Latin Lupe Lu*, their treatment of the Righteous Brothers' US hit of 14 months previously, makes US #46.
Oct *Death Of An Angel*, their cover of Donald Wood's original, makes US #42.
Nov ***The Kingsmen - Vol. 2*** reaches US #15, repeating the first album's formula of familiar cover versions.

1965

Mar *The Jolly Green Giant*, based on a canned produce TV commercial, hits US #4.
Apr ***The Kingsmen - Vol. 3*** reaches US #22.
May *The Climb*, written about a dance, peaks at US #65.
Sept *Annie Fannie*, celebrating a **Playboy**-magazine cartoon character, makes US #47.
Nov [15] The group guests on NBC-TV's "Hullabaloo", singing *Money*.
Dec Live album, ***The Kingsmen On Campus***, reaches US #68.

1966

Apr *Killer Joe*, reviving a 1963 Rocky Fellers US hit, makes US #77.
May A continuing seller since 1963 because it has been US radio's most-played "oldie", *Louie Louie* briefly re-enters the US chart at #97.
Sept ***15 Great Hits*** reaches US #87, their final chart entry.

1967

Easton leaves the Kingsmen, which has been through numerous other personnel changes. The band splits permanently six months later. (After a spell in the army, Ely will plays bass with the Portland Zoo Electric Band in 1968, followed by Phleobus Union and Briar Fox in the '70s.)

1989

July [14] Following Rhino Records (US) 1985 CD release of ***The Best Of The Kingsmen***, and after a new lineup of the Kingsmen, comprising Mitchell, Peterson, Curtis and bassist Marc Willett, recut *Louie Louie* for a California Cooler TV commercial in 1987, 432 axemen break the world record for most guitarists playing in unison for the longest period of time, at the "Peach Festival", Gaffney, SC, when they play *Louie Louie* for 30 minutes. Ely will participate in the *Louie Louie* 30th-anniversary tour at the 35th annual Auto Show, Hara Arena, Dayton, OH in January 1992.

1995

June [20] Los Angeles Federal Judge William D. Keller now awards the group's more than 100 recordings previously kept by Scepter-Wand, which had breached its contract by not giving royalties to the band. (Made public for the first time in January 1993 by the Freedom of Information Act, it becomes clear that the FBI undertook a substantial investigation in 1964 to figure out the lyrics to *Louie Louie*. Having played the record backwards, forwards, using computers, cryptographers and filters, they issued a 120-page report which concluded: nothing.)

THE KINKS

Ray Davies (vocals, guitar); **Dave Davies** (vocals, guitar); **Pete Quaife** (bass); **Mick Avory** (drums)

1962

Sept Ray Davies (b. June 21, 1944, Muswell Hill, London), who was given a guitar on his 13th birthday and was weaned on the music of Muddy Waters and Chuck Berry, persuaded his parents to buy one for his younger brother Dave (b. Feb. 3, 1947, Muswell Hill), in 1958. The brothers attended the William Grimshaw Secondary School, where Ray and classmates Quaife (b. Dec. 31, 1943, Tavistock, Devon) and drummer John Start formed a band, playing locally as the Ray Davies Quartet. Ray left school at 16 to work in an architect's office, and now begins studying at Hornsey Art College, Hornsey, London. Dave, meanwhile, has been expelled from school during the summer, having been caught inflagrante delicto with a girl. Ray meets Alexis Korner when the bluesman plays at the Hornsey Art College in December and, with his help, he joins the blues combo Hamilton King/Dave Hunt Band, gigging at the Piccadilly club in January 1963. Davies will leave Hornsey to attend the Croydon College of Art, studying theater design, while also continuing to play with Dave in the Ray Davies Quartet.

1963

Feb [16] The Quartet plays at the "St. Valentine's Carnival Dance" at Hornsey Town Hall and will soon name-change to the Ravens, after Dave sees the Vincent Price film "The Raven". Becoming part of London's growing R&B scene (led by the Rolling Stones), Ray splits his time between gigging with the Dave Hunt Band and the Ravens.
Sept The Ravens attract the interest of businessmen Robert Wace and Grenville Collins, who arrange a meeting with pop impresario Larry Page and become the group's managers, booking them for society gatherings and country parties. In exchange Wace, a frustrated singer, gets to sing a few numbers with the band at the gigs.
Nov Wace, who will rename the group the Kinks, meets Page, who is running music publisher Edward Kassner's Denmark Productions. He places Dave's *One Fine Day*, one of five tracks on the group's demo tape, with his own singer, Shel Naylor. While Decca and Philips have already turned down the group, Wace then meets American producer Shel Talmy, who is working at Mills Music and has connections at Pye Records. The Ravens, meanwhile, have placed ad in **Melody Maker**: "Drummer wanted for a smart go-ahead group." Avory (b. Feb. 15, 1944, Hampton Court, Surrey) fits the bill and is added as drummer.
Dec [31] The Kinks make their first appearance at the Lotus House restaurant, London, where they are seen by impresario Arthur Howes.

1964

Jan [23] With the Kinks management now including Wace, Collins, Page, tour promoter Howes and Talmy, the band signs a one-year contract to Pye, with options to renew, and records four songs within a week.
Feb Recorded at Howes' suggestion after he had seen the Beatles sing it at the Paris Olympia on January 17th, the group's debut single, *Long Tall Sally*, is released (issued on the Cameo label in the US).
[7] Intense hype earns the band an appearance on ITV's "Ready Steady Go!" and much press coverage.
[12] The group inks a five-year management contract with Wace and Collins' Boscobel Productions.
[26] Boscobel signs a deal with Denmark Productions, authorizing Page to manage the band with Kassner owning the group's publishing rights.
Apr Follow-up single, *You Still Want Me*, is issued, as the band is placed on a Dave Clark Five/Hollies UK package tour.
Aug [2] The Kinks supports the Beatles at the Gaumont Cinema, Bournemouth, Hants.
Sept [10] The group's third single, *You Really Got Me*, rockets to UK #1 and #7 in the US, where they are now signed to a long-term contract with Reprise Records. Penned by Ray, after Page had suggested that he try to write a song in the style of the Kingsmen's recent *Louie Louie* smash, its insistent riff lays the base for all Kinks singles during this period and will remain the group's most identifiable hit.
Oct Their debut album ***Kinks***, comprising R&B covers and Ray Davies compositions and featuring session help from Jimmy Page and Jon Lord, hits UK #3.
[9] They join a Billy J. Kramer UK tour.
[19] A six-date tour of Scotland begins at the Barrowlands, Glasgow, Scotland.
Nov *All Day And All Of The Night* hits UK #2.
Dec The band's debut album, released in the US as ***You Really Got Me***, reaches #29.
[6] The Kinks embarks on a one-week tour at the New Theatre, Oxford, Oxon., with Gene Pitney.
[11] They come second in the **New Musical Express** Poll Winners' Best New Group section and sixth in the British Vocal Group section.
[12] Ray marries 17-year-old Kinks fan, Lithuanian art student Rasa Didztpetris, in Bradford, Yorks., with brother Dave as best man.

1965

Jan [1] The group guests on BBC-TV's "Beat In The New Year".
[12] They fly to Paris, France, to appear in "Musicorama", a marathon three-day TV and radio show. (During the month, they also perform in Australia, returning by way of the US to appear on ABC-TV's "Shindig!", while Ray Davies and manager Larry Page pen *Revenge*, the new "Ready Steady Go!" theme.)
Feb [18] *Tired Of Waiting For You*, written by Ray on the London Underground's Metropolitan line between Isleworth and central London, is the band's second UK chart-topper, as *All Day And All Of The Night* hits US #7.
[23] They perform at the Olympia Theatre, Paris, France.
Mar Their sophomore album, ***Kinda Kinks***, hits UK #3.
[22] Quaife collapses in a cinema in Muswell Hill, and is taken to hospital, where he has stitches to a head wound, causing the cancellation of four concert dates. Further trouble follows during gigs in Europe, when the group is involved in a riot at the Tivoli Concert Hall, Copenhagen, Denmark.
Apr *Tired Of Waiting For You* hits US #6, as ***Kinks-Size*** reaches US #13.
[11] The band takes part in the annual "**New Musical Express** Poll Winners Concert" at the Empire Pool, Wembley, Middx., as *Everybody's Gonna Be Happy* peaks at UK #17. The single sees a change of style, influenced by Earl Van Dyke, who has recently toured with the group.
[30] The Kinks embark on a 21-date, twice-nightly UK package tour, with the Yardbirds, Goldie & the Gingerbreads and others, at the Adelphi Theatre, Slough, Bucks.
May [25] They pull out of the tour after Dave Davies receives ten stitches to head injuries, having been being hit by an errant Mick Avory cymbal during a concert in Cardiff, Wales. Davies apparently kicks Avory's drumkit after bad feeling between the two boils over. The Walker Brothers fill in for the remaining dates.
[31] The band continues its engagements with a TV show in Paris.
June *Set Me Free*, originally written for Cilla Black,

hits UK #9 and US #23.
[5] They perform their first stage show since Davies' injury, at the Astoria Theatre, Rawtenstall, Lancs.
[19] The Kinks makes their US live debut, with the Moody Blues, at the Academy of Music in New York, NY, although the rest of the tour is unsuccessful and is cancelled after five dates. Ray Davies and Page are involved in an altercation, with Davies refusing to go on stage at the Hollywood Bowl, on a bill shared with the Beach Boys, in the first week of July. He finally agrees to play, with Page retreating to England the next day. When Davies returns, he asks Wace and Collins to fire Page. The group's behavior on the US trek leads to a four-year ban by the American Federation of Musicians.
July [18] They begin a tour of Australia.
Aug ***Kinda Kinks*** makes US #60.
Sept *See My Friend* hits UK #10, while *Who'll Be The Next In Line* reaches US #34. With management affairs in disarray, the Kinks write a letter to Boscobel to end their contract, on the grounds that they were under the age of 21 when it was signed, allowing Boscobel to terminate its agreement with Denmark Productions. This leaves the band free to sign a new deal with Boscobel, with the proviso that Wace and Collins would not delegate their management responsibilities.
[2] The group embarks on a ten-day tour of Denmark, Finland and Sweden.
Oct [1] They begin an eight-day German tour in Munich.
Nov [10] Larry Page issues a statement confirming that he has served a writ against managers Wace and Collins over alleged breach of contract and to enforce his claim to part-management of group. The case will go on for five years, with Davies' royalties frozen, before finally being settled in the House Of Lords.
Dec ***Kinks Kontroversy*** hits UK #9, as ***Kinks Kinkdom*** reaches US #13.
[23] The group appears in the Christmas pantomime version of ITV's "Ready Steady Go!"

1966

Jan [8] The Kinks appear on the last broadcast of ABC-TV's "Shindig!"
[15] *Till The End Of The Day* hits UK #8.
Feb *A Well Respected Man* reaches US #13.
Mar [11-21] The group embarks on a tour of Belgium, with Mick Grace of the Cockneys deputizing for Ray Davies, who is suffering from flu and stress.
[31] Davies rejoins the band for the BBC-TV's "Top Of The Pops", but all other immediate UK dates are cancelled.
Apr In a softer songwriting style, the Ray Davies-penned *Dedicated Follower Of Fashion* hits UK #4, accompanied by a promo film lensed in the hip clothes shops of London's Carnaby Street. ***Kinks Kontroversy*** makes US #95.
[28] Avory falls ill with tonsilitis. Session drummer and former Tornado, Clem Cattini, deputises at a gig at the Mecca Ballroom, Nottingham, Notts.
May *Till The End Of The Day* peaks at US #50.
June *Dedicated Follower Of Fashion* makes US #36.
[4] Quaife breaks his right foot in a car crash. John Dalton, from the Mark Four, fills in as his replacement for six weeks.
[9] Dalton makes his BBC-TV "Top Of The Pops" debut with the band.
[12] The group embarks on an extensive European tour in Madrid, but is refused permission to work because Quaife's name, not Dalton's, is on the work permit.
July They sign a business management deal with Allen Klein.
[9] *Sunny Afternoon* hits UK #1, deposing the Beatles' *Paperback Writer.*
Aug ***The Kinks Greatest Hits!*** hits US #9.
Sept Budget compilation album, ***Well Respected Kinks***, hits UK #5. Quaife leaves temporarily, his absence covered by John Dalton.
[3] The group embarks on a tour of Holland, Italy, Germany, Norway, Denmark and Finland, set to end on the 25th.
[16] Quaife leaves the band, with Dalton staying on as a permanent member.
Oct *Sunny Afternoon* reaches US #14.
Nov Its parent album, ***Face To Face***, peaks at UK #12.
Dec *Dead End Street* hits UK #5, but falters at US #73. BBC-TV bans the promo film, which features the group leaping in and out of coffins.
[3] Quaife rejoins the band after a change of heart.

1967

Feb ***Face To Face*** peaks at US #135.
Apr UK concert performances are recorded for a future live album.
[15] Ray appears on the panel of BBC-TV's "Juke Box Jury".
May *Waterloo Sunset* hits UK #2.
[13] Ray Davies announces he is leaving the band to concentrate on writing and producing. He tells the **New Musical Express**, "There just isn't time to make personal appearances and work on the Kinks' records." Manager Wace issues a denial.
[16] Davies changes his mind about leaving.
July *Mr. Pleasant* peaks at US #80, their last US chart appearance for three years.
Aug Dave Davies, in brother Ray's shadow thus far, hits UK #3 with his solo, *Death Of A Clown* (nevertheless written by Ray).
Sept ***The Live Kinks*** climbs to US #162.
Oct ***Something Else***, containing *Waterloo Sunset, Death Of A Clown* and *David Watts*, makes UK #35, the group's last original album to chart in Britain.
Nov *Autumn Almanac* hits UK #3.
Dec Dave Davies' *Susannah's Still Alive* makes UK #20, as ***Sunny Afternoon***, a budget-priced Kinks compilation, hits UK #9.

1968

Jan ***Live At Kelvin Hall***, reflecting the raw edge of the Kinks' live performance, is released.
Feb [23] The Kinks play the Granby Halls, Granby, Leics., with Traffic and the Bonzo Dog Doo Dah Band.
Mar ***Something Else By The Kinks*** makes US #153.
Apr *Wonderboy* reaches UK #36.
[6] The group begins a 20-date, twice-nightly UK tour, with the Herd, the Tremeloes, Gary Walker & the Rain and others, at the Granada Theatre, Mansfield, Notts., set to end on the 28th at Coventry Theatre, Coventry, Warks.
Aug Lilting ballad, *Days*, peaks at UK #12.
Oct [20] The band begins a week-long cabaret engagement at the Fiesta, Stockton-on-Tees, Cleveland, regarded as a "cabaret-circuit graveyard".
Nov Ray's homage to England, ***(The Kinks Are) The Village Green Preservation Society***, comprising tracks from the never-released ***Four More Respected Gentlemen***, is issued.

1969

Apr *Plastic Man* makes UK #31, partly due to a BBC ban due to the inclusion of the word "bum" in the lyric. Quaife leaves the band permanently, and is again replaced by Dalton. Ray produces ***Turtle Soup*** for the Turtles, writes a song a week to feature in BBC-TV series "Where Was Spring?", starring Eleanor Bron, and co-writes the theme for the film version of "Till Death Us Do Part", as well as penning songs for the movie "The Virgin Soldiers".
Oct ***Arthur (Or The Decline And Fall Of The British Empire)*** is released. Commissioned as an ITV play written by Julian Mitchell, but never produced, its subject is an ordinary man reflecting on his life. It fails to chart in the UK, but makes US #105.
[17] The group supports Spirit at New York's Fillmore East, as they begin a six-week US tour, their first in four years, after resolving problems with the American Federation of Musicians.

1970

Jan *Victoria* makes UK #33.
Mar *Victoria* peaks at US #62.
June Ray flies from New York to London and back during the Kinks' US tour, to re-record a vocal line in *Lola*, changing "Coca-Cola" to "cherry cola" to appease the BBC and copyright holders.
July Once again, Ray announces he is quitting the band, but, as ever, will change his mind.
Aug The Kinks' transvestite-themed *Lola* hits UK #2 and matches *All Day And All Of The Night*'s 14-week stay on the chart.
Oct [15] Ray Davies stars in BBC-TV's Play For Today, "The Long Distance Piano Player".
Dec ***Lola Vs. Powerman And The Moneygoround, Part One*** reaches US #35, lyrically highlighted by Ray's attack on the increasingly litigious music business.

1971

Jan *Apeman*, another song with a re-recorded lyric, also spends 14 weeks on the UK survey, hitting #5 and climbing to US #45.
Mar Kinks-penned album soundtrack to ***Percy***, a film concerning a penis transplant, is released.
Apr John Gosling, who played keyboards on *Lola*, joins the band.
Oct Pye-issued retrospective, ***Golden Hour Of The Kinks***, reaches UK #21.
Nov The group signs a $1-million deal for five albums with RCA Records. Ray Davies is now the group's manager, following Collins' selling his interest in the band to Wace, who in turn quits.

1972

Jan ***Muswell Hillbillies***, eulogizing Ray's North London childhood, makes US #100. The group is now regaining a large US following, already nostalgic for the '60s.
Feb [25] The band embarks on a US tour, now augmented by a horn section and female backing vocalists.
Apr ***The Kinks Kronikles*** reaches US #94, a greatest-hits package reflecting the group's revived fortunes in the US.
May [6] The group takes part in the "Bickershaw Festival", near Wigan, Lancs.
June *Supersonic Rocket Ship* reaches UK #16.
Aug ***Everybody's In Showbiz, Everybody's A Star***, a double set with a live album showcasing their US oldies act and a studio album augmented by the Mike Cotton Sound brass ensemble, reaches US #70.
Oct The band previews a new work as a West End stage show, "The Kinks Are The Village Green Preservation Society", and plays London's Rainbow Theatre at the end of a short UK tour.

1973

Jan [14] The Kinks perform at London's Theatre Royal, Drury Lane.
Mar ***The Great Lost Kinks Album*** reaches US #145.
May The group opens its own Konk Studios in Hornsey, London.
June [20] Ray's wife Rasa walks out on him, taking their two children with her. (The following week, Davies is admitted to Highgate Hospital following an apparent drug-overdose suicide attempt.)
July [15] During a show at London's White City Stadium, on a bill with Edgar Winter's White Trash and Sly & the Family Stone, an emotional Ray announces he is quitting the music business, inevitably returning within a week. His brother Dave does leave the group, however, rejoining in 1975.
Dec ***Preservation Act I*** reaches US #177. The album is an extension of the themes first introduced in "Village Green". It will also make US #114 the following July, and in October the Kinks will launch their own short-lived label, Konk, with Claire Hammill's ***Stage Door Johnnies***.

1975

June ***Soap Opera***, based on a TV musical, "Starmaker", which Ray wrote last year, peaks at US #51.
Dec ***Schoolboys In Disgrace*** reaches US #45, the group's last original album for RCA.

1976

June RCA-released ***The Kinks Greatest - Celluloid Heroes*** climbs to US #144.
[23] A press release from Arista Records announces

that the Kinks have signed to the label.
Nov Dalton leaves, and is temporarily replaced by Andy Pyle.
Dec UK press reports a fight at London's Nashville club between Ray and Konk act, Café Society's Tom Robinson.

1977

Feb [26] The group appears on NBC-TV's "Saturday Night Live".
Mar With Dave Davies firmly back in the Kinks' fold, the group's Arista debut, ***Sleepwalker***, reaches US #21, their first US Top 20 outing in 11 years.
Apr [23] The Kinks performs at the Civic Center, San Diego, CA, during its US "Sleepwalker" tour.
May *Sleepwalker* makes US #48.
July Ray Davies announces - yet again - that he is quitting. He will of course return.
Nov Seasonal single, *Father Christmas*, is released.
Dec The group plays a Christmas show at London's Rainbow Theatre.

1978

Apr Pyle leaves. (He will form the group United with Gosling, temporarily replaced by a returning Dalton.)
May Dalton now leaves permanently, as does Gosling. They are replaced by former-Pretty Thing Gordon Edwards (keyboards) and Jim Rodford (b. July 7, 1945, St. Alban's) (bass), ex-Argent.
[26] The group begins a one-month US tour, set to end on June 25th to tie in with release of ***Misfits***.
June ***Misfits*** reaches #40 in the US, where the group remains most successful.
Sept The Kinks have their first US Top 40 Singles-chart success in eight years with *Rock'n'Roll Fantasy*, which reaches #30.
Oct [1] The band performs at London's Hammersmith Odeon.
[28] TV-advertised Ronco label-released ***20 Golden Greats*** reaches UK #19.

1979

Feb The Pretenders make UK #34 with their debut hit, *Stop Your Sobbing*, originally a Kinks album track. (They will also hit UK 7 with *I Go To Sleep* in 1981, another Kinks album track, originally covered by Peggy Lee.)
June *(I Wish I Could Fly Like) Superman* reaches US #41.
July Ian Gibbons replaces Edwards on keyboards.
Sept ***Low Budget*** makes US #11, and is certified gold.

1980

June ***One For The Road*** reaches US #14, also earning a gold disc.
July Dave releases his first solo album, ***PL 13603*** (released in the UK as ***AFL1-3603***, both titled after the disc's relevant catalog numbers).
Aug [11] The band performs at the San Diego Arena, CA, on a US tour.
Sept ***Second Time Around*** peaks at US #177.
Dec The Kinks, now comprising the Davies brothers, Avory, Rodford and Gibbons, begin a short UK tour.

1981

Apr [6] "Chorus Girls", a play by Barrie Keeffe with songs by Ray Davies, opens at the Theatre Royal, Stratford East, London.
July Dave's ***Glamour*** makes US #152, as the Kinks' single, *Better Things*, reaches US #46.
Sept Ray, currently romantically involved with Pretenders founder Chrissie Hynde, is divorced from his second wife, Yvonne.
Oct [3] The band plays at New York's Madison Square Garden for the first time.
Nov ***Give The People What They Want*** reaches US #15, with the extracted *Destroyer* peaking at US #85.

1982

Jan Ray begins work on "Return To Waterloo", which will be shown on C4-TV, and is subsequently released on video and as the RCA-released ***Return To Waterloo*** album in 1984.
Sept [3-5] The Kinks participate in the three-day "US Festival" in San Bernardino, CA.

1983

Jan [22] Ray and Hynde's daughter Natalie is born.
May Dance hall-styled *Come Dancing*, written about Ray's sister Gwen and her husband Brian, hits US #6, aided by exposure on MTV.
Aug Ray Davies-produced and written (as ever), ***State Of Confusion***, recorded at the group's own Konk Studio in London, reaches US #12.
Sept *Come Dancing* reaches UK #12, the group's first UK single success in 11 years.
Oct Reissued *You Really Got Me* makes UK #47, winning out over *Don't Forget To Dance*, which makes UK #58 (and also US #29).
Nov ***Kinks Greatest Hits - Dead End Street*** peaks at UK #96, while Dave releases his third solo effort, ***Chosen People*** on Warner Bros. Records.

1984

May Hynde leaves Ray for Simple Minds' Jim Kerr. An unofficial biography of the Kinks, by Johnny Rogan, is published.
Word Of Mouth makes US #57.
Nov The official biography of the Kinks, by Jon Savage, is published.

1986

Apr Julien Temple-directed film, "Absolute Beginners", premieres with Ray appearing as the father of Patsy Kensit's Crepe Suzette.
July ***Come Dancing With The Kinks - The Best Of The Kinks 1977-1986*** makes US #159, as the band signs a new deal with London Records in the UK and MCA in North America.

1987

Jan London/MCA debut, ***Think Visual***, makes US #81, as the band embarks on a US tour. During the year, Virgin Video releases a compilation of Kinks promotional videos, while PRT brings the Pye-label Kinks back catalog to compact disc. The following March the MCA US-released ***Live - The Road***, recorded during their US summer tour of 1987, will make US #110.

1989

Aug ***Shangri-La***, a various artists-compilation tribute of Kinks songs, featuring the Cardiacs, the Fleshtones, Cud and the Patch-Up Boys (a pseudonym for the Go-Betweens), is released.
Sept [23] ***The Ultimate Collection***, released by UK retrospective specialist label Castle Communications, makes UK #35.
Nov ***UK Jive*** steps to US #122 as the Kinks begin a US tour with new additions, keyboardist Mark Haley and drummer Bob Henrit (b. May 2, 1945).

1990

Jan [17] The Kinks are inducted into the Rock and Roll Hall of Fame at the fifth annual dinner, at New York's Waldorf Astoria Hotel. (The original line-up are all present, including Quaife, now an airbrush artist living in Ontario, Canada.)
Apr [2] Ray Davies and the Kinks are bestowed with the Special Contribution To British Music honor at the 35th annual Ivor Novello Awards, at London's Grosvenor House Hotel.

1991

July [30] "The Story Of The Kinks" documentary airs on C4-TV.
Sept MCA releases ***Lost & Found (1986-1989)***, a compilation comprising tracks from ***Think Visual***, ***The Road*** and ***UK Jive***.
Nov [22] The Kinks are backed by the Smithereens on *Lola* and *You Really Got Me*, during a gig at the Boston Garden, Boston, MA.
Dec CBS/Sony, to which the group signed in April, releases a new five-track Kinks EP, *Did Ya*.

1992

Apr [25] They perform at the Sound Action awareness and fundraiser, held to celebrate "Earth Day 1992" at Foxboro Stadium, Foxborough, MA.

1993

Mar As Rhino continues releasing the group's catalog on compact disc in the US, their Sony album, and '90s debut, ***Phobia***, is released, featuring the Davies brothers, Henrit and Rodford. Included is the song *Hatred (A Duet)*, with the chorus line, "Hatred is the only thing that keeps us together", a thinly-veiled reference to the turbulent relationship which endures between the Davies brothers.
[29] The group plays London's Clapham Grand during current UK dates.
Apr [30] They begin an eight-date US club tour at the Bayou, Washington, DC, set to end on May 10th at The Academy, Boston.
May [1] ***Phobia*** charts for a week at US #166.
[25] The group guests on NBC-TV's "The Tonight Show".
June [27] They play at the "Glastonbury Festival", Glastonbury, Somerset.
July [11] The band performs at London's Royal Albert Hall.
Sept [1] A US arena/theater tour ends at Los Angeles' Wiltern Theatre.
[18] Singles retrospective ***The Definitive Collection*** debuts at its UK #18 peak.

1994

Mar [26] The band performs at the Wembley Arena, during a four-date UK tour.
Oct [13] The Kinks guest on BBC1-TV's "Steve Wright's People Show".
[16] They embark on a 29-date UK/Eire tour at Rothes Hall, Glenrothes, Fire, set to end on November 23rd at the Opera House, Cork, Eire.

1995

July [16] The Kinks perform at the Valley Forge Music Fair, Devon, PA, during a brief US tour.
Sept Ray Davies' **X-Ray** autobiography, written in a fictional interview style, is published.
[2] He performs *All Day And All Of The Night* and *Lola* at the Concert for the Rock and Roll Hall of Fame at Cleveland Stadium, Cleveland, OH, wearing a reversible Union Jack/Stars And Stripes jacket.
Oct He takes his one-man show "To The Bone" on a US promotional visit, reading passages from his autobiography, delivering anecdotes and performing old and new material, much of it featured on a new album also titled ***To The Bone***.

KISS

Gene Simmons (bass, vocals); **Paul Stanley** (guitar, vocals); **Ace Frehley** (guitar, vocals); **Peter Criss** (drums, vocals)

1973

Jan [30] The band has been formed, originally as part-time rock outfit Wicked Lester, in 1972 in New York, NY by musician acquaintances Simmons (b. Chaim Witz, Aug. 25, 1949, Haifa, Israel), a teacher, and Stanley (b. Paul Stanley Eisen, Jan. 20, 1950, Queens, New York). Criss (b. Peter Crisscoula, Dec. 27, 1945, Brooklyn, New York) is contacted by the pair after placing his own ad in **Rolling Stone** ("Drummer willing to do anything to make it"), and they have rehearsed as a trio while continuing day jobs. Guitarist Frehley (b. Paul Frehley, Apr. 22, 1951, Bronx, New York) has completed the line-up, recruited via an ad in the **Village Voice**. The group now plays its first gig as Kiss at the Popcorn Club in Queens, with an emphasis on highly visual rock theatrics. Following a second performance at Manhattan's Hotel Diplomat, the band signs a management deal with Bill Aucoin.

Dec [31] Kiss makes its Academy of Music, New York debut with Blue Öyster Cult, Iggy Pop and Teenage Lust.

1974

Jan [8] Neil Bogart's fledgling Casablanca Records signs the band.
Feb Their debut album, ***Kiss***, launched with a nationwide promotion campaign including marathon kissing competitions, climbs to US #87, staying charted for 23 weeks, eventually earning the group its first gold disc.
June [22] Their debut chart single *Kissin' Time* makes US #83.
Nov The band's sophomore album, ***Hotter Than Hell***, burns out at US #100.

1975

Apr Through constant touring, Kiss has built a strong following, intrigued not least by the members' penchant for outrageous leather costumes, meticulously painted faces (a device successfully employed to disguise their real-life features) and stage-set pyrotechnics, spurring ***Dressed To Kill*** to climb to US #32.
June [14] *Rock'N'Roll All Nite* (studio version) stops at US #68.
Nov ***Alive!***, recorded on tour, hits US #9, earning a fourth gold disc.
[21] The Kiss Army fan club officially forms in Terre Haute, IN.

1976

Jan [24] Extracted from the album, the live *Rock 'N'Roll All Nite* reaches US #12.
Feb [20] Kiss members' footprints are placed on the pavement outside Grauman's Chinese Theater in Hollywood, CA.
Apr ***Destroyer*** reaches US #11 and is the group's first platinum-selling disc.
May [1] *Shout It Out Loud* is heard at US #31.
[15-16] The group plays at London's Hammersmith Odeon, during a brief, four-date UK visit.
June [16] *Flaming Youth* peaks at US #74.
[5] ***Destroyer*** reaches UK #22 and ***Alive!*** will make UK #49 on the 26th during a two-week chart stay.
Aug ***The Originals***, a repackaging of the first three hard-rock albums containing a comic-book history of Kiss, peaks at US #36.
Dec [4] Atypical ballad, *Beth*, written and sung by Criss with the B-side *Detroit Rock City*, hits US #7. The group returns for UK dates but interest is limited, their image taken less seriously as the band only conducts interviews in full make-up. ***Rock And Roll Over*** enters the US chart, set to make #11 during a platinum-earning, 45-week chart tenure.
[11] Frehley receives an electric shock during a concert at Lakeland, FL. He is not seriously hurt.

1977

Feb [26] *Hard Luck Woman* makes US #15.
May [14] *Calling Dr. Love* reaches US #16.
June [28] Marvel Comics publishes **The Kiss Comic Book**, based on the masked men.
Aug [25-27] Kiss plays three shows at the Great Western Forum, Inglewood, CA, which are recorded for the forthcoming ***Kiss Alive II***.
Sept [3] *Christine Sixteen* makes US #25 while ***Love Gun*** hits US #4.
Oct [15] Its title track *Love Gun* peaks at US #61.
Nov ***Alive II*** hits US #7 and becomes the group's fourth platinum disc. It also charts for a week at UK #60.

1978

Feb [11] A live version of their 1976 hit, *Shout It Out Loud*, peaks at US #54.
Apr [22] *Rocket Ride* flies to US #39.
May ***Double Platinum***, a two-record set of Kiss "classics", makes US #24, their fifth consecutive platinum release.
Oct The four members simultaneously issue eponymous solo albums which are launched in a high-profile campaign, with each cover featuring a matching portrait of the artist in full make-up. Each album is shipped platinum, but sales fail to match the expected demand. Simmons' ***Gene Simmons*** fares best, reaching US #22, followed by ***Ace Frehley*** (#26), ***Paul Stanley*** (#40) and ***Peter Criss*** (#43).
[30] NBC-TV airs the animated cartoon "Kiss Meets The Phantom Of The Park", in which the heroes foil a mad scientist who has gone beserk in an amusement park.

1979

May Kiss returns with *I Was Made For Lovin' You*, which makes US #11 and is the group's UK Singles chart debut, at #50.
June ***Dynasty*** hits US #9, eventually being certified platinum, spurred by a US "Dynasty Tour"
July Kiss is awarded the Gold Ticket for playing to over 100,000 fans at New York's Madison Square Garden.
[28] ***Dynasty*** makes UK #50.
Oct [20] The extracted *Sure Know Something* makes US #47.

1980

May [17] Musically at odds with his colleagues, Criss leaves the group to pursue a solo career (and will shortly release ***Out Of Control***, followed by ***Let Me Rock You*** in 1982, after which he will join Balls of Fire and marry **Playboy** centrefold, Debra Svensk.)
June ***Kiss Unmasked***, the first album to miss the US Top 30, peaks at #35 and makes UK #48 (July [5]). *Shandi*, from the album, reaches US #47.
July [25] The band plays at New York's Palladium, with newly recruited drummer Eric Carr (b. July 12, 1950, Brooklyn).
Aug Kiss embarks on a European tour.

1981

Jan [12] The RIAA donates some 800 rock albums, including Kiss' ***Alive!***, to the Library of Congress, while Casablanca releases ***Best Of The Solo Albums***.
Dec ***Music From The Elder***, a concept album unlike much of the band's previous material, peaks at US #75.
[5] ***Music From The Elder*** also makes UK #51, with *A World Without Heroes*, an unlikely collaboration with Lou Reed, reaching US #56 and UK #55.

1982

July [3] UK-only collection, ***Killers***, makes UK #42.
Nov [6] ***Creatures Of The Night*** reaches UK #22, and will make US #45. It is dedicated to Casablanca label boss Neil Bogart, who recently died from cancer.
Dec Following a serious car accident, Frehley leaves the group and is replaced by Vinnie Vincent (b. Vincent Cusano). (Frehley will spend four years overcoming drug addiction and will resurface with his own group, Frehley's Comet, in 1987 releasing the US #43 ***Frehley's Comet***, the US #84 ***Live + 1*** the following year, ***Second Sighting*** (US #81, same year and UK #79 (June [18], 1988)) and the solo ***Trouble Walkin'*** (US #102) in 1989.)

1983

Apr *Creatures Of The Night* makes UK #34.
Aug Kiss cancels a three-day tour of Argentina when the extremist Free Fatherland Nationalist Commando movement threatens to stop the tour, even if it "goes so far as to cost the very lives of that unfortunate band".
Sept [18] Kiss members finally reveal all, appearing on MTV without make-up for the first time.
Oct ***Lick It Up*** begins a new phase in the band's career. With the band now signed to the Mercury label, the album-cover photo features the group minus the usual camouflage. The album reaches US #24 (going gold), and hits UK #7.
Dec [17] *Lick It Up* makes US #66 having already made UK #31.

1984

Jan Mark St. John replaces the departing Vincent, who is allegedly fired for "unethical behavior". He will later form Vinnie Vincent's Invasion, releasing the US #64, ***Vinnie Vincent Invasion***, in 1986 and ***All Systems Go*** (US #64 in 1988).
Oct ***Animalize***, returns the group to platinum status, making US #19 and UK #11. *Heaven's On Fire* reaches US #49 and UK #43.
Dec Simmons stars as the villain, opposite Tom Selleck's hero, in the premiering film "Runaway".

1985

Oct ***Asylum*** makes US #20 and UK #12 and features Bruce Kulick, who has replaced St. John (who has Reiter's syndrome). The excerpted *Tears Are Falling* reaches US #51 and UK #57.

1986

May Kiss contributes *Runaway* to the various-artists album, ***Hear'N'Aid***, for heavy-metal music's fund-raising activities for famine relief.
June Simmons stars in the film "Never Too Young To Die", with Robert Englund and George Lazenby. (He will also appear, with Ozzy Osbourne in, "Trick Or Treat", and alongside Rutger Hauer in "Wanted Dead Or Alive".)

1987

Oct [30] *Crazy Crazy Nights* peaks at US #65.
Nov *Crazy Crazy Nights* is Kiss' biggest UK success, hitting #45.
[7] Its parent album ***Crazy Nights*** debuts at its UK #4 peak and will reach US #18.

1988

Jan [30] Ballad *Reason To Live* makes US #68 and UK #33.
July [8] The group embarks on a summer tour of North America, with Cheap Trick, at the Forum, Halifax, NS, Canada.
Aug Simmons establishes the Simmons record label.
[28] A 29-date North American tour ends at the Great Western Forum, Inglewood, CA.
Sept *Turn On The Night* makes UK #41. Kiss plays the opening night of the newly relocated Marquee club in London's Charing Cross Road.
[4] The group takes part in "Monsters Of Rock" package at Willem II Stadion, Tilburg, Germany, with Iron Maiden, Anthrax, Helloween, Great White and David Lee Roth.
Dec [10] Greatest hits collection, ***Smashes, Thrashes And Hits***, bows at its UK #62 peak during a two-week chart stay and will reach US #21.

1989

Jan [14] *Let's Put The X In Sex* makes US #97.
Nov *Hide Your Heart* peaks at UK #59, as their new studio album, ***Hot In The Shade***, reaches US #29 and UK #35 (Nov [4]), supported by the 132-date "Hot In The Shade" tour.
Dec [16] *Hide Your Heart*, originally recorded by Bonnie Tyler and then Mötley Crüe and Robin Beck, reaches US #66.

1990

Mar [31] Ballad *Forever*, written by Stanley with Michael Bolton, makes UK #65.
Apr [21] *Forever* hits US #8, the group's first Top 10 hit in 14 years.
May [4] The group begins a six-month North American tour, supported by Faster Pussycat and Slaughter, in Lubbock, TX.
June [30] *Rise To It* stalls at US #81.
July [5] Band has to cancel a New Haven concert, after Stanley sustains neck and back injuries in a July 4th car accident in Pelham, NY.

1991

Feb [5] Criss appears on US syndicated TV's "Donahue" show, together with the man who has claimed he was Criss (in a story for **The Star** tabloid - "Kiss Star Hits The Skids"), and Criss' ex-wife Debbie, who tells viewers she believes that her husband has never met Donahue's fourth guest, Cherylanne Thompson, who took in the impostor but also claims to have had a "very close relationship" with the real Criss (Thompson will reappear on the pop

front in 1992, alleging attempted rape by Billy Idol).
Aug [26] Criss files a libel lawsuit in Los Angeles, CA against **The Star**, for its January 8th, 1991, story which claimed he was a hopeless alcoholic living on the streets of Santa Monica, CA.
Nov [24] Carr dies of complications from cancer at Bellevue Hospital, New York, after suffering a cerebral haemorrhage two days after the MTV Awards in September.

1992

Jan [25] Kiss' cover of Argent's *God Gave Rock & Roll To You* (Kiss opened for the group in its early years), featured in "Bill And Ted's Bogus Journey", hits UK #4.
Mar [9] *Unholy* debuts at its UK #26 peak.
Apr [23] With its latest drummer, ex-Black Sabbath and Badlands Eric Singer, the group begins a low-key, ten-city tour at the Stone, San Francisco, CA, set to end on May 10th at L'Amour in Brooklyn, New York. The group issues a press release featuring quotes from Metallica's Lars Ulrich and even country star Garth Brooks who says: "My biggest influence through junior high was Kiss. That was my thing."
May [16] The band embarks on the eight-date UK leg of its "Revenge '92 Tour" at the SE&CC Glasgow, Scotland, set to end on the 26th at the National Exhibition Centre, Birmingham, W. Midlands.
[21] Kiss makes a special guest appearance at the official "Kiss Crazy Konvention" at London's Astoria Theatre.
[23] ***Revenge***, produced by Bob Ezrin and the band's first album since ***The Elder***, bows at its UK #10 peak.
June [6] ***Revenge*** bows at its US #6 peak.
July [26] Stanley marries actress-model Pamela Bowen in Los Angeles.
Oct [1] Further US dates, supported by Faster Pussycat and Trixter, begin at the Stabler Arena, Bethlehem, PA.
Nov [27] Their Palace of Auburn Hills, MI concert - in front of 9,880 fans - is filmed for a forthcoming full-length video and album ***Kiss Alive III***.

1993

Apr [6] Criss, shortly to release ***Criss***, his first solo album in 15 years, and **The Star** settle out of court, hours before the trial is about to start.
May [18] Kiss are inducted into Hollywood's Rock Walk, as Los Angeles' Mayor Tom Bradley proclaims "Kiss Day".
[29] ***Alive III*** debuts at its UK #24 peak, as Simmons continues working on a Kiss tribute album, set to include favorite tracks covered by Anthrax, Garth Brooks, Nirvana and Pearl Jam, among others.
June [5] ***Alive III*** bows at its US #9 peak.

1994

Feb [7] Simmons and Stanley present the Heavy Metal/Hard Rock New Artist trophy at the 21st annual American Music Awards, held at Los Angeles' Shrine Auditorium.
July [13] The group guests on NBC-TV's "The Tonight Show", performing *Hard Luck Woman* with Garth Brooks. Brooks' version of the Kiss song is included on the newly released ***Kiss My Ass*** tribute album with Kiss covers by the likes of Anthrax, Lenny Kravitz, Gin Blossoms, Toad The Wet Sprocket, Dinosaur Jr., Lemonheads, Extreme and other acts who claim the band were an influence on their youth.
[26] The band appears on CBS-TV's "Late Show With David Letterman", performing with Gin Blossoms.
Sept [8] The group performs at the Sports Palace, Mexico City, Mexico, during a tour of Central and South America.

1995

Jan [24] Kiss begins a tour of Japan. During their visit they will raise $10,000 for the victims of the Kobe earthquake.
Feb [4] The group embarks on first tour of Australia in 17 years, at the Entertainment Center, Perth. The band will play a total of six shows, accompanied by a nine-hour Kiss convention at each gig.
June [17] The first of 23 US city Kiss conventions begins in Los Angeles, uniquely choreographed and hosted by the band.
July [30] Stanley gives bride Corinda Clark away to groom Bill Rexer, with Simmons as best man, at a Kiss convention in New York City.
Aug [9] The group reunites with Criss to tape its MTV "Unplugged" session in New York, which also includes appearances by sometime members Singer and Kulick.

1996

Feb [28] The group, again in its original lineup and resplendent once more in full costume regalia and makeup, makes a surprise appearance alongside rapper 2Pac to present the Best Pop Vocal Performance trophy at the 38th annual Grammy Awards, held at the Shrine Auditorium. The group will shortly announce plans to undertake a US summer tour.
Mar [23] Acoustically reworking past glories, ***MTV Unplugged*** charts for a week at UK #74.
[30] ***Unplugged*** debuts at its US #15 peak.

KLF

Bill Drummond; Jimmy Cauty

1986

Nov Drummond (b. William Butterworth, Apr. 29, 1953, South Africa), who has already worked in Scotland as a set designer, carpenter and deep-sea trawlerman, joined Liverpool indie power-pop combo Big In Japan, which also included Jayne Casey, Ian Broudie (later of Lightning Seeds) and Holly Johnson (later of Frankie Goes To Hollywood), in May 1977. He co-founded Merseyside-based Zoo Records with Teardrop Explodes' keyboardist, Dave Balfe, going on to manage and produce the band and the also-signed Echo & the Bunnymen. Revealing an enduring character trait, Drummond refused to work with either band after 1986, believing that they were killing music. Working in an A&R capacity for WEA Records in 1985, he handled Pete Waterman act, Brilliant, whose membership included guitarist Cauty (b. 1954). Prior to forming the KLF partnership with Cauty, however, Drummond releases his folk-inflected, eclectic debut solo album, ***The Man***, for Creation (licensed to Bar None Records in the US), which includes the tracks *Julian Cope Is Dead* and a version of Goffin & King's *Goin' Back*. Recorded live at the McMillan Hall, Galloway, Scotland, it will be followed by a second solo outing, ***Bill Drummond***, in January the following year, released on Atlantic Records.

1987

May [30] Disgusted by what they had done to the music industry, Drummond and Cauty have teamed up to form an anarchic organization bent on guerilla warfare against the traditional music business fraternity. Known as KLF Communications, it will provide them with both a media voice and a label outlet for a number of music projects, which will include the duo's various incarnations: JAMs, Disco 2000, the Justified Ancients of Mu Mu, the Timelords and KLF. The first release is the JAMs' *All You Need Is Love*, an attack on the media's coverage of the AIDS health crisis which includes samples of Beatles records, BBC broadcasts and Page 3 model, Samantha Fox. Accompanying promotion by the band includes daubing regional police chief James Anderton's ("God's policeman") face with the phrase "Shag, Shag, Shag", on a **Today**-newspaper billboard.
July JAMs' debut album, ***1987: What The Fuck's Going On?***, continues the anti-establishment streak and features further pioneering sampling, particularly on *The Queen And I*, which, based on Abba's *Dancing Queen* hit, prompts immediate litigation by Abba's lawyers, requesting that all copies of the record be returned or destroyed (the case is finally settled when the masters are surrendered to the MCPS and Abba).
Sept Becoming temporarily obsessed with Whitney Houston's ***Whitney***, Drummond and Cauty release, again as the JAMs, the 12", one-sided *Whitney Joins The Jams*, mixing samples of *I Wanna Dance With Somebody* with the TV theme to "Mission Impossible", which is only made available in Scotland. Two remaining projects for the year are a further JAMs single, *Downtown*, their treatment of the Petula Clark classic (which includes the London Community Gospel Choir), and Disco 2000's *I Gotta CD*.

1988

Mar [5] Following a final JAMs single, *Who Killed The JAMs?*, in January, and re-incarnated as KLF, the moniker's debut, *Burn The Beat*, is released.
June [18] Mixing an original Cauty rhythm track with the theme to the BBC-TV series "Dr. Who" and Gary Glitter's *I'm The Leader Of The Gang*, in an attempt to deliberately create a chart-topping single using, the words of Drummond, "the lowest common denominator in every aspect", a further KLF Communications off-shoot, the Timelords' *Doctorin' The Tardis*, hits UK #1 for a week. Glitter himself is recruited for a 12" remix, *Gary In The Tardis*, version.
Aug The global success of the single enables Drummond and Cauty to buy their own recording studio in South London, which they name Trancentral, where they begin working on five 12"-single recordings, only two of which, *3 A.M. Eternal* and *What Time Is Love*, will be released, soon to become popular floor-fillers on the burgeoning UK rave scene.
Sept Under the Timelords' guise, the pair publish **The Manual**, a £5.99 instruction book on how to easily secure a number one record. (It includes a tribute to UK DJ Steve Wright: "You don't even have to like him to be awed by him. The man is a genius, he is the most popular DJ in the country and has been the heartbeat of the British psyche since 1985.") The rest of the year is spent filming a 50-minute KLF road movie, "The White Room", starring Paul McGann.

1989

Mar Disco 2000 (whose lead vocalist, Cressida, is Cauty's wife) releases its final effort, a cover of Stevie Wonder's *Uptight*.
July The debut KLF album ***The White Room*** is released, including the extracted *Kylie Said To Jason*, which fails to reach the UK chart, avoided not least by Radio 1, concerned about upsetting fans of the popular chart artists, Kylie Minogue and Jason Donovan.

1990

Feb KLF releases the self-proclaimed "world's first, biggest and best" ambient house album, ***Chill Out***, consisting of the sounds of bleating sheep mixed over music samples from Acker Bilk, Fleetwood Mac, Jesus Loves You and Elvis Presley.
June KLF Communications releases Cauty's first solo album (under his own name), ***Space***, which includes contributions from Alexander Paterson, with whom Cauty has also recorded a number of singles under the ambient production-team name, the Orb, over the past year.
Aug KLF's *What Time Is Love (Live At Trancentral)* hits UK #5 during a three-month chart stay, providing the first hit for Drummond and Cauty under the KLF moniker. It is co-credited as featuring the Children of the Revolution, an umbrella term which includes an ensemble of DJs, vocalists, engineers and producers who are involved in the breakthrough recording.
Dec KLF appears at the DMC European Convention, held at the Paridiso Club, Amsterdam, Holland, performing a 23-minute version of *What Time Is Love*, during which the group distributes most of the DJ mixing equipment on stage to members of the audience, much to the chagrin of its owners, the event's organizers, who subsequently ban the group from all future performances at the venue.

1991

Feb [2] A remix of *3 A.M. Eternal* by KLF featuring the Children of the Revolution hits UK #1. Hailed by

its fans as an era-defining rave classic, the song showcases the talents of guest vocalist Maxine Harvey and rapper Ricardo.
[5] The duo is arrested in Battersea, London, for painting a logo on a **Sunday Times** billboard ad. They are released after being questioned for four hours, and will subsequently pay £500 in compensation.
Mar [16] Re-recorded and reissued, ***The White Room***, featuring reggae and dub treatments of earlier cuts alongside current hits, peaks at UK #3, at the start of a 43-week chart stay.
May [11] *Last Train To Trancentral* hits UK #2, behind Cher's *The Shoop Shoop Song (It's In His Kiss)*, spurred by a promotional video (filmed at Pinewood Studios) depicting a huge-scale model of KLF's imaginary Lost Continent of Mu created by the duo with Cauty's brother, Simon.
June [23] Cauty and Drummond serve ice creams during the interval of comedian Emo Phillips' performance at the Liverpool Festival of Comedy as "The Lost Children Of Mu" sing on stage.
Sept [7] *3 A.M. Eternal* hits US #5, earning a gold sales disc.
[14] ***The White Room*** reaches US #39, also going gold.
Nov [16] *It's Grim Up North*, a remix no longer featuring ex-Wah! frontman Pete Wylie running through a list of northern UK towns as highlighted by the original version (recorded in 1990), released under the Justified Ancients of Mu Mu banner, hits UK #10.
[23] *What Time Is Love?*, sampling the MC5's *Kick Out The Jams*, makes US #57.

1992

Jan [4] Known on the original 1989 version of ***The White Room*** album as *Hey Hey We're Not The Monkees*, a re-recorded treatment now released as *Justified And Ancient* hits UK #2 and incongruously features "The First Lady Of Country, Miss Tammy Wynette". Encouraged to participate in its promotional video clip, Wynette appears as the Queen of the Lost Continent of Mu.
Feb [11] KLF shares the Best British Group trophy (with Simply Red) at the 11th annual BRIT Awards, at London's Hammersmith Odeon, but have already left the event before the presentation of the trophy. Prior to this, the band (joined by Extreme Noise Terror) performed a thrash-metal version of *3 A.M. Eternal*, immediately followed by an announcement over the PA system: "Ladies and gentlemen, the KLF have now left the music business." On the morning of the Awards, Drummond and Cauty collected a freshly killed sheep from a slaughterhouse and, persuaded not to disembowel the animal live on stage as originally planned, dump it instead outside the post-Awards party being held at the Royal Lancaster Hotel, with a note attached: "I died for you. Bon appetit!"
Mar [5] KLF appears on BBC1-TV's "Top Of The Pops".
[14] *America : What Time Is Love?* hits UK #4.
[15] The duo attends the fifth annual "Rock'n'Roll Banger Race" at Wimbledon Stadium, Wimbledon, London.
[21] *Justified And Ancient* reaches US #11.
May [16] A full-page ad, taken out by KLF Communications on the back page of the **New Musical Express**, states: "We have been following a wild and wounded, glum and glorious, shit but shining path these past five years; the past two of which have led us up onto the commercial highground. We are at a point now where the path is about to take a sharp turn from these sunny uplands down into a netherworld of we-know-not-what. For the forseeable future there will be no further record releases from the Justified Ancients of Mu Mu, the JAMs, the Timelords, the KLF and any past, present or future name attached to our activities." Confirming that all KLF-label record releases are now deleted, it ends: "There is no further information." An answerphone at KLF Communications' office states: "This is a recorded announcement ... Bill Drummond and Jimmy Cauty have now left the music business."
[19] Commenting on the apparent dissolution of the band, distraught UK DJ Steve Wright says: "We were all devastated when we heard about it. We thought they were the most exciting and original group around. It's definitely the worst news since Cliff Richard split with the Shadows." (Cauty and Drummond will re-appear in 1993, recording K Cera Cera, with the Red Army Choir - offering the track to the authorities at Wembley Stadium to use before the F.A. Charity Shield game - but never releasing it, and placing adverts for the public to vote for the 1993 Turner Awards, under the heading "Let The People Choose - Who Is The Worst Of Them All".)

THE KNACK

Doug Fieger (vocals, guitar); **Berton Averre** (guitar); **Prescott Niles** (bass); **Bruce Gary** (drums)

1979

Feb The group has formed in Los Angeles, CA, in May of the previous year, with the intention of presenting a tight update of the mid-'60s beat-group style - a sound which comes to be dubbed "power pop". Fieger (b. Aug. 20, 1952, Detroit, MI) is the former bassist of Detroit group Sky, while Gary (b. Apr. 7, 1952, Burbank, CA) is ex-Jack Bruce Band. Niles (b. May 2, New York, NY) and Averre (b. Dec. 13, Van Nuys, CA) are fellow veterans of Los Angeles session work. Huge live success on the Southern California club scene has 13 record labels bidding to sign the group, with Capitol succeeding. They are teamed with Blondie's producer, Mike Chapman, with whom they produce an album's worth of songs, with little overdubbing, in only 11 days and for $18,000.
Aug [25] The Knack's debut, *My Sharona*, is an instant US smash, topping the chart for the first of six weeks. It sells over a million copies inside two weeks, adding a second million in less than a month in the US, becoming the best-selling 45 of the year. It also hits UK #6. ***Get The Knack*** performs similarly, topping the US chart a week earlier for the first of five weeks. It will sell over five million copies worldwide by the end of 1979, though it has charted for only two weeks at UK #65 (Aug [4]).
Nov *Good Girls Don't*, also from the debut set, reaches US #11 and UK #66.

1980

Mar Constant Beatles comparisons contribute to an early critical backlash against the group, which in turn hits their record sales: ***But The Little Girls Understand*** reaches US #15, its 600,000 sales only a fraction of the first album's total. The extracted *Baby Talks Dirty* makes US #38.
Apr Hasty follow-up, *Can't Put A Price On Love*, stops at US #62.

1981

Nov *Pay The Devil (Ooo Baby Ooo)* reaches US #67. It is taken from ***Round Trip***, which peaks at US #93, convincing group members that they have lost the knack. They play a final US tour before disbanding, one of the fastest rise-and-fall acts in pop history. Fieger forms Taking Chances, his three colleagues staying together as the Game, but neither venture will renew commercial success. Fellow Detroiters Was (Not Was) will employ Fieger as a guest vocalist on their 1983 album, ***Born To Laugh At Tornados***.

1994

Apr [16] Reforming in 1987, with Fieger, Averre, Niles and new drummer Billy Ward, the Knack released its Charisma label debut, ***Serious Fun***, produced by Don Was, in February 1991, with promotion including a March appearance at New York's China Club, as part of a "pro-jam session" sponsored by WNEW, one of a monthly series of benefits for Nordoff-Robbins. Fieger has also been seen in the early '90s in a recurring role as one of Dan's poker-playing pals on ABC-TV's "Roseanne", and shopped a Don Was-helmed solo album to record labels in 1992, while Niles became a music teacher, Gary continued as a session player and Averre worked on writing a musical, "Critic At Small". *My Sharona*, given a resurgence by its exposure in the movie "Reality Bites", now re-debuts at its US #91 peak, urging the group back into activity once more, set to play at the Roseland Ballroom, New York on May 13th sharing the bill with Melissa Etheridge and Urge Overkill.

GLADYS KNIGHT & THE PIPS

Gladys Knight (vocals); **Merald "Bubba" Knight** (vocals); **William Guest** (vocals); **Edward Patten** (vocals)

1952

Sept [4] Knight (b. May 28, 1944, Atlanta, GA), whose parents are singers in the Wings Over Jordan Gospel Choir and who has herself already sung gospel widely around the South with the Morris Brown Choir, has won $2,000 for singing *Too Young* on NBC-TV's "Ted Mack's Original Amateur Hour" the previous year. After an impromptu performance together at a tenth birthday party for brother Merald (b. Sept. 4, 1942, Atlanta), Gladys, Merald and sister Brenda now form a vocal group with cousins William (b. June 2, 1941, Atlanta) and Elenor Guest, singing gospel and ballads at family gatherings, and church functions at the Mount Mariah Baptist Church in Atlanta.

1957

Having been persuaded by another cousin, James "Pips" Woods (whose nickname they purloin and who becomes their manager), to turn professional, the quintet cuts its first disc, *Whistle My Love*, for Brunswick Records. The Pips also tour with Sam Cooke, B.B. King and Jackie Wilson. Brenda Knight and Elenor Guest will both leave the group in 1959 to get married, and are replaced by two male vocalists: a further cousin, Edward Patten (b. Aug. 2, 1939, Atlanta), and Langston George.

1960

The group records a 1952 Johnny Otis song, *Every Beat Of My Heart*, for the Atlanta-based Huntom label, initially with little success, but eventually with enough sales interest for Huntom to sell the master to the larger R&B independent Vee-Jay label in Chicago, II.

1961

May The group is signed by Bobby Robinson's New York-based Fury label, and re-records *Every Beat Of My Heart*.
June Both versions of *Every Beat Of My Heart* chart at the same time. The newer recording (on Fury) peaks at US #45, but the Vee-Jay original, credited to the Pips, is still climbing.
July *Every Beat Of My Heart* on Vee-Jay hits US #6 and tops the R&B chart for a week, resulting in huge demand for tour and club dates.

1962

Feb With the group now billed as Gladys Knight & the Pips, *Letter Full Of Tears*, on Fury, reaches US #19 (while UK singer Billy Fury's cover will make UK #32 a few weeks later).
Apr *Operator* peaks at US #97 and, shortly afterwards, George quits, leaving the group as a permanent quartet. (Knight will depart for some two years to marry and start a family, while the Pips will work as back-up session singers.)

1964

July [4] With Knight returning and the group signed to another independent R&B label, Maxx Records, *Giving Up*, written by Van McCoy, makes US #38.
Sept [12] *Lovers Always Forgive* reaches US #89, following which the label goes bankrupt, leaving the group without an outlet.

1966

Oct Still busy on the live circuit, with a tight, sharply choreographed act behind Knight's gospel-influenced soul leads, Gladys Knight & the Pips are booked as special guests on a Motown touring package and, on the strength of audience reception, are offered a recording contract by label boss, Berry Gordy Jr. They sign to Motown Records, which places them on its Soul imprint, alongside Jimmy Ruffin and Junior Walker & the All-Stars, and release *Just Walk In My Shoes*, produced by Harvey Fuqua and Johnny Bristol.
Dec [23] Motortown Revue, with the Pips and many other Tamla acts, opens for the week at the Fox Theatre, Detroit, MI.

1967

May The group switches to producer Norman Whitfield for *Take Me In Your Arms And Love Me*, which makes US #98.
July Their UK chart debut is *Take Me In Your Arms And Love Me*, which, aided by massive airplay on UK pirate radio stations, reaches #13.
Aug *Everybody Needs Love* makes US #39.
Nov [29] They begin a UK promotion visit which will end on December 6th.
Dec [16] Gladys Knight & the Pips' major chart breakthrough comes with their original version of Whitfield and Barrett Strong's *I Heard It Through The Grapevine*, later one of the most successful and re-recorded songs in the Motown/Jobete publishing catalog, which hits US #2 for the first of three weeks, eventually selling over one million copies, held from the top by the Beatles' *Hello Goodbye*. It also tops the US R&B survey for six weeks and makes UK #47, while the act's first US hit album, ***Everybody Needs Love***, including *Grapevine*, peaks at #60.
[3] The group plays at London's Saville Theatre, supporting Joe Tex.

1968

Mar [9] Another Whitfield/Strong composition, *The End Of Our Road*, which like *Grapevine*, is subsequently covered by Marvin Gaye, reaches US #15.
July [6] *It Should Have Been Me* makes US #40, while ***Feelin' Bluesy*** peaks at US #158.
Sept [28] *I Wish It Would Rain*, released only seven months after the Temptations' US #4 version, makes US #41.

1969

Feb ***Silk'N'Soul*** peaks at US #136.
Mar [7] The quartet performs at the "Grand Gala Du Disque", Amsterdam, Holland, on a bill including the Moody Blues.
Apr [12] Ashford & Simpson-penned and-produced *Didn't You Know (You'd Have To Cry Sometime)* makes US #63.
Sept [13] The group's unexpected, gospel-tinged revival of Shirley Ellis' 1964 dance hit, *The Nitty Gritty*, reaches US #19.
Dec [27] Another gospel-based song, Whitfield/Strong's *Freedom Train*, reaches US #17. Both it and the previous hit are included on ***Nitty Gritty***, which climbs to US #81. *You Need Love Like I Do (Don't You)*, again penned by Whitfield and Strong, will makes US #25 in April the following year with the compilation album ***Gladys Knight & The Pips' Greatest Hits***, reaching US #55 in May.

1971

Feb [13] While the group has ceased working with Whitfield, the producer of nine of its last ten hits, it has teamed with producer Clay McMurray for *If I Were Your Woman*, which, written by McMurray with Pam Sawyer and Leon Ware, hits US #9 and becomes the group's second US million seller.
June [6] They guest on the final edition of CBS-TV's "The Ed Sullivan Show".
July [17] *I Don't Want To Do Wrong*, the first A-side to be part-written by group members (with producer Bristol and Catherine Schaffner), reaches US #17. It is taken from ***If I Were Your Woman***, which makes US #35 - their highest-placed album to date.

1972

Feb [5] McMurray-penned and-produced *Make Me The Woman That You Go Home To* climbs to US #27 while ***Standing Ovation*** sits at US #60.
Apr [29] *Help Me Make It Through The Night*, the group's soul revival of Kris Kristofferson's ballad and a million-seller for Sammi Smith in 1971, reaches US #33.
July Their first Motown single, *Just Walk In My Shoes*, is reissued in the UK, and reaches #35 - the group's first UK chart entry in four years.
Dec *Help Me Make It Through The Night* reaches UK #11, their biggest UK hit to date.

1973

Jan Increasingly concerned that they have not been getting the support and career-development that Motown has afforded its other leading acts, despite a string of hits, they decide to leave when their contract expires and are quickly signed by New York-based Buddah Records.
Mar A 1968 album track, the Bacharach/David ballad *The Look Of Love*, is picked by UK Motown as the follow-up to *Help Me Make It Through The Night*, and reaches UK #21.
Apr [7] A composition by Mississippi songwriter Jim Weatherly, *Neither One Of Us (Wants To Be The First To Say Goodbye)*, produced by Joe Porter, and released as the group leaves Motown, becomes their second-biggest success on the label, and third million seller, hitting US #2 behind Vicki Lawrence's *The Night The Lights Went Out In Georgia*.
May ***Neither One Of Us*** is their first Top 10 album, hitting US #9.
July [7] From the album, *Daddy Could Swear, I Declare*, co-written by Gladys and Bubba Knight with producer Bristol, reaches US #19, while *Neither One Of Us (Wants To Be The First To Say Goodbye)* makes UK #31.
[28] Their Buddah label debut is Weatherly's *Where Peaceful Waters Flow*, which reaches US #28.
Sept Another album on Soul, ***All I Need Is Time***, featuring tracks cut shortly before the group's Motown exit, clocks in at US #70, its title song *All I Need Is Time*, produced by Porter, making US #61.
Oct [27] *Midnight Train To Georgia*, another Weatherly-written song (originally named *Midnight Plane To Houston*, in which form he has cut it himself), tops the US chart for the first of two weeks and also spends four weeks at R&B #1. A soul classic and Knight-career highlight, it is another million seller and the first of four consecutive gold singles on Buddah.

1974

Jan [19] *I've Got To Use My Imagination*, a further million seller, hits US #4. It is taken from the group's Buddah debut album, ***Imagination***, which hits US #9, and also includes *Midnight Train To Georgia*. The album earns a gold disc for half a million sales and is the first to feature the group as co-producers, with Tony Camillo, Kenny Kerner and Richie Wise.
Mar [2] The group wins Best Pop Vocal Performance By A Duo, Group Or Chorus for *Neither One Of Us (Wants To Be The First To Say Goodbye)*, and Best R&B Vocal Performance By A Duo, Group Or Chorus for *Midnight Train To Georgia* categories at the 16th annual Grammy Awards.
[28] They embark on a European tour.
Apr [27] Similarly-styled ballad, *Best Thing That Ever Happened To Me*, another Weatherly song from ***Imagination***, hits US #3 and is a further million seller. A double compilation album, ***Anthology***, on Motown, reaches US #77, while Soul issues ***Knight Time***, containing unissued material by the group, which makes US #139.
May The group's soundtrack album for the film "Claudine", featuring songs written and produced by Curtis Mayfield, reaches US #35 and earns another gold disc.
July [13] *On And On*, taken from ***Claudine***, hits US #5 to become the group's fourth consecutive gold single.
[27] They perform a critically-revered set at Detroit's Pine Theater.
Aug [10] *Between Her Goodbye And My Hello* is the final single on Soul, and climbs to US #57.
Dec [14] *I Feel A Song (In My Heart)* reaches US #21, taken from ***I Feel A Song***, which peaks at US #17 and earns a gold disc.

1975

Feb [18] Knight & the Pips win the Favorite Band, Duo Or Group, Soul/R&B; Favorite Band, Duo Or Group, Pop/Rock, Favorite Single, Soul/R&B, and Favorite Album, Soul/R&B categories at the second annual American Music Awards, held at the Civic Auditorium, Santa Monica, CA.
Apr [12] *Love Finds Its Own Way* makes US #47. (Knight marries for the second time - her husband is ex-social worker Barry Hankerson. She moves her family home to Detroit.)
May The group's final Soul album, ***A Little Knight Music***, climbs to US #164.
June A medley of *The Way We Were/Try To Remember*, from the long-running off-Broadway musical "The Fantasticks!", recorded live at a club in Detroit and prefaced by a spoken passage from Knight, hits UK #4 and reaches US #11.
[21] ***I Feel A Song*** becomes the group's first UK chart album, reaching UK #20.
July [10] The group begins a four-week run of "The Gladys Knight And The Pips Show" on NBC-TV in a summer replacement slot. The one-hour shows mix music with comedy and guest stars.
Aug After the UK Top 10 success of *The Way We Were*, which sets the standard of sophisticated supper-club soul on which the group will concentrate for the rest of its Buddah career, the label's UK licensee begins re-issuing earlier US Buddah hits. The first of these, *Best Thing That Ever Happened To Me*, now hits UK #7.
Oct *Money* makes US #50.
Dec David Gates-penned *Part Time Love* reaches US #22 and UK #30, while ***2nd Anniversary***, a reference to completing two successful years with Buddah, reaches US #24.

1976

Jan [31] They nab the Favorite Band, Duo Or Group, Soul/R&B trophy at the third annual American Music Awards, held at the Santa Monica Civic Auditorium.
June *Midnight Train To Georgia* belatedly hits UK #10, after being extracted from the compilation album.
[19] ***The Best Of Gladys Knight And The Pips***, a compilation of Buddah 45s, hits UK #6 and will reach US #36.
Aug *Make Yours A Happy Home* reaches UK #35.
Oct Knight makes her movie-acting debut in "Pipe Dreams", a romantic drama set in the Alaskan oilfields, produced by, and co-starring, her husband Hankerson. The Pips do not feature in the film, but join her in singing eight songs on the soundtrack.
Nov Mournful soul ballad *So Sad The Song*, from ***Pipe Dreams***, makes US #47 and UK #20.
Dec The soundtrack set ***Pipe Dreams*** wafts to US #94.

1977

Jan *Nobody But You*, another song from ***Pipe Dreams***, reaches UK #34.
[7-9] Knight & the Pips perform at London's New Victoria Theatre.
June [10-11] They perform at the third "Kool Jazz Festival", in San Diego, CA.
July [23] ***Still Together*** makes UK #42 and will reach US #51. The title is ironic since - throughout 1977-79 - Gladys Knight & the Pips will be unable to record together, even though they continue to perform live as a team. The forced recording separation is due to complex legal problems involving several record labels. The group is trying to move to CBS/Columbia and still has a $1.7-million suit hanging over it from the end of the Motown days, as well as a dispute over royalties with Motown. Previously recorded material

is released and, the atypical and uptempo *Baby Don't Change Your Mind*, the group's last US hit single on Buddah, a blend of traditional Motown with a hint of the new disco style, reaches US #52 and hits UK #4, their biggest UK release.
Oct *Home Is Where The Heart Is* reaches UK #35.
Dec [17] TV-advertised double album, ***30 Greatest***, on K-tel, hits UK #3.

1978

Apr *The One And Only*, the theme song from the Henry Winkler film of the same title, reaches UK #32.
July *Come Back And Finish What You Started*, in the uptempo mode of *Baby Don't Change Your Mind*, reaches UK #15.
Aug [29-31] During current UK dates, the group performs three nights at the London Palladium.
Sept ***The One And Only*** peaks at US #145.
Oct *It's A Better Than Good Time* reaches UK #59.

1979

Knight records an enforced solo album, ***Miss Gladys Knight***, for Buddah, while the Pips secure a deal with Casablanca Records and release two albums, ***At Last ... The Pips*** and ***Callin'***, without her.

1980

July [26] With litigation finally resolved, Gladys Knight & the Pips have reunited for recording, having signed a new deal with CBS/Columbia. *Landlord*, one of only two Columbia US singles successes, peaks at US #46 and hits R&B #3, while their Ashford & Simpson-produced Columbia debut, ***About Love***, reaches US #48.
Sept Uptempo, disco-aimed *Taste Of Bitter Love* makes UK #35.
Oct [11] Ballads round-up, ***A Touch Of Love***, another UK TV-advertised compilation on K-tel, reaches UK #16.
Dec Dance-oriented track, *Bourgie Bourgie*, reaches UK #32, after finding considerable popularity in UK discos.

1982

Nov [25] While ***Touch*** has reached US #109 in October 1981, Knight appears at the "World Music Festival" at the Bob Marley Performing Center near Montego Bay, Jamaica, on a bill with Aretha Franklin, the Clash, Squeeze, the Grateful Dead and others.

1983

May [28] Leon Sylvers III-produced *Save The Overtime (For Me)* hits US R&B #1 for a week and makes US #66.
July ***Visions*** is the group's biggest-selling domestic album for eight years, reaching US #34 and earning a gold disc.

1984

Jan [16] Knight & the Pips win the Favorite Band, Duo Or Group, Soul/R&B category at the 11th annual American Music Awards, held at the Shrine Auditorium, Los Angeles, CA.
Feb A third UK TV-advertised compilation album, ***The Collection - 20 Greatest Hits***, on Starblend Records, reaches UK #43.

1985

Apr ***Life*** reaches US #126.
Sept [18] Sitcom "Charlie & Co.", in which Gladys stars as Diana Richmond with Flip Wilson, premieres on CBS-TV and will remain on air until July 23rd, 1986. (By year's end, the group leaves CBS and signs to MCA Records.)

1986

Jan [18] Knight, along with Stevie Wonder and Elton John, is one of the "friends" to contribute to Dionne Warwick's *That's What Friends Are For*, which begins a four-week stay atop the US chart, becoming the best-selling single of the year, with sales over one million (it also reaches UK #16).
June Knight teams with Bill Medley to sing *Loving On Borrowed Time*, the love theme from the Sylvester Stallone movie "Cobra", whose soundtrack makes US #100.
Dec [31] Knight & the Pips join Air Supply, Freddie Jackson and Melba Moore for CBS-TV's "Happy New Year America".

1987

Feb [24] Knight wins Best Pop Performance By A Duo Or Group With Vocal category with Dionne Warwick, Elton John and Stevie Wonder, for *That's What Friends Are For*, at the 29th annual Grammy awards at Los Angeles' Shrine Auditorium.
Sept [28] She joins Smokey Robinson to guest for a week on the syndicated TV show, "$10,000 Pyramid".

1988

Feb [27] Variously produced by Burt Bacharach and Carole Bayer Sager, Reggie Calloway, Sam Dees and Nick Martinelli, ***All Our Love*** tops the US R&B survey, makes US #39 and charts for a week at UK #80.
Mar *Love Overboard* reaches US #13, having topped the R&B chart on Jan [23].
[30] Gladys Knight & the Pips celebrate 30 years of recording by collecting the Heritage Award at the second annual Soul Train Music Awards, held at the Santa Monica Civic Center.

1989

Jan [14] They win Best Vocal Group category at the NAACP 21st Image Awards.
[30] The group is named the Favorite Soul/R&B Duo Or Group category at the 16th annual American Music Awards, staged at the Shrine Auditorium.
Feb [22] The group wins Best R&B Performance By A Duo Or Group With Vocal category for *Love Overboard* at the 31st annual Grammy awards. (This will effectively be the group's swan song, as Knight splits from the Pips. Patten and Guest will work in the ice-cream business, while brother Merald will continue to tour with Gladys.)
Mar [30] Knight makes her solo debut at Bally's in Las Vegas, NV.
July With Knight now signed as a solo artist to MCA, *Licence To Kill*, her Narada Michael Walden-produced title theme to the latest James Bond movie, hits UK #6.
Nov [11] 18-track, TV-advertised ***The Singles Album*** reaches UK #13.

1990

Nov [25] Knight & the Pips reunite only to perform on the "Motown 30 : What's Goin' On!" special which airs on CBS-TV.

1991

Jan [21] Knight is honored with the Creative Achievement award at the Congress Of Racial Equality - Living The Dream 1991 Awards Dinner at Sheraton Center Hotel & Towers, New York.
June [15] She appears at a Los Angeles benefit concert organized by actor/director Robert Townsend for the family of the late David Ruffin, with Dionne Warwick and Stevie Wonder.
July [27] Knight's solo album ***Good Woman***, including her treatment of Karyn White's *Superwoman* recorded with Dionne Warwick and Patti Labelle, makes US #45.
Sept [19] She sings *I Wish I'd Never Loved You At All* at the "Ray Charles : 50 Years In Music, Uh-Huh!" tribute, set to air on Fox-TV on October 6th.
Nov [26] The "Gladys Knight's Holiday Family Reunion", taped on September 21st at UCLA's Royce Hall, airs on ABC-TV.

1992

Apr [10] Knight is honored at the fifth annual **Essence** Awards, recognizing eight African-American women "who have enriched all of our lives through their contributions to education, to social policy, to public service and the arts", held at New York's Paramount.
[28] She participates in the recording of Quincy Jones' ***Hallelujah!***, a contemporary version of "The Messiah" at the A&M Studios, Hollywood.
Mar [22] Knight appears at the Westbury Music Fair, Westbury, NY, during her current US tour.
June William Guest sets up the Guest Shot record label in Atlanta.
July [4-5] During an eight-date UK visit, Knight plays at London's Hammersmith Odeon.
Oct [16] She participates in a tribute to the late Temptations singer Eddie Kendricks, at a concert in Redondo Beach, CA.
Nov [19] Knight guest stars with Dionne Warwick on Patti Labelle's "Out All Night" US TV sitcom.
Dec [7] She is featured on "The Winans' Real Meaning Of Christmas", which airs on syndicated TV.
[11-12] Knight performs a pair of dates at the Trump Taj Mahal, Atlantic City, NJ.

1993

Feb [19] She plays to a sellout crowd of 4,412 at the Fox Theatre, Detroit, during her current US tour.
May [5] Knight hosts the Atlanta Kids' Celebration at the Omni, Atlanta.
[30] She performs at the National Memorial Day Concert 1993 on the West Lawn in Washington, DC.
Nov Knight contributes *Go On And On*, written, played and produced by Stevie Wonder, to Elton John's newly released ***Duets*** album.

1994

Jan [30] Knight takes part in the "Great Georgia Music Makers" pre-game show at Superbowl XXVIII at Atlanta's Georgia Dome.
Feb [7] She performs *Ain't Nothing Like The Real Thing* with Vince Gill (which is also featured on the compilation ***Rhythm Country And Blues***) at the 21st annual American Music Awards held at the Shrine Auditorium.
[19] Knight participates in the much-hyped Jackson Family Honors show at the MGM Grand Hotel in Las Vegas, NV.
Mar [15] Knight co-hosts the eighth Soul Train Awards at the Shrine Auditorium, with Patti LaBelle and Johnny Gill.
[23] She takes part in "Rhythm Country And Blues - The Concert", benefitting the Country Music Foundation and the Rhythm And Blues Foundation, at the Universal Amphitheatre, Universal City, CA.
Sept [20] Aunt Jemima's Lite Maple Syrup TV ads, starring Knight, begin airing on US TV. A grandmother, Knight is criticized by some African-American groups for her role, being accused of perpetuating black racial stereotypes.
Oct [1] Her solo ***Just For You***, co-produced by Jam and Lewis and Babyface, debuts at its US #53 peak.
[21-22] Knight sells out the Cerritos Center for the Performing Arts, Cerritos, CA, sharing a bill with Michael McDonald.
Nov [15] Frank Sinatra's ***Duets II***, featuring a pairing with Knight and Stevie Wonder on For *Once In My Life*, is released.
Dec [11] During a current round of US dates, Knight sells out the Valley Forge Music Fair, Devon, PA.

1995

Apr [9] Knight performs at the Universal Amphitheatre, during current US tour.
May [24] She takes part in the five-day "1970s Soul Music Festival" in Saint Martin, Guadeloupe.
July [12] Knight sings at the "Let's Stamp Out AIDS" benefit at the Universal Amphitheatre.
Aug [6] She co-hosts the inaugural Soul Train Lady of Soul Awards, from the Santa Monica Auditorium.
Sept [29] Knight joins Aretha Franklin, the Isley Brothers and Kool & the Gang at KISS-FM's "Classic Soul" concert at New York's Madison Square Garden.

1996

Jan [16] Motown finally releases ***The Lost Live Album***, a critically-hailed recording, previously thought to be lost, of a performance the group made on July 27th, 1974 at Detroit's Pine Knob Theater.
[17] Mariah Carey inducts Gladys Knight & the Pips

into the Rock and Roll Hall of Fame at the 11th annual dinner, held at New York's Waldorf Astoria Hotel. The Pips have not performed with Knight since 1990: while Bubba remains her manager, Patten suffered a stroke in 1995 and now moves either with the help of a wheelchair or walker, while Guest is the vice-president of Crew Records in Detroit.

BUDDY KNOX

1956

Knox (b. Wayne Knox, Apr. 14, 1933, Happy, TX), Jimmy Bowen and Don Lanier, all students on athletics scholarships at West Texas State University, Canyon, TX, have formed the Rhythm Orchids the previous year to play college dances and parties, with Knox and Lanier on guitars and Bowen picking stand-up bass. In a three-day session at Norman Petty's recording studio in Clovis, NM, where they meet and recruit drummer Dave Alldred, the trio records three of its own songs. Local Dumas, TX businessman Chester Oliver presses 1,500 copies of a single, coupling *Party Doll*, sung by Knox, and written by him at the age of 15, and *I'm Sticking With You*, sung by Bowen. The record sells out around Dumas and Amarillo, TX, helped by Amarillo DJ Dean Kelly playing *Party Doll*, and the trio decides to form its own label, Triple-D (after KDDD in Dumas, where Bowen has been a DJ), to fill the continuing local demand for the cut.

1957

Jan Lanier's sister in New York sends a copy of the single to Phil Kahl at Roulette Records, which signs the group and flies it to New York to record additional tracks. Roulette markets both sides of the original separately with new B-sides, so *Party Doll* is released, credited to Buddy Knox & the Rhythm Orchids, while *I'm Sticking With You* credits Jimmy Bowen & the Rhythm Orchids.

Apr [12] The group stars in Alan Freed's "Rock'n'Roll Easter Jubilee" show at New York's Paramount Theater.

[13] *Party Doll* hits US #2, selling over a million copies. It is joined on the survey by three hasty cover versions by Steve Lawrence (#10), Wingy Manone (#56), and Roy Brown (#89). *I'm Sticking With You* reaches US #14.

[18] Knox joins the tank corps for six months' active duty as a US army reserve lieutenant. (Prior to this, Roulette organized a 20-song session in New York with him and the group, to avoid a future shortage of tracks.)

May *Party Doll* reaches UK #29.

June With Knox in the army, the follow-up is credited to "Lieutenant Buddy Knox". Another group original, *Rock Your Little Baby To Sleep*, reaches US #23.

Oct The Hawaiian-flavored *Hula Love*, written by Knox as a teenager and closely based on the 1911 song, *My Hula, Hula Love*, makes US #12.

Nov Knox & the Rhythm Orchids perform *Hula Love* in the rock'n'roll movie, "Jamboree".

Dec Alldred leaves the group to become "Dicky Doo" in Dicky Doo & the Don'ts, and is replaced by Chico Hayak.

1958

Mar *Swingin' Daddy* climbs to US #80.

Aug *Somebody Touched Me*, a revival of the 1954 Ruth Brown R&B hit, reaches US #22, the last single to credit the Rhythm Orchids. (Bowen will move to record production, initially with Chancellor. In the mid-'60s, he will become an MOR producer, working with Bing Crosby, Frank Sinatra, Dean Martin, Kenny Rogers and others, later running his own Amos label and, by the '80s becoming the Nashville president of MCA Records, and then Capitol/Liberty in the '90s.)

1959

Jan Double-sided *That's Why I Cry/Teasable Pleasable You*, with Bobby Darin guesting on piano, climbs to US #88/#85.

May *I Think I'm Gonna Kill Myself* peaks at US #55, his last hit for Roulette. A Knox original, it will be covered by Waylon Jennings.

1961

Jan After two commercial flops, Knox moves to Liberty, where Snuff Garrett produces a remake of the six-year-old Clovers R&B hit, *Lovey Dovey*, which reaches US #25.

Mar Knox unearths *Ling Ting Tong*, a 1955 Charms/Five Keys R&B novelty, which peaks at US #65 and is his last US chart appearance. He will make a surprise return to the UK survey with *She's Gone*, at #45 in August the following year.

1968

May After non-charting recordings for the Ruff and Reprise labels, Knox signs to United Artists, with his style more firmly aimed at the C&W market. *Gypsy Man* is a US country hit, without crossing to the pop chart, and a fair-selling album of the same title follows. He will appear in the 1972 country-music movie "Traveling Light", with Waylon Jennings, Bobby Bare, and Jerry Allison of the Crickets, with whom he also co-writes the soundtrack.

1977

Apr Having become a Canadian citizen in 1974 and settled on a farm near Winnipeg, also becoming an active businessman, co-owning a club in Vancouver, BC, Canada, and purchasing real estate in Seattle, WA, he now tours the UK with contemporaries Jack Scott, Warren Smith and Charlie Feathers, and is recorded live with them at London's Rainbow Theatre by EMI, for ***Four Rock'N'Roll Legends***. (He will later record for Redwood Records and his own Sunnyhill label, but releases will be sporadic. In the '80s he will work regularly - and successfully - as a live act in Canada, Europe and the US, notably joining a reunited Rhythm Orchids for a concert in Canyon, in 1989.)

KOOL & THE GANG

James "J.T." Taylor (lead vocals); **Robert "Kool" Bell** (bass); **Ronald Bell** (saxophones); **Claydes Smith** (guitar); **George Brown** (drums); **Dennis "Dee Tee" Thomas** (saxophones); **Robert "Spike" Mickens** (trumpet)

1964

The group is assembled by Robert Bell (b. Oct. 8, 1950, Youngstown, OH), whose father has played with jazz pianist Thelonious Monk, with fellow students at Lincoln High School, Jersey City, NJ, initially as jazz combo the Jazziacs. Its original line-up features Bell, his brother Ronald (b. Nov. 1, 1951, Youngstown), Brown (b. Jan. 5, 1949, Jersey City), Mickens (b. Jersey City) and Thomas (b. Feb. 9, 1951, Jersey City), with Woody Sparrow (guitar) and Rick Westfield (keyboards). In 1967 Sparrow leaves, and is replaced on guitar by Smith (b. Sept. 6, 1948, Jersey City). Finding little earning power in jazz, the band moves towards R&B, and a local Jersey City promoter finds the group regular gigs backing soul acts, under the name the Soul Music Review. Still playing jazz in its spare time, in churches and coffee bars, the group frequently jams with jazzmen Leon Thomas and Pharoah Saunders. The following year, the group becomes a popular R&B attraction, first as the New Dimensions, then the New Flames (known on the local scene as Kool & the Flames). To avoid confusion with James Brown's Famous Flames, a switch is made to Kool & the Gang, and the moniker sticks.

1969

May While playing New York, NY club dates, the band meets writer/producer Gene Redd, who is setting up his own De-Lite Records label. Impressed with the group's tightness as a live unit, and its original material, Redd offers a recording deal.

Oct With the youngest members just graduated from high school, the band debuts for De-Lite with the self-penned funk instrumental *Kool And The Gang*, which makes US #59 (and R&B #19).

1970

Jan Another instrumental, *The Gang's Back Again*, peaks at US #85, from their debut album, the funky jazz/R&B phrased, horns-led ***Kool And The Gang***.

July *Let The Music Take Your Mind* stops at US #78.

Oct *Funky Man* makes US #87.

1971

Apr The performance album, ***Live At The Sex Machine***, is the band's first chart album, at US #122. It includes group compositions, and versions of Dionne Warwick's *Walk On By* and Jim Webb's *Wichita Lineman*.

Oct ***The Best Of Kool And The Gang***, an optimistic early compilation of singles to date, peaks at US #157 and will be followed by the wholly instrumental album, ***Live At P.J.'s***, which reaches US #171 in January.

1973

Apr ***Good Times*** makes US #142.

Oct *Funky Stuff*, the band's first major commercial breakthrough, makes US #29 and R&B #5.

Dec ***Wild And Peaceful***, including *Funky Stuff*, entirely written, produced and arranged by the band, reaches US #33, earning a gold disc for half a million sales, during a 60-week chart stay.

1974

Jan Instrumental album, ***Kool Jazz***, gathering up the more jazz-oriented tracks from three previous albums, reaches US #187.

Mar From ***Wild And Peaceful***, the band's first million-selling single is *Jungle Boogie*, which hits US #4.

June *Hollywood Swinging* hits US #6, a second million seller.

Oct *Higher Plane*, from the band's forthcoming album, peaks at US #37.

Dec ***Light Of Worlds*** reaches US #63, earning the band's second gold album in a 34-week chart run.

1975

Jan The band visits Europe for the first time, playing at the MIDEM music-industry festival in Cannes, France, followed by a UK tour. Tracks from their Rainbow Theatre, London gig are recorded for future album use.

Feb *Rhyme Time People*, co-written by the band with their early live collaborators, Thomas and Saunders, and taken from ***Light Of Worlds***, peaks at US #63.

May Compilation ***Kool And The Gang Greatest Hits!*** reaches US #81.

July *Spirit Of The Boogie*, the title track from forthcoming album, reaches US #35. Its B-side *Summer Madness*, from ***Light Of Worlds***, collects airplay in its own right (and is featured in the movie "Rocky"). The tracks are later chart-listed as a double A-side.

Oct ***Spirit Of The Boogie***, again written and produced by the band, reaches US #48.

Dec Extracted *Caribbean Festival* makes US #55.

1976

May ***Love And Understanding***, which couples five new tracks with live versions of *Hollywood Swinging*, *Summer Madness* and *Universal Sound* from the early 1975 London Rainbow concert, reaches US #68, while the title cut, *Love And Understanding*, makes US #77. Otha Nash (trombone) and Larry Gittens (trumpet) join the band temporarily.

1977

Jan ***Open Sesame*** peaks at US #110, while the title track *Open Sesame* makes #55. (It is the group's last US hit single for three years - a symptom of their early sound now being eclipsed by the exploding disco genre.)

July [2-4] The group performs at the "Brute Music Festival", Callaway, MD, before an estimated 100,000 crowd.

1978

Jan The band's *Open Sesame* is included on the soundtrack album to "Saturday Night Fever", which hits US #1 for 25 weeks and UK #1 for 18 (eventually selling over 25 million copies).
Feb ***The Force*** peaks at US #142. Westfield leaves. As they search for a fresh dance direction, Bell meets soul vocalist James Taylor (b. Aug. 16, 1953, SC) and invites him to join the line-up. A chance meeting in the studio with jazz-funk keyboardist and producer Eumir Deodato (a 1973 hitmaker with *Also Sprach Zarathustra*), results in him becoming the group's new producer, a role he will hold through to 1982. Earl Toon, Jr. also joins the band (on keyboards) in Westfield's place (but will not remain a permanent member). These various changes will result in a simpler, more commercial sound, which includes ballads.

1979

Feb [15] ***Saturday Night Fever*** wins Album Of The Year at the 21st annual Grammy Awards.
Nov [15] Disco-styled *Ladies Night*, the title track from the group's current album, hits UK #9.
Dec [15] The first Deodato-produced, Taylor-fronted Kool & the Gang album, ***Ladies Night***, reaches US #13 and is the group's first platinum album.

1980

Jan [12] *Ladies Night* hits US #8, selling over a million to earn a gold disc.
Mar *Too Hot*, also from the album, hits US #5 and reaches UK #23.
July Third single from ***Ladies Night***, *Hangin' Out*, makes UK #52.
Dec Ronald Bell/Kool & the Gang-penned, pop/dance-fused *Celebration* hits UK #7.

1981

Feb [7] *Celebration* hits US #1 for the first of two weeks and is the band's biggest-selling single, earning a double platinum award for over two million US sales. The song has been used as the welcome-home anthem for the American hostages returned from captivity in Iran on January 26th and as the theme song of the 1981 Superbowl, later also becoming the theme for the Oakland Athletics' baseball team. ***Celebrate***, from which it is taken, hits US #10 and is also a platinum seller.
Mar Divorce-themed soul swayer, *Jones Vs. Jones*, also from ***Celebrate***, reaches UK #17.
June *Take It To The Top*, a third single from the million-selling album, stops at UK #15, while *Jones Vs. Jones* makes US #39.
Dec [5] *Steppin' Out* reaches UK #12
[26] *Take My Heart (You Can Have It If You Want It)* reaches US #17.

1982

Jan Uptempo *Get Down On It* hits UK #3, their first UK top-five success. ***Something Special***, which includes both this and the two December US/UK hit singles, reaches US #12 (the band's third consecutive platinum album).
[25] The group wins the Favorite Band, Duo Or Group, Soul/R&B category at the ninth annual American Music Awards, held at the Shrine Auditorium, Los Angeles, CA.
[30] ***Something Special*** hits UK #10 - their first British chart album.
Feb *Steppin' Out* peaks at US #89.
Mar *Take My Heart (You Can Have It If You Want It)* reaches UK #29.
May *Get Down On It* hits US #10.
Aug [28] Bell/Taylor/Gang-composed *Big Fun* peaks at UK #14.
Oct [9] ***As One***, their last Deodato-produced album, makes UK #49 and will go on to reach US #29 earning another gold disc.
[15-18] The band plays four nights at London's Apollo Victoria Theatre, followed by further UK dates in Manchester and Birmingham.
[16] Percolating *Big Fun* reaches UK #21.
Nov [10] ***As One*** is certified gold by the RIAA.
[13] *Ooh La La La (Let's Go Dancin')* hits UK #6.

1983

Jan *Hi De Hi, Hi De Ho* reaches UK #29, as *Ooh La La La (Let's Go Dancin')* makes US #30.
[17] Kool & the Gang nabs the Favorite Band, Duo Or Group, Soul/R&B category at the tenth annual American Music Awards, again held at the Shrine Auditorium.
June UK-only compilation, ***Twice As Kool***, compiling the group's UK hit singles to date, hits #4.

1984

Jan *Straight Ahead* reaches UK #15, taken from the band-produced ***In The Heart***, which makes US #29 (another gold disc) and UK #18.
Feb *Joanna*, a Taylor/Smith ballad from ***In The Heart***, hits US #2 (behind Culture Club's *Karma Chameleon*) and becomes a million seller, the band's biggest US Singles chart success after *Celebration*.
Mar *Joanna/Tonight* is released as a UK double A-side from the album and hits #2, the group's highest-placed UK single.
[24] ***In The Heart*** is certified gold by the RIAA.
May *Tonight* climbs to US #13, while *(When You Say You Love Somebody) From The Heart* hits UK #7.
Nov [25] While the band is on tour in the UK, Bell, Taylor and Thomas take part in the recording of Band Aid's *Do They Know It's Christmas?* to aid African famine relief.
Dec Jim Bonneford-produced light-dance/pop chugging *Fresh* reaches UK #11.

1985

Jan ***Emergency*** reaches US #28 and UK #47.
Feb [23] *Misled* reaches UK #28.
Mar [9] *Misled* hits US #10.
June *Fresh*, belatedly issued as a US single, hits #4.
Sept Bell/Taylor ballad, *Cherish*, hits US #2 for three weeks, despite a beach-located video promo clip featuring the band's latest fashion garb, behind Dire Straits' *Money For Nothing*. It is another million seller and also hits UK #4.
Nov Extracted title track, *Emergency*, reaches US #18 and UK #50.
Dec The band tours Britain, with major dates at the National Exhibition Centre, Birmingham, W. Midlands, the Brighton Centre, Brighton, E. Sussex and Wembley Arena, Wembley, Middx.

1986

Jan [27] They win the Favorite Band, Duo Or Group, Soul/R&B, and Favorite Album, Soul/R&B categories at the 13th annual American Music Awards, held at the Shrine Auditorium.
Mar [21] The RIAA certifies two million sales of ***Emergency***.

1987

Jan [12] ***Forever*** is certified gold by the RIAA.
[24] Taylor/Bell/Gang-written *Victory* hits US #10, having reached UK #30. It is taken from ***Forever***, which reaches US #25. Both are produced by Khalis Bayyan (who is actually Ronald Bell, having adopted a Moslem name in accordance with his faith - his brother Robert becomes Amir Bayyan). Curtis "Fitz" Williams is now on keyboards, with Clifford Adams and Michael Ray as trombonist and second trumpeter respectively. The album sleeve also notes the death of ex-member, Rick Westfield.
[26] They again collect the Favorite Video, Duo Or Group, Soul/R&B trophy at the 14th annual American Music Awards, held at the Shrine Auditorium.
Feb The group begins a US tour.
Mar *Stone Love* reaches UK #45.
May [2] *Stone Love* hits US #10.
July [25] *Holiday* peaks at US #66.
Oct [31] *Special Way* makes US #72, the group's final new chart single of the decade.

1988

Feb Taylor leaves the band to pursue a solo career, to be replaced by a succession of new lead singers - Gary Brown, Skip Martin (ex-Dazz Band) and Odeen Mays.
Aug Compilation album, ***Greatest Hits***, is released, including three new tracks, one of which is the band's new single, *Rags To Riches*.
Dec [3] UK-only ***The Singles Collection*** reaches #28.

1989

Jan [14] A remixed reissue of *Celebration* peaks at UK #56.
Mar Building his solo career as James "J.T." Taylor, the singer hits US R&B #2 with *All I Want Is Forever*, a duet ballad with soulstress Regina Belle, also included on the soundtrack to the current "Spinal Tap" movie. It is featured on his debut album, ***Master Of The Game***, released by MCA in December. He will also make UK #63 with *Long Hot Summer Night* and UK #57 with *Feel The Need* in 1991, taken from the album ***Feel The Need***, and UK #59 with *Follow Me* the following year.
Apr [3] Kool & the Gang begins a short UK tour at the Edinburgh Playhouse, Scotland, ending on the 8th at London's Hammersmith Odeon.
May [9] The RIAA certifies gold sales of *Cherish*, *Get Down*, *Joanna* and *Too Hot*.
July Now signed to Mercury Records, the Taylor-less Kool & the Gang struggles commercially, as ***Sweat*** fails to cross over.

1990

Sept [1-3] The group takes part in "Rock'n'Roll's Main Event" at Glen Helen Regional Park in San Bernardino, CA, with Jerry Lee Lewis, the Commodores, Fats Domino, Don McLean, Johnny Rivers, Rick Derringer and Edgar Winter and others.
Oct [27] Among four Kool & the Gang retrospectives issued during the year, ***Kool Love***, released by UK TV-advertising label Telstar, peaks at UK #50. A remixed *Get Down On It (Oliver Momm Mix)* will chart for one week at UK #69 on July [6] the following year.

1993

Apr [27] With Taylor releasing his third solo set ***Baby I'm Back***, and his 1988 departure having clearly affected the group's commercial success to a similar degree to that of Lionel Richie's exit from the Commodores, Kool & the Gang's first album in three years, ***Unite***, is released on the JRS/Mogull Entertainment label, featuring Kool and four other original members with new lead singer Odeen Mays.
July [5-10] The group performs at the Blue Note in Osaka, Japan, before moving on to the Blue Note in Fukuoka, Japan, to play from the 12th to the 17th.

1995

Sept [3] Having released ***NYC Cool*** the previous year, but now reformed with the original line-up including the much-missed Taylor, the group takes part in a Muscular Dystrophy benefit in Portland, OR, which grabs headlines because of support act the Golden Blades, whose lead singer, the ice-skating acid queen Tonya Harding, is showered with bottles and much booing for her vocal prowess.
[29] The group takes part in the "KISS-FM Classic Soul" concert with Aretha Franklin, Gladys Knight and the Isley Brothers, at New York's Madison Square Garden.
Nov Coolio's new single *Too Hot* samples Kool & the Gang's hit of the same name. The group's "Back Together Again" world tour, which will include package dates with similarly veteran disco/soul acts Gap Band and the S.O.S. Band, will get underway in February the following year.

1996

May Newly-signed to Curb Records (US), Kool & the Gang's ***State Of Affairs***, featuring a returning James Taylor, is released.

KRAFTWERK

Ralf Hutter (keyboards, drums, vocals, woodwind, strings); **Florian Schneider-Esleben** (keyboards, drums, vocals, woodwind, strings); **Wolfgang Flur** (electronic drums); **Klaus Roeder** (violin, guitar)

1970

Hutter (b. 1946, Krefeld, West Germany) and woodwind student Schneider-Esleben (b. Apr. 7, 1947, Düsseldorf, West Germany), having met two years earlier while majoring in improvised music at the Düsseldorf Conservatory, join Organisation, influenced by the new wave of German keyboard groups, including Tangerine Dream. The Organisation's debut album, ***Tone Float***, produced by Conny Plank and recorded at a studio inside a Düsseldorf oil refinery, is released through RCA Records. Hutter and Schneider-Esleben leave to form their own band, Kraftwerk (German for "power plant"), recruiting Klaus Dinger and Thomas Homann.

1971

With the economic and innovative use of drum and tape machines and synthesizers, the band's debut album, ***Highrail***, released on the German Philips label, attracts critical attention, but few sales, and Dinger and Homann leave to form Neu. The following year, ***Var*** is released in Germany, while in the UK Vertigo Records releases ***Kraftwerk***, a compilation of material from the group's first two albums.

1973

Nov ***Ralf And Florian*** is released. Self-produced, with help from Plank, it contains a mix of sparse, experimental synthesizer music and traditional string and woodwind parts. In preparation for their next project, the pair adds Flur and Roeder to create a four-piece unit.

1975

May Taken from ***Autobahn***, which has been released the previous November, the uniquely repetitive 22-minute, 30-second title track *Autobahn*, relaying a journey on the German highway system, has received unexpected airplay in both territories, and an edited version now reaches UK #11 and US #25, while ***Autobahn*** hits UK #4 and US #5. Its hi-tech, rhythmic-synthesized style will open doors for many futurist and Eurodisco acts over the next ten years.

Oct Reissued ***Ralf And Florian*** makes US #160. While Roeder is replaced by Karl Bartos, the band leaves Philips/Vertigo to form its own Düsseldorf-based Kling Klang label, licensed through EMI.

Nov ***Radio Aktivitaet*** is released in Germany.

1976

Jan Its English language equivalent ***Radio-Activity***, issued by Capitol, reaches US #140, as Vertigo releases the compilation album, ***Exceller 8***.

Oct The group performs at London's Camden Town Roundhouse.

1977

May ***Trans-Europe Express***, recorded at their own Kling Klang studio, peaks at US #119.

The band tours Britain once again, appearing on stage in typically generic robotic style, wearing mannequin outfits.

1978

May The self-written and self-produced six-track album ***The Man-Machine*** (German title: ***Mensch Maschine***) hits UK #9, selling over 100,000 copies, and climbs to US #130.

June *Trans-Europe Express* makes a belated US #67.

Nov *Neon Lights* peaks at UK #53.

1981

May After a two-year UK chart absence, *Pocket Calculator* makes UK #39. ***Computer World*** reaches UK #15 and US #72 (it will later influence Neil Young's ***Trans***), as the band embarks on a world tour with a transportable stage version of their Kling Klang studio.

July Double A-side, *Computer Love/The Model*, makes UK #36.

1982

Feb [6] Reissued, and by now both a dancefloor and an airplay favorite, *Computer Love/The Model* tops the UK chart, spurring ***Trans-Europe Express*** to make UK #49.

Mar *Showroom Dummies* reaches UK #25, as the group begins another British tour.

1983

Jan With the boom in rhythm boxes and portable tape machines, many electro-pop bands emulate Kraftwerk's rhythm patterns, one of the most successful singles being Afrika Bambaataa's current *Planet Rock*, which borrows the *Trans-Europe Express* riff.

Apr ***Techno Pop*** is scheduled for release (catalog number: EMC 3407), but it is cancelled without official reason, while the group also drops out of a UK tour without comment.

Aug *Tour De France*, commissioned by the organizers of the European bicycle race as its official theme, is released from the four-song album, ***Set***, and reaches UK #22. Following its subsequent exposure in the movie "Breakdance", a remixed version of *Tour De France* will re-chart at UK #24 in September the following year.

1986

Nov After ***Autobahn***, reissued by Parlophone, has made UK #61 in June 1985, its first album for the parent EMI label, ***Electric Café***, climbs to UK #58. Released in the US by Warner Bros., it peaks at #156. Its sleeve features computer graphics from the New York Institute, which subsequently produces an entirely computer-generated video for the title cut. Kraftwerk will perform well-received UK live dates in January the following year, as a second single from the album, *Telephone Call*, follows *Musique Non-Stop*.

1991

June [8] Following another traditionally lengthy activity gap, Kraftwerk has re-emerged to perform four dates in Genoa, Italy in February 1990 as *The Robots* now reaches UK #20.

[22] Remix collection, ***The Mix***, debuts at its UK #15 peak.

July [11] With Bartos and Flur having left to form Elektric with Kraftwerk lyricist Emil Schult, the group, with new recruits Fritz Hijbert and Fernando Fromm-Abrentes, embarks on a nine-date UK tour at Glasgow, Scotland's Barrowlands, set to end on the 20th at London's Brixton Academy.

Nov [2] *Radioactivity* makes UK #43.

1995

May While no official news of a Kraftwerk split has been announced, the group, which occasionally pops up to perform a sprinkling of live dates (including an appearance at the "Greenpeace Stop Sellafield" benefit concert, headlined by U2, at Manchester's G-Mex Centre on June 19th 1992 and a performance at the "Klang Art Music Festival" in Osnabruck, Germany in May 1993 (with another at the "Ars Electronica Festival" in Linz, Austria in June), Kraftwerk has not released a new album in nine years. Bartos is reportedly working on the new Electronic album with Bernard Sumner and Johnny Marr.

BILLY J. KRAMER & THE DAKOTAS

Billy J. Kramer (vocals); **Mike Maxfield** (lead guitar); **Robin MacDonald** (rhythm guitar); **Ray Jones** (bass); **Tony Mansfield** (drums)

1963

Jan [6] Kramer (b. William Howard Ashton, Aug. 19, 1943, Bootle, Lancs.), a British Rail apprentice fitter during the day and formerly a rhythm guitarist for the Phantoms, has been spotted the previous December by Brian Epstein singing at Liverpool's Cavern club with the Coasters, who were voted the #3 favorite group in the local **Mersey Beat** magazine poll. Epstein buys Kramer's contract from manager/promoter Ted Knibbs for £50, signing the artist to a six-year management deal with his NEMS company. The Coasters, who want to keep their day jobs, leave to team up with local singer Chick Graham. Failing to obtain the services of Liverpool's Remo 4 as a backing group, Epstein teams Kramer with Manchester group the Dakotas - Maxfield (b. Feb. 23, 1944, Manchester, Lancs.), MacDonald (b. July 18, 1943, Nairn, Highland, Scotland), Jones (b. Oct. 22, 1939, Oldham, Lancs.) and Mansfield (b. Anthony Bookbinder, May 28, 1943, Salford, Lancs.), who have been playing professionally since February 1962.

Feb After rapid rehearsals and a show at the Cavern, Kramer and the Dakotas leave for a three-week season at the Star-Club in Hamburg, West Germany. They hone their stage act before returning to UK.

Mar [7] Having played on Brian Epstein's package "Mersey Beat Showcase" concert at the Co-operative House, Nottingham, Notts., with the Beatles, Gerry & the Pacemakers and the Big Three, the group is signed to Parlophone by EMI's George Martin. Liverpool songwriter Ralph Bowdler offers *She's My Girl* to record but, because of the Epstein connection, the group has access to John Lennon and Paul McCartney's songs and chooses *I'll Be On My Way*, on which the Beatles have passed, and *Do You Want To Know A Secret?*, recently recorded by the Beatles for their first album.

[14] They cut *Do You Want To Know A Secret?* at Abbey Road Studios in London, but have to re-record the vocals on the 21st after the original version has been lost.

June *Do You Want To Know A Secret?* hits UK #2, behind the Beatles' own *From Me To You*. For its release, the "J." is inserted into Kramer's name for the first time, to distinguish him from other singers named Billy, an idea suggested by John Lennon.

Aug [22] *Bad To Me*, written by Lennon specifically for Kramer and recorded on June 27th, tops the UK chart for the first of three weeks, but is dethroned by the Beatles' *She Loves You*. The Dakotas hit UK #18 with the instrumental *The Cruel Sea*, written 18 months earlier by Maxfield, who chose the title at random when he spotted Nicholas Monserrat's novel on a bookshelf.

[10] The group appears on the 100th edition of ITV show "Thank Your Lucky Stars", with Cliff Richard, the Shadows, the Searchers, Brian Poole & the Tremeloes and Alma Cogan.

Sept Kramer wins a **Melody Maker** poll award as the UK's Best Newcomer Of The Year.

Oct [27] The group appears on ITV's variety show, "Sunday Night At The London Palladium", two weeks after the Beatles' debut.

Nov [5] Kramer visits New York, NY on a promotional visit with Epstein.

[30] *I'll Keep You Satisfied*, the group's third Lennon/McCartney-penned single, hits UK #4, promoted by a 20-date UK tour titled "The Billy J. Kramer Pop Parade", with the Fourmost and Johnny Kidd & the Pirates.

Dec ***Listen To Billy J. Kramer*** reaches UK #11.

[24] The group opens in "The Beatles Christmas

Show", with Rolf Harris, the Barron Knights, Tommy Quickly, the Fourmost and Cilla Black, mixing music and pantomime, at London's Finsbury Park Astoria, set to end on January 11th.

1964

Feb [29] The band begins a 20-date, twice-nightly UK package tour, with Gene Pitney and Cilla Black at the Odeon Cinema, Nottingham, Notts.

Mar [19] Released as a single against Epstein's advice but at Kramer's insistence, a US song by Mort Shuman and John McFarland, *Little Children*, gives the group its biggest UK seller so far, topping the chart after selling 78,000 copies in one day. It dethrones another of Epstein's acts, Cilla Black, and will be displaced by the Beatles' *Can't Buy Me Love*.

Apr [26] The band plays at the annual "**New Musical Express** Poll Winners Concert" at the Empire Pool, Wembley, Middx., with the Beatles, Cliff Richard & the Shadows and the Rolling Stones, among others.

June *Little Children* hits US #7 and is a worldwide million seller.

[7] The group makes its debut on CBS-TV's "The Ed Sullivan Show", during a US tour.

July *Bad To Me*, having originally flopped in the US, is reissued as the B-side to *Little Children*. It picks up airplay in its own right and replaces its A-side in the US Top 10, at #9. Jones leaves the Dakotas, MacDonald switches to bass and Mick Green, ex-Johnny Kidd & the Pirates, joins on rhythm guitar.

[9] The group plays before H.R.H. the Queen Mother at the Royal Agricultural Hall, Stoneleigh Abbey, Kenilworth, Warks.

Aug *From A Window*, a new Lennon/McCartney song, hits UK #10, while *I'll Keep You Satisfied* reaches US #30 and ***Little Children*** makes US #48.

Oct *From A Window* makes US #23.

Dec [16] Kramer guests in "The Music Of Lennon-McCartney", a 50-minute tribute also featuring Peter Sellers, Marianne Faithfull, Cilla Black, Peter and Gordon, Lulu, Esther Phillips and Richard Anthony, which airs on ITV in London. (The rest of the country will see the program the following night.)

1965

Jan *It's Gotta Last Forever* proves an ironic title as it fails to hit the UK chart.

Feb *Billy J. Plays The States*, a 4-track live EP recorded on stage at Long Beach, CA, is released in Britain to moderate sales, as *It's Gotta Last Forever* peaks at US #67.

May [25] They participate in the "British Song Festival" at the Dome, Brighton, East Sussex.

June The group's last hit is Burt Bacharach's *Trains And Boats And Planes*, which makes UK #12 (and US #47), losing out to Bacharach's own version, which hits UK #4.

Aug [22] Maxfield leaves the Dakotas to concentrate on songwriting activities, and signs with Brian Epstein. The Dakotas decide to remain as a trio after his departure.

Sept [18] The group's Blackpool North Pier summer season closes.

Oct [8] The band embarks on an 18-date, twice-nightly "Star Scene 65" UK tour, with bill-toppers the Everly Brothers, and Cilla Black and others, at Bedford Granada, Beds., set to close on the 28th at the ABC Cinema, Wigan, Lancs.

Nov *Neon City* fails to chart. Relying on outside songwriters for material and closely associated with the now-lapsed Mersey boom, the group is failing to keep up with the rapid changes on the pop scene.

Dec [27] They open in the "Mother Goose" pantomime at the Stockton Globe, performing for three weeks.

1966

May [30] The group begins a two-week tour of Poland.

Aug [7] "Gather No Moss", filmed before a live audience in Santa Monica, CA, premieres in the UK at the Futurist Cinema, Birmingham, Warks. The band finds more live work on the UK's northern club-and-cabaret circuit. Mansfield leaves, and Frank Farley, ex-Johnny Kidd sideman, joins. *You Make Me Feel Like Someone* is the last release credited to the group.

1967

Jan *Sorry*, a solo by Kramer (although he still plays live with the Dakotas), does not chart and his contract is not renewed by EMI.

[28] The Dakotas embark on nine-date, twice-nightly UK tour, with the headlining Four Tops, the Merseys, Madeleine Bell, the Remo Four and the Johnny Watson Band, at London's Royal Albert Hall, ending February 5th at the De Montfort Hall, Leicester, Leics.

Apr Kramer covers the Bee Gees' *The Town Of Tuxley Toy Maker* on a one-off release for Reaction Records (with the writers on backing vocals).

1968

Mar The Dakotas split, and Kramer continues his cabaret career as a soloist. He marries shortly afterwards and releases a cover of Nilsson's *1941* on NEMS Records, which gains much UK airplay but no chart place. (He will also revive Lennon and McCartney's *A World Without Love* on NEMS later in the year, before moving to MGM Records for another one-off, *The Colour Of My Love*). His cover of Neil Diamond's *And The Grass Won't Pay No Mind*, will be issued by Polydor in June 1971 under Kramer's real name, William Howard Ashton.

1973

Now signed to Decca Records, for whom he cuts two singles, Kramer tours the US with a new group of Dakotas as part of Richard Nader's "British Re-Invasion Show". Maintaining his performing career in clubs in the UK and Europe, and joining the occasional major nostalgia-concert package, Kramer remains an active performer. Despite lack of chart success, he continues to record: 11 singles appear on seven different UK labels, including two in a brief return to EMI in 1977, and a cover of Elvis Presley's *Blue Christmas* for Hobo, in 1979.

1993

Mar [1] Having recorded variously for the JM, Runaway, RAK and Mean labels during the '80s, Kramer, now settled in Long Island, NY, embarks on the 51-date "Solid Silver Sixties Show 30th Anniversary Tour", with the Searchers and Gerry & the Pacemakers, at the Beau Sejour Centre, Guernsey, set to end May 9th at the London Palladium. (By year's end, EMI releases ***The Best Of Billy J. Kramer & The Dakotas*** on compact disc.)

ALISON KRAUSS

1987

Influenced by the music of past-masters of the bluegrass genre, child-prodigy Krauss (b. July 23, 1971, Champaign, IL), the daughter of a guitar and banjo-playing mother and guitarist father, began playing the violin at age five, initially learning classical music but soon moving to bluegrass-based fiddling. Entering talent contests from the age of eight, she won her first State Fiddle Championship age 12 when she was also voted the Most Promising Fiddle Player by the Midwest Society for the Preservation of Bluegrass in America. Following a string of further fiddle awards and having linked with stand-alone bluegrass band Union Station, her first recordings have appeared on a 1985 album ***Different Strokes*** released by Fiddle Tunes Records which, together with her appearance at the 1986 "Newport Jazz & Folk Festival" has led to her being signed up by folk/roots label Rounder Records which now issues her maiden effort, ***Too Late To Cry*** while she is still just 16 years old. Showcasing her prodigious ability as a bluegrass fiddle-player and her uniquely fragile angelic soprano vocal style, the follow-up album, 1989's ***Two Highways*** (recorded with Union Station) will be nominated in the Best Bluegrass Recording category at the 32nd annual Grammy Awards.

1990

Having spent much of the previous year playing abroad, notably in Israel and Pakistan, Krauss and Union Station are invited to perform at the "International Folklore Festival" in Kiev, Russia, before returning home to tour in support of her their third album ***I've Got That Old Feeling***.

1991

Feb [20] ***I've Got That Old Feeling*** wins the Best Bluegrass Recording category at the 33rd annual Grammy Awards.

Sept [21] The extracted *Steel Rails* becomes her first US Country chart single, on its way to make #73.

1992

Mar ***Every Time You Say Goodbye***, produced by Krauss with the credited Union Station, which currently lines up as Tim Stafford (guitar and vocals), Barry Bales (bass), Adam Steffey (mandolin) and Ron Block (banjo), and including her version of Karla Bonoff's *Lose Again* and Lennon & McCartney's *I Will*, is released to its usual high critical praise.

1993

Feb [24] Krauss & Union Station nab the Best Bluegrass Album trophy (for ***Every Time You Say Goodbye***) at the 35th annual Grammy Awards held at Los Angeles, CA's Shrine Auditorium.

Mar [27] Dolly Parton's ***Slow Dancing With The Moon***, including a duet with Krauss on *More Where That Came From*, reaches US #16.

June [26] Krauss in inducted by Garth Brooks into the Grand Ole Opry in Nashville, TN, the first bluegrass performer to be so honored in 29 years.

Aug [3] Michael McDonald's ***Blink Of An Eye***, including Krauss' backing vocal on *Matters Of The Heart*, is released by Reprise Records.

1994

Oct [1] AIDS research-benefitting various artists album ***Red Hot + Country*** is released by Mercury (US) including Krauss' version of Crosby Stills Nash & Young's *Teach Your Children*, which she has recorded with Suzy Bogguss and Kathy Mattea and an all-star country chorus including Crosby, Stills & Nash.

June ***I Know Who Holds Tomorrow*** is released on Rounder, a collaboration between its producer Krauss and the gospel/country-based Cox Family.

Dec [3] Featured on Shenandoah's ***In The Vicinity Of The Heart***, Krauss' duet with the band on *Somewhere In The Vicinity Of The Heart* begins its US Country chart rise to #7.

1995

Mar [1] ***I Know Who Holds Tomorrow*** wins the Best Southern Gospel, Country Gospel or Bluegrass Gospel Album category at the 37th annual Grammy Awards, held at the Shrine Auditorium.

May [23] Rounder's retrospective of Krauss' best work to date, ***Now That I've Found You : A Collection*** is certified platinum by the RIAA.

June [10] Her first crossover success, *When You Say Nothing At All* makes US #53, as ***Now That I've Found You : A Collection*** reaches US #13.

July [24] She appears on NBC-TV's "The Tonight Show".

Aug [4-5] Krauss performs during Rounder Records Weekend at the Lincoln Center, New York, NY.

Oct [27] Her current US tour visits the Valley Forge Music Fair, Devon, PA, a bill grossing $43,777 from 2,105 enthusiasts.

Nov [20] Confirming her mainstream appeal, Krauss performs on CBS-TV's "Late Show With David Letterman".

Dec [19-21] She participates with Amy Grant, Vince Gill, Gary Chapman and the Nashville Symphony at its third annual holiday concert at the Grand Ole Opry House.

1996

Feb [28] Her version of *Baby, Now That I've Found You* is named Best Female Country Vocal Performance while *Somewhere In The Vicinity Of The Heart* (with Shenandoah) nabs the Best Country Collaboration trophy at the 38th annual Grammy Awards, staged at the Shrine Auditorium.
June Further confirming her appeal to non-country/bluegrass audiences, Krauss participates in this summer's US roots-rock "H.O.R.D.E." tour headlined by Blues Traveler.

LENNY KRAVITZ

1989

Jan An only child with a multi-cultural family heritage (his mother, Roxie, born in Miami, FL, to a Georgian woman (half black, half Cherokee) and a Bahamian father, met her Russian Jewish husband, Sy, while both were working at NBC-TV), Kravitz (b. Leonard Albert Kravitz, May 26, 1964, Brooklyn, New York, NY), who has grown up in New York City, teaching himself piano, guitar, drums and bass, moved with his parents to Los Angeles, CA, in 1977, after Roxie has been cast as Helen Willis in "The Jeffersons" CBS-TV series. Having himself secured a number of teen acting roles (including a "Bill Cosby" special and commercials for Burger King and action doll, Johnny West), Kravitz has joined the California Boys Choir while still attending Beverly Hills High (90210), with classmates Slash, Chynna Phillips and Maria McKee. Weaned on James Brown, Jimi Hendrix, Led Zeppelin and Bob Marley, he left home at age 16 and, determined on a musical career, initially under the name Romeo Blue, has recorded a 10-song demo with money from his father, which has interested I.R.S. Records, who schedule, but fail to release, one cut, *Romeo*. This now leads to a more permanent agreement with Virgin America, which signs him to cut a debut disc under his real name. (His parents split up in 1985.)
Nov [25] Having wed "The Cosby Show" starlet Lisa Bonet (whom he met at a New Edition gig), Kravitz's solo debut, the rock/soul meld ***Let Love Rule***, including *Fear* (with lyrics by Bonet), enters the US chart. The self-penned, produced-and-performed effort, heavily inspired by '60s culture, is conversely revered or criticized for being retrogressive, a musical obsession which will underpin his first three albums, complemented by his hippie image, which includes wearing flared Wrangler jeans, flowery shirts and tattoos, including a chrysanthemum on his backside.

1990

Jan [19] Kravitz begins a US tour, supporting Tom Petty, set to end on June 3rd.
Feb Title cut, *Let Love Rule*, peaks at US #89.
[10] ***Let Love Rule*** finally makes US #61.
May [14] Kravitz begins an eight-date UK tour at Glasgow, Scotland's Mayfair club, set to close on the 24th at London's Town & Country club, as ***Let Love Rule*** climbs to UK #56.
[26] He plays at Los Angeles' Dodger Stadium, opening for David Bowie.
June [2] The extracted *Mr. Cabdriver* peaks at UK #58.
[18] Kravitz guests on NBC-TV's "The Tonight Show".
July He begins recording his second album, at the Waterfront Studios in Hoboken, NJ.
Aug *Let Love Rule*, featuring a version of John Lennon's *Cold Turkey* on the B-side, makes UK #39.
Dec [15] Madonna's *Justify My Love*, co-written by Kravitz and ex-Prince associate Ingrid Chavez, though solely credited to Kravitz, and co-produced by him with Andre Betts, hits UK #2. (During recording sessions for the single, Madonna has given Kravitz a skull and crossbones ring.)
[21-22] Having completed a seven-night stretch at New York's Beacon Theatre, supporting Bob Dylan, Kravitz takes part in two John Lennon tribute concerts at the Tokyo Dome, Tokyo, Japan.

1991

Jan [5] *Justify My Love* tops the US Hot 100. Chavez subsequently sues Kravitz, in June, for a credit and royalty share. (Kravitz, currently going through a traumatic separation from Bonet, will subsequently say in **Details**: "I didn't want her name on it because I didn't want us associated. It wasn't something I wanted to put in my wife's face. It was out of respect.")
Mar [9] A benefit cover of the Plastic Ono Band's *Give Peace A Chance*, recorded by the Peace Choir, a one-off, all-star ensemble assembled by Kravitz (who has also added new lyrics and has produced the cut), and Sean and Yoko Ono Lennon, makes US #54.
[30] Previewing a forthcoming album, *Always On The Run* makes UK #41.
Apr [13] Kravitz' self-produced sophomore album, ***Mama Said***, featuring Slash and Sean Ono Lennon among its musical guests, and documenting the end of his marriage, enters the UK chart, set to hit #8 during a half-year residency.
[22] Kravitz guests on syndicated TV's "The Arsenio Hall Show".
May [2] He embarks on an eight-date UK tour at Manchester, Gtr. Manchester's Apollo Theatre, set to end on the 11th at London's Brixton Academy.
[30] Kravitz performs at Le Zenith, Paris, France, during European dates.
June [29] Bonet-aimed, '70s soul-tinged *It Ain't Over 'Til It's Over* reaches UK #11.
Aug [24] *It Ain't Over 'Til It's Over* is his US singles breakthrough, hitting #2 behind Bryan Adams' *(Everything I Do) I Do It For You*.
[31] ***Mama Said*** reaches US #39, earning his first gold disc.
Sept [21] *Stand By My Woman* peaks at UK #55.
Oct [31] Kravitz plays at New York's Beacon Theatre during US dates.
Nov [16] *Stand By My Woman* peaks at US #76.
[24] He begins a six-date UK tour at the Wembley Arena, Wembley, Middx, set to end at the Ice Bowl, Dundonald, Strathclyde, Scotland.
Dec [31] He plays a New Year's Eve concert at the Maple Leaf Gardens, Toronto, ON, Canada, during a major North American tour supporting the Cult.

1992

Feb [19] Still on the tour with the Cult, Kravitz plays to a sellout crowd at New York's Madison Square Garden.
Nov [14] Vanessa Paradis' *Be My Baby*, written and produced by Kravitz, together with her album, ***Vanessa Paradis*** (#45, Nov [7]), hits UK #6.

1993

Feb [6] Kravitz appears on C4-TV's "Saturday Zoo", during a round of UK TV appearances.
Mar [6] *Are You Gonna Go My Way* hits UK #4.
[27] He joins Prince on stage at the latter's Apollo Theatre, New York gig, singing the Purple One's *When You Were Mine*.
Apr [17] Kravitz guests on NBC-TV's "Saturday Night Live".
May [1] With Kravitz having recorded a version of Bill Withers' *Use Me* with Mick Jagger, for the veteran's current solo album, ***Wandering Spirit***, and having written *Line Up* with Aerosmith's Steve Tyler and Joe Perry for their forthcoming ***Get A Grip***, also working on cuts for Al Green and Curtis Mayfield, his third album, ***Are You Gonna Go My Way*** - self written and mainly self-performed, as ever (with help from his touring bassist, Tony Breit, and ex-Broken Homes guitarist, Craig Ross) - peaks at US #12, having already debuted at UK #1 on Mar [13]. It includes his first reggae outing, *Eleutheria*, named after the Bahamian island Eleuthera, where he has rented a house for the past six years and is now building a home, organic garden and recording studio.
[29] *Believe* reaches UK #30.
Kravitz begins a world tour with dates in Europe and Japan, including three sold-out concerts at Budokan, Tokyo, before returning for amphitheatre autumn dates in the US, while his current album goes to #1 in Australia, Belgium and Switzerland, top five across Europe, and platinum in Canada.
June [27] Kravitz performs at London's Brixton Academy before a short European tour, having played the Pyramid Stage at the "Glastonbury Festival", Glastonbury, Somerset, the day before.
July [3-4] He takes part in the Torhout and Wechter festivals in Belgium on successive days.
Aug [16] Kravitz performs at the New Pine Knob Music Theatre, Clarkston, MI, during selected US dates.
Sept [2] Kravitz wins the Best Male Video category (for "Are You Gonna Go My Way") and performs live at the tenth annual MTV Video Music Awards held at the Universal Amphitheatre, Universal City, CA.
[9] He guests on CBS-TV's "Late Show With David Letterman".
[11] *Believe* peaks at US #60.
[18] *Heaven Help*, featuring a video directed by Joel Schumacher, reaches UK #20.
Nov [27] Kravitz plays at Wembley Arena, during his "The Universal Love Tour".
Dec [11] *Is There Any Love In Your Heart* makes UK #52.

1994

Jan [18] ***Reality Blues*** soundtrack album, featuring the new Kravitz song *Spinning Around Over You*, is released. (The following month, Kravitz will contibute *Billy Jack* to the Curtis Mayfield tribute album ***All Men Are Brothers***.)
Feb [5] He opens a seven-date Australian tour at the Entertainment Centre, Brisbane.
[14] Kravitz wins the Best International Male Artist category at the 13th annual BRIT Awards, held at London's Alexandra Palace.
Mar [5] *Heaven Help*, coupled with *Spinning Around Over You*, debuts at its US #80 peak.
July [9] ***Kiss My Ass***, to which Kravitz and Stevie Wonder contribute *Deuce*, debuts at its US #19 peak.
Sept [11-12] Currently touring the US, supporting the Rolling Stones, Kravitz is seen by 90,303 people, breaking a house record at Soldier Field, Chicago, IL.

1995

Jan [25] The RIAA certifies two million sales of ***Are You Gonna Go My Way***.
May [3] ***Mama Said*** is confirmed platinum by the RIAA.
Aug [10] ***Let Love Rule*** is certified gold by the RIAA.
Sept [8] Kravitz guests on "Late Show With David Letterman".
[9] *Rock And Roll Is Dead* debuts at its UK #22 peak.
[23] Self-produced ***Circus***, an attempt to move away from his previously retro-based music, hits UK #5 in its week of entry.
[30] ***Circus*** debuts at its US #10 peak.
Oct [14] *Rock And Roll Is Dead* peaks at US #75.
Nov [13] ***Circus*** is certified gold by the RIAA.
Nov Kravitz joins George Clinton onstage for two of the latter's shows in Los Angeles.
Dec [2] During a brief UK promotional visit, Kravitz appears on ITV's "Scratchy & Co." His mother, Roxie Roker dies the same day age 66.
[8] Kravitz guests on "The Tonight Show".
[23] Title cut *Circus* debuts at its UK #54 peak.

1996

Jan [27] He plays a sellout date at Los Angeles' Wiltern Theatre, during a brief North American tour.
Feb [15] Kravitz returns to "Late Show With David Letterman".
[23] Visiting Europe for a round of promotional appearances, Kravitz guests on C4-TV's "TFI Friday".
Mar [9] *Can't Get You Off My Mind* makes UK #54 in its week of entry.
[23] He plays a one-off London show at Wembley Arena, during a short European tour, taking in Spain, Belgium and Denmark.

May [11] *Can't Get You Off My Mind* makes US #62.
June [6] The annual US "H.O.R.D.E." caravan tour, including Kravitz on its bill, opens its nine-week, 40-city trek in Minneapolis, MN.

KRIS KRISTOFFERSON

1958

Kristofferson (b. June 22, 1936, Brownsville, TX) leaves Pomona College with a Ph.D, to study in the UK at Oxford University on a Rhodes Scholarship, where he also becomes a Golden Gloves boxer. He starts writing songs while in Britain, cutting six tracks with producer Tony Hatch for Top Rank as Kris Carson, signing with Larry Parnes' talent stable. Upon returning home in 1960, Kristofferson joins the US army where he will learns to fly. He subsequently spends much time in Germany as a helicopter pilot. While there, he continues songwriting and performs in clubs at US bases. Several new songs are sent back to the US in 1963, to publisher Marijon Wilkin in Nashville, TN.

1965

He leaves the army with the rank of captain, with an invitation to take up a teaching post at West Point Military Academy. Now writing songs regularly, Kristofferson is about to take up the academic post teaching literature when he meets Johnny Cash, who encourages him to take his songwriting seriously. He moves to Nashville, living economically and working as a janitor at $58 a week for CBS Records Studios, while he tries to get his songs accepted by publishers and artists.

1969

Aug Cash has suggested to Roger Miller that he record Kristofferson's *Me And Bobby McGee*, which now reaches US Country #12 and helps (along with Cash's unpaid PR work) to establish the writer's name.

1970

June Having signed a recording deal with the Nashville-based Monument Records, his freshman album, ***Kristofferson***, is released.
Aug [26] He plays at the "Isle Of Wight Festival" at East Afton Farm, Godshill, Isle of Wight.
Oct [10] Cash's cover of Kristofferson's *Sunday Morning Coming Down* becomes the writer's first US Country #1.

1971

Mar Sammi Smith hits US #8 with Kristofferson's *Help Me Make It Through The Night*. It becomes his first million-selling composition, rapidly followed by Janis Joplin's career-highlight cover of his *Me And Bobby McGee*, which tops the US chart for two weeks, another million seller.
July Kristofferson makes his US chart debut with ***The Silver-Tongued Devil And I***, which peaks at #21 and will be certified gold.
Sept [25] Kristofferson takes part in the "Big Sur Folk Festival", Big Sur, CA, with Joan Baez, Taj Mahal and others.
Oct *Loving Her Was Easier (Than Anything I'll Ever Do Again)* makes US #26.
Nov ***Me And Bobby McGee***, with sleeve notes written by Cash, reaches US #43, earning a second gold disc.
Kristofferson makes his movie-acting debut, also singing four songs, in "Cisco Pike", co-starring Gene Hackman. (By the early '80s, he will be better known for his film acting than for his music.)

1972

Mar [14] Kristofferson wins the Best Country Song category for *Help Me Make It Through The Night* at the 14th annual Grammy Awards.
Apr *Josie* climbs to US #63, while Gladys Knight & the Pips' version of *Help Me Make It Through The Night* makes US #33 (and will reach UK #11 in November).
May ***Border Lord*** makes US #41 during a month when Kristofferson performs at London's Royal Albert Hall.

1973

Jan ***Jesus Was A Capricorn*** reaches US #31, earning another gold disc, while its title track *Jesus Was A Capricorn* makes US #91.
July Kristofferson co-stars with Bob Dylan in Sam Peckinpah's movie, "Pat Garrett And Billy The Kid".
Aug [19] Kristofferson marries singer Rita Coolidge, in Malibu, CA, with his father, a minister, presiding over the ceremony.
Oct Another extract from ***Jesus Was A Capricorn***, the ballad *Why Me* (later often revived by Elvis Presley in concert), reaches US #16, during a 38-week chart run (only a week shy of Johnny Mathis' *Wonderful, Wonderful* 39-week record) and is Kristofferson's only self-performed million-selling single.
Nov Kristofferson has teamed with his wife for ***Full Moon*** (on Coolidge's label, A&M), which reaches US #26.
[8] *Why* is certified gold by the RIAA.
[9] The RIAA certifies ***The Silver Tongued Devil And I*** gold.
[29] ***Jesus Was A Capricorn*** is certified gold by the RIAA.
Dec From the album, the duet *A Song I'd Like To Sing* makes US #49.

1974

Mar [2] Kristofferson and Coolidge win Best Country Vocal Performance By A Duo Or Group for *From The Bottle To The Bottom* at the 16th annual Grammy Awards.
Apr Duet, *Loving Arms*, peaks at US #86.
July Solo album, ***Spooky Lady's Sideshow***, reaches US #78.
Dec [18] ***Me And Bobby McGee*** is certified gold by the RIAA.

1975

Jan ***Breakaway***, again recorded with Coolidge, makes US #103.
May [5] Kristofferson guests on NBC-TV's "The Smothers Brothers Comedy Hour".
Oct [20] ***Full Moon*** is certified gold by the RIAA.

1976

Jan ***Who's To Bless ... And Who's To Blame*** peaks at US #105.
Feb [28] Kristofferson and Coolidge win Best Country Vocal Performance By A Duo Or Group category for *Lover Please* at the 18th annual Grammy Awards.
Kristofferson co-stars with Sarah Miles in the film "The Sailor Who Fell From Grace With The Sea", lensed in the UK. (Their explicit love scenes are rumored to cause trouble between him and Coolidge, particularly when photos of Kristofferson and Miles appear in a subsequent **Playboy** spread.)
Aug ***Surreal Thing*** peaks at US #180.
Dec Kristofferson co-stars with Barbra Streisand in a hit remake of "A Star Is Born". His performance will win him a Golden Globe award as Best Actor In A Motion Picture Comedy Or Musical.

1977

Feb [12] Film soundtrack album ***A Star Is Born***, on which Kristofferson sings five tracks, tops the US chart for the first of six weeks.
June *Watch Closely Now*, from the movie soundtrack, makes US #52 - his last US Singles chart entry.
July Early-material compilation, ***Songs Of Kristofferson***, reaches US #45, while ***A Star Is Born*** tops the UK chart for two weeks.
Sept Kristofferson participates in the "New York Pop Arts Festival" at Radio City Music Hall.
Nov He co-stars with Burt Reynolds in "Semi-Tough".

1978

Apr [18-19] Kristofferson and Coolidge finish a five-date UK tour at London's Royal Albert Hall. While in the UK, he also appears on BBC2-TV's "In Concert" and ITV's "The Muppet Show".
May ***Easter Island*** reaches US #86.
June Kristofferson stars as Rubber Duck in the movie "Convoy", based on C.W. McCall's hit of the same name.
Nov [9] ***Songs Of Kristofferson*** is certified gold by the RIAA.

1979

Jan [9] The "Music For UNICEF" concert, celebrating the International Year Of The Child, takes place in the General Assembly Hall of the United Nations in New York, where Kristofferson sings *Fallen Angels* with Coolidge, donating their royalties from the song to UNICEF. (NBC-TV will air "A Gift Of Song - The Music For UNICEF Concert" the following night.)
Mar ***Natural Act***, with Coolidge, reaches US #106. Kristofferson finally kicks a 20-year heavy-drinking habit, but also separates from his wife.
[2-4] He joins Coolidge, Bonnie Bramlett, Stephen Stills and others to participate in "Havana Jam", a joint US-Cuban concert at the Karl Marx Theater, Havana, Cuba, the first such event for 20 years.
May ***Natural Act*** makes UK #35 his only solo UK chart album.
Dec [2] His six-year marriage to Coolidge ends in divorce.

1983

Jan Having concentrated on acting, with roles in 1980's "Heaven's Gate" and "Rollover" the following year, playing a business mogul opposite Jane Fonda, Kristofferson releases ***The Winning Hand***, featuring duets with Brenda Lee, Willie Nelson and Dolly Parton.

1984

Aug He stars in "Flashpoint" with Treat Williams.
Sept Kristofferson is reunited with his "A Star Is Born" co-star Barbra Streisand on film, when he appears as a bartender in her video for the single *Left In The Dark*.
Nov He teams with Willie Nelson on ***Music From Songwriter*** (from the film "Songwriter", in which they co-star), which reaches US #152.

1985

Mar [18] Kristofferson is inducted into the Songwriters Hall of Fame at the 16th annual awards ceremony, held at the Waldorf Astoria Hotel, New York.
Sept ***Highwayman***, a collaboration with Johnny Cash, Waylon Jennings and Willie Nelson, tops the US Country chart, and makes US #92. The extracted Jimmy Webb-penned *Highwayman* is voted ACM Single Of The Year.
Dec Kristofferson stars in Alan Rudolph's film, "Trouble In Mind".

1986

Jan [27] As a Highwayman, Kristofferson wins the Favorite Video, Duo Or Group, Country, and Favorite Video Single, Country categories at the 13th annual American Music Awards, held at the Shrine Auditorium, Los Angeles, CA.
July [22] At a BMI lunch in Nashville, TN, it is announced that *Help Me Make It Through The Night* has now received its three-millionth play.

1987

Jan [13-18] Kristofferson and Coolidge reunite, professionally, for a week's residence at the Las Vegas, NV Hilton.
Mar Now signed to Mercury Records, Kristofferson issues a new country album with his backing band the Borderlords, ***Repossessed***, including *They Killed Him*, a tribute to Jesus Christ, Mahatma Gandhi and Martin Luther King Jr.
July [4] Kristofferson plays at the "Welcome Home" benefit for Vietnam Veterans, with John Fogerty, Neil Diamond and Stevie Wonder.

[6] He makes a public apology after a memorial plaque given to him by Veterans at the "Welcome Home" benefit is found in a trash can. (He will donate $1,000 to the Vietnamese Veterans Association.)

Sept [19] Kristofferson participates in the "Farm Aid II" charity benefit with Neil Young, John Cougar Mellencamp, Lou Reed and others, at Nebraska University's Memorial Stadium.

1989

Aug Playboy magazine reports that Kristofferson, Sting and Peter Coyote will star in the movie "Sandino", about the Nicaraguan general assassinated in 1934.

Nov His second Mercury-released album, ***Third World Warrior***, continues Kristofferson's country career.

1990

Feb Kristofferson embarks on the "Highwaymen 2" tour with Waylon Jennings, Johnny Cash and Willie Nelson, to support the quartet's ***Highwaymen 2***, which will make US #79 in April.

May The Highwaymen are allowed to continue using the moniker, after the '60s group of the same name has sought to block its use, despite the original group's lead guitarist and singer, Stephen Trott, who is now employed as a Federal Appeals Court judge. Kristofferson contributes *Walk Our Own Road* to Randy Travis' album of duets, ***Heroes & Friends***.

Sept *Help Me Make It Through The Night* is named one of the BMI's Most Performed Songs of 1940-1990.

1991

Apr [9] Kristofferson stars with Willie Nelson in CBS-TV's "Another Pair Of Aces: Three Of A Kind".

Nov [3] He takes part in the Bill Graham "Laughter Love & Music" memorial concert at San Francisco's Golden Gate Park Polo Field, before an estimated crowd of 350,000.

1992

Mar [14] The Highwaymen take part in "Farm Aid V" at the Texas Stadium, Irving, TX.

Apr [13] Kristofferson stars with Dyan Cannon and Tony Curtis in the Arnold Schwarzenegger-directed "Christmas In Connecticut" on the TNT cable channel.

Aug He is a featured performer on board the QE2 when it goes aground near Cuttyhunk off the Massachusetts coast. He also takes part in the third annual "Back To The Ranch" concert in Montauk, Long Island, NY, with Paul Simon, Jennings, Nelson and Cash.

Oct [16] Kristofferson sings *I'll Be Your Baby Tonight* with Willie Nelson at the "Bob Dylan Tribute" from New York's Madison Square Garden.

Nov Following news of Arkansas Governor Bill Clinton's presidential victory, Kristofferson says, "I think, between us, Bill Clinton and I have settled any lingering myths about the brilliance of Rhodes scholars."

1993

Feb [17] The Highwaymen is named Top Vocal Group at the first German American Country Music Federation Awards, held in Nashville, TN.

Apr [10] During a current British tour, the Highwaymen perform at Wembley Arena, Wembley.

May [22] Kristofferson guests on CBS-TV's "Willie Nelson The Big Six-O" birthday celebrations.

[23] The Highwaymen perform in New York's Central Park during the "Country Takes Manhattan" season.

Sept [27] Kristofferson takes part in Jimmy Webb's Avery Fisher Hall concert in New York, with David Crosby, Michael Feinstein and Glen Campbell.

1994

Jan Shanachie Records' ***Brace Yourself - A Tribute To Otis Blackwell***, to which Kristofferson has contributed *All Shook Up*, is released.

Feb [2] He takes part, with Lou Reed, Suzanne Vega and Victoria Williams, in "In My Own Words : A Bunch Of Songwriters Sittin' Around Singing" as part of the Bottom Line's 20th anniversary celebrations.

July [11] Kristofferson performs at the annual "Fleadh" Festival in London's Finsbury Park.

Sept [10] As he finishes a US tour with the Everly Brothers, Kristofferson takes part in "Farm Aid VII" in New Orleans, LA.

Oct [8] Kristofferson co-hosts and narrates "Elvis Aaron Presley : The Tribute", an all-star concert at the Pyramid Arena, Memphis, broadcast on pay-per-view.

1995

Mar Kristofferson is presented with the Roger Miller Songwriter Award for career achievement at the Music City New Country Songwriters Awards.

Apr [4] As the Highwaymen's new album ***The Road Goes On Forever*** is released, Kristofferson's version of *Paperback Writer* appears on the Beatles country tribute album, ***Come Together***.

June [4] The Highwaymen, currently on a US tour, play at the Universal Amphitheatre, Universal City, CA.

Aug [15] ***A Moment Of Forever***, produced by Don Was (who admits in its sleeve notes that "Kris is the most intelligent human I've ever met") and Kristofferson's best-received effort in many years, is released by Justice Records (US), as the Disney channel airs a one-hour BBC-produced documentary on Kristofferson.

Sept [30] He performs at the 35th anniversary concert at New York's Bitter End night spot.

1996

Apr [3] Kristofferson begins a one-week stretch in his Broadway music debut performing in "Joseph And Mary" at New York's Paramount.

L

PATTI LABELLE

1961

Having sung in her local church choir as a girl growing up in south-west Philadelphia, PA, LaBelle (b. Patricia Louise Holt, May 24, 1944, Philadelphia) forms the all-girl vocal group the Blue Belles in Philadelphia, with Nona Hendryx (b. Aug. 18, 1945, Trenton, NJ), Sarah Dash (b. Oct 4, 1942, Trenton) and Cindy Birdsong (b. Dec. 15, 1939, Camden, NJ). Holt and Birdsong have been members of the Ordettes in high school, while Dash and Hendryx have sung in the Del Capris. Now combined, they perform at local gigs organized by promoter Bernard Montague, which leads to them meeting producer Bobby Martin and signing, via Martin, to Newtown Records.

1962

May *I Sold My Heart To The Junkman*, first recorded by the Four Sportsmen for Newtown (whose vocal track Martin wipes from the original, adding new vocals by the girls), reaches US #15. Holt will gradute to lead vocal so Martin boosts her billing in the group and she becomes Patti LaBelle. A ballad, *Down The Aisle (The Wedding Song)*, duly credited to Patti LaBelle & the Blue Belles, will make US #37 in November the following year.

1964

Feb Newly signed to Parkway Records, part of Cameo, Philadelphia's leading independent label, LaBelle's version of the standard ballad *You'll Never Walk Alone*, from the musical "Carousel" (a UK chart-topper by Gerry & the Pacemakers only three months earlier), climbs to US #34.

Dec Another standard cover, *Irish Danny Boy (Londonderry Air)*, makes US #76.

1965

Nov [21] The group opens for the Rolling Stones at the Memorial Auditorium, Dallas, TX.

Dec After a year of recording inaction, the group has signed to Atlantic, their label debut, *All Or Nothing*, climbing to US #68.

1966

Jan [11] The Blue Belles begins a short UK tour at the Cromwellian club in London and will also appear on ITV's "Ready Steady Go!" on the 14th, and "Thank Your Lucky Stars" on the 22nd.

June [24] A 46-date US tour of one-nighters opens in Greensboro, NC, with Otis Redding, Sam & Dave, Percy Sledge, and others.

Dec *Take Me For A Little While* peaks at US #89. (It will be covered by several UK groups, including the Koobas, who just miss the UK Top 50 with it, and will also be revived by another Atlantic act, Vanilla Fudge.) In December the following year, Birdsong will leave the group to join the Supremes (in place of Florence Ballard). The Blue Belles continue as a trio, but leave Atlantic as the hits dry up.

1970

With the trio's career at a low ebb, Vicki Wickham, a UK expatriate who first met the girls as a "Ready Steady Go!" executive when they guested on the show during the 1966 promotional visit, becomes their manager. She abbreviates the group name to LaBelle and updates its image and material.

1971

Oct Having signed with Warner Bros. Records, the trio has cut ***LaBelle***, which gained good reviews but failed to chart, despite a US tour supporting the Who. More commercially successful is ***Gonna Take A Miracle***, on which they sing back-up vocals to Laura Nyro on a collection of group oldies, and which now reaches US #46. Their second Warner album, ***Moonshadow***, six of its songs written by Hendryx, with the group's sound developed into a sleek rock/funk hybrid, will be released the following year.

1974

July Having enveiled a new visual image of tight, shiny glam "space" suits, similar to the glitter-pop costumes sported by many groups currently on the UK chart, while headlining at New York, NY's Bottom Line club the previous year, and newly signed to Epic Records, sessions begin for ***Nightbirds*** with producer Allen Toussaint in New Orleans, backed by the Meters.

Dec ***Nightbirds*** is released in the US, including the funky *Lady Marmalade*, which becomes a substantial club and disco hit.

1975

Mar [29] *Lady Marmalade*, with its distinctive French-language chorus line, "Voulez-vous coucher avec moi ce soir?", tops the US chart for a week, having been certified gold by the RIAA on the 25th. It is written by Bob Crewe and Kenny Nolan (who have also penned the song it has deposed at US #1, Frankie Valli's *My Eyes Adored You*). Its success spurs ***Nightbirds*** to hit US #7.

Apr *Lady Marmalade* is the group's only UK hit, peaking at #17.

May [6] ***Nightbirds*** is also certified gold by the RIAA.

June *What Can I Do For You?* makes US #48.

Oct ***Phoenix*** peaks at US #44.

1976

Oct ***Chameleon*** stops at US #94, after which the trio splits. While LaBelle heads towards the AC/Soul market, Hendryx will conversely continue her R&B/rock leanings, charting in the US with ***Nona*** (#83 in 1983), ***The Art Of Defense*** (#167 the following year) and ***Female Trouble*** (#96 in 1987) followed by Private Music's US release of ***Skin Diver*** in 1989.

1977

Nov Remaining with Epic, Patti LaBelle's maiden solo album, ***Patti LaBelle***, reaches US #62 and is followed by three further Epic releases: ***Tasty*** (US #129 in July 1978), ***It's Alright With Me*** (US #145 in May 1979) and ***Released*** (US #114 in May 1980).

1981

Oct Newly signed to Gamble and Huff's Philadelphia International label and despite hometown support (LaBelle still lives in Philadelphia with her husband and three children), ***The Spirit's In It*** only climbs to US #156.

1982

Sept [9] She opens on Broadway, co-starring with Al Green in Vinnette Carroll's gospel musical, "Your Arm's Too Short To Box With God", at the Alvin Theatre. The scheduled limited engagement of 30 shows will be extended to 80 after rave reviews.

1984

Mar After LaBelle's lengthy recording absence, although she is still signed to Philadelphia International, *If You Only Knew* reaches US #46. Its parent album, ***I'm In Love Again***, makes US #40 and, in a 35-week chart stay, sells over half a million copies in the US, earning a gold disc.

Apr LaBelle guest duets with Bobby Womack on *Love Has Finally Come At Last*, extracted from his US #88 album, ***The Poet II***.

May [29] ***I'm In Love Again*** is certified gold by the RIAA.

Sept She plays Big Mary in the film "A Soldier's Story".

1985

May Newly signed to MCA Records, she has initially recorded two tracks for the soundtrack to "Beverly Hills Cop", the first of which, *New Attitude*, reaches US #17.

July [13] She performs prominently at the "Live Aid" benefit spectacular at the JFK Stadium, in her

hometown of Philadelphia.
Aug Her second "Beverly Hills" Cop track, *Stir It Up*, makes US #41.

1986

June [14] *On My Own*, a Burt Bacharach/Carole Bayer Sager ballad duetted with Michael McDonald (recorded in separate studios on separate coasts - they do not meet until they perform the song together on Johnny Carson's "The Tonight Show" on NBC-TV), heads the US chart for the first of three weeks (having topped the R&B chart on May [17] and been certified gold by the RIAA on May 23rd), while her MCA debut album, ***Winner In You***, showcasing her powerful R&B vocal style to full effect, tops the US R&B survey for eight weeks. The single also hits UK #2, behind Spitting Image's novelty, *The Chicken Song*, though it will hit #1 on the airplay-integrated Network chart.
[27] ***Winner In You*** is certified platinum by the RIAA.
July [19] ***Winner In You*** also tops the US chart for a week, and will make UK #30.
Aug *Oh, People*, its promo video shot by Godley & Creme, reaches UK #26.
Sept [26] *Oh People* peaks at US #29.
Oct LaBelle stars in the NBC-TV movie "Unnatural Causes".
Dec [1] She receives an Award Of Merit from the Philadelphia Art Alliance.
On My Own is named Top R&B Single on **Billboard** magazine's year-end survey.

1987

Feb *Something Special (Is Gonna Happen Tonight)*, from the Bette Midler/Shelley Long-starring film "Outrageous Fortune", is released.
Aug *Just The Facts*, written and produced by Jimmy Jam and Terry Lewis for the Dan Aykroyd/Tom Hanks film, "Dragnet", is issued.

1989

Aug [24] LaBelle plays the Acid Queen in an all-star performance of the Who's "Tommy" at the Universal Amphitheatre, Universal City, CA, with Elton John, Steve Winwood, Phil Collins and Billy Idol.
Oct [21] LaBelle-sung love theme, *If You Asked Me To*, from the soundtrack to the current James Bond movie "Licence To Kill", makes US #79 (and will be revived, with global success, by Celine Dion in 1992), while ***Be Yourself***, including songs by Prince, Diane Warren, and Bacharach and Sager, among others, peaks at US #86.
Nov [15] LaBelle undertakes an extensive US tour with James Ingram at the Orpheum Theatre in Minneapolis, MN, set to end March 11th, 1990, in New York, in support of her recent MCA release.

1990

Jan [15] She is honored with a Lifetime Achievement Award at the sixth annual CORE (Congress Of Racial Equality) awards dinner, at the Sheraton Center, New York.
[18-19] During a current US tour, LaBelle performs at the Fox Theatre, Atlanta, GA, with opener James Ingram.
Feb Motown releases *Forgotten Eyes*, a charity single featuring 100 artists, including Labelle. (All proceeds from the record will go to benefit Retinitis Pigmentosa International.)
Mar [24] She co-hosts the fourth annual Soul Train Awards at Los Angeles, CA's Shrine Auditorium, with Dionne Warwick and Luther Vandross.
Apr [16] LaBelle appears at "Nelson Mandela - An International Tribute For A Free South Africa" at Wembley Stadium, Wembley, Middx.
June [26] She wins the Public Choice Award for Outstanding Female Vocalist and an industry award for Best Rap/Urban Performer at the third annual Philadelphia Music Awards at the Academy, Philadelphia.
July [20] Gladys Knight's ***Good Woman***, on which LaBelle covers Karyn White's *Superwoman* in trio with Knight and Dionne Warwick, enters the US chart.
Oct [19] LaBelle is one of eight African-American women honored by **Essence** magazine, celebrating its 20th anniversary, at Radio City Music Hall, New York.
Nov [25] She performs at the "Motown 30 : What's Goin' On!" special, which airs on CBS-TV.
Dec [4] With her seasonal ***This Christmas*** album released in the US, LaBelle is inducted into Philadelphia's Music Foundation Hall of Fame and is also honored with a bronze plaque on Broad Street.
[29] She participates in the "Lou Rawls Parade Of Stars Telethon", raising money for the United Negro College Fund.
[31] She ends the year with a $113,260-grossing performance at the Fox Theatre, Detroit, IL, supported by Alexander O'Neal.

1991

Mar LaBelle duets with country star Ronnie Milsap for the track *Love Certified*, on his latest album ***Back To The Grindstone***.
[12] She co-hosts the fifth annual Soul Train Awards, at the Shrine Auditorium, with Dionne Warwick and Luther Vandross.
Apr [6] LaBelle takes part in NBC-TV's "Bob Hope's Yellow Ribbon Party", to celebrate the homecoming of American troops from the Gulf.
[19-20] Two dates at the Circle Star Theatre, San Carlos, CA, gross $215,000.
[28] She participates in the recording of Quincy Jones' ***Hallelujah!***, a contemporary version of "The Messiah", at A&M Studios, Hollywood.
May [16] GRP Records releases ***Am I Cool, Or What?***, a homage to cartoon feline Garfield, featuring LaBelle's *I Love It When I'm Naughty*.
June [8] LaBelle serves as MC at the first IAAAM '91 Celebration of African American Music Month dinner at the Wyndham Franklin Plaza Hotel in Philadelphia.
July [30] "The Arsenio Hall Show" syndicated TV program is entirely devoted to LaBelle.
Aug [28] "Going Home To Gospel With Patti LaBelle" from Chicago's Quinn Chapel, airs on PBS-TV.
Sept [7] LaBelle sings *Over The Rainbow* at the "Party For Richard Pryor" in Beverly Hills, CA, set to air on CBS-TV on November 23rd.
[20] "A Comedy Salute To Michael Jordan", with LaBelle one of the featured guests, airs on NBC-TV.
Nov [21] As she finishes a 90% sold-out 35-city US tour to promote ***Burnin'***, despite recently experiencing a heart murmur, and prior to commencing rehearsals for a US tour of the Truman Capote/Harold Arlen musical, "Heart Of Flowers", LaBelle guest-stars on NBC-TV's "A Different World".
[24] At Cyndi Lauper's wedding to actor David Thornton in Manhattan, New York, NY, officiated by Little Richard, LaBelle sings *A Whiter Shade Of Pale*.

1992

Jan [11] LaBelle is named Entertainer Of The Year at the 24th annual NAACP Image Awards, at the Wiltern Theatre, Los Angeles.
Feb [12-16] She plays five sellout dates at the Merriam Theatre, University of the Arts, Philadelphia.
[25] She shares the Best R&B Vocal Performance, Female (for ***Burnin'***) nod with Lisa Fischer, at the 34th annual Grammy Awards, from Radio City Music Hall, New York.
Mar [10] LaBelle hosts the sixth annual Soul Train Music Awards from the Shrine Auditorium.
[14] Released the previous October, ***Burnin'*** makes US #71.
Apr [28] ***Burnin'*** is certified gold by the RIAA, as LaBelle participates in the recording of Quincy Joes' recording of ***Hallelujah!***, a contemporary version of Handel's "Messiah", at A&M Studios in Hollywood.
May [31] LaBelle's recording of *You'll Never Walk Alone* is used to promote a fundraising New York AIDS walk (and will also be used for similar treks in San Francisco, CA on July 19th and Los Angeles on September 20th).
July [18] She attends the wedding ceremony of Whitney Houston and Bobby Brown in Mendham, NJ, before playing the first of three sellout shows at the Westbury Music Fair, Westbury, NY.
Aug [3] Current North American dates include a gig at the Ontario Place Forum, Toronto, ON, Canada.
Sept [19] LaBelle's TV sitcom, "Out All Night", premieres on NBC-TV, in which she plays singer Chelsea Paige, owner of a trendy Los Angeles club.
[24] She performs at the "Jean-Paul Gaultier In LA" fashion benefit for AMFAR AIDS Research at the Shrine Auditorium.
Nov [13] LaBelle is the musical guest on NBC-TV's "The Tonight Show".
[18] She takes part in the all-star "Commitment To Life VI" benefit for the AIDS Project Los Angeles, at the Universal Amphitheatre, honoring Barbra Streisand and David Geffen.
[28] Her performance set, ***Live!***, debuts at its US #135 peak.
Dec She is featured on the soundtrack to the Steve Martin-starring "Leap Of Faith" movie.

1993

Jan [16] LaBelle takes part in the 25th annual NAACP Image Awards ceremony at the Civic Auditorium, Pasadena, CA, set to air on NBC-TV on the 23rd.
[25] She collects the Favorite Female Artist, R&B/Soul trophy (her first ever) at the 20th annual American Music Awards, held at the Shrine Auditorium.
Feb [26] Having appeared on the "Arsenio Hall" show on the 11th, LaBelle now guests on the US syndicated TV show "Whoopi Goldberg".
Mar [4] Honored with a star on Hollywood Walk Of Fame, LaBelle proclaims, "I feel like a queen."
[9] She co-hosts the seventh annual Soul Train Music Awards with Luther Vandross and Natalie Cole, also at the Shrine Auditorium.
Apr [30] LaBelle hosts the sixth annual **Essence** Awards at the Paramount, New York.
May [23] She performs at the Valley Forge Music Fair, Devon, PA, during a current round of US dates.
Nov [2] LaBelle guests on "The Tonight Show".
Dec [12] She sings at the 12th annual "Christmas In Washington" benefit, set to air on NBC-TV on the 15th.

1994

Mar [15] LaBelle co-hosts the eighth annual Soul Train Awards at the Shrine Auditorium.
[23] She performs at "Rhythm Country And Blues - The Concert", benefitting the Country Music Foundation and the Rhythm and Blues Foundation, at the Universal Amphitheatre.
[26] ***Rhythm Country & Blues*** compilation, including LaBelle's duet with Travis Tritt on *When Something Is Wrong With My Baby*, reaches US #18.
May [25] LaBelle once again guests on the "Arsenio Hall" show.
June [25] Featuring her interpretations of some of her favorite songs, ***Gems*** debuts at its US #48 peak.
July [18] She guests on "The Tonight Show".
[28] During her current US tour, LaBelle is joined onstage at her Harborlights Pavilion concert in Boston, MA by Bette Midler and Ruth Pointer on *Over The Rainbow*.
[30] *The Right Kinda Lover* makes US #61.
Sept [3] *The Right Kinda Lover* debuts at its UK #50 peak.
Oct [6] LaBelle opens her own 300-seat cabaret venue, Chez LaBelle, in the Newmarket district of Philadelphia.
[9] She performs at Los Angeles' Greek Theatre at the start of another US tour.
Nov [26] Frank Sinatra's ***Duets II***, featuring a pairing with LaBelle on *Bewitched*, reaches US #29.
Dec [6] ***Gems*** is certified gold by the RIAA.
[28] CBS-TV airs "The 17th Annual Kennedy Center Honors", at which LaBelle performs a tribute to Aretha Franklin with the Four Tops and the choir of Detroit's New Bethel Baptist Church.

1995

Jan [10] She takes part in a tribute concert for Ella Fitzgerald at the Universal Amphitheatre.
Mar [13] LaBelle co-hosts the ninth annual Soul Train Music Awards.
Apr [26] She performs a benefit at the Performing Arts Center at the Manhattan Community College, Manhattan, NY, for the Richard J. Caron Foundation.
June [3] LaBelle performs at the inaugural Blockbuster Entertainment Awards from Hollywood, CA's Pantages Theater, set to air on CBS-TV on the 6th.
July [20] As LaBelle signs with Riverhead Books to write her autobiography, provisionally titled **Don't Block The Blessing**, she plays a sellout show at the Spreckels Theater, San Diego, CA, during a US summer tour.
Sept [30] She performs at the opening night celebrations of the FleetCenter in Boston, backed by the Boston Pops Orchestra, and also duets with James Taylor on *Shower The People*.
Oct [7] Reunited with her former partners for a one-off single under the group name LaBelle, *Turn It Out*, featured on the soundtrack album ***To Wong Foo, Thanks For Everything, Julie Newmar***, hits US #1 on the US Hot Dance Music Chart.
[16] Patti LaBelle sings *I Got Rhythm* with Tony Bennett at the "Tony Bennett : Here's To The Ladies" benefit at the Pantages Theater, set to air on CBS-TV on December 1st.
Nov [2] She is inducted into the Soul Train Hall of Fame and performs *Forever Young* at the 25th Soul Train anniversary from the Shrine Auditorium. (The show will on CBS-TV on the 22nd.)
[19] LaBelle performs at Frank Sinatra's 80th birthday tribute at the Shrine Auditorium.

1996

Jan [20] Soundtrack album ***Waiting To Exhale***, featuring LaBelle's *My Love, Sweet Love*, tops the US chart.
Feb [24] ***The Songs Of West Side Story***, a various artists update of the famous musical featuring a contribution by LaBelle, makes US #65.
Mar [29] LaBelle is honored with the Heritage Award for Outstanding Career Achievements, and performs *Over The Rainbow* at the tenth annual Soul Train Music Awards held at the Shrine Auditorium.
May [13] Having received an honorary degree at the Berklee College of Music commencement ceremonies in Boston the day before, LaBelle nows tapes a TV special with the Boston Pops Orchestra.
July [6] She performs at the Louisiana Superdome, New Orleans, LA, during her 1996 US summer tour.

k.d. lang

1983

lang (b. Kathryn Dawn Lang, Nov. 2, 1961, Consort, AB, Canada), always insisting on the lower-case version of her performing name, at five competing in couple of local festivals, winning one (singing *Robin In The Rain*), has become proficient as both a pianist and guitarist during her teens, also playing Gilbert Blythe in a high-school production of "Anne Of Green Gables" and being placed eighth in a national javelin competition, before leaving school to perform avant-garde and classical music, studying at Red Deer College and joining the musical production of "Country Chorale", eventually setting her sights on a career in country music. Forming a backing band comprising Mike Creber (piano), John Dymond (bass), Gordon Matthews (guitar), Ben Mink (violin) and Michel Pouliot (drums), lang releases her Canada-only maiden album, ***A Truly Western Experience***.

1987

Sept Having earned her performance spurs with five years of North American club dates, lang has been signed to Sire Records, which now releases her sophomore effort, ***Angel With A Lariat***, produced by Dave Edmunds. With a visual image defined by her short, spiky hair and a penchant for wearing men's clothing, the album is largely ignored by traditional US country radio, but lauded by fans of new country, who are also embracing Lyle Lovett and Nanci Griffith.
Dec [5] *Crying*, a powerful duet with Roy Orbison from the film soundtrack to "Hiding Out", enters the US Country chart on its way to #42, becoming a popular live highlight on future tours.

1988

Feb [28] lang performs at the closing ceremony of the 1988 Winter Olympics at the McMahon Stadium in Calgary.
May [28] She makes her pop-chart debut with ***Shadowland***. Produced by Owen Bradley and featuring Brenda Lee, the Jordanaires and Loretta Lynn, among others, it will make US #73.
July [7] lang guests on NBC-TV's "Late Night With David Letterman".

1989

Feb [22] *Crying* wins the Best Country Vocal Collaboration category at the 31st annual Grammy Awards.
June [17] Mostly self-penned, and produced by Ben Mink, ***Absolute Torch And Twang***, credited to k.d. lang & the Reclines (her backing band, named in honor of Patsy Cline), begins a year-long stay on the US chart, eventually reaching #69 on Mar [24], 1990.

1990

Feb [18] Hailed as a hot new artist, lang is pictured on the premiere cover of **Entertainment Weekly**.
[21] She collects the Best Country Vocal Performance, Female trophy for ***Absolute Torch And Twang*** at the 32nd annual Grammy Awards.
Mar [27] ***Absolute Torch And Twang*** is certified gold by the RIAA.
Nov [23] lang, currently featured on the "Dick Tracy" film soundtrack with *Ridin' The Rails*, returns to perform on "Late Night With David Letterman".

1991

Mar [25] ***Absolute Torch And Twang*** is named NARM's 1990 Best Seller and Best Selling Country Album, Female.
May [4] ***Tame Yourself***, a various-artists album to benefit the People for the Ethical Treatment of Animals, to which lang has contributed *Damned Old Dog*, peaks at US #165.
July [14] lang appears on C4-TV's "Town And Country". (By year's end, "Salmonberries", directed by Percy Adlon and co-starring Chuck Connors and lang, as an orphan girl working on the Alaska pipeline, in her first movie role, wins the Grand Prix prize at the 1991 "Montreal Film Festival" in Montreal, PQ, Canada.)

1992

Jan [16] ***Shadowland*** is certified gold by the RIAA.
Mar [28] ***Ingenue*** debuts at its UK #28 peak. A musical hybrid of pop and country, with the viola and vibraphone prominent, the critically-revered and award-winning set will confirm lang as a significant crossover artist.
Apr [3] lang guests on NBC-TV's "The Tonight Show".
May [1] She returns for another appearance on "Late Night With David Letterman".
[13] lang appears on BBC1-TV's "Wogan" at the end of a short UK tour.
[30] *Constant Craving*, extracted from the album, peaks at UK #52, and ***Ingenue*** hits UK #3.
June [5] She opens the first segment of a headlining US tour at the Memorial Auditorium, Burlington, VT, separated by European dates, and set to end on November 4th at the Tower Theatre, Upper Darby, PA.
Aug [10] lang performs on syndicated TV's "The Arsenio Hall Show".
[29] *Crying* finally reaches UK #13.
Sept [26] ***Ingenue***, described by its performer as "nouveau easy listening" and "post-nuclear cabaret", climbs to its US #44 1992 peak.
Oct [6] European dates are highlighted by a performance at London's Royal Albert Hall.
[10] Her breakthrough radio hit, *Constant Craving*, makes US #38.
Dec [10] lang performs on "The Tonight Show".

1993

Jan [19] She appears at PETA's "Animals Ball", during the Presidential Inauguration festivities in Washington, DC.
[25] lang collects the Favorite New Artist, Adult Contemporary trophy at the 20th annual American Music Awards, held at the Shrine Auditorium, Los Angeles, CA.
Feb [16] She sings *No More Tears (Enough Is Enough)* in duet with Erasure's Andy Bell at the 12th annual BRIT Awards, held at London's Alexandra Palace. (The track will subsequently see the light of day on the soundtrack album to the film "Coneheads".)
[24] lang collects the Best Pop Female Vocal trophy (her third win) and performs *Constant Craving* at the 35th annual Grammy Awards, held at the Shrine Auditorium. (In a **USA Today** interview, lang, who declared her lebianism in 1992, says: "In some instances it gets a little crazy, sort of like Beatlemania. I guess you have to expect that with being one of the first people to come out. I always thought of myself as someone like Ronstadt or Roy Orbison or even Elvis, whose association with country was very strong in the early part of their career and then they moved on as a vocalist. To me, its all just music.")
Mar [3] During a UK promotional stop, which has included C4-TV's "Saturday Zoo" and BBC1-TV's "Pebble Mill", lang performs on BBC1-TV's "Top Of The Pops".
[4] She is named Best Female Singer in **Rolling Stone**'s Music Awards Critics' Picks.
[10] ***Ingenue*** is certified platinum by the RIAA.
[13] ***Ingenue***, spurred by its award-winning streak, re-peaks, at US #18.
[20] *Constant Craving* reaches UK #15, as ***Ingenue*** hits UK #3.
[21] ***Ingenue*** wins Album Of The Year, while lang also nabs Songwriter Of The Year (with Ben Mink) and Producer Of The Year (with Mink and Greg Penny), for *Constant Craving* and *The Mind Of Love*, categories at the 22nd annual Juno Awards, at the O'Keefe Centre, Toronto, ON, Canada.
Apr [16] She performs at the "Earth Day" benefit concert headlined by Paul McCartney at the Hollywood Bowl, Hollywood, CA, with proceeds going to PETA, Greenpeace and Friends Of The Earth.
May [1] *The Mind Of Love* charts for a week at UK #72. She is controversially featured on the cover of this month's **Vanity Fair**, being shaved by model Cindy Crawford.
June [21] During her current UK visit, lang appears on BBC1-TV's "Bruce's Guest Night".
[26] *Miss Chatelaine* charts for two weeks at UK #68.
Sept [2] lang wins Best Female Video for "Constant Craving" at the tenth annual MTV Video Music Awards at the Universal Amphitheatre, Universal City, CA.
Nov [13] Her soundtrack to Gus Van Sant movie of the same name, ***Even Cowgirls Get The Blues***, debuts at its UK #36 peak.
[20] ***Even Cowgirls Get The Blues*** bows at its US #82 peak.
Dec [1] lang performs at the George Michael-organized "Concert Of Hope" benefit at the Wembley Arena, Wembley, Middx.
[4] Elton John's ***Duets*** album, to which lang has contributed a paired update of Womack & Womack's *Teardrops*, hits UK #4 in its week of entry, and will reach US #25 on the 11th.
[11] *Just Keep Me Moving* charts for a week at UK #59.

1994

Jan [15] lang guests on BBC2-TV's "Unplugged".
June [1] She duets with Tony Bennett on *Moonglow*

on the latter's "MTV Unplugged" show.
[24] lang takes part in the "LifeBeat" concert at the Beacon Theatre, New York, NY, with Melissa Etheridge, Jon Secada and Sarah McLachlan.
Sept [2] "Salmonberries" finally receives its US premiere.

1995

Feb [27] lang is named Best International Female Artist at the 13th annual BRIT Awards held at London's Alexandra Palace.
Mar [1] She performs *Moonglow* with Tony Bennett at the 37th annual Grammy Awards, held at the Shrine Auditorium.
Sept [30] *If I Were You* charts for a week at UK #53, as the ***Friends - The Album*** soundtrack, featuring a previously unreleased track by lang, is released.
Oct [1] She is featured on an ITV "South Bank" special.
[14] ***All You Can Eat***, a cross-genre album lasting a scant 34 minutes, hits UK #7 in its week of entry.
[16] lang cybertalks with fans on America OnLine.
[28] ***All You Can Eat*** debuts at its US #37 peak.
Dec [3] lang performs at the inaugural VH1 "Fashion And Music Awards", from Lexington Avenue, Manhattan.

1996

Feb [13] She plays to a sellout crowd of 3,496 at the Wang Center for the Performing Arts, Boston, MA.
Mar [7] lang guests on CBS-TV's "Late Show With David Letterman".
[8-10] She plays at New York's Radio City Music Hall.
Apr [7] lang begins an eight-date US tour at the Opera House, Seattle, WA, set to end on the 17th at Centennial Hall, Tucson, AZ.
[23] She embarks on an 11-date UK tour at the Academy, Birmingham, West Midlands, set to end at Wembley Arena on May 9th-10th.
May [18] *You're OK* bows at UK #44.

CYNDI LAUPER

1979

Lauper (b. Cynthia Anne Stephanie Lauper, June 20, 1953, New York, NY), who moved from a Williamsburg suburb to Queens with her mother, brother and sister in 1958, after her parents' divorce, left home in 1970 to hitch-hike through Canada with her dog, Sparkle. Spending the following year studying art at Vermont College, her musical career began in 1974, when she joined Long Island band Doc West as lead singer, before linking with covers band Flyer, with whom she spent the next three years. Losing her voice after intense vocal performing in 1977, doctors say she will never sing again. However, she regains her voice through vocal training with Katie Ayresta. With Lauper meeting sax/keyboards player John Turi the following year, they form Blue Angel, which is now signed to Polydor Records. Issuing ***Blue Angel*** in 1980, the band soon splits (after management and label squabbles), with Lauper going on to work in Screaming Mimi's clothes store. The following year she meets David Wolff, her future manager and beau, while working at Miho's bar in New York, singing current Top 40 songs.

1983

Mar After Lauper has been declared bankrupt in a court case relating to her Blue Angel days the previous year, Wolff secures the singer a deal with CBS/Columbia subsidiary, Portrait, and she begins work on her debut album, with help from Eric Bazilian and Rob Hyman of Philadelphia, PA-band, the Hooters.
Dec Her maiden album, ***She's So Unusual***, produced by Rick Chertoff, is released, showcasing her distinctively quirky, high-pitched pop vocal style.

1984

Mar [10] *Girls Just Want To Have Fun*, penned by Robert Hazard, hits US #2 for the first of two weeks, eventually earning a platinum disc, held off #1 by Van Halen's *Jump*, and UK #2, where it is topped by Frankie Goes To Hollywood's *Relax*.
Apr [5] "Girls Just Want To Have Fun" wins Best Female Video at the second annual American Video Awards.
June [9] Ballad *Time After Time*, co-written by Lauper and Hyman, hits US #1, earning a gold disc (and #3 in the UK where it is again held off #1 by Frankie Goes To Hollywood's *Two Tribes* and the still-hot *Relax*). Its video features her mother Catrine, boyfriend Wolff and mentor, wrestling administrator Lou Albano. (Her first two singles will also both be used in UK TV commercials.) The parent album, ***She's So Unusual***, hits US #4 and UK #16 and will eventually sell over five million US copies.
Sept [8] *She Bop* hits US #3, earning her third gold disc, and makes UK #46.
[18] She wins the Best Female Video category for "Girls Just Want To Have Fun" at the inaugural MTV Video Music Awards, held at Radio City Music Hall, New York, hosted by Dan Aykroyd and Bette Midler.
Dec [8] Her cover of Jules Shear's *All Through The Night* hits US #5, Lauper's fourth consecutive top-five US smash in one year, and peaks at UK #64. She is also named **Billboard**'s Top Pop New Artist.

1985

Jan [28] Following the 12th annual American Music Awards, at which she collects the Favorite Female Artist, Pop/Rock, and Favorite Female Video Artist, Pop/Rock trophies, Lauper joins 45 other artists as USA For Africa at the A&M Studios, Hollywood, CA, to record *We Are The World*.
Feb [9] *Money Changes Everything*, the fifth single from ***She's So Unusual***, reaches US #27.
[26] Lauper wins the Best New Artist category at the 27th annual Grammy Awards.
May [11] Shear's version of *Steady*, written by Shear and Lauper, when she was with Blue Angel, peaks at US #57.
July [13] *The Goonies 'R' Good Enough*, from the film soundtrack to "The Goonies", hits US #10.

1986

Aug Ballad *True Colors*, penned by Tom Kelly and Billy Steinberg, and the first single from the forthcoming ***True Colors***, reaches UK #12.
Sept ***True Colors*** hits US #4 and UK #25. It includes Lauper co-written originals and covers of *What's Going On* and *Iko Iko*. Lauper begins a tour of Australia and Japan.
Oct [25] *True Colors* tops the US chart for the first of two weeks.

1987

Jan [10] *Change Of Heart*, written with Essra Mohawk, and with the Bangles on backing vocals, peaks at UK #67.
Feb [14] *Change Of Heart* hits US #3.
Mar Lauper's cover of Marvin Gaye's *What's Going On* peaks at UK #57.
May [9] *What's Going On* reaches US #12.
June [20] *Boy Blue* peaks at US #71.
Aug Performance video, "Cyndi Lauper In Paris", filmed at Le Zenith concert hall, Paris, France, is released.
Sept [11] She performs at the fourth annual MTV Video Music Awards, held at the Universal Amphitheatre, Universal City, CA. (By year's end, Lauper becomes a born-again Christian, having spent two years heavily involved in the promotion of professional US wrestling.)

1988

June [27] She receives an honorary high-school diploma at Richmond Hill High School Class of 1988, in Queens.
July [39] *Hole In My Heart (All The Way To China)*, from the film "Vibes", in which she makes her acting debut, peaks at US #54.
Oct Lauper joins several US songwriters and performers including Michael Bolton and Holly Knight at the "Music Speaks Louder Than Words" summit in the USSR.

1989

Apr [17] The RIAA certifies gold sales of *She Bop* and *Time After Time* and platinum sales of *Girls Just Want To Have Fun*.
June *I Drove All Night* hits UK #7, her first UK Top 10 single for five years.
July ***A Night To Remember***, co-produced by the artist with Lennie Petze and Phil Ramone, and featuring guests Larry Blackmon, Eric Clapton and Bootsy Collins, among others, reaches US #37 and UK #9.
[8] Steinberg/Kelly-written *I Drove All Night* hits US #6.
Aug *My First Night Without You* peaks at US #62 and UK #53. The accompanying video is closed-captioned for the hearing impaired.
Dec [30] *Heading West* peaks at UK #68.

1990

Apr Now pursuing an acting career - she plays Mary in Disney Channel's Shelley Duvall-produced "Mother Goose Rock'n'Rhyme" and a mermaid in the movie "Paradise Paved" - Lauper returns to Richmond Hill School in Queens to collect her high-school diploma.
July ***Music Speaks Louder Than Words*** compilation, with Lauper's *Cold Sky*, recorded at the 1988 Moscow summit, is released.
[21] Lauper takes part in Roger Waters' performance of "The Wall" at the site of the Berlin Wall in Potzdamer Platz, Berlin, Germany. The event is broadcast live throughout the world and raises money for the Memorial Fund for Disaster Relief.

1991

Mar [9] The Peace Choir's fundraising remake of *Give Peace A Chance*, which features Lauper, makes US #54.
[20-21] She appears at the first "American Music Awards Concert Series" in Yokohama Arena, Tokyo.
Nov [24] Lauper marries actor David Thornton at a wedding in Manhattan, New York, officiated by Little Richard, with Patti LaBelle singing *A Whiter Shade Of Pale*.
Dec [4] The RIAA certifies sales of five million for ***She's So Unusual***.

1992

Apr [5] She sings at an abortion-rights march in Washington, DC.
June [3] She appears on BBC1-TV's "Wogan".
[12] The Lauper-starring comedy/thriller movie, "Off And Running" (originally filmed in 1990), makes its UK debut.
[13] Lauper is featured on BBC1-TV's "Top Of The Pops".
[20] She performs with the host on ITV's "Tom Jones : The Right Time", the same day that *The World Is Stone*, featured in the Tim Rice musical "Tycoon", reaches UK #15.

1993

Jan [25] Lauper sings at the 20th annual American Music Awards at the Shrine Auditorium.
Apr [6] Sony Kids' label releases ***Put On Your Green Shoes***, raising funds to benefit Songwriters and Artists for the Earth, the Earth Island Institute and Save The Children, and featuring a contribution from Lauper.
May [27] She appears on NBC-TV's "Late Night With David Letterman".
July [3] Her first album of the '90s, ***Hat Full Of Stars***, co-produced with Junior Vasquez and featuring the Hooters, debuts at its US #112 peak.
[7] Lauper guests on NBC-TV's "The Tonight Show".
Sept [2] She guests on CBS-TV's "Late Show With David Letterman".
[4] Lauper guests on ABC-TV's "In A New Light '93" two-hour AIDS special "A Beacon In The War Against AIDS".

Nov [13] *That's What I Think* debuts at its UK #31 peak.
[27] ***Hat Full Of Stars*** charts for a week at UK #56.

1994

Jan [15] The extracted *Who Let In The Rain* reaches UK #32.
Feb [7] Lauper presents the Favorite Soul/R&B New Artist Award at the 21st annual American Music Awards.
Aug In addition to directing a music video for her *Hey Now Girls (Girls Just Want To Have Fun)* remix, she also lenses RCA act Fury in the Slaughterhouse video "When I'm Dead And Gone".
Sept [3] Compilation album ***Twelve Deadly Cyns ... And Then Some*** hits UK #2 in its week of entry.
Oct [8] Revised mix now titled *Hey Now Girls (Girls Just Want To Have Fun)* hits UK #4.
[20] Lauper guests on C4-TV's "The Big Breakfast".
Nov [14] The RIAA certifies two million sales of ***True Colors***.

1995

Jan Playboy magazine reports that Lauper will be one of the voices of the three gargoyles in Disney's animated version of "The Hunchback Of Notre Dame".
Feb [11] *I'm Gonna Be Strong*, originally recorded in 1981 with Blue Angel, debuts at its UK #37 peak, as she plays the first of two nights at London's Royal Albert Hall, during her current 13-date UK tour, set to end on the 27th at the Symphony Hall, Birmingham.
July [18] Lauper performs a sellout show at The Academy, New York, the day after guesting on "Late Show With David Letterman".
Aug [18] She guests on "The Tonight Show".
[19] Following global sales of three million copies, ***12 Deadly Cyns ... And Then Some***, now released in the US, makes US #81.
[26] *Come On Home* debuts at its UK #39 peak.
Sept [23] *Hey Now (Girls Just Want To Have Fun)* peaks at US #87.

LED ZEPPELIN

Robert Plant (vocals); **Jimmy Page** (guitar); **John Paul Jones** (bass); **John Bonham** (drums)

1968

July [7] Highly rated UK blues/rock outfit the Yardbirds, whom Page (b. James Patrick Page, Jan. 9, 1944, Heston, Middx.) had joined in June 1966, splits after a gig in Luton, Beds., following a final US tour (during which they have performed *I'm Confused*, later titled *Dazed And Confused*, and *White Summer*, both becoming part of Led Zeppelin's repertoire). Already a guitar and harmonica-playing music veteran, Page joined Neil Christian & the Crusaders in 1960 and has performed on a number of seminal '60s recordings, including hits by Jet Harris & Tony Meehan (*Diamonds*), Them (*Here Comes The Night*), Lulu (*Shout*), the Who (*I Can't Explain*), Dave Berry (*The Crying Game*) and Brenda Lee (*Is It True*).) Together with Yardbirds' bassist, Chris Dreja, he forms the New Yardbirds, who are booked for a ten-day tour of Scandinavia, but Page decides to launch the group with a new line-up, and Dreja quits to become a photographer. Jones (b. John Baldwin, June 3, 1946, Sidcup, Kent), an ex-session man and arranger like Page, joins on bass. Terry Reid and B.J. Wilson of Procol Harum decline recruitment, but Reid recommends 19-year-old ex-Midlands R&B, ex-Listen vocalist, Plant (b. Aug. 20, 1948, West Bromwich, Warks). Page and group manager Peter Grant see Plant perform with a band called Hobbstweedle in Birmingham, Warks. He is invited to join and leaves the Midlands with only his rail fare in his pocket. Plant in turn suggests Bonham (b. May 31, 1948, Bromwich), who is backing acts like Joe Cocker, Chris Farlowe and Tim Rose on the club circuit. He joins, leaving his own group, Band Of Joy.
Sept The New Yardbirds tour Scandinavia, having recorded their first album in two weeks.
Oct [15] They make their live debut at Surrey University as Led Zeppelin. (The Who's drummer, Keith Moon, had often used the phrase "going down like a lead Zeppelin" to describe disastrous gigs: Page likes the phrase, drops the "a", and the group is renamed Led Zeppelin, after a short spell as the New Yardbirds featuring Led Zeppelin.)
[18] The band makes its London Marquee club debut, and will shortly appear on BBC-TV's "How It Is".
Dec [26] The group begins its first US tour in Boston, MA, backing Vanilla Fudge and the MC5, and is an immediate success.

1969

Jan [31] They open for Iron Butterfly, who are so unsettled by the crowd's positive reaction to Led Zeppelin, that they refuse to go on.
Feb With the group signed to Atlantic Records by Jerry Wexler at the recommendation of Dusty Springfield, ***Led Zeppelin***, produced by Page, begins its climb to US #10. Immediately showcasing the ideal rock/blues fusion of Plant's impressive and powerful vocal style and Page's accomplished guitar work, it includes several numbers already popular at their live gigs, including versions of Willie Dixon's *You Shook Me* and Otis Rush's *Can't Quit You*.
Apr *Led Zeppelin* hits UK #6. A decision not to release singles in Britain (at Grant's insistence) leads to a lack of exposure on UK radio and only rare TV appearances. As the group begins its second US tour, this time as bill-toppers, *Good Times Bad Times* makes US #80.
[24-27] A five-week, sell-out US tour opens with three nights at the Fillmore West, San Francisco, CA, on a bill with Julie Driscoll, Brian Auger & the Trinity.
June [13] A five-date UK tour starts at the Town Hall, Birmingham.
[27] The band performs at London's Playhouse Theatre, for BBC Radio's "In Concert".
[28] They play at the "Bath Festival of Blues and Progressive Music" at the Bath & West Royal Showground, Shepton Mallet, Somerset.
[29] Led Zeppelin tops the bill at the "Pop Proms" at London's Royal Albert Hall.
July They participate in the "Newport Jazz And Blues Festival", Newport, RI, despite promoter George Wein announcing that the group will not be appearing because of illness. In fact, the authorities had demanded the cancellation after trouble two nights earlier.
Oct The band appears at a "Sunday Lyceum" concert promoted by Tony Stratton-Smith, and receives the highest fee ever paid to a UK band for a one-off concert.
[17] Led Zeppelin plays at Carnegie Hall, New York, NY, at the start of a 3½-week US tour. It is the first rock concert held there since 1965, when the Rolling Stones caused a ban on future gigs.
Nov [6-8] The band performs at San Francisco's Winterland Ballroom, with the Bonzo Dog Band.
Dec [27] ***Led Zeppelin II*** tops the US survey during a 98-week chart tenure and will eventually sell over six million US units. Recorded and written in hotel rooms and during rehearsals on tour, it features *Whole Lotta Love*, which will become a group anthem (already a UK #13 hit cover for Alexis Korner's C.C.S. in November).
The Financial Times announces that the group has made $5 million in US sales, and comments that, unlike the Beatles, they have not been awarded MBEs for their export achievements. The band is, however, awarded two platinum discs and a gold disc at London's Savoy Hotel, by Mrs. Gwyneth Dunwoody, Parliamentary Secretary to the UK Board of Trade.

1970

Jan Zeppelin's *Whole Lotta Love* hits US #4 and earns the band its only US gold disc single, as the group begins a UK tour, including another date at the Royal Albert Hall.
[31] Plant discharges himself from Kidderminster General Hospital, Kidderminster, Worcs., after receiving facial injuries in a car crash.
Feb [7] ***Led Zeppelin II*** tops the UK chart during a 138-week visit.
[28] Following a threat by Eva von Zeppelin, a relative of airship designer Ferdinand von Zeppelin, to sue if her family name is used in Denmark, Led Zeppelin play a gig in Copenhagen as the Nobs.
Mar Led Zeppelin performs at the "Montreux Jazz Festival", Montreux, Switzerland.
Apr [6] Currently hailed as the world's top live attraction, the group is given the keys to the city of Memphis, TN, before a concert on their current US trek, following which they return home, after almost 18 months of touring and recording. *Living Loving Maid (She's Just A Woman)*, B-side of *Whole Lotta Love*, peaks at US #65.
[13] *Whole Lotta Love* is certified gold by the RIAA.
May [19] The group begins work on its third album, at the Headley Grange country estate.
June [27] Having toured Iceland and turned down $200,000 to play two US concerts, they appear again at the "Bath Festival of Blues and Progressive Music", Shepton Mallet.
Aug The group embarks on another US tour.
Sept Its appearances in New York's Madison Square Garden gross over $100,000 per performance. The band is voted Top Group in a **Melody Maker** poll, after years of Beatles' domination. With the Rolling Stones in tax exile and the Beatles disbanded, Led Zeppelin is currently considered Britain's hottest rock export.
Oct [31] ***Led Zeppelin III***, again produced by Page, and with an acoustic-based change of style, tops the US chart at the beginning of a four-week run, on its way to three platinum sales discs.
Nov [7] ***Led Zeppelin III*** hits UK #1 during a 40-week survey sit-in.

1971

Jan The extracted *Immigrant Song*, co-written, as with the majority of Zeppelin songs, by Page and Plant, reaches US #16.
[9] The group plays at London's Royal Albert Hall during a short UK tour.
Mar [5] Led Zeppelin begins a "thank you" tour for its British fans in the clubs and ballrooms of its early days in 1968, also agreeing to play for the original 1968 fee, if the promoter charges that year's admission fee.
Aug During a six-week stay in Jersey, the group plays impromptu gigs at the Jersey Folk & Blues Club at the Royal Hotel, St. Helier.
Sept A concert in Milan, Italy, ends in a riot, with police tear-gassing the crowd.
Dec [4] Their fourth album, untitled, hits UK #1, having hit US #2 in November. It becomes known as ***Led Zeppelin IV*** (or ***Four Symbols*** after the runic images on its inner sleeve), the group's selling power underlined by the lack of any title or name on the album cover. (In the US, it will stay charted for one week shy of five years, logging some 11 million sales.) Its musical highlight, *Stairway To Heaven*, though never released as a single, not least due to its 8 minute and 1 second length, becomes the group's most identifiable anthem, regarded as a landmark recording in rock history, which will populate "all-time" song polls and radio airwaves well into the '90s.
[20-21] They play Wembley Arena, Wembley, Middx., with circus and novelty acts, during an 11-date UK tour.

1972

Feb [12] *Black Dog*, written by Page, Plant and Jones, reaches US #15.
Apr [15] *Rock And Roll* makes US #47.
July Manager Grant fails to organize a planned Led Zeppelin concert at London's Waterloo train station.
Nov [30] A 24-date UK tour bows at Newcastle City Hall, Newcastle, Tyne & Wear, set to end the weekend before Christmas with two concerts at London's Alexandra Palace.

1973

Apr [14] ***Houses Of The Holy***, broadening the band's musical scope to incorporate elements of reggae, folk and soul, hits UK #1, its sleeve again showing no official title.
May [4] The group opens a 33-concert, 30-city US tour at Braves Stadium in Atlanta, GA, before a crowd of 49,236, grossing $246,180.
[12] ***Houses Of The Holy*** tops the US chart for the first of two weeks, ultimately certified with six platinum discs.
The Financial Times quotes Grant as saying that Led Zeppelin will earn $30 million in the US in the coming year. The group's concert, before 56,800 people, at Tampa Stadium, FL, grosses $309,000, breaking the US attendance and box-office record held by the Beatles for their 1965 Shea Stadium performance.
July [30] A Madison Square Garden concert is filmed for inclusion in the movie, "The Song Remains The Same". The band is robbed of $180,000 from New York's Drake Hotel deposit box, which is never recovered. Meanwhile, *Over The Hills And Far Away* makes US #51.
Oct The group works on fantasy film sequences for a forthcoming movie. Page appears on Maggie Bell's album, ***Suicide Sal***, and Jones writes, produces and plays on Madeleine Bell's album, ***Comin' Atcha***. (Years later Jones will reveal he came close to quitting the band at this time to become choirmaster of Winchester Cathedral.)
Dec *D'yer Mak'er* makes US #20.

1974

Apr [6] The formation of Led Zeppelin's own label, Swan Song, named after an unreleased Page instrumental, is announced. Releasing all subsequent Zeppelin material, its signings will include Bad Company, Maggie Bell, Dave Edmunds and the Pretty Things.
May Swan Song is launched with parties in the US and London.
Aug [15] The group performs in Central Park, New York.

1975

Jan [8] 60,000 tickets for three Led Zeppelin concerts at Madison Square Garden sell out in four hours.
Mar [22] Their first Swan Song album, the double set ***Physical Graffiti***, featuring frantic sitar work by Page on *Kashmir*, tops the US chart at the beginning of a six-week tenure (and will go on to receive four further platinum sales awards), having hit UK #1 the previous week.
Apr 51,000 tickets for three UK concerts at Earls Court, London, sell out in two hours.
May While US President Gerald Ford's daughter tells Dick Cavett on his US talk show that Led Zeppelin is her favorite group, *Trampled Underfoot* reaches US #38.
[17-18, 23-25] The band plays five four-hour shows at London's Earls Court.
June The band members go into tax exile in Switzerland.
Aug [5] Plant and his wife are badly injured in a car crash while on holiday in Rhodes, Greece. In plaster casts, he is flown to Britain for treatment, but is flown out again - on a stretcher - to Jersey, to recuperate, when the time limit on his UK visit (before paying full income tax for the year), expires.

1976

Apr [24] ***Presence***, including the ten-minute opus *Achilles Last Stand*, tops the UK chart for a week.
May [1] ***Presence*** hits US #1, earning double-platinum sales status.
Oct [20] Led Zeppelin's film, "The Song Remains The Same", premieres at the Cinema One in New York, raising $25,000 for the Save The Children Fund.
Nov [13] Soundtrack double album, ***The Song Remains The Same***, recorded live at Madison Square Garden, hits UK #1 and US #2. The group makes its first US TV appearance, performing *Black Dog* on "Don Kirshner's Rock Concert".

1977

Feb [1] The group postpones a US tour when Robert Plant contracts tonsilitis.
May [6] The band plays before a crowd of 76,000 in Michigan, breaking its own attendance record.
[12] Led Zeppelin receives the Outstanding Contribution To British Music award at the 22nd annual Ivor Novello Awards, at London's Grosvenor House Hotel.
July [23] During a US tour, Bonham, manager Peter Grant and a bodyguard are arrested and charged with assault on a security employee of promoter Bill Graham at the Oakland Coliseum, Oakland, CA.
[27] Plant's son Karac dies after falling ill with a stomach infection, causing the cancellation of the remaining dates. Plant flies home, as media reports suggest that the group, appalled by its bad luck, is about to split.

1978

July After a quiet year with his family, Plant re-emerges to play with local musicians, and Led Zeppelin regroups to prepare a new album.
Dec They record at Abba's Polar Studios, Stockholm, Sweden, during their ongoing tax exile.

1979

June The group plays dates in Switzerland, Belgium, Austria, Holland and Germany.
Aug [7] Playing its first UK gig in four years, Zeppelin tops the bill at the "Knebworth Fair", Knebworth, Herts., a major UK outdoor festival.
Sept [8] Released in six different sleeves, ***In Through The Out Door*** hits UK #1, Zeppelin's eighth, and last, consecutive UK chart-topper
[15] ***In Through The Out Door*** hits US #1, eventually selling over five million copies.
Dec Plant, Jones and Bonham join an all-star line-up for a UNICEF "Rock For Kampuchea" benefit concert at London's Hammersmith Odeon.

1980

Feb *Fool In The Rain* reaches US #21.
May The band announces its first full-scale European tour for seven years.
June [27] A concert in Nuremberg, West Germany, is halted after three numbers, when Bonham collapses.
July [7] Led Zeppelin plays what will be its final concert, closing with *Whole Lotta Love*, at the Eissporthalle, West Berlin, West Germany, at the end of the European tour, on the 12th anniversary of the Yardbirds' break-up which gave birth to the group.
Sept They meet at Page's Windsor, Berks. house to rehearse for a US tour.
[25] Bonham is found dead in bed, having choked in his sleep after a heavy drinking bout.
Oct [10] Bonham's funeral takes place at his local parish church in Rushnock, Hereford & Worcs.
Dec [4] A statement is released announcing the group's decision not to continue after "the loss of our dear friend".

1982

Feb Page-composed soundtrack album for Michael Winner's movie, "Death Wish II", reaches UK #40 and US #50.
Oct Page is given a conditional discharge at the Inner London Crown Court, after admitting cocaine possession. The judge hears that he risks losing millions in income if he is unable to tour the US and Japan with his new group in 1983.
Dec ***Coda***, compiled by Page from previously unissued band material, hits UK #4.

1983

Jan ***Coda*** hits US #6.
Feb [7] ***Coda*** is certified platinum - the group's 44th - by the RIAA.
Mar [17] Page performs at the second "Prince's Trust Rock Gala" at London's Royal Albert Hall, alongside fellow axemen, Jeff Beck and Eric Clapton.
Sept [20-21] Page appears at an ARMS fundraiser in aid of multiple sclerosis sufferers, at the Royal Albert Hall, with Beck, Clapton and Steve Winwood, performing *Stairway To Heaven*.
Dec [8] Page plays at a further ARMS fundraiser at Madison Square Garden, having performed at three likewise benefits at San Francisco's Cow Palace from the 1st to the 3rd.

1984

July Page appears with Roy Harper at the "Cambridge Folk Festival", Cambridge, Cambs.
Oct The Honeydrippers, an ad-hoc gathering of Page, Plant, Beck, and Chic's Nile Rodgers, release their only album, ***Volume One***, which will hit US #4 and UK #56, yielding the US #3 hit cover of *Sea Of Love* (which will make UK #56 the following February, when *Rockin' At Midnight* reaches US #25).
[30] The RIAA certifies two million sales of ***The Song Remains The Same***.

1985

Mar Page joins Harper for ***Whatever Happened To Jugula?***, which makes UK #44. Having formed a new combo, the Firm, with Bad Company's vocalist Paul Rodgers, bassist Tony Franklin and drummer Chris Slade, he releases ***The Firm***, which makes UK #15 and US #17.
Apr The Firm's *Radioactive* reaches US #28.
May Follow-up single *Satisfaction Guaranteed* stalls at US #73.
July [13] Zeppelin re-forms, with Phil Collins guesting on drums, for the "Live Aid" benefit extravaganza at JFK Stadium, Philadelphia, PA.
Nov Multinational group the Far Corporation takes *Stairway To Heaven* into the UK chart for the first time, hitting #8.

1986

Jan Led Zeppelin rehearses for a week, with Chic's Tony Thompson on drums, but decides not to re-form.
Mar [22] The Firm's *All The Kings Horses*, a trailer for its new album, peaks at US #61.
Apr Parent album ***Mean Business*** peaks at US #22 and UK #46.
Oct [18] Far Corporation's *Stairway To Heaven* makes US #89.

1987

A belated plagiarism suit filed by Willie Dixon, who claims similarities between his *You Need Love* and Zeppelin's *Whole Lotta Love* is settled out of court.

1988

May [14] Zeppelin regroups again, with Jason Bonham filling his father's role, and performs, reluctantly on Plant's part, *Stairway To Heaven* and *Whole Lotta Love* at Madison Square Garden, as part of Atlantic Records' 40th-year celebration concert.
Sept As Plant's summer tour closes, Page launches American dates (now employing Jason Bonham (drums), John Miles (vocals) and Durban Laverde (bass)) to promote his recent Geffen-released solo album, ***Outrider***, which reaches US #26, having been certified gold on August 23rd, and UK #27.

1989

Feb Los Angeles rock station KLOS begins playing an hour of Led Zeppelin music every night of the year.
Apr New band Dread Zeppelin starts playing reggae versions of Led Zeppelin classics throughout California.
May Long-time manager Peter Grant states that the band will never re-form for touring or any future recording work.
June [9] Page plays with Les Paul at his 72nd birthday party, at New York's Hard Rock Café.

1990

Jan [1] WKRL radio station in St. Petersburg, FL plays *Stairway To Heaven* for 24 hours, as a prelude to

an all-Led Zeppelin format.
[12] The station begins alternating Zeppelin's music with that of Pink Floyd.
May [5] Plant, Page and Jones join Jason Bonham, who is continuing his own career fronting Bonham, for a five-song set at a reception at the Heath Hotel, Bewdley, near Kidderminster, after Bonham's wedding to his childhood sweetheart, Jan Charteris.
Aug [18] Page joins Aerosmith on stage at the "Monsters Of Rock" festival at Castle Donington, Leics., before a crowd of 72,500, playing *Train Kept A-Rollin'*.
[20] Page joins them on stage again at their Marquee club, London gig, playing a blues jam which ends with *Immigrant Song*.
Oct ***Remasters***, a 26-cut, career-highlights collection, digitally remastered by Page, hits UK #10, its US release delayed for 18 months.
Nov Atlantic Records' issue of ***Led Zeppelin***, a 54-track boxed set chronicling the years 1968-78, makes US #18 and UK #48.
Dec [11] The RIAA certifies multi-platinum sales of ***Presence*** (two million), ***Led Zeppelin*** (four million), ***In Through The Out Door*** (five million) and ***Physical Graffiti*** (four million).

1991

Nov Still signed to Geffen Records, Page begins working with former Whitesnake vocalist David Coverdale, Bad English bassist Richie Phillips and Heart drummer Denny Carmasi, with a view to recording and touring in 1992. (Jones, now an in-demand producer, helms projects for Butthole Surfers, Stefan Grossman, Ben E. King, Mission and John Renbourn, arranges strings for R.E.M. and Raging Slab, guests on albums by Brian Eno and Peter Gabriel and writes movie scores and theater pieces.)

1992

Apr [4] Belatedly-released, ***Remasters*** makes US #47.
May ***Stairway To Heaven***, a 12-track various artists compilation of 12 different versions of the classic track, is released in Australia.
[23-24] The first official Zeppelin convention is held at the Royal National Exhibition Halls, Russell Square, London, staged by fanzine **Tight But Loose**.
Aug [11] ***Led Zeppelin II*** is certified multi-platinum by the RIAA for sales of six million.
[20] The RIAA also confirms ***Remasters*** gold and ***Led Zeppelin III*** multi-platinum (three million).
[27] The RIAA confirms sales of six million of ***Houses Of The Holy***.
Sept Stairway To Heaven - Led Zeppelin Uncensored, a chronicle of the legendary seedier side to the band's 12-year career written by Richard Cole, ex-tour manager and bouncer for the band, is published.

1993

Apr [3] 11-song ***Coverdale/Page***, released by Coverdale/Page and produced by Mike Frazier, debuts at its US #5 peak, having done likewise at UK #4 on Mar [27].
[12] The RIAA certifies the ***Led Zeppelin*** boxed set four times platinum.
July [3] Coverdale/Page's *Take Me For A Little While* debuts at its UK #29 peak.
Sept [25] Led Zeppelin's ***Remasters*** debuts at its UK #61 peak.
Oct [9] ***Boxed Set II*** charts for a week at UK #56 and debuts at its US #87 peak.
[23] Coverdale/Page's *Take A Look At Yourself* charts for a week at UK #43.
Nov Having sold over one million US copies of its first boxed venture, ***Led Zeppelin***, Atlantic Records releases the ten-CD boxed set, ***The Complete Studio Recordings***, containing all of Zeppelin's studio recordings, all mastered by Page from the original two track-stereo master tapes, amid rumors that the group is to re-form to appear on "MTV Unplugged".
[16] ***The Complete Studio Recordings*** are certified gold by the RIAA.
Dec [7] Page leaves his handprints in the Guitar Center in Los Angeles, as he is given a star on the Hollywood Rock Walk.

1994

Apr [9] ***Led Zeppelin IV*** re-charts, peaking at UK #48.
[23] Page joins Plant onstage at a Alexis Korner tribute concert at the Buxton Opera House, in Derby, Derbys., fuelling speculation of a reunion.
Aug [25-26] They reunite again at LWT Studios on the South Bank in London, to perform a set for MTV's "Unplugged" series, titled "Unledded".
Oct [12] The MTV 90-minute "Unledded" program, taped in London, Wales and Morocco, receives the series' highest-ever rating. In addition to acoustic versions of Led Zeppelin classics, the show also features eight new songs penned by Page and Plant. (Not invited to the reunion, Jones continues producing, currently for Heart and Diamanda Galas.)
Nov [10] Page and Plant guest on BBC Radio 1FM's "Soundbite".
[19] Page and Plant's ***No Quarter*** hits UK #7 in its week of entry.
[26] ***No Quarter*** debuts at its US #4 peak.
Dec [22] ***No Quarter*** is certified platinum by the RIAA.

1995

Jan [12] Page, Plant and Jones jam with Steve Tyler and Joe Perry on *Train Kept A-Rolling* and a 15-minute medley of *For Your Love*, *Bring It On Home To Me*, *Baby Please Don't Go* and *Long Distance Call*, after Led Zeppelin is inducted into the Rock and Roll Hall of Fame at the tenth annual dinner.
[30] Page and Plant perform *Black Dog* live via satellite from London, prior to receiving a lifetime achievement award at the 22nd annual American Music Awards held at Los Angeles' Shrine Auditorium. Jones accepts the award in Los Angeles.
Apr [8] ***Encomium : A Tribute To Led Zeppelin***, a various artists tribute to Led Zeppelin featuring Sheryl Crow, Stone Temple Pilots, Hootie & the Blowfish, Blind Melon, Duran Duran, 4-Non Blondes, Cracker, Big Head Todd & the Monsters, Rollins, Helmet, Never The Bride and a duet between Plant and Tori Amos, debuts at its US #17 peak.
Sept The Gibson Guitar company launches the Jimmy Page Les Paul guitar in the US.
Dec [4] Page and Plant attend the funeral of former manager Peter Grant in Hellingly, East Sussex.
[24] Page and Plant's *Gallows Pole* reaches UK #35.

1996

Jan [25] ***Encomium : A Tribute To Led Zeppelin*** is voted Best and Worst Tribute Album in **Rolling Stone**'s Readers' Poll.
[26] The RIAA confirms that ***Led Zeppelin IV*** is now the fourth biggest-selling album of all-time in the US with 16 million copies sold, behind ***Rumours*** (17m), ***Eagles Greatest Hits 1971-1975*** (22m) and ***Thriller*** (24m).
see also: **ROBERT PLANT, THE YARDBIRDS**

BRENDA LEE

1956

Mar [31] Lee (b. Brenda Mae Tarpley, Dec. 11, 1944, Lithonia, GA), after performing at many local talent contests including her first, at age five, singing *Take Me Out To The Ball Game* in her home town of Atlanta, GA, makes her debut, at age 11, on ABC-TV's "Ozark Jubilee" show, hosted by country singer Red Foley, who had first spotted her performing in Augusta, GA. With Lee offered a five-year management deal by Top Talent following the program, Dub Albritton becomes her personal manager, a position he will retain until his death in 1972, Lee also tours with Foley's road show, before making national TV appearances on NBC-TV's "The Perry Como Show" and CBS-TV's "The Ed Sullivan Show".
July She signs to Decca Records, which promotes her as "Little Miss Brenda Lee", highlighting her tender years and diminutive stature.
[30] Lee records *Jambalaya* during her first session for Decca.

1957

Mar After modest country success with *Jambalaya* and *I'm Gonna Lassoo Santa Claus*, her pop chart debut is *One Step At A Time*, backed by the Anita Kerr Singers, which makes US #43. (It will be her only single up to 1964 not to be recorded in Nashville, TN, taped instead at Decca's Pythian Temple Studios in New York, NY.)
Aug *Dynamite* makes US #72 and leads to her revamped billing as "Little Miss Dynamite", a reference to her dynamic stage presence, which will stay with her until the mid-'60s.

1959

Mar Lee is booked to play at the Olympia in Paris, France (partly to help drum up publicity in the US). The original show is cancelled when the promoter discovers her age, but her manager leaks a story to the local press alleging that she is a 32-year-old midget, and then gains publicity by denying it. Held over at the Olympia for five weeks, Lee becomes an in-demand name in Europe, performing shows in Germany, Italy and the UK.

1960

Apr After two hitless years, Lee's cover of Ronnie Self's rock ballad, *Sweet Nothin's*, hits US #4 and is a million seller.
May *Sweet Nothin's* hits UK #4.
July [18] The country-styled and self-penned *I'm Sorry* tops the US chart for the first of four weeks and will become another million seller, also reaching UK #12. (Its B-side, *That's All You Gotta Do*, hits US #6.)
Sept Lee embarks on "The Fall Edition Of The Biggest Show Of Stars For 1960" US tour, with Chubby Checker, Bobby Vinton, Fabian and Jimmy Clanton.
Oct [24] Italian-originated ballad, *I Want To Be Wanted*, tops the US chart for a week, her third consecutive million seller. Its B-side, *Just A Little*, also makes US #40, while her maiden album, ***Brenda Lee***, which includes the hit singles, hits US #5, and will spend 13 months on the survey.
Nov *I Want To Be Wanted* makes UK #31.
Dec *Rockin' Around The Christmas Tree* reaches US #14, and will become a Christmas standard. Originally released in 1958, when it sold 5,000 copies, the classic festive smash, with a sax solo by Boots Randolph, will ultimately sell over five million copies.

1961

Jan ***This Is ... Brenda*** hits US #4.
Feb Ballad *Emotions* hits US #7, while the B-side, *I'm Learning About Love*, peaks at US #33.
Mar An early rocker, *Let's Jump The Broomstick*, is reissued in Britain and reaches #12.
Apr *Emotions* reaches UK #45, reflecting the UK's declining interest in her ballad style, despite US Top-10 consistency.
May *You Can Depend On Me* hits US #6.
June ***Emotions*** reaches US #24.
[25] Lee performs in an Alan Freed package show at the Hollywood Bowl, Hollywood, CA, with Bobby Vee, Jerry Lee Lewis, the Shirelles and others.
Aug A return to uptempo material with the Jackie DeShannon-penned gimmick-rocker, *Dum Dum* hits US #4 and makes UK #22. Its ballad B-side, *Eventually*, reaches US #56.
Oct ***All The Way***, including *Dum Dum*, reaches US #17.
Nov Country ballad, *Fool #1*, hits US #3 (another gold disc) and makes UK #38. The uptempo B-side, *Anybody But Me*, climbs to US #31.
Dec The re-promoted *Rockin' Around The Christmas Tree* rolls to US #50.

1962

Mar Ballad *Break It To Me Gently* hits US #4 and UK #46, its uptempo B-side, *So Deep*, making US #52.
Apr ***Sincerely*** reaches US #29.
May Not released in the US, the uptempo *Speak To Me Pretty* is Lee's biggest UK hit, at #3. It is taken from children's movie "Two Little Bears", in which Lee has a cameo role. Meanwhile, the ballad *Everybody Loves Me But You* hits US #6, its rock B-side, *Here Comes That Feeling*, peaking at US #89.
Aug Uptempo *Here Comes That Feeling* is chosen, instead of the A-side, by Decca as a UK follow-up to *Speak To Me Pretty* and hits #5. Back home, a slow DeShannon song, *Heart In Hand*, reaches US #15, its brisk B-side, *It Started All Over Again*, making US #29. Lee performs in a production of the musical "Bye Bye Birdie" in Kansas City, MO.
Oct *It Started All Over Again* reaches #15.
Nov *All Alone Am I* hits US #3 and is another million seller, while the B-side, *Save All Your Lovin' For Me*, peaks at US #53. ***All The Way*** belatedly reaches UK #20.
Dec *Rockin' Around The Christmas Tree* is released in the UK for the first time and hits #6. On its fourth US outing, it makes #59, as ***Brenda, That's All*** reaches US #20.
[30] Lee is slightly hurt as fire guts her Nashville home and she tries to rescue her poodle, Cee Cee, who dies of smoke inhalation.

1963

Feb *All Alone Am I* breaks Lee's UK "ballad jinx", hitting #7, while the double A-side, *You Used To Be/ She'll Never Know*, makes US #32/#47. ***Brenda, That's All*** reaches UK #13.
Apr ***All Alone Am I*** makes US #25.
[24] Lee marries the considerably taller Ronnie Shacklett in Nashville.
May *Losing You* hits US #6 and UK #10, and ***All Alone Am I*** hits UK #8.
[3] After eight days' honeymoon, Lee opens at the Copacabana, New York.
June Lee receives a graduation diploma from a private school in California.
July She signs a 20-year contract with Decca, guaranteeing her $35,000 a year. It also includes a two-film deal with Universal Pictures.
Aug Double A-side, *My Whole World Is Falling Down/I Wonder*, reaches US #24/#25, as *I Wonder* makes UK #14.
Nov *The Grass Is Greener* reaches US #17, and the uptempo B-side, *Sweet Impossible You*, climbs to US #70 and UK #28.

1964

Jan ***Let Me Sing***, which includes *Break It To Me Gently* and *Losing You*, reaches US #39, while *As Usual* reaches US #12.
Feb *As Usual* hits UK #5.
Apr *Think* reaches US #25 and UK #26, the first indication that Lee's chart consistency is being affected by the rise of Merseybeat and group-oriented music which has swept many contemporaries from the chart.
[23] The NARM conference at the Eden Roc Hotel, Miami Beach, FL, presents Lee with the Best Selling Female Vocalist and Top Female Singles Artist awards.
July *Alone With You* stops at US #48, as ***By Request*** climbs to US #90.
Sept *When You Loved Me* makes US #47.
[19] Lee performs at the Paris Olympia, France.
Oct She records in Britain with the Animals' and Herman's Hermits' producer, Mickie Most, in an effort to meet the new musical trends head-on. *Is It True*, penned by UK writers John Carter and Ken Lewis, is rush-released and reaches UK #17.
Nov *Is It True*, featuring Jimmy Page on guitar, also makes US #17.
[2] Lee takes part in the "Royal Command Performance" at the London Palladium.
[14] She begins a 17-date, twice-nightly UK tour, with Manfred Mann, Marty Wilde, Johnny Kidd & the Pirates, Bern Elliott, Heinz, Wayne Fontana & the Mindbenders, and the John Barry Seven, at London's Finsbury Park Astoria, set to end on December 12th at Blackpool's Opera House.
Dec Extracted from ***Merry Christmas***, *Christmas Will Be Just Another Day* reaches UK #29.
[7] Lee performs in "Pop Beat" at London's Royal Albert Hall, with Dave Berry & the Cruisers, Brian Poole & the Tremeloes, the Nashville Teens, the Miracles, Wayne Fontana & the Mindbenders, and the Yardbirds.

1965

Feb A second Most production, *Thanks A Lot*, makes US #45 and UK #41. Its B-side, a cover of Dave Berry's 1964 UK hit *The Crying Game*, climbs to US #87.
May *Truly, Truly, True* peaks at US #54.
July A return to country-style ballad, *Too Many Rivers* reaches US #13, Lee's biggest hit single in over two years.
Aug *Too Many Rivers* makes UK #22, her final UK Singles chart entry.
Oct ***Too Many Rivers*** reaches US #36.
Nov *Rusty Bells* rings at US #33.
[16] Lee arrives in Britain for three weeks of TV and concert engagements.

1966

May She plays a two-week stint at the Cocoanut Grove in Hollywood.
[28] This week's **Billboard** includes a Brenda Lee special supplement.
July ***Bye Bye Blues*** makes US #94 and UK #21, while *Ain't Gonna Cry No More* peaks at US #77.
Aug Compilation album, ***10 Golden Years***, featuring a hit from each year 1956-65, reaches US #70.
Dec Uncharacteristic rock-styled *Coming On Strong* makes US #11.

1967

Feb ***Coming On Strong*** reaches US #94 and, taken from it, *Ride, Ride, Ride* stops at US #37.
June ***For The First Time***, with jazzman Pete Fountain, reaches US #187.
Nov [11] While Lee is in London cutting material with producer Mike Leander in Decca's Studios, she walks out on BBC1-TV's "Dee Time", after producer Terry Henebery refuses to allow her to promote her new single.

1969

Apr *Johnny One Time* makes US #41, after Lee's two-year chart absence. In her country-style ballad, it has much in common with mainstream late-'60s country music, to which Lee is inevitably drawn.
May *You Don't Need Me For Anything Anymore* makes US #84.
June ***Johnny One Time*** reaches US #98. The following year Lee will record ***Memphis Portrait*** with producer Chips Moman.

1973

Apr Kris Kristofferson-penned *Nobody Wins* is her last US Hot 100 entry, at US #70 (though it also tops the US Country chart). Lee will concentrate on country music for the remainder of her career. Released from Decca before her official contract expiry, Lee moves to Elektra in July 1977 (her only recording for the label is a country single), before re-signing to MCA in Nashville, in 1979.

1980

Nov TV-promoted compilation, ***Little Miss Dynamite***, on Warwick Records, reaches UK #15. The following March Lee will feature in the Burt Reynolds/Jackie Gleason film, "Smokey And The Bandit II", as the Nice Lady.

1984

Jan With Lee having been inducted into the Georgia Music Hall of Fame the prrevious year, the double compilation, ***25th Anniversary***, peaks at UK #65.
Mar [16-17] During a UK visit, Lee performs a pair of dates at Baileys, Watford, Herts. A further TV-promoted retrospective, ***The Very Best Of Brenda Lee***, will reach UK #16 in April the following year.

1988

May k.d. lang's ***Shadowland***, featuring backing vocals by Lee with Kitty Wells and Loretta Lynn, is released.
Aug [4] Lee files suit for $20 million against MCA Records in the Davidson County, TN Chancery Court, for failing to account for sales, licensing her records without her authorization, neglecting foreign licensing and blocking her attempts to make audits. The two parties will reach agreement on August 25th the following year.

1994

Oct [22] Featured on the soundtrack to the 1990 "Dick Tracy" movie and signed to Warner Bros. Records, the same year, Lee has continued to perform throughout the '90s, not least at the "Elvis Presley Birthday Banquet" at Graceland, Memphis, TN, to mark the 15th anniversary of his death on January 8th 1992, and regularly appears in the country veteran capital of Branson, MO. Her fourth UK-charting compilation, ***The Very Best Of Brenda Lee With Love*** now reaches UK #20.

THE LEFT BANKE

Michael Brown (keyboards);
Steve Martin (vocals); **Jeff Winfield** (guitar);
Tom Finn (bass); **George Cameron** (drums)

1964

Working in New York, NY as an assistant at his father Harry's World United recording studio and playing piano for Reparata & the Delrons, classically-trained musician Brown (b. Michael Lookofsky, Apr. 25, 1949, New York) first meets engineer's assistant Martin (who has just arrived in New York from Madrid, Spain), Cameron and Finn. The latter, recently in the Magic Plants (who have recorded at the studios), first met Cameron when, as a member of the Castels, he performed on the same bill as the drummer, who was playing with the Morticians. Blending classical influences with "British invasion"-style pop-rock, the newly-formed Left Banke begins experimenting and rehearsing Beatles, Rolling Stones and Zombies covers, while working on original material including *I've Got Something On My Mind* and *I Haven't Got The Nerve*, recorded towards the end of the 1965. Harry Lookofsky grooms their talent for harmony singing and unusual arrangements, and builds their tracks to professional production standards, but initially fails to interest record companies, causing the outfit to temporarily dissolve, with Brown heading to California.

1966

Mar With Brown joined in the Golden State by Cameron, Finn and Martin, the band adds vocals to the backing track of *Walk Away Renée*, a baroque-styled arrangement of a ballad co-written by Brown about Finn's girlfriend, Renée Fladen, which will prove sufficiently offbeat to be turned down by several labels before it is released by Mercury's subsidiary label, Smash Records, in July, at the instigation of the parent company's Charlie Fach.
Oct *Walk Away Renée* hits US #6.

1967

Feb *Pretty Ballerina* reaches US #15. Rick Brand (ex-Spyders) replaces Winfield on guitar. A rift in the group has developed and, as owner of the name Left Banke, Brown, unenthusiastic about touring, retires to the studio to record *Ivy Ivy* and *And Suddenly* with vocalist Bert Sommer. These will fail to chart in May, when Smash declines to promote them, while the two group factions are at loggerheads. By the time they reconcile, both *Ivy Ivy* and the rapidly-issued follow-up, *She May Call You Up Tonight*, are lost causes.

May ***Walk Away Renée/Pretty Ballerina***, recorded in January, peaks at US #67.

Sept Having temporarily reconciled, the group, with Brown, records *Desirée* and *In The Morning Light* at Capitol Studios in New York.

Oct *Desirée* peaks at US #98 and is their last chart entry. Brown leaves for good, followed by Brand. With the Left Banke name left to Finn, Martin and Cameron, they will record four more singles.

1968

Jan A cover version of *Walk Away Renée* by the Four Tops hits UK #3, and reaches US #14 in March.

Aug A more unexpected cover version of *And Suddenly* (the B-side of the ill-fated *Ivy Ivy*), by Cherry People, makes US #45.

Oct The trio returns to the studio to cut *Goodbye Holly* and *Sing Little Bird Sing* with *Green Tambourine*-producer, Paul Leka.

Nov ***Left Banke, Too*** is released, featuring future Aerosmith frontman, Steven Tyler, on backing vocals for three tracks, but its commercial failure results in the Left Banke splitting.

1969

Nov Martin and Brown team up to release the one-off, *Myrah/Pedestal*, following which Brown joins forces with Montage, writing, producing, playing keyboards and vocally arranging most of its only album, ***Montage***, released by Laurie Records.

1971

Martin releases *Two By Two/Love Songs In The Night*, both written by Brown, but it proves to be a one-off reunion. Brown and vocalist Ian Lloyd go on to form Stories, with Steve Love (guitar) and Brian Madey (drums), signing to Kama Sutra Records.

1973

Aug [25] After the band's *I'm Coming Home* has made US #42 with the accompanying debut album, ***Stories*** peaking at #182 in August 1972, Stories enjoy its biggest hit with a cover of Hot Chocolate's *Brother Louie*, which tops the US chart and sells over a million. Meanwhile Brown has left the group during the recording sessions for ***Stories About Us***, which reaches US #29.

1976

Brown forms the Beckies, who release ***The Beckies*** on Sire Records, with Mayo James McAllister and Gary Hodgden from Kansas City band Chesmann Square, and Scott Trusty. Tom Finn provides harmony vocals for one song on the album.

1978

Feb Martin, Finn and Cameron attempt to re-form the Left Banke. They record an album's worth of material, which will remain unreleased until 1986 (***Voices Calling***), and *And One Day*, a single issued in the US, during the autumn, by Camerica Records. (In the mid-'80s, US and UK archive labels Rhino and Bam Caruso will reissue all Left Banke's material, including originally unreleased tracks and obscurities, while PolyGram will release the definitive Left Banke-retrospective double CD, ***There's Gonna Be A Storm - The Complete Left Banke Recordings 1966-1969***, in 1991.)

THE LEMONHEADS

Evan Dando (vocals, guitar); **Nic Dalton** (bass); **David Ryan** (drums)

1986

Featuring a variable line-up during its first six years, the Lemonheads, always based around attorney's son Dando (b. Mar. 4, 1967, Boston, MA), is formed by the singer/guitarist/songwriter at the Commonwealth School, Boston, having previously played as the Whelps with Ben Deily and Jesse Peretz. The day after graduation, the band records four songs for $100, and releases a thousand 7" EPs under the title *Laughing All The Way To The Cleaners*. Subsequently signing to the independent Taang! label, the Lemonheads go on to record three albums, ***Hate Your Friends*** (1987), ***Creator*** (1988, which sees drummer John Strohm in the line-up and includes their cover version of Charles Manson's *Home*) and ***Lick*** (1989, which includes a well-received cover of Suzanne Vega's *Luke*) the last of which sees Deily and Peretz leave and Ryan (b. Oct. 20, 1964, Fort Wayne, IN) join, each garnering increasingly positive reviews and college radio attention in addition to strong early sales in Austria, West Germany and Switzerland.

1990

Aug With a burgeoning cult following and with Taang! having recently issued highlights from the first three albums on ***Create Your Friends***, Dando has signed the Lemonheads to Atlantic Records, which issues ***Lovey***, a pop/folk/heavy-rock meld. *Favorite Spanish Dishes*, a CD5 maxi-single comprising three quirky cover songs and two Dando originals and featuring ex-Blake Babies (in which Dando has previously and temporarily played in 1988, not least on the album ***Slow Learners***) bassist Juliana Hatfield, is released the following July.

1992

Feb Dando, as the Lemonheads, undertakes a solo tour of Australia.

July [20] Dando and Hatfield broadcast live on "Morning Becomes Electric" radio show on Los Angeles, CA's KCRW station.

Aug [1] Now joined by Ryan and new bassist Dalton (b. Nov. 14, 1964, Australia), the trio's ***It's A Shame About Ray***, produced by the Robb Brothers in Los Angeles and featuring musical guests Gunnar Nelson, Barry Goldberg and Jeff "Skunk" Baxter, initially charts for a week at UK #69.

Oct [17] *It's A Shame About Ray* charts for a week at UK #70, also becoming a hot college radio item in the US.

Nov [27] Dando plays a solo acoustic set at London's Ronnie Scott's club.

Dec [10] The band appears on BBC1-TV's "Top Of The Pops".

1993

Jan [2] Its cover of Simon & Garfunkel's *Mrs. Robinson*, coupled with *Bein' Around*, reaches UK #19. (The Lemonheads' version of *Mrs. Robinson* is included on the 25th-anniversary, wide-screen video release of "The Graduate", causing Dando to ruminate "Some people, probably wearing Italian shoes, said 'Hmmm, we need to get "The Graduate" out to more of a flannel-wearin' kind of audience'.")

[16] ***It's A Shame About Ray*** now makes UK #33.

[22] The group plays a short set, before signing copies of the album at London's Virgin Megastore.

Feb [6] *Confetti*, backed with *My Drug Buddy*, debuts at its UK #44 peak, as ***It's A Shame About Ray*** makes US #68.

Apr [5-6] Following a tour of Australia, the Lemonheads begin a short UK tour at London's Kilburn National Ballroom.

[7] The Lemonheads win Outstanding Modern Rock Act and Single Of The Year (for *It's A Shame About Ray*) at the Boston Music Awards, at the Wang Center, Boston.

[17] Double CD single, *It's A Shame About Ray*, bows at its UK #31 peak.

[27] They play a sellout date at New York's The Academy.

June [29] ***Sweet Relief***, a various-artists tribute/ benefit album for singer/songwriter Victoria Williams (now suffering from multiple scleroris), including the Lemonheads' *Frying Pan*, is released on the Thirsty Ear Recordings label.

Aug Dando performs at the opening of Johnny Depp's Sunset Strip club, the Viper Room, with Tom Petty & the Heartbreaks, Maria McKee and Shane McGowan.

Sept During a visit to the UK, the Lemonheads play at Minsthorp High School in Pontefract, W. Yorks., following the signing of a 450-strong petition from the school's pupils.

Oct [16] *Into Your Arms*, written by Robyn St. Clare of Australian group the Love Positions, debuts at its UK #14 peak.

[23] With Dando currently adopted by the UK's alternative music media as its poster-boy, ***Come On Feel The Lemonheads***, taking its title from a word-play on Slade's *Cum On Feel The Noize*, debuts at its UK #5 peak.

[30] ***Come On Feel The Lemonheads***, with contributions from Belinda Carlisle, Hatfield and Rick James, debuts at its US #56 peak.

Nov [27] *It's About Time* bows at its US #56 peak.

Dec [4] *Into Your Arms* peaks at US #67 during a nine-week stay at the top of the US Modern Rock survey.

[12] The Lemonheads play a sellout show at Bogart's in Cincinnati, OH.

1994

Jan [14] The Lemonheads, now no more than a vehicle for a solo Dando, begin a tour of Australia in Tasmania.

Mar [21] Dando, now revealing a shorn look, plays a set at Tower Records' Harvard Square in Cambridge, MA.

May [6] Dando guests on C4-TV's "The Big Breakfast".

[14] *Big Gay Heart* debuts at its UK #55 peak.

June [26] Dando plays on the last day of the annual "Glastonbury Festival".

July [8] The Lemonheads perform at the Roseland Ballroom, New York, during current US dates.

[9] Kiss tribute album, ***Kiss My Ass***, including Dando's version of *Plaster Caster*, reaches US #19 in its week of entry.

Aug [31] Following an appearance at the "Reading Festival" on the 26th, Dando plays a five-song solo set opening for Oasis in Newport, Gwent, Wales. (Dalton is planning on re-launching Godstar, while Ryan is currently playing in Fuzzy.)

Oct Richard Thompson tribute album, ***Beat The Retreat***, including Dando's duet with Syd Straw on *For Shame Of Doing Wrong*, is released by Capitol Records.

1995

Feb [18] Dando guests on BBC2-TV's "Later With Jools Holland".

Mar **Playboy** magazine reports that Dando is to be Liv Tyler's love interest in the movie "Heavy".

[11] Re-promoted ***It's A Shame About Ray*** reaches UK #33.

Apr [29] Dando, while visiting Martha's Vineyard, MA, plays an impromptu *Jumpin' Jack Flash* at the Lampost in Oak Bluffs.

June [24] *Perfect Day*, a Dando duet with Kirsty MacColl, charts for a week at UK #75.

Aug [22] ***Empire Records*** soundtrack, featuring a solo cut from Dando, is released.

JOHN LENNON

1968

Nov [29] The son of Fred and Julia Lennon (the latter having died on July 15th 1958), who separated when Lennon (b. John Winston Lennon, Oct. 9, 1940, Woolton, Liverpool, Lancs.) was only two years old, subsequently raised by his Auntie Mimi, has formed the Quarry Men Skiffle Group (named after his secondary school, Quarry Bank) in 1955. An introduction to fellow Liverpudlian Paul McCartney in the summer of 1957 has resulted in the formation of the most successful songwriting partnership in popular music history and their founding membership in most successful recording group, the Beatles. While still a member of the band, Lennon has made his first and only solo appearance, in the role of Private Gripweed, in a feature film, "How I Won The War", directed by Richard Lester, in October 1967, and now releases his first album, ***Unfinished Music No. 1 - Two Virgins***. A melange of sound effects and disjointed music, it is made famous by its cover, depicting Lennon and partner Yoko Ono (b. Feb. 18, 1933, Tokyo, Japan) in a naked, full-frontal pose. (They first met on November 9th, 1966, at the "Unfinished Paintings And Objects" private exhibition at the Indica art gallery in Mason's Yard, London.) Lennon took the photo himself on a delayed shutter release, reportedly too embarrassed to employ a professional photographer. EMI refuses to distribute the album and it is handled by Track, which wraps it in brown paper bags for retail.

Dec [10] Lennon makes his first scheduled solo TV performance, at the filming of "The Rolling Stones' Rock'n'Roll Circus", singing *'Yer Blues* (although the film will never be shown).

[18] John and Yoko hold a press conference while sitting inside a white bag at London's Royal Albert Hall, at the Underground Art Movement's Christmas party.

1969

Jan 30,000 copies of ***Two Virgins*** are seized by the police at Newark Airport, Newark, NJ. A Chicago, IL record store displaying the album is closed down by the vice squad.

Feb ***Unfinished Music No. 1 - Two Virgins*** makes US #124.

Mar [2] John and Yoko play a "natural music" concert at the Lady Mitchell Hall, Cambridge, Cambs.

[20] Lennon marries Ono in the British Consulate office in Gibraltar.

Apr [22] On the roof of the Apple building in Savile Row, London, Lennon changes his middle name from Winston to Ono by deed-poll. The Commissioner Of Oaths is Señor Bueno de Mesquita.

May ***Unfinished Music No. 2 - Life With The Lions*** makes US #174, released on Apple's avant-garde imprint, Zapple. A continuation of the first album, it features a free-form live concert on one side, while the other is recorded on a cassette player at the Queen Charlotte Hospital, Hammersmith, London, during Ono's pregnancy (which ends in miscarriage).

[26] The Lennons begin an eight-day "bed-in" in Room 1742 of the Hotel La Reine Elizabeth, Montreal, Canada, an event undertaken to promote world peace, and made open to the media.

July Recorded during the "bed-in" on May 31st, *Give Peace A Chance* hits UK #2 and becomes the definitive peace anthem for pacifists worldwide. The disc is credited to the Plastic Ono Band (a name Lennon will use for a musical aggregation with whom he will record over the next few years). Appearing on the cut are Lennon, Tommy Smothers, Petula Clark, Timothy Leary and Allen Ginsberg.

Sept [6] *Give Peace A Chance* reaches US #14.

[13] The Plastic Ono Band, with a line-up of Eric Clapton, Klaus Voorman and Alan White, appears in a hastily-arranged slot at the "Toronto Rock'n'Revival Show" held at the Varsity Stadium, Toronto University, Toronto, ON, Canada. The group rehearses on the flight to Toronto and performs a shaky set of rock'n'roll classics and Lennon originals.

Nov *Cold Turkey*, themed on the agonies of drug withdrawal, reaches UK #14.

[25] Lennon returns his MBE to Buckingham Palace with a note: "Your Majesty, I am returning this MBE in protest against Britain's involvement in the Nigeria-Biafra thing, against our support of America in Vietnam, and against *Cold Turkey* slipping down the charts. With love, John Lennon of Bag."

Dec ***The Wedding Album***, an avant-garde recording which includes souvenirs of Lennon's wedding, makes US #178. **Melody Maker**'s Richard Williams reviews a pre-release copy of the album, pressed on two discs, each with a blank B-side, and notes that these B-sides contain single tones maintained throughout, reproduced electronically and altering by a microtone or semitone to produce an uneven beat. (They are, in fact, an engineer's test signal.) Lennon and Ono send him a telegram saying: "We both feel that this is the first time a critic topped the artist."

[15] Lennon makes his last live appearance in Britain at a UNICEF "Peace For Christmas" benefit at London's Lyceum Ballroom.

1970

Jan [17] *Cold Turkey* peaks at US #30, as ***The Plastic Ono Band - Live Peace In Toronto 1969***, its sleeve an Yves Klein painting named "Blue", hits US #10.

[17] A London exhibition of Lennon lithographs is raided by police acting under the Obscene Publications Act.

[26] *Instant Karma* is written, recorded and mixed in one day's session.

Feb *Instant Karma*, produced by Phil Spector, hits UK #5 and US #3. It features George Harrison on guitar, Allen Klein, and assorted clubgoers from London's Hatchetts club on backing vocals.

Mar With the Beatles now officially defunct, Lennon and Ono begin an intensive six-month course of primal scream therapy conducted by its originator, Dr. Arthur Janov, during which Lennon writes most of the material for a forthcoming album.

[17] ***Live Peace - In Toronto*** is certified gold by the RIAA.

Dec [14] The RIAA also confirms *Instant Karma* gold.

1971

Jan ***John Lennon And The Plastic Ono Band*** traces themes from Lennon's troubled adolescence and topics brought to the surface during his primal therapy treatment. Subsequently hailed as a creative tour de force, it makes UK #11 and hits US #6, while *Mother* climbs to US #43.

[28] ***John Lennon And The Plastic Ono Band*** is certified gold by the RIAA.

Apr Anthemic *Power To The People* hits UK #7 and US #11.

June [6] The Lennons join Frank Zappa onstage at the Fillmore East, New York, NY.

July Lennon writes *God Save Us/Do The Oz* with Yoko and Phil Spector for Bill Elliott & the Plastic Oz Band to raise funds for the controversial **Oz** magazine court case.

Aug [13] Lennon flies from Heathrow Airport to New York. (He will never set foot on British soil again.)

Sept [21] The Lennons guest on US-TV's "The Dick Cavett Show".

Oct [30] ***Imagine***, commercially his most successful album, and highlighted by a consistently melodic pop/rock sound, tops both the US and UK charts in the same week and is acclaimed as his most rounded solo work. Containing two thinly-veiled attacks on Paul McCartney in *Crippled Inside* and *How Do You Sleep?*, the set, co-produced by John, Yoko and Phil Spector, features Badfinger, Harrison, Nicky Hopkins (piano), Jim Keltner and Alan White (drums), Mike Pinder and Voorman (bass).

Nov [13] Piano-led, peace-themed ballad, *Imagine*, hits US #3 and will be revered as the artist's seminal solo cut. (Its UK release will be resisted until 1975.)

Dec *Happy Xmas (War Is Over)* is released again only in the US, but fails to chart (which it continues to do on subsequent re-releases).

[17] The Lennons appear on stage at the Apollo Theatre, Harlem, New York, at a benefit concert for the wives of the victims of the Attica State Prison riot in September.

1972

Jan [29] Elephant's Memory becomes Lennon's new backing band.

Feb [15-18] Lennon and Ono co-host syndicated TV's "The Mike Douglas Show" for four days, during which Lennon jams with his rock'n'roll hero, Chuck Berry.

[29] Lennon's US immigration visa expires.

Mar [16] The Lennons lodge an appeal with the US Immigration & Naturalization Office in New York, after they are served with deportation orders arising from John's 1968 cannabis possession conviction.

June [10] *Woman Is The Nigger Of The World* makes US #57.

July For the US #48 double album, ***Some Time In New York City***, Lennon has teamed for one disc with Elephant's Memory (who contributed to the soundtrack of "Midnight Cowboy") to record overtly political comments on causes ranging from Northern Ireland to the imprisonment of radicals Angela Davis and John Sinclair. The other disc comprises concert recordings with the Mothers Of Invention. The Beatles' song-publishing arm, Northern Songs, refuses to recognize some of Yoko Ono's composer credits with Lennon, and the British release of the album is delayed.

Aug [13] John and Yoko play two Madison Square Garden concerts, raising $250,000 for retarded children.

[30] Regarded by some as his first completely solo performance, Lennon makes his only major appearance at a concert in Madison Square Garden, for the One To One charity, and is joined on stage by Stevie Wonder and Roberta Flack for the *Give Peace A Chance* finale.

Oct ***Sometime In New York City*** reaches UK #11.

Dec *Happy Xmas (War Is Over)* hits UK #4, making the first of many chart visits, having been initially held back from a UK release by the Ono song-credit dispute.

[23] "Imagine", a film based on Lennon's album of the same name and Ono's ***Fly***, receives its world premiere on US TV.

1973

Mar [23] Lennon is ordered to leave the US within 60 days by the Immigration Authorities and begins his long fight to gain the necessary green card to enable him to remain in the country. He issues a public statement - "Having just celebrated our fourth wedding anniversary, we are not prepared to sleep in separate beds. Love and peace, John and Yoko."

Oct [24] Lennon begins litigation against the US Government, accusing it of tapping his telephone.

Nov *Mind Games* climbs to UK #26 and US #18. ***Mind Games***, a return to the commercial texture of ***Imagine***, makes UK #13 and hits US #9.

[30] ***Mind Games*** is certified gold by the RIAA.

1974

Jan Lennon asks the Queen for a royal pardon in connection with his five-year-old UK drug conviction to enable him to go to and from the US.

Mar [12] Lennon, who has entered a dark period in his life, embarking on a drunken Los Angeles lifestyle after a temporary split from Ono, and currently seen in the company of his former personal assistant, May Pang, is involved in an infamous incident at Los Angeles' Troubadour club: with a tampon taped to his head, he hurls insults at the performing Smothers Brothers and punches their manager and a cocktail waitress, before being forcibly removed from the premises with pal Harry Nilsson. The episode makes headlines worldwide.

Aug He produces Nilsson's ***Pussycats***, a collection of cover versions.

[23] Lennon reports a UFO sighting in New York.

Sept [27] He guest-DJs on Los Angeles radio station KHJ-FM.

Oct Self-produced at the Record Plant, New York, and including musical guests Elton John, Nilsson and Julian Lennon (playing drums on *Ya Ya*), ***Walls And Bridges*** hits UK #6.

Nov [16] The extracted rocker, *Whatever Gets You Through The Night*, hits US #1, making him the last of the four ex-Beatles to secure a US chart-topper (in the same week that ***Walls And Bridges*** also tops the US Album survey), and makes UK #36. Elton John has played on the session for the single and, recognizing the song's potential, makes a deal with Lennon that if the disc gets to #1, Lennon will have to appear in concert with him. The singer accepts, confident of the record's lack of chart-topping potential.

[28] On Thanksgiving Night, Lennon makes what will be his final concert appearance, at Madison Square Garden, joining Elton John for three songs: *Whatever Gets You Through The Night*, *Lucy In The Sky With Diamonds* and *I Saw Her Standing There* (released as an EP in Britain in March 1981, making UK #40). Following the gig, he reunites with Yoko backstage.
Dec [9] Lennon shows up at ABC-TV's "Monday Night Football" booth during a game between the Los Angeles Rams and the Washington Redskins and talks with Howard Cosell and Frank Gifford. Ronald Reagan is also in attendance and explains the rules of the game to Lennon.

1975

Jan *Happy Xmas (War Is Over)* re-charts, at UK #48.
Feb [22] Ballad *#9 Dream* hits US #9.
Mar [8] *#9 Dream* reaches UK #23.
In ***Rock'n'Roll***, Lennon finally achieves his aim to record an album of his favorite rock'n'roll songs. The project was begun in 1973 with Phil Spector producing. After disagreements between the two, Spector disappeared with the master tapes and Lennon, unhappy with the production work, re-recorded the set. It is reported that Lennon has struck up an agreement with Morris Levy, Chuck Berry's publisher, that he would cover certain Berry songs for a new album as Levy threatened a lawsuit against Lennon for using Berry's song *You Can't Catch Me* in the shape of *Come Together* on ***Abbey Road***. Lennon subsequently gives Levy some master tapes of songs which, without Lennon's authorization, he releases as the TV-advertised mail-order ***Roots - John Lennon Sings The Great Rock & Roll Hits*** on the Adam VIII label. Apple promptly releases ***Rock'n'Roll*** to kill off the disc and Lennon successfully sues Levy, winning compensation of $45,000. The album hits both UK and US #6.
Apr [26] Lennon's remake of Ben E. King's *Stand By Me* reaches US #20.
May [24] *Stand By Me* reaches UK #30.
June [13] He makes his last TV appearance, on "Salute To Sir Lew Grade", performing *Slippin' And Slidin'* and *Imagine*.
Sept [20] David Bowie's *Fame*, co-written by the artist with Lennon and Carlos Alomar, tops the US chart (also reaching UK #17), while Lennon also plays guitar on Bowie's version of the Beatles' *Across The Universe*, both included on ***Young Americans***.
Oct [7] New York State Supreme Court votes by a two to one majority to reverse Lennon's deportation order.
[9] Sean Taro Ono Lennon is born. The birth of his only child by Ono has a profound effect on Lennon. (He retires for five years to become a househusband in his Manhattan apartment, in the Dakota building, while Ono runs their business empire.)
Nov [22] Greatest hits compilation, ***Shaved Fish***, hits UK #8. Released as a UK single for first time, *Imagine* hits #6.
Dec [13] ***Shaved Fish*** reaches US #12.

1976

July [27] Judge Ira Fieldsteel approves Lennon's application for his green card (no: A17-597-321), allowing him permanent residence in the US. Gloria Swanson, Norman Mailer, Geraldo Rivera and sculptor Noguchi appear at the hearing as character witnesses.

1977

Jan [20] The Lennons attend President Jimmy Carter's inaugural gala in Washington, DC.
May Lennon pays $6,795 to Chuck Berry's Big Seven Music company, after allegedly using *You Can't Catch Me* for *Come Together*.

1980

Aug After a lengthy recording hiatus, Lennon begins songwriting again, while vacationing in Bermuda, and records sessions at the Hit Factory in New York, for the forthcoming ***Double Fantasy*** (named after a flower Lennon saw in a botanical garden in Bermuda).
Sept [21] With all prior solo releases issued on the Beatles' Apple label, Lennon signs with Geffen Records, after David Geffen has offered to release the album without hearing any of the material.
Nov [29] ***Double Fantasy*** is released by John Lennon and Yoko Ono, receiving positive reviews, as Lennon returns to the limelight. Co-produced with Jack Douglas, it includes musical guests Hugh McCracken and Earl Slick (guitars), Tony Levin (bass), George Small (keyboards) and Andy Newmark (drums).
Dec [8] Lennon and Ono leave the Record Plant studio at 10:30 p.m. They enter the West 72nd Street entrance of the Dakota building and Lennon turns around when he hears a voice say, "Mr. Lennon". He is shot four times by 25-year-old Mark David Chapman, before struggling up six stairs to inside the alcove of the guard area, where he collapses at approximately 10:50 p.m. He is placed in the back seat of Police Officer James Moran's patrol car and driven to the Roosevelt Hospital 15 blocks away, where he is pronounced dead from a massive loss of blood at 11:30 p.m. (His killer had quit his job as a maintenance man in Honolulu, HI, in October. On the 27th of that month, he had purchased a five-shot Charter Arms .38 special from J&S Sales, Ltd. for $169. After a brief visit to Atlanta, GA, where he used to attend high school, he had returned to Hawaii, before finally leaving on December 5th. He had arrived in New York on the 6th, checking into a $16.50-a-night room at a YMCA, nine blocks from the Dakota. On the 7th, he had moved to the $82-a-day room at the Sheraton Centre Hotel. On the afternoon of the murder at around 5:00 p.m., Lennon had autographed his copy of ***Double Fantasy*** - "John Lennon 1980". Prior to all of this Chapman had married a Japanese woman several years his senior, covered his ID badge at his job with the name John Lennon and constantly played Beatle songs on his guitar - in the opinion of one forensic psychiatrist: "He had already tried to kill himself and he was unsuccessful, so he decided to kill Lennon. The homicide was simply a suicide turned backward.")
[14] Ono calls for a ten-minute silent vigil around the world at 2:00 p.m. EST.
[20] Public response to the slaying is overwhelming, not least spurring record sales: *(Just Like) Starting Over* hits UK #1.
[24] The still-climbing *(Just Like) Starting Over* is certified gold by the RIAA.
[27] ***Double Fantasy*** tops the US chart at the start of an eight-week run, as *(Just Like) Starting Over* begins a five-week stay at US #1.

1981

Jan [10] *Imagine* tops the UK chart after release-week retail orders of 300,000. With the reissued *Happy Xmas (War Is Over)* at #2, *Give Peace A Chance* reaches UK #33.
[22] A picture of a naked Lennon embracing a fully-clothed Ono appears in an obituary issue of **Rolling Stone** magazine.
Feb [7] *Woman* completes a hat-trick of Lennon UK #1s in a nine-week period, the same day that ***Double Fantasy*** also tops the UK Album chart for the first of two weeks.
Mar [14] Roxy Music's tribute version of Lennon's *Jealous Guy* hits UK #1, while *Woman* hits US #2.
Apr [1] *Woman* is certified gold by the RIAA.
May *Watching The Wheels* reaches UK #30 and US #10.
[19] Lennon is posthumously honored with the Outstanding Contribution To British Music at the 26th annual Ivor Novello Awards, held at London's Grosvenor House Hotel.
Aug [25] Chapman is sentenced to 20 years to life for Lennon's murder.
Dec *Happy Xmas (War Is Over)* makes UK #28.

1982

Feb [24] Lennon is honored at the first annual BRIT Awards, held at the Grosvenor House Hotel, for his Outstanding Contribution To British music on the same day that ***Double Fantasy*** is named Album Of The Year at the 24th annual Grammy Awards.
Apr [29] *Woman* wins the Outstanding British Lyric category at the 27th annual Ivor Novello Awards, at the Grosvenor House Hotel.
Nov *Love* climbs to UK #41, while the compilation ***The John Lennon Collection*** reaches US #33.
Dec [4] ***The John Lennon Collection*** hits UK #1 for the first of six weeks, as the reissued *Happy Xmas (War Is Over)* makes UK #56.

1984

Jan *Nobody Told Me* from the forthcoming ***Milk And Honey*** hits UK #6. ***Heart Play - Unfinished Dialogue***, a Polydor-released album featuring excerpts from a **Playboy** magazine interview given shortly before his death, reaches US #94.
Feb ***Milk And Honey***, featuring six of Lennon's songs recorded just before his death in 1980, and six additional cuts by Ono, hits UK #3 and US #11.
Mar *Nobody Told Me* hits US #5.
[21] Julian, Sean and Ono attend the opening ceremony of "Strawberry Fields", an area in Central Park Ono has bought in memory of her late husband.
Apr *Borrowed Time* makes UK #32, as *I'm Stepping Out* peaks at US #55.
[13] ***Milk And Honey*** is certified gold by the RIAA.
Oct [22] The RIAA ratifies sales of three million of ***Double Fantasy***.
Nov Lennon's first son Julian, from his marriage to Cynthia Twist, has his first hit with *Too Late For Goodbyes*, at UK #6 and ***Valotte***, which reaches UK #20 and US #17, many critics noting a similar vocal style to that of his late father, whose *Jealous Guy*, from ***Imagine***, peaks at UK #65.

1986

Feb [26] "Live In New York City" video is certified gold by the RIAA.
Mar ***Live In New York City***, recorded at Lennon's final live performance, in August 1972 at Madison Square Garden, makes UK #55 and US #41, accompanied by a similarly titled long-form video release.
Dec ***Menlove Avenue***, a compilation of unreleased studio sessions from the ***Rock'n'Roll*** and ***Walls And Bridges*** period named after the Liverpool street where he grew up, peaks at US #127.

1988

Sept Ono produces a syndicated series for radio on Lennon's life which features many unheard songs and interviews. A biography by Albert Goldman, who has previously written a book on Elvis Presley, outrages fans with its claims and is denounced by Ono.
[30] Lennon is given a star on Hollywood's Walk of Fame.
Oct [4] A movie and soundtrack, under the generic title "Imagine", produced by Ono, are simultaneously released, the film premiere taking place in New York. They include out-takes, videos, home movies and previously unheard material.
Nov ***Imagine : Music From The Motion Picture*** makes UK #64 and US #31.
Dec [3] Three-track single, *Imagine/Happy Xmas (War Is Over)/Jealous Guy*, peaks at UK #45.

1989

Jan [18] Sean and Yoko Ono attend as Lennon is inducted into the Rock and Roll Hall of Fame (as a Beatle) at the fourth annual dinner, at New York's Waldorf Astoria Hotel.
Apr His first wife, Cynthia Lennon opens Lennon's Restaurant in London, where dishes include Sgt. Pepper Steak and Penny Lane Pate. As Yoko embarks on a movie career, Sean spends time with David Bowie during the ***Tin Machine*** recording sessions in New York.
May "Imagine John Lennon" (the 1988 movie) and old live footage, compiled as "Sweet Toronto", are released as video cassettes.
Aug At a Julian Lennon concert at the Beacon Theatre, New York, his half-brother Sean comes on stage to duet on *Stand By Me*.

1990

May [5] The "John Lennon Tribute Concert" is held at the Pier Head Arena in Merseyside to celebrate the artist's songs: acts taking part, either live or on video, include Al Green (*All You Need Is Love* and *Power To The People*), the Christians (*Revolution*), Joe Cocker (*Come Together* and *Isolation*), Lenny Kravitz (*Cold Turkey*), Kylie Minogue (*Help*), Natalie Cole (*Lucy In The Sky With Diamonds* and *Ticket To Ride*), Wet Wet Wet (*I Feel Fine*), Ringo Starr with Jim Keltner, Jeff Lynne, Tom Petty and Joe Walsh (*I Call Your Name*), the Moody Blues (*Across The Universe*), Lou Reed (*Jealous Guy* and *Mother*), Terence Trent D'Arby (*You've Got To Hide Your Love Away*), Randy Travis (*Nowhere Man*), Cyndi Lauper (*Working Class Hero* and *Hey Bulldog*), Deacon Blue (*A Hard Day's Night*), Lou Gramm (*You Can't Do That*), Dave Stewart (*Instant Karma*), Ray Charles (*Let It Be*), Dave Edmunds (*A Day In The Life*, *Strawberry Fields Forever* and *Working Class Hero*), Daryl Hall & John Oates (*Don't Let Me Down* and *Julia*) and Roberta Flack (*In My Life*). Proceeds from the event go to the John and Yoko-established Spirit Foundation.

June [9] An international music festival "Muzeco '90" in Donetsk, Russia, is (prematurely) dedicated to the 50th anniversary of Lennon's birth.

Oct [9] *Imagine* is played simultaneously in 130 countries to commemorate what would have been Lennon's 50th birthday. A live worldwide broadcast is beamed from the United Nations, consisting of a short introduction by Marcela Pérez de Cuéllar, wife of the UN Secretary-General, and a taped message of Lennon followed by the playing of *Imagine*.

[10] George Martin presents the John Lennon Songwriting Awards to three students at Salford College of Technology.

Dec [21-22] Two Lennon tribute concerts take place at the Tokyo Dome, Tokyo, Japan, with Miles Davis (performing *Strawberry Fields Forever*), Natalie Cole & Toshinobu Kubota (*Ticket To Ride*), Linda Ronstadt (*Good Night*), Hall & Oates (*Julia* and *Don't Let Me Down*) and Sean Lennon (*You've Got To Hide Your Love Away*).

1991

Oct "Imagine" tops US MTV's Top 100 Videos Of All Time countdown.

Nov [15] The Great Gatsby auction house begins a two-day "The Lennon Collection" sell-off in Atlanta, GA. Items under the hammer include his earliest guitar, a Hofner Compensator, authenticated by a letter of provenance from George Harrison.

[26] The RIAA certifies ***Imagine*** double platinum and ***Rock'n'Roll*** gold.

[27] ***Shaved Fish*** is certified platinum.

1992

May The University of Liverpool announces details of the "John Lennon Memorial Scholarship", provided from a trust fund set up in his memory.

[7] Setting a new celebrity clothing record, Christies auction house in London accepts $43,500 for a leather jacket worn by Lennon, from an unidentified bidder.

June [22] Through the US Supreme Court, California history professor, Jonathan Wiener, wins the latest round in a nine-year legal battle with the FBI which should pave the way to open the agency's files on Lennon, which began at the instigation of the CIA in 1967.

July [16] With actor Mike McGann in the lead role, "Imagine - The John Lennon Story" opens at the Liverpool Playhouse, Liverpool, a few hundred yards from the Cavern club. The 46-song musical biography also features Karl Lornie as McCartney, Peter Ferris as Harrison and Paul Case as Ringo Starr, and is based on an idea by Bob Eaton, who also produced the 1986 documentary play, "Lennon".

1994

Jan [19] Lennon is posthumously inducted into the Rock and Roll Hall of Fame at the ninth annual dinner by McCartney at the Waldorf Astoria Hotel. He says "The thing you must remember is that I'm the number one John Lennon fan. I love him to this day and I always did love him. All these people assembled to thank you for everything that you mean to all of us. Tonight you're in the Rock and Roll Hall of Fame. God bless you."

1995

Oct [28] As *Love*, covered by reggae singer Janet Kay, is broadcast as the theme to a Sony TV commercial in Japan, ***Working Class Hero - A Tribute To John Lennon***, featuring Lennon covers by the Red Hot Chili Peppers, Sponge, Collective Soul, Candlebox, Mary-Chapin Carpenter, Blues Traveler, Flaming Lips, Toad, Cheap Trick, George Clinton and Mad Season, among others, reaches US #94 in its week of entry.

Nov [19] The first portion of "The Beatles Anthology" airs on ABC-TV. Including extensive new interviews with the remaining trio, edited in with old Lennon interviews, it attempts to build a definitive archival documentary of the Beatles' early years, with personal anecdotes, remembrances and observations. At the close of tonight's segment, the Beatles first "new" recording since their split, *Free As A Bird* receives its premiere airing. The track has been assembled around a previously unissued Lennon demo which Ono has passed to McCartney in 1993 (along with another Lennon cut *Real Love* which was originally featured in the 1988 "Imagine" soundtrack), to which the remaining members have added a relevant rhythm section, bridge and harmony vocal parts, under the guidance of co-producer Jeff Lynne.

see also: **THE BEATLES**

ANNIE LENNOX

1988

Dec Lennox (b. Dec. 25, 1954, Aberdeen, Grampian, Scotland), who has grown up in a two-room tenement apartment in Aberdeen, the daughter of a railways boiler-maker/shipyard welder father and housewife mother, having studied the flute from an early age and failed to complete a scholarship course at London's Royal Academy of Music, has met musician Dave Stewart in 1971 with whom she has begun a personal and professional liaison which has led the pair to success in the Catch, the Tourists (1979-1980) and as Eurythmics, the latter proving to be be one of the most successful pop/rock duos of the '80s. Still in the partnership, Lennox's first solo venture is a duet with soul legend Al Green, reviving Jackie De Shannon's 1969 US #4 hit, *Put A Little Love In Your Heart*, for the "Scrooged" soundtrack. The single climbs to UK #28 and will hit US #9, in January the following year.

1989

Feb [18] Having already won a clutch of BRIT and Ivor Novello awards as a vocalist and songwriter, Lennox accepts her fourth Best British Female Artist trophy at the ninth annual BRIT Awards, held at London's Dominion Theatre, during a month when she announces that she will be taking a two-year sabbatical. With Stewart going on to form the Spiritual Cowboys, Eurythmics' split will prove permanent.

1990

Oct Lennox contributes *Ev'ry Time We Say Goodbye* to ***Red Hot & Blue***, a covers anthology of Cole Porter songs released to benefit AIDS education. With the comprehensive ***Eurythmics Greatest Hits*** hitting UK #1 (and US #72) in March the following year, its release is confirmation that Lennox and Stewart have gone their separate ways.

1992

Mar [14] Lennox appears on ITV's "Aspel & Co", having performed on BBC1-TV's "Top Of The Pops" two days earlier.

Apr [11] Mournful ballad *Why* hits UK #5, during a month when Stewart buys Lennox's share in The Church Studio, which the pair had bought together in the '80s.

[18] Lennox guests on NBC-TV's "Saturday Night Live", as ***Diva*** enters the UK chart at #1. Featuring a studio band comprising producer Steve Lipson (guitars and keyboards), Peter-John Vettese (keyboards) and Marius de Vries (keyboards), the largely self-written 11-track set is released via a worldwide solo deal with Arista Records. Critically praised, it will become one of the year's biggest-selling albums in Europe.

[28] A Lennox rockumentary, "Diva", is broadcast on BBC2-TV.

May [8] She is the music guest on NBC-TV's "The Tonight Show".

June [13] *Precious* reaches UK #23.

July [3] Lennox's appearance at the "Montreux Jazz Festival", Montreux, Switzerland, is taped for an MTV "Unplugged" show, set to air on August 26th.

[18] *Why* makes US #34.

Aug [8] ***Diva*** peaks at US #23.

Sept [5] *Walking On Broken Glass*, spurred by a period-piece, costume-drama video clip featuring Hugh Laurie, hits UK #8.

[9] "Why" wins the Best Female Video category at the ninth annual MTV Video Music Awards held at the Pauley Pavilion, Los Angeles, CA.

Oct [6] Lennox is interviewed on syndicated TV's "Whoopi Goldberg" chatshow.

[31] *Cold* debuts at its UK #26 peak, while Lennox works with Lipson on material for the soundtrack to Francis Ford Coppola's "Bram Stoker's Dracula" at Townhouse Studios, London.

Nov [13] ***Diva*** is certified platinum by the RIAA.

[14] *Walking On Broken Glass* reaches US #14.

1993

Feb [13] *Little Bird*, backed with *Love Song For A Vampire*, which is featured in "Bram Stoker's Dracula", and helped by 30 Odeon cinemas showing the video before the movie for a month, bows at its UK #3 peak. The video clip is directed by Sophie Muller and based on Bob Fosse's "Cabaret", with eight Lennox lookalikes and the heavily-pregnant real singer.

[16] Lennox collects the Best British Female Artist and Best Album (for ***Diva***) trophies at the 12th annual BRIT Awards, held at the Alexandra Palace, London.

[24] "Diva" snares the Best Long Form Video category at the 35th annual Grammy Awards, held at the Shrine Auditorium, Los Angeles.

Mar [1] ***Diva*** returns to UK #1, eventually selling 5.5 million copies worldwide.

[4] Lennox is named Best Female Singer in **Rolling Stone**'s Music Awards Readers' Picks.

[13] *Little Bird* makes US #49.

May [26] She wins the Best Song Musically And Lyrically category for *Why* at the 38th annual Ivor Novello Awards, held at the Grosvenor House Hotel.

1995

Feb [18] Previewing her second album, her cover of Lover Speaks' 1986 UK #56 *No More 'I Love You's'* debuts at its UK #2 peak.

[28] Lennox backs Carly Simon on *You're So Vain* at Arista boss Clive Davis' pre-Grammy bash at the House of Blues with Melissa Etheridge and Sarah McLachlan.

Mar [1] Lennox and George Michael present Song Of The Year trophy to Bruce Springsteen at the 37th annual Grammy Awards at the Shrine Auditorium.

[18] She guests on NBC-TV's "Saturday Night Live", as ***Medusa***, a covers album produced by Stephen Lipson and featuring Procol Harum's *A Whiter Shade Of Pale* (the first record she ever bought at age 14), Al Green's *Take Me To The River*, Bob Marley's *Waiting In Vain*, Blue Nile's *Downtown Lights*, plus songs originally performed by the Temptations, Neil Young, the Clash, the Persuaders and Paul Simon, enters UK chart at #1.

(In the current edition of **Vanity Fair** and commenting on her former Eurythmics partner Stewart, Lennox

says: "I don't need any association with him any more than he needs it from me.")
Apr [1] ***Medusa*** debuts at its US #11 peak.
May [16] ***Medusa*** is certified platinum by the RIAA.
[27] *No More 'I Love You's'* reaches US #23.
June [10] *A Whiter Shade Of Pale* debuts at its UK #16 peak.
[22] Lennox is honored at the second annual "VH1 Honors" ceremony from the Shrine Auditorium.
[23] She guests on NBC-TV's "The Tonight Show".
July She takes part in the "Donna Sotto Le Stelle" fashion gala on the Spanish Steps in Rome, Italy.
Sept [8] Lennox performs her first New York concert since 1988 and her only scheduled US appearance of the year - a free concert in Central Park. 6,000 tickets have been given away in two New York stores in 15 minutes. (The performance is recorded for a limited edition eight-track live album ***Live In Central Park*** which will be paired with copies of ***Medusa*** worldwide by year's end (100,000 in the UK, 50,000 in Germany - the coupling will not emerge in the US until the following spring).)
[10] She joins Paul Simon on *Something So Right* at the latter's annual Children's Health Fund benefit concert at New York's Paramount.
[14] Lennox participates in the T.J. Martell Foundation 20th anniversary dinner, honoring Clive Davis with the 1995 Humanitarian Award.
[30] *Waiting In Vain* debuts at its UK #31 peak.
Oct [24] Female-only compilation, ***Ain't Nuthin' But A She Thing***, featuring a new cut by Lennox, is released in the US.
Dec [9] *Something So Right*, featuring its writer Paul Simon, debuts at its UK #44 peak.

1996

Feb [19] Lennox is once again named Best Female Artist at the 1996 BRIT Awards held at London's Exhibition Centre.
[28] Lennox wins Best Pop Vocal, Female for *No More 'I Love You's'* and performs the Clash's *Train In Vain (Stand By Me)* at the 38th annual Grammy Awards also joining Seal in a rendition of *What's Going On* in tribute to posthumous Lifetime Achievement Award recipient, Marvin Gaye.
see also: **EURYTHMICS**

LEVEL 42

Mark King (vocals, bass);
Mike Lindup (keyboards, vocals);
Boon Gould (guitar); **Phil Gould** (drums)

1980

May The band has been formed in London earlier in the year by King (b. Oct. 20, 1958, Cowes, Isle of Wight), Phil Gould (b. Feb. 28, 1957, Hong Kong), his brother Boon (b. Roland Gould, Mar. 4, 1955, Shanklin, Isle of Wight) and Lindup (b. Mar. 17, 1959, London), though three of its members have been brought up on the Isle of Wight, where King has been a drummer with various holiday-camp groups, before switching to bass and moving to the UK capital. Taking their name from Douglas Adams' book **The Hitch-Hiker's Guide To The Galaxy**, in which "42" is the answer to the question "What is the meaning of life?", their first London club gigs are played as a purely instrumental jazz-funk outfit, though their debut single, *Love Meeting Love*, features a vocal by King, urged by producer/label owner Andy Sojka as a vital selling-point, and is now released on Sojka's UK dance-oriented independent label, Elite Records. It receives strong UK dance-floor play and makes the Dance chart, attracting interest in the group from larger record companies.
Sept With the Elite pressing having sold out and now signed to Polydor, the reissued *Love Meeting Love* makes UK #61.
Nov *(Flying On The) Wings Of Love* is released as a popular dance-club follow-up.

1981

May *Love Games*, from the band's debut album, reaches UK #38.
Aug *Turn It On* reaches UK #57.
Sept [5] ***Level 42***, produced by Mike Vernon, peaks at UK #20.
Nov *Starchild*, also from the album, makes UK #47, as the band tours West Germany supporting the Police.
Dec Elite releases a limited-edition album, ***Strategy***, containing the rest of the material recorded prior to the band's Polydor signing.

1982

Apr ***The Early Tapes, July-August 1980***, a reissue by Polydor of the Elite limited-edition album, makes UK #46.
May *Are You Hearing (What I Hear?)* reaches UK #49.
Oct *Weave Your Spell* peaks at UK #43. It is taken from ***The Pursuit Of Accidents***, which makes UK #17, supported by the "Pursuit Of Accidents" tour of UK and Europe, which leads the group to meet Larry Dunn and Verdine White of Earth, Wind & Fire, who offer to produce the band's next album.

1983

Feb *The Chinese Way* is its first UK Top 30 single, reaching UK #24.
Apr *Out Of Sight, Out Of Mind*, written by all four band members, makes UK #41.
Aug Light funk *The Sun Goes Down (Living It Up)* hits UK #10.
Sept ***Standing In The Light***, produced in Los Angeles, CA, by Dunn and White, hits UK #9, once again highlighted by King's thumb-pumping bass-playing, and is followed by a six-week US tour.
Oct *Micro Kids*, taken from the album, reaches UK #37. Following the band's return from the US, Level 42 plays UK dates into the New Year.

1984

July King releases his debut solo album, ***Influences***, which makes UK #77. He also releases *Freedom*, with Lindup but credited to Thunderthumbs & the Toetsenman (their nicknames).
Oct *Hot Water*, which becomes a live highlight, reaches UK #18, taken from ***True Colours***, which makes UK #14.
Nov *The Chant Has Just Begun*, also from ***True Colours***, is heard at UK #41.

1985

July Double live album, ***A Physical Presence***, mostly recorded at small UK club venues during the tour, climbs to UK #28.
Oct *Something About You* hits UK #6, their best-selling UK single so far.
Nov The band-penned ***World Machine***, produced by Wally Badarou, broadens the group's sound into a more commercial pop vein and hits UK #3, during a 72-week chart stay.
Dec Ballad *Leaving Me Now*, from ***World Machine***, reaches UK #15. It prominently features Lindup's distinctive falsetto vocals alongside King's, a trend which will continue on most subsequent single releases.

1986

May [31] *Something About You* is the group's US chart debut, hitting #7, as the parent album, ***World Machine*** reaches US #18.
June *Lessons In Love*, with Gary Barnacle on saxophone, coupled with a live version of stage favorite *Hot Water*, hits UK #3. It is the group's highest chart placing and will be the second-biggest selling single of the year in Europe, reaching #1 in eight countries. It is followed by a successful long-running world tour.
[20] The group takes part in the fourth "Prince's Trust Rock Gala" at Wembley Arena, Wembley, Middx., with Eric Clapton, Phil Collins, Elton John, Paul McCartney and others.
Aug [2] *Hot Water* stalls at US #87, while the group tours the US supporting Steve Winwood.

1987

Jan King is voted Best Bass Player in **Making Music** magazine's poll.
Feb Uptempo *Running In The Family* hits UK #6. The group tours the UK and Europe promoting it.
Apr Ballad *To Be With You Again* hits UK #10.
June [5-6] King and Lindup perform at the fifth annual "Prince's Trust Rock Gala", for the second successive year, at the Wembley Arena.
[27] *Lessons In Love* reaches US #12, while ***Running In The Family***, including the two previous singles, and again produced by Badarou, hits UK #2 and US #23. In support, the band plays a UK tour, which includes two dates at the National Exhibition Centre, Birmingham, West Midlands, and eight at Wembley Arena, followed by other European and the US dates.
Aug [22] *Running In The Family* makes US #83.
Sept *It's Over*, another ballad, hits UK #10. As well as the usual 7" and 12" singles formats, 5,000 copies are released experimentally as one of UK's first CD video discs, predating both CD-ROM and DVD. The pressing sells out, despite the fact that CD video players are not available on the UK market.
Dec Both Gould brothers leave the group, Boon suffering from an ulcer and Phil from nervous exhaustion. (Boon Gould will later release a solo album.) Neil Conti from Prefab Sprout joins temporarily on drums. *Children Say*, another track from the album, promoted by a video which features just King and Lindup, reaches UK #22. Proceeds are donated to London's Great Ormond Street Children's Hospital Appeal Fund.

1988

Sept *Heaven In My Hands* reaches UK #12.
Oct ***Staring At The Sun***, featuring new recruits Gary Husband (drums) and Alan Murphy (guitar), hits UK #2 and will make US #128, while the extracted *Take A Look* makes UK #32.
[29] Level 42 begins a ten-date European tour in Hamburg, West Germany, set to end on November 12th in Barcelona, Spain.

1989

Feb *Tracie* reaches UK #25.
July [18-19] King, Lindup and Husband take part in the seventh annual "Prince's Trust Rock Gala", at the Birmingham National Exhibition Centre.
Oct [19] Murphy dies from AIDS.
Nov Career-hits retrospective, ***Level Best***, hits UK #5 and includes the current UK #39, *Take Care Of Yourself*.

1990

June [11] Lindup releases the solo album ***Changes*** on Polydor.
Nov [19] Pia King is granted an uncontested "quickie" divorce after her husband has run off with their children's nanny, and her best friend, Ria van de Brom.
Dec [5-8, 10-18] Level 42 plays 15 nights at London's Hammersmith Odeon to a total of 51,000 fans.

1991

Mar Level 42 and Polydor part company (the label unhappy with direction of the band's new album), while new guitarist Jakko Jakszyk, formerly with Tom Robinson, joins.
Aug [4] The band headlines the Crystal Palace Bowl, Crystal Palace, London, with Squeeze, Gary Clail, Big Dish and Witness also on the bill.
[17] Newly signed to RCA Records, the band's *Guaranteed* debuts at its UK #17 peak.
Sept [14] ***Guaranteed*** hits UK #3.
Oct [1] A month-long UK tour bows at the Corn Exchange, Cambridge, Cambs., set to end on the 30th at the Brighton Centre, Brighton, East Sussex.
Dec [2] *Something About You* is honored for one

million US performances, at the annual BMI Awards at London's Dorchester Hotel.
[19] *Overtime* debuts at its UK #62 peak.

1992

Jan [20] Following Polydor's recent issue of the nine-CD boxed set ***1980-1989 Complete***, comprising the group's entire album output with the company, the band performs at the annual "Midem Festival", held at Palm Beach, Cannes, France.
Feb [25] Level 42 is featured on C4-TV's "Return To The Dome".
Mar [19-21] They play three dates at the Town & Country club, London, during a month-long UK tour.
Apr [18] *My Father's Shoes* charts for a week at UK #55.

1994

Mar [5] *Forever Now* reaches UK #19.
[26] Produced by Julian Mendelsohn, at London's SARM Studios, ***Forever Now*** hits UK #8 in its week of entry.
Apr [17] The group guests on BBC2-TV's "The O Zone".
[30] *All Over You* debuts at its UK #26 peak.
July [19] The band guests on C4-TV's "The Big Breakfast".
Aug [6] *Love In A Peaceful World* debuts at its UK #31 peak, as superfan Antony Hicks changes his name to include the titles of all the band's album titles and the full names of all the band members.
Sept [29] The group embarks on 13-date UK tour at Portsmouth Guildhall, set to end on October 14th at London's Royal Albert Hall.

THE LEVELLERS

Mark Chadwick (lead vocal, guitar, banjo); **Simon Friend** (guitar); **Jeremy Cunningham** (bass); **John Sevink** (violin); **Charlie Heather** (drums)

1990

Apr Chadwick and Sevink, who have left Brighton, East Sussex-based band Fence following the group's only single *Frozen Water*, released in May 1987, have formed the folk-angst rock band (with post-punk sensibilities, its name taken from the pro-republican Puritan movement of the 17th century) in Brighton in February 1988, recruiting Cunningham, Heather and guitarist Alan Miles. Following the issue of two singles on the local Hag label (*Carry Me* and *Outside Inside*)in 1989, its self-penned debut album ***A Weapon Called The Word*** (which will also be the name of its web page in 1995), produced by Phil Tennant is now released by the French label, Musidisc. Folowing constant touring around the UK and rest of Europe over the next year (during which Miles quits after dates in Belgium), the Levellers will be picked up China Records having earned a small loyal following of new-age traveling hippies, mostly unemployed and homeless devotees.

1991

Sept With Friend having replaced Miles, *One Way*, issued by China, makes UK #51, taken from ***Levelling The Land***, to be released the following month.
Dec [7] *Far From Home* charts for a week at UK #71.

1992

May [8] The band plays at Leeds University, Leeds, West Yorks.
[23] Four-track EP *15 Years* debuts at its UK #11 peak.
June [13] The reissued, social-conscience themed ***Levelling The Land***, produced by Alan Scott, reaches UK# 22, the same day that *One Way* becomes the band's first US chart disc, entering the Modern Rock survey on its way to #11.
[27] The group appears at the "Glastonbury Festival". (During the month, the Levellers will make their US debut at the 13th annual New Music Seminar held at The Academy, New York, NY.)

1993

July [10] *Belaruse* bows at its UK #12 peak.
Sept [4] Following mediocre reviews, ***The Levellers*** nevertheless enters at its UK #2 high behind UB40's ***Promises And Lies*** (though its US sales total will be 12,000).
Nov [6] *This Garden* reaches UK #12.

1994

May [14] Five-track *Julie* EP debuts at its UK #17 peak.
June [24] The band plays on the opening day of the annual "Glastonbury Festival", Glastonbury, Somerset.

1995

Feb The group buys an abandoned clock factory in Brighton, converting it into The Metway, a studio with office space at a cost of £150,000 (to be used by management, and to run its various political interests, including its opposition to the Criminal Justice Act, and the production of **The Book**, a directory listing various action and anti-government pressure groups).
Aug [12] Ballad *Hope St* bows at its UK #12 peak.
Sept [16] Recorded at Metway and produced once more by Alan Scott, ***Zeitgeist*** (German for "spirit of the age") debuts at UK #1.
[18] A 14-date UK tour opens, set to end on October 6th.
Oct [14] *Fantasy* enters at its UK #16 peak.
Dec [18] The band participates in "Freakshow Christmas '95" with the Pogues, Dreadzone and others, at the Sheffield Arena, Sheffield, Yorks.
[23] *Just The One*, featuring Joe Strummer on piano, bows at its UK #12 peak.

1996

Jan Licensed to Elektra Records, ***Zeitgeist*** is issued in the US, where the band is reluctant to play. (Chadwick: "We're not very comfortable with the US. They have a different way of going about things over there.")

GARY LEWIS & THE PLAYBOYS

Gary Lewis (vocals, drums); **Al Ramsey** (guitar); **John West** (guitar); **David Costell** (bass); **David Walker** (keyboards)

1964

Aug Lewis (b. Gary Levitch, July 31, 1946, New York, NY), the son of movie comedian Jerry Lewis, in whose "Rock-A-Bye-Baby" film he appeared in 1957, having played drums since age 14 under the guidance of Buddy Rich, forms a band at a theatre-arts college in Pasadena, CA, with neighbors Ramsey (b. July 27, 1943, NJ), West (b. July 31, 1939, Uhrichsville, OH), Costell (b. Mar. 15, 1944, Pittsburgh, PA) and Walker (b. May 12, 1943, Montgomeryville, AL). Initially together to play at local parties, they audition at Disneyland and are hired for a summer season at the theme park. They also have a cameo musical role in the Raquel Welch movie, "A Swingin' Summer".

1965

Feb [20] With the group signed to Liberty Records by producer Snuff Garrett (who will employ the Eligibles - Ron Hicklin, Al Capps and Stan Farber - as session singers on all Playboys' subsequent hits), the debut is the Leon Russell-arranged *This Diamond Ring*, co-written by Al Kooper, previously turned down by Bobby Vee and recently cut as an R&B shuffler by Sammy Ambrose. An instant hit, it tops the US chart for the first of two weeks, is a million seller and secures an appearance on CBS-TV's "The Ed Sullivan" show.
May [8] *Count Me In*, written by the Crickets' Glen D. Hardin, hits US #2, behind Herman's Hermits' *Mrs. Brown You've Got A Lovely Daughter*. In a chart currently dominated by UK acts, Lewis is the only American artist on the survey. Their debut album, ***This Diamond Ring***, reaches US #26.
June [28] The group appears on the CBS-TV "It's What's Happening Baby" special.
Aug Sing-a-long *Save Your Heart For Me*, covering a 1963 Brian Hyland B-side (on which Lewis whistles as well as sings), hits US #2, behind Sonny & Cher's *I Got You Babe*.
Sept [17] The band guests on ITV's "Ready Steady Go!" during a UK visit, as well as appearing on BBC-TV's "Top Of The Pops" and ITV's "Thank Your Lucky Stars".
Oct *Everybody Loves A Clown*, a joint composition by Lewis, Garrett and Russell, hits US #4, while ***A Session With Gary Lewis & The Playboys***, which includes the previous two hit singles, reaches US #18.
Dec ***Everybody Loves A Clown*** makes US #44.

1966

Jan The Beach Boys-like *She's Just My Style*, again jointly-penned by its singer, producer and arranger but featuring Jim Keltner on drums, hits US #3, while the group is featured in the pop/espionage B-movie "Out Of Sight", with the Turtles, the Knickerbockers and Freddie & the Dreamers.
Apr *Sure Gonna Miss Her*, highlighted by sterling guitar work by Tommy Tedesco, hits US #9, as ***She's Just My Style*** reaches #71.
June *Green Grass*, a song by UK composers Roger Cook and Roger Greenaway, hits US #8 (the last of Lewis's seven consecutive US Top 10 smashes).
July ***Gary Lewis Hits Again!***, with Dave Pell having taken over from Garrett as producer, makes US #47. (The group is still little more than Lewis backed by a group of Los Angeles session singers led by Hicklin, with a session-team rhythm section.)
Aug *My Heart's Symphony*, another Hardin song, reaches US #13.
Oct Lewis plays the lead role in the musical "Bye Bye Birdie" in Kansas City, MO.
Nov *(You Don't Have To) Paint Me A Picture* makes US #15.
Dec Compilation album, ***Golden Greats***, collecting all of the group's Top 10 singles, hits US #10, becoming Lewis' most successful album, and staying charted for 46 weeks. The band also appears in Lewis' father Jerry's film, "Way Way Out".

1967

Jan [1] Lewis is drafted into the US army, and the band is forced to split. (Prior to his call-up, a "Why I Would Like To Give Gary Lewis His Last Kiss" contest is held, the winner presented with her prize on CBS-TV's "The Ed Sullivan" show.) Bitter at the interruption to his career, he will refuse to form a Special Services band to entertain troops and instead spends his time as a clerk/typist in Korea. *Where Will The Words Come From*, released just before his draft, reaches US #21.
Apr Liberty continues to issue earlier-recorded Lewis discs but, with the band off the road and unavailable for TV promotion, *The Loser (With A Broken Heart)* reaches only US #43, while ***You Don't Have To Paint Me A Picture*** peaks at #79.
[28] ***This Diamond Ring*** is certified gold by the RIAA.
June *Girls In Love* reaches US #39.
July ***New Directions*** peaks at US #185.
Sept [16] *Jill* makes US #52.

1968

Aug Out of the army and with a new group of Playboys, Lewis' revival of Brian Hyland's *Sealed With A Kiss* reaches US #19.
Sept Newly-recorded ***Gary Lewis Now!*** sells moderately, peaking at US #150, but will be Lewis' last chart album (followed by ***I'm On The Right Road Now***) before leaving Liberty Records.

1969

June Lewis tries another revival, this time the

Cascades' *Rhythm Of The Rain*, but it halts at #63, his final Hot 100 entry.
Sept ***Rhythm Of The Rain*** is released. (Lewis tries to escape the teenybop appeal of his earlier hits by evolving a more serious singer/songwriter style, but makes little headway.)
[29] ***Golden Greats*** is certified gold by the RIAA.

1975

Feb In an unexpected postscript, *My Heart's Symphony* is reissued in the UK, where Lewis & the Playboys made no impression during the '60s. After dancefloor success (as a "rare oldie") on the northern soul scene, it makes UK #36. With the advent of '60s-nostalgia shows and tours in the US, Lewis re-forms the Playboys to concentrate on playing his early hits on the oldies circuit, and finds regular touring work, while also running a music store in Los Angeles, and giving guitar and drum lessons.

1985

Apr Still touring - with a varying line-up of Playboys - and living in Cleveland, OH, having cut one-off singles for Scepter and Epic and an album of remakes for Gusto and then K-tel, Lewis joins the Turtles, Grass Roots, the Mamas & the Papas and the Buckinghams for a US revival "Happy Together" trek, continuing on the oldies circuit into the '90s. (He will battle an ongoing drink problem and enter a rehab program in 1987.)

HUEY LEWIS & THE NEWS

Huey Lewis (vocals, harmonica); **Sean Hopper** (keyboards); **Chris Hayes** (lead guitar); **Johnny Colla** (saxophone, guitar); **Mario Cipollina** (bass); **Bill Gibson** (drums)

1979

May Lewis (b. Hugh Cregg III, July 5, 1950, New York, NY) has been a latecomer member, on harmonica and occasional vocals, along with future News keyboardist Hopper (b. Mar. 31, 1953, CA) to San Francisco, CA good-time rock band Clover, when it signed to Vertigo Records in the UK in 1976, making his lead vocal debut on *Chicken Funk*, produced by Nick Lowe. Contributing to Elvis Costello's debut album, ***My Aim Is True***, and touring the UK behind Thin Lizzy and others, the band has gone on to release two albums in 1977, ***Unavailable*** and ***Love On The Wire***. With Clover founder John McFee leaving to join the Doobie Brothers, Clover now breaks up. Lewis plays briefly in London on sessions for Nick Lowe and on Dave Edmunds albums (***Labour Of Lust*** and ***Repeat When Necessary***), before returning to Mill Valley, CA, involving himself in a yoghurt business by day and joining regular Monday-night jam sessions at Uncle Charlie's club in Marin County with a group of musicians, who will form the core of his next band. They record a disco version of the "Exodus" theme, titled *Exodisco*, which is picked up by Mercury Records, and issued under the name American Express. It doesn't do very nicely.

1980

May After playing informally together for some months, the News is formed permanently when Chrysalis signs the group on the strength of demos recorded by the Monday-night jammers at the Different Fur Studio in Marin County, CA. Lewis and Hopper are joined by Hayes (b. Nov. 24, 1957, CA), who has been with California jazz bands, while Colla (b. July 2, 1952, CA), Gibson (b. Nov. 13, 1951, CA) and Cipollina (b. Nov. 10, 1954, CA) are all ex-members of Soundhole, which previously backed Van Morrison.
July The largely self-penned ***Huey Lewis And The News*** debut, produced by Bill Schnee, is released.

1982

Apr [17] *Do You Believe In Love*, written by Clover's producer, Robert John "Mutt" Lange, is the band's first US hit, at #7.
June ***Picture This***, once again highlighting the band's tight, no-nonsense, straight rock approach, reaches US #13. More covers oriented, it includes songs by Wet Willie, Phil Lynott and the Hollywood Flames (their 1957 hit, *Buzz Buzz Buzz*). The song from Wet Willie's Michael Duke, *Hope You Love Me Like You Say You Do*, is extracted and reaches US #36. Lynott's song, *Tattoo (Giving It All Up For Love)*, is also issued in Britain.
Sept *Workin' For A Livin'*, also from the second album, makes US #41.

1983

Sept Self-written and produced ***Sports***, featuring ex-Clover McFee, is released and initially hits US #6. (It is destined to be a long-term US seller, topping seven million sales.)
Nov *Heart And Soul*, a Nicky Chinn/Mike Chapman song originally recorded by Exile, hits US #8 (the first US hit from ***Sports***).

1984

Mar *I Want A New Drug (Called Love)* hits US #6. (Lewis later sues Ray Parker Jr., writer of the similarly-styled "Ghostbusters" theme, for alleged plagiarism of this song; the case will be settled out of court to Lewis' satisfaction.)
June [30] ***Sports*** hits US #1 for a week, while a third extract, *The Heart Of Rock And Roll*, hits US #6, where it will stay for four weeks.
July [24] The group performs at the North Dakota State Fair, before a crowd of over 18,000.
Sept *If This Is It*, also from ***Sports***, peaks at US #6 and finally gives Lewis a UK chart debut, reaching #39.
Dec Final ***Sports*** extract, *Walking On A Thin Line*, reaches US #18.

1985

Jan [28] Following the 12th annual American Music Awards, held at the Shrine Auditorium, Los Angeles, CA, where they collect the Favorite Video, Duo Or Group, Pop/Rock trophy, Lewis and the band participate in the recording of USA For Africa's *We Are The World* in Los Angeles, with Lewis taking a solo vocal role.
July Lewis opts out of playing at "Live Aid", allegedly resenting the hype surrounding the event.
Aug [24] *The Power Of Love*, written for the movie "Back To The Future" in which Lewis also has a cameo role as a music teacher, tops the US chart for the first of two weeks, becoming a million seller.
Sept ***Sports*** finally charts in the UK, reaching #23, while *The Power Of Love* is the band's first UK Top 20 hit, climbing to #11.
Oct [16] ***Picture This*** is certified gold by the RIAA.
Dec EP *Heart And Soul*, a compilation of US Top 10 hits *The Heart Of Rock And Roll* and the title track, plus *Hope You Love Me Like You Say You Do* and *Buzz Buzz Buzz* from the ***Picture This*** album, peaks at UK #61.

1986

Jan [27] The group wins the Favorite Single, Pop/Rock, and Favorite Video Single, Pop/Rock categories at the 13th annual American Music Awards, held at the Shrine Auditorium.
Feb [10] The band is named Best International Group at the fifth annual BRIT Awards, at London's Grosvenor House Hotel, and also performs live at the ceremony.
[25] "Huey Lewis & The News : The Heart Of Rock'n'Roll" wins Best Music Video, Long Form at the 28th annual Grammy Awards.
Mar Following the British premiere of "Back To The Future", *The Power Of Love* has been reactivated (as a double A-side with a reissue of the band's first US hit, *Do You Believe In Love*), and hits UK #9.
Apr [28] "Huey Lewis And The News" video is certified gold by the RIAA.
May *The Heart Of Rock And Roll*, released for the third time in the UK, finally makes #49.
Sept [20] Pop/rock based *Stuck With You*, aided by a desert-island video clip, begins a three-week stay at US #1, and reaches UK #12.
Oct [18] ***Fore!***, which includes *Stuck With You* and *The Power Of Love*, hits US #1 and UK #8.
Dec [6] *Hip To Be Square* hits US #3 and makes UK #41.
[7] Lewis & the News sing the US national anthem a cappella before the San Francisco 49ers vs. New York Jets football game at Candlestick Park, San Francisco.

1987

Jan [26] Huey Lewis & the News collect the Favorite Video, Duo Or Group, Pop/Rock, and Favorite Band, Duo Or Group, Pop/Rock trophies at the 14th annual American Music Awards, held at the Shrine Auditorium.
Mar [14] *Jacob's Ladder*, the fourth single from ***Fore!***, hits US #1. Written by Bruce and John Hornsby, whose first album Lewis has partly produced, and whose group has supported the News on tour, the song is a swipe at US TV evangelists.
Apr *Simple As That*, released in the UK instead of *Jacob's Ladder*, makes #47.
May [30] *I Know What I Like* hits US #9.
July [20] The RIAA certifies seven million sales of ***Sports***.
Sept [19] *Doing It All (For My Baby)* hits US #6, the sixth smash cut from ***Fore!***.

1988

July [25] The RIAA confirms three million sales of ***Fore!***
Aug Self-produced ***Small World*** is released, set to reach US #11 and UK #12.
Sept The extracted *Perfect World* hits US #3, but only makes UK #48, the band's last charting single of the '80s in Britain.
[27] ***Small World*** is certified platinum by the RIAA.
Nov [26] Title cut, *Small World*, featuring Stan Getz on tenor sax, reaches US #25.

1989

Jan [30] The RIAA certifies both *I Want A New Drug* and *The Power Of Love* gold.
Feb [11] Final album extract, *Give Me The Keys (And I'll Drive You Crazy)*, makes US #47.
May [18] The group takes part in an AIDS benefit concert with Tracy Chapman, the Grateful Dead, Los Lobos and Linda Ronstadt, at the Oakland-Alameda County Coliseum, Oakland, CA.
Sept [8-9] The band plays under the name the Sports Section at the Club Casino, Hampton, NJ, to try out new songs.

1991

May [18] Now signed to EMI Records, Lewis & the News' label debut, ***Hard At Play***, co-produced with Bill Schnee, debuts at its UK #39 peak and will do similarly at US #27 the following week.
June [15] *Couple Days Off* reaches US #11.
July [1] ***Hard At Play*** is certified gold by the RIAA.
Sept [14] *It Hit Me Like A Hammer* reaches US #21.
Oct [26] When flying home following his attendance at a Lewis & the News gig in Concord, CA, legendary American promoter Bill Graham dies in a helicopter crash (together with the pilot and Graham's companion, Melissa Gold), when the chopper hits a 200' utility tower in Sonoma County, CA.
[28] Lewis attends Graham's memorial service.
Nov [3] The band performs at the Arizona State Fair, Phoenix, AZ
[19] The group appears on NBC-TV's "The Tonight Show".

1992

Jan [25] They feature on cable channel TNT's "Super Bowl Saturday Night" (while Lewis is also currently seen playing Reba McEntire's husband in the video for her country hit *Is There Life Out There?*).
Feb [19] The band performs at the "Houston Livestock Show & Rodeo", the Astrodome, Houston,

TX, staged by the PRCA Rodeo.
Mar [7] With the group winning the Outstanding Group category and Colla nabbing the Outstanding Reeds/Brass Player trophy, they perform at the 15th annual Bay Area Music Awards, at the San Francisco Civic Auditorium.
Aug [10] The band plays at the Ohio State Fair, Columbus, OH, during its current US tour. (After only one album with EMI, the band now signs to Elektra Records.)
Nov [21] ***The Heart Of Rock & Roll - The Best Of*** collection bows at its UK #23 peak.

1993

Jan [25] The group performs at a tribute concert to Bill Graham, following the 20th annual American Music Awards, at which the late promoter was honored with the Award of Merit, with John Fogerty, Jerry Garcia, Eddie Money, Carlos Santana, Joan Baez, Stephen Stills and Grace Slick, at the Shrine Auditorium. (During the year, Lewis will appear in Robert Altman's "Short Cuts".)

1994

June [4] Nostalgic covers set ***Four Chords & Several Years Ago*** makes US #55.
July [2] *(She's) Some Kind Of Wonderful* makes US #44.
[27] They appear on CBS-TV's "Late Show With David Letterman".
Aug [8] The group guests on C4-TV's "The Big Breakfast".
Oct [8] They perform a cappella at "First Day Of Fall Fest 94" on Boston Common, Boston, MA.
[15] *But It's Alright* makes US #54.
Nov [19] The band plays a sellout date at the Star Plaza Theatre, Merrillville, IN, during a current US tour.

1995

Apr [22] ***Come Together : America Salutes The Beatles***, a country tribute to the Beatles including Lewis' version of *Oh! Darling*, released by Liberty, makes US #90 in its week of entry.
Aug [3] During a current US tour, the group grosses $125,066 from a performance at the Pine Knob Music Theatre, Clarkston, MI.

1996

Mar Originally recorded for the 1988 Disney animated feature "Oliver & Company", Lewis' *Once Upon A Time In New York City* is finally released as a single.
July [7] Huey Lewis & the News begin their 1996 summer tour at the Cape Cod Melody Tent in Hyannis, MA, set to end on September 20th at the Western Washington Fair, Puyallup, WA.

JERRY LEE LEWIS

1949

With Lewis (b. Sept. 29, 1935, Ferriday, LA) showing an early talent for music, his parents buy him a piano, which he teaches himself to play in two weeks. He is exposed to a rich mix of musical cultures - jazz (through his parents), hillbilly (and its more commercial offspring, country and western), gospel and cajun. He makes his first public performance at an auto show featuring the year's new-model Fords, in Natchez, LA. When he earns $9 singing *Hadacol Boogie* with a local C&W band, his father encourages his musical career, loading the piano on the family truck and driving his son to shows. The following year, Lewis attends the fundamentalist Assembly of God Institute Bible School in Waxahachie, TX, where he studies music and theology, though, displaying an early rebellious streak, he will later be expelled.

1952

Feb Lewis, at age 16, marries preacher's daughter Dorothy Barton whom he soon abandons in favor of club life. In September the following year, Lewis gets married, bigamously, to Jane Mitcham at a shotgun wedding, encouraged by her brothers. He will finally divorce Dorothy the following month when Jane gives birth to Jerry Lee Lewis Jr.

1956

Lewis and his father sell 33 dozen eggs to finance a trip to Memphis, TN, hoping to audition for Sun Records, but arrive only to find that label head Sam Phillips has just left for Nashville, TN. Lewis threatens to sit on the doorstep until he is allowed in to perform. Eventually, Jack Clement lets him in to cut a tape and tells him to return in a month. When he does so, Phillips invites him to record *Whole Lotta Shakin' Goin' On* and *Crazy Arms* for a Sun single. Released near the end of the year, it is promptly banned by most of the country's radio stations because of its vulgarity.
Dec [4] Lewis joins Elvis Presley and Carl Perkins in an impromptu recording session at Sun studios in Memphis. (These recordings will become known as "The Million Dollar Quartet". Johnny Cash leaves the session just before its start, at the insistence of his wife, who wants to go shopping.)

1957

Lewis, on an extensive US tour highlighted by his abrasive and wild stage antics (which will become legendary), meets Sam Phillips' brother Judd at a show in Alabama. He offers Lewis national TV exposure and takes him to New York, securing a contract for two appearances on NBC-TV's "The Steve Allen Show".
Mar [31] He begins a major tour of Southern states with Perkins and Cash in Little Rock, AR.
July [28] Lewis makes his US TV debut on "The Steve Allen Show". (His second appearance is the only time Allen's show ever tops Ed Sullivan's in the national ratings. Before it, *Whole Lotta Shakin' Goin' On* had sold about 30,000 copies, mainly in the South. Afterwards, it sells more than six million nationally, not hitting its #3 chart peak until September, when Sun is shipping 50-60,000 copies a day. It also simultaneously tops the C&W and R&B charts.) (Lewis first heard it sung by its co-writer, Roy Hall, at the Music Box in Nashville. Hall wrote it with David Williams, under the pseudonym Sonny David.)
Oct *Whole Lotta Shakin'*, released on the London label, hits UK #8.
Nov [12] Movie "Jamboree" (UK title: "Disc Jockey Jamboree"), with Lewis, Fats Domino, Carl Perkins and many others, premieres in the US.
Dec [11] Still married to Jane Mitcham, Lewis secretly marries his 13-year-old second cousin Myra Gale Brown, daughter of his bass player Jay, in Hernando, MS. (Lewis' other cousins include future country singer Mickey Gilley and TV evangelist-to-be Jimmy Swaggart.)

1958

Jan Seminal rock'n'roll smash, *Great Balls Of Fire*, hits US #2 for a month, kept from the top by Danny & the Juniors' *At The Hop*. It sells a million copies in its first ten days of release (and will sell over five million in the US). It also tops the UK chart, on the 10th.
Feb Lewis' cover of Hank Williams' *You Win Again* (a 1952 US #13 for Tommy Edwards), the B-side of *Great Balls Of Fire*, makes US #95.
[25] Lewis backs Buddy Holly at a Fort Lauderdale, FL gig, playing piano on *Drown In My Own Tears*.
Apr *Breathless* hits both US and UK #7, as Lewis is legally divorced from Mitcham.
May [22] Lewis' unorthodox marriage to Myra Gale Brown has earned condemnation from the Church in the US, but the real storm hits when he arrives for his first UK tour. Waiting reporters ask who his young companion is. He tells them she is his wife and cousin and that he has been married twice before. The resulting media and public hysteria leads to his being booed off stage and forced to cancel 34 of the scheduled 37 concerts. On his return to the US, he finds that Sun, panicked by the scandal, has not serviced his new record, *High School Confidential*, to DJs.
June [9] Lewis takes out a five-page trade ad to explain his recent divorce. He writes, "I hope that if I'm washed up as a performer, it won't be because of this bad publicity." He also re-weds Myra in a ceremony of impeccable legality. *High School Confidential*, from the film of the same name (in which Lewis appears), reaches US #21, selling half a million copies. (Sales of Lewis' subsequent Sun releases will be limited by lack of radio play and the label's hesitancy in promoting its artist.)
Sept *Break Up* makes US #52, as its B-side, *I'll Make It All Up To You*, peaks at US #85, both songs written by Charlie Rich.
Oct Sun releases his debut album ***Jerry Lee Lewis***.

1959

Jan *I'll Sail My Ship Alone* peaks at US #93.
Feb *High School Confidential* makes UK #12. Myra gives birth to Lewis' second son, Steve Allen.
May *Lovin' Up A Storm* reaches UK #28. In June the following year, *Baby Baby Bye Bye* will climb to UK #47, as the constantly touring Lewis develops a serious problem with alcohol and pep pills.

1961

May *What'd I Say* makes US #30 and UK #10.
June [25] Lewis takes part in Alan Freed's Spectacular at the Hollywood Bowl, Hollywood, CA, with Brenda Lee, Bobby Vee, B. B. King, the Shirelles and the Ventures, among others.

1962

Apr [24] Lewis' son Steve Allen drowns in their home swimming pool, as Myra fixes Easter dinner.
[29] Lewis returns to Britain for the first time in four years, amid favorable public response at the City Hall, Newcastle, Tyne & Wear.
June ***Jerry Lee Lewis Vol. 2*** reaches UK #14, his only UK Album chart appearance.
Sept Lewis' version of Chuck Berry's *Sweet Little Sixteen* peaks at US #95 and makes UK #38.

1963

Mar His cover of Little Richard's *Good Golly Miss Molly* makes UK #31.
Sept [6] Lewis leaves Sun and signs to Mercury Records subsidiary, Smash.

1964

Mar ***The Golden Hits Of Jerry Lee Lewis***, a re-recording of his Sun hits for Smash, becomes Lewis' first US chart album, reaching #116 during an eight-week chart stay.
Apr Lewis' first single for Smash, *I'm On Fire*, peaks at US #98.
Nov Live *High Heel Sneakers* steps to US #91.
[22] Lewis begins a UK tour with the Yardbirds, Twinkle, the Quiet Five and others, at the Hippodrome, Brighton, Sussex, set to end on December 7th at the Town Hall, Birmingham, Warks.
Dec ***The Greatest Live Show On Earth***, recorded in Birmingham, AL on July 1st, 1964, makes US #71.

1965

Mar [31] Lewis begins a European tour in Germany.
Apr [18] He appears in the film "Be My Guest", which goes on general release in the UK as a B-feature to the Morecambe & Wise picture, "The Intelligence Men".
June ***The Return Of Rock*** makes US #121.

1966

May ***Memphis Beat*** peaks at US #145.
July [1] Lewis begins a US tour with Herman's Hermits, the Animals and Lou Christie, in Honolulu, HI.
Aug [21] He is signed to play Iago in Jack Good's London stage production of "Catch My Soul", his rock-opera adaptation of Shakespeare's "Othello".
Oct [17] Lewis embarks on his first UK tour in two years in Bradford, Yorks., with two cabaret gigs at the Guiseley Paradise and the Lyceum Rainbow.

1968

Mar With Lewis having switched to country music, *Another Place, Another Time* peaks at US #97 but hits US C&W #1.

July *What Made Milwaukee Famous (Has Made A Loser Out Of Me)* makes US #94, but is another sizeable country hit (one of more than 30 by Lewis over the next ten years). ***Another Place, Another Time*** peaks at US #160, during a 12-week stay.

Aug Lewis takes part in the eighth annual "National Jazz & Blues Festival" in Richmond, Surrey.

1969

Feb ***She Still Comes Around (To Love What's Left Of Me)*** makes US #149.

Mar [1] *To Make Love Sweeter For You* tops the US Country survey.

Apr [14] The Monkees' NBC-TV special, "33⅓ Revolutions Per Monkee", featuring Lewis and others, including Little Richard, Fats Domino, the Clara Ward Singers, Brian Auger, Buddy Miles and Julie Driscoll, airs.

May Two Smash albums, ***Jerry Lewis Sings The Country Music Hall Of Fame, Volume 1*** and ***Volume 2***, reach US #127 and US #124.

Sept Two Sun compilation albums simultaneously make the US chart: ***Original Golden Hits Vol. 1*** (including the first three singles) reaches #119, while ***Vol. 2*** makes #122.

[13] Lewis takes part in "The Rock'n'Revival Concert" in Toronto, ON, Canada, with fellow rockers Chuck Berry, Gene Vincent, Bo Diddley, Little Richard and, making their live debut, John Lennon's Plastic Ono Band.

1970

Feb ***She Even Woke Me Up To Say Goodbye*** spends two weeks on the US chart, making #186.

May ***The Best Of Jerry Lee Lewis***, a collection of his country hits, peaks at US #114.

Sept [26] *There Must Be More To Love Than This* becomes Lewis' fourth US Country chart-topper.

Oct ***Live At The International, Las Vegas***, his first album on the main Mercury label, reaches US #149.

Nov [18] Myra and Jerry Lee divorce. She will later claim that she only spent three nights alone with Lewis in 13 years of marriage. He is shocked into embracing the Church and shunning alcohol, cigars and the pursuit of young women. (This abstinence will last two months.)

1971

Jan ***There Must Be More To Love Than This*** makes US #190.

Aug ***Touching Home*** climbs to US #152.

Dec ***Would You Take Another Chance On Me*** peaks at US #115, its title track topping the US Country chart on Jan [8] the following year.

1972

Jan Lewis' version of Kris Kristofferson's *Me And Bobby McGee* becomes his biggest pop hit in more than 13 years, climbing to US #40.

Apr He returns to rock'n'roll, covering the Big Bopper's *Chantilly Lace*, which reaches US #43 (also becoming his final US Country chart-topper). ***The "Killer" Rocks On*** ("The Killer" being Lewis' best-known nickname), begins a 12-week US chart run, peaking at #105.

May *Chantilly Lace* makes UK #33 (marking his first UK hit in nine years and his last to date).

July *Turn On Your Love Light* peaks at US #95.

Aug [5] Lewis participates in the first-ever "London Rock'n'Roll Festival" at Wembley Stadium, Wembley, Middx., on a bill with Bill Haley, Chuck Berry, Little Richard and Bo Diddley, among others.

1973

Mar ***The Session***, a collection of oldies recorded in London with the help of Peter Frampton, Rory Gallagher, Albert Lee, Alvin Lee and others, reaches US #37.

May Extracted from the album, *Drinkin' Wine Spo-Dee O'Dee*, a cover of the 1949 R&B #2 for Stick McGhee, and one of the first songs Lewis ever performed, reaches US #41 (and will be his last US pop hit).

Nov [13] Lewis' 19-year-old son Jerry Lewis Jr., the drummer in his band, is killed in an auto accident in DeSoto county, having recently been in mental hospitals and suffering from drug abuse.

1976

Sept [29] Lewis accidentally shoots his bass player Norman Owens in the chest, while blasting holes in his own office door during his own birthday party. Owens survives but sues his boss.

Nov [22] A notorious hell-raiser, Lewis drives his Rolls Royce into a ditch and is arrested for drunk driving.

[23] Ten hours later, he is arrested for brandishing a Derringer pistol outside Elvis Presley's Gracelands home in Memphis, demanding to see the "King".

1977

Mar Security guards quit a Lewis gig in Manchester, Gtr. Manchester, when knuckle duster-wielding teddy boys storm the stage. During a quieter UK tour the following year, Lewis will perform at London's Rainbow Theatre on November 19th. Signing with Elektra Records, his label debut ***Jerry Lee Lewis*** will make US #186 in May 1979.

1981

Apr [23] Following the release of the US #125 peaking "Roadie" film soundtrack the previous July, to which Lewis has contributed the ironically titled *(Hot Damn) I'm A One Man Woman*, a concert in Stuttgart for German TV reunites the three surviving members of Sun's 1956 "Million Dollar Quartet": Lewis, Carl Perkins and Johnny Cash, who this time is not whisked away by his wife to shop. (Recordings from the show will be released in 1982 on the CBS album ***The Survivors***.)

June [30] Lewis is hospitalized in Memphis Methodist Hospital with a haemorrhaging stomach ulcer. From his bed, he countersues Elektra Records for $5 million, as a label dispute ends his contract. (After two serious operations, doctors estimate his chances of survival at 50/50. He is back on the road within four months and recording for MCA Records.)

1982

Feb [24] Lewis appears on the year's Grammy Awards telecast with cousin Mickey Gilley, as ex-wife Myra's book, **Great Balls Of Fire**, is published. (Myra Williams, now remarried, is an Atlanta real estate broker.)

June [8] Lewis' estranged fourth wife drowns in a swimming pool.

1983

June [7] Still logging moderate country hits (and wives), Lewis gets married, for the fifth time, to his companion of two years, 25-year-old Shawn Michelle Stevens.

Aug [24] Shawn is found dead at Lewis' Mississippi home. An autopsy finds the cause of death to be a methadone overdose and a grand jury finds no reason to suspect foul play, despite widespread media interest.

1984

Feb [16] Lewis surrenders himself to federal authorities in Memphis for arraignment, and to plead not guilty to charges of evading federal income taxes between 1975-80.

Apr [24] Lewis marries wife number six, 22-year-old Kerrie McCarver.

Oct After a long battle with the Internal Revenue Service, a Federal Court jury acquits Lewis of tax evasion. A **Rolling Stone** article by Pulitzer Prize winner Richard Ben Cramer points to disturbing circumstantial evidence surrounding Shawn's death - broken glass on the floor, a sack of bloodstained clothes in the room where she died and blood and bruises on her body. Her mother claims Shawn had called her the day before her death and said she was going to leave Lewis after they had had physical fights. "The Killer" survives the scandal.

1985

Lewis recovers from another spell on the critical list, with two bleeding ulcers. Rhino Records releases ***Milestones***, a collection of Lewis' work from 1956 to 1977, while he begins recording an album with Gilley.

1986

Jan [23] Lewis is inducted into the Rock and Roll Hall of Fame at the inaugural induction dinner, at New York's Waldorf Astoria Hotel.

June [5] He joins Ray Charles as Fats Domino's guests at the Storyville Jazz Hall, New Orleans, LA, recording an HBO-TV special, "Fats Domino And Friends". Ron Wood plays guitar for Lewis.

Dec [2] Lewis checks into the Betty Ford Clinic to overcome his painkiller addiction.

1987

Jan [28] Kerrie gives birth to Jerry Lee Lewis III - Lewis' only surviving son - in Memphis.

1988

May Filming of the Lewis bio-flick, "Great Balls Of Fire", begins, starring Dennis Quaid, who receives piano lessons from Lewis, as "The Killer".

June He takes part in ceremonies for the Barcelona Olympics.

Dec Lewis, still under investigation by the IRS, appears in Memphis Federal Bankruptcy Court filing for protection, saying he owes over $3 million to some 22 creditors, including $2 million in back taxes.

1989

June [13] Lewis is awarded a star on the Hollywood Walk of Fame, Los Angeles.

July "Great Balls Of Fire" opens in US cinemas, dramatizing the early years of Lewis' career. Both Quaid and Lewis have already quibbled over who will sing the vocals on the film's songs. The result is a 50/50 arrangement with Lewis performing new versions of his old hits on the soundtrack album.

Nov At a concert at London's Hammersmith Odeon, Lewis is joined on stage by Van Morrison, Dave Edmunds, Brian May, John Lodge and others.

1990

Mar [8-10] US dates are highlighted by a three-night stint at the Fox Theatre, Detroit, MI, grossing $233,130.

Apr A European tour is cancelled when Lewis fails to turn up for six shows. Promoter Mervyn Conn threatens litigation.

[15] Conn persuades Lewis' wife to fly to the UK in the hope that Lewis will follow her and thereby honor his agreement. (On March 2nd the following year, Lewis will reportedly be too drunk to take the stage at a gig at the Typhoon Arena, Turku, Finland.)

June The "Dick Tracy" soundtrack, to which Lewis has contributed *It Was The Whiskey Talkin' (Not Me)*, reaches US #108.

1992

Apr [1] Jerry Lee Lewis' 1,300-seat Spot club opens on Beale Street, Memphis.

[25] IRS agents seize a $10,000 pay cheque that Lewis receives for performing at a Shriners' fundraising concert in Savannah, GA, which will go towards reducing his $2 million debt to the IRS (listed when he filed for bankruptcy in 1988).

May [1-2] He performs a pair of dates at London's Hammersmith Odeon.

Oct [10] He cancels a gig at Billy Bob's Texas in Fort Worth four hours before showtime.

1993

Mar [1] Lewis makes his first appearance at his own

Spot venue in Memphis.
Apr [20] ***All Killer No Filler***, a two-CD various labels career retrospective is released by vault specialists, Rhino Records.
July [10] Now domiciled in Eire (although he denies this is to avoid the taxman), he is booed offstage during an oldies concert in La Coruna, Spain.

1994

Mar [7] Lewis returns to the US after a year of IRS-induced exile.
July [25] His lawyer, David Monypeny announces that the singer has settled a $4.1 million disagreement with the IRS.
Oct [8] Lewis sings *See See Rider* at "Elvis Aaron Presley : The Tribute", an all-star music event held at the Pyramid Arena, Memphis, broadcast live on US pay-per-view TV.
Nov [8] He is taken to hospital in Southaven, MS, complaining of breathing problems after choking on some food the day before.

1995

Feb Lewis launches his own 1-900-988-FIRE telephone line featuring a personal message and marketing treats from wife Kerrie's mail order company, Kerrie Enterprises.
May [23] Elektra releases his first new studio effort in 12 years, ***Young Blood***, a set of covers of Hank Williams and Jimmie Rodgers songs, produced by Andy Paley.
[24] Lewis guests on NBC-TV's "The Tonight Show".
Sept [2] Lewis sings *Great Balls Of Fire* and *Whole Lotta Shakin'*, backed by the E. Street Band, at the Concert for the Rock and Roll Hall of Fame held at Cleveland Stadium, Cleveland, OH.

GORDON LIGHTFOOT

1958

Lightfoot (b. Nov. 17, 1938, Orillia, ON, Canada), having shown musical talent since age eight and later learning to play the piano, writing his first composition, *The Hula Hoop Song*, at age 17, has graduated from Orilla Collegiate Institute, and moves from his home town on the shore of Lake Simcoe to study orchestration and harmony at Westlake College of Music, Los Angeles, CA, but becomes homesick after 14 months and returns to Canada, where he joins square-dance ensemble the Swinging Singing Eight, not least for TV engagements. While also turning out piano pieces for a living, he begins to take a deep interest in folk and country music, taking up the guitar (both 6 and 12-string), inspired by listening to Pete Seeger and Bob Gibson. He goes on to team with Terry Whelan to form the Two Tones folk duo, releasing the Art Snider-produced ***The Two Tones Live At The Village Corner*** on Canatal Records, in 1960. He will make his US debut at La Cave in Cleveland, OH, sharing the bill with José Feliciano. in 1961.

1963

Having recorded his ten-track debut solo album for Snider's Chateau label (which releases three singles during the year *Negotiations*, *I'll Meet You In Michigan* and *The Day Before Yesterday*) and spent a year working in the UK, not least hosting an eight-week BBC-TV variety series, Lightfoot returns to Canada to perform with Oscar Brand on the CTV folk series "Let's Sing Out", and further hones his singer/songwriter skills performing folk-styled material around Toronto, ON, Canada clubs with his guitar. Hearing Bob Dylan for the first time on disc, he begins to absorb his influence.

1964

Singing upstairs at Steel's Tavern in Toronto, he meets Ian & Sylvia Tyson, a leading Canadian folk duo, who decide to record his *For Lovin' Me* and *Early Morning Rain*. (The two songs are passed on for consideration by Peter, Paul & Mary, who also record them and have US hits with both during 1965.) Lightfoot is signed by Albert Grossman and John Court, managers of the Tysons, Peter, Paul & Mary and Bob Dylan, to their production company, Groscourt Productions.

1965

He recruits two back-up musicians, Red Shea (guitar) and John Stockfish (bass), for live gigs, as Groscourt signs a lease deal with United Artists Records, which releases his label debut, the self-penned ***Lightfoot***.
June [19] Country singer Marty Robbins hits US C&W #1 with his treatment of *Ribbon Of Darkness*. (During the year, Lightfoot receives the first of many Canadian Juno music awards.)

1966

Feb [16] He begins a nine-date UK tour with the Ian Campbell Folk Group, Ian & Sylvia and the Settlers at the De Montfort Hall, Leicester, Leics., set to end on the 25th at Fairfield Halls, Croydon, Surrey.

1967

Having released ***The Way I Feel***, Lightfoot makes his debut at New York, NY's Town Hall. UA will release ***Did She Mention My Name*** the following year, further showcasing his literate writing style and distinctive baritone vocal.

1969

June [2] Lightfoot makes a one-off London appearance at London's Royal Festival Hall, supporting his latest album, ***Back Here On Earth***.
Dec His last set for UA, ***Sunday Concert***, is issued, recorded live at Massey Hall, Toronto. When Groscourt's lease ends with United Artists the following January, the production company signs to the Warner Bros. subsidiary label Reprise, with Lightfoot working with producer Lenny Waronker.

1971

Feb Lightfoot's Singles chart debut, the self-penned ballad, *If You Could Read My Mind*, hits US #5, while the Waronker and Joe Wissert co-produced album, ***If You Could Read My Mind***, originally called ***Sit Down Young Stranger*** and retitled after the single's success, reaches US #12.
June [14] ***If You Could Read My Mind*** is certified gold by the RIAA.
July *If You Could Read My Mind* reaches UK #30, while the follow-up, *Talking In Your Sleep*, peaks at US #64, with ***Summer Side Of Life*** making US #38. A United Artists compilation album, ***Classic Lightfoot (The Best Of Gordon Lightfoot, Vol. 2),*** also charts, at US #178.
Sept *Summer Side Of Life* peaks at US #98.

1972

May ***Don Quixote*** reaches US #42 and UK #44.
July *Beautiful*, taken from ***Don Quixote***, peaks at US #58.
Dec ***Old Dan's Records*** makes US #95.

1974

June [22] ***Sundown***, once again produced by Waronker, hits US #1 for the first of two weeks.
[29] *Sundown* tops the US chart.
Aug *Sundown* reaches UK #33, while ***Sundown*** makes UK #45. In the US, a further United Artists compilation, ***The Very Best Of Gordon Lightfoot***, makes US #155.
Nov *Carefree Highway*, another enduring radio favorite, taken from ***Sundown***, hits US #10.

1975

Apr ***Cold On The Shoulder***, with string arrangements by Nick DeCaro, hits US #10.
May [24] The extracted *Rainy Day People*, reaches US #26.

1976

Jan Double compilation, ***Gord's Gold*** (the first component album of the two has some re-recordings of songs from his United Artists days, because Lightfoot is unhappy with the original versions) reaches US #34 and earns a gold disc. By now, Lightfoot is playing some 70 concerts a year in the US and Canada, backed by a stage band consisting of Red Shea and Terry Clements (guitars), Pee Wee Charles (steel guitar) and Rick Haynes (bass). (There is no drummer on live shows, though Jim Gordon plays drums on recording sessions.)
Nov *The Wreck Of The Edmund Fitzgerald*, a dramatic tale chronicling the sinking of an ore vessel carrying 26,216 tons of taconite iron pellets on Lake Superior, WI, on November 11th, 1975 with the loss of all 29 crew members, hits US #2 for two weeks (behind Rod Stewart's *Tonight's The Night*), and is Lightfoot's second gold single.
Dec Co-helmed by Waronker and Lightfoot, ***Summertime Dream***, which includes *The Wreck Of The Edmund Fitzgerald*, hits US #12 (and will be certified as another million seller on February 7th, 1980). Lightfoot appears onstage with Bob Dylan's "Rolling Thunder Revue".

1977

Jan *The Wreck Of The Edmund Fitzgerald* makes UK #40.
Mar *Race Among The Ruins* peaks at US #65.

1978

Mar Lightfoot moves to the main Warner Bros. label for the Toronto-recorded ***Endless Wire***, which climbs to US #20.
Apr *The Circle Is Small (I Can See It In Your Eyes)*, taken from ***Endless Wire***, makes US #33.
[25] ***Endless Wire*** is certified gold by the RIAA.
Oct *Daylight Katy*, not issued as a US single, makes UK #41. The follow-up album ***Dream Street Rose*** will reach US #60 in May 1980.

1982

Mar With ***The Best Of Gordon Lightfoot*** released only in the UK the previous year, ***Shadows*** peaks at US #87.
May *Baby Step Back*, taken from ***Shadows***, makes US #50, and is Lightfoot's final US Hot 100 single of the decade. (By year's end he appears in the movie "Harry Tracy" with Bruce Dern.)

1985

Apr Lightfoot sings on *Tears Are Not Enough* by Northern Lights, the Canadian multi-artist recording in aid of the USA For Africa trust, sharing vocals with fellow Canadians Neil Young, Joni Mitchell, Bryan Adams, Baron Longfellow and others.
Aug ***Salute*** peaks at US #175.

1986

Sept ***East Of Midnight***, produced with help from compatriot David Foster, climbs to US #165 and includes the extract *Anything For Love*.
Oct [13] ***Sundown*** is certified platinum by the RIAA.

1988

Apr Having completed a Lightfoot ends a North American tour in Atlantic City, NJ in November the previous year, and now backed by the Lightfoot Band, now comprising Terry Clements, Rick Haynes and recent additions Barry Keane on drums and Mike Heffernan on keyboards, he begins re-recording 12 self-penned songs and the previously unrecorded *If It Should Please You*, at Eastern Sound studios, Toronto, which will be released as ***Gord's Gold Volume II*** at the end of the year.

1989

Oct [3] Recently married, Lightfoot, now alcohol-free after years of abuse, plays at the Westbury Music Fair, Westbury, NY, during an extended North American tour. His next US tour in the fall of '91 will be highlighted by a concert at New York's Carnegie Hall on September 27th.

1992

Sept [18] During Lightfoot's current US tour, his performance at the New Pine Knob Music Theatre, Clarkston, MI, grosses $99,728.
Dec [4-5] While ***The Original Lightfoot***, a 60-song boxed set including his albums for UA, has been issued only in Canada, Lightfoot plays at the State Theatre, Minneapolis, MN.

1993

Mar [23] Following a seven-year recording hiatus, he releases ***Waiting For You*** on Warners, including a cover of Dylan's *Ring Them Bells*. The largely acoustic album of one-take cuts, featuring Terry Clements (guitar), Rick Haynes (bass), Michael Heffenan (keyboards) and Barry Keane (drums), was recorded at Manta Eastern Sound in Toronto and is supported by a 36-date North American tour, beginning at the Civic Theatre, Des Moines, IA, and including a six-day stint at the Massey Hall.

1994

Mar [13] During current US dates, Lightfoot performs at the Powell Symphony Hall, St. Louis, MO.
Aug [4] The RIAA certifies two million sales of ***Gord's Gold***.
Nov [13] Lightfoot performs at the Westbury Music Fair, Westbury, NY.

1995

Mar [16-18, 23-25] He plays a week of concerts at Massey Hall, Toronto.
Apr [20] Lightfoot begins a US tour at Braden Auditorium, Normal, IL.
Aug [10-13] The 35th annual "Mariposa Folk Festival" in Orillia, ON, Canada, honors Lightfoot.

1996

Mar [10] Lightfoot performs at the 25th annual Juno Awards held at Copps Coliseum, Hamilton in his native Ontario.

THE LIGHTNING SEEDS

Ian Broudie (vocals, keyboards, guitar)

1989

Aug [12] Broudie (b. Aug. 4, 1958, Liverpool, Lancs.), already a veteran of several bands including Big In Japan between 1977-78 (a Liverpudlian combo which also included future Frankie Goes To Hollywood front man Holly Johnson) and the short-lived Secrets, has joined Original Mirrors in early 1979 (which released one album ***Original Mirrors*** on Mercury Records in 1980). Leaving the group, he has subsequently concentrated on production work, leading to highly rated collaborations with the likes of Echo & the Bunnymen (their first two albums), Icicle Works, Wah! and the Fall before forming the Care in 1983 (which issued three infectious pop singles including the UK #48 *Flaming Sword*, November 1983) with ex-Wild Swans Paul Simpson, before disbanding. Having spent the rest of the decade on further production chores, Broudie has also formed a named outlet for his own recordings, namely Lightning Seeds. Its first single *Pure*, released on indie Ghetto label, now reaches UK #16.

1990

Feb [10] Highly infectious, keyboard led, melodic pop outing ***Cloudcuckooland***, released by Ghetto, and featuring Simpson and Peter Coyle, debuts at its UK #50 peak.
May [5] Licensed to MCA in the US ***Cloudcuckooland*** enters the US chart on its way to #46.
July [28] The extracted *Pure* reaches US #31.

1992

Mar [28] Now signed to Virgin Records (UK), *Life Of Riley* reaches UK #28, backed with his cover of Thunderclap Newman's *Something In The Air*.
Apr [11] Mostly written by Broudie and co-produced with Simon Rogers, ***Sense***, and featuring guest vocalists Terry Hall, Icicle Works' Ian McNabb and Juliet Roberts (with the studio band of Mark Feltham (harmonica), Alan Dunn (accordion), Clive Layton (Hammond organ) and Roddy Lorimer (trumpet), makes US #154, while *Life Of Riley* peaks at US #98.
[18] ***Sense*** charts for a week at UK #53.
June [13] Title cut *Sense* peaks at UK #31.

1994

Aug With his '90s production credits now including Frazier Chorus, Northside, Terry Hall and the Primitives among many others, and having also written and performed the theme to BBC1-TV's "Match of the Day"'s "Goal Of The Month" feature, Broudie's Lightning Seeds is now signed to Epic Records worldwide.
[20] Its label debut *Lucky You*, written and co-performed with Hall reaches UK #43.

1995

Jan [21] *Change* reaches UK #21.
Feb [11] ***Jollification***, once again co-produced with Rogers and featuring guests (and co-writers) Hall, McNabb and Alison Moyet, having briefly charted in September 1994 at UK #60, now debuts at its UK #30 peak.
Apr [22] *Marvellous* reaches UK #24.
July [29] *Perfect* reaches UK #18.
Oct [28] *Lucky You* reaches UK #28.

1996

Mar [9] *Ready Or Not* reaches UK #20 in its week of entry.
May [18] ***Pure Lightning Seeds*** bows at its UK #27 peak.
June [1] *Three Lions (The Official Song Of The Football Team)*, a collaboration between the Lightning Seeds and BBC2-TV's "Fantasy Football League" hosts Baddiel & Skinner enters the UK chart at #1.

LITTLE FEAT

Lowell George (vocals, guitar); **Paul Barrere** (lead guitar); **Bill Payne** (keyboards); **Fred Tackett** (guitar); **Kenny Gradney** (bass); **Richie Hayward** (drums); **Sam Clayton** (percussion)

1970

Mar Having played flute in his Hollywood High School Orchestra and harmonica with his brother Hampton on US-TV's "Ted Mack's Amateur Hour" as a teenager, gaining his diploma in 1962 and going on to contribute oboe and saxophone parts to mid-60s recordings by Frank Sinatra, singer/songwriter/guitarist George (b. Apr. 13, 1945, Hollywood, CA), ex-folk rock combo Factory, the Standells and the Seeds, having briefly joined Frank Zappa's Mothers of Invention to replace Ray Collins (his rhythm guitar and vocals preserved on the Zappa track *Didja Get Any Onya* from ***Weasels Ripped My Flesh***), is encouraged by Zappa to form his own band, after he has heard George's song, *Willing*. George takes Zappa's advice and his bass player, Roy Estrada (b. Roy Ralph Estrada, Apr. 17, 1943, Santa Ana, CA). They link with the classically-trained keyboardist Payne (b. Mar. 12, 1949, Waco, TX), who has also been the musical director of the Santa Barbara-based Viscounts in the late '60s, and Hayward (b. Ames, IA) who has been in his first band at the age of nine and already played with George in Factory and has also been a member of Fraternity of Man. Jimmy Carl Black of the Mothers of Invention provides the band's name when laughing at George's small shoe size.
May Little Feat signs to Warner Bros. Records, and *Strawberry Flats/Hamburger Midnight* is released to critical acclaim and will both be featured on the group's debut album ***Little Feat***, produced by Russ Titelman, and with guests Ry Cooder and "Sneaky" Pete Kleinow, released in November. Their sophomore effort, ***Sailin' Shoes***, once again blending rock with soul, blues and country elements, will follow in May 1972, after which Estrada leaves to join Captain Beefheart's Magic Band.

1973

Feb Their third album, ***Dixie Chicken***, is released and includes Gradney (b. New Orleans, LA) on bass and ex-Soul Destroyers percussionist Clayton (b. New Orleans), both ex-Delaney & Bonnie. Ex-Lead Enema Barrere (b. July 3, 1948, Burbank, CA), who has been released from a California State Adult Authority facility in Chino, CA in 1971, also joins and the new line-up plays its first gig at the "Easter Festival" in Hawaii, HI. However the cycle of touring and destructive personal habits becomes too much and the band breaks up. Payne joins the Doobie Brothers, but quits mid-tour to join Bonnie Raitt's band. The rest of the band signs to Zappa's DiscReet label to provide backing for unknown Los Angeles, CA singer Kathy Dalton. Freddie White joins from Donny Hathaway's band, on drums. There are rumors that ex-Vinegar Joe singer Robert Palmer will be asked to replace the increasingly erratic George, who in turn is rumored to be forming a band with John Sebastian and Phil Everly.

1974

Nov Encouraged financially by Warner Bros. to re-form, the group has re-entered its Blue Seas Studio in Hunts Valley, MD, to cut ***Feats Don't Fail Me Now***, featuring Bonnie Raitt, Emmylou Harris and Van Dyke Parks, which reaches US #36, earning the band's first chart placing.

1975

Jan [12] The group begins a nine-city, 18-show European tour, under the banner "The Warner Brothers Music Show". The other bands on tour, the Doobie Brothers, Tower Of Power, Bonaroo, Montrose and Graham Central Station, are critically upstaged by Little Feat, which attracts rave reviews.
July As the band records ***The Last Record Album***, George contracts hepatitis.
Dec Jazz-leaning ***The Last Record Album***, mostly co-penned by Payne and Barrere, reaches US and UK #36.

1976

May [31] Little Feat is one of the support acts on "Who The Put The Boot In", the first of three Who headliners at London's Charlton Football Ground.
June [13] On a return UK visit, the band plays at the Odeon Theatre, Birmingham, West Midlands.

1977

June ***Time Loves A Hero*** reaches US #34 and hits UK #8 with George having only contributed one song.
Aug The band performs four nights at the Rainbow Theatre, London, during its UK summer tour.

1978

Mar Live shows supporting the double set ***Waiting For Columbus*** are considered lackluster, but it reaches US #18 and UK #43, becoming the band's second gold disc.

1979

Jan Grateful Dead's ***Shakedown Street***, produced by George, reaches US #41.
Apr Having recorded its final album, Payne announces that Little Feat has disbanded. George sets out on tour with the solo album ***Thanks, I'll Eat It Here***, featuring top sessioneers David Foster, Jim Keltner, David Paich and Jeff Porcaro, and singing guests Raitt and J.D. Souther, which makes US and UK #71.
June [29] Two months after Little Feat's break-up and

the day after a sell-out solo performance in Washington, DC, George, aged 34, is found dead from a heart attack brought on by drug abuse, in a motel in Arlington, VA.

Aug [4] The surviving members of Little Feat are joined by Jackson Browne, Emmylou Harris, Larson, Michael McDonald, Raitt and Linda Ronstadt in a benefit concert at the Great Western Forum, Inglewood, CA. The 20,000 crowd raises over $230,000 for George's widow.

Dec Little Feat album, ***Down On The Farm*** (originally titled ***Duck Lips***), reaches US #29 and UK #46.

1981

Aug Compilation album mixing live material with studio remnants, ***Hoy-Hoy!***, makes UK #76.

Sept ***Hoy-Hoy!*** reaches US #39. Hayward will become an in-demand backing performer for the likes of Robert Plant and Joan Armatrading, while Payne goes on to top session work in the studio. Barrere's debut solo album ***On My Own Two Feet***, will be released on the Mirage label in 1983.

1986

Apr [17] ***Feats Don't Fail Me Now*** is certified gold by the RIAA.

June UK-only ***As Time Goes By : The Best Of Little Feat***, a 12-track retrospective, is released by WEA.

1988

Aug The original line-up, now augmented by guitarists ex-Pure Prairie League's Craig Fuller (who also takes on the lead vocal slot) and Fred Tackett, has regrouped and re-signed with Warner Bros., releasing ***Let It Roll*** which makes US #36, earning the group's fourth gold disc.

1989

Feb [14] ***Let It Roll*** is certified gold by the RIAA.

Sept [12] The group ends a US tour at the Greek Theatre, Los Angeles, CA.

Nov [8] The RIAA certifies gold sales for ***Dixie Chicken*** and ***Time Loves A Hero*** and platinum sales for ***Waiting For Columbus***.

1990

May [19] ***Representing The Mambo***, co-produced by Payne with Bill Massenburg, reaches US #45.

[22] The group appears at the Fox Theatre, St. Louis, MO, during a US tour.

June [29] Now managed by Peter Asher, Little Feat plays at London's Hammersmith Odeon.

July [13] The band begins a further two-month US trek in Columbus, OH, set to end on September 18th in Los Angeles.

1991

Mar [30] The group, signed earlier in the month to Morgan Creek Records, is showcased on PBS-TV's "Austin City Limits".

Aug Having toured in his backing band on a 1987 trek, Payne and Tackett are featured on Bob Seger's newly released ***The Fire Inside***.

Oct [12] ***Shake Me Up*** debuts at its US #126 peak.

Dec [14] Little Feat grosses $33,489 at the Wicomico Youth & Civic Center, Salisbury, MD, during US dates.

1992

July [23] They perform at Chastain Park Amphitheatre, Atlanta, GA, grossing $171,014, during a US concert series.

Oct [11] The band appears at the "Healing The Sacred Hoop - The Next 500 Years" benefit at the Shoreline Amphitheatre, Mountain View, CA, on a bill with Raitt, Don Henley, Todd Rundgren, Ry Cooder and others, raising $240,518.

1993

Jan [20] The group performs at the "New England Ball" in Washington, DC, on the day of President Clinton's inauguration.

Mar [21] Little Feat headlines the "13th Musicians for UNICEF" benefit concert, at the Palomino Club, North Hollywood.

1994

Apr [9] The group's new singer Shaun Murphy, replacing the departed Fuller, makes her live debut with the band at a private taping at the Anaheim Marriott Hotel for National Public Radio's "E-Town" show. (Payne and Tackett had met her when they all played in Bob Seger's touring band in 1987.)

[29] The group appears at the 25th annual "New Orleans Jazz & Heritage Festival", at the Kiefer U.N.O. Lakefront Arena, New Orleans.

Sept [8-9] The "Blues Music Festival" package, with Little Feat, B.B. King and Dr. John, now plays a sellout show at the Filene Center for the Performing Arts, Wolf Trap Farm Park, Vienna, VA.

1995

May [13] Now signed to Zoo Records, ***Ain't Had Enough Fun*** debuts at its US #154 peak, as the group embarks on a US tour to promote the album.

Sept [13] Little Feat guests on NBC-TV's "The Tonight Show".

Nov [9] The group plays a sole London date at the Shepherd's Bush Empire.

Dec They continue working on a live double album (the first since 1978's ***Waiting For Columbus*** set), due for release the following year.

1996

Jan [19] During a band hiatus, Murphy opens in Charleston, SC as a backing singer on Bob Seger's first US tour since 1987.

LITTLE RICHARD

1950

Little Richard (b. Richard Wayne Penniman, Dec. 5, 1932, Macon, GA), having grown up with 11 brothers and sisters, the children of Charles and Leva Mae, and the Seventh Day Adventist faith (his father and grandfather are preachers), has sung in church with the family Penniman Singers, developing strong gospel links, as the Tiny Tots Quartet, after running off with Dr. Hudson's Medicine Show, selling snake oil at fairs and carnivals. Going on to sing with Sugarfoot Sam's Minstrel Show, Richard is adopted by the white family of Ann and Johnny Johnson, who run Ann's Tick Tock club in Macon, where he begins performing R&B numbers, having learned to play gospel piano from a character named Esquerita. He also appears at the Douglass Theater and the City Auditorium, picks up a job washing dishes in a bus station and sings with the B. Brown Orchestra.

1951

Oct [16] Richard makes his first recordings in Atlanta, GA, for RCA Camden, arranged after singer Billy Wright introduced him to a Georgia DJ with label connections, who entered him in a radio audition contest at Atlanta's Eighty One Theater. Wright, with his heavy make-up and gelled hair, is to be a major visual influence on Richard. (Tracks from this session and another, in January 1952, including *Every Hour* and *Get Rich Quick*, are released in 1952 on four US singles and on an album in both the US and UK in 1959 and 1970.)

1953

Richard moves to Houston, TX, to record eight tracks for Don Robey's Peacock label, initially credited to sessions vocal group, the Tempo-Toppers but, after 1955, the billing is changed to feature Little Richard. The following year Richard meets Lloyd Price, who suggests sending blues demos recorded at Macon radio station WBML to Art Rupe at Speciality Records in Los Angeles, CA.

1955

Feb Richard auditions for Specialty. Tracks recorded include the a cappella gospel piece, *He's My Star*, and piano boogie *Chicken Shack Baby*. He fronts the Johnny Otis Orchestra for two singles and tours small black nightclubs, where he mainly sings the blues.

Sept [14] Specialty contacts Richard, giving him half a cent for every record sold, while he is working in Fayetteville, TN, and he enters the studio for a 48-hour session in New Orleans, LA, with the Crescent City rhythm section (which features on many of Fats Domino's discs) and producer Robert "Bumps" Blackwell, who is also Richard's manager. Playing piano and singing, and after recording blues numbers *Kansas City* and *Directly From My Heart*, Richard records a version of a live number he has written - *Tutti Frutti*. (The lyrics are cleaned up by local songwriter Dorothy La Bostrie.) The histrionic vocal and bashing piano style set the mould for Little Richard's image, as Blackwell insists on a live feel to studio recordings.

1956

Feb *Tutti Frutti*, its publishing rights sold to Specialty for $50, reaches US #17, staying charted for 12 weeks and selling over three million copies.

Mar Richard enters the recording studio again. (He will record six more sessions between now and February 1957, using a band based around Earl Palmer (drums), Red Tyler and Lee Allen (saxes), Frank Fields (bass), Ernest McLean and Justin Adams (guitars) and supplementary pianists, Huey Smith, Edward Frank, Little Booker and Salvador Doucette.) Pat Boone's version of *Tutti Frutti* reaches US #12.

May *Long Tall Sally* makes US #13. Originally titled *The Thing*, then *Bald Headed Sally*, the song was sanitized for Boone to record his own version (US #8).

June B-side, *Slippin' And Slidin'*, based on the ribald New Orleans blues number, *I Got The Blues For You*, reaches US #33.

Aug *Rip It Up* makes US #17, as its B-side, *Ready Teddy*, peaks at US #44.

Dec *Rip It Up*, released on London label, is his UK chart debut, at #30.

1957

Feb Richard heads for Los Angeles with his own band, the Upsetters, beginning an intensive schedule of touring and film work (including the movie "Mr. Rock'n'Roll").

Mar *The Girl Can't Help It*, from the Jayne Mansfield-starring film of the same name, peaks at US #49. (Richard appears in the movie, and was also featured in the Bill Haley vehicle "Don't Knock The Rock", the previous year.) *Long Tall Sally* hits UK #3 during a 16-week stay, while the B-side, *Tutti Frutti*, spends a week at UK #29.

Apr *Lucille*, penned by Richard, peaks at US #27, its flip-side, *Send Me Some Lovin'*, climbing to US #54, while *She's Got It* reaches UK #15.

May *The Girl Can't Help It* hits UK #9, as its A-side, *She's Got It*, re-enters the UK chart for two weeks, reaching #28.

July *Jenny, Jenny* makes US #14, while the flip-side, *Miss Ann*, peaks at US #56.

Aug *Lucille* hits UK #10. Richard's only US chart album in the '50s, ***Here's Little Richard***, enters the chart, set to peak at #13 during a five-week run. (He will never secure a UK chart album.)

Sept *Jenny, Jenny* reaches UK #11.

Oct *Keep A Knockin'*, from the film "Mr. Rock'n'Roll", hits US #8.

[12] After a year of whirlwind success, Little Richard, in Sydney, New South Wales on the fifth date of a two-week Australian tour, publicly renounces rock'n'roll and embraces God. (He will later tell the story of dreaming of his own damnation and praying to God after one of the engines in a plane he was in caught fire.)

[13] On his return to the US, Specialty arranges a final eight-song session before he enters theological college. The label also tries to keep his conversion quiet. (Stable mate Joe Lutcher has been warning

Richard for some time that pop music is "evil", and the pair will later tour the US as the "Little Richard Evangelistic Team".)

Dec *Keep A Knockin'* reaches UK #21.

1958

Jan [27] Richard enters the Oakwood Theological College in Huntsville, AL, where he will receive a BA and become ordained as a Seventh Day Adventist minister.

Mar *Good Golly, Miss Molly*, from the final Specialty session, hits US #10 and UK #8. (Its B-side *Hey Hey Hey Hey*, will be revived in 1964 by the Beatles on ***Beatles For Sale***, in a medley with *Kansas City* which fails to credit Richard's song. Several years later, after strong words from the song's publisher, it is fully credited on the album and back royalties are paid by EMI.)

June *Ooh! My Soul* makes US #35.

July B-side, *True Fine Mama*, peaks at US #68.

Aug *Ooh! My Soul* reaches UK #22.

Oct Richard's version of *Baby Face*, written in 1926, peaks at US #41.

1959

Jan *Baby Face* hits UK #2, behind Elvis Presley's *I Got Stung/One Night*.

Apr His version of *By The Light Of The Silvery Moon* makes UK #17.

May *Kansas City*, his last US chart hit for five years, peaks at US #95, eclipsed by Wilbert Harrison's #1 version.

June *Kansas City* reaches UK #26. During the summer, Richard returns to the studio to record gospel tracks for Gone/End Records. (The basic vocal/piano/organ tracks are overdubbed with a choir, and have extra instrumentation added, when they are re-released on the Coral and Guest Star labels in the '60s.)

1960

Having sold an estimated 18 million singles during the '50s, Richard will spend the next two years recording 20 gospel songs, with Quincy Jones producing, for release on albums on the Mercury label. Seven more gospel tracks, including *Crying In The Chapel*, are also cut for Atlantic, with Jerry Wexler producing.

1962

Oct [7] Richard makes his UK debut on ITV's "Thank Your Lucky Stars".

[8] The Rev. Little Richard returns to rock'n'roll with a comeback tour, his first UK package tour, promoted by Don Arden. During the 20-date series, two people are treated in hospital after a Bristol, Somerset show, an attendant is injured when a crowd tries to storm the stage in Slough, Bucks., and police with dogs go on stage after a show in Walthamstow, London, to clear the audience.

[12] Richard headlines a five-and-a-half-hour package bill at the Tower Ballroom, New Brighton, Lancs., also featuring the Beatles, Billy Kramer & the Coasters, the Merseybeats, the Big Three and others. (Brian Epstein also books him into the Cavern.)

[27] On Mercury, *He Got What He Wanted* makes UK #38.

Nov [1-14] He plays a 14-day stint at the Star-Club, Hamburg, West Germany, sharing the bill with the Beatles. (Paul McCartney reportedly asks Richard to teach him his singing style.)

1963

Richard tours Europe with the Beatles (with whom firm, mutually respecting relationships have been formed), the Rolling Stones and others. He later notes that the young groups know his records better than he does.

Oct [5] Little Richard joins the Everly Brothers' UK tour, ostensibly to boost poor ticket sales.

1964

Mar He records the first of seven sessions for Vee-Jay. Early tapings produce versions of *Whole Lotta Shakin' Goin' On* and *Good Lawdy Miss Clawdy*.

May [8] Richard appears on ITV's "Ready Steady Go!" with Brian Poole, the Swinging Blue Jeans and Carl Perkins, during a short UK visit.

June On his second UK tour, *Bama Lama Bama Loo* reaches UK #20, his last UK hit for 13 years.

Aug *Bama Lama Bama Loo* peaks at US #82.

Oct [3] Richard fails to appear at the beginning of a UK tour at the Cellar Hall, Kingston, Surrey.

Dec He re-records his greatest hits for Vee-Jay. (In Britain, various combinations of the tracks appear on the Stateside, Fontana, Sue, President and Joy labels over the next four years.)

1965

Vee-Jay issues the albums ***Little Richard Is Back*** and ***Little Richard's Greatest Hits***, released in the UK on Fontana.

Nov *I Don't Know What You've Got But It's Got Me* is the only Vee-Jay single to chart, spending a week at US #92.

Dec Richard records seven studio tracks for Modern Records, including *Holy Mackerel*, *Don't You Want A Man Like Me* and *Baby What You Want Me To Do*.

1966

Jan He records the Modern-label released ***Little Richard Sings His Greatest Hits - Recorded Live***, combining studio tracks with overdubbed applause, released in the UK on the Polydor and Contour labels.

Mar Richard begins recording five sessions for soul label, Okeh.

Aug [29] At their final live concert at San Francisco, CA's Candlestick Park, the Beatles' farewell song is Richard's *Long Tall Sally*.

Dec [11] He makes a sole London appearance at the Saville Theatre.

1967

Aug Another live compilation, ***Little Richard's Greatest Hits***, on Okeh, peaks at US #184, and is his first chart album in ten years. (As a rock'n'roll revival in Europe gains momentum, Richard revisits for successful tours. He is also becoming increasingly involved in drug abuse, which will dog his career into the '70s).

1968

Richard records six tracks for Brunswick, which are released as US singles. The first two, *Try Some Of Mine* and *She's Together* (produced by Don Covay), are also issued (by MCA) in the UK.

Aug [18] He takes part in the "Schaefer Music Festival" in New York, NY's Central Park.

1969

Apr [14] The Monkees' NBC-TV special, "33⅓ Revolutions Per Monkee", featuring Little Richard and others, including Jerry Lee Lewis, Fats Domino, the Clara Ward Singers, Brian Auger, Buddy Miles and Julie Driscoll, airs.

Sept [13] Little Richard takes part in the "Rock'n'Revival Concert" at the Varsity Stadium in the University Of Toronto, Toronto, ON, Canada, with Chuck Berry, Fats Domino, Jerry Lee Lewis, Gene Vincent, Bo Diddley and John Lennon's newly-formed Plastic Ono Band. (Now living in Riverside, CA, he signs to Reprise Records.)

1970

July Reprise-issued ***Freedom Blues***, recorded at Muscle Shoals, makes US #47.

[18] Richard takes part in the "Randall Island Rock Festival" with Jimi Hendrix, Jethro Tull, Grand Funk Railroad, Steppenwolf and others.

Sept *Greenwood Mississippi* stalls at US #85. He appears at the "Toronto Pop Festival", documented in D.A. Pennebaker's film, "Keep On Rockin'". In November the following year, ***The King Of Rock'n'Roll*** will make US #184.

1972

Apr Richard sings on Canned Heat's *Rockin' With The King*, which makes US #88, contributes two cuts to the soundtrack of the Warren Beatty/Goldie Hawn-starring movie "$" (UK title: "The Heist"), and reunites with Blackwell, Earl Palmer and Lee Allen to record ***The Second Coming***.

June [2] He takes part in the 29th "Rock & Roll Spectacular", with Lloyd Price, Shirley & Lee, Danny & the Juniors, the Cleftones, the Exciters, and Dion & the Belmonts, who have re-formed specially for the date, at New York's Madison Square Garden. (He has been, and will be, a regular performer on this bill over the years.)

Aug [5] Richard is booed offstage at the first-ever "London Rock'n'Roll Festival" at Wembley Stadium, Wembley, Middx., which also features Bill Haley, Chuck Berry, Jerry Lee Lewis and Bo Diddley.

1973

After leaving Reprise, with an unissued country album ***Southern Child***, Richard records for ALA with Blackwell (his last work with the producer).

June [20] He rises from his sickbed to make an appearance on Dick Clark's retrospective 20th-anniversary "Bandstand" show on ABC-TV.

1976

Having recorded a one-off single, *Call My Name*, for Emerson, Lake & Palmer's Manticore label the previous year, he re-records 20 of his greatest hits in London for SJ Records. After the death of his brother Tony, Richard is re-born to Christianity for the second time and works temporarily for Memorial Bibles International. Creole Records' release of SJ recordings of *Good Golly Miss Molly/Rip It Up* will make UK #37 in July 1977.

1979

Richard becomes a fully-fledged evangelist, preaching the story of his salvation throughout the US, stating that "If God can save an old homosexual like me, he can save anybody". (He will relate the experience of his redemption in the lengthy *Little Richard's Testimony*, included on his gospel album ***God's Beautiful City***.)

1986

Jan [23] Little Richard is inducted into the Rock and Roll Hall of Fame at the inaugural induction dinner, at New York's Waldorf Astoria Hotel.

Apr [12] *Great Gosh A'Mighty (It's A Matter Of Time)*, from the forthcoming Richard Dreyfuss/Bette Midler-starring movie, "Down And Out In Beverly Hills", in which Little Richard also appears, makes US #42.

June *Great Gosh A'Mighty (It's A Matter Of Time)* peaks at UK #62.

Oct Newly signed to WEA Records, he releases ***Lifetime Friend***, the extracted *Operator* making UK #67. Concerted media promotion mixes his gospel attitudes with the legendary Little Richard flamboyance.

Dec He teams with the Beach Boys for *Happy Endings*, from the film "The Telephone", and will guest on New Edition's *Tears On My Pillow*, released in the US in the New Year.

1988

Sept Richard contributes *Rock Island Line* with Fishbone to the Woody Guthrie/Leadbelly tribute album, ***Folkways : A Vision Shared***.

Nov Now seen as a media evangelist, Richard duets with Philip Bailey on the title track for the Arnold Schwarzenegger/Danny DeVito film, "Twins".

1989

Jan [18] Richard inducts the late Otis Redding into the Rock and Roll Hall of Fame at the fourth annual dinner, at the Waldorf Astoria Hotel. He and Mick Jagger sing *I Can't Turn You Loose* at the after-dinner music bash.

Feb [7] Georgia State Representative Billy Randall introduces a bill to make *Tutti Frutti* the state's official rock song.

July [12] A press conference is held to announce Disney Channel's Shelley Duvall-produced "Mother Goose Rock'n'Rhyme", which includes Richard in the all-star line-up, in the role of Old King Cole.

1990

June [21] Richard is bestowed with a star on the Hollywood Walk of Fame on "Little Richard Day" in Los Angeles.
Sept He performs a guest rap on *Elvis Is Dead* from Living Colour's new album, ***Time's Up***.
[23] Richard plays at the City Auditorium, Macon - his first hometown concert in 35 years. (The town's Penniman Boulevard has been named after him.)

1991

Feb [10] Little Richard joins with nearly 100 celebrities in Burbank, CA, to record *Voices That Care*, a David Foster and fiancée Linda Thompson Jenner-composed and organized charity record to benefit the American Red Cross Gulf Crisis Fund.
Mar [9] The Peace Choir's *Give Peace A Chance* remake, featuring Richard, makes US #54.
June [4] He takes part in the "Celebrate The Soul Of American Music" at the Pantages Theater, Hollywood, CA, to benefit the Thurgood Marshall Scholarship Fund.
[22] Disney's ***For Our Children***, a benefit album for the Pediatric AIDS Foundation, which features Richard on *Itsy Bitsy Spider*, reaches US #31.
July [17] Currently touring the US with James Brown, Richard is quoted in **USA Today**: "If I had been born white, there never would have been an Elvis Presley."
Aug [26] His million-selling achievements never previously formally recognized, Richard receives his first ever gold disc, for ***For Our Children***, at the Walt Disney Studios, Hollywood.
Nov [24] Little Richard officiates the marriage between Cyndi Lauper and actor David Thornton at their wedding in Manhattan, New York.
Dec [3] He is present at the Hollywood Walk of Fame ceremony honoring pioneering DJ Alan Freed.

1992

Jan [15] Richard inducts the Isley Brothers into the Rock and Roll Hall of Fame at the seventh annual dinner, at the Waldorf Astoria Hotel, also joining the Isleys for *Shout* at the post-ceremony jam.
Feb [6] "Little Richard's Rock And Roll Reunion" takes place at the Universal Amphitheatre, Universal City, CA, to benefit the Lupus Foundation of America.
Mar [1] "Muhammad Ali's 50th Birthday", featuring a tribute from Richard, airs on ABC-TV.
May [30] He receives the first Lupus Foundation of America Platinum Star award at the Beverly Hilton Hotel, Los Angeles.
June [20] Richard grosses $53,853 performing at the Westbury Music Fair, Westbury, NY, during US summer dates.
Oct [20] ***Shake It All About***, another collection of children's tunes on Walt Disney Records, again featuring Richard, is released in the US.
Dec [5] "The Giants Of Rock'n'Roll" package concert takes place at the Wembley Arena, with Richard, Bobby Vee & the Ricochettes, Lloyd Price, Duane Eddy, Johnny Preston, Chris Montez and Little Eva.

1993

Jan [19] Richard performs *Reelin' & Rockin'* and *Good Golly Miss Molly* in an all-star band at "An American Reunion : The Fifty-second Presidential Gala", held at the Capital Centre, Landover, MD.
Feb [15] Reacting to news that he will receive a Lifetime Achievement Award at this year's Grammys on the 23rd, Richard is angry that it will be presented to him at a dinner the night prior to the Awards and not at the ceremony itself. "This is the crowning achievement of my career and they want to give it to me secretly. It's like I'm in the kitchen doing all the cooking and the waiters get all the credit. I cried (when I heard) - I've been waiting so long." NARAS president Michael Greene replies: "Everybody is always mad at us. We have over 400 nominees and just X amount of real estate."
[24] Having received his Grammy the night before, a still-upset Richard attends the 35th annual Grammy Awards, held at the Shrine Auditorium, Los Angeles, and says, prior to the show's start: "I'm the innovator. I'm the emancipator. I'm the originator. I'm the architect of rock'n'roll." Greene, who has earlier told Richard that there is not enough time in the live telecast for him to thank his peers, makes a rambling ten-minute speech during the ceremony.
Nov [3] Richard guests on CBS-TV's "Hearts Afire".
Dec [4] Elton John's ***Duets*** album, to which Richard contributes *The Power*, hits UK #5 in its week of entry and will reach US #25 the following week.
[29] Richard appears on CBS-TV's 16th annual "The Kennedy Center Honors" in a tribute to Marion Williams.

1994

Mar [2] Richard is presented with the Rhythm and Blues Foundation's Ray Charles Lifetime Achievement Award at the fifth annual Foundation Awards show, at New York's Roseland Ballroom.
[23] He takes part in "Rhythm Country & Blues - The Concert", benefitting the Country Music Foundation and the Rhythm and Blues Foundation, at the Universal Amphitheatre.
[26] Various artists compilation album ***Rhythm Country And Blues***, featuring Richard's duet with Tanya Tucker on *Somethin' Else*, reaches US #18.
Apr [22] Richard takes part in the 25th annual "New Orleans Jazz & Heritage Festival".
Oct [30] He performs at the "Gala For The President" at Washington's Ford Theatre, in the presence of President Clinton, set to air on ABC-TV on December 7th.

1995

Jan [19] Richard appears at the "Commitment To Life VIII" benefit for AIDS Project Los Angeles, honoring Elton John, Tom Hanks and Ron Meyer at the Universal Amphitheatre.
Mar [2] He introduces award winner Lloyd Price at the sixth annual Rhythm and Blues Foundation Pioneer Awards at Hollywood Palladium.
Apr [23] Richard joins Dolly Parton at the 1995 opening ceremonies of Dollywood in Pigeon Forge, TN, performing two shows.
May [16] During the show's week in London, Richard and Chuck Berry play in the band backing Elvis Costello on the "Late Show With David Letterman".
Sept [2] Richard sings *Good Golly Miss Molly* at the Concert for the Rock and Roll Hall of Fame at the Cleveland Stadium, Cleveland, OH.
Nov [19] He sings *That Old Black Magic* at Frank Sinatra's 80th birthday tribute at Los Angeles' Shrine Auditorium.

1996

Feb The all-star update of ***The Songs Of West Side Story***, to which Richard has contributed his version of *I Feel Pretty*, is released in the US.

THE LITTLE RIVER BAND

Glenn Shorrock (vocals); **David Briggs** (guitar); **Beeb Birtles** (guitar); **Graham Goble** (guitar); **George McArdle** (bass); **Derek Pellicci** (drums)

1975

Mar After London-based Australian band Mississippi has broken up after two years, in 1974, three of its members, Goble (b. May 15, 1947, Adelaide, South Australia, Australia), ex-Zoot guitarist Birtles (b. Gerard Birtlekamp, Nov. 28, 1948, Amsterdam, Holland) and Pellicci (b. Feb. 18, 1953) meet Shorrock (b. June 30, 1944, Rochester, Kent, raised in Elizabeth, South Australia, Australia), late of Esperanto who has lived in Australia since his teens and is a veteran of the indigenously popular Twilights '60s band, and fellow Australian Glenn Wheatley, working in management in London, decide to team up in Australia in the New Year, and now re-form as Mississippi, with Wheatley as manager. Criticized for having an American name, they become the Little River Band, a moniker chosen at random from a small community 30 miles outside Melbourne, Australia.
May Adding guitarist Rick Formosa and bassist Roger McLachlan, they cut their debut album ***Little River Band***. Initially released only in Australia, it will be voted Album Of The Year.

1976

Apr Now signed to EMI's Harvest label, the soft-rock based ***Little River Band*** is issued worldwide, as the group begins a global tour, without Formosa and McLachlan, who have left and have been replaced by Briggs (b. Jan. 26, 1951, Melbourne) and McArdle (b. Nov. 30, 1954, Melbourne).
Oct The band plays at London's Marquee club, having just completed a European tour supporting the Hollies, and before embarking on a US trek opening for the Average White Band.
Dec *It's A Long Way There* is the group's first US hit single, reaching #28, spurring ***Little River Band*** to make US #80.

1977

Mar *I'll Always Call Your Name* peaks at US #62, while ***Diamantina Cocktail***, an amalgam of two Australian albums (1976's ***After Hours*** and this year's ***Diamantina Cocktail***), reaches US #49, becoming the first US gold-certified album by an Australian group.
Aug The group plays at the annual "Reading Festival", Reading, Berks.
Nov *Help Is On Its Way*, taken from ***Diamantina Cocktail***, and produced by American John Boylan, reaches US #14.

1978

Mar *Happy Anniversary* reaches US #16.
Oct Smooth Goble-penned smash, *Reminiscing*, hits US #3, earning a gold disc, while ***Sleeper Catcher*** reaches US #16, and will earn a platinum disc. The band returns home from its second world tour, to find it has swept the first Australian Rock Awards and Wheatley has been named Manager Of The Year.

1979

Jan The group tours the US again, after which McArdle will leave, giving away all his money and retreating to the Blue Mountains to undertake a three-year Bible-study course. He is replaced on bass by Barry Sullivan, while New Zealander Mal Logan joins on keyboards.
Apr Goble-written *Lady* hits US #10.
Sept *Lonesome Loser*, written by Briggs and marking a change of label from Harvest to Capitol, hits US #6 where the band's light rock material is proving popular fare on radio.
Oct ***First Under The Wire***, on Capitol, and including *Lonesome Loser*, hits US #10, also achieving platinum status.

1980

Jan *Cool Change*, taken from ***First Under The Wire***, hits US #10.
Apr Briggs is replaced by Wayne Nelson (b. Chicago, IL), and guitarist Stephen Housden also joins.
May *It's Not A Wonder* peaks at US #51.
June Live double album, ***Backstage Pass***, makes US #44.
[6] The group plays a one-off UK concert at London's Rainbow Theatre, supporting Kevin Ayers.

1981

Nov *The Night Owls* hits US #6, taken from the George Martin-produced ***Time Exposure***, which makes US #21, earning a gold disc. *Take It Easy On Me*, also from ***Time Exposure***, will hit US #10 the following March, with a third extract, *Man On Your Mind*, reaching US #14 in May.

1983

Feb *The Other Guy* reaches US #11, while a compilation album, ***Little River Band/Greatest Hits***, makes US #33.

June *We Two* reaches US #22. Shorrock leaves to go solo, and is replaced by John Farnham (b. July 1, 1949).

Aug ***The Net***, which includes *We Two*, peaks at US #61.

Sept *You're Driving Me Out Of My Mind*, also taken from ***The Net***, makes US #35.

Oct With Shorrock signed to Capitol Records, his solo single, *Don't Girls Get Lonely*, peaks at US #69.

1985

Mar After more personnel changes, Goble is left as the only original member, and the band's credit changes to LRB on ***Playing To Win***, which makes US #75. The title track *Playing To Win* peaks at US #60. The Richard Dodd-produced ***No Reins*** will be its final original release on Capitol Records in April the following year, by which time Farnham will also quit for a solo career (his anthemic *You're The Voice* becoming an Australian chart-topper and hitting UK #6 in April 1987).

1988

Jan After a two-year recording hiatus, Little River Band signs to MCA, its renewed activity due largely to Shorrock rejoining. A new line-up appears on a TV concert from the "World Expo" in Brisbane, Australia.

Apr The band plays a concert in Melbourne to launch its comeback album, ***Monsoon***, reuniting the group with producer John Boylan, and single, *Love Is A Bridge*.

Aug Glenn Frey joins the band on stage at the Sydney Entertainment Centre, Sydney, New South Wales, Australia. The reunited LRB joins Frey on the Eagles' hits *Desperado*, *Lyin' Eyes* and *Take It Easy*, as well as their own *Cool Change* and *Night Owls*.

1990

Mar Dennis Lambert-produced ***Get Lucky***, with a line-up of Shorrock (vocals), Pellicci (drums), Nelson (bass), Houseden (guitar), Peter Beckett (guitar) and Richard Bryant (keys), is released on Curb Records.

May [18] A North American tour begins in Vancouver, BC, Canada.

1995

Sept [2] Following the 1991 release of ***Worldwide Love***, and still touring annually (now augmented by its latest recruit guitarist Tony Sciuto), the Little River Band celebrates its 20th year with the last date on its current US tour at Chanberg, IL, performing songs from the recently released Rhino Records restrospective ***Reminiscing - The 20th Anniversary Collection***, followed by a tour in Germany where the group remains a strong live draw.

LIVE

Ed Kowalczyk (vocals); **Chad Taylor** (guitar); **Patrick Dahlheimer** (bass); **Chad Gracey** (drums)

1991

Initially performing in its blue-collar hometown of York, PA, from 1985 as the U2/R.E.M.-influenced high school band Public Affection, the permanent nucleus of Kowalczyk (b. July 17, 1971, Lancaster, PA), Taylor (b. Nov 24, 1970, York), Dahlheimer (b. May 30, 1971, York) and Gracey (b. July 23, 1971, York) began playing as Live after band members graduated from high school. Local gigging included a residency at the Chameleon Club in Lancaster (where Kowalczyk still lives, his three colleagues remaining in York), performing self-written hard-rock material, lyrically led by Kowalczyk, who is inspired by the writings of Henry Miller and philosopher Jiddu Krishnamurti. Now performing farther afield, the band is spotted by a Radioactive Records A&R scout, who has brought them to the attention of label boss Gary Kurfirst who now signs the group after seeing it play at the famed CBGB club in New York, NY.

1992

Jan [25] Produced by ex-Talking Heads keyboardist Jerry Harrison, Live's first release, the four-track EP ***Four Songs*** is issued, its lead track *Operation Spirit* now entering the US Modern Rock chart set to hit #9.

Feb [8] Live's hard-driving debut album, again helmed by Harrison, ***Mental Jewelry*** makes US #73 helped by enthusiastic US college radio support. (Over the next year, the band will continue touring including a slot on MTV's "120 Minutes" US caravan with Big Audio Dynamite, Public Image Ltd. and Blind Melon, before returning to the studio to prepare its sophomore album.)

1994

July [23] Taken from the May-released ***Throwing Copper*** and heavily rotated on MTV (US), *Selling The Drama* makes US #43.

Aug [14] The group takes part in "Woodstock '94" at Winston Farm, Saugerties, NY. (During the year, the band's non-stop touring schedule also includes South American dates, including the "Hollywood Rock Festival", participation in the "WOMAD" tour of US, a club tour with labelmates Fatima Mansions and a December performance at KROQ-FM's Acoustic Christmas in Los Angeles, CA.)

1995

Jan [21] The band is the music guest on NBC-TV's "Saturday Night Live".

Feb [25] *I Alone* makes US #48, the same day that *Lightning Crashes* tops the US Modern Rock chart, its video-clip directed by Jake Scott.

Apr [6] ***Mental Jewelry*** is certified gold by the RIAA.

[19] The band's "MTV Unplugged" performance airs in the US, taped at the Brooklyn Academy of Music, New York.

May [6] In its 52nd week on the survey, ***Throwing Copper***, once again produced by Harrison, finally tops the US chart.

[13] The group's first US tour of the year ends at the Tri-Cities Coliseum, Kennewick, WA, on a bill grossing $62,138 from 3,537 fans.

July [1] During UK dates, including this summer's 25th "Glastonbury Festival", *Selling The Drama* bows at its UK #30 peak.

[15] ***Throwing Copper*** enters at its UK #7 high.

[21] Variously supported by Big Audio Dynamite, Buffalo Tom, Veruca Salt and P.J. Harvey, Live begins a headlining 33-date, 32-city US tour at Hersheypark Stadium, Hershey, PA, a $520,369 box-office from 25,558 attendees, set to end on September 20th at the CoreStates Spectrum, Philadelphia, PA. (It will include a $10-admission show at the Chameleon Club in Lancaster in July to help celebrate the tenth anniversary of the club that helped launch the band's career.)

Aug [10] The RIAA certifies five million US sales of ***Throwing Copper***.

Oct [7] *All Over You* charts for a week at UK #48.

Dec [6] Live is named Top Rock Artist at the sixth annual **Billboard** Music Awards, broadcast live on Fox-TV from the Coliseum, New York.

LIVING COLOUR

Corey Glover (vocals); **Vernon Reid** (guitar); **Doug Wimbish** (bass); **Will Calhoun** (drums)

1985

Reid (b. Aug. 22, 1958, London), born to West Indian parents and raised in Brooklyn, New York, NY from age two, the son of Post Office worker James and supermarket worker Mary, received his first guitar at age 15, from a cousin. Having gained informal instruction from Melvin the barber and subsequently Ted Dunbar and Rodney Jones, he has studied performing arts for two years at the Manhattan Community College, before earning his musical spurs with electric jazz outfit Defunk, and subsequently graduates from Ronald Shannon Jackson's avant-garde jazz-fusion collective, Decoding Society. Based in New York, NY, he now forms the power quartet Living Colour, taking the name from the pioneering NBC-TV announcement, "The following program is brought to you in living color", with drummer Calhoun (b. July 22, 1964, Bronx, New York), a 1986 graduate of the Berklee School of Music, Boston, MA, where he has won the Buddy Rich Award for percussion excellence and toured with Harry Belafonte, and bassist Muzz Skillings (b. Manuel Skillings, Jan. 6, 1960, Queens, New York), a graduate of City College. Intent on fusing dance, soul and jazz elements with hard rock and heavy metal, an innovative idea for an all-black group, they are joined by Glover (b. Nov. 6, 1964, Brooklyn) (having just completed work as an actor playing Francis, in Oliver Stone's movie "Platoon"), whom Reid has heard singing "Happy Birthday" at a mutual friend's party 18 months before. During the year, Reid also forms the Black Rock Coalition pressure movement with journalist Greg Tate.

1986

Having seen the band performing at CBGB's in New York, Mick Jagger invites them to play on his forthcoming solo album, ***Primitive Cool***. He will subsequently produce two demos for the group, *Glamour Boys* and *Which Way To America*, which will help them secure a recording deal with Epic Records. Jagger will continue to be a long-term champion of the band.

1988

Sept Their debut album, ***Vivid***, with Jagger-produced tracks, emerges, set to hit US #6 and stay on the survey for over a year. Constant touring to promote the project includes support slots for Cheap Trick, Robert Palmer, Anthrax and Billy Bragg.

Oct Reid features on the Keith Richard debut solo album, ***Talk Is Cheap***, a popular session choice, and will also guest on Bernie Worrell's ***Funk Of Ages***.

1989

Apr [1] The band is featured as the musical guest on NBC-TV's "Saturday Night Live".

May [6] Hard-funk, rock-driven *Cult Of Personality*, sampling part of a President John F. Kennedy speech, reaches US #13.

[31] The group performs live at the first International Rock Awards held in Lexington Avenue Armory, New York, and wins an Elvis Award as Best New Band.

July Reid co-hosts a benefit concert with Nona Hendryx at the Music Machine, Los Angeles, CA, for the local branch of the Black Rock Coalition.

[11] The group's "Primer" video is certified gold by the RIAA.

[22] Follow-up single, *Open Letter (To A Landlord)*, peaks at US #82.

Aug The group headlines a Beacon Theatre, New York concert to benefit the New York-based Partnership for the Homeless, raising $50,000. John Mellencamp joins them onstage for an electric version of *Pink Houses*.

[31] Living Colour embarks on the Rolling Stones' "Steel Wheels North American Tour 1989" at Veterans Stadium, Philadelphia, PA, before a sellout crowd of 55,000.

Sept [6] Mick Jagger presents the group with the Best New Artist, Best Group Video, and Best Stage Performance trophies at the sixth annual MTV Video Music Awards, backstage at the Three Rivers Stadium, Pittsburgh, PA.

Oct [21] Jagger-helmed *Glamour Boys* makes US #31.

1990

Feb [21] Living Colour wins Best Hard Rock Performance for *Cult Of Personality* at the 32nd annual Grammy Awards, at Los Angeles' Shrine Auditorium.

Mar [8] The group wins Best New American Band in

Rolling Stone magazine's Readers' Picks Music Awards, and Reid wins Best Guitarist in the magazine's Critics' Picks Music Awards. (Calhoun is named Best New Drummer by **Modern Drummer**.)
Apr [22] The band performs at an "Earth Day" celebration in New York's Central Park.
Aug [26] The group plays at the annual "Reading Festival", Reading, Berks.
Sept Reid writes and produces four tracks for a forthcoming album by B.B. King, on sessions which include Paul Griffin, Wilbur Bascomb and Living Colour's Calhoun.
Oct [6] Despite no Hot 100 extractions, their sophomore album, ***Time's Up***, clocks in at US #13, having already made UK #21 in September. Produced by Ed Stasium, the album features Little Richard rapping on *Elvis Is Dead*, Carlos Santana, rapper Queen Latifah and, of course, Jagger.
[11-12] Living Colour plays two nights at the Town & Country club, London, during selected UK dates.
[25] ***Time's Up*** is certified gold by the RIAA.
[27] *Type* anchors at UK #75.
Nov [3] "The Miracle Biscuit Tour" begins in Albany, NY.
Dec [11-13] During current US dates, the band plays three sellout shows at the New York Academy.

1991

Jan Skillings and Glover are invited to be guest professors at the PS20 Elementary School, Brooklyn.
[26] The group plays a sellout date at the Agora Arena, Cleveland, OH.
Feb [20] Living Colour wins the Best Hard Rock Performance, Vocal Or Instrumental category for ***Time's Up***, at the 33rd annual Grammy Awards, at New York's Radio City Music Hall.
Mar [7] The group is named Best Band in the annual **Rolling Stone** Critics' Picks Music Awards.
[16] Remixed by Soulshock and Cutfather from ***Time's Up***, *Love Rears Its Ugly Head* reaches UK #12, spurring the album to re-peak, at UK #20.
Apr [6] Reid marries Mia McLeod in Staten Island, New York.
May [17] The band is featured on C4-TV's "Friday At The Dome".
June [2] An eight-date UK tour ends at London's Brixton Academy.
[15] *Solace Of You* reaches UK #33.
July [19] The band performs on syndicated TV's "The Arsenio Hall Show".
[21, 23-4] Touring on the "Lollapalooza" alternative acts package, the band plays three dates at Irvine Meadows Amphitheatre, Laguna Hills, CA.
Aug [10] With personal divisions preventing the completion of a new studio effort, Epic issues the mini-album, ***Biscuits***, comprising six tracks recorded between April 1989 and May 1991, two of which are live, peaks at US #110.
Nov [2] Reissued *Cult Of Personality* peaks at UK #67.
[8] An exhibition of Reid's photographs, "Once Upon A Time, Called Now", is displayed at the World Tattoo Gallery, Chicago, IL.
[20] Living Colour is profiled on BBC2-TV's "Rapido".
[29] Skillings quits the band.
Dec [13] Reid, Calhoun and Eye & I's bassist Melvin Gibbs play at The Knitting Factory in New York City.

1992

Mar Garland Jeffreys' ***Don't Call Me Buckwheat***, featuring Reid, is released in the US. (He will also guest on *Cabbies On Crack* on the Ramones' ***Mondo Bizarro***, released later in the year.)
May Tackhead bassist Doug Wimbish (b. Sept. 22, 1956, Hartford, CT), also a session veteran for the Sugarhill label and former James Brown and George Clinton sideman, replaces Skillings, having first played with Living Colour at the "Hollywood Rock Festival" in Brazil, in January.

1993

Feb [11] The band performs a one-off date at London's Marquee club, its first UK date with Wimbish in the line-up, and will appear on C4-TV's "The Word" the following evening.
[20] *Leave It Alone* debuts at its UK #34 peak.
Mar [6] ***Stain*** bows at its UK #19 peak. With the group having dispensed with earlier producer Ed Stasium, the set is helmed by Ron St. Germain and includes the instrumental *WTFF* (also the group's unofficial monogram, standing for : "What The Fuck Factor").
[20] ***Stain*** debuts at its US #26 peak.
[26] An 11-date "Stained In The UK" tour opens at Leeds University, Leeds, Yorks., set to end on April 6th at the Guildhall, Portsmouth, Hants., before the group returns for a US theater and college tour in mid-April.
Apr [17] *Auslander* charts for a week at UK #53.
May [20] The band attends a celebration of the signing of the National Voter Registration Act on the South Lawn of the White House in Washington, DC.
[22] The group plays a sellout date at New York's Roseland Ballroom during the current North American tour.
July [16] They perform at "The Phoenix 1993" festival at Long Marston, Stratford-upon-Avon, Warks.
Nov [12] The group guests on CBS-TV's "Late Show With David Letterman".

1994

Apr [14] Glover opens in the musical "Fallen Angel", written by Billy Boesky (son of Ivan), at New York's Circle In The Square Theater.
May [26] Reid sings with Chuck Berry at the Apollo Theatre Hall of Fame Concert, which will air on NBC-TV on September 6th.
Nov [9] The RIAA certifies two million sales of ***Vivid***.

1995

Jan [27] **Performance** magazine reports that Living Colour are no more, quoting Reid : "It wasn't fun anymore. The magic was no longer there. I have not made this decision overnight. I've been struggling with it and searching my soul for well over a year. But at the same time that Living Colour's sense of unity and purpose was growing weaker and fuzzier, I was finding more and more creative satisfaction in my solo projects. Finally, it become obvious that I had to give up the band and move on".
Oct [24] RCA Hendrix tribute album ***In From The Storm***, featuring Glover (who is also a sometime VJ on the VH1 cable web), is released, as Reid continues work with his new band Masque, signed to 550/Epic.

L.L. COOL J

1984

Nov Raised by his grandparents, and having started rapping at the age of nine when his grandfather bought him some DJ equipment, L.L. Cool J (b. James Todd Smith, Jan. 14, 1968, St. Albans, Queens, New York, NY) is a street-wise 13-year-old when he starts sending out hip-hop demos taped in his home basement. Impressed by the demo cuts, Rick Rubin, a senior at New York University in the process of setting up his own pioneering Def Jam record label with Russell Simmons, signs L.L. Cool J and releases *I Need A Beat*, the label's first 12" single.

1985

Nov A distribution deal with CBS/Columbia Records sees the international release of his debut album, ***Radio***, while he also contributes *Can You Rock It Like This* to Run D.M.C.'s ***King Of Rock***. Having established his performing name, standing for Ladies Love Cool James, his *I Can't Live Without My Radio*, featured in the first rap movie, "Krush Groove", makes US R&B #15. This leads to a 50-city package tour with the "New York City Fresh Festival", also featuring Run D.M.C., the Fat Boys, Whodini and Grandmaster Flash.
Dec [23] A fight breaks out at a Baltimore, MD roller-rink during an L.L. Cool J show: one person is trampled underfoot, three are shot.

1986

Feb [15] On his first UK visit he is revered as a cutting-edge rap innovator by the music press and the media. *I Can't Live Without My Radio* fails to cross over, but ***Radio*** now makes UK #71 and #46 in the US, where it will earn him his first platinum disc.
Apr L.L. Cool J supports Run D.M.C. on their "Raising Hell" tour.

1987

June He headlines the "Def Jam '87" tour of the US and Britain with Public Enemy, Eric B., Doug E. Fresh and Whodini. A near-riot occurs at the sellout Hammersmith Odeon, London gigs, soliciting further media interest.
July [4] *I'm Bad* peaks at UK #71.
[11] Co-produced and co-written by L.L. Cool J and the L.A. Posse (Bobby Erving, Darryl Pierce and Dwayne Simon), ***Bigger And Deffer*** tops the US R&B chart at the beginning of an 11-week run.
[18] *I'm Bad* climbs to US #84.
Aug ***Bigger And Deffer*** hits US #3 and also makes UK #54. It includes the first-ever rap ballad, *I Need Love* recorded with the L.A. Posse. During the month, he is fined $250 for lewd behavior on stage at a Columbus, GA, gig.
Sept [12] *I Need Love* becomes his first major hit single, reaching US #14, topping the US R&B survey two weeks later.
Oct *I Need Love* hits UK #8, confirming L.L. Cool J as one of the leading voices in the progressive rap movement.
Nov [9] The RIAA certifies two million sales of ***Bigger And Deffer***.
[21] *Go Cut Creator Go* peaks at UK #66.

1988

Feb Double A-side, *Going Back To Cali/Jack The Ripper*, makes US #31 and UK #37, as L.L. Cool J continues to tour.
Mar [30] He collects the Best Rap Album and Best Rap Single trophies at the second annual Soul Train Music Awards, held at the Civic Center, Santa Monica, CA.
Apr [19] ***Radio*** is certified platinum by the RIAA.
Nov [30] He plays the first rap concert in Côte d'Ivoire, Africa. Halfway through the concert people faint, fights break out, the stage is stormed and the show ends abruptly.

1989

June *I'm That Type Of Guy* makes UK #43.
July ***Walking With A Panther***, with 16 tracks on the LP, 18 on the compact disc and 20 on the cassette format, makes UK #43.
[15] *I'm That Type of Guy* tops the US Rap chart.
[22] ***Walking With A Panther*** hits US R&B #1 and will hit US #6, becoming his third consecutive platinum certified album on August 10th.
[24] *I'm That Type Of Guy* is certified gold by the RIAA.
Aug [9] He begins a 21-date US tour at Bloomington, MN, set to end in Miami, FL, on September10th.
[11] Singer David Parker, band technician Gary Saunders, bodyguard Christopher Tsipouras, all members of L.L. Cool J's retinue, are charged with first-degree criminal sexual conduct after allegedly raping a 15-year-old girl who attends an after-concert party, having gone backstage with a pass won in a Minneapolis radio contest.
Sept L.L. Cool J is booed at a voting-registration rally in Harlem, alongside Chuck D, Doug E. Fresh and MC Lyte.

1990

Apr [7] Confirming his mainstream popularity beyond the genre confines of rap, L.L. Cool J takes part in "Farm Aid IV" at the Hoosier Dome, Indianapolis, IN.

June *To Da Break Of Dawn*, from the rap-themed "House Party" movie soundtrack, is released.
Oct [13] Co-produced by the rapper with Marley Marl, the well-received tough-rap set ***Mama Said Knock You Out*** debuts at its UK #49 peak.
Nov [3] ***Mama Said Knock You Out*** reaches US #16.
Dec [1] The extracted *Around The Way Girl/Mama Said Knock You Out* makes UK #41.
[11] L.L. Cool J kicks off the national "The Cool School Video Program", which encourages children to stay in school by taking part in a make-your-own video contest, at the Martin Luther King Jr. Middle School, in Dorchester, MA.

1991

Jan [15] The still-climbing *Around The Way Girl* is certified gold by the RIAA.
Mar [2] *Around The Way Girl* hits US #9.
[8] Michael J. Fox/James Woods movie "The Hard Way", in which L.L. Cool J plays a cop, opens in US theaters.
[9] The Peace Choir's all-star, including Cool J., remake of John Lennon's *Give Peace A Chance* makes US #54.
[16] Reissued *Around The Way Girl* now makes UK #36.
Apr [2] L.L. Cool J gives away a pair of sneakers to every student, teacher and staff member at Thompson Middle School in Dorchester, MA, to celebrate its winning the "Foot Locker Cool School Video" contest.
May [1] L.L. Cool J performs a sellout gig at New York's Beacon Theatre.
[15] *Mama Said Knock You Out* is certified gold by the RIAA.
[28] *Going Back To Cali* is also confirmed gold by the RIAA.
June [14] He joins other R&B/rap stars as part of a 13-city "Budweiser Superfest" US tour which begins in Charlotte, NC.
Aug [7] Simone Johnson sues him for palimony in the New York Family Court, claiming half of his earnings. He agrees to pay $1,650 a month in support.
Sept [5] "Mama Said Knock You Out" wins the Best Rap Video category and Cool J. performs *Don't Call It A Comeback* at the eighth annual MTV Video Music Awards, held at the Universal Amphitheatre, Universal City, CA.
[8] Currently featured in a five-page fashion spread in **Rolling Stone**, he performs *Don't Call It A Comeback* at the fifth annual MTV Awards, at the Universal Amphitheatre.
[14] *6 Minutes Of Pleasure*, with backing vocals by the Flex, peaks at US #95.
Oct [19] ***Simply Mad About The Mouse***, to which L.L. Cool J has contributed *Who's Afraid Of The Big Bad Wolf*, debuts at its US #160 peak, as Marley Marl's ***In Control Volume II - For Your Steering Pleasure***, featuring Cool J. as one of the featured rappers, bow at its US #152 peak.
Dec [3] He raps a medley of hits at the second annual **Billboard** Music Awards held at the Barker Hangar, Santa Monica Airport, Santa Monica, also winning the Top Rap Singles Artist category.
[8] During UK dates, he performs at London's Astoria Theatre.

1992

Jan [3] The RIAA certifies sales of two million of ***Mama Said Knock You Out***.
[17] L.L. Cool J participates in "A Call for Reunion - A Musical Celebration" at the Lincoln Memorial Hall, Washington, DC.
Feb [20] He holds a press conference outside New York City Hall to discuss his support for Increase The Peace Corps, a community-based youth organization emphasising racial harmony.
[25] L.L. Cool J wins Best Rap Solo Performance for *Mama Said Knock You Out* at the 34th annual Grammy Awards, from Radio City Music Hall, New York, at which he also performs.
Apr [2] He appears on syndicated TV's "The Arsenio Hall Show".
Aug He sets up Uncle Records, with Brian Latture as label chief.
Dec "Toys", marking L.L. Cool J's major film-acting debut, playing a demented general's son alongside Robin Williams, opens across the US. In this month's **Interview**, he says that the relative longevity of success he has enjoyed, unlike many other rap acts, is because: "I don't take it too serious and I don't believe my own hype."

1993

Jan [17] Cool J. performs at "A Call For Reunion : A Musical Celebration" during the Inaugural festivities at the Lincoln Memorial Hall.
Feb [12] He guests on syndicated TV's "Whoopi Goldberg".
[24] Together with basketball legend Magic Johnson, he presents the Best Rap Duo Or Group award to Arrested Development at the 35th annual Grammy Awards, held at the Shrine Auditorium, Los Angeles, CA.
Apr [3] *How I'm Comin'*, the first extract from ***14 Shots To The Dome***, debuts at its US #57 peak.
[10] *How I'm Comin'* bows at its UK #37 peak.
[12] A European promotional tour including Sweden, London, Germany and France begins, set to end on the 25th.
[17] ***14 Shots To The Dome***, variously produced by L.L. Cool J, Marley Marl, Q.D. III and Bobby "Bobcat" Ervin, debuts at its US #5 peak and charts for a week at UK #74.
May [20] L.L. Cool J guests on NBC-TV's "Late Night With David Letterman".
June [2] ***14 Shots To The Dome*** is certified gold by the RIAA.
July [3] *Pink Cookies In A Plastic Bag*, backed with *Back Seat Of My Jeep*, makes US #42.
Aug He opens his Camp Cool J. for children, designed to raise self-esteem and foster leadership skills.

1995

Aug [7] He marries his live-in girlfriend and mother of his two children at their New York City home.
Oct [25] Cool J. speaks to an assembly of students at the Jeremiah E. Burke High School in Dorchester, MA, encouraging them to stay in school and go to college.
Nov [1] He guests on NBC-TV's "The Tonight Show".
[23] Cool J. takes part in the 69th Macy's Thanksgiving Day Parade in New York.
Dec [2] With Cool J. now a TV star, featured in NBC-TV's sitcom "In The House", his new single, *Hey Lover*, featuring vocal assistance from Boyz II Men, hits US #3.
[18] Management company Nixon-Katz Associates files suit in Los Angeles Superior Court seeking $67,500 for services it claims it provided Cool J., following an alleged verbal management agreement made in April.

1996

Jan [20] *Hey Lover* debuts at its UK #17 peak.
Feb [10] His sixth album, ***Mr. Smith*** reaches US #20.
Mar [29] Cool J. co-hosts and performs *Loungin'* at the tenth annual Soul Train Music Awards from the Shrine Auditorium.
Apr [13] *Doin' It* hits US #9.

NILS LOFGREN

1969

Lofgren (b. June 21, 1952, Chicago, IL), of Italian and Swedish parents, having been a classical music student for ten years and played in Beatles and Kinks-influenced high-school bands, the Waifs and the Grass, in Maryland, before running away from home, or, more specifically, from school, with $100 in his pocket, and sleeping for two weeks in doorways in Greenwich Village, New York, NY, forms the band Paul Dowell & the Dolphin after returning home. They successfully audition for Sire Records and release two singles, but split after both fail commercially and the group is beset by management and contract problems. A new rock combo, Grin, is formed, with Lofgren on vocals, keyboards and guitar, Bob Berberich (b. 1949, Maryland), ex-Reekers, on drums, and Bob Gordon (b. 1951, Oklahoma), ex-Paul Dowell & the Dolphin, on bass.

1970

Feb Having seen him playing with Grin at the Cellar Door club in Washington, DC, in 1969, Neil Young invites Lofgren to play piano (and uncredited guitar) on his album, ***After The Goldrush***. He plays frequently with Young and his band Crazy Horse after the album, but does not join the group full time, remaining committed to making a success of Grin.

1971

Feb Lofgren writes and plays on songs for the eponymous debut album by Crazy Horse.
Aug With Grin having signed to Spindizzy/Columbia, its self-named debut album ***Grin*** reaches US #192, supported a tour with Edgar Winter. The follow-up Grin album, ***1+1***, also produced by David Briggs, will peak at US #180 next February, while the extracted *White Lies*, Grin's only US chart single, peaks at #75 on Mar [11].

1973

Mar Lofgren's younger brother, Tom, has been recruited on second guitar for Grin's third album, ***All Out***, which makes US #186.
Nov Having signed a new deal with A&M, the band records ***Gone Crazy***, but its commercial failure precipitates the end of the group. After playing briefly with the Dubonettes and producing their debut A&M album (released under a new name, Charlie & the Pep Boys), Lofgren accepts another invitation, joining Crazy Horse for Young's "Tonight's The Night" tour. He will leave the lineup the following year to pursue a solo path, when the press speculates that the Rolling Stones will recruit Lofgren as lead guitarist in place of the departed Mick Taylor.

1975

Apr Lofgren re-signs to A&M as a solo artist, and ***Nils Lofgren***, including a homage to Keith Richards in *Keith Don't Go (Ode To The Glimmer Twin)* and co-produced with Briggs, reaches US #141. He supports the release with extensive touring, including a UK visit, with a band including Tom Lofgren (guitar), Scotty Ball (bass) and Mike Zack (drums).
Nov [4] Lofgren appears on BBC2-TV's "The Old Grey Whistle Test".
[5] He begins a short UK tour, supporting Joan Armatrading, at Leeds University, Leeds, West Yorks.

1976

Jan An "official bootleg" album, ***Back It Up***, a recording of a live show broadcast on radio station KSAN in San Francisco, CA, is acclaimed by the press, despite limited availability.
Mar Lofgren starts a US club and concert tour, introducing his new studio album.
May ***Cry Tough***, part-produced by Al Kooper and Briggs, reaches US #32 and hits UK #8 and includes a revival of the Yardbirds' *For Your Love*.
[5] Lofgren begins a nine-date UK tour to promote ***Cry Tough*** at Colston Hall, Bristol, Avon, set to end on the 15th at Leeds University.

1977

Apr Co-produced by Lofgren and Andy Newmark, ***I Came To Dance*** reaches US #36 and UK #30, featuring Wornell Jones and Newmark as his new bass player and drummer. Patrick Henderson joins the live band on keyboards.
Nov [6] Live double album, ***Night After Night***, recorded on tour earlier in the year, reaches UK #38. ***Night After Night*** makes US #44.

1979

Aug ***Nils***, featuring three songs with lyrics by Lou Reed and a cover of Randy Newman's *Baltimore*,

makes US #54.
[19] Lofgren appears along with the Stranglers and AC/DC, supporting the Who in concert at Wembley Stadium, Wembley, Middx. (He will also perform at the annual "Reading Festival" during his visit.)

1981

Oct With Lofgren signed to the new MCA-distributed Backstreet label, ***Night Fades Away***, produced by Jeff Baxter and featuring music guests Nicky Hopkins, Jeff Porcaro and Del Shannon, makes US #99 and UK #50. An A&M compilation set, ***A Rhythm Romance***, will anchor at the UK Top 100 for one week on May 1st the following year.

1983

Feb He tours again with Neil Young, also playing on the latter's controversial, synthesizer-based ***Trans***.
Aug Co-produced by Lofgren, Kevin McCormick and Newmark, ***Wonderland*** is released and sells poorly, ending his Backstreet contract.

1984

May [15] Lofgren joins Bruce Springsteen's E. Street Band as guitarist, replacing Steve Van Zandt, and tours with Springsteen, whom he first met during a Fillmore East audition night in 1972, into 1985.

1985

June Now signed to UK independent label Towerbell, his solo career resumes with ***Flip***, recorded at Philadelphia, PA's Warehouse Studios with producer Lance Quinn, which reaches UK #36. Taken from it, *Secrets In The Street* makes UK #53.

1986

Apr Following the release of his third live set, double album ***Code Of The Road*** (which peaks at UK #86), the Towerbell label hits financial problems and folds, leaving Lofgren to put his solo projects on ice, returning to Springsteen's backing unit. He will appear on two tracks of Springsteen's ***Tunnel Of Love*** released in November 1987 and will remain a full stage member of the E. Street Band, playing on the early 1988 "Tunnel Of Love Express" US and European tour.

1989

July [23] Having performed at the "Human Rights Now!" Amnesty International tour opener at Wembley Stadium with Springsteen on September 2nd the previous year, Lofgren now joins Ringo Starr & His All-Starr Band on a 28-date, 27-city US tour, opening at the Park Central Amphitheater, Dallas, TX. Billed as the "Tour For All Generations", it is the first tour by a Beatle in 13 years. Also in the band are Dr. John, Billy Preston, Joe Walsh, Rick Danko, Levon Helm, Jim Keltner and Clarence Clemons.

1990

Nov [22] Lofgren plays the first of three UK dates, at the Manchester International 2, Manchester, Gtr. Manchester, supporting the UK issue of ***The Best Of Nils Lofgren - Don't Walk ... Rock*** on the UK Connoisseur label.

1991

Apr [27] ***Silver Lining***, Lofgren's first album in five years, with guest vocals by Bruce Springsteen on the extracted single, *Valentine*, charts for a week at UK #61.
May [3] Lofgren plays a sellout gig at The Ritz, New York, during a US tour to promote his new album. (He will beat the much taller radio personality Howard Stern 34-4 at one-on-one basketball, winning a $500 bet, at the Nassau Veterans Memorial Coliseum, Uniondale, NY. New York Knicks Hall of Famer Walt Frazier acts as referee.)
[18] ***Silver Lining***, released by Rykodisc, peaks at US #153.
Nov [23] Lofgren begins a six-date UK tour at Leicester University, Leicester, Leics., set to end on the 28th at London's Town & Country club.

1992

Feb [14] Lofgren guests on NBC-TV's "The Tonight Show".
Nov [23] He plays at the Town & Country club during a three-date UK visit, promoting his new Essential label album ***Crooked Line***.

1993

May [5] Lofgren takes part in PBS-TV's "A Beatles Songbook".
Oct [30] ABC-TV's "The Paula Poundstone Show", which features Lofgren as its musical director, premieres - but will be axed after its second broadcast.

1995

Aug [13] Having released ***Every Breath*** the previous October, featuring Foreigner's Lou Gramm, on Permanent Records in the UK and still with Rykodisc in the US, Lofgren performs at the Coca-Cola Starplex Amphitheatre, Dallas, TX, now opening for Ringo Starr on US dates.

KENNY LOGGINS

1971

June Loggins (b. Jan. 7, 1948, Everett, WA), having moved to California with his family as the son of a traveling salesman, and majored in music at Pasadena City College, Pasadena, CA where he also played in a folk group, has joined Mercury Records-signed studio group Gator Creek before playing in Second Helping in 1968. Following a 1969 one-off tour with ex-hitmakers the Electric Prunes, Loggins has gone on to become a full-time songwriter, earning $100 a week, at Wingate Music, a division of ABC Records, now scoring his first compositional success, *House At Pooh Corner* for the Nitty Gritty Dirt Band, which peaks at US #53. It is one of four Loggins songs cut by the band on its album, ***Uncle Charlie And His Dog Teddy***. Subsequently signed by A&R man Don Ellis, Loggins to CBS/Columbia Records as a solo performer, Loggins meets staff producer Jim Messina who works with him to prepare a debut solo album. The resulting ***Kenny Loggins With Jim Messina Sittin' In*** charts in May 1972, setting the stage for a five-year collaboration initially as Kenny Loggins Band With Jim Messina and subsequently Loggins & Messina. In April 1973, Loggins' next major songwriting success will see Anne Murray's version of *Danny's Song*, written by Loggins for his brother Dan's son, hit US #7.

1976

Jan Still with Messina, Loggins turns down an offer to co-star with Barbra Streisand in the film "A Star Is Born". Shortly after, he cuts his hand with a craft knife while practicising his wood-carving hobby at home - a serious injury which requires surgery.
July [16] Loggins & Messina split, following a final concert in Hawaii, with both artists remaining individually signed to CBS/Columbia. (During the month, Loggins marries Eva Ein, a long-time friend of Messina's wife, Jenny.)

1977

July The largely self-penned ***Celebrate Me Home***, Loggins' first solo album, produced by Phil Ramone and Bob James, reaches US #27 during a 33-week chart stay. He tours the US for the first time as a solo artist, backed by a new band featuring Mike Hamilton on guitar, Brian Mann on keyboards, Vince Denham on saxes, Jon Clarke on woodwinds, George Hawkins on bass and Tris Imboden on drums, supporting Fleetwood Mac.
Sept Loggins' first solo hit single, *I Believe In Love*, peaks at US #66.

1978

May Loggins wins the 50-yard men's freestyle in 29.3 seconds at the "Rock And Roll Sports Classic" at the Irvine Campus, UCLA, Orange County, CA.
Sept His sophomore set ***Nightwatch***, produced by Bob James, hits US #7, confirming Loggins as a major pop/rock singer-songwriter in his own right. It includes a revival of Billy Joe Royal's 1965 hit, *Down In The Boondocks*, and also the Loggins/Michael McDonald-penned *What A Fool Believes* (which will be a US #1 hit for McDonald's band the Doobie Brothers, in 1979).
Oct *Whenever I Call You Friend* with Stevie Nicks of Fleetwood Mac guest-duetting, co-written by Loggins with Melissa Manchester, hits US #5.
[13] ***Nightwatch*** is certified platinum by the RIAA. The following January, the extracted *Easy Driver* will peak at US #60.

1980

Feb Loggins' ***Keep The Fire***, recorded with producer Tom Dowd, reaches US #16 and yields the US #11, *This Is It*, written about Loggins' father. It includes songs co-written with Michael McDonald, Stephen Bishop and Loggins' wife Eva, and has guest appearances by McDonald and Michael Jackson.
[27] Loggins and McDonald win the Song Of The Year category for *What A Fool Believes* at the 22nd annual Grammy Awards.
Oct *I'm Alright*, the theme from the movie "Caddyshack", hits US #7. Loggins has also recorded much of the film's soundtrack album, which makes US #78.
Nov Live double album, ***Kenny Loggins : Alive***, reaches US #11.
[14] ***Kenny Loggins : Alive*** is certified gold by the RIAA.
Dec [22] His debut set ***Celebrate Me Home*** is confirmed platinum by the RIAA.

1981

Feb [25] Loggins wins Best Pop Vocal Performance, Male, for *This Is It* at the 23rd annual Grammy Awards.

1982

Oct Loggins' ***High Adventure***, co-produced with Bruce Botnick and featuring David Foster, McDonald and most of Toto, among others, reaches US #13, as the extracted *Don't Fight It*, a duet with Journey vocalist Steve Perry, makes US #17.
Nov [22] ***High Adventure*** is certified gold by the RIAA.

1983

Jan Enduring radio smash, *Heart To Heart*, reaches US #15.
May *Welcome To Heartlight*, a song inspired by the writings of children from the Heartlight School, reaches US #24.

1984

Mar [31] *Footloose*, the Loggins/Dean Pitchford-penned uptempo theme sung by Loggins from the film of the same title, tops the US chart for first of three weeks, and is a million seller. (The song was written in a hotel room in Lake Tahoe, NV, where Loggins was performing - despite recovering from broken ribs sustained after a fall off the stage at a concert in Provo, UT.)
Apr [21] Soundtrack album, ***Footloose***, which Loggins shares with Deniece Williams, Bonnie Tyler and others, tops the US chart at the start of a ten-week run and is a multi-million seller.
May *Footloose* hits UK #6, Loggins' first UK chart success, while the film soundtrack, ***Footloose***, hits UK #7.
July Also taken from the movie, *I'm Free (Heaven Helps The Man)* reaches US #22.

1985

Jan [28] Following the 12th annual American Music Awards celebrations, Loggins joins 45 other artists as USA For Africa at the A&M studios, Hollywood, CA, to record *We Are The World*.
May ***Vox Humana***, partly produced by David Foster,

makes US #41, while the extracted title track, *Vox Humana* (Latin for "Human Voice"), reaches US #29.
July *Forever* reaches US #40.
Oct *I'll Be There* climbs to US #88.
Nov [1] ***Keep The Fire*** is certified platinum by the RIAA.

1986

July [26] *Danger Zone*, the theme from the Tom Cruise movie "Top Gun", hits US #2, as the soundtrack album tops the US chart for five weeks.
Sept [13] *Playing With The Boys*, also from "Top Gun", peaks at US #60.
Nov Soundtrack album, ***Top Gun***, hits UK #4.
[21] *Full Sail* and *Loggins And Messina* are certified platinum by the RIAA.
Dec *Danger Zone* makes UK #45. Loggins' ballad, *Meet Me Half Way*, from Sylvester Stallone's "Over The Top", will reach US #11 on June 13th the following year.

1988

Sept ***Back To Avalon*** makes US #69, while the extracted *Nobody's Fool*, the theme from the film "Caddyshack 2", hits US #8.
Nov [1-6] Loggins performs eight shows at the Neil Simon Theatre on Broadway in New York.
[26] *I'm Gonna Miss You*, produced by Peter Wolf, peaks at US #82.

1989

Feb [25] *Tell Her* peaks at US #76. As Loggins rests from his recording career, he announces that he and his wife and sometime songwriting partner, Eva, intend to divorce.
July [24] ***Vox Humana*** is certified gold by the RIAA, followed by platinum certification for *Footloose* on January 17th the following year.

1991

Sept [10] Loggins performs on NBC-TV's "The Tonight Show".
[28] After a three-year recording hiatus, Loggins returns with ***Leap Of Faith***, co-produced with Terry Nelson and featuring David Foster, Siedah Garrett, Michael McDonald, Smokey Robinson and Mavis Staples, among others, which debuts at its US #71 peak.
Nov [23] Eco-themed *Conviction Of The Heart*, co-penned by Guy Thomas with Loggins, first performed at an "Earth Day" benefit the previous year, makes US #65.

1992

Jan [16-19] Loggins makes a four-date appearance at Caesar's Tahoe, Stateline, NV.
Apr [15] He performs on "What About Me? I'm Only Three", a CBS-TV environmental awareness program aimed at youngsters.
July [12] TV special, "Kenny Loggins : Going Home", premieres on the Disney cable channel.
Aug [8] US summer dates continue with a gig in the Kohala Coast resort, HI.
Nov [16] ***Leap Of Faith*** is certified gold by the RIAA.
[18] Loggins appears at "Commitment To Life VI" benefit for AIDS Project Los Angeles, at the Universal Amphitheatre, Universal City, CA, honoring Barbra Streisand and David Geffen.

1993

Jan [20] He participates in the "Arkansas Ball" on the day of Bill Clinton's presidential inauguration in Washington, DC, with the President-elect playing sax on Loggins' *Your Mama Don't Dance*.
Apr [16] Loggins performs at an "Earth Day" concert headlined by Paul McCartney, at the Hollywood Bowl, Hollywood, CA, with proceeds going to PETA, Greenpeace and Friends of the Earth (and is currently working on an album for the Sony Kids' label to benefit Songwriters and Artists for the Earth, the Earth Island Institute and Save The Children).
Sept [10] Loggins guests on NBC-TV's "The Tonight Show".
[25] Recorded on last year's US tour, Loggins' performance set ***Outside : From The Redwoods*** makes US #60.
Oct [30] Loggins takes part in a "Gala For The President" at Washington's Ford Theatre, in the presence of President Clinton, set to air on ABC-TV on November 24th.

1994

July [21] Loggins plays a sellout date at the Wolf Trap Farm Park for the Performing Arts in Vienna, VA, during his 1994 US summer tour.
Sept [10] Harking back to his 1971 compositional debut success, and aimed at both parents and kids, ***Return To Pooh Corner***, containing songs he has sung to his own children, makes US #65.
Oct [7-8] Loggins plays two dates at Los Angeles' Greek Theatre.
Dec [5] ***Return To Pooh Corner*** is certified gold by the RIAA.
[9] Loggins performs at the National Council of La Raza Awards in Los Angeles, set to air on Fox-TV on the 28th.

1995

June [3] Loggins performs at the Summer Pop Bowl Amphitheatre, San Diego, CA, during a current round of US dates.
July [21] Songwriter Guy Thomas files a $5 million lawsuit in Los Angeles against Garth Brooks claiming copyright infringement of his 1991 hit composition, written with Loggins, *Conviction Of The Heart* by Brooks' *Standing Outside The Fire*. Loggins does not participate in the suit.

1996

Feb [24] The all-star update ***The Songs Of West Side Story*** to which Loggins has contributed *Tonight* in duet with Wynonna, makes US #65.
see also: **LOGGINS & MESSINA**

LOGGINS & MESSINA

Kenny Loggins (vocals, guitar);
Jim Messina (vocals, guitar)

1967

Sept Messina (b. Dec. 5, 1947, Maywood, CA), having formed a high-school surf instrumental group, Jim Messina & the Jesters, which becomes popular on the California "Battle Of The Bands" circuit and records two albums, ***Jim Messina And The Jesters*** for Thimble Records and the hot rod-oriented ***The Dragsters*** for Audio Fidelity, with *Drag Bike Pookie* being a local California hit, has moved to studio work in Los Angeles, CA, as a guitarist, engineer and producer, when the surf craze evaporates, and, from being the group's studio engineer, Messina joins Buffalo Springfield on bass, in place of Bruce Palmer. Together with fellow ex-Buffalo Springfield member Richie Furay, he then forms Poco in August 1968, with George Grantham, Rusty Young and Randy Meisner. Messina also assembles ***Last Time Around*** from latter-day studio tapes, after Buffalo Springfield has split. Meanwhile Loggins (b. Jan. 7, 1948, Everett, WA), having majored in music at Pasadena City College, Pasadena, CA, joins studio group Gator Creek, which records for Mercury Records, before joining Second Helping in 1968. After joining (for one tour) ex-hitmakers the Electric Prunes, Loggins becomes a full-time songwriter, on $100 a week, at Wingate Music, a division of ABC Records in 1969, nabbing his first hit composition with *House At Pooh Corner* recorded by the Nitty Gritty Dirt Band, which peaks at US #53 in June 1971.

1971

Sept At the instigation of friend and A&R man Don Ellis, Loggins signs to Columbia as a solo artist where he meets Messina, who has left Poco the previous November to become a staff producer at the label, and who works with Loggins to prepare a debut solo album. Their collaboration is such that ***Kenny Loggins With Jim Messina Sittin' In*** is released as a joint effort and they decide to continue to work together, making their live debut at the Troubadour in Los Angeles, billed as the Kenny Loggins Band With Jim Messina.

1972

May ***Kenny Loggins With Jim Messina Sittin' In*** reaches US #70 during a 113-week chart stay, while the extracted *Vahevala* climbs to US #84. It also includes *Danny's Song* which Anne Murray will take to US #7 in April the following year.
June *Nobody But You*, written by Messina, makes US #86. Both this and the previous single are credited to Kenny Loggins With Jim Messina.

1973

Jan *Your Mama Don't Dance* hits US #4. (The song will be much covered, not least, by Elvis Presley) It is included on ***Loggins And Messina***, also produced by Messina, which reaches US #16.
Mar [7] *Your Mama Don't Dance* is certified gold by the RIAA.
Apr The pair tours the US on bills with Jim Croce and the Doobie Brothers.
May *Thinking Of You* reaches US #18 and is credited to Loggins & Messina, as are subsequent duo releases.
Dec ***Full Sail*** docks at US #10, as *My Music*, taken from it, reaches US #16.

1974

Mar *Watching The River Run*, a joint composition, peaks at US #71.
July Double live album, ***On Stage***, hits US #5.
Dec ***Mother Lode*** hits US #8, having been certified gold on November 25th.

1975

Feb *Changes*, taken from ***Mother Lode***, makes US #84.
May *Growin'* peaks at US #52.
Sept Their revival of the Chris Kenner/Dave Clark Five hit, *I Like It Like That*, climbs to US #84. It is extracted from ***So Fine***, a nostalgic set of R&B oldies from the '50s and early '60s, which reaches US #21.
Oct Also from the oldies album, their treatment of Clyde McPhatter's *A Lover's Question* makes US #89, the final Loggins & Messina hit single.

1976

Mar ***Native Sons*** reaches US #16. A lengthy tour begins, with a new back-up band, though Loggins, with a cast on his recently injured hand, is unable to play guitar.
July [16] The duo splits, following a final concert in Hawaii (both are, in any case, signed individually to Columbia, the hitmaking liaison always having been on an informal basis).
Aug [19] ***Native Sons*** is certified gold by the RIAA. ***The Best Of Friends***, compiling the duo's hit singles, will make US #61 in January the following year while a final remnant, and second live double album, assembled after the duo's break-up, ***Finale*** will peak at US #83 in January 1978.

1979

Nov Messina's solo career resumes with ***Oasis*** making US #58. Moving to Warner Bros. Records for his final chart album, ***Messina*** at US #95 in July 1981, Messina will take a break from performing, investing his money in his own Gateway Studios in Carpinteria, CA, before releasing the 1983 Warner Bros. album, ***One More Mile***.

1989

Apr Messina permanently rejoins Poco for its comeback ***Legacy*** album.
[15] Heavy-metal outfit Poison updates Loggins & Messina's 1973 US #4 hit, *Your Mama Don't Dance*, hitting US #10 (and UK #13).

1992

Oct [30] While earlier Loggins & Messina sets, ***On Stage*** and ***Sittin' In*** have both been certified platinum by the RIAA on July 22nd the previous year (with their best-seller, ***Best Of Friends*** eventually being ratified for two million US sales on November 21st 1994), Messina now plays at The Bottom Line, New York, as part of a month-long North American tour and, by year's end, will temporarily reunite with Loggins for a number of local benefit gigs in their home town of Santa Barbara, CA.
see also: **Kenny LOGGINS, BUFFALO SPRINGFIELD, POCO**

LOS LOBOS

David Hidalgo (guitar, accordion, vocals); **Cesar Rosas** (guitar, vocals); **Conrad Lozano** (bass); **Steve Berlin** (saxophone); **Luis Pérez** (drums)

1974

Hidalgo (b. Oct. 6, 1954, Los Angeles, CA) and Pérez (b. Jan. 29, 1953, Los Angeles), friends from an art class in Garfield High School in East Los Angeles, Rosas (b. Sept. 26, 1954, Los Angeles) and Lozano (b. Mar. 21, 1951, Los Angeles), all Spanish-Americans living in Los Angeles' Chicano community and refugees from Top 40-cover bands (Lozano has also been in future hitmaking group Tierra), decide to form an acoustic group to rediscover and revitalize traditional Chicano folk music. Their first recording is as a backup group to various singers on ***Si Se Puede (It Can Be Done)***, a benefit disc for the Hispanic United Farm Workers Union. They name the quartet Los Lobos Del Este de Los Angeles, quickly trimming it Los Lobos (Spanish for "The Wolves") and will spend the next two years researching and rehearsing, before making their debut at a Veteran of Foreign Wars hall in the Los Angeles suburb of Compton, then performing regularly at Chicano weddings, bars and benefits in the Los Angeles area. An immediate success with the older generation of Chicanos, Los Lobos also become popular among members of their own generation anxious to retain elements of Mexican culture. Released on the New Vista label, the group will record, and finances, with help from friends, its debut album, 1978's ***Just Another Band From L.A.***, selling the record at gigs.

1980

May In an incongruous billing, Los Lobos opens for Public Image Ltd. at a concert in Los Angeles. Its acoustic set receives a hostile reception from the hardcore punk audience (they are pelted with bottles, coins and spit and give up after about ten minutes). Unphased, the band continues performing locally and comes to the attention of the local Anglo-American music industry, as it integrates an electric sound into the previously acoustic-only Spanish and American tunes.

1982

Jan [22] Subsequently regarded by the band as a turning point, they receive an overwhelming and enthusiastic response opening for the Blasters at Los Angeles' Whisky club. (During the year they are asked by Paul Bartel to cut tracks for his forthcoming "Eating Raoul" movie, and contribute a Spanish version of *Devil With The Blue Dress On* and the Perez/Hidalgo original, *How Much Can I Do?*)

1983

Signing to Los Angeles independent label Slash, Los Lobos record the EP *And A Time To Dance*, on which labelmate Blasters' saxist, Steve Berlin (b. Sept. 14, 1955, Philadelphia, PA), plays and also co-produces with T-Bone Burnett. (Berlin, who moved west with the Soul Survivors, before they became the Beckmeier Brothers, cutting an album for Casablanca, then joined Top Jimmy & the Rhythm Pigs and the Plugz, before becoming a Blaster, has liked the band's work ever since they supported the Blasters at the Whisky club gig, and will join the band full time soon after. He has already played with the band at manager Gary Ibanez's Pico Rivera garage, which doubles as a rehearsal studio.) The EP will sell 50,000 copies and allow the band to buy a second-hand Dodge van in which to tour around the US.

1984

Feb [28] Los Lobos win the Best Mexican/American Performance category for *Anselma* at the 26th annual Grammy Awards.
Dec With Berlin fully on board, the critically-revered ***How Will The Wolf Survive?*** enters the US chart, set to reach #47.

1985

Mar *Will The Wolf Survive?* reaches US #78.
Apr Released in the UK via London Records, the double A-side, *Don't Worry Baby/Will The Wolf Survive?*, makes UK #57, while ***How Will The Wolf Survive?*** peaks at UK #77.
June Paul Simon's ***Graceland***, on which Los Lobos sings on *All Around The World Or The Myth Of Fingerprints*, is released.

1986

June Waylon Jennings' version of *Will The Wolf Survive?* hits US Country #5. During the year, the in-demand Tex-Mex pioneers, who are receiving increasing media attention in the US and UK, cited as a leading roots band, cut a cover of Fats Domino's *I'm Gonna Be A Wheel Someday* for the Blake Edwards' film "A Fine Mess", back T-Bone Burnette on his Dot label debut, ***T-Bone Burnett***, and contribute harmony vocals on *Lovable* for Elvis Costello's ***King Of America***.

1987

Mar Once again co-helmed by Burnette, ***By The Light Of The Moon*** makes US #47 and UK #77.
May [16] The group performs on NBC-TV's "Saturday Night Live".
June [19-21] Los Lobos perform at the annual "Glastonbury Festival", Pilton, Somerset.
July [24] The "La Bamba" movie, based on the life of '50s Chicano pop star Ritchie Valens, to whose soundtrack and subsequent album the band has contributed eight tracks, opens in the US. It includes the group's versions of the Valens compositions *Come On Let's Go*, *Ooh! My Head*, *Donna* and his 1959 hit, *La Bamba*, a traditional Mexican wedding song.
Aug [1] Los Lobos' version of *La Bamba* hits UK #1 for the first of two weeks, becoming the first all Spanish-sung record to do so. Valens' original version charts briefly at UK #49.
[29] *La Bamba* tops the US chart for the first of three weeks.
Sept [11] The group performs at the fourth annual MTV Video Music Awards, held at the Universal Amphitheatre, Universal City.
[12] Soundtrack album, ***La Bamba***, hits US #1 and makes UK #24.
Oct [31] The extracted *C'mon On, Let's Go* reaches UK #18.
Nov [7] *C'mon On, Let's Go* peaks at US #21.

1988

Sept [7] "La Bamba" wins the Best Video From A Film category at the fifth annual MTV Video Music Awards, held at the Universal Amphitheatre.
Oct ***La Pistola Y El Corazon*** (English translation: ***The Pistol And The Heart***), recorded in five days, is released. Containing traditional Mexican/American folk songs, it avoids deliberate commercial exploitation of the *La Bamba* success.

1989

May [18] Los Lobos take part in an AIDS benefit concert with Tracy Chapman, the Grateful Dead, Huey Lewis & the News and others, at the Oakland-Alameda County Coliseum, Oakland, CA.

1990

Feb [21] Los Lobos wins Best Mexican/American Performance for ***La Pistola Y El Corazon*** at the 32nd annual Grammy Awards, held at the Shrine Auditorium, Los Angeles.
June Buckwheat Zydeco's ***Where There's Smoke There's Fire***, produced by Hidalgo, is released.
Sept [11] The band plays at London's Town & Country club, during a short UK visit.
[29] ***The Neighborhood***, co-produced by the band with Larry Hirsch and featuring mainly English tracks with music guests Levon Helm, John Hiatt and Jim Keltner, peaks at US #103.
Oct [19] Back in the US, Los Lobos begin US dates at the Greek Theatre, Los Angeles.

1991

Apr The band performs at the 22nd annual "Jazz & Heritage Festival" in New Orleans, LA.
May [18] ***Deadicated***, a collection of Grateful Dead covers to which Los Lobos have contributed *Bertha*, reaches US #24. (Hidalgo also guests on Toni Childs' ***House Of Hope***, released the following month.)
Aug [21] They guest on NBC-TV's "Late Night With David Letterman".
July [20] The group appears at the "Telluride Midsummer Music Festival" at Telluride Town Park, Telluride, CO.
Nov [3] They play at the Bill Graham "Laughter Love & Music" memorial concert at San Francisco, CA's Golden Gate Park Polo Field, before an estimated 350,000 crowd.
[8-10] Los Lobos perform at the "Festival De Rock Iberoamericanca" at the Cinemobile Cafetal, Caracas, Venezuela, in front of 55,000 fans.

1992

Mar Soundtrack album, ***The Mambo Kings***, to which the group has contributed *Beautiful Maria Of My Soul*, makes US #50.
May [13] The band performs at London venue, the Borderline.
[18] They are featured on BBC2-TV's "The Late Show".
June [27] The critically-praised experimental set ***Kiko***, produced by Mitchell Froom, peaks at US #143.
July [11] During a European concert visit, they play at London's Town & Country club.
Aug [17] They win the Favorite Group Of The Year category at the fourth annual Desi Entertainment Awards, at the Wiltern Theatre, Los Angeles.
[19] The band performs on NBC-TV's "The Tonight Show".
[26] They gross $16,905 appearing at the Avalon Ballroom, Boston, MA, during US dates which will continue through November.
Sept Suzanne Vega's ***99.9° F***, with Hidalgo guesting on several tracks, makes US #86, while the group works on the soundtrack to "Annie Oakley", starring Keith Carradine, slated for release on the Rabbit Ears label.
Oct [14] "American Heroes & Legends", with music by Los Lobos, premieres on the Showtime cable channel.
[27] The group performs at Tipitina's in New Orleans, LA, during its current US tour.

1993

Jan [11] During further US dates, a Park West, Chicago, IL gig grosses $22,500.
[17-18] Los Lobos play at the Reunion Hall as part of the "America's Reunion On The Mall", during Presidential inauguration festivities in Washington, DC.
June [12] Los Lobos play a 20th anniversary concert at the Greek Theatre in Griffith Park, Los Angeles, with their guests John Hiatt, John Lee Hooker and Richard Thompson.
July [18] The group performs on the Mean Fiddler stage at "The Phoenix 1993 Festival", at Long Marston, Stratford-upon-Avon, Warks.
Sept [2] "Kiki And The Lavender Moon" wins the Breakthrough Video category at the tenth annual

MTV Video Music Awards, held at the Universal Amphitheatre.
[18] ***Just Another Band From L.A. : A Collection***, a two-CD career anthology including film soundtrack work, their first EP and 12 previously unreleased cuts, charts for a week at US #196.

1994

Feb [19] The group takes part in the "Artists Rights Foundation" benefit at the Shrine Auditorium, with Chris Isaak and Lou Reed.
May [23] Los Lobos, Big Head Todd & the Monsters and the Dave Matthews Band play to a sellout crowd of 18,061 at the Red Rocks Amphitheatre, Denver, CO.
June [18] They perform at the Sam Boyd Silver Bowl, University of Nevada, Las Vegas, NV, supporting the Eagles.
Oct Richard Thompson tribute album, ***Beat The Retreat***, including the band's version of *Down Where The Drunkards Roll*, is released in the US by Capitol. (Hidalgo and Perez are also currently busy with their extra-curricular side band, the Latin Playboys who release ***Latin Playboys***.)

1995

Mar [28] Rhino Records releases ***Till The Night Is Gone : A Tribute To Doc Pomus***, featuring Los Lobos' version of *Lonely Avenue*.
Sept [22] Los Lobos records *Midnight Shift* in Los Angeles, for the forthcoming Buddy Holly tribute album ***notfadeaway : remembering buddy holly***, to be released the following January.
Nov [12] The group performs a fund raiser at the Castaic Lake State Recreation Area, sponsored by Harley-Davidson of Glendale, CA, to benefit the Muscular Dystrophy Association.

1996

Feb [28] Los Lobos' *Mariachi Suite* is named Best Pop Instrumental at the 38th annual Grammy Awards held at the Shrine Auditorium.
Apr [6] Having spent much of the past 18 months also working on the film soundtracks to "Desperado", "Mi Vida Loca" and the forthcoming Keanu Reeves-starring "Feeling Minnesota", and having released the Grammy-nominated children's album ***Papa's Dream***, the band's label debut for Warner Bros. Records, ***Colossal Head***, co-produced by Froom with Tchad Blake, enters the US chart at its #81 peak.

LOVE

Arthur Lee (vocals, guitar); **Bryan MacLean** (vocals, guitar); **John Echols** (lead guitar); **Ken Forssi** (bass); **Alban "Snoopy" Pfisterer** (drums, keyboards)

1965

Apr Formed in Los Angeles, CA, initially as the Grass Roots, comprising ex-Arthur Lee & the LAGS frontman Lee (b. Mar. 7, 1945, Memphis, TN) who recorded one single *The Ninth Wave* released by Capitol in late '64, ex-Byrds roadie MacLean (b. 1947, Los Angeles), Echols (b. 1947, Memphis) who was also in the LAGS, Johnny Fleckenstein and Don Conka, they have name-changed to Love (the Grass Roots being taken up by another band). Original members Conka, who suffers from drug-induced unreliability, and Fleckenstein have already been replaced by former Surfaris bassist Forssi (b. 1943, Cleveland, OH) who first saw the band play at a Brave New World gig on Melrose, and Pfisterer (b. 1947, Switzerland), as the band now makes its live debut in Los Angeles, subsequently building a strong reputation playing clubs on Sunset Strip. Establishing itself as a leading West Coast underground rock act, Love takes up a residency at Bido Lito's club in Hollywood and, by the following year, becomes the first rock group to sign to Elektra Records.

1966

May Its debut album, ***Love***, a marriage of Beatles and Byrds-inspired rock, makes US #57.
[20-22] Love performs at San Francisco, CA's Avalon Ballroom with Captain Beefheart and Big Brother & the Holding Company.
June *My Little Red Book*, a Bacharach/David song originally cut by Manfred Mann for the film "What's New Pussycat?", peaks at US #52.
Sept *7 And 7 Is* makes US #33.
Dec [2-4] The group plays at the Fillmore West, San Francisco, with Moby Grape and Lee Michaels.

1967

Mar Love's more orchestral sophomore effort, ***Da Capo***, recorded with the addition of Tjay Cantrelli on flute and saxophone and Michael Stuart on drums, makes US #80. Pfisterer and Cantrelli depart, leaving the band as Lee, Forssi, MacLean, Echols and Stuart.
June [9] The group begins recording ***Forever Changes*** at Sunset Sound Recorders and Leon Russell's Skyhill Studios in Los Angeles.
Nov Critically-praised, ***Forever Changes***, widely regarded as the group's (and Lee's) masterwork, with nine of 11 cuts penned by Lee, reaches UK #24 and US #152.

1968

Jan Subsequently revered as the group's seminal recording, *Alone Again Or* makes US #99. Despite Love's identity being most closely associated with Lee, MacLean has been responsible for writing and singing the track.
Apr [18-20] The group performs again at the Fillmore West on a bill with the Staple Singers.
Aug Lee emerges with a restructured band, recruiting Frank Fayad (bass), George Suranovich (drums) and Jay Donnellan (lead guitar).

1969

Sept ***Four Sail***, the band's last outing for Elektra, makes US #102.
Dec Love moves to Blue Thumb Records and uses material remaining from the ***Four Sail*** sessions for the double set ***Out Here***, which reaches US #176. Suranovich is fired and replaced by Drachen Theaker, ex-Crazy World Of Arthur Brown, who leaves shortly thereafter.

1970

May ***Out Here*** reaches UK #29.
Sept Elektra compilation, ***Love Revisited***, comprising tracks from the first three albums, peaks at US #142.
Dec Lee has re-formed the band once again, with Fayad, Suranovich, and Gary Rowles and Nooney Rickett on guitars, for ***False Start***, with Jimi Hendrix guesting on one track, one of his final cameos performances. Soon after the album's release, Lee dismisses the rest of the group.

1972

Aug Lee releases his debut solo album, ***Vindicator***, on A&M Records. The following year the Love compilation ***Love Masters*** will be released while Lee records ***Black Beauty***, which will remain unissued.

1974

Dec Lee forms yet another version of Love, which includes Melvan Whittington (guitar), John Sterling (guitar) and Joe Blocker (drums), with Sherwood Akuna and Robert Rozelle sharing bass duties. The line-up records the soul-influenced ***Reel To Reel*** for RSO Records, after which Lee returns to playing occasional one-off dates.

1977

Sterling convinces Lee to re-form Love and attempt to recapture the spirit of earlier times. The band's line-up is Lee, MacLean, Sterling, Kim Kesteron (bass) and George Suranovich (drums), with the Knack's drummer, Bruce Gary, also playing at one point, but it never releases any recordings. (Subsequent Love reunions in the early '80s include one with Lee and MacLean on a southern California tour.)

1995

Aug While Love's cult status has guaranteed the release of original and previously unavailable material including ***Best Of Love*** (Rhino Records, 1980), ***Arthur Lee*** (Rhino/Beggars Banquet, 1981), ***Love Live*** (Rhino, 1982), ***Love*** (MCA, 1982)), the Damned reached UK #27 with its revival of *Alone Again Or* in 1987. Arthur Lee & various backing units of Love have continued to appear on nostalgia bills into the early '90s, while Lee has spent the last year performing well-received US club dates backed by Baby Lemonade on the West coast and members of Das Damen on the East. Elektra/Rhino Records (US) now releases the two-disc anthology, ***Love Story***.

LYLE LOVETT

1986

Sept Lovett (b. Nov. 1, 1957, Klein, TX, a town named after one of his great-great-grandfathers, a Bavarian weaver who helped found the outpost in the 1840s) has been raised on a family horse ranch, run track at high school and majored in journalism at Texas A&M, while performing in local Houston, TX clubs and folk festivals. Going on to study German at graduate school, he performed one song in a 1983 TV movie "Bill: On His Own", while his first recorded work, *If I Were The Man*, appeared in 1985 on an album accompanying **Fast Folk Musical Magazine, Vol. 2**. Having also contributed harmony vocals to Nanci Griffith's ***The Last Of The True Believers*** the same year, and influenced by Guy Clark, Townes Van Zandt, Randy Newman and Tom Waits, Lovett began hawking demos around Nashville, TN in the mid-'80s. Guy Clark has brought Lovett's songs to the attention of MCA A&R head Tony Brown, who has signed him to the label and remixed ten of the demo cuts, now released as ***Lyle Lovett*** by Curb/MCA.

1988

Mar The self-penned ***Pontiac***, once again co-produced with Brown, and featuring Vince Gill and Emmylou Harris, blending gospel, jazz, country, blues, swing and rock influences with a bitter-sweet rootsy traditionalism, peaks at US #117.

1989

Feb [22] Lovett sings *She's Hot To Go* at the 31st Grammy Awards held at Los Angeles, CA's Shrine Auditorium.
Mar Big-band, swing-tinged ***Lyle Lovett And His Large Band***, helmed by Brown, Lovett and Villy Williams, makes US #62.

1990

June [26] Lovett embarks on a 13-date US tour at the Poplar Creek Music Theatre, Hoffman Estates, IL, supporting Rickie Lee Jones.
Aug Walter Hyatt's MCA Master Series album, ***King Tears***, produced by Lovett, is released in the US.

1991

May [18] ***Deadicated***, a collection of Grateful Dead covers to which Lovett has contributed *Friend Of The Devil*, reaches US #24.
July Leo Kottke's ***Great Big Boy***, featuring Lovett singing backup vocals on three tracks, is released in the US. He has also recently contributed the Don Was-produced *You Can't Resist It* to the "Switch" movie soundtrack.

1992

Jan [15] Lovett inducts Johnny Cash into the Rock and Roll Hall of Fame at the seventh annual dinner, at New York's Waldorf Astoria Hotel.
Mar [4] He performs a one-off UK date at the Shaw

Theatre, London.
[25-26, 28] Lovett performs three dates at the Paramount Theatre, Austin.
Apr [2] He guests on NBC-TV's "Late Night With David Letterman", also promoting the Robert Altman-directed movie "The Player", which features Lovett is his movie debut, playing a cop.
[18] Lyrically barbed as ever, Lovett's fourth album, ***Joshua Judges Ruth***, recorded at Los Angeles' Ocean Way Studio, co-produced by Lovett, long-time cohort Billy Williams and George Massenburg, and including musical guests Sweet Pea Atkinson, Emmylou Harris, Rickie Lee Jones, Leo Kottke, Francine Reed and Was (Not Was)' Sir Harry Bowens, debuts at its US #57 peak.
May [6-9] During a US tour, Lovett resides at The Roxy, Los Angeles, for four nights.
[12] He performs on NBC-TV's "The Tonight Show".
June [11] A seven-date UK tour, partially supporting Dire Straits, kicks off at Cardiff Arms Park, Cardiff, Wales.
[27] Lovett performs with the host on ITV's "Tom Jones : The Right Time".
July [25] In between performing two songs on NBC-TV's "The Tonight Show", Lovett is mauled by fellow guest, radio personality Howard Stern.
Aug [3] A 35-date North American trek begins at the Artemus Ham Concert Hall, Las Vegas, NV, the same day ***Lyle Lovett And His Large Band*** is certified gold by the RIAA.
Sept [9] Lovett co-hosts, with Bonnie Raitt, a post-concert reception in Milwaukee, WI, raising funds to benefit the Lac Courte Oreilles Indian tribe from Wisconsin.
Oct [22] Lovett sings the "Star Spangled Banner" at a Toronto Blue Jays vs. Atlanta Braves game at the SkyDome, Toronto, during the World Series.
Nov [5] Lovett breaks his elbow while performing at the Arlene Schnitzer Concert Hall, Portland Center for the Performing Arts, Portland, OR, forcing him to cancel the remaining seven dates of his tour.
[18] He appears at the AIDS Project Los Angeles' "Commitment To Life VI" cocktail and dinner party, at the Universal Amphitheatre, Universal City, CA, honoring Barbra Streisand and David Geffen.
Dec [2] Currently featured on the soundtrack to the Steve Martin-starring "Leap Of Faith", performing *Pass Me Not* with George Duke, Lovett is interviewed on syndicated TV's "Whoopi Goldberg" show.

1993

Feb [17] He performs *Stand By Your Man*, a live favorite which is also featured as the closing song to the current hit movie "The Crying Game", with its originator Tammy Wynette on "The Tonight Show". Lovett is also currently filming "Short Cuts", Altman's follow-up to "The Player".
[26] Lovett & His Acoustic Quartet play a sellout show at the Chrysler Hall, Norfolk Scope Convention & Cultural Centre, Norfolk, VA, during his current North American tour.
Mar [25] ***Joshua Judges Ruth*** is certified gold by the RIAA.
May [22] He appears on CBS-TV's "Willie Nelson The Big Six-O" birthday celebrations.
June [16] Lovett guests on "Late Night With David Letterman".
[27] In one of the surprise celebrity events of the year, he marries actress Julia Roberts at the St. James Lutheran Church in Marion, IN. Roberts will later walk on stage at Lovett's Noblesville, IN concert in her wedding dress and kiss her new husband in front of 10,000 fans.
Oct [1] CBS-TV's "A Day In The Life Of Country Music", featuring what several country artists did on May 7th including Lovett, airs.
Nov [15] ***Pontiac*** is certified gold by the RIAA.

1994

Mar [26] Various compilation, ***Rhythm Country & Blues***, featuring Al Green and Lovett's *Funny How Time Slips Away*, reaches US #18.
Apr [19] Lovett guests on CBS-TV's "Late Show With David Letterman".
Sept [3-4] He plays at London's Royal Albert Hall during a brief UK visit.
Oct [8] ***I Love Everybody***, an 18-track self-penned album co-produced with Billy Williams and including guest backing vocalist, Julia Roberts, bows at its UK #54 peak.
[10] As he performs at the Joseph B. Gould Paramount Theatre in Denver, CO, Tammy Wynette's duets album ***Without Walls***, featuring a pairing with Lovett on *If You Were To Wake Up*, is released.
[15] ***I Love Everybody*** debuts at its US #26 high.

1995

Feb [2] Lovett guests on NBC-TV's sitcom "Mad About You".
[15] A 1980 graduate, Lovett performs on the Texas A&M University campus in College Station.
[25] As he prepares for an ESPN segment of "Moto World", he breaks his collarbone in a dirt bike accident in Baja, CA, preventing a scheduled appearance at the Grammys.
Mar [1] Lovett wins the Best Pop Vocal Collaboration category, with Al Green, for *Funny How Time Slips Away* and the Best Country Performance By A Duo Or Group With Vocal category with Asleep At The Wheel, for *Blues For Dixie*, at the 37th annual Grammy awards at the Shrine Auditorium.
[28] In a joint statement released by Roberts' publicist it is revealed that Lovett and Roberts are separating, adding "We remain close and in great support of each other".
May Ichiban Records releases Francine Reed's ***I Want You To Love Me***, including *Why I Don't Know*, a duet with Lovett.
Aug [9] Currently on tour with opening act Shawn Colvin, Lovett plays before a sellout crowd of 9,519 at Red Rocks Amphitheatre, Denver, CO.
Oct [7] Lovett performs at the sixth annual Music Festival at Verde Valley School, Sedona, AZ, in support of the school's Native American Scholarship Fund, founded by Jackson Browne.
Dec [7] Lovett and Randy Newman guests on "The Tonight Show", singing *You've Got A Friend* from the movie "Toy Story".

1996

Feb [10] ***Dead Man Walking*** soundtrack, featuring Lovett's *Promises*, written and performed by him specifically for the movie, makes US #61.
Mar [7] Lovett guests with Randy Newman on "Late Show With David Letterman".
[25] Lovett and Newman sing the Oscar-nominated *You've Got A Friend* from "Toy Story" at the 68th annual Academy Awards from Los Angeles' Dorothy Chandler Pavilion.
June [18] ***The Road To Ensenada***, featured Chris Hillman and Randy Newman, is released on MCA/Curb, supported by a US summer tour.

THE LOVIN' SPOONFUL

John Sebastian (vocals, guitar, harmonica, autoharp); **Zal Yanovsky** (guitar, vocals); **Steve Boone** (bass, vocals); **Joe Butler** (drums, vocals)

1964

Feb [9] Among friends invited to Cass Elliot's house to watch the Beatles' US TV debut on "The Ed Sullivan Show" are Sebastian (b. Mar. 17, 1944, New York, NY) and Yanovsky (b. Zalman Yanovsky, Dec. 19, 1944, Toronto, ON, Canada). They discuss the possibility of forming a rock group and play guitars until dawn. Sebastian, whose father recorded harmonica singles for Archie Bleyer's Cadence label in the '50s, is a college-dropout Greenwich Village folkie who backed local heroes Fred Neil and Tom Rush, and made sporadic appearances (including on their Elektra album) as a member of the Even Dozen Jug Band. Yanovsky is guitarist with the Halifax Three, a sharp-suited folk group from Nova Scotia, Canada.
June During the height of Beatlemania, the Halifax Three folds, with Yanovsky and founder member Denny Doherty joining Elliot and James Hendricks, ex-the Big Three, and Tim Rose. As the Mugwumps, they become prototypical electric folkies. Gigs are disastrous and recordings so inept that Warner Bros. releases their album only after they become famous elsewhere. Between studio stints backing Judy Collins, Jesse Colin Young and Tim Hardin, Sebastian becomes a Mugwump, but the group disbands.
Dec Doherty, having joined the Journeymen for seven months before they split, goes with Elliot to the Virgin Islands, where they join the Mamas & the Papas. Their song, *Creeque Alley*, chronicles the comings and goings of the clique.

1965

Jan With producer Erik Jacobsen, Sebastian and Yanovsky plan a new outfit - to be called the Lovin' Spoonful (after a phrase from Mississippi John Hurt's *Coffee Blues*). They find Boone (b. Sept. 23, 1943, Camp Lejeune, NC) and Butler (b. Sept. 16, 1943, Glen Cove, Long Island, NY) and rehearse in the basement of the rundown Albert Hotel. Early attempts at gigging and recording are unsuccessful.
June After a residency at the Night Owl in Greenwich Village, they work on Sebastian's innovative compositions, while Jacobsen secures a deal with the recently-formed Kama Sutra label.
July [24] At a Night Owl gig, the group is seen by audience members Phil Spector, Bob Dylan and the Byrds.
Oct [16] A celebration of rock'n'roll, *Do You Believe In Magic* hits US #9.
Dec Their debut album, ***Do You Believe In Magic***, makes US #32. They evolve their own style - a light, lyrical synthesis they call "good-time music". Others call it "folk rock". With their striped jerseys and mischievous image, they become America's mop tops from Manhattan.

1966

Jan [22] *You Didn't Have To Be So Nice* hits US #10.
Apr [9] *Daydream* hits US #2, behind the Righteous Brothers' *(You're My) Soul And Inspiration*, and is a million seller. ***Daydream*** hits US #10. A compilation, ***What's Shakin'***, on Elektra, includes four Spoonful tracks - given to them in early 1965 in return for musical equipment. One track *Good Time Music*, defines the group's raison d'être.
[13] The group appears on the ITV show "Ready Steady Go!", at the start of its first UK tour.
May [7] *Daydream* hits UK #2, behind Manfred Mann's *Pretty Flamingo*.
[28] ***Daydream*** hits UK #8.
June [11] Written in a taxi en route to the studio, *Did You Ever Have To Make Up Your Mind* hits US #2, behind the Rolling Stones' *Paint It Black*.
[25] The group plays on "The Beach Boys Summer Spectacular", with Chad & Jeremy, Percy Sledge and the Byrds, at the Hollywood Bowl, Hollywood, CA, the day after a playing a similar show at the Cow Palace in San Francisco.
Aug [13] Featuring atmospheric street noise and engineer Roy Halee's booming drum experiments (which he continues on Simon & Garfunkel's ***Bookends***), *Summer In The City* becomes the Lovin' Spoonful's biggest hit, beginning a three-week stay at US #1 and earning their second gold disc.
[20] *Summer In The City* hits UK #8. During the month, the band embarks on a State Fairs tour in the New York area, as "What's Up Tiger Lily?", starring Woody Allen and featuring the band, opens throughout US cinemas.
Sept [19] *Summer In The City* is certified gold by the RIAA.
Oct Soundtrack album for the movie "What's Up Tiger Lily?" makes US #126. The film, a Japanese thriller on to which Woody Allen and Louise Lasser have dubbed unrelated American dialogue, becomes a cult item.

Nov [4] The band embarks on a six-week US tour.
[19] *Rain On The Roof* hits US #10.
Dec Their third album of the year, ***Hums Of The Lovin' Spoonful***, makes US #14.

1967

Jan [21] *Full Measure*, the B-side of the still-climbing *Nashville Cats*, peaks at US #87.
[28] *Nashville Cats* becomes their sixth consecutive Top 10 success, hitting US #8, and making UK #26.
Mar [18] With full orchestral backing, *Darling Be Home Soon* reaches US #15 and UK #44 (their last UK hit). ***The Best Of The Lovin' Spoonful***, the first of many compilations, hits US #3 and will spend a year on the chart.
May Their second soundtrack album, for Francis Ford Coppola's "You're A Big Boy Now", makes US #118.
June [10] *Six O'Clock*, with new producer Joe Wissert, reaches US #18.
[24] Yanovsky quits after a performance at the "Forest Hills Music Festival", New York, following media indignation over a marijuana bust where he allegedly incriminated others to avoid prosecution. His replacement is Jerry Yester, ex-the Modern Folk Quartet.
July [7] ***The Best Of The Lovin' Spoonful*** is certified gold by the RIAA.
Sept Yanovsky debuts with *As Long As You're Here*.
Nov [18] *She's Still A Mystery* reaches US #27.

1968

Feb [3] *Money* makes US #48. ***Everything Playing*** peaks at US #118.
Apr ***The Best Of The Lovin' Spoonful Vol. 2*** makes US #156.
Aug [3] *Never Going Back* peaks at US #73, written by John Stewart and produced by Chip Douglas, fresh from their success with the Monkees' *Daydream Believer*.
Oct After "two glorious years and a tedious one", Sebastian leaves the group, which soon crumbles. Subsequent individual output confirms that, to all intents and purposes, he *was* the Lovin' Spoonful. Sebastian's first solo venture is writing songs for "Jimmy Shine", a Broadway play starring Dustin Hoffman.
Nov Their final album, ***Revelation Revolution 69***, credits only Joe Butler. Any Spoonful ingenuity is absent.

1969

Jan [25] *She's A Lady*, Sebastian's solo debut, reaches US #84.
Feb [8] The Lovin' Spoonful's *Me About You* peaks at US #91, a lackluster swan song for one of the era's top US pop groups.
Aug [16] Clad in the tie-dyes which will become his trademark, Sebastian appears at the "Woodstock Music & Art Fair" in Bethel, NY. He performs the Spoonful song *Younger Generation*, which becomes a highlight of the "Woodstock" movie, and *I Had A Dream*, the opening track on ***Woodstock***.

1970

Mar While MGM and Warner/Reprise argue about who owns his contract, Sebastian's first album, the Paul Rothchild-produced ***John B. Sebastian*** (issued on both labels!) rises to US #20.
Sept At the UK's "Isle Of Wight Festival", Sebastian reunites with Yanovsky, attending as part of Kris Kristofferson's band. (Yanovsky's solo, ***Alive And Well In Argentina***, co-produced with Jerry Yester, finds only cult acceptance. He returns to Ontario, to open his Chez Piggy's restaurant. Yester cuts albums with his wife, Judy Henske (***Farewell Aldebaran***) and the group Rosebud (***Rosebud***), before joining his brother Jim in the Association for a brief spell. He will re-form the Modern Folk Quartet in the '80s, but wins more acclaim as a producer for the likes of Aztec Two Step and Tom Waits, and as a string arranger in Los Angeles. Butler appears on Broadway in "Hair", and Boone moves to Baltimore, MD, where he works as a musician.)
Oct Loser in the contract battle, MGM issues the unauthorized live album ***John Sebastian Live***, recorded during Lovin' Spoonful days, which peaks at US #129.

1971

Apr Reprise retaliates with a bona fide live album, ***Cheapo Cheapo Productions Presents ...***, which makes US #75.
Sept Sebastian's ***The Four Of Us***, inspired by a cross-country vacation, reaches US #93. (Sebastian will spend time touring as a one-man show and playing the occasional harmonica session on albums by Stephen Stills, Ohio Knox, Rita Coolidge and the Everly Brothers, before releasing his first album in three years, ***The Tarzana Kid***, in September 1974 which marks a reunion with Spoonful producer Erik Jacobsen.)

1976

May [8] After five singles have failed to chart, Reprise are on the point of dropping Sebastian when his song *Welcome Back*, for John Travolta's ABC-TV series, "Welcome Back Kotter", hits US #1. Meanwhile, the double album, ***The Best Of The Lovin' Spoonful***, peaks at US #183, while Sebastian's ***Welcome Back*** makes US #79.
Aug [7] Sebastian's *Hideaway* peaks at US #95.

1980

Oct 15 years after the Lovin' Spoonful's inception, the four original members reunite for a cameo appearance in Paul Simon's now premiering movie, "One Trick Pony". (During the rest of the decade, Sebastian will continue to tour regularly, with friends and as a solo act, and write for TV and films including "The Care Bears", "Strawberry Shortcake" and NBC-TV's "The Jerk II".)

1996

May [12] While the Lovin' Spoonful, minus Sebastian, has reformed for nostalgia work in 1991, with the line-up of Butler, Boone and the Yester brothers, Sebastian, who hosted "The Golden Age Of Rock'n'Roll" TV series on the A&E-TV cable channel in January 1991, and appeared in an episode of Fox-TV's "Married With Children" in November 1992, before releasing ***Tar Beach*** on the Shanachie label, his first album in 17 years in March 1993. With *Summer In The City* featured on last year's soundtrack to "Die Hard With A Vengeance", and reissued as a single for the first time in stereo, Sebastian's latest album ***I Want My Roots***, credited to John Sebastian & the J-Band (which comprises Jimmy Vivino, Fritz Richmond and James Wormworth) is now issued by Musicmasters in the US.

NICK LOWE

1965

As a bassist, Lowe (b. Mar. 24, 1949, Woodchurch, Suffolk) joins Kippington Lodge, a group based in Tunbridge Wells, Kent, with Bob Andrews (keyboards), Brinsley Schwarz (guitar), Pete Whale (drums) and Barry Landerman (keyboards). Lowe and Schwarz have previously been together in schoolboy groups, Sounds 4 Plus 1 and Three's A Crowd. Signed to Parlophone Records the following year, the band will release five singles over four years, none of which charts. With Landerman and Whale leaving and with Billy Rankin on drums, the group changes its name to Brinsley Schwarz in 1969, before signing to the Famepushers management company in February the following year, which helps them secure a recording contract with United Artists Records.

1970

Apr [4] As ***Brinsley Schwarz*** is released, containing six Lowe compositions, Famepushers tries to launch the group by flying a planeload of UK rock writers to New York, NY, to see them play support to Van Morrison at the Fillmore East, at a cost of £120,000, which turns out to be a legendary tactical disaster, involving 26 limousines and 133 journalists, photographers and TV crew personnel.

Nov ***Despite It All***, with seven Lowe songs and one by Andrews, also fails.

1972

Feb With Brinsley Schwarz now featuring additional singer/guitarist Ian Gomm, ***Silver Pistol***, mainly composed of songs by Lowe and Gomm, and recorded in their own house, which is pictured on the sleeve, is released, quickly followed by the September issue of ***Nervous On The Road***.

1973

Oct Their fifth album, ***Please Don't Ever Change***, fares no better than its predecessors, although a measure of the group's status within the music industry is that they appear on two of the most collectible compilation albums of the year, ***Greasy Truckers Party*** and ***Glastonbury Fayre***.

1974

Mar Budget-priced compilation album, ***Original Golden Greats***, includes a track earlier issued incognito (as "the Hitlers") on single and two previously unreleased items, one of which (*Run Rudolf Run*) is a live recording from a tour on which the band played as support to Paul McCartney & Wings.
July ***The New Favourites Of Brinsley Schwarz***, produced by Dave Edmunds, is released but, by now unsurprisingly, fails to chart. It includes Nick Lowe's *(What's So Funny 'Bout) Peace, Love And Understanding*, which will later be recorded by Elvis Costello.
Nov The group appears, with Dave Edmunds, as the Electricians in the feature film "Stardust", starring David Essex.

1975

Mar Brinsley Schwarz splits, having cut several critically-praised albums but with little commercial recognition. Schwarz and Rankin briefly join another "pub-rock" band, Ducks DeLuxe. (Schwarz and Andrews will then join the Rumour, which becomes Graham Parker's backing band; Rankin will rarely be heard of, while Gomm will launch a solo career, scoring a US #18 hit in 1979 with *Hold On*.)
July Lowe concentrates on production, working over the next nine months on the Kursaal Flyers' ***Chocs Away***, Dr. Feelgood's second album, ***Malpractice***, and Graham Parker's ***Howling Wind***. He also records two glam-rock one-off singles under pseudonyms the Disco Brothers and the Tartan Horde (whose single, *Rollers Show*, is a parody of current teen-rage act, the Bay City Rollers).

1976

Aug [14] Lowe's debut single, *So It Goes*, co-produced with Jake Riviera, is the first release, with the catalog number BUY 1, on the seminal UK independent label Stiff, where Lowe becomes an in-house producer. (He will be responsible for the Damned's debut album and Elvis Costello's first single, *Less Than Zero*. Aside from label duties, he also produces Clover's (including Huey Lewis) *Chicken Funk* and Dave Edmunds' ***Get It***.)

1977

May On Stiff, Lowe releases the four-track EP, *Bowi*, the title a tongue-in-cheek response to David Bowie's ***Low***.
June Edmunds' UK #26, *I Knew The Bride*, has been written by Lowe in the style of Chuck Berry's *You Never Can Tell*.
July Lowe joins Edmunds' group Rockpile, while continuing his parallel solo career, often using the same musicians, and producing Costello's debut album, ***My Aim Is True***, and the Rumour's ***Max***, among others.
Oct Lowe revives Billy Fury's *Halfway To Paradise* on Stiff. He also performs in the Stiff tour package, "Live Stiffs", with labelmates Costello, Ian Dury and Wreckless Eric, following which he leaves the label with Costello and Riviera, moving to Riviera's newly formed Radar Records.

1978

Mar ***Jesus Of Cool***, illustrating his bass guitar collection on the sleeve, is Lowe's first solo effort (US title: ***Pure Pop For Now People***) and reaches UK #22 and US #127. Taken from it, the first Radar single, *I Love The Sound Of Breaking Glass*, hits UK #7. (For Radar he also produces Costello's second album, ***This Year's Model***.)

May Lowe's *Little Hitler*, co-written by Dave Edmunds, is released, while Mickey Jupp's ***Juppanese***, a Lowe co-production, is his last Stiff assignment.

July Retrospective ***Fifteen Thoughts Of Brinsley Schwarz*** is released.

Sept [9] Lowe performs at the "Knebworth Rock Festival", Knebworth, Herts, before embarking on a UK tour with Dave Edmunds and the Smirks.

Nov *American Squirm* is issued, while Lowe contributes to the soundtrack of the film "Rock'N'Roll High School".

1979

Jan Lowe produces the Pretenders debut, *Stop Your Sobbin'*, and another Costello album, ***Armed Forces***.

June *Crackin' Up* makes UK #34, while ***Labour Of Lust***, recorded in London and Helsinki with Rockpile, peaks at UK #43 and US #31.

July [4] Rockpile opens a two-month US tour supporting Blondie, at the Central Youth Centre, Scranton, PA.

Aug [15] The movie "Americathon", with soundtrack contributions from Lowe, premieres.

[18] Lowe marries Johnny Cash's step-daughter, Carlene Carter, in Los Angeles, CA.

Sept [1] Documentary "Born Fighters", devoted to Lowe and Dave Edmunds, is shown on UK TV.

Cruel To Be Kind, a re-recording of an old B-side (co-written with ex-Brinsley Schwarz colleague Ian Gomm), makes #12 in both the UK and US.

1980

During a year spent mostly working on the road and in the studio with Rockpile, Lowe also produces Costello's ***Get Happy*** and his wife Carlene's ***Musical Shapes***.

Oct Rockpile releases its only album, ***Seconds Of Pleasure***.

1981

Jan Costello's ***Trust*** is released, the last of his which Lowe will produce for five years.

Feb Rockpile splits, leaving Lowe working solo before forming his own touring and recording band, Nick Lowe & the Chaps with ex-Ace keyboard player Paul Carrack, ex-Rumour guitarist Martin Belmont and Bobby Irwin on drums.

Sept Lowe produces Carlene Carter's ***Blue Nun***.

1982

Feb Nick Lowe & the Chaps tour the US, then change their name to Noise To Go. ***Nick The Knife*** is Lowe's first album for F-Beat Records and uses an assortment of musicians from Rockpile and Noise To Go. It spends two weeks at UK #99 and makes US #50.

Oct Lowe produces the Fabulous Thunderbirds' ***Rhythm***.

1983

June ***The Abominable Showman***, co-produced by Roger Bechirian, with Simon Climie (later of Climie Fisher) among its guests, makes US #129.

1984

Jan John Hiatt's ***Riding With The King*** is released, co-produced by Lowe.

June Lowe's *Half A Boy, Half A Man* peaks at UK #53.

July ***Nick Lowe And His Cowboy Outfit***, featuring *L.A.F.S. (Love At First Sight)* and a duet with Costello on *Baby It's You* peaks at US #113.

Sept Lowe's compilation album, ***Sixteen All-Time Hits***, is released on Demon Records.

1985

Sept ***Rose Of England*** is issued, Lowe's last album for F-Beat and also his final recording with Cowboy Outfit.

1986

Jan [11] *I Knew The Bride (When She Used To Rock And Roll)*, produced by Huey Lewis and backed by the News, peaks at US #77.

Mar Another Lowe compilation album, ***Nick's Knack***, is released in Britain by Demon Records.

Sept Costello's ***Blood And Chocolate***, reuniting with Lowe, is issued on Demon Records.

1988

Feb ***Pinker And Prouder Than Previous*** is released featuring material recorded over an 18-month period, its guest musicians include Lowe's long-time collaborator, Edmunds.

July [29-31] Lowe takes part in the three-day "Cambridge Folk Festival" at Cherry Hinton Hall, Cambs. Another Demon retrospective, ***Basher : The Best Of Nick Lowe***, the most comprehensive to date, will be released the following year.

1990

Apr [14] Now signed to Reprise Records, Lowe's ***Party Of One*** peaks at US #182.

July Katydids' album, ***Katydids***, helmed by Lowe, is issued.

Sept [6] During a short Californian sweep, he performs in San Francisco.

1992

Feb [29] Still an in-demand producer (he recently helmed Rain's 1991 debut set), Lowe has teamed with Ry Cooder, John Hiatt and Jim Keltner to form Little Village, whose first album, ***Little Village***, bows at its UK #23 peak and makes US #66 on Mar [14], spurred by UK and US live dates.

1994

Sept Arthur Alexander tribute album ***Adios Amigo***, to which Lowe has contributed *In The Middle Of It All*, is released in the US.

Nov [26] Lowe guests on BBC2-TV's "Later With Jools Holland".

Dec His latest album ***The Impossible Bird***, a mix of originals and covers, is released in the US on Upstart Records.

1995

Jan [25] Lowe begins a month-long US tour with the Impossible Birds (Geraint Watkins (keyboards), Paul Riley (bass) and Robert Trehern (drums)) at Toad's Place, New Haven, CT. (During the tour, Lowe will admit that his songwriting royalties from Curtis Stigers' version of *(What's So Funny 'Bout) Peace, Love And Understanding*, included on ***The Bodyguard*** soundtrack, has, after 30 years in the industry, made him a millionaire.)

July [5] Upstart releases the three-track live EP *Live! On The Battlefield*.

L7

Donita Sparks (guitar, vocals); **Suzi Gardner** (guitar, vocals); **Jennifer Finch** (bass, vocals); **Dee Plakas** (drums)

1990

Jan L7, its name a slang expression meaning "square", has been formed in Los Angeles, CA in 1985 by transplanted Chicago, IL surburbanite Sparks (b. Apr 8, 1963, Chicago) and Gardner (b. Aug 1, 1960, Altus, OK) who recruit Finch (b. Aug 5, 1966, Los Angeles) in 1986 and the first of a number of drummers, Roy Koutsky. Having released their debut set, the grunge/punk/metal-fused set ***L7*** for Epitaph Records, produced by label-head Brett Guretwitz, also a member of Bad Religion, in December 1987, and with a second drummer, Anne Anderson having been replaced by Plakas (b. Demetra Plakas, Nov. 9, 1960, Chicago), the all-girl outfit has signed a short-term deal with the emerging indie label Sub Pop, whose Jonathan Poeman calls the band "a real primal rock machine", which issues *Shove*, to be followed by the nine-track EP ***Smell The Magic*** in November, both of which find a popular home at US college radio. The following year, L7 will ink a more lasting deal with Slash Records, released via the London label in the UK.

1992

Apr [8] An 11-date UK tour gets underway at the The Junction, Cambridge, Cambs.

[21] Hailed as an instant indie classic, *Pretend We're Dead* (with *Shit List* on the B-side) reaches UK #21.

May [2] The 11-track ***Bricks Are Heavy***, helmed by Nirvana producer Butch Vig, debuts at its UK #24 peak.

[30] *Everglade* bows at its UK #27 peak.

Aug [16] The band embarks on a US tour opening for the Beastie Boys at the Cleveland Agora Theatre, a bill grossing $28,050 from 1,700 attendees.

Sept [5] ***Bricks Are Heavy*** makes US #160.

[8] L7 performs *Pretend We're Dead* on NBC-TV's "Late Night With David Letterman'.

[12] *Monster* debuts at its UK #33 peak.

Oct [28] European dates begin in Helsinki, Finland, supporting label-mates Faith No More, set to end on December 19th in Zurich, Switzerland.

Nov [20] The band's appearance on C4-TV's "The Word" is highlighted by Sparks taking off her jeans to reveal that she does not wear panties.

Dec [5] Re-issued *Pretend We're Dead* makes UK #50.

1993

Mar [9] L7 supports Pearl Jam at a concert at the Pensacola Civic Center, Pensacola, FL.

1994

June [16] The group performs at London's Astoria Two venue, as part of the "MTV 120 Minutes" music festival.

July [9] *Andres* debuts at its UK #34 peak.

[23] Produced by Garth Richardson, ***Hungry For Stink*** enters at its UK #26 high during a two week chart stay.

[30] ***Hungry For Stink*** debuts at its US #117 peak.

Aug [1] The group embarks on the "Lollapalooza" alternative festival tour at the FDR Park, Philadelphia, PA.

1995

Jan [14-15] The group performs at two benefit concerts for Rock for Choice (a women's rights organization which the band members helped found) at the DAR Constitution Hall, Washington, DC, headlined by Pearl Jam and also featuring Neil Young.

Feb [2] London Records announces that the scheduled single *Stuck Here Again* will not be released today because the master-tape for the intended B-side (*Bloodstains*) was recently lost in transit between Los Angeles and London, and a new replacement track is not available.

[9] An eight-date UK visit, with Wool opening for L7, ends with a gig at London's Astoria Theatre.

Aug During a US tour the band appears as Camel Lips at a gig in Emo's Austin, TX (which is also the name it performed under in the 1994 John Waters-directed movie "Serial Mom", also contributing *Gas Chamber* to the soundtrack).

Sept During the month the band plays at Seattle's "Bombershoot Festival", at the Seattle Arena, WA.

LULU

1963

Having made her stage debut in 1957 at Bridgeton Public Hall in Scotland, Lulu (b. Marie McDonald

McLaughlin Lawrie, Nov. 3, 1948, Lennoxtown, Strathclyde, Scotland), still only 15 years old joins Glasgow, Scotland group the Gleneagles, which begins to play regularly at the Lindella and Le Phonographe clubs. The latter's owner, Tony Gordon, impressed by audience reaction, introduces the group to his sister Marion Massey, who is in showbiz management in London. Massey becomes the group's manager and changes the name to Lulu & the Luvvers, which lines up as Lulu (vocals), Ross Nelson (lead guitar), Jim Dewar (rhythm guitar), Alec Bell (keyboards), Jimmy Smith (saxophone), Tony Tierney (bass) and David Miller (drums).

1964

May [16] The group debuts on ITV's "Thank Your Lucky Stars".

June Massey has negotiated a contract with Decca Records, and the group's first disc is a revival of the Isley Brothers' *Shout*, which hits UK #7. It is quickly followed by the similarly-styled *Satisfied*.

Aug *Shout* makes a minor US chart showing at #94.

Nov With Lulu now billed as a solo artist, *Here Comes The Night*, a UK #2 hit for Them, also on Decca, a few months later, charts briefly at UK #50.

Dec [26] Lulu opens in the role of Witch Hazel in the pantomime "Once Upon A Fairytale", at the Gaumont Theatre, Doncaster, Yorks. Partly thanks to her musical versatility and her easy TV demeanor, Lulu begins attracting bookings as a solo act, while still performing regular club and package-show gigs with the Luvvers who are no longer credited on disc.

1965

May [25] Lulu performs *Leave A Little Love* at the televised "Brighton Song Festival" at the Dome, Brighton, East Sussex. The Les Reed-penned song is placed second, behind Kenny Lynch's *I'll Stay By You*, and hits UK #8.

Sept *Try To Understand* reaches UK #25.

Oct [4] Lulu heads the cast of a new BBC-TV 13-part series, "Stramash" (a Scottish word meaning riot or disturbance).

[22] Lulu & the Luvvers embark on 28-date, twice-nightly UK package tour with Gene Pitney, Peter & Gordon, the Rockin' Berries and others, at London's Finsbury Park Astoria, set to end on November 21st at the Odeon Cinema, Leeds, Yorks.

Dec [16] Lulu is featured in the ITV airing of a tribute to "The Music Of Lennon & McCartney".

[20] She flies to the US to appear in "Murray The K's Christmas Show" at New York's Brooklyn Fox, set to open on the 24th.

1966

Jan [5] Lulu & the Luvvers appear in the first broadcast of BBC-TV's "The Whole Scene Going" teenage magazine series.

Mar [8] Lulu becomes the first British female singer to appear behind the Iron Curtain, when she begins a Polish tour with the Hollies in Warsaw.

[19] She returns from the tour, at which point Lulu & the Luvvers split.

[25] Lulu embarks on her first solo trek, a 31-date, twice-nightly UK package tour with Roy Orbison, the Walker Brothers and others at London's Finsbury Park Astoria which will close on May 1st at the Coventry Theatre, Coventry, Warks.

May [31] Lulu begins filming "To Sir With Love" on location and at Pinewood Studios, with Sidney Poitier in the lead role.

Nov [6] She begins a seven-date, twice nightly UK tour with the Beach Boys, David & Jonathan and others again at the Astoria Theatre, set to close on the 13th at the Birmingham Theatre, West Midlands.

Dec [24] Lulu opens in the "Babes In The Wood" pantomime at the Wimbledon Theatre, Wimbledon, London.

1967

Feb Lulu signs a five-year recording deal with producer Mickie Most.

Apr [16] She appears at the **Daily Express** "Record Star Show" at the Empire Pool, Wembley, Middx.

[23] The first of six 30-minute BBC2-TV shows titled "Three Of A Kind" airs.

[24] She performs at an Empire Pool Wembley charity show with Paul Jones, the Alan Price Set, the Kinks, the Move, Cream and the Tremeloes, among many others.

May Moving from Decca to Columbia Records with Most, their first collaboration, on a cover of a Neil Diamond B-side, is *The Boat That I Row*, which hits UK #6, as Lulu tours the UK supporting the Beach Boys.

June [4] Lulu attends the world premiere of "To Sir With Love" in New York.

July *Let's Pretend* reaches UK #11. Its B-side is the Don Black/Mark London song, *To Sir With Love*, which is not promoted in Britain, despite good box-office returns for the film.

Oct [21] *To Sir With Love*, issued as a US A-side to coincide with the release of the movie, tops the US chart for the first of five weeks.

Nov *Love Loves To Love Love* makes UK #32, while a reissued *Shout* makes US #96.

[2] *To Sir With Love* is certified gold by the RIAA.

[9] Lulu is a special guest presenter on the 200th edition of BBC1-TV's "Top Of The Pops".

[13] She participates in the "Royal Variety Show" at the London Palladium.

[28] Lulu guests on NBC-TV's "The Tonight Show", at the start of a US promotional tour which also takes in appearances on "The Joey Bishop Show" and "The Red Skelton Show".

Dec ***To Sir With Love*** peaks at US #24.

1968

Feb *Best Of Both Worlds* makes US #32.

[12] Lulu opens at London's Talk Of The Town, before embarking a month of cabaret dates at Hollywood's Coconut Grove and Miami's Diplomat Hotel.

Mar *Me The Peaceful Heart* hits UK #9.

June *Boy* reaches UK #15.

[17] While on tour in North America, Lulu appears at Issy's Club in Vancouver, BC, Canada, wearing an eye patch, after receiving a black eye while travelling on a boat that morning.

July [5] Lulu begins a week-long engagement at Disneyland in Anaheim, CA.

Aug [31] "Hold On - It's The Dave Clark Five", on which she guests, airs on ITV.

Sept Her cover of Tim Rose's *Morning Dew* makes US #52.

Nov *I'm A Tiger* hits UK #9.

Dec [27] Lulu hosts her own musical variety show on BBC1-TV, with special guests the Jimi Hendrix Experience. Hendrix causes production consternation when he switches - in mid-act - to an unscheduled number, Cream's *Sunshine Of Your Love*.

1969

Jan [11] Lulu sings the first of six Eurovision Song Contest UK entry nominations on BBC1-TV's "Happening For Lulu" show, singing one song each week for the next five, reprising all of the cuts on her February 22nd broadcast, including *I Can't Go On Living Without You*, penned by new writing team Elton John and Bernie Taupin.

Mar [29] She represents the UK in the Eurovision Song Contest with *Boom-Bang-A-Bang*. In the most bizarre result in the history of the contest, it ties for first place with the entries from France, Spain and Holland.

Apr [12] *Boom-Bang-A-Bang* hits UK #2, behind Marvin Gaye's *I Heard It Through The Grapevine*.

[18] Lulu marries Maurice Gibb of the Bee Gees, at Gerrards Cross, Bucks., with Robin Gibb as his brother's best man.

Aug [11] Barry and Maurice Gibb begin filming "Cucumber Castle" with a host of guest stars, including Lulu, who will sing *Mrs. Robinson* in the TV movie.

Nov Lulu leaves Mickie Most and Columbia, and signs to Atlantic subsidiary Atco Records, debuting with *Oh Me Oh My (I'm A Fool For You Baby)*, penned by Glaswegian Jim Doris, and recorded in Muscle Shoals, AL, with production by Jerry Wexler, Tom Dowd and Arif Mardin. It makes UK #47.

1970

Feb *Oh Me Oh My (I'm A Fool For You Baby)* climbs to US #22.

Mar ***New Routes***, released on Atco, makes US #88.

May Lulu teams with the Dixie Flyers on *Hum A Song (From Your Heart)*, which reaches US #54.

June [20] NBC-TV show "Andy Williams Presents Ray Stevens", with Lulu and Mama Cass as regular guests, premieres.

1971

July Talking about the early part of her career, Lulu is quoted in the **Radio Times** : "I must have been a revolting little cow".

Aug [28-29] Lulu takes part in the "Berlin Disc Gala" with Ray Charles, Nancy Wilson, Henry Mancini and Gilbert Becaud in Berlin, West Germany.

Oct Compilation album, ***The Most Of Lulu***, reaches UK #15.

1974

Feb Having separated from Gibb the previous year (they will later divorce, Lulu subsequently marrying hairdresser John Frieda in 1976), and now signed to Polydor Records, her treatment of David Bowie's *The Man Who Sold The World*, with Bowie both producing and featured on saxophone and back-up vocals, hits UK #3. *Take Your Mama For A Ride*, on Wes Farrell's Chelsea label, will make UK #37 in April 1975, her last chart disc of the decade, despite recording a one-off album Elton John's Rocket label, ***Don't Take Love For Granted***, released in June 1978.

1981

Feb [23] Following the issue of ***The Very Best Of Lulu***, a re-recording of her hits produced by Mark London, released on Warwick Records the previous year, Lulu takes part in the "25 Years Of British Pop" segment at the "Royal Variety Performance" in London.

Oct Newly signed to Alfa Records (licensed to CBS), Lulu's *I Could Never Miss You (More Than I Do)* reaches US #18, while ***Lulu***, produced by Mark London and featuring Alan Tarney and Trevor Spencer, peaks at US #126.

Nov She appears at the "Royal Variety Show" in London.

Dec *I Could Never Miss You (More Than I Do)* makes UK #62.

1982

Jan *If I Were You* makes US #44, taken from ***Take Me To Your Heart Again***. For the remainder of the decade, Lulu will mostly concentrate on stage and TV work, including productions of "Guys And Dolls" and "Song And Dance" and ITV's "The Secret Diary Of Adrian Mole, Aged 13¾".

1985

Dec Lulu takes part in "Carol Aid", an all-star Christmas carol concert to raise money for the Band Aid Trust, at London's Heaven nightclub, also featuring Chris De Burgh, Sandie Shaw and Cliff Richard.

1986

Aug Newly signed to Jive records, her revision of *Shout*, in a similar but updated arrangement of the original, hits UK #8. The original version is later reissued by Decca, and the sales of this are controversially added to those of the new recording for UK chart collation.

1992

Oct Now signed to Dome Records (licensed to SBK/EMI Records) and newly separated from husband Frieda, Lulu begins working on her first album in ten years at the Intimate Studios and Caledonian Road Studios in London, having been encouraged by Barry Gibb to resume her recording career.

1993

Jan [28] She performs on BBC1-TV's "Top Of The Pops", the only female artist to appear on the long-running show in each of the last four decades.
Feb [6] *Independence* reaches UK #11.
[16] Lulu presents the Best Female Artist award at the 12th annual BRIT awards at London's Alexandra Palace.
Mar [6] Her comeback album, the contemporary R&B-tinged set ***Independence***, variously produced by Barry Gibb, Errol Henry, Nick Martinelli and Mike Ward, charts for a week at UK #67.
[25] Lulu appears again on "Top Of The Pops", duetting with Bobby Womack on *I'm Back For More*, which will bow at its UK #27 peak on Apr [3].
June [2] She guests on Soul Asylum's MTV "Unplugged" program, singing *To Sir With Love* with the group, as Tina Turner's *I Don't Want To Fight*, written by Lulu and Steve DuBerry, continues its climb up the UK and US charts.
Sept [4] *Let Me Wake Up In Your Arms* debuts at its UK #51 peak.
Oct [9] Take That's *Relight My Fire*, featuring a guest vocal from Lulu, enters the UK chart at #1.
Dec [4] *How 'Bout Us*, reviving Champaign's 1981 US #12/UK #5 hit, makes UK #46.
[31] "Lulu's Big Show" airs on BBC2-TV.

1994

Aug [27] *Goodbye Baby And Amen* debuts at its UK #40 peak.
Oct [23] *I Don't Wanna Fight* is named of the Most Performed Songs of the Year at the annual BMI Awards Ceremony at the Dorchester Hotel.
Nov [5] Lulu guests on BBC1-TV's "Steve Wright's People Show".
[26] *Every Woman Knows* debuts at its UK #44 peak.

FRANKIE LYMON & THE TEENAGERS

Frankie Lymon (lead vocals); **Sherman Garnes** (vocals); **Joe Negroni** (vocals); **Herman Santiago** (vocals); **Jimmy Merchant** (vocals)

1955

Lymon (b. Sept. 30, 1942, Washington Heights, New York, NY), already a performer with his brothers Howie and Lewis in the Harlemaires Jr. (their father, Howard is in the senior Harlemaires) and currently working part time in a local grocery store, is a student at the Edward W. Stitt Junior High in the Bronx, New York, where he joins the Premiers, a quartet formed at the school, consisting of two black singers, tenor Merchant (b. Feb. 10, 1940, New York) and bass man Garnes (b. June 8, 1940, New York), and two Puerto Ricans, lead singer Santiago (b. Feb. 18, 1941, New York) and baritone Negroni (b. Sept. 9, 1940, New York). They are also variously called the Coupe De Villes and the Ermines.
Nov The Premiers impress A&R scout Richard Barrett, leader of the Valentines, who use the same school for rehearsals, who introduces them to record executive George Goldner.
Dec Goldner, a dance instructor and multiple label owner, signs the group to Gee, named after his recent Crows' smash. The soprano-voiced Lymon assumes the lead vocal role and the group records *Why Do Fools Fall In Love*. Santiago has added to the song after Garnes' apartment neighbor, Richard White, has offered the group the poem **Why Do Birds Sing So Gay**, which, with some music and lyrical changes by Merchant and Santiago becomes *Why Do Fools Fall In Love*, after Lymon has also contributed.)

1956

Feb Credited to the Teenagers, a name suggested by a session saxophonist, featuring Frankie Lymon, *Why Do Fools Fall In Love* tops the R&B chart and crosses into the pop list, hitting US #7, with sales exceeding a million.
Apr Sidelining academic pursuits, the group embarks on a hectic, non-stop touring schedule, including an Alan Freed package trek. A second single, *I Want You To Be My Girl*, giving Lymon billing over the group, reaches US #17.
July *I Promise To Remember* peaks at US #57 and *Why Do Fools Fall In Love* hits UK #1, as the 13-year-old Lymon becomes a teen heart-throb.
Oct *The ABCs Of Love*, the group's fourth release, climbs to US #77.

1957

Mar Written as a riposte to the growing body of rock'n'roll detractors, *I'm Not A Juvenile Delinquent* fails to chart domestically, despite promotion in the Alan Freed movie "Rock Rock Rock", but reaches UK #12. The group's British tour includes two weeks topping the bill at the London Palladium. At 14, Lymon is the youngest-ever headliner, having already been the youngest UK chart-topper, at 13.
Apr *Baby Baby*, the flip of *I'm Not A Juvenile Delinquent*, also in the Freed film, attracts UK airplay in the wake of the Teenagers' tour and outsells the A-side, hitting UK #4.
July Lymon is encouraged by Goldner to break from the Teenagers, and his first solo effort, *Goody Goody*, recorded in England, reaches US #22 and #24 in the UK, where it is his last hit. (The Teenagers will continue with new lead singer Billy Lobrano, initially embarking on a US tour with singer Roy Hamilton and releasing *Flip Flop*. He will subsequently make way for ex-Jimmy Castor & the Juniors singer, Kenny Bobo, in the spring of 1960, by which time the Teenagers will have left Roulette, signing to Goldner's End label. Their final lead vocalist, Johnny Houston will record two sessions with the group for Columbia Records, before being dropped, marking the demise of the band.)
Sept [6] "The Biggest Show Of Stars For 1957" package tour, with the Teenagers, Buddy Holly & the Crickets, Chuck Berry, Paul Anka, the Drifters, the Everly Brothers, Clyde McPhatter and others, opens at the Syria Mosque, Pittsburgh, PA, set to close on November 24th at the Mosque, Richmond, VA. (The white artists on the bill are unable to play on several dates because of segregation laws which forbid black and white acts to perform on the same stage.)

1959

Oct A Lymon recording session is cancelled when the singer's voice begins to break, an enforced silence which will last until May the following year.

1960

Aug After three years in the doldrums, during which time Roulette absorbs the bankrupt Goldner's labels, *Little Bitty Pretty One*, originally recorded for a 1958 album, returns Lymon to the US chart, at #58. The comeback is short-lived as his broken voice has robbed him of his major asset. The following year, and on the advice of distraught friends, Lymon submits to a drug rehabilitation program. In 1964, following his failure as a restyled nightclub act, Lymon is arrested and found guilty of narcotics offenses.

1968

Feb [28] On leave from his army post in Georgia, and scheduled to begin a recording session with Roulette the following day, Lymon's body is discovered in his grandmother's 165th Street, New York house in which he grew up. A nearby syringe figures in every news report. A star at 13, all but spent at 14, he is dead at 25.

1981

Oct Diana Ross' revival of *Why Do Fools Fall In Love* hits US #7 and will hit UK #4 the following month, also dedicating her current album to Lymon's memory. (The original endures as one of rock's most popular oldies, and a reconstituted group of Teenagers, led by Santiago and Merchant (both Negroni and Garnes died in the late '70s, Garnes dying in prison in 1977, Negroni suffering a cerebral haemorrhage in 1978), with Pearl McKinnon duplicating Lymon's soprano, continues to gather momentum on the rock-revival and lounge circuits. Subsequently named Frankie Lymon's Original Teenagers, the nostalgia act's line-up will also include Lois Alston and Lewis Lymon.)

1992

Nov [17] Following a suit filed in October 1987, a New York federal district court jury finds that Merchant, currently employed as a cabbie, and Santiago are entitled to royalties from *Why Do Fools Fall In Love* backdated to 1969. On April 16th Lymon's widow, Emira had been awarded a 50% royalty share of the song by US District Judge Vincent L. Broderick, this final decision meaning that Merchant and Santiago will share the remaining 50%. At the end of the four-day trial, Magistrate Judge Naomi Reice Buchwald hears attorney Ira G. Buchwald claim that rights belong to his clients, which include the estate of the late Morris Levy (who had acquired them from Goldner, who had originally filed the copyright for himself and Lymon in 1955), his Roulette Records and Big Seven Music. (Levy had allegedly threatened Merchant and Santiago with "physical force", which had caused them to remain silent until 1987.) Merchant and Santiago's attorney, Carl E. Person, states that his clients had not received any royalties, estimated at $4 million in 38 years.

1993

Jan [12] Stevie Wonder inducts Frankie Lymon & the Teenagers into the Rock and Roll Hall of Fame at the eighth annual awards dinner, held at the Century Plaza Hotel, Los Angeles, CA.
Mar [20] The group participates in the "Moondog Coronation Ball '93", celebrating what was billed at the first rock'n'roll concert, at the Public Hall, Cleveland, OH. (US vault specialists Rhino Records have recently brought Frankie Lymon & the Teenagers highlights to compact disc with its release of ***Best Of***, the same company reporting in 1994 that it plans to develop a movie biography of Lymon.)

LYNYRD SKYNYRD

Ronnie Van Zant (vocals); **Gary Rossington** (guitar); **Allen Collins** (guitar); **Billy Powell** (keyboards); **Leon Wilkeson** (bass); **Artimus Pyle** (drums)

1964

Jacksonville, FL junior school classmates Rossington (b. Dec. 4, 1951, Jacksonville), Larry Jungstrom (bass) and Bob Burns, already playing in Me, You & Him, members of the Lakeshore Rebels little league baseball team, first meet Van Zandt (b. Jan. 15, 1948, Jacksonville), currently in the combo Us, after he knocks Burns out at a baseball game. Deciding to form a band together Burns has a drum kit and Rossington has bought a guitar with money earned from his paper route, they recruit Collins (b. July 19, 1952, Jacksonville), who was previously in the Mods, and begin performing under several names, including the Noble Five, its first gig being at a barbecue house at Christmas, the Wildcats, Sons Of Satan, One Percent and My Backyard, during the remainder of the decade. Honing their style as a southern-boogie blues/rock outfit, they go on to release their debut single, *Need All My Friends*, in 1968 on the Jacksonville-based Shade Tree label.

1970

Building a strong regional reputation through concerted gigging in the late '60s, the group now changes its name to Lynyrd Skynyrd, immortalizing their old school gym teacher, Leonard Skinner, a legendary antagonist of long-haired students. Still with the line-up of Rossington, Van Zant, Collins, Burns and Jungstrom, they record demos in Sheffield, AL, and will issue a second single, *I've Been Your Fool*, in 1971.

1972

Al Kooper (ex-Blood, Sweat & Tears) is touring with Badfinger and looking for suitable talent for his new Sounds Of The South label, licensed to MCA, when he spots the group playing at Funocchio's bar in Atlanta, GA. Impressed by Skynyrd's "Dixie rock" style, he signs the band (for $9,000), which is now augmented by Wilkeson (b. Apr. 2, 1952), who has replaced Jungstrom, but will temporarily quit after six months, replaced by ex-Strawberry Alarm Clock guitarist, Ed King and Powell (b. June 3, 1952). (Jungstrom will eventually team with Van Zant's brother Donnie in .38 Special, in 1979.)

1973

July [28] MCA holds a press launch for band, which is followed by a US tour supporting the Who on its "Quadrophenia" outing, opening at the Cow Palace, San Francisco, CA.

Nov Their debut album, ***Pronounced Leh-Nerd Skin-Nerd***, reaches US #27 and earns a gold disc. Produced by Kooper, it uniquely features three guitarists: King, who has switched from bass following Wilkeson's return, Rossington and Collins. The album's highlight, and most enduring radio favorite, is the rock classic *Free Bird*, a tribute to the late Duane Allman of the Allman Brothers Band.

1974

Oct [26] *Sweet Home Alabama* is the group's first US chart single, hitting #8. The song is seen as a Southerners' riposte to Neil Young's redneck-criticizing 1971 cut, *Southern Man*. It is taken from ***Second Helping***, again produced by Kooper, which reaches US #12 and earns a second gold disc.

[4] The band performs at the Denver Coliseum, Denver, CO, during current US dates.

Dec Burns leaves, and is replaced on drums by Pyle (b. July 15, 1948, Spartanburg, SC).

1975

Jan [25] *Free Bird*, belatedly issued as a single (soon to become the band's anthem and a perennial on FM rock radio), reaches US #19.

May With the group now signed directly to MCA Records, ***Nuthin' Fancy*** hits US #9, earning another gold disc, and makes UK #43, following the group's UK live debut as the support act to Dutch group Golden Earring. King exits midway through the "Torture Tour", as drug and alcohol problems come to the fore.

July [1] During non-stop US touring, throughout which the group is breaking box-office records not least at the Nashville State Fairground and the Macon Coliseum, Lynyrd Skynyrd plays at the Coliseum, Jackson, MS, with Peter Frampton.

Aug [2] *Saturday Night Special* reaches US #27.

1976

Feb [10] The group, now managed by Englishman Peter Rudge (who also handles the Who), begins a five-date UK tour at Colston Hall, Bristol, Avon.

Mar *Double Trouble* makes US #80, while ***Gimme Back My Bullets***, produced by Tom Dowd, reaches US #20 (their fourth gold disc) and UK #34. As the band develops a rowdy rock'n'roll reputation, Van Zant is continually arrested for brawling - usually in bar fights.

Aug [21] The group appears at the "Knebworth Festival", Knebworth, Herts., alongside the Rolling Stones, 10cc, Todd Rundgren's Utopia, Hot Tuna and the Don Harrison Band.

Sept Three-track EP, comprising *Free Bird*, *Sweet Home Alabama* and *Double Trouble*, reaches UK #31.

[5] Rossington is injured in a car crash in Jacksonville.

Nov Double live set, ***One More For The Road***, recorded at the Fox Theatre, Atlanta, over three nights the previous year, features a new third guitarist, Steve Gaines (b. Sept. 14, 1949, Seneca, MO), and a female back-up vocal trio. It hits US #9 and UK #17 and is the group's biggest seller, earning a platinum disc for million-plus US sales.

Dec Live version of *Free Bird*, from the double album, makes US #38.

1977

Feb [29] At the beginning of a month-long UK concert visit, highlighted by three opening dates from the 28th-30th at London's Rainbow Theatre, the band is involved in a scuffle with guests at the Royal Lancaster Hotel, London, and then clash with members of the Metropolitan Police Boxing Team, which is holding its annual dinner at the venue. Rossington and Pyle are both knocked unconscious during the melée and need medical treatment.

Apr [15] Van Zant and Collins present a gold disc for ***One More For The Road*** to Maynard Jackson, Mayor of Atlanta, and another to the Fox Theatre, Atlanta, where the album was recorded. Several group members, plus James Brown and other celebrity Georgians, are honored at a ceremony in the Atlanta Braves' baseball stadium, prior to the team's opening home game.

Oct [20] Van Zant, Steve Gaines, his sister Cassie Gaines, one of the three back-up singers, and personal manager Dean Kilpatrick are among six passengers killed when Skynyrd's rented, twin-engined, propeller-driven Convair 240 plane, leased from Falcon Airways and short of fuel, crashes into a swamp in Gillsburg, MS, while en route from Greenville, SC, to Baton Rouge, LA, where the group is scheduled to play at Louisiana University. Rossington, Collins, Powell and Wilkeson are all seriously injured, but will eventually recover. MCA withdraws the sleeve of ***Street Survivors***, released just three days earlier, which pictures the group standing amid flames.

Nov ***Street Survivors***, a second platinum disc, hits US #5 and UK #13.

1978

Mar *What's Your Name*, taken from ***Street Survivors***, reaches US #13.

Apr [29] The group's last US hit single is *You Got That Right*, which makes #69.

Nov ***Skynyrd's First And Last***, containing previously unreleased 1970-72 recordings, reaches US #15 and UK #50.

[10] ***Skynyrd's First And Last*** is certified platinum by the RIAA.

1979

Oct With the exception of Pyle, the surviving Lynyrd Skynyrd members form a new group, the Rossington-Collins Band, with female lead vocalist Dale Krantz, who has earlier been a back-up singer for .38 Special, the band fronted by Van Zant's brother, Donnie. Guitarist Barry Harwood, added to give a three-guitar line-up again, and drummer Derek Hess also join, as the new band signs to MCA. (During the year, Pyle, Powell and Wilkeson release their album ***Alias Contraband***.)

1980

Jan EP *Free Bird* re-charts in the UK, at #43.

Feb Double compilation, ***Gold And Platinum***, reaches US #12 and UK #49.

Aug The first Rossington-Collins Band album, ***Anytime, Anyplace, Anywhere***, reaches US #13, and earns a gold disc, while the extracted *Don't Misunderstand Me* is the band's only hit single, peaking at US #55. On stage, the group plays an instrumental version of *Free Bird* to close its act, the song now dedicated to Ronnie Van Zant.

1981

Jan [20] ***Gimme Back My Bullets*** is certified gold by the RIAA.

Nov ***This Is The Way***, by the Rossington-Collins Band, makes US #24. It is dedicated to Collins' wife Katy, who died a year earlier. Shortly after, the band breaks up.

1982

Feb [13] The inscribed 300lb marble slab is stolen from the grave of Ronnie Van Zant in a cemetery at Orange Park, FL. Police will find it two weeks later, in a partially dried-up river bed.

Mar Pyle forms a new quintet, the Artimus Pyle Band, which begins touring the US. (It will release ***A.P.B.***, followed by 1983's ***Nightcaller***, both on the Clouds label through MCA.)

June EP *Free Bird* charts for the third time in the UK, now flying to its #21 peak.

Dec ***Best Of The Rest***, a compilation of Skynyrd rarities and out-takes, reaches US #171.

1986

Jan [26] Collins' car runs off the road, crashing into a culvert, paralysing him from the waist down and killing his girlfriend, Debra Jean Watts. (During the year, Rossington releases the album ***Returned To The Scene Of The Crime***, while Powell joins a Christian band, Vision, which will release ***Vision***, after being released from 30 days in jail. The group will join ex-Grand Funk Railroad singer Mark Farner on a club tour the following year. They perform Lynyrd Skynyrd material and the audience response convinces members that Skynyrd should re-form.)

1987

July [21] The RIAA certifies platinum sales for ***Nuthin' Fancy*** and multi-platinum sales for ***Gold And Platinum*** (three million), ***One More From The Road*** (three million), ***Pronounced Leh-nerd Skin-nerd*** (two million), ***Second Helping*** (two million) and ***Street Survivors*** (two million).

Sept A new Lynyrd Skynyrd lineup is assembled, comprising Rossington, Powell, Pyle, Wilkeson, King, Steve's younger brother Johnny Van Zant (vocals) (who has already released four solo albums ***No More Dirty Deals*** (1980), ***Round Two*** (1981), ***The Last Of The Wild Ones*** (1982) and ***Van-Zant*** (1985), and Randall Hall (guitar), with Dale Krantz Rossington and Carol Bristow (The Honkettes) on backing vocals. The group plays at Charlie Daniels' 13th "Volunteer Jam Reunion" in Georgia and a 32-date reunion tour, marking the tenth anniversary of the fatal plane crash.

Nov MCA-issued ***Legend***, comprising previous B-sides, unreleased and uncompleted songs by the original Lynyrd Skynyrd, produced by Dowd with the surviving members, makes US #41.

1988

Apr New line-up's double live album, ***Southern By The Grace Of God/Lynyrd Skynyrd Tribute Tour***, makes US #68, containing tracks recorded on their September 1987 reunion tour.

July Having trimmed its name to the Rossington Band, with the splinter Allen Collins Band also formed, and still recording as a parallel concern to Skynyrd, ***Love Your Man*** peaks at US #140.

Dec [3] Will To Power tops the US chart, with a medley reviving Peter Frampton's *Baby I Love Your Way* and Lynyrd Skynyrd's *Freebird*.

1990

Jan [23] Hospitalized since September, Collins dies at Jacksonville's Memorial Medical Center.

June [15] "The Tribute Tour" video is certified gold by the RIAA.

Sept Johnny Van Zant releases his fifth solo album ***Brickyard Road***, on Atlantic Records.

Dec [31] Lynyrd Skynyrd ends the year performing at San Francisco's Cow Palace.

1991

June [29] Newly signed to Atlantic Records (and East West in Britain), the group's ***Lynyrd Skynyrd 1991*** debuts at its US #64 peak, supported by a world tour beginning on the 14th anniversary of the plane crash.

Aug [31] Their latest US trek ends at the Shoreline Amphitheatre, Mountain View, CA.

Sept [27] A fall US tour begins in Louisville, KY.

1992

Feb [11-12] The group performs two sellout gigs at London's Town & Country club, during a UK visit which also includes a further pair of dates at the capital's Hammersmith Odeon on the 27th and 29th.
Mar [14] Performing at "Farm Aid V", the band is joined on stage by Kris Kristofferson.
May [25] During its now annual US tour, the group takes $122,640 at the Coca-Cola Star Lake Amphitheatre, Burgettstown, PA box office.
Sept [26] The group plays at the Cal Expo Amphitheatre, Sacramento, CA, during its second US tour of the year.
Nov Pyle, who has returned to his own Artimus Pyle Band the previous year, is arrested at his Jacksonville Beach home on a charge of sexually assaulting a four-year-old girl and is held without bail, pending a December 12th court appearance.

1993

Feb [10] ***Skynyrd's Innyrds*** is certified platinum by the RIAA.
[19] The group, comprising Rossington (who has recently written songs with Tom Kiefer of Cinderella, and with Travis Tritt), Powell, Wilkeson, King and Van Zant, with guitarist Randy Hall and drummer Kurt Custer, celebrates its 20th anniversary with a "Lynyrd Skynyrd & Friends LYVE (Pronounced Live)" pay-per-view TV performance from the Fox Theatre, Atlanta, with guests Peter Frampton, Brett Michaels, Keifer, Zakk Wylde and Charlie Daniels. It marks the start of an international tour supporting ***The Last Rebel***, produced by Barry Beckett, which debuts at its US #64 peak on Mar [6].
Mar [13] They perform at the inaugural "Freebird Festival" at the Naval Air Station, Jacksonville, to raise funds for the Ronnie Van Zant Memorial Park.
May [6] The group's "The Last Rebel Tour" opens at the UTC Arena, Chattanooga, TN, with Bad Company and Drivin'n'Cryin'.
[18] The Ronnie Van Zant Park opens in Clay County, FL, a memorial recreation area for the children of the area where he grew up.
July [7] The group plays a preview concert at the yet-to-be-opened Glen Helen Blockbuster Pavilion, San Bernardino, CA.
Sept [10] A three-date UK tour, rescheduled because of an injury to Randall Hall, opens at London's Hammersmith Apollo, set to end on the 14th at the Apollo Theatre, Manchester, Gtr. Manchester.
Dec [24] Pyle is sentenced to eight years probation for molesting two sisters after pleading guilty to attempted capital battery and lewd and lascivious assault.

1994

June [2] The Allman Brothers embark on the "Endangered Species 1994" tour, with support act Ted Nugent, at the Coca-Cola Starplex Amphitheatre, Dallas, TX.
Aug [27] ***Endangered Species***, an acoustic-based remake of Skynyrd standards, debuts at its US #115 peak.
Nov [19] ***Skynyrd Frynds***, a country-style tribute album, featuring Travis Tritt, Alabama, Sammy Kershaw, the Mavericks, Steve Earle, Charlie Daniels and Wynonna, among others, makes US #56.
Dec [19] Released in 1992, ***The Boxed Set*** retrospective is certified gold by the RIAA.

1995

July [11] The group plays a sellout date at the Sunrise Musical Theatre, Sunrise, FL, at the close of a three-month US tour.
Sept [25] Midway through another US trek, Ed King is admitted to Piedmont Hospital, Atlanta, and treated for congestive heart failure. Released on the 29th, the tour will go on without him.
Dec [29] The "Freebird Fest" weekend, including a "Freebird - The Jam" concert the day before at the Fox Theatre, Atlanta, continues with the premiere of "Freebird ... The Movie", featuring concert footage and video clips, including an in-plane film shot by a surviving roadie who was aboard the fateful 1977 flight.

1996

Aug [22] Lynyrd Skynyrd ends a US summer tour with the Doobie Brothers at the Oak Mountain Amphitheatre Birmingham, Alabama.

M

MADNESS

Suggs (vocals); **Mike Barson** (keyboards); **"Chrissie Boy" Foreman** (guitar); **"Bedders"** (bass); **Lee "Kix" Thompson** (saxophone, vocals); **"Woody" Woodgate** (drums); **Chas Smash** (horns)

1977

June [30] Barson (b. May 21, 1958, London), Thompson (b. Oct. 5, 1957, St. Pancras, London) and Foreman (b. Christopher Foreman, Aug. 8, 1958, London), all from Gospel Oak School in Camden and living in Kentish Town, London, have formed the bluebeat-based the Invaders in 1976 with an initial lead vocalist known only as Dikron, and now makes its first public appearance with John Hasler on drums and Smash (b. Cathal Smyth, Jan. 14, 1959) on bass, introducing its ska-derived "nutty sound". Dikron is replaced by Suggs (b. Graham McPherson, Jan. 13, 1961, Hastings, Sussex) in February the following year, but only in September will the variable line-up become permanent with the original trio augmented by Suggs, Bedders (b. Mark Bedford, Aug. 24, 1961, London) and Woodgate (b. Daniel Woodgate, Oct. 19, 1960, London).

1979

Jan [1] The Invaders play their last gig at the London Film-makers Co-op, after which they change their name to Madness.
Mar Suggs strikes up a friendship with members of the Specials after seeing them perform at the Hope & Anchor pub, Islington, London, and Madness signs to Specials' leader Jerry Dammers' ska-revival devoted 2-Tone label.
Oct Their debut disc *The Prince*, a tribute to ska innovator Prince Buster written by Thompson and 2-Tone's second release, makes UK #16. The band then signs to Dave Robinson's Stiff Records in Britain (after a wedding party) and Sire in the US. (Years later, Suggs, in a **Daily Express** interview, will cite the reason for signing with Stiff was because they didn't want their royalties spent on tropical plants in the office.)
[22] The group embarks on a 21-date 2-Tone UK tour at Exeter University, set to end on November 14th at the Pavilion, Ayr, Strathclyde, Scotland.
Nov ***One Step Beyond***, produced by Clive Langer and Alan Winstanley, who will produce most of the band's records, hits UK #2 during a 78-week chart stay. Meanwhile, the band completes a three-week US tour of New York, California and Texas.
Dec *One Step Beyond*, a Prince Buster cover of the B-side to his *Al Capone*, hits UK #7.
[30] Madness headlines a concert at London's Lyceum Ballroom.

1980

Jan *My Girl* hits UK #3. (It is later covered by another Stiff artist, Tracey Ullman, as *My Guy*.)
Feb Madness returns from a European tour and plays a Saturday morning gig at London's Hammersmith Odeon for "under 16s".
Mar The group's progress is marred by the unwanted attentions of National Front extremists while on tour with the Specials. ***One Step Beyond***, released on Sire Records, peaks at US #128.
Apr *The Work Rest And Play EP* hits UK #6, featuring *Night Train To Cairo* as the lead track and a cut rebutting the National Front.
July The band begins a 30-date tour of Europe.
Oct *Baggy Trousers*, written with trademark London wit by Foreman and Suggs, hits UK #3, spurred by a Dave Robinson-produced video featuring "flying" sax player Thompson, as its parent album, ***Absolutely***, again helmed by Langer and Winstanley, hits UK #2, during a 46-week chart stay.
[8] A UK tour begins in Blackpool, Lancs.
Nov ***Absolutely*** makes US #146. The group is subsequently released from Sire in the US, under an

agreement which stated that if the second album did not sell a certain amount, Madness could leave the label. They begin a "Twelve Days Of Madness" UK tour with each date including an "under-16s" matinee, where all tickets sell for £1, in addition to an evening show. The trek ends with five sell-out gigs at London's Hammersmith Odeon, among them a Christmas Eve charity show.

Dec *Embarrassment*, penned by Foreman and Thompson, hits UK #4, as Madness are voted Singles Artists of the Year by the **New Musical Express**, having spent 46 weeks on the chart during 1980.

1981

Feb Instrumental, *Return Of The Los Palmas Seven*, hits UK #7, as the group appears in the 2-Tone movie "Dance Craze".

Mar Madness begin work on full-length feature film "Take It Or Leave It", directed by Stiff Records' boss Robinson. They also embark on the "Absolutely Madness One Step Beyond Far East Tour" of Australasia, Japan and US.

May *Grey Day* hits UK #4.

Oct *Shut Up* hits UK #7, as its parent album, ***Seven***, recorded at Compass Point Studios in Nassau, Bahamas, hits UK #5. Their "Take It Or Leave It" movie premieres to poor reviews.

[8] The group sets out on a 36-date UK tour in Bradford, S. Yorks.

1982

Jan The band's revival of Labi Siffre's 1972 hit, *It Must Be Love*, hits UK #4, its backing track recorded in nine hours in a living room studio in a house in Durham. (Siffre makes a cameo appearance on the video and children are warned on BBC1-TV's "Top Of The Pops" by DJ Jimmy Savile not to copy the group who jump into a swimming pool clutching electric guitars in the clip.) Suggs marries singer Bette Bright at St. Luke's Church, Highgate, London. Chas Smash flies to Italy to rescue his brother Brendan from the clutches of the Foreign Legion.

Mar *Cardiac Arrest* reaches UK #14, their first single since *The Prince* not to make the Top 10.

May [22] Early-hits compilation, ***Complete Madness***, hits UK #1, while a video collection of the same title also becomes a best-seller.

[29] *House Of Fun* tops the UK chart for the first of two weeks spurred by another highly original video filmed at a fun fair, toppling Eurovision winner Nicole's *A Little Peace*.

July *Driving In My Car* hits UK #4.

Aug The group plays at the Bull & Gate pub in Kentish Town, London, as a warm-up for their appearance at the "Prince's Trust Royal Gala" at London's Dominion Theatre.

Nov ***The Rise And Fall*** hits UK #10.

Dec *Our House* hits UK #5.

1983

Feb [21] Madness begins its annual UK tour.

Mar *Tomorrow's (Just Another Day)* hits UK #8.

Apr The group, now with Geffen Records in the US, makes US #41 with ***Madness.***

May [5] *Our House* wins the Best Pop Song category at the 28th annual Ivor Novello Awards at London's Grosvenor House Hotel.

July [23] *Our House* becomes the group's biggest US hit at #7.

Sept *Wings Of A Dove* hits UK #2, held off the top spot by UB40's *Red Red Wine*.

Oct [8] *It Must Be Love* makes US #33.

Nov *The Sun And The Rain* hits UK #5.

Dec The group performs at London's Lyceum Ballroom, to benefit Greenpeace.

[21] Founding member and writer Barson announces his intention to leave and settle in Holland with his Dutch wife, Sandra.

1984

Feb *Michael Caine*, with a guest appearance by the actor, reaches UK #11.

Mar Its parent album, ***Keep Moving***, hits UK #6. *The Sun And The Rain* peaks at US #72.

Apr ***Keep Moving*** peaks at US #109, and is their US chart swan song.

June *One Better Day* makes UK #17, and is the group's last release for Stiff, on which they hit the Top 20 with every UK release.

Oct Having formed its own label Zarjazz, derived from its favorite comic **2000 AD**, through Virgin Records, the first release is Feargal Sharkey's *Listen To Your Father*, written by Madness and originally intended as a group single, which makes UK #23.

1985

Feb Smash and Suggs as the Fink Brothers (characters in **2000 AD**), peak at UK #50 with *Mutants In Mega City*.

Mar Madness, with UB40, the Specials, General Public and others, assembled as Starvation, make UK #33 with *Starvation Tam-Tam Pour L'Ethiope*, to raise funds for the starving in Ethiopia, Eritrea and the Sudan.

Sept Madness' *Yesterday's Men*, their first on Zarjazz, reaches UK #18.

Oct ***Mad Not Mad***, still produced by Langer and Winstanley, makes UK #16.

Nov *Uncle Sam*, with a return to their "nutty sound" video style, makes UK #21 - their first to fail to make the Top 20 in 21 attempts.

Dec [21] Madness participates in the Greater London Council Christmas party for the unemployed with Marc Almond, Ian Dury and others.

[31] The band appears on BBC2-TV's "Old Grey Whistle Test" New Year concert into the small hours.

1986

Feb *Sweetest Girl*, their revival of Scritti Politti's 1981 UK #64, makes UK #35.

July The group plays its final gig of the decade at a docklands festival in Hartlepool, Cleveland.

Sept [1] Madness officially announces that it will split.

Nov *Waiting For The Ghost Train* reaches UK #18.

Dec A second hits album, ***Utter Madness***, makes UK #29. The following March, Voice Of The Beehive's *Just A City*, featuring Bedders and Woody, will be released. (Bedders will subsequently begin work on film scores.)

1988

Feb Madness, re-formed as four-piece The Madness, signs to Virgin.

Mar Sitar-fused *I Pronounce You* peaks at UK #44.

May ***The Madness*** makes US #65.

June *What's That* is the first Madness disc to fail to chart in Britain. (Suggs will become a regular comedy host at the Mean Fiddler club in North London before becoming manager of the Farm, having produced their first single in 1985, and will guest on harmonica and backing vocals on Morrissey's UK #18, *Piccadilly Palare*, in October 1990, while Thompson and Foreman will resurface as the Nutty Boys on Street Link Records releasing the reggae album, ***Crunch***, in May 1990. Smash will fill an A&R role at Go! Discs in 1991, Barson remains in semi-retirement in Holland, Bedders becomes a graphic design student while Woody continues to collaborate with Voice Of The Beehive.)

1992

Mar The reformed group inks a new songwriting deal with EMI Publishing and recording contract with Go! Discs.

[7] Reissued *It Must Be Love* hits UK #6.

[14] ***Divine Madness***, their third hits compilation, hits UK #1.

Apr [25] Re-released, *House Of Fun* debuts at its UK #40 peak.

Aug [8] Reissued, *My Girl* bows at its UK #27 peak.

[8-9] Under the banner "Madstock!", Madness plays two open air concerts at Finsbury Park, London, with guests Morrissey, Ian Dury & the Blockheads and Flowered Up. At the second gig, Prince Buster joins the band for *One Step Beyond* and *Madness*. (Foreman has announced of their comeback: "We will reform at 9:30 p.m. on August 8th and plan to split up again an hour-and-a-half later and then at midnight we'll turn back into pumpkins. And it's my birthday that day so if anyone wants to buy me a drink please form an orderly queue after the show".)

Nov [14] ***Madstock!***, recorded live at the group's reunion gigs, debuts at its UK #22 peak.

[28] New recording, *The Harder They Come*, makes UK #44.

Dec [15-16] The group begins a seven-date UK comeback tour at the Wembley Arena, Wembley, Middx., set to end on the 22nd at the National Exhibition Centre, Birmingham, West Midlands.

1993

Jan [1] "Madstock : The Movie", the film of the group's Finsbury Park concerts, airs on C4-TV.

Feb [16] Madness perform *Night Boat To Cairo* at the 12th annual BRIT Awards, held at the Alexandra Palace, London.

[27] Reissued *Night Boat To Cairo* debuts at its UK #56 peak.

Oct [9] *The 2-Tone EP*, with Madness as one of the featured artists, debuts at its UK #30 peak.

Dec [22-23] The group perform festive concerts at Wembley Arena.

1994

Aug [6] Madness performs at another "Madstock!" show at Finsbury Park.

1995

Aug [12] Newly signed as a solo artist to East West Records, Suggs' *I'm Only Sleeping*, his re-working of the Beatles song and coupled with *Off On Holiday*, debuts at its UK #7 peak.

Oct [14] Suggs' *Camden Town* enters at its UK #14 high.

Dec [16] Suggs' *The Tune* bows at its UK #33 peak.

1996

May [11] Suggs' revival of Paul Simon's Cecilia, featuring Louchie Lou and Michie One, hits UK #4.

MADONNA

1977

Raised, along with her five brothers and sisters, by her Chrysler auto engineer father from the age of six when her mother died, and having initially studied piano before switching to ballet, but finding drama her forté when studying at Rochester Adams High School, playing lead roles in school productions, and after a year at the University of Michigan, to which she has earned a scholarship and begun dancing in a troupe headed by John Flynn, Madonna (b. Madonna Louise Veronica Ciccone, named after her mother, Aug. 16, 1958, Bay City, MI) heads for New York, NY, at the urging of her ballet teacher. Subsequently moving to university in North Carolina, she is awarded another scholarship, having completed a six-week dance workshop, to Alvin Ailey's prestigious New York studio, to work with choreographer Pearl Lang. While in New York, she will also take a number of jobs, including modeling and working in a doughnut shop in Times Square.

1979

She lands a place in the "Patrick Hernandez Revue", after auditioning for producers Jean Claude Pellerin and Jean Van Lieu, working in Paris, France. (Hernandez is a disco star looking to capitalize on his worldwide hit, *Born To Be Alive*.) She stays for six months before leaving the troupe to form a band with her boyfriend Dan Gilroy. Calling the group the Breakfast Club, they play local venues, with Madonna starting behind the drum kit, but soon stepping out front to sing.

1980

Madonna leaves the band and starts her own group Emmenon, shortened later to Emmy. When the first drummer is replaced by an old boyfriend from Detroit, MI, former waiter Steve Bray, who she had met at the Blue Frogge disco in Ann Arbor, MI while they were at the University of Michigan, she leaves the dance company and begins working with him on demo tapes at his home studio. She also lands a part in Stephen Jon Lewicki's low-budget 60-minute movie thriller "A Certain Sacrifice". Late in the year she signs to rock manager Adam Atler's Gotham Productions, taking a series of odd jobs to pay her way, including part-time nude modeling for photographers and art students. She will also begin recording as a backing vocalist for Otto Von Wernherr and Steve Bentzel at Mindfield Records in New York contributing to *Cosmic Climb*, *We Are The Gods* and *Wild Dancing*. (A 12" single from these sessions will be released in 1986 as by Madonna & Von Wernherr.)

1982

She splits from Gotham, having spent a year recording in studios and waiting for a record deal. (Gotham will later sue her and receive an insubstantial settlement.) Madonna's break comes when she gives DJ/producer Mark Kamins at the Danceteria club, a tape of the dance material she has made with Bray. Kamins introduces her to Sire Records' executive Michael Rosenblatt, who hears the cassette and agrees to sign her - subject to label boss Seymour Stein's approval. Stein, hospitalized, agrees and the deal is signed. Kamins produces *Ain't No Big Deal*, intended as the first single but dropped in favor of *Everybody*, which breaks on dance radio stations and climbs the dance chart, promoted via lip-synching performances at clubs including the Danceteria. *Everybody* is also released in the UK in December.

1983

June Following another club hit, *Physical Attraction*, penned by Reggie Lucas, the pop/dance confection *Holiday*, written by current flame and producer John "Jellybean" Benitez, is released. During a UK promo trip, Madonna lip-synchs to the cut at London's Music Machine.

Sept Her maiden album, ***Madonna***, produced by Lucas, enters the US chart to eventually hit #8 (and sell four million US units), as *Lucky Star* is released in Britain.

Oct *Holiday*, which had been turned down by Phyllis Hyman and Mary Wilson, reaches US #16.

1984

Feb *Holiday* hits UK #6 spurred by her performance on BBC1-TV's "Top Of The Pops", as ***Madonna*** hits UK #6.

Apr Re-released, *Lucky Star* reaches UK #14.

June *Borderline* hits US #10 and peaks at UK #56.

Sept [18] Madonna performs live at the inaugural MTV Video Music Awards held at Radio City Music Hall, New York.

Oct *Lucky Star* hits US #4, giving a boost to the album and pushing its sales over a million. Madonna begins work on her first major film role, in Susan Seidelman's "Desperately Seeking Susan", alongside Rosanna Arquette.

Nov Dance-dominated ***Like A Virgin***, which includes a cover version of the Rose Royce hit-ballad *Love Don't Live Here Anymore*, produced by Nile Rodgers and featuring Chic's rhythm section, enters the UK chart. (With its release, Madonna begins a concerted marketing campaign built around the image of herself as a coy but lacily-trussed "virgin", a ploy she will vary, with an increasingly outrageous expression of sexual freedom, with each subsequent album, skillfully manipulating the media at large.)

Dec [22] Having premiered the single during the live telecast of the inaugural MTV Video Music Awards on September 18th, *Like A Virgin*, written by Tom Kelly and Billy Steinberg, and suggested to Madonna by Warner Bros. A&R head Mo Ostin, tops the US chart for the first of six weeks, the longest span since Olivia Newton-John's *Physical*.

1985

Jan *Like A Virgin* hits UK #3.

[10] *Like A Virgin* is certified gold by the RIAA.

Feb [9] ***Like A Virgin*** begins a three-week stay at US #1 and will become her most successful album, staying charted for over two years and selling over nine-million domestic copies alone. (Its success will see Madonna's face reach the cover of **Time** magazine and inspire Madonnaland, a clothing concession in Macy's US stores.)

[13] Madonna and actor Sean Penn have their first date at the Private Eyes club in New York.

Mar *Material Girl* hits US #2 and UK #3, aided not least by a Marilyn Monroe-pastiche video (featuring Keith Carradine), an image Madonna will persist with through the decade.

[29] "Desperately Seeking Susan" premieres in the US.

Apr Madonna begins her first concert series. Titled "The Virgin Tour", it plays to 355,000 fans in 27 cities with up-and-coming rap pack the Beastie Boys as her support act. On the final tour date, she is carried off-stage by her father, Tony.

May [11] Jon Lind/John Bettis-penned ballad *Crazy For You* from the Matthew Modine-starring film "Vision Quest", tops the US chart.

June *Angel* hits US #5, as *Crazy For You* hits UK #2.

July [13] With early-career (1977) nude snaps of her featured in this month's **Penthouse** and **Playboy**, Madonna performs both solo (*Holiday*, *Into The Groove* and *Love Makes The World Go Round*) and with the Thompson Twins in the Philadelphia, PA leg of "Live Aid" at the JFK Stadium. She is introduced by Bette Midler who claims that Madonna is "a woman who pulled herself up by her bra-straps". (The movie release of other early work, the soft-porn "A Certain Sacrifice", is also planned against her wishes.)

[16] *Crazy For You* is certified gold by the RIAA.

[30 *Angel/Into The Groove* 12" single is also confirmed gold by the RIAA.

Aug [3] Taken from the "Desperately Seeking Susan" movie and co-written by Madonna and Bray, the uptempo dance-smash *Into The Groove* is Madonna's first UK chart-topper. (In the US, it will only appear on the B-side of the 12" *Angel* so will never make **Billboard** Hot 100.) Sire later adds the song to ***Like A Virgin*** and also repackages ***Madonna*** as ***The First Album***. *Holiday* re-enters the UK chart, this time hitting #2 - kept out by *Into The Groove* (only the Beatles, John Lennon and Frankie Goes To Hollywood have also filled the top two places simultaneously).

[16] Madonna marries actor Sean Penn on her 26th birthday. As the cliffside coastal wedding takes place, news crews buzz overhead in a fleet of helicopters.

[17] *Dress You Up* enters the US chart to hit #5. After her honeymoon, she begins working on a new album which she will dedicate to her husband, "the coolest guy in the universe".

Sept [21] After nearly a year on chart, ***Like A Virgin*** hits UK #1 while *Angel* hits UK #5.

Oct *Gambler* hits UK #4.

Dec *Dress You Up* hits UK #5 and becomes Madonna's eighth Top 10 hit of the year. She becomes the only woman to have three discs in the UK top 15 since Ruby Murray 30 years earlier.

[3] "The Virgin Tour - Madonna Live" is certified platinum by the RIAA.

1986

Jan *Borderline* and *Gambler* both re-enter the UK chart, hitting #2 and #61 respectively as "Like A Virgin The Video EP" wins top honors at the British Video Awards. Madonna and Penn travel to China to film scenes for a new movie.

Feb [2] Producer and ex-boyfriend Jellybean Benitez hits US #18 with *Sidewalk Talk*, written by and featuring Madonna.

Mar While filming "Shanghai Surprise", press harassment causes much-publicized Mr. and Mrs. Penn reaction. After **The Sun**'s photographer Dave Hogan is knocked down by the Penn's car, the UK tabloid press picks up on the incident and on rumblings of discontent on the film set. Producer George Harrison calls a press conference to defuse the situation.

Apr Due to recording commitments Madonna is unable to appear opposite Bruce Willis in scheduled movie "Blind Date". The "Like A Virgin - Live" video documentary is released.

June [7] Cementing their songwriting and production partnership which will steer Madonna's career to the end of the decade, the Patrick Leonard/Madonna-written *Live To Tell*, a ballad from the film "At Close Range", starring Sean Penn, hits US #1, having already hit UK #2. (Leonard has previously been the musical director for the Jacksons' "Victory" tour and arranged instrumental music for "At Close Range".)

July [12] Produced by Madonna, with Stephen Bray and Leonard, ***True Blue*** enters the UK chart at #1 where it will stay for a further five weeks and earn multi-platinum status. On the same day, the father/daughter relationship themed *Papa Don't Preach* tops the UK singles survey.

Aug [16] ***True Blue*** begins a five-week stay at US #1, eventually selling over seven million US copies on the same day that *Papa Don't Preach* heads the US Hot 100, boosted by a video clip starring Danny Aiello and UK youngster Felix Howard.

Sept [15] Madonna collects the prestigious Video Vanguard trophy at the third annual MTV Video Music Awards broadcast simultaneously from the Universal Amphitheatre, Universal City, CA and the Palladium, New York.

Oct [11] *True Blue* tops the UK chart, tying Sandie Shaw's record of most UK number #1s (three) by a female act.

Nov [15] *True Blue* hits US #3 as "Shanghai Surprise" premieres to savage reviews.

Dec Co-written by Madonna, Gardner Cole and Peter Rafelson, *Open Your Heart* hits UK #4 while Nick Kamen's *Each Time You Break My Heart*, co-written, arranged and produced by the diva with Stephen Bray, hits UK #5.

1987

Jan [26] She wins the Favorite Female Video Artist, Pop/Rock category at the 14th annual American Music Awards, held at the Shrine Auditorium, Los Angeles, CA.

Feb [7] *Open Your Heart* becomes Madonna's fifth US chart-topper, and her third from ***True Blue***.

Mar Madonna receives the dubious distinction of being voted "Favorite Artist Of Record Pirates" by a special **Billboard** panel, a measure of her worldwide popularity.

Apr [25] Madonna becomes the only female artist to have four UK #1s when *La Isla Bonita* tops the chart.

May [2] *La Isla Bonita* hits US #4.

June [9] Madonna guests on NBC-TV's "The Tonight Show".

[14] A record-breaking Japanese tour begins in Osaka.

July [25] *Who's That Girl*, also the title of the new movie in which she stars with Griffin Dunne and Sir John Mills, hits UK #1. Again critically mauled, the film fails to match the single's success. Madonna tours Britain for the first time, playing a show in Leeds, W. Yorks and three at Wembley Stadium, Wembley, Middx., under the banner "Who's That Girl Tour".

Aug [22] *Who's That Girl* tops the US chart.

Sept [11] She performs at the fourth annual MTV Video Music Awards, held at the Universal Amphitheatre.

[29] ***Who's That Girl*** is certified platinum by the RIAA.

Soundtrack ***Who's That Girl*** hits US #7 and UK #4.

Oct [24] *Causin' A Commotion* hits US #2 and UK #4.

Dec *The Look Of Love* hits UK #9 while an album of dance remixes, ***You Can Dance***, hits UK #5. Madonna is also featured on A&M's current ***A Very Special Christmas*** compilation, reviving Eartha Kitt's *Santa Baby*.

[4] Madonna files for divorce from Sean Penn in Malibu, CA, but will change her mind a week later.

1988

Jan *You Can Dance* reaches US #14.
[5] Madonna serves divorce papers on Sean Penn.
[20] ***You Can Dance*** is certified platinum by the RIAA.
Mar [23] The RIAA certifies four million sales of ***Madonna***.
[29] "The Virgin Tour - Madonna Live" video reaches the RIAA-certified 100,000 sales plateau.
May [3] Madonna opens at the Royale Theatre on Broadway in "Speed The Plow" with Joe Mantegna and Ron Silver.
Sept Against her wishes, a video of film "A Certain Sacrifice" becomes publicly available as a new Patrick Leonard produced-album is recorded in Los Angeles.
Oct Press reports state that Meryl Streep wins the title role in the film version of "Evita", after Madonna is turned down for demanding a $5 million fee and refusing to do a screen test. (The on-off project will return to Madonna's camp in 1991.)
[4] "Ciao Italy - Live From Italy" video is certified platinum by the RIAA.
Dec [12] She signs a two-year, five-film deal with Columbia Pictures.

1989

Jan [25] Madonna files for divorce for the second time from Penn at Los Angeles County Superior Court while assault charges against Penn, filed by Madonna at Malibu Sheriff's office on December 28th, are dropped. She moves into a new three bedroom house in Hollywood Hills, CA.
Feb She appears unannounced at the "AIDS Dance-a-thon" at the Shrine Auditorium.
Mar [2] Madonna begins a $5 million sponsorship deal with Pepsi-Cola. For the first time, a major star uses a song for a TV commercial ahead of its retail release, when *Like A Prayer* airs during NBC-TV's "The Cosby Show".
[3] Italian TV refuses to air the clip on the grounds that it is blasphemous. Pepsi begins reassessing its deal with Madonna.
[25] Gospel-tinged *Like A Prayer* tops the UK chart for the first of three weeks. Its promo video causes a worldwide media and religious storm, and is banned by the Vatican. Because of its strong religious imagery, Pepsi drops its commercial and withdraws Madonna's sponsorship claiming consumer confusion between the commercial and the video. Her proposed 1989 tour is also cancelled.
Apr [1] ***Like A Prayer***, co-produced with Leonard and including *Love Song*, a duet with Prince, tops the UK chart.
[22] *Like A Prayer* hits US #1 at the beginning of a three-week run, the same day that its parent album, ***Like A Prayer***, tops the US albums survey for the first of six weeks, eventually earning three platinum discs.
May Madonna takes part in the ecological awareness benefit "Don't Bungle The Jungle" at the Brooklyn Academy of Music, New York, duetting with galpal Sandra Bernhard on *I Got You Babe*.
[16] *Like A Prayer* is certified platinum by the RIAA.
July [15] *Express Yourself*, supported by a typically steamy video directed by David Fincher, hits US #2. (Madonna overtakes the Beatles on the list of all-time consecutive top five hits. Her total of 16 is now only surpassed by Elvis Presley's 24.)
Aug [11] *Express Yourself* is certified gold by the RIAA.
Sept [6] "Like A Prayer" wins the Best Viewer's Choice Video category at the sixth annual MTV Video Music Awards ceremony at the Universal Amphitheatre, while "Express Yourself" nabs Best Art Direction, Best Cinematography and Best Direction.
Oct [7] *Cherish* hits US #2.
Dec [23] Dreamy child-themed *Dear Jessie* hits UK #5, as Madonna wins Top Adult Contemporary Artist in **Billboard**'s Year In Music annual survey. (By year's end, Madonna will also have completed the filming of "Bloodhounds On Broadway".)

1990

Jan [6] *Oh Father* reaches US #20.
[23] The RIAA certifies three million sales of ***Like A Prayer***.
Mar [8] Madonna wins Worst Female Singer and Worst Video ("Like A Prayer") in **Rolling Stone**'s Readers Poll and Best Video ("Like A Prayer") in the magazine's Critics Awards.
[31] *Keep It Together* hits US #8.
Apr [11] *Keep It Together* is certified gold by the RIAA.
[13] Her 54-date worldwide "Blonde Ambition" tour opens at the Chiba Marine Stadium in Tokyo, Japan, featuring traditionally-revealing costumes designed by Jean Paul Gaultier.
[14] From a forthcoming album, *Vogue* hits UK #1 and will earn a gold disc.
May [4-5] The US leg of the "Blonde Ambition" tour opens at The Summit in Houston, TX, before a sellout crowd of 31,427 paying $881,235. (She will cancel a concert at the Rosemont Horizon, Rosemont, IL, suffering from infected vocal chords. Subsequent concerts will also have to be called off.)
[12] *Vogue*, which via its accompanying video, begins a mini-fad for dance stance "vogueing", hits US #1 for the first of three weeks.
[26] As *Vogue* holds at #1, the US top five are all female artists, the first time since June 1979 when Anita Ward was in pole position.
[29] Toronto, ON, Canada police "review" her third SkyDome concert, citing a complaint of "lewdness".
June [2] Marketed in line with her current role as Breathless Mahoney in Warren Beatty's "Bugsy", ***I'm Breathless*** debuts at its UK #2 peak.
[20-21 24-25] Madonna grosses $3,357,500 from four sellout dates at the Meadowlands Arena, East Rutherford, NJ.
[23] ***I'm Breathless*** hits US #2, unable to dislodge MC Hammer.
13-year-old Keith Sorrentino files a $500,000 lawsuit against Madonna, claiming he suffers nightmares and bed-wetting problems from an incident that occurred in May 1988 outside Madonna's Central Park West apartment in New York. The complaint charges that Madonna grabbed his camera, flung him to the ground and choked him after he asked to take her photo. Madonna, in response, files a third-party countersuit against Sorrentino's older sister, Darlene, claiming her to be an obsessive fan who has subjected Madonna to "threatening, abusive, vexatious and obscene statements" over the years.
[25] She donates profits from the Brendan Byrne Arena gig, her last on the "Blonde Ambition" tour, to the American Foundation for AIDS Research.
[28] The RIAA certifies two million sales of *Vogue*.
[30] The European leg of the "Blonde Ambition" trek opens in Gothenburg, Sweden.
July The Italian Bishop's Conference campaigns to ban her from playing three dates in Italy issuing the statement: "Her new show, with the symbols it uses and the values it expresses, is an offense to good taste".
[6] Generally praised for her teasing role as Breathless Mahoney in current beau Warren Beatty's "Dick Tracy" movie, the film makes its European premiere in Leicester Square, London.
[11] Madonna's second scheduled show at the Flaminio Stadium, Rome, Italy, is cancelled, reportedly due to poor ticket sales and a general laborers' strike.
[18] Dogged by the UK gutter press, Madonna goes jogging in Hyde Park, causing criticism in the media, which states that she had previously agreed to help launch the fundraising ***Nobody's Child*** album to benefit Romanian orphans.
[20-22] Madonna performs at Wembley Stadium, at the start of the UK leg of her world tour.
[28] *Hanky Panky* hits US #10 and UK #2.
[30] The RIAA certifies two million sales of ***I'm Breathless***.
Aug [5] "Madonna - Live! Blonde Ambition World Tour '90" concert airs on HBO, and becomes the most watched show in the station's 18-year history.
Sept [7] In addition to Madonna performing a period costume-enhanced live performance of the song, "Vogue" scoops the Best Editing, Best Cinematography and Best Direction trophies at the seventh annual MTV Video Music Awards at the Universal Amphitheatre. (She will also perform the same song at a benefit for AIDS Project Los Angeles at the Wiltern Theatre, Los Angeles.)
[19] *Hanky Panky* is certified gold by the RIAA.
Nov [21] Madonna is sued by her next door neighbor for having a hedge which blocks his view.
[23] MTV announces a ban on the video, filmed at the Royal Monceau Hotel in Paris, France, for the newly-released *Justify My Love*, which as a result will be lucratively released as a video sales cassette.
[24] Greatest hits collection ***The Immaculate Collection***, marking the commercial debut of the "Q Sound" recording technique, concurrently released with a similar video package, but not including the album's *Justify My Love*, immediately hits UK #1, where it will stay for nine weeks on its way to five platinum UK sales discs.
Dec [3] ABC-TV airs the video in full on "Nightline", with anchorman Forrest Sawyer quizzing Madonna on its subject matter.
[15] *Justify My Love* hits UK #2.

1991

Jan Rabbi Abraham Cooper of the Simon Wiesenthal Center in Los Angeles wants copies of ***The Immaculate Collection*** removed from record stores, because one of the tracks has lyrics of biblical reference which the Center believes could incite anti-semitism.
[5] Co-written by Madonna and Lenny Kravitz and produced by Kravitz, the partly-spoken *Justify My Love* hits familiar US #1, still boosted by the banning of the accompanying steamy hotel bedroom-shot black and white video co-starring current beau Tony Ward.
[26] ***The Immaculate Collection*** hits US #2, with domestic sales eventually topping six million.
[28] Madonna wins the Favorite Dance/Music Single category for *Vogue* at the 18th annual American Music Awards at the Shrine Auditorium.
Feb [22] "Justify My Love" video is certified platinum by the RIAA.
Mar [2] *Rescue Me* enters the US Hot 100 at #15, the highest-debuting single by a female artist in rock history. (The previous record was held by Joy Layne, whose *Your Wild Heart* entered at #30 in 1957.) The single will, however, only peak at US #9. On the same day, a remixed *Crazy For You* bows at its UK #2 peak behind the Simpsons' *Do The Bartman*.
[3] *Vogue* wins International Single Of The Year at the 20th annual Juno Awards, at the Queen Elizabeth Theater, Vancouver, BC, Canada.
[7] *Vogue* is named Best Single and Best Video in the annual **Rolling Stone** Readers' Picks music awards. Madonna's "Blonde Ambition Tour" is named Best Tour and she wins Best Dressed Female Artist and Sexiest Female Singer categories. "Justify My Love" wins Best Video and Hype Of The Year in the Critics' Picks.
[20] "Madonna - Four Clips" video passes the 100,000 sales mark.
[23] *Rescue Me* hits US #9.
[25] She sings Stephen Sondheim's "Dick Tracy"-featured *Sooner Or Later (I Always Get My Man)* at the 63rd annual Academy Awards ceremony, at the Shrine Auditorium. The song will win this year's Oscar for Best Song. Her escort for the evening's festivities is Michael Jackson.
Apr [20] *Rescue Me* hits UK #3.
May Cardinal O'Connor calls upon the Pope to excommunicate Madonna for her blasphemous performances and abuse of Catholic imagery.
[6] "Truth Or Dare : On The Band Behind The Scenes, And In Bed With Madonna", a revealing Madonna-commissioned warts-and-all roving bio-documentary, directed by Alek Keshishian, premieres in Los Angeles.
[13-14] Regis Philbin and Madonna conduct a one-on-one interview on the balcony of her Los Angeles hotel

room on syndicated TV's "Regis & Kathie Lee" show.
[24] *Rescue Me* is certified gold by the RIAA.
June [15] Reissued *Holiday*, originally a 1984 UK #2, hits UK #5.
July [17] "In Bed With Madonna" premieres at London's Marble Arch Odeon.
[22] Madonna guests on BBC1-TV's "Wogan" from the "Cannes Film Festival".
Dec The Boring Institute of Maplewood, NJ names Madonna Most Boring Personality Of 1991, claiming that "she's parlayed a bad attitude into superstardom".
[10] She contributes to an all-star benefit auction for American AIDS Research in Beverly Hills, CA.

1992

Jan [29] Musician actress Ingrid Chavez will receive co-songwriting recognition and back-royalties with Lenny Kravitz who originally claimed sole credit for penning *Justify My Love* following a ruling in her favor. Chavez has alleged that Kravitz persuaded her to relinquish any credit or royalties in return for $500. Madonna is not involved in the testimony.
Feb Dancers Oliver Crumes, Kevin Shea and Gabriel Trupin file suit over the release of "Truth Or Dare" movie.
[22] Madonna makes a surprise guest appearance on NBC-TV's "Saturday Night Live" "Coffee Talk" segment as Liz Rosenberg, coincidentally the name of Warner Bros. Records' New York Vice-President of Publicity.
[25] "Madonna : Blonde Ambition World Tour Live" wins Best Music Video - Longform at the 34th annual Grammy Awards from Radio City Music Hall.
Apr [20] Warner Bros.' parent company Time Warner Inc. announces a new seven-year multi-media contract with Madonna under her newly formed Maverick group of companies (a name derived from the first two letters in her two names (Madonna Veronica) and the last three of her manager's, Frederick Demann), with a record label, publishing company, book, TV, merchandising and motion picture subsidiaries all under the collective Maverick umbrella, to be run from Los Angeles, New York and London. Despite the fact that each of her last five albums has sold less than the previous one in the US, media estimates suggesting that the deal is worth $60 million to the industry's latest mogul are described by DeMann as "low". Early Maverick-planned projects include Madonna's ninth solo album (and will include signing Alanis Morissette), her production of the debut set by Jose & Luis, a coffee table sex-photo book by photographer Steven Meisel, an HBO cable TV biography of Mexican artist Frida Kahlo and the Maverick Picture Co. debut film, the $10-million project "Snake Eyes" directed by Abel Ferrara with the diva starring.
May [29] Following a sting operation, the FBI recovers 44 nude photographs of Madonna stolen from a collection by fashion lensman Steven Meisel. Meanwhile, the June issue of **Playboy** features naked shots of the star from the same beach location session.
June [16] The first International "Madonna Appreciation Convention" (the Madonnathon) kicks off at the Holiday Inn, Southfield, MI on her 34th birthday.
Aug [1] Ballad, *This Used To Be My Playground*, hits UK #3.
[8] *This Used To Be My Playground*, featured in the screen-only film soundtrack to "A League Of Their Own" and only available on the summer Olympics-celebrating ***Barcelona Gold*** compilation, tops the US chart.
Sept [10] *This Used To Be My Playground* is certified gold by the RIAA.
[17] The bed used as a prop in the "In Bed With Madonna" film is bought by a 15-year old Dutch girl at a UNICEF fundraising auction for $7,700.
[24] Madonna exposes her breasts during AMFAR AIDS "Jean-Paul Gaultier In LA" fashion benefit before 6,000 people at the Shrine Auditorium.
Oct [15] Her "Sex" party to promote her forthcoming album and book (also called "Sex", a metal-covered collection of provocative photographs featuring Madonna) is held at Manhattan's Industria Super-studio for 800 invited guests. Ever the media chameleon, Madonna arrives carrying a toy lamb and dressed as Little Bo Peep. The book reportedly sells 500,000 copies in its first week.
[24] Breathy *Erotica* hits US #3, once again spurred by a risqué bondage-themed video clip. ***Erotica*** debuts at its UK #2 peak (on its way to double platinum certification) behind Simple Minds' ***Glittering Prize 81-92***.
[31] *Erotica* hits UK #3.
Nov [7] ***Erotica*** bows at its US #2 pinnacle behind Garth Brooks' ***The Chase***.
Dec [10] *Erotica* is certified gold by the RIAA.
[19] '70s-disco retro-styled *Deeper And Deeper* hits UK #6.

1993

Jan [6] The RIAA certifies two million sales of ***Erotica***.
[16] Guesting on NBC-TV's "Saturday Night Live", she tears up a picture of blue-collar celebrity Joey Buttafuoco á la Sinead O'Connor after singing *Bad Girl*. The show has its biggest rating since 1981.
[30] *Deeper And Deeper* hits US #7.
Mar [13] *Bad Girl* hits UK #10.
[27] *Bad Girl* reaches US #36.
Apr [3] Her cover of *Fever*, originally a 1956 hit for Little Willie John, bows at its UK #6 peak.
May [13] Madonna tapes a performance on syndicated TV's "Arsenio Hall Show"'s 1000th performance at the Hollywood Bowl, Hollywood, CA, which airs on the 14th.
June Maverick Television Corp. signs a deal with ABC-TV to jointly develop and produce specials, movies and the mini-series "Madonna : The Early Years".
July [31] *Rain* debuts at its UK #7 peak.
Sept [11] *Rain* reaches US #14.
[25] Madonna performs at Wembley Stadium during her current world tour.

1994

Apr [9] Ballad *I'll Remember*, from the movie "With Honors", hits UK #7.
May [28] *I'll Remember*, co-penned by Madonna, Leonard and Richard Page, hits US #2, behind All-4-One's *I Swear*.
June [14] *I'll Remember* is certified gold by the RIAA.
Sept [20] The RIAA certifies 300,000 sales of "The Immaculate Collection" video.
Oct [8] *Secret* debuts at its UK #5 peak.
Nov [5] *Secret* hits US #3, as its parent album ***Bedtime Stories*** hits UK #3 in its week of entry.
[12] ***Bedtime Stories*** debuts at its US #3 peak.
Dec [24] Co-written, co-produced and co-sung with Babyface, *Take A Bow* reaches UK #16.

1995

Jan [5] *Secret* is certified gold by the RIAA.
[30] Madonna performs *Take A Bow* with Babyface at the 22nd annual American Music Awards, from the Shrine Auditorium.
Feb [9] The RIAA certifies multi-platinum sales of ***True Blue*** (seven million) and ***Like A Virgin*** (nine million) and gold sales of "The Girlie Show - Live Down Under" video.
[20] Madonna opens the 14th annual BRIT Awards at London's Alexandra Palace, singing *Unconscious*.
[25] *Take A Bow* tops the US chart, as *Bedtime Story* , with remixes by Junior Vasquez and Orbital, debuts at its UK #4 peak. (Madonna becomes the first female artist to have 11 US chart-toppers, and now stands at #5 on the all-time list behind the Beatles, Elvis Presley, the Supremes and Michael Jackson.)
[27] The RIAA certifies gold sales for *Take A Bow* and and two million sales for ***Bedtime Stories***.
Mar Playboy reports that Madonna has signed to star in Quentin Tarantino's next film, as her latest movie, "Blue In The Face", starring Harvey Keitel, Roseanne and Lou Reed, is set for release by Miramax.
[16] The RIAA certifies six million sales of ***The Immaculate Collection***.
[18-19] Telecast live on MTV-US, Madonna reads a bedtime story from David Kirk's **Miss Spider's Tea Party** to a throng of 1,500 pyjama-clad fans at New York's Webster Hall night club to promote her new Mark Romanek-directed "Bedtime Story" video.
Apr [25] Having switched to the William Morris Agency for personal representation on March 13th, Madonna now moves to ICM.
[29] *Bedtime Story* reaches US #42.
May [6] Dropping to #52, *Bedtime Story* breaks Madonna's run of 32 consecutive Top 40 hits.
[29] 37-year-old Robert Hoskins is shot in the left arm and pelvis by private security guard Basil Stephens after scaling a fence at Madonna's Hollywood Hills home and lunging for the latter's gun. He is booked on stalking charges while in Cedars-Sinai Hospital receiving treatment. (Madonna is not at home at the time.)
July [15] *Human Nature* makes US #46.
Aug [26] *Human Nature* debuts at its UK #8 peak.
Sept [7] Madonna collects the Best Female Video trophy for "You Don't Know How It Feels" at the 11th annual MTV Video Music Awards held at Radio City Music Hall.
Oct [20] Madonna is named as a co-defendant as CEO of Maverick in a $750,000 wrongful termination suit filed in Los Angeles Superior Court by former company receptionist and assistant Sonji Shepherd, alleging the label failed to "protect its female employées from unwelcome sexual advances".
Nov [2] Madonna makes her first appearance on BBC1-TV's "Top of The Pops" in 11 years.
[4] Marvin Gaye tribute album, ***Inner City Blues - The Music Of Marvin Gaye***, to which Madonna has contributed *I Want You*, a collaboration with Massive Attack, peaks at its US #106 debut.
[18] Ballad *You'll See*, written with producer David Foster, hits UK #5, as a full ballads retrospective ***Something To Remember***, including three new cuts, hits UK #3 in its week of entry.
[25] ***Something To Remember*** debuts at its US #6 peak.
Dec [3] Madonna is presented with the Most Fashionable Artist Award by former husband Sean Penn at the first "VH1 Fashion Awards" at Lexington Avenue, Manhattan.
[16] *You'll See* hits US #6.

1996

Jan [3] Madonna gives evidence in Courtroom 116 at the Los Angeles Criminal Courts Building against alleged stalker Robert Hoskins who will be found guilty on the 8th. Judge Andrew Kauffman had threatened her with arrest if she didn't testify.
[6] *Oh Father* bows at its UK #16 peak.
Feb [6] Madonna holds a press conference in Buenos Aires, Argentina, as she begins location work on the much-delayed movie "Evita", directed by Alan Parker and co-starring Jonathan Pryce and Antonio Banderas.
[24] This week's edition of **Billboard** includes a full-page advertisement attack on Madonna by animal rights group PETA including: "Dear Madonna, Bravo for putting your knife-wielding stalker behind bars. Might you now become more sensitive to defenseless animals suffering comparable terror, by no longer promoting bullfighting in your videos ("Take A Bow" and "You'll See")."
Mar [10] Amid strong local protests, and having personally convinced President Carlos Saul Menem to grant permission to film at the historic site (he had earlier been quoted: "A total and utter disgrace. Pornographic and blasphemous - an insult to Argentine women"), Madonna lip-synchs to *Don't Cry For Me Argentina* in her role as Eva Peron on the balcony of the presidential palace where the first lady of Argentina told a devoted crowd she was dying in 1951.
[23] *One More Chance*, once again co-written with Foster, reaches UK #11 in its week of entry.
Apr [20] Her publicist announces that Madonna is pregnant, the father-to-be being her personal trainer of the past 18 months, Carlos Leon.
May [18] *Love Don't Live Here Anymore* peaks at US #78.

THE MAMAS & THE PAPAS

John Phillips (vocals); **Denny Doherty** (vocals); **Cass Elliot** (vocals); **Michelle Gilliam** (vocals)

1964

The group initially comes together as trio the New Journeymen in St. Thomas in the Virgin Islands, when Doherty (b. Nov. 29, 1941, Halifax, NS, Canada) teams with Phillips (b. Aug. 30, 1935, Parris Island, SC) and Gilliam (b. Holly Michelle Gilliam, Apr. 6, 1944, Long Beach, CA), who married in 1962 after meeting at San Francisco, CA's Hungry I club. Phillips, as a member of folk trio the Journeymen, with Scott McKenzie and Dick Weissman, released three albums on Capitol Records while Doherty has sung with similar group the Halifax Three, recording for Epic Records, before joining Elliot (b. Ellen Cohen, Sept. 19, 1941, Baltimore, MD), ex-lead singer of the Big Three, in the Mugwumps (with Zalman Yanovsky and John Sebastian, who form the Lovin' Spoonful). The Mugwumps release *I Don't Wanna Know*, on Warner Bros., cut some more material not issued at the time and, after working on the "Freak Out" movie soundtrack, split. The New Journeymen rehearse to fulfill contractual obligations.

1965

Jan Elliot has become a waitress, but joins them briefly in the Virgin Islands, where they receive rent-free accomodation in exchange for singing at the Lark nightclub, before becoming a full-time member when the group relocates to California. Here they meet up with an old friend, ex-New Christy Minstrel Barry McGuire, who introduces them to his producer, and owner of the new Dunhill label, Lou Adler.

Oct Adler hires them to sing back-up vocals on sessions for McGuire's *This Precious Time* and also uses Phillips' song *California Dreamin'* for McGuire. The New Journeymen sign to Dunhill in their own right and after toying with the name the Magic Circle, they become the Mamas & the Papas.

Dec *Go Where You Wanna Go* is recorded as a debut single, but Adler releases the group's own version of *California Dreamin'* instead (using the same backing track as featured on McGuire's album version).

1966

Mar [12] *California Dreamin'*, immediately showcasing the quartet's effortless harmony style, hits US #4 and will earn a gold disc for a million-plus US sales.

May [7] The follow-up, *Monday Monday*, another Phillips song (which everyone in the group dislikes apart from him) tops US chart for the first of three weeks, and is another million-seller while *California Dreamin'* reaches UK #23.

[21] ***If You Can Believe Your Eyes And Ears***, which contains both songs, tops the US chart for a week during a 105-week chart stay.

June *Monday Monday* hits UK #3.

[10] *California Dreamin'*, *Monday Monday* and ***If You Can Believe Your Eyes And Ears*** are certified gold by the RIAA.

July [8] Gilliam is fired from the group, and is replaced temporarily by Jill Gibson, long-time girlfriend of Jan Berry from Jan & Dean.

[30] Co-penned by Doherty and John Phillips, *I Saw Her Again* hits US #5, while the album, retitled ***The Mamas And The Papas*** in the UK, hits UK #3.

Aug Phillips and Gilliam reconcile, and she returns to the group, replacing Gibson.

Sept *I Saw Her Again* reaches UK #11.

Oct [14] The group performs at New York, NY's Carnegie Hall.

[22] The group's second album ***The Mamas And The Papas*** hits US #4. They also make a US TV special.

Nov [26] *Look Through My Window* reaches US #24.

Dec [1] ***The Mamas And The Papas*** is certified gold by the RIAA.

1967

Jan [21] John Phillips-written *Words Of Love*, a lead vocal showcase for Elliot, hits US #5 and is a third million-selling single while its B-side, their revival of Martha & the Vandellas' *Dancing In The Street* peaks at US #73.

Feb Their sophomore album (retitled ***Cass, John, Michelle And Denny*** in the UK) reaches UK #24. *Words Of Love* makes UK #47.

Mar [2] *Monday Monday* wins Best Contemporary (Rock'n'Roll) Group Performance Vocal Or Instrumental Of 1966 at the ninth annual Grammy Awards.

[25] Their treatment of the Shirelles' *Dedicated To The One I Love* hits US #2 for the first of three weeks behind the Turtles' *Happy Together*, and becomes the group's fourth million-selling single. It is taken from ***The Mamas And The Papas Deliver***, which spends seven weeks also at US #2.

[20] ***The Mamas And The Papas Deliver*** is certified gold by the RIAA.

[26] Mama Cass gives birth to a daughter, Owen Vanessa, in a Los Angeles, CA hospital.

May *Dedicated To The One I Love* also hits UK #2, while the uptempo *Creeque Alley*, the story-song of the group's history up to its first successes, hits US #5.

June [18] The group is the closing act of third and final evening of the "Monterey International Pop Festival", at the Monterey County Fairgrounds, Monterey, CA, also notable as the last time the original quartet will sing live together. Filmed by D.A. Pennebaker for the movie "Monterey Pop", the group has been the prime mover in the organization of the event with Lou Adler.

July ***The Mamas And The Papas Deliver*** hits UK #4 while, Phillips' composition *San Francisco (Be Sure To Wear Some Flowers In Your Hair)*, recorded by ex-Journeyman Scott McKenzie, hits US #4.

Aug *Creeque Alley* hits UK #9 (and is the group's last UK chart single), as McKenzie's *San Francisco* tops the UK chart for four weeks.

Sept [16] *Twelve Thirty (Young Girls Are Coming To The Canyon)* reaches US #20.

Oct [7] Elliot spends the night in jail in London, accused of stealing from a hotel, causing the cancellation of UK concert and TV appearances.

Nov [25] *Glad To Be Unhappy*, originally recorded by the group for a Rodgers and Hart TV tribute show, makes US #26.

Dec Compilation, ***Farewell To The First Golden Era***, hits US #5, and is the group's last gold album, while *Dancing Bear* is their first disc not to make the US Top 50, peaking at #51.

1968

Feb [9] ***Farewell To The First Golden Era*** is certified gold by the RIAA.

[12] Gilliam gives birth to Chynna Phillips (who will form one third of Wilson Phillips in 1987).

Mar [8] While Cass has recently co-produced, with Steve Barri, Canadian group 3's A Crowd's only album, ***Christopher's Movie Matinee***, on the Dunhill label, the group is included for the first time in the new publication of **Who's Who In America**.

June *Safe In My Garden* peaks at US #53.

[28] Phillips, Doherty and Elliot write to Gilliam informing that she is fired from the group.

July ***The Papas And The Mamas*** reaches US #15 as the group officially dissolves at a time when Phillips and Gilliam also head for a personal split.

Aug A live track with Elliot taking a solo vocal, *Dream A Little Dream Of Me*, and credited to Mama Cass, reaches US #12 and UK #11.

Sept Movie theme *For The Love Of Ivy* peaks at US #81.

[29] Elliot guests on CBS-TV's "The Smothers Brothers Comedy Hour".

Oct Dunhill Records sues Phillips, Doherty and Gilliam, charging that they have not met their contractual obligations to the label since disbanding the group.

[8] Elliot opens as a soloist at Caesar's Palace in Las Vegas, NV, but collapsing with a throat haemorrhage on the debut night of a six-week season, the stint is cancelled as she undergoes a major throat operation.

Nov Second compilation album, ***Golden Era, Vol. 2***, makes US #53, while Mama Cass' maiden solo album, ***Dream A Little Dream***, makes US #87, and her second solo single *California Earthquake* rumbles to US #67.

Dec Mamas & the Papas' revival of Bobby Freeman's *Do You Wanna Dance* makes US #76.

1969

Apr As the remaining members record as a trio for Warwick, Phillips' own company, UK compilation, ***Hits Of Gold***, hits UK #7 while Mama Cass' *Move In A Little Closer, Baby* peaks at US #58.

June Mama Cass' ***Bubblegum, Lemonade, And ... Something For Mama*** peaks at US #91. (During the year, Cass also records with the group Electric Flag, but the results of the sessions are never released.)

Aug Mama Cass' *It's Getting Better* reaches US #30 and hits UK #8 (her last UK hit).

Nov US compilation, ***16 Of Their Greatest Hits***, makes US #61, while Mama Cass' *Make Your Own Kind Of Music* reaches US #36. On this, and subsequent singles, she is billed as Mama Cass Elliot.

Dec ***Make Your Own Kind Of Music***, a reissue of Cass' previous solo set plus the hit title track, peaks at US #169.

1970

Feb Mama Cass' *New World Coming* makes US #42.

May Phillips' solo album, ***John Phillips (John The Wolfking Of L.A.)***, peaks at US #181.

July *Mississippi*, from Phillips' album, climbs to US #32, his only solo hit single. Phillips also co-produces, with Lou Adler, Robert Altman's film "Brewster McCloud", while Elliot appears in the movie "Pufnstuf".

Aug Mama Cass' *A Song That Never Comes* peaks at US #99, her last US solo entry.

Oct [31] After Gilliam and Phillips have divorced, she marries actor Dennis Hopper, though wedded bliss will only last for eight days.

1971

Mar Mama Cass' compilation, ***Mama's Big Ones***, peaks at US #194.

Apr ***Dave Mason And Mama Cass***, duetted by Elliot with the ex-member of Traffic, makes US #49. Doherty's solo album, ***Whatcha Gonna Do?***, is released.

Nov The group's attempted reunion on ***People Like Us*** peaks at US #84. After lukewarm reviews they decide to split again. *Step Out*, taken from the reunion album, will make US #81 the following February.

1973

Mar Double compilation, ***20 Golden Hits***, reaches US #186.

July [30] At a press conference organized by New York Senator James Buckley, the former group members announce a $9 million suit against ABC-Dunhill Records. Phillips claims in a press statement that the label has been guilty of "systematic, cold-blooded theft of perhaps up to $60 million, stolen from each and every artist who recorded for it during a seven-year period". The label says the charges are "without foundation".

1974

July [29] Elliot dies while staying in London at singer Harry Nilsson's flat, aged 32, from a heart attack while choking on food and inhaling vomit.

1977

While John has contributed tracks to Nicolas Roeg's 1975 movie "The Man Who Fell To Earth" starring David Bowie, Michelle Phillips, who has kept her original married surname as her professional name, becomes a successful actress initially appearing in feature films (such as the Hopper-directed "The Last Movie", "Dillinger", "Bloodline" (1979) "The Man With Bogart's Face" (1980) "Savage Harvest" (1983)

"American Anthem" (1986) and "Let It Ride" (1989) among others) and on TV, most notably as a regular on "Knot's Landing" during the '80s. She also records the solo album, ***Victim Of Romance***, for A&M.

July TV-promoted compilation, ***The Best Of The Mamas And The Papas***, hits UK #6.

1981

Apr [20] Having been arrested in Los Angeles on July 30th the previous year by federal narcotics agents for possession of cocaine, Phillips is now jailed for five years after pleading guilty to the charges in a Los Angeles court. The sentence will be suspended after 30 days, in exchange for 250 hours of community service by Phillips and he will tour the US, lecturing against drugs.

1982

Mar [3] Phillips and Doherty re-form the group for a reunion tour which opens at New York's Other End club. The female group members are both new: Phillips' daughter MacKenzie (b. Nov. 10, 1959) (who has starred in the hit film "American Graffiti") and ex-lead singer of Spanky & Our Gang, Spanky McFarlane (b. June 19, 1942, Peoria, IL). This new line-up releases nothing new on disc but remains on the oldies touring circuit in the US.

1986

July Having been included on the "Happy Together Tour" across the US in April 1985 with the Turtles, Grass Roots, Gary Lewis, the Buckinghams and others, the re-formed Mamas & the Papas are hired by the Florida Panhandle real estate company to play a beach gig at Destin, FL, in order to attract prospective condominium buyers. (Doherty performs with group from 1982 to 1987, but will then return to Canada and begin acting.)

1988

Nov [5] The Beach Boys hit US #1 with *Kokomo*, co-penned by Phillips. The Mamas and the Papas, now comprising John and MacKenzie Phillips, Spanky McFarlane and Scott McKenzie (b. Philip Blondheim, Oct. 1, 1944, Jacksonville, FL) will embark on "An Evening Of California Dreamin' - The Tour" with Brewer & Shipley, Maria Muldaur, Canned Heat and the New Riders of the Purple Sage, throughout the US the following year.

1995

Jan [28] After Michelle Phillips sought a court order in July 1991 to prevent an alleged film producer (and alleged ex-beau) George Miller from organizing a movie project based on her book **California Dreamin'**, the same year MCA released the anthology ***Creeque Alley : The History Of The Mamas and the Papas***, and John Phillips received a liver transplant at the University of California, Los Angeles Medical Center, Los Angeles on July 4th 1992, a fresh compilation ***California Dreamin'*** reaches UK #14 in its week of entry.

MANFRED MANN

Paul Jones (vocals, harmonica); **Manfred Mann** (keyboards); **Mike Vickers** (guitar); **Tom McGuinness** (bass); **Mike Hugg** (drums)

1962

Dec The group is initially formed in London as the Mann-Hugg Blues Brothers, after Mann (b. Manfred Lubowitz, Oct. 21, 1940, Johannesburg, South Africa) and Hugg (b. Aug. 11, 1942, Andover, Hants.), have met in the summer while playing piano and vibes respectively in the Ken Goddard Quartet at the South Seas Bar at Butlin's Holiday Camp in Clacton-on-Sea, Essex. They recruit Jones (b. Paul Pond, Feb. 24, 1942, Portsmouth, Hants.), having been introduced to him by the Marquee club's Bill Carey, Vickers (b. Apr. 18, 1941, Southampton, Hants.), and Dave Richmond on bass, with an occasional horn section comprising Ian Fenby (trumpet), Tony Roberts (tenor sax) and Don Fay (baritone sax). Jones has been a member of the Oxford based Odin & the Big Secret which became the Roosters (also including Ben Palmer (piano), future Rolling Stone Brian Jones (guitar), who was replaced by Eric Clapton, Robin Mason (drums) and Tom McGuinness (bass).

1963

Mar [11] The group's Marquee club debut in London is one of a series of notable engagements, including gigs at the Studio 51 and Crawdaddy Clubs, which attract record company interest.

May With a change of name to Manfred Mann at the suggestion of producer John Burgess, the band signs to EMI's HMV imprint, after recording six demos for the label, and being turned down by Pye and Decca. United Artists subsidiary Ascot will sign the group for the US.

July Their debut single, the jazz/R&B instrumental *Why Should We Not?*, is released.

Oct *Cock-A-Hoop*, with an uptempo R&B vocal, is the follow-up.

1964

Jan Richmond leaves for session work, and is replaced by ex-Roosters and Casey Jones & the Engineers' bassist McGuinness (b. Dec. 2, 1941, Wimbledon, London), who, at the time of joining, is lugging furniture for Bentalls department store. (Jones and McGuinness have played one gig in a band in summer 1964, before splitting up.) The group is asked to write a new theme tune for the ITV pop show "Ready Steady Go!", replacing the Surfaris' *Wipe Out*, and comes up with *5-4-3-2-1*.

Feb Exposed as the weekly program theme (on which the group also frequently guests), *5-4-3-2-1* hits UK #5. (Its lyric reverses several thousand years of Greek mythology - in this song, Trojans wait at the gates of Troy, while the Greeks are inside!)

May Uptempo R&B-style *Hubble Bubble Toil And Trouble* reaches UK #11.

Aug [13] The group's cover of *Do Wah Diddy Diddy*, an obscure Jeff Barry/Ellie Greenwich song originally cut without chart success by the Exciters, deposes the Beatles' *A Hard Day's Night*, to top the UK survey for the first of two weeks, eventually selling 650,000 copies in Britain.

Oct Their debut album ***The Five Faces Of Manfred Mann***, mainly a collection of R&B covers with a few originals, hits UK #3.

[17] *Do Wah Diddy Diddy*, their US chart debut, begins a two-week spell at US #1.

Nov Their revival of the Shirelles' *Sha La La* hits UK #3.

Dec US compilation, ***The Manfred Mann Album***, reaches US #35.

1965

Jan *Sha La La* makes US #12.

Feb The group's first down-tempo A-side, *Come Tomorrow*, hits UK #4.

Mar *Come Tomorrow* makes US #50, while ***The Five Faces Of Manfred Mann*** peaks at US #141.

May *Oh No Not My Baby*, a revival of Maxine Brown's US hit, reaches UK #11.

June The band appears in the televised "Brighton Song Festival", Brighton, Sussex, performing the autobiographical *The One In The Middle*. It also contributes Bacharach/David's *My Little Red Book* to the soundtrack of movie "What's New, Pussycat?", released as a US single.

July *The One In The Middle* is the title song of a four-track EP, which sells as strongly as a single in the UK, and hits #6, its main selling point being the inclusion of a version of Bob Dylan's *With God On Our Side*, which receives extensive airplay.

Sept Jones announces his intention to pursue a solo career, but will stay until they find a replacement.

Oct Another Dylan song, *If You Gotta Go, Go Now*, hits UK #2 behind Ken Dodd's *Tears*, despite TV bans from "Crackerjack" and "Gadzooks".

Nov ***Mann Made***, again a mix of covers and originals, hits UK #7. Vickers leaves to concentrate on arranging and studio work, and McGuinness switches to guitar as the group recruits new bassist Jack Bruce (b. May 14, 1943, Glasgow, Scotland), after he has worked out a month's notice with John Mayall, so Pete Burford and David Hyde each fill in on bass for two weeks. The band also experiments with a two-piece horn section of Henry Lowther on trumpet and Lyn Dobson on sax to augment its sound.

1966

Jan [26] The Animals' Eric Burdon sings lead vocals for Manfred Mann at a London gig, while Paul Jones is recovering from a minor car crash.

May [5] *Pretty Flamingo*, written by Mark Barkan, tops the UK chart for the first of three weeks.

July *You Gave Me Somebody To Love* peaks at UK #36.

[31] Jones leaves the band, having given a year's notice of his intention. Bruce departs at the same time to form Cream with Eric Clapton and Ginger Baker.

Aug After the group has considered Rod Stewart, Long John Baldry and Wayne Fontana, Jones is replaced by Mike D'Abo (b. Mar. 1, 1944, Betchworth), ex-A Band Of Angels, and Bruce by Klaus Voorman (b. Apr. 29, 1942, Berlin, Germany) from Paddy, Klaus & Gibson. *Pretty Flamingo* peaks at US #29. Meanwhile, the group changes record labels in Britain from HMV to Fontana, and links with producer Shel Talmy.

Sept Their treatment of Bob Dylan's *Just Like A Woman*, from his album ***Blonde On Blonde***, is the group's first Fontana single, and its first with D'Abo on lead vocals, and hits UK #10, but is not released in the US where Dylan scores his own hit, while the composer's version is unavailable as a UK single.

Oct Compilation, ***Mann Made Hits***, on HMV, reaches UK #11.

Nov *Semi-Detached Suburban Mr. James* hits UK #2. (The title originally used a more common name, Jones, which was changed during recording in case it should be interpreted as a reference to Paul Jones.) Meanwhile, Jones, who has remained contracted to HMV as a soloist, releases his first single, *High Time*, which hits UK #4. Manfred Mann's first Fontana album ***As Is*** reaches UK #22.

1967

Jan ***Soul Of Mann***, an HMV compilation of the group's instrumental tracks, makes UK #40.

Feb Jones' solo, *I've Been A Bad Bad Boy*, hits UK #5.

Apr [1] Manfred Mann guests on the BBC Light Programme's "Saturday Club" radio show with Jimi Hendrix, Helen Shapiro and Vince Hill.

[15] **Disc And Music Echo** runs a competition to give away six pedigree Siamese kittens owned by D'Abo, under the heading "Mike D'Abo's Kitten Contest".

[22] The group's *Ha! Ha! Said The Clown* hits UK #4.

May Jones stars in Peter Watkins' film "Privilege", with model Jean Shrimpton, while an EP of songs from the movie tops the UK EP chart.

June Manfred Mann's instrumental revival of Tommy Roe's *Sweet Pea* makes UK #36.

Sept Jones' *Thinkin' Ain't For Me* reaches UK #32, while the group's version of Randy Newman's *So Long Dad* is released.

1968

Jan UK movie "Up The Junction" premieres with songs and music written and performed by the group.

Feb [14] The band's cover of another Dylan song, as yet unrecorded by him, *The Mighty Quinn (Quinn The Eskimo)*, tops the UK chart for the first of two weeks.

Apr [13] *The Mighty Quinn* hits US #10.

June ***The Mighty Quinn*** makes US #176, released in Britain as ***Mighty Garvey***.

July A cover of John Simon's *My Name Is Jack*, which the group has seen featured in the film "You Are What You Eat", hits UK #8.

Sept Mann and Hugg visit Las Vegas, NV, to discuss writing the score for the movie "Venus In Furs", as well as discussing songs for a film starring Barbara McNair, before flying to New York for talks on writing jingles for US TV commercials.

1969

Jan [25] *Fox On The Run* peaks at US #97.
Feb *Fox On The Run* hits UK #5, while Jones' final UK solo chart success, at UK #45, is *Aquarius*, taken from the musical "Hair". (He subsequently drops out of music to concentrate on theater work for the next ten years, including appearances in "Conduct Unbecoming", "Hamlet" and "Joseph And The Amazing Technicolor Dream Coat".)
May Manfred Mann's *Ragamuffin Man* hits UK #8.
June [5] The group splits after a series of farewell gigs. Mann forms a jazz group, named Emanon ("no name" backwards), but this soon disbands before he works with Hugg on advertising jingles for Michelin, Ski Yogurt and others.
Oct McGuinness forms McGuinness Flint, with Hughie Flint (drums), Benny Gallagher (guitar, vocals), Graham Lyle (guitar, vocals) and Dennis Coulson (keyboards, vocals). (Their chart highlight will be the UK #2 smash *When I'm Dead And Gone* in December 1970, followed by ***McGuinness Flint*** which hits UK #9 and US #155 in February 1971 when *When I'm Dead And Gone* makes US #47. Their remaining chart achievements will be: *Malt And Barley Blues* (UK #5, May 1971) and ***Happy Birthday, Ruthy Baby*** (US #198, September, 1971). McGuinness and keyboards player Lou Stonebridge (a latter-day replacement for Coulson) will continue as Stonebridge McGuinness in 1975.)
Nov Mann and Hugg have re-grouped with session musicians (including Steve York (b. Apr. 24, 1948) (bass) and Dave Quincy (b. Sept. 13, 1939) (keyboards)) as the experimental jazz/rock Manfred Mann Chapter Three, issuing ***Manfred Mann Chapter Three*** on Philips' "progressive" Vertigo label, to be followed by ***Manfred Mann Chapter Three, Volume Two*** released the following October.

1971

June Mann forms Manfred Mann's Earth Band in a more progressive rock style with Mick Rogers (b. Michael Oldroyd, Sept. 20, 1946) (vocals/guitar), ex-Playboys, Bulldog and Procession, Colin Pattenden (bass), and ex-Squires drummer Chris Slade (b. Oct. 30, 1946). Slade suggests the new group name during a flight to Dublin, Eire.

1972

Mar Signed to Polydor Records and having undertaken its first UK tours with Free and Deep Purple, now followed by the first of three coast-to-coast US treks with Savoy Brown, Manfred Mann's Earth Band's debut album, ***Manfred Mann's Earth Band***, makes US #138.
Apr Earth Band's *Living Without You* climbs to US #69.
Dec [24] Following noise-level complaints by local residents at a gig at the University of Florida in Miami, FL, the police cut off the power during the band's encore, resulting in a two-hour on-campus riot.

1973

June Earth Band's ***Get Your Rocks Off*** peaks at US #196.
Oct The group hits UK #9 with *Joybringer*, instrumentally based on *Jupiter*, from Holst's "The Planets". Subsequently signing a new long-term recording deal with Bronze Records in the UK, ***Solar Fire***, still on Polydor in the US and including a version of Dylan's *Father Of Day*, will reach US #96 the following April before ***The Good Earth***, marking a new US deal with Warner Bros. Records, peaks at US #157 in December.

1976

Apr Extracted from ***Nightingales And Bombers***, which has already made US #120 the previous October, the band's version of Bruce Springsteen's *Spirit In The Night* peaks at US #97.
Sept With Rogers having left to form Aviator, replaced by ex-Hillbury Walker and Central Park Reunion-vocalist Chris Thompson (b. Mar. 9, 1948, New Zealand) and with Dave Flett having also joined, another Springsteen cover, *Blinded By The Light*, hits UK #6. Having performed at the annual "Reading Rock Festival" in August, in Reading, Berks., the band tours Europe on a twin-bill with Blue Öyster Cult.
Oct The first Earth Band album to chart in the UK is ***The Roaring Silence*** (including *Blinded By The Light*), which hits UK #10.

1977

Feb [19] *Blinded By The Light* tops the US chart for a week and becomes a million-seller.
Mar ***The Roaring Silence*** hits US #10.
[1] *Blinded By The Light* is certified gold by the RIAA.
Apr [5] The RIAA certifies gold sales of ***The Roaring Silence***.
June *Spirit In The Night*, issued in a remixed version, climbs to US #40. During a year mostly spent touring Europe and the US, including a co-headlining appearance at the "Pink Pop Festival" in Holland with the Kinks, Pattenden quits, replaced by session bassist Pat King while Mann is co-opted as fellow to teach music theory at Goldsmith's College, Lewisham, London.

1978

Apr ***Watch*** reaches US #83.
[7] The band's 14-date UK tour begins at Newcastle City Hall, Tyne & Wear set to end on the 23rd at the Fairfield Halls, Croydon, Surrey.
June *Davy's On The Road Again*, written by Robbie Robertson and John Simon, hits UK #6, as ***Watch*** makes UK #33. (By year's end, Mann dissolves the current line-up with Slade going on to form Terra Nova with Pattenden, who will subsequently hook up with Beggars Opera.)

1979

Feb Jones and McGuinness reunite to form the Blues Band, initially only part-time, with Dave Kelly on guitar and vocals, Gary Fletcher on bass and Hughie Flint on drums. (Rob Townsend will replace Flint midway through the band's existence.) They will make UK #40 with the ***Official Bootleg Album*** in March 1980, followed by *The Blues Band EP* (UK #68, July 1980), ***Ready*** (UK #36, November 1980) and ***Itchy Feet*** (UK #60, October 1981).
Mar With the new line-up of Mann, Thompson, King and Steve Waller (guitar/vocals) and Geoff Britton (b. Aug. 1, 1943), ex-Gun, East of Eden and Wild Angels (drums), the Earth Band's version of Dylan's *You Angel You* peaks at UK #54, as its parent album ***Angel Station*** reaches UK #30.
Apr The group performs in Paris, France, during a 60-date European tour.
June *You Angel You* makes US #58, while ***Angel Station*** peaks at US #144.
[7] An 11-date UK segment of their European trek begins, set to end on the 22nd.
July *Don't Kill It Carol*, also from ***Angel Station***, peaks at UK #45.
Oct TV-advertised ***Semi-Detached Suburban***, a compilation of Manfred Mann's '60s hits, demonstrates their enduring appeal by hitting UK #9.
Nov [25] The Earth Band takes part in "**The Sun/** Goaldiggers Five-A-Side Soccer" tournament at Empire Pool, Wembley, Middx., with Status Quo and ELO. The following October, the non-charting ***Chance*** will be released.

1981

Mar While Thompson having left to form Night the previous year with Stevie Lange, Robbie McIntosh and Nicky Hopkins (b. Feb. 24, 1944, London) (which then becomes Island, before splitting in 1983, when McIntosh joins the Pretenders) and with Matt Irving having replaced King, the Earth Band's ***Chance*** climbs to US #87.

1982

Dec After four years of over 600 gigs in Europe and North America, the Blues Band splits following farewell concerts at the Venue in London. (Jones will return to stage work, appearing in "Cats" in 1982, followed by long residencies in "Guys And Dolls" and "The Beggar's Opera".)

1983

Feb Earth Band's ***Somewhere In Africa***, a concept album about Mann's homeland of South Africa, makes UK #87. (An amended version of ***Somewhere In Africa***, released via the band's new US deal with Arista Records, will peak at US #40 in March the following year, when *Runner* will also reach US #22.)
Apr [30] The original Manfred Mann reunites for the 25th anniversary of London's Marquee club. (During the year, the band undertakes a European tour which includes three sellout shows in Budapest, Hungary, which will yield the live album ***Budapest***, after which Waller and Irving leave and Rogers rejoins.)

1986

July With Bronze Records having gone into liquidation two years earlier, the band re-emerges after a lengthy silence on 10 Records in the UK with ***Criminal Tango***, consisting of oldies revivals. (A second effort for 10, ***Masque***, will be released in November 1987.)
Aug [19] Manfred Mann's Earth Band plays its last ever gig at the Old School House, Woking, Surrey.

1991

Dec [7] While Mann has released a new-age effort, ***Manfred Mann's Plain Music***, on the Rhythm Safari label in the US with help from Noel McCalla (vocals), Barbara Thompson (sax), Peter Sklair (bass) and Ian Hermann (drums) in October, McGuinness, Jones, Hugg, D'Abo and Vickers, together with Benny Gallagher, Graham Lyle, Hughie Flint, Tom Robinson, Dave Kelly and others now perform at McGuinness' 50th birthday bash at the Town & Country club, London. (Mann is touring Europe at the time.)

1994

Sept [10] While an earlier compilation, ***Ages Of Mann*** has debuted at its UK #23 peak on Jan [23] the previous year, followed by the June 1993 EMI release of the comprehensive ***Manfred Mann's Best Of The EMI Years*** (with Ascot issuing a similar package in the US), a further collection ***The Very Best Of Manfred Mann's Earth Band*** now makes UK #69 in its week of entry.

THE MANHATTAN TRANSFER

Tim Hauser (vocals); **Alan Paul** (vocals);
Janis Siegel (vocals); **Cheryl Bentyne** (vocals)

1972

Ex-Viscounts member Hauser (b. 1940, Troy, New York, NY), ex-Young Generation, a mid-'60s group on Leiber and Stoller's Red Bird label, the only remaining member of an earlier Manhattan Transfer formed in 1969 which included Gene Pistilli and recorded one jug-band album (which will be reissued in 1975 as ***Jukin'***) for Capitol Records having taken its name from a John Dos Passos novel set in the 1920s, assembles a new quartet with Laurel Massé (b. 1954), Paul (b. 1949, Newark, NJ) and Siegel (b. 1953, Brooklyn, NY) in New York, devoted to a tight vocal harmony style. Hauser has been in teenage doo-wop groups in New York, while Paul has been a child actor, played on Broadway in "Oliver", toured in "Grease", and featured in TV commercials. Siegel, a former member of Young Generation, and Massé have sung commercials music and session vocal work. A sound incorporating elements from, and material out of, several vocal-group genres, plus a visual style embodying '30s and '40s swing era kitsch, is first honed in New York's gay clubs and baths (the same circuit which recently launched Bette Midler's career). Mainstream cabaret work, developing the group's spectacularly-staged live performances, will lead to their signing to Atlantic Records in 1974.

1975

Jan [22] The group guests on Mary Tyler Moore TV special.
July Their debut album, ***The Manhattan Transfer***, co-produced by Hauser and label boss Ahmet Ertegun, reaches US #33, during a 38-week chart stay.
Aug [10] The group's music and comedy variety show "Manhattan Transfer" begins a four-week run on CBS-TV on Sunday evenings.
Nov Taken from the debut album, *Operator* reaches US #22, their only US chart single of the decade.

1976

Feb *Tuxedo Junction* reaches UK #24.
Oct ***Coming Out***, produced by Richard Perry, makes US #48.

1977

Feb [23-24] The group performs at London's New Victoria Theatre, during a UK visit.
Mar [12] Taken from ***Coming Out***, the group's revival of Art & Dotty Todd's 1958 US Top 10 hit *Chanson D'Amour*, sung in French, tops the UK chart for the first of three weeks (having dethroned another Perry production, Leo Sayer's *When I Need You*). It is also a major hit in France, and establishes the group's reputation throughout Europe.
Apr ***Coming Out*** makes UK #12, while ***Manhattan Transfer*** belatedly charts at UK #49.
June *Don't Let Go*, also from ***Coming Out***, climbs to UK #32.

1978

Mar ***Pastiche*** reaches US #66 and hits UK #10.
[13] They perform at the London Palladium.
Apr *Walk In Love*, from ***Pastiche***, reaches US #12.
[27] The group ends a UK tour at the Hippodrome, Birmingham, West Midlands.
June From the album, *On A Little Street In Singapore* makes UK #20.
Sept Double A-side extract from ***Pastiche***, a revival of the Supremes' *Where Did Our Love Go* and the French-sung *Je Voulais Te Dire (Que Je T'Attends)*, climbs to UK #40.
Dec Performance set ***Live***, recorded in Manchester, Gtr. Manchester, Bristol, Avon and London during the group's April/May tour, hits UK #4.

1979

Jan Again from ***Pastiche***, *Who What When Where Why* makes UK #49. Recently injured in a car accident, Massé leaves the group, and is replaced by Cheryl Bentyne (b. Jan. 17, 1954, Mount Vernon, WA).
Nov ***Extensions***, produced by Jay Graydon, and including *Birdland*, a vocal interpretation of Weather Report's tribute to Charlie Parker and a highlight of the group's stage act, makes UK #63. *Birdland* will also be used for an Akai TV commercial jingle.

1980

Jan ***Extensions*** peaks at US #55, with the group updating its sound and image from pure swing to a more contemporary slick chic.
June *Twilight Zone-Twilight Tone*, incorporating the instrumental riff from the old TV series theme, peaks at US #30 and UK #25.
Dec *Trickle Trickle* makes US #73, as **Downbeat** magazine names them the Best Vocal Group Of 1980 in its annual poll.

1981

Feb [25] The group wins the Best Jazz Fusion Performance Vocal Or Instrumental category for *Birdland* at the 23rd annual Grammy Awards.
Aug ***Mecca For Moderns*** reaches US #22, while their revival of the Ad Libs' 1965 US Top 10 hit *Boy From New York City* hits US #7, their biggest-selling US single.

1982

Jan Compilation, ***The Best Of The Manhattan Transfer***, peaks at US #103.
Feb [24] The group wins the Best Pop Performance By A Duo Or Group With Vocal for *Boy From New York City* and Best Jazz Vocal Performance By A Duo Or Group categories for the album track *Until I Met You (Corner Pocket)* at the 24th annual Grammy Awards.
June Their revival of *Route 66*, featured in Burt Reynolds film "Sharkey's Machine", makes US #78.

1983

Feb [23] The group once again scoops the Best Jazz Vocal Performance Duo Or Group category for *Route 66* at the 25th annual Grammy Awards.
Oct Disco-flavored club favorite, *Spice Of Life*, penned by Rod Temperton and Derek Bramble, makes US #40.
Dec ***Bodies And Souls***, produced by Richard Rudolph and including *Spice Of Life*, peaks at US #57, during a six-month chart stay.

1984

Feb *Spice Of Life* reaches UK #19, as ***Bodies And Souls*** makes UK #53.
[28] They again win the Best Jazz Vocal Performance Duo Or Group category, this time for *Why Not!* at the 26th annual Grammy awards.

1985

Feb The group's last chart single of the decade is *Baby Come Back To Me (The Morse Code Of Love)* at US #83. It is taken from the part-live, part-studio recorded ***Bop Doo-Wop***, which climbs to US #127.
Oct ***Vocalese***, featuring the lyrics of Jon Hendricks, makes US #74.

1986

Feb [25] ***Vocalese*** is named Best Jazz Vocal Performance Duo Or Group at the 28th annual Grammy Awards, a category they have now made their own.

1987

May The group guests on Bobby McFerrin's US #103 ***Spontaneous Inventions***.
June ***Live***, recorded in Tokyo, Japan, in 1986, peaks at US #187.
Oct [7] The RIAA certifies gold sales of ***Manhattan Transfer*** .

1989

Feb [22] With the latin-flavored album having made US #98 in January the previous year, ***Brasil*** is named Best Pop Vocal Performance By A Duo Or Group With Vocal at the 31st annual Grammy Awards.
May The Manhattan Transfer contributes *I Wanna Be Your Girl* to the newly released Richard Perry-produced ***Rock, Rhythm & Blues*** compilation.

1991

May Following the Manhattan Transfer's appearance on CBS-TV's "Sinatra 75 : The Best Is Yet To Come" broadcast on December 16th the previous year, the Alec Baldwin/Kim Basinger-starring movie soundtrack to "The Marrying Man", featuring solo cuts by Paul (*You're Driving Me Crazy (What Did I Do?)*) and Hauser (*Mama Look A Boo Boo*), is released.
Sept [21] Now signed to Columbia Records, the group's label debut, ***The Offbeat Of Avenues***, featuring musical guest Michael McDonald, bows at its US #179 peak.
Oct [14] The group sings on NBC-TV's "The Tonight Show".

1992

Feb [25] They win the Best Contemporary Jazz Performance category for *Sassy* from ***The Offbeat Of Avenues*** at the 34th annual Grammy Awards, held at Radio City Music Hall, New York.
June Bentyne releases her solo album, ***Something Cool***, on Columbia Records.
July [25-26] Manhattan Transfer performs at the Westbury Music Fair, Westbury, NY, during a US summer tour.
Oct [30] The group sings at London's Royal Festival Hall during its latest UK visit.
Dec [16] They guest on ABC-TV sitcom "Home Improvement".
[26] Festive set ***Christmas Album*** peaks at US #120.
[31] They end a month-long US tour with the first of three performances at Harvey's Resort Hotel, Stateline, NV. ***The Best Of Manhattan Transfer*** will be certified platinum by the RIAA the following November 30th.

1994

Aug [26] The group performs to a 7,035 sellout crowd at the Filene Center, Wolf Trap Farm Park Performing Arts Center, Vienna, VA, during its US summer tour with George Benson.
Dec [2] They sing at New York's Avery Fisher Hall, during a round of year-end US dates.

1995

Jan [30] Frankie Valli and the Manhattan Transfer present the Favorite Pop/Rock Female trophy at the 22nd annual American Music Awards.
Mar [11] Covering standards from 1959-1969, ***Tonin'***, featuring guest performances from Phil Collins, Chaka Khan, Bette Midler, Laura Nyro, Ben E. King, Valli, Felix Cavaliere and Smokey Robinson, among others, makes US #123.
May [15] The group performs at the first annual Musicians Assistance Program benefit concert, held at the House of Blues in Los Angeles, CA.
Sept [2] ***The Very Best Of The Manhattan Transfer*** charts for a week at US #157.

BARRY MANILOW

1961

Manilow (b. Barry Alan Pinkus, June 17, 1946, Brooklyn, New York, NY), raised by his mother and grandparents, having acquired a stepfather, Willie Murphy, and taken piano and accordian lessons from the age of seven, and having left Eastern District High School in Brooklyn where he was voted best musician, moves to Greenwich Village, marries and goes to work in the CBS-TV mailroom in Manhattan. He enters New York City College to study advertising, with the aim of becoming a television executive, but within a year moves to the New York College Of Music, which leads to a further two-year course at the Juilliard School of Music. Spending a short time as a film editor at CBS-TV in 1962, Manilow is asked by an off-Broadway producer to compose music arrangements for current projects including an original score for the off-Broadway show "The Drunkard". Divorced by 1967, Manilow is asked by CBS to be musical director on the show "Callback", a syndicated showcase for newcomers, which will occupy him through the end of the decade during which time he will also write dozens of TV and radio commercials.

1972

Mar Having spent two seasons working as one half of the duo Jeanne & Barry in cabaret at Upstairs At The Downstairs in New York, opening for Joan Rivers and playing piano for auditioning actors, Manilow is about to quit when a girl singer asks him to accompany her audition at the Continental Baths, a nightclub set up in the basement by a Turkish Bath establishment. She fails the audition, but Manilow is taken on as house pianist on Saturday nights. Two weeks later, young singer Bette Midler turns up for an audition which leads to his arranging and producing Midler's *Boogie Woogie Bugle Boy* single and its parent album ***The***

Divine Miss M. He also cuts his own four-cut demo, including *Could It Be Magic*, which he sells to Bell Records, on the condition that he will tour to promote a debut album.
Oct Manilow meets his subsequent long-term co-producer Ron Dante at a soft-drink jingle session for Shasta Cola with Melissa Manchester and Valerie Simpson.

1973

Midler asks Manilow to be her musical director on a US tour. Manilow, his debut album ***Barry Manilow*** already released by Bell, obliges, opening the second half of her show with three of his own songs.

1974

Apr While Midler takes a year's sabbatical, Manilow tours the US and, without a hit single, performs some of the material his audience may be familiar with including self-penned or performed commercials for companies including McDonalds, Kentucky Fried Chicken, Pepsi, Dr. Pepper and many others.

1975

Jan [18] Melodramatic ballad, *Mandy* (originally titled *Brandy* when its lyricist Scott English made US #91 with it in March 1972), firmly establishing Manilow's romantic lush love-song style, hits US #1 for a week.
[31] *Mandy* is certified gold by the RIAA.
Feb ***Barry Manilow II***, originally issued on Bell in 1973, but now released on Arista Records (with whom he will remain into the '90s), hits US #9.
Mar *Mandy* makes UK #11, Manilow's UK chart debut.
Apr *It's A Miracle*, written about his experiences on tour with Midler, reaches US #12.
Aug *Could It Be Magic*, based on Chopin's "Prelude In C Minor", hits US #6.
Oct His revitalized debut album, ***Barry Manilow I***, now reaches US #28.
Dec [31] Manilow plays a New Year's Eve show at New York's Beacon Theatre.

1976

Jan [6] Still-climbing *I Write The Songs* is certified gold by the RIAA.
[17] *I Write The Songs*, written by the Beach Boys' Bruce Johnston, tops the US chart, for a week. Arista president Clive Davis had heard David Cassidy's version during a UK visit and suggested it to Manilow.
Feb ***Tryin' To Get The Feelin'***, again co-produced with Dante, hits US #5, and will become Manilow's longest charted US album at 87 weeks.
May Title cut ballad, *Tryin' To Get The Feelin'*, hits US #10.
July [30] Manilow begins an eight-month 98-city US tour.
Oct *This One's For You* makes US #29.
[22] ***Barry Manilow I*** is certified gold by the RIAA.
Dec [21] "Barry Manilow On Broadway" opens for a two-week sold-out season at New York's Uris Theatre, set to end on January 2nd. The show will receive a special Tony award.

1977

Feb *Weekend In New England*, penned by Randy Edelman, hits US #10.
[19] *I Write The Songs* wins Song Of The Year at the 19th annual Grammy Awards.
Mar [2] ABC-TV airs "The Barry Manilow Special".
Apr [13] Manilow ends another US tour at the MGM Grand Hotel, Las Vegas, NV as ***This One's For You*** hits US #6.
July [16] Eventually selling over three million domestic copies, ***Barry Manilow Live***, recorded at the Uris Theatre, hits US #1 and, as his only US chart-topper, confirms that his greatest and most enduring appeal will lie in the live arena. He currently has five albums on the chart and by the year's end will have sold seven million albums in a year in US.
[23] Richard Kerr/Will Jennings-penned ballad, *Looks Like We Made It*, becomes his third US chart-topper.
Sept [7] *Looks Like We Made It* is certified gold by the RIAA.
[11] "The Barry Manilow Special" wins an Emmy Award in the Comedy, Variety Or Music Special category.
Nov *Daybreak* reaches US #23.

1978

Jan [16] He wins the Favorite Male Artist, Pop/Rock category at the fifth annual American Music Awards, held at the Civic Auditorium, Santa Monica, CA.
Feb ***Even Now*** enters the US chart set to hit #3.
[24] ABC-TV airs "The Second Barry Manilow Special" from the Pantages Theater, Hollywood, CA, with guest Ray Charles.
Apr [6] Still-climbing *Can't Smile Without You* is certified gold by the RIAA.
May Jaunty *Can't Smile Without You*, written by UK team Chris Arnold, David Martin and Geoff Morrow, hits US #3 and makes UK #43.
July *Even Now*, co-penned by Manilow with Martin Panzer, reaches US #19.
[29] He performs at the Forest Hills Tennis Stadium, New York.
Aug Uptempo party-popping *Copacabana (At The Copa)*, from the Chevy Chase/Goldie Hawn film "Foul Play", hits US #8 and #42 in the UK, where it is paired as a double A-side with *Somewhere In The Night*.
Sept [7] *Copacabana (At The Copa)* is certified gold by the RIAA.
Oct He has his first album success in Britain with ***Even Now*** reaching #12.
[7] Manilow begins a European tour with a concert at London's Royal Albert Hall, followed by four dates at the London Palladium (9-12th).
Nov *Ready To Take A Chance Again*, also from "Foul Play" and an Academy Award nominee, reaches US #15.
[27] ***Greatest Hits*** is certified platinum by the RIAA.

1979

Jan *Could It Be Magic* belatedly reaches UK #25.
[12] He nabs the Favorite Male Artist, Pop/Rock trophy at the sixth annual American Music Awards held at the Santa Monica Civic Auditorium.
Feb *Somewhere In The Night*, written by Richard Kerr and Will Jennings, hits US #9.
[15] Manilow wins the Best Pop Vocal Performance, Male category for *Copacabana (At The Copa)* at the 21st annual Grammy Awards.
Mar Hits collection, ***Manilow Magic***, hits UK #3 during a 151-week chart stay, while a double compilation album, ***Greatest Hits***, hits US #7.
Apr Ray Stevens makes US #49 with *I Need Your Help Barry Manilow*, an affectionate send-up of Manilow's schmaltzy style.
May [23] ABC-TV broadcasts "The Third Barry Manilow Special".
June [12, 19] BBC2-TV airs two Manilow specials.
Nov *Ships* hits US #9, as its parent album ***One Voice*** peaks at UK #18.

1980

Jan [18] He wins the Favorite Male Artist, Pop/Rock category for the third consecutive year at the seventh annual American Music Awards, held at the ABC-TV Studios, Hollywood, CA.
[28] ***One Voice*** is certified platinum by the RIAA.
Feb *When I Wanted You* reaches US #20 taken from ***One Voice*** which hits US #9. (Its title cut will become a popular live number as successive audiences learn to light candles during its opening bars. Manilow will also contribute the song as the national theme for United Way of America.)
May *I Don't Want To Walk Without You* reaches US #36.
Aug [22] Manilow receives a star on the Hollywood Walk of Fame.
Oct He writes and performs *We Still Have Time* for the Jack Lemmon film "Tribute".
Nov *Lonely Together* reaches UK #21.

1981

Jan *I Made It Through The Rain* hits US #10, as its parent album, ***Barry***, reaches US #15 and hits UK #5. Manilow embarks on "In The Round World Tour".
Feb *I Made It Through The Rain* makes UK #37.
[4] ***Barry*** becomes Manilow's sixth consecutive platinum album.
Apr *Lonely Together* breaks a run of 18 consecutive Top 40 hits, stopping at US #45. The boxed album, ***Gift Set***, makes UK #62.
May Uptempo *Bermuda Triangle* reaches UK #15.
Oct His revival of the Four Seasons' *Let's Hang On* makes UK #12, as its parent album, ***If I Should Love Again***, the first solely produced by Manilow, hits UK #5.
Nov *The Old Songs* reaches US #15, as the parent album, ***If I Should Love Again***, makes US #14.
[24] ***If I Should Love Again*** is certified gold by the RIAA.
Dec *The Old Songs* peaks at UK #48.

1982

Jan Manilow sells out five nights at London's Royal Albert Hall at the start of a 15-date UK tour. Manchester councillors will threaten a High Court injunction against the singer during his current UK tour if he is unable to restrain his fans from using lighters or candles during his Apollo Theatre shows. The crowd-swaying flame-lighting ritual has become a popular audience habit at Manilow concerts.
Feb *Somewhere Down The Road* reaches US #21, as *If I Should Love Again* peaks at UK #66. ***Greatest Hits*** makes US #147.
Apr [19, 26] BBC-TV airs two "Barry In Britain" TV specials.
May [1] ***Barry Live In Britain*** tops the UK chart for a week, while *Stay*, taken from the album, heads to UK #23. *Let's Hang On* makes US #32.
Sept *Oh Julie!* reaches US #38.
Oct *Oh Julie!* stops at US #69.
[6] Manilow begins his "Around The World In 80 Dates" tour, including 95 sellout dates in 52 US cities and first visits to Japan and Australia.
Nov *I Wanna Do It With You* hits UK #8, as its parent album, ***I Wanna Do It With You***, hits UK #7.
Dec *I'm Gonna Sit Right Down And Write Myself A Letter* peaks at UK #36.
[31] Manilow and Bette Midler perform as Father Time and Baby New Year at a New Year's Eve celebration at the Universal Amphitheatre, Universal City, CA.

1983

Jan [15] *Memory*, from the musical "Cats", reaches US #39, and ***Here Comes The Night*** makes US #32.
[17] ***Here Comes The Night*** is certified gold by the RIAA.
May US TV cable web Showtime airs "Barry Manilow : The Concert At Blenheim Palace".
June *Some Kind Of Friend* makes UK #48.
Aug [27] Manilow embarks on the UK leg of "Around The World" tour, performing before 40,000 housewives and fans at an outdoor concert at Blenheim Palace, Oxon.
Sept *You're Looking Hot Tonight* makes UK #47.
Oct Further retrospective, ***A Touch More Magic***, hits UK #10.
[6] His world tour ends with a gala charity concert for the Royal College Of Music and the British Fund for World Jewish Relief at London's Royal Albert Hall in the presence of H.R.H. the Prince and Princess of Wales.

1984

Jan *Read 'Em And Weep*, written and produced by Jim Steinman (and originally recorded by Meat Loaf), reaches US #18 and UK #17 as its parent album, ***Barry Manilow/Greatest Hits, Volume II*** makes US #30.
[22] Manilow sings the American national anthem before "Super Bowl XVIII" between the Los Angeles Raiders and the Washington Redskins, at Tampa Stadium, Tampa, FL.
Dec Jazz-tinged ***2.00 AM Paradise Café***, with guests Sarah Vaughan, Mel Tormé and Gerry Mulligan, makes UK #28.

1985

Jan ***2.00 AM Paradise Café*** reaches US #28.
[14] ***2.00 AM Paradise Café*** is certified gold by the RIAA.
July Compilation album, ***The Manilow Collection - 20 Classic Hits***, reaches US #100. (Manilow has been quoted as saying: "I wanted to write music that would be played in elevators for ever and ever. When you get played in elevators, you know you've made it.")
Nov ***Manilow*** climbs to US #42 and UK #40.

1986

Jan [4-6] Manilow plays three sellout dates at Wembley, Middx., during a UK tour.
July [26] *I'm Your Man* peaks at US #86.
He releases his first Spanish-language album, ***Barry Manilow, Grandes Exitos En Espanol***.

1987

Sept [2] The RIAA certifies gold sales of ***The Manilow Collection - 20 Classic Hits***, platinum sales of ***Barry Manilow II***, and multi-platinum sales of ***Barry Manilow Live*** (three million), ***Even Now*** (three million), ***Greatest Hits*** (three million), ***This One's For You*** (two million) and ***Tryin' To Get The Feeling*** (two million).
Nov Having had a tumor on his tongue removed by surgery, Manilow's TV special "Big Fun On Swing Street" with Kid Creole, Gerry Mulligan, Stanley Clarke and Phyllis Hyman, and produced by Steve Binder, airs.
[25] Manilow begins his "Big Fun Tour De Force" tour in Milwaukee, WI.

1988

Feb His second jazz-laced effort, ***Swing Street***, featuring Kid Creole, Stan Getz, Phyllis Hyman and Diane Schuur, reaches US #70 and UK #81.
Nov [11] Manilow continues his world tour with the European leg in Mainz, Germany. A fan in East Germany writes to Manilow: "Please tell me when you're coming to West Germany. I plan to steal a hot-air balloon and sail over the Berlin Wall."
[27] Manilow takes part in the fifth anniversary, and final, edition of ITV's variety show "Live From The Palladium", before playing a week of sellout concerts at London's Alexandra Palace.

1989

Apr [18] "Barry Manilow At The Gershwin" opens on Broadway running until June 10th, grossing $3,177,150, during a hiatus from his world tour.
May ***Songs To Make The Whole World Sing*** reaches UK #20, as the extracted *Please Don't Be Scared* makes UK #35, and Manilow returns for another British tour.
June Released in the US as ***Barry Manilow***, the album peaks at US #64.
Dec [26-31] Manilow plays six sellout dates at the Universal Amphitheatre, during a current US tour, grossing $1,208,425.

1990

Mar Recorded on December 2nd-3rd, 1989, ***Live On Broadway*** makes UK #19.
[17] Manilow takes part in Arista Records' 15th Anniversary at the "That's What Friends Are For" Radio City Music Hall concert, raising more than $2 million, the proceeds going to Gay Men's Health Crisis and other AIDS organizations. The show will air on CBS-TV on April 17th.
June [8] Manilow guests on NBC-TV's "The Tonight Show".
[30] ***Live On Broadway*** makes a one week US chart visit at #196, while the UK-issued comprehensive double-album retrospective, ***The Songs 1975-1990***, reaches UK #13.
Sept [14] His "Live On Broadway" video is certified platinum by the RIAA.
Dec [12] Still-climbing ***Because It's Christmas*** is confirmed gold by the RIAA.
[22] ***Because It's Christmas***, featuring duets with K.T. Oslin (*Baby, It's Cold Outside*) and Exposé (*Jingle Bells*), makes US #40.

1991

May [29] He receives the Hitmaker Award at the 22nd annual Songwriters Hall of Fame Induction Ceremony & Awards Dinner, held at the New York Hilton.
June Manilow produces a Nancy Wilson album of Manilow music set to Johnny Mercer lyrics at Rumbo Studios, Los Angeles.
Sept [12] A US tour begins in San Diego, CA.
[25-28] Manilow headlines the re-opening of the Madison Square Garden Felt Forum, now known as The Paramount.
Oct [12] ***Showstoppers***, a collection of Broadway show tunes, debuts at its US #68 peak.
[24-26] Manilow plays sellout dates at Wembley Arena, Wembley, grossing £484,044, during his current UK tour.
Nov [2] ***Showstoppers*** bows at its UK #53 peak. Manilow is also featured on the newly released ***The Christmas Album ... A Gift Of Hope***, a benefit album produced by the San Diego Children's Hospital.
[15-17] He plays sellout dates at the Fox Theatre, St Louis, MO, during his latest US dates.
Dec [23] "Because It's Christmas" video is certified gold by the RIAA.
[31] Manilow guests on "Dick Clark's New Year's Rockin' Eve '92" on ABC-TV.

1992

Feb [19] He appears in front of the House Intellectual Property Subcommittee in Washington, DC, testifying in favor of record industry royalties from sales of digital recorders and blank tapes.
[27] Manilow emcees and sings *I Made It Thru The Rain* at Elizabeth Taylor's 60th birthday party at Disneyland, Anaheim, CA.
June [12] He sings a hits medley and a new song, *Enter Clive*, at the New York Friars Club annual testimonial dinner honoring Arista boss Clive Davis as Man Of The Year, at the Waldorf Astoria Hotel.
[14] Manilow participates in the "All-Star Fiesta At Ford's", taped at the Ford Theatre, Washington. (ABC-TV will air the show on July 11th.)
Nov [7-8] He performs before 94,000 people at the ULTRA Football Stadium, Manila in the Philippines, during a seven-date visit.
Dec [7] Manilow participates in the "Royal Variety Performance" at London's Dominion Theatre in the presence of their Royal Highnesses The Prince and Princess of Wales. The show will air on BBC1-TV on the 12th. Arista provides the perfect Christmas gift for Manilow's loyal fans, releasing the career-retrospective boxed set, ***The Complete Collection And Then Some ...***.

1993

Jan [2] He takes part in NBC-TV's "Dame Edna's Hollywood Special", as ***The Complete Collection And Then Some ...*** charts for a week at US #182.
Mar [24-25] Manilow embarks on a 17-date UK tour at the National Exhibition Centre, Birmingham, West Midlands, set to end on April 14th at the SE&CC, Glasgow, Scotland.
Apr [3] ***Hidden Treasures*** debuts at its UK #36 peak.
[4] Manilow guests on BBC2-TV's "The O Zone".
[10] *Copacabana (At The Copa) (1993 Remixes)* bows at its UK #22 peak.
May [17] He plays himself on CBS-TV's "Murphy Brown".
June [14] Manilow guests on "The Tonight Show".
[17] 30-city "Greatest Hits And Then Some" tour opens in Anaheim, CA, set to end August 8th in Houston, TX.
Sept [4] ABC-TV airs the two-hour "In A New Light '93" special, "A Beacon In The War Against AIDS", including Manilow's performance of *I Am Your Child*.
Nov [17] ***Greatest Hits Volume II*** is certified gold by the RIAA.
[27] Revised version *Could It Be Magic 1993* reaches UK #36.
Dec [4] Latest compilation, ***The Platinum Collection*** makes UK #37.
[11] "Barry Manilow : The Best Of Me" airs on PBS TV.
[23] Manilow performs at the Tucson Community Center Arena, Tucson Convention Center, Tucson, AZ, during a current round of US dates.

1994

Jan [15] He cancels a headline appearance at the Inaugural gala for New Jersey Governor-Elect Christie Whitman at the Atlantic City Convention Center, saying he thought the show was part of the "Ethnic Pride & Heritage Festival" and that he did not want to appear to be endorsing the Republican Governor. Paul Anka will take his place.
[17] Manilow holds auditions in London for a forthcoming stage musical version of "Copacabana". (When the show opens in June, the **Daily Express** will describe it as a "nerve-shattering, stunningly bad experience", while **Today** writes this "witless musical is a new Mani-low".)
Feb He files suit in Orange County Superior Court against Los Angeles radio station KBIG, seeking $13 million in damages and $15 million in punitive damages, charging that the station's TV ads pledging not to play any of his songs is causing irreparable damage to his reputation.
Mar [30] Manilow embarks on a European tour at the Musikhalle in Hamburg, Germany.
May [7] He headlines the 1994 Rita Hayworth Gala to benefit the Alzheimer's Association at the Chicago Hilton & Towers Hotel.
[17] Manilow is joined onstage by Dame Edna Everage while performing in Sydney, Australia.
Aug [6] *Let Me Be Your Wings*, with Debra Byrd, charts for a week at UK #73.
[12] Manilow begins a month-long US tour at the Wisconsin State Fair Grandstand in West Allis, WI, set to end on September 18th at the Starlight Theatre, Kansas City, MO.
Sept [8] He cancels his remaining shows at the State Theatre, Cleveland, OH, following the death of his mother at age 70.
Oct [10] Manilow guests on CBS-TV's "Late Show With David Letterman".
Nov [3] He embarks on a seven-date UK tour, grossing a total of £1,253,010, at the Scottish Exhibition & Conference Centre, Glasgow.
[19] Big-band based ***Singin' With The Big Bands*** makes UK #54.
[22] Manilow makes a return visit to "The Tonight Show".
Dec [13] Still-climbing ***Singin' With The Big Bands*** is certified gold by the RIAA.
[14] Manilow's star is unveiled in an augural ceremony with 15 other artists at the "Sidewalk of the Stars" outside New York's Radio City Music Hall.
[27] He plays a sellout date at the Symphony Hall, San Diego, CA.
[31] ***Singin' With The Big Bands*** makes US #59.

1995

Apr [10] Manilow guests on the "Late Show With David Letterman".
June [8-9] Following a series of US dates in May, Manilow now plays to two sellout crowds of 28,525 at the National Auditorium, Mexico City, Mexico, grossing 4,938,382 pesos.
Aug [4] He performs a sellout show at the I.C Light Amphitheatre, Pittsburgh, PA, at the beginning of another series of North American dates.
Nov [22, 24-25] Manilow plays his final dates of 1995 at the Sunrise Musical Theatre, Sunrise, FL.

1996

Feb [20] Involved in a five-car pile-up on Interstate 10 in Los Angeles, Manilow signs autographs for fans and police while waiting for his Range Rover to be towed.
Apr [5-6] He begins a nine-date UK tour at the Wembley Arena, set to end on the 17th-18th at the National Exhibition Centre, Birmingham.

THE MARCELS

Cornelius "Nini" Harp (lead vocals, guitar); **Ronald "Bingo" Mundy** (first tenor vocal); **Gene Bricker** (second tenor vocal); **Dick Knauss** (baritone vocal); **Fred Johnson** (bass vocal)

1961

Feb The multi-racial vocal quintet, three black and two white singers, with a name taken from a hairstyle, is based in Pittsburgh, PA, where its club act consists mainly of cover versions of R&B and doo-wop group oldies. It disbands and re-forms more than once before manager Julius Kruspir sends a sampler tape of the group's vocal efforts to producer Stu Phillips at New York, NY-based Colpix Records. Phillips now calls them in for an after-hours recording session and after cutting three tracks, they experiment with the Rodgers and Hart oldie *Blue Moon* (which has become a standard in 1935 when three different versions all hit the US top ten), turning in an outrageous version which kicks the tempo up and buries the original melody with bass singer Johnson performing an exaggerated parody of the traditional bass doo-wop role. This proves to be the gimmick which hooks first radio DJs and then record buyers. Murray The K, at station WINS in New York, plays a borrowed advance tape 26 times in one show, creating overnight demand in the city.

Apr [3] *Blue Moon* tops the US chart for the first of three weeks, displacing Elvis Presley's *Surrender*, and will become a US million seller. It also hits US R&B #1 for two weeks.

May [4] Licensed by Pye International Records, *Blue Moon* also tops the UK survey, despite criticism from panelists on BBC-TV's "Juke Box Jury" and in much of the music press.

June A straighter, gimmick-free revival of George Gershwin's *Summertime* peaks at US #78 and UK #46. The group's two white vocalists (Bricker and Knauss) leave, and are replaced by Walt Maddox and Fred Johnson's brother Allen while their next single, a revamp of another oldie, *You Are My Sunshine*, is released.

Dec Their revival of Ted Weems' 1947 million seller, *Heartaches*, given the *Blue Moon* treatment, hits US #7. The group appears alongside Chubby Checker and Dion in the low-budget twist-craze exploitation movie "Twist Around The Clock", singing *Merry Twistmas*.

1962

Feb *My Melancholy Baby* (on which the Marcels parody themselves, starting with a *Blue Moon* bass man intro, halting proceedings with a hammy "oh no, not that ole thing again - sing *Melancholy Baby*", and then doing just that, but in *Blue Moon* style), makes US #58. The gimmick approach is wearing thin, and it will be the group's last hit. Mundy leaves, followed by Harp, as they encounter managerial problems. A final Colpix single, *I Wanna Be The Leader*, has the once-again highlighted bass vocalist bewailing his restriction to singing "ba-ba-ba's" - he wants to be lead vocalist and handle more sophisticated lyrics.

1963

Apr After the the group has cut its final single, *How Deep Is The Ocean*, for the Kyra label, and disbanded shortly thereafter, Johnny Cymbal pays tribute to the Marcels' sound on his *Mr. Bass Man*, which reaches US #16 and UK #24.

1993

While the five original Marcels have reunited on several occasions in the '70s for Ralph Nader's "Rock'n'Roll Revival" shows and are still active on the nostalgia circuit, and with *Blue Moon* remaining a perennial favorite oldie, being used, for example, over the closing credits of John Landis' 1980 movie, "An American Werewolf In London", Rhino Records brings their career highlights to CD with the US issue of ***The Best Of The Marcels***. Allen Johnson dies on September 28, 1995.

MARILLION

Fish (vocals); **Steve Rothery** (guitar); **Mark Kelly** (keyboards); **Peter Trewavas** (bass); **Ian Mosley** (drums)

1979

Aug Formative unit Silmarillion, named after the novel by J.R.R. Tolkien, has been founded in Aylesbury, Bucks., by Doug Irvine (bass) and Mick Pointer (b. July 22, 1956) (drums) as an instrumental group, playing a one-hour set at the Hanborough tavern in Southall, Middx. in December 1978. Rothery (b. Nov. 25, 1959, Brampton, Yorks.), now answering a music paper ad, is chosen from 30 applicants and joins the band on guitar. Brian Jelliman is added on keyboards in October as the group shortens its name to Marillion. Irvine quits in November 1980 and, while the group advertises for a bassist/vocalist, it records instrumental *The Web* at Leyland Studio in Buckingham, Bucks., and sends the tape to two musicians from Scotland, who had been in touch with them.

1981

Jan [2] Fish (b. Derek Dick, Apr. 25, 1958, Dalkeith, Lothian, Scotland) and bassist Diz Minnitt, both members of Nottingham band the Stone Dome, arrive, with lyrics to *The Web*, to audition. Fish, the son of a garage proprietor, having left school to do a four-year degree course with the Forestry Commission in Cumbria, has sung with small bands in Scotland. His nickname has stuck when a landlady accuses him of wallowing in the bath like a fish.

Mar [14] The new line-up debuts at the Red Lion pub, Bicester, Oxon.

July Marillion records a three-track demo, comprising *Garden Party*, *He Knows You Know* and *Charting The Single* at Roxon Studio, Oxon, which is later sold at gigs.

Aug The band supports Spirit at local venue, the Friars, Aylesbury.

Nov Kelly (b. Apr. 9, 1961, Dublin, Eire), playing with Romford, Essex band Chemical Alice, replaces Jelliman.

1982

Jan [25] Marillion plays its first headlining gig at London's Marquee club.

Feb The group records a session for BBC Radio 1's Tommy Vance's "The Friday Rock Show". A Marillion fan club called "The Web" is established.

Mar Minnitt quits and is replaced by Trewavas (b. Jan. 15, 1959, Middlesborough, Cleveland) from local group the Metros.

May Marillion begins a 25-date, six-week tour of Scotland.

July The group headlines at the Friars, Aylesbury, the first unsigned band to do so.

Aug During constant UK gigging, the band takes part in the Theakston and Reading festivals, and opens for Jethro Tull at the "Nostell Priory Festival".

Sept Marillion signs a worldwide contract with EMI Records.

Nov Its debut single, *Market Square Heroes*, peaks at UK #60.

Dec Marillion plays three sellout dates at London's Marquee.

1983

Feb *He Knows You Know* reaches UK #35. The readers of UK music paper **Sounds** vote Marillion Best New Band Of 1982.

Mar Confirming their status as the leading UK progressive rock-reviving act, ***Script For A Jester's Tear***, recorded at London's Marquee studios in December with producer Nick Tauber, hits UK #7, its lyrics all penned by Fish, who has now adopted a central live role, often appearing in heavily made-up stage guises, clearly influenced vocally and visually by Peter Gabriel's early presence in Genesis.

[15] Marillion begins a 29-date UK tour, supported by Peter Hammill, at Norwich University, Norwich, Norfolk, set to end on April 18th with a sellout date at London's Hammersmith Odeon.

Apr *Market Square Heroes* re-enters at UK #53. The group sacks Pointer, replacing him with former Camel drummer Andy Ward.

May [20] The group makes its BBC-TV debut on "The Old Grey Whistle Test".

June *Garden Party* reaches UK #16, spurred by Marillion's first appearance on BBC1-TV's "Top Of The Pops".

[17] The group headlines the "Glastonbury Festival", Glastonbury, Somerset.

July Marillion embarks on a five-week tour of North America, during which, ***Script For A Jester's Tear***, released through Capitol Records, peaks at US #175. The tour is curtailed when Ward leaves the band.

Aug The band appears at the "Reading Festival" for the second year, with John Marter temporarily sitting in on drums.

Sept Marillion opens for Rush for five nights at New York's Radio City Music Hall.

Oct Video "Recital Of The Script", filmed at an April 18th Hammersmith Odeon concert, is released. Jonathan Mover is temporarily recruited as drummer.

Nov The group starts work on its new album at Manor Studios, Oxon., with permanent new drummer Mosley (b. June 16, 1953, Paddington, London), who has studied at the Guildhall School of Music, before playing with Curved Air, the Gordon Giltrap Band and Steve Hackett and as a member of the orchestras for both "Hair" and "Jesus Christ Superstar" in London's West End.

Dec Taking a break from recording, Marillion plays a five-date "Farewell To '83" tour and invites Mosley to join the band full time.

1984

Feb *Punch And Judy* reaches UK #29.

Mar ***Fugazi***, again produced by Tauber, hits UK #5 while the video package "Grendel And The Web" is released.

Apr The group begins a 24-date sell-out tour of Britain before touring Europe and North America.

May *Assassing* reaches UK #22.

July [21] Marillion plays at the Milton Keynes Bowl, Milton Keynes, Bucks., on a bill with Status Quo, Nazareth and Jason & the Scorchers.

Aug The band tours Europe, playing a series of festivals in West Germany, returning to the UK to headline the final day of the "Nostell Priory Festival".

Nov Budget-priced live album, ***Real To Reel***, recorded in Leicester, Leics., and Montreal, PQ, Canada, hits UK #8, released to counter the many bootlegs available and in response to requests from Marillion's fan club "The Web".

[3] Marillion performs at the Royal Court Theatre, Liverpool, Merseyside, at the start of 14-date UK "Real To Reel" tour, set to end on December 22nd at the familiar Friars club, Aylesbury.

1985

Mar The group begins work on its new album at Hansa Studios in Berlin, West Germany, with producer Chris Kimsey.

May [25] Marillion starts a European tour.

June Ballad, *Kayleigh*, hits UK #2, behind the Crowd's charity chart-topper, *You'll Never Walk Alone*

[29] Its parent album, ***Misplaced Childhood***, recorded in West Germany and the last of a trilogy of concept albums, enters the UK chart at #1.

Aug [17] The group plays the Z.Z. Top-headlined "Monsters Of Rock Festival" at Castle Donington, Leics.

Sept *Lavender* hits UK #5, while Fish loses his voice, causing the cancellation of a 23-date UK tour.

Oct *Kayleigh* peaks at US #74.

Nov *Heart Of Lothian* reaches UK #29, as the group postpones its US tour after Fish is advised to rest his vocal chords, while ***Misplaced Childhood*** makes US #47.

1986

Jan [8-10] The band plays three nights at London's

Hammersmith Odeon, at the start of a month-long UK tour, before beginning a three-month trek of North America, promoting ***Brief Encounter***, a mini-album of live tracks and B-sides, which makes US #67.
Feb [6] The group appears at benefit gig at the Hammersmith Odeon, with the proceeds going to Pete Townshend's Double-O project for drug rehabilitation.
[9] Marillion takes part in the "Colombian Volcano Appeal Concert" at London's Royal Albert Hall, with Annie Lennox, Chrissie Hynde, David Gilmour, Pete Townshend, the Communards and Working Week, before embarking on a three-month US tour.
June Promo clips package, "1982-1986 The Videos", featuring seven of the band's hits and a B-side, *Lady Nina*, is released.
[28] Marillion plays the "Welcome To The Garden Party" at Milton Keynes Bowl.
Oct Fish and Tony Banks, from Genesis, team for *Shortcut To Somewhere*, which makes UK #75.
Dec The band ends the year with a short series of sellout Christmas shows.

1987

May *Incommunicado* hits UK #6.
June Its parent album, ***Clutching At Straws***, hits UK #2, as the band sets off on a nine-month world tour which will include an appearance at the TV special "Ibiza '92" at the Ku Club, Ibiza.
July *Sugar Mice* makes UK #22, while ***Clutching At Straws*** peaks at US #103.
Sept [18] Marillion begins a US tour.
Nov *Warm Wet Circles* reaches UK #22 as the performance video "Live At Loreley" is released.

1988

July ***B-Sides Themselves***, a CD-only collection of non-album material, makes UK #64, while the band meets in Scotland to discuss Fish's increasing disagreement over Marillion's musical direction.
Sept Marillion and Fish announce they are to split.
Nov *Freaks (Live)* reaches UK #24.
Dec ***The Thieving Magpie***, recorded during their 1984 "Fugazi" and 1987 "Clutching At Straws" tours and named after Rossini's "La Gaza Ladra", with which they open their live shows, reaches UK #25.

1989

Jan With Marillion's new album half finished and several auditioned singers proving unsuitable, the band's management receives a tape sent by Steve Hogarth's publishers.
Apr [1] Hogarth, ex-Europeans and How We Live, officially replaces Fish as Marillion's lead singer.
Sept *Hooks In You*, Hogarth's debut with the band, makes UK #30.
Oct ***Season's End***, with lyrics mostly written by Hogarth and John Helmer, hits UK #7 as Marillion embarks on a tour of Europe. Fish's debut solo single, *State Of Mind*, makes UK #32. (His subsequent chart action will be: 1990's *Big Wedge* (UK #25, 1990), ***Vigil In A Wilderness Of Mirrors*** (UK #5, February, his first and only solo album for EMI), *A Gentleman's Excuse Me* (UK #30, March), 1991's *Internal Exile*, his debut for Polydor Records (UK #37, September), ***Internal Exile*** (UK #21, November), 1992's *Credo* (UK #38, January), his cover of Thunderclap Newman's *Something In The Air* (UK #51, June), 1993's #46 debut-peaking ***Songs From The Mirror*** (January), 1994's *Lady Let It Lie* (UK #46, April), *Fortunes Of War* (UK #67, October) and ***Suits*** (UK #18, June), and 1995's *Just Good Friends*, with Sam Brown (UK #63, August), ***Yang*** (UK #52, September) and ***Yin*** (UK #58, September).)
Dec Extracted from ***Season's End***, *Uninvited Guest* peaks at UK #53.
[3] Marillion begins a 12-date UK tour at City Hall, Newcastle, Tyne & Wear, set to end on the 18th at the Hammersmith Odeon.

1990

Apr [14] *Easter* makes UK #34.
July [12] Marillion performs at the Wembley Arena, Wembley, Middx.
Dec [18] The group begins a short five-date Christmas tour at Rock City, Nottingham, Notts., ending on the 22nd at London's Town & Country club.

1991

June [15] *Cover My Eyes (Pain And Heaven)* reaches UK #34.
July [6] Produced by Chris Neil, ***Holidays In Eden*** debuts at its UK #7 peak.
[30] The group plays at the Hammersmith Odeon.
Aug [17] *No One Can* reaches UK #33.
Sept [17] The band embarks on an 11-date UK tour in Liverpool, set to close on the 30th, again at the Hammersmith Odeon.
Oct [5] *Dry Land* bows at its UK #34 peak.

1992

Apr [14] The group plays a sellout date at the Variety Arts Center, Los Angeles, CA, during its current North American tour.
May [23] *Sympathy* reaches UK #17.
June [20] Marillion hits-retrospective, ***A Singles Collection 1982-1992***, bows at its UK #27 peak.
Aug [1] *No One Can* makes UK #26.
Sept [5] The group plays a one-off date at the Wembley Arena, to celebrate the tenth anniversary of its signing with EMI.
[18-19] Marillion embarks on an eight-date South American tour in Sao Paolo, Brazil, set to end on October 1st in Caracas, Venezuela.

1994

Feb [19] Recorded at the Chateau de Marouatte in France and co-produced with Dave Meegan, ***Brave*** hits UK #10 in its week of entry.
[22] The group begins the nine-date UK leg of its "The Brave Tour" at St. David's Hall, Cardiff, South Glamorgan, Wales, set to end on March 4th-5th at London's Kentish Town Forum, before embarking on the European leg on March 15th at the Aladin in Bremen, Germany.
Mar [26] *The Hollow Man* debuts at its UK #30 peak.
May [8] They begin another short UK "Brave Tour" at the Civic Hall, Guildford, Surrey, a nine-date trek set to end on the 18th at Labatt's Hammersmith Apollo.
[14] *Alone Again In The Lap Of Luxury* makes UK #53.
Sept [2] Following a tour of North America, Marillion now plays a sellout show at the National Auditorium, Mexico City, Mexico.

1995

June [10] *Beautiful* enters at its UK #29 high.
July [8] Once again co-helmed with Meegan, ***Afraid Of Sunlight***, including several lyrical references to the late Kurt Cobain, reaches UK #16 in its week of entry.

1996

Apr [20] ***Made Again*** debuts at its UK #37 peak.

BOB MARLEY & THE WAILERS

Bob Marley (vocals, guitar); **Peter Tosh** (vocals, guitar); **Bunny Wailer** (vocals, percussion); **Carlton Barrett** (drums); **Aston "Family Man" Barrett** (bass)

1961

Marley (b. Robert Nesta Marley, Feb. 6, (though his passport date will indicate: Apr. 6), 1945, Nine Miles, Rhoden Hall, St. Ann's, Jamaica), the son of English army captain Norval Sinclair Marley from Liverpool, Lancs. who is a superintendent for the Crown lands, and Jamaican Cedella Booker, comes to the attention of Kingston, Jamaica, label owner and producer Leslie Kong and records the original pop song *Judge Not (Unless You Judge Yourself)* for Kong's Beverley label, credited to Bob Morley, followed by *One Cup Of Coffee*. Forming the Wailin' Wailers (as Marley will later state "because we started out crying") in 1964 with childhood friends from the Trenchtown ghetto of West Kingston, Tosh (b. Winston Hubert McIntosh, Oct. 19, 1944, Church Lincoln, Westmoreland, Jamaica), Bunny Livingston (soon known as Bunny Wailer, b. Neville O'Riley, Apr. 10, 1947, Kingston), Junior Braithwaite, Cherry Smith and Beverley Kelso, the group will begin a prolific four-year recording relationship with top Kingston producer Clement Seymour (Sir Coxsone) Dodd, owner of the Studio One label.

1965

Feb The Wailin' Wailers' first Studio One single, *Simmer Down*, is a big Jamaican hit, estimated to eventually sell 80,000 copies on the island. (Recording as the Wailin' Wailers and the Wailin' Rudeboys, the group will cut some 80 sides for Studio One between now and 1966 - notably *Put It On*, *The Ten Commandments Of Love* and *Love And Affection*.)

1966

Feb [10] Marley marries Alpharita Constantia Anderson. (Known as Rita, the ex-member of the Soulettes will go on to join the I-Threes.)
[11] He leaves Kingston for the US to visit his mother in Wilmington, DE, finding work as a waiter, lab assistant for DuPont, forklift driver on a nightshift in a warehouse, and assembly line worker in the Chrysler plant, using the name Donald Marley.

1967

He returns to Kingston with $700 savings with which he sets up his own Wailin' Soul label, and signs a deal with Johnny Nash, releasing *Reggae On Broadway*. (Nash will later have hits with *Stir It Up* and *Guava Jelly*, both written by Marley.) He reunites with Tosh and Wailer and will record 11 singles for Kong's Beverley label from late 1967 to early 1968. Wailer serves 14 months in jail after being convicted of marijuana possession.

1968

Oct [17] Rita gives birth to Ziggy (b. David) Marley in Kingston. (Together with his younger brother Stephen (b. Apr. 20, 1972, Wilmington, DE) and sister Cedella (b. Aug. 23, 1967, Kingston), Ziggy will form Ziggy Marley & the Melody Makers in 1982). (During the year Marley will reportedly get his hair cut for the last time, subsequently growing dreadlocks in the Rastafarian tradition.)

1969

The Wailers become committed Rastafarians and leave Kong to work with similarly-inclined producer, Lee "Scratch" Perry, on their newly-formed Tuff Gong label. (With Perry, the Wailers will record a number of reggae standards including *Soul Rebel*, *Duppy Conqueror*, *400 Years* and *Small Axe*, and their debut set, ***The Wailing Wailers***.)

1972

Island Records head Chris Blackwell signs the group, an unprecedented move for both a major label and a reggae act, aiming to break it in the international market. With the rhythm section of the Barrett brothers, Aston "Family Man" (b. Nov. 22, 1946, Kingston) and Carlton (b. Dec. 17, 1950, Kingston), who have been working with the group since the Perry sessions, the Wailers release ***Catch A Fire*** which, with unprecedented promotional support, establishes them as strong contenders for mainstream pop stardom - a promise fulfilled later in the year with their second Island album ***Burnin'***. The following year Marley & the Wailers will be dropped as the support act on a Sly & the Family Stone US tour for allegedly upstaging the headlining act.

1974

Sept [14] Eric Clapton tops the US chart with Marley's *I Shot The Sheriff* (originally on ***Burnin'***). (During the year, and despite growing international recognition, Tosh and Wailer leave the Wailers, unhappy with the Island-generated public perception of Bob Marley & the Wailers. Female vocal trio the I-Threes (Judy Mowatt, Marcia Griffiths and Marley's wife, Rita), Bernard "Touter" Harvey and Earl "Wire" Lindo (keyboards) and Al Anderson (guitar) join.)

1975

May Their international breakthrough comes with the group's third Island album, ***Natty Dread***, which makes US #92.

July [18-19] The group plays at the Mecca Lyceum, The Strand, London.

Aug Bob Marley & the Wailers begin a UK tour with a new line-up of Tyrone Downie (keyboards), Alvin "Seeco" Patterson (percussion) and Julian "Junior" Murvin (guitar), who replace Harvey and Lindo.

Oct *No Woman No Cry*, extracted from forthcoming ***Live!***, reaches UK #22. A career and genre-defining reggae classic, it is curiously Marley's only UK chart single not to be self-penned (written by Vincent Ford). ***Natty Dread*** makes UK #43 while ***Burnin'*** peaks at US #151.

[11] The Wailers, performing their last gig in their original line-up, are on the same bill with Stevie Wonder at the National Arena, Kingston, with Wonder playing piano on *I Shot The Sheriff*.

Nov ***Catch A Fire*** peaks at US #171.

Dec ***Live!***, recorded at London's Lyceum Ballroom on July 18th, makes UK #38.

1976

May ***Rastaman Vibrations*** reaches UK #15, including *War*, with lyrics taken from a speech by Emperor Haile Selassie.

June The group plays at London's Hammersmith Odeon during a current UK visit.

July *Roots Rock Reggae*, again written by Vincent Ford, makes US #51, Marley's only US chart single, as ***Rastaman Vibrations*** hits US #8, during a 22-week stay on chart.

Dec [3] An attempt is made on Marley's life when seven gunmen burst into his Kingston home, and injure Marley, his wife and his manager, Don Taylor. (Believing it to be politically motivated, Marley will leave Jamaica for an 18-month exile in Miami, FL, where ***Exodus*** will be partly recorded.)

[4] ***Live!*** makes US #90.

[5] Marley participates in the "Smile Jamaica Concert" at the National Heroes Circle Stadium, Kingston.

1977

June Self-produced ***Exodus*** hits UK #8. During the year he has an operation at Cedars of Lebanon Hospital, Miami, to remove a toe after a cancerous growth is found. The media is informed that he has received a foot injury while playing his favorite game, soccer.

July Title cut, *Exodus*, reaches UK #14.

Aug ***Exodus*** makes US #20.

Oct *Waiting In Vain* reaches UK #27, as the group plays a week's residency at the Rainbow Theatre, Finsbury Park, London.

1978

Feb Double A-side, *Jamming/Punky Reggae Party*, hits UK #9.

Apr *Is This Love* hits UK #9 taken from the self-produced ***Kaya***, featuring a rejoined Lindo, hits UK #4.

[22] Returning to Jamaica, the group headlines the "One Love Peace Concert" in Kingston, where Marley unites Prime Minister Michael Manley and his opponent Edward Seaga on stage in avowals of unity and common purpose.

May ***Kaya*** makes US #50.

June [22] The group plays at Bingley Hall, Stafford, Staffs., during its current British tour.

July *Satisfy My Soul*, featuring ska-based horns, reaches UK #21.

Dec Live double album, ***Babylon By Bus***, recorded during their June 1978 world tour at the Pavilion, Paris, makes UK #40, while Marley makes a short trip, his first, to Kenya and his avowed spiritual home, Ethiopia.

1979

Feb ***Babylon By Bus*** peaks at US #102. The group headlines at New York's Apollo Theatre in Harlem, the first reggae band to do so.

Sept [24] They perform at a benefit concert for Rastafarian children at the National Heroes Stadium, Kingston.

Oct Black-emancipation themed ***Survival*** reaches UK #20.

Nov *So Much Trouble In The World* peaks at UK #56.

[22] The group returns to perform at the Apollo Theatre.

Dec ***Survival*** makes US #70.

1980

Apr [17] Marley performs at the Independence Day celebrations in Salisbury, Zimbabwe, in front of H.R.H. Prince Charles and President Mugabe. Shortly afterwards, the group begins a major European tour, in Dublin, Eire, which will encompass West Germany, France, Norway, Sweden, Denmark, Belgium, Holland, Spain and Ireland, including a 100,000 sell-out show in Milan, Italy.

June [7] Marley headlines the "Summer Of '80 Garden Party" at the Crystal Palace Concert Bowl, London, with the Average White Band, Q-Tips and Joe Jackson.

July *Could You Be Loved* hits UK #5, as its parent album, ***Uprising***, co-produced with Chris Blackwell, hits UK #6.

[13] Their European tour ends at Bingley Hall, Stafford.

Aug ***Uprising*** reaches US #45.

Sept [20] Marley & the Wailers play the first of two nights at New York's Madison Square Garden with the Commodores.

[21] Marley collapses jogging in Central Park, New York. Cancer is subsequently diagnosed and Marley attends Sloan-Kettering Hospital in New York as an out-patient. The tour is cancelled, though tonight's second Madison Square Garden gig goes ahead.

Oct *Three Little Birds*, prominently featuring the I-Threes, reaches UK #17.

Nov [4] Marley is baptised at the Ethiopian Orthodox Church, Kingston, converting to a Christian Rastafarian and taking the new name Berhane Selassie.

Dec Marley flies to Dr. Josef Issels Clinic in Rottach-Egern, Bavaria, West Germany, for treatment. Stevie Wonder hits US #5 with his tribute to Marley, *Master Blaster (Jammin')*.

1981

Apr Marley is awarded Jamaica's Order of Merit, accepted in his absence by his son Ziggy.

May [11] Marley dies of lung cancer and a brain tumor, age 36, at the Cedars of Lebanon Hospital, having flown to his mother's home in Miami.

[20-21] His body lies in state at the National Arena in Kingston.

[21] A Jamaican legend, Marley is buried with full state honors in St. Ann's, after an Ethiopian Orthodox Festival funeral is held in Kingston, attended by thousands.

July Reissued, *No Woman No Cry* hits UK #8, while the live, re-titled ***Live At The Lyceum*** re-enters the UK chart at #68.

Aug [6] The "Fourth International Reggae Sunsplash Festival" in Jarrett Park, Montego Bay, Jamaica, billed as a tribute to Marley, is attended by 20,000 people. Four of Marley's children appear as the Melody Makers.

Nov ***Chances Are***, on Cotillion, collecting archive tracks recorded between 1968 and 1972, peaks at US #117.

1982

Feb The London Borough of Brent dedicates Marley Walk, a path on a Willesden Green Estate.

Dec [29] Jamaica issues a Bob Marley commemorative stamp. The following year *Buffalo Soldier* will hit UK #4 in June when ***Confrontation*** also hits UK #5. The album will peak at US #55 the following month.

July ***Confrontation*** makes US #55.

1984

May [19] Island's compilation album (and accompanying video package), ***Legend***, to commemorate the third anniversary of Marley's death, hits UK #1 in its week of entry and will stay there for 12 weeks during a 129-week chart tenure. Double A-side, *One Love/People Get Ready*, hits UK #5.

July *Waiting In Vain*, originally from ***Exodus***, reaches UK #31.

Oct ***Legend*** makes US #54 and will also spend over two years on the survey, earning triple-platinum status.

Dec Reissued *Could You Be Loved* peaks at UK #71. A 10-track rarities set, ***Rebel Music***, will make UK #54 in July 1986.

1987

Apr [17] Carlton Barrett is shot dead outside his home in Kingston.

May [19] The Wailers, having ousted Rita Marley as executor of Marley's will, call for an investigation of his estate.

Sept [11] Tosh is murdered by burglars at his Jamaican home.

1989

Mar New label Slam Records announces plan to issue previously unreleased 1967-1972 Marley material originally recorded for Tuff Gong label. His son, Ziggy, increasingly assuming the Marley mantle, returns to the studio to record a follow-up to his successful ***Conscious Party***.

1990

Feb [6] To commemorate the birth of Bob Marley, today is proclaimed a national holiday in Jamaica.

June Blackwell inaugurates the Bob Marley Memorial Fund in New York by presenting a check for $75,000 to Amnesty International. (The donation will be given annually for ten years at the Penta Hotel in New York.) Island reissues CD versions of 13 Marley albums in the US.

Sept [1] Re-promoted and issued on CD, ***Legend*** peaks at US #72 beginning another lengthy chart tenure.

[30] Alvin Patterson suffers an aneurysm while the Wailers are performing in Curitida, Brazil.

Nov [27] "The Bob Marley Story" video is certified gold by the RIAA.

1991

May [18] ***Talkin' Blues***, another compilation of unreleased material and interviews conducted in 1973, peaks at US #103.

May [25] *One Love/People Get Ready* makes UK #42.

June [8] ***Legend*** re-charts to reach UK #11.

[26] A tribute concert is held at Villa Borghese in Rome, Italy, to commemorate the tenth anniversary of his death.

July [2] Reggae veteran Eddy Grant joins the heated competition to wrest control of Marley's recording and publishing legacy by bidding $13.5 million for the rights which have also attracted a $15.2 million bid by MCA and a joint offer by Rita Marley and Blackwell. Rita issues the statement: "We are completely incensed as a family at the idea of Eddy Grant trying to take our heritage away." The Jamaican Supreme Court continues to consider the various tenders.

[29] The court session is adjourned until October, with the ruling that the three offers were too disparate for comparison.

Oct [18] Carlton Barrett's wife Tina, Glenroy Carter and Junior Neil are sentenced for conspiring in a murder-for-hire case. Tina receives a seven-year sentence.

Dec [9] Jamaican Supreme Court Justice Clarence Walker, ending a decade of legal wrangles, directs that Marley's assets be sold for $11.5 million to his widow, children and Blackwell's Island Logic Ltd., despite MCA's higher offer. Ziggy Marley names his daughter, born today, Justice.

1992

Apr [11] ***Legend*** begins another UK chart stretch, reaching #18, while spending a further 47 weeks on the survey.
[27] Island Visual Arts bows the theatrical release of live concert footage, including the 1980 Independence Day gig in Zimbabwe, collected for the film "Time Will Tell" at the Prince Charles Theatre, London. C4-TV will air the movie on May 23rd while the US premiere will air on July 11th on pay-per-view.
Oct [3] *Iron Lion Zion* hits UK #5, as ***Songs Of Freedom*** debuts at its UK #10 peak. A four-CD retrospective collection featuring Marley's first recordings in 1962, a live version of *Redemption Song*, recorded at his final concert in Pittsburgh, PA in September 1980, his numerous hits and previously unavailable cuts unearthed by Rita, the 78-track release, accompanied by a 64-page tribute booklet written by **Billboard** editor Timothy White (also the author of **Catch A Fire**, a definitive Marley tome), has been simultaneously released in 54 countries.
[31] ***Songs Of Freedom*** makes US #86.
Nov [28] *Why Should I/Exodus* bows at its UK #42 peak.

1993

Feb [12-14] Cutty Ranks, Maxi Priest, Lady Levi and bill-toppers the Wailers perform at the 12th annual "Bob Marley Day Festival" tribute, held at the Long Beach Arena, Long Beach, CA.

1994

Jan [19] Marley is posthumously inducted into the Rock and Roll Hall of Fame by U2's Bono at the ninth annual dinner held at New York's Waldorf Astoria Hotel.
Feb [6] A year of festivities to celebrate the 50th anniversary of Marley's birth begins at the Bob Marley Museum in Kingston with the Marley Foundation's Tribute Concert with performances by the Wailers and Rita and Ziggy Marley.
May [23] The RIAA certifies five million sales of ***Legend***, easily the best-selling reggae album of all-time.
Sept [28] ***Songs Of Freedom*** is certified platinum by the RIAA for sales of two million.

1995

May [20] *Keep On Moving* debuts at its UK #17 peak.
June [3] Follow-up to ***Legend***, a further collection overseen by Blackwell, ***Natural Mystic : The Legend Continues*** hits UK #5 in its week of entry.
[10] ***Natural Mystic : The Legend Continues*** debuts at its US #67 peak.

1996

Feb [6] Rita Marley announces plans to create the permanent "Bob Marley - A Tribute To Freedom" exhibit at Universal Studio's new Orlando, FL-based entertainment "E-Zone" complex, which will include a recreation of his Jamaican house complete with artifacts, set to open in 1998. Meanwhile Graphix Zone (US) reveals details for its forthcoming release of a multimedia enhanced-CD of Marley's life and music, set to include nine songs including the rare recording *Selassie In The Chapel*.
June [8] *What Goes Around Comes Around* reaches UK #42.

MARMALADE

Dean Ford (lead vocals, harmonica); **Patrick Fairley** (guitar); **Junior Campbell** (guitar, piano, vocals); **Graham Knight** (bass); **Alan Whitehead** (drums)

1961

The group is formed in the Glasgow, Strathclyde, Scotland, suburb of Springburn by friends Fairley (b. Apr. 14, 1946) and Campbell (b. Wullie Campbell Jr., May 31, 1947, Glasgow), who has spent two years playing clarinet in local East Bank Academy Orchestra. Apprentice plater Ford (b. Thomas McAleese, Sept. 5, 1946, Coatbridge, Strathclyde, Scotland), who has first played at dances at Whifflet Parish church hall with the Tonebeats at age 13, before joining the Monarchs, where he is seen by Fairley and Campbell at Glasgow's Barrowlands Ballroom and asked to join as lead singer. Trainee chef Raymond Duffy soon joins on drums, while shipping clerk Knight (b. John Graham Knight, Dec. 8, 1946, Glasgow) answers an advertisement in the **Glasgow Evening Citizen** for a bass guitarist at the end of 1964, and auditions in a YMCA hall for Campbell, Fairley, Ford and Duffy. He has been playing in the recently-split group the Vampires of Springburn. He completes the line-up which now calls itself the Gaylords (occasionally prefacing this with Ford's name) and, concentrating on Cliff Richard & the Shadows as role models for image and repertoire, they begin gigging in Scotland.

1965

With the beat group boom in full swing, they broaden their output to US soul covers, hiring Brian Poole & the Tremeloes' manager, Peter Walsh, to oversee all business matters, and begin playing in England, primarily at US Air Force bases. They are voted #1 group in Scotland in 1964 (a title they will retain in 1965 and 1966), and their professionalism draws attention from major record companies. Norrie Paramor, Cliff Richard's mentor and head of EMI's Columbia label, is the first to sign them. Their debut single, a cover of Chubby Checker's *Twenty Miles*, backed with an example from the Campbell/McAleese catalog, *What's The Matter With Me*, sells strongly in Scotland as the group continues touring, releasing *Mr. Heartbreak's Here Instead* and a workout of Shirley Ellis' nonsense-rhyme novelty, *The Name Game*.

1966

Their fourth and final Columbia single *He's A Good Face, But He's Down And Out* receives wider appreciation, but still fails to chart. Disillusioned, the band decides to change its name, manager, record company and relocate to London. Duffy declines and quits, later to re-surface in Matthews Southern Comfort while the remaining quartet becomes Marmalade, at manager Walsh's suggestion, and places an ad for a drummer in **Melody Maker** magazine which brings in Alan Whitehead (b. July 24, 1946), a work-study trainee from Orpington, Kent.

1967

The group earns a solid reputation in London, but is unable to interest anyone in its own compositions. Despite a well received showing at the "Windsor Jazz Festival", Windsor, Berks., and a Thursday night residency at London's Marquee club, the group still has only support slots on tours and plays others' hits on the ballroom circuit. The members agree to "sell out" - going totally commercial in an attempt to break into the big time. They sign to CBS Records, releasing *It's All Leading Up To A Saturday Night*.
May [15] The group appears in Alun Owen's BBC2-TV play "The Fantastist", performing *Can't Stop Now*.
Dec *I See The Rain*, makes the Dutch chart, peaking at #23 during a five-week showing. Jimi Hendrix expresses the opinion that it is the best single of 1967, but the British public remains unimpressed. Marmalade sets off on a tour of Holland.

1968

June Following the release of *Man In A Shop*, their next single, a cover of the Grass Roots' current US #49 *Lovin' Things*, written by Jet Loring and Arthur Scroeck, and already covered by another Scottish group, with Campbell and Knight on backing vocals, hits UK #6.
Aug [10] The group appears at the eighth "National Jazz & Blues Festival" at the Kempton Park racecourse, Sunbury-on-Thames, Middx.
Oct *Wait For Me Marianne* peaks at UK #30 during a five-week chart run.

1969

Jan [1] Marmalade's cover of a bouncy reggae-tinged track from ***The Beatles***, *Ob-La-Di Ob-La-Da*, tops the UK chart for the first of three weeks (though interrupted for one week by the rise of the Scaffold's *Lily The Pink*), despite competition from the Bedrocks' #20 version. ***There's A Lot Of It About It*** is released.
May [10] The group takes part in an open-air pop festival at Notts County Football ground, Nottingham, Notts., with the Tremeloes, the Move, Georgie Fame, Jethro Tull, Status Quo and Love Sculpture.
July *Baby Make It Soon*, the group's final single for CBS, hits UK #9.
Nov [14] They sign to Decca Records with a deal allowing them complete freedom to write, arrange, produce and record whatever material they wish, free from corporation interference. The Campbell/McAleese-written *Reflections Of My Life* is released the same day.

1970

Jan *Reflections Of My Life* hits UK #3.
May *Reflections Of My Life*, released through sister company London, hits US #10.
June ***Reflections Of The Marmalade*** is issued (US title: ***Reflections Of My Life***), climbing to US #71.
Sept Follow-up single, *Rainbow*, hits UK #3 and US #51, as Campbell assumes studies at the Royal College of Music.

1971

Apr *My Little One* reaches UK #15. As the group's virtual music director, Campbell quits shortly after the group triumphs in Thailand at the "Bangkok Music Festival", frustrated at the restrictions imposed by working within a group. Guitarist/composer Hughie Nicholson, ex-Decca-signed Scots group the Poets, is recruited. Whitehead also quits and is replaced by a second ex-Poet, Dougie Henderson.
Oct *Cousin Norman*, written by Nicholson, hits UK #6.
Nov Fairley announces his "retirement" as a performer, to work as promotion manager for the group's three music publishing companies, Catrine, Carnbro and J.G.K., before joining RSO as general manager of publishing affairs. Marmalade remains a quartet. *Reflections Of My Life* earns a gold disc and will ultimately sell over two million copies.
Dec *Back On The Road* makes UK #35, taken from their new album, ***Songs***.

1972

May While the band has recently been exposed by the **News Of The World** for backstage shenanigans involving female fans, *Radancer* hits UK #6. Nicholson quits to join Cody.
Oct Junior Campbell signs to Decca offshoot, Deram, and hits UK #10 with his own *Hallelujah Freedom* (followed up by the UK #15 *Sweet Illusion* in June 1973).

1974

Oct Ford, Knight and Henderson, the only remaining members of the group, issue ***Our House Is Rockin'*** for EMI. Knight departs and Marmalade is joined by Mike Japp (guitar, keyboards, vocals), Joe Breen (bass) and Howie Casey (drums).

1975

Ford quits and emigrates to the US, where he cuts an eponymous album with Alan Parsons including extracted single, a cover of Jimmy Webb's *Crying In My Sleep*. A critical but not commercial success, both are released in the UK by EMI. Fairley also goes to US where he stays in publishing, not least working with Yes. Knight and Whitehead will resurrect the name Marmalade in 1976, bringing in guitarist/keyboardist Sandy Newman, from Scottish group the Chris McClure Section.

1977

Mar Signed to Tony Macaulay's Target Records, Marmalade's *Falling Apart At The Seams* hits UK #9. Released on Ariola America in the US, it makes #49, though further singles and ***Only Light On My Horizon Now*** all fail to follow-up successfully. Garth Watt-Roy joins the group on vocals and keyboards before becoming a member of the Q-Tips the following year, to be replaced by ex-Federation member, Bristol-born Alan Holmes. In 1978, Marmalade's ***Doing It All For You***, will be released by Sky Records. Lining up as Knight, Newman, Holmes and ex-Love Affair drummer Glenn Taylor in 1980, Marmalade will flourish on the cabaret circuit during the '80s, recording albums and singles sporadically for the European market, where a loyal following is maintained.

1991

Oct [6] Having established their own Just Songs record label in 1984, and releasing the Newman composition *Heartbreaker* the same year (a song which will be covered not least by the Tremeloes' lead singer Chip Hawkes, under the pseudonym Maxwell Silver), the band has continued to successfully tour Britain with White Plains and other acts, on the nostalgic "Sound Of The 60s" package shows, and now move into the '90s in similar fashion, performing at "The Biggest '60s Party In Town" at London's Olympia Hall.

MARTHA & THE VANDELLAS

Martha Reeves (lead vocals); **Annette Sterling** (vocals); **Rosalind Ashford** (vocals)

1961

Oct Having already sung in her first vocal group, the Fascinations and with ex-high school friends Sterling (b. Annette Beard), and Ashford (b. Sept. 2, 1943, Detroit) as vocal trio the Del-Phis (trimmed from its earlier quartet after former lead singer Gloria Williamson has departed), recording *I'll Let You Know* for the Chess imprint Checkmate label in 1961, Reeves (b. July 18, 1941, Eufaula, AL), having moved to Detroit, MI in her teens, undertakes solo club dates singing as Martha LaVelle, now winning top prize in a local talent contest which awards three nights of singing during happy hour at Detroit's 20 Grand Club. On her final night, she is spotted by Tamla Motown Records' executive Mickey Stevenson who asks Reeves to audition, which she eagerly tries to do the following day, only to be told that auditions are only held on the third Thursday of each month. Spending the rest of the day answering Stevenson's phone, Reeves becomes secretary to Stevenson, Smokey Robinson, Robert Bateman and Holland/Dozier/Holland in the A&R department earning $35 a week. Among other tasks, and since she is known to possess a good voice, one of her jobs is to sing new song lyrics onto tapes for artists, normally back-up singers, who need to learn the words prior to recording sessions. When a female backing singer is absent from a recording session through illness, the producer, familiar with Reeves' voice from demo tapes, suggests she fills the role, the first of many such appearances.

1962

July Getting regular studio opportunities, Reeves has mentioned her two former partners, and Motown tries out all three as an integrated back-up trio. The first session on which they sing is for Marvin Gaye's *Stubborn Kind Of Fellow*, which also becomes his first hit single, making US #46.
Sept After also backing Gaye on *Hitch Hike* (which will make US #30 in March 1963), the trio is signed as an act in its own right, to Motown's Gordy label, and renamed Martha & the Vandellas (named as a monikered hybrid of Van Dyke Street in Detroit and because they liked singer Della Reese). Their maiden single *I'll Have To Let Him Go* is released.

1963

June Their sophomore 45, a mid-tempo beat-ballad, *Come And Get These Memories*, reaches US #29, taken from their debut album, ***Come And Get These Memories***.
Sept Bounding dance number, *Heat Wave*, written by Holland/Dozier/Holland, hits US #4 and tops the R&B chart for five weeks (replacing fellow Motown freshman Stevie Wonder's *Fingertips*), to sell over one million copies.
Dec Same writing team's *Quicksand*, in a similar dance-oriented style, hits US #8 while ***Heat Wave*** makes US #125. In spite of their new-found success, Sterling leaves to get married, and is replaced by Betty Kelly (b. Sept. 16, 1944, Detroit).

1964

Mar *Live Wire* reaches US #42.
May *In My Lonely Room* makes US #44.
Sept The trio plays a ten-day engagement at the Fox Theater in Brooklyn, New York, in Murray The K's "Rock'n'Roll Extravaganza", along with Marvin Gaye, the Supremes, the Searchers, the Shangri-Las and many others.
Oct The group's version of *Dancing In The Street*, co-written by Marvin Gaye and turned down by Mary Wells, becomes one of the most consistently-played dance records of all time. Their second million seller, it hits US #2 for two weeks, behind Manfred Mann's *Do Wah Diddy Diddy*.
Nov *Dancing In The Street* is their UK chart debut, reaching #28, helped by a promotional visit which sees the trio on "Top Of The Pops" (4th) and "Ready Steady Go!" (6th).

1965

Jan *Wild One* makes US #34.
Mar [20] The trio begins a 21-date, twice-nightly UK Tamla Motown package tour at Finsbury Park Astoria, London, with labelmates the Supremes, the Miracles, Stevie Wonder, the Temptations and special guests Georgie Fame & the Blue Flames, set to end on April 12th at the Guildhall, Portsmouth, Hants.
Apr The trio returns to US Top 10 with *Nowhere To Run*, which hits US #8 and UK #25, one of the first batch of three singles released in the UK launch of the Tamla Motown label.
June ***Dance Party*** (including *Dancing In The Street* and *Nowhere To Run*) makes US #139.
[28] The group guests on CBS-TV's "It's What's Happening Baby" special.
Sept *You've Been In Love Too Long* reaches US #36.
Dec After many DJs have flipped the A-side, *You've Been In Love*, over, its B-side, the Holland/Dozier/Holland's ballad *Love (Makes Me Do Foolish Things)*, peaks at US #70.

1966

Mar *My Baby Loves Me* reaches US #22.
[29] The group begins a UK tour.
June *What Am I Gonna Do Without Your Love?* peaks at US #71.
July ***Greatest Hits***, a compilation of singles to date, makes US #50.
Sept [5] The trio performs at the Fillmore Auditorium, San Francisco.
Dec *I'm Ready For Love*, written by Holland/Dozier/Holland for the Supremes but turned down, hits US #9 and reaches UK #29.
[23] The group begins a week-long engagement at the Fox Theatre, Detroit, as part of the Motortown Revue, with the Temptations, Stevie Wonder, Gladys Knight & the Pips, Jimmy Ruffin, the Underdogs, Chris Clark, J.J. Barnes and the Earl Van Dyke Band.

1967

Feb ***Watchout!***, including *I'm Ready For Love*, peaks at US #116.
Apr *Jimmy Mack*, extracted from ***Watchout!***, hits US #10, and tops the R&B survey for a week, becoming another million seller. It also reaches UK #21 (and will be a consistent seller in Britain over the next two decades because of its inherent danceability and the equal popularity of the B-side *Third Finger, Left Hand*).
May [19-20] The group plays at the Fillmore West, San Francisco, CA.
Sept *Love Bug Leave My Heart Alone* reaches US #25.
Oct Performance set ***Martha And The Vandellas Live!*** peaks at US #140.
Dec The group's name is amended to Martha Reeves & the Vandellas on *Honey Chile*, which climbs to US #11.

1968

Jan Hampered by partial hearing loss, Kelly leaves and is replaced by Reeves' younger sister Lois, previously with the Orlons.
Feb *Honey Chile* reaches UK #30.
May Double A-side, *I Promise To Wait, My Love/Forget Me Not*, makes US #62 and #93 respectively.
June ***Ridin' High*** peaks at US #167.
Sept *I Can't Dance To That Music You're Playin'* reaches US #42.
[15] The trio appears on the first edition of NBC-TV's black audience-targeted music show "Soul", alongside Lou Rawls and comedian Red Foxx.
Nov *Sweet Darlin'* peaks at US #80.

1969

Feb *Dancing In The Street* is reissued in the UK and, with the particular patronage of Alan Freeman's major national radio show "Pick Of The Pops", now hits #4.
Apr *Nowhere To Run*, reissued as a UK follow-up, reaches #42.
May *(We've Got) Honey Love*, from the parent album ***Sugar'n'Spice***, makes US #56. *Jimmy Mack* will re-chart in the UK, at #21 in September 1970, after which *I've Gotta Let You Go* reaches US #93 in November, taken from ***Natural Resources***.

1971

Mar Following the birth of Reeves' son, which has caused her to take time off, Martha and Lois have re-grouped, minus Ashford, who has left and been replaced by Sandra Tilley from ex-Motown group the Velvelettes. *Forget Me Not*, a minor 1968 US hit, now climbs to UK #11.
May The group plays a comeback show at P.J.'s club in Los Angeles, CA.
Nov *Bless You* makes US #53, their last US chart single.
Dec [2] The group plays its farewell concert at the Cobo Hall, Detroit. (Reeves will begin a solo career, while her sister Lois joins Quiet Elegance, recording for the Hi label in Memphis, TN.)

1972

Jan [22] *Bless You* is also their final UK chart entry, reaching #33.
Apr ***Black Magic*** becomes their last US chart album and reaches #146.

1974

Apr Having signed as a solo artist to MCA Records, and worked the previous year with J.J. Johnson on the music for the black action movie "Willie Dynamite" including *Willie D*, *King Midas* and *Keep On Movin' On*, backed by the Sweet Things, Reeves' only solo hit single is *Power Of Love*, on MCA, which now makes US #76. It is taken from ***Martha Reeves***, produced by Richard Perry, and featuring Billy Preston, Joe Sample, Nicky Hopkins and Ralph McDonald. (It will be followed by ***The Rest Of My Life***, released by Arista Records in 1976 and the disco-oriented ***We Meet Again*** issued by Fantasy Records in 1978, reuniting her with Motown producer Henry Cosby.)

1978

July [1] The original Martha & the Vandellas re-form for the first time in ten years at a benefit concert for actor Will Geer at the Catalyst, Santa Cruz, CA. (Reeves will resume her solo career with ***Gotta Keep Moving*** in 1980 before entering into semi-retirement.

She will also sing *Heatwave* solo at the 25th Motown Anniversary TV show broadcast on NBC-TV on May 16th 1983.)

1989

Oct [21] The reunited trio (Tilley has died in 1982) begins a UK tour at the Talk Of The Town, Manchester, Gtr. Manchester. (They will return to the UK as part of the "Giants Of Motown Show" with the Four Tops, the Temptations, the Supremes and the Marvelettes, at the Wembley Arena, Wembley, Middx., on April 5th 1992, while performing regularly in the US, brought out of retirement by Reeves, but keeping their day jobs, Sterling working in a hospital and Ashford working for a phone company.)

1993

Feb [25] Reeves is inducted into the Rhythm and Blues Foundation at the fourth annual Pioneer Awards, at the Palace Theater, Los Angeles.

1994

Aug Hyperion publishes Reeves' biography, **Dancing In The Street : Confessions Of A Motown Diva**, as her former employer brings her debut album ***Come And Get These Memories*** to compact disc.

1995

Jan [12] Martha & the Vandellas are inducted into the Rock and Roll Hall of Fame by B52's Kate Pierson and Fred Schneider at the eighth annual dinner, from New York's Waldorf Astoria Hotel, singing *Dancing In The Streets* at the perfunctory post-dinner jam.
Sept [2] Reeves sings with John Mellencamp at the Concert for the Rock and Roll Hall of Fame at Cleveland Stadium, Cleveland, OH.

JOHN MARTYN

1968

Feb Singer-songwriter Martyn (b. Sept. 11, 1948, Glasgow, Scotland), musically guided as a teenager by folk artist Hamish Imlach, has re-located from Glasgow to London two years earlier, where he is spotted and urgently signed by Island Records' founder Chris Blackwell as the first solo white artist to the fledgling label, which now releases his critically well-received jazz-tinged folk debut, ***London Conversation***. His sophomore effort, ***The Tumbler***, produced by Al Stewart and featuring flautist Harold McNair, released just ten months later, further challenges the boundaries of traditional folk.

1969

Having married singer Beverly Kutner, the newly-weds, inspired by the "Woodstock Music & Art Fair", which they attend, and by the Band's 1968 ***Music From Big Pink*** album, record ***Stormbringer*** in the US with help from the group's Levon Helm, to be released in the UK in February the following year, credited as John & Beverly Martyn. Returning to London, the Martyns record a second album together, ***The Road To Ruin***, enlisting the bass talents of Danny Thompson, who becomes a close companion to John not least as a drinking buddy, which is issued by Island in November 1970. With Beverly subsequently pregnant, Martyn, who is building a solid cult club following, releases the solo ***Bless The Weather***, further showcasing his technical Echoplex guitar skills, in November 1971.

1973

Feb The critically-praised release of his follow-up set ***Solid Air*** (its title track written for close friend Nick Drake), highlighted by Martyn's distinctive bluesy vocal style, elevates him to concert hall status in the UK. ***Inside Out***, reflecting a free-form jazz style and featuring Thompson, Steve Winwood, Bobby Keyes and Traffic's Chris Wood, follows in 1974.

1975

Jan The mellow, folk-returning ***Sunday's Child*** is issued, to be followed by an official bootleg, ***Live At Leeds***, initially sold by mail order from his Hastings, Sussex house, but subsquently afforded a release by Island. Eric Clapton's ***Slowhand***, including a cover version of Martyn's *May You Never*, will emerge in November 1977.

1978

Feb [4] Having spent time in Jamaica the previous year, where he has worked with Lee Perry, the Blackwell-produced ***One World***, prominently featuring Winwood, is his commercial breakthrough, entering at its UK #54 peak.

1980

Nov [1] The break-up of his marriage and an ongoing battle with alcohol and drug abuse autobiographically underscores the release of ***Grace And Danger***, produced by Martin Levan and featuring Phil Collins on drums and vocals, which also reaches UK #54. (Martyn will subsequently state: "Some people keep diaries - I make records".)

1981

Sept [26] Newly signed to WEA Records, the Collins-produced ***Glorious Fool*** enters the UK chart, set to reach #25 as Martyn undertakes a UK tour with a band including keyboardist Max Middleton, drummer Jeff Allen and bassist Alan Thompson.

1982

Sept His second and final WEA outing, the equally rock-tinged ***Well Kept Secret***, helmed by Sandy Roberton and featuring Pete Wingfield and Lee Kosmin, peaks at UK #20.

1984

Nov [17] Having issued a second live DIY mail-order album, ***Philentrophy***, the previous year, ***Sapphire***, self-produced and recorded at Compass Point Studios in the Bahamas, marks his return to Island and shines at UK #57, accompanied by a European tour.

1986

Mar Self-helmed ***Piece By Piece***, with sleeve note thanks to his second wife Annie, peaks at UK #28, his final UK chart appearance of the decade. (By year's end, Martyn also completes the soundtrack to the Tyne-Tees TV environmental series "Turning Of The Tide". In October the following year, Island will release his third live set, ***Foundations***, recorded at London's Town & Country club.)

1990

Apr With a late '80s album rejected by Island, Martyn has signed to Permanent Records which releases the self-produced ***The Apprentice***, featuring saxophonist Andy Shephard.
June [3] Martyn participates in "The Big Day", a festival in Glasgow, airing live on C4-TV.

1991

Sept Permanent issues ***Cooltide***, co-produced with Brian Young and Spencer Cozens, as Martyn undertakes a UK concert and radio promotion tour.

1992

Oct [10] His 21st album, ***Couldn't Love You More***, released by Permanent, debuts at its UK #65 peak, a re-recorded collection of his career highlights, produced by Matt Butler and featuring guest musicians David Gilmour, Shephard and old friend Phil Collins, all of whom will collaborate on a similar Martyn project in 1993.

1993

Jan [26] Martyn performs at the Fairfield Halls, Croydon, Surrey, prior to the release of a second Permanent re-cut collection of earlier compositions, ***No Little Boy*** in June, licensed in the US to Mesa Blue Moon Records. Island will issue the retrospective ***Sweet Little Mysteries - The Island Anthology*** in June the following year.

RICHARD MARX

1984

Nov At age 18, Marx (b. Sept. 16, 1963, Chicago, IL), having been brought into performing music from an early age by his father, Richard Sr., a jazz pianist and top jingle writer and mother, a jingles singer, and sung on TV commercials himself since the age of five, has been contacted by Lionel Richie in 1982. Richie had heard a demo tape of four Marx songs, and invited him to sing backing vocals for his forthcoming album including the subsequent hits *All Night Long*, *You Are* and *Running With The Night*. Richie also introduced Marx to a number of the industry's movers and shakers. With Canadian producer David Foster and Kenny Rogers, he has gone on to co-write *What About Me?* which now makes US #15 by Rogers with Kim Carnes and James Ingram, and the January 1985 Rogers' solo cut *Crazy*, which peaks at US #79. (From this highly successful springboard, Marx will collaborate with many artists over the next two years, writing for Chicago (***We Are The World*** album track *Good For Nothing*), Philip Bailey (***The Goonies*** album cut *Love Is Alive*), and others.)

1986

A friend, Bobby Colomby (ex-Blood, Sweat & Tears, now an A&R executive), introduces Marx to the president of EMI Manhattan who sees solo artist potential in his songs and signs Marx to the label worldwide. Colomby also teams him with producer David Cole, who will co-produce his debut album.

1987

Aug Marx begins a lengthy US tour supporting R.E.O. Speedwagon.
[29] *Don't Mean Nothing*, with Joe Walsh guesting, is his US chart debut, hitting #3.
Dec [12] *Should've Known Better* hits US #3 and will earn a Grammy Award nomination for Best Rock Vocal Performance, Male.

1988

Mar *Should've Known Better* makes UK #50, while *Endless Summer Nights* hits US #2.
Apr His self-written AOR/AC-mixed debut, ***Richard Marx***, co-helmed with Cole, peaks at UK #68, and reaches US #19 during an 86-week chart lease, eventually selling over two million domestic units.
May *Endless Summer Nights* makes UK #50.
July [23] Rock ballad, *Hold On To The Nights*, tops the US chart and Marx becomes the first male singer to notch four top three hits from a debut album. With his solo career soaring, he continues to write and produce projects with other artists, including Randy Meisner (ex-Eagles), Fee Waybill (ex-Tubes), and new all-girl rock group Vixen.

1989

Jan [8] Marx marries actress/singer Cynthia Rhodes.
Mar [11] Ann Wilson and Robin Zander's *Surrender To Me*, written by Marx, hits US #6.
June [24] The first single from his recently released sophomore effort, ***Repeat Offender***, *Satisfied* hits US #1 and makes UK #52.
Aug [12] Piano-led ballad, self-penned and co-produced with David Cole, *Right Here Waiting*, also tops the US survey and will hit UK #2.
Sept [2] ***Repeat Offender*** heads the US chart, having already hit UK #8.
Oct [16] *Right Here Waiting* is certified gold by the RIAA.
Nov [1] The RIAA confirms three million sales of ***Repeat Offender***. (It will sell six million copies worldwide.)

Dec [2] Further ballad, *Angelia*, hits US #4.

1990

Jan [24] Marx begins the year on the road in Pittsburgh, PA.
Mar [3] *Too Late To Say Goodbye*, written with former Tubes lead singer Fee Waybill, reaches US #12 and UK #38.
[8] Marx wins the Worst Male Singer category in **Rolling Stone**'s 1989 Critics' Award.
May [3] His "Richard Marx Volume 1" video is certified platinum by the RIAA.
[10] Marx donates $52,000 to the Children Of The Night organization to help teenage runaways and under-age prostitutes at the site of a planned children's shelter in Los Angeles, CA. (Marx has now donated $100,000 royalties from his current single *Children Of The Night*.)
June [23] Fifth extract, *Children Of The Night*, reaches US #13.
July [7] *Children Of The Night* peaks at UK #54.
[10] Marx sings the national anthem at Major League Baseball's All Star game at Wrigley Field, Chicago.
Aug Further Marx-produced tracks appear on a Vixen album, ***Rev It Up***. Other current production and songwriting credits include projects by Animotion, Poco (*Nothin' To Hide*) and Kevin Cronin.
[31] A North American tour ends in Honolulu, HI.
Sept [1] The reissued pairing of *Endless Summer Nights* and *Hold On To The Night* peaks at UK #60.
Dec [5] Marx performs on CBS-TV's "1990 Grammy Legends Show".

1991

Mar Marx teams with David Crosby, Chicago's Bill Champlin and REO Speedwagon lead vocalist Kevin Cronin to record the Persian Gulf War-themed *Hard To Believe*.
Apr Marx, and four other acts, are released by EMI Records, following a dispute with his Left Bank Management company. EMI President Sal Licata is quoted as saying: "The reasons behind my decision are multi-fold, but were based on business logic."
[15] President/CEO of Capitol Industries, Joe Smith, announces that Marx will be switched from EMI to Capitol.
Oct [19] *Keep Coming Back* debuts at its UK #55 peak.
Nov [9] Marx embarks on a day-long, five-city "Rush-In, Rush-Out, Rush Street Tour", playing gigs in Baltimore, MD, New York City, NY, Cleveland, OH, Chicago and ending with a show at Burbank Airport, Los Angeles, between 9:00 a.m. and midnight.
[16] Self-produced ***Rush Street***, featuring Luther Vandross, Billy Joel and Motley Crue's Tommy Lee, charts for a week at UK #60.
Dec [3] Marx guests on NBC-TV's "The Tonight Show".
[21] *Keep Coming Back*, featuring Vandross on backing vocals, reaches US #12.

1992

Mar [14] Marx participates in "Farm Aid V" from Texas Stadium, Irving, TX.
Apr [12] He finishes a two-week Canadian tour at the Ottawa Congress Centre, Ottawa, Canada.
[25] Murder-story telling *Hazard* hits US #9, as Marx performs in an all-star concert at the Irvine Meadows Amphitheatre, Laguna Hills, CA, to benefit the Pediatric AIDS Foundation.
May [2] ***Rush Street***, reaches US #35.
[14] He performs *Hazard* at the fourth annual World Music Awards at the Sporting Club, Monte Carlo, Monaco.
June [13] ***Rush Street*** re-charts, now hitting UK #7.
[19] Marx guests on "The Tonight Show".
[27] *Hazard* hits UK #3.
July [15] He performs at the Greek Theatre, Los Angeles, during a US summer tour, set to end on August 30th at the Minnesota State Fair Grandstand, St. Paul, MN.
[22] ***Rush Street*** is certified platinum by the RIAA.
Aug [22] *Take This Heart* reaches US #20.
Sept [5] *Take This Heart* reaches UK #13.
Nov [14] *Chains Around My Heart* stops at US #44.
[29-30] Marx plays two dates at London's Hammersmith Odeon.
Dec [5] *Chains Around My Heart* reaches UK #29.

1993

May [22] Marx helps out at a record store counter in Los Angeles to benefit LIFEbeat's CounterAid, a one day fundraiser for people with HIV/AIDS, as he still works on his fourth album, ***Paid Vacation***, set for release in February 1994.
Nov [16] Marx participates in a tribute to the Eagles with Randy Meisner as part of NBC-TV's "A '70s Celebration : The Beat Is Back", taped at Los Angeles' Wiltern Theatre.
[23] The RIAA certifies sales of three million of ***Richard Marx***.

1994

Jan [26] Marx guests on ITV's "Des O'Connor Tonight".
Feb [5] *Now And Forever*, featured in the Alec Baldwin/Kim Basinger movie "The Getaway", reaches UK #13.
[7] Marx participates in the 21st American Music Awards at Los Angeles' Shrine Auditorium.
[19] Co-produced by Marx with Terry Thomas and featuring a host of music talent including Vandross, Richie, Bill Champlin, Vince Gill and Timothy B. Schmidt, ***Paid Vacation*** hits UK #11 in its week of entry.
Mar [5] ***Paid Vacation*** reaches US #37.
[19] *Now And Forever* hits US #7.
May [7] *Silent Scream* reaches UK #32.
June [17] He gives a World Cup pre-game performance at Chicago's Soldier Field.
July [27] Marx plays to a sellout crowd of 2,870 at the Westbury Music Fair, Westbury, NY, during his US summer tour.
Aug [20] *The Way She Loves Me* reaches UK #39.
[27] *The Way She Loves Me* reaches US #20.
Dec [14] ***Paid Vacation*** is certified platinum by the RIAA.

1995

Feb [23] Currently his hottest market, Marx begins a six-date Asian tour in Bangkok, Thailand.
Mar [3] Now more popular in Far-Eastern Asia than any other territory, his live event "V At The Hard Rock", held in Singapore during the tour, is filmed for broadcast through Asia in December on STAR TV's V Music Channel. His Asia-only compilation, ***Ballads***, with two bonus cuts, will sell over 300,000 copies in the territory by year's end.
Nov [11] Marx performs at the 11th annual Adam Walsh Dinner & Auction, benefitting the National Center for Missing and Exploited Children, at the Radisson Hotel, Rochester, NY.

1996

Apr Marx puts the finishing touches to his next album, ***Flesh And Bone***, scheduled for release in the US in July.

MASSIVE ATTACK

3-D (vocals); **Mushroom** (keyboards); **Daddy G** (keyboards)

1990

The Massive Attack R&B ensemble, which will always revolve around the trio nucleus of graffiti artist, songwriter and singer, 3-D (b. Robert Delnaja, 1966), Daddy G (b. G. Marshall, 1959) and Mushroom (b. A. Vowles, 1968), has first come together in 1987, though all its members are veterans of an earlier mid-'80s hip-hop/soul collective known as the Wild Bunch, which also featured Nellee Hooper and Milo Johnson in its floating roster, and which emerged as part of the burgeoning Bristol, Avon rap scene in the mid-'80s, becoming regionally popular with regular gigs at the city's Dugout club and urban-themed single releases including *Tearing Down The Avenue* and *Fucking Me Up*. Recruiting soul vocalist Shara Nelson in 1986, and with Hooper departing to join Soul II Soul the following year, though he will remain on the periphery of the group not least as a remixer of singles, Massive Attack, having already released a one-off single (*Any Love* through Warner Bros. (UK), in July 1988), has linked with Neneh Cherry's producer and husband Cameron McVey, after 3-D has co-written Cherry's May 1989 hit *Manchild*, and is now signed to Circa Records via its own Wild Bunch label, releasing the debut single *Daydreaming*.

1991

Mar Innovative R&B cut *Unfinished Sympathy*, co-written and sung by Nelson and promoted via a ground-breaking video clip directed by Baillie Walsh, reaches UK #13. (It is their only single to be released under the edited moniker, Massive, done so to ensure airplay of the single which has been issued during the Gulf War.)
[28] Massive Attack's critically-revered debut set ***Blue Lines***, co-produced by McVey, including three collaborative Tricky tracks, makes UK #67, showcasing soulful, urban-themed, slick beat grooves, with vocals by Nelson, reggae singer Horace Andy and Tony Bryan. It will be nominated for a BRIT Award and named as Album Of The Year by **The Face**.
June *Safe From Harm*, again featuring Nelson, reaches UK #25.

1992

Jan [25] U2's *Mysterious Ways*, with a remix version by Massive Attack available, hits US #9, having already reached UK #13 in November.
Feb [29] EP *Massive Attack*, including the group's cover of William DeVaughn's *Be Thankful For What You've Got*, reaches UK #27.

1993

Following her exposure with the band, Nelson is signed to Cooltempo Records for a solo career which will begin with the Mercury Prize-nominated ***What Silence Knows*** (followed by ***Friendly Fire*** in 1996). Meanwhile, Massive Attack's core trio regroups at Mushroom's Wild Bunch Studio and Antenna Studios, Bristol to patiently create a follow-up set.

1994

Oct [8] ***Protection***, co-produced by Hooper and the band and featuring Everything But The Girl's Tracey Thorn, Andy and Jungle pioneer Tricky among others, hits UK #4 in its first chart week.
[29] *Sly*, featuring Nigerian vocalist Nicolette on lead vocal, debuts at its UK #24 peak. Meanwhile the band is midway through its first ever live tour, with eight dates in the UK and four others in the rest of Europe.

1995

Jan [21] Slow-jammed *Protection*, featuring co-writer Thorn on lead vocal, bows at its UK #14 peak.
Mar [4] A remixed and augmented dub version of the group's second album, ***Protection/No Protection*** hits UK #10.
Apr [8] *Karmacoma*, featuring rapping by Tricky (an alternative version will appear on his forthcoming solo album), reaches UK #28.
July [25] Massive Attack performs at The Supper Club, New York, NY during a US promotional trip.
Nov [7] ***Something To Remember***, Madonna's ballad retrospective collection, including a new collaboration with Massive Attack on a version of Marvin Gaye's *I Want You* (which is also featured on the recently issued Gaye-tribute album ***Inner City Blues***) is released worldwide by Maverick Records.

1996

Feb [19] Massive Attack is named Best Dance Act at the 1996 BRIT Awards held at London's Earl's Court

Exhibition Centre.
May [20] RCA Records (UK) releases the Euro '96 soccer championship-themed various artists compilation, ***The Beautiful Game***, including a previously released cut by Massive Attack.

DAVE MATTHEWS BAND

Dave Matthews (vocals, guitar); **LeRoi Moore** (reeds); **Carter Beauford** (drums); **Boyd Tinsley** (violin); **Stefan Lessard** (bass)

1993

Sept Matthews (b. Johannesburg, South Africa), who has moved with his family from South Africa to New York, NY in 1969, after his physicist father has landed a job with IBM, has returned to finish high school in Johannesburg, before settling in Charlottesville, VA in 1986, where he meets Beauford and Moore, who become members of his locally gigging backing unit. He also performs with regular cohort and guitarist Tim Reynolds whom he has met in 1987 (though Reynolds will never join the Dave Matthews Band). Having built a loyal regional following and recruited Tinsley and Lessard, the group now releases its first album, ***Remember Two Things***, on a US indie label, which quickly leads to its signing to RCA Records.

1994

Oct [15] A US tour opening for Phish reaches the Oak Mountain Amphitheatre, Pelham, AL, a bill grossing $143,722 from 9,979 attendees. (The group also makes its first UK date, a showcase at London's Borderline club.)

1995

Feb [24] Dave Matthews Band guests on CBS-TV's "Late Show With David Letterman".
Apr [15] The group appears on NBC-TV's "Tonight Show".
May [19-21] US tour dates are highlighted by three concerts opening for the Grateful Dead at the Sam Boyd Stadium, University of Nevada, Las Vegas, shows grossing $3,765,990 from 125,533 fans.
June [10] Produced by Steve Lillywhite, the band's sophomore set, ***Under The Table And Dreaming***, a musical amalgamation of rock, jazz, folk, reggae and world beats, reaches US #11.
[24] The band appears at the "Glastonbury Festival", Glastonbury, Somerset, two days prior to a performance at the Forum in London.
July [20] Set to end in September, US dates resume at Mud Island Amphitheatre, Memphis, TN, a bill grossing $104,200 from a crowd of 5,210.
Aug [14] The group makes a return visit to "The Tonight Show".
Oct [1] The band plays at "Farm Aid" held at the Cardinal Stadium, Kentucky Fair & Expo Center, Louisville, on a bill with founder Willie Nelson, John Mellencamp, Neil Young, John Conlee, Hootie & the Blowfish and others.
Dec [5] The group participates in WBCN's "Xmas Rave" at the Orpheum Theatre, Boston, MA.
[30-31] The Dave Matthews Band ends its breakthrough year with a pair of dates during a further US trek at the Coliseum, Hampton, VA, grossing $604,025 from a total of 25,371 fans.

1996

Jan [11] ***Under The Table Dreaming*** is certified for three million US sales by the RIAA. Having completed the recording of the new album, Matthews undertakes a short solo acoustic tour of the northeastern US with longtime sideman, guitarist Tim Reynolds.
Mar [12] Philips Media releases ***All Access : The H.O.R.D.E. Festival CD-ROM*** culled from performances on last year's "H.O.R.D.E." tour including one by the Dave Matthews Band.
May [18] The group's second RCA album, ***Crash***, debuts at US #2, behind Hootie & the Blowfish's ***Fairweather Johnson***. Promotion will include a headlining US tour, beginning on June 4th in Virginia Beach, VA, plus appearances on this summer's "H.O.R.D.E." caravan tour, set to begin on June 6th in Minneapolis, MN.

MATTHEWS SOUTHERN COMFORT

Ian Matthews (vocals, guitar); **Mark Griffiths** (guitar); **Carl Barnwell** (guitar); **Gordon Huntley** (pedal steel); **Andy Leigh** (bass); **Raymond Duffy** (drums)

1969

Jan Matthews (b. Ian Matthew McDonald, June 30, 1946, Lincs.), an alumnus of London-based mid-'60s harmony vocal group Pyramid which released *Summer Of Last Year* on Deram Records in January 1967, having previously turned down a career as a professional soccer player, has quit the group in November '67 to join UK folk pioneers Fairport Convention as joint lead vocalist. Staying with the group for 14 months, he now leaves, having contributed to two Fairport albums and recruits Griffiths, Barnwell, Huntley, Leigh and Duffy to form his own Matthews Southern Comfort outfit, which is signed to EMI Records.

1970

Jan Its debut album, ***Matthews Southern Comfort***, is released and shows Matthews veering away from his previous folk-rock inclinations toward a country style.
July ***Second Spring***, again largely witten by Matthews, makes UK #52.
Oct [31] A smooth, steel guitar-backed country style version of Joni Mitchell's *Woodstock* tops the UK chart for the first of three weeks (having already been a US Top 20 hit in the spring for Crosby, Stills, Nash & Young).
Nov Marshall Chess, head of administration for the Rolling Stones' proposed new label, is keen to sign the band, but Jagger turns it down, reportedly on the grounds that it "is not funky enough".
Dec Matthews leaves the group, after failing to turn up for a gig, just before the last Matthews Southern Comfort album, ***Later That Same Year***, is released.

1971

Jan Matthews now signed solo to Vertigo, releases the self-penned and produced ***If You Saw Thru' My Eyes***.
Mar *Woodstock* reaches US #23.
Apr The band becomes Southern Comfort following Matthews' departure, signing to Harvest Records for the album ***Southern Comfort***. Meanwhile, ***Later That Same Year*** makes US #72.
July ***Frog City*** by Southern Comfort makes US #196 including *Mare, Take Me Home* which peaks at US #96.
Aug The group performs at the annual "Reading Festival", Reading, Berks.
Oct *Tell Me Why* by Southern Comfort reaches US #98.

1972

Feb Matthews' ***Tigers Will Survive*** climbs to US #196, while his a cappella revival of the Crystals' *Da Doo Ron Ron* peaks at US #96. He forms Plainsong, with singer/guitarist Andy Roberts, keyboards player Dave Richards and bassist Bobby Ronga.
Sept Plainsong's ***In Search Of Amelia Earhart*** is issued on Elektra Records while Southern Comfort's ***Stir Don't Shake*** is its last album, after which the group disbands.
Dec Ronga leaves Plainsong as the group records a second album for Elektra (which is never released, although five tracks will be heard on Matthews' solo albums). Plainsong splits after the sessions and Matthews moves, at the suggestion of Elektra boss Jac Holzman, to Los Angeles, CA, to work with Michael Nesmith.

1973

Sept His first solo Elektra album, ***Valley Hi***, produced by Nesmith at his Countryside Studios, reaches US #181. Matthews tours the US, supporting America, with his own band comprising ex-Nazz drummer Tom Mooney and the Curtis brothers from Crazy Horse.

1974

June ***Some Days You Eat The Bear ... Some Days The Bear Eats You*** is Matthews' last album for Elektra as he continues touring the US under the name Ian Matthews & Another Fine Mess, with a band comprising Tommy Nunes (guitar), Joel Tepp (harmonica), Don Whaley (bass) and John Ware (drums).
Aug ***Journey From Gospel Oak***, a compilation of unreleased 1971-72 material recorded in November 1972 and scheduled for release by Vertigo, is issued by Mooncrest in the UK, with Matthews unaware of its release.
Oct ***The Best Of Matthews Southern Comfort*** is released, again without Matthews' knowledge.

1976

May After his contract with Elektra has expired in August 1975, and failing to sign a proposed deal with Arista Records, ***Go For Broke***, Matthews' first for CBS/Columbia Records, produced by Norbert Putnam, is released.
Oct ***Distilled***, a Southern Comfort compilation, is released by Harvest in the UK. ***Hit And Run***, Matthews' second and final album for Columbia, including a remake of *Tigers Will Survive*, will be issued in May the following year.

1978

Sept [3] Matthews embarks on a UK tour, supporting Renaissance, at the Gaumont Theatre, Southampton, Hants., set to end on the 25th with the last of a series of solo dates at Dingwalls, London.
Oct ***Stealin' Home***, issued by Mushroom Records, reaches US #80 while folk label Rockburgh, owned by Sandy Roberton, releases the set in the UK. *Shake It* becomes a prominent turntable favorite and reaches US #13, his first hit for eight years.

1979

Jan [31] Matthews plays at the Venue, London.
Mar *Give Me An Inch* (later a hit for Robert Palmer) peaks at US #67.
Aug ***Siamese Friends*** is released. The following March ***Discreet Repeat***, a double compilation of solo material, is Matthews' last recording for Mushroom and Rockburgh, while a one-off deal with RSO Records results in the release of ***A Spot Of Interference*** in June.

1981

Matthews, living in Seattle, WA, is involved in a legal dispute with Mushroom, which he claims owes him more than $500,000 in royalties. He subsequently releases ***Moods For Mallard*** and ***Shook*** (the latter recorded for Polydor in Germany in 1983) after which he abandons his own recording career, moves to Los Angeles and takes up a post as A&R executive for Island Records in 1984, before switching to a similar position at the pioneering new age Windham Hill label in 1986.

1987

Aug Matthews participates in Fairport Convention's 20th-anniversary celebrations by appearing live with the band. ***Meet Southern Comfort*** and Fairport Convention's ***Heydays***, an album of UK BBC radio broadcasts from 1968-69, both featuring Matthews' work, are released during the year in the UK, while Moore leaves his post at Windham Hill to begin recording a new album for the same label - a move which some view as perfect A&R.

1988

Apr ***Walking A Changing Line - The Songs Of Jules Shear*** is released on Windham Hill, the label's first all-vocal set, and receives significant critical acclaim.

1990

Aug Having relocated to Austin, TX the previous year, Matthews, now signed to Gold Castle, releases ***Pure And Crooked***, reverting to the original Gaelic spelling of his first name, Iain, and issued in the UK via a label license with Virgin.

1995

Aug Having reunited Plainsong for 1992's one-off set ***Dark Side Of The Room***, Moore's solo career has resumed with ***Skeleton Keys*** on Mesa/Rhino Records in the US in 1993 and ***The Dark Ride*** on the Watermelon label the following year. Now teamed with Mark Hallman and Michael Fracasso, Moore has formed Hamilton Pool which issues its debut album ***Return To Zero***, also on Watermelon. (MCA has issued ***The Best Of Matthews Southern Comfort*** in 1992, while Elektra has collected Moore's solo highlights with the label on 1993's ***The Soul Of Many Places***.)

see also: **FAIRPORT CONVENTION**

JOHN MAYALL

1963

July Mayall (b. Nov. 29, 1933, Macclesfield, Cheshire), having taken the George Formby Teach Yourself Ukelele correspondence course in his teens and studied at Manchester Art College, completed National Service in the British army, including a tour of duty in Korea, and then worked in a Manchester, Lancs. art studio attached to an advertising agency, formed his first group, the Blues Syndicate in 1962. Gigging mostly at Manchester's Twisted Wheel club, the group, a quintet featuring guitar, piano, trumpet, alto sax and Hughie Flint on drums, played raw R&B, inspired by Alexis Korner's London-based Blues Incorporated. Encouraged by Korner, Mayall has moved to London in January, where he has worked as a draughtsman, while trying to assemble a new R&B outfit. After trying out many musicians, Mayall now debuts the Bluesbreakers with himself on vocals, keyboards and harmonica, Bernie Watson on guitar, John McVie on bass and Peter Ward on drums, to be replaced once full-time gigging starts by Martin Hart.

Aug The Bluesbreakers begin a Thursday-night residency at the Scene, Great Windmill Street, London.

1964

Apr Mayall signs a short-term deal with Decca Records, and records *Crawling Up A Hill*. Shortly after, the band's personnel changes, reducing to a quartet comprising Mayall, McVie, Roger Dean on guitar and a returning Flint.

May [8] *Crawling Up A Hill* is released.

1965

Mar [26] His debut album, ***John Mayall Plays John Mayall***, recorded live at Klook's Kleek R&B club on December 7th, 1964, in West Hampstead, London, is issued along with the extracted *Crocodile Walk*, after which the Decca deal expires and is not renewed.

Apr Hearing that Eric Clapton has left the Yardbirds, impressed with his playing on *Got To Hurry* the B-side of *For Your Love*, Mayall invites him to join the Bluesbreakers. Clapton, keen to play blues, the reason he split from the Yardbirds, agrees. He is hired in place of Dean, who is dismissed in a fashion which will become a Mayall trademark. Clapton's presence in the group is sufficient to substantially boost the audience numbers at Mayall's gigs.

[23] The group appears on ITV's "Ready Steady Goes Live!".

June [19] The Bluesbreakers play at the "Uxbridge Blues And Folk Festival", Uxbridge, Middx., alongside the Who, Long John Baldry, the Spencer Davis Group, and others.

Aug Clapton, tired of one-night gigs and wanting some sunshine, departs without notice, with a car full of friends, for three months in Greece. Mayall muddles through with temporary replacement guitarists, but audience attendances begin to wane as word spreads of Clapton's exit.

Oct McVie is fired by Mayall for allegedly being drunk once too often, and Jack Bruce, ex-Graham Bond Organisation, replaces him on bass.

Nov With the Bluesbreakers proving to be an apprentice stop for some of tomorrow's more notable musicians, Mayall finds Peter Green, a guitarist good enough to step into Clapton's shoes, when Clapton himself returns with a tan and slips back into his job. Green is forced out after only three days as a Bluesbreaker. Shortly after Clapton's return, Bruce leaves because Mayall is unable to pay him enough and McVie rejoins the line-up. With Clapton, the Bluesbreakers record *I'm Your Witchdoctor* in a one-off deal with Immediate Records.

1966

Mar Producer Mike Vernon convinces Decca that Mayall should be re-signed, and the group cuts its first studio album ***Blues Breakers*** (having also made another one-off single, *Lonely Years*, for the small Purdah label between contracts).

July ***Blues Breakers***, credited to John Mayall with Eric Clapton for maximum commercial appeal, becomes Mayall's first major success, hitting UK #6. While the album is in the Top 10, Clapton leaves for the second and final time, to join Jack Bruce and Ginger Baker in Cream.

[17] Mayall persuades an initially uncertain Peter Green to replace Clapton, this time on a firm basis.

Sept [18] Flint leaves, and is replaced on drums by Aynsley Dunbar, ex-the Mojos.

Oct Two singles on Decca, *Parchman Farm* and *Looking Back* (the first featuring Clapton, the second Green), are issued in rapid succession.

1967

Mar ***A Hard Road***, the only studio album featuring Green, with a sleeve painting by Mayall, hits UK #10.

Apr Dunbar leaves to join Jeff Beck's group, and is replaced first by Mickey Waller, then by ex-Shotgun Express drummer Mick Fleetwood.

June [15] Fleetwood is fired by Mayall, also for alleged excessive drinking, and Green follows him, to subsequently form Fleetwood Mac. Mayall, left with just himself and McVie, who has already been approached about joining Fleetwood Mac, but initially refused, hires several new musicians: Mick Taylor (ex-Gods) on guitar, Chris Mercer on sax, Keef Hartley (ex-Artwoods) on drums and second sax player Rip Kant (who vanishes after two months). This line-up is the first to tour the US.

Aug [13] Mayall plays on the final day of the seventh "National Blues Festival" at Balloon Meadow on the Royal Windsor Racecourse, Windsor, Berks.

Sept ***Crusade*** hits UK #8. McVie is tempted away to Fleetwood Mac and is followed in the Bluesbreakers by a succession of short-lived bassists lasting eight months between them: Paul Williams, Keith Tillman and Andy Fraser. At the same time, the brass section of the band is enlarged, as Henry Lowther on trumpet and Dick Heckstall-Smith on sax join existing sax player Mercer.

Dec ***The Blues Alone***, a solo by Mayall, with Hartley playing drums on some tracks, makes UK #24.

1968

Jan The band begins a US tour at the Café Au-Go-Go club in New York.

Feb [1-4] The group plays at the Fillmore West, San Francisco, CA, with Jimi Hendrix.

Mar ***Diary Of A Band Vol. 1***, recorded live on the road during 1967, reaches UK #27 while its companion volume, ***Diary Of A Band Vol. 2***, makes UK #28. Meanwhile, Mayall has his first US chart album with ***Crusade***, which peaks at #136.

[25] Mayall refuses to play at the Top Rank Ballroom, Woverhampton, West Midlands, when 30 fans are barred for not wearing ties.

Apr [21] Hartley leaves to form his own band. Mayall asks an initially sceptical Jon Hiseman (ex-Graham Bond Organisation) to replace him on drums for an extended US tour. Tony Reeves from the New Jazz Orchestra joins on bass after Fraser leaves, going on to form Free.

June Solo album, ***The Blues Alone***, peaks at US #128.

July [7] The group takes part in the "Woburn Festival of Music", Woburn Abbey.

Aug ***Bare Wires***, recorded by the extended, brass-featuring band line-up, hits UK #3.

[11] They take part in the eighth "National Jazz & Blues Festival", before embarking on a lengthy US tour, at the end of which Mayall breaks up the band and settles in Los Angeles, CA, retaining Taylor on guitar, and recruiting bassist Steve Thompson and drummer Colin Allen to return to his old quartet format.

Oct ***Bare Wires*** reaches US #59.

1969

Jan ***Blues From Laurel Canyon***, recorded in Los Angeles by the quartet, reaches UK #33.

Apr ***Blues From Laurel Canyon*** makes US #68.

[6] Mayall's band plays at the "Palm Springs Pop Festival" in Palm Springs, CA, where a riot breaks out when police helicopters try to disperse an audience too large for the festival site.

[8] They open at the Whisky A-Go-Go in Los Angeles.

May Taylor leaves to join the Rolling Stones, and Allen departs to Stone The Crows.

June Mayall forms a new band, dropping the Bluesbreakers tag, featuring a revolutionary line-up without drums. Thompson remains on bass, while Marianne Faithfull's former stage guitarist, Jon Mark, is recruited, with Duster Bennett (guitar) and Johnny Almond (sax).

July [3-6] The group takes part in the four-day "Newport Jazz Festival" in Newport, RI.

[11-12] They perform at the Fillmore East in New York, with Spooky Tooth.

Aug Compilation album, ***Looking Back***, with tracks recorded between 1964 and 1967 (including some with Clapton), reaches UK #14.

Oct *Don't Waste My Time* peaks at US #81, Mayall's only US chart single, taken from ***The Turning Point***.

Nov ***The Turning Point***, recorded by the drumless line-up at the Fillmore East, and the first result of a new recording deal with Polydor, peaks at UK #11 and US #32. During a 55-week US chart stay, it becomes Mayall's only gold disc. He announces the launch of his own Crusade label.

[10] He embarks on an eight-date UK tour at the Free Trade Hall, Manchester, set to end on the 29th at the Granada Theatre, Walthamstow, London.

1970

Apr ***Empty Rooms*** hits UK #9, while ***Diary Of A Band*** (the same as the UK-issued ***Diary Of A Band, Vol. 1***) makes US #93.

May ***Empty Rooms*** reaches US #33.

June The band splits, with Mark and Almond forming the duo Mark-Almond, and the others moving to sessions or solo work.

[26] Mayall performs again at the "Bath Festival of Blues & Progressive Music", Shepton Mallet, Somerset.

Nov [20] A UK tour opens at the Fairfield Halls, Croydon, Surrey.

Dec ***U.S.A. Union***, on which Mayall collaborates with an entirely US-originated group (Harvey Mandel on guitar, Larry Taylor on bass and Don "Sugarcane" Harris on violin) for the first time, reaches UK #50 and US #22.

1971

Apr [11-18] The group plays at the Fillmore West, San Francisco, with Johnny Winter and Grand Funk Railroad.

May ***John Mayall - Live In Europe*** (equivalent to the UK-issued ***Diary Of A Band, Vol. 2***) stops at US #146.
June Double set, ***Back To The Roots***, a reunion with previous Bluesbreakers Clapton, Taylor and Hartley, alongside Mayall's current US members, makes UK #31 (his final UK charting album) and US #52.
Dec The double compilation album, ***Thru The Years***, containing mostly unreleased '60s Bluesbreakers material, peaks at US #164, while a new studio album, ***Memories***, cut by a trio comprising Mayall, Larry Taylor on bass and ex-Ventures lead guitarist Jerry McGee on guitar, climbs to US #179.

1972

Jan 200 youths attempting to crash a Mayall gig at the Bayfront Center, St. Petersburg, FL, are scalded with hot water.
July Live ***Jazz Blues Fusion***, recorded in New York and Boston with guitarist Freddie Robinson, trumpeter Blue Mitchell and standup bassist Victor Gaskin, reaches US #64.
Nov ***Moving On***, with Robinson and Mitchell, makes US #116.

1973

Mar Double album, ***Down The Line***, combining an album of mid-'60s studio cuts with the original ***John Mayall Plays John Mayall*** live album, peaks at US #158.
Oct Further double set, ***Ten Years Are Gone***, makes US #157.

1974

Mar Mayall cuts ***The Latest Edition*** with Hightide Harris and Randy Resnick (lead guitar), Red Holloway (saxes/flute) and Soko Richardson (drums).
Apr [14] Mayall, with a band comprising Jesse Ed Davis, Larry Taylor (bass), Holloway and Richardson, begins a UK tour at the Town Hall, Birmingham, West Midlands.

1975

Mar Mayall has signed to ABC/Blue Thumb Records for ***New Year, New Band, New Company***, which makes US #140, his final US chart entry. The new band of the title includes earlier cohorts Taylor and Don Harris, plus Rick Vito (guitar), Jay Spell (keyboards), Richardson, and for the first time, a female vocalist, Dee McKinnie.

1979

May After several further album releases (***Time Expired Notice To Appear*** (1975), ***John Mayall*** (1976), ***A Banquet Of Blues*** (1976), ***Lots Of People*** (1977) and ***Blues Roots*** (1978)), Mayall signs to DJM Records, issuing ***Bottom Line***. This is followed by two further DJM projects, ***No More Interviews*** (later in the year) and ***Road Show Blues*** (1980).

1984

Having reunited with Mick Taylor and John McVie for US and Australian tours in 1982, Mayall now puts together a new Bluesbreakers with Coco Montaya, Walter Trout (guitars), Bobby Haynes (bass), Joe Yuele (drums), releasing ***Behind The Iron Curtain*** on GNP Crescendo in 1986. The following year Mayall signs to German label Entente for the live ***The Power Of The Blues***.

1988

Dec Newly signed to Island Records, he releases ***Chicago Line***, supported by a now rare European tour. (During the year PolyGram issues vintage Mayall from the '60s as the album ***Archives To Eighties : Featuring Eric Clapton And Mick Taylor***.)

1990

June ***A Sense Of Place*** is released on Island, as Mayall, still a California resident, embarks on major US tour.
Sept [22] Mayall returns to the US chart for the first time in more than 15 years, with ***A Sense Of Place*** making #170.

1991

Feb [8] Mayall appears on NBC-TV's "The Tonight Show", as he continues to tour the US, playing his own unique brand of blues.
Apr [22-23] He joins Z.Z. Top's US tour at the Reunion Arena, Dallas, TX, replacing the just-fired Black Crowes.

1992

June [29] Mayall makes a rare live appearance in the UK at London's Town & Country club.

1993

Apr [17] With Mayall now signed to Silvertone (UK), ***Wake Up Call***, his first album of the '90s, charts for a week at UK #61.
May [4] During current US dates, Mayall plays at Toad's Place, New Haven, CT.

1994

Mar [10] Mayall guests on "The Tonight Show".
July [31] Currently on tour with Z.Z. Top, he plays a sell-out date at the Arena, La Crosse Center, La Crosse, WI.

1995

Oct [7] Following the release of his latest Silvertone album ***Spinning Coin***, featuring new Bluesbreaker find, Texan Buddy Whittington, the group plays at the Universal Amphitheatre, Universal City, CA, on a bill with Robert Cray, John Lee Hooker and Buckwheat Zydeco.

CURTIS MAYFIELD

1970

Oct [1] Having formed his first group the Alphatones while attending Chicago, IL's West Side Grammar School with Al Boyce, James Weems and Dallas Dixon before joining the gospel group the Northern Jubilee Gospel Singers with his three cousins Sam, Tommy and Charles Hawkins, in which he tours as part of his grandmother the Reverend A.B. Mayfield's Traveling Soul Church where he met Jerry Butler, R&B innovator Mayfield (b. June 3, 1942, Chicago), for 13 years a member of the Impressions, 11 of them spent as its leader, chief songwriter and producer, now leaves the group for a solo career - after finding his own replacement, Leroy Hutson. The Impressions remain on his Curtom label (whose motto is "We're A Winner") and he will continue to direct their career. (As a songwriter and producer, Mayfield has also written a string of R&B hits for artists on the Okeh label, notably those for Gene Chandler and Major Lance and for other artists including the Fascinations, the Five Stairsteps and Cubi on his own earlier labels Mayfield and Windy C.)
Dec His debut solo album, ***Curtis***, reaches US #19, and includes two lengthy funk pieces, *Move On Up* and the protest song *(Don't Worry) If There's A Hell Down Below, We're All Going To Go* which, edited as a US single, reaches US #29.

1971

July Live double album ***Curtis/Live!***, with a mixture of new and recent songs and Impressions oldies, recorded at the Bitter End in New York, NY, reaches US #21. (In contrast to his rich studio productions, Mayfield's '70s live band will be his own guitar and vocals, plus drummer, percussionist and bass player, and occasionally a second guitarist.)
Aug *Move On Up*, from the first album, becomes a UK dancefloor hit and his UK chart debut, reaching #12.
Dec ***Roots*** makes US #40. It contains the anti-war song *We Got To Have Peace*, but is mostly concerned with romantic themes. The extracted *Get Down* peaks at US #69. Mayfield devotes the next few months to work on his first film soundtrack.

1972

Sept [7] The still-rising ***Superfly*** is certified gold by the RIAA.
Oct [21] ***Superfly***, the film soundtrack album to "Superfly", one of the rash of "blaxploitation" movies which appear in the wake of 1971's highly successful "Shaft" with its innovative Isaac Hayes score, tops the US chart for the first of four weeks, and earns a gold disc. Much of the music is downbeat, despairing at the violence and drug culture in the film rather than glorifying it. A cautionary tale, *Freddie's Dead*, is extracted and hits US #4, his first solo million seller.
[31] *Freddie's Dead* is certified gold by the RIAA.

1973

Jan Title track, *Superfly*, hits US #8, a second million-seller.
[18] *Superfly* is also confirmed gold by the RIAA.
Mar ***Superfly*** reaches UK #26, his only UK chart album.
Apr When Mayfield appears on syndicated TV's "Soul Train", performing *Pusherman*, references to drugs in the lyrics are deleted.
June [6] The RIAA ratifies gold sales of ***Back To The World*** and ***Curtis***.
Aug ***Back To The World***, featuring mainly social consciousness songs, imbued with a rich, layered production, reaches US #16, and is his third and final gold album. Taken from it, *Future Shock* makes US #39.
Oct Chicago's WTTW-TV produces a musical special based around Mayfield, titled "Curtis In Chicago". It features both original and current Impressions line-ups, plus Jerry Butler, Gene Chandler and other artists with whom Mayfield has been involved. Following various solo and group spots, the show ends with an ensemble rendition of the Impressions' *Amen*.
Nov *If I Were Only A Child Again*, from the TV show, peaks at US #71.
Dec ***Curtis In Chicago***, the soundtrack from the broadcast, makes US #135.

1974

Jan *Can't Say Nothin'* peaks at US #88.
May Mayfield produces and plays on Gladys Knight & the Pips' soundtrack album, ***Claudine***, which reaches US #35.
Aug ***Sweet Exorcist*** makes US #39 and contains a collaboration with Donny Hathaway on *Suffer*, while the extracted *Kung Fu*, referencing the current martial arts craze, makes US #40.
Dec ***Got To Find A Way*** peaks at US #76.

1975

July ***There's No Place Like America Today***, a downbeat set dealing with racial prejudice, violence and deprivation, stops at US #120.
Oct From it, a uniquely upbeat ballad, *So In Love*, peaks at US #67, his last US chart single.
Dec Mayfield works with the Staple Singers on their soundtrack album ***Let's Do It Again***, which reaches US #20.

1976

July Disco aimed ***Give, Get, Take And Have*** peaks at US #171.
Aug Aretha Franklin's ***Sparkle***, produced by Mayfield, reaches US #18.

1977

Apr ***Never Say You Can't Survive*** (featuring his own version of *Sparkle*) peaks at US #173.
Oct Soundtrack album, ***Short Eyes***, from the low-budget prison movie featuring both Mayfield and Tex-Mex country singer Freddy Fender and based on Miguel Pinero's prize-winning play, follows the ***Superfly*** mould, but with no commercial success.

1978

June ***Almighty Fire***, another Mayfield-helmed album by Aretha Franklin, makes US #63, but marks the final

collaboration between them.
Oct ***Do It All Night***, entirely disco-styled, is released.
Dec *No Goodbyes*, a lengthy disco track which is Mayfield's first UK single for three years, is issued only on 12" and peaks at UK #65.

1979

Apr His Curtom label hits financial difficulties and Mayfield sells out to RSO Records, which insists he find an outside producer for his next disc. He chooses Philadelphia team Norman Harris, Ronald Tyson and Bunny Sigler.
Sept ***Heartbeat***, part-produced by the trio, with three self-produced tracks, makes US #42 and includes *Between You Baby And Me*, a duet with his recent discovery Linda Clifford.

1980

July ***The Right Combination***, again with Clifford, peaks at US #180.
Aug Mayfield's solo ***Something To Believe In*** reaches US #128, his last album with RSO, and his final US chart entry. (By year's end, Mayfield and his family will move from Chicago to Atlanta, GA.)

1981

Sept Mayfield has transferred to Neil Bogart's Boardwalk label, where disco producer Dino Fekaris produces Mayfield's newly-released ***Love Is The Place***, which is only issued in the US. Mayfield's prospects with the label further decline when Bogart dies shortly after its release.

1983

Mar The self-produced ***Honesty***, released on Boardwalk in the US the previous October, mixing political comment and romantic soul cuts, is now issued by Epic Records in the UK, where reviews are positive, and he tours twice in quick succession, his concerts featuring only pre-***Superfly*** material. (Later in the year, both Mayfield and Jerry Butler rejoin the Impressions for a brief US tour. A studio album from the reunion is rumored, but none emerges.)

1985

Sept Having performed a pair of dates on February 5th-6th the previous year at London's Venue during another UK tour, and with Curtom defunct, Mayfield has formed CRC Records which releases his US-only ***We Come In Peace With A Message Of Love***. A new single *Baby It's You* will be released in both territories on the 98.6 label in November the following year, but a planned album does not appear.

1987

May Having released *Baby It's You* the previous November, but now without a recording contract, Mayfield makes a short UK tour when he is invited to record with the Blow Monkeys, one of a current crop of UK groups who regard his early '70s work as inspirational.
June The Blow Monkeys' *Celebrate (The Day After You)*, featuring Mayfield, is released. (As an apparent pre-election attack on Prime Minister Margaret Thatcher, it is banned by the BBC as possibly prejudicial, until after the event, and peaks at UK #52.)

1988

June Mayfield tours the UK, Switzerland, Austria, West Germany, Holland and France, as the Curtom label is revived internationally by independent soul label Ichiban Records. The soundtrack album ***Superfly*** is reissued in the UK.
July *Move On Up*, always Mayfield's most popular recording in Britain (and subsequently repromoted by Mayfield fan Paul Weller, who revived it with the Jam), is reissued as a UK 12" single, and charts briefly at #87.

1990

Aug [13] Mayfield is crushed when a strong gust of wind blows a lighting rig on him during a rainstorm at an outdoor concert at Wingate High School Football Field in Flatbush, Brooklyn, New York.
[24] Paralysed from the neck down, Mayfield is transferred from King's County Hospital to Shepherd Spinal Center near his Atlanta, GA, home. Doctors fear he will remain paralysed. (Shortly after the tragedy, Mayfield's house burns down.)
Sept Recorded before his accident, a fashionably updated version of *Superfly*, namely *Superfly 1990*, featuring rap insertions by co-credited hip-hop star Ice-T, makes UK #48 and is featured on the accompanying ***Return Of Superfly*** soundtrack.

1991

Feb [28] Curtis Mayfield Day is declared in Los Angeles, CA, at a ceremony held in the rain outside the Ivar Theatre and the Inner City Cultural Center.

1993

Mar [15] ***People Get Ready : A Tribute To Curtis Mayfield***, a benefit album containing covers of Mayfield classics by the likes of Jerry Butler, Huey Lewis, Bunny Wailer and Living Colour's Vernon Reid is released, with half the proceeds going directly to the disabled star. Mayfield and his son Todd have recently formed the new indie rap label Conquest, also distributed by Ichiban.

1994

Jan [5] Mayfield is enshrined into the Hall of Fame at the NAACP's 26th annual Image Awards in Pasadena, CA.
Mar [1] He receives the Grammy Legend Award at the 36th annual Grammy Awards, held at New York's Radio City Music Hall, as Steve Winwood, Bruce Springsteen, Bonnie Raitt, B.B. King and others join in an all-star tribute to Mayfield.

1995

Mar [1] Mayfield and Me'Shell N'degeocello present the Best R&B Duo Or Group trophy to Boyz II Men at the 37th annual Grammy Awards held at Los Angeles' Shrine Auditorium.
July Newly signed to Warner Bros. Records, Mayfield begins work on a new album with producers Jimmy Jam & Terry Lewis, Daryl Simmons, Don Was and Narada Michael Walden.
Sept [21] Mayfield is part of a class action law suit beginning today in Atlanta whereby a number of veteran soul acts are seeking back-dated pension fund remuneration from allegedly unscrupulous record labels.
Nov [2] He is inducted into the Soul Train Hall of Fame at the 25th Soul Train Anniversary, staged at the Shrine Auditorium.

1996

Feb [27] Following the release of ***Curtis Mayfield & The Impressions : The Anthology 1961-1977*** by MCA in 1992 and Curtom's ***Living Legend*** last year, Rhino Records now issues the definitive Mayfield appraisal, the three-CD boxed set ***People Get Ready! The Curtis Mayfield Story***.
see also: THE IMPRESSIONS

PAUL McCARTNEY

1970

Apr [9] Having made his debut with the Quarry Men skiffle group on October 18th 1957, McCartney (b. James Paul McCartney, June 18, 1942, Liverpool, Lancs.), the son of Mary (who died from cancer in 1956) and sometime jazz-band leader James McCartney, has gone on to form, with Quarry Men founder John Lennon, the most successful songwriting partnership in popular music history and become the co-founder, bassist and co-lead vocalist of the most successful recording group of all-time, the Beatles. While the group has recently wrapped up the recording of its final album, ***Let It Be***, McCartney, who married Linda Eastman (b. Sept. 24, 1942, Scarsdale, New York, NY) at Marylebone Register Office, London on March 12th the previous year, has already finished sessions for his debut solo project, and now announces that he will not record with John Lennon again, as the acrimonious Beatles split is made official.
May [23] Released at the same time as ***Let It Be***, McCartney's home-studio recorded, self-penned, produced and performed solo debut, ***McCartney***, tops the US chart for the first of three weeks, will earn two platinum discs, and hits UK #2.
Sept [12] Producer Mickie Most meets McCartney in Scotland to offer him the role of poet Lee Simmons in the movie "The Second Coming Of Suzanne".

1971

Apr [17] His debut solo single, *Another Day*, hits UK #2 and US #5.
June [5] His sophomore set, ***Ram***, credited to Paul & Linda McCartney, hits UK #1 and US #2 (where it earns another platinum sales disc). While his former writing partner Lennon bases his early solo career on songs of personal angst and political commentary, McCartney settles into a simpler pop groove which will remain a constant for most of his recording career, much to the eager chagrin of rock critics.
Aug [3] McCartney announces the formation of his new band, Wings, comprising Paul and Linda McCartney, ex-Moody Blue guitarist Denny Laine (b. Brian Hines, Oct. 29, 1944, off the Jersey coast in a boat) on guitars and vocals, and Denny Seiwell on drums.
Sept [4] *Back Seat Of My Car* makes UK #39 as the US-only released *Uncle Albert/Admiral Halsey* tops the US chart.
[21] *Uncle Albert/Admiral Halsey* is certified gold by the RIAA.
Nov [8] He launches the album ***Wings Wildlife*** at the Empire Ballroom, Leicester Square, London, with Ray McVay & His Band Of The Day and the Frank & Peggy Spencer Formation Team.
Dec ***Wings Wildlife*** reaches UK #11 and US #10. His second album in six months, it is savaged by critics.

1972

Jan [13] ***Wings Wildlife*** is certified gold by the RIAA.
[29] Henry McCullough, ex-Grease Band, joins Wings.
Feb [9] The group embarks on a UK tour at Nottingham University, Nottingham, Notts., arriving at colleges unannounced and asking social secretaries if they would like Wings to perform in their hall that evening. The 11-date series will end on the 23rd at Oxford University, Oxford, Oxon.
Mar [14] *Uncle Albert/Admiral Halsey* wins the Best Arrangement Accompanying A Vocalist category at the 14th annual Grammy Awards.
Apr [8] Highly political *Give Ireland Back To The Irish* reaches UK #16 and US #21. Written after the "Bloody Sunday Massacre" in Northern Ireland in January, it is banned by the BBC and the IBA.
June Embittered by the ban on his single, McCartney puts music to a nursery rhyme, with the resulting *Mary Had A Little Lamb* hitting UK #9.
July [9] Wings makes its formal concert debut at the Theatre Antique, Chateauvallon, France, at the start of a 25-date European and Scandinavian tour, set to end on August 24th at the Deutschlandhalle, West Berlin, West Germany.
[22] *Mary Had A Little Lamb* reaches US #28.
Aug [10] Paul and Linda are fined £800 for possession of cannabis in Gothenburg, Sweden.
Sept [20] They are arrested again for possession at their Scottish farmhouse in Campbeltown.
Nov [30] BBC Radio One bans the newly released *Hi Hi Hi*, after it is played once on the "Tony Blackburn Breakfast Show".

1973

Jan [13] Its B-side, *C Moon*, now the preferred airplay cut, hits UK #5.
Feb [3] *Hi Hi Hi* hits US #10.
Mar [8] An ITV special, "James Paul McCartney", is filmed at Borehamwood Studios, Herts, the same day McCartney is fined £100 for growing cannabis on his

Campbeltown farm.
Apr Ballad *My Love* hits UK #9 as McCartney hints at a possible Beatles reunion.
May ***Red Rose Speedway***, credited to Paul McCartney & Wings, hits UK #5.
[10] "James Paul McCartney" special airs. A musical extravaganza, it features McCartney in a crowded Liverpool pub for a singalong, performing a Fred Astaire-style dance routine and ending with a solo performance of *Yesterday*.
[11] Wings embark on their first major UK tour at the Hippodrome, Bristol, Avon, a 15-date trek set to end on 27th at London's Hammersmith Odeon.
[25] The still-climbing ***Red Rose Speedway*** is certified gold by the RIAA.
June [2] On the same day that ***Red Rose Speedway*** tops the US chart, *My Love* hits US #1, deposed four weeks later by George Harrison's *Give Me Love (Give Me Peace On Earth)*, while *Live And Let Die*, McCartney's theme to the forthcoming James Bond film, hits UK #9. Music producer George Martin has played the song in its finished form to the film's producer Harry Saltzmann, who assumes it is a demo and suggests that Thelma Houston should cut it. Martin reassures Saltzmann that this is a finished item by an ex-Beatle. (The song stands but Brenda Arnau will cover it on the film's soundtrack album.)
July [6] *My Love* is certified gold by the RIAA.
Aug [9] McCullough and Seiwell quit Wings as the remaining trio flies to Ginger Baker's ARC Studios in Lagos, Nigeria, to record ***Band On The Run***.
[11] *Live And Let Die* hits US #2, kept off the top by Diana Ross' *Touch Me In The Morning* and then by Stories' *Brother Louie*.
[31] *Live And Let Die* is confirmed gold by the RIAA.
Dec *Helen Wheels*, a song written about McCartney's Landrover jeep, affectionately known as "Hell On Wheels", reaches UK #12.
[26] Paul and Linda present BBC1-TV's "Disney Time".

1974

Jan [12] *Helen Wheels* hits US #10.
Mar [30] *Jet*, inspired by McCartney's pet labrador puppy, hits both UK and US #7.
Apr [13] ***Band On The Run*** begins a four-week stay atop the US chart, after receiving rave reviews. It will sell 6,000,000 copies worldwide and spend over two years on both the UK and US surveys. Its celebrity-filled cover features Michael Parkinson, James Coburn, Kenny Lynch, Clement Freud, Christopher Lee and John Conteh posing with the group as escaped convicts caught in a searchlight. (McCartney had invited them to lunch, and then asked them to pose for the photo.) After many refusals, due to drug convictions, McCartney finally gets a US visa.
May The group becomes a five-piece again with Jimmy McCulloch (b. June 4, 1953, Glasgow, Strathclyde, Scotland), ex-Thunderclap Newman and Stone The Crows, joining on guitar and vocals, and former UK karate champion Geoff Britton (b. Aug. 1, 1943) on drums.
June McCartney-produced *Liverpool Lou*, released by his brother Mike McGear's group, Scaffold, hits UK #7.
[4] Still-climbing title cut *Band On The Run* is certified gold by the RIAA.
[8] *Band On The Run* tops the US chart for the first of three weeks. The group travels to Nashville, TN, to record, and for McCartney to produce Peggy Lee's ***Let's Love***.
July [13] ***Band On The Run*** tops the UK survey.
Aug *Band On The Run* hits UK #3, backed with his theme to the ITV series "The Zoo Gang".
Oct Wings release *Walking In The Park With Eloise*, written by McCartney's father James, under the pseudonym the Country Hams. (When McCartney appears on the BBC radio program "Desert Island Discs", he chooses it as one of his favorite records.)
Nov [27] Paul and Linda sing backing vocals on *Mine For Me* at a Rod Stewart concert at the Lewisham Odeon, London.
Dec *Junior's Farm*, written during McCartney's stay in Nashville at Junior Putnam's farm, reaches UK #16.

1975

Jan [11] *Junior's Farm* hits US #3.
Feb Joe English (b. Feb. 7, 1949, Rochester, NY) replaces Britton on drums.
[22] *Sally G* makes US #39.
Mar [1] At the 17th annual Grammy Awards, *Band On The Run* nabs the Best Pop Vocal Performance By A Duo, Group Or Chorus category.
June *Listen To What The Man Said* hits UK #6.
[14] ***Venus And Mars***, containing a version of the theme to popular ITV soap opera "Crossroads", tops the UK chart.
[26] McCartney's "Crossroads" theme airs for the first time on ITV.
July [19] *Listen To What The Man Said* and ***Venus And Mars*** simultaneously head respective US listings.
Sept [5] *Listen To What The Man Said* is certified gold by the RIAA.
[9] Wings begin a 13-month tour of ten countries at the Gaumont Cinema, Southampton, Hants. They will play to over two million people. (During Australian dates, faux chat-show host Norman Gunston asks Linda McCartney whether the only reason she is in the band is because she sleeps with the group's lead singer.)
Oct [25] *Letting Go* makes UK #41 and US #39.
Dec [13] *Venus And Mars Rock Show* reaches US #12, but fails to chart in the UK, his first miss in 13 years.

1976

Apr [3] ***Wings At The Speed Of Sound*** hits UK #2, behind the soundtrack to the ITV show "Rock Follies". McCartney's democratic approach to Wings affords each member a lead vocal cut and shared songwriting credits.
[24] ***Wings At The Speed Of Sound*** begins an eight-week run at US #1.
May [3] The Wings world tour arrives in the US as "Wings Over America", and McCartney makes his first US stage appearance in ten years at the Tarrant County Convention Center, Fort Worth, TX, as ***Wings At The Speed Of Sound*** is certified platinum by the RIAA.
[22] Pop ditty, *Silly Love Songs*, tops the US chart.
June [2] Wings establish a new world attendance record for an indoor crowd as 67,100 paying customers see them at the Kingdome in Seattle, WA.
[11] *Silly Love Songs* is confirmed gold by the RIAA.
[12] *Silly Love Songs* hits UK #2, kept from the top by labelmates the Wurzels with the novelty *Combine Harvester*.
July Boosting his burgeoning publishing interests, McCartney buys Edwin H. Morris Music, which includes the entire Buddy Holly catalog which McCartney has often quoted as a seminal inspiration on his own songwriting.
Aug [11] EMI inks a deal with Soviet company Melodiya to release ***Band On The Run*** in the Soviet Union.
[14] *Let 'Em In* hits US #3.
[28] *Let 'Em In* hits UK #2.
Sept [7] McCartney commemorates Holly's 40th birthday by instituting an annual "Buddy Holly Week".
[25] Wings play a UNESCO concert in St. Mark's Square, Venice, Italy, to draw attention to the decay and neglect in the historic city. The concert is a success but the weight of equipment used by the group causes areas of subsidence damage in the Square.
Oct [19-21] Wings' world tour comes to an end with three sellout shows at the Empire Pool, Wembley, Middx.
[25] *Let 'Em In* is certified gold by the RIAA.
Dec [20] The RIAA also ratifies platinum sales of ***Wings Over America***.

1977

Jan [22] ***Wings Over America***, a triple-set, 30-track documentary of the group's US tour, including five Beatles songs, tops the US chart and hits UK #8.
Mar [5] *Maybe I'm Amazed*, a live version of a song from McCartney's debut solo album, reaches UK #28.
Apr [2] *Maybe I'm Amazed* hits US #10.
[29] ***Thrillington***, an orchestral interpretation of McCartney's ***Ram***, is released, featuring orchestra leader Percy "Thrills" Thrillington, a pseudonym for McCartney.
Sept [8] McCulloch quits Wings to join a re-formed Small Faces, while English joins Sea Level, once again reducing Wings to a trio.
Dec [3] Waltz *Mull Of Kintyre* tops the UK chart for the first of nine weeks. It is co-written with Laine about the southern tip of the Kintyre peninsula, 11 miles from McCartney's farmhouse in Campbeltown. (Laine will later sell McCartney his rights to the song after being declared bankrupt.)
[10] Wings film an appearance for BBC1-TV's "The Mike Yarwood Christmas Show", singing *Mull Of Kintyre* amidst a cloud of dry ice. The show will air on Christmas day.
[17] Mr. David Ackroyd purchases the one millionth copy of *Mull Of Kintyre* in the UK and becomes the first record buyer in the world to receive a gold disc for his purchase. (It will be the biggest-selling UK single of all time at 2.5 million, replacing the Beatles' *She Loves You*, until Band Aid's 1984 *Do They Know It's Christmas?*)

1978

Jan [14] *Mull Of Kintyre* fails to score in the US, though its B-side, *Girls School* makes US #33.
Mar [30] ***London Town*** is certified platinum by the RIAA.
Apr *With A Little Luck* hits UK #5, as its parent album, ***London Town***, recorded in London and on the yacht "Fair Carol" in the Virgin Islands, hits UK #4 and US #2. It features *Girlfriend*, later covered by Michael Jackson on ***Off The Wall***.
May [12] *Mull Of Kintyre* wins the Best Selling A-Side category at the 23rd annual Ivor Novello Awards, at the Grosvenor House Hotel, London.
[20] Proving to be an enduring radio favorite, *With A Little Luck* becomes McCartney's sixth US chart-topping solo single.
July *I've Had Enough* makes UK #42, as Wings becomes a five-piece, joined by Laurence Juber on guitar and vocals and ex-sessionman Steve Holly on drums.
Aug [5] *I've Had Enough* reaches US #25.
Sept Title cut *London Town* peaks at UK #60.
Oct [14] *London Town* makes US #39.
Dec Compilation album ***Wings Greatest*** hits UK #5 and US #29.
[6] ***Wings Greatest*** is certified platinum by the RIAA.

1979

Mar [16] "Wings Over The World" airs on US TV.
May [5] *Goodnight Tonight* hits UK #5.
[15] Still-rising *Goodnight Tonight* is confirmed gold by the RIAA.
[19] Paul joins George Harrison and Ringo Starr for an impromptu jam session at the wedding reception of Eric Clapton and Patti Harrison, as *Goodnight Tonight* hits US #5, where it is released on the Columbia label, with which McCartney signs a deal, worth a reported $2 million per album for three albums in three years, $2 million for the catalog and a 22% royalty rate.
June [30] *Old Siam Sir* makes UK #35 as its parent album, ***Back To The Egg***, hits UK #6 and US #8. His ninth album to achieve million-plus sales in the US (certified on July 18th), it also marks the final set credited to Wings.
July [28] *Getting Closer* reaches US #20.
Aug *Haven't We Met Somewhere Before?*, written by McCartney for the film "Heaven Can Wait" but rejected, is featured as the opening song in the film "Rock'n'Roll High School", performed by the Ramones. Linda McCartney releases *Seaside Woman*, under the name Suzy & the Red Stripes. Despite McCartney's production, the single fails to chart.
Sept *Getting Closer/Baby's Request* makes UK #60.
[14] Wings appear on stage at the Hammersmith Odeon with the Crickets, as part of the fourth annual "Buddy Holly Week" festivities.
Oct [13] *Arrow Through Me* reaches US #29.
[24] McCartney receives a medallion cast in rhodium

from the UK Arts Minister at a **Guinness Book Of Records** reception at Les Ambassadeurs Club, London, after being declared the most successful composer of all time. From 1962 to 1978, he has written or co-written 43 songs that have sold over one million copies each and has sold over 100 million singles and 100 million albums to date.
Nov [24] Wings open an 18-date UK tour at the Royal Court Theatre, Liverpool, set to end on December 17th at the Apollo Theatre, Glasgow, Scotland.
Dec [20] Paul and Linda announce on Tom Snyder's "Tomorrow" show on US TV that the Beatles will never reunite.
[29] Wings play the last night of the "Concerts For The People Of Kampuchea" at the Hammersmith Odeon, with *Rockestra Theme* revived with an all-star band, most of whom featured on the disc.

1980

Jan [5] Festive *Wonderful Christmastime*, McCartney's first solo single since 1971, hits UK #6.
[16] McCartney is jailed in Tokyo for marijuana possession, after being found with 219g of marijuana on his arrival at Narita International Airport. (Laine later sympathetically relates McCartney's experience in *Japanese Tears*.)
[25] He is released and extradited from Japan. He is not keen to return.
Feb [26] McCartney receives the Outstanding Music Personality award at the British Rock and Pop Awards at London's Café Royal.
[27] *Rockestra Theme* wins the Best Rock Instrumental Performance for Wings at the 22nd annual Grammy Awards.
May [3] *Coming Up* hits UK #2, behind Dexy's Midnight Runners' *Geno*. In its accompanying video clip, McCartney takes on the role of five stars - Frank Zappa, Ron Mael, Buddy Holly, Andy Mackay and himself as a Beatle with a collarless suit, in a group dubbed the Plastic Macs.
[8] McCartney receives the Special Award For International Achievement at the 25th annual Ivor Novello Awards, held at the Grosvenor House Hotel.
[31] ***McCartney II*** begins a two-week stay atop the UK chart. Like his solo debut album, the set has been recorded at home, using microphones plugged directly into tape machines.
June [28] B-side, *Coming Up*, featuring a live version, recorded at the Glasgow Apollo in December 1979, which has become popular on US radio, tops the US chart, as different forms of the same song are currently ranked in both the US and UK.
July [19] Ballad *Waterfalls* hits UK #9.
[21] *Coming Up* is certified gold by the RIAA.
[25] ***McCartney II*** is also confirmed gold by the RIAA.
Sept *Temporary Secretary* is released as a limited edition 12" single.
Oct [31] McCartney records with producer George Martin for the first time in eight years, when they cut *We All Stand Together* at AIR Studios, London.
Nov [26] Film "Rockshow", a Wings concert from their 1976 US tour, premieres at New York's Ziegfeld Theatre.
Dec [8] John Lennon, is murdered in New York, as he returns home from a recording session. McCartney, describing him as "a great man who will be sadly missed", says that he will mourn in private.

1981

Feb ***McCartney Interview***, originally a promotional record for US radio stations, is released due to public demand and peaks at US #158. It is deleted on the day of release in Britain, but still reaches #34.
Apr [27] He attends the wedding of Ringo Starr and Barbara Bach at Marylebone Register Office, London.

1982

Jan [30] McCartney guests on BBC Radio's "Desert Island Discs". His eight selections are Elvis Presley's *Heartbreak Hotel*, Chuck Berry's *Sweet Little Sixteen*, Gene Vincent's *Be Bop A Lula*, John Lennon's *Beautiful Boy*, the Coasters' *Searchin'*, Little Richard's *Tutti Frutti*, the Country Hams' *Walking In The Park With Eloise* and Julian Bream's *Courtly Dances* from Benjamin Britten's *Gloria*.
Apr [24] *Ebony And Ivory*, calling for racial harmony and written by McCartney as a duet with Stevie Wonder, tops the UK chart. (McCartney becomes first of the Beatles to gain an entry in **Who's Who**.)
May [8] ***Tug Of War***, recorded with help from Stevie Wonder, Eric Stewart, Ringo Starr and Carl Perkins, hits UK #1.
[15] *Ebony And Ivory* also heads the US survey for the first of seven weeks, set to become the year's most successful single.
[29] ***Tug Of War*** begins a three-week run atop the US chart.
June [7] *Ebony And Ivory* is certified gold by the RIAA.
[29] ***Tug Of War*** is confirmed platinum by the RIAA.
Aug [21] Horns-backed *Take It Away* reaches UK #15 and US #10.
Oct [23] *Tug Of War* makes both UK and US #53.
Nov [20] *The Girl Is Mine*, a duet with Michael Jackson from his album ***Thriller***, hits UK #8.

1983

Jan [8] *The Girl Is Mine* hits US #2.
Feb [8] McCartney wins Best British Male Artist and the Sony Trophy For Technical Excellence at the second annual BRIT Awards, at the Grosvenor House Hotel.
May [5] *Ebony And Ivory* nabs International Hit Of The Year at the 28th annual Ivor Novello Awards, also at the Grosvenor House Hotel.
Oct McCartney makes a cameo appearance driving a Robin Reliant in Tracey Ullman's video for her UK #2 smash, *They Don't Know*.
Nov [19] *Say Say Say*, another duet with Jackson promoted by a $500,000 video, hits UK #2, behind Billy Joel's *Uptown Girl*, as McCartney's album ***Pipes Of Peace*** hits UK #4 and US #15. Produced by ex-Beatles producer George Martin, the album includes music guests Andy McKay, Stanley Clarke, Ringo Starr, Steve Gadd, Eric Stewart and Michael Jackson. (By year's end, McCartney also writes the main theme to Richard Gere film "The Honorary Consul".)
Dec [10] *Say Say Say* begins a six-week run atop the US chart.

1984

Jan [14] *Pipes Of Peace*, spurred by another costly video, this time recreating the famous Christmas Day truce during the Great War in 1914, becomes his second solo UK chart-topper.
[16] Paul and Linda are again arrested for drug possession in Barbados and will each receive a $200 fine.
Feb [11] *So Bad*, with *Pipes Of Peace* on the B-side, makes US #23.
[17] ***Pipes Of Peace*** is certified platinum by the RIAA.
Oct [27] *No More Lonely Nights*, previewing McCartney's first feature film, hits UK #2, behind Wham!'s *Freedom*. The B-side features a uptempo version of the A-side ballad.
Nov [3] ***Give My Regards To Broad Street*** hits UK #1, the soundtrack to a film starring McCartney, based on his script and described as a "musical fantasy drama". The album comprises re-recordings of Beatles tracks and McCartney hits and is once again overseen by Martin. The film is a critical and box-office failure, but reaches US #21.
[16] McCartney co-hosts NBC-TV's "Friday Night Videos" with Julian Lennon.
[28] He is awarded the Freedom of Liverpool in a ceremony at his home city's Picton Library.
Dec [8] *No More Lonely Nights* hits US #6. McCartney, who now owns rights to the Rupert Bear cartoon stories, which have appeared in the UK's **Daily Express** newspaper for over 50 years, has made a short pilot film featuring the song *We All Stand Together*, credited to Paul McCartney & the Frog Chorus. It hits UK #3, and will become an annual Christmas favorite, while the animated video will also become a UK best seller.
[26] ***Give My Regards To Broad Street*** is certified gold by the RIAA.

1985

Mar [13] *We All Stand Together* is named Best Film Theme Or Song at the 30th annual Ivor Novello Awards, at the Grosvenor House Hotel.
July [13] McCartney sings *Let It Be* as the climax to the "Live Aid" benefit spectacular at Wembley Stadium, Wembley.
Aug [10] Michael Jackson, formerly McCartney's friend and music collaborator, outbids the ex-Beatle in the acquisition of the ATV music publishing catalog, which includes a large portion of the Lennon and McCartney composition songbook. Seen by McCartney as an act of betrayal, relationships with Jackson are permanently soured.

1986

Jan [4] *Spies Like Us*, the theme to the Dan Aykroyd/Chevy Chase film of the same name, reaches UK #13, as *We All Stand Together*, repromoted at Christmas, reaches UK #32.
[27] McCartney is honored with the Special Award Of Merit at at the 13th annual American Music Awards, held at the Shrine Auditorium, Los Angeles, CA.
Feb [8] *Spies Like Us* hits US #7.
June [20] McCartney participates in the "Prince's Trust Birthday Party" at the Wembley Arena.
Aug [16] *Press* reaches UK #25.
[29] BBC1-TV airs the "McCartney" special.
Sept [13] *Press* reaches US #21. ***Press To Play*** hits UK #8 and US #30.
Nov [24] McCartney takes part in the annual "Royal Variety Performance" at London's Theatre Royal, Drury Lane.
[29] *Stranglehold* peaks at US #81.
Dec The McCartneys escape injury when their car bursts into flames on the way to a recording of C4-TV show "The Tube" in Newcastle, Tyne & Wear.
[20] *Only Love Remains* reaches UK #34.

1987

Nov 17-track greatest hits album, ***All The Best!***, hits UK #2.
Dec [12] *Once Upon A Long Ago* hits UK #10. (The CD version of the single harks back to McCartney's first love with versions of *Don't Get Around Much Anymore* and *Kansas City* while the vinyl single's B-side, *Back On My Feet*, is co-written with Elvis Costello.)

1988

Jan ***All The Best!***, with a different track listing from the UK version, makes US #62.
[20] Claiming he still has business differences with the rest of the group, McCartney does not attend the induction of the Beatles into the Rock and Roll Hall of Fame at the third annual induction dinner, at New York's Waldorf Astoria Hotel.
June It is reported that McCartney has been asked to record an album of his rock'n'roll favorites for exclusive release in USSR on the state Melodiya label.
[24] McCartney receives the Silver Clef Award for Outstanding Achievement In The World Of British Music at the annual Nordoff Robbins Music Therapy Centre lunch, at London's Inter-Continental Hotel.
July [12] McCartney is bestowed a honorary doctorate from the University of Sussex, Brighton, East Sussex.
Aug **Moscow News** reports that plans are being laid for McCartney to play eight concerts in Moscow in 1989, as work continues on a new album.
Sept [7] McCartney joins the Crickets on stage at the "Buddy Holly Week" festival in London.
Nov McCartney produces *Let The Children Play* (profits of which will go to the annual Children In Need fundraising event).

1989

Feb USSR's Melodiya label presses 40,000 copies of ***Back In The USSR***, featuring McCartney's interpretations of several classic rock'n'roll hits, including *Kansas City*, *Lawdy Miss Clawdy*, *Lucille*,

That's All Right Mama and *Ain't That A Shame*.
Mar *Veronica* cements a new co-writing relationship with Elvis Costello. Forthcoming albums from both artists will feature co-written songs and McCartney claims in interviews that the collaboration reminds him of working with Lennon.
Apr [4] McCartney receives a standing ovation when collecting the Outstanding Services To British Music award at the 34th annual Ivor Novello lunch, at the Grosvenor House Hotel. Accepting the statuette, he performs an impromptu rap in front of many peers.
[20] He teams with fellow Liverpudlians Gerry Marsden, Holly Johnson and the Christians to record *Ferry 'Cross The Mersey* in aid of the Hillsborough Disaster Fund (hitting UK #1 on May 20th).
May [27] McCartney embarks on major promotion in support of *My Brave Face*, which reaches UK #18, and a forthcoming album, including appearances on BBC1-TV's "Wogan" chat show, a **Rolling Stone** magazine front cover, and an eight-part BBC Radio 1 series, "Paul McCartney Story".
June [24] ***Flowers In The Dirt*** hits UK #1 and begins a US rise to #21. Containing Costello collaborations, including a vocal duet, its producers include Trevor Horn, Neil Dorfsman, Chris Hughes and David Foster with musical assistance from Nicky Hopkins and David Gilmour. Plans are announced for a six-month world tour, starting in Scandinavia in September. The backing band will be Hamish Stuart (ex-Average White Band), Robbie McIntosh, Chris Whitten, Paul Wickens and Linda McCartney. Press reports that McCartney and Sting will lead a UK BBC radio campaign to raise listeners' awareness of environmental issues.
July [8] *My Brave Face* reaches US #25.
[27] McCartney announces the world tour at a press conference at London's Playhouse Theatre, and treats 400 fan club members to a 90-minute set previewing the live show.
Aug [7] ***Flowers In The Dirt*** is certified gold by the RIAA.
[12] *This One* reaches UK #18.
[21] He begins four days of rehearsal at the Lyceum Theatre, New York.
Sept [16] *This One* peaks at US #94.
[21] McCartney performs at Studio 6, Goldcrest studios, Elstree, Herts., for winners of a BBC Radio 1 contest.
[28] McCartney's first world tour in 13 years opens at the Scandinavium, Gothenburg, Sweden.
Nov [23-24, 27, 29] The North American leg of the trek begins at the Great Western Forum, Inglewood, CA. During the third show, Stevie Wonder joins McCartney on stage to sing *Ebony And Ivory*.
Figure Of Eight makes UK #43.
Dec [11-14] McCartney performs four sellout shows before 62,351 at New York's Madison Square Garden, grossing $1,759,290 and is awarded the Gold Ticket for playing to over 100,000 fans.
[15] A committed vegetarian and environmental awareness campaigner, McCartney donates $100,000 to Friends of the Earth.
[19] McCartney is honored by the PRS for his "unique achievement in popular music" at a luncheon at Claridge's Hotel, London - the first time in the body's 75-year history that an individual has been so honored.

1990

Jan [2] He begins the British leg of his world tour at National Exhibition Centre in Birmingham, West Midlands. It is his first UK concert appearance in a decade.
[5] At a further concert at the National Exhibition Centre, a man turns up backstage claiming to be Father McKenzie (McCartney's fictional character in *Eleanor Rigby*). McCartney is heard to respond, "Where's Mr. Kite and Billy Shears? Are they here too?"
[11] McCartney plays the first of 11 concerts at the Wembley Arena, before crowds totalling 137,000.
[13] *Figure Of Eight* peaks at US #92.
[16] McCartney meets 21-year-old Polish teacher Agnieska Czarniecka, who for four years has run the Paul McCartney Kindergarten in Cracow, where 200 children are taught English through McCartney's songs.
[25] CBS-TV's "48 Hours", following McCartney at his Rosemont Horizon, Chicago, IL gig, airs.
Feb McCartney contributes a cover of *It's Now Or Never* to the compilation album ***The Last Temptation Of Elvis***, to benefit the Nordoff Robbins Music Therapy charity.
[17] *Put It There* makes UK #32.
[21] McCartney is presented with NARAS' Lifetime Achievement Award at the 32nd annual Grammy Awards by rock legend Meryl Streep, noting that McCartney "as a member of the Beatles, had an impact not only on rock'n'roll but also on Western culture, and, as a solo performer and songwriter, continues to develop and grow after three decades".
Mar [9] McCartney donates $250,000 to the Sloan-Kettering Cancer Centre and Friends of the Earth during an 11-date stint at the Dome, Tokyo, Japan.
[31-**Apr** 1] He records the highest grossing concert of the year when 118,352 fans pay $3,550,560 to see him at the Memorial Stadium, University of California-Berkeley, Berkeley, CA.
Apr [21] McCartney gains a place in **The Guinness Book Of Records** when he plays before the largest-paying attendance of a 184,000 people at a public event at the Maracana Stadium, Rio de Janeiro, Brazil. It breaks the record of 175,000 set by Frank Sinatra at the same venue on January 26th, 1980.
June Harold "Ness" Rynard of Carlisle, PA, begins collecting 500,000 signatures to petition H.R.H. Queen Elizabeth II demanding that McCartney be knighted. Based at Friends of Paul, PO Box 368, Carlisle, PA 17013, he will accumulate 10% of his target by June 1991.
July [29] McCartney's world trek ends at Chicago's Soldier Field in front of 55,630 fans, grossing $1,807,975. The tour has lasted 45 weeks, during which he has played 102 concerts in 46 cities.
Sept [4] The 15th annual "Buddy Holly Week" begins with a performance at the Lone Star Roadhouse in New York, with Dave Edmunds, Steve Forbert, Joe Ely, Max Weinberg and the Crickets. Special guests are Maria Elena Holly and New York mayor David Dinkins.
Oct [27] *Birthday* reaches UK #29.
Nov Performance set, ***Tripping The Live Fantastic***, recorded during his recent world sojourn, reaches UK #17.
[18] McCartney's birth certificate is sold for $18,000 in Houston, TX, despite allegations of auction-rigging to get an inflated price for the document.
Dec [1] ***Tripping The Live Fantastic*** reaches US #26.
[8] *All My Trials* makes UK #35.

1991

Jan [5] ***Tripping The Live Fantastic - Highlights***, a special limited-edition version of the album, peaks at US #141.
[25] McCartney records an acoustic set before a small audience for the embryonic US-MTV program "Unplugged" at London's Limehouse Studios. The show will premiere in the US on April 3rd.
Mar [7] He is named Best Bassist in the annual **Rolling Stone** Readers' Picks music awards.
May [10] McCartney plays at London's Mean Fiddler, the smallest concert venue he has performed at since playing the Cavern for the last time on August 3rd, 1963.
June [1] ***Unplugged - Official Bootleg***, documenting his January 25th MTV performance and the first in a highly successful series of spin-off albums from the "Unplugged" series, debuts at its UK #7 peak.
[22] ***For Our Children***, to which McCartney has contributed *Mary Had A Little Lamb*, reaches US #31.
[22] ***Unplugged (The Official Bootleg)*** bows at its US #14 peak.
[27] McCartney's classical work, the semi-autobiographical "Liverpool Oratorio", is performed by the Royal Liverpool Philharmonic Orchestra in Liverpool Cathedral.
[28] He takes Michael Portillo, Minister for Inner Cities, on a tour of the abandoned Liverpool Institute.
Aug [12] ***Tripping The Live Fantastic - Highlights!*** is certified platinum by the RIAA.
Sept [18] "Get Back", the movie of McCartney's world tour, receives its world premiere at the Passage Hotel, Hamburg, Germany. (It will receive its UK premiere the following night in Liverpool, Birmingham, Leeds and Glasgow, before opening in London on the 20th.)
Oct [12] ***Choba B CCCP (The Russian Album)*** charts for a week at UK #63.
Nov [16] ***Choba B CCCP (The Russian Album)***, originally released in the Soviet Union in 1988, debuts at its US #109 peak.
[18] "Liverpool Oratio" makes its US premiere at New York's Carnegie Hall with the Royal Liverpool Philharmonic again conducted by Carl Davis.
[27] The RIAA certifies platinum sales of ***Venus And Mars*** and multi-platinum sales of ***Band On The Run***, now standing at three million.
Dec [13] ***McCartney*** is confirmed by the RIAA for sales of two million.
[21] ***Paul McCartney's Liverpool Oratorio Conducted By Carl Davis***, featuring Kiri Te Kanawa, Sally Burgess, Jerry Hadley and Willard White, peaks at US #177, and topples José Carreras, Placido Domingo and Luciano Pavarotti from atop the **Billboard** Classical chart after more than a year at #1.

1992

Feb [5] ***Ram*** is certified platinum by the RIAA.
[21] At a PRS lunch, he announces plans to open a "Fame"-style school, the Liverpool Institute for the Performing Arts.
May The MPA donates £500,000 to McCartney's Liverpool Institute. The Beatle has now reportedly contributed £1.5 million.
[5] *Say Say Say* is certified platinum by the RIAA.
[18] Sweden's King Carl Gustaf presents the first Polar Music Prize to McCartney, cited for his "creativity and imagination as a composer and artist which has revitalised popular music over the last 30 years" by the Royal Swedish Academy of Music. McCartney also receives one million Kronor (approx £110,000), part of which he uses to establish the Liverpool Institute and a Liverpool hospital fundraising campaign.
Aug While staying in New York's Hamptons, he joins G.E. Smith's band at Stephen Talk House, Amagansett, to sing *Blue Suede Shoes*.
Sept McCartney finishes a new album with producer Julian Mendelsohn at The Mill in Rye, East Sussex.
Dec [3] At a luncheon to preview his new album in the US, Capitol president/CEO Hale Milgrim announces the signing of McCartney "for the rest of his recording career".
[10] At a press conference to announce his first tour of Australia since 1975, McCartney says that the remaining Beatles are working together on a forthcoming documentary and that there is a good chance they will also perform together.
[11] McCartney tapes an "Up Close" special for MTV, set to air on February 3rd, at the Ed Sullivan Theater, New York. (During the year, McCartney also sings on Eddie Murphy's *The Yeah Yeah Song* for the comedian's ***Love's Alright*** album, in exchange for Murphy becoming a vegetarian for a week.)

1993

Jan [23] *Hope Of Deliverance* reaches UK #18.
Feb [13] McCartney guests on NBC-TV's "Saturday Night Live", as ***Off The Ground*** debuts at its UK #5 peak.
[27] Pop-returning ***Off The Ground*** bows at its US #17 peak.
Mar [5] McCartney's latest world tour opens at the Subiaco Oval, Perth, Australia. His Melbourne Cricket Ground 51,000-seater concert sells out in eight hours.
[6] *C'mon People* bows at its UK #41 peak.
[13] *Hope Of Deliverance* stops at US #83.
Apr [8] McCartney announces at a press conference that $9 million had been promised for his show-business school in Liverpool.

[12] ***Off The Ground*** is certified gold by the RIAA.
[14] The US leg of the world trek opens at the Sam Boyd Silver Bowl, Las Vegas, NV, set to end on June 4th at the Silverdome, Detroit.
[16] McCartney headlines an "Earth Day" concert at the Hollywood Bowl, with Steve Miller, 10,000 Maniacs, Kenny Loggins, Bruce Cockburn, PM Dawn and k.d. lang with funds going to PETA, Greenpeace and Friends of the Earth. He is joined on stage by Ringo Starr for *Hey Jude*.
May [18] In a **USA Today** interview he says about the 1985 Michael Jackson publishing takeover of the Lennon and McCartney songwriting legacy: "I've written to him three times" (and not received a reply.) "You know what's upsetting? I'm the only living writer in the company! I reckon it's time to negotiate what reflects (my) success. I'm still on the little kid's deal. Now Michael Jackson picks up more for that song (*Yesterday*) ... than I do."
June [15] "Paul McCartney Live In The New World", his first televised live concert, is broadcast on Fox-TV from the Blockbuster Pavilion, Charlotte, NC.
Nov [20] Performance set ***Paul Is Live*** debuts at its UK #34 peak.
Dec [4] ***Paul Is Live*** bows at its US #78 peak.

1994

Jan [19] McCartney inducts John Lennon into the Rock and Roll Hall of Fame at the ninth annual dinner, held at New York's Waldorf Astoria Hotel. He says "The thing you must remember is that I'm the number one John Lennon fan. I love him to this day and I always did love him. All these people assembled to thank you for everything that you mean to all of us. Tonight you're in the Rock and Roll Hall of Fame. God bless you."
Feb [22] With no label credit to reveal the artist's identity, the pseudonymic *The Fireman*, recorded by McCartney, with Youth, in 1993, is issued in the US by Capitol, following its earlier UK release.
Mar [4] ***All The Best*** is certified platinum by the RIAA.
[12] McCartney receives the Doris Day Music Award at the Genesis Awards.
Nov He appears as a Shakespearean actor in a TV commercial to promote the Liverpool Institute of the Performing Arts.

1995

Mar [23] McCartney performs *Lady Madonna* backed by the Brodsky Quartet, plus excerpts from the "Liverpool Oratorio" at a £250 head-per-ticket dinner benefit at St. James Palace to raise money for London's Royal College of Music, at the request of its president, H.R.H. the Prince of Wales. His 10 minute, classical piano piece, "The Leaf", is performed by former student, Anya Alexeyev.
May [29] A 13-part multigenre McCartney-directed radio series "Oobu Joobu" premieres in the US via the Westwood One radio network. It includes never-before heard McCartney recordings and rehearsal, Beatles soundchecks and interviews.
June [12] His daughter Stella's premiere fashion collection takes place in London with a new song *Stella May* written by her father included as part of the runway music.
July [15] Paul and Linda head a parade through Rye to celebrate the opening of a 16-bed hospital fund-raising drive.
Sept [4] McCartney, Paul Weller and Oasis' Noel Gallagher, with help from Beautiful South, Black Grape and Dodgy, cut *Come Together*, as the Smokin' Mojo Filters, for the ***Help!*** War Child benefit album.
[14] His hand-written lyrics for *Getting Better* sell for $249,200 at a Sotheby's auction in London.
Oct [16] He joins Allen Ginsberg onstage at the Royal Albert Hall.
Nov [8] McCartney becomes the first pop musician to be made a Fellow of the Royal College of Music, receiving his award for distinguished services to music from H.R.H. the Prince of Wales.
[19] The first portion of "The Beatles Anthology" airs on ABC-TV. Including extensive new interviews with the remaining trio, edited in with old Lennon interviews, it attempts to build a definitive archival documentary of the Beatles' early years, with personal anecdotes, remembrances and observations. At the close of tonight's segment, the Beatles first "new" recording since their split, *Free As A Bird* receives its premiere airing. The track has been assembled around a previously unissued Lennon demo which Yoko Ono has passed to McCartney in 1993 (along with another Lennon cut *Real Love* which was originally featured in the 1988 "Imagine" soundtrack), to which the remaining members have added a relevant rhythm section, bridge and harmony vocal parts, under the guidance of co-producer Jeff Lynne.
Dec [13] While McCartney is with Linda during an operation to remove a lump in her breast, their London home is burglarized.

1996

Jan [30] He cuts a huge cake as the doors of the Liverpool Institute of the Performing Arts open for the first time, a ceremony also attended by the Environment Minister Sir Paul Beresford, producer Martin and LIPA CEO Mark Weatherstone-Witty.
see also: **THE BEATLES**

THE McCOYS

Rick Zehringer (lead guitar, vocals); **Bobby Peterson** (organ); **Randy Hobbs** (bass); **Randy Zehringer** (drums)

1965

June The group has been formed in Union City, IN, in 1962 by brothers Rick (b. May 8, 1947, Fort Recovery, OH) and Randy Zehringer (b. 1951, Union City, IA), with friends Dennis Kelly (bass) and Ronnie Brandon (keyboards), while at high school and naming themselves after the Ventures' 1960 rock instrumental *The McCoy*, B-side of the US #2 hit, *Walk Don't Run*. After performing as Rick & the Raiders and the Rick Z Combo, under which they release *You Know That I Love You* during early post-high-school gigs, they now revert to being the McCoys, with Hobbs and Peterson replacing college-bound Kelly and Brandon and sign to songwriter/producer Bert Berns' new New York, NY label Bang Records, after opening for Bang artists the Strangeloves (producers Feldman/Goldstein/Gottehrer) at a gig in Dayton, OH. (The Strangeloves are touring with the Dave Clark Five and are driving back to New York following tornado warnings which ground their flight, when their agent suggests they stop off and do the Dayton gig.) The Strangeloves invite Rick & the Raiders to record *Hang On Sloopy* in New York, one of Berns' own songs and a 1964 US hit for the Vibrations as *My Girl Sloopy*. A regular in the Strangeloves live set, which Dave Clark is just about to record, the track has already been cut and they add Zehringer's guitar and the group's vocals.
Sept [16] The group is featured on the season premiere of ABC-TV's "Shindig".
Oct [2] *Hang On Sloopy* tops the US chart, selling over one million copies, and hits UK #5 as the first release on the independent label Immediate Records, owned by the Rolling Stones' manager Andrew Loog Oldham.
Dec Their revival of Peggy Lee's 1958 hit *Fever* in a *Hang On Sloopy*-style arrangement hits US #7 and reaches UK #44. (Its B-side, *Sorrow*, will be covered in the UK a few months later by the Merseys and hit UK #4. David Bowie will revive it again in 1973.) ***Hang On Sloopy*** climbs to US #44.
[9] While on tour in the UK, Rick Zehringer is admitted to the National Temperance Hospital suffering from a severe reaction to a smallpox inoculation.

1966

Feb *Up And Down* makes US #46.
Mar Their treatment of Ritchie Valens' *Come On Let's Go* reaches US #22, the group's last US Top 30 hit.
Aug Their second album, ***(You Make Me Feel) So Good***, fails to chart, but the title track climbs to US #53.
Oct Eschewing their previous R&B-based style in an attempt to expand their image, the McCoys have recorded the psychedelic *Don't Worry Mother, Your Son's Heart Is Pure*, which stops at #67. Its follow-up, *I Got To Go Back* recalling *Sloopy*'s R&B style, will make US #69 the following January, with *Beat The Clock* peaking at US #92 in May, after which the group splits from Bang Records.

1968

Oct Signed to Mercury Records in search of wider artistic freedom, the group issues ***Infinite McCoys***. Fashionably psychedelic, it features Blood, Sweat & Tears' brass section and is produced by Rick Zehringer. *Jesse Brady*, which makes a brief showing at US #98, is the last McCoys chart entry.

1969

Following the release of a second Mercury album, ***Human Ball***, and after the group has become a regular feature at Steve Paul's Scene club in New York, Paul takes over the McCoys' management and teams them, minus a departing Peterson, with albino blues guitarist Johnny Winter, whom he also manages.

1970

Oct Rick Zehringer has changed his surname to Derringer to produce ***Johnny Winter And ...***, which reaches US #154 and UK #29 with Rick, Randy and Hobbs the featured backing group (and on Winter's follow-up album, ***Live - Johnny Winter And ...***, also produced by Derringer, which will climb to US #40 and UK #20 in 1971).

1971

Oct Rumors abound of the group rehearsing in Laurel Canyon, Los Angeles, CA, with Rick Derringer, Danny Whitten, "Whitey" Glan (drummer from Bush) and Nick St. Nicholas, ex-Steppenwolf, but nothing comes of the liaison.

1972

May When Winter stops touring to cure a drug habit, Derringer joins brother Edgar Winter's band White Trash on the road and performs on ***Roadworks*** which makes US #23. (Derringer will also helm Edgar Winter's May 1973 US chart-topper *Frankenstein* and the parent US #3 album ***They Only Come Out At Night***.)

1973

Dec Signed to Steve Paul's Blue Sky label as a solo artist, Derringer's ***All American Boy*** reaches US #25 and yields his only US chart solo single, the US #23 *Rock And Roll Hoochie Koo*. While recording solo, he continues to play with and produce albums for both Winter brothers.

1976

Aug Following his ***Spring Fever*** which peaked at US #141 in May the previous year, he has formed the hard-rock quartet Derringer, with Danny Johnson (guitar), Kenny Aaronson (bass) and Vinnie Appice (drums), but ***Derringer*** makes only US #154. (Later albums ***Sweet Evil*** and ***Live*** (both 1977), and ***If I Weren't So Romantic, I'd Shoot You*** (1978) will follow.)

1979

Derringer returns to solo recording with the release of ***Guitars And Women*** and ***Face To Face*** and turns to smaller club venues. (He will continue to get credits as a well-respected session musician, appearing not least on albums by Steely Dan, who wrote their 1974 hit *Rikki Don't Lose That Number* about Derringer, Donald Fagen, Todd Rundgren, Bette Midler and others.)

1984

Apr While Derringer has released his final solo effort

of the decade, ***Good Dirty Fun***, on Passport Records the previous year, Weird Al Yankovic's ***In 3-D***, a selection of hit parody/pastiches produced by Derringer reaches US #17. Taken from it, *Eat It* (a parody of Michael Jackson's *Beat It*), hits US #12 and UK #36. (Derringer will produce five albums for Yankovic.)

1993

Having played guitar in Cyndi Lauper's 1986 touring band and produced Yankovic's *Fat*, a parody of Michael Jackson's *Bad*, timed to coincide with Jackson's 1988 world tour, Derringer has remained an in-demand session musician and producer, also embarking on a major US tour with Edgar Winter and writing *Real American* (subsequently used as World Wrestling Federation Champion Hulk Hogan's theme song), by the end of the '80s, and now resumes his solo career with the release of ***Back To The Blues*** on his own Blues Bureau Records.

MICHAEL McDONALD

1972

McDonald (b. Dec. 2, 1952, St. Louis, MO), son of a St. Louis bus driver, has formed his first band, Mike & the Majestics, while still attending high school in 1964, which proved popular at local fraternity parties and was the first of a string of bands McDonald played with during the '60s including Jerry Jay & the Sheratons, the Del Rays and Blue. Now signed to his first recording deal with RCA Records, the self-penned *God Knows I Love My Baby* is released to little notice and RCA passes on the option to release an album. His current session work includes songs and vocals for acts including David Cassidy (*Hold On Me* for Cassidy's forthcoming ***Dreams Are Nuthin' More Than Wishes***) and Jack Jones. The following year, signed to Bell Records, McDonald will release the Rick Jarrard-produced singles *Dear Me* and *When I'm Home*, but once again, the label fails to issue an album.

1974

Aug Without a solo contract, and at the instigation of drummer Jeff Porcaro, who is also in the new line-up, McDonald joins Steely Dan as a keyboardist and backing vocalist, having already performed live with the group earlier in the year. (McDonald will recall: "If there was ever anybody who had a huge influence on my life, it was Jeff. It was literally him who got me the job with Steely Dan. All of a sudden I went from playing the Trojan Room on Glendale Boulevard to walking on stage with Steely Dan".)

1975

Apr He auditions for the Doobie Brothers in New Orleans, LA, and is chosen to replace the exiting Tom Johnston. McDonald is required to learn and rehearse the live Doobies repertoire for a solid 48 hours prior to an immediate band tour. During his seven-year stay with the group, his lead vocal work, songwriting and keyboard playing will dominate the Doobie Brothers' output and he will be largely credited with reviving the act's fortunes, not least writing and fronting the US Top 10 hits, the 1979 chart-topper *What A Fool Believes* (for which he will win two Grammy awards with co-writer Kenny Loggins) and the 1980 US #5 *Real Love*.

1978

June [24] Always looking to collaborate his songwriting skills (including efforts with Loggins, Michael Johnson, Brenda Russell and others), McDonald has co-written, via the US mail service, *You Belong To Me* with and for Carly Simon, which now hits US #6.

1979

Aug He provides vocal assistance on Christopher Cross' newly released successful debut album ***Christopher Cross***, particularly prominent on the US #2 hit *Ride Like The Wind*.

[4] McDonald joins Jackson Browne, Emmylou Harris, Nicolette Larson, Bonnie Raitt, Linda Ronstadt and members of Little Feat in a benefit concert in aid of Lowell George's widow at the Great Western Forum, Inglewood, CA. The 20,000 crowd raises over $230,000.

Oct ***Together***, the film soundtrack to the Jacqueline Bisset-starring movie of the same name, featuring McDonald and Jackie De Shannon on *I've Got My Mind Made Up*, is released.

1980

Feb [23] His first non-band recording success is a duet with Nicolette Larson on his *Let Me Go Love*, which reaches US #35.

He cuts the original track *If You Remember Me* for the Jon Voight/Faye Dunaway-starring movie "The Champ", which will later be a hit for Chris Thompson.

Oct McDonald co-produces, with Patrick Henderson, the debut album for his wife, Amy Holland, titled ***Amy Holland***.

1982

Mar Arista album, ***That Was Then - The Early Recordings Of Michael McDonald***, is released. Collecting material from his days at Bell, it features seven previously-released cuts and rough versions of four unreleased tracks, including his cover of the Allman Brothers' *Midnight Rider*.

[31] The Doobie Brothers announce they are splitting. McDonald will immediately sign a deal with Warner Bros. Records and resume his solo career.

Oct [23] His first strictly solo success, *I Keep Forgettin' (Every Time You're Near)*, hits US #4. (He will later be sued by Leiber and Stoller for "using" their Chuck Jackson hit *I Keep Forgettin'* - he loses the case and future royalties will be split as Leiber/Stoller/McDonald/Sanford.) His debut album, ***If That's What It Takes***, has been released simultaneously and begins a 32-week chart stay, hitting US #6. Showcasing his distinctive soul vocal style, the album has been produced by Ted Templeman and Lenny Waronker, and features top-drawer session players, including members of Toto and Steve Gadd, Greg Phillinganes, Willie Weeks, Loggins and Lenny Castro.

Oct [13] ***If That's What It Takes*** is certified gold by the RIAA.

Nov [6] The Quincy Jones-created Donna Summer's *State Of Independence*, including McDonald in an all-star chorus, reaches US #42, also climbing to UK #14.

Dec From his solo album, *I Gotta Try* makes US #44, while McDonald is prominently featured on Kenny Loggins' current album, ***High Adventure***, not least co-writing and singing on the US #15 extract *Heart To Heart*.

1983

May Spending much of the year composing and collaborating, McDonald has written and produced a second Amy Holland album, ***On Your Every Word***, for Capitol and now joins Chris Thompson to help ex-Doobie Brother Patrick Simmons revive the Chi-Lites' *Have You Seen Her* on his solo debut album, ***Arcade***.

1984

Feb His duet with James Ingram for his debut album, the inspirational *Yah Mo B There*, reaches US #19 and initially makes UK #44. A "Jellybean" Benitez remix of *Yah Mo B There* will reach UK #12 the following January.

1985

Feb [26] McDonald and Ingram win the Best R&B Performance By A Duo Or Group With Vocal category for *Yah Mo Be There* at the 27th annual Grammy Awards.

July *No Lookin' Back* reaches US #34.

Sept His sophomore album, ***No Lookin' Back***, begins a four-month US chart stay during which it will peak at #45. Produced by McDonald and Templeman, it features a similar session line-up to the first Warner Bros. album. *Our Love*, also featured in Richard Gere/Kim Basinger movie "No Mercy", is released as a single.

1986

June [14] McDonald's duet with Patti LaBelle, the Bacharach/Sager-penned ballad *On My Own* hits US #1. It is included on LaBelle's ***The Winner In You***, for which she cut her vocal track in Philadelphia, PA, and sent the tape to McDonald to add vocals in Los Angeles, CA. They have yet to meet and even tape the promotional video on opposite coasts. It also hits UK #2 behind Spitting Image's *The Chicken Song*, though UK #1 on the airplay-integrated Network Chart survey.

July UK re-issued *I Keep Forgettin'* makes #43.

Aug [30] Released on MCA for the film soundtrack of "Running Scared", starring Billy Crystal and Gregory Hines, *Sweet Freedom*, penned by Rod Temperton, hits US #7.

Sept *Sweet Freedom* reaches UK #12, prompting a UK promotional visit including a BBC1-TV "Top Of The Pops" appearance. McDonald also links with Ingram again as they join ex-Ambrosia front-man David Pack on his *I Can't Let Go* from the Warner album, ***Anywhere You Go***.

Nov McDonald's unmistakable voice is heard on Toto's current US #11 hit ballad, *I'll Be Over You*.

Dec A UK-only compilation album, ***Sweet Freedom***, hits UK #6, during a 35-week chart run. A premature greatest hits package, it includes the Doobie Brothers' *What A Fool Believes*, plus the specially-licensed *On My Own* and *Sweet Freedom*, from MCA, and *Yah Mo B There*, from Qwest.

1987

Apr McDonald visits the UK for sell-out dates, including two nights at London's Hammersmith Odeon, where he is joined by UK singer Jaki Graham for *On My Own* (prompting McDonald to provide her with a song for her next album) and encores with the soul classic *When A Man Loves A Woman*.

[15] *Sweet Freedom* is named Best Film Theme Or Song at the 32nd annual Ivor Novello Awards lunch, at the Grosvenor House Hotel, London.

Oct Gospel group the Winans' ***Decisions*** album, featuring McDonald on shared lead vocals on *Love Has No Color*, makes US #109.

Dec [29] McDonald becomes a father to son Dylan Michael.

1988

Aug Having contributed backing vocals to his first three albums, McDonald is featured on Christopher Cross' fourth outing, ***Back Of My Mind***.

Nov [12-13] McDonald returns to Britain for two concerts in preparation for the recording of a third album for Warner Bros. The Richard Perry-produced ***Rock, Rhythm & Blues*** compilation, including McDonald's *For Your Precious Love* will be released the following May.

1990

Feb [24] McDonald participates in the "Roy Orbison All-Star Benefit Tribute" at the Universal Amphitheatre, Universal City, CA, alongside Bonnie Raitt, Bob Dylan and many others, raising $500,000 for the Shelter Partnership and the National Coalition for the Homeless.

Apr A McDonald co-produced (with Grady Walker) track, *Don't Cry For Me*, appears on the Virgin Soundtrack for the Anne Archer-starring movie soundtrack, ***Love At Large***.

May [26] ***Take It To Heart***, variously co-produced with Gardner Cole, David Gamson, Ted Templeman and Don Was and featuring David Lasley, Don Was, Jeff Porcaro and Abraham Laboriel, among others, reaches UK #35.

June [9] *Take It To Heart*, the title cut from new album, co-written with Diane Warren, peaks at US #98.

[21] McDonald undertakes a world tour beginning in North America. His live band includes Bernie Chiaravalle (lead guitar, vocals), Charles Frichter (bass, vocals) Chuck Sabatino (keyboards, vocals), Tim Heintz (keyboards), George Perilli (drums) and Vince Denham (saxophone).

July [11] His tour reaches the UK, including selected dates as the special guest on Tina Turner's farewell trek.
[14] ***Take It To Heart*** peaks at US #110.
Aug [4] His concert trek returns to the US until month's end.
Sept [23] McDonald begins a week of concerts in Japan.
Nov [23-24] He ends his six-month live sojourn with dates at London's Hammersmith Odeon.

1991

Mar [1-2] McDonald performs at the second "Rock'n'Soul Revue" at the Beacon Theatre, New York, alongside organizer Donald Fagen, Boz Scaggs, Patti Austin and others.
[9] The Peace Choir's *Give Peace A Chance*, to which McDonald contributes vocal support, makes US #54.
July [30] McDonald guests on syndicated TV's "The Arsenio Hall Show" Patti LaBelle special.
Sept Manhattan Transfer's ***The Offbeat Of Avenues***, featuring McDonald on *A World Apart*, is released.
Oct [6] "Ray Charles : 50 Years In Music", for which McDonald sings *I Got A Woman*, airs on Fox TV.

1992

Jan [30] McDonald takes part in the "Friends Of Smitty" benefit for musician and writer William Smith, suffering a stroke, at the Palace Theatre, Burbank, CA
Feb [8] ***The New York Rock And Soul Revue - Live At The Beacon***, to which McDonald has contributed *Knock On Wood*, *Lonely Teardrops*, *Minute By Minute* and *Pretzel Logic* (with Donald Fagen), peaks at US #170.
Mar [21] McDonald and the Doobie Brothers reunite for the Memphis Horns 25th anniversary show at the Pyramid, Memphis, TN, sharing a bill with Robert Cray, Boz Scaggs and Johnny Rivers.
Dec [7] He is featured on "The Winans Real Meaning Of Christmas", which airs in US TV syndication, appearing with Bonnie Raitt, Kenny Loggins and Gladys Knight.
[14] McDonald plays at a benefit at the Universal Amphitheatre, to establish an education trust fund for the children of Toto drummer Jeff Porcaro, who died in August.

1993

Jan [20] McDonald participates in the Arkansas Ball in Washington, DC, on President Clinton's Inaugural day.
Aug [3] Including a cover of Goffin and King's *Hey Girl*, his otherwise self-penned fourth album, ***Blink Of An Eye***, co-produced with Russ Titelman and featuring guests Benmont Tench, Vince Gill, Alison Krauss and Mike Campbell among others, is released.
Dec [31] McDonald guests on NBC-TV's "The Tonight Show" New Year's Eve show, performing *Higher Ground*.

1995

July [14] McDonald rejoins the Doobie Brothers for a six-week US shed tour. Later in the year he will contribute *Maria* in collaboration with Ingram and David Pack to the all-star musical update ***The Songs Of West Side Story***, to be released in the US the following February, two months prior to a solo appearance at Nashville, TN's "Tin Pan South" songwriters' week, an annual event in which he regularly participates.

REBA McENTIRE

1975

Oct Influenced not least by the music of her heroine Patsy Cline, McEntire (b. Reba Nell McEntire, Mar. 28, 1954, Chockie, OK), the daughter of Clark, a champion steer-roping rodeo cowboy father and Jacqueline, a teacher mother, began her entertainment career as a hometown rodeo performer (in barrel races) and singer. While also traveling with the rodeo, her mother taught Reba, sister Susie and brother Pake, who will go on to his own solo career signing with RCA in 1986, to sing in harmony, resulting in the siblings performing as the Singing McEntires at schools and clubs and signing to the Boss label in 1972 (they will stay together until the start of her solo career). In 1974, while in her second year at Southeastern Oklahoma State University in Durant, OK, studying education, McEntire has sung the national anthem at the National Rodeo finals in Oklahoma City, OK, impressing singer Red Steagall, who encourages her to go to Nashville, TN, helping her to now sign a solo deal with Mercury Records. Initially teaming her with producer Jerry Kennedy, McEntire's US Country debut will be the #88 peaking *I Don't Want To Be A One Night Stand* in July the following year, the same month she marries her first husband, rodeo champion Charlie Battles on the 21st. In spite of her well-received 1977 album debut ***Reba McEntire***, released the same year she makes her debut at the Grand Ole Opry, McEntire will have to wait until 1980 to first hit the Country Top 10 with *(You Lift Me) Up To Heaven* at #8 in July.

1983

Jan [8] Having released the increasingly popular albums ***Feel The Fire*** (1980), ***Heart To Heart*** (1981) and ***Unlimited*** (1982) and having already notched up 15 US Country chart singles, *Can't Even Get The Blues* becomes her first #1 record, followed by another Country chart-topper, *You're The First Time I've Thought About Leaving* on April 30th, taken from this year's album ***Behind The Scenes***. (She will score 11 further US Country #1s during the rest of the decade, although none of them will cross over onto the Hot 100, or score in the UK, where she will remain chart-less.)

1985

Having signed with MCA Records the previous year, her label debut ***Have I Got A Deal For You*** is released, during a year in which she also becomes a member of the Grand Ole Opry, to be followed by two US Country Album chart-toppers, ***Whoever's In New England*** and ***What Am I Gonna Do About You*** (both produced by Jimmy Bowen and issued in 1986).

1987

Feb [24] *Whoever's In New England* brings McEntire her first Grammy for Best Country Vocal Performance, Female at the 29th annual Grammy Awards.
Apr [21] ***What Am I Gonna Do About You*** is certified gold by the RIAA.
June [6] An early round-up of ten MCA chart singles, ***Reba McEntire's Greatest Hits*** becomes her first entry on the Top 200, on its way to a #139 peak.
Nov [102] ***The Last One To Know*** begins a US chart rise to #102.

1988

Apr [20] ***The Last One To Know*** is certified gold by the RIAA.
May [21] ***Reba*** enters the US chart on its way to #118.

1989

Apr [2-4] A relentless live performer, McEntire's current US trek is highlighted by three nights in Palm Desert, CA.
June [3] Her sixteenth album release, ***Sweet Sixteen*** enters the US chart set to make #78.
Oct [14] ***Live***, recorded earlier in the year, begins a US chart climb to #124. (During the year, McEntire will marry her second husband Narvel Blackstock.)

1990

Mar [9] "Reba", a video collection, is certified gold by the RIAA.
Sept [22] ***Rumor Has It*** begins an 89-week chart tenure during which it will reach US #39.
(During the year, McEntire's acting career gets underway with a cameo in the movie "Tremors", to be followed by an appearance in the Kenny Rogers TV movie "Luck Of The Draw : The Gambler Returns".)

1991

Mar [16] Her manager Kirk Cappello and seven members of her backing band, Chris Austin, Joey Cigainero, Paula Kaye Evans, Jim Hammon, Terry Jackson, Tony Saputo and Michael Thomas, are all killed when their twin-engine plane, taking them to a show in Texas, flies into a mountain.
Aug [7] ***My Kind Of Country*** is certified gold by the RIAA.
Nov [9] Lyrically reflecting the recent loss of her musician friends, ***For My Broken Heart*** reaches US #13 during a two-year plus chart tenure.

1993

Jan [7] ***Sweet Sixteen*** is certified platinum by the RIAA.
[23] ***It's Your Call***, co-produced by McEntire and Tony Brown and featuring the duet *The Heart Won't Lie*, with her frequent vocal collaborator Vince Gill, hits US #8.
Feb [9] ***Reba*** is certified platinum by the RIAA.
Apr [23] The RIAA also certifies sales of two million of ***Rumor Has It***.
July [6] ***Whoever's In New England*** is confirmed platinum by the RIAA.
[8] ***Merry Christmas To You*** is ratified gold by the RIAA.
Oct [23] ***Greatest Hits Volume Two*** hits US #5. (During the year her songs are featured on the film soundtracks to "North", in which she also appears, and "The Little Rascals".)

1994

Mar [1] Ballad *Does He Love You?*, a duet with Linda Davis, wins the Best Country Vocal Collaboration category at the 36th annual Grammy Awards held at New York's Radio City Music Hall.
Apr [15] ***Best Of Reba McEntire*** is certified gold by the RIAA.
May [21] ***Read My Mind*** hits US #2.
June [28] ***Read My Mind*** is confirmed platinum by the RIAA.
Nov [1] Her day is highlighted by the launch of three million Fritos snacks featuring with her face on the front of the packet.
[15] McEntire appears on NBC-TV's "Tonight Show".
[25] A live concert event, "Reba" airs on NBC-TV.
Her best-selling autobiography **Reba : My Story**, published by Bantam and written with Tom Carter, hits the **New York Times**' best-seller list.
Dec [7] She is named Top Female Artist Of The Year in the Country category at the fifth annual **Billboard** Music Awards held at the Universal Amphitheatre, Universal City, CA.
[19] The RIAA certifies sales of three million of ***It's Your Call***.

1995

Jan [7] *Till You Love Me*, becomes her first ever Hot 100 entry, peaking at US #78.
Feb [27] ***Have I Got A Deal For You*** is certified gold and ***Greatest Hits*** platinum by the RIAA.
May [10] McEntire becomes the first woman to be named Entertainer Of The Year since Barbara Mandrell won in 1980, at the 30th annual Academy of Country Music Awards, held at the Universal Amphitheatre.
[25] ***Rumor Has It*** reaches US #39.
June [3] She sings at the inaugural Blockbuster Entertainment Awards held at Hollywood's Pantages Theater, set for broadcast on CBS-TV on June 6th, also collecting the Top Country Artist (female) trophy.
Aug [11] The RIAA certifies platinum sales for ***The Last One To Know*** and multi-platinum sales for ***For My Broken Heart*** (three million), ***Read My Mind*** (three million), ***Greatest Hits*** (three million) and ***Greatest Hits Volume II*** (four million).
[25] ***Reba McEntire Live*** is also confirmed platinum by the RIAA.
Sept [19] Her recent TV movie "Buffalo Girls" is released on video (US).

Oct [3] Celebrating 20 years in the business with today's release of her 16th MCA album ***Starting Over***, McEntire is confirmed by the RIAA as the third best-selling female artist, with 28 million albums sold in US recording history, behind Barbra Streisand and Linda Ronstadt.
[21] Produced by Tony Brown, ***Starting Over***, her interpretations of songs that have influenced her career including *Talking In My Sleep*, *You Keep Me Hangin' On* and *On My Own* bows at its US #5 peak, the same day her current North American tour plays at the Copps Coliseum, Hamilton, ON, a concert grossing $453,796 (Canadian) from 11,942 fans. (During the year she will perform 120 US dates which will take some $19 million at the box-office, her live entourage including 13 trucks, five buses and her own private plane)
Nov [24] "Reba : Starting Over" is broadcast as a CBS-TV special.
Dec [4] She once again appears on "The Tonight Show".

1996

Jan [30] McEntire is named Favorite Female Country Artist for an unprecedented tenth consecutive year at the 23rd annual American Music Awards held at Los Angeles' Shrine Auditorium. (She was also voted the Country Music Association's Female Vocalist Of The Year from 1984-1987.)
Mar [14] Her Starstruck Entertainment company moves into a 25,000 square-foot building on Nashville's Music Row.

MC5

Rob Tyner (vocals); **Fred "Sonic" Smith** (guitar); **Wayne Kramer** (guitar); **Michael Davis** (bass); **Dennis Thompson** (drums)

1964

Guitarist Kramer (b. Apr. 30, 1948, Detroit, MI) and Smith form the Bounty Hunters in Lincoln Park, MI, and link with Tyner (b. Robert Derminer, Dec. 12, 1944, Detroit) who wants to become the group's manager, but instead ends up as bassist. Name-changing initially to Motor City Five, Tyner quits the band, only to return as its lead singer the following year, by which time Davis and Thompson have also been recruited on bass and drums respectively. Managed by John Sinclair, the group takes an increasingly anti-establishment lyrical position underscored by a music bed of loud, experimental, jazz/rock/R&B fusion. By 1967, revered as Detroit's leading cult group, MC5 becomes the house band for the radical White Panther Party and associated Trans Love Commune, led by Sinclair.

1968

Apr [17-21] The group performs at the Avalon Ballroom, San Francisco, CA, on a bill with Cream and the Psychedelic Stooges.
June Having released two singles (*One Of The Guys* in 1967 and the recent *Borderline*) and an album on E.S.P. Records, MC5 appears at the Democratic National Convention in Chicago, IL.
Oct [30-31] The band's raucous performance at the Grande Ballroom, Detroit is recorded for the subsequent ***Kick Out The Jams*** album.

1969

Mar [8] Signed to Elektra Records for $10,000 after label publicist Danny Fields has introduced the group to label founder Jac Holzman, ***Kick Out The Jams*** enters the US chart on its way to #30. The band's career highlight, it will be regarded as a seminal underground release and yields the US #82 *Kick Out The Jams*. (The band is dropped from the label after they write an expletive on company notepaper and personally deliver the stationery to stores that refused to stock the album, after they had already deleted an expletive from *Kick Out Of Jams*.)
Aug [26] The group embarks on a US tour with Iggy & the Stooges in New York.

1970

Mar ***Back In The USA***, a studio set produced by Jon Landau and released on Atlantic Records, peaks at US #13.
July [24-26] The group performs at the Mick Farren-organised "Phun City Festival" in London.
With Davis departed, MC5 enlist the help of a number of Detroit jazz musicians to record and release the avant-garde ***High Time*** the following year.

1972

Feb [11] Relocated to Europe, where they sometimes play under the pseudonym Rohan O'Rahilly, MC5 performs at the Friars Club, Aylesbury.
Aug [5] They perform at the "London Rock'n'Roll Festival" at Wembley Stadium, Wembley, Middx., with Little Richard, Gary Glitter, Wizzard, Jerry Lee Lewis, Bill Haley, Billy Fury, Bo Diddley, Emile Ford and Heinz backed by Dr. Feelgood.
Dec [31] The group plays its last-ever gig, fittingly at the Grande Ballroom, Detroit, after which the unit permanently dissolves, though Tyner will subsequently form the short-lived New MC5.

1980

Mar [1] With the group's stature confirmed as an influence on the late '70s UK punk/new-wave movement, and with Davis playing in Destroy All Monsters, Thompson in New Race and Kramer in Gang War, Smith marries rock poetess Patti Smith.

1991

Sept [17] Tyner, who released the solo album ***Blood Brothers*** on the Birmingham, AL R&A label the previous year, dies of heart failure in the driveway at his home after returning from a grocery store in the Detroit suburb of Berkley. He is buried in an MC5 T-shirt.
Nov [18] ***Kick Out The Jams***, recorded at the Grande Ballroom in 1968, is released as a UK-only digitally remastered CD, while UK duo KLF's current global smash, *What Time Is Love?*, is highlighted by the sampling of MC5's seminal *Kick Out The Jams*.

1992

Feb [22] "Kick Out The Jams : A Tribute To Rob Tyner" is held at the State Theater, Detroit, to benefit the Tyner Scholarship Fund and the Center For Creative Studies. Relocated to Nashville, Kramer, currently working in an off-Broadway musical "The Last Words of Dutch Schultz" and recording the solo ***Wayne Kramer's Deathtongue***, Davis, now living in Phoenix, AZ, and playing with his own Michael Davis Group, Smith, performing in the Sonic Rendezvous Band, and Thompson (who has remained in Detroit), are joined by Dee Dee Ramone and a number of local bands.

1994

Nov [5] Smith dies from a heart attack in Detroit, at age 45. A public memorial will be held on the 8th at Mariner's Church, Detroit. (He has been working on his wife's comeback album and recently contributed to the soundtrack of Wim Wender's movie "Until The End Of The World".) (Kramer continues his solo career releasing the albums ***The Hard Stuff*** in 1995 and ***Dangerous Madness*** in 1996.)

SARAH McLACHLAN

1989

Aug Singer-songwriter and 12-string guitar player McLachlan (b. Jan. 28, 1968, Halifax, NS, Canada), having begun playing on the Canadian folk circuit in 1987, an apprenticeship interrupted only by her participating in a World Vision charity assignment to the Far East, has been signed up by Arista Records, which now releases her maiden album, the self-penned, haunting ***Touch*** recorded at three studios in Vancouver, BC, Canada and produced by Greg Reely. The Celtic-tinged folk pop album, showcasing her introspective mature lyrics, gains critical acclaim in her native Canada.

1991

Sept [10] Her self-written (except a cover of Donovan's *Wear Your Love Like Heaven*) sophomore album ***Solace***, produced by keyboardist Pierre Marchand, is released in the US, to wider, still positive reviews. (During the year she will also contribute vocal work to folk/rock outfit Balloon's debut album ***Gravity***.)

1992

Feb [15] Taken from ***Solace***, *Into The Fire*, popular on US college radio and triple-A formats, enters the Modern Rock chart set to hit #4.
Mar [24] McLachlan appears on NBC-TV's "Late Night With David Letterman".
Apr [25] ***Solace*** finally charts at US #167.
[28] She performs on Dennis Miller's short-lived, US-TV syndicated "Dennis Miller Show".
Nov [10] Arista releases the various artists ***No Alternative*** AIDS-research benefit album which includes McLachlan's self-penned *Hold On*, inspired by the film documentary "A Promise Kept" about a woman who discovers her fiancé has AIDS (the cut will also enter the US Modern Rock chart in February 1995, set to reach #29).

1994

June [4] Once again a self-written set produced by Marchand, the breakthrough album ***Fumbling Towards Ecstasy***, inspired by two years of personal growth and highlighted as ever by her alternately intimate and passionate vocal style, makes US #50.
[18] The extracted *Possession* peaks at US #73.
[24] McLachlan appears at a LifeBeat benefit concert at the Beacon Theatre, New York, NY, alongside Melissa Etheridge, k.d. lang and Jon Secada.
Nov [5] *Good Enough* peaks at US #77.

1995

Jan [19] ***Fumbling Towards Ecstasy*** is certified platinum by the RIAA.
Mar [28] Available in Canada since January, ***The Freedom Sessions*** mini-album is released in the US, including re-take versions of cuts from her recent album, plus her cover of Tom Waits' *Ol '55* and a bonus multi-media track.
Apr [15] ***The Freedom Sessions*** bows at its US #78 peak.
July [13] She performs at LIFEbeat's second "The Beat Goes On" benefit at New York's Beacon Theatre (airing on VH1 in August).
[15] Her ten-date US tour begins opening for the Chieftains at the Jones Beach Theatre, Wantagh, NY (a $223,323-grossing bill from a crowd of 6,785) set to end on August 1st at the Cynthia Woods Mitchell Pavilion, The Woodlands, TX.
Aug [8] Sony 550 Music (US) releases the multi-artist compilation ***Spirit of '73 : Rock For Choice*** including McLachlan's version of Joni Mitchell's *Blue* while Arista issues the CD Plus multimedia enhanced version of ***The Freedom Sessions***, which includes home videos, photos, art, lyrics and interviews.
Sept [2] McLachlan plays at the "Kumbaya Festival '95" held at the Molson Amphitheatre, Toronto, ON, Canada, to a crowd of 4,829.
[21] She performs on the "Horizons : An Inaugural Celebration" bill at the General Motors Place, Vancouver, Canada, an event including David Foster, Blue Rodeo, Michelle Wright, Shania Twain, the Nylons and others.

1996

Jan [20] Ballad *I Will Remember You*, taken from the movie "The Brothers McMullen" and written by McLachlan with Seamus Egan and Dave Merenda, makes US #65.

DON McLEAN

1969

Singer/songwriter/guitarist McLean (b. Oct. 2, 1945, New Rochelle, NY), an asthmatic child who has been interested in music from an early age, decided to pursue a career in music after the death of his father in 1961. In 1964, having performed at concerts while at high school and as a student at Villanova University (where he played with Jim Croce), he began working in clubs around New York, NY, having met Judy Collins' manager Harold Lenthal whose assistant Charles Close has secured him dates at the city's Gas Light venue, followed by shows at the Potting Shed in Lenox, MA and the Second Fret in Philadelphia, PA, before gigging farther afield in Baltimore, MD, and Canada, where he subsequently works with Lee Hays, Brownie McGhee and Josh White. Having returned to three years of studying in 1965 at Iona College, he has also continued to perform, beginning to play his own compositions in 1967, when he signed to a management deal by Herb Gart and performs his first college concert at Boston University, before making Saratoga Springs, NY's Caffé Lena his base in 1968. Through the club's owner, Lena Spencer, he has been appointed "The Hudson River Troubadour" by the New York State Council on the Arts, playing in 50 river communities three times a day for a month, earning $200 a week. Having heard about McLean hitch-hiking from Mount Marcy in the Adironacks to Riverside Park on 125th St., New York, giving impromptu concerts on the way, folk pioneer Pete Seeger now invites him to join an expedition to sail the Hudson River, to tell people living on the waterway about the dangers of industrial pollution. The sloop *Clearwater*, with McLean as a crew member and part of the Sloop Singers, sails from South Bristol, ME, to New York in six weeks, giving 25 concerts. A TV special, "The Sloop At Nyack", chronicling the trip, airs on US NET's "Sounds Of Summer" series.

1970

McLean spends six weeks singing at elementary schools in Massachusetts. While staying at Mrs. Sedgewich's lodging house, he reads a book about painter Vincent Van Gogh and, inspired by the subject, writes *Vincent*, one of only six songs penned during the year. His debut album ***Tapestry***, rejected by 34 labels, is released on the Mediarts label, produced by the Youngbloods' Jerry Corbitt, and dedicated to the Weavers. Though it fails to chart, it secures the artist a contract with United Artists Records.

1971

June [26] The title track from his forthcoming ***American Pie***, an 8-minute 36-second track divided into two parts against all convention, documenting rock'n'roll Americana and most notably referencing Buddy Holly's death as "the day the music died", receives its first radio play on New York's WNEW. (At the end of the year, radio station WABC in New York names it the most-played record of the year.)

1972

Jan [3] With both still rising on the charts, the RIAA certifies gold sales of *American Pie* and ***American Pie***.
[15] *American Pie* tops the US chart for the first of four weeks.
[22] Dedicated to Holly, the self-penned ***American Pie*** also hits US #1 at the beginning of a seven-week run. The Ed Freeman-produced set immediately show-cases McLean's effortless vocal quality and literate songwriting style.
Mar Van Gogh-inspired ballad, *Vincent*, coupled with *Castles In The Air*, reaches US #12 as McLean's freshman album, ***Tapestry***, belatedly peaks at US #111. *American Pie* hits UK #2, kept from the top by Chicory Tip's *Son Of My Father*, while ***American Pie*** hits UK #3.
June [17] *Vincent*, also played daily at the Van Gogh Museum in Amsterdam, Holland, tops the UK chart for the first of two weeks. Performing at the Troubabour in Los Angeles, McLean is seen by singer Lori Lieberman. Inspired by his performance, she asks her writers/producers Charles Fox and Norman Gimbel to write a song about him, resulting in *Killing Me Softly With His Song*, which she records for her debut album, ***Lori Lieberman***. (The song is subsequently a US chart-topper for Roberta Flack in 1973).
July ***Tapestry*** reaches UK #16 as McLean concludes a European tour.

1973

Feb *Dreidel* makes US #21 as its parent album, the Freeman-produced ***Don McLean***, reaches US #23.
Apr His revival of Buddy Holly's *Everyday*, from the forthcoming ***Playin' Favorites***, makes UK #38.
May *If We Try*, from ***Don McLean***, peaks at US #58.
June Perry Como makes US #29 with the McLean-penned ballad *And I Love You So*, having hit UK #3 in May.
Oct Having toured for most of the year in Australia, New Zealand, Japan, the US, Europe and Scandinavia, and having taken a sabbatical from writing and performing, and returning to Caffé Lena to do a one-off show with friend Frank Wakefield, McLean begins writing again.
Nov ***Playin' Favorites***, a collection of non-originals, makes UK #42, with the extracted *Mountains O' Mourne* topping the chart in Eire.

1974

Dec ***Homeless Brother***, produced by Joel Dorn with top New York session musicians, Richard Tee, Hugh McCracken, David Spinozza and Willie Weeks, peaks at US #120 and includes covers of George Harrison's *Sunshine Life For Me (Sail Away Raymond)* and *Crying In The Chapel*, a US #3 in 1965 for Elvis Presley, with vocals from the Persuasions.

1975

May [5] He sings *And I Love You So* on NBC-TV's "The Smother Brothers Comedy Hour".
[13] McLean embarks on a 15 date UK tour at London's Royal Albert Hall, set to end on the 29th at the De Montfort Hall, Leicester, Leics.
[31] McLean performs a free concert to 85,000 people in London's Hyde Park - the tenth act to have played at the venue.
June *Wonderful Baby*, later recorded by Fred Astaire, peaks at US #93.

1976

Sept *Solo*, a live double album recorded on his 1975 UK tour is released. His next studio set, ***Prime Time***, which includes *The Pattern Is Broken* also featured in film "Fraternity Row", will be issued the following April.

1978

May [1] A 15-date UK tour opens at London's Royal Albert Hall, set to end on the 16th at Manchester's Free Trade Hall.
June [26] Newly signed to Millennium Records, McLean begins work on a new album at the Jack Clement recording studio, Nashville, TN.

1980

June [21] *Crying*, reviving Roy Orbison's 1961 US #2, tops the UK chart for the first of three weeks while its parent album, the EMI-released ***Chain Lightning***, produced by Larry Butler two years earlier and featuring the Jordanaires, heads to UK #19.
Sept 15-track compilation, ***The Very Best Of Don McLean***, hits UK #4, as McLean tours extensively in Britain.

1981

Mar [21] *Crying* hits US #5 for the first of three weeks, as ***Chain Lightning*** reaches US #28.
May [30] *Since I Don't Have You*, reviving the Skyliners' 1959 US #12, makes US #23.
Aug [15] *It's Just The Sun* peaks at US #83.
Dec [26] *Castles In The Air*, a new recording of his 1972 hit, makes US #36.

1982

Jan ***Believers***, dedicated to the Weavers' Lee Hays, who died in August 1981 after a long battle with diabetes, peaks at US #156.
May *Castles In The Air* makes UK #47.

1984

Jan "The Music Of Don McLean" video, featuring McLean in concert and being interviewed by DJ Paul Gambaccini, is released.
Apr [18] McLean begins a UK tour in Cardiff, S. Glamorgan, Wales, set to end at London's Royal Festival Hall on May 12th.

1987

Apr EMI America releases ***Don McLean's Greatest Hits - Then And Now***, coupling five McLean hits with five new tracks recorded in New York and Berkeley, CA, with producer Dave Burgess (ex-member of the Champs), who is now acting as McLean's manager. The extracted *He's Got You* makes #73 on the US Country chart.
Nov McLean concludes another sellout UK tour at London's Royal Festival Hall. (He will have played in Britain almost every other year since his first visit in 1972.)

1988

June Now firmly settled in the country field, McLean, signed to Capitol Records, releases the Burgess-produced ***Love Tracks***, recorded at Nightingale studios, Nashville, which unusually for the artist features new songs by outside writers.

1990

Sept Newly signed to Gold Castle, and having released ***For The Memories Volumes 1 & 2*** which features standards from the '30s, '40s and '50s, McLean's ***Greatest Hits Live!***, recorded at London's Dominion Theatre during his autumn 1980 UK tour, is issued.

1991

Oct [10] With a two-CD career retrospective, ***Favorites And Rarities***, recently released, McLean's 16-date UK tour opens at London's famed Hackney Empire, set to end on the 25th at the Regent Theatre, Ipswich, Suffolk.
Nov [9] *American Pie*, originally a 1972 UK #2 and now reissued as part of EMI's Classic Tracks promotion, reaches UK #12, as Curb Records in the US releases his seasonal covers album, ***Don McLean Christmas***.

1995

After a theater group in Sheffield, S. Yorks has staged "'Til Tomorrow", a musical comprising 20 of McLean's songs in 1992, and having sung at Buddy Holly tribute concerts at London's Victoria Palace and the Surf Ballroom in Clear Laker, IA, in February the following year, McLean, now residing in Maine with his wife of eight years and two children and working on his autobiography, releases ***River Of Love*** on Curb Records.

MEAT LOAF

1969

Born to a gospel-singing family, Marvin Lee Aday (b. Sept. 27, 1951, Dallas, TX, a date that he will insist is the correct one despite numerous reports that it is 1947), nicknamed "Meatloaf" after stepping on the foot of his high school football coach in 1961, left his home in Dallas to go to Los Angeles, CA, in 1966, and established a reputation as a strong lead vocalist with Los Angeles band Meat Loaf Soul, which became the psychedelic rock outfit Popcorn Blizzard the following year. Staying together for three years, the band opened for acts including the Who, Ted Nugent, Iggy Pop and Johnny & Edgar Winter. Now living in a communal home in Echo Park, Los Angeles, he applies for a job as a parking-lot attendant at the Aquarius Theatre, when he meets an actor appearing in musical "Hair". Auditioning at the actor's suggestion, he is cast as Ulysses S. Grant in the Los Angeles production.

1970

June "Hair" opens at the Vest Pocket Theatre, Detroit, MI, where he meets female singer Stoney who is cast as Sheila in the show and with whom he will record one eponymous album for the Rare Earth label, and tour with Alice Cooper and labelmates Rare Earth. The duo splits shortly after (Stoney later joins Bob Seger's band as a backing singer).

1971

Mar Meat Loaf rejoins the road tour of "Hair" at the Hanna Theatre, Cleveland, OH.
June While still with the show, Meat Loaf makes his US chart debut (with Stoney), as *What You See Is What You Get* peaks at US #71.
Sept He has moved to New York with "Hair", when the show closes. In December the following year Meat Loaf will be cast as Buddha in the musical "Rainbow".

1974

Jan "More Than You Deserve", a musical written by Jim Steinman, opens off-Broadway, with Meat Loaf in the roles of Perrine and Rabbit. (Steinman, a New Yorker raised in California, is in high-school band, Clitoris That Thought It Was A Puppy, when he writes the play "Dream Engine", which impresses New York producer Joseph Papp, prompting Steinman to relocate to New York to work frequently with Papp.)

1975

Mar [10] Meat Loaf opens at the Belasco Theatre on Broadway in Richard O'Brien's "The Rocky Horror Show" as Eddie and Dr. Scott. (He will recreate the role for the film "The Rocky Horror Picture Show".) By year's end, Meat Loaf and Steinman tour the US with the "National Lampoon Road Show".

1976

Feb [17] Meat Loaf opens in "Rockabye Hamlet", a musical version of "Hamlet" in which he plays a priest, at New York's Minskoff Theatre.
Oct Ted Nugent's ***Free For All***, featuring Meat Loaf on lead vocals, is released, set to hit US #24.

1977

Jan Steinman and Meat Loaf start rehearsing at the Ansonia Hotel, New York, on songs Steinman has written for the musical "Neverland", a futuristic version of "Peter Pan", which has recently been presented at Washington's Kennedy Center. After extensive rehearsals, they sign a deal with RCA Records, but pull out when the label refuses to include producer Todd Rundgren as part of the package. Rundgren's own Bearsville Records funds the project for a period before Warner Bros. Records steps in and agrees to release the album, but with limited promotion. Meat Loaf, Steinman and Rundgren reject the offer. In desperation, manager David Sonenberg plays the tapes to the fledgling Cleveland International company, which persuades Epic Records to release the project. Meat Loaf performs at the CBS/Epic Records convention in New Orleans, LA, an appearance which results in the company commissioning promo films for the tracks *Bat Out Of Hell*, *Paradise By The Dashboard Lights* and *You Took The Words Right Out Of My Mouth*.
Oct [29] ***Bat Out Of Hell*** enters the US chart set to reach #14 during an 82-week chart stay. (One of the most consistent rock catalog items over the next ten years, it will eventually sell over seven million copies in the US alone.)

1978

Jan ***Bat Out Of Hell*** is released in Britain. Sales soar after a promo video clip of its title track is shown on BBC2-TV's "The Old Grey Whistle Test".
Mar [11] ***Bat Out Of Hell*** begins an astonishing 471 weeks on the UK chart, during which it will hit #9, pass two million sales, and be hailed as a rock-opera classic.
June *You Took The Words Right Out Of My Mouth* reaches UK #33.
[6] He plays at London's Hammersmith Odeon during a UK visit.
July Meat Loaf tours Australia, where ***Bat Out Of Hell*** knocks ***Saturday Night Fever*** off the top of the chart. The extracted *Two Out Of Three Ain't Bad* reaches US #11.
[20] *Two Out Of Three Ain't Bad* is certified gold by the RIAA.
Aug *Two Out Of Three Ain't Bad* reaches UK #32.
Sept *Paradise By The Dashboard Lights*, with Ellen Foley on female vocals and Phil Rizzuto as the baseball announcer, makes US #39.
Oct Meat Loaf ends his North American tour in Cleveland, OH, his 170th date in under a year as the album goes platinum. In Toronto, an over-exuberant Meat Loaf falls off stage and tears ligaments in his leg, leaving him in a wheelchair for a month.

1979

Jan *You Took The Words Right Out Of My Mouth* makes US #39.
Feb *Bat Out Of Hell* reaches UK #15.
June [13] Film "Roadie", in which Meat Loaf stars with Blondie's Debbie Harry, premieres in the US.
Aug [15] Meat Loaf's second film of the year, "Americathon", opens in Los Angeles.

1981

May Intended as follow-up to ***Bat Out Of Hell***, Steinman releases the solo album ***Bad For Good***, having tired of waiting for Meat Loaf, who has had vocal chord problems brought about through too much touring, to lay down vocal tracks. It reaches US #63 and hits UK #7.
Sept [12] Meat Loaf's second album, ***Deadringer***, with all songs written by Steinman, enters the UK chart at #1 and will reach US #45 while the extracted *I'm Gonna Love Her For Both Of Us* heads to US #84 and UK #62.

1982

Feb *Dead Ringer For Love*, a duet with Cher, hits UK #5 as Meat Loaf begins a major tour.

1983

Mar [12] Now pursued by other acts, the Steinman written-and-produced Bonnie Tyler smash, *Total Eclipse Of The Heart*, tops the UK chart (and will hit US #1 in October).
May Meat Loaf's ***Midnight At The Lost And Found***, produced by Tom Dowd without Steinman, hits UK #7, as the extracted *If You Really Want To* peaks at UK #59.
Oct *Midnight At The Lost And Found* reaches UK #17.

1984

Jan *Razor's Edge* makes UK #41.
Meat Loaf appears on UK TV's "Rebellious Jukebox" with Jools Holland.
Oct Newly signed to Arista Records in the UK and RCA in the US, his label debut, *Modern Girl*, reaches UK #17.
Nov ***Bad Attitude***, with Roger Daltrey guesting, hits UK #8, as Meat Loaf begins a tour.

1985

Jan *Nowhere Fast* peaks at UK #67, while Epic's compilation ***Hits Out Of Hell*** hits UK #2, as a simultaneous video package also sells.
Apr With ***Bad Attitude*** peaking at US #74 his last US charting album of the decade, the extracted *Piece Of The Action* peaks at UK #47.

1986

July Meat Loaf appears as Gil in the film "Out Of Bounds".
Sept *Rock'n'Roll Mercenaries*, a duet with John Parr, reaches UK #31.
Oct ***Blind Before I Stop***, recorded in Rosbach, West Germany, with producer Frank Farian, reaches UK #28.

1987

June Increasingly a UK TV media favorite, Meat Loaf plays for the Duchess of York's team in the fundraising "The Grand Knockout Tournament" at Alton Towers, Alton, Staffs.
Nov ***Live At Wembley*** makes UK #60, as his Arista contract expires. In August the following year, and responding to a hail of plastic bottles being launched at him at a UK concert, Meat Loaf says, "Do you wanna rock'n'roll or do you wanna throw shit?" The crowd responds with "Throw shit!"

1990

Jan Meat Loaf begins a public Ultra SlimFast diet.
Sept [24] He plays at New York's Madison Square Garden on a bill with the Allman Brothers Band.

1991

June [22] *Dead Ringer For Love*, originally a 1981 UK #5, debuts at its UK #53 peak.
Aug Recording sessions, tentatively titled ***Back Into Hell*** with Meat Loaf reunited with writer Steinman, get underway at the Ocean Way Recording in Los Angeles.
Sept [7] ***Bat Out Of Hell*** re-charts at UK #14.

1992

Feb [14] "Wayne's World", in which Meat Loaf cameos, premieres in the US.
Apr He appears in an anti-drink-driving Star G.A.S. (Stars Against Alcohol Behind The Wheel) publicity campaign in West Germany.
June It is reported that Meat Loaf has shed 84lb on his Ultra SlimFast Diet and is $1 millon richer because of it.
[27] Reissued *Two Out Of Three Ain't Bad* charts for one week at UK #69.
Aug [29] Having re-charted yet again, ***Bat Out Of Hell*** reaches UK #24, during a further 14-week stay on the chart.
Sept [6] Meat Loaf sings the national anthem before a "Field of Dreams" charity baseball game, featuring baseball greats Reggie Jackson, Vida Blue, Ferguson Jenkins and Bob Gibson, in Dyersville, IA.
Dec Having appeared in "The Diary Of The Hurdy-Gurdy Man" earlier in the year (and set to act in the forthcoming "The South Philadelphia Story"), he is featured on the "Leap Of Faith" film soundtrack.

1993

Sept [18] Newly signed to MCA Records, Meat Loaf stages one of the biggest pop music comebacks, as his ***Bat Out Of Hell II : Back Into Hell*** sequel enters UK chart at #1, where it will spend a further ten weeks during 1993, the day after his "Everything Louder" world tour opens in the US.
Oct [1] Meat Loaf guests on NBC-TV's "The Tonight Show".
[16] Reissued ***Hits Out Of Hell*** reaches UK #26.
[23] With its video costing $565,000 to produce, *I'd Do Anything For Love (But I Won't Do That)* tops the UK chart, where it will stay for seven weeks.
[30] ***Bat Out Of Hell II : Back Into Hell*** tops the US chart.
Nov [5] *I'd Do Anything For Love (But I Won't Do That)* is certified platinum by the RIAA.
[6] *I'd Do Anything For Love (But I Won't Do That)* begins a five-week stay at US #1.
[13] ***Bat Out Of Hell*** reaches UK #19.
[19] Meat Loaf guests on CBS-TV's "Late Show With David Letterman".
Dec [25] *Bat Out Of Hell* hits UK #8.

1994

Jan [4] Meat Loaf and Jim Steinman discuss the "Bats Out Of Hell" projects on Radio 1FM with Bob Harris.
[27] As he guests on BBC1-TV's "Jonathan Ross ... Presents", Loaf is named Most Unwelcome Comeback in **Rolling Stone**'s 1994 Music Awards Critics' Picks. ***Bat Out Of Hell II : Back Into Hell*** is named Worst Album and "I'd Do Anything For Love (But I Won't Do That)" Worst Video. *I'd Do Anything For Love (But I Won't Do That)* is also voted Worst Record at the **New Musical Express** BRAT Awards.
Feb [7] He sings *That's When Rock'n'Roll Dreams Come True* at the 21st annual American Music Awards.
[9] During continuing world tour, Meat Loaf plays before a sellout crowd of 15,083 at New York's Madison Square Garden.
[14] ***Bat Out Of Hell II : Back Into Hell*** is named Highest Selling Album at the 13th annual BRIT Awards at London's Alexandra Palace, and also receives a special award for five platinum sales awards for the album. In addition he sings *I'd Do Anything For Love (But I Won't Do That)* with Rozalla, replacing a sick Cher, at the ceremonies.
[26] *Rock And Roll Dreams Come Through* reaches UK #11.
Mar [1] *I'd Do Anything For Love (But I Won't Do That)* wins Meat Loaf Best Rock Solo Performance, Male at the 36th annual Grammy Awards at New York's Radio City Music Hall.
[12] *Rock And Roll Dreams Come Through* reaches US #13.
[18] Meat Loaf begins the nine-date UK leg of his world tour at Aberdeen's Exhibition & Conference Centre, set to end on April 2nd at the National Exhibition Centre, Birmingham.
Apr [4] The European leg of his tour opens at the Forest National, Brussels, Belgium, set to end on May 3rd at Le Zenith, Paris, France.
May [4] He wins the World's Best Hard Rock Artist of the Year at the World Music Awards at Monte Carlo's Sporting Club.
[14] *Objects In The Rear View Mirror May Appear Closer Than They Are* reaches UK #26.
[28] *Objects In The Rear View Mirror May Appear Closer Than They Are* peaks at US #38.
June [5] Meat Loaf plays a sellout gig at the Meadowlands Arena, East Rutherford, NJ, as his world tour returns to the US.
July [19] Songwriter Jordan Sage files suit in a Milwaukee federal court for copyright infringement, claiming that *Objects In The Rear View Mirror* is based on one of his own songs.
Sept [30] The RIAA certifies 12 million sales of ***Bat Out Of Hell***.

1995

Apr [7] The RIAA confirms five million sales of ***Bat Out Of Hell II : Back Into Hell***.
Aug [29] Crew members, Henry Urgoti and Michael Shea, die in a helicopter crash on a shoot for the video for *I'd Lie For You (And That's The Truth)*.
Sept [12] Meat Loaf sings at Luciano Pavarotti's annual War Child charity benefit at Novi Sad Park in Modena, Italy, a performance which will be included on the subsequent ***Pavarotti & Friends Together For The Children Of Bosnia***, released the following March.
[18] Cleveland International files suit against Sony Music for $5.2 million in back royalties relating to Meat Loaf's early releases on the label.
Oct [27] The online site (http://www.meat-loaf.mca.com) is launched to promote the release of ***Welcome To The Neighbourhood***.
[28] *I'd Lie For You (And That's The Truth)*, written by Diane Warren and featuring a vocal pairing with Patti Russo, debuts at its UK #2 peak.
Nov [11] ***Welcome To The Neighbourhood***, produced by Ron Nevison, hits UK #3 in its week of entry.
[18] *I'd Lie For You (And That's The Truth)* reaches US #13.
Dec [2] ***Welcome To The Neighbourhood*** debuts at its US #17 peak.
[5] Meat Loaf performs at Wembley Arena, Wembley, Middx.
[13] He guests on NBC-TV's "The Tonight Show".

1996

Feb [3] The extracted *Not A Dry In The House* hits UK #7.
[9] Following Cleveland Entertainment's litigation against Sony Music the previous September, Meat Loaf now files suit in Southern District Court, New York, against the former, seeking to regain the masters from ***Bat Out Of Hell*** claiming that Cleveland has failed to pay him back royalties.
Mar [2] *Not A Dry In The House* peaks at US #82.
Apr [1] His open-ended "Welcome To The Neighbourhood" world tour opens in the UK at Westpoint Park, Exeter, Devon, its UK leg set to end with a pair of dates at the Wembley Arena on the 29th and 30th.
[27] *Runnin' For The Red Light (I Gotta Live)* reaches UK #21 in its week of entry.

MEGADETH

Dave Mustaine (lead vocals, guitar); **Marty Friedman** (guitar); **Dave Ellefson** (bass); **Nick Menza** (drums)

1985

May Outspoken group leader Mustaine (b. Sept. 13, 1961, La Mesa, CA), having grown up in a troubled family environment in the California suburb of La Mesa, has already played lead guitar with pioneering thrash-metal band Metallica between 1981-1983, and gone on to form Megadeth with Ellefson (Nov. 12, 1964, MN) in Los Angeles, CA in 1983, initially recruiting drummer Gar Samuelson and guitarist Chris Poland. Securing a one-off deal with the independent Combat label, the group releases its uncompromising thrash debut, ***Killing Is My Business ... And Business Is Good!***, featuring a cover of Nancy Sinatra's *These Boots Are Made For Walking*.

1986

Nov Signed to Capitol Records on the strength of its first album, Megadeth's politically vitriolic ***Peace Sells ... But Who's Buying?*** makes US #76 and will earn a gold disc. It is supported by a massive 72-week headlining tour.

1987

Mar [31] Sued by another band calling itself Megadeath, Mustaine says, "Money and muscle gets rid of them."
June Samuelson and Poland are asked to leave, and are replaced by Jeff Young (guitar) and Chuck Behler (drums).
Dec *Wake Up Dead* makes UK #65.

1988

Feb ***so far, so good ... so what!***, including their UK #45 thrash treatment of the Sex Pistols' *Anarchy In The UK*, reaches US #28.
Mar [18] ***so far, so good ... so what!*** enters at its UK #18 peak.
May [21] The extracted *Mary Jane* reaches UK #46.
Aug [20] The band ends its "so far so good ... so what!" world tour at Castle Donington's "Monsters Of Rock" festival, the group's last gig for two years (due, not least, to Mustaine's reported drug-addiction problems).

1990

Jan The group's cover of Alice Cooper's 1973 hit, *No More Mr. Nice Guy*, climbs to UK #13.
Feb [16] ***so far, so good ... so what!*** is certified gold by the RIAA.
Sept Previewing a new album, *Holy Wars ... The Punishment Due* peaks at UK #24.
Oct [14] With Mustaine now reportedly "clean", he band performs on the "Clash Of The Titans" metal fest at the Wembley Arena, Wembley, Middx. with Slayer, Testament and Suicidal Tendencies.
[27] Mike Clink-produced ***Rust In Peace***, featuring new guitarist Friedman (b. Dec. 8, 1962, Washington, DC), who has already released three solo albums on the Schrapnel label, and drummer Menza (b. July 23, 1964, West Germany) who have replaced the exiting Young and Behler, reaches US #23 and hits UK #8.

1991

Jan They appear at the "Rock In Rio II" festival, Rio De Janeiro, Brazil, while ***Rust In Peace*** is certified gold in the US.
Mar [23] *Hangar 18* reaches UK #26.
May [16] A further "Clash Of The Titans" tour begins in Dallas, TX, with Anthrax, Slayer and Alice In Chains in the US.

1992

June [27] *Symphony Of Destruction* debuts at its UK #15 peak.
July [18] Anti-nuclear themed ***Countdown To Extinction***, co-produced by Mustaine, debuts at its UK #5 peak, while Mustaine covers the Democratic Party Convention for MTV.
Aug [1] ***Countdown To Extinction*** bows at its US #2 peak, behind Billy Ray Cyrus' ***Some Gave All***.
Sept [29-30] During a major European tour, Megadeth plays a pair of dates at London's Hammersmith Apollo.
Oct [22] The group performs on BBC1-TV's "Top Of The Pops".
[24] *Skin O' My Teeth* debuts at its UK #13 peak.
[31] Megadeth begins a US tour initially set to end on December 8th at the Tingley Coliseum, New Mexico State Fair, Albuquerque, NM.
Nov [11] ***Peace Sells ... But Who's Dying?*** is certified platinum by the RIAA.
Dec [5] *Symphony Of Destruction* peaks at US #71.

1993

Jan [3] A further US tour re-opens at the Thomas & Mack Center, University of Nevada, Las Vegas, NV, set to end on February 21st, followed by visits to Australia and Japan.
Mar [26-28] The band performs at the Obras Arena, Buenos Aires, Argentina, having recently received the Genesis Awards' Doris Day Music Award for the anti-hunting message expounded on ***Countdown To Extinction***.
May [29] *Sweating Bullets* debuts at its UK #26 high.
June Having been featured on the "Super Mario Brothers" soundtrack, Megadeth now contributes *Angry Again* to Arnold Schwarzenegger-starring "The Last Action Hero" soundtrack.
[5] Megadeth plays at the National Bowl, Milton Keynes, Bucks., on a bill with Metallica.
Nov [23] ***The Beavis And Butt-Head Experience***, featuring Megadeth's *99 Ways To Die*, is released in the US.

1994

Nov [5] ***Youthanasia*** hits UK #6 in its week of entry, with a limited number made available in blue vinyl LPs.
[19] ***Youthanasia*** bows at its US #4 peak.
Dec [1-5] The group plays a week of dates at the Obras Stadium in Buenos Aires, Argentina.
[13] The RIAA certifies platinum sales of ***Rust In Peace*** and multi-platinum sales of ***Countdown To Extinction*** (two million).

1995

Jan [5] ***Youthanasia*** is also confirmed platinum by the RIAA.
[7] The extracted *Train Of Consequences* debuts at its UK #22 peak.
[13] A 35-date "Feed The Hungry" North American tour opens at the Grady Gammage Memorial Auditorium, Arizona State University, Tempe, AZ, set to end on February 25th in Los Angeles. (By tour's end, the band will have collected 35 tons of food for

local distribution.)
Mar [9] The European leg of the world tour opens at Ulster Hall, Belfast, Northern Ireland, set to end on April 30th in Bourges, France.
[25] ***Youthanasia/Hidden Treasure*** reaches UK #28 in its week of entry.
July [16] Following dates in Australia and Japan, the US tour continues with a sellout date at the Newport Music Hall, Columbus, OH.
Aug [5] ***Hidden Treasures*** EP debuts at its US #90 album peak.
see also: **METALLICA**

MELANIE

1967

The daughter of Ukranian-Italian parents, singer/ songwriter folk artist Melanie (b. Melanie Safka, Feb. 3, 1947, Astoria, Long Island, NY), having made her first public performance at the age of four on the radio show "Live Like A Millionaire", is a student at New York's Academy of Fine Arts and, having begun singing in the Quay bar in Seabright, NJ after college hours, and as an occasional singer/ guitarist in clubs in Long Branch, NJ (where the family moved during her teens), and Greenwich Village, New York, signs her first publishing agreement and cuts her debut single *Beautiful People*, for CBS/Columbia Records. Following another cut for Columbia, she confronts label boss Clive Davis and quits when told that the company is grooming Michele Lee as a priority over her.

1969

May Misdirected when going to audition for a part in a production of "Dark Side Of The Moon", and allegedly going into the wrong office, she has met Peter Schekeryk, who invites her to perform an impromptu vocal audition. He is sufficiently impressed to become her manager (and later producer and husband), and has secured her a deal with Neil Bogart's Buddah label which now releases her maiden album ***Born To Be*** and the extracted *Beautiful People*.
Aug [16] She appears during a rainstorm at the "Woodstock Music & Art Fair" in Bethel, NY, where she is as appreciative of the audience as they are of her (the inspiration for her song *Lay Down (Candles In The Rain)*).
Nov Her second album, ***Affectionately Melanie***, makes US #196.

1970

July Melanie's first chart single, the hymnal *Lay Down (Candles In The Rain)*, backed by the Edwin Hawkins Singers, hits US #6. It is taken from ***Candles In The Rain***, which reaches US #17 and will earn a gold disc.
Sept *Peace Will Come (According To Plan)* reaches US #32.
Nov Live album, ***Leftover Wine***, recorded at New York's Carnegie Hall, reaches US #39. Following a highly successful UK tour, Melanie's revival of the Rolling Stones' *Ruby Tuesday* hits UK #9.
Dec *Candles In The Rain* hits UK #5. Spurred by its UK success, *Ruby Tuesday* is issued as a US single and makes #33. Her soundtrack album from the movie "All The Right Noises" is also released.

1971

Jan Previously a minor UK hit as a cover version by the New Seekers four months earlier, Melanie's own version of her *What Have They Done To My Song Ma* makes UK #39.
Feb *Leftover Wine* climbs to UK #22.
Mar *The Good Book* peaks at US #80. (She becomes noted for her musical adaptations of children's stories, including Alexander Beetle and Christopher Robin, and becomes an active ambassador for UNICEF, touring the world on its behalf.)
June *The Good Book* hits UK #9. Meanwhile, Melanie, at odds with Buddah Records and its insistence that she deliver albums on demand, forms her own label, Neighborhood Records, in partnership with Schekeryk to whom she is now married.
Dec [9] Melanie performs at London's Rainbow Theatre.
[13] ***Candles In The Rain*** is certified gold by the RIAA.
[16] The still-climbing *Brand New Key* is certified gold by the RIAA.
[25] Her first Neighborhood release, the light-hearted *Brand New Key*, tops the US chart for the first of three weeks. Written in 15 minutes and intended as an uptempo concert relief ditty, its lyric nonetheless attracts misinterpretations of its overt innocence, and even sparks some radio bans. ***Gather Me***, also on Neighborhood and including the single, reaches US #15 and earns a gold disc. Former label Buddah gathers up previously unissued tracks as ***Garden In The City*** in competition, which peaks at US #115 but, in a novel marketing move, is packaged in a flower-scented "scratch-and-sniff" sleeve.
[9] Melanie performs at London's Rainbow Theatre during UK visit.

1972

Jan *Brand New Key* hits UK #4, as ***Gather Me*** makes UK #14. (In 1975, UK West Country rural novelty band the Wurzels will take their comic adaptatation of *Brand New Key*, titled *Combine Harvester*, to UK #1.)
Mar Competing Melanie singles, *The Nickel Song* (on Buddah) and *Ring The Living Bell* (on Neighborhood), peak at US #35 and #31.
Apr Buddah double album, ***The Four Sides Of Melanie***, a compilation of her earliest material, peaks at US #103, while ***Garden In The City*** makes UK #19.
June [3] Melanie participates in the Crystal Palace Garden Party, Crystal Palace, London with the Beach Boys, Joe Cocker, Richie Havens, Sha Na Na and David Blue.
[13] ***Gather Me*** is certified gold by the RIAA.
Oct *The Four Sides Of Melanie* reaches UK #23.
Nov *Together Alone* peaks at US #86.
Dec *Stoneground Words* climbs to US #70.

1973

Mar *Bitter Bad* makes US #36.
June Live double album, ***Melanie At Carnegie Hall***, her second performance set to be recorded at the New York venue, stops at US #109. (She has now retreated from full-time performing to spend time at home in New Jersey and will become a mother three times in three years.)
Dec *Will You Love Me Tomorrow*, her remake of the Shirelles 1961 classic, peaks at US #82.

1974

Mar *Will You Love Me Tomorrow* makes UK #37.
May *Madruguda* peaks at US #192, her final chart entry.
[9] With Bob Dylan, Pete Seeger and others, she takes part in "Friends Of Chile" benefit concert at New York's Felt Forum, raising $30,000 towards legal aid fees for Chilean refugees and political prisoners.

1975

With her career noticeably slowing, Melanie releases two albums, ***As I See It Now*** and ***Sunset And Other Beginnings***, after which the Neighborhood label closes. Subsequently signing a one-off deal with Atlantic Records, ***Photograph***, co-produced by Ahmet Ertegun, will be released the following year.

1977

Photogenic - Not Just A Pretty Face is issued on Midland International label, while a second new album, ***Ballroom Streets***, is released by the independent label Tomato. (Melanie will retreat from the recording scene for five years but will continue to play live.)

1983

Sept Following the release of her comeback album, ***Arabesque*** by RCA Records in August the previous year, *Every Breath Of The Way*, issued on the revitalized Neighborhood label, peaks at UK #70. This minor success leads to some UK live dates though a show at London's Royal Albert Hall is cancelled due to poor ticket sales, prompting Melanie to perform outside the venue to an enthusiastic audience.
Nov *Seventh Wave* is her last Neighborhood release.

1989

Sept Following the 1987 Canada-only release of ***Am I Real Or What***, UK label Food For Thought issues ***Cowabonga***, as Melanie receives an Emmy Award for her lyrics to the TV series "Beauty And The Beast" theme. During the year she also joins the "Woodstock 20th Anniversary" reunion tour and, based in Clearwater, FL, will continue performing into the '90s (sometimes joined on stage by her daughters, Jeordie and Leilah, who also perform as the Denver, CO-based Safkab folk group).

1994

Aug [13] Having released ***Precious Cargo*** on the label of the same name in 1991, followed by ***Freedom Knows My Name*** on Lonestar Records in 1993, and this year's ***Silver***, Melanie spearheads an alternative, and free, "Woodstock '94" concert at the original Bethel, NY site.

JOHN MELLENCAMP

1962

Mellencamp (b. Oct. 7, 1951, Seymour, IN), the second of five children of an electrical engineer father and a 1946 "Miss Indiana" runner-up mother, born with a tumor in his neck which doctors remove along with two vertebrae (resulting in a 4-F draft deferment), joins his first band in fifth grade, miming to current hits. Spending 18 months with his first live band, Crepe Soul beginning in 1965, he goes on to join Snakepit Banana Barn the following year, playing at college fraternities for $30 a weekend. Buying his first acoustic guitar in 1967, and graduating from Seymour High School in 1970, Mellencamp leaves the family home, moving to an apartment in the small town of Valonia. He marries and becomes a father, finds work as a carpenter's helper, while his wife Priscilla works as a telephone operator. The following year he forms glitter-rock group Trash, with guitarist friend Larry Crane, which performs locally, covering mainly '60s hits.

1975

After graduating from Vincennes University, Mellencamp (now separated from his wife and child) works for a telephone company, before being laid off. With a year's severance pay, he sets out for New York, NY with a demo he has made of Paul Revere & the Raiders' *Kicks*. An admirer of David Bowie, Mellencamp calls his management company, MainMan. He meets Tony De Fries, who offers to record him and arranges a deal with MCA Records.

1976

Mellencamp records his first album, ***Chestnut Street Incident***, mainly comprising cover versions. When it is released, still in demo form, Mellencamp discovers that De Fries has re-named him Johnny Cougar, and he has to participate in a De Fries-conceived "Johnny Cougar Day", driving through hometown Seymour, in an open-top car motorcade.

1977

Parting company with MainMan, he moves to Bloomington, IN, where he rehearses self-written material with his newly-formed band, the Zone, records demos for Gulcher label and cuts a second album, ***The Kid Inside***. He meets Billy Gaff, president of Riva Records and manager of Rod Stewart, who signs him to the label.

1978

Apr Cougar performs at the Marquee during a visit to London.

June [1] He embarks on A 15-date UK tour at the Bristol Granary, set to end on the 20th at the Newport Stowaway, Gwent, promoting ***A Biography*** (not released in the US), heralded by Gaff as the next Springsteen. Despite a massive publicity campaign (posters spring up bearing the legend "Cougar" and little else), the disc and promotion fail.

1979

Aug ***John Cougar***, featuring some material from ***A Biography***, makes US #64.

Dec *I Need A Lover* reaches US #28 and will top the singles chart in Australia.

1980

Feb *Small Paradise* peaks at US #87. After nearly three years on the road, Mellencamp returns to the studio to cut a new album.

Oct Still billed as John Cougar, ***Nothin' Matters And What If It Did***, produced by Steve Cropper, reaches US #37.

Dec *This Time* makes US #27. *Ain't Even Done With The Night* will reach US #17 the following May.

1982

Apr Having divorced and remarried, he begins a major US tour with his own band, comprising Larry Crane, Mike Wanchic (guitar), Toby Meyers (bass) and Kenny Aronoff (drums), supporting Heart, before headlining later in the year.

July [3] He gives a free concert for 20,000 high-school students in Fort Wayne, IN, who had sandbagged for eight days in March 1982, during the state's worst flood crisis.

Aug [7] *Hurts So Good* hits US #2 for the first of four weeks and becomes a million seller, kept off the top by Human League's *Don't You Want Me*.

Sept [11] As the self-penned, co-produced (with Don Gehman) ***American Fool*** tops the US chart, the mid-western adolescent tale, *Jack And Diane*, moves up to US #4 and *Hurts So Good* falls to US #8, making Mellencamp the only male artist to have two US Top 10 hits and a #1 album simultaneously. ***American Fool*** stays at US #1 for nine weeks, achieving platinum sales.

Oct [2] *Jack And Diane* hits US #1 for the first of four weeks.

Nov *Jack And Diane* reaches UK #25, while ***American Fool*** makes UK #37. It becomes the biggest-selling album of the year in the US, selling over three million copies.

1983

Jan *Hand To Hold On To* hits US #9. Mellencamp cancels an appearance at the "US Festival", after promoters insist on all video rights to his performance.

[17] He ties, with Rick Springfield, to win the Favorite Male Artist, Pop/Rock category at the tenth annual American Music Awards held at the Shrine Auditorium, Los Angeles, CA.

Nov [26] *Crumblin' Down* hits US #9, as he changes his name to John Cougar Mellencamp. Its parent album ***Uh-huh*** hits US #9, becoming his second platinum seller.

1984

Feb [11] *Pink Houses* hits US #8.

Mar ***Uh-huh*** peaks at UK #92.

May [19] *Authority Song* reaches US #15.

July Susan Miles wins MTV's "Party House With Mellencamp" competition, subsequently choosing to paint her house pink. (During the year, he writes a screenplay "Ridin' The Cage" in which Warner Bros. shows interest and also produces Mitch Ryder's comeback album ***Never Kick A Sleeping Dog***.)

1985

Mar The Blasters' ***Hard Line*** album, including the Mellencamp-produced *Colored Lights*, is released.

July [13] He turns down the opportunity to participate in "Live Aid", stating "Concerts that just raise money aren't a good idea."

Sept [22] He organizes the inaugural "Farm Aid" fundraiser with Willie Nelson and Neil Young, held in Champaign, IL. During the show he asks the audience to write to their congressmen demanding action to help American farmers.

Oct [12] *Lonely Ol' Night* hits US #6.

[26] Mellencamp guests on NBC-TV's "Late Night With David Letterman".

Nov Recorded in his newly-built studio, ***Scarecrow***, dedicated to his grandfather Speck, hits US #2. His final album for Riva, it will eventually sell over three million domestic copies.

Dec [6] At a concert at New York's Madison Square Garden, the sound system breaks down twice. Mellencamp waits patiently for the problem to be resolved. When he returns to the stage, he plays for two hours and tells the audience that anyone with a ticket stub can get their money back if they so wish.

[28] Home-themed *Small Town* hits US #6.

1986

Feb Continuing to depict life in mid-western America, *Small Town* makes UK #53.

Apr [5] *R.O.C.K. In The USA* hits US #2.

May *R.O.C.K. In The USA* peaks at UK #67.

June [14] *Rain On The Scarecrow* makes US #21.

July [4] Mellencamp participates in "Farm Aid II" at Manor Downs, Austin, TX.

Aug [16] *Rumbleseat* makes US #28.

Sept Mellencamp and his band start work with producer Don Gehman on a new album at Belmont Hall Studio, IN.

1987

Sept [19] Mellencamp appears at "Farm Aid III" at the University of Nebraska's Memorial Stadium.

Oct [3] *Paper In Fire*, his first release on Mercury Records and, in part, inspired by the film "Hud", as are other songs of his, hits US #9 as its parent album ***The Lonesome Jubilee*** hits US #6 and UK #31.

[30] Mellencamp begins a six-week US tour in Terre Haute, IN, set to end on December 15th.

Dec He contributes *I Saw Mama Kissing Santa Claus* to the newly released various artists' Special Olympics charity album ***A Very Special Christmas***.

[16] Mellencamp performs two free concerts for the people of Chilicothe, OH, after local radio station WFBC has initiated a petition.

1988

Jan [9] *Cherry Bomb* hits US #8.

[25-26] Mellencamp returns to the UK to play two concerts at London's Hammersmith Odeon.

Apr *Check It Out* reaches US #14.

May [26] He opens a US tour at Irvine Meadows Amphitheatre, Laguna Hills, CA, set to end in July in Milwaukee, WI.

June *Rooty Toot Toot* peaks at US #61.

Aug [13] Mellencamp appears with Paul Simon on NBC-TV's "Coca Cola Presents Live : The Hard Rock".

[14] He becomes a grandfather at 37 when his 18-year-old daughter from his marriage to Priscilla, Michelle, gives birth to Elexis Suzanne Peach.

[18] His current wife Victoria files for divorce in Monroe Superior Court, after eight years of marriage, and seeks custody of their two children.

Sept Mellencamp contributes *Do Re Mi* to the newly released Woody Guthrie/Leadbelly tribute album, ***Folkways : A Vision Shared***. He also produces ***Too Long In The Wasteland*** the debut album from James McMurtry (son of **The Last Picture Show** author Larry McMurtry).

Nov He directs a video for Bob Dylan's *Political World* in Bloomington.

1989

May ***Big Daddy*** reaches UK #25.

June [17] Anti-fame single, *Pop Singer*, reaches US #15, aided by an appropriately disdainful video clip.

July ***Big Daddy*** hits US #7.

[10] ***Big Daddy*** is certified platinum by the RIAA.

Aug [12] *Jackie Brown* makes US #48.

1990

Apr [7] He participates in "Farm Aid IV", singing *Paper In Fire*, *Rain On The Scarecrow* and *Pink Houses*.

July [23] Mellencamp begins filming his screen debut as a singer returning home to celebrate his grandfather's 84th birthday in rural Indianapolis in "Souvenirs". He also records the soundtrack album with John Prine, Dwight Yoakam, Joe Ely and James McMurtry.

1991

Mar After a two-year recording hiatus, Mellencamp returns to the studio with his current band Toby Myers, John Kascella, David Grissom (who has replaced Larry Crane), Mike Wanchic and Kenny Aronoff, having completed his own movie project "Falling From Grace".

Sept Having spent much of the last three years painting, Mellencamp (who estimates in a **USA Today** interview that, as a committed smoker, he has puffed some 46,000 cigarettes since his last tour in 1988) puts the results on show at an art exhibition in Hilton Head, SC.

[16] Mellencamp plays a show at New York's Carnegie Hall to promote his new album.

Oct [17] He faints at at a radio station in Seattle, WA, and is rushed to hospital where Dr. John Olsen, Seattle Heart Clinic cardiologist said his heart rate had dropped to 20-25 bpm.

[19] Self-produced ***Whenever We Wanted*** debuts at its UK #39 peak.

[26] ***Whenever We Wanted*** bows at its US #17 high.

Nov [14] Mellencamp is honored at the fourth annual Nordoff Robbins Silver Clef dinner and benefit auction at the Roseland Ballroom, New York.

[23] *Get A Leg Up* reaches US #14.

Dec [3] Mellencamp leads off the second annual **Billboard** Music Awards with a performance of *Love And Happiness*.

1992

Jan [6] ***Whenever We Wanted*** is certified platinum by the RIAA.

[7] Mellencamp begins his "Whenever We Wanted" North American tour, his first in four years, at the Martin Luther King Arena, Savannah Civic Center, Savannah, GA, before a sellout crowd of 6,792. (His current tour band is Aronoff (drums), Wanchic (guitar), Myers (bass), Lisa Germano (fiddle), Grissom (guitar), and Pat Peterson and Jenny Douglas McRae (backing vocals).)

Feb [5] He holds a free concert in Johnson City, TN before a crowd of 3,500, protesting the cancellation of MTV by the Sammons Communications cable company, a cost-cutting decision by the Dallas-based corporation who pulled the music channel from their cable systems on January 1st. Sammons will relent on March 19th.

[18, 20] Mellencamp plays two sellout shows at the Great Western Forum, Inglewood, CA, grossing $494,275.

Mar [14] He takes part in "Farm Aid V" at the Texas Stadium, Irving, TX.

[21] *Again Tonight* hits US #3.

Apr [11] Mellencamp plays at Wembley Arena, Wembley, Middx., the final date of the UK leg of his current trek.

July He cancels dates in Detroit, MI and Pittsburgh, PA because of exhaustion. Further dates will be axed after bassist Myers severs part of his big toe in a boating accident.

[4] "Ain't That America : A July 4th Celebration" TV show, which features Mellencamp, airs live from the Deer Creek Music Center, Indianapolis.

Aug [12] Mellencamp is featured on "MTV Unplugged".
Sept [5] He weds model Elaine Irwin in his rustic cabin along the White River near his hometown of Seymour. They met while shooting his "Get A Leg Up" video earlier in the year.
[26] ***Honeymoon In Vegas*** soundtrack, to which Mellencamp has contributed *Jailhouse Rock*, reaches US #18.
Oct [16] Mellencamp performs *Like A Rolling Stone* at the Bob Dylan 30th anniversary tribute at Madison Square Garden, with Al Kooper reprising his original organ role. (During the year Mellencamp's directorial film debut, "Falling From Grace" premieres in the US, starring himself opposite Mariel Hemingway. The accompanying soundtrack album ***Falling From Grace*** includes three new cuts by the singer with other contributions from the likes of Nanci Griffith, Janis Ian and John Prine.)

1993

Jan [22] Mellencamp plays a benefit for band member John Cascella, who had died of a heart attack on November 14th while driving home after watching the Evander Holyfield-Riddick Bowe heavyweight fight in Indiana, at the Murat Theatre, Indianapolis.
July [28] He plays a "Concert For The Heartland" benefit at the World Music Theater, Chicago, IL.
Aug [31] Mellencamp guests on the second broadcast of CBS-TV's "The Late Show With David Letterman".
Sept [18] Variously produced by Mellencamp with Michael Wanchic, David Leonard and Malcolm Burn, ***Human Wheels***, including *All Roads To The River* co-written with Janis Ian, debuts at its UK #37 peak.
[25] ***Human Wheels*** bows at its US #7 peak.
Nov [10] ***Human Wheels*** is certified platinum by the RIAA.
[13] *Human Wheels* makes US #48.

1994

Feb [17] Agreement is reached in Marion Superior Court, Indianapolis, that Mellencamp must attend at least one therapy session with his daughters and can only visit them under supervision at his ex-wife's home.
July [9] Co-produced with Wanchic and featuring guest vocalist Lisa Germano, ***Dance Naked*** bows at its US #13 peak.
Aug [8] Mellencamp suffers a mild heart attack after a show at the Jones Beach Theatre, Wantagh, NY, during his current summer tour.
Sept [3] His treatment of Van Morrison's *Wild Night*, duetted with bassist and singer Me'shell Ndegeocello, hits US #3 and reaches UK #34.
[7] Mellencamp cancels the rest of his current US tour after being diagnosed with a clogged artery by doctors at Bloomington Hospital.
Nov [14] ***Dance Naked*** is certified platinum by the RIAA.
Dec [17] Its title cut *Dance Naked* makes US #41.

1995

Jan [27] The RIAA certifies multi-platinum sales of ***The Lonesome Jubilee*** (three million), ***Uh-Huh*** (three million), ***American Fool*** (four million) and ***Scarecrow*** (four million).
Feb [16] ***John Cougar*** is confirmed gold by the RIAA.
July [17] ***Nothing Matters And What If It Did*** is ratified platinum by the RIAA.
Sept [2] Mellencamp sings a medley of *Rockin' In The USA* and *Little Latin Lupe Lu*, *Ring Of Fire* with Johnny Cash and *Dancing In The Street* with Martha Reeves at the Concert for the Rock and Roll Hall of Fame at Cleveland Stadium, Cleveland, OH.
Oct [1] Mellencamp performs on an all-star bill at "Farm Aid VIII", held at Cardinal Stadium, Kentucky Fair & Expo Center, Louisville, KY.

MEN AT WORK

Colin Hay (vocals); **Ron Strykert** (guitar); **Greg Ham** (sax, keyboards, flute); **John Rees** (bass); **Jerry Speiser** (drums)

1979

Men At Work forms in Melbourne, Victoria, Australia, after Hay (b. June 29, 1953, Scotland), who emigrated at the age of 14 with his parents to Australia, and Strykert (b. Aug. 18, 1957, Australia), who have met while performing in the musical "Heroes" in Sydney, intially decide to form an acoustic duo. They are joined first by Rees and then by Hay's old friends from Melbourne's La Troube University, Speiser and Ham (b. Sept. 27, 1953, Australia). The following year they work regularly as the house band at the Cricketer's Arms, a Richmond, Melbourne pub, where they are noted by customer Peter Karpin, who works for CBS Records and through his persistence, the label signs to the band.

1982

Mar Their debut single, *Who Can It Be Now?*, written by Hay, as with all subsequent hit singles, and ***Business As Usual***, produced by American, Peter Mclan, both top the Australian charts (the album for ten weeks, beating a record established by Split Enz's ***True Colours***) as Men At Work becomes the highest-paid band in Australia.
Oct [30] Following a US tour supporting Fleetwood Mac, *Who Can It Be Now?*, with its promo video receiving saturation MTV play, tops the US chart for one week and will become a million seller.
Nov [13] ***Business As Usual*** begins a 15-week hold on US #1. Its chart-topping run is a new record for a debut album (beating the 12 weeks established by the Monkees in 1967), before surrendering to Michael Jackson's ***Thriller***. The group begins a 50-date headlining US tour, supported by fellow Australians Mental As Anything. Meanwhile their UK debut is *Who Can It Be Now?*, which makes UK #45.
Dec The band evicts a drunk from the stage during a gig in Perth, Australia, only to discover it is national cricket hero, Dennis Lillee.

1983

Jan [15] *Down Under*, another Australian #1 during 1982, tops the US chart for the first of four weeks, becoming another platinum seller.
[29] ***Business As Usual*** begins a six-week reign at UK #1, the same week that the extracted *Down Under* tops the UK singles survey. For two weeks, the group has both the best-selling single and album in the US and UK simultaneously - a feat previously achieved by only a few, including the Beatles, Rod Stewart and Simon & Garfunkel.
Feb [23] Men At Work wins Best New Artist category at the 25th annual Grammy Awards.
[25] *Down Under* is certified gold by the RIAA.
May Hay-penned ***Cargo***, originally cut the previous summer in Melbourne with producer Mclan, but held over because of the success of its predecessor, hits US #3 and UK #8, while *Overkill*, taken from it, makes UK #21.
[28] The group appears on first day of the three-day "US '83 Festival" in San Bernardino, CA, co-headlining the day's bill with the Clash and the Stray Cats.
June *Overkill* hits US #3.
July Also extracted from their second album, the anti-war themed *It's A Mistake* makes UK #33.
Aug *It's A Mistake* is their fourth consecutive US Top 10 hit at #6.
Oct *Dr. Heckyll And Mr. Jive*, third single from Cargo, reaches US #28 and UK #31, the group's last UK chart entry.

1985

June After a lengthy recording hiatus during which Rees and Speiser have left the band, with session men taking the bass and drum roles for the band's third album, the group makes US #47 with Hay's *Everything I Need.*
July ***Two Hearts***, containing the hit single, reaches US #50.
Sept [11] ***Two Hearts*** is certified gold by the RIAA.
Nov The group, with Hay (the only original member remaining), James Black, ex-Mondo Rock, Colin Bayley, ex-Mi-Sex, Jeremy Alsop and Chad Whackerman, tours Japan and also performs three concerts in China. Soon after, Men At Work will split.

1987

Mar Still signed to CBS/Columbia, and recorded in London with producer Robin Millar, Hay's solo album, ***Looking For Jack***, released under the name Colin James Hay, reaches US #126 including the US #99 peaking *Hold Me*. His solo career will continue with the issue of ***Wayfaring Sons*** on MCA in 1990.

1994

Oct [21] The RIAA certifies sales of six million copies of ***Business As Usual***.
Nov [21] ***Cargo*** is certified multi-platinum (three million) by the RIAA.

1996

Apr Unable to secure a US recording contract following the 1993 release of his last solo album ***Peaks And Valleys***, Hay has set up his own Australian label Lazy Eye for last year's ***Topanga*** (named after the Californian town where he now spends half his time, commuting from Melbourne), while the album was issued in the UK on Direct Topic Records. Hay has also embarked on an acting career, appearing not least in "Raw Silk", "Wills And Burke" and "Georgia", and is currently featured as a psychotic musician in the premiering Australian movie "Cosi". Meanwhile, Sony's Legacy imprint releases ***Contraband : The Best Of Men At Work*** in the US.

NATALIE MERCHANT

1993

Aug [28] Former church choirist and current vegetarian Merchant (b. Oct. 26, 1963, Jamestown, NY) who has joined Still Life members and fellow Jamestown Community College students Steven Gustafson, Dennis Drew and Robert Buck to form 10,000 Maniacs in January 1981, has successfully fronted the folk/rock band as its lyricist and lead singer for twelve years (including her final studio album with the group, ***Our Time In Eden*** issued in February of this year, and ***Unplugged*** which is due for release in October) attracting a loyal college-based following at alternative radio, and has recently announced that she is leaving the line-up saying "being in a band for me was like having five husbands. The divorce was pretty amicable." She now plays her first gig as a solo artist, although she has performed alone previously while still a member of 10,000 Maniacs, at the "Shake-A-Leg" charity benefit concert held at the Fort Adams State Park, Newport, RI, at which she also duets with Billy Bragg.
Nov [4] Merchant appears on CBS-TV's "Late Show With David Letterman".
[13] Taken from the various artists benefit album ***Born To Choose***, Merchant's duet with R.E.M. (she is a longtime friend of the band's Michael Stipe), *Photograph* begins a US Modern Rock chart climb to hit #9.

1995

July [8] Having signed a solo deal with Elektra Records, her maiden album ***Tigerlily***, hailed by the **Wall Street Journal** (and they should know) as "A gem. ***Tigerlily*** has the presence of a timeless classic", debuts at its US #13 peak, having entered at its UK #39 high on the 1st. Produced with John Holbrook, featured musicians include Jennifer Turner (guitar), Barrie Maguire (bass), Peter Yanwitz (drums) and

Adrian Guevarra (percussion).
Oct [28] *Carnival* hits US #10.
Nov [21] Elektra Records US releases its first E-CD, Merchant's multimedia enhanced single *Wonder*.
Dec [19] Merchant performs on CBS-TV's "Late Show With David Letterman".

1996

Feb [21] ***Tigerlily*** is certified platinum by the RIAA.
Mar [17] Her first solo world tour begins which will include special appearances with Sting and headlining US summer dates.
Apr [28] Merchant participates in "VH1 Honors - Witness" benefit, a concert for human rights broadcast live on the US cable network from the Universal Amphitheatre, Universal City, CA.
May [18] *Wonder* reaches US #20.
see: **THE 10,000 MANIACS**

METALLICA

James Hetfield (vocals, guitar); **Kirk Hammett** (guitar); **Jason Newsted** (bass); **Lars Ulrich** (drums)

1981

July Having left his family in Los Angeles, CA, where they emigrated in August 1980 from Denmark and encouraged him to pursue his father's vocation as a professional tennis player, Ulrich (b. Dec. 26, 1963, Gentoss, Denmark) goes to London and tours the UK with New Wave British Heavy Metal outfit Diamond Head Ulrich has already been instrumental in compiling the various artists album ***The New Wave Of British Heavy Metal*** with **Kerrang!** magazine editor Geoff Barton in 1979, a movement which will influence a whole generation of hard rockers. Returning to the US in October, Ulrich determines to form a band to record a track offered him by Metal Blade label owner Brian Slagel for a forthcoming compilation, ***Metal Massacre***. From a Los Angeles magazine ad, Ulrich recruits Hetfield (b. Aug. 3, 1963, Los Angeles), ex-Obsession and Leather Charm and the son of an opera-singing mother, and records *Hit The Lights* with lead guitarist Lloyd Grant. As Metallica, a name suggested by friend Ron Quintana in San Francisco, CA, who has the same title in mind for a fanzine, they will re-record the same cut for a Canadian release of the album with Dave Mustaine (b. Sept. 13, 1961, La Mesa, CA) on lead and Ron McGovney, Hetfield's room-mate, on bass.

1982

Mar [14] Following the recording of a seven-track demo, ***No Life Till Leather***, McGovney has quit, replaced by Cliff Burton (b. Clifford Lee Burton, Feb. 10, 1962), who Ulrich has spent four months trying to persuade to leave his existing band, Trauma, who are based in San Francisco (to where Metallica now relocates). The new line-up now makes its stage debut at Radio City, Anaheim, CA.

1983

Mar At the instigation of Megaforce label boss John Zazula, who offers the group a management and record deal, Metallica relocates to New Jersey, living in Jamaica, Queens, New York.
Apr [11] Mustaine is fired (and will cut his debut solo album, ***Killing Is My Business ... And Business Is Good***, before forming Megadeth) and is replaced by ex-Exodus guitarist Hammett (b. Nov. 18, 1962, San Francisco, CA), ex-Exodus, who has also played with mentor Joe Satriani.
May After a series of New Jersey gigs, the group begins recording its debut album ***Kill 'Em All*** (working title: ***Metal Up Your Ass***) at the Music America Recording Studios, which is licensed, with great cult interest in the UK, to fledgling independent heavy metal label, Music for Nations. It is produced by Paul Curcio and will be supported by a short UK tour with Raven.

1984

Aug Their second effort, ***Ride The Lightning***, is released on Megaforce in the US, but picked up by Elektra Records three months later, a result of moves by the major label's A&R man Michael Alago. Its reviews, particularly in the UK, confirm Metallica as the pioneering force in the thrash/speed metal movement. The album will sell half a million copies by year's end and reaches US #100 (though will eventually earn multi-platinum status). Still on Music For Nations in Europe, it reaches UK #87 as the group signs with Peter Mensch and Cliff Burnstein of management team Q-Prime, which also handles Def Leppard.

1985

Aug [17] Spending much of the year preparing its follow-up album, Metallica performs at the annual "Monsters Of Rock" heavy-metal bash at Castle Donington, Leics.

1986

Mar ***Master Of Puppets*** climbs to US #29 and UK #41, despite an absence of hit singles, while the group spends six months as guests on Ozzy Osbourne's US tour. Unusually for a metal band in the age of MTV, they achieve all this without the aid of a promo video. The tour's only hitch comes when Hetfield breaks his wrist skateboarding, a favored band activity. Roadie James Marshall deputizes.
Apr With touring reviving sales interest in the earlier albums, ***Kill 'Em All*** makes US #155.
Sept Metallica begins a European trek including successful UK dates.
[27] Between Scandinavian gigs, the tour bus leaves the road, killing Burton instantly. No one else is seriously injured. (The band returns to California and attends Burton's funeral in San Francisco.)
Nov [15] Bass player Jason Newsted (b. Mar. 4, 1963, Battle Creek, MI), from Phoenix-based Flotsam and Jetsam, makes his Metallica debut in Tokyo, Japan, during the band's US and Far East tour.

1987

Jan Metallica returns to Europe to complete re-scheduled dates.
Feb [13] "Master Of Puppets" world tour finally ends in Gothenburg, Sweden.
Mar The group enters an expensive Marin County, CA rehearsal studio to demo material for a new album. Unaccustomed to the plush environment, the band elects to play outside the studio, instead of inside, and Hetfield breaks his arm, again skateboarding in an empty pool. The group leaves the studio and decides to soundproof Ulrich's home garage in San Francisco. When Hetfield is fit to play, rather than writing songs, they work on covers of their favorite UK metal tracks.
July The band moves into Ulrich's garage and cut five tracks in six days, covering band favorites Budgie, Diamondhead, Killing Joke and the Misfits. Released as *The $5.98 EP - Garage Days Revisited*, it reaches UK #27, on the singles chart, the first fruit of the band's new UK deal with rock-oriented Vertigo label.
Aug [22] Metallica returns to perform at the "Monsters Of Rock Festival" at Castle Donington. After two more "Monsters Of Rock" dates at German festivals it returns to Ulrich's garage to work on a new album.
Oct ***The $5.98 EP - Garage Days Revisited*** makes US #28 on the Albums survey.

1988

May Metallica joins Van Halen, the Scorpions and others as part of a further "Monsters Of Rock" package tour in US and Europe. They also play two warm-up gigs at the Troubadour club, Los Angeles, under the pseudonym Frayed Ends.
Sept [3] *Harvester Of Sorrow* enters the UK chart at #20, but drops 12 places the following week.
[17] ***... And Justice For All***, released simultaneously in the US and UK, precedes a headlining US tour scheduled to begin mid-November. The album hits UK #4 immediately, but will rise to hit US #6 during a one-year chart residence.

1989

Feb [22] Metallica performs *One* at the 31st annual Grammy Awards at the Shrine Auditorium, Los Angeles, though Jethro Tull will controversially beat them to win the Best Hard Rock/Heavy Metal category.
Apr Spurred by a disturbing anti-war themed video clip, *One* debuts at UK #13 peak, and will make US #35, as the band embarks on a major "Damaged Justice Tour" of North America.
Dec [6] "$19.98 Home Video - Cliff 'Em All" video reaches the RIAA-certified 200,000 sales plateau.

1990

Feb [21] Metallica wins the Best Metal Performance category for *One* at the 32nd annual Grammy Awards, at Shrine Auditorium.
May [19] Vertigo's issue of six 12" singles of early Metallica material under the collective album title ***The Good, The Band And The Live*** peaks at UK #56.
July [23] The RIAA certifies gold sales of *One* and platinum sales of the ***Garage Days Revisited*** EP.
Oct [31] ***N.W.O.B.H.M. - '79 Revisited***, compiled by Ulrich and Geoff Barton, is released on Metal Blade Records in the UK.
Nov [3] ***Rubáiyát***, Elektra's 40th anniversary compilation, to which Metallica has contributed a cover of *Stone Cold Crazy*, makes US #140.

1991

Jan [10] "2 Of One" video is certified by the RIAA for sales of 100,000.
Feb [20] Metallica wins the Best Metal Performance (Vocal Or Instrumental) category for *Stone Cold Crazy* from ***Rubáiyát*** at the 33rd annual Grammy Awards, staged at New York's Radio City Music Hall.
Aug The group performs two shows at the Phoenix Theater, Petaluma, CA to prepare for an upcoming tour, with Faith No More's Jim Martin and Mike Bordin guesting with the band on the first night.
[3] Elektra Entertainment invites fans to the world-premiere listening party at Madison Square Garden for their new album, with 19,000 tickets given away.
[10] *Enter Sandman* debuts at its UK #5 peak, as the group embarks on another "Monsters Of Rock" package tour with Mötley Crüe, Black Crowes and Queensryche, in Copenhagen, Denmark.
[17] The band again performs at the annual "Monsters Of Rock" festival at Donington Park before a 72,500 capacity crowd (paying some $2.74 million).
[24] ***Metallica*** enters the UK chart at #1.
[31] ***Metallica*** also debuts at the top spot in the US.
Sept [5] The band appears live at the seventh annual MTV Video Music Awards, at the Universal Amphitheatre, Universal City, CA, singing *Enter Sandman*.
[28] They perform at the Tushino Air Field, Moscow, Russia, before a crowd of 500,000.
[30] The still-climbing *Enter Sandman* is certified gold by the RIAA.
Oct [12] The group takes part in "Bill Graham's Day On The Green Festival", at the Oakland-Alameda County Stadium, Oakland, CA, before a sellout crowd of 50,271, as *Enter Sandman* reaches US #16.
[29] Their world tour kicks off in Peoria, IL
Nov [16] *The Unforgiven* reaches UK #15.
Dec [22-23] The group closes out the year with sellout dates at the Centrum in Worcester, MA, grossing $473,320.

1992

Jan [6-8] Metallica plays three sellout shows at the Great Western Forum, Inglewood, CA.
[11] *The Unforgiven* reaches US #35.
Feb [25] Metallica wins the Best Metal Performance With Vocal category for ***Metallica*** at 34th annual Grammy Awards, from Radio City Music Hall. They also perform *Metallica*.
Mar ***Metallica*** is also named Outstanding Album and Outstanding Metal Album at the Bay Area Music Awards, as *Enter Sandman* wins Outstanding Song

and Ulrich nabs the Outstanding Drummer/Percussionist category.
[16] Fans dangle an usher by his ankles from the balcony at Metallica's Orlando Arena, Orlando Centroplex, Orlando, FL, during crowd trouble at a Metallica gig. The band will pay $38,000 for repairs and cleaning, after the audience trashes the building. Arena director Joanne Grant says "This stuff doesn't happen at a Kenny Rogers concert, but the band was very gracious."
Apr [1] The RIAA certifies three million sales of ***... And Justice For All***.
[20] Hetfield sings *Stone Cold Crazy* at the Freddie Mercury tribute at Wembley Stadium, Wembley, Middx.
May [2] *Nothing Else Matters* makes US #34.
[9] *Nothing Else Matters* hits UK #6.
July [22] Concerned about the recent appointment of Al Gore as Bill Clinton's vice-presidential running mate in the US election (and the subsequent heightened profile of Gore's music censorship-heralding wife, Tipper), Hetfield is quoted in **USA Today**, saying: "Her re-emergence 'makes me want to clean my guns'".
[26] Metallica, now on tour with Guns N' Roses and Faith No More, plays before a sellout 49,345 crowd at Three Rivers Stadium, Pittsburgh, PA.
Aug [8] Hetfield receives injuries after a stage prop explodes during a concert at the Olympic Stadium, Montreal, PQ, Canada. He is rushed to hospital and treated for second and third-degree burns on his left hand, and first-degree burns on his right arm. The band cuts short its set. Metal Church guitarist John Marshall, who had filled in for Hetfield on eight dates of their 1986 Ozzy Osbourne support slot tour, joins for remaining dates. *Wherever I May Roam* peaks at US #82.
Sept [9] "Enter Sandman" wins the Best Metal/Hard Rock Video category at the ninth annual MTV Video Music Awards held at the Pauley Pavilion, Los Angeles.
Oct [22] Metallica embarks on the European leg of its world trek at the Flanders Expo, Ghent, Belgium.
[31] *Sad But True* charts for a week at US #98.
Nov [7] *Wherever I May Roam* reaches UK #25.
Dec [18] European tour leg ends at the Globen, Stockholm, Sweden. The group has grossed $40 million domestically during the year.

1993

Jan [25] Metallica collects the Favorite Artist, Heavy Metal/Hard Rock trophy at the 20th annual American Music Awards, held at the Shrine Auditorium.
[26] Their tour resumes in the US before a sellout crowd of 7,889 at the Hersheypark Arena, Hershey, PA.
Feb [25] The group begins a five-date stint at the Sports Palace, Mexico City, Mexico, grossing $3,562,734 before crowds totalling 101,722.
[27] *Sad But True* reaches UK #20.
Mar [4] The band wins the Best Heavy Metal Band category in **Rolling Stone**'s 1993 Music Awards Readers' and Critics' Picks.
[8] Metallica wins the Outstanding Group, Outstanding Guitarist (Hammett), Outstanding Bassist (Newsted) and Outstanding Drummer/Percussionist (Ulrich) categories at the 1993 Bay Area Music Awards, at the Bill Graham Civic Auditorium, San Francisco.
[27] A three-date stint opens at the Sydney Entertainment Centre, Australia, during the antipodean leg of its tour.
Apr [10] A riot erupts outside the group's Jakarta, Indonesia concert at the Lebakbulus Stadium after fans are denied entrance. More than 80 injuries are reported.
June [5] The group plays its "Nowhere Else To Roam" concert at Milton Keynes Bowl, Milton Keynes, Bucks.
July [3-4] Metallica performs at the Torhout and Wechter festivals in Belgium on successive days.
Dec [11] Three CD/cassette, video boxed set, ***Live Shit : Binge And Purge***, including an entire Mexico City concert recorded in 1991 in support of the ***Metallica*** album, debuts at its US #26 peak and charts for a week at UK #54.

1994

Jan [27] The group is named Best Heavy Metal Band in **Rolling Stone**'s 1994 Music Awards Readers' Picks.
May [30] Metallica begins a US tour at the Lakeside Amphitheatre, Darien Lake Theme Park, Darien Center, NY.
June [28] The RIAA certifies three million sales of ***Master Of Puppets***, as the band plays a sellout date at the Riverport Amphitheatre, Maryland Heights, MO.
July [20] A month after the previous tour ends, Metallica now begins its "Shit In The Sheds Tour" at Portland Meadows, Portland, OR, set to end in Miami, FL on August 21st.
Sept [27] Metallica files suit against Elektra Entertainment in San Francisco County Superior Court, asking to be dismissed from its ten-year contract based on California's Labor Code 2855. (They will settle their dispute in December and remain with the label.)

1995

Feb [2] ***Metallica*** is certified for eight million sales by the RIAA.
June [6] The RIAA also confirms multi-platinum sales for ***Kill 'Em All*** (two million), ***Ride The Lightning*** (three million) and ***... And Justice For All*** (four million).
[21] Their "Live Shit : Binge And Purge" video surpasses 900,000 US sales level.

1996

Feb [26] Hammett performs with honoree Carlos Santana, as the NARAS Foundation holds its first salute to an individual act at the Universal Amphitheatre.
Mar [3] With its first new studio album in nearly five years, ***Load***, finally due for a June 4th release, Lollapalooza tour organizers announce that Metallica will top the bill for this summer's US rock caravan.
June [1] Written by Hetfield and Ulrich, *Until It Sleeps*, the first single from the album, enters at its UK #5 high.
[8] *Until It Sleeps* hits US #10 in its week of entry.
[22] Having shifted over 680,000 domestic copies in its first seven days at retail, ***Load***, co-produced by Bob Rock with Hetfield and Ulrich, debuts at US #1.

GEORGE MICHAEL

1983

Aug Having grown up in the London suburbs of Finchley, Burnt Oak and Radlett with his two sisters Melanie and Yioda, Michael (b. Georgios Kyriacos Panayiotou, June 25, 1963, Finchley, London), having met future music partner Andrew Ridgeley at Bushey Meads Comprehensive School, Herts., in 1975, forming with him their first band, the Executive, in 1979, signing a long-term publishing deal with Morrison Leahy in 1982 (not least for *Careless Whisper*, written by the duo when Michael was 18), has already sought and found global success as the creative force and lead vocalist of Wham!, which will prove to be Britain's most successful pop duo of the '80s. With Wham!-mania currently gripping Europe, Michael travels to Muscle Shoals Studios in Muscle Shoals, AL, to record a solo version of *Careless Whisper*, with Jerry Wexler producing. Sessions are instructive, but unsuccessful, and Michael returns to London to re-record the ballad for later release.

1984

June He flies to Miami, FL to cut his first solo video for *Careless Whisper*.
July His friend David Austin's *Turn To Gold*, co-penned and produced by Michael, peaks at UK #68.
Aug [18] Still a member of Wham! and released on CBS/Columbia's Epic label (to whom Wham! is signed), Michael's solo debut, *Careless Whisper*, begins a three-week run atop the UK chart after Ridgeley and Michael decide that song, strikingly opposed to Wham!'s fun uptempo style, will benefit as a solo release. It will sell over one million UK copies, and become an enduring worldwide radio favorite. Michael dedicates the song to his parents, to whom he will remain very close: "Five minutes in return for 21 years."
Nov [25] Invited by Bob Geldof to sing on Band Aid's *Do They Know It's Christmas?*, Michael records a lead vocal section at the all-star gathering at London's SARM Studio, Notting Hill.

1985

Feb [16] With Wham! at the peak of its success, the duo has elected to release *Careless Whisper* in the US credited to "Wham! featuring George Michael" which now begins three weeks at US #1.
Mar [13] Michael is named Songwriter Of The Year at the 29th annual Ivor Novello awards, at London's Grosvenor House Hotel. Presented with the award by Elton John, which he accepts with great emotion, Michael becomes its youngest ever recipient.
May Increasingly musically independent from Ridgeley, Michael sings two duets with Smokey Robinson and Stevie Wonder at a Motown celebration in New York, NY.
July [13] Pre-dating a future recorded collaboration, Michael sings lead vocals to Elton John's performance of *Don't Let The Sun Go Down On Me* at the "Live Aid" spectacular at Wembley Stadium, Wembley, Middx.
Nov Continuing the association, Michael completes falsetto backing on John's hit *Nikita* and duets on *Wrap Her Up*, both for John's album ***Ice On Fire***.
Dec Michael and Ridgeley decide to split Wham! in 1986, leaving both free to pursue solo paths.
[28] Michael features on four Top 20 records in the UK Christmas chart: Wham!'s *I'm Your Man*, Wham!'s re-entered *Last Christmas*, Band Aid's re-entered *Do They Know It's Christmas?* and as backing vocalist on Elton John's still charting *Nikita*.

1986

Feb [28] Michael announces that Wham! will officially split in the summer.
Apr [19] His second solo single, the self-penned ballad *A Different Corner*, chronicling Michael's current fragile emotional state, tops the UK chart for the first of three weeks.
June [14] *A Different Corner* hits US #7.
[20] Michael performs at the fourth annual "Prince's Trust Rock Gala" at the Wembey Arena, Wembley.
[28] Wham! plays "The Final" date at Wembley Stadium. (Following a rest, Michael will begin work on his debut solo album, recording in SARM studios, Notting Hill, London, and PUK Studios, Denmark, and will sign with US management team Michael Lippman and Rob Kahane.)
Sept Michael flies to the US to record a duet with Aretha Franklin and film the accompanying video. The song will appear on her new album.
Nov [25] In a move which will have serious repercussions for both parties, CBS/Epic Records exercises its option to receive five more albums from Michael.

1987

Feb [7] Michael and Franklin's *I Knew You Were Waiting (For Me)*, written by Simon Climie and Dennis Morgan, produced by Narada Michael Walden, and released by Epic in Britain, tops the UK chart.
Apr [18] Released on Arista (Franklin's label) in the US, *I Knew You Were Waiting (For Me)* tops the US Hot 100 for the first of two weeks.
June The first post-Wham! Michael solo single, the funky *I Want Your Sex*, is released ahead of his debut album. Featured on the soundtrack album ***Beverly Hills Cop II***, the song causes protest, particularly in the UK where reactionary radio prohibits airplay in the AIDS era. (BBC Radio 1 will only air the cut after 9:00 p.m.) US MTV re-edits the video three times before it is deemed acceptable. Michael insists that the

lyrics promote monogamous relationships and spells this out on the accompanying video which stars his current girlfriend, US make-up artist Kathy Jueng. Despite the radio ban, it hits UK #3.

July Speculation in the UK that Michael is at least a backing vocalist on a version, reportedly recorded by his cousin, of the Bee Gees *Jive Talkin'* released under the name Boogie Box High, will remained unconfirmed. The single hits UK #7.

Aug [8] *I Want Your Sex*, with all instruments and vocals completed by Michael, hits US #2.

Oct *Faith*, the title cut from his forthcoming album, hits UK #2.

Nov [14] His debut solo album, ***Faith***, written, arranged and produced by Michael and featuring him on most instruments, though Wham! bassist Deon Estus remains as a regular sideman, enters at UK #1 and will stay charted for 72 weeks.

Dec [12] Benefitting from heavy US MTV rotation of the video, *Faith* hits US #1 for the first of four weeks.

1988

Jan On discovering that his accountants are investing in a US arms company, he instructs all stock to be sold.

[4] Michael re-negotiates his contract with Epic Records.

[16] *Father Figure* reaches UK #11 as Michael prepares for forthcoming live work. ***Faith*** tops the US chart for the first of 12 weeks during an 87-week survey tenure, eventually selling over nine million US copies.

Feb [8] Michael is named Best British Male Artist at the seventh annual BRIT Awards, held at London's Royal Albert Hall.

[19] Michael opens his "Faith" world tour at Budokan, Tokyo, Japan, to a wildly enthusiastic reception.

[27] In only its seventh week on the chart, *Father Figure* hits US #1, as ***Faith*** holds for its fifth consecutive week on the US album list. Including his earlier Wham! hits, *Father Figure* becomes Michael's sixth US #1.

Mar During Australian dates, Michael unveils a giant white stage cage which opens and closes the show in dramatic fashion. He can only use the device at appropriate venues, including all US gigs, which are divided between spring and fall.

[2] Michael wins the Best R&B Performance By A Duo Or Group With Vocal category with Aretha Franklin for *I Knew You Were Waiting (For Me)* at the 30th annual Grammy Awards.

May Ballad *One More Try* hits UK #8.

[28] *One More Try* becomes the third US chart-topper from his debut album, which has also returned to pole position, quadruple platinum in six months.

June [11] Having resumed the tour at Earls Court in London, Michael plays an early slot for "Nelson Mandela's 70th Birthday Tribute" concert at Wembley. He performs only cover versions by black artists including Marvin Gaye's *Sexual Healing*. Six hours later, Michael is performing at another sold-out Earls Court solo date.

[18] *One More Try* tops the US R&B chart.

[29] As the tour reaches Europe, some dates are cancelled and postponed when Michael is admitted to hospital to have a benign vocal chord cyst removed.

July Fifth extracted single, *Monkey*, remixed by producers Jimmy Jam and Terry Lewis reaches UK #13.

Aug [27] *Monkey* tops the US chart becoming his eighth US #1 of the '80s, a record beaten only by Michael Jackson with nine.

The second section of his US tour begins with sold-out dates and more rave reviews. Michael announces that he will donate proceeds of his forthcoming single, *If You Were My Woman*, a remake of Gladys Knight's *If I Were Your Woman*, to anti-apartheid groups. (The record will, however, not be released.)

Sept [7] "Father Figure" wins the Best Direction category at the fifth annual MTV Video Music Awards held at the Universal Amphitheatre, Universal City, CA.

Oct [12] The financial conditions of Michael's January 4th, 1988 CBS contract are revised.

[31] The "Faith" tour ends at Pensacola, FL.

Dec Another ballad from his album, *Kissing A Fool*, reaches UK #18 and hits US #5. "Faith", a collection of video clips, becomes an instant best-seller, rounding off one of the most successful debut album promotions in pop history.

1989

Jan [30] Michael collects the Favorite Male Artist, Pop/Rock, Favorite Album, Soul/R&B and Favorite Male Artist, Soul/R&B trophies at the 16th annual American Music Awards, held at the Shrine Auditorium, Los Angeles, CA.

Feb [2] Michael wins the Album Of The Year category for ***Faith*** at the 31st annual Grammy Awards.

Michael accepts undisclosed damages in excess of £100,000 from **The Sun** newspaper in the High Court in a libel action over articles printed on October 13th and 15th, 1986, which stated that he gatecrashed a party being given by Andrew Lloyd Webber and was drunk and abusive.

Apr [4] *Faith* is named International Hit Of The Year, while Michael is named Songwriter Of The Year (for the second time) at the 34th annual Ivor Novello Awards lunch, at London's Grosvenor House Hotel.

May Long-time Michael cohort, Estus, benefits from the Michael-produced and co-written *Heaven Help Me*, which makes UK #41 and hits US #5. (He is also featured on Jody Watley's current album, ***Larger Than Life***.)

June [23] Michael is honored with the Silver Clef Award, at the 14th annual Nordoff Robbins benefit lunch in London.

Sept [6] Madonna presents the prestigious Video Vanguard Award to Michael at the sixth annual MTV Video Music Awards ceremony at the Universal Amphitheatre.

Nov [28] The RIAA certifies gold sales of *Faith* and *One More Try* and platinum sales of *I Want Your Sex*.

1990

Apr Sunday Times magazine, in its annual "Britain's Rich - The Top 200", places Michael at #128 with £65 million.

July [26] The financial conditions of Michael's Sony deal are revised again after the company receives ***Listen Without Prejudice***.

Aug [21] Michael is interviewed by Steve Wright on BBC Radio 1.

Sept [1] Previewing his second solo album, his social awareness-themed ballad, *Praying For Time*, hits UK #6. Its B-side is a live cover of Stevie Wonder's *If You Were My Woman* from Michael's appearance at the 1988 Nelson Mandela show.

[2] Michael is the subject of an introspective documentary on Melvyn Bragg's ITV "The South Bank Show", which will be subsequently edited for video release.

[15] ***Listen Without Prejudice, Vol. 1***, again written, arranged and produced by Michael (a second volume is reportedly already in the can), immediately hits UK #1 and begins a multi-platinum stay on both the UK and US charts. With its launch, and that of his autobiography **Bare**, Michael announces that he is rejecting much of the traditional rock-star lifestyle, not least appearing in videos and performing world tours, and intends to concentrate more on songwriting than success.

Oct [13] *Praying For Time*, boosted as it connects with many military personnel leaving the US for Gulf duty, hits US #1, ousting Maxi Priest's *Close To You*.

[20] ***Listen Without Prejudice, Vol. 1*** hits US #2, held off pole position by MC Hammer's ***Please Hammer Don't Hurt 'Em***.

Nov [10] *Waiting For That Day* reaches UK #23.

Dec [22] *Freedom!* hits US #8 and UK #28. Also known as *Freedom! '90* to distinguish it from Wham!'s 1985 hit *Freedom*, it benefits from a super-model (Christy Turlington, Linda Evangelista, Naomi Campbell, Cindy Crawford and Tatiana Patiz)-starring video in which Michael's biker jacket, synonymous with his "Faith" period image is symbolically burnt.

1991

Jan [4] *Freedom* is certified gold by the RIAA.

[9] His "George Michael" video is certified platinum by the RIAA.

[15] Michael performs the first of two nights at the National Exhibition Centre, Birmingham, West Midlands, at the beginning of his "Cover To Cover" tour. Playing mini-tours in selected territories over the next few months, the majority of his set is devoted to his interpretations of some of his favorite songs, which include many Stevie Wonder and Elton John hits, and even Adamski's *Killer*.

[25] He makes his first live appearance since 1988 on the seventh day of the "Rock In Rio II" festival at the Maracana soccer stadium in Rio de Janeiro, Brazil.

[28] Michael reunites with Ridgeley to close the "Rock In Rio II" festival.

Feb [10] ***Listen Without Prejudice, Vol. 1*** is named Best British Album at the tenth annual BRIT Awards, at London's Dominion Theatre. Collecting the award, Michael dedicates the trophy to Epic Records marketing manager Ronnie Fischer, who died, age 34, in November 1990.

[23] *Heal The Pain*, an early-Beatlesque acoustic cut, makes UK #31, becoming Michael's first UK solo single not to make the Top 30.

Mar [2] *Waiting For That Day* reaches US #27. Following its release, the B-side ballad *Mother's Pride*, rapidly makes airplay gains and becomes the second Michael cut to become an unwitting Gulf War favorite and, in a rare '90s Hot 100 practice, charts separately from its A-side, peaking in the same week at US #46.

[7] Michael is named Best Male Singer and Sexiest Male Artist in the annual **Rolling Stone** Readers' Picks music awards.

[22-23] His "Cover To Cover" tour returns to the UK for sold-out concerts at Wembley Arena.

[26] The "Faith" video reaches 150,000 US sales.

Apr [6] Jazz-phrased *Cowboys And Angels* makes UK #45.

Oct [1] His "Cover To Cover" US leg opens at the Oakland-Alameda County Coliseum, Oakland, CA.

[25-26] During his US tour, Michael plays two sellout dates at New York's Madison Square Garden, grossing $752,685. The varied 2½ hour set mixes Michael standards together with covers including *Ain't Nobody*, *Back To Life* and *Ain't No Stopping Us Now*.

Nov [27] ABC-TV's "MTV 10" tribute airs, with Michael contributing *Freedom '90*.

Dec [7] *Don't Let The Sun Go Down On Me*, recorded live with its writer, Elton John, enters the UK chart at #1. The track will also be included on Elton John's 1993 ***Duets*** album. (Proceeds from the single will go to the London Lighthouse and Rainbow Trust children's charities.)

1992

Jan [11] ***Two Rooms - Celebrating The Songs Of Elton John & Bernie Taupin***, to which Michael has contributed his treatment of *Tonight*, reaches US #18.

[22] The still-climbing *Don't Let The Sun Go Down On Me* is certified gold by the RIAA.

Feb Michael is presented with the Golden Note Award at an ASCAP reception, becoming its youngest ever recipient. He also files a $1-million lawsuit against Chancery Financial Management, accusing them of poor investment advice on his pension fund.

[1] *Don't Let The Sun Go Down On Me*, with Elton John, tops the US chart, his tenth US chart-topper. (Proceeds from US sales will go to the Dana Farber Cancer Institute's Jimmy Fund.)

Apr [20] Michael performs the Queen cuts *Year Of 39*, *These Are The Days Of Our Lives*, a duet with Lisa Stansfield and *Somebody To Love*, with the London Community Gospel Choir, at "A Concert For Life" fundraiser organized by the remaining Queen members in tribute to Freddie Mercury at Wembley Stadium, Wembley.

[23] He announces the donation of $500,000 royalties from the sale of *Don't Let The Sun Go Down On Me* to

various British and American AIDS and children's educational charities. Current world sales exceed 1.7 million.
June Michael begins working on the concept album ***Trojan Souls*** project in Los Angeles tentatively planned for release through his cousin Andros Georgiou's new label Hardback Records (though it will not emerge). While not performing himself, not least due to percolating legal wrangles, Michael invites guest vocalists including Elton John, Anita Baker, Bryan Ferry, Stevie Wonder and Aretha Franklin to contribute.
[13] *Toofunky* debuts at its UK #4 peak.
Aug [4] *Toofunky* is certified gold by the RIAA.
[8] *Too Funky*, backed with also previously unissued *Crazy Man Dance*, a new R&B number from the ***Red Hot + Dance*** various artists compilation benefitting AIDS charities, hits US #10.
Oct [11] Michael participates in an Elizabeth Taylor AIDS Foundation benefit at Madison Square Garden with Elton John, Lionel Richie and Bruce Hornsby.
[21] Disputing both the creative and marketing abilities of Epic Records, Michael's lawyer Tony Russell informs Sony Entertainment (the newly named parent of Epic Records) that Michael is not bound by his contract and owns his masters, beginning a lengthy court case between artist and label.
[27] Mr. Justice Knox says that the case will not come to court until at least October 1993.
[30] Russell files a High Court writ, against Sony Entertainment, which disputes Michael's claims. (The following month, Michael issues the following statement: "Since Sony Corporation bought my contract, along with everything and everyone else at CBS, I have seen the great American company that I proudly signed to as a teenager become a small part of the production line for a giant electronics corporation which, quite frankly, has no understanding of the creative process. Sony appears to see artists as little more than software.")

1993

Mar [11] Michael attends the American Film Institute's dinner at the Beverly Hilton Hotel, Los Angeles, to bestow Elizabeth Taylor with its Life Achievement Award.
[20] P.M. Dawn's *Looking Through Patient Eyes*, incorporating Michael's *Father Figure*, reaches UK #11.
Apr [27] He participates in "Aretha Franklin : Duets", the diva's first TV special, taped at New York's Nederlander Theatre. The show will air on the Fox network on May 9th.
May [1] His *Five Live EP*, with tracks from the 1992 Freddie Mercury tribute concert including *Somebody To Love*, *These Are The Days Of Our Lives* (with Lisa Stansfield) plus a *Papa Was A Rolling Stone/Killer* medley from his own "Covers" tour and *Calling You*, covering a song originally written for the film "Baghdad Cafe", enters the UK chart at #1. With his legal dispute still raging, the EP has been released by Hollywood Records, with proceeds once again going to various AIDS charities.
[8] ***Five Live*** debuts at its #46 peak on the US Album survey.
[29] The extracted *Somebody To Love*, with Queen, reaches US #30.
July [24] A second extract, *Killer/Papa Was A Rollin' Stone*, makes US #69.
Sept [2] Michael wins the German International Viewers Choice category at the tenth annual MTV Video Music Awards, held at the Universal Amphitheatre.
Oct [4] Michael's High Court case begins with opening comments from his QC Mark Cran.
[28] Michael goes into the witness box to give evidence.
Dec [1] Also one of its organizers, Michael performs at the "Concert Of Hope" benefit held at the Wembley Arena on a bill with David Bowie, Simply Red's Mick Hucknall and k.d. lang.

1994

Jan [17] The trial resumes after a Christmas break.
Apr [13] The High Court case ends after 74 days of hearing.
June [21] Justice Jonathan Parker delivers his 273 page ruling in favor of Sony. After the verdict, Michael's answer-phone message is "I'm never going to sing again. Bastards! Bastards!" to the the tune of *Careless Whisper*.
[23] Michael is ordered to pay both sides' costs, estimated at £3 million.
July [7] "George Michael : A Television Interview With Sir David Frost", recorded on June 27th, airs on ITV. On his relationship with Sony, he says : "If Sony were to come to me at this stage and say 'OK, George, we've made our point, you can go, we really don't need you ... you can continue your career elsewhere, you know we don't want this mess to continue'. I have to be honest. If they were going to do that unconditionally, I'd have to say 'OK, I'm not going to be a martyr, I have my own life to think about, and I can't fight for the whole industry at the risk of losing the rest - or the next ten years - of my life as an artist'. And I would probably accept that, but I think that is so unlikely".
Aug [8] After already having spent a reported $4 million in total legal fees, Michael files an appeal in London to overturn the recent ruling in Sony's favor.
Sept [27] The RIAA certifies sales of two million of ***Listen Without Prejudice***, seven million less than his debut, a disparity which became a central issue in the court case with Michael having claimed that Sony did little in the way of marketing or promotion of the album in the US.
Nov [1] Kahane steps down as Michael's manager.
[24] Michael performs *Jesus To A Child*, his first new song in five years, at the inaugural MTV European Music Awards at the Pariser Platz, against the backdrop of the Brandenburg Gate in Berlin, Germany.
Dec [12] The Court of Appeal's Master of the Rolls, Sir Thomas Bingham, tells Michael that he will have to wait until 1996 to have his appeal heard.
[13] The RIAA certifies sales of nine million of ***Faith***.

1995

Jan [19] Michael appears at "Commitment To Life VIII" benefit for AIDS Project Los Angeles, honoring Elton John, Tom Hanks and Ron Meyer, at the Universal Amphitheatre.
Mar [1] He presents the Song Of The Year trophy, with Annie Lennox, to Bruce Springsteen at the 37th annual Grammy Awards, held at the Shrine Auditorium.
Apr [16] Michael raises $112,000 by giving his forthcoming single *Jesus To A Child* a sole airing on Capital Radio's "Help A London Child".
July [13] Sony announces that Michael has won his freedom from the company, freeing him to sign as the first music act to Dreamworks SKG in the US and Virgin Records for the rest of the world in a two-album deal. Sony will get an estimated $40 million plus 3% of retail sales of his next two albums, his back catalog and a ***Greatest Hits*** album.
[20] Andy Stephens, vice-president of marketing for Sony Music Europe, becomes his manager for the world outside North America.
Nov [23] Michael presents the Free Your Mind Award to Greenpeace at the second annual MTV Europe Awards in Paris, France, criticising Prime Minister John Major for his support of French premier Jacques Chirac's nuclear policy: "If business means looking the other way while your partners endanger the planet, we are better off on our own".
Dec [12] *Jesus To A Child* is serviced digitally via satellite to stations between 8:00 a.m. and 8:15 a.m.

1996

Jan [20] Comeback ballad *Jesus To A Child* enters the UK chart at #1.
Feb [24] *Jesus To A Child* hits US #7 in its week of entry, previewing his first album in six years, the self-penned ***Older***.
May [4] *Fastlove* enters the UK chart in pole position before repeating the same feat throughout much of the rest of Europe.
[25] Written, arranged and produced by Michael, ***Older***, co-dedicated to Antonio Carlos Jobim "who changed the way I listened to music", begins its UK chart residence at #1.
June [1] ***Older*** bows at its US #6 peak as *Fastlove* simultaneously hits US #8.
see also: **WHAM!**

BETTE MIDLER

1965

Midler (b. Dec. 1, 1944 Paterson, NJ), named after Bette Davis by her film fan mother, and raised in Oahu, HI, where her father works as a civilian painter for the US Navy, harbors acting ambitions while studying at the University of Hawaii, and gains her first part as an extra, playing a missionary's wife, in the locally-filmed movie "Hawaii". Moving to New York, NY, the following year, she earns a living from bit stage parts, before auditioning for the Broadway production of "Fiddler On The Roof" in which she takes a long-running chorus line role. Performing *Matchmaker* at the annual Tony Awards in April 1968, she leaves the show in 1969 after advancing to the role of Tzeitel, and begins a parallel singing career, while appearing in the rock musical "Salvation", honing her act as a song stylist, with small gigs in Greenwich Village, New York clubs.

1970

One of her drama teachers at the Herbert Berghof studio, Bob Elston, helps her obtain a regular singing engagement in the offbeat venue of the Continental Baths, a Turkish bath with a largely gay male clientele. She creates a multi-element act, which includes earthy comedy with a variety of musical styles, from show tunes to Andrews Sisters pastiches and '60s girl groups repertoire. Her piano accompanist is Barry Manilow.

1971

Cult fame at the Turkish baths attracts the US media and Midler appears on TV on both David Frost's and Johnny Carson's shows - initially as a novelty act and then as a guest vocalist. She also plays Mrs. Walker and the Acid Queen in a stage production of the Who's "Tommy" by the Seattle Opera Association in Seattle, WA.

1972

Dec [31] Having moved into mainstream cabaret and widespread TV slots, and signed to Atlantic Records, she marks the end of her "arrival" year with two capacity major-venue concerts at the Philharmonic Hall in Lincoln Center, New York.

1973

Mar Her maiden album, ***The Divine Miss M***, largely produced by Joel Dorn and featuring accompaniment by Manilow, hits US #9, while the extracted *Do You Want To Dance?*, her revival of Bobby Freeman's hit, reaches US #17.
July Also taken from her debut album, her treatment of the Andrews Sisters' *Boogie Woogie Bugle Boy* hits US #8.
Nov *Friends*, coupled with Midler's revival of the Dixie Cups' *Chapel Of Love*, makes US #40.
Dec [3-23] Midler plays a 19-performance engagement, with musical director Barry Manilow, at Broadway's Palace Theatre, unperturbed with topping fashion maven Mr. Blackwell's Worst Dressed Women Of The Year list.
[12] The still-rising ***Bette Midler*** is certified gold by the RIAA.

1974

Feb ***Bette Midler*** hits US #6, while the extracted revival of Glenn Miller's *In The Mood* makes US #51. Manilow has also played piano on this album, but starts his own solo career soon after.
Mar [2] Midler wins the Best New Artist category at the 16th annual Grammy Awards.

1975

Feb [16] She guest stars, with Elton John, on the first edition of Cher's weekly CBS-TV series.
Dec [1] Midler is hospitalized on her birthday to undergo an emergency appendectomy.
[10] She begins a 20-city, 80-performance US tour.

1976

Feb [17] Harvard University's Hasty Pudding Theatrical Society honors Midler as Woman Of The Year. Her acceptance speech claims that her award "characterizes what the American male wants in a woman - brains, talent and gorgeous tits".
[28] Her third album ***Songs For The New Depression***, reaches US #27.
Mar [1] Midler is featured in **Time** magazine.

1977

June After a three-year absence from the singles chart, *You're Moving Out Today*, co-written with Bruce Roberts and Carole Bayer Sager, makes US #42 (while Sager's version hits UK #6).
July Performance double album, ***Live At Last***, makes US #49.

1978

Feb *Storybook Children (Daybreak)* climbs to US #57, while its parent album, ***Broken Blossom***, produced by Brooks Arthur and featuring Brenda Russell, Russ Kunkel and Tom Waits among others, reaches US #51.
Sept [3] "Old Red Hair Is Back", a Midler special airs on ITV
[21-23] She makes her UK concert debut at the London Palladium, at the start of a British tour.
Nov [25] Midler hosts "Rolling Stone ... The 10th Anniversary" special on CBS-TV.

1979

July *Married Men*, her cover of Bonnie Tyler's UK hit, reaches US #40.
Oct [10] "The Rose", in which Midler stars in the rags-to-riches-to-rags story of a Janis Joplin-type rock singer, opens in cinemas across the US. Midler's performance as the central character is highly rated and will bring her an Oscar nomination.
Nov ***Thighs And Whispers*** makes US #65.

1980

Feb Her revival of Percy Sledge's *When A Man Loves A Woman*, featured in "The Rose", climbs to US #35 while the soundtrack album, ***The Rose***, reaches US #12, and becomes Midler's first platinum disc.
Midler's first book, **A View From A Broad**, is published.
June Title track, *The Rose*, becomes Midler's biggest single to date, hitting US #3.
July [25] *The Rose* is certified gold by the RIAA.
Sept [17] "Divine Madness", a movie built around a Midler concert in 1979 at the Civic Auditorium, Pasadena, CA, premieres in Los Angeles.

1981

Jan *My Mother's Eyes*, from "Divine Madness", reaches US #39, while the movie's live soundtrack album ***Divine Madness*** makes US #34.
Feb [25] Midler wins the Best Pop Vocal Performance, Female category for ***The Rose*** at the 23rd annual Grammy Awards, following which, she has the additional accolade of appearing on the cover of **Newsweek**.

1982

Dec [31] Midler and Barry Manilow appear as Baby New Year and Father Time respectively at a New Year's Eve celebration at the Universal Amphitheatre, Universal City, CA. (This year's Midler movie will be the Don Siegel-directed movie "Jinxed".)

1983

Apr Midler grosses $,1327,020 from seven sellout shows at New York's Radio City Music Hall.
Sept Barry Mann/Cynthia Weil/Tom Snow ballad, *All I Need To Know*, peaks at US #77. (The song will be a US #2 hit in 1989 as *Don't Know Much* by Linda Ronstadt and Aaron Neville.)
Oct ***No Frills***, produced by Chuck Plotkin and including the single, reaches US #60.
Nov Another ***No Frills*** extract, *Favorite Waste Of Time*, peaks at US #78.

1984

Mar Her update of the Rolling Stones' *Beast Of Burden*, boosted by a Mick Jagger cameo in its video, peaks at #71.
Sept [14] Midler co-hosts, with Dan Aykroyd, the inaugural MTV Video Music Awards from New York's Radio City Music Hall.
Dec Midler weds Martin von Haselberg, also known as Harry Kipper.

1985

Jan [28] She is one of a host of US stars contributing vocals to USA For Africa's recording *We Are The World*, in aid of African famine relief.
Feb Having completed recording for this year's ***Mud Will Be Flung Tonight!***, Midler's music career takes a back seat once more, as she signs a contract with Touchstone Pictures to make a series of films. The first three, "Down And Out In Beverly Hills" (with Richard Dreyfus and Nick Nolte), "Ruthless People" (with Danny De Vito and Judge Rheinhold) and "Outrageous Fortune" (with Shelley Long), are major hits, and will reinstate her box-office prowess. In November the following year, Mrs. von Haselberg becomes a mother for the first time at age 40, giving birth to daughter, Sophie, while in November 1988, Disney's "Oliver And Company", which features the voice of Midler, will open in US movie theaters.

1989

June [10] Without a Top 10 record in nine years, Midler hits US #1 with her version of the Larry Henley/Jeff Silber-penned ballad, *The Wind Beneath My Wings*. It is prominently featured in her current film "Beaches", the first project released by her newly-formed All Girls Production company, for which she has now also recorded the entire soundtrack. Released as ***Beaches***, it also hits US #2 and will make UK #21.
July *The Wind Beneath My Wings* hits UK #5.
Sept [25] The trial commences in Midler's $10-million lawsuit against the Ford Motor Co. and the Young & Rubicam advertising agency for using a soundalike (earlier Midler backing singer Ula Hedwig) to impersonate Midler singing *Do You Want To Dance* in a 1985 Mercury Sable commercial.
Oct [31] Midler is awarded $400,000 in damages in the case.

1990

Jan [18] ***The Divine Miss M*** is certified gold by the RIAA.
Feb [21] *The Wind Beneath My Wings* wins Record Of The Year and Song Of The Year at the 32nd annual Grammy Awards ceremonies at the Shrine Auditorium, Los Angeles. Her performance of the hit closes the show.
Apr [22] Midler takes part in ABC-TV's "Earth Day Special" also featuring Robin Williams, Quincy Jones and Barbra Streisand, among others.
Dec [15] Taken from her current album, Midler's version of Julie Gold's *From A Distance* captures the heart of state-of-war America and hits US #2, behind Stevie B.'s *Because I Love You (The Postman Song)*. Produced by Arif Mardin, it has stalled at UK #45, where it has been in competition with a simultaneously-released version by Cliff Richard. (This year's Midler film is "Stella", to be followed in 1991 by a co-starring picture with Woody Allen in "Scenes From A Mall".)

1991

Jan [2] *From A Distance* is certified platinum by the RIAA.
[5] Its parent album ***Some People's Lives***, helmed by Mardin, hits US #6.
Feb [20] Midler opens the 33rd annual Grammy Awards ceremony, at Radio City Music Hall, New York, with a live version of *From A Distance*, which also wins Song Of The Year for its writer Gold.
[23] *Night And Day* makes US #62.
Mar [12] The RIAA certifies two million sales of ***Some People's Lives***.
June [7] Midler guests on BBC1-TV's "Wogan".
[22] ***For Our Children***, to which Midler has contributed *Blueberry Pie*, reaches US #31.
[29] Reissued *From A Distance* hits UK #6.
July [20] ***Some People's Lives*** hits UK #5.
Aug [29] The RIAA confirms three million sales of ***Beaches***.
Sept [15] Midler is honored at the "Commitment To Life V" AIDS Project Los Angeles' benefit at the Universal Amphitheatre.
Oct [24] *The Wind Beneath My Wings* is certified platinum by the RIAA.
Nov She becomes the 236th Adopt-A-Highway volunteer, hiring a company to clear trash and graffiti along Ventura freeway in Los Angeles. Her sign reads "Litter Removal Next 2 Miles, Bette Midler".
[5] Midler guests on ABC-TV "Barbara Walters" special.
[14] She makes a rare 40-minute live performance to an invited, industry audience at the world premiere of her latest film "For The Boys" at the Academy Of Motion Picture Arts & Sciences, her first stage set in seven years (aside from charity appearances).
[22] She appears on NBC-TV's "The Tonight Show".
Dec [21] ***For The Boys*** soundtrack reaches US #22.
[27] ***For The Boys*** is certified gold by the RIAA.

1992

Jan [18] *Every Road Leads Back To You*, from the movie "For The Boys" for which Midler will earn her second Oscar nomination, peaks at US #78.
Feb [15] ***For The Boys*** charts for a week at UK #75.
Mar [23] US Supreme Court lets the 1989 $400,000 award for the soundalike commercial stand.
May [21] Midler serenades TV legend Johnny Carson with *One For My Baby (And One More For The Road*, on his penultimate "Tonight" show as host.
Aug [30] The May 21st "Tonight" show, featuring Midler, wins the Best Performance, Variety Or Music Program category at the annual Emmy Awards, in Pasadena, CA.
Oct [3] Midler attends the biannual Children's Diabetes Foundation benefit, at the Beverly Hilton, Beverly Hills, CA.
Dec [23] She takes part in CBS-TV's "HBO's 20th Anniversary" special.

1993

Jan [17] Midler performs at "A Call For Reunion" at the Lincoln Memorial, Washington, DC, during Presidential Inaugural week.
July [31] As her latest movie, "Hocus Pocus", is now in cinemas throughout the US, a 14-track hits collection, ***Experience The Divine : Greatest Hits*** makes US #50.
Aug [18] Midler is featured on NBC-TV's "Now".
Sept [14] Sellout "Nobody Beats The Wiz Concert Series, Live At Radio City" opens at Radio City Music Hall, set to end on October 23rd. (It is her first concert appearance in ten years, and she is given a $25,000 Tiffany diamond band to mark the anniversary.)
Nov [3] ***Experience The Divine : Greatest Hits*** is certified gold by the RIAA.
[6] ***Experience The Divine : Greatest Hits*** hits UK #3.
[30] The RIAA certifies two million sales of ***The Rose***.
Dec [12] CBS-TV airs "Gypsy", in which Midler stars as Mama Rose.
[14] Midler's star is unveiled in an augural ceremony with 15 other artists at the Sidewalk of the Stars in

front of Radio City Music Hall.
[15-23] With her sellout shows at the Universal Amphitheatre, Midler becomes the highest-grossing artist in the 21 year history of the venue, earning $2,200,000.

1994

Feb [23] A $5 million breach of contract suit filed by Martha Raye is dismissed by a Los Angeles Superior Court Judge. (She had claimed that "For The Boys" was biographical.)
May [13] Midler guests on CBS-TV's "Late Show With David Letterman".
[27] She embarks on a US summer tour at the ThunderDome, St. Petersburg, FL.
Sept [3-4] Midler makes her first appearance in Las Vegas, NV since 1976, at the MGM Grand Garden.

1995

Mar [11] The Manhattan Transfer's ***Tonin'***, featuring Midler along with guest performances from Phil Collins, Chaka Khan, Laura Nyro, Ben E. King, Frankie Valli, Felix Cavaliere and Smokey Robinson, among others, makes US #123.
June [12] Midler is joined by local officials and schoolchildren at the Little Red Lighthouse beneath the George Washington Bridge to announce the cleanup of seven miles of the Hudson River.
[22] She is honored at the "VH1 Honors" ceremony at the Shrine Auditorium.
Dec [22] Arson destroys Midler's beachfront home on the island of Kauai, HI.
[30] ***Bette Of Roses***, her first non-soundtrack album in five years, now makes US #45 and UK #55.

1996

Feb [23] She guests on CBS-TV's "Wynonna : Revelations" special on Wynonna Judd.

MIDNIGHT OIL

Peter Garrett (vocals); **Jim Moginie** (guitar); **Martin Rotsey** (guitar); **Dwayne "Bones" Hillman** (bass); **Rob Hirst** (drums)

1976

Sydney, New South Wales, Australia schoolboy friends Moginie, Hirst and Rotsey, playing on low-budget tours in the group Farm, place a newspaper ad for a lead singer. Garrett, on a sabbatical from his law studies at the Australian National University in Canberra, and a member of local band Rock Island Line, is the only reply and is recruited. Hillman, New Zealand-born, ex-the Swingers, joins on bass the following year and Midnight Oil's name is chosen by a keyboard player who is briefly in the line-up. In the summer of 1977, Garrett receives his law degree from the University of New South Wales.

1978

Now playing clubs and pubs five nights a week mostly in New South Wales, the group establishes its own Powderworks label, having been rejected by every major record company in Australia. They are becoming one of the hottest and most articulate bands and begin to forge links with a number of ecological and charitable causes including Greenpeace, the Movement Against Uranium and the Tibet Council.

1979

As one of Australia's most popular live acts, Midnight Oil, angered by the monopoly of booking agencies and promoters, establishes its own agency and blacklists 22 Australian venues which refuse to exert reasonable limitations on door prices. By year end, the band's debut album ***Head Injuries*** earns a gold disc in Australia.

1980

Further establishing itself as a pioneering spirit in environmental health with Garrett taking an increasingly political stance, Midnight Oil's follow-up, the Australia-only released album ***Bird Noises*** again achieves gold status. Hirst wins the first of eight consecutive Best Drummer Awards in the annual **Ram** magazine readers' poll. Their third Powderworks album, ***Place Without A Postcard***, recorded in Sussex, England, with producer Glyn Johns, will achieve Australian platinum success the following year, and will result in the group signing a worldwide contract with CBS/Columbia Records.

1983

June Having undertaken its first major US dates the previous year, in support of ***Red Sails In The Sunset***, produced by Nick Lounay, and also performed in Japan, during which time Garrett has visited Hiroshima, the group's countdown-to-destruction-titled ***10, 9, 8, 7, 6, 5, 4, 3, 2, 1*** is released, again to great domestic success, and is promoted with live dates.

1984

Feb [4] ***10, 9, 8, 7, 6, 5, 4, 3, 2, 1*** makes an international breakthrough at US #178. Politically more prominent than ever, Garrett is asked to run for a six-year senate seat in the Australian Senate for the newly-formed Nuclear Disarmament Party. He receives 200,000 votes.

1985

Jan [1] Midnight Oil kicks off the New Year with a live simulcast on the Australian Broadcasting System and FM radio with a performance from an island near Sydney Harbour, Australia.
Aug The critically-revered ***Red Sails In The Sunset*** makes US #177.
Dec Garrett contributes to the Artists United Against Apartheid album, which spawns the hit single *Sun City*.

1986

Diesel And Dust is certified Australian gold in 17 hours, platinum in three days and is confirmed as the largest ship-out in Australian record history. The following year Garrett will be made president of the Australian Conservation Foundation.

1988

Feb [13] ***Diesel And Dust*** is finally released worldwide and enters the US survey, set to make #21 during a 21-week chart stay.
July [2] The extracted *Beds Are Burning* reaches US #17, having already made its UK debut at #48.
Aug *The Dead Heart*, extracted from ***Diesel And Dust***, peaks at UK #68, written for the Australian movie "Uluru - An Anangu Story".
Sept [17] *The Dead Heart* rises to US #53.
Nov [21] ***Diesel And Dust*** is certified platinum by the RIAA.

1989

Apr The reissued *Beds Are Burning* hits UK #6.
July Re-released *The Dead Heart* makes UK #62. Midnight Oil spends much of the year recording its next album, and only performs two gigs, for the Aboriginal Rights Association and the Tibet Council.

1990

Feb [10] *Blue Sky Mine*, trailering a forthcoming album project, and focusing on the plight of post-war immigrants to Western Australia, who became victims of blue asbestos cancer (8,000 are still suffering) working as miners, peaks at UK #66.
[18] The band participates in an eight-hour benefit concert for victims of the December 28th, 1989 New South Wales earthquake, alongside Crowded House and others at the International Sports Centre, Newcastle, New South Wales, Australia.
Mar [10] Its parent album ***Blue Sky Mining***, including some of the band's most politically-scathing work to date, reaches UK #28.
[24] *Blue Sky Mine* makes US #47.
Apr [14] ***Blue Sky Mining*** reaches US #20. Its US issue by Columbia uses recycled paper for the controversial "long box" CD display pack. The follow-up single, *Forgotten Years*, theming on the wastes of war and promoted via a video lensed at a cemetery in Verdun, France, where 700,000 perished during World War I, is released.
[16] European leg of their "Blue Sky Mining Tour" begins, set to end May 12th.
[24] ***Blue Sky Mining*** is certified gold by the RIAA.
May [15] "The Blue Sky Mining" North American leg begins in Charlotte, NC, set to end June 26th at Thunderbird Stadium, Vancouver, BC, Canada.
[30] In New York, NY to perform at Radio City Music Hall gigs, Midnight Oil plays a noontime concert in front of the Exxon Building on 6th Avenue in Manhattan to protest at the company's global-polluting activities, not least the Exxon Valdez oil spill in Alaska. 10,000 attend the free agit-pop event which features a large back-drop reading "Midnight Oil Makes You Dance ... Exxon Oil Makes Us Sick".

1991

Mar [25] The group boycotts the fifth annual Australian Record Industry Association Awards at the Darling Harbour Convention Centre, Sydney. Their Best Group, Best Album (***Blue Sky Mining***), Best Cover Work and Best Video ("Blue Sky Mine") trophies are accepted by manager Gary Morris.
Apr They receive the Crystal Globe, Sony Music International's own award to acts who have sold five million units worldwide outside their own territory.
May [18] ***Deadicated***, a collection of Grateful Dead songs recorded by various artists, to which Midnight Oil has contributed *Wharf Rat*, with a portion of the proceeds from the sale of the album going to the Rainforest Action Network & Cultural Survival, reaches US #24.

1992

Apr [25] Garrett performs solo at "Earth Day Sound Action 1992" benefit at Foxboro Stadium, Foxborough, MA, sharing the bill with Steve Miller, Indigo Girls, Bruce Cockburn, the Kinks and Joan Baez.
May [30] ***Scream In Blue : Live***, a 12-track collection of live recordings from concert dates in New York and Australia between 1982-1990, debuts at its US #141 peak.

1993

Mar [19-20] The group performs at the Obras Arena, Buenos Aires, Argentina.
Apr [18] They play a show at the Ritz, New York as part of Earth Day celebrations.
[22] Midnight Oil performs at the Sound Action awareness fund-raiser, another Earth Day benefit at the Merriweather Post Pavilion, Columbia, MD.
[24] *Truganini*, from the band's forthcoming album, reaches UK #29.
May [1] The band's ninth album, ***Earth & Sun & Moon***, produced by Nick Launay, debuts at its UK #27 peak, and will do likewise at US #49 on the 8th.
[8] The group appears on NBC-TV's "The Tonight Show".
June [3] Midnight Oil is featured on MTV's "Unplugged".
[22] They play a one-off London date at the Brixton Academy.
July [3] *My Country* charts for a week at UK #66.
[15] The group performs an early morning outdoor concert before 2,000 protesters at Clayoquat Sound in British Columbia, the site of 850,000 acres of rainforest.
Aug [4] "The Outbreak Of Love Tour" opens in Minneapolis, MN.
Sept [6] Midnight Oil guests on CBS-TV's "Late Show With David Letterman".
Nov [4-5] They play two London shows at The Forum.
[6] *In The Valley* charts for a week at UK #60.

1994

July [16] Midnight Oil plays at Jones Beach Theatre, Wantagh, NY, as part of the W.O.M.A.D. summer tour.

1995

Jan [13-14] The group plays at the "Mountain Rock Festival" in New Zealand, before embarking on a five-date tour of Australia.

ROGER MILLER

1958

Miller (b. Roger Dean Miller, Jan. 2, 1936, Fort Worth, TX), raised in Erick, OK by his mother after his father died when he was one, and where he began writing songs at the age of five before buying his first guitar when 12, after three years serving in the US Army in Korea, in which he has been assigned to Special Services and played in a country band, has settled in Nashville, TN, in 1957, attempting to become a successful songwriter. While working at various day jobs, including bellhop at the Andrew Jackson Hotel, and serving backing-band apprenticeships with the likes of Ray Price, Faron Young and Minnie Pearl, he now begins recording for RCA Records, but initially finds better luck with his compositions, not least *Invitation To The Blues* for Ray Price (US #92 in 1958) and *(In The Summertime) You Don't Want My Love* for Andy Williams (US #64 in 1960 - Miller's own version becomes his US Country chart debut the same year at #14) among others.

1962

Nov Following the US #6 Country survey success with *When Two Worlds Collide* the previous year, Miller has joined Faron Young's band as drummer and back-up vocalist, while his song *Swiss Maid* recorded by Del Shannon now hits UK #2.

1964

Mar He is taking acting lessons and preparing to move to Los Angeles, CA, in an attempt to break into films when he signs to Mercury Records' Smash imprint, and his debut label release, the self-penned novelty *Dang Me*, starts to accumulate airplay and sales.

July [18] *Dang Me*, produced in Nashville by Jerry Kennedy, tops the US Country chart for the first of six weeks and hits US #7.

Aug ***Roger And Out*** makes US #37 during a 46-week survey tenure, earning a gold disc for a half million US sales.

Oct Taken from it, the novelty country-rocker *Chug-A-Lug* hits US #9.

Dec *(And You Had A) Do-Wacka-Do* makes US #31.

1965

Mar [20] *King Of The Road*, in a more restrained, jazzy style, sells 550,000 copies in its first 18 days on release. His most enduring song, it hits US #4 and will spend five weeks heading the US Country chart.

Apr [13] Miller wins the Best C&W Song, Best C&W Single and Best C&W Vocal Performance, Male for *Dang Me*, Best C&W Album for ***Dang Me/Chug-A-Lug*** and Best New C&W Artist categories, at the seventh annual Grammy Awards.

May [13] *King Of The Road*, released on the Philips label in Britain, tops the UK chart for one week. (Miller will later open a hotel in Nashville, named "The King Of The Road"). ***The Return Of Roger Miller*** hits US #4.

[19] *King Of The Road* is certified gold by the RIAA.

June *Engine Engine No. 9*, a close melodic relative of the Everly Brothers' *Walk Right Back*, hits US #7 and makes UK #33.

Aug *One Dyin' And A Buryin'* makes US #34, while ***The 3rd Time Around*** reaches US #13.

Sept [1] ***The Return Of Roger Miller*** is confirmed gold by the RIAA.

Oct Bittersweet *Kansas City Star* rises to US #31 and UK #48.

Dec *England Swings*, naively-written but catchily commercial, about London trendiness, hits US #8. ***Golden Hits***, a compilation of his singles to date, hits US #6 and will remain on the chart for 13 months.

1966

Jan Despite UK reviews dismissing it as "pure corn", *England Swings* makes UK #13.

Feb [11] ***Golden Hits*** is certified gold by the RIAA.

Mar Introspective *Husbands And Wives* climbs to US #26.

[15] Miller wins Best Contemporary (Rock'n'Roll) Single, Best Contemporary (Rock'n'Roll) Vocal Performance, Male, Best C&W Single, Best C&W Song and Best C&W Vocal Performance, Male for *King Of The Road* and Best C&W Album for ***The Return Of Roger Miller*** at the eighth annual Grammy Awards.

July Nonsense song *You Can't Roller Skate In A Buffalo Herd* peaks at US #40.

Aug [4] ***Dang Me*** is certified gold by the RIAA.

Sept [12] "The Roger Miller Show", a musical variety half-hour on NBC-TV, begins a weekly run on Monday evenings.

Oct Another novelty, *My Uncle Used To Love Me But She Died*, reaches US #58.

Nov His revival of Elvis Presley's *Heartbreak Hotel*, peaks at US #84, Miller's first non self-written hit.

Dec [26] His US TV show ends its run after moderate success, while ***Words And Music*** peaks at US #108.

1967

Apr *Walkin' In The Sunshine* reaches US #37.

July ***Walkin' In The Sunshine*** makes US #118, as Miller's record sales enter a steep decline from their 1964/65 peak.

1968

Apr Reflectively sentimental *Little Green Apples*, written by Bobby Russell, reaches US #39. (It will win two Grammy Awards as Best Song and Best Country Song.)

May *Little Green Apples* reaches UK #19, after a two-year UK chart absence, but will be his last UK hit.

Sept ***A Tender Look At Love*** peaks at US #173.

Dec *Vance* peaks at US #80, and will be Miller's last US Hot 100 entry (although he will continue to make the C&W chart). *Little Green Apples* will re-enter the UK chart to reach #39 in May the following year when ***Roger Miller*** peaks at US #163 in September.

1970

Feb ***Roger Miller 1970*** spends two weeks at US #200. (It will be his last US chart album but he will be an active songwriter and live performer in the US throughout the '70s and '80s, despite a lack of hits.)

1985

Apr [25] "Big River", a musical written by Miller, based on Mark Twain's **Huckleberry Finn**, opens at the Eugene O'Neill Theatre on Broadway, New York, and will win a Tony Award as Best Musical, among seven Tony nods, as Miller continues to have recording success in the country field.

1992

Oct [25] Having spent the late '80s performing with a symphony orchestra and on the supper-club circuit, and with many of his 800-plus compositions still covered by numerous artists (not least Scottish twinset the Proclaimers, whose treatment of *King Of The Road* hit the UK Top 10 in 1990), Miller dies of cancer in Century City Hospital, Los Angeles, survived by his wife, four daughters and three sons.

1995

Oct [4] Miller is posthumously inducted into the Country Music Hall of Fame at the annual Country Music Association Awards in Nashville.

Nov CD boxed-set, ***King Of The Road : The Genius Of Roger Miller***, comprising 28 rare photographs, an 8,000 word booklet and previously unreleased material, is released on Mercury.

THE STEVE MILLER BAND

Steve Miller (vocals, guitar); **James "Curley" Cooke** (guitar, vocals); **Lonnie Turner** (bass, vocals); **Tim Davis** (drums, vocals)

1965

Miller (b. Oct. 5, 1943, Milwaukee, WI), son of a pathologist raised in Dallas, TX, who received his first guitar lesson from family friend Les Paul in 1948 and recorded a jam with his father's friend T-Bone Walker in 1952 at the age of 11, formed his first band the Marksmen Combo while still attending Woodrow Wilson High School in 1955 with schoolfriend Boz Scaggs (b. William Scaggs, June 8, 1944, OH), playing around Texas, Louisiana and Oklahoma and, at age 14, backed blues legend Jimmy Reed in a Dallas bar. Going on with Scaggs to Wisconsin University, Madison, WI, in 1961, they played in R&B/Motown covers band, the Ardells, which transformed into the Fabulous Night Train with Ben Sidran. Leaving college in 1963, Miller returned to Texas to write songs, many of which form the basis for ***Children Of The Future***, before studying literature at Copenhagen University, Denmark. Returning to the US the following year, he moved to Chicago, IL, where he worked with Muddy Waters, James Cotton, Howlin' Wolf and the Butterfield Blues Band, among others, before now joining Barry Goldberg to form the World War Three Band, which becomes the Goldberg Miller Blues Band, releasing *The Mother Song* for Epic Records.

1966

Nov Miller moves to San Francisco, CA, forming the Miller Band, with Cooke, Turner (b. Feb. 24, 1947, Berkeley, CA) and Davis. The group begins gigging, making its live debut at the Matrix club.

1967

Mar [22-23] The group plays at the Avalon Ballroom, San Francisco, with the Quicksilver Messenger Service.

Apr The band participates in the "San Francisco Stage College Folk Festival", as Jim Peterman joins on organ and vocals.

[28-30] The group plays at the Fillmore West, San Francisco, with Buffalo Springfield.

June [1-4] They perform again at the Avalon Ballroom on a bill with the Doors.

[17] The group is the seventh act of the afternoon on the second day of the "Monterey International Pop Festival", at the Monterey County Fairgrounds, Monterey, CA.

Sept Scaggs re-teams with Miller and joins the band, which backs Chuck Berry on his live album ***Live At The Fillmore***, while Cooke leaves to form Curley Cooke's Hurdy Gurdy Band.

Oct The group signs to Capitol Records, before starting a major US tour.

1968

Jan The Steve Miller Band arrives in Britain to record its debut album with producer Glyn Johns, at Olympic Studios in Barnes, London.

Feb Three Steve Miller Band tracks are featured on the newly-released soundtrack to the movie "Revolution" on United Artists.

May [18] The band appears at the "Northern California Folk-Rock Festival", on a bill with the Doors, the Grateful Dead and others.

June The Johns-helmed ***Children Of The Future*** peaks at US #134.

Aug Scaggs leaves shortly after completion of the group's new album, ***Sailor***, as does Peterman, leaving the group to continue as a trio, though Miller's earlier cohort Sidran will join briefly on keyboards.

Nov *Living In The USA* peaks at US #94, as the parent album, ***Sailor***, reaches US #24.

Dec [26-29] They play again at the Fillmore West, San Francisco, with Sly & the Family Stone and Pogo.

1969

Mar Nicky Hopkins, ex-Jeff Beck's group, joins on keyboards.
May [29-**June** 1] The Fillmore West once again hosts the band on a bill with Chicago.
June ***Brave New World***, like the previous two albums, recorded in the UK with Glyn Johns, reaches US #22, with Paul McCartney playing bass on *My Dark Hour*, using the pseudonym Paul Ramon.
Sept [11-14] They perform four further dates at the Fillmore West.
Nov ***Your Saving Grace*** makes US #38. Turner and Hopkins both leave, the latter to join Quicksilver Messenger Service while Bob Winkelman becomes Miller's new bassist.

1970

Jan [29-**Feb** 1] The group performs at the favored Fillmore West, with Sha Na Na.
May [22-24] They participate in the three-day "Hollywood Music Festival" at Newcastle-under-Lyme, near Stoke, Staffs.
July ***Number Five***, recorded in Nashville, TN, and produced by the band, reaches US #23. Davis leaves for a solo career (and will cut two albums for Metromedia).
[16-19] Another series of dates at the Fillmore West sees them sharing a bill with Bo Diddley.
Aug Miller recruits Ross Valory (b. Feb. 2, 1949, San Francisco) on bass and vocals and Jack King on drums.
Sept *Going To The Country* peaks at US #69. ***Rock Love*** will make US #82 in October the following year, two months before Valory quits (to subsequently re-emerge in Journey.)

1972

Jan Miller augments the group with keyboardist Dicky Thompson, bassist Gerald Johnson and second drummer Roger Alan Clark.
Feb The band performs at London's Rainbow Theatre, where it previews its forthcoming album.
Mar Clark and King both leave, the latter being replaced by namesake John King.
Apr ***Recall The Beginning ... A Journey From Eden*** peaks at US #109. Already recovering from a serious auto accident, Miller contracts hepatitis, forcing a six-month layoff.
Oct The Steve Miller Band begins a 50-city US tour, for which Turner returns, replacing Johnson, who leaves to join Boz Scaggs' band. Cooke joins for some gigs towards the end of the tour.
Dec Capitol's retrospective double, ***Anthology***, climbs to US #56.

1973

Apr The band returns to London to play at the Rainbow Theatre.
Oct [20] ***The Joker***, with distinctive cover art by John Van Hamersveld and Norman Seeff, enters the US survey and will prove to be Miller's trump card, eventually hitting US #2.

1974

Jan [11] The still-climbing *The Joker* is certified gold by the RIAA.
[12] Miller-penned title cut, *The Joker*, featuring an innovative acoustic guitar track, becomes a huge US radio hit and displaces Jim Croce's *Time In A Bottle* to top the US chart.
Apr *Your Cash Ain't Nothing But Trash* peaks at US #51.
May Thompson and King leave the line-up.
June Reissued *Living In The USA* makes US #49. Miller takes a sabbatical, buying a 312-acre farm in Medford, OR, and installing a 24-track studio.

1975

July [5] Miller, making his first live appearance in 14 months, assembles a new Steve Miller Band, comprising Turner, Les Dudek on guitar and vocals and Doug Clifford on drums, for the "Knebworth Festival", Knebworth, Herts., where Pink Floyd tops the bill.
Oct The band reverts to a trio with Miller and Turner and new drummer Gary Mallaber (b. Oct. 11, 1946, Buffalo, NY).

1976

May Having formed his own Sailor Records, licensed to Capitol in the US and Mercury in Europe, ***Fly Like An Eagle***, Miller's first album in two years, hits US #3 during a 97-week chart stay and will eventually become his best-selling album.
June ***Fly Like An Eagle*** reaches UK #11, his first British album success.
[7-8] The group embarks on a 16-date "Summer Serenade '76" tour in Dallas, TX, set to end on the 30th in San Diego, CA.
July Outlaw-themed *Take The Money And Run* reaches US #11.
Oct Miller assembles yet another Steve Miller Band, comprising Turner, Mallaber, David Denny (b. Feb. 5, 1948, Berkeley) (guitar), Norton Buffalo (harmonica, vocals), Greg Douglas (b. Oct. 11, 1949, Concord, CA) (guitar, vocals) and Byron Allred (b. Oct. 27, 1948, Logan, UT) (keyboards).
Nov [6] *Rock'n'Me* becomes his second US #1 and will reach UK #11, as **Rolling Stone** votes ***Fly Like An Eagle*** Best Album Of The Year by year's end.

1977

Mar *Fly Like An Eagle* hits US #2, kept off the top by Barbra Streisand's *Evergreen*.
Apr [18] *Fly Like An Eagle* is certified gold by the RIAA.
May ***Book Of Dreams***, recorded at the same sessions as ***Fly Like An Eagle*** hits US #2, and will be Miller's last new album release of the decade.
[28, 30] Steve Miller Band plays two concerts at the Oakland-Alameda County Stadium, Oakland, CA, in front of 100,000 people on a bill with Heart, the Eagles and Foreigner.
June ***Book Of Dreams*** reaches UK #12.
July *Jet Airliner*, another staple on US rock radio, hits US #8.
[24] Miller begins a US tour at the Omni, San Francisco, ending August 18th.
Oct *Jungle Love* reaches US #27.
Nov [4] ***Anthology*** is certified gold by the RIAA.
Dec *Swingtown* peaks at US #17. ***Greatest Hits 1974-1978*** will wind up the decade's chart action climbing to US #18 in December the following year.

1981

Nov Despite a four-year lay-off, the self-produced ***Circle Of Love***, devoting an entire side to the extended *Macho City*, reaches US #26.
Dec The extracted *Heart Like A Wheel* reaches US #24.
[30] ***Circle Of Love*** is confirmed gold by the RIAA for 500,000 US sales.

1982

Feb Title cut *Circle Of Love* peaks at US #55.
June ***Abracadabra***, produced by Miller and Mallaber, hits US #3 and UK #10.
[19] Miller begins an extensive US tour with new guitarists Kenny Lewis and John Massaro, recruited to the live line-up.
Aug One of only two Miller-penned cuts from the parent album, *Abracadabra* hits UK #2, held off the top by Captain Sensible's *Happy Talk*.
[23] The RIAA awards gold status to the still-climbing *Abracadabra*.
Sept [4] *Abracadabra* becomes Miller's third US chart-topper, in an edited form, while *Keeps Me Wondering Why* peaks at UK #52.
Nov *Cool Magic* climbs to US #57.
[16] ***Abracadabra*** is certified platinum by the RIAA.

1983

Jan *Give It Up* peaks at US #60.
May ***The Steve Miller Band Live!***, recorded on a UK tour in 1982, peaks at US #125 and UK #79. A live video is simultaneously issued. ***Italian X-Rays*** will make US #101 in November the following year but will not place in the UK where it is his last Mercury release and will be his last release in the UK on Mercury. It includes *Shangri-La* which peaks at US #57 the month before and *Bongo Bongo* which will stop at US #84 in February 1985.

1986

Nov [22] Miller-written *I Want To Turn The World Around*, from a forthcoming album, makes US #97.
Dec ***Living In The 20th Century*** is released, climbing to US #65. Produced by Miller and featuring Kenny G and James Cotton among its guests, the album is dedicated to Jimmy Reed with whom Miller had played as a teenager. His first for Capitol in the UK under a new Sailor licensing deal, it includes familiar Miller associates, among them Mallaber, Buffalo and guitarist Les Dudek, with one side devoted to covers of blues classics.

1987

July [8] ***The Joker*** is certified platinum by the RIAA.
[14] Miller is bestowed a star on the Hollywood Walk of Fame in Los Angeles, CA. (His only release of the year is the 14-track UK Mercury issued ***Greatest Hits 1976-1986***.)

1988

Oct ***Born 2 B Blue*** peaks at US #108. It celebrates his 20th year at Capitol with a set of blues and jazz standards, recorded with help from Sidran, Phil Woods on sax and Milt Jackson on vibes, and includes a jazz version of *Zip-A-Dee-Doo-Dah* and a cover of Lee Dorsey's *Ya Ya*.
Nov [10] Miller begins his first tour in six years in Burlington, VT.

1990

June [1] He embarks on a major US tour, with former Foreigner lead vocalist Lou Gramm supporting, in Bloomington, MN, set to end on September 12th at the Coliseum, Seattle, WA.
Sept [15] *The Joker* belatedly tops the UK chart during its use on a Levi's jeans TV commercial. In the first publically-admitted case in UK chart history, chart compilers Gallup confirm that two singles tied for this week's #1, achieving identical panel sales tallies: Deee-Lite's *Groove Is In The Heart* is pipped by Miller's oldie by the subsequently much-criticized ruling that *The Joker*'s panel sales increase over its previous week's performance was greater than Deee-Lite's.
Oct [6] ***The Best Of Steve Miller 1968-1973*** makes UK #34.
[20] The band performs before a sellout crowd of 74,100 at the Cotton Bowl, Fair Park, Dallas, to benefit the Texas Special Olympics.
[26] Miller plays at the fourth annual Bridge School benefit held at the Shoreline Amphitheatre, Mountain View, CA, on a bill with Neil Young, Elvis Costello, Jackson Browne and Edie Brickell.
Nov [18] The band plays a date at Wembley Arena, Wembley, Middx., during a brief UK visit.

1991

July [20] The Pine Knob Music Theatre, Clarkston, MI, hosts a sellout date by the band on a bill with Bad Company and Damn Yankees.
Aug [10] Z.Z. Top, the Steve Miller Band, Extreme and Eric Johnson play a sellout show at the Spartan Stadium, San Jose State University, San Jose, CA, grossing $1,033,097.
Sept [16] The RIAA certifies multi-platinum sales of ***Book Of Dreams*** (three million) and ***Fly Like An Eagle*** (four million).

1992

Mar [7] The group takes part in the 15th annual Bay Area Music Awards from the San Francisco Civic Auditorium.
Apr [25] During his current US tour, Miller plays at the "Earth Day Sound Action 1992" benefit at Foxboro Stadium, Foxborough, MA, sharing the bill with Midnight Oil's Peter Garrett, Indigo Girls, Bruce Cockburn, the Kinks and Joan Baez.

May [24] Montgomery, AL police search for a man who has been posing as Miller and has fled a local motel, where the touring Neville Brothers are staying, owing $600 in unpaid lodging, limousine and champagne charges. The impostor did, however, leave a $73 tip on an $8 drinks bill earlier in the day when mingling with unsuspecting members of the band prior to tonight's gig.
June [20] Miller plays before a sellout crowd of 57,425 at the Robert F. Kennedy Memorial Stadium, Washington, DC, during a short series of dates supporting the Grateful Dead.
[30] The RIAA certifies six million sales of ***Greatest Hits 1974-1978***, confirmation of the enduring appeal, not least on US radio, of his earlier work.
July [5] His North American "Lost Cities" tour opens at the Pacific Amphitheatre, Costa Mesa, CA.
Aug [26] The group, sharing billing with Bryan Adams and Extreme, plays before a sellout crowd of 18,950 at Lansdowne Park Grandstand, Central Canada Exhibition, Ottawa, ON, Canada, during the Canadian leg of the trek.
Oct [10] Miller participates in the "All Our Colors - The Good Road Concert" benefit at the Shoreline Amphitheatre, Mountain View, CA, with Santana, Jackson Browne, John Lee Hooker and others.

1993

Apr [16] Miller plays at an "Earth Day" concert headlined by Paul McCartney at the Hollywood Bowl, Hollywood, CA, with proceeds going to PETA, Greenpeace and Friends of the Earth.
Mar [23] The Paul Rodgers-assembled ***Tribute To Muddy Waters***, featuring fret work from Miller, is released on Victory Music.
June [4] A 46-date US tour opens at the Target Center, Minneapolis, set to end on August 18th at the Waikiki Shell, Honolulu, HI.
July [28] Miller guests on NBC-TV's "The Tonight Show".
Aug [7] *Wide River*, the title track from Miller's new album, peaks at US #64.
[14] Self-written and produced ***Wide River*** makes US #85.

1994

June [4] Miller takes part in the "Living Legends Concert", to celebrate Gibson Guitars' centenary, at New York, NY's Beacon Theatre.
Aug [16] He plays a sellout date at The Aladdin, Las Vegas, NV, during his current US summer tour. (During the year Capitol will release the three-CD retrospective ***Steve Miller Band Box Set*** which includes his first recording as a five year-old.)

1995

July [14] Miller embarks on a 32-date US tour, with the Doobie Brothers, at Deek Creek Music Center, Noblesville, IN, set to end the Cal Expo Amphitheatre, Sacramento, CA on September 9th.
Nov [18] Miller plays a sellout date at the Paramount Theatre, Seattle, WA, during a further short US tour.

1996

Apr [10] Miller embarks on a 16-date US trek at the Northrop Auditorium, Minneapolis, MN, set to end on May 6th at the Orlando Arena, Orlando, FL.

MILLI VANILLI

KYLIE MINOGUE

1987

July Minogue (b. May 28, 1968, Melbourne, Victoria, Australia), daughter of Australian accountant Ron and Welsh mother Carol, has secured her first acting role, as a Dutch girl in the Australian TV soap opera "The Sullivans" in March 1979, before undertaking the character of Robin in another soap, "Skyways", in October, which also features future acting and recording collaborator Jason Donovan. Having successfully completed her High School Certificate in 1984, Minogue joins another soap, "The Hendersons", as Charlotte Kernow. Two further TV parts, in "Fame And Misfortune" and "The Zoo Family" were completed in 1985, before she quit school the following year to accept the role of Charlene Mitchell in the new Australian soap "Neighbours", again co-starring with Donovan. Winning the Australian TV Logie award for her role in the top-rated show in April this year, Minogue is now invited to sing at an Australian Rules Football game in Sydney, and performs Little Eva's 1962 hit *The Locomotion*. It attracts the attention of Australian label Mushroom, which signs her to record the song.
Aug *The Locomotion* hits #1 in Australia for seven weeks, before being deposed by Los Lobos' *La Bamba*.
Sept Spotted by UK producer Pete Waterman, Minogue is invited to record at Stock/Aitken/Waterman's London studios during a ten-day UK visit and cuts *I Should Be So Lucky*. Meanwhile, UK ratings of "Neighbours" approach 14 million viewers per episode.
Nov *The Locomotion* is certified as Australia's biggest-selling single of the '80s and is a hit in New Zealand and the Far East.

1988

Jan Light pop dance-ditty *I Should Be So Lucky*, written and produced by SAW, is released on its own independent PWL label, after all major record companies have turned it down.
Feb [20] *I Should Be So Lucky* hits UK #1, on its way to becoming the UK's first gold single of the year. It also hits tops the chart in Australia, where Minogue is awarded four further TV Logie awards.
May As *I Should Be So Lucky* tops charts in 12 other territories, the follow-up, *Got To Be Certain*, hits UK #2, held off the top by Wet Wet Wet's *With A Little Help From My Friends*.
July Her maiden album, ***Kylie***, written and produced by SAW, enters at UK #1, on its way to platinum sales. With Minogue signed to Geffen in US, *I Should Be So Lucky* reaches US #28.
Aug Remixed by SAW for UK and US consumption, *The Locomotion* hits UK #2 in its first week of release.
Sept Minogue begins a US promotional visit.
Oct Fourth single from debut album, *Je Ne Sais Pas Pourquoi*, hits UK #2, behind Enya's *Orinoco Flow* (confirming Minogue as the most successful debut solo female singer ever on the British survey).
Nov [12] *The Locomotion* hits US #3, as ***Kylie*** makes US #53 and her first video-hits collection, "Kylie : The Videos", tops the UK video rankings.
[21] She takes part in the "Royal Variety Performance" in London.
Dec Minogue is only the third woman to achieve the best-selling album of the year in the UK (joining Barbra Streisand (***Love Songs***) and Madonna (***True Blue***)).

1989

Jan [7] *Especially For You*, a kiss'n'cuddle ballad duet with Jason Donovan, tops the UK chart.
Feb [11] *It's No Secret* makes US #37.
Mar [1] ***Kylie*** is certified gold by the RIAA.
May [13] Another typically commercial uptempo SAW pop-dance confection, *Hand On Your Heart*, hits UK #1.
Aug [5] *Wouldn't Change A Thing* hits UK #2, her seventh straight top two UK smash, behind Jive Bunny & the Mastermixers' *Swing The Mood*.
Oct [21] Her sophomore set, ***Enjoy Yourself***, completely created at PWL studio by the SAW team, debuts at UK #1, on its way to multiplatinum UK sales awards.
Nov [4] The extracted *Never Too Late* hits UK #4, breaking her top two run. (None of her 1989 UK releases have charted in the US.) Right on cue, "Kylie : The Videos 2" tops the UK video surveys.
Dec [23] Peter Waterman-instigated Band Aid II's re-recording of *Do They Know It's Christmas?*, including vocal support from Minogue and Donovan, hits UK #1. Minogue appears in the Australian movie "The Delinquents".

1990

Jan [27] Her remake of Little Anthony & the Imperials 1958 US #4, *Tears On My Pillow*, hits UK #1, her fourth chart-topper.
Feb Minogue opens her Australian debut tour in Brisbane.
Apr Video, "Live In Japan", is released by Video Collection.
May [19] Returning to uptempo SAW dance material, *Better The Devil You Know*, featured in movie "If Looks Could Kill", hits UK #2, behind Adamski's *Killer*.
June [18] During a UK tour, Minogue performs at the Wembley Arena, Wembley, Middx.
Oct [10] '70s soul retrospective, *Step Back In Time*, aided by similar era-styled video, hits UK #4.
Nov [24] As rumors circulate that Minogue has left the SAW stable, a decision influenced, not least, by her close liaison with current beau fellow Australian and INXS lead singer Michael Hutchence, her SAW-dominated third album, ***Rhythm Of Love***, marking a deliberate attempt to harden her previously candy-coated image into a sexier adult projection, hits UK #9, though renewed US success remains elusive.

1991

Feb [16] *What Do I Have To Do* hits UK #6.
June [8] *Shocked* hits UK #6, as she guests on ITV's "Ghost Train".
[15] "The 1991 World Music Awards", featuring a Minogue performance, airs on ITV.
Sept [14] *Word Is Out* reaches UK #16.
Oct [26] Minogue begins a short UK tour at the

National Exhibition Centre, Birmingham, West Midlands, set to end on November 4th at the Playhouse, Edinburgh, Scotland.
[26] ***Let's Get To It*** debuts at its UK #15 peak.
[27] Minogue wins the Worst Female Solo Singer category at the **Smash Hits** Poll Winners Awards.
Nov [16] *If You Were With Me Now*, a duet with Keith Washington, hits UK #4.

1992

Feb [1] Her update of Chairmen Of The Board's 1970 UK #3 *Give Me Just A Little More Time*, also used for an Accurist TV commercial, hits UK #2, behind Wet Wet Wet's *Goodnight Girl*.
May [2] *Finer Feelings*, remixed by the Brothers In Rhythm (Steve Anderson and Dave Seaman), reaches UK #11.
Aug [29] *What Kind Of Fool* reaches UK #14.
Sept [5] ***Kylie Greatest Hits*** enters the UK chart at #1.
Nov [28] Covering Kool & the Gang's 1980 disco smash *Celebration*, Minogue's version debuts at its UK #20 peak, as she appears on BBC1's "Going Live!".

1993

Feb Minogue signs with BMG subsidiary label deConstruction worldwide, except the US, where she inks with Terry Ellis' Imago Records, and Australia, where she remains with Mushroom, as she is rumored to be working with St. Etienne's Pete Wiggs and Bob Stanley on new material.
[9] *The Locomotion* is certified gold by the RIAA.
[16] Minogue presents the Best International Solo Artist trophy at the 12th annual BRIT Awards in London.

1994

Sept [10] *Confide In Me* debuts at its UK #2 peak.
Oct [1] ***Kylie Minogue***, with collaborations with Brothers In Rhythm, Jimmy Harry and Farley & Heller, hits UK #4 in its week of entry.
Nov [5] She appears on BBC1-TV's "Steve Wright's People Show".
Dec [3] *Put Yourself In My Place*, remixed by David Morales and Drizabone, reaches UK #11.

1995

Jan [24] Minogue is named Most Desirable Human Being at the **New Musical Express** BRAT Awards.
Feb [2] She hosts BBC1-TV's revamped "Top Of The Pops".
July [22] *Where Is The Feeling?* debuts at its UK #16 peak, as she appears on ITV's "Scratchy & Co.".
Aug [6] Minogue performs at the "T In The Park" festival at Strathclyde Country Park, Hamilton, Strathclyde, Scotland.
Oct [14] *Where The Wild Roses Grow*, an unlikely duet with fellow-Australian Nick Cave, debuts at its UK #11 peak. Of the collaboration, Cave says: "I've always wanted to write Kylie a song, to have her sing something sad and slow." (Having appeared in the movie "Streetfighter" with Jean Claude van Damme, Minogue now stars in "Biodrome" co-starring Stephen Baldwin and Pauly Shore.)

THE MIRACLES

see: SMOKEY ROBINSON & THE MIRACLES

THE MISSION

Wayne Hussey (guitar, vocals); **Simon Hinkler** (guitar); **Craig Adams** (bass); **Mick Brown** (drums)

1986

May Hussey (b. Jerry Lovelock, May 26, 1958, Bristol, Avon) and Adams (b. Apr. 4, 1962, Otley, Yorks.), after the break-up of the Sisters of Mercy, planned a follow-on band named the Sisterhood, but legal disputes with their ex-colleague Andrew Eldritch will ultimately prevent the use of this moniker. Ex-Artery guitarist Hinkler and ex-Red Lorry Yellow Lorry drummer Brown have been recruited to complete the post-punk goth-rock quartet which has played its first dates, still billed as Sisterhood, supporting the Cult on a European tour in January, and performed its first radio sessions for Janice Long's BBC Radio 1 show in February. Now renamed the Mission, they sign to the independent label Chapter 22, based in Solihull, West Midlands, and begin their first headlining UK tour "Expedition 1 - Keeping The Faith", supported by Pauline Murray and the Storm.
June Their debut single, *Serpents Kiss*, tops the UK Independent chart, and peaks at UK #70.
July Several major UK labels show interest and their contract is bought from Chapter 22 by Mercury Records, as they tour Italy and Germany.
Aug Double A-side, *Garden Of Delight*, paired with their revival of Neil Young's *Like A Hurricane*, released on Chapter 22 prior to the new deal, tops the Independent chart and makes UK #50. The band plays a mini-tour of Holland and Belgium, and appears at the 24th annual "Reading Festival", Reading, Berks.
Oct *Stay With Me*, the group's debut on Mercury, reaches UK #30.
Nov The Mission embarks on a UK tour to launch its debut album, ***God's Own Medicine***, which reaches UK #14.

1987

Jan *Wasteland*, edited from its album version, reaches UK #11, as the band plays overseas dates titled "The World Crusade".
Mar *Severina*, also from the album, peaks at UK #25 as the group returns to tour Britain.
Apr The band makes its live US debut on a two month coast-to-coast tour, billed as Mission UK to avoid a name-clash with an existing US band, as ***God's Own Medicine*** makes US #108. Adams will be sent home early during the tour suffering from physical and mental exhaustion.
July The group tours Europe briefly between two major UK dates supporting U2 in Leeds, West Yorks. and Edinburgh, Scotland. Compilation album, ***The First Chapter***, rounding up nine tracks recorded for Chapter 22, including the first two hit singles, makes UK #35.
Aug The band plays again at the "Reading Festival", this time as headliners, before recording a new album at Richard Branson's Manor Studios near Oxford, Oxon, with ex-Led Zeppelin John Paul Jones producing.

1988

Feb *Tower Of Strength* reaches UK #12.
Mar ***Children*** hits UK #2, supported by a UK tour.
Apr The Mission begins a ten-month headlining world trek, while *Beyond The Pale*, taken from the album, reaches UK #32.
May ***Children*** peaks at US #126.
Oct Goth-heavy video collection, "From Dusk To Dawn", is released in the UK by Channel 5.
Dec Closing its world tour, the Mission plays sellout dates at the Wembley Arena, Wembley, Middx., and the National Exhibition Centre, Birmingham, West Midlands.

1989

May Devoting much of the year to recording a new album, the group participates in two benefit concerts, one for the Lockerbie Air Disaster Fund, the other for the relatives of the Hillsborough soccer tragedy. They will also perform again at the annual "Reading Festival" in August.

1990

Jan [20] Ballad, *Butterfly On A Wheel*, reaches UK #12.
Feb [17] Tim Palmer-produced ***Carved In Sand*** hits UK #7, as the concurrent video collection, "Waves Upon The Sand", is released.
Mar [10] *Deliverance* reaches UK #27, as the Mission embarks on a one-month major-venue UK tour.
Apr [22] North American tour opens at the Metropolis in Montreal, Canada, after the first five dates are cancelled when Hinkler is struck down with rheumatic fever, set to end in New York City, NY, on May 25th.
[28] ***Carved In Sand*** peaks at US #101, though a major breakthrough US hit single remains elusive.
May Hinkler leaves the band, replaced for the tour by Dave Wolfenden, causing Hussey to leave the stage in tears at a Toronto, ON, Canada, gig after announcing his departure.
June [2] *Into The Blue* makes UK #32.
Nov [2] Out-takes and remixes associated with the last album project, collected as ***Grains Of Sand***, reaches UK #28.
[17] The extracted *Hands Across The Ocean*, produced by Andy Partridge, also reaches UK #28.
[24] The group performs at the "Rocknight Festival", Dusseldorf, Germany.
Dec [11-12] The band ends its European tour with two shows at London's Brixton Academy.
Merry Christmas Everybody, recorded by the Metal Gurus (the Mission in glam-rock disguise) and produced by Slade's Noddy Holder and Jim Lea, is released.

1991

May [14] Hussey guests on C4-TV's "Star Test".
June [1] The group, now augmented by new guitarist Paul Etchells, makes its only UK live appearance of the year at London's Finsbury Park with New Model Army and Killing Joke.

1992

Feb The band puts the finishing touches to its new album at Comforts Place Studios.
Mar [15] The group appears on ITV's "Cue The Music".
May [2] *Never Again* makes UK #34.
June [17] The Mission plays at Rock City, Nottingham, Notts., the first of nine party nights where fans can listen to a playback of the new album, ***Masque***, some of which are attended by Hussey, Adams and Brown.
[20] *Like A Child Again* debuts at its UK #30 high.
July [4] ***Masque,*** featuring a song by Wonder Stuff's Miles Hunt, two co-written tracks by former Waterboy Anthony Thistlewaite, and string arrangements by Killing Joke's Jaz Coleman, enters at its UK #23 peak.
Oct [17] *Shades Of Green* stops at UK #49.
Dec The group works on new material at its home studios with Joe Gibb producing.

1993

Aug [21] Eldritch and Hussey reunite for the "Off The Street" benefit at London's Town & Country club.
Sept [25] The group begins rescheduled 12-date UK tour at the Newcastle Riverside, set to end on October 8th-9th at London's Mean Fiddler, Harlesden. (New bassist Andy Hobson has not worked out, so Andy Cousin, formerly of All About Eve, takes his place.)

1994

Jan [8] *Tower Of Strength*, with new East India Trans Cairo and Bombay mixes by Youth, debuts at its UK #33 peak.
Feb [12] The group, temporarily comprising Hussey, Brown, Cousin, ex-Spear Of Destiny guitarist Mark Thwaite and former Pendragon keyboardist Rik Carter, begins a six-date UK tour at the Barrowlands, Glasgow, Strathclyde, set to end on the 18th at the Forum, London.
[19] Compilation set ***Sum And Substance***, closing the group's account with Mercury, makes UK #49 in its week of entry.
Mar [26] *Afterglow* charts for a week at UK #53.

1995

Feb [4] *Swoon* also charts for a week at UK #75.
[25] ***Neverland***, issued on its own Neverland label, makes UK #58 in its week of entry, as the Mission, now a duo of Hussey and Brown, embarks on an 11-date UK tour at the UEA, Norwich, Norfolk, set to end on March 10th at London's Shepherd's Bush Empire.
Apr [1] The Mission begins an eight-date tour of

Germany in Munchen, set to end on the 18th at the Batschkapp, Frankfurt.
see also: **THE SISTERS OF MERCY**

JONI MITCHELL

1966

Growing up in an apartment above a drug-store on Main Street in Fort McLeod, AB, Canada, the daughter of Royal Canadian Air Force lieutenant William Anderson and his bank clerk wife Myrtle (née Myrtle Marguerite McKee) and having been stricken with polio at the age of nine, Mitchell (b. Roberta Joan Anderson, Nov. 7, 1943, Fort McLeod) who entered the Alberta College of Art, Calgary in 1962, having worked as a model and shown an early aptitude for visual arts, aiming for a career as a commercial artist, also sings and plays a $36 baritone ukelele, which she learnt from a Pete Seeger teach-yourself record. As music gradually becomes more important than her art studies, and at a friend's suggestion, she began singing at the local Depression coffee house with Peter Albling. On her way to perform at the "Mariposa Folk Festival" in Ontario in 1964, Mitchell wrote her first song, a blues number, *Day After Day*. After the festival, instead of returning to school, she entered Toronto's Yorktown folk scene and started playing in local coffee bars. Pregnant with her last boyfriend's baby (who will be placed in foster care before being adopted, never to see her real mother) and marrying fellow folk singer Chuck Mitchell in June 1965, they worked as a duo on the northeastern US circuit before relocating to Detroit, MI, where their marriage dissolved. Keeping her married name, she now moves to New York, NY, while Tom Rush, having met Mitchell in Detroit, records her *Urge For Going*, after Judy Collins has rejected the composition.

1967

Still in New York, Mitchell arranges her own bookings and finances until she meets Elliot Roberts, who sees her opening for Richie Havens at the Café Au Go Go in Greenwich Village and who becomes her manager, quitting his job at the William Morris Agency, securing a deal with Reprise Records through the label's A&R executive Andy Wickham and his boss Mo Ostin. After a period in London at the invitation of producer Joe Boyd and a UK tour supporting the Incredible String Band, Mitchell moves to Los Angeles, CA, to record an album produced by David Crosby, who had "discovered" her singing at the Gaslight Club in Coconut Grove, FL. (Judy Collins records Mitchell's *Both Sides Now* and *Michael From Mountains* on her album ***Wildflowers***.)

1968

June Mitchell's maiden album, the poetically self-penned ***Joni Mitchell*** (also known as ***Song For A Seagull***), produced by Crosby and featuring Mitchell on piano and guitar with Stephen Stills on bass, peaks at US #189.
Sept Mitchell appears at London's Royal Albert Hall with Al Stewart and Fairport Convention in "An Evening Of Contemporary Song".
Dec [28] She participates in the "Miami Pop Festival" at the Gulfstream Racing Park in Hallandale, FL, with Fleetwood Mac, Marvin Gaye, Three Dog Night and Canned Heat. It is the start of a 40-week spell on the road, playing festivals in Atlanta, Newport, Big Sur, New York and Monterey and opening for Crosby, Stills & Nash.

1969

Feb [1] Mitchell makes her debut at New York's Carnegie Hall.
May [1] She guests on ABC-TV's "The Johnny Cash Show", set to air on June 7th.
Aug [18] Scheduled to take part in the "Woodstock Music & Art Fair" in Bethel, NY, Mitchell pulls out on the advice on David Geffen because of a commitment to appear on Dick Cavett's TV talk show. Instead of appearing at the momentous event, Mitchell writes *Woodstock*.
Oct Her self-penned sophomore set, ***Clouds***, featuring Mitchell's own versions of *Both Sides Now* and *Chelsea Morning*, reaches US #31, aided by her appearances on Johnny Cash's TV show, where she meets Bob Dylan for the first time.

1970

Feb [17] Mitchell announces that she is quitting live performance, during a concert at London's Royal Albert Hall.
Mar [11] She wins the Best Folk Performance category for ***Clouds*** at the 12th annual Grammy Awards.
May ***Ladies Of The Canyon***, recorded while she is living with Graham Nash in Laurel Canyon, reaches US #27 and is her first gold album, while Crosby, Stills, Nash & Young make US #11 with Mitchell's *Woodstock*.
July *Big Yellow Taxi* reaches UK #11, as its parent album, ***Ladies Of The Canyon***, hits UK #8.
Aug *Big Yellow Taxi* makes US #67.
[29] Mitchell plays on the fourth day of the "Isle Of Wight Festival" at the East Afton Farm, Godshill, Isle of Wight. During her set a man jumps onstage and yells "This is just a hippie concentration camp".
Oct [31] Matthews Southern Comfort tops the UK chart with the Mitchell-penned festival-chronicling *Woodstock*.
Nov [21] Mitchell performs at London's Royal Festival Hall.

1971

July Mitchell tours the US and Europe with Jackson Browne, and is featured on backing vocals on James Taylor's US #1 *You've Got A Friend*.
Aug ***Blue***, recorded at A&M studios Los Angeles with Stephen Stills (bass), James Taylor (guitar), Russ Kunkel (drums) and "Sneaky" Pete Kleinow (pedal steel), reaches US #15 and hits UK #3, once again highlighting Mitchell's highly literate and reflective composition skills and distinctive vocal and acoustic guitar styles.
Sept *Carey*, from ***Blue***, charts for a week at US #93.

1972

Dec After a sabbatical, spent in the woods of Canada where she writes material for her new album, she releases the self-penned (as ever) ***For The Roses***, her first album for David Geffen's Asylum Records, which features guests Stills and Nash, drummer Russ Kunkel and Crusader Wilton Felder.
[22] ***For The Roses*** is certified gold by the RIAA.

1973

Jan *You Turn Me On, I'm A Radio*, from ***For The Roses***, makes US #25.
Feb ***For The Roses*** reaches US #11.
Nov Nazareth's version of her *This Flight Tonight* reaches UK #11.

1974

Jan *Raised On Robbery*, featuring Robbie Robertson on guitar, peaks at US #65.
Feb [27] The still-rising jazz-phrased ***Court And Spark*** is certified gold by the RIAA.
Mar ***Court And Spark***, Mitchell's first fully-electric album, with help from Larry Carlton, Joe Sample, Felder, Robbie Robertson and the L.A. Express, reaches UK #14.
May *Help Me* hits US #7 as its parent album, ***Court And Spark***, hits US #2 for four weeks.
Aug [14-17] Four dates at the Universal Amphitheatre, Universal City, CA, are recorded for editing as ***Miles Of Aisles***.
Sept *Free Man In Paris*, with José Feliciano guesting on guitar, reaches US #22.
[14] Mitchell performs at Wembley Stadium, Wembley, Middx., on a bill with Crosby, Stills, Nash & Young and the Band.
Nov [27] Still-climbing ***Miles Of Aisles*** is certified gold by the RIAA.
Dec [24] Mitchell joins Linda Ronstadt, Carly Simon and James Taylor singing Christmas carols on the streets of Los Angeles.

1975

Feb A live version of *Big Yellow Taxi* makes US #24, taken from the double performance set ***Miles Of Aisles***, recorded last August with the L.A. Express - Tom Scott (woodwinds/reeds), Robben Ford (guitar), Larry Nash (piano), Max Bennett (bass) and John Guerin (drums) - which hits US #2 and makes UK #34. (The concert comprises familiar Mitchell material with only two new songs, *Love Or Money* and *Jericho*.)
Mar [1] Mitchell and Tom Scott win the Best Arrangement Accompanying Vocalists category for *Down To You* from ***Court And Spark***, at the 17th annual Grammy Awards.
She joins Bob Dylan's "Rolling Thunder Revue", initially as a spectator, and subsequently as a performer.
Dec [4] The still-climbing ***The Hissing Of Summer Lawns*** is certified gold by the RIAA.

1976

Jan Somehow hailed by **Rolling Stone** as the Worst Album of the Year in its annual critics' roundup, ***The Hissing Of Summer Lawns***, again using the L.A. Express, hits US #4 and reaches UK #14.
Feb The extracted *In France They Kiss On Main Street* peaks at US #66.
Nov ***Hejira***, mostly written in her car while driving through the US and strongly jazz-oriented, is released.
[20] Mitchell, with John Sebastian, Country Joe McDonald and Fred Neil, takes part in "California Celebrates The Whales Day" at the Memorial Auditorium, Sacramento, CA.
[25] She participates in the Band's farewell concert, "The Last Waltz", at the Winterland Ballroom, San Francisco, singing *Helpless* with Neil Young, performing *Coyote* with Dr. John and joining an all-star cast on *I Shall Be Released*.
Dec Featuring drummer John Gerin and bassist Jaco Pastorius, ***Hejira*** reaches UK #11.

1977

Jan ***Hejira*** peaks at US #13, having become her seventh consecutive gold album on December 23rd. (During the year, Mitchell will attend the Rio Carnival in Brazil, a trip which provides musical inspiration for her next album.)

1978

Feb Double album, the Latin-Afro phrased ***Don Juan's Reckless Daughter***, with guests Chaka Khan, Wayne Shorter, Pastorius, Glenn Frey and J.D. Souther, reaches US #25, and reaches UK #20.
[13] ***Don Juan's Reckless Daughter*** is certified gold by the RIAA.
Apr Impressed by her recent release, jazz giant Charles Mingus, fighting Lou Gehrig's disease, contacts Mitchell to ask whether she would assist him on a project based on T.S. Eliot's "Four Quartets". It comes to nothing, but Mitchell agrees to write and sing lyrics to six melodies he has written, and begins work in her Regency Hotel apartment in New York.

1979

Jan [5] Charles Mingus dies, age 56, in Cuernavaca, Mexico.
June [15] Mitchell performs at the "Playboy Jazz Festival" at the Hollywood Bowl, Hollywood, CA.
July ***Mingus***, using jazz musicians Gerry Mulligan, John McLaughlin, Jan Hammer and Stanley Clarke, is released. Mitchell is quoted as saying: "Mingus wanted his stock to go up before he died, there was an element of choosing me to write his epitaph, help ensure he got a bigger funeral." It makes US #17 and UK #24.
Sept A concert at the County Bowl, Santa Barbara, CA, is recorded for the forthcoming album ***Shadows And Light*** with the backing band comprising Pat Metheny (lead guitar), Pastorius (bass), Don Alias

(drums), Lyle Mays (keyboards), Michael Brecker (sax) and the Persuasions (vocals).

1980

Oct Live double set, ***Shadows And Light***, makes US #38 and UK #63.
Dec [2] Her "Shadows And Light" concert special airs on Showtime-TV. (The following February 5th, Canadian Prime Minister Pierre Trudeau will induct Mitchell into Canada's Juno Hall of Fame.)

1982

Mar Now signed to David Geffen's Geffen label, and during sessions for her new album, ***Wild Things Run Fast***, she parts company with Roberts, her manager for 17 years. After a few weeks' handling her own affairs, she teams with Peter Asher.
Nov [21] Mitchell marries her bassist, Larry Klein, at Roberts' home in Malibu, CA.
Dec *(You're So Square) Baby, I Don't Care*, originally sung by Elvis Presley in the 1957 film "Jailhouse Rock", makes US #47 as its parent album, the self-produced ***Wild Things Run Fast***, with guest vocalists Lionel Richie and James Taylor, heads to US #25 and UK #32. The following year, Mitchell will undertake a US tour, her last of the decade.

1985

Nov Changing direction yet again, using UK synthesizer boffin Thomas Dolby as co-producer and with actor Rod Steiger featured as an evangelist on the track *Tax Free*, ***Dog Eat Dog*** peaks at UK #57.
Dec ***Dog Eat Dog*** makes US #63.

1986

Jan [11] The extracted *Good Friends*, with guest vocalist Michael McDonald, peaks at US #85.
June [15] Mitchell sings three songs at the Amnesty International Concert at Giants Stadium, East Rutherford, NJ.
Oct [13] The RIAA certifies platinum sales of ***Blue*** and ***Ladies Of The Canyon***.

1988

Apr ***Chalk Mark In A Rainstorm***, co-produced with Klein and recorded in the US and UK, and featuring guests Peter Gabriel, Don Henley, Dolby, Tom Petty, Willie Nelson, Wendy & Lisa and Billy Idol, makes US #45 and UK #26.

1990

July [21] Mitchell takes part in Roger Waters' staging of "The Wall" at the site of the Berlin Wall in Potzdamer Platz, Berlin, Germany, singing *Goodbye Blue Sky*. The event is broadcast live throughout the world, and raises money for the Memorial Fund For Disaster Relief.
Sept [10-21] Mitchell's paintings, now her main interest, form a major part of "Canada In The City", an exhibition of Canadian art, music and culture at the Broadgate Centre in London.

1991

Mar [9] The Mitchell and Klein-produced, self-penned as ever, ***Night Ride Home***, atypically recorded without celebrity guests, debuts at its UK #25 peak.
Apr [27] ***Night Ride Home*** makes US #41. Her final outing with Geffen, Mitchell enters into a dispute with the label which has allegedly placed a lien on her publishing royalties in an effort to recoup its investment in her recordings, a tactic which the company subsequently drops.

1993

June [5-6] Mitchell takes part in the "Troubadours Of Folk Festival" at UCLA's Drake Stadium, Los Angeles.
Nov [14] She receives the Lifetime Achievement Award from the Saskatchewan Recording Industry Association in Saskatoon, SK, Canada.

1994

Nov [5] Co-produced again with Klein and featuring music guests Seal, Wayne Shorter and Carlos Vega among others, ***Turbulent Indigo***, seeing Mitchell's return to Reprise after 23 years, makes UK #53 in its week of entry.
[12] ***Turbulent Indigo*** debuts at its US #47 peak.
[21] Mitchell performs an acoustic showcase for the album at 41 Queensgate Terrace, London - her first UK appearance in 12 years.

1995

Jan [19] She appears at the "Commitment To Life VIII" benefit for AIDS Project Los Angeles, honoring Elton John, Tom Hanks and Ron Meyer at the Universal Amphitheatre.
[26] Mitchell performs at the Gene Autry Western Heritage Museum in Los Angeles, before 240 invited fans.
Feb [3] She appears on NBC-TV's "The Tonight Show" - her first TV appearance, by her recollection, since the "Johnny Cash Show" in 1970.
Apr [24] Mitchell guests on CBS-TV's "Late Show With David Letterman".
May [6] She performs at the 26th annual "New Orleans Jazz & Heritage Festival".
Sept Reprise releases ***Friends - The Albums***, featuring a previously unreleased Mitchell cut.
Nov [6] Mitchell plays a surprise show at Greenwich's Village Fez Club in New York, in front of 200 fans, including Chrissie Hynde, Carly Simon, Natalie Merchant and Marc Cohn.
Dec [6] She accepts the prestigious Century Award at the 1995 **Billboard** Music Awards, broadcast live on Fox-TV from New York's Coliseum.
[12] She guests again on "The Tonight Show".

1996

Jan [3] CBS-TV airs a one-hour "CBS This Morning" special, including an interview and live performance from Mitchell.
Feb [28] Mitchell edges hot competition from the Eagles, Mariah Carey and Madonna to clinch the Best Pop Album category for ***Turbulent Indigo*** at the 38th annual Grammy Awards held at Los Angeles' Shrine Auditorium. Surprised and grateful in receipt, Mitchell thanks co-recipient Klein (from whom she is now separated, though remains friends), while her artwork for the album, created with Robbie Cavolina, is named Best Recording Package.

MOBY GRAPE

Alexander "Skip" Spence (guitar, lead vocals); **Peter Lewis** (guitar, vocals); **Jerry Miller** (guitar); **Bob Mosley** (bass); **Don Stevenson** (drums)

1966

Aug The band, which takes its name from the punch line to the joke "What's purple and lives at the bottom of the sea?", is formed in San Francisco, CA, by Lewis (b. July 15, 1945, Los Angeles, CA), son of movie star Loretta Young, and Mosley (b. Dec. 4, 1942, Paradise Valley, CA), who has recorded a single with the Misfits and recently been leading Peter & the Wolves, with Joel Scott Hill (guitar) and Kent Dunbar (drums). The latter pair drops out replaced by Spence (b. Apr. 18, 1946, Windsor, ON, Canada), ex-Jefferson Airplane and Quicksilver Messenger Service, Stevenson (b. Oct. 15, 1942, Seattle, WA) formerly with the Continentals and the Frantics, and Miller (b. July 10, 1943, Tacoma, WA), also an ex-Frantic (who has also played with the Searchers, the Kingsmen and Bobby Fuller and in various bar bands in the Pacific North-West with Stevenson, most recently the short-lived Marsh Gas).
Nov [4] The group makes its live debut at the California Hall, San Francisco, before a reported audience of five.
Dec [2-4] After two months rehearsing at The Ark in Sausalito, CA, and developing a strong local reputation, the group plays at the Fillmore West, San Francisco, with Love and Lee Michaels.
[30-31] The group plays two year-end shows at the Avalon Ballroom, San Francisco, on a bill with Country Joe & the Fish.

1967

Feb [24-26] The group performs again at the Fillmore West, with the Chambers Brothers.
Mar [12] Moby Grape having signed with CBS/Columbia Records at the instigation of producer David Rubinson, in the face of enormous interest from 14 other labels, including cutting a demo with Elektra's Paul Rothchild, now begins recording its debut album at Columbia Records Studios on Santa Monica Blvd., Los Angeles.
[24-25] They play at San Francisco's Winterland Ballroom.
June [6] Columbia lays on a press junket for the band at the Avalon Ballroom to promote its debut album. In the early hours of the following morning, Lewis, Miller and Spence are arrested for contributing to the delinquency of minors, after being caught with three underage girls in Marin County, CA. Although the charges are later dropped, the damage has been done.
[7] Their debut album, ***Moby Grape***, recorded at a cost of $11,000, is released accompanied by a publicity hype involving the simultaneous release of five singles. The album will reach US #24.
[17] The group is the first act of the evening session of the second day of the "Monterey International Pop Festival", at the Monterey County Fairgrounds, Monterey, CA.
July [15] *Omaha*, one of the five 45s, charts briefly at US #88, as the group tours the US with the Mamas & the Papas and the Buckinghams.
Aug [10-13] They play at the Avalon Ballroom with Canned Heat and Vanilla Fudge.
Nov After disastrous Los Angeles sessions for a follow-up album, the band is sent to record ***Wow*** in New York, NY, where Columbia insists on discipline.

1968

Feb [11-12] Moby Grape performs at Greenwich Village's Village Theatre, on a bill with the Jefferson Airplane, Procol Harum and Move.
Mar [21-23] The group appears again at the Fillmore West, this time on a bill with Traffic.
June ***Wow***, with one track playing at 78rpm, plus the bonus live album ***Grape Jam***, and guests Al Kooper and Mike Bloomfield, reaches US #20. Shortly after its release, Spence leaves with drug problems and checks into Bellevue Hospital for six months. (He will re-emerge with the solo ***Oar*** in October 1969.)
July [23-28] The remaining quartet performs at the favored Fillmore West with the Jeff Beck Group.

1969

Feb Moby Grape undertakes a short UK and European tour. On their return to the US they move to Boulder Creek, near Santa Cruz, CA, with Miller, still a Grape, set on joining the Rhythm Dukes with John Barret and John Oxendine.
Mar Mosley leaves, joining the marines. (He will last nine months before being discharged for fighting an officer.) ***Moby Grape '69*** peaks at US #113.
Apr The remaining trio records a contractual obligation-filling album in Nashville, TN, in three days, with session man Bob Moore playing bass, before splitting with Miller and Stevenson both joining Bill Champlin's Rhythm Dukes.
Oct ***Truly Fine Citizen***, from the April recordings, peaks at US #157.

1970

Dec [6] A fake Moby Grape, put on the road by manager Matthew Katz, who owns the name, performs a few dates including a gig outside the gates of the Rolling Stones/Jefferson Airplane concert at the Altamont Speedway, Livermore, CA.

1971

Apr The original quintet reunites, adding Gordon Stephens (viola, mandolin) and signs to Reprise Records.
Aug The band dissolves again without playing any live gigs.
Oct ***20 Granite Creek***, titled after the house where it was recorded, produced by David Rubinson, and released six weeks after the band's final split, peaks at US #177.

1973

Oct Lewis, Mosley, who released ***Bob Moseley*** on Reprise in March the previous year, and Miller team again, with drummer Johnny Craviotto and guitarist Jeff Blackburn, who have both been with Miller for two years in Silver Wings, based in Santa Cruz. Since Katz still owns the Moby Grape name, having just won a lawsuit to the rights, the band calls itself the (Original) Grape.

1975

May Having played small-time live dates but unable to attract a record deal (while ***Great Grape*** has been issued the previous year by a fake Katz-backed aggregation),the group splits again with Mosley, Miller and Craviotta forming Fine Wine with ex-H.P. Lovecraft guitarist Michael Been, recording ***Fine Wine***, released only in West Germany.

1977

May Mosley, Craviotta and Blackburn link as Ducks and are joined briefly by Neil Young, gaining live notoriety in Santa Cruz but not recording.
July Spurred by the Ducks' growing reputation, Lewis and Miller form yet another Grape, joined by the long-absent Spence, plus drummer John "Fuzzy" Oxendine, who played with Miller in the Rhythm Dukes in 1969, Christian Powell on bass, and Cornelius Bumpus (who will join the Doobie Brothers late on in their career) on sax.

1978

Feb Mosley rejoins after the Ducks folds.
Apr ***Live Grape*** is released by the new group in US on Escape label but it finds little commercial success. Lewis and Spence will leave during the year but with an ever-fluctuating personnel, Grape plays into '80s obscurity in minor Southern California live circuits, also recording ***Moby Grape '83***, released that year on Katz's San Francisco Sound label, featuring Mosley, Lewis, Stevenson and Miller.

1989

The original Moby Grape, minus Spence, reunites as the Melvilles, still legally prevented from using the valuable moniker. Meanwhile, a tribute band, Grape Escape, with Craig Juan (bass), Mark Lashlly and Lynn Giles (guitars), George Hastings (drums) and Grant Ewald (keyboards), releases *Paint The White House Black* with Jerry Miller guesting on lead guitar. Mosley releases ***Live At Indigo Ranch*** as Mosley Grape on Katz's label, while Miller, now gigging as the Jerry Miller Band, releases *Now I See* on the Herman label.

1991

Apr [26] While the original line-up of Miller, Mosley, Lewis and Stevenson, still minus Spence but with Don Abernethy drummer Kirt Tuttle, released a 1990 album on their own Herman label, cut in a Seattle studio (and released by the Melvilles with a second pressing credited to the Legendary Grape), their nine-date Legendary Moby Grape 1991 Spring Tour West USA now opens at the Blue Max, Chico, CA, set to end on May 10th at the Dakotas, Portland, OR. (Sony/Legacy will release the retrospective twofer, ***Vintage - The Very Best Of Moby Grape***, in June 1993.) Mosely, who was diagnosed schizophrenic in 1970 is reportedly homeless around the San Diego area in 1994 while Spence, who has also been diagnosed with the same condition, lives in a residential care facility in Northern California.

EDDIE MONEY

1977

Singer/guitarist Money (b. Edward Mahoney, Mar. 2, 1949, Brooklyn, New York, NY), the son of a New York policeman, himself attending the NYPD police academy where he works as a clerk, has simultaneously fronted a Long Island, NY, rock band by night, under the pseudonym of Eddie Money, having begun his music apprenticeship as a member the Grapes Of Wrath during his mid-teens. Faced with a choice of careers, he has quit the force and moved to Berkeley, CA, where he becomes a regular vocalist on the San Francisco Bay, CA bar circuit. Concert promoter Bill Graham spots his potential and becomes his manager, now negotiating a recording deal with CBS/Columbia.

1978

May His mostly self-penned rock debut, ***Eddie Money***, produced by Bruce Botnick, reaches US #37, and will initially sell over a million copies to earn a platinum disc after almost a year on the chart, boosted by the extracted *Baby Hold On*, which reaches US #11. Following this success, Money begins touring the US tour as support act to the Rolling Stones, Ted Nugent, and Cheap Trick, before embarking on a headlining jaunt of his own.
Sept *Two Tickets To Paradise*, also from the album, reaches US #22.

1979

Jan His revival of the Miracles' *You've Really Got A Hold On Me* peaks at US #72.
Feb Money performs at The Venue, London, during a brief UK visit.
Mar *Maybe I'm A Fool* reaches US #22 taken from his sophomore set, the Bruce Botnick-produced ***Life For The Taking***, which climbs to US #17 and earns a platinum disc for a million sales.
June *Can't Keep A Good Man Down*, also from ***Life For The Taking***, peaks at US #63.
Sept Money records *Get A Move On* for the film soundtrack to "Americathon", which makes US #46.

1980

Sept *Runnin' Back* peaks at US #78, the first single from his third album ***Playing For Keeps***, which makes US #35 and confirms the formula from which Money will rarely deviate, namely hook-filled pop/rock songs aimed squarely at US AOR radio.
Nov His duet with Valerie Carter on *Let's Be Lovers Again* peaks at US #65.

1982

Sept Money returns to the US chart after a two-year absence with *Think I'm In Love*, which reaches #16, trailering his forthcoming album.
[3-5] Money plays at the three-day "US Festival", financed by Apple Computers founder Steven Wozniak, in San Bernardino, CA, with Jackson Browne, the Cars, Fleetwood Mac, the Grateful Dead, Police, Santana, Talking Heads and many others.
Oct ***No Control***, produced by Tom Dowd, reaches US #20 and earns a gold disc.
Nov [13] Taken from the album, *Shakin'* peaks at US #63.

1984

Jan After its parent album ***Where's The Party?*** has made US #67 the previous December, *The Big Crash* peaks at US #54.
Mar Also from ***Where's The Party?***, *Club Michelle* stops at US #66.

1986

Nov [15] Following another lengthy recording hiatus, during which he battles to overcome a drug problem, Money returns with his biggest-selling single, as the Leeson & Vale-penned *Take Me Home Tonight* hits US #4. It features guest vocalist Ronnie Spector, singing the opening line of *Be My Baby*, her 1963 million seller with the Ronettes.
Dec ***Can't Hold Back***, co-produced by the artist with Richie Zito and including the top five single, reaches US #20.

1987

Mar [14] Radio-ready *I Wanna Go Back*, taken from ***Can't Hold Back***, makes US #14.
June [27] *Endless Nights* reaches US #21.
Aug [11] The RIAA certifies platinum sales of ***Can't Hold Back*** and ***No Control***.
Sept [26] *We Should Be Sleeping* peaks at US #90.

1988

Oct [6] Money guests on NBC-TV's "Late Night With David Letterman".
Dec [24] *Walk On Water*, written by John Harms, hits US #9, taken from ***Nothing To Lose***, again co-produced with Zito, which makes US #49.

1989

Mar [18] *The Love In Your Eyes* reaches US #24.
May [13] *Let Me In* peaks at US #60.
July [6] The RIAA certifies two million sales of ***Eddie Money***.

1990

Feb [10] *Peace In Our Time*, written by UK hit writers Andy Hill and Pete Sinfield, reaches US #11, as the hits collection ***Greatest Hits ... Sound Of Money*** makes US #53.
Oct [31] ***Greatest Hits ... Sound Of Money*** is certified gold by the RIAA.
Dec [28] Money plays a year-end sellout show at the Luther Burbank Center For The Arts, Santa Rosa, CA.

1991

Oct [12] His treatment of Romeo Daughter's *Heaven In The Back Seat* makes US #58.
Dec [27] Money plays before sellout crowd of 1,361 at the Symphony Hall, San Diego, CA.

1992

Jan [7] He guests on NBC-TV's "The Tonight Show".
Feb [8] ***Right Here*** peaks at US #160.
Mar [7] *I'll Get By* reaches US #21.
[29] During his current US tour, Money plays a sellout show at the Eastbrook Theatre, Grand Rapids, MI.
Apr [8] Money guests on "Late Night With David Letterman".
[25] He participates in an all-star concert at Irvine Meadows Amphitheatre, Laguna Hills, CA, to benefit the Pediatric AIDS Foundation.
June [20] *Fall In Love Again* peaks at US #54.
Oct [24] On tour with the Greg Kihn Band, Money performs at the Palace Of Auburn Hills, Auburn Hills, MI.
Nov Acoustic EP, ***Unplug It In***, recorded at clubs in Houston, TX, and Austin, TX and, co-produced with Mony Byrom, will be issued the following year.

1993

Mar [8] Money performs at the 1993 Bay Area Music Awards at the Bill Graham Civic Auditorium, San Francisco.
Apr [3] He performs at The Boathouse, Norfolk, VA, during current US dates.

1994

Feb [7] Money presents the Favorite Pop/Rock Single trophy at the 21st annual American Music Awards.
June [24] Currently on a summer tour with REO Speedwagon and Foghat, Money performs at the Riverport Amphitheatre, Maryland Heights, MO.
Nov [14] ***Life For The Taking*** is certified platinum by the RIAA.

1995

Jan [4] Money conducts his first online chat, hosting a session on the Prodigy network.
[13] During current live dates, Money plays at The

Joint, Hard Rock Hotel, Las Vegas, NV.
Apr [22] Money performs at an Earth Day Celebration concert at the MDC Hatch Shell, Boston, MA.
May Newly signed to Bill Graham's reactivated Wolfgang label, Money releases ***Love And Money*** featuring a large host of guest musicians including Sheila E., Timothy B. Schmit and Robin Beck.
July [2] He embarks on a US summer tour in Fort Madison, IA, set to end on August 27th at the Merriweather Post Pavilion, Baltimore, MD.
Sept [14] During another round of shows, Money plays at the Tulane County Fair, Tulane, CA.

1996

May [17-18] Still touring annually, Money performs at the "Strawberry Fest" in Oxnard, CA, during selected US dates.

THE MONKEES

Davy Jones (vocals, guitar); **Mike Nesmith** (vocals, guitar); **Peter Tork** (vocals, keyboards, bass, guitar); **Mickey Dolenz** (vocals, drums)

1965

Writer/director/producer Bob Rafelson, who, while working as associate producer on NBC-TV's "The Wackiest Ship In The Army", thinks about a TV series based around a folk group and teams with Bert Schneider, son of the president of Columbia Pictures, to form Raybeat company in the US to produce, for Jackie Cooper, head of Screen Gems, a pilot episode of a sitcom based around a Beatles-type group using Richard Lester's film "A Hard Day's Night" as its framework.
Sept [9] An ad appears in the **Hollywood Reporter** (followed the next day by the same ad in **Daily Variety**): "Madness!! Folk & ROLL Musicians Singers for acting roles in new TV series. Running parts for 4 insane boys, age 17 to 21. Want spirited Ben Frank's types. Have courage to work. Must come down for interview. Call: HO 6-5188". 437 hopefuls are auditioned including Stephen Stills, who is allegedly turned down because of bad teeth, Paul Williams, Keith Allison, Jerry Yester and the future leader of Three Dog Night, Danny Hutton, who makes the last eight. (Reports that Charles Manson auditions are inaccurate. He is serving time at Terminal Island prison and will not be released until March 21st, 1967.)
Oct The four signed are Jones, Nesmith, Dolenz and Tork. Jones (b. Dec. 30, 1945, Manchester, Lancs.), ex-apprentice jockey and actor, has made his TV debut in the BBC play "June Evening"; starred as Ena Sharples' grandson Colin Lomax in the ITV show "Coronation Street" in 1961; in the first episode of "Z-Cars" in 1962; in both London and New York, NY productions of "Oliver" as the Artful Dodger (for which he received a Tony nomination) and "Pickwick" and had TV roles in "Ben Casey" and "Farmer's Daughter". He has also appeared as part of the "Oliver" cast on the CBS-TV "The Ed Sullivan Show" broadcast which sees the Beatles make their US TV debut. He is already a minor-teen sensation in the US, where he has made an album and hit US #93 with *What Are We Going To Do?* Nesmith (b. Robert Michael Nesmith, Dec. 30, 1942, Houston, TX), a member of Los Angeles, CA's folk circuit, has released singles for the Colpix label under the name Michael Blessing. Dolenz (b. George Michael Dolenz Jr., Mar. 8, 1945, Tarzana, Los Angeles), son of Hollywood character actor George Dolenz, and child star of NBC/ABC-TV show "Circus Boy", under the name Mickey Braddock playing the lead role Corky, and acted in "Peyton Place", "Route 66" and "Mr. Novak", has been a member of Micky & the One Nighters and the Missing Links and made an unsuccessful single. Tork (b. Peter Thorkelson, Feb. 13, 1944, Washington, DC), recommended to the producers by his friend Stephen Stills, has also drifted around the Los Angeles' folk circuit playing in the Au Go Go Singers with Richie Furay.
Nov [13] Filming begins on the pilot episode, its mixture of silent comedy and slow and fast motion film technique, a big success with a test audience of teenagers.

1966

Jan [17] NBC-TV buys "The Monkees" series, placing it in its 1966 fall schedule.
Mar As acting and grooming lessons begin, the group members are encouraged to record and write themselves, but their efforts are found wanting. Songwriters Tommy Boyce and Bobby Hart, who have already written *Last Train To Clarksville* and *The Monkees Theme*, are overlooked as musical producers for the show. UK producer Mickie Most passes, and attempts with Snuff Garrett and Goffin and King don't pan out.
Apr [3] Tork makes his solo debut at Los Angeles' Troubadour, on a bill headed by Muddy Waters.
May [31] "The Monkees" TV series begins filming.
July With the show due to start in September, Screen Gems music chief Don Kirshner takes over and appoints Boyce and Hart as producers, and, with Lester Sill, is responsible for moulding the Monkees' sound and musical persona. Gerry Goffin and Carole King, Neil Diamond, Barry Mann and Cynthia Weil and Neil Sedaka, all signed to Kirshner's Aldon Music company, are brought in to write songs.
Sept [1] The Monkees make a personal appearance at a Screen Gems press party in Los Angeles at the beginning of a ten-day promotional tour to launch the TV series.
[12] "The Monkees" TV show premieres on NBC-TV.
Oct [27] The RIAA certifies gold sales of the still-climbing *Last Train To Clarksville* and ***The Monkees***.
Nov [5] Despite a hesitant start for the series, the group's debut single, *Last Train To Clarksville*, with Louie Shelton's distinctive opening guitar line, hits US #1, providing the perfect counterpoint to the Beatles' "yeah yeah yeah" with "no no no".
[12] Their debut album, ***The Monkees***, released on Colgems, tops the US chart for the first of 13 weeks, selling 3,200,000 copies in three months.
[26] *I'm A Believer*, written by Neil Diamond, is released. With advance orders of 1,051,280 it will be confirmed gold by the RIAA two days later.
Dec [3] The Monkees make their live debut before a sellout crowd of 8,364 at the International Center Arena, Honolulu, HI, with fan response confirming Beatlemania-like success.
[26] The band begins a 12-date concert tour promoted by Dick Clark Productions at the Denver Coliseum, Denver, CO, set to end on January 22nd at the Cow Palace, San Francisco, CA.
[31] The group hits US #1 with Jeff Barry-produced *I'm A Believer*, recorded at the RCA Studios in New York, as "The Monkees" TV show premieres on BBC1-TV.

1967

Jan [6] Based on advance orders, ***More Of The Monkees*** is certified gold by the RIAA.
[14] *(I'm Not Your) Steppin' Stone* reaches US #20.
[21] *I'm A Believer* tops the UK chart where it will stay for four weeks, selling over 750,000 copies.
Feb [4] ***The Monkees*** also hits UK #1.
[6] Dolenz arrives in Britain.
[7] Nesmith arrives in the UK. He and Dolenz appear on BBC1-TV's "Top Of The Pops" and, during media interviews, announce that in future they will play on their own records and not use session men.
[11] ***More Of The Monkees***, released with advance orders of over 1.5 million, begins an 18-week stay at US #1, toppling ***The Monkees***, which lodges at #2 for a month.
[13] Jones arrives in Britain and visits his family in Manchester.
[25] *Last Train To Clarksville* belatedly reaches UK #23, while a successful US concert tour gives the group more confidence as musicians in a real band. Nesmith insists that the Monkees should be allowed to play on their own records with more of their own songs (at this point, James Burton, Glen Campbell, Leon Russell, David Gates, Jim Gordon and Hal Blaine are regular session players on their discs) and insists that either he or Don Kirshner goes. Schneider gives him backing and Kirshner resigns as chief executive of Screen Gems Music. During the month, a UK fan magazine, **Monkees Monthly**, is launched.
Mar [2] The Monkees' *Last Train To Clarksville*, nominated in the Best Contemporary Rock'n'Roll Group Performance and Best Contemporary Rock'n'Roll Recording categories, loses to the Mamas & the Papas' *Monday Monday* and the New Vaudeville Band's *Winchester Cathedral* respectively at the ninth annual Grammy Awards.
[8] *A Little Bit Me A Little Bit You* is certified gold by the RIAA.
[13] NARM honors the band as the Best Selling American Vocal Group with the Best Selling Album (***The Monkees***) and Top Single (*I'm A Believer*) at its annual convention.
[15] Kirshner files a $35.5-million lawsuit in New York against Screen Gems-Columbia for being fired without cause from his position as President of Colgems Records.
[25] Jones announces the formation of his record company, Davy Jones Presents. His first signing will be Vinnie Basile.
[30] Jones is featured on the BBC Home Service's "Pop Goes A Person" radio program with Paul Jones, Pete Murray, Alan Freeman and Simon Dee.
Apr [1-2] The band plays two dates in Canada, at the Arena, Winnipeg, MB, and Maple Leaf Gardens, Toronto, ON.
[5] Monkees fans walk from London's Marble Arch to the US Embassy in Grosvenor Square to protest Davy Jones' planned call-up.
[6] The group appears again on "Top Of The Pops".
[10] Tork plays a short acoustic set on Hootenanny Night at the Troubadour club in Los Angeles.
[22] In a "Most Popular Monkee" poll conducted in UK music paper **Disc & Music Echo**, Jones receives 63% of the votes, Dolenz 22%, Tork 8% and Nesmith 7%.
[29] Their treatment of another Neil Diamond composition, *A Little Bit Me, A Little Bit You*, hits US #2 (and becomes a third million-selling single) and UK #3.
May [13] ***More Of The Monkees*** tops the UK chart, unseating ***The Sound Of Music*** (which had dethroned ***The Monkees***).
[16] ***Headquarters***, their third consecutive album to sell over one million copies, is released. While Nesmith has brought in producer Chip Douglas, the group plays on the album supplemented by only three outsiders.
[23] Nesmith has his tonsils removed, causing the cancellation of a concert in San Jose, CA, on the 27th.
June [4] The Monkees win an Emmy Award for Outstanding Comedy Series 1966-67.
[9] The group plays at the Hollywood Bowl, Hollywood, CA.
[10] Jones is exempted from call-up because he is deemed responsible for supporting his father.
[24] ***Headquarters*** hits US #1 for one week, before being displaced by the Beatles' ***Sgt. Pepper***.
[30] They play the first of three sold-out concerts at the Empire Pool, Wembley, Middx.
July [7] The group appears again on "Top Of The Pops".
[8] The Monkees begin a 29-date US tour at the Sports Coliseum, Jacksonville, FL, with the Jimi Hendrix Experience as opening act (though they will quit the tour within two weeks.)
[14] The still-climbing *Pleasant Valley Sunday* is certified gold by the RIAA.
[29] *Alternate Title* hits UK #2. (Its original title *Randy Scouse Git* had been heard by Dolenz on the BBC1-TV show "Till Death Us Do Part".) ***Headquarters*** hits UK #2, kept from the top by the Beatles' ***Sgt. Pepper***.
Aug [2] A scheduled concert in Milwaukee, WI, is cancelled due to fan violence.
[4] After a performance in Minneapolis, MN, a fan stows away on the band's plane headed for St. Louis, MO. The girl's father threatens to bring charges for

transporting a minor across state lines.
[19] Sunny *Pleasant Valley Sunday* hits US #3.
Sept [2] *Pleasant Valley Sunday* reaches UK #11, as the B-side, *Words*, reaches US #11.
[11] The second season of "The Monkees" TV series begins on NBC-TV.
[30] The follow-up series starts on BBC-TV.
Oct [20] Jones opens his own Zilch boutique, in Greenwich Village, New York.
Nov [14] Still-rising *Daydream Believer* is certified gold by the RIAA.
[18-19] Nesmith assembles 58 of Los Angeles's top session men to give his songs a big band treatment and self-finances ***The Wichita Train Whistle Sings***, to the tune of $75,000, to be released on Dot Records.
Dec [2] ***Pisces, Aquarius, Capricorn & Jones Ltd.*** begins a five-week stay atop the UK chart as *Daydream Believer*, written by ex-Kingston Trio member John Stewart, hits US #1, where it will remain for four weeks. (Jones had trouble interpreting the lyrics, so engineer Hank Cicalo used a code to number different takes. Jones asks at the beginning of the record "What number is this?" to which everyone in the studio replies, "7a".) The band completes filming of the second television series with Tim Buckley and Frank Zappa making guest appearances.

1968

Jan [27] *Daydream Believer* hits UK #5.
Feb [9] Hal Cone, former manager and head of Davy Jones Records, against whom the singer had filed a $150,000 damages suit, is found guilty of grand theft, forgery, receiving stolen property and conspiracy.
[15] Shooting begins for the Monkees feature film "Head", directed by Bob Rafelson.
[17] ***Pisces, Aquarius, Capricorn & Jones Ltd.*** hits UK #5.
[26] Still-climbing *Valleri* is certified gold by the RIAA.
[29] The Monkees, nominated in two categories, lose to the 5th Dimension's *Up Up And Away* at the tenth annual Grammy Awards.
Mar [25] The 58th, and final, episode of their TV series is broadcast.
[30] *Valleri* becomes the band's sixth million-selling single, hitting US #3, as its B-side, *Tapioca Tundra*, makes US #34. The Monkees collect their tenth gold disc in 18 months.
Apr [20] *Valleri* reaches UK #12.
May [18] ***The Birds, The Bees And The Monkees***, on which each group member contributes individual tracks, hits US #3.
[21] The band performs a free concert in Salt Lake City, UT, to be filmed for live segments of "Head".
June The TV series (along with "Batman") is axed. *I'm A Believer* and *A Little Bit Me, A Little Bit You* receive awards from the BMI as the Most Performed BMI Songs of 1967.
July [6] The Monkees' revival of the Coasters' *D.W. Washburn* reaches US #19, as its B-side, *It's Nice To Be With You*, peaks at US #51.
[12] Dolenz and Samantha Juste, whom he met when she was working on "Top Of The Pops", are married at their Laurel Canyon home by Dolenz's stepfather.
[20] *D.W. Washburn* reaches UK #17.
Aug [10] Nesmith's ***The Wichita Train Whistle Sings*** peaks at US #160.
[19] "The Monkees" final TV episode airs on prime-time TV.
Sept [18] The group performs the first of seven concerts in Australia at the Festival Hall, Melbourne.
Oct [8] They play the last of five dates in Japan at the Festival Hall, Osaka, their last performance as a quartet.
[19] *Porpoise Song*, the theme song from "Head", peaks at US #62.
Nov [6] "Head" premieres in New York. Given a budget of $750,000 by Columbia Pictures, Rafelson, expected to deliver a standard teen flick, has instead, with Jack Nicholson, who has become part of the Monkees' clique, created a film about the manipulation of the Monkees, mixed in with a tribute to classic Hollywood movies. The resultant bizarre potpourri features a variety of guest appearances, from boxer Sonny Liston to Victor Mature as the Big Victor, representing capitalism. It includes scenes of the Monkees committing suicide by jumping from a bridge, and a concert intercut with Vietnam war atrocities. (It is a box-office disaster and will not be shown in Britain until March 1977.)
Dec [30] Tork quits, buying out his contract for $160,000 and, after years of conspicuous living, is left completely broke. The remaining members are also keen to call it a day, but are scared off by Tork's highly-priced contract buy-out. Tork forms a new group Release with Ripley Wildflower (bass and vocals) and girlfriend Reine Stewart (drums).

1969

Feb [5] The three-piece Monkees guest on CBS-TV's "The Glen Campbell Goodtime Hour".
[8] Soundtrack album, ***Head***, makes US #45.
[16] Jones guests on ABC-TV's "This Is Tom Jones", singing *Consider Yourself* from "Oliver!"
Mar [15] *Tear Drop City* peaks at US #56.
[26] *Tear Drop City* makes UK #46.
[29] The Monkees embark on a North American tour at the Coliseum, Vancouver, Canada.
Apr [12] ***Instant Replay*** makes US #32.
[14] NBC-TV special "33⅓ Revolutions Per Monkee", recorded in 1968 before Tork left the band, with Little Richard, Jerry Lee Lewis, Fats Domino, the Clara Ward Singers, Brian Auger, Buddy Miles and Julie Driscoll, airs. (The show will be broadcast on BBC2-TV on May 24th.)
May [17] *Someday Man* peaks at US #81.
June [16] The trio guests on NBC-TV's "The Tonight Show".
[21] A scheduled appearance at the 1969 "Forest Hills Music Festival" is cancelled due to poor ticket sales.
[25] *Someday Man* makes UK #47.
July [19] *Listen To The Band*, written by Nesmith, and using musicians who will become Area Code 615, peaks at US #63, as the group guests on ABC-TV's "Johnny Cash Show", singing *Everybody Loves A Nut* with the host.
[26] ***The Monkees Greatest Hits*** makes US #89.
Oct [6] The trio guest stars on NBC-TV's "Rowan & Martin's Laugh-In".
[18] *Good Clean Fun* peaks at US #82.
Nov [30] The group makes its last live appearance (for 15 years) at the Oakland-Alameda County Coliseum, Oakland, CA, before a crowd of 2,000. During the performance, Nesmith announces his plans to form a new group called the First National Band, while Dolenz and Jones state their intention to continue as the Monkees.
Dec [6] ***The Monkees Present*** makes US #100.

1970

Jan [3] Jones announces his intention to leave the Monkees.
Mar [1] Nesmith, his contractual obligations complete, quits the Monkees. He signs a solo deal with RCA Records, receiving a $20,000 advance, while Dolenz and Jones carry on recording ***Changes***, but it fails to sell. (The industry joke is that the next album will be by the Monkee.)
May The First National Band, comprising Nesmith, John London, John Ware and "Red" Rhodes, makes its debut at the Ice House in Pasadena, CA.
June [8] Dolenz opens in the play "Remains To Be Seen" at the Pleasant Run Theatre, near Chicago, IL, set to end on July 27th.
[13] *Oh My My* peaks at US #98 as Dolenz and Jones decide to end the Monkees.
Oct [3] Nesmith's solo, *Joanne*, reaches US #21 and his album, ***Magnetic South***, released via solo deal with RCA Records, peaks at US #143.

1971

Jan [9] Nesmith's *Silver Moon* makes US #42, while its parent album, ***Loose Salute***, peaks at US #159.
May [8] *Nevada Fighter*, also by Nesmith, peaks at US #70 taken from the non-charting ***Nevada Fighter***. He performs solo on "American Bandstand".
July [31] Jones, signed as a solo artist to Bell, makes US #52 with *Rainy Jane*, penned by Neil Sedaka for the Monkees in 1967, but never recorded.
Oct Dolenz, now working in TV and film, releases his first solo single, *O Someone*, on MGM.

1972

Feb ***Tantamount To Treason, Volume 1*** is issued by Michael Nesmith & the Second National Band.
Apr Dolenz guests stars on an episode of CBS-TV's "My Three Sons".
June Dolenz's second MGM single, *Unattended In The Dungeon*, is released, as Jones also signs to the label, releasing *Who Was It?*, shortly thereafter.
July Nesmith becomes president of his own Countryside label, signed to Elektra Records.
Aug Nesmith's solo, ***And The Hits Just Keep On Comin'***, is released.
Sept Bell issues ***Refocus***, a Monkees' greatest hits collection, to tie in with ABC-TV's Saturday morning re-runs of "The Monkees" TV series.
Oct Dolenz and writer/producer Michael Lloyd release *Johnny B Goode* as Starship, on Lion Records. The following October Dolenz will audition for the role of Fonzie in the forthcoming ABC-TV series "Happy Days" while in September 1974, **The Prison**, a book and an accompanying record, will be released on Nesmith's newly-formed Pacific Arts Corporation.

1975

Mar After McDonald's have offered a TV commercial, the group meets to discuss re-forming, though Tork, who has served four months in federal prison in the early '70s after being found guilty of possession of hashish, declines as he is a vegetarian. Nesmith, who has just finished his next solo project ***Pretty Much Your Standard Ranch Stash***, is only interested if a feature film is part of the package. Dolenz and Jones re-form the band with writers Tommy Boyce and Bobby Hart, and begin a two-year tour, "The Golden Great Hits Of The Monkees Show - The Guys Who Wrote 'Em And The Guys Who Sang 'Em".
July [4] Dolenz Jones Boyce & Hart make their live debut before a crowd of 12,500 at Six Flags Over Mid-America in St. Louis, MO. (Following the success of their appearance, they sign a deal with Capitol, which issues ***Dolenz, Jones, Boyce And Hart***.)

1976

July [4] Dolenz Jones Boyce & Hart are joined onstage at Disneyland in Anaheim, CA, by Tork, now working as a school teacher in Pacific Hills School, Santa Monica, CA.
Oct [2] ***The Monkees Greatest Hits***, a reissue of ***Refocus***, capitalizing on the group's reactivity, makes US #58.
Dec Dolenz, Jones and Tork record *Christmas Is My Time Of Year* with producer Chip Douglas, who releases the track on his own label.

1977

Apr [16] Nesmith's first UK success is with *Rio* at #28, in part due to the 1974 creation of his Pacific Arts Corporation, a video company which films a promo for the single. (Also releasing ***From A Radio Engine To A Photon Wing*** and next year's ***Live At The Palais***, he will subsequently produce films including "Elephant Parts", "Time Rider" and "Repo Man". The National Film Theatre in Britain imports a copy of "Head" to meet cult demand. It runs for a season at the Electric Cinema in Notting Hill, London.)
July Tork makes several well-received solo appearances at CBGB's in New York.

1979

Feb [23] After Dolenz and Jones have opened together in the stage version of Harry Nilsson's "The Point" at London's Mermaid Theatre on December 22nd the previous year, the show now closes, after which Dolenz decides to stay in Britain, to work as a freelance director in TV ("Metal Mickey") and stage

("Bugsy Malone"). (Nesmith's mother Bette sells her patent for Liquid Paper to the Gillette Corporation for $47 million. She will die in 1980, leaving Nesmith as her sole beneficiary.)
May [12] *Hey Ra Ra Ra, Happy Birthday Mickey Mouse*, by Davy Jones & A Million Kids, is released on Warner Bros. as the official theme song for the 50th birthday gala celebration of the legendary Disney character.
Aug [25] Nesmith's album, ***Infinite Rider On The Big Dogma***, peaks at US #151.

1980

Apr [19] Four-track EP, *The Monkees*, containing *I'm A Believer*, *Daydream Believer*, *Last Train To Clarksville* and *A Little Bit Me, A Little Bit You*, reaches UK #33. (During the year, Jones tours Japan after *Daydream Believer* is used in a Kodak commercial, and Monkeemania breaks loose once again in Japan. Meanwhile Nesmith releases ***Elephant Parts***.)

1981

Nov Retrospective, ***The Monkees***, makes UK #99. During the year, Tork tours Japan with his group the New Monks, after working as a waiter and telling the **National Enquirer** that he is a "professional has-been".

1986

Feb [22-23] To celebrate the 20th anniversary of the group, MTV airs "Pleasant Valley Sunday", a 22-hour broadcast of every "Monkees" TV episode.
Rhino Records US inadvertently creates the foundation for a Monkees revival, reissuing all of the band's albums along with much previously unavailable material. Dolenz, Jones and Tork re-form the group to begin a US summer tour, as ***The Monkees Greatest Hits*** re-charts to make US #69.
May [24] The Monkees begin a 145-date US leg of "The Monkees 20th Anniversary World Tour", with Gary Puckett & the Union Gap, Herman's Hermits and the Grass Roots, at the Concord Hotel, Kiamesha Lake, NY, set to end on December 3rd at the Stabler Arena, Bethlehem, PA.
June [22-23] MTV repeats "Pleasant Valley Sunday".
Aug Mini-Monkeemania explodes in the US again with the group occupying six positions on the album chart: ***The Monkees*** (#92), ***More Of The Monkees*** (#96), ***Headquarters*** (#121), ***Pisces, Aquarius, Capricorn & Jones Ltd.*** (#124), ***The Birds, The Bees And The Monkees*** (#145) and ***Changes*** (#152), featuring only Dolenz and Jones.
[1-3] "The Monkees Convention" is held in Philadelphia, PA.
[12] Auditions are held for the New Monkees. Jason Nesmith and Bobby Darin's son Dodd both fail to make the final four.
[30] New recording *That Was Then This Is Now* reaches US #20.
Sept [4] The Monkees receive the key to the city of Hollywood from honorary mayor Johnny Grant on "Monkee Day".
[7] During a performance at the Greek Theatre in Los Angeles, Nesmith joins the group on stage for *Pleasant Valley Sunday* and *Listen To The Band*.
[13] ***Then And Now ... The Best Of The Monkees*** continues the revival as it reaches US #21. Comprising all Monkees hits, it also includes three new songs by Tork and Dolenz.
[15] They perform live at the third annual MTV Video Music Awards broadcast simultaneously from the Universal Amphitheatre, Universal City, CA, and the Palladium, New York.
Oct [18] As the group plays in Atlanta, Mayor Andrew Young declares it "Monkees Day". *That Was Then This Is Now* peaks at UK #68.
Nov [8] Reissued *Daydream Believer* peaks at US #79.

1987

Jan [15] ***Then And Now ... The Best Of The Monkees*** is certified platinum by the RIAA.
Sept While Rhino releases two further albums of rare material, ***Missing Links*** and ***Live 1967***, a newly-recorded album, ***Pool It!***, produced by Roger Bechirian, makes US #72.
Oct [10] *Heart And Soul* peaks at US #87. (During their current US tour, music satirist "Weird" Al Yankovic appears onstage with the band, dressed in a wooly hat and sideburns.)

1989

Mar Following US cable web VH1 December airing of a "Monkees Week Marathon", broadcasting all "The Monkees" TV episodes. the group embarks on its first-ever UK tour.
Apr EP *The Monkees*, issued by Arista, peaks at UK #62, while a TV-advertised K-tel compilation, ***Hey Hey It's The Monkees - Greatest Hits***, reaches UK #12.
May [4] Columbia Pictures serves a court order on Jones, Dolenz and Tork to stop them using the name the Monkees.
July [9] During the Monkees summer tour, Nesmith joins them on stage, for a rare original line up performance.
[10] The group receives a star on the Hollywood Walk of Fame.
Sept After a poorly attended US tour, the band splits, vowing never to work together again.

1991

Nov [26] Rhino Records' (which will shortly issue a comprehensive 80-track, four-CD/cassette boxed set retrospective, ***Listen To The Band***, chronicling the group's career) off-shoot Kid Rhino releases ***Mickey Dolenz Puts You To Sleep***, a selection of classic pop songs revised as children's lullabies. Dolenz will embark on the "Rockin' Back To The '60s" US package tour the following year with the Chiffons, the Grass Roots, Gary Puckett, the Turtles, the Buckinghams and Cannibal & the Headhunters before having his **I'm A Believer : My Life Of Monkees, Music And Madness** published in August 1993. Jones, who commutes between his homes in England, Santa Barbara, CA, and Pennsylvania, has recently starred with Susannah York and David McCallum in BBC1-TV's "Trainer", having come in second at a Sandown race meeting in England, riding Gilded Chief, and will tour with the "Brady Bunch" stage show in 1992, while Nesmith's entire solo catalog is set for release by Awareness Records in Britain as he continues solo recording. Tork is composing songs for his first solo album, scheduled for release on Beachwood Records.
Dec [16] ***The Monkees Greatest Hits*** is certified platinum by the RIAA.

1994

Aug [17] With Nesmith having released his latest solo work, ***The Garden*** in June and Jones set to begin a national US tour in the part of Vince Fontaine in the "Grease" musical on September 27th, the RIAA certifies platinum sales of ***The Birds, The Bees And The Monkees*** and multi-platinum sales of ***Headquarters*** (two million), ***Pisces, Aquarius, Capricorn And Jones Ltd.*** (two million), ***The Monkees*** (five million) and ***More Of The Monkees*** (six million).

1995

June [29] At the end of a month which has seen the release of Tork's latest album ***Stranger Things Have Happened***, Dolenz, Jones, Tork and Ringo Starr feature in the premiere showing of a US TV Pizza Hut commercial. After Rhino has issued the legendary Monkees movie "Head" in January, a roll-out of all 58 original "The Monkees" television episodes also gets underway. The following February, 36 years after failing as to start a career as an apprentice jockey (a career lasting for three weeks when he was 14), Jones will finally win his first horse race at Britain's Lingfield Park riding Digpast in the one mile Ontario Amateur Riders' Handicap. The same month, the Monkees also announce plans to undertake a summer UK tour.

THE MOODY BLUES

Justin Hayward (guitar, vocals);
Mike Pinder (keyboards); **Ray Thomas** (flute, harmonica, vocals); **John Lodge** (bass, vocals);
Graeme Edge (drums)

1964

May [4] Denny Laine (b. Brian Hines, Oct. 29, 1944, Tyseley, Birmingham, Warks. during an air raid, though legend will also indicate birth in a boat off the coast of Jersey, Channel Islands) disbands Denny Laine & the Diplomats and forms a new group in Birmingham, Warks., comprising Thomas (b. Dec. 29, 1942, Stourport-on-Severn, Hereford) and Pinder (b. Dec. 27, 1941, Birmingham), who have been playing at the Top Ten club in Hamburg, West Germany for nearly a year with the Crewcats, and now both from local rock group El Riot & the Rebels, and Edge (b. Mar. 30, 1942, Rochester, Staffs.), from Gerry Levene & the Avengers and Clint Warwick (b. Clinton Eccles, June 25, 1940, Birmingham), from the Rainbows. They secure a residency at the Carlton Ballroom in Birmingham. The club owners get £2,000 from brewers Mitchell & Butler for publicity purposes, so the band, in deference to the brewers, adopts the name the MB Five. They soon decide that the M should stand for Moody and the B for Blues, becoming the Moody Blues Five. They sign with London manager Tony Secunda, who secures them a season of Monday nights at the Marquee, which in turn leads to a contract with Decca Records.
Aug The group performs its debut single, *Lose Your Money*, on ITV's "Ready Steady Go!".
Sept [11] The group plays at the Birmingham Town Hall, supporting Alexis Korner's Blues Incorporated.

1965

Jan [8] They begin a 24-date, twice-nightly UK tour, with Chuck Berry, at the Odeon Theatre, London, set to end on the 31st at the Regal Theatre, Edmonton, London.
[28] *Go Now*, their cover of Bessie Banks' US R&B hit, tops the UK chart. (New York, NY DJ B. Mitchell Reed had given the group a copy of the record on a visit to London.)
Mar *I Don't Want To Go On Without You*, their revival of a Drifters' B-side and competing with rival cover versions by the Searchers and the Escorts, makes UK #33.
[5] The group makes its first live broadcast on the BBC Radio's "Joe Loss Pop Show".
Apr [11] The Moody Blues take part in the annual "**New Musical Express** Poll Winners Concert" at the Empire Pool, Wembley, Middx., with the Beatles, the Rolling Stones, the Kinks, the Animals and many others.
[17] *Go Now* holds down the anchor position in a unique US Top 10 in which nine of the singles are from the UK.
May [24] The band appears at the "British Song Festival" at the Dome, Brighton, Sussex.
June [5] They guest on ITV's "Thank Your Lucky Stars".
[19] The Moody Blues make their US debut, with the Kinks, at the Academy of Music in New York.
July *From The Bottom Of My Heart* reaches UK #22 and US #93, while ***The Magnificent Moodies***, produced by Denny Cordell, is released.
Aug [6] They play on opening day of the fifth annual "National Jazz & Blues Festival" at the Richmond Athletic Ground, Richmond, Surrey.
Sept [6] The band signs a management contract with NEMS.
[21] The group participates in "Pop From Britain" concert at London's Royal Albert Hall, with Cliff Bennett & the Rebel Rousers, Georgie Fame & the Blue Flames and the Fourmost.
Nov *Everyday* makes UK #44.
Dec [3] The group embarks on a nine-date, twice-nightly tour supporting the Beatles during their last-ever UK concerts, beginning at Glasgow's Odeon, Scotland.

[19] The band appears on CBS-TV's "The Ed Sullivan Show".

1966

Apr *Stop!* spends one week on US Hot 100, at #98.
June Warwick leaves the group (and will quit the music business).
July [14] His replacement, Rod Clarke, from Les Garçons, plays his first date with the group at the Locarno, Coventry, Warks.
Aug [6] The group begins a nine-day tour of Denmark.
Oct [12] The band splits, after its only release of the year *Boulevard De La Madelaine* fails to chart and Laine leaves to sign a solo deal with Deram, before joining ex-Move member Trevor Burton in the band Balls (and Paul McCartney's Wings in 1973).
Nov After the quickest reunion in rock'n'roll history, Pinder, Thomas and Edge recruit two new members. John Lodge (b. July 20, 1945, Birmingham), has been in El Riot & the Rebels with Thomas and Pinder, before playing with the Carpetbaggers, the John Bull Breed and the Falcons. Justin Hayward (b. David Justin Hayward, Oct. 14, 1946, Swindon, Wilts.), who after leaving school, spent six months as a trainee salesman with a building firm, before working in a theatrical repertory company and joining the Offbeats theatre ensemble in Jersey. He then joined Marty Wilde's Wildecats for two days, before forming a trio with Marty and his wife. They worked in cabaret before Hayward went solo, signing with Pye A&R chief Alan Freeman and manager Lonnie Donegan. Hayward, also with releases on Parlophone and Decca, has written to Eric Burdon who is forming the New Animals. Burdon, already with his band signed up, passes his name on to Thomas who asks him to join as lead guitarist and vocalist. The new line-up moves to Belgium, to avoid the UK taxman.

1967

Apr [14] Laine releases his first solo single, *Say You Don't Mind* (subsequently a hit for Colin Blunstone).

1968

Jan Hayward-penned *Nights In White Satin* reaches UK #19. It is taken from their first LP ***Days Of Future Passed***, a concept album based around a theme of different times of the day and night, which makes UK #27. The London Festival Orchestra, a group of session musicians conducted by Peter Knight, also plays a major part, though its orchestrated passages are edited between and around the Moody Blues tracks so the orchestra does not actually accompany the group. (The original idea, abandoned early on, was for band and orchestra to record Dvorak's "New World Symphony" together as a stereo sampler for Decca sales reps.) The album is also the start of a long-term relationship between the Moody Blues and producer Tony Clarke.
May [4] ***Days Of Future Passed*** enters the US chart set to reach #27, earning the group its first gold disc, during a 102-week chart run.
June [29] The band makes a rare concert appearance in London, at the Queen Elizabeth Hall.
Aug *Voices In The Sky* reaches UK #27, as its parent album, ***In Search Of The Lost Chord***, another concept album, hits UK #5.
Sept *Tuesday Afternoon*, taken from ***Days Of Future Passed***, makes US #24, while ***In Search Of The Lost Chord*** makes US #23 and earns a second gold disc.
Nov *Ride My See Saw*, extracted from ***In Search Of The Lost Chord***, peaks at US #61.
[29-30] The group, whose performances are now highlighted by the harmonic vocal exchange between Lodge and Hayward, plays the Shrine Auditorium, Los Angeles, CA, during a current US tour.
Dec *Ride My See Saw* makes UK #42. Its B-side is the little heard *A Simple Game* (later a UK #3 for the Four Tops with Clarke producing).

1969

Mar [7] The band performs at the "Grand Gala Du Disque", Amsterdam, Holland.
Apr [22] They guest on ITV's "Pop Scotch".
May [10] ***On The Threshold Of A Dream*** tops the UK chart for the first of two weeks and reaches US #20 during a 136-week chart run, their third gold disc.
July *Never Comes The Day* peaks at US #91.
Aug [30] The group plays on the opening day of the "Isle Of Wight Festival" at Woodside Bay, near Ryde, Isle of Wight.
Oct *Watching And Waiting* is the first single release on the band's own Threshold label.
Dec ***To Our Children's Children*** hits UK #2. The band moves to Cobham, Surrey, and opens a chain of Threshold record stores.
[12] The group performs at London's Royal Albert Hall, during a UK tour. The concert is recorded (and released as part of ***Caught Live + 5*** in June 1977).

1970

Jan ***To Our Children's Children*** reaches US #14 and is the group's fourth gold album.
May Hayward, needing to finish a song in his Barnes, London flat before new recording sessions, has joined two different compositions, one fast and philosophical, the other a love ballad, both in the key of C, which has resulted in the dramatic pairing released as *Question*, the group's first release on its own Threshold label, which hits UK #2, kept off the top by the England World Cup Squad's *Back Home*.
June *Question* reaches US #21.
July [22] ***To Our Children's Children*** is certified as the group's fourth gold album by the RIAA.
Aug [22] ***A Question Of Balance***, written and recorded in five weeks, hits UK #1 for the first of three weeks.
[30] The band plays on the final day of the "Isle Of Wight Festival" at the East Afton Farm, Godshill, Isle of Wight.
Sept ***A Question Of Balance*** hits US #3.
Oct [30] The Moody Blues perform at London's Royal Festival Hall.
Dec [3] The group embarks on a US tour, making its Carnegie Hall, New York debut on the 14th.
[9] ***In Search Of The Lost Chord*** is certified gold by the RIAA.

1971

Aug [14] ***Every Good Boy Deserves Favour***, named after the lines on a treble stave, tops the UK chart.
Sept *The Story In Your Eyes* reaches US #23 (the UK equivalent is withdrawn, at the band's request), while its parent album, ***Every Good Boy Deserves Favour***, hits US #2.
[10] ***Every Good Boy Deserves Favour*** is confirmed gold by the RIAA.
Oct During a US visit, the band is presented with the relevant sixth gold disc. Given the choice by the record company to select the presenter of the award, they decide on actor Jay Silverheels (Tonto in "The Lone Ranger" TV series).

1972

June Lodge-penned dreamy ballad, *Isn't Life Strange*, reaches UK #13 and US #29.
Nov Re-issued *Nights In White Satin* hits US #2, passing a million sales, as its parent album, ***Days Of Future Passed***, finally hits its US peak of #3, while the group tours North America, including sellout dates at the Great Western Forum, Inglewood, CA, and Long Beach Arena, Long Beach, CA. ***Seventh Sojourn*** hits UK #5.
Dec [9] ***Seventh Sojourn*** tops the US chart for five weeks having been confirmed gold on November 21st.
[18] *Nights In White Satin* is certified gold by the RIAA for one million sales.

1973

Jan *Nights In White Satin* hits UK #9, ten places higher than its previous appearance five years earlier.
Feb *I'm Just A Singer (In A Rock'n'Roll Band)* makes UK #36. (This will be their last new release until 1978.)
Mar *I'm Just A Singer (In A Rock'n'Roll Band)* reaches US #12.
Oct [25] The group embarks on a 13-date US tour at the Civic Center, Pittsburgh, PA, set to end on November 8th at the University of Michigan, Ann Arbor, MI.

1974

Feb The band ends a nine-month world trek in the US, during which it has used its own 707 touring plane.
June Hayward and Lodge start recording at the Moody Blues' new, as yet unopened, studio backed by three-piece Idaho group Providence.
July [17] The Moody Blues open their own studio, the first quadrophonic facility in the world, in West Hampstead, London.
Nov Double compilation album, ***This Is The Moody Blues***, reaches UK #14 and US #11.
Dec [2] ***This Is The Moody Blues*** is certified gold by the RIAA.

1975

Mar [10] Hayward and Lodge's ***Blue Jays*** is launched in the US at a listening party in New York's Carnegie Hall and will hit UK #4 and US #16.
Apr Pinder releases his solo debut ***The Promise***.
Aug Thomas' solo album, ***From Mighty Oaks***, makes UK #23 and US #68.
Oct Hayward and Lodge's *Blue Guitar*, co-produced by 10cc, hits UK #8 while the Graeme Edge Band featuring Adrian Gurvitz makes US #107 with ***Kick Off Your Muddy Boots***.

1977

Feb After Thomas' sophomore effort, ***Hope Wishes And Dreams***, has peaked at US #147 the previous August, Lodge's solo, ***Natural Avenue***, reaches UK #38 (and will stop at US #121 in May).
Mar Hayward's ***Songwriter*** makes UK #28 and US #37.
Apr The group closes down its Threshold label.
June Double album ***Caught Live + 5***, featuring three sides of the December 1969 Royal Albert Hall concert and a fourth side of unreleased studio recordings from the late '60s, reaches US #26, and is the group's first album not to reach gold certification.
July A second Graeme Edge Band album, ***Paradise Ballroom***, peaks at US #164.

1978

June Having reunited for their first new recording in six years, the Moody Blues release ***Octave***, with Decca organizing a celebratory garden party at which the band receives 42 platinum and five gold discs from label boss Sir Edward Lewis. Recorded at the Record Plant in Los Angeles, the sessions have been partly produced by Clarke (who has effectively been the sixth Moody Blue for over a decade and closely identified with the development of the group's symphonic sound) who has left midway through the project. ***Octave*** is also notable as the last recording with Pinder in the lineup.
July ***Octave*** hits UK #6 and reaches US #13. Pinder's replacement is Patrick Moraz (b. June 24, 1948, Morges, Switzerland), ex-Mainhorse, Refugee and Yes keyboardist. Hayward's solo, *Forever Autumn*, extracted from Jeff Wayne's concept album, ***War Of The Worlds***, hits UK #5.
Aug *Steppin' In A Slide Zone*, written by Lodge, makes US #39.
Oct The group begins its first live appearances in four years, for a sellout world tour. *Driftwood* peaks at US #59.
Nov [14] They appear on ITV's "Get It Together".

1979

Jan [26] ***Octave*** is certified platinum by the RIAA.
Dec *Nights In White Satin* is re-issued a second time, making UK #14, while the TV-promoted K-tel compilation, ***Out Of This World***, reaches UK #15.

1980

July Following rumors that he is to star in a movie version of "Gulliver's Travels" written by Larry Gelbart with music by Lionel Bart, Hayward's second solo album, ***Night Flight***, produced by Jeff Wayne, reaches UK #41 and US #166.

1981

May ***Long Distance Voyager***, on Threshold, hits UK #7.

July [25] ***Long Distance Voyager*** tops the US chart for the first of three weeks.

Aug *Gemini Dream*, written by Lodge about the experience of performing as a Moody Blue and taken from ***Long Distance Voyager***, reaches US #12.

[18] ***Long Distance Voyager*** is certified platinum by the RIAA.

Oct *The Voice* reaches US #15.

Dec *Talking Out Of Turn* peaks at US #65. (By year's end the band's 11-date sixth US tour will have grossed $571,000.)

1983

Sept *Blue World* makes UK #35, as its parent album, ***The Present***, reaches UK #15 and US #26.

Oct *Sitting At The Wheel* reaches US #27.

Dec *Blue World* peaks at US #62.

1985

Mar [13] The Moody Blues are presented with the award for Outstanding Contribution To British Music at the 30th annual Ivor Novello Awards lunch, at London's Grosvenor House Hotel.

Apr Retrospective album, ***Voices In The Sky/The Best Of The Moody Blues***, featuring the group's hits from 1967-83, reaches US #132.

Oct Hayward's third solo album, ***Moving Mountains***, on Towerbell Records, reaches UK #78.

1986

May Newly signed to Polydor Records, the group's ***The Other Side Of Life*** makes UK #24 and hits US #9.

June [19] The Moody Blues open a major US tour at Chastain Park, Atlanta, GA, set to end on October 7th.

July [12] *Your Wildest Dreams* hits US #9.

Sept [2] Hayward is hospitalized having collapsed from exhaustion after a concert in Los Angeles.

[20] *The Other Side Of Life*, its video clip lensed in London's Soho, peaks at US #58. (Hayward's *It Won't Be Easy* theme to the BBC-TV series "Starcops" will be released the following July.)

1988

July ***Sur La Mer*** reaches US #38, having made UK #21.

Aug *I Know You're Out There Somewhere* makes US #30 and UK #52.

1989

Oct Hayward has linked with producer/arranger Mike Batt to record the UK #47 album, ***Classic Blue***, with the London Philharmonic Orchestra, released by the UK-only Trax Records.

1990

Feb [3] Threshold retrospective, ***Greatest Hits***, peaks at US #113.

May [22] ***Days Of Future Passed*** is certified platinum by the RIAA.

July [21] The Moody Blues close the "Goodwill Games" in Seattle, WA, at the end of a 33-city US tour.

Aug [2] The group tapes a show at the Garden State Arts Center, Holmdel, NJ for the "SRO" TV series.

1991

June [4] Hayward participates in a Mike Batt-conducted Royal Philharmonic Pops Orchestra concert at London's Barbican Theatre, with proceeds going to the Save The Children fund.

[9] The group sings the national anthem before the "World Bowl '91" at Wembley Stadium between the London Monarchs and the Barcelona Dragons.

July [13] ***Keys Of The Kingdom*** debuts at its UK #54 peak.

[13] ***Keys Of The Kingdom*** bows at its US #94 peak.

Aug [3] The group plays a sellout show at the Jones Beach Theatre, Wantagh, NY, during a US tour delayed by two weeks because Lodge has flu. Additional musicians Bias Boshell and Paul Bliss currently augment the band's live line-up.

Sept Moraz files a $500,000 lawsuit against the band and Threshold Records seeking compensation for breach of verbal contract, claiming that he was unfairly excluded from their current tour.

Nov [5] The Moodies embark on seven-date UK tour at the City Hall, Newcastle-upon-Tyne, Tyne & Wear, set to end on the 13th at the National Exhibition Centre, Birmingham.

Dec [10-11] The group, having delayed its US tour by two weeks because Lodge has 'flu, plays before two sellout crowds totalling 9,334 at the "WNEW-FM Christmas Concert" at The Paramount, New York.

1992

May [22] On another US trek, sharing the bill with Chicago, the Moody Blues perform at the Blockbuster Pavilion, Charlotte, NC.

Sept [9-10] They play two sellout shows at the Red Rocks Amphitheatre, Denver, CO, accompanied by the Colorado Symphony Orchestra. (These shows will constitute their forthcoming 1993 live album.)

Nov [6] The group, currently in litigation against Decca Records, reportedly attempting to secure the rights to their back catalog, embarks on a 12-date Canadian leg of the tour at the Massey Hall, Toronto, ON, set to end on the 19th at the Orpheum Theatre, Vancouver, BC. The 12 dates will gross in excess of CAN $700,000.

1993

Apr [3] ***Live At Red Rocks***, recorded in Denver, CO, the previous September, makes US #93.

Nov [10] The RIAA certifies platinum sales of ***The Other Side Of Life*** and ***The Story of The Moody Blues ... Legend Of A Band***.

Dec [17] The group performs at Wembley Arena, during a four-date UK tour.

1994

Mar [17] During another US visit, the Moody Blues play a sellout date at the Coliseum, Greensboro, NC. (During a show in Wallingford, CT, Hayward experiences hearing loss, and on leaving the stage discovers a large Japanese beetle is his ear.)

Apr [20] Their "One Night At Red Rock" video is certified gold by the RIAA.

June [24] The Moody Blues perform with the Long Island Philharmonic Orchestra at the Jones Beach Theatre, Wantagh, NY, during another summer tour of the US. (Many of the shows will be performed with the local symphony orchestra.)

Sept [8] A further US mini-tour opens at the Red Rocks Amphitheatre, Denver, CO, set to end on October 8th at Port St. Lucie, FL.

[27] The Moody Blues are inducted into Hollywood's Rock Walk.

Oct ***Time Traveller***, an 80-track boxed set retrospective including a fifth bonus disc ***Encore - Live At Red Rocks***, is released.

Nov [17] ***A Question Of Balance*** is certified platinum by the RIAA for one million US sales.

[18] ***On The Threshold Of A Dream*** is also confirmed platinum by the RIAA, for one million sales.

1995

Feb [20] The group guests on NBC-TV's "The Tonight Show", as the US One Step label releases Mike Pinder's ***Among The Stars*** - only his second album in 18 years following the 1993 issue of ***Off The Shelf***.

Nov [13] The Moody Blues take part in 92.3 KROCK's "Hungerthon '95" at the Beacon Theatre, New York.

1996

May [17] The Moody Blues begin a North American summer tour at the Nat Bailey Stadium, Vancouver.

GARY MOORE

1968

Moore (b. Apr. 4, 1952, Belfast, Northern Ireland), already proficient on his Les Paul guitar, having played in his school group Granny's Intentions, forms his first professional band, the blues/rock outfit Skid Row, in Belfast with ex-school mate Noel Bridgeman (drums), Phil Lynott (vocals) and Brendan Shields (bass), which, reduced to a three-piece following Lynott's departure to start Thin Lizzy the following year, relocates to London in 1970, recording the first of two albums for CBS, ***Skid Row***, followed by ***34 Hours*** in 1971. Quitting the band the same year, Moore briefly links with folk/rock outfit Dr. Strangely Strange before forming his own Gary Moore Band in 1973, showcasing his considerable guitar virtuosity on its debut release ***Grinding Stone***.

1974

Jan Lynott recruits Moore as the temporary replacement in Thin Lizzy for departed guitarist Eric Bell, his engagement initially lasting four months. (Moore will then spend the next 18 months as an increasingly in-demand session guitarist, before joining Jon Hiseman's reincarnated jazz/rock combo Colosseum II in 1975, with whom he will record ***Strange New Flesh***, and ***Electric Savage*** (1976).)

1977

Jan Moore temporarily rejoins Thin Lizzy for a ten-week US tour, now deputizing for Brian Robertson who has injured his hand following a brawl at London's Speakeasy club.

May Moore returns to Colosseum II, to record its final album, ***Wardance***.

1978

Aug With Robertson having left Thin Lizzy, Moore joins full time, contributing to the band's ***Black Rose*** album released the following year, while simultaneously completing his first solo project.

1979

Feb [3] His freshman set, ***Back On The Streets***, released on MCA Records, makes UK #70.

May The extracted rock-ballad, *Parisienne Walkways*, weaving Moore's soaring guitar around guest vocals by Lynott, hits UK #8.

July [17] At the instigation of Lizzy's management, Moore and Thin Lizzy part company for the last time, midway through a US tour. Moore goes on to Los Angeles, CA, where he forms the hard-rock outfit G-Force with Willie Dee (bass), Tony Newton (vocals) and Mark Nausseef.

1980

Sept Signed to Jet Records, the band's only album, ***G-Force***, is released, including the excerpted singles *You* and *White Knuckles*, supported by a small-venue west-coast US tour. The following year Moore will play briefly with the Greg Lake Band.

1982

Oct Newly signed to Virgin Records, Moore finally begins his solo career in earnest, releasing ***Corridors Of Power*** featuring the backing unit of keyboardist Tommy Eyre, bassist Neil Murray, drummer Ian Paice and vocalist Charlie Huhn, which reaches UK #30 (and will climb to US #149 the following May).

1984

Jan *Hold On To Love*, featuring his own vocal, makes UK #65.

Mar Moved to Virgin imprint 10 Records, his third

solo venture, ***Victims Of The Future***, continuing his melodic hard-rock inclination, peaks at UK #12 and US #172.
Aug The extracted *Empty Rooms* initially reaches UK #51.
Oct Live set, ***We Want Moore!***, peaks at UK #32.

1985

June A second duet with Lynott, *Out In The Fields*, hits UK #5.
Aug Reissued *Empty Rooms* now makes UK #23.
Oct ***Run For Cover***, featuring Paul Thompson, ex-Deep Purple Glenn Hughes and drummer Ted McKenna, stops at UK #12 (and will move to US #146 the following April, released on the Mirage label). Its follow-up set ***Rockin' Every Night*** will roll to UK #99 for one week on July [12] the following year, with the extracted *Over The Hills And Far Away* peaking at UK #20 in December.

1987

Mar ***Wild Frontier*** becomes Moore's biggest success of the decade, hitting UK #8 (and US #139 in June), yielding the UK #35 *Wild Frontier*, *Friday On My Mind* (UK #26 in May) and *The Loner* (UK #53 in September).
Dec [5] Double EP, *Take A Little Time* (including *Out In The Fields*), peaks at UK #75.

1989

Mar Celtic-tinged ***After The War***, including musical guests Ozzy Osbourne and Sisters of Mercy, reaches UK #23 and US #114, its title cut *After The War* also making UK #37.

1990

Apr [7] Rejecting hard rock for the first time and finally finding his most popular niche, Moore's blues guitar-drenched ***Still Got The Blues***, co-produced with Ian Taylor and featuring Albert Collins and Albert King, enters the UK chart. Eventually hitting UK #13 and US #83 (on Feb [16], 1991), it will sell over three million copies worldwide, going platinum in Germany, Sweden, Holland, Japan, Australia and gold in the UK and US. (It includes his UK #48, *Oh Pretty Woman*, with King guesting.)
May *Still Got The Blues (For You)* peaks at UK #31.
Dec [15] Further excerpt, *Too Tired*, makes UK #71 for one week.

1991

Feb [5] Moore guests on NBC-TV's "Late Night With David Letterman".
[16] *Still Got The Blues* peaks at US #97.
Sept Moore begins recording a follow-up album in the US and Paris, France, once again with co-producer Taylor.

1992

Feb [29] *Cold Day In Hell*, previewing the new set, reaches UK #24.
Mar [21] ***After Hours,*** a second blues outing but now heading in a soul direction and featuring the Memphis Horns, B.B. King (duetting on *Since I Met You Baby*) and Albert Collins, debuts at its UK #4 peak.
[28] ***After Hours*** debuts at its US #145 peak.
May [16] *Story Of The Blues* makes UK #40.
[20] Moore performs one of only two US dates this year (the other set in New York, NY in seven days time) at the Universal Amphitheatre, Universal City, CA, with his backing Midnight Blues Band, grossing $127,700.
June [7-8] He plays his first UK dates since August 1990 at London's Hammersmith Odeon.
[28] Moore returns to the same venue to perform on "National Music Day" with Mick Jagger, Charlie Watts, Pop Staples and Ronnie Wood.
July [25] *Since I Met You Baby*, with B. B. King, peaks at UK #59.
Oct [4-5] Moore plays a pair of dates at London's Royal Albert Hall.
[24] *Separate Ways* charts for a week at UK #59.

1993

May [8] The Paul Rodgers-assembled ***Tribute To Muddy Waters*** album, with fret work from Moore, makes US #91.
[15] Revised version *Parisienne Walkways '93* reaches UK #32.
[22] Virgin-released live-performance set, ***Blues Alive***, bows at its UK #8 peak.

1994

June Moore has joined Ginger Baker and Jack Bruce in BBM for the album ***Around The Next Dream***, now released by Virgin.
Nov [26] Compilation set, ***Ballads And Blues 1982-1994***, makes UK #33 in its week of entry.

1995

Apr [27] Moore previews tracks from his new album at London's Shepherd's Bush Empire, with ex-Fleetwood Mac co-founder Peter Green making a rare public appearance at the end of the set.
June [10] A tribute to Green, ***Blues For Greeney*** reaches UK #14 in its week of entry.
[17] Extracted *Need Your Love So Bad* debuts at its UK #48 peak, during a two-week chart stay.
Nov [16] ***Still Got The Blues*** is certified gold by the RIAA.
see also: **THIN LIZZY**

ALANIS MORISSETTE

1990

Morissette (b. June 1, 1974, Ottawa, ON, Canada), whose family has moved to West Germany when she was three years old (her parents teaching the children of military personnel), before returning to Canada when she was six, has written her first tunes at the age of nine, having begun playing the piano three years earlier. Just one year later in 1984, she has taken an acting part in the Nickelodeon US cable network show "You Can't Do That On Television", a role which leads to her appearing in a movie playing a singer called Alanis (opposite future "Friends" TV star Matt LeBlanc as her boyfriend). With money saved from her acting work, Morissette has recorded her first single at the age of 11 with keyboardist Lindsay Morgan and guitarist Rich Dodson (of Canadian band the Stampeders) - 2,000 copies of the resulting *Fate Stay With Me* are released on her own Lamor label (established by her parents), subsequently gaining the attention of MCA Publishing in Toronto, ON, Canada which signs her to a song-publishing agreement at the age of 14, which in turn lands her a recording deal with MCA Records (Canada). Her debut album is now released, the dance-based ***Alanis*** which will sell over 100,000 copies in her home country and win her a domestic Juno Award as Canada's Most Promising Female Artist. Her live dates to promote the album will include an opening slot for white rap novelty act Vanilla Ice. Moving to Toronto in 1991 after graduating from high school and linking with new manager Scott Welch, her maiden effort will be followed by the Paula Abdul-esque, pop/soul-based ***Now Is The Time*** in 1992 which will sell 50,000 domestic copies. (Following her future success in the alternative music genre, Morissette will ensure that MCA is prevented from reissuing her markedly different MCA projects.)

1994

Feb Having moved to Los Angeles, CA the previous year, when she secured an acting role opposite Corey Haim in Fox-TV's short-lived sitcom "Just One Of The Girls", Morissette, earnestly set on a new direction as a serious singer-songwriter, though currently without a new label deal, now teams with successful rock/pop producer Glen Ballard to whom she has been introduced through a song-publishing contact. Together, they write and record an album's worth of material at his home studio in San Fernando Valley, CA, which they shop to major record labels, who are universally disinterested in the project. However, following a 15-minute meeting with 21-year old Guy Oseary, an A&R scout for the Madonna-owned Maverick label, a deal is forthcoming within days.

1995

June [13] Her critically-acclaimed label debut, ***Jagged Little Pill*** is released by Maverick in the US, revealing a frank, rebellious and impulsive songwriting and performing style which will immediately connect with Generation X-ers. During the month Morissette performs her first live appearance in the UK at a showcase for the new album held at London's Hanover Grand.
Aug [19] The album's first single *You Oughta Know* featuring the Red Hot Chili Peppers' Flea and Dave Navarro, and already climbing the US chart, reaches UK #22.
Sept [9] During US tour dates, she performs at the Blossom Music Center, Cuyahoga Falls, OH, on a bill grossing $73,760 from a 10,890 crowd. Her live band comprises Jesse Tobias (guitar), Nick Lashley (guitar), Taylor Hawkins (drums) and Chris Chaney (bass).
[17-18] She appears on consecutive nights at the John Anson Ford Theatre, Hollywood, CA.
Oct [7] ***Jagged Little Pill*** tops the US chart, making Morissette the first Canadian female artist to achieve a #1 album in the States.
[28] Morissette is the music guest on NBC-TV's "Saturday Night Live" the same day that *Hand In My Pocket* debuts at its UK #26 peak.
Nov [16] The RIAA certifies four million sales of ***Jagged Little Pill.***
[26] Further US tour dates include tonight's gig at the Egyptian Room, Murat Centre, Indianapolis, IN.
Dec [13] She opens for David Bowie at "The Greatest Music Party In The World" held at the National Exhibition Centre, Birmingham, West Midlands.

1996

Feb [19] Morissette sings *Hand In My Pocket* at the 15th annual BRIT Awards, held at London's Earl's Court Exhibition Centre.
[27] The RIAA now certifies ***Jagged Little Pill*** for six million US sales.
[28] She performs a stripped-down version of *You Oughta Know*, with its notoriously included f-word edited out in a seven-second delay by live broadcaster CBS-TV, at the 38th annual Grammy Awards held at Los Angeles' Shrine Auditorium, at which she also collects the Album Of The Year, Best Rock Album (***Jagged Little Pill***), Best Rock Song (with co-writer Ballard) and Best Female Rock Vocal (both for *You Oughta Know*) statuettes.
Mar [10] A leather-clad Morissette plays her current single *Ironic* at her native 25th annual Juno Awards held at the Copps Coliseum, Hamilton, ON, Canada, at which she also lifts trophies for Best Album, Best Single, Best Female Vocalist, Best Songwriter and Best Rock Album.
Apr [13] *Ironic* hits US #4.
[20] *Ironic* bows at its UK #11 peak.
May [4] ***Jagged Little Pill*** finally tops the UK chart.
June [29] Morissette takes part in the "MasterCard Masters of Music Concert for the Prince's Trust" at London's Hyde Park.

VAN MORRISON

1966

June Morrison (b. George Ivan, Aug. 31, 1945, Belfast, Northern Ireland), having left school at the age of 15 to concentrate on a career in music, influenced not least by the recordings of Hank Williams and Leadbelly, and encouraged from an early age by his parents to have an interest in blues and jazz, being weaned on his father's extensive record collection, has begun playing guitar and soprano sax with local rock'n'roll and jazz groups at the turn of the decade, including the country-rock group Deanie Sands & the Javelins. Touring the UK and the rest of Europe playing sax and harmonica with local R&B group the Monarchs in 1961 (which cut an instrumental single for CBS Records in Germany, *Twingy Baby*), Morrison has gone on to form Them in 1963, from members of the Monarchs and the Gamblers, including guitarist Billy Harrison and some old schoolfriends. Fronted by Morrison as its lead vocalist and principal songwriter, not least penning the much-revered *Gloria*, the group has scored two Top 10 UK hits and one US chart album by the time he decides to leave the band, now returning to Belfast at the end of a grueling US tour.

1967

Mar He signs a solo contract with producer/songwriter Bert Berns (who has steered Them), traveling to New York, NY to record for his Bang label, while the re-assembled group continues without Morrison, replacing him with vocalist Ken McDowell.
Sept [30] *Brown Eyed Girl*, the first of four Berns/Morrison singles, hits US #10, and marks the beginning of Morrison's solo career.
Oct Berns has issued an album of Morrison's recordings, ***Blowin' Your Mind***, without the singer's knowledge, which reaches US #182.
[20-22] Morrison performs at the Avalon Ballroom, San Francisco, CA.
Dec Berns dies of a heart attack. Morrison, now living in Cambridge, MA, and playing in a bass, flute and guitar jazz-blues trio, negotiates with other companies and signs a solo contract with US Warner Bros. Records after the label's vice president Joe Smith has extracted Morrison from his contract with Bang.

1968

Sept [25] Teamed with producer Lewis Merenstein, he spends the first of two days recording ***Astral Weeks*** at Century Sound Studios in New York City. He will finish the album on October 15th. (Without a hit single, the set will take time to generate sales, but will move into the US charts by the end of the year, and become regarded as a seminal '60s album.)

1970

Apr Critically acclaimed ***Moondance***, including the popular track *Into The Mystic*, never to be released as a single, peaks at US #29 and UK #32, aided in the US by *Come Running*, which makes #39. The self-written and produced album, which showcases the artist's oft-repeated lyrical themes of mysticism, romance and the personal quest, features steady band members John Platania (guitar), Jeff Labes (keyboards) and Jack Shroer (drums).
[23, 26] Morrison plays the Fillmore West, San Francisco, CA, with Joe Cocker, bookending dates at the Winterland.
Sept ***His Band And The Street Choir*** is released to poor reviews (and will climb to US #32 in 1971).

1971

Jan [2] From the album, *Domino* hits US #9, as Morrison moves to live in California.
Apr [3] *Blue Money* makes US #23. Morrison becomes a much-respected live act in the US, assembling an 11-piece Caledonia Soul Orchestra, including string players and guitarist John Platania, a mainstay of his studio work.
June [12] *Call Me Up In Dreamland* peaks at US #95.
Oct Morrison is featured on the Band's ***Cahoots*** album, co-writing *4% Pantomime* with Robbie Robertson.
Dec [4] *Wild Night* reaches US #28, while the Ted Templeman-produced ***Tupelo Honey***, featuring John McFee and Ronnie Montrose guesting on guitars, makes US #27. It is conceived as a suite of love songs to Morrison's wife, Janet Planet. During its recording, Morrison has jammed for two days with John Lee Hooker, results of which will only appear on two Hooker tracks, featured on the latter's ***Never Get Out Of These Blues Alive*** and 1973's ***Born In Mississippi, Raised In Tennessee***.

1972

Feb [12] Title track, *Tupelo Honey*, peaks at US #47.
June Morrison performs several dates in California, including cover versions of Bob Dylan's *Just Like A Woman* and Doris Day's *Que Sera Sera* in the repertoire.
Sept [9] Morrison's tribute to soul legend Jackie Wilson, *Jackie Wilson Said (I'm In Heaven When You Smile)* peaks at US #61. Critically revered as another milestone work, its parent album, ***St. Dominic's Preview***, enters the US chart, and, during a six month stay, will reach #15.
Nov [4] *Redwood Tree* stops at US #98.

1973

July [23-24] Morrison plays two nights at the Rainbow Theatre, Finsbury Park, London.
Aug Prior sessions producing Jackie De Shannon are followed by the release of ***Hard Nose The Highway***, featuring the Oakland Symphony Orchestra and including the ten-minute *Autumn Song*, which makes UK #22 and US #27. Morrison's personal life, always kept from public view, hits trouble and he is divorced. Following a popular European tour backed by the Caledonia Soul Orchestra, he returns to Ireland to write songs.

1974

Jan ***T.B. Sheets***, comprising tracks from the ***Blowin' Your Mind*** sessions, is released and peaks at US #181.
Mar Performance double album, ***It's Too Late To Stop Now***, documenting his much-celebrated live work, with Morrison accompanied by the Caledonian Soul Orchestra, makes US #53. Morrison disbands the orchestra and tours Europe with a five-piece band, playing sax and harmonica himself.
June Morrison records two tracks in Holland, a cover of Fleecie Moore's *Caledonia*, to be released as a single with the B-side, *What's Up Crazy Pup*.
July [20] He performs at the "Knebworth Festival", Knebworth, Herts., sharing the bill with the Allman Brothers and the Doobie Brothers.
Nov ***Verdon Fleece***, an intensely personal record of songs written in Ireland in 1973, makes US #53 and UK #41, and marks the beginning of a three-year reclusive period of reflection, away from touring or record releasing though he will spend much time in the studio.

1976

Mar Morrison guests on harmonica and guitar for Bill Wyman's newly-released album ***Stone Alone***. He will also contribute a song for Sammy Hagar's ***Nine On A Scale of Ten***.
Nov [25] Morrison is one of many special guests at the Band's farewell concert, "The Last Waltz", singing *Tura Lura Lural* and *Caravan* and joining an all-star cast on *I Shall Be Released*.

1977

May After scrapping a tentatively titled album, ***Mechanical Bliss***, and experimental sessions with Crusader Joe Sample, Morrison's "comeback" album, ***A Period Of Transition***, makes UK #23 and US #43 and features co-producer Dr. John on piano.
June Morrison plays a surprise gig at London's Speakeasy with Dr. John, Mick Ronson and Eric Burdon.
Dec [10] Re-released *Moondance* makes US #92.
[13] ***Tupelo Honey*** is certified gold by the RIAA.

1978

Oct The self-produced ***Wavelength*** makes US #28 and UK #27, and includes a Jackie DeShannon co-penned number, *Santa Fe*. The studio band for the album is ex-Them colleague Peter Bardens (keyboards), Mickey Feat (bass), Peter Van Hooke (drums) and Bobby Tench (guitar).
Nov [11] Its title track, *Wavelength*, makes US #42, while *Bright Side Of The Road*, Morrison's first solo UK chart single, peaks at #63.

1979

Sept ***Into The Music***, including his revival of Tommy Edwards' 1958 *It's All In The Game*, makes UK #21 and US #43 (his records are now distributed by Warner Bros. in the US and by PolyGram for the rest of the world).

1980

Sept ***Common One***, with Morrison edging further towards renewed spiritualism and Celtic musical traditions, reaches UK #53 and US #73.

1982

Feb After another break of more than a year, ***Beautiful Vision***, with Morrison again the soul mystic and heavily themed on his Belfast memories, reaches UK #31 and US #44.
June Morrison performs at the annual "Glastonbury Fayre", Glastonbury, Somerset.

1983

Mar ***Inarticulate Speech Of The Heart*** is released. Striking a chord with fans of his earlier solo recordings, and aided by the instrumental *Celtic Swing*, for which Morrison makes a promo video, it makes UK #14 and US #116.

1984

Mar ***Live At The Grand Opera House***, recorded in Belfast, reaches UK #44, further evidence of his still sell-out live status.
July He receives a big reception when he joins Bob Dylan at Wembley Stadium, Wembley, Middx., in front of 72,000 people. They perform Dylan's *It's All Over Now, Baby Blue*, a song Morrison recorded in the early '60s.
[7] Morrison plays at the annual "Montreux Jazz Festival" in Montreux, Switzerland.
Nov Morrison leaves his base in Marin County, CA, to begin nomadic travelling between Dublin, Belfast and London.

1985

Feb ***A Sense Of Wonder***, returning further to the realms of poetry and spirituality, including a musical backdrop for the William Blake poem **Let The Slave (Price Of Experience)**, reaches UK #25 and US #61. (The credits include a thank you to Church of Scientology founder L. Ron Hubbard.)

1986

May [17] He joins U2, Elvis Costello and the Pogues for Dublin's "Self Aid" concert, a post "Live Aid" effort at raising funds for the unemployed in Eire.
July ***No Guru, No Method, No Teacher***, the title representing Morrison's rebuttal of press attempts to characterize his spirituality and cast him as a devotee of Scientology, peaks at UK #27 and US #70.
Oct [13] ***Moondance*** is certified platinum by the RIAA.

1987

June [19-21] Morrison takes part in the "Glastonbury Festival", Glastonbury, Somerset.
Sept Self-penned and produced as ever, ***Poetic Champions Compose***, recorded with a studio line-up of Neil Drinkwater (keyboards), Steve Pearce (bass), Roy Jones (drums), Mick Cox (guitar) and Martin Drover (horns), reaches UK #26 and US #90.

1988

July ***Irish Heartbeat***, an exploration of Morrison's Celtic musical roots recorded with the Chieftains, Ireland's top traditional music group, makes UK #18 and US #102. Morrison is in his most cheerful form and is even seen to smile in concert, during regular tour outings.

1989

June With Morrison now signed to PolyGram's Polydor imprint in Britain and Mercury Records in the

US, ***Avalon Sunset***, featuring Georgie Fame on keyboards (now a regular member of his musical troupe) and guest Cliff Richard, reaches UK #13 and US #91.
July [1] The extracted ballad, *Have I Told You Lately*, makes UK #74.
[18-19] Morrison takes part in the seventh annual "Prince's Trust Rock Gala" at the National Exhibition Centre, Birmingham, West Midlands.
Nov He is joined on stage by John Lee Hooker at the Beacon Theatre, New York, performing *Boom Boom* and *It Serves Me Right To Suffer*.
Dec Spiritual brothers Van Morrison and Cliff Richard duet on *Whenever God Shines His Light*, released for the festive season to good effect at UK #20.
[1] Morrison and Fame guest on NBC-TV's "Late Night With David Letterman".

1990

Apr [7] ***The Best Of Van Morrison***, an incomprehensive Polydor anthology, hits UK #4 and #50 in the US (Aug [11]) (where it will earn his second platinum disc as a consistent catalog seller, logging over three years on the survey).
June [3] Morrison participates in the "Fleadh 1990 Festival" in Finsbury Park, London, with a host of Irish acts.
July [21] He takes part in Roger Waters' performance of "The Wall" at the site of the Berlin Wall in Potzdamer Platz, Berlin, Germany. The event is broadcast live throughout the world, and raises money for the Memorial Fund For Disaster Relief.
Aug [27] He performs before a sellout crowd of 13,589 at the Grandstand, CNE, Toronto, ON, Canada.
Oct [18] Morrison plays at the Apollo Theatre, Manchester, Gtr. Manchester, during a current UK tour, again with Fame.
[20] Increasingly popular once more, traditionally self-composed and produced ***Enlightenment*** hits UK #5 and will climb to US #62 on Feb [9] the following year. It includes the extracted *In The Days Before Rock'n'Roll*, a notable ode to radio somehow including a reference not only to music legends of the past but also race jockey Lester Piggott.

1991

Mar [16] BBC2-TV's "Arena" series broadcasts "One Irish Rover", a Morrison documentary.
[23] Morrison penned-and-produced Tom Jones single, *Carrying A Torch*, peaks at UK #57. It is one of four tracks on which they have collaborated live for Jones' forthcoming album, also titled ***Carrying A Torch***, recorded at the Townhouse studios, London.
Apr [14-15] Morrison plays before a sellout crowd of 15,418 at the Greek Theatre, University of California-Berkeley, CA, grossing $330,189.
June [2] He takes part in "Fleadh '91" at London's Finsbury Park Astoria.
Aug [4] Morrison participates in the "Feile '91 Festival" at the Semple Stadium, Thurles, Co. Tipperary, with the Pogues, Nanci Griffith and the Wonder Stuff.
Sept He guests on John Lee Hooker's Charisma debut, ***Mr. Lucky***.
[21] ***Hymns To The Silence*** debuts at its UK #5 peak.
Nov [16] ***Hymns To The Silence*** makes US #99.

1992

Jan [9] ***Hymns To The Silence*** is certified gold by the RIAA.
Apr [26] Morrison plays two sellout shows at The Paramount, New York, grossing $340,500, during his latest US tour.
May [24] He performs at the "Scottish Fleadh" at Glasgow Green, Glasgow, Scotland.
June [28] Morrison performs at the annual "Glastonbury Festival".
July Morrison receives an honorary Doctor of Letters degree from University of Ulster in Jordanstown, honored because his "Belfast childhood and the city's atmosphere, streets, scenes and people were reflected throughout his work".
Dec Despite being a legendary and disdainful adversary of the media, Morrison participates in a concert to celebrate the 20th anniversary of San Francisco critic Joel Selvin, with Chris Isaak, Todd Rundgren and Bonnie Raitt.

1993

Jan Having begun work on a new album at The Wool Hall studio in October, Morrison continues recording at his traditional base, the Townhouse Studios.
[12] He fails to turn up at the eighth annual Rock and Roll Hall of Fame induction dinner held at the Century Plaza Hotel, Los Angeles, CA, becoming the first living inductee to miss the event. The honor is accepted on his behalf by Robbie Robertson.
Feb During a show in Dublin, Morrison is joined on stage during his singing of *Gloria* by Bono, Larry Mullen, Johnny Cash, Bob Dylan, Elvis Costello, Steve Earle, Steve Winwood, Chrissie Hynde, Nanci Griffith, Jerry Lee Lewis and Kris Kristofferson.
[27] ***The Best Of Van Morrison Vol. 2*** debuts at its UK #31 peak.
Apr [3] ***The Best Of Van Morrison Vol. 2*** stops at US #176.
[25-26] Morrison plays two sellout dates at the Wang Center for the Performing Arts, Boston, MA, grossing $240,041 from a combined 7,072 audience.
May [4] Morrison performs at the opening night of new London venue, The Forum. (He had also been the last act to play there on March 21st when it closed its doors as the Town & Country club.)
[15] *Gloria*, teaming Morrison with blues veteran John Lee Hooker, bows at its UK #31 peak.
June [12] While Rod Stewart's version of Morrison's *Have I Told You Lately* climbs the UK and US charts, the self-produced ***Too Long In Exile***, including *Gloria* and guests Georgie Fame and Candy Dulfer, debuts at its UK #4 peak. (It will do likewise in the US on the 26th at #29.)
Dec [13-14] The Van Morrison Soul and R&B Review plays at the Berkeley Community Theater, Berkeley, CA.

1994

Feb [11] He begins an eight-date UK tour at the Royal Centre, Nottingham, Notts, set to end on March 5th at the City Hall, Sheffield, S. Yorks.
[14] Morrison is presented with the Outstanding Contribution To British Music honor by former Beirut hostage John McCarthy at the 13th annual BRIT Awards, at London's Alexandra Palace. He closes the show with *Gloria*.
Apr [30] ***A Night In San Francisco***, a 22-track live album recorded in December 1993 with guests Hooker, Junior Wells, Fame and Dulfer, hits UK #8 in its week of entry.
June [4] ***A Night In San Francisco*** debuts at its US #125 peak.
Sept [3] Once again proving the endurance of his compositions, Morrison's *Wild Night* is taken to US #3 in a treatment by John Mellencamp and Me'Shell NdegeOcello.
Oct [23] *Have I Told You Lately* is named one of the Most Performed Songs Of The Year at the annual BMI Awards Ceremony at London's Dorchester Hotel.
Nov [21] The RIAA certifies two million sales of ***The Best Of Van Morrison***.

1995

Mar [18] His revised version of *Have I Told You Lately?*, now paired with the Chieftains, charts for a week at UK #71.
May [23] Morrison is honored with the Lifetime Achievement Award at the 40th annual Ivor Novello Awards at London's Grosvenor House Hotel.
June [10] *Days Like This* charts for a week at UK #65, as Morrison performs at the annual "Fleadh Festival" at London's Finsbury Park.
[24] ***Days Like This***, its front cover featuring a photo of Morrison and his girlfriend Michelle Roca, a former Miss Ireland, hits UK #5 in its week of entry.
[29] He guests on CBS-TV's "Late Show With David Letterman".
[30] Morrison plays a sellout date at The Paramount, New York, during a North American mini-tour.
July [8] ***Days Like This*** debuts at its US #33 peak.
Nov Morrison performs in Belfast on the day of President Clinton's visit to the city. (He gives permission for *Brown Eyed Girl* to be used in a commercial promoting peace in Northern Ireland.)
[7] He is named Best Songwriter at the annual **Q** Awards at London's Park Lane Hotel.
[9] Morrison attends a memorial service for fellow Irishman Rory Gallagher.
[14] He plays a rare UK date at Leeds' Town & Country Club 3.
Dec [2] *No Religion* charts for a week at UK #54.
[9] He guests on BBC2-TV's "Later With Jools Holland".
[28] Morrison is featured in BBC2-TV's "A River Of Sound", a three-part documentary on the origins of traditional Irish music.

1996

Feb [3] Serving up his first jazz-phrased set ***How Long Has This Been Going On***, recorded with Georgie Fame who has recruited top-flight jazz musicians including Pee Wee Ellis, and released on the Verve label, makes US #55.
June [19] Morrison performs at the Wembley Arena, during a four-date UK tour with Ray Charles.
see also: **THEM**

MORRISSEY

1987

Aug Son of a hospital porter and librarian, Morrissey (b. Stephen Patrick Morrissey, May 22, 1959, Davyhulme, Lancs.) has entered the music world as a would-be music journalist, contributing, as a freelancer, to **Record Mirror** in the late '70s and writing the Babylon Books-published tome **James Dean Isn't Dead** while UK president of the New York Dolls fan club, and performer, initially with the Nosebleeds, going on to find considerable critical and commercial success as the anti-hero lead singer and lyricist of UK alternative outfit the Smiths, which he formed with fellow Mancunian guitarist Johnny Marr in 1982. With their personal and professional relationship now soured, however, Morrissey signs a solo deal with EMI Records, permanently dissolving the Smiths.
Sept He is reportedly mulling over an offer to make a cameo appearance in C4-TV soap "Brookside" as a potential purchaser of Harry Cross' bungalow.

1988

Jan Morrissey records a set for BBC Radio 1 but, unhappy with the results, subsequently asks for it to be canned.
Mar [26] His debut solo, ***Viva Hate***, enters the UK chart at #1, and, released in the US by Sire Records, will make #48. Produced by co-writer Stephen Street and featuring Durutti Column guitarist Vini Reilly, it includes *Suedehead*, which, reactivating EMI's HMV label imprint and taking its title from Richard Allen's 1971 novel about black-hating, gay-bashing, post-skinhead gangs, hits UK #5, spurred by a video clip showing Morrissey at play in James Dean's hometown.
June [18] Follow-up, the typically doom-laden *Everyday Is Like Sunday*, hits UK #9.
Dec [22] As a farewell gesture, Morrissey performs a final Smiths gig with Andy Rourke and Mike Joyce, augmented by Craig Gannon, replacing the noticeably absent Marr, at the Wolverhampton Civic Hall, West Midlands.

1989

Feb [11] *Last Of The International Playboys* hits UK #6.
Apr [29] *Interesting Drug* debuts at its UK #9 peak.
Nov [25] Seance-themed *Ouija Board, Ouija Board*, featuring Joan Sims in its promotional video, is heard at UK #18.

1990

May [5] Having recorded and canned a new album, Morrissey continues to release one-off singles: *November Spawned A Monster* peaks at UK #12.
Oct [20] *Piccadilly Palare* reaches UK #18.
[27] Rounding up his recent singles and once again referencing the characters Julian and Sandy from early '60s BBC Radio comedy show "Round The Horne" (as has the recent single), his sophomore effort, ***Bona Drag***, hits UK #9.
Dec [1] ***Bona Drag*** makes #59 in the US, where Morrissey remains the darling of the college/alternative music scene.

1991

Jan [18] His "Hulmerist" video is certified gold by the RIAA.
Feb [23] *Our Frank* reaches UK #26.
Mar [16] Much of it co-penned with ex-Fairground Attraction's Mark Nevin, ***Kill Uncle***, featuring ex-Madness keyboardist Mark "Bedders" Bedford and produced by Clive Langer and Alan Winstanley, debuts at its UK #8 peak.
[30] ***Kill Uncle*** makes US #52.
Apr [13] The extracted *Sing Your Life* reaches UK #33.
[27] A seven-date European tour begins at the Dublin Stadium set to end on May 6th at the Hamburg Docks, Hamburg, West Germany.
May [29] His first US solo trek opens at the Sports Arena, San Diego, CA.
June [14] Morrissey is the music guest on NBC-TV's "The Tonight Show".
July [13] He plays at New York, NY's Madison Square Garden, as part of the New Music Seminar, grossing $301,450.
[20] Morrissey performs his first UK gig since December 1988 at Wembley Arena, Wembley, Middx, at the start of a seven-date UK tour.
Aug [3] *Pregnant For The Last Time* reaches UK #25.
Sept Morrissey cancels a five-date Australian tour after coming down with viral flu after the first gig in Brisbane, Queensland.
Oct [1] He begins a six-date UK tour at the Victoria Hall, Hanley, Staffs, set to end on the 8th at the De Montfort Hall, Leicester, Leics.
[12] *My Love Life* debuts at its UK #29 peak.
Dec [28] He appears at Amnesty International's "Big 30" concert broadcast on ITV.

1992

Apr [30] Much to Morrissey's chagrin, Omnibus publishes Johnny Rogan's book **Morrissey & Marr - The Severed Alliance**.
May [7] He appears on BBC1-TV's "Top Of The Pops".
[9] *We Hate It When Our Friends Become Successful* debuts at its UK #17 peak.
June [26] He appears at the annual "Glastonbury Festival", Glastonbury, Somerset.
July [18] *You're The One For Me, Fatty* debut at its UK #19 peak.
[28] Morrissey makes a midnight store appearance at Vinyl Solution, Grand Rapids, MI, which sells 557 copies of his new album in 1 hour and 38 minutes.
Aug [8] He is pelted by missiles while singing *Glamorous Glue* draped with a Union Jack around his body, performing on the bill at Madness' reunion concert at Finsbury Park, London, as his fourth solo outing, ***Your Arsenal***, produced by Mick Ronson, debuts at its UK #4 peak.
[9] After Morrissey has pulled out of a second Madness gig, lead singer Suggs comments, "A fag paper blew on stage last night and nearly took one of his ears off."
[15] Glam rock-inspired ***Your Arsenal*** bows at its US #21 peak.
Sept [14] Picketers, organized by Tunde Osho, protest outside EMI's offices objecting to Morrissey's supposed use of nationalist imagery on recent European dates.
Oct [10-11] He grosses $839,855 for two shows at the Hollywood Bowl, Hollywood, CA, during a US tour.
Nov [14] He is the musical guest on NBC-TV's "Saturday Night Live"
Dec [11] An eight-date UK tour commences at the Sheffield City Hall, Yorks.
[19] *Certain People I Know* debuts at its UK #35 peak, as Morrissey plays a gig at London's Alexandra Palace, having offered ticket concessions to those who bought stubs for the second Madness date.

1993

May [22] ***Beethoven Was Deaf***, a 16-track live set recorded at Le Zenith, Paris, France, the previous December, and released in Europe only, bows at its UK #13 peak.
Nov [16] ***Viva Hate*** is certified gold by the RIAA.

1994

Mar [12] *The More You Ignore Me, The Closer I Get* debuts at its UK #8 peak.
[26] Produced by Steve Lillywhite, ***Vauxhall And I*** tops the UK chart in its first week.
Apr [9] ***Vauxhall And I*** debuts at its US #18 peak.
May [21] *The More You Ignore Me, The Closer I Get* makes US #46.
June [11] *Hold On To Your Friends* bows at its UK #47 peak.
Aug [20] *Interlude*, a duet with Siouxsie, enters at its UK #25 high.

1995

Jan [28] *Boxers* bows at its UK #23 peak.
Feb [2] Morrissey embarks on 18-date UK leg of European tour to promote his new album at the Barrowlands, Glasgow, Strathclyde, Scotland, set to end on the 26th at London's Theatre Royal, Drury Lane.
[18] ***World Of Morrissey***, a compilation of B-sides, live tracks and selected hits, reaches UK #15 in its week of entry.
Mar [11] ***World Of Morrissey*** charts for a week at US #134.
Sept [2] *Dagenham Dave* bows at its UK #26 peak.
[9] Once again helmed by Lillywhite, ***Southpaw Grammar*** enters at its UK #4 high.
[30] ***South Paw Grammar*** debuts at its US #66 peak.
Nov [11] Morrissey guests on BBC2-TV's "Later With Jools Holland."
[14-15, 17-18] 15-date "The Outsiders" UK tour, with Morrissey opening for David Bowie, opens at Wembley Arena, set to end on December 8th at the Manchester Nynex Arena.
[29] Morrissey pulls out of "The Outsiders" tour after being hospitalized, following a performance at the Aberdeen Exhibition Centre, Aberdeen, Grampian, Scotland.
Dec [8] Morrissey is released from hospital, following his undiagnosed "illness".
[9] *The Boy Racer* bows at its UK #36 peak.
[23] *Sunny* debuts at its UK #42 high.
see also: **THE SMITHS**

THE MOTELS

Martha Davis (vocals); **Jeff Jourard** (guitar); **Marty Jourard** (keyboards, sax); **Michael Goodroe** (bass); **Brian Glascock** (drums)

1978

July The new-wave rock group is formed in Los Angeles, CA, by Davis (b. Jan. 15, 1951, Berkeley, CA), who married at the age of 15 and is the mother of two daughters, who has led a three-piece version for some five years, initially as the Warfield Foxes and the Angels of Mercy in Berkeley, and then as the Motels based in Los Angeles, and Jeff Jourard (though other early members including Dean Chamberlain, later of Code Blue, and Richard Andrea, later of the Know, will come and go). They recruit the latter's brother, ex-classical guitarist-turned-jazz/rock bassist Goodroe and, after rejecting dozens of other drummers, UK-expatriate Glascock, once in Toe Fat with Cliff Bennett, and since a session man for Joan Armatrading, the Bee Gees and others.

1979

Jan Regular work at the Whisky A-Go-Go, and as the house band at Madame Wong's in Hollywood, CA, and dates around other Los Angeles clubs, attract a strong live following, and also initiate record company interest.
Mar Capitol Records signs the group on Mother's Day.
Sept The group's debut album, the new wave based ***Motels***, including the cult success *Total Control*, produced by John Carter, is released.
Oct The band begins an extensive tour in support of the album, playing in Canada, Australia (where they will always achieve popular success, returning for four more treks before 1985), the UK and US.
Dec ***Motels*** belatedly reaches US #175 following well-received US dates. Jeff Jourard leaves after disagreements with Davis, replaced on lead guitar by Tim McGovern from the Pop.

1980

Sept Their second album, the Carter-produced ***Careful***, dedicated to Glascock's brother John, Jethro Tull's bassist, who died aged 26 on November 17, 1979, after open heart surgery, reaches US #45.
Oct *Whose Problem?*, taken from ***Careful***, peaks at UK #42, following a successful British tour and strong radio play.

1981

Jan *Days Are O.K.*, also from the album and written by McGovern, makes UK #41, completing the band's UK singles chart career before its US equivalent has even begun.
Mar [31] The group begins recording ***Apocalypso***, but Capitol rejects it and tells them to return to the studio to record it again.

1982

Mar [7] New album, now retitled ***All Four One***, is completed. Producer Val Garay has recruited Kim Carnes' backing band to play on the set and, during the sessions, McGovern has left to be replaced by ex-Elephant's Memory guitarist Guy Perry.
July ***All Four One*** reaches US #16, during a 41-week chart run while the extracted, Davis-written *Only The Lonely* is their US Singles chart debut, hitting #9.
Oct *Take The L (Out Of Lover)*, also from ***All Four One***, peaks at US #52.
[13] ***All Four One*** is certified gold by the RIAA.
Dec *Forever Mine* stops at US #60.

1983

Jan [30] The group, with additional guitarist and keyboard player Scott Thurston, begins recording a new album at Record One Studios in Los Angeles.
Nov *Suddenly Last Summer* hits US #9, helping its parent album, ***Little Robbers***, also produced by Garay, to US #22.
Dec [21] ***Little Robbers*** is certified gold by the RIAA.

1984

Jan *Remember The Nights*, extracted from ***Little Robbers***, makes US #36.
Apr [4] Tina Turner's version of the Motels' *Total Control* is included on USA For Africa's fund-raising ***We Are The World*** album.

1985

Sept *Shame* reaches US #21, taken from the band's fifth album, ***Shock***, which climbs to US #36.
Nov Extracted title track, *Shock*, peaks at US #84.

1987

Dec [12] Having overcome cancer, which had

contributed to the break-up of the Motels, Davis, still signed to Capitol, returns with *Don't Tell Me The Time*, which makes US #80 and is taken from her maiden solo album, ***Policy*** (many tracks of which were originally recorded at earlier Motels' sessions), which reaches US #127. (A 19-track CD retrospective, ***No Vacancy - The Best Of The Motels***, will be issued by Capitol in 1990.)

THE MOTHERS OF INVENTION

Frank Zappa (guitar; vocals); **Ray Collins** (vocals); **Jim 'Motorhead' Sherwood** (guitar); **Don Preston** (keyboards); **Roy Estrada** (bass); **Bunk Gardner** (saxophone); **Jimmy Carl Black** (drums)

1964

Having graduated through a series of bands including high school units the Black Outs and the Ramblers, followed by the Soots (also featuring early cohort Don Van Vliet (aka Captain Beefheart), and most recently the Masters and the Soul Giants, and financed the establishment of his own Studio Z in Cucamonga, CA, Zappa (b. Francis Vincent Zappa, Dec. 21, 1940, Baltimore, MD) has moved to Los Angeles, CA and assembled a new group named the Muthers from the remains of the Soul Giants, comprising Collins (b. Nov. 19, 1937), Dave Coronada (saxophone), Estrada (b. Apr. 17, 1943, Santa Ana, CA) and Black (b. Feb. 1, 1938, El Paso, TX). With Elliott Ingber (guitar) joining and Estrada departing the following year, the risk-taking, innovative combo, always led by Zappa's ever-changing and demanding musical visions, signs a management contract with Herb Cohen, and begins a residency at Los Angeles' Whisky A-Go-Go club, its name amended to the Mothers.

1966

Jan MGM Records' producer, Tom Wilson, more interested in the group's R&B strengths than its musical social satire, signs the Mothers to MGM's jazz/R&B Verve label, for a $2,500 advance.

June [3-4] The group plays at the Fillmore Auditorium, San Francisco, on a bill with Grateful Dead and Quicksilver Messenger Service.

July Verve has prevailed upon Zappa that he should extend the group's name to the Mothers Of Invention for its debut album, the Wilson-produced, acerbic double set, ***Freak Out!***.

Sept [9-10] The Mothers Of Invention perform another pair of gigs at the Fillmore Auditorium. By year's end, Ingber leaves to link up with Beefheart's band, with the ever-variable and expanding Mothers Of Invention aggregate now accommodating Gardner (b. John Leon Gardner, May 2, 1933), Sherwood (b. Euclid James Sherwood, May 8, 1942), drummer Billy Mundi and keyboardist Don Preston (b. Sept. 21, 1932, Flint, MI).

1967

Feb After much underground media promotion (instigated by Zappa), ***Freak Out!*** climbs to US #130, during a 23-week chart stay.

Apr [25] The Mothers Of Invention are featured on CBS-TV's "Inside Pop - The Rock Revolution" special, also appearing with Leonard Bernstein.

July The critically-revered ***Absolutely Free***, once again showcasing the group's eclectic creativity, mixing free-form rock with classical elements, and wrapped in Zappa's savage lyrical wit, makes US #41.

Aug Ian Underwood joins on keyboards.

Sept [23] The Mothers Of Invention, backed by a 15-piece orchestra, make their UK debut at London's Royal Albert Hall.

1968

Feb [14] Zappa announces that the Mothers Of Invention are to film and record "Uncle Meat", a group-focusing documentary.

Mar ***We're Only In It For The Money***, its sleeve parodying the Beatles' ***Sgt. Pepper's Lonely Hearts Club Band***, while musically mocking the prevailing hippy psychedelia of 1967, reaches US #30. The Mothers Of Invention undertake a lengthy residency at the Garrick Theater in Greenwich Village, New York, to where they have now relocated.

Apr [12] The group plays at the US Record Industry's NARAS annual dinner in New York, with a performance which pokes barbed fun at the assembled diners.

June ***Lumpy Gravy***, the first album released under Zappa's own name but featuring various band members, peaks at US #159, a largely instrumental collage recorded with a 50-piece orchestra. Mundi leaves the band.

July ***We're Only In It For The Money*** makes UK #31.

Oct [25] The group plays the first of two concerts at London's Royal Festival Hall.

1969

Jan ***Cruising With Ruben And The Jets***, a doo-wop pastiche credited to the group of its title, but in reality a thinly-disguised Zappa & Mothers, peaks at US #110.

Apr An early retrospective, ***Mothermania/The Best Of The Mothers***, makes US #151. Compiled by Zappa, it fulfills his contractual obligation to Verve.

June The jazz-rock fused extended double album, ***Uncle Meat***, released by the Zappa-created Bizarre Records in the US (and the Transatlantic label in the UK), and billed as "the soundtrack for a movie you will probably never get to see" (though not actually a soundtrack recording) reaches US #43, while the group relocates, at Zappa's behest, to Los Angeles.

[27] The group plays at the Denver Pop Festival held at Mile High Stadium, CO, sharing a bill with Jimi Hendrix, Creedence Clearwater Revival, and others, before a 50,000 crowd.

July [3-6] The band takes part in the four-day Newport Jazz Festival, in Newport, RI.

Aug [20] Zappa temporarily disbands the Mothers Of Invention (whose line-up had recently included guitarist Lowell George (b. Apr. 13, 1945, Hollywood, CA) and drummer Art Tripp III (b. Arthur Dyer Tripp, Sept. 10, 1939) at the end of a short tour of Canada, reportedly "tired of playing for people who clap for all the wrong reasons" (and also because of the burdensome expense of keeping the large cast on the road). (Estrada and George will go on to form Little Feat, Gardner and Black assemble Geronimo Black while Tripp joins Beefheart's band.)

Dec ***Hot Rats***, released under Zappa's own name on Bizarre, and featuring guest appearances by Captain Beefheart and violinist, Jean-Luc Ponty, makes US #173 (and will hit UK #9 in March the following year).

1970

Mar The Mothers Of Invention's mostly-instrumental ***Burnt Weeny Sandwich*** reaches US #94 and UK #17.

May [11] A re-formed Mothers Of Invention, featuring Zappa and Underwood, with newcomers George Duke (keyboards), Jim Pons (b. Mar. 14, 1943, Santa Monica, CA) (bass) and Aynsley Dunbar (drums), with ex-Turtles Howard Kaylan (b. Howard Kaplan, June 22, 1947, New York) and Mark Volman (b. Apr. 19, 1947, Los Angeles) on vocals, perform at the Fillmore East in New York.

[15] They premiere ***200 Motels***, recorded with Zubin Mehta and the Los Angeles Philharmonic Orchestra (though subsequently released as a Zappa solo set).

June [27] The band takes part in the Bath Festival of Blues & Progressive Music, in Shepton Mallet, Somerset, part of a weekend bill costing punters £2.10 shillings.

Oct The group's second album release of the year, ***Weasels Ripped My Flesh***, a combination of unissued live and studio material from the previous three years, makes UK #28, having reached US #189 in July.

1971

Feb [8] Zappa is forced to cancel a planned UK concert by the band with the Royal Philharmonic Orchestra at London's Royal Albert Hall after venue officials have declared the libretto "200 Motels" (the score to which was to have been featured) to be obscene, and refused to allow its performance. Undaunted, Zappa procedes with the movie "200 Motels", a fictionalized documentary of the Mothers, at UK's Shepperton Studios, with guest appearances by Ringo Starr and Keith Moon of the Who, among others. (Critical and audience response to the film will be muted.)

Aug With the group having reverted to the shortened Mothers moniker, ***Live The Mothers/Fillmore East - June 1971*** climbs to US #38.

[7] The Mothers play at UCLA, Los Angeles, the show being recorded for future release as ***Just Another Band From L.A.***

Dec [3] The band is performing at Montreux Casino, Switzerland, when the venue burns to the ground (an event subsequently recounted in Deep Purple's legendary cut, *Smoke On The Water*). No-one is hurt, but the Mothers lose $50,000-worth of equipment in the blaze, which is reputedly started by a hippie, listening to the music while perched atop the casino roof.

[10] The group plays a concert at London's Rainbow Theatre, at which Zappa is pushed off the stage into the orchestra pit, breaking a leg and ankle in several places, and suffering a fractured skull.

1972

May The Mothers' ***Just Another Band From L.A.*** makes US #85.

Sept Zappa's solo instrumental set, ***Waka/Jawaka - Hot Rats***, featuring various Mothers, peaks at US #152.

Dec The group's ***The Grand Wazoo***, featuring the latest ad-hoc recruits including Tony Duran (guitar), trombonists Ken Shroyer and Bill Byers, Ernie Watts (saxophone) and wind instrumentalists Mike Altschul, Tony Ortega, Fred Jackson and Earl Dumler, enlisted to impart a big-band sound, is released.

1973

Dec The Mothers, currently comprising Zappa, Ponty, Bruce Fowler (trombone), Tom Fowler (bass), Ian and Ruth Underwood (marimba, vibes), Duke and Ralph Humphrey (drums), issue ***Over-Nite Sensation***, the first release on Zappa's new DiscReet label, which makes US #32 (and will be certified gold by the RIAA on November 9th, 1976).

1974

May [12] The Mothers, now featuring Zappa, Duke, Humphrey, the Fowlers, Napoleon Murphy Brock (saxophone), Preston, Jeff Simmons, drummer Chester Thompson and ex-Cream bassist, Jack Bruce, play at the University of Notre Dame, Notre Dame, IN.

Nov With Zappa now determined on a largely solo-credited career which has already seen ***Apostrophe*** hit US #10 in July, the Mothers' live album, ***Roxy And Elsewhere***, reaches US #27. A further Mothers performance set, ***One Size Fits All*** (featuring Johnny "Guitar" Watson among others) will reach US #26 in September the following year while ***Bongo Fury***, variously credited to Zappa, Captain Beefheart and the Mothers will be the last original effort to bear the group's name, peaking at US #66 in November the same year, the same month Zappa's solo ***Zoot Allures*** resumes his solo path in earnest. As a fluid and ground-breaking ensemble, the Mothers Of Invention/ Mothers unit has proved a fertile apprenticeship for a large number of innovative and subsequently well-known performers, while allowing its front man to experiment freely with multi-genre expertise, a talent which develops further, often aided by ex-Mothers, throughout his subsequently prolific solo sojourn. (Zappa's litigious efforts to win back the rights to the entire Mothers Of Invention catalog will prove successful, making way for the re-release in the late

'80s of the group's archive material through his own Barking Pumpkin label, collected not least on ***Old Masters - Box One, Two*** and ***Three***, and a host of vintage material brought to compact disc in the '90s. Assorted ex-Mothers including Gardner, Preston and Black, will perform as the Grandmothers throughout the '80s, featuring past material written by the group's absent originator in their set.)
see also: **Frank ZAPPA**

MÖTLEY CRÜE

Vince Neil (vocals); **Mick Mars** (guitar); **Nikki Sixx** (bass); **Tommy Lee** (drums)

1981

Jan [13] Frank Carlton Serafino Ferrano (b. Dec. 11, 1958, San Jose, CA) who, deciding to call himself Nikki Sixx, has left US group London who became the house band at Los Angeles, CA club, The Starwood, and, having also started the short-lived band Christmas with Lee (b. Thomas Lee Bass, Oct. 3, 1962, Athens, Greece, to a Greek mother and US military father) from local Los Angeles band, Suite 19, now forms Mötley Crüe. They link with guitarist Bob Deal (b. Apr. 3, 1955, Terre Haute, IN), whom they meet after he has placed an ad in Los Angeles newspaper **Recycler**: "loud, rude, aggressive guitarist available" and who changes his name to Mick Mars. After original lead vocalist O'Dean is fired just two days into the job, Neil (b. Vincent Neil Wharton, Feb. 8, 1961, Hollywood, CA), is recruited from Cheap Trick-covers group, Rock Candy, after Sixx, Lee and Mars had gone to see its rhythm guitarist James Alverson.
May The group makes its debut opening for Y&T at the Starwood in Hollywood, followed by a gig at Pookie's sandwich shop in Pasadena, attended by 12 people.
June Demo single, *Stick To Your Guns*, backed with *Toast Of The Town*, and recorded at Crystal Sound Studios, is handed out at gigs. Funded by construction-company owner Allan Coffman, 1,000 are copies pressed.
Dec ***Too Fast For Love***, recorded at Hit City West Studio over three days at a reported cost of $7,000, is released on the Leathur label.

1982

Mar With an increasingly outrageous stage act which includes chainsawing mannequins and setting their pants on fire, and following sellout Los Angeles gigs at the Roxy and the Troubadour and three dates at the Whisky, Mötley Crüe plays at the Civic Auditorium, Santa Monica, CA, and comes close to selling out the 3,500-seat venue.
June The group embarks on a disastrous tour of Canada, ominously started when Neil's stage attire of belts, chains, etc. are confiscated at customs as deadly weapons. Meanwhile, Tom Zutant signs the band to Elektra Records, following a counter offer to beat out Virgin Records.
Aug Elektra reissues ***Too Fast For Love*** after Leathur has sold out of the original 20,000 copies.
Oct [31] The group headlines a Halloween Special in Los Angeles with Y&T and Randy Hansen.
Dec [13] Having invited every manager they know to come and see them perform at the Santa Monica Civic Auditorium, the Crüe signs with Doc McGhee and Doug Thaler of McGhee Enterprises Inc.

1983

Mar [26] The group begins a US tour as support act on Kiss' "Creatures Of The Night" trek.
May [23] They perform second to bottom on the "Heavy Metal Day" bill at the "US Festival" in San Bernardino, CA.
Oct [31] The band plays at the Limelight Club, Chicago, IL, for MTV's "Halloween Horror Show".
Nov Their second album, ***Shout At The Devil***, helmed by veteran rock producer Tom Werman, is released, peaking at US #17 and eventually earning triple platinum status.
[11] The group embarks on a 78-date North American headlining tour at the Orange Pavilion in San Bernardino, CA, set to end in Phoenix, AZ, on April 1st, 1984.
Dec Their debut album, ***Too Fast For Love***, now licensed to Elektra, makes US #77.

1984

Jan [12] The group performs at New York, NY's Madison Square Garden, supporting Ozzy Osbourne on his current US tour.
Feb *Looks That Kill* makes US #54.
June *Too Young To Fall* peaks at US #90.
Aug [18] The group makes its UK debut at the "Monsters Of Rock Festival", bottom of the bill to headliners Iron Maiden, at Castle Donington, Leics. They continue on to Europe, supporting Iron Maiden, during which Lee and Sixx set fire to a hotel room in France with flare guns.
Dec [8] Neil, while driving a 72 Ford Pantera sports car, is involved in a fatal accident in Redondo Beach, CA, which kills Hanoi Rocks member Nick "Razzle" Dingley and injures two others. (Neil is charged with vehicular manslaughter and released on $2,500 bail. He will serve 20 days in jail, pay $2.6 million compensation to the injured parties, serve 200 hours of community service and undertake school and college lectures on the dangers of drugs and alcohol.) (During the recording of ***Shout At The Devil***, Sixx had smashed his car into a telephone pole, which required a steel pin to be implanted into his shoulder.)

1985

Feb ***Shout At The Devil*** is voted #1 album by readers of **Circus** magazine.
Apr The band begins recording a new album at Pasha Music House, Record Plant West and Cherokee studios, Los Angeles.
June ***Theatre Of Pain***, with the group reunited, ships gold in the US, eventually hits US #6 and makes UK #36 (their UK chart debut). (The album's liner notes convey the message: "To all Crüe fans - if, and or when, you drink, don't take the wheel. Live and learn so we can all rock our asses off together for a long time to come. The Crüe. We love you!")
July Their revival of Brownsville Station's *Smokin' In The Boys Room* reaches US #16 and UK #71. Neil and Mars participate in the heavy-metal benefit single *Stars*, to raise money for Ethiopian famine relief.
Sept Mötley Crüe begins its "Theatre Of Pain" world tour, and drops *Kill 'Em Dead Kid* from its live act. (At the conclusion of the tour, Sixx undergoes drug and alcohol rehabilitation.)
Oct The band donates $17,500 to an anti-drunk driving organization and appears in several PSAs. The San Antonio, TX council drafts legislation restricting behaviour at rock concerts, citing Mötley Crüe as an example of bad influences on local youth.
Nov Japanese dates sell out, as *Home Sweet Home* peaks at US #89.

1986

Feb [6] The group begins a nine-date UK tour at the Apollo Theatre, Manchester, Gtr. Manchester, with special guests Cheap Trick, set to end on the 14th and 15th with dates at London's Hammersmith Odeon.
Mar *Home Sweet Home*, a double A-side in the UK with the reissued *Smokin' In The Boys Room*, makes UK #51.
[7] Their "Theatre Of Pain" world tour finally ends in Italy.
May [10] Tommy Lee marries Heather Locklear from ABC-TV show "Dynasty" and has "Heather" tattooed on his left forearm.
June Neil enters Gardena City jail, where he will serve 18 days, reduced because of good behavior.
Oct Six months of recording begins at the One On One, Rumbo and Conway studios.

1987

May Epitomizing the group's musical and personal attitude, ***Girls Girls Girls*** is released and will hit US #2 and UK #14. Its title track *Girls Girls Girls*, aided by a hotly rotated babe-heavy video clip, reaches US #12 and UK #26.
June Embarking on a world "Girls Girls Girls" tour, they use their own Lear jet for US dates. The 100-show series grosses $21,100,000, but is truncated and finally scrapped after Sixx's reported drug overdose. This dramatic event prompts each member to enter drug and alcohol abuse rehabilitation programs in the coming months, after which members will report for work as "clean".
[17] Vittoria Hohman files suit against Mötley Crüe and promoters Beach Club Promotions after allegedly suffering permanent damage after a December 1985 St. Petersburg's Bayfront Center concert she had gone to with her daughter. She will settle out of court.
July Sixx announces plans to marry Vanity, an ex-girlfriend of Prince, in December.
[22] ***Too Fast For Love*** is certified platinum by the RIAA.
Dec [12] *You're All I Need* peaks at US #83.
[22] Just back from the Far East, Sixx checks into a clinic, after ingesting drugs and alcohol and having technically died in a hotel room at Hollywood's Franklin Plaza. Guns N' Roses Steven Adler calls paramedics, who pronounce him DOA in the ambulance when his heart stops beating for two minutes, but give him two needles of adrenalin inserted into his chest to revive him. Fellow band members are prematurely informed of his death. After his release from hospital, he will hitch-hike home.

1988

Jan Matthew John Trippe sues the group's management, claiming he was asked to masquerade as Sixx after the latter was injured in the car accident in 1983. Trippe claims he wrote and performed as Sixx for two years before Sixx rejoined the group in summer 1985 and demands royalty payments for songs he has written under Sixx's name. *You're All I Need/Wild Side* reaches UK #23.
[19] Manager Doc McGhee pleads guilty to importing more than 40,000 lb of marijuana. (His other act, Bon Jovi, was one of the first to make Rock Against Drugs commercials.)
Feb [17] A 12-year-old fan sets his legs on fire while trying to imitate a stunt shown in the group's "Live Wire" video.
Aug The group begins recording its new album, provisionally titled ***Monstrous***, in Vancouver, BC, Canada, with producer Bob Rock. (After another name-change to ***Sex Sex And Rock And Roll***, the band will settle on ***Dr. Feelgood***.)

1989

May During the month Lee attends a Barry Manilow concert in New York.
Aug McGhee's partner, Doug Thaler, takes over management of the group.
[12-13] Mötley Crüe participates in the "Moscow Music Peace Festival" at Lenin Stadium with Bon Jovi, Ozzy Osbourne, the Scorpions, Cinderella, Skid Row and from USSR Gorky Park, Nuance, CCCP and Brigada S. All proceeds go to programs that fight drug and alcohol abuse in the US and USSR.
Sept ***Dr. Feelgood***, featuring contributions from Bryan Adams, Steven Tyler and Cheap Tricksters Robin Zander and Rick Nielsen, hits UK #4.
[6] The group presents the Heavy Metal trophy at the sixth annual MTV Video Music Awards at the Universal Amphitheatre, Universal City, CA, during which Neil and Guns N' Roses' Izzy Stradlin get into a fight backstage.
Oct [5] The band plays a warm-up tour date at the Whisky, Los Angeles, as the Foreskins.
[14] ***Dr. Feelgood***, tops the US chart, the group's first #1 album.
[28] Its title cut *Dr. Feelgood* hits US #6.

Nov *Dr. Feelgood* makes UK #50.
[2] *Dr. Feelgood* is certified gold by the RIAA.
[15] The RIAA certifies three million sales of ***Shout At The Devil***.
Dec [10] The group plays a sellout show at the Meadowlands Arena, East Rutherford, NJ, during the North American leg of another world tour, with Warrant supporting.

1990

Jan [27] *Kickstart My Heart* reaches US #27.
[28] The band walks off stage for 20 minutes at the Rushmore Plaza Civic Center, Rapid City, SD, concert after Neil is hit in the face by a cup of ice.
Feb [12-13] The group plays two sellout dates at the Great Western Forum, Inglewood, CA, grossing $570,900 as they continue US dates.
Mar [25] Lee is arrested by detective D.N. Bourbo in Augusta, GA, for mooning to the audience during the Augusta-Richmond County Civic Center concert. He is charged with indecent exposure and performing a sexually implicit act.
Apr [7] Lee is injured during a New Haven Coliseum, CT, concert, receiving mild concussion after falling 20 feet from a rope unsecurely fixed to a lighting scaffold during a stunt that goes wrong, and spends the night in the Yale-New Haven hospital.
[28] *Without You* hits US #8, as the band completes its first tour of Australia, including five sellout dates in Sydney, Melbourne and Brisbane.
May [12] *Without You* makes UK #39.
[30] "The Adventures Of Ford Fairlane" movie, in which Neil plays a rock star, premieres in the US.
July [21] *Don't Go Away Mad (Just Go Away)* reaches US #19.
Aug [2] The North American leg of a $25 million-grossing tour ends at the McNichols Sports Arena, Denver, CO.
Sept [19] Mars marries Crüe backing singer Emi Canyn.
[29] *Same Old Situation (S.O.S.)* peaks at US #78.
Dec [17] "Dr. Feelgood The Videos" is certified platinum by the RIAA.

1991

Jan [16] The RIAA confirms four million sales of ***Dr. Feelgood***.
[28] The band collects the Favorite Album, Heavy Metal/Hard Rock trophy at the 18th annual American Music Awards, held at the Shrine Auditorium, Los Angeles.
Feb [12] "Uncensored" reaches the RIAA-certified 200,000 sales plateau.
Mar [7] The group is named Best Heavy Metal Band in the annual **Rolling Stone** Readers' Picks music awards.
Apr [13-14] Mötley Crüe plays sellout dates at the Civic Center, Providence, RI, during another round of US dates.
Aug [17] Having played a low-key at London's Marquee club as the Foreskins on the 14th, they perform at the "Monsters Of Rock Festival", Donington Park, Leics., before a capacity crowd of 72,500.
Sept The band inks a reported $35-million five-album deal with longtime label home, Elektra.
[7] *Primal Scream* debuts at its UK #32 peak.
Oct [5] *Primal Scream* makes US #63.
[19] Compilation, ***Decade Of Decadence - '81-'91***, bows at US #2, behind Guns N' Roses' ***Use Your Illusion II***, and peaks at UK #20.
Nov Rehearsals begin for their seventh album. Lee tells **Circus**, "If one member were to leave or die, this would be the only Mötley Crüe that ever was."
[22] ***Decade Of Decadence*** is certified platinum by the RIAA.

1992

Jan [11] *Home Sweet Home ('91 Remix)* debuts at its UK #37 peak, as Lee participates in the third annual MTV "Rock'n'Jock" softball game held to benefit the T.J. Martell Foundation For Leukemia.
[18] *Home Sweet Home '91*, a remix of their 1985 US #89 release, reaches US #37.
Feb [11] Neil turns up for rehearsal and is promptly fired.
[14] Elektra issues a press release announcing, "Race car driving has become a priority in Vince Neil's life, and because of this, the rest of the band felt Neil didn't share their determination and passion for music." Neil rejects this version of events and says he was fired for taking a stand against the group's new musical direction.
Mar Kik Tracee's Stephen Shareaux auditions for Crüe, but is rejected.
May Neil releases his debut single, *You're Invited But Your Friend Can't Come*, with Damn Yankees' Jack Blades and Tommy Shaw. It is the lead-off cut on the soundtrack to the Pauly Shore-starring movie "Encino Man".
July [14] John Corabi (b. Apr. 26, 1959, Philadelphia, PA), formerly of Scream, begins writing and rehearsing with band. During the band's sabbatical, Mars helps his wife Emi Canyn assemble her group Alice In Thunderland.
Oct [3] Neil's *You're Invited* charts for a week at UK #63.
[22] Neil files a lawsuit in California state court seeking reinstatement in the band and at least $5 million in damages.
Nov [13] "Crüe Ball", a video pinball game designed by Electronic Arts for the Sega Genesis System and featuring three Crüe songs, is released.
Dec The group completes its new album at Devonshire Sounds with Bob Rock at the production desk.

1993

May [15] Neil's debut solo album, ***Exposed***, released world wide on Warner Bros. Records, debuts at its US #13 peak, having charted for a week at UK #44 on the 8th.
June [11] Mars accidentally shoots Rebecca Mettling during target shooting in a desert to the north of Los Angeles.

1994

Feb [8] Lee is charged with possession of a concealed and loaded firearm after trying to walk through a metal detector at Los Angeles Airport with a semi-automatic pistol.
Mar [3] He is sentenced to one year's probation after pleading no contest to the firearms charge. He also pays a $200 fine and $340 in penalties.
[5] *Hooligan's Holiday* debuts at its UK #36 high.
[26] The Bob Rock-helmed ***Mötley Crüe*** reaches UK #17 in its week of entry.
[2] ***Mötley Crüe*** debuts at its US #7 peak.
May [3] ***Mötley Crüe*** is certified gold by the RIAA.
June [22] The band breaks furniture at a club and Corabi utters obscenities during an on-air night club promotion for Dallas radio station KEGL.
July [4] They play an Independence Day concert at the Coca-Cola Star Lake Amphitheatre, Burgettstown, PA, during a US summer tour.
Sept [22] Lee is shot with pepper spray and handcuffed by Sheriff's deputies after a brawl at a West Hollywood nightclub.
Dec [21] Lee is arrested for investigation of spousal abuse and released on $50,000 bail, after his live-in girlfriend Bobbie Brown flags down a Sheriff's deputy and accuses him of beating her. (The following year, Lee will marry bouncing "Baywatch" barbie-babe Pamela Anderson.)

1995

June [6] The RIAA certifies four million sales each of 1987's ***Girls, Girls, Girls*** and 1985's ***Theatre Of Pain***.
Sept [30] Neil's second solo album, ***Carved In Stone***, charts for a week at US #139. (It includes *Skylar's Song* written about his four-year old daughter, who is currently in Los Angeles' Children Hospital, suffering from cancer.)

MOTÖRHEAD

Lemmy (bass, vocals); **Eddie Clarke** (guitar); **Phil Taylor** (drums)

1964

Lemmy (b. Ian Kilmister, Dec. 24, 1945, Stoke-on-Trent, Staffs.), a vicar's son who has abandoned a career in horsebreaking, inspired by hearing a Little Richard record, having begun his musical career in Blackpool, Lancs., as a member of soul bands the Rainmakers and the Motown Sect, and subsequently the Rockin' Vickers, wearing dog collars and Finnish national costume, moves to London, initially staying at Ron Wood's mother's house, playing in bands Sam Gopal's Dream and Opal Butterfly, and also spends time as a roadie for Jimi Hendrix. Joining pioneering heavy-rock outfit Hawkwind in August 1971 to replace bassist Dave Anderson, initially for six months, he ends up staying for nearly four years, singing on their biggest hit, 1972's UK #3 *Silver Machine*.

1975

May Lemmy is dismissed from Hawkwind after spending five days in a Canadian jail for drug possession.
June On his return to Britain, Lemmy announces plans for a new band, initially to be called Bastard, but subsequently named Motorhead, the title of the last song he wrote for Hawkwind, and a cut which will become his new outfit's popular live anthem. Formative members are Larry Wallis (still with the Pink Fairies) on guitar and Lucas Fox on drums. Lemmy's description of his musical approach is: "We're the kind of band that if we moved in next to you, your lawn would die."
July Motorhead debuts at London's Roundhouse, supporting Greenslade.
Sept At odds with producer Dave Edmunds in studio sessions for its debut album on United Artists, Fritz Fryer takes over.
Oct They support Blue Öyster Cult at London's Hammersmith Odeon.
Dec Fox is replaced by Lemmy's friend Philthy Animal (b. Philip Taylor, Sept. 21, 1954, Chesterfield, Derbys.), who has not played professionally before.

1976

Jan United Artists rejects Motorhead's debut album. (The tapes will be released in 1979 as ***On Parole***.)
Feb Ex-Blue Goose and Continuous Performance member "Fast" Eddie Clarke (b. Oct. 5, 1950) joins as second guitarist, and after one rehearsal as a four-piece Wallis walks out. (The remaining trio, generally regarded as the definitive Motorhead line-up, will stay together for six years.) For seven months, the group has no manager, no recording contract and no income.
Dec Two tracks, *White Line Fever* and *Leavin' Here*, are recorded for Stiff Records (which will release the cuts two years later in a singles box set, and on the compilations ***A Bunch Of Stiffs*** and ***Hits Greatest Stiffs***).

1977

Apr The band records a gig at London's Marquee club, though a recording hitch renders the tapes unusable. Chiswick Records boss Ted Carroll offers them two days in the studio as consolation and they record 11 songs as Chiswick puts up the money to finish an album.
June Motorhead supports Hawkwind on tour. Taylor breaks bones in his hand punching someone in a fight after the third gig, but carries on. Chiswick releases *Motorhead/City Kids* and then ***Motorhead***, which makes UK #43 and establishes the band's unique brand of uncompromising and deafening heavy metal, led by Lemmy's distinctively throaty vocal style.
Aug On a headlining UK tour, Taylor breaks bones again when he hits the tour manager's face in a Plymouth hotel, causing the cancellation of remaining dates.

1978

July While Taylor, Clarke, Speedy Keen and Billy Rath have recently moonlighted as the Muggers, Motorhead signs to Bronze Records, as part of a deal which includes Hawkwind and Girlschool.
Sept Their first Bronze single, a cover of *Louie Louie*, peaks at UK #68.
Oct [29] The group ends a month-long UK tour at the City Hall, Newcastle, Tyne & Wear.

1979

Mar ***Overkill*** reaches UK #24 with its title track *Overkill* making UK #39.
[24] The group embarks on a 17-date UK tour at City Hall, St. Alban's, Herts., set to end on the 12th at the St. George's Hall, Bradford, Yorks.
July *No Class* peaks at UK #61.
Oct ***Bomber*** reaches UK #12, while the title cut *Bomber* makes UK #34.
Dec Liberty/UA's release of the rejected 1976 album, ***On Parole***, stops at UK #65.

1980

May EP *The Golden Years* hits UK #8.
July [26] Motorhead headlines the "Heavy Metal Barn Dance" at Bingley Hall, Stafford, Staffs.
Oct Furiously-paced, hard-rock guitar-driven, as is all Motorhead material, *Ace Of Spades* reaches UK #15, while its parent, ***Ace Of Spades***, hits UK #4.
[22] They begin a 33-date UK tour at the Gaumont Theatre, Ipswich, Suffolk, set to close on November 29th with the last of four dates at London's Hammersmith Odeon.
Dec Chiswick-released EP of early material, *Beer Drinkers And Hell Raisers*, makes UK #43.
[20] Taylor accidentally breaks a bone in his neck while partying after a show in Belfast. (By year's end Lemmy will have to fly to Britain in mid-tour after infection sets in in a bone on the back of his hand after a coin has been thrown at him during a gig in Ljubljana, Yugoslavia. He will spend six days in hospital.)

1981

Feb Motorhead has teamed with its feminine counterpart, Girlschool, as Headgirl, and covered each other's songs (*Bomber* and *Emergency*) and Johnny Kidd & the Pirates' *Please Don't Touch* on the EP *St. Valentine's Day Massacre*, which hits UK #5. Lemmy also collaborates with the Nolan Sisters, Cozy Powell and others on *Don't Do That*.
Apr The group begins its first US tour.
June [27] ***No Sleep Till Hammersmith***, a performance album recorded at the Hammersmith Odeon in 1980, enters the UK chart at #1, becoming a rare live chart-topper, and career peak.
July Live single, *Motorhead/Over The Top*, hits UK #6. Motorhead has become the clear ascendant of New Wave Of British Heavy Metal (NWBHM), a movement which will inspire US bands like Metallica.

1982

Feb The group cancels a gig at Cardiff's Sophia Gardens after the roof collapses because of snow, relocating the show to Talbot's Afan Lido.
Mar *Iron Fist* reaches UK #29.
Apr ***Iron Fist*** hits UK #6.
May Motorhead begins a major US tour. Lemmy's plan to record a version of Tammy Wynette's *Stand By Your Man* with the Plasmatics' Wendy O. Williams is the final straw for Clarke, who quits the tour. (He will later form Fastway.) Brian Robertson (b. Sept. 12, 1956, Glasgow, Scotland), ex-Thin Lizzy, is brought in as his replacement.
June ***Iron Fist*** peaks at US #174.

1983

Feb Big Beat label-released ***What's Words Worth***, recorded live at London's Roundhouse early in the band's career, reaches UK #71.
May *I Got Mine* makes UK #46.
June ***Another Perfect Day*** reaches UK #20.
July *Shine* makes UK #59.
Aug ***Another Perfect Day*** peaks at US #153 as Robertson and Taylor both leave. Following auditions Lemmy selects Phil Campbell (b. May 7, 1961, Pontypridd, M. Glamorgan, Wales) and Wurzel (b. Michael Burston, Oct. 23, 1949, Cheltenham, Gloucs.) with ex-Saxon drummer Pete Gill also joining the new four-piece Motorhead.

1984

May The new line-up debuts at the Hammersmith Odeon.
Sept *Killed By Death* peaks at UK #51 while a double album compilation of mainly old material, ***No Remorse***, reaches UK #14. The group leaves Bronze, which serves an injunction on them, resulting in Motorhead being unable to record for nearly two years.
Oct Lack of funds causes the band to temporarily stop touring as they move into a house in suburban London, next door to a clergyman. The following June, Lemmy will record a single with 19-year-old UK model Samantha Fox (her first), but an injunction will prevent its release.

1986

May Motorhead contributes to the post-"Live Aid" heavy-metal fundraising ***Hear N' Aid***, which makes UK #50 and US #80.
June *Deaf Forever* peaks at UK #67, the first collaboration with producer Bill Laswell and new label GWR, which also re-releases the Motorhead back catalogue.
July ***Orgasmatron***, written in two days and recorded in three weeks, reaches UK #21.
Aug [16] Motorhead takes part in the seventh annual "Monsters Of Rock" festival at Castle Donington, Leics.
Dec ***Orgasmatron*** peaks at US #157.

1987

Apr Lemmy contributes to Ferry Aid's *Let It Be*, released to benefit those bereaved by the Zeebrugge ferry disaster. The record sells over half a million copies, topping the UK chart for three weeks.
Sept Lemmy appears in the Comic Strip movie "Eat The Rich". His performance wins no acting awards but the Motorhead theme tune for the film appears on Motorhead's ***Rock'n'Roll***, which makes UK #34 and US #150. The group's second live album, ***No Sleep At All*** will close its chart account for the decade peaking at UK #79 on Oct [15] the following year.

1990

Feb Lemmy & the Upsetters, with Mick Green, contribute a cover of *Blue Suede Shoes* to the compilation album ***The Last Temptation Of Elvis***, to benefit the Nordoff Robbins Music Therapy charity.
June Motorhead signs to WTG Records, and records a new album with Ed Stasium and Dave Edmunds (neither of whom last the distance) in Los Angeles, CA, where Lemmy is now fully resident, though the state's health and fitness lifestyle makes little impression on the hardened, non-stop drinking party machine.

1991

Jan [12] With a current line-up of Wurzel, Campbell, a re-joined Taylor and Lemmy, and licensed to Epic Records, Motorhead's uncompromising consistency continues to be rewarded as *The One To Sing The Blues* makes UK #45.
Feb [2] Its parent album, ***1916***, including a rare cello-backed ballad, produced by Peter Solley, reaches UK #24. On the group's 16th anniversary, Lemmy is quoted as saying: "We've been going four years longer than the Third Reich."
Apr [27] ***1916*** peaks at US #142.
May [10] Motorhead appears on C4-TV's "Friday At The Dome".
[16] In an effort to "blow the roof off the dump", the group guests on NBC-TV's "Late Night With David Letterman".
[20] North American tour opens at the Concert Hall, Toronto, Canada.
Aug After a Great Woods Center For The Performing Arts, Mansfield, MA concert, Lemmy slips backstage, breaking two ribs and causing the cancellation of the rest of the tour.

1992

May Mikkey Dee (b. Oct. 31, 1963, Olundby, Sweden), formerly of Dokken and King Diamond, replaces the departed Philthy Animal Taylor for the group's upcoming US tour.
Aug [8] ***March Or Die***, featuring Slash and Ozzy Osbourne, charts for a week at UK #60.
Oct [3] They play before a sellout crowd of 66,639 at the Rose Bowl, Pasadena, CA, during a current US tour with Guns N' Roses and Metallica.
[12] The group guests on NBC-TV's "The Tonight Show", reportedly the first metal band to do so.
Nov [8] They begin an eight-date UK tour at the Sheffield City Hall, set to end on the 16th at the Guildhall, Portsmouth, Hants.
[14] EP *'92 Tour* stops at UK #63.
Dec [23] Motorhead plays a festive gig at the recently renamed Hammersmith Labatt's Apollo.

1993

July Having been dropped by Epic Records, Lemmy responds in **Pulse** magazine: "I couldn't give a fuck. They can't hurt me. I've demonstrated that. Now it's time to rock the boat a little. Because the boat stinks at the moment. I've never seen a more cock-handed lot of assholes."
Sept [18] Revised update of *Ace Of Spades (The CCN Remix)* reaches UK #23, ahead of the forthcoming release of their ***Bastards*** album on their own umlaut-friendly Motörhead label.

1994

Feb [8] Motörhead embarks on a North American club tour with Black Sabbath and Morbid Angel at The Sting in New Britain, CT.
Dec [10] *Born To Raise Hell*, with Ice T and Ugly Kid Joe's Whitfield Crane on vocals and featured in the movie "Airheads", debuts at its UK #47 peak.

1995

June Lemmy signs on to CompuServe to interact with his fans.
July [4] They play an Independence Day show with Black Sabbath at the Pine Knob Music Theatre, Clarkston, MI, during a US tour.
Nov [2] Motörhead performs at London's Kentish Town Forum.
Dec [24] Having earlier cameod in "John Wayne Bobbit Uncut" as a passerby hit in the face by Bobbit's separated appendage, Lemmy celebrates his 50th birthday at the Whisky in Los Angeles, with Metallica and 15 bottles of bourbon.

1996

Jan [12] Motörhead perform at The Vic, Chicago, IL.
see also: **HAWKWIND**

MOTT THE HOOPLE

Ian Hunter (vocals, guitar); **Mick Ralphs** (guitar); **Verden Allen** (keyboards); **Overend Watts** (bass); **Dale "Buffin" Griffin** (drums)

1969

May [13] Watts (b. Peter Watts, May 13, 1949, Birmingham, Warks.), Griffin (b. Oct. 24, 1948, Ross-on-Wye, Hereford), Allen (b. May 26, 1944, Hereford, Hereford) and Ralphs (b. May 31, 1944, Hereford) have come together as the Shakedown Sound the previous year after meeting as members of the Doc Thomas Group. After the band has changed its name to Silence (previously used by Watts and Griffin for a post-school band), and with vocalist Stan Tippins on board, Ralphs has sent a demo tape to Guy Stevens at Island Records, who becomes their manager and producer. Tippins is sacked and Stevens places an ad in UK music paper **Melody Maker** for a new singer/keyboards player. Hunter (b. June 3, 1946), a veteran of clubs in Hamburg, West Germany, who has played on singles by the 1958 Rock'n'Roll Show including 1967's *I Can't Drive*, and Charlie Wolfe in 1968, replies and wins the audition. Stevens now auditions them and renames them Mott The Hoople after a 1967 novel by Willard Manus.

Oct Their first single on Island is *Rock'n'Roll Queen*.

Nov The band's debut album, ***Mott The Hoople*** (originally to have been titled ***Talking Bear Mountain Picnic Massacre Disaster Dylan Blues*** but overruled by Island), includes covers of the Kinks, Sonny Bono and Doug Sahm (Sir Douglas Quintet) material, and highlights Hunter's distinctive vocal style. (In 1970, it will make UK #66 and US #185.)

1970

Oct *Mad Shadows* makes UK #48 as the band tours widely in Britain, becoming a major live attraction to a degree not reflected by early record sales. Rather more chaotic US visits help promote the group in the US.

1971

Apr ***Wild Life*** climbs to US #44 and includes a live version of Little Richard's *Keep A Knockin'*.

June [3-6] The group plays at the Fillmore West, San Francisco, CA, on a bill with Albert King and Freddie King.

July [8] They perform at London's Royal Albert Hall and cause a minor riot, which leads to two people being injured and damages to two boxes, leading to a temporary ban on rock gigs at the venue. The group is also ordered to pay a "damages to property" bill of £1,467.

Aug ***Brain Capers***, produced by George "Shadow" Morton and the band's last album for Island, is released.

[28-29] The group takes part in the August Bank Holiday "Weeley Festival" at Weeley, Essex.

1972

Mar [26] After a show in Zurich, Switzerland, they decide to split. Long-time Mott fan David Bowie, hearing of the decision, offers them one of his new songs to continue recording. After turning down *Suffragette City*, they choose *All The Young Dudes*.

July Extracting itself from the Island contract, the band signs a new deal with CBS/Columbia Records.

Sept Career highlight, *All The Young Dudes*, produced by Bowie, hits UK #3, causing a minor controversy over the line "Stealing clothes from Marks and Sparks" (later changed to "unmarked cars").

Oct ***All The Young Dudes*** reaches UK #21 and includes contributions from both Bowie and his guitarist, Mick Ronson. Island issues ***Rock'n'Roll Queen***, a compilation of earlier tracks.

Nov As *All The Young Dudes* makes US #37 and the ***All The Young Dudes*** album reaches US #89, the group begins its first major US tour, which Hunter chronicles in a diary.

[25] The band plays at the "Woodstock Of The West Festival" in Los Angeles, CA, with Stevie Wonder, the Eagles and the Bee Gees, among others.

Dec On their return from the US, Allen quits to pursue solo projects but will not be immediately replaced as the band temporarily continues as a quartet.

1973

Jan *One Of The Boys*, taken from the album, makes US #96. The band plays its first UK gigs as a four-piece.

July *Honaloochie Boogie*, their first release with new members Morgan Fisher (ex-Love Affair) (piano) and Mick Bolton (organ) makes UK #12. Ralphs leaves to form new band Bad Company, and is replaced by Luther Grosvenor (b. Dec. 23, 1949, Evesham, Worcs.) from Spooky Tooth, now calling himself Ariel Bender.

Aug The band headlines a highly successful US tour, including a sellout week at Broadway's Uris Theatre, New York, NY. ***Mott*** hits UK #7 and reaches US #35.

Sept Hunter-written *All The Way From Memphis* hits UK #10.

Dec *Roll Away The Stone*, again penned by Hunter, hits UK #8.

[14] The group ends a 22-date UK tour at London's Hammersmith Odeon.

1974

Apr *The Golden Age Of Rock And Roll* reaches UK #16 while ***The Hoople*** makes UK #11.

June ***The Hoople*** reaches US #28, while *The Golden Age Of Rock And Roll* peaks at US #96 (the band's last US chart single). Hunter's book, the revealing **Diary Of A Rock'n'Roll Star**, based on the band's touring exploits, is published.

July *Foxy Foxy* reaches UK #33. Bolton leaves, apparently on religious grounds, and is replaced by ex-Amen Corner keyboardist Blue Weaver. Meanwhile, an early compilation, ***Rock'n'Roll Queen***, issued in the US on Atlantic Records, makes US #112.

[6] The group co-headlines the "Buxton Festival", Buxton, Derbys., with the Faces and Humble Pie.

Sept [20] Bender quits, to be replaced on guitar by Mick Ronson (b. May 26, 1949, Hull).

Oct Hunter collapses from exhaustion in the US, prior to planned European dates.

Nov *Saturday Gigs* reaches UK #41, while their album, ***Mott The Hoople - Live***, recorded in November 1973 at the Hammersmith Odeon and in New York in May 1974, heads to UK #32 and US #23.

Dec [16] With Hunter not fully recovered, and problems looming over the rescheduling of gigs, the band decides to split.

1975

Jan Hunter and Ronson form the Hunter-Ronson Band, designed as a touring unit to promote solo albums on which both are working.

Mar Ronson's solo, ***Play, Don't Worry***, reaches UK #29 and US #103.

[20] The Hunter-Ronson Band begins a 13-date tour in Sheffield, S. Yorks.

May [17] Buffin, Watts and Fisher regroup under the truncated name Mott, adding new members Ray Major (guitar) and Nigel Benjamin (vocals), while Hunter's solo ***Ian Hunter*** reaches UK #21 and US #50. The Hunter-Ronson Band plays a sellout UK tour, and then makes a short visit to the US, before splitting.

June Hunter's solo single, *Once Bitten, Twice Shy*, with its memorable opening lyric, "'allo", reaches UK #14.

Oct Mott's ***Drive On*** peaks at UK #54 and US #160, and will be the group's last chart success.

1976

June Hunter's ***All American Alien Boy*** makes UK #29 and US #177, while Mott's ***Shouting And Pointing*** is released.

Nov Benjamin leaves Mott and the band splits.

1977

Feb Hunter and members of his group escape a house fire in Montreal, PQ, Canada, where they are living while recording an album. They are left standing naked in snow in 4-below temperatures as the entire house and contents are destroyed.

Oct Mott members, minus Hunter, regroup again, adding John Fiddler from Medicine Head, as British Lions. (They will last some two years and two albums, ***British Lions*** and ***Trouble With Women***, after which Fisher will form his own Pipe label, and Buffin and Watts their own Grimstone Productions, producing Slaughter & the Dogs and Department S, among others. Buffin will revert to his real name and occasionally produce live sessions for BBC's Radio 1. Allen and Grosvenor will release material through Jet and Spinet Records over the next five years.)

After two years' living and working in the US (re-publishing an updated version of his book, as **Reflections Of A Rock'n'Roll Star**), Hunter returns to Britain with a new four-piece backing band, named Overnight Angels (after his new album ***Overnight Angels***). The band plays ten well-received dates in the UK, but the album fails to chart and is not issued in the US. (Hunter will follow it with an 18 months pause in New York, though he will produce Generation X's ***Valley Of The Dolls*** during 1978.)

1979

May Hunter's ***You're Never Alone With A Schizophrenic***, his first for Chrysalis Records, reaches UK #49 and US #35.

June [28] Hunter appears at New York's Palladium Theatre with Ronson and Ellen Foley.

Sept Hunter's *Just Another Night* peaks at US #68. A live double album, ***Ian Hunter Live : Welcome To The Club***, recorded during a record-breaking seven-night sellout at Los Angeles' Roxy club, will reach UK #61 and US #69 the following April.

1983

Aug Having released ***Short Back And Sides***, with help from Todd Rundgren and two members of the Clash, which reached UK #79 and US #62 the previous September, Hunter switches back to CBS/Columbia for ***All Of The Good Ones Are Taken***, which now makes US #125.

1990

Jan [6] After a long period out of the public eye, Hunter has re-teamed with Ronson for a reactivated Hunter-Ronson Band which, signed to Mercury Records, returns with the new Bernard Edwards-produced ***Y U I ORTA*** making US #157. It will be released in the UK the following month supported by selected sellout dates.

1993

Apr [29] Ronson dies of cancer in London. His last live performance had been a year previously at the Freddie Mercury tribute concert. Def Leppard's Joe Elliott says, "If there's a God up there why does he do this? It can only be because he's trying to put together the ultimate band".

June While Atlantic has brought ***Mott The Hoople*** and ***Rock And Roll Queen*** to compact disc in 1991, the same year Castle Communications UK issued the Hunter anthology ***The Collection***, CBS now releases ***The Ballad Of Mott***, a boxed-set retrospective.

THE MOVE

Carl Wayne (vocals); **Roy Wood** (vocals, guitar); **Trevor Burton** (lead guitar); **Ace Kefford** (bass); **Bev Bevan** (drums)

1966

Feb The group is formed in Birmingham, Warks., by members of three of the city's best existing beat groups: Wood (b. Nov. 8, 1947, Birmingham, not as Ulysses Adrian Wood, a legend subsequently established after Wood had jokingly provided the name to a teen magazine) ex-Mike Sheridan & the Nightriders, Wayne (b. Aug. 18, 1944, Moseley, Warks.), Kefford (b. Christopher Kefford, Dec. 10, 1946, Moseley), Bevan (b. Nov. 24, 1944, Birmingham), ex-Carl Wayne & the Vikings, Denny Laine & the Diplomats and Danny King & the Mayfair Set, and Burton (b. Mar. 9, 1944, Aston, Warks.) ex-Danny King & the Mayfair Set. Stabilizing as a quintet after initial jams at Birmingham's Cedar club, the band builds a strong local reputation, links with manager Tony Secunda and moves to London.

July [30] The group performs at the sixth annual "National Jazz & Blues Festival", Windsor, Berks. (and set off distress flares during its act).

Dec With a cult following gained by several Secunda-initiated PR stunts and from regular outrageous behaviour during a residency at London's Marquee club (taken over from the Who), the group signs with producer Denny Cordell, and via him to Deram Records. At one of the Marquee gigs, after further pyrotechnics, three fire engines are called to the venue.

1967

Jan *Night Of Fear*, a Roy Wood song with a riff based on Tchaikovsky's "1812 Overture", hits UK #2.
Apr The band offers a £200 reward for information leading to the recovery of tapes stolen from their agent's car in London's Tin Pan Alley. (They will subsequently be found on a building site in North London by a laborer who duly receives £200).
Supporting the Rolling Stones at the Olympia, Paris, France, the group lets off naval distress signals outside the venue.
[14-15] The group plays at the "Arts Festival Ball" all-nighter at the Hotel Metropole, Brighton, Sussex.
[29] The band performs during a 14-hour "Technicolour Dream" concert in the Great Hall of the Alexandra Palace, London, on a bill with Pink Floyd, Tomorrow and John's Children (featuring Marc Bolan).
May *I Can Hear The Grass Grow*, developing Wood's flirtation with psychedelia, hits UK #5. The group begins to gain a reputation for Who-type destruction (usually smashing TV sets or obliterating effigies of people like Adolf Hitler) on its stage act and on TV appearances.
Sept [30] BBC Radio 1 is launched in Britain, with the Move's *Flowers In The Rain* as the first disc played.
Oct *Flowers In The Rain* hits UK #2. The group has switched, with other Cordell-produced acts, to Regal Zonophone Records, a label previously reserved for Salvation Army music.
Nov The Move is successfully sued by UK Prime Minister Harold Wilson over a nude caricature of him on a promotional postcard for *Flowers In The Rain*, with all royalties earned by the record going to charity as part of the settlement. *Cherry Blossom Clinic*, scheduled as the next single, is dropped since its lyric, concerning a mental asylum, is considered likely to create more unfavorable publicity. (The track will appear on the group's first album.)
Dec [11] The band embarks on a week-long Scandinavian tour, with dates in Helsinki, Stockholm, Gothenburg, Malmo and Copenhagen.
[22] They perform at London's Olympia Hall.

1968

Mar *Fire Brigade* hits UK #3.
Apr Their debut album, ***Move***, reaches UK #15. It had earlier been reported that Marlon Brando was to narrate a monologue on the album. Kefford leaves the group due to illness and will not return, subsequently pursuing a solo career. (He will record a single as the Ace Kefford Stand for Atlantic, reviving the Yardbirds' *For Your Love*.) Burton switches to bass as the group continues as a quartet. Richard Tandy (who will later play with Burton in Balls and with Wood and Bevan in ELO) occasionally joins on keyboards and bass. Secunda also quits as manager.
July *Wild Tiger Woman* is released.
Aug The group appears at the first "Isle Of Wight" festival.
Sept Live *Something Else* is released, an unusual, five-track 33rpm 7" EP, later to become an expensive collector's item.
[16] More than 200 fan club members are invited to the group's first recording session with new producer Jimmy Miller at London's Olympic Studios, Barnes.
Dec [26] The band begins a week-long tour of West Germany.

1969

Feb [5] Wood-penned *Blackberry Way* tops the UK chart for a week, the Move's only #1 hit. Burton, tired of the group's commercial material, quits on the eve of a US tour, which has to be cancelled. (He will join the Uglys and then form Balls with ex-Moody Blues' vocalist Denny Laine.)
Mar Jeff Lynne (b. Dec. 30, 1947, Birmingham) of the Idle Race and Rick Price (b. June 10, 1944, Birmingham) of Sight and Sound are invited to join the Move. Lynne decides against it, but Price comes in as bassist.
July Wood-written *Hello Susie*, covered by Amen Corner, hits UK #4.
Aug *Curly* reaches UK #12.
Oct The Move's only US tour is unsuccessful and the Northern UK cabaret gigs which follow cause a rift between Wayne and the others.

1970

Jan [31] Wayne leaves for a solo cabaret and TV career which will see moderate success during the '70s. Lynne agrees to join in his place (having taken over from Roy Wood in the Nightriders), admitting to being more interested in the Electric Light Orchestra project currently being mooted by Wood.
May *Brontosaurus*, taken from ***Shazam*** which was released in February, an uncharacteristically heavy rocker, hits UK #7.
June [1] Rick Price signs a solo recording and production deal with President Records.
Oct ***Looking On*** is released along with the extracted *When Alice Comes Back To The Farm*.

1971

July With the band moved to EMI's Harvest label, and with Wood and Lynne jointly producing, *Tonight* reaches UK #11, taken from ***Message From The Country***.
Oct The Move makes its final live appearances, after which Price leaves. (He will form Sheridan/Price and then Mongrel, but will later rejoin Wood in Wizzard. The only Move performances will be on UK TV, promoting its final two singles.)
Nov *Chinatown* reaches UK #23. Plans are made for transforming the Move into the Electric Light Orchestra (later known as ELO), with the recruitment of five musicians, including ex-Move part-timer Richard Tandy.

1972

Feb Wood releases the solo *When Grandma Plays The Banjo*.
Apr [16] The first live appearance of ELO, at the Greyhound pub in Croydon, London, marks the demise of the Move.
May The final Move single, *California Man*, hits UK #7.
Aug Wood leaves ELO to form Wizzard.
Nov *Do Ya*, written by Lynne, on the UK B-side of *California Man*, is issued as an A-side in the US and gives the Move its only US chart entry, peaking at #93 (and subsequently revived to greater success by ELO). (EMI will bring Move's career highlights to compact disc with the 1993 release of ***Great Move : The Best Of The Move***.)
see also: **THE ELECTRIC LIGHT ORCHESTRA, WIZZARD**

ALISON MOYET

1983

July Moyet (b. Genevieve Alison Jane Moyet, June 18, 1961, Basildon, Essex), nicknamed "Alf" from childhood by her French father and having sung with Southend R&B groups the Vicars and the Screaming Abdabs, joined ex-Depeche Mode keyboardist and songwriter Vince Clarke to form Yazoo (known in the US as Yaz) in January 1982 (the same year she also contributed her considerable vocal talent to Fad Gadget's ***Under The Flag***). The unlikely combination of Moyet's bluesy vocals and Clarke's synthesizer wizardry proved successful, yielding an 18-month run of UK hit singles and albums. With Yazoo now splitting after completing its second album. Clarke remains with Mute Records but Moyet signs as a solo artiste to CBS Records, under the name Alison Moyet. Recording is delayed until contractual difficulties are resolved with US Sire, to which Moyet is still tied via Yazoo's North American deal.

1984

Aug With Moyet having married long-time boyfriend Malcolm Lee and moved from Essex to Hertfordshire, her CBS debut, *Love Resurrection*, with a lusher sound than the sparse electronic style of Yazoo, hits UK #10.
Nov Soul-styled *All Cried Out* reaches UK #8.
Dec *Invisible*, penned by Lamont Dozier, reaches UK #21.

1985

Jan [19] Her maiden solo album, ***Alf***, produced and largely written by Tony Swain and Steve Jolley, tops the UK chart and will stay on the survey for a year as Moyet begins a major UK tour to promote the album.
Feb [10] She heads the bill of a benefit concert at the London Palladium for the National Jazz Centre, on a varied line-up which includes Jools Holland from Squeeze and the Humphrey Lyttleton Band.
[11] Moyet is named Best British Female Artist at the fourth annual BRIT Awards, at London's Grosvenor House Hotel.
Apr In a change of style to acknowledge her early musical influences, Moyet's revival of Billie Holiday's jazz standard, *That Ole Devil Called Love*, proves to be her biggest UK hit, at #2. She gives birth to her first child (though her marriage will fail within the year).
June She follows her Billie Holiday revival with a UK tour accompanied by a jazz band, but receives much criticism for over-reaching herself, and does not commit the stage set to record.
July [13] She appears at the historic "Live Aid" benefit at Wembley Stadium, Wembley, Middx., duetting with Paul Young on *That's The Way Love Is*. James Brown's album ***Gravity***, featuring a Moyet duet with the soul legend, will be released in October the following year.

1987

Jan After a lengthy hiatus, *Is This Love?*, written by Moyet and Jean Guiot, reaches UK #3.
Apr ***Raindancing***, produced by Jimmy Iovine, hits UK #2, while the extracted *Weak In The Presence Of Beauty* hits UK #6.
June *Ordinary Girl* makes UK #43.
July ***Raindancing*** makes US #94.
Dec Her revival of the Ketty Lester oldie, *Love Letters*, remaining true to Lester's hit arrangement, hits UK #4, aided by a popular domestic-scene video co-starring UK comediennes French & Saunders.

1988

Feb [8] Moyet wins the Best British Female Artist category for the second time at the seventh annual BRIT Awards, at London's Royal Albert Hall. (On May 19th the following year Moyet will be granted an uncontested divorce from hairdresser husband Malcolm Lee after a five-year marriage, on the grounds they have lived apart for more than two years.)

1991

Apr [5] Moyet performs live on BBC1-TV's "Wogan".
[13] *It Won't Be Long* makes UK #50.
May [4] The largely self-written ***Hoodoo***, produced by Pete Glenister and featuring Fine Young Cannibals' Cox and Steele, debuts at its UK #11 peak.
[12] Moyet performs at "The Simple Truth - A Concert For Kurdish Refugees" benefit at the Wembley Arena, Wembley, singing *Chain Of Fools*.
June [1] *Wishing You Were Here* charts for a week at UK #72.
[5] Moyet makes a rare live appearance at London's Town & Country club.
Oct [26] *This House* reaches UK #40.
Nov [20] Moyet begins a seven-date UK tour at the

Riverside, Newcastle, Tyne & Wear, set to end on the 26th at Reading University.
[24] She takes part in a "Children In Need" benefit at London's Borderline with Kirsty MacColl, Ian McNabb and Thomas Lang.

1992

Feb [11] Moyet guests on C4-TV's "Return To The Dome".
Mar [2] She begins an eight-date North American tour, supporting Jules Shear at the 9.30 Club, Washington, DC, set to close on the 15th at Slim's, San Francisco, CA.
Apr [3] She plays a one-off London date at the Mean Fiddler.
Aug Moyet begins new sessions at Townhouse Studios with Glenister once again producing.
Sept [8] She sings at the Mercury Music Prize awards ceremony at London's Savoy Hotel.
Nov [29] Moyet performs acoustically at an Amnesty International concert for human rights at London's Royal Albert Hall, sharing the bill with David Byrne & the Pro Arte Orchestra and the Balanescu Quartet.
Dec She continues to work on her fourth album at Mayfair Studios, now with production help from Lightning Seeds' Ian Broudie. (During the year, Moyet has also contributed vocal work to Ocean Colour Scene's ***Ocean Colour Scene*** album.)

1993

Jan [30] Moyet performs at a tribute to celebrate the 29th anniversary of the US pro-choice legal ruling "Roe vs. Wade" at the Ritz, New York, NY with Joan Jett, Joey Ramone, Lunachicks and Fluid.
June [26] She participates in the "Glastonbury Festival", Glastonbury, Somerset, on the acoustic Pyramid stage.
Oct [23] *Falling* makes UK #42.

1994

Feb [17-19] Moyet takes part in the Gavin Seminar industry convention in San Francisco, CA. She says of her intermittent live appearances: "I've always been a bit of a lazy cow. I won't go on tour for longer than two weeks. It doesn't bother me if I sell 500,000 records or five million".
Mar [26] *Whispering Your Name*, released in 12" and CD formats with a mix of the song by erstwhile colleague Vince Clarke, their first collaboration since the break-up of Yazoo, reaches UK #18.
Apr [2] Co-produced by Glenister and Broudie, ***Essex*** reaches UK #24 in its week of entry.
[9] ***Essex*** charts for a week at US #194.
May [28] *Getting Into Something* debuts at its UK #51 peak.
June [14] Moyet plays at The Vic, Chicago, IL, during a short US club date tour.
Sept Broudie's Lightning Seeds' new project, ***Jollification***, including *My Best Day* co-written with Moyet, is released.
Oct [22] *Ode To Boy*, with a dance remix by Junior Vasquez, charts for a week at UK #59.
[23] Moyet takes part in the "Stonewall Equality" show, at London's Royal Albert Hall, with Sting, Elton John, Melissa Etheridge and Lily Savage.

1995

June [3] Combining both her career highlights in Yazoo and her subsequent solo successes, the compilation album ***Singles*** tops the UK Chart in its first week on sale.
Aug [26] *Solid Wood* debuts at its UK #44 peak.
Nov [27] Moyet embarks on an eight-date UK tour at Oxford's Apollo Theatre, set to end on December 7th at London's Royal Albert Hall.

1996

Apr [5] Trip-hop messiah Tricky's album, ***Nearly God***, credited to Nearly God the artist, hits UK #10, and includes a duet with Moyet on the bluesy *Make a Change*.
[13] Reactivated by Sony and augmented with a selection of live highlights, ***Singles*** now reaches UK #17.
see also: YAZOO

MUD

Les Gray (vocals); **Rob Davis** (lead guitar, vocals); **Ray Stiles** (bass, vocals); **Dave Mount** (drums, vocals)

1968

Apr Gray (b. Apr. 9, 1946, Carshalton, Surrey), a veteran of skiffle and trad jazz bands, and Mount (b. Mar. 3, 1947, Carshalton), both from different local groups, team to form the pop outfit Mud, recruiting local musicians, Davis (b. Oct. 1, 1947, Carshalton) and Stiles (b. Nov. 20, 1946, Carshalton), ex-Trolls and Remainder. Making its first live appearance in April at the Streatham Ice Rink, London, and releasing a one-off debut single, *Flower Power*, for CBS Records, the band makes its radio debut on BBC's "Monday Monday" in October. Signing with Pye Records in April 1967 following their victory in the national "Search For Sound" contest and gigging as a semi-professional band, Mud now finally turn pro, re-signing to CBS and releasing *Up The Airy Mountain*. After the group makes its UK TV debut on BBC1's "The Basil Brush Show" in May the following year, Philips Records will release the band's third single, *Shangri-La*, followed by *Jumping Jehosaphat* in June 1970.

1973

Feb Mud begins a UK tour opening for US crooner Jack Jones.
Apr Newly signed to Mickie Most's RAK label, *Crazy* is their UK chart debut, reaching #12.
July *Hypnosis* makes UK #16.
Dec *Dyna-Mite*, produced and written, like many of Mud's early successes, by song-writing team Nicky Chinn and Mike Chapman, hits UK #4.

1974

Jan [26] *Tiger Feet* tops the UK chart for the first of four weeks, and starts a short-lived UK dance craze. Labelmate Suzi Quatro will knock them off the top spot with *Devil Gate Drive*.
Mar [15] The group begins a 30-date UK tour at the Coventry College Of Education, West Midlands.
May *The Cat Crept In* hits UK #2.
Aug *Rocket* hits UK #6.
Sept Chinni-Chap-created ***Mud Rock*** hits UK #8. Mud signs to Private Stock Records (though their first single for the label will not be released until October 1975).
Dec [21] Chinni-Chap-penned ballad, *Lonely This Christmas*, on which Gray indulges his passion for Elvis Presley vocal inflections, begins a festive four-week run at the top of the UK chart.

1975

Mar *The Secrets That You Keep*, another Presley pastiche, released on Valentine's Day, hits UK #3.
May [3] *Oh Boy*, Mud's revival of the Crickets 1957 UK #3, tops the UK chart, deposing the Bay City Rollers' *Bye Bye Baby*.
July *Moonshine Sally* hits UK #10, while ***Mud Rock Vol. 2*** hits UK #6.
Aug *One Night* makes UK #32.
Oct *L-L-Lucy*, the group's first release on Private Stock, hits UK #10.
Nov RAK compilation, ***Mud's Greatest Hits***, reaches UK #25.
Dec Ballad, *Show Me You're A Woman*, hits UK #8 and ***Use Your Imagination*** makes UK #33.

1976

June *Shake It Down* reaches UK #12.
Dec *Lean On Me*, a 1972 UK #18 for its writer Bill Withers, hits UK #7. (This will end Mud's chart-making career, though the group is signed to RCA, which issues ***It's Better Than Working***.

1977

Mar Gray, signed to Warner Bros. as a solo artist, reaches UK #32 with his revival of the Mindbenders 1966 UK #2, *A Groovy Kind Of Love*.
Dec The group plays at London's Rainbow Theatre.

1978

Apr [6] RCA throws a tenth-anniversary party for Mud and releases ***Mudpack***.
June [2] The group embarks on 15-date UK tour at the Top Rank, Brighton, Sussex, including a week's stint in cabaret at Baileys, Watford, set to end on the 30th at the Wakefield Theatre Club.

1985

Dec While three further Mud albums have been released (***Rock On*** (1979), ***As You Like It*** (1979) and ***Mud*** (1983)), the re-issued *Lonely This Christmas* peaks at UK #61, as the group continues to perform on the UK cabaret circuit. (Stiles will make his first BBC1-TV's "Top Of The Pops" appearance in almost 12 years in September 1988 as a member of the Hollies, performing *He Ain't Heavy, He's My Brother*.)

1991

Oct [18-21] Following the release of the nostalgic ***Let's Have A Party*** the previous year, Mud performs at the "2nd Hemsby '70s & Glam Rock Weekender" at Pontins Holiday Centre in Hemsby, Norfolk, sharing the bill with Showaddywaddy, the Sweet, the Glitter Band, Alvin Stardust, Mungo Jerry and the Rubettes. The original versions of the group's bubble-gum pop hits will reach compact disc in Europe with the 1994 release of the 20-track ***Dynamite*** retrospective on the BR Music label.

N

RICK NELSON

1957

Apr [10] Ricky Nelson (b. Eric Hilliard Nelson, May 8, 1940, Teaneck, NJ), second son of US showbiz couple Ozzie and Harriet Nelson (formerly a bandleader and band vocalist), has played himself in the family radio show "The Adventures Of Ozzie And Harriet" since March 1949 and since its switch to ABC-TV in October 1952, and appeared in the movies "The Story Of Three Loves" and "Here Comes The Nelsons". He sings Fats Domino's *I'm Walking* for the first time on the show, eliciting a huge teenage response. In real life, Nelson has told a girlfriend he intends to record a single, as a defensive reaction to her adulation of Elvis Presley. Through contacts at Verve Records, Ozzie Nelson arranges to have the song recut in a studio session, arranged by guitarist Barney Kessel, along with two other tracks.

May Verve releases the single, *A Teenager's Romance*, coupled with *I'm Walking* and, with instant television exposure, it sells 60,000 copies in just three days.

June *A Teenager's Romance* hits US #8 and *I'm Walking* reaches US #17, with total sales topping one million.

Sept The third track from his debut session, *You're My One And Only Love*, is issued, coupled with Kessel's instrumental *Honey Bop*, and reaches US #14. No contract has been signed with Verve and, when it becomes clear that the label is withholding royalties, Ozzie Nelson initiates legal proceedings, and agrees to Lou Chudd of Imperial Records (which had released Fats Domino's original *I'm Walking*) signing Ricky. Additionally, one of his songs is included in each subsequent episode of "The Adventures Of Ozzie And Harriet" (which will guarantee maximum exposure through to 1966, when the series ends).

Oct *Be-Bop Baby*, his Imperial debut (a self-confessed stab at a Carl Perkins-type rockabilly track), hits US #5, and is his second million seller. Its B-side cover of Elvis Presley's recent version of *Have I Told You Lately That I Love You* reaches US #29.

1958

Jan Uptempo *Stood Up* hits US #5 (earning another gold disc), while the B-side, *Waiting In School*, written by Johnny and Dorsey Burnette, makes US #18.

[20] His debut album, ***Ricky***, a mixture of familiar rock songs and ballads, tops the US chart for the first of two weeks.

Feb Nelson forms his own full-time band for live work and for recording sessions as well as "Ozzie And Harriet" TV slots. He recruits James Burton (guitar) and James Kirkland (bass), after hearing them play in the studio with Bob Luman, plus Gene Garf (piano) and Richie Frost (drums). (Kirkland will later be replaced by Joe Osborn.) Meanwhile, *Stood Up* is his UK chart debut, at #27.

Apr *Believe What You Say*, another Johnny and Dorsey Burnette composition, hits US #8, and is coupled with the country-flavored *My Bucket's Got A Hole In It*, which reaches US #18.

Aug [4] *Poor Little Fool*, written by Sharon Sheeley, becomes Nelson's first #1 single, topping the US chart for the first of two weeks, and selling well over one million domestic units.

Sept His sophomore set, ***Ricky Nelson***, including *Poor Little Fool*, hits US #7.

Oct *Poor Little Fool* hits UK #4.

Nov Introspective ballad, *Lonesome Town*, the first song submitted to Nelson by songwriter Baker Knight, hits US #7, while its B-side, *I Got A Feeling*, also penned by Knight, hits US #10, combining to make a further million seller.

Dec UK follow-up to *Poor Little Fool* is the familiar oldie *Someday (You'll Want Me To Want You)*, which competes with a UK chart version by Jodi Sands. It hits UK #9, while the flip, *I Got A Feeling*, reaches UK #27.

1959

Jan Nelson co-stars in the Howard Hawks-directed western "Rio Bravo", with John Wayne and Dean Martin.

Mar ***Ricky Sings Again***, another compendium of rockers and country-style ballads, reaches US #14.

Apr Two tracks taken from the album form the next million-selling double A-side single: Knight's ballad *Never Be Anyone Else But You* hits US #6, while rocking Dorsey Burnette composition *It's Late* hits US #9.

May *It's Late* hits UK #3.

June *Never Be Anyone Else But You* reaches UK #14.

Aug Another double A-side US Top 10 has both *Sweeter Than You* (a Knight ballad), and *Just A Little Too Much* (a Burnette rocker), independently hitting US #9.

Sept *Sweeter Than You* makes UK #19, as *Just A Little Too Much* reaches UK #11.

Nov ***Songs By Ricky***, including both sides of his recent hit, reaches US #22.

Dec Offbeat and laid-back *I Wanna Be Loved* reaches US #20, while the B-side, *Mighty Good*, makes US #38.

1960

Jan *I Wanna Be Loved* reaches UK #30.

May *Young Emotions* makes US #12, with its B-side, *Right By My Side*, peaking at US #59.

July *Young Emotions* stops at UK #48.

Sept *I'm Not Afraid* peaks at US #27, coupled with Nelson's revival of *Yes Sir, That's My Baby* at US #34.

Oct ***More Songs By Ricky*** makes US #18. He appears in the comedy film "The Wackiest Ship In The Army", with Jack Lemmon.

1961

Jan *You Are The Only One* reaches US #25, while the flip-side, *Milk Cow Blues* (one of the earliest songs recorded by Elvis Presley), peaks at US #79.

May [8] On his 21st birthday, Nelson officially changes his performing name from Ricky to Rick.

[29] Jerry Fuller-penned *Travelin' Man* (originally offered to Sam Cooke, but rejected) begins two weeks at US #1, giving Nelson another million-seller after a long run of smaller successes. Its B-side, *Hello Mary Lou*, a Gene Pitney composition, hits US #9.

July ***Rick Is 21***, containing both sides of the recent single, hits US #8, while *Hello Mary Lou* gets A-side promotion in the UK and hits #2.

Nov *A Wonder Like You* makes US #11, with its B-side, *Everlovin'*, making US #16.

Dec *Everlovin'*, a UK A-side, reaches #23.

1962

Apr *Young World*, written by Fuller, hits US #5, while its flip-side revival of Gershwin's *Summertime* reaches US #89.

May *Young World* makes UK #19.

June ***Album Seven By Rick*** reaches US #27.

Sept *Teenage Idol*, a pseudo-autobiographical lament on the isolation caused by fame, hits US #5 and climbs to UK #39.

1963

Feb Nelson's last new single for Imperial, *It's Up To You*, another Fuller song, hits US #6 and makes UK #22. Nelson signs a new $1 million contract with Decca Records, set to last 20 years.

Mar Compilation, ***Best Sellers By Rick***, makes US #112.

Apr Both sides of his Decca debut single, *You Don't Love Me Anymore/I Got A Woman*, chart, at US #47 and #49, while Imperial's *That's All/I'm In Love Again* makes US #48 and #67. Nelson has time to promote neither: he marries Kristin Harmon, daughter of American football star Tom Harmon, and she joins him, playing his wife, in the cast of "Ozzie And Harriet". (They will divorce in 1981.)

May ***It's Up To You***, his final outing for Imperial, peaks at US #128.

June *String Along*, previously recorded by Fabian, and given the same guitar riff by Burton as *Poor Little*

Fool, reaches US #25.
July ***For Your Sweet Love*** makes US #20.
Oct His first major Decca hit is a Latin-rhythm revival of Glenn Miller's *Fools Rush In*, which makes both US and UK #12.

1964

Jan Imperial's issue of an old album track, the Gene Pitney song *Today's Teardrops*, reaches US #54.
Feb Another revival on Decca, the 1930 song *For You*, repeating the Latin arrangement, hits US #6 and UK #14. It is his last US Top 10 disc, and last UK chart entry for eight years. ***Rick Nelson Sings For You*** makes US #14, and will be his last album chart entry until 1970.
May Another Latin revival, *The Very Thought Of You*, reaches US #26.
Sept *There's Nothing I Can Say* peaks at US #47.
Nov He features in the movie "Love And Kisses" (adapted from a Broadway play), co-starring with wife Kristin. It arouses little attention in an age where the Beatles and the "British invasion" have swept aside much of the entertainment world's establishment.
Dec *A Happy Guy* makes US #82. A Billy Vera composition, *Mean Old World*, will peak at US #96 the following March, his last US Single chart entry for almost five years.

1966

May Still signed to Decca, Nelson enters the country-music phase of his career with the critically-acclaimed ***Bright Lights And Country Music***.
Sept [3] "The Adventures Of Ozzie And Harriet" finally ends its US TV run after 14 years.

1967

Apr His second country effort, ***Country Fever***, again reaps critical plaudits but few sales. It will be followed by ***Another Side Of Rick***, with folkier country material including a trio of Tim Hardin compositions, released in November 1968.

1969

May Having recently released ***Perspective***, Nelson forms a new road and recording band, with Allen Kemp (guitar), Tom Brumley (steel guitar), ex-Poco member Randy Meisner (bass), and Pat Shanahan (drums), which will become the Stone Canyon Band.

1970

Jan ***Rick Nelson In Concert*** features the still-unnamed Stone Canyon Band. Recorded at the Troubadour in Los Angeles, CA, it includes three Bob Dylan songs, plus Nelson's own oldies, *I'm Walking* and *Hello Mary Lou*. Dylan's *She Belongs To Me* is also released in a studio-recorded version, and puts Nelson back on the US Singles map at #33.
Apr Nelson's own composition, *Easy To Be Free*, makes US #48.
Nov ***Rick Sings Nelson*** peaks at US #196.

1971

June ***Rudy The Fifth*** is regarded as one of his best releases, highlighted by his cover of the Rolling Stones' *Honky Tonk Women* (a Nelson concert favorite around this time), and *Gypsy Pilot*, which is also issued as a single. Meisner leaves the Stone Canyon Band after the recording, to co-found the Eagles.
Oct [15] Booed at the seventh annual "Rock'n'Roll Revival" concert at New York, NY's Madison Square Garden, on a bill with Gary U.S. Bonds, the Coasters, the Shirelles, Bobby Rydell, Bo Diddley and Chuck Berry, when he plays new material alongside his early hits, Nelson pens *Garden Party* as a response.

1972

Feb [25] Nelson embarks on a four-date UK tour at the Odeon Cinema, Birmingham, West Midlands, set to end on the 28th at London's Royal Albert Hall.
Oct *Garden Party* hits US #6 (in a Top 10 which currently includes Elvis Presley and Chuck Berry), and becomes Nelson's first million seller since 1961.
Nov *Garden Party* makes UK #41 - his first UK hit single for eight years, but also his last. He makes his first visit to the UK, playing mainly at US bases with the Stone Canyon Band.
[24] *Garden Party* is certified gold by the RIAA.

1973

Jan ***Garden Party*** reaches US #32.
Feb *Palace Guard*, taken from the album, peaks at US #65. Signing with MCA Records later in the year, his first and last album for the label (despite having reportedly signed a nine-album deal), ***Windfall***, also marking his last album with the Stone Canyon Band, will make US #190 in March 1974.

1977

Aug [10] *Travelin' Man* is certified gold by the RIAA.
Sept Newly signed to Epic Records, Nelson releases the self-produced ***Intakes***. (His short period with Epic is commercially unsuccessful, but he experiments with material from a wide range of sources including John Fogerty and Gallagher & Lyle. His follow-up album, ***Back To Vienna***, produced by Al Kooper and featuring Dr. John, Michael McDonald and Jeff Baxter is never released.)

1981

Feb Having signed yet another deal, this time with Capitol Records, his label debut ***Playing To Win*** (produced by Jack Nitszche) becomes his last US chart entry, at #153. (He will continue to gig widely, both in the US and overseas, during the early to mid-'80s, mixing new material with old in audience-pleasing fashion. He also has guest acting roles on various TV drama series, including "McCloud" and "Petrocelli" and will feature in the 1983 NBC-TV movie "High School USA", playing a school principal, with his mother Harriet portraying his secretary.)

1985

Aug [22] Nelson co-stars with Fats Domino in a live spectacular at the Universal Amphitheatre, Universal City, CA. (The show is taped as a TV special for syndicated US airing in January 1986. Following his death, it will be re-edited as a tribute show. A subsequent program will feature Nelson singing John Fogerty's *Big Train (From Memphis)* with Johnny Cash, Jerry Lee Lewis, Roy Orbison and Carl Perkins.)
Nov He tours the UK on a well-received nostalgia package "The Regal Rock'n'Blues Reunion", which co-stars Bobby Vee, Bo Diddley and Del Shannon.
Dec [31] Nelson dies, along with his fiancée Helen Blair, his sound engineer Clark Russell and band members Bobby Neal, Patrick Woodward, Rick Intveld and Andy Chapin, when a chartered DC3 carrying them between concert dates in Guntersville, AL, and Dallas, TX, catches fire and crashes near De Kalb, TX. (Rumors ensue that the fire was caused by the plane's occupants freebasing cocaine. This allegation later proves to be without foundation.)

1986

Jan [6] A memorial service for Nelson is held in the Church Of The Hills at Forest Lawn Memorial Park, Hollywood, CA.
A posthumous album, ***All The Best***, is released, consisting of recent re-recordings of his hits.

1987

Jan [21] Nelson is posthumously inducted into the Rock and Roll Hall of Fame at the second annual ceremony, held at New York's Waldorf Astoria Hotel.

1991

Aug [31] After several attempts, Nelson's twin sons, Matthew and Gunnar, have found commercial success the previous year as lite-metal duo Nelson, while his daughter, Tracy, is successfully pursuing an acting career, starring in ABC-TV's "Father Dowling Mysteries" and "Glitter"; and CBS-TV's sitcom "Square Pegs". Rick Nelson's *Hello Mary Lou (Goodbye Heart)*, originally a 1961 UK #2 and released as part of EMI's Classic Tracks promotion, now makes UK #45. During the year, the same label will bring his considerable hit portfolio to compact disc with the issue of ***Ricky Nelson Volume 1 : The Legendary Master Series*** and ***The Best Of Rick Nelson Volume 2***.

SANDY NELSON

1958

Nelson (b. Sander Nelson, Dec. 1, 1938, Santa Monica, CA), inspired at the age of seven to play drums after seeing Gene Krupa perform live, is a neighbor of Dean Torrence, later of Jan & Dean, and is in a high school-based group with Jan Berry, Torrence and future Beach Boys member Bruce Johnston, though he leaves before the recording of the Jan & Arnie-credited hit *Jennie Lee*. With Johnston, he joins local club/dance band Kip Tyler & the Flips as its drummer, and plays on a few singles recorded for the Ebb and Challenge labels. He begins regular session work on small-label productions around Los Angeles, CA (notably those involving the Kim Fowley/Bruce Johnston/Gary "Skip" Paxton "brat pack"), and makes his first major hit appearance drumming on Phil Spector's first disc, the Teddy Bears' *To Know Him Is To Love Him*.

1959

July Nelson finances the recording of his own instrumental, *Teen Beat* (with Johnston playing piano), which highlights his percussion repertoire, at DJ Art Laboe's Original Sound Studio in Hollywood, CA. Laboe, who has just launched Original Sound Records (and has a current US #14 hit with its fourth release, Preston Epps' *Bongo Rock*), hears commercial potential and decides to release *Teen Beat* as a one-off.
Aug [3-6] As part of a session band including Jackie Kelso (sax) and Red Callender (bass), Nelson backs Gene Vincent on tracks for his ***Crazy Times*** album at the Capitol Tower Studios, Hollywood.
Oct *Teen Beat* hits US #4 and becomes a million seller, interesting other labels in Nelson (who has no contract with Laboe), leading him to sign to Imperial Records.
Nov His Imperial debut *Drum Party* fails to chart in the US (as will three singles which follow during 1960-61).
Dec *Teen Beat* hits UK #7.

1960

Jan Gene Vincent's *Wild Cat*, with Nelson on drums, reaches UK #21. Meanwhile, Nelson's first album, ***Teen Beat***, features a re-recording of the title track (Original Sound holds on to the hit version, and will continue to profit from it via reissues and compilation albums for the next two decades), plus a mixture of Nelson originals and cover versions.
July [11] The Hollywood Argyles' *Alley-Oop*, featuring Nelson on drums and (screaming) back-up vocals, tops the US chart and becomes a million seller.

1961

Dec *Let There Be Drums*, featuring Richie Allen (who later becomes better known as record producer Richard Podolor) on guitar, hits US #7 and becomes Nelson's second million seller.

1962

Jan *Let There Be Drums* hits UK #2, behind Cliff Richard's *The Young Ones*.
Mar *Drums Are My Beat* reaches US #29, while its B-side, *The Birth Of The Beat*, at US #75, is edited from its ten-minute version on Nelson's ***Let There Be Drums***, which is his best-selling album, hitting US #6 during a 46-week chart tenure.
Apr *Drums Are My Beat* climbs to UK #30.
May *Drummin' Up A Storm* makes US #67 while the flip-side, *Drum Stomp*, peaks at US #86. ***Drums Are My Beat!*** reaches US #29.
July *All Night Long* makes US #75 and *Drummin' Up A Storm* UK #39.

Aug Both feature on ***Drummin' Up A Storm***, which peaks at US #55.
Oct *And Then There Were Drums* reaches US #65.
Nov ***Compelling Percussion***, including *And Then There Were Drums* and the off-beat *Drums - For Strippers Only*, peaks at US #141.
Dec ***Golden Hits***, not a compilation of his own successes but a collection of instrumental versions of oldies like *Splish Splash*, *Kansas City* and *What'd I Say*, makes US #106.

1963

Following a motorcycle accident, Nelson has his right foot and part of his leg amputated. After recuperation, he returns to drumming despite this disability. (His 1963 album ***Beat That Drum***, released by Imperial during his absence, contains earlier tracks which are reissued under new titles to give the impression of being new material.)

1964

Oct *Teen Beat '65*, an update of his original hit, with a dubbed-on audience to give it a live feel, makes US #44.
Dec ***Live! In Las Vegas***, despite its title, dubbed in Los Angeles, peaks at US #122.

1965

Mar ***Teen Beat '65*** makes US #135.
July Another "live" album, ***Drum Discotheque***, including the updated *Let There Be Drums '66*, peaks at US #120.
Oct ***Drums A-Go-Go*** (the title track has hovered just below the US Hot 100 with the original version by the Hollywood Persuaders) makes US #118.

1966

Jan ***Boss Beat***, containing mainly covers of recent pop hits, peaks at US #126.
Apr Nelson's final US chart entry is ***"In" Beat***, another set of pop covers, which makes #148. (He will remain with Imperial until the early '70s, releasing two or three albums per year of either current cover versions, stylistic themes like jazz or country, or revivals of the big band sound - as with ***Manhattan Spiritual*** in 1969.)

1972

June Nelson visits the UK with producer Nik Venet, to record in London, and gives a detailed radio interview to DJ Charlie Gillett about his career, on BBC Radio London's show "Honky Tonk".

1982

After a decade of playing regularly around Los Angeles, usually with a small jazz group in which he is able to improvise on drums more freely than within earlier rock/pop constraints, Nelson returns to recording via his own label, Veebltronics. *A Drum Is A Woman* becomes a cult favorite in rock instrumental circles (notably in the UK, where it is imported), but runs foul of a feminist organization in Los Angeles. Nelson, taken aback ("I only meant a drum is sensual and sexy"), reissues it under the less controversial title *Drum Tunnel*. (His small group work will continue through the '80s, with occasional releases for devotees on his own label, while UK combo Boss Beat will release a cover of *Let There Be Drums* in a contemporary vein in 1988.)

WILLIE NELSON

1939

At age six, and surrounded by the influence of music at home, Nelson (b. Apr. 30, 1933, Abbott, TX) is bought a Stella guitar by his mother. His grandparents, who are helping to raise him following the divorce of his parents Ira and Myrtle, are learning music through mail-order courses and passing their knowledge on to Willie and his older sister, Bobbie Lee. Willie begins writing songs at age seven, and spends much time listening to the radio, favoring the Grand Ole Opry concerts and Texas western swing (particularly Bob Wills). His family's dedication to the church and gospel music will also make a profound impression. Joining John Paycheck's Bohemian Polka Band on a part-time basis at age ten, and with his sister Bobbie (who marries fiddle player Bud Fletcher), he goes on to play with Fletcher's friend Bud Wills in 1946. Nelson joins the airforce in 1952, serving in Korea for a short period, but has to leave the same year with a bad back, shortly thereafter studying agriculture and business at Baylor University, Waco, TX. Marrying Martha Matthews, and becoming a father to their first daughter, Lana, Nelson continues composing, and starts playing in small clubs and bars in Fort Worth, TX.

1955

He begins broadcasting a radio show in Washington state which features a half-hour live set by his own band. A second daughter, Susie, is born the following year, and with his composing skills maturing, Nelson finances his own recording of *No Place For Me*, which he sells to his radio listeners (2,000 copies) in Vancouver, WA, where he has become a successful DJ.

1958

After three years away from Texas trying various jobs, ranging from DJ to encyclopedia and vacuum-cleaner salesman, Nelson returns to Houston, TX, where he works as a DJ and also performs at the Esquire nightclub. His songwriting has become prolific, but his dire financial position forces him to sell songs cheaply, including future country standard *Family Bible* for $50, and *Night Life* (later a hit for Ray Price) for $150. His son Billy is born.

1960

The Nelsons move to Nashville, TN, where Willie meets other struggling musicians, including Mel Tillis, Roger Miller and Kris Kristofferson, who hang out in Tootsie's Orchid Lounge.

1961

Dec With the help of Hank Cochran, Nelson has signed a publishing contract with Pamper Music. His song, *Crazy*, is picked up by Patsy Cline and now hits #2 on the US Country chart and later hits US #9, her first Top 10 crossover record (it will become one of Nelson's most enduring compositions). Earlier in the year he penned *Hello Walls*, a US #2 for Faron Young, the biggest hit of the latter's career, and one which affords its writer his first royalty check for $40,000. With his songwriting a success, Nelson, again aided by Cochran, secures a recording deal with Liberty Records.

1962

His debut album, ***... And Then I Wrote***, is released. Nelson has further success on the Country chart with Shirley Collie on *Willingly*, and the solo *Touch Me*. As other artists, including Perry Como, Eydie Gorme and Jimmy Elledge, enjoy hits with Nelson material, crossover success currently eludes him. He replaces Danny Young in Ray Price's Cherokee Cowboys as a working musician, but the strains of touring result in divorce for Willie and Martha.

1963

Jan His sophomore album, ***Here's Willie Nelson***, is released, featuring Leon Russell on piano. It achieves little in sales, and Nelson moves to Monument Records, while Liberty closes down its country operations.
Dec Nelson's *Pretty Paper* is a big Christmas hit for Roy Orbison, reaching US #15 (and UK #6 a year later).

1964

Nov [28] Nelson achieves a childhood ambition by making his debut at Nashville's Grand Ole Opry, performing initially as an opening act for Roger Miller, and later forming a band with Wade Ray.
Dec Newly signed to RCA Records, which insists that he conforms to its traditional country output, Nelson's label debut, ***Country Willie - His Own Songs***, is released.

1965

Nelson marries Shirley Collie and they settle in Ridgetop, TN, taking up hog-farming. (Ray Price asks Nelson to raise one of his fighting roosters, but Nelson shoots it when it kills two of his hens and Price refuses to record any Nelson song again.) RCA album, ***Country Favorites Willie Nelson Style***, achieves few sales. A performance at Panther Hall, Fort Worth the following year will be recorded for release as ***Country Music Concert***.

1968

Having released two more RCA albums, ***Make Way For Willie Nelson*** and ***The Party's Over*** prior to this year's ***Texas In My Soul*** and ***Good Times***, and having divorced Collie (who had become a martial arts expert) the previous year, Nelson marries glass-factory worker Connie Koepke, whom he met at a concert in Cut'n'Shoot, TX. They will have a daughter, Paula, in 1969.

1970

June Through showbusiness lawyer Neil Rushen, Nelson has signed to Atlantic Records, which allows him the creative freedom that had frustrated him at RCA. His label debut is the gospel-tinged ***The Troublemaker*** (later issued by CBS/Columbia in 1976).
Dec [23] The Nelsons' house in Ridgetop, on the outskirts of Nashville, TN, burns to the ground. (Nelson will move his family back to Texas and will live there, and in Colorado, for the next 20 years.)

1971

May Atlantic releases ***Shotgun Willie***, which becomes his best-selling vocal project to date and includes a version of Leon Russell's ballad *A Song For You*. Nelson begins his biggest US tour with a major concert in every state.

1972

July [4] Nelson inaugurates his annual "Fourth Of July Picnic" (which will be held every year until 1980 at different Texas locations), at Dripping Springs, TX. The following year, still without a solo hit single or album, Nelson is inducted into the Nashville Songwriters Hall of Fame. Depressed at turning 40 next April, an inebriated Nelson lies down in the middle of the road hoping that a truck will run him over.

1975

July After 14 years of only specialist success on disc, Nelson has signed to CBS/Columbia Records for whom his debut set, ***Red Headed Stranger***, climbs to the top of the US Country chart, while *Blue Eyes Crying In The Rain* crosses over to reach US #21. Its success will help the album climb to US #28. As Nelson's pioneering and innovative "outlaw" country-style becomes more popular, ***Red Headed Stranger*** begins a run of US album popularity which will see at least one project chart every year for 14 years. The set's simple instrumentation and sparse production flies against current Nashville trends and the album will spend 43 weeks on the pop chart.
Oct [4] His 27th US Country single, *Blue Eyes Crying In The Rain* finally gives Nelson his first Country chart-topper.
Nov RCA begins extensive re-releasing and repackaging of old Nelson material: ***What Can You Do To Me Now*** peaks at US #196, while ***Wanted : The Outlaws***, a ground-breaking project recorded with Waylon Jennings, Tompall Glaser and Jessi Colter, is the first country album to be a million seller, topping the genre's survey.

1976

Jan *Remember Me* makes US #67.
Feb [28] Nelson wins the Best Country Vocal Performance, Male category for *Blue Eyes Crying In The Rain* at the 18th annual Grammy Awards, as the Columbia album, ***The Sound In Your Mind***, is

released, making US #48. Meanwhile, an RCA single, *Good Hearted Woman*, recorded with Waylon Jennings, climbs to US #25.

Mar [11] ***Red Headed Stranger*** is certified gold by the RIAA.

May [8] Nelson performs at Bob Dylan's second benefit gig for convicted boxer Rubin "Hurricane" Carter. Following the Houston concert, Nelson is served with a subpoena for grand jury investigation into drug offences.

RCA-released album, ***Willie Nelson Live*** (a reissue of the 1966 album ***Country Music Concert***), peaks at US #149.

June Atlantic-issued ***Phases And Stages***, originally recorded in 1964, produced by Jerry Wexler, makes US #187.

Oct His fourth chart album of the year, the newly-licensed ***The Troublemaker***, climbs to US #60.

1977

Jan [31] He collects the Favorite Single, Country trophy at the fourth annual American Music Awards, held at the Civic Auditorium, Santa Monica, CA.

May ***Before His Time***, released by RCA, is a compilation of earlier recordings remixed by Waylon Jennings, which peaks at US #78.

July His Columbia album, ***To Lefty From Willie***, a tribute to Lefty Frizzell, who died in 1975, makes US #91.

1978

Feb Nelson has teamed with Jennings for ***Waylon And Willie***. Released through Jennings' RCA contract (Columbia will be flexible with Nelson's contract for many years), it benefits from the US #42 single, *Mamas Don't Let Your Babies Grow Up To Be Cowboys*, and heads to US #12. Nelson sets up his own short-lived label, Lone Star, to record other artists.

May Columbia album, ***Stardust***, featuring a US #84-peaking version of Hoagy Carmichael's *Georgia On My Mind*, is released. An album of pop standards produced by Booker T. Jones, it begins a two-year chart stay during which it will reach US #30 (and will reside on the Country survey for over 500 weeks).

[5] ***The Sound In Your Mind*** is certified gold by the RIAA.

Dec Recorded live at Harrah's, Lake Tahoe, NV, the double album, ***Willie And Family Live***, begins its rise to US #32 and a one-year chart stay.

1979

Feb [15] Nelson wins the Best Country Vocal Performance, Male, for *Georgia On My Mind* and Best Duo Or Group Vocal Performance, for *Mamas Don't Let Your Babies* categories at the 21st annual Grammy Awards. He also nabs CMA's Entertainer Of The Year honor. An RCA album, ***Sweet Memories***, peaks at US #154.

June New collaborative studio effort, ***One For The Road***, by Nelson and Leon Russell, peaks at US #25.

Aug [2] ***One For The Road*** is certified gold by the RIAA.

Nov Columbia album, ***Willie Nelson Sings Kristofferson***, unites him with another old friend and makes US #42.

Dec Seasonal album, ***Pretty Paper***, hits **Billboard**'s Top 10 Christmas chart and US #73.

1980

Jan Nelson makes his movie debut, alongside Robert Redford and Jane Fonda, in "Electric Horseman". The soundtrack album, ***Electric Horseman***, featuring a side of Nelson songs and another of instrumental themes by Dave Grusin, makes US #52.

Feb A single from the film, digging at his 1978 hit, *My Heroes Have Always Been Cowboys*, reaches US #44.

Mar Finding ever-inventive ways of using old material, RCA has invited Danny Davis to score orchestral backing for earlier Nelson recordings. The subsequent album, ***Danny Davis And Willie Nelson With The Nashville Brass***, peaks at US #150.

June Nelson and Ray Price have finally settle their 15-year feud, recording ***San Antonio Rose*** together, which begins a 25-week run peaking at US #70.

Sept Nelson appears in a second movie, the country-themed "Honeysuckle Rose", while his *On The Road Again*, from the film, climbs to US #20. The soundtrack album, featuring a Nelson duet with Emmylou Harris, will make US #11.

1981

Feb [25] Nelson wins the Best Country Song category for *On The Road Again*, at the 23rd annual Grammy Awards. The studio album, ***Somewhere Over The Rainbow***, is released, rising to US #31.

Mar [21] *Angels Flying Too Close To The Ground* becomes Nelson's tenth US Country chart-topper.

June Nelson is taken sick in Hawaii with a collapsed lung, spending his hospital stay writing songs.

July [4] His annual "Fourth Of July Picnic" is held at Caesar's Palace, Las Vegas, NV.

Aug RCA issues ***The Minstrel Man***, which peaks at US #148.

[13] ***Somewhere Over The Rainbow*** is certified platinum by the RIAA.

Sept Willie Nelson's ***Greatest Hits (And Some That Will Be)*** is released by Columbia. During a 93-week chart stay, it will make US #27.

1982

Jan [25] He wins the Favorite Male Artist, Country, and Favorite Single, Country (tieing with Anne Murray) categories at the ninth annual American Music Awards, held at the Shrine Auditorium, Los Angeles, CA.

Mar ***Always On My Mind*** is released. The title track, his version of Presley's live favorite, becomes the biggest success of Nelson's career, hitting US #5 and propelling sales of the parent album to hit US #2 for four weeks during a 99-week chart stay.

June Nelson appears with Gary Busey in the movie "Barbarosa", and in the TV movie "In The Jailhouse Now", with John Savage. Two albums are released for the country market, ***Old Friend***, with Roger Miller, and the ***In The Jailhouse Now*** soundtrack recorded with Webb Pierce.

July His only solo UK chart single is *Always On My Mind*, which makes UK #49 during a three-week stay. (None of Nelson's albums will make the UK survey.)

Aug *Let It Be Me* makes US #40. Nelson is now performing as many as 250 concerts per year, including dates with Frank Sinatra, Waylon Jennings, the Stray Cats, Z.Z. Top, Neil Young, Dolly Parton and Linda Ronstadt, with worldwide live success.

Oct Jennings and Nelson reappear on RCA for ***WWII***, which makes US #57 and includes *Just To Satisfy You* (a US #52 item in March).

Dec Nelson wins the Top Artists Country, Top Country Album (***Always On My Mind***) and Top Country Singles (*Always On My Mind*) categories in **Billboard**'s Year In Music survey. (Nelson will also be voted ACM's Entertainer Of The Year.)

1983

Jan Nelson contributes to Kris Kristofferson's newly released duets album, ***The Winning Hand***.

[17] He wins the Favorite Album, Country, and Favorite Album, Pop/Rock categories at the tenth annual American Music Awards held, as ever, at the Shrine Auditorium.

Feb ***Poncho And Lefty***, on Epic Records through Merle Haggard's new contract, is credited to Haggard/Nelson and tops the US Country chart, also making US #37.

[23] Nelson wins the Best Country Vocal Performance, Male category for *Always On My Mind* at the 25th annual Grammy Awards. (It will also win an award as CMA's Single Of The Year.) Meanwhile, his new solo studio album, ***Tougher Than Leather***, is released, set to make US #39.

Mar [7] Nelson receives a Lifetime Achievement award from the Songwriters' Hall of Fame.

Apr Third album with Waylon Jennings, ***Take It To The Limit***, their first for Columbia, makes US #60.

May Nelson becomes the first country artist to receive the National Academy Of Popular Music's Lifetime Achievement award.

July [4] After a three-year gap, Nelson reinstates his annual "Fourth Of July Picnic", but will extend it to a three-day event held in different US locations, including Syracuse, NY, and Atlanta, GA.

Oct [3] ***San Antonio Rose*** is certified gold by the RIAA.

Nov ***Without A Song*** reaches US #54 and features Nelson's first duet with Julio Iglesias on their version of *As Time Goes By*.

Dec More RCA songs reappear on ***My Own Way***, which peaks at US #182.

1984

Jan [9] *Without A Song* is certified gold by the RIAA.

[16] Nelson wins the Favorite Male Artist, Country, category at the 11th annual American Music Awards, held at the Shrine Auditorium.

May Another duet with Iglesias, the ballad *To All The Girls I've Loved Before*, hits US #5 and UK #17. (The record will win the Academy of Country Music Single Award and the **Billboard** Country Top Single Award by year's end.)

June ***Angel Eyes***, featuring guitarist Jackie King, peaks at US #116.

Aug ***City Of New Orleans*** makes US #69, during a six-month chart stay.

Oct [7] "Songwriter", starring Nelson and Kristofferson, has its Nashville premiere, while the album soundtrack, ***Music From Songwriter***, released as a collaborative effort, climbs to US #152.

1985

Jan [28] Following the 12th annual American Music Awards at the Shrine Auditorium, at which Nelson collects the Favorite Male Video Artist, Country, trophy, he joins 44 other artists at A&M Studios, Hollywood, to record *We Are The World*, to raise funds to help feed the starving in Africa and the US.

Mar ***Me And Paul***, referring to his long-serving drummer Paul English, peaks at US #152 as the year's collaborative album, ***Funny How Time Slips Away***, with Faron Young, makes the Country survey.

Apr Nelson and Iglesias win the CMA Vocal Duo Of The Year award for *To All The Girls I've Loved Before*.

Sept [22] Inspired by "Live Aid", Nelson becomes a main organizer and the president of "Farm Aid", created to raise funds and help the plight of US farmers. "Farm Aid I" is held amid massive US media interest, will pool over $10 million in donations, and become an annual music festival into the '90s.

Meanwhile, ***Highwayman***, a collaboration between Nelson, Johnny Cash, Waylon Jennings and Kristofferson, tops the US Country chart and climbs to US #92. (*The Highwayman* will be voted ACM Single Of The Year.)

Oct ***Half-Nelson***, comprising only duets, peaks at US #178.

Nov His *Time Of The Preacher* is used in the BBC-TV nuclear-thriller "Edge Of Darkness". He writes *They're All The Same* for Johnny Cash, having been told by Cash that he dreamt Nelson had written a song with that title.

1986

Jan [27] As a Highwayman, Nelson wins the Favorite Video, Duo Or Group, Country, and Favorite Video Single, Country, categories at the 13th annual American Music Awards, held at the Shrine Auditorium, at which he also collects the Favorite Male Artist, Country, Favorite Single, Country, and Special Award Of Appreciation trophies for himself.

May ***The Promiseland*** hits C&W #1, joining five Nelson albums still on the survey.

June He begins sold-out UK dates, including a performance attended by H.R.H. Prince Charles.

July [4] His annual "Fourth Of July Picnic" turns into a "Farm Aid II" benefit concert in Austin, TX.

Sept Nelson receives the Roy Acuff Community Service Award from the Country Music Federation.

Nov [7] He appears as a corrupt lawman in NBC-TV's "Miami Vice".
[21] The RIAA certifies sales of two million of ***Red Headed Stranger***.
Dec [16] ***The Troublemaker*** is certified gold by the RIAA.

1987

Jan [26] Nelson nabs the Favorite Male Artist, Country trophy at the 14th annual American Music Awards, held at the Shrine Auditorium.
Feb He appears in a film based on his early Columbia concert album, ***Red Headed Stranger***.
Apr [6] ***Half Nelson*** is certified gold by the RIAA.
July [4] The "Fourth Of July Picnic" is held at Carl's Corner, TX. His live band is still Bobbie Nelson (piano), Jody Payne (guitar), Grady Martin (guitar), Mickey Raphael (harmonica), Bee Spears (bass) and Paul English (drums). ***Island In The Sea*** is released.
Sept Nashville's Country Hall of Fame opens a multi-media exhibition of the life and career of Willie Nelson.

1988

Sept Nelson contributes *Philadelphia Lawyer* to the newly released Woody Guthrie/Leadbelly tribute albums ***Folkways : A Vision Shared***.
Oct ***What A Wonderful World***, comprising cover versions, is released, set to hit US Country #6, as an extracted duet with Iglesias, *Spanish Eyes*, will hit US Country #8. It is his 30th album for Columbia in 13 years, of which 15 have earned gold discs, eight having gone on to be certified platinum.

1989

Jan [30] Nelson is presented with a Special Merit Award for his contribution to the music industry at the 16th annual American Music Awards, at the Shrine Auditorium.
July [25] He heads a fundraiser at the Bellevue Hotel, Washington, DC, for the family of Dixon Terry, president of the Family Farm Coalition, killed by lightning while baling hay on his farm in Greenfield, IA, Memorial Day weekend, leaving his wife and two children and a $300,000 debt over his farm.
Aug ***A Horse Called Music*** hits US #2 on the Country chart, spawning the US Country #1 smash, *Nothing I Can Do About It Now*.
Sept Aptly-titled Columbia album, ***Born For Trouble***, is released. (Before year's end, Nelson will receive the Governor's Award from the Nashville chapter of NARAS, and will host a 24-hour wild west show on the Cowboy Television Network, a cable channel Nelson has been instrumental in establishing.)
[16] *Nothing I Can Do About It Now* becomes Nelson's 20th US Country chart-topper.
[18] The RIAA certifies gold sales of ***Take It To The Limit*** and platinum sales of ***Pretty Paper***.

1990

Jan [9] The RIAA ratifies four million sales of ***Stardust***.
Feb Nelson embarks on the "Highwaymen 2" tour with Waylon Jennings, Johnny Cash and Kris Kristofferson to support ***Highwayman 2***, which will make US #79 on Apr [7].
Apr [1] Nelson's tour bus crashes into a car in Riverdale, Canada, on the way to concerts in Newfoundland. The car driver dies.
[7] Nelson appears at "Farm Aid IV" at the Hoosier Dome, Indianapolis, IN, before a sellout crowd of 43,000.
May The group is allowed to continue performing under the Highwaymen name, after '60s group the Highwaymen has sought to block its use. The original group's lead guitarist and singer is now Federal Appeals Court Judge Stephen Trott. During the month Nelson contributes *Birth Of The Blues* to Randy Travis' newly released album of duets, ***Heroes & Friends***. *Always On My Mind* is voted Country Single Of The Decade by **Billboard**.
Aug [22] The RIAA certifies two million sales of ***Willie And Family Live***.
Sept [28] The Highwaymen perform at the Concord Pavilion, Concord, CA, during current dates.
Nov [9] The Internal Revenue Service seizes Nelson's bank accounts and real estate holdings to satisfy a $16.7 million tax debt. (In response, Nelson sues former accounting firm Price Waterhouse in Dallas Federal Court, seeking $45 million in damages.)

1991

Jan [4] As all of Nelson's material wealth begins to go under the hammer, the Revenue auctions his three-bedroomed house, valued at $72,000, in Yakima, WA, for $50,500. (Nelson had never lived in it.)
[29] Nelson's 44-acre Dripping Springs ranch and house in San Marco, TX, are sold for the minimum required bid of $203,840.
Mar [5] Former Texas university football coach Darrell Royal pays $117,375 for Nelson's 76-acre spread, comprising a golf course, country club, and Nelson's Pedernales recording studio. (Personal items from the property raise a further $68,000.)
Apr [9] Nelson stars with Kris Kristofferson in CBS-TV's "Another Pair Of Aces: Three Of A Kind".
[18] The Revenue sells Nelson's 22-acre fishing camp, on a 668-acre spread which also includes a wild west movie set, to George and Mary Larson for $86,100.
[20] Nelson takes part in the "Earth Day 1991 Concert" at Foxboro Stadium, Foxborough, MA, with Billy Bragg, Jackson Browne, Rosanne Cash, Bruce Cockburn, Bruce Hornsby & the Range, Indigo Girls, Queen Latifah, Ziggy Marley and 10,000 Maniacs.
June [3] Nelson continues in his efforts to pay his $16 million IRS debt by releasing ***Who'll Buy My Memories***.
Aug [10] Waylon & Willie's ***Clean Shirt*** debuts at its US #193 peak.
Sept Nelson signs a deal to become star-in-residence at the Ozarks Theatre, Branson, MO. He is scheduled to perform ten shows a week from May 1992.
[16] He marries make-up artist Ann-Marie D'Angelo, whom he met on the "Red Headed Stranger" set in 1986, and with whom he already has two children, in Dallas. It is his fourth marriage.
[19] Nelson sings *Busted* with Ray Charles for the "Ray Charles : 50 Years In Music"TV special, which will air on Fox-TV on October 6th.
Oct [7] *Always On My Mind* is confirmed gold by the RIAA.
Dec [21] Roy Rogers' ***Tribute*** album, on which Nelson is featured, peaks at US #113.
[25] His son William Hugh Nelson Jr. hangs himself.

1992

Mar [10] The RIAA certifies platinum sales of ***Willie Nelson Sings Kristofferson*** and three million sales of ***Willie Nelson's Greatest Hits (And Some That Will Be)***.
[14] The Highwaymen, currently on a US tour, perform at "Farm Aid V" at the Texas Stadium, Irving, TX, an event also featuring John Mellencamp, Neil Young and the Black Crowes among others.
Apr [15] The Highwaymen gross £158,255 before a sellout crowd of 7,446 at the Point Theatre, Dublin, Eire, at the start of a European trek.
May [11] The RIAA confirms two million sales of ***Honeysuckle Rose***.
Aug The Highwaymen take part in the third annual "Back To The Ranch" concert in Montauk, Long Island, NY.
[11] The "Honeymoon In Vegas" soundtrack, to which Nelson had contributed *Blue Hawaii*, is released.
Sept [20] Nelson joins Charlie Daniels on *Blue Eyes Crying In The Rain*, *Night Life* and other standards at the 11th "Volunteer Jam" at the Starwood Amphi-theatre, Nashville, TN.
Oct [16] He sings *What Was It You Wanted* and, with Kristofferson, *I'll Be Your Baby Tonight*, at the Bob Dylan 30th anniversary concert at New York, NY's Madison Square Garden.
[29] Nelson guest stars as himself on ABC-TV's "Delta".

1993

Jan [20] Nelson performs at the "Southern Ball" in Washington, DC, following President Clinton's inauguration.
Feb [2] He reaches a settlement with the IRS, paying $9 million of the outstanding $16.7 million owed (he has already paid $3.6 million). His case against accounting firm, Price Waterhouse, alleging they gave him bad financial advice, continues.
[6] CMA's 35th anniversary show "A Country Celebration", in which Nelson duets with Bob Dylan, airs on CBS-TV.
[16] Nelson takes part in NBC-TV's "Academy Of Country Music's Hits" special.
[17] The Highwaymen win the Vocal Group category at the first German American Country Music Federation Awards in Nashville, TN.
Mar [28] Nelson performs in Hillsboro, TX, near his Abbott birthplace, to raise funds to help rebuild the century-old Hill County Courthouse, gutted by fire on New Year's Day. A 6,000 crowd attends, as Hill County designates it "Willie Nelson Day".
Apr [10] His latest album, ***Across The Borderline***, marking a departure from country, debuts at its US #75 peak. The Don Was-produced set, on which Nelson tackles songs by Peter Gabriel, Lyle Lovett, Willie Dixon and John Hiatt and others, features musical guests Bob Dylan, Sinead O'Connor, Paul Simon and Bonnie Raitt. (During his career, Nelson has duetted with over 75 different artists.)
May [15] Nelson guests on NBC-TV's "Saturday Night Live".
[22] CBS-TV airs "Willie Nelson The Big Six-O" birthday celebrations.
[23] The Highwaymen perform in New York's Central Park as part of the "Country Takes Manhattan" season.
June [25] Nelson guests on NBC-TV's "The Tonight Show".
Oct [1] CBS-TV's "A Day In The Life Of Country Music", featuring what several country artists did on May 7th, including Nelson, airs.

1994

Jan [23] Following an appearance on CBS-TV's "Late Show With David Letterman" on the 20th, Nelson plays a sellout show at New York's Beacon Theatre.
Mar [8] EMI Nashville releases the two-CD, 61 track set, ***Willie Nelson : The Early Years (The Complete Liberty Recordings Plus More)***.
[23] Nelson guests on "The Tonight Show".
[26] Released by Justice Records, ***Moonlight Becomes You*** charts for a week at US #188.
Apr [28] He takes part in the 25th annual "New Orleans Jazz & Heritage Festival".
May [3] Nelson performs at James Brown's birthday party at the Civic Center, Augusta, GA.
[10] Police find Nelson sleeping in his Mercedes by the roadside on Interstate 35 in Hewitt, TX, and arrest him on a misdemeanor drug charge after finding marijuana in the car.
Aug [7] During a current US tour with Waylon Jennings, Nelson plays to a 3,400 sellout crowd at the Star Plaza Theatre, Merrillville, IN.
Sept [18] He takes part in Farm Aid VII in New Orleans.
Oct [7] ***City Of New Orleans*** is certified platinum by the RIAA.
[21] The RIAA certifies four million sales of ***Always On My Mind***.
Nov [14] ***Without A Song*** is certified platinum by the RIAA.
[26] Frank Sinatra's ***Duets II***, featuring a pairing with Nelson on *Foggy Day In London Town*, reaches US #29.
Dec [31] ***Healing Hands Of Time*** makes US #103.

1995

Jan [12] Nelson inducts the Allman Brothers Band into the Rock and Roll Hall of Fame at the tenth annual dinner at New York's Waldorf Astoria Hotel. He sings *Funny How Time Slips Away*, with Al Green,

at the traditional post-dinner jam.
[28] ***Super Hits*** peaks at US #193.
Feb [14] Nelson performs, backed by a full orchestra, at New York's Beacon Theatre.
Apr [1] He plays at a family farm benefit concert before 2,000 people in a muddy field in Unionville, MO.
[4] As the latest Highwaymen album, ***The Road Goes On Forever***, is released, ***Come Together***, a Beatles tribute album by country artists, including Nelson's version of *One After 909*, is also released.
May [10] Nelson performs live at the 30th annual Academy of Country Music Awards from Universal Studios, Hollywood, CA.
June [5] A teary-eyed Nelson accepts the Minnie Pearl Award at the TNN/Music City News Awards in Nashville.
[8] The Highwaymen, currently on a US tour, perform at the Pine Knob Music Theatre, Clarkston, MI.
July [4] As Nelson holds his annual July 4th picnic, Rhino releases ***Willie Nelson : A Classic And Unreleased Collection***, while Justice Records releases his new Grady Martin-produced set ***Just One Love***.
Aug [15] Nelson guests on CBS-TV's "Late Show With David Letterman".
[18] He plays a sellout date at the Valley Forge Music Fair, Devon, PA, during US summer dates.
Oct [1] The annual Nelson-organized "Farm Aid" takes place at Lousville's Cardinal Stadium, with Nelson, Neil Young, John Mellencamp, Hootie & the Blowfish and others.
[14] A&M (US)-released ***Tower Of Song : The Songs Of Leonard Cohen***, featuring Nelson's version of *Bird On A Wire*, charts for a week at US #198.
Nov [14] Nelson's second boxed set of the year, ***Revolutions Of Time ... The Journey 1975-1993***, chronicling his Columbia career, is released by Sony Legacy.

1996

Feb [20] Nelson guests on "The Tonight Show".
Mar The follow-up set to the 1976 Outlaw project, ***Nowhere Road For The Outlaws : 20th Anniversary***, is recorded in Nashville by Nelson and Jennings, the sessions produced by Steve Earle.
June [4] As the first country artist ever signed to Island Records, Nelson's label debut, the self-penned ***Spirit*** is released, a sparse set recording featuring only his sister Bobbie and Jody Payne on guitar and Johnny Gimbel on fiddle. (A second album for Island, already in the can and scheduled for release in September, is Nelson's first attempt at reggae, produced by Don Was, which the performer will preview as an unlikely headliner at this summer's "Sunfest" in Jamaica.)
[22] As Nelson continues to tour the length and breadth of the US, he now performs at Opryland USA in Nashville.

AARON NEVILLE

1960

Oct The third of four singing brothers raised in New Orleans, LA (of which he will later say "New Orleans is the true music. It's been in my heart all my life and nothing can turn me around from it because it's freedom music"), encouraged to sing by his high-school teacher Solomon Spencer, Neville (b. Jan. 24, 1941, New Orleans), influenced by the vocal style of the Spaniels' Pooky Hudson, has joined vocal group the Avalons in 1955 at the age of 14. When his eldest brother Art joined the US Navy in 1958, Neville has taken his place in R&B combo the Hawketts. By the end of the decade, Neville has also married and spent six months in prison for car theft. Out of jail and having been on the road with Larry Williams, Neville's first solo success, *Over You*, recorded with Allen Toussaint for the Minit label, begins a long-term working relationship between the artist and producer/arranger Toussaint (who even pens early cuts under the pseudonym Naomi Neville) and now reaches US R&B #21, with the artist credited as Arron Neville.

1966

Oct Having spent much of the first half of the decade in an early sibling unit, the eight-piece New Orleans circuit band Neville Sounds (although he has also continued to record for Minit up to 1963), Neville now records a solo blues ballad, *Tell It Like It Is*, for New Orleans label, Par-lo. Written by Lee Diamond and ex-Hawketts member George Davis, it reputedly sells 40,000 copies in New Orleans in its first week of release. (It will later be adapted as an anthem for the US Black Power movement.)

1967

Jan [7] Soul classic, *Tell It Like It Is*, tops the US R&B chart for the first of five weeks and also hits US #2, becoming a million seller.
Feb On the strength of his hit, Aaron begins several months of live work around the US, including an appearance at the prestigious Apollo Theatre in Harlem, New York, NY, and a national tour with Otis Redding. His backing band for the tour is the Neville Sounds, with brother Art on keyboards.
Apr Neville's follow-up, *She Took You For A Ride*, reaches US #92. Its 1968 follow-up, *Where Is My Baby* will fail to score and with the Neville Sounds dissolving in the same year, Neville and his younger brother Cyril will branch off as Soul Machine, spending the next seven years performing in New Orleans, Nashville, TN and New York, interrupted by Neville's drug bust in 1973 resulting in his second incarceration. That same year Neville, once again in collaboration with Toussaint, will record a one-off single *Hercules* for Mercury Records.

1977

Oct Following a spell with his brothers (who are winding up their concurrent involvement in the Meters) in Wild Tchoupitoulas the previous year, and now performing with them as the newly formed and permanent Neville Brothers for Capitol Records, Neville's cover of Joe South's *The Greatest Love* is released by Polydor, once again produced by Toussaint.

1980

Feb While his long-term involvement as lead singer of the Neville Brothers will continue into the '90s, his tandem solo career resumes with his contribution of *I Love Her Too* to the newly-released film soundtrack for "Heartbeat".

1984

June Linda Ronstadt meets Neville during the World's Fair in New Orleans. She has finished performing with Nelson Riddle, and goes to Pete Fountain's club to see the Neville Brothers' act.
Oct Passport Records in the US releases Neville's six-track solo mini-album ***Orchid In The Storm***, showcasing his unique, other-worldly treble vocal skill, produced by Joel Dorn. His only solo set of the decade, it will be licensed to Demon Records in the UK for issue the following year.

1988

Aug Rob Wasserman's ***Duets***, featuring Neville's vocal interpretation of *Stardust*, is released.
Dec [10] Neville's son Ivan, having learnt his musical skills playing in Keith Richards' backing band, makes US #26 with *Not Just Another Girl* from his debut album, ***If My Ancestors Could See Me Now*** (US #107).
Oct [27] Neville sings *Amazing Grace* and *How Great Thou Art* at the wedding of actor John Goodman to fine arts student Annabeth Hartzog at the St. Charles Avenue Presbyterian Church, New Orleans.
Dec With the Neville Brothers currently reaping belated critical and commercial success with ***Yellow Moon***, Neville enjoys his biggest hit in 23 years, as his duet on Linda Ronstadt's *Don't Know Much*, produced by Peter Asher from her current US # 7, UK #43 album, ***Cry Like A Rainstorm - Howl Like The Wind***, which prominently features Neville on three further duet cuts, hits both US and UK #2.

1990

Jan [28] He sings the national anthem at "Superbowl XXIV" between the San Francisco 49ers and the Denver Broncos at the Superdome, New Orleans.
Feb Neville contributes a cover of *Young And Beautiful* to the newly-released compilation album ***The Last Temptation Of Elvis***, to benefit the Nordoff Robbins Music Therapy charity. (He is also featured on Daniel Lanois' recently issued ***Acadie*** on the tracks *Amazing Grace* and *The Maker*.)
[21] While the siblings win the Best Pop Instrumental Performance for *Healing Chant*, Neville and Ronstadt nab the Best Pop Performance By A Duo Or Group With Vocal trophy for *Don't Know Much* at the 32nd annual Grammy Awards, held at the Shrine Auditorium, Los Angeles, CA.
Mar Neville's "Tell It Like It Is" video, with guests Bonnie Raitt, Gregg Allman, John Hiatt, Buckwheat Zydeco and Dennis Quaid, is released in the US. (Aaron has appeared as a heavy in Quaid's film "Everybody's All-American", and will also cameo in Spike Lee's "Malcolm X" in 1992.)
[8] Neville is voted Best Male Singer in **Rolling Stone** magazine's 1989 Critics' Awards.
Mar [31] Ronstadt and Neville's *All My Life*, written by Karla Bonoff, reaches US #11.
May [6] He performs solo at the 21st annual "Jazz & Heritage Festival" at the Fair Grounds Race Track, New Orleans.
June [2] Ronstadt and Neville's update of Sam & Dave's 1967 US #42 hit *When Something Is Wrong With My Baby* makes US #78.

1991

Feb [20] Neville and Ronstadt win the Best Pop Performance By A Duo Or Group With Vocal category for the second consecutive year, for *All My Life*, at the 33rd annual Grammy Awards, at Radio City Music Hall, New York.
Mar [3] He sings *Bird On A Wire* at the induction of its writer, Leonard Cohen, into the Juno Hall of Fame at the 20th annual Juno Awards, at the Queen Elizabeth Theatre, Vancouver, BC, Canada.
[7] He is once again named Best Male Singer in the **Rolling Stone** Critics' Picks 1990 music awards.
Apr [24] Neville performs at the tenth anniversary of "The Arts At St. Ann's" series at St. Ann's Church, Brooklyn Heights, NY, with John Cale, Dr. John and others.
May Neville nears completion of a Ronstadt co-produced solo project and guests on his son Ivan's forthcoming sophomore album, ***Sound Of Love***.
July [20] Signed to A&M Records, his first solo album of the '90s, ***Warm Your Heart***, co-produced by Ronstadt and George Massenberg with choice covers including songs by Randy Newman and John Hiatt, makes US #44.
Aug[17] Neville sings the American national anthem and serves as guest ringmaster at the Ringling Brothers & Barnum & Bailey Circus at the New Orleans Superdome.
[22] He guests on NBC-TV's "Late Night With David Letterman".
Oct [12] Robbie Robertson's ***Storyville*** featuring Neville, is released set to reach UK #30 and US #69.
[19] *Everybody Plays The Fool*, Neville's first solo hit in almost a quarter of a century and a cover of the Main Ingredient's 1972 US #3, hits US #8.
Nov [3] He performs at the late Bill Graham "Laughter Love & Music" memorial concert at San Francisco's Golden Gate Park Polo Field before an estimated 350,000-strong crowd. (Both the Neville Brothers and Aaron are steered by Bill Graham Management.)
Dec [12] He guests on NBC-TV's "Tonight" show.

1992

Jan [28] ***Warm Your Heart*** is certified gold by the RIAA.
Apr Aaron and Art Neville perform at the New Orleans Artists Against Hunger and Homelessness

benefit at the Lakefront Airport, New Orleans.
Oct Maria Muldaur's ***Louisiana Love Call***, featuring guest vocalist Neville, is released in the US.
Nov Neville and Kenny G's *Even If My Heart Would Break* duet is featured on Kenny G's ***Breathless***, and the "The Bodyguard" film soundtrack.
[18] He participates in the "Commitment To Life VI" benefit for AIDS Project Los Angeles, honoring Barbra Streisand and David Geffen, at the Universal Amphitheatre, Universal City, CA.

1993

Jan [20] Neville performs at the Western Ball on Inauguration Day in Washington, DC.
July [8] Having recently been seen in cinemas playing the leader of a chain gang in Melvin Van Peebles' film "The Posse", Neville guests on "The Tonight Show".
[17] *Don't Take Away My Heaven*, the Diane Warren-penned first single from his forthcoming album ***The Grand Tour***, makes US #56, during a five-month stay on the Hot 100.
Oct [9] ***The Grand Tour***, produced by Steve Lindsey and including musical guests Ronstadt and brothers Art and Charles, plus songs by Leonard Cohen, Bob Dylan, Marvin Gaye and George Jones, reaches US #37, as its title track *The Grand Tour* debuts at its US #90 peak.
Dec [12] He takes part in the 12th annual "Christmas In Washington" concert, set to air on the 15th on NBC-TV.
[24] He guests on "Harry Connick Jr. Christmas Concert", singing *The Christmas Song* and, duetting with Connick on *I Pray For Christmas*.
[25] Festive solo album ***Aaron Neville's Soulful Christmas*** climbs to US #36.

1994

Jan [19] ***The Grand Tour*** is certified platinum by the RIAA.
Feb [7] Neville takes part in the 21st annual American Music Awards.
Mar [23] He performs at "Rhythm Country And Blues - The Concert", benefitting the Country Music Foundation and the Rhythm and Blues Foundation, at the Universal Amphitheatre.
[26] ***Rhythm Country & Blues***, featuring his duet with Trisha Yearwood on *I Fall To Pieces*, reaches US #18.
Apr [9] Neville takes part in the fifth annual "Rainforest Benefit Concert" at New York's Carnegie Hall, with Elton John, Sting, James Taylor, Tammy Wynette, Luciano Pavarotti, Branford Marsalis and Whitney Houston.
Aug [12] Aaron performs at the Grandstand, Indiana State Fair, Indianapolis, IN, supporting Wynonna.
Oct Tammy Wynette's album, ***Without Walls***, featuring a duet with Neville, is released.
[8] He sings *Young And Beautiful* at "Elvis Aaron Presley : The Tribute", an all-star event at the Pyramid Arena, Memphis, TN, broadcast live on pay-per-view TV in the US.
Nov [23] He embarks on a 15-city "Northwest Airlines Christmas On Ice" US tour, to benefit the Toys For Tots and Special Olympics organizations, with ice-skater Nancy Kerrigan, at the Cumberland County Civic Center, Cumberland, ME, set to end on December 18th at West Palm Beach Auditorium, West Palm Beach, FL.

1995

Feb ***Till The Night Is Gone : A Tribute To Doc Pomus***, including Neville's interpretation of *Save The Last Dance For Me*, is released by Rhino.
Mar [1] *I Fall To Pieces*, his duet with Trisha Yearwood, wins the Best Country Vocal Collaboration category at the 37th annual Grammy Awards from Los Angeles' Shrine Auditorium.
Apr [18] He guests on CBS-TV's "Late Show With David Letterman".
May [6] His third solo album in four years, ***Tattooed Heart***, including material by Diane Warren and Andrew Gold and backing guests Waddy Wachtel, Dean Parks and Steve Cropper, makes US #64.
July [29] The extracted *Can't Stop My Heart From Loving You (The Rain Song)* bows at its US #99 peak.
Sept [14] Aaron guests on NBC-TV's "The Tonight Show".
Oct [14] A&M (US)-released ***Tower Of Song : The Songs Of Leonard Cohen***, featuring Neville's version of *Ain't No Cure For Love*, charts for a week at US #198.
Dec [18] He again guests "Late Show With David Letterman".
[20] CBS-TV's "Kathie Lee : Home For Christmas", featuring Aaron as one of Kathie Lee Gifford's guests, airs.

1996

Feb [2] Neville guests on CBS-TV's 45th annual "Miss USA Pageant" from South Padre Island, TX.
Mar [14] Having wrapped recordings with his brothers for a new group project due in May, Neville appears on Fox-TV's "New York Undercover".
see also: **THE NEVILLE BROTHERS**

THE NEVILLE BROTHERS

Art Neville (vocals, piano);
Aaron Neville (vocals); **Charles Neville** (sax);
Cyril Neville (vocals, percussion)

1954

All four brothers grow up in a home and city environment rich in music in New Orleans, LA, sons of a merchant seaman father and dancer mother. Eldest sibling Art (b. Dec. 17, 1937, New Orleans), weaned on the songs of local legends Fats Domino and Professor Longhair, records *Mardi Gras Mambo*, as vocalist and pianist with a seven-piece New Orleans R&B band, the Hawketts, which has been initially formed at his high-school, which becomes a local standard, reissued annually by Chess for the Mardi Gras celebrations. Shortly afterwards, and prompted by his high-school teacher Solomon Spencer, younger brother Aaron (b. Jan. 24, 1941, New Orleans) will join R&B vocal group the Avalons.

1957

Still performing with the Hawketts, Art signs a solo deal with Specialty Records and releases several singles (including *Zing Zing* and the two-chord *Cha Dooky-Doo*), which are popular in the R&B market. Third brother Charles (b. Dec. 28, 1938, New Orleans), who left home at age 14 to get married, joins the house band at New Orleans' Dew Drop Inn club, touring the South with various blues players, including Jimmy Reed and Little Walter. The following year Art joins the US Navy and Aaron fills his place in the Hawketts. Aaron's adventures outside the band will include getting married and serving six months in prison for car theft. He will go on to begin a parallel solo career in 1960 beginning a long term association with producer Allen Toussaint.

1962

Jan Back with the Hawketts after military service, Art has a regional hit with *All These Things*. He will follow Aaron to Toussaint as a soloist but neither will have any major chart success with Minit. Charles leaves New Orleans to play in New York, NY with Joey Dee & the Starliters, while baby brother Cyril (b. Jan. 10, 1948, New Orleans) starts showing an interest in music. He will shortly join Art and Aaron in an eight-piece New Orleans circuit band named the Neville Sounds.)

1968

The Neville Sounds splits, with Aaron and Cyril branching off as the Soul Machine, and Art keeping the rhythm section ("Ziggy" Modeliste on drums, George Porter on bass, Leo Nocentelli on guitar, and himself on keyboards) to form the Meters, who rapidly become New Orleans' equivalent of Memphis' Booker T. & the MG's, playing as house band behind many Allen Toussaint and Marshall Sehorn productions, and performing as the resident combo at the city's Ivanhoe Bar.

1969

Mar Toussaint and Sehorn decide to emulate Booker T. by recording the Meters as an R&B instrumental group in its own right and leasing it to New York's Josie Records. Their debut, *Sophisticated Cissy*, makes US #34.
June The Meters' *Cissy Strut* reaches US #23.
July ***The Meters***, a wholly instrumental collection, peaks at US #108.
Aug The Meters' *Ease Back* reaches US #61. The following year, the hits continue with *Look-Ka Py Py* climbing to US #56 in January the same month ***Look-Ka Py Py*** stops at US #198, *Chicken Strut* reaching US #50 in May, *Hand Clapping Song*, the last Sehorn and Toussaint single, making US #89 in July, when ***Struttin'*** also peaks at US #200.

1972

The Meters sign to Reprise, releasing ***Cabbage Alley***. (The Meters' own hit career begins to fade, but its session work will include stints with major acts like Dr. John on ***In The Right Place***, ***Desitively Bonaroo***, and his 1973 US Top 10 hit, *Right Place, Wrong Time*, Robert Palmer on his first solo album, ***Sneakin' Sally Through The Alley***, and LaBelle, on their 1974 smash, *Lady Marmalade*.)

1974

With Charles given a three-year prison sentence for drug possession the previous year and Aaron also incarcerated for a similar bust, the Meters' ***Rejuvenation*** is issued, including slide guitar from Lowell George of Little Feat.

1975

Sept While Soul Machine has spent stints in Nashville, TN, and New York, Cyril now splits to join Art in the Meters as percussionist/vocalist, and the band tours Europe as support to the Rolling Stones, while ***Fire On The Bayou*** reaches US #179.

1976

With the four brothers now united as the Wild Tchoupitoulas, the self-titled ***Wild Tchoupitoulas***, its name taken from the Mardi Gras tribe of their Indian uncle, recorded with their uncle George Landry, is released. They also record *Trick Bag* as the Meters. A final Meters album, ***New Direction***, will be released with the extracted *Be My Lady* reaching US #78 in October the same year.

1978

Mar Having changed their name to the Neville Brothers and newly signed to Capitol Records, the quartet's debut album, ***The Neville Brothers***, is released.

1981

Sept After Bette Midler has lobbied A&M Records to sign the band, its label debut ***Fiyo On The Bayou***, a play on an earlier Meters title, is released, dedicated to Landry, who died on August 9th, 1980, peaks at US #166, highlighted by the unique, golden-voiced Aaron's treatment of *Mona Lisa*. Gaining a strong cult following, they are also increasingly popular with their musical peers, not least undertaking opening slots for the Rolling Stones on its current US tour.

1984

June ***Neville-ization***, recorded live in 1982 at New Orleans' Tipitina's, is released.
Linda Ronstadt meets Aaron during the World's Fair in New Orleans. She has finished performing with Nelson Riddle, and goes to Pete Fountain's club to see the Neville Brothers' act. (Later in the decade she will invite him to team up for an album resulting in a string of hit singles and a pair of Grammys, a project which re-launches Aaron into a successful parallel solo career in the '90s as a pop balladeer.)

1986

June Having released a second performance album ***Live At Tipitina's*** the previous year on the local Spindletop label, the Neville Brothers participate in an Amnesty International benefit concert, alongside Sting, Joan Baez, Peter Gabriel and Bryan Adams, during the various artists' "A Conspiracy Of Hope" two-week tour.

1987

Apr ***Treacherous : A History Of The Neville Brothers 1955-1985***, a 30-year retrospective double album of the brothers' career, released by Rhino Records, peaks at US #178 (and will be followed by a further archive anthology ***Treacherous Too*** in 1991).
May ***Uptown***, featuring a more mainstream soul music production than previous releases, with guests Jerry Garcia, Keith Richards, Carlos Santana and others, makes US #155.

1989

Apr As the band is increasingly "discovered" by a young rock/soul audience, ***Yellow Moon***, produced by Daniel Lanois and featuring his long-time collaborator Brian Eno, enters the US survey on a 24-week ride during which it makes #66, as the group embarks on a UK tour.
July [15] The brothers embark on major US dates, supporting Jimmy Buffett on his "Off To See The Lizard Tour '89".
Dec Extracted ballad from ***Yellow Moon***, *With God On Our Side*, makes UK #47.

1990

Feb [21] The group wins the Best Pop Instrumental Performance for *Healing Chant* at the 32nd annual Grammy Awards, held at the Shrine Auditorium, Los Angeles, CA.
Mar [8] The Neville Brothers are voted Best Band in **Rolling Stone** magazine's 1989 Critics' Awards.
Apr [16] The group participates in the "Nelson Mandela - An International Tribute To A Free South Africa" concert at Wembley Stadium, Wembley, Middx.
June [22-24] The brothers participate in the three-day "Glastonbury Festival of Contemporary Performing Arts", at Worthy Farm, Pilton, Somerset, as a third Ronstadt/Aaron pairing, *When Something Is Wrong With My Baby*, halts at US #78.
July [7] The brothers' *Bird On The Wire*, featured in the Mel Gibson/Goldie Hawn movie of the same name, peaks at UK #72.
Aug Celebrating ten years with A&M, the latest Neville Brothers album, co-produced by Dave Stewart, ***Brother's Keeper***, makes UK #35.
[30] The Neville Brothers, as special guests of long time supporter Linda Ronstadt on her current US tour, play to a sellout crowd of 10,216 at the Jones Beach Theatre, Wantagh, NY.
Sept [8] ***Brother's Keeper*** peaks at US #60.
Oct The group contributes *In The Still Of The Night*, written for the 1937 movie "Rosalie", to the newly released ***Red Hot + Blue***, an anthology of Cole Porter songs to benefit AIDS education.
Dec [15] The Neville Brothers guest on NBC-TV's "Saturday Night Live".

1991

May [5] The band performs at the 22nd annual "New Orleans Jazz & Heritage Festival", at the Fair Grounds Race Track, as part of its 24-date US tour.
June [16] The group makes an appearance at the "Playboy Jazz Festival" at the Hollywood Bowl, Hollywood, CA.
Aug [8] The Nevilles, Joe Cocker, Jack Bruce and Ginger Baker play to a sellout crowd of 27,000 at Park Hayarkon, Tel Aviv, Israel.
[25] The group plays on the second day of the "Gold Coast Concert Bowl", Squaw Valley, CA, with Booker T. & the MG's and Jerry Garcia.
Nov [14] The Nevilles finish their New Orleans' Municipal Auditorium show with a funeral march in honor of their manager, the late Bill Graham.
Dec [27-28] The group plays two sellout shows at the Wiltern Theatre, Los Angeles.

1992

Jan [15] The band inducts the late Professor Longhair into the Rock and Roll Hall of Fame, at the seventh annual dinner at New York's Waldorf Astoria Hotel. Aaron calls the legendary piano player "The grandfather of rock'n'roll. Where did rock'n'roll come from? It's the baby of R&B".
Apr Aaron and Art perform at the New Orleans Artists Against Hunger and Homelessness benefit at the Lakefront Airport, New Orleans.
May [2] A man fools the Nevilles into thinking he is Steve Miller, quitting town with an unpaid $600 motel bill in Montgomery, AL.
June [13] Co-produced by the brothers with Hawk Wolinski and David Leonard, ***Family Groove*** peaks at US #103.
July [11] The group takes part in the "American Music Festival" at the Winter Park Ski Resort, CO.
Aug [13] They perform at New York's Central Park Summer Stage '92 concert series.
[26] The Neville Brothers, currently on a North American tour with Joe Cocker, play at the Mann Music Center, Philadelphia, PA.
Sept [1] The group guests on NBC-TV's "Late Night With David Letterman".
[27] They perform at a Berloni Foundation benefit for leukaemia patients, in Luciano Pavarotti's horse stables in Modena, Italy (to be released as ***Pavarotti & Friends*** the following March).
Oct [3] They play at London's Hammersmith Odeon.
Nov [13] Art Neville reunites with fellow Meters, Porter, Nocentelli and Modelesti, at a Nocentelli gig at Jimmy's Music Club, New Orleans, joining in for an encore of *Hey Pocky Way*.

1993

Jan [11] The group plays a sellout show at the Sweeney Convention Center, Santa Fe, NM, during its current US tour. The first of the brothers to record, Art's earliest work is collected in a Specialty Records release, ***Art Neville : His Specialty Recordings 1956-1958***.
Mar [10] The Neville Brothers are profiled on CBS-TV's "48 Hours".
Dec [30-31] The group plays year-end shows at San Francisco's Warfield Theatre.

1994

Apr [22] The band performs at the 25th annual "New Orleans Jazz & Heritage Festival".
May [21] The Nevilles' ***Live On Planet Earth*** debuts at its US #126 peak.
[26] They take part in the "Apollo Theatre Hall Of Fame" concert, set to air on NBC-TV on September 6th.
June [21] Currently on tour with Crosby Stills & Nash, the Nevilles play a sellout date at the James L. Knight Center, Miami, FL.
July [7] The group guests on NBC-TV's "The Tonight Show".
[12] ***Yellow Moon*** is certified gold by the RIAA.
Aug [14] The group plays at "Woodstock II", at Winston Farm, Saugerties, NY.
Sept [18] They take part in "Farm Aid VII" in New Orleans.

1995

Feb [17] The band plays at the Majestic Theatre, San Antonio, TX.
May [31] The siblings play the first of two dates at New York's Irving Plaza.
July [7] The Neville Brothers perform at the annual "Montreux Jazz Festival", Montreux, Switzerland.
Sept [20] The group plays at the Northwest Concert Center, The Puyallup Fair, Puyallup, WA.

1996

Mar [30] The Neville Brothers take part in the "Uptown Street Festival" in New Orleans having wrapped recordings for ***All My Relations***, co-produced with James Stroud, and due for release on May 14th, supported by six months of touring.
see also: **Aaron NEVILLE**

NEW EDITION

Bobby Brown (vocals); **Ricky Bell** (vocals); **Ralph Tresvant** (vocals); **Michael Bivins** (vocals); **Ronald DeVoe** (vocals)

1983

Feb [5] Having established itself over two years as Boston, MA talent show champs and with several lip-synching gigs in the northeastern states under its belt, the five-member R&B teen unit New Edition (all are aged between 13 and 15) lining up as Bell (b. Sept. 18, 1967, Boston), Tresvant (b. May 16, 1968, Boston), Bivins (b. Aug. 10, 1968, Boston), DeVoe (b. Nov. 17, 1967, Boston) and Brown (b. Robert Brown, Feb. 5, 1969, Roxbury, MA) makes its residency debut at New York, NY's Copacabana Club, under the wing of pop entrepreneur, manager, and producer Maurice Starr, who has already secured a recording deal with the local independent Streetwise label.
May [28] Moulded by Starr as an '80s version of the Jackson 5, New Edition hits UK #1, via a Streetwise license to London Records, and makes US #46 with the sugar-coated pop/R&B confection *Candy Girl*.
Aug UK follow-up, *Popcorn Love*, makes UK #45.
Oct *Is This The End* peaks at US #85, while parent album, ***Candy Girl***, climbs to US #90 (the group will never score a UK chart album).

1984

May The group splits acrimoniously from Starr and signs to MCA Records, as a five-year legal wrangle begins over the rights to use the New Edition name.
Nov Their breakthrough US MCA hit, *Cool It Now*, hits US #4, as their second album, ***New Edition***, begins a US rise to hit #6.

1985

Jan [4] *Cool It Now* is certified gold by the RIAA.
Feb The extracted *Mr. Telephone Man* reaches US #12 and UK #19, the group's last UK chart entry. A further single from their album, *Lost In Love*, will also make US #35.
Dec *Count Me Out* peaks at US #51 as their second MCA outing, ***All For Love***, begins a climb to US #32.

1986

Apr *A Little Bit Of Love (Is All It Takes)* makes US #38.
June [2] ***All For Love*** is certified platinum by the RIAA.
July *With You All The Way* peaks at US #51.
Oct Their revival of the Crewcuts' 1955 US #3, *Earth Angel*, reaches US #21, aided by its inclusion on the "Karate Kid II" movie soundtrack.
Dec New Edition releases its final album with Brown in the line-up: ***Under The Blue Moon***, including the recent *Earth Angel*, is a collection of updated '50s and '60s pop/R&B standards which will make US #43.

1987

Jan [23] ***Under The Blue Moon*** is certified gold by the RIAA.
[26] New Edition wins the Favorite Band, Duo Or Group, Soul/R&B, category at the 14th annual American Music Awards, held at the Shrine Auditorium, Los Angeles, CA.
Brown signs a solo deal, also with MCA, which will supersede New Edition's achievements towards the end of the decade. Meantime, the band recruits former gospel singer and Stacy Lattisaw-session vocalist Johnny Gill (b. May, 22, 1966, Washington, DC) who, at 22, is the oldest member. (He has already charted with the Lattisaw-paired US #139 album, ***Perfect Combination***, in 1984.)

July ***Dragnet***, the soundtrack to the Dan Aykroyd/Tom Hanks movie, including New Edition's *Helplessly In Love*, is released in the US.

1988

Sept [17] New Edition makes an impressive return to chart form as *If It Isn't Love* hits US #7. It is taken from the US #12 album ***Heart Break***, which is mostly written and produced by hit-machine R&B duo Jimmy Jam and Terry Lewis, although two cuts are co-written and co-produced with New Edition and Tresvant. The album also marks a concerted effort to shed their teeny-bop image and head for the adult market. The group begins a US tour supporting Brown, who also appears for ten minutes with his old line-up as part of a contractual obligation (band members, old and new, remain good friends).

Nov [19] *You're Not My Kind Of Girl* peaks at US #95.

1989

Feb The group is awarded the Gold Ticket for playing to over 100,000 fans at New York's Madison Square Garden.

Mar [11] New Edition's *Can You Stand The Rain* makes US #44 having already topped the US R&B survey. (While Bobby Brown's solo career goes multi-platinum, New Edition members elect to divide amicably, on the provision that the central team will continue to operate, with additionally recruited members if necessary, whenever it needs to. The result is a new R&B/hip-hop trio, Bell Biv DeVoe (clearly combining Bell, Bivins and DeVoe), and two solo careers for Tresvant and Gill, who is already the featured vocalist on the George Howard single *One Love* (a US R&B #77 in January).

Apr [12] New Edition wins the R&B/Urban Contemporary Album Of The Year, Group category, at the third annual Soul Train Music Awards, held at the Shrine Auditorium.

July [9] Still touring as New Edition, the group's production manager, Ronald Byrd, 30, is charged with criminal homicide after allegedly chasing support group Guy's security chief, Anthony Bee, from the Civic Arena to the Hyatt Hotel in Pittsburgh, PA, and shooting him prior to the two groups' appearances that night (subsequently postponed) at the Budweiser Summerfest concert series. Recent New Edition recruit Michael Clark is also listed in critical condition at Pittsburgh Allegheny Hospital, with facial injuries suffered from a beating from four Guy stagehands armed with baseball bats. (The dispute had begun in Greensboro, NC, on July 8th, when Guy played over its time limit.)

1990

Jan Reuniting with Lattisaw, the Gill duet, *Where Do We Go From Here*, hits US R&B #1.

Apr [19] "Past And Present" video is certified gold by the RIAA.

July [28] ***Johnny Gill*** hits US #8.

Aug [4] During a year in which all three New Edition splinter acts will dominate US R&B and pop charts (Bell Biv Devoe's success is already underway), Gill, signed to Motown, the only New Edition-related act (including Brown) not to remain with MCA, hits US #3 with *Rub You The Right Way*, while his debut album, ***Johnny Gill***, including guest producers Jam and Lewis and L.A. Reid and Babyface, hits US #8.

Sept [7] New Edition re-forms for a one-off live performance at the seventh annual MTV Awards at the Universal Amphitheatre, Universal City, CA.

[29] Gill's *My, My, My* hits US #10.

Dec [15] L.A. Reid and Babyface-produced *Fairweather Friend* reaches US #28 for Gill.

[19] Gill embarks on the "Triple Threat North American Tour" with Bell Biv Devoe, Keith Sweat and Monie Love at the Onondaga County War Memorial, Syracuse, NY.

1991

Jan [22] Gill performs at the 23rd Annual NAACP Image Awards, which airs on NBC-TV.

[26] Tresvant's solo career kick-starts with the soulful *Sensitivity* finally hitting US #4.

[28] With all three acts swarming the US surveys, New Edition reunites with all original members, including Brown, to perform at the 18th annual American Music Awards, held at the Shrine Auditorium, where Bell Biv DeVoe also wins Best New Artist.

Feb [2] Produced by Jam and Lewis, Tresvant's MCA solo debut album, ***Ralph Tresvant***, peaks at US #17, while the platinum ***Johnny Gill*** is still at #67 in the same week. *Sensitivity* also reaches UK #18.

[23] Gill's *Wrap My Body Tight* debuts at its UK #57 peak, as ***Ralph Tresvant*** bows at UK #37.

Mar [12] Gill wins the Best R&B/Urban Contemporary Single, Male category, at the fifth annual Soul Train Music Awards, held at the Shrine Auditorium.

[30] *Wrap My Body Tight*, remixed by Vaughn Halyard, peaks at US #84.

Apr [13] Tresvant's *Stone Cold Gentleman*, with Bobby Brown guest-rapping, makes US #34. With a third Bobby Brown solo album due in the summer, New Edition is responsible for five US Top 10 acts in eight years.

[16] Gill guests on NBC-TV's "The Tonight Show".

June [14] Gill and Tresvant (together with Bell Biv Devoe) embark on the 13-city US "Budweiser Superfest" revue, together with other R&B acts, in Charlotte, NC.

Aug Gill and Tresvant contribute to the video of Marvin Gaye's "Mercy Mercy Mercy", a tie-up between Motown and the Audubon Society to increase awareness of the nation's environmental problems.

[3-4] Tresvant takes part in the all-star KMEL Jam at the Shoreline Amphitheatre, Mountain View, CA.

Oct [19] ***New Edition's Greatest Hits, Volume One*** debuts at its US #99 peak.

1992

June Gill's *There U Go* is featured on the just-released "Boomerang" film soundtrack.

Aug [15] Tresvant's *Money Can't Buy You Love*, from the movie "Mo' Money", makes US #54.

Nov [28] Shabba Ranks' *Slow And Sexy*, featuring Gill, reaches UK #17.

1993

Jan [9] *Slow And Sexy* reaches US #33.

June [19] Gill's *The Floor* makes US #56.

[24] Gill guests on syndicated TV's "The Arsenio Hall Show".

[26] ***Provocative***, Gill's sophomore effort on Motown, debuts at its US #14 peak, having done likewise in the UK the previous week, at #41.

July [17] The extracted *The Floor* charts for a week at UK #53.

1994

Jan [22] Tresvant's ***It's Goin' Down*** makes US #131.

[29] Gill's *A Cute, Sweet, Love Addiction* debuts at its UK #46 peak.

Mar [15] Gill co-hosts, with Gladys Knight and Patti LaBelle, the eighth annual Soul Train Music Awards at the Shrine Auditorium, during which he performs a medley tribute to Heritage Award recipient, Barry White.

July [19] The RIAA certifies two million sales of ***Heart Break***.

1995

July Gill forms his own Diesel label.

Oct [13] The RIAA certifies two million sales of ***New Edition***.

see also: **BELL BIV DEVOE; Bobby BROWN**

NEW KIDS ON THE BLOCK

Donnie Wahlberg (vocals); **Danny Wood** (vocals); **Jordan Knight** (vocals); **Jonathan Knight** (vocals); **Joey McIntyre** (vocals)

1984

Music veteran and entrepreneur Maurice Starr, ex-Johnson Brothers with his brother Michael Jonzun, has also cut two solo albums for RCA, ***Flaming Starr*** and ***Spicey Lady***, already responsible for finding and promoting R&B teen unit New Edition in 1981, is keen to find a "white New Edition", and enlists the help of old friend, talent agent Mary Alford, also a personnel officer at the Massachusetts Department of Education. (During the search, Starr receives a call from the FBI inquiring why he had given his phone number to a young boy in a flower shop.) Alford discovers Wahlberg (b. Aug. 17, 1969, Dorchester, MA) at the local Dorchester Copley Square High School, one of nine children of a divorced working mother and a bus driver. Wahlberg, in turn, suggests auditioning former classmates from William M. Trotter Elementary School in nearby Roxbury, MA, where he, Wood (b. Daniel Wood, May 14, 1971, Boston, MA), Jordan (b. May 17, 1971, Worcester, MA), former head chorister of All Saints Episcopal Church Choir, and Knight (b. Nov. 29, 1968, Worcester, MA) were all bussed to school. Starr moulds and trains the group, initially known as Nynuk, over a year during which early member Jamie Kelley will drop out to be replaced by McIntyre (b. Joseph McIntyre, Dec. 31, 1972, Needham, MA). Donnie's brother Mark and friend Pete Fitzgerald will also drop out of the original line-up. In March 1985 Nynuk will perform its first gig at the Joseph Lee School, Dorchester, lip-synching to early demo tapes.

1986

Jan They sign to CBS Records' Black division, who are interested in the idea of a commercial rap/dance pop mix, as showcased in their four-song demo tape, and persuade Starr to use the revised name, New Kids On The Block.

Apr Their debut release, *Be My Girl*, fails to attract interest.

July [4] New Kids perform at the "City Kids Speak On Liberty" program at Battery Park, New York, NY. They will subsequently support the Four Tops at the "Dorchester Kite Festival" and open for Lisa Lisa & Cult Jam at the 9 Lansdowne Club, Boston.

1988

Mar Following a year of intermittent and largely unnoticed club and PA engagements to promote their debut album ***New Kids On The Block***, which initially sells just 5,000 copies, program director Randy Kabrich of WRBQ, Tampa, FL radio station begins playing the group's fourth single *Please Don't Go Girl*, originally recorded by Starr-created trio Irving & the Twins. It is added by many other pop stations as the ball starts rolling.

June New Kids start a six-week US tour supporting teen-queen Tiffany, followed by a month-long headliner of their own.

Nov [21] Returning from their Japanese trip, during which they film TV commercials, the band plays a benefit for the Police Athletic League in Boston, on a bill featuring Jeffrey Osborne and the Pointer Sisters.

1989

Jan [4-5] The New Kids On The Block take part in the annual United Cerebral Palsy telethon for the third year running.

Feb [16] The group embarks on what will seem a never-ending tour at the Westport Playhouse, St. Louis, MO, the first four months of which they will be supported by the equally-popular bubblegum diva, Tiffany.

Mar [11] During a half-year chart residence, pop rap *You Got It (The Right Stuff)* hits US #3 as the New

Kids teen-throb mania explodes across North America. Its parent album ***Hangin' Tough***, helmed by Starr, also hits US #4, and will remain charted for over two years, accumulating eight RIAA platinum discs, launching the hottest US teen-idol group phenomenon of the decade.
[29] *You Got It (The Right Stuff)* is certified gold by the RIAA.
Apr [24] Massachusetts Governor Michael Dukakis designates today "New Kids On The Block Day" (the Kids will also perform at a Dukakis-formed Alliance Against Drugs benefit later in the year), one day ahead of the Boston Music Awards at which the Beantown boys win the Outstanding R&B Single and Outstanding Music Video categories while Starr is named Producer Of The Year.
June [13] The still-climbing *I'll Be Loving You (Forever)* is certified gold by the RIAA.
[17] During summer engagements at Disneyland, CA and Disneyworld, FL, their ballad, *I'll Be Loving You (Forever)*, hits US #1.
Aug Revived and re-promoted debut, ***New Kids On The Block***, peaks at US #25, eventually selling over three million domestic units.
Sept [9] ***Hangin' Tough*** and its title song *Hangin' Tough* hit US #1 simultaneously, aided by a now familiar teen-screaming promo clip featuring the band's synchronized dance-troupe style and white rap antics.
[23] The UK campaign begins with *Hangin' Tough* making #52, while the band visits for a four-day promotional tour, including an appearance on the **Smash Hits**' TV awards show.
Nov [4] *Cover Girl* hits US #2.
[10] *Cover Girl* is certified gold by the RIAA.
[11] B-side of *Hangin' Tough*, a cover of the Delfonics' *Didn't I (Blow Your Mind)*, hits US #8.
[25] *You Got It (The Right Stuff)* tops the UK survey for the first of three weeks as ***Hangin' Tough*** begins a lengthy UK chart residence, hitting #2.
[26-27] The group grosses $1,058,616 at sellout dates at the Spectrum, Philadelphia, PA.
[28] *Hangin' Tough* is certified platinum by the RIAA.
Dec While the seasonal US-only ***Merry, Merry Christmas*** hits US #9, the group ends the year having completed 250 nights on the road, with three albums in the US Top 30 and as victors in **Billboard**'s Year In Music survey for Top Pop Singles Artists and Duos/Groups.
[13] The RIAA certifies two million sales of ***Merry, Merry Christmas***.
[27] New Kids present the Boston Against Drugs group with a $25,000 check at the World Trade Center, Boston. (A further $25,000 is earmarked for the Governor's Alliance Against Drugs.)

1990

Jan [6] Starr-penned and produced lush sentimental ballad, *This One's For The Children*, hits US #7, with all profits set to go to the United Cerebral Palsy charity, as ***New Kids On The Block*** reaches US #25.
[9] *This One's For The Children* is certified gold by the RIAA.
[13] *Hangin' Tough* hits UK #1 for the first of two weeks.
[22] They collect the Favorite Band, Duo Or Group, Pop/Rock and Favorite Album, Pop/Rock trophies at the 17th annual American Music Awards, held at the Shrine Auditorium, Los Angeles, CA.
Feb [5] During another major US tour, Hasbro, a Rhode Island-based toy manufacturer, unveils its New Kids On The Block dolls at a press conference at the Hard Rock Café, New York. (When they hit the stores in December, over one million will be sold.)
[6] Disney Channel airs New Kids' "Hangin' Tough In Concert" TV special.
Mar [8] **Rolling Stone** magazine's Readers' Picks vote New Kids the Worst Band, the Worst Tour, *Hangin' Tough* the Worst Single and ***Hangin' Tough*** Worst Album in its annual poll.
[10] **Billboard** reports that the group's 1-900 telephone number currently receives 125,000 calls a day.
[15-16] The group plays two sellout shows at Nassau Veterans Memorial Coliseum, Uniondale, NY, the second of which is shown on pay-per-view TV.
Apr [26] During the band's first European tour, Wood injures his ankle in Manchester, Gtr. Manchester, when he trips over a stuffed toy animal thrown on stage by a fan. He flies back to Boston to receive treatment from Boston Celtics' trainer Ed Lacerte.
May [2] The RIAA certifies eight million sales of ***Hangin' Tough***.
[12] *Cover Girl* hits UK #4.
[24] The RIAA confirms 1.2 million sales of the "Hangin' Tough - Live" video.
June [16] *Step By Step* hits UK #2.
[24] During the band's "Magic Summer '90" US tour, sponsored by McDonald's, Wahlberg falls through an unlocked trapdoor mid-concert at the Saratoga Raceway, Saratoga Springs, NY. The trek is set to close on September 15th at Dodger Stadium, Los Angeles.
[30] ***Step By Step*** debuts at UK #1, and hits US #1 in its second week of release, as its title cut *Step By Step*, originally recorded by another Starr group the Superiors, also tops the US Hot 100.
July [10] *Step By Step* is certified platinum by the RIAA.
[13] The world's first heart/liver recipient, 13-year-old Stormie Jones, meets the band backstage after their Hanover Township, TX, show.
[21] Wahlberg's duet with Japanese singing starlet Seiko, *The Right Combination*, makes US #54. (Jordan will also duet during the year with teen star Ana for *Angel Of Love*.)
Aug [1] The RIAA certifies three million sales of ***Step By Step***.
[3] They play to a sellout crowd of 63,510 at the Exhibition Place Stadium, Toronto, ON, Canada.
[4] During a gig at the Olympic Stadium, Montreal, PQ, Canada, three armed robbers steal souvenir sales proceeds valued at $260,000.
[8] Jordan Knight is involved in an incident in an Atlanta, GA bar, after his bodyguard Steven Chandler allegedly assaults two people.
[18] Harmonious and melodic *Tonight* hits UK #3.
Sept [2] Wahlberg allegedly assaults 20-year-old **Harvard Crimson** editor Benjamin Dattner aboard Delta Airlines flight 1140 from Salt Lake City, UT, to Atlanta. Dattner is treated for a scratched cornea and head injuries at Fulton County Hospital, Atlanta.
[8] *Tonight* hits US #7, as ABC-TV airs the first New Kids cartoon series.
[14] They play to a sellout crowd of 55,003 at Dodger Stadium, Los Angeles.
[15] New Kids' business manager James Rossi has his briefcase, containing $100,000 in cash, stolen as he checks out of the Bel Air Hotel, Hollywood, CA.
Oct [1] **Forbes** magazine lists the group as the fifth richest entertainers in the US with pre-tax income of $78 million.
[12] The band performs at the Amnesty International benefit concert at the National Stadium, Santiago, Chile, alongside Sting, Sinead O'Connor and Peter Gabriel, among others.
[13] *Let's Try It Again/Didn't I (Blow Your Mind)* hits UK #8.
Nov [3] The belated UK issue of the debut ***New Kids On The Block*** album, already markedly out-dated in contrast to their current urban, streetwise dude style, nevertheless hits UK #6. *Let's Try It Again* hints at a burst bubble, stopping at US #53.
[6] The RIAA certifies three million sales of ***New Kids On The Block***.
[7] The Knight brothers appear on NBC-TV's "Unsolved Mysteries", urging fans to help find teenager Cari Lynn Nixon, a missing teenager from Ausable Forks, NY. (Someone watching the New Kids video "Hangin' Tough Live" thinks she has seen Nixon in the audience on the video.)
[15-18] They play four sellout shows at Joe Louis Arena, Detroit, MI, grossing $1,809,225.
[21] At the second of two sellout dates at the Nassau Veterans Memorial Coliseum, Uniondale, they meet backstage with Amnesty International USA executive director Jack Healey who signs them as members of the organization.
[30] The RIAA confirms domestic sales of 1,050,000 of the "Step By Step" video and 1,150,000 of the "Hangin' Tough" video.
Dec [7] US cable subscribers are offered pay-per-view broadcast of the group's "Live No More Games" concert.
[14-16] The New Kids play their final dates of 1990 in their home state at the Centrum in Worcester, MA, on a tour which will gross $74.1 million.
[15] *This One's For The Children* hits UK #9, while the now UK issued ***Merry, Merry Christmas*** reaches #13. By the end of the year one of the most successful marketing stories of pop history will be complete: in addition to the record sales (all five of their albums are still charted on the **Billboard** Top 200 Album survey), New Kids will have notched up the three best-selling music video collections of all time in the US ("Hangin' Tough" 1.2 million, "Step By Step" 1 million and "Hangin' Tough Live" 1.25 million), launched best-selling dolls, Simon & Schuster books, comics, a Saturday morning TV cartoon show, tour merchandise and a 1-900-9095 KIDS recorded telephone message line. A conservative estimate of the income generated by the group for the year is reported at $861 million.

1991

Jan [5] ***No More Games/Remix Album,*** with remixes by producers Arthur Baker, Clivilles and Cole, Mark Liggett and Chris Barbosa and Freddy Bastone, reaches US #19.
[15] ***No More Games/The Remix Album*** is certified gold by the RIAA.
The band performs at the multi-artist "Rock In Rio II" festival at the Marcana Stadium, Rio de Janeiro, Brazil.
[27] The group provides half-time entertainment, performing *A Small World Salute To 25 Years Of The Super Bowl* alongside 2,000 children, at Superbowl XXV.
[28] They perform at the 18th annual American Music Awards, which airs on ABC-TV.
[29] The RIAA certifies 100,000 sales of the "In Step ... Out Of Time", "Sheik Of My Dreams" and "The New Kid In The Class" videos.
[31] The group performs at the Tokyo Dome, Tokyo, Japan.
Feb [16] *Games* reaches UK #14.
[23-24] As the group's never-ending cash-cow tour continues, they play sellout dates at the Oakland-Alameda County Coliseum, Oakland, CA.
Mar [2] ***No More Games/Remix Album*** debuts at its UK #15 peak.
[7] New Kids are voted Worst Band, *Step By Step* is voted Worst Single and ***Step By Step*** Worst Album in the annual **Rolling Stone** magazine Readers' Picks music awards.
[27] Wahlberg is arrested after allegedly setting fire to the carpet outside Rooms 942 and 944 in the Seelbach Hotel, Louisville, KY. (He will plead guilty to a charge of criminal mischief.)
Apr Amy Omvig and her mother Paula, Erin McCauley and Dena Houser file suit in Polk County District Court, IA, after a gig in November 1990, at which a stampede caused 17 concert-goers to be taken to hospital. The three girls and mother are suing the band for "pain and suffering".
May [12] The group appears by satellite from the Ahoy, Rotterdam, Holland in "The Simple Truth" benefit concert for Kurdish refugees at Wembley Arena, Wembley, Middx, at the start of eight nights at the venue, from which they will gross £1,513,471, seen by 104,844 people.
[25] *Call It What You Want*, remixed by Clivilles and Cole, reaches UK #12.
July [30] Wood is presented with a cheque for the Dorchester Youth Collaborative by **TeenVid** magazine at the Hard Rock Café in Boston.
Sept Forbes magazine's annual list has the group as the top entertainment money-making act of year with earnings of $115 million.
Oct [5] *Good Vibrations*, co-written and produced by Wahlberg for his rising-star brother Marky Mark, tops

the US chart, taken from Mark's Wahlberg-helmed US #21-peaking freshman album ***Music For The People***.
[30] Latest leg of the never-ending tour opens at the Forum in Copenhagen, Denmark.
Nov [14] 1,000 fans require medical attention after an audience melée during a show in Berlin, West Germany.
Dec [2-3] The group begins a 13-date UK tour at the Manchester G-Mex, set to end on the 15th at the National Exhibition Centre, Birmingham, West Midlands.
[14] *If You Go Away* debuts at its UK #9 peak.
[21] ***H.I.T.S.*** makes UK #50 in its week of entry.

1992

Jan [8] Jordan Knight pleads innocent in Roxbury District Court to the charge that he ordered his bodyguard to assault North Eastern graduate Seamus McHugh at the Axis Nightclub in Boston on June 19th, 1991.
[15-17] The group performs three sellout dates at Palacio De Los Deportes, Mexico City, Mexico.
[24] University of Massachusetts music instructor Greg McPherson files suit in Suffolk Superior Court for $12 million in damages for not being paid for his work on the "Hangin' Tough Live" video and "Magic Summer" commercial for Coca-Cola. He also alleges that the band only sings 20% of its own vocals on their albums.
Feb During a show at a gymnastics hall in Olympic Park, Seoul, South Korea, before a crowd of 16,000, a stampede occurs 40 minutes into the show, leaving some 30 teenagers injured, one of whom will die a few days later.
[10] The band files countersuit against McPherson in Suffolk Superior Court seeking unspecified damages.
Apr Wahlberg signs a production deal with Interscope Records.
[16] McPherson drops his lawsuit, after reportedly receiving a financial settlement from Maurice Starr.
June [12] Jordan Knight and Wood are cleared of copyright infringement. George Soule had claimed the chorus of Tommy Page's 1990 US chart-topper *I'll Be Your Everything*, which Knight and Wood had penned, was the same as his song of the same name, recorded by Percy Sledge in 1974. Judge Miriam Goldman Cederbaum tells jurors a song title is not subject to copyright.

1993

June The group's manager Dick Scott issues a statement confirming that their name has been officially shortened to New Kids, although a month later this will be changed to NKOTB. No longer under the production guidance of Starr, the group continues to work on its first album in nearly three years at a Virginia Beach studio with various producers including Narada Michael Walden and Joe Public.
July The soundtrack to the movie "Free Willy", on which NKOTB's *Keep On Smiling* is featured, is released.

1994

Jan [24] The group receives a star on Tower Records' Walk of Fame in Boston, followed by an in-store autograph session.
[29] *Dirty Dawg* makes US #66.
Feb [7] NKOTB presents the Favorite Pop Rock Album trophy at the 21st annual American Music Awards held at the Shrine Auditorium.
[12] ***Face The Music***, the band's first album under its new moniker, bows at its US #37 peak, at the start of a six week chart stay.
[19] *Dirty Dawg* debuts at its UK #27 high.
Mar [12] ***Face The Music*** makes UK #36 in its week of entry.
[26] *Never Let You Go* enters at its UK #42 peak.
[31] McIntyre suffers a slipped disc when thrown from his horse Shakespeare, near his Essex, MA home.
Apr [1] With the bubble now burst, the group, minus McIntyre, begins its last 27-city US club tour in Philadelphia, PA.

1995

Nov [17] The US District Court rules that some profits made by the band should be paid to alleged Mafia member James Martorano, who had originally provided a $60,000 loan to get the band started. (Following the demise of the once hot group, Jordan Knight is preparing for his first solo album release, Wahlberg and Wood become producers, McIntyre makes his acting debut in the movie version of "The Fantasticks", while Jonathan Knight quits the business altogether.)

NEW ORDER

Barney Sumner (guitar, vocals);
Peter Hook (bass); **Stephen Morris** (drums);
Gillian Gilbert (keyboards)

1980

May [18] Seminal UK indie outfit Joy Division comes to a sudden end with the suicide of its lead singer Ian Curtis. During the weeks ahead, the remaining group members, Sumner (b. Bernard Dicken, Jan. 4, 1956, Salford, Lancs., known as Bernard Albrecht in Joy Division), Hook (b. Feb. 13, 1956, Salford) and Morris (b. Oct. 28, 1957, Macclesfield, Cheshire) resolve to continue, recording under a new name, though remaining on Tony Wilson's Factory label. While the previously completed and scheduled Joy Division recordings, *Love Will Tear Us Apart* and ***Closer*** are released, they decide on the moniker New Order, despite claims of Nazi connotations by some in the UK music press.
July [29] The trio performs its debut gig at the Beach Club in their home base of Manchester, Gtr. Manchester.
Sept [20] New Order plays the first of four US East Coast dates, which Joy Division had been booked to play in May, at Maxwell's, Hoboken, NJ.
Oct Gilbert (b. Jan. 27, 1961, Manchester), ex-all-girl punk band the Inadequates and long-time friend of Morris, joins New Order on keyboards and occasional guitar. She has recently studied at Stockport Technical College, Stockport, Gtr. Manchester.
[25] The band plays its first gig as a quartet at the Squat Club, Manchester.
Dec They enter Strawberry Studios, Stockport, to record debut material.

1981

Jan New Order begins a series of UK dates between recording sessions.
[25] Hook records a five-minute interview for BBC Radio 1's "Walters Weekly".
Feb [9] Their first London date is a supposedly secret gig at the Heaven club for which 1,000 tickets instantly sell out. Supporting acts include Section 25 and the Stockholm Monsters.
[16] The group's debut UK radio session is broadcast on "The John Peel Show" on BBC Radio 1.
Mar *Ceremony*, released by Factory reaches UK #34.
Apr [24] The group begins two weeks' recording at Strawberry Studios with producer Martin Hannett, for its first album, and films a TV special for Granada Television from whom Factory supremo Tony Wilson moonlights.
May A short European tour takes in France, Belgium, West Germany, Denmark, Sweden and Norway.
June [18] New Order documentary "Celebration" is broadcast on ITV.
[20] The band plays at the "Glastonbury Fayre", Glastonbury, Somerset, benefitting the Campaign For Nuclear Disarmament.
Oct Double A-side, *Procession/Everything's Gone Green*, peaks at UK #38.
Dec Their debut album, ***Movement***, reaches UK #30 and, in common with the majority of their releases throughout the decade, enjoys a lengthy chart-topping residence on the UK Independent chart. Another ITV performance sees band members dressed in Santa Claus outfits.

1982

Jan [4] They appear on BBC2-TV's "Riverside", playing *Temptation* and *Death Rattle*.
Mar [6] The group is interviewed on Irish radio RTE2.
Apr [8] On a European mini-tour, a riot occurs at a New Order gig in Rotterdam, Holland. Hook is knocked unconscious.
June [1] A session by the band on BBC Radio 1's "John Peel Show" includes the unrecorded *Turn The Heater On* (subsequently released as part of the Strange Fruit series), penned by reggae artist Keith Hudson.
[12] *Temptation*, released as a 33rpm 12"-only single, reaches UK #29.
[16-22] The group plays a mini-tour of Italy.
[26] The Hacienda club in Manchester, owned by Factory Records, and in which New Order has a financial interest, opens with a free members' evening highlighted by a performance by the group.
Sept [11] The group headlines the first day of fourth "Futurama Festival" in Leeds, West Yorks.
[19] New Order plays in a basketball stadium in Athens, Greece, as part of the first "Festival Of Independent Rock'n'Roll".
Oct [22] Recordings begin for their second album at London's Britannia Row Studios.
Nov Six-track mini-set ***New Order, 1981-1982***, compiling tracks from UK and Belgian singles, is released in North America.
[25] The band begins a ten-date tour of Australia and New Zealand, opening at the Palais Theatre, Melbourne, Victoria, Australia.

1983

Feb The group records for two weeks in New York, NY with US dance producer and mix-master Arthur Baker.
Apr *Blue Monday*, released only as a 12" single, climbs to UK #12.
May Synth-dominated ***Power, Corruption And Lies***, produced by the group, hits UK #4.
Sept 12"-only single, *Confusion*, produced and co-written by Baker, reaches UK #12. The group is now increasingly popular on the US new rock/dance market, aided by the release of *Blue Monday*, on Baker's dance-oriented Streetwise label.
Oct Having remained in the UK Top 100 since its release, *Blue Monday* now hits UK #9. (By 1987, the UK 12"-only release will have sold over 600,000 copies to become Britain's biggest-selling 12" single, with a global tally of over three million.)

1984

Apr The group makes its first visit to Japan playing sell-out shows in Tokyo and Osaka. A brief recording session in Tokyo produces *State Of The Nation* for future release.
May *Thieves Like Us* reaches UK #18, again produced and co-written with Baker. Factory's European off-shoot label, Factory Benelux releases New Order's *Murder* for the Belgium market.

1985

Feb New Order is signed to Quincy Jones' Qwest Records in the US.
May The group embarks on Far Eastern tour.
[25] *The Perfect Kiss* (which will reach UK #46) is simultaneously released with its parent album ***Low Life***, which immediately hits UK #7.
July ***Low Life*** marks their US chart debut at #94.
Aug Currently touring North America where *Perfect Kiss* is top five on **Billboard**'s Dance chart, the group is featured on BBC2-TV's marathon music video show "Rock Around The Clock".
Sept Factory reportedly draws up its first formal recording contracts. New Order's deal stipulates that the band only has to give six months' notice if it wishes to leave the label.
Nov *Sub-Culture* stops at UK #63.

1986

Feb [8] New Order takes part in a benefit at the Royal Court Theatre, Liverpool, for the city's 48 Labour councillors, who are facing legal action over the Rate Cap dispute.
Apr *Shellshock* (with *Shellcock* on the B-side), featured as one of three New Order tracks on the soundtrack to the John Hughes-directed movie "Pretty In Pink", reaches UK #28. Factory's Ikon video label releases long-form home video, controversially titled "Pumped Full Of Drugs".
July The group performs at the "Festival of the Tenth Summer" in Manchester.
Sept With their current Factory release, *State Of The Nation*, peaking at UK #30, the June 1982 "John Peel Show" radio session, released as a 12" EP for part of an archive series by Strange Fruit Records, makes UK #54.
Oct ***Brotherhood***, recorded in London, Dublin and Liverpool, hits UK #9.
Nov *Bizarre Love Triangle* makes UK #56 during a two-week chart stay, despite the aid of a Shep Pettibone remix, as ***Brotherhood*** makes US #117.

1987

Apr In between tours of the US and South-East Asia, New Order records cuts for the movie soundtrack to "Salvation", which is to be released later in the year on Les Disques De Crépuscule, a Belgian indie label.
June [19-21] They take part in the three-day "Glastonbury Festival", Glastonbury, Somerset.
Aug *True Faith*, released to worldwide critical and commercial enthusiasm, hits UK #4. Produced by Stephen Hague, it is a major international breakthrough, aided by an innovative accompanying video, directed by Jean Baptiste Mondino.
[29] ***Substance***, recalling all the band's 1980-87 UK 12" singles, hits UK #3 on release. (It will eventually sell over 400,000 copies in Britain alone, though only a few of these will be on the DAT (digital audio tape) format for which ***Substance*** is one of the earliest releases.)
Nov ***Substance*** climbs to US #36, while a second Strange Fruit 12" EP *Peel Sessions Volume II* is released. Sumner announces his intention to work as a soloist during 1988.
Dec [26] *True Faith*, written by the band and Hague, becomes its US singles chart debut, reaching #32, while *Touched By The Hand Of God* peaks at UK #20. European dates include sell-out shows in London, Dusseldorf and Paris.

1988

Feb [8] "True Faith" is named Best British Music Video, at the seventh annual BRIT Awards, at London's Royal Albert Hall.
The group appears at the "San Remo Festival" in Italy where they "mime" for the first time.
Mar New Order performs before their Royal Highnesses the Duke and Duchess of York at the Stock Exchange nightclub in Los Angeles, CA, during UKLA Week, a festival aimed at strengthening UK/US business ties.
May Perennial *Blue Monday* is reissued, remixed by John Potoker and overseen by Quincy Jones, and retitled *Blue Monday 1988*. It hits UK #3 while peaking at US #68.
June The group begins three months of recording in Ibiza and Bath, Avon.
Nov Film producer Chris Bernard commissions New Order to record the soundtrack for a forthcoming BBC-TV series, "Making Out".
Dec *Fine Time*, the first single from their forthcoming album, peaks at UK #11, much to the chagrin of their manager Rob Gretton who had bet each member of the band £250 that it would hit the Top 10. The group sets off on tour of South America, following their only UK concert of the year at the G-Mex Centre, Manchester, where they are supported by labelmates Happy Mondays.

1989

Jan [20] The group plays first of two dates in Southern France.
Feb [11] Its sixth album ***Technique***, co-produced with Hague, debuts at UK #1 and will peak at US #32.
[21] The group appears live on C4-TV's "Big World Café".
Mar *Round And Round* reaches UK #21, aided by a rare live performance on BBC1-TV's "Top Of The Pops". (Wilson temporarily resigns as Factory chairman over a bet with manager Gretton that it would make the top five.) Its B-side features their theme tune to current ITV soccer series "Best And Marsh". They also perform two concerts in Glasgow, Scotland, and Birmingham, West Midlands.
Apr [8] The band kicks off the first stage of a North American tour at San Juan, Puerto Rico.
June The group returns to Europe to attend the Hacienda's seventh birthday party held at the Roxy club, Amsterdam, Holland.
[14] A 21-date "Monsters Of Art Tour", with Public Image Ltd. and the Sugarcubes, restarts at Shoreline Amphitheatre, Mountain View, CA.
Aug New Order plays at the annual "Reading Festival", Reading, Berks.
Sept *Run 2* from ***Technique*** makes UK #49.
Dec Sumner releases the first fruits of his side-project from New Order, linking with the Pet Shop Boys' Neil Tennant and the Smiths' Johnny Marr in ad-hoc outfit Electronic. The resulting *Getting Away With It*, released on Factory, reaches UK #12.
[7] ***Technique*** is certified gold by the RIAA.

1990

Feb [14] "Substance" video is certified gold by the RIAA.
May While Morris and Gilbert have continued soundtrack work (not least for two series of the TV hit "Making Out" and a BBC-TV play "Shooting Stars"), Hook forms Revenge with Dave Hicks and Chris Jones, releasing their debut album, ***One True Passion***, on Factory in the UK and Capitol in the US.
[19] Electronic's *Getting Away With It* makes US #38.
June [9] Under the one-off band name, England New Order, the group has combined with the England World Cup Football Squad to hit UK #1 with *World In Motion ...*, the team's officially commissioned World Cup theme. The song, and accompanying soccer-based video, includes a rap by UK soccer hero John Barnes. The hit is written by New Order (its rhythm track originally penned by Gilbert and Morris as the TV theme to "Reportage") and UK comedian/actor Keith Allen.
Aug Sumner joins Marr and both Pet Shop Boys for Electronic's first live performance at Los Angeles' Dodger Stadium. They support Depeche Mode in a slot originally booked for the Jesus & Mary Chain, who have withdrawn.

1991

Jan [18] ***Substance*** is certified platinum by the RIAA.
May [11] Electronic's *Get The Message* hits UK #8.
June [8] ***Electronic*** debuts at its UK #2 peak behind Seal's ***Seal***.
Aug [3] ***Electronic*** stops at US #109.
[4] Electronic takes part in the "Cities In The Park Festival", Heaton Park, Prestwich, with the Pet Shop Boys joining them onstage.
Sept [5] Electronic is featured in **Rolling Stone**'s fall fashion layout.
[28] Electronic's *Feel Every Beat* reaches UK #39.
Oct [28] Morris and Gilbert, billed as the Other Two, release *Tasty Fish* on London Records.
Nov [25] Factory Records releases a four-volume boxed set, ***Palatine***, comprising tracks by New Order and Electronic.
Dec [12] Electronic plays a one-off date at Wembley Conference Hall, Wembley, Middx.

1992

Feb [15] Revenge, which released the EP *Gun Porn World* in December, counters with a one-off gig at Witchwood, Ashton-under-Lyne.
[22] New Order's ***BBC Radio 1 Live In Concert*** debuts at it UK #33 peak.
July [4] New Order's *Disappointed* debuts at its UK #6 peak.
Nov [21] *How Does It Feel?* bows at UK #27, as the band puts the finishing touches to new album at RAK Studios with producer Stephen Hague.

1993

Jan Following the demise of Factory Records (in part due, allegedly, to the late delivery of New Order's new album), the band signs to London Records, but remaining with Qwest in the States.
Apr [24] *Regret*, from the group's forthcoming ***Republic*** album, hits UK #4.
May [15] ***Republic*** enters at UK #1.
[29] ***Republic*** debuts at its US #11 peak.
July [3] *Ruined In A Day* bows at its UK #22 high.
[10] *Regret* reaches US #28.
[17] ***Substance 1987*** enters at its UK #32 peak.
Sept [11] *World (The Price Of Love)* reaches UK #13 and debuts at its US #92 pinnacle.
Dec [18] *Spooky* bows at its UK #22 high.

1994

Feb Continuing in tandem as The Other Two, Gilbert and Morris' ***The Other Two And You*** is released.
Mar [8] ***Republic*** is certified gold by the RIAA.
Nov [19] Revised *True Faith - 94*, featuring remixes by Mike "Spike" Drake, Paul Oakenfold and Steve Osborne, debuts at its UK #9 peak.
Dec [3] ***(The Best Of) New Order*** hits UK #4 in its week of entry.

1995

Jan [28] *Nineteen63*, accompanied by the previously unreleased *Let's Go* and with mixes by Arthur Baker, Justin Robinson, Tall Paul and Joe T. Vanelli, reaches UK #21.
Apr [8] Fending off import demand from the UK, ***(The Best Of) New Order***, with slightly altered content and remixes to the UK version, makes US #78.
May BBC-TV documentary "Prozac Diary" airs featuring Sumner experimenting with the drug to see if it enhances the creative process. (He is currently working in the studio with Johnny Marr, working on the next Electronic album.)
July [22] Revised *Bizarre Love Triangle* bows at its US #98 peak.
Aug [5] *Blue Monday - 95* debuts at its UK #17 peak.
Sept [2] With Hook leading the house band on BBC2-TV's "The Mrs. Merton Show", with his wife Caroline as the aforementioned Mrs. Merton, a further compilation ***(The Best Of)/? (The Rest Of)*** hits UK #5 in its week of entry.
see also: **JOY DIVISION**

RANDY NEWMAN

1961

Songwriter, pianist and vocalist Newman (b. Randolph Newman, Nov. 28, 1943, New Orleans, LA), nephew of Alfred and Lionel Newman (heads of music at 20th Century-Fox Pictures), and a graduate in music composition at UCLA, releases his US debut *Golden Gridiron Boy* on Dot Records, produced by Pat Boone. Finding greater success as a songwriter after joining the staff at Liberty Records' music publishing division, Metric Music, the following year, earning $50 per week, he writes the Fleetwoods' *They Tell Me It's Summer*, the B-side of their 1962 US #36 hit *Lovers By Night, Strangers By Day*; *Somebody's Waiting*, the B-side of Gene McDaniels' *Spanish Lace*, which makes US #31 in the same year, and his first A-side compositional hit, Jerry Butler's version of *I Don't Want To Hear It Anymore*, at US #95 in July 1964.

1965

May His first song to chart in the UK is Cilla Black's recording of *I've Been Wrong Before*, which reaches UK #17. (Over the next two years, he continues to establish himself as a major songwriter, with hit covers of his songs by Alan Price (*Simon Smith And His Amazing Dancing Bear*) and Gene Pitney (*Nobody Needs Your Love* and *Just One Smile*), as well as recordings by Judy Collins, Manfred Mann, Frankie Laine, Jackie DeShannon, the Walker Brothers, the Nashville Teens, Harpers Bizarre, and many more.)

1966

He releases the instrumental album, ***The Randy Newman Orchestra Plays Music From The Hit Television Series "Peyton Place"***, on US Epic, with help from his uncles at 20th Century-Fox. The following year, and with help from producer friend Lenny Waronker, Newman becomes a staff arranger-producer at Warner Bros. Records, working with the Beau Brummels, Van Dyke Parks and Harpers Bizarre.

1968

June Newman's debut vocal album, ***Randy Newman***, is released on Warner's Reprise label, along with the extracted *Bee Hive State*. It includes already-covered songs like *Love Story* and *So Long Dad*, plus *Cowboy* (which Newman has submitted unsuccessfully after being invited to write a theme song for the film "Midnight Cowboy"). Many copies of the album are allegedly given away as a loss-leader publicity stunt by Warner, and the album fails to chart.

1970

Mar Following Newman's success as the arranger of Peggy Lee's Leiber/Stoller-penned, *Is That All There Is?*, which has hit US #10 the previous November, Harry Nilsson releases ***Nilsson Sings Newman***, with covers of ten Newman songs, including some not yet recorded by the writer, who guests on vocals on two tracks.

Apr Uniquely sardonic, his self-penned ***Twelve Songs***, originally a demo set, produced by Lenny Waronker, features guest musicians Ry Cooder, Clarence White and Gene Parsons of the Byrds among others, and includes *Mama Told Me (Not To Come)*, left off the previous album because Newman did not rate it highly enough.

July [11] His first #1 composition is Three Dog Night's version of *Mama Told Me (Not To Come)*, which tops the US chart for the first of two weeks. Meanwhile, Newman contributes to the film soundtrack to "Performance", starring Mick Jagger, on which Newman also sings *Gone Dead Train*, and to the Dick Van Dyke/Bob Newhart comedy "Cold Turkey", for which he writes the score.

1971

Oct Performance set, ***Randy Newman Live***, recorded at New York, NY's Bitter End club, is his US chart debut, at #191. It is enlivened by his humorous song-intros and spoken interjections, a hallmark of his live work.

1972

July Co-produced by Waronker and Russ Titelman and featuring music guests Ry Cooder, Jim Keltner and Wilton Felder among others, ***Sail Away***, with its much-covered title track, peaks at US #163, selling over 100,000 copies during an 18-week chart stay, furthering his reputation as a highly original songsmith.

1974

June Newman makes his UK live debut at London's Theatre Royal Drury Lane.

Oct [5] He plays at the Atlanta Symphony Hall, GA, accompanied by an 87-piece orchestra conducted by another uncle, Emil Newman.

Dec ***Good Old Boys***, again co-helmed by Waronker and Titelman, featuring guest backing vocals by Glenn Frey and Don Henley of the Eagles, reaches US #36. It is his biggest-selling album to date, staying charted for five months, and will be promoted by a 20-city US tour, accompanied by the Atlanta Symphony Orchestra.

1978

Jan *Short People*, his Hot 100 chart performance debut, hits US #2 behind medium-height band the Bee Gees at #1 with *Stayin' Alive*, and is a million seller. A parody on bigotry (a familiar Newman theme), it ironically makes him a target for hatred by short people throughout the US for a while, though Newman (measuring 5' 11") is publicly unrepentant. The song is taken from ***Little Criminals***, written, arranged and conducted by the artist, his first album to hit the US Top 10, at #9. Album guests include members of the Eagles. (Neither the album nor single charts in the UK, but Newman makes a UK tour during the year, and his live set is taped for a BBC-TV show.)

[24] The RIAA certifies gold sales of both *Short People* and ***Little Criminals***.

1979

Sept ***Born Again***, one of the first digitally-recorded albums (and for which he has commuted to Los Angeles, CA and written the songs in an office, 9-5 fashion), peaks at US #41. It features guest vocals by Stephen Bishop, and includes the non-charting single, *Story Of A Rock'n'Roll Band*, a send-up of the Electric Light Orchestra story, in theatrical Jeff Lynne-style.

1980

July UB40's revival Newman's haunting *I Think It's Going To Rain Today*, from his first album, released as a double A-side with the group's own *My Way Of Thinking*, hits UK #6.

1982

Feb His soundtrack to the Milos Forman movie, "Ragtime", starring James Cagney, is released on Elektra, and peaks at US #134. (*One More Hour* will be nominated for an Oscar as Best Original Song.)

1983

Feb A duet with Paul Simon, *The Blues*, reaches US #51.

Mar ***Trouble In Paradise*** reaches US #64. Including the recent Simon collaboration, it also features guest appearances by Bob Seger, Rickie Lee Jones, Linda Ronstadt, Jennifer Warnes, Don Henley, Lindsay Buckingham and Christine McVie.

1984

Aug His song, *I Love L.A.*, from ***Trouble In Paradise***, is used for US TV commercials promoting the Los Angeles Olympics.

Oct He writes and performs the soundtrack to the Robert Redford movie "The Natural", released as an album on Warner Bros. The following September 22nd, Newman will participate in Willie Nelson's inaugural "Farm Aid" benefit.

1986

Nov He writes and records the soundtrack music for the Steve Martin/Chevy Chase comedy film "The Three Amigos" (which also features his first screenplay work, in collaboration with Martin). His first compilation album, ***Lonely At The Top***, surveying a variety of his work, is released in Europe-only to promote a tour the following May.

1988

Oct ***Land Of Dreams***, Newman's first album in five years, part-produced by Jeff Lynne and Mark Knopfler, is released, and is set to make US #80, while the typically barbed extract, *It's Money That Matters*, peaks at US #60.

1990

June [9-10] Newman, with Paula Abdul, B.B. King, Alice Cooper, Kenny Loggins and Quincy Jones, film a video at A&M studios promoting recycling based on *Yakety Yak*. Sponsored by the Take It Back Foundation, "Yakety Yak, Take It Back!" also features Bugs Bunny, and will be released in April 1991. (By year's end, and having contributed *Falling In Love* to the Tom Selleck movie "Her Alibi", and *Burn On* to "Major League", Newman scores the soundtrack to the Robin Williams/Robert De Niro hit movie "Awakenings". Newman is also featured on ***The Simpsons Sings The Blues*** album, with *I Love To See You Smile*.)

1991

Jan [11] Newman writes the Gulf War-themed *Lines In The Sand*, recording it two days later.

Mar [9] The Peace Choir's *Give Peace A Chance*, which features Newman among its all-star cast, makes US #54.

May [7] Newman begins a short US tour, playing the first of two nights with the Boston Pops Orchestra performing selections from his film music.

Aug [26] He wins an Emmy for his music for the ABC-TV series "Cop Rock".

1992

July [11] Newman performs at the "American Music Festival" on a bill with the Neville Brothers, Warren Zevon, Leon Russell, the BoDeans and NRBQ at the Winter Park Ski Resort, CO.

Nov [12] He guests on NBC-TV's "Late Night With David Letterman".

[20] Newman plays two sellout shows at the Great American Music Hall, San Francisco, CA, during his latest US tour.

1994

Apr [30] He takes part in the 25th annual "New Orleans Jazz & Heritage Festival".

June [9] Newman guests on CBS-TV's "Late Show With David Letterman".

1995

Mar [27] He performs his Oscar-nominated theme to "The Paper" at the 67th annual Academy Awards held at Los Angeles' Shrine Auditorium.

Apr [28-29] Newman performs at the Cerritos Center for the Performing Arts, Cerritos, CA with Buffy Sainte-Marie. (During the month, the tribute album ***For The Love Of Harry (Everybody Sings Nilsson)***, to which Newman has contributed *Remember*, is released.)

Aug [6] He takes part in the annual "Newport Folk Festival" at Fort Adams State Park, Newport, RI.

Sept [2] Newman's new project, the concept album ***Faust***, a musical featuring James Taylor, Don Henley, Elton John, Bonnie Raitt, Linda Ronstadt and Newman as the Devil, is released. The work concurrently opens on stage at the La Jolla Playhouse in San Diego on the 24th, running through to the 29th. (The CD-Plus release the following January, featuring the entire album score, lyrics and interviews, will Reprise's first ever in that format.)

Nov [11] Newman guests on BBC2-TV's "Later With Jools Holland".

1996

Mar [25] Newman sings his Oscar-nominated song *You've Got A Friend* from his soundtrack to "Toy Story" with co-vocalist Lyle Lovett at the 68th annual Academy Awards ceremony held at Los Angeles' Dorothy Chandler Pavilion.

Apr [9] Featuring his latest film score and five new songs, the Disney soundtrack to its animated feature, the Tim Burton-directed "James And The Giant Peach" hits US stores, as Newman announces a string of forthcoming US summer tour dates.

[23] Newman receives the Henry Mancini Award for lifetime achievements at the 11th annual ASCAP Film and TV Awards, staged at the Beverly Hilton, Beverly Hills, CA.

OLIVIA NEWTON-JOHN

1964

Newton-John (b. Sept. 26, 1948, Cambridge, Cambs.), having moved to Melbourne, Victoria, Australia, with her family at the age of five, and having sung in a folk vocal group in her early teens, becoming a frequent performer on local TV with singing partner Pat Carroll, wins a Johnny O'Keefe national talent contest, for which the prize is a trip to the UK. Postponing the visit for a year to complete school, she travels to the UK with Carroll, to perform as a duo in pubs and clubs. After Carroll's visa expires in early 1966 and she returns to Australia, Newton-John remains in the UK performing solo, and cuts a one-off single for Decca Records in May, recording Jackie DeShannon's *Till You Say You'll Be Mine*. In September the same year she meets Bruce Welch of the Shadows at a concert in Bournemouth, Dorset, who offers her the chance to star in Cliff Richard and the Shadows' London Palladium pantomime, "Cinderella", though she declines in order to return to Australia for Christmas. Back in the UK in 1968, she sets up home with Welch in West London and will be cited in his divorce proceedings the following year.

1970

Aug She is recruited by producer Don Kirshner to join Toomorrow, with Ben Thomas, Karl Chambers, Vic Cooper and Chris Slade, a group formed to star in a movie of the same title. A pair of Toomorrow singles are issued simultaneously in the UK, on different labels, Decca and RCA.

[27] "Toomorrow" (a science fiction musical comedy) opens in cinemas throughout the UK, and RCA releases a soundtrack album by the group. Both fail commercially and, after spending time on promotional work for the film, the quartet disbands.

1971

Jan Newton-John duets with Cliff Richard on *Don't Move Away*, the B-side of his UK hit, *Sunny Honey Girl*, after which she joins Richard's tour of Holland, Belgium, West Germany and Switzerland.

Apr Her belated second solo single, recorded for UK Pye International via a deal signed with Festival Records in Australia, covers Bob Dylan's *If Not For You*, and hits UK #7. It is produced by John Farrar, now married to her ex-partner Pat Carroll, and also a member of Marvin, Welch & Farrar with Bruce Welch, to whom she is engaged.

Aug [30] She appears on BBC1-TV guesting in Cliff Richard's holiday special, "Getaway With Cliff".

Sept *If Not For You* is her US debut at #25.

Oct [25] She begins a season at the London Palladium on a bill topped by Cliff Richard.

Dec Her revival of the folk standard *Banks Of The Ohio*, produced by Welch and Farrar, hits UK #6, and stops at US #94, while ***If Not For You*** makes US #158.

1972

Jan She begins a 13-week guest residency on Cliff Richard's BBC1-TV series, "It's Cliff Richard".

Apr Her cover of George Harrison's *What Is Life* reaches UK #16. Shortly after, Newton-John and Welch break up.

Aug *Just A Little Too Much* is released.

1973

Feb Another cover, of John Denver's *Take Me Home, Country Roads*, reaches UK #15.

June *Let Me Be There*, written by ex-Shadows member John Rostill, is released.

Aug She plays solo recorder on Marvin, Welch & Farrar's *Music Makes My Day*.

1974

Feb *Let Me Be There* hits US #6 (after topping the US Country chart), her first major US success, and the first of five consecutive US million seller singles, and spurs ***Let Me Be There*** to US #54.

[8] *Let Me Be There* is certified gold by the RIAA.

Mar Her third album, ***Music Makes My Day***, is the first to chart in the UK, reaching #37.

[2] She wins the Best Country Vocal Performance, Female category for *Let Me Be There*, at the 16th annual Grammy Awards.

Apr [6] She represents the UK in the Eurovision Song Contest, held in Brighton, East Sussex, with *Long Live Love*. The song fails in the competition (won by Abba with *Waterloo*), but reaches UK #11.

June ***Long Live Love*** marking a move to EMI Records in the UK, peaks at UK #40. *If You Love Me (Let Me Know)* fails to chart in the UK, but after the US success of *Let Me Be There* it hits US #5, earning another gold disc on the 26th.

Sept [9] The still-climbing album ***If You Love Me, Let Me Know*** is certified gold by the RIAA.

Oct Ballad *I Honestly Love You* reaches UK #22.

[5] *I Honestly Love You* is her first chart-topper, holding at #1 for two weeks.

[9] *I Honestly Love You* is certified gold by the RIAA.

[12] Her US album, ***If You Love Me, Let Me Know***, also tops the US chart for one week.

[14] ***Let Me Be There*** is also confirmed gold by the RIAA.

1975

Jan Newton-John, her new boyfriend Lee Kramer (who becomes her manager in the US, at the suggestion of original manager Peter Gormley) and her writer/producer John Farrar, move from the UK to the US, to capitalize on her huge 1974 US success. (She will take up residence in Malibu, CA.)

Feb [18] She collects the Favorite Female Artist, Pop/Rock, Favorite Album, Country, Favorite Female Artist, Country, and Favorite Single, Pop/Rock, trophies at the second annual American Music Awards, held at the Civic Auditorium, Santa Monica, CA.

[26] The still-climbing ***Have You Never Been Mellow*** is certified gold by the RIAA.

Mar [1] *I Honestly Love You* is named Record Of The Year and Newton-John wins the Best Pop Vocal Performance, Female category at the 17th annual Grammy Awards. (She is also voted Female Vocalist Of The Year by the Country Music Association, the first UK performer to be so honored. The choice angers many prominent CMA members, who leave to form the Association of Country Entertainers. She answers the criticism by playing the country music circuit heavily, and recording in Nashville, TN.)

[8] Already confirmed gold three days earlier, *Have You Never Been Mellow*, written and produced by Farrar, tops the US chart for one week.

[15] Its parent album, ***Have You Never Been Mellow***, also hits US #1 for a week.

Apr *Have You Never Been Mellow* makes UK #37.

Aug *Please Mr. Please*, written by Welch and originally his only solo single in 1974, hits US #3, becoming her fifth million-selling single in a row on September 16th.

Sept ***Clearly Love*** is certified gold by the RIAA, set to reach US #12 in November when the extracted *Something Better To Do* makes US #13.

1976

Jan *Let It Shine/He Ain't Heavy ... He's My Brother* climbs to US #30. Her duet with John Denver on *Fly Away* also rises to US #13.

[31] She takes home the Favorite Female Artist, Pop/Rock, Favorite Album, Pop/Rock, and Favorite Female Artist, Country, trophies at the third annual American Music Awards, held again at the Santa Monica Civic Auditorium.

Apr [27] The still-rising ***Come On Over*** is certified gold by the RIAA.

May ***Come On Over*** makes US #13 and UK #49, as the title cut, *Come On Over*, reaches US #23. Kramer resigns as her manager, and the couple's personal relationship also dissolves.

Sept *Don't Stop Believin'* makes US #33.

Nov [17] Her first US TV special is aired on ABC-TV, with guests including Elliot Gould and Lynda Carter.

Dec ***Don't Stop Believin'***, certified gold on the 8th, reaches US #30, with *Every Face Tells A Story* climbing to US #55.

1977

Jan [31] She collects the Favorite Female Artist, Pop/Rock, trophy at the fourth annual American Music Awards, again held at the Santa Monica Civic Auditorium.

Apr Ballad *Sam*, taken from ***Don't Stop Believin'***, reaches US #20.

[14] Newton-John begins a US tour.

May [8] She makes her New York, NY live debut at the Metropolitan Opera House, and is approached to play the lead role of Sandy in a movie adaptation of the Broadway hit musical of '50s nostalgia, "Grease".

[28] As part of the Queen's Silver Jubilee celebrations, she stars in "The Big Top Show" at Windsor Castle, Windsor, Berks., with Elton John and Leo Sayer.

June *Making A Good Thing Better* stalls at US #87.

July *Sam* hits UK #6.

Aug ***Making A Good Thing Better*** peaks at US #34 and UK #60.

Oct Newton-John and Kramer are reunited, both professionally and personally.

Dec A reissue of *I Honestly Love You* peaks at US #48.

1978

Jan Compilation album, ***Olivia Newton-John's Greatest Hits***, makes US #13 and UK #19, initially selling over one million units in the US.

May US television special "Olivia" airs on ABC-TV. She sues her US label, MCA Records, for $10 million, alleging "failure to adequately promote and advertise" her records.

June [10] Written and produced by John Farrar, *You're The One That I Want*, a duet with co-star John Travolta from the movie "Grease", tops the US chart for one week, eventually selling over two million copies to earn a platinum disc.

[16] Movie "Grease" opens across the US.

[17] *You're The One That I Want* also hits UK #1 for the first of nine weeks, selling over 1,870,000 copies, making it the third best-selling single in UK pop history to date.

July [29] Soundtrack album, ***Grease***, begins a 12-week hold at US #1, and is a multi-million seller.

Aug [31] The still-climbing *Hopelessly Devoted To You* is certified gold by the RIAA.

Sept *Summer Nights*, a second "Grease" duet with Travolta, hits US #5, topping a million sales.

[30] *Summer Nights* heads the UK chart for the first of seven weeks, eventually selling over 1,500,000 copies, and giving the duo a second entry among Britain's ten best-selling singles of all time. Her solo from "Grease", the ballad *Hopelessly Devoted To You*, hits US #3, and is a further million seller.

Dec *Hopelessly Devoted To You* hits UK #2 while Newton-John performs UK dates including London's Rainbow Theatre.

[5] Yet to peak, ***Totally Hot*** is certified platinum by the RIAA.

1979

Jan *A Little More Love* hits US #3 and UK #4, while its parent album, ***Totally Hot***, hits US #7. It also makes UK #30.

[9] The "Music For UNICEF Concert", featuring Newton-John singing *Rest Your Love On Me* with Gibb and *The Key*, donating the royalties from the song to UNICEF, staged to celebrate the International Year Of The Child, takes place in the General Assembly Hall of the United Nations in New York, to be broadcast the following day on NBC-TV as "A Gift Of Song - The Music For UNICEF Concert".

Feb [12] *A Little More Love* is confirmed gold by the RIAA.

June *Deeper Than The Night* climbs to US #11 and UK #64.

Aug *Totally Hot*, the title track from her most recent album, makes US #52 while its B-side, *Dancin' Round And Round*, reaches US #82.

1980

May Her duet with Andy Gibb on *I Can't Help It* makes US #12. (She is also featured on Gibb's current release ***After Dark***.)

July [12] Newton-John stars with Gene Kelly in the fantasy musical movie, "Xanadu", which is

slaughtered by the critics and proves a box office failure, but spins off a highly successful music soundtrack. The title track, *Xanadu*, recorded with the Electric Light Orchestra, now tops the UK chart for the first of three weeks, and the movie's soundtrack album also hits UK #2 for two weeks.
[15] *Magic* is certified gold by the RIAA.
Aug [2] Her solo *Magic*, from ***Xanadu***, begins a month long stay atop the US survey.
Sept Soundtrack album, ***Xanadu***, shared between Newton-John and ELO, hits US #4, while *Magic* peaks at UK #32.
Nov *Suddenly*, a ballad duet with Cliff Richard from ***Xanadu***, reaches UK #15.

1981

Jan *Suddenly* reaches US #20.
Aug [5] Newton-John receives a star on the Hollywood Walk of Fame in Hollywood, CA.
Nov [21] *Physical*, written by Steve Kipner and Terry Shaddick, and banned by some radio stations for its supposed sexual innuendo, hits US #1 for the first of ten weeks, equalling the second longest holding chart-topper in pop history behind Elvis Presley's 11-week *Hound Dog*. It will also hit UK #7, and become one of the first and most identifiable aerobic themes.
Dec ***Physical***, promoted by a US TV special based around the songs on the album (her fourth such TV vehicle), hits US #6, and is another million seller, also making UK #11.

1982

Jan [5] *Physical* is certified platinum by the RIAA.
Feb *Landslide* reaches UK #18.
Apr *Make A Move On Me* hits US #5, and peaks at UK #43.
May [22] She performs on NBC-TV's "Saturday Night Live".
July *Landslide* makes US #52. She makes a rare US tour, partly filmed for video release.
Nov *Heart Attack* hits US #3 and makes UK #46, while the TV-promoted compilation, ***20 Greatest Hits***, hits UK #8. A different collection, ***Olivia's Greatest Hits, Vol. 2***, reaches US #16.

1983

Jan Reissued *I Honestly Love You*, from the compilation, makes UK #52.
[17] She wins the Favorite Female Artist, Pop/Rock, category, at the tenth annual American Music Awards, held at the Shrine Auditorium, Los Angeles, CA.
Feb *Tied Up* peaks at US #38.
[23] "Physical" is named Best Video at the 25th annual Grammy Awards.
Nov David Foster-written *Twist Of Fate*, from the film, "Two Of A Kind", in which she again co-stars with Travolta (although this time the fare is non-musical), reaches UK #57.

1984

Jan Soundtrack album, ***Two Of A Kind***, containing four Newton-John cuts, peaks at US #26, while *Twist Of Fate* hits US #5.
[16] ***Two Of A Kind*** is certified platinum by the RIAA.
Mar Also from the movie, *Livin' In Desperate Times*, peaks at US #31.
Aug She hosts a reception in Los Angeles for the Australian Olympic team.
Oct [12] The RIAA certifies two million sales each of ***Greatest Hits***, ***Greatest Hits Vol. 2***, ***Physical*** and ***Xanadu***.

1985

Nov *Soul Kiss* reaches US #20, while the album, ***Soul Kiss***, peaks at US #29.
Dec [19] ***Soul Kiss*** is certified gold by the RIAA.

1986

Jan [17] Having married actor/dancer Matt Lattanzi the previous year, whom she first met while working on "Xanadu", she gives birth to daughter, Chloe.
Mar ***Soul Kiss*** makes UK #66, her final '80s UK chart appearance.
July [5] David Foster's *The Best Of Me*, featuring Newton-John, makes US #80.

1988

Sept ***The Rumour***, largely produced by Davitt Sigerson, makes US #67 while the title cut, *The Rumour*, produced and co-written by Elton John, reaches US #62.

1989

Newton-John is appointed Goodwill Ambassador for the United Nations Environment Program.
Dec Newton-John is warned to increase security after Ralph Nau, having stalked her since 1981, seeks release from the Elgin Mental Health Center, IL.

1990

Jan [6] Still running her own Koala Blue Australian-style clothing business, started in 1984 with Farrar's wife Pat, and now signed to Geffen Records, Newton-John's ***Warm And Tender***, a collection of favorite nursery rhymes, lullabies and standards she sings to her daughter Chloe, makes US #124.
Dec [17] Newton-John appears in NBC-TV's "A Mom For Christmas".

1991

Jan [12] Re-hashed Travolta and Newton-John's *Grease Megamix* hits UK #3.
Mar [23] Travolta and Newton-John's *Grease - The Dream Mix* debuts at its UK #47 peak.

1992

May [14] Newton-John and Cliff Richard co-host the third annual World Music Awards, held at the Sporting Club, Monte Carlo, Monaco.
June [27] ***Back To Basics : The Essential Collection 1971-1992***, a best-of set including four new songs, *Not Gonna Be The One*, *I Want To Be Wanted*, *Deeper Than A River*, and the single, *I Need Love*, bows at its US #121 peak.
July [4] *I Need Love* charts for a week at UK #75.
[11] Newton-John takes part in ABC-TV's "A Call To Action In The War Against AIDS" special, as *I Need Love* stops at US #96.
[14] She reveals she is battling breast cancer, declaring "I am making this information public myself to save enquiring minds 95 cents". She also postpones her upcoming concert tour.
[25] ***Back To Basics : The Essential Collection 1971-1992*** reaches UK #12.

1993

Apr [6] Sony Kids' various artists, ***Put On Your Green Shoes***, album, to which Newton-John contributes a track, is released in the US as she recuperates from recent cancer treatment.

1994

Sept [7] Newton-John performs at the "Best For The Bush" concert, at the Melbourne Sports & Entertainment Centre to benefit Queensland farmers. She will also appear in the CBS-TV movie "A Christmas Romance" on December 18th.

1995

Feb [11] Her first new studio set in five years, ***Gaia (One Woman's Journey)*** reaches UK #33.
Dec [9] *Had To Be*, a duet with Cliff Richard from his current musical project "Heathcliff", debuts at its UK #22 peak.

NILSSON

1967

Nov Nilsson (b. Harry Edward Nilsson III, June 15, 1941, Brooklyn, New York, NY), having lived in California since childhood, is a computer specialist under his given name at the Security First National Bank in Van Nuys, CA working the night shift between 5:00 p.m. - 1:00 a.m., sunlighting during the day at an office shared with George Tipton and Perry Botkin Jr. on Vine and Selma in Hollywood, CA, as Nilsson, part-time songwriter. He has successfully hawked *Paradise* and *Here I Sit* to Phil Spector for the Ronettes and *This Could Be The Night* for the Modern Folk Quartet (also produced by Spector), and also released his own single on Mercury Records under a third name, Johnny Niles, before securing the largely-ignored mid-decade release of his first solo album as Nilsson on ***Spotlight On Nilsson***, issued by the Tower label. One of his compositions, *Cuddly Toy*, is now included by the Monkees on their ***Pisces, Aquarius, Capricorn & Jones Ltd.*** With interest in his material running high, RCA Records signs him as a singer/songwriter.

1968

Mar His label debut, ***Pandemonium Shadow Show***, produced by Rick Jarrard, includes six Nilsson originals (including *Cuddly Toy*), plus covers including the Beatles' *You Can't Do That* (in which he incorporates many Beatles' song titles into the lyrics) and *She's Leaving Home*, and a carbon-copy of Phil Spector's arrangement of Ike & Tina Turner's *River Deep, Mountain High*. The album does not chart, but gets wide airplay: John Lennon hears it and names Nilsson his favorite US singer. Three of the new songs are quickly covered: *1941* (Tom Northcott and Billy J. Kramer), *Without Her* (Jack Jones) and *It's Been So Long* (Kenny Everett).
Sept ***Aerial Ballet*** contains all Nilsson originals apart from Fred Neil's *Everybody's Talkin'*, which is issued as a single, gaining much airplay, as will Sandie Shaw's cover of the album's *Together*.

1969

Jan He writes the score for Otto Preminger's film "Skidoo", including a vocal version of the movie's credits, also taking a small role in the movie (starring Jackie Gleason and Carol Channing), as a security guard.
June Three Dog Night's revival of *One*, a Nilsson composition from *Aerial Ballet*, hits US #5, becoming his first million selling composition.
July The Turtles' *The Story Of Rock And Roll*, a Nilsson song on which he has also played piano, which makes US #48.
Sept ***Harry*** is his first album to chart, peaking at US #120. Mainly self-produced, it contains *The Puppy Song* (later a hit for David Cassidy) and his first Randy Newman cover, *Simon Smith And The Amazing Dancing Bear*. He writes *Best Friend*, the theme for new TV comedy series, "The Courtship Of Eddie's Father", and also composes incidental music for the show.
Oct Nilsson's version of Fred Neil's *Everybody's Talkin'*, from ***Aerial Ballet***, has been chosen as the theme tune to the film "Midnight Cowboy", despite prospective songs having been commissioned from several writers, including Bob Dylan's *Lay Lady Lay* and Nilsson's own *I Guess The Lord Must Be In New York City* (included on ***Harry***). The resulting exposure belatedly turns it into his first US chart single, hitting #6.
Nov *Everybody's Talkin'* reaches UK #23, while its follow-up, *I Guess The Lord Must Be In New York City*, makes US #34.

1970

Mar He releases the self-produced ***Nilsson Sings Newman***, an interpretative collection of ten songs written by Randy Newman who is also featured on piano.
[11] *Everybody's Talkin'* wins the Best Contemporary Vocal Performance, Male category at the 12th annual Grammy Awards.

1971

Apr Nilsson has written, narrated and sung the songs in "The Point", an animated children's fantasy produced by Murakami-Wolf Films for US TV. Its accompanying soundtrack, ***The Point***, reaches US #25, his biggest-selling album to date.

May *Me And My Arrow*, from ***The Point***, reaches US #34.
July ***Aerial Pandemonium Ballet***, a compilation of tracks from the first two albums, peaks at US #149.

1972

Jan ***The Point*** makes UK #46.
Feb [19] While recording in the UK the previous year with producer Richard Perry, Nilsson has heard Badfinger's *Without You*, written by the group's Pete Ham and Tom Evans, and determines to record his own version. Released as a single, the epic ballad now tops the US chart for the first of four weeks. Its Perry-helmed parent album, ***Nilsson Schmilsson***, hits US #3.
Mar [3] The RIAA certifies gold sales of both *Without You* and ***Nilsson Schmilsson***.
[11] *Without You* begins a five-week run at UK #1, selling almost 800,000 copies in Britain, while ***Nilsson Schmilsson*** hits UK #4.
Apr *Jump Into The Fire*, makes US #27.
June *Coconut*, a third single from ***Nilsson Schmilsson***, peaks at UK #42.
Aug ***Son Of Schmilsson***, a second gold album, makes US #12 and UK #41, while *Coconut* hits US #8.
Nov Self-penned *Spaceman*, from ***Son Of Schmilsson***, reaches US #23.
Dec [30] ***Son Of Schmilsson*** is certified gold by the RIAA.

1973

Jan *Remember (Christmas)*, also self-written, makes US #53.
Mar Nilsson wins Best Male Pop Vocal Performance Of 1972 for *Without You*, at the 15th annual Grammy Awards.
Aug ***A Little Touch Of Schmilsson In The Night***, a set of standard ballad revivals with an orchestra conducted by Gordon Jenkins, reaches US #46 and UK #20, his last UK chart album.
Sept Taken from the album, his version of *As Time Goes By* peaks at US #86.

1974

Mar [12] Nilsson and John Lennon are thrown out of Los Angeles, CA's Troubadour club after heckling the Smothers Brothers' act.
May Self-penned *Daybreak* reaches US #39, his last US chart single. It is taken from the film soundtrack to "Son Of Dracula", a horror-spoof-musical directed by Freddie Francis in which Nilsson and Ringo Starr appear. The soundtrack album, ***Son Of Dracula***, containing Nilsson's songs and Paul Buckmaster's incidental music, makes US #160.
Oct ***Pussy Cats***, produced by Lennon, reaches US #60. It includes offbeat revivals of rock standards like *Rock Around The Clock*, and Bob Dylan's *Subterranean Homesick Blues*.

1976

Feb After ***Duit On Mon Dei*** has made US #141 the previous April which has included *Good For God*, also included in the film soundtrack to "In God We Trust", ***Sandman*** now peaks at US #111.
Aug ***Nilsson ... That's The Way It Is*** stops at US #158.
Nov Reissued *Without You* climbs to UK #22.
Dec Adapted for the stage, "The Point" runs successfully at London's Mermaid Theatre. (The show had originally begun a stage run in 1975 for the Boston Repertory Theater.)

1977

Aug Ballad *All I Think About Is You* makes UK #43, and is Nilsson's last UK chart entry. It is taken from ***Knnillssonn***, which makes US #108, his final studio set for RCA. A compilation ***Greatest Hits***, which will become his final US chart album, makes #140 in July the following year, when he also records an album for United Artists which will remain unreleased.

1980

Sept Having signed a new deal with Mercury Records, Nilsson releases (for the first time credited to his full name Harry Nilsson) ***Flash Harry***, produced by Steve Cropper. It features song collaborations with John Lennon, Ringo Starr and Van Dyke Parks, among others, plus two items by new acquaintance Eric Idle. One track, *Harry*, is a tribute to Nilsson, sung by Idle and Charlie Dore.

1981

Apr [27] He attends the wedding of Ringo Starr and Barbara Bach. Stunned by the recent death of Lennon, Nilsson will devote much of his time lobbying for US gun-control, helping establish the National Coalition to Ban Handguns, and also recording the single *With A Bullet* in 1982 which will be sold at Beatles' conventions. Retiring from the music scene for a good part of the decade, he will establish a film distribution company in Los Angeles. In December 1988, his only release of the '80s will be ***A Touch More Schmilsson***, featuring previously unreleased out-takes from the original ***Schmilsson*** sessions.

1990

Sept *Everybody's Talkin'* is named one of BMI's Most Performed Songs Of 1940-1990, having passed the four million performance plateau.
Oct An up-dated collection of past glories, ***Without Her - Without You***, is released by BMG Enterprises.

1991

June [22] ***For Our Children***, the Pediatric AIDS Foundation charity album, to which Nilsson has contributed *Blanket For A Sail*, reaches US #31.

1992

Sept [4] Having recently contributed to the film soundtrack to "The Fisher King", and performed three songs at a Beatlefest weekend in Chicago, IL on August 22nd, he sings *Without You* at a Ringo Starr show at Caesar's Palace, Las Vegas, NV.

1994

Jan [15] Having suffered a heart attack on February 14th the previous year, which required hospitalization in the intensive care unit of Cedars-Sinai Hospital, Los Angeles, Nilsson, who has just completed his first new collection of songs in 13 years, dies in his sleep at his Agoura Hills home.
Mar [5] Reissued *Without You* makes UK #47 (while Mariah Carey's update hits US #3).

1995

Feb [18] ***Personal Best : The Harry Nilsson Anthology***, a 48-track twin-CD covering the period 1967-1977, personally selected by Nilsson prior to his death and including four never-before-released cuts, is released by RCA.
Apr Musicmasters releases ***For The Love Of Harry (Everybody Sings Nilsson)***, a 23-track tribute album of Nilsson songs sung by Brian Wilson, Aimee Mann, the Roches, Ringo Starr and Stevie Nicks, Randy Newman, Jellyfish, Marc Cohn, Joe Ely, Marshall Crenshaw, Joe Ely, Gerry Beckley, Robert Lamm and Carl Wilson and Jimmy Webb, among others.

NINE INCH NAILS

Trent Reznor (vocals, guitar, keyboards, bass, drums)

1988

Aug Multi-instrumentalist Reznor (b. Michael Trent Reznor, May 17, 1965, Mercer, PA), who began playing classical piano at five, the same age from which he was raised by his maternal grandparents in rural Mercer, has also proved proficient on the sax and tuba by the time he plays in a high school band, Option 30. After graduating at the local Allegheny College in computer engineering he has moved to Cleveland, OH, working at a musical instrument store, Pi Corporation, and successfully auditions for local band, Innocent, becoming its keyboardist on the album ***Livin' On The Streets***. After the band splits, Reznor has teamed with Urge before joining the Exotic Birds, a group formed by three Cleveland Institute of Art percussion majors, releasing the vinyl-only EP *L'Oiseau* on the local Pleasureland label. Thereafter, Reznor has been a member of the group Problems, featured in the 1987 movie "Light Of Day" performing *True Love Ways*, joined Slam Bam Boo, appearing on the group's 1988 Slack label issued single *White Lies/Cry Like A Baby*, and temporarily been a member of Kevin McMahon's band Lucky Pierre (he will later engineer and program four tracks for McMahon's new combo, Prick's debut album). Having also spent time as an engineer at Right Track Studios in Cleveland where he has recorded three demo songs in the summer of '88, he has formed Nine Inch Nails, now signing a recording deal with TVT Records, better known as a label releasing television themes compilation albums, whose boss, Steve Gottleib is unimpressed by Reznor's debut effort, ***Industrial Nation***, a raging and uncompromising wall of dark industrial rock which will hallmark most of his future work. Reznor begins an uncomfortable relationship with the label, which nevertheless continues to release his unique self-written, performed and produced vision of angst and despair.

1989

Jan Having been asked to leave an opening slot for Skinny Puppy after performing ten shows with them the previous year, Nine Inch Nails (whose live lineup will constantly alter around Reznor (with the exception of drummer Chris Vrenna), begins three years of constant gigging, supporting the Jesus & Mary Chain on a US tour set to end in March (to be followed by a stint opening for Peter Murphy which will close on April 14th in Washington, DC). (Other members of NIN's live band currently include ex-Exotic Bird guitarist Richard Patrick, and David Hamas (keyboards).)
Dec [16] Having sung on Pigface's *Suck* and on 1,000 Homo DJ's cover of Black Sabbath's *Supernaut* earlier in the year, Nine Inch Nails' *Down In It*, finding airplay on the more adventurous US college radio stations, enters the US Modern Rock survey set to reach #16. (Out-takes from its controversial MTV-rejected video will be investigated by the F.B.I. which is concerned that they contain excerpts from a snuff movie.)

1990

Feb [10] ***Pretty Hate Machine***, variously co-produced by Reznor with Flood, Adrian Sherwood, Keith LeBlanc and John Fryer, enters the US chart at the beginning of a two year-plus residence.
Mar [31] A second extract, *Head Like A Hole* charts for a week at #28 on the US Modern Rock chart.
June [21] Nine Inch Nails' "Hate '90 North America" tour opens in St. Louis, set to end on August 4th in Cleveland.
Aug [7] Reznor joins Revolting Cocks on stage in Cleveland, subsequently teaming with them on a US tour up to a Florida show a few weeks later.

1991

Sept [21] *Head Like A Hole* makes UK #45.
Nov [16] *Sin*, its video clip featuring images of gay men smearing blood on their bodies and acts of genitalia piercing, debuts at its UK #35 peak.
[23] ***Pretty Hate Machine*** finally makes US #75, the reward for two years of constant live gigs which have included UK dates supporting Wonder Stuff and European shows opening for Guns N' Roses.

1992

Jan Prevented from recording his next album while an escalating dispute with TVT remains unresolved, Reznor and his manager John A. Malm Jr. form the Nothing record label for future Nine Inch Nails releases (which will be licensed to Interscope Records, but still tied to TVT, and which will also sign Pop Will Eat Itself, Prick and Marilyn Manson among others).

Mar [3] ***Pretty Hate Machine*** is certified gold by the RIAA.
Oct [10] EP ***Broken***, including the singles *Happiness In Slavery* and *Wish*, debuts at its US #7 peak. (It has been released in two CD versions - one with 8 tracks, the other with 99, with 7 to 97 left blank.)
[17] Licensed in the UK to Island Records, ***Broken*** enters at its UK #18 high.
Dec [18] ***Broken*** is certified platinum by the RIAA.

1993

Feb [24] Nine Inch Nails' *Wish* is named Best Metal Performance at the 35th annual Grammy Awards held at Los Angeles, CA's Shrine Auditorium. (Reznor will spend much of the year writing and recording his next album.)

1994

Mar [19] Previewing the forthcoming album, *March Of The Pigs* makes US #59.
[26] Influenced by David Bowie's ***Low*** and co-produced by Reznor and Flood in Beverly Hills, CA, the unremittingly dark ***The Downward Spiral***, featuring Adrian Belew and Porno For Pyros drummer Steve Perkins, bows at its US #2 peak having entered at it UK #9 high the previous week.
Apr [9] *March Of The Pigs* debuts at its UK #45 peak.
May [20] Nine Inch Nails embark on a six-date UK tour at the Civic Hall, Wolverhampton, W, Midlands, set to end on the 26th at the Forum, London.
June [4] Singer/songwriter Tori Amos' *Past The Mission*, featuring Reznor and recorded at 10050 Cielo Drive, the house in which Sharon Tate was murdered in 1969, reaches UK #31. On the same day, "The Crow" film soundtrack which includes Nine Inch Nails' cover of Joy Division's *Dead Souls*, hits US #1. (Reznor's other recent collaborations include production or remix work for Megadeth, Machines of Loving Grace and Wolfgang Press and two tracks as part of Hollywood Records (US) Queen albums reissue program.)
[18] *Closer* bows at its UK #25 pinnacle.
Aug [6] With a line-up of Reznor, Robin Finck (guitar), Danny Lohner (guitar, bass, keyboards), James Woolley (keyboards) and Vrenna, Nine Inch Nails' "Self Destruct Tour" begins at Molson Park, Barrie, ON, Canada, a bill grossing $569,994 (Canadian) from 24,870 attendees, set to end on February 18th 1995 at the Kiefer U.N.O. Lakefront Arena, New Orleans, LA (Reznor's new home town). An 83-date trek, it will include two nights at New York, NY's Madison Square Garden on December 8th-9th (to 24,120 fans), with sold-out concerts in 71 cities grossing more than $10 million.
[13] The band performs at "Woodstock II" at Winston Farm, Saugerties, NY.
Sept [19] ***Natural Born Killers***, the soundtrack to the controversial Oliver Stone-directed movie, entirely produced by Reznor, released on his Nothing label and including Nine Inch Nails' *Something I Can Never Have* and *Burn*, enters the US chart on its way to #19.
Oct [15] *Closer* makes US #41.
[18] ***The Downward Spiral*** is certified platinum by the RIAA.
Nov [13] Reznor's dog Maide dies after falling 50' from the third floor balcony at a Columbus, OH concert held at the Greater Columbus Convention Center in front of 5,215 fans.
Dec [28] Nine Inch Nails perform a special holiday show at the Odeon Concert Club, Cleveland, OH before 900 fans, with proceeds going to a local charity.

1995

Jan [5] Adam Ant joins Reznor onstage at the Centrum in Worcester, MA, singing *Physical (You're So)*, *Red Scab* and *Beat My Guest*.
May Nine Inch Nails plays its first gigs in Australia.
June [17] A remixed version of the last album (by Rick Rubin, Foetus's Jim Thirwell, Aphex Twin, Coil and NIN) ***Further Down The Spiral*** EP debuts at its US #23 peak (and will be released as a 60-minute plus set in the UK with a different track listing).
July [17] The RIAA certifies sales of two million copies of ***The Downward Spiral***.
Sept [14] Nine Inch Nails begins a six-week US trek opening for David Bowie on "The Outside Tour" at the Meadows Music Theatre, Hartford, CT, a double-bill taking $251,025 at the box-office from 10,838 attendees, set to close on October 29th, the last of two dates at the Great Western Forum, Inglewood, CA.
[20] The RIAA certifies sales of two million copies of ***Pretty Hate Machine***.

1996

Feb [28] *Happiness In Slavery* is named the Best Metal Performance at the 38th annual Grammy Awards held again at the Shrine Auditorium.

NIRVANA

Kurt Cobain (vocals, guitar);
Chris Novoselic (bass); **Dave Grohl** (drums)

1987

The band is initially formed as covers combo Skid Row in Seattle, WA, by Cobain (b. Kurt Donald Cobain, Feb. 20, 1967, Hoquiam, WA) on drums (currently living with his cocktail waitress mother in an Aberdeen trailer park), and Novoselic (b. Krist Anthony Novaselic, May 16, 1965, Compton, CA), the son of Croatian immigrants, on guitar, who have met through Melvins' singer Buzz Osbourne while Cobain is hauling gear for that group. The Melvins' Dale Crover soon joins on drums, switching Cobain to guitar and Novoselic to bass as the unit name-changes to Ed Ted & Fred and Fecal Matter, before settling on Nirvana. They begin performing Cobain-penned material at local gigs around Seattle and at the Evergreen State College in Olympia, WA, while he and Melvins drummer Dale Crover cut ten demos in an afternoon session with producer Jack Endino, who plays the results to independent label Sub Pop's Jonathan Poneman. He signs the band, which will release its debut single, a cover of Shocking Blue's *Love Buzz*, in December 1988.

1989

Mar Nirvana's first album, ***Bleach***, is issued by Sub Pop (and licensed to Tupelo Records in the UK), recorded on eight-track for $600 in three days, and featuring temporary second guitarist, Mindfunk's Jason Everman, who also plays on Nirvana's upcoming first west coast and national tours. The album proves popular on college radio, not least on KCMU, the 401 watt University of Washington radio station, which is also the first to air cuts by concurrently emerging Seattle bands, Soundgarden and Mudhoney. Fire Ant's Chad Channing (b. Jan. 31, 1967, Santa Rosa, CA) replaces Crover on drums (the group also temporarily enlisting Dinosaur Jr.'s J. Mascis).
Nov Following a European tour, Everman plays his final gig with the band in New York, NY.

1990

July Nirvana's only release of the year, *Silver*, featuring Mudhoney's Dan Peters on drums, is issued.
Aug Ex-Dave Bramage Band drummer Grohl (b. Jan. 14, 1969, Warren, OH) replaces Channing, recruited from his existing group, Scream. With a strong regional buzz, and having hawked a six-track demo recorded with producer Butch Vig, Nirvana signs with David Geffen's DGC label, receiving $287,000 in advance money. They approach Scott Litt and Don Dixon to produce their label debut, but eventually stick with Vig.

1991

Aug During a European tour supporting Sonic Youth, Nirvana plays at the annual "Reading Festival", Reading, Berks.
Oct [12] Their sophomore album, the punk/metal fused grunge-pioneering ***Nevermind***, enters the US chart.
Nov [5] The band performs at London's Astoria Theatre during a short UK tour.
[27] ***Nevermind*** is certified platinum by the RIAA.
[29] The group begins another seven-date UK visit at Carlton Studios, Edinburgh, Scotland, set to end with a pair of dates on December 4-5th at London's Kilburn National Ballroom.
Dec [7] Subsequently revered as a genre classic, *Smells Like Teen Spirit*, named after a deodorant, hits UK #7.
[18] The band is featured on BBC2-TV's "Rapido", while they have to cancel two Irish dates and a handful of European shows after playing at the "Transmusicales Festival", Rennes, France, when Cobain goes down with a viral infection.
[31] Nirvana performs a New Year's Eve gig at the Cow Palace, San Francisco, CA.

1992

Jan [11] The group guests on NBC-TV's "Saturday Night Live", as the hotly MTV-rotated *Smells Like Teen Spirit* hits US #6 and ***Nevermind***, featuring four-month old Spencer Elden on its sleeve, tops the US chart. Critically regarded as a seminal alternative rock classic for Generation X, the album's success opens the door for Pearl Jam, Mudhoney and Soundgarden and inaugurates the '90s Seattle "grunge" rock wave. (The CD format of ***Nevermind*** features an additional track: at the album's close, after ten minutes of silence, a 13th song, *Endless, Nameless*, magically appears.)
Feb Having toured Australia in January, the band plays dates in New Zealand and Japan.
[1] ***Nevermind*** hits UK #7.
[3] The RIAA announces that ***Nevermind*** has reached the three million sales plateau in the US (where it will eventually top seven million).
[22] Revived ***Bleach*** finally makes US #89.
[24] Cobain weds Hole diva Courtney Love, after a five-month courtship, in Waikiki, HI. They expect a baby on September 10th, amid press concern that Love is allegedly using heroin.
Mar [7] ***Bleach*** debuts at its UK #33 peak.
[14] *Come As You Are* bows at its UK #9 peak.
[20] Aimed at limiting freedom of speech on recordings, the Date House Bill 2554 is signed by Washington Governor Booth Gardener. In protest, the Washington Music Industry Coalition, supported by Nirvana, will hold a press conference on June 11th before filing a complaint on the 23rd for a declaratory judgement and injunctive relief against the Bill.
Apr [1] *Smells Like Teen Spirit* is certified platinum by the RIAA.
May [2] *Come As You Are* makes US #32.
UK duo, Nirvana (Patrick Campbell-Lyons and Alex Spyropoulos), files suit against the American band and Geffen Records, alleging that they have been performing and recording under the disputed name since 1968. (The dispute will eventually be settled out of court in the British band's favor, though allowing the US Nirvana to continue with the moniker.)
June [22] Cobain is rushed to hospital after a concert at King's Hall, Belfast, Northern Ireland, allegedly suffering from acute stomach pains brought on by ulcers.
Aug [1] *Lithium* reaches UK #11.
[15] *Lithium* peaks at US #64.
[18] A daughter, Frances Bean, is born to Cobain and Courtney Love at Cedars Sinai Hospital, Los Angeles, CA.
[23] A Seattle Coliseum concert is cancelled at the last minute, apparently beause of **Vanity Fair**'s interview with Courtney Love, which suggests that she was using heroin during her pregnancy. Cobain will subsequently speak of exacting revenge on the article's author.
[30] The group plays on the final day of the 20th annual "Reading Festival".
Sept [9] "Smells Like Teen Spirit" wins the Best Alternative Music Video, and Best New Artist Video, categories at the ninth annual MTV Video Music Awards, held at the Pauley Pavilion, Los Angeles. During the band's performance of *Lithium*, Novoselic

is rendered unconscious after being hit by his own guitar having lobbed it skywards, while Cobain has an argument backstage with Axl Rose.
[11] Nirvana headlines a benefit concert for the Washington State Music Coalition.
Oct The band begins recording sessions for a new album with producer Jack Endino.
Dec [19] *In Bloom* reaches UK #28, while UK outfit Killing Joke file a lawsuit claiming that *Come As You Are* uses the same guitar riff as their 1985 single, *Eighties*.

1993

Jan [16] ***Incesticide***, a collection of early recordings, archive oddities and BBC radio sessions and out-takes, including covers of the Vaseline's *Molly Lips* and Devo's *Turn Around*, reaches US #39 and UK #14.
Feb [16] Nirvana wins the Best International Newcomer category, at the 12th annual BRIT Awards, held at the Alexandra Palace, London.
Mar [6] Nirvana's *Oh, The Guilt*, coupled with Jesus Lizard's *Puss*, bows at its UK #12 peak during a two-week chart stay. (Chicago indie label Touch And Go will release a 100,000 special edition in the US.)
Apr [9] The band plays a benefit concert at San Francisco's Cow Palace for the Tresnjevka Women's Group in Bosnia-Herzegovina, at Novoselic's instigation.
May The group continues recording a new album in Minnesota with producer, Steve Albini (ex-Big Black Rapeman), which is allegedly causing friction with Geffen Records who are unhappy with its progress. Albini will subsequently tell the **Village Voice** that "the record label and management company didn't want me to produce the album. If everyone feels like taking the band's time and money and wasting it, my conscience is clear"). Novoselic files a report for **Spin** magazine from Zagreb, Croatia, for its current issue.
[2] A police report states that Cobain had injected himself with $30 to $40 worth of heroin, and that Love had injected him with buprenorphine at a party. He is taken to Seattle's Harborview Medical Center, before voluntarily checking himself into a California rehab facility.
June [4] Police go to Cobain and Love's home in Seattle and break up a dispute. Cobain is arrested and spends three hours in jail. The disagreement allegedly concerns Cobain's collection of firearms.
July [23] Cobain overdoses in the bathroom of his New York hotel, before performing at the New Music Seminar at the Roseland Ballroom in the evening.
Aug [14] The group plays at a Pro-Choice rally in Washington, DC, with Pearl Jam.
Sept [2] Nirvana wins the Best Alternative Video category for "In Bloom" at the tenth annual MTV Video Music Awards, held at the Universal Amphitheatre, Universal City, CA.
[11] *Heart-Shaped Box* debuts at its UK #5 peak.
[25] Their second studio album for Geffen, ***In Utero***, debuts at UK #1, as the group guests on the season premiere of NBC-TV's "Saturday Night Live". At the same time Michael Azerrad's biography, **Come As You Are**, written with the full co-operation of the band, is published. The graphic account has been rush-released in order to nullify the impact of a book by Britt Collins and Victoria Clarke, to which Nirvana vehemently objects. After legal representations to potential publishers, the project fails to see the light of day.
Oct [9] ***In Utero*** debuts at US #1.
Nov [23] ***The Beavis And Butt-Head Experience***, to which Nirvana has contributed *I Hate Myself And Want To Die*, is released.
Dec [18] *All Apologies/Rape Me* debuts at its UK #32 peak.
[30] The group plays a sellout date at the Great Western Forum, Inglewood, CA.

1994

Jan [8] Nirvana plays what will be its last-ever US date at the Center Arena, Seattle.
[27] **Rolling Stone** names Nirvana Best Band and ***In Utero*** Best Album in the 1994 Music Awards Critics' Picks.
Feb [5] Nirvana begins a European tour in Lisbon, set to end on April 1st at the Cardiff International Arena, Cardiff, South Glamorgan, Wales.
Mar [1] The group plays its final show in Munich, Germany.
[2] Cobain checks into Suite 541 at the Excelsior Hotel in Rome, Italy. After taking a combination of prescription drug Rohypnol, chlorylhydrate, a prescription anesthetic and some champagne, he slips into a coma, and is rushed to the Umberto I Polyclinic Hospital, where he has his stomach pumped, after Love has found him at about 5:30 a.m. He is subsequently transferred to Rome American Hospital, until his discharge on the 8th.
[28] Cobain checks into the Exodus Recovery Center, Daniel Freeman Marina Hospital, Marina del Rey, CA. (Grohl and Novoselic have threatened to disband Nirvana if he doesn't enter a rehab facility.)
[31] He walks out of the Center.
Apr [4] Cobain's mother, Wendy O'Connor, files a missing persons report.
[5] Cobain shoots himself with a Remington 20-gauge shotgun recently obtained from Stan's Gun Shop, with longtime friend Dylan Carlson, because of alleged trespassers on his property.
[8] Gary Smith, a 50-year old electrician contracted to install a burglar alarm, finds Cobain's body at approximately 8:40 a.m. on the floor of his garage apartment. Nearby is a suicide note, which quotes Neil Young's *My My, Hey Hey (Out Of The Blue)* - "It's better to burn out than fade away".
[10] A public memorial service for Cobain is held at Seattle Center's Flag Pavilion. Fan Daniel Kaspar kills himself.
July [12] Grohl and Novoselic sit in with the Stinky Puffs at the "Yoyo A Go Go Festival" in Seattle.
Aug [24] Geffen Records announces the release of the 30-track ***Verse Chorus Verse***, an album of live recordings, in November.
Sept [8] Nirvana wins the Best Alternative Video and Best Art Direction categories (both for "Heart Shaped Box") at the 11th annual MTV Video Music Awards, held at New York's Radio City Music Hall.
Nov [12] ***Unplugged In New York*** tops the UK chart in its week of entry.
[19] ***MTV Unplugged In New York*** debuts at US #1.

1995

Jan [13] The RIAA certifies three million sales of ***MTV Unplugged In New York***.
[20] The RIAA certifies 100,000 sales of the "Live! Tonight! Sold Out!" video.
[30] Nirvana wins the Favorite Artist/Heavy Metal - Hard Rock category at the 22nd annual American Music Awards held at the Shrine Auditorium.
Feb [7] JAMPAC (Joint Artists and Music Promotions Political Action Committee), an organization fronted by Novoselic, is unveiled in Seattle, dedicated to fighting the planned Erotic Music Bill.
[10] The RIAA certifies four million sales of ***In Utero*** and seven million of ***Nevermind***.
[27] ***Bleach*** is confirmed platinum by the RIAA.
Mar [3] Grohl's new band, Foo Fighters for which he has switched to lead guitar and lead vocal, with Pat Smear (guitar), Nate Mendel (bass) and William Goldsmith (drums), makes its debut at the Satyricon, Portland, OR.
May [16] *All Apologies* is named Most Performed Song on college radio at the 1995 BMI Pop Awards held at the Beverly Wilshire, Los Angeles.
July As Foo Fighters releases the Grohl-penned ***Foo Fighters***, Novoselic returns with his new band, Sweet 75, at a JAMPAC fundraiser in a barn in Bremerton, WA.
Nov [7] ***Incesticide*** is certified platinum by the RIAA.
Dec ***Singles***, a Geffen-released CD boxed set of the group's singles, is released in the UK.

1996

Feb [14] Foo Fighters' video for its forthcoming single *Big Me*, a visual pastiche on the currently camp popular "Mentos" candy TV commercial, receives its premiere on MTV-US.
[28] ***MTV Unplugged In New York*** is named Best Alternative Music at the 38th annual Grammy Awards held at the Shrine Auditorium.
Apr Foo Fighters' *Big Me*, a short burst of Beatlesque pop/rock, a far cry from Nirvana, begins a rise up both the UK and US charts. A new cut by Foo Fighters is also included on the newly released ***Songs In The Key Of X***, music from and inspired by the Fox-TV show "The X-Files".

TED NUGENT

1967

An enthusiastic game-hunter even as a boy, Nugent (b. Dec. 13, 1948, Detroit, MI), having played guitar since the age of nine, and led local Detroit bands the Royal High Boys and the Lourdes in his early and mid-teens, has graduated from his third band Cobo Hall (which opened for the likes of the Beau Brummels and the Supremes) to form heavy-rock garage band the Amboy Dukes in Chicago, IL the previous year, with himself and Steve Farmer on guitars, John Drake on vocals, Rick Lober on keyboards, Bill White on bass, and Dave Palmer on drums, although the personnel will change frequently throughout the group's existence as the vehemently anti-drugs Nugent will summarily dismiss any group member he suspects of indulging. The group signs to Mainstream Records, and now finds local success with its first single, a revival of Them's *Baby Please Don't Go*.

1968

Feb Band's first album, ***The Amboy Dukes***, is also its US chart debut, peaking at #183.
Aug *Journey To The Center Of The Mind* is the group's only US hit single, reaching #16, while its parent album, ***Journey To The Center Of The Mind***, makes US #74. A third album for Mainstream, ***Migration***, will fail to chart. The band tours almost continuously, with some 150 dates a year, mostly in the Northwest and in the South with a stage act which starts out as quasi-psychedelic punk rock, but will become ever more dominated by Nugent's flashy, Jimi Hendrix-inspired guitar fireworks.

1970

Mar Newly signed to Polydor Records, ***Marriage On The Rocks/Rock Bottom*** peaks at US #191. Their live ***Survival Of The Fittest***, recorded at the Eastown Theater in Detroit, will reach US #129 the following March, credited to Ted Nugent & the Amboy Dukes.

1973

In an ongoing campaign of self-publicity while touring between record deals, Nugent stages live "guitar battles" with other heavy feedback merchants including Iron Butterfly's Mike Pinera (currently with the New Cactus Band), the MC5's Wayne Kramer, and Frank Marino of Mahogany Rush.

1974

With another label switch to Frank Zappa's DiscReet label, and credited as Ted Nugent's Amboy Dukes, two albums, ***Call Of The Wild*** and ***Tooth, Fang And Claw***, are released. (Both titles are indicative of Nugent's highly-publicized passion for blood-sports and hunting. He is adept with firearms and bow and arrow, and an active supporter of the National Rifle Association. From his Michigan farm he frequently hunts wild game which becomes food for the Nugent household.)
Oct Nugent wins the US National Squirrel-Shooting Archery Contest, downing a squirrel at 150 yards. Over the three-day event, he also guns down over two dozen other live moving targets.

1975

July The Amboy Dukes split, and Nugent is signed to a solo deal by Epic Records, teaming-up with producer Tom Werman, retaining bass player Rob Grange from the final Dukes line-up, and adding Derek St. Holmes, from Detroit band Scott, on rhythm guitar and vocals, and Cliff Davies on drums, to make up his new backing band. He is also taken over by Aerosmith's managers, Leber-Krebs, who organize his blitzkreig live tours into commercially successful operations.

Dec [28] He is threatened on stage in Spokane, WA, by audience member David Gelfer, who aims a .44 Magnum at him before being taken away to be charged with "intimidating with a weapon".

1976

Apr Nugent's first solo chart single is *Hey Baby*, which peaks at US #72, taken from his debut Epic album, ***Ted Nugent***, which provides his first US Top 30 album, peaking at #28, and collecting a gold disc during its 62-week chart run.

Aug Nugent makes his UK debut at the annual "Reading Festival", Reading, Berks.

Sept ***Ted Nugent*** makes UK #56, his UK chart bow.

Nov ***Free For All***, with guest vocals by Meat Loaf, reaches US #24 and UK #33, and becomes Nugent's first million seller, earning a platinum disc. *Dog Eat Dog*, taken from the album, makes US #91.

1977

Feb [23] Nugent embarks on his first UK tour at the Free Trade Hall, Manchester, Gtr. Manchester.

July ***Cat Scratch Fever*** peaks at US #17 (his second platinum album), and UK #28.

Sept Title track, *Cat Scratch Fever*, is Nugent's biggest-selling solo single, reaching US #30.

1978

Jan Nugent causes controversy when he signs his autograph on a fan's arm with the tip of a Bowie knife.

Feb Instrumental single, *Home Bound*, reaches US #70.

Mar His double performance set ***Double Live Gonzo!*** makes US #13 (his third in a row to go platinum) and UK #47.

[18] He plays at the "California Jam II" in Ontario, CA, before an audience of 250,000, alongside Heart, Santana, Aerosmith, Dave Mason and others.

Apr *Yank Me, Crank Me*, from the live album, climbs to US #58.

July [20] ***Double Live Gonzo!*** is certified platinum by the RIAA.

Nov [16] The still-climbing ***Weekend Warriors*** is also confirmed platinum.

Dec ***Weekend Warriors*** reaches US #24.

1979

Jan *Need You Bad*, taken from ***Weekend Warriors***, peaks at US #84.

Apr [7] Nugent performs at the "California Music Festival", at the Memorial Coliseum, Los Angeles, CA, to 110,000 people, sharing the bill with Van Halen, Cheap Trick, Aerosmith and the Boomtown Rats.

June ***State Of Shock*** peaks at US #18.

[7] ***State Of Shock*** is certified gold by the RIAA.

July [28] Nugent appears at the "World Series Of Rock" concert at Cleveland Stadium, OH, with Aerosmith, Journey and Thin Lizzy.

1980

June ***Scream Dream*** reaches US #13 and UK #37.

July [6] More than 30 members of the audience at a Nugent concert in Hollywood are arrested, for violence and drug offenses.

[23] ***Scream Dream*** is certified gold by the RIAA.

Aug *Wango Tango*, extracted from ***Scream Dream***, makes US #86, and is Nugent's final solo hit single. A live album, ***Intensities In 10 Cities***, will peak at US #36 and UK #75 the following April.

1982

Jan Compilation album, ***Great Gonzos! The Best Of Ted Nugent***, makes US #140. It is Nugent's final release on Epic, as he signs a new deal with Atlantic Records. He also revamps his band, bringing in one-time Vanilla Fudge drummer Carmine Appice, and recruiting previous accompanists Derek St. Holmes (vocals) and Dave Kiswiney (bass).

Aug His debut Atlantic album, ***Nugent***, makes US #51.

1984

Jan [10] Nugent appears in NBC-TV series "Miami Vice".

Apr ***Penetrator***, on Atlantic, peaks at US #56.

1986

Apr He plays on *Stars*, recorded by heavy-metal aggregation Hear'n'Aid, to profit the USA for Africa Foundation, as his own ***Little Miss Dangerous*** makes US #76.

[20] Nugent strips a 19-year-old fan down to her underwear, but is not arrested by police. He later states, "I did such a good job, they didn't have the heart to arrest me."

May [13] Nugent, appearing on sex therapist Dr. Ruth Westheimer's TV show, says, "life is one big female safari and Dr. Ruth is my guide".

Nov [21] The RIAA certifies two million sales of ***Ted Nugent***.

1987

Dec [25] Nugent guests on NBC-TV's "Late Night With David Letterman", singing *The Christmas Song* with a bogus Letterman.

1988

Mar His final solo album for Atlantic, ***If You Can't Lick 'Em ... Lick 'Em***, makes US #112. He also currently featured singing *Love Is Like A Chain Saw* in the horror film "State Park".

Dec [31] Nugent participates in the third annual "Whiplash Bash" at Cobo Arena, Detroit.

1989

Nugent forms new heavy-metal battalion Damn Yankees with ex-Styx guitarist Tommy Shaw, ex-Night Ranger Jack Blades and drummer Michael Cartellone, signing to Warner Bros. Records.

1990

Mar [3] A Lansing, MI benefit for Nugent's various hunting projects features an acoustic set from Nugent. (He has started the monthly hunting magazine, **Ted Nugent's World Bowhunters**, and also sells 20,000 copies of *Fred Bear - American Hunter's Theme Song*, through his mail-order business.)

May [19] Damn Yankees' *Coming Of Age* peaks at US #60.

[26] Ron Nevison-produced ***Damn Yankees*** initially makes US #30.

July [17] The band undertakes the first leg of a US tour with Bad Company in Burlington, VT.

1991

Jan [12] *High Enough* hits US #3, with songwriting credited to Tom, Jack and Ted.

Feb [9] In its 46th charted week, ***Damn Yankees*** re-peaks at US #13, as they play in Birmingham, AL, during a US tour.

Apr [20] Damn Yankees headline a welcome-home concert for returning Gulf War troops at the Norfolk Naval Air Station in Norfolk, VA, during their "Operation Rock'n'Roll Storm Tour", as it is now dubbed.

May [4] The group takes part in "Volunteer Jam XIV" at the Starwood Amphitheatre, Nashville, TN.

June [1] Damn Yankees' *Come Again* makes US #50.

[27] The group guests on NBC-TV's "Late Night With David Letterman".

July [12] Damn Yankees, Bad Company and the Steve Miller Band perform at the Alpine Valley Music Theatre, East Troy, WI.

Dec [26] In an anti-drug message to 50 fans while the stage crew set up at a Saginaw, MI gig, Nugent says Jimi Hendrix "thought I was stupid, and I thought he was a god. Now he's dead, and I'm still Ted".

[31] Nugent dishes out 200lbs of venison donated by the Michigan Sportsmen Against Hunger program at a Salvation Army center soup kitchen in Detroit, with the greeting "I kill it, you grill it".

1992

Apr [12] *High Enough* is named Outstanding National Rock/Pop Single at the Motor City Music awards in Detroit.

Aug [11] The RIAA certifies two million sales each of ***Cat Scratch Fever*** and ***Free For All***.

[29] Damn Yankees' ***Don't Tread*** debuts at its US #22 peak.

Dec [19] Their *Where You Goin' Now* reaches US #20 as Nugent is currently seen on US TV commercials as a pitch-man for Energizer batteries.

[31] A sellout crowd of 12,380 attends Ted Nugent's Seventh Annual New Year's Eve Whiplash Bash at the Cobo Conference & Exhibition Center Arena, Detroit.

1993

Jan [11] After shooting off two flaming arrows during a Cincinnati Gardens set, Nugent is fined $1,000 and given a three-day suspended sentence for a misdemeanor fire-code violation.

Mar [20] Damn Yankees play to a 4,195 sellout crowd at the A.J. Palumbo Center, Duquesne University, Pittsburgh, PA, during their current tour.

May [15] *Silence Is Broken*, from "Nowhere To Run", peaks at US #62.

June [15] Sony Legacy retrospective imprint issues ***Out Of Control***, a two CD/cassette boxed set Nugent retrospective.

1994

Mar Wyoming Senator, Malcolm Wallop, proclaims Nugent "a great American" for his work with children, his leadership in the anti-drug movement and pro-hunting stance, and for launching Wyoming's Hunters for the Hungry, donating thousands of pounds of game to needy families.

May [20] Performing solo once again, Nugent plays a sellout date at the Starwood Amphitheatre, Antioch, TN, during a current US tour with Lynyrd Skynyrd.

Aug [11] As the tour continues, Nugent now performs at the Darien Lake Performing Arts Center in Holmdel, NJ.

Dec [30] On the eve of Nugent's annual New Year's Eve Cobo Arena "Whiplash Bash", he plays at the Wings Stadium, Kalamazoo, MI.

1995

May [11] Nugent embarks on a four-month US tour with Bad Company at the Sunrise Musical Theatre, Sunrise, FL.

[20] ***Spirit Of The World*** debuts at its US #86 peak.

June [1] Nugent receives a star on the Hollywood Rock Walk of Fame.

Sept [4] Nugent plays the Meadows Music Theatre, Hartford, CT with Bon Jovi and Bad Company.

Dec [31] Nugent's tenth annual "Whiplash Bash" plays at the Cobo Arena, Detroit, MI.

GARY NUMAN

1977

Numan (b. Gary Webb, Mar. 8, 1958, Hammersmith, London), the son of a British Airways bus driver, whose former groups have included Meanstreet, who appeared on the punk compilation album ***Live At The Vortex***, assumes the group name Tubeway Army, calling himself "Valerium", drafting in Paul Gardiner, aka "Scarlett" (bass), and Numan's uncle, Gerald Lidyard, aka "Rael" (drums), for live appearances. As he discovers synthesizers, his sound moves away from guitars towards electronic rock, influenced musically by Kraftwerk and visually by David Bowie. Signed to the Beggars Banquet label, Numan quits his job at W.H. Smith on the day the first Tubeway Army single, *That's Too Bad* (which has been funded by his father Tony), is released the following February. It will be followed by a second single, *Bombers*, in August 1978, at which time Numan is also featured singing on a TV commercial for Lee Cooper jeans.

1979

Apr *Down In The Park* is issued.
May Numan makes his BBC1-TV "Top Of The Pops" debut, performing the synthesizer-based, self-penned, *Are Friends Electric?*
June [30] *Are Friends Electric?*, from Tubeway Army's ***Replicas***, tops the UK chart for the first of four weeks, boosted by its first pressing of 20,000 picture discs. Numan assembles a touring band: Paul Gardiner (bass), Rrussell *(sic)* Bell (guitar, synthesizer), Chris Payne (synthesizer), Cedric Sharpley (drums) and Ultravox moonlighter, Billy Currie (keyboards, synthesizer).
July [21] ***Replicas***, credited to Tubeway Army, tops the UK chart for a week.
Sept [20] Numan begins a 13-date UK tour at the Apollo Theatre, Glasgow, Scotland. After selling out London's Hammersmith Odeon, he announces a second show there, with proceeds going to the Save The Whales Fund.
[22] With the Tubeway Army name dropped in favor of Gary Numan, *Cars* also hits UK #1 as his ***The Pleasure Principle*** enters the UK chart in pole position, and one week after ***Tubeway Army***, Numan's 1978 debut album, has reached UK #14.
Oct ***Replicas***, released in the US on Atco Records, peaks at US #124.
Dec *Complex* hits UK #6.

1980

May As Numan's world tour continues through Europe, US, Japan, Australia and New Zealand, *We Are Glass* hits UK #5 as ***The Pleasure Principle*** reaches US #16. A video, "The Touring Principle", filmed at Numan's Hammersmith Odeon concert on September 28th, 1979, is released.
June *Cars*, Numan's only US singles chart success, hits #9.
Sept *I Die : You Die*, premiered on BBC1-TV's "Kenny Everett Video Show", hits UK #6. (Numan is also featured on the current Robert Palmer UK #31 album, ***Clues***, notably on the hit *Johnny And Mary* (UK #44).)
[4] Numan embarks on his second UK tour, a 17-date trek titled "The Gary Numan Teletour 80", at the Odeon Cinema, Birmingham, West Midlands, set to end on the 29th at the City Hall, Newcastle, Tyne & Wear. Numan and accompanists are all dressed in modernist boiler-suit uniforms and remain static throughout the robotic performance.
[13] ***Telekon*** enters the UK chart at #1.
Nov ***Telekon*** makes US #64.

1981

Jan *This Wreckage* reaches UK #20.
Apr [26-28] He plays three sell-out shows at the Wembley Arena, Wembley, Middx., and on the final night announces his retirement from live work.
May Boxed album, ***Living Ornaments 1979-1980***, hits UK #2, while the individually split ***1979*** makes UK #47, and ***1980*** reaches UK #39.
July Paul Gardiner's *Stormtrooper In Drag* hits UK #49, featuring Numan on vocals.
Sept *She's Got Claws* hits UK #6. ***Dance***, written about the aftermath of his first real love, hits UK #3, with guests Mick Karn of Japan and Roger Taylor from Queen.
[18] Numan embarks on a round-the-world trip in his single-engine Cessna plane. The attempt ends in India, when he is forced to make an unscheduled landing, which leads to him and his co-pilot being placed under house arrest, finally arriving back in the UK on Christmas Eve.
Nov ***Dance*** peaks at US #167.
Dec His touring backing band Dramatis' *Love Needs No Disguise*, featuring Numan on vocals, reaches UK #33.

1982

Jan [29] Returning from a meeting in Cannes, France, Numan's plane makes a forced landing at an RAF base near Southampton, Hants. The ever-inventive UK press claims that he has landed on the A3057 between Southampton and Andover after running low on fuel.
Mar *Music For Chameleons*, with Dollar's Therese Bazar guesting, reaches UK #19.
[9] Numan appears at Uxbridge Magistrates Court, London, cited with carrying an offensive weapon, a baseball bat, while queuing at a hamburger stand. The charges will be dropped.
Apr He announces that he is quitting the UK to concentrate on breaking into the US market.
June *We Take Mystery (To Bed)* hits UK #9.
Aug *White Boys And Heroes* reaches UK #20.
Sept ***I, Assassin*** hits UK #8, though will only stay charted for six weeks.
Oct [8] Numan returns to the live arena, opening an 18-date US tour at Perkins Palace in Pasadena, CA, set to end on November 8th in Chicago, IL.
Nov Dramatis makes UK #57 with *I Can See Her Now*.
Dec Compilation album, ***New Man Numan - The Best Of Gary Numan***, peaks at UK #45.

1983

Sept *Warriors* makes UK #20 as the ***Warriors*** album, produced by Bill Nelson, reaches UK #12, aided by a 40-date UK tour, now dressed in Mad Max mode.
Oct *Sister Surprise*, his last release for Beggars Banquet, makes UK #32.

1984

Mar Numan forms his own label, Numa Records, signing Hohokam, Steve Braun, John Webb (Numan's brother), and actress/model Caroline Munro. *Venus In Furs*, by Paul Gardiner, who has recently died from a drug overdose, will be the label's first release.
Oct ***The Plan***, credited to Tubeway Army & Gary Numan, makes UK #29.
Nov The first Numan release on his own label, *Beserker*, reaches UK #32, as the ***Beserker*** album climbs to UK #45.
Dec *My Dying Machine* peaks at UK #66.

1985

Mar Shakatak member Bill Sharpe's *Change Your Mind*, a teaming with Numan from Sharpe's forthcoming Polydor album, ***Famous People***, makes UK #17.
Apr Numan's performance set, ***White Noise Live***, peaks at UK #29.
May EP *The Live EP* reaches UK #27.
Aug *Your Fascination* makes UK #46.
Sept *Call Out The Dogs* climbs to UK #49, as its parent album, ***The Fury***, reaches UK #24, supported by a 17-date "The Fury" tour.
Nov *Miracles* makes UK #49.

1986

Apr *This Is Love* reaches UK #28.
June *I Can't Stop* makes UK #27.
Oct Sharpe and Numan's *New Thing From London Town* peaks at UK #52.
Nov [8] ***Strange Charm*** peaks at UK #59, in its week of entry.
Dec [6] *I Still Remember*, with all proceeds going to the Royal Society For The Prevention Of Cruelty To Animals (RSPCA), charts for a week at UK #74.

1987

Feb Numan closes down the Numa label.
Apr UK group Radio Heart, featuring Numan as a guest vocalist, reaches UK #35 with *Radio Heart*.
June A second Radio Heart single featuring the artist, *London Times*, makes UK #48.
Sept *Cars (E Reg Mix)*, a remix of Numan's 1979 #1, reaches UK #16.
[7] Numan embarks on an 18-date "Exhibition" tour at St. David's Hall, Cardiff, South Glamorgan, Wales, set to end on the 26th at London's Hammersmith Odeon.
Oct Double album, ***Exhibition***, a Beggars Banquet compilation of hits, makes UK #43, as early Numan albums are released on CD.

1988

Feb Sharpe and Numan's *No More Lies* reaches UK #34, aided by an appearance on ITV's "The Roxy".
Oct Newly signed to Miles Copeland's Illegal label, Numan makes UK #48 with ***Metal Rhythm***, while the extracted *New Anger* makes UK #46, as Numan embarks on 19-date UK tour.
Nov *America* peaks at UK #49.

1989

June Sharpe and Numan's *I'm On Automatic* makes UK #44.
Oct Numan undertakes 14-date "The Skin Mechanic" tour as the I.R.S.-released ***Skin Mechanic*** makes UK #55.

1990

Sept Numan and Mike Smith are asked to write music for Rodman Flender's movie, "The Unborn".
Dec Numan is made an Air Display Pilot Evaluator by the Civil Aviation Authority.

1991

Mar [16] Still with I.R.S., *Heart* enters at its UK #43 peak.
[30] Self-produced ***Outland***, still perpetuating his robotic synthesizer sound, makes UK #39, as he finishes a 12-date UK tour, with a freshly boiler-suited ex-Kajagoogoo member Nick Beggs, now in Numan's touring troupe.
Sept [14] An 18-date European "Emotion" tour, his first such dates in ten years, opens at the Ancienne Belgique in Brussels, Belgium, set to end on October 4th at King George's Hall, Blackburn, Lancs.

1992

Mar [21] *The Skin Game*, including his cover of Prince's *U Got The Look* on the CD format, charts for a week at UK #68.
[22] Numan begins 13-date "Isolate" tour, to promote the compilation album ***Isolate***, at the Liverpool Empire, set to end on April 4th at the Hammersmith Odeon.
Apr [3-4] Still playing annual UK tours, Numan performs at London's Hammersmith Odeon.
Aug [1] *Machine + Soul* spends a week at UK #72.
[22] Its parent album, ***Machine + Soul***, including a cover of Prince's *1999* on the CD version, debuts at its UK #42 peak, as the first Gary Numan convention is held at the Regent's Palace Hotel, Piccadilly Circus, London.

1993

Sept [4] Reissued *Cars*, extracted from his forthcoming best of compilation, charts for a week at UK #53.
Oct [2] ***Best Of 1979-83*** charts for a week at UK #70.
[23] Numan embarks on a 14-date "Corrosion" tour at the Brentwood Leisure Centre, set to end on November 6th at London's Hammersmith Apollo.
Dec [7] He begins another UK tour, a seven-date jaunt supporting Orchestral Manoeuvres In The Dark, at the Scottish Exhibition & Conference Centre, Glasgow, Strathclyde, Scotland, set to end on the 12th at Wembley Arena.

1994

Nov [2] He embarks on a ten-date UK tour, to promote his new album ***Sacrifice***, at the Civic Hall, Guildford, Surrey, set to end on the 12th at London's Astoria 2. The following August, Numan will win **Music Week**'s Racing Challenge at the Thunder Road Kart Track in Croydon, Surrey.

1996

Mar [16] Originally a hit 17 years ago, a revised *Cars (Premier Mix)*, currently used in a Carling Premier TV ad, bows at its UK #17 peak.
[30] A further compilation of remixed past glories, ***The Premier Hits*** reaches UK #21 in its week of entry.

O

OASIS

Liam Gallagher (lead vocal); **Noel Gallagher** (guitar); **Paul "Bonehead" Arthurs** (guitar); **Paul "Guigs" McGuigan** (bass); **Tony McCarroll** (drums)

1991

Aug [18] Manchester City soccer club supporters and brothers Noel Gallagher (b. May 29, 1967, Burnage, Manchester, Lancs.), younger brother Liam (b. Sept. 21, 1972, Burnage, Manchester) and their older brother Paul have been raised during their teenage years by their Irish Catholic mother Margaret (who has separated from their father, a sometime country & western DJ) in the bleak Manchester suburb of Burnage. Noel, a punk enthusiast who received a six-month probation sentence for robbing a local store at the age of 13, when he also started playing the guitar, musically inspired by the Smiths' Johnny Marr, has, together with Liam, set his sights on a career in music after attending a February 1989 gig by the Manchester-based Stone Roses. Subsequently failing an audition to join the Inspiral Carpets as lead singer, he is nevertheless invited to become the band's guitar technician and roadie and, leaving his job as a storeman for British Gas, has spent the next two years touring the world with the band, and practising his own demos with the group's sound engineer Mark Coyle. Meanwhile Liam has joined a local outfit Rain as its lead singer (not to be confused with the Liverpool combo of the same name), which has been formed by Arthurs (b. June 23, 1965, Manchester), McGuigan (b. May 9, 1971, Manchester) and McCarroll. Changing its name to Oasis (taking its name from the Swindon Oasis venue) and with Noel, returned from abroad with the Inspiral Carpets, sitting in the audience, the quartet, now plays its first gig under the new moniker at Manchester's Boardwalk club, second on a bill featuring the Catchmen and Sweet Jesus. Unimpressed by their performance, Noel offers to join the group on the condition that they only perform his songs and that he retains complete control over the band's progress, conditions they eagerly agree to after hearing his self-performed demo of *Live Forever*.

Oct [19] With its members on the dole, except for Noel who is still employed by Inspiral Carpets, Oasis performs its first gig as a quintet, again at the Boardwalk, where it also rehearses in the venue's basement on weekends, subsequently recording a demo tape which it sends to local magazine **City Life** and Manchester DJ Craig Cash.

1992

Apr [19] Following further local gigs, the band plays its first show in the South at the Dartford Polytechnic, Dartford, Kent. During the rest of the year, Noel insists that the band steps up rehearsals to five days a week and begins sending demo tapes to all and sundry, not least Factory boss Tony Wilson (who rejects it as being too "baggy"), Northside's manager Macca and local DJs Mark Riley and Mark Radcliffe.

Nov [22] Highlighted by what will become highly marketable sibling in-fighting between Noel and Liam, the group performs its last gig of the year, once again at the Boardwalk. (In December, Noel meets up with his hero Johnny Marr after Marr's brother has been given an Oasis demo to pass onto him, resulting in a telephone call from the ex-Smith to Noel and the pair swapping notes at a Doncaster guitar shop.)

1993

May [31] Attending the gig to see 18 Wheeler, Creation Records label boss Alan McGhee is impressed by Oasis' five-song performance at the King Tut's Wah Wah Club, Glasgow, Strathclyde, Scotland and immediately offers to sign the band, convinced he has found a hybrid of the Sex Pistols and the Beatles. (The band, who were not officially asked to perform at the club, reportedly threaten to trash the place if not offered a chance to play.)

Sept [14] Still officially unsigned, Oasis performs at the Canal Bar, Manchester as part of the second "In The City" music festival.

Oct [22] Creation signs the band.

Nov [3] Sony Music US A&R executive Dave Massey sees the band play at the group's first London gig at the Powerhaus club, and agrees with McGhee's decision (Creation is now licensed via Sony), signing Oasis for the rest of the world to Sony.

Dec [16] Oasis plays its last gig of the year opening for Verve at the Krazy House, Liverpool, Lancs., before completing four days of recording at the city's Pink Museum studios.

1994

Feb [8] The band's planned live debut outside the UK, at a concert at the Sleepin Arena in Amsterdam, Holland, is scrapped following a melée on board the ferry taking them there from Harwich, involving Liam and Arthurs, which results in their immediate return to Britain.

Mar [23] A UK tour co-headlining with Whiteout begins at the Bedford Angel, Bedford, Beds., set to end on April 13th at the Lomax, Liverpool, highlighted by increasingly controversial behavior both onstage and off, to the delight of the scandal-hungry UK music media.

Apr [7] Oasis takes part in the six-day "Sound City '94" festival at the Tramway, Glasgow.

[23] Having completed recordings for most of its debut album at sessions in Monmouth, Gwent, Wales and Golant, Cornwall, Oasis' first single *Supersonic* enters at its UK #31 peak, helped by an appearance on C4-TV's "The Word" and Single Of The Week nods in both the **New Musical Express** and **Melody Maker**.

[29] The group embarks on its second UK tour of the year at the Adelphi, Hull, Humberside, a 12-date trek set to end on May 14th at the Leadmill, Sheffield, S. Yorks.

June [1] They begin a third tour at Edwards, Birmingham, W. Midlands, a nine-date trek set to end on June 12th at the Cathouse, Glasgow.

[4] Oasis takes part in "Undrugged - A Pure Celebration, Ten Years Of Creation" at London's Royal Albert Hall.

[22] They tape a four-song set for broadcast on BBC 1FM's "Evening Session" show.

[26] The group performs to its biggest crowd of the year (over 30,000) on the NME Stage on the final day of the annual "Glastonbury Festival", Glastonbury, Somerset.

July [2] *Shakermaker* bows at its UK #11 high.

[21] Oasis performs its first US gig at the New Music Seminar held in New York, NY, going onstage at the Wetlands club at midnight.

[30-31] Oasis plays during the "Tennants In The Park" festival, in Hamilton, Glasgow.

Aug [9] During further now sold-out UK dates, their show at London's Riverside is stopped short after a fan jumps onstage and hits Noel in the face.

[13] Following tonight's gig at the "Hultsfred Festival" in Sweden, during European dates, the group is arrested for its latest fracas, while Liam will also break his foot jumping off the top of a moving tour bus.

[20] Soaring rock ballad *Live Forever* bows at its UK #10 pinnacle, its promo video partly shot in New York's Central Park.

Sept [5] During further UK dates the band appears at Manchester's Hacienda club.

[10] Now hailed as the pioneers of BritPop, the group's debut album ***Definitely Maybe***, produced by the group with Mark Coyle, and featuring half a picture of Burt Bacharach on its cover, enters the UK chart at #1.

Oct [22] *Cigarettes And Alcohol* (with the band's live cover of the Beatles' *I Am The Walrus* on the CD-single format) enters at its UK #7 peak, while the group completes a five-week tour of the US.

Nov [2-6] The band performs during the "FNAC Inrockuptibles Festival" held in Lille, France

[24] Oasis wins the Best UK Band category at MTV's first annual European Music Awards held at the Pariser Platz, Berlin, Germany against the backdrop of the Brandenberg gate.

[30] A ten-date UK swing begins at the Guildhall, Southampton, Hants., set to end at the Manchester Academy on December 18th, but marred by two cancelled shows in Middlesbrough and Liverpool, after Liam loses his voice.
Dec [10] Oasis performs *I Am The Walrus* and *Whatever* on BBC2-TV's "Later With Jools Holland".
[31] *Whatever* hits UK #3 in its week of entry.

1995

Jan [6] A second US tour begins at the Cat's Cradle, Carrboro, NC, set to end on March 25th at the Eagles Auditorium, Milwaukee, WI, a final gig which will gross $10,500 from 1,500 fans.
[24] The group wins the **New Musical Express** Album of the Year, Best New Band and Best Single (*Live Forever*) categories at the magazine's Brat Awards held at London's New Empire.
Feb [20] Oasis is named Best Newcomer at the 13th annual BRIT Awards, held at London's Alexandra Palace.
Mar [9] The group makes its US network television debut appearing on CBS-TV's "Late Show With David Letterman".
[18] At the Tyndale Armory, Indianapolis, IN gig, Liam walks offstage after playing four of five songs, when an audience member throws wire-rimmed prescription glasses at him.
Apr [1] ***Definitely Maybe***, recorded at a cost of £75,000, makes US #58. (Its release in Japan has been preceded by a six-cut mini-album, ***Supersonic***, released last July.)
[17] The band appears on C4-TV's "The White Room".
[20] During European dates and increasingly at odds with his notoriously antagonistic band mates, drummer McCarroll is involved in a fracas with the Gallagher 'Bruise Brothers' after a gig in Paris, France. The weekend following the group's appearance on BBC1-TV's "Top Of The Pops" on the 26th, he will be fired.
May [6] *Some Might Say* bows at UK #1.
[13] *Some Might Say (12 Inch Format)* charts for a week at UK #71, the same day that Paul Weller's ***Stanley Road***, featuring Noel as a guest, hits UK #1.
June [22] ***Definitely Maybe*** is certified gold by the RIAA for 500,000 US sales.
[23] Oasis' new drummer Alan White (b. May 26, 1972, London) makes his debut with the band at the 25th annual "Glastonbury Festival" held at Worthy Farm, Pilton, Somerset.
July [22] The band plays to 78,000 people at Slane Castle, Dublin, Ireland on a £1,796,667-grossing bill with R.E.M and Spearhead.
[25-26] The group appears at Kirklees Stadium, Huddersfield, Yorks., a concert also featuring R.E.M., Beautiful South and Belly.
Aug [26] At the height of a bitter media-fed feud between BritPop champs Blur and Oasis, and selling 274,000 copies in its first week, Blur's *Country House* enters the UK chart at #1, outsmarting Oasis' *Roll With It* (at sales of 216,000) which enters at #2.
Sept [4] Noel, Weller and Paul McCartney record a cover of the Beatles' *Help*, for inclusion as the title track of Go! Discs' forthcoming benefit album for the children of war in Bosnia.
Oct [1] Having postponed UK dates in September because McGuigan is allegedly suffering from exhaustion, the Gallaghers and White perform a 40-minute live acoustic set for 500 people at midnight at London's Virgin Megastore to launch the group's new album (which will reportedly sell 250,000 copies in its first four days of release).
[14] Oasis' sophomore set ***(What's The Story) Morning Glory?*** debuts at UK #1. (During the month, the rivalry between Oasis and Blur reaches a new peak when Noel in quoted in **The Observer** as allegedly saying that he hopes Blur's Damon Albarn and Alex James catch AIDS and die.)
[19] The band makes a second appearance on "Late Show With David Letterman" during further US tour dates (during which Scott MacLeod of the Ya Ya's, stands in for McGuigan).
Nov [7] Following two sold-out nights at London's Earl's Court Stadium on the 4th and 5th, Oasis is named Best Live Act in the **Q** Awards, held at the Park Lane Hotel, London.
[11] Sweeping rock anthem *Wonderwall* bows at its UK #2 peak.
[25] Interview single *Wibbling Rivalry (Interviews With Noel And Liam Gallagher)*, credited to Oas*s, bows at its UK #52 peak.
Dec [2] Oasis once again appears on a pre-taped "Later With Jools Holland", the same night it performs at "Deck The Hall Ball" at the Mercer Arena, Seattle Center, Seattle, WA, on a bill with Porno For Pyros, Sonic Youth, Everclear and others.
[28] Noel tells Radio 1FM listeners that he cried upon hearing Manchester City soccer club supporters singing *Wonderwall* on the terraces.
[31] "The White Room New Year Special" featuring Oasis, David Bowie, Stevie Wonder and others, airs on C4-TV.
(With the band huge down under, but refusing to tour, Sony Music Australia begins a petition drive to get Oasis to visit. Noel's reported response (to **Billboard**'s Christie Eliezer) is: "We don't fuckin' wanna fly to the other fuckin' end of the world and play like fuckin' shit".)

1996

Jan [14] The group's European tour reaches Berlin, Germany.
Feb [19] Oasis takes home the Best Video (for "Wonderwall"), Best Group, and Best Album (***(What's The Story) Morning Glory?***) trophies at the 1996 BRIT Awards held at London's Earl's Court Exhibition Centre. A surly acceptance speech by the band refers to record industry-types as "corporate pigs".
[24] ***(What's The Story) Morning Glory?*** hits US #4.
Mar In an interview with this month's **Q** magazine (made in December of last year), and commenting on the ongoing feud with Oasis, Blur's Albarn states: "The only thing we've got in common with Oasis is the fact that we're both doing shit in America". (Blur's most recent album peaked at US #150, while Oasis is currently at #5 on the US album survey with two million-plus Stateside sales.)
[2] *Don't Look Back In Anger* debuts at UK #1.
[9] *Wonderwall* hits US #8.
Apr Greater Manchester police confirms that it is investigating allegations made by Noel Gallagher in **Melody Maker** that he and Liam would burgle houses and steal car stereos as youths.
May [3] Noel Gallagher's management company issues a statement that he has turned down the Ivor Novello Songwriter Of The Year award, because it was being shared with Blur, accusing BASCA (the "Ivors" governing body) of trying to get publicity by resurrecting the Oasis/Blur feud.

BILLY OCEAN

1974

Ocean (b. Leslie Sebastian Charles, Jan. 21, 1950, Trinidad, West Indies), having become interested in music at the age of four when he is given a toy ukelele, has moved with his family, including five brothers and sisters, to London in 1958. On leaving Stepney Green School, he became an apprentice tailor's cutter, and his boss, Benjamin Sollinger, lent him £30 to buy a piano. Ocean has sung with local London East End band Shades of Midnight at a pub in Petticoat Lane, and with groups the Go and Dry Ice, and as a solo act in his own right using pseudonyms, including Joshua and Sam Spade. Working at a Savile Row tailors in London, he releases his first single under the group name Scorched Earth, before working at Ford Motors in Dagenham, Essex, where he moonlights so he can write and record during the day.

1976

Apr Having quit his Ford job and signed to Dick Leahy's GTO label the previous year, teaming up with producer Ben Findon, his first single, *Whose Little Girl Are You*, has already been released in December, followed by the disco-soul driven *Love Really Hurts Without You*, which now hits UK #2 and reaches US #22.
Aug *L.O.D. (Love On Delivery)* makes UK #19 and will become his first US R&B showing at #55.
Dec *Stop Me (If You've Heard It All Before)* peaks at UK #12.

1977

Apr He meets Laurie Jay, who becomes his manager. GTO has rejected his latest song, *Who's Gonna Rock You* (which will become a 1980 UK #12 for the Nolan Sisters), preferring *Red Light Spells Danger* which hits UK #2. *American Hearts* will peak at UK #54 in September 1979 with *Are You Ready* making UK #42 the following February. La Toya Jackson's debut album, released in October 1980, will include two Ocean-penned songs, *Are You Ready*, and *Stay The Night*.

1981

May Having self-financed the GTO-rejected *Nights (Feel Like Getting Down)*, it makes the US R&B #7, licensed to Epic Records. (It will later appear without permission on Jane Fonda's first workout album, for which Ocean will be awarded substantial royalties.)
July ***Nights (Feel Like Getting Down)*** peaks at US #152, his previous two albums having failed to chart in either territory. ***Inner Feeling***, also released by Epic, will following in 1982.

1984

May After two years of inactivity, but now signed to Jive Records where he is teamed with producer and fellow Trinidadian, Keith Diamond, their first collaboration, the pop-dance nugget *European Queen (No More Love On The Run)*, is released.
Oct [31] The still-rising revised version *Caribbean Queen* is certified gold by the RIAA.
Nov [3] *European Queen*, retitled, at his manager's suggestion, and reissued as *Caribbean Queen (No More Love On The Run)* hits US #1, US R&B #1 and #1 on the dance chart. (It will also receive a third title and version as *African Queen* for relevant territories.) Its parent album, ***Suddenly***, hits both US #9 and UK #9, while *Caribbean Queen (No More Love On The Run)* hits UK #6.

1985

Feb *Loverboy*, penned by Ocean with producer Robert "Mutt" Lange, hits US #2, held off #1 by Foreigner's *I Want To Know What Love Is*. Ocean begins a two-month US tour, playing his first live dates with a band in ten years. *Loverboy* makes UK #13.
Mar Ocean wins the Best R&B Vocal Performance category at the 27th annual Grammy Awards.
May He begins his first major tour, "Ocean Across America", which will include a performance at "Live Aid", Philadelphia, PA, in July.
June Ballad title track, *Suddenly*, hits #4 in both the UK and US.
July *Mystery Lady* peaks at US #24.
Aug *Mystery Lady* stops at UK #49.
Sept [5] The RIAA certifies two million sales of ***Suddenly***.

1986

Feb [8] Further pop/dance outing, *When The Going Gets Tough, The Tough Get Going*, featured on the soundtrack to the Michael Douglas/Kathleen Turner movie "The Jewel Of The Nile", begins a four-week run at UK #1, despite a UK video ban for featuring US non-Musicians Union members Douglas, Turner and Danny De Vito.
[15] *When The Going Gets Tough, The Tough Get Going* hits US #2.
May Ballad *There'll Be Sad Songs (To Make You Cry)* reaches UK #12.
[17] ***Love Zone*** hits UK #2.
June [28] *There'll Be Sad Songs (To Make You Cry)*

tops the US R&B chart.
July [5] Written by Wayne Braithwaite with Ocean and Diamond, who have contributed nine of the ten songs on the parent album, *There'll Be Sad Songs (To Make You Cry)* is Ocean's second US #1, and will be nominated for a Grammy Award.
Aug *Love Zone* peaks at UK #49 while ***Love Zone*** hits US #6.
Sept [27] *Love Zone* hits US #10.
Oct *Bittersweet* makes UK #44, as Ocean begins a sellout UK tour.
Dec [23] The RIAA certifies two million sales of ***Love Zone***.
[27] *Love Is Forever* reaches US #16.

1987

Jan *Love Is Forever* makes UK #34.
[26] Ocean wins the Favorite Male Video Artist, Pop/Rock, and Favorite Single, Pop/Rock categories at the 14th annual American Music Awards, held at the Shrine Auditorium, Los Angeles, CA.

1988

Mar Co-penned with Lange, *Get Outta My Dreams (Get Into My Car)* hits UK #3.
[19] ***Tear Down These Walls***, variously helmed by writer/producers Lange, Diamond and Wayne Braithwaite, hits UK #3.
Apr [9] Ocean's third US chart-topper, *Get Outta My Dreams*, deposes Michael Jackson's *Man In The Mirror*.
[16] *Get Outta My Dreams* heads the US R&B survey.
May ***Tear Down These Walls*** makes US #18. Ocean begins a UK tour, leading up to major world venues until the winter, as *Calypso Crazy* climbs to UK #35.
June *The Colour Of Love* reaches US #17 and peaks at UK #65, as the tour reaches North America.
July [21] ***Tear Down These Walls*** is certified platinum by the RIAA.

1989

Nov [18] *Licence To Chill*, unrelated to the current James Bond movie, peaks at US #32, as the Ocean retrospective, ***Greatest Hits***, covering the period 1984 to 1989, makes US #77, already hitting UK #4.

1990

Jan Hip-hop extraction, *I Sleep Much Better (In Someone Else's Bed)*, featuring the Fresh Prince and Mimi, is released.
July [17] ***Greatest Hits*** is certified gold by the RIAA.

1991

Nov Nattily dread-locked Ocean is arrested in London's Notting Hill on suspicion of selling cannabis. The charges will be dropped.

1993

Feb [6] *Pressure* bows at its UK #55 peak.
June [13] Ocean appears on ITV's "Cue The Music as his first album in four years, ***Time To Move On***, produced by Steely & Clevie and featuring R. Kelly on keyboards, is released by Jive.

SINEAD O'CONNOR

1982

O'Connor (b. Dec. 12, 1966, Glenageary, Eire), having grown up the third of four children in suburban Dublin, Eire, and been placed in a Dominican residential center run by nuns, for girls with behavioral problems after having been caught shoplifting (her parents split up when she was eight, her mother subsequently dying in a car crash in 1985), has been asked, at age 14, by a teacher at the Mayfield College, Drumcondra, Eire, to sing at her wedding. Her performance of *Evergreen* is heard by the bride's brother, Paul Byrne, drummer with Irish band In Tua Nua, for whom O'Connor will later co-write their first single, *Take My Hand*. Going on to further education at a Waterford boarding school before running away to Dublin where she attends the Dublin College of Music and finds part-time jobs including one, as a kiss-o-gram French maid, O'Connor begins performing solo gigs in 1985, mainly comprising Bob Dylan covers in Dublin pubs. She then joins local band Ton Ton Macoute, and links with future manager and boyfriend Fachtna O'Ceallaigh, who has persuaded U2 guitarist The Edge to feature her vocals on the soundtrack album he is working on for the film "Captive".

1986

While performing with Ton Ton Macoute, she is spotted by Ensign Records executives Nigel Grainge and Chris Hill. She tells Grainge she is leaving the band and he invites her to London with a complimentary plane ticket to begin a contract with Ensign, contrary to the advice of U2's Bono. The agreement allows for her to serve an apprenticeship at the label's office prior to beginning her recording career.
Sept Virgin Records release *Heroine* as the main theme single from "The Captive" soundtrack, featuring O'Connor on vocals.

1987

Apr O'Connor, who is currently featured on labelmate World Party's debut album, ***Private Revolution***, begins work on her own project, self-producing, following unsuccessful sessions with producer Mick Glossop.
June O'Connor and boyfriend John Reynolds, who is drumming on the current recordings, parent a son, Jake.
Oct Ensign releases O'Connor's first single, *Troy*.
Dec O'Connor plans to sue the Adelphi Hotel in Liverpool, Merseyside, after she is allegedly assaulted by a member of the security staff, after being refused entrance to the disco for wearing jeans.

1988

Jan Her breakthrough single, *Mandinka*, set to make UK #17, launches O'Connor's career. Her striking, closely-shaved head and stridently-voiced opinions immediately attract media interest - visual and mental projections she will persist with for some years. Her debut album, the self-produced ***The Lion And The Cobra***, including guests Enya and ex-Ant Marco Pirroni, is also released, set to make UK #27 (on Feb [27] and US #36, where the album will be a popular spin on college and alternative radio, during a 28-week chart residence. O'Connor spends much of the year touring Britain, the US and Europe in support of the album, which is issued on Chrysalis Records outside the UK.
June [3] During her current UK tour, a gig at London's Dominion Theatre is filmed for subsequent TV broadcast and video release.
Sept *Jump In The River*, released in two versions (one a duet with Karen Finley), fails to score in the UK, as has *I Want Your Hands On Me* (in April), which featured rapper MC Lyte. *Jump In The River*, also featured in the Jonathan Demme-directed movie, "Married To The Mob", reaches #17 on **Billboard**'s Modern chart, though she has yet to secure a Hot 100 hit.

1989

Feb [22] O'Connor performs *Mandinka* at the 31st annual Grammy Awards ceremony held at the Shrine Auditorium, Los Angeles, CA, having been nominated for the Best Female Vocalist category.
Mar O'Connor and Reynolds are married.
Apr John Maybury-directed screening of last year's Dominion Theatre performance is released on video as "The Value Of Ignorance".
May The The's album, ***Mind Bomb***, featuring O'Connor duetting with Matt Johnson on *Kingdom Of Rain*, hits UK #4.
Nov [10] ***The Lion And The Cobra*** is certified gold by the RIAA.
Dec O'Connor splits with ex-boyfriend and manager O'Ceallaigh, two days prior to the filming of a video for her forthcoming single, which she will later claim made her feel tearful during filming.

1990

Jan [20] Previewing her second album, *Nothing Compares 2 U* is released, a cover version of a Prince song featured on a 1985 self-titled album by Paisley Park act Family. With an arrangement by Soul II Soul's Jazzie B and Nellee Hooper, and produced by O'Connor with Hooper, the melancholic ballad of lost-love becomes one of the fastest-selling singles in chart history worldwide.
Feb [3] *Nothing Compares 2 U* hits UK #1, where it will stay for five weeks.
[21] O'Connor makes her acting debut in the subsequently-screened C4-TV film, "Hush-A-Bye-Baby", playing a 15-year old schoolgirl, also called Sinead, which premieres at the Dublin Film Festival".
Mar [24] Her second album, ***I Do Not Want What I Haven't Got***, immediately hits UK #1. Including performances from husband Reynolds, ex-Smith Andy Rourke and Jah Wobble, it is co-produced by O'Connor and Hooper and will remain charted for the rest of the year as it begins to top charts in 13 worldwide territories.
Apr [14] A world trek kicks off in Cornwall, under the banner "Year Of The Horse Tour".
[20] One day prior to its US peak, *Nothing Compares 2 U* is certified platinum by the RIAA.
[21] On its way to #1 in 18 territories, *Nothing Compares 2 U* begins a month-long stay at US #1. Its sales are boosted not least by an innovative John Murphy-directed video, during which O'Connor cries to great dramatic effect in a continuous face-to-camera shot, intercut with somber walking scenes. It becomes MTV's most requested video of the year, and together with the single, will win a clutch of awards over the next 12 months.
[28] ***I Do Not Want What I Haven't Got*** begins a six-week stay at the top of the US album chart on its way to triple platinum sales.
May The US leg of her world tour starts in Atlanta, GA.
[11] The RIAA certifies two million sales of ***I Do Not Want What I Haven't Got***.
[12] With ever-increasing media notoriety, O'Connor refuses to appear on NBC-TV's "Saturday Night Live" show in protest at the inclusion of guest host, the equally controversial comedian, Andrew "Dice" Clay.
June [23] During the three-day "Glastonbury Festival Of Contemporary Performing Arts" on Michael Eavis' farm in Pilton, near Glastonbury, Somerset, O'Connor and her band perform on a bill featuring Happy Mondays, De La Soul, the Cure, Jesus Jones, Del Amitri and labelmates World Party.
[26] O'Connor returns home to perform at the Dublin Point.
July [21] She participates in Roger Waters' performance of "The Wall" at the site of the Berlin Wall in Potzdamer Platz, Berlin, Germany. The event, also released as an album and video, is broadcast live throughout the world, and raises money for the Memorial Fund for Disaster Relief.
[28] Uptempo *The Emperor's New Clothes* peaks at US #60 and UK #31.
Aug [1] Her US tour resumes in St. Paul, MN (during which she reportedly checks into a Minneapolis Hospital to have an abortion).
[24] O'Connor refuses to perform her scheduled gig at New Jersey's Garden State Arts Center in Holmdel, NJ, if the American national anthem is played, initially in protest at the idea of US patriotism, and subsequently in protest at the current wave of music censorship prevailing in the US. The incident becomes a major international news story, amid rumors that O'Connor has left her husband and is involved with her support act, UK soul singer Hugh Harris.
[29] While some US radio stations ban O'Connor records, the bewigged and made-up artist joins an anti-O'Connor patriotic demonstration being staged outside her own concert prior to her evening performance in Saratoga Springs, NY.
Sept [7] O'Connor wins three Silver Astronauts trophies for Best Video Of The Year, Best Female Video and Best Post Modern Video categories at the

seventh annual MTV Video Music Awards. At the backstage party, she is reported to have asked Living Colour's Vernon Reid "Will you marry me and have my love child?", to which he replied: "Mmm ... OK."

Oct [2] Mike Reichtien, working in the meat section of Mrs. Gooch's Natural Food store in Beverly Hills, CA, sings the American national anthem to O'Connor while she is in the store, and is subsequently fired.

[12-13] O'Connor performs at the Amnesty International benefit, "From Chile ... An Embrace of Hope", alongside Sting, New Kids On The Block, Crosby, Stills & Nash, Ruben Blades, Wynton Marsalis, Jackson Browne and others, duetting on vocals with Peter Gabriel for *Don't Give Up*.

[27] Third album extract, the ballad *Three Babies*, promoted by a sleeping white horse-featured video clip, makes UK #42.

Nov [3] O'Connor contributes a version of *You Do Something To Me*, written for the 1929 stage musical, "Fifty Million Frenchmen", to ***Red Hot + Blue***, an anthology of Cole Porter songs to benefit AIDS education. She will also perform live at the album's press launch.

[6] O'Connor performs at London's Royal Albert Hall.

[26] During World AIDS week, O'Connor presents a series of five minute TV shorts entitled "AIDS Updates".

Dec Press reports state O'Connor's claims that on a visit to Prince's home, she was physically threatened by him. In a December issue lunch-time interview in **Q** magazine, O'Connor is quoted as saying "They stuff the meat full of hormones and all sorts of chemicals and it tastes delicious, but when I'm getting my period, I'm like Freddy Krueger".

[10] *Nothing Compares 2 U* is named Top Worldwide Single at the inaugural **Billboard** Music Awards, at which O'Connor sings *You Do Something To Me*.

1991

Jan [9] O'Connor, now living in a rented Hollywood Hills, CA house with her son Jake and long-time friend and assistant Ciara O'Flanagan, tops the annual list of US fashion doyen Mr. Blackwell's worst-dressed women of the year, calling her the "bald-headed banshee of MTV".

Feb [1] Having also announced that she is pulling out of the forthcoming annual BRIT Awards in London, O'Connor says she will not attend the Grammy Awards in a letter sent to the National Academy of Recording Arts & Sciences (NARAS), stating that she does not like the music industry's values and that "I signed my record deal when I was 17 and it has taken me this time to gather enough information and mull it over and reach a conclusion. We are allowing ourselves to be portrayed as being in some way more important, more special than the very people we are supposed to be helping - by the way we dress, by the cars we travel in, by the 'otherworldliness' of our shows and by a lot of what we say in our music". (NARAS' Michael Greene will respond caustically in future interviews, questioning O'Connor's motives, noting that she did not have any problem with attending both the MTV and the American Music Awards.)

[10] O'Connor is named Best International Artist, Female, at the tenth annual BRIT Awards, at the Dominion Theatre, London. In her absence, and as a tribute to her, organizer Jonathan King plays a video clip from another nominee in the category, Whitney Houston, singing her current single, *The Star Spangled Banner*.

[15] As a climax to her increasingly bad press, UK tabloid newspaper **The Sun** publishes a story about O'Connor's alleged lack of patriotism over the current Gulf Crisis (even though she is Irish), with the front page headline: "Sinead The She Devil".

[20] Expected to win a clutch of awards, O'Connor nabs Best Alternative Music Performance (Vocal Or Instrumental), for ***I Do Not Want What I Haven't Got***, at the 33rd annual Grammy Awards, at New York, NY's Radio City Music Hall.

Mar [7] O'Connor is named Artist Of The Year and Best and Worst Female Singer in the annual **Rolling Stone** Readers' Picks. ***I Do Not Want What I Haven't Got*** wins Best Album. She also tops the Artist Of The Year, Best Female Singer, Best Single and Best Album categories in the Critics' Picks.

May [12] O'Connor appears by satellite from the Hague, Holland, at "The Simple Truth" concert for Kurdish refugees at Wembley Arena, Wembley, Middx.

June [15] The self-penned ballad, *My Special Child*, makes UK #42, as press reports reveal that O'Connor will play the lead role in "Joan Of Arc", with filming due to begin in early 1992 in France.

Dec O'Connor shares this year's Sour Apple Award, presented by the Hollywood Women's Press Club, and given to celebrities who "most believe his or her own publicity", with actors Alec Baldwin and Kim Basinger.

[14] Festive release, *Silent Night*, debuts at its UK #60 peak.

[25] "The Ghost Of Oxford Street", directed by Malcolm McLaren, airs on C4-TV, with O'Connor playing a ghostly waif, singing *Silent Night*.

1992

Jan [11] The tribute album, ***Two Rooms - Celebrating The Songs Of Elton John & Bernie Taupin***, to which O'Connor has contributed *Sacrifice*, reaches US #18.

Jah Wobble's *Visions Of You*, featuring O'Connor and from his Mercury Prize-nominated ***Rising Above Bedlam*** album on which she also guests on *Sweet Divinity*, is released in the UK.

Sept [3] She previews her forthcoming album by performing a track live from New York, backed by a 45-piece orchestra, an unusual broadcast for BBC1-TV's "Top Of The Pops".

[19] *Success Has Made A Failure Of Our Home* reaches UK #18, as BBC2-TV airs "Sinead O'Connor - Coffee And Cigarettes", a 40-minute program on the making of her new album.

Oct [3] O'Connor guests on NBC-TV's "Saturday Night Live", singing *Success Has Made A Failure Out Of Me*, and a venomous a cappella version of Bob Marley's *War*. To a reaction of stunned audience silence, O'Connor tears up a picture of the Pope at the end of the song and proclaims "Fight the real enemy". It will cause uproar in the Catholic community and result in her lifetime ban from the program. The show's producer Lorne Michaels says of the incident: "We were sort of shocked, the way you would be at a house guest pissing on a flower arrangement in the dining room". ***Am I Not Your Girl?***, featuring a picture of Guatemalan street child Carmona Lopez, who was beaten by police officers in 1990 and later died of his injuries, hits UK #6.

[10] Her standards-covering torch album, ***Am I Not Your Girl?***, bows at its US #27 peak.

[13] O'Connor releases a written statement offering no apologies for her "Saturday Night Live" performance.

[16] Scheduled to sing *I Believe In You* at the "Bob Dylan 30th Anniversary Celebration" concert from New York's Madison Square Garden, she is booed by the audience, and instead sings *War*, eventually exiting the stage in tears.

[21] The National Ethnic Coalition of Organizations smashes more than 200 albums, CDs and cassettes, provided by people incensed with her "Saturday Night Live" appearance, as a steam roller crushes the offending articles in Manhattan, New York.

[25] The "Sinead Brigade", mostly wearing O'Connor face-masks, assembles outside St. Patrick's Cathedral in New York City, tearing up pictures of the Pope.

Nov O'Connor donates her Los Feliz, CA home, valued at $800,000, to the Red Cross, after Peter Egan had called for donations to the Red Cross Somalia relief fund.

[9] She continues her attacks on the Catholic Church in a **Time** magazine interview.

[27] O'Connor guests on BBC1-TV's "Terry Wogan's Friday Night".

Dec [12] *Don't Cry For Me Argentina*, originally a UK #1 for Julie Covington in 1976, debuts at its UK #53 peak. (She will return to Dublin to live at Christmas, and, as she takes stock of her career, begins singing lessons at the Parnell School of Music with Frank Merriman.)

1993

Jan O'Connor is featured on *Be Still*, released to benefit the Peace Together project for the youth in Northern Ireland. It is also reported that she is writing the soundtrack to "Proved Innocent", the story of pardoned Guildford Four prisoner, Gerry Conlon, and also penning a song for James Brooks' musical film "I'll Do Anything".

Mar [21] O'Connor sings *Make Me A Channel Of Your Peace* at the end of a peace demonstration in Dublin.

Apr [10] Willie Nelson's ***Across The Borderline*** album, featuring an O'Connor duet on *Don't Give Up*, debuts at its US #75 peak.

June [10] O'Connor takes out a full-page ad in the **Irish Times** explaining her reason for pulling out of the forthcoming "Peace Together" concert. (She will also pull out of the play "Hamlet's Nightmare" in Dublin in July, citing emotional exhaustion, although she is set to begin filming "Where No Birds Sing" in Ireland with Gabriel Byrne during the summer.)

Sept [7] O'Connor reportedly attempts suicide by taking an overdose of vodka and pills, after which she sends her son Jake to temporarily live with his father.

1994

Feb [12] O'Connor guests on CBS-TV's "Late Show With David Letterman".

[19] Featured on the film soundtrack to "In The Name Of The Father", O'Connor's *You Made Me The Thief Of Your Heart* debuts at its UK #42 peak.

[23] She sings the Who's *Baba O'Riley* with Roger Daltrey at his Carnegie Hall, New York gig.

Aug [23] ***No Prima Donna - The Songs Of Van Morrison***, a various artists tribute to Van Morrison, to which O'Connor has contributed *You Make Me Feel*, is released.

Sept [5] **Time** magazine reports that O'Connor is in a drug and alcohol rehabilitation clinic in London.

Oct [1] ***Universal Mother***, featuring guests Germaine Greer, the Irish Chamber Orchestra and co-producer Phil Coulter, reaches UK #19 and debuts at its US #36 peak.

[22] O'Connor guests on BBC1-TV's "The Danny Baker Show".

Dec [3] *Thank You For Hearing Me*, accompanied by two CD versions, one with a 15-minute remix of *Fire On Babylon*, the other her version of the Animals' *The House Of The Rising Sun*, reaches UK #13. (During the month O'Connor sings *Make Me A Channel Of Your Peace* and *Thank You For Hearing Me* at the Nobel Peace Committee gala at the National Theatre, Oslo, Norway.)

1995

Apr [29] *Haunted*, a duet with ex-Pogue Shane McGowan, debuts at its UK #30 peak.

June [10] O'Connor takes part in the annual "Fleadh Festival" at London's Finsbury Park.

[15] She hits two Israeli photographers and damages their equipment during a visit to Jerusalem's Holy Sepulchre Church.

[23] She performs at the 25th annual "Glastonbury Festival", Worthy Farm, Pilton, Somerset.

July [4] O'Connor embarks on "Lollapalooza '95" at the Gorge, George, WA, with Sonic Youth, Hole, Cypress Hill, Pavement, Beck, Jesus Lizard and the Mighty Mighty Bosstones.

[15] After just eight dates, a pregnant O'Connor pulls out of "Lollapalooza '95" and flies home to Dublin.

Aug [26] *Famine* charts for a week at UK #51.

Sept [4] O'Connor records a track for Go! Discs' War Child charity album ***Help***.

1996

Mar During the month, O'Connor gives birth to her second child, a girl.

THE O'JAYS

Eddie Levert (vocals); **Walter Williams** (vocals); **William Powell** (vocals)

1961

While Levert (b. June 16, 1942, Canton, OH) and Williams (b. Aug. 25, 1942, Canton) have already sung as a gospel duo, they added Powell (b. Jan. 20, 1942, Canton), Bobby Massey and Bill Isles to form the R&B/doo-wop quintet the Triumphs at McKinley High School, Canton, in 1958. Name-changing to the Mascots the following year, they performed to regional success around Cleveland, OH, before recording for the first time, cutting *Miracles* for the Wayco label, having come under the wing of Cleveland DJ Eddie O'Jay, who hones their stage act to professionalism, and gives career guidance. As a return gesture, they rename themselves the O'Jays as further singles follow on the King label.

1963

Sept Newly signed to Imperial Records, *Lonely Drifter* is their US chart debut at #97, produced by label owner H.B. Barnum, though the O'Jays will have to wait nearly two years before their next cross-over success.

1965

June Their revival of Benny Spellman's 1962 hit *Lipstick Traces (On A Cigarette)* makes US #48.
Aug *I've Cried My Last Tear* peaks at US #94.
Nov The O'Jays' debut album, ***Comin' Through***, is released on Imperial.

1966

Aug Isles leaves to work as a songwriter, but maintains links with the group, which continues performing as a quartet and moves back to Cleveland.
Oct *Stand-In For Love* peaks at US #95. The group leaves Imperial, moving to the associated Minit label on which their sophomore set, ***Soul Sounds*** will be issued in May the following year.

1968

Jan Newly signed to New York, NY-based Bell Records, *I'll Be Sweeter Tomorrow (Than I Was Today)* climbs to US #66.
July *Look Over Your Shoulder* makes US #89.
Sept Their last success on Bell is *The Choice*, which peaks at US #94.

1969

Mar The group plays at the Apollo Theatre in Harlem, New York, with the Intruders, who are working with Kenny Gamble and Leon Huff, and recommend their producers to check out the O'Jays.
Sept Having teamed with Gamble and Huff's short-lived Philadelphia-based Neptune label production company, *One Night Affair*, makes US #68 followed by *Deeper (In Love With You)* which climbs to US #64 in May 1970 with *Looky Looky (Look At Me Girl)* peaking at US #98 in September, their last Neptune release. Massey will leave to go into record production in 1971 (finding early success with Cleveland group the Ponderosa Twins), with the O'Jays continuing as a trio.

1972

Apr Gamble and Huff form their own label, Philadelphia International Records, and suggest to Levert that he might like to sign to it as a soloist. Levert is only interested in working as part of the group, so the O'Jays are signed as a unit, having rejected similar approaches by Motown and Invictus Records.
Sept [1] The still-climbing *Backstabbers,* their debut release on the label, becomes the group's first RIAA certified gold disc.
Oct [10] *Backstabbers*, a departure for the group into a hard-hitting, socially-aware lyric penned by Huff, Gene McFadden and John Whitehead, hits US #3 and reaches UK #14. The album, ***Backstabbers***, hits US #10.
Dec Taken from the album, *992 Arguments* makes US #57.

1973

Feb [9] *Love Train* is certified gold by the RIAA.
Mar [24] The group tops the US chart for a week with the R&B smash, *Love Train*, written and produced by Gamble and Huff, and also taken from ***Backstabbers***.
Apr *Love Train* hits UK #9.
May ***The O'Jays In Philadelphia***, rounding up the group's Neptune recordings, peaks at US #156.
[8] ***Backstabbers*** is certified gold by the RIAA, the O'Jays' and Philadelphia International's first gold album.
July *Time To Get Down* reaches US #33.

1974

Jan ***Ship Ahoy***, written and produced by Gamble and Huff, reaches US #11, and earns another gold disc.
Mar *Put Your Hands Together*, taken from ***Ship Ahoy***, hits US #10.
June Also from the album *For The Love Of Money*, which hits US #9.
[12] *For The Love Of Money* is certified gold by the RIAA.
Aug Performance set, ***The O'Jays Live In London***, recorded on their first UK and European tour, reaches US #17.

1975

Jan *Sunshine* peaks at US #48.
June *Give The People What They Want* makes US #45, taken from ***Survival***, which reaches US #11.
[12] The RIAA confirms gold status for ***Survival***.
[19] ***Live In London*** is also certified gold by the RIAA.
Aug *Let Me Make Love To You* peaks at US #75.

1976

Jan [24] The group's fourth million-selling single (already certified on the 4th), *I Love Music (Part 1)* hits US #5, taken from ***Family Reunion***, which hits US #7, showing both the group and the Gamble & Huff production team to be at the top of their game.
Feb *I Love Music (Part 1)* reaches UK #13. Prior to the group's biggest US tour, Powell leaves, diagnosed as having cancer. His replacement is Sammy Strain (b. Dec. 9, 1941, Brooklyn, NY), who has previously sung for 12 years with Little Anthony & the Imperials. The group also forms its own Shaker Records in Cleveland, designed as a "community-style" label to help nurture new talent in its home region.
Apr *Livin' For The Weekend* reaches US #20.
Oct *Message In Our Music* makes US #49, while its parent album, ***Message In The Music***, reaches US #20.
[21] ***Message In The Music*** is certified gold by the RIAA.

1977

Feb *Darlin' Darlin' Baby (Sweet Tender Love)* makes US #72 and UK #24.
May [26] Powell dies of cancer at his Canton home.
July ***Travelin' At The Speed Of Thought*** reaches US #27.
[12] ***Travelin' At The Speed Of Thought*** is certified gold by the RIAA.

1978

Jan Double compilation album, ***The O'Jays : Collectors' Items***, peaks at US #132.
Apr A remixed disco version of *I Love Music* makes UK #36.
May [31] The still-climbing ***So Full Of Love*** is confirmed platinum by the RIAA.
June ***So Full Of Love*** hits US #6.
[16] Still-rising *Use Ta Be My Girl* is ratified gold by the RIAA.
July [8] Gamble & Huff-penned, R&B swinging *Use Ta Be My Girl*, taken from their recent album, hits US #4, and reaches UK #12.
[12] The group celebrates its 20th anniversary performing at the Greek Theatre, Los Angeles, CA.
Oct Ballad *Brandy*, written by Joseph Jefferson and Charles Simmons, makes US #79 and UK #21. *Sing A Happy Song* will peaks at UK #39 the following October, while its parent album, ***Identify Yourself***, becomes another platinum disc-earner (on December 26th), reaching US #16.

1980

Feb *Forever Mine* makes US #28.
Oct The group has switched from Philadelphia International to the associated TSOP label for *Girl, Don't Let It Get You Down*, which is its last US singles chart entry, at #55. On the same label, ***The Year 2000***, makes US #36. Its follow-up album ***My Favorite Person*** will climb to US #49 in July 1982.

1983

Aug While the group celebrates its 25th anniversary playing a 75-city US tour on a bill with Rufus and Johnny "Guitar" Watson, *Put Our Heads Together* reaches UK #45, while ***When Will I See You Again*** makes US #142.

1986

Sept [13] *(Pop, Pop, Pop, Pop) Goes My Mind* by Levert, a group comprising Eddie Levert's sons Gerald and Sean, and friend Marc Gordon, tops the US R&B chart.
Nov [21] The 1976 album ***Family Reunion*** is certified platinum by the RIAA.

1987

Nov The group makes its first UK visit in 15 years, playing three nights at London's Hammersmith Odeon.
[7] The O'Jays return to top the US R&B survey with *Lovin' You*.
Dec Newly signed to EMI Manhattan Records, ***Let Me Touch You*** climbs to US #66. Their '80s chart career will wrap with ***Serious*** peaking at US #114 in June 1989, including the US R&B #1 *Have You Had Your Love Today*, which features a rap solo by Jaz.

1990

Jan [22] They collect the Favorite Band, Duo Or Group, Soul/R&B trophy, at the 17th annual American Music Awards, held at the Shrine Auditorium, Los Angeles.
Nov [2-3] Currently touring with Regina Belle, they play at the Tropworld Showroom, Tropworld Casino & Entertainment Resort, Atlantic City, NJ.
Dec [31] They take part in "Dick Clark's New Year's Rockin' Eve" on ABC-TV.

1991

Mar [9] Nathaniel Best (b. Dec. 13, 1960, Miami, FL) having replaced Strain, the EMI-released ***Emotionally Yours***, its title track penned by Bob Dylan, peaks at US #73, while the related Levert unit's latest album, ***Rope A Dope Style***, stands at US #161.
Aug [29] ***Emotionally Yours*** is certified gold by the RIAA.

1992

Jan [11] The O'Jays win the Outstanding Vocal Group category for ***Emotionally Yours*** and are inducted into the Image Hall of Fame at the 24th NAACP Image Awards, at the Wiltern Theatre, Los Angeles.
July [26] On tour with the Whispers, they play two sellout shows at the Valley Forge Music Fair, Devon, PA.
Aug [11] ***Ship Ahoy*** is certified platinum by the RIAA.
Oct [16] The group sings *Emotionally Yours* at the "Bob Dylan 30th Anniversary Concert Celebration" at New York's Madison Square Garden.

1994

Apr [1] After ***Heartbreaker*** has debuted at its US #75 peak the previous Aug [14], and still active on the US tour circuit, the group performs at the Westbury Music Fair, Westbury, NY, on a bill with the Whispers, Levert and Terry Hodges.

1995

July [12] They sing at the "Let's Stamp Out AIDS" benefit at the Universal Amphitheatre, Universal City, CA.
Sept [14] The O'Jays participate in the T.J. Martell Foundation 20th anniversary dinner honoring Clive Davis with the 1995 Humanitarian Award.
Oct [14] Gerald and Eddie Levert's self-explanatory ***Father And Son*** set debuts at its US #20 peak.

MIKE OLDFIELD

1968

Nov At the age of 15, multi-instrumentalist Oldfield (b. May 15, 1953, Reading, Berks.) releases ***Children Of The Sun*** on the UK label Transatlantic Records, under the name Sallyangie, recorded with his older sister Sally, for whom he has already played guitar when she performed as a folk artist in Berkshire pubs. Forming his own short-lived outfit, Barefeet, in September the following year, Oldfield goes on to join Kevin Ayers' backing band, the Whole Wide World, as bass player in March 1970, appearing on Ayers' ***Shooting At The Moon***, released in October the same year and on ***Whatevershebringswesing***, released in August 1971, after which he elects to pursue a solo career.

1972

With financial backing from Virgin record shops' owner Richard Branson, who is planning his own label, Oldfield, at age 19, begins work at Abbey Road Studios in London on a 50-minute quasi-classical instrumental composition. Virgin signs him to its fledgling label, also providing studio time at the newly-opened Manor recording complex.

1973

May The Virgin label launches with Oldfield's lengthy and unique ***Tubular Bells***, which will enter the UK chart on July 14th. Not entirely solo (it has contributions from Jon Field on flute, Steve Broughton on drums and ex-Bonzo Dog Doo-Dah Band vocalist Viv Stanshall as occasional narrator, among others), the album also features hundreds of studio overdubs by Oldfield playing different parts, and is co-produced by its creator with Simon Heyworth and Tom Newman.

1974

Mar [26] Still-rising in both the UK and US, ***Tubular Bells*** is certified gold by the RIAA.
Apr ***Tubular Bells*** hits US #3 and will eventually selling three million US copies.
May A segment from side one of ***Tubular Bells***, currently used as the main theme to horror movie, "The Exorcist", and subsequently released as a US single, hits US #7 (Oldfield's only US singles showing).
July Bowing to public demand, Virgin issues *Mike Oldfield's Single*, containing an edit from ***Tubular Bells*** similar to the US release which reaches UK #31. Meanwhile, the album, after an initial year on the UK chart, much of it in the Top 10, reaches its highest placing to date - #2 behind Paul McCartney & Wings' ***Band On The Run***.
Sept [14] Having signed a 17-year contract with Virgin, Oldfield's second album, the similarly-constructed ***Hergest Ridge***, enters the UK chart at #1.
Oct [5] After three weeks, it is deposed by ***Tubular Bells***, finally peaking in pole position after 16 months on sale. (It will spend a total of 264 weeks on the UK chart during the decade, before re-charting in the '90s.) ***Hergest Ridge*** makes US #87.
Nov Oldfield plays guitar on his friend David Bedford's ***Stars End***, performed by the Royal Philharmonic Orchestra.

1975

Feb ***The Orchestral Tubular Bells***, arranged by Bedford and played by the Royal Philharmonic Orchestra, with Oldfield on guitar, reaches UK #17. A second Oldfield single, *Don Alfonso*, is released.
Mar [1] ***Tubular Bells*** is named Best Instrumental Composition Of 1974 at the 17th annual Grammy Awards.
Nov ***Ommadawn***, incorporating wider influences than the two previous works, including Celtic and African phrasings, hits UK #4.

1976

Jan Seasonal double A-side, combining the traditional *In Dulce Jubilo* with the vocal *On Horseback*, hits UK #4, while ***Ommadawn*** peaks at US #146.
Dec ***Boxed***, a four-album boxed-set, containing remixed versions of his first three albums and a compilation of singles and guest appearances, reaches UK #22. *Portsmouth*, a traditional tune arranged by Oldfield, will hit UK #3 the following January. Two subsequent singles - Oldfield's arrangement of the *William Tell Overture* and *The Cuckoo Song* - will both fail to chart.

1978

Dec Self-penned as ever, the double album, ***Incantations***, three years in the making, reaches UK #14. For the first time, Oldfield is willing to give interviews and spend time promoting an album, after receiving a course of Exegesis training in self-assertiveness.

1979

Jan Four-track *Take Four*, reprising *Portsmouth*, *In Dulce Jubilo* and two traditional re-arrangements, peaks at UK #72.
May ***Guilty***, recorded with a New York, NY rhythm section, surprises many with its disco leanings, and reaches UK #22. Its release is followed by Oldfield's first tour, with a 50-piece accompaniment which includes string players and a choir. The shows are audio/visual events, incorporating films by Ian Eames.
Aug Live double album, ***Exposed***, recorded during the tour, reaches UK #16.
Dec ***Platinum***, a less earnest and more varied collection than its predecessors, peaks at UK #24.

1980

Jan Oldfield's version of the theme from the BBC1-TV children's show "Blue Peter" reaches UK #19.
July Live group, Oldfield Music, is formed for a UK and European tour to promote ***Platinum***.
Sept Oldfield's version of Abba's *Arrival*, with a pastiche of Abba's "helicopter" album sleeve, is released.
Nov *QE2* reaches UK #27, featuring the extracted revival of the Shadows' *Wonderful Land*.

1981

July *QE2*, released on Epic Records in the US, peaks at #174. Virgin announces that worldwide sales of ***Tubular Bells*** have passed ten million. (Oldfield will subsequently sue Richard Branson over royalty payments from his time with Virgin, differences which will be settled out of court. Later, commenting on his lengthy contract, Oldfield will say: "There will always be an element of bitterness there. The gentlemanly thing would have been to let me go.") Oldfield is entered in the UK edition of **Who's Who** - the only rock musician included, apart from Paul McCartney.
[28] Oldfield plays a free concert in London on the eve of H.R.H. Prince Charles and Lady Diana Spencer's wedding, composing new music for the occasion. (This helps him gain the Freedom of the City of London in 1982 in recognition for both his charity work and his export contribution from overseas sales and earnings.)

1982

Mar The Mike Oldfield Group is formed for live work, with Maggie Reilly (vocals), Tim Cross (keyboards), Maurice Pert (percussion, keyboards), Rick Fenn (bass) and Pierre Moelen (drums).
Apr ***Five Miles Out***, partly inspired by his experiences as a private pilot, hits UK #7, while the extracted title track, *Five Miles Out*, makes UK #43.
May ***Five Miles Out*** peaks at US #164.
June *Family Man*, a vocal track from ***Five Miles Out***, reaches UK #45. (The song will be revived as a US #6 and UK #15 hit in 1983 by Daryl Hall & John Oates.)

1983

June ***Crises*** hits UK #6.
July *Moonlight Shadow*, a thinly-disguised reference to John Lennon's murder, extracted from ***Crises***, and featuring a vocal by Maggie Reilly, hits UK #4.
Sept *Shadow On The Wall*, also from ***Crises***, with a guest vocal by ex-Family singer Roger Chapman, is released.

1984

Jan *Crime Of Passion* makes UK #61.
July ***Discovery*** reaches UK #15, while *To France*, taken from it, makes UK #48.
Dec Oldfield's soundtrack album of his music from the movie "The Killing Fields" peaks at UK #97.

1986

Apr *Shine*, with Yes singer Jon Anderson on guest vocals, is released. (Oldfield will spend the rest of the year producing a video album, which will eventually appear in 1988 as "Wind Chimes".)
[7] With excerpts from ***Tubular Bells*** used on Paul Hardcastle's 1985 UK #1, *19*, Oldfield wins an Ivor Novello Award by default as the song nabs the International Hit Of The Year trophy at the 31st annual lunch, at London's Grosvenor House Hotel.

1987

Oct [10] ***Islands*** reaches UK #29, its title track, also issued as a UK single, featuring guest vocals by Bonnie Tyler. The album, also featuring Ayers and Roger Chapman, will peak at US #138 the following March. ***Earth Moving*** will complete his '80s album releases reaching UK #30 on July [22] 1989.

1990

June [9] With no pre-release hit singles, ***Amorok*** makes UK #49 and will prove Oldfield's least successful album to date with only a two-week chart stay.
Dec *Etude* is released in the UK, not least due to its extensive use as a TV advertising theme for Nurofen painkillers.

1992

Mar Newly signed to WEA, Oldfield begins work on ***Tubular Bells II*** at his home studio in Los Angeles, CA, with producer Trevor Horn.
Sept [4] Oldfield premieres ***Tubular Bells II*** at an Edinburgh Castle, Edinburgh, Scotland charity concert, to be broadcast on BBC2-TV, also meeting H.R.H. Prince Charles after the performance.
[12] ***Tubular Bells II***, featuring Susannah Melvoin, Edie Lehman and Sally Bradshaw on vocals, John Robinson on drums and Jamie Muhoberac on various instruments, enters the UK chart at #1.
[19] ***Tubular Bells*** re-charts, peaking at UK #48, on the strength of the success of its sequel. Oldfield comments: "If I can achieve anything with ***Tubular Bells II*** it is to escape the New Age rack in record stores".
[27] Oldfield performs at a benefit for leukemia patients in Luciano Pavarotti's horse stables in Modena, Italy, with an all-star cast (released the following year as ***Pavarotti & Friends***.)
Oct [1] He makes a rare appearance on BBC1-TV's "Top Of The Pops".
[10] *Sentinel* hits UK #10.
Dec [26] *Tattoo* reaches UK #33.

1993

Mar [1] He plays a sellout show at New York's Carnegie Hall.
Apr [5-8] Oldfield performs four nights at London's Royal Albert Hall.
[24] *The Bell*, with MC Viv Stanshall, makes UK #50.
June [6] Oldfield guests on BBC2-TV's religious

program "Faith & Music".
Oct [2] Career retrospective ***Elements - The Best Of Mike Oldfield*** hits UK #5.
[9] The extracted and reissued *Moonlight Shadow* debuts at its UK #52 peak.

1994

Dec [3] Based on Arthur C. Clarke's book of the same name, the self-produced ***The Songs Of Distant Earth***, including Gregorian and Sami chant elements, and featuring an extra CD-ROM track, reaches UK #24 in its week of entry.
[17] The excerpted *Hibernaculum* debuts at its UK #47 peak.

1995

Sept [2] Still commuting between his homes in Chalfont St. Giles, Bucks. and Hollywood, CA, with his Spanish girlfriend Rosa, following two marriages and five children, his latest single *Let There Be Light* charts for a week at UK #51.

1996

Feb Reprise in the US finally issues ***The Songs Of Distant Earth***, its additional CD-ROM segment encouraging users to decipher a code to enter the multimedia content.

ALEXANDER O'NEAL

1978

Raised and based in Minneapolis, MN, an ex-North Natchez High School footballer and active civil rights supporter, O'Neal (b. Nov. 14, 1954, Natchez, MS) has settled on a career in music, starting out on the local club scene in 1972. He now teams up with the burgeoning R&B Minneapolis music elite to form Flyte Time, whose co-members include future production force Jimmy Jam and Terry Lewis. Prince, already leading the local music scene, invites them to become his full-time backing band. Apparently due to his arrogance and unwillingness to conform, O'Neal is fired and sets up a temporary and unsuccessful rival band, and will release his debut single, the largely unnoticed *Playroom*, in 1980.

1984

Maintaining an association with Jam and Lewis, O'Neal, now solo, accepts their offer to write and produce a debut album to be released on their Tabu label (licensed through CBS/Columbia). The producers invite label colleague, and ex-Time member, Monte Moir, to oversee three cuts while Moir, Jam and Lewis also form O'Neal's backing band, the Secret, for the album.

1985

Apr His freshman album, ***Alexander O'Neal***, recorded at Creation Audio, Minneapolis, largely produced and written by Jam and Lewis, is released, peaking at US #91. It features three US Hot Black Singles hits (*Innocent*, a duet with labelmate Cherrelle, *A Broken Heart Can Mend*, and *If You Were Here Tonight*), but none crosses over.
June ***Alexander O'Neal*** climbs to UK #19 after strong import demand.
Dec His duet with soulstress Cherrelle on her *Saturday Love* hits UK #6, but fails again to lift O'Neal out of the US specialist rankings.

1986

Feb *If You Were Here Tonight*, written and produced by Moir, reaches UK #13.
Apr *A Broken Heart Can Mend* makes UK #53.
[19] *Saturday Love* reaches US #26.
July Suffering from severe cocaine and alcohol addiction, O'Neal enters Minnesota's Hazelden Clinic. During his treatment, Jam and Lewis promise they will produce a follow-up album after his rehabilitation and also contribute half the cost of O'Neal's hospital bills.

1987

Aug Having recovered and married for a second time (O'Neal already has three children), his sophomore album, ***Hearsay***, is released. All tracks, bar one, are written and produced by Jam and Lewis who are coming off their recent success with Janet Jackson. It will hit UK #4 and US #29. The first cut from the album, the crisply-funked *Fake*, reaches US #25, having already topped the US R&B chart, and UK #33, helped by an energetic black and white video.
Sept [16] O'Neal begins a co-headlining US tour with the Force MD's.
Oct Co-written by O'Neal and Jellybean Johnson, *Criticize* hits UK #4.
[20] ***Hearsay*** is certified gold by the RIAA.
Dec O'Neal performs soldout dates in London.
[19] *Criticize* peaks at US #70.

1988

Feb *Never Knew Love Like This*, a duet with Cherrelle, from ***Hearsay***, climbs to UK #26 and US #28, while "The Voice On Video" hits #3 on the UK Music Video chart.
Mar [26] ***Hearsay/All Mixed Up*** hits UK #4.
May Ballad *The Lovers* reaches UK #28.
July *What Can I Say To Make You Love Me*, released to coincide with standing-room-only UK dates, makes UK #27. One of his Wembley Arena, Wembley, Middx. performances is filmed for later TV showing.
Oct With its parent album ***Hearsay***, now on the US and UK charts for over a year, the UK-only reissue and remix of *Fake*, titled *Fake '88*, reaches UK #16. BBC-TV airs the full Wembley concert recorded in July.
Nov Seasonal album, ***My Gift To You***, featuring traditional Christmas songs and Jam/Lewis originals, is released, set to make US #149 and UK #53. O'Neal also guests on Cherrelle's new album, ***Affair***, on the tracks *Keep It Inside* and *Everything I Miss At Home*. Meanwhile, the UK-only issued, ***Hearsay All Mixed Up***, featuring remixed tracks from his second album, ***Hearsay***, is released.
Dec [17] Festive set ***My Gift To You*** debuts at its UK #53 peak and includes the UK #30 double A-side *Christmas Song/Thank You For A Good Year*

1989

Feb From the UK remix project, *Hearsay '89* peaks at UK #56.
July [18-19] O'Neal takes part in the seventh annual "Prince's Trust Rock Gala" at the National Exhibition Centre, Birmingham, West Midlands.
Sept *Sunshine*, released two years after the issue of its parent album, peaks at UK #72. The ***Hearsay/All Mixed Up*** combination has now remained on the UK survey for over two years.
Dec Not satisfied with releasing remixed versions, those remixes are now segued into *Hitmix (Official Bootleg Mega-Mix)*, which reaches UK #19.

1991

Jan [19] Having performed a pair of year-ending dates on December 30th-31st the previous year at the famed Fox Theatre in Detroit, MI, on a bill with soul veteran Patti LaBelle, new material emerges, his first in three years, in the shape of the album-previewing *All True Man*, which reaches UK #18.
Feb [1] O'Neal embarks on major UK tour dates, supported by UK soul troupe the Pasadenas.
[2] Parent album, ***All True Man***, again mostly written and produced by Jam and Lewis, debuts at its UK #2 peak, behind Sting's ***Soul Cages***.
Mar [16] ***All True Man*** makes US #49.
[30] *What Is This Thing Called Love* peaks at UK #53.
Apr [13] *All True Man* reaches US #43.
[19] O'Neal begins a series of dates at London's Royal Albert Hall, during a current UK tour set to end on the 30th at the Brighton Centre, Brighton, East Sussex.
May [11] *Shame On Me* debuts at its UK #71 peak.
[12] O'Neal appears at "The Simple Truth" benefit concert for Kurdish refugees at Wembley Arena, Wembley.
Aug [26] ***All True Man*** is certified gold by the RIAA.
Oct [3-8] He participates in the "World Song-Stylist Live Series I" at the Tokyo Metropolitan Art Space, Tokyo, Japan.

1992

May [30] ***This Thing Called Love - Greatest Hits*** bows at its UK #4 peak.
Nov [14] *Sentimental* charts for a week at UK #72.
Dec O'Neal puts the finishing touches to his new album at Elumba Recording, Los Angeles, CA.

1993

Jan [21] He is ordered to pay a $5,000 fine and undergo chemical-dependency treatment after pleading guilty to drug possession, following his arrest in Minneapolis in June 1992.
[30] *Love Makes No Sense* debuts at its UK #26 peak.
Feb [20] Newly signed to A&M Records, his label debut, ***Love Makes No Sense***, debuts at its UK #14 peak.
[27] ***Love Makes No Sense*** bows at its US #89 peak.
July [3] Second extract, *In The Middle*, debuts at its UK #32 peak, as O'Neal makes a brief UK visit, appearing on BBC1-TV's "Top Of The Pops" and C4-TV's "The Big Breakfast".
Sept [25] *All That Matters To Me* charts for a week at UK #67.

1994

Feb Tabu releases ***This Thing Called Love : The Greatest Hits Of Alexander O'Neal***, comprising his mostly Jam & Lewis-helmed highlights with the label.

ROY ORBISON

1954

After his family has spent the war in Fort Worth, TX, Orbison (b. Apr. 23, 1936, Vernon, TX) has been raised in Wink, TX from the age of ten, and made his first public appearance representing Texas at the International Lions Club Convention in Chicago, IL, before gaining a Saturday afternoon radio show on KERB in Kermit, TX, with Charline Arthur. Having also performed with local hillbilly group the Wink Westerners in his teens, winning a talent contest organized by the Pioneer Furniture Company in Midland, TX, which led to an appearance on a KMID television show, he now studies geology at North Texas State University in Denton, TX. (While there, Orbison's classmate Pat Boone has his first hit, *Two Hearts*.) Going on to sing with the Teen Kings in 1955, he records at Norman Petty's studio in Clovis, NM, and releases *Trying To Get To You* on Je-Wel Records.

1956

July Having auditioned, at the suggestion of Johnny Cash, in Memphis, TN, for Sam Phillips at Sun Records, his first Sun single, the uptempo rockabilly number, *Ooby Dooby*, written by two college mates, Wade Moore and Dick Penner, at North Texas State, peaks at US #59. Together with the Teen Kings, Orbison hits the road on a US package tour with Cash and Carl Perkins, though the group will split after recording their third single, *Devil Doll* in December. Three further solo singles will be released on Sun the following year, all in the rockabilly mode, which is not the forté for Orbison's high, expressive vocal style. He subsequently moves to Nashville, TN, to concentrate on his songwriting.

1958

May Writing compositions for Acuff-Rose Music publishers, he has placed *Claudette*, written for his wife Claudette Frady (which he has recorded as a demo at Sun, but will be released two decades later), with the Everly Brothers. Released as the B-side of the duo's *All I Have To Do Is Dream*, it reaches US #30 and shares in worldwide sales of several million.

1959

Jan Still in Nashville, and having bought himself out of his Sun contract, he signs to RCA Records (a deal secured by his manager Wesley Rose), but *Seems To Me* and *Almost 18* fail to register and, guided by Rose, he parts from the label to sign to the newer, smaller outfit, Monument Records, owned by Fred Foster.

1960

Feb Orbison's second Monument single, *Up Town*, with an Anita Kerr string arrangement, charts at US #72.

July Written by the artist with Joe Melson, who is the former leader of Midland band the Cavaliers, *Only The Lonely*, originally offered to both Elvis Presley and the Everly Brothers, is his major breakthrough, hitting US #2 eventually selling over one million copies. Its wordless vocal accompaniment becomes a much-covered gimmick.

Oct [20] *Only The Lonely*, showcasing his dramatically distinctive vocal skill, is his UK chart debut, topping the survey for the first of two weeks, dethroned by the year's biggest-seller, Elvis Presley's *It's Now Or Never*.

Nov *Blue Angel*, similarly styled to *Only The Lonely*, hits US #9.

Dec *Blue Angel* reaches UK #11.

1961

Jan *I'm Hurtin'* rises to US #27.

Apr Orbison is treated for a duodenal ulcer.

June [5] Starkly melodramatic *Running Scared* is another million seller, topping the US chart for one week, and will hit UK #9.

Oct *Crying*, again written with Melson, and his third million seller, hits US #2 and UK #25. Its B-side, *Candy Man*, penned by Fred Neil, reaches US #25. (Both titles will be much revived by other acts, not least Don McLean's 1980 UK chart-topping revival of the former.)

1962

Mar Orbison's fourth million seller is the uptempo, and also frequently revived, *Dream Baby*, which hits US #4.

[8] The Beatles make their radio debut on the BBC program "Teenager's Turn", singing Orbison's *Dream Baby*.

Apr Cindy Walker-penned *Dream Baby* hits UK #2, behind the Shadows' *Wonderful Land*.

June ***Crying*** is his first album to chart, reaching US #21.

July Less commercial *The Crowd* makes US #26 and UK #40.

Nov Double A-side ballad/beat combination, *Leah/ Working For The Man*, reaches US #25 and #33. In Britain, only *Working For The Man* is promoted, peaking at UK #50. Meanwhile, the compilation album, ***Roy Orbison's Greatest Hits***, reaches US #14.

1963

Mar Self-penned ballad, *In Dreams*, which will become one of Orbison's most enduring songs, hits US #7.

Apr *In Dreams* hits UK #6.

May Orbison, who wears glasses to see properly, leaves his only regular pair on a plane while flying to Alabama to perform, and has to wear his dark-tinted shades. Immediately due to fly on to Britain for a tour, he has to keep on wearing these and they become such a trademark during his widely-photographed and reported trek with the Beatles that Orbison accepts them as his new image.

[18] He begins a UK tour with the Beatles and Gerry & the Pacemakers, opening at the Granada Cinema, Slough, Bucks.

June After the UK trek, ***Lonely And Blue*** reaches UK #15, while ***Crying*** makes UK #17.

July *Falling* reaches US #22 and hits UK #9, entering the Top 20 while *In Dreams* is also still present. (*Falling*'s B-side, *Distant Drums*, will be a posthumous hit for Jim Reeves.)

Sept [11] Orbison embarks on a 23-date, UK package tour with Brian Poole & the Tremeloes, the Searchers and Freddie & the Dreamers, set to end on October 6th at King George's Hall, Blackburn, Lancs.

Oct Another double A-side couples the Elvis Presley oldie, *Mean Woman Blues*, which hits US #5, with the Orbison/Melson penned ballad, *Blue Bayou*, which reaches US #29. Meanwhile, ***In Dreams*** peaks at US #35, as Orbison tours Canada.

Nov *Blue Bayou* hits UK #3, while the rock side peaks at UK #19. ***In Dreams*** hits UK #6.

Dec Seasonal ballad, *Pretty Paper*, recorded in London, reaches US #15 but is not released in the UK at this time, due to the continuing success of *Blue Bayou*.

1964

Jan Orbison embarks on a tour of Australia with the Beach Boys, Paul & Paula, the Surfaris and the Joy Boys.

Mar *Borne On The Wind*, issued only in the UK as a single, reaches #15.

Apr [18] Orbison embarks on another British tour with Freddie & the Dreamers at the Adelphi Theatre, Slough, Bucks., set to end on May 16th at the City Hall, Newcastle, Tyne & Wear.

[26] He celebrates his 28th birthday with a party attended by the Beatles.

May [17] Orbison performs on the bill of Brian Epstein's "Pops Alive" at London's Prince of Wales Theatre.

[23] *It's Over*, another enduring ballad written by Orbison with Bill Dees, hits US #9.

June [25] *It's Over* tops the UK chart for the first of two weeks - the first time a US act has had a UK #1 since the beginning of August 1963, when Elvis Presley topped with *(You're The) Devil In Disguise*.

July ***Exciting Sounds Of Roy Orbison***, a compilation of his early Sun tracks on Ember Records, reaches UK #17.

Sept [26] Distinctive uptempo arrangement of *Oh, Pretty Woman*, again written by Orbison and Dees, whom he had met when Dees was in the Five Bops, begins a three-week run atop the US chart and will go on to sell seven million copies worldwide.

Oct [8] *Oh, Pretty Woman* tops the UK chart for the first of three weeks, while still heading the US survey.

[30] *Oh Pretty Woman* is certified gold by the RIAA.

Nov Orbison divorces Claudette on the grounds of cruelty. She had been having an affair with their builder, Braxton Dixon. Compilation album, ***More Of Roy Orbison's Greatest Hits***, reaches US #19, while ***Early Orbison***, which compiles tracks from his first two Monument albums, peaks at US #101.

Dec *Pretty Paper*, released one Christmas later in the UK, hits #6. ***Oh, Pretty Woman***, a compilation of singles tracks released only in Britain, hits UK #4.

1965

Jan Orbison tours Australia with the Rolling Stones.

Feb [16] He begins a 30 date, twice-nightly package trek with Marianne Faithfull, the Rockin' Berries, Cliff Bennett & the Rebel Rousers and others, at the Adelphi Theatre, Slough, set to close on March 21th at the Empire Theatre, Liverpool, Lancs.

Mar *Goodnight* reaches US #21 and UK #14.

June [30] Orbison's contract with Monument expires. He signs a new US deal with MGM Records for a guaranteed $1 million, which offers movie as well as recording opportunities. He is satisfied with the way London Records has marketed his Monument repertoire in the UK and many other territories around the world and signs a new direct international deal with London, which automatically gives them the product recorded for MGM.

July [17] An 18-date Irish tour begins in Bray, ending in Waterford on August 1st.

Aug Latin-styled *(Say) You're My Girl* makes US #39 and UK #23. *Ride Away*, the first single under the new arrangement with MGM and London, reaches US #25 and UK #34, while ***There Is Only One Roy Orbison***, his first for MGM, reaches US #55 and hits UK #10.

Nov His revival of the R&B standard, *Let The Good Times Roll*, released by Monument in competition with newer releases, peaks at US #81.

Dec Ballad *Crawling Back* reaches US #46 and UK #19, as a Monument compilation, ***Orbisongs***, makes US #136.

1966

Feb Uptempo *Breakin' Up Is Breakin' My Heart* reaches US #31 and UK #22, while ***The Orbison Way*** peaks at US #128 and UK #11.

Mar [20] Orbison tops the bill at ITV's "Sunday Night At The London Palladium".

[24] ***Roy Orbison's Greatest Hits*** is certified gold by the RIAA.

[25] He begins a 31 date, twice-nightly UK concert series with the Walker Brothers, Lulu and others, at the Astoria Theatre, Finsbury Park, London, set to end on May 1st at the Coventry Theatre, Coventry, Warks.

[27] Orbison falls off his motorcycle while scrambling at Hawkstone Park, Birmingham, Warks. He fractures his foot and is taken to Thorpe Coombe General Hospital, London, and will continue the tour sitting on a stool onstage and walking on crutches.

Apr Orbison and Claudette re-marry in Nashville. *Twinkle Toes*, another uptempo rocker, reaches US #39 and UK #29.

[24] He takes part in the London to Brighton vintage car rally.

May [1] Orbison performs at the "**New Musical Express** Poll Winners Concert" at the Empire Pool, Wembley, Middx., with an all-star cast.

June [6] Tragedy strikes when the Orbisons are returning from the National Drag Races meeting near Bristol, TN. A truck pulls out from a side road near Gallatin, TX, and hits Claudette on her motorcycle. She dies, age 25, an hour later at Sumner Memorial Hospital.

July *Lana*, previously an album track, now issued as a UK single, reaches #15.

Aug *Too Soon To Know*, a highly personal ballad, widely recognized as referring to the loss of his wife, hits UK #3 but stops at US #68. ***The Classic Roy Orbison*** reaches UK #12.

[7] Orbison begins pre-recording of "The Fastest Guitar Alive" movie soundtrack in Nashville.

Sept Compilation album, ***The Very Best Of Roy Orbison***, makes US #94.

[7] He begins filming "The Fastest Guitar Alive" at MGM'S Hollywood studios, in a role originally intended for Elvis Presley.

1967

Jan *There Won't Be Many Coming Home*, taken from the film, reaches UK #18, while, *Communication Breakdown* makes US #60.

[22] A tour of Australia and the Far East, with the Walker Brothers and the Yardbirds, begins at Sydney Stadium, Sydney, New South Wales, Australia.

Mar *So Good* makes UK #32.

[3] Orbison embarks on a 32-date, twice-nightly UK trek with the Small Faces, Paul & Barry Ryan, Jeff Beck and others at the Astoria Theatre, Finsbury Park, London, set to end on April 9th at the ABC Theatre, Romford, Essex.

Apr [8] He spends the day at the US Embassy in London trying to resolve work permit problems for his British nanny, Australian secretary and Samoan housekeeper/cook.

July ***Orbisongs*** peaks at UK #40.

Aug *Cry Softly Lonely One*, which sees a reconciliation with songwriter Joe Melson, reaches US #52.

Sept Compilation album, ***Roy Orbison's Greatest Hits***, climbs to UK #40.

1968

July [28] Orbison makes his UK club debut at the Stockton Fiesta.

Aug *Walk On*, a dramatic ballad, makes UK #39.

[5] Orbison opens for a one-month season at the Talk of the Town, London.

Sept [14] More tragedy strikes while Orbison is touring Britain, performing in Birmingham, Warks., his home in Nashville catches fire, and the two eldest

of his three sons, Roy Jr. and Tony, die in the blaze.
Oct *Heartache* makes UK #44.

1969

Mar [25] Orbison marries German-born Barbara Wellhonen, whom he met at a club in Leeds, S. Yorks.
Apr He deputizes for an ailing Engelbert Humperdinck on two dates of a Humperdinck/Mary Hopkin tour, though the final three dates of the tour are cancelled.
May *My Friend* climbs to UK #35, taken from ***Roy Orbison's Many Moods***.
[18] Orbison performs at London's Hammersmith Odeon during his current UK tour.
Oct Gimmicky, uptempo *Penny Arcade* reaches UK #27.

1970

Apr *So Young*, the love theme from the movie "Zabriskie Point", is released. The Orbisons move to Bielfeld near Dusseldorf, West Germany, Barbara's birthplace. (He will continue to release one album a year for the next five years: this year's ***The Big O*** followed by ***Hank Williams : The Roy Orbison Way*** (1971), ***Roy Orbison Sings*** (1972), ***Memphis*** (1973) and ***Milestones*** (1974).)

1973

Jan Compilation album, ***All-Time Greatest Hits***, makes UK #39.
Orbison leaves MGM to sign a one-year deal with Mercury Records (before returning to Monument), releasing ***I'm Still In Love With You***.

1976

Jan [31] TV-promoted compilation album, ***The Best Of Roy Orbison***, tops the UK chart for a week.
Apr [23] At the nadir of his career, Orbison plays at the Van-a-Rama auto exposition in Cincinnati Gardens, Cincinnati, OH, before a crowd of less than 100.

1977

Mar [14] Orbison opens for the Eagles, who are currently at US #1 with ***Hotel California***.
[27] He performs at London's Theatre Royal Drury Lane promoting his latest album, ***Regeneration***.
Apr Orbison records a message for Michelle Booth, a teenager who idolizes "The Big O", after she had been left in a coma having been thrown from a London train during an assault.

1978

Jan [18] Orbison undergoes coronary by-pass surgery at St. Thomas' Hospital in Nashville.
During the year, he signs to Elektra/Asylum Records, releasing the album ***Laminar Flow*** the following year.

1980

July He returns to the US singles chart for the first time in 13 years (at #55), duetting with Emmylou Harris on *That Lovin' You Feelin' Again*, from the soundtrack to "Roadie", in which he also makes a cameo appearance.
Sept [5] Orbison plays at the second annual "Buddy Holly Memorial Concert" at the Civic Center, Lubbock, TX.(A projected movie biography "The Living Legend", with Martin Sheen as "The Big O", is scrapped after Orbison withdraws his support for the film.)

1981

Feb [25] *That Lovin' You Feelin' Again* wins the Best Country Performance By A Duo Or Group With Vocal category at the 23rd annual Grammy Awards.
July [18] ***Golden Days*** makes UK #63.
[19] Odessa, TX proclaims "Roy Orbison Day". He plays there for the first time in 15 years, and is given the keys to the city.

1983

Mar Having sued Acuff-Rose publishers for $50 million the previous September, claiming mismanagement and under-accounting of royalties, and after a four-year recording gap, his ***Big O Country*** is released, followed by ***Problem Child*** in 1984.

1986

Sept Now living in Malibu, CA (where his home will be featured on the TV program "Lifestyles Of The Rich And Famous" in 1987), Orbison experiences a major career resurgence when film director David Lynch uses *In Dreams* as a central theme in his movie "Blue Velvet". Orbison is apparently opposed to its inclusion in the film, but Lynch uses it anyway.

1987

Jan [21] He is inducted into the Rock and Roll Hall of Fame at the second annual induction dinner, at New York, NY's Waldorf Astoria Hotel, and is joined by Bruce Springsteen, who inducts him, singing *Oh, Pretty Woman*.
Apr [23] Orbison re-records some of his greatest hits with producer T-Bone Burnett at Oceanways Studios in Los Angeles, CA.
May [22] He guests on NBC-TV's "Saturday Night Live" with host, "Blue Velvet"-star, Dennis Hopper.
July [11] Newly signed to Virgin Records in the UK the re-recorded T-Bone Burnett sessions, released as ***In Dreams : The Greatest Hits***, makes UK #86.
Aug [14] Orbison embarks on a US tour at the Paul Masson Winery, Saratoga, CA, set to end on September 4th at the Hilton Ballroom, Eugene, OR.
Sept [30] "A Black And White Night", a club concert at which Orbison is backed by a cast of star admirers, including Bruce Springsteen, Elvis Costello, Bonnie Raitt, k.d. lang, Jackson Browne, J.D. Souther, Jennifer Warnes and Tom Waits, takes place at the Coconut Grove, Ambassador Hotel in Los Angeles. The musical content mostly features his familiar hits of the '60s.

1988

Jan Orbison's duet with lang on *Crying* is featured in the film "Hiding Out", and makes #42 on the US Country chart.
Apr [23] Orbison celebrates his 52nd birthday at a Bruce Springsteen concert during which the audience sings *Happy Birthday*.
Nov Orbison, in the guise of Lefty, participates in the all-star recording ensemble the Traveling Wilburys, which also features Bob Dylan, Tom Petty, and Jeff Lynne of the Electric Light Orchestra. ***The Traveling Wilburys***, with major contributions from Orbison, races up both US (#3) and UK (#16) charts, as does the extracted single, *Handle With Care* at US #45 and UK #21.
[19] He makes his last TV appearance at the "Diamond Awards Festival" in Antwerp, Belgium.
Dec [4] Orbison makes what will be his last performance at the Front Row Theatre, Highland Heights, near Cleveland, OH.
[6] He is rushed to Hendersonville Hospital, after suffering a heart attack at 11:00 p.m. in his mother's bathroom, where he dies within minutes of admittance, at 11:54 p.m.
[9] Wink mayor Maxie Watts declares "Roy Orbison Memorial Day".
[13] "Celebration Of Life", a tribute to Orbison, with Bonnie Raitt, J.D. Souther, the Stray Cats and others, takes place at the Wiltern Theatre, Los Angeles.

1989

Jan *You Got It*, co-penned with fellow Wilburys Jeff Lynne and Tom Petty, hits UK #3 as a Rhino Records anthology, ***For The Lonely : An Anthology, 1956-1965***, peaks at US #110 and ***In Dreams : The Greatest Hits*** makes US #95.
[21] Telstar TV-advertised compilation, ***The Legendary Roy Orbison***, tops the UK chart.
Feb [11] ***Mystery Girl***, recorded before his death for Virgin, hits UK #2, and will hit US #5.
[22] *Crying*, his re-made duet with k.d. lang, wins Best Country Vocal Collaboration at the 31st annual Grammy Awards.
Mar [29] ***Mystery Girl*** is certified platinum by the RIAA.
Apr *You Got It* hits US #9, as *She's A Mystery To Me*, written by U2's Bono and the Edge, reaches UK #27.
[23] "Roy Orbison Day" is declared in Texas.
May [11] Orbison is posthumously inducted into the Songwriters' Hall of Fame at its 20th anniversary ceremonies, held at Radio City Music Hall, New York.
July [11] ***In Dreams : The Greatest Hits*** is confirmed gold by the RIAA.
Dec [2] From the September 1987 event, ***A Black And White Night Live*** makes UK #51. Wink's mayor Maxie Watts launches the Roy Orbison Memorial Monument Fund to erect a monument to the singer. By year's end, Acuff-Rose Music sues Orbison's estate over ownership of songs including those on ***Mystery Girl*** and ***Traveling Wilburys***. The suit alleges Barbara Orbison persuaded Orbison to break his 1985 five-year contract to write songs for the firm annually.

1990

Jan [6] ***A Black And White Night Live*** makes US #123.
Feb [24] The "Roy Orbison Concert Tribute To Benefit The Homeless", with host Whoopi Goldberg and Dwight Yoakam, k.d. lang, Bruce Hornsby, Gary Busey, Dean Stockwell, Roger McGuinn, David Crosby, Chris Hillman, Bob Dylan, Bonnie Raitt, Was (Not Was) and B.B. King, among others, takes place at the Universal Amphitheatre, Universal City, CA.
Apr ***Pretty Woman***, a various artists film soundtrack for the Julia Roberts/Richard Gere-starring film of the same name, with Orbison's *Pretty Woman* as its recurrent theme, begins a 91-week stay on the US chart, eventually hitting #4.
July [13] ***All Time Greatest Hits Of Roy Orbison - Volume I*** is certified gold by the RIAA.
Nov [27] ***Ballads - 22 Classic Love Songs*** reaches UK #38.

1991

Feb [20] Orbison wins the Best Pop Vocal Performance, Male category for *Oh, Pretty Woman*, from ***A Black And White Night Live***, at the 33rd annual Grammy Awards, at Radio City Music Hall, New York.
July [16] ***All Time Greatest Hits Of Roy Orbison - Volume II*** is also certified gold by the RIAA.

1992

Aug [1] *I Drove All Night* hits UK #7 (and will re-chart at UK #47 on Nov [13] the following year).
[29] *Crying*, the five-year old duet with lang, reaches UK #13.
Nov [7] *Heartbreak Radio* debuts at its UK #36 peak.
[28] ***King Of Hearts***, comprising further cuts recorded for Virgin, makes UK #23 in its week of entry.
Dec [26] ***King Of Hearts*** peaks at US #179.

ORCHESTRAL MANŒUVRES IN THE DARK

Andy McCluskey (vocals);
Paul Humphreys (synthesizers)

1977

Sept Liverpool, Merseyside schoolfriends McCluskey (b. June 24, 1959, Wirral, Cheshire) and Humphreys (b. Feb. 27, 1960, London), having played together and separately in various short-lived school bands including Hitlerz Underpantz and Equinox, for whom McCluskey has written *Orchestral Manœuvres In The Dark*, jointly form Id, with Gary Hodgson (guitar), Steve Hollis (bass), and Malcolm Holmes (drums). The group performs several songs which will later emerge in the OMD repertoire, and boasts eight transient members during its year of existence. One Id track, *Julia's Song* (with lyrics by ex-member Julia Kneale), is recorded for inclusion on the Open Eye label compilation, ***Street To Street - A Liverpool Album*** which will be released in July 1979.

1978

Aug The Id splits, and McCluskey joins local

experimental band Dalek I Love You as vocalist, but will stay for only a month before becoming disillusioned by the band's chaotic approach, and leaves to work in the Customs and Excise office at Liverpool Docks, following which he and Humphreys decide to start a new group, initially named VCL XI after the valve number depicted on a Kraftwerk album.
Oct [12] Their first gig - regarded by the duo more as a self-indulgent, synthesizer-led experiment in non-group music - is at the seminal Liverpool club Eric's. They perform with the help of Paul Collister and backing tracks provided by their tape recorder "Winston", as Orchestral Manœuvres In The Dark (after McCluskey's old song), chosen as the most self-indulgent name they can think of. Their first recordings are made on Collister's TEAC 4-track tape deck.

1979

June OMD's *Electricity* is released on the Manchester-based independent Factory label in a 5,000 pressing, which quickly sells out and leads to a more permanent contract with DinDisc, a label set up by Virgin Records' boss Richard Branson to have an all-female staff, which will immediately reissue *Electricity*.
Aug OMD plays at an all-day open air concert in Leigh, Gtr. Manchester, with A Certain Ratio, Echo & the Bunnymen, Joy Division and Teardrop Explodes, before an estimated audience of 300.
Sept [8-9] They take part in the "Futurama" festival at the Queens Hall, Leeds, S. Yorks.
[20] The group begins a 13-date UK tour supporting Gary Numan at the Apollo Theatre, Glasgow, Scotland.
Dec [7-8] They support Talking Heads at London's Electric Ballroom.

1980

Feb OMD's second single, *Red Frame White Light*, debuts at UK #67.
[15] The group's first headlining tour opens at Eric's, Liverpool.
Mar Their debut album, the synth-dominated ***Orchestral Manœuvres In The Dark***, recorded in their own Liverpool studio, peaks at UK #27.
May *Messages* reaches UK #13.
[9] The group begins a ten-date UK tour at Manchester's Russell Club, ending at the Cedar Ballroom, Edinburgh, Scotland, on the 23rd.
Oct Self-penned (as with all of its hit material) *Enola Gay*, titled after the plane which dropped the atomic bomb on Hiroshima, hits UK #8.
Nov Its sophomore effort, ***Organisation***, hits UK #6. Augmented by Dave Hughes on synthesizer and Malcolm Holmes on drums, OMD tours Britain, the rest of Europe and the US through early 1981, during which Hughes leaves and is replaced by Martin Cooper.

1981

Oct *Souvenir* hits UK #3.
Nov ***Architecture And Morality***, co-produced by the band with Richard Manwaring, also hits UK #3, during a 39-week chart run.
Dec Anthemic, synthesizer-heavy *Joan Of Arc* hits UK #5.

1982

Feb *Maid Of Orleans*, a sequel to *Joan Of Arc*, hits UK #4. Released on Epic Records in the US, ***Architecture And Morality*** peaks at US #144. McCluskey and Humphreys will spend much of the year in their studio, working on a fourth album.

1983

Mar *Genetic Engineering* reaches UK #20, as ***Dazzle Ships*** hits UK #5. (DinDisc is now absorbed by Virgin, which releases all of the band's future product in Britain.)
Apr *Telegraph* makes UK #42.
May ***Dazzle Ships*** peaks at US #162.

1984

May *Locomotion* hits UK #5, as ***Junk Culture*** begins a 27-week UK chart run, during which it hits #9.
July *Talking Loud And Clear* reaches UK #11.
Sept *Tesla Girls* makes UK #21. (Nikolai Tesla is one of the pioneers of electrical technology.)
Nov *Never Turn Away* peaks at UK #70 as ***Junk Culture***, released via their new US deal with A&M Records, makes US #182.
Dec After touring Europe, the US, Japan and Australia in the past two years, Humphreys decides the pressure is too great and that he will quit and settle down with his American wife. Ten days later he has changed his mind and is back in OMD.

1985

June Ballad *So In Love* reaches UK #27, as ***Crush***, featuring latest recruits, brothers Graham and Neil Weir, and produced by Stephen Hague, makes UK #13.
July [7] OMD, with Aswad and Working Week, performs a free concert in London's Battersea Park, as part of Greater London Council's "Jobs For A Change" scheme.
Aug *Secret* makes UK #34. The group becomes more popular in the US, partly as a result of support tours for acts including the Thompson Twins and Power Station.
Oct *So In Love* is OMD's first US singles success, peaking at #26. The group begins a series of anti-racism concerts with other artists in Europe.
Dec *La Femme Accident* makes UK #42.

1986

Feb [1] *Secrets* peaks at US #63, as ***Crush*** makes US #38.
[2] A 17-date UK tour begins at the Empire Theatre, Liverpool, set to end on the 24th and 25th with dates at London's Hammersmith Odeon.
May *If You Leave* makes UK #48. McCluskey says in an interview, "America is the only place where we're still hip."
[31] *If You Leave*, featured on the soundtrack of John Hughes' film "Pretty In Pink", hits US #4.
July Band performs at the "Festival Of The Tenth Summer" in Manchester.
Oct *(Forever) Live And Die* makes UK #11. Once again helmed by Hague, ***The Pacific Age*** reaches UK #15 and US #47, after which the Weir brothers leave the line-up.
Nov *We Love You* peaks at UK #54.
Dec [6] *(Forever) Live And Die* reaches US #19. *Shame* will peak at UK #52 the following May.

1988

Feb *Dreaming* makes UK #50, and #60 when reissued six months later. Virgin Video releases "The Best Of OMD" video clips package.
Mar [19] ***In The Dark - The Best Of OMD*** begins a 30-week UK chart run, hitting #2, and makes US #46.
May [21] *Dreaming* reaches US #16.

1989

Sept McCluskey guests on producer Arthur Baker's newly-released album, ***The Message Of Love***. (Humphreys leaves the band and will form his own group, the Listening Pool, with former bandmates Martin Cooper and Martin Holmes and will release the album ***Still Life*** on its own Telegraph label, leaving McCluskey as the only Orchestral Manœuvre.)

1991

Mar [11] ***The Best Of OMD*** is certified gold by the RIAA.
May [11] *Sailing On The Seven Seas*, OMD's first outing with McCluskey as sole custodian, hits UK #3.
July [1] OMD, now comprising McCluskey, Abe Juckes (drums), and Nigel Ipinson and Phil Coxon (keyboards), begins a UK tour at the Apollo Theatre, Oxford, Oxon., set to end on the 20th at the Empire Theatre, Liverpool.
[3] The band guests on BBC1-TV's "Wogan".
[27] *Pandora's Box* hits UK #7.
Aug [3] OMD takes part in the "Cities In The Park Festival" at Heaton Park, Prestwich, Lancs.
[17] ***Sugar Tax***, produced by OMD with Andy Richards and Howard Gray, hits UK #3.
[24] The group supports Simple Minds at the Milton Keynes Bowl, Milton Keynes, Bucks.
Sept [15] A North American tour opens at the Concert Hall, Toronto, ON, Canada.
[21] *Then You Turn Away* makes UK #50.
Oct [15] An 11-date UK series begins at the Newport Centre, Newport, Gwent, Wales, set to end on the 29th at the Northgate Arena, Chester, Cheshire.
Dec [7] *Call My Name* debuts at its UK #50 peak.

1993

Apr [30] McCluskey joins with Kirsty MacColl on a duet of Mott The Hoople's *Roll Away The Stone* at a party to celebrate the launch of Virgin Radio, at the Piccadilly Theatre, London.
May [22] *Stand Above Me* reaches UK #21.
June [26] Co-produced by McCluskey with Phil Coxon at Liverpool's Amazone Studio, ***Liberator*** debuts at its UK #14 peak.
July [17] ***Liberator*** charts for a week at US #169.
[24] *Dream Of Me*, based on Barry White's *Love's Theme*, reaches UK #24.
Sept [18] *Everyday* debuts at its UK #59 peak.
Dec [4] A seven-date UK tour opens at the Glasgow SE&CC, set to end on the 12th at Wembley Arena.

TONY ORLANDO & DAWN

Tony Orlando (vocals); **Joyce Vincent Wilson** (vocals); **Telma Hopkins** (vocals)

1960

Orlando (b. Michael Anthony Orlando Cassivitis, Apr. 3, 1944, Manhattan, New York, NY), of Greek/Puerto Rican heritage, has been singing with local doo-wop group the Five Gents, and has cut demos for a music publisher in the late '50s. Having met Don Kirshner at Aldon Music, Orlando is now teamed with young writer Carole King to sing demos of her compositions. An early King song, *Halfway To Paradise*, written with Gerry Goffin, is sold to Epic Records.

1961

June Epic's release of Orlando's demo of *Halfway To Paradise*, produced by Kirshner, makes US #39 (while in the UK, Billy Fury will hit #3 with his version).
Oct Barry Mann/Cynthia Weil-penned *Bless You* reaches US #15.
Nov *Bless You* hits UK #5.
Dec *Happy Times (Are Here To Stay)*, Orlando's last for Epic, peaks at US #82.

1962

Feb [9] Orlando begins a 15-date, twice-nightly UK tour with Bobby Vee, Clarence "Frogman" Henry, the Springfields and others, at the Gaumont Cinema, Doncaster, S. Yorks, set to end on the 25th at the Winter Gardens, Bournemouth, Dorset.

1963

Having had little further success, Orlando finds work at music publishers Robbins, Feist and Miller, and also gets married. Spending the next seven years in the music publishing world, he will work for Clive Davis at April-Blackwood publishers from 1968, where he is involved with writers James Taylor and Laura Nyro.

1970

May Bell Records is interested in releasing *Candida*, produced by Hank Medress and Dave Appell, by the unknown trio Dawn (named after Bell boss Wes Farrell's daughter), but are unhappy with the lead singer. They keep the backing vocal track by session singers Hopkins (b. Oct. 28, 1948, Louisville, KY) and ex-Debonaires Wilson (b. Dec. 14, 1946, Detroit, MI), and Medress and Appell ask Orlando to record the lead vocal. He hears the results two months later on New York radio as the disc is taking off.
Sept [30] *Candida* is certified gold by the RIAA.
Oct *Candida* hits US #3.

Dec *Candida* reaches US #35.
[16] The still-rising *Knock Three Times* is also confirmed gold by the RIAA.

1971

Jan [23] Follow-up *Knock Three Times*, written by Irwin Levine and L. Russell Brown, hits US #1 for the first of three weeks. It features Orlando on lead vocals and has been released under the group name Dawn, though Orlando has still not met Hopkins and Wilson, who recorded the backing vocals in California. Orlando finally meets the girls through producer Tony Camillo, and insists on forming a full-time unit for promotion and touring.
Feb *Candida* hits UK #9.
Apr *I Play And Sing* makes US #25.
May [15] *Knock Three Times* tops the UK chart for the first of five weeks during a 27-week survey stay.
July *Summer Sand* reaches US #33.
Aug *What Are You Doing Sunday* hits UK #3.
Sept [20] The trio makes its UK cabaret debut with a week-long stint at the Talk of the Town, Manchester, Gtr. Manchester.
Nov *What Are You Doing Sunday* makes US #39.
Dec ***Dawn Featuring Tony Orlando*** stops at US #178. *Runaway/Happy Together* will reach US #79 the following February with *Vaya Con Dios* peaking at US #95 in July.

1973

Jan *You're A Lady* peaks at US #70, pipped by Peter Skellern's original version at US #50.
Mar ***Tuneweaving*** reaches US #30.
Apr [2] The still-rising *Tie A Yellow Ribbon Round The Old Oak Tree* is certified gold by the single.
[21] Dawn has recorded *Tie A Yellow Ribbon Round The Old Oak Tree*, based on a true tale of a convict returning home to White Oak, GA, hoping to see a sign that his wife still loves him, which begins a four-week stay atop both the US and UK charts. (It will be the year's best-selling single, with sales of over six-million copies internationally, and will produce over 1,000 cover versions.)
Sept *Say, Has Anybody Seen My Sweet Gypsy Rose* hits US #3 and reaches UK #12.
Oct ***Dawn's New Ragtime Follies*** makes US #43.
[9] *Say, Has Anybody Seen My Sweet Gypsy Rose* is certified gold by the RIAA.
Dec *Who's In The Strawberry Patch With Sally* reaches US #27.

1974

Feb [19] They collect the Favorite Single, Pop/Rock trophy at the inaugural American Music Awards, held at the Civic Auditorium, Santa Monica, CA.
Mar [2] Fred Silverman, head of programming for CBS-TV, sees Dawn perform *Tie A Yellow Ribbon Round The Old Oak Tree* at the 16th annual Grammy Awards, and subsequently offers the trio a four-week summer tryout variety series. ("Tony Orlando And Dawn" will air for two seasons.)
[9] Now credited as Tony Orlando & Dawn, *Who's In The Strawberry Patch With Sally* makes UK #37.
Apr *It Only Hurts When I Try To Smile* peaks at US #81.
May [18] ***Golden Ribbons*** makes UK #46.
Oct *Steppin' Out (Gonna Boogie Tonight)* hits US #7, as its parent album, ***Prime Time***, climbs to US #16, bringing the group's worldwide sales to over 25 million.

1975

Jan The trio's first two albums, combined as ***Candida & Knock Three Times***, are reissued, making US #170, while ***Tony Orlando & Dawn II*** stops at US #165.
Feb *Look In My Eyes Pretty Woman* reaches US #11.
Apr [1] ***Tuneweaving*** is confirmed gold by the RIAA.
May [3] Dawn has moved with Bell promotion man and friend Steve Wax to Elektra Records, as the group's cover of Jerry Butler's 1960 US Top 10 smash, *He Don't Love You (Like I Love You)*, tops the US chart for the first of three weeks. ***He Don't Love You (Like I Love You)*** is also released, reaching US #20.
June ***Tony Orlando And Dawn's Greatest Hits*** reaches US #16.
[9] *He Don't Love You (Like I Love You)* is certified gold by the RIAA.
Aug *Mornin' Beautiful* reaches US #14.
Sept *You're All I Need To Get By*, a 1968 US #7 for Marvin Gaye and Tammi Terrell, makes US #34.
[24] ***Tony Orlando And Dawn's Greatest Hits*** is certified gold by the RIAA.
Nov ***Skybird*** peaks at US #93, as its extracted title track, *Skybird*, makes US #49.

1976

Jan [31] They win the Favorite Band, Duo Or Group, Pop/Rock category at the third annual American Music Awards, again held at the Santa Monica Civic Auditorium.
Mar Their cover of Sam Cooke's 1961 US #7, *Cupid*, reaches US #22.
Apr ***To Be With You*** makes US #94.

1977

Apr [23] *Sing* peaks at US #58.
May [30] Orlando participates in the "Muhammad Ali Invitational Track Meet" at Cerritos College, Norwalk, CA, aired on CBS-TV, with Ali, Angel Cordero and Marvin Gaye, who wins the event.
July [22] During a performance at "The Music Show" in Cohasset, MA, Orlando stuns Hopkins and Wilson, announcing to the audience that "this is my last day as a performer". (His close friend, comedian Freddie Prinze, has recently committed suicide, and his 21-year-old sister Rhonda has also died.)
Nov No longer with Dawn, Orlando returns to playing the Las Vegas, NV circuit.

1979

Aug Orlando, now signed to Casablanca Records, makes US #54 with *Sweets For My Sweet*.
Sept Hopkins embarks on a TV acting career in ABC-TV's "A New Kind of Family" (and will also appear regularly in "Bosom Buddies" and "Gimme A Break"), as Orlando makes his acting debut in the TV movie "Three Hundred Miles For Stephanie" and guests on "The Cosby Show".

1981

Jan When American hostages are returned from 444 days in captivity in Iran, the American public revives Dawn's lasting image of welcoming them home with yellow ribbons.
Orlando takes over the leading role in "Barnum" on Broadway, while Jim Dale is on vacation.
Nov [15] Orlando joins a star cast in "Hey, Look Me Over!", a one-off benefit for the American Musical and Dramatic Academy at the Avery Fisher Hall, New York.

1990

Sept While Orlando, Hopkins and Wilson re-formed to perform at Trumps in Atlantic City, NJ, in August 1988 (though Hopkins will continue her acting career, starring in the ABC-TV series "Family Matters") and the trio continues to appear as a nostalgia act, *Tie A Yellow Ribbon Round The Old Oak Tree* is named one of the BMI's Most Performed Songs Of 1940-1990, when it surpasses the three million performance plateau.

JEFFREY OSBORNE

1970

Osborne (b. Mar. 9, 1948, Providence, RI), having been a regular at the Ebony Lounge, New London, CT nightspot, and taught himself to play drums at the age of 15, then singing and drumming with local bands, is offered the chance to join R&B troupe L.T.D. (Love, Togetherness and Devotion), a ten-man funk group from Greensboro, NC, after he sits in with the group on a tour date in Providence, following an incident when their original drummer has been hauled off to jail for fighting. Despite being married with two young daughters, he follows his mother's advice to grab the opportunity and becomes L.T.D.'s lead singer. Initially touring on the US R&B circuit, Osborne supplements his income in the early '70s with session work for the likes of Smokey Robinson and the Sylvers, before L.T.D. signs a production deal with Jerry Butler's Foundation Records and, signed to A&M Records, releases ***Love, Togetherness And Devotion*** in 1974, followed by ***Gettin' Down*** in 1975. With their opening chart salvo, *Love Ballad* (US #20 in 1976), the group begins five years of US R&B and pop success including five further chart singles, including the US #4 *(Every Time I Turn Around) Back In Love Again*, and five US chart albums: ***Love To The World*** (#52, 1976), ***Something To Love*** (#21, 1977), ***Togetherness*** (#18, a platinum seller the following year), ***Devotion*** (1979) and ***Shine On*** (#28, 1980). The extracted title track and soul ballad *Shine On*, on which Osborne's vocals gleam, will reach US #40 in January 1981, the group's last chart single.

1982

Jan ***Love Magic*** makes US #83, following which Osborne, clearly established as the leading voice in the group, leaves, replaced by Leslie Wilson and André Ray. He remains with A&M as a solo artist.
Aug His debut solo album, ***Jeffrey Osborne***, produced by George Duke, makes US #49 as the extracted *I Really Don't Need No Light* reaches US #39.
Dec Also from the album, his soaring ballad, *On The Wings Of Love*, reaches US #29.

1983

Apr *Eenie Meenie* peaks at US #76.
Sept *Don't You Get So Mad*, from Osborne's sophomore album ***Stay With Me Tonight***, reaches US #25 and UK #54, his first solo UK chart entry.

1984

Jan Funky *Stay With Me Tonight*, the Raymond Jones-penned title cut, reaches US #30.
Mar ***Stay With Me Tonight***, again helmed by Duke, reaches US #25 after more than six months on the chart, becoming his first solo gold album.
Apr *We're Going All The Way*, written by Barry Mann and Cynthia Weil, and taken from the album, makes US #48.
May *Stay With Me Tonight* reaches UK #18, while the parent album ***Stay With Me Tonight*** makes UK #56.
July *On The Wings Of Love* belatedly reaches UK #11.
Oct Osborne's duet with Joyce Kennedy, on *The Last Time I Made Love*, makes US #40. (She is ex-soul group Mother's Finest, whose first solo album, ***Lookin' For Trouble***, is Osborne's first venture into production. The album peaks at US #79, and will earn him a producer's Grammy nomination.) *Don't Stop* peaks at UK #61, while its parent set, ***Don't Stop***, makes UK #59.
Dec ***Don't Stop*** and *Don't Stop* peak at US #39 and #44 respectively. A second cut from the album, *The Borderlines*, will reach US #38 in March the following year.

1986

Aug Politically-themed *Soweto* makes UK #44, taken from ***Emotional***, on which Osborne has worked with producers Richard Perry, Michael Masser and Rod Temperton, in addition to long-time collaborator George Duke. Three of the tracks are also self-produced, as Osborne builds on the studio experience gained from working with Kennedy. The album peaks at US #26, becoming his third US gold disc.
[23] *You Should Be Mine (The Woo Woo Song)*, written by Andy Goldmark and Bruce Roberts, reaches US #13.

1987

Feb Osborne sings a spine-tingling a cappella *The Star-Spangled Banner*, prior to the NBA All-Star game in Seattle, WA.
Aug [29] *Love Power*, duetting with Dionne Warwick, reaches US #12.

1988

Aug After a two-year recording hiatus, during which Osborne has spent more time with second wife Sheri and daughter Tiffany, he returns with ***One Love - One Dream***, again with a variety of co-producers, including Roberts, who also co-writes with Osborne, Goldmark, Ross Vannelli and David "Hawk" Wolinski.

Sept [24] The dance-tempo *She's On The Left* tops the US R&B chart, while ***One Love - One Dream*** climbs to US #86.

1989

June [22] Osborne duets with Michael Bolton on *You've Lost That Lovin' Feelin'* at the Songwriters' Hall of Fame Awards, held at New York, NY's Radio City Music Hall.

Sept Osborne is featured on the movie soundtrack, ***Rooftops***.

Nov Now signed to Clive Davis' Arista Records, Osborne is initiated via a duet with labelmate Dionne Warwick on the ballad, *Take Good Care Of You And Me*.

1990

Feb [14] "In Performance At The White House" from the East Room, and as part of the President's Day celebration, featuring Osborne and others, airs on PBS-TV.

[16] His debut Arista solo album, ***Only Human***, peaks at US #95. Mainly produced and arranged by Barry Eastmond, it includes guest appearances from Joey Diggs, Vincent Henry and Grover Washington Jr.

Mar [17] Osborne and a host of labelmates take part in Arista Records 15th Anniversary at Radio City Music Hall's "That's What Friends Are For" concert, raising more than $2 million, the proceeds going to Gay Men's Health Crisis and other AIDS organisations. (The show will air on CBS-TV on April 17th.)

1991

Feb [10] Osborne joins with nearly 100 celebrities in Burbank, CA, to record *Voices That Care*, a David Foster and fiancée Linda Thompson Jenner-composed and organized charity record, to benefit the American Red Cross Gulf Crisis Fund.

[19] He performs at an Arista Records' dinner at New York's Plaza Hotel, and is joined by Lisa Stansfield and Michael Bolton on *You Should Be Mine (The Woo Woo Song)*.

Apr [9] Osborne sings the National Anthem on the opening day of the Oakland A's 1991 baseball season against the Minnesota Twins, at the Oakland-Alameda County Coliseum, Oakland.

May [28] He plays a one-off London date at the Town & Country Club.

Dec [11] Osborne is the guest performer at the Brotherhood Crusade Black United Fund ceremony, at the Beverly Hilton Hotel, Beverly Hills, CA.

1992

Jan [7] An all-star cast records Osborne's *The Heart Of A Hero* in Los Angeles, CA, to raise money for AIDS research.

Feb [19] He performs at the first annual Pro Set Los Angeles Music Awards, at the Civic Auditorium, Santa Monica, CA.

Apr [28] Osborne participates in the recording of ***Hallelujah!***, Quincy Jones' contemporary reading of Handel's "The Messiah", at A&M Studios, Hollywood.

June He guests on *Loving Every Moment* from Najee's current ***Just An Illusion*** album.

1993

Apr [5] Osborne sings the national anthem at the Oakland A's vs. Detroit Tigers season opener at the Oakland-Alameda County Coliseum.

1994

Apr [30] Having toured as part of last December's "The Colors Of Christmas" US R&B package tour with Roberta Flack, Peabo Bryson and Patti Austin, Osbourne, who has not released an album since 1990, performs in an all-star version of *Get On Up*, with the likes of Bruce Springsteen, Steve Cropper and noted singers Magic Johnson and Woody Harrelson, at the end of the opening night of the House of Blues on Los Angeles' Sunset Boulevard.

JOAN OSBORNE

1994

Nov One of six children born to their building contractor father Jerry and seamstress mother Ruth, singer-guitarist Osborne (b. 1963, Anchorage, KY) first sung in her local church-choir in the bible-belt town of Anchorage as a child. Studying at the film school of New York University, NY, she has dropped out in 1986. Two years later, and taking a bet from friends, Osborne goes onstage at the Abilene club in New York and sings *God Bless The Child*, the only song she and the piano player knew. Spending the next six years singing and playing gospel-tinged blues in Manhattan clubs and recording her debut album, a live set released on her own Womanly Hips label in 1992, she has been spotted performing in Philadelphia, PA by the Hooters' Rob Hyman who contacts Rick Chertoff, senior VP at Polygram Holdings. Chertoff promptly signs her to his recently formed imprint, Blue Gorilla label, pairing her with Hyman and fellow Hooter Eric Bazilian to record her label debut.

1995

May [10] Osborne performs at the PNE Coliseum, Vancouver, BC, Canada, opening for Melissa Etheridge.

Aug Recorded at Big Blue studio, Katonah, NY, her 12-track album ***Relish*** is released. Produced by Rick Chertoff, it mostly co-written with him, keyboardist Hyman and guitarist/harmonica player Bazilian, and includes *Ladder* which samples Marc Bolan's *Mambo Sun*.

Oct [16] A US tour with Rusted Root reaches the Symphony Hall, Civic Center, Springfield, MA, a bill grossing $48,204 from a 2,472 crowd.

1996

Jan [13] Osborne is the music guest on NBC-TV's "Saturday Night Live".

[17] She sings *I Heard It Through The Grapevine* in duet with Stevie Wonder at the traditional post-dinner jam following the 11th annual Rock and Roll Hall of Fame induction dinner, held at New York's Waldorf Astoria Hotel.

[30] Once again opening for Etheridge, Osborne plays at London's Shepherd's Bush Empire.

Feb [3] Swarming US radio, her breakthrough hit *One Of Us*, written solely by Bazilian, hits US #4.

[6] Hollywood Records (US) releases the soundtrack to "Mr. Wrong", including *Strenuous Acquaintances*, a new cut by Osborne.

[28] She performs the nominated *One Of Us* at the 38th annual Grammy Awards held at Los Angeles, CA's Shrine Auditorium, but will lose out in all of her five nominated categories.

Mar [9] ***Relish*** bows at its UK #5 peak.

[16] In its 28th chart week, ***Relish*** finally hits US #9.

Apr [28] Already a supporter of various causes including Rock For Choice, Planned Parenthood and the Brooklyn-based Park Slope Safe Homes Project, Osborne performs at the 1996 VH1 Honors event, a live broadcast concert to benefit human rights organization Witness held at the Universal Amphitheatre, Universal City, CA.

OZZY OSBOURNE

1967

Osbourne (b. John Osbourne, Dec. 3, 1948, Aston, Warks.), one of six children raised in the industrial North of England by his mother and factory-working father, whose early career as a burglar is halted by two months served in Winson Green Prison at age 17, takes a job in a slaughterhouse, but soon becomes unemployed. With three other Birmingham youths, Tony Iommi, Terry Butler and Bill Ward, and as its lead singer, he forms Polka Tulk, which becomes Earth before taking its permanent name from one of their early songs, *Black Sabbath*. After the release of their eponymous debut album in 1970, Black Sabbath will become a hugely successful rock act, helping to define the new genre of heavy metal. The group, and Osbourne in particular also set new standards for the hard-rock lifestyle with their voluminous consumption of alcohol and drugs.

1978

Osbourne leaves Black Sabbath after seven albums, following a major row with group member Tony Iommi. He is replaced by ex-Savoy Brown vocalist Dave Walker, before returning briefly later in the year after plans to form a band with guitarist Gary Moore and ex-Deep Purple bassist Glenn Hughes fall through.

1980

July Now permanently split from Sabbath, Osbourne signs a solo deal with Jet Records, with an album already recorded with his new band, the Blizzard of Ozz, comprising ex-Quiet Riot guitarist Randy Rhoads, ex-Rainbow bassist Bob Daisley, and ex-Uriah Heep drummer Lee Kerslake. Jet is owned by Don Arden, who has recently ceased to handle Black Sabbath.

Aug [14] The group begins a UK mini-tour, which will include an appearance at the annual "Reading Festival", Reading, Berks. at the Nite Club, during the "Edinburgh Rock Festival" in Edinburgh, Scotland.

Sept *Crazy Train* makes UK #49, as its parent album, the self-penned ***Ozzy Osbourne's Blizzard Of Ozz***, hits UK #7.

Nov *Mr. Crowley*, written about occultist Aleister Crowley, makes UK #46, spurred by warm-up gigs under the name Law.

1981

Apr ***Blizzard Of Ozz*** enters the US chart, where it will stay for two years and peak at #21, also earning platinum status in the process.

May Osbourne begins a US tour with a new Blizzard of Ozz. Kerslake and Daisley have left to join Uriah Heep, and are replaced by Tommy Aldridge (b. Aug. 15, 1950, Nashville, TN), Florida-raised, ex-Black Oak Arkansas, Pat Travers Band and Gary Moore's band, on drums, and Rudy Sarzo (b. Nov. 9, 1952, Havana, Cuba), ex-Quiet Riot and Angel, on bass. (In a notorious incident Osbourne bites the head off a live dove before assembled CBS/Columbia executives at a meeting in Los Angeles, CA.)

Aug The group returns to Britain to headline the "Heavy Metal Holocaust" at Stoke-On-Trent, Staffs., following Black Sabbath's withdrawal.

Nov Osbourne's second album, ***Diary Of A Madman***, the title taken from Crowley's autobiography, reaches UK #14 and US #16, earning a second US platinum disc.

Dec He cancels a UK tour because of strain and personal problems.

1982

Jan Daisley returns, replacing Aldridge, and Don Airey (ex-Rainbow) is added on keyboards.

[20] At the beginning of a US tour, Osbourne bites the head off a bat during a show in Des Moines, IA - the bat bites back and Osbourne reportedly has to undergo a rabies injection.

Mar [19] During high jinks near Orlando, FL, the party's tour plane is buzzing their bus, making mock dive-bomb runs. On the last run the wing of the plane clips the bus and it is thrown out of control and crashes into a house, killing 25-year-old Randy Rhoads, Osbourne's hairdresser Rachel Youngblood, and pilot Andrew Aycock. (Osbourne decides to complete the tour, bringing in ex-Gillan guitarist Bernie Torme as a temporary replacement for Rhoads.)

May ***Mr. Crowley***, a picture-disc live EP, enters the US album chart, reaching #120 during an 18-week stay. Black Sabbath is preparing to release ***Live At Last***, which features performances of old songs with Dio on vocals, who claims the songs are his own. Osbourne books two nights at The Ritz in New York, NY, with Aldridge, Sarzo and Brad Gillis (guitar), and records a double album's worth of old Sabbath numbers, which will be released as ***Talk Of The Devil***.
June Jake E. Lee, ex-Los Angeles band Rough Cutt, joins Osbourne's group on guitar.
July [4] Osbourne marries Don Arden's daughter Sharon, who is now his personal manager (having left his wife Thelma in 1981), in Maui, HI. Aldridge is best man.
Nov ***Talk Of The Devil*** enters the UK chart, peaking at #21.
Dec [10] The seven-date "Talk Of The Devil" tour begins at the St. Austell Coliseum, St. Austell, Cornwall, set to end on the 20th at the Royal Court Theatre, Liverpool, Merseyside.

1983

Jan ***Talk Of The Devil*** reaches US #14.
May [28] The Ozzy Osbourne Band plays at the "US Festival' in CA. Following a tour and new recording sessions, Aldridge leaves again, replaced by Carmine Appice, ex-Vanilla Fudge, as Sharon and Don Arden quarrel over management issues. She assumes full management control of Osbourne's affairs, encouraging him to sign with CBS/Columbia in the US and Epic in the UK. Family relations will remain strained.
Dec *Bark At The Moon* enters the UK chart, to peak at #21, aided by a werewolf transformation video, a device which also becomes popular on stage. Its parent album, ***Bark At The Moon***, reaches US #19 and UK #24.

1984

Feb During the month, splintered glass from a broken mirror used in the filming of the video for the single *So Tired* lodges in Osbourne's throat, but there are no permanent ill effects, although he will postpone eight dates of a US tour.
Mar Appice leaves the group and Aldridge returns for another extensive tour.
June Ballad *So Tired* reaches UK #20, as Osbourne is urged by his wife to enter the Betty Ford Clinic for treatment of drug and alcohol dependency.

1985

Jan Osbourne and the Blizzard of Ozz play at the "Rock In Rio" festival at the Barra da Tijua, Rio de Janeiro, Brazil. Airey is no longer with the group and, after the festival, Aldridge quits, never to return. Daisley follows, but will continue to help in studio recordings. Osbourne recruits drummer Randy Castillo, from Lita Ford's band, and bassist Phil Soussan, with recent recruit San Diegan Don Costa (guitar).
July [13] Osbourne, Tony Iommi, Geezer Butler and Bill Ward re-form for a day as Black Sabbath to play at the "Live Aid" benefit in Philadelphia, PA. (The day before the concert Osbourne was served with a writ from Don Arden, charging that he is trying to re-form Sabbath as a performing unit and claiming $1.5 million in damages. The band plays on and Arden loses the suit.)

1986

Jan Ozzy Osbourne's autobiography, **Diary Of A Madman**, is published.
Feb *Shot In The Dark* reaches UK #20, as parent album, ***The Ultimate Sin***, hits UK #8.
[12] Osbourne begins his first full UK tour in three years at City Hall, Newcastle, Tyne & Wear, set to end 15 dates later on March 4th at St. George's Hall, Bradford, S. Yorks.
Apr [26] *Shot In The Dark* peaks at US #68.
May Osbourne embarks on tours of the US and Japan.
June ***The Ultimate Sin*** hits US #6.
Aug Title track, *The Ultimate Sin/Lightning Strikes*, spends a week at UK #72 as Osbourne takes a break from his US tour to appear at the "Monsters Of Rock" heavy metal festival at Castle Donington, Leics.
Dec [19] A California Superior court judge denies a motion to reinstate a lawsuit served on January 13th against Osbourne and CBS Inc., which had sought to implicate Osbourne in the suicide of Californian teenager John McCollum, who it was claimed had been influenced by the lyrics of Osbourne's *Suicide Solution*. Judge John L. Cole states that the case involved areas "clearly protected by the First Amendment".

1987

Mar In a parody of the attention he has received from fundamentalist US Christian groups, Osbourne plays a Bible-bashing preacher in the premiering heavy metal film "Trick Or Treat".
Apr Osbourne is mugged in New York's Times Square, by a thief who thrusts a knife through the open window of the taxi he is in.
[3] "The Ultimate Ozzy" video is certified gold by the RIAA.
May [23] Double album, ***Tribute***, dedicated to Randy Rhoads and consisting of live recordings from 1981 featuring Rhoads' guitar playing, reaches UK #13.
June ***Tribute*** hits US #6.
July [17] Osbourne begins a 16-week tour of prisons, highlighted by a heavy metal version of *Jailhouse Rock*.

1988

Feb Osbourne recruits a new guitarist, 21-year-old Zakk Wylde (b. Jan. 14, 1967, NJ), who has been teaching guitar in New Jersey. During preparations for a new album Soussan quits, leaving Castillo on drums, John Sinclair on keyboards, and Daisley as a studio-only bassist.
Apr [10] Osbourne announces he would like to tour the world's insane asylums.
July [18] A California appeals court upholds a decision to dismiss a wrongful death suit brought against the singer by the parents of a suicide victim.
Oct [22] ***No Rest For The Wicked***, produced by Roy Thomas Baker, reaches UK #23 in its week of entry, and will reach US #13. Osbourne embarks on a two-month US tour, opening in Omaha, NE (and ending in Long Beach, CA), after which he will return to domestic life with his wife and three children at their 18th-century Buckinghamshire home.
Dec [8] Osbourne plays at the Meadowlands Arena, East Rutherford, NJ, during a major US tour, with current band line-up Zakk Wylde, Geezer Butler and Randy Castillo.

1989

Mar [29] "Wicked Videos" is certified gold by the RIAA.
Apr [17] ***No Rest For The Wicked*** is certified platinum by the RIAA.
June [4] Osbourne donates $15,000 to AIDS research after a concert in Philadelphia.
[17] Heavy metal ballad duet with peroxide axeiste Lita Ford, *Close My Eyes Forever*, hits US #8, having spent a week at UK #75 last December.
Aug [12-13] Osbourne participates in the "Moscow Music Peace Festival" at Lenin Stadium with Bon Jovi, Mötley Crüe, the Scorpions, Cinderella, Skid Row, and from the USSR, Gorky Park, Nuance, CCCP and Brigada S. All proceeds go to programs that fight drug and alcohol abuse in the US and USSR.
Sept [2] He is charged with threatening to kill his wife, but is released on condition he immediately go into detox and stay away from her. The case is dropped when the couple decide to reconcile.

1990

Mar Osbourne guest stars in Sam Kinison's "Under My Thumb" video as the Judge. (Paul Williams acts as defense attorney.)
[17] Live album ***Just Say Ozzy***, recorded at London's Brixton Academy, makes UK #69 and US #58.
Aug [18] Old material issued on Priority, released as ***Ten Commandments***, debuts at its US #163 peak.
Oct Butler leaves the band.
[4-5] Two cases are filed in Macon, GA against Osbourne and CBS by the parents of teenagers Michael Waller and Harold Hamilton, who shot themselves in the head, Waller in May 1986 and Hamilton in March 1988.
Nov [14] A motion is filed to dismiss the suit.
He joins Frank Bruno and Billy Connolly for the newly released single *The Urpney Song*, from ITV's cartoon series "The Dreamstone".
Dec Speaking at the Foundation Forum's censorship panel, Osbourne states "if I wrote music for people who shot themselves after listening to my music, I wouldn't have much of a following".
[16] Osbourne makes a cameo appearance on Fox-TV's "Parker Lewis Can't Lose".

1991

Feb [8] Osbourne takes part in KNAC radio station's fifth anniversary concert at the Long Beach Convention & Entertainment Center, Long Beach, with new guitarist Michael Inez making his debut, and supported by Alice In Chains and L.A. Guns.
May [6] Atlanta US District Court Judge Duross Fitzpatrick rules that *Suicide Solution* cannot be proven to have caused Waller to have committed suicide, and is also protected by the First Amendment.
Oct [3-5] Osbourne headlines the Foundations Forum hard rock heavy metal convention at the Los Angeles' Airport Marriott Hotel.
[5] ***No More Tears***, produced by Duane Baron and John Purdell, debuts at its US #7 peak, as the extracted title track, *No More Tears*, reaches UK #32.
[19] ***No More Tears*** bows at its UK #17 pinnacle.
[26] Osbourne breaks his foot onstage during a show on his current "Theater Of Madness" tour at the Aragon Ballroom, Chicago, IL. He plays on in Cleveland, Buffalo and New York, developing an infection in his ankle, which will cause him to cancel the remaining dates.
Nov [30] Autobiographical *Mama I'm Coming Home*, about his unhappy childhood, debuts at its UK #46 peak.

1992

Jan [4] *No More Tears*, co-penned with Motorhead's Lemmy, makes US #71.
[5] Osbourne resumes his "Theater of Madness" tour before a sellout crowd of 4,005 at the Sunrise Musical Theatre, Sunrise, FL.
Mar [20] He performs at London's Brixton Academy, during current UK dates.
[28] Osbourne receives bruises when he invites the first two rows of his audience to join him on stage, but several more rows gate-crash his invitation during the Randy Rhoads memorial concert at the Irvine Meadows Amphitheatre, Laguna Hills, CA. (While he crawls offstage, the mob causes an estimated $100,000 worth of damage.)
Apr [18] *Mama, I'm Coming Home* reaches US #28.
June [9] US leg of the "No More Tours Tour" opens at the Memorial Coliseum, Portland, OR.
July [27] On his demonic public reputation, Osbourne is quoted in **USA Today** saying: "It's a wonder I haven't been blamed for the outbreak of AIDS", while on the subject of drinking he adds "When I hit the bottle the first time, I hated the taste, but the feeling was what I had been looking for all my life".
Aug [11] The RIAA certifies platinum sales of ***Speak Of The Devil*** and ***Tribute*** and two million sales of ***Bark At The Moon***.
[25] Osbourne plays to a sellout crowd of 14,742 at the New Pine Knob Music Theatre, Clarkston, MI.
Sept [25] Two fans are stabbed and 20 arrested at the State Fair Grandstand, Oklahoma City, OK gig. (Sharon Osbourne blames the availability of alcohol at the event.)
Oct [1] The Supreme Court lets stand rulings that Osbourne's free speech rights protect him against lawsuits which allege his music encourages suicides.
[1-2] Osbourne performs at the Joe & Harry Freeman Coliseum, San Antonio, TX, his first concerts in that city in ten years, following an incident when he urinated on a wall at the Alamo. Mayor Nelson Wolff, presumably referring to the decision to let him

perform, says "I think it stinks".
[31] "Halloween Jam At Universal Studios" concert special with Osbourne, the Black Crowes, En Vogue, Slaughter, AC/DC, Jodeci, Sir Mix-A-Lot, Spinal Tap and Cracker airs on ABC-TV.
Nov [14-15] Billed as his last ever live performances, Osbourne's final U.S. dates at the Pacific Amphitheatre, Costa Mesa, CA end with an original Black Sabbath reunion. A thirty-minute Sabbath set features Osbourne, Iommi, Butler and Vinny Appice (minus Dio who "flatly refused" to take part). He is also honored with a star on the Rock Walk on Sunset Boulevard, Hollywood, CA. (In a subsequent quote on retirement, Osbourne will say : "Who wants to be touring at 46? I screwed all the groupies when it was safe ... It's time to go home".)

1993

May [16] Osbourne guests on BBC2's religious program, "Faith & Music".
June [5] He attends the wedding of Mariah Carey and Tommy Mottola at the St. Thomas Episcopal Church on 5th Avenue, New York.
July [3] Two-CD/cassette performance set, ***Live And Loud*** (from the "Theater Of Madness" and "No More Tours" tours), debuts at its US #22 peak.
[21] ***Just Say Ozzy*** is certified gold by the RIAA.
Aug [9] ***Live And Loud*** is also confirmed gold by the RIAA.
Oct [23] Osbourne participates in the recording of "Halloween Jam II" ABC-TV special from Universal Studios.

1994

Mar [1] He wins the Best Metal Performance category for *I Don't Want To Change The World* at the 36th annual Grammy Awards, held at New York's Radio City Music Hall.
[16] Osbourne orders his insurance company to pay $60,000 to electrician Kenneth Allan Winkler, who suffered a shoulder injury at the March 28th, 1992 Newport Beach, CA concert.
[22] The RIAA certifies three million sales of ***Blizzard Of Oz***.
June Osbourne is awarded **Kerrang!**'s Kudos Awards at the inaugural "Kerrang! Great British Heavy Metal Awards" at the Notre Dame Hall in London's Leicester Square. Taking Osbourne's retirement protestations seriously, Wylde releases his first album with his new band, Pride & Glory.
Sept [27] ***Kermit Unpigged***, featuring Osbourne duetting with Miss Piggy on *Born To Be Wild*, is released by Jim Henson Records.
Oct [26] The RIAA certifies multi-platinum sales of ***Diary Of A Madman*** (three million), ***No More Tears*** (three million) and ***The Ultimate Sin*** (two million).
Dec [10] Osbourne invites eight radio contest winners to have dinner at his home in England to celebrate the success of the tribute album ***Nativity In Black : A Tribute To Black Sabbath***.

1995

Aug [26] The no longer retired Osbourne begins his first Latin and South American tour in Monterey, Mexico.
Oct [27] Osbourne plays a sellout show at the Hollywood Palladium, Hollywood, CA, during a short US tour.
Nov [4] ***Ozzmosis***, produced by Michael Beinhorn, reaches UK #22 in its week of entry.
[8] He begins the UK leg of his tour at the Regent Theatre, Ipswich, Suffolk. (The following night's show in Portsmouth will be cancelled when Castillo comes down with tennis elbow, and a show on the 17th will also be cancelled when Osbourne succumbs to laryngitis.)
[11] ***Ozzmosis*** debuts at its US #4 peak.
[25] The extracted *Perry Mason* debuts at its UK #23 peak.
Dec [31] Osbourne's "Retirement Sucks" tour opens at the McNichols Sports Arena, Denver, CO, following a 16-US city and 28-European city warm-up tour.

1996

Jan [7] Following a show at The Summit in Houston, TX, Osbourne gets whiplash and knocked unconscious after his car is rear-ended.
Feb [29] The "Retirement Sucks" tour plays a sellout show at the Great Western Forum, Inglewood, CA.
see also: **BLACK SABBATH**

THE OSMONDS

Alan Osmond (vocals); **Wayne Osmond** (vocals); **Merrill Osmond** (vocals); **Jay Osmond** (vocals); **Donny Osmond** (vocals)

1962

Dec [20] The group has been formed in 1959 as a barber-shop style harmony quartet, by four of the sons of devoted Mormons, George and Olive Osmond - Alan (b. June 22, 1949, Ogden, UT), Wayne (b. Aug. 28, 1951, Ogden), Merrill (b. Apr. 30, 1953, Ogden) and Jay (b. Mar. 2, 1955, Ogden) in their hometown, Ogden, where they sang at their Mormon church's Family Nights. On a visit to Los Angeles, CA, the group has met a professional barber-shop quartet in Disneyland and, after performing impromptu harmonies with them, have been introduced to the park's talent booker, who signs the brothers for the "Disneyland After Dark" show. As the Osmond Brothers, the group now appears for the first time on the new, weekly "Andy Williams Show" on NBC-TV, harmonizing on *I'm A Ding Dong Daddy From Dumas* and *Side By Side*. Six-year-old Donny (b. Donald Osmond, Dec. 9, 1957, Ogden) will joins his siblings the following December, singing with his brothers on their numbers and soloing on *You Are My Sunshine* on the "Andy Williams Show". (They will remain regulars on the show throughout its first five-year run.)

1967

May The weekly "Andy Williams Show" comes to an end.
Sept The group begins regular guest appearances on ABC-TV's "The Jerry Lewis Show" (which will last until mid-1969). In 1968 the Osmonds become the first signing to Andy Williams' Barnaby label, before moving to Uni Records.

1971

Feb [4] The still-rising *One Bad Apple* is already certified gold by the RIAA.
[13] Now known as the Osmonds, they have debuted on the US chart after being signed to MGM Records by president Mike Curb, who sees their potential as an answer to the Jackson 5. Curb has sent them to Fame Studios in Muscle Shoals, AL, where producer Rick Hall has recorded them on the Jacksons-cloning *One Bad Apple*, written by George Jackson, which now tops the US chart for the first of five weeks. ***Osmonds***, which includes the hit, reaches US #14.
Mar *I Can't Stop*, a reissue from their previous label Uni, peaks at US #96.
June Aware of the teen-idol appeal of his youthful good looks (he has had the major share of US teen magazine coverage since the success of *One Bad Apple*), MGM records Donny as a solo act, beginning with *Sweet And Innocent*, which hits US #7, and will become the first solo million seller by a member of the family.
July *Double Lovin'* makes US #14.
Aug ***Homemade*** reaches US #22, and earns a gold disc, while Donny's first solo album, ***The Donny Osmond Album***, which includes *Sweet And Innocent*, makes US #13.
Aug [30] *Sweet And Innocent* is certified gold by the RIAA.
Sept [11] A revival of the Goffin and King-penned Steve Lawrence/Mark Wynter 1963 hit *Go Away Little Girl*, recorded solo by Donny, begins a three-week run at US #1.
[13] ***Osmonds*** is certified gold by the RIAA.
Oct *Yo-Yo*, written by Joe South, hits US #3.
[13] *Go Away Little Girl* is certified gold by the RIAA.
Nov [17] *Yo-Yo* is also confirmed gold by the RIAA.
Dec Donny's album, ***To You With Love, Donny***, reaches US #12.
[13] ***The Donny Osmond Album*** is confirmed gold by the RIAA.

1972

Jan Donny's treatment of Freddie Scott's *Hey Girl*, released as a double A-side with a new version of Billy Joe Royal's *I Knew You When*, hits US #9.
[20] ***Homemade*** is certified gold by the RIAA.
[26] ***To You With Love*** is certified gold by the RIAA.
Mar *Down By The Lazy River*, written by Merrill and Alan, hits US #4, while the group's album, ***Phase III***, including both this hit and *Yo-Yo*, hits US #10.
[24] The still-climbing *Puppy Love* and the already peaked *Down By The Lazy River* are both certified gold by the RIAA.
Apr *Down By The Lazy River* is the group's UK chart debut, reaching #40, while in the US, Donny's revival of Paul Anka's 1960 million-seller, *Puppy Love*, hits #3.
May ***Portrait Of Donny*** is released, set to hit US #6.
[29] ***Phase III*** is certified gold by the RIAA.
June Little Jimmy Osmond (b. Apr. 16, 1963, Canoga Park, CA), the youngest of the family (and notably overweight though he will lose the surplus pounds in his teenage years), makes his recording debut on a solo novelty, *Long-Haired Lover From Liverpool*, which climbs to US #38, but will score its biggest sales in Britain at the end of the year. (Interviewed, the nine-year-old admits that he has no idea where Liverpool actually is.)
July [8] Donny's *Puppy Love*, his UK solo chart debut, tops the survey in its second week, holding at #1 for a further four weeks, as Osmond-mania becomes an adolescent rash over Britain's youth, a teen phenomenon which will outstrip its US counterpart and give the group and solo members huge UK live, TV and record success over the next five years. Donny's revival of Nat "King" Cole's *Too Young* reaches US #13, while its parent album ***Too Young*** enters the US chart and is set to rise to #11.
[28] *Hey Girl* is confirmed gold by the RIAA.
Aug The group's *Hold Her Tight* makes US #14, while the performance set, ***The Osmonds Live***, reaches US #13 and earns a gold disc.
Sept Donny's album, ***Portrait Of Donny***, hits UK #5.
[16] The Osmonds cartoon TV series starts on ITV.
Oct Donny's *Too Young* hits UK #5, while his double A-side, *Why/Lonely Boy* (revivals of Frankie Avalon and Paul Anka hits respectively), reaches US #13.
Nov ***Osmonds Live*** reaches UK #13, while the group sings guest vocals (and is dually credited) on Steve Lawrence & Eydie Gormé's *We Can Make It Together*, which reaches US #68.
Dec [23] Little Jimmy tops the UK chart for the first of five weeks with *Long-Haired Lover From Liverpool*, which becomes the year's biggest UK seller, shifting over 985,000 copies and makes him the youngest individual (age nine) ever to hit UK #1. The group's rock original, *Crazy Horses*, lines up at UK #2 behind it, also reaching US #14. Donny's *Why* hits UK #3 as the group's album, ***Crazy Horses***, makes US #14 and hits UK #9. Donny's solo album, ***Too Young***, hits UK #7, as his album, ***My Best To You***, begins a climb to US #29.
[30] ***Portrait Of Donny*** and ***Osmonds Live*** are certified gold by the RIAA.

1973

Jan [24] *Crazy Horses and* ***Too Young*** are also ratified gold by the RIAA.
Feb Little Jimmy's album, ***Killer Joe***, reaches UK #20 and peaks at US #105, while his revival of LaVern Baker's '50s hit, *Tweedle Dee*, makes US #59.
Mar [31] Donny's revival of *The Twelfth Of Never* (already successful for both Johnny Mathis and Cliff Richard) tops the UK chart and will hit US #8, selling over one million copies, while Little Jimmy's *Tweedle Dee* hits UK #4.

May Donny's ***Alone Together*** makes US #26 and hits UK #6.
July The group's rocker, *Goin' Home*, reaches US #36.
Aug *Goin' Home* hits UK #4, while the group's concept album, ***The Plan***, an expression of their Mormon faith, hits US #58 and UK #6.
[25] Donny's update of Tab Hunter's *Young Love* begins a four-week run atop the UK chart, having peaked at US #23, where it is released as a double A-side with a revival of Jimmy Charles' *A Million To One*.
Sept [14] The RIAA certifies gold sales of *Twelfth Of Never* and ***My Best To You***.
Oct The group's harmony ballad, *Let Me In*, written by Alan, Wayne and Merrill, reaches US #36.
Nov Marie Osmond (b. Oct. 13, 1959, Ogden), the group's younger sister, who has recently begun singing in concert with her brothers, debuts on the US chart, hitting US #5 with a million selling country-style ballad (produced by country star Sonny James), reviving Anita Bryant's 1960 million-seller, *Paper Roses*, as her maiden album ***Paper Roses*** makes US #59.
Dec *Let Me In* hits UK #2 behind David Cassidy's *Daydreamer/Puppy Song*. Marie's *Paper Roses* hits UK #2 for Christmas (behind Gary Glitter's *I Love You Love Me Love*). Donny's *When I Fall In Love* hits UK #4, and his solo album, ***A Time For Us***, also hits UK #4, while heading for US #58.
[7] *Paper Roses* is certified gold by the RIAA.

1974

Jan Donny's double A-side revival of Elvis Presley's *Are You Lonesome Tonight?* and Nat "King" Cole's *When I Fall In Love* reaches US #14.
Feb Marie's ***Paper Roses*** peaks at UK #46.
[19] Donny co-hosts the inaugural American Music Awards with Michael Jackson, at the Aquarius Theater, Hollywood, CA.
Apr Little Jimmy's treatment of Eddie Hodges' 1961 hit, *I'm Gonna Knock On Your Door*, reaches UK #11.
May The Osmond's *I Can't Stop* climbs to UK #12.
July Marie's ***In My Little Corner Of The World*** enters the US chart, set to make #164.
Aug Osmonds' ***Our Best To You*** hits UK #5.
[12] The group begins six evenings of live BBC-TV shows, aired at peak time from the BBC Television Theatre, Shepherd's Bush, London.
[31] The Osmonds' *Love Me For A Reason*, a ballad co-penned by Johnny Bristol, tops the UK chart for the first of three weeks. Donny & Marie begin a series of duets with a revival of Dale & Grace's *I'm Leaving It (All) Up To You*, which hits US #4 and UK #2. Donny & Marie's ***I'm Leaving It All Up To You*** enters both surveys, set to reach US #35 and UK #13.
Sept [20] *I'm Leaving It All Up To You* is certified gold by the RIAA.
Oct *Love Me For A Reason* hits US #10.
Dec Donny's *Where Did All The Good Times Go* makes UK #18, while ***Love Me For A Reason*** makes US #47 and UK #13. ***Donny*** enters the US chart set to reach #57.

1975

Jan The group embarks on a tour of Australia.
Donny & Marie's *Morning Side Of The Mountain*, a revival of Tommy Edwards' 1959 success, hits US #8 and UK #5.
Feb ***Donny*** makes UK #16.
[21] ***I'm Leaving It All Up To You*** is certified gold by the RIAA.
Mar The group's *Having A Party*, not released as a US single, reaches UK #28, while Donny's solo *I Have A Dream* makes US #50.
Apr Marie's treatment of Connie Francis' *Who's Sorry Now* reaches US #40, as the ***Who's Sorry Now*** album makes US #152.
June ***I'm Still Gonna Need You*** makes UK #19.
July The Osmonds' update of Frankie Valli's *The Proud One* hits UK #5, while Donny & Marie's update of Eddy Arnold's country ballad, *Make The World Go Away*, makes US #44 and UK #18, and the duo's ***Make The World Go Away*** makes US #133 and UK #30.
Sept *The Proud One* reaches US #22, while the group's ***The Proud One*** peaks at US #160.
Dec *I'm Still Gonna Need You* reaches UK #32.

1976

Jan ***Around The World - Live In Concert*** peaks at US #148 and UK #41.
[16] "Donny & Marie", a one-hour musical/comedy/ variety show, heavily featuring all the Osmond family, debuts on ABC-TV.
[31] Donny & Marie collect the Favorite Band, Duo Or Group, Country trophy at the third annual American Music Awards, held at the Civic Auditorium, Santa Monica, CA.
Feb Donny & Marie's cover of Nino Tempo & April Stevens' *Deep Purple* reaches US #14 and UK #25.
May ***Donny & Marie - Featuring Songs From Their Television Show*** makes US #60.
June Donny & Marie's ***Deep Purple*** makes UK #48, while the group's latest BBC-TV series runs through July.
July Donny's version of the Four Seasons' *C'mon Marianne* makes US #38.
Oct Donny's trend-influenced ***Discotrain*** makes US #145 and UK #59, while the group tapes another short UK BBC-TV series (through December).
Nov The group's *I Can't Live A Dream* reaches US #46 and UK #37, and is the Osmonds' last singles chart entry. ***Brainstorm*** peaks at US #145.
Dec [23] ***Donny & Marie - Featuring Songs From Their Television Show*** is certified gold by the RIAA.

1977

Jan ***Donny & Marie - A New Season*** makes US #85, while the festive ***The Osmonds Christmas Album*** peaks at US #127.
Feb Donny & Marie's revival of the Marvin Gaye/Tammi Terrell duet, *Ain't Nothing Like The Real Thing*, reaches US #21.
May ***This Is The Way That I Feel***, by Marie, peaks at US #152.
June Marie's *This Is The Way That I Feel* reaches US #39, and is her last solo US hit single.
[6] A US group tour begins in Tucson, AZ.
Oct Aiming at an older market, Donny's ***Donald Clark Osmond*** peaks at US #169.
Dec The "Donny & Marie" TV show, previously made in Hollywood, originates, in a Christmas Special edition, from the family's present home town of Orem, UT, where the Osmonds have built their own $2 million studio facility to house all their subsequent film, TV and video projects. This show features 28 Osmond family members, and has the somewhat-larger Mormon Tabernacle Choir guesting.

1978

Jan Donny & Marie's revival of the Righteous Brothers' *(You're My) Soul And Inspiration* reaches US #38, while ***The Osmonds Greatest Hits*** peaks at US #192.
[12] ***New Season*** is confirmed gold by the RIAA.
Mar ***Winning Combination***, by Donny & Marie, makes US #99.
Nov Donny & Marie's *On The Shelf* is their final duetted chart entry, reaching US #38.
[6] The still-climbing ***Goin' Coconuts*** is certified gold by the RIAA.
Dec Soundtrack album, ***Goin' Coconuts***, from the feature film starring Donny & Marie, makes US #98.

1980

Feb The group's final BBC-TV series airs in the UK.
Aug The Osmonds officially break up.
Dec [12] Marie begins her own NBC-TV series, "Marie", produced by Osmond Productions. The music/comedy hour will run for two months, and will briefly return to screens the following September, but will not find the success of the "Donny & Marie" show.

1982

Mar [21] While the four older Osmonds re-form to concentrate on country music, signing to Elektra Records, Donny stars in the title role of a Broadway revival of the musical "Little Johnny Jones" at the Alvin Theater, New York, NY. (It closes after only one performance.)

1983

The Osmond family's film and video studio center in Utah is sold to a Texan banker. (It will be re-purchased five years later by Jimmy Osmond, from the profits of his many successful businesses - including promoting Prince's Far East tour).

1984

Apr The Osmonds, their repertoire now wholly country music (and signed to Warner Bros.), visit Britain to play at Mervyn Conn's annual "Country Music Festival" at Wembley, Middx., and perform a six night residency at Baileys in Watford, Herts.

1985

Apr The group, now known as the Osmond Brothers and newly signed to EMI America, returns to play the Wembley "Country Music Festival" for the second year running. (During the year, Donny will incongruously make a cameo appearance in a promo video for Jeff Beck's *Ambitious*.) Marie, who releases this year's country outing ***There's No Stopping Your Heart*** on Curb Records, will marry her engineer/producer, Brian Blosil, on October 28th the following year.

1987

Sept Having married Debra Glenn and the couple having three children, now living in Provo, UT, and spent the past few years as a TV producer, fronting his own production company Night Star, as director and satellite TV entrepreneur, Donny, having not recorded for a decade, signs a new recording deal, only for UK releases, with Virgin Records. Having auditioned to be lead singer of David Foster's group Airplay, he has a chance meeting at a UNICEF function with Peter Gabriel which has led to him recording at Gabriel's Box, Wilts. studios with producer George Acogny, a Senegal-born jazz guitarist living in Queens, New York, NY. His first single, *I'm In It For Love*, now peaks at UK #70. Marie, now signed to Capitol Records, following a stint at Elektra, as a major country artiste, releases ***I Only Wanted You***. Jimmy has become a rock impresario, not least assisting Michael Jackson on his forthcoming "Bad" world tour, restaurateur and owner of the Oz-Art advertizing and design company.

1988

Feb [22] Donny begins his comeback tour, with a band comprising Rory Kaplan, Jeffrey Suttles, Jenny Douglas, Oneida James, Ron Reinhardt and Jon Clarke, at the Crazy Horse Saloon in Los Angeles.
Sept With a new image aimed squarely at the George Michael market, Donny's *Soldier Of Love* reaches UK #29 - the first Top 30 pop hit by any of the Osmonds in the '80s.
Nov Donny's *If It's Love That You Want* peaks at UK #70.
Dec Marie, who has recently released ***All In Love***, wins the 1988 Roy Acuff Community Service Award.

1989

June [3] Hailed by the US media as one of the most surprising comebacks in pop history, Donny's *Soldier Of Love* hits US #2, kept off the top by Michael Damian's *Rock On*. Osmond has been signed for his US releases by Capitol.
Aug [3] The Federal Deposit Insurance Corporation (FDIC) files suit against the Osmond brothers, alleging they owe $150,000 on a 1980 loan from the now-closed Utah First Bank.
[26] The non-fluke follow-up, *Sacred Emotion*, reaches US #13, while parent album ***Donny Osmond*** enjoys a 33-week ride to US #54. (Meanwhile Marie releases her latest country foray, ***Steppin' Stone***.)

1990

Mar [8] Donny is voted Most Unwelcome Comeback

in **Rolling Stone** magazine's 1989 Music Awards.
Apr Looking to a new generation to assume the famous Osmond mantle, four of Alan Osmond's eight offspring are launched as the Osmond Boys, and release a re-make of *Hey Girl*, produced by Alan Osmond, on the ARO label in the US.
July The Osmond Boys - Michael, Nathan, Douglas and David, debut with ***Osmond Boys*** on Reprise.
Aug [29] Marie collapses during a county fair in Canton, OH, and requires hospital treatment for a stomach virus.
Nov [17] Donny's ***Eyes Don't Lie*** peaks at US #177.
Dec [8] His *My Love Is A Fire* reaches US #28.

1991

Feb [10] Donny joins with nearly 100 celebrities in Burbank, CA, to record *Voices That Care*, a David Foster and fiancée Linda Thompson Jenner composed and organized charity record, to benefit the American Red Cross Gulf Crisis Fund.
[16] Donny's *My Love Is A Fire* peaks at UK #64.
[23] His *Sure Lookin'* makes US #54.
Mar [13] Marie appears on CBS-TV's "48 Hours".
Apr [6] She guests on NBC-TV's "Bob Hope's Yellow Ribbon Party", as Donny forms an unlikely duet with Dweezil Zappa on the latter's remake of the Bee Gees' *Stayin' Alive*.
[28] Donny guests on Fox-TV's "Parker Lewis Can't Lose".

1992

Jan [7] The Osmonds participate in an all-star recording of Jeffrey Osborne's *The Heart Of A Hero* to raise money for AIDS research.
June [24] Donny begins a year-long run in the musical "Joseph And The Amazing Technicolor Dreamcoat" in Toronto, Canada. (He will return to the show, touring the US in 1996.)
July With her husband Brian Blosil, Marie sues the **Globe** US tabloid for $18 million over an article disputing the paternity of their one-year-old son, Michael.
Sept [1] The Osmond Family Theater opens at the Bob-O-Link Theater, Branson, MO, country music's fast-growing second city.

1993

Jan While Curb Records in the US has recently issued the only, and incomplete, CD group retrospective : the ten-track ***Greatest Hits***, the 31-strong Osmond clan sell their homes in Provo, UT, and move en masse to Branson.

1994

Jan [17] Donny fights former Partridge Family alumnus Danny Bonaduce in a three-round charity boxing match in Chicago, IL at the China Club nightclub, to determine which former teen idol had grown into the more macho adult. Bonaduce wins a 2-1 decision.

1995

Sept [23] Reissued *Crazy Horses* charts for a week at UK #50, before pent-up demand for a comprehensive CD collection of Osmond highlights, ***The Very Best Of The Osmonds*** also brings the group back to the UK album chart at #17 the following April.

GILBERT O'SULLIVAN

1970

Singer/songwriter O'Sullivan (b. Raymond O'Sullivan, Dec. 1, 1946, Waterford, Eire), having moved to Swindon, Wilts., with his family at age 13, where he played in bands the Doodles and Rick's Blues (led by future Supertramp founder Rick Davies), and had his songs *You* and *Come On Home* covered by the Tremeloes on their 1967 album, ***Here Comes The Tremeloes***, has released his first single, *What Can I Do*, for CBS Records UK, under the name Gilbert in April 1968, while still attending Swindon Art College studying graphic design. After releasing a second one-off single, *Mr. Moody's Garden*, on Major Minor, O'Sullivan now sends a demo tape and a photo of himself, looking unusual enough to be sure to attract attention, to Gordon Mills, manager of Tom Jones and Engelbert Humperdinck. Mills is impressed, signs him to his newly-formed MAM record label, changes Ray's name to Gilbert, and becomes his producer on disc.
Dec His debut MAM single with his surname added, the self-penned (as will be all his subsequent hits) social-awareness ballad, *Nothing Rhymed*, hits UK #8. O'Sullivan begins to make TV and personal appearances with a strikingly obtuse visual image: short trousers, sleeveless sweater, flat cap and pudding basin haircut (the image in the photo which had caught Mills' attention, but will be retained only for the first couple of releases).

1971

Apr *Underneath The Blanket Go* makes UK #40, while EMI's Columbia label reissues the Major Minor single as by Gilbert O'Sullivan, but flipped over to feature *I Wish I Could Cry*.
Sept *We Will* reaches UK #16. (American singer Andy Williams will subsequently ask O'Sullivan if he can record the song, but wants to change the colloquial lyric "I bagsy be in goal", which he does not understand.)
[29] O'Sullivan makes his concert debut in aid of the World Wildlife Fund at London's Royal Albert Hall, with Dave Edmunds' Rockpile, the Sweet and Ashton Gardner & Dyke.
Oct ***Gilbert O'Sullivan - Himself*** hits UK #5, during an 82-week chart run.
Dec *No Matter How I Try* hits UK #5.

1972

Apr Ballad *Alone Again (Naturally)*, chronicling the death of his parents, hits UK #3.
July Uptempo *Ooh-Wakka-Doo-Wakka-Day* hits UK #8.
[29] *Alone Again (Naturally)*, his US debut, complete with new, longer-haired, college sweater image, begins a six-week stay at US #1.
Aug [9] *Alone Again (Naturally)* is certified gold by the RIAA.
Sept ***Gilbert O'Sullivan - Himself***, amended to include *Alone Again (Naturally)*, not on the UK version a year earlier, hits US #9.
Nov [11] *Clair* tops the UK chart for the first of two weeks. The song is written about manager Mills' daughter for whom O'Sullivan used to babysit.
Dec *Clair* hits US #2, held off the top by Billy Paul's *Me And Mrs. Jones*, and then by Carly Simon's *You're So Vain*.

1973

Jan [20] ***Back To Front*** hits UK #1 for a week, and will stay on the survey for 64 weeks. O'Sullivan hosts his own BBC-TV special in Britain, to coincide with its release.
Feb ***Back To Front*** reaches US #48.
Mar [22] *Clair* is certified his second gold disc by the RIAA.
Apr [7] He has switched from acoustic to electric piano for *Get Down*, which tops the UK chart for the first of two weeks. ("Get down" is an admonition to his dog with regard to furniture, not an instruction for dancers.)
May *Out Of The Question*, not released as a UK single, and taken from ***Back To Front***, makes US #17.
[3] Despite his Irish nationality, O'Sullivan is named Songwriter Of The Year, at the 18th annual Ivor Novello Awards, held at London's Connaught Rooms.
[25] O'Sullivan embarks on an 18-date UK tour at London's Royal Festival Hall, set to end on June 19th at the Carlton, Dublin, Eire.
Aug *Get Down* hits US #7, and will become O'Sullivan's third US gold disc on September 18th.
Sept *Ooh Baby* reaches UK #18.
Oct ***I'm A Writer Not A Fighter***, as with all early efforts produced by Gordon Mills, hits UK #2.
Nov *Ooh Baby* reaches US #25, while ***I'm A Writer Not A Fighter*** stops at US #101, O'Sullivan's final US chart album.
Dec Heart-broken ballad, *Why Oh Why Oh Why*, hits UK #6.

1974

Mar *Happiness Is Me And You* reaches UK #19.
Apr *Happiness Is Me And You* peaks at US #62, and is O'Sullivan's final US chart 45.
May [16] *Get Down* wins the Most Performed British Song category, at the 19th annual Ivor Novello Awards, again held at the Connaught Rooms.
Aug O'Sullivan incurs the wrath of the feminist movement with *A Woman's Place*, which makes UK #42.
Nov ***Stranger In My Own Back Yard*** hits UK #9.
Dec Seasonal *A Christmas Song* reaches UK #12. The perky *I Don't Love You But I Think I Like You* will peak at UK #14 the following July.

1976

Dec Compilation album, ***Greatest Hits***, reaches UK #13. His last outing for MAM, ***Southpaw*** will be issued the following November when O'Sullivan launches a comeback tour.

1979

June [8] O'Sullivan begins legal proceedings against MAM and Mills for unpaid royalties.

1980

Oct Newly signed to CBS Records and a resident of Jersey in the Channel Islands, his label debut, *What's In A Kiss?*, reaches UK #19, taken from ***Off Centre***. The compilation album, ***20 Golden Greats***, a TV-promoted release on K-tel, will make UK #98 the following September.

1982

May During the case of O'Sullivan versus MAM/Mills, the judge rules in favor of the plaintiff, agreeing that his original contract with Mills had been unreasonable, and that he had not received his due share of the revenue created by his songs and records. The court awards him payment of substantial back royalties. (Mills will die in 1986.)
Oct ***Life And Rhymes***, produced by Graham Gouldman, is released on CBS.

1989

Nov After a long absence from record and retirement from live performances, ***Frobisher Drive***, named after his old address in Swindon, has been released in West Germany the previous year. Now signed to Chrysalis Records UK, ***In The Key of G***, depicting O'Sullivan carrying an upright piano up a street on the front cover, is released, still within his pleasing, understated melodic style.

1990

Feb [24] In an unlikely UK #72 chart entry, Chrysalis remixes the extracted *So What*, promoting it, prior to release, as a rare Italian house dance cut, thereby exciting moderate sales interest.
June [18] Further extraction, *At The Very Mention Of Your Name*, re-recorded and mixed by David Foster, is released.
July [7] O'Sullivan makes a rare TV appearance on ITV's "Cannon And Ball" show.

1991

Mar O'Sullivan undertakes a poorly-attended UK tour with his piano, a string section, and a small troupe of actors. During the concerts the actors dramatise scenes from O'Sullivan's life, intercut with performances of his most memorable songs.
May [25] Compilation ***Nothing But The Best***, released by Castle Communications, debuts at its UK #50 peak.
Dec [18] In an historic case, O'Sullivan is granted an injunction by Manhattan Federal Judge Kevin Duffy in District Court Southern District of New York, NY to prevent rap-star Biz Markie from sampling *Alone Again (Naturally)* for his single, *Alone Again*. The lawsuit is settled in O'Sullivan's favor on the 31st.

1995

Nov [28] Following the March 1993 release of ***Sounds Of The Loop***, his first album of the '90s, released on Park Records in the UK, and remaining most popular in Japan where the self written-and-produced ***The Little Album*** has recently been issued, O'Sullivan plays a rare gig at London's Camden Jazz Café.

JOHNNY OTIS

1941

Of Greek-American parentage, the Berkeley, CA-raised Otis (b. John Veliotes, Dec. 29, 1921, Vallejo, CA), a musician since his teens, continues an extensive musical apprenticeship, begun with Willard Marsh's Collegians, now securing his first professional gig as the drummer in Count Otis Matthews' West Oakland House Rockers, in West Oakland, CA, which gains a residency at a gambling casino in Reno, NV, paying $45 per week for the three of them (Otis, Count Matthews and bassist Bob Johnson), after which Matthews splits, while Otis and Johnson drive to Denver, CO, where they play with George Morrison's band. When Omaha, NE-based Lloyd Hunter's band's drummer is drafted, Otis is invited to replace him and will go on to team up with fellow group member Preston Love to form the Love-Otis group. When Love joins Count Basie's band, Otis goes to Los Angeles, CA, to join Harlem Leonard's combo, before playing with Bardu Ali's band. Forming his own, 16-piece jazz-swing band in 1945, they become the house band at Club Alabam and, when Excelsior Records owner Otis Rene hears them at the venue, he invites the group to cut four tracks incuding *Harlem Nocturne*, though the first of a dozen singles released is *Fla-G-L-Pa*. Touring the US with Louis Jordan, Nat Cole, the Ink Spots and others the following year, Otis returns to Los Angeles in 1947 and forms an R&B combo. Pioneering the development of west coast R&B, Otis, who also records two singles for Modern Records in 1949, opens two Barrelhouse venues in Watts, Los Angeles, in 1948, the city's first major venues to exclusively feature R&B music, mostly local acts whom Otis - with an unerring ear for talent - has discovered. These include the teenage Little Esther (Phillips) and the Robins (later to become the Coasters).

1950

Mar [4] Scoring the first in a series of blues hits on the Savoy label as *Double Crossing Blues*, credited to the Johnny Otis Quintette and featuring Little Esther, tops the US R&B chart for the first of nine weeks, he tours with the Johnny Otis Rhythm & Blues Caravan Show, an R&B revue featuring the pick of talent from the Barrelhouse. Several R&B-oriented record companies have noted Otis' ear for finding strong performers, and he becomes a travelling talent scout while on the road with his show. (Legend has him note and recommend to King Records three future major acts in one night while visiting Detroit, MI: Jackie Wilson, Little Willie John and the Royals, later to become Hank Ballard & the Midnighters.)
Apr [15] Otis replaces himself at US R&B #1 with *Mistrustin Blues* (both hits credited to the Johnny Otis Orchestra).
July [8] His third and final US R&B chart-topper (all in the same year) is *Cupid's Boogie*, once again featuring Little Esther. (Between 1950-1951, Otis will also cut nine 78s for the Regent label.)

1952

Through the next three years, Otis, also recording six singles for Mercury Records, four for Peacock Records and five for the Dig label, discovers and works with (among others) Big Mama Thornton (producing and co-writing her original version of *Hound Dog* which will result in legal action with Leiber & Stoller when Elvis Presley subsequently makes the song an international smash), Bobby Bland, Little Richard and Johnny Ace (producing *Pledging My Love*).

1957

Having formed his own short-lived Dog Records in 1955 and released ***Mel Williams And Johnny Otis***, he signs to Capitol, to record as the Johnny Otis Show, with various featured singers taking the vocals.

1958

Jan *Ma! He's Making Eyes At Me*, with Marie Adams on lead vocal, hits UK #2.
Feb *Bye Bye Baby* reaches UK #20.
Aug *Willie And The Hand Jive* hits US #9, taken from ***The Johnny Otis Show***. (This will be covered in 1960 by Cliff Richard and the Shadows, and become a UK and international hit.)
Nov *Crazy Country Hop* peaks at US #87. *Castin' My Spell*, featuring the singing of Marci Lee, will reach US #52 the following May.

1960

Feb *Mumblin' Mosie* peaks at US #80, but his run of Capitol hits ceases. (Otis, who severed three fingers in his right hand the previous year, will move to King Records, but will not chart again in the '60s, spending much of his time at the label as a producer from 1961 onwards.)

1969

Blues-based album, ***Cold Shot***, recorded for Kent Records and highlighting Otis' son Shuggie (a talented slide guitarist) and blues vocalists Gene Connors and Delmar "Mighty Mouth" Evans, gains positive reviews and good sales, and includes the R&B hit, *Country Girl*. The same team, thinly anonymous, concocts a pornographic blues album, ***Snatch And The Poontangs***.

1970

Mar ***Here Comes Shuggie Otis*** peaks at US #199.
The Otis band plays at the "Monterey Jazz Festival", Monterey, CA, which is recorded for ***Live At Monterey***, to be released the following year by Epic Records.

1975

Mar Having launched his own Blues Spectrum label the previous year, concentrating on R&B recordings, including Charles Brown and Joe Turner, backed by the Otis band, ***Inspiration Information*** by Shuggie Otis now peaks at US #181.

1982

After a lengthy absence from disc, Otis signs to US independent Alligator label with a new version of the Johnny Otis Show, releasing ***The New Johnny Otis Show***. The new line-up includes Shuggie and Delmar Evans, plus drummer Nicky Otis, two new vocalists (Barbara Morrison and Charles Williams), and guest players like Plas Johnson on sax. The revue continues to tour and record (notably 1985's ***Big Time Scoop***) in an ensemble-fashion much as it did in the '50s.

1994

Jan [19] Etta James inducts Otis into the Rock and Roll Hall of Fame as a "non-performer" at the ninth annual dinner at New York, NY's Waldorf Astoria Hotel.
Mar [2] Otis receives the Pioneer Award at the fifth annual Rhythm and Blues Foundation Awards at New York's Roseland Ballroom.

1995

Apr Having opened the Johnny Otis Market & Deli in Sebastopol, CA in 1990, where he has performed regularly into the mid-'90s in the market's nightclub on weekends with band members including vocalists Jackie Payne, Gail Muldrow & the Dangerous Divas, horn section Ronald Wilson, Larry Douglas and Danny Armstrong, drummer Nicky Otis, bassist and grandson John 'Lucky' Otis III and Brad Pie, his guitar-playing nephew, and following 1993's ***Spirit Of The Black Territory Bands*** on Arhoolie Records, Night Train now releases his latest set ***Too Late To Holler***.

P

Q

ROBERT PALMER

1969

Nov After a Services' childhood based mostly in Malta, and a post-schooldays' apprenticeship in a semi-pro Scarborough, Yorks. rock'n'roll band Mandrake Paddle Steamer at age 15, Palmer (b. Alan Palmer, Jan. 19, 1949, Batley, Yorks.) has resigned as a graphic designer and moved to London to join the Alan Bown Set as its vocalist, replacing Jess Roden, and now appears on Bown's Deram-label single, *Gypsy Girl*, having also recorded new vocals to replace Roden's original on ***The Alan Bown!*** (though the US release on Music Factory retains Roden's vocals). The following year, he joins avant-garde jazz rockers DaDa in place of Paul Korda, who has sung (with Elkie Brooks) on their album, ***DaDa***, for Atco Records, though the group will splinter before recording again.

1972

Apr Palmer has stuck with ex-DaDa musicians to form Vinegar Joe the previous year, aimed in a more blues-rock direction. Sharing vocal duties with Brooks, his other band-mates are Pete Gage (guitar), Mike Deacon (keyboards), Steve York (bass), and Pete Gavin (drums). Signed to Island Records, they release ***Vinegar Joe***, but like all their subsequent albums, it fails to chart.

1974

Mar [9] After much live acclaim, particularly in Europe, but poor sales for two albums ***Rock'n'Roll Gypsies***, and ***Six-Star General***, Vinegar Joe plays its last UK gig at St. Paul's College, Cheltenham, Gloucs., followed by a two-week tour of Yugoslavia.

Sept Retained by Island as a solo artist, Palmer records the Steve Smith-produced ***Sneakin' Sally Through The Alley*** in New Orleans, LA, with assistance from the Meters and Little Feat's Lowell George. (The album's distinctive sleeve is shot in the approach tunnel to Heathrow Airport.) It receives much US airplay, and will eventually climb to US #107 in July the following year.

1975

Dec Having relocated with his wife to New York, NY, his sophomore set, ***Pressure Drop***, released after a US tour as support and back-up singer with Little Feat, and featuring the group and a Motown rhythm section, with string settings by Barry White's arranger Gene Page, peaks at US #136.

1976

Nov ***Some People Can Do What They Like*** peaks at US #68, and is a UK chart debut at #46. His first chart single will be the extracted, *Man Smart, Woman Smarter*, which reaches US #63 in January the following year. (Palmer moves from New York to Nassau, Bahamas, where he will be based until 1987.)

1978

Apr The mostly self-penned and produced, ***Double Fun*** makes US #45.

June *Every Kinda People*, written by Free's Andy Fraser and the first extracted single from ***Double Fun***, is Palmer's breakthrough 45, reaching US #16, and gives him a UK singles chart debut at #53.

Sept Palmer undertakes his first solo European tour.

1979

July ***Secrets*** reaches UK #54, while *Bad Case Of Loving You (Doctor Doctor)*, from the album, makes #61.

Sept ***Secrets*** makes US #19, as *Bad Case Of Loving You (Doctor Doctor)* reaches US #14.

Nov Palmer performs at London's Hammersmith Odeon during current UK dates.

1980

Feb His revival of Todd Rundgren's *Can We Still Be Friends* makes US #52.

Sept ***Clues***, which includes collaborations with Gary Numan, reaches UK #31, his highest album-chart placing yet in the UK, while the extracted *Johnny And Mary* makes UK #44.
Nov ***Clues*** reaches US #59. A concert at London's Dominion Theatre is recorded for a live album project.
Dec *Looking For Clues*, from ***Clues***, makes UK #33.

1982

Apr Combined concert (from the November 1980 recording) and studio-recorded, ***Maybe It's Live***, reaches UK #32. One of the non-live tracks revives the Persuaders' 1973 US hit *Some Guys Have All The Luck*, which reaches #16.
May ***Maybe It's Live*** peaks at US #148.

1983

Apr Self-written and produced ***Pride***, recorded again at Nassau's Compass Point Studio, Bahamas, reaches UK #37 and US #112, and contains the UK #53 extract, *You Are In My System*, a cover of a US #64 dance hit by the System.
June *You Can Have It (Take My Heart)* reaches UK #66.
July He returns to the US Singles chart as *You Are In My System* makes #78.

1985

Jan He joins Duran Duran's John and Andy Taylor, and Chic's drummer Tony Thompson, providing vocals on a temporary basis in Power Station, designed as a one-album studio project.
Apr Power Station's ***The Power Station*** reaches UK #12 and goes on to hit US #6, spawning the hit singles: *Some Like It Hot* (US #6, UK #14), *Get It On* (US #9, UK #22) and *Communication* (US #34, UK #75).
July He leaves Power Station after a dispute with other members, who want to continue the project, particularly for touring, not least to appear at "Live Aid" in Philadelphia, PA. Michael Des Barres replaces him.
Nov *Discipline Of Love (Why Did You Do It)* makes US #82, while ***Riptide***, produced by Chic's Bernard Edwards, makes a poor initial UK showing, reaching #69.

1986

May [3] Palmer-penned *Addicted To Love*, from ***Riptide***, and with vocal arrangements by Chaka Khan, hits US #1, and is his first worldwide million-selling single, aided by a striking testosterone-inducing, Terence Donovan-lensed video featuring black mini-skirted models strumming instruments, which is hotly rotated on MTV, becoming one of the decade's most enduring audio visual clips. ***Riptide***, boosted by *Addicted To Love*'s presence, hits US #8.
June *Addicted To Love* hits UK #5, reactivating ***Riptide*** to hit UK #5.
July [19] *Hyperactive* reaches US #33.
Aug Jimmy Jam/Terry Lewis-penned *I Didn't Mean To Turn You On*, originally a US #79 in 1984 for Cherrelle, hits UK #9, once again aided by his girl-model video backing band, while ***Riptide***, boosted back into the UK chart by the singles' success, finally hits #5.
Sept [15] "Addicted To Love" wins the Best Male Video category at the third annual MTV Video Music Awards (at which he also performs), broadcast simultaneously from the Universal Amphitheatre, Universal City, CA, and the Palladium, New York.
[17] ***Riptide*** is certified platinum by the RIAA for million-plus sales.
Nov [8] *I Didn't Mean To Turn You On* hits US #2. *Discipline Of Love (Why Did You Do It)*, reissued in the UK, stops at #68.

1987

Feb [24] Palmer wins the Best Rock Vocal Performance, Male category for *Addicted To Love* at the 29th annual Grammy Awards, at the Shrine Auditorium, Los Angeles, CA.
Sept Palmer and his family move to Lugano, Switzerland, where he works on music for the film soundtrack to "Sweet Lies", commuting to the Logic Studios in Milan, Italy.

1988

Apr As the Island-released *Sweet Lies* reaches UK #58, having already peaked at US #94, EMI Manhattan Records confirms Palmer as its latest signing.
July [9] His EMI debut, the self-produced ***Heavy Nova***, with contributions from Band members Garth Hudson and Rick Danko, enters at its peak of UK #17, and will climb to US #25, while the self-written *Simply Irresistible* reaches UK #44.
[15] Palmer guests on NBC-TV's "Late Night With David Letterman".
Sept [10] *Simply Irresistible* hits US #2.
Nov [3] ***Heavy Nova*** is confirmed platinum by the RIAA.
[12] The extracted ballad *She Makes My Day* hits UK #6.
Dec [17] His faithful update of Gap Band's 1982 US #24, *Early In The Morning*, reaches US #19.

1989

Jan [17] *Addicted To Love* is certified gold by the RIAA.
Feb [22] Palmer wins (his second) Best Rock Vocal Performance, Male trophy for *Simply Irresistible* at the 31st annual Grammy Awards.
June *Change His Ways* reaches UK #28.
Aug [5] From a forthcoming album, *Tell Me I'm Not Dreaming*, featuring female vocalist B.J. Nelson, peaks at US #60, while *It Could Happen To You* peaks at UK #71 three weeks later.
Dec [2] ***Addictions : Volume 1***, a greatest hits retrospective of his Island days, hits UK #7.

1990

Jan [6] ***Addictions : Volume 1*** makes US #79.
Mar [8] The ever-stylish Palmer wins Best Dressed Male Rock Artist in **Rolling Stone** magazine's 1989 Music Awards.
Apr Richard Gere/Julia Roberts hit movie soundtrack album, ***Pretty Woman***, featuring Palmer's *Life In Detail*, begins multi-platinum success.
Nov [17] His cover version, with UB40, of Dylan's *I'll Be Your Baby Tonight* hits UK #6, as his second EMI album, the 18-track self-helmed ***Don't Explain***, reaches UK #25.
Dec [22] ***Don't Explain*** peaks at US #88.

1991

Jan [19] Self-produced and co-written *You're Amazing* reaches US #28.
[26] A medley update of Marvin Gaye's *Mercy Mercy Me (The Ecolgy)* and *I Want You* hits UK #9.
Mar [1] Palmer embarks on a UK tour.
[19] He guests on syndicated TV's "The Arsenio Hall Show".
Apr [20] *Mercy Mercy Me (The Ecology)/I Want You* reaches US #16.
May [30] He performs at London's Town & Country club.
June [15] *Dreams To Remember* charts for a week at UK #68.
July [12] A US tour opens at Caesar's Palace, Lake Tahoe, NV.

1992

Mar [14] Reissued *Every Kinda People* makes UK #43.
Apr [4] ***Addictions Vol. 2***, a second compilation issued by Island, simultaneously released with "Addictions - The Videos" featuring the landmark "Addicted To Love" promo clip, debuts at its UK #12 peak.
Aug [7] Brent Bourgeois' ***A Matter Of Feel***, for which Palmer has sung and co-written *I'm Down With You*, is released.
Oct [7] Palmer guests on ITV's "Des O'Connor Tonight" show.
[19-24] He sails on the QE2 to New York, performing nightly on his way.
[24] *Witchcraft* makes UK #50.
[28] Palmer guests on NBC-TV's "The Tonight Show".
[31] ***Ridin' High***, an album of big band standards, bows at its UK #32 peak.
Nov [14] ***Ridin' High*** charts for a week at US #173.
[17-18] Palmer performs tracks from his latest nostalgic project with a 40-piece orchestra at London's Royal Albert Hall.
[20] He participates in the annual "Children In Need" telethon on BBC1-TV.
Dec [23] "Robert Palmer - Ridin' High", filmed at the Royal Albert Hall, airs on BBC1-TV.

1993

Jan [24] He performs at a Marvin Gaye tribute at MIDEM, France, with Chaka Khan, George Duke, Al Jarreau and others.

1994

May [23] ***Addictions, Vol. 1*** is certified gold by the RIAA.
July [9] Previewing a new album, *Girl U Want* debuts at its UK #57 peak.
Aug [24] Palmer guests on ITV's "Michael Ball" show.
Sept [10] *Know By Now* reaches UK #25.
[24] Recorded in Milan, Italy, and featuring his girlfriend Mary on the front cover, ***Honey*** reaches UK #25 in its week of entry.
Oct [5] Palmer guests on syndicated TV's "Regis And Kathie Lee" promoting ***Honey***.
[13] He guests on NBC-TV's "The Tonight Show".
Dec [17] *You Blow Me Away* debuts at its UK #29 peak.

1995

Oct [14] *Respect Yourself* debuts at its UK #45 peak.
[28] A further compilation ***The Very Best Of Robert Palmer*** hits UK #4 in its week of entry.

1996

Jan [20] Palmer guests on C4-TV's "The White Room".

GRAHAM PARKER & THE RUMOUR

Graham Parker (vocals); **Brinsley Schwarz** (guitar); **Bob Andrews** (keyboards); **Andrew Bodnar** (bass); **Steve Goulding** (drums)

1975

Having returned to the UK from a tomato-picking and drug-abusing stay in Guernsey, Channel Islands, following a slew of factory jobs in England, Parker (b. Nov. 18, 1950, London) is introduced to his eventual backing band, the Rumour, which includes members from UK roots bands Ducks DeLuxe, Brinsley Schwarz and Bontemps Roulez, by future Stiff Records boss, Dave Robinson, whom Parker has met through slide guitarist Noel Brown (who had answered an advert placed by Parker in **Melody Maker** in 1974). Already a veteran of R&B/rock outfits the Black Rockers and Deep Cut Three, Parker has sent a demo tape of original R&B cuts to the Hope & Anchor pub, above which Robinson runs a small studio and where the group begins rehearsing.

1976

Jan [9] Parker signs to Vertigo Records, after A&R chief Nigel Grainge has heard *Between You And Me* on Charlie Gillett's BBC Radio London show "Honky Tonk".
Mar [26] His debut single, *Silly Thing*, is released as Parker begins a UK tour with Thin Lizzy.
Apr His debut album, ***Howlin' Wind***, produced by Nick Lowe and featuring the Rumour, Noel Brown and Dave Edmunds, is released to much critical acclaim, not least for his compositional and R&B vocal skills, and is accompanied by a well-received soldout club tour, spurring 30,000 album sales.
Sept Official bootleg album, ***Live At Marble Arch***, secures a US deal with Mercury. With only 1,000 copies pressed, it is itself much bootlegged.
Oct His third album of the year, ***Heat Treatment***,

produced by Robert John "Mutt" Lange, and featuring a semi-permanent brass section, sells 60,000 copies.

1977

Jan ***Heat Treatment*** makes US #169.
Mar EP *The Pink Parker* is his first UK singles success at #24, its lead track a cover of the Trammps' disco classic *Hold Back The Night*, featuring guest guitarist - Thin Lizzy's Brian Robertson.
Apr *Hold Back The Night* peaks at US #58 during a US college tour.
May Lowe-produced ***Stick To Me***, featuring nine Parker-penned songs, peaks at US #125.
July The Rumour releases its first Parker-less album, ***Max***.
Oct ***Stick To Me*** reaches UK #19.

1978

May *Don't Ask Me Questions* makes UK #32, as the double parent album, ***The Parkerilla***, comprising three sides of live studio material with a 12" single on the fourth side, reaches UK #14.
July ***The Parkerilla*** peaks at US #149.
[15] Parker and the Rumour open for Bob Dylan at an open-air concert at Blackbushe Aerodrome, near Camberley, Surrey.

1979

Feb The Rumour releases a cover of Duke Ellington's *Do Nothing Till You Hear From Me*. They are signed to Stiff, while Parker remains at Vertigo and releases *Frozen Years*.
Mar ***Squeezing Out Sparks***, a ten-track, Parker-penned album, produced by Jack Nitzsche, regarded as Parker and the band's most accomplished studio recording to date, makes UK #18 and, through a new deal with Arista Records in the US, climbs to #40, with the aid of a promo album, ***Live Sparks***, a concert version of the studio disc. Graham Parker & the Rumour begin a major US tour suppporting Cheap Trick, including a sellout date at New York, NY's Palladium. During the tour, Parker dedicates the anti-Mercury Records song, *Mercury Poisoning*, to his new record boss, Arista's Clive Davis. The Rumour releases its second album without Parker on Stiff, ***Frogs, Sprouts, Clogs And Krauts***.
May *Emotional Traffic*, pressed in red, amber and green vinyl, is later flipped, but *Hard Enough To Show* also fails to chart.
Nov ***Issues***, under the pseudonym the Duplicates, is released on Stiff.

1980

Apr Parker signs to Stiff Records and releases *Stupefaction*, and the Jimmy Iovine-produced ***The Up Escalator***, which includes Bruce Springsteen on backing vocals on the cut *Endless Night*. The album reaches UK #11 - Parker's biggest UK success, and begins a rise to US #40.
Aug ***Purity Of Essence***, the Rumour's third and last album, is released, along with the single, *My Little Red Book*. With Andrews already gone, the group splits from Parker and disbands after backing US singer/songwriter Garland Jeffreys on his album, ***Escape Artist***. Parker publishes sci-fi book **The Great Trouser Mystery**.

1982

Mar Self-penned ballad, *Temporary Beauty*, makes UK #50, as his RCA debut, ***Another Grey Area***, his first solo outing without the Rumour and produced by Jack Douglas, reaches UK #40.

1983

Sept ***The Real Macaw***, produced by David Kershenbaum and featuring Schwarz, Graham Small (keyboards), Kevin Jenkins (bass) and Gilson Lavis (drums), makes US #59 while the extracted *Life Gets Better* peaks at US #94.

1985

Apr Newly signed to Elektra Records, Parker releases ***Steady Nerves***, recorded with backing band the Shot (which includes Schwarz).
June [22] *Wake Up (Next To You)* makes US #39, Parker's only US Top 40 single.

1986

June He begins a European tour, backed by Schwarz and Bodnar.
Aug [22-24] Parker takes part in the three-day, 24th annual "Reading Rock Festival", Reading, Berks.

1988

May At Atlantic's 40th anniversary concert at New York's Madison Square Garden, Bob Geldof performs Parker's abortion-themed song, *You Can't Be Too Strong*, from ***Squeezing Out Sparks***.
July ***The Mona Lisa's Sister***, with help from Schwarz, Bodnar and drummer Pete Thomas, appears on Demon Records in the UK (and RCA in the US), having been rejected by Elektra. It has cost $60,000 to record, less than his last video with Elektra, and makes US #77.
Sept [24] Parker begins a solo US acoustic tour at Rhode Island University, Providence, RI.

1989

Mar [17] Co-produced by Parker, Schwarz and Jon Jacobs, ***Human Soul*** peaks at US #165.
June Parker embarks on a rock'n'roll revue US tour alongside Dave Edmunds, Steve Cropper, Kim Wilson and Dion.
July He releases ***Live! Alone In America***, recorded on his 1988 tour, and featuring a gospel version of Sam Cooke's *A Change Is Gonna Come*.

1991

Apr [9] Parker guests on NBC TV's "Late Night With David Letterman".
[13] 15-track RCA album, ***Struck By Lightning***, featuring John Sebastian on harmonica and Garth Hudson on organ and accordion, peaks at US #131.
May Among Parker's desert island disc list featured in Tower Records' **Pulse** magazine: *This Is How It Feels* by Inspiral Carpets, *Cuyahoga* by R.E.M. and his favorite, *Try A Little Tenderness* by Otis Redding.

1992

Feb Parker signs a new recording deal with Capitol Records.
July [11] He performs before a sellout crowd of 30,000 at Prince George's Equestrian Center, Upper Marlboro, MD, with the Charlatans, the Soup Dragons, They Might Be Giants, Catherine Wheel and others, as his Capitol debut, ***Burning Questions***, is released.
Sept [30] Parker guests on NBC-TV's "The Tonight Show".
Oct [16-17] He performs at the 9:30 Club, Washington, DC, during his current US tour.

1993

Sept Rhino issues career retrospective, ***Passion Is No Ordinary Word - The Graham Parker Anthology 1976-1991***.

1994

Jan Shanachie Records' ***Brace Yourself - A Tribute To Otis Blackwell***, to which he has contributed *Paralyzed*, is released as Parker continues work on the novel **Hatemail**.
Sept The Arthur Alexander tribute album, ***Adios Amigo***, including a cover version by Parker, is issued.

1995

Mar [14] Following the release of one-off EP *Graham Parker's Christmas Cracker* on the Dakota Arts label, Razor & Tie releases Parker's first new album in three years, ***12 Haunted Episodes***, a 12-cut album recorded in one five-hour session.
Dec Parker teams up with Mavis Staples, Felix Cavaliere, Dennis Edwards, Johnny Colla, Chuck Jackson and Bobby Womack to record *Holiday Heroes* for the Chicago-based Soul Purpose Records.

RAY PARKER JR.

1970

Parker (b. May 1, 1954, Detroit, MI), having played the guitar since age 12, and toured supporting the (Detroit) Spinners with his post-high school group Jeep Smith & the Troubadours, becomes a guitarist in the house band, with Michael Henderson, Hamilton Bohannon and Ollie Brown, at Detroit's biggest club, the Twenty Grand, which leads to studio sessions for Motown Records (including his first for Marvin Gaye) and for Holland/Dozier/Holland's Invictus and Hot Wax labels. After working with Parker in the studio on sessions for the album ***Talking Book***, Stevie Wonder subsequently invites him to join the road band for his North American tour with the Rolling Stones in May 1972. After playing on Stevie Wonder's follow-up album, ***Innervisions***, Parker moves to Los Angeles, CA, in 1973, where he begins songwriting in earnest (inspired by working with Wonder), and becomes a regular session guitarist, playing with Barry White and White's various offshoots, and Boz Scaggs, Chaka Khan, Herbie Hancock and LaBelle, among others.

1974

Dec Parker's first hit composition is *You Got The Love*, recorded by Rufus, which reaches US #11. He also has a bit part in the movie "Uptown Saturday Night". Barry White's *You See The Trouble With Me*, which Parker co-writes and plays on, will hit UK #2 in April 1976.

1977

Parker opens his own Ameraycan recording studio in Los Angeles. A demo tape impresses Arista Records chief Clive Davis, and he is signed to the label. He forms the R&B band Raydio, with himself on vocals and guitar, Arnell Carmichael on synthesizer, Charles Fearing on guitar, Vincent Bonham on keyboards, Jerry Knight on bass and Larry Tolbert on drums - all ex-studio cohorts from the early '70s in Detroit.

1978

Apr Raydio's debut single, *Jack And Jill*, a pop/soul fusion written and produced by Parker, hits US #8 and will become a million seller, while ***Raydio*** makes US #27 and earns a gold disc for half a million sales. Bonham leaves the group, which tours the US with Bootsy Collins.
May *Jack And Jill* reaches UK #11.
Aug *Is This A Love Thing*, also from the album, makes UK #27.

1979

Aug Raydio's second album, the largely Parker-penned ***Rock On***, makes US #45 (also a gold disc), while the extracted *You Can't Change That* hits US #9.

1980

June The group changes its name to Ray Parker Jr. & Raydio for its third album, ***Two Places At The Same Time***, which reaches US #33 and is Parker's third gold album. Its title cut, *Two Places At The Same Time*, makes US #30.

1981

June ***A Woman Needs Love***, his fourth consecutive gold disc, reaches US #13, while *A Woman Needs Love (Just Like You Do)* hits US #4, his highest-placed single yet.
Sept *That Old Song*, also from the fourth album, reaches US #21. Parker produces soulstress Cheryl Lynn's *Shake It Up Tonight*, which makes US #70, and her album, ***In The Night***, which peaks at US #104.

1982

June Parker has disbanded the group to record solo, and his ***The Other Woman*** reaches US #11, again earning a gold disc. The title track, *The Other Woman*, inspired, according to Parker, by listening to Rick Springfield's *Jessie's Girl*, hits US #4.
Aug *Let Me Go*, also from the album, peaks at US #38.

1983

Jan Third single from ***The Other Woman***, *Bad Boy*, reaches US #35. A compilation ***Greatest Hits***, covering both Raydio and Parker's solo career to date, makes US #51.

1984

Jan *I Still Can't Get Over Loving You* reaches US #12, taken from ***Woman Out Of Control***, which peaks at US #30, as usual, produced and written by the artist.
Aug [11] Parker's theme for the Bill Murray/Dan Aykroyd film "Ghostbusters", written and recorded within two days, tops the US chart for the first of three weeks and is Parker's second US million-selling single. Its promo video is directed by Ivan Reitman and includes Murray and Aykroyd, plus guest cameos by Danny De Vito, Peter Falk and others. (The song will earn Parker an Academy Award nomination, although he will be successfully sued by Huey Lewis for plagiarising his *I Want A New Drug*.)
Sept *Ghostbusters* hits UK #2 for three weeks, behind Stevie Wonder's million-selling *I Just Called To Say I Love You*.

1985

Jan *Jamie* reaches US #14, taken from Parker's ***Ghostbusters***, which makes US #60 (but is overshadowed by the movie soundtrack album, which as well as his theme song has tracks by Elmer Bernstein, the Thompson Twins, Air Supply and others, and hits US #6 and UK #24). (Parker is also featured acting in the current NBC-TV series, "Berrenger's", which runs through March.)
Dec *Girls Are More Fun* reaches US #34, as ***Sex And The Single Man*** makes US #65.

1986

Jan As the film opens in Britain to repeat its US box office success, *Ghostbusters* re-charts at UK #6, lifting its UK tally to 800,000 sales.
Feb Parker's duet with UK singer Helen Terry on *One Sunny Day/Dueling Bikes*, from the film soundtrack to "Quicksilver", is released on Atlantic and peaks at US #96, while *Girls Are More Fun* makes UK #46.

1987

Sept [19] Newly signed to Geffen Records, his debut single, *I Don't Think That Man Should Sleep Alone*, peaks at US #68.
Oct Geffen-released album, the largely self-written and produced ***After Dark*** makes US #86 and UK #40.
Nov *I Don't Think That Man Should Sleep Alone*, from ***After Dark***, reaches UK #13. *Over You*, a duet with Natalie Cole written by Burt Bacharach and Carole Bayer Sager, will peak at UK #65 in January the following year.

1991

Sept Newly signed to MCA Records and having contributed to Glenn Medeiros' *All I'm Missing Is You* the previous year, Parker releases ***I Love You Like You Are***, his first album in four years, co-produced with Father MC and Gary Taylor. Thereafter Parker will move back to becoming an in-demand session performer, contributing guitar work not least to SMW's 1993 hit *Always On My Mind*, Norman Connors' ***Remember Who You Are***, and Omar's ***For Pleasure*** released in 1995.

THE ALAN PARSONS PROJECT

1974

Parsons (b. 1949, UK), who has joined BBC television, working in the tape duplication department before moving to London's Abbey Road Studios where he has assistant-engineered the Beatles' ***Abbey Road***, and engineered the Hollies' *He Ain't Heavy, He's My Brother*, Pink Floyd's ***The Dark Side Of The Moon***, Wings' ***Wildlife*** and ***Red Rose Speedway*** among others, forms a group with his partner, lyricist, singer and keyboard player, Eric Woolfson. (Parallel with his recording career, Parsons will also become an in-demand producer, working with Al Stewart, John Miles, Pilot and Steve Harley's Cockney Rebel among many others.)

1976

July Signed to Arista Records in the UK, his first album as an artist/producer, two years in the making and intended as a one-off project, is ***Tales Of Mystery And Imagination***, based on Edgar Allan Poe's book. Like all subsequent Parsons releases, it is a concept album packaged in an elaborate sleeve and instrumentally synthesizer-based, but features Woolfson on vocals with a selection of guest vocalists, this time using Arthur Brown, John Miles and the Hollies' Terry Sylvester. Released on 20th Century in the US, it reaches US #38, after being premiered at Griffith Park Observatory's planetarium, Los Angeles, CA, accompanied by one of the first specially-commissioned laser shows.
Aug ***Tales Of Mystery And Imagination*** makes UK #56.
Sept Taken from the album, *(The System Of) Doctor Tarr And Professor Fether* reaches US #37.
Oct *The Raven*, also from ***Tales Of Mystery And Imagination***, peaks at US #80.

1977

Aug ***I, Robot***, inspired by a concept from science-fiction writer Isaac Asimov, and titled after his book, makes UK #30.
Oct *I Wouldn't Want To Be Like You*, with vocals by Lenny Zakatek, makes US #36, taken from ***I, Robot***, which hits US #9, and earns Parsons his first platinum disc.

1978

Jan *Don't Let It Show*, with vocals by David Townshend, peaks at US #92.
June ***Pyramid*** makes UK #49.
Aug ***Pyramid*** reaches US #26, eventually earning a gold disc.
Sept *What Goes Up*, taken from ***Pyramid***, peaks at US #87.

1979

Sept ***Eve***, evoking a musical battle of the sexes, makes UK #74. The music is supplied by a nucleus of ex-Pilot players David Paton (bass) and Ian Bairnson (guitar), Cockney Rebel's Stuart Elliott (drums), with Lesley Duncan as a featured vocalist.
Oct ***Eve*** reaches US #13, earning another gold disc.
Dec *Damned If I Do*, with Zakatek on vocals, is taken from ***Eve*** and makes US #27.

1981

Feb Having already reached UK #38 the previous November, ***The Turn Of A Friendly Card*** makes US #13 and earns Parsons a second platinum disc for a million-plus sales. Zakatek has contributed lead vocals to *Games People Play*, which is extracted to reach US #16.
Aug Ballad *Time*, with Woolfson at the mike, reaches US #15.
Nov *Snake Eyes*, with vocals by Chris Rainbow, climbs to US #67.

1982

June ***Eye In The Sky***, concerned with the misuse of technology, its title taken from a Philip K. Dick novel, reaches UK #28 with Colin Blunstone among its featured vocalists.
Oct ***Eye In The Sky*** hits US #7 and is a third platinum seller. The title track, *Eye In The Sky*, with Woolfson singing, hits US #3.
Dec *Psychobabble*, with vocals by Elmer Gantry, makes US #57.

1983

Jan *Old And Wise*, a third extract from ***Eye In The Sky***, peaks at UK #74.
Nov Compilation album, ***The Best Of The Alan Parsons Project***, makes UK #99.
Dec *You Don't Believe*, with Zakatek out front, makes US #54.

1984

Jan Compilation ***The Best Of The Alan Parsons Project*** reaches US #53.
Mar Ballad *Don't Answer Me*, with co-writer Woolfson on vocals, makes UK #58, with its parent album, ***Ammonia Avenue***, reaching UK #24.
May *Don't Answer Me* reaches US #15, as does ***Ammonia Avenue***, which earns a gold disc.
June *Prime Time*, with Woolfson again on vocals, makes US #34.

1985

Feb ***Vulture Culture*** makes UK #40.
Mar Taken from the album, *Let's Talk About Me*, with vocals by David Paton, makes US #56.
Apr ***Vulture Culture*** swoops to US #46.
May *Days Are Numbers (The Traveller)*, with vocals by Rainbow, peaks at US #71.

1986

Feb Parsons and his label Arista are in dispute over royalty payments for scheduled CD releases, delaying his back-catalog reissues by a year. ***Stereotomy***, the title another Edgar Allan Poe reference, features Procol Harum's singer Gary Brooker, among others, and makes US #43.
Mar [1] *Stereotomy*, with John Miles on lead vocals, peaks at US #82.

1987

Feb ***Gaudi***, based on the life of the Spanish architect/painter Antonio Gaudi, makes UK #66 and US #57, while most of Parsons' back-catalog is finally released on CD by Arista.
Apr A second compilation, ***Limelight : The Best Of, Vol. 2***, featuring ten tracks from previous albums, most of them also former US hit singles, is released.
June Parsons and Woolfson digitally re-master the original album ***Tales Of Mystery And Imagination*** for CD release by Mercury Records, adding some new touches with synthesizer and guitar, and a narration by Orson Welles (commissioned at the time of the original release).
Arista will issue ***Instrumental Works***, a non-vocal Alan Parsons Project compilation, in November the following year.

1995

June While "Freudiana", written with Eric Woolfson, received its premiere at the Theatre An Der Wien, Vienna, Austria in 1990 (when Arista also issued the ***Alan Parsons Box Set***), UK retrospective label Castle Communications issued the more modest 15-track ***Anthology*** collection in November 1991. Following Parsons' first new album in six years, ***Try Anything Once*** in 1993, and having dropped the Project appendage, Parsons, having completed rare European dates, now undertakes his first ever US tour to promote his latest project, ***The Very Best Live***, released by RCA Victor.

GRAM PARSONS

1968

Feb Weaned on the music of his hero, country legend Hank Williams, singer/guitarist Parsons (b. Cecil Connor III, Nov. 5, 1946, Winter Haven, FL), who joined his first band, the Pacers, at high school before playing in the Legends with Jim Stafford in the early '60s, linked with popular college folk act the Shilohs in 1963 alongside Joe Kelly, Paul Surratt and George Wrigley. Quitting the group to study at Harvard College, Cambridge, MA, in 1965, Parsons subsequently abandoned further education to form the

International Submarine Band, recruiting Ian Dunlop (bass), Mickey Gauvin (drums) and John Neuse (guitar). Based in Los Angeles, CA and fusing country/rock, a genre which Parsons is largely credited with creating, with folk, the group has cut ***Safe At Home*** in 1967, though its release comes three months after the band folds, as Parsons now joins the Byrds as its keyboardist.

July Having contributed vocals (which are subsequently erased and replaced) to the Byrds' forthcoming ***Sweetheart Of The Rodeo***, on the eve of the South African leg of the band's world tour, Parsons, refusing to play to segregated audiences, checks out of a London hotel and ends his brief tenure with the group.

Oct Parsons teams with ex-Byrds' guitarist Chris Hillman to form the country-rock devoted Flying Burrito Brothers, enlisting "Sneeky" Pete Kleinow (pedal steel guitar) and Chris Ethridge (bass), and signs to A&M Records.

1969

May The Parsons-led Flying Burrito Brothers debut album, ***The Gilded Palace Of Sin***, peaks at US #164. After contributing to the band's second album, ***Burrito Deluxe*** released in April the following year and troubled by increasing drug dependency, Parsons will elect to pursue a solo career.

1972

Sept Signed to Reprise Records, Parsons, unable to interest Merle Haggard in producing his debut album, begins recording sessions co-helmed with Rik Grech at Los Angeles' Capitol and Wally Heider studios.

1973

Jan His freshman effort, ***GP***, a ground-breaking country rock meld featuring sessioneers James Burton (guitar), Buddy Emmons (pedal steel) and Glen D. Hardin (keyboards) among others, is released to critical acclaim.

Feb [21] Having formed a backing tour band, the Fallen Angels, comprising Neil Flanz, Gerry Mule, N.D. Smart II, Kyle Tullis and his girlfriend Emmylou Harris (recruited as a leading harmony vocalist), Parsons performs at the Armadillo World Headquarters, TX.

Apr They play before a live audience at WLIR radio station, Hempstead, NY (subsequently released as ***Gram Parsons And The Fallen Angels Live, 1973***), during a US tour.

June Following appearances at country rock festivals in Baltimore, MD and Philadelphia, PA, Parsons returns to the studio with Harris to self-produce his sophomore album.

Sept [19] Having already indicated that "If I go, I want to be in Joshua Tree and my ashes scattered there", Parsons dies age 26 from a heroin overdose. (Following the funeral, his body mysteriously disappears, and is duly cremated by his manager Philip Kaufman in the California desert, in line with those wishes.)

1974

Feb His posthumously-released second album, ***Grievous Angel***, including a Grammy-nominated duet rendition with Harris of Boudleaux Bryant's *Love Hurts*, peaks at US #195, once again commercially belying its subsequent influence on the burgeoning country rock scene.

1990

Following the 1982 release of his career highlights package, ***Gram Parsons***, by Warner Bros. (with tribute sleeve notes by Elvis Costello: "If it should fail to move you - then you have a big problem."), Reprise collects Parsons' solo material with the single CD release of ***GP/Grievous Angel***. Rhino Records will assemble ***Commemorativo : A Tribute To Gram Parsons*** for US release in January 1994.

see also: **THE BYRDS; THE FLYING BURRITO BROTHERS**

DOLLY PARTON

1962

Raised in the Smokey Mountains, Parton (b. Jan. 19, 1946, Locust Ridge, Sevier County, TN), the fourth of Robert and Avie Lee Parton's 12 children (delivered by Dr. Robert F. Thomas, whom she later immortalizes in song and who the family had to pay with a sack of corn meal, such was their economic plight), having made her own guitar at the age of five and already appeared on Cass Walker's Knoxville, TN radio show at 10, took a Greyhound bus to Lake Charles, LA, in 1955 to record her first single, *Puppy Love*, penned with her uncle Bill Owens, for the local Gold Band label, which also released her follow-up, *Girl Left Alone*. Drumming with the Sevier County High School marching band, Parton has made her debut at "The Grand Ole Opry" in 1958 and now records *It's Sure Gonna Hurt* for Mercury Records, credited to Dolly Parton with the Merry Melody Singers, which includes three members of the Jordanaires.

1964

June [1] Parton relocates to Nashville, TN, the day following her high school graduation, staying with relatives. She then signs with Monument Records, which, with Ray Stevens producing, initially aims her at the pop market.

1966

Apr Her first success, however, is as a songwriter with Bill Phillips' US Country #6 hit *Put It Off Until Tomorrow*, on which she also sings.

May [30] Parton weds Carl Dean (whom she met in the Wishy Washy laundromat on her first day in Nashville), in Catoosa County, GA. (Despite persistent media scrutiny and rumor, she will remain married to her reclusive partner into the '90s.)

1967

Jan [21] Released by Monument her first recording chart disc is the typically self-effacing *Dumb Blonde* which now enters the US Country chart set to make #24.

Oct [7] "Dolly Parton Day" is celebrated in Sevier County. 7,000 locals attend her concert at the courthouse to celebrate her signing to RCA and replacing Norma Jean, to whom she had earlier sent some songs, on "The Porter Wagoner Show" TV program.

1968

June [29] Her RCA debut *Just Because I'm A Woman* enters the US Country survey set to reach #17. During the year Parton becomes a regular on "The Grand Ole Opry" show and she and Wagoner are named Best Duet Of The Year by the Country Music Association (CMA), and receive the first of three Grammy nominations.

1969

Jan [4] Parton becomes an inducted member of the Grand Ole Opry.

Mar ***Just The Two Of Us***, with Porter Wagoner, peaks at US #184. (The partnership will produce 18 country hits – the first a cover of Tom Paxton's *The Last Thing On My Mind*.)

Aug Parton/Wagoner album, ***Always, Always***, peaks at US #162.

Nov Her solo album, ***My Blue Ridge Mountain Boy***, climbs to US #194.

1970

Apr Parton/Wagoner album, ***Porter Wayne And Dolly Rebecca***, peaks at US #137.

Aug ***A Real Live Dolly***, recorded at her high school, makes US #154.

Oct ***Once More***, again with Wagoner, peaks at US #191.

1971

Feb [6] *Joshua* becomes Parton's first US Country chart-topper.

Mar ***Two Of A Kind***, Parton's last chart album with Wagoner, climbs to US #142.

June Solo album ***Joshua*** peaks at US #198.

1974

Mar The jealous girlfriend-themed, self-penned *Jolene* makes US #60 and tops the US Country chart. (With her striking bewigged, large-chested image firmly established, Parton says of her appearance: "When I wear fancy outfits and hairdos and sparkling jewelry, people might think I'm showing off. But I'm not. When I was a little girl, I liked toys but I didn't have any. I was always very impressed when I saw someone dressed real fine. I used to sigh and say: someday, girl, someday.")

Apr [21] Parton and Wagoner perform their last live show together in Salinas, KS.

June [8] Parton-written *I Will Always Love You*, tops the US Country survey (and will be revived to global success by Whitney Houston in 1992).

She forms the Traveling Family Band, which includes four siblings and two cousins.

1975

Apr Parton takes part in the annual "Country Festival" at Wembley, Middx.

Oct Having been nominated on five previous occasions, she is voted Female Vocalist Of The Year by the CMA.

1976

Feb Syndicated TV series, "Dolly", recorded in Nashville and featuring country stars, airs in the US.

June *Jolene* hits UK #7. Vocal problems will result in her cancelling 65 dates in the latter part of the year.

Oct Parton is named CMA Female Vocalist Of The Year for a second successive year.

1977

May Newly signed to west coast management team Ray Katz and Sandy Gallin, Parton participates in a concert in Scotland at Glasgow's King Theatre to celebrate H.R.H. Queen Elizabeth II's Silver Jubilee, at which she is introduced to H.R.H. Prince Philip, the Duke of Edinburgh, backstage.

[6] She makes her New York, NY debut at the Bottom Line club.

July *Light Of A Clear Blue Morning* peaks at US #87, while its parent album, ***New Harvest ... First Gathering***, a shift away from country to pop, makes US #71.

1978

Jan Mainstream pop song, *Here You Come Again*, written by Barry Mann and Cynthia Weil, hits US #3 as ***Here You Come Again*** reaches US #20.

[16] She wins the Favorite Album, Country category at the fifth annual American Music Awards, held at the Civic Auditorium, Santa Monica, CA.

Feb [1] *Here You Come Again* is confirmed gold by the RIAA.

Apr [28] ***Here You Come Again*** is certified platinum by the RIAA, her first.

May Parton-penned *Two Doors Down* reaches US #19.

June [12] ***The Best Of Dolly Parton*** is ratified gold by the RIAA.

Aug [16] ***Heartbreaker*** is certified gold by the RIAA.

Sept *Heartbreaker* makes US #37.

Oct Parton appears on the front cover of **Playboy** magazine, in a bunny costume. She is named Entertainer Of The Year by the CMA, as *Heartbreaker* makes US #27.

Nov [20] She concludes a three-week European tour, with a performance at London's Hammersmith Odeon.

Dec Compilation album, ***Both Sides***, makes UK #45.

1979

Feb [15] Parton wins the Best Country Female Vocal Performance category at the 21st annual Grammy Awards.

[17] Parton becomes the first country artist to have a

disco hit, with the self-written, *Baby I'm Burnin'*, which also makes US #25 and tops the Country chart.
July [21] *You're The Only One* peaks at US #59 as its parent album, ***Great Balls Of Fire***, makes US #40.
[28] *You're The Only One* becomes Parton's tenth solo US Country chart-topper (not including an 11th with Porter Wagoner, *Please Don't Stop Loving Me Now* in 1974).
Oct [13] *Sweet Summer Lovin'* peaks at US #77.
Nov [13] ***Great Balls Of Fire*** is certified gold by the RIAA.

1980

May *Starting Over Again* makes US #36, while its parent album, ***Dolly Dolly Dolly***, makes US #71.
Dec [19] "Nine To Five", in which Parton makes her movie debut, as a secretary, with Jane Fonda and Lily Tomlin, premieres in the US.

1981

Feb [19] The still-rising *9 To 5* is certified gold by the RIAA.
[21] Self-penned *9 To 5*, written for the movie, tops the US chart and makes UK #47.
Mar ***9 To 5 And Odd Jobs*** reaches US #11.
[6] ***9 To 5 And Odd Jobs*** is confirmed gold by the RIAA.
May *But You Know I Love You* makes US #41.
Sept Her treatment of the Animals' *The House Of The Rising Sun* peaks at US #77.
Dec ***9 To 5*** is named Top Country Album in **Billboard**'s Year In Music survey.

1982

Feb [24] Parton wins the Best Country Vocal Performance category for the second time, for *9 To 5* at the 24th annual Grammy Awards.
Mar [25] The TV version of "9 To 5" airs, with Parton's sister Rachel Dennison reprising her role.
May ***Heartbreak Express***, co-produced with Gregg Perry featuring a cover photo by Herb Ritts, makes US #106.
June Parton embarks on her first major US tour in three years.
July She stars as a madam with Burt Reynolds in the premiering movie, "The Best Little Whorehouse In Texas".
Sept Ballad *I Will Always Love You*, from "The Best Little Whorehouse In Texas" and her re-make of her own 1974 Country chart-topper, makes US #53, and is her 15th Country #1 as her ***The Best Little Whorehouse*** soundtrack album climbs to US #63, on which Parton duets with Burt Reynolds on *Sneakin' Around*.
Dec ***Greatest Hits*** makes US #77.

1983

June ***Burlap And Satin***, helmed by Gregg Perry, makes US #127.
Oct [29] *Islands In The Stream*, a duet with Kenny Rogers, written by the Bee Gees and co-produced by Barry Gibb, tops the US chart, the only platinum selling single of the year. (It will go on win a clutch of awards, including the American Music Awards' Favorite Country Single and the Academy of Country Music's Single Record Of The Year.)

1984

Jan *Save The Last Dance For Me* makes US #45 as its parent album ***The Great Pretender***, reprising hits of the '50s and '60s and produced by Val Garay, reaches US #73.
[16] She wins the Favorite Single, Country category (with Kenny Rogers) for *Islands In The Stream* at the 11th annual American Music Awards, held at the Shrine Auditorium, Los Angeles, CA.
Apr *Downtown* reaches US #80, as *Here You Come Again* makes UK #75.
June [18] Sylvester Stallone/Dolly Parton-starring picture, "Rhinestone", based on Larry Weiss' song *Rhinestone Cowboy*, premieres in the US. (The project is Parton's first since major stomach surgery.) The soundtrack album, ***Rhinestone***, featuring Parton songs, makes US #135.
Dec Festive album, ***Once Upon A Christmas***, with Kenny Rogers, and produced by David Foster, is released, set to make US #31.

1985

Jan *The Greatest Gift Of All*, from a Parton and Rogers' Christmas TV special, makes US #81, as they prepare for a paired US tour.
[28] *Islands In The Stream* again wins the Favorite Single, Country category at the 12th annual American Music Awards, held at the Shrine Auditorium, the first time that the same disc has won twice.
June *Real Love*, another duet with Rogers, peaks at US #91. Construction begins on Dollywood, an 87-acre theme park in Pigeon Forge, TN, near her birthplace in the Smokey Mountains.
Aug Further Rogers duet, *Real Love*, peaks at US #91.
Sept ***Greatest Hits*** makes UK #74.
Dec ABC-TV airs "A Smoky Mountain Christmas", which becomes the network's highest-rated Sunday night program in over two years.

1986

Jan [19] Parton begins work on an often-postponed album project with Emmylou Harris and Linda Ronstadt, as her country smash, *Think About Love*, hits US Country #1.
Oct [7] ***Greatest Hits*** is certified platinum by the RIAA.

1987

Mar [21] Parton's country collaboration with Emmylou Harris and Linda Ronstadt, ***Trio***, produced by George Massenberg, makes UK #60.
May ***Trio*** tops the US Country survey for five weeks, and is set to hit US #6. The extracted *To Know Him Is To Love Him* also tops the Country chart.
July [14] ***Trio*** is certified platinum by the RIAA.
Sept [27] As the Dolly Parton Wellness and Rehabilitation Center of Sevier County Medical Center now opens, ABC-TV premieres "Dolly", a variety show scheduled as the network's prime-time Sunday evening show. (Despite attempts to re-vamp the program, it fails to achieve good ratings, and ABC will pull it.)
Dec ***Rainbow***, a mainstream pop album produced by Steve Goldstein, and Parton's first for CBS/Columbia Records, peaks at US #153 and US Country #18.

1988

Feb [20] Parton and Porter Wagoner perform on "Dolly", together for the first time since their 1974 break-up.
Mar Parton visits the UK to promote ***Rainbow*** and appears on the ITV show "Aspel & Co."
[2] ***Trio*** wins Parton, Ronstadt and Harris a Grammy for Country Vocal, Duo Or Group at the 30th annual Awards. It is Parton's fourth.
May Parton's ballad duet with Smokey Robinson, *I Know You By Heart*, is released. (By year's end, Parton will have lensed "Steel Magnolias" with fellow actresses Sally Field, Shirley MacLaine, Julia Roberts, Daryl Hannah and Olympia Dukakis, and established the Dollywood Foundation program that promises a college scholarship to every student who graduates from any of the three high schools in Parton's home county in Tennessee.)

1989

June Returning to country flavors, ***White Limozeen*** hits US Country #3 and spawns her 22nd and 23rd US Country #1 singles, *Why'd You Come In Here Lookin' Like That* and *Yellow Roses*.
July [13] During a Los Angeles concert, Parton is surprised when her backing singer on *Islands In The Stream* turns out to be Kenny Rogers.

1990

Jan [8] Parton visits Carl Perkins at his house in Jackson, MS, and co-writes four songs.
Mar She buys WSEV (pending FCC approval), her hometown radio station in Sevierville, TN, the first station she ever sang on, with the intention of moving it to Dollywood and making it an attraction at her Pigeon Forge theme park.
Aug [16-17] During a current US tour with Kenny Rogers, Parton performs at the Entertainment Center, California Mid-State Fair, Paso Robles, CA.
Sept Parton is fined $20,000 by the US Department Of Labor for making her teenage staff put in longer than to 9 to 5 hours at Dollywood.
Parton guests on *Do I Ever Cross Your Mind*, from Randy Travis' newly-released duets album, ***Heroes & Friends***.
Dec [14] She guests on NBC-TV's "The Tonight Show".
[21 ABC-TV airs the "Dolly Parton Christmas At Home" special.
[31] Parton performs her final shows of the year with two sellout performances, at the Riverside Theatre, Milwaukee, WI, grossing $210,460.

1991

May [4] *Rockin' Years*, a duet with Ricky Van Shelton becomes her first US Country #1 of the '90s.
[25] ***Eagle When She Flies*** reaches US #24.
Sept [23] NBC-TV movie, "Wild Texas Wind", starring Parton and Gary Busey with a special guest appearance by Willie Nelson, airs.
Dec [6] ***White Limozeen*** is certified gold by the RIAA.

1992

Apr [8] Parton guests on NBC-TV's "Tonight" show promoting her latest movie, "Straight Talk" (starring opposite James Woods).
[24] CBS-TV's "Conversations With ..." focusing on Parton airs from the Ryman Auditorium, Nashville.
May [2] Soundtrack album written and performed by Parton, ***Straight Talk***, peaks at US #138.
[16] She takes part in NBC-TV's "Bob Hope's America Red White & Beautiful - The Swimsuit Edition".
June [5] Parton appears on BBC1-TV's "Wogan".
Aug [2] During her current US tour, Parton performs at the Garden State Arts Center, Holmdel, NJ.
[3] She donates $500,000 to improve public education in the Sevier County Schools system.
[4] ***Eagle When She Flies*** is certified platinum by the RIAA.
Oct [26] Parton takes part in cable station TNN's "Hats Off To Minnie : America Honors Minnie Pearl" special.
Dec Whitney Houston's version of Parton's *I Will Always Love You* tops charts around the world, becoming the country artist's most successful composition.

1993

Feb [17] Her new single, *Romeo*, is launched on the Billy Ray Cyrus ABC-TV special.
Mar [16] Parton guests on NBC-TV's "Late Night With David Letterman".
[27] While Dolly prepares a second "trio" effort, her latest offering, ***Slow Dancing With The Moon***, reaches US #16, and features Billy Ray Cyrus, Mary-Chapin Carpenter, Tanya Tucker, Vince Gill and Chet Atkins, as she performs before a sellout crowd of 3,876 at the Sunrise Musical Theatre, Sunrise, FL.
Apr [10] *Romeo*, credited to Dolly Parton & Friends, makes US #50.
[27] RCA releases a double CD retrospective, ***The RCA Years, 1967-1986***, in the US.
[30] Parton takes part in the Kentucky Derby Festival's USA Harvest Hunger Relief Concert at Louisville Gardens, Louisville, KY.
May [12] She attends a benefit at the Lincoln Center, New York, at which Sony Corp. president Norio Ohga conducts members of the Metropolitan Opera Orchestra.
[14] Parton performs a sellout show at New York's Carnegie Hall during the "Country Takes Manhattan" concert series.
Oct [5] ***Slow Dancing With The Moon*** is certified

platinum by the RIAA.
Nov [20] ***Honky Tonk Angels***, recorded with Loretta Lynn and Tammy Wynette, debuts at its US #42 peak. With the extracted *Silver Threads And Golden Needles* reaching #68 on the US Country survey, Parton is now just five discs short of charting 100 US Country singles.

1994

Jan The Dolly Parton Beauty Confidence Collection, a cosmetics line created by Revlon, infomercial debuts on US TV.
[5] ***Honky Tonky Angels*** is certified gold by the RIAA.
[17] Parton guests on NBC-TV's "The Tonight Show".
Mar [21] She performs *The Day I Fall In Love*, a duet with James Ingram from the movie "Beethoven's 2nd", at the 66th annual Academy Awards at Los Angeles' Dorothy Chandler Pavilion.
Apr [16] *The Day I Fall In Love* debuts at its UK #64 peak.
Sept [12] AIDS benefit album ***Red Hot + Country***, featuring Parton's *You've Gotta Be My Baby*, is released.
Oct [29] ***Heartsongs - Live From Home*** reaches US #87, as ***Greatest Hits*** makes UK #65.
Dec [27] ***Home For Christmas*** is certified gold by the RIAA.

1995

May Walt Disney Television executives confirm that Parton's half-hour comedy for CBS-TV's "Heavens To Betsy" will never air.
July [17] Parton attends the opening of Dollywood Co.'s $14.5 million Branson Dixie Stampede Dinner Attraction.
Oct [21] ***Something Special***, including a new version of *I Will Always Love You* with Vince Gill, reaches US #54.

1996

Jan [4] "The Grand Ole Opry 70th Anniversary", featuring Parton, airs on CBS-TV.

PAVEMENT

Stephen Malkmus (guitar, vocals);
Scott "Spiral Stairs" Kannberg (guitar vocals);
Mark Ibold (bass); **Stephen West** (drums);
Bob Nastanovich (percussion)

1992

Jan Initially formed as a part-time garage band in Stockton, CA in 1989 by University of Virginia history major Malkmus (b. Santa Monica, CA), who has also worked as a guard at New York, NY's Whitney Museum, and his friend Kannberg (b. Stockton,) the pair have recorded and self-distributed, on their Treble Kicker label, the Malkmus-penned, five-cut *Slay Tracks: (1933-1969)* single for $800 at the small Louder Than You Think studio in Stockton during their first year together. Subsequently teamed with the studio's owner (and first drummer) Gary Young (b. 1953, Stockton), Pavement has gone on to issue the quirky, feedback-laced *Demolition Plot J-7* in 1990, the mini-album ***Perfect Sound Forever*** the following year and now the last of its own Drag City indie label releases, the EP *Summer Babe*, material mostly featuring two-minute slices of chaotic noise. Having recently signed to the Atlantic Records-licensed Matador label, the lineup has also expanded to include Ibold (b. Cincinnati, OH) (who joined in 1991) and Nastanovich (b. Rochester, NY), who came onboard in August the previous year.
Apr [25] Critically well-received by the alternative music press (which dubs their music "low-fi"), the distortion-filled ***Slanted And Enchanted***, a seemingly unstructured avant-garde rock set, charts for a week at UK #72, and, though uncharted in the US will shift some 100,000 copies.
Nov [28] EP *Watery Domestic* also charts briefly at UK #58.

1993

Apr [3] Rounding up an eclectic selection of earlier material, ***Westing (By Musket & Sextant)*** debuts at its UK #30 peak.
June West (b. Richmond, VA) replaces Young (who will commence a solo career with the release of *Planet Man*).

1994

Feb [12] Finding a home at US college radio - it will hit US #10 on the Modern Rock survey in April - *Cut Your Hair* charts for a week at UK #52.
[17] Pavement embarks on a ten-date UK tour at the Assembly Rooms, Edinburgh, Lothian, Scotland, set to end on the 28th at The Forum, London.
[26] Laid-back, pop-tinged ***Crooked Rain Crooked Rain***, again warmly greeted by the music media, enters at its UK #15 high.
Mar Recording sessions for Pavement's next album get underway in New York before completion in Memphis, TN later in the year. (During the year, Malkmus will also collaborate on a side project band Silver Jew (with his friend David Berman) releasing ***Starlight Walker*** on Drag City.)
Aug [26] The group takes part in the annual "Reading Festival", Reading, Berks.

1995

Apr [29] Now signed to Warner Bros. Records, Pavement's label debut ***Wowee Zowee*** charts briefly at US #117 having entered at its UK #18 peak the previous week.
July [4] Pavement embarks on the "Lollapalooza '95" package tour at the Gorge, George, WA, with Sonic Youth, Hole, Cypress Hill, Sinead O'Connor, Beck, Jesus Lizard and the Mighty Mighty Bosstones.
[27] The group performs at the annual "Reading Festival", Reading, Berks.

1996

May Matador Records releases the band's new four-track EP ***Pacific Trim***.
June [15-16] Pavement appears at the Tibetan Freedom Concert held in San Francisco to benefit the Milrepa Fund, an organization co-founded by hosts for the evening, the Beastie Boys.

PEARL JAM

Eddie Vedder (vocals); **Mike McCready** (guitar);
Stone Gossard (guitar); **Jeff Ament** (bass);
Dave Krusen (drums)

1990

June Following the death of Mother Love Bone's lead vocalist Andrew Wood from a heroin overdose on March 19th earlier this year, bassist Ament (b. Mar. 10, 1963, Big Sandy, MT) and guitarist Gossard (b. July 20, 1966, Seattle), both also ex-Green River, now continue as a Seattle, WA-based unit, joined by local veteran musician and current Shadow member McCready (b. Apr. 5, 1965, Seattle). Assembling a demo tape and in search of a lead singer, the three-track tape reaches the San Diego, CA-based Vedder (b. Edward Mueller, Dec. 23, 1966, Evanston, IL) via Red Hot Chili Peppers' Jack Irons. After writing lyrics and completing the vocal to the demos, Vedder is asked to complete the line-up by year's end. The combo, augmented by Soundgarden's Matt Cameron and Chris Cornell also completes a tribute album to Wood, ***Temple Of The Dog*** (recorded under the same moniker and due for release by A&M the following year). Vedder also suggests Pearl Jam's name, which legend alternately suggests is named either after his great-grandmother or from a hallucinogenic jam recipe. On their sixth day together they play at Seattle's Off Ramp club, calling themselves the New Jersey Nets after point guard Mookie Blaylock, whose sports card has been found in the same box as their demo tape.

1991

Jan Managed by Kelly Curtis and augmented by Krusen, Pearl Jam's live reputation, including a 12-date opening slot for Alice In Chains and demo tapes secure a contract with Epic Records.
Mar Pearl Jam begins two months of recording sessions for its first album at London Bridge Studios in Seattle.
June Following its completion, Krusen leaves, temporarily replaced by New Bohemians drummer Matt Chamberlain for a short US tour which includes a gig at New York, NY's Wetlands club.
Sept With Chamberlain short tenure in the drum seat over (he will go on to join NBC-TV's "Saturday Night Live" house band), ex-Dr. Tongue member Dave Abbruzzese (b. May 17, 1964) joins.

1992

Feb [29] Written by Vedder and Gossard, the group's first single *Alive* reaches UK #16.
Mar [7] Co-produced by the band with keyboardist Rick Parashar, the critically-hailed ***Ten***, named after Blaylock's uniform shirt number, debuts at its UK #18 peak.
Apr [11] The group is the music guest on "Saturday Night Live".
[18] *Even Flow* debuts at its UK #27 peak.
June Stardog Records releases ***Temple Of The Dog***, the collaborative tribute album by members of Soundgarden and Pearl Jam for Wood, which will hit US #5, earning a platinum disc.
July [18] Pearl Jam embarks on a multi-artist, 34-date "Lollapalooza Festival '92" tour at the Shoreline Amphitheatre, Mountain View, CA. The trek will end on September 13th at the Irvine Meadows Amphitheatre, Laguna Hills, CA, after 32 sellout dates before crowds totalling 740,794, grossing $18,627,212 at the box office. (During a week's break from "Lollapalooza", the band heads to Atlanta, GA, to record *Sonic Reducer*, with producer Brendan O'Brien mixing. 14,000 copies of the cut will be mailed to fan club members.) ***Singles***, the Seattle grunge-rock soundtrack album to the current Matt Dillon-starring movie, to which Pearl Jam (who form Dillon's backing band, Citizen Dick in the movie) have contributed *Breath* and *State Of Love And Trust*, enters the US chart, set to hit #6.
Aug [22] ***Ten*** hits US #2 on its way to ten million-plus US sales behind Billy Ray Cyrus' ***Some Gave All***. Its phenomenal domestic sales tally will be helped by the absence of any extracted US singles releases.
Sept [9] The band performs *Jeremy* at the "MTV Video Music Awards", held at the Pauley Pavilion, Los Angeles, CA.
[20] The group gives a free "Drop In The Park" concert in Magnuson Park, Seattle, with 20,000 tickets given away in two hours and 3,000 "Rock The Vote" registrations collected.
[26] *Jeremy* bows at its UK #15 peak during a European tour.
Oct [16] Vedder and McCreedy sing *Masters Of War* at the "Bob Dylan 30th Anniversary Celebration" concert at New York's Madison Square Garden, while the Stardog Records-reissued Mother Love Bone's only album, 1990's ***Apple***, now including the band's five song EP *Shine* and the previously unavailable *Lady Godiva Blues*, climbs to US #77.
Nov [1] The group participates in Neil Young's sixth annual "Bridge School Benefit" with Elton John, Sammy Hagar and James Taylor at the Shoreline Amphitheatre, Mountain View, CA, raising $434,210 from the 20,000 sellout crowd.
Dec [31] Pearl Jam opens a New Year's eve gig for Keith Richards & the Expensive Winos at the Academy, New York.

1993

Jan [12] Inducting the Doors into the Rock and Roll Hall of Fame at the eighth annual dinner, at the Century Plaza Hotel, Los Angeles, Vedder, now compared to Jim Morrison himself, has been asked to

perform *Roadhouse Blues, Break On Through* and *Light My Fire* with the remaining Doors members, and states "I figured it was either me or William Shatner".
[23] Vedder headlines a "Rock For Choice" benefit at Los Angeles' Hollywood Palladium with Screaming Trees, Mary's Danish and others.
[25] Pearl Jam wins the Favorite New Artist categories for both Pop/Rock and Heavy Metal/Hard Rock at the 20th annual American Music Awards, held at the Shrine Auditorium, Los Angeles.
Mar [4] Pearl Jam is named Best New American Band, Vedder named Best New Male Singer and "Jeremy" chosen as Best Video in **Rolling Stone**'s 1993 Music Awards Readers' Picks, while the band begins recording its second album in San Francisco, CA, with producer Brendan O'Brien.
Apr Gossard's side band, Shame, forced to re-name to Brad because of an existing Shame, with Jeremy Toback (bass), Regen Hagar (drums) and Shawn Smith (vocals), releases its debut album, ***Shame***.
May [23] Pearl Jam members take part in celebrity softball games at the T.J. Martell Foundation and Neil Bogart Memorial Fund 1993 Rock 'N Charity Celebration, at the Blair Field, Long Beach, CA.
July [13-14] Having played a couple of surprise gigs, one in Missoula, MT, and the other at an American Music Club gig at Slim's in San Francisco (the $5 ticket proceeds going to Navy sailor Aaron Ahearn who is facing court martial for allegedly refusing to dump trash in the ocean), where they perform AC/DC's *Highway To Hell* and AMC's *Bad Liquor*, the group plays two London dates at the Brixton Academy, during a tour of Europe.
Sept [2] The group wins the Best Video Of The Year, Best Group Video, Best Metal Hard Rock Video and Best Director categories (all for "Jeremy"), at the tenth annual MTV Video Music Awards, held at the Universal Amphitheatre, Universal City, at which they also perform *Keep On Rockin' In The Free World* with Neil Young.
[25] ***Sweet Relief***, a benefit album for singer/songwriter Victoria Williams, diagnosed with multiple sclerosis, including Pearl Jam's *Crazy Mary*, makes US #131.
Oct [15] The group plays an unannounced gig at the Off Ramp in Seattle.
[23] Produced by Brendan O'Brien, ***Vs.*** debuts at its UK #2 peak.
Nov [6] ***Vs.*** enters the US chart at #1, recording the highest-selling one week total in history (950,378 - enough to make it the 38th best-selling album of the year), where it will stay for five weeks. With the alternative music media drooling, Pearl Jam, together with city-mates Nirvana, are hailed as the champions of the Seattle-based grunge phenomenon.
[18] Vedder is arrested in New Orleans, LA. and charged with public drunkenness and disturbing the peace after a fight with waiter James Gorman in a French Quarter bar. Chicago White Sox pitcher Jack McDowell is knocked unconscious in the melée.
[27] During a concert at the University of Colorado, Vedder chases security guards from the slam-dance arena. He is issued with a summons, alleging he obstructed government operations.

1994

Jan [1] *Daughter* debuts at its UK #18 peak.
[27] The group is named Artist Of The Year, Best Band and Brightest Hope for 1994, Vedder is named Best Male Singer and Best Songwriter and "Jeremy" named Best Video in **Rolling Stone**'s 1994 Music Awards Readers' Picks. In the Critics' Picks list, ***Vs.*** is named Best Album, Vedder named Best Male Singer and the group is named Artist of the Year.
Feb [23-24] Vedder sings *Let My Love Open The Door, Squeeze Box* and *My Generation* at Roger Daltrey's Carnegie Hall shows.
Mar [22] The group is named Best-selling Artist of the Year and ***Vs.*** is named Best-selling Alternative Recording and Best-selling Rock Recording at NARM's 1993-4 Best Seller Awards in San Francisco, as they perform at the Convocation Centre, Cleveland State University, during a tour beleaguered by problems caused by the group's refusal to use Ticketmaster to sell tickets.
Apr [16] Pearl Jam guests on "Saturday Night Live".
[17] They sell out New York's Paramount, during their current tour.
May [6] The group files a memorandum with the Antitrust Division of the US Department of Justice charging that Ticketmaster has a monopoly.
June [4] *Dissident* reaches UK #14.
[30] Gossard and Ament testify before a House of Representatives subcommittee, after the group's May 6th memorandum.
Aug [16] New Orleans Municipal Judge John Shea dismisses Vedder's public drunkenness and disturbing the peace charges arising from the November 18th, 1993 incident.
[22] Manager Curtis announces on a Seattle radio station that Abbruzzese has decided to leave the band to study music formally.
[26] Abbruzzese denies he left of his own accord. "For reasons that I don't completely understand, the other members of the band decided that it was necessary to fire me".
Oct [1] Pearl Jam plays an acoustic set at the eighth annual Bridge School benefit at Shoreline Amphitheatre, Mountain View, CA.
Nov [26] *Spin The Black Circle* debuts at its UK #10 peak, and coupled with *Tremor Christ*, reaches US #18.
Dec [10] Again helmed by O'Brien, ***Vitalogy*** hits UK #4.
[24] ***Vitalogy*** tops the US chart, having sold 877,001 copies on CD and cassette in its first seven days on sale. The vinyl format has been issued two weeks earlier prompting an initial and rare vinyl-only US chart peak of #55 prior to its pole position full-format roll-out.

1995

Jan [8] Vedder plays DJ on four-plus hours of late-night radio self-titled "Self Pollution Radio". The group sings ten songs in an adjacent studio.
[12] Pearl Jam inducts Neil Young into the Rock and Roll Hall of Fame at tenth annual dinner, staged at New York's Waldorf Astoria Hotel.
[14-15] The group headlines two benefit concerts for Voters For Choice at Washington's Constitution Hall, marking former Red Hot Chili Pepper Jack Irons' (b. July 18, 1962, Los Angeles) debut on drums.
Feb [5-6] Pearl Jam plays two unannounced private shows, at the Moore Theater, Seattle - the first one for 1,400 fan club members, the second, where they are joined onstage by Neil Young for *Peace And Love*, for regional fans and underprivileged youngsters.
[25] *Not For You* debuts at its UK #34 peak.
[28] MTV honors Pearl Jam with its Rock The Vote award.
Mar [16] The RIAA certifies six million sales of ***Vs.***
[25] Karekare Surf Club senior lifeguard Eric Davis rescues Vedder when a riptide carries him about 250' offshore in New Zealand. (He had been swimming with Crowded House's Tim Finn.)
Apr [13] Vedder makes a surprise appearance at Mike Watt's show at the Dingo Bar, Albuquerque, NM, before a crowd of approximately 300.
[26] He plays drums with his wife, Beth Leibling's band Hovercraft in Philadelphia, wearing dark glasses and a wig.
June [6] The RIAA certifies nine million sales of ***Ten***.
[16] Further to their ongoing battle against Ticketmaster, they kick off a US tour at Boise State University Pavilion, Boise, ID. All tickets for the tour are being distributed by California-based start-up company, ETM Entertainment Network, a task which will soon prove too great causing the cancellation of a number of dates on the problem-plagued trek.
[24] Neil Young takes over from Vedder at the group's Golden Gate Park, San Francisco gig when Vedder falls ill six songs into the set and requires treatment at a hospital emergency room.
July [15] Recorded live in the studio with Pearl Jam his backing band and overseen by producer O'Brien, the collaborative Neil Young ***Mirror Ball*** album hits US #5, having peaked at its UK #4 debut on the 8th.
Aug [19] *Jeremy*, backed with *Yellow Ledbetter*, peaks at US #79.
Oct [13] The RIAA certifies five million sales of ***Vitalogy***.
Nov [6-7] Pearl Jam plays sellout shows at the Sports Arena, San Diego, CA, with the Ramones opening.
Dec [16] *Merkinball* debuts at its UK #25 peak.
[23] *I Got ID*, coupled with *Long Road*, bows at its US #7 peak.

1996

Jan [9] Columbia Records releases the soundtrack to "Dead Man Walking", including two new cuts by Vedder in collaboration with Pakistani artist Nusrat Fateh Ali Khan, *The Long Road* and *The Face Of Love*.
[30] Pearl Jam win the Favorite Artist, Heavy Metal and Favorite Artist, Alternative categories at the 23rd annual American Music Awards, held at the Shrine Auditorium.
Feb [3] Pearl Jam's *Daughter/Yellow Ledbetter* makes US #97.
[26] Calling into question why they are even attending, Pearl Jam is collectively bored and dismissive of the event upon collecting the Best Hard Rock Performance trophy for *Spin The Black Circle* at the 38th annual Grammy Awards also held at the Shrine Auditorium, with Vedder saying from the podium "I don't think it means anything".

TEDDY PENDERGRASS

1969

Pendergrass (b. Theodore Pendergrass, Mar. 26, 1950, Philadelphia, PA), whose mother was a Philadelphia nightclub performer notably at the popular Skioles venue, has taught himself the drums in his early teens after a childhood steeped in gospel music, and is drumming with local group the Cadillacs, when they are invited to become the instrumental back-up team for Harold Melvin & the Blue Notes, a Philadelphia R&B/doo-wop group with a 13-year history (and a 1960 US #78 hit with *My Hero*). During a French West Indies tour the following year, the Blue Notes lead singer John Atkins leaves and Pendergrass replaces him as front man.

1971

Harold Melvin & the Blue Notes sign to Kenny Gamble and Leon Huff's Philadelphia International label, based in its own home city. Over the next five years the band will achieve substantial R&B/pop success, mostly written and produced by Gamble & Huff, all of which will be prominently led by Pendergrass' deep soul vocal tones. *I Miss You* opens their chart account reaching US #58 in August 1972, and will be followed by the million-selling, seminal soul ballad, *If You Don't Know Me By Now*, a US #3 smash in December the same year (and UK #9). Thereafter ***Harold Melvin And The Blue Notes*** makes US #53 also in December, *Yesterday I Had The Blues* peaks at US #63 in March 1973, with *The Love I Lost* hitting US #7 in December (and UK #21 the following February) - the group's second million seller, as ***Black And Blue*** makes US #57. *Satisfaction Guaranteed (Or Take Your Love Back)* makes US #58 and UK #32 in May 1974, while the Gene McFadden and John Whitehead-penned, *Where Are All My Friends*, peaks at US #80 in November. ***To Be True*** reaches US #26, earning a gold disc for half a million sales during its 32-week chart run in May 1975, yielding the US #15 *Bad Luck* and *Get Out* (UK #35) (both in June), and *Hope That We Can Be Together Soon*, featuring guest vocalist Sharon Paige duetting on lead vocals with Pendergrass, which makes US #42 in August.

1976

Feb The group's last major US hit single is the social awareness-themed ballad, *Wake Up Everybody* (penned by McFadden and Whitehead), which reaches US #12. The album, ***Wake Up Everybody***, hits US #9 earning a second gold disc.

Mar *Wake Up Everybody* reaches UK #23.

Apr *Tell All The World How I Feel About 'Cha Baby* peaks at US #94. It is the group's last single for Philadelphia International and also the last with Pendergrass' defining lead vocal. He leaves for a solo career, staying with Gamble and Huff's label, while Harold Melvin & the Blue Notes move to ABC Records, with their new lead singer David Ebo.

Aug The group compilation album, ***All Their Greatest Hits***, reaches US #51.

1977

Mar To compete with Thelma Houston's revival, Harold Melvin & the Blue Notes' version of Gamble/Huff/Gilbert song, *Don't Leave Me This Way*, previously an album track, is issued as a UK single, and outsells Houston's, hitting UK #5.

July Pendergrass' first solo hit single is Gamble and Huff's *I Don't Love You Anymore*, which makes US #41. It is taken from his debut solo album, ***Teddy Pendergrass***, which reaches US #17 and spends 35 weeks on the chart. A different single, *The Whole Town's Laughing At Me*, is extracted in the UK and reaches #44. Having taken a year's hiatus from live performance after splitting with Melvin, he begins to tour with the 15-piece Teddy Bear Orchestra (the moniker taken from Pendergrass' nickname). His sultry ballads, addressed directly to the females in the audience, quickly bring him a reputation as a ladies' man entertainer.

Aug Pendergrass joins Lou Rawls, Billy Paul, Archie Bell and others on the Philadelphia All-Stars' *Let's Clean Up The Ghetto* (all profits will go to a five-year charity project in areas of urban decay) which reaches US #91 and UK #34.

[22-27] Pendergrass participates in "Let's Clean Up The Ghetto Week" in Los Angeles, CA, at the instigation of Mayor Tom Bradley.

1978

June [21] ***Teddy Pendergrass*** is certified platinum by the RIAA.

Aug [25] The still-rising ***Life Is A Song Worth Singing*** is also confirmed platinum by the RIAA.

Sept His sophomore set, ***Life Is A Song Worth Singing***, and the extracted *Close The Door* respectively reach US #11 and #25.

[2] Pendergrass performs a "For Women Only" midnight concert at Avery Fisher Hall, New York, NY. The audience are handed white chocolate, teddy bear-shaped lollipops. Further "ladies only" concerts, invariably standing-room-only affairs, follow, a PR exercise by manager Shep Gordon to capitalize on the perception of Pendergrass as an aural seducer.

Oct [25] *Close The Door* is certified gold by the RIAA.

Nov *Close The Door*, a double A-side with *Only You*, makes UK #41.

1979

Jan [12] He wins the Favorite Male Artist, Soul/R&B category (tieing with Lou Rawls) at the sixth annual American Music Awards, held at the Civic Auditorium, Santa Monica CA.

Aug ***Teddy*** hits US #5 having already earned another platinum disc on July 27th, while the extracted *Turn Off The Lights* peaks at US #48.

1980

Feb Performance double album, ***Teddy Live! Coast To Coast***, with three sides recorded in concert and a fourth containing interviews and new studio tracks, makes US #33, reaching gold status. A UK tour is cancelled, partly because of Pendergrass' reported liaison with the wife of Marvin Gaye - who is touring Britain for the same promoter at the same time.

Mar [13] ***Teddy Live! Coast To Coast*** is confirmed gold by the RIAA.

Sept ***T.P.*** reaches US #14, and is Pendergrass' fourth album to turn platinum with US sales of over one million. It includes a duet with Stephanie Mills on *Feel The Fire*.

[19] ***T.P.*** is certified gold by the RIAA.

Oct *Can't We Try*, taken from ***T.P.***, climbs to US #52.

1981

Jan Another extract from the album, *Love T.K.O.*, co-written by Cecil Womack, reaches US #44.

Apr He tours the UK for the first time as a soloist, once again wowing female audiences in particular.

July Pendergrass duets again with Stephanie Mills on her single, *Two Hearts*, on 20th Century, which peaks at US #40 and UK #49.

Oct ***It's Time For Love*** reaches US #19, earning another gold disc on December 23rd.

1982

Feb *You're My Latest, My Greatest Inspiration* makes US #43. He makes his movie debut in "Soup For One", also contributing *Dream Girl* to the soundtrack which is produced by Chic's Nile Rodgers and Bernard Edwards. He also makes a second successful UK visit.

Mar [18] On the way home from a basketball game in Philadelphia, Pendergrass crashes his Silver Spirit Rolls Royce, hitting a guardrail, crossing over into the opposite lane before hitting two trees. He is pulled from the wreck with a severely injured spinal chord, and hospitalized in critical condition. (He is paralysed from the neck down for some time and gradually recovers only partial movement, but it will keep him from recording and performing for over two years.) His passenger, Tenika Watson, turns out to be a transsexual nightclub performer by the name of John Watson.

Oct ***This One's For You***, consisting of material recorded before the accident, makes US #59.

1984

Jan ***Heaven Only Knows***, his last for Philadelphia International, peaks at US #123.

July Signed to Asylum Records, Pendergrass, now permanently confined to a wheelchair, has returned with ***Love Language*** rising to US #38.

Aug From the album, *Hold Me*, a duet with Whitney Houston and marking her first chart entry, makes US #44.

Sept [17] ***Love Language*** is certified gold by the RIAA.

1985

July [13] Pendergrass makes his comeback to the live arena, performing at "Live Aid" at the JFK Stadium in Philadelphia.

1986

Jan ***Workin' It Back*** makes US #96.

Feb *Hold Me*, having failed to chart in 1984, is reissued in Britain after Whitney Houston has topped the chart with *Saving All My Love For You*, this time climbing to UK #44.

1988

May [21] Having married Karen Still on June 20th the previous year, and now signed to Elektra Records, his label debut, ***Joy***, variously produced by the artist with Reggie and Vincent Calloway, Nick Martinelli and Miles Jaye, reaches UK #45.

June [25] Reggie Calloway-penned soul shuffler, *Joy*, tops the US R&B chart.

July Title single and album, ***Joy***, make US #77 and US #54 respectively.

Aug [23] ***Joy*** is certified gold by the RIAA.

1990

June [30] Soundtrack to the Andrew Dice Clay movie, "The Adventures Of Ford Fairlane", featuring Pendergrass duetting with Lisa Fisher on *Glad To Be Alive*, is released.

Nov [3] ***Rubáiyát***, Elektra's 40th anniversary compilation, to which Pendergrass has contributed a cover of Bread's *Make It With You*, makes US #140.

1991

Mar [13] Pendergrass appears on syndicated TV's "The Arsenio Hall Show", promoting his current album, ***Truly Blessed***.

Apr [27] Largely co-produced and co-written with Terry Price, ***Truly Blessed*** makes US #49.

June [7-9] Pendergrass co-chairs the first IAAAM '91 Celebration Of African American Music Month at the Wyndham Franklin Plaza Hotel in Philadelphia.

1993

June [15] Pendergrass sings *Close The Door* at the "Apollo Theatre Hall of Fame" concert, set to air on NBC-TV on August 4th.

Oct [23] Featuring Patti LaBelle, Gerald Levert and Barry White among a host of guests, ***A Little More Magic*** debuts at its US #92 peak.

Nov [2] Pendergrass guests on NBC-TV's "The Tonight Show".

1994

Nov [19] KWS' *The More I Get, The More I Want*, featuring Pendergrass on lead vocals, debuts at its UK #35 peak.

1995

June [1] He takes part in a fund-raising benefit for his self-created Pendergrass Institute for Music and Performing Arts held at the Valley Forge Music Fair, Devon, PA.

CARL PERKINS

1952

Jan [24] Perkins (b. Carl Perkings, Apr. 9, 1932, Ridgely, near Tiptonville, TN), from a poor sharecropping family, whose father Buck is an invalid with a lung disorder, who, while still in fourth grade at school, was driven 70 miles by his teacher to sing *Home On The Range* and *Billy Boy* on radio station WTJS, has begun to play bars and honky tonks around Tennessee in 1950, with brothers Jay and Clayton as the Perkins Brothers Band, to earn extra money. He now marries Valda Crider in Corinth, MS, who encourages him to make a career in music. (During their first year together, he picks cotton while Valda, who gives birth to their first child, Stan, on November 11th, takes in laundry to make ends meet.)

1954

Feb Perkins begins to play professionally, still on the honky-tonk circuit, singing and playing electric guitar with his brothers backing him on acoustic guitar and double bass. They mix country and hillbilly music with the occasional blues and uptempo R&B number, and earn around $30 a month. Perkins relocates to Jackson, MS, where he and his wife move into a government housing project.

Aug He hears Elvis Presley's first single, *Blue Moon Of Kentucky*, on the radio, and recognizes a similar blend of styles to those he is playing himself. After watching Presley at a high school dance in Betthel Springs, MS, the Perkins Brothers Band travels to Memphis, TN, to audition for Presley's record company, Sun.

Oct The three brothers, with new drummer W.S. Holland, impress owner Sam Phillips at Sun, particularly with Perkins' original material, offering him a contract if he can come up with more new songs.

1955

Jan [22] The first Sun recording session produces *Movie Magg* and *Turn Around*, which are issued as a single on Phillips' new label, Flip Records, to little attention.

Feb Perkins supports Elvis Presley on a tour of the South.

July [11] Uptempo rockabilly *Gone Gone Gone* is recorded for Perkins' second single, released on the main Sun label.

Oct [11] Perkins begins an 11-date "Jamboree" tour in Abilene, TX, set to end on the 22nd in St Louis, MO, with Johnny Cash and Elvis Presley.
Nov When Presley's contract is sold to RCA Records, Phillips decides to mould Perkins into a suitable replacement, and encourages him to play up the emerging rock'n'roll elements in his writing and recording. The band is signed to Phillips' Stars Inc. promotional agency.
Dec [19] Perkins and the band record his own composition, *Blue Suede Shoes* (based on a true incident spotted in a gig audience). Sensing its commercial potential, Phillips rush-releases it with heavy promotion.

1956

Mar [3] *Blue Suede Shoes* enters the US Top 100 simultaneously with Presley's first national hit, *Heartbreak Hotel.*
[17] Perkins makes his first TV appearance, on Red Foley's country show, "Ozark Jubilee".
[22] The Perkins brothers are driving to New York, NY, from Norfolk, VA, where they have played a concert on a bill with Gene Vincent and Johnny Burnette, for appearances on "The Perry Como Show" on NBC-TV and "The Ed Sullivan Show" on CBS-TV, when their car hits a pick-up truck near Dover, DE. Perkins and brother Jay are both hospitalized with their injuries, and media promotion made possible by *Blue Suede Shoes*' success slips away while they are recovering.
Apr *Blue Suede Shoes* hits US #3, and will sell over a million copies. Presley's cover is released as the lead song on an EP after he, rather than Perkins, sings it on national TV, and it reaches US #24.
[10] When Perkins leaves hospital and returns to Memphis, he is presented with a new 1956 Cadillac Fleetwood by Sam Phillips, in celebration of *Blue Suede Shoes*' seven-figure sales success.
June *Blue Suede Shoes* hits UK #10 (his only UK chart single), though Presley's cover simultaneously hits UK #9.
July Perkins' follow-up, *Boppin' The Blues*, peaks at US #70.
Sept He begins a three-month US tour on a bill featuring Gene Vincent and Johnny & Dorsey Burnette.
Dec [4] While Perkins and the band are in the Sun Studio in Memphis recording *Matchbox* (with label newcomer Jerry Lee Lewis playing piano on the session), they are visited by Johnny Cash (on the way downtown to shop for Christmas presents with his wife), and then by Presley, who has just returned to Memphis for the holiday season. After Cash leaves, the other three settle down to a studio jam session on familiar gospel, country and R&B numbers, while Phillips leaves the tape running. (These impromptu recordings become legendary as "The Million Dollar Quartet" tapes and segments will be released in the late '70s and mid-'80s, after Presley's death, reaching compact disc in 1990 as ***The Million Dollar Quartet***.)

1957

Mar *Your True Love* peaks at US #67, and is Perkins' last hit for Sun.
[31] Perkins opens a tour of the South, co-headlining with Johnny Cash (and supported by Jerry Lee Lewis, among others), in Little Rock, AR.
Nov [12] Rock'n'roll movie, "Jamboree", opening as "Disc Jockey Jamboree" in the UK, premieres in Hollywood, and features Perkins performing *Glad All Over*.

1958

Feb [19] After the label has issued ***Dance Album Of Carl Perkins***, the artist leaves Sun to sign a new recording deal with CBS/Columbia Records. (Johnny Cash will follow within months.)
May *Pink Pedal Pushers*, taken from his Columbia debut ***Whole Lotta Shakin'***, peaks at US #91.
Oct [22] Jay Perkins, never fully recovered from the car crash two years before, dies from a malignant brain tumor sustained in the accident.

1959

June *Pointed Toe Shoes* peaks at US #92, and will be Carl Perkins' last US pop chart entry. He will subsequently switch to Decca Records but will have no chart success with the label.

1964

May [9] Having toured Europe for the first time the previous year, playing US bases in France, Italy and Germany, he now begins his first major UK tour, co-headlining with Chuck Berry, at Finsbury Park Astoria, London. Also on the bill are the Animals and the Nashville Teens. (His arrival at London airport has been greeted by fans holding a banner proclaiming "Welcome Carl 'Beatle Crusher' Perkins". In fact, the Beatles are ardent fans and play a jam session with him the first time their touring paths cross, which inspires the group to cut three Perkins compositions (of the many they have traditionally played on stage) before the end of the year.
Perkins records *Big Bad Blues*, with backing by the Nashville Teens, in London.
June [1] Perkins attends the Beatles' recording of *Matchbox* at Abbey Road Studios, London. (The single will reach US #17.)
Oct [18] Perkins begins a 28-date, twice-nightly UK tour, with the Animals, Gene Vincent, the Nashville Teens and others, at the Odeon Cinema, Liverpool, Lancs., set to end on November 15th at the Winter Gardens, Bournemouth, Dorset.
Dec The Beatles revive two more Perkins songs - *Honey Don't* (the original B-side of *Blue Suede Shoes*) and *Everybody's Trying To Be My Baby* - on their chart-topping ***Beatles For Sale*** (***Beatles '65*** in the US). These covers earn Perkins more in songwriter royalties than he has earned from all his own post-*Blue Suede Shoes* recordings.

1966

Perkins signs to country label Dollie Records, where he will cut a series of highly-rated, but non-charting singles like *County Boy's Dream* and *Lake County Cotton Country*.

1967

He joins Johnny Cash's touring revue (and will spend several years playing back-up guitar for Cash and performing in his own right in the shows, also providing Cash will the February 1969 US #42 hit *Daddy Sang Bass*). He is also featured in Cash's weekly TV show, and in his documentary movie and million selling album recorded at San Quentin prison, among other notable appearances. Both Cash and Perkins forswear alcohol and pills which have been threatening to blight their lives, and support each other with a joint "dry" pact. They also become born-again Christians.

1970

Jan Back with CBS/Columbia which released ***Carl Perkins On Top*** the previous year, he works on ***Boppin' The Blues***, a collaboration with rock revival band NRBQ, which backs him on several re-makes of his early hits. The following year he will write songs for the soundtrack to the Robert Redford movie, "Little Fauss And Big Halsy".

1973

Nov Newly signed to Mercury Records' country division, ***My Kind Of Country*** is released and includes a revival of Kenny Rogers' *Ruby (Don't Take Your Love To Town)* and the US Country #61 extract *(Let's Get) Dixiefried* a remake of his 1956 original.

1974

Dec His brother Clayton, troubled with a severe drink problem, takes his own life (shortly before Perkins' father dies of cancer).

1976

He launches his own production company and label, Suede Records, in the US. He also leaves the Johnny Cash troupe after nine years on the road, and launches his own new road band which includes his two sons (Stan and Gregory). Following Elvis Presley's death, he will release the tribute single, *The EP Express* in October 1977, largely made up from titles of Presley hits.

1978

Apr In a brief deal with the UK label Jet, Perkins records ***Ol' Blue Suedes Is Back***, containing remakes of his early material, which, with TV promotion and an accompanying tour, reaches UK #38 - the only hit album of his career.

1981

Apr [23] Perkins, Johnny Cash and Jerry Lee Lewis record a joint session in Stuttgart, West Germany, which will result in ***The Survivors***. (During a year in which Perkins establishes the Carl Perkins Center for the Prevention of Child Abuse, Paul McCartney invites Perkins to the sessions for his ***Tug Of War*** album, writing one song, *Get It*, as a duet for the pair.)

1985

Feb Perkins appears as Mr. Williams, a nightclub bouncer, in John Landis' premiering film "Into The Night".
Mar He cuts a new version of *Blue Suede Shoes* for the soundtrack to the film, "Porky's Revenge", backed by Lee Rocker and Slim Jim Phantom of the Stray Cats.
Oct [21] At Limehouse Studios, London, a TV special is taped to mark the 30th anniversary of *Blue Suede Shoes*. It consists of a performance by "Carl Perkins And Friends", the latter including George Harrison, Ringo Starr, Eric Clapton, Dave Edmunds (who co-ordinates the band and music), and the Stray Cats' Rocker and Phantom.

1986

Jan [1] "Blue Suede Shoes" TV special has its first showing, on C4-TV. (It will also be released as a home video.)
June ***Class of '55***, recorded by Perkins, Cash, Roy Orbison and Lewis is released.
Dec [1] A Coca-Cola commemorative bottle goes on sale in Perkins' hometown of Jackson at $10 apiece, with proceeds going to the Carl Perkins Center for the Prevention of Child Abuse, an organization he founded in 1982.

1987

Jan [21] Perkins is inducted into the Rock and Roll Hall of Fame at the second annual dinner, at the Waldorf Astoria Hotel, New York.

1989

Aug [10] Cable station TBS airs "Coming Home - A Rockin' Reunion" filmed in 1985 as the class of '55 reunion with Roy Orbison, Jerry Lee Lewis and Johnny Cash. (Perkins continues to tour regularly with his sons Greg and Stan in his backing band.)
Sept [30] The Judds' *Let Me Tell You About Our Love*, co-written by Perkins who is also featured on guitar, tops the US Country chart for a week. (The following January, among other activities. Perkins will write four songs with Dolly Parton at his Jackson home.)

1992

Jan [21] Perkins is honored at the eighth annual Hard Rock Café Industry Party in New York.
July He joins George Harrison onstage at the Hard Rock Café 21st anniversary party in London, singing *Everybody's Trying To Be My Baby*, while his latest album, ***Friends Family & Legends***, is released on the Platinum label, featuring harpist Johnny Neel and keyboardists Paul Shaffer and George Small.
Aug Recovering from throat cancer (which has included 37 cobalt radiation treatments), Perkins is too ill to headline a two-month reunion tour of the UK, which also showcases ex-Presley sidemen, guitarist Scotty Moore with whom Perkins has cut the album ***706 Reunion***, drummer D.J. Fontana and the Jordanaires.

1994

June [1] Having released ***Carl Perkins & Sons*** on BMG Records the previous year and recently completed two further projects, ***Disciple In Blue Suede Shoes*** and ***Take Me Back***, Perkins participates in "The Roots Of Country", a celebration of the re-opening of Nashville's Ryman Auditorium, the former home of the Grand Ole Opry, set to air on the 25th.
Oct [8] He takes part in "Elvis Aaron Presley : The Tribute", an all-star concert staged at the Pyramid Arena, Memphis, TN, broadcast live on pay-per-view throughout the US.

THE PET SHOP BOYS

Neil Tennant (vocals); **Chris Lowe** (keyboards)

1981

Aug Tennant (b. Neil Francis Tennant, July 10, 1954, Gosforth, Tyne & Wear), who has already played in Newcastle-based folk outfit Dust and has a degree in history, is assistant editor of UK pop magazine, **Smash Hits**, having already worked as editor for comic hero publishers **Marvel**, when, in a hi-fi shop in London's King's Road, he meets Lowe (b. Christopher Sean Lowe, Oct. 4, 1959, Blackpool, Lancs.), son of a jazz trombonist, who has been in the seven-piece band One Under The Eight, where he learned keyboards, but is currently studying architecture at Liverpool University. They write songs and record demos for the next two years, naming themselves the Pet Shop Boys after friends who worked in an Ealing pet shop.

1983

Aug On assignment to interview Sting for **Smash Hits** in New York, Tennant meets long-time hero, disco producer Bobby "O" Orlando, who offers to produce the duo.

1984

June The duo's Orlando-produced debut, *West End Girls*, becomes a cult success in France and Belgium but its UK release on Epic Records goes un-noticed and the pair is dropped by the label.
Nov They sign with manager Tom Watkins.

1985

Feb After competitive bidding over new demos, EMI Records signs the duo to its UK Parlophone imprint.
July *Opportunities (Let's Make Lots Of Money)* fails to chart, despite strong airplay.
Aug The duo makes its first live appearance at the ICA, London, being interviewed by Max Headroom on the TV program of the same name.
Oct A re-recorded version of *West End Girls*, now produced by Stephen Hague, is released and will take three months to make a Top 10 breakthrough.

1986

Jan [11] *West End Girls* tops the UK chart for the first of two weeks, knocking Shakin' Stevens' *Merry Christmas Everyone* from the top, and selling over 700,000 copies in Britain.
Mar [29] *Love Comes Quickly* reaches UK #19.
Apr [5] Their debut album, the self-penned, synthesizer-dominated, dance/pop based ***Please***, produced by Hague, hits UK #3.
May Remixed *Opportunities (Let's Make Lots Of Money)* reaches UK #11.
[10] *West End Girls* soars to US #1, becoming a chart-topper in eight countries.
Aug [2] *Opportunities (Let's Make Lots Of Money)* hits US #10, as ***Please*** hits US #7. (Despite pressure from the public, press and record company, the group refuses to tour anywhere, a policy it will maintain for three years.)
Sept Extracted from ***Please***, a fourth single, *Suburbia*, hits UK #8.
[15] They perform live at the third annual MTV Video Music Awards, broadcast simultaneously from the Universal Amphitheatre, Universal City, CA, and the Palladium, New York, NY.
[29] ***Please*** is certified platinum by the RIAA for one-million plus US sales.
Oct [4] *Love Comes Quickly* peaks at US #62.
Nov Six special 12" mixes of hits from ***Please*** have been repackaged as the mini-album, ***Disco***, which reaches UK #15.

1987

Jan "Television", a video collection of promo clips, tops the UK Music Video ranking as ***Disco*** makes US #95.
[24] *Suburbia* peaks at US #70.
Feb [9] *West End Girls* is named Best Single Of The Year at the sixth annual BRIT Awards, at London's Grosvenor House Hotel. Tennant receives their award from Boy George, while traditionally shy-boy Lowe watches the show from home on television.
Apr [15] *West End Girls* is named International Hit Of The Year at the 32nd annual Ivor Novello Awards, also held at the Grosvenor House Hotel.
July [4] After six months' writing and recording an album, the duo's synth-swept, melodramatic, hi-nrg-tinged *It's A Sin* tops the UK chart for the first of three weeks, and will go on to similar success worldwide.
Aug [14] The duo performs a cover version of *Always On My Mind* on the ITV special, "Love Me Tender", marking the tenth anniversary of Elvis Presley's death.
[29] A collaboration with Dusty Springfield on a three-year old Tennant/Lowe composition, *What Have I Done To Deserve This?*, produced by Hague, hits UK #2.
Sept [19] ***Actually*** hits UK #2, at the beginning of a 59-week multi-platinum chart tenure.
Oct *Rent*, the Pet Shop Boys' fifth UK top tenner, hits #8, while they spend two weeks promoting their new album in Japan.
Nov [14] *It's A Sin* hits US #9 as ***Actually*** climbs to US #25.
[23] ***Actually*** is certified gold by the RIAA for five-hundred thousand US sales.
Dec [19] *Always On My Mind*, the duo's first non-original single, begins a four-week stay atop the UK chart.

1988

Jan The duo writes and produces Eighth Wonder's debut single, *I'm Not Scared*. Led by vocalist Patsy Kensit, it will hit UK #7 in February.
Feb [8] The Pet Shop Boys win the Best British Group category at the seventh annual BRIT Awards, held again at the Grosvenor House Hotel. Dusty Springfield joins them to sing *What Have I Done To Deserve This?* live at the ceremony.
[20] *What Have I Done To Deserve This?* hits US #2.
Apr [9] *Heart* tops UK chart for the first of three weeks.
May *Always On My Mind* hits US #4. A repackaged US version of ***Actually*** is issued in the UK, with the previously omitted *Always On My Mind* included.
June They appear live at a benefit concert at the Piccadilly Theatre, London, after being persuaded to do so by actor Ian McKellen.
July A Pet Shop Boys feature film, "It Couldn't Happen Here", co-starring Joss Ackland, Neil Dickson, Barbara Windsor and Gareth Hunt, is released in the UK, but interest is short-lived.
Sept *Domino Dancing* hits UK #7, and is followed by the six-track album ***Introspective***, containing their own version of *I'm Not Scared*, a Frankie Knuckles house mix of *I Want A Dog*, a new version of *Always On My Mind*, and two tracks produced by Trevor Horn.
Oct The duo appears on BBC1-TV's "Wogan" to promote *Domino Dancing*.
[22] ***Introspective*** hits UK #2 at the beginning of a 39-week chart stay.
Nov Horn-produced *Left To My Own Devices* hits UK #4, as recent promo clips video collection "Show-business" hits the best seller lists.
Dec [22] Having peaked at US #34 earlier in the month, ***Introspective*** is certified gold by the RIAA.

1989

Feb A second collaboration with Dusty Springfield produces *Nothing Has Been Proved*. Used over the end titles of the film "Scandal", it reaches UK #16 for the '60s star.
[4] *Left To My Own Devices* peaks at US #84.
June [29] The Pet Shop Boys embark on their first tour, taking in Hong Kong, Japan and the UK. Admittedly nervous about the venture, their performances, prominently featuring a number of visual art enchancements, are well received.
July The duo's *It's Alright* hits UK #5.
Aug Their production of Liza Minnelli's *Losing My Mind*, giving the diva her UK chart debut, hits #6. (Two minor hits will follow from this liaison, *Don't Drop Bombs* and *So Sorry I Said*, and ***Results***, which hits UK #6.)
Dec As a side project, Tennant has teamed with New Order's Bernard Sumner and ex-Smiths guitarist Johnny Marr to form Electronic. The combo's debut *Getting Away With It* reaches UK #12.

1990

May [19] *Getting Away With It* makes US #38.
July [7] Dusty Springfield's ***Reputation***, which features *Nothing Has Been Proved* and four other tracks produced by the Pet Shop Boys and Julian Mendelsohn, reaches UK #18.
Aug Tennant and Lowe make their US debut guesting on two songs during an Electronic concert at Dodger Stadium, Los Angeles, CA, supporting Depeche Mode.
Oct [6] *So Hard*, from their forthcoming ***Behaviour***, hits UK #4 in its first week on the chart.
Nov [3] ***Behaviour***, co-produced with Harold Faltermeyer, hits UK #2, unable to dislodge Paul Simon's ***The Rhythm Of The Saints***.
The Pet Shop Boys play their first ever full US gig at the Mayan club, Los Angeles.
[24] *So Hard* peaks at US #62, in the same week that parent album, ***Behavior***, reaches its US #45 peak.
Dec [1] *Being Boring* reaches UK #20, despite a highly physical black and white promo video, featuring a half-naked model.

1991

Feb [23] *How Can You Expect To Be Taken Seriously?* peaks at US #93.
Mar [19] A 17-date North American tour opens at the James L. Knight Center in Miami, FL, set to end on April 14th at the Massey Hall, Toronto, Canada.
[30] *Where The Streets Have No Name/Can't Take My Eyes Off You*, an uptempo Euro-disco coupling of the U2 song with the Frankie Valli 1967 US #2, hits UK #4, issued as a double A-side with *How Can You Expect To Be Taken Seriously?*
June [7-9] The Pet Shop Boys close a short UK tour with two nights at Wembley Arena, Wembley, Middx.
[15] *Jealousy* reaches UK #12.
[22] *Where The Streets Have No Name (I Can't Take My Eyes Off You)* peaks at US #72.
Oct [15] The duo plays a benefit for St. Mary's Hospital's HIV unit, at London's Heaven club before a crowd of 1,200.
[26] *DJ Culture* debuts at its UK #13 peak.
Nov [16] Greatest hits collection, ***Discography***, bows at its UK #3 peak.
[23] *DJ Culture Mix* makes UK #40.
[30] Compilation ***Pet Shop Boys Discography - The Complete Singles Collection*** peaks at US #111.
Dec [21] *Was It Worth It?* debuts at its UK #24 high, as the duo guests on BBC1-TV's "Going Live".

1992

Jan [27] **The Sun** reports that the duo is splitting, "bored witless with just being pop stars after 11 years of hits." Tennant appears on BBC Radio 1's Simon Bates show to deny the story.
Feb [16] The Pet Shop Boys are featured on ITV's "South Bank Show".
Mar They co-produce tracks for Cicero, recording for their newly-formed Spaghetti label.

May [13] The duo performs at the Hacienda, Manchester, Gtr. Manchester.
June [8] They headline a LIFEbeat benefit concert at the Roseland Ballroom, New York.
July [4] Electronic's *Disappointed* bows at its UK #6 peak.
[27-31] Tennant and Lowe fill in for Simon Bates as DJs on Radio 1.
Sept They begin work on new material at London's Sarm West Studios, and produce Boy George's forthcoming UK and US hit version of Dave Berry's *The Crying Game* for the soundtrack to the film of the same name.

1993

June [6] The duo guests on BBC2's "The O Zone".
[12] *Can You Forgive Her?* debuts at its UK #7 peak.
Sept [18] *Go West*, the duo's cover of Village People's camp 1979 US #45/UK #15, debuts at its UK #2 peak, behind Culture Beat's *Mr. Vain*.
Oct [9] Continuing the Boys' successful self-penned synth-based formula, the sel-produced ***Very*** enters the UK chart at #1. Early copies include the limited edition bonus set ***Relentless***.
[23] ***Very*** debuts at its US #20 peak.
Dec [18] The extracted *I Wouldn't Normally Do This Kind Of Thing* reaches UK #13.

1994

Feb [14] The Pet Shop Boys perform *Go West* at the 13th annual BRIT Awards at London's Alexandra Palace.
Apr [16] *Liberation* debuts at its UK #14 peak.
Sept [10] *Yesterday, When I Was Mad* debuts at its UK #13 peak.
[24] Compiled by producer Danny Rampling, a second collection of remixes ***Disco 2*** hits UK #6 in its week of entry.
Oct The Pet Shop Boys take part in the "Stonewall Equality" show at London's Royal Albert Hall, with Elton John, Sting and Alison Moyet.
[8] ***Disco 2*** debuts at its US #75 peak.
Nov [20-21] The duo plays two sellout dates at the National Auditorium, Mexico City, Mexico.

1995

Feb [8] The RIAA certifies gold sales of ***Discography*** and ***Very***.
Aug [12] *Paninaro '95* reaches UK #15.
[19] ***Alternative***, a two-disk round-up of the duo's B-sides, hits UK #2 in its week of entry.
Sept [16] ***Alternative*** bows at its US #103 peak, during a two week chart stay.

1996

May [4] The Pet Shop Boys return with *Before*, which debuts at its UK #7 peak.

PETER & GORDON

Peter Asher (vocals, guitar);
Gordon Waller (vocals, guitar)

1964

Jan Asher (b. June 22, 1944, London), already an established child actor, having played Jennings on BBC radio and appeared in several movies, and Waller (b. June 4, 1945, Braemar, Grampian, Scotland), both sons of doctors, first met at Westminster boys' school in 1959 where they were part of a quasi-Shadows trio, playing at school events and coffee bars, and have left school determined to pursue a music career together. EMI's A&R chief Norman Newell now hears them during a two-week booking at London's Pickwick club, and they are summoned to EMI to record one of their own compositions, *If I Were You*.
[21] Inviting Paul McCartney, then Asher's sister Jane's boyfriend, to help finish a song he had started, the duo rushes to record it at EMI.
Apr [23] This debut release, *A World Without Love*, credited as a Lennon and McCartney composition, tops the UK chart for the first of two weeks.
June [19] The duo begins a US tour at New York, NY's World Fair, set to end on July 5th.
[27] *A World Without Love* hits US #1 and will head charts in nine other countries.
July [3-4] Towards the end of the trek, the pair takes part in "A Million Dollar Party" presented by KPOI at the International Center Arena, Honolulu, HI, an event headlined by the Beach Boys.
[4] *Nobody I Know*, also written by McCartney (and still co-credited to Lennon), hits UK #10.
Aug [1] *Nobody I Know* reaches US #12 as ***A World Without Love***, released by Capitol Records in the US, reaches US #21 and ***Peter And Gordon*** makes UK #18.
Oct *I Don't Want To See You Again*, penned by McCartney, reaches US #16.
Nov Peter & Gordon appear on CBS-TV's "The Ed Sullivan Show".
Dec ***In Touch With Peter And Gordon*** is released in the UK, while ***I Don't Want To See You Again*** makes US #95.

1965

Jan [7] The duo flies to South Africa for tour dates, amid harsh criticism from the Musicians' Union.
Feb *I Go To Pieces*, given to them by Del Shannon while on tour together in Australia, hits US #9.
Apr Their cover of Buddy Holly's *True Love Ways* hits UK #2 and reaches US #14. ***I Go To Pieces*** is released in the US and climbs to #51.
July [2] They headline Dick Clark's "Caravan Of Stars" tour throughout the US, set to close on September 6th.
[10] *To Know You Is To Love You* hits UK #5.
Aug [7] *To Know You Is To Love You* reaches US #24.
Oct [2]***True Love Ways***, a US-only release makes #49.
[22] Following the release of ***Hurtin' 'n' Lovin'***, the duo embarks on a 28-date, twice-nightly UK package tour, with headliner Gene Pitney, Lulu & the Luvvers, the Rockin' Berries and others, at the Finsbury Park Astoria, London, set to end on November 21st at the Odeon Cinema, Leeds, Yorks.
Nov Van McCoy song *Baby I'm Yours* reaches UK #19. A Barbara Lewis #11 hit three months earlier in the US, it is the flipside of *Don't Pity Me*, which peaks at US #83.
Dec [15] They fly to Nashville, TN, to cut a country and western album, before flying to New York to begin dates with DJ Murray The K.
[16] The duo is featured in the previously taped ITV broadcast of a tribute to "The Music Of Lennon & McCartney".
[24] Murray The K's "Christmas Show", with Peter & Gordon one of the featured acts, opens at New York's Brooklyn Fox Theater.

1966

Feb US-only ***Peter And Gordon Sing And Play The Hits Of Nashville*** is released.
Mar The duo releases *Woman*. McCartney, growing tired of people assuming his songs are only hits because his name appears on the credits, has penned the song as Parisian student Bernard Webb for the UK, where it reaches #28, and added the co-writing credit of A. Smith for the US, where it climbs to #14.
The album of the same name, ***Woman***, only released in the US, peaks at #60.
Apr [11] The duo appears on the final episode of NBC-TV's "Hullabaloo", singing *Looking For Tears*.
June [11] *There's No Living Without Your Love* makes US #50.
Don't Pity Me and ***Peter And Gordon*** are released.
July ***The Best Of Peter And Gordon*** stops at US #72, while *To Show I Love You* peaks at US #98.
Oct *Lady Godiva*, co-written by Mike Leander, reaches UK #16, despite being banned in Lady Godiva's hometown of Coventry, Warks., and being branded obscene by the city's mayor.
Nov *Lady Godiva* hits US #6. Its sales will top seven figures by 1967, the duo's fourth million seller.
Dec ***Somewhere ...*** is released.

1967

Jan *Knight In Rusty Armour* reaches US #15, as ***Lady Godiva*** makes US #80.
[7] The duo guests on the first edition of ITV's "Doddy's Music Box".
Feb Peter & Gordon announce that they are splitting as a full-time act, although they will continue to occasionally record together.
Mar ***Knight In Rusty Armour*** is released in the US.
Apr *Sunday For Tea* makes US #31 and *The Jokers* peaks at US #97. They are the duo's final US chart entries and neither charts in Britain.
May [15] Waller plays a DJ in the BBC2-TV play "The Fantasist".
June ***In London For Tea*** is issued in the US, while Waller releases a US solo single, *Speak For Me*.

1968

July Following Waller's solo singles, *Rosecrans Boulevard* (January) and *Every Day* (June), the duo releases *You've Had Better Times*. (It will be released in the US at Christmas, where it is taken from ***Hot, Cold And Custard***. Waller's *Weeping Analeah* will receive a domestic release at the same time.)
Sept The duo permanently splits - their final UK single release, *I Can Remember (Not Too Long Ago)*, emerging in May the following year. Asher becomes A&R manager at the Beatles' Apple Records, having begun a production career, helming three singles for Paul Jones.
Dec James Taylor's eponymous debut album is released, produced by Asher following which he leaves Apple to develop his career as a manager and producer, initially in-house at MGM Records in Los Angeles, CA. Waller releases a second US solo single, *Every Day*, followed by *I Was A Boy When You Needed A Man* for Bell Records in April 1969, and his final single, *You're Only Gonna Hurt Yourself*, in May the following year, preceding his only solo album, ***Gordon*** (***... And Gordon*** in the US) in 1972. (Waller, who will be cast as Pharaoh in the London production of Tim Rice and Andrew Lloyd Webber's musical "Joseph And The Amazing Technicolor Dreamcoat" in May 1973, will retire from the music scene.)

1990

Feb [21] Asher, now living in Malibu, CA, with his wife Wendy, wins his second Producer Of The Year trophy (his first has come in 1978) at the 32nd annual Grammy Awards, at the Shrine Auditorium, Los Angeles. (Starting with James Taylor in the '60s, through a host of artists in the '70s and '80s, most notably Linda Ronstadt, Asher is still producing and managing acts in the '90s, including 10,000 Maniacs and Randy Newman. Waller, who moved to Fowey, Cornwall, in 1987 to run a gift store and dinghy repair shop, will be cleared of sending an indecent fax message at Bodmin magistrates court in Cornwall on April 4th, 1992.)

TOM PETTY & THE HEARTBREAKERS

Tom Petty (vocals, guitar); **Mike Campbell** (guitar); **Howard Epstein** (bass); **Benmont Tench** (keyboards); **Stan Lynch** (drums)

1971

The son of an insurance salesman, singer-songwriter/guitarist Petty (b. Oct. 20, 1952, Gainesville, FL), inspired by Elvis Presley whom he saw filming "Follow That Dream" on location in Ocala, FL, near his Gainesville home at the age of seven, also seeing the Beach Boys, Searchers and Zombies at his first ever gig, formed his first band the Sundowners (name-changing to the Epics) with three schoolfriends upon graduating from Gainesville High School in 1968. Now calling themselves Mudcrutch, the band, comprising Petty (bass, guitar), Tommy Leadon, brother of Eagle Bernie Leadon (lead guitar), Campbell (b. Feb. 1, 1954, Panama City, FL) (guitar) and Randall Marsh (drums), makes its first recordings, financed by Gerald Maddox, a bell pepper farmer from Bushnell, FL, at Criteria Studios, Miami, FL, with producer Ron Albert.

1974

Apr [1] Petty leaves Gainesville and heads to Los Angeles, CA, with a Mudcrutch demo tape, and finds interest from seven labels, including Denny Cordell's Shelter Records, which signs the band.

1975

The only Mudcrutch single, *Depot Street*, is released, but after permanently relocating to Los Angeles and recording an album for Shelter, the band breaks up. (The album will remain unreleased.) Cordell retains Petty on Shelter and suggests working solo, but he forms new back-up band the Heartbreakers, with ex-Mudcrutch members Campbell and Tench (b. Sept. 7, 1954, Gainesville) and recruits Ron Blair (b. Sept. 16, 1952, Macon, GA) and Jeff Jourard, both playing in Gainesville band RGF, and Lynch (b. May 21, 1955, Gainesville), drummer with another Gainesville band, Road Turkey. (With a surfeit of guitarists, Jourard will soon leave and form the Motels with brother Marty.)

1976

Nov Written by Petty and produced by Cordell, their debut album, ***Tom Petty And The Heartbreakers***, is released, selling 6,500 after three months of retail.

1977

Apr Petty & the Heartbreakers support Nils Lofgren on a UK tour.

May Petty's song, *American Girl*, is recorded by ex-Byrds member Roger McGuinn (another of Petty's early influences). The group works hard on the road to promote its debut album (playing over 200 dates around US, Europe and UK during the year).

June ***Tom Petty And The Heartbreakers*** reaches UK #24.

July *Anything That's Rock'n'Roll*, from the album, makes UK #36.

Aug *American Girl*, also from the debut set, climbs to UK #40.

1978

Feb A further album extract, *Breakdown*, is the group's US chart debut at #40, while ***Tom Petty And The Heartbreakers***, having entered the chart in September, finally makes US #55.

May The group appears in the movie "FM", about a California radio station, while the Petty track *Breakdown*, included on the soundtrack album, hits US #5 and makes UK #37.

June [24] The band performs at the "Knebworth Festival", Knebworth, Herts.

July Their second album, ***You're Gonna Get It!***, once again showcasing the outfit's guitar-based straight-ahead rock approach, reaches UK #34.

[7] The still-climbing ***You're Gonna Get It!*** is certified as Petty's first gold disc by the RIAA.

Aug ***You're Gonna Get It!*** makes US #23, while the extracted *I Need To Know* peaks at US #41.

Oct *Listen To Her Heart* reaches US #59.

1979

May [23] Petty files for Chapter 11 Bankruptcy (the right to work out a re-organization of his debts). This has partly arisen out of a record company dispute: Shelter has been sold to ABC, which has now been bought by MCA Records, and Petty is said to owe MCA $575,000, which will only be automatically repaid if he remains one of its acts and cuts six further albums. MCA sues for breach of contract, but the bankruptcy declaration, revealing assets of only $56,000, causes the suit to be withdrawn as pointless. A solution is reached via the formation of the new MCA-controlled label, Backstreet Records, to be run by Danny Bramson and devoted wholly to Petty & the Heartbreakers.

Sept Petty hands over the tapes for a new album and tours the US under the banner "Why MCA?"

[19-23] The band plays at the "Musicians United For Safe Energy" (MUSE) anti-nuclear concerts at New York, NY's Madison Square Garden, alongside Bruce Springsteen, Jackson Browne, Carly Simon, the Doobie Brothers and others.

Nov ***Damn The Torpedoes***, written by Petty and co-produced with Jimmy Iovine, peaks at UK #57.

1980

Feb *Don't Do Me Like That* hits US #10, while parent album, ***Damn The Torpedoes***, hits US #2 for seven weeks (behind Pink Floyd's ***The Wall***) and will be certified for two million sales by the RIAA on October 12th 1984.

Mar *Refugee*, taken from the album, reaches US #15.

May A third extract, *Here Comes My Girl*, peaks at US #59.

1981

May ***Hard Promises*** makes UK #32. Petty has initially withheld the tapes for this, until MCA agrees not to implement a proposed $1 price rise to $9.98 on the US release. Petty, whose sales have accounted for almost 25% of MCA's 1980 profits, has accused the label of greed, and it backs down.

June *The Waiting* reaches US #19 as its parent album, ***Hard Promises***, once again co-helmed by Iovine and featuring Stevie Nicks on *Insider*, hits US #5.

Aug *A Woman In Love (It's Not Me)* peaks at US #79.

[10] ***Hard Promises*** is certified platinum by the RIAA.

Sept Returning the favor, Stevie Nicks' *Stop Draggin' My Heart Around* with Petty & the Heartbreakers backing her, hits US #3 and makes UK #50.

1982

Mar Blair, tired of touring, leaves, to be replaced by Howard Epstein (b. July 21, 1955, Milwaukee, WI), who has played in John Hiatt's band and toured with Del Shannon.

June [6] Petty plays at "Peace Sunday : We Have A Dream", an anti-nuclear concert to launch Peace week, at the Rose Bowl, Pasadena, CA, sharing the bill with Bob Dylan, Jackson Browne, Stevie Wonder and many more.

Sept [1] Epstein makes his live debut with the Heartbreakers at the Santa Cruz Auditorium, Santa Cruz, CA.

[5] Petty performs at the "US Festival" in San Bernadino, CA, alongside Fleetwood Mac, the Police, Talking Heads and a host of others.

Nov ***Long After Dark***, again co-produced with Iovine, makes UK #45.

1983

Jan ***Long After Dark*** hits US #9, while the extracted *You Got Lucky*, co-written by Petty and Campbell, reaches US #20.

[4] ***Long After Dark*** is confirmed gold by the RIAA.

Apr *Change Of Heart*, also from ***Long After Dark***, makes US #21.

May Del Shannon releases ***Drop Down And Get Me***, produced by Petty and backed by the Heartbreakers.

1985

Apr ***Southern Accents***, co-produced by Petty, Iovine and Dave Stewart of Eurythmics, reaches UK #23. *Don't Come Around Here No More*, taken from it and written with Stewart, makes UK #50.

May ***Southern Accents*** hits US #7, while *Don't Come Around Here No More* reaches US #13.

July [6] *Make It Better (Forget About Me)* peaks at US #54.

[13] Petty & the Heartbreakers perform at the "Live Aid" benefit at the JFK Stadium in Philadelphia, PA.

Sept [7] *Rebels* peaks at US #74.

[13] "Don't Come Around Here No More"' wins the Best Special Effects category at the second annual MTV Video Music Awards, held at Radio City Music Hall, New York.

[20] ***Southern Accents*** is certified platinum by the RIAA.

[22] Petty performs at the inaugural "Farm Aid" fundraiser in Champaign, IL.

1986

Jan [25] Rosanne Cash's *Never Be You*, written by Petty and Tench, tops the US Country chart.

Feb [24-25] The group performs in Sydney, Australia, during a tour of Australia, New Zealand and Japan, supporting Bob Dylan, as the live double album, ***Pack Up The Plantation***, reaches US #22.

Mar [1] *Needles And Pins*, with Stevie Nicks, makes US #37. Meanwhile, Dylan, with Petty & the Heartbreakers backing, releases *Band Of The Hand*, the theme song to the movie of the same title, on MCA.

June Petty begins a 40-date US "True Confessions" tour with Dylan, preceded by a major concert for Amnesty International.

1987

Mar [4] Petty obtains a restraining order against the B.F. Goodrich Tire Company from using a song similar to Petty's *Mary's New Car*.

May [2] ***Let Me Up (I've Had Enough)*** peaks at UK #59 in its week of entry.

[17] Fire destroys Petty's house in Los Angeles with damage estimated at $800,000.

June [20] *Jammin' Me* reaches US #18.

July ***Let Me Up (I've Had Enough)*** reaches US #20.

[21] ***Let Me Up (I've Had Enough)*** is ratified gold by the RIAA.

Oct Petty & the Heartbreakers open a tour with Dylan in Israel, moving on to dates in Europe.

1988

Jan [25] ***Tom Petty And The Heartbreakers*** is certified gold by the RIAA.

Nov Petty, as alter-ego Charlie T. Wilbury Jr., has joined George Harrison, Bob Dylan, Roy Orbison and Jeff Lynne as the Traveling Wilburys, hitting US #3 and UK #16 with ***Volume 1***.

Dec [12] Petty attends a memorial for Orbison, with Don Henley, Graham Nash, Bonnie Raitt and others.

1989

May *I Won't Back Down*, the first single from the forthcoming album, ***Full Moon Fever***, reaches UK #28.

July ***Full Moon Fever***, credited as a Petty solo album and co-written and produced with Lynne and Campbell, with the Heartbreakers (minus Lynch) playing on most tracks, hits US #3, while *I Won't Back Down* reaches US #12.

[5] Petty begins a 44-date US tour at Miami Arena, Miami, FL. (He will refuse to perform at the Garden State Arts Center, Holmdel, NJ, when he discovers Greenpeace officials have been denied access.)

[6] On the second night of the tour at Bayfront Center, St. Petersburg, FL, Petty is joined on stage by Roger McGuinn for four Byrds' numbers.

[8] ***Full Moon Fever*** hits UK #8 in its week of entry.

Aug *Runnin' Down A Dream* peaks at UK #55.

Sept [23] *Runnin' Down A Dream* reaches US #23.

Nov *Free Fallin'* peaks at UK #64.

1990

Jan [27] *Free Fallin'*, written by Petty and Lynne, hits US #7.

Feb [20] He plays a sellout show at the Met Center, Bloomington, MN, during current US tour, supported by Lenny Kravitz.

Mar [1] During a concert at Great Western Forum in Inglewood, CA, Petty is joined on stage by Bob Dylan and Bruce Springsteen, singing Creedence Clearwater Revival's *Travelin' Band* and the Animals' *I'm Crying*.

[13] The RIAA certifies three million sales of ***Full Moon Fever***.

[24] *A Face In The Crowd* makes US #46.

Aug [27] "Full Moon Fever - The Video" is certified gold by the RIAA.

Nov [17] A second Wilburys outing fittingly titled

Vol. 3, with Petty now appearing as Muddy Wilbury, enters the US chart set to reach #11.

1991

Mar [9] The Peace Choir's *Give Peace A Chance*, with Petty one of the all-star contributors, makes US #54.
July [6] *Learning To Fly*, again written with Lynne, makes UK #46.
[20] ***Into The Great Wide Open***, co-helmed by Lynne, debuts at its UK #3 peak.
[27] ***Into The Great Wide Open*** reaches US #13.
Aug [24] *Learning To Fly* lands at US #28.
[29] Petty embarks on a US tour in Denver, CO.
Oct [12] He guests on NBC-TV's "Saturday Night Live".
Nov [23] Title cut, *Into The Great Wide Open*, peaks at US #92.
[24] Petty plays before a sellout crowd of 12,307 at the Oakland-Alameda County Coliseum, Oakland, CA.

1992

Mar [23-25, 27-28] He performs at Wembley Arena, Wembley, Middx., during his current UK tour.
Apr He signs a three-year deal with Warner Bros. Records.
[4] *Too Good To Be True* bows at its UK #34 peak.
Oct [16] Petty participates in the Bob Dylan 30th anniversary tribute concert at New York's Madison Square Garden, singing *Mr. Tambourine Man* with Roger McGuinn as well as performing solo on *License To Kill* and *Rainy Day Women*, and backing Dylan on *My Back Pages* with Eric Clapton, George Harrison and McGuinn.
Dec [9] He presents **Billboard**'s first Century Award to George Harrison at the 1992 Billboard Music Awards.

1993

Aug Petty performs at the opening of Johnny Depp's Sunset Strip Club, the Viper Room, with Evan Dando, Maria McKee and Shane McGowan.
Oct [30] *Something In The Air*, his revival of Thunderclap Newman's 1969 UK #1/US #37, and one of two new tracks included on the forthcoming ***Greatest Hits*** package, debuts at its UK #53 peak.
Nov [4] The group plays a date in Petty's home town of Gainesville, broadcast live on the Westwood One radio network.
[13] ***Greatest Hits***, featuring the two new cuts produced by Rick Rubin, Petty and Campbell, debuts at its UK #10 peak.

1994

Feb [5] ***Greatest Hits*** hits US #5.
Mar [12] The extracted *Mary Jane's Last Dance* debuts at its UK #52 peak.
[19] *Mary Jane's Last Dance* reaches US #14.
Aug [30] A Petty tribute album by various underground acts, ***You Got Lucky***, is released in the US.
Sept [8] Petty performs at the 11th annual MTV Video Music Awards, held at Radio City Music Hall. He also picks up the lifetime achievement Video Vanguard award, while "Mary Jane's Last Dance" is named Best Male Video.
Oct [1] Petty performs at the eighth Bridge School benefit at the Shoreline Amphitheatre, Mountain View, CA.
[2] Lynch plays his last show with the band after 19 years. He will go on to pursue a career in producing.
Nov [12] ***Wildflowers***, released as a Petty solo album, though Heartbreakers Tench, Epstein and Campbell all appear, makes UK #36 in its week of entry.
[19] ***Wildflowers*** debuts at its US #8 peak, the same day Petty guests on "Saturday Night Live", with Dave Grohl filling in on the drum stool.
[21] Petty appears on CBS-TV's "Late Show With David Letterman".

1995

Feb [4] *You Don't Know How It Feels* reaches US #13.
Apr [28] The RIAA certifies four million sales of ***Greatest Hits***.
June [3] *It's Good To Be King* makes US #68.
Aug [10] The RIAA certifies three million sales of ***Wildflowers***.
Sept [7] Petty wins the Best Male Video category for "You Don't Know How It Feels" at the 12th annual MTV Video Music Awards, held at New York's Radio City Music Hall.
Nov A six-CD, 92-track boxed-set retrospective, ***Playback 1973-1993***, is released in the US. One disc is devoted to 15 B-sides, another to previously unreleased live performances and a third comprises previously unissued studio material.

1996

Feb [28] *You Don't Know How It Feels* is named Best Rock Vocal Performance, Male at the 38th annual Grammy Awards held at the Shrine Auditorium.
Apr [26] Not expected to play and attending to receive the George and Ira Gershwin Award for Lifetime Musical Achievement at Los Angeles' UCLA, Petty performs a new song *Angel Dream* on an amp and guitar belonging to one of the students, to the assembled 4,000-strong crowd, one of six new cuts he has written for the forthcoming Edward Burns-directed movie "She's The One".

WILSON PICKETT

1963

May Pickett (b. Mar. 18, 1941, Prattville, AL), having moved to Detroit as a teenager in 1955, has sung in gospel groups, before joining R&B band the Falcons in 1961, veterans of the 1959 US #17 hit, *You're So Fine*, after he is heard singing and playing his guitar on the front porch of his home by Falcon member and neighbor Willie Schofield. With Pickett on lead vocal, having replaced Eddie Floyd, they have scored a second US hit with the #75-peaking *I Found A Love* in May the following year. Falcons producer Robert Bateman has suggested that Pickett should go solo and arranged an audition with singer Lloyd Price, owner of the Double L label. Price signs him, and *If You Need Me*, a Bateman/Pickett composition, now peaks at US #64 (a cover by the better-known Solomon Burke makes US #37).
Sept *It's Too Late*, his second on Double L, makes US #49.
Nov *I'm Down To My Last Heartbreak*, also on Double L, climbs to US #96.

1965

May Atlantic Records buys Pickett's contract and after two non-charting releases under the guidance of Bert Berns (*I'm Gonna Cry* and *Come Home Baby*), producer Jerry Wexler records him at Stax Studios, Memphis, TN, with Booker T. & the MG's.
Sept *In The Midnight Hour*, written by Pickett and MG's guitarist Steve Cropper, reaches US #21, subsequently becoming a highly-regarded and much-covered soul classic. Pickett gains the nickname "The Wicked Pickett" at Atlantic (often used in his publicity) - supposedly because of his interest in the ladies at the record company.
Oct *In The Midnight Hour* is his UK chart debut, at #12.
Nov [9] Pickett makes his live bow in the UK at the Scotch Of St. James club in London, backed by three members of the Animals, before embarking on a 17-date UK tour.
Dec *Don't Fight It* makes US #53 and UK #29, while ***In The Midnight Hour*** peaks at US #107.

1966

Jan *634-5789* reaches US #13 and UK #36, and is Pickett's first US R&B #1 (for seven weeks).
Mar Pickett begins his second UK tour, causing a sensation among the burgeoning British mod and R&B audience.
July Staying with numbers for titles, *Ninety Nine And A Half (Won't Do)* makes US #53.
Sept Recorded at Muscle Shoals Studios, Muscle Shoals, AL, Pickett's revival of Chris Kenner's *Land Of 1,000 Dances* (also a 1965 US Top 20 for Cannibal & the Headhunters) is the only Top 10 hit of this much-covered song, at US #6, also climbing to UK #22.
Oct ***The Exciting Wilson Pickett*** reaches US #21.
Dec *Mustang Sally*, written by Mack Rice (ex-the Falcons), peaks at US #23 and UK #28.

1967

Mar ***The Wicked Pickett*** makes US #42, while his revival of Solomon Burke's *Everybody Needs Somebody To Love* reaches US #29.
[28-**Apr** 2] Pickett participates in Murray The K's Easter Show, "Music In The 5th Dimension", at Manhattan RKO Theatre, New York, NY.
Apr Pickett's solo version of his Falcons success, *I Found A Love*, makes US #32.
July US radio airplay is divided on the double-sided *Soul Dance Number Three/You Can't Stand Alone*, which peaks at US #55/#70.
Sept Pickett's cover of Dyke & the Blazers' *Funky Broadway* (a minor hit in the spring) hits US #8 and R&B #1 (for a week). ***The Sound Of Wilson Pickett***, containing the hit, reaches US #54.
Oct *Funky Broadway* makes UK #43.
Nov His revival of former mentor Price's million seller, *Stag-O-Lee*, reaches US #22, but is replaced by radio DJs spinning its B-side, *I'm In Love*, which climbs to US #45. These are among several tracks cut at renewed sessions in Memphis, in partnership with Bobby Womack.
Dec ***The Best Of Wilson Pickett***, a compilation of hit singles to date, peaks at US #35 during a year-long chart run.

1968

Mar *Jealous Love* makes US #50, while ***I'm In Love*** reaches US #70.
May *She's Lookin' Good* reaches US #15.
July *I'm A Midnight Mover*, in *Midnight Hour* style, makes US #24.
Aug ***The Midnight Mover*** peaks at US #91.
Oct *I Found A True Love* (not to be confused with *I Found A Love*) makes US #42, while *I'm A Midnight Mover* makes UK #38 (after a year's absence on the UK rankings).
Dec *A Man And A Half* makes US #42.

1969

Jan Recording again at Muscle Shoals, Pickett's cover of the Beatles' *Hey Jude* (at the suggestion of Duane Allman of the Allman Brothers, who plays guitar on the cut), reaches US #23 while the original version is still charting. It also rises to UK #16 (and is Pickett's final UK chart entry).
Apr ***Hey Jude*** peaks at US #97 while *Minnie Skirt Minnie* makes US #50.

1970

May Pickett's rock cover (again with Duane Allman) of Steppenwolf's *Born To Be Wild* peaks at US #64.
June His version of the Archies' *Sugar Sugar*, a double A-side with the tribute song, *Cole, Cooke And Redding*, reaches US #25.
Aug A further rock update, *Hey Joe*, peaks at US #59, but its follow-up, a revival of *You Keep Me Hanging On*, stops at US #92, taken from ***Right On***.
Nov Recorded in Philadelphia, PA, with producers Kenny Gamble and Leon Huff and with a sharp new Pickett sound on original material, *(Get Me Back On Time) Engine Number 9* reaches US #14 (and R&B #3). From these sessions, ***Wilson Pickett In Philadelphia*** makes US #64.

1971

Mar Another Philadelphia production, *Don't Let The Green Grass Fool You*, reaches US #17 (and R&B #2).
[22] *Don't Let The Green Grass Fool You* is his first RIAA-certified gold disc.
Apr Pickett headlines with other artists on a tour of Ghana, Africa, to celebrate the country's independence. (He also features prominently in the movie and album of the event, ***Soul To Soul***.)

June Taken from ***Don't Knock My Love***, *Don't Knock My Love, Pt. 1*, recorded with Brad Shapiro and Dave Crawford in Miami, FL, reaches US #13.
[22] *Don't Knock My Love* is certified gold by the RIAA.
July Compilation album ***The Best Of Wilson Pickett, Vol. II*** reaches US #73.
Sept *Call My Name, I'll Be There* peaks at US #52.

1972

Feb His cover of UK band Free's *Fire And Water* rises to US #24, while ***Don't Knock My Love*** makes #132.
July *Funk Factory* peaks at US #58.
Nov Pickett's revival of Randy Newman's (and Three Dog Night's million seller) *Mama Told Me Not To Come* charts briefly at US #99, after which Pickett and Atlantic Records part company.

1973

Apr Newly signed to RCA Records, *Mr. Magic Man* manages a week at US #98, while the album ***Mr. Magic Man*** makes US #187.
Oct *Take A Closer Look At The Woman You're With* makes US #90 (Pickett's last US Top 100 entry). (Three albums ***Tonight I'm My Biggest Audience*** (1974), the critically-revered ***Pickett In The Pocket***, another Pickett/Shapiro Miami production (1974), and ***Join Me And Let's Be Free*** (1975) and many singles, will follow on RCA over the next three years.)

1974

Nov [21] Pickett is arrested in Andes, New York, for possession of a dangerous weapon, after he pulls a gun during an argument. Frequently temperamental, especially when indulging his appetite for alcohol, Pickett has an off-stage reputation to match his fiery passion while performing.

1978

Sept Following the 1976 release of ***Peace Breaker*** on his own Wicked label, Pickett, making widely vocal his contempt for the disco explosion, for its emasculation of the traditional soul style, attempts to blend artistic preference with commercial necessity on ***A Funky Situation***, produced by Rick Hall in Muscle Shoals and issued on Big Tree Records.

1979

Apr Newly signed to EMI America Records ***I Want You*** is released, to be followed by 1981's ***The Right Track***, neither finding commercial favor. He is more successful on the US live circuit, reverting to his best-known material, and often touring with "The Soul Clan", an aggregation of his '60s contemporaries like Eddie Floyd, Don Covay and Joe Tex.

1986

Jan [15] Continuing to tour but currently label-less, Pickett guests on NBC-TV's "Late Night With David Letterman". In July the following year he will face a five-year jail-term when a New Jersey court hears how he brandished a firearm after a fight in a local bar.

1988

Oct Newly signed to Motown Records, his new version of *In The Midnight Hour* peaks at UK #62, taken from ***American Soul Man***, his first album in seven years.

1991

Jan [16] Pickett is inducted into the Rock and Roll Hall of Fame at the sixth annual ceremony, held at New York's Waldorf Astoria Hotel.

1992

Apr [24] Pickett is arrested for striking 86-year old Pepe Ruiz with his car, and charged with driving with open bottles of alcohol, namely six empty vodka miniatures and six empty beer cans. Ruiz is in guarded condition in an Englewood hospital. (A week earlier, Pickett had been ordered to move out of his house. He is also currently charged with damaging the lawn of his neighbor, Mayor Donald Aronson.)
May [4] He agrees to pay $6,500 and enter an alcohol rehabilitation program as part of an agreement to get his former girlfriend Jean Cusseaux to drop charges against him. Judge Lawrence D. Smith in Hackensack, NJ, also orders him to pay $3,500 to the battered women's shelter where she stayed.
[5] Pickett pleads innocent to charges stemming from the April 24th incident.

1993

Feb [25] He is inducted into the fourth Rhythm and Blues Foundation Pioneer Awards at the Palace Theater, Los Angeles, CA. (Pickett's career comes to compact disc as ***A Man And A Half - The Best Of Wilson Pickett*** is issued by Rhino Records in the US.)
Mar Pickett strikes a deal with Englewood mayor Donald Aronson, who will drop charges against him in exchange for a free concert. Aronson says "I've always said Wilson Pickett's worst enemy is Jack Daniels".
June [30] He pleads guilty to reduced charges of assault.
Oct [1] Pickett is sentenced to one year in jail and five years probation for the 1992 drinking offence, and also pays a $5,000 fine, has to undergo treatment for alcoholism and do 200 hours of community service.

1994

Jan [3] He begins serving his jail term in Bergen County Jail, Hackensack, NJ.
Aug [4] Judge Andrew P. Napolitano rules that former companion Jean Marie Cusseaux can claim battered-woman syndrome compensation from Pickett.

1996

Apr [4] Out of jail but still on five years probation, Pickett is arrested again at his Englewood, NJ home and charged with possession of two grams of cocaine and being under the influence of a controlled substance, with bail subsequently set at $6,500. With his current girlfriend, Elizabeth Trapp, bleeding, police also found a blood-splattered broken glass table.

PINK FLOYD

Roger Waters (vocals, bass); **Rick Wright** (keyboards); **David Gilmour** (vocals, guitar); **Nick Mason** (drums)

1965

Waters (b. Sept. 6, 1944, Great Bookham, Surrey), Wright (b. July 28, 1945, London), and Mason (b. Jan. 27, 1945, Birmingham, Warks.) meet as students all studying architecture at Regent Street Polytechnic in London and form Sigma 6 with Clive Metcalf (bass), Juliette Gale (the future Mrs. Wright) and Keith Noble (vocals), shortly name-changing to Architectural Abdabs. Waters invites former next-door neighbor and Camberwell Art School student Syd Barrett (b. Roger Keith Barrett, Jan. 6, 1946, Cambridge, Cambs.) to join the trio in a new band, which Barrett names the Pink Floyd Sound after Georgia bluesmen Pink Anderson and Floyd Council. Barrett's music apprenticeship has been served in Geoff Mott & the Mottoes, followed by the Hollering Blues. Late in the year the group, having dropped Sound from its moniker, plays its first gig, a mix of R&B and 12-bar blues, at the Countdown club in London.

1966

Mar [13] London's Marquee club begins the "Spontaneous Underground", a Sunday afternoon psychedelic groove with Pink Floyd as regulars. The group drops its blues sound and begins playing extended musical numbers mostly written by Barrett. They quickly become the hippest band among London's early psychedelic set and experiment with feedback and electronic sound, with back-projected film shows and lights.
Oct [15-16] The band plays at the "All-Night Rave Pop Op Costume Masque Drag Ball Et Al", on the opening night of the Roundhouse in Chalk Farm, London, for which they are paid £15. **The San Francisco Examiner** review of the show is not even aware that Floyd had played, thinking them to be "a large pick-up band of assorted instruments on a small central platform."
[31] They sign a deal with the management team of Peter Jenner and Andrew King, creating a six-way partnership called Blackhill Enterprises.
Dec [23] The group's reputation for experimentation and innovation continues as it makes its debut at the UFO club which becomes the focal point of British psychedelia. Despite the name, the club is an Irish dance hall on other nights, called the Blarney club, in a basement on London's Tottenham Court Road. Here the group verifies its future recorded sound with songs like *Interstellar Overdrive* and *Astronomie Domine*.

1967

Feb [18] They play at the California Ballroom, Dunstable, Beds.
[27] Pink Floyd records its first single, *Arnold Layne*, at Sound Techniques Studio with producer Joe Boyd, but still has no record contract.
Mar EMI signs the group and purchases *Arnold Layne*. (Legend has it that when introduced to label executives, one asked 'Which of you is "Pink?"' - referred to on the later album, ***Wish You Were Here***.)
[5] The band supports Lee Dorsey at London's Saville Theatre.
[6] They guest on the Move's ITV show "The Rave".
[16] They record *Interstellar Overdrive* with producer Hurricane Smith at London's Abbey Road Studios.
Apr *Arnold Layne* reaches UK #20. Surprisingly, despite its transvestite subject matter, BBC radio continues to play the record while pirate station Radio London bans it.
[29] The group takes part with other acts in a 14-hour, all-night "Technicolour Dream" concert, in the Great Hall of Alexandra Palace, London.
May [12] They play at the newly opened Queen Elizabeth Hall, London.
[29] Pink Floyd performs at "Barbeque '67" at the Tulip Bulb Auction Hall, Spalding, Lincs., with Jimi Hendrix, Cream, the Move, Geno Washington and Zoot Money.
July *See Emily Play* hits UK #6 despite British DJ Pete Murray describing the group as a "con" on BBC-TV's "Juke Box Jury". They will not have another hit single for 12 years.
[29-30] They take part in an all-night "International Love-In" at London's Alexandra Palace.
Aug Their debut album, ***The Piper At The Gates Of Dawn***, hits UK #6.
Sept The group begins a short tour of Ireland with shows at the Ballymena Flamingo and Cork Arcadia.
Oct [1] They arrive in New York, NY for their first US dates.
[24] The US tour is cancelled when Barrett refuses to move his lips in time to *Arnold Layne* when they lip-synch it on ABC-TV's "American Bandstand". (During further "promotion", Barrett, who is developing an LSD drug dependency, being interviewed on "The Pat Boone Show", responds to questions with a blank stare.)
Nov *Apples And Oranges* is released.
[14] The group embarks on a package tour at London's Royal Albert Hall with Amen Corner, the Move, and headliners the Jimi Hendrix Experience, set to end on December 5th at Green's Playhouse, Glasgow, Scotland, with Barrett becoming increasingly unstable.

1968

Jan Barrett's behavior causes concern, and Waters invites a friend, David Gilmour (b. Mar. 6, 1947, Cambridge), to join the group, excusing Barrett from live appearances to concentrate on songwriting. Gilmour has been a member of local band the Ramblers which became Jokers Wild, who once appeared with the Pink Floyd Sound and Paul Simon.
Apr [6] Barrett is asked to leave (going into immediate seclusion in Cambridge) as the group

reverts to a four-piece, minus its main songwriter. Jenner and King also quit as managers, viewing Barrett as the main creative force.
It Would Be So Nice is released.
May The group embarks on a short European tour, playing at the "Rome International Pop Festival", Italy. They also record the soundtrack to the Peter Sykes movie, "The Committee".
June ***A Saucerful Of Secrets*** hits UK #9.
[29] Pink Floyd plays the first-ever large-scale free rock concert in London's Hyde Park with Jethro Tull, Tyrannosaurus Rex and Roy Harper.
July [4] The group embarks on a US tour, through to September.
Oct The "Tonite Let's All Make Love In London" movie, which features three Floyd songs, opens in the UK.
Dec *Point Me At The Sky* is released.

1969

July Having appeared at the "More Furious Madness From The Massed Gadgets Of Auximenes" concert at the Royal Festival Hall and toured Sweden, Holland, Ireland and the UK earlier in the year, the group's ***More*** soundtrack to Barbet Schroeder's film, "More", hits UK #9.
[20] Pink Floyd performs *What If It's Just Green Cheese?* live in the studio during BBC1-TV's "Omnibus" Apollo 11 space mission special.
Aug [8] The group takes part in the ninth "National Jazz, Pop, Ballads & Blues Festival" at Plumpton Racecourse, near Lewes, Sussex.
Sept [17] Pink Floyd performs in Amsterdam, Holland, at the start of a further two-month European tour.
Oct Double set, ***Ummagumma***, consisting of one record of live performances and the other contributions from each member of the group, hits UK #5.
Dec [6] The band plays at the Indoor Sports Centre, Port Talbot, Wales, with Fairport Convention, East of Eden and Sam Apple Pie.
Barrett is retained as a solo act by EMI's Harvest label, and *Octopus* is released as a first sample of his new material.

1970

Jan Barrett's debut album, ***The Madcap Laughs***, with help from Gilmour and Waters, reaches UK #40 as ***Ummagumma*** makes US #74.
[23] Pink Floyd performs its forthcoming album, ***Atom Heart Mother***, under the title ***The Amazing Pudding*** in Paris, France.
Feb [7] The group plays at the Royal Albert Hall, London, during a short UK tour.
Mar They contribute three songs to the soundtrack of Michaelangelo Antonioni's film, "Zabriskie Point".
Apr [29] The group plays at the Fillmore West, San Francisco.
June [27] They perform ***Atom Heart Mother*** at the "Bath Festival Of Blues & Progressive Music", Shepton Mallet, Somerset.
July [18] Pink Floyd gives a free concert in London's Hyde Park, with Edgar Broughton, Deep Purple, Third Ear and Formerly Fat Harry.
Oct [24] ***Atom Heart Mother*** tops the UK chart and defines the sound which will elevate Pink Floyd to worldwide superstar status in the next decade, also making US #55. Waters' ***Music From The Body***, created with his golfing partner Ron Geesin for a Roy Battersby documentary film "The Body", is released on Harvest.
Nov Barrett releases ***Barrett***, but does no promotion for the album, staying in seclusion except when in the recording studio. It proves to be his swan song and he returns to his hometown of Cambridge to become a recluse, resisting all efforts by Pink Floyd members and others to entice him back into the limelight.

1971

July [31] The group leaves for a tour of the Far East.
Aug Budget-priced compilation album, ***Relics***, released by EMI in April on its Regal-Starline label and containing their first two singles, which had been deleted, makes UK #32 and US #152.
[15] The group performs at the Randwick Racecourse, Sydney, New South Wales, one of two Australian shows during the 1970s.
Sept [17] Pink Floyd, the only non-classical act at the music festival in Montreux, Switzerland, performs ***Atom Heart Mother***.
Oct [4-7] They perform at the Roman Amphitheatre, Pompeii, Italy.
[15] They set out on another US tour.
Nov ***Meddle*** hits UK #3 and heads to US #70. Side two is taken up by *Echoes*, which becomes a live favorite. In a **Melody Maker** poll, the group is voted second in Best Group category behind Emerson, Lake & Palmer.

1972

Jan A 14-date "Tour '72" begins at the Dome, Brighton, East Sussex, set to end with three nights at the Rainbow Theatre, Finsbury Park, London, on February 17th-19th, premiering ***Eclipse***, which will become ***The Dark Side Of The Moon***.
Feb Barrett makes a brief reappearance in Stars, a Cambridge-based trio featuring Jack Monk (bass) and Twink (drums), at the Corn Exchange, Cambridge, but after three local appearances they split without recording, and Barrett becomes a recluse again. Renewed critical interest in him prompts EMI to reissue Barrett's two earlier albums as a double pack. Pink Floyd begins recording sessions for "The Valley" movie soundtrack at Strawberry Studios, Chateau D'Herouville, France.
Mar The group begins a 17-city US tour at Fort Hesterly Armory, Tampa, FL.
June ***Obscured By Clouds***, their soundtrack to Barbet Schroeder's film, "The Valley", hits UK #6 and becomes Pink Floyd's highest-charting album to date in the US, at #46. During the month, the band enters Abbey Road Studios to begin recording ***The Dark Side Of The Moon***.
Sept "Pink Floyd Live At Pompeii", a movie made for European television, receives its premiere at the Edinburgh Theatre, Edinburgh, Scotland. (It will be released in 1974 to cinema screens.)
[22] The group performs at the Hollywood Bowl, Hollywood, CA.
Oct They embark on a three-month tour of Europe.

1973

Jan [14] French TV films Roland Petit's re-staging of his ballet "Le Pink Floyd Ballet" in Paris, France.
Mar [31] With lyrics by Waters and music by the band, ***The Dark Side Of The Moon*** hits UK #2, behind ***20 Flashback Greats Of The Sixties***. It will never top the chart despite charting for an initial 310 weeks, while the record which keeps it off the top will only remain charted for a further 10 weeks. The band-produced concept project engineered by Alan Parsons, dealing with madness, whose sound effects and music are moulded into Pink Floyd's most commercial outing, will sell more than 20 million copies worldwide, becoming a landmark rock work.
Apr [28] ***The Dark Side Of The Moon*** tops the US chart for a week during a record breaking 741-week US chart stretch. (In the '80s CD boom, it is reported that there is a pressing plant in Germany that only produces ***The Dark Side Of The Moon*** and no other CDs.) The group spends the rest of the year touring to perform the album in its entirety, with an appropriately grandiose stage production.
May [19] The band plays at London's Earls Court during current UK dates.
June [16] They embark on a US tour at the Roosevelt Stadium in New Jersey.
July The extracted *Money*, is released in the US (but not Britain), making #13.

1974

Jan ***A Nice Pair***, a re-package of their first two albums, makes UK #21 and US #36.
July The group begins a short tour of France.
Oct Pink Floyd is set to work on ***Household Objects***, an album without any musical instruments, but recordings are abandoned.

1975

Jan They begin working on a new album project, ***Wish You Were Here***.
Apr The group takes a break from recording to tour the US for two weeks.
July [5] In its first UK appearance of the year, Pink Floyd headlines the "Knebworth Festival", Knebworth, Herts.) and performs one of its most spectacular shows including real Spitfire planes and quadrophonic sound.
Oct [4] ***Wish You Were Here*** tops both the UK and US charts. It contains a tribute to Syd Barrett, *Shine On You Crazy Diamond*, sung by Roy Harper. (Barrett visits the band in the studio while the album is made, but he is never again tempted from his self-induced seclusion into any active part in music.) Violinist Stephane Grappelli also makes an uncredited contribution on the album.
Dec In the US, CBS/Columbia Records signs the band away from Capitol for $1 million.

1976

Apr The group begins working on its latest project, the ***Animals*** album.
Dec [3] They make headlines when a film shoot for the sleeve of ***Animals*** goes disastrously wrong. A 40'-tall inflatable pig, moored above Battersea Power Station, breaks loose from its mooring. The Civil Aviation Authority issues a warning to all pilots in London airspace that a pig is on the loose. It is last sighted at 18,000' over Chatham, Kent.

1977

Jan [23] Their "Animals" tour opens in West Germany, set to finish on July 6th at the Olympic Stadium, Montreal, PQ, Canada. (At the conclusion of the sojourn, Mason produces the Damned's second album ***Music For Pleasure***, and co-helms Steve Hillage's ***Green***, Gilmour makes a solo debut and Wright records ***Wet Dream***. They will reconvene in April 1979.)
Feb ***Animals*** hits UK #2 and US #3.

1978

May Solo album, ***David Gilmour***, recorded with friends Willie Wilson and future Foreigner bassist Rick Wills, reaches UK #17 and subsequently US #29. (Gilmour is also currently featured on protegée Kate Bush's maiden album, ***The Kick Inside***.)
Nov Rick Wright's solo debut, ***Wet Dream***, is released on Harvest.
Dec [9] Gilmour performs a solo set, although he names his studio trio as Bullit, on BBC2-TV's "The Old Grey Whistle Test".

1979

Feb Despite enormous earnings, the group is in a perilous financial state due to the collapse of investment company, Norton Warburg, which has handled its business affairs. Waters comes to the forefront as a writer, composing almost all of the group's forthcoming album, ***The Wall***.
Dec Concept double album, ***The Wall***, hits UK #3.
[15] Taken from it, *Another Brick In The Wall (Part II)*, begins a five-week run at UK #1.

1980

Jan [19] ***The Wall*** tops the US chart for the first of 15 weeks (where it will eventually sell over eight million US copies), as the group tours with a show which explores the theme of the group's alienation from its audience. One of the most celebrated stage spectaculars in rock history, a 160' long, 30'-high wall is built between group and audience and then ceremoniously destroyed after the intermission. Due to its enormous financial outlay, the show is only performed 29 times at a financial loss. Wright leaves the band after the tour due to personal differences with Waters.
Feb [7] The US leg of "The Wall" tour begins,

including five nights apiece at the Sports Coliseum, Los Angeles, CA, and the Nassau Veterans Memorial Coliseum, Uniondale, NY.

Mar [22] *Another Brick In The Wall* tops the US chart for the first of four weeks.

May *Run Like Hell* makes US #53.

June [27] Pink Floyd is awarded the Silver Clef Award at the annual Nordoff Robbins Music Therapy Centre lunch in London.

Aug The group performs six nights at Earls Court, London.

1981

Feb During the German leg of the tour, they play eight shows at the Westfalenhalle, Dortmund.

May Mason's ***Nick Mason's Fictitious Sport*** collaboration with jazz musician/composer Carla Bley, featuring Robert Wyatt on vocals, peaks at US #170.

June [17] The group finishes a further five-night stint at Earls Court.

Dec A greatest hits collection, ***A Collection Of Great Dance Songs***, makes UK #37 and US #31.

1982

July [14] Movie version of "The Wall", directed by Alan Parker and starring Bob Geldof, premieres in London.

Aug *When The Tigers Break Free* makes UK #39. A 17-year old San Antonio, TX youth is charged with killing his aunt, with his lawyers citing his mental instability aggravated by listening to too much Pink Floyd music.

1983

Apr [2] ***The Final Cut*** becomes the group's third UK #1 and will hit US #6. The album, co-produced with Michael Kamen, has an anti-war theme and is almost entirely the work of Waters.

May The extracted *Not Now John* makes UK #30. In a career spanning 16 years, it is only Pink Floyd's fifth UK singles chart hit. The division between Waters and the other two members proves divisive and they split acrimoniously.

[23] ***The Final Cut*** is certified platinum by the RIAA.

1984

Mar Gilmour's second solo album, ***About Face***, including lyrical contributions from Pete Townshend, makes UK #21 and US #32.

[30] Gilmour makes a promotional appearance on C4-TV's "The Tube", as a prelude to a solo world tour in which he will include the popular Floyd classic, *Money*, in his repertoire.

[31] He begins a solo tour to promote ***About Face***, performing in Europe for a month, before playing North America until July 16th, when he will perform his last show at the Beacon Theatre, New York.

Apr Recording with ex-Fashion frontman Dee Harris under the collective name Zee, Wright releases ***Identity***, on the day that Waters releases his first solo single, *5.01 A.M. (The Pros And Cons Of Hitch-Hiking)*.

May Waters' solo opus, ***The Pros And Cons Of Hitch -Hiking***, featuring guests Eric Clapton, Ray Cooper, Michael Kamen and David Sanborn, climbs to UK #13 and US #31.

July [16] Waters embarks on a world tour, playing one set of self-penned Floyd standards and a second half of solo material. With sets designed by Gerald Scarfe, visuals by film director Nicholas Roeg and a large backing-band, including Clapton, and lacking the Pink Floyd brand name, it proves a great personal financial strain. (By year's end, Gilmour plays on a variety of sessions including Bryan Ferry's ***Bete Noire***, Grace Jones' ***Slave To The Rhythm*** and Arcadia's ***So Red The Rose***.)

1985

June Waters dismisses Steve O'Rourke as his manager, against Gilmour and Mason's wishes, even offering them the legal entitlement to the name Pink Floyd.

July [13] Gilmour plays guitar for Bryan Ferry appearance at "Live Aid" at Wembley Stadium, Wembley, Middx.

Sept Mason's second album, ***Profiles***, emerges, a collaboration with Rick Fenn, credited as Mason & Fenn, released simultaneously with a 30-minute autobiographical film, "Life Could Be A Dream", an account of his double career as a drummer and racing driver.

Dec Waters notifies EMI and CBS/Columbia that he is no longer a member of Pink Floyd.

1986

Feb [6] Gilmour, fresh from a stint in Pete Townshend's solo project band, Deep End, forms David Gilmour & Friends, with several Deep End members including Kamen, Simon Phillips and Bad Company's Mick Ralphs.

[9] They perform at the "Colombian Volcano Appeal" concert at London's Royal Albert Hall, with Annie Lennox, Chrissie Hynde, Pete Townshend, Marillion, the Communards and Working Week.

Apr Gilmour and Waters begin work on new projects independently of each other.

Oct Waters releases ***When The Wind Blows***, the soundtrack to the Raymond Briggs/Jimmy Mukarami's movie-length cartoon of the same name. The project, which mainly consists of performances by his current group, the Bleeding Heart Band, also includes David Bowie and other various artist tracks.

[31] Waters brings suit in the Chancery Division of the High Court in London, asking the court to dissolve the partnership and, as band leader and creator of the most successful Pink Floyd recordings, to block Gilmour and Mason from using the band name for future recording and touring.

Nov [11] Gilmour, Mason and Wright, the latter now a salaried member of Pink Floyd, issue a press release stating that the group has no intention of disbanding and is currently working on a new album. They decide their project should be under the Pink Floyd banner, but Waters claims in court they have no right to use the name. They win temporary rights against Waters to continue using the much coveted moniker.

1987

May [30] Waters' *Radio Waves* spends a week at UK #74.

June [27] His ***Radio K.A.O.S.*** reaches UK #25 in its week of entry and will make US #50.

Aug [15] Waters opens the US leg of a world tour in Hartford, CT. During the tour, with his Bleeding Heart Band, Waters installs temporary phone booths throughout concert halls enabling fans to call him on stage and make song requests. Each concert, often playing in direct competition to Gilmour's Pink Floyd sojourn, is previewed by a video film of Pink Floyd's 1967 standard, *Arnold Layne*.

Sept [7] Despite threats to promoters from Waters that he will stop any shows given by Pink Floyd, the band's 200-date "The Momentary Lapse Of Reason" world tour starts in Ottawa, Canada.

[19] Pink Floyd's ***A Momentary Lapse Of Reason*** hits UK #3 in its week of entry and will hit US #3. The extracted *Only Learning To Fly* is released on CD only in the UK, but fails to chart.

Oct [31] *Learning To Fly* peaks at US #70.

Nov [7] Waters' performance in Quebec, PQ, Canada, is recorded by Westwood One for later broadcast throughout North America.

[21] Waters' live concert at the Wembley Arena, is recorded for broadcast by Capital Radio next April.

Dec *On The Turning Away*, extracted from ***A Momentary Lapse Of Reason***, peaks at UK #55.

1988

Jan Waters makes UK #54 with *The Tide Is Turning (After Live Aid)*.

May A 20-minute Waters' video, "Radio K.A.O.S.", is released. (Waters is rumored to have recorded an anti-Pink Floyd song, *Amused To Death*, but elects not to issue it.)

June *1 Slip*, from ***A Momentary Lapse Of Reason***, makes UK #50.

Aug "The Momentary Lapse Of Reason" tour visits Britain with sold-out dates at Wembley Stadium. At Manchester City Football Club's Maine Road concert, video cameras spy on the crowd to spot drug use, resulting in nine arrests.

Sept Their latest trek concludes at the Nassau Veterans Memorial Coliseum. In the 12 months on the road, the band has been seen by more than ten million people at 155 concerts in 15 different countries, as a new generation of Pink Floyd fans tune in to their music.

[7] "Learning To Fly" wins the Best Group Video category at the fifth annual MTV Video Music Awards, held at the Universal Amphitheatre, Universal City, CA.

Dec [3] Performance album ***Delicate Sound Of Thunder*** reaches UK #11 in its week of entry and will make US #11.

1989

Jan [23] ***Delicate Sound Of Thunder*** is certified platinum by the RIAA.

July [6] ***A Collection Of Great Dance Songs*** is also confirmed platinum by the RIAA.

[22] The band plays a concert, which is televised worldwide, on a giant barge moored off St. Mark's Basilica, Venice, Italy.

1990

June [30] Pink Floyd takes part in the Silver Clef award winners show at Knebworth Park, with Phil Collins, Paul McCartney, Status Quo, Tears For Fears and others.

July [21] An estimated 200,000 people attend Waters' most ambitious solo project to date, a complete performance of "The Wall" at the site of the Berlin Wall in Potzdamer Platz, Berlin, West Germany. Highlighted by the destruction of an artificial wall during the concert, featured performers include Bryan Adams, the Band, James Galway, the Hooters, Cyndi Lauper, Ute Lemper, Joni Mitchell, Van Morrison, Sinead O'Connor, the Scorpions, Marianne Faithfull, actors Tim Curry and Albert Finney and long-time Floyd collaborator and ex-Thin Lizzy guitarist Snowy White. The event is broadcast live throughout the world, and raises money for the Leonard Cheshire-established Memorial Fund for Disaster Relief. (Waters' father had been a pilot killed during World War II before he was born.)

Aug [4] ***The Wall***, the original Floyd double set, re-charts at UK #52 and US #120.

Sept [29] Waters' ***The Wall - Live In Berlin*** reaches UK #27 in its week of entry and makes US #56. Recorded using state-of-the art technology, it is issued simultaneously with a same-titled video.

Oct Previously unissued *Nick's Boogie* track is released on CD as part of the ***Tonight Let's All Make Love In London*** soundtrack. The 11-minute cut was recorded with Joe Boyd in 1966 in Chelsea, before the group had become Pink Floyd.

1991

Mar [26] Floyd's "Delicate Sound Of Thunder" video reaches the 200,000 RIAA-certified sales plateau.

Oct [10] Pink Floyd is inducted into the National Association of Brick Distributors' second annual Brick Hall of Fame gala in New York, in recognition of services to the brick industry through ***The Wall***.

[18] Waters performs at the "Guitar Legends"axe-fest in Seville, Spain.

[28] Gilmour suffers facial cuts and Mason minor injuries when their Jaguar goes over an embankment 12 miles from the north-central Mexican city of San Luis Potosi, during the Pan-American Rally.

1992

Mar [10] The RIAA certifies three million sales of ***A Momentary Lapse Of Reason***.

Apr [15] Pink Floyd is bestowed the Outstanding Contribution To British Music award at the annual Ivor Novello Awards ceremonies, at London's Grosvenor House Hotel.

Sept [12] Waters' *What God Wants, Part 1* reaches

UK #35.
[19] Waters' ***Amused To Death***, produced with Patrick Leonard, and featuring Don Henley, Andy Fairweather-Low, Steve Lukather, Randy Jackson, Marv Albert and a major contribution from Jeff Beck, debuts at its UK #8 and US #21 peak.
Nov [24] Floyd boxed set, ***Shine On***, is released.

1993

Mar [20] ***The Dark Side Of The Moon*** re-hits UK #4, re-promoted in a 20th anniversary 5" x 5" cardboard box CD.
[23] The Paul Rodgers assembled ***Tribute To Muddy Waters*** album, featuring fret-work from Gilmour among others, is released.
Apr EMI (UK) issues a Syd Barrett retrospective, a three CD/cassette boxed set, ***Crazy Diamond***, including his three solo albums, ***The Madcap Laughs***, ***Barrett*** and ***Opel***.
[2] ***Shine On*** is certified gold by the RIAA.

1994

Mar [7] ***The Dark Side Of The Moon*** reaches the RIAA-certified 13 million sales mark.
[11] The RIAA certifies gold sales of ***Atom Heart Mother***, ***A Nice Pair***, ***Obscured By Clouds***, ***Piper At The Gates Of Dawn*** and ***Saucerful Of Secrets***, platinum sales of ***Ummagumma*** and multi-platinum sales of ***Meddle*** (two million).
[30] Pink Floyd embarks on a 59-date North American "Division Bell" tour at Joe Robbie Stadium, Miami, FL, set to end on July 9th-10th at the Robert F. Kennedy Memorial Stadium, Washington, DC.
Apr [23] Named after the parliamentary bell rung in Britain's House of Commons when a vote is cast, ***The Division Bell***, featuring material co-written by Gilmour with his girlfriend Polly Samson, debuts at US #1.
June [4] The extracted *Take It Back* debuts at its UK #23 high, as the band plays the last of three sellout dates at the Veterans Stadium, Philadelphia, PA, breaking both the highest grosser and house records.
July [2] *Take It Back* peaks at US #73.
[9-10] North American tour ends at the Robert F. Kennedy Memorial Stadium. The trek has been seen by 3,043,233 people, selling out 52 of the 59 shows and grossing $103,666,142.
[22] The group's European and Scandinavian tour opens in Lisbon, Portugal, before travelling through Spain, France, Germany, Austria, Denmark, Sweden, Norway, Finland, Holland, the Czech Republic, Italy and finally England.
Sept [6] The band members have dinner with Czech President Vaclav Havel.
[7] They play in front of the biggest audience of the tour, a 120,000 capacity crowd at the Strahov Stadium, Prague, the Czech Republic.
Oct [19] "The Division Bell" UK tour opens at London's Earls Court, but is marred by several injuries to fans when an area of seating collapses a minute into the opening number. (By tour's end, Pink Floyd will have played 110 dates.)
[29] *High Hopes*, coupled with *Keep Talking*, debuts at its UK #26 peak.
Nov [1] "The Dark Side Of The Moon" concert, recently taped at Earls Court and the first time the band has played the entire album in concert, airs on pay-per-view TV.

1995

Jan [31] The RIAA certifies four million sales of ***Animals***.
Mar [1] Pink Floyd wins the Best Rock Instrumental Performance category for *Marooned*, from ***The Division Bell***, at the 37th annual Grammy Awards, held at Los Angeles' Shrine Auditorium.
May [2] The RIAA certifies multi-platinum sales of ***The Wall*** (10 million) and ***Wish You Were Here*** (five million).
June [10] Live album chronicling the band's last tour, ***Pulse*** tops the UK chart in its week of entry.
[24] ***Pulse***, the first album to be released with a flashing light built into its packaging, debuts at US #1.
July [31] The RIAA certifies two million sales of ***Pulse***.
Aug [14] "Pulse" video is certified platinum by the RIAA.
Oct [10] The tribute album ***Us And Theme : Symphonic Pink Floyd***, interpreted by the London Philharmonic Orchestra and members of Killing Joke, is released by Point Music in the US.

1996

Jan [17] Smashing Pumpkins' Billy Corgan inducts Pink Floyd into the Rock and Roll Hall of Fame at the 11th annual induction dinner at New York's Waldorf Astoria Hotel. At the perfunctory post-dinner jam, he sings *Wish You Were Here* with the band.
Mar [9] Reissued ***Relics***, now available for the first time on CD, debuts at its UK #48 peak.

GENE PITNEY

1960

Nov Pitney (b. Feb. 17, 1941, Hartford, CT), having grown up in Rockville, CT, and learnt to play the drums, guitar and piano as a child, has begun writing songs while still at Rockville High School, fronting Gene Pitney & the Genials for high school dances, and cut his first single - the self-penned, *Classical Rock And Roll*, in 1959 - as one-half of the duo Jamie & Jane, with Ginny Mazarro, on Decca Records. Regularly making demos of his songs and sending them to a New York, NY music publisher, Pitney has secured his first cover, when the Kalin Twins (of *When* fame) recorded *Loneliness*, and now his *Today's Teardrops* is recorded by Roy Orbison as the B-side of *Blue Angel*, which hits US #9.

1961

Jan His first Top 10 success as a writer is with *Rubber Ball*, recorded by Bobby Vee. The song is credited to "Orlowski" (his mother's maiden name), because of publishing complications.
Feb He quits the University of Connecticut, where he has been studying electronics, to concentrate on music. *(I Wanna) Love My Life Away*, recorded as a demo on four-track equipment, with Pitney singing all of the parts and playing most of the instruments (and costing $30 - the session fee to the bass player), has been placed with Musicor Records, distributed through United Artists. It is Pitney's US chart debut, reaching #39 after heavy promotion touring around radio and TV stations.
Apr *(I Wanna) Love My Life Away* reaches UK #26.
May Ricky Nelson has a US and UK Top 10 hit with Pitney's song, *Hello Mary Lou*. (It will become one of his most revived compositions.)
Sept Goffin/King composition, *Every Breath I Take*, co-produced at Bell Sound Studios in New York, by Phil Spector, part of a fully orchestral four-song session costing an astronomical $13,000, makes US #42, and will be best remembered for its extended falsetto ending - a product of Pitney's heavy cold during the session.

1962

Jan *Town Without Pity*, the Ned Washington/Dmitri Tiomkin-penned theme from the Kirk Douglas film of the same name, reaches US #13.
Feb [4] Pitney appears on ITV's "Thank Your Lucky Stars", at the start of his first UK visit.
Mar *Town Without Pity* makes UK #32.
June *(The Man Who Shot) Liberty Valance*, written by Bacharach and David as the theme to the John Wayne/James Stewart western (but not used on the soundtrack because the film is released early without it), hits US #4.
Nov Another Bacharach/David song, *Only Love Can Break A Heart*, hits US #2, and is Pitney's first million seller. It is kept from the top by his own composition, *He's A Rebel*, given to Phil Spector for the Crystals. *Only Love*'s B-side, *If I Didn't Have A Dime (To Play The Jukebox)*, peaks at US #58.

1963

Feb *Only Love Can Break A Heart* reaches US #48, while *Half Heaven - Half Heartache*, co-written by Pitney's publisher Aaron Schroeder, reaches US #12.
May *Mecca* makes US #12, while ***Gene Pitney Sings Just For You*** peaks at US #85.
Aug *True Love Never Runs Smooth*, another Bacharach/David ballad, reaches US #21, while ***World Wide Winners*** climbs to US #41.
Dec *24 Hours From Tulsa* reaches US #17, as ***Blue Gene*** makes US #105.

1964

Jan Boosted by a UK promotional visit, in which Pitney appears widely on TV, Bacharach/David's *24 Hours From Tulsa* becomes his first major UK success, hitting UK #5. After returning to the US due to illness, he visits Britain again after the single is established on the chart for a full UK tour.
Feb *That Girl Belongs To Yesterday*, written by Keith Richard and Mick Jagger, makes US #49. (Pitney has met the Rolling Stones via their manager Andrew Oldham, who is also his UK publicist, and has been present at sessions for their first album and played piano on *Little By Little*.)
[29] Pitney embarks on a 20-date, twice-nightly UK tour, with Cilla Black, Billy J. Kramer & the Dakotas, the Swinging Blue Jeans and others, at the Odeon Cinema, Nottingham, Notts., set to end at the Odeon Cinema, Guildford, Surrey, on March 21st.
Apr *That Girl Belongs To Yesterday* hits UK #7, as does ***Blue Gene***. The compilation, ***Gene Pitney's Big Sixteen***, makes US #87.
May *Yesterday's Hero* peaks at US #64, and is not released in the UK. (Its substitute, *I'm Gonna Find Myself A Girl*, fails to chart in Britain.)
June [26] Pitney performs at the Allentown Fair Grounds Grandstand, Allentown, PA, during the "Dick Clark & His Caravan Of Stars" package tour, also featuring the Shirelles, Brian Hyland, the Supremes, the Rip Chords and Major Lance, among others.
Oct *It Hurts To Be In Love* hits US #7 and makes UK #36.
Nov ***It Hurts To Be In Love*** climbs to US #42.
[7] Pitney begins a 26-date, twice-nightly UK tour, with Gerry & the Pacemakers, the Kinks, Marianne Faithfull and others, at the Granada Cinema, Walthamstow, London, set to close on December 6th at the Futurist, Scarborough, Yorks. During a concert in Birmingham, Warks., his head is cut open by some castanets thrown by a member of the audience.
Dec *I'm Gonna Be Strong*, written by Barry Mann and Cynthia Weil, hits US #9 and UK #2, held off the top by the Rolling Stones' *Little Red Rooster*, and then the Beatles' *I Feel Fine*. It becomes one of his most celebrated records because of its top register final notes (which Pitney will always reproduce on stage).

1965

Feb Compilation album, ***Gene Pitney's Big 16***, reaches UK #12.
[5] Pitney arrives in London for a three-day promotional stop, during which he appears on "Ready Steady Go!", "Top Of The Pops", "Juke Box Jury" and "Thank Your Lucky Stars".
Mar *I Must Be Seeing Things* makes US #31 and hits UK #6. ***I'm Gonna Be Strong*** reaches UK #15, while a Nashville-recorded album of country songs duetted with George Jones, ***George Jones And Gene Pitney***, makes US #141.
[8] Pitney begins a tour of Australia and New Zealand with Freddie & the Dreamers, ending on the 25th.
Apr *I've Got Five Dollars And It's Saturday Night*, a duet with Jones from the album, peaks at US #99.
June *Last Chance To Turn Around* reaches US #13.
July Another Mann/Weil song, *Looking Through The Eyes Of Love* (with B-side *Last Chance To Turn Around*), hits UK #3. ***I Must Be Seeing Things*** peaks at US #112.
Aug *Looking Through The Eyes Of Love* makes US #28.

Sept ***Looking Through The Eyes Of Love*** climbs to US #43 and heads for UK #15.
Oct [17] Pitney appears on ITV's "Sunday Night At The London Palladium".
[22] He begins a 28-date, twice-nightly UK package tour, with Lulu & the Luvvers, Peter & Gordon, the Rockin' Berries and others at London's Finsbury Park Astoria, set to end at the Odeon Cinema, Leeds, Yorks., on November 21st.
Dec *Princess In Rags* makes US #37 and hits UK #9.

1966

Jan Pitney comes second in the "San Remo Song Contest" in Italy, with *Nessuno Mi Puo Guidicare*.
Feb [12] Pitney begins a further 14-date, twice-nightly UK tour with Dave Dee, Dozy, Beaky, Mick & Tich, Len Barry and others, at the Gaumont Cinema, Ipswich, Suffolk, set to close on the 27th at the ABC Cinema, Southampton, Hants.
Mar *Backstage* hits UK #4, as the compilation, ***Big Sixteen, Volume 3***, peaks at US #123.
May *Backstage* reaches US #25. A film role is mooted for Pitney in the movie, "Sweet Wind Of Spring", but the Italian-based production does not materialize.
July Having failed to chart in the US, *Nobody Needs Your Love*, written by Randy Newman, hits UK #2, behind the Kinks' *Sunny Afternoon*.
Oct ***Nobody Needs Your Love*** reaches UK #13.
Nov [14] Pitney appears in the "Royal Variety Show" at the London Palladium.
Dec A second Newman composition, *Just One Smile*, hits UK #8, while a new compilation, ***Greatest Hits Of All Times***, makes US #61.

1967

Jan *Just One Smile* peaks at US #64. Meanwhile, Pitney marries childhood sweetheart Lynn Gayton in the Roman Catholic church at Ospedaletti near San Remo, Italy, where he is representing the US in the annual song festival. (They will have two sons, Christopher and Todd.)
Feb [17] Pitney embarks on a 28-date, twice-nightly UK tour, with the Troggs, David Garrick, Sounds Incorporated, the Loot and Normie Rowe & the Playboys, at London's Finsbury Park Astoria, set to end on March 19th at the Coventry Theatre, Coventry, Warks.
Mar [4] *(In The) Cold Light Of Day* makes UK #38, as ***Young, Warm And Wonderful*** makes UK #39.
Apr [22] Compilation album, ***Gene Pitney's Big Sixteen***, peaks at UK #40.
Aug [4] Pitney begins a US tour, with the Easybeats, the Buckinghams, the Happenings and the Music Explosion, at the Bushnell Memorial Auditorium in Hartford.
Nov [11] During a UK promotional tour, with appearances on "Top Of The Pops" on the 9th and "The Joe Loss Pop Show" on the 10th, Pitney now guests on BBC1-TV's "Dee Time".
Dec *Something's Gotten Hold Of My Heart*, written by Roger Cook and Roger Greenaway, hits UK #5.

1968

Apr [5] Pitney begins another 28-date, twice-nightly UK trek with Amen Corner, Status Quo, Don Partridge, Simon Dupree & the Big Sound and others, at Odeon Cinema, Lewisham, London, set to finalé on May 7th at the Granada Cinema, Walthamstow, London.
May [1] *Somewhere In The Country* makes UK #19.
July *She's A Heartbreaker*, an R&B performance of a song written by Charlie Foxx and Jerry Williams, reaches US #16.
Sept ***She's A Heartbreaker*** peaks at US #193.
Nov *Billy You're My Friend* peaks at US #92, while *Yours Until Tomorrow*, a Goffin/King song, makes UK #34.

1969

Feb [7] Pitney begins a 27-date, twice-nightly UK tour (his sixth), with the Marmalade, Joe Cocker, the Iveys and others, at Odeon Cinema, Birmingham, set to end on March 9th at the ABC Cinema, Blackpool, Lancs.
Mar Tony Hazzard-penned *Maria Elena* reaches UK #25.
Oct Compilation album, ***Best Of Gene Pitney***, hits UK #8.

1970

Jan *She Lets Her Hair Down (Early In The Morning)*, an adaptation of a Silvikrin shampoo TV ad, peaks at US #89.
Mar *A Street Called Hope*, another Cook/Greenaway song, makes UK #37, as Pitney begins another UK tour, with Badfinger and Clodagh Rodgers.
Oct *Shady Lady* reaches UK #29.

1974

May After *24 Sycamore*, written by Les Reed and Barry Mason, and previously recorded by UK singer Wayne Fontana, has made UK #34 the previous May, Pitney signs a new worldwide recording deal with UK label Bronze Records.
Aug His first Bronze release, *Blue Angel*, makes UK #39. After voice strain and bouts of ill-health, he cuts down on his previously almost continuous worldwide touring to six months in each year, to spend the other half at home with his family.

1975

Apr [10] The Gene Pitney Appreciation Society presents him with a plaque in honor of his regular twice-annual UK tours. The presentation is made during a tour, on stage at the Fiesta club, Sheffield, S. Yorks.
Oct Alan O'Day-penned *Train Of Thought* is released, taken from ***Pitney '75***.
Nov He opens a UK concert tour to promote both records, at the Batley Variety Club, Batley, Yorks.

1976

Oct TV-promoted compilation, ***His 20 Greatest Hits***, hits UK #6. Signing to Epic Records the following January, three subsequent singles will fail to score, and the deal is not extended. (Still a twice-annual UK visitor, he will play at the London Palladium in December 1978, supported by Co-Co, the group which performs the UK's entry in that year's "Eurovision Song Contest".)

1989

Jan [28] After many years away from recording, though still touring all over the world for six to eight months each year, Pitney has added guest vocals to a new version of his hit *Something's Gotten Hold Of My Heart*, by UK singer Marc Almond, formerly of Soft Cell, which now hits UK #1. It is nearly 28 years since Pitney first charted in the UK.
July [10] Pitney, B.J. Thomas and the Shirelles appear in Nashville, TN federal court as a trial begins in a lawsuit against Gusto Records and GML over alleged improper payment of royalties of re-released hits.

1990

May [2] Pitney is awarded $187,762 by US District Court Judge Thomas Higgins in the case against Gusto Records.
Oct [7] He embarks on a 13-date UK tour at the Fairfield Halls, Croydon, Surrey, set to end on the 21st at the Hippodrome, Birmingham, W. Midlands.
[27] Pitney, always more popular in Britain than the US, returns to the UK chart with ***Backstage - The Greatest Hits And More***, a collection of his hits and eight new tracks produced by David Courtney, which reaches UK #17.

1992

Jan [25] Pitney performs a 4,000 seat sellout show at the Wang Center for the Performing Arts, Boston, MA, grossing $64,009.
Oct [2] He embarks on a 21-date UK tour at the Ipswich Regent, set to end on the 25th at the London Palladium.

1995

Aug With Pitney still a popular live draw whose performances in the '90s thus far have been highlighted by an appearance at New York's Carnegie Hall on February 26th, 1993, and following the release of ***The Ultimate Anthology*** on the One Way label in April of this year, Tomato Records issues the 51-track two-CD retrospective ***The Great Recordings***.

THE PIXIES

Black Francis (vocals, guitar); **Joey Santiago** (lead guitar); **Kim Deal** (bass, vocals); **David Lovering** (drums, vocals)

1986

Francis (b. Charles Michael Kitteridge Thompson IV, 1965, Long Beach, CA), aka Black Francis, an anthropology major at the University of Massachusetts, Amherst, MA, studying Spanish on an exchange program in Puerto Rico, drops out with the intention of forming a band. He persuades college room-mate Santiago (b. June 10, 1965, Manila, Philippines) to quit as well and relocate with him to Boston, MA. Placing an ad for a bassist "into Hüsker Dü and Peter, Paul and Mary", they hire the only respondent, Deal (b. June 10, 1961, Dayton, OH), aka Mrs. John Murphy, a former high-school cheerleader in Ohio. At her suggestion they recruit Lovering (b. Dec. 6, 1961, Boston), and begin performing a mostly experimental, chaotic set around the Boston club scene, most often at the Green Street Station, the Rat and T.T. The Bear's, calling themselves the Pixies, a name chosen by Santiago flicking through a dictionary.

1987

Oct Having sent a demo tape to London-based independent label 4AD head Ivo Watts-Russell, via Throwing Muses' manager Ken Goes, the company releases the songs as the eight-track mini-album, ***Come On Pilgrim***, which receives European critical raves and tops the UK Independent Album chart.

1988

Mar Their second album for 4AD, the Steve Albini-produced ***Surfer Rosa***, is hailed as an underground classic, and again tops the UK Independent Album survey. Its CD release includes the ***Come On Pilgrim*** set.
Apr [8] The Pixies sell out the Mean Fiddler, the first date of a European tour supporting Throwing Muses, while US labels jostle to sign them.
Aug The four-track EP, *Gigantic*, again a hit UK indie item, is released to coincide with the group's first full British tour.

1989

Apr [1] Trailering a forthcoming album, *Monkey Gone To Heaven* peaks at UK #54.
[29] Gil Norton-produced, and subsequently more commercially framed third project, ***Doolittle***, marks the Pixies debut for US Elektra Records, while 4AD is rewarded in Britain as the album immediately hits UK #8. During a six-month US chart residence, it will make #98, while extracts, the recent and forthcoming UK chosen singles, will also prove popular US modern and college tracks. The Pixies begin the 50-date, "Sex And Death" European leg of a 150-date world tour. During the Manchester, Gtr. Manchester gig, Francis will slice his finger.
July [1] *Here Comes Your Man* peaks at UK #54.
Aug Pixies contribute their version of *Winterlong* to the compilation album, ***The Bridge : A Tribute To Neil Young***, as the US leg of the tour begins.
[15] The group plays the Paradise, Boston, during current US dates.
Oct [31] A second US "Doolittle" tour begins in Eugene, OR.

1990

Mar [8] Pixies are named Best New American Band in **Rolling Stone**'s 1989 Critics Award.
Apr [19] Further honors are collected at their homebase

SKC Boston Music Awards, held at the Wang Center, as the band wins the Outstanding Debut Pop/Rock Album category for ***Doolittle***, their first US release.

June [9] Deal, still very much a Pixie, launches off-shoot unit the Breeders, with Throwing Muses' Tanya Donnelly (guitar), ex-Perfect Disaster Josephine Wiggs (bass) and sole male member, drummer Shannon Doughton. Their debut album, ***Pod***, immediately reaches UK #22, released by 4AD, and recorded in Edinburgh, Scotland, with Albini producing.

July [28] Pixies' *Velouria* reaches UK #28, and becomes another hot US alternative radio add-on.

Aug [25] With its lead-off track, *Cecilia Ann*, an unusual cover of an early '60s Surftones disc, the fourth Pixies album, ***Bossanova***, hits UK #3.

[26] The band headlines the final day at the annual "Reading Festival" at Little John's Farm, Reading, Berks.

Sept [5] Their extensive European tour continues with a first German date in Linz.

[15] Again produced by Gil Norton, ***Bossanova***, peaks at US #70.

Oct [1] The group embarks on a 17-date British and Irish trek at Dublin Stadium, Dublin, Eire, set to end on the 21st at London's Brixton Academy.

Nov [3] ***Rubáiyát***, Elektra's 40th anniversary compilation, to which the group contributes a cover of *Born In Chicago*, makes US #140.

[10] Second ***Bossanova*** extract, *Dig For Fire*, peaks at UK #62.

[30] The Pixies play to a sellout crowd of 2,575 at The Ritz, New York, NY, during their current US tour.

Dec [15] Appearing on a bill with Jane's Addiction and Primus, the band plays at San Fransico's Civic Auditorium.

1991

June [8] The group performs at the Crystal Palace Bowl, Crystal Palace, London, as *Planet Of Sound* debuts at its UK #27 peak.

[21] A performance at the Glasgow SE&CC is curtailed when a safety barrier collapses.

July [14] They return to play at London's Mean Fiddler.

Oct A Leonard Cohen tribute album, ***I'm Your Fan***, to which the band has contributed *(I Can't Forget)*, is released.

[5] ***Trompe Le Monde***, with 15 new songs written by Francis, except *Head On* penned by Jim and William Reid of the Jesus & Mary Chain, hits UK #7.

[26] ***Trompe Le Monde*** bows at its US #92 peak.

Nov [27] The group plays a sellout concert at the Orpheum Theatre, Boston, during its current North American tour, set to end on December 22nd at the Palladium, Los Angeles, CA.

1992

Jan [31] The Pixies appear at the Mandell Hall, Chicago, IL, on the latest leg of their US tour.

Feb [6] The band appears on NBC-TV's "Late Night With David Letterman".

Apr [18] Breeders' EP, *Safari*, charts for a week at UK #69, as the Pixies continues its US tour opening for U2 at the Oakland-Alameda County Coliseum, Oakland, CA.

1993

Jan [14] Francis confirms on Radio 5's "Hit The North" show that the group is no more, following disagreements with Deal. Santiago begins recording with Francis while Deal works on a new Breeders album, and Lovering records with Nitzer Ebb.

Mar [20] ***Frank Black***, a nomenclature for Thompson (who is now claiming to be the "Ernest Hemingway of indie rock"), debuts at its UK #9 peak. The following week in the US, it will enter at its #117 high.

Sept [11] Following the EP *Cannonball* debuting at its UK #40 peak on Aug [21], the Breeders' ***Last Splash***, co-produced by Deal with Mark Freegard, bows at its UK #5 pinnacle, and will do the same in the US at #33 on Feb [5] 1994. (Subsequent chart singles will be *Divine Hammer* (UK #59 - Nov [6]) and *Cannonball* (US #69 - Dec [25] and again US #44 - Feb [26], 1994).)

1996

Feb [3] Following Frank Black's second outing, the 62-minute ***Teenager Of The Year*** co-produced by Black, Eric Drew Feldman and Al Clay which debuted at its US #131 peak on June [11], 1994, and following RIAA gold certification of the Pixies' 1989 album ***Doolittle*** on November 10th last year, Black's third outing, the self-written and produced ***The Cult Of Ray***, debuts at its UK #39 peak.

[17] ***The Cult Of Ray***, released in the US via his new deal with American Recordings, charts for a week at US #127, where Black's cult status assures strong airplay at college and alternative radio.

ROBERT PLANT

1966

Nov Plant (b. Aug. 20, 1948, West Bromwich, Warks.), after abandoning a chartered accountancy course two years earlier, while living in Walsall, Warks., and having sung with several local R&B and blues groups including Black Snake Moan, the Banned and the Crawling King Snakes, makes his recording debut as a member of Birmingham, Warks.-based band Listen, on *You Better Run*, for CBS Records. Cutting two further 45s for the label the following year (*Our Song* and *Long Time Coming*), and singing on the Exceptions' *The Eagle Flies On Friday,* he joins Birmingham group Band Of Joy, along with John Bonham, which releases no records (though an album of its archive material will be issued by Polydor in 1978).

1968

Aug While debating whether to join Alexis Korner's new band as singer, he is asked by Jimmy Page to join the New Yardbirds, which becomes Led Zeppelin. Plant will remain lead singer with the pioneering hard-rock quartet for the next 12 years, until they split after the death of drummer John Bonham in December 1980, instrumental as both a writer and vocal focus in establishing the group as the most successful global rock act of the '70s.

1979

Dec [29] He sings with Dave Edmunds' band Rockpile in the third "Concert For The People Of Kampuchea" at London's Hammersmith Odeon.

1981

Apr Plant begins a solo career, playing live with his part-time band, the Honeydrippers, which makes occasional appearances in London and Birmingham, playing R&B and blues covers. (During the year, he will also work with the Big Town Playboys.)

Sept Plant begins solo recordings at Edmunds' Rockfield Studios, Monmouth, Gwent, Wales.

1982

July His debut solo album, ***Pictures At Eleven***, released on Led Zeppelin's SwanSong label, hits UK #2 and US #5.

Oct The extracted *Burning Down One Side* makes UK #73 and US #64.

Nov *Pledge Pin* peaks at US #74. (By year's end, Plant returns to Rockfield for further recordings, now with Phil Collins, Robbie Blunt (guitar), Jezz Woodroffe (keyboards), Paul Martinez (bass) and Barriemore Barlow (drums).)

1983

June Due to have his live set shown on C4-TV show "The Tube", Plant, dissatisfied with his performance, vetoes its transmission.

July *Big Log* reaches UK #11, spurred by a BBC1-TV "Top Of The Pops" appearance (which Led Zeppelin had never done), and US #20, while his sophomore effort, ***The Principle Of Moments***, co-produced with Benji LeFeure and Pat Moran, hits UK #7 and US #8.

1984

Jan *In The Mood* reaches US #39.

[12] ***The Principle Of Moments*** is certified platinum by the RIAA.

Nov After Plant tours with the Honeydrippers, their mini-album, ***The Honeydrippers, Vol. 1***, hits US #4 and UK #56. The project lines up as Plant, Jimmy Page, Jeff Beck and Chic's Nile Rodgers, who also produces the set.

Dec [15] The Honeydrippers perform on NBC-TV's "Saturday Night Live".

1985

Jan Their revival of Phil Phillips' *Sea Of Love*, from the mini-album, hits US #3 and makes UK #56.

Feb The Honeydrippers' *Rockin' At Midnight* reaches US #25.

June Musically diverse solo album ***Shaken 'n' Stirred***, featuring Little Feat's Richie Hayward, makes UK #19 and US #20.

July *Little By Little*, taken from the album, reaches US #36.

[13] Plant plays at "Live Aid" at the JFK Stadium in Philadelphia, PA, in a one-off Led Zeppelin reunion with Phil Collins filling in on drums.

[18] ***Shaken 'n' Stirred*** is certified gold by the RIAA.

1986

Jan Plant, Page, bassist Charlie Jones and drummer Tony Thompson, rehearse in a small hall near Bath, Avon, with the idea of reviving Led Zeppelin, but after a few days the project is abandoned.

Mar With several other Birmingham-based acts, he participates in the "Heartbeat 86" benefit show for a children's hospital.

1988

Feb Plant performs in Folkestone, Kent, with his new band, credited as the Band of Joy (for one night only), with a line-up of Doug Boyle (guitar), Phil Johnstone (keyboards) and Chris Blackwell (drums). All are young Led Zeppelin fans who have sent Plant a demo tape which impressed him. (Johnstone is also the writer of the group's material, collaborating with Plant on *Heaven Knows* and *Tall Cool One* for the singer's new album.) *Heaven Knows* reaches UK #33.

Mar [12] ***Now And Zen***, produced by Plant, Johnstone and Tim Palmer, with a guest appearance from Jimmy Page and sampled Led Zeppelin tracks, hits UK #10 in its week of entry and will hit US #6.

May [9] ***Now And Zen*** is certified platinum by the RIAA.

[14] Plant plays with Led Zeppelin at another one-off reunion at Atlantic Records' 40th anniversary concert at New York, NY's Madison Square Garden (with John Bonham's son Jason on drums).

July He guests on Page's newly-released ***Outrider***. Plant's *Tall Cool One*, featuring a Page guitar solo and used in US TV ads for Coca-Cola, reaches US #25.

Sept [3] Ballad *Ship Of Fools* peaks at US #84.

Dec [12] "Mumbo Jumbo" video is certified gold by the RIAA.

1989

Dec Plant has collaborated with Ian Gillan, Brian May and Bruce Dickinson in the one-off benefit group Rock Aid Armenia, with a re-make of *Smoke On The Water*, which makes UK #39, with all profits from the record going to the victims of the Armenian earthquake disaster.

1990

Feb Plant contributes a cover of *Let's Have A Party* to the newly-released compilation album, ***The Last Temptation Of Elvis***, to benefit the Nordoff Robbins Music Therapy charity.

Mar [31] Co-produced with Johnstone, ***Manic Nirvana*** reaches UK #15 having been recorded with the studio line-up of Plant, Johnstone, Doug Boyle (guitars),

Charlie Jones (bass) and Chris Blackwell (drums).
Apr *Hurting Kind (I've Got My Eyes On You)* makes UK #45 and US #46.
[28] ***Manic Nirvana*** reaches US #13.
June [22] He is presented with the Silver Clef award at the annual Nordoff Robbins Music Therapy Centre lunch in London.
July [5] His "Manic Nirvana" tour begins in Albany, NY, set to end November 26th in Muskogee, OK, and features his now regular backing band of Blackwell, Boyle, Johnstone and Jones, supported variously by Alannah Myles, the Black Crowes, then Faith No More.
Dec [12] Plant begins a six-date UK tour at the City Hall, Newcastle-upon-Tyne, Tyne & Wear, set to close on the 18th and 19th at London's Town & Country club, as he signs a solo deal with Fontana.

1992

Apr [20] He sings *Crazy Little Thing Called Love* at the Freddie Mercury tribute at Wembley Stadium, Wembley, Middx.
Sept Plant begins working on a new album at RAK Studios with producer Chris Hughes.

1993

May [15] *29 Palms*, the first single from his forthcoming Fontana label debut, reaches UK #21.
June [5] ***Fate Of Nations***, featuring his long-term backing band augmented by guitarists Francis Dunnery and Kevin Scott MacMichael, and featuring guests Nigel Kennedy, Richard Thompson and Clannad's Maire Brennan, bows at its UK #6 peak, and will reach US #34 on June 19th.
[25] Plant performs at the "Glastonbury Festival", Glastonbury, Somerset.
July [3] *I Believe* debuts at its UK #64 peak.
[16] He plays a one-off London concert at the Brixton Academy.
Sept [10] Plant guests on CBS-TV's "Late Show With David Letterman".
Nov [26-27] He plays two sellout shows at the Tower Theatre, Upper Darby, PA, during a short North American tour.
Dec [7] ***Fate Of Nations*** is certified gold by the RIAA.
[23] Plant plays his last date of the year at the Brixton Academy, London.
[25] His revival of Tim Hardin's *If I Were A Carpenter* debuts at its UK #63 peak.

1994

Jan [22] Having performed on the 15th in Sao Paolo, Plant now performs in Rio de Janeiro, both concerts part of the "Hollywood Rock Festival".
Apr [23] Plant is joined onstage by Jimmy Page at the Alexis Korner tribute concert at the Buxton Opera House in Derby, Derbys.
Aug [25-26] They reunite again at LWT Studios on the South Bank in London, to perform a set for MTV's "Unplugged" series, titled "Unledded".
Oct [12] The MTV 90-minute "Unledded" program, taped in London, Wales and Morocco, receives the series' highest-ever ratings. In addition to acoustic versions of Led Zeppelin classics, the show also features eight new songs penned by Page and Plant.
Nov [10] Page and Plant guest on Radio 1 FM's "Soundbite".
[26] Page and Plant's ***No Quarter***, featuring a similar mix of Zeppelin updates and new material, much of it with an Arabic/World music influence, debuts at its US #4 peak.
Dec [22] ***No Quarter*** is certified platinum by the RIAA.
[24] Page and Plant's *Gallows Pole* reaches UK #35.

1995

Apr [8] ***Encomium : A Tribute To Led Zeppelin***, featuring Plant's duet with Tori Amos on *Down By The Seaside*, reaches US #17.
Dec [4] Having spent the earlier part of the year touring with Page in support of their reunion album, Plant attends the funeral of former Led Zeppelin manager Peter Grant in Hellingly, East Sussex.
see also: **LED ZEPPELIN**

THE PLATTERS

Tony Williams (lead vocals);
David Lynch (vocals); **Paul Robi** (vocals);
Herb Reed (vocals); **Zola Taylor** (vocals)

1954

Feb [15] The group has been formed the previous year as a harmony-led doo-wop quartet in Los Angeles, CA, by lead singer Williams (b. Apr. 5, 1928, Elizabeth, NJ), who was working as a parking lot attendant by day, Lynch (b. 1929, St. Louis, MO), Reed (b. 1931, Kansas City, MO) and Alex Hodge, and while performing in Los Angeles clubs they have met manager/producer Buck Ram (b. Samuel Ram, Dec. 18, 1908, Chicago, IL), with whom they now sign a management agreement.
May At Ram's instigation, female singer Taylor (b. 1934), from the Teen Queens, joins the group to widen and sweeten the vocal blend.
July Hodge has a run-in with the law and leaves. Ram recruits Robi (b. 1931, New Orleans, LA), completing the line-up of the Platters, which will become the most successful black group of the '50s. The group signs to Federal Records, an R&B subsidiary of King, but its debut release, *Only You (And You Alone)*, fails to chart. Ram provides the group with excellent live bookings, and their financial success persuades another Los Angeles vocal group, the Penguins, to also sign to Ram's stable.

1955

Sept After the Penguins score a million seller on the independent Dootone label with *Earth Angel*, Mercury Records approaches Ram to sign them. He agrees, provided Mercury also takes the Platters.
Nov The group's Mercury debut, a new version of the Ram-co-penned *Only You (And You Alone)*, hits US #5, also a US R&B chart-topper, promoted notably by DJ Hunter Hancock.

1956

Feb [18] *The Great Pretender* tops the US chart for the first of two weeks, eventually selling over one million copies, while its B-side, *I'm Just A Dancing Partner*, peaks at US #87. (Ram has told Mercury that *The Great Pretender* will be the next hit, before he has even written a song to go with the title.)
May *(You've Got) The Magic Touch*, once again written by their manager, hits US #4 and is a second million seller. The B-side, *Winner Take All*, makes US #50.
July The group's debut album, the Ram-arranged ***The Platters***, hits US #7, showcasing the group's seemingly effortless gift for sweet soul/pop harmony.
Aug [4] *My Prayer*, offered by its English lyricist Jimmy Kennedy to Ram after he has heard *The Great Pretender*, begins a five-week run at US #1, earning another gold disc, while the B-side, *Heaven On Earth*, makes US #39.
Sept *The Great Pretender* coupled with *Only You* is the group's UK debut at #5.
Nov *You'll Never Never Know* reaches US #11, as its flip-side, *It Isn't Right*, makes US #23. Meanwhile, *My Prayer* hits UK #4.
[18] The group performs at the Forum, Wichita, KS, on a tour with Bill Haley & the Comets, Frankie Lymon, Clyde McPhatter, Chuck Berry and the Clovers, among others.

1957

Jan *On My Word Of Honor* reaches US #20 and the B-side, *One In A Million*, makes US #31. The UK pairing of *You'll Never Never Know/It Isn't Right* peaks at #23.
Feb ***The Platters, Volume Two*** reaches US #12.
Apr *I'm Sorry* reaches US #19, its B-side *He's Mine* rising to US #23.
June *I'm Sorry* makes UK #18.
July *My Dream* climbs to US #24.
Nov *Only Because*, peaking at US #65, is the group's first US Top 50 failure since signing to Mercury.

1958

Mar *Helpless* stops at US #56.
Apr [21] *Twilight Time*, co-written by Ram with the Three Suns, who had a major hit with the song in 1944, and originally issued as the flip-side of *Out Of My Mind*, having been premiered on "Dick Clark's Saturday Night TV Show", now tops the US chart for a week and becomes another million seller. Mercury also produces a film clip, which it uses to promote the song to US TV shows - an early ancestor of the music video.
[28] *Twilight Time* becomes the group's fourth and final US R&B chart-topper.
July Its B-side, *You're Making A Mistake*, makes US #50, as *Twilight Time* hits UK #3.
Oct The group undertakes an extended European tour and records *Smoke Gets In Your Eyes* while performing in Paris, France. Meanwhile, *I Wish* makes US #42 and the B-side, *It's Raining Outside*, peaks at US #93.

1959

Jan [19] *Smoke Gets In Your Eyes*, originally a 1934 hit for Paul Whiteman (and a Jerome Kern/Otto Harbach song from the 1933 musical "Roberta"), is another million seller, topping the US chart for the first of three weeks and becoming the definitive version of the standard.
Mar [21] *Smoke Gets In Your Eyes* topples Shirley Bassey's *As I Love You* from the top of the UK charts, during a 17-week tenure in the Top 10.
Apr ***Remember When?*** reaches US #15.
May *Enchanted* rises to US #12.
July Title track, *Remember When*, makes US #41.
Aug *Remember When* reaches UK #25.
[10] The four male members of the group are arrested in Cincinnati, OH, having been found inflagrante delicto with four 19-year-old women (three of them white). Wide media coverage of the scandal results in radio stations across the US removing the Platters records from playlists.
Oct *Where*, an adaptation of Tchaikovsky's "Symphonie Pathétique", makes US #44 with its B-side, *Wish It Were Me*, from the film "Girls' Town", peaking at US #61.
Dec [10] The male group members are acquitted of charges of lewdness, assignation, and aiding and abetting prostitution, arising from their August arrest. Judge Gilbert Bettman lectures them in court about responsibility to their public.

1960

Jan [13] The Platters embark on a UK tour in Sheffield, Yorks.
Feb Another oldie, *Harbor Lights*, hits US #8 and UK #11, as its B-side, *Sleepy Lagoon*, peaks at US #65. Compilation album, ***Encore Of Golden Hits***, enters the US chart, set to hit #6 during a 174-week stay, during which it is certified gold.
May *Ebb Tide*, credited to The Platters featuring Tony Williams, makes US #56.
Aug *Red Sails In The Sunset* reaches US #36.
Nov *To Each His Own* makes US #21.
Dec Further compilation, ***More Encores Of Golden Hits***, reaches US #20.

1961

Jan Williams leaves the group (and will sign as a soloist to Frank Sinatra's Reprise label later in the year), and is replaced by Sonny Turner (b. Charles Turner) as lead vocalist.
Feb *If I Didn't Care* makes US #30.
[14] Ram and the group file a lawsuit against Mercury Records for refusing to accept recordings without Williams' lead vocal. Ram states that the contract does not stipulate who should sing lead, and that other members have previously done so on some 25 Platters tracks.

Apr *Trees* peaks at US #62.
Sept *I'll Never Smile Again* makes US #25.
Dec [7] ***Encore - Golden Hits*** is certified gold by the RIAA.

1962

Feb *It's Magic* at US #91 is the group's last Top 100 entry for Mercury and its last chart score for over four years. Helen Williams (who had replaced Taylor in October 1957, and is the wife of Tony Williams) and Robi leave to go solo and are replaced by Sandra Dawn (b. New York City, NY) and Nate Nelson (b. Apr. 10, 1932, New York City), ex-Flamingos.
The Platters tour Poland becoming the first American group to appear there without a Government subsidy. They also announce they will never again play in Atlanta, GA, if audiences are segregated.

1965

Sept [1] ***More Encore Of Golden Hits*** is certified gold by the RIAA.

1966

June Now signed to Musicor Records, and with their traditional ballad style modified to more contemporary soul, the Platters make US #31 with *I Love You 1,000 Times* (also a US R&B #6 success).
July Musicor-released album, ***I Love You 1,000 Times***, including new versions of previous hits, peaks at US #100.
Dec *I'll Be Home*, their update of a 1956 Moonglows/ Pat Boone hit, peaks at US #97.

1967

Apr Motown-influenced *With This Ring* is the biggest chart success for the new-style Platters, reaching US #14, taken from ***Going Back To Detroit***.
Aug Also uptempo, *Washed Ashore (On A Lonely Island In The Sea)* makes US #56.
Oct [18] The group appears at Richard Nader's first "Rock'n'Roll Revival Concert" at Madison Square Garden, New York, NY, alongside Chuck Berry, Bill Haley & His Comets, and others.
Nov *Sweet, Sweet Lovin'* peaks at US #70, and is the final Platters US chart entry. (The group, with various personnel changes and even ad-hoc rival outfits will continue as a worldwide live nightclub attraction through the next two decades, still guided by Ram, and, in addition to this year's ***I Get The Sweetest Feeling***, will release ***Sweet Sweet Lovin'*** in 1968, ***Encore Of Broadway Golden Hits*** (1972) and ***Live*** (1974.)

1978

Apr UK compilation, ***20 Classic Hits***, featuring '50s Mercury repertoire, and promoted via a nostalgic TV campaign, hits #8.

1989

Feb [1] Having recently been awarded $3.5 million against Ram and others, for threatening and harassing him over the ongoing dispute involving rights to the Platters' name, Robi dies at the age of 58.

1990

Jan [17] The Platters are inducted into the Rock and Roll Hall of Fame with the Four Seasons, the Who, Bobby Darin, the Kinks, Simon & Garfunkel, the Four Tops and Hank Ballard at the fifth annual dinner, at the Waldorf Astoria Hotel, New York. (The current line-up features the return of Tony Williams, alongside Taylor, Reed and Rosalyn Atkins, and still performs throughout the US, mainly in cabaret. Lynch and Nelson have both died of cancer on January 2nd, 1981 and June 1st, 1984 respectively.)

1992

Aug [14] After Ram has died in Las Vegas, NV on January 1st the previous year, Tony Williams dies in his sleep at his Manhattan penthouse, suffering from diabetes and emphysema, survived by his wife Helen, a son and four sisters. (He had toured Thailand and Japan in 1991 with Tony Williams & the Platters with wife Helen and son Ricky, performing for the last time on New Year Eve's in Thailand.) In 1995, Robi's widow will win the latest round to recover royalty rights over the Platters' recordings and publishing interests from Ram's estate. Meanwhile, Rhino Records and Mercury continue to bring the group's hit repetoire to compact disc.

P.M. DAWN

Prince Be (vocals);
DJ Minutemix (sampling, turntables)

1989

Brothers Attrell (b. Attrell Cordes, May 19, 1970, Jersey City, NJ) and Jarrett Cordes (b. July 17, 1971, Jersey City), whose father died of pneumonia when both were boys, and younger brother Duncan drowned in a park at age two, have been raised by their step-father (who was a percussionist member of Kool & the Gang) and mother in New York, NY, now calling themselves Prince Be (Attrell) and DJ Minutemix (Jarrett) respectively, have begun fusing melodic pop with rap lyrics and while still in their teens record their first song, *Check The Logic*, at a Long Island studio, the beginning of a demo process which will lead to their signing to the dance/rap label, Gee Street.

1991

Jan With their chosen name of P.M. Dawn (meaning "from the darkest hour comes the light"), the duo releases *Ode To A Forgetful Mind.*
June *A Watcher's Point Of View* makes UK #36 as the duo develops their dreamy, melody-laden brand of hip-hop which will be termed "daisy-age rap".
Aug *Set Adrift On Memory Bliss*, based on the fake guitar chords of Spandau Ballet's *True*, hits UK #3.
Sept [14] Recorded in London, their sample-filled (including Doobie Brothers, Dr. John and Chick Corea snippets among others) debut album, ***Of The Heart, Of The Soul And Of The Cross : The Utopian Experience*** hits UK #8 in its week of entry.
Oct [19] ***Of The Heart, Of The Soul And Of The Cross : The Utopian Experience*** enters the US chart on its way to #48, as a fourth UK extract, *Paper Doll*, peaks at UK #49.
Nov [30] *Set Adrift On Memory Bliss* tops the US chart for a week.
Dec One month after an interview in **Details** magazine in which Prince Be, an African-American, stated: "I don't like black people actually. I don't like black people. I don't like white people. The prejudice thing is so stupid. Public Enemy and people like that - they just make mountains out of mole-hills. KRS-1 wants to be a teacher, but a teacher of what?", he is attacked onstage by KRS-1 and entourage who also break the record being spun by Minutemix.
[19] The RIAA certifies gold sales of *Set Adrift On Memory Bliss* and ***Of The Heart, Of The Soul And Of The Cross***.

1992

Feb [15] *Paper Doll* peaks at US #28.
[29] *Reality Used To Be A Friend Of Mine* reaches UK #29.
Oct [31] *I'd Die Without You*, also featured in the soundtrack to the Eddie Murphy-starring "Boomerang", hits US #3. (Prince Be is currently featured in a Nike US TV shoe commercial.)
Nov [13] *I'd Die Without You* is certified gold by the RIAA.
[21] *I'd Die Without You* reaches UK #30.

1993

Feb [27] The duo is featured on C4-TV's "Saturday Zoo".
Mar [6] They appear on BBC1-TV's "Going Live!".
[20] *Looking Through Patient Eyes*, incorporating George Michael's *Father Figure*, reaches UK #11.
[25] The duo performs on syndicated TV's "The Arsenio Hall Show".
Apr [3] The duo's sophomore effort, ***The Bliss Album ...? (Vibrations Of Love And Anger And The Ponderance Of Life And Existence***, including its treatment of the Beatles' *Norwegian Wood*, debuts at its UK #9 peak, as Minutemix now goes under the name J.C. the Eternal.
[16] They participate in an Earth Day concert headlined by Paul McCartney at the Hollywood Bowl, with proceeds going to PETA, Greenpeace and Friends of the Earth, before embarking on the summer WOMAD caravan tour.
May [8] ***The Bliss Album ...?*** reaches US #30.
[22] The brothers help out at a record store counter in Los Angeles, CA to benefit LIFEbeat's CounterAid, a one day fund raiser for people with HIV and AIDS.
[29] *Looking Through Patient Eyes* hits US #6.
June [1] ***The Bliss Album ...?*** is certified gold by the RIAA.
[4] They perform *Looking Through Patient Eyes* on NBC-TV's "The Tonight Show".
[19] *More Than Likely*, featuring Boy George, reaches UK #40.
Sept [4] *The Ways Of The Wind* peaks at US #54.
Nov [27] ***Stone Free: A Tribute To Jimi Hendrix***, to which the group has contributed *You've Got Me Floating*, released by Reprise Records, reaches US #28.
Dec [11] Elton John's ***Duets***, to which P.M. Dawn contributes *When I Think About Love (I Think About You)*, reaches US #25.

1994

Oct [19] P.M. Dawn guests on BBC2-TV's "Black Tracks".

1995

Aug Jarrett is arrested in Burlington County, NJ, on charges that he sexually assaulted and abused his 14-year old cousin. He is freed on $10,000 bail.
Sept [30] *Downtown Venus* debuts at its UK #58 peak.
Oct [7] *Downtown Venus* makes US #48.
[21] Receiving P.M. Dawn's strongest reviews to date, the self-produced ***Jesus Wept***, eclectically sampling cuts by Deep Purple, Joni Mitchell, Al B. Sure! and Talking Heads, bows at its US #119 peak.
Dec [30] *Sometimes I Miss You So Much (Dedicated To The Christ Consciousness)* peaks at US #95.
[31] PM Dawn guests on C4-TV's "The White Room New Year Special" with Oasis, David Bowie, Stevie Wonder, Pulp and Jimmy Cliff.

1996

Feb [19] The duo discusses ***Jesus Wept*** online on Prodigy's Jump : Chat line.
Mar [26] Warner Bros. Records (US) releases ***Songs In The Key Of X***, music from and inspired by the Fox-TV show "The X Files", including a new cut by P.M. Dawn written by Don Was.
Apr [6] *Sometimes I Miss You So Much (Dedicated To The Christ Consciousness)* charts for a week at UK #58.

POCO

Richie Furay (guitar, vocals); **Jim Messina** (guitar, vocals); **Rusty Young** (pedal steel); **Randy Meisner** (bass, vocals);
George Grantham (drums, vocals)

1968

Aug After the break-up of Buffalo Springfield, a new country-rock outfit forms as Pogo, in Los Angeles, CA, around Springfield alumni Furay (b. May 9, 1944, Yellow Springs, OH) and Messina (b. Dec. 5, 1947, Maywood, CA), who join Young (b. Feb. 23, 1946, Long Beach, CA), Grantham (b. Nov. 20, 1947, Cordell, OK), both ex-Colorado band Boenzee Cryque, and Meisner (b. Mar. 8, 1946, Scottsbluff, NE), ex-Poor. Young has rejected an offer from Gram Parsons to join his new Flying Burrito Brothers outfit, preferring instead to join the ex-Springfield members,

who were his favorite band of the time.
Nov [18] After rehearsing in Topanga Canyon for several weeks, the band makes its debut at the Troubadour, Los Angeles' "hoot night". They play a five-song set, including Furay's *Nobody's Fool* and *What A Day* and Young's instrumental *Grand Junction*.
Dec [26-27] They perform at the Fillmore West, San Francisco, CA, sharing the bill with Steve Miller and Sly & the Family Stone.

1969

Jan [15] Pogo signs to Epic Records after Atlantic agrees "to assign to CBS all right, title, etc., to the exclusive services of Richard Furay" in exchange for acquiring the rights to Graham Nash, who is still signed to Epic through the Hollies. (This releases Furay to record for Epic as part of Pogo.)
Mar Because of threatened court action by **Pogo** comic-strip creator Watt Kelly, the band changes its name to Poco.
Apr During debut recording sessions, Meisner quits after a personality clash, and will return home to Scottsbluff and work at a John Deere tractor factory, before joining Rick Nelson's Stone Canyon Band. Timothy Schmit (b. Oct. 30, 1947, Sacramento, CA) is invited to replace him, but turns the offer down to stay in college and avoid the draft. Poco continues as a four-piece.
June [13] The group plays at the Hollywood Palladium, sharing the bill with the Bonzo Dog Doo Dah Band.
[20] They appear at the three-day "Newport Festival" at San Fernando Valley State College, Devonshire Downs, Northridge, CA.
Sept [20] Poco's debut album, ***Pickin' Up The Pieces***, makes US #63, and will sell over 100,000 copies.

1970

Feb Invited a second time, Schmit now joins. (He has been in Sacramento folk trio, Tim, Tom & Ron in 1962, becoming surf band the Contenders in 1963, before joining New Breed and then Glad, who name-changed to Redwing.)
May [14-17] Poco plays four nights at the Fillmore West, San Francisco, CA, on a bill with Spirit.
July Their Furay-produced second album, ***Poco***, dedicated to David Geffen, though they will shortly sign a management deal with Shiffman & Larson, reaches US #58.
[3-5] They appear at the three-day "Atlanta Rock Festival", alongside Johnny Winter, Jimi Hendrix and others, in Byron, GA.
Aug [6] Poco appears alongside Paul Simon, Janis Joplin and others at the 12-hour anti-war "Concert For Peace" at New York, NY's Shea Stadium, 25 years after the bombing of Hiroshima.
Nov [21] *You Better Think Twice* peaks at US #72. Messina leaves for a solo career, replaced by Paul Cotton (b. Feb. 26, 1943, Los Angeles), who joins from Illinois Speed Press, at the recommendation of Chicago's Peter Cetera.

1971

Feb Live album, ***Deliverin'***, produced by Messina prior to his exit and recorded at the Boston Music Hall and New York Felt Forum, reaches US #26.
May [1] *C'mon* peaks at US #69.
Dec The Steve Cropper-produced ***From The Inside***, the group's first with Cotton, makes US #52.

1972

Feb [10] Poco makes its live UK debut at Loughborough University, before playing two dates at London's Rainbow Theatre on the 11th and 12th.
Nov [21] The band appears on the first broadcast of ABC-TV's "In Concert".

1973

Jan ***A Good Feelin' To Know***, produced by Jack Richardson and Jim Mason, peaks at US #69.
Feb Recording begins on Poco's next album, whose title track, *Crazy Eyes*, is a song Furay has written about Gram Parsons four years previously. The set will also include a Parsons' cut, *Brass Buttons*.
Aug [10] Poco performs at San Francisco's Winterland Ballroom, in what will be one of Furay's last appearances with the band.
Sept Furay leaves to co-form the Souther-Hillman-Furay Band.
Nov Richardson-helmed ***Crazy Eyes*** reaches US #38.

1974

June Again produced by Richardson, ***Seven***, with the band now reduced to a four-piece, makes US #68.
Nov [9] During a current US tour, the band performs at Yale University, New Haven, CT.
Dec The band-written and produced ***Cantamos***, recorded at the Record Plant, Los Angeles, and its last for Epic, peaks at US #76.

1975

July Newly signed to ABC, ***Head Over Heels***, produced by Poco with Mark Harman, reaches US #43.
Aug Epic releases the double album, ***The Very Best Of Poco***, which climbs to US #90.
Nov [15] ABC-issued *Keep On Tryin'* makes US #50, their first chart single in four years.

1976

Apr [17] Also on Epic, ***Poco Live***, recorded during their 1974 winter tour, peaks at US #169.
June [26] ***Rose Of Cimarron*** makes US #89, promoted by a major US tour, supporting the Stills-Young band. When Rusty Young causes the tour to close and new member Al Garth quits, Poco comes close to disbanding once again.
Aug [14] The Young-penned title track, *Rose Of Cimarron*, peaks at US #94, but will become an enduring US airplay favorite.
Dec The group starts recording at the Scoring Two Studios, but leaves three weeks later to assess its future.

1977

July [9] ***Indian Summer***, with Poco's country roots replaced by the synthesizer playing of Steely Dan's Donald Fagen, reaches US #57.
Sept [17] Schmit leaves to join the Eagles (once again replacing Meisner), as *Indian Summer* makes US #50.

1978

Jan Grantham also leaves, to join Secrets. (He will then move to Nashville, TN, working as Ricky Skaggs' drummer for some years, then joining Steve Wariner.)
Mar After exhaustive auditions, British musicians Charlie Harrison and Steve Chapman are recruited.
Dec Kim Bullard (b. Atlanta, GA), who has toured with Crosby, Stills & Nash, also joins on keyboards.

1979

Jan Produced by Richard Sanford Orshoff, ***Legend*** reaches US #14, while CBS issues the retrospective ***Poco : The Songs Of Richie Furay***.
Mar [31] The extracted acoustic guitar-led ballad, *Crazy Love*, penned by Young, is the band's biggest hit at US #17.
Apr [12] ***Legend*** becomes the group's first RIAA-certified gold disc.
June [14] Poco takes part in a "MUSE (Musicians for Safe Energy)" benefit concert at the Hollywood Bowl, Hollywood, CA, with Jackson Browne, Crosby Stills & Nash and others.
July [21] Cotton-written *Heart Of The Night* makes US #20.

1980

July The band, now with MCA Records which has absorbed the ABC label, releases the Mike Flicker-produced ***Under The Gun***, which reaches US #46.
Aug [30] *Under The Gun*, spurred by a Michael Nesmith-lensed video, makes US #48.
Oct [25] Cotton-penned *Midnight Rain* peaks at US #74.

1982

Mar [13] After ***Blue And Gray*** has made US #76 the previous July, ***Cowboys And Englishmen***, again helmed by Flicker and largely a collection of covers, by writers including Hal David, J.J. Cale, Gordon Lightfoot and Tim Hardin, peaks at US #131.
Dec [4] Having moved to Atlantic Records, ***Ghost Town***, recorded in Silverlake, CA, and co-produced by the band with John Mills, makes US #195. The extracted Young ballad, *Shoot For The Moon*, will reach US #50 on Feb [19] the following year.

1984

May [19] *Days Gone By* peaks at US #80.
June With a reunited line-up including both Furay and Schmit, its parent album ***Inamorata***, co-produced by Young and Cotton, makes US #167. (Shortly after, the group will break for a five-year hiatus during which time Young and Grantham will reunite to back former Pure Prairie Leaguer, Vince Gill, on a 1986 US tour.)

1989

Apr After Messina has approached Young with a view to reforming Poco the previous year
the reunited band, now lining up as Furay (who is now also a minister in a Boulder, CO church), Young, Messina, Grantham and Meisner, signs to RCA Records.
Nov [4] Young-written *Call It Love* reaches US #18, Poco's biggest hit in ten years. It is taken from ***Legacy***, largely produced by David Cole, which rises to US #40.
[30] In a rare UK TV appearance, Poco guests on BBC1's "Wogan", performing *Follow Your Dreams*.

1990

Jan [20] *Nothin' To Hide*, co-penned and produced by Richard Marx, makes US #39, as the group embarks on a major US tour with Marx. A Paul Cotton solo album, ***Changing Horses***, is released on the Sisapa label, while early Poco material retrospective double CD, ***Poco : The Forgotten Trail (1969-74)***, is released via the Legacy series.
Mar [9] ***Legacy*** is certified gold by the RIAA.
Apr [7] Poco takes part in "Farm Aid IV" at the Hoosier Dome, Indianapolis, IN, performing a medley of *A Good Feelin' To Know*, *Take It To The Limit*, *Your Mama Don't Dance* and *Crazy Love*.

1993

Jan [7] As the group, now including Young, Cotton, Tim Smith (percussion) and Richard Neville (bass), continues to tour North America, they play a WBOS radio station free concert at South Station, Boston, MA. Meanwhile Young is working on new album with Doobie Brother Patrick Simmons as Four Wheel Drive.
Apr [17] Poco plays at the USF Soccer Field, University of South Florida, Tampa, FL, during a tour with John Kay & Steppenwolf, Edgar Winter and Dave Mason.
see also: **BUFFALO SPRINGFIELD, THE EAGLES, LOGGINS & MESSINA**

THE POGUES

Shane MacGowan (guitar, vocals); **Jem Finer** (banjo); **Philip Chevron** guitar); **James Fearnley** (accordion); **Spider Stacy** (tin whistle); **Caitlin O'Riordan** (bass); **Andrew Ranken** (drums)

1983

The band falls together in London, led by MacGowan (b. Shane Patrick Lysaght MacGowan, Dec. 25, 1957, Tunbridge Wells, Kent, but growing up in Tipperary, Eire), ex-punk band the Nipple Erectors (later the Nips) who went on to join Stacy (b. Peter Stacy, Dec. 14, 1958, London) in the Chainsaws, before linking with Finer (b. Jeremy Max Finer, July 20, 1955, Stoke-on-Trent, Staffs.), with whom MacGowan has also busked at London's Finsbury Park tube station, to play a punk/folk mix of Irish rebel songs at the Cabaret Futura club, London, originally under the name Pogue Mo Chone ("kiss my arse" in Gaelic). Adding two drinking partners from King's Cross pubs, Ranken (b. Nov. 13, 1953, London) and ex-Nip Fearnley (b. Oct. 9, 1954, Manchester, Lancs.), the band plays a mixture of country, rockabilly and assorted Scottish and Irish folk. O'Riordan is recruited as the group's early gigs include playing at the Irish Centre, Camden, London, and supporting psychobilly act King Kurt.

1984

May Forming its own Pogue Mahone label, with independent distribution by Rough Trade, the band releases its debut single, *The Dark Streets Of London*, which is banned from daytime BBC radio play when the meaning of the group's name becomes apparent.
June Stiff Records picks up the single and signs the band, reputedly for half a crate of Guinness beer, but persuades the group to abridge its name to the Pogues.
Oct [31] The group embarks on a 26-date British tour, suppporting Elvis Costello.
Nov The band's debut album, ***Red Roses For Me***, produced by Stan Brennan, mixes group originals with traditional folk songs, and charts briefly at UK #83, featuring the extracted *Boys From The County Hell*.

1985

Apr MacGowan-penned *A Pair Of Brown Eyes*, produced by Elvis Costello, peaks at UK #72, its promo video filmed by Alex Cox (with whom the band will make a feature film).
June *Sally Maclennane* makes UK #51, aided by a special limited-edition pressing in the shape of a shamrock.
Aug [24] Following a successful "Cambridge Folk Festival" appearance and a headlining slot at a benefit concert for Nicaragua in Brixton, London, the Costello-produced ***Rum, Sodomy And The Lash*** (a title taken from Winston Churchill's description of life in the Royal Navy) reaches UK #13.
Sept Their revival of a Ewan MacColl folk song, *Dirty Old Town*, produced by new member, ex-Radiators From Space guitarist Chevron (b. June 17, 1957, Dublin, Eire), subbing for Finer who is on maternity leave, makes UK #62.

1986

Jan The band makes its US live debut with a short tour - during which O'Riordan briefly walks out between New York shows, leaving Pogues roadie Darryl Hunt (b. May 4, 1950, Nottingham, Notts.) to temporarily deputize on bass.
Mar A plan to revive the Lovin' Spoonful's *Do You Believe In Magic?* is shelved, as the band releases the four-track EP, *Poguetry In Motion*, which climbs to UK #29.
Apr MacGowan is hit by a London taxicab as he leaves a restaurant and suffers a fractured arm and torn ligaments, though his already-inconsistent front row of teeth, for which he has become notorious, is thankfully unharmed.
May [16] O'Riordan marries Elvis Costello in Dublin, Eire.
[17] The band appears in Dublin at the "Self Aid" concert (raising funds to help the young Irish unemployed to set up in business), with U2, Van Morrison, Elvis Costello, Chris De Burgh and others.
June [20] The group plays at the "Glastonbury Fayre", Glastonbury, Somerset, on a bill with the Cure, Level 42 and the Housemartins, among others.
Sept *Haunted*, written by O'Riordan and originally used on the soundtrack to the Cox-directed film "Sid And Nancy", makes UK #42 while most of the band are in Spain's Sierra Nevada with Cox, filming the surreal western "Straight To Hell", co-starring Joe Strummer (they play the homicidal McMahon gang).
Nov O'Riordan leaves the group and Hunt takes over permanently on bass.

1987

Mar [6] The group appears on Irish TV, with U2 and other guests, in a 25th anniversary celebration of Irish folk group the Dubliners.
Apr *The Irish Rover*, teaming the Pogues and the Dubliners, hits UK #8.
June The band has contributed four songs to the soundtrack album from "Straight To Hell". The movie is released to mixed reviews. *The Good, The Bad And The Ugly* (from the film) is scheduled as a single, but then cancelled. Pogues manager Frank Murray persuades a close friend, veteran Irish musician Terry Woods (b. Dec. 4, 1947, Dublin, Eire) who has retired from the music business and is working in a plastics factory, to join the band on mandolin and concertina.
Nov After the collapse of Stiff, and its absorption by Trevor Horn's ZTT Records, the band's Pogue Mahone label is revived within the new set-up to release its records.
Dec *A Fairytale Of New York*, written by MacGowan and Finer with seasonal lyrics (and some ripe language), intended as a MacGowan/O'Riordan duet two years earlier, but now featuring Kirsty MacColl guesting in the female vocal slot, hits UK #2 during Christmas week, kept off the top by the Pet Shop Boys' *Always On My Mind*.

1988

Jan [30] ***If I Should Fall From Grace With God***, produced by Steve Lillywhite (MacColl's husband), hits UK #3 in its week of entry. The band is on a three-week US tour on which ex-Clash frontman Joe Strummer (b. John Mellor, Aug. 21, 1952, Ankara, Turkey), joins as a temporary member - adding the Clash hits *London Calling* and *I Fought The Law* to the Pogues' on stage repertoire.
Mar Title track, *If I Should Fall From Grace With God*, peaks at UK #58.
Apr ***If I Should Fall From Grace With God*** makes US #88.
July *Fiesta* reaches UK #24. MacGowan collapses at Heathrow Airport en route to San Francisco, CA, to support Bob Dylan. He misses ten days of concerts and the band plays on without him.
Dec *Yeah Yeah Yeah Yeah Yeah* makes UK #43.

1989

July *Misty Morning, Albert Bridge* makes UK #41.
[10] Their "Slaughtered Lambs Of New Wave Tour" with Violent Femmes begins at the Poplar Creek Music Theatre, Hoffman Estates, IL.
[29] ***Peace And Love*** hits UK #5 and will go on to make US #118.
Oct [7] Fearnley marries actress Danielle Von Zerneck.

1990

Feb The group contributes a cover of *Got A Lot O' Livin' To Do* to the newly released compilation album, ***The Last Temptation Of Elvis***, to benefit the Nordoff Robbins Music Therapy charity.
June Once again featuring the Dubliners, the double A-side *Jack's Heroes*, the unofficial theme for the Irish World Cup soccer team, and *Whiskey In The Jar*, peaks at UK #63.
Sept *Summer In Siam* makes UK #64.
Oct The Pogues and Kirsty MacColl contribute *Miss Otis Regrets/Just One Of Those Things* to the newly-released ***Red Hot + Blue***, an anthology of Cole Porter songs to benefit AIDS education.
[7] The group embarks on a 12-date UK tour at the City Hall, Newcastle-upon-Tyne, Tyne & Wear, set to end on the 26th at Wembley Arena, Wembley, Middx.
[13] Largely MacGowan-penned ***Hell's Ditch***, produced by Strummer, reaches UK #12.
Dec [15] ***Hell's Ditch*** debuts at its US #187 peak.

1991

Mar [17] The group plays a St. Patrick's Day gig at Glasgow's Barrowlands.
Apr *Birmingham Six* is declared eligible for airplay after the convictions have been quashed.
June [2] They take part in "Fleadh '91" at the Finsbury Park Astoria, London.
[29] BBC2-TV airs "Bringing It All Back Home", a five-part look at the roots of Irish music and the role America has played in its history, featuring among others, the Pogues.
July [9] "The Pogues - Completely Pogued" airs on C4-TV.
[15] The group performs at London's Brixton Academy as part of the "Chieftains Music Festival 1991".
Aug [4] They participate in the "Feile '91 Festival" at the Semple Stadium, Thurles, Co. Tipperary.
Sept [21] *A Rainy Night In Soho* charts for a week at UK #67.
[26-27] The Pogues perform at the Beacon Theatre, New York, on a bill with Strummer.
Oct [12] The 14-track ***The Best Of The Pogues*** debuts at its UK #11 peak.
Nov [29-30] The group, with Strummer now a full-time member having replaced the increasingly unreliable MacGowan as lead singer (who has been fired after a sake-drinking binge in Japan left him incapable of playing a gig), embarks on an 11-date UK tour at the Corn Exchange, Cambridge, Cambs., set to end on December 12th at London's Town & Country club.
Dec [25] "The Ghost Of Oxford Street", with the group playing robbers and directed by Malcolm McLaren, airs on C4-TV.

1992

Jan [4] Reissued *Fairytale Of New York*, originally a 1987 UK #2 hit, reaches UK #36.
May [30] Their version of the Rolling Stones' *Honky Tonk Women* debuts at its UK #56 peak.
Aug [23] The group performs at WOMAD's tenth birthday party at the World in the Park, Royal Victoria Park, Bath, Avon.
Oct [4] They begin another UK tour at Manchester Academy. The 11-date series will end on December 10th at the Brixton Academy.
Dec [12] MacGowan, now pursuing a solo career, has teamed with Nick Cave to cover Louis Armstrong's *What A Wonderful World*, which charts for a week at UK #72.

1993

Jan MacGowan is reportedly close to signing a solo deal with ZTT Records.
Aug [28] The Pogues' *Tuesday Morning* reaches UK #18.
Sept [11] ***Waiting For Herb***, featuring founding member Spider Stacy as the band's new lead vocalist, in place of the now-departed Strummer, debuts at its UK #20 peak.
Dec [1] The group, with newcomers James McNally (accordion/whistle) and David Coulter (mandolin/fiddle) in the line-up, plays live at Tower Records' Piccadilly Store on National AIDS Day.
[17] MacGowan joins the band onstage at its Kentish Town Forum show, encouraging rumors that he is set to rejoin the band.

1994

Jan [22] *Once Upon A Time* makes UK #66.
Mar [17] The Pogues plays the RPM in Toronto, ON, Canada, during its current North American tour, as MacGowan's new band, the Popes which includes Paul McGuinness (guitar), Bernie France (bass), Danny Pope (drums) and Tom McManamon (banjo), performs at the Clapham Grand in London.
July [15] The Pogues take part in "The Phoenix 1994" festival, at Long Marston, near Stratford-upon-Avon, Warks.
Aug [18-21] They perform at the "Heineken Music Festival", Castle Field, Portsmouth, Hants.

1995

June Shane MacGowan & the Popes' debut album ***The Snake***, including a duet with Sinead O'Connor

and another with Clannad's Maire Brennan, is released by ZTT in the UK and will be promoted with selected European dates including an appearance during July's "Montreux Jazz Festival", Switzerland.
Dec [22-23] The Pogues play year-end dates at London's Shepherd's Bush Empire.

1996

Apr [20] MacGowan's inimitable interpretation of *My Way* debuts at its UK #29 peak.
[25] They end a month-long North American tour, at the Fillmore, San Francisco, CA.
see also: **THE CLASH**

THE POINTER SISTERS

Ruth Pointer (vocals); **Anita Pointer** (vocals); **Bonnie Pointer** (vocals); **June Pointer** (vocals)

1971

Sisters Bonnie (b. July 11, 1951, East Oakland, CA) and June Pointer (b. Nov. 30, 1953, East Oakland), daughters of a minister at East Oakland Church Of God, with a strong grounding in religious music, began performing as an R&B duo around San Francisco, CA clubs in 1969, calling themselves Pointers, and were soon joined by sister Anita (b. Jan. 23, 1948, East Oakland), who left her day job as a secretary. San Francisco promoter Bill Graham now becomes the trio's manager, and local producer David Rubinson begins to hire them. They work extensively over the next two years as stage and session back-up vocalists for Elvin Bishop, Boz Scaggs, Dave Mason, Taj Mahal and others.

1972

Ruth Pointer (b. Mar. 19, 1946, Oakland) leaves an office job to complete the R&B vocal quartet and Atlantic Records signs them to a recording deal after the company's Jerry Wexler spotted them opening for Bishop at Los Angeles, CA's Whisky A Go-Go club, releasing *Don't Try To Take The Fifth*, produced by Wardell Quezergue. A follow-up single will remain unreleased.

1973

Oct Freed from both Atlantic and Bill Graham, the group has been signed by David Rubinson to Blue Thumb Records, a subsidiary of ABC.
[13] *Yes We Can Can*, written by Allen Toussaint and produced by Rubinson, reaches US #11, while the group's first album, ***The Pointer Sisters***, will reach US #13.

1974

Jan [2] The group performs at the annual "Midem Festival" in France.
Feb [2] Their revival of Willie Dixon's standard, *Wang Dang Doodle*, peaks at US #61.
[7] ***The Pointer Sisters*** is certified gold by the RIAA.
Apr ***That's A Plenty***, again produced by Rubinson, makes US #82. They perform extensive TV bookings, with a visual image based on '40s-style fashions.
July [25] ***That's A Plenty*** is also confirmed gold by the RIAA.
Sept Double performance set ***Live At The Opera House***, recorded at the San Francisco Opera House, at which the group has been the first pop act ever to play, peaks at US #96.
Dec [14] Country-styled *Fairytale*, atypical of their previous or future R&B work, written by Anita and Bonnie, reaches US #13 and makes US Country #37 (with the group playing Nashville's Grand Ole Opry as part of a tour).

1975

Mar [1] *Fairytale* wins Best Country Vocal Performance By A Duo Or Group at the 17th annual Grammy Awards.
[15] *Live Your Life Before You Die* peaks at US #89.
Oct [4] *How Long (Betcha' Got A Chick On The Side)* makes US #20 (having topped the US R&B chart for two weeks), while its parent album, ***Steppin'***, reaches US #22.
Dec [27] *Going Down Slowly* peaks at US #61.

1977

Feb [4] With June having suffered from exhaustion the previous year, when their only chart action was the double album, ***The Best Of The Pointer Sisters*** making US #164 on December 25th, the group now takes part in the 25th anniversary edition of Dick Clark's "American Bandstand" on ABC-TV.

1978

Jan ***Having A Party*** peaks at US #176, as the group leaves Rubinson and Blue Thumb, suing the label for unpaid royalties. Meanwhile, Bonnie leaves her sisters to go solo, and signs to Motown.

1979

Feb [24] The remaining trio has signed to Richard Perry's new Planet label, where their debut, *Fire*, written by Bruce Springsteen and produced by Perry (as will be the remainder of the group's hit output), hits US #2, behind Rod Stewart's *Da Ya Think I'm Sexy?*, with its parent album ***Energy*** reaching US #13. Bonnie's Motown solo debut, *Free Me From My Freedom/Tie Me To A Tree (Handcuff Me)*, peaks at US #58, while her maiden album, ***Bonnie Pointer***, makes US #96. *Everybody Is A Star*, the group's revival of Sly & the Family Stone's 1970 hit, is the group's UK chart debut, at #61.
[5] *Fire* is certified gold by the RIAA.
[13] ***Energy*** is also confirmed gold by the RIAA.
Apr *Fire* reaches UK #34.
May [5] *Happiness*, written by Toussaint and taken from ***Energy***, makes US #30.
Oct The sisters' ***Priority*** peaks at US #72 (failing to yield hit singles, though it includes songs by Bob Seger, Graham Parker, Springsteen and Jagger/Richard), while Bonnie's revival of the Elgins' *Heaven Must Have Sent You* reaches US #11.

1980

Feb Her update of the Four Tops' *I Can't Help Myself (Sugar Pie, Honey Bunch)*, Bonnie's final solo hit, makes US #40, while her second album, also titled ***Bonnie Pointer II***, peaks at US #63. (She enters a legal dispute with Motown, which will prevent the release of further solo material on the label.) Jerry Weintraub takes over the sisters' management.
Oct [25] Written by Tom Snow and Cynthia Weil *He's So Shy* hits US #3 for the first of three weeks, while its parent album ***Special Things***, with session contributions from Ollie Brown, Nate Watts and Greg Phillinganes, makes US #34.
Nov [25] *He's So Shy* is certified gold by the RIAA.
Dec [6] *Could I Be Dreaming*, also from ***Special Things***, peaks at US #52.

1981

Aug [29] Smooth soul-tinged *Slow Hand*, written by Michael Clark and John Bettis, with Anita on lead vocal, hits US #2 (behind Diana Ross and Lionel Richie's *Endless Love*), taken from ***Black And White***, which reaches US #12.
Sept [2] *Slow Hand* is certified gold by the RIAA.
[26] *Slow Hand* hits UK #10.
[16] ***Black And White*** is also certified gold by the RIAA.
Oct [3 ***Black And White*** reaches UK #21.
Dec [12] Also from the album, *Should I Do It* peaks at UK #50.

1982

Apr [3] *Should I Do It* reaches reaches US #13, during a 16-week chart run.
Aug [28] *American Music* makes US #16, featured on ***So Excited!***, which peaks at US #59, and also includes a version of Prince's *I Feel For You*, later a hit for Chaka Khan.
Nov [27] Jittery *I'm So Excited*, co-written by the sisters, and extracted from its near-namesake album, reaches US #30, while a compilation album, ***The Pointer Sisters' Greatest Hits***, on Planet, peaks at US #178.

1983

Apr [16] *If You Wanna Get Back Your Lady* peaks at US #67.
Nov [26] *I Need You* heralds a new album, and makes US #48. (During the year, June releases ***Baby Sitter***, her first solo outing.)

1984

Apr [14] The synthesizer-based *Automatic*, co-written by Mark Goldenberg and Brock Walsh and featuring Ruth's lead vocal, hits US #5. It is also taken from ***Break Out***, which hits US #8 (which will become the sisters' only multi-platinum certified album) and UK #9. The set, produced as ever by Perry, includes guest musicians Glen Ballard, Paulinho Da Costa, Lee Ritenour, Greg Phillinganes and Bruce Roberts.
May *Automatic* hits UK #2, behind Duran Duran's *The Reflex*.
July [7] *Jump (For My Love)*, with June out front, also from ***Break Out***, hits US #3 and UK #6.
Aug *I Need You*, belatedly released in the UK, reaches #25. (Bonnie, now signed to Private I records, releases ***If The Price Is Right***.)
Oct [27] *I'm So Excited*, a remix of their 1982 chart success, hits US #9.
Nov *I'm So Excited* reaches UK #11.
Dec The trio wins the Top Dance Singles/Albums category in **Billboard**'s Year In Music.

1985

Jan Uptempo dance cut, *Neutron Dance*, from ***Break Out***, and also heard in the film "Beverly Hills Cop", makes UK #31.
[28] Having collected the Favorite Video, Duo Or Group, Soul/R&B and Favorite Band, Duo Or Group, Soul/R&B trophies at the 12th annual American Music Awards, held at the Shrine Auditorium, Los Angeles, earlier in the evening, the Pointer Sisters take part in the recording of USA For Africa's *We Are The World*.
Feb [16] *Neutron Dance* hits US #6.
[26] The Pointer Sisters win Best Performance By A Duo Or Group with Vocal category for *Jump (For My Love)*, and Best Vocal Arrangement For Two Or More Voices for *Automatic*, at the 27th annual Grammy Awards.
Apr [27] *Baby Come And Get It* makes US #44.
Aug ***Contact*** makes UK #34.
Sept [3] ***Contact*** is certified platinum by the RIAA on its way to reach US #24.
[21] *Dare Me* reaches US #11 and UK #17, taken from ***Contact***.
Nov [30] *Freedom* peaks at US #59.
Dec [5] The RIAA certifies three million sales of ***Break Out***.

1986

Jan [20] The Pointer Sisters join Eddie Murphy, Bill Cosby, Bob Dylan and Stevie Wonder in concerts to celebrate the first observance of Martin Luther King Jr.'s birthday as a US national holiday.
[27] They win the Favorite Video, Duo Or Group, Soul/R&B category at the 13th annual American Music Awards, again held at the Shrine Auditorium.
Mar [15] *Twist My Arm*, from ***Hot Together***, peaks at US #83.
Aug Anita hits #2 on the US Country chart, duetting with Earl Thomas Conley on *Too Many Times*.
Dec [20] With June's lead vocal, *Goldmine* makes US #33, as ***Hot Together*** reaches US #48.

1987

Feb [21] *All I Know Is The Way I Feel* peaks at US #93.
Sept [5] *Be There*, from the soundtrack to "Beverly Hills Cop II", makes US #42 as Anita, still in the trio, releases her maiden solo effort, ***Love For What It Is***,

produced by Preston Glass.
Dec The Pointer Sisters contribute *Santa Claus Is Coming To Town* to the newly-released Special Olympics charity album, ***A Very Special Christmas***.

1988

Apr Including songs written by Diane Warren, Siedah Garrett, Jonathan Butler and Matthew Wilder, and proving to be their final album for RCA, ***Serious Slammin'*** peaks at US #152, while the extracted *He Turned Me Out* is featured in the movie "Action Jackson".
Dec Ruth contributes *Streets Of Gold* to the soundtrack to the Disney cartoon movie "Oliver And Company", with fellow artists Billy Joel, Huey Lewis and Bette Midler, among others.

1989

May The Richard Perry-created ***Rock, Rhythm & Blues*** compilation is released featuring the Pointers Sisters' *Mr. Lee*.
Aug [19] ***Jump - The Best Of The Pointer Sisters*** reaches UK #11.

1990

July Now signed to Motown and under the new production wing of Levi Seacer Jr., ***Right Rhythm*** is released.
Sept [8] Ruth marries her personal trainer, Michael Sayles, in her garden in Malibu, CA.

1991

Apr [14] Having joined Bob Hope's entertainment troupe to the US troops serving in the Gulf before Christmas, and contributed to *Voices That Care*, the Sisters appear on ABC-TV's "Welcome Home, America!" forces tribute.
May [14] The Pointer Sisters contribute *Nine Alive* to the newly-released cartoon cat Garfield homage album, ***Am I Cool, Or What?***, released by GRP.
Nov [23] CBS-TV's "Party For Richard Pryor", taped in Beverly Hills on September 7th and including the Pointer Sisters singing *Hot Together*, airs.

1992

July [14] The group plays at the Valley Forge Music Fair, Devon, PA, during a series of summer dates.
Nov [26] They perform at a Thanksgiving Day Parade in Houston, TX.
Dec [31] Still touring regularly, they see out the year with the first of three shows at Bally's Grand Hotel, Atlantic City, NJ.

1993

Jan [24] The group takes part in a tribute to Marvin Gaye, in support of the fight against AIDS at the "Midem Festival".
July [13] Now signed to SBK Records by Fred Davis, their label debut, ***Only Sisters Can Do That***, is released.

1994

Jan [5] The sisters are enshrined in the Hall of Fame at the NAACP 26th annual Image Awards in Pasadena, CA.
[20] The Pointer Sisters become only the second all-girl group (after the Supremes) to receive a star on the Hollywood Walk of Fame.
Feb [7] The sisters present the Favorite Male Country Artist trophy at the annual American Music Awards, held at the Shrine Auditorium.
Mar [23] They take part in the "Rhythm Country And Blues - The Concert", benefitting the Country Music Foundation and the Rhythm and Blues Foundation, at the Universal Amphitheatre, Universal City, CA.
[26] ***Rhythm And Blues***, featuring the Pointers' duet with Clint Black on *Chain Of Fools*, reaches US #18.
Aug [15] The group performs at the Pine Knob Music Theatre, Clarkston, MI, during summer US dates.

1995

Sept The Pointer Sisters begin a 47-city tour appearing in the musical "Ain't Misbehavin'" in Green Bay, WI.
Dec [24] Bonnie's husband Jeffrey Bownes is arrested for alleged battery, following a scuffle at a Christmas party at June's house in the Hollywood Hills.

POISON

Bret Michaels (vocals); **C.C. DeVille** (guitar); **Bobby Dall** (bass); **Rikki Rockett** (drums)

1984

Michaels (b. Bret Michael Sychak, Mar. 15, 1963, Pittsburgh, PA) and Rockett (b. Richard Ream, Aug. 8, 1959, Mechanicsburg, PA) have already formed the Spectres in hometown Pittsburgh, and gone on to join up with licensed cosmetologist Dall (b. Robert Kuy Kendall, Nov. 2, 1965, Miami, FL, but settled in Mechanicsburg at age eight) and Matt Smith to form Paris, playing mostly rock covers in local bars, when they decide to relocate to Hollywood, CA, driving cross-country in a $700 ambulance Michaels has bought, in an effort to succeed as a heavy-metal band. The following year, guitarist Smith is replaced by DeVille (b. Bruce Anthony Johannesson, May 14, 1962, Brooklyn, New York, NY), a clinical psychology major at NYC and veteran of many rock outfits, including Lace, the Broken Toys, the Shears, Screaming Mimi & Saint James, Van Gogh's Ear and Roxx Regime, the forerunner of Stryper. His experience enables the quartet to hone its hard-rocking, glam heavy-metal style as the band prominently gigs around the Los Angeles, CA, club circuit in search of a record deal.

1986

Aug [2] Having secured a contract with Enigma Records, licensed to Capitol, Poison's debut album, ***Look What The Cat Dragged In*** begins the first of 101 weeks on the US Album chart during which it will hit #3 and rack up multi-platinum status. The band also embarks on a US tour opening for Ratt and Cinderella.

1987

May [16] As word spreads and gig venues get larger, *Talk Dirty To Me*, aided by what will become a typically peroxide-drenched, babe-heavy promo video clip, popular with MTV US viewers, hits US #9 and UK #67.
June The group participates in the TV special "Ibiza '92", at the Ku Club, Ibiza.
July [25] Follow-up, *I Want Action*, makes US #50.
Nov [21] Third extract, *I Won't Forget You*, reaches US #13. (By year's end, Poison is voted Best New Artist Or Group in specialist US rock magazine **Circus**' Readers Poll.)

1988

May [21] Their second album, ***Open Up And Say ... Aah!***, produced by Tom Werman, reaches UK #18 in its week of entry and begins a quintuple-platinum rise to hit US #2, while Poison supports David Lee Roth on his US trek, until August. In its concert contract, the band demands, and receives, ample dressing-room supplies of Kentucky Fried Chicken, Reese's Peanut Butter Cups, shrimp cocktails, Domino's pepperoni pizza and a tour total of 876 boxes of Trojan condoms, at each venue.
July [9] *Nothin' But A Good Time*, having already made UK #35 in May, hits US #6.
Aug Poison makes its UK debut on the "Monsters Of Rock" festival bill at Castle Donington, Leics.
Oct [8] *Fallen Angel* reaches US #12.
Nov [5] *Fallen Angel* reaches UK #59.
Dec [24] As Poison is inducted into **Circus** magazine's Hall of Fame, the ballad, *Every Rose Has Its Thorn*, tops the US chart for the first of three weeks. Written by the four group members, it will become the second biggest-selling single of the year, behind Steve Winwood's *Roll With It*.

1989

Jan [26] *Every Rose Has Its Thorn* is certified gold by the RIAA.
Feb *Every Rose Has Its Thorn* is their UK singles breakthrough, reaching #13.
[28] Poison wins the Most Underrated Group category in **Circus**' Readers Poll.
Apr [15] Still from ***Open Up*** album, their update of Loggins & Messina's *Your Mama Don't Dance* hits US #10.
May [13] *Your Mama Don't Dance* reaches UK #13.
Sept UK reissued *Nothin' But A Good Time* makes UK #48, as the band prepares its third album.

1990

Apr The group members guest on comedian Sam Kinison's newly-released album, ***Leader Of The Banned***.
July [21] ***Flesh And Blood*** hits UK #3 in its week of entry.
Aug [7] The RIAA certifies three million sales of ***Look What The Cat Dragged In***.
[18] On the same day that the band appears for the second time at Castle Donington's "Monsters Of Rock" festival, and within only four weeks of release, the Bruce Fairbairn and Mike Fraser-produced ***Flesh And Blood*** hits US #2, behind MC Hammer's ***Please Hammer Don't Hurt 'Em***.
Sept [1] Lead-off single, *Unskinny Bop*, hits US #3, having already reached UK #15.
[5] *Unskinny Bop* is certified gold by the RIAA.
[19] Headlining "Flesh And Blood" US tour, supported by Warrant, opens at the Brown County Arena, Green Bay, WI, set to extend into 1991.
Oct [27] *Something To Believe In* makes UK #35.
Nov [3] While Michaels has recently co-written and produced much of his girlfriend and Giant Records' signing Susie Hatten's debut album, DeVille's axework can currently be heard on Warrant's US #10 smash, *Cherry Pie*.
[19] Police are called in to aid crowd control for a small venue gig at the Academy Theatre, New York.
Dec [1] DeVille spends six hours in a Louisville, KY jail, following a public drunkenness and criminal mischief arrest, after the group's Louisville Gardens concert.
[8] Ballad *Something To Believe In*, written about the death of the group's security guard, Kimo, hits US #4.

1991

Jan [19] Having cancelled five US dates and a festival appearance in Iceland amid rumors of a drug-induced break-up, although management states that any problems are due to Dall breaking two fingers of his left hand in a slammed car door, the group embarks on the Canadian leg of its tour, supported by Don Dokken, at the PNE Pacific Coliseum, Vancouver, BC, Canada.
[28] They perform at the 18th annual American Music Awards, held at Los Angeles' Shrine Auditorium.
Feb [14] The RIAA certifies three million sales of ***Flesh And Blood***.
Mar [23] *Ride The Wind* makes US #38.
[25] ***Flesh And Blood*** is named the Best Selling Heavy Metal Album at the NARM 1990 Best Seller Awards.
Apr [9] Increasingly at odds, Michaels and DeVille have a punch up in a New Orleans hotel room.
May [12] The latest leg of tour opens at the Selland Arena, Fresno, CA, on a bill with Slaughter and BulletBoys.
June [9-15] The group cancels five dates because Michaels has a viral infection of his vocal chords and Dall a pinched back nerve.
[19] One year into the tour, the "Flesh And Blood" trek is cancelled.
[29] *Life Goes On* makes US #35.
Aug [19] Remaining a member of the band, Michaels signs a separate solo contract with Capitol Records.
Sept [5] The group performs at the eighth annual MTV Video Music Awards, held at the Universal Amphitheatre, Universal City, CA.
Oct [8] Billed as Bret Michaels & the Hollywood

Gutter Cats, the frontman sets out on a six-week solo trek starting in Columbus, OH, performing acoustic versions of Poison hits and classic-rock cover versions, with each gig opening with the audio broadcast of the forthcoming Poison double live set.
[21] The RIAA certifies five million sales of ***Open Up And Say ... Ahhh***.
Nov [23] *So Tell Me Why* debuts at its UK #25 peak, as Michael issues a public warning to DeVille and Dall, who have recently entered drug rehab, to "get it together or split".
[30] The self-produced ***Swallow This Live*** performance album, including four new studio cuts, bows at its US #51 peak.
Dec [14] ***Swallow This Live*** makes UK #52 in its week of entry.

1992

Jan [11] Michaels participates in the third annual MTV US cable network's "Rock'n'Jock" softball game, held to benefit the T.J. Martell Foundation for Leukemia charity.
[27] DeVille's departure from Poison is officially announced as he forms the C.C. DeVille Experience.
May [20] Richie Kotzen (b. Feb. 3, 1970, Birdsboro, PA), having already released three solo albums for the Shrapnel label - ***Richie Kotzen***, ***Fever Dream*** and ***Electric Joy***, and now signed to Roadrunner as a solo artist, officially joins Poison as its new lead guitarist.
June [4] The group participates in Capitol Records' 50th anniversary all-star gala at the Capitol Tower on Sunset and Vine in Hollywood, CA.

1993

Jan [16] The band warms up the 400,000-strong crowd at the Lincoln Memorial, Washington, DC, at the start of the week-long Presidential Inaugural festivities.
Feb [13] *Stand*, from the group's forthcoming album, bows at its UK #25 peak.
[19] Michaels takes part in the 20th anniversary "Lynyrd Skynyrd & Friends LYVE (Pronounced Live)" pay-per-view concert from the Fox Theatre, Atlanta, GA.
Mar [6] Having already sold 15 million albums worldwide, Poison's fifth effort, ***Native Tongue***, produced by Richie Zito, and featuring the Tower of Power Horns, Sheila E., Timothy B. Schmit and a gospel choir, debuts at its US #16 and UK #20 peaks.
[13] *Stand* makes US #50.
Apr [18] The UK leg of its "Native Tongue" tour opens at the Newport Centre, Newport, Gwent, Wales.
[21] ***Native Tongue*** is certified gold by the RIAA for 500,000 US sales.
[24] *Until You Suffer Some (Fire And Ice)* debuts at its UK #32 peak.
May [7] The group guests on NBC-TV's "The Tonight Show".
July [26-27] Poison performs in Santiago, Chile, during its current tour of South America.

1994

Jan [14] Poison, with new guitarist Blues Saraceno (b. Oct. 17, 1971) having replaced Kotzen who was fired last summer, plays the first of two "Hollywood Rock Festival" gigs at Sao Paolo, Brazil. (They will follow this up with a concert in Rio de Janeiro on the 21st, before returning home to the US.)
May [24] Michaels breaks his thumb, nose and collar-bone, loses four teeth, cracks his sternum, receives a hairline fracture of his upper jawbone in addition to contusions and lacerations after he loses control of his Ferrari and crashes into a telephone pole in Burbank, CA.

1996

Apr [11] Michaels files suit against Capitol Records in Los Angeles Superior Court seeking compensatory damages of $20 million, claiming that the label has reneged on a verbal agreement to extend the time period allowed to deliver solo product, a schedule which allegedly has advance monies attached, all pursuant to his solo contract signed in 1991. The ongoing dispute has also prevented the release of a new Poison album.

THE POLICE

Sting (vocals, bass); **Andy Summers** (guitar, vocals); **Stewart Copeland** (drums, percussion, vocals)

1977

Jan [9] The son of a CIA agent, Copeland (b. Stewart Armstrong Copeland, July 16, 1952, Alexandria, VA), who spent part of his youth in the Middle East where his father was working, drumming in the UK with progressive rockers Curved Air, which is managed by Copeland's brother Miles has first met Sting (b. Gordon Matthew Sumner, Oct. 2, 1951, Wallsend, Tyne & Wear), an ex-primary school teacher whose nickname is derived from a regularly worn, bee-like black-and-yellow-striped jersey, while the latter is playing in the jazz combo Last Exit at a gig nearby the Newcastle Polytechnic students' party where Curved Air has appeared earlier one evening in December 1976, the pair being introduced by local journalist Phil Sutcliffe. They now meet again in London, set on forming a new band.
[12] They begin rehearsing with guitarist Henri Padovani (b. Corsica), at Copeland's studio in his Mayfair apartment.
Feb [12] The Police records its first single, *Fall Out*, backed by *Nothing Achieving*, at Pathway studios, with the two sides costing £150 to record.
[21] The band begins rehearsals with New York, NY singer Cherry Vanilla, to back her on a UK tour.
Mar [3] Cherry Vanilla, Johnny Thunders & the Heartbreakers and the Police start their tour at London's Roxy club in Covent Garden.
[19] The Police begins a tour of Holland and France, supporting Wayne County & the Electric Chairs.
May *Fall Out* is released on Copeland's Illegal label, selling out its initial pressing of 2,000 copies immediately, and entering the UK Independent chart.
[28] After original Gong members reunite to play at the Circus Hippodrome in Paris, France, ex-Gong member Mike Howlett invites Copeland and Sting to join guitarist Summers (b. Andrew James Summers, Dec. 31, 1942, Poulton-Le-Fylde, Lancs.) to play as Strontium 90. (Summers is ex-New Animals, Soft Machine and Kevin Ayers, and has contributed to Neil Young's ***Everybody Knows This Is Nowhere***.)
June The Police plays at London's Marquee club, after which Summers is formally added to the line-up. He adds a guitar echo unit which, combined with Copeland's inverted reggae drum style, will provide a trademark minimalist rhythm bed to Sting's vocals.
July [25] Summers plays with the band at the Music Machine - the first of only two gigs the Police play as a quartet.
Aug [10] The group records a session with producer John Cale.
[12] Padovani quits the band.
[18] The group plays its first gig as a trio at Rebecca's, Birmingham, W. Midlands.
Oct [22] The Police travels to Munich, West Germany, to record and play with Eberhard Schoener, for his EMI album, ***Video Flashback***.

1978

Jan [13] The group begins recording its first album at Surrey Sound Studios with Nigel and Chris Gray engineering.
Feb [22] The Police appear in a Wrigley's Chewing Gum commercial for US TV, having to dye their hair blond for it. (Mistakenly associated with the UK punk movement, the blond visual image will give the group a strong identity for the next two years.)
Mar [11] The Police support US group Spirit at London's Rainbow Theatre, at the start of a UK tour promoted by Miles Copeland.
[22] Miles Copeland secures an option deal with A&M Records to release *Roxanne*.
Apr *Roxanne* is released in Britain but initially fails to chart, as the band, currently working with Schoener's Laser Theatre in Germany, is unable to promote it.
July Copeland releases *Don't Care* under the name of Klark Kent. An eponymous 10" album, on green vinyl, is also issued.
Oct The group's second single for A&M, *Can't Stand Losing You*, makes UK #42.
[16] The Police appears on BBC Radio 1's "Kid Jensen Show", before setting off on its first US tour.
[20] Having flown to New York on the budget Laker Skytrain airline, carrying their instruments as hand luggage, the group makes its US debut at New York's CBGB's, at the start of a 23-date North American trek.
Nov Their debut album, the self-produced ***Outlandos D'Amour***, recorded for £3,000, and set to hit UK #6, is released, together with the extracted *So Lonely*.
Dec The band begins a UK tour, supporting Alberto Y Lost Trios Paranoias.

1979

Feb [13] The group starts work on its second album at Surrey Sound Studios.
Mar [1] They embark on a 29-date US tour at the Whisky, Los Angeles.
Apr [25] The band makes its debut on BBC1-TV's "Top Of The Pops", as the re-released Sting-penned *Roxanne* climbs the UK chart.
[28] Roxanne reaches US #32, as the band then heads back to the US for its third tour.
May *Roxanne* makes UK #12 as parent album, ***Outlandos D'Amour***, hits UK #6 and US #23.
June The Police begin its first headlining UK tour.
July [24] The band headlines the first day of the 19th annual "Reading Rock Festival", Reading, Berks.
Aug Re-released, Sting-written *Can't Stand Losing You* hits UK #2, behind the Boomtown Rats' *I Don't Like Mondays*.
[11] Sting appears on BBC-TV's "Juke Box Jury".
[16] "Quadrophenia", featuring Sting in the role of Ace, premieres in the UK, though he rejects numerous other current film offers, including the villain in the Bond movie "For Your Eyes Only".
Sept [10] *Message In A Bottle* is released as the group begins an 11-date UK tour, at the Assembly Rooms, Derby, Derbys., set to end at London's Hammersmith Odeon. It tops the UK chart after two weeks of release.
[27] The Police plays New York's Diplomat Hotel at the start of a two-month US tour which will include a visit to Kennedy Space Center in Houston to film a video for the forthcoming single, *Walking On The Moon*.
Oct [13] Their second album, ***Reggatta De Blanc***, co-produced by the group with Nigel Gray, at a cost of £6,000, hits UK #1 for the first of four weeks. It will also reach US #25, where it will be issued as a double 10" album and earn a gold disc.
Nov *Fall Out*, originally released through the Illegal label in 1977, makes UK #47.
Dec [1] *Walking On The Moon* hits UK #1. Like every Police single released on A&M, it is written by Sting, who now visually and musically dominates the line-up.
[18] In the middle of a German and UK tour, the Police play at London's Hammersmith's Palais and Odeon on the same night, making the short journey between venues in an army personnel carrier, with 40 police officers on standby to maintain order.
[22] *Message In A Bottle* peaks at US #74.

1980

Jan [20] The group performs at the State University of New York, Buffalo, NY, at the start of its first world tour (which takes in 37 cities in 19 countries, ending in Sting's home town Newcastle, where it plays two charity concerts for the Northumberland Association of Boys' Clubs). The band sets up its own charity, the Outlandos Trust, headed by Conservative Member of Parliament Anthony Steen.
Mar Re-issued *So Lonely*, the group's fourth UK Top 10 success, hits #6.
[25] The Police become the first Western group to

perform in Bombay, India, at the Homi Bha Bha Auditorium.
June *Six Pack*, a collection of Police singles, now issued on blue vinyl, reaches UK #17, as Sting and Summers exit to Eire for tax purposes.
July [7] The band begins work on its third album at Wisseloord Studio in Hilversum, Holland.
[26] The group headlines the "Reggatta De Bowl" charity gig at Milton Keynes, Bucks.
[28] They play at the "Dalymount Festival" in Dublin, Eire, with U2 and Squeeze.
Aug [9] The band begins a month's tour of Europe at the "Wechter Festival" in Belgium.
Sept [27] The teacher-themed *Don't Stand So Close To Me* hits UK #1, where it will remain for four weeks.
Oct [3] BBC-TV airs the "Police In The East" documentary.
[11] ***Zenyatta Mondatta***, co-produced by the trio with Nigel Gray, begins a four-week stay at UK #1.
[21] The Police begins a 33-date North American tour at the Winnipeg Arena, Winnipeg, MB, Canada.
Dec [14-16] The Police plays three concerts at Buenos Aires and Mar Del Plata in Argentina.
[20] *De Do Do Do, De Da Da Da* hits UK #5.

1981

Jan [10] The band sells out its first concert at New York's Madison Square Garden at the start of a two-month tour of North America, Japan, Australia and New Zealand.
[17] *De Do Do Do, De Da Da Da* hits US #10 as ***Zenyatta Mondatta*** is the group's first US top album at #5.
Feb [25] ***Reggatta De Blanc*** wins the Best Rock Instrumental Performance category at the 23rd annual Grammy Awards.
[27] ***Zenyatta Mondatta*** is certified platinum by the RIAA.
Mar [1] Sting begins acting work on the BBC-TV play "Artemis 81".
Apr [11] *Don't Stand So Close To Me* hits US #10.
May [19] Sting is named Songwriter Of The Year at the 26th annual Ivor Novello Awards, held at London's Grosvenor House Hotel.
June [10] ***Reggatta De Blanc*** is certified gold by the RIAA.
[15] The group begins recording its fourth album at AIR studios in Montserrat in the Caribbean, with Hugh Padgham co-producing, on the recommendation of XTC's Andy Partridge. The project is again filmed by BBC-TV. (Hosted by Squeeze member and TV presenter Jools Holland, it will air in the UK at Christmas.)
Oct [3] *Invisible Sun*, inspired by the troubles in Northern Ireland, hits UK #2, kept off the top by Adam & the Ants' *Prince Charming*.
[10] Its parent album, ***Ghost In The Machine***, co-helmed by Padgham, hits UK #1 at the start of a three-week run.
Nov [14] *Every Little Thing She Does Is Magic* tops the UK chart, the only cut from the album to be recorded at Le Studio, Quebec, PQ, Canada.
Dec [5] *Every Little Thing She Does Is Magic* hits US #3.
[26] *Spirits In The Material World* reaches UK #12. (During the year, the group plays a secret gig at London's Marquee, but because of blizzard-like weather conditions, few turn up. Organizers try to attract passers-by, but few believe that the band is playing there.)

1982

Jan ***Ghost In The Machine*** begins a six-week run at US #2.
Feb They donate proceeds from a Fillmore Stadium concert in San Francisco, CA, to help save Sir Freddie Laker's beleaguered airline.
[24] The Police is named Best British Group at the first annual BRIT Awards, at London's Grosvenor House Hotel, and hours later wins the Best Rock Vocal Performance By A Duo Or Group for *Don't Stand So Close To Me* and Best Rock Instrumental Performance for *Behind My Camel* categories at the 24th Grammy Awards.
Mar [13] *Spirits In The Material World* reaches US #11.
Apr [29] *Every Little Thing She Does Is Magic* wins the Best Pop Song category at the 27th annual Ivor Novello Awards, again held at the Grosvenor House Hotel.
May [15] *Secret Journey* makes US #46.
July Copeland scores Francis Ford Coppola's movie "Rumble Fish". The group plays an arena concert at Gateshead Athletics Stadium, Gateshead, Tyne & Wear, with support acts the Beat and U2.
Sept Sting's first solo single, a revival of *Spread A Little Happiness* from the soundtrack of "Brimstone And Treacle", reaches UK #16, the start of an increasingly successful solo career.
[3-5] The band plays at the three-day "US Festival", financed by Apple Computers founder Steven Wozniak, in San Bernardino, CA, to 400,000 people, along with Jackson Browne, the Cars, Fleetwood Mac, the Grateful Dead, Eddie Money, Santana, Talking Heads and many others.
Oct Summers releases an instrumental album, ***I Advance Masked***, with King Crimson's Robert Fripp, as Copeland writes a ballet score for the San Francisco Ballet's production of "King Lear".

1983

June [4] *Every Breath You Take*, a Sting song about obsessive love, hits UK #1 for the first of four weeks.
[25] Its parent album, ***Synchronicity*** (Swiss psychologist Carl Jung's theories of the collective unconsciousness and mystical coincidence), most of which Sting wrote at Ian Fleming's former Jamaican home and again recorded in Montserrat and Le Studio, Quebec, enters the UK chart at #1, where it will stay for two weeks. Sting bases its lyrical direction on written works by Arthur Koestler.
July [9] *Every Breath You Take* hits US #1 for the first of eight weeks, spurred by a Godley & Creme-shot black and white video currently on heavy US MTV rotation.
[23] ***Synchronicity*** tops the US chart for the first of 17 weeks, achieving quadruple-platinum status.
Aug *Wrapped Around Your Finger* hits UK #7 and US #8.
[15] *Every Breath You Take* is certified gold by the RIAA.
[18] The group plays before a 70,000 crowd at New York's Shea Stadium.
Oct [8] *King Of Pain* hits US #3.
Nov *Synchronicity II* reaches UK #17.
Dec [10] *Synchronicity II* makes US #16. (*Every Breath You Take* is named Top Single in **Billboard**'s Year In Music survey.)

1984

Jan [21] *King Of Pain* peaks at UK #17. During the month Copeland's soundtrack album ***Rumble Fish*** is released by A&M.
Feb [28] *Every Breath You Take* is named Song Of The Year and Best Pop Performance By A Duo Or Group With Vocal, and ***Synchronicity*** is named Best Rock Performance By A Duo Or Group With Vocal, at the 26th annual Grammy Awards.
Mar [3] *Wrapped Around Your Finger* hits US #8.
Apr [5] "Every Breath You Take" is named Best Group Video at the second annual American Video Awards.
[19] *Every Breath You Take* nabs the Best Song Musically & Lyrically and Most Performed Work categories at the 29th annual Ivor Novello Awards, held at the Grosvenor House Hotel.
Aug [15] ***Outlandos D'Amour*** is certified platinum by the RIAA.
Sept Summers and Fripp release their second collaboration ***Bewitched***.
[18] "Every Breath You Take" wins the Best Cinematography category at the inaugural MTV Music Video Awards, held at Radio City Music Hall, New York, NY, hosted by Dan Aykroyd and Bette Midler.
Nov [14] The RIAA certifies two million sales of ***Ghost In The Machine*** and four million sales of ***Synchronicity***.

1985

Feb [11] The Police wins the Outstanding Contribution To British Music honor at the fourth annual BRIT Awards, at London's Grosvenor House.
May Copeland releases the African-influenced album, ***The Rhythmatist***.
June Increasingly independent from the rest of the band, Sting releases his first solo album, ***Dream Of The Blue Turtles***.

1986

June [11] The Police reunites at an Amnesty International concert in Atlanta, GA, performing five songs.
July [21] The group begins rehearsing for the follow-up to ***Synchronicity***, but abandons the sessions soon after, as Sting insists on pursuing solo musical and acting interests.
Oct A revised edition of the earlier hit, *Don't Stand So Close To Me '86*, makes UK #24, as a prelude to a greatest hits package.
Nov [8] ***Every Breath You Take - The Singles***, reprising the group's career, is its fifth successive UK #1, and hits US #7.
[29] *Don't Stand So Close To Me '86* makes US #46.
Dec [22] "Every Breath You Take Videos" is certified gold by the RIAA.

1987

July Summers' ***XYZ*** is released, the first to feature his vocals. (Further albums will follow - ***Mysterious Barricades*** (1988), ***Golden Wire*** (1989), ***Charming Snakes*** (1990) and ***World Gone Strange*** (1991), before he serves a stint as the live music director on US syndicated TV's "The Dennis Miller Show" in January 1992. He also scores the movies "Weekend At Bernie's" and "2010".)

1988

Jan Copeland releases the instrumental album, ***The Equalizer And Other Cliff Hangers***, which includes US TV's "The Equalizer" theme, as a prelude to future new age albums on brother Miles' newly-established specialist label, No Speak. He will continue to be successful as a composer, writing the scores for films "Wall Street", "Talk Radio", "Hidden Agenda", "First Power" and "Men At Work" and others, and composing the opera "Holy Blood And Crescent Moon", for the Cleveland Opera in 1989, before forming Animal Logic with Deborah Holland and Stanley Clarke (whose ***Animal Logic*** makes US #106 in December 1989, followed by ***Animal Logic II*** in 1991).

1992

Aug [22] Copeland and Summers (who himself took the plunge on September 30th the previous year) attend Sting's marriage to Trudie Styler, and at the reception at the couple's Wiltshire home, they reconvene for a couple of numbers.
Oct [10] A further Police compilation, ***Greatest Hits***, debuts at its UK #10 peak. (***Message In A Box : The Complete Recordings***, a four-CD boxed set retrospective, including all five studio albums plus rarities, will be released in September 1993, charting at US #79 on Oct [16], and being confirmed gold by the RIAA on January 19th the following year.)
Nov [19] The RIAA certifies three million sales of ***Every Breath You Take - The Singles***.

1995

May [13] *Can't Stand Losing You (Live)* debuts at its UK #27 peak.
June [10] Performance hits set, ***Live*** reaches UK #25 in its week of entry and will do the same at US #86 on July [1]. With Sting's solo career in full flow, Summers, who has recorded ***Invisible Threads*** with John Etheridge for Mesa Blue Moon records in 1993, will issue his new instrumental set, ***Synaethesia***, featuring music guests drummer Ginger Baker and bassist Jerry Watts on CMP Records in the US in February 1996, while Copeland's latest soundtrack

work will be for the April 1996-premiering Winona Ryder-starring movie "Boys", preceding a commission by US cable network, the Discovery Channel to compose the score for its first theatrical motion picture, "The Leopard Son", scheduled to open later in the year.
see also: **STING**

BRIAN POOLE & THE TREMELOES

Brian Poole (vocals); **Rick West** (lead guitar); **Alan Blakley** (rhythm guitar); **Alan Howard** (bass); **Dave Munden** (drums)

1959

The group is formed in Dagenham, Essex, by ex-schoolfriends Poole (b. Nov. 2, 1941, Barking, Essex), on vocals and guitar, Blakley (b. Apr. 1, 1942, Bromley, Kent) on drums, Howard (b. Oct. 17, 1941, Dagenham) on saxophone and Brian Scott on lead guitar, before Munden (b. Dec. 12, 1943, Dagenham) joins on drums, allowing Blakley to switch to rhythm guitar and Poole to sing. Howard changes from sax to bass guitar, and the group begins as a dancehall band playing cover versions, including impersonations of Buddy Holly & the Crickets (with Poole wearing Holly-type horn-rimmed glasses). Their first public appearance is at the Ilford Palais, Ilford, Essex.

1961

July After two years of solid gigging, during which West (b. Richard Westwood, May 7, 1943, Dagenham) has joined as lead guitarist making the group a quintet, BBC radio producer Jimmy Grant spots them playing in Southend, Essex, and books them for featured spots on the Light Programme's popular "Saturday Club" show. The group also plays a summer season as a successful rock-ballroom band, at Butlin's holiday camp at Ayr, Strathclyde, Scotland, billed as Brian Poole & the Tremilos.

1962

Jan They are signed to Decca, after being selected in preference to the Beatles, both groups auditioning on New Year's Day, but local availability swings it for producer Mike Smith when he has to choose.
Mar Their debut single, *Twist Little Sister*, fails to chart, but picks up UK airplay and earns them a spot on TV's "Thank Your Lucky Stars".
Sept An album of cover versions, ***Big Hits Of '62***, is released on Decca's low-price Ace of Clubs label. The group backs the Vernons Girls on their cover of Little Eva's *The Loco-Motion*. (The Tremeloes also back Mike Sarne on *Come Outside* and John Leyton on *Wild Wind*.)

1963

Mar With the advent of the Merseybeat boom, they adopt a harder rocking stance. Poole abandons his Holly specs for contact lenses, and through energetic marketing by Decca, they become part of the new R&B/beat movement, but *Keep On Dancing*, featured in the British pop movie, "Just For Fun", fails to score.
Aug The group hits UK #5 with its cover of *Twist And Shout*, hugely popular on the Beatles debut album but not available as a Beatles single. Further progress is halted by the Beatles' EP, *Twist And Shout*, which is a bigger seller.
Sept [11] The band embarks on 23-date UK package tour with Roy Orbison, the Searchers and Freddie & the Dreamers.
Oct [10] Their revival of the Contours' *Do You Love Me?* tops the UK chart for the first of three weeks, fighting off the Dave Clark Five version.
Nov [8] They begin another UK tour, with the Searchers, Freddie & the Dreamers, Dusty Springfield and Dave Berry, in Halifax, Yorks.
Dec *I Can Dance*, almost a clone of *Do You Love Me?*, makes UK #31.

1964

Mar Their fast-rocking revival of a Roy Orbison B-side, *Candy Man*, hits UK #6.
Apr [4] They begin a tour of Australia and New Zealand with Gerry & the Pacemakers.
[26] The band appears at the annual "**New Musical Express** Poll Winners Concert" at the Empire Pool, Wembley, Middx., with the Beatles, Cliff Richard and many others.
June Their first ballad hit, a revival of a Crickets B-side, *Someone Someone*, hits UK #2. The group spends time in Ireland filming a spot in the movie, "A Touch Of Blarney".
Sept Return-to-the-beat *Twelve Steps To Love* makes UK #32, as *Someone Someone* peaks at US #97 - the group's only US chart entry with Poole.

1965

Feb Another ballad, updating the Browns' *The Three Bells*, featuring Norman Petty on piano, reaches UK #17.
Mar [1] The group embarks on a 15-date, twice-nightly UK tour of independent theatres known as "The P.J. Show", with P.J. Proby and the Fourmost, at London's Finsbury Park Astoria, set to end on the 16th at the Usher Hall, Edinburgh, Scotland.
Aug Their treatment of the Strangeloves' US hit *I Want Candy* reaches UK #25, and will be the group's last hit in its present form.
Sept [30] The band begins a rescheduled 15-day Scandinavian tour.
Nov *Good Lovin'* (subsequently a US #1 for the Young Rascals) is released.
Dec [31] They begin their third successive New Year tour of Scandinavia.

1966

Jan Poole and Howard return to Britain after being arrested in Finland over a disputed £200 Helsinki hotel bill.
[28] Poole and the Tremeloes announce they are splitting.
May Mickie Clark, from Dagenham, replaces Alan Howard who leaves the music business to establish a dry-cleaning business. Poole releases the solo *Hey Girl*, which fails to chart.
June [6] Poole begins a solo tour of Denmark, Sweden and Norway.
[10] The Tremeloes' solo career also starts unremarkably, as a Poole-less cover of Paul Simon's *Blessed* fails to chart.
July The group moves to CBS releasing a cover of the Beatles' *Good Day Sunshine* from ***Revolver***. Its new front-man, Len "Chip" Hawkes (b. Nov. 11, 1946, London), replacing Clark on bass, helps develop a strong harmony vocal blend which will highlight subsequent records. (The Fortunes' Dave Carr had previously been rumored a hot favorite to join.)

1967

Mar A "good-time" cover of Cat Stevens' *Here Comes My Baby* begins the group's second and stronger lease of chart-life, hitting UK #4.
[11] The band begins a 21-date UK tour with the Spencer Davis Group, the Hollies and Paul Jones at the Granada Cinema, Mansfield, Notts.
[23] Poole releases his solo debut on CBS, a David & Jonathan song, *That Reminds Me Baby*.
Apr [2] The Tremeloes' tour ends at the Empire Theatre, Liverpool, Lancs.
May [18] Their revival of a Four Seasons B-side, *Silence Is Golden*, released because of the popular response to it on the Hollies package tour, and showcasing the group's perfected harmony vocals, is its biggest-seller, topping the UK chart for the first of three weeks. Meanwhile, *Here Comes My Baby* reaches US #13.
June [30] The Tremeloes embark on their debut US tour in Ohio. (On their arrival at Kennedy Airport, New York, NY, their plane lands under full emergency conditions. During the tour, they are made freemen of Jersey Shore, PA, and receive golden keys from the mayor.)
July ***Here Come The Tremeloes***, re-titled ***Here Comes My Baby*** in the US, makes UK #15 and US #119 (the group's only album success).
Aug Uptempo *Even The Bad Times Are Good* hits UK #4, as *Silence Is Golden* makes US #11 and becomes a million seller.
Oct *Even The Bad Times Are Good* makes US #36.
Nov Although the group is now a familiar sight on UK TV and on the live circuit, record success varies, its material aligning it away from the progressing rock scene. The more subtle and less commercial ballad, *Be Mine*, makes UK #39.

1968

Feb *Suddenly You Love Me*, identifying the group's pop market by blending strongly commercial ingredients, hits UK #6.
Mar *Suddenly You Love Me* reaches US #44, the group's final US chart entry. The Tremeloes tour South America, playing 14 shows in Argentina and six in Uruguay.
Apr They begin a UK package tour with the Kinks, the Herd and others. Munden misses the start suffering from chickenpox.
May Latin-tinged, uptempo *Helule Helule* reaches UK #14.
June The group's visit to the US is cancelled when they are refused TV work visas.
Oct *My Little Lady*, another exuberant harmony rocker, hits UK #6. The band signs a £25,000 deal to appear in cabaret at Northern Clubs operated by the Bailey Organisation.
[22] The group begins a two-week tour of Israel, the first by a UK group since Cliff Richard & the Shadows in 1965.
Nov [12] They start another South American trek with TV and radio dates in Rio de Janeiro, Brazil.
[28] The Tremeloes' North American tour begins in Toronto, ON, Canada.
Dec The band changes pace with a more serious cover of Bob Dylan's *I Shall Be Released*, reaching UK #29.
[28] The group guests on BBC1-TV's "Happening For Lulu".
[31] They perform in Stockholm at the start of a six-day tour of Sweden and Denmark.

1969

Mar Poole bows with his new backing-group, the Seychelles, on the President label with *Send Her To Me*. (His solo career fails to take off, and he returns to the family's butchery business in Dagenham.)
Apr *Hello World* reaches UK #14.
May [11] The Tremeloes perform at the 17th annual "**New Musical Express** Poll Winners Concert".
Oct West misses Hawkes' wedding to TV personality Carol Dilworth after he is "kidnapped" by students.
Nov *(Call Me) Number One* hits UK #2, and is one of the group's biggest UK sellers. *By The Way* will make UK #35 the following April before *Me And My Life* hits UK #4 in October, the group's final Top 10 entry.

1971

July *Hello Buddy* makes UK #32, the band's last hit single, as it becomes eclipsed by newcomers in the British teen market, like T. Rex, Sweet and Slade. With almost a decade's worth of familiar hits to draw upon, the Tremeloes join the cabaret and northern UK club circuit, where the nostalgia factor ensures a consistently lucrative living.

1974

Nov Hawkes leaves for a solo vocal career performing country music, in a year when he also recovers from a car accident. After the group releases its last album ***Shiner*** on the DJM label, Blakley will also quit in January the following year. (Hawkes' son Chesney is passed the torch, hitting UK #1 in 1991 with *The One And Lonely*.)

1989

June The Tremeloes, having made a brief recording comeback covering F.R. David's hit, *Words*, have maintained a modest presence on the cabaret circuit and '60s nostalgia tours around Britain, sometimes with their original leader as Brian Poole & the Tremeloes, performing early beat-era material, and sometimes as the Tremeloes, playing later hits. Poole now joins the Troggs' Reg Presley, the Searchers' Mike Pender, Clem Curtis from the Foundations and the Merseybeats' Tony Crane, to temporarily form the Corporation (aka the Travelling Wrinklies). They perform hit medleys from the '60s on a UK summer tour and release a version of *Ain't Nothing But A House Party* on their own label. Ultimately, all return to their day jobs, though the Tremeloes will occasionally turn up at nostalgia events such as "The Biggest '60s Party In Town" at London's Olympia Hall on October 6th 1991. Castle Communications will bring the bands hits to compact disc with the May 1990 release of ***The Ultimate Collection***, while US fans have to wait for Rhino Records to issue ***The Best Of The Tremeloes*** in 1992.

IGGY POP

1964

Raised in a trailer park, Pop (b. James Jewel Osterberg, Apr. 21, 1947, Muskegan, MI) joins the Iguanas as drummer and singer, and also has one-off jobs drumming for Junior Wells, Buddy Guy, the Shangri-Las and others. The Iguanas release a cover of Bo Diddley's *Mona* the following year, of which 1,000 copies are made and sold at gigs. He meets ex-Dirty Shames member Ron Asheton (b. July 17, 1948, Washington, DC) and James Williamson, and leaves the Iguanas to join the Prime Movers Blues Band with Asheton on bass (who is sacked after two weeks and later joins the Chosen Few) which will make its vinyl debut with the 1965 single *Mona/I Don't Know Why*. He adopts the name Iggy Pop: Iggy after the Iguanas, Pop after local junkie Jim Popp, and moves to Chicago, IL in 1966 with friend Sam Lay, drummer with the Butterfield Blues Band.

1967

Oct [31] Having returned to Michigan, he has formed the Psychedelic Stooges with Asheton and his brother Scott (b. Aug. 16, 1949, Waashington) on drums. Iggy & the Stooges now make their live debut at an Ann Arbor, MI Halloween party.

Dec Also ex-Dirty Shames, Dave Alexander (b. June 3, 1947, Ann Arbor, MI) joins on bass as Pop appears in an obscure art movie with Nico. The following year, the band continues to play live, mostly around Michigan, supporting Blood, Sweat & Tears at one gig, while Pop, whose live antics will become legendary and involve partial nudity, cutting his skin onstage and smearing food over his body, is also busted for indecent exposure.

1969

Apr Elektra A&R scout Danny Fields, in Detroit, MI, to sign the MC5, sees the group, now abbreviated to the Stooges, and signs it, advancing $25,000 to record a debut album.

Aug Raw-rock based debut set ***The Stooges***, produced by John Cale and recorded in four days, peaks at US #106.

1970

May [10-24] With Steve Mackay added on sax and ex-roadie Bill Cheatham on guitar, ***Fun House*** is recorded at Elektra Sound Recorders in Los Angeles, CA, produced by Don Gallucci. Earlier cohort James Williamson also joins as an additional guitarist.

Aug Alexander and Cheatham quit, while Zeke Zettner, another ex-roadie, joins. The band will split the following year with Pop determined to break a reported heroin addiction. He will move to Florida to improve his golf and also spend time cutting lawns for a living.

1972

Apr After turning down an offer to return to Elektra Records, he meets admirer David Bowie and his then manager Tony DeFries in New York. They persuade Pop to sign with MainMan Management and he re-forms the Stooges.

July Iggy & the Stooges, featuring Pop, the Asheton brothers and Williamson, make their UK debut at a King's Cross cinema, London, and begin sessions for a new album.

1973

Apr ***Raw Power***, the first of a two-album deal with CBS/Columbia, peaks at US #182. A new album is planned, but disagreements between the band and management prevent its release. (Out-takes and sessions from it are later issued by US Bomp and French Siamese Records in the late '70s.) DeFries sacks Williamson over drug problems and Scott Thurston joins on keyboards.

Oct The band moves back to the US for a tour which ends in violence at two gigs in Detroit. One of the shows, recorded on a cassette machine, is issued as ***Metallic K.O.***

Dec [31] The band plays a New Year's Eve gig at the Academy of Music in Los Angeles, CA.

1974

Feb Pop quits the Stooges prior to an East Coast tour.

July [3] He performs at a tribute concert to Jim Morrison at Los Angeles' Whisky club.

1975

Feb [10] Alexander dies in Detroit.

Williamson becomes a recording engineer in Los Angeles, CA, while Asheton forms a new short-lived US band the New Order, and later Destroy All Monsters, with ex-MC5 members.

May New sessions for Pop are sponsored by rock journalist Bob Edmonds and songwriter Jimmy Webb, who donates his home for the recordings which are made on Pop's weekend leave from the Neuro-psychiatric Institute in Los Angeles. Pop, Williamson and Thurston nail nine tracks before Pop returns to the institute for drug rehabilitation. Reportedly David Bowie is his only visitor.

1976

Mar [21] Pop and Bowie are involved in a drug bust in their hotel room in Rochester, NY.

June Pop and Bowie vacation at Chateau d'Herouville, France, and enter the studio to begin working on a Pop solo album.

Oct [1] Bowie and Pop relocate to the Schöneberg district of West Berlin, Germany, where they will be based for nearly three years.

1977

Jan Bowie's ***Low***, featuring Pop, hits UK #2 and US #11.

Feb Pop signs with RCA Records.

Mar [5] He performs at London's Rainbow Theatre, with Bowie on keyboards.

Apr [5] In an unlikely clash of cultures Pop and Bowie guest on US TV's "The Dinah Shore Show".

[9] Pop's first solo album, ***The Idiot***, "recorded" by Bowie, rather than produced, reaches UK #30. It includes the first version of future Bowie hit *China Girl*, co-written by the pair. Pop tours, with Bowie again playing keyboards, supported by Blondie. Throughout the summer, old Stooges numbers become regular features of punk live sets including those by the Sex Pistols, the Damned and others.

May [14] ***The Idiot*** makes US #72.

June [4] Re-issued ***Raw Power*** debuts at its UK #44 peak. (The track *Hard To Beat* is re-titled *Your Pretty Face Has Gone To Hell.*)

Oct [1] ***Lust For Life***, again produced by Bowie, reaches UK #28. It was recorded and mixed in 13 days in Berlin, and includes *The Passenger*, inspired by a Jim Morrison poem.

[8] ***Lust For Life*** makes US #120.

[30] Pop performs at London's Rainbow Theatre in Finsbury Park.

1978

June He plays shows at London's Music Machine, prior to a tour of France and Germany. During the year, ***Skydog In France*** and ***Kill City***, from the May 1975 sessions are released on Bomp in the US and Radar in Britain. A live album, taken from the two most recent tours, is issued as ***TV Eye (1977 Live)*** on RCA, once again helmed by Bowie.

1979

Mar Newly signed to Arista Records, he forms a new touring band, including ex-Sex Pistol Glen Matlock, ex-Ike & Tina Turner band-leader Jackie Clark, and regular Pop keyboardist sideman Thurston.

Oct ***New Values*** peaks at US #180 and UK #60. It is produced by Williamson and reunites Pop with Thurston, Scott Asheton, Williamson and MC5's guitarist, Fred "Sonic" Smith. They tour Britain with Matlock on bass. The inclusion of an ex-Sex Pistol leads to a ban by Dunstable Council, which has still not lifted an existing one on the Sex Pistols.

1980

Mar ***Soldier*** peaks at US #125 and UK #62. XTC's Barry Andrews replaces Thurston, who leaves to join the Motels. Other guests include Simple Minds, Bowie, Ivan Kral of the Patti Smith Group and Matlock.

May [30-31] Pop performs at the Music Machine in London, following a German tour.

Aug ***No Fun***, a Stooges compilation on Elektra, is released.

Sept [26] During current US dates, Pop plays at Detroit's Bookie's club.

1981

Sept ***Party***, his last for Arista, makes US #166, while the extracted *Bang Bang* becomes a popular US dance hit.

Dec Pop, supporting the Rolling Stones on a US tour, is booed offstage at the Silverdome, Pontiac, MI.

1982

Sept ***Zombie Birdhouse*** is issued on Blondie Chris Stein's Animal label. Pop and Stein also work on the movie soundtrack to "Rock'n'Rule". Pop will also contribute the title song on the soundtrack to the Alex Cox movie, "Repo Man", the following year when he also undertakes his first tour of Australia and Japan, though these will be his last live appearances in three years. Marrying in 1984, he will make a cameo appearance in Cox's "Sid And Nancy" in 1985, relocate to Brooklyn, NY, and also spend time in hospital suffering from pneumonia and injuries sustained in an accident, during which time he will write a book of anecdotes with Anne Wehrer, titled **I Need More**.)

1986

Oct Newly signed to A&M Records, his label debut is *Cry For Love*, co-written with Steve Jones.

[11] His most accessible outing to date, ***Blah Blah Blah***, co-produced by Dave Richards and Bowie, reaches UK #43 and will make US #75.

1987

Jan His cover of Johnny O'Keefe's 1957 song, *Real Wild Child*, is Pop's first major single success, hitting UK #10. He also makes a cameo appearance in the Paul Newman film, "The Color Of Money".

1988

July [21] ***Instinct***, produced by Bill Laswell and still featuring Jones on guitar (who also co-writes four songs), bows at its UK #61 peak and will reach US #110, as Pop guests on NBC-TV's "Late Night With

David Letterman". He is also currently featured on the soundtrack to "Dogs In Space".

1990

Feb *Livin' On The Edge* makes UK #51.
[24] Pop takes part in the "Roy Orbison Concert Tribute To Benefit The Homeless" at the Shrine Auditorium, Los Angeles.
Apr [6] John Waters movie, "Cry Baby", in which Pop stars, opens in US cinemas.
[16] He guests in the NBC-TV premiere "Shannon's Deal", having appeared in "Tales From The Crypt" and "Miami Vice".
July [21] ***Brick By Brick***, produced by Don Was, debuts at its UK #50 peak. The track *My Baby Wants To Rock'n'Roll* is penned with Slash of Guns N' Roses, who plays on four tracks on the album, alongside fellow Gunner Duff.
Aug [18] ***Brick By Brick*** makes US #90.
Oct [6] Pop participates in the "A Gathering Of Tribes" festival held at the Shoreline Amphitheatre, Mountain View, CA.
[13] *Candy*, a duet with the B52's Kate Pierson, peaks at UK #67.
Nov [19] Pop plays a sellout show at Toad's Place, New Haven, CT, during his current US club tour.

1991

Jan [19] Pop and Debbie Harry's duet, *Well Did You Evah*, written for the 1940 stage musical "DuBarry Was A Lady", rewritten for 1956 film "High Society", and now from ***Red Hot + Blue***, an anthology of Cole Porter songs to benefit AIDS education, makes UK #42.
Feb *Candy* reaches US #28.
Mar Pop takes the role of famed Los Angeles District Attorney Vincent Bugliosi in John Moran's opera, "The Manson Family".
[9] The Peace Choir's *Give Peace A Chance*, with Pop making a contribution with a host of other artists, makes US #54.
Aug [23] Having already taken part in the Roskilde, Leysin and "Bizarre" festivals, Pop performs at the annual "Reading Festival", Reading, Berks.
Oct [10] Pop is inducted into the National Association of Brick Distributors' second annual Brick Hall of Fame gala in New York, in recognition of services to the brick industry, for the title of his album, ***Brick By Brick***. He receives a trophy made of brick.

1992

Nov He begins work on a new album with producer Malcolm Burns. During the year he has toured the US once and Europe twice, and also played a series of dates in Buenos Aires as well as penning three songs for the movie "American Dreamer".

1993

May [26] Pop guests on NBC-TV's "Late Night With David Letterman", having completed work on Jim Jarmusch's short movie, "Coffee And Cigarettes", with Tom Waits.
July [27] Newly signed to Virgin Records, Pop makes a rare five-date UK visit beginning at the Corn Exchange, Cambridge, Cambs., promoting his forthcoming album, ***American Caesar***.
Sept [4] *The Wild America* EP charts for a week at UK #63.
[25] ***American Caesar*** charts for a week at UK #43.

1994

Mar [3] Pop guests on NBC-TV's "The Tonight Show".
[7] He plays a sellout show at the Commodore Ballroom, Vancouver, BC, Canada, during a North American tour.
May [21] *Beside You* debuts at its UK #47 peak.
July [17] Pop takes part in "The Phoenix 1994" festival at Long Marston, Stratford-upon-Avon, Warks.
Oct [8] Pop sings *Rip It Up* at "Elvis Aaron Presley : The Tribute", an all-star music event staged at the Pyramid Arena, Memphis, TN, broadcast live on pay-per-view in the US.

1995

Mar [10] He performs at the opening night gala of the Hard Rock Hotel & Casino in Las Vegas, NV.
Sept [2] Pop sings *Back Door Man* with Soul Asylum at the Concert for the Rock and Roll Hall of Fame at Cleveland Stadium, Cleveland, OH.

1996

Mar [5] Having recently completed further acting roles in Jarmusch's "Dead Man", "City Of Angels" and a sequel to "The Crow", and finished the soundtrack score to "The Brave", Pop's new album ***Naughty Little Doggie*** is released by Virgin.
Apr [8] Pop plays at New York's Roseland Ballroom, during a brief northeast tour of the US to promote his latest album.

PORTISHEAD

Beth Gibbons (lead vocals); **Geoff Barrow** (multi-instrumentalist/producer); **Adrian Utley** (guitar); **Dave McDonald** (sound engineer)

1992

May Barrow (b. Dec. 9, 1971, Walton-In-Gordano, Avon) who has grown up in the small village of his birth, in between the Avon towns of Portishead and Clevedon, has learned to play the drums as a boy and has moved with his mother to live in Portishead as a teenager, when she separated from his father. Inspired to begin breakdancing when the electro and hip-hop era arrived, Barrow has subsequently attended a graphic design course in 1988, but dropped out in search of a career in music production. Subsequently employed as a one of the builders of the Coach House Studio, home to the burgeoning Bristol, Avon music scene of producers Smith & Mighty and R&B aggregate Massive Attack among others, Barrow has been promised a job at the studio once it is finished, resulting in his working as a tea-boy and part-time tape-operator, notably on Massive's 1991 debut ***Blue Lines***. After also working on Neneh Cherry's ***Homebrew*** album, and having met Gibbons (b. Jan. 4, 1965, Devon), who has left Devon for Bristol at the age of 21, while both are on the government-run Enterprise Allowance job creation scheme in Bristol, Avon in February 1991, the pair is now invited to spend time in Cherry and husband Cameron McVey's London-based home studio, resulting in a nine-month stay, which fails, however, to bear fruit. Subsequently teaming with Caroline Killoury and Debbie Swainson who are forming their own Fruit management company (which will also handle Bristol-based act Tricky), Barrow and Gibbons return to the Coach House and record a session with Adrian Utley (b. 1958) an R&B/jazz session guitar veteran, which initially yields *Sour Times*, indicating to all concerned that they have finally found their groove. Gibbons quits her job at a Bristol advertising agency, and the newly-named Portishead is formed in the spring of '93, based around Barrow and Gibbons but including Utley and sound engineer Dave McDonald (b. 1964) as integral members, who together prepare a three-track demo.

1993

Aug Having approached six record companies, Barrow has been invited by A&R scout Ferdy Unger-Hamilton to London to play the three-song demo (*Sour Times, It's A Fire* and *It Could Be Sweet)* to Go! Discs R&B imprint, Go! Beat, resulting in a recording contract (though only Gibbons and Barrow will ink as Portishead). With Barrow musically influenced by '60s soundtrack composers, producer Giorgio Moroder, soul-man Isaac Hayes and '80s jazz-hop band A Tribe Called Quest, while Gibbons has been weaned on the music of Astrud Gilberto, Janis Joplin, Janis Ian and Elizabeth Fraser, the group begins recording its first album, simultaneously working on a side project to provide the music bed to a film-short directed by film school graduate Alexander Hemmings.

1994

May [4] A mini-album taster ***Numb*** is released by Go! Beat.
June [2] The ten-minute black and white film "To Kill A Dead Man", prominently led by Portishead's soundtrack, receives its premiere at London's Prince Charles Cinema (and will subsequently "open" for major movie releases including "Reservoir Dogs", "The Last Seduction" and "Pulp Fiction").
Aug [13] Sampling Lalo Schifrin's *More Mission Impossible*, *Sour Times* charts for a week at UK #57. The group make its first and only live appearance of the year at London's Blue Note's Athletico club.
Sept [3] Some 45-minutes in length, ***Dummy***, mixing retro-sounding cinematic themes with hip-hop, soul, jazz and blues and showcasing Gibbons' powerful blues vocal chops, initially makes UK #32 (and will be voted album of the year by **The Face**, **Melody Maker**, **Mix Mag**, **ID** and **The Daily Telegraph** among other critical nods). Upon the album's release the band has placed painted mannequins at highly visible traffic junctions around London.

1995

Jan [6] ***Dummy*** is certified gold by the BPI.
[14] Featuring a sample of *Ike's Rap III* by Isaac Hayes, *Glory Box* bows at its UK #13 peak.
[24] Portishead is named Best Dance Act at the **New Musical Express**' BRAT Awards held in London.
[28] ***Dummy*** hits UK #3.
Feb [25] The extracted *Sour Times (Nobody Loves Me)* makes US #53.
Mar [11] ***Dummy*** makes US #79.
[18] The group performs on BBC2-TV's "Later With Jools Holland".
Apr [22] The re-promoted *Sour Times* debuts at its UK #13 peak, as Portishead begins its first full tour, a 27-date swing taking in eight countries.
[29] During maiden US dates, the group plays at the Avalon in Boston, MA.
May [12] The band holds a multimedia event at London's South Bank complex including a further showing of "To Kill A Dead Man".
Sept [4] Portishead records *Mourning Air* for inclusion on the hastily-issued War Child benefit album ***Help!***
[12] ***Dummy*** wins the hotly-contested Mercury Music Prize at a presentation held at London's Savoy Hotel.

PREFAB SPROUT

Paddy McAloon (guitar, vocals); **Martin McAloon** (bass); **Wendy Smith** (vocals, guitar)

1982

Aug Prefab Sprout has formed earlier in the year as a quartet in Consett, Durham, based around Newcastle University English Literature graduate, Paddy McAloon (b. June 7, 1957, Consett) who has wanted to use the band name since he first thought of it in 1973. The early line-up, performing only McAloon songs, includes his brother Martin (b. Jan. 4, 1962, Durham, Durham), Smith (b. May 31, 1963, Durham) and drummer Mick Salmon, and plays local pub gigs in the Durham area. Rejected by all the major labels they approach, Prefab Sprout releases 1,000 copies of *Lions In My Own Garden* on its own Candle label, which attracts the attention of Newcastle record store owner and label head Keith Armstrong. Signing the band to his Kitchenware Records the following March, the group's label debut *The Devil Has All The Best Tunes* becomes a UK Independent hit in October.

1984

Jan *Don't Sing*, with Kitchenware signing the band to a distribution deal with Epic, peaks at UK #62.
Mar With Graham Lant having replaced Salmon, their debut album, the McAloon-penned ***Swoon*** reaches

UK #22, co-produced by Prefab Sprout and David Brewis, and yields *Couldn't Bear To Be Special*.
Nov *When Love Breaks Down* is released, featuring another new drummer, Neil Conti (b. Feb. 12, 1959, London).

1985

Mar A re-mixed *When Love Breaks Down* is issued, but still fails to chart.
June The critically-revered, sensitive pop-rock sophomore album ***Steve McQueen***, literately written by Paddy and produced by Thomas Dolby, reaches UK #21. Including two extra cuts, it is re-titled ***Two Wheels Good*** in the US, after objections to the original title from McQueen's daughter.
July From the album, *Faron Young* peaks at UK #74.
Nov Following the release of *Appetite* in September, *When Love Breaks Down* reaches UK #25 at the third attempt. *Johnny Johnny* will peak at UK #64 the following February, when the group plays a one-off gig at London's Hammersmith Odeon, before starting a tour of Japan.

1988

Feb After a two-year recording hiatus, *Cars And Girls*, a McAloon commentary on Bruce Springsteen songs, makes UK #44.
Mar [26] ***From Langley Park To Memphis*** hits UK #5, in its week of entry. Produced by Paddy McAloon with Jon Kelly, Andy Richards and Thomas Dolby (who was scheduled to produce the whole album but could not because of illness), it features Stevie Wonder, Pete Townshend and the Andrae Crouch Gospel Singers. The album sells half a million copies in Europe in its first ten weeks of release.
Apr *The King Of Rock'n'Roll* hits UK #7, but the band is unwilling to tour.
June McAloon, still living in his parents' home in Consett, begins work on the soundtrack to an unwritten movie, "Zorro The Fox".
July *Hey Manhattan!* peaks at UK #72.
Nov Ballad *Nightingales*, featuring Stevie Wonder on harmonica, is released in the UK.

1989

July [1] ***Protest Songs***, comprising material recorded in September 1985, reaches UK #18 in its week of entry.

1990

Aug [25] *Looking For Atlantis* peaks at UK #51.
Sept [8] The 19-track, critically-revered, ***Jordan : The Comeback***, again produced by Dolby, and featuring percussionist Luis Jardim, harmonica by Judd Lander and voices from actress Jenny Agutter, hits UK #7 in its week of entry.
Oct [5] The group embarks on a 15-date UK "The Comeback Tour", its first in five years, at the Guildhall, Portsmouth, Hants., set to end with a pair of dates on the 22nd and 23rd at London's Hammersmith Odeon.
[27] *We Let The Stars Go* makes UK #50 (and will become one of the final nominations for the 1990 Ivor Novello Awards in the Best Song Musically & Lyrically category).

1991

Jan [12] *Carnival 2000*, one track on *Jordan : The EP*, promoted by an unlikely appearance on the BBC1-TV kids' show "Going Live", makes UK #35.

1992

Apr The group works on new tracks with producer Stephen Lipson at the Metropolis Studios.
June [20] *The Sound Of Crying* reaches UK #23, during a five-week chart stay.
July [11] ***A Life Of Surprises - The Best Of Prefab Sprout***, a 16-track compilation featuring two new tracks, the recent single and *If You Don't Love Me*, debuts at its UK #3 peak.
Aug [15] *If You Don't Love Me* reaches UK #33.
Oct [3] *All The World Loves Lovers* bows at its UK #61 peak.

1993

Jan [16] *Life Of Surprises* reaches UK #24 following an appearance on BBC1-TV's "Top Of The Pops" on the 7th. (McAloon will resurface the following year contributing two new songs to Jimmy Nail's UK TV series, as a five-year gap between original Prefab Sprout studio albums lengthens.)

THE PRESIDENTS OF THE UNITED STATES OF AMERICA

Chris Ballew (vocals, two-string guitar); **Dave Dederer** (three string-bass); **Jason Finn** (drums)

1994

Dec [31] Both sons of wealthy Seattle, WA, socialite families, Ballew first met Dederer at the city's Bush prep school, but only played together once at an ad-hoc alumni bash before attending separate East Coast universities. After Ballew has graduated from the University of New York, he relocated to Boston, MA, and teamed with Morphine's Mark Sandman, learning to play two-string guitar and performing with him in the ad-hoc combo Supergroup in 1992. Meanwhile, Dederer has graduated from Brown University where he played in punk/R&B covers band Big Heads of Pluternis and, having stayed in touch with Ballew, they have both returned to Seattle in 1992, forming Go! trio with Ballew's school-mate Dave Thiele on drums (the latter subsequently known as the "fourth President"). After Thiele has moved to Boston to study, Ballew and Dederer have formed the Presidents of the United States of America in 1993, and secured a residency at Seattle's Crocodile Cafe, where they are spotted by the venue's booking agent Scott McCaughey Finn, a seven-year veteran of Seattle grunge outfit Love Battery. The band, which claims never to rehearse, now plays its first New Year's eve gig, at Seattle's Moe's club. The group will record its first album for $4,000 for the small Seattle-based indie label PopLlama Records the following year.

1995

Sept [2] On the eve of releasing its debut solo album, the group has been snapped up by Sony Music's Columbia imprint on the understanding that the label will release the debut set as is. With the band marketed as "three guys, five strings, one nation under God", a reference to Ballew's two string guitar and Dederer's three string bass, ***The Presidents Of The United States Of America*** enters the US chart at #185, introducing the group's quirky new-punk leanings.
Oct [12] On its way to eventual multiplatinum status, ***The Presidents Of The United States Of America*** is certified gold by the RIAA and will be nominated for a Grammy Award as Best Alternative Music Performance.
Nov [17] The group is the music guest on CBS-TV's "Late Show With David Letterman".
Dec [27] The band records what will be billed as a New Year's Eve gig at Moe's club in Seattle, which will be shown on the giant Sony Jumbo Tron screen on the 31st in New York's Times Square.

1996

Jan [7] The group enters Heart's Bad Animals studio in Seattle to begin recording its sophomore album, which will be delayed for release until 1997 to allow sales of its debut to peak.
[13] Written about a fat lady sitting in a swamp, *Lump* reaches UK #15.
[27] ***The Presidents Of The United States Of America*** peaks at UK #18 during a six-week chart stay.
Feb [19] On Presidents Day, the group performs in front of Mount Rushmore national monument, airing live on MTV (US).
Mar [9] ***The Presidents Of The United States Of America*** hits US #6, having already been certified double platinum by the RIAA. Cosmic Records releases *It's Not Like That Anymore*, by Supergroup, the still-active ad-hoc collaboration between Morphine's Sandman and the Presidents' lead singer Ballew.
Apr [13] The Dederer-penned *Peaches* hits US #29.
[20] *Peaches* hits UK #8 in its week of entry.
July [8] During its second UK tour of the year, following a first trip in April, the Presidents perform at London's Brixton Academy.

ELVIS PRESLEY

1945

Oct [3] At the age of ten, Presley (b. Elvis Aaron Presley, Jan. 8, 1935, East Tupelo, MS, his middle name, taken from his father Vernon's friend Aaron Kennedy, is mis-spelled on his birth certificate, a mistake he will rectify as an adult), one of twin sons (born after brother Jesse Garon, who is stillborn) is attending Lawhon Grammar School where his fifth grade teacher, Mrs. Oleta Bean Grimes, recommends Presley's singing to principal Mr. J.D. Cole, who enters him in the music contest at the 38th annual Mississippi-Alabama Fair & Dairy Show in Tupelo. Before an audience of 5,000, he comes second to Shirley Jones Gallentine singing *Old Shep*, a performance aired live on WELO radio.

1949

Sept [20] Having moved with his parents to Memphis, TN, in September 1948, to a one-bedroom apartment at 572 Poplar Ave., where his father finds a job at the United Paint Company and his mother, Gladys, works at a hospital as a nurse's aide, Presley attends L.C. Humes High School by day (where his music teacher, Miss Marmann, gives him a C grade and tells him he can't sing), mowing lawns or cinema ushering in his off-school time, earning $14 per week. The family now qualifies for federal housing, moving to a two-bedroom apartment in the Lauderdale Courts at 185 Winchester Street. Presley, naturally shy, makes few friends at school and does not shine academically.

1952

Apr [17] Following a month's employment at the Precision Tool Company during the previous summer, and now at a $12.75 a week part-time job at Loew's State Theater, Presley is fired for punching out a fellow usher who had told the manager that Elvis was getting free candy from the girl at the concession stand. (He will begin working at the Upholsteries Specialities Co. on August 6th.)

1953

June [14] Having become noted in his final year as a performer in the Christmas 1952 school show, and as an eye-catching dresser, Presley gains his high school diploma and leaves.
July [18] Employed by Crown Electric Co. earning $35 a week as a truck driver, he calls at Memphis Recording Service ("We record anything - anywhere - anytime") at 706, Union Ave., paying $4 to make a private recording. Marion Keisker, office manager for Sam Phillips, who owns the company and the associated Sun Records label, finds his voice interesting, and keeps a tape of *My Happiness*, a reworking of a major 1948 hit for several artists, and *That's When Your Heartaches Begin*, a country song recorded by Bob Lamb, to play for Phillips, writing down his address, a neighbor's phone number and the note "Elvis Pressley. Good ballad singer. Hold." on a piece of paper.

1954

Jan [4] Presley returns to cut a second private record, singing *Casual Love Affair* and *I'll Never Stand In Your Way* on a 10" acetate. This time, Phillips asks for Presley's address and a phone number, promising to

contact him to try something in the studio.
Apr Looking for a vocalist to record *Without You*, a song he has received on an anonymous Nashville, TN, demo, Phillips agrees to Keisker's suggestion of Presley, who has visited the studio several times since January, to try out songs. He makes several attempts but finds no empathy with the song, so Phillips lets Presley try out his gospel, country, R&B and Dean Martin-ballad material, and suggests some rehearsal sessions with other musicians.
June [27] Phillips calls guitarist Scotty Moore (b. Winfield Scott Moore III, Dec. 27, 1931, Gadsen, TN) who runs the local club band Doug Poindexter's Starlite Wranglers, who have just cut *My Kind Of Carrying On* for Sun and, with the band's bass player Bill Black (b. Sept. 17, 1926, Memphis), they begin practice sessions with Presley at Moore's house.
July [5] Phillips tries a recording session with Presley, Moore and Black on Leon Payne's country ballad, *I Love You Because*. During a break, Presley fools about with an uptempo romp through Arthur Crudup's blues number, *That's All Right*, and is joined, first by Black, and then by Moore in an impromptu jam session. Phillips, hearing the individual "something" for which he has been searching in vain with Presley, has them repeat it with tapes running, and after a handful of run-throughs, a satisfactory master is made.
[6] Similar experimentation marks the next day's song - Bill Monroe's bluegrass *Blue Moon Of Kentucky*, which is accelerated to a racing tempo. Moore suggests the strange hybrid of (black) blues and (white) country will offend the Southern radio and musical community, but Phillips hears commercial potential, and couples *That's All Right* with *Blue Moon Of Kentucky* as the first Sun single. They also cut *Harbor Lights* during these sessions.
[10] Phillips takes acetates of the recorded tracks to DJ Dewey Phillips at Memphis radio station WHBQ. The DJ rates *That's All Right* and plays it on his R&B show, "Red Hot And Blue", at just after 9:30 p.m. The switchboard immediately lights up with requests for repeat spins. Phillips phones Presley's apartment building to ask him to come to the studio for an interview but Presley, forewarned by Sam Phillips of the single's likely airing, is at the Suzore No. 11 Theatre watching the double-bill "Goldtown" and "Ghost Riders", unable to face the embarrassment of hearing his voice on the radio. His parents seek him out and take him to WHBQ, where Phillips puts him at his ease, and Memphis learns that this hot new R&B singer is a local white 19-year-old, who is almost immediately given the title "King Of Western Bop".
[12] Presley signs a recording contract with Sun and a one-year personal management deal with Scotty Moore, in which Moore will receive "10% of all earnings from engagements, appearances and booking made by him", and gives notice to quit Crown Electric.
[19] With over 5,000 orders from the Memphis area, the single is released as Presley's Sun debut. (It will top the local chart by the end of the month, with action on both sides: Dewey Phillips plays *That's All Right*, while Sleepy Eye John on WHEM and Uncle Richard and most other Memphis DJs play *Blue Moon Of Kentucky*.)
[20] The trio's first public performance, as the Blue Moon Boys, sees them playing on a flatbed truck outside a new drugstore on Lamar Ave., Memphis, to mark its opening, to a swelling and increasingly excited crowd. (Local engagements at the Eagle's Nest and Bel Air clubs follow, sometimes performing with the Starlite Wranglers, but Moore and Black soon leave the band to work with Presley full-time.)
[30] Local agent Bob Neal books Presley low on the bill of a two-performance show at Overton Park Shell auditorium in Memphis, headlined by Slim Whitman. After a polite reception to two country ballads during the afternoon show, he is advised by Dewey Phillips to perform uptempo material in the evening. He sings *Good Rockin' Tonight* and *That's All Right*, complete with rhythmic leg and body movements. The sensual performance drives the audience wild. Presley exits the stage bewildered by screams and shouts which all but drown the music and is pushed back by Phillips to encore, to a similar reception. Established country artist Webb Pierce, waiting to follow him, stands stunned and uncomprehending.
Aug [19] Presley returns to Sun Studios to record *Blue Moon*.
[21] He plays his first gig outside Tennessee in Gladewater, TX.
Sept [25] *Good Rockin' Tonight*, a 1948 hit for Wynonie Harris, backed with *I Don't Care If The Sun Don't Shine*, from Walt Disney's "Cinderella", is released as a follow-up single.
Oct [2] Phillips gains a booking for Presley on Nashville's "Grand Ole Opry", aired live from Ryman Auditorium. He is introduced by Hank Snow and sings *Blue Moon Of Kentucky*, but fails to impress the staid audience, or the talent booker Jim Denny, who suggests he takes up truck driving again.
[16] He gets a better reception on country music radio show, "Louisiana Hayride", from the Shreveport Municipal Auditorium, and broadcast on KWKH in Shreveport, LA. After he sings *That's All Right* and *Blue Moon Of Kentucky* to an enthusiastic live audience, he is asked back the following week. Prior to his third appearance, station director Horace Logan signs Presley to a year's contract, at $18 per weekly slot (with Black and Moore earning $12 each per show). He is also contracted to sing a radio commercial for one of the show's sponsors, Southern Made Doughnuts.
Nov [23] Neal, with Moore's agreement, takes over management, taking 15% of Presley's earnings and books the trio (billed as Elvis Presley, the Hillbilly Cat, & His Blue Moon Boys), initially at Nashville's annual Country Convention and then into a series of one-night dates all over the South.
Dec [18] His third single, Kokomo Arnold's *Milkcow Blues Boogie*, coupled with Jack Sallee's *You're A Heartbreaker*, is recorded at Sun, with several versions of *I'm Left, You're Right, She's Gone*.

1955

Jan Oscar Davis, right-hand man to talent entrepreneur Col. Tom Parker (manager of Eddy Arnold and Hank Snow), is impressed by Presley's power over an audience having seen him at Memphis Airport Eagle's Nest Inn in November, while visiting Neal (although some sources claim that he had seen him in New Boston, TX, at the insistence of Tommy Sands). He reports the local phenomenon back to Parker, who negotiates with Neal to have Presley on his "Hank Snow Jamboree" package shows of country acts playing the Southern states. Parker sets up a meeting in Memphis with Neal and Presley, where he offers guidance and suggests that Presley should be recording elsewhere than Sun - a notion rejected both by Neal and Presley.
[8] His third single, *Milkcow Blues Boogie*, couple with *You're A Heartbreaker*, is released.
Feb [5] Presley records a cover of Arthur Gunter's *Baby Let's Play House*, for which he invents a hiccuping rockabilly vocal style, which will characterize many later impersonations of his singing, and also cuts *I Got A Woman* and *Trying To Get To You*.
[14] Presley performs in Carlsbad, NM, at a show reportedly booked by Parker.
Mar [5] He makes his TV debut on the weekend edition of "Louisiana Hayride", broadcast by Shreveport's CBS affiliate, KWKH-TV.
[14] Presley is interviewed, but does not sing, on Jimmy Dean's "Town & Country Jubilee" TV show, broadcast on WMAL-TV in Washington, DC. The trio then travels to New York to audition for CBS-TV's "Arthur Godfrey's Talent Scouts" show in New York. Having to fly to the audition un-nerves Presley, and his performance of *Good Rockin' Tonight* is below par. Godfrey's producers turn him down (and will pick up instead on his biggest '50s rival in popularity, Pat Boone).
Apr [1] *Baby Let's Play House/I'm Left, You're Right, She's Gone* is released by Sun, to better sales than its predecessor.
[5] Parker pays for Presley's parents to travel to see him on a "Hank Snow Jamboree" in Chattanooga, TN, and suggests that their son is being over-worked (having previously ascertained Gladys Presley's fears on this), and that he needs more professional management. Gladys is cautious, mentioning Presley's obligations to Neal, Sun and the "Louisiana Hayride" (a contract now extended to 18 months), but Parker finds an ally in Vernon Presley (who will later give him signed permission to negotiate a new recording deal on his son's behalf).
[16] Presley makes his first appearance on the "Big D Jamboree" on Dallas station KRLD, with Sonny James, Hank Locklin and the Maddox Brothers and Rose.
May [13] Presley's stage act causes an audience riot for the first time, in Jacksonville, FL. He has much of his clothing ripped off, but escapes uninjured. (Years later, singer Johnny Tillotson, an audience member that day, says this did not happen and was merely a PR story conceived by Parker.)
June [18] Presley makes his second appearance on the "Big D Jamboree".
July *Baby Let's Play House* is Presley's first national chart entry, hitting #10 on **Billboard**'s Country chart, and Presley buys his first Cadillac. Parker begins to promote Presley outside the South, impressing New York music publisher Arnold Shaw with Presley's records and reputation, and via Shaw, top Cleveland, OH, DJ Bill Randle, who gives him heavy airplay which slowly spreads to New York.
Aug [6] *Mystery Train*, which Phillips had originally cut with Little Junior Parker & the Blue Flames, and *I Forgot To Remember To Forget*, Presley's final Sun single, is released.
[15] Presley finally signs a formal management contract with Colonel Parker who spreads word that Presley's contract with Sun may be for sale. Decca Records bids $5,000 and is turned down by Phillips, as is Dot Records' offer of $7,500. Parker hears that Mercury Records is considering a $10,000 bid, and makes it known to CBS/Columbia's Mitch Miller, who says he will up it to $15,000. Parker hints that RCA is considering $20,000, and Miller intimates that "no singer is worth that much". Ahmet Ertegun of Atlantic disagrees, and is willing to risk $25,000, but Parker insists that nearly twice as much is "more realistic".
Oct [15] Presley plays at The Cotton Club in Lubbock, TX, where the opening act is local hillbilly duo Buddy (Holly) & Bob.
[20] He performs before Brooklyn High School students in Cleveland in a show filmed for the documentary "The Pied Piper Of Cleveland : A Day In The Life Of A Famous Disc Jockey", about Bill Randle. Bill Haley & His Comets, Pat Boone and the Four Lads also take part.
Nov [12] Presley is voted Most Promising Country And Western Artist in the annual US DJ poll, and Parker has him prominently attend at the Country Music DJ's Convention in Nashville.
[20] With Neal's management contract about to formally expire, Parker takes up the negotiating power granted him by Presley's parents and works out a deal in New York with RCA Records and Aberbach's publishing subsidiary, Hill & Range, which will pay Sun and Phillips' Hi-Lo Music $35,000 for the Presley contract and all previously-recorded material, and Presley himself $5,000 for future royalties on past Sun singles. In need of expansion capital (and with only a year of Presley's contract still to run), Phillips accepts. (Phillips begins investing in the fledgling Holiday Inn hotel chain, which will make him a bigger fortune than the record industry.) The deal is signed at the Warwick Hotel, New York City.
[22] Neal's contract with Presley expires, and RCA/Aberbach/Parker's offer to Sam Phillips becomes official. RCA will reissue all five Presley singles on its own label, though Sun still has a sell-off period for existing stock.
Dec [31] *I Forgot To Remember To Forget* tops the US Country chart.

1956

Jan [10-11] Presley records his first RCA sessions, at

the RCA-leased Methodist Television, Radio & Film Commission Studios in Nashville. His first cut is a cover of Ray Charles' *I Got A Woman*, while the second is a new song, *Heartbreak Hotel*, penned by Tommy Durden and Mae Boren Axton, the Colonel's public relations representative in Florida - she has given Presley the Glenn Reeves-recorded demo in her suite at the Andrew Jackson Hotel during the Disc Jockey Convention in Nashville. He also cuts *Money Honey*, *I'm Counting On You* and *I Was The One*. The session uses more musicians than the Sun recordings, including Moore, Black, Chet Atkins on guitar, Floyd Cramer on piano, Dominic ("D.J.") Fontana (ex-house-drummer with "The Louisiana Hayride", who has also been touring regularly with Presley) on drums, and brothers Ben and Brock Speer and Jordanaire Gordon Stoker on backing vocals.
[27] *Heartbreak Hotel* is issued to tie in with his US network TV debut the next day.
[28] Presley guests on the first of four weekly slots (for $1,250 each) on the Jackie Gleason Enterprises-produced, Tommy and Jimmy Dorsey-hosted "Stage Show", aired live from CBS' Studio 50 in New York. He is introduced by Bill Randle, performing *Shake Rattle And Roll* with *Flip, Flop and Fly* and *I Got A Woman*. Gleason states after the show "He can't last. I tell you flatly, he can't last." (His four appearances will be increased to six by popular demand.)
[30] In RCA's New York studios, Presley begins recording his own version of Carl Perkins' *Blue Suede Shoes*, plus seven more tracks for his debut album. (Sessions will end on February 3rd.)
Feb [4] On his second "Stage Show" appearance he sings *Baby, Let's Play House* and Little Richard's *Tutti Frutti*.
[11] On "Stage Show" he performs *Heartbreak Hotel*, backed by the Dorsey Brothers Orchestra, and *Blue Suede Shoes*.
[18] Another "Stage Show" slot features *I Was The One* and a repeat of *Tutti Frutti*.
Mar [3] *Heartbreak Hotel* debuts on the US chart at #68.
[17] Presley returns to "Stage Show", singing *Blue Suede Shoes* and *Heartbreak Hotel*.
[24] His final "Stage Show" appearance features *Money Honey* and *Heartbreak Hotel*. (This show is in competition with NBC-TV's "The Perry Como Show", on which Carl Perkins was scheduled, but is unable to perform *Blue Suede Shoes*, having been involved in car smash on the way to New York.)
Apr [1] A screen test is filmed at Paramount Studios in Hollywood, CA, with Presley acting the role of Jimmy Curry in a scene from "The Rainmaker", with veteran actor Frank Faylen.
[3] Presley appears on NBC-TV's "The Milton Berle Show", aired live from the aircraft carrier USS Hancock, moored in San Diego, CA. 25,000 people apply for tickets, and an estimated 40 million (a quarter of the US population) watch him sing *Heartbreak Hotel*, *Shake Rattle And Roll* and *Blue Suede Shoes*. He earns $5,000 from the show. (He performs two versions of *Blue Suede Shoes*, the second with Milton Berle playing his brother Melvin.)
[4-5] He makes his concert debut in California, playing two nights at the San Diego Sports Arena.
[6] Producer Hal B. Wallis signs Presley to a three-film, seven-year contract with Paramount Pictures, worth $450,000.
[7] *I Was The One*, the B-side of the still-climbing *Heartbreak Hotel*, makes US #23.
[10] Presley buys a $40,000 home in Audubon Drive, Memphis. He will live there with his parents until March 1957.
[11] He is flying from Amarillo to Nashville for a recording session when his plane develops engine trouble, and has to make an emergency landing in El Dorado, AR. Shaken, he records *I Want You, I Need You, I Love You* later in the day, but the incident creates an aversion to flying.
[23] Presley makes his debut in Las Vegas, NV, - two weeks at the Venus Room of the New Frontier Hotel, earning $8,500 a week, billed as "The Nation's Only Atomic Powered Singer" opening for headliners Freddie Martin & His Band and comedian Shecky Greene. The middle-aged audience's reaction is cool and he will only perform the first week, not returning to Vegas for 13 years. However, he appropriates an uptempo arrangement of R&B oldie *Hound Dog* from the hotel's lounge group, Freddie Bell & the Bell Boys.
[28] The March of Dimes presents Presley with the King of Hearts Award.
May [5] *Heartbreak Hotel* tops the US chart, becoming Presley's first million seller (it also hits C&W #1 and R&B #5) becoming the biggest-selling single of 1956, as *Blue Suede Shoes*, released as the lead track on an EP, makes US #24 (Carl Perkins' original hits #4). On the same day, his debut album, ***Elvis Presley***, also tops the US survey for the first of ten weeks (with advance orders of 362,000, making it RCA's first million-dollar album by a solo artist, and biggest-selling album to date before it is even issued).
[12] Presley makes his UK chart bow at #15 with *Heartbreak Hotel*.
[26] His cover of the Drifters' *Money Honey*, the lead track on Presley's second EP, peaks at US #76.
June [5] On a second "The Milton Berle Show", Presley performs a comedy routine with Berle, singing *I Want You, I Need You, I Love You* and *Hound Dog*, in a hip-shaking performance which invites a storm of protest. The show features the Jordanaires backing Presley on TV for the first time. It will also be the last Milton Berle TV show for a decade.
[16] *Blue Suede Shoes* hits UK #9, one place ahead of Carl Perkins' original, while *My Baby Left Me* (like *That's All Right Mama*, an Arthur Crudup song), B-side of the still climbing *I Want You, I Need You, I Love You*, reaches US #31.
[23] *Heartbreak Hotel* hits #2 (behind Pat Boone's *I'll Be Home*), and will stay in the Top 10 for 16 weeks.
July [1] Presley returns to NBC-TV on "The Steve Allen Show" in New York, where the producers attempt to quieten the criticism by involving him in more comedy, and insisting on more sedate performances of *I Want You, I Need You, I Love You* and *Hound Dog* (the latter sung in white tie and tails to an actual (unmoved) Bassett hound, by the name of Sherlock). Allen presents Presley with 18,000 signatures from Tulsa, OK, requesting him to be on TV again. He also appears in "Range Roundup", a sketch with Allen and fellow guests Imogene Coca and Andy Griffith. (After the show he appears on local WRCA-TV's "Hy Gardner Calling" show from his hotel room.)
[2] Presley records *Hound Dog* at RCA's New York studio, finally satisfied after 31 takes. He also cuts quicker final versions of *Don't Be Cruel* and *Any Way You Want Me (That's How I Will Be)*, with the Jordanaires (Gordon Stoker, Neal Matthews, Hoyt Hawkins and Hugh Jarrett) who have started out as a gospel group in Springfield, MO, supplying backing vocals for the first time.
[4] He returns to Memphis by train to appear at a charity concert for the **Memphis Press-Scimitar**'s Milk Fund, and the Variety Club's Home for Convalescent Children, at the 14,000-seater Russwood Park, the home of a minor league baseball team.
[28] *I Want You, I Need You, I Love You* hits US #3, his second million-selling single.
[31] Policeman Charles Ward gives Presley a ticket for speeding in Hattiesburg, MS, as he is driving to Memphis.
Aug [3] Presley opens a week-long tour of Florida (performing 24 shows in seven cities) at the Olympic Theatre, Miami.
[22] Filming begins in Hollywood on "The Reno Brothers", for which Hal Wallis "loans" his new movie property to 20th-Century Fox. A Civil War western starring Richard Egan and Debra Paget, Maurice Geraghty's novel is adapted to feature Presley, playing Clint Reno, and is set to include four period-style songs, written by Ken Darby whose trio backs Presley on the recordings. The ballad, *Love Me Tender* (based on the 1861 folk ballad, *Aura Lee*), is sufficiently strong for the producers to re-title the movie after it. Presley's parents stay with him at Hollywood's Knickerbocker hotel during filming.
[24] He records *We're Gonna Move* and *Love Me Tender* at 20th Century Fox, Stage 1, in Hollywood
Sept [1] *Hound Dog*, originally recorded by Big Mama Thornton in 1953, hits US #2, behind the Platters' *My Prayer*. US sales of *Hound Dog*, and its flip-side, *Don't Be Cruel*, will top five million.
[1-3] At Radio Recorders studios in Hollywood, with his usual backing musicians, Presley records 13 songs for his sophomore album.
[8] *I Want You, I Need You, I Love You* reaches UK #14.
[9] A Presley segment aired from Hollywood is slotted into the New York-transmitted "The Ed Sullivan Show" on CBS-TV. (Sullivan is originally on record as saying he would never have Presley on his show, but Steve Allen's success in direct competition has changed his mind, and Parker negotiates $50,000 for three slots.) It is watched by an estimated 54 million people (a third of the US population and an 82.6% viewing share), and features *Don't Be Cruel*, *Love Me Tender*, *Ready Teddy* and *Hound Dog*. Sullivan himself is ill, injured in a car crash three days previously, and the show is hosted by Charles Laughton.
[10] On the Monday after the show, record stores are deluged with requests for *Love Me Tender*, not scheduled for release for many weeks.
[15] *Don't Be Cruel* tops the US chart, where it will stay for five weeks, and becomes the first of three Presley hits to also head both the US Country and R&B surveys.
[26] He returns to Tupelo, to perform at the annual Mississippi-Alabama Fair and Dairy Show. The town declares "Elvis Presley Day" in his honor, as Mayor James Ballard presents him with the key to the city, and he plays afternoon and evening open-air shows, donating his $10,000 fee to the Elvis Presley Youth Foundation. (He will donate $100,000 annually to the charity.)
Oct [13] *Blue Moon*, one of seven simultaneously-released singles comprising the whole debut album, plus *Shake Rattle And Roll* and *Lawdy Miss Clawdy*, in 45rpm form, makes US #55.
[20] *I Don't Care If The Sun Don't Shine*, a Sun track released by RCA on an EP, peaks at US #74. RCA, unable to resist huge advance orders (856,237 by the end of September), releases *Love Me Tender* before the movie premiere.
[27] *Hound Dog* hits UK #2, where it will stay for three weeks behind Frankie Laine's *A Woman In Love*.
[28] Presley makes his second appearance on "The Ed Sullivan Show", performing *Don't Be Cruel*, *Love Me Tender*, *Hound Dog* and *Love Me*. Sullivan presents him with a gold disc for *Love Me Tender*.
Nov [10] **Billboard**'s national DJ poll reveals that Presley is the most-played male artist and country artist of 1956.
[15] "Love Me Tender" premieres at New York's Paramount Theater. A 50' cardboard cut-out of Presley adorns the front of the cinema. Critics slay the movie, but it recoups its $1-million production costs in little more than a week and 20th Century Fox releases a record 550 prints across the US.
[17] *Love Me Tender*, penned by Ken Darby, but credited to his songwriter-wife Vera Matson and Presley, tops the US chart, as *Blue Moon* hits UK #9.
[23] Unemployed sheet-metal worker Louis Balint punches Presley at Toledo's Commodore Perry Hotel, claiming that his wife's love for Presley has caused his marriage to break up. He will later be fined $19.60 for assault and then be jailed because he is unable to pay the penalty.
Dec [1] *Any Way You Want Me*, the B-side of *Love Me Tender*, reaches US #27.
[4] At home in Memphis for Christmas, Presley wanders into Sun studios in the afternoon where Carl Perkins and his group are recording a session, with Jerry Lee Lewis guesting on piano. Johnny Cash is also present, but his wife draws him away to go shopping. The others settle down to a jam session, mostly on gospel songs and recent hits. Phillips tapes what will become known as the legendary "Million Dollar Quartet Session" (issued on disc after Presley's death). The "Million Dollar Quartet" phrase is coined

by **Memphis Press Scimitar** entertainment editor Robert Johnson.
[8] His sophomore set, ***Elvis***, begins a five-week stay at US #1.
[13] "Love Me Tender" premieres in London.
[16] Presley makes his fiftieth and final appearance on the "Louisiana Hayride", a benefit concert for the Shreveport YMCA at the Louisiana Fairgrounds.
[22] *I Don't Care If The Sun Don't Shine*, the B-side of *Blue Moon*, peaks at UK #23.
[29] Sentimental ballad, *Old Shep*, from the EP *Elvis, Vol. 2* (extracted from the album), makes US #47 as *Love Me Tender* reaches UK #11.

1957

Jan [4] Presley has a pre-induction medical check-up at Kennedy Veterans Hospital, Memphis, a preliminary to his call-up by the US Army.
[5] *Love Me*, the lead track from *Elvis, Vol. 1*, another EP of album extracts, hits US #6.
[6] Presley makes what will be his last appearance on network TV for some years on "The Ed Sullivan Show" slot in New York. During uptempo numbers, he is shown on screen only from the waist up. Sullivan tells the audience that he's "never had a pleasanter experience on our *shew* with a big name than we've had with you", and that Presley is a "real decent, fine boy".
[12-24] Sessions at Radio Recorders produce several new tracks, including *Peace In The Valley* and *All Shook Up*, plus all the material for his forthcoming "Loving You" movie.
[19] *Paralyzed* makes US #59.
[21] Presley's second film, his first contracted movie for Hal Wallis, begins production at Paramount Studios: "Loving You" (originally titled "The Lonesome Cowboy", and subsequently "Running Wild"), sees Elvis, playing Deke Rivers, co-starring with Lizabeth Scott and Wendell Corey. Presley receives his first screen kiss from Jana Lund.
[26] *When My Blue Moon Turns To Gold Again* reaches US #27 and *Poor Boy*, from the EP of songs from "Love Me Tender", rises to US #35.
Feb [16] *Playing For Keeps*, the B-side of the still-climbing *Too Much*, makes US #34.
Mar [2] *Too Much*, recorded in 1954 by Bernard Hardison, handed to Presley by its co-writer Lee Rosenberg as the singer was boarding a train in Los Angeles, and introduced on his last Ed Sullivan appearance, hits US #2 behind Tab Hunter's *Young Love*.
[9] Sun single, *Mystery Train*, released for the first time in Britain, reaches #25, as *Rip It Up*, from ***Elvis***, also extracted as a UK single, makes #27.
[19] Presley buys Graceland, a 23-room, two-storey mansion in 13.8 acres of ground at 3764, South Bellevue Boulevard in the Memphis suburb Whitehaven. He pays $102,500 for the property, built of Tennessee limestone and previously used as a church by the Graceland Christian Church. The original house had been built by S.E. Toof, who named it after his daughter Grace. Grace's niece Ruth Moore and her husband Dr. Thomas Moore had rebuilt the house in the late '30s, which is now sold to Elvis by Moore's daughter Ruth Marie.
Apr [13] The B-side ballad of the still-rising *All Shook Up*, *That's When Your Heartaches Begin* (which includes a short spoken recitation), makes US #58.
[20] *All Shook Up*, written by Otis Blackwell (who also penned *Don't Be Cruel*) and allegedly penned after a challenge by Shalimar Music executive Al Stanton while he is drinking a Pepsi in Blackwell's presence (after debuting two weeks earlier at #26, before jumping to #6), tops the US chart where it will stay for eight weeks, selling two million copies and becoming the biggest-selling single of 1957.
[27] Presley performs at Maple Leaf Gardens, Toronto, ON, Canada, his first concert outside the USA, during a week-long tour which takes in Detroit, MI, Buffalo, NY, Ottawa, ON, Canada, Philadelphia, PA and Wichita Falls, TX.
[29] *Peace In The Valley*, now on an EP of four religious songs, reaches US #39.
[30] The songs for his forthcoming movie, "Jailhouse Rock", are cut at Radio Recorders Studios, with song-writers Jerry Leiber and Mike Stoller participating.
May [13] Production begins on "Jailhouse Rock" at MGM's Culver City Studios, Los Angeles. Co-starring Judy Tyler, Mickey Shaughnessy, Dean Jones and Jennifer Holden, Presley plays Vince Everett, a misfit convicted of manslaughter who becomes a rock star.
[14] Presley is rushed to Cedars of Lebanon Hospital, Los Angeles, suffering from chest pains. (A porcelain cap from one of his front teeth, swallowed during filming, had become lodged in a lung.)
June [1] *Too Much* hits UK #6.
[15] *All Shook Up* charts in the UK at #24, a week before its official release date, due to copies of the edition pressed for US servicemen at bases in the UK, being made available to HMV-Appointed Stockists and sold over the counter. It will disappear the following week, before then re-charting at #7 when the official HMV pressing appears.
[24] ***Peace In The Valley*** EP hits US #3 on the Album chart.
July [9] Presley attends the premiere of "Loving You" at the Strand Theater, Memphis, with his parents.
[15] *(Let Me Be Your) Teddy Bear*, from "Loving You", and penned by Cameo-Parkway founders Kal Mann and Bernie Lowe, begins a seven-week stay at US #1, and is another two-million-plus seller, as *All Shook Up* hits UK #1, becoming Presley's first UK chart-topper, where it will also stay for seven weeks, selling over half a million copies.
Aug The British outlet for Presley's recordings changes, as RCA's own label is launched through Decca. EMI, which has previously issued RCA product on the HMV label, has a lengthy sell-off period for recordings already licensed, and for several months the UK chart is flooded by competing Presley singles on two labels.
[2] The Official UK Elvis Presley Fan Club is launched by Jeanne and Doug Saward. (In the US, there are already thousands of Presley fan clubs.)
[3] *(Let Me Be Your) Teddy Bear*, one of the first UK RCA singles released, hits UK #3, during a nine-week spell in the Top 10.
[19] Ballad title-song, *Loving You*, the flip-side of *(Let Me Be Your) Teddy Bear*, reaches US #28.
[23] "Loving You" opens in London.
Sept [2] EP ***Loving You Vol II*** a four-song extract from the soundtrack, reaches #18 in the US Album, while the ***Love Me Tender*** soundtrack EP makes #22.
[5-7] Presley cuts seasonal tracks for a forthcoming Christmas album at Radio Recorders.
[14] *Paralyzed*, from ***Elvis***, and released by HMV in its sell-off period, hits UK #8, giving Presley three simultaneous UK Top 20 entries.
[21] Black and Moore quit over a salary dispute with Colonel Parker. Black will form the Bill Black Combo, although he will play on three more Presley sessions in 1958.
[27] Presley, backed by Hank Garland and Bob Moore, plays a benefit at the annual Mississippi-Alabama Fair and Dairy Show in Tupelo for the Elvis Presley Youth Recreation Center.
[29] ***Loving You***, which has the soundtrack recordings on one side and a second side of new non-movie songs (including a cover of the Bing Crosby/Grace Kelly hit ballad, *True Love*), hits US #1 for the first of ten weeks, earning a gold disc for half a million sales.
[30] EP ***Just For You***, which has four songs from the album's non-film side, makes US #16 on the Album survey.
Oct [17] "Jailhouse Rock" premieres at Loew's State Theater, Memphis (where Presley worked back in 1952).
[26] *Party*, another rocker from ***Loving You***, hits UK #2, behind Paul Anka's *Diana*, during a nine-week stay in the Top 10. (With the movie not yet scheduled for UK release, RCA holds *Jailhouse Rock* back until the New Year in Britain.)
[28-29] Presley performs at the Pan Pacific Auditorium, Hollywood, while filming "King Creole".
Nov [2] *Loving You*, the B-side of *Teddy Bear*, peaks at UK #24. (Presley has six other singles in the chart this week - a new UK record for simultaneous hits by one artist.)
[9] *Jailhouse Rock*, the Leiber/Stoller-written title song from the film, begins a six week tenure at US #1, selling over two million units. Also from the movie, its B-side *Treat Me Nice* reaches US #27, as *Got A Lot O' Livin' To Do*, B-side of *Party*, reaches UK #17.
[10] Presley makes his first concert appearance outside Continental North America at Honolulu Stadium, Honolulu, HI.
[16] *Trying To Get To You*, on HMV, makes UK #16.
[23] *Lawdy Miss Clawdy*, the flipside of *Trying To Get To You*, reaches UK #15.
Dec [12] Al Priddy, a DJ at radio station KEX in Portland, OR, is fired for playing Presley's version of *White Christmas*. The station's management says "It is not in the spirit we associate with Christmas".
[14] *Santa Bring My Baby Back (To Me)* hits UK #7.
[19] Amid nationwide teenage protest, Presley's draft notice for the US army is served on him (at Graceland, where he has returned for Christmas with his parents) by Milton Bowers, chairman of the Memphis Draft Board #86.
[21] Frank Freeman, Paramount Studios production chief, petitions the army for a 60-day deferment on Presley's induction date, so that the movie, "King Creole", can be completed. Freeman is told Presley will have to ask for the deferment personally. The draft board agrees to a two-month delay, which incurs a barrage of public comment alleging "special treatment".
[26] Presley donates thousands of teddy bears to the National Foundation for Infantile Paralysis.
[30] ***Elvis' Christmas Album*** tops the US chart, where it will stay for four weeks. Initially packaged as a deluxe gift item, with a sleeve incorporating ten pages of photos, it has a side of secular Christmas material (including *Blue Christmas* and an appropriation of Clyde McPhatter and the Drifters' arrangement of *White Christmas*), and a side of carols and hymns which incorporates the songs from the EP ***Peace In The Valley***. It earns a gold disc (and over two decades of repeat Christmas sales will sell well over one million copies).

1958

Jan [10] *Jailhouse Rock*, due for release as a UK single on this day, is put back for a week because Decca's pressing plant is unable to meet advance orders of 250,000.
[16] "Jailhouse Rock" premieres in London.
[18] The last UK HMV-released single, the early Sun track *I'm Left, You're Right, She's Gone*, reaches UK #21.
[20] Production begins on "King Creole", based on Harold Robbins' novel "A Stone For Danny Fisher", and co-starring Walter Matthau and Carolyn Jones, on the day he had been scheduled to enter the Army.
[25] *Jailhouse Rock* enters the UK chart at #1 (the first time this feat has been achieved), and will stay at the summit for three weeks, selling 750,000 copies.
Feb [1] His last recording session prior to Army induction produces four songs - *Your Cheatin' Heart* (not issued until 1965), *Wear My Ring Around Your Neck* (his next single), *Doncha' Think It's Time* and *My Wish Came True*.
[15] Five-song EP *Jailhouse Rock*, joins the single of the same title on the chart, reaching UK #18, as *I Beg Of You*, B-side of the still-climbing *Don't*, hits US #8.
[17] Movie "Jailhouse Rock" goes on general UK release, while in the US, production of "King Creole" moves to New Orleans, LA for location filming, where Presley takes over a floor of the Roosevelt Hotel with his entourage. The city declares "Elvis Presley Day" as he arrives, and the streets are so choked with people that filming is initially impossible.
Mar [15] He plays two concerts at Russwood Park, Memphis. They will be his last live performances in close to three years. *Don't*, Presley's first ballad A-side since *Love Me Tender*, tops the US chart, heading for two million sales.
[24] Presley is sworn in as US private 53310761 at the Local Draft Board 86 Memphis draft office, then

leaves by Greyhound bus for Fort Chaffee, AR, for full induction. He will be paid $78 per month as a private.
[25] Presley receives a regulation short back and sides from army barber, James Peterson.
[27] He is given inoculations against Asian flu, tetanus and typhoid. After four days at Chaffee, he begins his basic training at Fort Hood, TX, in A Company Second Medium Tank Battalion Second Armored Division.
[29] *Don't* hits UK #2, behind Perry Como's *Magic Moments*.
Apr [28] ***Elvis' Golden Records***, a compilation of singles from *Heartbreak Hotel* to *Jailhouse Rock*, hits US #3, earning a gold disc, and lodging in the US top 25 for 74 weeks.
May [10] *Doncha' Think It's Time*, B-side of the still-rising *Wear My Ring Around Your Neck*, reaches US #21.
[24] *Wear My Ring Around Your Neck* hits US and UK #3.
June [10-11] On his first weekend's furlough from the Army, Presley records two sessions at RCA Studios in Nashville (which will provide his hit singles of late 1958 and 1959).
[25] Presley's parents celebrate their 25th wedding anniversary while living in a house he has rented for them, close to Fort Hood.
July [2] "King Creole" opens across the US.
[26] *Hard-Headed Woman*, from the soundtrack to "King Creole", hits US #2, selling over one million copies. In keeping with the movie's setting, its arrangement incorporates elements of Dixieland jazz against a rock backing. Its B-side, *Don't Ask Me Why*, also from the film, reaches US #28.
Aug [2] *Hard-Headed Woman* hits UK #2, held off the top by the Everly Brothers' *All I Have To Do Is Dream/Claudette*.
Gladys Presley falls ill, and is returned to Memphis and admitted to the Methodist Hospital where the family doctor and four specialists diagnose acute hepatitis. After three days, her condition worsens and the hospital advises Presley to return home. After initial reluctance (the Army fearing press allegations of "preferential treatment"), he is granted compassionate leave. Against Gladys' wishes, he flies from Texas.
[12] He visits his mother in hospital, staying the night and much of the following day.
[14] He has returned home to rest when Gladys dies of heart failure at 3:15 a.m., with Vernon Presley at her bedside.
[16] Her funeral is held at the National Funeral Home in Forest Hill, Memphis. Presley is so overcome with grief that he is unable to stand for much of the proceedings and has to be supported. 500 policeman keep a gigantic crowd at bay.
[28] "King Creole" opens in London.
Sept [22] After giving a press conference at the Military Ocean Terminal Brooklyn Army Terminal, New York (by special dispensation of the US Army), Presley sets sail for Bremerhaven for a tour of duty in Germany, on the troop-ship USS General Randall.
[30] Its sell-off period expired, EMI deletes all Presley and other RCA product from its HMV catalog.
Oct [1] Presley arrives in Germany at Bremerhaven and is transported to the US Army base at Friedberg, near Frankfurt, where he joins his unit - Company D, 32nd Tank Battalion, 3rd Armor Corps. On the base, he will be a jeep driver for his platoon sergeant, Billy Wilson. (He will buy a house in nearby Bad Neuheim, taking advantage of a military rule which allows him to live off camp if he has family to support, moving his father, grandmother, some friends and staff into it.)
[11] Soundtrack album, ***King Creole***, hits US #2, unable to usurp Frank Sinatra's ***Only The Lonely***.
[18] The extracted title cut, *King Creole*, hits UK #2, behind Connie Francis' *Stupid Cupid/Carolina Moon*.
[29] Presley sees Bill Haley & the Comets in concert in Stuttgart, West Germany.
Nov [8] The introduction of a UK album chart sees ***Elvis' Golden Records*** and ***King Creole*** hit UK #3 and #4 respectively, behind ***South Pacific*** and Frank Sinatra's ***Come Fly With Me***.
[27] Presley is given the rank of private first class.
[29] Frantic rocker *I Got Stung* hits US #8.
Dec [20] Its flipside, *One Night*, a heavy blues-rock treatment of a 1956 Smiley Lewis R&B hit (with lyrics altered from the suggestive originals to ensure radio play), hits US #4, with sales yet again topping one million.

1959

Jan [31] *I Got Stung/One Night* tops the UK chart, where it will stay for three weeks.
Mar RCA releases the pre-Germany press conference and interviews as a spoken-word EP, *Elvis Sails*.
Apr [4] Compilation ***For LP Fans Only***, rounding up singles B-sides and EP tracks, including some Sun recordings, reaches US #19.
[11] ***Elvis***, a 14-track expansion of ***For LP Fans Only***, hits UK #4.
[25] Another double A-side release, the wild rocker *I Need Your Love Tonight*, hits US #4.
May [2] B-side, *(Now And Then There's) A Fool Such As I* (his revival of a 1953 country hit by Hank Snow), hits US #2, behind the Fleetwoods' *Come Softly To Me*, selling over two million copies on home turf.
[16] *A Fool Such As I/I Need Your Love Tonight* tops the UK chart, dethroning Buddy Holly's *It Doesn't Matter Anymore*, and will enjoy a 13-week run in the Top 10, including five in pole position.
June [1] Presley is promoted to specialist Fourth Class Corporal.
[3] He develops an abscessed tonsil, and will spend a week in Frankfurt Military Hospital. (After treatment, he travels to Paris, France, where he will give an impromptu performance for the staff of the Lido night club, during a two-week leave in the city.)
Aug [8] *A Big Hunk O' Love*, one of Presley's fastest-paced rockers, hits UK #4.
[15] *A Big Hunk O' Love* tops the US chart for the first of two weeks, selling over a million.
[22] Its B-side ballad, *My Wish Came True*, reaches US #12. These are the last of the June 1958 recordings to be issued on single. (A dearth of new Presley records will follow until after his 1960 Army release - with the approval of Parker, who wants fans sufficiently starved of product to prepare for the post-Army material.) ***A Date With Elvis***, with a calendar for counting down the days to Presley's US Army release enclosed, hits UK #4.
Sept At the U.S. servicemen's Eagle's Club in Wiesbaden, US Airman Currie Grant introduces Presley to a young American girl, 14-year-old Priscilla Beaulieu, step-daughter of a US Air Force captain, who lives nearby.
Oct [10] Compilation ***A Date With Elvis***, another gathering of singles and EP tracks including five Sun recordings, makes US #32.

1960

Jan [20] Presley is promoted to Sergeant, getting a $22.94 per month raise.
Feb The first edition of **Elvis Monthly** is published, edited from Heanor, Derbys., by Albert Hand. The magazine will continue to be published into the '90s.
[13] Four-song EP *Strictly Elvis*, featuring the sentimental *Old Shep* (unavailable in Britain since 1958), reaches UK #26.
[17] ***Elvis*** is certified gold by the RIAA.
Mar [1] The US Army hosts a "Farewell Elvis" press conference at the Friedburg base in Germany, organized by Captain Marion Keisker, who is working with the Armed Forces Network in Germany.
[2] He flies home for demobilization from Frankfurt. The plane makes a refuelling stop at Prestwick Airport, Scotland, and while it is on the ground, Presley talks to fans through an airport fence. This is the only occasion on which he sets foot on UK soil. (The main reason that Elvis will never play abroad is because Colonel Parker is living as an illegal alien (from Holland) in the US and will not risk having to re-enter the US.)
[3] At 7:42 a.m., he lands in a snowstorm at McGuire Air Force Base, NJ. Nancy Sinatra is the official greeter as he steps off the plane.
[5] Presley is demobbed from the US Army at Fort Dix, NJ, ranked a buck sergeant. Tennessee senator, Estes Kefauver, places a tribute to Presley in the Congressional Record.
[7] He arrives home in Memphis, having come from Fort Dix by private train.
[20-21] His first post-Army recording session takes place at RCA Studios in Nashville, with Moore back in the band (Black will never again play with Presley). His regular studio pianist is now Floyd Cramer (who will become a hitmaker in his own right). Six tracks are nailed down, including *Stuck On You* and *Fame And Fortune*, which are rush-scheduled by RCA.
[23] He travels by train from Nashville to Miami, FL, to tape a TV show slot with Frank Sinatra.
[26] The Timex-sponsored Sinatra show, "Welcome Home Elvis", is recorded in the Grand Ballroom of the Fontainebleau Hotel, Miami Beach. Presley guests with Sammy Davis Jr. and Sinatra's daughter, Nancy. He sings *Fame And Fortune* and *Stuck On You* in a solo slot, and teams with Sinatra on a traded duet of *Love Me Tender* and *Witchcraft*. Parker has negotiated $125,000 for the appearance. (He also sings *It's Nice To Go Traveling* in army uniform with the rest of the cast.) It will be his last TV appearance for eight years.
Apr [3-4] A longer Nashville session is later rated one of Presley's most artistically successful, producing material for ***Elvis Is Back***, and two million-selling singles, *It's Now Or Never* and *Are You Lonesome Tonight*.
[18] He travels with his father from Memphis to Hollywood, on Missouri Pacific Railroad's Texas Eagle Express, to begin filming "G.I. Blues".
[23] *Stuck On You* hits UK #3.
[30] *Stuck On You*, released with advance US orders of 1,275,077, and Presley's first single issued in stereo, dethrones Percy Faith's *Theme From A Summer Place* atop the US chart, where it will remain for four weeks.
May [2] Filming begins at the Paramount Studios lot on "G.I. Blues", which co-stars Juliet Prowse, and typecasts Presley as Tulsa McLean, a young US soldier in Germany (though in an entertainment unit, from which the Army had withheld Presley for fear of more "special treatment" accusations).
[7] Compilation ***50 Million Elvis Fans Can't Be Wrong - Elvis Gold Records, Vol. 2***, reaches US #31, earning a gold disc.
[12] "The Fourth Frank Sinatra Timex Show" airs on ABC-TV.
[15] *Fame And Fortune*, the flip-side of *Stuck On You*, reaches US #17.
June Presley has his tonsils removed in a Memphis hospital.
[6] ***Elvis Is Back***, with tracks from the April Nashville session, hits US #2 (behind the Kingston Trio's ***Sold Out***) and earns a gold disc.
[30] ***Elvis Is Back*** hits UK #1, as compilation album, ***Elvis' Golden Records, Vol. 2***, hits UK #4.
July [3] Vernon Presley marries divorcee Dee Stanley, whom he has met while living in Germany (her ex-husband having been a master sergeant in the US Army and formerly a bodyguard to General Patton), in Huntsville, AL.
Aug Presley is named Public Enemy #1 by the East German communist newspaper, **Young World**, following a riot for which he is blamed. Six Elvis fans are jailed for between one and two years for forming an Elvis fan club and singing rock'n'roll songs in the street.
[8-12] Four songs intended for the film "Flaming Star" are recorded at 20th Century Fox Studios, Hollywood, though only the title song and one other will make the final cut.
[16] Production begins on "Flaming Star" at 20th Century Fox Studios in Hollywood. Co-starring Steve Forrest and Barbara Eden, it is a western directed by Don Siegel, with Presley in the role (turned down by Marlon Brando) of a troubled half-breed.
[20] *It's Now Or Never*, recorded at the April 3rd session, but not used on the album, knocks Brian Hyland's *Itsy Bitsy Teenie Weenie Yellow Polka Dot Bikini* from the top of the US chart, where it will stay for five weeks. It is an adaptation of the 1899 Italian

song, *O Sole Mio*, written by Eduardo di Capua with English lyrics by Aaron Schroeder and Wally Gold, and, with its semi-operatic Latin sound, stands apart from anything Presley has recorded before (worldwide, it will become his biggest-selling single, with total sales over 20 million). Its B-side, the contrasting *A Mess Of Blues*, reaches US #32. (In Britain, a publishing wrangle over *It's Now Or Never*, due to *O Sole Mio*'s copyright, temporarily prevents its release, so RCA promotes *A Mess Of Blues* and pairs it with *The Girl Of My Best Friend* from ***Elvis Is Back***.)
Sept [17] *A Mess Of Blues* hits UK #2, behind the Shadows' *Apache*.
Oct [28] Copyright problems resolved, *It's Now Or Never* is released in Britain, having built up advance orders of 500,000, the largest known in the UK to date.
[30-31] In Nashville, Presley records his first lengthy gospel music session which will form much of his 1961 inspirational set, ***His Hand In Mine***.
Nov [5] *It's Now Or Never* enters the UK chart at #1, where it will stay for nine weeks. On the Saturday following the single's Friday release, many UK shops report selling more copies of the single than everything else in stock combined.
[7-8] Songs for the film "Wild In The Country" are recorded at Radio Recorders in Hollywood.
[10] "G.I. Blues" premieres in London.
[11] Filming begins on "Wild In The Country", in which Presley stars as Glenn Tyler with Hope Lange and Tuesday Weld, at the Victorian Ink House in St. Helena, CA, (during which Presley receives a platinum watch from RCA for having sold 75 million records).
[12] Former bass player Bill Black reaches US #11, with his Combo's own instrumental version of Presley's *Don't Be Cruel*.
[15] "G.I. Blues" premieres at the Fox Wilshire Theatre, Los Angeles, prior to a nationwide release on the 23rd.
Dec With her parents' permission, Priscilla Beaulieu flies to Memphis to spend Christmas with Presley and his family at Graceland.
[3] *Are You Lonesome Tonight*, a 1927 US #4 hit for Vaughn Deleath, but originally recorded by Al Jolson, vaults to US #1, after entering at #35 two weeks earlier. It will stay at the summit for six weeks, selling two million copies. On it, Presley updates the mid-song narration technique originally employed on *That's When Your Heartaches Begin* in 1957, which splits listeners into love-or-hate camps.
[10] Soundtrack album, ***G.I. Blues***, tops the US chart, where it will stay for ten weeks, earning a gold disc.
[13] *It's Now Or Never* passes the million sales mark in Britain in six weeks: the one-millionth copy leaves Decca's pressing plant at 3:30 p.m. This is a new record time for a disc achieving this total in the UK - the previous holder, Harry Belafonte's *Mary's Boy Child* in 1957, took eight weeks.
[17] *Are You Lonesome Tonight*'s B-side *I Gotta Know* reaches US #20.
[21] "Flaming Star" premieres in Los Angeles, to disappointing box office returns compared with "G.I. Blues", on the same day that Chief Wah-Nee-Ota inducts Presley into the Los Angeles Indian Tribal Council.
[31] ***Elvis Christmas' Album*** re-charts for one week at US #33.

1961

Jan [13] "Flaming Star" opens in London.
[14] ***G.I. Blues*** tops the UK chart, where it will remain for 25 weeks.
[28] *Are You Lonesome Tonight?* begins a four-week run at UK #1, having entered the previous week at #2.
Feb [13] ***His Hand In Mine***, his first wholly religious album (made up of most of the gospel songs recorded at the end of October and covering most of the material from the Golden Gate Quartet's 1953 Columbia mini-album), reaches US #13 and will earn a gold disc for half a million sales.
[25] Presley makes his first concert appearance since 1958, performing at a benefit on "Elvis Presley Day" at Ellis Auditorium in Memphis in aid of local charities including the Elvis Presley Youth Center in Tupelo, raising $51,000. During the show, he is presented with a plaque by RCA to mark record sales of 76 million worldwide.
Mar Presley signs a five-year movie contract with Hal Wallis.
[8] Tennessee Governor Buford Ellington confers upon Presley the honorary title of colonel, before the General Assembly of the State's legislature.
[17] Filming begins on "Blue Hawaii" in Hawaii.
[25] Presley plays another benefit show, at Bloch Arena in Pearl Harbor, HI, with Minnie Pearl and James Stewart, raising $62,000 for the USS Arizona Memorial Fund. (His 17-song set will be his last stage appearance for more than eight years.) *Surrender*, another dramatic adaptation of a 1911 Italian ballad, *Come Back To Sorrento* (*Torna A Sorrento*), and the only secular recording from the October 1960 gospel session, hits US #1, displacing Chubby Checker's *Pony Time*. It will stay on top for two weeks and become a further million seller, while its B-side, *Lonely Man*, written for "Wild In The Country", but cut from the completed film, makes US #32. *Wooden Heart*, from "G.I. Blues", released as a single throughout most of the world but not in the US, tops the UK chart where it will remain for six weeks, staying in the UK Top 50 for 27 weeks.
May [20] *Flaming Star*, the lead cut from the EP *Elvis By Request*, an experimental four-track release at 33rpm, reaches US #14.
June [3] *Surrender* tops the UK survey for the first of four weeks while the gospel-themed ***His Hand In Mine*** hits UK #3.
[10] *I Feel So Bad*, his revival of Chuck Willis' 1954 US R&B #8, hits US #5.
[15] "Wild In The Country", a drama co-starring Presley with Tuesday Weld and Hope Lange, premieres in Memphis. Like "Flaming Star", it has few songs and is serious in intent. (It is also not a huge money-maker, inevitably leading Col. Parker back to lighter, more lucrative "G.I. Blues"-style films.)
July [1] *I Feel So Bad*'s B-side, the ballad title song, *Wild In The Country*, reaches US #26.
[11] Filming begins on "Follow That Dream" on location in Crystal River, FL, although Presley won't make his presence felt for a further two weeks.
Aug [26] ***Something For Everybody***, divided into ballad and beat sides, and recorded with *I Feel So Bad* in Nashville on March 12th and 13th, tops the US chart, where it will stay for three weeks, earning a gold disc. At the last minute, *I Slipped, I Stumbled, I Fell*, an aggressive rocker recorded for "Wild In The Country", is added.
Sept [2] Joe Dowell's version of *Wooden Heart* tops the US chart - the most successful contemporary cover version of a Presley song.
[16] *Wild In The Country/I Feel So Bad* hits UK #4.
[23] *(Marie's The Name) His Latest Flame*, hits US #4.
Oct [7] *Little Sister*, the flip of *His Latest Flame*, hits US #5, familiarly heading for one million plus sales.
Nov [9] *(Marie's The Name) His Latest Flame/Little Sister* begins a four week stay at UK #1. ***Something For Everybody*** hits UK #2 (behind ***Another Black And White Minstrel Show*** by the George Mitchell Minstrels).
[22] The film "Blue Hawaii", a romantic musical originally titled "Hawaii Beach Boy" with 14 songs and co-starring Presley with Joan Blackman and Angela Lansbury, is released in the US. (It will be a huge box-office success, setting the seal on a money-making Presley movie formula.)
Dec [16] Soundtrack album, ***Blue Hawaii***, tops the US chart for the first of 20 weeks, and is Presley's biggest-selling album to date, topping two million sales.

1962

Jan [6] *Rock-A-Hula Baby*, coupled with the still climbing *Can't Help Falling In Love* from "Blue Hawaii", reaches US #23. ***Blue Hawaii*** holds at UK #1 for 18 weeks (and will remain in the UK Top 20 for 65 weeks).
[13] ***Elvis' Christmas Album*** re-charts at US #120.
Feb [3] *Can't Help Falling In Love*, also from the movie, hits US #2 (behind Joey Dee & the Starliters' *Peppermint Twist*), and is another million seller. (This will become one of Presley's most enduring and much-covered ballads, and during the '70s will be the song with which he will invariably close his live appearances.)
[24] *Rock-A-Hula Baby/Can't Help Falling In Love* hits UK #1.
Apr [9] Filming begins on "Girls! Girls! Girls!" on location in Hawaii.
[11] "Follow That Dream", a romantic comedy partly filmed on location in the rural deep South, opens in Ocala, FL, again to good box office receipts. It co-stars Presley with Anne Helm and Arthur O'Connell, and features only five songs.
[21] Loping rockaballad, *Good Luck Charm*, displaces future movie co-star Shelley Fabares' *Johnny Angel* at US #1. The two-week chart-topper will be Presley's last US #1 single for nine years. Its sales top one million, while its B-side ballad, *Anything That's Part Of You*, reaches US #31.
May Priscilla moves into Graceland living under the supervision of Vernon and attending the Immaculate Conception High School, where she will graduate in June 1963.
[26] *Good Luck Charm* begins a five-week stay at UK #1.
June [16] EP *Follow That Dream*, with four cuts from the movie, reaches US #15. (25 years later, *Follow That Dream* will often be revived in concert by Bruce Springsteen. Presley will never sing it in performance.)
[30] EP *Follow That Dream* reaches UK #34. (The following week, **Record Retailer** will state that it is no longer collating sales on the EP and it drops out of the chart. It will, however, reach UK #11 in the **New Musical Express** chart.)
July [28] *Pot Luck* tops the UK chart.
[27] "It Happened At The World's Fair" begins filming at MGM's Culver City Studios. (Most of the subsequent shooting will be done on location in Seattle, WA, at the World's Fair.)
Aug [11] ***Pot Luck*** hits US #4.
[29] The film "Kid Galahad", a re-make of the 1937 Humphrey Bogart/Edward G. Robinson movie, and starring Presley as a potential boxing champion (featuring Gig Young, Lola Albright and Charles Bronson), opens in the US.
Sept [1] *Just Tell Her Jim Said Hello*, the B-side of the still climbing *She's Not You*, makes US #55.
[8] *She's Not You* hits US #5, becoming another million seller.
[15] *She's Not You* begins a three-week stay atop UK chart.
Oct [20] Rocking *King Of The Whole Wide World*, the lead track from six-song soundtrack EP *Kid Galahad*, reaches US #30.
[27] Ballad *Where Do You Come From*, from the movie "Girls! Girls! Girls!", and the B-side of *Return To Sender*, peaks at US #99.
[31] "Girls! Girls! Girls!", a romantic musical co-starring Presley with Stella Stevens, Jeremy Slate and Laurel Goodwin, receives its world premiere in Honolulu, HI.
Nov [17] *Return To Sender*, a traditionally-styled (Otis Blackwell co-penned), medium-pace Presley rocker also from the movie hits US #2 for the first of five weeks (unable to usurp the Four Seasons' *Big Girls Don't Cry*), its sales topping two million.
[21] "Girls! Girls! Girls!" opens in US mainland theatres.
[30] "Kid Galahad" premieres in the UK, at the London Pavilion.
Dec [15] *Return To Sender* tops the UK chart, where it will stay for three weeks, selling 700,000 copies.
[29] ***Elvis' Christmas Album*** re-charts at US #59.

1963

Jan [12] Soundtrack album, ***Girls! Girls! Girls!***, hits US #3 and earns a gold disc.
[26] His second album, ***Elvis*** (subtitled in the UK, ***Rock 'N' Roll No. 2***), is reissued after some years' unavailability since deletion by HMV, hitting UK #3.
[28] Production begins on "Fun In Acapulco" at

Paramount Studios in Hollywood.
Feb [9] Soundtrack album, ***Girls! Girls! Girls!***, hits UK #2, behind Cliff Richard's soundtrack album, ***Summer Holiday***.
Mar [9] Ballad *They Remind Me Too Much Of You*, from "It Happened At The World's Fair" and the B-side of *One Broken Heart For Sale*, makes US #53.
[16] Blackwell/Scott-penned *One Broken Heart For Sale*, also from the movie, reaches US #11 and UK #12. (It is Presley's first single since *Blue Moon* not to make the US Top 10 and at 1 minute 34 seconds, is Presley's shortest hit).
Apr [3] "It Happened At The World's Fair", featuring Presley with Joan O'Brien and Gary Lockwood in another romantic musical, opens in Los Angeles.
May [25] Soundtrack album, ***It Happened At The World's Fair***, hits US and UK #4.
June [14] Beaulieu graduates from the Immaculate Conception Cathedral High School, receiving a congratulatory Corvair from her boyfriend. She will enroll at the Patricia Stevens Finishing School.
July [15] Filming begins on "Viva Las Vegas".
Aug [3] *(You're The) Devil In Disguise* hits UK #1 for a week. (It will be Presley's last UK chart-topper until mid-1965, and the last single by any US act to reach UK #1 until Roy Orbison's *It's Over* in 1964.)
[10] *(You're The) Devil In Disguise* hits US #3 and is a million seller.
[13] ***Girls! Girls! Girls!*** is certified gold by the RIAA.
Oct Filming begins on "Kissin' Cousins" at MGM's Culver City Studios.
Nov [2] Leiber/Stoller's *Bossa Nova Baby*, taken from the film "Fun In Acapulco", reaches UK #13.
[16] *Bossa Nova Baby* hits US #8 and tops a million sales, while its B-side, R&B-rocker *Witchcraft* (a revival of a little-known 1956 US #5 R&B hit by the Spiders), reaches US #32. ***Elvis' Gold Records, Volume 3***, a compilation of most of the hit singles from *Stuck On You* to *She's Not You*, hits US #3 and earns a gold disc.
[27] "Fun In Acapulco" opens in the US, co-starring Presley with Ursula Andress and Elsa Cardenas.

1964

Jan Presley buys Potomac, the yacht previously owned by President Roosevelt, for $55,000 and then donates it to the March of Dimes charity, which then gives it to the St. Jude's Hospital, Memphis, founded by Danny Thomas.
[4] *Kiss Me Quick*, from ***Pot Luck***, belatedly issued as a single after being a major hit in Eire and several European countries, reaches UK #14.
[18] Soundtrack album, ***Fun In Acapulco***, almost entirely Latin-influenced, hits US #3, earning another gold disc.
Feb [8] ***Fun In Acapulco*** hits UK #9.
Mar [6] His latest movie, "Kissin' Cousins", a hillbilly comedy in which Presley plays dual roles as an air force officer and his mountain boy cousin (the latter in a blond wig), opens in Phoenix, AZ. In Britain, the location-filmed "Viva Las Vegas", which has also been completed for the same company (MGM), is released instead, with the title amended to "Love In Las Vegas". (A musical titled "Viva Las Vegas" has been released in the UK in the early '50s by MGM.) Presley's "Las Vegas" co-star is Ann-Margret, better-known than most of his leading ladies. (Off-screen, a romance between them is rumored, which comes to nothing, though both will remain close friends. She will attend his funeral.)
[9] Filming begins on "Roustabout".
[21] *Kissin' Cousins*, title song from the film, reaches US #12.
[28] Its B-side soul-style ballad (later regarded a Presley classic), *It Hurts Me*, makes US #29. It is one of just three songs cut recently in a now-infrequent Nashville studio session, on January 12th.
Apr [11] *Viva Las Vegas* reaches UK #17.
[18] Compilation ***Elvis' Golden Records, Vol. 3***, released belatedly in UK, hits #6.
[20] "Viva Las Vegas" premieres in New York City (both it and "Kissin' Cousins" will show in the Top 20 US box-office hits of 1964).
May [2] Soundtrack album, ***Kissin' Cousins***, hits US #6.
[23] *Kiss Me Quick*, released in the US as special double A-side "Gold Standard Series", coupled with *Suspicion* (to catch spin-off sales from Terry Stafford's US #3 hit revival of the latter), reaches US #34.
June [13] His treatment of Ray Charles' *What'd I Say*, cut in gospel-rock style with the Carol Lombard Quartet on back-up vocals, taken from "Viva Las Vegas", reaches US #21, while its B-side, *Viva Las Vegas*, reaches US #29.
[22] Shooting begins on "Girl Happy" at MGM Studios.
July [4] Four-track soundtrack EP, *Viva Las Vegas* (excluding the two songs already on a single), charts for one week at US #92.
[11] *Kissin' Cousins* hits UK #10.
Aug [8] Soundtrack album, ***Kissin' Cousins***, hits UK #5.
[22] *Such A Night*, a revival of a 1954 Johnnie Ray hit which Presley had recorded in April 1960 (and originally issued on ***Elvis Is Back***), reaches US #16.
Sept [4] *Such A Night* climbs to UK #13.
Oct Filming begins on "Tickle Me".
Nov [11] "Roustabout", a romantic drama teaming Presley with established actress Barbara Stanwyck, opens in the US and at London's Columbia Theatre the following day. (Raquel Welch makes her movie debut in the film.) Much of it features Presley riding a motorcycle and a minor accident while shooting has to be written into the script to accommodate a facial cut.
[14] *Ain't That Loving You Baby*, recorded during Presley's Army leave weekend session in June 1958, (along with *I Got Stung*, *A Fool Such As I* and others), reaches UK #15.
[21] *Ain't That Loving You Baby* reaches US #16.
[28] Organ-backed ballad, *Ask Me*, an Italian-originated song recorded in January at the same time as *It Hurts Me* and coupled with *Ain't That Loving You Baby*, reaches US #12. (It is the first time since 1961 that both sides of a Presley single reach the US Top 20, while the combined sales give Presley another million seller.)
Dec [26] *Blue Christmas*, extracted from the 1957 Christmas album, climbs to UK #11.

1965

Jan [2] Soundtrack album, ***Roustabout*** (which does not spin off a single release), tops the US chart for one week (to be dethroned by ***Beatles '65***), earning another gold disc.
[16] ***Roustabout*** reaches UK #12.
Mar Presley and Parker note the tenth anniversary of their partnership, with the announcement that they have made $150 million from sales of 100 million records, and a further $135 million from Presley's first 17 movies.
[15] Filming begins on "Harum Scarum" at MGM Studios.
[20] *Do The Clam*, a dance number from the forthcoming movie, "Girl Happy", hits UK #19.
Apr [3] *Do The Clam* reaches US #21.
[14] Movie "Girl Happy", co-starring Presley with actress/singer Shelley Fabares (whose *Johnny Angel* Presley's *Good Luck Charm* replaced at US #1 in 1962), opens in the US.
May [8] ***Girl Happy*** hits UK #7.
[25] Filming begins on "Frankie And Johnny".
[28] "Tickle Me" premieres in Atlanta, GA.
June [12] His revival of the Orioles' 1953 million-selling gospel ballad, *Crying In The Chapel*, originally issued to coincide with Easter, and recorded in 1960 with the tracks which formed ***His Hand In Mine***, but held for release until now, hits US #3. In the process it becomes his first US Top 10 hit since *Bossa Nova Baby*, and sells one million copies. The soundtrack album, ***Girl Happy***, also hits US #8.
[19] *Crying In The Chapel* tops the UK chart.
[27] "Tickle Me" opens in London.
July [17] *It Feels So Right*, originally a 1960 cut from ***Elvis Is Back***, now included in "Tickle Me" and the B-side of the still climbing *(Such An) Easy Question*, makes US #55.
[24] *(Such An) Easy Question*, originally from ***Pot Luck*** and now also in "Tickle Me", reaches US #11.
Aug [7] Staying at the Ilikai Hotel, Waikiki, Presley begins filming "Paradise Hawaiian Style" at Hanauma Bay, HI.
[14] EP *Tickle Me*, comprising five tracks all from earlier Presley albums, peaks at US #70. (It will be his last EP to make the US chart - the format is all but dormant in the US by now).
[18] Herman's Hermits' lead singer Peter Noone interviews Presley for the **New Musical Express** at a party held at the Polynesian Cultural Center in Hawaii.
[27] Presley plays host to the Beatles, who are on a break in Los Angeles during a US tour, at his rented house in Perugia Way, Bel Air. They talk and play together for hours late into the night, jamming along to records, while managers Tom Parker and Brian Epstein play pool in an adjoining room.
Oct [9] *I'm Yours*, from "Pot Luck" but also revived for "Tickle Me", reaches US #11, with a narration on the original cut removed. ***Flaming Star And Summer Kisses***, a UK compilation comprising tracks from the deleted ***Loving You*** and the unissued (in the UK) EP, *Elvis By Request*, reaches UK #11.
[21] Bill Black dies at Baptist Memorial Hospital Memphis, four months after receiving surgery to remove a brain tumor.
[23] ***Elvis For Everyone***, a collection of unreleased studio and film recordings cut between Presley's Sun days and 1964, and retailed to mark his tenth anniversary with RCA, hits US #10.
Nov [24] "Harum Scarum", which co-stars Presley and Mary Ann Mobley in an unlikely "Desert Song"-type setting, premieres in Los Angeles with a nationwide release set for December 15th. (In Britain, where it is re-titled "Harem Holiday", the film is ill-received even by fans and the UK publication **Elvis Monthly** advises Presley followers to complain to producer Sam Katzman about the poor quality of the production.)
Dec [4] *Tell Me Why*, an unreleased song recorded in 1957 (at the same session as *All Shook Up*), reaches UK #15, as ***Elvis For Everyone*** debuts at its UK #8 peak.
[24] Presley proposes to Priscilla Beaulieu.
[25] *Puppet On A String*, a light ballad from "Girl Happy", which has sustained airplay ever since the movie soundtrack's release and has finally been issued as a US single for the Christmas market, reaches #14.

1966

Jan Having left Graceland to live with her parents after graduating from high school, Priscilla Beaulieu returns, to live again with Presley's grandmother. Rumors of a secret engagement ensue when she is seen regularly with Presley on his between-films breaks throughout the year.
[1] Soundtrack album, ***Harum Scarum***, hits US #8, as *Blue River* peaks at US #95.
[22] ***Harem Holiday*** reaches UK #11.
[29] *Blue River*'s A-side, *Tell Me Why*, reaches US #33.
Feb Filming begins on "Spinout" at MGM Studios with President Lyndon Johnson visiting the set during shooting.
Mar [12] *Blue River* reaches UK #22.
[31] "Frankie And Johnny", a romantic musical/comedy based on the 19th-century traditional song directed by Fred De Cordova co-starring Presley as Johnny with Donna Douglas (from TV's "The Beverly Hillbillies") as Frankie, premieres at the Gordon Theatre, Baton Rouge, LA.
Apr [8] "Frankie And Johnny" opens at the Victoria Theatre, London.
[23] *Please Don't Stop Loving Me*, from the movie and the B-side of the title track, makes US #45.
[30] *Frankie And Johnny* reaches US #25.
May [7] *Frankie And Johnny* reaches UK #21.
[14] Soundtrack album, ***Frankie And Johnny***, reaches UK #11.
[25] At a four-day recording session in Nashville, Presley works with producer Felton Jarvis for the first time.
[28] ***Frankie And Johnny*** reaches US #20.
June [9] "Paradise, Hawaiian Style", a largely location-shot romantic musical designed to re-create

the magic (and money-making power) of "Blue Hawaii", opens in Memphis, featuring Presley with UK actress Suzannah Leigh. With inferior songs and dulled charisma, the movie does only a fraction of the earlier Hawaiian picture's box office gross.
[11] Filming begins on "Double Trouble" at MGM Studios, Culver City.
July [23] *Love Letters*, one of 18 tracks cut in a productive return to the Nashville studios at the end of May, and a revival of Dick Haymes 1945 US #11 hit, though virtually an exact copy of Ketty Lester's distinctive voice/piano arrangement of 1962, reaches US #19.
Aug [6] *Love Letters* hits UK #6.
[13] Soundtrack album, ***Paradise, Hawaiian Style***, hits UK #7.
Sept [3] ***Paradise, Hawaiian Style*** reaches US #15.
[12] Production begins on "Easy Come, Easy Go".
Nov [5] *Spinout*, the movie title song, makes US #40, while *All That I Am* reaches UK #18.
[19] A-side coupling, *All That I Am*, also from the film, makes US #41. (It is the first Presley recording to feature strings in the accompaniment.)
[23] Musical comedy film, "Spinout", co-starring Shelley Fabares again, opens in the US (retitled "California Holiday" in Britain).
Dec [10] ***California Holiday*** reaches UK #17. It includes three non-movie bonus tracks: a revival of the Clovers' R&B rocker, *Down In The Alley*, Hawaiian ballad *I'll Remember You*, and a lengthy version of Bob Dylan's *Tomorrow Is A Long Time* (which Dylan will, three years later, quote as being his favorite cover version of one of his songs).
[17] Soundtrack album, ***Spinout***, makes US #18.
[31] *If Every Day Was Like Christmas*, a new seasonal song recorded in Nashville on June 10th, hits UK #9. (It does not chart in the US because of a policy of restricting Christmas records to a special Christmas survey.)

1967

Feb [9] Presley buys the 163-acre Twinkletown Farm, near Walls, MS, re-naming it the Circle G Ranch.
[18] *Indescribably Blue*, recorded at the same June session as *If Every Day Was Like Christmas*, reaches UK #21.
[25] *Indescribably Blue* reaches US #33.
Mar [22] "Easy Come, Easy Go", co-starring veteran actress Elsa Lanchester, opens nationwide in the US, while Presley begins work on "Clambake", delayed by two weeks after he has suffered concussion from hitting his head on a bathtub.
Apr [5] "Double Trouble", a comedy thriller, is released in the US. Much of it is set in Europe (though shot in Hollywood), and features UK supporting actors Norman Rossington and leading lady Annette Day.
[27] "Easy Come, Easy Go" premieres in the UK at London's Plaza cinema.
May [1] Presley marries Priscilla Beaulieu at the Aladdin Hotel, Las Vegas, in the private suite of its owner Milton Prell, at 9:41 a.m., before 100 invited guests, in an eight-minute civil ceremony conducted by Nevada Supreme Court Justice David Zenoff. Presley's assistant, Joe Esposito, is best man, and the bride's sister, Michelle, is maid of honor. After a reception in the hotel, they fly in Frank Sinatra's Lear jet "Christina" to Palm Springs, CA, to begin their honeymoon.
[4] After a day in Hollywood where Presley puts finishing touches to the movie "Clambake", they fly home to Memphis to complete their honeymoon.
[13] Presley's second religious album, ***How Great Thou Art***, including *Crying In The Chapel*, and recorded in Nashville alongside *Love Letters*, reaches US #18 (and UK #11), earning a gold disc.
[27] *That's Someone You Never Forget*, from ***Pot Luck***, charts for one week at US #92. Double A-side, *You Gotta Stop/Love Machine*, taken from "Easy Come, Easy Go", makes UK #38.
[29] A second wedding reception is held at Graceland, for 125 friends and relatives unable to attend in Las Vegas.
June [10] *Long Legged Girl (With The Short Dress On)*, a novelty rocker from ***Double Trouble***, and the A-side of *That's Someone You Never Forget*, peaks at US #63.
[12] Filming begins on "Speedway".
Aug *Long Legged Girl (With The Short Dress On)* makes UK #49.
[19] Soundtrack album, ***Double Trouble***, reaches US #47.
Sept [2] ***Double Trouble*** charts for one week at UK #34.
[16] *There's Always Me*, taken from his 1961 album, ***Something For Everybody***, peaks at US #56.
[29] Governor Buford Ellington declares "Elvis Presley Day" in Tennessee.
[30] *Judy*, coupled with *There's Always Me*, and also from ***Something For Everybody***, peaks at US #78.
Oct [18] Filming begins on "Stay Away, Joe" on location near Sedona, AZ.
Nov [4] His revival of bluesman Jimmy Reed's *Big Boss Man*, cut at a rare Nashville studio session of R&B and country numbers on September 10-11th, with Charlie McCoy playing harmonica, reaches US #38.
[18] From the same session, its B-side, *You Don't Know Me*, a 1962 hit for Ray Charles, makes US #44.
[22] "Clambake" opens in the US, co-starring Shelley Fabares for the third time with Presley, plus TV actors Will Hutchins and Bill Bixby.

1968

Jan Parker announces that the Singer Sewing Machine Company is to sponsor Presley's first TV spectacular, to be made by NBC TV for a year-end telecast.
Feb [1] A daughter, Lisa Marie, is born at 5:01 p.m. at Baptist Memorial Hospital, Memphis.
[8] Presley is inducted into **Playboy** magazine's Hall of Fame.
[10] Soundtrack album ***Clambake*** (which also includes a side of non-movie bonus songs, including *Guitar Man, You Don't Know Me* and *Big Boss Man*), reaches US #40.
[24] *Guitar Man*, written by country-rock singer-guitarist Jerry Reed (and featuring him on guest guitar), reaches US #43.
[29] ***How Great Thou Art*** wins Presley his first Grammy for Best Sacred Performance Of 1967 at the tenth annual awards.
Mar [8] "Stay Away Joe", a comedy western made on location in Arizona, and starring Presley as an American Indian, opens in the US.
[11] Presley records four songs for the film, "Live A Little, Love A Little", at MGM Sound studios in Hollywood. (One of these, *Wonderful World*, by UK songwriting team Guy Fletcher and Doug Flett, has also just been recorded by Cliff Richard with slightly different lyrics as one of Britain's six short-listed songs for the "Eurovision Song Contest".)
[30] *Guitar Man* reaches UK #19.
Apr [6] *Stay Away*, taken from the film "Stay Away Joe", and sung to the traditional tune of *Greensleeves*, peaks at US #67.
[9] ***Loving You*** is certified gold by the RIAA.
[20] Released as a special single for Easter, Presley's revival of the inspirational *You'll Never Walk Alone* (originally from the musical "Carousel", but best known via Gerry & the Pacemakers' interpretation), peaks at US #90. The soundtrack album, ***Clambake***, charts for one week at UK #39.
May [11] *U.S. Male*, the A-side of *Stay Away* and another Reed song in similar style to *Guitar Man* (and again with him playing guitar), reaches US #28.
[30] "Clambake" opens at London's New Victoria Cinema.
June [1] Compilation ***Elvis' Gold Records, Volume 4***, anthologizing mostly post-1962 hit singles, reaches US #33.
[8] *U.S. Male* reaches UK #15.
[12] Movie "Speedway", co-starring Presley with Nancy Sinatra (as a tax inspector, out to get him), premieres in Charlotte, NC. They duet on one song on the soundtrack.
[27] Work begins at 6:00 p.m. at NBC's Studio 4 in Burbank on the Singer-sponsored NBC-TV special, produced and directed by Steve Binder (whose previous credits include the all-star "T.A.M.I. Show" in 1964). Binder has won a lengthy battle with Parker over the format of the show, which he sees as an opportunity to relaunch the magnetism of Presley as a live performer. (Parker had wanted Presley to sing 20 Christmas songs and say goodnight.)
[28] Taping continues for the special, where for two extended sessions, Presley, Scotty Moore, Charlie Hodge and D.J. Fontana play in the round with an audience gathered about them, jamming on familiar material. These sessions continue the next day, interspersed with choreographed set pieces involving such Presley songs as *Trouble*, *Guitar Man*, *It Hurts Me*, *Little Egypt* and a gospel medley. A new song, *If I Can Dream*, is specifically written for the show's finalé by Earl Brown. (By June 30th, Binder and NBC have hours of tape to edit into a one-hour program.)
July [4] An avid car collector, Presley donates a Rolls Royce to auction for SHARE, a Hollywood women's charity, with the $35,000 proceeds going to retarded children.
[7] Presley cuts the title song from "Charro", with a backing track by the Hugo Montenegro Orchestra, in Hollywood. (It will be released in 1969 as the B-side to *Memories*.)
[13] Coupled *Let Yourself Go* and *Your Time Hasn't Come Yet, Baby*, from "Speedway", peak at US #71 and #72 respectively.
[21] "Speedway" receives its European premiere at the "Elvis Convention '68" at the De Montfort Hall, Leicester, Leics.
[22] Filming begins on "Charro" near Apache Junction, AZ.
Aug [24] Soundtrack album, ***Speedway***, makes US #82. This is unique in being the only Presley album on which a track is sung entirely by somebody else - in this case, co-star Nancy Sinatra's *Your Groovy Self*.
[31] *Your Time Hasn't Come Yet, Baby* reaches UK #22.
Oct *You'll Never Walk Alone*, appearing some months after its US release, makes UK #44.
[5] *Almost In Love*, from "Live A Little, Love A Little", peaks at US #95.
[19] *A Little Less Conversation*, also from "Live A Little, Love A Little", and the A-side of *Almost In Love*, makes US #69.
[23] His latest movie, "Live A Little, Love A Little" opens in the US, a slightly more adult comedy than usual, co-starring Presley (as a photographer) with Michele Carey and veteran actors Rudy Vallee and Sterling Holloway.
[28] Filming begins on "The Trouble With Girls (And How To Get Into It)" at MGM Studios.
Dec [8] The Singer-sponsored TV special, "Elvis", airs on NBC-TV. It draws rave critical reactions, has the year's largest viewing figures for a musical special and is the highest-rated show of the week.
[31] The "Elvis" special airs on BBC2-TV.

1969

Jan [13] He begins lengthy recording sessions at Chips Moman's American Sound Studio in Memphis, the first time he has recorded in his home town since working with Sam Phillips on the Million Dollar Quartet tapes in December 1956. Between January 16th-17th and 20th-23rd, he will record 20 songs which will form the basis of a highly-rated series of singles and an album.
[25] Recording complete, Presley flies to Aspen, CO, with his wife and entourage, for a skiing vacation.
Feb [1] *If I Can Dream*, the critically-rated closing number from the TV special, restores Presley to the US Top 20, reaching #12.
[8] ***Elvis***, the soundtrack from the NBC-TV special, hits US #8, his highest-placed album in the US since 1965, and the first since ***How Great Thou Art*** to pass half a million sales to earn a gold disc.
[17-22] More recording sessions at American Sound Studio produce a further 14 new tracks, including revivals of many favorites from other artists' repertoires.
Mar [13] "Charro", a dramatic Western, featuring incidental music by Hugo Montenegro, and co-starring Ina Balin and Victor French, opens nation-

wide in the US.
[22] *If I Can Dream* reaches UK #11.
Filming begins on "Change Of Habit" at Universal Studios, Los Angeles.
Apr [12] *Memories*, an orchestra-backed ballad extracted from the TV show, reaches US #35.
May After completing work on "Change Of Habit" in Hollywood, Presley and Priscilla vacation for two weeks in Honolulu, HI.
[17] ***Elvis : NBC TV Special*** hits UK #2.
June [10] Presley flies to Las Vegas to discuss arrangements for what is to be his comeback to the live stage after eight years.
[14] *In The Ghetto*, Mac Davis' stark social-conscience song with a subtle, arresting arrangement and the first release from the Memphis sessions, hits US #3 (becoming his first Top 10 success in four years), selling over one million copies (his first single to do so since *Crying In The Chapel*, four years earlier). ***Elvis Sings Flaming Star***, a collection of tracks either unissued or (like the title track) not previously on an album, is released at low price and reaches US #96. (This is actually a reissue by RCA of an album titled ***Singer Presents Elvis***, pressed up for sale only through Singer Sewing Machine shops at the time of the TV special, as a promotional tie-in. Copies of the original album will become high-priced collectors' items, because of scarce availability.)
July [5] *In The Ghetto* hits UK #2 for three weeks, behind Thunderclap Newman's *Something In The Air*. Presley flies to Las Vegas to begin rehearsals for his comeback show.
[19] ***From Elvis In Memphis***, a varied collection from the January session, receives the best reviews of a Presley album since ***Elvis Is Back*** and reaches US #13, earning another gold disc. ***Flaming Star*** hits UK #2.
[22] ***Elvis*** NBC-TV special is certified gold by the RIAA.
[31] In his first live concert since March 25th, 1961, Presley opens at the Showroom of the International Hotel, Las Vegas, the beginning of a four-week engagement of 57 shows which will net him $1.5 million. (The concerts are universally acclaimed as a triumph, with the magnetic stage presence of old still intact and Presley doing justice to both '50s material and new songs.) His new live back-up band includes Rick Nelson's ex-guitarist James Burton, bassist Jerry Scheff, guitarists John Wilkinson and Charlie Hodge, keyboards player Larry Muhoberac (who will be replaced on future engagements by ex-Cricket Glen D. Hardin) and drummer Ronnie Tutt. Back-up vocal groups are the Imperials (the Jordanaires having turned down the gig because of Nashville commitments) and the Sweet Inspirations.
Aug [9] *Clean Up Your Own Back Yard*, taken from the film, "The Trouble With Girls", reaches US #35.
[17] The TV special is re-shown on NBC-TV, with *Blue Christmas* edited out and replaced by *Tiger Man*, in deference to the midsummer season.
[28] Presley's season at the International closes. He and Priscilla fly to Palm Springs for a three-week vacation.
[30] ***From Elvis In Memphis*** tops the UK chart for one week.
Sept [3] "The Trouble With Girls (And How To Get Into It)", co-starring Marlyn Mason, receives its American premiere. Featuring cameo appearances by John Carradine and Vincent Price, it once again sees little action at the box office, as the low-budget Presley movie era comes to an end.
[27] *Clean Up Your Own Back Yard* reaches UK #21.
Nov [1] Mark James-penned *Suspicious Minds*, another recording from the January Memphis session, heads the US chart for a week, giving Presley his first Hot 100 chart-topper in seven years. It will sell almost two million copies (but will be his last US #1).
[10] "Change Of Habit", in which Presley co-stars as a ghetto doctor with Mary Tyler Moore as a nun, opens in the US.
[27] Double album, ***From Memphis To Vegas/From Vegas To Memphis***, featuring two sides of live performance and two from the Memphis sessions, reaches US #12.
Dec [12] ***From Memphis To Vegas/From Vegas To Memphis*** is confirmed gold by the RIAA.

1970

Jan [17] *Suspicious Minds* hits UK #2 (behind Rolf Harris' *Two Little Boys*). It is the first UK Presley single to feature a picture sleeve.
[26] Presley returns to the International Hotel for a second season, opening with *All Shook Up* and closing with *Can't Help Falling In Love*, earning $1 million for a month's shows, set to end on February 23rd.
[28] ***From Elvis In Memphis*** is certified gold by the RIAA.
[31] *Don't Cry Daddy*, penned by Mac Davis and coupled with *Rubberneckin'* from "Change Of Habit", hits US #6 and is another million seller.
Feb [27] He begins three days of performances at the Astrodome, Houston, TX, to a total of 200,000 people.
[28] German import album, ***Portrait In Music***, charts for one week at UK #36.
Mar Presley enters Baptist Memorial Hospital, Memphis, suffering from glaucoma of the left eye. He will remain hospitalized for three days.
[21] *Kentucky Rain*, penned by Eddie Rabbitt, reaches US #16, as *Don't Cry Daddy* hits UK #8 while ***From Memphis To Vegas/From Vegas To Memphis*** hits UK #3.
May [23] Budget album, ***Let's Be Friends***, makes US #105.
June [20] *Kentucky Rain* reaches UK #21.
[27] *The Wonder Of You*, a live revival of an old Ray Peterson hit, recorded in Las Vegas and coupled with *Mama Liked The Roses*, hits US #9, and earns a gold disc for a million US sales.
July Filming begins on "Elvis - That's The Way It Is" at MGM Studios.
[25] Live album, ***On Stage - February 1970***, recorded at the second International Hotel season, reaches US #13, earning a gold disc.
Aug [1] *The Wonder Of You* tops the UK chart, where it will stay for six weeks, selling over 700,000 copies.
[10] Presley begins a third month-long season of 58 shows at the International Hotel, Las Vegas, set to end on September 7th. (During one performance, Presley sings *Along Came Jones* to audience member Tom Jones.)
[14] *The Wonder Of You* is certified gold by the RIAA.
[15] ***On Stage*** hits UK #2.
[22] It is announced that Presley will undertake his first US tour since the mid-'50s, a six date trek opening in Phoenix, AZ.
[29] Double A-side, *I've Lost You/The Next Step Is Love*, reaches US #32.
Oct [10] Four-album boxed set compilation, ***Worldwide 50 Gold Award Hits, Vol. 1***, containing most of his major hits, reaches US #45, earning a gold disc.
Nov [10] Presley begins a week-long tour of the West Coast at the Oakland-Alameda County Coliseum, Oakland, CA, set to end at the Denver Coliseum, Denver, CO, on the 17th.
[11] "Elvis - That's The Way It Is", a documentary of his summer 1970 Las Vegas shows, opens nationwide in the US.
[28] A live, recorded revival of Dusty Springfield's *You Don't Have To Say You Love Me*, coupled with *Patch It Up*, reaches US #11, while *I've Lost You* hits UK #9.
Dec [5] ***Elvis Back In Memphis***, previously released as the second part of ***From Memphis To Vegas/From Vegas To Memphis***, makes US #183.
[12] Budget album, ***Almost In Love***, mostly collecting film songs from earlier EPs, reaches US #65.
[15] "Elvis - That's The Way It Is" is released in the UK.
[21] Presley, staying at a Washington, DC hotel under the name of Joe Burrows, meets President Richard Nixon in the Oval Office of the White House, Washington.
[30] He returns to Washington with Shelby County, TN sheriff William Morris to tour the FBI headquarters.
Elvis' Golden Records, Vol. 1, reissued in Britain, reaches UK #21, and ***Worldwide 50 Gold Award Hits Vol. 1*** makes UK #49.

1971

Jan [9] Presley receives the Jaycee's Award as one of the Ten Outstanding Young Men Of The Year. (The other winners are all from outside the entertainment field and include President Nixon's press secretary, Ronald Ziegler.) Soundtrack album, ***Elvis : That's The Way It Is***, reaches US #21, and earns another gold disc.
[23] *You Don't Have To Say You Love Me* hits UK #9. ***Elvis : That's The Way It Is*** reaches UK #12.
[26] He begins another month-long, 57-show season at the International Hotel, Las Vegas, set to end on February 23rd.
Feb [6] From the forthcoming ***Elvis Country***, his update of Les Paul & Mary Ford's 1954 US #11 hit *I Really Don't Want To Know*, backed with *There Goes My Everything*, reaches US #21.
[23] ***On Stage - February 1970*** is certified gold by the RIAA.
[27] ***Elvis Country (I'm 10,000 Years Old)***, recorded during a lengthy Nashville session in June 1970, reaches US #12, earning a further gold disc.
Apr [10] *Where Did They Go, Lord?*, coupled with *Rags To Riches* (originally a 1953 R&B hit for the Dominoes, and a pop #1 for Tony Bennett), makes US #33. ***Elvis Country*** hits UK #6.
[17] Religious compilation, ***You'll Never Walk Alone***, released for Easter, makes US #69. His revival of Engelbert Humperdinck's *There Goes My Everything* (the B-side of *I Really Don't Want To Know* in the US) hits UK #6.
June [1] The two-room shack in Tupelo, Presley's birthplace, is opened as a tourist attraction.
[5] *Rags To Riches* hits UK #9.
[12] *Life/Only Believe* peaks at US 53.
July [10] ***Love Letters From Elvis***, recorded at the same sessions as ***Elvis Country***, reaches US #33.
[31] ***Love Letters From Elvis*** hits UK #7.
Aug [21] Unusual folk-styled *I'm Leavin'* makes US #36. *Heartbreak Hotel*, reissued on a maxi-single and coupled with *Hound Dog* and *Don't Be Cruel*, hits UK #10. Budget album, ***C'mon Everybody***, with more tracks from earlier film EPs, makes US #70. ***C'mon Everybody*** hits UK #5 and ***You'll Never Walk Alone*** reaches UK #20.
Sept [8] Presley receives the Bing Crosby Award, from the National Academy of Recording Arts and Sciences, given to people who "during their lifetimes, have made creative contributions of outstanding artistic or scientific significance to the field of phonograph records". (He is the sixth recipient, predecessors being Bing Crosby, Frank Sinatra, Duke Ellington, Ella Fitzgerald and Irving Berlin.)
[11] Four-album boxed compilation, ***Worldwide Gold Award Hits, Vol. 2*** (each copy containing a small rectangle cut from an item of Presley's clothing), makes US #120.
Oct [2] Budget album, ***Almost In Love***, makes UK #38.
Nov [1] "Elvis On Tour" opens nationwide, documenting an earlier trek from April 5th-19th. The Hollywood Foreign Press Association hails the film the Best Documentary Of 1972.
[5] Presley embarks on an 11-day tour at the Metropolitan Sports Center, Minneapolis, MN, set to end on the 16th at the Salt Palace, Salt Lake City, UT.
[6] *It's Only Love* makes US #51.
[23] *I'm Leavin'* reaches UK #23.
Dec [11] ***Elvis' Christmas Album***, reissued in the UK at budget price, hits UK #7.
[18] A further mid-price selection, ***I Got Lucky***, with another set of film EP tracks, reaches US #104. UK maxi-single reissue of *Jailhouse Rock*, in the wake of *Heartbreak Hotel*'s success, makes UK #42.

1972

Jan [1] ***I Got Lucky*** reaches UK #26.
[18] Part of Bellevue Boulevard, Memphis, is re-named Elvis Presley Boulevard. (The northern section is not re-named following protests from the Bellevue Baptist Church.)
[22] His treatment of B.J. Thomas' *I Just Can't Help Believing*, taken from the soundtrack of "Elvis : That's

The Way It Is", hits UK #6.
[26] Presley begins his annual month-long season at the Hilton Hotel (no longer named the International Hotel), Las Vegas, set to end on February 23rd.
Feb [16] A show at the Hilton Hotel, Las Vegas, is recorded.
[23] Presley and Priscilla are legally separated. (She will become involved with karate instructor Mike Stone.)
Mar [11] His treatment of Buffy Saint-Marie's ballad, *Until It's Time For You To Go*, reaches US #40.
[14] Presley is honored by NARAS at the 14th Grammy Awards with a Lifetime Achievement Award, "in recognition of his artistic creativity and his influence in the field of recorded music upon a generation of performers and listeners whose lives and musical horizons have been enriched and expanded by his unique contributions".
[18] ***Elvis Now*** peaks at US #43.
Apr [5] He embarks on a 15-day tour at the Memorial Auditorium, Buffalo, set to end on the 19th at the Tingley Coliseum, Albuquerque, NM.
[22] *Until It's Time For You To Go* hits UK #5.
May [13] His third gospel album, ***He Touched Me***, makes US #79.
[27] Live, recorded revival of Mickey Newbury's *An American Trilogy* (combining traditional standards *Dixie*, *All My Trials* and *Battle Hymn Of The Republic*), makes US #66.
June [3] A reissue of ***Elvis For Everyone*** charts for one week at UK #48.
[9-11] He plays his first concerts in New York - four shows at Madison Square Garden to a total of 80,000 people, earning $730,000 - at the start of a 12-date tour set to end on the 20th at the Civic Assembly Center, Tulsa, OK.
[10] ***Elvis Now*** reaches UK #12 and ***Rock And Roll***, a reissue of his first UK album, ***Rock 'N' Roll No. 1***, makes UK #34.
July [1] *An American Trilogy* hits UK #8.
[22] ***Elvis As Recorded At Madison Square Garden*** hits UK #3.
Aug [4] He begins a second season at the Hilton Hotel, Las Vegas, set to end on September 4th.
[11] Divorce proceedings begin between Elvis and Priscilla.
[12] Low-price compilation, ***Elvis Sings Hits From His Movies, Volume 1***, peaks at US #87.
[19] ***He Touched Me*** makes UK #38.
Sept [9] ***Elvis As Recorded At Madison Square Garden*** reaches US #11, earning a gold disc.
[16] The **New Musical Express** reports "Elvis Says No To Britain", with Colonel Parker giving unsuitability of venues as the reason.
Oct [21] Dennis Linde-penned R&B rocker, *Burning Love*, hits UK #7.
[28] *Burning Love* hits US #2, behind Chuck Berry's *My Ding-A-Ling*, giving Presley has his first US Top 10 and million-selling single since *The Wonder Of You* in 1970.
Nov [8] Presley begins a ten-date tour at the Municipal Coliseum, Lubbock, set to end on the 18th at the Honolulu International Center, Honolulu, HI.
[20] Presley announces plans for a "Aloha From Hawaii" concert, at a press conference in the Hilton Hawaiian Village, Waikiki. It is to be a benefit show for the family of Kuiokalakani Lee, a Hawaiian writer and singer who had died of cancer in 1966.

1973

Jan [6] Budget set ***Burning Love And Hits From His Movies, Vol. 2***, combining the recent hit with earlier film songs, reaches US #22.
[14] The "Elvis : Aloha From Hawaii" TV show is aired live via the Intelsat IV satellite from Honolulu International Center Arena, to Japan, Australia, New Zealand, South Vietnam, Thailand, Philippines, Hong Kong, Singapore and Malaysia. (The US and Europe see a taped version, but Britain declines to take it. Its total worldwide audience is estimated as one billion - the largest ever for any TV show.) The concert raises $75,000 for the Kuiokalakani Lee Cancer Fund, and Presley sings Lee's best-known song, *I'll Remember You*, during the telecast.
[20] *Always On My Mind*, the flip-side of the still climbing US hit *Separate Ways*, hits UK #9.
[26] Presley begins his annual month-long season at the Hilton Hotel, Las Vegas, set to end on February 23rd.
Feb [3] Ballad *Separate Ways*, from "Elvis On Tour" (and widely interpreted as having been recorded because of his recent separation from Priscilla), reaches US #20.
[13] Presley falls ill during a concert appearance in Las Vegas, and is attended to by physician Dr. Sidney Bowers (who will receive a white Lincoln Continental in appreciation). The still-climbing ***Aloha From Hawaii Via Satellite*** is certified gold by the RIAA.
Mar [3] ***He Touched Me*** wins Presley his second Grammy Award (and second for a religious album), as Best Inspirational Performance Of 1972.
[10] Double album, ***Aloha From Hawaii Via Satellite***, a recording of the January telecast, reaches UK #11.
[17] Budget collection, ***Separate Ways***, again coupling the recent hit with earlier material, makes US #46.
Apr [4] "Aloha From Hawaii", sponsored by Chicken-of-the-Sea Tuna Companies, airs on NBC-TV.
[22] Presley embarks on a nine-date tour at the Veteran's Memorial Stadium, Phoenix, set to end on the 30th at the Denver Coliseum.
May [4] He begins a 25-show engagement at the Sahara Tahoe Hotel, Stateline, NV, which is cancelled after Presley falls ill.
[5] ***Aloha From Hawaii Via Satellite*** tops the US chart for one week, Presley's first #1 album in nine years - and his last.
[13] Presley's Mother's Day concert at Lake Tahoe, NV, is held in memory of Gladys Presley, with the show's proceeds going to the Barton Memorial Hospital.
June [2] A live version of James Taylor's *Steamroller Blues*, from the "Aloha From Hawaii" show, coupled with *Fool*, reaches US #17.
[6] Movie "Elvis On Tour", filmed on the road the previous year, opens in the US. (It will win a Golden Globe award as Best Documentary Of The Year.)
[9] A UK-only released live update of Tony Joe White's *Polk Salad Annie*, an on-stage favorite, reaches #23.
[20] Presley embarks on a 14-date tour at the Municipal Auditorium, Mobile, AL, set to end on July 3rd at The Omni, Atlanta, GA.
[28] ***Elvis : That's The Way It Is*** is certified gold by the RIAA.
July [21-25] Presley cuts sessions at Stax Recording Studios in Memphis.
Aug [6] He begins a month-long, 59 show season at the Hilton Hotel, Las Vegas.
[18] ***Elvis***, with recently-recorded material, makes US #52.
Sept [15] *Fool* reaches UK #15, as ***Elvis*** peaks at UK #16.
Oct [11] Presley and Priscilla are finally divorced at a courthouse in Santa Monica, CA. Remaining close friends, they walk out of the court arm-in-arm. She receives a lump sum of $2 million plus alimony, child support and incidentals.
[15] Presley is admitted to Baptist Memorial Hospital, Memphis, suffering from pneumonia and will remain hospitalized for two weeks.
[27] *Raised On Rock*, penned by Mark James, coupled with the Tony Joe White-authored *For Ol' Times Sake*, makes US #41.
Dec [8] *Raised On Rock* peaks at UK #36.
[10-16] Presley conducts further sessions at Stax Recording Studios.

1974

Jan [5] ***Raised On Rock/For Ol' Times Sake***, combining recently-cut rock and country material, makes US #50.
[8] ***Elvis - A Legendary Performer Vol. 1*** is certified gold by the RIAA.
[26] Presley begins his fifth successive New Year season at the Hilton Hotel, Las Vegas, set to end on February 9th.
Feb [23] ***Elvis - A Legendary Performer Vol. 1***, compiled as a historical overview and combining notable hits with unreleased material and interviews, reaches UK #20.
Mar [1] He embarks on a 20-date tour at Oral Roberts University, Tulsa, OK, set to end on the 20th at Mid-South Coliseum, Memphis.
[2] ***Elvis - A Legendary Performer, Vol. 1*** makes US #43, earning a gold disc.
[23] A revival of Billy Lee Riley's *I've Got A Thing About You, Baby*, coupled with *Take Good Care Of Her*, reviving Adam Wade's 1961 US #7, reaches US #39.
Apr [6] *I've Got A Thing About You, Baby* makes UK #33.
May [4] ***Good Times*** peaks at US #90.
[16-26] Presley performs a season of shows at the Sahara Tahoe Hotel, Stateline.
[25] ***Good Times*** charts for one week at UK #42.
June [15] He embarks on an 18-date tour at the Tarrant County Convention Center, Fort Worth, TX, set to close on July 2nd at the Salt Palace, Salt Lake City.
July [20] *If You Talk In Your Sleep* makes UK #40.
Aug [3] *If You Talk In Your Sleep* reaches US #17.
[19] Presley begins his 11th season at the Hilton Hotel, Las Vegas. Two shows are cancelled due to his having 'flu.
[24] ***Elvis Recorded Live On Stage In Memphis*** reaches US #33. (During the month, he also receives his 8th Degree Black Belt in Karate (and is increasingly incorporating elements of the martial art into his stage routines).)
Sept [7] ***Elvis Recorded Live On Stage In Memphis*** charts for one week at UK #44.
[27] Presley embarks on a 21-date tour at the Maryland Fieldhouse, College Park, MD, set to end with a short eight-show season at the Sahara Tahoe Hotel, Stateline.
Nov A UK-only released double album, ***40 Greatest Hits***, marketed by Arcade Records, is a best seller, but is kept out of the chart until July 1975 by a rule which excludes TV-advertised compilations.
[23] ***Having Fun With Elvis On Stage***, containing clips of Presley's between-songs stage patter and jokes, makes US #130. (It had originally been sold by Parker on his own Boxcar label as a souvenir item at concerts.)
Dec [14] His hard-rocking revival of Chuck Berry's *Promised Land* reaches US #14.

1975

Jan [4] Presley's update of the ballad, *My Boy*, produced by its English lyricist Bill Martin and originally recorded in English by Richard Harris, hits UK #5.
Presley is hospitalized at Baptist Memorial Hospital, Memphis, where he will remain for two weeks, diagnosed with hypertension and an impacted colon, and is ordered to take a special diet and a treatment of cortisone, which has the side-effect of causing notable weight gain. (He will fight to maintain a balance between his health and weight for the rest of his life, with prescription drugs in often grossly over-prescribed amounts.)
Feb [1] *Promised Land* hits UK #9.
Mar [1] Presley wins his third Grammy Award, as his 1974 live version of *How Great Thou Art*, from ***Elvis Recorded Live On Stage In Memphis***, is named Best Inspirational Performance. ***Promised Land***, including the title track and *My Boy*, reaches UK #21.
[8] *My Boy* rises to US #20.
[15] ***Promised Land*** makes US #47.
[18] He begins another season at the Hilton Hotel, Las Vegas. The 29-show series is set to end on April 1st.
Apr [18] Presley buys a 1958 Convair 880 plane (Delta Airship #912) for $250,000, and, after an $800,000 customization, will name it the "Lisa Marie". (In September, he will purchase a second plane, a 550mph Jet Star he nicknames "Hound Dog" for $899,702.)
[24] Presley embarks on a major series of one-night dates at the Coliseum, Macon, GA, which will include 43 dates through to July 24th at the Civic Center, Asheville, NC.
May [31] *T-R-O-U-B-L-E* reaches UK #31.

June [14] *T-R-O-U-B-L-E* peaks at US #35, as ***Today*** makes UK #48.
[18] Presley undergoes a face-lift at Mid-South Hospital, Memphis.
Aug [2] ***Today*** climbs to US #57.
[18-20] A five-show stint at the Hilton Hotel, Las Vegas, is cancelled with Presley suffering from exhaustion. He will be hospitalized at Baptist Memorial Hospital, Memphis, for two weeks. (While in hospital, Presley will pledge $5,000 to Jerry Lewis' Labor Day Muscular Dystrophy Association Telethon.)
Sept ***The Elvis Presley Sun Collection*** (the first time the early tracks have all been released on one album) makes UK #16.
Nov [15] *Bringing It Back* peaks at US #65.
Dec [2-15] Presley plays 17 further shows at the Hilton Hotel, Las Vegas.
[13] *Green, Green Grass Of Home*, his version of Tom Jones' hit, issued as a UK-only single, reaches #29.
[31] Presley rips his pants onstage during a concert in Pontiac, MI. Unrelated to this, he breaks the record for a solo artist, grossing $816,000 for a single performance.

1976

Jan [17] ***40 Greatest Hits***, a TV-advertised album on Arcade, now chart-eligible, reaches UK #16.
Feb [10] As well as adding to his gun collection, Presley is made a Police Reserve for the Memphis Police.
Mar [6] ***Elvis - A Legendary Performer, Vol. 2***, another historical overview, reaches US #46 and earns a gold disc.
[17] Presley embarks on six-date tour at Freedom Hall, Johnson City, TN, set to end at Kiel Auditorium, St. Louis, MO, on the 22nd.
Apr [21] He begins a short trek at the Kemper Arena, Kansas City, MO, set to end with 15 shows at the Sahara Tahoe Hotel, Stateline, on May 9th.
[29] Bruce Springsteen, on tour in Memphis, attempts to see Presley by climbing the fence at Graceland. He is escorted off the premises by security guards while still trying to explain who he is.
May [8] *Hurt*, reviving Timi Yuro's 1961 US #4 hit, makes UK #37.
[29] *Hurt*, coupled with the Dennis Linde-penned *For The Heart*, reaches US #28, as compilation album, ***The Sun Sessions***, makes US #76.
June [12] ***From Elvis Presley Boulevard, Memphis, Tennessee***, recorded in February at his new studio at Graceland, reaches UK #29.
July [5] Presley will make his last live appearance in his adopted hometown, at the Mid-South Coliseum.
[17] ***From Elvis Presley Boulevard, Memphis, Tennessee*** reaches US #41, earning another gold disc.
Oct [16] *The Girl Of My Best Friend*, reissued in the UK, hits #9.
[29-31] Presley records tracks at his home studio in Graceland.
Nov [23] Jerry Lee Lewis is arrested outside Graceland when he appears, drunk, and with a .38 Derringer pistol, demanding to see Presley.
Dec [8] At a Las Vegas Hilton show before 200 members of his British fan club, Presley says that "plans are under way now for a visit to London".

1977

Feb [5] Another reissue, the 1962 track *Suspicion*, hits UK #9.
Mar [5] Mark James-penned *Moody Blue*, coupled with *She Thinks I Still Care* (a 1962 Country chart-topper for George Jones), reaches US #31.
Apr [1] Presley re-enters Baptist Memorial Hospital, Memphis, suffering from fatigue and intestinal flu and will remain hospitalized for five days.
[2] *Moody Blue* hits UK #6.
[25] He makes his final recordings, in a session following a concert at the Civic Center, Saginaw, MI.
May [28] Compilation album, ***Welcome To My World***, mixing live and studio country songs, makes US #44. (It will earn a platinum disc for million-plus sales after his death.)
[29] Presley stops during a concert at the Civic Center, Baltimore, MD. He returns 30 minutes later after being attended to by a physician.
June [18] **Photoplay** magazine awards Presley its Gold Medal Award For Favorite Variety Star and Favorite Rock Music Star.
[26] Presley plays his 55th concert of the year at the Market Square Arena, Indianapolis, IN. It will be his last live performance. A commemorative RCA two billionth label-pressing copy of *Moody Blue* is presented to Presley at the steps of his Lisa Marie jet, in which he has flown to Indianapolis for the evening performance.
Aug [1] Book **Elvis : What Happened?**, written by former Presley payroll members Red and Sonny West and Dave Hebler with tabloid journalist Steve Dunleavy, exposing the apparent darker side of Presley's private personality, is published.
[12] The Angola Coach Company sells Presley's former tour bus, a Flxible VL 100 coach originally bought by Elvis in 1959 and often driven by him until 1968 when he sold it to "Hoosier Hotshot" Herb Shrinner. The original equipment in the vehicle included a trash compactor, rotisserie and a four slice toaster.
[16] Just after midnight, as Presley drives through the gates of Graceland (for what will be the last time) in his 1973 Stutz Blackhawk, a fan shoots what will become the final photo ever taken of Elvis alive. At 2:20 p.m., Presley is discovered lying on the floor in a bathroom on the second floor at Graceland by girlfriend Ginger Alden. (They had reportedly been scheduled to marry on the 27th during a concert in Memphis.) He had been seated on the toilet reading **The Scientific Search For The Face Of Jesus**. Although Alden will later claim a idfferent version: "I thought at first he might have hit his head because he had fallen out of his black lounging chair and his face was buried in the carpet". She calls bodyguard Al Strada and aide Joe Esposito, who had been playing racquet ball with Presley earlier in the day, but he fails to respond to resuscitation attempts and is rushed to Baptist Memorial Hospital, but pronounced dead at 3:30 p.m. His death by heart failure (cardiac arrythmia) at age 42 makes major headlines throughout the world. (Bio Science Laboratories will reveal that at the time of his death, Presley's body contained butabarbital, codeine, morphine, pentobarbital, Placidyl, Quaalude, Valium and Valmid.)
[17] Thousands of fans from all over the US, and even overseas, arrive in Memphis to pay their respects (25,000 file past his coffin at Graceland during the afternoon). In Washington, DC, President Jimmy Carter issues a tribute statement: "Elvis Presley's death deprives our country of a part of itself. He was unique and irreplaceable." Carter notes how Presley's unique meld of styles "changed the face of American popular culture ... he was a symbol to people the world over, of the vitality, rebelliousness and good humor of this country".
[18] Presley's funeral service, arranged by singer J.D. Sumner and conducted by the Reverend C.W. Bradley, is held at Graceland, with 150 people attending, and 75,000 more outside the gates. His body is moved by hearse in a 19-Cadillac cortege to Memphis' Forest Hill cemetery, for entombment at 4:30 p.m. in a mausoleum alongside his mother. With two prayers, one poem and 150 mourners, the legend is laid to rest in a grey marble crypt, 9' long, 27" high, surrounded by thousands of floral tributes which have required over 100 vans to take them from Graceland to the burial site. The King is buried still wearing his TCB ("taking care of business") ring. Teenagers Alice Hovatar and Juanita Johnson are killed during an all-night vigil at Graceland after a car ploughs into the assembled crowd.
[27] Ten re-charting Presley albums peak in the UK - ***40 Greatest*** tops the chart, with ***Welcome To My World*** (#7), ***Elvis In Demand***, a UK fan club-compiled set of hard-to-find tracks initially charting in February, (#12), ***G.I. Blues*** (#14), ***Elvis' Golden Records Vol. 1*** (#21), ***Live At Madison Square Garden*** (#26), ***Elvis' Golden Records Vol. 2*** (#27), ***Hits Of The 70s*** (#30), ***Elvis' Golden Records Vol. 3*** (#49) and ***Pictures Of Elvis*** (#52).
Sept [3] *Way Down*, featuring Sumner's distinctive bass vocals, tops the UK chart, where it will stay for five weeks, selling more than 600,000 copies. Seven other singles also re-chart in Britain - *It's Now Or Never* (#39), *All Shook Up* (#41), *Crying In The Chapel* (#43), *Jailhouse Rock* (#44), *Are You Lonesome Tonight* (#46), *The Wonder Of You* (#48) and *Wooden Heart* (#49). ***The Elvis Presley Sun Collection***, another re-charted album, reaches UK #16.
[10] ***Moody Blue*** hits UK #3 as ***Blue Hawaii*** peaks at UK #26.
[12] The still-climbing *Way Down* is certified gold by the RIAA.
[17] ***Moody Blue***, containing his final recordings (including *Way Down*), hitting US #3, is also a million seller. *Return To Sender* makes UK #42, as ***That's The Way It Is*** makes UK #34.
[24] *Way Down* reaches US #18, while ***The Sun Years*** makes UK #31.
Oct [1] ***Elvis' Golden Records Vol. 1*** climbs to US #63, as ***Loving You*** reaches UK #24.
[2] The bodies of Presley and his mother are removed from Forest Hill cemetery and re-buried side-by-side in the Meditation Garden at the rear of Graceland, because of an attempt to steal his body from the public cemetery.
[3] CBS-TV broadcasts "Elvis In Concert", a special filmed during his final tour in June in Omaha and Rapid City. It features an emotional preface by Vernon Presley.
[7] ***From Elvis Presley Boulevard, Memphis, Tennessee*** is confirmed gold by the RIAA.
[14] The still-climbing ***Elvis In Concert*** is certified platinum by the RIAA.
[22] ***Elvis' Golden Records Vol. 3*** makes US #64, as Ronnie McDowell's *The King Is Gone*, the most successful of what will eventually be hundreds of Elvis tribute records, reaches US #13.
[25] ***Elvis - A Legendary Performer, Vol. 2*** is certified gold by the RIAA.
Nov [5] Double album, ***In Concert***, combining the soundtrack from the TV show with June 1977 tour recordings, reaches UK #13.
[12] ***Les 40 Grands Plus Succes***, a French pressing of ***40 Greatest***, charts for a week at UK #56.
[19] ***Elvis In Concert*** hits US #5.
[27] The Meditation Gardens at Graceland are opened to the public.
Dec [1] ***Elvis Country*** is certified gold by the RIAA.
[24] *My Way*, a 1977 live recording of the Frank Sinatra standard, reaches US #22.

1978

Jan [7] *My Way* hits UK #9.
[13] *My Way* is certified gold by the RIAA.
Mar [11] ***Aloha From Hawaii Via Satellite*** re-charts at UK #35.
Apr [8] ***He Walks Beside Me*** charts for one week at UK #37.
May [20] A UK compilation of early tracks, ***Elvis - The '56 Sessions, Vol. 1***, makes UK #47.
June [10] Gospel collection, ***He Walks Beside Me***, reaches US #113.
July [29] *Don't Be Cruel*, reissued as a UK single to tie in with the ***'56 Sessions*** album, reaches #24.
Aug [19] ***Elvis : NBC TV Special*** peaks at UK #50.
Sept [1-10] A 10-day Elvis Convention is held at the Las Vegas Hilton Hotel, promoted by Col. Parker, with Priscilla and Vernon Presley in attendance.
[30] ***Sings For Children And Grown Ups Too*** makes US #130.
Dec [2] ***Elvis - A Canadian Tribute***, which includes all his recordings by Canadian writers, peaks at US #86.
[16] Reissued ***Elvis' 40 Greatest*** makes UK #40.
[18] The still-rising ***Elvis - A Legendary Performer, Vol. 3*** is certified gold by the RIAA.

1979

Jan [27] ***Elvis - A Legendary Performer, Vol. 3*** makes US #113.
Feb [10] ***Elvis - A Legendary Performer Vol. 3*** makes

UK #43.
[11] The Dick Clark-produced biopic, "Elvis", with Kurt Russell in the title role, Shelley Winters as Gladys Presley and directed by John Carpenter, airs on ABC-TV.
Mar [31] ***Our Memories Of Elvis***, on which producer Felton Jarvis re-edits tapes to remove horns and strings and highlight Presley's voice against small-group accompaniment, makes US #132.
Apr [21] ***Our Memories Of Elvis*** charts for one week at UK #72.
June [26] Vernon Presley dies in Tupelo of a heart attack, aged 63. (He will be buried beside his wife and son at Graceland.)
Sept [1] ***Our Memories Of Elvis Volume 2*** peaks at US #157.

1980

Jan [5] Seasonal *It Won't Seem Like Christmas (Without You)* reaches UK #13, as the TV-promoted double compilation, ***Love Songs***, hits UK #4.
Mar At a Sotheby's auction in London, a paper napkin from the Las Vegas Riviera Hotel with Presley's authenticated signature on it, sells for $500.
May [16] Dr. George Nichopoulous is indicted in Memphis on 14 counts of over-prescription of drugs, notably to Presley, Jerry Lee Lewis, and nine other patients.
July Compilation album, ***Elvis Presley Sings Leiber And Stoller***, makes UK #32.
Aug Boxed set, ***Elvis Aron Presley***, reaches UK #21, as the re-issued ***Paradise Hawaiian Style*** charts briefly at UK #53.
[14] The Statue of Presley, sculpted by Eric Parks, is unveiled in Elvis Presley Plaza, Memphis.
Sept [20] An eight-album boxed set, ***Elvis Aron Presley***, reaches US #27. It consists largely of previously unheard material, including Presley's April 1956 Las Vegas appearance and the 1961 charity concert in Hawaii. Only 250,000 copies are produced worldwide. *It's Only Love*, released on single for the first time in Britain after inclusion on the boxed set, backed with *Beyond The Reef*, is his final UK Top 10 hit, at #3.
Dec TV-promoted K-tel-released gospel compilation, ***Inspirations***, hits UK #6.
[20] Seasonal *Santa Claus Is Back In Town* (from the 1957 Christmas album), makes UK #41.

1981

Jan [8] On what would have been Presley's 46th birthday, the Governors of Alabama, Florida, Georgia, Illinois, Kansas, North and South Carolina, Pennsylvania and Virginia declare "Elvis Presley Day" in their respective states.
Feb [7-8] "Elvis And Me", with Dale Midkiff as Elvis and Susan Walters as Priscilla, airs on ABC-TV. It is based upon Priscilla Presley's book of the same title.
[21] *Guitar Man*, in a version with updated accompaniment added by Jarvis shortly before his death on January 3rd, makes UK #43.
Mar [1] David Gerber-produced "Elvis And The Beauty Queen", with Don Johnson as Presley and Stephanie Zimbalist as Linda Thompson, airs on NBC-TV.
[21] ***Guitar Man***, also with updated accompaniment, makes UK #33.
[24] The Felton Jarvis-remixed *Guitar Man*, peaks higher than its original 1968 appearance, reaching US #28.
[28] ***Guitar Man*** reaches US #49.
Apr [1] ***The Million Dollar Quartet*** album is released for the first time on Sun in the UK.
[3] Warner Bros. film, "This Is Elvis", a David Wolper-produced documentary of his life using original concert and movie footage, plus specially-filmed linking material using actors, has its press premiere at the Memphian Theater, Memphis. The following day, the film has its world premiere in Dallas at the "USA Film Festival". Elvis-soundalike vocalist Ral Donner narrates.
May [9] *Lovin' Arms*, reviving Dobie Gray's 1973 US #61 (from ***Guitar Man***), and album ***This Is Elvis Presley***, both make UK #47.
[16] Double soundtrack album, ***This Is Elvis***, peaks at US #115.
Dec [5] ***The Ultimate Performance***, a compilation of live tracks from various earlier albums, climbs to UK #45.

1982

Jan [9] ***Elvis - Greatest Hits, Volume One*** peaks at US #142.
Feb [20] ***Elvis Presley EP Pack*** charts for one week at UK #97.
[27] Compilation ***The Sound Of Your Cry***, rounding up rare tracks, makes UK #31.
Apr [10] A live version of *Are You Lonesome Tonight*, recorded at Las Vegas International on July 31st, 1969, on which Presley breaks up laughing mid-song, reaches UK #25.
June [7] At the instigation of Priscilla and Jack Soden (an executive director of Elvis Presley Enterprises Inc.), the Graceland mansion is opened to the public, though Presley's aunt Delta Boggs will continue to live there until Lisa Marie inherits the estate on her 25th birthday. Approximately 750,000 people will visit each year.
July [3] *The Sound Of Your Cry*, backed by the Imperials Quartet, makes UK #59.
Sept [4] ***Romantic Elvis/Rockin' Elvis*** peaks at UK #62.
Dec [11] *The Elvis Medley*, assembled from clips taken from *Jailhouse Rock*, *Teddy Bear*, *Hound Dog*, *Don't Be Cruel*, *Burning Love* and *Suspicious Minds*, rises to US #71, but will be Presley's final US chart single of the decade. ***The Elvis Medley***, coupling the medley with nine hits, reaches US #133.
[18] ***It Won't Seem Like Christmas Without You*** makes UK #80.

1983

Jan [14] ***Welcome To My World*** is certified platinum by the RIAA.
Feb [19] A further UK reissue of *Jailhouse Rock* on its 25th anniversary, re-charts at UK #27.
Apr ***Jailhouse Rock/Love In Las Vegas***, compiling songs from both films on a picture disc, reaches UK #40.
May [14] Taken from it, *Baby I Don't Care*, makes UK #61.
June [11] ***I Was The One***, with additional modern accompaniment to several '50s hits, makes US #103.
Aug [20] ***I Was The One***, with *The Elvis Medley*, peaks at UK #83.
Dec [3] ***A Legendary Performer Vol. 4*** charts for one week at UK #91.

1984

Jan [14] Presley's version of Billy Swan's *I Can Help*, released as a single for the first time, reaches UK #30.
Apr [7] ***Elvis - The First Live Recordings***, gathering extremely early tapes of Presley performing on "Louisiana Hayride", peaks at US #163. ***I Can Help*** makes UK #71.
July ***Elvis - The First Live Recordings*** rises to UK #69.
Nov His version of Roger Whittaker's ballad, *The Last Farewell*, peaks at UK #48.

1985

Jan [12] ***Rocker*** makes US #154.
[26] A six-album boxed set, ***Elvis - A Golden Celebration***, issued to mark the 50th anniversary of Presley's birth, makes US #80. It concentrates on 1956-1957 unreleased live and TV show material, together with posthumously-discovered tapes of Presley singing at home with friends. ***20 Greatest Hits Volume 2*** charts for one week at UK #98.
Priscilla Beaulieu, now a successful actress (and a star of TV show "Dallas") publishes **Elvis And Me**, her account of love and life with Presley.
Feb *The Elvis Medley* finally appears as a UK single, making #51.
Mar [9] ***A Valentine Gift For You***, compiling Presley love songs, peaks at US #154.
May [25] ***Reconsider Baby***, a collection of his notable blues recordings, charts for a week at UK #92.
Aug A little-heard version of *Always On My Mind*, from the soundtrack of ***This Is Elvis***, reaches UK #59.
Oct UK TV-advertised compilation on the Telstar label, ***Ballads***, reaches UK #23.

1986

Jan [23] Presley is inducted into the Rock and Roll Hall of Fame at the inaugural dinner, staged at the Waldorf Astoria Hotel, New York.
Mar [31] ***Crying In The Chapel*** is certified gold by the RIAA.
July [16] "'68 Comeback Special" and "Aloha From Hawaii" videos are confirmed gold and platinum respectively by the RIAA.

1987

Jan [26] He is posthumously honored with the Special Award Of Merit at the 14th annual American Music Awards, held at the Shrine Auditorium, Los Angeles.
Apr [18] *Bossa Nova Baby*, backed with *Ain't That Lovin' You Baby*, reissued in Britain to tie in with a Latin music fad in dance clubs, makes UK #47, aided by a new extended mix by UK DJ/producer Simon Harris.
Aug [16] Cinemax-TV premieres "Elvis '56", narrated by Levon Helm.
[29] To mark the tenth anniversary of Presley's death, the double album, ***Presley - The All-Time Greatest Hits***, compiling 45 hit tracks, hits UK #4. (A similar US double album, ***The Top Ten Hits***, peaks at #117.) *Love Me Tender/If I Can Dream* is extracted as a double A-side and makes UK #56.
Oct ***The Number One Hits*** peaks at US #143.

1988

Jan Following its use on a TV ad for glue, Presley's *Stuck On You* is reissued and charts at UK #58.
Mar [2] *Hound Dog* is inducted into the NARAS Hall of Fame at the 30th annual Grammy Awards.
May [20] The RIAA certifies gold sales of ***Roustabout*** and two million sales each of ***Aloha From Hawaii Via Satellite*** and ***Elvis Sings The Wonderful World Of Christmas***.

1989

Jan Retired airline pilot Ed Leek is offered over $1 million for the acetate of Presley's 1953 recording of *That's When The Heartaches Begin*.
[28] ***Stereo '57 (Essential Elvis Vol. 2)*** makes UK #60. It includes previously undiscovered early stereo recordings made at Radio Recorders Studios.
Liverpool solicitor David Deacon's company Park McMaddy signs with the Presley estate to build the Elvis Presley Centre at Blackpool's Golden Mile, Lancs.
Feb At the height of the "I've seen Elvis" rumors spread by the world's tabloid press, UK newspaper **The Sun** offers £1 million to anyone who can bring a live Presley to its offices.
Apr Sun Records signs a deal with Ed Leek, owner of the purported first Elvis acetate, to release it as a single.
May [29] Lisa Marie, married since October 1988 to musician Danny Keough, gives birth to 7lb 2oz girl Danielle Riley at St. John's Hospital, Santa Monica, CA.
June Priscilla, as chief executive of his increasingly valuable estate, commissions a new US TV program concentrating on Elvis' early rock'n'roll years.
July Officials at Graceland deny a request from the Mississippi Tournament of Roses Association to use a giant likeness of Presley's head spinning on a record on the float for the "1990 Rosebowl Parade". Other Mississippi natives B.B. King, Conway Twitty and Tammy Wynette will be featured.
[15] His white suit and cape worn during the "Aloha From Hawaii" 1973 TV concert is stolen from the Los Gatos, CA home of Presley impersonator Charlie Stickerod. (The thief leaves behind 24-carat gold Elvis discs and other memorabilia.)
[27] Destitute Louisiana woman Rhonda Boler, 20, auctions a Diamond Medallion Cross given to her by Elvis during his 1974 comeback concert in Monroe, LA, on syndicated TV show "A Current Affair".
Aug [10] A colorized version of "Jailhouse Rock" airs

for the first time on the TBS cable network.

1990

Feb New Musical Express-originated compilation, ***The Last Temptation Of Elvis***, including a previously-unreleased take of *King Of The Whole Wide World*, plus various cover versions of Presley hits from such artists as Bruce Springsteen, Robert Plant, Jesus & Mary Chain, Daryl Hall & John Oates and others, is released to benefit the Nordoff Robbins Music Therapy Charity.

[6] "Elvis", focusing on the period 1954-5 with Michael St. Gerard as the King, airs on ABC-TV. Although critically well-received, it will be cancelled on May 19th.

July [21] ***Hits Like Never Before***, another ***Essential Elvis*** compilation full of rare out-takes, makes UK #71.

Sept [1] ***The Great Performances*** climbs to UK #62 and includes *My Happiness*, the first ever issue of his debut recording from 1953.

Nov [6] The RIAA certifies 150,000 sales of both "Great Performances Volume 1 : Center Stage" and "Great Performances Volume 2 : Man And Music" Buena Vista videos, which both include never-before-seen footage.

Dec While the trustees of Presley's estate continue to manage and market a multitude of Presley promotions, the latest, "Elvis - the Cologne", is launched with the ad-line "America has had 41 Presidents ... but only one King."

1991

Jan [8] On what would have been Presley's 56th birthday, the Hard Rock Café in Orlando, FL, serves its memorial meal, supposedly the King's favorite, comprising a 6lb beef roast, creamed potatoes with butter, mixed vegetables with butter, peas with salt pork and cornbread, followed by banana pudding.

[22] ***Elvis' Golden Records*** is released in China, on cassette only, selling for nine yuan (approximately $1.73).

Aug [17] *Are You Lonesome Tonight (Live)*, originally a 1983 UK #27, debuts at its UK #68 peak.

[24] ***Collectors Gold***, a three-CD boxed set released to mark the 14th anniversary of Presley's death, and containing rare studio, movie and live out-takes, charts for a week at UK #57.

Oct The city of Ottawa names a street "Elvis Lives Lane", nearby the 15-member-strong Elvis Sighting Society, which devotes itself to tracking Elvis sightings and raising money for charity.

[3] Presley's first guitar, a blond and brown Martin D18, used during his Sun days and displayed in the Country Music Hall of Fame for 17 years, is auctioned at the Red Baron Antique auction gallery, Atlanta, GA. Despite asking for an opening bid of $5 million, it goes for $180,000 to Englishman Dickey Wakefield.

Nov Graceland gains a spot on the National Register Of Historic Places.

Dec [6] ***Memories At Christmas*** is certified gold by the RIAA.

1992

Jan [1] The Rodgers & Hammerstein Organization takes over exclusive US and Canadian administration for the Elvis Presley music catalogs through a deal with the Presley estate and Gary Horey and Julian and Jean Aberbach.

[7] US Postmaster General Anthony M. Frank announces on CNN's "Larry King Live" that a commemorative Presley stamp will be issued on the King's birthday in 1993.

[22] "The Elvis Conspiracy" airs in syndication on US-TV.

Feb [22] ***From The Heart - His Greatest Love Songs*** debuts at its UK #4 peak.

Mar [27] Updating his sales achievements, the RIAA certifies a slew of Presley records : *(Marie's The Name) His Latest Flame, A Big Hunk O' Love, Ain't That Loving You Babe, Blue Christmas, Bossa Nova Baby, Clean Up Your Backyard, Devil In Disguise, Frankie And Johnny, I Feel So Bad, I'm Yours, I've Lost You, If I Can Dream, Kentucky Rain, Kissin' Cousins, One Broken Heart For Sale, Puppet On A String, Really Don't Want To Know, Separate Ways, She's Not You, Tell Me Why, Viva Las Vegas, You Don't Have To Say You Love Me, Elvis Presley (EP), Elvis Volume 1 (EP), Heartbreak Hotel (EP), Kid Galahad (EP), Loving You, Volume 1 (EP)*, ***Burning Love And Hits From His Movies, Volume 2***, ***Elvis In Person***, ***Elvis Now***, ***Elvis' Golden Records, Volume 4***, ***He Touched Me***, ***He Walks Beside Me - Favorite Songs Of Faith And Inspiration***, ***The Number One Hits***, ***Top Ten Hits***, ***You'll Never Walk Alone*** (gold), *A Fool Such As I, Burning Love, Can't Help Falling In Love, Crying In The Chapel, Don't, Don't Cry Daddy, Good Luck Charm, Hard Headed Woman, Heartbreak Hotel, I Got Stung, I Want You, I Need You, I Love You, In The Ghetto, It's Now Or Never, Return To Sender, Stuck On You, Surrender, Suspicious Minds, Teddy Bear, Too Much, Wear My Ring Around Your Neck, Elvis Sings Christmas Songs (EP), Elvis Volume 1 (EP), Follow That Dream (EP), Jailhouse Rock (EP), King Creole Volume 1 (EP), King Creole Volume 2 (EP), Love Me Tender (EP), Loving You, Volume 2 (EP), Peace In The Valley (EP), The Real Elvis (EP)*, ***Elvis' Golden Records, Volume 2***, ***Elvis' Golden Records, Volume 3***, ***G.I. Blues***, ***His Hand In Mine*** (all platinum), and multi-platinum - *All Shook Up* (two million), *Are You Lonesome Tonight* (two million), *Hound Dog* (three million), *Jailhouse Rock* (two million), *Love Me Tender* (two million), ***Blue Hawaii*** (two million), ***Elvis As Recorded At Madison Square Garden*** (two million), ***Elvis' Christmas Album*** (two million), ***Elvis' Golden Records, Volume 1*** (five million), ***How Great Thou Art*** (two million), ***Moody Blue*** (two million) and ***Pure Gold*** (two million).

Apr [24] CBS-TV airs "Elvis - The Great Performances", hosted by Priscilla from Graceland.

May [12] Dr. Nichopoulos, long-suspected of over-prescribing medication to Elvis, and previously cleared of any wrong-doing, faces renewed and similar allegations from other patients at a hearing before the Tennessee Board of Medical Examiners.

June [4] The US Post Office announces the winning design of the forthcoming Elvis stamp.

[17] The RIAA confirms platinum sales of ***Elvis Aron Presley*** and two million sales of ***World Wide 50 Gold Award Hits, Volume 1***.

Aug [12] RCA and the RIAA present his estate with 110 gold and platinum records, the most ever awarded simultaneously, for Presley titles which continue to pile up sales, fifteen years after his death.

[16] Among events staged for the 15th anniversary of his death (Elvis International Tribute Week), Memphis residents hold the annual Dead Elvis Ball.

[29] *Don't Be Cruel* bows at its UK #42 pinnacle, as ***The All Time Greatest Hits*** charts for a week at UK #75.

Sept [5] ***The King Of Rock'n'Roll - The Complete 50's Masters***, a five-CD boxed set containing newly-remastered versions of every Presley 1950s recording, peaks at US #159.

[26] Soundtrack album, ***Honeymoon In Vegas***, reaches US #18. The movie, starring Nicolas Cage, Sarah-Jessica Parker and James Caan and featuring a group of sky-diving Elvis impersonators, features cover versions of Presley hits from Billy Joel (*All Shook Up* and *Heartbreak Hotel*), Ricky Van Shelton (*Wear My Ring Around Your Neck*), Amy Grant (*Love Me Tender*), Travis Tritt (*Burning Love*), Bryan Ferry (*Are You Lonesome Tonight?*), Dwight Yoakam (*Suspicious Minds*), Trisha Yearwood (*(You're The) Devil In Disguise*), Jeff Beck and Jed Leiber (*Hound Dog*), Vince Gill (*That's All Right*), John Mellencamp (*Jailhouse Rock*), Willie Nelson (*Blue Hawaii*) and Bono (*Can't Help Falling In Love*).

Oct [21] Lisa Marie gives birth to 7lb 8oz son Benjamin Storm Keough at an undisclosed Florida hospital.

Nov [20] ***The King Of Rock'n'Roll - The Complete 50's Masters*** is certified platinum by the RIAA.

1993

Jan [8] The Presley postage stamp, designed by Mark Stutzman, issued after years of campaigning by Pat Geiger, goes on sale. (It is made available at 12:01 a.m. at Graceland and noon throughout the rest of the country.) Many fans will deliberately address letters to false destinations so that they will be returned stamped "Return To Sender".

[23] ***From The Heart - His Greatest Hits*** and ***The All Time Greatest Hits*** re-chart at UK #34 and #58 respectively.

Mar [4] ***The King Of Rock'n'Roll - The Complete 50's Masters*** is named Best Reissue Album in **Rolling Stone**'s 1993 Music Awards Critics' Picks.

Sept [28] Boxed CD-set, ***From Nashville To Memphis : The Essential '60s Masters 1***, rounding up in remastered form all Presley's 1960-1969 studio recordings, excluding gospel, live and Hollywood-recorded material, is released.

Nov [30] ***From Nashville To Memphis : The Essential '60s Masters 1*** is certified gold by the RIAA.

1994

May [26] The daughter of the King of Rock'n'Roll marries the King of Pop in a secret ceremony in the Dominican Republic.

Aug [16] Light Year Entertainment releases three-video boxed set "Elvis : The Concert Collection", comprising "Aloha From Hawaii", "The '68 Comeback Special" and "One Night With You".

Sept [17] ***The Essential Collection*** hits UK #6.

Oct Peter Guralnick's much-praised biography **Last Train To Memphis** is published by Little Brown.

[8] "Elvis Aaron Presley : The Tribute", a multi-star music event staged at the Pyramid Arena, Memphis, is broadcast live on pay-per-view in the US. Scotty Moore and the Jordanaires are the house band.

Dec [15] "Elvis : The Tribute" airs on ABC-TV.

[24] ***If Every Day Was Like Christmas*** makes US #94.

1995

Mar [1] *Heartbreak Hotel* is inducted into the NARAS 22nd annual Hall of Fame at the 37th Grammy Awards.

Apr [19] "Elvis : The Lost Performances" video reaches the RIAA-certified 100,000 sales plateau.

June The RIAA certifies total US sales of Presley records at 48.5 million.

Nov [11] *The Twelfth Of Never* debuts at its UK #21 peak.

1996

Apr [2] Reprising Jack Good's '70s musical, "Elvis" opens in London at the Prince of Wales Theatre with Alexander Bar as a young Presley, Timothy Whitnall portraying the '60s Elvis and P.J. Proby taking on his later years.

May [11] Following the April 29th issue of "Elvis 56", a video documentary narrated by Levon Helm, ***Elvis 56***, comprising 22 classic tracks from 1956, bows at its UK #42 peak.

[18] *Heartbreak Hotel*, coupled with *I Was The One*, make UK #45 in their week of entry.

THE PRETENDERS

Chrissie Hynde (vocals, guitar); **Pete Farndon** (bass); **James Honeyman-Scott** (guitar); **Martin Chambers** (drums)

1973

Hynde (b. Sept. 7, 1951, Akron, OH), heavily influenced by mid-'60s US soul stars (having attended a Mitch Ryder & the Detroit Wheels concert at a local amusement park in 1965), has already learnt to play a baritone ukelele before playing guitar with the Akron-based combo Saturday Sunday Matinee, which included future Devo keyboardist Mark Mothersbaugh, in 1967. Subsequently spending three years at Kent State University, studying art, she now leaves for London where she sells leather handbags in

Oxford Street and models at St. Martin's School of Art. She also meets **New Musical Express** magazine journalist Nick Kent, who invites her to become a contributing writer. Her first review is of a Neil Diamond album.

1974

Nov [1] Having worked part-time at future punk guru Malcolm McLaren's London clothes shop Sex, Hynde has relocated to Paris, France, to join the Frenchies, linking with session guitarist Chris Spedding. The band now performs its first gig with Hynde on vocals, supporting the Flamin' Groovies at the Olympia, Paris. The following year, Hynde will move to Cleveland, OH, and join R&B group Jack Rabbit, before returning to Britain in 1976 to play in the short-lived, Berk Brothers, though she is deposed as lead singer by Johnny Moped.

1977

Feb Spedding's *Hurt*, produced by Chris Thomas and featuring Hynde on backing vocals, is released in the UK.

Aug She cuts a demo tape of *The Phone Call* and links with Anchor Records' Dave Hill, who is forming Real Records and invites her to join on an ad-hoc basis and helps fund further demo sessions.

1978

Mar Hynde assembles a band with Hereford-based musicians Farndon (b. June 12, 1952, Hereford, Hereford), ex-Bushwackers on bass, drummer Gerry Mackleduff (who will be replaced by Chambers (b. Sept. 4, 1951, Hereford) following the recording of the first single) and Honeyman-Scott (b. Nov. 4, 1956, Hereford) on guitar. The group, still nameless, records Ray Davies' *Stop Your Sobbing*, with producer Nick Lowe for the Real label. Hynde settles on the name Pretenders, inspired by the Platters hit, *The Great Pretender*.

1979

Feb *Stop Your Sobbing* is their UK chart debut at #34, as the group begins club touring, including dates at London's Marquee and Moonlight clubs.

July Produced by Thomas, the follow-up, *Kid* (allegedly inspired by UK DJ David "Kid" Jensen), climbs to UK #33, as the group begins a month's UK tour, including a headline concert at London's Lyceum Ballroom.

Oct [22] The Pretenders begin four consecutive Monday night gigs at the Marquee club, as the Hynde /Honeyman-Scott-penned pop-rock outing *Brass In Pocket* begins its climb to UK #1.

Dec Christmas is celebrated with two festive dates at the favored Marquee venue. The band also performs at the "Concert For Kampuchea" at London's Hammersmith Odeon.

1980

Jan [19] As *Brass In Pocket* tops the UK chart for the first of two weeks, Hill leaves Real to become the Pretenders' full-time manager (the label is bought by US company Sire, which retains the band). As the group begins a 30-date UK tour, its debut album, ***Pretenders***, largely produced by Chris Thomas, enters the UK chart at #1 and begins a US rise to hit #9.

Apr *Talk Of The Town* hits UK #8 as the Pretenders visit the US for the first time and Hynde meets former hero Ray Davies at a New York, NY club (they begin a three-year relationship). The band plays at the 3,500-seater Civic Auditorium, Santa Monica, CA, which is sold out in two hours, and a benefit gig for the United Indian Development Association in Hollywood, CA.

May Towards the end of a US mini-tour, Hynde is involved in a fight with a Memphis, TN bouncer and spends a night in jail.

[31] *Brass In Pocket (I'm Special)* reaches US #14.

July [5] *Stop Your Sobbing* peaks at US #65.

[26] Grace Jones cover of Hynde's *Private Life* enters the UK chart set to reach #17.

Aug [23] A North American tour includes a performance before 50,000 at the "Heatwave Festival" in Mosport Park, Toronto, ON, Canada.

Oct [6] A 15-date UK tour begins in Newcastle, Tyne & Wear.

1981

Feb [21] Hynde-penned *Message Of Love* reaches UK #11.

Apr US-only released EP ***Extended Play***, featuring *Message Of Love*, *Talk Of The Town*, *Porcelain*, *Cuban Slide* and *Slide*, reaches #27 on the Album survey.

[10] Honeyman-Scott marries US model Peggy Sue Fender, in London.

May [16] Chambers ties the knot with Tracey Atkinson.

Aug [15] ***Pretenders II***, again helmed by Thomas, set to reach US #10, hits UK #7, as the group begins a three-month US tour.

Sept [5] During a show at Perkins Cow Palace, Pasadena, CA, the group is joined onstage by Bruce Springsteen to sing Jackie Wilson's *(Your Love Keeps Lifting Me) Higher And Higher*.

[19] *Day After Day* makes UK #45.

Oct [1] Chambers puts his hand through a window pane while on tour in Philadelphia, PA, severing tendons and arteries, causing cancellation of the final quarter of the tour.

Dec [5] *I Go To Sleep*, covering another Davies song, hits UK #7. (Shortly before planned UK Christmas dates, Chambers damages his other hand and more concerts are postponed.)

1982

Jan The Pretenders resume US dates, followed by concerts in Japan, Hong Kong and Australia.

Apr On their planned wedding day, Davies and Hynde are turned away by a registrar concerned that they are arguing too much.

May Honeyman-Scott plays for the Beach Boys on a US tour.

June [15] Farndon is fired, now viewed as incompatible with the other members.

[16] Honeyman-Scott dies following sustained cocaine and heroin addiction.

July Hynde flies to the US to be with Davies on the Kinks' US tour.

Aug [11] ***Pretenders*** is certified platinum by the RIAA.

Sept Tony Butler (b. Feb. 13, 1957, Ealing Gtr. London) temporarily fills in on bass (he will re-join Big Country), while Billy Bremner (b. 1947, Scotland) (ex-Rockpile) joins on lead guitar.

Nov [6] Spurred by its Don Letts-lensed promo clip, *Back On The Chain Gang* reaches UK #17.

1983

Feb Hynde gives birth to her and Davies' daughter, Natalie. Mick Green of the Pirates helps audition new guitarists and Robbie McIntosh (ex-Manfred Mann's Earth Band and Night) becomes the new lead guitar while he recommends Malcolm Foster, who is hired as bassist.

Mar [19] *Back On The Chain Gang* hits US #5 (where it is used in Martin Scorsese's film, "King Of Comedy").

Apr [14] Farndon, who had been in the process of forming a group with Rob Stoner and ex-Clash drummer Topper Headon, dies of a drug overdose in the bathtub.

May [28] The Pretenders participate in the three-day "US Festival" at San Bernardino, CA.

Dec Festive *2000 Miles* reaches UK #15.

1984

Jan *Learning To Crawl* makes UK #11 and is set to hit US #5.

[6] The group embarks on a six-date UK leg of "The Pretenders World Tour" at the Gaumont Theatre, Ipswich, Suffolk, set to end on the 16th at London's Hammersmith Odeon. Natalie joins her mother on the trek, but Davies' Kinks commitments keep the family apart. (An MTV-sponsored concert at New York's Radio City Music Hall sells out in one hour.)

Feb [11] *Middle Of The Road* reaches US #19.

Apr [18] *Learning To Crawl* is certified platinum by the RIAA.

May [5] *Show Me* reaches US #28 as, following a whirlwind romance, Hynde (having dumped Davies), marries Simple Minds vocalist Jim Kerr.

July [7] *Thin Line Between Love And Hate*, reviving the Persuaders 1971 hit, now with Paul Carrack on keyboards, peaks at US #83 and UK #49.

1985

July [13] The Pretenders perform at the "Live Aid" benefit spectacular at the JFK Stadium, Philadelphia, following Simple Minds.

Aug [31] A duet teaming Hynde with UB40 on a revival of Sonny & Cher's *I Got You Babe* tops the UK chart, and will reach US #28.

1986

Nov [1] Following a lengthy recording session featuring a variety of musicians, based around Hynde, ***Get Close*** produced by Jimmy Iovine, hits UK #6 and will reach US #25.

Dec The extracted Hynde-written *Don't Get Me Wrong*, aided by an "Avengers" TV show-style black and white video, hits UK #10.

[22] ***Get Close*** is confirmed gold by the RIAA.

[27] *Don't Get Me Wrong* hits US #10.

1987

Jan *Hymn To Her* hits UK #10.

[14] The Pretenders begin an eight-month world tour in Plattsburgh, NY, with the Hynde-assembled lineup of Robbie McIntosh (guitar), T.M. Stevens (bass), Bernie Worrell (keyboards) and Blair Cunningham, ex-Haircut 100, (drums).

Mar [7] *My Baby* (following an addition to the Kerr family), peaks at US #64.

Sept *If There Was A Man*, recorded for the soundtrack album to the James Bond movie "The Living Daylights", under the name Pretenders For 007, makes UK #49.

Nov [14] 16-track compilation, ***The Singles***, hits UK #6 and will make US #69, as a remixed version of *Kid* is released.

1988

July A second collaboration between UB40 and Hynde, after performing together in June at "Nelson Mandela's 70th Birthday Tribute" concert at Wembley Stadium, Wembley, Middx., *Breakfast In Bed*, hits UK #6.

1989

June [8] At a Greenpeace Rainbow Warriors press conference in London, noted vegetarian Hynde says she once firebombed McDonalds.

[9] McDonalds in Milton Keynes, Bucks., is firebombed. McDonalds threatens legal action against Hynde and asks her to sign a written document agreeing not to repeat her statements. She signs. (The following year she will be honored at the People for the Ethical Treatment of Animals (PETA) tenth anniversary Humanitarian Awards Gala in Washington, DC.)

1990

Apr [7] Chambers, now an in-demand player, drums with Guns N' Roses at "Farm Aid IV", amid rumors that he is joining the band.

[16] Hynde takes part in "Nelson Mandela - An International Tribute For A Free South Africa" at Wembley Stadium.

May [26] ***Packed!***, featuring Bremner and Dominic Miller (guitars), John McKenzie (bass) and Cunningham (drums), reaches UK #19, while the extracted singles, *Never Do That* and *Sense Of Purpose*, fail to chart, despite a video appearance for the latter by Hynde's current beau, UK boxer Gary Stretch.

June [16] ***Packed!*** makes US #48.

1991

May [4] The various artists album, ***Tame Yourself***,

benefitting PETA, and featuring Hynde on *Born With A Purpose*, makes US #165.

1992

Jan [4] A committed vegetarian, Hynde eats a groenteburger (vegetable burger) at a McDonalds in Amsterdam, Holland.
May She continues working on a new album at West Side Studios with Lenny Kaye producing.
June [28] The **Daily Mail** reports that Peggy Honeyman-Scott is suing Hynde for failing to make royalty payments. She has received £30,000 since her husband's death in June 1982.
Oct [16] Hynde sings *I Shall Be Released* and duets with Lou Reed on *Foot Of Pride* at the "Bob Dylan 30th Anniversary Celebration" concert at New York's Madison Square Garden.

1993

Jan [19] Hynde performs at PETA's 1993 Animals Ball during Inauguration festivities in Washington, DC.
[23] The Moodswings' *Spiritual High*, to which Hynde contributes guest vocals, makes UK #47.
Feb [16] Hynde presents the Best International Act trophy at the 12th annual BRIT Awards.
June The Pretenders cover of 10cc's 1975 UK #1, *I'm Not In Love*, is featured on the film soundtrack to the Robert Redford/Demi Moore movie, "Indecent Proposal".
Sept During the month Hynde joins Urge Overkill onstage in Las Vegas and New York City.
Nov [27] ***Stone Free : A Tribute To Jimi Hendrix***, to which Hynde has contributed *Bold As Love*, released by Reprise Records, debuts at its US #28 peak.

1994

Apr [18] Hynde guests on C4-TV's "The Big Breakfast".
[25] The Pretenders, now comprising, Hynde, Chambers, guitarist Adam Seymour (ex-Katydids) and bassist Andy Hobson (ex-Primitives), embark on a four-date UK tour (their first since 1987), at The Garage, Glasgow, Strathclyde, Scotland, set to end on the 29th at London's W1 Astoria.
[30] Ballad *I'll Stand By You* hits UK #10.
May [7] The group guests on NBC-TV's "Saturday Night Live".
[21] Critically revered as a return to form, ***Last Of The Independents*** hits UK #8 in its week of entry.
[28] ***Last Of The Independents*** debuts at its US #41 peak.
June [11] Following an appearance at the "Live 105 BFD" concert at the Shoreline Amphitheatre, Mountain View, CA on the 10th, the Pretenders now take part in KROQ's "Weenie Roast" at the Irvine Meadows Amphitheatre, Irvine, CA.
[24] The Pretenders play on the NME Stage on the opening day of the annual "Glastonbury Festival", Glastonbury, Somerset.
[25] *Night In My Veins* peaks at US #71.
[27] ***The Singles*** is certified gold by the RIAA.
July [9] *Night In My Veins* reaches UK #25.
Sept [19] The Pretenders embark on a nine-date UK tour at the Civic Hall, Wolverhampton, West Midlands, set to end on the 29th at Newport Centre, Newport, Gwent, Wales.
Oct [8] The group guests on BBC1-TV's "The Danny Baker Show".
[15] *977* debuts at its UK #66 peak.
[18] The Pretenders embark on a US tour before a sellout crowd of 1,500 at the Coca-Cola Roxy Theatre, Atlanta, GA, set to end on November 21st at the Arlene Schnitzer Concert Hall, Portland Center for the Performing Arts, Portland, OR.
[14] They guest on NBC-TV's "The Tonight Show".
Nov [16] ***Last Of The Independents*** is certified gold by the RIAA.
[26] Frank Sinatra's ***Duets II***, with the Chairman of the Board paired with Hynde on *Luck Be A Lady*, reaches US #29.
Dec [3] *I'll Stand By You* reaches US #16.

1995

Apr [15] Recently murdered Latino star Selena's Spanish version of *Back On The Chain Gang* tops **Billboard**'s Hot Latin Tracks Singles chart.
Mar [4] The "Boys On The Side" film soundtrack, including Hynde's cover of Morrissey's *Every Day Is Like Sunday*, reaches US #17.
[25] Comic Relief-benefitting single covering the Judds' country classic *Love Can Build A Bridge*, recorded by Hynde, Cher, Neneh Cherry and Eric Clapton, tops the UK chart.
June The group, augmented by the Duke (string) Quartet and Blur's Damon Albarn on piano, performs and records an acoustic show at Jacob Street Studios in Bermondsey, London for future album release and TV broadcast. Percussionist Wiff augments the line-up.
Sept [2] The Pretenders perform *My City Was Gone* at the Concert for the Rock and Roll Hall of Fame at Cleveland Stadium, Cleveland, OH.
Oct During the month Hynde sings the National Anthem at the third game of the World Series between the Cleveland Indians and the Atlanta Braves at Jacobs Field, Cleveland.
[14] Reissued *Kid* charts for a week at UK #73.
[17] Documentary "The Pretenders : No Turn Left Unstoned" airs on C4-TV.
[28] The Pretenders performs at the ninth annual Bridge School Benefit concert held at the Shoreline Amphitheatre, Mountain View, CA, with Bruce Springsteen, Neil Young, Hootie & the Blowfish and Blind Melon, among others.
Nov [2] Hynde guest-stars on NBC-TV's "Friends".
[3] She appears on CBS-TV's "Late Show With David Letterman".
[4] Produced by Stephen Street and comprising effortless acoustic reworkings of the group's career highlights recorded live in June, ***The Isle Of View*** reaches UK #23.
[5] The Pretenders play the second of two sellouts at the Symphony Space, New York, NY.
[18] ***The Isle Of View*** makes US #100.

THE PRETTY THINGS

Phil May (vocals); **Dick Taylor** (lead guitar);
Brian Pendleton (rhythm guitar);
John Stax (bass); **Viv Prince** (drums)

1963

Dec Taylor (b. Jan. 28, 1943, Dartford, Kent), while studying at Sidcup Art College, Sidcup, Kent, with Keith Richard, has been an early member of Little Boy Blue & the Blue Boys (an embryonic Rolling Stones) the previous year, but has quit to begin a course at the Royal College of Art, as the group changes its name to Rollin' Stones and is about to turn professional. Going on to form the Pretty Things (taking the name from Bo Diddley's *Pretty Thing*) with fellow R&B devotee May (b. Nov. 9, 1944, Dartford), they add Prince (b. Aug. 9, 1944, Loughborough, Leics.), Pendleton (b. Apr. 13, 1944, Wolverhampton, Warks.) and Stax (b. John Fullegar, Apr. 6, 1944, Crayford, Kent), now signing to Fontana Records after a gig at London's Central School of Art, and in the next few months will appear on ITV's "Ready Steady Go" and feature in **The Sunday Times** color supplement.

1964

June The group creates media interest with its no-holds-barred style of R&B, a long-haired, unkempt image which takes the Rolling Stones persona one step further (May holds claim to having the longest hair on a man in Britain). Bryan Morrison and James Duncan take over the group's management while their Duncan-penned debut hit, *Rosalyn* (based on Benny Spellman's *Fortune Teller*), makes UK #41.
Nov *Don't Bring Me Down* hits UK #10 as the group's image reaches its peak of notoriety when attempts are made to evict the members from their communal home in Belgravia. Newspapers print tales of their exploits on the road and moral outrage is voiced by the establishment.

1965

Mar ***The Pretty Things*** hits UK #6, as the extracted *Honey I Need* reaches UK #13.
Apr [24] The group embarks on the second half of a Billy Fury tour at the ABC Cinema, Gloucester, Gloucs., with Brian Poole & the Tremeloes, Dave Berry and the Zephyrs, set to end on May 9th at the Colston Hall, Bristol, Somerset.
July *Cry To Me*, written by Bert Berns, reaches UK #28.
Sept The Pretty Things appear on the ABC-TV show "Shindig!" alongside the Yardbirds, Jerry Lee Lewis and Raquel Welch.
Oct [7] The group embarks on a week-long Scandinavian tour.
Nov Skip Alan (b. Alan Skipper, June 11, 1948, London), formerly with Them, replaces Prince who claims he has been asked to leave because he has been involved in so much bad publicity.
Dec ***Get The Picture*** fails to chart as the group's popularity begins to wane together with the R&B boom.

1966

Jan *Midnight To Six Man* makes UK #46.
[6] The band begins location filming on the 15-minute feature "A Day In The Life Of The Pretty Things".
May *Come See Me* makes UK #43.
July The group makes its final UK chart entry at #50 with the Ray Davies-penned *A House In The Country*.
Dec Pendleton is taken sick and the band continues as a four-piece.

1967

Apr [29] The band takes part in a 14-hour all-night "Technicolour Dream" concert in the Great Hall of Alexandra Palace, London.
May ***Emotions*** completes their contract with Fontana, with basic tracks heavily overdubbed with strings, against the group's wishes. The band then signs to EMI, and will release three singles without success. Stax leaves and is replaced by two former members of Bern Elliott's Fenmen, organist/pianist Jon Povey (b. Aug. 20, 1944, London) and bassist Wally Allen, as the group reverts to a five-piece.

1968

Mar John "Twink" Alder replaces Alan.
July The group plays a free concert in London's Hyde Park with the Nice and Traffic.
Dec Its critically-acclaimed rock opera, ***SF Sorrow***, is released. The group is now involved in London's flourishing psychedelic underground scene, far removed from its R&B origins.

1969

Jan The Pretty Things perform "SF Sorrow" in its entirety at London's Camden Roundhouse, and are also currently featured in a cameo role in the Norman Wisdom film "What's Good For The Goose".
Nov Taylor quits to become a producer with drummer Alder. (They will later work together when Alder becomes a member of the Pink Fairies.) Alan returns and Vic Unitt, from the Edgar Broughton Band, replaces Taylor. ***Parachute***, a critical success which will be voted Album Of The Year by **Rolling Stone**, will make UK #43 the following June.

1971

May The group embarks on a UK tour with the Pink Fairies.
Nov Having split in June, the Pretty Things are prompted to re-form by manager Bill Shepherd and sign to Warner Bros. Records. May, Povey and Alan are joined by Peter Tolson (b. Sept. 10, 1951, Bishops Stortford, Herts.) on guitar, Stuart Brooks on bass and Gordon Edwards (b. Dec. 26, 1946, Southport, Merseyside) on keyboards.

1973

Nov During a year in which the band tours the US for the first time, David Bowie pays homage to the group on his newly released album of cover versions, ***Pin Ups***, which includes *Rosalyn* and *Don't Bring Me Down*.

1974

Oct Newly signed to Led Zeppelin's Swan Song label, ***Torpedo*** makes US #104.
Dec Jack Green (b. Mar. 12, 1951, Glasgow, Scotland) replaces Brooks and the group undertakes a lengthy US tour.

1976

Mar [27] ***Savage Eye*** peaks at US #163.
June [18] The Pretty Things disband for a second time, when May, the only surviving original member, quits, having played a few final gigs supporting Uriah Heep and Bad Company at the Empire Pool, Wembley, Middx.
July May forms Phil May & the Fallen Angels which includes Bill Lovelady and ex-T. Rex bongo player Mickey Finn, with ex-Pretty Thing Wally Allen. The group releases an album in Holland only, where the Pretty Things still enjoy cult status. The remaining members will continue under the name Metropolis, until quitting at the end of the following year.

1980

Aug The band re-forms to work part-time, playing clubs and pubs and releases ***Cross Talk***. (During the year they will also appear performing the title theme in the Vincent Price horror movie, "The Monster Squad".)

1984

Aug The group begins a residency at a club in London's Little Venice and records the performance set, ***Live At Heartbreak Hotel***, in front of an invited audience. (During the year, members of the group provide music for an episode of the ITV series "Minder" under the name Zac Zolan & Electric Banana.)

1995

Sept [26] With their last new album, ***Out Of The Island***, recorded in Germany in 1987 and released the following year, a reunited Pretty Things have performed selected dates during the '90s, and sued both EMI, for alleged non-payment of North American royalties, and PolyGram, over its acquisition of the group's royalties collection company in the mid-'70s, in 1993. While Fontana Records has issued ***Get A Buzz : The Best Of The Fontana Years*** in 1992, Brian Pendleton, who hasn't been heard of in 30 years, now turns up at the group's latest reunion gig.

LLOYD PRICE

1952

July [12] Pianist, composer and vocalist Price (b. Mar. 9, 1933, Kenner, LA) began leading an R&B quintet in New Orleans, LA, in 1950, also writing and performing jingles and songs for local radio station, WBOK. One of these, *Lawdy Miss Clawdy*, has resulted in Price signing to Specialty Records (having been rejected by the Imperial label in favor of Fats Domino). The re-recorded seminal R&B cut, with Domino on piano, now hits US R&B #1 for the first of seven weeks (and will spawn numerous cover versions, including one by Elvis Presley). It will be followed up by two further US R&B top 5 hits, *Oooh, Oooh, Oooh* and *Restless Heart*.

1953

Feb *Ain't It A Shame* is another Top 10 R&B success before Price is drafted into the US Army, where he will form a band which entertains troops in Japan, Korea and the Far East. Prior to his service, Price advises fellow singer Little Richard to send tapes to his producer Art Rupe. Discharged from the Army in 1956, Price moves to Washington, DC, where he sets up his own Kent Record Company.

1957

Apr [18] *Just Because*, leased to ABC-Paramount, reaches US #29. Like every further chart success, except *Never Let Me Go* and *Misty*, *Just Because* is an original Price composition.
Oct [5] *Lonely Chair*, on KRC, peaks at US #88.

1959

Feb [14] On ABC-Paramount, Price's *Stagger Lee*, his R&B rewrite of the folk tune *The Ballad Of Stack-O-Lee*, hits US #1 for four weeks, also holding the top spot on the US R&B survey for the same length of time.
Mar *Stagger Lee* hits UK #7. With Bo Diddley, the Coasters, Clyde McPhatter and Little Anthony & the Imperials, Price begins a seven-week "Biggest Show Of Stars" package tour in Richmond, VA.
Apr [4] *Where Were You (On Our Wedding Day)* reaches US #23.
May *Where Were You* reaches UK #15.
June *Personality* hits UK #9 (and will re-chart at UK #25 in August).
[20] *Personality*, another US R&B chart-topper, hits US #2 for three weeks, held from the top by Johnny Horton's *The Battle Of New Orleans*.
Sept [19] *I'm Gonna Get Married* hits US #3, his final US R&B chart-topper, and makes UK #23.
Nov [21] *Wont'cha Come Home* reaches US #43.
Dec [12] Its A-side, *Come Into My Heart*, makes US #20, as Price completes a year filled with US R&B package tours and TV appearances.

1960

Mar [12] *Never Let Me Go*, the B-side of the still-climbing *Lady Luck*, peaks at US #82.
Apr [23] *Lady Luck* makes UK #45.
[26] *Lady Luck* reaches US #14.
[27] Price performs at the Lauderdale County Coliseum, Florence, AL as part of the "Biggest Show Of Stars For '60" tour, with Clyde McPhatter, Bo Diddley, the Coasters, Little Anthony & the Imperials and Jimmy Reed, among others.
May [21] *For Love* makes US #43.
June [4] Its reverse side, *No Ifs No Ands*, climbs to US #40.
Aug [13] *Question* reaches US #19.
Oct [1] *Just Call Me (And I'll Understand)* climbs to US #79.
Dec [17] *(You Better) Know What You're Doin'* peaks at US #90.

1963

Nov [16] His cover of Errol Garner's standard, *Misty*, is Price's first US Hot 100 single in almost three years, at #21. It is released on his own Double-L label, which also issues the first solo recording by Falcons' lead vocalist Wilson Pickett.

1964

Jan [25] *Billie Baby*, also on Double-L, peaks at US #84. (Price concentrates on other music business interests and investments and establishes a fund, providing black students with scholarships to attend college.) Among ongoing covers of Price material by other artists, Wilson Pickett's re-make of *Stag-O-Lee* will reach US #22 in December 1967.

1969

Price, now based in New York, NY, establishes a new label, Turntable, and opens a club of the same name, at former jazz venue Billboard. (This follows the murder of his Double-L partner Harold Lugan at their New York office - his body is found while the record player spins a Lloyd Price disc.)

1972

Mar After *Stagger Lee* has reached the US chart at #25 for a third time with Tommy Roe's cover in October the previous year, Price releases ***To The Roots And Back*** on the GSF label.

1976

Having co-promoted the three-day "Zaire 74" music festival in Zaire, Africa, with boxing promoter Don King in September of that year, Price and King now form the LPG label in New York, having unsuccessfully dabbled in Muscle Shoals soul (on Scepter) and versions of Broadway hits (on the Ludix label), and will release ***The Nominee*** in 1978.

1995

Mar [2] After Kenner City Council has renamed 4th Street, Lloyd Price Avenue on March 18th the previous year, Price now receives the Pioneer Award at the sixth annual Rhythm and Blues Foundation ceremonies held at the Hollywood Palladium, Los Angeles.

PRIMAL SCREAM

Bobby Gillespie (vocals); **Robert Young** (guitar); **Andrew Innes** (guitar); **Henry Olsen** (bass); **Tobay Toman** (drums)

1987

Oct [17] Inspired by Love, the Rolling Stones, Sly Stone, the Stooges and Johnny Thunders, the group has been formed in Glasgow, Scotland, in 1984 by Gillespie (b. June 22, 1964, Scotland), who will remain the only constant member until the line-up stabilizes by the decade's end. While Gillespie has spent much of the band's first year touring as the drummer of the Jesus & Mary Chain, Primal Scream has released its first single, *All Fall Down*, in 1985, with *Crystal Crescent* emerging the following year, both on manager Alan McGee's seminal UK alternative label Creation. Having also contributed the 80-second *Velocity Girl* to the **New Musical Express** indie compilation cassette ***C86***, the band's debut album, ***Sonic Flower Groove***, both raw and energetic and conversely moody and melodic, is released on McGee's Elevation label through WEA (a short lived arrangement), now making UK #62 for a week.

1989

Sept Experimenting with a raw guitar sound, the band's follow-up, ***Primal Scream***, and the extracted *Ivy Ivy Ivy*, are released on Creation, becoming fixtures on the UK Independent chart.

1990

Mar Shifting direction once again, having become involved in the dance club scene (notably at Shoom) and linking with emerging producer Andy Weatherall, the hedonistic rock/dance crossover anthem *Loaded*, written by Gillespie, Innes and Young, reaches UK #16.
Aug Follow-up, *Come Together*, makes UK #26.

1991

Apr Following a winter of non-stop partying, the band begins recording an album which will take six weeks to complete.
June [22] Blues-tinged *Higher Than The Sun*, mixed by the Orb, makes UK #40 as the group undertakes its first UK tour in 18 months, its line-up augmented by Boys Own's Hugo Nicolson, ex-Felt keyboardist Martin Duffy, vocalist Denise Johnson and DJs Weatherall and the Orb.
Aug [24] *Don't Fight It Feel It* debuts at its UK #41 peak.
Oct [5] Fusing '90s dance energy with a late '60s psychedelic rock style, ***Screamadelica*** hits UK #8 upon release.

1992

Feb [15] EP *Dixie-Narco* reaches UK #11.
Sept [8] Amid chaotic scenes, Primal Scream receives the Mercury Music Prize for ***Screamadelica*** from George Martin at the inaugural dinner held at

London's Savoy Hotel.
Nov [28] The group headlines the "Miners Benefit Trust Concert" at the Sheffield Arena, Sheffield, Yorks, having returned from recording sessions in Nashville, TN.

1994

Mar [12] *Rocks*, coupled with the George Clinton mix of *Funky Jam*, debuts at its UK #7 peak. (Prior to its release, the band has junked an estimated 100,000 sleeves because of a printing error.)
[24] The group, now comprising Gillespie, Innes, Young, Duffy and Johnson, embarks on a 15-date UK and Irish tour (its first the miners' benefit concert in 1992) at the Ulster Hall, Belfast, Northern Ireland, set to end on April 11th at Brighton Event, Brighton, East Sussex.
Apr [9] ***Give Out, But Don't Give Up***, produced by George Drakoulias after unsuccessful sessions with Tom Dowd and Jimmy Miller, hits UK #2 in its week of entry, behind Pink Floyd's ***The Division Bell***.
May [17] Primal Scream plays at The Aladdin, Las Vegas, NV, at the start of a US tour supporting Depeche Mode, set to end on July 8th at the Deer Creek Music Center, Noblesville, IN.
June [18] *Jailbird* bows at its UK #29 peak.
July [30] They play on the first day of a two-day festival at Strathclyde Park in Glasgow.
Aug [27] The group plays on the second day of the annual "Reading Festival", Reading, Berks.
Dec [10] *(I'm Gonna) Cry Myself Blind* debuts at its UK #49 high, as they play the second of two gigs at Glasgow Barrowlands, Glasgow, Strathclyde, Scotland, at the end of a year which has seen the group play 110 dates.

1995

Jan [22] The band performs at the "Big Day Out" at the Royal Showgrounds, Melbourne, Victoria, Australia.
Spending much of the year preparing its fifth album, a new cut by the group will emerge on the film soundtrack to "Trainspotting", released at year's end.

PRINCE/♀

1970

Prince (b. Prince Rogers Nelson, June 7, 1958, Minneapolis, MN), named after the Prince Rogers Trio, led by his jazz-pianist father John Nelson and occasionally featuring his mother Mattie as a vocalist, began teaching himself the piano and performed in school talent shows, and was taken by his step-father, Hayward Baker, to see James Brown in concert in 1968, a seminal musical experience which will permeate into Prince's own recordings and live performances as an adult artist. Now at age 12, Prince, experiencing problems with his step-father, runs away from home and drifts, sometimes staying with his father (who buys him a guitar which he teaches himself to play). He is eventually adopted by the Anderson family, whose son André (later André Cymone) becomes a close friend and future musical collaborator. Prince begins writing songs and starts to play saxophone, drums and bass guitar, eventually mastering over two dozen instruments.

1972

Drummer Charles Smith, a cousin, invites Prince to play guitar, with Cymone on bass, in his junior high school-based band, Grand Central, which also has Cymone's sister Linda on keyboards. Their repertoire is mainly current hit covers, which Prince arranges.

1973

Prince attends Minneapolis Central High School, where fellow students include Mark Brown (later bassist Brown Mark) and Terry Lewis (later of Time). Grand Central becomes Champagne, Morris Day replaces Smith on drums, and Prince becomes the band's leader, although most of his own songs fall flat with audiences. His writing influences include, alongside several major R&B names, folk-singer Joni Mitchell.

1974

Even before he leaves school at 16, Prince and his cohorts have developed their own Minneapolis musical scene and sound, known to its young adherents as "Uptown", around Prince's outfit Flyte Tyme, which includes drummer Jellybean Johnson, bassist Terry Lewis and singer Alexander O'Neal. (The influential "Minneapolis Sound" of the '80s is rooted here.)

1976

Prince is invited to play guitar on sessions at Sound 80 studios in Minneapolis by Brooklyn artist Pepe Willie, produced by Motown's Hank Cosby, and also featuring Colonel Abrams. (This is the source of the instrumental out-takes album, ***The Minneapolis Genius : 94 East***, released in 1986 by Willie on the Hot Pink label.)
Meanwhile, a demo tape is produced by sound engineer Chris Moon, who recognizes Prince's talent and teaches him studio technique in return for half the proceeds from items on which they collaborate, mainly lengthy funk workouts on sexual themes.
June While Prince heads for New York to seek a recording deal, Moon's demo attracts the attention of Minneapolis businessman Owen Husney.
Sept Prince returns to Minneapolis, and Husney forms the management company American Artists with attorney Gary Levinson. Convincing Prince to mould his songs into a more accessible form, he puts up money for the recording of high-quality demos.

1977

Mar Record company negotiations start from the premise that Prince will produce himself. After a studio audition, Warner Bros. Records offers a long-term contract.

1978

Nov His debut album, ***For You***, which has taken five months to produce (and used double the money advanced by Warner for three albums), is almost entirely written, sung and played by Prince, with synthesizers heavily featured, and peaks at US #163.
[25] The extracted *Soft & Wet* (a title many radio stations are wary of), reaches US #92 and US R&B #12, selling almost 350,000 copies, mainly in the R&B market. (Its follow-up, *Just As Long As We're Together*, also from the album, fails to chart.)

1979

Jan At Minneapolis' Capri Theatre (and chiefly to assembled Warner executives), Prince debuts the band he has formed after completing the first album (with Cymone on bass, keyboard player Gayle Chapman and drummer Bobby Z, plus rock guitarist Dez Dickerson and keyboardist Matt Fink, the result fusing rock and funk styles).
Feb Prince leaves Husney and American Artists, turning variously and unsatisfactorily for management to Hollywood-based Perry Jones and Bob Marley's ex-manager, Don Taylor, before his Warner-appointed agent, Steve Fargnoli, introduces him to Cavallo & Ruffalo (managers of Earth, Wind & Fire and Ray Parker Jr.).
June Recording begins for a new album which this time will be completed in six weeks.
Oct ***Prince*** peaks at US #22, initially selling half a million copies. From it comes another R&B (but not crossover) hit (#13), *Why You Wanna Treat Me So Bad?*, and also contains *I Feel For You* (which Chaka Khan will revive for a UK #1 and US #3 hit in 1984).
Dec [1] The extracted *I Wanna Be Your Lover* tops the R&B chart for the first of two weeks.

1980

Jan Prince tangles with Motown funk artist Rick James while supporting him on a US tour.
[26] *I Wanna Be Your Lover* reaches US #11 and his UK chart debut at #41.
Feb Chapman leaves and is replaced by Lisa Coleman (daughter of Los Angeles session veteran Gary Coleman), who has auditioned via a demo (and will stay with Prince for six years).
[9] Prince performs a showcase in Minneapolis, but the venue is far from full and reactions to his overtly sexual stage antics are mixed.
[21] ***Prince*** is certified platinum by the RIAA.
Mar Always a prolific songwriter, often creating tracks on his Fender Telecaster guitar, Prince begins recording another album, a rough-edged, mostly solo affair cut on his own 16-track equipment, which emerges as ***Dirty Mind***.
[18] *I Wanna Be Your Lover* is certified gold by the RIAA.
Dec After being remixed in Los Angeles, ***Dirty Mind*** makes US #45. It breaks Prince to a wider audience but is criticized by some as being too sexual, particularly on cuts like *Head* and *Sister*. From it, *Uptown* hits US R&B #5, but fails to cross over.

1981

Jan Prince and his backing band, soon to be known as the Revolution, begin to tour widely in the US.
June [2] Prince makes his British debut at London's Lyceum Ballroom. The attendance is poor and the rest of the tour is cancelled. (He will not play in the UK again for five years.)
On returning to the US, Cymone quits the band for solo projects. (He will sign with American Artists and will release two albums, before concentrating on production.)
July Warner Bros. release an eponymous album by Minneapolis group Time, with all songs credited to Jamie Starr, an early Prince pseudonym. The album had originated when Prince invited Morris Day to sing over six tracks he had already completed. The band has been formed only after the album was completed and includes former Flyte Tyme members Lewis and Johnson, plus keyboardists Jimmy Jam and Monte Moir. (The members will later pay tribute to Prince's role as motivator in shaping the group.)
Nov [21] *Controversy*, the extracted title track from his forthcoming album, peaks at US #70. (Another cut, *Let's Work* hits R&B #9, but fails to cross over.)
Time backs Prince on his US tour.
Dec Prince's fourth album, ***Controversy***, reaches US #21.

1982

Mar He buys a mansion in suburban Minneapolis, where he will permanently reside.
Oct A six-month tour begins in support of ***1999***. It is a Minneapolis revue, with Prince & the Revolution following Time and Prince's new all-girl group, Vanity 6 (blonde Bostonian Brenda Bennett, Canadian Dee Dee Winters aka Vanity, and 16-year-old Minneapolis native, Susan Moonsie).
Dec The title track, *1999*, makes US #44. The double album begins a slow US chart rise (but will be a major seller during 1983). Although Prince has played and produced most of its tracks, the album is credited to Prince & the Revolution for the first time.

1983

Jan Prince is added to the white act-dominated MTV playlist with his video for *Little Red Corvette*, from ***1999***. Always uneasy with interviews, he begins almost blanket press silence, which he will always maintain.
Feb ***1999*** finally picks up momentum, aided by wide exposure for *Little Red Corvette*, now issued as a single.
[12] *1999* makes UK #25. However, the tour does not go well. Time, despite a successful second album, ***What Time Is It?*** (which has reached US #26), is relegated to backing Vanity 6 from behind a curtain, while Jam and Lewis are fired by Prince after missing a show (through being stranded by snow in Atlanta, GA, where they were producing the S.O.S. Band).
Apr The tour finishes and Prince begins work on a film with Hollywood scriptwriter William Blinn, while UCLA film graduate, Albert Magnoli, is brought to Minneapolis to discuss directing the

project. Dickerson leaves the Revolution, and is replaced by Wendy Melvoin (daughter of session keyboardist Mike Melvoin), who will also appear in the film. Prince cancels already-scheduled sellout dates at London's Dominion Theatre.
May [21] *Little Red Corvette* hits US #6, while ***1999*** finally hits US #9, and will stay on the chart for more than two years.
[28] *Little Red Corvette* makes UK #54.
July [23] Title song, *1999*, re-charts at US #12.
Aug Prince premieres some of his forthcoming project, ***Purple Rain***, at the First Avenue club in Minneapolis.
Oct [22] *Delirious*, the third single from the album, hits US #8.
Nov Filming of "Purple Rain" begins (and will take seven weeks, at a cost of $7 million). Wendy and Lisa begin contributing as a songwriting team as part of the project. *Purple Rain*, *Baby I'm A Star* and *I Would Die 4 U* are recorded live at the First Avenue club, where the movie's performance scenes are filmed.
[26] Reissued *Little Red Corvette* peaks at #66.

1984

Jan [28] Double A-side, *Let's Pretend We're Married /Irresistible Bitch*, climbs to US #52.
June [20] *Dirty Mind* is certified gold by the RIAA.
July [7] Recorded at Sunset Sound Studio, Los Angeles, the self-penned, self-produced *When Doves Cry*, taken from the forthcoming movie and album ***Purple Rain***, gives Prince his first chart-topper, hitting US #1 for the first of five weeks (it will be the biggest-selling single of 1984).
[27] Semi-autobiographical "Purple Rain" opens nationwide in the US (and in Britain four days later), its plot taking romantic liberties with Prince's past, his relationship with his parents and his rise through the Minneapolis scene. It is well received despite its cast of non-actors, and takes $60 million in two months at the US box office.
[28] In the UK, it is also his biggest success to date, hitting #4.
Aug [4] Soundtrack album, ***Purple Rain***, produced, arranged, composed and performed by Prince & the Revolution, begins a 24-week run atop the US chart (eventually selling over ten million domestic copies) and will hit UK #7, one of the decade's best-selling albums.
[21] *When Doves Cry* is certified gold by the RIAA.
Sept [29] *Let's Go Crazy*, also from ***Purple Rain***, tops the US chart for the first of two weeks (but is not issued in Britain at this time).
Oct [6] Title song, the anthemic ballad *Purple Rain* hits UK #8.
Nov [17] *Purple Rain* hits US #2.
Nov A 100-date US tour gets underway. (By the time it ends in April 1985 over 1,692,000 tickets will have been sold while throughout the schedule Prince plays unpublicized free concerts for handicapped children.) The two-hour show features his latest protegée, percussionist/singer Sheila E. (daughter of Santana percussionist Pete Escovedo, and introduced to Prince by Carlos Santana), with whom he has already recorded ***The Glamorous Life*** in June 1984.
[7] *Let's Go Crazy* is certified gold by the RIAA.

1985

Jan [5] *I Would Die 4 U* makes UK #58.
[11] His 1981 album ***Controversy*** is confirmed platinum by the RIAA.
[26] Double A-side, *1999/Little Red Corvette*, becomes Prince's most successful UK single to date, hitting #2 (behind Elaine Paige and Barbara Dickson's *I Know Him So Well*), while ***1999*** makes UK #30.
[28] Prince wins the Favorite Single, Soul/R&B, Favorite Album, Soul/R&B, and Favorite Album, Pop /Rock categories at the 12th annual American Music Awards, held at the Shrine Auditorium, Los Angeles. Although expected to join the all-star session for USA For Africa's *We Are The World*, recorded after the Awards ceremony, he declines on the grounds that he does not record with other acts - but offers to donate an exclusive track (*4 The Tears In Your Eyes*) to the follow-up benefit album, ***We Are The World***.
Feb [2] *I Would Die 4 U*, also from the movie, hits US #8 (and continues the artist's preference for using numbers and single letters in place of words in both song titles and reprinted sleeve lyrics).
[11] Prince is named Best International Solo Artist, and ***Purple Rain*** wins the Best Film Soundtrack category at the fourth annual BRIT Awards, held at London's Grosvenor House Hotel.
Mar [2] Prince wins the Best Group Rock Vocal Performance category for *Purple Rain* and R&B Song Of The Year for *I Feel For You* at the 27th annual Grammy Awards.
[9] *Take Me With You*, issued as a double A-side with *Let's Go Crazy*, hits UK #7.
[23] *Take Me With You*, duetted with another female protegée, Apollonia (who replaces Vanity, to lead Apollonia 6) reaches US #25, and is the only single from ***Purple Rain*** not to hit the US Top 10. It is bettered by Scottish singer Sheena Easton's *Sugar Walls*, which Prince has written for her under the pseudonym Alexander Nevermind, hitting US #9.
[25] Prince wins the Best Original Score Oscar for "Purple Rain" at the Academy Awards.
June [1] ***Around The World In A Day*** tops the US chart for the first of three weeks and hits UK #5. The album has evolved from rehearsals for Prince's next tour, and has been recorded at the newly-built Paisley Park studios at his Minneapolis HQ, the Warehouse. In contrast to its predecessor, it is released with minimal promotion, and Prince reportedly has to be persuaded by Warner Bros. into releasing singles from it. Tracks include the spiritual *The Ladder* (co-written with his father) and *Temptation*, which purportedly features a conversation with God. Prince instructs Fargnoli to announce that he is retiring from live performance. Paisley Park, his studio complex and also now the name of his label, will become the center of Prince-orchestrated projects and acts, including the Family (featuring his regular sax player, Eric Leeds and Susannah Melvoin) and Madhouse (a jazzy project, also featuring Leeds), in addition to independent protegées including Sheila E. and Jill Jones.
Prince visits Paris, France, to plan and write songs for a new movie, after which he and Fargnoli travel to the South of France to schedule shooting for his next film, "Under The Cherry Moon". When work starts, Prince relegates director Mary Lambert to an advisory role, and takes full control.
[29] *Paisley Park* reaches UK #18.
July [2] The RIAA certifies two million sales of ***Around The World In A Day***.
[20] The first US extract from ***Around The World In A Day***, *Raspberry Beret*, hits US #2 (behind Duran Duran's *A View To A Kill*), and is the first single released on his own Paisley Park imprint.
[22] ***1999*** is confirmed multi-platinum by the RIAA for sales of three million.
Aug [17] *Raspberry Beret* makes UK #25.
Sept [21] *Pop Life*, from ***Around The World In A Day***, hits US #7. Prince breaks his press silence to talk to Neal Karlen for **Rolling Stone**, though the interview, vetted by Prince and his management, is largely unrevealing.
Oct [26] *Pop Life* peaks at UK #60.
Nov [2] *America*, a further single from the album, stops at US #46.

1986

Mar [22] *Kiss* hits UK #6.
Apr [5] *Kiss* tops the US R&B survey.
[19] *Kiss*, its video directed by Rebecca Blake, taken from the forthcoming movie and soundtrack album, ***Parade***, heads the US chart for the first of two weeks. Behind it at #2 is *Manic Monday* by the Bangles, written by Prince under the pseudonym Christopher Tracy.
May ***Parade - Music From Under The Cherry Moon*** hits US #3 and UK #4. Prince decides to return to live work and the "Parade" tour is launched, with a big band, and dazzling choreography replacing technoflash, and a greater R&B emphasis. Reviews are ecstatic.
[5] *Kiss* is certified gold by the RIAA.
June Lisa Barber, a Sheridan, WY motel chambermaid, is the 10,000th caller to an MTV contest number. She wins a date with Prince to attend the premiere of "Under The Cherry Moon" in her hometown.
[3] ***Parade*** is confirmed platinum by the RIAA.
[7] Prince's birthday show in Detroit is filmed.
[14] *Mountains*, written by Wendy and Lisa and taken from ***Parade***, makes UK #45.
July [1] "Under The Cherry Moon" film premieres in Sheridan. Barber tells Prince she enjoys the movie. After the showing, at the party at the Holiday Inn, Prince plays an impromptu 45-minute set.
[2] "Under The Cherry Moon" opens nationwide at 941 US theatres.
[5] *Mountains* reaches US #23.
Aug Prince submits a song to one of his long-time favorite artists, Joni Mitchell, but she finds it unsuitable and declines to record it.
[9] *Anotherloverholenyohead*, from ***Parade***, peaks at US #63.
[12-14] Prince plays three sellout nights at Wembley Arena, Wembley, Middx., his first UK dates in five years. (These are among his final live appearances with the Revolution, which he will disband before the end of the year.)
[23] UK-only issued *Girls And Boys* reaches #11.
Sept [15] "Raspberry Beret" wins the Best Choreography category at the third annual MTV Video Music Awards broadcast simultaneously from the Universal Amphitheatre, Universal City, CA, and The Palladium, New York.
Nov [8] *Anotherloverholenyohead* makes UK #36.

1987

Mar Prince prepares a new stage show, recruiting musicians and dancers. He retains Fink, Leeds, Greg Brooks and Wally Safford from the Revolution, recalls Sheila E. and adds guitarist Mico Weaver, keyboardist Boni Boyer, bassist Seacer and dancer/singer Cat Glover.
[28] *Sign O' The Times* UK #10.
Apr [11] Stark, urban-themed *Sign O' The Times* tops the US R&B chart, as ***Sign O' The Times*** hits UK #4 in its week of entry.
[25] *Sign O' The Times* hits US #3, as rehearsals for a European tour take place at the National Exhibition Centre, Birmingham, West Midlands.
May Double album, ***Sign O' The Times***, as ever produced, arranged, composed and performed by Prince, hits US #6.
June [20] *If I Was Your Girlfriend*, on which Prince's alter-ego "Camille" is credited with lead vocal, makes US #67, as the European tour begins.
July Prince's two Wembley Stadium dates are cancelled. The official reason given is poor weather (and hoped-for alternative dates at the indoor Earl's Court arena cannot be arranged in time), but rumors cite inter-promoter politics as a factor. No attempt is made to stage the "Sign O' The Times" tour in the US (because, it is assumed, of the large costs involved), but a movie of the same title, largely consisting of the tour show as filmed in Rotterdam, Holland, serves as a substitute for both US and UK audiences. (It will also be issued as a home video.)
[2] ***Sign O' The Times*** is certified platinum by the RIAA.
[4] *If I Was Your Girlfriend* reaches UK #20.
Sept [5] *U Got The Look*, a duet from ***Sign O' The Times*** with Sheena Easton, and aided by a steamy performance video clip (rumors of a romantic liaison between them persist), hits US #2.
[11] He performs at the fourth annual MTV Video Music Awards held at the Universal Amphitheatre.
Oct [17] *U Got The Look* reaches UK #11.
Dec [5] *I Could Never Take The Place Of Your Man*, another track from ***Sign O' The Times***, reaches UK #29. Meanwhile, the music press runs stories concerning a mysterious Prince album, featuring back-to-his-roots raw sex and funk tracks, which he is apparently asking Warner to rush out on their carefully-planned Christmas release schedules. Label staff admit to

knowing less about the project than the press, but rumors persist that Prince wants the album released in plain black sleeves with no recording credits.

1988

Jan [1] Prince performs an after-midnight concert to benefit the Minnesota Coalition for the Homeless, joined on stage by Miles Davis. Wendy and Lisa's ***Sideshow*** is released by Virgin Records. The ***Black Album***, as it will become known, fails to officially materialize. Several thousand are pressed in Europe and, when the recall notice comes, 100 copies slip out of WEA Records' German pressing plant. These (directly or via a German radio broadcast) and advance promo cassettes, are the sources for a flood of ***Black Album*** bootlegs. The album is a series of hardcore erotic funk out-takes; track listing is: *Le Grind, Cindy C, Dead On It, When 2 R In Love, Bob George, Supercalifragisexi, 2 Nigs United 4 West Compton* and *Hard Rock In A Funky Place*.
Feb [6] *I Could Never Take The Place Of Your Man* hits US #10.
[20] Its B-side, *Hot Thing*, peaks at US #63.
May [14] *Alphabet St.*, from the album (which is announced as definitely not being the ***Black Album***), hits UK #9.
[21] ***Lovesexy***, an unlikely blend of sexy R&B and spiritual concerns, becomes his first UK chart-topper and is heading for US #11. It also concerns itself with the "battle" between Camille (the good or positive side of Prince's personality) and Spooky Electric (the bad). A Prince-penned Warner press release suggests that the ***Black Album*** was Spooky Electric's idea, but that Camille won over and stopped the "evil" record. (Some critics suggest that the whole business of the mystery album was merely an elaborate pre-release scam for ***Lovesexy***.) Meanwhile, Prince's sister, Tyka Nelson, signs to Chrysalis Records, and releases an album, to little interest.
June [25] *Alphabet St.* hits US #8.
July The "Lovesexy" tour begins in Paris, France, and includes seven nights at Wembley Arena. In a return to a flashier stage style, Prince enters the circular stage on an out-size pink Cadillac. His latest female cohort, Cat, disrobes him on a neon bed and then ties him to a chair. (After some of the gigs, Prince adjourns to small clubs, where he performs an additional late-night three-hour set for invited guests.)
[23] *Glam Slam*, from ***Lovesexy***, reaches UK #29.
Aug [9] His "Prince And The Revolution" video reaches the the RIAA-certified 100,000 sales plateau.
Sept [7] "U Got The Look" wins the Best Male Video and Best Stage Performance categories at the fifth annual MTV Video Music Awards, held again at the Universal Amphitheatre.
[14] A 20-date US tour, Prince's first in four years, starts at the Met Center, Bloomington, MN, set to end in Worcester, MA, on October 22nd. (Prince will play a benefit concert in Boston, MA, to establish a scholarship in the name of 17-year-old Frederick Weber, who was killed when hit by an automobile while waiting in line for Prince concert tickets outside Boston's Tower Records store.)
Nov [19] *I Wish U Heaven*, from ***Lovesexy***, reaches UK #24. Prince ends the year collaborating with other artists, working with Sheena Easton, duetting with Madonna on her forthcoming album and signing George Clinton to Paisley Park (having helped pay off the latter's tax bill).
Dec [5] ***Lovesexy*** is certified gold by the RIAA.

1989

Jan [10] "Sign O' The Times" video is confirmed platinum by the RIAA.
[23] Dave Hill's biography, **Prince : A Pop Life**, is published in Britain.
Apr Prince's half-sister, Lorna Nelson, loses a court battle insisting that he stole her lyrics for use in *U Got The Look.*
July [1] *Batdance*, a stuttered and sampled house /dance cut, including dialog snippets from the forthcoming film "Batman" by its stars Michael Keaton and Jack Nicholson, hits UK #2, behind Soul II Soul's *Back To Life*.
Aug [5] *Batdance*, the first cut from the Prince-composed and produced soundtrack which forms part of the massive multi-entertainment Warner Bros. project, based around the summer's hot movie, hits US #1, and is the third Prince US #1 as a performer. Its parent album, ***Batman***, is also in its third of six weeks at US #1, having already hit UK #1 on July 1st.
[11] *Batdance* is certified platinum by the RIAA.
[29] The RIAA confirms two million sales of ***Batman***.
Sept [16] Follow-up, *Partyman*, reaches UK #14.
[24] Prince opens the 15th anniversary NBC-TV "Saturday Night Live" special.
Oct [7] *Partyman* reaches US #18.
Nov [8] *Partyman* is certified gold by the RIAA.
Dec [16] Further ***Batman*** extract, *The Arms Of Orion*, a duet with Easton, makes US #36, having already made UK #27 on the 2nd. (By year's end, Prince will have begun work on his next film project, "Graffiti Bridge", written and produced an album, released on Paisley Park, for Mavis Staples, and completed further production work for Morris Day, Jerome Benton and even rumored-to-be short-term belle, "Batman" actress Kim Basinger.)

1990

Jan [22] Prince is honored with the Special Award Of Achievement at the 17th annual American Music Awards, held at the Shrine Auditorium.
Feb [3] *Nothing Compares 2 U*, Sinead O'Connor's cover of a Prince-penned track which was featured on a 1985 album by Paisley Park act the Family, tops the UK chart (and will hit US #1 on April 21st before winning a batch of awards).
[18] ***Batman*** is named Best Soundtrack at the ninth annual BRIT Awards held at London's Dominion Theatre.
Apr [30] He previews his forthcoming "Nude Tour" at the 650-ticket Rupert's Nightclub in Golden Valley, Minneapolis, with the $100-a-head proceeds going to the family of his former bodyguard, Charles "Big Chick" Huntsberry, who died on April 2nd of heart failure at age 49.
June [19] The 17-date UK leg of his "Nude Tour" tour opens with 16 sellout shows, before crowds totalling 184,000, at Wembley Arena, set to end on August 24th.
Aug Prince files a civil lawsuit against promoter Francesco Sanavio of Avantguarde for breach of contract concerning alleged non-payment for his shows in Italy.
[11] *Thieves In The Temple* hits UK #7.
[30] The Japanese leg of his world tour begins, set to end on September 10th.
Sept [1] ***Graffiti Bridge*** tops the UK chart.
[22] *Thieves In The Temple* and ***Graffiti Bridge*** both hit US #6.
Oct [2] *Thieves In The Temple* is certified gold by the RIAA.
[6] Minneapolis Mayor Don Fraser declares "Prince Day", though the star is reported to be in Los Angeles.
Nov [1] ***Graffiti Bridge*** is certified gold by the RIAA, as the movie premieres in New York.
[17] *New Power Generation* peaks at US #64 and UK #26.

1991

Jan [6] Prince premieres his latest backing band, the New Power Generation: Tony M (rapper), Rosie Gaines (six octave range singer), Michael Bland (drums), Levi Seacer Jr. (guitar), Kirk Johnson (guitar), Damon Dickson (dancer), Sonny T (bass) and Tommy Barbarella (keyboards) at the Glam Slam club in Minneapolis.
[18] Prince performs at the opening night of the "Rock In Rio II" festival at the Maracana soccer stadium in Rio de Janeiro, Brazil, before an estimated crowd of 60,000.
Feb [1] Having been fired in 1988, Prince's ex-managers Joseph Ruffalo, Robert Cavallo and Steve Fargnoli, bring a lawsuit against their former boss in Los Angeles Superior Court, suing for severance pay and punitive damages, claiming he owes them $600,000.
Mar [7] Prince is named Best Songwriter in the annual **Rolling Stone** Readers' Picks music awards.
[23] Elisa Fiorillo's *Oooh This I Need*, written and produced by Prince, peaks at US #90.
Apr [13] From "Graffiti Bridge", teen-star Tevin Campbell reaches US #12 with the Prince-penned and produced *Round And Round*.
Aug [15] ABC-TV airs "The International Special Olympics All-Star Gala" special, at which Prince sings *Diamonds And Pearls* and *Baby I'm A Star*.
[31] ***Gett Off*** import reaches UK #33.
Sept [5] Prince performs *Gett Off* at the eighth annual MTV Video Music Awards, held at the Universal Amphitheatre.
[7] *Gett Off*, the accompanying video directed by Randee St. Nicholas, hits UK #4.
[9] Prince guests on syndicated TV's "The Arsenio Hall Show".
[28] *Cream* reaches UK #15.
Oct [12] ***Diamonds And Pearls***, recorded with the New Power Generation, debuts at its UK #2 peak behind Simply Red's ***Stars***. *Gett Off* reaches US #21.
[23] *Gett Off* is certified gold by the RIAA.
Nov DC Comics publish the first **Prince** comic.
[9] Smooth sex-filled R&B swinger *Cream* becomes his fifth US chart-topper as ***Diamonds And Pearls*** hits US #3.
[13] "Gett Off" video is certified gold by the RIAA.
Dec [6] Steve Fargnoli files a $5 million suit in Los Angeles Superior Court alleging the track *Jughead* is about him.
[7] Title cut *Diamonds And Pearls* bows at its UK #25 peak.
[13] BBC1-TV airs the documentary, "Omnibus - The Prince of Paisley Park".

1992

Jan [11] *Insatiable* peaks at US #77. Prince plays a surprise two-hour gig at the Glam Slam Club previewing his upcoming tour.
[16] *Cream* is certified gold by the RIAA.
[30] The RIAA also confirms two million sales of ***Diamonds And Pearls***.
Feb [12] Prince is again named Best International Artist at the 11th annual BRIT Awards, held at London's Hammersmith Odeon.
Apr [3] His latest tour, with the New Power Generation, kicks off at the Tokyo Dome, Tokyo, Japan.
[4] *Money Don't Matter 2 Night*, its video directed by Spike Lee, reaches UK #19.
[24] Prince plays the first of six sellout concerts at the Sydney Entertainment Centre, Sydney, New South Wales, Australia, before 66,222 people.
May [16] *Money Don't Matter 2 Night* reaches US #23, its profits being donated to the United Negro College Fund.
[22] "Thunder", an 18-minute ballet by the Joffrey Ballet, based on *Thunder* from ***Diamond And Pearls*** premieres in Los Angeles.
June [15-17, 19-24] Prince performs at London's Earls Court during the UK leg of his current tour.
[27] *Thunder* debuts at its UK #28 peak.
July [25] *Sexy MF* stops at US #66. *Sexy MF/Strollin'*, banned by all radio stations in the UK, hits UK #4.
Sept [9] "Cream" wins the Best Dance Video category at the ninth annual MTV Video Music Awards, held at the Pauley Pavilion, Los Angeles, at which he also performs the song.
Oct [17] ♀ enters the UK chart at #1 and will earn a platinum disc for 300,000 sales. The self-proclaiming *My Name Is Prince* hits UK #7.
[24] *My Name Is Prince* makes US #36.
[31] ♀ debuts at its US #5 pinnacle.
Nov [14] *My Name Is Prince (Remixes)* charts for a week at UK #51.
Dec [12] *7* reaches UK #27.
[17] ♀ is certified platinum by the RIAA.

1993

Jan [27] The Joffrey Ballet's "Billboards" opens at the University of Iowa's Hancher Auditorium, Iowa City,

IA. (There will be four sold out shows at Chicago's Civic Opera House on March 16th-21st.)
Feb [16] He wins the Best International Solo Artist category at the 12th annual BRIT Awards, held at the Alexandra Palace, London.
[25] Prince is jostled onstage at a taping of "The Arsenio Hall Show", after he invites audience members to join him after singing *The Max*.
[27] *7* hits US #7.
Mar [8-9] Having played a two-hour warm-up show at his new Glam Slam club in Los Angeles earlier in the week, Prince kicks off his first North American tour in five years at the Sunrise Musical Theatre, Sunrise, FL, a ten-city trek backed by the NPG, before two sellout crowds of 7,589 paying $267,068.
[10] *7* is certified gold by the RIAA.
[13] *The Morning Papers* debuts at its UK #52 peak.
[24-26] Prince performs for a sellout crowd of 17,188 at New York's Radio City Music Hall.
[27] He performs for the first time at the famed Apollo Theatre in Harlem, New York, before a specially invited audience of under-privileged children's groups from the local community.
Apr [27] Reach Media Relations Inc., his PR firm, issues a statement that Prince is retiring from studio recordings to concentrate on theatre, film and other ventures.
May [15] *The Morning Papers* makes US #44.
June [7] On his 35th birthday, Prince announces he is changing his name to ♀, leaving the media to subsequently refer to him as the Artist Formerly Known As Prince.
July [26] UK leg of European summer tour opens at the National Indoor Arena, Birmingham, W. Midlands.
Sept [25] Career compilations ***The Hits/The B Sides*** and ***The Hits 1*** debut at their respective UK #4 and #5 peaks.
Oct [2] *Pink Cashmere* makes US #50, as ***The Hits/The B Sides*** and ***The Hits 1*** debut at their US #19 and #46 peaks.
[9] ***The Hits 2*** hits UK #5 and US #54.
[23] *Peach* reaches UK #14.
Dec [11] *Controversy* debuts at its UK #5 peak, as several US publications, including **Entertainment Weekly** and **The Village Voice**, print ads, placed by ♀, featuring his shadowed face with the plea: "Eligible bachelor seeks the most beautiful girl in the world to spend holidays with".

1994

Feb [1] Warner Bros. and Paisley Park Enterprises release a statement announcing the end of their joint venture.
[11] ♀'s new single, *The Most Beautiful Girl In The World*, receives its premiere on CBS-TV's "Miss USA Pageant".
[13] 600-strong crowd gather at Paisley Park Studios for a 70-minute set to celebrate the release of the new single.
Apr [23] *The Most Beautiful Girl In The World* tops the UK chart.
[30] *The Most Beautiful Girl In The World*, distributed through the indie Bellmark Records following the break with Warners, hits US #3.
May [4] ♀ is awarded the Outstanding Contribution to the Music Industry and sings *The Most Beautiful Girl In The World* at the sixth annual World Music Awards at the Sporting Club, Monte Carlo, Monaco.
[26] *The Most Beautiful Girl In The World* is certified gold by the RIAA.
June [4] *The Beautiful Experience* debuts at its UK #18 peak.
[18] *The Beautiful Experience* EP makes US #92 on the Album chart.
[26] Stevie Wonder joins ♀ onstage for *Maybe Your Baby* at the Glam Slam. (During the month, Comptons NewMedia launches ***Interactive***, ♀'s first CD-ROM, set to become one of the format's most successful titles.)
July [11] The RIAA certifies 11 million sales of ***Purple Rain***.
[12] ♀ duets with Nona Gaye on *Love Sign*, as they guest on NBC-TV's "The Tonight Show".
Aug [27] Collecting archive material under his old name, ***Come*** enters the UK album chart at the summit.
Sept [3] ***Come*** debuts at its US #15 peak.
[10] The extracted *Letitgo* bows at its UK #30 high.
[24] *Letitgo* reaches US #31.
Oct [7] ♀ flicks the switch at London's Roundhouse to launch VH1 in the UK. The first video to air is "Dolphin".
[18] ***Come*** is certified gold by the RIAA.
[25] ♀ reportedly signs an agreement letting Warners release ***The Black Album***.
Nov [24] ♀ performs *Peach* at MTV's inaugural European Music Awards, against the backdrop of the Brandenburg Gate at the Pariser Platz in Berlin, Germany.
Dec [3] The infamous ***The Black Album*** reaches UK #36 in its week of entry.
[10] ***The Black Album*** bows at its US #47 peak.
[13] ♀ previews a track from his forthcoming ***The Gold Experience*** album on CBS-TV's "Late Show With David Letterman".

1995

Jan [30] In typically flamboyant style, ♀ performs a hits medley and sucks a lollipop throughout the event finalé rendition of *We Are The World* at the 22nd annual American Music Awards, held at the Shrine Auditorium.
Feb [27] ♀ again wins the Best International Male Artist trophy at the 14th annual BRIT Awards held at London's Alexandra Palace.
Mar [3] ♀ embarks on an 11-date UK and Irish tour at Wembley Arena, set to end on the 30th at The Point, Dublin, Eire.
[18] *Purple Medley* bows at its UK #33 peak.
Apr [1] *Prince Medley* peaks at US #84.
June [17] He performs at an open-house evening with a $5 cover admission at his Paisley Park Studios in Hanhassen, MN, an event including use of a recreation center with late-night dancing and music videos.
Aug [10] The RIAA certifies platinum sales of ***The Hits I*** and ***The Hits II***.
Sept [23] *Eye Hate U* debuts at its UK #20 peak.
Oct [7] *I Hate U* reaches US #12, as ***The Gold Experience*** hits UK #4 in its week of entry.
[14] ***The Gold Experience*** debuts at its US #6 peak.
Dec [9] The extracted pop/R&B meld *Gold* bows at its UK #10 peak.
[23] *Gold* peaks at US #88.

1996

Feb [14] On Valentine's Day, longtime bachelor ♀ marries his fiancée, dancer Mayte Garcia, at a Minneapolis church (not in Paris as originally planned).
[19] ♀ is once again named Best International Male Artist at the 15th annual BRIT Awards held at London's Earl's Court Exhibition Centre.
Apr [17] The soundtrack album to Spike Lee's latest film, ***Girl 6***, comprising material by Prince & the New Power Generation, is released in the US.

JOHN PRINE

1970

Dec Prine (b. Oct. 10, 1946, Maywood, IL), learning music from visits to his grandparents in Kentucky, and introduced by his brother David to folk artists at the Earl of Oldtown folk club in Chicago, IL, recorded his first two songs, written when he was 14, *Sour Grapes* and *The Frying Pan*, along with *Twist And Shout*, on his sister-in-law's tape recorder. After graduating from high school in 1964, he worked for the US Postal Service for six years, because "you got health insurance and start accumulating great vacation time", interrupted only by being drafted into the military between January 1966 and December 1967 to serve in West Germany. Becoming a regular on the Chicago club circuit, where he meets fellow singer/songwriter Steve Goodman, he quits his job at the Post Office, now making more from playing three nights a week than he does on his round. Apparently bolstered by liquor, Prine performs at an open-mike night at the Fifth Peg club in Chicago.

1971

During the summer, Kris Kristofferson, in Chicago for a concert, goes to the Earl of Oldtown, with Paul Anka also in attendance. The club is closed but Prine does an impromptu set for Kristofferson and Anka. Shortly thereafter, Goodman and Prine are invited by Anka to New York, NY to cut some demos, also going to see Kristofferson perform at the Bitter End, who invites them up on stage. Prine sings three songs and is seen by Jerry Wexler, who talks to him in the dressing room and the next morning offers him a $25,000 recording contract with Atlantic Records. Prine has been in New York for less than 24 hours. After some consideration, Prine signs and is sent to American Recording Studios in Memphis, TN, to cut his debut album.

1972

Mar With both Prine and Goodman managed by Al Bunetta, the former releases his country/folk debut, ***John Prine***, which peaks at US #154.
Nov His sophomore effort, once again highlighted by his Dylan-esque vocal delivery, ***Diamonds In The Rough***, climbs to US #148.

1973

Dec Having completed a US tour which has included a one-week residence at Los Angeles, CA's Troubadour club, the self-penned ***Sweet Revenge***, produced by Arif Mardin and featuring session musicians David Briggs, Goodman, Cissy Houston and Ralph MacDonald among others, peaks at US #135. ***Common Sense***, cut with Steve Cropper at Ardent Studios, Memphis, will make US #66 in May 1975.

1977

Jan [22] ***Prime Prine - The Best Of John Prine*** peaks at US #196, but will eventually earn a gold disc as a strong selling catalog item. (Having bought himself out of his Atlantic contract the previous year, Prine signs a three album deal with David Geffen's Asylum Records and begins summer sessions with producer Jack Clement which come to naught.)

1978

July His Asylum debut, ***Bruised Orange***, recorded from January through March at the Chicago Recording Company and produced by Steve Goodman, peaks at US #116.

1979

Sept ***Pink Cadillac***, taped January through May at Sam Phillips' Recording Studio in Memphis and produced by his sons, Knox and Jerry Phillips, with two tracks, *Saigon* and *How Lucky*, produced by Sam himself, peaks at US #152.

1980

July [2] With his compositions increasingly in demand by other artists, *Love Is On A Roll*, written by Prine with Roger Cook, hits US Country #1 for Don Williams.
Sept ***Storm Windows***, produced by Barry Beckett at Muscle Shoals Studios, peaks at US #144. No longer with a recording deal, Prine moves to Nashville and founds his own Oh Boy label, with Dan Einstein and manager Al Bunetta.

1984

Apr Having issued *I Saw Mommy Kissing Santa Claus* on the Oh Boy label, only available by mail order and at Ernest Tubb's record store in Nashville the previous December, his Oh Boy debut album, ***Aimless Love***, featuring guest vocalist Jennifer Warnees, is released.
Sept [20] Prine's long-time cohort and friend, Steve Goodman, dies of leukaemia.

1985

Jan [26] Prine performs at a Steve Goodman tribute concert at the Arie Crown Theatre in Chicago, with David Bromberg, the Nitty Gritty Dirt Band, Bonnie Raitt, Arlo Guthrie, Richie Havens, John Hartford and others. Following the release of 1986's ***German Afternoons*** which includes *Speed Of The Sound Of Loneliness*, a Prine nugget which will be definitively covered by Nanci Griffith, Prine will issue ***John Prine Live***, mostly recorded at the Coach House in San Juan Capistrano, CA, in 1985.

1990

Nov Having scrapped earlier sessions with Keith Sykes in Memphis, Prine begins work on a new album produced by Heartbreakers bassist Howie Epstein, which will last through July the following year.

1991

Sept [16] Critically lauded ***The Missing Years*** is issued on his own Oh Boy label, including songs co-penned with Roger Cook, John Mellencamp and Mike Campbell, and guests Phil Everly, Albert Lee, David Lindley, Tom Petty, Bonnie Raitt, Bruce Springsteen and Benmont Tench. It is followed by a six-week US tour, supporting Raitt.

1992

Feb [19] Prine guests on NBC-TV's "Late Night With Davd Letterman".
[25] He wins the Best Contemporary Folk Album category for ***The Missing Years*** at the 34th annual Grammy Awards, held at New York's Radio City Music Hall.
Mar Prine appears in a cameo role (as a member of the Buzzin' Cousins group) in John Mellencamp's premiering debut motion picture, "Falling From Grace", to which he has also co-penned the cut *Take A Look At My Heart*.
July [31] Prine plays at the "Abbot Ale 28th Cambridge Folk Festival" in the Cherry Hinton Hall Grounds, Cambridge, Cambs.
Aug [16] He performs during New York's Central Park "Summer Stage '92" concert series.
Nov [11] Prine plays a one-off UK date at London's Clapham Grand. (During the year he also presents "Town And Country" for C4-TV.)

1993

Jan [26] ***The Best Of John Prine*** is certified platinum by the RIAA.
Feb Prine begins recording the follow-up to ***The Missing Years***.
Mar [4] During a brief trip to Hawaii, Prine performs at the Hawaiian Ballroom, Honolulu, HI.
June [5] Prine takes part in the "Troubadours Of Folk Music" concert with Joni Mitchell, Arlo Guthrie, Richie Havens and others, at UCLA.
Sept Arthur Alexander's tribute album ***Adios Amigo***, including a contribution by Prine, is released on Rhino.
Dec ***A John Prine Christmas*** is issued on his Oh Boy label, following the October release of a Rhino career retrospective, ***The John Prine Anthology - Great Days*** double CD.

1995

May [27] Once again highly praised by critics, ***Lost Dogs And Mixed Blessings***, again produced by Epstein and featuring guests Carlene Carter, Marianne Faithful, Sass Jordan and Waddy Wachtel among many others, makes US #159.

P.J. PROBY

1958

Proby (b. James Marcus Smith, Nov. 6, 1938, Houston, TX), after an education at military school, has moved to Los Angeles, CA, the previous year with ambitions to become a star. Taking the name Jett Powers, he has taken singing and acting lessons and picked up bit parts in B-movies and on TV. As Powers, he now records two solo singles (*Go Girl Go* and *Loud Perfume*) for small Los Angeles' labels, without commercial success. He also forms the Moondogs with Marshall Leib (later one of Phil Spector's Teddy Bears), Larry Taylor (later of Canned Heat) and Elliott Ingber (later in Frank Zappa's Mothers of Invention); despite its later credentials, this quartet achieves little. Working as a demo singer, he signs to Liberty Records the following year as a songwriter (his *Clown Shoes* will be Johnny Burnette's last UK hit in 1962). Also recording for Liberty in 1961, both as Jett Powers and as Orville Wood, a series of singles will fail to make any impression.

1963

Fellow songwriter Jackie DeShannon introduces him to UK TV producer Jack Good (of "Oh Boy!" fame), currently working in Hollywood, CA. Good earmarks him for the role of Iago in a rock version of "Othello", which he is hoping to stage with Cassius Clay in the title role, but the project flounders.

1964

Apr Good is commissioned by Brian Epstein to produce a Beatles special in London for BBC-TV, and invites Powers - now using the name P.J. Proby, which meets with Good's approval - to Britain as a guest act for the show. Good, who engineered Gene Vincent's moody black-leather image for UK TV five years earlier, moulds a startling visual appearance for Proby, with tight trousers, loose smock top, and an 18th-century-type pony-tailed hairstyle.
May [6] The show "Around The Beatles" is screened in the UK, and Proby's rocking guest slot arouses great interest. In anticipation, Good produces *Hold Me*, a 1939 ballad revived as a raucous rave-up, with Proby self-duetting in abandoned style. He sells it to Decca Records for release.
July *Hold Me* hits UK #3, rocketing Proby to stardom in Britain, where he settles, to take advantage of a flood of TV and live work.
Sept [12] Marketed in the US as part of the "British Invasion", *Hold Me* peaks at US #70.
Oct *Together*, a 1961 Top 20 hit for Connie Francis, is rocked up in similar style to *Hold Me*, with Jimmy Page, later of Led Zeppelin, on guitar, and hits UK #8. Liberty Records, to which Proby is still contracted in the US, enforces its rights and wins a court action to prevent Decca releasing further Proby material. He also transfers to Liberty in the UK. (The label has already issued *Try To Forget Her*, from his Jett Powers days, in competition with *Together*. Despite a reported large advance order figure, it failed to chart.)
[3] He records an edition of the ABC-TV show "Shindig" with the Beatles headlining at the Granville Theatre, Fulham, singing *You'll Never Walk Alone* and *Hold Me*.
Nov [6] Proby embarks on a UK tour in Edmonton.

1965

Jan His first new Liberty recording, *Somewhere*, from "West Side Story", a melodramatic arrangement with Proby in quivering, over-the-top ballad vocal form, hits UK #6.
[29] Proby begins a 22-date, twice-nightly package tour with Cilla Black, the Fourmost, Tommy Roe & the Roemans, Tommy Quickly and Sounds Incorporated at the ABC Cinema, Croydon, Surrey.
Feb [1] After Proby performs his first number during which his trousers split, the manager of the ABC Luton, Beds., draws the curtain and refunds the audience's money. Concerts at Croydon, Surrey and Walthamstow, London, also end in controversy, resulting in a near-blanket ban on Proby in UK concert halls.
[8] ABC-TV follows its theatre chain namesake with a ban on Proby screen appearances, because of the trouser-splitting incident.
[13] *Somewhere* peaks at US #91.
[24] BBC-TV bans Proby from appearing on any shows.
Mar His revival of Billy Eckstine's *I Apologise*, with another exaggeratedly dramatic vocal performance, reaches UK #11, while ***I Am P.J. Proby*** climbs to UK #16 (his only chart album).
[1] A 15-date, twice-nightly UK tour of independent theaters, where he is not banned, known as "The P.J. Show", with the Fourmost and Brian Poole & the Tremeloes, opens at Finsbury Park Astoria, London.
[9] Proby is taken ill in Manchester. Tom Jones deputises the following two nights and, when Proby fails to resume the tour, it is cancelled.
June Affected by the bans, Proby begins to lose his performing reliability and becomes eccentric off-stage, with a penchant for outrageous pronouncements to the media (he informs a **Sunday Times** interviewer that he aims to star in a movie "about a pop star who goes off his head and believes he's Jesus Christ").
July *Let The Water Run Down*, in rocking R&B style, reaches UK #19.
[23] Proby announces he will not appear on ITV's "Ready Steady Go!" again, after he is faded out in the middle of his second number on the show.
Oct A Lennon/McCartney ballad, *That Means A Lot*, reaches UK #30.
Nov [6] Proby splits with his manager of a year, John Heyman.
[10] He signs a management deal with Bertie Green and Mel Collins (which will be ended by mutual agreement within a week).
[29] Tito Burns becomes Proby's agent.
Dec His straight and sensitive version of *Maria*, from "West Side Story", hits UK #8.
[4] Proby's work permit expires, and shortly afterwards he is told to leave his Chelsea house when his lease runs out, after complaints from neighbors.

1966

Feb *You've Come Back* makes UK #25.
Mar Proby refuses to enter the recording studio until a royalty dispute he has with Liberty is settled.
[12] He begins a six-date, twice-nightly farewell UK tour with the Searchers and others, at the Town Hall, Birmingham, Warks., set to end on the 27th at the Empire Theatre, Liverpool, Lancs.
[29] Proby leaves Britain when his permit expires.
Apr [18] He begins a US tour with Gene Pitney.
May His latest manager, Terence Hillman, returns to London after terminating his contract by mutual agreement.
June *To Make A Big Man Cry*, having failed as a single for Adam Faith, makes UK #34.
Nov *I Can't Make It Alone*, a Goffin/King ballad with Spectoresque production by Jack Nitzsche, makes UK #37.

1967

Feb Proby files for bankruptcy in Los Angeles, listing debts of £180,000.
[13] He is granted a two-week work permit to perform in the UK.
Mar [25] *Niki Hoeky*, an R&B-rocker written by Pat and Lolly Vegas (later to find fame as Redbone with *Witch Queen Of New Orleans*), reaches US #23. It is Proby's biggest but last US hit (and fails to chart in the UK).
June The **New Musical Express** reports that Proby has been added to the cast of "Finian's Rainbow".

1968

Mar MOR/country ballad, *It's Your Day Today*, makes UK #32, his final UK hit. Shortly afterwards, he is declared a bankrupt, with debts of £60,000, and returns to the US, reputedly to Texas to breed horses, a venture which also fails. (He will continue recording for Liberty, much of it country-styled material, with the occasional oddity like the seven-minute *Mery Hopkins Never Had Days Like These*.)

1970

Aug *It's Goodbye* is, appropriately, Proby's last Liberty release.
Oct Proby returns to Britain, at Jack Good's request, to play Cassio in Good's rock musical version of "Othello", titled "Catch My Soul", in the '69 Theatre Company production at the University Theatre,

Manchester, Lancs. The show transfers to London's West End, where it enjoys a successful run.

1972

Mar A one-off single for EMI's Columbia label, coupling the standard *We'll Meet Again* with his own song *Clown Shoes*, makes no impact. (Similar one-offs for a variety of labels like Ember, Seven Sun and Rooster will characterize his sparse recorded output through the next decade. His live work will mainly be in UK cabaret, playing a nostalgic show to appeal to those with memories of the mid-'60s. In contrast to his earlier public eccentricities, he will be reclusive off stage.)

1977

Proby is signed, again by Jack Good, to portray the '70s Elvis Presley in the stage musical, "Elvis" in London's West End. (Presley at younger periods of his life is played by other singers, including Shakin' Stevens. The musical will run successfully for 19 months and pick up a theatre award as Best Musical Of The Year. Proby's performance will deteriorate after excellent initial reviews, and he will be sacked.)

1985

Sept After living in Britain in comparative obscurity for several years (though regularly playing small club and cabaret dates), Proby signs to Manchester independent label Savoy Records, releasing a revival of Soft Cell's *Tainted Love* on a 12"-only single, which generates music press interest, but is not a hit.
Nov A rapid follow-up on Savoy, his revival of Joy Division's *Love Will Tear Us Apart*, again has more positive reviews than sales. (Further, often eccentric, releases on the label – including *Anarchy In The UK* and a recitation from T.S. Eliot's poem "The Waste Land" - will also only remain cult items, despite the fact that in the late '80s Proby is recording more regularly than at any time since his chart heyday.)

1991

Apr [15] Having released a three-track single, *Hot California Nights*, on the Da Doo Ron Ron label (billed as "From Houston Texas - the new voice of new country") in 1990, and this year's nine-track CD, ***Thanks***, on the J'Ace label, Proby suffers a heart attack in his room at Blackpool's Lansdowne Hotel after playing the first night of a comeback season (but will discharge himself from Victoria Hospital within two days). He will continue living in a terraced house in Bolton, often in an alleged alcoholic haze, as Ron Ellis prepares a biography on the singer.

1996

Apr [2] The seemingly indestructable Proby, having returned to the London stage the previous year in a Roy Orbison bio-musical, now reprises his role in Jack Good's revived '70s musical, "Elvis" which opens in London at the Prince of Wales Theatre with Alexander Bar as a young Presley, Timothy Whitnall portraying the '60s Elvis and Proby taking on his later years.

PROCOL HARUM

Gary Brooker (vocals, piano); **Matthew Fisher** (keyboards); **Robin Trower** (guitar); **Dave Knights** (bass); **Barry J. Wilson** (drums)

1962

While Brooker (b. May 29, 1945, Southend, Essex), Trower (b. Mar. 9, 1945, Southend) and bass player Chris Copping (b. Aug. 29, 1945, Southend) were still at secondary school in Southend in 1959, they teamed with singer Bob Scott and drummer Mick Brownlee to form the Paramounts. The group became popular locally, playing covers of rock hits in local youth clubs, and when Scott dropped out, pianist Brooker took over the lead vocal slot. Now, after the group leaves school and gains a manager, Peter Martin, its gigs (still semi-professional) expand, as does the repertoire, which includes covers of US R&B singles by Ray Charles, James Brown, Bobby Bland and others. The group also becomes the resident band at Southend's Shades club.

1963

Jan Brownlee, the only one who does not wish to turn professional, leaves (to become a bricklayer), and is replaced by Wilson (b. Mar. 18, 1947, Southend) on drums, recruited through a classified ad in **Melody Maker**.
Sept Copping leaves to go to Leicester University, and is replaced on bass by Diz Derrick.
Oct A demo, coupling covers of the Coasters' *Poison Ivy* and Bobby Bland's *Further On Up The Road*, gains the group an EMI audition, and it signs to the Parlophone label, working with the Hollies' producer, Ron Richards.

1964

Jan *Poison Ivy* is released as their first single, and hits UK #35. It receives a boost from the Rolling Stones, who name the Paramounts their favorite UK R&B group after the two bands have worked together on ITV's "Thank Your Lucky Stars" pop show.
Mar Their revival of Thurston Harris' *Little Bitty Pretty One* is plugged via an ITV "Ready Steady Go!" appearance, but fails to chart (as will three more singles released to the end of 1965).

1966

Sept The group splits after its live gigs have reduced in quality (i.e. backing Sandie Shaw and Chris Andrews on tours of Europe). Derrick leaves the music business, Trower and Wilson play with other R&B circuit bands, and Brooker decides to concentrate on songwriting, teaming with lyricist Keith Reid (b. Oct. 19, 1945), whom he has met via a mutual acquaintance, R&B producer Guy Stevens.

1967

Apr With a batch of material in need of a band to play it, Brooker and Reid advertise for musicians in **Melody Maker**, and the first version of Procol Harum (which legend alternately suggests is named after the Latin (procul) for "far from these things" or after impresario Guy Stevens pedigree cat's birth certificate, Procol Harun) is formed calling themselves the Pinewoods, with Brooker on piano and vocals, Fisher (b. Mar. 7, 1946, Croydon, Surrey) on organ, Ray Royer (b. Oct. 8, 1945) on guitar, Knights (b. June 28, 1945, Islington, London) on bass and Bobby Harrison (b. June 28, 1943, East Ham, London) on drums. Producer Denny Cordell, a long-time acquaintance of Brooker, oversees the first recording, Reid's surreal poem, *A Whiter Shade Of Pale*, set by Brooker to music adapted from one of the movements of Bach's "Suite No. 3 in D Major".
May The band performs *A Whiter Shade Of Pale* at London's Speakeasy club, and Cordell places the record with Decca's Deram label, also sending a demo to pirate radio ship Radio London to see how it sounds on the radio.
[12] Rave listener reaction to the first few exclusive plays of it on "Big L" prompt Deram to rush-release it in Britain.
June [4] The group makes its London concert debut supporting Jimi Hendrix at the Saville Theatre, London.
[8] *A Whiter Shade Of Pale* tops the UK chart for the first of six weeks, eventually selling 606,000 copies, dethroned by the Beatles' *All You Need Is Love*. Procol Harum becomes only the sixth act to hit UK #1 with its debut release.
[17] They appear on the first edition of new BBC1-TV series, "Billy Cotton's Music Hall".
July [29] *A Whiter Shade Of Pale* hits US #5, taking its sales over one million (eventual worldwide sales will top six million). Meanwhile, after dissension within the group (plus panic that there is no act and no other repertoire with which to tour on the back of the hit), Royer and Harrison are asked to leave (they form their own band, Freedom), and Brooker recruits his old Paramounts cohorts Trower and Wilson to take over on guitar and drums.
Oct Cordell's production company moves its outlet from Deram to EMI's Regal Zonophone label (Brooker's father Harry once recorded for the label when a member of Felix Mendelsohn's Hawaiian Serenaders), and *Homburg*, in similar grandiose style to the first single, hits UK #6. Meanwhile, ***Procol Harum***, not a chart item in the UK, reaches US #47 where its pressing includes *A Whiter Shade Of Pale* among the tracks, unlike the UK version, and all but one of the other tracks are Brooker/Reid collaborations.
Nov [18] *Homburg* reaches US #34.

1968

Mar [26] *A Whiter Shade Of Pale* wins the International Song of the Year honor at the 13th annual Ivor Novello Awards, held at the Playhouse Theatre, London.
Apr *Quite Rightly So* makes UK #50.
May [29] They embark on an eight-day Italian tour in Milan with Herman's Hermits.
Nov The group is signed to A&M Records in the US for its second album, ***Shine On Brightly***, which reaches US #24, but on Regal Zonophone in the UK, it fails to chart.
Dec [28] On tour in the US, the group plays at the "Miami Pop Festival", at the Gulfstream Racing Park, Hallandale, FL, to 100,000 people, along with Chuck Berry, Fleetwood Mac, the Turtles, Canned Heat, and many more.

1969

Mar Knights and Fisher both leave, to take up management and production respectively. Copping, his university studies at Leicester complete, rejoins his former Paramounts co-members, on both bass and organ. The line-up of early 1969 Procol Harum is now the same as early 1963 Paramounts.
Apr [6] The group plays with Ike & Tina Turner, John Mayall and others at the "Palm Springs Pop Festival", Palm Springs, CA, where an audience too large for the drive-in car park venue riots when police helicopters try to disperse it.
June ***A Salty Dog*** (recorded before the departure of Fisher and Knights, and produced by the former) reaches US #32, while the title track, *A Salty Dog*, makes UK #44.
[22] The band performs at the "Toronto Rock Festival", Toronto, ON, Canada, to 50,000 people, alongside the Band, Chuck Berry, Steppenwolf and Blood, Sweat & Tears.
July ***A Salty Dog*** is the first Procol Harum album to chart in the UK, at #27.
Aug [1] The group plays at the "Atlantic City Pop Festival", Atlantic City, NJ, with Creedence Clearwater Revival, Janis Joplin, B.B. King, the Byrds and others, to 110,000 people.

1970

June ***Home***, on which Chris Thomas takes over as producer (as he will for the next few albums), makes UK #49.
July The band plays at the three-day "Atlanta Pop Festival" in Byron, GA, to a 200,000-strong crowd, on a bill with Jimi Hendrix, Captain Beefheart, Jethro Tull, the Allman Brothers Band and others.
Aug ***Home*** makes US #34.
[28] Procol Harum appears on the second day of UK's "Isle Of Wight Festival", East Afton Farm, Godshill, Isle of Wight.

1971

July Having signed a new contract with Chrysalis Records (via Island) in the UK, ***Broken Barricades*** makes UK #41 and US #32.
[16] Trower leaves for a solo career. (He will become popular as a guitarist heading his own group through the '70s, with particular album sales success in the US.) Dave Ball (b. Mar. 30, 1950) joins on guitar, while Alan Cartwright (b. Oct. 10, 1945) comes in on

bass to allow Copping to concentrate on keyboards.
Aug [6] The group performs a concert with the Edmonton Symphony Orchestra and the Da Camera Singers, in Edmonton, AB, Canada. Mostly consisting of newly-arranged versions of earlier album tracks, the show is recorded for a live album release.

1972

Apr [17] They embark on a 13-city US tour.
May Live set, ***Procol Harum In Concert With The Edmonton Symphony Orchestra***, from the Canadian concert, makes UK #48. A double-pack reissue combining ***A Whiter Shade Of Pale*** (the debut album with the title track added) and ***A Salty Dog*** reaches UK #26.
June Reissued *A Whiter Shade Of Pale*, the lead track on a maxi-single (with *Homburg* and *A Salty Dog*), climbs to UK #13.
July ***Procol Harum In Concert With The Edmonton Symphony Orchestra*** becomes the group's best-selling album in the US, hitting #5 and earning a gold disc for half a million-plus sales.
[29] Taken from it, a new orchestra-backed version of *Conquistador* (originally a track on their debut set) makes US #16.
Aug Live *Conquistador* reaches UK #22.
[28] ***Procol Harum In Concert With The Edmonton Symphony Orchestra*** is certified gold by the RIAA.
Sept Ball leaves to work with Long John Baldry and is replaced by ex-Plastic Penny and Cochise member Mick Grabham.

1973

May ***Grand Hotel***, featuring guest backing vocals by the Swingle Singers, reaches US #21.
Nov US compilation, ***The Best Of Procol Harum***, on A&M, peaks at US #131. ***Exotic Birds And Fruit***, its title a reference to the sleeve painting by Jakob Bogdani, will make US #86 the following May.

1975

Mar [16] Along with Kevin Coyne and John Martyn, Procol Harum headlines "Over The Rainbow", the closing-down concert at London's Rainbow Theatre in Finsbury Park.
Sept ***Procol's Ninth*** reaches UK #41 and US #52. It is produced, at Brooker's request, by Jerry Leiber and Mike Stoller, and includes their song, *I Keep Forgettin'* (formerly a hit for Chuck Jackson), as well as a revival of the Beatles' *Eight Days A Week*. Extracted from it, *Pandora's Box* reaches UK #16.

1977

Apr [23] After Cartwright has left the previous July, with Copping moved back to bass, and Pete Solley joining on keyboards, ***Something Magic*** reaches US #147, and is the final Procol Harum album for 14 years. The group decides to split, considering that its particular strand of music has been fully explored, and recognising a less favorable musical climate as punk rock catches hold in Britain. A round of live dates supporting the last album becomes a farewell tour.
May [15] Procol Harum plays its last full concert for 14 years at New York City's Academy of Music.
Oct [18] *A Whiter Shade Of Pale* is named joint winner (with Queen's *Bohemian Rhapsody*) as Best British Pop Single 1952-1977, at the British Record Industry Britannia Awards, to mark the Queen's Silver Jubilee, held at the Wembley Conference Centre, Wembley, Middx., (and shown on ITV two days later). Procol Harum re-forms for the occasion to perform the song live.

1979

Brooker, the most prominent post-Procol solo artist, releases the George Martin-produced solo album, ***No Fear Of Flying***, on Chrysalis. (It will be followed by ***Lead Me To The Water***, featuring Eric Clapton and Phil Collins among others, in 1982 on Mercury Records, and ***Echoes In The Night***, co-produced with Fisher in 1985, also on Mercury. He will go on to join Clapton's backing band in the late '80s before concentrating on writing ballet scores.) Chrysalis will release ***Portfolio***, an 18-track Procol Harum hits and highlights retrospective in May 1988.

1990

Aug [18 -19] Brooker sings *A Whiter Shade Of Pale* at the annual "Cropredy Folk Festival", Cropredy, Oxon, backed by Fairport Convention.

1991

Aug Having completed "Delta", his latest ballet score premiered by the Royal Danish Ballet in December 1990, and spoken to Reid at his New York city home about writing together again, Brooker has reformed Procol Harum with the studio line-up of himself, Trower, Fisher, Reid and Mark Brzezicki (drums), which has recorded ***The Prodigal Stranger***, now released by Zoo Entertainment. (Wilson died in Oregon in 1989.)
Sept An 11-city North American tour, their first in 14 years, opens at the Winter Gardens Theatre in Toronto, for which Trower, unable to tour, is replaced by Tim Renwick.
Oct [9] The group guests on NBC-TV's "Late Night With David Letterman".
Dec [13] They appear on NBC-TV's "The Tonight Show".

1992

May [19] Procol Harum, now only Brooker and sidemen Geoffrey Whitehorn (guitar), Don Snow (b. Jan. 13, 1957, Kenya) (keyboards) and Brzezicki (b. June 21, 1957, Slough, Bucks.) (drums), plays at The Academy, New York, during latest US dates.

1995

Aug [12] After Brooker has sung the three-verse version of *A Whiter Shade Of Pale* with the 1992 Procol line-up but augmented by Andy Fairweather-Low and bassist Dave Bronze, at his annual charity Christmas concert at Chiddingfold Club in Surrey the previous December, Procol Harum, now comprising Brooker, Fisher, Whitehorn and Matt Pegg, performs at Shepherd's Bush Empire, their first London show in 18 years.

PUBLIC ENEMY

Chuck D; Flavor Flav; Terminator X; Professor Griff

1982

Nov Future Public Enemy managers and producers, Hank Shocklee and Bill Stephney, are classmates at the Adelphi University, Long Island, New York, NY, where Chuck D (b. Carlton Ridenhour, Aug. 1, 1960, Roosevelt, Long Island) is studying graphic design. College radio station WBAU program director, Stephney, invites Chuck D and Shocklee to mix a show which leads to their own three hour "Super Special Mix Show" in January the following year. In November 1983, Flavor Flav (b. William Drayton, Mar. 16, 1959, Roosevelt), who used to work with Chuck D for D's father's V-Haul company, who had been ringing up the station incessantly, joins, hosting the first half of Chuck's show. By 1984 Shocklee and Chuck D will record their own basement tapes for broadcast on WBAU, including the track, *Public Enemy Number 1*, from which they will name their group.

1986

Assembled as a performing group and producing a steady diet of early hip-hop rap mixed with their own aggressive DJ style, their cult success attracts Def Jam record-label entrepreneur Rick Rubin. Chuck D and Shocklee recruit a flexible roster of members, including Flav, DJ Terminator X (b. Norman Lee Rogers, Aug. 25, 1966, New York) and Professor Griff, Minister of Information (b. Richard Griffin) and others, S1WS Roderick Chillous, James Allen and James Norman. Chuck D and Shocklee also run a mobile deejay and concert promotion company called Spectrum City, broadcast the UHF-TV show "Word - The World Of Rock And Dance", and manage Long Island's first hip-hop venue, the Entourage in Bayshore, NY, where Chuck D handles promotion, Shocklee organizes gigs, Terminator X spins the wheels of steel, Flav MCs, and the S1WS martial arts team handles security.

1987

May Augmented by hip-hop activist Harry Allen as spokesperson and "media assassin", and signed to Def Jam by Rubin (who had tried to sign the band in 1985, but been turned down by Chuck D), Public Enemy's innovative, aggressive urban rap (they are described by Stephney as "the black panthers of rap") is trademarked with the release of their debut album, ***Yo! Bum Rush The Show***, which makes US R&B #28, spurred by a US tour supporting the Beastie Boys. The title cut is a reworking of the demo track, *Public Enemy No. 1*.
Nov Following a European tour opening for label-mate L.L. Cool J, during which their live performance attracts headlines and tight police security, their debut UK single, *Rebel Without A Pause*, makes UK #37.

1988

Jan Two fans are crushed to death at a post-gig reception after a Public Enemy concert in Tennessee.
Feb *Bring The Noise* climbs to UK #32, while ***Yo! Bum Rush The Show*** peaks at US #125.
July [9] *Don't Believe The Hype* makes #18 in the UK, where repeated short live visits prop sales for their social/political-based rap anthems.
[30] Their second album, ***It Takes A Nation Of Millions To Hold Us Back***, immediately hits UK #8 and begins a US chart rise to #42 and becomes their first platinum disc.
Sept The group performs at New York's notorious Rikers Island Prison.
[24] ***It Takes A Nation Of Millions To Hold Us Back*** hits US R&B #1.
Oct The extracted *Night Of The Living Baseheads* peaks at UK #63 and US R&B #62, where a mainstream Hot 100 showing is prevented due to poor airplay ratings beyond the specialist hip-hop outlets.

1989

May *Black Steel In The Hour Of Chaos* peaks at US R&B #86.
June [21] Chuck D announces the dismissal from the group of Professor Griff after a May 22nd interview with **Washington Post** reporter David Mills (reprinted on June 14th in the **Village Voice**), in which he allegedly made anti-Semitic statements including, "Jews are responsible for the majority of wickedness that goes on across the globe".
[22] Chuck D again prematurely announces the break-up of Public Enemy on New York radio station WLIB. In a subsequent MTV interview, he guardedly retracts the statement.
[24] Featured as the repetitive central theme to Spike Lee's hit urban jungle movie, "Do The Right Thing", *Fight The Power* reaches UK #29. Released from the hip-hop Motown soundtrack album, it will also reach US R&B #20, aided by a video partly filmed in Riker's Island jail.

1990

Jan [20] *Welcome To The Terrordome* reaches UK #18.
Mar [21] An eight-day visit to the UK for selected live dates begins, supported by labelmate hip-hoppers 3rd Bass, and includes two dates at London's Brixton Academy. Griff makes his last appearance with the group, having allegedly insulted MC Serch on the eve of their European tour. His place will temporarily be taken by former Unity Force producer James Norman.
Apr [7] Police emergency line call-up-attacking *911 Is A Joke* makes UK #41, while Griff, now signed to Skywalker Records, releases his debut album, the

hard-core rapping ***Pawns In The Game***.
[28] Third Public Enemy album, ***Fear Of A Black Planet***, instantly hits UK #4.
May [26] ***Fear Of A Black Planet*** hits US #10, a major sales breakthrough, though consistent lack of mainstream radio support means that all single extracts will fail to crack the Hot 100.
June [7] ***Fear Of A Black Planet*** is certified platinum by the RIAA.
[23] *Brothers Gonna Work It Out* makes UK #46.
[27] The US leg of their "Tour Of A Black Planet" opens at the Coliseum, Richmond, VA, their first US trek in two years.
Aug [25] Mid-tour, their concert at the Shoreline Amphitheatre, Mountain View, CA, erupts into an open audience brawl.
Sept The group reportedly appears in an FBI report to Congress examining "Rap Music And Its Effects On National Security".
Nov [3] *Can't Do Nuttin' For Ya Man* makes UK #53, as Terminator X begins his solo career with the Def Jam single, *Want To Be Dancin'*. The group performs at the Docklands Area in London during its current UK visit.

1991

Jan [1] Sister Souljah temporarily replaces Griff as Minister of Information.
Feb [9] Flavor Flav is arrested at his Long Island home on charges of assaulting his live-in girlfriend, and mother of his three children, Karen Ross. (He will plead guilty to third degree assault. Nassau District Court Judge Richard LaPera sentences him to serve 30 days, orders him to pay $334 for medical expenses and grants Ross a permanent order of protection against Flav.)
Mar [7] The band is named Best Rap Group in the annual **Rolling Stone** magazine Readers' Picks music awards.
Apr Public Enemy's future is once again cast in doubt as Stephney and Shocklee split over business differences. Chuck D also announces that there will not be any group live dates in the near future.
June The group records a new album at Record Plant Studios, New York, produced by the Bomb Squad.
Sept Chuck D files a $5 million lawsuit against the marketing company promoting St. Ides malt liquor for sampling his voice.
[24] Their "Apocalypse '91" tour with Anthrax plays at the Mid-Hudson Civic Center, Poughkeepsie, NY, with a line-up of Hank and Keith Shocklee, Chuck D and Gary (G-Wiz) Rinaldi. (During the tour, the group organizes lunches, celebrity basketball games, and talks to children at inner-city schools.)
[28] The group guests on NBC-TV's "Saturday Night Live".
Oct [12] *Can't Truss It* debuts at its UK #22 peak.
[19] ***Apocalypse 91 ... The Enemy Strikes Back*** debuts at its US #4 peak and UK #8.
Nov [26] ***Apocalypse 91 ... The Enemy Strikes Back*** is certified platinum by the RIAA.
[30] *Can't Truss It* makes US #50.
Dec [3] *Can't Truss It* is confirmed gold by the RIAA.

1992

Jan Flavor is arrested for driving without a licence and non-payment of child support.
[3] "The World's Greatest Rap Show Ever" tour, headlined by Public Enemy and with Queen Latifah, Naughty By Nature, MC Lyte and the Geto Boys, plays at New York's Madison Square Garden before a sellout crowd of 14,118.
[7] "By The Time I Get To Arizona" video, with a scene in which fictitious characters responsible for thwarting the creation of Martin Luther King Jr.'s official holiday are assassinated, is unveiled at a Sheraton Hotel, New York press conference.
[25] *Shut 'Em Down* debuts at its UK #21 peak.
Mar [12] The group wins the Best Rap Album category at the sixth annual Soul Train Music Awards, held at the Shrine Auditorium, Los Angeles, CA.
Apr [11] *Nighttrain* debuts at its UK #55 peak.
May A scheduled 14-date "Tour Of Hell" South African trek is postponed until November.
June [19] The group takes part in U2's "Greenpeace Stop Sellafield" concert at the G-Mex, Manchester, Gtr. Manchester, during a current UK tour.
Aug [29] Public Enemy performs on the second day of the 20th annual "Reading Festival", Reading, Berks.
Sept [6] They participate in KISS-FM's birthday jam at London's Brixton Academy.
Oct [3] Compilation ***Greatest Misses*** debuts at its US #13 and UK #14 peaks.
[23] Now supporting U2 on their "Zooropa" tour, Public Enemy cuts short a performance at the Sun Devil Stadium, Tempe, AZ, singing *By The Time I Get To Arizona* and one other song, in protest at the state's refusal to grant Martin Luther King Jr. Day the status of an official holiday.
Nov [18] ***Greatest Misses*** is certified gold by the RIAA.

1993

Mar [1] Professor Griff's ***The X Minista*** is released in the US (and will be released in the UK on the Musicdisc label), to be followed by Flavor Flav's solo debut, ***Flavor Flav***, on Def Jam, due in September.
Nov [1] Flav is arrested in the Bronx, New York, charged with attempted murder for allegedly shooting at his neighbor Thelouizs English near their Brooklyn homes. Flav claims English had sex with his girlfriend. (Flav will subsequently book himself into the Betty Ford Clinic to overcome a cocaine addiction.)

1994

Aug [13] *Give It Up* debuts at its UK #18 peak.
[19] Flav is arrested again for allegedly assaulting Hope Dooner, who photographed his daughter on a New York street.
[20] *Give It Up* reaches US #33.
Sept [3] ***Muse Sick-N-Hour Mess Age*** reaches UK #12 in its week of entry.
[10] ***Muse Sick-N-Hour Mess Age*** debuts at its US #14 peak.
[23] The group guests on CBS-TV's "Late Show With David Letterman".
Oct [3] ***Yo! Bum Rush The Show*** is certified gold by the RIAA.
[19] Chuck D announces on BET cable channel's "Teen Summit" that he will leave the group in January 1995 to work on his community-based youth organization and to develop new music projects. The following day, his publicist Ursula Smirth refutes the story.
[25] ***Muse Sick-N-Hour Mess Age*** is confirmed gold by the RIAA.
Dec [26] The group performs a year-end show at the Roxy in Phoenix, AZ.

1995

May [26] Flav is sentenced to 90 days in jail for firing a gun at English in the November 1st 1993 incident.
June [1] The group appears again on "Late Show With David Letterman".
July Flav breaks both his arms in a motorcycle accident in Milan, Italy.
[29] *So Whatcha Gonna Do Now?* charts for a week at UK #50.

PUBLIC IMAGE LTD.

John Lydon (vocals); **Keith Levene** (guitar); **Jah Wobble** (bass); **Jim Walker** (drums)

1978

Apr After the Sex Pistols split at the end of their December 1977 US tour, lead singer Johnny Rotten reverts to his real name, John Lydon (b. Jan. 31, 1956, Finsbury Park, London), and, having taken a short holiday in Jamaica, returns to Britain to form a new band with ex-Clash member Levene, novice bass-player Wobble (b. John Wardle) and Canadian Walker, who has played drums with the Furys, and is recruited through an ad and subsequent auditions. With the quartet's name chosen as a sanitized anti-rock'n'roll statement, Public Image Ltd. signs to Virgin Records (for whom the Sex Pistols' also recorded).
July [25] The formation of the group is officially announced by Lydon.
Nov Its debut single, *Public Image*, released in a mock-newspaper sleeve, hits UK #9 with the group billed as Public Image Ltd. (though most subsequent singles will simply credit PiL).
Dec ***Public Image Ltd.*** reaches UK #22.
[25] Their first live gig is a Christmas Day showcase at London's Rainbow Theatre. (Scattered live dates will follow in early 1979, but PiL will not mount a full tour until the late '80s. Walker will leave, to be replaced on drums by Richard Dudanski and then by Martin Atkins.)

1979

June [30] Lydon guests on BBC1-TV's "Juke Box Jury", on a panel with Joan Collins.
July *Death Disco* reaches UK #20.
Sept [8-9] PiL performs at the two-day Futurama Festival at the Queens Hall, Leeds, W. Yorks.
Oct *Memories* peaks at UK #60.
Dec ***Metal Box*** reaches UK #18, so titled because the original release is packaged in a round 12" metal container with the album inside in the form of three 12" singles.

1980

Feb [13] Lydon's London house is raided by the police, who smash open the front door to find him waving a ceremonial sword at them from the top of the stairs. The only illegal item found on the premises is a canister of tear gas, claimed to be for defense against intruders.
Mar ***Metal Box*** is reissued in conventional form as the double album, ***Second Edition***, and reaches UK #46. The band plays selected European dates, including a Paris, France concert which is recorded for a future live album.
May ***Second Edition*** peaks at US #171.
[17] The band performs *Poptones* on ABC-TV's "American Bandstand".
June Returning from a short US tour which has had a mixed reception, the band announces that it will not play live again, and Atkins leaves to join Brian Brain.
Aug Wobble departs for a solo career (and will later form Human Condition, and more successfully in the '90s - after working for London Underground - Jah Wobble's Invaders Of The Heart).
Oct [6] Lydon is arrested for assault, after a pub brawl in Dublin, Eire. (Sentenced to three months in jail for disorderly conduct, he will be acquitted on appeal.)
Nov Live album, ***Paris Au Printemps (Paris In The Spring)***, from the concert earlier in the year (and released mainly to counter bootleg albums of PiL's live show), makes UK #61. Jeanette Lee joins the group for "visual assistance", organizing its visual elements.

1981

Apr [18] From new recordings by Lydon, Levene and Lee, *Flowers Of Romance* reaches UK #24.
[25] ***The Flowers Of Romance***, with Atkins drumming on three tracks, reaches UK #11.
May [15] PiL plays a show at New York's Ritz club (deputising for Bow Wow Wow), posing behind a video screen while the music is played from tapes. They are showered with missiles and booed off stage by the 1,500 audience, whom Lydon insults in return. (The band considers the event successful, having video taped the debacle for movie use.) A second show the following night is cancelled.
June ***The Flowers Of Romance*** peaks at US #114.

1982

Feb Lydon dismisses rumors that the group has split, following an article in **Sounds**. Lydon says "the tosspot was desperate for a story last week so he made one up". (While he relocates to New York, Lee quits the band.)

1983

July Levene now departs, leaving the pivotal Lydon as PiL's only full-time member.
Oct *This Is Not A Love Song* hits UK #5, the group's biggest hit single, while the double album, ***Live In Tokyo***, its second performance set, makes UK #28. Lydon appears in the movie "Cop Killer" with Harvey Keitel.

1984

May Lydon assembles a new band for *Bad Life*, which peaks at UK #71.
July ***This Is What You Want ... This Is What You Get*** makes UK #56. Lydon will subsequently team with New York hip-hop pioneer, Afrika Bambaataa, under the one-off name Time Zone for *World Destruction*, which makes UK #44 the following February.

1986

Feb *Rise*, on which Ginger Baker plays drums, reaches UK #11. It is taken from ***Album*** (the cassette release is titled ***Cassette*** and the CD ***Compact Disc***), produced by Material member Bill Laswell (and also featuring Baker on drums and percussion), which makes UK #14 and US #115. PiL tours to promote the release.
May *Home*, also from ***Album***, peaks at UK #75.
Dec Virgin Video releases "Public Image Ltd. : The Videos", comprising promotion clips to date.

1987

Sept *Seattle* reaches UK #47 as its parent album, the Gary Langan-produced ***Happy?***, makes UK #40 and US #169, recrediting one Johnny Rotten.

1988

Aug PiL, comprising Lydon with ex-Siouxsie & the Banshees, Magazine and the Armoury Show John McGeogh (guitar), ex-Damned Lu Edmonds (keyboards, guitar), Alan Dias (bass) and Bruce Smith (drums), embarks on a tour supporting Big Country which will include the 200,000-attended "Soviet Peace Festival" held in Tallinn, Estonia.
Sept 500 fans storm the stage in Athens, Greece, during a PiL set, destroying equipment and setting fire to trees in the park. Greek anarchists join in throwing rocks and petrol bombs while a reported £1 million-worth of damage is caused.

1989

May PiL's *Disappointed* charts at UK #38. Edmunds quits, citing ear problems.
June [10] Stephen Hague-produced ***Nine*** (PiL's ninth release) reaches UK #36 and will make US #106, as Lydon embarks on another round of provocative promotion including a US tour with New Order and the Sugarcubes.

1990

Nov [10] ***Greatest Hits ... So Far*** reaches UK #20 in its week of entry, while *Don't Ask Me* makes UK #22.

1992

Jan Following termination of their Virgin contract, PiL regroups with Lydon, Levine, Russell Webb (bass), formerly of the Skids and the Armoury Show, replacing Alan Dais, and new drummer Mike Joyce (b. June 1, 1963, Manchester), ex-Smiths and Buzzcocks.
Feb [22] *Cruel* debuts at its UK #49 peak.
Mar Lydon buys Mae West's former home in Hollywood.
[7] ***That What Is Not*** makes UK #46.
May [2-3] The group plays at London's Town & Country club during a current UK tour.
Aug [9] Lydon joins Ian Dury onstage at the "Madstock" gig at Finsbury Park, playing guitar on *Sex And Drugs And Rock'n'Roll*.
[28] PiL performs on the first day of the 20th annual "Reading Festival", Reading, Berks.
Sept [13] The group appears at The Ritz, New York, during its latest North American tour.

1993

Mar Lydon now signs a solo deal with Atlantic Records.
Nov [13] A one-off collaboration between Lydon and and techno production unit Leftfield, credited as Leftfield Lydon, debuts at its UK #13 peak with *Open Up* on the Hard Hands label.

1994

Sept Still preparing his solo debut album, Lydon's autobiography **Rotten : No Irish, No Blacks, No Dogs**, co-authored with Kent and Keith Zimmeman, is published.
see also: **THE SEX PISTOLS**

PULP

Jarvis Cocker (vocals); **Russell Senior** (guitar); **Candida Doyle** (keyboards); **Steve Mackey** (bass); **Nick Banks** (drums)

1983

Apr Originally called Arabacus Pulp, the group has been formed in Sheffield, S. Yorks. in 1979 while its leader and frontman Cocker is still attending school, performing its earliest shows during lunch breaks in the school canteen and cutting its first music as a soundtrack to fellow student Glen Marshall's school film project. Making its professional debut at a 1980 gig at Rotherham Arts Centre, followed by an appearance at the "Bouquet Of Steel" festival at the Leadmill club in Sheffield in August the same year, Pulp evolves through a variable lineup which sees bassists David Lockwood, Philip Thompson and drummers Mark Swift and Jimmy Sellers come and go. With the lineup of Jarvis, Pete Dalton (guitar), Jamie Pinchbeck (bass) and Wayne Furniss (drums), Jarvis has given BBC Radio 1's John Peel a demo tape in 1981 while the DJ is doing a Radio 1 Roadshow in Sheffield, and has been invited two weeks later to record a session for his program, an event which only proves to be a false start. The band has split, however, after its members' final school exams in July 1982 with Pinchbeck and Dalton going off to university. Jarvis has subsequently assembled a new backing crew of local musicians including Simon Hinkler and Cocker's sister Saskia, and signed with the York-based Cartel indie distribution label, Red Rhino which now releases Pulp's debut album ***It***. In January 1984 Cocker then teams with his guitar-playing friend Senior and recruits keyboardist Tim Allcard, bassist Pete Mansell and drummer Magnus Doyle, though this version alters by the summer, after gigs at Brunel University and another in Leeds, with Magnus Doyle's sister Candida replacing Allcard. Recording *Little Girl (With Blue Eyes)* for the London-based indie Fire Records in December 1985, the group's progress is stunted again in early '86, when Cocker injures himself after jumping out of a window (allegedly to impress a girlfriend), and ends up in a wheelchair for a year. Moving through further lineup changes, Magnus Doyle leaves in 1987 to travel abroad, replaced by Banks, with temporary bassist Anthony Genn also performing with the group during the year. In May of '87, the group's second album ***Freaks***, recorded in one week for £600, is released by Fire, before Cocker undertakes film studies at London's St. Martin's Art College, where he meets and recruits permanent bassist Mackey.

1993

Sept After Fire has issued ***Separations*** in July the previous year amid much rancor with Cocker, which has resulted in a two-year retail delay, and in the band signing with Sheffield-based indie Gift Records (releasing *O.U.*, *Babies* and *Razzmatazz* between June '92 and February of this year), Pulp's fortunes change as it now inks a more permanent deal with Island Records, with the settled lineup of Cocker, Senior, Doyle, Mackey and Banks.
Nov [27] Following the October release of the mini-album ***Pulpintro - The Gift Recordings***, a collection of highlights originally recorded for Gift and licensed by Island, *Lip Gloss* bows at its UK #50 peak, a chart debut some 13 years after the band's first gig.

1994

Apr [2] *Do You Remember The First Time?* enters at its UK #33 high.
[30] Its parent album ***His 'N' Hers***, produced by Ed Buller, bows at its UK #9 peak. Their fourth original album, it will be nominated for the third annual Mercury Music Prize.
May [6] Pulp plays a one-off London date at The Forum.
June [4] *The Sisters EP* bows at its UK #19 peak.
[17] Fire releases a collection of Pulp's earlier work for the label as ***Masters Of The Universe - Pulp On Fire 1985-86*** (and will also reissue ***It*** in November).
[26] They play on the final day of the "Glastonbury Festival", Glastonbury, Somerset.
Aug [27] The group performs at the annual "Reading Festival", Reading Berks.
Oct [31] They appear at "Live At The Lighthouse" AIDS benefit at London's Lighthouse AIDS Centre, set to air on Carlton-TV in January and the general ITV network in the spring.
Dec During UK dates, Pulp plays at London's Theatre Royal, Drury Lane.

1995

June [3] The class-system themed *Common People* bows at its UK #2 peak.
[24] Pulp performs a well-received set having replaced bill-topper Stone Roses, who have pulled out of the 25th anniversary Glastonbury Festival at Worthy Farm, Pilton, Somerset.
July [22] The band plays at the Heineken Music Festival at Roundhay Park, Leeds.
Oct [1] A UK tour begins at the Barrowlands, Glasgow, Strathclyde, Scotland, set to end October 22nd in Sheffield.
[7] *Mis-Shapes*, coupled with drug-glamorizing *Sorted For Es And Wizz*, enters at its UK #2 peak, behind Simply Red's *Fairground*.
Nov [2] Cocker throws a tantrum on Norwegian television show "ZTV" in Oslo after the band's equipment breaks down, also injuring his foot when he kicks his microphone across the stage.
[11] Pulp appears on BBC2-TV's "Later With Jools Holland" the same day the Chris Thomas-produced ***Different Class*** enters the UK chart at #1, being confirmed platinum for 300,000 UK sales within two weeks and finally bringing Pulp to the front ranks of Brit Pop.
Dec [2] The group is featured on BBC1-TV's "Live And Kicking".
[5] The band performs in Paris, France.
[9] *Disco 2000* debuts at its UK #7 peak.
[18] BBC2-TV airs "No Sleep Till Sheffield : Pulp Go Public".

1996

Feb [19] After Pulp has already performed earlier in the evening, Michael Jackson's performance of *Earth Song* at the 1996 BRIT Awards at London's Earl's Court Exhibition Centre, is interrupted when Cocker walks onstage, causing a melée during which it is claimed some of the children sharing the stage with Jackson, are injured. Cocker claims that his behavior, for which he will be arrested but not charged, was "a form of protest at the way Michael Jackson sees himself as some Christ-like figure with the power of healing". Jackson states afterwards that he was "immensely proud that the show went on despite (Cocker's) disgusting and cowardly behavior", a comment for which Cocker momentarily considers suing Jackson for defamation of character.
[27] ***Different Class*** is released in the US.
The ***Trainspotting*** film soundtrack, including a new cut by Pulp, is also released Stateside.
Mar [1] The group ends an eight-date UK tour at the Wembley Arena, Wembley, Middx.

[11] Cocker is cleared of any wrongdoing at the recent BRITS' fracas.
[23] ***Countdown 1992-1983*** debuts at its UK #10 peak.
Apr [6] *Something Changed* hits UK #10 in its week of entry.

SUZI QUATRO

1965

Quatro (b. Suzi Quatrocchio, June 3, 1950, Detroit, MI), having been taught to play drums and piano by her father, who made sure his four daughters and one son received a good grounding in music, played bongos in her father's semi-professional Art Quatro Trio at age eight, and formed her own group at school in 1958. Determined to make a career in music, she left school in 1964 and formed the Pleasure Seekers with her sisters, Arlene, Patti and Nancy, appearing on local TV as Suzi Soul. Having become regulars at Detroit's Hideout club, the main venue for new young rock talent, the Pleasure Seekers' *Never Thought You'd Leave Me* is now released on Dave Leone and Punch Andrews' (later Bob Seger's manager) Hideout label, but not distributed outside Michigan. (A second and final cut by the group, *Light Of Life*, will be issued by Mercury Records the following March, before Quatro and her sisters travel to Vietnam to tour casualty wards in 1967.)

1969

After Suzi and Nancy have formed hard-edged progressive rock act Cradle the previous year, UK producer Mickie Most, in Detroit to work with Jeff Beck at Motown Studios, sees the group at a local club and, impressed by Suzi, invites her to come to Britain and record for his RAK label. Cradle splits the following year, and Quatro takes up Most's offer to relocate. She arrives in London with Arlene, who is acting as her manager, but who returns to Detroit after Most signs her sister.

1973

June [16] After 18 months of writing and rehearsing, Quatro's debut cut, *Rolling Stone* has been released the previous July. Quatro's second single, *Can The Can*, a pop/rock concoction penned for her by RAK's newly-signed writing team, Nicky Chinn and Mike Chapman, now hits UK #1 for a week. Playing bass in addition to singing, she tours Britain, supporting Slade with a backing band comprising Len Tuckey (guitar), Dave Neal (drums) and Alastair McKenzie (keyboards), who is soon replaced by Mike Deacon from Vinegar Joe.
Aug *48 Crash* hits UK #3.
Oct Her maiden album, ***Suzi Quatro***, written by Chinn and Chapman, and produced by Chapman, makes UK #32, as her leather cat-suit-clad image becomes familiar to fans.
Nov *Daytona Demon* reaches UK #14.

1974

Feb [23] *Devil Gate Drive* is her second UK #1 for the first of two weeks, dethroning label-mate Mud's *Tiger Feet*.
Apr ***Suzi Quatro*** makes US #142.
July *Too Big* reaches UK #14.
Sept [14] *All Shook Up*, released on Bell in the US, peaks at #85. (She receives a message from Elvis Presley complimenting her on the cover version and inviting her to Graceland - an offer she does not have the nerve to take up.)
[30] She begins a tour of West Germany, supported by the Arrows.
Oct ***Quatro***, once again helmed by Chapman, peaks at US #126.
Nov *The Wild One* hits UK #7.

1975

Feb *Your Mama Won't Like Me* reaches UK #31.
Apr After seven consecutive chart singles, *I Bit Off More Than I Could Chew* fails to score.
May ***Your Mama Won't Like Me*** reaches US #146 as Quatro undertakes a three-month US tour, supporting Alice Cooper. Nearly three years after its UK release, *Can The Can*, released on Big Tree, will make US #56 the following February 14th.

1977

Feb [12] Quatro embarks on her first UK tour in two years at Sheffield University, Sheffield, S. Yorks.
Apr [2] *Tear Me Apart*, Quatro's first release since August 1975, reaches UK #27. The producers of the ABC-TV series "Happy Days", having spotted Quatro on the cover of **Rolling Stone**, cast her as female rocker Leather Tuscadero. She is written into further episodes, but declines the offer to star in a spin-off series to stay in Britain with her husband, Len Tuckey.

1978

Apr After another non-chart single, Quatro hits UK #4 with yet another ChinniChap pop smash, *If You Can't Give Me Love*.
July *The Race Is On* reaches UK #43.
Nov *Stumblin' In*, a duet with Smokie's lead singer, Chris Norman, makes UK #41.

1979

May [12] Country-pop based *Stumblin' In*, released on RSO, hits US #4.
June ***If You Knew Suzi***, a Chapman-produced album which contains *Stumblin' In*, reaches US #37.
[23] *If You Can't Give Me Love* makes US #45.
[7] *Stumblin' In* is certified gold by the RIAA.
Oct [6] *I've Never Been In Love* peaks at US #44 as ***Suzi ... And Other Four Letter Words*** climbs to US #117.
Nov *She's In Love With You* reaches UK #11.

1980

Jan *Mama's Boy* reaches UK #34.
[19] *She's In Love With You* makes US #41.
Apr TV-advertised, 14-track ***Suzi Quatro's Greatest Hits***, hits UK #4. *I've Never Been In Love* makes UK #56.
Oct After leaving RAK and signing to Chinn and Chapman's new Dreamland label, *Rock Hard*, featured in the movie "Times Square", peaks at UK #68.
Nov ***Rock Hard*** reaches US #165. *Lipstick* will make US #51 the following February 28th.

1982

Nov [20] Having quit touring, given birth to a daughter, Laura, and signed with Polydor Records following the demise of Dreamland, *Heart Of Stone* peaks at UK #60, taken from ***Main Attraction***. (During the following year, she will re-sign to RAK , perform at the annual "Reading Festival", Reading, Berks., in August, and begin hosting the UK daytime program, "Gas", subsequently remaining a TV personality through much of the '80s.)

1994

Jan [27] After EMI has issued the career-retrospective collection, ***Wild One : The Greatest Hits*** in May 1990, Quatro, involving herself mostly in the visual arts, spending the early part of the decade working on ITV, also opened in a four-week stint in February 1991 playing scandalous actress Tallulah Bankhead in the musical "Tallulah Who?", which she co-penned with Willy Russell, following a nine-month run in London's West End in "Annie Get Your Gun". Now married to German promoter Rainer Haas, and still performing occasional live dates in the UK, Quatro guests on BBC1-TV's popular comedy series "Absolutely Fabulous". Razor & Tie Records will issue her glam-rock highlights Stateside in April 1996 as ***The Wild One : Classic Quatro***.

QUEEN

Freddie Mercury (vocals); **Brian May** (guitar); **John Deacon** (bass); **Roger Taylor** (drums)

1967

May (b. July 19, 1947, Hampton Hill, Twickenham, Surrey), with help from his father, made his first guitar in 1963, hand-carving the instrument from a 19th-century fireplace. Using a moving pick-up arrangement, he created a wide range of tones and echoes and, using a coin as a pick, honed guitar skills which would become the genesis of the future distinctive Queen guitar sound. Leaving school with ten "O-level" and three "A-level" examination passes, he went on to study astronomy and physics at Imperial College, London (and was also in teenage band the Others, which released *Oh Yeah* in both the UK and US on Fontana.) Invited by Sir Bernard Lovell to work at Jodrell Bank in 1966, May chooses a music career instead and now forms Smile with Taylor (b. Roger Meddows-Taylor, July 26, 1949, King's Lynn, Norfolk) and Tim Staffell, whom he met at Imperial College, on bass.

1970

Having released the US-only Smile single, *Earth*, on Mercury Records the previous year, Staffell leaves to join ex-Bee Gee Colin Petersen's group, Humpy Bong, but persuades his flat-mate Mercury (b. Frederick Bulsara, Sept. 5, 1946, Zanzibar, Tanzania) to join May and Taylor. Ex-Sour Milk Sea and Wreckage vocalist Mercury, his father a government accountant, has moved to England in 1959 with his family, living less than 100 yards from May's home in Feltham, Middx., although they do not meet until this year. Having graduated from Ealing College of Art, London, with a diploma in Graphic Art and Design, he has set up an art and fashion stall in London's Kensington Market with Taylor. Queen is formed, but the group still seeks a regular bass player, and is temporarily using both Mike Grose and Barry Mitchell.

1971

June With science student Deacon (b. Aug. 19, 1951, Leicester, Leics.), who has graduated with first class honors in electronics, having joined on bass in February, Queen plays its first gig at Hornsey's College of Estate Management at Hornsey Town Hall, London, before performing regularly in clubs and colleges while continuing to pursue their own ambitions: May is working towards a doctorate, Taylor is reading for a biology degree and Deacon is teaching.

1972

Aug Queen is invited to showcase new recording hardware at De Lane Lea Studios. Present while they record a demo tape are engineers Roy Thomas Baker and John Anthony (who had worked on the Smile single). They are impressed with the group and suggest to their employers, Trident Audio Productions, that Queen should be signed.
Nov After Trident executives have attended a Queen concert, the company signs the band to a production, publishing and management deal. While Baker and Anthony start work on a debut album at Trident's studios, recording in vacant studio time, the company employs US A&R man Jack Nelson to negotiate a record deal. He hawks a 24-track demo and EMI Records signs the group.

1973

Feb [5] The band records its first session for BBC Radio 1.
Apr [9] EMI launches Queen with a gig at London's Marquee.
June While Queen awaits the launch of its first album, Mercury, as Larry Lurex, releases a revival of the Beach Boys' *I Can Hear Music*.
July EMI releases Queen's debut single, *Keep Yourself Alive*, and first album, ***Queen***. The band supports

Sparks, again at London's Marquee club.
Nov [12] Queen begins a UK tour as support to Mott The Hoople at Leeds Town Hall, Leeds, W. Yorks.

1974

Mar [1] The group begins its first headlining British tour at Blackpool's Winter Gardens set to end with a gig at London's Rainbow Theatre, as the flamboyant Mercury quickly becomes the central character in the line-up.
Apr [6] ***Queen 2***, recorded with state-of-the-art technology, hits UK #5 during a 29-week chart stay.
[12] Queen begins a US tour, again supporting Mott The Hoople, in Denver, CO, as its debut set, ***Queen***, released on Elektra Records in the US, makes #83.
[13] *Seven Seas Of Rhye*, a re-working of a track from the first album, hits UK #10. (Queen makes its BBC1-TV "Top Of The Pops" debut when a David Bowie promo film is unavailable and the group is slotted into the show, making a major impact.)
May [16] Abandoning a US tour, May is flown back to Britain after collapsing with hepatitis in New York, and then develops a duodenal ulcer. ***Queen 2*** makes US #49.
Nov [30] With May fully recovered, ***Sheer Heart Attack*** hits UK #2 during 42-week chart run. The extracted *Killer Queen* also hits UK #2 (behind David Essex's *Gonna Make You A Star*), as the group begins another UK tour, at Manchester's Palace Theatre (ending with a performance at London's Rainbow Theatre).

1975

Feb [5] Queen begins a US trek in Columbus, OH.
[15] *Now I'm Here* peaks at UK #11 as Queen is voted "Band Of The Year" in Britain by **Melody Maker**.
May [17] *Killer Queen*, Queen's first US hit single, reaches #12, as does parent album ***Sheer Heart Attack***. After touring the US and Far East (a territory to which Queen will pay much attention), the group begins recording a new album, with Baker once again producing, using six different studios.
July [3] Mountain Studios, Montreux, Switzerland, which the group has bought from Alex Grob and Anita Kerr, opens.
Sept [19] The group splits acrimoniously with Trident, and signs with Elton John's manager, John Reid.
Nov [1] The first product of the new sessions is the classical pastiche, *Bohemian Rhapsody*, the pinnacle of Baker's lavish production and Mercury's rock operatic writing and performance style. EMI had been reluctant to issue the seven-minute single, but after a copy has been leaked to DJ Kenny Everett at London's Capital Radio, creating a sales demand through heavy airplay, today's release becoming inevitable.
[18] ***Sheer Heart Attack*** is certified gold by the RIAA.
[29] *Bohemian Rhapsody*, now edited to 5 minutes 52 seconds, tops the UK chart for the first of nine weeks, the longest run at #1 since Paul Anka's *Diana* in 1957. Bruce Gowers' innovative promotional video film also boosts the single's sales performance throughout the world. (Although the promo has cost only £5,000, it heralds a new era in the music industry utilizing videos to promote records.)
Dec [14] A UK tour begins at the Empire Theatre, Liverpool, Merseyside.
[24] The group's most successful year ends with a simultaneous live broadcast on BBC1-TV and Radio 1 of its Hammersmith Odeon, London show.
[27] ***A Night At The Opera*** hits UK #1 in a chart run of nearly a year.

1976

Jan [27] Queen begins a four-month tour of US, Japan and Australia at the Palace Theatre, Waterbury, CT.
Feb [7] Its debut album, ***Queen***, reaches UK #24, more than two years after its release.
Mar [9] ***A Night At The Opera*** is certified gold by the RIAA.
Apr [17] ***A Night At The Opera*** hits US #4.
[24] *Bohemian Rhapsody* hits US #9. "Queen At The Rainbow" film is released to UK cinemas, supporting Burt Reynolds' "The Hustle".
May [24] *Bohemian Rhapsody* wins the Best Selling British Record category at the 21st annual Ivor Novello Awards, held at London's Dorchester Hotel.
June [3] *Bohemian Rhapsody* is confirmed gold by the RIAA.
July [17] The second single from the current album, *You're My Best Friend*, hits UK #7, as fresh sessions get underway.
[31] *You're My Best Friend* reaches US #16.
Sept [17] The group gives a free concert in London's Hyde Park with Kiki Dee and Supercharge, before an estimated crowd of 150,000.
Dec [1] Queen, scheduled to appear on ITV show "Today", pulls out at the last minute. EMI replaces the group with recent signing the Sex Pistols, who make a lewd and legendary appearance with host Bill Grundy.
[11] *Somebody To Love* hits UK #2. (Group members have moved into other activities during the year: Mercury producing Eddie Howell's ***Man From Manhattan*** (on which he and May also play), and all members, bar Deacon, playing on Ian Hunter's ***All American Alien***.)
[29] ***A Day At The Races*** is certified gold by the RIAA.

1977

Jan [8] ***A Day At The Races*** tops the UK chart, as Queen begins a North American tour, in an outrageous visual style led by Mercury's flamboyant stage costumes. *Somebody To Love* reaches US #13.
Feb [12] ***A Day At The Races*** hits US #5.
Mar [29] ***Queen*** is certified gold by the RIAA.
Apr [2] *Tie Your Mother Down* reaches UK #31.
[9] *Tie Your Mother Down* makes US #49.
June [17] The band members announce that they are to become tax exiles.
July [2] As the group tours Europe, *Queen's First EP*, with lead track, *Good Old Fashioned Lover Boy*, reaches UK #17. (Taylor, the first group member to cut a solo disc, releases *I Wanna Testify*.)
Oct With its new album completed, Queen begins a US tour that will end at Christmas.
[18] *Bohemian Rhapsody* ties with Procol Harum's *A Whiter Shade Of Pale* as Best British Pop Single, 1952-1977, at the British Record Industry Britannia Awards, honoring the Queen's Silver Jubilee and the centenary of recorded sound at Wembley Conference Centre, Wembley, Middx.
Nov [19] *We Are The Champions* hits UK #2, released as a double A-side with the equally anthemic *We Will Rock You* while parent album, ***News Of The World***, hits UK #4, and starts a climb to US #3, as rumors circulate that Mercury is to go solo.
Dec [28] ***News Of The World*** is certified gold by the RIAA.

1978

Feb *Spread Your Wings* reaches UK #34.
[4] *We Are The Champions* hits US #4. (Both this song and *We Will Rock You* will become enduring crowd chants at US sports events well into the '90s.) Meanwhile, Queen completes a tour of Europe, including only two major UK dates. May contributes guitar to one-time skiffle king Lonnie Donegan's comeback album, ***Puttin' On The Style***.
Apr [25] *We Are The Champions* is certified platinum by the RIAA.
May [27] *It's Late* peaks at US #74, as the band plays a series of UK gigs at Wembley.
July The band begins a three-month stay at Montreux, recording a new album at its own studio.
Nov Double A-side, *Bicycle Race/Fat Bottomed Girls*, reaches UK #11. Queen starts a six-month tour of US, Japan and Europe. ***Jazz*** hits UK #2 and, eventually, US #6.
[16] The audience at New York's Madison Square Garden is treated to the sight of semi-nude female cyclists during Queen's performance of *Fat Bottomed Girls* (a visual device also used in the video). The group is also awarded the Gold Ticket for playing to over 100,000 fans at the venue.
[28] ***Jazz*** is certified platinum by the RIAA.

1979

Jan [13] *Bicycle Race/Fat Bottomed Girls* reaches US #24, as the group begins a UK tour. The US picture sleeve for the single differs from its UK counterpart in that it has a strategically placed bikini on the featured model.
Mar *Don't Stop Me Now* hits UK #9.
[3] *Don't Stop Me Now* stalls at US #86.
July Performance set, ***Live Killers***, recorded at British dates, is released, with the extracted *Love Of My Life*, hitting UK #3 and #63 respectively. (During the month, Mercury dances with Derek Dean and Wayne Eagling at London's Royal Ballet.)
[24] The still-climbing ***Live Killers*** is certified gold by the RIAA.
Aug ***Live Killers*** reaches US #16.
Nov Written by Mercury while taking a bath in Munich's Hilton Hotel, Germany, the light-hearted, rockabilly-sytled *Crazy Little Thing Called Love* hits UK #2. It represents a musical departure for Queen, including Mercury's debut as a rhythm guitarist, and was recorded in Munich with producer Mack, the first outside producer other than Baker to work with Queen to date.
[20] The group embarks on a 14-date UK and Irish tour in Cork, Eire, set to end on December 9th at the Bristol Hippodrome.
Dec Elektra finally releases *Crazy Little Thing Called Love* after US stations begin playing imported copies.
[26] Queen plays at a Kampuchea benefit concert at London's Hammersmith Odeon.

1980

Feb [16] *Save Me* reaches UK #11.
[23] *Crazy Little Thing Called Love* tops the US chart.
May [12] *Crazy Little Thing Called Love* is certified gold by the RIAA.
July *Play The Game* reaches UK #14.
[26] *Play The Game* makes US #42, as Queen begins a US tour that will last until September.
[19] Its parent album, ***The Game***, heads the UK survey for the first of two weeks.
Sept Third single from ***The Game***, Deacon's *Another One Bites The Dust*, with its distinctive Chic-style disco bass line, hits UK #7.
[20] ***The Game*** begins a five-week run atop the US chart.
Oct [1] ***The Game*** is confirmed platinum by the RIAA.
[4] *Another One Bites The Dust* tops the US chart for the first of three weeks. Unexpected support for the single has come from R&B/urban radio stations as it also hits US R&B #2.
Nov [25] *Another One Bites The Dust* is certified platinum by the RIAA.
Dec [27] *Need Your Loving Tonight* makes US #44 as the group tours the UK and Europe.
Flash Gordon, Queen's soundtrack for the futurist film of the same name, hits UK #10 and makes US #23. (During the year, they become the first band to be included in a list in **The Guinness Book Of Records** of Britain's highest paid executives.)

1981

Jan [10] The extracted *Flash* hits UK #10.
[30] *Another One Bites The Dust* wins the Favorite Single, Pop/Rock category at the eighth annual American Music Awards, held at the ABC-TV Studios, Hollywood, CA.
Feb Queen performs again in Japan before setting off on a groundbreaking South American tour, taking in Argentina and Brazil, under the banner "Gluttons For Punishment Tour". (Their South American popularity will soar throughout the decade. A concert in São Paulo is performed before a world-record paying audience of 231,000.)
[14] *Flash* makes US #42.
Apr Taylor's second solo single, *Future Management*, peaks at UK #49, as its parent album, ***Fun In Space***,

reaches UK #18 and US #121.
Nov [14] Queen's ***Greatest Hits*** tops the UK chart, beginning an initial 312-week chart run, and reaches US #14.
[21] *Under Pressure*, Queen's collaboration with David Bowie hits UK #1 (the group's first UK chart-topper since *Bohemian Rhapsody*). *Under Pressure* was recorded so spontaneously that there was no B-side, and as Queen's *Soul Brother* makes the flip, they receive top billing on the single. Its success is also only the second occasion that two previous UK chart toppers have teamed for a #1, the other coupling being Frank and Nancy Sinatra. Queen also becomes the first group to top the Singles, Albums and Video Sales charts simultaneously in Britain.
Dec [30] ***Greatest Hits*** is certified platinum by the RIAA.

1982

Jan [9] *Under Pressure* reaches US #29.
May [8] Queen's *Body Language* reaches UK #25 and US #11.
[15] The dance-based ***Hot Space*** hits UK #4 and US #22. The group, in the middle of a European tour, plays a concert at Milton Keynes Bowl, Milton Keynes, Bucks., which is filmed by C4-TV. (The tour will continue to North America, followed by Japan in the fall.)
June [19] *Body Language* reaches US #11.
July [10] *Las Palabras De Amor* reaches UK #17.
[12] ***Hot Space*** is confirmed gold by the RIAA.
Aug [21] *Calling All Girls* peaks at US #60.
[28] *Back Chat* makes UK #40.
Sept [15] Queen plays what will be its last ever US show at the Great Western Forum, Inglewood, CA.

1983

Apr [21-22] During a year-long Queen sabbatical, May gathers a group of friends for a session at Record Plant Studios in Los Angeles, CA, including Eddie Van Halen (guitar), Fred Mandel (keyboards), Phil Chen (bass) and REO Speedwagon drummer Alan Gratzer.
Nov The first fruit of May's star-session is *Star Fleet*, based on a Japanese children's puppet sci-fi series theme, which peaks at UK #65. The mini-album, ***Star Fleet Project***, reaches UK #35 and US #125. (During the year a change of US distribution to EMI-owned Capitol Records is negotiated.)

1984

Feb Queen's *Radio Ga Ga* enters the UK chart at #4 and climbs to #2, held off the top by Frankie Goes To Hollywood's *Relax*, which is boosted by a further 12" remix to increase its sales for the week. The single is an apparent criticism of contemporary radio programming, while its video effectively integrates a backdrop of scenes from the film "Metropolis". Composed by Taylor, this hit completes a unique chart feat, as all four group members have now individually penned a Top 10 record.
Mar ***The Works***, once again co-produced with Mack, hits UK #2 and US #23, and will stay on the UK chart for 93 weeks.
Apr *I Want To Break Free* hits UK #3 (and will subsequently be adopted by Shell for TV commercials).
[7] *Radio Ga Ga* reaches US #16.
[24] ***The Works*** is certified gold by the RIAA.
May [26] *I Want To Break Free*, which will be adopted by the ANC party in South Africa despite the group's forthcoming visit to Sun City, makes US #45.
June [28] Queen is honored with the Silver Clef award at the annual Nordoff Robbins Music Therapy Centre lunch in London.
July *It's A Hard Life* hits UK #6. Taylor's second solo album, ***Strange Frontier***, reaches UK #30.
Aug After a month of rehearsals, Queen begins a European tour which will include four nights at Wembley Arena. The European dates are followed by a controversial eight-show visit to Sun City in South Africa, putting them on the United Nations cultural blacklist.
[11] *It's A Hard Life* peaks at US #72.
Oct *Hammer To Fall*, the fourth single from ***The Works***, reaches UK #13. Mercury's first solo effort (under his own name) *Love Kills*, taken from the new soundtrack by Giorgio Moroder to Fritz Lang's classic 1926 film "Metropolis", hits UK #10.
Dec Queen's seasonal *Thank God It's Christmas* reaches UK #21.

1985

Jan Queen plays at the "Rock In Rio" festival in Rio de Janeiro, Brazil, as local clergy issue a statement that the group's show will corrupt the nation's youth.
May Mercury's second solo single, *I Was Born To Love You*, reaches UK #11 and US #76. (While the other band members' solo releases have been with EMI, he has signed to CBS.) His solo album, ***Mr. Bad Guy***, also self-written and produced, including *Foolin' Around* from the movie soundtrack to "Teachers", hits UK #10. Taylor produces actor Jimmy Nail's UK #3, *Love Don't Live Here Anymore*, a revival of Rose Royce's 1978 hit.
July [13] Queen performs at "Live Aid" at Wembley Stadium, Wembley, regarded by many as the highlight of the UK end of the benefit spectacular. Organizer Bob Geldof later says "It was the perfect stage for Freddie. He could ponce about in front of the whole world".
Mercury's second single from ***Mr. Bad Guy***, *Made In Heaven*, peaks at UK #57. Taylor, meanwhile, has co-produced Feargal Sharkey's current UK #26 hit *Loving You*.
Sept Mercury's *Living On My Own* makes UK #50.
Nov Queen's *One Vision*, from the soundtrack of the film, "Iron Eagle", hits UK #7. May and Deacon guest on Elton John's ***Ice On Fire***.
Dec ***The Complete Works***, a 14-album boxed set, containing all the group's albums except ***Greatest Hits***, plus a bonus disc of previous single-only tracks, is released.

1986

Jan [11] *One Vision* makes US #61.
Apr Mercury contributes three tracks to the cast recording of Dave Clark's newly-released stage musical, "Time".
[25-27] Queen's first ever fan club convention is held at Great Yarmouth, Norfolk.
[26] *A Kind Of Magic* hits UK #3. (The song and its flipside, *A Dozen Red Roses For My Darling*, are written for the film "Highlander".)
May Deacon has temporarily formed the Immortals, to provide *No Turning Back* for the movie "Biggles".
June [7] Mercury's *Time*, from the album, makes UK #32.
[14] ***A Kind Of Magic***, co-produced by the band with either Mack or David Richards, and featuring Joan Armatrading on *Don't Lose Your Head*, enters the UK chart at #1, and makes US #46.
[28] The extracted *Friends Will Be Friends* reaches UK #14.
July A Wembley Stadium concert is taped for simultaneous broadcast on UK independent TV and radio. Mercury releases a video EP of his four singles to date.
[27] Queen performs at Budapest's Nepstadion in Hungary in front of 80,000 fans during a European tour. The concert, filmed as "Magic In Budapest", is the first by a Western act since Louis Armstrong in 1964, and the first concert to be filmed in Eastern Europe.
Aug [9] Queen returns to Britain to appear at the "Knebworth Festival", Knebworth, Herts., as *A Kind Of Magic* makes US #42. It will be the group's 658th and last concert.
Oct [4] *Who Wants To Live Forever*, with a string arrangement by Michael Kamen, reaches UK #24.
[25] "Real Magic" is broadcast live by satellite on UK Independent television and radio simultaneously, the first such achievement.
Dec Performance album ***Live Magic*** hits UK #3.

1987

Mar [14] Mercury's version of the Platters' *The Great Pretender* hits UK #5.
Apr [15] The group is honored with the Outstanding Contribution To British Music trophy at the 32nd annual Ivor Novello Awards, held at London's Grosvenor House Hotel.
June Mercury participates in the TV special, "Ibiza '92", at the Ku Club, Ibiza.
Oct Taylor, playing guitar rather than drums, has formed the Cross, with Clayton Moss (guitar), Spike Edney (keyboards), Peter Noone (bass) and Josh Macrae (drums). Signed to Virgin Records, their *Cowboys And Indians* makes UK #75.
Nov [14] Increasingly operatic over the years, Mercury's duet with Spanish opera singer Monserrat Caballé, *Barcelona*, hits UK #8.
Dec A three-volume video compilation, "The Magic Years", chronicling Queen's extensive recording and visual career, superseding previous Queen video collections, all of which have been worldwide best-sellers, is released.

1988

Feb [6] The Cross album, ***Shove It!***, peaks at UK #58 in its week of release, as the off-shoot begins a mini-tour. May produces a cover of *Bohemian Rhapsody* by Bad News, the Young Ones comic troupe heavy metal alter egos. (He will also produce singles for current flame, actress Anita Dobson.)
Oct [8] Mercury and Caballé highlight a star-studded show to launch Barcelona's successful bid for the 1992 Olympic Games at the Avinguda De Maria Cristina stadium. The pair's album, also titled ***Barcelona***, reaches UK #25.

1989

May [13] *I Want It All* heralds Queen's collective return, hitting UK #3 and beginning a US climb.
June [3] Its parent album, ***The Miracle***, recalls an earlier Queen sound and hits UK #1. Co-produced with Dave Richards, it also includes follow-up UK hit, *Breakthru'*.
[17] *I Want It All* makes US #50, as ***The Miracle*** goes on to US #24.
July [8] *Breakthru'* hits UK #7.
Aug [26] *The Invisible Man* reaches UK #12.
Oct [28] *Scandal* climbs to UK #25.
Dec [9] *The Miracle* reaches UK #21. May has collaborated with Ian Gillan, Robert Plant and Bruce Dickinson as Rock Aid Armenia, with a remake of *Smoke On The Water*, which makes UK #39, with all profits from the record going to the victims of the Armenian earthquake disaster.
[16] ***At The Beeb***, collecting Queen's BBC radio sessions highlights, peaks at UK #67.

1990

Feb [18] Queen collects the BPI Award for Outstanding Contribution To British Music at the ninth annual BRIT Awards, at the Dominion Theatre, London.
May Cross' second and final album, ***Mad, Bad And Dangerous To Know*** is released by Virgin.
Nov May composes the score for the Red & Gold Theatre Company's production of "Macbeth".
(During the year, the band signs a new US deal including its substantial back catalog, reportedly worth $10million, with Walt Disney's fledgling Hollywood Records.)

1991

Jan [26] *Innuendo* tops the UK chart in its week of release. (At 6 minutes 32 seconds, it is the third longest UK #1 of all time, behind the Beatles' *Hey Jude* and Simple Minds' *Belfast Child*.)
Feb [16] ***Innuendo*** also enters the UK chart at #1. Produced by the band with David Richards, it also begins a rapid US chart rise.
Mar Brian May has co-produced, co-written and performed on the UK Comic Relief 1991 charity single, *The Stonk*, recorded by Hale & Pace & the Stonkers.
[2] ***Innuendo*** reaches US #30.
[23] *I'm Going Slightly Mad* reaches UK #22.
Apr [3] ***Innuendo*** is certified gold by the RIAA.
June [1] *Headlong* reaches UK #14.
Oct [19] May takes part in the closing night of the

"Guitar Legends" series in Seville, Spain, peforming *Now I'm Here*, *Tie Your Mother Down*, and *Driven By You*.

Nov [2] *The Show Must Go On* reaches UK #16.

[9] ***Greatest Hits II*** enters the UK chart at #1.

[24] Mercury dies of complications from AIDS at his Holland Park home, London. A statement is issued by the group and Jim Beach: "We have lost the greatest and most beloved member of our family. We feel overwhelming grief that he has gone, sadness that he should be cut down at the height of his creativity, but above all great pride in the courageous way he lived and died. It has been a privilege for us to have shared such magical times. As soon as we are able we would like to celebrate his life in the style to which he was accustomed". (The group's publicist, Roxy Meade requests that donations be sent to the Terrence Higgins Trust, PO Box 40, London, WC1X 8JU.)

Dec [7] ***Live Magic*** (#51), ***A Kind Of Magic*** (#66) and ***Innuendo*** (#34) all re-chart in the UK.

[14] May's *Driven By You*, helped by its use in a Ford car commercial, hits UK #6.

[21] *Bohemian Rhapsody/These Are The Days Of Our Lives* re-enters the UK chart at #1, as ***Greatest Hits*** hits UK #8. (*Bohemian Rhapsody* sells the most UK copies in its first week since Band Aid's chart-topper in 1984.)

1992

Feb [12] *Bohemian Rhapsody* wins the Best British Single category at the 11th annual BRIT Awards at London's Hammersmith Odeon (presented by DJ Simon Mayo), and Mercury is posthumously honored with the Outstanding Contribution To British Music Special Award

Apr [15] *Bohemian Rhapsody* is named Best Selling A-Side, and May's *Driven By You* Best Theme From A TV/Radio Commercial at the annual Ivor Novello Awards, at London's Grosvenor House. The group donates $1.76 million to the Terrence Higgins Trust from the profits of the reissued *Bohemian Rhapsody*.

[20] May, Deacon and Taylor stage "A Concert For Life" before a crowd of 70,000 at Wembley Stadium, as a tribute to Mercury and a fundraiser for AIDS Awareness. Broadcast to an unprecedented 70 countries worldwide, the event features a plea by Elizabeth Taylor and performances by Metallica, Extreme, Bob Geldof, Spinal Tap, Def Leppard, Guns N' Roses and U2 (via satellite from Sacramento, CA), a first-ever live concert link with South Africa and versions of Queen-backed songs by: George Michael (*Year Of 39*, *These Are The Days Of Our Lives*, with Lisa Stansfield, and *Somebody To Love* with the London Community Gospel Choir), David Bowie (*Under Pressure* with Annie Lennox) and Elton John, performing *Bohemian Rhapsody* with help from Axl Rose, and *The Show Must Go On*, a Mercury song which Queen never played live. Liza Minnelli leads the all-star choral finalé of *We Are The Champions*. May closes an emotional night providing the guitar part to *God Save The Queen* with vocals supplied by the audience. (Spinal Tap introduce their performance, resplendent in regal outfits, declaring that they will cut short their set by 35 songs "because we know Freddie would have wanted it this way".)

May [6] The RIAA certifies gold sales of *The Show Must Go On* and platinum sales of ***Classic Queen***.

[9] *Bohemian Rhapsody*, already extensively featured in the hit movie "Wayne's World", hits US #2, behind Kris Kross' *Jump*, as the compilation, ***Classic Queen***, hits US #4. (All profits from the sale of the single will go to the Earvin "Magic" Johnson AIDS Foundation.)

[23] In a statement released by attorneys, Mercury has bequeathed the majority of his estate (approximately £10 million) to long-time friend Mary Austin.

[26] "Queen - Live At Wembley" is released on video.

[29] Following concerns by their Principal, Donald Quinlan, that his pupils are overly identifying with Freddie Mercury, eighth graders at the Sacred Heart School in Clifton, NJ, decide not to sing *We Are The Champions* at their graduation ceremony. Quinton's objection, mainly due to the fact that Mercury had died from AIDS, leads the students to begin requesting the song on WHTZ (Z100) radio station in New York. When other students hear and request it, it becomes Z100's most requested record, which leads Hollywood Records to release it as a single.

June [6] ***Live At Wembley '86*** debuts at its UK #2 peak, behind Lionel Richie's ***Back To Front***.

[20] ***Live At Wembley*** makes US #53 in its week of entry.

Aug [8] Reissued *We Will Rock You*, backed with *We Are The Champions*, makes US #52.

[15] Mercury and Caballé's reissued *Barcelona* now hits UK #2, behind Snap's *Rhythm Is A Dancer*.

[22] Parent album, ***Barcelona***, debuts at its UK #15 peak.

Sept [9] May and Taylor present a cheque for $300,000 to Magic Johnson for his Magic Johnson Foundation for AIDS Research, at the ninth annual MTV Awards, at the Pauley Pavilion, Los Angeles, at which "Bohemian Rhapsody" wins the Best Video From A Film category.

[19] May's *Too Much Love Will Kill You* hits UK #5.

[27] He performs at a benefit for leukemia patients in Luciano Pavarotti's horse stables in Modena, Italy, with Pavarotti, Sting, Suzanne Vega, Aaron Neville & the Neville Brothers, Mike Oldfield, Bob Geldof, Gipsy Kings, Ute Lemper and Zucchero.

Oct [10] May's ***Back To The Light*** hits UK #6 in its week of entry, as Queen's ***Greatest Hits*** reaches US #11.

[17] Hank Marvin's *We Are The Champions*, featuring Brian May, charts for a week at UK #66.

Nov [9] "Queen : Days Of Our Lives" airs on MTV Europe.

[13] Taylor and Jim Beach open the first Freddie Mercury Building for AIDS Research in Holland.

[28] May's *Back To The Light* reaches UK #19, as the Mercury compilation ***The Freddie Mercury Album*** debuts at its UK #4 peak.

Dec [19] Mercury's *In My Defense* hits UK #8.

1993

Jan [9] Reactivated ***Greatest Hits*** and ***Greatest Hits II*** reach UK #33 and #25 respectively.

[13] ***Greatest Hits*** is certified platinum by the RIAA.

[16] ***Classic Queen*** makes US #94.

Feb [6] Mercury's reissued *The Great Pretender*, currently featured in the movie "Night In The City", bows at its UK #29 peak.

[20] May's ***Back To The Light*** debuts at its US #159 peak.

[23] Brian May's band, comprising Cozy Powell (drums), Neil Murray (bass), Spike Edney (keyboards), Mike Caswell (guitar), Chris Thompson, Maggie Ryder and Miriam Stookloy (vocals), opens for Guns N' Roses in Austin, TX.

Mar [23] The Paul Rodgers-assembled ***Tribute To Muddy Waters***, featuring May, is released by Victory Music.

May [1] Queen and George Michael's EP *Five Live*, from 1992's "A Concert for Life", enters the UK chart at #1, where it will stay for three weeks.

[8] ***Five Live***, issued as a mini-album in the US, debuts at its #46 peak.

[29] The extracted *Somebody To Love*, with Michael, reaches US #30.

June [4] Following US dates supporting Guns N' Roses, the Brian May Band embarks on a ten-date "Back To The Light" UK tour at the Playhouse Theatre, Edinburgh, Scotland, set to end on the 19th at the Bournemouth International Centre, Bournemouth, Dorset.

[26] May's *Resurrection*, with Cozy Powell, reaches UK #23.

Aug [14] Mercury's *Living On My Own* tops the UK chart.

Dec [18] May's *Last Horizon* debuts at its UK #51 peak.

1994

Feb [19] May's ***Live At Brixton Academy*** reaches UK #20 in its week of entry.

May [14] Taylor's *Nazis* debuts at its UK #22 peak.

[25] Mercury posthumously wins the International Hit of the Year category for *Living On My Own* at the 39th annual Ivor Novello Awards, at London's Grosvenor House Hotel.

Sept [17] Taylor's ***Happiness*** reaches UK #22 in its week of entry.

Oct [1] Taylor's *Foreign Sand*, recorded with Yoshiki, debuts at its UK #26 peak, during a two-week chart stay.

Nov [19] ***Greatest Hits I*** and ***II***, re-released by Parlophone in a boxed set in a gold slip case with a full-color 40-page booklet, limited edition, debuts at its UK #37 peak. (The 50,000 CDs are gold colored.)

[26] Taylor's *Happiness?* debuts at its UK #32 peak.

1995

Nov [4] Credited to Queen and featuring Mercury, *Heaven For Everyone*, originally included on Taylor's 1988 Cross album ***Shove It!***, hits UK #2 in its week of entry.

[18] Assembling and revising tracks cut prior to Mercury's death, Queen's ***Made In Heaven*** tops the UK chart in its first sales week.

[25] ***Made In Heaven*** debuts at its US #58 peak.

Dec [23] The extracted *A Winter's Tale* debuts at its UK #6 peak.

1996

Mar [16] *Too Much Love Will Kill You* reaches UK #15.

QUEENSRYCHE

Geoff Tate (lead vocal); **Chris DeGarmo** (guitar); **Eddie Jackson** (bass); **Scott Rockenfield** (drums); **Michael Wilton** (guitar)

1983

Nov The hard-rock quintet has been formed in 1981 in the Seattle, WA suburb of Bellevue by 16-year old Tate (b. Jan. 14, 1959, Stuttgart, West Germany) who links with school friends Wilton (b. Feb. 23, 1962, San Francisco, CA), DeGarmo (b. June 14, 1963, Wenatchee, WA) and Rockenfield (b. June 15, 1963, Seattle), who lived in the same apartment building as DeGarmo and Jackson (b. Jan. 29, 1961, Robstown, TX), all five already veterans of local covers bar-combos. They have already recorded and released their self-written and self-financed 1982 debut EP, *Queen Of The Ryche*, which has led to a contract with EMI America Records, who promptly reissues the set as ***Queensryche***, which, supported by a US tour, now makes US #81.

1984

Dec Their second album, ***The Warning***, reaches US #61 spurred by extensive touring opening for the likes of Bon Jovi and Kiss, earning the group's first gold disc, having already made UK #100 on Sept [24].

1986

Sept Produced by Neil Kernon, ***Rage For Order***, once again showcasing Tate's formidable vocal range set amid the band's progressive-rock style, climbs to US #47, promoted via another US trek opening for Metallica, having already peaked at UK #66 on July [26].

1988

May [21] ***Operation : mindcrime***, a concept album based on the science-fiction writings of George Orwell and produced by Peter Collins, enters the US chart where it will stay for exactly one year, peaking at #50, earning the group's first platinum sales award. It will also climb to UK #58 the following month. The extracted *Eyes Of A Stranger* will spend a week at UK #59 on May [13] the following year.

1990

Sept [22] Marking a softer direction with the inclusion of ballads and orchestration by Michael Kamen, ***Empire***, once again helmed by Collins, debuts at its UK #13 peak.

Oct [6] ***Empire*** hits US #7 on the US survey where it will remain for over two years, exceeding two million sales.
Nov [10] Its title cut, *Empire*, bows at its UK #61 peak.

1991

May *Silent Lucidity* initially reaches UK #34 (but upon reissue, will rise to #18 on Aug [15] the following year).
June [1] Rock ballad, *Silent Lucidity*, hotly rotated by US MTV, hits US #9, the group's first domestic Top 100 single.
July [6] *Best I Can* debuts at its UK #36 peak.
Aug [10] Queensryche embarks on the "Monsters Of Rock" metal package tour also featuring Metallica, Mötley Crüe and Black Crowes, in Copenhagen, Denmark.
Sept [5] Also performing the song, "Silent Lucidity" wins the Viewers Choice category at the eighth annual MTV Video Music Awards, held at the Universal Amphitheatre, Universal City, CA.
[7] *Jet City Woman* bows at its UK #39 peak.
Nov [23] ***Operation : livecrime***, a live souvenir package including the album, a 44-page booklet and a one hour video filmed on location in Wisconsin, peaks at US #38.
Dec [10] The group's current US tour arrives at the Tuscon Community Center, Tuscon, AZ, a bill grossing $131,250 from 7,490 attendees.

1993

June *Real World* is featured in the premiering Arnold Schwarzenegger-starring movie dud, "The Last Action Hero".

1994

Oct [3] The RIAA confirms three million US sales for ***Empire***.
[22] The group's sixth album, ***Promised Land*** enters at its UK #13 high.
Nov [5] Co-produced by the band with James 'Jimbo' Burton, ***Promised Land*** debuts at its US #3 peak.
Dec [13] ***Promised Land*** is certified platinum by the RIAA.

1995

Feb [9] A European tour begins at Glasgow's Barrowland, Scotland, moving on to dates in Germany, France, Belgium and Scandanavia, before climaxing at London's Royal Albert Hall on March 10th.
Mar [16] Their "Promised Land" tour reaches the Koseinekin Hall, Tokyo, Jaoan.
Apr [14] The US leg of its world tour gets underway at the Wings Stadium, Kalamazoo, a bill grossing $97,656 from 4,069 fans.
July EMI Records releases a multimedia version of ***Promised Land***, a two-disc CD-ROM, the labels first such venture.

QUICKSILVER MESSENGER SERVICE

Gary Duncan (guitar); **John Cipollina** (guitar); **David Freiberg** (bass); **Greg Elmore** (drums)

1964

Dec The group forms in San Francisco, CA, with Jim Murray on vocals and harmonica, Cipollina (b. Aug. 24, 1943, Berkeley, CA) on guitar, Freiberg (b. Aug. 24, 1938, Boston, MA) on bass and Casey Sonoban on drums. Skip Spence is briefly involved during early rehearsals at the Matrix club, while Dino Valenti (b. Chester Powers, Nov. 7, 1943, Danbury, CT) is lead vocalist, but a drug-bust and imprisonment quickly put him out of the picture. Elmore (b. Sept. 4, 1946, San Diego, CA) and Duncan (b. Gary Grubb, Sept. 4, 1946, San Diego), both ex-Brogues, join in a new version of the group the following June. After several months of rehearsal in a North Beach basement, Quicksilver Messenger Service will give its first public performance in December 1965.

1966

Feb [26] On a bill with Big Brother & the Holding Company and Great Society, the band performs at the Fillmore Auditorium, San Francisco.
June [3-4] They play again at the Fillmore Auditorium, this time alongside the Grateful Dead and Mothers of Invention.
Nov [18-19] The group performs at the Avalon Ballroom, San Francisco, for the third time during the year.

1967

Jan [14] They appear at the first "Human Be-In" at the Polo Fields, Golden Gate Park, San Francisco, alongside Jefferson Airplane and Big Brother & the Holding Company.
Mar [22-23] They perform at the Avalon Ballroom, on a bill with Steve Miller.
June [17] The band is the sixth act of the second day at the "Monterey International Pop Festival" at the County Fairgrounds, Monterey, CA.
July Having become a huge live attraction around San Francisco (with some 75 gigs at the Avalon Ballroom alone), the group makes a cameo appearance performing two songs in the hippie exploitation movie, "Revolution".
Oct Murray leaves and the group signs to Capitol Records, one of the last current Bay Area bands to sign a recording contract, having held out until Capitol has agreed to all its conditions.
[27-29] They play at the Avalon Ballroom with Taj Mahal and the Sons Of Champlin.

1968

May [10-12] The group performs again at the Avalon Ballroom, this time on a bill with the Ace of Cups and the Flamin' Groovies.
June [21-23] They play at the Fillmore West with Sly & the Family Stone.
Aug Their debut album, ***Quicksilver Messenger Service***, strong on jams and extended instrumental passages due to the lack of a notable lead vocalist, makes US #63. The group appears at the two-day "Newport Festival" in Costa Mesa, CA.

1969

Jan Duncan leaves to form a band with Valenti.
May ***Happy Trails***, including live performances from the Fillmores East and West, with Cipollina and Duncan guitar-led improvizations on Bo Diddley's *Who Do You Love* and *Mona*, makes US #27.
Aug Nicky Hopkins (b. Feb. 24, 1944, London), ex-Steve Miller band and Rolling Stones sideman, joins on piano, just in time to prevent the remaining three-piece band from splitting.
[23] *Who Do You Love*, extracted in shortened form from the previous album, makes US #91.
Dec ***Shady Grove***, featuring Hopkins, makes US #25.
[31] The group plays a New Year's Eve show at San Francisco's Winterland.

1970

Jan [1] Valenti re-joins permanently, and Duncan returns, after playing a New Year's Eve reunion gig.
July Hopkins leaves, and is replaced on keyboards by Mark Naftalin, ex-Paul Butterfield.
Oct ***Just For Love***, recorded in Hawaii and displaying a new, more vocal style, reaches US #27, as Cipollina, disillusioned by the new Valenti-dominated direction, leaves to produce a Jim Murray solo album, the sessions for which result in new band Copperhead.
Nov [7] *Fresh Air*, taken from the album, is the group's biggest US hit single, making #49.

1971

Mar [6] ***What About Me*** reaches US #26, while the extracted *What About Me* (later covered by Moving Hearts) anchors at US #100.
July Freiberg is arrested for drug possession, fined $5,000 and jailed for two months. He is replaced on bass by Mark Ryan. (Freiberg will join Jefferson Airplane in August 1972.)
Oct Naftalin leaves and is replaced by Chuck Steales.
Dec ***Quicksilver*** peaks at US #114.

1972

May ***Comin' Thru*** makes US #134.
Aug The band is again scheduled to play a British tour but for the third time it is cancelled, as the members consider splitting up after playing a week-long "closing down celebration" concert series in San Francisco. Triple set, ***Last Days Of The Fillmore***, includes three Quicksilver tracks and reaches US #40.

1973

June The group does not split but virtually ceases activity, while the compilation, ***Anthology***, peaks at US #108. Ryan leaves and John Nicholas (ex-It's A Beautiful Day) joins on bass. A seven-man version of the group maintains a low live profile the following year and does not record. New members are Harold Aceves (drums), Bob Hogan (keyboards) and Bob Flurie (bass), with Duncan, Elmore and Valenti remaining.

1975

Dec [20] In another line-up change, Valenti, Duncan and Elmore have reunited, now with Skip Olsen on bass and Michael Lewis on keyboards, to record ***Solid Silver***, which now makes US #89. After this, they finally disband. Gary Duncan will exhume the Quicksilver Messenger Service name with Michael Lewis and Sammy Piazzza for ***Peace By Piece*** released in 1987.

1989

May [29] Having spent time in a number of bands over the past 15 years including the Dinosaurs and Man, Cipollina dies from emphysema in Greenbrae, CA.
June [16] Freiberg, Duncan, Elmore, Peter Albin, Spencer Dryden, Robert Hunter, Pete Sears, Mickey Hart, Bob Weir and Huey Lewis & the News' Gibson, Hayes and Mario Cipollina (John's brother), participate in a tribute concert at the Fillmore West, San Francisco.

1994

Nov [16] With ***Happy Trails*** having been certified gold by the RIAA on May 7th 1992, the same year Rhino Records released ***Sons Of Mercury : The Best Of Quicksilver Messenger Service*** on CD (UK reissues label See For Miles followed with its 1993 issue of ***The Ultimate Journey***), Valenti now dies in Santa Rosa, CA.

R

RADIOHEAD

Thom E. Yorke (vocals, guitar, piano); **Ed O'Brien** (guitar); **Jonny Greenwood** (guitar); **Colin Greenwood** (bass); **Phil Selway** (drums)

1991

June Yorke (b. Oct. 7, 1968, Wellingborough, Northants.) having grown up in Scotland before his family moved, when he was eight, to Oxford, Oxfordshire, has formed his first band at the age of ten before moving on to boarding school in Abingdon, Oxfordshire two years later. Subsequently dropping out of further education, he has assembled the group earlier in the year with former classmates and school band members O'Brien (b. Edward John O'Brien, Apr. 15, 1968, Oxford) and Colin Greenwood (b. June 26, 1969, Oxford), and now completes the quintet with Selway (b. May 23, 1964, Hemingford Grey, Cambs.) and Greenwood's brother Jonny (b. Jonathan Greenwood, Nov. 5, 1971, Oxford). Built around self-written material and a three-guitar sound, and quickly dismissing its first name On A Friday, the group settles on Radiohead, taken from a Talking Heads track on ***True Stories***. Based on strong word-of-mouth early gigs and its first demo tape, the group is promptly signed to EMI Records' Parlophone imprint in September.

1992

May Radiohead's debut release, the *Drill EP*, comprising *Prove Yourself*, *Stupid Car*, *Thinking About You* and *You*, is issued by Parlophone to positive UK music media reviews.
Sept The dark, self-deprecating *Creep* is released.

1993

Feb [13] The group's chart debut, *Anyone Can Play Guitar* bows at its UK #32 peak.
Mar [6] Co-produced by Sean Slade, Chris Hufford and Paul Kolderie, their alternative rock-based, well-received freshman set, ***Pablo Honey*** reaches UK #25 in its entry week, eventually earning gold certification from the BPI.
May [22] *Pop Is Dead* enters at its UK #42 peak.
[29] With a strong buzz created by live dates and hot activity on MTV, ***Pablo Honey***, released in the US by Capitol Records, enters the US chart at #184.
Aug [7] ***Pablo Honey*** reaches US #32 and will eventually sell over two million copies worldwide.
Sept [4] *Creep* reaches US #34, having become a mainstay on US college radio, also hitting #2 on the Modern Rock survey.
[18] The reissued *Creep* hits UK #7 in its week of entry.
[27] ***Pablo Honey*** is certified platinum by the RIAA.

1994

May [25] Radiohead plays the first of three UK dates at Manchester University, Manchester, Gtr. Manchester.
June [26] The band plays on the closing day of the annual "Glastonbury Festival", Worthy Farm, Pilton, Somerset.
Aug [27] Radiohead performs on the second day of the annual "Reading Festival", Reading, Berks.
Sept [27] They begin a ten-date UK tour at The Plaza, Glasgow, Strathclyde, Scotland, set to end on October 8th at London's Shepherd's Bush Empire.
Oct [8] *My Iron Lung* EP debuts at its UK #24 peak, as the group begins recording its second album at the Manor, Abbey Road and RAK studios.

1995

Mar [11] *High And Dry*, coupled with *Planet Telex*, bows at its UK #17 peak.
[25] ***The Bends*** enters at its UK #6 high.
May [26] A US tour opens in Boston, set to close on June 15th at the Palace, Los Angeles, CA.
[27] Taped prior to departure, the band is featured on BBC2-TV's "Later With Jools Holland".
June [3] Ballad *Fake Plastic Trees* reaches UK #20.
[24] Produced by John Leckie, the critically-revered ***The Bends*** initially makes US #147. By year's end it

will appear in a host of magazine Top 10 year's best lists including those in **People**, **Melody Maker**, **New Musical Express**, **Musician**, **Billboard** and **Options**.
July [29-30] Radiohead performs at the National Bowl, Milton Keynes, Bucks., a two-day festival headlined by R.E.M, and also including the Cranberries and Blur, which grosses £2,997,728.
Sept [2] *Just*, its Jamie Thraves-directed video clip depicting a man lying down on a pavement (which will draw massive viewer response on MTV-US in November), bows at its UK #19 peak.
[8] Having already supported them on summer Euro-dates, the group begins a US tour opening for R.E.M. at the Miami Arena, Miami, FL, a gig which takes $487,477 at the box office.
[19] Go Discs! releases ***Help!***, a various artists album to benefit the War Child charity, recorded just five days earlier under the direction of prime-movers Brian Eno and Yorke. Controversially excluded from the main UK album chart (which does not include various artists projects), it will immediately head to pole position on the Compilations survey.
Nov [4] With the group currently warming up audiences for Soul Asylum on further US dates, the various artists *Help!* EP taken from the ***Help!*** sessions, and led by Radiohead's *Lucky* hits UK #51.
[7] Radiohead's UK tour comes to a close at the Guildhall, Southampton, Hants.

1996

Feb [19] Together with co-producer Eno, Yorke collects the Freddie Mercury Award for ***Help!*** at the 1996 BRIT Awards held at London's Earl's Court Exhibition Centre.
[4] *Street Spirit (Fade Out)* hits UK #5 in its week of entry.
Mar [16] A month-long US club tour begins.
Apr [4] ***The Bends*** is certified gold by the RIAA.
[6] *High And Dry* makes US #78.
[20] ***Bends*** now peaks at US #88.
July [13] They perform at the third annual "T In The Park" festival staged in Strathclyde, Scotland.
Aug [12] The group begins a 13-date US tour opening for Alanis Morissette at the Darien Lake Performing Arts Center, Darien Center, NY, set to close on the 29th at the Pine Knob Theatre, Clarkston, MI.

GERRY RAFFERTY

1968

Singer/songwriter/vocalist Rafferty (b. Apr. 16, 1947, Paisley, Strathclyde, Scotland), quits the last of a series of Scottish-based rock cover groups, and joins the Humblebums, a folk-based group featuring singer/comedian Billy Connolly and Tam Harvey, which signs to Transatlantic Records and will record two Bill Leader-produced albums, ***The New Humblebums*** (1969) and ***Open Up The Door*** (1970), before splitting. Staying on Transatlantic as a solo artist, Rafferty's first solo effort, ***Can I Have My Money Back?***, emerges in 1971.

1972

In London, he forms Stealers Wheel, conceived as "a Scots version of Crosby, Stills, Nash & Young", with ex-Big Three Joe Egan (b. Oct. 18, 1949, Paisley), a colleague from Paisley, Rab Noakes (guitar), Ian Campbell (bass) and Roger Brown (drums, vocals). By the time the group is signed to A&M Records, this line-up has already splintered, and the debut album, ***Stealers Wheel***, produced by Jerry Leiber and Mike Stoller, features Rafferty and Egan as joint lead vocalists, playing guitar and keyboards respectively, Rod Coombes (drums), Tony Williams (bass) and ex-Big Three guitarist Paul Pilnick. Rafferty leaves the group shortly after the album is recorded and, dissatisfied with the music business, returns to Scotland with his wife and baby. He is replaced by Luther Grosvenor, ex-Spooky Tooth, and Delisle Harper replaces Williams.

1973

May *Stuck In The Middle With You*, co-written by Rafferty and Egan, hits US #6, taken from the similarly co-penned ***Stealers Wheel***, which makes US #50.
June *Stuck In The Middle With You* hits UK #8 and Rafferty is persuaded to rejoin the group.
Sept *Everyone's Agreed That Everything'll Turn Out Fine* reaches US #49 and UK #33. It proves inappropriate, as Pilnick, Coombes and Williams all leave the band. Rafferty and Egan record a second album as a duo, with session help from Joe Jammer (guitar), Gary Taylor (bass) and Andrew Steele (drums).

1974

Feb *Star*, written by Egan from the forthcoming album, reaches UK #25 and US #29.
Apr ***Ferguslie Park***, named after a district of Paisley, peaks at US #181. *Right Or Wrong*, released the following March, recorded by Rafferty and Egan with Bernie Holland (guitar) and Dave Wintour (bass), and produced by Mentor Williams, will fail to chart as Rafferty and Egan permanently split.

1978

Feb Rafferty resurfaces after an enforced absence through management and label problems. Signed to United Artists as a solo artist, he now releases ***City To City***, co-produced with Hugh Murphy and featuring top UK session help including Andy Fairweather-Low and Barbara Dickson.
Apr [1] Following the release of the title track, *City To City*, the self-penned *Baker Street*, driven by an arresting sax riff from session player Raphael Ravenscroft, and helped by saturation UK airplay, hits #3 behind Kate Bush's *Wuthering Heights* and Blondie's *Denis (Denee)*, as ***City To City*** hits UK #6. (Its total worldwide sales will top five million copies.)
June *Baker Street* hits US #2 for six weeks behind Andy Gibb's *Shadow Dancing*. In the UK, the ballad *Whatever's Written In Your Heart* is released as the follow-up, but fails to chart despite strong airplay (as does a competing reissue of old Transatlantic track, *Mary Skeffington*).
[20] ***City To City*** is certified platinum by the RIAA.
July [8] Following his appearance on the "David Frost" US TV show, ***City To City*** tops the US chart, displacing the ***Saturday Night Fever*** soundtrack (which has held at #1 for almost six months). He makes a US promotional visit, but declines (and will continue to refuse) to tour North America.
[12] *Baker Street* is confirmed gold by the RIAA.
Oct *Right Down The Line*, the US follow-up, reaches US #12.

1979

Jan *Home And Dry*, the third US single from ***City To City***, makes #28.
Feb Richard & Linda Thompson's ***Sunny Vista***, partly produced by Rafferty, is released. (Further recording sessions later in the year between Richard Thompson and Rafferty will be canned, but issued for the first time on the 1993 album ***Watching The Dark : The History Of Richard Thompson***.)
May [4] Rafferty wins the Best Song Musically And Lyrically and Best Pop Song categories at the 24th annual Ivor Novello Awards, held at London's Grosvenor House Hotel.
June Rafferty's second United Artists album, ***Night Owl***, again co-helmed with Murphy, hits UK #9.
July ***Night Owl*** reaches US #29, having already earned a gold disc on June 1st for half a million US sales. The title track, *Night Owl*, extracted as a UK single, hits #5, while in the US, *Days Gone Down (Still Got The Light In Your Eyes)* reaches #17.
Sept *Get It Right Next Time*, also from ***Night Owl***, reaches UK #30 and US #21.

1980

Apr *Bring It All Home*, from Rafferty's forthcoming album, peaks at UK #54, as Rafferty performs at London's Royal Albert Hall.
May ***Snakes And Ladders***, recorded at George Martin's Montserrat studio, reaches UK #15.
June *The Royal Mile (Sweet Darlin')*, taken from ***Snakes And Ladders***, peaks at UK #67 (his last UK hit single of the decade).
July ***Snakes And Ladders*** makes US #61.
Aug *The Royal Mile (Sweet Darlin')* peaks at US #54 (his final US hit).

1982

Oct Having built a home recording studio at his Kent farm, ***Sleepwalking*** reaches UK #39. The following February, Mark Knopfler's soundtrack to the movie "Local Hero" featuring Rafferty as a music guest, will be released. (During a lengthy recording sabbatical, Rafferty will subsequently travel with his family to spend a year in Italy before driving across North America.)

1988

May [21] Having signed a new recording deal with London Records and found success as the producer of the Proclaimers' UK #3 hit *Letters From America* the previous November, his label debut, ***North And South***, makes UK #43 in its first sales week. Recorded with long-term friend and producer Hugh Murphy, it yields *Shipyard Town*.

1990

Mar [24] A remixed version of *Baker Street* peaks at UK #53, taken from the 15-track ***Right Down The Line - The Best Of Gerry Rafferty*** retrospective, issued simultaneously by EMI.

1995

Oct [28] Following PWL-signed act Underground's UK #2 revival of Rafferty's *Baker Street* in September 1992, and subsequently signed to A&M Records, Rafferty's ***A Wing And A Prayer***, co-produced as always with Murphy and including three songs co-written with his singer-songwriting brother Jim, charted for a week at UK #73 on Feb [13] 1993, followed by a seven-date UK tour at the Brighton Dome, Brighton, East Sussex which ended on the 28th of that month at London's Hammersmith Apollo. A further CD collection, ***One More Dream - The Very Best Of Gerry Rafferty*** now reaches UK #17 in its week of entry.

RAGE AGAINST THE MACHINE

Zack de la Rocha (lead vocals); **Tom Morello** (guitar); **Timmy C** (bass); **Brad Wilk** (drums)

1992

July [13] With its roots in Orange County, CA, but based in Los Angeles, CA, the group has been assembled the previous year by former Lock Up guitarist (who recorded one album for Geffen Records in 1989) and 1986 Harvard graduate Morello (b. 1964, New York, NY), whose father fought as part of the Kenyan Mau Maus guerilla movement which opposed British rule, while his mother is a co-founder of the anti-censorship pressure group, Parents For Rock And Rap, and ex-Lock Up colleague Wilk (b. Portland, OR) who have successfully auditioned Timmy C and ex-Inside Out frontman and eye-catchingly dreadlocked Rocha (b. 1970, Long Beach, CA), who lives in Irvine, CA and is the son of a Spanish mural painter. As a punk-inspired, hardcore metal/hip-hop fused quartet, and on the strength of raucous early live shows around Los Angeles and 5,000 12-cut cassette tapes which it has sold at gigs, the band has been eagerly snapped up by Epic Records, after rejecting overtures from Madonna's Maverick-owned label among others. Fuelled by Rocha's confrontational lyrics and vocal style and Morello's shrieking guitar play, the band quickly earns a devoted live following opening for the likes of Body Count, Public Enemy, Pearl Jam, Tool, and now supporting Porno For Pyros at the latter's debut gig in Los Angeles.

Sept [11] Rage Against The Machine performs on the second stage at "Lollapalooza II", also held in Los Angeles.

Oct [1] The group begins its first European tour opening for Suicidal Tendencies, controversial dates set to end on the 24th.

1993

Jan [23] The band headlines a "Rock For Choice" benefit at the Palladium, Hollywood, CA, also featuring Eddie Vedder, Screaming Trees and Mary's Danish, among others.

Mar [6] *Killing In The Name* makes UK #25.

[8] The group begins a US tour with House Of Pain.

[20] Co-produced by the band with Garth Richardson, their venomous and uncompromising debut album, ***Rage Against The Machine***, spurred by glowing reviews from the relevant alternative music media and a controversial cover photograph depicting a self-immolating Buddhist monk protesting the Vietnam war, reaches UK #17. It will enter the US chart on May [1], but will take nearly one year to peak.

May [8] Following an appearance on C4-TV's "The Word", *Bullet In The Head* enters at its UK #16 high.

July [18] Appearing completely nude at a Lollapalooza gig in Philadelphia, PA, the group spends 25 minutes in silent protest (wearing duct tape across their mouths), refusing to play a single note, with the initials P-M-R-C (Parents Music Resource Center, the pro-censorship pressure group) scrawled across their chests.

Sept [4] *Bombtrack* bows at its UK #37 peak during a UK tour.

[11] The band headlines an Anti-Nazi League benefit at London's Brixton Academy.

Oct [14] The group begins a headlining US tour at Hollyood's Palladium.

Nov [17] Further US dates opening for Cypress Hill begin in Denver, CO.

Dec [19] MTV's "120 Minutes" program (US) airs the first showing of the band's "Freedom" video which combines live footage with text from Peter Matthiessen's book **In The Spirit Of Crazy Horse**.

1994

Feb [19] ***Rage Against The Machine*** finally peaks at US #45 during an 89-week chart run.

Apr [28] A Rage-organized benefit concert "For The Freedom Of Leonard Peltier", also featuring Cypress Hill, Mother Tongue and X, raises $75,235.91 for the Leonard Peltier defense fund, at California State University, Dominguez Hills, CA.

June [24] The band plays on the first day of the "Glastonbury Festival", Worthy Farm, Pilton, Somerset.

July [30] The group plays at the "T In The Park" festival Strathclyde Country Park, Hamilton, Strathclyde, Scotland.

Aug [17] Already confirmed platinum in Australia, Canada, the UK, France, Belgium and Chile, ***Rage Against The Machine*** is certified platinum by the RIAA.

Oct [22] The group performs at "Latinpalooza", another fund-raiser, this time for United Farm Workers and Para Los Ninos, at the Grand Olympic Grounds, Los Angeles.

Dec [30] The film soundtrack ***Higher Learning***, including the new Rage cut *Year Of The Boomerang*, is released by Epic.

1995

Aug [13] The group's own headlining benefit concert for the International Concerned Friends And Family Of Mumia Abu-Jamal, also featuring Chuck D, the Sullivan Brothers and Handsome among others, takes place at the Capitol Ballroom, Washington, DC.

1996

Apr [13] The band's US network TV debut on NBC-TV's "Saturday Night Live" is cut short by one song after its stage crew has attempted to drape inverted US flags on the amplifiers. *Bulls On Parade* hits UK #8 in its week of entry.

[14] The Peter Christopherson-directed video for "Bulls On Parade" receives its premiere on MTV's "120 Minutes" (US).

[19] The group plays a secret gig at Hollywood's Dragonfly club, Hollywood, CA.

[20] The band performs another Los Angeles date at the Velodrome, Dominquez Hills.

[27] The group's sophomore album, ***Evil Empire*** hits UK #4 in its week of entry.

May [3] Rage begins a headlining European tour in Madrid, Spain.

[4] ***Evil Empire*** enters the US chart at #1 having sold 250,000 in its first week.

[11] The band's first UK dates in three years bow at London's Brixton Academy.

June [15-16] The group participates in the Tibetan Freedom Concert in San Francisco, CA, a benefit concert organized by the Beastie Boys for the Milarepa Fund.

Aug [23] The band performs at the annual Reading Festival, Reading, Berks.

RAINBOW

Ritchie Blackmore (lead guitar); **Ronnie James Dio** (vocals); **Tony Carey** (keyboards); **Jimmy Bain** (bass); **Cozy Powell** (drums)

1975

Apr [7] Rock guitarist Blackmore (b. Apr. 14, 1945, Weston-super-Mare, Somerset) leaves Deep Purple after a show in Paris, France. He has become disillusioned by the band's direction, despising the just-completed ***Stormbringer***, and has recorded *Black Sheep Of The Family*, rejected by Deep Purple, with American band Elf, which has toured as Purple's support band and recorded its second album, ***Carolina County Ball***, for Purple records.

May After Elf has completed its final album, ***Trying To Burn The Sun***, with producers Roger Glover and Martin Birch, the group, minus its guitarist Steve Edwards, who departs to Florida, with Dio (b. July 10, 1949, Cortland, NY) on vocals, Mickey Lee Soule on keyboards, Craig Gruber on bass and Gary Driscoll on drums, teams with Blackmore as Ritchie Blackmore's Rainbow. He takes the band to Musicland Studios, Munich, West Germany, to record ***Ritchie Blackmore's Rainbow***.

July Gruber leaves as soon as the album sessions are complete, and is replaced on bass by Bain, ex-Harlot.

Sept ***Ritchie Blackmore's Rainbow***, released on Purple's offshoot Oyster label, reaches UK #11 and US #30.

Oct Soule and Driscoll leave the band, and Blackmore recruits Powell (b. Dec. 29, 1947, Cirencester, Gloucs.) (ex-Bedlam and solo success with *Dance With The Devil*, but more recently driving racing cars for Hitachi) and Carey (b. Oct. 16, 1953, Fresno, CA), from Los Angeles, CA country group Blessings, to join himself, Dio and Bain.

1976

July ***Rainbow Rising***, recorded by the new line-up, reaches UK #11, where it is released on Polydor Records, and US #48, still on Oyster.

Aug [31] The group makes its UK stage debut to promote the album and will tour US, Canada, Europe and Far East for the remainder of the year.

1977

Jan Bain is fired by Blackmore for being musically out of step with the band (or at least with its leader). His replacement on bass is Mark Clarke, ex-Uriah Heep, among others.

May The band records a new album at Le Chateau Studio in Paris, France. During the sessions, Blackmore becomes disenchanted with both Carey and Clarke, and elbows both from the band. Studio recordings are halted and Blackmore decides to assemble a live album instead.

July David Stone, keyboards player with Canadian band Symphonic Slam, joins after auditioning in Los Angeles for Blackmore, while Australian bassist Bob Daisley, ex-Steve Ellis' band Widowmaker, is also recruited.

Aug Live double album, ***On Stage***, recorded by the band's second line-up during its late 1976 tours, with the billing shortened to Rainbow, hits UK #7 and makes US #65.

Sept *Kill The King* is Rainbow's first chart single, making UK #44. A UK tour is postponed until November while the new players are being broken in.

Nov The group plays four nights at London's Rainbow Theatre during its British tour.

Dec The band returns to the Paris studios to complete a third studio album.

1978

Jan Rainbow tours Japan before further North America dates through much of the rest of the year.

Apr *Long Live Rock'n'Roll*, trailering the new album, reaches UK #33.

May Produced by Martin Birch, ***Long Live Rock'n'Roll*** hits UK #7 and reaches US #89.

Oct Extracted from the album, and marketed on red vinyl, *L.A. Connection* reaches UK #40.

Nov After a lengthy period on the road, perfectionist Blackmore has become more disillusioned with most of his band. At the end of a US tour, he unloads everybody but Powell (Dio will re-emerge as vocalist with Black Sabbath). He settles in his US home in Connecticut before renewed auditioning.

Dec Blackmore plays at London's Marquee club with ex-Deep Purple colleague Ian Gillan's band over Christmas. He fails to persuade Gillan to become Rainbow's vocalist, but recruits Don Airey, ex-Colosseum, on keyboards.

1979

Apr Blackmore brings in vocalist Graham Bonnet, one-time hitmaker as half of the Marbles, but later less successful as a solo singer, and Roger Glover (b. Nov. 30, 1945, Brecon, Powys, Wales), ex-Deep Purple with Blackmore, and now mainly producing, joins on bass.

Sept ***Down To Earth***, recorded by the new line-up and produced by Glover, hits UK #6 and reaches US #66.

Oct The extracted *Since You Been Gone*, written by ex-Argent singer/writer Russ Ballard (and a 1978 US chartmaker for Head East), hits UK #6.

Dec *Since You Been Gone* peaks at US #57.

1980

Mar *All Night Long*, a Blackmore/Glover composition, also from ***Down To Earth***, hits UK #5.

Aug [16] Powell quits the band following its headlining appearance at the first "Monsters Of Rock Festival" in Castle Donington, Leics.

Oct [1] Bonnet also leaves, to pursue a solo career signed to Vertigo Records. Joe Lynn Turner, ex-US group Fandango, joins as lead singer, while Bobby Rondinelli is recruited on drums.

1981

Feb *I Surrender*, another Russ Ballard song, gives Rainbow its highest singles hit at UK #3. It is taken from ***Difficult To Cure***, produced by Glover, which also hits UK #3.

Apr ***Difficult To Cure*** makes US #50, spurred by a US tour.

July *Can't Happen Here*, a remixed version of a Blackmore/Glover song from ***Difficult To Cure***, reaches UK #20.

Aug Polydor UK reissues both the band's first hit single, *Kill The King*, and its original album, ***Ritchie Blackmore's Rainbow***, which re-chart at UK #41 and #91 respectively.

Nov Airey leaves (later to join Ozzy Osbourne's group), and is replaced on keyboards by Dave Rosenthal, in time for a UK tour.

Dec Compilation album, ***The Best Of Rainbow***, reaches UK #14, while the four-track 12" EP *Jealous Lover*, its title track having been the UK B-side of

Can't Happen Here, recorded at a leisurely, tour break session in a church hall, peaks at US #147.

1982

Apr *Stone Cold* climbs to UK #34, taken from ***Straight Between The Eyes***, which hits UK #5.
June *Stone Cold* makes US #40, and ***Straight Between The Eyes*** US #30. The band plays a world (excluding Britain) tour to promote the album.

1983

Sept Rondinelli has been replaced by former Brand X drummer Chuck Burgi for ***Bent Out Of Shape***, which reaches UK #11. Taken from it, *Street Of Dreams* peaks at UK #52. MTV in the US bans its promo video, which visually demonstrates hypnosis.
Oct The band plays its first UK tour since 1981, playing a set drawn mainly from the recent album.
Nov *Can't Let You Go*, also from ***Bent Out Of Shape***, makes UK #43, while ***Bent Out Of Shape*** reaches US #34.
Dec *Street Of Dreams* peaks at US #60.

1984

Mar [14] In Rainbow's final live show, in Japan, they are accompanied by a Japanese symphony orchestra, and the set includes Blackmore's adaptation of Beethoven's "Ninth Symphony". Following the Japanese tour, he decides to fold the band as both he and Glover are invited to re-join the most successful line-up of Deep Purple (with Jon Lord, Ian Gillan and Ian Paice).
Apr Deep Purple officially re-forms, with Blackmore and Glover as members.

1986

Mar Double Rainbow compilation, ***Finyl Vinyl***, remixed for release by Glover, and containing many unheard live items by Rainbow, plus scarce tracks previously only on singles B-sides, reaches UK #31 and US #87, a successful coda to the band's career.
see also: **DEEP PURPLE**

BONNIE RAITT

1969

Raitt (b. Nov. 8, 1949, Burbank, CA), daughter of Broadway musical star John Raitt ("Oklahoma", "Carousel" and "Kiss Me Kate"), has grown up in Los Angeles, CA since 1957 with her Quaker family, who also take a liberal and pacifist political stance, which will influence much of her benefit and charity work in the future. She has taken up guitar at the age of eight, when she received a $25 Stella instrument as a Christmas gift, and, encouraged by her father, has become a proficient blues and folk guitarist by the time she relocated to Radcliffe College in 1967 to read African studies. Now leaving Radcliffe, she begins playing blues guitar at small coffee houses, like Club 47, in the Boston, MA area, after her boyfriend, musician Dick Waterman, has introduced her to Otis Rush, Fred McDowell and Son House, and promoted her early shows. Over the next two years, Raitt will enjoy increasing cult success on the burgeoning East Coast folk and blues scene, regularly playing at such venues as The Gaslite, New York, NY, and Main Point, Philadelphia, PA. Influenced not least by the recordings of Joan Baez, Bob Dylan, Muddy Waters and John Hammond, Raitt performs with her regular sideman, bassist Freebo.

1971

Nov Signed to Warner Bros. Records, Raitt's maiden album, ***Bonnie Raitt***, is released, showcasing her musical range with blues material from Robert Johnson and Sippie Wallace, sitting alongside early R&B and country.

1972

Sept [10] Raitt participates in the "Ann Arbor Jazz & Blues Festival", in Ann Arbor, MI, with Sippie Wallace.
Dec Her sophomore album, ***Give It Up***, produced by Michael Cuscuna and including three self-penned songs and contributions from Jackson Browne and Eric Kaz, gives her a US chart debut, peaking at #138.

1973

Dec Having moved back to Los Angeles, CA, ***Takin' My Time*** reaches US #87, aided by constant US touring. Produced by John Hall (of Orleans), it features Lowell George, Bill Payne, Jim Keltner and Taj Mahal among many session luminaries. It also includes an early recording of the Kaz-penned *Cry Like A Rainstorm* (to become the title album cut for Linda Ronstadt's platinum album of 1989) and *Guilty*, inked by Randy Newman.

1974

May During the month Raitt performs in Cambridge, MA, supporting Bruce Springsteen.
Dec Now firmly set in the alternate pattern of touring and recording, ***Streetlights***, produced at the Hit Factory in New York by R&B veteran Jerry Ragavoy, with the help of top local session players, peaks at US #80.

1975

Dec Her fifth album, ***Home Plate***, produced in Los Angeles by Paul Rothchild and featuring her growing family of guest musicians and friends (not least Freebo), including John Hall, J.D. Souther, Bill Payne, Tom Waits and Browne, reaches US #43, prompting her first appearance on the cover of **Rolling Stone** magazine. Now performing up to 100 concerts per year, Raitt will embark on a US tour supporting Little Feat the following May.

1977

July Her most commercially-successful Warner Bros. album, ***Sweet Forgiveness***, reaches US #25. With her regular touring band of Will McFarlane (guitar), Jef Labes (keyboards), Dennis Whitted (drums) and Freebo (bass), and additional vocalists Michael McDonald and J.D. Souther, the Rothchild-produced set includes a revival of Del Shannon's *Runaway*, which gives Raitt her first chart single at US #57.
Aug Raitt performs at London's Hammersmith Odeon during current UK dates.

1979

Aug [4] Raitt joins Browne, Emmylou Harris, Nicolette Larson, McDonald, Ronstadt and members of Little Feat in a benefit concert in aid of Lowell George's widow, at the Great Western Forum, Inglewood, CA. The 25,000 audience raises $230,000.
Sept [19-23] Raitt co-organizes and performs at the Musicians United For Safe Energy (MUSE) anti-nuclear concerts at New York's Madison Square Garden, alongside Bruce Springsteen, Jackson Browne, Carly Simon, the Doobie Brothers and others.
Oct [13] Following a one-year recording hiatus, ***The Glow*** is released, set to make US #30. Co-produced by Val Garay and Peter Asher, it again showcases the depth and variety of Raitt's musical style, and highlights both her electric and slide steel guitar experience and expertise.

1980

Jan The extracted Robert Palmer-penned *You're Gonna Get What's Coming* peaks at US #73, while ***No Nukes***, the triple-set recording of last September's MUSE concerts featuring Raitt, reaches US #19.
Oct [24] ***Sweet Forgiveness*** is certified gold by the RIAA.

1982

Mar [6] ***Green Light*** is released, featuring a new backing group, the Bump Band, including keyboardist Ian McLagan (ex-Small Faces), drummer Ricky Fataar (ex-Beach Boys), bassist Ray Ohara and guitarist Johnny Lee Schell. Marking a move towards a rockier, more pop-oriented sound, the album will reach US #38.

1985

Dec [3] ***Give It Up*** is confirmed gold by the RIAA.
[14] Following a period of semi-retirement (during which Raitt has continued her battle with alcohol and drug abuse), Artists Against Apartheid, comprising 49 acts including Raitt, makes US #38 and UK #21, with *Sun City*.

1986

Sept ***Nine Lives***, Raitt's ninth and last album for Warner Bros., peaks at US #115. Produced by Billy Payne and George Massenburg, it includes songs from Karla Bonoff, Tom Snow, Bryan Adams, Will Jennings, Richard Kerr and, as on each of her albums to date, Kaz. It also features her old friend and blues mentor, Sippie Wallace, singing on her revival of Toots & the Maytals' *True Love Is Hard To Find*.
Dec Still consistently touring, Raitt performs at Los Angeles' Beverly Theater.

1987

Apr Having recently joined a program for recovering alcoholics, Raitt spends two days in recording sessions in Minneapolis, MN, with Prince, who had seen her perform in December 1986.
July [4] She participates in "The July Fourth Disarmament Festival" in the Soviet Union with James Taylor, Santana, the Doobie Brothers and several Russian groups.
Dec By year's end, her increasing involvement in charity, political and benefit causes will see her organize the "Stop Contra Aid" concert, featuring herself along with Don Henley, Herbie Hancock and others, participate in Amnesty International and Farm Aid annual gatherings, and film a homeless awareness video, "Wake Up America", with Bonnie Bramlett and Rita Coolidge.

1988

During a year in which she signs a new recording contract with Capitol Records, and begins taping her label debut, Raitt also contributes her version of the "Dumbo" classic, *Baby Mine*, to Hal Wilner's A&M compilation of Disney standards, ***Stay Awake***, and another song to the Marlo Thomas-organized project-for-children album, ***Free To Be A Family***. Both tracks are produced by Don Was (of Was (Not Was)), who will be recruited to oversee production of her forth-coming album.
Dec [12] Raitt attends a memorial tribute to Roy Orbison with Tom Petty, Graham Nash, and Don Henley, among others.

1989

Apr [15] Raitt's Capitol label debut, ***Nick Of Time***, produced by Was, enters the US album chart. It will be regarded as her most consistent work to date and will stay charted for exactly two years. It includes guest contributors Was (Not Was) vocalists Sweet Pea Atkinson and Sir Harry Bowens, Crosby & Nash, Kim Wilson, Herbie Hancock, David Lasley and regulars Fataar and Schell.
Oct While album cuts *Thing Called Love* and *Love Letter* prove popular on US radio, Raitt is featured on John Lee Hooker's newly released ***The Healer***. A long-standing and popular recording guest, Raitt's other recent contributions include projects by David Crosby, Colin James, Emmylou Harris, B.B. King, Ivan Neville, Little Feat and Jackson Browne.
Nov Raitt performs a week-long series of concerts benefitting the National Sanctuary Defense Fund, an organization aiding Central American refugees.
Dec [27-28, 30-31] Raitt plays before four sellout crowds at the Oakland-Alameda County Coliseum, Oakland, CA, supporting the Grateful Dead.

1990

Feb [21] At her career peak, Raitt sweeps the 32nd annual Grammy Awards, held at the Shrine Auditorium, Los Angeles, winning Album Of The

Year (***Nick of Time***), Best Pop Vocal Performance, Female (*Nick Of Time*), Best Rock Vocal Performance, Female (*Nick Of Time*), and Best Traditional Blues Recording (*I'm In The Mood* from John Lee Hooker's ***The Healer***).

[24] Raitt takes part in the "Roy Orbison Concert Tribute To Benefit The Homeless", with host Whoopi Goldberg and Dwight Yoakam, k.d. lang, Bruce Hornsby, Gary Busey, Dean Stockwell, Roger McGuinn, David Crosby, Chris Hillman, Bob Dylan, Was (Not Was) and B.B. King, among others, at the Universal Amphitheatre, Universal City, CA.

Mar [8] Raitt wins the Best Female Singer category in **Rolling Stone** magazine's Critics Awards.

Apr [7] In its 52nd chart week, ***Nick Of Time*** finally hits US #1, and the extracted *Have A Heart*, featured in the Bob Hoskins/Denzil Washington-movie "Heart Condition", peaks at US #49. Raitt takes part in "Farm Aid IV" at the Hoosier Dome, Indianapolis, IN.

[16] Raitt participates in the "Nelson Mandela - An International Tribute To A Free South Africa" concert at Wembley Stadium, Wembley, Middx., singing *Blowin' In The Wind* with Anita Baker, Mica Paris and Natalie Cole.

[24-25] Raitt joins a host of celebrities at Don Henley's benefit concerts to preserve the historic Walden Woods, at the Centrum, Worcester, MA.

May [5] ***Nick Of Time*** also gives Raitt her UK chart debut at #51.

[26] *Nick Of Time* peaks at US #92.

July [25] A sellout US tour begins at Poughkeepsie, NY, where Raitt had attended summer camp as a child, supported by blues guitarist Jeff Healey and R&B piano legend Charles Brown.

Aug [25] Warner Bros.-issued retrospective, ***The Bonnie Raitt Collection***, compiled by Raitt herself, peaks at US #61, and includes a previously unavailable live duet with Sippie Wallace of her *Women To Be Wise*.

[31] Raitt sings *Amazing Grace* with Jackson Browne and Stevie Wonder at the memorial service for Stevie Ray Vaughan, at the Laurel Land Memorial Park, Oak Cliff, Dallas, TX.

Oct [4] Raitt joins Rickie Lee Jones, Melissa Etheridge and Dianne Reeves at a "Vote Choice" concert to benefit the pro-choice activism of the Hollywood Women's Political Committee, at the Wadsworth Theater, Los Angeles.

Nov [16-17] Raitt joins Bruce Springsteen and Browne in two all-acoustic benefit concerts at the Shrine Auditorium, the proceeds of which will go to the Christic Institute to finance a lawsuit claiming that the US government sanctioned illegal arms sales and drugs trafficking to finance covert operations in the Iran-contra affair.

Dec [16] Raitt and Browne perform at a concert in Sioux Falls, ND, to commemorate the 100th anniversary of the massacre of Sitting Bull at Wounded Knee.

[25] Raitt and actor Michael O'Keefe announce their engagement.

1991

Jan [16] Raitt inducts John Lee Hooker into the Rock and Roll Hall of Fame at the sixth annual ceremony, held at New York's Waldorf Astoria Hotel, and also performs *In The Mood* with Hooker and Robert Cray, and *Mustang Sally* with John Fogerty, Chaka Khan and Bruce Springsteen at the traditional post-dinner jam.

Mar [9] The Peace Choir's *Give Peace A Chance*, to which Raitt contributes, peaks at US #54.

Apr [28] Raitt and O'Keefe marry at the Union Church, Tarrytown, NY. The bride is given away by her father.

July [6] Raitt's second outing for Capitol, ***Luck Of The Draw***, with guests Richard Thompson, Bruce Hornsby and John Hiatt among others, and co-produced with Was, debuts at its UK #38 peak.

[12] Raitt performs at the annual "Montreux Jazz Festival" in Switzerland.

[14] She plays at London's Hammersmith Odeon during a short UK tour.

[26] A US trek, with Chris Isaak supporting, opens in Park City, UT.

Aug [17] ***Luck Of The Draw*** hits US #2, behind Natalie Cole's ***Unforgettable With Love***.

Sept [1] Raitt donates a percentage of profits from her Saratoga Springs, NY concert to environmental groups battling a proposed coal-burning power plant in upstate New York.

[17] She guests on NBC-TV's "The Tonight Show".

Oct [4] Now touring with John Prine, Raitt performs at the State Fair of Texas at the Starplex Amphitheatre, Dallas, TX.

[19] *Something To Talk About* hits US #5.

[26] Raitt is the musical guest on NBC-TV's "Saturday Night Live".

Nov [25] She appears on BBC1-TV's "Wogan" as she prepares for a UK tour.

Dec [6] Raitt ends her UK visit at the Free Trade Hall, Manchester, Gtr. Manchester.

[14] *I Can't Make You Love Me*, a ballad co-written by former Cincinnati Bengal defensive end Mike Reid, and featuring Bruce Hornsby's trademark piano, debuts at its UK #50 peak.

1992

Jan [29] Raitt attends the ceremony honoring her father's addition to the Hollywood Walk of Fame.

Feb [15] *I Can't Make You Love Me* reaches US #18.

[21] "Bonnie Raitt & A Gathering of Friends" acoustic show is held at the Orpheum Theatre, Boston, to raise funds to find a bone marrow donor for musician Reeve Little.

[22] Raitt is named MusiCares 1992 Person of the Year at their annual NARAS MusiCares Foundation dinner at the Waldorf Astoria, which also features performances by Jackson Browne, Natalie Cole and David Crosby.

[25] She wins Best Pop Vocal Performance, Female for *Something To Talk About*, Best Rock Performance By A Duo Or Group with Vocal for *Good Man, Good Woman* with Delbert McClinton, and Best Rock Vocal Performance, Solo for her ***Luck Of The Draw*** album at the 34th annual Grammy Awards, from Radio City Music Hall, New York, at which she also performs *I Can't Make You Love Me* with Hornsby.

Apr [16] Raitt wins Outstanding Female Vocalist at the Boston Music Awards, at the Wang Center, Boston.

[18-19] Her concerts in Santa Rosa, CA, raise $80,000 for Democratic congressional candidate Dan Hamburg's campaign to preserve California's Pacific coastline.

May [2] Raitt accepts an honorary doctorate degree in music from the Berklee College of Music in Boston.

[16-17] She performs with her father and the Boston Pops at Boston's Symphony Hall during which they sing *Hey There* and *Blowin' Away*.

[23] Raitt plays a benefit gig for California congress-woman Barbara Boxer in Los Angeles.

July [13] *Not The Only One* makes US #34.

[26-28] She supports Eric Clapton and Elton John at Wembley Stadium, Wembley, Middx.

Aug [10] Raitt, Gary Busey and Hoyt Axton come onstage to sing *With A Little Help From My Friends*, at a Ringo Starr concert at the Greek Theatre, Los Angeles.

[20] She guests on NBC-TV's "Late Night With David Letterman".

Sept [6] Back on the road, Raitt plays to a sellout crowd of 5,301 at the Mud Island Amphitheatre, Memphis, TN, with support act Lyle Lovett.

[15] Prior to a Hollywood Bowl show with Robert Cray, she says she will donate part of the proceeds from the concert to the "Rebuild L.A." organisations.

[16] Raitt attends a fundraiser for presidential hopeful Bill Clinton, at Ted Field's Beverly Hills estate, spon-sored by the Hollywood Women's Political Committee.

Oct [11] She participates in "Healing The Sacred Hoop - The Next 500 Years" benefit for the Inter-national Indian Treaty Council, at the Shoreline Amphitheatre, Mountain View, CA. (The following day, some acts on the bill give a free concert in downtown San Francisco.)

Nov [8] Raitt participates in the "Imua Hawaii" benefit at the NBC Arena, Honolulu, HI, to help victims of Hurricane Iniki, with Crosby Stills & Nash, Jackson Browne and Jimmy Buffett.

Dec [7] She is one of the featured guests on "The Winans Real Meaning Of Christmas" which airs in syndication on US TV.

[11] Raitt makes a return visit to "The Tonight Show".

1993

Feb [25] She co-hosts the fourth annual Rhythm and Blues Foundation's Pioneer Awards at the Hollywood Palace, Hollywood.

Apr [10] Willie Nelson's ***Across The Borderline***, featuring Raitt's vocals on *Getting Over You*, debuts at its US #75 peak.

[27] Raitt participates in "Aretha Franklin : Duets", the diva's first TV special, taped at New York's Nederlander Theatre, singing *Since You've Been Gone* with Franklin and *Natural Woman* with Franklin and Gloria Estefan. (The show, which benefits the Gay Men's Health Crisis, will air on Fox-TV on May 9th.)

May [22] She guests on CBS-TV's "Willie Nelson The Big Six-O" birthday celebrations.

[24] Raitt presents writers Mike Reid and Allen Shamblin with an award for *I Can't Make You Love Me*, at the 10th annual ASCAP Pop Awards dinner at the Beverly Hilton Hotel, Beverly Hills, CA.

June [29] The 1990 Warner compilation, ***The Bonnie Raitt Collection***, is certified gold by the RIAA.

Nov [5] Raitt performs at the seventh annual Bridge School benefit at the Shoreline Amphitheatre, Mountain View, CA.

Dec [4] Elton John's ***Duets*** album, featuring *Love Letters* with Raitt, debuts at its UK #4 peak, reaching US #25 a week later.

1994

Jan [26] The RIAA certifies five million sales of ***Luck Of The Draw***.

Feb [23] Raitt performs at the "No Nukes On The River" concert at the University of Minnesota, Minneapolis, MN with Soul Asylum's Dave Pirner and Dan Murphy.

Mar [1] She performs a medley in tribute to Curtis Mayfield at the 36th annual Grammy Awards with Bruce Springsteen, Steve Winwood, B.B. King and others.

[2] Raitt guests on CBS-TV's "Late Show With David Letterman" in tandem with Jerry Butler and Ben E. King.

Apr [9] *Love Sneakin' Up On You* charts for a week at UK #69.

[16] Co-produced with Was and featuring the Memphis Horns, David Lasley and Richard Thompson among many others, ***Longing In Their Hearts*** tops the US chart and reaches UK #26 in its week of entry.

May [7] *Love Sneakin' Up On You* reaches US #19.

June [18] Ballad *You*, written by Bob Thiele Jr., John Shanks and Tonio K, debuts at its UK #31 peak, during a two-week chart stay.

July [9] Raitt embarks on a summer tour of North America, at the Pine Knob Music Theatre, Clarkston, MI.

Aug [13] *You* peaks at US #92.

Oct [1] Raitt guests on NBC-TV's "Saturday Night Live". (A Richard Thompson tribute album ***Beat The Retreat***, to which Raitt has contributed *When The Spell Is Broken* is released.)

Nov [21-22] Having completed the second leg of her North American tour, with Hornsby in support, Raitt now plays two sellout dates at the Arlington Theatre, Santa Barbara, CA, with her father and John Lee Hooker guesting.

[23] The RIAA confirms two million sales of ***Longing In Their Hearts***.

Dec [13] The RIAA certifies four million sales of ***Nick Of Time***.

1995

Feb [27] Raitt performs at the annual MusiCares benefit, with Tony Bennett, Natalie Cole and David Crosby.

Mar [1] She wins the Best Pop Album category for ***Longing In Their Hearts*** and performs *Love Sneakin' Up On You* at the 37th annual Grammy Awards, held at the Shrine Auditorium.
[2] As the organization's vice-chairman, Raitt attends the sixth annual Rhythm and Blues Foundation Pioneer Awards, to bestow $220,000 in grants to Cissy Houston, Darlene Love, Junior Walker and others.
[22] Raitt begins a 12-date tour of New Zealand, Australia and Japan, at the Town Hall, Wellington, North Island, New Zealand.
[25] *You Got It*, faithfully reviving Roy Orbison's 1989 US #9 hit and featured in the movie "Boys On The Side", reaches US #33.
May [11] Raitt takes part in PBS station KLRU's in its tribute to Stevie Ray Vaughan at Austin's Music Hall for broadcast on "Austin City Limits".
[24] She begins a North American tour at Hardee's Walnut Creek Amphitheatre, Raleigh, NC.
July [14] Raitt participates in the Joy Community Outreach to end Homelessness celebrity auction fundraiser at the Hollywood Athletic Club, Universal City, CA.
Oct [24] She guests with her father on "Late Show With David Letterman".
Nov [11] *Rock Steady*, a duet with Bryan Adams, enters at its UK #50 high.
[25] Recorded in July at the Paramount Theatre, Oakland, CA, the live album ***Road Tested*** debuts at its US #44 and UK #69 peaks.
Dec [2] *Rock Steady* makes US #73.
[3] Raitt performs a medley of B.B. King's hits with Etta James and Dr. John at the 18th annual Kennedy Center Honors in Washington.

1996

Jan [23] She guests on NBC-TV's "The Tonight Show".
Feb [28] She performs briefly with her father at the 38th annual Grammy Awards held at the Shrine Auditorium.
Apr [19] Her first multimedia work, ***Burning Down The House*** E-CD is released by Capitol in the US, featuring five full-length live clips, interviews, lyrics and one music video.
Aug [6] ***A Tribute To Stevie Ray Vaughan***, including a performance by Raitt, is released by Epic Records (US).

THE RAMONES

Joey Ramone (vocals); **Johnny Ramone** (guitar); **Dee Dee Ramone** (bass); **Tommy Ramone** (drums)

1974

Aug [16] After a first gig at a private party, the Ramones, having formed in Forest Hills, New York, NY, begin a residency at New York's seminal new-wave venue CBGB's club. The original line-up is Johnny Ramone (b. John Cummings, Oct. 8, 1951, Long Island, New York), Ritchie Ramone, soon to be replaced by Dee Dee Ramone (b. Douglas Colvin, Sept. 18, 1952, Fort Lee, VA) and Joey Ramone (b. Jeffrey Hyman, May 19, 1952, Forest Hills). Tommy Ramone (b. Thomas Erdelyi, Jan. 29, 1952, Budapest, Hungary) takes over on drums to let Joey sing. They all adopt the working surname Ramone.

1975

June The band auditions for Rick Derringer and Blue Sky Records by opening for Johnny Winter at Waterbury, CT, in front of a 20,000 audience, though the label will not sign them.
Nov Danny Fields becomes the band's manager, and negotiates a recording contract with Sire Records.

1976

Feb The group records its debut album on a $6,400 budget.
May *Blitzkrieg Bop*, their debut single, is released, taken from ***The Ramones***, a furiously-paced punk set which peaks at US #111.
July [4] The group celebrates the US bicentennial by making its debut at London's Roundhouse with fellow patriots the Flamin' Groovies and the Stranglers. They are also currently featured in the punk film, "Blank Generation".
Nov The Ramones pull out of a UK tour twin-headlining with the Sex Pistols. The Damned and the Clash replace them.

1977

Mar ***Leave Home*** peaks at US #148, once again comprising short, high-octane punk cuts.
May ***Leave Home*** makes UK #45, while the group begins its first UK tour, popularizing its no-frills "1-2-3-4" intros to every song, and its "Gabba gabba hey!" catchphrase.
June *Sheena Is A Punk Rocker* reaches UK #22.
[6] The group plays two shows at London's Roundhouse with Talking Heads.
July The Heartbreakers release *Chinese Rocks*, co-written by Dee Dee Ramone. The band is invited to Phil Spector's home, as its winter UK tour is cancelled.
Aug *Swallow My Pride* makes UK #36.
Sept *Sheena Is A Punk Rocker* peaks at US #81.
Dec ***Rocket To Russia*** reaches US #49 and UK #60. (During the year, Joey is hospitalized in New York after suffering second degree burns to his face, neck and upper chest after he drops a teapot.)

1978

Jan *Rockaway Beach* peaks at US #66.
May Tommy Ramone leaves the band (but remains their producer, credited as T. Erdelyi). He is replaced by Marc Bell (b. July 15, 1956, New York) from Richard Hell's Voidoids, who takes the name Marky Ramone. *Do You Wanna Dance* peaks at US #86.
Oct *Don't Come Close* makes UK #39 while ***Road To Ruin***, on which the group makes an effort to write songs lasting more than their usual two minutes, reaches US #103 and UK #32.

1979

Apr [25] Roger Corman's film, "Rock'n'Roll High School" premieres in Los Angeles, CA. The band is featured in the film, performing the title track and a new Paul McCartney song, *Did We Meet Somewhere Before*.
June Live album, ***It's Alive***, recorded at London's Rainbow Theatre, reaches UK #27.
Aug Soundtrack album, ***Rock'n'Roll High School***, with the Ramones tracks re-mixed by Phil Spector, is released.
Sept *Rock'n'Roll High School* peaks at UK #67. (Spector has reportedly listened to the opening chord for ten hours.)

1980

Jan ***End Of The Century***, produced by Spector, makes US #44 and UK #14. Recorded in five different studios, the band will later denounce ***Century*** as its worst album.
Feb *Baby I Love You*, their cover of the Spector-produced Ronettes hit from 1964, hits UK #8.
Apr *Do You Remember Rock'n'Roll Radio* peaks at UK #54.
Aug [18] The group begins a six-week European tour at the Assembly Rooms, Derby, Derbys. They will play London's Hammersmith Odeon the following night and the Playhouse, Edinburgh, Scotland, on the 24th during "Edinburgh Rock Festival" week.

1981

Aug ***Pleasant Dreams***, produced by Graham Gouldman in New York and England, makes US #58.
Sept [3-5] The Ramones perform in front of almost 500,000 during the three-day "US Festival" in San Bernardino, CA. (The following year, Joey will cut *I Got You Babe* with Holly Beth Vincent of Holly & the Italians.)

1983

Apr ***Subterranean Jungle***, produced by Beserkley Records' Ritchie Cordell and Glen Kolotkin, makes US #83. Marky Ramone leaves the group and is replaced by Richard Beau from the Velveteens, who becomes the second Ritchie Ramone.
Aug [21] Joey Ramone is found at 3:30 a.m. by police on East 10th St. and rushed to St. Vincent's Hospital, New York, where he undergoes four hours of emergency brain surgery to remove blood clots. (He was in a fight with fellow musician Seth Micklaw of Sub Zero Construction over his girlfriend, Cynthia Whitney.)

1985

Jan Signed to Beggars Banquet in the UK, the Ramones' ***Too Tough To Die***, with contributions from Talking Heads' Jerry Harrison and Tom Petty & the Heartbreakers' Benmont Tench, makes UK #63 having already peaked at US #171 the previous November.
Feb *Howling At The Moon*, co-produced by Eurythmics' Dave Stewart, peaks at UK #85.
June *Bonzo Goes To Bitburg*, a reference to a controversial visit by US President Ronald Reagan to a Nazi war grave, is released.
[22] The Ramones perform at Milton Keynes Bowl, Milton Keynes, Bucks., supporting bill-toppers U2.
Dec [14] Artists United Against Apartheid, comprising 49 artists including Joey Ramone, make US #38 and UK #21 with *Sun City*.

1986

May *Somebody Put Something In My Drink/ Something To Believe In* peaks at UK #69, taken from ***Animal Boy***, which reaches US #143 and UK #38. ***Halfway To Sanity*** will make UK #78 in its week of entry on Oct [10] the following year and will peak at US #172, as Marky re-joins the band.

1989

June After the retrospective album, ***Ramones Mania***, has made US #168 the previous June and Johnny Ramone has joined Debbie Harry for the August-released duet, *Go Lil' Camaro Go*, the ***Brain Drain*** now peaks at US #122.
Aug Dee Dee leaves the group to become rap performer Dee Dee King, replaced by C.J. Ramone (b. Christopher Joseph Ward, Oct. 8, 1965, Long Island). Meanwhile, Joey appears as himself in the film "Roadkill".
[19] ***Brain Drain*** anchors at UK #75.
The group contributes music to the film of Stephen King's "Pet Semetary", with help from Debbie Harry and Chris Stein.

1990

Jan Joey tears ligaments in his ankle at New York's Ritz club, causing the cancellation of February dates.
June [12] A best-of CD, ***The Ramones ... All The Stuff Plus More***, is released by Sire.
[28] "The Escape From New York" world tour with Jerry Harrison, Deborah Harry and Tom Tom Club begins in Columbia, MD.
Sept [27] Dee Dee is arrested on a marijuana possession misdemeanor charge, in a drug sweep of Greenwich Village's Washington Square Park area in New York.
Dec [8-9] The group performs at London's Brixton Academy during its current UK visit.
[29] They play to a sellout crowd of 2,575 at The Ritz, New York.

1991

May Joey launches "Spring Offense At CBGB's", a two-day festival of new bands.
Oct [21] Chrysalis Records releases ***Loco Live***, a 33-track live album recorded at Barcelona's Sala Zeleste in early 1991.
Dec [2] The group begins a seven-date UK tour with the Damned at the Hummingbird, Birmingham, West Midlands, set to end on the 7th and 8th at Brixton Academy.

[30] The Ramones play a year-end date at Toad's Place, New Haven, CT, during a US club tour.

1992

Mar Dee Dee, no longer rapping, forms Dee Dee Ramone & the Chinese Dragons with Ritchie Screech (guitar), Alan Bama (bass) and Scott Goldstein (drums).
June [9-10] The group plays at the RPM, Toronto, during a Canadian tour.
Sept C.J. breaks his arm while riding a Harley Davidson round the stage before a performance at a festival in Germany.
[26] Now signed to Radioactive Records, ***Mondo Bizarro***, featuring Vernon Reid, Joe McGinty, Andy Shernoff and Flo & Eddie, and including a cover of the Doors' *Take It As It Comes*, and *Censorshit*, a riposte to Tipper Gore, the former chairperson of the PMRC, charts for a week at US #190.
Oct [8] The Ramones play a sellout show at the Roseland Theater, Portland, OR, at the start of a US tour, supported by Social Distortion, set to end on November 13th at the Orpheum Theatre, Boston, MA.
[16] The group guests on NBC-TV's "The Tonight Show".
Dec [13] They embark on a six-date UK visit at the Rainbow, Bristol, Avon, set to close on the 20th at the Brixton Academy.
[26] *Poison Heart* peaks at UK #69.

1993

Jan [30] Joey takes part in a 29th anniversary celebration of the Roe vs. Wade abortion ruling at The Ritz, New York, with Joan Jett, Alison Moyet, Lunachicks and Fluid. (He will also join with General Johnson to perform *Rockaway Beach* for ***The Godchildren Of Soul : Anyone Can Join*** compilation.)
Oct [21] The group sings *Happy Birthday* on Fox-TV's "The Simpsons".

1994

Jan [28] The Ramones perform in Sydney, New South Wales, Australia, during the four-date third annual "Big Day Out" Festival.
[29] ***Acid Eaters***, an album of cover versions including their version of the Who's *Substitute*, with Pete Townshend on backing vocals, is released on the Radioactive label, charts for a week at US #179.
Feb [2] They begin an eight-date Japanese tour in Tokyo.
Mar [10] The group embarks on another US tour, before a sellout crowd of 3,500 at the Hollywood Palladium, Hollywood, CA, with Frank Black supporting.
June [3] Joey Ramone throws himself a 42nd birthday party in Manhattan. Debbie Harry sings *Happy Birthday*, while Joey and his brother Michael Hyman run through a selection of Ramones songs.
[27] ***Ramones Mania*** is certified gold by the RIAA.

1995

Apr [7] The Ramones play a sellout club date at Toad's Place, New Haven, CT.
May [29] They take part in the all-star "New Rock 102.1 Fest" at the Marcus Amphitheatre, Milwaukee, WI, with Duran Duran, Faith No More, Bush, Violent Femmes and others.
July [8] ***Adios Amigos*** makes UK #62 in its week of entry.
[11] Joey reiterates, in a **USA Today** interview, that the group's new album will be its swan song, disappointed with the band's modest commercial success after 21 years, particularly in light of the current popularity enjoyed by current young pretenders Green Day and Offspring.
[22] ***Adios Amigos*** bows at its US #148 peak, during a two-week chart stay.
Aug [2] Their "Adios Amigos" farewell tour, which the group insists will be its last, opens at the Strand Theater, Providence, RI, set to close in the US on September 17th at the Ted Gormley Stadium, New Orleans, LA, before a five-date jaunt in Buenos Aires, Argentina.
Nov [18] Their farewell retirement tour continues at the Palace of Auburn Hills, Auburn Hills, MI, with White Zombie.

1996

Feb [3] The Ramones perform a one-off retirement date in the UK at the Brixton Academy.
[9] They guest on CBS-TV's "Late Show With David Letterman".
[14] The group plays another farewell concert at the Avalon Ballroom, Boston, MA.
Mar [3] "Lollapalooza" tour organizers announce that the Ramones will be on the bill for this summer's annual US rock caravan trek.

SHABBA RANKS

1980

Ranks (b. Rexton Fernando Gordon, Jan. 17, 1966, Sturgetown, Jamaica), inspired by the Jamaican dancehall roots toasting of Yellowman, Charlie Chaplin and Josey Wales, has moved to the tough streets of Kingston, and begins singing and recording in small local Jamaican clubs and studios under the name DJ Don, moulding a unique new vocal style, which will mix rap with Jamaican dancehall reggae swing (raggamuffin), increasingly veering towards a "slackness" (X-rated) hip-hop style. Following work at the Jammys studio/label in the mid-'80s, Ranks goes on to record with Bobby Digital for the Digital B label, and, by decade's end, is turning out a prodigiously large number of locally-released product (including *Are You Sure*, *Best Baby Girl*, *Maama Man*, *Get Up Stand Up* and *Golden Touch*), amassing a significant regional following which is spreading to the Caribbean communities in both London and New York.

1990

Following the huge regional success of the blatantly sexual *Wicked In Bed*, on Digital B, Ranks, managed by the Specs Shang agency, is signed to Epic Records, while specialist UK reggae label Greensleeves releases ***Golden Touch***, rounding up Ranks' recent 12" singles and an earlier album, ***Rapping With The Ladies***.

1991

Apr [6] *She's A Woman*, recorded with the credited Scritti Politti, reaches UK #20.
May [25] *Trailor Load A Girls* peaks at UK #63.
June [29] ***As Raw As Ever***, bringing his innovative drum-machine dancehall/rap/reggae fusion, based largely on sexual themes, to a wider audience, peaks at UK #51.
Sept [14] The extracted *Housecall (Your Body Can't Lie To Me)*, a duet with Maxi Priest, makes UK #31.
Nov [23] ***As Raw As Ever*** makes US #89.
Dec [7] *Housecall (Your Body Can't Lie To Me)* reaches US #37.

1992

Jan [30] ***As Raw As Ever*** is certified gold by the RIAA.
Feb [25] ***As Raw As Ever*** wins Best Reggae Album category at the 34th annual Grammy Awards, held at the Radio City Music Hall, New York, NY. (Ranks is the first reggae artist to win a Grammy, an honor never bestowed even upon Bob Marley.) Encouraged by his win, and amid rumors that he is now a millionaire, burglars empty Ranks' Jamaican home, while, during a busy month, Ranks also becomes a father to his first child, Shabboo.
Apr He collects six trophies at the International Reggae Awards ceremony in Jamaica, having nabbed two Caribbean Music Awards in March.
Aug [1] *Mr. Loverman*, from the movie soundtrack ***Deep Cover***, makes US #40.
[8] An early greatest hits collection, ***Rough And Ready Vol. 1***, makes US #78, with sales eventually topping 250,000.
[15] *Mr. Loverman* reaches UK #23.
[22] ***Rough And Ready Vol. 1*** debuts at its UK #71 peak.
[29] Ranks performs at the closing ceremonies of Sony Music Distribution marketing meetings at the Westin Harbour Castle Hotel, Toronto, ON, Canada.
Sept He is accused of rape by a woman who appeared in his "Trailer Loada Girls" video, the fourth time he has been accused of such a crime.
[29] Ranks is hailed in a **USA Today** lead article as the new Bob Marley.
Oct He embarks on a US tour supporting Bobby Brown, but will pull out in February 1993, after collapsing at a video shoot.
Nov [14] ***Xtra Naked***, featuring Queen Latifah, Chubb Rock and Johnny Gill, makes US #64.
[28] Promoted by a burlesque-style promo clip, *Slow And Sexy*, featuring Johnny Gill and produced by Jimmy Jam and Terry Lewis, bows at its UK #17 peak.
Dec Ranks appears on C4-TV's "The Word" saying that "gays deserve crucifixion", the latest in the controversial artist's outspoken statements on sexuality.
[30] The still-climbing *Slow And Sexy* is certified gold by the RIAA.

1993

Jan [9] *Slow And Sexy* reaches US #33.
[16] Ranks wins the World Male Artist category at the 25th annual NAACP Image Awards at the Pasadena Civic Auditorium, Pasadena, CA, set to air on the 23rd.
[20] ***X-Tra Naked*** is certified gold by the RIAA.
Feb [24] He snares his second consecutive Grammy for Best Reggae Album (***X-Tra Naked***), at the 35th annual Grammy Awards held at the Shrine Auditorium, Los Angeles, CA.
Mar [2] Scheduled to appear on the next night's NBC-TV's "The Tonight Show", Ranks is axed from the program following complaints by GLAAD (Gay and Lesbian Alliance Against Defamation) over his recent comments on homosexuality. Commenting further on his alleged gay-bashing comments, Ranks says: "Everybody has their own beliefs in life. If they say Shabba is anti-gay, that's their belief. If they say Shabba is gay, that's their belief. Each to his own."
[3] Organizers of the "Fun-d Fest" charity benefit at the Pasadena Rose Bowl, Pasadena, CA, set for April 3rd, withdraw an invitation for Ranks to appear as co-headliner.
[6] *I Was A King*, duetted with actor Eddie Murphy, charts for a week at UK #64.
[20] *Mr. Loverman* hits UK #3.
Apr [24] Reactivated ***Xtra-Naked*** re-charts at UK #38.
May [22] *Housecall (Remix)* hits UK #8.
[28] Ranks performs at the Hummingbird, Birmingham, West Midlands, during current UK dates.
June [26] *What'cha Gonna Do?*, featuring Queen Latifah, debuts at its UK #21 peak.

1994

Jan [8] *Family Affair*, Ranks' cover of Sly & the Family Stone's 1971 US #1/UK #15, and featured in the film "Addams Family Values", reaches UK #18.
Feb [19] *Family Affair* debuts at its US #84 high.

1995

Apr [1] *Let's Get It On* makes US #81.
[29] *Let's Get It On* enters at its UK #22 peak.
June [30] Ranks performs on the "Hot 97 Summer Jam" bill at the Byrne Meadowlands Arena, East Rutherford, NJ, on a bill with Brandy, Notorious B.I.G., Method Man, Naughty By Nature, Soul For Real and Blackstreet.
July [1] Featuring guests Sly & Robbie and Steely & Clevie among many others, ***A Mi Shabba*** debuts at its US #13 peak.
Aug [5] *Shine Eye Gal*, featuring Mykal Rose, debuts at its UK #46 peak.

1996

Aug [12] He embarks on a US tour with Maxi Priest

and Shaggy under the collective banner "Reggae Madness".

THE (YOUNG) RASCALS

Felix Cavaliere (vocals, keyboards);
Eddie Brigati (vocals, percussion);
Gene Cornish (guitar); **Dino Danelli** (drums)

1964

Feb The group forms as a trio, comprising ex-Joey Dee & the Starliters' Cavaliere (b. Nov. 29, 1944, Pelham, New York, NY), Brigati (b. Oct. 22, 1946, Garfield, NJ) and Cornish (b. May 14, 1946, Ottawa, ON, Canada) (an ex-member of the Unbeatables who released one album on the Fawn label in 1964, and the single *I Wanna Be A Beatle*), in Garfield, and their first gigs as a rock/R&B trio are at the local Choo Choo club. Having begun in the high-school singing group the Stereos, Cavaliere went on to form Felix & the Escorts with Mike Esposito (later called the Blues Magoos), while they attended Syracuse University, Syracuse, NY, releasing one single, *The Syracuse*, on the Jag label, before being asked to tour Europe with Joey Dee & the Starliters. He first met Brigati when the latter came backstage to see his brother, David Brigati, also a member of the Starliters. (David will later sing backing vocals in the studio with the Rascals.) Shortly after, Danelli (b. July 23, 1945, New York), an old friend of Cavaliere's (they have been in Sandu Scott & Her Scotties together), who has played jazz with Lionel Hampton and in various New York and Las Vegas club house bands, joins on drums as the quartet becomes the Rascals.

July The Rascals become the resident band at the Barge, a floating, fashionable nightclub off Southampton, Long Island, NY. A 45-minute set of familiar and self-penned R&B, interspersed with rock oldies, is honed, with the group wearing choirboy shirts and knickerbockers.

Aug New York promoter Sid Bernstein becomes interested in the group, and takes over as manager. He turns down offers from Red Bird and Phil Spector's Philles Records, and signs them (now as the Young Rascals and minus the uniforms) to Atlantic Records for a $10,000 advance, and an agreement that they could use the studio whenever it was available, free of charge.

1965

Aug [15] They perform on the Beatles bill at Shea Stadium, New York, before playing a four-week engagement at New York's Harlow club. They have become regulars on the New York club scene, also playing at Tom Jones, the Phone Booth and Steve Paul's The Scene.

Nov [2] The group cuts its first single, *I Ain't Gonna Eat Out My Heart Anymore*.

1966

Jan *I Ain't Gonna Eat Out My Heart Anymore*, written by Pam Sawyer and Lori Burton, and heavily supported (due to the group's overtly black sound) by R&B radio stations, makes US #52.

Apr [30] *Good Lovin'*, a Rudy Clark/Artie Resnick song, originally an R&B hit for the Olympics in 1965, tops the US chart for a week, boosted by four appearances on CBS-TV's "The Ed Sullivan Show" and an April 14th slot on NBC-TV's "Hullabaloo", and is the group's first million seller.

July *You Better Run*, the first self-penned A-side (by Cavaliere and Brigati), reaches US #20, while their debut album, ***The Young Rascals***, heavy on R&B cover versions from the group's stage act, reaches US #15 during an 84-week chart stay.

Oct Cavaliere's composition, *Come On Up*, makes US #43.

Nov [29] The group arrives in Britain for a brief visit which will include appearances on "Ready, Steady, Go!" and "Saturday Club", and a live appearance on December 1st at Blaises, London, before flying to Paris, France, on their way home to the US.

1967

Mar *I've Been Lonely Too Long*, another Cavaliere/Brigati collaboration, with a Motown dance feel (aiding its progress on the US R&B chart), makes US #16. ***Collections*** reaches US #14.

May [4] *Groovin'*, the first self-produced effort by the band, with assistance from Atlantic's Tom Dowd and Arif Mardin, signals a move towards a more uniquely Young Rascals sound than their R&B style, fusing Latin influences and a cool jazz sensitivity. Written by Cavaliere and Brigati about a woman Cavaliere loves by the name of Adrian, and a euphemism for Sunday afternoon sex, it tops the US chart for the first of four weeks. (DJ Murray The K had been at the session when the group recorded the cut, and went to the Atlantic brass, demanding that they release it.)

June [13] *Groovin'* is certified gold by the RIAA.

July *Groovin'* is the band's UK chart debut, hitting #8.

Aug *A Girl Like You* hits US #10 and makes UK #37, the group's UK chart swan song.

Sept ***Groovin'***, featuring the previous two singles and the forthcoming release, hits US #4.

Oct *How Can I Be Sure* is another change of pace, inspired by romance in Cavaliere's life (he will marry shortly). Wrapped in a loping arrangement, with French accordion and strings, it hits US #4.

[4] The band embarks on a UK tour, with Traffic, at Finsbury Park Astoria, London.

1968

Jan The psychedelia-inflected *It's Wonderful* reaches US #20. The group has become absorbed in the "Summer Of Love" philosophy, and Cavaliere adopts Indian philosopher Swami Satchidananda as his guru, with the whole band becoming involved in the latter's Integral Yoga Institute.

Mar On tour in Florida, the group's trailer breaks down outside Fort Pierce, and the Young Rascals encounter heavy anti-rock and racist harassment from rednecks. In response to this, they announce they will play no further live bills which do not include at least one black act.

Apr ***Once Upon A Dream***, an effects-laden concept album in *It's Wonderful*-style, hits US #9. While on tour, Cavaliere is admitted to San Diego Hospital, San Diego, CA, with an internal complaint keeping him hospitalized for two weeks. Remaining West Coast dates are cancelled.

May The group persuades Atlantic to drop the "Young" from its name, and *A Beautiful Morning* appears as by the Rascals. Their third million selling single, it hits US #3.

June The Rascals participate in a "Soul Together" concert at New York's Madison Square Garden with Aretha Franklin, Sonny & Cher, Joe Tex, King Curtis and Sam & Dave.

[28] *Beautiful Morning* is certified gold by the single.

July [22] ***Groovin'*** is confirmed gold by the RIAA, as will be ***Collections*** a week later.

Aug [17] *People Got To Be Free* tops the US chart for the first of five weeks, set to become their fourth and last million-selling single. Written by Cavaliere and Brigati, the song is the former's reaction to the assassinations of Martin Luther King and Robert Kennedy, whose campaign the band had worked for, earlier in the year.

[23] *People Got To Be Free* is certified gold by the RIAA.

Sept [4] ***The Young Rascals*** and the still-rising ***Time Peace/The Rascals Greatest Hits*** are both certified gold by the RIAA.

[28] Compilation album, ***Time Peace/The Rascals' Greatest Hits***, heads the US chart for a week during a 58-week chart stay.

Dec *A Ray Of Hope*, the last Rascals A-side co-written by Brigati and Cavaliere, and a deliberate sequel to *People Got To Be Free* (dedicated to Senator Edward Kennedy who responds with an appreciative letter to the group), reaches US #24.

1969

Feb The Rascals perform at London's Royal Albert Hall.

Mar *Heaven*, penned by Cavaliere (as are the remainder of the group's chart hits) in waltz-time, makes US #39.

Apr [21] Still-climbing ***Freedom Suite*** is certified gold by the RIAA.

May Double album, ***Freedom Suite***, reaches US #17 and includes the wholly-instrumental *Music Music*, a new departure for the group.

June *See* climbs to US #27.

[20] The Rascals play at the "Newport '69 Rock Festival" at Devonshire Downs, Northridge, CA, alongside Jimi Hendrix, Jethro Tull and Creedence Clearwater Revival, among others.

Oct *Carry Me Back* reaches US #26.

Dec [15] The group plays a rare UK gig, supporting John Lennon's Plastic Ono Supergroup at London's Lyceum Ballroom, at a benefit for UNICEF.

1970

Jan [28] The Rascals take part in a seven-hour benefit concert at Madison Square Garden, along with Judy Collins, Peter, Paul & Mary, and others, for the Vietnam Moratorium Committee.

Feb ***See*** makes US #45, while the extracted *Hold On* peaks at US #51.

[5] Eddie quits the band on the day they sign a five-year, $1million deal with CBS/Columbia.

Aug The gospel-flavored *Glory Glory*, with vocal backing from the Sweet Inspirations, peaks at US #58.

1971

Mar ***Search And Nearness*** charts for a week at US #198. It is their final album for Atlantic and the last to feature Cornish, who leaves after its completion. He and Brigati are replaced by Buzzy Feiten (b. New York City, NY) (guitar) and Robert Popwell (Daytona, FL) (bass), while vocalists Ann Sutton and Molly Holt also join, expanding the line-up to a sextet.

July *Love Me* peaks at US #95, the group's only singles chart entry on Columbia, and its final US Hot 100 single. It is taken from their debut Columbia album, ***Peaceful World***, which makes US #122.

1972

May ***The Island Of Real*** peaks at US #180. Soon after, the group disbands.

Dec Cornish and Danelli have formed Bulldog, with John Turk (vocals/keyboards), Eric Thorngren (guitar) and Billy Hocher (bass). Signed to Decca Records, they chart in the US with ***No*** (#44) and ***Bulldog*** (#176), but this initial impetus is not followed up, and the group will split. (Brigati is engaged mostly on session work, while Cavaliere concentrates on production, notably with Laura Nyro.)

1974

Cavaliere signs to Bearsville Records as a solo artist, releasing the Todd Rundgren-produced ***Felix Cavaliere***, followed by ***Destiny*** in September the following year. Brigati will record ***Brigati*** for Elektra in 1976 with his brother David, including a disco-style version of *Groovin'*.

1978

May Cornish and Danelli are reunited in the band Fotomaker and with Atlantic Records. *Where Have You Been All My Life* peaks at US #81, while ***Fotomaker*** climbs to US #88.

Dec Fotomaker's *Miles Away* makes US #63, but is the group's last chart success. (Two further albums, ***Vis A Vis*** and ***Transfer Station***, will follow in 1979 before the band splits.)

1980

Apr Four years since the release of his last outing ***Treasure*** (also the name of his mid-'70s band), Cavaliere has his only solo hit with *Only A Lonely Heart Sees*, on Epic, which makes US #36, and is taken from ***Castles In The Air***. (Danelli will join

Steve Van Zandt's Little Steven & the Disciples of Soul in 1982.)

1988

May [14] Without Brigati, the group has re-formed for a "Good Lovin' 88" US tour earlier in the year, with Tommy James & the Shondells, and now performs at Atlantic Records' 40-year anniversary concert at New York's Madison Square Garden. (*Good Lovin'* has recently been featured in a highly-rated episode of ABC-TV series, "Moonlighting".)

1989

Danelli and Cornish sue Cavaliere to prevent him from calling his band the Young Rascals. A New York judge rules that Danelli and Cornish can call themselves the New Rascals and Cavaliere "formerly of the Young Rascals." (The New Rascals are Danelli, Cornish, Benny Harrison (vocals/keyboards), Kevin Osborne (vocals/trombone) and Tony Mercadante (vocals/bass).)

1992

Feb [8] ***The New York Rock And Soul Revue - Live At The Beacon***, to which Eddie and David Brigati have contributed *Groovin'*, peaks at US #170. (During the year, Rhino Records issues a two-CD career retrospective, ***The Rascals Anthology 1965-1972***, matched by a similar UK collection ***In Retrospective***.)

1994

Jan Having contributed to the Peace Choir's *Give Peace A Chance*, a US #54 benefit single in March 1991, Cavaliere releases ***Dreams In Motion***, his first album in more than a decade on Don Was' new Karambalage label. (Was had originally contacted Cavaliere in 1990 by calling their mutual friend John Sebastian.)

CHRIS REA

1977

Aug Inspired by the music of Joe Walsh and Ry Cooder, among others, singer-songwriter/guitarist Rea (b. Mar. 4, 1951, Middlesbrough, Cleveland), while working in his family's ice cream parlor in Middlesbrough, and doing part-time laboring, bought his first guitar at the age of 19, becoming proficient enough to join local professional band, Magdelene, in 1973, whose singer David Coverdale has just left to join Deep Purple, when he also began honing his songwriting skills. Cutting a one-off single, *So Much Love*, for Magnet Records in May the following year, Magdelene changed its name to the Beautiful Losers in 1975, and won **Melody Maker**'s Best Newcomers Of 1975 award, though little further progress was made. Rea now splits from the group, to sign to Magnet as a solo artist, and works with producer Gus Dudgeon on a debut album. The Beautiful Losers dissolve (and Rea will later estimate that by the end of the band's career, around 30 members have passed through its ranks).

Nov He is one of many guitarists guesting on ***The Hank Marvin Guitar Syndicate***, a solo instrumental project by the Shadows' lead guitarist.

1978

Apr *Fool (If You Think It's Over)* is released.

June His Dudgeon-produced debut set, the self-penned ***Whatever Happened To Benny Santini?***, with session contributions from Pete Wingfield, Rod Argent and others, is released. (The title refers to a proposed Magnet marketing ploy, which has earlier considered re-christening Rea, Benny Santini.)

Sept In the less new wave-obsessed US radio market, *Fool (If You Think It's Over)*, released on United Artists, climbs to US #12, spurring ***Whatever Happened To Benny Santini?*** to reach US #49. Rea is offered a major US tour, but turns it down to concentrate on further recording in Britain.

Oct The single's US success has prompted Magnet to re-promote it in the UK, with *Fool (If You Think It's Over)* now making UK #30. (Elkie Brooks' 1982 cover will reach UK #17.)

[26] ***Whatever Happened To Benny Santini?*** is certified gold by the RIAA.

Nov Title track, *Whatever Happened To Benny Santini?*, peaks at US #71.

[30] Rea performs on the second day of the "Great British Music Festival" at Wembley Arena, Wembley, Middx.

1979

Feb [15] Though nominated, *Fool (If You Think It's Over)* fails to win a Grammy Award at the 21st annual ceremony.

Apr *Diamonds*, a track taken from Rea's second album, ***Deltics***, makes both UK and US #44.

May ***Deltics***, again produced by Dudgeon, is Rea's UK album chart debut at #54.

1980

Apr Rea's first self-produced album, ***Tennis***, reaches UK #60, featuring the extracted singles, *Tennis* and *Dancing Girls*. (He spends much of the next two years on the road in Britain, continuing to write songs, but eschewing recording in favor of stage work. He also marries his long-time girlfriend Joan.)

1982

Mar ***Chris Rea***, co-produced with Jon Kelly at both AIR and Abbey Road studios, makes UK #52, while in the US, its release marks a new deal with CBS/Columbia.

Apr *Loving You*, the opening track from ***Chris Rea***, is his first chart single in three years, reaching UK #65 and US #88.

1983

June ***Water Sign***, co-helmed with Dave Richard and self-written (as ever), makes UK #64.

Oct *I Can Hear Your Heartbeat*, taken from ***Water Sign***, peaks at UK #60, but is a bigger hit in Eire and Europe, hitting the Top 20 in several countries, as does the album. This helps build his European reputation to a level far exceeding his still cult-sized British following. He undertakes a successful tour of Europe, and West Germany - in particular - affords him near-superstar status.

1984

Mar *I Don't Know What It Is But I Love It*, a taster from his next album, peaks at UK #65.

May ***Wired To The Moon***, co-produced with Dave Richards and featuring a studio band of Kevin Powell (bass), Jeff Seopardi (drums) and Jerry Stevenson (guitar), reaches UK #35.

1985

May *Stainsby Girls*, following strong UK airplay, reaches UK #27.

June Again co-produced with Richards, ***Shamrock Diaries***, which includes *Stainsby Girls*, is Rea's first UK Top 20 album, reaching #15.

July *Josephine* peaks at UK #67.

1986

Mar *It's All Gone* stops at UK #69.

Apr [26] ***On The Beach*** becomes Rea's best-seller in the UK to date, bowing at its #11 peak, during a 24-week chart run.

June A remixed version of *On The Beach*, title song from the album, peaks at UK #57.

Nov [8] Rea begins a 35-date European tour in Stuttgart, West Germany, set to end on December 28th at London's Hammersmith Odeon.

1987

June Rea participates in the TV special, "Ibiza '92", at the Ku Club, Ibiza.

July His self-penned *Let's Dance* (the third different UK hit single by this title, following Chris Montez's 1962 #2, and David Bowie's 1983 #1) reaches UK #12, to become his biggest-selling British single.

Aug *Loving You Again* makes UK #47.

Sept [26] The self-produced ***Dancing With Strangers***, which includes *Let's Dance*, debuts at UK #2, behind Michael Jackson's ***Bad***, earning a gold disc in its first week of release, and confirming Rea's star status in the UK, now comparable to that which he enjoys in the rest of Europe.

[5] In the US, *Let's Dance*, Rea's first release via a new deal with Motown, peaks at US #81. Meanwhile, he makes his first concert tour of Australia, followed by another European trek, supported by a now-regular road band: Robert Ahwaii (guitar), Max Middleton (keyboards), Kevin Leach (keyboards), Dave Kemp (saxophone), Eogham O'Neil (bass), Dave Mattacks (drums) and Rea's brother, Kevin (percussion/vocals).

Dec The seasonal *Joys Of Christmas* is released.

1988

Feb *Que Sera* peaks at UK #73.

Aug *On The Beach Summer '88*, a remixed version of the earlier hit, is Rea's first single for WEA, which has acquired Magnet, and reaches UK #12. WEA re-promotes ***On The Beach*** which makes UK #37.

Oct *I Can Hear Your Heartbeat* peaks at UK #74.

Nov [12] Compilation album, ***New Light Through Old Windows***, hits UK #5, becoming a chart mainstay.

Dec *Driving Home For Christmas* peaks at UK #53.

1989

Feb *Working On It* stops at UK #53.

Mar ***New Light Through Old Windows***, released through Geffen Records, makes US #92.

Apr [15] *Working On It* peaks at US #73.

Oct *The Road To Hell (Part 2)*, concerning itself with traffic on the Greater London ring-road, the M25, hits UK #10.

Nov [11] ***The Road To Hell*** enters the UK chart at #1, where it will stay for three weeks (and will peak at US #107 on Apr [21] the following year).

Dec [23] Band Aid II's *Do They Know It's Christmas*, featuring Rea, tops the UK chart. His child abuse-themed ballad, *Tell Me There's A Heaven* will reach UK #24 on Feb [24] the following year, with *Texas* peaking at UK #69 on May [5].

1991

Mar [2] Previewing a forthcoming album, *Auberge* reaches UK #16.

[9] With all 11 tracks written by Rea and produced by Jon Kelly, ***Auberge*** enters the UK chart at #1.

Apr [6] *Heaven* debuts at its UK #57 peak.

May [18] ***Auberge*** charts for a week at US #176.

July [6] Easy pop-rock swaying *Looking For The Summer* makes UK #49.

Nov [16] *Winter Song* reaches UK #27.

[23] Rea begins a 12-date UK tour at the G-Mex, Manchester, Gtr. Manchester, set to end on December 17th at Wembley Arena.

1992

Aug Rea records new material at The Mill Studio.

Oct [24] *Nothing To Fear* bows at its UK #16 peak.

Nov [14] Self-written and produced, ***God's Great Banana Skin*** enters at UK #4.

[28] *God's Great Banana Skin* debuts at its UK #31 peak.

Dec [2] Rea guests on ITV's "Des O'Connor Tonight".

1993

Jan [3] He embarks on a 23-date UK tour at the Sheffield Arena, Sheffield, S. Yorks., set to end on February 18th at the International Riverside Bowl Supertent, Gateshead, Tyne & Wear.

[15] Movie "Soft Top, Hard Shoulder", for which Rea has composed the score, opens in London.

[30] *Soft Top, Hard Shoulder* bows at its UK #53 peak.

Apr [1-4] Rea performs four concerts in Paris, France.

Oct [30] *Julia* reaches UK #18.

[31] Rea participates in the 30-lap TOCA Shoot-Out at Donington Park racetrack, but is eliminated after the first round.

Nov [13] Having recently contributed *If You Were Me* to Elton John's ***Duets*** album, his own ***Espresso Logic*** debuts at its UK #8 peak, featuring his mainstay backing musicians Max Middleton and Robert Ahwai, and music guest Davy Spillane on uillean pipes.

1994

Mar [22] Rea plays a sellout date at the Music Hall, Toronto, ON, Canada, during a North American tour.
Nov [5] His second compilation, the 17-track ***The Best Of Chris Rea*** enters at its UK #3 peak.
[12] *You Can Go Your Own Way*, featured in an ad campaign for the Ford Probe car, debuts at its UK #28 peak.
Dec [24] Reissued ballad *Tell Me There's A Heaven* charts for a week at UK #70.

RED HOT CHILI PEPPERS

Anthony Kiedis (vocals); **John Frusciante** (guitar); **Flea** (bass); **Chad Smith** (drums)

1983

The group has originally formed in 1978 as Los Faces, and then Anthem, at Fairfax High School, Los Angeles, CA, by Kiedis (b. Nov. 1, 1962, Grand Rapids, MI), the son of actor Blackie Dammett, who replaces original vocalist Allen Misholski, Flea (b. Michael Balzary, Oct. 16, 1962, Melbourne, Australia), who has played first trumpet in the Los Angeles Junior Philharmonic, guitarist Hillel Slovak (b. Apr. 13, 1962 Haifa, Israel), and Jack Irons (b. July 18, 1962, Los Angeles) on drums. After graduating from Fairfax, Kiedis has enrolled at UCLA as a political science major, while Flea has quit to join hardcore garage punk outfit, Fear. Slovak and Irons formed the short-lived What Is This?, but are now invited by Kiedis and Flea to start the Red Hot Chili Peppers, playing an early gig as Tony Flow & the Miraculous Majestic Masters of Mayhem, at Los Angeles' Kit Kat Strip Club, during which the band inaugurates its legendary stage stunt of performing nude wearing socks over their genitalia. Going on to play regularly at the Cathay de Grand club, the band is signed to EMI America, though, with Irons and Slovak still under a separate contract with What Is This?, the group's first album has to be recorded with Jack Sherman on guitar and ex-Weirdos' Cliff Martinez filling in on drums.

1984

Apr Their raucous debut album, ***The Red Hot Chili Peppers***, produced by Gang of Four's guitarist Andy Gill, is released by EMI. Fully complemented by Irons and Slovak, ***Freaky Styley***, produced by George Clinton and featuring James Brown backing members Maceo Parker and Fred Wesley, will follow in June 1985 as the group continues forging its innovative funk/punk/thrash fusion.

1987

Dec Including *Party On Your Pussy*, which will become a popular anthem (with fans), the group's third album, ***The Uplift Mofo Party Plan***, produced by Michael Beinhorn, opens its US chart account, peaking at #148.

1988

Jan [20] The band performs a radio station-sponsored gig at Palomino, North Hollywood.
May [16] EMI releases *The Abbey Road EP*, its cover sleeve aping the famous Beatles album jacket, but with the Chili Peppers appearing without clothing, albeit with socks firmly in place.
June [25] Slovak dies from a heroin overdose in Los Angeles.
July Disturbed by his colleague's death, Irons quits the band (and will re-emerge in Eleven and then Pearl Jam in 1994), to be temporarily replaced by Dead Kennedys' drummer D.H. Peligro. While P-Funk guitarist Duane "Blackbyrd" McKnight also joins, the chemistry is wrong and the line-up dissolves. Subsequently auditioning 30 drummers, they settle on Chad Smith (b. Oct. 25, 1962, St. Paul, MN), while Kiedis, himself recovering from drug dependency, and invited by his friend Bob Forrest to audition for his band Thelonius Monster, meets guitarist John Frusciante (b. Mar. 5, 1970, New York, NY) and asks him to join the re-grouped Red Hot Chili Peppers. (Flea, currently moonlighting as a trumpet player in Trulio Disgracias, an aggregation of Fishbone and Thelonius Monster members, and Frusciante, will also start up ad-hoc punk band Hate to play Hollywood clubs.)

1989

Sept [16] ***Mother's Milk***, also produced by Beinhorn, begins an eight-month US chart stay on its way to #52 and includes the group's first US Modern Rock charting single *Knock Me Down* which will hit #6, followed by a second extraction, their version of Stevie Wonder's 1973 US #4/UK#29 *Higher Ground*.

1990

Feb [21] The band performs at Hamburg Docks, Hamburg, West Germany.
Mar [14] During a spring-break concert in Daytona Beach, FL, Flea and Smith are arrested and charged with battery for sexually harassing a woman. (Subsequently pleading guilty, they are told to apologize and pay a $1,000 fine, donate $5,000 each to a rape crisis center, and give $300 to the State Attorney's Office for prosecution costs.)
[29] ***Mother's Milk*** is certified gold by the RIAA.

1991

Jan [7] Their "Psychedelic Sex Funk Live From Heaven" video is certified gold by the RIAA.
Mar [9] Frusciante and Flea are featured on the Peace Choir's *Give Peace A Chance*, which makes US #54.
Oct [11] The group performs on NBC-TV's "Late Night With David Letterman".
[12] Newly signed to Warner Bros. Records, and already moving up the US survey, the Rick Rubin-produced ***Blood Sugar Sex Magik***, recorded in a Hollywood Hills house, debuts at its UK #25 peak, but will not peak in the US until May the following year.
Nov [11-12, 15-16] During its current US tour, the group plays four sellout dates at the Roseland Ballroom, New York City, NY.
[20] The band is featured on BBC2-TV's "Rapido".
[26] The still-climbing ***Blood Sugar Sex Magik*** is certified gold by the RIAA.
Dec [31] The band ends the year with a 14,522 sellout show (also featuring Nirvana and Pearl Jam) at the Cow Palace, San Francisco, CA, grossing $399,355. (By year's end, Kiedis, who made his acting debut as Sylvester Stallone's son in the 1976 film "F.I.S.T.", appears in the movie "Point Blank", while other film cameos from group members include "Thrashin'" and "Tough Guys" (with Burt Lancaster and Kirk Douglas), with Flea having lensed the Penelope Spheeris-directed "The Decline of Western Civilization" and "Suburbia", and also set to play a busboy in the 1992 movie "Motorama".)

1992

Jan [11] The extracted and repetitively phrased *Give It Away*, with an eye-catching video directed by Stephane Sednaoui, peaks at US #76.
Feb [22] The group guests on NBC-TV's "Saturday Night Live" (and are currently featured on the soundtrack to "Wayne's World", singing *Sikamikanico*).
[27] They perform at the Kongresshalle, Frankfurt, West Germany, during European dates.
Mar [4] The band embarks on an eight-date British tour at the Hummingbird, Birmingham, West Midlands, set to end on the 13th and 14th at London's Brixton Academy.
[6] They appear on C4-TV's "The Word".
[12] The group performs *Under The Bridge* on BBC1-TV's "Top Of The Pops".
[14] *Under The Bridge* debuts at its UK #26 peak.
Apr [1] The still-climbing ***Blood Sugar Sex Magik*** becomes the band's first RIAA certified platinum album (going on to top the three-million sales plateau by 1993).
May [7] Frusciante announces he is quitting, in a Tokyo, Japan hotel room, during a four-date Japanese tour. (He will release the solo effort ***To Clara*** in 1994.)
[16] Funk/thrash melding ***Blood Sugar Sex Magik*** finally hits US #3, seven months after first charting.
[27] The still-rising *Under The Bridge* is certified gold by the RIAA.
[28] Hearing that the band is looking for a new guitarist, Brent Paschke of Brooklyn Park, MN, heads west to contact their management. Getting nowhere, he finds Flea's address, camps outside and auditions for him (unsuccessfully) the next day in his garage. Meanwhile, ex-Circle Jerks, Thelonius Monster and Two Free Stooges guitarist, Zander Schloss, joins the group in rehearsals for their forthcoming "Lollapalooza II" summer tour.
June [6] *Under The Bridge*, hits US #2, behind Kris Kross' *Jump*.
July [18] 34-date alternative acts package "Lollapalooza Festival '92" tour opens at the Shoreline Amphitheatre, Mountain View, CA, headlined by the Red Hot Chili Peppers with Pearl Jam, the Jesus & Mary Chain, Soundgarden, Ministry, Ice Cube and Lush. The tour will end on September 13th at the Irvine Meadows Amphitheatre, Laguna Hills, CA, after 32 sellout dates before crowds totalling 740,794, grossing $18,627,212 at the box office. Following the trek, Frusciante's permanent replacement, Arik Marshall (b. Feb. 13, 1967, Los Angeles), ex-Marshall Law, joins the line-up, replacing Schloss.
Aug [15] *Breaking The Girl* debuts at its UK #41 peak.
Sept [9] "Give It Away" wins the Best Art Direction and Breakthrough Video categories, while "Under The Bridge" collects the Viewers Choice trophy at the ninth annual MTV Video Music Awards, held at the Pauley Pavilion, Los Angeles, CA.
[23] The group is featured on MTV's "Rock The Vote", and will perform at a "Rock For Choice" movement benefit at New York's Palladium the following month.
[24] Kiedis and Balzary catwalk at a Jean-Paul Gaultier fashion benefit for AMFAR AIDS research, at the Shrine Auditorium, Los Angeles, as the RIAA certifies three million sales of ***Blood Sugar Sex Magik***.
Oct [9-10] The group embarks on an 11-date tour of Australia and New Zealand, at the Hordern Pavilion, Sydney, Australia, set to end on the 28th in Auckland, North Island, New Zealand.
[17] EMI-issued retrospective, ***What Hits!?***, bows at its UK #23 peak.
[24] ***What Hits!?*** reaches US #22.
Dec [13] Flea guest-hosts on Fox-TV's "The Ben Stiller Show".
[31] The group cancels a show in San Francisco, after Kiedis is hospitalized with dysentery which he caught in Borneo.

1993

Jan [22] The group performs until the early hours of the first day of the "Hollywood Rock Festival" in Rio de Janeiro, Brazil.
Feb [24] They collect the Best Hard Rock Song trophy for *Give It Away*, which they also perform with George Clinton's P-Funk All-Stars, at the 35th annual Grammy Awards, held at the Shrine Auditorium.
Mar [4] Flea is named Best Bassist in **Rolling Stone**'s 1993 Music Awards Readers' Picks.
[15] Former guitarist Jack Sherman files a breach-of-contract, fraud and malpractice suit in Los Angeles Superior Court, charging the terms of his partnership agreement with the band were fraudulently violated after he was fired from the group in February 1985. The group's attorney Eric Greenspan says "the case is completely without merit."
May [14] Kiedis guests on the 1,000th edition of syndicated TV's "The Arsenio Hall Show".
[27] ***What Hits!?*** is certified platinum by the RIAA.

June [26] The group performs on the Pyramid Stage at the annual "Glastonbury Festival", Worthy Farm, Pilton, Somerset.
Aug A month after joining the group as its new guitarist (Marshall having recently quit), Jesse Tobias, from Los Angeles band Mother Tongue, quits by mutual decision. (They had placed an ad to recruit Marshall's replacement in the **Los Angeles Weekly**, getting more than 3,000 calls in three days, after which they have to disconnect the phone.)
Sept [5] Dave Navarro (b. June 7, 1967, Santa Monica, CA), formerly of Jane's Addiction, replaces Tobias.
Oct [23] *Soul To Squeeze*, from the soundtrack to "Coneheads", reaches US #22 during a five-week spell atop the US Modern Rocks survey.
[31] Flea is at the scene of actor's River Phoenix fatal collapse outside The Viper Room club in Los Angeles, and rides with him in the ambulance to the hospital.
Nov [23] ***The Beavis And Butt-Head Experience***, featuring the Chili Peppers' *Search And Destroy*, is released in the US.

1994

Jan [7] The US Government pulls a radio ad featuring Kiedis promoting condoms to prevent AIDS, after learning of his sexual battery and indecent exposure conviction.
Feb [5] Reissued *Give It Away* debuts at its UK #9 peak.
Mar [8] Their "Funky Monks" video is certified gold by the RIAA.
[22] A Superior Court judge dismisses Sherman's suit citing the statute of limitations.
Apr [30] Re-released *Under The Bridge* re-charts, bowing at its UK #13 peak.
Aug [14] The group performs at "Woodstock '94" at Winston Farm, Saugerties, NY.
[28] They headline the final day of the annual "Reading Festival", Reading, Berks.
Oct [19, 22] They play two sellout shows, supporting the Rolling Stones, at the Rose Bowl, Pasadena, CA.
Nov [19] Comprising out-takes, remixes and previously unreleased cuts, ***Out In L.A.*** debuts at its US #82 peak, during a two-week chart stay, and its UK #61 high.

1995

Aug [19] Alanis Morissette's *You Oughta Know*, featuring Flea and Navarro reaches UK #22.
Sept [2] *Warped* enters at its UK #31 peak.
[23] ***One Hot Minute*** debuts at its UK #2 peak.
[30] ***One Hot Minute*** enters at its US #4 pinnacle.
Oct [21] The excerpted *My Friends* debuts at its UK #29 peak.
[28] John Lennon tribute album ***Working Class Hero***, including the band's cover of *I Found Out*, enters at its US #94 peak.
Nov [9] Smith breaks his wrist playing baseball, causing the group to postpone its forthcoming tour.
[16] ***One Hot Minute*** is certified platinum by the RIAA.
Dec [12] Smith chats on America OnLine.

1996

Feb [6] The Red Hot Chili Peppers begin their postponed tour at CoreStates Spectrum, Philadelphia, PA, set to end on April 16th at the Sports Arena, San Diego, CA.
[13] The group guests on CBS-TV's "Late Show With David Letterman".
[17] ***Aeroplane*** reaches UK #11 in its week of entry.
May [1] ***Blood Sugar Sex Magik*** is certified for four million US sales by the RIAA.
[3] The band begins the New Zealand and Australian leg of its tour at the Supertop, Auckland.

OTIS REDDING

1959

Having dropped out of Ballard-Hudson Senior High School in the tenth grade, R&B singer and son of a Baptist minister, Redding (b. Sept. 9, 1941, Dawson, GA), heavily influenced by Little Richard, begins performing on "The Teenage Party" talent show, broadcast on radio on Saturday mornings, on which he finds success with his Little Richard imitation, and meets his future wife, Zelda. After being spotted at the Douglass Theater, Macon, GA, by Johnny Jenkins, who, unimpressed by Otis' backing band, asks whether he can back him instead, Redding begins gigging regularly in clubs with Johnny Jenkins & the Pinetoppers, and makes his first recording locally with the group backing him on *She's Alright*, a Little Richard pastiche (having already cut a single as Otis & the Shooters on the California label, Finer Arts).

1960

Sept After six months in Los Angeles, CA, looking for a break in music (but finding only a car wash job), Redding returns to Macon and records *Shout Bamalama* (again in Little Richard style), for the Confederate label, distributed by King Records.

1961

Redding gains a residency at Macon's Grand Dukes club, and cuts another single, *Gettin' Hip*, for Alshire Records. Phil Walden, the Pinetoppers' manager, meets Redding at a Pinetoppers gig at the Lakeside Amusement Park, and becomes his manager.
Aug Redding marries Zelda and they set up home in Macon.

1962

Feb Still associated with the Pinetoppers, regularly chauffeuring the group to gigs and given vocal spots in its act, Redding accompanies Jenkins and the group on a college tour of Tennessee and Alabama. In Atlanta, GA, they record *Love Twist* for the local Gerald label, which is picked up by Atlantic Records and sells well in Southern states.
Oct At the suggestion of Atlantic's Joe Galkin, Jenkins & the Pinetoppers, with Redding again driving, travel to Memphis, TN, to record a session at the Atlantic-distributed Stax Records. At the end of the (unproductive) Jenkins session, with studio time in hand, Redding persuades Stax's owner Jim Stewart to have him record two of his own songs: the Little Richard-styled *Hey Hey Baby*, and the slow, pleading *These Arms Of Mine*, backed by Steve Cropper, Johnny Jenkins, Al Jackson and Lewis Steinberg, in which Stewart hears commercial potential. Atlantic (which has paid for the session, and technically has Redding contracted) allows Stax to issue it as a single on the new Volt label.

1963

Mar Following local Memphis success, *These Arms Of Mine* reaches US R&B #20.
June *These Arms Of Mine* debuts Redding on the US Hot 100, peaking at #85.
[24] With his first national hit finally peaking, Redding's second recording session is held at Stax. He is now officially an Atco (Atlantic subsidiary) artist, but by special arrangement, records as part of the Stax set-up, and continues to have feature releases issued on Volt.
Oct *That's What My Heart Needs*, cut in June, makes US R&B #27, but fails to cross over.
Nov On the strength of two hits and the fast-climbing third release, *Pain In My Heart*, Redding is invited to play, for $400, one week at New York's Apollo Theatre in Harlem (his performance being recorded for Atco's live compilation, ***Saturday Night At The Apollo***, released in 1964).

1964

Feb *Pain In My Heart*, an adapted cover of Irma Thomas' current Southern R&B hit, *Ruler Of My Heart*, makes US #61, and is his biggest seller to date.
Apr Redding/Walden song, *Come To Me*, recorded with Booker T. & the MG's rhythm section (as will be virtually every Redding track), but with Jenkins playing additional guitar, peaks at US #69.
May His debut album, ***Pain In My Heart***, makes US #103, while the extracted *Security* peaks at US #97 (though it will be much-covered by UK R&B groups). Redding embarks on the "Hot Summer Revue Tour" throughout the US with Solomon Burke, Garnett Mimms, Joe Tex, Wilson Pickett, Don Covay, Arthur Conley, Ben E. King, all members of the "Soul Clan".
Nov The self-penned *Chained And Bound* peaks at US #70.

1965

Mar *Mr. Pitiful*, the nickname Memphis DJ Moohah Williams had given Redding, makes US #41, as its B-side, *That's How Strong My Love Is*, peaks at US #74.
Apr ***The Great Otis Redding Sings Soul Ballads*** makes US #147.
[19] Redding begins recording ***Otis Blue*** at Stax Studios, Memphis.
June Deep soul ballad, *I've Been Loving You Too Long (To Stop Now)*, becomes his breakthrough release on the US pop chart, reaching US #21 (and R&B #2).
July [3] Though Redding has not yet had a British hit, when the UK R&B chart is launched he has two Top 20 placings, with *Mr. Pitiful* (#6) and *Pain In My Heart* (#16).
Oct Uptempo *Respect*, penned by Redding with Speedo Simms of the Premiers in mind, makes US #35 (and R&B #4). (Two years later, the song will be revived in a still more commercial arrangement by Aretha Franklin and become a million-selling US chart-topper.)
Nov ***Otis Blue/Otis Redding Sings Soul***, often cited by critics as one of the all-time great soul albums, makes US #75.
Dec *Just One More Day* peaks at US #85.

1966

Jan UK Atlantic's Tony Hall selects Redding's version of the Smokey Robinson-penned *My Girl* (a US #1 for the Temptations in 1965, but not a big UK seller) as a UK single from ***Otis Blue***. Gaining strong airplay it becomes his UK chart debut, reaching #11.
Mar ***Otis Blue/Otis Redding Sings Soul*** gives him his first British chart album, hitting UK #6, during a 21-week Top 30 stay.
Apr ***The Great Otis Redding Sings Soul Ballads*** finds belated UK sales, peaking at #30. Meanwhile, Redding's version of the Rolling Stones' *(I Can't Get No) Satisfaction* reaches US #31 (R&B #4) and UK #33. (Redding will tour Britain and Europe to great success later in the year, and will record "Ready Steady Otis!", an entire edition of ITV pop show "Ready Steady Go!")
June *My Lover's Prayer* peaks at US #61 (and R&B #10), while ***The Soul Album***, from which it is taken, makes US #54.
[24] Redding begins a 46-date US tour of one-nighters, with Sam & Dave, Patti LaBelle & the Blue-belles, Percy Sledge, Garnett Mimms and others, in Greensboro, NC.
Aug ***The Soul Album*** makes UK #22 and *My Lover's Prayer* climbs to UK #37. Redding launches his own label, Jotis Records. Among its acts is Arthur Conley, for whom Redding writes and produces *Sweet Soul Music* (a reworking of Sam Cooke's *Yeah Man* which will hit US #2 and UK #7 in 1967).
Sept R&B dance track, *I Can't Turn You Loose*, makes UK #29 (having hit US R&B #11).
Nov *Fa-Fa-Fa-Fa-Fa (Sad Song)*, also used as CBS-TV's "The $64,000 Question" theme, reaches US #29 and UK #23.
Dec [20-22] Redding appears at the Fillmore Auditorium, sharing the bill with the Grateful Dead.

1967

Jan ***Complete And Unbelievable ... The Otis Redding Dictionary Of Soul*** makes US #73 and UK #23 while, taken from it, his revival of the standard ballad, *Try A Little Tenderness*, is his second-biggest US hit single to date, reaching #25.

Feb A UK reissue of ***Otis Blue*** (following a change of Atlantic's UK licensee), after an extended absence from retail, hits UK #7, while *Try A Little Tenderness* makes UK #46.
Mar [17] Redding begins a 13-date UK "Soul Concert Sensation '67" tour with Sam & Dave, Eddie Floyd, Arthur Conley, Carla Thomas, the Markeys and Booker T. & the MG's, at Finsbury Park Astoria, London, set to end on April 8th at London's Hammersmith Odeon.
Apr *I Love You More Than Words Can Say* peaks at US #78, while his revival of the Beatles' *Day Tripper* reaches UK #43. Redding's live performance at Los Angeles' Whisky A-Go-Go club is recorded by Atlantic (and will be released after his death).
May Redding's debut album, ***Pain In My Heart***, is belatedly released for the first time in Britain and reaches #28, while *Let Me Come On Home* peaks at UK #48.
June Redding duets with Stax artist (and daughter of Rufus *Walking The Dog* Thomas), Carla Thomas, on an adaptation of Lowell Fulson's *Tramp*, which reaches US #26, while his solo revival of Sam Cooke's *Shake!* makes US #47. Redding's collaborative album with Thomas, ***King And Queen***, climbs to US #36.
[17] Redding is the closing act on the second evening of the "Monterey International Pop Festival" at the County Fairgrounds, Monterey, CA, at which he is backed by Booker T. & the MG's. Taking the stage after Jefferson Airplane, his appearance is seen as a deliberate move to capture the attention of the predominantly young, white, rock audience. Redding's biggest asset is the passionate strength of his live performance, and he gets a rapturous reception from the largely hippy audience. (Part of his set will be included in D.A. Pennebaker's film, "Monterey Pop".)
July *Shake* reaches UK #28.
Aug *Glory Of Love* peaks at US #60, while ***King And Queen***, with Carla Thomas, reaches UK #18, and their duetted single, *Tramp*, makes UK #18.
Sept Performance set, ***Otis Redding Live In Europe***, recorded on the Stax/Volt tour, reaches US #32. Meanwhile, Redding's second duet single with Thomas, a version of Eddie Floyd's much-covered *Knock On Wood*, reaches US #30.
Oct *Knock On Wood* makes UK #35.
[14] His second UK tour of the year, the "Soul Explosion", with Sam & Dave, Percy Sledge, Arthur Conley, Eddie Floyd, Carla Thomas, Booker T. & the MG's, opens at London's Finsbury Park Astoria, set to end on November 6th at the Fairfield Halls, Croydon, Surrey. (Redding has been off the road for two months to remove throat polyps.)
Dec [7] Redding enters the studio to record a song he has written with Stax guitarist Steve Cropper, *(Sittin' On) The Dock Of The Bay*. (A relaxed soul ballad, it will become his biggest hit, but Redding will not live to see its release.)
[9] Redding flies to Cleveland, OH, in his new twin-engined Beechcraft plane to appear on "Upbeat", a syndicated TV show hosted by Don Webster.
[10] En route to a concert at The Factory in Madison, WI, the plane carrying Redding and his road band, the Bar-Kays, goes down at 3:28 p.m. in the icy waters of Lake Monoma, near Madison. The only survivor is Memphis-born Ben Cauley - at 20, the oldest of the Bar-Kays. (At Redding's funeral at Macon's City Auditorium, the pall-bearers will be fellow soul singers Joe Tex, Joe Simon, Johnnie Taylor, Solomon Burke, Percy Sledge, Don Covay and Sam Moore, of Sam & Dave.)

1968

Jan Compilation album, ***History Of Otis Redding***, hits US #9, a bigger seller than any album during his lifetime.
Mar [11] Five days from its US chart peak, *(Sittin' On) The Dock Of The Bay* is certified gold by the RIAA.
[16] The posthumously-released *(Sittin' On) The Dock Of The Bay* tops the US chart for the first of four weeks, selling over a million copies, and hits UK #3. Meanwhile, another Otis and Carla Thomas single, *Lovey Dovey*, makes US #60, while a UK reissue of *My Girl* reaches #36.
Apr ***History Of Otis Redding*** hits UK #2 (behind Bob Dylan's ***John Wesley Harding***), while the live set, ***Otis Redding In Europe***, reaches UK #14.
May ***Dock Of The Bay***, a collection of tracks from his final sessions in late 1967, hits US #4 while, taken from it, *The Happy Song (Dum Dum)*, reaches US #25.
June [22] ***Dock Of The Bay*** tops the UK chart for a week, while *The Happy Song (Dum Dum)* reaches UK #24.
July Also taken from the album, his treatment of the Impressions' *Amen* makes US #36 and its B-side, *Hard To Handle*, peaks at US #51. This, like subsequent posthumous singles, is released on Atco rather than Volt.
Aug *Hard To Handle*, elevated to the A-side in the UK, makes #15, while ***The Immortal Otis Redding***, assembling more of his last recordings, reaches US #58.
Nov Ballad, *I've Got Dreams To Remember*, makes US #41, while its parent album, ***The Immortal Otis Redding***, reaches UK #19.
Dec ***Otis Redding In Person At The Whisky A-Go-Go***, recorded in April 1967, makes US #82, while his revival of James Brown's *Papa's Got A Brand New Bag* makes US #21 - his biggest US hit since *(Sittin' On) The Dock Of The Bay*.

1969

Mar His cover of Clyde McPhatter's '50s hit, *A Lover's Question*, makes US #48.
[12] *(Sittin' On) The Dock Of The Bay* is named Best R&B Vocal Performance, Male, and Best R&B Song Of 1968, at the 11th annual Grammy Awards.
June *Love Man* peaks at US #72.
July *Love Man* makes UK #43 (Redding's final UK chart single), while ***Love Man*** makes US #46.

1970

Aug ***Tell The Truth***, containing Redding's last unissued recordings from 1967, anchors at US #200.
Nov Reprise Records issues ***Monterey International Pop Festival***, comprising one side of Redding and the other of Jimi Hendrix performing at the June 1967 festival. It climbs to US #16. A double anthology, ***The Best Of Otis Redding***, will peak at US #76 in October 1972, his final US chart entry. Redding's 12-year-old son, Dexter, will releases *God Bless*, on Phil Walden's Capricorn label the following year in November.

1980

Dec Brothers Dexter (vocals, bass) and Otis Redding III (guitar), and their cousin, Mark Locket (vocals, drums, keyboards), now a trio named the Reddings and signed to the Believe label, have their first chart entry with *Remote Control*, which makes US #89. (It will be followed by ***The Awakening*** (US #174 in January the following year), ***Class*** (US #106 in August), their own version of *(Sittin' On) The Dock Of The Bay* (US #55 in July 1982), and ***Steamin' Hot*** (US #153, the same month).)

1989

Jan [18] Little Richard inducts Redding posthumously into the Rock and Roll Hall of Fame at the fourth annual dinner, held at New York's Waldorf Astoria Hotel.

1994

June [1] Following the issue by the UK Ace label in January 1992 of ***Not Sentimental***, a collection of tracks recorded just before his death, and Atlantic's UK #50 peaking ***Dock Of The Bay - Definitive Collection*** on Sept [11] the following year, the comprehensive four-CD/cassette boxed set, ***Otis! The Definitive Otis Redding***, has been issued in November the same year by US vault specialist label Rhino Records. Redding is now posthumously inducted into the Songwriters Hall of Fame at the 25th annual ceremony held at New York's Sheraton Hotel and Towers. A further collection of career highlights will be issued in 1995 as ***The Very Best Of Otis Redding, Volume 2***.

JIMMY REED

1955

Feb Having moved to Gary, IN, after a spell in the Navy and then to Chicago, IL, where his laid-back, boogie-influenced style has made him a popular figure on the Southside club and bar scene, singer-songwriter/blues harmonica player Reed (b. Mathis James Reed Leland, Sept. 6, 1925, Dunleith, MS), one of ten children born into a sharecropping family, signed to the newly formed Vee-Jay label two years earlier, hits US R&B #5 with *You Don't Have To Go Boogie In The Park*. Reed had gone to Vee-Jay with his best friend and co-worker in a local steel foundry, Eddie Taylor, who was auditioning, but A&R man Calvin Carter was more interested in Reed and signed him instead. Its success is followed by seven further Top 20 R&B hits including *Ain't That Loving You Baby* (#3) and *You've Got Me Dizzy* (#3), both in 1956.

1957

July Reed's first Top 100 pop hit is *The Sun Is Shining*, at US #65.
Nov *Honest I Do* makes US #32. Reed is now the biggest draw on the Southside club scene, eclipsing even Muddy Waters. During the year his debut album ***I'm Jimmy Reed*** is also issued by Vee-Jay.

1958

Apr [5] Irvin Feld's "Greatest Show Of Stars" opens its 80-date US tour in Norfolk, VA, with Reed performing on a package with Sam Cooke, the Everly Brothers and Clyde McPhatter, among others.
Aug *Down In Virginia* peaks at US #93.

1959

May [29] Reed performs in pouring rain at an outdoor festival in the Herndon Stadium, Atlanta, GA. Other artists on the bill include Ray Charles, the Drifters and B.B. King.

1960

Mar *Baby What You Want Me To Do* makes US #37 (subsequently covered by Elvis Presley).
May *Found Love* peaks at US #88.
Oct *Hush-Hush* reaches US #75.

1961

June *Big Boss Man*, also the name by which Reed will become known, reaches US #78, followed by the September-peaking *Bright Lights Big City* at US #58. Both are also big R&B hits as blues' popularity declines in favor of R&B/soul and the emerging UK R&B/beat boom.
Oct [16] The double album, ***Jimmy Reed At Carnegie Hall***, comprising a studio re-creation of Reed's Carnegie Hall concert and a "best of" selection, enters the US chart set to make #46. The following year *Aw Shucks, Hush Your Mouth* will peak at US #93 in February, *Good Lover* makes US #77 in June, with ***Just Jimmy Reed*** reaching US #103 in October.

1964

Sept *Shame Shame Shame* makes UK #45 having peaked at US #52 in April the previous year.
Oct Reed begins an extensive UK club and concert tour while the Rolling Stones cover his *Honest I Do* on their first album. Other British groups to cover Reed tracks include the Pretty Things, the Animals (both recording *Big Boss Man*) and Them (*Bright Lights Big City*). Reed is unable to capitalize on this due to increasing ill-health (epilepsy and alcoholism), and will remain inactive for most of the late '60s and early '70s.

1976

Aug [29] He dies from an epileptic seizure in San

Francisco, CA, after completing a three-night engagement at the Bay Area's Savoy club. He is survived by his wife and eight children.

1991

Jan [16] After his widow has successfully negotiated an out-of-court royalty settlement with publisher Arc Music in 1988, when she alleged that the company took advantage of an uneducated Reed in a 1967 agreement, whereby he assigned all of his song rights for a total of $10,000, and following the Chameleon label's 1988 release of the CD compilation ***Bright Lights, Big City***, Reed is inducted into the Rock and Roll Hall of Fame, at the sixth annual dinner, at New York's Waldorf Astoria Hotel.

LOU REED

1965

Growing up in Freeport, Long Island, NY, the son of Toby and Sidney Reed who sent him to a psychiatrist at the age of 17 where he received eight weeks of shock treatment in an attempt to cure him of severe mood swings, Reed (b. Louis Firbank, Mar. 2, 1943, Freeport), after playing in local teenage bands including the Shades, studying journalism and creative writing at Syracuse University, Syracuse, NY, and working for Pickwick Records as a writer and recorder of low-budget cash-in records for supermarket racks (and scoring a near-hit single in New York with *The Ostrich* by the Primitives), becomes a founder member of the Velvet Underground with fellow student John Cale and Sterling Morrison. During his time with the band, Reed will be its lead singer and most prominent songwriter.

1970

Aug [23] After playing his last gig with the Velvet Underground at Max's Kansas City club in New York, NY, Reed's parents pick him up and take him home to Freeport, Long Island, where he will stay for next two years, working as a typist in his father's accountancy firm for $40 a week. Reed continues to write poetry and songs and is persuaded to sign a solo contract with RCA Records.

1972

June Helmed by Flamin' Groovies' producer Richard Robinson, his debut solo album, ***Lou Reed***, recorded in London with Yes members Steve Howe and Rick Wakeman among others, reaches US #189, and includes old Velvet Underground material.

July [8] Reed joins David Bowie onstage during a Save The Whale benefit at London's Royal Festival Hall.

[14] During further UK dates backed by his band the Tots, Reed performs at London's King's Cross Cinema and will return to play further shows in December.

1973

Jan [9] Reed marries a cocktail waitress, Betty, in New York.

Mar [24] He is bitten on the posterior by a fan who leaps on stage at a concert in Buffalo, NY, shouting "Leather!" The man is seized and ejected from the theater, leaving Reed to end the show and contemplate a sore bottom.

Apr ***Transformer***, produced in London by label-mate, and self-confessed Reed fan, Bowie, and his sideman Mick Ronson, reaches US #29. (Three songs on the album were commissioned by Andy Warhol for a Broadway musical he was intending to produce with Yves Saint Laurent.)

[23] The extracted, self-penned *Walk On The Wild Side*, for which session bassist Herbie Flowers is paid £17 for his defining bass line contribution, reaches US #16, is Reed's only solo US chart single and will remain his most enduring song.

May [18] Reed supports the Who at Charlton Athletic Football Club, Charlton, London.

June *Walk On The Wild Side* hits UK #10, and does not draw the anticipated BBC radio ban over its lyrics, because the producers fail to understand idioms like "giving head". As in the US, it will be his only UK chart single. (Regarded as a rock classic, it will be much covered, even as a dance/hip-hop version by Tabu artist Jamie J. Morgan in 1990.) ***Transformer*** makes UK #13 during a six month-chart stay.

Sept [22] Reed headlines the annual "Crystal Palace Garden Party" in London, during a world tour.

Nov ***Berlin***, his third consecutive album to be recorded in London, produced this time by Bob Ezrin, and featuring Steve Winwood and Jack Bruce among others, makes US #98 and hits UK #7.

1974

Apr Live album, ***Rock'n'Roll Animal***, recorded at New York's Academy of Music, with a line-up of Reed (guitar, vocals), Dick Wagner (guitar), Steve Hunter (guitar), Prakash John (bass), Josef Chirowsky (keyboards) and Whitney Glen (drums), climbs to US #45 and UK #26, and with consistent sales will earn Reed his first gold disc.

May [18] Reed supports the Who at Charlton Athletic Football Club, The Valley, Charlton, London.

Nov ***Sally Can't Dance*** hits US #10, his only US Top 20 effort.

1975

Apr Further performance set, ***Lou Reed Live***, contains another section of the previous year's Academy of Music concert, and is a companion to the live album, ***Rock'n'Roll Animal***, from the same occasion.

July Double set, ***Metal Machine Music***, is the most controversial of Reed's career, and the least accessible, revealing four sides of white noise, whines, whistles, feedback and screams, though the sleeve implies that it is a live set. Originally to have been released by Red Seal (RCA's classical music division) as an experimental piece of music, the set fails to sell after poor and bewildered reviews, and is withdrawn by RCA within a few months.

Aug Reed performs at the annual "Reading Festival", Reading, Berks.

1976

Mar ***Coney Island Baby***, returning to Reed's quirky-rock style, peaks at US #41 and UK #52, his last for RCA.

Nov Newly signed to Arista Records, his label debut, ***Rock And Roll Heart***, makes US #64, and includes the 11-minute saga, *Street Hassle*.

1977

Mar [20] Reed is banned from performing at the London Palladium because of his "punk image".

May Compilation album, ***Walk On The Wild Side : The Best Of Lou Reed***, on RCA, peaks at US #156.

1978

May ***Street Hassle***, featuring an uncredited Bruce Springsteen, makes US #89.

[1] ***Rock'n'Roll Animal*** is certified gold by the RIAA.

[17] Reed begins a week of concerts at New York's Bottom Line club, which are recorded for a planned live album, ***Take No Prisoners***.

1979

Mar Performance double set, ***Take No Prisoners***, including his persistent berating of the audience, is released by Arista in the US and by RCA elsewhere (due to a contractual wrangle).

June Arista-issued ***The Bells*** has a brief four-week US chart run, peaking at #130, but is critically panned as being his strangest effort since ***Metal Machine Music***.

1980

Feb [14] On St. Valentine's Day, Reed marries Sylvia Morales, in a ceremony at his apartment on Christopher Street, Greenwich Village, New York. (His previous marriage had foundered early on.)

May ***Growing Up In Public***, his second album release inside 12 months, peaks at US #158.

Oct Reed has a cameo role as a record producer in Paul Simon's premiering film, "One Trick Pony".

Dec His final Arista outing, ***Rock And Roll Diary, 1967-80***, a history of Reed's earlier career, with most tracks by the Velvet Underground, peaks at US #178.

1982

Mar He returns to RCA for ***The Blue Mask***, which makes US #169, and features guitarist Robert Quine. It is dedicated to long-time Reed inspiration, the poet Delmore Schwartz under whom he studied at Syracuse University.

July ***Transformer***, reissued in the UK at mid-price, re-charts at #91.

1983

Apr ***Legendary Hearts*** peaks at US #159, featuring popular alternative radio cuts, *New Sensation* and *I Love You Suzanne* (which is accompanied by a comic promo video). Its follow-up set ***New Sensations***, co-produced with John Jansen and recorded at New York's Skyline Studios, will make US #56 and UK #92 in August the following year.

1985

Oct Reed's version of *September Song* is released on A&M, taken from the Kurt Weil-tribute compilation, ***Lost In The Stars***.

Dec He appears with 48 other acts on the Artists United Against Apartheid single, *Sun City*, on Manhattan Records, which reaches US #38 and UK #21.

1986

May Straight rock-aimed ***Mistrial***, featuring the extracted *The Original Wrapper*, makes US #47 and UK #69.

Nov [15] He performs on NBC-TV's "Saturday Night Live". His duet with Sam Moore on a re-working of Sam & Dave's million seller, *Soul Man*, used as the theme to the movie of the same name, will reach UK #30 the following February.

1989

Jan [7-8] Having contributed to Rob Wasserman's ***Duets*** album and co-written three tracks with Rubén Blades on the latter's album, ***Nothing But The Truth*** the previous year, Reed now works with John Cale on two shows at St. Ann's Church, New York, as a tribute to Andy Warhol.

Feb [4] Newly signed to Sire Records, his back-to-the-basics set ***New York***, with Reed and Mike Rathke (guitars), Wasserman (bass), Fred Maher (drums and co-producer) and Maureen Tucker on two tracks, reaches UK #14 and will make US #40.

Mar Reed performs six nights at the St. James Theatre, Broadway, New York.

May [4] He guests on NBC-TV's "Late Night With David Letterman".

Aug [19] During a major US tour, Reed breaks his ankle after a sound-check in Cleveland, OH, and has to cancel the remainder of the dates.

Oct [21] The 17-track anthology, ***Retro***, reaches UK #29.

Nov [29] ***Songs For 'Drella : A Fiction***, a 50-minute suite written with Cale as a tribute to Warhol, is performed at the Brooklyn Academy of Music, Brooklyn, NY.

1990

Apr [16] Reed participates in the "Nelson Mandela - An International Tribute To A Free South Africa" concert at Wembley Stadium, Wembley, Middx.

May [5] Reed sings *Jealous Guy* and *Mother* at the "John Lennon Tribute Concert", held at the Pier Head Arena in Merseyside to celebrate the songs of Lennon, as the Reed/Cale album, ***Songs For 'Drella***, reaches UK #22 and will make US #103.

Dec During the bitter **New York Daily News** workers' strike, Reed performs at a $55,000-raising benefit, "News Aid", with Pete Seeger, the Roches and others.

1991

Feb [12] Reed lectures at the New School for Social Research, in New York.
July During the month he reads selections from his forthcoming book of poems, **Between Thought And Expression**, at New York's Central Park Summerstage.
Dec [10] Reed participates in the fourth annual Reebok Human Rights Award ceremony at the Park Plaza Castle, Boston, MA.

1992

Jan [14] He performs again on NBC-TV's "Late Night With David Letterman".
[25] ***Magic And Loss***, inspired by the recent deaths of two friends, Rotten Rita and Doc Pomus, debuts at its UK #6 peak.
Feb [1] ***Magic And Loss*** debuts at its US #80 peak.
[18] Reed is made a Knight of the French Order of Arts and Letters, by Culture Minister, Jack Lang, in Paris, France.
Mar [15] He embarks on his first British tour in over two years at the Palace Theatre, Manchester, Gtr. Manchester, set to end with the last of five dates at London's Hammersmith Odeon on the 27th.
[24] He reads extracts from **Between Thought And Expression** at the Lyttleton Theatre, London.
May [9] Reed plays to a sellout crowd of 2,626 at the Orpheum Theatre, Minneapolis, MN, during his current North American tour.
June [26-28] He takes part in the three-day "Glastonbury Arts & Music Festival" at Shepton Mallet, Somerset.
Oct He sings *Walk On The Wild Side* at a New York party to celebrate a ruling which stops religious fundamentalist Donald Wildmon from getting the "Damned In The USA" movie banned.
[16] Reed duets with Chrissie Hynde on *Foot Of Pride*, at the "Bob Dylan 30th Anniversary Celebration" concert, at New York's Madison Square Garden.

1993

Jan [20] He performs at the Tennessee Ball on Inauguration Day in Washington, DC.
Feb [19] Reed plays at New York's Bottom Line with Luka Bloom, David Byrne and Rosanne Cash.
May [1] *Walk On The Wild Side* is the featured song on BBC2-TV's "Tales Of Rock'n'Roll".
June [6] A re-formed Velvet Underground plays at the Wembley Arena, Wembley, Middx., following two shows at the Playhouse, Edinburgh, Scotland, on the 1st and 2nd and The Forum, London, on the 5th.
Sept [25] Reed is featured on Victoria Williams' benefit album ***Sweet Relief***, singing one of her songs. which now makes US #131. (Williams has been diagnosed with multiple sclerosis in 1992.)

1994

Feb [2] "In My Own Words : A Bunch Of Songwriters Sittin' Around Singing", with Reed, Kris Kristofferson, Suzanne Vega and Williams, takes place at New York's Bottom Line, as part of the venue's 20th anniversary celebrations.
[21] Reed guests on CBS-TV's "Late Show With David Letterman".
[23-24] He sings *Now And Then* at Roger Daltrey's anniversary special at New York's Carnegie Hall.
Aug [11] Reed plays a sellout show at New York's Beacon Theatre with Peter Gabriel.
Nov [12] Warner Bros. release, ***Bright Red***, the new album by Reed's latest love Laurie Anderson, including a spoken word duet by the couple, charts for a week at US #195.

1995

Jan [12] He inducts the late Frank Zappa into the Rock and Roll Hall of Fame at the tenth annual induction dinner at New York's Waldorf Astoria Hotel.
Mar [15] Reed attends a news conference at New York's Planet Hollywood to launch the Liverpool Institute for Performing Arts.
[25] He joins Victoria Williams onstage at New York's Town Hall for a rendition of *Sweet Jane*.
Till The Night Is Gone : A Tribute To Doc Pomus, to which Reed has contributed *This Magic Moment* is released.
Aug A biography **Transformer : The Lou Reed Story** by Victor Bockris is published in the US by Simon & Schuster.
Sept [2] Reed sings *Sweet Jane* with Soul Asylum at the Concert for the Rock and Roll Hall of Fame at Cleveland Stadium, Cleveland, OH.
As Reed continues to work with Robert Wilson on the musical "Time Rocker", based on H.G. Wells' **The Time Machine**, Luaka Bop Records releases the soundtrack to "Blue In The Face", a film starring Harvey Keitel, Roseanne, Madonna and Reed, with a new cut by him.
Nov [4] Combining solo and group highlights, the compilation album ***The Best Of Lou Reed And The Velvet Underground*** makes UK #56.

1996

Jan He attends a reading by Salman Rushdie of his latest novel, **The Moor's Last Sigh**, at the New York Public Library.
Feb [22] Reed guests again on "Late Show With David Letterman".
Mar [2] Newly-signed to Warner Bros. Records, and recorded entirely as his home studio, The Roof, ***Set The Twilight Reeling***, including the anti-right wing Christian movement-attacking *Sex With Your Parents (Motherfucker)*, reaches UK #26 in its week of entry.
[9] ***Set The Twilight Reeling*** bows at its US #110 peak.
[19] Reed guests on NBC-TV's "The Tonight Show".
[31] He performs at New York's Beacon Theatre.
Apr [15] Reed plays a sole Swiss date at the Kongresshaus in Zurich, during his 12-country swing of Europe.
May [6] He begins a four-date UK tour at Labatt's Apollo, Manchester, Gtr. Manchester, set to end on the 11th at the Birmingham Academy.
July [20] During European dates, Reed performs at the "Beach Festival", Zeebrugge, Belgium.
see also: **THE VELVET UNDERGROUND**

R.E.M.

Michael Stipe (vocals); **Peter Buck** (guitar); **Mike Mills** (bass); **Bill Berry** (drums)

1980

Feb A student of painting and photography at the University of Georgia, Athens, GA, the band's future lyricist and lead singer, Stipe (b. John Michael Stipe, Jan. 4, 1960, Decatur, GA), who contracted scarlet fever at the age of two, nicknamed Mr. Mouse by his father, but called Mike Stipe the Shining Light at kindergarten, has already sung in garage band 1066, performing punk covers in St. Louis, MO., has met Buck (b. Peter Lawrence Buck, Dec. 6, 1956, Berkeley, CA) in Athens record store, Wuxtry Records, in 1978, where Buck worked (and kept a guitar behind the counter, eagerly learning licks in between serving customers). Both share an interest in British new wave music and now form R.E.M. with like-minded Berry (b. William Thomas Berry, July 31, 1958, Duluth, MN) and Mills (b. Michael Edward Mills, Dec. 17, 1956, Orange County, CA), whom they met at a party. Mills, who quits his day job running an inserting machine at an Athens newspaper, and Berry have already played together in a number of short-lived local rock bands. The new group's initials stand for Rapid Eye Movement - a physiological term for the sleep-cycle stage in which dreaming occurs.
Apr [5] R.E.M. makes its concert debut as the Twisted Kites at Kathleen O'Brien's party at the Steeplechase, the converted St. Mary's Episcopalian church, on Oconee Street in Athens.

1981

Feb [8] The band records its first session at Bombay Studios in Smyrna, GA.
July Now managed by Jefferson Holt, who has invited ex-Sneaker Mitch Easter to produce debut recordings, 1,000 copies of the band's first single, *Radio Free Europe*, are released on the local Hib-Tone label. It is picked up by the US college radio network and becomes an airplay favorite. **Village Voice** magazine votes it Best Independent Single Of The Year. Easter also records their second track, *Sitting Still*.

1982

Mar Impressed by *Radio Free Europe*, Miles Copeland signs the band to his I.R.S. label. The five-track mini-album, ***Chronic Town***, produced by Easter, is heavily praised by rock critics. Dense layers of guitar add to Stipe's often inaudibly sung lyrics, adding an air of mystique to the band, which is already developing cult status.

1983

May Their full-length debut, the dreamlike ***Murmur***, co-produced by Easter and Don Dixon, is released on I.R.S. It peaks at US #36 during a 30-week chart stay, as the band becomes a popular college radio item. Live performances now mix original material with covers of songs including *Born To Run*, *In The Year 2525*, and *Paint It Black*.
Aug [13] A re-recorded version of *Radio Free Europe* is R.E.M.'s US chart single debut, at #78.
The group plays a series of seven stadium dates opening for Copeland-managed band, the Police.
Nov [18] R.E.M. makes its European debut on C4-TV's "The Tube".

1984

May Recorded in 12 days, the band's self-penned ***Reckoning***, featuring a more straightforward, Byrds-influenced, guitar-jangling alternative folk/rock style, more accessible for mainstream US radio play, begins a one year-plus stay on the US chart, peaking at #27, and is their UK debut at #91. As with all their '80s releases, R.E.M. embarks on extensive touring to support the album.
June The extracted *So. Central Rain (I'm Sorry)* peaks at US #85, and is followed by *(Don't Go Back To) Rockville* (which will be covered by 10,000 Maniacs in 1993).
[9] During the band's current US tour, the Byrds' Roger McGuinn joins them onstage to sing *So You Want To Be A Rock'n'Roll Star*.
Nov [21] They perform at the Rock City, Nottingham, Notts., during a UK tour.
Dec ***Reckoning*** extract, *Windout*, is incongruously included in the "Bachelor Party" movie soundtrack.

1985

Jan R.E.M. travels to Britain for further live dates and to record a new album with veteran folk/rock producer, Joe Boyd, though Stipe reportedly suffers a mental and physical breakdown during the sessions.
June ***Fables Of The Reconstruction*** enters the US chart, selling over 300,000 copies in three months and reaching US #28. All attempts at hit singles fail, but with a growing fan following (with particular adulation from a group of "Distiples", who believe, sophomorically, that Stipe is a guru) and critical praise, it makes UK #35.

1986

Sept The rock-based ***Life's Rich Pageant***, produced by John Cougar Mellencamp's collaborator Don Gehman, reaches US #21 and UK #43.
[13] They play at Mud Island Amphitheatre, Memphis, TN, during their latest US tour.
Oct [11] *Fall On Me*, its accompanying video directed by Stipe, peaks at US #94.

1987

Jan R.E.M. begins a successful US tour.

[23] ***Life's Rich Pageant*** is certified gold by the RIAA.
May [16] A collection of out-takes and B-side material released as ***Dead Letter Office*** (with its CD format also including the ***Chronic Town*** mini-album tracks) bows at its UK #60 peak, during a two-week chart stay, and will reach US #52, selling over 250,000 copies. In its sleeve-notes, Buck writes "listening to this album should be like browsing through a junk-shop". (All band members, except Stipe, are currently featured on Warren Zevon's ***Sentimental Hygiene***.)
Sept [26] Their fifth album, ***Document***, recorded in Nashville, TN, co-produced with long-time collaborator Scott Litt, and the last new material for I.R.S., reaches UK #28 in its week of entry, and will hit US #10. "Succumbs", a collection of plot-free videos, tops Billboard's video ranking.
Oct The band plays its first UK concerts in two years, while two R.E.M. recordings, *Swan Swan H*, and their cover of the Everly Brothers' classic, *All I Have To Do Is Dream*, are included on the I.R.S.-released compilation, ***Athens GA : Inside Out***.
Dec [5] The melodic, folk-rock leaning *The One I Love*, from ***Document***, hits US #9 and makes UK #51.

1988

Jan UK magazine **New Musical Express** readers vote four R.E.M. albums into its all-time Top 100. **Rolling Stone** magazine devotes its front cover to R.E.M., with the heading "America's Best Rock'n'Roll Band".
[25] ***Document*** is certified platinum by the RIAA.
Feb [20] Belatedly released, *It's The End Of The World As We Know It* peaks at US #69.
Apr *Finest Worksong* makes UK #50.
May [11] R.E.M. (minus Stipe), back McGuinn in Atlanta, as the Southern Gentlemen, playing seven Byrds songs and *Knockin' On Heaven's Door*.
June Following seven I.R.S. album releases, R.E.M. signs worldwide to Warner Bros. Records for a reported six million dollars.
Oct Stipe, with 10,000 Maniacs' singer Natalie Merchant and the Roches, contributes *Little April Shower* to the newly-released various artists Walt Disney compilation, ***Stay Awake***.
[29] The I.R.S.-released R.E.M. label retrospective, ***Eponymous*** (including the rare and original version of their debut single, *Radio Free Europe*), makes UK #69 and will reach US #44.
Nov [27] The group's Warner debut ***Green***, once again co-helmed with Litt and recorded at the Ardent Studios, Memphis, TN, reaches UK #27 in its week of entry and will reach US #12, as the band undertakes an exhaustive tour, which will be its last of the decade.

1989

Feb The extracted *Stand* peaks at UK #51.
Mar [1] "Green World Tour", the group's first arena trek, opens at the Louisville Gardens, KY, supported by Indigo Girls.
Apr [21] Stipe and Buck take part in the first Earth Day concert, at Merriweather Post Pavilion, Columbia, MD.
[8] *Stand* hits US #6, and will subsequently be featured as the theme to Fox TV's Chris Elliott-starring comedy, "Get A Life".
Berry collapses in Munich from bronchial infection, reported as Rocky Mountain Spotted Fever, forcing the cancellation of the rest of their German tour.
June [17] *Orange Crush* reaches UK #28, its promo clip directed by Matt Mahurin.
[24] *Pop Song '89* peaks at US #86.
Aug *Stand* re-charts at UK #48. (During an R.E.M. recording hiatus, Mills scores music for a movie by friend Howard Libov, Buck tours with friend Kevin Kenney, with local band Drivin'n'Cryin', and teams with Robyn Hitchcock under the name the Crosses to cut a track for the Byrds tribute album, ***Time Inbetween***, while Stipe produces local band the Chickasaw Muddpuppies' debut album, ***White Dirt***, duets with Syd Straw on *Future 40's* from Straw's debut album, ***Surprise***, and forms his own film and video company, C-OO, which films and releases "R.E.M.: Tourfilm", and opens his own vegetarian restaurant in Athens, called The Grit.)
Sept [6] "Orange Crush" wins the Best Post Modern Video category at the sixth annual MTV Video Music Awards, held at the Universal Amphitheatre, Universal City, CA.

1990

Apr [21] Stipe participates in "A Performance For The Planet" at the Merriweather Post Pavilion. (During the year, he also conceives a series of public service commercials on AIDS, abortion, the environment and racism. Natalie Merchant and rapper KRS-One are among artists who contribute.)
May [22] The group's "Pop Screen" video is certified gold by the RIAA.
Nov [30] "R.E.M. Tourfilm" video is also confirmed gold by the RIAA.
Dec [8] Having formed an ad-hoc offshoot in 1986 known as the Hindu Love Gods, which released the singles *Narrator* and *Good Time Tonight*, Buck, Mills and Berry, now teamed with Warren Zevon, for whom they have played on two of his last three albums, release a loose collection of blues covers, ***Hindu Love Gods***, under the same band name, which peaks at US #168. (By year's end, the band has received many honors, including the Earth Day 1990 Award for Environmentally Responsible Business, and the Athens-Clarke Heritage Foundation Inc. Award for support of historic preservation in Athens (their attorney Bertis Downs is president of the local historic society). Stipe has produced all-girl outfit Swell, Opal Fox Society, the Beggarweeds and Hetchy Hetchy. Still firmly based at the R.E.M./Athens Ltd. headquarters in Georgia, where they work in management and rehearsal rooms, they also complete their second album for Warner Bros.)

1991

Mar [14-15] The group plays two sets at London's Borderline under the pseudonym Bingo Hand Job. Billy Bragg also plays a mini-set.
[16] Career highlight *Losing My Religion*, the first single from their new album, makes UK #19.
[23] Its Litt co-produced parent album, the baroque-tinged, love-themed, strings-laden ***Out Of Time***, which includes guest KRS-One, with whom Stipe has recently recorded the hip-hop single, *The Greenhouse Effect*, and B-52's bomber Kate Pierson, enters the UK chart at #1.
Apr 10,000 postcards are received from fans supporting passage of the National Voter Registration Act. (The cards had been inserted into the CD longbox of ***Out Of Time***.)
[10] R.E.M.'s " Unplugged" show for MTV is recorded at New York's Chelsea Studios. The show will air on the 24th.
[13] R.E.M., with Pierson as added vocalist, appears as the musical guest on NBC-TV's "Saturday Night Live".
[28] The band plays its only concert of 1991 in Charlotte, WV.
May [18] ***Out Of Time*** tops the US chart, becoming the first album by a rock band to hit US #1 since Mötley Crüe's ***Dr. Feelgood*** in October 1989, as *Losing My Religion*, now at US #21, continues to climb the Hot 100. Unlike previous releases, R.E.M. elects not to tour in support of the project.
June [15] While R.E.M. members are currently writing and playing on a new Troggs album, *Shiny Happy People* hits UK #6.
[22] *Losing My Religion* hits US #4.
[24] The RIAA certifies gold sales of ***Fables Of The Reconstruction*** and ***Reckoning***.
Aug [17] *Near Wild Heaven* debuts at its UK #27 peak.
Sept [5] "Losing My Religion" wins the Best Video, Best Group Video, Best Art Direction, Best Editing, Best Direction and Breakthrough Video categories at the eighth annual MTV Video Music Awards, held again at the Universal Amphitheatre.
[7] Billy Bragg's *You Woke Up My Neighbourhood*, co-written by and featuring Stipe, makes UK #54.
[8] Stipe guests on Nickelodeon cable channel's "The Adventures Of Pete And Pete".
[12] *Losing My Religion* is certified gold by the RIAA.
[24] ***Tom's Album***, a various artists collection of cover versions of Suzanne Vega's *Tom's Diner*, including an R.E.M. treatment with Bragg on vocals, is released.
[28] *Shiny Happy People* hits US #10.
[30] A Leonard Cohen tribute album, ***I'm Your Fan***, to which R.E.M. has contributed *First We Take Manhattan*, is released in Britain on East West.
Oct [5] *The One I Love* reaches UK #16.
[10] ***Murmur*** is certified gold by the RIAA.
[12] I.R.S.-issued, ***The Best Of R.E.M.***, hits UK #7 in its week of entry.
Nov [16] Media-slaying *Radio Song* debuts at its UK #28 peak.
[26] "This Film Is On" video is certified gold by the RIAA.
[27] Introduced by fellow Georgian, actress Kim Basinger, the band takes part in ABC-TV's "MTV 10" special, offering a pre-taped live version of *Losing My Religion*.
Dec [3] The group tops the Modern Rock Artist and Top World Album categories at the second annual **Billboard** Music Awards, held at the Barker Hangar, Santa Monica, CA.
[14] Reissued *It's The End Of The World As We Know It* bows at its UK #39 pinnacle.

1992

Jan [31] R.E.M. plays a benefit for a mental health organization in Athens.
Feb [12] Stipe and Mills collect the Best International Group trophy at the 11th annual BRIT Awards, held at London's Hammersmith Odeon.
[25] R.E.M. wins the Best Pop Performance By A Duo Or Group With Vocal for *Losing My Religion*, Best Alternative Music Album for ***Out Of Time***, and Best Music Video - Shortform, for "Losing My Religion" categories at the 34th annual Grammy Awards, held at Radio City Music Hall, New York.
Mar [7] The soundtrack to Wim Wenders' new film, "Until The End Of the World", featuring R.E.M.'s *Fretless*, makes US #114.
[19] The group wins the Outstanding Act Of The Year, Outstanding Rock Album (***Out Of Time***) and Outstanding Video ("Losing My Religion") categories at the first annual Coca-Cola Atlanta Music Awards, held at the Fox Theatre.
June [5] The RIAA certifies four million sales of ***Out Of Time***.
Sept [23] The band is featured on MTV's "Rock The Vote" special.
Oct Neneh Cherry's new album, ***Homebrew***, featuring Stipe on *Trout*, is released.
[10] *Drive* reaches UK #11, as ***Automatic For The People***, with string arrangements by former Led Zeppelin John Paul Jones, enters the UK chart at #1. Its title is taken from Weaver D's soul food diner in Athens, whose orders are always met with "automatic". The eatery's "Delicious Fine Foods - Automatic For The People" sign is stolen when the album is released, but returned four days later with a note of apology and $10 to cover costs.
[15-16] The group plays in London, during a European tour which takes them to Germany, Holland, Italy, Spain, France and Sweden.
[24] ***Automatic For The People*** debuts at its US #2 peak behind Garth Brooks' ***The Chase***. (The sleeve of the CD has a letter for the consumer to send to General Than Shwe of the Myanmar Defense Ministry, requesting the release of Nobel Peace Prize winner Aung Sung Suu Kyi, held under house arrest since July 1989.)
Nov [12] Stipe joins 10,000 Maniacs onstage in Atlanta, singing John Prine's *Hello In There*, and duetting with Merchant on *A Campfire Song*.
[19] The group plays before 500 fan club members at the 40 Watt Club, Athens, GA, to record *Drive* for an upcoming Greenpeace benefit album.
Dec [5] *Man On The Moon*, lyrically penned by Stipe about the late comedian Andy Kaufman, reaches UK #18, spurred by a Peter Care-directed video.

[26] *Drive* reaches US #28. (During a year in which Buck has produced an album for Uncle Tupelo on Rockville Records, and Stipe has worked as co-producer with Oliver Stone on the movie "Desperation Angels", Staplegun Records releases the various artists compilation, ***Surprise Your Pig : A Tribute To R.E.M.***)

1993

Jan [20] Stipe and Mills combine with U2's Adam Clayton and Larry Mullen Jr. as Automatic Baby to sing *One*, and Stipe joins 10,000 Maniacs on *To Sir With Love* and *Give Them What They Want*, at the MTV 1993 Rock & Roll Inaugural Ball, in Washington, DC.
Feb [16] R.E.M. wins the Best International Group category at the 12th annual BRIT Awards, held at London's Alexandra Palace.
[27] *The Sidewinder Sleeps Tonite* reaches UK #17.
Mar [4] ***Automatic For The People*** is named Best Album, the group ties with U2 as Best Band and Stipe is named Best Male Singer in **Rolling Stone**'s 1993 Music Awards Critics' Picks.
[20] ***Out Of Time*** reaches UK #29, two years after it originally charted.
[27] *Man On The Moon* reaches US #30.
Apr [14] The group is named International Band, and ***Automatic For The People*** named International Album, at the annual IRMA (Irish Recorded Music Industry) Awards, held at the National Concert Hall in Dublin. Mills is present to receive the awards.
[24] Vigilantes of Love album, ***Killing Floor***, co-produced by Buck, is released in the US. ***Automatic For The People*** is confirmed double platinum in Britain (600,000 sales), as the album hits UK #1 again.
May [15] Mournful ballad *Everybody Hurts* hits UK #7.
[20] Stipe, Mills and Berry attend a celebration of the signing of the National Voter Registration Act on the South Lawn of the White House.
July The soundtrack to "Coneheads" is released in the US, featuring an R.E.M. out-take of *It's A Free World Baby*.
[24] *Nightswimming* debuts at its UK #27 peak.
Sept [2] R.E.M. performs *Everybody Hurts* at the tenth MTV Video Music Awards, held at the Universal Amphitheatre, Universal City, CA.
Nov [6] *Everybody Hurts* reaches US #29.
Dec [8] Stipe performs *We Shall Overcome* with Peter Gabriel and Merchant at the annual Reebok Human Rights at the Hynes Auditorium in Boston, MA.
[11] *Find The River* charts for a week at UK #54.

1994

Jan ***In Defense Of Animals*** to which Stipe has contributed *Arms Of Love*, is released in the US, while Mills wraps up production of three walls down album ***Building Our House*** for March release on Rust Records.
Feb [28] R.E.M. is the first recipient of the Patrick Lippert Award at the Rock The Vote benefit in New York.
May [7] ***Backbeat***, the soundtrack album to the movie recording the early days of the Beatles in Hamburg, West Germany, with Mills, Dave Grohl, Dave Pirner and Thurston Moore the featured band, charts for a week at US #190.
Aug [17] The RIAA certifies two million sales of ***Green***.
Sept [8] A shaven-headed Stipe collects four trophies for "Everybody Hurts" at the 11th annual MTV Video Music Awards held at Radio City Music Hall in the Best Direction, Editing, Cinematography and Breakthrough categories.
[17] Referencing a famous Dan Rather broadcast line, *What's The Frequency, Kenneth?* debuts at its UK #9 peak.
Oct [1] Returning to a hard-rock based sound ***Monster***, featuring Sonic Youth's Thurston Moore, Stipe's sister Lynda, and Rain Phoenix, sister of River Phoenix, to whom the album is dedicated, having notched up the biggest first week UK sales in five years, debuts at UK #1.
[15] ***Monster*** also enters at US #1.
A Richard Thompson tribute album, ***Beat The Retreat***, including R.E.M.'s version of *Wall Of Death*, is released.
Nov [5] *What's The Frequency, Kenneth?* reaches US #21.
[12] *Bang And Blame* debuts at its UK #15 peak, as the group guests on NBC-TV's "Saturday Night Live".

1995

Jan [13] R.E.M. embarks on its first world tour in more than five years at the Entertainment Center, Perth, Western Australia, Australia. Scott McCaughey and Nathan December are added to provide extra guitar and bass. (During one of the band's Myer Music Bowl, Melbourne concerts, tennis star Jim Courier plays drums on an encore of *Wichita Lineman*.)
[26] They are named Best Band in **Rolling Stone**'s 1995 Music Awards Critics Picks.
Feb [4] *Bang And Blame* reaches US #19.
[9] The RIAA confirms four million sales of ***Automatic For The People***.
[11] *Crush With Eyeliner* reaches UK #23.
[27] R.E.M. is once again named Best International Act and performs live at the 13th annual BRIT Awards, held at London's Alexandra Palace.
Mar [1] Berry leaves the stage midway through *Tongue* during a concert at the Patinoire De Malley Auditorium, Lausanne, Switzerland, complaining of a migraine headache. The band plays a couple of acoustic numbers, before Grant Lee Buffalo's Joey Peters takes over the drum stool for the remaining hour of the set.
[3] Diagnosed with a ruptured aneurysm on the outside surface of his brain, Berry undergoes a craniotomy at the University Hospital Center of Vaud, Lausanne.
[6] The band cancels its remaining European dates.
[11] ***Fables Of The Reconstruction*** re-charts at UK #58.
Apr [15] *Strange Currencies* debuts at its UK #9 peak.
May [15] The group's world tour resumes at the Shoreline Amphitheatre, Mountain View, CA.
June [3] *Strange Currencies* makes US #47.
[22-24] R.E.M. ends the North American leg of the world tour before sellout crowds totalling 56,694 at New York's Madison Square Garden.
[28] The European leg of the tour re-convenes in Berlin, Germany.
July [11] Mills has abdominal surgery to remove an intestinal tumor, causing the further cancellation of six European dates.
[22] In the latest incident in R.E.M.'s troubled world trek, two teenagers drown in the Boyne River during the group's concert at Slane Castle, County Meath, Eire - the first such fatal incident since a David Bowie concert there in 1987.
[25-26] R.E.M. plays the first-ever rock concerts at the Alfred McAlpine Stadium, Huddersfield, W. Yorks, grossing £1,610,000.
[29] *Tongue* bows at its UK #13 peak.
Aug [10] The RIAA certifies four million sales of ***Monster***.
[11] Stipe is diagnosed with an inguinal hernia before the band's concert in Prague, Czechoslovakia. (He will undergo surgery the next day at the Emory University Hospital in Atlanta.)
[21] R.E.M. files a trademark infringement suit in US District Court in Atlanta, against the Hershey Foods Corp. for launching an unauthorized "Kit Kat/R.E.M. Concert" for free tickets and trips, alleging injury to business reputation, false advertising and deceptive practices.
Sept [7] The band performs and collects the lifetime achievement Video Vanguard honor at the 12th annual MTV Video Music Awards, held at Radio City Music Hall.
[8] Its US tour resumes at the Miami Arena, Miami, FL, before a sellout crowd of 15,822.
Nov [21] R.E.M. finishes its world tour with the last of three sellout dates at The Omni, Atlanta. (The 69 North American dates have grossed in excess of $45 million.)
Dec [5] Stipe co-hosts a cocktail party with initiator Peter Gabriel in Los Angeles, CA, to provide an update on Witness, a program to provide video equipment to human-right activists around the world.

1996

Jan [25] R.E.M. wins Best Band and Best Tour categories in the **Rolling Stone** Readers' Poll and Best Band in the Critics' Poll.
Mar [26] Warner Bros. releases ***Songs In The Key Of X***, music from and inspired by the Fox-TV show "The X-Files", including a collaboration between R.E.M. and William S. Burroughs.
Apr [28] Stipe, rumored to be moving towards movie work (having already formed his Single Cell Pictures film production company with New Line Cinema in September 1994), performs at VH1 Honors, a live concert held to benefit the Witness organization at the Universal Amphitheatre.
May [22] The group releases a press statement announcing it has split from its longtime manager Jefferson Holt, who is leaving to "pursue other interests". It is subsequently revealed that he is leaving amid alleged sexual harassment charges made against him by an employee at the group's company offices.
July [22] *Sponge*, R.E.M.'s contribution to the recently released various artists, Vic Chesnutt-tribute album, ***Sweet Relief II: Gravity Of The Situation***, is released in the US.
Sept [10] Featuring Patti Smith among its guests, R.E.M.'s ***New Adventures In Hi-Fi*** is scheduled for release by Warner Bros.

REO SPEEDWAGON

Kevin Cronin (vocals); **Gary Richrath** (guitar); **Neal Doughty** (keyboards); **Bruce Hall** (bass); **Alan Gratzer** (drums)

1968

Named after a make of fire engine, REO Speedwagon is formed in Champaign, IL, by local Illinois University students Gratzer (b. Nov. 9, 1948, Syracuse, NY) and Doughty (b. July 29, 1946, Evanston, IL), who recruit the band's chief songwriter, Richrath (b. Oct. 18, 1949, Peoria, IL), vocalist Terry Luttrell and bass player Craig Philbin. The group becomes the town's most popular live band and, by the turn of the decade, is managed by Irving Azoff, who secures the melodic rock-based group a deal with Epic Records, which releases their debut album, ***REO Speedwagon***, in 1971.

1972

Feb Cronin (b. Oct. 6, 1951, Evanston), whom Richrath has discovered via a "Musicians' Referral Service" in Chicago, IL, replaces Luttrell on lead vocals. The band begins to tour extensively (as it will throughout the '70s, often sharing major treks with fellow midwestern acts like Bob Seger's Silver Bullet Band and Kansas).
Dec ***R.E.O. T.W.O.***, featuring Cronin on lead vocals for the first time, is released. Following differences with Richrath, however, Cronin departs for a solo career (which will last for the next three band projects), replaced by Mike Murphy.

1974

Feb ***Ridin' The Storm Out*** is their first album to chart in the US, peaking at #171.
Dec ***Lost In A Dream***, their second album of the year, reaches US #98. ***This Time We Mean It***, the last to feature Murphy as lead vocalist, will make US #74 the following August as the band splits from manager Azoff.

1976

July Hall (b. May 3, 1953, Champaign) has replaced Philbin on bass and Cronin has rejoined on lead vocals for ***R.E.O.***, which peaks at US #159. Cronin and Richrath will co-produce the group from here on, and jointly provide most of its songs.

1977

Apr The live double album, ***You Get What You Play For***, reaches US #72. Staying charted for two weeks shy of a year, it will earn the band's first platinum album for a million-plus sales. The heavy touring schedule continues.
June Their first US chart single is a live version of *Ridin' The Storm Out*, taken from the double album, which peaks at US #94.

1978

May The group makes a cameo appearance in the premiering movie, "FM", performing *Ridin' The Storm Out*.
June ***You Can Tune A Piano, But You Can't Tuna Fish***, makes US #79, eventually spending 11 months on the chart and spawning *Roll With The Changes*, which makes US #58.
Aug *Time For Me To Fly* peaks at US #56.
Dec [14] ***You Get What You Play For*** is certified platinum by the RIAA. ***Nine Lives*** (also the band's ninth album) will reach US #33 the following September and be confirmed gold by the RIAA on December 5th.

1980

June A double compilation, ***A Decade Of Rock'n'Roll, 1970 To 1980***, rounding up tracks from the group's first ten years, makes US #55 while a reissue of *Time For Me To Fly* (also on the compilation) from two years earlier, peaks at US #77.

1981

Feb [21] ***Hi Infidelity*** finally achieves the band's major chart breakthrough, toppling John Lennon's ***Double Fantasy*** from US #1, and holding pole position for a total of 15 weeks to the end of June (in three separate runs). It will eventually sell over nine million domestic copies.
Mar [21] Cronin-penned power-rock ballad, *Keep On Loving You*, the first single from ***Hi Infidelity***, also tops the US chart (for a week) and is another million seller. After a decade as one of the busiest and most continually-mobile tour support bands in the US, REO Speedwagon is now a bill-topping stadium-filler in its own right.
May *Take It On The Run*, also from ***Hi Infidelity***, hits US #5, while *Keep On Loving You* is their UK chart debut, hitting #7.
July Third single from the album, *Don't Let Him Go*, makes US #24.
Aug [8] MTV features REO Speedwagon live from Denver, CO, for its first stereo concert broadcast.
[13] Their 1972 album ***R.E.O./T.W.O.*** is certified gold by the RIAA.
[22] *Take It On The Run* reaches UK #19, while ***Hi Infidelity*** hits UK #6 during a 29-week chart run.
Oct *In Your Letter* reaches US #20.

1982

Aug ***Good Trouble*** hits US #7 and reaches UK #29. Taken from it, *Keep The Fire Burnin'* also hits US #7.
Oct Also from the album, *Sweet Time* reaches US #26.
[1] ***Good Trouble*** is confirmed platinum by the RIAA.

1985

Jan After *I Do Wanna Know* has reached US #29 a month earlier, ***Wheels Are Turnin'*** hits US #7.
Mar [9] *Can't Fight This Feeling*, written by Cronin on the Hawaiian island Molokai, and taken from ***Wheels Are Turnin'***, hits US #1 for the first of three weeks.
Apr *Can't Fight This Feeling* reaches UK #16.
June Another track from the album, *One Lonely Night*, reaches US #19.
Aug *Live Every Moment* makes US #34.
Nov UK-only compilation album, ***Best Foot Forward***, is released.

1987

Feb Their first new album in nearly two years, ***Life As We Know It***, enters the US chart, set to reach #28, during a 48-week chart stay.
Apr [4] *That Ain't Love* reaches US #16.
June [6] *Variety Tonight* peaks at US #60.
Aug [11] ***Life As We Know It*** is certified gold by the RIAA.
Oct [24] *In My Dreams*, co-written by Cronin with Tom Kelly, reaches US #19. (A 14-track US compilation retrospective, ***The Hits*** will make US #61 the following August.)

1989

Apr [17] The RIAA certifies gold sales of *Take It On The Run* and *Can't Fight This Feeling* and platinum sales of *Keep On Loving You* and ***Ridin' The Storm Out***.

1990

Sept [9] The group headlines an anti-drug "Users Are Losers" concert in Miami, FL, organized by the Metro-Dade County Police.
[15] With the band now lining up as Cronin, Doughty, Hall, Dave Amato (b. Mar. 3, 1953) (ex-Ted Nugent band, lead guitar), Bryan Hitt (b. Jan. 5, 1954) (ex-Wang Chung, drums) and Jesse Harms (b. July 6, 1952) (keyboards), ***The Earth, A Small Man, His Dog And A Chicken*** climbs to US #129.
Oct [12] The RIAA certifies two million sales of ***Wheels Are Turnin'***.
[25] ***You Can Tune A Piano, But You Can't Tuna Fish*** reaches the RIAA-certified two million sales plateau.
Nov [3] *Love Is A Rock* peaks at US #65.
[10] The group plays a sellout show at the Chicago Theatre, Chicago, during a current US tour.

1992

Jan While Cronin has recently written *Hard To Believe* to benefit the Home Front Trust, for families of Gulf War casualties, recording the track with Bill Champlin, David Crosby and Richard Marx, Richrath now works on an album with a new band at Sherwood Studios, Los Angeles.
[31] The group plays to a sellout crowd of 6,096 at the Veterans Memorial Arena, Brown County Expo Centre Complex, Green Bay, WI.
Feb Richrath's new band, Richrath, debuts with ***Only The Strong Survive***, released by GNP/Crescendo.
Aug [11] The 1980 compilation ***A Decade Of Rock And Roll*** is certified platinum by the RIAA.
[27] REO Speedwagon performs at the New Pine Knob Theatre, Clarkston, MI, during its current US tour.

1994

Aug [7] The group performs at the Pine Knob Music Theatre, Clarkston, MI, with fellow dinosaurs rockers, Blue Oyster Cult, during US summer dates with Cheap Trick, Foghat, Starship, Eddie Money, Survivor and Kansas.
Nov [9] The RIAA certifies two million sales of ***The Hits***.

1995

Mar [7] With US radio play of its enduring hit singles having kept the album alive as a strong catalog item, ***Hi Infidelity*** is certified for nine million sales.
July [27] Currently on tour with Fleetwood Mac, Pat Benatar and Orleans, REO Speedwagon plays a sellout date at the Garden State Arts Center, Holmdel, NJ. Still a popular draw on US summer package tours, the group will participate in next year's "Can't Stop Rockin' '96" caravan with Foreigner and Peter Frampton, beginning July 3rd at Darien Lake, NY.

THE REPLACEMENTS

Paul Westerberg (vocals, guitar);
Bob Stinson (guitar); **Tommy Stinson** (bass);
Chris Mars (drums)

1979

The son of a car salesman, Westerberg (b. Dec. 31, 1960, Minneapolis, MN), inspired by the music of the Sex Pistols and working at various jobs including one as a janitor and another at a steel foundry, forms the Impediments with Bob Stinson (b. Dec. 17, 1959, Mound, MN), his 12-year old brother Tommy (b. Oct. 6, 1966, San Diego, CA) and Mars (b. Apr. 26, 1961, Minneapolis), playing, usually inebriated, on the local Minneapolis club scene. Attracting the interest of local Twintone Records' boss Peter Jesperson and a change of name to the Replacements results in the group's punk-styled debut ***Sorry Ma, Forgot To Take Out The Trash*** emerging in 1981, with each of its tracks lasting an average of two minutes. A second rapid-fire set, ***Stink***, also co-produced by Jesperson, Steve Fjelstad and the band, garners attention from the alternative music press, impressed by titles including *Fuck School*, with its 1982 release, as the band also gains a well-earned reputation for a drugs and booze-filled lifestyle and similarly affected live performances.

1985

Nov Following one further outing for Twin Tone, the country/punk-tinged ***Hootenay***, co-produced by the band, Jesperson and Paul Stark and released in 1983, and the critically-praised ***Let It Be***, issued by Zippo Records in October the following year (the first Replacements album to reach the UK), and showcasing, for the first time, Westerberg's earnest songwriting talent, the Replacements have been signed to Sire Records which now releases ***Tim***, produced by Tommy Erdelyi.

1986

Feb [1] ***Tim***, featuring Alex Chilton on *Left Of The Dial*, enters the US chart on its way to #183. (By year's end, Bob Stinson will be ejected from the group for ongoing substance abuse, to be replaced by guitarist Slim Dunlap (b. Robert Dunlap, Aug. 14, 1951, Plainview, MN).)

1987

May [30] The genre-mixed ***Pleased To Meet Me***, featuring the Memphis Horns and produced by Jim Dickinson, enters the US survey, set to make #131 during a 19-week chart tenure, and includes the much-praised ode to suicide, *The Ledge*.

1988

Dec Having contributed their version of the "101 Dalmations" song to ***Stay Awake : Interpretations Of Music From Vintage Disney Films***, *Cruella De Ville* marks the group's debut on the US Modern Rock chart, peaking at #11.

1989

Mar [11] *I'll Be You* tops the US Modern Rock survey for a week.
May [13] *I'll Be You* makes US #51 spurring its parent album, the Big Star-influenced ***Don't Tell A Soul*** to US #57. Featuring vocal guest Tom Waits and co-produced by the band with Matt Wallace, it will eventually sell over 250,000 domestic copies. (During the year, Westerberg weans himself from alcohol addiction.)
July [5] The Replacements begin a US tour at the Miami Arena, FL, opening for Tom Petty.

1990

Oct [13] With Mars having departed, allegedly concerned about Westerberg's domination of the group, *Merry Go Round* begins the first of four weeks atop the US Modern Rock survey. (Mars will re-emerge in 1992 with his solo debut, ***Horseshoes And Hand Grenades***, followed by ***75% Less Fat*** in 1993

and ***Tenterhooks*** two years later.)
[20] Featuring replacement drummer, ex-Routine 11 and Things Fall Down's Steve Foley, ***All Shook Down***, dominated as ever by Westerberg's lyrical vision and featuring guests Benmont Tench and John Cale, makes US #69.

1991

Jan [18] During a headlining US tour, the group plays to a sell-out crowd of 3,600 at the Hollywood Palladium, Hollywood, CA.
June [22] The Replacements perform at New York, NY's Madison Square Garden, opening for Elvis Costello, a bill grossing $362,225.
Sept The band dissolves with Westerberg, clearly the most prominent ex-member, remaining with Sire, though Dunlap will release ***The Old New Me***, for the Replacements' early label, Twin Tone in 1993 (featuring Westerberg among its guests), with Tommy Stinson going on to form Bash And Pop, also staying on Sire for ***Friday Night Is Killing Me***, issued the same year.

1993

July [3] Having contributed his first solo cut, *Dyslexic Heart* to last year's US #6 peaking ***Singles*** soundtrack, Westerberg's debut album, ***14 Songs***, relatively subdued by comparison to his Replacements outings, enters the US chart, set to reach #44 during a 10-week ride. Co-produced with Wallace, the well-received, self-penned set includes music guests Joan Jett and keyboardist Ian McLagan.

1995

Feb [18] Former lead guitarist, Bob Stinson dies from a drug overdose at his Minneapolis apartment. His brother Tommy will assemble his latest outfit, Perfect, by year's end.
Dec [2] The television soundtrack album, ***Friends***, including the new Westerberg cuts, *Sunshine* and *Stain Yer Blood*, hits US #41.

1996

May [18] Westerberg's sophomore solo set, ***Eventually***, enters at its US #50 peak, with several of its 12 tracks recorded on the first or second takes, and including the ballad, *Good Day*, written about the death of his ex-colleague Stinson the previous year. Westerberg also begins auditioning for a live backing band, having already recruited ex-New Power Generation drummer Michael Bland, for live shows later in the year.

PAUL REVERE & THE RAIDERS

Paul Revere (keyboards); **Mark Lindsay** (vocals, saxophone); **Drake "Kid" Levin** (guitar); **Philip "Fang" Volk** (bass); **Mike "Smitty" Smith** (drums)

1959

Lindsay (b. Mar. 9, 1942, Eugene, OR), working in a bakery by day and singing with his own high school band by night, is watching a band at a local Elks Hall gig, when he plucks up courage to ask if he can sing with them. They accept and he performs Jerry Lee Lewis' *Crazy Arms*. Group leader, Revere (b. Jan. 7, 1938, Harvard, NE), an ex-hairdresser raised in Boise, ID, now running the Reed'n'Bell drive-in restaurant in Caldwell, ID, invites Lindsay to replace lead vocalist Red Hughes, as they name-change to the Downbeats, comprising Robert White (lead guitar), Richard White (rhythm guitar), William Hibbard (bass guitar) and Jerry Labrum (drums). Going on to cut half a dozen instrumentals at IMM Productions studios in Boise the following year, Revere takes the tapes from the sessions to Los Angeles, CA, where he meets John Guss at the Gardena pressing plant. Guss cuts a record from tape, re-naming the band Paul Revere & the Raiders, and releasing its debut single, *Beatnik Sticks*.

1961

Apr The group's local hit, *Like, Long Hair*, another instrumental, makes US #38. Shortly after, Revere will be drafted and the group disbands. An album and four follow-up singles, on Gardena, fail to chart through lack of live promotion.

1963

Mar Revere and Lindsay regroup in Portland, OR, where Smith (playing at teen club Headless Horseman), Volk and Levin join the re-vamped line up. The group becomes part of the buoyant Portland/Seattle live scene, alongside bands like the Wailers, the Sonics and the Kingsmen, which leads to their signing to northwestern label Jerden which issues *So Fine*. This in turn brings the group to the notice of CBS/Columbia Records, which buys its contract.
June The first Columbia single is their version of the staple of every northwestern band's live act, Richard Berry's *Louie Louie*, with a vocal by Lindsay. (The Kingsmen's version is released nationally by Wand Records almost simultaneously and, despite Columbia's promotion, the Kingsmen's will hit US #2 and sell over a million.) Lindsay will leave the next year, when the follow-up, *Louie - Go Home*, also fails to chart.

1965

Apr The Raiders have moved to Los Angeles with Lindsay re-joined, as the group releases a version of *Ooh Poo Pah Doo*.
June Impressed by their showmanship, teen appeal and their startling Revolutionary War stage outfits, a band trademark, "American Bandstand" presenter Dick Clark adopts the group as the house band for his new ABC-TV show, "Where The Action Is", which launches on June 27th. (This constant national exposure turns them into teen idols, and guarantees excellent promotion for subsequent records with the photogenic Lindsay becoming a pin-up heart-throb in the US.)
Oct Columbia has paired the group with producer Terry Melcher for *Steppin' Out* which makes US #46. ***Here They Come***, featuring mostly familiar rock standards and released to coincide with the TV show launch, peaks at #71 - the group's first chart album.

1966

Jan [18] The Kinks-influenced *Just Like Me*, its cover of a local record by Rick Dey & the Wild Knights, reaches US #11.
Apr Levin is drafted, and is replaced on guitar by Jim Valley, ex-Viceroys and Don & the Goodtimes.
May [10] Propelled by an arresting guitar riff, *Kicks*, an anti-drug song originally penned by Barry Mann and Cynthia Weil with UK group the Animals in mind, hits US #4, and ***Just Like Us!*** hits US #5. It will stay charted for 43.
July [25] The group performs *Kicks* and *Just Like Me* on NBC-TV's "Hullabaloo".
[26] *Hungry*, another Mann/Weil song in hard-rock style, hits US #6, while the mostly group-written album ***Midnight Ride*** hits US #9.
Oct [25] The first group-penned hit single is *The Great Airplane Strike*, by Lindsay and producer Melcher, which makes US #20.
Nov [2] They guest star on ABC-TV's "Batman", in an episode titled "Hizzoner The Penguin".

1967

Jan [6] ***Just Like Us!*** is certified gold by the RIAA, the first Columbia album by a rock group to sell one million copies.
[10] Lindsay and Melcher's *Good Thing* hits US #4.
Feb ***The Spirit Of '67***, including *Hungry* and *Good Thing*, hits US #9, their third consecutive Top 10 album.
[16] The group guest stars on CBS-TV's "Coliseum" with Woody Allen.
Mar [5] They appear on CBS-TV's "The Smothers Brothers Comedy Hour".
[14] *Ups And Downs* reaches US #22. Meanwhile, Volk and Smith leave to join Levin (now out of the service) to form Brotherhood, while Valley departs to work as a soloist.
[20] ***Midnight Ride*** is confirmed gold by the RIAA.
Apr [17] ***Spirit Of '67*** is also certified gold by the RIAA.
[30] Freddy Weller (b. Wilton Frederick Weller, Sept. 9, 1947, Atlanta, GA), whom Revere had spotted in Ohio while working for Billy Joe Royal, joins for the band's appearance on CBS-TV "The Ed Sullivan Show", to promote *Him Or Me - What's It Gonna Be?* Then bassist Charlie Coe (b. Nov. 19, 1944), who had been in the original line-up in Boise, but left to continue education, majoring in music at Boise College, and drummer Joe Correro (b. Nov. 19, 1946, Greenwood, MS), who had played at high school with Bobbie Gentry and in Memphis-based Flash & the Board of Directors (who had done a two-week tour with the Raiders), both join.
June [6] *Him Or Me - What's It Gonna Be?* hits US #5. With influences from the Monkees and the Rolling Stones clearly showing, this is later rated by critics as the group's finest moment.
July Compilation album, ***Paul Revere And The Raiders Greatest Hits***, reaches US #15.
Aug [25] ***Paul Revere And The Raiders Greatest Hits*** is certified gold by the RIAA.
Sept [19] *I Had A Dream*, a heavy rocker with a hint of psychedelia, makes US #17.
Oct ***Revolution!***, highlighted by *Him Or Me - What's It Gonna Be?* and featuring session musicians Ry Cooder, Van Dyke Parks, Hal Blaine and Glen Campbell among others, reaches US #25.
Dec *Peace Of Mind* peaks at US #42, the group's last single produced by Melcher.

1968

Jan The band's own Saturday morning Dick Clark-produced ABC-TV show, "Happening '68", begins airing, and will run until September 1969. Their still-strong teen appeal makes them more unfashionable with rock fans drifting in the direction of West Coast, psychedelic and progressive sounds, but the music is much less out on a limb, credibility-wise, than the group's image and presentation suggest.
Mar [12] The Lindsay produced Rolling Stones-influenced *Too Much Talk* reaches US #19. He will continue to be the group's producer until the end of its chart days, but will also have a parallel solo vocal career.
[20] The group appears on NBC-TV's "Jack Benny's Carnival Nights".
Apr ***Goin' To Memphis***, recorded with producer Chips Moman, makes US #61.
July [23] *Don't Take It So Hard* reaches US #27.
Aug Coe leaves and is replaced by "Where The Action Is" regular, Keith Allison.
Oct *Cinderella Sunshine* peaks at US #58, while ***Something Happening*** climbs to US #122.

1969

Apr *Mr. Sun, Mr. Moon* reaches US #18.
May *Hard'n'Heavy (With Marshmallow)* makes US #51. Lindsay announces plans for his solo career.
July *Let Me* reaches US #20.
Aug Lindsay's first solo single, *First Hymn From Grand Terrace*, part of Jimmy Webb's epic *Hymn From Grand Terrace* featured on Richard Harris' ***The Yard Went On Forever***, peaks at US #81.
Oct ***Alias Pink Puzz***, named after they use the pseudonym Pink Puzz in an affort to get radio stations, turned off by the Paul Revere name, to play their records, reaches US #48, while from it, the Weller-penned *We Gotta All Get Together* makes US #50, the last discs to be credited to Paul Revere & the Raiders.

1970

Feb *Just Seventeen*, credited to the Raiders, peaks at US #82. Lindsay's biggest solo success is *Arizona*, a song recorded by Steve Rowland's UK group Family Dogg as the follow-up to their 1969 hit, *Way Of Life*. Lindsay's revival hits US #9, and earns a gold disc for million-plus sales. (It is also a typical example of Lindsay's solo output, which tends towards tuneful ballads in Glen

Campbell mould, which would not fit into the invariably uptempo and rocking Raiders group style.)
Apr Lindsay's first solo album, ***Arizona***, makes US #36.
May ***Collage***, the first album credited just to the Raiders, peaks at US #154, while Lindsay's solo *Miss America*, from ***Arizona***, reaches US #44.
July Lindsay's *Silver Bird* makes US #25.
Oct His solo album, ***Silver Bird***, climbs to US #82.
Nov Lindsay's version of Neil Diamond's *And The Grass Won't Pay No Mind* reaches US #44.

1971

Jan *Problem Child*, another Lindsay solo, stops at US #80.
Feb Lindsay embarks on a solo tour of the US, supporting the Carpenters.
June His cover of Bread's *Been Too Long On The Road* peaks at US #98.
[30] The still-rising *Indian Reservation* is certified gold by the RIAA.
July [20] Musical variety show, "Make Your Own Kind Of Music", headlined by the Carpenters with Lindsay a regular feature, airs on NBC-TV, set to end on September 7th.
[24] The group's revival of John D. Loudermilk's *Indian Reservation (The Lament Of The Cherokee Reservation Indian)*, previously a US and UK Top 20 hit for Don Fardon, and recommended to the group by Columbia A&R man Jack Gold, hits US #1 for a week, the Raiders' only US chart-topper. Weller sings lead vocal (he will later have a successful career as a solo country singer) and Lindsay still produces. (The group has now split as a live unit, and has session men playing most of the instrumental parts on current recordings.)
Aug ***Indian Reservation*** reaches US #19. Correro leaves the band, and Smith returns in his place while Omar Martinez and Robert Woolley are added to the line-up.
Oct The group's version of Joe South's *Birds Of A Feather* reaches US #23, while Lindsay's solo album, ***You've Got A Friend***, makes US #180, and *Are You Old Enough* peaks at US #87.

1972

Feb The Raiders' *Country Wine* climbs to US #51.
June *Powder Blue Mercedes Queen* makes US #54.
Aug Double compilation album, ***All-Time Greatest Hits***, rounding up their chart singles, makes US #143.
Nov *Song Seller* peaks at US #96.
Dec Smith quits the band again.

1973

Feb The last Raiders chart single is *Love Music*, which peaks at US #97.
May Weller leaves, and Revere recruits Doug Heath, from Merrilee Rush's backing band.
June [20] The group appears on the 20th anniversary special edition of Dick Clark's "American Bandstand", alongside Little Richard, Three Dog Night and others. Lindsay will quit the band in January 1975, with Revere promoting drummer Omar Martinez to lead vocalist. Allison will leave in April of the same year, replaced by Ron Foos.

1976

June [26] *Ain't Nothin' Wrong*, written by KC and Richard Finch, is released on Drive/TK.
July ***The British Are Coming*** is released on 20th Century during the USA's bicentennial celebrations. Revere and Lindsay take full advantage of the promotion the bicentennial is giving to the group, touring through the summer, but Revere will disband the group by year's end. He will re-join the group, lining up as Martinez, Foos, Woolley and led by Heath, on New Year's Eve 1978, as it embarks on a 250 to 300 date-a-year schedule, with this line-up remaining together to the present.

1985

July [17] While Revere and Lindsay have enjoyed many successful years singing TV and radio jingles, and continue touring regularly on the rock'n'roll/ oldies circuit, and following the US release of ***Paul Revere Rides Again*** on Hitbound in 1983 (the same year that Edsel in the UK issued the compilation album, ***Kicks***), Paul Revere & the Raiders begin a regular slot on "Rock'n'Roll Summer Action", broadcast for the first time on ABC-TV, set to end on August 28th.

TONY RICH

1993

The son of José, his piano-playing father, Rich, (b. Anthony Jeffries, Nov. 19, 1971, Detroit, MI), raised in Detroit and weaned on a rainbow of music genres including R&B, rock, folk, pop and hip-hop, has taught himself to play acoustic guitar in his early teens, subsequently mastering his brother, Joe's keyboard. Invariably as their youngest member, Rich has gone on to serve his musical apprenticeship as a singer and keyboard player for several local R&B and jazz/fusion bands, before working with, and often fronting, gospel groups and choirs. Recording demos for and with a number of Detroit-based songwriters, one of them has come to the attention of Detroit Pistons basketball star John Salley, who has paid Rich to contribute to sessions at his own studio for his production company. With Salley encouraging him to pursue a solo career, Rich has met hot R&B producer Dallas Austin through Tim and Bob, a production duo who are working at Salley's company, and via Austin, Rich plays a song down the telephone to R&B performer/producer Pebbles, who invites him to take his first ever plane flight to meet with her in Atlanta, GA. Subsequently recording four Rich compositions for her own solo album, Pebbles introduces Rich to her husband, songwriter/producer and LaFace Records co-founder L.A. Reid, who now invites Rich to relocate to Atlanta and become part of the label's fertile songwriting, session playing, mixing and production crew.

1994

Mar [12] The various artists album ***A Tribute To Curtis Mayfield***, to which Elton John has contributed a track featuring Rich's session work, enters the US chart, set to reach #56.
May [28] His work during the year for the LaFace label's R&B roster includes a remix of Toni Braxton's *You Mean The World To Me* which now hits US #7 (and UK #30 on July [9]).
Sept [17] Boyz II Men's sophomore album, ***II***, which includes the Rich composition *I Sit Away*, enters the US chart at #1.
Nov Having completed a remix of TLC's *Red Light Special* (which will hit US #2 and UK #18 in April the following year), Rich is given the green light by Reid to begin work on his solo debut album.

1995

Oct Rich undertakes a promotional tour of Europe to introduce his forthcoming debut album, including an appearance on the new-talent German TV entertainment show "Geldoderliebe".
Dec [5] Rich performs a showcase in New York, NY, before playing a similar album preview in Los Angeles, CA on the 12th.
[16] His freshman single, *Nobody Knows*, a Babyface-sounding ballad based around his acoustic guitar playing, begins a six-month plus residence on the US Hot 100.

1996

Feb [3] His debut album, ***Words***, a largely acoustic-based R&B, folk and pop meld credited to the Tony Rich Project, though entirely written, performed and produced by Rich and released by LaFace, enters the US chart.
[28] He performs *Superstition* with R&B contemporary D'Angelo in tribute to Lifetime Achievement Award recipient Stevie Wonder at the 38th annual Grammy Awards held at the Shrine Auditorium, Los Angeles, CA.
Mar [7] Rich sings *Nobody Knows* on CBS-TV's "Late Show With David Letterman".
[19] ***Words*** is confirmed gold by he RIAA.
[23] Co-written by his brother Joe, *Nobody Knows* finally hits US #2 as ***Words*** reaches US #31.
Apr [22] *Nobody Knows* is certified platinum by the RIAA for one million US sales.
Apr [28] He performs at the "VH1 Honors", a live concert held at the Universal Amphitheatre, Universal City, CA to benefit the Witness organization, singing duets with Joan Osborne on versions of the Rolling Stones' *Beast Of Burden*, and Al Green's *Let's Stay Together*.
May [31] Questioned on his rapid rise to front-rank R&B status, Rich responds in this week's **Entertainment Weekly**: "I knew it would happen. I put a lot of work into my music, and when you put a lot of work into anything, you expect returns."
June [1] *Nobody Knows* hits UK #4.
[8] ***Words*** makes UK #27. Rich withdraws from the bill of the forthcoming "Smokin' Grooves" US R&B/rap caravan tour, not wishing to restrict himself to a rap-only audience, believing his appeal to be more wide-stream.
July [6] *Nobody Knows* celebrates its 30th consecutive week on the US Hot 100 survey, still at #10, as Toni Braxton's sophomore album, ***Secrets***, which includes her version of Rich's *Come On Over Here*, enters at its US #2 peak.
[22] The Tony Rich Project's first US tour opens at the Cal Expo Amphitheatre, Sacramento, CA, a 31-date swing set to close on September 2nd at the Blockbuster Pavilion, Devore, CA.

CLIFF RICHARD

1948

Sept Richard (b. Harry Rodger Webb, Oct. 14, 1940, Lucknow, India) arrives in England for the first time on the wartime troopship SS Ranghi to live in Carshalton, Surrey, with his parents, Rodger (who has been running Kellner's restaurant in Lucknow) and Dorothy, and sisters, Donella and Jacqueline. His family moves to Enfield, Middx. in 1952 where he attends Cheshunt Secondary Modern School, and forms a five-piece vocal group, the Quintones, which splits when the three girl members go to secretarial college. After leaving school with an "O-level" pass in English in the summer of 1957, he finds work as a credit control clerk at Atlas Lamps factory in Enfield. He also joins the Dick Teague Skiffle Group, playing pubs in Ware, Cheshunt and Hoddesdon. During the first half of 1958, he and the group's drummer, Terry Smart, leave to form a rock'n'roll band with Norman Mitham on guitar, calling themselves Harry Webb & the Drifters. Teddy Boy John Foster, employed at the local sewage works, sees the band at the Five Horseshoes pub in Hoddesdon and offers to manage them. Foster persuades his parents to finance the recording of a demo and, for £10, they cut *Breathless* and *Lawdy Miss Clawdy* at HMV Records store in London's Oxford Street. They subsequently play a week's engagement at the 2I's coffee bar in London's Soho district. After a gig they are approached by Ian Samwell, wishing to join the group as its lead guitarist. He is accepted, also proving to have songwriting talent. Promoter Bob Greatorex books the group for a one-night stand at a dance hall in Ripley, Derbys., but is unhappy with the lead singer's name. After a discussion at the Swiss pub near the 2I's, they settle upon Cliff Richard & the Drifters. (Samwell suggests leaving the "s" off Richards, the initial suggestion, pointing out that when Richard corrects people who get it wrong, they will keep his name in mind.)

1958

June [14] Foster arranges for Richard & the Drifters

to take part in a talent contest at the Gaumont Cinema on Shepherd's Bush Green in London. He persuades variety agent George Ganjou to see the band and Ganjou takes Richard's demo tape to Norrie Paramor, head of A&R at EMI Records' Columbia label, who invites the group to audition for him.

July [24] *Move It* and *Schoolboy Crush* are recorded in number two studio at the Abbey Road Studios, London.

Aug [9] Richard signs to EMI's Columbia imprint and leaves his job at Atlas. With the Drifters, he begins a four-week residency at Butlins holiday camp in Clacton-on-Sea, Essex. Mitham quits the band, Samwell switches to bass and Ken Pavey, a professional player working at the holiday camp, fills in the guitar slot.

[29] His debut single, *Schoolboy Crush*, a cover of a US release by Bobby Helms, backed with *Move It* (a rock number written by Samwell in response to an article by Steve Race in **Melody Maker** and completed on a bus on the way to the studio) is released. Two session players, guitarist Ernie Shears and bassist Frank Clarke, are on the tracks at Paramor's insistence, to ensure a strong sound.

Sept The group is signed to appear on a UK package tour headed by *When* hitmakers, the Kalin Twins. Minus a lead guitarist since Mitham's departure, Foster visits the 2I's to recruit singer/guitarist Tony Sheridan, but cannot find him. Instead, he spots Hank Marvin, a regular at the club and known to be an excellent player. Marvin agrees to join Richard on tour provided his rhythm guitar-playing partner, Bruce Welch, is taken on too.

[13] Richard makes his British TV debut on Jack Good's "Oh Boy", on which he will become a program resident. Good has heard the single, disregarded *Schoolboy Crush*, but raved over *Move It*. He orders Richard to sing without his customary guitar and minus his sideburns. (He also encourages a sexy stage act which will have newspapers complaining about TV depravity and the corruption of the young.) At the same time, *Move It*, now promoted to the A-side after most radio DJ's have shared Good's judgement, makes its debut on the UK chart.

Oct [5] Richard & the Drifters, comprising Marvin (lead guitar), Welch (rhythm guitar), Samwell (bass) and Smart (drums), make their concert bow at the Victoria Hall, Hanley, Staffs., at the start of the Kalin Twins' UK tour, which also features trumpeter Eddie Calvert and the Most Brothers. (Teen reaction to Richard will be such that, almost from the outset, the Kalin Twins will find him a hard act to follow.)

[25] *Move It* hits UK #2, behind Connie Francis' *Stupid Cupid*, as Richard makes his UK radio debut, on the BBC Light Programme's "Saturday Club".

Nov By the end of the tour, Samwell has been eased to a songwriting/management role to make way for a stronger bass player - Jet Harris, who was touring with the Most Brothers but has been helping the Drifters on most dates. Smart leaves, feeling he is not up to the standard of the more recent recruits, and announces his intention to join the Merchant Navy. He is replaced by Harris' drummer friend, Tony Meehan.

[17] Richard & the Drifters open a variety season at the Metropolitan Theatre in the Edgware Road, London (followed by two weeks at London's Chiswick Empire and Finsbury Park Empire).

Dec [13] Follow-up, *High Class Baby*, another Samwell composition, hits UK #7, though Richard hates the song (and will never perform it again). On a tour of one-nighters, Richard loses his voice and, so as not to disappoint fans at a concert in Hull, he mimes while Wee Willie Harris stands in the wings, providing a vocal impersonation of Richard.

1959

Jan [24] Richard, with the new line-up, begins his first headlining UK tour at the Rialto Theatre, York, Yorks., on a bill with Wee Willie Harris and Tony Crombie & His Rockets.

Feb [14] *Livin' Lovin' Doll*, written by Norrie Paramor and Bunny Lewis under the names Johnny May and Jim Gustard, reaches UK #20, as Richard wins the Best New Singer award in the annual **New Musical Express** poll.

Apr [27] Richard & the Drifters begin a twice-nightly week long run at London's Chiswick Empire with the Five Dallas Boys, Kay & Kimberley, Tommy Wallis & Beryl, Jean & Peter Barbour, Ray Alan & Steve and Des O'Connor.

May [14] The film, "Serious Charge", starring Anthony Quayle, premieres in London, featuring Richard (who sings three songs) as a young semi-delinquent trying to make it as a rock singer.

[16] *Never Mind*, B-side of the still-climbing *Mean Streak*, reaches UK #21.

[23] *Mean Streak* hits UK #10, both sides having been written by Samwell. His debut album, ***Cliff***, hits UK #4.

[30] Richard & the Drifters top the bill on the last-ever broadcast of "Oh Boy".

June [23] They take part in the "Oh Boy" segment at the "Royal Variety Performance".

Aug [1] *Living Doll*, written by Lionel Bart for "Serious Charge", but revamped for single release as a mid-tempo, country-style song, tops the UK chart for the first of five weeks, selling over 500,000 copies. The song will win an Ivor Novello award, and the single, on international sales, earns him his first gold disc.

Oct [17] Rocking B-side of the still-rising *Travellin' Light*, Samwell's *Dynamite*, reaches UK #16 (and will be a popular concert item throughout Richard's career and be re-recorded more than once).

[31] *Travellin' Light*, in similar style to *Living Doll*, tops the UK chart, where it will remain for five weeks.

Nov His sophomore album, ***Cliff Sings***, hits UK #2.

[23] *Living Doll*, issued in the US on ABC Records, reaches US #30.

[27] Film, "Expresso Bongo", premieres in London. Based on Wolf Mankowitz' stage play, it stars Laurence Harvey, with Richard as the manipulated teenage rock star, Bongo Herbert.

Dec Richard & the Shadows (to which the Drifters have changed their name to avoid confusion with the US Drifters) open at Stockton's Globe Theatre in the pantomime, "Babes In The Wood".

1960

Jan [17] Richard & the Shadows top the bill on ITV's "Sunday Night At The London Palladium", viewed by a 19 million audience - the highest ever for a light entertainment show.

[21] Richard guests on ABC-TV's "The Pat Boone Show", singing five songs, including *Living Doll*.

[22] Richard & the Shadows begin a five-week North American package tour, with Freddy Cannon, Bobby Rydell, Clyde McPhatter and bill-topper Frankie Avalon, in Montreal, PQ, Canada.

Feb [6] *A Voice In The Wilderness*, a ballad from "Expresso Bongo", hits UK #2 for the first of three weeks, held from the top by Anthony Newley's *Why*, while the EP, *Expresso Bongo*, featuring four songs from the film, reaches UK #14 (representing uncommonly large sales for the time by an EP).

[21] Richard wins the Top British Male Singer award in the **New Musical Express** poll, and takes a two-day break from the US tour to attend the presentation in London.

Apr [16] *Fall In Love With You* hits UK #2. Meanwhile, Richard and his family move into their first owned home in Percy Road, Winchmore Hill, London.

May [16] Richard participates in the "Royal Variety Performance" at London's Victoria Palace, in the presence of the Queen, appearing in a "youth" segment, alongside Adam Faith and Lonnie Donegan.

[23] Fan club members preview 21 newly-recorded songs in the conference room of EMI's new Manchester Square headquarters in London.

June Richard & the Shadows open a six-month season at the London Palladium, in "Stars In Your Eyes", with Russ Conway, Billy Dainty, Edmund Hockridge, David Kossoff, Des O'Connor and Joan Regan.

July [28] *Please Don't Tease*, written by Bruce Welch with Pete Chester (son of comedian Charlie), is chosen by members of Richard's fan club, invited to a preview hearing of recently-recorded tracks, as the best bet for a hit single.

Aug [13] *Please Don't Tease* begins a four-week hold on UK #1, before being deposed by the Shadows' first instrumental hit, *Apache*.

Oct [8] Fast rocker, *Nine Times Out Of Ten* (the fans' third choice), hits UK #3.

[14] Richard receives more than 5,000 cards on his 20th birthday.

Nov ***Me And My Shadows*** hits UK #2, behind the soundtrack album, ***South Pacific***.

Dec [31] *I Love You* begins a two-week stay at UK #1.

1961

Feb [4] It is announced that Richard and his manager Tito Burns are parting, amicably. (The following month, Australian Peter Gormley, who is already handling the Shadows, becomes Richard's manager.)

Mar [18] *Theme For A Dream* hits UK #3.

Apr [8] Richard sits on the panel of BBC-TV's "Juke Box Jury".

May [6] *Gee Whiz It's You* (from ***Me And My Shadows***), pressed as a single for export, hits UK #4, while *Theme For A Dream* is still in the Top 20. Meanwhile, ***Listen To Cliff*** hits UK #2.

[15] Richard's father dies in hospital, aged 56.

[20] Richard makes his debut on ITV's "Thank Your Lucky Stars", singing *A Girl Like You*.

July [22] *A Girl Like You* hits UK #3.

Aug [17] Richard & the Shadows begin a European tour at the Tivoli Gardens, Copenhagen, Denmark.

[28] He opens a six-week summer season at the Opera House, Blackpool, Lancs.

Nov [4] *When The Girl In Your Arms Is The Girl In Your Heart*, a ballad from his forthcoming film, "The Young Ones", hits UK #3.

Nov [4] ***21 Today*** tops the UK chart for a week.

Dec [10] "The Young Ones" premieres in London.

1962

Jan [11] As the movie opens throughout Britain (it will be the second-biggest box office grosser of the year, after "The Guns Of Navarone"), its title song, *The Young Ones*, written by Sid Tepper and Roy C. Bennett, enters the UK chart at #1, where it will stay for six weeks, eventually selling more than one million copies.

[15] The soundtrack album, ***The Young Ones***, knocks Elvis Presley's ***Blue Hawaii*** from UK #1, at the beginning of a six-week run, before surrendering again to the Presley soundtrack. Press reports that Richard is to marry 17-year-old Valerie Stratford are quickly dismissed.

[28] A UK package tour headlined by Richard opens at the Gaumont Cinema, Derby, Derbys.

Feb Richard wins **New Musical Express**' Top British Male Singer award for the second consecutive year.

Mar [13] He receives an award as Show Business Personality Of The Year from the Variety Club of Great Britain.

May [5] Richard is awarded a gold disc for one million UK sales of *The Young Ones*.

[13] Richard and the Shadows are presented with the Special Award at the seventh annual Ivor Novello Awards, held at London's BBC Television Centre.

June [2] *I'm Looking Out The Window*, his revival of a Peggy Lee ballad, backed with an update of Bobby Freeman's *Do You Wanna Dance?*, hits UK #2 (behind Elvis Presley's *Good Luck Charm*).

Sept [21] Richard pays a brief visit to the US to appear on CBS-TV's "The Ed Sullivan Show".

[28] He appears on BBC-TV's (pre-taped) "The Billy Cotton Band Show", singing *It'll Be Me*.

[29] His treatment of Jerry Lee Lewis' rocker, *It'll Be Me*, hits UK #2, behind Presley's *She's Not You*.

Nov His US visit comes to an end in Miami, FL before a convention for the Theatre Owners of America.

[3] Richard begins a week of concerts at the London Palladium, while ***32 Minutes And 17 Seconds With Cliff Richard*** hits UK #3.

[30] Richard & the Shadows begins a UK tour at the

Gaumont Cinema, Doncaster, Yorks.
Dec On ITV's "Sunday Night At The London Palladium", Richard premieres both sides of *The Next Time/Bachelor Boy*, the latter Richard's first co-writing credit, and both taken from his forthcoming film, "Summer Holiday".

1963

Jan [5] *The Next Time/Bachelor Boy* tops the UK chart for a week (before being deposed by the Shadows' *Dance On*), eventually selling 950,000 copies.
[10] "Summer Holiday", filmed largely on European locations in summer 1962 and directed by Peter Yates, premieres in London.
[21] Radio Luxembourg devotes its entire "ABC Of The Stars" program to Richard.
Feb [2] Soundtrack album, ***Summer Holiday***, tops the UK chart for the first of 14 weeks.
[11] Richard appears at a charity concert for underprivileged African children in Nairobi, Kenya, Africa, after a promise made to Kenya's African Nationalist leader, Tom Mboya.
[23] Richard and the Shadows begin a six-week 36-date UK tour of one-nighters at Sophia Gardens, Cardiff, South Glamorgan, Wales, set to end on April 7th in Brighton, Sussex.
Mar [14] Title song, *Summer Holiday*, begins two weeks atop the UK chart, replacing Frank Ifield's *The Wayward Wind*.
Apr [14] Richard & the Shadows appear on CBS-TV's "The Ed Sullivan Show", singing *Summer Holiday*.
May [3] Richard wins another Ivor Novello Award as one of eight writers of ***Summer Holiday***, which nabs the Year's Outstanding Score Of A Musical category, at the eighth annual ceremony, held at London's BBC Television Centre.
[25] His treatment of Ruth Brown's *Lucky Lips* hits UK #4.
June Richard & the Shadows star in "Holiday Carnival", a summer variety show at Blackpool (set to end in September).
Aug US teen magazine, **16**, votes Richard Most Promising Singer in its annual poll.
[10] Richard & the Shadows appear on the 100th edition of "Thank Your Lucky Stars", with Alma Cogan, Billy J. Kramer, Brian Poole & the Tremeloes and the Searchers.
[17] ***Cliff's Hit Album***, a compilation of singles from *Move It* to *Do You Want To Dance?*, hits UK #2, behind the Beatles' ***Please Please Me***.
Sept [14] His cover of Tommy Edwards' *It's All In The Game* hits UK #2, behind the Beatles' *She Loves You*, while in the US, where he is now signed to Epic, *Lucky Lips* becomes Richard's first chart single since *Living Doll*, peaking at #62.
Oct ***When In Spain***, recorded in Spanish in Barcelona, hits UK #8.
[20] Richard appears again on "The Ed Sullivan Show", singing *It's All In The Game*.
Nov [3] Richard & the Shadows appear on ITV's "Sunday Night At The London Palladium", singing *Don't Talk To Him*.
Dec [2] Richard & the Shadows begin filming "Wonderful Life" in the Canaries.
[7] *Don't Talk To Him* hits UK #2, held from the top by the Beatles' *She Loves You* (enjoying its second run at #1).

1964

Feb [15] *It's All In The Game* reaches US #25 - his biggest US hit to date.
[22] *I'm The Lonely One* hits UK #8.
Mar [28] Richard & the Shadows begin a 22-date, twice-nightly UK tour at the ABC Cinema, Southampton, Hants, ending at the Odeon Cinema, Leeds, Yorks., on April 19th.
Apr [18] *I'm The Lonely One* peaks at US #92.
May Richard & the Shadows begin a European tour with a week of concerts at the Olympia, Paris, France.
[26] They perform at the annual "**New Musical Express** Poll Winners Concert" at the Empire Pool, Wembley, Middx.
June [6] *Constantly*, his English-lyric version of an Italian ballad, hits UK #4, while the US-compiled ***It's All In The Game*** makes US #115.
July [2] Richard attends the world premiere of his new film, "Wonderful Life", at the Empire Theatre, Leicester Square, London.
[18] The soundtrack album, ***Wonderful Life***, hits UK #2, behind ***The Rolling Stones***.
Aug [1] *Bachelor Boy* charts for a week at US #99.
[8] *On The Beach*, from the film "Wonderful Life", hits UK #7.
[10] Richard receives a gold disc for one million sales of *The Next Time/Bachelor Boy* on "Thank Your Lucky Stars".
[19-21] At the invitation of Epic Records, Richard records in Nashville, TN, with producer Billy Sherrill and vocal backing from the Jordanaires.
Oct [25] Richard & the Shadows take part in "The Greatest Pop Concert Of 1964" at the Empire Pool, Wembley, with the Dave Clark Five, the Seekers and others, with comperes DJ Pete Murray and actor Roger Moore.
[31] His revival of Johnny Mathis' *The Twelfth Of Never* hits UK #8.
Nov [2] Richard & the Shadows perform at the "Royal Variety Show" in London.
Dec [19] *I Could Easily Fall (In Love With You)* hits UK #9, taken from the London Palladium pantomine, "Aladdin And His Wonderful Lamp", which stars Richard & the Shadows with Arthur Askey and Una Stubbs.

1965

Jan [16] ***Aladdin And His Wonderful Lamp*** reaches UK #13.
Feb Richard denies rumors that he is quitting show business.
Apr [17] *The Minute You're Gone*, cut in Nashville, tops the UK chart for a week. (Its B-side, *Just Another Guy*, is one of the first covers of a song by Neil Diamond.) Meanwhile, ***Cliff Richard*** hits UK #9.
June [8-14] Richard & the Shadows play a week of concerts in Birmingham, Warks.
July [3] *On My Word* reaches UK #12.
[9] Richard & the Shadows begin an eight-date Scandinavian tour in Copenhagen, ending on the 20th in Gothenburg, Sweden.
Aug [7] They embark on the second leg of a Continental tour at Frejus, France.
[14] Compilation album, ***More Hits By Cliff***, reaches UK #20.
Sept [11] *The Time In Between* reaches UK #22, while ***When In Rome***, sung in Italian, fails to chart.
Oct [3] Richard & the Shadows open a UK tour in Derby.
[9] Richard comperes ITV's "Sunday Night At The London Palladium".
Nov Richard & the Shadows participate in the annual "Royal Variety Show". They record four tracks for a Walt Disney-style album, including *Chim Chim Cheree* and *Zip A Dee Doo Dah*, but give up after one session.
Dec [7] Richard appears on ITV show "Cinema", discussing his films.
[25] *Wind Me Up (Let Me Go)*, another ballad from the Nashville sessions, hits UK #2 for the first of three weeks, behind the Beatles' *We Can Work It Out/Day Tripper*.

1966

Jan [8] ***Love Is Forever***, a collection of romantic ballads, charts for a week at UK #19.
Feb [21] Richard & the Shadows make their cabaret debut at London's Talk Of The Town.
Apr [3] They take part in the "Stars' Organisation For Spastics" concert at the Empire Pool, Wembley.
[9] *Blue Turns To Grey*, written by Mick Jagger and Keith Richard, reaches UK #15.
May [1] The team participates in the annual "**New Musical Express** Poll Winners Concert", at the Empire Pool, on a bill with the Beatles, the Rolling Stones, Roy Orbison, Dusty Springfield, the Yardbirds, the Spencer Davis Group and many others.
[28] ***Kinda Latin*** hits UK #9.
June [16] Richard joins evangelist Billy Graham on stage at Earls Court, London, and talks of his discovery of the Christian faith, before singing *It Is No Secret*.
Aug [20] Ballad, *Visions* (later used as the closing theme for his TV series), hits UK #7.
Oct [8] Richard attends the premiere of his film, "Finders Keepers", in London.
Nov [5] *Time Drags By*, from "Finders Keepers", hits UK #10.
Dec [10] Richard opens in the London Palladium pantomime, "Cinderella", with music entirely written by the Shadows. (The show will end on April 1st, 1967.)
[12] Richard & the Shadows attend the premiere of the film, "Thunderbirds Are Go!" in which their puppet likenesses appear, singing *Shooting Star*.

1967

Jan Richard states in a **New Musical Express** article that he intends to give up show business and teach religious instruction in school.
[21] *In The Country*, taken from "Cinderella", hits UK #6, while ***Cinderella*** reaches UK #30.
[28] Soundtrack album, ***Finders Keepers***, hits UK #6.
Apr [15] *It's All Over*, previously cut by the Everly Brothers, hits UK #9.
May [6] ***Don't Stop Me Now*** reaches UK #23.
[7] Richard participates in the annual "**New Musical Express** Poll Winners Concert", at the Empire Pool, on a bill with the Beach Boys, Stevie Winwood, Georgie Fame, Lulu and Dusty Springfield.
[24] ITV airs a "Cliff" special.
July [1] *I'll Come Running*, penned by Neil Diamond (as is the B-side, *I Got The Feeling*), reaches UK #26.
Sept [23] Richard is voted Top Male Singer by readers of **Melody Maker**.
[30] *The Day I Met Marie*, written by Hank Marvin, hits UK #10. (For many years, Richard will cite this as his favorite of his own recordings.)
Oct [18] Richard performs at the Shibuya Public Hall, Tokyo, Japan.
Nov [11] Gospel album, ***Good News***, his first religious release, charts for a week at UK #37.
Dec [6] He is confirmed into membership of the Church of England by Graham Leonard, Bishop of Willesden, at St. Paul's Church, Finchley, London.
[30] Ballad, *All My Love*, hits UK #6.

1968

Feb Richard fills in on drums for the Shadows at the Talk Of The Town, London, when Brian Bennett falls sick.
Apr [1] Richard appears in the ITV drama, "A Matter Of Diamonds".
[6] He sings Bill Martin/Phil Coulter's *Congratulations* in the "Eurovision Song Contest", held at London's Royal Albert Hall, coming second to Spain's Massiel, with *La La La*.
[13] *Congratulations* tops the UK chart for the first of two weeks - his first #1 hit in three years (and last until 1979). It will be a worldwide million-seller, partly thanks to the availability of multi-lingual versions.
May Richard & the Shadows participate in the annual "**New Musical Express** Poll Winners Concert", at the Empire Pool, on a bill with Lulu, the Rolling Stones, Dusty Springfield, Scott Walker and others.
June [8] Live album, ***Cliff In Japan***, recorded at Sankei Hall, Tokyo, reaches UK #29.
[22] *Congratulations* peaks at US #99.
[28] He appears in a concert special on ITV's "Talk Of The Town", taped at the London venue of the same name.
July [6] *I'll Love You Forever Today*, co-written by Richard for his forthcoming film, "Two A Penny", reaches UK #27.
[11] UK TV airs a "Cliff Richard And The Shadows"

special to celebrate their ten years together.
Aug ***Two A Penny*** is released. It is partly the soundtrack of the film, a morality drama, which Richard has made, without a fee, for the Billy Graham organization.
Oct [11] Richard & the Shadows begin a season at the London Palladium.
[26] *Marianne*, written by actor Bill Owen (later notable for his role in BBC1-TV's "Last Of The Summer Wine") reaches UK #22.
Nov [30] ***Established 1958***, comprising half Cliff Richard and half Shadows tracks, celebrating their tenth anniversary in show business, reaches UK #30.

1969

Jan [4] *Don't Forget To Catch Me*, from the tenth anniversary album, reaches UK #21.
Mar [29] *Good Times (Better Times)* climbs to UK #12.
May [12] Richard guests on UK children's TV show, "Sooty".
June [21] *Big Ship*, written by Raymond Froggatt, hits UK #8.
July [19] Compilation album, ***The Best Of Cliff***, hits UK #5.
Oct [4] *Throw Down A Line*, a duet with Hank Marvin, hits UK #7, while ***Sincerely*** reaches UK #24.
[7] Richard & the Shadows begin a Japanese tour at the Alaska, Tokyo.
Nov [7] They commence a UK tour in Finsbury Park, London.
Dec [10] He participates in a special gala midnight performance at the London Palladium in aid of the Royal Society for the Prevention of Cruelty to Animals (RSPCA).
[20] *With The Eyes Of A Child* reaches UK #20.

1970

Jan [3] Richard's own "It's Cliff Richard" TV series begins on BBC1-TV.
Mar [7] A second duet with Marvin, *The Joy Of Living* (also the theme of the TV series), reaches UK #25.
May [11] Richard makes his straight stage acting debut in Peter Shaffer's "Five Finger Exercise", at the New Theatre, Bromley, Kent.
July [4] *Goodbye Sam, Hello Samantha*, widely promoted as his 50th single, hits UK #6, while the performance set, ***Cliff Live At The Talk Of The Town***, fails to chart.
Aug [31] BBC-TV airs a Cliff Richard special with guest Aretha Franklin.
Sept [26] *I Ain't Got Time Anymore* reaches UK #21.
Oct Religious album, ***About That Man***, is released.
[12] Richard receives the National Viewer's Association Award from Malcolm Muggeridge and Mary Whitehouse.
[21] Richard & the Shadows begin a UK tour in Golders Green, London.
Dec [19] ***Tracks'n'Grooves*** makes UK #37.

1971

Jan [2] BBC-TV airs the first of a 13-week series, "It's Cliff Richard", with resident guests Marvin and Una Stubbs.
Feb [20] *Sunny Honey Girl* reaches UK #19.
Apr [24] Marvin-penned, ecological-themed *Silvery Rain* reaches UK #27.
May [17] Richard opens at the Sadlers Wells Theatre in London in the play "The Potting Shed". (The show had been scheduled to open a week earlier at Bromley, but the New Theatre was gutted by fire before the opening night.)
June [13] Richard & the Shadows take part in "A Night With The Stars", a tribute to the recently-deceased UK singer Dickie Valentine, at the London Palladium. (Richard joins Petula Clark in a duet of *I Want To Hold Your Hand.*)
July [5] Richard receives an Ivor Novello award for Outstanding Services To British Music, at the "Rose D'Or Festival" in Juan Les Pins, at which he also performs with Olivia Newton-John.
Aug [7] *Flying Machine* makes UK #37.
Oct [25] Richard & the Shadows start a season at the London Palladium.
Dec [4] *Sing A Song Of Freedom* reaches UK #13.

1972

Jan BBC1-TV airs the first of a second 13-week series, "It's Cliff Richard", with resident guests Newton-John and the Flirtations.
Mar [11] *Jesus* makes UK #35.
Apr [14] Richard is voted the Top Male Pop Personality by **The Sun** newspaper for the third year running.
Sept [2] UK TV airs "The Case", a musical comedy-thriller starring Richard, Newton-John and comedian Tim Brooke-Taylor.
[16] *Living In Harmony* reaches UK #12.
Nov [17] Richard begins a UK tour, at Fairfield Halls, Croydon, Surrey, where he is joined onstage by Olivia Newton-John.
Dec [23] ***The Best Of Cliff, Volume Two*** makes UK #49, while *A Brand New Song* becomes his first single not to make the UK Top 50.

1973

Jan [10] Richard appears on BBC1-TV's "Cilla Black Show", singing six entries chosen to represent Britain in the Eurovision Song Contest. *Power To All Our Friends* is chosen as the entry by TV viewers.
Mar [24] *Power To All Our Friends* hits UK #4.
Apr [7] *Power To All Our Friends* comes third in the Contest.
May [26] *Help It Along*, a four-track EP containing the Eurovision entry songs, reaches UK #29.
Nov [26] Richard takes part in the "Royal Variety Performance" in London.

1974

Jan The soundtrack album, ***Take Me High***, makes UK #41.
Feb [2] *Take Me High* reaches UK #27, the theme from Richard's movie of the same title, co-starring Debbie Watling and George Cole, and filmed on location in Birmingham, West Midlands.
Mar Richard is awarded the Silver Clef for Outstanding Services To The Music Industry by the Nordoff Robbins Music Therapy charity.
Apr [3-11] He plays at the London Palladium, but will fall ill, with Rolf Harris deputizing for three performances.
June [15] *(You Keep Me) Hangin' On* reaches UK #13. Meanwhile, the live album, ***Help It Along***, is released with all profits going to the TEAR Fund (an international Christian aid organization), but does not chart.
July [3] Richard plays Bottom in a production of "A Midsummer Night's Dream", with past and present members of his old school in Cheshunt.
[9] The International Cliff Richard Movement meets for the first time at the United Reform Church in Crouch End, London.
Oct [27] Richard & the Shadows play together for the first time in six years in a charity concert at the London Palladium.
Nov ***The 31st Of February Street***, produced by Dave Mackay, is released.

1975

Jan Richard appears "In The Name Of Jesus" concert at the Royal Albert Hall.
Mar *It's Only Me You've Left Behind* is released.
June [5] Richard participates in a charity concert at the Free Trade Hall, Manchester, Gtr. Manchester, for the families of two policemen who died in the course of duty.
July [9] BBC1-TV airs "Jim'll Fix It", in which fan Helen Moon from Cromer, Norfolk, meets Richard.
Sept [6] BBC1-TV series "It's Cliff And Friends" premieres.
Oct *(There's A) Honky Tonk Angel (Who Will Take Me Back In)* does not chart, after Richard belatedly becomes aware of the implications of the song's lyric, and refuses to promote it.

1976

Feb EMI Records releases ***I'm Nearly Famous*** and ***The Best Of Cliff Richard*** in the USSR, becoming the third UK artist to achieve such an honor.
Mar [27] Mournful ballad *Miss You Nights*, with Bruce Welch taking over as Richard's producer, reaches UK #15, restoring him to the UK singles chart after a 20-month absence.
June [5] *Devil Woman* hits UK #9.
[12] Welch-produced ***I'm Nearly Famous***, including the two recent Top 20 singles, hits UK #5.
Sept [16] Richard begins a USSR tour with a concert at the Hall of the October Revolution, Leningrad, to a rapturous reception.
[25] He is invited to a reception at the British Embassy in Moscow, as *I Can't Ask For Anymore Than You*, also from ***I'm Nearly Famous***, reaches UK #17 and *Devil Woman* becomes his first US Top 10 success, hitting #6 (higher than it attained domestically).
Oct [16] ***I'm Nearly Famous*** makes US #76.
[20] *Devil Woman* is certified gold by the RIAA, his first and only US million-selling single.
Dec [7-8] He appears in concert at the Kalamandir Auditorium, New Delhi, India. (During his visit to his birth-nation, he also meets Mother Theresa.)
[11] *Hey, Mr. Dream Maker* reaches UK #31.
[25] *I Can't Ask For Anymore Than You* peaks at US #80.

1977

Apr [2] ***Every Face Tells A Story*** hits UK #8.
[9] *My Kinda Life* reaches UK #15.
July [2] *Don't Turn The Light Out* peaks at US #57.
[23] Ballad, *When Two Worlds Drift Apart*, makes UK #46.
Sept [5] Richard's book, **Which One's Cliff?**, written with Bill Latham, is published.
Oct [18] The British Phonographic Institute (BPI) awards Richard the Britannia Award as Best British Male Solo Artist Of The Last 25 Years, to coincide with the Queen's Silver Jubilee celebrations.
[28] Richard receives the Gold Badge Award from the Songwriters' Guild of Great Britain.
Nov [5] TV-advertised double compilation album, ***40 Golden Greats***, tops the UK chart for a week - his first #1 album since ***Summer Holiday***.

1978

Jan Richard is presented with a personally inscribed Shure SM58 microphone by the company.
Feb [27] Richard & the Shadows begin two weeks of reunion concerts at the London Palladium.
Mar Gospel album, ***Small Corners***, makes UK #33, but *Yes! He Lives*, taken from it, fails to chart.
June [29] Richard & the Shadows are presented with the Silver Clef Award for Outstanding Services To British Music by H.R.H. the Duchess of Gloucester, at the second annual Nordoff Robbins Music Therapy charity lunch in London.
Aug *Please Remember Me*, coupled with a new version of the former #1 hit, *Please Don't Tease*, is released.
Oct ***Green Light*** reaches UK #25 in a month when Richard performs at the Royal Albert Hall "Help, Hope And Hallelujah" concert.
Nov The extracted *Can't Take The Hurt Anymore* is released.
Dec [11] Richard performs again at the Royal Albert Hall, at the end of his 20th anniversary sellout tour.

1979

Feb [1] EMI Records organizes a special lunch at Claridge's, London, to celebrate its 21-year association with Richard.
[13] Richard & the Shadows receive a special award at the annual **Music Week** awards, celebrating 21 years as hit-making artists.
Mar TV-promoted live album, ***Thank You Very Much***, featuring highlights of the previous year's

Palladium concerts with the Shadows, hits UK #5.
Apr Title song, *Green Light*, peaks at UK #57.
July [5] Richard is guest of honor at the Variety Club of Great Britain lunch at the Dorchester, London.
Aug [25] *We Don't Talk Anymore*, an Alan Tarney composition produced by Welch, tops the UK chart where it will stay for four weeks, his first UK #1 in more than 11 years. It will become his biggest-selling single worldwide, with total sales exceeding five million.
Sept [8] ***Rock'n'Roll Juvenile*** hits UK #3. Norrie Paramor, Richard's original producer, dies.
[22] Richard participates in "Hosannah '79", an anti-racist festival in Birmingham.
Oct [4] Richard and Kate Bush perform with the London Symphony Orchestra at the Royal Albert Hall, as part of the venue's 75th birthday appeal.
Nov *Hot Shot*, from ***Rock'n'Roll Juvenile***, makes UK #46.
Dec [2] Richard participates in a carol concert in Camberley, Surrey, in aid of the International Year Of The Child.
[16] He leads an estimated 30,000 people in carol singing outside Buckingham Palace, as part of the International Year Of The Child activities.

1980

Jan [1] Richard is included in the Queen's New Year Honours List, being awarded an OBE (Order of The British Empire).
[19] *We Don't Talk Anymore* hits US #7, while the album, ***We Don't Talk Anymore*** (a revised version of ***Rock'n'Roll Juvenile***), makes US #93.
Mar [1] *Carrie*, from the album, hits UK #4.
Apr [16] Mother-of-two Kim Kayne pays £1,400 for the privilege of having lunch with Richard as part of the fund-raising activities of London's Capital Radio "Help A London Child" charity.
[19] *Carrie* makes US #34.
July [23] Richard receives his OBE from the Queen at Buckingham Palace.
Sept [13] *Dreamin'* hits UK #8. Its parent album, ***I'm No Hero***, produced and mostly penned by Tarney, hits UK #4.
Oct Richard plays three nights at London's Apollo Theatre.
Nov *Suddenly*, a ballad duet with Olivia Newton-John from the film soundtrack to "Xanadu", reaches UK #15.
[22] *Dreamin'*, co-written by Tarney with Leo Sayer, hits US #10.

1981

Jan [17] *Suddenly* reaches US #20, as Richard embarks on a US promotional tour with appearances on Merv Griffin's and Dionne Warwick's shows.
Feb [7] Tarney-penned *A Little In Love* reaches UK #15, while ***I'm No Hero*** makes US #80.
[23] Richard & the Shadows take part in the "25 Years Of British Pop" segment at the "Royal Variety Performance".
[24] Richard receives the **Daily Mirror** newspaper's readers' award as Outstanding Music Personality Of The Year at London's Café Royal.
Mar [3] Richard begins a seven-week, 35-date North American tour, opening in Seattle, WA.
[14] *A Little In Love* reaches US #17.
[16] Richard appears on syndicated TV show "Solid Gold".
[20] While he is away, "Cliff In London" airs on BBC-TV.
Richard's first home video, "The Young Ones", is released by Thorn EMI Video.
Apr [18] Richard ends his US tour in Los Angeles, CA.
May The "Cliff Richard Rock Special" takes place at London's Hammersmith Odeon - all audience members dress in '50s clothes.
June [6] *Give A Little Bit More* makes US #41.
July [11] Compilation album, ***Love Songs***, featuring familiar ballads, tops the UK chart for the first of five weeks.
Sept [12] *Wired For Sound* hits UK #4.
Oct [3] ***Wired For Sound***, again helmed and mostly written by Tarney, hits UK #4 and US #132.
[24] *Wired For Sound* peaks at US #71.
Dec [12] *Daddy's Home*, his update of Shep & the Limelites' 1961 US smash recorded live in concert, hits UK #2, behind the Human League's *Don't You Want Me*.

1982

Feb [24] Richard wins the Best British Male Artist category at the inaugural BRIT Awards at London's Grosvenor House.
Mar [20] *Daddy's Home* reaches US #23.
Aug [7] *The Only Way Out* hits UK #10.
Sept [4] ***Now You See Me ... Now You Don't***, including his previous and next singles, hits UK #4.
Oct *Where Do We Go From Here?* peaks at UK #60.
[23] *The Only Way Out* makes US #64.
Dec [25] The seasonal *Little Town*, a new uptempo arrangement of the Christmas carol "O Little Town Of Bethlehem", reaches UK #11.

1983

Mar [19] Richard's duet with Phil Everly on the Stuart Colman-produced rocker, *She Means Nothing To Me*, hits UK #9.
Apr [30] His cover of Buddy Holly's *True Love Ways*, recorded live with the London Philharmonic Orchestra, hits UK #8, taken from the live album, ***Dressed For The Occasion***, which hits UK #7.
June [4] *Drifting*, a ballad duetted with Christian singer Sheila Walsh, peaks at UK #64.
Sept [24] Dance-oriented *Never Say Die (Give A Little Bit More)* reaches UK #15. This is the first Richard single to have an extended 12" dance version.
Oct ***Silver***, marking 25 years as a recording artist, hits UK #7 (and is briefly available as a boxed set which includes a second album, ***Rock'n'Roll Silver***, with versions of several '50s oldies).
Nov [12] *Never Say Die (Give A Little Bit More)* peaks at US #73.
Dec [17] *Please Don't Fall In Love*, taken from ***Silver***, hits UK #7.

1984

Apr [14] *Baby You're Dynamite*, a rocker from the album, reaches UK #27.
May [19] After heavy radio play, its B-side ballad, *Ocean Deep*, charts at UK #72 in place of the A-side.
July ***20 Original Greats***, with Richard & the Shadows, makes UK #43.
Sept *Two To The Power*, a duet with Janet Jackson on her label A&M, is released.
Nov *Shooting From The Heart* peaks at UK #51.
Dec ***The Rock Connection***, including several rock tracks first heard on ***Rock'n'Roll Silver***, plus *She Means Nothing To Me*, makes UK #43. (This compilation is released because his lapsed EMI contract will take time to renegotiate; meanwhile, he is not available for recording.)

1985

Feb *Heart User* makes UK #46.
July [13] Richard performs at the Wembley Stadium end of the "Live Aid" benefit spectacular.
Sept It is announced that Richard is to star in London's West End in 1986, in the first stage production of Dave Clark's musical, "Time".
[21] The first recording of a song from the show, *She's So Beautiful*, produced by Stevie Wonder and featuring him on all instruments, with Richard handling the vocals and with a video directed by Ken Russell, reaches UK #17.
Dec *It's In Every One Of Us*, penned by US writer David Pomeranz several years earlier but from "Time", makes UK #45.
[19] Richard joins Chris De Burgh, Lulu, Sandie Shaw and others for Carol Aid, a carol-singing event at London's Heaven club, to raise funds for the Band Aid appeal.

1986

Mar [29] He returns to UK #1 with a spoof revival of his own former chart-topper *Living Doll*, recorded with alternative TV comedy team the Young Ones, with all proceeds going to the Comic Relief charity. With Hank Marvin guesting on guitar, it tops the UK chart for three weeks and sells over 500,000 copies.
Apr [9] Richard opens at London's Dominion Theatre in the lead role in Dave Clark's musical, "Time" (which also features an electronic/holographic "cameo" by Lord Olivier). The show and star are well reviewed and initially draw capacity audiences. Richard will stay in the musical for a year, after which David Cassidy will take over.
May *Born To Rock'n'Roll*, taken from "Time", fails to chart, while ***Time***, the original all-star album of the show, featuring Richard and other guest performers including Freddie Mercury, Dionne Warwick and Julian Lennon, reaches UK #21.
Sept *All I Ask Of You*, from a rival West End musical (Andrew Lloyd Webber's "The Phantom Of The Opera"), Richard's duet with the show's female lead Sarah Brightman, hits UK #3.
Dec *Slow Rivers*, a teaming with Elton John (on whose Rocket label Richard's US hits were issued in the mid-'70s), makes UK #44.

1987

June EMI celebrates the 15th anniversary of its Hayes, Middx., pressing plant as Richard re-signs with the label.
July [11] *My Pretty One* hits UK #6.
Sept [26] *Some People* hits UK #3, while its parent album, ***Always Guaranteed***, produced again by Tarney, hits UK #5 - eventually outselling all previous Richard albums to turn platinum.
Oct A 50-date "Always Guaranteed" European tour is followed by six sellout nights at the National Exhibition Centre, Birmingham.
Nov [7] *Remember Me*, also from ***Always Guaranteed***, makes UK #35.
Dec He hosts a Pro-Celebrity charity tennis tournament.

1988

Feb [20] *Two Hearts*, a final extract from the album, makes UK #34.
Sept The 30th anniversary of his first hit with *Move It*, is noted by tributes in a variety of media, and a 30th anniversary 47-date UK tour begins at the end of September, ending mid-December. Every ticket sells out within three days, giving a combined tour audience of over 200,000.
Nov [21] Richard performs at the "Royal Variety Performance".
Dec [10] Richard's 99th single, the seasonal *Mistletoe And Wine*, tops the UK chart, where it will stay for four weeks, to become the biggest-selling UK single of the year.
[24] ***Private Collection***, a double compilation album rounding up a decade of hits from *We Don't Talk Anymore* to the new *Mistletoe And Wine* (and including most of Richard's duets with other artists), tops the UK chart and turns quadruple platinum, with sales of over a million.

1989

Feb Richard is honored for his Outstanding Contribution To British Music, at the eighth annual BRIT Awards, held at the Royal Albert Hall.
Apr Following the success of his greatest hits video package, "Private Collection", the performance video "Guaranteed Live '88" is released.
June [10] His 100th hit single, *The Best Of Me*, written by David Foster, Richard Marx and Jeremy Lubbock, debuts at its UK #2 peak, held off the top by Jason Donovan's *Sealed With A Kiss*.
[16-17] "Cliff Richard - The Event" takes place before two capacity crowds of 72,000 at Wembley Stadium. Support acts are all chosen by Richard and include Aswad (with whom he duets on *Share A Dream With Me*), Gerry & the Pacemakers, the Searchers, the Kalin Twins (with whom he toured as support in 1958) and the Shadows. Richard also performs a

forthcoming Stock/Aitken/Waterman single, *I Just Don't Have The Heart*.
Sept [2] *I Just Don't Have The Heart* hits UK #3.
Oct [21] *Lean On You* reaches UK #17.
Nov [25] ***Stronger*** hits UK #7.
Dec [23] Richard's duet with Van Morrison, *Whenever God Shines His Light*, reaches UK #20, the same week that Band Aid II's update of *Do They Know It's Christmas?*, featuring Richard, enters the UK chart at #1.

1990

Mar [3] *Stronger Than That* reaches UK #14.
Apr [2] He receives the Lifetime Achievement Award for services to British music (an extraordinary honor for a non-songwriter), at the 35th Ivor Novello Awards, held at London's Grosvenor House Hotel.
June [30] Richard appears with the Shadows, at the Nordoff Robbins Music Therapy Silver Clef charity concert, at Knebworth, Herts.
Sept [1] *Silhouettes* hits UK #10.
Oct [20] Richard's cover of the Julie Gold standard, *From A Distance*, reaches UK #11.
Nov [1] Richard begins 38-date "From A Distance" UK tour with 12 shows at the National Exhibition Centre, Birmingham, ending at the Wembley Arena, selling 207,000 tickets for 18 nights, on January 3rd.
Dec [29] *Saviour's Day* tops the UK chart as ***From A Distance ... The Event*** hits UK #3.

1991

June [15] Richard takes part in the second annual World Music Awards, held at the Sporting Club in Monte Carlo, Monaco.
Aug [17] He is featured on Andrew Lloyd Webber's ***The Premiere Collection***, which peaks at US #130.
Sept [14] *More To Life* debuts at its UK #23 peak.
Dec [11] Richard guests on ITV's "Des O'Connor Tonight".
[14] ***Together With Cliff Richard*** hits UK #10.
[21] *We Should Be Together*, Richard's 60th charted single, hits UK #10, as "Cliff At Christmas" airs on BBC Radio 2.
[22] "Joy To The World" and "Together With Cliff Richard" are broadcast on BBC1-TV.

1992

Jan [11] *This New Year* bows at its UK #30 pinnacle.
May [14] Together with earlier singing partner Olivia Newton-John, Richard co-hosts the third annual World Music Awards, held again at the Sporting Club, as he continues working on new material at R.G. Jones Studios with Paul Moessl co-producing.
June [28] Richard leads off National Music Day from the roof of Broadcasting House, London.
Oct [1] Richard embarks on his 37-date "Access All Area '92" tour, including 13 dates at the National Exhibition Centre Birmingham, five at the Sheffield Arena, three at Glasgow's SE&CC and 16 dates at Wembley Arena, where the trek will end on November 29th.
Dec [4] He guests on BBC1-TV's "Terry Wogan's Friday Night".
[12] *I Still Believe In You* hits UK #7.

1993

Mar [27] *Peace In Our Time*, originally a US 1990 #11 hit for Eddie Money, debuts at its UK #8 peak.
May [1] Following a 45-date UK pop tour earlier in the year, and recent gospel-fundraising charity dates, ***Cliff Richard - The Album***, his 56th project, featuring songs by Nik Kershaw, Leeson & Vale, and Pete Sinfield, among others, enters the UK chart at #1.
June [19] *Human Work Of Art* reaches UK #24.
Oct [2] *Never Let Go* debuts at its UK #32 peak.
Dec [24] Richard is profiled on ITV's "South Bank Show".
[25] *Healing Love* reaches UK #19.

1994

May [25] Richard presents Sir Tim Rice with the Outstanding Contribution to British Music award at the 39th annual Ivor Novello Awards, held at London's Grosvenor House Hotel.
July First ever US CD collection ***The Cliff Richard Collection 1976-1994*** is released by Razor Tie Records.
Oct [15] ***The Hit List*** hits UK #3 in its week of entry.
Nov [8] Previewing a major new project, his 31-date "Heathcliff" UK tour, opens at the National Exhibition Centre, Birmingham, set to end on December 23rd at Wembley Arena. (Four people will be taken to hospital with secondary burns and five others treated for scalding after a heating pipe bursts under their seats at Wembley.)
Dec [10] His treatment of the Everly Brothers' standard *All I Have To Do Is Dream*, coupled with a reissued *Miss You Nights*, debuts at its UK #14 peak.

1995

May [8] Richard sings at Buckingham Palace as part of the VE Day celebrations.
Oct [21] *Misunderstood Man* debuts at its UK #19 peak.
[25] Sir Cliff Richard receives his knighthood from H.R.H. Queen Elizabeth II, the same day he also attends Jerry Lordan's memorial service at St. Martins-in-the-Fields, London.
[27] He is presented with the Pied Piper Award for his contribution to the songwriter at the annual PRS/ASCAP Awards held in London.
Nov BBC Radio 2 music programs editor Brian Stephens drops Richard's new single from its playlist for being "too raucous".
[9] Police raid Richard's holiday home, arresting his caretaker Clive Williamson for possession of drugs with intent to supply.
[11] Previewing his forthcoming musical, ***Songs From Heathcliff*** reaches UK #15 in its week of entry.
Dec [9] The extracted *Had To Be*, a duet with Olivia Newton-John, debuts at its UK #22 peak.

1996

Mar [30] *The Wedding*, a duet with Helen Hobson, charts for a week at UK #40. During the month Richard sets a new record when £2,305,000-worth of tickets are sold on the first day of availability for his forthcoming musical "Heathcliff", based on Emily Bronte's "Wuthering Heights" character, to be staged in London's West End. Sir Cliff has funded 75% of the production himself, and will also feature in the lead role.
July [3] During a rain delay at the All England Tennis Championships held at Wimbledon, Sir Cliff spontaneously appears in the stands with a microphone, singing *Congratulations* backed by an ad-hoc vocal group including Gigi Fernandez, Pam Shriver and Virginia Wade, and *Bachelor Boy* backed by Martina Navratilova. The heavens miraculously clear within 20 minutes, allowing defending champion Pete Sampras to continue his centre court match. **The Daily Telegraph** reports in tomorrow's edition that the event will go down in history as "Cliffstock".
see also: THE SHADOWS

LIONEL RICHIE

1967

Richie (b. June 20, 1949, Tuskegee, AL), the son of a retired army captain and a teacher, having been raised in a religious environment, singing in his local Episcopal Church choir, is encouraged to seek a career in the ministry, but his Uncle Bertram buys him a saxophone and his grandmother encourages him to practice the piano. Now studying economics at the predominantly black Tuskegee Institute (where he was born - his grandfather having worked on campus), he meets other ambitious musicians including Thomas McClary and William King to form the Commodores (and also meets his future wife, Brenda Harvey). Becoming a popular funk/R&B outfit in the early '70s, the group, increasingly led by Richie's knack for writing and singing classic soul ballads, achieves multi-platinum chart-topping success by the end of the decade, with a string of global hit singles, notably *Sweet Love*, *Three Times A Lady*, *Sail On* and *Still*.

1980

Nov [15] Richie's first non-Commodores composition hit, *Lady*, sung by Kenny Rogers, tops the US chart for the first of six weeks, and will reach UK #12. Richie has also produced the disc, which was recorded in only four hours, and has led to his meeting Rogers' manager Ken Kragen.

1981

Mar Still with the Commodores, but increasingly in demand as a solo producer and writer, Richie enters the studio with Rogers to helm ***Share Your Love*** (US #6), which spawns the US #3 hit, *I Don't Need You*.
Apr While working on the Rogers' project and a new Commodores album, Richie is contacted by film producer, Franco Zeffirelli, who needs a song for his forthcoming Brooke Shields movie, "Endless Love". He offers Diana Ross as a possible co-vocalist. Richie accepts and flies to Reno, NV, for a 3:00 a.m. recording session with Ms. Ross.
July He appears on his final Commodores studio album, ***In The Pocket***. From it, the Richie-penned and performed ballad, *Oh No*, will hit US #4 and makes UK #44 in November.
Aug [15] The Richie/Ross ballad duet, *Endless Love*, hits US #1, where it will stay for nine weeks, and UK #7. (The song becomes the most successful Motown and soundtrack single to date. Its achievements coincide with Richie signing a solo management deal with Kragen, although he is still officially with the Commodores.)

1982

Jan [25] He wins the Favorite Single, Pop/Rock, and Favorite Single, Soul/R&B categories (both for *Endless Love* with Ross), at the ninth annual American Music Awards, held at the Shrine Auditorium, Los Angeles, CA.
Mar Richie begins work in Los Angeles on his debut solo album with Commodores' producer James Anthony Carmichael, who enlists a top session crew including Greg Phillinganes, Paulinho DaCosta and Michael Boddicker. Joe Walsh, Kenny Rogers and even tennis star Jimmy Connors also guest. On many tracks Richie plays on the same studio piano used by Carole King on her album, ***Tapestry***.
[29] Richie performs *Endless Love* at the 55th annual Academy Awards ceremony, in Los Angeles.
Aug With his debut album completed, Richie and the Commodores, still theoretically together, mourn the death of their manager Benny Ashburn at the age of 54.
Oct Formally marking the end of his association with the Commodores, his first solo single, *Truly*, is released, a ballad from the Motown-issued ***Lionel Richie***. The self-penned album will hit US #3 and UK #9, and is dedicated to Ashburn.
Nov [27] *Truly* tops the US chart for the first of two weeks and hits UK #6.
Dec [9] *Truly* is certified gold by the RIAA.

1983

Jan [17] He wins the Favorite Single, Pop/Rock, and Favorite Male Artist, Soul/R&B categories at the tenth annual American Music Awards, held at the Shrine Auditorium.
Feb *You Are* makes UK #43.
[23] With 17 previously unsuccessful nominations, Richie finally wins the Best Pop Vocal Performance, Male, for *Truly*, at the 25th annual Grammy Awards.
Mar *You Are* hits US #4.
May Ballad, *My Love*, hits US #5 and makes UK #70. Richie is already recording a follow-up album, and planning a first solo tour.
[16] Richie sings *You Mean More To Me* at the "25th Motown Anniversary" TV special.
Sept He begins a 48-date world trek, including three weeks in the Far East, opening at Lake Tahoe, NV. Supported by the Pointer Sisters, his backing band includes Prince percussionist Sheila E. For *Endless*

Love, Richie uses a life-like Diana Ross laser projection.
Oct [29] The Mayor of Tuskegee, AL proclaims "Lionel Richie Day".
Nov [12] Uptempo dance cut, *All Night Long (All Night)*, hits US #1 during a five-month chart stay (including four weeks at #1) and UK #2. It outsells *Endless Love*, to become Motown's biggest single worldwide to date, and is spurred by a promo video produced by ex-Monkee Mike Nesmith. On the same day, its parent album, ***Can't Slow Down***, also heads the UK chart.
[22] Los Angeles' Mayor Tom Bradley pronounces it "Lionel Richie Day".
Dec [3] ***Can't Slow Down*** begins a three-week run atop the US survey on its way to eight million-plus US sales during a three year-plus chart tenure. Once again co-produced with Carmichael, it features co-written tracks with Cynthia Weil and David Foster, and includes top flight session help from Toto's Steve Lukather and Jeff Porcaro, among others.
[12] *All Night Long* is certified gold by the RIAA.
Richie and his wife move house from Kenny Rogers' estate to a Bel Air, Los Angeles, mansion. During tour dates, Richie's plane crash-lands in Phoenix, AZ, though no one is hurt.

1984

Jan *Running With The Night*, aided by a Bob Giraldi-directed video, hits US #7 and UK #9.
[16] Richie co-hosts the 11th annual American Music Awards held at the Shrine Auditorium, also winning the Favorite Single, Soul/R&B category.
Mar Pepsi-Cola announces an $8.5 million sponsorship deal with Richie, for which he will record a series of song-associated TV commercials, while they fund two tours over the next two years.
[24] Familiar self-penned ballad, *Hello*, begins a six-week run atop the UK chart (his first solo UK #1).
May [12] With a second major tour underway, with opening act Tina Turner, *Hello* hits US #1. (Originally slated for inclusion on the debut album, the typical Richie ballad is supported by an emotive video using the dramatic effect of a blind girl, again directed by Giraldi. Richie plays the part of Mr. Reynolds, a teacher.)
[30] *Hello* is confirmed gold by the RIAA.
Aug [4] Album extract, *Stuck On You*, hits US #3 and UK #12.
[12] Richie has been asked by Los Angeles XXIII Olympic Games producer David Wolper to perform the final song at the closing ceremony. In a larger-than-life extravaganza, Richie performs *All Night Long*, featuring an occasion-written extra verse. Helped by 200 dancers, he is seen by an estimated worldwide TV audience of 2.6 billion.
Oct [19] The RIAA certifies four million sales of ***Lionel Richie*** and eight million sales of ***Can't Slow Down***.
Nov From ***Can't Slow Down***, *Penny Lover*, co-written with his wife Brenda, hits US #8 and UK #18.
Dec Diana Ross hits US #10 with the Richie-written and produced *Missing You*, a tribute to the late Marvin Gaye.

1985

Jan Encouraged by Kragen, Richie is asked by Quincy Jones to co-write a song with Michael Jackson for the USA For Africa all-star effort, to raise money for famine relief. Prepared over a three-day period, they take only two hours to write *We Are The World* - a worldwide #1 which also features Richie's vocal contributions.
[28] He collects the Favorite Male Artist, Pop/Rock, Favorite Male Artist, Soul/R&B, Favorite Male Video Artist, Soul/R&B, Favorite Male Video Artist, Pop/Rock, Favorite Video Single, Soul/R&B, and Favorite Video Single, Pop/Rock trophies, at the 12th annual American Music Awards, held at the Shrine Auditorium.
Feb [26] ***Can't Slow Down*** wins Album Of The Year category, while Richie and Carmichael tie with David Foster for Producer Of The Year, at the 27th annual Grammy Awards.
July [13] Richie performs at the JFK Stadium, Philadelphia, PA end of the "Live Aid" benefit spectacular.
Dec [21] Peaking at UK #8, *Say You Say Me* hits US #1 for the Christmas period. Although not written specifically for the movie, it features as the theme to the Gregory Hines/Mikhael Baryshnikov film, "White Nights", though Motown does not allow the song to appear on the Atlantic movie soundtrack album. The US chart-topper sets a new record as Richie becomes the only songwriter in history to achieve nine #1s in nine consecutive years.

1986

Jan Richie returns to the studio to cut his long-awaited third album.
[21] *Say You, Say Me* is certified gold by the RIAA.
Mar [24] *Say You, Say Me* wins an Oscar for Best Original Song, at the Academy Awards ceremony.
May Richie is named ASCAP's Writer Of The Year.
Aug [23] *Dancing On The Ceiling* hits UK #7.
[30] ***Dancing On The Ceiling***, repeating his proven formula, with Richie adding the talents of Eric Clapton, Alabama and others, hits UK #2, behind ***Now! That's I Call Music 7***. The "Dancing On The Ceiling" video, featuring gravity-defying Richie dancing round all four sides of a room, is directed by Stanley Donen.
Sept [13] *Dancing On The Ceiling* hits US #2 behind Berlin's *You Take My Breath Away*.
[27] ***Dancing On The Ceiling*** tops the US chart.
Nov [29] *Love Will Conquer All* hits US #9 and makes UK #45.
Dec Ballad, *Ballerina Girl*, reaches UK #17.

1987

Jan [26] Richie wins the Favorite Male Artist, Pop/Rock, Favorite Male Artist, Soul/R&B, Favorite Male Video Artist, Soul/R&B, and Favorite Video Single, Pop/Rock categories, at the 14th annual American Music Awards, held at the Shrine Auditorium.
Feb Richie ends a three-month US tour, seen by over one million people.
[14] Unusual for the '80s, the B-side of *Ballerina Girl*, the country-flavored *Deep River Woman*, peaks at US #71 (and US Country #10), having been flipped by US radio stations. The song features Alabama on backing vocals.
[21] *Ballerina Girl* hits US #7.
Mar Richie embarks on the UK leg of "The Outrageous Tour", his first ever UK solo concert dates.
May [16] *Sela*, the final extract from the ***Ceiling*** project, reaches US #20 and UK #43.
[21] The RIAA certifies four million sales of ***Dancing On The Ceiling***.

1988

Apr [1] "The Making Of Dancing On The Ceiling" video is certified platinum by the RIAA.
June Richie's wife Brenda is arrested for "investigation of corporal injury to a spouse, resisting arrest, trespassing, vandalism, battery and disturbing the peace". Ms. Richie is apparently upset when she discovers her husband with model-actress Diane Alexander, in the latter's apartment.

1989

May [11] Richie performs at the Songwriters' Hall of Fame 20th Anniversary, before retreating once again to work on a new album. The following year, Richie will separate from his wife of 17 years, also having to cope with the death of his father, and the appearance of polyps on his vocal cords.

1991

Oct He suffers from haemorrhaging of his left vocal cord, having already had two operations in the past three years.
Nov [12] He is cleared of plagiarizing songs written by Tracy Singleton and Gene Thompson on *Deep River Woman*, *Stuck On You* and *Sela*.

1992

May [16] *Do It To Me* makes UK #33.
[27] Richie guests on BBC1-TV's "Wogan".
June [5] He makes his first live US concert performance in five years as part of a token five-shows-in-five-countries mini-tour at The Ritz, New York, to promote his final Motown album release.
[6] ***Back To Front***, a greatest hits compilation with three new tracks, enters the UK chart at #1, where it will stay for six weeks.
[27] *Do It To Me* reaches US #21, as ***Back To Front*** reaches US #19.
Aug Richie signs a new five-album deal with Mercury Records, reportedly worth $30 million.
Oct [3] Still on Motown, *My Destiny* hits UK #7.
[11] Richie participates in the Elizabeth Taylor AIDS Foundation benefit at Madison Square Garden, with Elton John, George Michael and Bruce Hornsby.
[20] ***Back To Front*** is certified platinum by the RIAA.
Nov [28] The included *Love, Oh Love* debuts at its UK #52 peak.

1994

May Richie's new girlfriend Diane Alexander gives birth to their son, Miles.
June [1] Richie is inducted into the Songwriters Hall of Fame at the 25th annual ceremony held at New York's Sheraton Hotel and Towers.
Sept Luther Vandross and Mariah Carey's update of Richie's *Endless Love* hits UK #3, set to hit US #2 two weeks later.

1996

Jan [30] Richie performs his new single *Don't Wanna Lose You* at the 23rd annual American Music Awards held at the Shrine Auditorium.
Apr [6] *Don't Wanna Lose You* bows at its UK #17 peak.
[20] His first new album in ten years, ***Louder Than Words***, still combining his knack for radio friendly R&B swingers and ballads, released by Mercury and produced with Jimmy Jam & Terry Lewis, reaches UK #11 in its week of entry. Earlier in the month Richie has begun filming the Penny Marshall-directed "The Preacher's Wife" co-starring Whitney Houston and Denzel Washington.
May [4] *Don't Wanna Lose You* reaches US #39.
[11] ***Louder Than Words*** reaches US #28.
May [31] He sings three songs and co-emcees WXFS-FM's KISS concert at Boston's Four Seasons hotel as part of the preview evening for the annual Genesis fundraiser the following day.
see also: **THE COMMODORES**

JONATHAN RICHMAN

1971

Mar Richman (b. May 16, 1951, Boston, MA), a writer for Boston-based music papers **Vibrations** and **Fusion**, put together his first group, which will usually be called the Modern Lovers, in 1969, influenced by mid-'60s US garage rock and the hard, monotone style of Lou Reed with the Velvet Underground. The first stable version of the Modern Lovers is now formed in Boston, where the group will be based, although playing often in New York, where its reputation initially takes off, with Richman on vocals and guitar, Ernie Brooks on bass, Jerry Harrison (later to join Talking Heads) on keyboards, John Felice (subsequently of the Real Kids) on rhythm guitar and David Robinson (later of the Cars) on drums. The group is flown to Los Angeles, CA, the following April at the joint expense of A&M and Warner Bros. Records to record demos with Kim Fowley producing (to be released years later on Bomp Records), before signing up with Warners.

1973

Nov An album has been recorded for Warner Bros.,

with John Cale producing, though Richman feels that the sessions are unsatisfactory. There is some dissension within the group, and the label, sharing the uncertainty, has decided not to release the album and now parts company with the band. Robinson leaves and is replaced by Bob Walker on drums for only a few final gigs. The Modern Lovers will disband in January with Richman returning to Boston.

1975

June Richman has signed to the new independent label Beserkley Records, based in Berkeley, CA, debuting with the self-penned two-part *Roadrunner* (to be released via United Artists in the UK).
July Beserkley has bought the tapes of the John Cale-produced recordings from Warner, which are released as ***The Modern Lovers***. Richman is also currently featured on the label's seminal compilation album ***Beserkley Chartbusters***.

1976

Oct ***Jonathan Richman And The Modern Lovers***, not to be confused with the previous Beserkley album, is released, consisting of new acoustic-based recordings produced by Beserkley's directors Greg Kolotkin and Matthew "King" Kaufman, for which Richman assembles a new line-up of the Modern Lovers, comprising Leroy Radcliff on guitar, Greg "Curly" Kerane on bass and David Robinson back on drums.

1977

June The Beserkley label is launched in Britain with Richman's reissued *Roadrunner*, which, with critically-acclaimed music press reviews, climbs to UK #11, the group's first singles chart entry (he will remain chart-less in his home country).
Sept [10] ***Rock'n'Roll With The Modern Lovers*** is the group's only UK chart album, reaching #50.
[18] The group plays at London's Hammersmith Odeon, during its first tour, with a new line-up including D. Sharpe on drums and Asa Breuner on bass.
Dec [17] *Egyptian Reggae*, an offbeat but highly-commercial guitar instrumental from ***Rock'n'Roll With The Modern Lovers***, hits UK #5.

1978

Feb *The Morning Of Our Lives*, a live-recorded single credited to just the Modern Lovers, reaches UK #29. (It is Richman's final chart entry. Subsequent singles released during the year by Beserkley, New England, Abdul & Cleopatra and Buzz Buzz Buzz, will all sell poorly.)
Richman disbands the Modern Lovers, ostensibly to begin a solo career. (Although he continues to record on his own for a while, he will effectively retire from live work for two years.)

1979

Jan ***The Modern Lovers Live***, an onstage set recorded on the group's late 1977 UK tour, is released.
Feb Following the break-up of the group, an album, to have been titled ***Modern Love Songs*** before the split, is released as the Richman solo album ***Back In Your Life***. *Lydia*, Richman's final Beserkley single, is also issued.

1980

Jan The compilation set ***The Jonathan Richman Songbook*** is Richman's final album for Beserkley.
Mar Following a two-year period of self-imposed seclusion in New England, Richman tours the US with a new-look Modern Lovers, including two female back-up singers.

1982

Aug Following the October 1981 release by Bomp Records of ***The Original Modern Lovers***, comprising archive material recorded in 1972 with Kim Fowley producing, Richman's solo return is ***Jonathan Sings!***, his first album for Sire Records (issued in the UK by Rough Trade).

1985

June Once again backed by the Modern Lovers, now lining up Ellie Marshall (backing vocals), Michael Guardabascio (drums) and Andy Paley (piano), ***Rockin' And Romance*** is released, including the extracted *That Summer Feeling* and *I'm Just Beginning To Live*. A final set for Sire, ***It's Time For Jonathan Richman*** will be issued the following February.

1988

Jan The Modern Lovers play live dates in the UK, with a new trio line-up of Richman on vocals and guitar, Brendan Totten on guitar and Johnny Avila on drums.
Mar ***Modern Lovers '88***, by the new line-up, is released by the Rounder label in the US and by Demon in Britain. Reverting permanently to his solo career, Richman's ***Jonathan Richman*** will be issued by Rounder in August the following year.

1990

Apr [19] Increasingly celebrated in New England, and still recording for the Cambridge, MA-based Rounder label, but forgotten elsewhere, Richman wins the Outstanding Pop/Rock Album (Indie Label) category for ***Jonathan Richman*** at the SKC Boston Music Awards at the Wang Center, Boston.
Aug [26] Richman takes part in the annual "Reading Festival" on the Mean Fiddler Stage in Reading, Berks.
Sept The self-explanatory ***Jonathan Goes Country*** is released in Britain on the Special Delivery label, having already been issued in the US by Rounder.

1992

Mar [11] Having performed at London's Mean Fiddler during a short UK visit the previous May 30th, Richman now embarks on a further week-long UK tour at London's Clapham Grand, set to end on the 18th at the Metronome, Folkestone, Kent.
July [19] Richman takes part in the tenth "WOMAD Festival" at Reading's Rivermead site.
Sept [26] During a current North American tour, Richman plays at the famed El Mocambo, Toronto, Canada. (At a Lone Star Roadhouse, New York, gig, ex-Modern Lovers Michael Guardabascio (drums) and singers Ellie Marshall and Beth Harrington join him onstage.)

1994

May [7] He plays a UK date at The Grand, Clapham.

1995

Aug Having released ***I, Jonathan, Te Vas A Emocionar*** in June 1993, entirely written and sung in Spanish and featuring Richman's 17-year old son playing drums on one track, and following Castle Communications' 1994 UK retrospective ***Collection*** and Rhino Records' ongoing reissue of his Beserkley catalog (with and without the Modern Lovers), Richman's latest Rounder effort, ***You Must Ask The Heart*** is released in the US.

RIDE

Mark Gardener (vocals, rhythm guitar); **Andy Bell** (lead guitar, vocals); **Steve Queralt** (bass); **Laurence Colbert** (drums)

1988

Teenage students attending Banbury Art College, Banbury, Oxfordshire, Bell (b. Aug. 11, 1970, Cardiff, Wales), Gardener (b. Dec. 6, 1969, Oxford, Oxfordshire), and Colbert (b. June 27, 1970, Kingston, Surrey) form Ride, with Queralt (b. Feb. 4, 1968, Oxford), who has been introduced to the trio by his brother, completing the permanent quartet which begins rehearsing in Colbert's parents' garage in the village of Ramsden, Oxfordshire. Musically influenced by the Stooges and mid-'80s alternative UK bands including My Bloody Valentine and the Jesus & Mary Chain, the group, showcasing a self-penned, droning, psychedelic wall of guitars sound and frequently encoring with the song *Drive Blind* at most early concerts, spends much of the following year gigging around Oxford and teams with its manager, local promoter Dave Newton. With live performances and a bursting reputation reaching London by the end of 1989, label interest peaks with their signing to the seminal UK indie stable, Creation Records.

1990

Feb [3] Ride's debut recording *Ride EP*, comprising *Drive Blind*, *Chelsea Girl*, *All I Can See* and *Close My Eyes*, makes UK #71, its cover art depicting flora, in keeping with the group's practice of throwing expensive flowers into the audience during concerts.
Apr [14] *Play EP*, collecting *Like A Daydream*, *Silver*, *Furthest Sense* and *Perfect Time*, enters at its UK #32 high.
Sept [29] Having completed recording its debut album during the summer, the band's third four-track EP release of the year, *Fall EP*, including *Dreams Burn Down*, *Taste*, *Here And Now* and *Nowhere*, debuts at its UK #34 peak.
Oct [27] Their freshman album, the critically revered, group-written ***Nowhere***, reaches UK #11 in its first chart week.

1991

Feb [9] Released via its US deal with Sire Records, the extracted *Taste* begins its rise on the US Modern Rock chart, set to make #24.
Mar [14] Ride, with Gardener playing a Rickenbacker guitar borrowed from Paul Weller, performs *Unfamiliar* on BBC1-TV's "Top Of The Pops".
[16] *Today Forever EP*, with *Unfamiliar* as its lead cut, bows at its UK #14 peak.
June [8] The group appears second on a bill topped by the Pixies at the Crystal Palace Bowl, Crystal Palace, London.

1992

Feb [15] The eight-minute plus *Leave Them All Behind* hits UK #9 in its week of entry.
During the month, Bell marries Swedish singer-songwriter Idha Ovelius (who will also sign to Creation, subsequently releasing the husband-guesting album ***Melody Inn***).
[14] *Leave Them All Behind* enters the US Modern Rock chart, set to reach #20.
Mar [21] Ride's self-penned sophomore effort, ***Going Blank Again***, co-produced by the group with Alan Moulder, immediately hits UK #5 after mixed reviews, supported by a UK tour climaxing with a pair of dates at London's Brixton Academy.
Apr [25] The extracted *Twisterella* enters at its UK #36 peak as the band embarks on a world concert trek.
May [16] During US dates, *Twisterella* begins its US Modern Rock chart climb to #12.
Aug During the month, Ride plays at the annual Reading Festival, Reading, Berks. Rehearsals for their third album will begin the following January.

1994

Apr Viewed as something of a comeback recording after an absent year during which Bell and Gardener have become increasingly disparate, *Birdman*, the first Ride release written by solely by Bell, debuts at its UK #38 high.
June [25] *How Does It Feel* charts for a week at UK #58.
July [2] Comprising six songs by Bell, four by Gardener, one by Colbert and another credited to "The Creation", ***Carnival Of Light***, co-produced by John Leckie and George Drakoulias and featuring Deep Purple's Jon Lord on keyboards, hits UK #5 in its week of entry.
Oct [8] The excerpted *I Don't Know Where It Comes From*, featuring Oxford's Christchurch Cathedral Choir, spends a week at UK #46.

1995

Aug [4] The group performs what will prove to be its final concert at the "Benicassim Festival", an event headlined by the Charlatans, at the Belodromo Municipale, Benicassim, Spain.
Sept With growing friction between Gardener and Bell hinting at Ride's dissolution, the group records its final studio album at Matrix Studios in London.
Nov [7] The performance set ***Live Light***, taped on the band's last European tour, is released in the US only by Mutiny Records.
Dec The group decides to permanently disband, not least following Gardener's decision to pursue a new musical direction.

1996

Jan [29] Bell plays a one-off acoustic gig at London's Borderline club.
Feb [24] Ride's *Black Nite Crash* charts for a week at UK #67.
Mar [11] Their final studio album ***Tarantula***, produced by the band with Digby Smith, is released by Creation in the UK and by Sire in the US.
[18] ***Tarantula*** is deleted by Creation.
[23] ***Tarantula*** bows at its UK #21 peak. Gardener subsequently forms a new band, initially named Exile, a moniker he soon scraps after discovering the existence of a veteran US country/pop outfit of the same name, with George Vjestica (guitar), Gary Stonage (bass) and ex-BAD drummer Chris Kavanagh. With Colbert joining the Oxford-based band Twist, Bell is the only ex-member to retain a recording deal with Creation.

THE RIGHTEOUS BROTHERS

Bill Medley (vocals); **Bobby Hatfield** (vocals)

1962

Already a veteran of the Romancers, Medley (b. Sept. 19, 1940, Santa Ana, CA), currently a member of the Paramours and who have recorded *There She Goes* on Moonglow, meets Hatfield (b. Aug. 10, 1940, Beaver Dam, WI), who is with the Variations and has already released a solo single, *Hot Tamales*, also on Moonglow. At the suggestion of label man John Wimber, the two combos initially combine (still as the Paramours) but soon pair down to a Medley/Hatfield duo, making their live debut at a high school prom in Anaheim, CA. (They are dubbed the Righteous Brothers by black marines who see them perform at the Black Derby in Santa Ana - the name sticks.)

1963

June Moonglow releases *Little Latin Lupe Lu*, a Medley-penned R&B/dance number, which makes US #49, after being used as an ad by Los Angeles, CA radio station KRLA. Two further Moonglow singles, *Koko Joe* and *My Babe* follow the latter peaking at US #75 in September.

1964

June Phil Spector expresses an interest in producing them, after seeing their performance on a package bill at the Cow Palace, San Francisco, CA, but they are still contracted to Moonglow. Spector strikes a deal whereby they appear on his own Philles label in the US and on London Records in the UK, while other territories receive their masters through Moonglow. They become Philles' first white act. Spector commissions husband and wife team Barry Mann and Cynthia Weil to write a song for them.
Aug [19] The Righteous Brothers support the Beatles as they begin a US tour at the Cow Palace.
Sept [16] They are featured with real-life brothers, Don and Phil Everly, and Sam Cooke on the premiere of the ABC-TV show "Shindig!"
Dec [12] Their first Philles single, *You've Lost That Lovin' Feelin'*, enters the US survey. Becoming one of the most enduring classics of the pop era and a showcase for the duo's considerable vocal talent (Medley's rich bass tones constrasting with Hatfield's high tenor voice), the song will later become a hit for Dionne Warwick, Daryl Hall & John Oates and actor Telly Savalas, among others, while many critics view this original as the definitive Spector "Wall of Sound" disc.

1965

Jan [11] The duo arrives in Britain for a promotional visit, performing on TV shows "Scene At 6.30", "Ready Steady Go!" and "Discs A Go-Go".
You've Lost That Lovin' Feelin' is featured on BBC-TV's "Juke Box Jury", but is dismissed by the four panelists, one questioning whether it has been played at the right speed, who vote it a "miss". A UK cover by Cilla Black charts the following week, but producer Andrew Loog Oldham places a self-paid ad in the UK music press extolling the virtues of the original over the cover.
Feb [4] The ad works as the Righteous Brothers leapfrog Black's version to hit UK #1, halting Black's cover at #2.
[6] *You've Lost That Lovin' Feelin'* begins a two-week stay atop the US chart while its parent album, ***You've Lost That Lovin' Feelin'***, hits US #4. Moonglow releases their early material on ***Right Now!***, which reaches US #11, and the extracted *Bring Your Love To Me* climbs to US #83. (Moonglow follows with the albums ***Some Blue-Eyed Soul*** (US #14) and ***This Is New!*** (US #39).)
[13] Medley is operated on for an injured spleen at the Martin Luther Hospital in Anaheim, CA.
May The duo's legitimate follow-up to *Lovin' Feelin'*, *Just Once In My Life*, penned by husband and wife team Gerry Goffin and Carole King, hits US #9. (Two further Moonglow singles chart: *You Can Have Her* (US #67) and *Justine*, from the film, "A Swingin' Summer" (US #85).)
June ***Just Once In My Life*** hits US #9.
[28] The duo appears on CBS-TV's "It's What's Happening Baby" special.
Aug Another Goffin/King song, *Hung On You*, makes US #47, but DJs prefer its B-side, Hatfield's solo interpretation of the '50s smash *Unchained Melody*, which hits US #4 and UK #14.
Dec MGM Records offers $1 million for the Righteous Brothers' contract and Spector, now interested in Ike & Tina Turner, sells.

1966

Jan Spector-helmed *Ebb Tide* hits US #5, and makes UK #48 as ***Back To Back*** reaches US #16. (Moonglow has its final success with the duo, as *Georgia On My Mind* peaks at US #62.)
Apr [9] Their MGM debut, on its Verve subsidiary, *(You're My) Soul And Inspiration*, which Mann and Weil had intended as a follow-up to *You've Lost That Lovin' Feelin'*, tops the US chart for the first of three weeks and makes UK #15. Medley's production, to some, differs little from Spector's work. ***Soul And Inspiration*** hits US #7.
May [9] *(You're My) Soul And Inspiration* is certified gold by the RIAA.
June Moonglow-issued ***The Best Of The Righteous Brothers***, compiled from four albums recorded between 1962 and 1963, makes US #130.
July *He* reaches US #18, while its B-side, *He Will Break Your Heart*, peaks at US #91.
[5] Medley has an operation to remove nodes from his vocal cords in a Los Angeles hospital.
[25] The Righteous Brothers appears on NBC-TV's "Hullabaloo", singing *Let The Good Times Roll*, *(You're My) Soul And Inspiration*, and a Beatles medley with Nancy Sinatra.
Sept *Go Ahead And Cry* reaches US #30, taken from ***Go Ahead And Cry***, which climbs to US #32.
Nov *White Cliffs Of Dover*, a reissue of a Philles album track, makes UK #21, as *On This Side Of Goodbye* reaches US #47.
[28] ***Soul And Inspiration*** is confirmed gold by the RIAA.
Dec *Island In The Sun* makes UK #36.

1967

Apr ***Sayin' Somethin'*** peaks at US #155.
May *Melancholy Music Man* reaches US #43.
June *Stranded In The Middle Of No Place*, their last hit for Verve, peaks at US #72.
Oct ***Greatest Hits*** reaches US #21, while ***Souled Out*** spends two weeks at US #198.
Nov Medley leaves to pursue a solo career (on MGM/Verve until 1969, but he will have little commercial success). Hatfield re-forms the duo with Jimmy Walker, ex-Knickerbockers. For legal reasons, the new pairing is not allowed to use the name the Righteous Brothers on record for a year.

1968

Oct Medley's debut album, ***100%***, on MGM, peaks at US #188, having already had three minor solo hits with *I Can't Make It Alone* (US #95), *Brown Eyed Woman* (US #43) and *Peace Brother Peace* (US #48).
[13] Medley guests on CBS-TV's "The Smothers Brothers Comedy Hour".
Dec Live album, ***One For The Road***, peaks at US #187. (During the year, Verve issues two albums by the Righteous Brothers featuring unreleased titles and singles. Hatfield records solo singles for Verve, while he waits out the legal delay.)

1969

Jan Reissued in the UK, *You've Lost That Lovin' Feelin'* hits #10. Medley releases two further albums. Hatfield and Walker, now recording as the Righteous Brothers, release ***Re-Birth***.
Mar Hatfield's solo effort, *Nothing Is Too Good For You*, makes US #84.
Apr ***Greatest Hits, Vol. 2*** reaches US #126 while Medley's solo album, ***Soft And Soulful***, peaks at US #152.
May [29] ***The Righteous Brothers Greatest Hits*** is certified gold by the RIAA.

1971

May Medley releases the Herb Alpert-produced, Michel Colombier-arranged ***A Song For You***, for A&M, which despite its impressive title track, *The Long And Winding Road*, and a new, slower version of *You've Lost That Lovin' Feelin'*, fails to chart. It will be followed by a second set for A&M, ***Smile***, issued in 1973.

1974

July [20] With the production team of Lambert and Potter behind them, Medley and Hatfield have re-formed and now hit US #3 with the Alan O'Day/John Stevenson-penned *Rock'n'Roll Heaven*, a tribute to dead rock'n'roll stars, released on Capitol's Haven subsidiary.
Aug ***Give It To The People*** reaches US #27.
Oct [19] The extracted title track, *Give It To The People*, reaches US #20.
Dec [21] *Dream On* reaches US #32. The following February 23rd, the Righteous Brothers will make a sole UK appearance at London's New Victoria Theatre.

1977

Nov *You've Lost That Lovin' Feelin'*, reissued again, makes UK #42. The following year, Medley's label debut for United Artists, ***Another Beginning***, will be released.

1981

Feb Medley resumes his solo recording career after a four-year absence to record ***Sweet Thunder*** in Berry Hill, TN, with producers Michael Lloyd, Brent Maher and Randy Goodrum for Liberty Records, having also signed with top management team Kragen & Company. The extracted *Don't Know Much* peaks at US #88. (The song will win Linda Ronstadt and Aaron Neville a Grammy Award for their version in 1990.)

1982

Oct Medley releases ***Right Here And Now***, produced by Richard Perry on the latter's Planet label. Its title track, *Right Here And Now*, makes US #58. He opens Medleys club in Los Angeles and he and Hatfield re-form again for an ABC-TV special celebrating the 30th anniversary of "American Bandstand", singing an updated version of *Rock'n'Roll Heaven*. (Medley's next solo album, ***I Still Do*** will be released by RCA Records two years hence, followed a year later by ***Still Hung Up On You***.)

1986

Sept [13] Berlin's *Take My Breath Away*, with *You've Lost That Lovin' Feelin'* on the B-side, tops the US chart. Both are featured prominently in the Tom Cruise film, "Top Gun".

1987

Sept *(I've Had) The Time Of My Life*, a Bill Medley/Jennifer Warnes duet from the movie, "Dirty Dancing", hits UK #6.

Nov [28] *(I've Had) The Time Of My Life* tops the US chart as the film's popularity soars. The album is the most successful soundtrack since ***Saturday Night Fever***, selling more than 14 million copies worldwide.

1988

Mar [2] Medley wins the Best Pop Performance By A Duo Or Group With Vocal category with Warnes, for *(I've Had) The Time Of My Life*, at the 30th annual Grammy Awards.

Aug Medley's cover of *He Ain't Heavy He's My Brother*, included on the soundtrack to Sylvester Stallone's "Rambo III", reaches UK #25, while the Hollies' reissued original tops the UK chart. (He has already recorded a duet with Gladys Knight for a previous Stallone movie, "Cobra".)

1990

Jan [25] Medley makes the first of two appearances, as himself, on NBC-TV's "Cheers".

Oct [20] Reissued *Unchained Melody*, spurred by its inclusion in the hit movie "Ghost", reaches US #13, as a different and newly recorded Medley-produced version on Curb Records also enters the Top 30, becoming the first time that two versions of the same song by the same act have charted since Bobbie Gentry's *Ode To Billie Joe* in 1967. ***The Righteous Brothers Greatest Hits*** makes US #31.

[27] Rhino Records-released compilation, ***Anthology (1962-1974)***, peaks at US #178.

Nov [3] As "Ghost" becomes the biggest-grossing movie of the year in Britain, *Unchained Melody* tops the UK chart, where it will stay for four weeks, as the re-recorded Curb version of *Unchained Melody* reaches US #19. The duo performs before a sellout crowd of 4,933 at the Mark G. Ettis Arena, Trump Taj Mahal, Atlantic City, NJ.

[24] Comprising new versions of their staple hits, ***The Best Of The Righteous Brothers***, also on Curb, debuts at its US #161 peak.

Dec [1] An original versions UK compilation ***The Very Best Of The Righteous Brothers*** reaches UK #11 with the reissued *You've Lost That Lovin' Feelin'* hitting UK #3 on the 22nd. *Unchained Melody* will be certified platinum by the RIAA on January 10th the following year, with Medley's duet with Jennifer Warnes, *(I've Had) The Time Of My Life*, re-hitting UK #8 on the 26th, spurred by the movie's recent UK TV exposure (Hatfield will also make his "Cheers" debut on the 31st singing *Unchained Melody*, much to the chagrin of Dr. Frazier Crane.) A four-date Righteous Brothers UK tour will open in Manchester on February 28th, set to end on March 3rd at the BIC, Bournemouth, Dorset, as the Righteous Brothers head toward mid-decade undertaking regular US tours each summer, when Medley also hosts an annual golf tournament in his name at the Los Coyetes Country Club, Irvine, CA to benefit Lupus disease awareness. ***Unchained Melody - The Best Of The Righteous Brothers*** will be certified platinum by the RIAA on June 2nd, 1992, with Rhino's ***Anthology (1962-1974)*** certified gold on November 30th the same year.

JOHNNY RIVERS

1961

Rivers (b. John Ramistella, Nov. 7, 1942, New York, NY), having grown up in Baton Rouge, LA, where he formed his first rock'n'roll groups in high school, then commuted in his later teens between New York and Nashville, TN, trying to gain an entry into the music business, has met DJ Alan Freed, who has been impressed by his songs and helped him secure a one-off deal with Gone Records, also suggesting the new name Rivers, from the river bayou country of his upbringing. After playing in Las Vegas, NV, and Lake Tahoe, NV, with Louie Prima's band, he has moved to Los Angeles, CA, where he has had his *I'll Make Believe* recorded by Ricky Nelson in 1958. His revival of *Blue Skies* for the Chancellor label in 1961 gains airplay, but fails to chart, while a live residency, at Los Angeles' Gazzari's club during 1963 begins to establish his name as a performer.

1964

Mar Rivers has moved to the newly-opened Whisky A Go-Go club, where his live rock-oldie sets intersperse record sessions, all the music being aimed primarily at the dancefloor. He becomes a success with regular patrons and the buzz reaches Imperial Records, which now signs him to a recording contract and tapes his live stage act.

June His live debut album, ***Johnny Rivers At The Whisky A Go-Go***, reaches US #12.

July The extracted update of Chuck Berry's *Memphis* (also a major hit in instrumental form for Lonnie Mack a year previously) hits US #2, behind the Four Seasons' *Rag Doll*.

Sept Another Berry live revival, *Maybelline*, reaches US #12.

Oct *Here We A Go Go Again!*, another set of mainly oldies from his club act, makes US #38.

Nov [12] Rivers arrives in London for a short promotional visit.

Dec Rivers' revival of Harold Dorman's R&B oldie, *Mountain Of Love*, hits US #9.

1965

Feb ***Johnny Rivers In Action!*** peaks at US #42.

Mar *Midnight Special*, his rocked-up version of Paul Evans' 1960 US hit, reaches US #20 (and in 1973 will be used as the theme to NBC-TV's music series of the same title), while its B-side revival of Sam Cooke's *Cupid* peaks at US #76.

May Rivers debuts at New York's Copacabana night-club.

June ***Meanwhile Back At The Whisky A Go-Go*** reaches US #21.

[28] Rivers appears on CBS-TV's "It's What's Happening Baby" special.

July *Seventh Son* becomes his third US Top 10 hit, at US #7.

Sept ***Johnny Rivers Rocks The Folk*** makes US #91.

Nov Taken from the folk/rock album, his treatment of the Kingston Trio's *Where Have All The Flowers Gone?* makes US #26.

1966

Jan *Under Your Spell Again* reaches US #35.

Apr Rivers' recording of *Secret Agent Man*, the theme from the Patrick McGoohan TV spy series "Secret Agent" (a re-titling of the UK series "Danger Man"), hits US #3, as "***... and I know you wanna dance***" peaks at US #52.

July His revival of *(I Washed My Hands In) Muddy Water*, cut by Charlie Rich as the B-side to his 1965 hit *Mohair Sam*, reaches US #19.

Sept ***Johnny Rivers' Golden Hits***, a compilation of his hit singles to date, reaches US #29.

Nov [12] *Poor Side Of Town*, an original ballad written by Rivers and producer Lou Adler, is his all-time biggest-selling single, topping the US chart for a week, and eventually selling over a million copies.

Dec ***Changes***, featuring *Poor Side Of Town* and other material with a similar, more contemporary sound, makes US #33. Rivers sets up his own music publishing company, Rivers Music (signing Jim Webb, among others), and, while in re-negotiation of his recording contract with Imperial, launches his own Liberty/Imperial-distributed label, Soul City Records, which will be a production base for Rivers' talent-scouting, including the 5th Dimension in 1967. He also assembles a regular studio band of acclaimed sessioneers Hal Blaine (drums), Joe Osborn (bass - an old friend from Baton Rouge) and Larry Knechtel (keyboards).

1967

Jan Rivers participates in the "San Remo Song Festival" in San Remo, Italy.

Mar Passing over Webb's song *By The Time I Get To Phoenix* as a single (which he suggests instead for Glen Campbell), Rivers' lush revival of the Four Tops' *Baby I Need Your Lovin'* hits US #3.

June ***Rewind*** reaches US #14.

[16] Rivers is the fifth act to perform on the first day of the "Monterey International Pop Festival" at the County Fairgrounds, Monterey, CA, an event he has co-organized, with Lou Adler and the Mamas & the Papas.

July His second Motown cover, of the Miracles' *The Tracks Of My Tears*, hits US #10.

1968

Jan *Summer Rain*, with hints of flower-power in its arrangement and lyric (which refers to the Beatles' ***Sgt. Pepper's Lonely Hearts Club Band***), reaches US #14.

Feb [29] He wins a Grammy Award as co-producer of the 5th Dimension's *Up, Up And Away*, which is named Record Of The Year For 1967 at the tenth annual ceremony.

May *Look To Your Soul* makes US #49.

June ***Realization*** hits US #5.

Dec *Right Relations*, with a socially-conscious lyric, peaks at US #61. (Rivers retires almost completely from live concert appearances to spend more time at his retreat in Carmel, CA.)

1969

Mar His cover of Joe South's *These Are Not My People* peaks at US #55.

June ***A Touch Of Gold*** reaches US #26.

Aug *Muddy River* makes US #41.

Sept [29] ***Realization*** is certified gold by the RIAA.

Nov *One Woman*, an excursion into soul music, peaks at US #89. Rivers sells Soul City Records for $2 million. (Now a rare performer, he will spend much time travelling in India and Japan, investigating disciplines such as yoga, transcendental meditation and vegetarianism.)

1970

June His treatment of Van Morrison's *Into The Mystic* makes US #51.

Aug ***Slim Slo Slider***, featuring songs by Gram Parsons, Van Morrison and John Fogerty, reaches US #100.

Sept *Fire And Rain*, his cover of James Taylor's ballad, peaks at US #94.

1971

May His revival of Frankie Ford's *Sea Cruise*, back in his original straightforward-rock style, peaks at US #84, Rivers' first release on United Artists, which has absorbed Imperial and Liberty Records.

Sept *Think His Name*, an inspirational number backed by the Guru Ram Das Ashram Singers, peaks at US #65, while ***Home Grown*** makes US #148.

Dec He sells his Rivers Music publishing house, with a stock of valuable copyrights, for over $1 million. ***L.A. Reggae***, on which he is backed by members of the Crickets and other guests, and which showcases mainly rock and R&B covers, will make US #78 the following November.

1973

Jan From the album, his revival of Huey "Piano" Smith's *Rockin' Pneumonia And The Boogie Woogie Flu* hits US #6.

[29] *Rockin' Pneumonia And The Boogie Woogie Flu* is certified gold by the RIAA.

May In similar style, his update of Carl Perkins' *Blue Suede Shoes* makes US #38 (though the album of the same title, a mixture of new and old songs, fails to chart).

1975

Mar [6] The RIAA confirms gold sales of ***Johnny Rivers' Golden Hits*** and ***A Touch Of Gold Volume II***.

Aug Having left UA, after disagreements with the label over contracts leave him disinclined to re-sign, to record on a one-off basis for Atlantic, and now signed to Epic Records, his version of *Help Me Rhonda*, a revival of the Beach Boys' 1965 US #1, on which Brian Wilson assists with back-up vocals, reaches US #22, and ***New Lovers And Old Friends*** makes US #147.

1977

Feb *Ashes And Sand*, issued on his own revived Soul City label, to which he has re-acquired the title rights, peaks at US #96.

[4] Rivers takes part in the all-star celebrity band with Chuck Berry, Gregg Allman and others, on the 25th anniversary special of Dick Clark's "American Bandstand" on ABC-TV.

Oct His cover of Jack Tempchin & the Funky Kings' *Swayin' To The Music (Slow Dancin')*, recorded for the Big Tree label, hits US #10.

Nov [29] *Swayin' To The Music* is his final RIAA certified gold disc.

1978

Jan ***Outside Help*** released on Big Tree peaks at US #142.

Feb Rivers' final US chart entry is a revival of a Major Lance hit, *Curious Mind (Um, Um, Um, Um, Um, Um)*, which makes US #41. He will subsequently take little active part in music-making, releasing only ***Borrowed Time*** on RSO Records in 1980 and the religious ***Not A Through Street***, in 1983, content in retirement with having sold some 30 million records over 15 years and in discovering a whole generation of successful songwriters and acts for whom he was an original sponsor and champion. Occasionally performing at one-off events into the '90s, including 1992's Memphis Horns 25th Anniversary Show in Memphis, TN, and a "Rock Against Hunger" benefit at the Count Basie Theatre, Red Bank, NJ, his career highlights will be brought to compact disc with the 1990 Rhino Records compilation ***Johnny Rivers : Anthology 1964-1977***.

SMOKEY ROBINSON & THE MIRACLES

Smokey Robinson (lead vocals); **Claudette Rogers** (vocals); **Ronnie White** (vocals); **Pete Moore** (vocals); **Bobby Rogers** (vocals)

1954

Robinson (b. William Robinson, Feb. 19, 1940, Detroit, MI) assembles the Matadors R&B vocal group from friends at Detroit's Northern High School: Ronnie White (b. Apr. 5, 1939, Detroit), Bobby Rogers (b. Feb. 19, 1940, Detroit) and Pete Moore (b. Nov. 19, 1939, Detroit), plus guitarist Marv Tarplin. Becoming established on the Detroit club scene over the next three years, and changing their name to the Miracles when Rogers' sister Claudette (b. 1942) joins, replacing another brother, Emerson, who goes into the US Army, they audition for Jackie Wilson's manager (who turns them down) at his office in 1957, where Robinson first meets Berry Gordy Jr., who has just written *Reet Petite* for Wilson, but who is still working at Ford Motors while trying to break into the music business full-time. He sees potential in the young group and helps it secure a deal with End Records.

1958

Feb [19] On Robinson's 18th birthday, End releases the Miracles' first single, *Got A Job*, a Robinson/ Gordy/ Tyrone Carlo-penned "answer" to the Silhouettes' hit, *Get A Job*.

1959

Oct Gordy, now closely involved with the group, has leased the Robinson-penned ballad, *Bad Girl*, to Chess Records, which becomes the Miracles' US pop chart debut at #93.

Nov [7] Robinson marries Claudette. (They will have two children, Berry and Tamla.)

1960

Using royalties from work with Jackie Wilson and Marv Johnson, and a loan of $800, Gordy forms his own company, Motown Records, and sets up the Tamla label to feature the Miracles. The first Tamla release is the Miracles' dance tune, *Way Over There*, which fails to chart.

1961

Feb *Shop Around*, written by Robinson and Gordy and an early model of the ultra-commercial R&B dance sound (and later much-covered), hits US #2 (and US R&B #1), and is the group's and Motown's first million seller, as the Miracles become the first Motown act to appear on ABC-TV's "American Bandstand". The hit is taken from the group's debut album ***Hi, We're The Miracles***.

Apr Follow-up, *Ain't It Baby*, makes US #49.

Aug *Mighty Good Lovin'* peaks at US #51.

Nov *Everybody Gotta Pay Some Dues* peaks at US #52 (but like all immediate post-*Shop Around* releases, is a bigger hit on local R&B charts), taken from their sophomore set ***Cookin' With The Miracles***. Robinson is, by now, becoming an increasingly important part of the growing Motown operation, both arranging and writing for young artists on the label, and Gordy makes him company vice-president.

1962

Feb *What's So Good About Goodbye* makes US #35.

June *I'll Try Something New* reaches US #39, taken from ***I'll Try Something New***.

Sept A reissue of *Way Over There* now peaks at US #94.

Nov [2] The first live Motortown package revue, featuring the Miracles, opens at the Boston Arena, Boston, MA.

1963

Feb Robinson-penned *You've Really Got A Hold On Me* is the group's second US Top 10 hit, at #8. (It will be covered by the Beatles on their second album, and become a staple of UK beat groups' repertoires.)

May *A Love She Can Count On* makes US #31.

June Their first chart album, ***The Fabulous Miracles*** peaks at US #118.

Sept Robinson-inked dance number, *Mickey's Monkey*, hits US #8 (and, reportedly, is also the first disc bought by Michael Jackson).

Oct Live set, ***The Miracles On Stage***, reaches US #139.

Dec Seasonal set ***Christmas With The Miracles*** is released.

1964

Jan *I Gotta Dance To Keep From Crying* makes US #35, while ***Doin' Mickey's Monkey*** peaks at US #113. Claudette Robinson retires from performance with the group, to look after home and family (though she will later guest with them on occasion and continue to sing on their records).

Apr Now adept at writing songs for other Motown acts, Robinson has penned the Temptations' first major hit, *The Way You Do The Things You Do*, which reaches US #11. At the same time, the Miracles' *(You Can't Let The Boy Overpower) The Man In You* peaks at US #59.

May [16] Robinson has his first #1 as a writer, with Mary Wells' version of his and Ronnie White's *My Guy* topping the US chart.

Aug *I Like It Like That* reaches US #27.

Oct *That's What Love Is Made Of* makes US #35.

[28-29] The Miracles perform on the "TAMI Show" at the Civic Auditorium, Santa Monica, CA, on a bill also featuring the Beach Boys, Chuck Berry, Marvin Gaye, the Supremes, the Rolling Stones and others.

Nov ***The Fabulous Miracles*** is issued.

Dec [1] They arrive in Britain for a short promotional tour, which will include appearances on the TV shows "Ready Steady Go!", "Thank Your Lucky Stars" and BBC Radio's "Saturday Club".

1965

Jan *Come On Do The Jerk* makes US #50.

Mar [6] Another Temptations' release of a Robinson/White song, *My Girl*, tops the US chart and becomes a million seller (though most of Motown's '60s catalog will remain officially uncertified by the RIAA). (On various songs, both for the Miracles and other acts, Robinson collaborates with group members: Moore, White or Tarplin. Like all the label's chief writers, he also oversees production and arrangement, using the Hitsville USA house band.)

[20] The group begins a 21-date, twice-nightly UK tour, set to end on April 12th at the Guildhall, Portsmouth, Hants., at Finsbury Park Astoria, London, to launch Tamla Motown's own identity in Britain, with labelmates the Supremes, Martha & the Vandellas, Stevie Wonder, the Temptations and special guests Georgie Fame & the Blue Flames.

Apr [17] Tamla Motown spectacular, featuring the Miracles, airs on ITV.

May Ballad, *Ooh Baby Baby*, reaches US #16.

June Double compilation, ***Greatest Hits From The Beginning***, is the group's first big album seller, reaching US #21.

Sept Another Robinson ballad, *The Tracks Of My Tears*, reaches US #16 (and will become a much-covered R&B standard).

Nov *My Girl Has Gone* reaches US #14.

1966

Feb A return to the dance idiom, *Going To A Go-Go* reaches US #11, and is the group's UK chart debut, making #44, while ***Going To A Go-Go*** hits US #8. Robinson begins to produce Marvin Gaye, renewing Gaye's US Top 10 status with *Ain't That Peculiar*.

July Another dance number, *Whole Lot Of Shakin' In My Heart (Since I Met You)*, makes US #46.

Dec *(Come Round Here) I'm The One You Need* reaches US #17 and UK #45.

1967

Jan *Away We A Go-Go* makes US #41.

[13] The Miracles perform at the re-opening of the Whisky A Go-Go in Hollywood, CA.

Mar [28] They play in Murray The K's week-long Easter show, "Music In The 5th Dimension", at the Manhattan RKO Theater, New York.

Apr Robinson's status within the group is recognized by Motown when, with the US #20 hit *The Love I Saw In You Was Just A Mirage*, the billing becomes Smokey Robinson & the Miracles.

July *More Love* (later revived by Kim Carnes) reaches US #23.

Nov ***Make It Happen*** reaches US #28.

Dec *I Second That Emotion*, later also much covered, is the group's first US Top 10 hit in four years, at #4.

1968

Jan *I Second That Emotion* is their first Top 30 UK hit, reaching #27.

Apr *If You Can Want* reaches US #11 and UK #50, while the compilation, ***Greatest Hits, Vol. 2***, hits US #7. (Robinson's golden songwriting period of the '60s is now drawing to a close, as his Motown corporate duties draw him away from composition. The group's later albums will contain many songs from outside sources.)
July *Yester Love* makes US #31.
Sept *Special Occasion* reaches US #26.
Nov ***Special Occasion*** climbs to US #42.

1969

Mar *Baby, Baby Don't Cry* hits US #8, while ***Live!*** makes US #71.
June *The Tracks Of My Tears*, not a hit first time round in Britain, is reissued and becomes the group's biggest UK success to date, hitting #9.
July *Doggone Right* makes US #33 while the group's rush-released version of the Dion hit, *Abraham, Martin And John*, originally an album track, also makes US #33 (in competition with a simultaneous US #35 version by comedienne, Moms Mabley).
Sept ***Time Out For Smokey Robinson And The Miracles*** makes US #25.
Oct *Here I Go Again*, the B-side of *Doggone Right*, reaches US #37.

1970

Jan *Point It Out* also makes US #37, while ***Four In Blue*** reaches US #78.
Feb The group records a "This Is Tom Jones" TV special in London.
June *Who's Gonna Take The Blame* makes US #46, while ***What Love Has Joined Together*** climbs to US #97.
Sept [12] *The Tears Of A Clown*, originally recorded in 1967 and released on ***Make It Happen***, tops the UK chart for a week, selling almost 900,000 copies.
Nov ***A Pocketful Of Miracles*** peaks at US #56.
Dec [12] Released by Motown in the US on the strength of its UK success, *The Tears Of A Clown* tops the US chart for the first of two weeks (their first US #1), and sells well over a million, becoming the group's most successful single ever.

1971

Feb Another former UK non-hit, *(Come 'Round Here) I'm The One You Need*, is reissued as a follow-up to *The Tears Of A Clown*, making UK #13.
May New recording, *I Don't Blame You At All*, climbs to US #18 and UK #11.
July Dance song, *Crazy About The La La La*, peaks at US #56.
Oct ***One Dozen Roses*** makes US #92.

1972

Jan *Satisfaction* makes US #49.
July [16] At the end of a six-month farewell US tour, Robinson, who has wanted to leave the group to pursue his own projects since 1970, makes his last appearance with the Miracles at the Carter Barron Amphitheater in Washington, DC, prior to launching his solo career via Motown. William Griffin (b. Aug. 15, 1950, Detroit) will replace him.
Aug *We've Come Too Far To End It Now* makes US #46, while ***Flying High Together*** reaches US #46.

1973

Jan *I Can't Stand To See You Cry*, the last single released by Robinson with the Miracles, makes US #45. The double compilation album, ***1957-1972***, reaches US #75.
Sept The Miracles' *Don't Let It End ('Til You Let It Begin)* peaks at US #56 (the first of only four hit singles the group will have without Robinson). Robinson's first solo album, ***Smokey***, peaks at US #70, though critics feel it lacks the assurance of his best work with the Miracles. The extracted *Sweet Harmony* makes US #48.

1974

Feb *Baby Come Close* is his first solo Top 30 hit, reaching US #27, while *Just My Soul Responding* makes UK #35.
June ***Pure Smokey***, an overtly romantic set, reaches US #99, while the extracted *It's Her Turn To Live* peaks at US #82.
Oct The Miracles' *Do It Baby* reaches US #13 (spurring ***Do It Baby*** to US #41).
Nov *Virgin Man* peaks at US #56.

1975

Jan The Miracles' *Don't Cha Love It* stops at at US #78 (previewing the forthcoming US #96 ***Don't Cha Love It***), while Robinson's *I Am I Am* climbs to US #56.
June *Baby That's Backatcha* reaches US #26, and tops the US R&B survey for a week.
[14] Its parent album, ***A Quiet Storm***, makes US #36.
Nov Also from the album, *The Agony And The Ecstasy* makes US #36.

1976

Feb [7] The Miracles' ***City Of Angels*** reaches US #33.
[21] Title song, *A Quiet Storm*, peaks at US #61.
Mar [6] *Love Machine* by the Miracles tops the US chart, eventually selling over one million copies, having hit UK #3 on Feb [7], the group's final hit single. They will secure two further US chart albums: ***The Power Of Music*** (#178 in Oct [30]) and ***Love Crazy*** (#117 in Ape [2] the following year).
Apr [4] Robinson begins a 14-date UK tour at the Locarno, Portsmouth, Hants, set to end on the 18th at the Top Rank Suite, Reading, Berks.
[24] ***Smokey's Family Robinson*** makes US #57.
July [3] *Open* peaks at US #81.
Oct [30] Reissued *The Tears Of A Clown* makes UK #34.

1977

Apr [2] ***Deep In My Soul*** peaks at US #47.
[23] The extracted *There Will Come A Day (I'm Gonna Happen To You)* makes US #42.
Aug Robinson is executive producer of, and writes and produces the music for, the premiering movie "Big Time".

1978

May *Love Breeze* makes US #75.
July *Daylight And Darkness* peaks at US #75.
Nov [6] Robinson performs at London's Palladium during a current UK visit.

1979

Feb Live double album, ***Smokin'***, makes US #165, while Robinson has teamed with Diana Ross, Marvin Gaye and Stevie Wonder on *Pops We Love You*, a tribute for Berry Gordy's father's 90th birthday, which peaks at US #59 and UK #66.
Oct ***Where There's Smoke*** reaches US #17.

1980

Feb The extracted *Cruisin'* is Robinson's first Top 10 solo hit, at US #4.
May ***Warm Thoughts*** reaches US #14 while, taken from it, *Let Me Be The Clock* makes US #31.

1981

May [23] *Being With You*, produced by George Tobin (to whom Robinson has originally submitted it for Kim Carnes, after she revived *More Love* successfully) hits US #2, coincidentally behind Carnes' *Bette Davis Eyes*, while ***Being With You*** heads to US #10.
June [13] *Being With You* tops the UK chart for the first of two weeks.
[27] ***Being With You***, his first UK chart album, reaches UK #17.
July *You Are Forever* peaks at US #59.
[7] *Being With You* is certified gold by the RIAA.
Dec [12] ABC-TV's "American Bandstand" airs the "Smokey Robinson 25th Anniversary Special". ***Yes It's You Lady*** will reach US #33 the following March, as will the extracted *Tell Me Tomorrow* (which also peaks at UK #51). *Old Fashioned Love* will stop at US #60 in May.

1983

Mar ***Touch The Sky*** makes US #50.
May [16] Robinson is reunited with the Miracles on the "Motown 25th Anniversary" NBC-TV special, singing *Shop Around*, *Tears Of A Clown* and *Going To A Go Go*, and duetting with Linda Ronstadt on *Ooh Baby*.
Aug *Blame It On Love*, a duet with Barbara Mitchell of High Inergy, makes US #48.
Sept Robinson's compilation album, ***Blame It On Love And All The Great Hits***, peaks at US #124. His duet with fellow Motown hit-maker Rick James on *Ebony Eyes* will make US #43 the following January with ***Essar*** peaking at US #141 in July.

1986

Mar Having taken part in the historic recording of USA For Africa's single, *We Are The World* on January 28th the previous year, ***Smoke Signals***, mostly produced by Steve Barri and Tony Peluso, and featuring Herb Alpert and the Temptations, now peaks at US #104.

1987

Jan [21] Robinson is inducted into the Rock and Roll Hall of Fame at the second annual dinner, at New York's Waldorf Astoria Hotel.
Apr *Just To See Her* makes UK #32, following Robinson's performance of the song at the TV-aired "Montreux Rock Festival", from Montreux, Switzerland.
July [4] *Just To See Her* hits US #8, Robinson's first Top 10 outing in six years, while ***One Heartbeat*** reaches US #26 and tops the US R&B survey.
Sept [8] ***One Heartbeat*** is certified gold by the RIAA.
[28] Robinson and Gladys Knight guest on the syndicated TV show, "$10,000 Pyramid", for a week.
Oct [3] Title cut, *One Heartbeat*, hits US #10.
Dec [12] *What's Too Much* peaks at US #79.

1988

Mar [2] Robinson wins the Best R&B Vocal Performance, Male, for *Just To See Her*, at the 30th annual Grammy Awards - his first Grammy nod.
Love Don't Give No Reason makes US R&B #35, while Robinson features in a duet with Dolly Parton on *I Know You By Heart*.
Aug Robinson guests as Chicago commodities trader Link Greer on the day-time TV soap, "Generations".
Nov [19] ***Love Songs***, combining individual Robinson and Marvin Gaye ballads, makes UK #69. *We've Saved The Best For Last*, with Kenny G, makes US #47 the following Mar [4], before NARAS honors Robinson as a Grammy Living Legend in November.

1990

Mar [24] ***Love, Smokey*** makes US #138.
May [6] He tapes a show at the Opera House, Bally's Grand Hotel Casino, Atlantic City, NJ, for the "SRO" US TV series.
[30] Robinson is inducted into the Songwriters Hall of Fame by Whitney Houston, at the 21st annual induction dinner, held at the Hilton Hotel, New York.
Nov [25] He takes part in CBS-TV's "Motown 30: What's Goin' On!" special.
Dec [5] Robinson performs at NARAS "1990 Grammy Legends Show".

1991

Mar [12] Robinson receives the Heritage Award for Outstanding Career Achievments In Music And Entertainment, at the fifth annual Soul Train Awards, held at the Shrine Auditorium, Los Angeles, CA.
Apr [27] He performs at the T.J. Martell Foundation for Leukemia & AIDS Research dinner in New York.
Nov [23] Newly signed to SBK Records after thirty years with Motown, *Double Good Everything* peaks at US #91, taken from the forthcoming ***Double Good Everything***.
[26] Robinson guests on NBC-TV's "The Tonight Show".

1992

Jan [21] He performs at the annual "Midem Festival" at the Palais des Festivals, Cannes, France.
Feb [26] Robinson guests on NBC-TV's "Late Night With David Letterman".
Apr [12] He is honored with the Lifetime Achievement Award at the first Motor City Music Awards, at Detroit's Music Hall.
June [4] His half-sister, Rose Ella Jones, files a suit against Robinson in a Los Angeles Superior Court, claiming that he has cheated her out of royalty payments due from her contribution to his songs written between 1980 and 1988.
Oct [3] Robinson plays at the Celebrity Theatre, Phoenix, AZ, during current US dates.
[23] He embarks on his first British tour in a decade, a 19-date jaunt, at the Derngate, Northampton, Northants., set to end on November 14th at the Villa Marina, Douglas, Isle of Man, including two dates at London's Hammersmith Odeon on the 30th and 31st.
Nov [14] Smokey Robinson & the Miracles' compilation, ***The Greatest Hits***, debuts at its UK #65 peak.
Dec [4-5] Robinson appears at the Trump Taj Mahal, Atlantic City, NJ.

1993

Jan [17] He participates in "An American Reunion : The People's Inaugural Celebration" at the Lincoln Memorial, Washington, DC, during inaugural week.
Apr [27] Robinson sings *Just To See Her* with the star of "Aretha Franklin : Duets", the diva's first TV special, taped at New York's Nederlander Theatre, to benefit the Gay Men's Health Crisis, and set to air on Fox-TV on May 9th.
June [15] He sings *Bring It On Home To Me* with Bryan Adams at the first "Apollo Theatre Hall of Fame" concert, recorded at the landmark theater, and set for broadcast on NBC-TV on August 4th.

1996

Mar [8] While Motown has issued a four-CD/cassette boxed set career anthology, ***The 35th Anniversary Collection*** in February 1994, Robinson has continued to turn up at industry gatherings and tribute events (including one for Ella Fitzgerald at the Universal Amphitheatre, Universal City, CA on January 10th 1995), and contributed vocals to a number of projects, including Tammy Wynette's 1994 duets album, ***Without Walls***, performing on an update of his own *I Second That Emotion* and reprising the same song with Manhattan Transfer for their 1995 set, ***Tonin'***. He has been honored for his support of the United Negro Fund at the second annual VH1 Honors concert on June 22nd 1995, the same year his former colleague, Ronnie White died of leukemia in Detroit's Henry Ford Hospital on August 26th. Robinson now receives the Pioneer In Music Award at the National Association of Black Owned Broadcasters' annual ceremony held in Washington, DC.

TOMMY ROE

1960

Roe (b. May 9, 1943, Atlanta, GA) has formed rock'n'roll combo Tommy Roe & the Satins, while still at Brown High School, Atlanta, in 1958. Heavily influenced by Buddy Holly & the Crickets, they earn their musical spurs playing at school hops and fraternity parties at Georgia University. Offered a recording deal by the local Judd Records, run by Judd Phillips, brother of Sun Records' Sam Phillips, the band now records *Sheila*, written by Roe at the age of 14, which gains local sales, but is not promoted nationally.

1961

Roe graduates from school and works as a technician for the General Electric company, still performing evenings and weekends. Atlanta DJ Paul Drew (with whom the Satins have played many live gigs) recommends him to Felton Jarvis, a producer at ABC/Paramount Records (and later to produce Elvis Presley), who likes his style and self-penned material, and signs him.

1962

June *Sheila* is re-recorded for ABC (originally as a B-side), in an arrangement similar to Holly's *Peggy Sue*, also in line with Roe's Holly-like vocal treatment. When it picks up major airplay in the US, the label advances him $5,000 to quit his GE job and tour to promote it.
Sept [1] *Sheila* tops the US chart for the first of two weeks, and will become Roe's first million seller.
Oct *Sheila* hits UK #2, behind the Tornados' *Telstar*, having aroused interest in Britain by entering the Top 30 simultaneously with Buddy Holly's posthumous *Reminiscing*.
Nov His revival of Robin Luke's *Susie Darlin'* reaches US #35, while ***Sheila*** peaks at US #110.
Dec *Susie Darlin'* makes UK #37.

1963

Mar [9] Roe begins a month-long UK tour at East Ham Granada, London, set to end at the Granada Cinema, East Ham, London, on the 31st, co-headlining with *Let's Dance*-hitmaker Chris Montez. The Beatles are the main support act.
Apr Rush-released in Britain because of the tour, Merle Kilgore's ballad, *The Folk Singer*, hits UK #4.
May *The Folk Singer* peaks at US #84. His next two singles, including a revival of Russ Hamilton's 1957 hit, *Rainbow*, will fail to chart.
Oct *Everybody*, a gospel-style rocker written by Roe on his UK tour, is also released first in Britain, where it hits #9.
Nov [9] Roe begins another UK tour with Freddie & the Dreamers, the Searchers and Brian Poole & the Tremeloes, at the Odeon Cinema, Bolton, Lancs.
Dec *Everybody* hits US #3.

1964

Feb *Come On*, in similar style to *Everybody*, reaches US #36.
May *Carol* makes US #61.
Dec *Party Girl* also peaks at US #61.

1965

Jan [29] After a two-year spell in the US Army reserves, Roe embarks on a 22-date, twice-nightly package tour with Cilla Black, the Fourmost, P.J. Proby, Tommy Quickly and Sounds Incorporated at the ABC Cinema, Croydon, Surrey, set to end on February 21st at the Empire Theatre, Liverpool, Lancs.

1966

July The self-penned *Sweet Pea*, recorded in a chunky, pop style (presaging the "bubblegum" pop phase two years later), hits US #8.
Nov *Hooray For Hazel*, in similar style, hits US #6.
Dec Compilation album, ***Sweet Pea***, rounding up the year's two hits and earlier singles back to *Everybody*, makes US #94.

1967

Feb *It's Now Winter's Day* reaches US #23.
Apr [8] *Sing Along With Me* charts for a week at US #91.
June [10] *Little Miss Sunshine* stops at US #99, while ***It's Now Winter's Day*** peaks at US #159. The following year, Roe will tour in Dick Clark's "Caravan Of Stars".

1969

Mar [7] *Dizzy* is certified gold by the RIAA.
[15] Steve Barri has become Roe's producer, with the intention of resurrecting his "Buddy Holly" sound, but instead the two have concocted *Dizzy*, co-written by Roe with hometown friend Freddy Weller (a member of Paul Revere & the Raiders), while they were on tour together in 1968. Driven by a sledgehammer Hal Blaine drum track, and an off-beat sawing violin arrangement by Jimmie Haskell, the song is a very sophisticated bubblegum blend which begins a four-week run atop the US chart. It is Roe's biggest seller, eventually topping two million copies in the US, with similar sales worldwide.
[25] The RIAA certifies gold sales of *Sheila* and *Sweet Pea*.
May *Heather Honey* makes US #29, as ***Dizzy*** reaches US #25.
June [4] *Dizzy* tops the UK chart for a week, deposing the Beatles' *Get Back*, and being replaced by the Beatles' *The Ballad Of John And Yoko*.
Aug *Heather Honey* reaches UK #24 (his last UK hit).
Oct *Jack And Jill* peaks at US #53.
Dec *Jam Up Jelly Tight* hits US #8.

1970

Jan [19] His fifth and final million-seller, *Jam Up And Jelly Tight* is certified gold by the RIAA.
Feb Compilation album, ***12 In A Roe : A Collection Of Tommy Roe's Greatest Hits***, reaches US #21.
Mar *Stir It Up And Serve It* makes US #50.
July *Pearl* also peaks at US #50.
Oct *We Can Make Music* makes US #49, while ***We Can Make Music*** peaks at US #134.

1971

Oct Following a summer US tour with long-time friends Joe South and Billy Joe Royal, Roe has his last hit for ABC, and his last US Top 30 entry, a revival of Lloyd Price's *Stagger Lee*, makes US #25.

1972

Sept Dissatisfied with West Coast life, and no longer with ABC Records, Roe has returned to Georgia, and, signed to Atlanta-based MGM South, makes US #92 with *Mean Little Woman, Rosalie*. *Working Class Hero*, also on MGM South, will peak at US #97, Roe's final chart single, in May the following May.

1976

Returning to Los Angeles, CA, after four years in Atlanta, Roe records two albums for Monument Records, ***Energy*** and ***Full Bloom***, but neither is commercially successful. He will subsequently drift out of the public eye, but will have success on the US Country charts in 1986 and 1987, signed to Mercury Records.

1991

The Best Of Tommy Roe : Yesterday, Today And Tomorrow is released on Curb. (Roe's career highlight, *Dizzy*, will be successfully revived by the Wonder Stuff and comedian Vic Reeves, topping the UK chart on November 9th.)

KENNY ROGERS

1958

Rogers (b. Kenneth Donald Rogers, Aug. 21, 1938, Houston, TX) earned his first dollars as a six-year-old, singing *You Are My Sunshine* for the residents of a nursing home near his home in Houston, in 1944. While attending Jefferson Davis High School in 1955, Rogers formed doo-wop combo the Scholars, who recorded *Poor Little Doggie* and *Spin The Wheel* for Jimmy Duncan's local Cue label, and *Kangewah*, written by Hollywood gossip columnist Louella Parsons, for Imperial Records. Through his brother Lelan, a promoter for Decca Records, Rogers now meets Ray Doggett (who has recently had success writing *On My Mind Again* for Gale Storm) and records Doggett's *That Crazy Feeling* at ACA Recording Studio in Houston. Originally released on the local Lynn label, Carlton Records picks it up and has Rogers make a major promotional tour billed as Kenny Rogers The First, which includes an appearance on Dick Clark's ABC-TV show, "American Bandstand". 19-year-old Rogers also marries his first wife, Janice, on May 15th.

1959

Sept Having cut further Carlton singles concurrently with releases on Ken-Lee, a label set up with brother Lelan, Rogers joins the jazz-styled Bobby Doyle Trio (its front man is a blind pianist) as a stand-up bassist and singer. With Janice filing for divorce on January 26th 1960, 22-year-old Rogers will marry a second time, to Jean Laverne Massey in October. The following year, the Bobby Doyle Trio tours the US extensively, frequently as support to the Kirby Stone Four and will begin work in New York, NY on its first album for CBS/Columbia in March 1962, resulting in the July release of ***In A Most Unusual Way***.

1965

June Having married for a third time on October 22nd 1963 (to Margo Gladys Anderson), Rogers cuts the solo *Take Life In Stride* for Mercury.

[24] With Don Russell, a fellow Bobby Doyle member, and Anthony Navarro, Rogers opens the Act Three club on Main Street in Houston, where the trio will play regularly.

Dec Rogers and Russell decide not to renew their license for the club.

1966

Having spent a short period with four-part harmony group the Lively Ones (Rogers, Russell, Paula Chase and Paul Mussarra), and working at the Houstonaire supper club, Rogers joins the New Christy Minstrels, earning $750 a week, and records one album with the group, ***New Kick! (The New Christy Minstrels Sing The Hits Of Today And Tomorrow)***.

1967

July Ken Kragen, co-manager of the Smothers Brothers and co-producer of their CBS-TV show "The Smothers Brothers' Comedy Hour", sees the group at Ledbetter's in Los Angeles, CA, and signs them to a management deal.

[10] The contracts of Rogers and fellow Minstrels Mike Settle, Terry Williams (his father was Tommy Dorsey's first-chair trombonist and vocalist) and Thelma Camacho expire.

[11] The start recording a debut album as the First Edition, for Reprise Records, having auditioned for producer Jimmy Bowen during their time with the Minstrels.

Nov [5] The band makes its first appearance on CBS-TV's "The Smothers Brothers Comedy Hour".

Dec ***The First Edition*** is released.

1968

Mar *Just Dropped In (To See What Condition My Condition Was In)*, with a heavy-rock arrangement and mock-"psychedelic" lyric, written by Mickey Newbury (and rejected by Jerry Lee Lewis), hits US #5, while their debut album, ***The First Edition***, peaks at US #118.

1969

Jan Mary Arnold replaces Camacho in the First Edition. (Karen Carpenter also auditioned for the slot.)

Mar *But You Know I Love You*, written by Settle in a more country style, reaches US #19.

Apr ***The First Edition '69*** peaks at US #164.

Aug *Ruby, Don't Take Your Love To Town*, concerning a disabled Korean War veteran, written several years earlier by country singer, Mel Tillis, hits US #6. Highlighting Rogers' distinctive solo vocal, it credits the group for the first time as Kenny Rogers & the First Edition.

Nov *Ruben James*, in similar style to *Ruby*, makes US #26.

Dec *Ruby, Don't Take Your Love To Town* hits UK #2 for five weeks, behind Rolf Harris' *Two Little Boys*, while ***Ruby, Don't Take Your Love To Town*** (the first album credited to the extended group name) reaches US #48.

1970

Feb *Something's Burning*, penned by Mac Davis, reaches US #11 and hits UK #8.

June ***Something's Burning***, with Settle now replaced by Kin Vassy, makes US #26.

Aug *Tell It All Brother* reaches US #17.

Nov *Heed The Call* makes US #33.

Dec Featuring both the previous hit singles, ***Tell It All Brother*** peaks at US #61.

1971

Apr *Someone Who Cares*, from the James Caan/Katharine Ross film "Fools", peaks at US #51 as the group's compilation album, ***Greatest Hits***, makes US #57.

July The gospel-flavored, Rogers-penned *Take My Hand* peaks at US #91.

Sept Canadian-produced syndicated TV program, "Rollin' On The River", starring the First Edition, airs on US TV. Filmed in a riverboat setting, it features several music guests, including Kris Kristofferson, Mac Davis and B.J. Thomas.

Oct ***Transition*** peaks at US #155.

1972

Apr *School Teacher*, with Vassy on lead vocal, peaks at US #91, taken from the double set, ***The Ballad Of Calico***, a concept album concerning the 1889 mining town of Calico, CA, which makes US #118. (The compilation album, ***Greatest Hits***, will be certified gold more than two years after its release on March 27th the following year, before the First Edition splits in 1974, leaving Rogers $65,000 in debt.)

1975

Mar Newly signed as solo artist to United Artists, his label debut, *Love Lifted Me*, peaks at US #97 taken from ***Love Lifted Me***.

1977

June [18] Story-telling country smash, *Lucille*, written by Roger Bowling and Hal Bynum, hits US #5, having become his first US Country chart-topper on April 2nd and tops the UK chart.

[22] *Lucille* is certified gold by the RIAA.

June [25] His sophomore solo album, ***Kenny Rogers***, reaches US #30.

July [2] ***Kenny Rogers*** reaches UK #14.

Aug [10] ***Kenny Rogers*** is ratified gold by the RIAA.

Sept [24] *Daytime Friends* makes UK #39.

Oct [1] The country-pop *Daytime Friends* reaches US #28, while its parent album, ***Daytime Friends***, peaks at US #39. Rogers gets married for the fourth time, to Marianne Gordon, an actress on the US TV show "Hee Haw". He also has his first book, **Making It With Music**, co-authored with Len Epand, published.

Nov Rogers begins a British concert tour with UA label-mate Crystal Gayle.

Dec [15] ***Daytime Friends*** is certified gold by the RIAA.

1978

Jan Ballad *Sweet Music Man* peaks at US #44.

[16] He collects the Favorite Single, Country trophy (for *Lucille*), at the fifth annual American Music Awards, held at the Civic Auditorium, Santa Monica, CA.

Feb [23] Rogers wins Best Country Vocal Performance, Male category for *Lucille*, at the 20th annual Grammy Awards, his first such nod.

Apr ***Ten Years Of Gold***, one side featuring re-recorded solo versions of the First Edition hits, reaches US #33 during a 103-week chart run.

July *Love Or Something Like It* reaches US #32.

[20] ***Ten Years Of Gold*** is certified gold by the RIAA.

Sept ***Love Or Something Like It*** makes US #53, confirmed gold on the 15th.

1979

Jan [12] He wins the Favorite Male Artist, Country, and Favorite Album, Country categories, at the sixth annual American Music Awards, held again at the Santa Monica Civic Auditorium.

Feb [27] The still-rising album ***The Gambler*** is certified platinum by the RIAA.

Mar *The Gambler* reaches US #16, while its parent set, ***The Gambler***, rolls to US #12.

June ***Classics***, an album of duets between Rogers and country singer, Dottie West, makes US #86.

July Steve Gibb-penned ballad, *She Believes In Me*, taken from ***The Gambler***, hits US #5 and peaks at UK #42.

[2] ***Classics*** is confirmed gold by the RIAA.

Aug [6] *She Believes In Me* is certified gold by the RIAA.

[16] Rogers performs at the Ohio State Fair, OH, to 80,000 fans.

Sept [14] "Kenny Rogers Day" is proclaimed in Los Angeles, as Rogers receives a star on the Hollywood Walk of Fame.

Nov Ballad *You Decorated My Life* hits US #7, while the parent album, ***Kenny***, hits US #3, subsequently becoming another million seller. Rogers' footprints are immortalized in cement at the Country Palace in Toledo, OH.

[12] Rogers begins filming "The Gambler", a TV movie based on the song of the same title, which marks his acting debut.

Dec A UK-only compilation, ***The Kenny Rogers Singles Album***, makes #12. CBS-TV airs the documentary "Kenny Rogers And The American Cowboy".

1980

Jan ***Every Time Two Fools Collide***, another duetted set with West, peaks at US #186.

[16] ***Kenny*** is certified platinum by the RIAA.

[18] He nabs the Favorite Male Artist, Country, and Favorite Album, Country categories, at the seventh annual American Music Awards, held at the ABC-TV Studios, Hollywood, CA.

Feb Story-telling *Coward Of The County*, taken from ***Kenny***, hits US #3.

[16] *Coward Of The County* tops the UK chart for the first of two weeks.

[27] Rogers wins his second Grammy Award for Best Country Vocal Performance, Male, for *The Gambler* at the 22nd annual ceremony.

Mar [7] *Coward Of The County* is certified gold by the RIAA.

Apr TV movie "The Gambler" airs on CBS-TV.

May *Don't Fall In Love With A Dreamer*, a duet with Kim Carnes, hits US #4. It is taken from **Gideon**, an entirely Carnes/Dave Ellingson penned set, co-produced by Larry Butler and Rogers, which reaches US #12. Meanwhile, ***Kenny*** hits UK #7.

[28] ***Gideon*** is confirmed platinum by the RIAA.

Aug *Love The World Away* reaches US #14.

Nov [15] Ballad *Lady*, penned by Lionel Richie, begins a six-week run atop the US chart, selling over one million units, and also hits #1 on the US R&B, C&W and Adult Contemporary charts. It will also reach UK #12, and is Rogers' first release on the Liberty label (renamed from United Artists).

[25] *Lady* is certified gold by the RIAA.

Dec Rogers shares the Top Male Vocalist Of 1980 award with Michael Jackson in **Record World** magazine.

[2] Still climbing the US survey, ***Kenny Rogers' Greatest Hits*** is certified platinum by the RIAA.

[13] Compilation album, ***Kenny Rogers' Greatest Hits***, of hit singles up to *Lady*, tops the US chart for the first of two weeks, staying charted for 181 weeks.

1981

Jan [30] He wins the Favorite Male Artist, Pop/Rock, Favorite Male Artist, Country, Favorite Album, Country, and Favorite Single, Country categories, at the eighth annual American Music Awards, held again at the ABC-TV studios, Hollywood.

Feb [7] A UK-only compilation ***Lady***, makes UK #40.

June *What Are We Doin' In Love*, a duet with West, reaches US #14.

Aug Written by Rick Christian, *I Don't Need You* hits

US #3, taken from ***Share Your Love***, produced by Richie, which also hits US #3. Rogers also stars in the TV movie, "Coward Of The County", in which he plays a Southern preacher.
[17] Rogers headlines at a Nassau Veterans Memorial Coliseum, Uniondale, NY, benefit concert for singer Harry Chapin, killed one month earlier in a car crash.
[28] ***Share Your Love*** is certified platinum by the RIAA.
Oct *Share Your Love With Me*, from his recent album, reaches US #14.
Dec [12] *Blaze Of Glory*, again from the album, peaks at US #66, while the self-produced seasonal ***Christmas*** makes US #34.

1982

Jan [5] ***Christmas*** is confirmed platinum by the RIAA.
[25] He collects the Favorite Album, Country, Favorite Album, Pop/Rock, and Favorite Male Artist, Pop/Rock trophies, at the ninth annual American Music Awards, held at the Shrine Auditorium, Los Angeles.
Mar [6] *Through The Years*, from ***Share Your Love***, reaches US #13.
Aug The film "Six Pack", starring Rogers, opens in US theaters.
[28] From the movie, *Love Will Turn You Around* reaches US #13 (and becomes his tenth US Country chart-topper).
[30] Still-climbing ***Love Will Turn Your Around*** is certified gold by the RIAA.
Sept [18] ***Love Will Turn You Around***, peaks at US #34.
Nov [13] *A Love Song* peaks at US #47.
[23] Rogers and his wife Marianne present the first World Hunger Media Awards at the UN in New York.
Dec ***Christmas*** re-charts at US #149, passing the platinum sales mark.

1983

Jan [17] He collects the Favorite Single, Country, and Favorite Male Artist, Country trophies, at the tenth annual American Music Awards, again held at the Shrine Auditorium. He is also presented with the Special Award Of Merit.
Feb He embarks on a US tour at the Special Events Center, University of New Mexico, Albuquerque, NM.
Mar Rogers' duet with Sheena Easton on their revival of Bob Seger's *We've Got Tonight* hits US #6 and UK #28.
Apr ***We've Got Tonight***, variously helmed by David Foster, Lionel Richie, Randy Goodrum and others, reaches US #27. This is his last new material for Liberty, as he signs to RCA Records in a deal reportedly worth more than $20 million.
[14] ***We've Got Tonight*** is certified gold by the RIAA.
June *All My Life*, from ***We've Got Tonight***, makes US #37.
Aug *Scarlet Fever*, also from the album, and Rogers' last Liberty single, peaks at US #94.
Sept [18] Kenny Rogers' special airs on HBO-TV.
Oct [29] *Islands In The Stream*, a duet with Dolly Parton, written by the Bee Gees, tops the US chart and becomes the only platinum single of the year. It will also nab the Vocal Duet Of The Year and Single Record Of The Year categories at the forthcoming Academy Of Country Music Awards. The single is taken from his debut RCA album ***Eyes That See In The Dark***, co-produced and co-written by Barry Gibb, which hits US #6 and makes UK #53 with its title track, *Eyes That See In The Dark*, stopping at UK #61. During the month, Rogers and Parton also host the annual CMA Awards.
[31] ***Eyes That See In The Dark*** is certified platinum by the RIAA.
Nov *Islands In The Stream* hits UK #7. The TV movie, "The Gambler II", starring Rogers, Bruce Boxleitner and Linda Evans, airs on US TV.
Dec [7] *Islands In The Stream* is certified gold by the RIAA with the still-climbing ***20 Greatest Hits*** confirmed platinum on the 21st.

1984

Jan A US Liberty compilation, ***20 Greatest Hits***, makes US #22.
[16] He wins Favorite Single, Country category (with Parton) for *Islands In The Stream*, at the 11th annual American Music Awards, held at the Shrine Auditorium.
Mar *This Woman*, from ***Eyes That See In The Dark***, reaches US #23.
May Title track, *Eyes That See In The Dark*, peaks at US #79.
June Liberty album, ***Duets***, compiling Rogers' hits with Sheena Easton and Kim Carnes with eight cuts duetted with Dottie West, makes US #85.
Oct ***What About Me?*** charts at US #31 and makes UK #97.
Nov *What About Me?*, sung in trio with Kim Carnes and James Ingram, reaches US #15.
Dec [2] Rogers and Dolly Parton's "A Christmas To Remember" special airs on US TV. The duo's album of seasonal duets, ***Once Upon A Christmas***, produced by David Foster, reaches US #31, while the extracted *The Greatest Gift Of All* makes US #81.
[3] ***What About Me*** is certified platinum by the RIAA.

1985

Jan [28] Following his win in the Favorite Single, Country category again, for *Islands In The Stream*, at the 12th annual American Music Awards, held at the Shrine Auditorium (the first time that the same disc has won twice), and in the Favorite Male Artist, Country, and Favorite Album, Country categories, Rogers takes part in the recording of USA For Africa's *We Are The World* in Los Angeles, the session having been largely co-ordinated by his manager Ken Kragen, after initial approaches by Harry Belafonte. The disc will top the US and UK charts, selling several million worldwide.
Feb *Crazy* makes US #79, as Rogers and Parton begin a joint US tour.
May ***Love Is What We Make It***, a Liberty compilation of previously unreleased material, makes US #145.
June Rogers/Parton duet, *Real Love*, the title cut from Parton's new album, peaks at US #91.
Aug A UK TV-promoted compilation album, the 20-track ***The Kenny Rogers Story***, on Liberty, hits UK #4.
Oct ***The Heart Of The Matter*** enters the US chart, set to make #51.
Nov [26] Rogers guests on NBC-TV's "Late Night With David Letterman".
Dec *Morning Desire* peaks at US #72, his last Hot 100 chart placing of the decade.
[5] ***Heart Of The Matter*** is certified gold by the RIAA.

1987

Jan ***They Don't Make Them Like They Used To***, largely produced by Jay Graydon, makes US #137.
Sept [12] *Make No Mistake, She's Mine*, a duet with country singer Ronnie Milsap, tops the US Country chart for a week, his 20th Country chart-topper, and his last.
Oct ***I Prefer The Moonlight***, a strictly country set, stops at US #163.

1988

Mar [2] Rogers wins Best Country Vocal Performance, Duet, for *Make No Mistake, She's Mine*, with Ronnie Milsap, at the 30th annual Grammy Awards.

1989

June Rogers has returned to Reprise and makes US #141 with his label solo debut, the Jim Ed Norman-produced ***Something Inside So Strong***, featuring a further duet with Parton on a cover of Mickey & Sylvia's *Love Is Strange*, and pairings with Gladys Knight, Anne Murray and Holly Dunn.
Sept [10] NBC-TV broadcasts the first annual "International Very Special Arts Festival" from the lawn of the White House, celebrating the accomplishments of physically and mentally handicapped artists from around the world. In addition to Rogers, other performers include U2, Mikhail Baryshnikov, Lauren Bacall and Michael Douglas.
Oct [25] The RIAA certifies two million sales of ***Once Upon A Christmas***.
Dec [5-11] Rogers plays seven sellout shows with support acts the Oak Ridge Boys and Garth Brooks, at the Westbury Music Fair, Westbury, NY, grossing $715,641.

1990

Jan [6] His third yuletide album, ***Christmas In America***, makes US #119.
Mar [3] He performs the first-ever concert at the Suncoast Dome, St. Petersburg, FL, selling out the 29,336 seater venue.
[27] ***Something Inside So Strong*** is certified gold by the RIAA.
May [5] He shares a bill with Dolly Parton at the Charlotte Coliseum, Charlotte, NC.
June [26] "Great Video Hits" is certified gold by the RIAA.
July [21] Rogers performs at the Goodwill Games opening ceremonies in Seattle, WA.
Nov [29] His "Gathering Around The Tree With Kenny" Christmas shows, with Baillie & the Boys and Jennifer McCarter & the McCarter Sisters, begin a six-date sellout stint at the Fox Theatre, Detroit, MI. (Further shows at the Westbury and Valley Forge Music Fairs will also be sold out.)

1991

Feb [10] Rogers joins with nearly 100 celebrities in Burbank, CA, to record *Voices That Care*, a David Foster and fiancée Linda Thompson Jenner composed-and-organized charity record, to benefit the American Red Cross Gulf Crisis Fund.
Mar [16] He takes part in the American Music Awards Concert Series, at the Yokohama Arena, Yokohama, Japan.
Apr [14] Rogers guests on ABC-TV's "Welcome Home, America!"
[22] He takes part in a benefit concert at Nashville's Municipal Auditorium for the families of Reba McEntire's band and crew, who have recently perished in a plane crash.
Nov [3-4] NBC-TV airs "The Gambler Returns : The Luck Of The Draw".
[24] Rogers takes part in the premiere of NBC-TV's prime-time country music show, "Hot Country Nights".
Dec [15-18] He takes his festive show, this year titled "Christmas In America", to the Valley Forge Music Fair, Devon, PA, for five sellout shows with Mark Chestnutt and the McCarters in support.

1992

Feb [29] Rogers acts as grand marshal of the Krewe of Endymion's 1992 parade at the Superdome, New Orleans, LA.
Apr [1] He participates in the silver anniversary of the County Music Hall of Fame from the Grand Ole Opry, Nashville. (CBS-TV will air the proceedings on May 20th.)
Sept [17] A 13-part documentary, "The Real West", hosted by Rogers, premieres on US cable-web A&E.
Nov [21] In the midst of a three-month US tour supporting his latest country album ***Back Home Again***, co-produced by Jim Ed Norman, Rogers plays at the Area Landmark Theatre, Syracuse, NY, with Emmylou Harris.
Dec Miami-based Clucker's Wood Roasted Chicken Inc. seeks $10 million in punitive damages against Fort Lauderdale-based Roasters Inc, which developed the Kenny Rogers Roasters Wood Roasted Chicken chain, claiming it stole its menu, recipe and layout.
[18] Kenny Rogers' "Christmas In The Ozarks", with Boyz II Men, Garth Brooks and Trisha Yearwood, airs on CBS-TV. (His Christmas show plays in the traditional venues in Detroit, Westbury and Devon.)

1993

Jan [6] ***Christmas In America*** is certified gold by the RIAA.
[20] Rogers hosts the American Music Awards 20th Anniversary show held at the Shrine Auditorium.
[13] He performs on CBS-TV's "A Country Music Celebration", from the Grand Ole Opry.
Feb [11] As Rogers confirms rumors of an impending divorce, the tabloid syndicated TV show "A Current Affair" broadcasts the alleged dirty phone-call tapes between Rogers and a number of women - Lori Walker, Sue Ann Lenderman and Lisa Applewhite - who filed a suit against him in the autumn of 1992 alleging that Rogers and his stockbroker coaxed them into playing kinky phone sex games and recorded sexually explicit messages on a private 1-800 number. The tabloid print media also makes hay of the story with headlines including "Kenny Rogers In Love Nest With Sexy Blonde Who Wrecked His Marriage", "Kenny Rogers Pawed Me And Asked Me To Make Dirty Phone Calls" and "Rogers Sexually Assaulted Me In His Hotel Suite". Spokesman for Rogers, Cheryl Kagen, responding for her client who is fighting the suit, says the singer "finds it disheartening that three consenting adults would take what were clearly private conversations and place them in the public arena".
[13-14] Rogers grosses $185,501 from two concerts at the Circle Star Theatre, San Carlos, CA, during current US dates.
[28] CBS-TV's "Rio Diablo" movie with Rogers, Travis Tritt and Naomi Judd, is broadcast.
Apr [3] He hosts CBS-TV's "11th Annual Country Showdown".
[20] Newly signed to Giant Records, Rogers' ***If Only My Heart Had A Voice*** is released, co-produced by James Stroud and Larry Butler.
May [22] Rogers guest stars on CBS TV's "Dr. Quinn - Medicine Woman".
Oct [1] CBS-TV airs "A Day In The Life Of Country Music", a documentary featuring several country artists, including Rogers, and what they did on May 7th.
[2] Compilation ***Daytime Friends - The Very Best Of Kenny Rogers*** reaches UK #16.

1994

Jan [7] Rogers performs at the King Center for the Performing Arts, Brevard Community College, Melbourne, FL, at the start of another year of regular live work.
Feb [11] Following an appearance on "The Tonight Show" on the 7th, Rogers guests on NBC-TV's "MacShayne : Winner Takes All".
July [15-16] Rogers plays at the Valley Forge Music Fair, Devon, PA, during summer dates.
Sept [2] A woman dressed as a chicken tries to throw a pie in Rogers' face during the Walworth County Fair in Elkhorn, WI, protesting the planned opening of the Kenny Rogers Roasters franchise.
Dec [2-4] Rogers' annual Christmas show now plays at the Fox Theatre. Detroit, MI.

1995

Jan [14] Having recently released a torch album of ballad standards, ***Time Piece***, produced by David Foster, He plays the opening performance at the new 6,000 seat Star of the Desert Arena at Buffalo's Bill Resort, Jean, near Las Vegas, NV.
Apr [13] He christens his new $13 million Showboat Branson Belle in Branson, MO.
Aug [18] Rogers and QVC announce the shopping channel's "Vote For Love Sweepstakes". Election results show that *Lady* is the number one love song of all time. The event will also spawn the network's music label onQ's first release, the twin-CD Rogers collection ***Vote For Love***, available only by mail-order from QVC the following January.
Nov [13] ***20 Great Years*** is certified gold by the RIAA.
Dec [19] Rogers' Christmas show plays at the Municipal Auditorium, Sioux City, IA.

1996

June He signs a new label deal with Nashville-based Magnatone Records.

THE ROLLING STONES

Mick Jagger (vocals, harmonica); **Keith Richard** (rhythm guitar); **Brian Jones** (lead guitar); **Bill Wyman** (bass); **Charlie Watts** (drums)

1960

Jagger (b. Michael Phillip Jagger, July 26, 1943, Dartford, Kent), a student at the London School of Economics and Richard (b. Keith Richards, Dec. 18, 1943, Dartford), who has been part of a choir that sang Handel's "Messiah" at Westminster Abbey, in the presence of H.R.H. Queen Elizabeth II, and is attending Sidcup Art School, renew their acquaintance, accidentally meeting on a train. They had first met in February 1951, while both were at Maypole County Primary School in Wilmington, Kent, but had since lost contact. The friendship is rekindled when they discover a joint love of R&B, and a passion for records on the Chess label, particularly Chuck Berry. Richard and Jagger subsequently join R&B group, Little Boy Blue & the Blue Boys, with Dick Taylor, Bob Beckwith and Allen Etherington. (Richard's only other job, working for the Post Office, will last for four days in December the following year, using his wages to buy his mother a record.)

1962

Mar [17] Alexis Korner's Blues Incorporated, featuring Korner on guitar, Dave Stevens on piano, Andy Hoogenboom on bass, Cyril Davies on harmonica, Dick Heckstall-Smith on tenor sax and Charlie Watts (b. Charles Watts, June 2, 1941, Islington, London) on drums, begins a regular Saturday night gig at the Ealing Jazz club, a residency which will often feature Jones (b. Lewis Brian Hopkin-Jones, Feb. 28, 1942, Cheltenham, Gloucs.). (After a brief spell in hometown band, the Ramrods, Jones, an all-round musician who has met Korner at a concert in Cheltenham, has moved to London and found a job in a department store, and under the alias of Elmo Lewis, advertised in **Jazz News** for R&B musicians to form a band. Pianist Ian Stewart answers the ad, and begins to rehearse with Jones. Through Stewart, Jones meets singer, Andy Wren, and guitarist, Geoff Bradford.)
Apr [7] Jagger, Richard and Dick Taylor bump into Jones, now playing in his own band with Stewart, Bradford and singer P.P. Bond (later to find success with Manfred Mann as Paul Jones), again at the Ealing Jazz Club. Jagger and Richard become friendly with Jones, and the nucleus of a new outfit is formed, comprising Jagger, Richard, Jones, Stewart, Bradford and Taylor, with a variety of drummers sitting in. Jagger also becomes vocalist with Blues Incorporated and plays with the group on his nights off from Alexis Korner's troupe.
June Tony Chapman, drummer with the Cliftons, auditions for the newly-named Rollin' Stones, taking their name from a Muddy Waters song.
July Blues Incorporated is booked to appear on BBC Radio's "Jazz Club", broadcast live on Thursday evenings, but the BBC deems Jagger unsuitable as a vocalist and Long John Baldry takes his place. Blues Incorporated, however, needs a group to sub for its Thursday night Marquee club sessions and Jagger and cohorts eagerly accept the gig.
[12] The Rollin' Stones, comprising Jagger, Richard, Jones, Taylor, and Stewart, with future Kink Mick Avory on drums, make their debut at the Marquee Jazz club.
Oct [27] The group, comprising Jagger, Richard, Jones, Stewart and Chapman, makes its first studio recordings, at Curly Clayton Studios in Highbury, London, taping covers of Muddy Waters' *Soon Forgotten*, Jimmy Reed's *Close Together* and Bo Diddley's *You Can't Judge A Book (By Looking At The Cover)*, which are submitted to record companies with little success.
Dec [7] Wyman (b. William Perks, Oct. 24, 1936, Lewisham, London), a former Royal Air Force AC1 Air Craftsman First Class, and in the Cliftons with Chapman, auditions for the Stones at the Wetherby Arms at World's End in Chelsea, London.
[15] Wyman makes his debut with the group at the youth club, Church Hall, Putney, London.

1963

Jan [14] Jagger, Richard, Jones, Wyman, Stewart and new recruit Watts, a designer with a Regent Street ad agency, who has been a regular drummer with Blues Incorporated and approached several times to join the fledgling Stones, but resisted for financial security, now replaces Chapman, and the new line-up plays together for the first time at the Flamingo Jazz club in Soho, London.
[28] The Stones record five tracks at IBC studios with engineer, Glyn Johns.
Feb [24] They begin a Sunday residency at the Station Hotel, Richmond, Surrey, earning £24 and attracting an audience of 66.
Mar [3] The Stones now start a weekly daytime residency at Studio 51, Ken Colyer Club, London, which will continue until September 23rd.
Apr [14] The group begins to attract large audiences at the Crawdaddy club and receives its first press write-up in the **Richmond & Twickenham Times** by Barry May. Tonight's gig is attended by members of the Beatles.
[23] The band, without Wyman and Watts, auditions for BBC Radio's "Jazz Club" program.
[28] Andrew Oldham, age 19, an ex-PR man for the Beatles, travels to Richmond with business associate Eric Easton to see the band, on the recommendation of **Record Mirror** journalist, Peter Jones.
May [1] Oldham and Easton sign a management contract with the group to their newly formed Impact Sound company, effective May 6th. The band becomes the Rolling Stones (adding the "g") at Oldham's insistence. (Stewart, pushed to the back-seat role of roadie and backing musician in the studio, with his straight image seen by Oldham to be at odds with the style he intends to create for the group, becomes an integral part of the band, unseen by the public, and is known as the sixth Stone until his death in 1985.)
[4] They play at a **News Of The World** charity gala in Battersea Park, London.
[9] They sign a three-year recording contract with Impact, which signs a tape/lease agreement with Decca Records, which has recently rejected the Beatles.
[10] The group enters Olympic Sound Studio to record an obscure Chuck Berry song, *Come On*. Decca rejects the recording as "dreadful".
[11] **New Record Mirror** writer, and R&B fan, Norman Jopling, writes a piece entitled "The Rolling Stones - Genuine R&B".
June [7] The group's first single, the re-recorded *Come On*, is released in the UK. The line "Some stupid jerk" is altered to "Some stupid guy" to ensure radio play.
[20] They begin a four-week Thursday residence at the Scene club, London.
July [7] The band makes its TV debut on ITV's "Thank Your Lucky Stars", coerced into wearing uniform check velvet collared jackets with matching ties and trousers, performing *Come On*.
[19] A performance at the coming-out party of Lord and Lady Killernan's daughter, Roxanna, in Hastings, Sussex, is cancelled when Jones falls ill on the way to the booking.
[20] The group makes its ballroom bow at the Corn Exchange, Wisbech, Cambs.
Aug [11] They play at the third "National Jazz & Blues Festival" at the Athletic Grounds, Richmond.
[28] The band makes its debut on ITV's "Ready Steady, Go!"
Sept [7] *Come On* reaches UK #21.
[10] With the Rolling Stones unable to decide on a

second single, a chance meeting between Oldham and his former employers, the Beatles' John Lennon and Paul McCartney, who have just left the Variety Club lunch, leads to their visiting the Studio 51 jazz club, where the Stones are rehearsing. The duo play part of a new song they have written, *I Wanna Be Your Man*, and within minutes complete the rest of the number, putting the Stones in the rare and privileged position of recording an unreleased Lennon/McCartney composition.
[15] The band plays at the "Great Pop Prom" at London's Royal Albert Hall.
[20] *Poison Ivy*, the scheduled follow-up to *Come On*, and allocated catalog number F11742, is withdrawn.
[29] The group starts its first British tour, a 32-date package supporting the Everly Brothers and Bo Diddley at London's New Victoria Theatre. The trek, with Little Richard joining midway through, will end on November 3rd at London's Hammersmith Odeon.
Oct [5] BBC Radio's "Saturday Club", on which Jones, Wyman and Watts back Bo Diddley, airs.
Nov [17] Jagger and Richard meet Gene Pitney at the recording of ITV's "Thank Your Lucky Stars", and present him with *That Girl Belongs To Yesterday*, which hits the US and UK charts, and marks the beginning of a songwriting partnership which will provide other artists with songs, though it will be almost a year before they write an original for the Stones.
Dec [20] The group is voted Sixth Best British Vocal Group in **New Musical Express** annual readers' poll.
[28] *I Wanna Be Your Man* (now also sung by Ringo on ***With The Beatles***) reaches UK #12, in a hard-driving R&B style, with whining steel guitar.

1964

Jan [2] The Stones sing *I Wanna Be Your Man* on the first edition of BBC-TV's "Top Of The Pops".
[6] The band begins its second UK tour, its first as bill-toppers, a 14-date "Group Scene 1964" package, supported by the Ronettes, Marty Wilde, the Swinging Blue Jeans, Dave Berry & the Cruisers, the Cheynes and compere Al Paige, at the Granada Theatre, Harrow-on-the-Hill, Middx., set to end on the 27th at the Colston Hall, Bristol, Somerset. The Stones are now attracting a major following with screaming fans and press reports of their wild concerts (the **New Musical Express** describes the group as a "caveman-like quintet"). The image of long-haired tearaways becomes compounded as an antidote to the Beatles clean showbiz image.
Feb [1] The group plays at the "Valentine Charity Pop Show" at the Royal Albert Hall, on a bill with Dusty Springfield, the Swinging Blue Jeans and Brian Poole & the Tremeloes.
[8] They begin another UK concert series, a 28-date package with John Leyton, Mike Berry, Jet Harris, Billie Davis, the Innocents, Don Spencer, the LeRoys and Billy Boyle, at the Regal Theatre, Edmonton, London, set to close on March 7th at the Winter Gardens, Morecambe, Lancs.
Mar [21] The group's revision of Buddy Holly's *Not Fade Away*, in Bo Diddley style, with Phil Spector lending a hand on maracas and co-writing the B-side, *Little By Little*, with Jagger, hits UK #3.
Apr [8] They cause a minor riot at the "Ready Steady, Go! Mad Mod Ball" before an audience of 8,000, at the Empire Pool, Wembley.
[22] The **Daily Mirror** reports that the president of the National Federation of Hairdressers is offering a free haircut to the next group to reach #1, claiming the Rolling Stones are the worst of the lot - "one of them looks as if he's got a feather duster on his head".
[26] The Rolling Stones take part in the annual "**New Musical Express** Poll Winners Concert" at the Empire Pool, Wembley.
May [2] Released with 100,000 advance orders, their debut album, ***The Rolling Stones***, tops the UK chart, replacing ***With The Beatles*** (the first time in just under a year that the Beatles are not at #1). Oldham makes the first of many marketing ploys by leaving the group's name off the album's front cover, unheard of in the history of record releases. The group also makes its first appearance on the US chart, at #98, with *Not Fade Away*.
[11] In the midst of another UK tour, the group is refused lunch at the Grand Hotel, Bristol, Somerset, where they are staying, because they are not wearing jackets and ties.
[27] 11 boys are suspended at a school in Coventry, Warks., for having Mick Jagger haircuts.
[31] The group takes part in the "Pop Hit Parade" concert at the Empire Pool, Wembley.
June [1] The Stones arrive at Kennedy airport, New York, on BA flight 505, for their first US tour.
[2] They make their US TV debut on "The Les Crane Show".
[5] A nine-date US tour opens at the Swing Auditorium in San Bernardino, CA, their first concert outside Britain. The visit will end on June 20th at Carnegie Hall, New York.
[10-11] The Stones record at Chess studios in Chicago, IL, where they meet Chuck Berry, Muddy Waters and Willie Dixon.
[13] The group appears on ABC-TV's "The Hollywood Palace", performing *I Just Wanna Make Love To You*, following Bertha the Elephant and her daughter Tina, and is subsequently subjected to quips from host Dean Martin. After comic acrobat Larry Griswold's act, Martin tells the audience: "That's the father of the Rolling Stones; he's been trying to kill himself ever since." He also comments "They're challenging the Beatles to a hair-pulling contest. I could swear Jackie Coogan and Skippy were in that group somewhere."
[22] On the day they return from the US tour, they play at a Commemoration Ball at Magdalen College, Oxford, Oxon, fulfilling an engagement booked a year earlier.
July [4] The Stones appear on BBC-TV's "Juke Box Jury", the only time the show has five panelists rather than four, and cause controversy over their languid comments and appearance.
[18] Their cover of the Valentinos' *It's All Over Now*, recorded at Chess Studios, tops the UK chart. With assistance from engineer Ron Malo, the Rolling Stones begin to define a harder rock sound which will become their trademark. *Not Fade Away* peaks at US #48.
[24] They cause a riot at Blackpool's Empress Ballroom, during a series of UK dates. 30 fans and two policemen are treated in hospital, with four fans appearing in court the following day, charged with assault and carrying offensive weapons.
Aug [8] *Tell Me (You're Coming Back)* reaches US #24.
[10] Jagger is fined £32 in Liverpool, Lancs., for driving without insurance and breaking the speed limit. His solicitor explains "Mr. Jagger was on an errand of mercy visiting two fans injured in a car crash."
[22] US-only released ***England's Newest Hit Makers - The Rolling Stones***, the UK debut album with the added single, *Not Fade Away*, reaches US #11.
Sept [5] The group begins a 31-date, twice-nightly UK tour with Inez & Charlie Foxx, the Mojos, Mike Berry, Billie Davis and Simon Scott, at London's Finsbury Park Astoria, set to end on October 11th at the Hippodrome, Brighton, Sussex.
[11] 16-year-old Laurie Yarham wins the Mick Jagger impersonation contest at a concert at the Town Hall, Greenwich, London, only to reveal his true identity - Jagger's younger brother, Chris.
[19] Jagger's girlfriend, Marianne Faithfull, hits UK #9 with the Jagger and Richard-penned, *As Tears Go By*, while *It's All Over Now* reaches US #26.
Oct [9] The Stones announce the cancellation of their South African tour, complying with the wishes of the Musicians' Union and its opposition to apartheid.
[14] Watts and Shirley Ann Shepherd are married by Registrar Mr. J.H. Hinkins in Bradford, Yorks.
[20] They play at the Olympia Theatre, Paris, France, as 150 are arrested for damage caused both inside and outside the venue.
[24] The Stones begin their second US tour with two shows at New York's Academy Of Music, set to close on November 15th at the Arie Crown Theatre, McCormick Place, Chicago, IL.
[25] The group makes its debut on CBS-TV's "The Ed Sullivan Show". After riotous scenes in the audience, Sullivan announces: "I promise you they'll never be back on our show. It took me 17 years to build this *shew*; I'm not going to have it destroyed in a matter of weeks."
[28-29] The Stones record the "TAMI Show" (Teen Age Music International Show) at the Civic Auditorium in Santa Monica, CA, performing *Reelin' And Rockin'*, *Time Is On My Side* and *It's All Over Now*, an event also featuring the Barbarians, Chuck Berry, the Beach Boys, James Brown, Marvin Gaye, Gerry & the Pacemakers, Lesley Gore, Jan & Dean, Billy J. Kramer & the Dakotas, Smokey Robinson & the Miracles and the Supremes. (The show will open in the UK at the Futurist, Birmingham, Warks. as "Gather No Moss" on August 7th, 1966.)
Nov [3] A 17-year-old falls from the balcony during a Stones' concert at the Public Hall, Cleveland, OH. Mayor Ralph Locker says, in banning them, "such groups do not add to the community's culture or entertainment".
[13] The group's official biography, **Our Own Story**, is published.
[15] Jones is admitted to Passavant Hospital in Chicago with a 105°F temperature, after missing the group's last four concerts.
[20] On their return to Britain, the group plays at the "Glad Rag Ball", with Long John Baldry, the Animals, the Pretty Things, Gene Vincent and Cliff Bennett, at the Empire Pool, Wembley.
[27] In Jagger's defence for further driving offences in Tettenshall, Staffs., Dale Parkinson, his solicitor, tells the court not to be prejudiced by his client's long hair, advising them "The Duke of Marlborough had much longer hair than my client and he won some famous battles. He powdered his too, because of the fleas. My client has no fleas. The Emperor Caesar Augustus also had rather long hair. He won many great victories. Barristers, too, wear long hair in the shape of wigs with curled-up ends. A lost licence will seriously affect Jagger's mobility and that of the Rolling Stones group. Britain needs every dollar she can earn, and the Rolling Stones earn more dollars than many professional exporters. Put out of your minds the nonsense talked about these young men, the Rolling Stones. They are not long-haired idiots, but highly intelligent university men." Jagger is fined £16.
Dec [5] The group's revival of Willie Dixon's *Little Red Rooster*, despite critics' scepticism that a purist blues record will be a hit, tops the UK chart, as a cover of Irma Thomas' *Time Is On My Side* hits US #6.
[6] The Stones are voted #1 UK R&B group and Best New Group in the **New Musical Express** annual readers' poll. Jagger is voted Best New Disc Or TV Singer.
[12] ***12 x 5*** hits US #3.
[21] Watts' book, **Ode To A High Flying Bird**, a tribute to jazz giant Charlie Parker, is published in the US.
[26] In a **New Musical Express** ad, the group wishes starving hairdressers and their families a Happy Christmas.

1965

Jan [9] Marianne Faithfull reaches US #22 with *As Tears Go By*.
[20] The group appears on the season premiere of ABC-TV's "Shindig!", inviting Howlin' Wolf to be its special guest, and sits at his feet while he plays.
[21] 3,000 fans greet the Stones as they arrive at the airport in Sydney, New South Wales, Australia.
[22] The group begins a 16-date tour of Australia, New Zealand and the Far East, with Roy Orbison, Rolf Harris and Dionne Warwick, at the Manufacturers' Auditorium, Agricultural Hall, Sydney, Australia. The tour, covering 36 shows in 16 days, will end on February 16th at Badminton Stadium, Singapore.
Feb [6] ***The Rolling Stones No. 2***, again with no title or artist name on the sleeve, hits UK #1, replacing ***Beatles For Sale***. It includes covers of US R&B hits including Otis Redding's *Pain In My Heart*, and Solomon Burke's *Everybody Needs Somebody To Love*, but also a greater number of Jagger/Richard compositions than their debut set. Jack Nitzsche contributes keyboards with the ever-present Stewart.
[20] *Heart Of Stone* reaches US #19.

Mar [5] The group begins a 14-date, twice-nightly UK tour, with Dave Berry & the Cruisers, Goldie & the Gingerbreads, the Konrads, the Checkmates, and special guests the Hollies, at the Regal Theatre, Edmonton, London, set to end on the 18th at the ABC Theatre, Romford, Essex.
[7] A teenage girl falls from the dress circle at the Palace Theatre, Manchester, Lancs., onto the audience below, breaking only a few teeth.
[11] Portuguese pianist Sergio Varella-Cid vents his anger to the press after his recital is drowned out by the Stones playing in another part of the City Hall, Sheffield, S. Yorks.
[19] The **Tailor And Cutter** magazine carries a plea to the Rolling Stones to wear ties to save tie-makers from financial disaster. (Years later the magazine will name Jagger one of the Hot Hundred Best Dressed Men.)
[20] *The Last Time*, recorded at RCA's Hollywood studios with engineer Dave Hassinger (and with Phil Spector and Jack Nitzsche providing production assistance), tops the UK chart.
[26] On the opening night of a seven-date Scandinavian tour at the Fyns Forum in Odense, Denmark, Wyman is knocked unconscious by a 220 volt shock on stage.
Apr [9] Band makes its live debut on ITV's "Ready Steady Goes Live!"
[10] A schoolteacher in Wrexham denounces parents who allow their children to wear Rolling Stones' "corduroy" trousers.
[11] The Stones make their second appearance at the annual "**New Musical Express** Poll Winners Concert" at the Empire Pool.
[16-18] They play three dates at the Olympia Theatre, Paris.
[23] The group begins a 21-date tour of North America at the Maurice Richard Arena, Montreal, PQ, Canada, set to close on May 29th at the Academy of Music, New York.
[24] US only-released, ***The Rolling Stones, Now!***, hits US #5.
[26] During a concert at the Treasure Island Gardens in London, ON, Canada, the chief of police unplugs mikes and amps to stop the show.
May [1] *The Last Time* hits US #9.
[2] Despite its host's previous comments, the Stones appear on CBS-TV's "The Ed Sullivan Show", on a bill with Tom Jones, Dusty Springfield and Morecambe & Wise, performing *The Last Time*, *Little Red Rooster*, *Everybody Needs Somebody* and *2120 South Michigan Avenue*. (They will also make appearances on "Hollywood A Go-Go" and "Shindig".)
[22] *The Last Time*'s B-side, *Play With Fire*, peaks at US #96.
June [24] A four-date Scandinavian tour begins in Oslo, Norway.
July [10] *(I Can't Get No) Satisfaction*, held back in the UK because of the EP's success, tops the US chart for the first of four weeks, the group's debut US #1. Based around a definitive riff which entered Richard's head after waking up in the middle of the night in his room at the Gulf Motel, Clearwater, FL, it is notable for its use of a fuzz box distorting the sound, and its risqué lyrics about menstrual cycles. (Richard will later claim this famous riff is based on Martha & the Vandellas' *Dancing In The Street*.)
[19] *(I Can't Get No) Satisfaction* is certified gold by the RIAA.
[22] Jagger, Wyman and Jones are fined £5 each with joint costs of 15 guineas at East Ham Magistrates' Court, London, after being found guilty of insulting behavior on March 18th when, denied use of the private toilet at the Francis Service Station on the Romford Road in East Ham by mechanic, Charles Keely, they urinated against the garage wall and drove off "making a well-known gesture".
[28] Watts buys a 16th-century timbered mansion in Sussex from Lord Shawcross. Watts' father comments "We can't understand why he prefers an old place like this to something modern."
[30] The group re-signs with Decca in the UK. (They do not however, sign with London in the US.)
Aug [1] The band makes its London Palladium debut, playing two shows supported by the Walker Brothers, the Moody Blues, the Fourmost, Steam Packet, the Quiet Five and Julie Grant.
[21] ***Out Of Our Heads***, the first Stones album to be recorded in stereo, begins a three-week run at US #1.
[28] Allen Klein becomes co-manager of the group with Oldham, as the Stones sign a £1.7 million contract with Decca to make five movies.
Sept [4] The group flies directly from a concert at the ABC Theatre in Belfast, Northern Ireland, to Los Angeles, to record *Get Off Of My Cloud*, returning for a concert at the Palace Ballroom, Douglas, Isle of Man, where they have to climb in through a toilet window to avoid fans.
[10] ITV's "Ready Steady, Go!" airs, devoted entirely to the Stones, who act as interviewers and hosts, with their guests Manfred Mann, Goldie & the Gingerbreads and the Preachers, who play their current single, the Wyman-produced, *Hole In My Soul*.
[11] *(I Can't Get No) Satisfaction* tops the UK chart.
[18] Wyman's wife Diane (whom he married in Penge, Kent, in 1959) writes "My Life As A Stone's Wife" for UK music paper, **Disc**.
[24] They begin their sixth UK tour, a 24-date, twice-nightly package with the Spencer Davis Group, Unit 4+2, Mike Sarne, the Checkmates, Charles Dickens, the Habits, the End and Ray Cameron, at the Finsbury Park Astoria, set to climax on October 17th at the Granada Theatre, Tooting, London. (The group's scheduled October 16th date at the Odeon Theatre, Southend, Essex, will be cancelled, when local authorities state that the police will be too busy controlling the crowds at the town's illuminations to concentrate on the Stones.)
Oct [16] ***Out Of Our Heads***, their first album recorded entirely in the US and featuring covers of soul classics rather than R&B cuts, and four Jagger/Richard originals, hits UK #2, held off the top by ***The Sound Of Music*** soundtrack.
[29] The group's 37-date North American tour begins at the Forum, Montreal, set to end on December 5th at the Sports Arena, Los Angeles.
Nov [1] A concert at the Memorial Auditorium, Rochester, NY, is stopped by police after seven minutes, when 3,000 fans try to storm the stage.
[6] *Get Off Of My Cloud* tops both the UK and US charts.
[15] The group sings *She Said Yeah* and *Get Off Of My Cloud* on NBC-TV's "Hullabaloo".
[29] Colorado's Governor John A. Love declares "Rolling Stones Day" throughout the state, as the group plays a sellout concert at the Coliseum in Denver that evening.
Dec [3] Richard is knocked unconscious by an electric shock on stage at the Memorial Hall in Sacramento, CA, when his guitar makes contact with his microphone during *The Last Time*.
[10] *Satisfaction* is voted Best Record Of The Year in the annual **New Musical Express** Readers' Poll.

1966

Jan [8] US-only released ***December's Children (And Everybody's)*** hits US #4.
[15] ***December's Children (And Everybody's)*** is certified gold by the RIAA.
[29] From the US album, the group's version of *As Tears Go By* hits US #6. It is intended as lead track on the next UK EP, but is withdrawn.
Feb [1] An announcement is made that the Stones will begin shooting their first feature film, "Back Behind And In Front", on April 10th.
[19] After five successive #1s, *19th Nervous Breakdown* is held at UK #2 for three weeks, by Nancy Sinatra's *These Boots Are Made For Walkin'*.
[18] The group begins an 11-date tour of Australia and New Zealand in Sydney. The 20-show tour will end on March 2nd at the Capitol Theatre, Perth, W. Australia, Australia.
Mar [10] Decca vetoes the release of the projected album, ***Could You Walk On The Water***. The original track line-up is also abandoned, and the project develops into ***Aftermath*** (hence its title).
[19] *19th Nervous Breakdown* hits US #2, held off the top for three weeks by S/Sgt. Barry Sadler's *The Ballad Of The Green Berets*.
[26] The group begins a seven-date, 11-show European tour in The Hague, Holland, set to end on April 5th in Copenhagen, Denmark.
[21] They win Most Outstanding Group Of 1965 at the annual Carl-Alan Awards in London.
Apr [30] ***Aftermath***, the first Stones album composed entirely of Jagger/Richard songs, tops the UK chart, where it will remain for eight weeks. Notable is the track *Going Home*, which lasts 11 minutes 35 seconds, the final seven minutes studio-improvized while the tapes still rolled. Produced by Oldham, Jones begins to add sitar and dulcimer on some tracks.
[30] Otis Redding names the Stones his favorite group (he covers *Satisfaction*).
May [1] The band makes its third consecutive appearance at the annual "**New Musical Express** Poll Winners Concert" at the Empire Pool.
[14] Compilation ***Big Hits (High Tide And Green Grass)*** hits US #3 and will eventually sell over two million US copies.
[28] *Paint It Black* hits UK #1.
June [11] *Paint It Black* tops the US survey.
[21] The Stones sue 14 New York hotels for a total of £1,750,000 over an alleged booking ban injurious to the group's reputation, and discriminatory in violation of New York's Civil Rights law.
[24] The group begins another North American tour, with the Standells and the McCoys at the Manning Bowl in Lynn, MA. The crowd is subdued with tear gas making it the last rock concert at the venue until 1985, when Aerosmith and Mötley Crüe perform. The 31-date trek will end on July 28th at the International Sports Center, Honolulu, HI.
July [23] *Sittin' On The Fence* by Twice As Much, written by Jagger and Richard, and released on Immediate, reaches UK #25.
[29] Jagger/Richard's *Out Of Time* hits UK #1 for Chris Farlowe.
Aug [13] US-only release, *Mother's Little Helper*, hits US #8. Its B-side ballad, *Lady Jane*, makes US #24, as ***Aftermath*** hits US #2 for two weeks behind the Beatles' ***Yesterday And Today***.
Sept [23] A 12-date, twice-nightly "Rolling Stones '66" tour with Ike & Tina Turner, the Yardbirds, Peter Jay & the Jaywalkers, the Kings of Rhythm Orchestra, the Ikettes, Jimmy Thomas, Bobby John and Long John Baldry, opens at the Royal Albert Hall, amidst scenes which see hundreds of screaming teenagers rushing on to the stage at the start of the group's performance. The band leaves the stage and an announcement is made that unless everyone returns to their seats, the show will be cancelled. Order is restored and the group plays its set. The tour will end on October 9th at the Gaumont Theatre, Southampton, Hants.
Oct [7] The group makes its last appearance on ITV's "Ready Steady, Go!"
[15] *Have You Seen Your Mother, Baby, Standing In The Shadow?*, suffering from a bad studio mix due to Decca's haste to release it, hits UK #5. (The Stones appear in drag, at a photo call to promote the single, on New York's Park Avenue.)
[29] *Have You Seen Your Mother, Baby, Standing In The Shadow?* hits US #9.
Nov Belatedly released in the UK, their first Decca compilation, the 14-track, ***Big Hits (High Tide And Green Grass)***, hits UK #4.
Dec [23] Jagger appears on the final edition of ITV's "Ready Steady, Go!"
[24] **Melody Maker** reports that rumors are spreading throughout the US that Jagger is dead.

1967

Jan [15] The Stones appear on the "The Ed Sullivan Show" but are forced to change the lyrics of *Let's Spend The Night Together* to "Let's Spend Some Time Together".
[19] The still-rising ***got LIVE if you want it!*** is certified gold by the RIAA.
[21] Live album, ***got LIVE if you want it!***, recorded at

the Royal Albert Hall, on September 23rd during the band's recent UK tour, hits US #6.
[22] They make their first and last appearance on ITV's "Sunday Night At The London Palladium", singing *Let's Spend The Night Together*, *Ruby Tuesday*, *It's All Over Now* and *Connection*. Showbiz tradition in Britain dictates that artists wave to the audience on a revolving stage during the program's fade-out. The Stones refuse and incur the wrath of press and public alike.
[29] Comedians Peter Cook and Dudley Moore, at the close of "Sunday Night At The London Palladium", wave to the audience with paper dummies of the group.
Feb [4] ***Between The Buttons*** hits UK #3. Featuring Watts' cartoon drawings on its back cover, it is the last to be produced by Oldham and points towards a greater self-sufficiency.
[5] The **News Of The World**, names Mick Jagger in an article about drug-taking pop stars. Jagger, appearing on ITV's "Eamonn Andrews Show", announces a writ for libel is to be served.
[11] *Let's Spend The Night Together*, backed by *Ruby Tuesday*, hits UK #3.
[12] Richard's Sussex home, "Redlands", is raided by 15 policemen with a warrant under the Dangerous Drugs Act. Charges are made against Richard and Jagger.
[24] The still-rising ***Between The Buttons*** is certified gold by the RIAA.
Mar [4] *Ruby Tuesday* tops the US chart, as its B-side, *Let's Spend The Night Together*, makes US #55.
[11] ***Between The Buttons*** hits US #2 for the first of four weeks, behind the Monkees' ***More Of The Monkees***.
[25] The group begins a 16-date European tour in Malmo, Sweden, set to end on April 17th in Athens, Greece.
Apr [13] The Stones play their first gig behind the Iron Curtain at the Palace of Culture, Warsaw, Poland. Police break up a crowd of 3,000, using batons and tear gas.
May [1] *Ruby Tuesday* is confirmed gold by the RIAA.
[10] Jagger and Richard appear in Chichester Crown Court, Chichester, Sussex, charged with being in possession of drugs. They elect to go to trial, pleading not guilty, and are granted £1,000 bail each. Jones is arrested in his London flat, charged with unlawful possession of drugs, and released on £250 bail.
[16] The group enters Olympic Studios to begin a four-day recording session.
June [8] Jones plays alto sax on the Beatles' *You Know My Name (Look Up The Number)*, at Abbey Road Studios.
[18] Jones introduces the Jimi Hendrix Experience on the final day of the "Monterey International Pop Festival", at the County Fairgrounds, Monterey, CA.
[25] Jagger and Richard are among a group of friends who take part in the live recording of the Beatles' *All You Need Is Love*, for the TV show, "Our World", broadcast from Abbey Road Studios to an estimated 400 million people across five continents.
[27] Jagger is tried at West Sussex Quarter Sessions in Chichester, on a charge of unlawfully possessing four benzedrine tablets containing amphetamine sulphate and methyl amphetamine hydrochloride, which he had bought, legally, in Italy. The jury finds him guilty after a six-minute deliberation, once the judge has ruled that his defense is not admissible. He is remanded in Lewes Jail overnight.
[29] Richard is tried on a charge of allowing his house to be used for the illegal smoking of cannabis. He too is found guilty. Judge Leslie Block sentences Richard to one year in jail and a £500 fine, and Jagger to three months in jail and £100 costs. Jagger goes to Brixton Jail, London, Richards to Wormwood Scrubs, London.
[30] Jagger and Richard are released by the High Court on bail of £7,000 each, and given leave to appeal their sentences.
July [1] **The Times** newspaper prints an editorial by William Rees-Mogg headlined "Who breaks a butterfly on a wheel?", protesting against the punishment meted out to the two group members.
[6] Jones collapses, waiting for his trial to start, and is admitted to hospital for nervous strain.
[31] Richard's conviction is quashed after some of the evidence against him had been deemed inadmissible. Jagger's sentence is reduced to a conditional discharge.
Aug [12] ***Flowers***, comprising singles and studio outtakes, hits US #3.
[16] The RIAA certifies ***Flowers*** gold.
[26] Jagger and girlfriend Marianne Faithfull visit the Maharishi Mahesh Yogi with the Beatles.
Sept [9] *We Love You*, the group's thank you to fans after the events of the last few months, backed with *Dandelion*, hits UK #8. It opens with the sound of footsteps and cell doors being slammed, and features backing vocals from Lennon and McCartney. They make a promotional film for it based on "The Trials Of Oscar Wilde", but it is banned by the BBC.
[29] It is announced that Oldham and the Stones are parting company.
Oct [7] *We Love You* makes US #50.
[14] A-side, *Dandelion*, reaches US #14.
[30] Jones is found guilty of drug possession and allowing his flat to be used for drug-taking at the Inner London Sessions, and sentenced to nine months in jail.
[31] Pending an appeal against his sentence, Jones is released from Wormwood Scrubs, on £750 bail.
Dec [3] Their forthcoming ***Their Satanic Majesties Request*** album is previewed on Radio 1's "Top Gear".
[6] Based on pre-orders ***Their Satanic Majesties Request*** is certified gold by the RIAA.
[12] Jones' sentence is quashed, in favor of a £1,000 fine and three years probation, after three psychiatrists concur he is in a poor mental state and has suicidal tendencies.
[14] Jones collapses and is rushed to St. George's Hospital, London, though he discharges himself shortly thereafter.
[16] **New Musical Express** reports that Marianne Faithfull is the first signing to the Stones' new Mother Earth label.

1968

Jan [6] Now split from Oldham, the self-produced, hallucinatory-influenced, ***Their Satanic Majesties Request***, hits UK #3. (This contribution to psychedelia is delivered months after the "Summer Of Love", and suffers from comparison with the Beatles' ***Sgt. Pepper***.) The album's complex 3-D sleeve photo is designed to outdo the recent Beatles effort. It also hits US #2 for six weeks, behind the Beatles' ***Magical Mystery Tour***, as Wyman makes US #87 with *In Another Land*, also from the album.
[27] *She's A Rainbow*, featuring a John Paul Jones string arrangement, reaches US #25.
May [12] The band makes its first live appearance in more than a year at the annual "**New Musical Express** Poll Winners Concert" at the Empire Pool.
[21] Jones appears at Great Marlborough Street Magistrates Court, London, on a charge of possession of marijuana, and is released on £200 bail.
June [4] Jones elects for trial by jury, and is remanded on bail to Inner London Sessions on June 25th. On the same day, the roof catches fire at Olympic Studios while the group is filming a sequence for its "One By One" documentary.
[6] The group inserts new lyrics to *Sympathy For The Devil*, which they record, following Robert Kennedy's death a day earlier.
[22] *Jumping Jack Flash* tops the UK chart, their first #1 in two years. The Stones team with Traffic producer Jimmy Miller and return to R&B/rock-based recordings.
July [6] *Jumping Jack Flash* hits US #1.
[26] Decca withdraws ***Beggars Banquet*** from its scheduled release, objecting to the sleeve which depicts a graffiti-covered toilet. (Jagger is incensed by the company's double standard, citing the earlier release of Tom Jones' ***A-tom-ic Jones***, which features the singer standing in front of a nuclear explosion.)
Sept [26] Jones is found guilty of possession of cannabis and fined £50 with 100 guineas costs.
Oct [5] *Street Fighting Man*, banned by many US radio stations fearing that the lyrics may incite civil disorder, makes US #48.
Nov [13] Jones buys Cotchford Farm in Hartfield, Sussex, former home of **Winnie The Pooh** author A.A. Milne.
Dec [11-12] The TV show "Rock And Roll Circus", created by the group, is filmed at Intertel Studios, Wembley, Middx., by director Michael Lindsay-Hogg, with performances from artists including the Who, Jethro Tull, Eric Clapton and John Lennon. (The show is never transmitted.)
[28] ***Beggars Banquet***, released in a plain white sleeve depicting an invitation, hits UK #3. (The press launch for the album at the Queensgate Hotel, London, is an actual banquet, which degenerates into a custard-pie fight between those present, which does not include a sick Richard, who is deputized for by Lord Harlech.) Produced by Miller and engineered by Glyn Johns, with mainly acoustic overtones, the album will be regarded by many as their finest achievement and includes critics' favorite *Sympathy For The Devil*. Jones is gradually being excised from the group's activities, with drug abuse and life in the fast lane having taken their toll. Since the sleeve dispute, the group's relationship with Decca has also worsened (when the album is re-promoted in the '80s by Decca, it will only be available in the toilet sleeve).

1969

Jan [11] ***Beggars Banquet*** hits US #5, with initial sales eventually topping one million.
May [28] Jagger and Faithfull are arrested at their London home, charged with possession of cannabis and released on £50 bail each.
June [8] Jones, in poor mental and physical shape, quits the group. He is quoted as saying "I no longer see eye to eye with the discs we are cutting", at a time when the group is recording some of its purest blues sounds (Jones' first love).
[9] The Rolling Stones announce Jones will be replaced by Mick Taylor (b. Michael Taylor, Jan. 17, 1948, Welwyn Garden City, Herts.), guitarist with the John Mayall Band.
July [3] Jones is found dead in his swimming pool at Hartfield by girlfriend Anna Wohlin after taking a midnight swim. (The coroner records a verdict of misadventure: "drowning while under the influence of alcohol and drugs.")
[5] The Rolling Stones, with Taylor making his debut, play a free concert in Hyde Park, London, attended by 250,000 fans. Jagger pays tribute to Jones by reciting Shelley's **Adonais**, and 3,000 butterflies are released. The event is filmed by ITV as "The Stones In The Park", and will be broadcast on September 2nd.
[6] Jagger flies to Australia with Faithfull to begin work on the film, "Ned Kelly".
[8] Faithfull attempts suicide after Jagger says their relationship is over, and will lie in a coma for eight days.
[10] Jones' funeral takes place at Hatherley Road Parish Church, Cheltenham, after which he is buried in the Priory Road Cemetery. The other Stones, excluding Jagger, are present. Canon Hugh Evan Hopkins reads Jones' own epitaph: "Please don't judge me too harshly."
[26] *Honky Tonk Women* begins a five-week stay at UK #1.
Aug [10] Richard's girlfriend, Anita Pallenberg, gives birth to a son, Marlon. (Richard and Pallenberg will be seen starring with David Warner in the film, "Michael Kohlhaas", which will be withdrawn shortly after release.)
[23] *Honky Tonk Women* tops the US chart, where it will stay for four weeks, being certified gold by the RIAA three days later.
Sept ***Through The Past Darkly (Big Hits Volume 2)***, a second greatest hits set, dedicated to the memory of Brian Jones, hits UK #2. Jean-Luc Godard's impressionistic film of the group at work, "Sympathy For The Devil", premieres at the "Edinburgh Festival" in Edinburgh, Scotland.
Oct [11] ***Through The Past Darkly (Big Hits Volume 2)*** hits US #2, behind Creedence Clearwater Revival's ***Green River***.

Nov [7] The Stones begin their sixth US tour at the State University, Fort Collins, CO. The 17-date trek will end on the 29th at Boston Garden, Boston, MA. Writer (and later rock biographer) Albert Goldman compares Jagger to Adolf Hitler in **The New York Times**.
[30] The group plays at a festival at the International Raceway, West Palm Beach, FL.
Dec [6] Aiming to repeat their successful Hyde Park concert, the Stones close their US tour with a free concert at the Altamont Speedway track, Livermore, CA. (The intended venue for the concert had been the Sears Point Raceway, but was made unavailable 20 hours before the scheduled start.) Having employed British Hell's Angels to act as security men in London, the group hire their San Francisco counterparts, who prove to be less placid and, due to a mixture of drink and drugs, provoke angry scenes. In a confused atmosphere, 18-year-old black youth Meredith Hunter is stabbed to death by bikers when he pulls a gun out at the front of the stage midway through the Stones' set. The group rushes through its numbers before escaping in a helicopter. The disastrous concert is seen by many as an epitaph to the peace and love aura of the late '60s and the end of an era.
[19] Jagger and Faithfull appear at Great Marlborough Street Magistrates Court. Jagger is found guilty and fined £200 with 50 guineas costs. Faithfull is acquitted.
[20] ***Let It Bleed*** enters the UK chart at #1, replacing the Beatles' ***Abbey Road***, which returns to the top the following week. It includes guest artists ranging from Ry Cooder to Merry Clayton, and is highlighted by *Midnight Rambler*, with Jagger portrayed in the role of the Boston Strangler, Albert de Salvo, and closes with the London Bach Choir singing the introduction to *You Can't Always Get What You Want*. It also includes the original country conception of *Honky Tonk Women*, recorded as *Country Honk*.
[27] ***Let It Bleed*** hits US #3, behind ***Led Zeppelin II*** and ***Abbey Road***.

1970

Feb [19] Residents and landowners of Altamont file a £375,000 suit claiming damage to their land.
Mar [11] Band documentary, "One Plus One", opens in the US.
July [28] "Ned Kelly" film premieres in Australia.
[30] The group announces that Allen Klein no longer represents them, beginning a round of litigation between the parties.
[31] The Stones' contract with Decca ends. (Still to deliver a single to complete the deal, they offer the unreleasable *Cocksucker Blues*.)
Aug [1] The movie "Performance" premieres, having been delayed for two years because of worries over its excessive violence. Jagger receives critical accolades for his performance as retired rock star Turner.
Sept [3] Jagger is cited in the divorce proceedings of Marianne Faithfull and her husband John Dunbar.
[19] Live album, ***Get Yer Ya-Ya's Out!***, recorded at New York's Madison Square Garden on November 27th-28th, 1969, hits UK #1 for the first of two weeks, fulfilling the band's final contractual obligation to Decca.
[23] Jagger meets Bianca Rose Perez Moreno de Macias after a concert at Paris Olympia.
Oct [1] A riot breaks out outside the Palazzo Del Sport, Milan, Italy. Police, using batons and tear gas, arrest 63 people.
[5] The group hires Prince Rupert Lowenstein as its financial adviser.
[7] "Ned Kelly" premieres in the UK.
[24] ***Get Yer Ya-Ya's Out!*** hits US #6.
[26] Meredith Hunter's mother files a £28,000 suit against the Stones and others.
[30] Jagger is ordered to pay £200 costs as Dunbar is granted a divorce from Faithfull.
Nov [28] Jagger's solo release, *Memo From Turner*, taken from the ***Performance*** soundtrack, reaches UK #32.
Dec [6] "Gimme Shelter" concert film opens in New York, documenting their 1969 US tour, ending with the events at Altamont.

1971

Jan [4] "Performance" premieres in London.
Mar [4] The Stones begin a British tour at the City Hall, Newcastle, Tyne & Wear, and announce their decision to live in the South of France as tax-exiles.
[14] Ticket touts charge up to £10 for tickets at their "farewell" concert at the Roundhouse, London.
[26] They perform at London's Marquee club for a US TV special.
Apr [3] ***Stone Age*** hits UK #4 as Decca begins repackaging Stones' material. (This will extend into the mid-'70s, and cause anger from the group, which publicly decries the process.)
[6] The band forms its own label, Rolling Stones Records, to be distributed worldwide by the Kinney group (via a $5 million deal with Atlantic Records), now owners of Warner Bros. Records. Marshall Chess is chosen to run the label, while Andy Warhol designs its logo.
May [8] ***Sticky Fingers***, with a Warhol-designed sleeve of a male torso from the waist down clad in jeans, complete with a real zip-fastener, and musically using a horn section to fill out their sound with heavy brass inflections, tops the UK chart. Again produced by Miller, it includes guests Billy Preston, Jim Price, Bobby Keyes, Ry Cooder, Nitzsche and Stewart.
[11] ***Sticky Fingers*** is certified gold by the RIAA.
[12] Jagger and Bianca marry at the Town Hall in St. Tropez, France.
[15] *Brown Sugar*, the first single release on the Rolling Stones label, and in the UK backed with *Bitch* and *Let It Rock*, hits UK #2, held off the top by Dawn's *Knock Three Times*. (It is the group's first hit in two years, and will come to be considered another rock classic.)
[22] ***Sticky Fingers*** tops the US chart, where it will stay for four weeks.
[29] The extracted *Brown Sugar* also heads the US survey.
July [23] The group, and Brian Jones' father, file a $29 million lawsuit against Klein, alleging "mis-management of funds", and failure to represent their interests.
[24] Acoustic guitar-led *Wild Horses* reaches US #28.
[31] The Decca-released *Street Fighting Man* reaches UK #21.
Aug [31] The Stones and Jones' father file a High Court writ against Andrew Oldham and Eric Easton for "royalty deprivation".
Sept [25] ***Gimme Shelter***, a Decca compilation released against the group's wishes, but issued to tie in with the film premiere of the same name and featuring one side of a live Albert Hall performance, reaches UK #19.
Oct [21] Jade, a daughter to Mick and Bianca Jagger, is born in Paris.

1972

Feb [12] Double retrospective album, ***Hot Rocks 1964-1971***, compiled by Klein, hits US #4, where it will eventually sell over six million units.
[16] Shirley Watts is arrested at Nice airport, for hitting and swearing at French Customs officials. (She will receive a suspended sentence.) A Hell's Angel is acquitted for the murder of Meredith Hunter, and immediately sues the Stones for £20,000 for invasion of privacy.
Mar [18] ***Milestones***, another Decca collection, reaches UK #14.
Apr [17] Richard's and Pallenberg's daughter, Dandelion, is born.
May [10] A press release is issued stating that the group and Klein have settled their differences, and will co-operate with each other in their claim against Easton.
[13] *Tumbling Dice*, from a forthcoming album, hits UK #5.
[27] *Tumbling Dice* hits US #7.
June [3] The group begins a North American tour with Stevie Wonder and Martha Reeves in Vancouver, BC, Canada. 30 police are injured by gatecrashers.
[10] ***Exile On Main Street***, the group's only double studio set, and recorded mainly in the Stones' mobile studio unit in France, under Richard's creative guidance, tops the UK chart. Clean-up TV campaigner Mary Whitehouse claims BBC radio should not air the album due to its obscene nature. Chairman Lord Hill listens to the disc and claims to hear nothing wrong, although it is littered with swear words.
[17] Already certified gold by the RIAA on May 30th, ***Exile On Main Street*** begins a four-week stay at US #1.
July [17] A bomb explodes, believed to be the work of French separatists, under the group's equipment van before a concert at the Montreal Forum, Montreal. More than 3,000 holders of fake tickets are also turned away as the angry mob hurl rocks, bottles and what appear to be smoke bombs.
[23] Jagger, Richard and Stanley Moore, Marshall Chess and Robert Frank, all members of the group's retinue, are arrested at Green Airport, Warwick, RI, on their way to a concert at the Boston Garden, after an altercation with **Providence Journal** photographer Andy Dickerman. Boston Mayor Kevin White intercedes on their behalf and phones the Rhode Island Governor to have them released on bail, resulting in the show starting at 12:30 a.m. Richard and Moore will file suit against the newspaper.
Aug [19] *Happy* reaches US #22.
Oct [10] The lawsuits between the Rolling Stones, ABKCO, Decca, Eric Easton and Andrew Oldham are all settled.
Nov [6] Wyman appears at Chelmsford Magistrates Court, Chelmsford, Essex, where he is fined £20 and loses his license for speeding in his Mercedes on the A12.
[11] The Decca-released compilation album, ***Rock'n'Rolling Stones***, makes UK #41.
Dec [6] Nice, France Public Prosecutor's Office confirms that arrest warrants have been issued for Richard and Pallenberg with regard to violating French drug laws. Richard states: "The first that I heard of the warrant for my arrest was when I read it in the newspaper here this morning".
[26] The Jaggers fly to Nicaragua to search for Bianca's relatives, missing after an earthquake.

1973

Jan [4] An entry ban is placed on an un-named Stone by the Immigration Ministry in Australia, where the group is to tour shortly. Five days later the ban will be lifted, without the Stone in question being named.
[6] Carly Simon's *You're So Vain*, on which Jagger adds a notable back-up vocal, tops the US chart.
[17] The still-climbing ***More Hot Rocks (big hits & fazed cookies)*** is certified gold by the RIAA.
[18] The group plays a benefit concert at the Great Western Forum, Inglewood, CA, in aid of victims of the Nicaraguan earthquake disaster which raises over $200,000, with the Stones contributing a further $150,000.
Feb [13] Another Klein double compilation album, ***More Hot Rocks (big hits & fazed cookies)***, hits US #9.
Apr [7] A Warwick judge refuses a motion to dismiss the charges arising from the July 23rd, 1972 incident, announcing that Jagger and Richard will stand trial the next time they set foot on US soil.
May [8] The Jaggers are honored in Washington, DC, with a Golden Key for their efforts toward the Nicaraguan Earthquake Relief.
June [9] *You Can't Always Get What You Want* (the B-side of 1969 #1 *Honky Tonk Women*) makes US #42.
[18] Marsha Hunt files an affiliation order at Marylebone Court, London, alleging that Jagger is the father of her two-year-old daughter.
[26] Richard and Pallenberg are arrested at their Cheyne Walk house on charges of possession of cannabis and a Smith & Wesson revolver.
[27] They appear at Marylebone Court and are freed on £1,000 bail.
July [31] Richard's house, "Redlands", is razed to the ground.
Aug Richard falls asleep in his room at the

Londonderry House Hotel in Hyde Park, London, and accidentally sets fire to himself. All group members are subsequently banned from staying there.

Sept [11] The group begins a UK tour.

[15] *Angie*, an acoustic ballad, hits UK #5, amid great press interest in its alleged subject, David Bowie's wife Angie.

[22] ***Goat's Head Soup***, recorded at Byron Lee's Dynamic Sound Studios in Kingston, Jamaica, tops the UK chart and is the last Jimmy Miller-produced Stones album.

[25] ***Goat's Head Soup*** is confirmed gold by the RIAA.

Oct [10] Jagger and Taylor perform with Billy Preston & the God Squad at the Rainbow Theatre, Finsbury Park.

[13] ***Goat's Head Soup*** begins a four-week stay at US #1.

[15] Richard is found guilty of use, supply and trafficking of cannabis in a Nice court. He receives a one-year suspended sentence and a 5,000-franc fine for similar charges involving heroin, and is banned from entering France for two years.

[20] *Angie* hits US #1 for a week.

[24] Richard appears in Great Marlborough Street Magistrates Court and is given a conditional discharge and a £205 fine for possession of cannabis, Mandrax tablets, Chinese heroin, firearms and ammunition, at his Cheyne Walk home.

Nov [15] *Angie* is certified gold by the RIAA.

1974

Feb [23] *Doo Doo Doo Doo Doo (Heartbreaker)*, also from ***Goat's Head Soup***, reaches US #15.

Mar [27] The group turns down a $100,000 request to play for a week at the Tropicana Hotel in Las Vegas, NV.

June [8] Wyman, the first Stone to release a solo album, makes UK #39 with ***Monkey Grip*** (also heading to US #99).

July [13-14] Richard joins Faces' guitarist Ron Wood's band at the Kilburn State Theatre, London.

Aug [17] *It's Only Rock'n'Roll* hits UK #10. Its release is heralded by an outbreak of graffiti across London bearing the title, and marks the debut of production credits for "The Glimmer Twins" - a pseudonym for Jagger and Richard.

Sept [21] *It's Only Rock'n'Roll* reaches US #16.

Oct [26] The Glimmer Twins-produced ***It's Only Rock'n'Roll*** hits UK #2, held off the top by the Bay City Rollers' ***Rollin'***. Recorded in Munich, West Germany, its guest musicians include Nicky Hopkins, percussionist Ray Cooper, Willie Weeks and Kenney Jones.

Nov [23] Already certified gold (its 21st consecutive million-selling album) by the RIAA on October 31st, ***It's Only Rock'n'Roll*** tops the US chart.

Dec [12] After over five years with the group, Taylor quits, suffering from the pressure of being a member of the world's most popular group, as the Stones prepare to start work on their new album in Munich. "The last 5½ years with the Stones have been very exciting and proved to be a most inspiring period. And as far as my attitude to the other four members is concerned, it is one of respect for them, both as musicians and people. I have nothing but admiration for the group, but I feel now is the time to move on and do something new." Jagger adds "After 5½ years, Mick wishes a change of scene and wants the opportunity to try out new ventures, new endeavours. While we are all most sorry that he is going, we wish him great success and much happiness." (Taylor will join the Jack Bruce Band with Carla Bley and Max Middleton before playing on two albums by Gong, touring in Bob Dylan's backing band in the early '80s, and will cut two solo albums, ***Mick Taylor*** (1979) and ***Stranger In This Town*** (1990).)

[14] Their revival of the Temptations' *Ain't Too Proud To Beg*, from ***It's Only Rock'n'Roll***, reaches US #17.

[31] Having released his debut solo set ***I've Got My Own Album To Do*** in October, Ron Wood (b. Ronald Wood, June 1, 1947, Hillingdon, London) of the Faces denies rumors that he is joining the group, stating the Faces are more important to him. Jagger says "No doubt we can find a brilliant 6' 3" blond guitarist who can do his own make-up."

1975

Apr [14] Wood is confirmed as Taylor's replacement for touring purposes only.

May [31] During a press conference at the Fifth Avenue Hotel in New York to announce a Stones US tour, the group comes into view performing live on a flat-bed truck.

June [1] The group, augmented by Wood, begins a US tour in Baton Rouge, LA (though he will return for a final Faces North American trip at the end of the Stones dates, before becoming a permanent Stone).

[14] The Decca-released ***Metamorphosis***, mainly a collection of Jagger/Richard songs demoed for other artists during the '60s, though it includes a rare Wyman-penned cut, *Downtown Suzie*, makes UK #45.

[28] The first Rolling Stones Records-issued compilation, ***Made In The Shade***, reaches UK #14.

July [6] Richard is charged with reckless driving and carrying an offensive weapon, a 7" hunting knife, in Fordyce, AR, and released on $162 bail. Richard, who is accompanied by Wood, states that he "bent down to change the waveband on the radio, and the car swerved slightly. A police patrol vehicle then pulled out from a lay-by and stopped us. I was also questioned about having a concealed weapon, which turned out to be a penknife complete with tin-opener and a device for removing stones from horse's hooves." (He will subsequently be cleared.)

[12] Their cover of Stevie Wonder's *I Don't Know Why*, from ***Metamorphosis***, peaks at US #42, as the album, with fewer tracks than the UK version, and released on Klein's ABKCO label, hits US #8.

[19] ***Made In The Shade*** hits US #6 the same week Wood's second solo album ***Now Look***, released by Warner Bros., enters the US survey set to make #118.

Aug [7] ***Made In The Shade*** is certified gold by the RIAA.

Sept [6] *Out Of Time*, also from the ABKCO album, featuring a Jagger solo over the backing track to his 1966 production for Chris Farlowe, climbs to US #81.

[20] *Out Of Time* makes UK #45.

Nov [22] The Decca-issued double compilation album, ***Rolled Gold - The Very Best Of The Rolling Stones***, debuts at its UK #7 peak.

Dec [6] A preacher in Tallahassee, FL, pronounces the Stones records "sinful", after concluding a survey of 1,000 unmarried mothers and discovering that 984 of them had conceived to the sound of rock music, although not necessarily the Stones. His congregation enjoys a bonfire fuelled by Rolling Stones and Elton John records.

1976

Apr [1] More than one million postal ticket applications are received for the group's forthcoming Earls Court, London gigs in May.

[6] "Ladies And Gentlemen : The Rolling Stones", the first motion picture in quadrophonic sound, opens in New York.

[17] Wyman's ***Stone Alone*** peaks at US #166.

[24] ***Black And Blue***, written and produced by Jagger and Richard and more dance-slanted than usual, hits UK #2.

May [10-12] The group begins a 13-date UK tour with three performances at the Apollo Centre, Glasgow, Scotland, set to end on the 27th with six nights at London's Earl's Court.

[15] ***Black And Blue*** tops the US chart, where it will enjoy a four-week run.

[19] Richard falls asleep at the wheel of his car and crashes on the M1 near Newport Pagnell, Bucks. Cocaine and marijuana are found in the vehicle (resulting in yet another fine).

June [5] The extracted ballad, *Fool To Cry*, hits UK #6 and US #10.

[6] Richard's ten-week-old son, Tara, dies from pneumonia in Geneva, Switzerland, while the Stones perform in Paris, France.

[23] ***Black And Blue*** is certified platinum by the RIAA.

July [17] US B-side, *Hot Stuff*, makes US #49.

Aug [21] The Stones headline the "Knebworth Festival", Knebworth, Herts., in front of 200,000 fans, and perform a retrospective set tracing their roots back to their debut album in 1964.

Nov [25] Wood, who released ***Mahoney's Last Stand***, a collaboration with ex-Face Ronnie Lane in September, joins an all-star cast on *I Shall Be Released* at the Band's "The Last Waltz" Farewell Concert, at San Francisco's Winterland Ballroom.

1977

Jan [10] Richard appears at Aylesbury Crown Court, Aylesbury, Bucks., charged with cocaine and LSD possession. He is found guilty of possessing cocaine and fined £750 with £250 costs, but acquitted on the charge of LSD possession. (He is also fined £25 for driving without an MOT or car tax.)

Feb The group wins an injunction against the **News Of The World** preventing the publication of stills from the 1972 tour movie "Cocksucker Blues".

[5] Following speculation at the MIDEM festival that they are to sign with PolyGram, it is announced that the Rolling Stones have signed a distribution deal with EMI for their next six albums. Jagger announces "In this Silver Jubilee Year, I feel it is only fitting we sign with a British company".

[24] Richard and girlfriend Anita Pallenberg are stopped at customs when they arrive in Toronto, ON, Canada.

[29] Richard is arrested by the Royal Canadian Mounted Police at Toronto's Harbour Castle Hotel, for possession of 22g of heroin and 5g of cocaine. A charge of trafficking in heroin will hang over him for 18 months with bail set at $25,000.

Mar [4-5] The group performs two gigs at the 300-capacity El Mocambo night club in Toronto. (The second set is recorded, and later appears as ***Love You Live***.)

[14] Richard makes his second court appearance, and is remanded on bail until June 27th.

[18] Wood, in the audience with Jagger and Wyman, joins the Eagles on stage for an encore at the latter's Madison Square Garden concert.

Apr [1] The Stones re-sign with Atlantic for North American distribution of Rolling Stones Records, in a deal reportedly worth $21 million for six albums.

June [27] Richard fails to show up for his latest Toronto court appearance.

Sept [20] BBC2-TV's "The Old Grey Whistle Test" airs an hour-long film of a 1976 Paris concert.

[23] "Ladies And Gentlemen, The Rolling Stones" movie premieres at the Rainbow Theatre, London.

[24] The performance set, ***Love You Live***, hits UK #3.

Oct [4] The still-rising ***Love You Live*** is certified gold by the RIAA.

[29] ***Love You Live*** hits US #5.

Dec [2] Richard appears in a Toronto court, and is remanded once again.

[17] Quickly-deleted, UK-only issued, TV-advertised double anthology, ***Get Stoned***, hits UK #8.

1978

Jan [26] Wood signs a solo deal with CBS Records at MIDEM in Cannes, France.

Apr [1] The Philadelphia Furies, a soccer team co-owned by Jagger, Peter Frampton, Paul Simon and Rick Wakeman, loses its first match of the North America Soccer League, 3-0 to the Washington Diplomats.

June [10] The Stones open a 25-date tour of North America, their ninth, at the Civic Center, Lakeland, FL, set to end at the Oakland-Alameda County Coliseum, Oakland, CA, on July 26th.

[15] The Glimmer Twins-produced ***Some Girls***, causing some controversy for its attitude towards women and use of photos of Lucille Ball, Raquel Welch and Farrah Fawcett-Majors in a mock-wig ad on the sleeve (changed after litigation threats), tops the US chart for the first of two weeks.

[17] *Miss You*, influenced by the current disco trend and the group's first 12" single, backed with the jangling country-ballad, *Far Away Eyes*, hits UK #3, as parent album, ***Some Girls***, hits UK #2.

[29] A fan is shot and 17 are arrested at the group's Rupp Arena, Lexington, KY, concert.
July [9] The Stones, minus Wyman, jam with Muddy Waters on stage at the Chicago nightclub, The Quiet Knight.
[10] Wyman is knocked unconscious when he falls off stage at a concert at the Coliseum, St. Paul, MN.
[26] The yet-to-peak *Miss You* is confirmed gold by the RIAA.
Aug [5] *Miss You* tops the US chart.
Oct [6] Jagger apologizes to the Rev. Jesse Jackson for offensive lyrics in *Some Girls*, but refuses to re-record the song.
[7] The Stones guest on the season premiere of NBC-TV's "Saturday Night Live", during which Jagger also joins Dan Aykroyd as Tom Snyder in a "Tomorrow" parody sketch.
[24] Richards (having reverted to his given name) pleads guilty in a Toronto court, to possession of heroin. Judge Lloyd Graburn imposes a one-year suspended sentence, and orders him to continue his addiction treatment and to play a benefit concert at the Canadian National Institute for the Blind within the next six months.
[28] Rolling Stones Records' reggae artist Peter Tosh's *(You Got To Walk And) Don't Look Back*, a duet with Jagger, makes UK #43.
Nov [4] *Respectable* reaches UK #23.
[11] *Beast Of Burden* hits US #8.
[25] *(You Got To Walk And) Don't Look Back* peaks at US #81.

1979

Feb [3] *Shattered* reaches US #31. Richards releases a solo single, his revival of Chuck Berry's *Run Rudolph Run*.
Apr [22] The Stones and the New Barbarians, a group assembled by Richards for the occasion with Wood (guitar), Ian McLagan (keyboards), Stanley Clarke (bass), Ziggy Modeliste (drums) and Bobby Keyes (sax), perform at the Civic Auditorium, Oshawa, ON, for the Canadian National Institute for the Blind, fulfilling Richards' judicial obligation.
[24] The New Barbarians begin an 18-date US tour in Ann Arbor, MI, set to close on May 21st at the Great Western Forum.
May [12] Wood's solo ***Gimme Some Neck*** enters the US chart set to make #45.
Aug [11] The New Barbarians play at the "Knebworth Festival", Knebworth.
Sept [2] Wyman joins Kiki Dee, Dave Mason, Todd Rundgren and Ringo Starr in a band raising funds for the Jerry Lewis Muscular Dystrophy Telethon, broadcast from Las Vegas, NV.

1980

Jan [13] Fans riot in Milwaukee, WI, when the New Barbarians play a concert, without Richards.
Feb [18] In an interview in the **Daily Express**, Wyman says that he intends to leave the Stones in 1982, on the group's 20th anniversary.
[22] Wood and girlfriend Jo Howard are arrested for cocaine possession on St. Martin in the Dutch Antilles, and will spend five days in jail.
July [3] Richards and Pallenberg separate. (He begins a new relationship with Patti Hansen.)
[5] ***Emotional Rescue***, continuing the band's dance-oriented foray, tops the UK survey.
[26] ***Emotional Rescue*** heads the US chart, where it will stay for seven weeks, as the extracted title-track, *Emotional Rescue*, hits UK #9.
Sept [6] *Emotional Rescue* hits US #3.
[10] ***Emotional Rescue*** is certified platinum by the RIAA.
Oct [3] Wyman begins work on the soundtrack to the Ryan O'Neal/Omar Sharif movie, "Green Ice".
[18] *She's So Cold* makes UK #33.
Nov [5] The Jaggers are divorced.
[8] *She's So Cold* reaches US #26.

1981

Jan [20] Richards' New York neighbors try to get him evicted for playing music too loudly late at night.
Feb Jagger walks out of the filming of Werner Herzog's "Fitzcarraldo" in Peru, after five members of the crew are killed.
Apr [18] Compilation album ***Sucking In The Seventies***, reaches US #15.
June Richards sees Chuck Berry's set at The Ritz in New York, after which Berry punches him in the eye.
[3] ***Sucking In The Seventies*** is certified gold by the RIAA.
Aug [22] Wyman's *(Si Si) Je Suis Un Rock Star* reaches UK #14. (It will be revived in the '80s as a TV commercial theme.)
[14] The Stones begin rehearsals at Long View Farm, Brookfield, MA, for an as-yet-unannounced US tour.
Sept [9] Wood's solo set ***1, 2, 3, 4*** enters the US chart set to make #164.
[12] ***Tattoo You*** hits UK #2, as the extracted *Start Me Up* hits UK #7.
[14] The group plays a warm-up gig as Blue Monday & the Cockroaches, at the 350-capacity Sir Morgan's Cave, Worcester, MA. Word of the show leaks out, and more than 4,000 fans turn up, resulting in 11 arrests.
[19] ***Tattoo You*** begins a nine-week stay at US #1.
[25] The group begins its tenth US tour at JFK Stadium, Philadelphia, PA, before a crowd of 90,000. The 50-date sojourn, attended by more than two million people and grossing over $50 million, will end on December 19th at the Hampton Coliseum, Hampton Roads, VA.
Oct [17] Thieves trying to steal tickets for a forthcoming Stones concert in Maryland shoot one man dead and injure another.
[28] 22-year-old Wesley Shelton is murdered by a 16-year-old outside the Astrodome, Houston, TX, where the Stones are playing.
[31] *Start Me Up* hits US #2 for the first of three weeks, held off the top by Christopher Cross' *Arthur's Theme (Best That You Can Do)*, and then Daryl Hall & John Oates' *Private Eyes*.
Nov [9] 12 people are hurt and 56 arrested at a Civic Center, Hartford, CT, concert.
[22] Jagger, Richards and Wood jam with Buddy Guy and Muddy Waters at the Checker Board Lounge, Chicago.
Dec [14] Mick Taylor joins the band for its Kemper Arena, Kansas City, MO, concert.
[19] Easy-flowing ballad, *Waiting On A Friend*, makes UK #50.

1982

Feb [6] *Waiting On A Friend* reaches US #13.
Mar [27] Wyman's *A New Fashion* makes UK #37.
Apr [10] His third solo album, ***Bill Wyman***, peaks at UK #55.
May [8] *Hang Fire* reaches US #20.
[26] The Stones begin a European tour at the Capitol Theatre, Aberdeen, Grampian, Scotland, supported by the J. Geils Band, set to close on July 25th at Roundhay Park, Leeds, W. Yorks.
[31] The group gigs at the 100 club in London's Oxford Street, to an audience of 400.
June [19] ***Still Life (American Concert 1981)***, with highlights of their 1981 US tour, hits UK #4.
[25] The Rolling Stones receive the Silver Clef Award for Outstanding Achievement To British Music from the Nordoff Robbins Music Therapy charity, in London. Stone alone Wyman accepts the award on the group's behalf from Dame Margot Fonteyn, before the band plays at Wembley Stadium in the evening.
[26] *Going To A Go-Go*, their revival of the Miracles hit, reaches UK #26.
July [10] ***Still Life*** hits US #5.
[17] *Going To A Go-Go* reaches US #25.
Aug [7] Import album, ***In Concert***, makes UK #94.
Oct [9] *Time On My Side*, taken from the live album, peaks at UK #62.
Dec [25] UK TV-promoted compilation album, ***Story Of The Stones***, makes UK #24.

1983

Jan [14] Jagger films his part as the Chinese Emperor in "The Nightingale", as part of Showtime TV's "Faerie Tale Theatre" series.
[18] ***Still Life*** is certified gold by the RIAA.
Feb [11] "Let's Spend The Night Together", the Hal Ashby-directed documentary of the group's 1981 tour, premieres at the Loew Theater in New York.
Mar [24] "Let's Spend The Night Together" is released in the UK.
Aug [25] Jagger and Richards reach agreement with CBS head Walter Yetnikoff to sign with the label at 3:00 a.m. in the Ritz Hotel, Paris. Reportedly worth $28 million, the deal calls for four Stones albums.
Sept [20-21] Wyman and Watts join Jeff Beck, Eric Clapton, Jimmy Page, Steve Winwood, Joe Cocker, Paul Rodgers, Kenney Jones, Andy Fairweather Low, Ray Cooper and Ronnie Lane (himself a sufferer), in a benefit concert at the Royal Albert Hall, in aid of ARMS (Action for Research into Multiple Sclerosis). The second show will be performed in the presence of their Royal Highnesses, the Prince and Princess of Wales.
Oct [28] Jagger guests on the first edition of C4-TV's "The Tube".
Nov [19] *Undercover Of The Night*, despite a Julien Temple-lensed gun-toting video ban by BBC1-TV's "Top Of The Pops", reaches UK #11, as its parent album, ***Undercover***, hits UK #3.
[28] Wyman and Watts begin a nine-date, four-city US tour, in aid of the ARMS charity, at the Reunion Arena, Dallas, TX, with Ron Wood joining the same group of musicians featured at the Royal Albert Hall on September 20th.
Dec [10] ***Undercover*** hits US #4.
[18] Richards marries long-time belle, 27-year-old model Patti Hansen at Cabo San Lucas, Mexico, on his 40th birthday. (He already has a son, Marlon, born in 1969, and a daughter, Dandelion, born in 1972, both by Anita Pallenberg).
[23] Jagger guests in Bette Midler's video for her forthcoming single, a cover of *Beast Of Burden*.
[24] *Undercover Of The Night* hits US #9.

1984

Jan [4] ***Undercover*** is certified platinum by the RIAA.
[20] Press reports state that Jagger has donated £32,000 to Great Britain's gymnastic hopefuls for the forthcoming Olympic Games in Los Angeles.
Feb [25] *She Was Hot* makes UK #42.
Mar [2] Jerry Hall gives birth to Elizabeth Scarlett Jagger.
[3] *She Was Hot* makes US #44.
May [6-10] Jagger records *State Of Shock* with the Jacksons at New York's A&R studio.
June [14] The Rolling Stones become the first act to be inaugurated into the Madison Square Garden Hall of Fame.
July [21] The Jacksons' *State Of Shock*, with Jagger trading lead vocals with Michael Jackson, reaches UK #14, while another Stones retrospective, ***Rewind 1971-1984 (The Best Of The Rolling Stones)***, reaches UK #23.
[28] The extracted re-issue, *Brown Sugar*, peaks at UK #58.
Aug [4] *State Of Shock* hits US #4.
[18] ***Rewind*** makes US #86.
Oct [30] The RIAA certifies four million sales of ***Some Girls*** and three million of ***Tattoo You***.
Nov [13] Stones' compilation video "Rewind" is released, and becomes the first music video in the UK to receive an "18" certificate.

1985

Mar Wyman begins sessions for ***Willie And The Poor Boys*** album and video project to benefit ARMS. Andy Fairweather Low, Kenney Jones, Jimmy Page, Chris Rea, Paul Rodgers, Ringo Starr, Charlie Watts and Terry Williams also contribute.
[9] Jagger launches a long-awaited solo career with *Just Another Night*, which reaches UK #32.

[16] Jagger's solo album, ***She's The Boss***, produced with Bill Laswell and Nile Rodgers and recorded at Compass Point Studios, Nassau, Bahamas, debuts at its UK #6 peak.
[30] *Just Another Night* reaches US #12.
Apr [20] ***She's The Boss*** reaches US #13.
June [1] *Lucky In Love*, Jagger's second solo single, makes US #38.
July [13] Jagger performs at "Live Aid" at the JFK stadium, Philadelphia, PA, backed by Daryl Hall & John Oates, and is joined by Tina Turner on a medley of *State Of Shock* and *It's Only Rock'n'Roll*. Wood and Richards join Bob Dylan for his set at the conclusion of the event. Earlier in the day, a video of Jagger and Bowie's duet, *Dancing In The Street*, recorded on June 29th, is premiered.
Sept [7] *Dancing In The Street* enters the UK chart at #1, going gold in a week and becoming the fastest-selling single of the year.
Oct [12] *Dancing In The Street* hits US #7.
Nov [18] Charlie Watts & His Big Band begin a week of performances at Ronnie Scott's jazz club, London.
Dec [12] Ian Stewart dies of a heart attack in his doctor's Harley Street, London reception room, while waiting to see him.

1986

Jan [23] Richards inducts Chuck Berry at the inaugural Rock and Roll Hall of Fame ceremony at the Waldorf Astoria Hotel in New York. Richards says "I lifted every lick he ever played."
Feb [23] The Stones play at the 100 club in Oxford Street, London, in memory of Ian Stewart.
[25] Having never won an individual Grammy category (or, indeed, a BRIT Award or Ivor Novello trophy), the Rolling Stones are honored by NARAS at the 29th annual Grammy Awards with a Lifetime Achievement Award, citing the band "who poured the foundation for modern pop and rock performers and writers to build their careers upon; who through their abilities to grow and to change with society's dynamics both musically and lyrically awakened the senses and consciousness of America and the world."
Mar [22] *Harlem Shuffle*, a re-make of Bob & Earl's 1964 US #44, reaches UK #13.
[23] The Charlie Watts Orchestra makes its debut at the Town Hall, Fulham, London. (During April, the orchestra plays a one-week stint at Ronnie Scott's jazz club.)
Apr [5] ***Dirty Work***, dedicated to the memory of Ian Stewart, and the group's first album for CBS, though still via their own Rolling Stones imprint, hits UK #4.
May [3] ***Dirty Work***, co-produced by the Glimmer Twins with Steve Lillywhite, hits US #4, as the extracted *Harlem Shuffle* hits US #5.
June [6] Richards joins Chuck Berry on stage at the third annual "Chicago Blues Festival" in Grant Park, Chicago.
[10] ***Dirty Work*** is certified platinum by the RIAA.
[20] Jagger and David Bowie perform *Dancing In The Street* at the Prince's Trust charity concert at the Empire Pool, Wembley.
[28] *One Hit (To The Body)*, accompanied by a Russell Mulcahy-directed video, reaches US #28, but is the group's first UK chart miss.
July [5] Wood and Wyman join Rod Stewart on stage at the end of Stewart's Wembley Stadium concert.
[7] Richards produces Aretha Franklin's version of *Jumpin' Jack Flash*, at Detroit's Tamla Motown United Sound studio. Wood plays guitar on the session.
Aug [3] The **News Of The World** prints an exclusive interview with 16-year-old model, Mandy Smith, who reveals she has been having an affair with Bill Wyman for 2½ years.
[30] Jagger's solo *Ruthless People*, from the film of the same name, and written with Dave Stewart and Daryl Hall, peaks at US #51.
Sept [15] "Dancing In The Streets" wins the Best Overall Performance category at the third annual MTV Video Music Awards, broadcast simultaneously from the Universal Amphitheatre, Universal City, CA, and The Palladium, New York.
[16] Jagger punches a photographer while dining at a Los Angeles restaurant with Eurythmic Dave Stewart.
Oct [16] After a week of rehearsals at Chuck Berry's farm in Wentzville, MO, Richards joins Eric Clapton, Julian Lennon, Linda Ronstadt, Etta James and Chuck Berry on stage at the Fox Theatre, St. Louis, MO, for a concert being filmed for Taylor Hackford's Berry documentary, "Hail! Hail! Rock'n'Roll".
Nov [15] Jagger begins recording a new album at Wisseloord Studio, Hilversum, Holland.
[23] Richards joins Eric Clapton on stage at The Ritz in New York, for *Cocaine* and *Layla*.
[29] The Charlie Watts Orchestra begins a five-date US tour at the West Hartford Music Hall, Hartford, CT, promoting its newly-released album ***Live At Fulham Town Hall***, issued by CBS/Columbia.

1987

Apr [13] Wyman launches his AIMS Project (Ambition, Ideas, Motivation, Success) at a press conference at the Champagne Exchange, London. The plan is to travel the UK with the Stones' mobile studio and record unknown bands.
Sept [26] Jagger's sophomore set, ***Primitive Cool***, featuring Vernon Reid from Living Colour whom Jagger promotes and produces over the next two years, reaches UK #26.
Oct [17] ***Primitive Cool*** makes US #41.
[24] The extracted *Let's Work*, written and produced with Dave Stewart, makes UK #31 and US #39.
Nov [4] Wood and Bo Diddley, collectively known as the Gunslingers, open a North American tour at the Newport Music Hall, Columbus, OH, set to end on the 25th at The Ritz, New York.
Dec [19] Jagger's *Throwaway* peaks at US #67.

1988

Jan [20] Jagger inducts the Beatles at the third annual Rock and Roll Hall of Fame dinner at the Waldorf Astoria Hotel, in New York, before taking part in a jam session with Bob Dylan, George Harrison, Elton John and Bruce Springsteen.
Feb [20] Wyman and Wood join Phil Collins, Elvis Costello, Ian Dury, Chris Rea, Eddy Grant, Terence Trent D'Arby and Kenney Jones at a benefit concert, organized by Wyman, at the Royal Albert Hall, to raise money for the Great Ormond Street Hospital for Sick Children's "Wishing Well Appeal".
Mar [2] Wood begins a two-week tour of Japan with Bo Diddley, again as the Gunslingers.
[15] Jagger plays his first-ever Japanese concert at the Castle Hall, Osaka, in front of 11,000 people at the start of his solo tour.
[23] Tina Turner joins Jagger on stage at the Kerakuen Dome in Tokyo, Japan, duetting with him on *Brown Sugar* and *It's Only Rock'n'Roll*.
Apr [18-26] Jagger attends a lawsuit case in White Plains Court in New York, brought by reggae musician Patrick Alley, who claims Jagger has plagiarized the song *Just Another Night*. Jagger will win the case.
May [18] All five group members reconvene for the first time in two years at London's Savoy Hotel.
June [28] The Gunslingers play at the Hammersmith Odeon, before embarking on a month-long tour of Germany, Italy and Spain.
Sept *(I Can't Get No) Satisfaction* is voted #1 by **Rolling Stone** magazine in its Top 100 Singles Of All Time list.
[17] Jagger plays a warm-up gig at the 400-capacity Kardomah Cafe in Sydney, Australia.
[22] He begins his Australasian tour at the Boondall Entertainment Centre, Brisbane, Queensland, Australia, set to end on November 5th at the Western Spring Stadium, Auckland, North Island, New Zealand.
Oct [8] Richards performs on NBC-TV's "Saturday Night Live".
[15] Richards debut solo album, ***Talk Is Cheap***, co-written and produced with Steve Jordan and featuring Ivan Neville, Patti Scialfa and Mick Taylor among others, makes UK #37 in its week of entry.
[16] Richards, his own Jamaican home damaged by the recent hurricane, takes part in the "Smile Jamaica" benefit to aid its victims, at the Dominion Theatre, London.
Nov [9] Wood jams with Jerry Lee Lewis at his recently-opened Woody's On The Beach club in Miami, FL.
[19] ***Talk Is Cheap*** reaches US #24.
[24] Richards embarks on a 15-date US tour at the Fox Theatre, Atlanta, GA, through to December 17th. His back-up band, called the X-Pensive Winos, comprises Ivan Neville, Bobby Keys, Sarah Dash, Steve Jordan, Charley Drayton and Waddy Wachtel.

1989

Jan [13] Jagger and Richards meet in Barbados to start writing material for a new album.
[18] The group is inducted into the Rock and Roll Hall of Fame at the fourth annual dinner, at the Waldorf Astoria Hotel. At the perfunctory after-ceremony jam, Jagger joins Stevie Wonder on a medley of *Uptight* and *Satisfaction*, and Tina Turner on a duet of *Honky Tonk Women*. Little Richard joins Richards, Wood and Mick Taylor on *Can't Turn You Loose* and *Bony Maronie*, before Jagger, Richards, Wood and Taylor perform *Start Me Up*.
[21] Wood jams with Bo Diddley, Willie Dixon, Percy Sledge, Koko Taylor and Republican Party Chairman Lee Atwater, at one of President-Elect George Bush's inauguration parties at the Convention Center in Washington, DC.
Mar [9] Wyman and Wood arrive in Barbados to join the other Stones as they start work on a new album at Eddy Grant's studio.
[15] The Stones sign a $70 million contract, the largest in rock history, with Michael Cohl, of Canadian-based Concert Promotions International, to play 50 North American dates. (MTV will sponsor the American dates, while Labatt will sponsor the Canadian leg.)
Apr [29] The Stones finish recording at AIR studios in Montserrat.
May [17] Wyman's Sticky Fingers restaurant opens in Kensington, London.
[31] Richards is inducted as a Living Legend, receiving his Elvis statuette from Eric Clapton at the first International Rock Awards, at the Armory in New York.
June [2] 52-year-old Wyman, who married for the first, and only previous time in 1959, secretly marries Mandy Smith, now 19, in Bury St. Edmunds, Suffolk, three days ahead of the press-reported date. His 28-year-old son Stephen is best man. The couple appear on the BBC1-TV chat show, "Wogan", that evening.
[5] The couple's marriage is blessed at St. John the Evangelist, Hyde Park Crescent, London, followed by a reception at the Grosvenor House Hotel, attended by all the Stones and their wives. Wyman makes full use of a walking frame given to him as a wedding present by comedian Spike Milligan.
[20] Richards' ***Talk Is Cheap*** is certified gold by the RIAA.
July The group arrives in Washington, CT, to commence rehearsals for its upcoming US tour, the first in eight years, at Wykeham Rise, a former girls' boarding school.
[11] A press conference is held off Track 42 in New York's Grand Central Station. The Stones step off a Metro North train boarded at 125th Street, to announce full details of the tour and album release. Jagger previews ***Steel Wheels*** on a boombox in front of 500 assembled journalists.
[19] Residents in Washington form a "Roll The Stones Out Of Town" action committee, denouncing the band for having "ruined their tranquility".
Aug [12] As a warm-up to the tour, the group plays Toad's Place, New Haven, CT, a club with a 700 capacity and $3 admission. Their set, lasting 56 minutes, features 11 songs.
[31] The "Steel Wheels North American Tour 1989" opens at Veterans Stadium, Philadelphia, PA, before a sellout crowd of 55,000. The tour line-up includes

Bobby Keys (sax), Chuck Leavell and Matt Clifford (keyboards), Cindy Mizelle, Bernard Fowler and Lisa Fischer (backing vocals), with US band Living Colour the support act.

Sept [6] During a concert at Three Rivers Stadium in Pittsburgh, PA, the Stones, linked by satellite to MTV's studios in New York, perform *Mixed Emotions*, for the MTV Awards ceremony.

[16] *Mixed Emotions* makes UK #36.

[23] ***Steel Wheels*** hits UK #2, behind Eurythmics' ***We Too Are One***.

[30] A three-CD/cassette boxed-set retrospective of earlier hits, ***Singles Collection : The London Years***, makes US #91.

Oct [7] ***Steel Wheels*** hits US #3.

[14] *Mixed Emotions* hits US #5.

[18-19, 21-22] The group plays four sellout shows at the Los Angeles Memorial Coliseum, Los Angeles, grossing $9,166,937.

[20] In a slew of US sales updates, the RIAA certifies ***The Rolling Stones Now***, ***The Rolling Stones*** and ***12 x 5*** gold, platinum totals for ***Through The Past Darkly***, ***Aftermath***, ***Beggars Banquet***, ***Get Yer Ya Ya's Out*** and ***Out Of Our Heads*** and multi-platinum sales of ***Let It Bleed*** and ***Big Hits (High Tide And Green Grass)***, both at two million.

[28] Eric Clapton joins the band on stage at New York's Shea Stadium, playing lead guitar on *Little Red Rooster*.

Nov [4] Jagger spends an hour in Watsonville, CA, with victims of the earthquake, prior to the group's concert at the Oakland-Alameda County Stadium. The band donates $500,000 to the Red Cross Disaster Relief Fund.

Dec [2] *Rock And A Hard Place* peaks at UK #63.

[13-14] The group plays two sellout dates at the Montreal Olympic Stadium, Montreal, at the end of the North American leg of the tour, which has grossed $98 million.

[23] *Rock And A Hard Place* reaches US #23.

1990

Jan [9] The RIAA certifies two million sales of ***Steel Wheels***.

Feb [14] The band plays the first of ten sellout dates at the Tokyo Dome.

Mar [8] The group wins the Artist Of The Year, Best Band Of 1989, Best Tour, Worst Album Cover (***Steel Wheels***), Comeback Of The Year nods in the annual **Rolling Stone** magazine Music Awards Of 1989. They also win Artist Of The Year, Best Tour and Best Drummer (Charlie Watts) in the Critics' Award list.

[10] Ballad extract, *Almost Hear You Sigh*, makes US #50.

May [18] A 22-date "Urban Jungle Europe 1990" tour opens in Rotterdam, Holland.

June [18] Wyman's video, "Digital Dream", is released.

[29] "25 x 5 : The Continuing Adventures Of The Rolling Stones" video reaches the RIAA-certified 100,000 sales plateau.

[30] Reissued *Paint It Black* peaks at UK #61.

July [7] Richards pricks his finger on a steel guitar string, which is subsequently diagnosed as being septic at a Wembley Stadium show, causing the postponement of concerts at Cardiff and others at Wembley. *Almost Hear You Sigh* reaches UK #31.

[14] Re-charting ***Hot Rocks 1964-1971*** hits UK #3.

Aug Covers album, ***Stoned Again - A Tribute To The Stones***, featuring the Shop Assistants, Dave Kusworth, Death Of Samantha, the Henry Kaiser Band and others, is released.

[18] The group ends its "Urban Jungle Europe 1990" tour at the Startakiadni Stadium, Prague, Czechoslavakia, at the invitation of Vlacek Havel, to benefit the Czechoslovak Childrens' Foundation. (Their only other Eastern European appearances were in Poland in 1964 and April 1967.)

[24-25] They play the re-scheduled dates at Wembley Stadium. By tour's end, the group has given 116 concerts before an estimated six million people.

Nov [12] Wood breaks both his legs after being hit, trying to wave traffic away from his broken down car on the M4 motorway, near Marlborough, Wilts.

[21] After a lengthy and exhaustive courtship, Mick Jagger and Jerry Hall finally marry in Bali, while on vacation. (The validity of the ceremony will subsequently be questioned however.)

[22] Wyman's lawyer, Wright Webb Syrett, announces the end of his 17-month marriage to Mandy Smith.

Dec [31] Woody's, Wood's club in New York's East Village, closes.

1991

Feb Klein, president of ABKCO publishing, accepts an offer from the "Snickers" candy bar makers to use *Satisfaction* as its theme tune for advertising purposes, after persistently rejecting similar bids for years. He finally gives way when the company offers $4 million. Jagger and Richards' reported share is $2.8 million. The commercial will not, however, be permitted to use the original recording.

Mar [30] *Highwire* makes US #57, and debuts at its UK #29 peak.

Apr [20] Live album, recorded during the 1990 "Steel Wheels/Urban Jungle" world tour, ***Flashpoint***, bows at its UK #6 high. (Jagger begins filming "Free Jack" in Atlanta with Emilio Estevez, Anthony Hopkins and David Johansen, as Richards plays on albums by John Lee Hooker and Johnnie Johnson.)

May [2] The Rolling Stones are honored with the Outstanding Contribution To British Music award at the 36th annual Ivor Novello Awards (even though Jagger and Richards have never been previously recognized at the British Academy of Songwriters Composers and Authors' prestigious ceremony).

[4] ***Flashpoint*** reaches US #16 and will be certified gold by the RIAA on the 28th.

June [1] *Ruby Tuesday (Live)* peaks at UK #59.

Aug Watts' ***From One Charlie*** is released by Continuum Records.

Oct [25] "At The Max", a film documentary from the last world tour presented in state-of-the-art IMAX wide screen format, opens in selected cinemas in North America.

Nov [20] An announcement is made that the Rolling Stones have signed a six-year, three-album deal with Virgin Records (which this month issues Richards' ***Live At The Hollywood Palladium*** recorded with the X-Pensive Winos) worth a reported £20 million, in a further bid by the label to bolster the superstar ranks of its roster, prior to a much-rumored company sale.

Dec Watts is fined £350 for failing to fill out his census form for his Halsdon House at Dalton, near Winkworth, Devon.

1992

Jan [12] A third child for Jagger and Jerry Hall, daughter Georgia May Ayeesha, is born in London.

[13] "Freejack", in which Jagger stars as futuristic bad guy Vacendak, opens in US theatres.

[15] Richards inducts Leo Fender into the Rock and Roll Hall of Fame at the seventh annual dinner, at New York's Waldorf Astoria Hotel.

Feb [16] Jagger is refused entry into Japan because of his 1969 drug record and has to stay at a hotel near Tokyo's Narita airport, to appeal against the decision. (He had been banned in 1973, but allowed entry in March 1988 and February 1990.)

Mar Wyman, who has once again announced his intention to quit the Stones (this time living up to his promise), works on a solo project with co-producer Terry Taylor at Maison Rouge Studios.

[23] At a cost of £1,750, Jagger provides satellite coverage of the World Cup cricket final to England's "A" team, on tour in St. Vincent, where he has a home.

May The **New York Daily News** reports that one-time Animal, Danny McCulloch, will replace Wyman.

[26] Charlie Watts' Quintet's ***A Tribute To Charlie Parker With Strings*** is released on the Continuum label.

June [23] ABKCO Video issues the digitally-restored film "Gimme Shelter", available for the first time on video.

[28] Jagger makes his first live appearance of the year playing with Gary Moore & the Midnight Blues Band, at the National Music Day Celebration of the Blues, at London's Hammersmith Odeon. Pops Staples, Buddy Guy, Otis Rush, Jimmy Rogers, Ron Wood and Charlie Watts also participate.

July [1] ***Singles Collection - The London Years*** is certified platinum by the RIAA.

[2] Jagger becomes a grandfather (on Hall's 35th birthday) when daughter Jade gives birth at the Dorset cottage she shares with the father, Piers Jackson. (While UK press rumors detail a temporary Jagger/Hall split, author Victor Bockris issues **Keith Richards : The Biography**.)

Sept [9] In presenting the Video Of The Year Award to Van Halen at the ninth annual MTV Video Music Awards, Jagger thanks Woody Allen and Mia Farrow for "making our rock'n'roll marriages seem so blissful".

[26] Tom Waits' ***Bone Machine***, featuring co-writing and guitar contributions from Richards, makes US #176.

Oct [16] Wood sings *Seven Days* at the "Bob Dylan 30th Anniversary Celebration" concert, from Madison Square Garden.

[28] Wood kicks off a North American tour at The Sting, New Britain, CT, promoting his new album, ***Slide On This*** which features Watts.

[31] Richard's solo set, ***Main Offender***, featuring Waddy Wachtel (guitar), Charley Drayton (bass), Steve Jordan, Ivan Neville (keyboards) and Sarah Dash (vocals), charts for a week at UK #45.

Nov [7] Richards' ***Main Offender*** debuts at its US #99 peak.

[24] Wyman's divorce is finalized, with the High Court awarding Mandy Smith £580,000.

Dec [3] Jagger, interviewed on MTV Europe, says: "Bill has decided he doesn't want to carry on because he's done it for too long. You'll have to ask Bill why, because I don't really know why."

[17-18] Keith Richards & the X-Pensive Winos perform at London's Town & Country club, during a European tour.

[31] While the Stones are still negotiating a $30 million advance to tour in 1993-94, Richards & the X-Pensive Winos headline at The Academy, New York, supported by Pearl Jam.

1993

Jan Wyman confirms that he is leaving the group on ITV's "Tonight" show.

[21] Richards & the X-Pensive Winos play before a sellout crowd of 5,048, at the Bill Graham Civic Auditorium, San Francisco.

Feb [6] Jagger guests on NBC-TV's "Saturday Night Live", expertly impersonating Keith Richards in a skit which has Mike Myers impersonating Jagger, as his solo effort, *Sweet Thing*, debuts at its UK #24 peak.

[9] Jagger plays a free gig at the Webster Hall dance club in New York.

[13] *Sweet Thing* bows at its US #84 high.

[16] Wyman plays bass in Rod Stewart's one-night reformed Faces, at the 12th annual BRIT Awards, held at London's Alexandra Palace.

[19-20, 22-24] Richards & the X-Pensive Winos play five sellout dates at New York's Beacon Theatre, grossing $418,200.

[20] Jagger's third solo album ***Wandering Spirit***, on which he is backed by Los Angeles blues band, the Red Devils, and produced by Rick Rubin, bows at its UK #12 peak, and will do likewise the next week at US #11. (Wyman's solo album, ***Stuff***, including his cover of Randy Newman's *Leave Your Hat On*, is also released, in Japan, on the Victor label, and will retail in Europe in July 1993.)

Mar [6] A previously taped New York showcase concert by Jagger airs on ABC-TV's "In Concert".

Apr [21] Wyman marries 33-year old American fashion designer Suzanne Accosta, in St. Paul de Vence, France. Watts releases his latest solo album ***Warm And Tender***.

[24] *Gimme Shelter*, reissued with 11 other versions of the song by various artists on a benefit single for the Putting Our House In Order charity, debuts at its UK #32 peak.

June [2] Jagger and Richard are inducted into the Songwriters Hall of Fame at the 24th annual ceremonies at the Sheraton Hotel & Towers, New York, as the RIAA certifies multi-platinum sales of ***Hot Rocks*** now standing at six million US sales.
Aug The band begins rehearsing for its new album at a 17th century farmhouse in County Kildare. Jagger says "We're on a promise not to scare the horses, so Keith is only playing on volume eight". (Recording will start with producer Don Was in Dublin at the end of October.)
Oct [9] Early anthology ***Hot Rocks 1964-1971*** re-charts at UK #66.
Dec [11] UK compilation ***Jump Back - The Best Of The Rolling Stones*** reaches UK #16.

1994

Apr Virgin reissues the band's catalog from 1971 on CD as collector's editions.
May [3] The Rolling Stones hold a press conference to announce its forthcoming "Voodoo Lounge" tour on board the Honey Fitz yacht on the Hudson River.
July [16] *Love Is Strong* debuts at its UK #14 peak.
[19] The band plays a 16-song, 90-minute warm-up gig at the RPM in Toronto.
[23] Co-produced with Was, the generally-praised ***Voodoo Lounge*** enters the UK chart at #1, featuring session bassist Darryl Jones, who will also complete the rhythm section for the band's forthcoming world tour.
[29] Jagger answers questions about the "Voodoo Lounge" tour from fans on the Prodigy online network.
[30] ***Voodoo Lounge*** hits US #2.
Aug [1] The "Voodoo Lounge" tour opens with the first of two sellout shows at the Robert F. Kennedy Memorial Stadium, Washington, DC.
Sept [3] *Love Is Strong* peaks at US #91.
[8] The band performs two songs at the 11th annual MTV Video Music Awards at New York's Radio City Music Hall - the first time the group has performed at any awards show.
[22] As they play the first of two sellout shows at the Veterans Stadium, Philadelphia, PA, the National Affinity Cards and the Maryland-based Chevy Chase Savings Bank introduces the Rolling Stones master-card and visa card complete with the Stones' seminal red tongue logo, available at 1-800 615 ROCK.
Oct [4] As the "Voodoo Lounge" tour crosses north of the border to the Commonwealth Stadium, Edmonton, AB, Canada, the band's publicists announce the tour has become the highest-ever grossing with ticket sales of $114 million.
[8] *You Got Me Rocking* debuts at its UK #23 peak.
[11] George Jones album ***The Bradley Barn Sessions*** is released in the US featuring Richards on *Say It's Not You*, while the latter with Wood and Watts have also contributed to Bobby Womack's ***Resurrection***, also issued this month.
[23] One-time Stones producer Jimmy Miller dies at the University Hospital, Denver, CO.
Nov [13] An interview with Ed Bradley airs on CBS-TV's "60 Minutes".
[18] The Rolling Stones become the first major band to have a segment of a gig broadcast live on the Internet. At 10:30 p.m. ET, with the worldwide Web address : http:/www.stones.com., 20 minutes of tonight's show at the Cottown Bowl, Fair Park in Dallas is made available by multi-media company Thinking Pictures.
[22] Jagger beats out Mother Theresa and Carlos the Jackal in a London School of Economics students' poll to elect a new honorary president.
[26] Ballad *Out Of Tears* makes US #60.
Dec [7] Beamed in via satellite from the Olympic Stadium in Montreal, the Stones perform live on the fifth annual **Billboard** Music Awards, also accepting an award for Artistic Excellence.
[10] *Out Of Tears* debuts at its UK #36 peak.
[21] The RIAA certifies two million sales of ***Voodoo Lounge***.

1995

Jan [14] The Rolling Stones play the first of four sellout shows before a total of 204,020 people at the Hermanos Rodriguez Autodromo, Mexico City, Mexico, at the start of the Central and South American part of the "Voodoo Lounge" tour.
Feb [4] Soundtrack album to Robert Altman's "Ready To Wear", featuring the previously unissued Stones cut *Jump On Top Of Me*, makes US #29.
[24-25] They play two sellout dates in South Africa at the Ellis Park Stadium, Johannesburg.
Mar [1] ***Voodoo Lounge*** is named Best Rock Album and "Love Is Strong" nabs Best Music Video Shortform at the 37th annual Grammy Awards, held at Los Angeles' Shrine Auditorium.
[15] Steve Tisch announces that he and Jagger have formed film production company, Lip Service.
[17] The band finishes a seven-date stint at the Tokyo Dome, Tokyo, Japan, grossing more than $27 million from a combined audience of 285,294.
[27] The group plays the first of two sellout dates at the Cricket Ground, Melbourne, Victoria, Australia, at the beginning of the Australian and New Zealand leg of the "Voodoo Lounge" tour - it is the band's first visit Down Under since 1973.
May [25] Jagger/Richard's first recording on reel-to-reel tape from 1961 including *Around And Around*, *Little Queenie* and *La Bamba*, is auctioned at Christie's in London. The anonymous winning bid is made by Jagger.
[25-26] The band tapes two warm-up gigs for the forthcoming European leg of the tour at the Paradiso Club, Amsterdam, Holland.
July [15] *I Go Wild* debuts at its UK #29 peak.
[19] The band plays a secret show at London's Brixton Academy.
[27] Bob Dylan joins the Rolling Stones on stage at the Grammont, Montpelier, France.
Aug [24] Microsoft's TV commercials for their "Windows '95" software launch premiere simultaneously in the US, UK, Australia and Canada, using *Start Me Up* as its background theme. (Bill Gates' company has reportedly paid $12 million for the privilege.)
Sept [7] "Love Is Strong" wins the Best Cinematography category at the 12th annual MTV Video Music Awards, held at Radio City Music Hall.
Nov [7] The band's first CD-ROM ***Voodoo Lounge***, developed by the group with Second Vision New Media, is released by GTE Entertainment in the US and by Virgin Interactive worldwide.
Jagger has formed the Jagged Films production company which now pays $650,000 for the movie rights to UK novelist Robert Harris' **Enigma**, the tenth project now in development at the company, to be co-produced with "Saturday Night Live" creator Lorne Michaels.
[11] The band's live cover of Dylan's *Like A Rolling Stone* debuts at its UK #12 peak.
[25] Performance album ***Stripped***, recorded at the Paradiso Club on May 25th-26th, hits UK #9 in its week of entry.
Dec [2] ***Stripped*** debuts at its US #9 peak.

1996

Mar [1] Already grossing more than $300 million, the final leg of the "Voodoo Lounge" world tour begins in Bombay, India.
see also: **THE FACES**

HENRY ROLLINS

1987

Apr Having left the Washington, DC-based band SOA to become lead singer for ultra hardcore punk protagonists Black Flag in July 1981, Rollins (b. Henry Garfield, Feb. 13, 1961, Washington, DC), has stayed with the outfit through its most prolific period, featuring on ***Damaged*** (1981), ***Everything Went Black*** (1983), ***My War***, ***Family Man*** and ***Slip It In*** (all 1984), ***Loose Nut***, ***The Process Of Weeding Out*** and ***Live '84*** (all 1985) and ***In My Head*** (1986). With the band's dissolution, and having already toured as a spoken-word solo artist since 1983, often reciting his own poetry (a parallel vocation which he will maintain throughout his recording career, much of it published by his own 2.13.61 company, named after his birth-date, which he has established in 1984), Rollins, cutting an imposingly muscular and heavily tattooed figure, will tour heavily to promote his first solo first project, ***Hot Animal Machine***, released in August, which sets the tone for his post-punk angst and political/social-themed, full-throttle attack. In September, the hard-working Rollins will also release the EP ***Drive By Shooting***, a collaboration with Henrietta Collins and the Wifebeating Childhaters, while ***Big Ugly Mouth***, a spoken-word album recorded in February will be issued in December, all on the Texas Hotel label.

1988

Having formed the Rollins Band with Chris Haskett (guitar), Andrew Weiss (bass), Sim Cain (drums) and soundman Theo Van Rock, the group releases ***Life Time***. Subsequently issuing albums both as a solo artist and spoken-word performer, and separately with the constantly touring Rollins Band, his ***Sweat Box*** and ***Do It*** solo efforts will follow in 1989, the same year the Rollins Band's ***Over*** and ***Hard Volume*** are released. 1990 will see further aural assaults with the group's ***Turned On*** (recorded live in Vienna, Austria in 1989), and another Rollins collaboration, ***Fast Food For Thought***, recorded with Wartime for Chrysalis Records. In July the following year, another one-off project, the 12" single *Let There Be Rock*, with Rollins backed by Australian musicians assembled as the Hard-Ons, will emerge, with his solo effort, ***Human Butt*** released on the Quarterstick label.

1992

Apr [25] After five years of independently, mostly self-released product, and following his mass audience exposure through the group's participation in last year's inaugural Lollapalooza alternative music US caravan tour, Rollins has signed to Imago Records. His label debut, ***The End Of Silence***, credited to the Rollins Band and mixing elements of blues and jazz into an otherwise uncompromisingly intense punk-metal set, bows at its US #160 peak, his first chart showing.
May Quarterstick releases a six-CD boxed-set anthology of Rollins spoken-word highlights, collected as ***Deep Throat***.
Sept [12] Extracted from ***The End Of Silence***, *Tearing* debuts at its UK #54 high.

1994

Apr [22] Rollins embarks on an 11-date UK/Irish tour at the Tivoli, Dublin, Eire, set to end at the Leicester De Montfort University, Leicester, Leics.
[23] Following his 1993 story-telling spoken-word solo release ***The Boxed Life***, a two-CD set also released by Imago, the Rollins Band's ***Weight***, produced by Van Rock, with Melvin Gibbs having replaced Weiss and musically reflecting a funk edge, enters at its UK #22 pinnacle during a two-week stay.
[30] ***Weight*** debuts at its US #33 peak.
Aug [28] Rollins performs on the last day of the annual "Reading Festival", Reading, Berks.
Sept [10] *Liar*, couple with *Disconnect*, bows at its UK #27 peak.
Nov His latest spoken-word effort, ***Henry : Portrait Of A Singer Singer*** is released by Imago.

1995

Mar [1] Rollins performs *Liar* with the Rollins Band at the 37th annual Grammy Awards held at Los Angeles' Shrine Auditorium and also wins the Best Spoken Word or Nonmusical Album category for ***Get In The Van : On The Road With Black Flag***, released the previous year.
Apr [18] ***Encomium : A Tribute To Led Zeppelin***, featuring the Rollins Band's cover of *Four Sticks*,

enters at its US #17 peak.
May The film soundtrack to "Johnny Mnemonic", including a new cut by the Rollins Band, is released in the US. (Rollins also acts in the film, the latest cameo in a burgeoning acting career which includes roles in last year's "The Chase" and the forthcoming "Heat".)
June Ever restless, he launches a new audiobook label, 213CD, while still running his 11-year old book publishing company 2.13.61. (By year's end, his latest spoken-word album, ***Ball-Hog Or Tugboat*** will be released.)

1996

Jan [5] His "Public Insomniac Tour" reaches London's The Forum. During the year, Rollins will become the second artist, after George Michael, to be signed to David Geffen/Steven Spielberg/Jeffrey Katzenberg's Dreamworks SKG label, with his company debut due in January 1997.
June [11] Imago Records files a $50m breach of contract suit against both DreamWorks' SKG Records and Rollins for the artist's recent signing to the latter company, alleging he was unfairly poached while still under contract.

THE RONETTES

Veronica Bennett (lead vocals);
Estelle Bennett (vocals); **Nedra Talley** (vocals)

1961

June Bennett sisters Veronica (b. Aug. 10, 1943, New York, NY) and Estelle (b. July 22, 1944, New York), with cousin Talley (b. Jan. 27, 1946, New York), have become resident dancers at the Peppermint Lounge, the focus of the Twist dance craze in New York, earlier in the year. Earning $10 a night, they have then toured with Joey Dee, dancing on DJ Clay Cole's "Twist Package", as the Dolly Sisters, and have also appeared with Cole in the dance exploitation movie, "Twist Around The Clock". After appearing with DJ Murray The K as dance regulars in his Brooklyn Fox stage shows, the trio is now signed by Colpix Records.
Aug *I Want A Boy* is released on Colpix, with the group credited as Ronnie & the Relatives.

1962

Apr They become the Ronettes on their second single, *Silhouettes*, which is issued on the subsidiary May label. (Two further small-selling releases, *I'm On The Wagon* and *Good Girls*, will follow during the next 12 months.)

1963

June Georgia Winters of **16** magazine invites Phil Spector to meet the trio when he is talent-scouting in New York, and Spector is particularly impressed by Veronica's (generally known as Ronnie) voice. Via a subterfuge involving a professed desire to return to school and complete their education, the girls obtain a release from the Colpix contract.
Aug Spector signs the trio to his Philles label, and spends a month assembling *Be My Baby* and *Baby I Love You*.
Oct The group's Philles debut, *Be My Baby*, glossed in an archetypal Spector "Wall Of Sound" production, hits US #2 (behind Jimmy Gilmer & the Fireballs' *Sugar Shack*).
Nov [13] The Ronettes open in Teaneck, NJ, as part of Dick Clark's "Caravan Of Stars" tour.
[23] *Be My Baby* hits UK #4.
Dec The group appears on Spector's various-artists seasonal compilation, ***A Christmas Gift For You***, singing *Frosty The Snowman*, *Sleigh Ride* and *I Saw Mommy Kissing Santa Claus*, tracks which will be airplayed as a Christmas radio tradition every subsequent Yuletide.

1964

Jan *Baby I Love You* reaches US #24 as the group begins a UK "Group Scene 1964" tour, supporting the Rolling Stones.
Feb [8] After returning to New York, the Ronettes greet the Beatles on their first visit to the US, and ask them questions in a radio interview.
[29] *Baby I Love You* reaches UK #11.
Apr Ronnie Bennett cuts the solo effort, *So Young*, which Spector places on his new subsidiary label, Phil Spector Records, but does no more than test-market the cut on a limited basis.
May *(The Best Part Of) Breaking Up*, written by Spector with Pete Anders and Vinnie Poncia, makes US #39.
Aug Pounding *Do I Love You?*, from the same songwriting team, reaches US #34, while *(The Best Part Of) Breaking Up* makes UK #43.
Oct [17] *Do I Love You?* reaches UK #35, the trio's final British hit.
Dec *Walking In The Rain*, a dramatic Spector/Mann/Weil-penned ballad with heavy Spector dressing, climbs to US #23. In the UK it is released as *In The Rain*, to avoid a copyright wrangle, but fails to chart. The record will earn a Grammy Award for its special sound effects.

1965

Jan Their debut album ***Presenting The Fabulous Ronettes, Featuring Veronica*** makes US #96.
Feb *Born To Be Together* peaks at US #52.
June *Is This What I Get For Loving You?* (later revived by Marianne Faithfull in 1967, when her version will reach UK#43) makes US #75.
[28] The Ronettes appear on CBS-TV's "It's What's Happening Baby" special.
Aug [14] The Ronettes 14-city US tour, opening for the Beatles - though without Ronnie, who has left the group to be with Spector (whom she shortly marries) - opens at the International Amphitheater, Chicago, IL. Cousin Elaine joins in her place.
Dec [6] The trio appears on NBC-TV's "Hullabaloo".

1966

Oct After a lengthy silence, the group returns with the Jeff Barry-produced *I Can Hear Music* (revived by the Beach Boys and others), but it stops at US #100 and is the Ronettes' last US chart entry. The group disbands almost immediately after this: both Estelle and Talley leave the music business, and will marry and settle into family life.

1969

Mar With Spector recording again via a production deal with A&M Records (which brings him three hits by Sonny Charles & Checkmates Ltd.), he cuts a single by Ronnie Spector: *You Came, You Saw, You Conquered*, credited to "The Ronettes, featuring the voice of Veronica".

1971

Mar Ronnie records tracks for her first solo album, at Abbey Road Studios, London, with her husband producing, and George Harrison (who has invited her on to the Apple label) contributing and writing songs.
May *Try Some, Buy Some* by Ronnie Spector, a Harrison composition, released on Apple, peaks at US #77.

1973

Mar Ronnie appears at a Richard Nader Rock'n'Roll Revival show at New York's Madison Square Garden, performing with new back-up singers Denise Edwards and Chip Fields as Ronnie & the Ronettes.
Nov Signed to Buddah Records by producer Stan Vincent, Ronnie & the Ronettes release *Lover, Lover*, produced by Vincent. Ronnie will separate from Spector during the year. Her second Buddah release is a Vincent-produced version of *I Wish I Never Saw The Sunshine* issued the following April, originally recorded by Spector with the Ronettes in 1965, but not released. During 1974 her divorce from Spector will become final (she will allegedly receive her first alimony payment of $1,300 delivered in nickels). In November 1976, Ronnie will provide back-up vocals for Bruce Springsteen, when he and the E. Street Band play six nights at the Palladium in New York, while the following year Little Steven Van Zandt will produce her treatment of Billy Joel's *Say Goodbye To Hollywood*, a song itself inspired by Ronnie.

1981

Jan She finally records a solo album, ***Siren***, produced by Genya Ravan and released on independent labels Polish in the US, and Red Shadow in Britain. Her only other major recording presence during the decade will be on Eddie Money's November 1986 US #4 hit, *Take Me Home Tonight*, featuring Ronnie reprising her famous *Be My Baby* line throughout the song, and signed to CBS/Columbia Records in 1987, another solo set, ***Unfinished Business***, signalling a determined return to recording and performance, released in July of that year.

1995

Mar Following the 1990 publication of her autobiography, **Be My Baby** (written with Vince Waldron), revealing, amongst other notable events, that as a 12-year-old she had to fend off the advances of a 13-year-old Frankie Lymon and that her ex-husband allegedly refused to let her leave their Los Angeles, CA home. Ronnie Spector has moved into the '90s as an occasional performer at benefit concerts and nostalgia events, including her 1992 participation in the US touring "Let The Good Times Roll" package. While the Ronettes 1961-62 recordings have found their way onto compact disc via Rhino Records' release of ***Early Years '61-'62***, a ruling in the New York State Supreme Court from Judge Ira Grammerman now dictates that American Express and the advertising agency Ogilvy & Mather violated the Ronettes' rights under the Screen Actors Guild contract regarding permission to use their voices in a commercial.

LINDA RONSTADT

1964

Ronstadt (b. July 15, 1946, Tucson, AZ) the daughter of Mexican/German parents, whose hardware store-owner father sings and plays Mexican songs in his spare time, having at the age of 14 sung with brother Mike and sister Suzi as the Three Ronstadts, and then as the New Union Ramblers, drops out of the University of Arizona, after one semester, to join guitarist Bob Kimmel, with whom she has performed with Mike and Suzi in local clubs, in Los Angeles, CA, as a member of the Kimmel Brothers. When the Kimmels break up, three of their number, Kimmel, Ronstadt and guitarist Kenny Edwards, form folk trio the Stone Poneys (named after Charley Patton's song *The Stone Poney Blues*). Performing regularly at Los Angeles' Troubadour club in 1965, the group is seen by promoter Herb Cohen, who is keen to manage Ronstadt as a solo act, but is persuaded by her to take on the trio. Mercury Records offers a deal if the group will switch to a surf repertoire and name-change to the Signets, but the band's fortunes decline and they revert to their original moniker. In 1966 Cohen recommends them to Nik Venet, a staff producer at Capitol Records, who signs them to the label, following which their debut album, ***The Stone Poneys***, is released.

1968

Jan [27] *Different Drum*, written by Mike Nesmith of the Monkees, previously recorded by the Greenbriar Boys and extracted from the Stone Poneys' ***Evergreen, Volume 2***, reaches US #13. It features Ronstadt singing solo, with studio musicians backing her.
Mar [2] ***Evergreen, Volume 2*** makes US #100, supported by a US tour opening for the Doors, with Ronstadt and Kimmel joined by session men.

(Edwards has already quit by this time and travelled to India.)
[30] *Up To My Neck In High Muddy Water*, credited to Linda Ronstadt & the Stone Poneys, peaks at US #93. Ronstadt is left as a solo artist with Capitol and records her maiden album ***Hand Sown, Home Grown*** to be released in April the following year.

1970

Oct ***Silk Purse*** peaks at US #103, while the extracted *Long Long Time* makes US #25 and is nominated for a Grammy Award. During the month she also appears at the Joan Baez-organized "Big Sur Folk Festival", also featuring the Beach Boys, Kris Kristofferson and others.

1971

Feb *(She's A) Very Lovely Woman/The Long Way Around* peaks at US #70.
Apr She recruits a group of musicians from the Troubadour club as her tour band, including Bernie Leadon (guitar), Glenn Frey (guitar), Randy Meisner (bass) and Don Henley (drums), who will become the Eagles.

1972

Mar ***Linda Ronstadt***, with backing by the road band, peaks at US #163, while the extracted *Rock Me On The Water* makes US #85.
[11] Neil Young's ***Harvest***, featuring Ronstadt's backing vocal on *Heart Of Gold* and *Old Man*, tops the US and UK chart.
Dec She works on ***Don't Cry Now*** with producer John Boylan for David Geffen's Asylum Records, but the project flounders, with Ronstadt heavily in debt, and Capitol also demanding a further contracted album. In the middle of recording the album, Ronstadt embarks on a three-month US concert tour with Neil Young.

1973

May Peter Asher, ex-Peter & Gordon, takes over Ronstadt's management and production after seeing her perform at New York, NY's Bitter End club, and steers ***Don't Cry Now*** to completion, after it has taken a year of sessions, three producers, and $150,000 in costs. (Asher has become her manager after his other act, Kate Taylor, retired from the music business two days after finishing an album.)
Dec ***Don't Cry Now***, with a production credit to J.D. Souther, makes US #45 during a 56-week chart stay.

1974

Jan Ballad *Love Has No Pride*, written by Eric Kaz, and taken from ***Don't Cry Now***, makes US #51.
Mar ***Different Drum*** on Capitol, a compilation of five Stone Poney cuts and early solo tracks, makes US #92.
May From the Asylum album, *Silver Threads And Golden Needles*, her update of a 1962 hit by the Springfields, peaks at US #67.
Dec [24] Ronstadt, Joni Mitchell, Carly Simon and James Taylor are sighted singing Christmas carols together in Los Angeles.

1975

Feb [15] With Asher producing, she has recorded her contractual obligation album for Capitol, ***Heart Like A Wheel***. Establishing what will be a familiar Ronstadt pattern of mixing carefully chosen oldie revivals with new songs, it tops the US chart for a week while, taken from it, her revival of Betty Everett's *You're No Good* (with Andrew Gold playing most of the instruments) also tops the US chart in the same week, and earns a gold disc.
June *When Will I Be Loved*, her treatment of the Everly Brothers' 1960 smash, also taken from ***Heart Like A Wheel***, hits US #2, behind Captain & Tennille's *Love Will Keep Us Together*. Its B-side, reviving Buddy Holly's *It Doesn't Matter Anymore*, makes US #47. Meanwhile, Capitol issues another compilation of early material, ***The Stone Poneys Featuring Linda Ronstadt***, which peaks at US #172.
Aug [25] ***Don't Cry Now*** is certified as Ronstadt's first gold by the RIAA.
Nov Recording for Asylum again, with Asher (who will remain her producer hereafter), Ronstadt's ***Prisoner In Disguise***, featuring longtime studio cohorts Gold, Edwards, Russ Kunkel, David Lindley and David Campbell, hits US #4. The extracted *Heat Wave/Love Is A Rose*, coupling an early Motown (Martha & the Vandellas) hit with a folky Neil Young-penned ballad, hits US #5.

1976

Feb Also from ***Prisoner In Disguise***, her revival of the Miracles' 1965 hit, *The Tracks Of My Tears*, reaches US #25.
[28] Ronstadt wins Best Country Vocal Performance, Female category for *I Can't Help It (If I'm Still In Love With You)*, at the 18th annual Grammy Awards.
May *The Tracks Of My Tears* is her UK chart debut at #42.
Aug [1] Ronstadt embarks on a US tour. (During the year, she is paid $500,000 to perform six concerts in Sun City, South Africa.)
Sept ***Hasten Down The Wind***, once again helmed by Asher, and including three Karla Bonoff songs, makes UK #32.
Oct Another Buddy Holly revival, *That'll Be The Day*, reaches US #11, taken from ***Hasten Down The Wind***, which hits US #3.
[28] ***Hasten Down The Wind*** is certified platinum by the RIAA.
Dec [2] Ronstadt is featured on the cover of **Rolling Stone** magazine.

1977

Jan The extracted Bonoff-penned *Someone To Lay Down Beside Me* peaks at US #42, while the compilation album, ***Greatest Hits***, which includes hit singles from both Capitol and Asylum, hits US #6.
[19] Ronstadt, currently in the company of California governor Jerry Brown, participates in the Inaugural Eve Gala Performance fundraiser for President-Elect, Jimmy Carter.
Feb [19] Ronstadt wins Best Pop Vocal Performance, Female for ***Hasten Down The Wind***, at the 19th annual Grammy Awards.
Mar [5] ***Hasten Down The Wind*** wins NARM trophies for Best Album By A Female Artist and Best Album By A Female Country Artist.
May [23] Ronstadt begins recording material for the forthcoming ***Simple Dreams*** (and is currently featured on backing vocals on Andrew Gold's *Lonely Boy*, which hits US #7).
June *Lose Again* peaks at US #76, while the double compilation, ***A Retrospective***, on Capitol, reaches US #46.
July [21] Ronstadt duets with Mick Jagger on *Tumbling Dice* at a Rolling Stones concert at the Community Center, Tucson.
Sept [20] She performs at the Universal Amphitheatre, Universal City, CA, wearing a cub scout uniform.
Oct [1] Bonoff's maiden solo album ***Karla Bonoff***, featuring Ronstadt on *Home* and *Rose In The Garden*, enters the US chart set to make #52.
During the month, Ronstadt sings *The Star Spangled Banner* at Game 1 of Major League Baseball's World Series between the Los Angeles Dodgers and the New York Yankees.
Dec [17] Her revival of Roy Orbison's *Blue Bayou* hits US #3 one week after her simultaneously-released cover of Buddy Holly's *It's So Easy* has hit US #5.
[3] ***Simple Dreams***, from which both are taken, tops the US chart for the first of five weeks and reaches UK #15.

1978

Jan *Poor, Poor Pitiful Me*, also from ***Simple Dreams***, makes US #31, while *Blue Bayou* peaks at UK #35.
[10] Ronstadt comes second on Mr. Blackwell's list of Worst Dressed Women Of 1978, behind Farrah Fawcett Majors.
[16] On a more positive note, she wins the Favorite Female Artist, Pop/Rock category at the fifth annual American Music Awards, held at the Civic Auditorium, Santa Monica CA.
Feb [25] Warren Zevon's ***Excitable Boy***, featuring Ronstadt on its title track, peaks at US # 189.
Apr [3] The film, "FM", in which Ronstadt is featured singing *Love Me Tender* premieres in Los Angeles. (Continuing a current trend, a DJ will take Ronstadt's cover of the song and splice it with Elvis Presley's version to create a "duet".)
May Her treatment of the Rolling Stones' *Tumbling Dice*, also featured on the ***FM*** soundtrack, reaches US #32.
Sept [22] The still-climbing ***Living In The USA*** is certified platinum by the RIAA.
Oct *Back In The USA*, her treatment of a Chuck Berry song included on her new album, peaks at US #16.
Nov [4] ***Living In The USA*** tops the US chart for a week, and makes UK #39.
[13] The 1977 compilation ***A Retrospective*** is certified gold by the RIAA.
[18] Nicolette Larson's ***Nicolette***, featuring Ronstadt on *Mexican Divorce*, *Give A Little* and *Come Early Morning*, enters the US chart set to reach #37.

1979

Jan Her cover of Smokey Robinson's *Ooh Baby Baby*, taken from ***Living In The USA***, hits US #7.
[12] Ronstadt nabs the Favorite Female Artist, Pop/Rock, and Favorite Single, Country trophies at the sixth annual American Music Awards, again held at the Santa Monica Civic Auditorium.
[16] She meets Dolly Parton and Emmylou Harris in Nashville, TN, at Parton's house.
[18] The trio records material in the Enactron Truck Studio in Los Angeles with producer Brian Ahern.
Mar Her revival of Doris Troy's *Just One Look* makes US #44.
Apr Ronstadt goes on safari with reported current beau, politician Jerry Brown.
May Her version of Elvis Costello's *Alison* makes UK #66.
Aug [4] Ronstadt joins Jackson Browne, Emmylou Harris, Nicolette Larson, Michael McDonald, Bonnie Raitt and members of Little Feat in a benefit concert in aid of Lowell George's widow, at the Great Western Forum, Inglewood, CA. The 20,000 crowd raises over $230,000.
Oct [24] She begins recording for the forthcoming ***Mad Love*** project.
Dec [21-22] Ronstadt is joined by Chicago and the Eagles to play two benefit concerts in San Diego, CA, and Las Vegas, NV, raising $150,000 for presidential candidate, Jerry Brown.

1980

Mar *How Do I Make You* hits US #10.
[29] Ronstadt takes part in a benefit on the steps of Pennsylvania's state capitol building after the Harrisburg Three Mile Island nuclear incident.
Apr Harder new-wave edged ***Mad Love***, recorded with backing from Los Angeles group the Cretones and featuring her treatment of Elvis Costello's *Alison*, and including *How Do I Make You*, hits US #3, and also makes UK #65.
[21] During current US dates, Ronstadt plays at the Five Seasons Center, Cedar Rapids, IA, donating the proceeds to Gary Hart's senatorial bid in Colorado.
May Her revival of Little Anthony & the Imperials' *Hurt So Bad*, taken from ***Mad Love***, hits US #8.
[12] ***Mad Love*** is certified platinum by the RIAA.
July [15] Ronstadt makes her acting debut as Mabel in the New York Shakespeare Festival's production of "The Pirates Of Penzance", at the Delacorte Theater in New York's Central Park, earning $400 a week.
Aug *I Can't Let Go*, a third single from ***Mad Love***, reaches US #31.
Nov [29] Emmylou Harris' ***Light Of The Stable***, featuring Ronstadt on the title cut, enters the US chart set to make #102. During the year she has also contributed vocals to Nicolette Larson's forthcoming ***Radioland*** (on *Ooo-Eee*) and Zevon's ***Bad Luck Streak In Dancing School*** (*Empty-Handed Heart*).

1981

Jan [8] "The Pirates Of Penzance" moves to Broadway, opening at the Uris Theatre (and will win a Tony award).
Feb [1-2, 8] The "Pirates" soundtrack is recorded at Columbia 30th Street Recording Studio.
June Ronstadt leaves the "Pirates" cast, replaced by Karla DeVito.
Dec Compilation album, ***Greatest Hits, Volume 2***, reaches US #26.

1982

Feb Ronstadt begins filming the movie version of "The Pirates Of Penzance", at Shepperton Studios in England.
June [12] She joins Jackson Browne, Bruce Springsteen and others to perform at a Peace Rally in New York's Central Park.
[30] She begins recording ***What's New***, a collection of standards.
Nov ***Get Closer***, produced as ever, by Asher, and featuring stalwart sidemen Edwards, Gold and Kunkel, and guest vocalists Emmylou Harris, Dolly Parton, J.D. Souther and James Taylor, makes US #31, while its title track, *Get Closer*, reaches US #29.
[23] ***Get Closer*** is confirmed gold by the RIAA.

1983

Feb Her treatment of Billy Joe Royal's *I Knew You When*, taken from ***Get Closer***, makes US #37.
[18] "The Pirates Of Penzance" movie opens at the Public Theater, New York.
May *Easy For You To Say*, written by Jimmy Webb, and also from ***Get Closer***, peaks at US #54.
[16] She appears as a special guest on Motown's 25th Anniversary special on NBC-TV, duetting with Smokey Robinson on *The Tracks Of My Tears* and *Ooh Baby Baby*.
Sept Ronstadt, Nelson Riddle and a 47-piece orchestra embark on a US tour, with performances at New York's Radio City Music Hall, New Orleans, LA's World's Fair Amphitheatre, and the Copa Room at the Sands Hotel, Atlantic City, NJ.
Dec In a departure from her traditional pop/rock/country mix, ***What's New***, comprising standards arranged by Riddle and recorded with his orchestra, hits US #3, while the extracted title track, *What's New*, reaches US #53.

1984

Feb ***What's New*** makes UK #31.
May [27] "Linda Ronstadt In Concert With the Nelson Riddle Orchestra" airs on US cable-TV's Cinemax.
Aug [24] Running through to October 5th, Ronstadt begins recording a second album with Riddle.
Oct [30] Ronstadt makes her operatic debut in "La Boheme", at New York's Public Theater. (The show will run for 30 previews and 38 performances, and transfer to the Anspacher Theater before closing on December 30th.)

1985

Jan ***Lush Life***, also with the Nelson Riddle Orchestra, reaches US #13 and UK #100.
[17] ***Lush Life*** is certified platinum by the RIAA.

1986

Jan [19] She begins recording the album, ***Trio***, with Emmylou Harris and Dolly Parton.
Apr Philip Glass' ***Songs From Liquid Days***, featuring Ronstadt's vocals on two cuts, makes US #91.
Sept Paul Simon's ***Graceland***, featuring Ronstadt on *Under African Skies*, is released.
Oct [13] Ronstadt, Harris and Parton sing *My Dear Companion*, at the Grand Ole Opry, Nashville.
[16] After a week of rehearsals at Chuck Berry's farm in Wentzville, MO, Ronstadt joins Eric Clapton, Julian Lennon, Etta James, Chuck Berry and ringmaster Keith Richard on stage at the Fox Theatre, St. Louis, MO, for a concert being filmed for Taylor Hackford's Berry documentary, "Hail! Hail! Rock'n'Roll".
Nov ***For Sentimental Reasons***, once again arranged and conducted by Riddle, reaches US #46, as ***'Round Midnight***, a deluxe boxed-set comprising ***What's New***, ***Lush Life*** and ***For Sentimental Reasons***, makes US #129.
Dec Ronstadt sings with Glass in concert in New York City, San Francisco and Los Angeles.
[8] ***For Sentimental Reasons*** is certified gold by the RIAA.

1987

Mar [14] Co-written by Barry Mann, Cynthia Weil and James Horner, *Somewhere Out There*, a ballad duet with James Ingram from the Spielberg-produced animated feature, "An American Tail", hits US #2, Huey Lewis & the News' *Jacob's Ladder*.
May ***Trio***, the much-anticipated country collaboration with Dolly Parton and Emmylou Harris, hits US #6 and peaks at UK #60. From it, their revival of the Teddy Bears' *To Know Him Is To Love Him* hits US C&W #1, but fails to cross over (two more tracks from the album, *Telling Me Lies* and *Those Memories Of You*, will also be top five US Country hits).
July [4] Ronstadt and Ingram sing *Somewhere Out There* at the "Welcome Home" benefit in Washington, DC, for Vietnam vets, broadcast on HBO-TV.
[14] ***Trio*** is certified platinum by the RIAA.
Aug *Somewhere Out There* hits UK #8.
Dec [19] Ronstadt is the music guest on NBC-TV's "Saturday Night Live".

1988

Feb ***Canciones De Mi Padre (My Father's Songs)***, an entirely Spanish-sung collection of 13 traditional Mexican songs which Ronstadt learned as a child from her father, reaches US #42.
[8] "Canciones De Mi Padre", a major international tour with a Spanish-language only repertoire, begins.
Mar [2] Ronstadt wins her third Grammy, for Best Country Vocal, Duo Or Group, for her work with Dolly Parton and Emmylou Harris on ***Trio***, at the 30th annual Grammy Awards.
July [11] She takes part in the first "International Festival Of Arts" in New York's Central Park with Placido Domingo, with whom she sings two duets, and Gloria Estefan.
[12-30] The "Canciones De Mi Padre" tour plays at Broadway's Minskoff Theatre.

1989

Feb [22] Ronstadt performs at the 31st annual Grammy Awards held at Los Angeles' Shrine Auditorium.
Mar She begins recording new material at Skywalker Ranch with Asher at the desk.
May [6] Ronstadt performs at UCLA's Mexican Arts Series benefit.
Aug [3] She is nominated for an Emmy Award for Individual Performance In A Variety Or Musical Program for PBS TV's "Great Performances : Canciones De Mi Padre".
Sept [13] The RIAA certifies platinum sales of ***Prisoner In Disguise*** and ***Greatest Hits Volume II***.
Oct [21] Neil Young's ***Freedom***, with Ronstadt featured on *Hangin' On A Limb*, enters the US chart set to reach #35.
Nov ***Cry Like A Rainstorm - Howl Like the Wind***, featuring four duets with Aaron Neville, and cameos from Brian Wilson, Jimmy Webb and the Oakland Interfaith Gospel Choir, hits US #7.
Dec [6] The still-rising *Don't Know Much* is certified gold by the RIAA.
[9] Ronstadt guests on NBC-TV's "Saturday Night Live" with Neville, as ***Cry Like A Rainstorm - Howl Like the Wind*** makes UK #43.
[23] *Don't Know Much*, one of the parent album's four duets with Neville and previously a 1981 US #88 for Bill Medley, hits US #2, behind Phil Collins' *Another Day In Paradise*, having also missed UK #1 by one place in November.

1990

Feb [21] *Don't Know Much*, performed by the duo during the ceremony, wins Best Pop Performance By A Duo Or Group With Vocal category at the 32nd Grammy Awards, held at the Shrine Auditorium. ***Cry Like A Rainstorm - Howl Like The Wind*** also wins Best Engineered Recording, for George Massenburg.
Mar [31] Bonoff-penned *All My Life*, a further duet with Neville, reaches US #11.
June [2] Again with Neville, *When Something Is Wrong With My Baby*, reviving Sam & Dave's 1967 US #42, peaks at US #78.
[8] Ronstadt performs at the T.J. Martell Foundation for Leukemia Cancer & AIDS Research 1990 Humanitarian Award concert, at Avery Fisher Hall, Lincoln Center, New York City.
Aug [9] She begins a major US tour, with the Neville Brothers in support, in Austin, TX, set to end on October 28th at the Concord Pavilion, Concord, CA.
Nov [3] ***Rubáiyát***, Elektra's 40th anniversary compilation, to which Ronstadt has contributed a cover of *The Blacksmith*, makes US #140.
[27] The RIAA certifies platinum sales of ***Blue Bayou*** and multi-platinum sales of ***Simple Dreams*** (three million) and ***Cry Like A Rainstorm, Howl Like The Wind*** (two million).
Dec [21-22] Ronstadt performs *Good Night* at two John Lennon tribute concerts, at the Tokyo Dome, Tokyo, Japan, on a bill with Miles Davis, Natalie Cole, Daryl Hall & John Oates and Sean Lennon.

1991

Feb [20] Ronstadt and Neville win Best Pop Performance By A Duo Or Group With Vocal category, for the second consecutive year, for *All My Life*, at the 33rd annual Grammy Awards, at Radio City Music Hall, New York.
Nov [27] ***Heart Like A Wheel*** is certified platinum by the RIAA.
Dec [23] She appears on PBS-TV's "Great Performances : La Pastorela", and has also recently contributed *Dreams To Dream* to the ***An American Tail : Fievel Goes West*** soundtrack. (During the year, Ronstadt has adopted a daughter, Mary Clementine.)

1992

Jan [4] ***Mas Canciones***, her second Spanish-language outing, makes US #88.
[16] *Somewhere Out There* is certified gold by the RIAA.
Apr Ronstadt's *Perfidia* and *Quiereme Mucho* appear on the newly-released "Mambo Kings" film soundtrack.
Aug [27] ***Canciones De Mi Padre*** is certified platinum by the RIAA.
Sept [17] Ronstadt guests on NBC-TV's "The Tonight Show".
Oct [3] ***Frenesi***, a further Spanish-only set, recorded with Ray Santos and his orchestra, charts for a week at US #193.
[22] She co-headlines a concert with Bruce Hornsby held for presidential candidate Bill Clinton, at the Pacific Amphitheatre, Costa Mesa, CA.
Nov [5-6] Ronstadt performs at the Hollywood Palladium, Hollywood, CA, during current US dates.
[19] She guests on Fox-TV's "The Simpsons", helping promote Barney's snow-ploughing business.

1993

Jan [17-18] She takes part in the "America's Reunion On The Mall" celebration in Washington, DC, during Inaugural festivities.
[20] Ronstadt performs at the Western Ball on Inauguration Day in Washington.
Feb [24] ***Frenesi*** wins the Best Tropical Latin Album category, while ***Mas Canciones*** is named Best Mexican American Album at the 35th annual Grammy Awards, held at the Shrine Auditorium.
Apr [30] She sings at the "Anheuser-Busch Companies Present A Night Of Music & Laughter" concert at the Wiltern Theatre, Los Angeles, to benefit

the National Hispanic Scholarship Fund.
May [6] Ronstadt guests on CBS-TV's "The Women Of Country", as she spends the next few weeks recording with Randy Newman.
[28] The RIAA certifies three million sales of ***What's New***.
Sept [7] Jimmy Webb's ***Suspending Disbelief***, his first solo album in 16 years, produced by Ronstadt and George Massenburg, is released in the US.
Dec [11] Co-produced with Massenburg (her first pop outing not to be helmed by Asher), ***Winter Light***, Ronstadt's latest solo offering, with material by Burt Bacharach and Hal David, Webb and Brian Wilson, debuts at its US #92 peak.

1994

Feb [24] Ronstadt guests on CBS-TV's "Late Show With David Letterman".
June [28] The RIAA certifies five million sales of ***Greatest Hits Volume I***.
July [12] During a current series of US dates, Ronstadt performs at the Hollywood Bowl, with Itzhak Perlman, John Williams and the Los Angeles Philharmonic Orchestra.
Sept [27] ***Kermit Unpigged***, to which Ronstadt has contributed a duet with the Muppet, is released by Jim Henson Records.
Dec [10] Frank Sinatra's ***Duets II***, to which Ronstadt and the Chairman of the Board pair on *Moonlight In Vermont*, hits US #9 in its week of entry, having made UK #29 on Nov [26].

1995

Apr [22] With its title cut written by Randy Newman from his forthcoming opus ***Faust***, Ronstadt's ***Feels Like Home***, co-produced again with Massenburg, makes US #75.
[27] Appearing on "The Tonight Show", Ronstadt takes umbrage with fellow guest Robin Quivers for her working with Howard Stern.
May [13] Ronstadt performs at New York's Radio City Music Hall, during a month-long US tour.
Sept Ronstadt has contributed *A Dream Is A Wish Your Heart Makes* to Disney's newly-released "Cinderella", while Newman's Asher-produced concept album ***Faust***, with Ronstadt featured singing *My Hero*, is also issued. She also appears in Don Was' currently televised Brian Wilson documentary "I Just Wasn't Made For These Times".

1996

July [3] PBS-TV airs "Performance At The White House", a pre-taped co-headlining event starring Ronstadt performing live with Neville for President Clinton and assorted dignitaries.
[13] ***Dedicated To The One I Love***, Ronstadt's collection of pop/rock lullabies, makes US #78.
[15] A 26-date US tour opens at the Interlochen Center-Kresge Auditorium, Interlochen, MI, set to end on September 1st at Fiddler's Green Amphitheatre, Englewood, CO.

ROSE ROYCE

Gwen Dickey (vocals); **Kenji Chiba Brown** (guitar); **Mike Nash** (keyboards); **Kenny Copeland** (horns); **Michael Moore** (horns); **Freddie Dunn** (horns); **Lequeint "Juke" Jobe** (bass); **Terral Santiel** (percussion); **Henry "Hammer" Garner** (drums)

1976

Sept The group has been formed in 1972 as the eight-piece R&B instrumental Total Concept Unlimited in Los Angeles, CA, by Motown producer Norman Whitfield to back artists and groups under his production wing, initially backing Edwin Starr live on stage, and has gone on to become the road band for the Temptations and then the Undisputed Truth, having also backed Yvonne Fair as Magic Wand. When Whitfield left Motown to work independently and launch his own Whitfield label, licensed to Warner Bros. Records, the combo has moved with him. Having been introduced to Dickey while the band was on on tour in Florida backing the Undisputed Truth, he recruits her as a lead vocalist, and names them Rose Royce, the intention being to turn the backing crew into a hitmaking unit. Whitfield is now contracted to write and provide the music for Michael Shultz's comedy film "Car Wash", starring Richard Pryor. Rose Royce, augmented by Melvin "Wah-Wah" Ragin on guitar, and Ben Wilber and Mark David on keyboards, plays the whole soundtrack, including some cuts with vocals by the Pointer Sisters.

1977

Jan [29] Soul/funk title song *Car Wash* tops the US chart for a week, deposing Stevie Wonder's *I Wish*.
Feb *Car Wash* is also their UK chart debut, hitting #9. Another song, *Put Your Money Where Your Mouth Is*, extracted earlier as the first UK single, now reaches UK #44, while the parent soundtrack double album ***Car Wash*** reaches US #14, having been certified gold on December 21st.
[22] *Car Wash* is certified platinum by the RIAA.
May Ballad *I Wanna Get Next To You*, also written and produced by Whitfield from the movie soundtrack, hits US #10 and UK #14.
July The last "Car Wash" single, *I'm Going Down*, peaks at US #70. Meanwhile, an abridged single-album version of the "Car Wash" soundtrack, released as ***The Best Of Car Wash*** in the UK, reaches #59.
Oct *Do Your Dance* makes US #39 and UK #30, while the group's first non-soundtrack project ***Rose Royce II/In Full Bloom*** hits US #9.
Nov ***Rose Royce II/In Full Bloom*** makes UK #18.
Dec [6] ***Rose Royce II/In Full Bloom*** is certified platinum by the RIAA.

1978

Jan Ballad *Ooh Boy* peaks at US #72.
Mar Further soulful love song *Wishing On A Star*, taken from ***Rose Royce II/In Full Bloom***, hits UK #3 but fails to chart in the US.
May Returning to a dance beat, *It Makes You Feel Like Dancin'* reaches UK #16.
Sept [20] Still climbing ***Rose Royce III/Strikes Again!*** is certified gold by the RIAA.
Oct Another ballad, *Love Don't Live Here Anymore*, taken from the group's forthcoming third album, is its biggest UK single, hitting #2 behind the million-selling *Summer Nights* by John Travolta and Olivia Newton-John. (The song will later be revived by Madonna on her album ***Like A Virgin***.)
Nov ***Rose Royce III/Strikes Again!***, makes US #28 and hits UK #7.

1979

Jan In the wake of its huge UK success, *Love Don't Live Here Anymore* makes US #32, but is the group's final US chart single.
Feb *I'm In Love (And I Love The Feeling)* stops at UK #51.
Sept ***Rose Royce IV/Rainbow Connection*** makes US #74 and UK #72.

1980

Jan Uptempo *Is It Love You're After?*, from the ***Rainbow Connection*** album, reaches UK #13.
Mar *Ooh Boy* belatedly makes UK #46.
Apr [19] TV-promoted compilation ***Rose Royce's Greatest Hits*** hits UK #1 for the first of two weeks (deposing Genesis' ***Duke***), during a 34-week chart spell.

1981

Feb With Dickey having left for a solo career (replaced by Richee Benson) and Brown making way for Walter McKinney, ***Golden Touch***, showcasing a harder urban-funk sound, peaks at US #160 - their last US chart appearance.
Nov *Rose Royce Express* returns the group to the UK singles chart at #52.

1984

Oct Following the release of ***Jump Street*** in 1982 and ***Stronger Than Ever*** the following year, ***Music Magic***, recorded for the US Montage label and produced by Bobby Eli and Michael Nash, is released in the UK by the dance-oriented Streetwave label and reaches UK #69 while the extracted *Magic Touch* is a UK disco success and charts at UK #43. *Love Me Right Now*, also on Streetwave, will make UK #60 the following April, taken from the forthcoming ***The Show Must Go On***.

1988

Apr [30] While Rose Royce's ***Fresh Cut*** has been released by Omni Records the previous June, UK dance outfit S-Express now tops the UK chart with *Theme From S-Express*, liberally sampling the opening riff of Rose Royce's *Is It Love You're After*.
June The MCA-reissued *Is It Love You're After*, a double A-side with *Car Wash*, reaches UK #20. The current line-up makes a UK tour on the strength of the single's success, while Dickey continues to release solo recordings. Following the March 1989 release of ***Perfect Lover***, co-produced by Steven Bernstein and Alan Rubens, the group will continue touring into the mid-'90s, usually as part of R&B package tours including 1991's "The Best Of The '80s" UK caravan.

DIANA ROSS

1970

Mar [8] Growing up in Detroit, MI's Brewster housing projects and joining local R&B vocal quartet the Primettes while still in high school, and following ten years in the spotlight as the lead vocalist of the Supremes, the most successful female trio of the '60s (being replaced by Jean Terrell whom Ross has introduced onstage at her final concert with the Supremes on January 14th), and seven weeks after leaving her ex-colleagues, Ross (b. Diane Ernestine Ross, Mar. 26, 1944, Detroit) makes her solo stage debut, in Framingham, MA. She remains signed to Motown Records, which makes an initial $100,000 investment in one of its most visible stars.
June After recordings tracks with various producers (including Bones Howe, with whom she cuts Laura Nyro's *Stoney End*, several months before Barbra Streisand takes her version of it into the US Top 10), her debut solo single, *Reach Out And Touch (Somebody's Hand)*, written and produced by Ashford & Simpson, reaches US #20.
Aug [1] *Reach Out And Touch (Somebody's Hand)* makes UK #33.
Sept [19] Ashford & Simpson-produced and penned *Ain't No Mountain High Enough* is Ross' first solo US chart-topper, holding at #1 for three weeks and selling one million copies. It also hits UK #6. (The song had originally been a hit duet for Marvin Gaye & Tammi Terrell in 1967, but Ross' version is a complete re-arrangement, making notable use of spoken passages.) Both this and the previous single are included on her maiden solo set, ***Diana Ross***, which climbs to US #19.
Nov ***Diana Ross*** makes UK #14.

1971

Jan Her second solo effort, ***Everything Is Everything***, reaches US #42.
Feb Taken from the album, *Remember Me* reaches US #16.
May [8] *Remember Me* hits UK #7, during a month when Ross marries Robert Silberstein.
Her revival of the Four Tops' *Reach Out I'll Be There* makes US #29, while the soundtrack album, ***Diana***, from the TV special "Diana" (which also includes Bill Cosby, Danny Thomas and the Jackson 5) makes US #46.
June ***Everything Is Everything*** reaches UK #31.
Aug [21] Released as a UK single from the album, at the urging of BBC Radio 1 breakfast show DJ, Tony Blackburn, who plugs it incessantly, *I'm Still Waiting*,

written by Deke Richards, tops the UK chart for the first of four weeks.
Sept ***Surrender*** makes US #56, as the extracted *Surrender* reaches US #38.
Oct The TV soundtrack album, ***Diana!***, makes UK #43. Ross is named chairman of the NAACP's annual Image Awards show, at the Beverly Hilton Hotel in Los Angeles, CA.
Nov [27] *Surrender* hits UK #10, as does ***I'm Still Waiting*** (which is the US album ***Surrender*** with the UK #1 smash added). Meanwhile, *I'm Still Waiting*, released as a US single on the strength of its UK success, stops at US #63.

1972

June [17] *Doobedood'ndoobe Doobedood'ndoobe* reaches UK #12.
Nov UK compilation album, ***Greatest Hits***, makes UK #34.
Dec Ross makes her major movie acting debut opposite Billy Dee Williams in the role of Billie Holiday, in the premiering Motown co-production, "Lady Sings The Blues", a dramatization of Holiday's life. She is nominated for (though does not win) an Oscar for her critically-lauded performance.

1973

Mar *Good Morning Heartache*, from "Lady Sings The Blues", makes US #34.
Apr [7] The soundtrack double album, ***Lady Sings The Blues***, including two Michel Legrand instrumentals, tops the US chart for the first of two weeks, subsequently earning a gold disc.
Aug [18] Ballad *Touch Me In The Morning*, the first song written for her by Michael Masser (with Ron Miller), tops the US chart for a week and becomes a million seller, and will also hit UK #9).
Sept ***Touch Me In The Morning*** hits US #5 and UK #7, during a month when Ross appears at London's Royal Albert Hall.
Oct ***Lady Sings The Blues*** makes UK #50, following a moderate reception for the movie's British release.
Nov *You're A Special Part Of Me*, duetted with Marvin Gaye, reaches US #12.
Dec Motown-paired album, ***Diana And Marvin***, variously produced by Hal Davis, Berry Gordy, Bob Gaudio and Ashford & Simpson, reaches US #26.

1974

Feb *Last Time I Saw Him* reaches US #14.
[9] *All Of My Life* hits UK #9. Both are taken from ***Last Time I Saw Him***, which makes US #52 and UK #41. Meanwhile, ***Diana And Marvin*** hits UK #6.
[19] She collects the Favorite Album, Pop/Rock trophy at the inaugural American Music Awards, held at the Aquarius Theater, Hollywood, CA.
Apr [20] An update of the Stylistics' *You Are Everything*, again with Gaye, hits UK #5.
May Also from the album with Gaye, *My Mistake (Was To Love You)* makes US #19, while the belatedly-released ***Last Time I Saw Him*** reaches UK #35.
June *Sleepin'* peaks at US #70.
July Performance set, ***Diana Ross Live At Caesar's Palace***, a recording of her club act from Las Vegas, NV, makes US #64 and UK #21.
Aug *Don't Knock My Love*, with Marvin Gaye, peaks at US #46.
[17] Another Stylistics revival with Gaye, *Stop, Look, Listen (To Your Heart)* makes UK #25.
Oct [12] *Love Me* reaches UK #38.

1975

Feb [18] Ross wins the Favorite Female Artist, Soul/R&B category at the second annual American Music Awards, held at the Civic Auditorium, Santa Monica, CA.
May [10] *Sorry Doesn't Always Make It Right* makes UK #23.
Dec Her second feature film, "Mahogany", directed by Berry Gordy Jr., with music by Michael Masser, and again co-starring Billy Dee Williams, premieres in the US. Its soundtrack album, ***Mahogany***, with Ross singing the title song, plus incidental music, reaches US #19.

1976

Jan [24] *Theme From Mahogany (Do You Know Where You're Going To)*, written by Masser and Gerry Goffin, tops the US chart for a week, eventually selling over one million copies, and will be nominated for Best Song at the forthcoming Academy Awards.
Apr *I Thought It Took A Little Time (But Today I Fell In Love)* makes US #47, while *Theme From Mahogany (Do You Know Where You're Going To)* hits UK #5. ***Diana Ross***, containing the two previous hit singles, hits US #5 and UK #4.
May [29] *Love Hangover*, a long, disco-driven track from ***Diana Ross***, having gained wide airplay, and already covered on single by the 5th Dimension, has been rush-released by Motown and now tops the US chart for the first of two weeks, becoming another million seller.
June [14-26] "An Evening With Diana Ross", directed by Joe Layton, runs for 16 performance at New York, NY's Palace Theatre. (Following its New York run, it will tour the US for the rest of the year, during which time she will also be divorced from Silberstein.)
July *I Thought It Took A Little Time* makes UK #32.
Sept [18] Ross co-hosts the "Don Kirshner Rock Awards" with Alice Cooper.
Oct *One Love In My Lifetime* makes US #25, while ***Diana Ross' Greatest Hits*** reaches US #13 and hits UK #2.
Nov The UK reissue of her former chart-topper, *I'm Still Waiting*, peaks at UK #41.

1977

Mar [6] "An Evening With Diana Ross", a 90-minute spectacular incorporating much of the stage show, airs on US TV.
Apr Live double set, ***An Evening With Diana Ross***, recorded in 1976 at the Ahmanson Theater, Los Angeles, makes US #29 and UK #52.
Oct She stars as Dorothy in the premiering film, "The Wiz", directed by Sidney Lumet. It is a black version of "The Wizard Of Oz", adapted from the successful Broadway stage musical (and also features close friend Michael Jackson as the Scarecrow). Original director John Badham has reportedly quit the project rather than accept Ross in the role of Dorothy.
Nov ***Baby It's Me*** reaches US #18.
Dec Taken from it, *Gettin' Ready For Love* reaches US #27 and UK #23.

1978

Apr *Your Love Is So Good For Me*, also from the album, makes US #49.
Aug *You Got It* peaks at US #49, while *Lovin' Livin' And Givin'* stops at UK #54.
Oct *Ease On Down The Road*, a bubbly duet with Jackson taken from the soundtrack of "The Wiz", released by MCA, reaches US #41.
Nov *Ease On Down The Road* makes UK #45, while ***Ross*** reaches US #49.

1979

Feb *Pops, We Love You (A Tribute To Father)*, sung with Marvin Gaye, Smokey Robinson and Stevie Wonder, in honor of Berry Gordy's father's 90th birthday, peaks at US #59 and UK #66.
Aug ***The Boss***, produced by Richard Perry, reaches US #14 and UK #52, while the extracted title song, *The Boss*, makes US #19 and UK #40.
Oct *No One Gets The Prize*, from ***The Boss***, peaks at UK #59.
Dec *It's My House*, also from the recent album, makes UK #32, while a TV-advertised UK compilation album, ***20 Golden Greats***, including all her UK chart singles, hits UK #2.

1980

July ***Diana***, written and produced by Nile Rodgers and Bernard Edwards of Chic, hits US #2 and reaches UK #12.
[17] ***The Boss*** Is certified gold by the RIAA.
Sept [6] Taken from ***Diana***, *Upside Down* begins a four-week run at US #1, also selling over a million, and hits UK #2.
Oct Also from the album, *My Old Piano* hits UK #5.
Nov *I'm Coming Out*, again from ***Diana***, hits US #5 and UK #13.

1981

Jan *It's My Turn*, the ballad theme from the Michael Douglas/Jill Clayburgh movie of the same title, hits US #9 and UK #16.
[30] She collects the Favorite Female Artist, Soul/R&B and Favorite Single, Soul/R&B trophies at the eighth annual American Music Awards, held at the ABC-TV studios, Hollywood, CA.
Feb [3] ***Diana*** is confirmed platinum by the RIAA.
[19] Price Waterhouse CPA, Glenn Kannry, pleads guilty to siphoning cash from Ross' bank account.
Apr *One More Chance* peaks at UK #49 and US #79, taken from ***To Love Again***, which makes US #32 and UK #26.
June *Cryin' My Heart Out For You* peaks at UK #58.
Aug [15] *Endless Love*, duetted with the song's writer/producer, Lionel Richie, tops the US chart for the first of nine weeks, eventually selling over two million copies. It is the theme from the film of the same name, starring Brooke Shields, and was recorded in a rapid early-morning session in Reno, NV - the two vocalists meeting briefly amid heavy schedules elsewhere. The single is released on Motown even though Ross has just left the label after two decades, signing a new North American deal with RCA Records and an international contract with EMI/Capitol, worth a reported $20 million.
Oct *Endless Love* hits UK #7.
[16] *Endless Love* is certified platinum by the RIAA.
Dec Her first RCA/Capitol single is the self-produced revival of Frankie Lymon & the Teenagers' 1956 million seller, *Why Do Fools Fall In Love*, which hits US #7 and UK #4. It is taken from the self-helmed ***Why Do Fools Fall In Love***, which makes US #15 and UK #17. Meanwhile, another double compilation set, ***All The Greatest Hits***, on Motown, makes US #37 and UK #21, collecting together her singles up to *Endless Love*.
[16] *Upside Down* is certified gold by the RIAA.

1982

Jan *Tenderness*, on Motown, makes UK #73.
[22] ***Why Do Fools Fall In Love*** is certified platinum by the RIAA.
[24] Ross sings the National Anthem at Superbowl XVI at the Pontiac Silverdome, Pontiac, MI.
[25] She nabs the Favorite Single, Pop/Rock and Favorite Single, Soul/R&B categories (both for *Endless Love* with Richie) at the ninth annual American Music Awards, held at the Shrine Auditorium, Los Angeles.
Feb *Mirror, Mirror*, taken from the RCA/Capitol album, hits US #8 and makes UK #36.
May Disco-aerobic styled, *Work That Body* makes US #44 and hits UK #7.
July [4] Ross opens a world tour at the Meadowlands, East Rutherford, NJ, with Miles Davis the support act.
Aug *It's Never Too Late* peaks at UK #41.
Nov *Muscles*, written and produced by Michael Jackson, hits US #10 and makes UK #15. It is taken from ***Silk Electric***, otherwise produced by Ross, which reaches US #27 and UK #33.
Dec TV-promoted compilation album, ***Love Songs***, compiled by K-tel in the UK from Motown recordings, hits UK #5.
[14] ***Silk Electric*** is certified gold by the RIAA.

1983

Jan Ross earns a reported $2,500,000 for a six-week season in Las Vegas.
[17] She wins the Favorite Female Artist, Soul/R&B category at the tenth annual American Music Awards, held at the Shrine Auditorium, at which she is also

presented with the Special Award of Merit. (She will, however, remain Grammy-less well into the '90s.)
Feb *So Close* peaks at US #40 and UK #43.
Mar [15] ***All The Great Hits*** is certified gold by the RIAA.
May [16] Ross reunites with Mary Wilson and Cindy Birdsong as the Supremes, during the "Motown 25" NBC-TV spectacular to celebrate the label's 25th birthday.
July [22] Ross gives a free concert in New York's Central Park, abandoned the previous night after only three songs, due to a torrential downpour and strong winds.
Aug ***Ross*** makes US #32 and UK #44 while *Pieces Of Ice* peaks at US #31 and UK #46. Yet another double compilation, ***Diana Ross Anthology***, on Motown, reaches US #63.

1984

Jan TV-advertised collection, ***Portrait***, hits UK #8, while *Let's Go Up* peaks at US #77.
Sept *All Of You*, a ballad duet with Julio Iglesias, reaches US #19, while *Touch By Touch* stops at UK #47.
Oct *Swept Away*, written and produced by Daryl Hall, makes US #19. It is taken from ***Swept Away***, variously produced by Ross, Hall, Richie, Perry, Arthur Baker and Bernard Edwards, which reaches US #26 and UK #40.
Nov [5] ***Swept Away*** is confirmed gold by the RIAA.

1985

Jan [28] She participates in USA For Africa's historic recording of *We Are The World*.
Apr Ballad, *Missing You*, taken from ***Swept Away***, hits US #10. The song, dedicated to the memory of Marvin Gaye, is written and produced by Lionel Richie.
Oct *Eaten Alive*, featuring Michael Jackson on backup vocals, makes US #77 and UK #71.
Nov ***Eaten Alive***, produced and largely co-penned by Barry Gibb, reaches US #45 and UK #11.
Dec *Chain Reaction*, written by the Bee Gees, peaks at US #95.

1986

Jan [21] ***Diana Ross Anthology*** is certified gold by the RIAA.
Feb [1] Ross marries Norwegian shipping magnate Arne Naess, in Geneva, Switzerland, before a gathering of 240 people with the Norwegian Silver Boys Choir singing. Stevie Wonder also performs at the reception.
Mar [8] *Chain Reaction*, Ross' biggest British success since *I'm Still Waiting*, tops the UK chart for the first of three weeks, helped by a black and white video including mock '60s footage.
Apr [14] "Vision Of Diana Ross" video is certified gold by the RIAA.
May Ballad *Experience*, also from ***Eaten Alive***, makes UK #47.
[24] A new mix of *Chain Reaction* peaks at US #66.
Nov Compilation, ***Diana Ross And Others : Their Very Best Back To Back***, makes UK #21.

1987

Jan [26] Ross hosts the 14th annual American Music Awards, again held at the Shrine Auditorium.
May [30] ***Red Hot Rhythm'n'Blues***, containing versions of R&B oldies, makes UK #47 in its week of entry and will make US #73, while the extracted *Dirty Looks* makes US R&B #12, failing to cross over, but reaches UK #49.
Oct Ross gives birth to her fourth child, Ross Arne.

1988

Oct Ross' treatment of the Bobettes' '50s hit, *Mr. Lee*, taken from ***Red Hot Rhythm'n'Blues***, makes UK #58.
Nov With Peter Asher producing, Ross contributes *If We Hold On Together* as the theme to the Steven Spielberg-produced cartoon film, "The Land Before Time". A UK remix of *Love Hangover* anchors at UK #75.

1989

Feb [4] While a reissue of the Supremes' *Stop! In The Name Of Love* makes UK #62, a UK TV compilation, ***Love Supreme***, by Diana Ross & the Supremes, hits UK #10.
Apr [20] Ross warms up for her UK tour, lip-synching at London's Brixton Academy on an Aswad bill.
[23] She begins the UK leg of her European trek, set to include dates at the Scottish Exhibition & Conference Centre, Glasgow, Strathclyde, Scotland, the National Exhibition Centre, Birmingham, West Midlands, and Wembley Arena, Wembley, Middx.
May [27] ***Workin' Overtime***, produced by Nile Rodgers and released on the newly-formed Ross Records (but also marking a return to Motown as its licensor), reaches UK #23 in its week of entry and will peak at US #116. The US release is delayed to gauge reaction to the first single on the label, the title track *Workin' Overtime*, which makes UK #32.
June [23] Ross participates in a worldwide ecological-awareness broadcast, "Our Common Future".
[24] She begins a two-month North American tour as *Workin' Overtime* fails to make the Hot 100.
July The extracted *Paradise* peaks at UK #61.
Nov [25] ***Greatest Hits Live***, on EMI UK, makes UK #34, in its week of entry.

1990

Feb [9-11] Ross plays three sellout shows at the Fox Theatre, Detroit, during her current US tour, grossing $711,440 from audiences totalling 23,761.
July An unnecessarily updated remix of the classic *I'm Still Waiting*, by Phil Chill, reaches UK #21.

1991

Apr Ross appears in Herb Ritts-lensed Gap commercials, with her daughter Tracee, who is launching a solo music career.
May [31] On the opening night of her world tour, Ross breaks the house record, previously held by John Denver, at the Mid-Hudson Civic Center, Poughkeepsie, NY.
July [24] Ross guests on NBC-TV's "The Tonight Show".
[25-28] She plays three sellout shows at the Universal Amphitheatre, Universal City, CA, grossing $493,759.
Sept [19-21] She performs another SRO triple-set at New York's Radio City Music Hall, before crowds totalling 17,820.
[28] ***The Force Behind The Power***, largely produced by Peter Asher, but including two cuts independently helmed by James Anthony Carmichael and Stevie Wonder, debuts at its US #102 peak.
[30] Ross speaks before a House Select Committee on Children, Youth & Families, in her capacity as spokeswoman for the National Children's Day Foundation, in Washington, DC.
Nov [14-16] Three Wembley Arena shows gross £793,500 during sellout UK dates.
[25] Ross headlines the "Royal Variety Show" at the London Palladium.
Dec [14] Ballad *When You Tell Me That You Love Me*, written by John Bettis and Albert Hammond, hits UK #2, behind George Michael and Elton John's *Don't Let The Sun Go Down On Me*.
[21] ***The Force Behind The Power*** reaches UK #11.

1992

Jan [1] Ross opens the annual Harrods' January sale in London. After touring the store with owner Mohamed Al Fayed, she is served a breakfast of scrambled eggs, bacon, tomatoes, sausage, toast, croissants and tea sweetened with honey. (While in London, she also records tracks at Mayfair Studios with producer Louis Jardin.)
Feb [15] *The Force Behind The Power* bows at its UK #27 peak.
[29] ***Motown's Greatest Hits***, another Ross collection, reaches UK #20.
Mar [16] Ross plays at the Entertainment Centre, Sydney, New South Wales, during the Australian leg of her tour.
June [2] She embarks on another British tour at The Point, Dublin, Eire, set to end on the 10th at the Glasgow Scottish Exhibition & Conference Centre.
July [4] *One Shining Moment* hits UK #10.
[6-10] Ross fills in for Simon Bates as a DJ on BBC Radio 1.
Dec [4] "Diana Ross Live ... The Lady Sings", a show in which Ross performs jazz and blues numbers in a New York club setting with a jazz/blues backing band, including Ron Carter, Roy Hargrove and Bobby Tucker, airs on US cable pay-per-view.
[23] BBC2-TV airs "Christmas In Vienna", with Ross, José Carreras and Placido Domingo, from Vienna City Hall. PBS-TV stations will air the show on the 24th.

1993

Jan [2] *If We Hold On Together* reaches UK #11.
[17] Ross performs at "A Call For Reunion : A Musical Celebration" during Inaugural festivities at the Lincoln Memorial, Washington.
Mar [13] *Heart (Don't Change My Mind)* debuts at its UK #31 peak.
Apr [24] ***Live ... Stolen Moments*** (subtitled ***The Lady Sings ... Jazz & Blues)***, from the December 4th show, bows at its UK #45 peak.
June [15] Ross sings *God Bless The Child* at the first "Apollo Theatre Hall of Fame" concert, from the landmark New York theater. (The show will air on NBC-TV on August 4th.)
Oct [9] *Chain Reaction*, issued as a trailer from the forthcoming career retrospective, re-charts at its UK #20 peak.
[30] ***One Woman - The Ultimate Collection*** debuts at its UK #2 peak, behind Meat Loaf's ***Bat Out Of Hell II - Back Into Hell***.
Dec [14] Her star is unveiled in an inaugural ceremony with 15 other artists at the "Sidewalk Of The Stars" outside Radio City Music Hall.
[25] ***Christmas In Vienna***, featuring Ross with Placido Domingo and Jose Carreras, enters chart at UK #71 and climbs to US #154.
[31] Ross guests on the pre-recorded "Clive James New Year's Eve" on both UK and US TV.

1994

Jan [1] *Your Love* reaches UK #14.
[16] Ross stars in the ABC-TV drama "Out Of Darkness".
Feb [2] She is the guest of honor at Midem '94 in France, where she is awarded the Commander in the Order of Arts and Letters from the French Minister of Culture, Jacques Toubon and also receives the City of Cannes Gold Medal from Mayor Michel Moulliet. In response, Ross performs a 40-minute show with "Lady Sings The Blues" collaborator Michel Legrand and ponders : "to think I've been doing this for 30 fuckin' years".
Apr [2] *The Best Years Of My Life* debuts at its UK #28 peak.
[23] Self-explanatory ***Diana Extended - The Remixes*** makes UK #58 in its week of entry.
June [17] Ross headlines the pre-game show at a World Cup match at Chicago's Soldier Field.
July [16] Reissued coupling *Why Do Fools Fall In Love*, paired with *I'm Coming Out*, reaches UK #36.
Dec [10] Ross winds up an Amway convention with a performance at the Tokyo Dome, Tokyo, Japan.
[17] Festive collection ***A Very Special Season*** reaches UK #37.

1995

Jan [18] She guests at the National Football League's 75th anniversary from New York City, set to air on ABC-TV on the 26th.
Mar [13] Ross is presented with the Heritage Award for Career Achievement by Berry Gordy at the ninth annual Soul Train Music Awards, held at the Shrine Auditorium.
June [16-17] She performs two concerts at the Kremlin Palace of Congresses in Moscow, Russia.
Aug [21-22] Ross plays two sellout shows at the Fox Theatre, Detroit, during her current US tour.
Sept [2] *Take Me Higher* debuts at its UK #32 peak.
[14] Ross guests on CBS-TV's "Late Show With

David Letterman".
[16] ***Take Me Higher***, variously produced by Narada Michael Walden, Nick Martinelli, Brenda Russell, Jon John and the Boom Brothers, hits UK #10 in its week of entry.
Oct [13] Ross plays the first of two sellout dates at Radio City Music Hall.
[14] ***Take Me Higher*** debuts at its US #114 peak, during a two week chart stay.
Nov [2] Ross is inducted into the Soul Train Hall of Fame at the 25th Soul Train Anniversary from the Shrine Auditorium, set to air on the 22nd on CBS-TV, at which she also sings *Take Me Higher* and *Voice Of The Heart*.
[25] *I'm Gone* debuts at its UK #36 peak.
Dec [8] She visits a sick Michael Jackson at the Beth Israel Medical Center North, New York.
[17] Ross headlines the "Greatest Music Party In The World", from the National Exhibition Centre, Birmingham, West Midlands, set to air on BBC1-TV on Christmas Day.

1996

Jan [28] Ross supplies the half-time entertainment at Super Bowl XXX in Tempe, AZ.
Feb [17] Her cover of Gloria Gaynor's 1979 UK and US chart-topper, *I Will Survive* debuts at its UK #14 peak.
Mar [10] Ross performs at the Festival Hall, Tampa Bay Performing Arts Center, Tampa, FL, during selected US dates.
June [10] One day after performing at the Harbor Lights venue in Boston, MA, Ross makes a benefit appearance at the city's Symphony Hall for the Anti-Defamation League raising $450,000.
see also: **THE SUPREMES**

ROXETTE

Per Gessle (guitar, vocals);
Marie Fredriksson (vocals)

1986

Both friends since 1979 and veterans of the Swedish music scene, Gessle (b. Feb. 12, 1959, Halmstad, Sweden), who has already fronted the successful rock group Gyllene Tider, until its split in 1984, going on to concentrate on a solo career and songwriting (including one track, *Threnody*, on Abba's Frida Lyngstad's 1982 album, ***Something's Going On***) links with Fredriksson (b. May 29, 1958, Östra Ljungby, Sweden), who is established as one of the country's top songwriter/performers, with over 300,000 copies already sold of her three solo albums, to form straight-rock duo Roxette, taking their name from a Dr. Feelgood song. They release their debut set, ***Pearls Of Passion***, recorded at Gessle's studio in Halmstad, which is only available in Sweden. Roxette will undertake a debut tour of its native turf in June 1987, when ***Pearls Of Passion*** earns a Swedish platinum (100,000) disc, and having spun-off two gold (25,000) singles.

1988

Oct Their sophomore set, ***Look Sharp!***, co-produced by permanent Roxette collaborator Clarence Ofwerman, is released in Sweden, hitting #1 for an initial three-month run, eventually selling close to 500,000 copies and becoming the second best-selling album in Sweden, behind Abba's ***The Album***. While on holiday in Scandinavia, a US college student on an exchange visit, hooked on the Roxette tracks he has heard on Swedish radio, takes a copy of the CD back home to Minneapolis, MN, and suggests to his local station that they play one of the tracks, *The Look*. After overwhelming listener response, the track, copied on cassette and distributed to other US stations, becomes a much requested airplay favorite.

1989

Feb [11] Still without an official US record deal, saturation airplay alone brings *The Look* onto the Hot 100. It is subsequently snapped up by EMI USA, and begins a steady rise to hit US #1, eventually becoming the eighth most successful single of the year in US.
Apr [4] Peaking four days later, *The Look* is already certified gold by the RIAA.
[8] *The Look* tops the US chart for a week.
[22] Its parent album, ***Look Sharp!***, enters the US chart set to make #23, and initially UK #45, during a 71-week chart stay.
May *The Look* hits UK #7, as the band continues on a non-stop worldwide promotional trip.
July [29] Punchy rock follow-up, *Dressed For Success*, reaches US #14, having made UK #48.
Nov [4] Power ballad, *Listen To Your Heart*, again written by the duo, hits US #1, the first chart-topper available in cassette form only, and peaks at UK #62.
Dec Roxette ends the year with a three-week European tour, their first live dates performed outside Sweden.

1990

Jan [18] ***Look Sharp!*** is certified platinum by the RIAA.
Feb [24] Fourth extract from ***Look Sharp!***, *Dangerous*, rises to hit US #2 for the first of two weeks, behind Janet Jackson's *Escapade*.
Apr [24] "Look Sharp Live" video is certified gold by the RIAA.
June [5] The still-climbing *It Must Have Been Love* is also confirmed gold by the RIAA.
[16] While Fredriksson and Gessle begin recording the follow-up to the multi-platinum ***Look Sharp!*** at EMI's Stockholm studios, their ballad, *It Must Have Been Love*, prominently featured in the Richard Gere/Julia Roberts hit movie, "Pretty Woman", tops the US chart. It also hits UK #3, spurring revived interest in the ***Look Sharp!*** album which now hits UK #4.
Oct Reissued *Listen To Your Heart*, twinned with *Dangerous*, hits UK #6.
Nov Re-released *Dressed For Success* reaches UK #18.

1991

Apr [6] Inspired by the Paul McCartney quote: "... writing songs with John Lennon was like being on a joyride", Beatles-fan Gessle-penned *Joyride* hits UK #4. It will also hit #1 in most European territories, including Sweden, Germany, and the Netherlands, and top surveys in Australia and Canada.
[13] ***Joyride***, featuring production and programming by Ofwerman and guest guitar work from Jonas Isacsson, debuts at its UK #2 peak, behind Eurythmics' ***Greatest Hits***.
May [4] ***Joyride*** reaches US #12.
[11] Title cut, *Joyride*, hits US #1.
[18] *Fading Like A Flower* reaches UK #12.
[31] The duo appears on NBC-TV's "The Tonight Show" as they prepare to embark on their first world tour.
July [12] ***Joyride*** is certified platinum by the RIAA.
Aug [31] *Fading Like A Flower (Every Time You Leave)* hits US #2, behind Bryan Adams' *(Everything I Do) I Do It For You*.
Sept [14] *The Big L* reaches UK #21.
Oct [19-20] They play at the Wembley Arena, Wembley, Middx., during the UK leg of their world trek.
Nov [30] *Spending My Time* peaks at UK #22.

1992

Jan [4] *Spending My Time* reaches US #32.
[21] The duo performs during the SBK-EMI Records evening at the Palais des Festivals, Midem, Cannes, France.
Feb [17] Roxette plays to a sellout crowd of 8,062 at the Olympic Saddledome, Calgary, Canada, during the current leg of its North American tour.
Mar [25-26] During 13 SRO dates in Central and South America, before crowds totalling 347,000, Roxette grosses $586,633 from a sellout audience of 18,800, at the National Auditorium, Mexico City, Mexico.
Apr [4] *Church Of Your Heart* reaches UK #21 and US #36.
June [25] The duo plays at Wembley Arena, supporting U2 on their UK dates. (By the end of their "Joyride World Tour", they will have played 108 shows to 1.5 million fans.)
Aug [8] *How Do You Do!* reaches UK #13.
Sept [12] ***Tourism*** bows at its UK #2 peak, behind Mike Oldfield's ***Tubular Bells II***.
Oct [29] They guest on NBC-TV's "The Tonight Show".
Nov [14] *Queen Of Rain* reaches UK #28, while ***Tourism*** peaks at US #117 and *How Do You Do!* makes US #58.

1993

Feb [22] Now self-proclaimed in music trade ads as "The World's No. 1 Duo!" (having already sold 21 million albums and 12 million singles worldwide to date), MTV UK's "MTV Unplugged" airs the duo in concert, at Stockholm's Cirkus Theatre.
Apr [29] Fredricksson gives birth to a daughter, Inex Josefin, in Stockholm.
June [19] *Almost Unreal*, featured on the film soundtrack to "Super Mario Brothers", stops at US #94.
July [24] *Almost Unreal* debuts at its UK #7 peak.
Oct [2] *It Must Have Been Love* hits UK #10.

1994

Mar [26] *Sleeping In My Car* reaches UK #14 in its week of entry.
Apr [23] Once again produced by Ofwerman and featuring the Swedish Radio Symphony Oechestra, ***Crash! Boom! Bang!*** hits UK #3 in its week of entry.
June [11] The extracted title ballad *Crash! Boom! Bang!* reaches UK #26.
[12] Roxette appears on BBC2-TV's "The O Zone".
July [23] *Sleeping In My Car* makes US #50.
Sept [17] *Fireworks* debuts at its UK #30 peak.
Dec [10] *Run To You* reaches UK #27.

1995

Feb [19] Roxette performs in Beijing, the first Western rock act to play in China since Wham! in 1986.
Apr [8] A second ballad from the album, *Vulnerable* debuts at its UK #44 peak.
May [1-2] The duo plays its last dates of a nine-month, 85 sellout, world tour at the Olympic Stadium, Moscow, Russia, the first concert allowed in the Russian capital since 1917.
Nov [4] Self-aware compilation ***Don't Bore Us, Get To The Chorus! - Greatest Hits*** hits UK #5 in its week of entry.
[13] Roxette appears on BBC2-TV's "The O Zone".
[25] Revised and reissued *The Look '95* debuts at its UK #28 peak.

1996

Mar [30] *You Don't Understand Me* makes UK #42 in its week of entry.

ROXY MUSIC

Bryan Ferry (vocals, keyboards); **Andy Mackay** (saxophone, woodwinds); **Phil Manzanera** (guitar); **Brian Eno** (synthesizers)

1971

Jan A fine arts graduate and former vocalist in the Banshees and the Gas Board, Ferry (b. Sept. 26, 1945, Washington, Co. Durham), the son of a coal miner, having already linked with ex-university colleague and bass player Graham Simpson to form a band to play Ferry compositions the previous November, has recently lost a job teaching ceramics at a girls school, and auditioned to take Gordon Haskell's place in King Crimson in December. Although he fails to get the gig, the group's Robert Fripp has been impressed enough to recommend him to Crimson's management team. Mackay (b. July 23, 1946, London), introduced to Ferry by a mutual friend, joins and brings with him electronics expert and synthesizer player Eno (b. Brian Peter George St. John le Baptiste de la Salle Eno, May 15, 1948, Woodbridge, Suffolk), an acquaintance from Reading University. With Simpson in the background, Ferry, Eno and Mackay record demos on Eno's tape recorder.

June Following ads in the UK music paper **Melody Maker**, Roger Bunn joins on guitar and classically-trained American tympanist, Dexter Lloyd, on drums. The band, initially named Roxy (but extended to Roxy Music upon noting the existence of a US Roxy), plays no live dates, but records demos of Ferry's material, which he hawks, initially without success, around London record companies.

July Bunn and Lloyd leave. Ferry recruits a guitarist he has long admired, Davy O'List (b. Dec. 13, 1950), formerly with Keith Emerson in the Nice, while another **Melody Maker** ad brings in drummer Paul Thompson (b. May 13, 1951, Jarrow, Tyne & Wear), who has backed Billy Fury.

Dec Following positive press coverage from **Melody Maker**'s Richard Williams on the strength of the early demos, Roxy Music plays two try-out gigs, at the Friends of the Tate Gallery Christmas show in London, and the Union Ball at Reading University, Reading, Berks.

1972

Jan [21] The band records a session for BBC Radio 1's "Sounds Of The Seventies", the early demo tape having impressed presenter John Peel.

Feb O'List leaves. Manzanera (b. Philip Targett-Adams, Jan. 31, 1951, London), who has been mixing the group's sound, but was previously guitarist with experimental band, Quiet Sun, joins in his place. E.G. Management signs the group to a contract which includes recording and leasing product to a record company.

Mar Their debut album is recorded for £5,000 at Command Studios, London, with ex-King Crimson lyricist Pete Sinfield producing.

May Simpson is dismissed from the project and Rik Kenton (b. Oct. 31, 1945), a bass-playing friend of Sinfield, replaces him.

[30] The band plays its first major gig with Kenton, at the "Great Western Express Festival" in Lincolnshire.

June Roxy Music's first tour is as support to Rory Gallagher around the North of England.

[20] The group makes its TV debut on BBC2-TV's "The Old Grey Whistle Test".

July The band supports Alice Cooper at the Empire Pool, Wembley, Middx., with press reviews applauding Roxy Music's act at Cooper's expense.

Aug Following a release deal signed by E.G. with Island Records, their critically-revered debut album, ***Roxy Music***, introducing Ferry's distinctive vocal style and the band's reliance on rock electronics, hits UK #10.

Sept Ferry-penned *Virginia Plain* (not on the album) hits UK #4.

Oct During Roxy Music's first headlining British trek, Ferry's voice begins to suffer (he has a history of tonsilitis) and a break in the tour follows, while he is hospitalized to have his tonsils removed.

Dec The band embarks on its first US tour, opening for Jo Jo Gunne, Edgar Winter and others.

1973

Jan Kenton is fired and not replaced, and during recordings for the second album, session player John Porter takes the bass role.

Apr [14] *Pyjamarama* hits UK #10, though the band claims it is a hasty release, pressured by Island. It is not included on ***For Your Pleasure***, which hits UK #10, promoted by a sellout UK tour.

July Eno quits the band to begin solo recording and a highly successful production career, after personality clashes with Ferry, who recruits Curved Air's violinist Eddie Jobson (b. Apr. 28, 1955, Billingham, Cleveland) as a replacement (initially a controversial move, as he does not consult the rest of the band).

Aug Licensed to Warner Bros. Records in the US, ***For Your Pleasure*** is the band's US chart debut at #193.

Oct Ferry releases his first solo album ***These Foolish Things*** (for some time his solo projects will continue in tandem with Roxy Music).

Nov The band tours Britain, with Jobson handling all keyboards (Ferry and Eno had previously shared them), and Ferry moves to centre stage as vocalist without an instrument.

Dec [8] The Chris Thomas-produced ***Stranded*** tops the UK chart for a week, including, for the first time, two co-written tracks (by Manzanera and Mackay). Bass player on the album is John Gustafson, ex-Big Three and the Merseys, while the sleeve model is **Playboy**'s Playmate Of The Year, Marilyn Cole. A successful European tour follows.

[15] *Street Life*, extracted from ***Stranded***, hits UK #9.

1974

May Mackay releases a largely-instrumental solo album, ***In Search Of Eddie Riff***, featuring Roxy Music in support, without Ferry.

June The band plays another US tour, where its appeal is still that of a cult fashion rather than a mainstream act. ***Stranded***, beginning a six-album US license deal with Atco Records, peaks at US #186.

Nov [9] *All I Want Is You*, heralding a new album (recorded in August with John Porter, who has produced Ferry's solo albums), reaches UK #12, as the band plays another soldout UK tour, with John Wetton (b. July 12, 1949, Derby, Derbys.) joining temporarily on bass. Ferry introduces new stage images, appearing in gaucho attire and US military-style uniform.

Dec ***Country Life***, again with Ferry co-writing material with other members of the band, hits UK #3. Its sleeve, showing two scantily-clad models (one of whom is Constanze Karoli, sister of Can guitarist Michael Karoli), causes controversy, notably in the US where it has to be sold in an opaque green shrink-wrap.

1975

Feb The band begins a tour of US, Japan, Australia and New Zealand, retaining Wetton on bass. While the band is on the road in the US, ***Country Life*** becomes its first major US seller, reaching #37.

May [24] Manzanera's solo debut, ***Diamond Head***, released by Island (and Atco in the US), makes UK #40. In August another Manzanera project, ***Mainstream***, a collaboration with former band Quiet Sun (Dave Jarrett (keyboards), Bill McCormick (bass) and Charles Hayward (drums)), will also be issued.

Oct A UK trek is mounted to promote the next album, this time without Wetton (who has joined Uriah Heep). Gustafson plays bass and will stay in the group on a semi-permanent basis for several months.

Nov ***Siren***, produced again by Thomas, and with co-writing credits for Mackay, Jobson and Manzanera, hits UK #6. The sleeve photo is of Texan fashion model Jerry Hall (with whom Ferry will later become romantically linked).

[8] The extracted *Love Is The Drug*, an R&B-based dance number, hits UK #2, - the band's biggest hit single to date - behind David Bowie's *Space Oddity*.

Dec The band tours North America again, as ***Siren*** climbs to US #50.

1976

Jan [24] *Both Ends Burning*, also from ***Siren***, makes UK #25.

Mar *Love Is The Drug*, the band's first US hit single, reaches US #30, as Roxy Music returns for more US dates.

May On returning to Britain, Mackay completes music for the ITV series, "Rock Follies", Manzanera works with new outfit 801 (which will release ***801 Live*** in October followed by ***Listen Now!!*** in 1977), Ferry completes more solo work and Jobson returns to the US to play with Frank Zappa.

June [26] After persistent press rumors, the band finally announces: "We have all decided to go our separate ways, for the rest of the year at least, to have a rest from Roxy Music for a while."

Aug With the group still inactive, a live album, ***Viva! Roxy Music***, assembled from concert recordings made between 1972 and 1975, hits UK #6, and will make US #81.

1977

Nov E.G. transfers the Roxy Music catalog from Island to Polydor Records in Britain. Earlier material is re-promoted, and *Virginia Plain*, reissued as a single (coupled with *Pyjamarama*), reaches UK #11.

Dec Compilation album, ***Greatest Hits***, reaches UK #20.

1978

Oct Mackay's sophomore solo set ***Resolving Contradictions*** is released by Island, while EG. Records issues Manzanera's ***K-Scope***.

Nov After an 18-month hiatus (recent months having seen Ferry's solo chart success dwindle), Ferry, Mackay, Manzanera and Thompson re-group to cut a new Roxy Music album at Basing Street Studios, London. Keyboards player Paul Carrack (b. Apr. 22, 1951, Sheffield, Yorks.) (ex-Ace) and, sharing bass chores, Gary Tibbs (b. Jan. 25, 1958, Northwood, Middx.) (ex-Vibrators) and Alan Spenner (ex-Kokomo) are recruited, with Jobson and Wetton forming UK.

1979

Mar *Trash*, heralding the new album, makes UK #40.

Apr The band-produced ***Manifesto*** hits UK #7, supported by a reunion tour of the UK and Europe (with Tibbs on bass and David Skinner on keyboards), before dates in the US and Japan.

May ***Manifesto*** reaches US #23.

June From the album, *Dance Away*, spurred by a performance on BBC1-TV's "Top Of The Pops" on the 7th, hits UK #2 and makes US #44.

Sept *Angel Eyes*, a disco-flavored excerpt from ***Manifesto***, and also available in a dance-floor-aimed extended 12" version, hits UK #4 (charting at the same time as Abba's entirely different *Angeleyes*).

1980

Jan A new album is recorded in London by Ferry, Mackay and Manzanera, who co-produce with Rhett Davies, with other players (including Tibbs, Carrack, guitarist Neil Hubbard, and drummers Andy Newmark and Allan Schwartzberg) being hired for session work. Two oldies, Wilson Pickett's *In The Midnight Hour* and the Byrds' *Eight Miles High*, are included among the new Ferry and Ferry/Manzanera songs.

May *Over You* hits UK #5.

June [28] ***Flesh And Blood*** tops the UK chart for a week as the group begins a 60-date European tour. The live band retains Carrack, Hubbard and Tibbs, while Andy Newmark deputizes for Thompson, who breaks his hand in a motorcycle accident on the eve of the tour.

July [14] Ferry collapses in his hotel room at Port Barcares in southwest France. He is flown by charter plane to a London hospital the following day with a kidney infection.

[23] The band resumes its UK tour at the Conference Centre, Brighton, East Sussex, set to close on August 2nd at Wembley Arena, Wembley.

Aug *Oh Yeah (On The Radio)* hits UK #5.

[23] ***Flesh And Blood*** returns to UK #1 for the first of three weeks, and makes US #35, while *Over You* peaks at US #80, the band's third and final US Hot 100 entry.

Nov *The Same Old Scene*, a third extract from the album, reaches UK #12.

Dec Manzanera and Mackay, credited as the Players, release ***Christmas*** on US indie label Rykodisc, and are also behind the Dumbells release, *Giddy Up/A Christmas Dream*.

1981

Mar [14] The band's version of John Lennon's *Jealous Guy*, cut as a tribute following Lennon's murder, tops the UK chart for the first of two weeks - Roxy Music's only #1 single.

1982

Mar Manzanera's ***Primitive Guitars*** is released by E.G.

Apr After a lengthy recording hiatus, *More Than This* hits UK #6, heralding what will be the band's last studio album of the decade, again recorded by the nucleus of Ferry, Mackay and Manzanera, with session musicians added. Mackay publishes a book, **Electronic Music**, written while the group was inactive.

June [5] ***Avalon***, produced by Davies, begins a three-week run atop the UK survey, its sleeve featuring Lucy Helmore, whom Ferry marries on the 26th.

July The extracted title song, *Avalon*, reaches UK #13.

Aug ***Avalon*** makes US #53 as the group embarks on a tour of Ferry, Mackay and Manzanera, the trio augmented by Spenner, Hubbard, Newmark, Jimmy Maelen and Guy Fletcher.

Oct *Take A Chance With Me*, also from the album, reaches UK #26.

1983

Mar Mini-album, ***Musique/The High Road***, recorded live at the Apollo Theatre, Glasgow, Strathclyde, Scotland, and the soundtrack to a live home video of the same title, reaches UK #26.

May ***Musique/The High Road*** makes US #67, as the band tours North America for the last time, in an eight-piece line-up. (This effectively ends all Roxy Music activities, as the three remaining core members turn to solo projects again.)

Nov Compilation album, ***The Atlantic Years 1973-1980*** (originated by the band's US label Atlantic), reaches UK #23.

1985

June Mackay and Manzanera have re-emerged to form the Explorers the previous year, with Ferry-like vocalist James Wraith handling lead vocal. Signed to Virgin Records, their only album ***The Explorers*** is now released, while Ferry re-launches his solo career, with ***Boys And Girls*** topping the UK chart. (Dissolving the Explorers, Manzanera will release the solo albums ***Guitarissimo***, a 1975-82 retrospective, the following year, and ***Southern Cross*** in 1987.)

1986

Apr [26] TV-promoted double compilation album, ***Street Life - 20 Great Hits***, containing both Roxy Music and Ferry highlights, tops the UK chart for the first of five weeks, and will earn a platinum disc during its 77-week survey stay. During the year, Manzanera's latest collaborative effort, now with John Wetton, is released as ***Wetton/Manzanera*** by Geffen Records.

1988

Nov [19] Following Mackay and Manzanera's June release of their collaborative ***Crack The Whip***, a second TV-promoted anthology, ***The Ultimate Collection***, again mixing Roxy Music and Ferry solo material, hits UK #6 in its week of entry. Mackay's ***Christmas*** will be issued in December the following year.

1995

Dec [4] After the Roxy Music performance set, ***Heart Still Beating***, recorded in Frejus, France, on August 27th 1982, has been released in September 1990, followed in November by Manzanera & Mackay's second album ***Manzanera & Mackay***, issued on the former's own Expression label (which has also released his ***Southern Cross*** and Mackay's ***Resolving Contradictions*** on CD for the first time), and following platinum certification by the RIAA of ***Avalon*** on December 2nd, 1992, and Virgin's issue of ***The Manzanera Collection***, a two-CD anthology in May of this year, a CD boxed-set retrospective ***The Thrill Of It All*** is now released.

1996

Apr [27] Reissued *Love Is The Drug* enters at its UK #33 peak.

see also: **Brian ENO, Bryan FERRY**

JIMMY RUFFIN

1963

R&B vocalist Ruffin (b. May 7, 1939, Collinsville, MS) having moved to Detroit, MI with his family to work in a car assembly plant in 1960, was recommended to label boss Berry Gordy Jr. at Motown Records by a member of the Contours and, signed to the subsidiary Miracle label, releasing the self-penned *Don't Feel Sorry For Me* in 1961, and spending much of the early '60s singing back-up for other acts. Following the release of his second single, *Since I Lost You,* on the Soul label, Motown now offers him the opportunity to replace Elbridge Bryant in the Temptations. He turns it down and instead recommends his brother David. He continues to work in the foundry of the Ford motor plant, taking time off to contribute to Motown package tours.

1966

Oct [29] After five years of waiting for the Motown promotional machine to roll around to him, Ruffin, still with the Soul label (alongside Jr. Walker & the All-Stars), has recorded the epic R&B ballad *What Becomes Of The Broken Hearted*, written by Paul Riser, James Dean and William Weatherspoon, which hits US #7.

Dec [31] *What Becomes Of The Broken Hearted* hits UK #8.

1967

Jan [28] *I've Passed This Way Before*, written and produced by Weatherspoon and Dean, reaches US #17.

Feb [18] *I've Passed This Way Before* climbs to UK #29.

Apr [22] *Gonna Give Her All The Love I've Got*, produced and co-penned (with Barrett Strong) by Norman Whitfield, makes US #29.

May [13] *Gonna Give Her All The Love I've Got* reaches UK #26.

The Jimmy Ruffin Way reaches UK #32.

June ***Top Ten***, containing the hits to date plus new material, peaks at UK #133.

Aug [12] *Don't You Miss Me A Little Bit Baby*, again helmed by Whitfield, makes US #68.

1969

Sept [6] Having already peaked at US #77 in April the previous year, *I've Passed This Way Before*, reissued in Britain as part of a campaign to re-promote Motown oldies, makes UK #33.

1970

Jan ***Ruff'N Ready*** peaks at US #196.

May [2] *Farewell Is A Lonely Sound*, once again written and produced by Weatherspoon and Dean, hits UK #8.

Aug [8] *I'll Say Forever My Love* hits UK #7.

Nov His duet with brother David (now a soloist, having left the Temptations) on a revival of Ben E. King's *Stand By Me*, makes US #61, taken from Jimmy's album of duets, ***I Am My Brother's Keeper***.

[21] *It's Wonderful (To Be Loved By You)*, another Witherspoon/Dean composition, hits UK #6.

1971

Feb *Maria (You Were The Only One)* stops at US #97, his last US success on Soul, after which he will record for Atlantic Records in Philadelphia, PA (releasing ***Jimmy Ruffin*** in 1973).

1974

June Compilation ***Jimmy Ruffin's Greatest Hits*** reaches UK #41.

Aug [24] Ruffin's seminal recording, *What Becomes Of The Broken Hearted*, is pulled from ***Greatest Hits*** and hits UK #4, his all-time highest chart placing, with aggregate sales now well over one million.

Nov [16] *Farewell Is A Lonely Sound*, also reissued, charts for the second time in the UK, reaching #30 and coincides with the release of Ruffin's debut for Polydor Records, to which he has signed while based in Britain.

[23] The debut single *Tell Me What You Want* makes UK #39. (An album, ***Love Is All We Need***, will be issued the following year.)

1980

Apr *Hold Onto My Love*, recorded for RSO Records and written and produced by Robin Gibb of the Bee Gees, hits US #10 and UK #7, but will be Ruffin's final US chart single. Its success prompts the Motown release of the comprehensive ***20 Golden Classics***.

June ***Sunrise*** on RSO, containing the hit, peaks at US #152.

1985

Jan Having participated in the Paul Weller-assembled Council Collective, which reached UK #24 with *Soul Deep* in December the previous year, Ruffin re-emerges after four years' silence, signed to EMI in the UK. *There Will Never Be Another You* is a UK club hit, spending a week at UK #68. (Ruffin, unable to find the momentum or the material to maintain his career, is dropped by EMI, though he will resurface on the Motor City label in 1988, cutting a couple of sides with Brenda Holloway.)

RUN D.M.C.

Jason Mizell aka "Jam Master Jay" (DJ);
Joseph "Run" Simmons (voice);
MC Darryl "D" McDaniels (voice)

1983

Apr Having all grown up in the New York, NY suburb of Hollis, Simmons (b. Nov. 24, 1966, New York), McDaniels (b. May 31, 1964, New York) and Mizell (b. Jan. 21, 1965, New York) have formed the rap trio Run D.M.C. the previous year, after graduating from St. Pascal's Catholic School, New York. (Mizell and McDaniels had also both attended St. Pascal kindergarten together up to eighth grade, while Simmons and Mizell were childhood neighbors.) Managed by Simmons' brother, Russell, who has set up Rush Productions, after rejections by a number of major labels, Run D.M.C. signs a recording deal with Profile Records in New York for $2,500, which now releases their debut cut, *It's Like That/Sucker M.C.'s*.

June Their first hip-hop set, ***Run - D.M.C.*** is released, set to reach US #53, and will spend over a year on the chart.

July Run D.M.C. embarks on a rap package tour which includes L.L. Cool J.

1984

Dec [17] ***Run - D.M.C.*** becomes the first rap album to reach RIAA gold certification.

1985

Feb Still without crossover hit singles, their sophomore effort, ***King Of Rock***, is released, set to peak at US #52, establishing the trio as pioneers of the rap genre, on its way to gold sales status.

May Run D.M.C. appears in the first rap movie, "Krush Groove". It is based on the life-story of Russell Simmons, who has now also become co-chairman of Run D.M.C. producer Rick Rubin's new label, the rap pioneering Def Jam Records.

Nov The trio contributes to the Artists Against Apartheid protest song and video, *Sun City*, which makes US #38 and UK #21.

1986

Jan Run D.M.C. teams with El DeBarge, Whitney Houston, Stacy Lattisaw, Lisa & Full Force, Teena Marie, Menundo, Stephanie Mills, New Edition, James "J.T." Taylor, Kurtis Blow, the Fat Boys, Grandmaster Melle Mel and Whodini as the King Dream Chorus & Holiday Crew, for *King Holiday*, a tribute to Martin Luther King Jr., with all proceeds benefitting the Martin Luther King Jr. Center for Non-Violent Social Change. The record reaches #30 on the US R&B chart.

July Run D.M.C., having become fashionably allied to training shoe manufacturer Adidas, debuts on the UK chart at #62 with *My Adidas/Peter Piper*.

Aug At the end of a short promotional summer European visit, Run D.M.C. signs a six-figure sponsorship-update deal with Adidas in Munich, West Germany.

[16] ***Raising Hell*** tops the US R&B chart - the first rap album to do so.

[17] Following five 1986 US gigs where crowd trouble has been prevalent (Pittsburgh, PA, Cleveland, OH, Atlanta, GA, Cincinnati, OH, and New York), a riot between rival gangs erupts at a Long Beach, Los Angeles, CA concert, with 42 of the 14,500 audience seriously injured. The incident sparks outbursts and future bans from many other US venues.

Sept ***Raising Hell*** hits US #3, the first rap album to make the Top 10, with sales eventually topping three million in the US, and UK #41. They become the first rap act to land a platinum album when ***Raising Hell*** is simultaneously certified gold and platinum. During the month, the group appears on NBC-TV's "Saturday Night Live", and co-raps with the hostess on "The Late Show Starring Joan Rivers". The City of Los Angeles rescinds an invitation for Run D.M.C. to take part in the "Los Angeles Street Scene Festival", because of recent troubles at the trio's gigs.

[27] Their update of heavy-metal outfit Aerosmith's *Walk This Way*, a collision of Run D.M.C. rap and heavy metal, as provided by the original band's vocalist Steve Tyler and guitarist Joe Perry, attracts saturated MTV rotation and hits US #4.

Oct *Walk This Way* hits UK #8, as mini-tour dates sellout in the UK.

Nov Run D.M.C. accepts an invitation from Michael Jackson to have dinner at his studio to discuss possible collaboration on his forthcoming album, but plans will be shelved. Run D.M.C. contribute with fellow rappers to ***Rap's Greatest Hits*** album, which makes US #114.

Dec Strengthening group resolve to make teenagers more aware of gang and drug-related problems, Run D.M.C. travels to Los Angeles to hold street seminars, some of which are co-hosted by the group's hero, Barry White.

[20] *You Be Illin'* reaches US #29.

1987

Jan Run D.M.C. begins writing and producing its own feature length movie, "Tougher Than Leather", planned as a rapping adventure thriller, in which they appear as rappers hunting down a drug-dealing record producer who has shot their roadie, and will also finance the project at an unexpected cost of $10 million.

Feb [18] ***King Of Rock*** is certified platnium by the RIAA.

Mar [23] They collect the Best Rap Single and Best Rap Album trophies at the inaugural Soul Train Music Awards, staged at the Civic Center, Santa Monica, CA.

Apr As a prelude to a UK tour with the similar-styled, Rubin-produced Beastie Boys, both bands appear at the "Montreux Pop Festival", Montreux, Switzerland.

[11] *It's Tricky* peaks at US #57.

[24] The RIAA certifies three million sales of ***Raising Hell***.

May *You Be Illin'* reaches UK #16.

Sept [11] They perform *Walk This Way* with Aerosmith at the fourth annual MTV Music Video Awards, held at the Universal Amphitheatre, Universal City, CA.

Dec Run D.M.C. contributes nativity rap song, *Christmas In Hollis*, to producer Jimmy Iovine's newly released seasonal compilation album, ***A Very Special Christmas*** (UK #56 and US #20).

1988

Jan The release of their movie project and accompanying album are delayed as a legal dispute opens between the band and its label, Profile.

Feb [11] The group performs at Eastside High School, Paterson, NJ, in honor of principal Joe Clark.

May *Run's House* makes UK #37.

June [4] With the dispute settled (Run D.M.C. have to pay legal costs, but are now tied to a ten-album deal with Profile), ***Tougher Than Leather*** reaches UK #13 in its week of entry and is set to hit US #9.

July Run D.M.C. headlines the "Run's House" US tour with DJ Jazzy Jeff & Fresh Prince, Public Enemy and others. At a Los Angeles gig, Run D.M.C. is joined on stage by the Beastie Boys.

[17] They receive the keys to Kansas City, MO, and Independence, MO, in honor of their support of the Work Works Campaign.

[19] ***Tougher Than Leather*** is certified platinum by the RIAA.

Aug *Mary Mary*, their cover of the Mike Nesmith-penned Monkees song, peaks at US #75.

1989

Sept With their *Ghostbusters* track currently featured on the US #14-peaking ***Ghostbusters II*** film soundtrack, *Pause* also makes UK #65.

1990

June [20] Run D.M.C. joins fellow rappers KRS-1, Public Enemy's Chuck D, Queen Latifah, MC Lyte, L.L. Cool J, Big Daddy Kane, Rebel MC and Ziggy Marley to record *H.E.A.L.*, for KRS-1's HEAL (Human Education Against Lies) campaign at Power Play studios in Long Island, New York.

Dec [1] *What's It All About* makes UK #48.

1991

Jan Run D.M.C. performs *Walk This Way* at the "Rock In Rio II" festival, Rio De Janeiro, Brazil, with New Kids On The Block.

[5] ***Back From Hell*** makes US #81.

Mar [9] The Peace Choir's *Give Peace A Chance*, with Simmons one of its featured artists, makes US #54.

[15] The rap trio appears on syndicated TV's "The Arsenio Hall Show".

Apr [17] Run D.M.C. embarks on a US tour, supported by EPMD, in Richmond, VA.

June [8] The group receives the Diamond Award for Excellence at the first IAAAM '91 Celebration of African American Music Month, at the Wyndham Franklin Plaza Hotel in Philadelphia, PA.

Aug [15] Cleveland police seek a grand-jury indictment against Simmons after he allegedly rapes a woman in his hotel room after the UrbanFest gig on the 9th. He will plead innocent on the 30th to rape charges, and be freed on a $10,000 bond.

Nov [14] Run D.M.C. guests on NBC-TV's "Late Night With David Letterman".

Dec [7] ***Greatest Hits 1983-1991*** charts for a week at US #199.

1992

Feb [20] Simmons' rape trial opens in Cleveland. The following day the case is dropped when his accuser refuses to testify. The former Bowling Green State University student, Monica Thomas, admits under oath that "there was never any basis" for the allegations.

May The group works on tracks at New York's Rawiston Recording Studio, with Jam Master Jay and Larry Smith producing.

1993

Jan [25] They break from recording their forthcoming album, to attend the 20th American Music Awards, held at Los Angeles' Shrine Auditorium, where they present the Favorite New Rap Artist trophy.

Mar [16] Run D.M.C. performs at New York's Radio City Music Hall, before a sellout crowd of 5,707.

Apr [3] *Down With The King* peaks at UK #69.

May [1] *Down With The King* reaches US #21.

[3] The group plays a one-off UK date at London's Ladbroke Grove Subterania.

[8] Run D.M.C. performs a benefit show for UNICEF in Switzerland.

[11] *Down With The King* is certified gold by the RIAA.

[15] Their seventh album, ***Down With The King***, released by Profile, and variously produced by Pete Rock, EPMD, the Bomb Squad and Jermaine Dupri, including the hit title track and featuring Neneh Cherry and KRS-1, debuts at its UK #44 peak.

[21] *Walk This Way* is confirmed gold by the RIAA.

[22] ***Down With The King*** hits US #7 in its week of release.

June [18] The group takes part in "Russell Simmons' Phat Jam - Live!", broadcast from the Academy Theater, New York, on US cable pay-per-view.

July [20] ***Down With The King*** is certified gold by the RIAA.

Nov [23] ***The Beavis And Butt-Head Experience***, to which Run D.M.C. has contributed *Bounce*, is released in the US.

1995

Sept [20] Simmons, now an ordained minister at Zoe Ministries Church in Manhattan, NY, releases the various artists ***REV RUN Presents***, the first album on his new gospel label REV RUN Records.

Oct [5] Run D.M.C. performs at New York's Madison Square Garden on a bill with Wu-Tang Clan, Brandy, Jodeci, Salt-n-Pepa, Mary J. Blige, Naughty By Nature, Soul IV Real and Notorious B.I.G.

Nov [7] With the trio preparing its next album for release in the summer of 1996, Profile releases a 12" vinyl-only boxed set of 10 classic Run D.M.C. cuts for $39.95 in the US, all in their original artwork.

THE RUNAWAYS

Cherrie Currie (vocals); **Lita Ford** (lead guitar); **Joan Jett** (rhythm guitar); **Jackie Fox** (bass); **Sandy West** (drums)

1976

Aug The all-girl teen rock'n'roll group has been formed by record producer and entrepreneur Kim Fowley (b. July 27, 1942, Los Angeles, CA) and teen lyricist Kari Krome, who, looking for a female Ramones, has introduced Jett (b. Sept. 22, 1960, Philadelphia, PA) to West (b. 1960) and subsequently recruited Currie (b. 1959, Los Angeles), Ford (b. Rosanna Ford, Sept. 23, 1959, London) and Fox (b. Jacqueline Fuchs, 1959) who replaced early bassist (and subsequent Bangle), Micki Steele. After a showcase gig on the roof of a Los Angeles apartment block, the Runaways have signed to Mercury Records which now releases their maiden set, the glam-rock, pop-fused ***The Runaways***, produced and co-written by Fowley, which peaks at US #194.

Sept The group makes its New York, NY headlining debut at CBGB's.

[23] They open their first British tour at the Apollo Theatre, Glasgow, Strathclyde, Scotland.

[27] The group is held overnight by police in Dover, Kent, following complaints from the manager of London's White House Hotel concerning the theft of hotel keys and a hairdrier.

Oct [1] They headline at London's Roundhouse in Chalk Farm.

1977

Feb Fowley/Earle Mankey-produced ***Queens Of Noise*** peaks at US #172.

June With a substantial fan-following already in place, the group tours Japan (which will produce ***Live***

In Japan).
July [1] Fox leaves the band for personal reasons, to be replaced by Laurie McAllister. (Fox will go on take a post in Ariola Records' West Coast promotion department in February 1978 before embarking on a legal career, leading to a position with law-firm Townsend & Townsend in San Francisco, CA in the '90s.)
Aug [13] Currie quits the group with Jett taking over as lead vocalist and Vicki Blue joining on guitar. (Currie will release the solo ***Beauty Is Only Skin Deep*** the following year, before forming a duo with sister Marie and recording for Capitol Records, achieving some success in Japan. After the sisters split, she will pursue an acting career which will include "Foxes" with Jodie Foster in 1980, the horror film "Parasite" in March 1982.)
Dec ***Waitin' For The Night***, again produced by Fowley, is released.

1978

Dec [31] The band plays its final concert in San Francisco. With no funds and no recording deal, Jett wants to keep the band strictly rock'n'roll, while Ford favors a move towards heavy metal. They are due to appear in the semi-documentary movie "We're All Crazy" but will split prior to the project getting underway (only Jett will appear). Jett will move to London, where she cuts tracks with ex-Sex Pistols Paul Cook and Steve Jones towards the end of the following year, during which Cherry Red Records (UK) will release ***And Now ... The Runaways*** (to be retitled by Rhino Records as ***Little Lost Girls*** in 1981).

1980

Feb Cherry Red issues ***Flaming Schoolgirls*** a half live/half studio set from the original line-up.
July [15-16] Jett performs at the two-day new wave festival "Urgh!" in Santa Monica, CA. Her performance is filmed for the movie "Urgh! A Music War".
Aug Jett, having been in hospital suffering from a heart-valve infection and pneumonia, forms her own backing band the Blackhearts, with Ricky Byrd (guitar), Gary Ryan (bass) and Lee Crystal (drums) and records ***Joan Jett*** with producers Kenny Laguna and Ritchie Cordell. With no initial US record company interest, Laguna releases the album himself, licensing the project to Ariola Records in Europe.

1981

Jan Joan Jett & the Blackhearts sign to Boardwalk Records.
Feb Jett opens at New York's Peppermint Lounge as a prelude to a US tour to promote her forthcoming album.
Apr ***Joan Jett***, now renamed ***Bad Reputation*** for US release on Boardwalk, reaches US #51.

1982

Mar [20] Jett's anthemic rock cover of the Arrows' *I Love Rock'n'Roll*, which she had seen them perform on UK TV during a British tour (but had earlier failed to convince the Runaways of its potential), begins a seven-week run atop the US chart (on its way to platinum sales status) while ***I Love Rock'n'Roll*** begins a rise to hit US #2.
May *I Love Rock'n'Roll* hits UK #4 as parent album ***I Love Rock'n'Roll*** reaches UK #25.
June For a follow-up, Jett's version of Tommy James & the Shondells' 1969 chart topper *Crimson And Clover* hits US #7 and UK #60.
Sept Her version of Gary Glitter's *Do You Wanna Touch Me (Oh Yeah)* is Jett's third US hit at #20.

1983

Aug Jett's *Fake Friends*, the first release on her own Blackheart Records, reaches US #35, taken from ***Album*** which makes US #20, earning a gold disc.
Oct Her treatment of Sly & the Family Stone's 1969 US chart-topper, *Everyday People*, climbs to US #37.

1984

May [26] Ford's second solo album (following last year's Mercury issued glam-metal debut ***Out For Blood***), ***Dancin' On The Edge*** makes UK #96 (and will climb to US #66 in October).
Nov Jett's ***Glorious Results Of A Misspent Youth*** reaches US #67.

1986

Oct [25] Jett's *Good Music*, with backing vocals from the Beach Boys, peaks at US #83 as its parent album ***Good Music*** climbs to US #105.

1987

Apr [4] Jett's *Light Of Day*, written by Bruce Springsteen and featured in the movie of the same name co-starring Jett (as leader of rock band, the Barbusters) and Michael J. Fox, reaches US #33.
Sept Ever the opportunist, Fowley has resurrected the Runaways name with an entirely new all-girl line-up which releases ***Young And Fast***, before quickly dissolving.

1988

June [18] Newly signed to RCA Records, Ford reaches US #12 with *Kiss Me Deadly*, taken from the platinum-selling ***Lita*** which peaks at US #29.
July Jett solo album ***Up Your Alley*** reaches US #19.
Oct [1] Jett's *I Hate Myself For Loving You* hits US #8 and UK #46.
Dec [17] Ford's hard-rocking *Kiss Me Deadly* peaks at UK #75.

1989

Jan [21] *Little Liar* reaches US #19 for Jett.
Feb Jett plays five sell-out concerts at Lunt-Fontanne Theatre, New York.
May Ford's metal ballad duet with Ozzy Osbourne, *Close My Eyes Forever*, makes UK #47.
June [17] *Close My Eyes Forever* hits US #8.
[26] Ford marries W.A.S.P. guitarist Chris Holmes at Lake Tahoe, CA.
Sept [28] Jett abruptly ends a gig after being hit in the face by a bracelet thrown from the crowd.

1990

Feb Having signed to SBK Records in 1989 and appearing in the movie "Rich Girl", Currie, now a member of hard rock combo Redd Kross, begins filming "Natural Born Killers", as she prepares her autobiography **Neon Angel : The Cherie Currie Story**. (She will re-emerge in 1993 with the Cherie Currie Band.)
[24] Jett's ***The Hit List***, an album of cover versions including *Dirty Deeds*, *Tush*, *Have You Seen The Rain*, *Love Me Two Times* and *Time Has Come Today*, among others, makes US #36.
[28] Ford is inducted into **Circus** magazine's Hall of Fame.
Mar [10] Jett's *Dirty Deeds* reaches US #36.
July [27] Ford's ***Stiletto*** makes US #52 and UK #66, as she tours with Motley Crue.

1991

Nov [6] Ford performs at The Roxy, West Hollywood, CA.
[23] Ford's *Shot Of Poison* makes US #45.
[30] Its parent album ***Dangerous Curves*** debuts at its US #132 peak (and will bow at its UK #51 peak on Jan [25], one week after *Shot Of Poison* has stopped at UK #63). (During the year, Jett's non-charting ***Notorious*** is released with RCA issuing ***The Best Of Lita Ford*** in 1992.)

1995

Aug [8] After Ford has launched Lita Ford Body Wear manufactured by Glamorous Appeal in Miami, FL, in the summer of 1993 and Jett's *I Love Rock And Roll* has charted for a week at UK #75 on Feb [19] 1994, re-exposed via its inclusion in the movie "Wayne's World", prior to her Warner Bros. Records label debut ***Pure And Simple*** in November, Ford, Jett, Currie and West have filed a $70,000 claim for unpaid royalties against Polygram and Fowley in Los Angeles Superior Court on November 18th last year. With Ford having released ***Black*** on the ZYX label in the US in January of this year, Sony's 550 label now issues ***Spirit Of '73 : Rock For Choice***, including Jett's new version of the Runaways' *Cherry Bomb*, recorded with L7.

TODD RUNDGREN

1967

Rundgren (b. June 22, 1948, Upper Darby, PA), who has already played guitar in a high-school group, Money, a UK-style R&B band, in 1965, has gone on to join Woody's Truck Stop the following year, a blues-based outfit in the Paul Butterfield mould, performing in Philadelphia, PA. With the group's bassist, Carson Van Osten, Rundgren now leaves to form the Nazz (the name's probable inspiration being the Yardbirds' B-side, *The Nazz Are Blue*). Designed to inherit a pre-psychedelic sound, notably the British influence of the Beatles, the Small Faces and the Move, the group includes Robert "Stewkey" Antoni on vocals and keyboards, and Thom Mooney on drums, and makes its live debut supporting the Doors.

1968

Nov Signed to Screen Gems/Columbia (which also rosters the Monkees), the Nazz has been placed on new subsidiary label, SGC, which releases their debut, ***Nazz***. It will peak at US #118 during a 26-week chart run.

1969

Jan The group visits the UK for promotion and to cut a second album in London, but because of problems with clearances from the UK Musicians' Union, work permits are declared invalid, and the Nazz flies to Los Angeles, CA to record instead.
Mar Their debut single, *Open My Eyes*, a riff-driven rocker released prior to the album without charting, is overtaken in US airplay by its Association-styled, harmony ballad B-side, *Hello It's Me*, at US #71.
June The group's second set, ***Nazz Nazz***, compiled from two albums-worth of material cut at the Los Angeles sessions, reaches US #80, but following continual disagreements with Mooney, Rundgren has left before the album's release (along with Van Osten). He returns for a promotional US tour before being replaced by future Cheap Trick member, Rick Nielsen.

1970

Feb *Hello It's Me* is released again as an A-side, following continuing airplay, and climbs to US #66. Rundgren becomes an in-house producer for Albert Grossman's Bearsville Studios, and engineers the Band's ***Stage Fright***.
Nov After producing Bearsville's first album, by the American Dream, Rundgren is given studio time as payment, and cuts ***Runt*** for Bearsville subsidiary, Ampex, with the aid of Tony Sales (bass) and Hunt Sales (drums), both subsequent members of David Bowie's Tin Machine. ("Runt" is a nickname given to Rundgren by Patti Smith.) From the album, *We Gotta Get You A Woman*, his first solo single, reaches US #20.

1971

Jan ***Runt***, showcasing both his technical expertise and penchant for melody, peaks at US #185, while the final Nazz album, ***Nazz III***, featuring the leftover second album tracks, is also released.
May The second album credited to Runt, ***The Ballad Of Todd Rundgren***, sells poorly, but the extracted *Be Nice To Me* makes US #71.
Sept *A Long Time, A Long Way To Go*, also from the album, peaks at US #92. He visits the UK to take over production of Badfinger's ***Straight Up*** from George Harrison.

1972

Apr Bearsville signs for distribution to Warner Bros., with Rundgren moved from Ampex to Bearsville itself, where he begins to record under his own name, starting with the double album, ***Something/Anything***, on which three sides are recorded solo, while the fourth

features a studio group playing live with no overdubs.
June ***Something/Anything*** peaks at US #29, earning Rundgren a gold disc, and *I Saw The Light*, taken from it, reaches US #16.
Aug Also from ***Something/Anything***, *Couldn't I Just Tell You* peaks at US #92. Rundgren's credits as a producer and engineer continue as he works extensively with Bearsville acts including Foghat, Jesse Winchester, Ian & Sylvia and Paul Butterfield.

1973

June ***A Wizard, A True Star***, recorded at his own Secret Sounds Studios in New York, is a near-psychedelic pot-pourri, with 26 songs presented in a style similar to ***Abbey Road***'s side two. It makes US #86, and includes the extracted Philly-soul single, *Sometimes I Don't Know What To Feel*.
July [14] *I Saw The Light* is Rundgren's only solo UK hit single, reaching #36.
Sept The Rundgren produced Grand Funk single and similarly-titled album, ***We're An American Band***, hit US #1 and #2 respectively, both becoming million sellers.
Dec Rundgren's solo revival of the Nazz song, *Hello It's Me*, taken from ***Something/Anything***, becomes his biggest-seller, hitting US #5.

1974

May Another two-album set, ***Todd***, half-solo and half-group, climbs to US #54 and includes *Sons Of 1984*, recorded live in New York's Central Park, and featuring a 3,000-strong chorus, overdubbed from the New York audience and another at San Francisco's Golden Gate Park, recorded in September 1973.
June Beach Boys-styled ballad, *A Dream Goes On Forever*, from ***Todd***, peaks at US #69.
Dec Rundgren has formed Utopia, with Mark Klingman and Ralph Shuckett on keyboards, Roger Powell on synthesizer, John Siegler on bass, John Wilcox on drums and Kevin Elliman on percussion, to develop his symphonic art-rock ideas and more metaphysical lyrical concerns. Their debut album, ***Todd Rundgren's Utopia***, an hour-long set, reaches US #34.

1975

Feb [26] ***Something/Anything*** is certified gold by the RIAA.
May *Real Man*, heralding a new solo album, peaks at US #83.
June His solo set, ***Initiation***, is a 68-minute single album, with cosmically-inclined songs (including *Real Man*) on one side, and a 30-minute instrumental on side two. Players include members of Utopia, plus Edgar Winter, Rick Derringer and Dan Hartman.
Dec Utopia's live second album, ***Another Live***, includes a version of the Move's *Do Ya*, plus a song from "West Side Story". Reaching US #66, this is the last album to feature the original Utopia line-up. Rundgren makes his first playing visit to the UK to promote the album with a series of successful concerts.

1976

July ***Faithful***, credited as a Rundgren solo set, but featuring future "Utopians", includes one side of close re-creations of six '60s classics, including two Lennon/McCartney songs, and one each by Bob Dylan, the Yardbirds and Jimi Hendrix, plus the Beach Boys' *Good Vibrations*, which is released as a single, and reaches US #34.
Aug [21] Rundgren performs at the "Knebworth Festival", Knebworth, Herts., with 10cc, Lynyrd Skynyrd, and bill-toppers, the Rolling Stones.

1977

Mar A new line-up of Utopia has been assembled for the Egyptology/pyramids-obsessed ***Ra***, comprising Rundgren (vocals and guitar), Kasim Sulton (bass and vocals), Roger Powell (keyboards and vocals) and John "Willie" Wilcox (drums). The album becomes the group's biggest UK hit, reaching UK #27, and peaks at US #79. (Rundgren has planned to release it on his own label, Etheric Records, but does not get the label beyond the planning stage.)
Oct Utopia album, ***Oops! Wrong Planet***, featuring shorter, more radio-oriented songs (including *Love Is The Answer*, later a hit for England Dan & John Ford Coley), reaches US #73 and UK #59. Rundgren produces Meat Loaf's ***Bat Out Of Hell***. (Becoming a rock staple, it will hit both the US and UK Top 10 in 1978, selling over 15 million copies worldwide, staying on the UK chart for seven years, and will be Rundgren's most successful production project, for which he will receive a producer's royalty.)

1978

May He returns to solo recording with the self-produced (as ever) ***Hermit Of Mink Hollow***, on which he also plays all instruments.
July From the album, Rundgren's first US Top 30 single since *Hello It's Me* in 1973 is *Can We Still Be Friends?* (later covered by Robert Palmer), which reaches US #29.

1979

Jan Live double album, ***Back To The Bars***, credited as a Rundgren solo, but featuring a variety of group line-ups including guests Hall & Oates (for whom he had previously produced ***War Babies***), Stevie Nicks of Fleetwood Mac and Spencer Davis, makes US #75.
Press reports state that Rundgren is to take the UK Musicians' Union to court over its "restrictive strangle-holds" over visiting musicians. (The union had refused him permission to broadcast a live show from London's The Venue.)
Mar [31] The Tubes' ***Remote Control***, produced by Rundgren, enters the US chart set to make #46, while in the UK, the Tom Robinson Band's ***TRB2***, also helmed by him, reaches UK #18.

1980

Feb Utopia album, ***Adventures In Utopia***, conceived as the soundtrack to a TV/video special, reaches US #32 and UK #57, the group's final UK chart entry.
Apr *Set Me Free*, from ***Adventures In Utopia***, is the group's first US hit single, making #27.
June Also from the album, *The Very Last Time* peaks at US #76.
Aug [13] Rundgren's home in Woodstock, NY, is broken into by four masked men, who bind and gag Rundgren, his girlfriend and three guests, then strip the house of valuable art treasures and stereo equipment.
Nov Utopia's ***Deface The Music***, entirely consisting of '60s Beatles pastiches, written and recorded in two weeks, peaks at US #65.

1981

Apr ***Healing***, totally solo and quasi-religious, reaches US #48. It includes a free single, *Time Heals* (which some months later is released in its own right, without success, despite being regarded as one of his best singles, though its Rundgren-produced promotional video will win Flo & Eddie's Golden Hippo Award).

1982

Mar Utopia album, ***Swing To The Right***, is the band's last for Bearsville, peaking at US #102.
Apr Rundgren undertakes a solo US tour to promote the album, despite it being a band recording.
Dec With the band newly signed to the US Network label, ***Utopia***, which is made into a double package by including a five-track 12" single, makes US #84. In the UK, it is issued as a single album by Epic with a free 7" single instead.

1983

Jan Taken from the album, *Feet Don't Fail Me Now* peaks at US #82, Utopia's last hit single.
Mar Rundgren's final solo Bearsville album, ***The Ever Popular Tortured Artist Effect***, makes US #66. He releases a 90-minute video special based on the album, recorded in his own computer-video studio in Woodstock.
May Taken from the album, *Bang The Drum All Day* is Rundgren's last solo US hit single, peaking at #63.
Oct Will Powers' *Kissing With Confidence*, co-written by Rundgren, reaches UK #17.

1985

May With a change of label to US Passport, ***Utopia Oblivion*** has made US #74, in March the previous year, a second Utopia album for the company, ***P.O.V.***, is now released and includes the group's version of *Mated*, later a UK #20 hit single for David Grant & Jaki Graham.
Nov Rundgren's ***A Cappella***, recorded for Warner Bros., uses just his voice, with help from the keyboard emulator, to make a variety of vocal-based sounds. The extracted *Something To Fall Back On* gains much radio play as he tours the US with a gospel-style vocal group in support.
Dec Rundgren's duet with Bonnie Tyler, *Loving You Is A Dirty Job (But Somebody's Gotta Do It)*, peaks at UK #73.

1986

May [3] Rundgren also features on guest vocals with Tyler on *If You Were A Woman (And I Was A Man)*, which peaks at US #77.
July [17] Rundgren guests on NBC-TV's "Late Night With David Letterman".
Utopia splits as ***Trivia***, a compilation of tracks from earlier albums, is released.

1987

Aug Rhino Records in the US (having previously re-released rare Nazz albums) begins a re-issue program covering all Rundgren and Utopia Bearsville releases, bringing Rundgren's work to CD for the first time.

1989

June ***Nearly Human***, which features *Parallel Lines* from the musical "Up Against It", makes US #102.
Aug "Up Against It" opens at New York, NY's Public Theater. Rundgren has written the score to Joe Orton's original script, intended as the Beatles' follow-up movie to "Help!"
Oct Rhino releases the Utopia/Rundgren retrospective ***Anthology***.

1990

Jan Rundgren plays four nights at Nakano Sun Plaza, Tokyo, Japan (videotaped for subsequent release as "Live In Japan").
[17] He begins a US tour in Los Angeles.
June Rundgren produces Jill Sobule's ***Things Here Are Different***, and the Pursuit Of Happiness' ***One Sided Story***.
July [6-7, 9, 11-12] He performs at the Palace of Fine Arts Theatre, San Francisco, recording the concerts for an intended future album.
Oct Rundgren invents Flowflazer, a software package for the Apple Mac computer, which generates a stream of psychedelic graphics.

1991

Mar [2] ***2nd Wind***, recorded live before an audience of 2,000 at the Palace of Fine Arts Theater, makes US #118.
Apr [17] Rundgren begins a US tour in Wilkes-Barre, PA.
[26] He guests on NBC-TV's "Late Night With David Letterman". (He has always been a particular Letterman favorite, not least for providing leggy backing singers.)
July His nineteen year association with Warner Bros. Records ends, as Rundgren enters into a new venture, NuTopia with NuTek, whose first product is the Video Toaster, a $4,000 "mini TV studio in a box", symptomatic of his increasing and pioneering involvement in multi-media.
Sept [8] He attends the renewal of marriage vows of manager Eric Gardner and wife Janis, with Little Richard and Phil Spector, who plays *The Anniversary Waltz* on accordion, also in attendance.
Nov [6] Rundgren makes the keynote speech at the

13th annual **Billboard** Music Video Conference in Los Angeles, heralding the dawn of interactive multi-media and its future fusion with music.

1992

Feb [2] A son Rebop is born, his third child, and first by singer Michele Gray.
Oct [11] Rundgren participates in the "Healing The Sacred Hoop - The Next 500 Years" benefit at the Shoreline Amphitheatre, Mountain View, CA , with Bonnie Raitt, Don Henley, Little Feat, Ry Cooder & David Lindley and others.
Dec He takes part in a concert to celebrate the 20th anniversary of San Francisco critic Joel Selvin, with Chris Isaak, Van Morrison and Bonnie Raitt.

1993

May Credited to TR-I (Todd Rundgren Interactive), ***No World Order***, the world's first conventional music CD with interactive CD counterpart, is released on Rhino's Forward label and Philips' CD-I system, having been available from Pony Canyon in Japan since the beginning of the year. He embarks on a 20-city promotional mini-tour, while Rhino Records also releases the live Utopia set, ***Redux '92 - Live In Japan***.
Dec [11-12] Rundgren plays two sellout shows at the Grays Harbor County Fair, Cleveland, OH, during his latest US tour.

1994

Apr It is reported that Rundgren is selling his royalties to ***Bat Out Of Hell*** to finance his new interactive label, Waking Dream.
Oct [6-7] Rundgren performs at London's Kentish Town Forum, during selected UK dates.

1995

Sept As Rundgren wraps up a 38-city US tour, while still a consultant to online service, CompuServe, his latest project, ***The Individualist***, is released in the US by ION as a multi-media CD-Plus title.

1996

Mar [9] He collects the Arthur M. Sohcut Award for his public service contribution to San Francisco at the 19th annual Bammie Awards held at the city's Warfield Theatre, before beginning a series of in-store presentations of ***The Individualist*** around the US.

RUSH

Alex Lifeson (guitar); **Geddy Lee** (vocals, bass); **Neil Peart** (drums)

1973

Lifeson (b. Aug. 27, 1953, Fernie, BC, Canada) and Lee (b. July 29, 1953, Willowdale, Canada), having met in the Toronto, Canada suburb of Sarnia while at high school, have teamed with drummer John Rutsey to form Rush in 1969, playing Cream, Hendrix and Led Zeppelin-influenced music, and began regular performing on the bar and club circuit when the legal drinking age was reduced from 21 to 18, graduating to a support slot for the New York Dolls in Toronto. They recruit producer Terry Brown (who has worked with Procol Harum and fellow Canadians, April Wine), and cut an album for $9,000 at Toronto's Sound Studios. Unable to interest record companies, they set up their own Moon label to release their debut album, ***Rush***, a copy of which is sent to Cleveland, OH radio station WMMS DJ, Donna Halper, who brings the band to the attention of Mercury Records, which signs them up for a two-album deal worth $200,000.

1974

July The self-produced ***Rush*** is re-released by Mercury as Rutsey quits and Peart (b. Sept. 12, 1952, Hamilton, ON, Canada) successfully auditions to take his place. The new trio lineup will endure as the permanent Rush unit into the '90s.
Aug [19] Rush embarks on its debut US tour, playing support dates until Christmas.
Oct ***Rush*** peaks at US #105.

1975

Jan The group begins work on its second album at Toronto Sound Studios.
Feb Rush is named Most Promising Group at the annual Juno Awards in Canada.
Mar The eight-song ***Fly By Night***, co-produced by the group with Terry Brown and featuring Lee playing classical guitar, once again showcasing their self-penned progressive rock style, and interest in science fiction/fantasy themes, makes US #113, as the group begins a US tour supporting Aerosmith and Kiss.
Nov Once again co-helmed with Brown, ***Caress Of Steel*** peaks at US #148.

1976

May Their fourth album in two years, ***2112***, co-produced with Brown and augmented by keyboardist Hugh Syme, a futuristic-themed set based on the work of novelist Ayn Rand, makes US #61.
June [11-13] Rush plays three sellout nights at Toronto's 4,000-seater Massey Hall.
Sept The group begins a domestic tour of Canada.
Nov Double performance album, ***All The World's A Stage***, recorded live in Toronto, makes US #40.
Dec The band plays selected US dates in New York, NY, Chicago, IL, Indianapolis, IN and Boston, MA.

1977

Jan *Fly By Night/In The Mood* peaks at US #88.
Apr The group begins a US tour of the northeast and midwest.
June [2] Rush opens on its first UK dates, the first seven of which are sellouts, at the Free Trade Hall, Manchester, Gtr. Manchester.
July Work commences on a new album at Rockfield Studios, Monmouth, Gwent, Wales.
Oct Comprising six extended pieces once again co-produced with Brown, ***A Farewell To Kings*** reaches US #33, and marks the group's UK chart debut at #22.
Nov ***2112***, ***All The World's A Stage*** and ***A Farewell To Kings*** are all certified gold.
Dec *Closer To The Heart* peaks at US #77.

1978

Jan The group's first UK chart single, *Closer To The Heart*, reaches UK #36.
Feb Rush wins the Best Group category at the annual Juno Awards.
[12] The group opens its second sellout UK tour at the Odeon Cinema, Birmingham, West Midlands.
Apr ***Archives***, a triple-set reissue of the group's first three albums, peaks at US #121.
Oct Rush embarks on its 113-date "Hemispheres" tour covering North America and Europe.
Dec The nine-song ***Hemispheres***, including the popular FM cut *The Trees* which lyrically concerns itself with the question of Quebec's secession from Canada, reaches US #47 and UK #14.

1979

Jan [8] The Canadian Government names Rush "Official Ambassadors Of Music".
Feb Rush wins another Best Group trophy, at the annual Juno Awards.
Apr The band embarks on a three-month tour of the UK and the rest of Europe.

1980

Jan Rush sets out on a five-month "Permanent Waves" tour of the US.
Feb Their breakthrough album ***Permanent Waves***, featuring shorter songs more suited to mainstream radio once again co-produced with Brown, hits US #4 and UK #3.
Mar The extracted *Spirit Of The Radio* peaks at US #51 and UK #13.
June Rush visits Britain for another sellout tour, including five nights at London's Hammersmith Odeon.

1981

Feb The band starts its "Moving Pictures" US tour to promote a new album.
Mar Again augmented by Hyme on keyboards, ***Moving Pictures***, featuring the popular instrumental *YYZ*, hits both US and UK #3.
[4] Their 1976 album ***All The World's A Stage*** is certified platinum by the RIAA.
Apr *Limelight* reaches US #55, while *Vital Signs/A Passage To Bangkok* makes UK #41.
Aug *Tom Sawyer* climbs to US #44.
Nov *Tom Sawyer* reaches UK #25. ***Exit ... Stage Left***, a second live double set, hits US #10 and UK #6.

1982

Jan A live version of *Closer To The Heart* peaks at US #69.
Mar Lee guests on vocals for fellow Canadians Dave Thomas and Rick Moranis (Bob and Doug McKenzie from Canadian TV comedy show, "SCTV") on *Take Off*, which reaches US #16 (its parent album, ***Great White North***, hitting US #8).
Oct *New World Man* reaches US #21 and UK #42, taken from the eight-song ***Signals***, also signalling the group's last collaboration with producer Brown, which hits US #10 and UK #3.
Nov The extracted *Subdivisions* peaks at UK #53.
[10] ***Signals*** is certified platinum by the RIAA. A further excerpt *Countdown*, with a live version of *New World Man* on the flipside, will make UK #36 the following May.

1984

May *The Body Electric* peaks at UK #56, and is featured on the Peter Henderson co-produced ***Grace Under Pressure***, which hits US #10 and UK #5.
June [26] ***Grace Under Pressure*** is certified platinum by the RIAA.

1985

Oct *The Big Money* makes UK #46.
Nov Augmented by keyboardist Andy Richards, ***Power Windows***, co-produced by the band with Peter Collins, hits US #10 and UK #9.

1986

Jan [11] *The Big Money* makes US #45.
[27] ***Power Windows*** is certified platinum by the RIAA.
Feb [19] Their "Exit ... Stage Left" video is confirmed gold by the RIAA.

1987

Oct *Time Stand Still*, with a guest vocal by Til Tuesday's Aimee Mann, makes UK #42.
Nov [9] The RIAA ratifies gold sales of ***Hold Your Fire*** and platinum sales of ***Exit ... Stage Left*** and ***Permanent Waves***.
[21] ***Hold Your Fire***, recorded in England, Montserrat, Toronto and Paris, France, with Collins again producing with the band, hits UK #10 in its week of entry, and will reach US #13.

1988

Apr *Prime Mover* makes UK #43.

1989

Jan [28] The self-produced ***A Show Of Hands***, a live album encapsulating their 1986 and 1988 world tours with eight of its 15 tracks recorded at Birmingham's National Exhibition Centre the previous year, reaches its UK #12 peak, and will make US #21.
Mar [9] ***A Show Of Hands*** is certified gold by the RIAA.
June [9] "A Show Of Hands" video is confirmed platinum by the RIAA.
Dec [9] Newly signed to Atlantic Records after 15 years with Mercury, Rush's label debut, ***Presto***, revealing a more straight-ahead rock approach, reaches UK #27 in its week of entry, and will reach US #16.

1990

Jan [11] ***Presto*** is certified gold by the RIAA.
Mar [30-31] During a six-month North American tour, the group plays two sellout dates at the Oakland-Alameda County Coliseum, Oakland, CA, grossing $509,438.
Oct [6] The Mercury-issued retrospective collection, ***Chronicles***, makes US #51.
[13] ***Chronicles*** debuts at its UK #42 peak.

1991

Apr [2-3] Rush, on its latest North American trek, plays before sellout crowds of 28,000 at the Great Western Forum, Inglewood, CA.
Sept [14] Co-produced by Rush with Rupert Hine, who also helmed the group's last outing, ***Roll The Bones*** hits UK #10.
[21] ***Roll The Bones*** debuts at its US #3 peak.
Oct [25] ***Roll The Bones*** is certified gold by the RIAA.
Dec [6-7] The group performs sellout dates at New York's Madison Square Garden, and are presented with the Gold Ticket Award for more than 100,000 tickets sold at the venue between 1981-1991.
[16] They play their last gig of the year, during a current tour, at the Maple Leaf Gardens, Toronto, grossing $295,303 from the 11,906 sellout crowd.

1992

Jan [2] The group resumes its tour at the Selland Arena, Fresno Convention Center, Fresno, CA, set to end on March 15th at the Nassau Veterans Memorial Coliseum, Uniondale, NY.
Mar [7] *Roll The Bones* charts for a week at UK #49.
Apr ***Roll The Bones*** is named Best Hard Rock Album, at the annual Juno Awards.
[10] The six-date UK leg of their "Roll The Bones" tour begins at the Sheffield Arena, set to end on the 18th at Wembley Arena, Wembley, Middx. (These are the group's first British dates since its 1988 "Hold Your Fire" tour).
May [21] The third segment of the "Roll The Bones" North American tour opens at Mid-South Coliseum, Memphis, TN.

1993

Oct [30] Reprising co-production chores with Collins, ***Counterparts***, featuring keyboardist John Wester with string arrangements by Michael Kamen, debuts at its UK #14 peak.
Nov [6] ***Counterparts*** bows at its US #2 peak.
Dec [1] The RIAA certifies gold sales of ***Caress Of Steel*** and platinum sales of ***A Farewell To Kings***, ***Fly By Night*** and ***Hemispheres***.
[7] ***Counterparts*** is confirmed gold by the RIAA.

1994

Jan [22] Their North American "Counterparts Tour 94" opens at the Pensacola Civic Center, Pensacola, FL.
May [7] Rush plays a sellout date at Maple Leaf Gardens, Toronto, at the end of its North American trek.
Nov [6] Following the release of his ***Burning For Buddy : A Tribute To The Music Of Buddy Rich*** project, Peart receives the Buddy Rich Lifetime Achievement Award.

1995

Jan [27] The RIAA certifies four million sales of ***Moving Pictures***.
Feb [1] ***Rush*** is confirmed gold by the RIAA, for 500,000 US sales.
[3] ***Archives*** is ratified platinum by the RIAA.
Nov [17] The RIAA certifies three million sales of ***2112*** with ***Chronicles*** confirmed at two million sales four days later.

1996

Jan [9] Lifeson's first side-project, ***Victor***, recorded by a group of musicians assembled by him under the same name, is released by Atlantic Records.

LEON RUSSELL

1958

Leaving home at the age of 17, Russell (b. Hank Wilson, Apr. 2, 1941, Lawton, OK), a child piano prodigy who has learned to play the trumpet and formed his own band with future Bread-maker David Gates in Tulsa, OK, in his mid-teens (and lying about his age to get a job in a Tulsa nightclub, playing with a visiting Ronnie Hawkins and Jerry Lee Lewis), moves to Los Angeles, CA, to continue club-performing, still using an older friend's I.D. until he turns 21. Still hiding the truth about his age, Russell begins a career as a multi-instrumental session man, learning guitar from James Burton, and playing in studio sessions alongside Glen Campbell, Dorsey Burnette and others. He will also regularly perform as a pianist on ABC-TV's pioneering "Shindig!" series.

1962

He becomes a regular member of Phil Spector's "Wall Of Sound" session crew, playing on hits by the Crystals, Bob B. Soxx & the Blue Jeans and others, sometimes using the pseudonym Russell Bridges. He also plays on Herb Alpert's *A Taste Of Honey*, and the Byrds' *Mr. Tambourine Man*.

1965

Feb [20] At Liberty Records, Russell begins arranging for Gary Lewis & the Playboys, whose first single, *This Diamond Ring*, now tops the US chart.

1967

With his own recording career getting off to a false start the previous year with the release of a one-off single for A&M, Russell builds his own recording studio, while current session work includes playing on ex-Byrd Gene Clark's solo album, and arranging *Feelin' Groovy* for Harpers Bizarre.

1968

Russell teams with guitarist Marc Benno for ***Asylum Choir***. Released on Mercury Records subsidiary Smash, it is critically rated, but fails commercially. He joins the Delaney & Bonnie and Friends tour and comes to the attention of Joe Cocker's manager and producer, Denny Cordell, after which Cocker's second album is recorded at Russell's studio (and includes *Delta Lady*, originally written by Russell for Rita Coolidge).

1969

Apr A second Asylum Choir album is recorded, but Smash declines to release it. Cordell suggests that Russell records with him in Britain, before they return to California to apply finishing touches to the album, and set up their own Shelter Records.

1970

June Russell organizes the band for Cocker's "Mad Dogs And Englishmen" US tour. His high profile in these live shows establishes a personal following, which benefits the critically-lauded ***Leon Russell***, Shelter's first release, which reaches US #60 (and includes the subsequently celebrated ballad, *A Song For You*, which will be covered by a host of artists including Donny Hathaway, and the Carpenters). His own show airs on National Educational TV in the US - a relaxed affair filmed in his recording studio and featuring a variety of friends, musicians, girlfriends and children. (He also plays with Bob Dylan, the Rolling Stones and Eric Clapton during the year.)

1971

Jan [22] The movie, "Mad Dogs And Englishmen", documenting the tour of the same name, with Russell in a prominent role, premieres in London.
July ***Leon Russell And The Shelter People***, recorded throughout 1970 and featuring *Beware Of Darkness*, co-written with George Harrison, climbs to US #17 and also reaches UK #29 - his only UK chart entry.
Aug [1] He plays guitar behind Bob Dylan at George Harrison's "Concert For Bangla Desh" at New York's Madison Square Garden.
Oct The Carpenters' version of *Superstar*, co-written by Russell and Bonnie Bramlett, hits US #2.

1972

Jan Having bought the tapes of ***Asylum Choir II*** from Smash, Russell has released the album on Shelter, which now reaches US #70.
Feb [3] ***Leon Russell And The Shelter People*** is certified gold by the RIAA.
Sept ***Carney*** is Russell's most successful album, hitting US #2 for four weeks during a 35-week chart stay.
[19] ***Carney*** is confirmed gold by the RIAA.
Oct *Tight Rope*, taken from ***Carney***, reaches US #11.
Nov Russell finishes a 58-city US tour, seen by some 600,000 people, which grosses $2.8 million.

1973

June [26] The still-climbing ***Leon Live*** is certified gold by the RIAA.
Sept Triple-live album, ***Leon Live***, recorded at Long Beach Arena, CA, in front of 70,000 people, hits US #9. From the set, *Queen Of The Roller Derby* peaks at US #89.
Oct Double A-side Hank Wilson single, *Roll In My Sweet Baby's Arms/I'm So Lonesome I Could Cry*, makes US #78. Both come from Russell's "pseudonymous" (it uses his real name) country set ***Hank Wilson's Back***, which climbs to US #28. (His future wife Mary McCreary's ***Butterflies In Heaven*** is also released on Shelter.)

1974

May Russell's revival of Tim Hardin's *If I Were A Carpenter* peaks at US #73.
Aug ***Stop All That Jazz***, recorded with help from J.J. Cale, Willie Nelson and Pete Drake, reaches US #34.

1975

July ***Will O' The Wisp***, with actor Gary Busey playing drums on *Bluebird*, makes US #30.
Nov *Lady Blue*, extracted from ***Will O' The Wisp***, reaches US #14.

1976

Jan *Back To The Island* makes US #53. Russell marries McCreary, who is currently a vocalist with the Sly & the Family Stone spin-off group, Little Sister. He also cuts his ties with Shelter Records and establishes a new label, Paradise Records.
Mar [9] ***Will O' The Wisp*** is certified gold by the RIAA.
July ***The Wedding Album***, released on Paradise and recorded with his wife, reaches US #34.
Sept *Rainbow In Your Eyes*, by Leon and Mary Russell, peaks at US #52. (This will be Russell's last chart single, though, as a writer, he is currently riding high as George Benson's version of his *This Masquerade* hits US #10).
Dec [29] Shelter compilation ***Best Of Leon*** is certified gold by the RIAA, having already made US #40 earlier in the month.

1977

Feb [19] Russell's *This Masquerade* wins Record Of The Year (by way of Benson's version), at the 19th annual Grammy Awards.
July Another duetted album with Mary Russell, ***Make Love To The Music***, peaks at US #142. Russell's next solo project, ***Americana***, will make US #115 in September the following year.

1979

Aug Russell moves closer to his country-blues roots on a double album, ***Willie And Leon***, recorded with Willie Nelson for his label, Columbia. It reaches US #25. ***The Live Album***, recorded by Russell with bluegrass band the New Grass Revival, will peak at US #187, his last chart album, in April 1981.

1984

Mar Russell releases his only other album of the decade, ***Hank Wilson Volume II*** (before involving himself for the remainder of the '80s in his own video production company).
June [19] Russell guests on NBC-TV's "Late Night With David Letterman".

1991

Apr Re-emerging into the music arena, Russell performs at the 22nd annual "New Orleans Jazz & Heritage Festival", at the Fair Grounds Race Track, New Orleans, LA. (During a year in which Russell is preparing a comeback album in collaboration with Bruce Hornsby for Virgin Records, he also sings and co-writes (with David Keith) the theme to NBC-TV's "Flesh And Blood".)

1992

July [11] Russell appears at the "American Music Festival" with the Neville Brothers, Warren Zevon, BoDeans, Randy Newman, and NRBQ at Winter Park Ski Resort, CO, a bill which grosses $175,944.
[16] He performs to a sellout crowd at the Roxy Theatre, Los Angeles, promoting his first album in eight years, the Hornsby co-produced, ***Anything Can Happen***, which includes backing vocals from his 12-year old daughter, Tina, and a guitar solo from his 14-year old son, Teddy Jack. In the UK, Castle Communications brings his career highlights to compact disc with the release of ***The Collection***. Russell will undertake two further US tours into mid-decade, in February 1993 and the same month in 1995, before EMI (US) issues the comprehensive retrospective, the three-CD ***Gimme Shelter*** boxed set in June 1996.

THE RUTLES

Ron Nasty (rhythm guitar, vocals); **Dirk McQuickly** (bass, vocals); **Stig O'Hara** (lead guitar, vocals); **Barry Wom** (drums, vocals)

1959

Jan [21] Nasty and McQuickly meet at 43, Egg Lane, Liverpool, Lancs., when McQuickly knocks Nasty to the floor. Soon joining with O'Hara, a guitarist of "no-fixed hairstyle", they will gig for 18 months as a trio before discovering Wom (b. Barrington Womble) hiding in their van. Arthur Scouse becomes their manager the following year, and sends them to Hamburg, West Germany, to play various clubs on the infamous Reeperbahn. On this trip a fifth member, Leppo, joins the group, mainly standing at the back as he cannot play guitar. He is lost in transit when the group returns to Liverpool. The group, however, will claim his influence as being immeasurable.

1961

Oct While the group has returned to the Liverpool club circuit, Leggy Mountbatten, a one-legged retail chemist from Bolton, Lancs., accidentally falls down the steps to the local Cavern venue and falls in love with the fit of the boys' trousers. He smartens up their image and does the rounds of London record companies.

1962

The group signs to Parlourphone after a recommendation from music publisher Dick Jaws, who signs their publishing rights for the rest of their natural lives.

1963

Nov Following the release of their debut album (which was recorded in 20 minutes) and with Rutlemania breaking out in the UK, Nasty causes a controversy at the "Royal Variety Show" when he bows to the Royal Box, and dedicates the next number to a very special lady in the audience, "Barry's mum".
Dec The nation takes the Rutles to its heart, with the Top 20 containing 19 of their records, including *Rut Me Do*, *Twist And Rut* and *Please Rut Me*.

1964

Feb The Rutles arrive to conquer the US with 10,000 fans awaiting their arrival at Kennedy Airport, though their plane lands at La Guardia. 73 million people see the group perform live on CBS-TV's "The Ed Sullivan Show", while New York DJ, Bill Murray The K, stakes a claim as the fifth Rutle.
Mar Nasty has his first book of comic prose, **Out Of Me Head**, published to worldwide acclaim.
July [10] Their debut feature film, "A Hard Day's Rut", directed by Richard Leicestershire, premieres in London.
Nov Mountbatten's autobiography, **A Cellarful Of Goys**, is published.

1965

July Their second feature film, "Ouch!", opens.
Aug [14] The group plays at Ché Stadium (named after Cuban guerilla leader, Ché Guevara) in New York, NY, arriving at the gig a day early to enable them to leave before the audience arrives.

1966

Aug Nasty is widely quoted in an interview that the Rutles are bigger than God. The story makes the front page all over the US and fans turn against the group. At a hurriedly arranged press conference, Nasty claims he has been misquoted, and actually said that the Rutles are bigger than Rod - the singer, Rod Stewart, who will not be famous for another five years.

1967

June The group claims it is influenced by the effects of tea, to which it was introduced two years earlier by Bob Dylan. McQuickly makes public his tea addiction and admits to enjoying biscuits too. Nasty is arrested for possession of tea by Detective Inspector Brian Plant, causing a national outcry. In London, **The Times** prints an editorial calling for the legalization of tea.
[1] Their meisterwerk, ***Sgt. Rutter's Only Darts Club Band***, is released, and re-shapes the world's attitude to pop music.
Aug O'Hara falls under the spell of Surrey mystic, Arthur Sultan. He convinces the rest of the group to join him at Sultan's retreat in Bognor, Sussex. While there, they hear the shock news that Mountbatten has resigned as their manager and accepted a teaching post in Australia.
Dec [26] The group faces its first failure when its TV film about four Oxford history professors on a tour of English tea shops, "The Tragical History Tour", is panned by the critics, despite the soundtrack's classic *W.C. Fields Forever* and *I Am The Waitress*.

1968

Apr Nasty and McQuickly launch the Rutle Corps at a press conference in New York. Its aim is to promote new artists. Early signings include Les Garçons de la Plage and Arthur Hodgeson & the Kneecaps. The company fails, its only success being the animated feature film, "Yellow Submarine Sandwich".
Dec Wom completes a year in bed as a tax dodge.

1970

May The group falls into disarray. The Rutle Corps crumbles. Nasty calls in the world's most feared promoter, Ron Decline, to settle their financial affairs. Their last album, ***Let It Rot***, is released with an accompanying film, which documents the group's sad break-up.
Dec The final split occurs. McQuickly sues Nasty and O'Hara, Wom sues McQuickly, Nasty sues O'Hara and Wom, and O'Hara accidentally sues himself. McQuickly joins Punk Floyd and releases *White Dopes On Punk*. Wom releases the solo album, ***When You Find The Girl Of Your Dreams In The Arms Of Some Scotsman From Hull***. After this, the group members drift into obscurity.

1978

Mar [22] Interest is re-awakened in the group through the NBC-TV documentary, "All You Need Is Cash", assembled by Eric Idle, former Monty Python and UK comedy series, "Rutland Weekend Television" actor, and ex-Bonzo Dog Doo-Dah Band member, Neil Innes. Despite claims made in the film by blues singers, Blind Lemon Pye and Rambling Orange Peel, that the Rutles stole their music, ***The Rutles***, a 20-track hits anthology, reaches UK #12 and US #63, with the extracted oldie, *I Must Be In Love*, making UK #39.

1991

Jan ***Rutles Highway Revisited (A Tribute to The Rutles)***, with covers of the Rutles' greatest music by Syd Straw, Marc Ribot, Das Damen, Shonen Knife, Pussywillows and others, is released. ***The Rutles : All You Need Is Cash***, already issued as a home video in 1990, will be brought to compact disc by Rhino Records in February 1996. Rumors of an anthologizing and anecdotal career documentary for television and home video release and an accompanying series of double-CD releases comprising out-takes, previously unissued material and past glories, remain entirely unconfirmed.

BOBBY RYDELL

1957

Having attended the same boys club as Frankie Avalon and Fabian, Rydell (b. Robert Ridarelli, Apr. 26, 1942, Philadelphia, PA), who entered Paul Whiteman's amateur talent TV show at the age of nine (and clipped the performer's name to Rydell) and became a regular singing and playing drums for three years, joins local Philadelphia rock band, Rocco & His Saints, as its drummer, whose line-up includes Avalon on trumpet. Leaving the Saints the following year to pursue a solo career as a vocalist, Rydell is rejected by Capitol, Decca and RCA Records, and now releases his first two singles (including his debut, *Fatty Fatty*) on manager Frankie Day's Veko label. Neither charts and Rydell signs to the Cameo label.

1959

June His sixth single (and fourth for Cameo), *Kissin' Time*, reaches US #11, and is the start of a successful four year period (Rydell will have 19 US Top 30 entries).
Sept [4-7] He performs at Dick Clark's four-day Michigan State Fair, which also features teen idols Frankie Avalon and Freddy Cannon.
Dec *We Got Love/I Dig Girls* hit US #6 and #46 respectively.

1960

Feb *Wild One*, written by Bernie Lowe, Kal Mann and Dave Appell, hits US #2.
Mar [26] Wild One also hits UK #2, behind Johnny Preston's *Running Bear*, where it is his first success on EMI's Columbia label. The B-side, *Little Bitty Girl*, reaches US #19.
May *Swinging School*, taken from the movie "Because They're Young", hits US #5, while the B-side, *Ding-A-Ling*, reaches US #18.
July His version of the Italian standard, *Volare*, hits US #4.
[2] *Swinging School* makes UK #44.
Sept [24] *Volare* reaches UK #22.
Dec *Sway* makes US #14, its flipside, *Groovy Tonight*, reaching US #70. Rydell appears with a host of stars in the "Christmas Rock'n'Roll Show" at the Paramount Theater, Brooklyn, New York, NY.

1961

Jan *Good Time Baby/Cherie* reach US #11 and #54 respectively.
[24] Rydell represents the US at the first "French International Rock'n'Roll Festival" in Paris, France.
[28] *Sway* reaches UK #12.

Feb ***Bobby's Biggest Hits*** reaches US #12.
Apr [1] *Good Time Baby* makes UK #42.
May *That Old Black Magic*, his cover of Glenn Miller's hit, makes US #21.
July *The Fish* reaches US #25.
[29] Dick Clark's "Caravan Of Stars" opens at Steel Pier, Atlantic City, NJ. During its six-week run ending in Detroit, MI, in September, Rydell plays selected dates.
Oct Live album, ***Rydell At The Copa***, makes US #56.
Dec *I Wanna Thank You* reaches US #21, while the B-side, *The Door To Paradise*, peaks at US #85 and *Jingle Bell Rock*, a seasonal duet with Chubby Checker, makes US #21. Following its success, they release ***Bobby Rydell/Chubby Checker***, which hits US #7.

1962

Feb *I've Got Bonnie* makes US #18, while its flipside, *Lose Her*, peaks at US #69.
June *I'll Never Dance Again* reaches US #14.
Sept ***All The Hits*** collection peaks at US #88.
Oct *The Cha-Cha-Cha*, co-penned by Kal Mann and Dave Appell, hits US #10.
Dec ***Biggest Hits Volume 2*** makes US #61.

1963

Feb *Butterfly Baby* reaches US #23.
May *Wildwood Days* climbs to US #17. Rydell stars in the films "Bye Bye Birdie" and "That Lady From Peking".
July [6] *Forget Him*, written and produced by Tony Hatch, reaches UK #13.
Sept *Let's Make Tonight* stops at US #98.
Nov *Forget Him* is Rydell's last major hit, at US #4, taken from ***Forget Him***.
[10] Rydell begins a British tour with Helen Shapiro at the Embassy Cinema, Peterborough, Cambs., set to end on December 15th at the ABC Cinema, Hull, Humberside.

1964

Jan ***The Top Hits Of 1963*** reaches US #67.
Mar *Make Me Forget* makes US #43, while *Forget Him* peaks at US #98.
May His cover of Peter & Gordon's *A World Without Love* stops at US #80.
Sept Rydell is one of many acts on the bill which re-opens New York's Paramount Theater, Brooklyn.
Dec Newly signed to Capitol Records, his label debut, *I Just Can't Say Goodbye*, spends a week at US #94.

1965

Feb *Diana* peaks at US #98, his chart swan song. (Hereafter, Rydell, whose success as a teen-idol is now eclipsed by the British beat invasion, will continue to record, with little commercial reward, for the RCA, Reprise, Pickwick and Perception labels. In 1978 Rydell has the honor of having the high school in the film, "Grease", named after him. He will enjoy many successful years on the US oldies circuit with his contemporary teen idols (notably Avalon and Fabian as part of the 1985 "Golden Boys of Bandstand" package tour), and will perform into the '90s on similar nostalgia caravans, also keeping his modest acting career alive.

MITCH RYDER & THE DETROIT WHEELS

Mitch Ryder (vocals); **Jim McCarty** (guitar); **Joe Kubert** (guitar); **Jim McCallister** (bass); **John Badanjek** (drums)

1963

Having left earlier R&B vocal groups Tempest and more recently the Peps, Ryder (b. William Levise Jr., Feb. 26, 1945, Detroit, MI) forms Billy Lee & the Rivieras, with Badanjek, McCarty, Kubert, and Earl Elliott on bass, in Detroit. They headline regularly at the Village club and record *Fool For You* for the local gospel-oriented Carrie Records. With Ryder building a strong reputation as a white soul singer, the group becomes the house band at Detroit's Walled Lake Casino the following year, attracting audiences of 3,000, and records a version of *Do You Want To Dance* for another local label, Hyland Records. Following a recommendation by local DJ Dave Prince, producer Bob Crewe signs the Rivieras to his New Voice label in January 1965, taking them to New York, NY for six months to rehearse and adapt their live repertoire for recording. The name Mitch Ryder is picked out of a phone book and the group becomes the Detroit Wheels in order to sound more "contemporary", with their debut single *I Need Help* released in July the same year.

1966

Jan Blue-eyed soul medley, *Jenny Take A Ride*, combining two rock oldies, *See See Rider* and Little Richard's *Jenny Jenny*, hits US #10.
Mar [5] *Jenny Take A Ride* reaches UK #27, while ***Take A Ride*** makes US #78. Kubeck and Elliot are drafted into the US Army, replaced by Mark Manko and Jim McCallister.
Apr Their revival of the Righteous Brothers' *Little Latin Lupe Lu* reaches US #17.
June *Break Out* peaks at US #62. (It will become a cult favorite on Northern UK dancefloors in the mid-'70s, but will never chart in Britain.)
July *Takin' All I Can Get* stops at US #100.
Sept ***Breakout...!!!*** reaches US #23. (During the month Ryder is sidelined by a bout of mono-nucleosis, brought about through overwork.)
Nov *Devil With A Blue Dress On/Good Golly Miss Molly*, another medley taken from ***Breakout...!!!***, is the band's biggest hit at US #4, and becomes a million seller. Crewe decides that Ryder's future is as a solo artist, and he splits singer and band after the sessions which produce the next album and two hit singles.

1967

Mar *Sock It To Me - Baby!* hits US #6.
[28] Ryder participates in Murray The K's Easter "Music In The 5th Dimension" show, at the Manhattan RKO Theater, New York.
May ***Sock It To Me!*** makes US #34, while a further medley single, *Too Many Fish In The Sea/Three Little Fishes*, reaches US #24. Crewe puts Ryder on the road as a solo act, resplendent in extravagant costumes, with a 40-piece orchestra, grooming him for the Las Vegas circuit. (The Detroit Wheels, without Ryder, will release three further singles before disbanding.)
July Ryder's first solo single, *Joy*, a more subdued production than the exuberant group efforts, peaks at US #41.
Oct His revival of *What Now My Love* reaches US #30.
Nov Another cover, *You Are My Sunshine*, peaks at US #88, taken from the non-charting ***What Now My Love***.
Dec ***All Mitch Ryder Hits!***, rounding up both group and solo singles, reaches US #37.

1968

Feb Ryder returns to the medley formula with two 1959 revivals for the US #87-peaking *(You've Got) Personality/Chantilly Lace*, his last Crewe-produced solo, following which he signs to Dot Records. The critically praised ***The Detroit-Memphis Experiment***, produced by Steve Cropper of Booker T. & the MG's, will be released the following year, featuring the extracted, *Sugar Bee*.

1972

Feb Reunited with Detroit Wheels drummer Badanjek in 1970, Ryder has formed the seven-man hard-rock band Detroit, signing to Dot associate label, Paramount Records. ***Detroit***, the band's only album release, now peaks at US #176.

1978

With a new eight-piece backing band, Ryder releases the critically hailed ***How I Spent My Vacation*** on the US independent label, Seeds & Stems, and German reissue specialists, Line Records. (Staying with Seeds & Stems in the US, and having become a cult favorite in West Germany via Line, the two labels will issue the live EP, *Rock'n'Roll Live*, in 1979, ***Naked But Not Dead*** and the *We're Gonna Win* EP in 1980, and the double-album set, ***Live Talkies***, which includes a bonus maxi-single, the following year.)

1983

Following the release of ***Got Change For A Million*** in 1981, and Ryder's September 1982 solo album, ***Smart Ass***, released on Line and in the UK by Safari Records, and after more than 15 chart-less years, Ryder returns to the US survey at #120 with ***Never Kick A Sleeping Dog***, produced by John Cougar Mellencamp for Riva Records. The extracted *When You Were Mine*, written by Prince, peaks at US #87.

1985

Aug [21] Ryder guests on NBC-TV's "Late Night With David Letterman". ***Detroit*** will be reissued on CD in 1988, including previously unreleased material, to be followed by ***Red Blood And White Mink***, his first new recording in five years, released in 1989.

1990

Nov Detroit US District Judge Horace Gilmore rules in favor of Molson Breweries, for allegedly using a Ryder sound-alike on *Devil With A Blue Dress On* beer commercials. During the year, Ryder's ***The Beautiful Toulang Sunset*** will be released. (Cubert will die the following year from liver cancer, while Badanjek now fronts his own band, the Notorious Johnnies.)

1994

Mar Still touring annually, and following the release of the 1991 CD compilation ***The Best Of Mitch Ryder & the Detroit Wheels*** and his 1992 album, ***La Gash***, Ryder's latest album, ***Rite Of Passage*** featuring the controversial track *Mercy*, inspired by Jack Kevorkian's crusade to legalize assisted suicide, is issued.

S

SADE

Sade Adu (vocals); **Stewart Matthewman** (sax); **Paul Denman** (bass); **Andrew Hale** (keyboards)

1980

The daughter of a Nigerian economics professor father, Sade Adu (b. Helen Folasade Adu, Jan. 16, 1959, Ibadan, Nigeria), brought with her family by her English mother, who is a nurse, to Clacton, Essex, in 1963, where she has been raised, and working part-time at London rock venue, the Rainbow, and now attending St. Martin's School of Art, joins her first group, Arriva, having written songs for some years (her first is *Kisses From The Karma Sutra*). One of the group's most popular live numbers will be *Smooth Operator*, penned by Adu and guitarist Ray St. John. Going on to join the eight-piece North London funk band Pride the following year, she links with manager Lee Barrett and future Sade band members Denman, Hale and Matthewman.

1983

With little record company interest, she quits Pride and forms her own band, Sade, inviting drummer Paul Cook to join the other three members. Barrett invests £8,000 in the project and secures enthusiasm from several labels, particularly Virgin, helped by gigs at Ronnie Scott's club, Soho, London, a venue well suited to the band's smokey, jazz-tinged soul material.

1984

Jan She signs to CBS/Epic Records as a solo artist (and to its Portrait imprint in the US) for a £60,000 advance and 14½% royalty from album sales. The Sade band members in turn sign to her.
Feb Sade's debut single, *Your Love Is King*, is released and hits UK #6, spurred by the group's BBC1-TV "Top Of The Pops" appearance.
Mar The band begins recording its debut album with producer Robin Millar, as Adu moves into a converted fire station in North London with current beau, journalist Robert Elms.
May Follow-up, *When Am I Gonna Make A Living*, makes UK #36.
June Sade appears at the "Prince's Trust" concert at the Royal Albert Hall.
July The debut album, ***Diamond Life***, hits UK #2 during a 98-week chart spell. One of the most successful female artist debuts of all-time, the band-penned, cool, sultry set, will eventually sell over six million copies worldwide and establish Adu as one of the most distinctive and stylish talents of the decade.
Aug Starting with selected UK dates, the band begins a hectic promotional tour of Europe, taking in Switzerland (including an appearance at the 18th annual "Montreux Jazz Festival"), West Germany and Italy. During the month Sade also donates money to striking UK coal miners' families.
Sept As *Smooth Operator* reaches UK #19 and becomes a substantial European hit, the band performs five shows in Tokyo, Japan. During her stay, Sade experiences an earthquake in bed. The earth moves, but she is unhurt.
Nov She sings and chats on BBC1-TV's "Wogan". She also moves apartments to Camden, London.
Dec She returns to Nigeria for Christmas to see her 82-year-old grandmother.

1985

Feb [23] ***Diamond Life*** enters the US chart, set to hit #5.
[11] ***Diamond Life*** wins Best British Album, at the fourth annual BRIT Awards, held at London's Grosvenor House Hotel.
Apr The band turns down an offer to perform at the annual "Montreux Pop Festival" to concentrate instead on recording its follow-up album.
May *Smooth Operator* finally hits US #5 after months of multi-format airplay.
July [13] Sade performs at the "Live Aid" benefit spectacular at Wembley Stadium, Wembley, Middx., as *Your Love Is King* peaks at US #54.
Sept "Diamond Life" video-clips package is released in the US.
Nov Sade begins a UK tour, followed by selected gigs at small US venues, as a taster from the new album, *Sweetest Taboo*, makes UK #31.
[16] The sophomore set, ***Promise***, again featuring group originals and produced by Millar, tops the UK chart for the first of two weeks, and will collect a platinum UK sales award.
Dec Sade performs at London's Royal Albert Hall.

1986

Jan The band begins a lengthy world tour to support the album (including major US dates in May).
Feb *Is It A Crime* makes UK #49.
[15] ***Promise*** begins a fortnight atop the US chart (and will also spend 11 weeks at #1 on the US R&B survey).
[25] Sade wins the Best New Artist category, at the 28th annual Grammy Awards in Los Angeles, CA.
Mar [1] *The Sweetest Taboo* hits US #5.
[12] The RIAA certifies two million sales of ***Promise***.
Apr She joins a select number of music performers who have featured on the front cover of US magazine, **Time**. As elsewhere, it is assumed that Sade is not a band, but a solo performer.
May [17] *Never As Good As The First Time* reaches US #20.
June [28] Sade takes part in a 250,000-attended anti-apartheid concert on Clapham Common in London, featuring Elvis Costello, Peter Gabriel, Boy George, Sting, Billy Bragg, Hugh Masekela, and others.
July [29] "Diamond Life" video is certified gold by the RIAA.

1987

Apr She appears in the premiering cult film, "Absolute Beginners", as torch singer Athene Duncannon, and contributes *Killer Blow* to the soundtrack. (By year's end, she will relocate to Spain and begin work with the band on its third album.)

1988

Apr Sade re-emerges with *Love Is Stronger Than Pride*, making UK #44.
May [3] ***Stronger Than Pride***, self-produced, written and arranged at Compass Point Studios, Bahamas, and at France's Miraval and Marcadet facilities, hits UK #3, in its week of entry.
June The extracted *Paradise* reaches UK #29.
July Sade begins a 40-date US tour, joined by vocalist Leroy Osbourne. *Paradise* reaches US #16, as ***Stronger Than Pride***, hits US #7.,
[9] *Paradise* tops the US R&B chart.
Nov [21-22] Sade plays soldout dates at Wembley Arena, Wembley, as part of the European leg of a world tour.

1989

Feb [11] Now permanently based in Spain, Sade Adu marries Spanish music video producer, Carlos Scola, in Vinuelas Castle, outside Madrid.

1992

Oct [10] Following a four-year gap between projects, during which time, Adu has divorced Scola and returned to London to build her own recording studio, and recently performed a few select gigs in Paris, France, *No Ordinary Love* debuts at its UK #26 peak.
Nov [7] Continuing the group's tasteful jazz-inflected smooth groove formula, ***Love Deluxe*** bows at its UK #10 pinnacle.
[21] Sade appears on NBC-TV's "Saturday Night Live", as ***Love Deluxe*** debut at its US #3 peak.
Dec Sade is named Best Artist at the first Black Music Awards, held at London's Hippodrome.
[5] *Feel No Pain* peaks at UK #56.

1993

Jan [23] Also currently featured in the Robert Redford/Demi Moore film, "Indecent Proposal", *No Ordinary Love* reaches US #28, and will become a mainstay on US AC and light jazz radio.
Feb [23-24] Sade embarks on a 24-date, 17-city North American tour at the Paramount Theatre in Seattle, WA, set to end on April 2nd in Fort Lauderdale, FL.
Mar [22] The group plays at The Paramount, New York, NY, with a bare-feet, elegant Adu performing 18 songs and three encores, the band augmented by horn player Rick Braun.
Apr [15] A 35-date European tour begins in Copenhagen, Denmark, set to close on June 3rd in London.
May [8] *Kiss Of Life* debuts at its UK #44 peak and makes US #78.
June [19] Reissued *No Ordinary Love*, tying in with the UK release of "Indecent Proposal", now reaches UK #14.
July [9] Sade performs on NBC-TV's "The Tonight Show".
[31] *Cherish The Day* debuts at its UK #53 peak.

1994

Mar [1] Sade wins the Best R&B Performance By A Duo Or Group With Vocal category for *No Ordinary Love* at the 36th annual Grammy Awards, held at New York's Radio City Music Hall.
Oct [23] *No Ordinary Love* is named one of the Most Performed Songs fo the Year at the annual BMI Awards ceremony, held at London's Dorchester Hotel.
Nov [9] The RIAA certifies four million sales of ***Love Deluxe*** and three million of ***Stronger Than Pride***.
[12] Compilation set ***The Best Of Sade*** hits UK #6 in its week of entry.
[26] ***The Best Of Sade*** debuts at its US #9 peak.

1995

Feb [2] The RIAA confirms sales of four million of ***Diamond Life***.
June [5] Former drummer Paul Cook issues a writ against Sony Music and Sade, seeking a share in the royalties of 11 songs written when he was in the band.
Aug [22] The RIAA certifies sales of two million of ***The Best Of Sade***.

SALT-N-PEPA

Salt (rap vocal); **Pepa** (rap vocal); **Spinderella** (rap vocal)

1985

Oct With their sights set on becoming nurses, the Brooklyn, NY-raised Salt (b. Cheryl James, Mar. 28, 1969, Bushwick, Brooklyn) and Pepa (b. Sandra Denton, Nov. 9, 1969, Kingston, Jamaica), former telephone sales girls working in Queens, NY, have been invited by colleague, and sometime R&B producer, Hurby Azor, to rap on *The Show Stoppa* (an answer record to Doug E. Fresh's current US hip-hop smash, *The Show*), a class project he is producing at New York, NY's Center for Media Arts (which will earn him an A grade). Released under the name Super Nature on the Pop Art label it reaches US R&B #46. Inspired by the experience, and taking their name from a line in *The Show Stopper*, the duo, still under Azor's direction, forms Salt-n-Pepa, signing to the innovative rap label Next Plateau the following year.

1987

Mar Backed by the disc-spinning female DJ, Dee Dee "Spinderella La Toya" (b. Deidre Roper, Aug. 3, 1971, New York), Salt-n-Pepa release their debut single, *My Mike Sounds Nice*, which makes an immediate impression on the New York rap scene, and hits the US R&B survey as will follow-ups *Tramp* (July) and *Chick On The Side*.
Aug [1] Their maiden album, and breakthrough set, ***Hot, Cool & Vicious***, produced by Azor, enters the US chart, where it will remain for over one year, eventually peaking at #26.

1988

Jan The extracted hip-hop/pop crossover *Push It*, remixed by DJ Cameron Paul, reaches US #19, confirming Salt-n-Pepa as the leading female act of the genre (and will be certified platinum by the RIAA on October 13th the following year).
Mar [23] ***Hot, Cool & Vicious*** is certified platinum by the RIAA.
Apr *Push It*, paired in the UK with *I Am Down*, makes UK #41.
July Reissued by the Champion label, *Push It*, now twinned with *Tramp*, hits UK #2.
Aug Their sophomore effort, ***A Salt With A Deadly Pepa***, enters the US album survey, set to make #38, and includes the rap hits *Shake Your Thang* (featuring E.U.), *Get Up Everybody (Get Up)* and the duo's hip-hop cover of the Isley Brothers' *Twist And Shout*.
[13] ***A Salt With A Deadly Pepa*** reaches UK #19.
Sept *Shake Your Thang (It's Your Thing)* reaches UK #22.
Nov *Twist And Shout* hits UK #4.
Dec [1] ***A Salt With A Deadly Pepa*** is certified gold by the RIAA.

1990

May [5] Variously produced by Salt, Azor and Steevee-O, ***Blacks' Magic*** reaches US #38, and will make UK #70 a week later.
[19] The extracted *Expression* peaks at US #26 (and UK #40), also notching up an eight-week tenure atop the US Rap chart.
[25] The RIAA confirms gold sales of ***Blacks' Magic*** and platinum sales of *Expressions*.

1991

May [11] Dance-diva Pebbles' *Backyard*, featuring Salt-n-Pepa, peaks at US #73.
June *Do You Want Me*, with guest rapper Alpha Omega, hits UK #5 and US #21.
[21] *Do You Want Me* is certified gold by the RIAA.
July [6] In the absence of a new album, London Records (to whom the trio is signed in Britain) issues the remix set, ***A Blitz Of Salt-n-Pepa Hits***, which makes UK #70.
Aug [3-4] The trio performs at two sellout shows at the "KMEL Summer Jam '91" with Tara Kemp, Jasmine Guy, Heavy D, Monie Love and others, at the Shoreline Amphitheatre, Mountain View, CA. (While Pepa has had her first child the previous year, Salt gives birth to a baby girl, as *Let's Talk About Sex*, featuring Psychotropic, hits UK #2.)
Oct [19] A second London compilation, ***The Greatest Hits***, hits UK #6, in its week of entry.
Nov [23] *Let's Talk About Sex* reaches US #13.
Dec [10] *Let's Talk About Sex* is certified gold by the RIAA.
[14] *You Showed Me* reaches UK #15.

1992

Mar [28] *Expression* re-charts at UK #23.
Apr [14] ***Blacks' Magic*** is ratified platinum by the RIAA.
[25] ***Rapped In Remixes*** bows in at its UK #37 peak.
Oct [3] *Start Me Up* debuts at its UK #39 peak.

1993

Jan [17] Salt-n-Pepa perform at the "Youth Ball" in Washington, DC, on the US presidential inauguration Day.
Feb A woman named Sandy Denton, posing as a fake Pepa, is at large in Virginia Beach, VA, trying to secure a record deal.
Mar [31] The trio attends an AIDS awareness seminar in Boston, MA.
May [22] They participate in LIFEbeat's Counteraid benefit, to raise funds for AIDS patients.
Oct [9] *Shoop* debuts at its UK #29 peak.
[19] The trio guests on syndicated TV's "The Arsenio Hall Show".
Nov [22] *Shoop* is certified gold by the RIAA.
Dec [4] *Shoop* hits US #4.

1994

Feb [5] Salt-n-Pepa guests on NBC-TV's "Saturday Night Live".
[7] They present the Favorite Adult Contemporary Artist award at the 21st annual American Music Awards, held at Los Angeles' Shrine Auditorium.
[26] *Whatta Man*, featuring En Vogue, hits US #3.
Mar [5] Having split from Azor, the self-directed ***Very Necessary*** hits US #4.
Apr [2] *Whatta Man* hits UK #7.
[13] *Whatta Man* is certified platinum by the RIAA.
May [27-28] As the trio winds down its US tour with R. Kelly, they play two dates at New York's Radio City Music Hall.
June [4] The re-charting *Shoop* reaches UK #13.
Aug [13] Salt-n-Pepa performs at "Woodstock II" at Winston Farm, Saugerties, NY.
Sept [8] They perform at the 11th annual MTV Video Music Awards from Radio City Music Hall, also winning the Best Dance Video, Best R&B Video and Best Choreography categories for *Whatta Man*.
Nov [12] *None Of Your Business* debuts at its UK #19 peak, and coupled with *Heaven Or Hell*, reaches US #32.

1995

Jan [7] *None Of Your Business* charts for a week at UK #64.
[19] Salt-n-Pepa appear at the "Commitment To Life VIII" benefit for AIDS Project Los Angeles, honoring Elton John, Tom Hanks and Ron Meyer, at the Universal Amphitheatre, Universal City.
[26] They are named Best Rap Group in **Rolling Stone**'s 1995 Music Awards - Critics' Picks.
Feb [11] The trio guests on CBS-TV's "Late Show With David Letterman".
Mar [1] Salt-n-Pepa performs *Whatta Man* and *None Of Your Business* at the 37th annual Grammy Awards, held at the Shrine Auditorium, while *None Of Your Business* collects the Best Rap Performance By A Duo Or Group trophy.
Apr [23] ***Very Necessary*** bows at its UK #36 peak.
May [3] They take part in the seventh annual World Music Awards at the Sporting Club, Monte Carlo, Monaco, set to air on ABC-TV on the 30th.
Aug [6] The trio receives the Entertainer Of The Year award at the inaugural Soul Train Lady of Soul Awards, held at the Santa Monica Auditorium, Santa Monica, CA.
Sept [11] The RIAA certifies five million sales of ***Very Necessary***.
[30] Soundtrack album ***To Wong Foo, Thanks For Everything, Julie Newmar***, including the new Salt-n-Pepa cut *I Am The Body Beautiful*, reaches US #108.
Oct Salt-n-Pepa signs an international deal with MCA Records, while also announcing the formation of its own Jireh Records, through the label.
[5] The trio appears at New York's Madison Square Garden, with Wu-Tang Clan, Run D.M.C., Brandy, Jodeci, Mary J. Blige and others.
[25] They guest on CBS-TV's "Late Show With David Letterman".
Nov [4] *Ain't Nuthin' But A She Thing* reaches US #38.
[19] They sing *Whatta Man* at Frank Sinatra's 80th birthday celebrations at the Shrine Auditorium, with an appropriate change of lyric.
Dec [7] Having performed at the Massachusetts State House in Boston during the day, after they are named Honorary Co-chairs of the Massachusetts/National Status of Girls' Conference and honored by Governor William Weld with a citation for portraying positive images of women, Salt-n-Pepa performs at the "Super Jam '95" at the FleetCenter, to benefit Project Bread, on a bill with Coolio, Brandy, Silk, Montell Jordan, After 7, Shai, Soul For Real and Brian McKnight.

1996

Aug Having contributed their version of *Gee, Officer Krupke*, a duet with Def Jef to the Feb [24] US #65 all-star ***The Songs Of West Side Story*** musical update, the trio's sixth album, having changed from its working title ***The Clock Is Ticking*** to ***Flavor In Your Ear***, is released by MCA and features Sheryl Crow on *I Can't Breathe*.

SAM & DAVE

Sam Moore (vocals); **Dave Prater** (vocals)

1961

Moore (b. Samuel David Moore, Oct. 12, 1935, Miami, FL), son of a Baptist deacon and ex-member of gospel group the Melonaires, now a secular soloist, is joined spontaneously on stage at the King of Hearts club in Miami by Prater (b. May 9, 1937, Ocilla, GA), a jobbing vocalist working at the club as a chef. Audience reaction is favorable, prompting them to form a duo. Signed by Morris Levy of Roulette Records in New York, NY the following year, the duo records gospel-flavored R&B for four years (also on the Alston label and mostly with producer Henry Glover), with little commercial success. (An eponymous album will be compiled from these Roulette singles after Sam & Dave have become successful.)

1965

Mar Having left Roulette to sign with Atlantic Records, Jerry Wexler arranges recording sessions in Memphis, TN, at Stax Records, resulting in a deal with Stax owner Jim Stewart whereby their records are to be released on his label. The duo is perfectly teamed with songwriters Isaac Hayes and David Porter, with backing provided by the Memphis Horns.

1966

Jan *You Don't Know Like I Know* peaks at US #90 and R&B #7.
June Horns-led *Hold On, I'm Comin'* reaches US #21, also topping the US R&B chart for a week and subsequently becoming a soul standard.
[24] The duo begins a 46-date US tour, with Otis Redding, Patti LaBelle & the Bluebelles, Percy Sledge, Garnett Mimms and others, in Greensboro, NC.
Sept ***Hold On, I'm Comin'*** reaches US #45.
Oct *Said I Wasn't Gonna Tell Nobody* peaks at US #64.
Dec *You Got Me Hummin'* makes US #77.

1967

Feb ***Double Dynamite*** peaks at US #118.
Mar [17] Now signed to Otis Redding's manager Phil Walden, Sam & Dave embark on the 13-date Stax/Volt UK "Soul Concert Sensation '67" tour, with Otis Redding, Eddie Floyd, Arthur Conley, Carla Thomas, the Markeys and Booker T. & the MG's, at the Finsbury Park Astoria, London, set to end on April 8th at London's Hammersmith Odeon. The success of these dates puts ***Hold On, I'm Comin'*** on the UK chart at #37. *When Something Is Wrong With My Baby*, an intense soul ballad, in contrast to previous uptempo funk hits, makes US #42.
May [6] Their revival of Sam Cooke's *Soothe Me* is the duo's first UK chart single at #35.
Double Dynamite reaches UK #28.
July *Soothe Me* peaks at US #56.
Oct [14] Becoming another staple of the genre, *Soul Man* begins a seven-week run atop the US R&B chart, and also hits US #2.
Nov [22] *Soul Man* is certified gold by the RIAA.
[25] *Soul Man* reaches UK #24.

1968

Jan ***Soul Men*** makes US #62.
Feb [29] *Soul Man* wins the Best R&B Group Performance Vocal Or Instrumental (Two Or More) category, at the tenth annual Grammy Awards.
Mar *I Thank You* hits US #9 and is another international million seller.
[30] *I Thank You* reaches UK #34, while ***Soul Men*** reaches UK #32.
May Stax splits from Atlantic after its distribution

deal expires, and the duo's recordings revert to the Atlantic label, with its recording sessions relocating to Miami. Prater shoots his wife during a domestic argument but, because of the circumstances of the incident, he avoids prosecution or imprisonment.
June *You Don't Know What You Mean To Me* makes US #48, taken from the non-charting ***I Thank You***. The duo takes part in the "Soul Together" concert at New York's Madison Square Garden, with Aretha Franklin, Sonny & Cher, the Rascals, Joe Tex and King Curtis.
Aug *Can't You Find Another Way (Of Doing It)* peaks at US #54.
Nov *Everybody Got To Believe In Somebody* stops at US #73.

1969

Jan *Soul Sister, Brown Sugar* makes US #41.
Mar *Born Again* peaks at US #92 and is Sam & Dave's last US chart single (though Atlantic will release a further eight, after the duo itself splits, up to June 1971). Compilation, ***The Best Of Sam And Dave***, winds up their US chart career, reaching #87.
[8] *Soul Sister, Brown Sugar* is their last, but biggest, UK hit, at #15.
June Sam & Dave appear at the "Soul Bowl '69 Festival" at the Astrodome, Houston, TX, alongside Aretha Franklin, the Staple Singers, Ray Charles and other major R&B names.

1970

Jan [22] The duo opens in the "Soul Together" UK package tour with Joe Tex, Arthur Conley and Clarence Carter at London's Royal Albert Hall, London, set to end on February 11th at the Finsbury Park Astoria. Now on notoriously bad terms with each other, Sam & Dave will split up for solo careers. Moore will stay with Atlantic and release three solo singles - none of them hits, while Prater will sign to Alston. With little commercial solo success, the duo will reunite, signing to United Artists in 1972 and releasing ***Back Atcha'*** in 1975 before the duo drifts apart once again.

1979

Feb With renewed interest in Sam & Dave, not least due to the Blues Brothers' revival of *Soul Man* (which reaches US #14), the duo is reactivated again.
Sept Sam & Dave tour the US, incongruously opening for the Clash. ***Sweet And Funky Gold***, consisting of re-recordings of their (and others') hits, is released on the Gusto label in the US.

1981

Having appeared as themselves in Paul Simon's semi-autobiographical movie, "One Trick Pony" the previous October, the partnership is now permanently dissolved after enduring a decade of on-off relationship. (Prater will tour with singer Sam Daniels, as Sam & Dave, the following year.)

1987

Feb Moore's re-recording of *Soul Man* with Lou Reed, released as the title theme to a teen-comedy film, reaches UK #30.
June Prater is arrested for selling crack to an undercover cop. He is sentenced to three years probation, a $2,500 fine and 150 hours of community service.

1988

Apr [9] Prater is killed when his car leaves the road and hits a tree near Syracuse, GA.
May [14] Moore appears at Atlantic Records' 40th anniversary show staged at Madison Square Garden, New York, duetting with "Blues Brother" Dan Aykroyd.

1989

Jan [21] Moore participates in a celebration for "Young Americans For President Bush" at the Presidential inauguration, at the Convention Center, Washington, DC.

1992

Jan [15] While Moore has recently become a Rhythm and Blues Foundation Pioneer Award Honoree, Sam & Dave are inducted into the Rock and Roll Hall of Fame at the seventh annual dinner, at New York's Waldorf Astoria Hotel.
Feb Moore signs a deal with AOC Music, a new label set up by Jean Karakos in Paris, France.
[26] He hosts the third annual Rhythm and Blues Foundation Pioneer Awards, at New York's Rainbow Room.
Apr [4] Bruce Springsteen's ***Human Touch***, featuring Moore among its guests, enters the UK chart at #1, and will hit US #2.

1993

June [7] Moore attends the ground-breaking ceremony of the Rock and Roll Hall of Fame in Cleveland, OH.
July [20] Twin-CD retrospective set, ***Sweat'n'Soul : The Anthology***, including three previously unreleased cuts, is issued by Rhino Records in the US.

1994

Mar [23] Moore performs at "Rhythm Country And Blues - The Concert", benefitting the Country Music Foundation and the Rhythm and Blues Foundation, at the Universal Amphitheatre, Universal City, CA.
[26] ***Rhythm Country And Blues***, including the pairing of Moore and Conway Twitty on *Rainy Night In Georgia*, recorded just prior to Twitty's death, reaches US #18.
Oct [8] Moore performs *Are You Lonesome Tonight* at "Elvis Aaron Presley : The Tribute", an all-star event held at the Pyramid Arena, Memphis, TN.

1995

July [17] *Hold On, I'm Coming* is finally certified gold by the RIAA.
Sept [2] Moore sings *Something's Wrong With My Baby*, *Hold On I'm Coming* and *In The Midnight Hour*, with John Fogerty harmonizing, at the Concert for the Rock and Roll Hall of Fame at Cleveland Stadium, Cleveland, OH.

SANTANA

Carlos Santana (guitar, vocals);
Neal Schon (guitar); **Gregg Rolie** (keyboards);
David Brown (bass); **Michael Shrieve** (drums)

1968

May [17-19] Santana (b. July 20, 1947, Autlán de Navarro, Mexico), having grown up in Tijuana, Mexico, and then San Francisco, CA (where he first discovers R&B and the blues), met keyboard player Rolie (b. June 17, 1947, Seattle, WA) after leaving high school, and with him formed the Santana Blues Band in October 1966, which included Brown (b. Feb. 15, 1947, New York, NY) (bass), Tom Frazer (rhythm guitar) and Rod Harper (drums). Playing extensively at San Francisco club and park gigs over the next two years, the band now makes its debut at the city's Avalon Ballroom, on a bill with Junior Wells and the Sons of Champlin. Shortening its name to Santana, and undergoing personnel shifts, the group's sound begins to incorporate the Latin music of Santana's own background into its blues-based approach. Percussionists Mike Carabello (b. Nov. 18, 1947, San Francisco) and José Chepito Areas (b. July 25, 1946, Léon, Nicaragua) are added to the line-up. Frazer and Harper leave, and Shrieve (b. July 6, 1949, San Francisco) joins on drums.
Sept [2] Santana appears during the three-day "Sky River Rock Festival and Lighter-Than-Air Fair", in Sultan, WA, with the Grateful Dead, Muddy Waters, Country Joe & the Fish, the Youngbloods and others.
Dec [19-22] They play at the Fillmore West, San Francisco.

1969

Feb Carlos Santana contributes to ***The Live Adventures Of Al Kooper And Mike Bloomfield***.
Mar [13] Santana makes the first of several appearances at the Fillmore West during the year, with Creedence Clearwater Revival and Jethro Tull.
Aug [1] The band takes part in the "Atlantic City Pop Festival" in Atlantic City, NJ, alongside Jefferson Airplane, B.B. King, Creedence Clearwater Revival and others.
[15] Now signed to CBS/Columbia, the band appears at the "Woodstock Music & Art Fair", in Bethel, NY, a performance which attracts national notice. (*Soul Sacrifice*, from the festival, is included in the ***Woodstock*** triple album and movie.)
[30] The group plays at its third major festival of the month at the "Texas International Pop Festival", at Dallas International Motor Speedway, Lewisville, TX, followed by an immediate appearance at the "New Orleans Pop Festival", New Orleans, LA.
Nov Their debut album, ***Santana***, co-produced by Brent Dangerfield and Santana, and boosted by their Woodstock appearance and positive critical response, hits US #4, during a two-year spell on the US chart.
Dec *Jingo*, a percussive highlight from the album, peaks at US #56.
[6] Santana play on the bill of the Rolling Stones' concert at Altamont Speedway, Livermore, CA, where a murder is committed during the Stones' act.

1970

Mar *Evil Ways*, also from the debut album, hits US #9.
Apr [18] Santana plays at London's Royal Albert Hall, with It's A Beautiful Day and Taj Mahal.
May ***Santana*** reaches UK #26.
June [27] The group performs at the "Bath Festival of Blues & Progressive Music", Shepton Mallet, Somerset.
Oct [24] Their second album, ***Abraxas***, co-helmed by Santana with Fred Catero, tops the US chart for the first of six weeks.
Dec ***Abraxas*** hits UK #7 (and will spend one year on the UK survey).

1971

Jan Their cover of Fleetwood Mac's *Black Magic Woman*, from ***Abraxas***, hits US #4, and is the band's biggest hit single. Neal Schon (b. Feb. 27, 1954, San Mateo, CA) joins on guitar and vocals.
Apr *Oye Como Va*, also from ***Abraxas***, and a Latin-rock adaptation of a salsa number by Tito Puente, reaches US #13.
Oct Brown and Carabello leave the band, joining forces with ex-Santana members Areas, Thomas Escovedo and Reyes. Santana, Rolie, Schon and Shrieve remain.
Nov [13] The self-produced ***Santana III*** tops the US chart for the first of five weeks and hits UK #6.
Dec The band breaks up as a live unit, although it will re-group for recording, as founder member Rolie and Schon leave. (After an 18-month rest, Rolie will join Schon in Journey.) Meanwhile, *Everybody's Everything*, taken from ***Santana III***, reaches US #12.

1972

Mar *No One To Depend On*, also from the third album, makes US #36.
Sept Carlos Santana has cut a live album at Hawaii's Diamond Head volcano, with drummer Buddy Miles, from which the double A-side, *Evil Ways/Them Changes*, makes US #84. Meanwhile ***Carlos Santana And Buddy Miles, Live!*** hits US #8 and reaches UK #29.
Dec ***Caravanserai***, moving the band's music into looser, jazzier forms, hits US #8 and UK #6.

1973

Jan [18] The group plays with the Rolling Stones at the latter's Great Western Forum, Inglewood, CA benefit concert for victims of the Nicaraguan earthquake, to a sellout crowd of 19,000.
Apr Carlos Santana marries Urmila, a Sri Chinmoy

adherent.

Aug ***Love Devotion Surrender***, a duetted instrumental fusion album between Carlos Santana and guitarist Mahavishnu John McLaughlin, reaches US #14 and hits UK #7. (Like his wife and McLaughlin, Santana has now become a devotee of Sri Chinmoy, and taken the additional religious name Devadip - which means "The light of the lamp of the Supreme".)

Sept [17] ***Love Devotion Surrender*** is certified gold by the RIAA.

Nov [29] The still-climbing ***Welcome*** is certified gold by the RIAA.

Dec ***Welcome*** reaches US #25 and hits UK #8. The band's personnel is changing extensively with every new album, but its music continues in to take an increasingly jazz-based direction.

1974

Sept Compilation ***Santana's Greatest Hits***, reaches US #17 and UK #14.

Oct [12] *Samba Pa Ti*, a Carlos Santana-penned instrumental from ***Abraxas***, reaches UK #27.

Nov A Carlos Santana collaboration with Alice Coltrane, another disciple of Sri Chinmoy, for the instrumental album ***Illuminations***, makes UK #40.

Dec ***Borboletta***, with guest appearances from Stanley Clarke and Brazilian musicians Airto Moriera and Flora Purim, reaches US #20 and UK #18.

1975

Mar [23] Santana performs at a benefit at San Francisco's Kezar Stadium, to raise funds to make up for a shortfall in the school system budget.

June Bill Graham, the first agent to book the band in the '60s, becomes the group's manager.

Dec Triple live-album, ***Lotus***, a deluxe package recorded and originally only released in Japan, appears belatedly in the US and UK.

1976

Jan [25] Carlos Santana guests with Bob Dylan's "Rolling Thunder Revue" at the "Night Of The Hurricane II" concert at the Astrodome, Houston, TX, a benefit show for imprisoned boxer Ruben "Hurricane" Carter. He duels on guitar with fellow guest Stephen Stills on *Black Queen*.

May ***Amigos*** hits US #10 and reaches UK #21. Taken from the album, *Let It Shine* makes US #77.

June [11] ***Amigos*** is confirmed gold by the RIAA.

Aug [7] The group plays at Wembley Arena, Wembley, Middx., on a bill with the Grateful Dead and the New Riders Of The Purple Sage.

Dec They perform at the Royal Albert Hall, London, the concert broadcast simultaneously by BBC-TV and stereo radio.

1977

Feb ***Festival*** reaches both US and UK #27.

Apr The band plays with Joan Baez and others, at a free concert for the inmates of Soledad prison in California, organized by the Bread & Roses charitable foundation.

[26] ***Festival*** is certified gold by the RIAA.

Sept [10] They co-headline the Crystal Palace Garden Party, Crystal Palace, London, with Elvis Costello.

Nov The group's revival of the Zombies' 1964 hit, *She's Not There*, becomes their biggest UK hit at #11.

Dec *She's Not There* reaches US #27, while the live double album, ***Moonflower***, hits US #10 and UK #7.

1978

Mar The band plays at California Jam II in Ontario, CA, to 250,000 people, alongside Ted Nugent, Aerosmith, Heart, and others.

Oct After a summer US tour, Santana begins a European trek.

[27] The still-rising ***Inner Secrets*** is certified gold by the RIAA.

Dec ***Inner Secrets*** reaches US #27 and UK #17. Taken from it, an update of Buddy Holly's *Well All Right* peaks at US #69 and UK #53.

1979

Feb Also from ***Inner Secrets***, their revival of Classics IV's *Stormy* makes US #32.

Apr Carlos Santana's instrumental solo duet, ***Oneness/Silver Dreams - Golden Reality***, comprising half studio cuts and half live recordings from Osaka, Japan, peaks at UK #55.

May *One Chain (Don't Make No Prison)*, extracted from ***Inner Secrets*** (and a 1974 US #41 for the Four Tops), peaks at US #59.

Nov ***Marathon*** reaches US #25 and UK #28.

1980

Feb *You Know That I Love You*, taken from ***Marathon***, makes US #35.

Mar *All I Ever Wanted*, also from the album, peaks at US #57.

Sept Another Carlos Santana instrumental solo double set, ***The Swing Of Delight***, with guest appearances by jazz-men Herbie Hancock, Wayne Shorter and Ron Carter, makes US #74.

1981

Apr ***Zebop!*** reaches UK #33.

June ***Zebop!*** hits US #9, earning gold certification by the RIAA on the 22nd.

July *Winning*, a Russ Ballard song from ***Zebop!***, reaches US #17.

Aug Also from the album, *The Sensitive Kind* peaks at US #56.

Oct Santana performs at London's Royal Albert Hall.

1982

Sept [3-5] Following a summer tour with Journey, Sammy Hagar and Point Blank, the band plays at the three-day "US Festival", financed by Apple Computers' founder, Steven Wozniak, in San Bernardino, CA, to 400,000 people, along with Jackson Browne, the Cars, Fleetwood Mac, the Grateful Dead, Eddie Money, Police, Talking Heads and many others.

Oct *Hold On*, featuring lead vocalist Alex Ligertwood, reaches US #15, taken from ***Shango***, which reaches US #22 and UK #35.

Dec *Nowhere To Run*, also from ***Shango***, peaks at US #66.

1983

Apr ***Havana Moon***, a Carlos Santana solo album with guest support from Willie Nelson, Booker T. Jones and the Fabulous Thunderbirds, makes UK #84.

1984

June [11] Santana plays at "Open Air '84" in Offenbach, West Germany with Bob Dylan and Joan Baez, during a European tour with Dylan.

1985

Apr ***Beyond Appearances*** makes US #50 and UK #58, while the extracted *Say It Again* climbs to US #46.

July [13] Santana appears at the "Live Aid" benefit spectacular in Philadelphia, PA.

1986

July [20] Santana celebrates its 20th anniversary with a concert in San Francisco, with all previous group members coming on stage to play as a 17-piece ensemble.

Nov The UK-only, TV-promoted ***Viva! Santana - The Very Best*** makes #50. Carlos Santana produces the music for the Ritchie Valens biopic, "La Bamba".

[21] The RIAA certifies platinum sales of ***Caravanserai*** and ***Carlos Santana And Buddy Miles, Live!***, four million sales of ***Abraxas*** and two million sales of ***Santana***.

1987

Apr ***Freedom*** peaks at US #95, supported by a lengthy "Freedom World Tour", with founder member Rolie rejoining the current line-up of Carlos Santana (guitar), Chester Thompson (keyboards), Alfonso Johnson (bass), Tom Coster (synthesizers), Graham Lear (drums), Armando Peraza, Raul Rekow and Orestes Vilato (all percussion) and Buddy Miles (vocals).

July [4] The group participates in a peace concert in Moscow, USSR, with the Doobie Brothers, Bonnie Raitt and James Taylor.

Nov [7] Carlos Santana's instrumental solo set, ***Blues For Salvador***, makes US #195.

1988

July Santana undertakes a 1988 summer tour with jazz saxophonist Wayne Shorter as a guest player.

Nov Twin-CD anthology ***Viva Santana***, including live material recorded between 1969 and 1987, makes US #142.

1989

Feb [22] Carlos Santana wins the Best Rock Instrumental Performance, Orchestra, Group Or Soloist category, for ***Blues For Salvador***, at the 31st annual Grammy Awards. (He is also featured on John Lee Hooker's newly-released ***The Healer***.)

Aug Carlos Santana launches his own Guts & Grace records.

[9] The 1974 album ***Borboletta*** is certified gold by the RIAA.

Nov [4] Carlos Santana joins Living Colour on stage during its set in Oakland, CA.

1990

May [30] Santana performs the first of three nights at London's Hammersmith Odeon.

July [13-15] The group plays sellout dates at the Greek Theatre, Los Angeles, before crowds totalling 18,544.

[14] ***Spirits Dancing In The Flesh***, recorded with the current line-up of Thompson (keyboards), Peraza (percussion), Ligertwood (guitar, vocals), Benny Rietveld (bass) and Walfredo Reyes (drums), peaks at UK #68.

Aug [1] ***Spirits Dancing In The Flesh*** makes US #85, including the extracted cover of Curtis Mayfield's *Gypsy Woman*.

[21] The 1977 album ***Moonflower*** is certified platinum by the RIAA.

Oct [20] Santana joins Steve Miller, Z.Z. Top and Colin James in a sellout concert to benefit the Texas Special Olympics at the Cotton Bowl, Fair Park, Dallas, TX.

Nov [5-6] During a current US tour, Santana plays to sellout crowds totalling 8,133 at the Beacon Theatre, New York.

1991

Jan [20] Santana appears at the "Rock In Rio II" festival in Brazil.

Apr [29] ***Santana's Greatest Hits*** is finally certified platinum by the RIAA.

June [15-16] They perform before 31,577 fans at the Sports Palace, Mexico City, Mexico.

[27] Carlos Santana is arrested at Houston Intercontinental Airport for allegedly having five grams of cannabis stashed in a film canister.

July [10] The group performs at Wembley Arena, Wembley.

Aug [8] Carlos pleads no contest and receives a six-month deferred sentence, community service and an insistence that he performs an anti-drug fundraising concert, following the drug-possession incident on June 27th.

Oct [28] Carlos Santana performs at former manager Bill Graham's funeral at Temple Emanuel in San Francisco.

Nov Carlos Santana, Gregg Rolie, Michael Shrieve and other songwriting ex-members sell the Santana music publishing catalog, Pertra Music, to BMG Music Publishing, via the group's Santana Blues Band Partnership.

[3] The group performs at the Bill Graham "Laughter Love & Music" memorial concert at San Francisco's Golden Gate Park Polo Field, before an estimated 350,000 crowd.

1992

Jan Carlos Santana signs a new recording deal with Polydor Records, which will include the license of his own Guts & Grace label.

[15] He performs *I Love You Much Too Much* as a musical tribute to Bill Graham, who had taught him the song, at the seventh annual Rock and Roll Hall of Fame induction dinner, at New York's Waldorf Astoria Hotel.

Mar [7] Carlos Santana is named Outstanding Guitarist at the 15th Bay Area Music Awards, held at the San Francisco Civic Auditorium.

[21] He plays the first of two homecoming concerts at the Bullring By The Sea in Tijuana, Mexico, where he began his career, becoming the first musical act to perform at the venue since Chicago, in 1967. His opening act is a mariachi band featuring his father, José.

June [5] Carlos is bestowed with the Legend Award at the 22nd annual Nosotros Golden Eagle Awards (dedicated to raising the image of Latinos in the media), at the Beverly Hilton, Los Angeles.

[6] With a spoken-word introduction by the late Bill Graham, ***Milagro*** peaks at US #102.

[17-18] Santana performs at London's Hammersmith Odeon during a UK visit.

Aug [13-15] The group plays three sellout dates at the Greek Theatre, Los Angeles, CA, grossing $502,312.

Oct [10] Santana participates in the "All Our Colors - The Good Road Concert" benefit for the Traditional Circle of Elders & Youth cultural organization, a Native American group, at the Shoreline Amphitheatre, Mountain View, CA.

Nov [5-6] Santana wraps up its North American tour with two shows at New York's Paramount.

1993

Mar [6] Carlos Santana is named Musician Of The Year at the 16th annual Bay Area Music Awards, at the Bill Graham Civic Auditorium, San Francisco.

[20] Santana plays a sellout show at the Waikiki Shell, Honolulu, in the midst of a short Hawaiian tour.

[23] The Paul Rodgers-assembled ***Tribute To Muddy Waters***, featuring fret-work from Carlos Santana, is released by Victory Music.

Sept [18] Santana, now touring again on a bill with Dylan, plays a sellout show at the candle-lit Chastain Park Amphitheatre, Atlanta, GA.

Nov [20] ***Sacred Fire***, a live album recorded in South America, charts for a week at US #181.

1994

Mar [25] Santana takes part in KLOS radio station's 25th anniversary concert at the Great Western Forum, Inglewood, CA, before a sellout crowd of 17,064.

July [9] They play a date at the Polaris Amphitheatre, Columbus, OH, during the current US tour.

Aug [14] 25 years after appearing at the original event, Santana performs at "Woodstock II" at Winston Farm, Saugerties, NY.

Oct [15] Newly signed to Polygram's Island imprint, ***Santana Brothers*** charts for a week at US #191. (Carlos has recently issued ***Live Forever*** on his own Guts And Grace label, a various artists selection compiled by him featuring original recordings by the likes of Jimi Hendrix, Marvin Gaye, John Coltrane, Bob Marley and Stevie Ray Vaughan, all taken from his own expansive record collection.)

[28] The 1979 album ***Marathon*** is certified gold by the RIAA.

Nov [15] Santana appears on CBS-TV's "Late Show With David Letterman".

[17] The group takes part in the "92.3 FM K-Rock Presents Hungerthon '94" benefit before a 2,937 capacity house at New York's Beacon Theatre.

1995

June [8] Santana, now comprising Santana, Thompson, Rekow, Myron Dove (bass), Karl Perazzo (timbales), Billy Johnson (drums) and vocalist Tony Lindsay, replacing Ligertwood, who has left for a solo career, plays at the Festival Hall, Tampa Bay Performing Arts Center in Tampa, FL, during its current month-long US concert swing.

July [31] The group embarks on a major US summer tour, sharing a bill with Jeff Beck, playing to 14,064 capacity crowd at the Filene Center, Wolf Trap Farm Park, Vienna, VA.

Aug [8] ***Dance Of The Rainbow Serpent***, a 34-track, three-CD boxed set retrospective starting with *Soul Sacrifice* recorded at the original Woodstock and ending with *Chill Out*, the title cut of John Lee Hooker's 1995 album featuring Carlos Santana on guitar, complete with a 64-page booklet, is released.

Oct [8] The Santana/Jeff Beck tour comes to end at the Paramount, New York, before a capacity 4,877 crowd.

[24] RCA releases the Jimi Hendrix tribute album, ***In From The Storm***, including a contribution by Carlos Santana.

Nov DCI Music releases "Carlos Santana : Influences", a three-part video documentary hosted by Carlos and focusing on three artists who influenced him - Bola Sete, Gabor Szabo and Wes Montgomery.

Dec [30] Santana plays its last gig of the year, on a bill with War, at the Arrowhead Pond, Anaheim, CA.

1996

Jan [5] As Carlos celebrates 30 years since the formation of the Santana Blues Band, Santana plays The Aladdin in Las Vegas, NV.

Feb [25] The NARAS Foundation holds its first salute to an individual act as it honors Carlos Santana at the Universal Amphitheatre, Universal City, CA. The band performs with him all evening in pairings with the likes of Herbie Hancock, Hooker, Metallica's Kirk Hammett and Buddy Guy, an event which Santana calls "a 4½ hour spiritual orgasm that felt like 4½ minutes".

Apr [25] Santana begins the seven-date New Zealand and Australian leg of its world tour at the Queen's Wharf in Wellington, North Island, NZ.

June [24] Following further dates in Indonesia, Malaya, Singapore, Thailand, China, Taiwan, Korea and Hawaii, Santana now embarks on the European leg of its current tour at the Forest National, Brussels, Belgium, set to end on July 25th at the Stadtpark, Hamburg, Germany.

Dec Santana becomes the fifth recipient of the prestigious Century Award for lifetime achievement at the fifth annual **Billboard** Music Awards, broadcast live on Fox-TV.

LEO SAYER

1972

Sayer (b. Gerard Hugh Sayer, May 21, 1948, Shoreham-by-Sea, Sussex), having studied at Worthing Art College, Sussex, and worked in London as a magazine illustrator, playing harmonica in folk clubs by night, returned to Sussex in 1968 after a nervous breakdown, and worked in a factory while starting to write songs. Having been a member of the Terrorplane Blues Band, he has formed his own group, Jester, and now Patches. David Courtney, an ex-drummer for Adam Faith, places an ad in the **Brighton Evening Argus** auditioning singers, bands and comedians at the Pavilion Theatre, Brighton, Sussex. 50 groups turn up, with Patches the last to audition. Courtney signs the band and becomes Sayer's co-writer. Patches record a one-off single, *Living In America*, though it is never released. Courtney and Sayer take their songs and the group to Faith, who signs them to a management contract and, when Patches splits, takes over Sayer as a solo artist. Gerard becomes Leo from a nickname given him by Faith's wife, Jackie: with his wide mane of thick curly hair, she calls him the "little lion" (he is only 5' 4" tall).

1973

Mar Faith and Courtney record Sayer at a studio owned by the Who's Roger Daltrey. Daltrey's own debut album, ***Daltrey***, is almost entirely written by Sayer (lyrics) and Courtney (music). (It provides Daltrey with his biggest solo hit, at UK #5, with *Giving It All Away*.)

Aug With Faith having secured Sayer a solo deal with Chrysalis Records, his debut single, the ballad *Why Is Everybody Going Home*, is released. Sayer marries a librarian, Janice.

1974

Jan [19] His second single, *The Show Must Go On*, hits UK #2 (Three Dog Night's cover will hit US #4 in May), and is extensively promoted by Sayer on TV and live appearances (with Roxy Music), during which he wears a pierrot clown costume and make-up designed by Kursty Clino.

Feb His debut album, ***Silver Bird***, hits UK #2. He makes a promotional US tour, after which the pierrot costume is abandoned because of negative US reaction.

June [29] The extracted *One Man Band* hits UK #6.

Oct *Long Tall Glasses* (originally written as *I Can Dance*, but amended in the studio after he has forgotten some of the original lyrics) hits UK #4, taken from his second album, ***Just A Boy*** (the title comes from a line in *Giving It All Away*), which hits UK #4.

1975

Feb He begins a two-month US tour, where he is signed to Warner Bros., which releases ***Just A Boy***.

May Sayer's US chart debut is ***Just A Boy***, which reaches US #16, and *Long Tall Glasses (I Can Dance)*, which hits US #9.

June *One Man Band* peaks at US #96.

Sept [20] *Moonlighting* hits UK #2, behind Rod Stewart's *Sailing*.

Oct ***Another Year***, featuring Sayer's by-now regular band of Chris Stainton (keyboards) and Grahame Jarvis (drums), hits UK #8. Courtney leaves as Sayer's producer and co-writer to work solo, replaced by ex-Supertramp bassist, Frank Farrell.

[1] A 12-date UK tour opens at the Winter Gardens, Bournemouth, Dorset, set to end on the 17th at the City Hall, Sheffield, S. Yorks.

Nov ***Another Year*** peaks at US #125. Sayer has to cancel a follow-up US tour, when he is hospitalized for a wisdom-tooth operation.

1976

Apr [8] Sayer embarks on a nine-date UK tour at the Gaumont Cinema, Ipswich, Suffolk, set to close at the Opera House, Blackpool, Lancs.

May [1] Another nine-date UK tour begins at the Apollo Theatre, Glasgow, Strathclyde, Scotland, set to end on the 10th at the ABC Cinema, Peterborough, Cambs.

Nov *You Make Me Feel Like Dancing*, an R&B-styled pop song written by Sayer with Vini Poncia, and recorded in Los Angeles, CA, with new producer Richard Perry, hits UK #2 spurred by a UK tour and subsequent dates in Australia.

Dec [28] The still-rising *You Make Me Feel Like Dancing* is certified gold by the RIAA.

1977

Jan [15] *You Make Me Feel Like Dancing* tops the US chart for a week.

Feb [19] *When I Need You*, a ballad written by Albert Hammond and Carole Bayer Sager, tops the UK chart for the first of three weeks, becoming Chrysalis Records' first ever #1.

[19] Its parent album, ***Endless Flight***, hits UK #4, during a 66-week chart stay.

Apr The all-star ***All This And World War II*** album/movie project, which features cover versions of Beatles songs including Sayer's treatment of *I Am The Walrus*, is released.

May [10] Still-climbing *When I Need You* is certified gold by the RIAA.

[14] *When I Need You* heads the US chart for a week, while the perky *How Much Love* hits UK #10. Sayer plays a 56-city US tour, which grosses $2 million.

June ***Endless Flight*** hits US #10.

Aug *How Much Love* reaches US #17.

Sept [19] ***Endless Flight*** is confirmed platinum by the RIAA.
Oct *Thunder In My Heart* makes UK #22, while parent album, ***Thunder In My Heart***, hits UK #8.
Nov *Thunder In My Heart* makes US #38, as ***Thunder In My Heart*** makes US #37.

1978

Jan *Easy To Love* makes US #36.
Feb [23] *You Make Me Feel Like Dancing* wins the Best Rhythm & Blues Song category, at the 20th annual Grammy Awards.
July Sayer hosts NBC-TV's "Midnight Special".
Sept ***Leo Sayer*** reaches UK #15 and peaks at US #101. He also begins a weekly TV series, "Leo", on BBC1-TV.
Oct *I Can't Stop Lovin' You (Though I Try)* hits UK #6, as Sayer appears at the London Palladium.
Nov His revival of Buddy Holly's *Raining In My Heart* makes US #47.
Dec *Raining In My Heart* reaches UK #21.
[14] Sayer guests on the "Perry Como Christmas Show", on US TV.

1979

Apr [28] Compilation, ***The Very Best Of Leo Sayer***, begins a three-week run atop the UK chart.
Oct ***Here*** makes UK #44.

1980

Aug His update of Bobby Vee's 1961 UK #4, *More Than I Can Say*, produced by Alan Tarney, hits UK #2.
Sept ***Living In A Fantasy***, helmed and mostly co-written by Tarney, reaches UK #15.
Dec [6] *More Than I Can Say* hits US #2.
[24] *More Than I Can Say* is certified gold by the RIAA. *Living In A Fantasy* will reach US #23 the following March when its parent album, ***Living In A Fantasy***, also makes US #36.

1982

Apr *Have You Ever Been In Love*, co-written by Andy Hill and Pete Sinfield, hits UK #10.
July The Bee Gees-penned *Heart (Stop Beating In Time)* reaches UK #22.
Aug ***World Radio***, produced by Arif Mardin and recorded in New York, NY and Los Angeles, reaches UK #30.

1983

Jan Sayer begins another BBC1-TV series, "Leo Sayer".
Apr Ballad *Orchard Road* reaches UK #16.
Oct *Till You Come Back To Me* peaks at UK #51.
Nov ***Have You Ever Been In Love***, promoted by a TV campaign, reaches UK #15.

1984

May Sayer embarks on a 50-date two-month UK tour. His revival of the Righteous Brothers' *Unchained Melody*, included on the soundtrack to the film "Car Trouble", will peak at UK #54 in February 1986.

1988

July Currently without a recording contract, Sayer embarks on a self-financed UK tour.
Nov His former manager Faith pays Sayer a reported £650,000. Details are not revealed, but the payment appears to be in settlement of owed earnings and record royalties.

1993

Mar [13] Having returned with his first album in seven years, the Tarney-produced ***Cool Touch*** released by EMI in July 1990, and won back worldwide rights to his masters from Chrysalis after a five-year dispute in December 1992 (a resolution which also requires the label to spend at least £125,000 to promote a greatest hits collection), Sayer's most enduring hit, the reissued *When I Need You* has peaked at UK #65 on Feb [20], and remains a popular AC radio oldie in the US. The Chrysalis-issued definitive hits CD collection, ***All The Best***, now reaches UK #26.

BOZ SCAGGS

1959

Scaggs (b. William Royce Scaggs, June 8, 1944, OH), having grown up in Texas, meets Steve Miller at St. Mark's Preparatory School in Dallas, TX, and joins his band, the Marksmen, on vocals and tambourine, while Miller also teaches him guitar. Going on to attend Wisconsin University, Madison, WI, together in 1961, they play in R&B/Motown covers group the Ardells, which becomes the Fabulous Night Train. Scaggs then returns to Texas in 1963 and forms R&B outfit the Wigs with John "Toad" Andrew on guitar, Bob Arthur on bass and George Rains on drums. The following year, and after the band has unsuccessfully tried to make an impression in Britain, they split, leaving Scaggs to relocate to Europe.

1965

He arrives in Stockholm, Sweden, where he records his debut album, ***Boz***, for Polydor, released only in Europe. Scaggs continues his world sojourn which reaches India before returning to the US.

1967

Sept [1] On his arrival back in San Francisco, CA, he rejoins the Steve Miller Band, replacing singer/guitarist James Cooke. The following year Scaggs is featured on the Steve Miller Band's two US chart albums, ***Children Of The Future*** (#134) and ***Sailor*** (#24), both recorded in the UK with producer Glyn Johns. After the sessions, he leaves the band due to musical differences with Miller.

1969

Feb With the help of **Rolling Stone** editor Jann Wenner, Scaggs gains a solo deal with Atlantic Records, and records at Muscle Shoals Studios in Muscle Shoals, AL, with top session players, including Duane Allman.
Aug ***Boz Scaggs***, produced by Wenner, is released to critical acclaim, but few sales, and he is subsequently dropped by the label.

1971

May After several months in the Southern states the previous year, Scaggs has moved back to the West Coast and formed the Boz Scaggs Band, which has been signed to CBS/Columbia at the end of the year. His label debut, the Glyn Johns-produced ***Moments***, reaches US #124, while the extracted *We Were Always Sweethearts* makes US #61.
July *Near You*, also from the album, peaks at US #96.
Dec ***Boz Scaggs And Band***, recorded in London, peaks at US #198.

1972

Oct *Dinah Flo* peaks at US #86, while its parent album, ***My Time***, co-produced with Roy Halee, reaches US #138 as Scaggs tours the US with guest band members Steve Miller and drummer George Rains.
Dec He forms a new band, with Les Dudek (guitar), Tom Rutley (bass), Jimmy Young (keyboards), Rick Schlosser (drums) and Jack Schroer (sax).

1974

Apr [27] Scaggs plays at the "Cherry Blossom Music Festival" in Richmond, VA, alongside the Steve Miller Band.
May The critically-revered ***Slow Dancer***, produced and partly co-written by Johnny Bristol, reaches US #81.
July Capitalizing on Scaggs' recent success, Atlantic reissues his only album for the label, ***Boz Scaggs***, which peaks at US #171.

1976

Apr [16] When he attempts to see Bobby Bland backstage after a show at Antone's club in Austin, TX, Scaggs is thrown out by bouncers.
May *It's Over*, from his forthcoming album, makes US #38.
Sept With back-up session players include future members of Toto, the soul-pop fused ***Silk Degrees***, produced by Joe Wissert and arranged by David Paich, becomes Scaggs' most commercially-successful album, hitting US #2 during a 115-week chart run.
Oct *Lowdown*, from the album, hits US #3.
[29] *Lowdown* is certified gold by the RIAA.
Nov *Lowdown* is Scaggs' UK chart debut, at #28, while a further extract, *What Can I Say?* , reaches US #42.

1977

Feb [19] *Lowdown* wins the Best Rhythm & Blues Song category, at the 19th annual Grammy Awards.
Mar *What Can I Say?* hits UK #10.
May *Lido Shuffle*, the fourth single from the album, reaches US #11 and UK #13.
July ***Silk Degrees*** reaches UK #20, more than a year after its release.
[13] A Scaggs concert at New York, NY's Avery Fisher Hall is ended midway through by a city-wide power cut.
Aug Rita Coolidge's cover of *We're All Alone*, a Scaggs ballad from ***Silk Degrees***, hits US #7 and UK #6, her biggest solo single.
Nov *Hard Times* peaks at US #58.
Dec ***Down Two Then Left***, its title originally announced as ***Still Falling For You***, reaches US #11and UK #55.
[9] ***Down Two Then Left*** becomes his second RIAA certified platinum album. The excerpted *Hollywood* will make US #49 and UK #33 (his last UK chart single), in January.

1979

June [3] Scaggs and Rickie Lee Jones join Bruce Springsteen and the E. Street Band for a jam session on stage at the Whisky A-Go-Go in Los Angeles, CA, at the wedding reception of Springsteen's lighting man, Mark Brickman.

1980

May *Breakdown Dead Ahead* reaches US #15.
June ***Middle Man*** hits US #8 and makes UK #52.
Aug *Jo Jo*, taken from ***Middle Man***, reaches US #17.
Oct *Look What You've Done To Me* makes US #14.

1981

Feb Compilation album, ***Hits***, dominated by tracks from ***Silk Degrees***, reaches US #24. Scaggs' last US chart single for seven years is *Miss Sun*, a duet with Lisa Dal Bello, which reaches US #14.
[6] ***Middle Man*** is certified platinum by the RIAA.

1982

May [28] Scaggs plays a benefit concert for the Vietnam Veterans Project at Moscone Center, San Francisco, with Jefferson Starship and the Grateful Dead. (The following year, Scaggs will retire from the music scene, and open his own Southern-style restaurant in San Francisco.)

1988

Apr Recently persuaded by CBS/Columbia to return to the studio to record a new album, Scaggs appears at the "Montreux Pop Festival" in Switzerland.
July His comeback effort, ***Other Roads***, is released. The set includes three songs co-written with singer/poet Jim Carroll, and features assistance from members of Toto. It climbs to US #47, while the extracted *Heart Of Mine* makes US #35. Scaggs announces plans to open Slim's, a jazz/blues club in San Francisco.
Nov [23] He makes a rare TV appearance, guesting on NBC-TV's "Late Night With David Letterman".

1989

Aug **Playboy** reports that Scaggs is set to play a detective in the film "Indigo", directed by Francis Ford Coppola's son Roman. The following year, and during another recording hiatus, Scaggs will produce San Francisco's Smoking Section's debut album for RCA

1991

Mar [1-2] Donald Fagen's second "Rock And Soul Revue II" with Scaggs, Michael McDonald, Phoebe Snow and Charles Brown, takes place at New York's Beacon Theatre.

Aug [9] The RIAA certifies gold sales of ***Slow Dancer*** and platinum sales of ***Hits***.

1992

Jan [30] Scaggs takes part in the "Friends of Smitty" benefit for musician William Smith, suffering from the effects of a stroke, at Palace Theatre, Burbank, CA.

Feb [8] ***The New York Rock And Soul Revue - Live At The Beacon***, to which Scaggs has contributed *Drowning In The Sea Of Love*, peaks at US #170.

Mar [21] He takes part in the "Memphis Horns 25th Anniversary Show" at The Pyramid, Memphis, TN, on a bill with Robert Cray, Johnny Rivers, the Doobie Brothers and Michael McDonald.

Aug [10] Scaggs sings *The Lord's Prayer* at the funeral of Toto's Jeff Porcaro.

Dec [14] Newly signed to Virgin Records, Scaggs participates in a Universal Amphitheatre, Universal City, CA benefit to establish a trust fund for Porcaro's children.

1994

Apr [7] Scaggs guests on CBS-TV's "Late Show With David Letterman".

[23] He takes part in the 25th annual "New Orleans Jazz & Heritage Festival".

May [21] Produced by Ricky Fataar, ***Some Change***, Scaggs' first album in six years, makes US #91.

Aug [6] Scaggs first album on his first US concert tour in 14 years at the House of Blues in Los Angeles, set to end on September 20th at the Majestic Theatre, Dallas, TX.

Sept [28] He performs on NBC-TV's "The Tonight Show".

Nov [14] The RIAA certifies five million sales of his career highlight, ***Silk Degrees***.

1995

July [22] He plays at the Hearst Greek Theatre, University of California-Berkeley, following an appearance at the Greek Theatre, Los Angeles the day before.

Sept [2] Scaggs and Slash perform Red House at the Concert for the Rock and Roll Hall of Fame at Cleveland Stadium, Cleveland, OH.

1996

Sept [2] Scaggs performs at the Hard Rock Café in Las Vegas, NV, during a short west coast tour of the US.

THE SCORPIONS

Klaus Meine (lead vocals); **Rudolf Schenker** (guitar); **Matthias Jabs** (guitar); **Francis Buchholz** (bass); **Herman Rarebell** (drums)

1975

Formed as a five-piece rock outfit in 1971 by Hanover, West Germany suburbanites Meine (b. May 25, 1948, Hanover) and Schenker (b. Aug. 31, 1948, Hildesheim, West Germany), with his younger brother Michael (b. Jan. 10, 1955, Savstedt, West Germany) on lead guitar and Rudy Lenners on drums, the Scorpions are signed to the German Metronome label and, deciding to record their hard-rock albums in English from the outset, have released their debut effort, ***Lonesome Crow***, in 1972 (issued in the US on the Billingsgate label, eventually selling 25,000 copies), a year in which they play 136 gigs, mostly in their home territory. Still self-managed, the band signs with RCA Records and, having released a second album, ***Fly To The Rainbow***, in 1974, following Michael Schenker's departure, to join UFO in 1973, replaced by Uli Roth on lead guitar, and also joined in 1974 by bassist Buchholz (b. Feb. 19, 1950, West Germany), the Scorpions now venture outside Germany for the first time, setting out on a club tour of Britain, followed by treks around France, Belgium and Luxembourg, to promote their third album, ***In Trance***. Meine later reflects: "We had to do everything ourselves. We booked the gigs, dealt with the record company and so on. Our deal with the label was that if we played gigs in countries outside Germany, then we'd get our records released in those countries." Using this incentive, the band builds a strong following in both Europe and Japan.

1976

Nov ***Virgin Killer***, their fourth album, goes gold in Japan in its first week of release, as the Scorpions' cancel a UK tour, unhappy with the itinerary. Following a UK trek to promote ***Taken By Force*** the following year, drummer Lenners quits and is replaced by Rarebell (b. Nov. 18, 1949, Lubeck, West Germany).

1978

During the year, they sell out a five-day tour of Japan where they remain highly successful. Recordings of two gigs at the Sun Plaza, Tokyo, are subsequently released as ***The Tokyo Tapes***. (By year's end, Roth quits to form Electric Sun.)

1979

Apr Following unsuccessful London auditions for a new lead guitarist (more than 100 try), they have chosen Hanover musician, Jabs (b. Oct. 25, 1955, Hanover). Now signed to Mercury in the US and EMI imprint Harvest Records in Britain, their label(s) debut, ***Lovedrive***, also featuring a temporarily returned Michael Schenker, reaches UK #36.

June The extracted *Is There Anybody There/Another Piece Of Meat* makes UK #39.

July Promoting the album, which is on its way to US #55, the group makes its US live debut in Cleveland, OH, at the "World Series of Rock" festival, in front of 70,000 people, before touring as the support act to Ted Nugent.

Aug Title cut, *Lovedrive*, peaks at UK #69.

1980

May ***Animal Magnetism*** is released, set to make UK #23 and US #52, yielding the UK #72 *Make It Real*, and is followed by extensive European and US live jaunts.

Sept [20] *The Zoo* peaks at UK #75.

Nov RCA-issued retrospective, ***Best Of Scorpions***, climbs to US #180.

1981

June Meine develops a throat infection, rendering him unable to perform. Following a successful operation, they complete ***Blackout***, once again based around Schenker's songwriting.

1982

Apr ***Blackout*** hits US #10, and reaches UK #11, also spawning the UK #64 and US #65 *No One Like You*. A seven-month world tour ensues, with the group performing to 1.5 million fans.

July *Can't Live Without You* reaches UK #63.

Aug A second RCA vaults collection, ***Best Of Scorpions Volume 2***, peaks at US #175.

1983

May [30] The Scorpions are co-headliners at the second "US Festival", playing before 300,000 in San Bernadino, CA.

Aug The band performs at the annual "Reading Rock Festival", Reading, Berks.

1984

Mar [8] ***Blackout*** is certified platinum by the RIAA for one million sales.

Apr The group releases its most successful album to date, ***Love At First Sting***, which makes UK #17 and hits US #6, during a 63-week chart tenure. It is followed by a world concert trek, during which they will open for Bon Jovi on a US arena tour.

May From the album, *Rock You Like A Hurricane* blows out at US #25.

July Rock ballad, *Still Loving You*, reaches US #64.

1985

Jan The band plays at the "Rock In Rio" festival at Barra da Tijua, Rio de Janeiro, Brazil.

July ***Worldwide Live***, a performance double album taped in 1984, makes US #14 and UK #18.

1986

May [28] ***Lovedrive*** is confirmed gold by the RIAA for 500,000 US sales.

Aug The Scorpions headline the "Monsters Of Rock" festival in Germany.

Sept [4] ***World Wide Live*** is certified platinum by the RIAA.

Dec [16] The accompanying "World Wide Live" video is ratified gold by the RIAA.

1988

May [14] ***Savage Amusement***, the last Scorpions album to be produced by long-time band cohort Dieter Dierks, reaches UK #18 in its week of entry and will eventually hit US #5. The group undertakes its last North American tour of the decade as part of the "Monsters Of Rock" package, followed by 50 headlining dates.

June The extracted *Rhythm Of Love* peaks at US #75 and UK #59.

[20] ***Savage Amusement*** is certified platinum by the RIAA.

Nov Invited to perform ten concerts to a 15,000 crowd per night in Leningrad, USSR, supported by Russian rockers Gorky Park, Meine says of the gigs: "We had never experienced anything like it - Russian kids, soldiers cried when we played *Holiday*. We could have easily sold out another ten nights." Returning a week later for the "Moscow Music Peace Festival", Meine is emotionally inspired to write *Wind Of Change*, his first composition for the group.

1989

Feb [18] *Passion Rules The Game* peaks at UK #74.

May [9] From their Russian experience, "To Russia With Love" video is certified gold by the RIAA.

1990

Feb [10] Mercury compilation, ***Best Of Rockers'N'Ballads***, reaches US #43.

July [21] The band participates in Roger Waters "The Wall" spectacular at the site of the Berlin Wall, Potsdamer Platz, Berlin, one hundred miles from where the band grew up.

Nov A world tour kicks off with warm-up dates in Poland and Czechoslovakia.

Dec [26-30] The group performs German dates in Frankfurt, Munich and Stuttgart.

[31] The band appears on MTV's "New Year's Eve World Party" staged at the Deutschlandhalle, in Berlin.

1991

Jan [12] They play the last of three UK gigs at the Wembley Arena, Wembley, Middx.

Feb [20] Their "Hit Between The Eyes" North American tour, with Great White and Trixter, opens at the Tingley Coliseum in Albuquerque, NM. (The group will donate $1 for each ticket sold at their North Carolina shows to the "Make A Difference Foundation".)

Mar [8-9] At sellout dates at the Irvine Meadows Amphitheatre, Laguna Hills, CA, the group is joined by guest jammers Jon Bon Jovi, Def Leppard's Phil Collen, Michael Schenker and Ratt's Steven Pearcy.

June [1] Whistle-led rock anthem, *Wind Of Change,* inspired by the dramatic social and political changes which have swept across Eastern Europe, debuts at its initial UK #53 peak, during a year-long run on the German chart.

[20] The group plays to a sellout crowd of 14,368 at the Great Western Forum, Inglewood, CA.
July [24] ***Crazy World*** is certified platinum by the RIAA.
Aug [31] Becoming a worldwide smash, *Wind Of Change* hits US #4.
Sept [4] *Wind Of Change* becomes the group's first RIAA certified gold single.
Oct [11] The group begins a four-date French tour at the Palais des Sports Bordeaux, Bordeaux.
[12] *Wind Of Change* now hits UK #2, behind Bryan Adams' *(Everything I Do) I Do It For You*. (The group records a Russian language version of *Wind Of Change*, which has rapidly become a global pop/rock standard.)
[28] ***Animal Magnetism*** is certified platinum by the RIAA.
Nov [2] Spurred by the global success of *Wind Of Change*, ***Crazy World***, produced by Keith Olsen, and featuring Jim Vallance, finally reaches UK #27 and US #21 on July [6] 1991, eventually selling over five million copies worldwide.
[30] Taken from ***Crazy World***, *Send Me An Angel* reaches UK #27.
Dec [14] Impressed by the "Cold War end" lyrical content of their worldwide hit anthem, *Wind Of Change*, besieged Soviet Union president Mikhail Gorbachev invites the band to meet him at the Kremlin, where they present him with a plaque of the song's lyrics.

1992

Jan [25] *Send Me An Angel* makes US #44.
Apr [6] EMI releases a Scorpions power-ballads collection, ***Still Loving You***.
May Bucholz quits the band to be replaced by Ralph Rieckermann (b. Aug. 8, 1958, Lubeck).
[14] The group takes part in the fourth annual World Music Awards at the Sporting Club in Monte Carlo, Monaco.
Dec [13] The Scorpions perform at an anti-hate event in Frankfurt, protesting against the current wave of right-wing violence in Germany.

1993

Jan They begin work on a new album with Bruce Fairbairn in Vancouver, Canada.
May [24] Meine receives an award from ASCAP for the performance success of *Winds Of Change*, at the society's tenth annual Pop Awards ceremony, at the Beverly Hilton Hotel, Los Angeles.
Sept [25] ***Face The Heat***, including the extracted German unification-themed *Alien Nation*, charts for a week at UK #51, as the band undertakes its "Face The Heat" world tour.
Oct [9] ***Face The Heat*** peaks at US #24 in its week of entry.
[21] ***Best Of Rockers'N'Ballads*** is certified platinum by the RIAA.

1994

Mar [22-23] The group plays two sellout shows at the Sports Palace, Mexico City, during the Mexican leg of its current North and Central American tour, set to end in July.
May [4] The Scorpions are named the World's Best-selling German Recording Artists of the Year at the sixth annual World Music Awards held at the Sporting Club, Monte Carlo, set to air on ABC-TV on the 31st.
Oct [8] They perform *(Marie's The Name) His Latest Flame* at "Elvis Aaron Presley : The Tribute", an all-star event at the Pyramid Arena, Memphis, TN, broadcast live in the US on pay-per-view TV.

1995

May ***Live Bites***, a performance album with three previously unreleased studio cuts, is released.
Aug [7] The RIAA certifies two million sales of ***Crazy World*** and three million of ***Love At First Sting***.

1996

May The Scorpions' latest album ***Pure Instinct*** is released.

SCRITTI POLITTI

Green Gartside (vocals); **David Gamson** (keyboards); **Fred Maher** (drums, backing vocals)

1977

Preferring to be called under the single name Green, Gartside (b. Green Strohmeyer-Gartside, June 22, 1956, Cardiff, South Glamorgan, Wales), an ex-schoolmate of Soft Cell's Marc Almond, has been inspired to begin a career in music after attending a Sex Pistols' concert in Leeds, W. Yorks. He now forms Scritti Politti with bassist Nial Jinks and drummer Tom Morley, all friends at Leeds Art School. With a fluid line-up (including keyboardist and manager Matthew Kay), the politically-motivated Scritti Politti moves to London the following year and begins low-key gigging at mainly punk venues, also releasing its debut single *Skank Bloc Bologna* on its own St. Pancras indie label, which in turn gains them a session on BBC Radio 1's "John Peel Show".

1979

July The band supports Joy Divison and Gang Of Four on a UK tour, but suffers a setback when Green collapses with a heart complaint.
Sept [8-9] They perform at the "Futurama Festival" at the Queen's Hall, Leeds.
Oct EP *Four 'A' Sides* is released on Scritti Politti's own St. Pancras label, complete with a photocopied sleeve, but goes unnoticed.
Nov Further EP, *John Peel Session*, drawn from the DJ's alternative music show, is released. (Green will spend the following year convalescing at home with his parents, and begins writing new songs, now heavily influenced by R&B music. Meanwhile, Jinks leaves the band.)

1981

Nov While the group's *The Sweetest Girl*, featuring Robert Wyatt on piano, has appeared earlier in the year on a free **New Musical Express** cassette, leading UK independent label Rough Trade has released the track as a single, which peaks at UK #64.

1982

May *Faithless* makes UK #56 and tops the UK Independent chart.
Aug Double A-side, *Asylums In Jerusalem/Jacques Derrida*, with guest Robert Wyatt on keyboards, is the group's first UK Top 50 entry at #43.
Sept Their debut album, the Green-penned, Rough Trade-released ***Songs To Remember***, a jazz/soul-tinged pop outing highlighted by his distinctive falsetto vocal style, produced by Adam Kidron and featuring temporary band members Joe Cang (bass), Mike MacEvoy (keyboards), Steve Sidwell (trumpet) and Jamie Talbot (saxophone), reaches UK #12, and again tops the UK Independent survey.
Nov Morley quits the group.

1984

Apr After Green has signed the group to Virgin Records the previous year, and moved to New York, NY to work on an album with new members Gamson (keyboards) and Maher (drums), and producer Arif Mardin,*Wood Beez (Pray Like Aretha Franklin)*, also featuring session talent Marcus Miller, Paul Jackson Jr., and Steve Ferrone, hits UK #10.
July The airy pop/soul tryout, *Absolute* reaches UK #17.
Nov *Hypnotise*, completing a trio of Green-written, synthesizer-dominated singles, peaks at UK #68.

1985

May *The Word Girl* hits UK #6.
June Mardin-produced ***Cupid And Psyche '85***, containing the 1984 singles, hits UK #5 and makes US #50. It is described by Green as a: "very super, hyper, syncopated, ping-ponged bif pow zip thing".
Sept *The Perfect Way* is the group's first US hit, at #11 (later covered by Miles Davis).

1986

Feb Madness' version of *The Sweetest Girl* makes UK #35.
[10] *Wood Beez (Pray Like Aretha Franklin)* peaks at US #91.
Aug Chaka Khan makes US #53 and UK #52 with the Green-penned *Love Of A Lifetime*. (Green and Gamson also write the title cut for Al Jarreau's forthcoming ***L Is For Lover***.)
Dec "Scritti Politti" video collection is released by Virgin. The band's *Best Thing Ever* will appear on Madonna's ***Who's That Girl*** film soundtrack released the following August.

1988

Mar The group takes part in the annual "Montreux Pop Festival" in Montreux, Switzerland.
May *Oh Patti (Don't Feel Sorry For Loverboy)*, with Miles Davis guesting on trumpet, reaches UK #13.
June [18] ***Provision***, recorded in New York, and written and produced by Green and Gamson, hits UK #8 in its week of entry and will make US #113. It has taken three years to complete, delayed by Green's need to always use the latest state-of-the-art studio technology.
July *First Boy In This Town (Lovesick)* stops at UK #63.
Aug *Boom! There She Was* peaks at US #53.
Oct Maher produces Information Society's US #3, *What's On Your Mind (Pure Energy)*, having also produced Marlon Jackson's debut album.
Nov *Boom! There She Was* peaks at UK #55. Green will subsequently retreat to his Welsh hideaway for two years to work on new material and experiment with the latest technology.

1991

Apr [6] A cover version of Lennon/McCartney's *She's A Woman*, with toasting assistance from ragga-reggae star Shabba Ranks, reaches UK #20.
Aug [10] *Take Me In Your Arms And Love Me*, Green's revival of Gladys Knight's hit with Sweetie Irie guesting, makes UK #47.
Sept [9] British Electric Foundation's ***Music Of Quality & Distinction Volume 2***, with Green contributing *I Don't Know Why I Love You*, is released.

SEAL

1990

May [12] Given up at birth by his wig-making mother Adebisi to a white foster family in Essex, though she subsequently reclaimed him at the age of four, Seal (b. Sealhenry Samuel, Feb. 19, 1963, Kilburn, London), one of six children from a Nigerian, Brazilian and West Indian ancestry, went to live with his father Francis Samuel, an interior decorator, when he was six after his mother was taken ill. Having been beaten by his father with whips and fists into his teenage years, Seal, who has begun singing while attending secondary school, making his first stage appearance at the age of 11 performing *I Can See Clearly Now* at a school talent show, has run away from home in 1978 at the age of 15, and linked with the short-lived outfit Stay Brave, subsequently spending much of the early '80s performing in London pubs and clubs around Soho and Camden while working at various jobs including clothes designing and electrical engineering. Contracting lupus at the age of 23 (which has left him with distinctive facial scars), and after singing on UK beer commercials, he has gone on to record demos, and signed a production deal in 1987 which came to naught. Having spent six months travelling around Asia towards the end of the decade including performances in Japan with funk combo Push, he has returned to Britain and, through rapper Chester Kamen, links with techno-pop artist Adamski, with whom he has co-written *Killer*, which he performs on and now tops the UK chart for the first of four weeks. After ten years of trying, Seal suddenly becomes a hot artist, inking a publishing deal with Trevor Horn's Beethoven Street company, and signing to the producer's ZTT label.

1991

Jan Having entered the UK chart the previous December, Seal's self-penned debut cut, *Crazy*, hits UK #2, spurred by Horn's production and an innovative special-effects promo clip.

June [1] His soul/rock-fused freshman album, ***Seal***, highlighted by his distinctive soul vocal style and produced by Horn with string arrangements by Anne Dudley, and featuring Wendy & Lisa on backing vocals, hits UK #1 in its week of entry.

Apr [7] He is named Best UK Male Artist at the UK-held DMC World DJ Awards.

[22] Seal appears on BBC1-TV's "Wogan".

May [2] He wins his first Ivor Novello award as co-author of *Killer*, which is named Best Contemporary Song, at the 36th annual lunch held at London's Grosvenor House Hotel.

[4] Follow-up, *Future Love EP*, climbs to UK #12.

July [20] Signed to Sire in the US, ***Seal*** begins a 63-week US chart run to #24, while *The Beginning* enters the UK survey, set to reach #24.

Sept [7] *Crazy* hits US #7, as ***Seal*** reaches US #24.

Oct [20] A seven-date UK tour opens at the Sunderland Empire, set to close on the 28th at London's Hammersmith Odeon. (It is followed by a European trek during which his truck blows over on a Swedish motorway. A local butcher lends Seal and the crew a van to continue on to Denmark.)

Nov [23] *Killer*, an EP featuring his solo re-cut of the Adamski smash, and Seal's cover of Jimi Hendrix's *Hey Joe*, hits UK #8, spurred by the first ever 3-D video promo clip.

[30] He performs at the "Red, Hot + Dance" AIDS benefit concert at the Brixton Academy, London.

Dec [12-13] Seal, currently featured on the movie soundtrack to "Toys", plays two further gigs at the Brixton Academy.

[28] He is featured on Amnesty International's "Big 30" fundraiser, broadcast on ITV.

1992

Feb [12] Seal collects the Best Male Artist, Best British Album (presented by Cilla Black) and Best British Video trophies at the 11th annual BRIT Awards, held at the Hammersmith Odeon, London, at which he also performs. (He will also be honored during the month as the Recording Artist Of 1991 by the Variety Club of Great Britain, at a Hilton Hotel bash in London.)

[14] He sings at a Valentine's Day AIDS benefit concert at the Hammersmith Odeon.

[25] Seal performs *Crazy* at the 34th annual Grammy Awards, at New York, NY's Radio City Music Hall, but fails to win an award for either of his nominations.

[29] His self-produced *Violet : The Acoustic EP* (including *Violet*, *Whirlpool*, *Wild* and *Show Me*) debuts at its UK #39 peak.

Apr [15] *Crazy* wins the Best Contemporary Song and International Hit Of The Year categories at the 37th annual Ivor Novello Awards, again held at the Grosvenor House Hotel.

[20] He joins Queen on *Who Wants To Live Forever* at "A Concert For Life", a Freddie Mercury tribute, at Wembley Stadium, Wembley, Middx.

1993

Apr Having begun work on his sophomore album at Chapel Studios, Los Angeles the previous June, with Nick Launay producing (an early cut appearing on the spring 1993 film soundtrack to "Indecent Proposal"), Seal resumes recordings with Trevor Horn at the SARM Studio in west London. (The sessions had been put on hold after Seal had almost been killed when his Range Rover rolled over at a hairpin bend on Mulholland Drive in Los Angeles, been stricken with pneumonia and Chronic Fatigue Syndrome and then has been at the scene of a shooting in a pool hall on Sunset Boulevard.)

Nov [27] A Jimi Hendrix tribute album, ***Stone Free***, to which Seal has contributed on Jeff Beck's version of *Manic Depression*, enters the US chart at its #28 peak.

1994

Apr [29] ***Seal*** is certified platinum by the RIAA.

May [28] *Prayer For The Dying* reaches UK #14.

June [4] Having taken two years, three months, one week and two days to complete, his sophomore album, ***Seal*** enters UK at #1 and features guest appearances by Joni Mitchell and Jeff Beck among others.

Aug [6] With its video clip filmed on New York's Lower West Side, *Kiss From A Rose* initially reaches UK #20 as *Prayer For The Dying* peaks at US #21.

Oct [12] Seal plays a sellout club date at Toad's Place, New Haven, CT, as a warm-up for his first US tour.

[26, 28-29, 31] As the support act for the Rolling Stones, Seal is seen by 199,285 people over four days of sellout shows at the Oakland-Alameda County Stadium, Oakland, CA.

Nov [5] *Newborn Friend* debuts at its UK #45 peak.

[12] Joni Mitchell's ***Turbulent Indigo***, featuring Seal on *How Do You Stop*, debuts at its US #47 peak having made UK #53 the previous week.

Dec [7-9] Seal ends his North American tour to capacity crowds at the Wiltern Theatre, Los Angeles.

1995

Mar [1] Seal performs *Feet On The Ground* at the 37th annual Grammy Awards, held at Los Angeles' Shrine Auditorium.

May [13-14] He embarks on a second North American tour at the Sunrise Musical Theatre, Sunrise, FL.

June [8] Seal guests on CBS-TV's "Late Show With David Letterman".

Aug [5] Reissued *Kiss From A Rose*, now featured in the movie "Batman Forever" and coupled with *I'm Alive*, hits UK #4.

[25] The RIAA certifies gold sales of *Kiss From A Rose* and two million sales of ***Seal***.

[26] *Kiss From A Rose* tops the US chart.

Sept [7] In between presentation duties, Seal collects the award for Best Video From A Film for "Kiss From A Rose", at the 12th annual MTV Video Music Awards, held at New York's Radio City Music Hall.

[9] ***Seal*** reaches US #15, more than 15 months after its chart debut.

Dec [9] *Don't Cry*, coupled with *Prayer For The Dying*, debuts at its UK #51 peak.

[31] Seal plays a New Year's Eve show at The Joint in the Hard Rock Hotel, Las Vegas, NV.

1996

Feb [17] *Don't Cry* debuts at its US #33 peak.

[25] The ATP Tennis tour announces it has licensed Seal's *Bring It On* as its commercial theme for the next two years.

[28] Seal takes home the Best Pop Vocal, Male, Record Of The Year and Song Of The Year categories, all for *Kiss From A Rose*, at the 38th annual Grammy Awards held at the Shrine Auditorium, at which he also performs the song and duets with Annie Lennox on *What's Going On* in tribute to Marvin Gaye.

SEALS & CROFTS

Jim Seals (vocals, guitar, saxophone, violin);
Dash Crofts (vocals, guitar, mandolin)

1966

Seals (b. Oct. 17, 1941, Sidney, TX) and Crofts (b. Darrell Crofts, Aug. 14, 1940, Cisco, TX), playing guitar and drums respectively in the backing band of rock singer/pianist Dean Beard (cutting some non-charting singles with him for the Edmoral and Atlantic labels), who was invited to join the Champs in 1958 (who had a million-selling rock instrumental with *Tequila* earlier in the year), joined the group with him, relocating from Texas to Los Angeles, CA. Leaving the fragmenting Champs in 1965, Seals has stayed in California to write songs and play sessions, while Crofts has returned to Texas. Seals now teams with guitarist Louie Shelton, bassist Joseph Bogan and, in need of a drummer, lures Crofts back to Los Angeles. This quartet becomes the Dawnbreakers, which is augmented by the three Day sisters as vocalists, one of whom, Billie Lee Day, Crofts marries.

1969

Following the example of group manager Marcia Day, the Dawnbreakers are converted to the Baha'i faith (founded by Persian prophet Baha'u'llah in the 19th Century). Seals marries Ruby Anderson, a member of the community living with the group at its manager's Los Angeles home.

1970

Mar The Dawnbeakers have split, with Shelton turning to production and Bogan to studio engineering. With their help, Seals and Crofts have remained together as a duo, and recorded ***Seals & Crofts***, now released by the Talent Associates label. It fails to chart, but their extensive live work gains a burgeoning following.

Nov ***Down Home***, their second and last on Talent Associates, makes US #122, and attracts the attention of Warner Bros. Records, which signs them.

1972

Jan Their Warner debut, ***Year Of Sunday***, produced by Shelton, and augmenting the duo's harmony-vocal blend with horn and string accompaniment, peaks at US #133.

Feb [25] Seals & Crofts embark on a four-date UK tour supporting Rick Nelson & the Stone Canyon Band at the Odeon Birmingham, set to end on the 28th at London's Royal Albert Hall.

Nov *Summer Breeze* (which will be successfully revived by the Isley Brothers in 1974) is their first Singles chart entry, hitting US #6, taken from ***Summer Breeze***, which hits US #7.

Dec [14] ***Summer Breeze*** is certified gold by the RIAA.

1973

Mar *Hummingbird*, with lyrics strongly influenced by Baha'i, reaches US #20.

June Soft-rock/pop follow-up, ***Diamond Girl***, self-penned as ever, and again produced by Shelton, hits US #4.

[19] The duo guests on ABC-TV's "Roberta Flack ... The First Time Ever".

[25] ***Diamond Girl*** is confirmed gold by the RIAA.

July The extracted title cut, *Diamond Girl* (jointly written in tribute to their wives, both new mothers) hits US #6.

Nov Proving to be an enduring radio cut, *We May Never Pass This Way (Again)* reaches US #21.

1974

Feb [8] The duo embarks on a 41-date US tour at Brigham Young University, Provo, UT, set to end on April 21st at Corpus Christi College, Corpus Christi, TX.

Mar [12] The still-climbing ***Unborn Child*** is certified gold by the RIAA.

Apr ***Unborn Child*** makes US #14, while its title track, *Unborn Child*, peaks at US #66.

June *King Of Nothing*, also from ***Unborn Child***, makes US #60. The duo tours constantly, punctuating its middle-of-the-road harmony material on stage with mandolin features by Crofts, and sax pieces and dance reels on the violin by Seals.

Sept Warner acquires the release rights to the duo's first two albums from Talent Associates, and reissues them as the double ***Seals And Crofts I And II***, which makes US #86.

1975

May ***I'll Play For You*** reaches US #30.

June Its extracted title track, *I'll Play For You*, reaches US #18.

Sept [29] ***I'll Play For You*** is ratified gold by the RIAA.
Dec ***Seals And Crofts' Greatest Hits***, a compilation of hit singles to date, reaches US #11, and will be certified for two million sales by the RIAA on October 13th 1986.

1976

July *Get Closer*, featuring Carolyn Willis (from hit-making group Honey Cone), hits US #6, and will become another longterm AC radio favorite.
Aug [25] ***Get Closer*** is certified gold by the RIAA before peaking at US #37 in September.
Dec *Baby, I'll Give It To You*, from ***Get Closer***, makes US #58.

1977

Jan ***Sudan Village***, featuring guest vocalist Willis on three cuts, peaks at US #73.
Feb [9] Seals & Crofts take part in ABC-TV's "American Bandstand's 25th Anniversary Special".
Nov *My Fair Share*, from the film "One On One", reaches US #28, while the Seals & Crofts-composed and performed soundtrack album, ***One On One***, peaks at US #118.

1978

Feb 32-track Dawnbreaker Studio, financed by Seals & Crofts' earnings, is completed to the duo's specifications at the HQ of manager Marcia Day's management company, Day Five Productions, in San Fernando Valley, CA. (The Baha'i religious community is also based there.)
June ***Takin' It Easy***, the first recorded at Dawnbreaker Studios, makes US #78, and is the duo's last album to chart, while *You're The Love*, taken from it, reaches US #18.
Sept Title song, *Takin' It Easy*, peaks at US #79, the duo's last chart entry.
[9] Drama series "The Paper Chase", a spin-off from the film of the same title, first airs on CBS-TV, with Seals & Crofts performing its theme song, *The First Years*. (Following the 1980 release of the non-charting 1980 album ***The Longest Road***, which features Stanley Clarke and Chick Corea among its guests, Seals & Crofts will quit the music business to initially devote their full-time efforts to the Baha'i community.)

1992

Aug [2] With Crofts now living in Nashville, TN, after spending much of the '80s in Australia and Mexico, and Seals running a coffee-bean farm in Costa Rica, and following constant rumors that the duo is set to come out of retirement to record a new album, they play at the Star Plaza Theatre, Merrillville, IN, while on a US reunion tour, on a bill with the Little River Band.

THE SEARCHERS

Mike Pender (vocals, lead guitar); **Tony Jackson** (vocals, bass); **John McNally** (vocals, rhythm guitar); **Chris Curtis** (vocals, drums)

1961

McNally (b. Aug. 30, 1941, Liverpool, Lancs.) and Pender (b. Michael Prendergast, Mar. 3, 1942, Liverpool) form an instrumental duo and perform at their local pub in Kirkdale, Liverpool, naming themselves the Searchers after John Ford's classic western. They meet Jackson (b. July 16, 1940, Liverpool) and drummer Norman McGarry, and the group begins regular work backing singer Johnny Sandon. Sandon will leave to front the Remo Four in March the following year, and they continue as a quartet, perfecting their harmony-vocal style. Regularly playing clubs including the Cavern, the Casbah, and the Hot Spot, they build a reputation at the Iron Door, whose owner becomes their manager. In September 1962, McGarry leaves to replace Ringo Starr in Rory Storm & the Hurricanes, and Curtis (b. Christopher Crummy, Aug. 26, 1941, Oldham, Lancs.) joins on drums. While playing clubs in Hamburg, West Germany, several tracks are recorded live at the Star-Club by Philips Records.

1963

May Having heard a demo by the group, Pye Records A&R man Tony Hatch views them in action at the Iron Door, and signs them to Pye.
Aug [10] Their debut single, reviving the Drifters' *Sweets For My Sweet*, tops the UK chart for the first of three weeks, deposing Elvis Presley's *Devil In Disguise*, as the group appears on the 100th edition of commercial TV show "Thank Your Lucky Stars", with Cliff Richard & the Shadows, Billy J. Kramer, Brian Poole and Alma Cogan.
[31] The band performs at "B-Day", a 13-hour outdoor rock festival in Liverpool, with the Hollies, Billy J. Kramer & the Dakotas and more than 20 other groups.
Sept ***Meet The Searchers*** hits UK #2.
[11] The group begins a 23-date UK package tour with Roy Orbison, Brian Poole & the Tremeloes, Freddie & the Dreamers and others, set to end on October 6th at King George's Hall, Blackburn, Lancs.
Oct [19] *Sweet Nothin's*, from the live Hamburg recordings released on Philips, makes UK #48.
Nov ***Sugar And Spice*** hits UK #5.
[8] The group begins another British tour, with Dusty Springfield, Freddie & the Dreamers, Brian Poole & the Tremeloes and Dave Berry, in Halifax, Yorks.
[16] *Sugar And Spice* hits UK #3.

1964

Jan [24] The group starts its own 15-minute weekly show on Radio Luxembourg.
Feb [1] *Needles And Pins*, their cover of Jackie DeShannon's minor US hit, written by Jack Nitzsche and Sonny Bono, begins a three-week run atop the UK chart, and will be the group's biggest hit, with total UK sales of over 850,000.
[11] McNally is taken ill with a septic throat.
[29] The band begins a 29-date twice nightly UK package trek with Dusty Springfield, Bobby Vee and Big Dee Irwin, at the Adelphi Cinema, Slough, Bucks., set to end on March 29th at the Empire Theatre, Liverpool.
Apr [5] The Searchers guest on CBS-TV's "The Ed Sullivan Show", during a five-day US stay.
[11] Signed to Kapp Records in the US, *Needles And Pins* reaches US #13, taking sales over one million.
[26] The group appears in the annual "**New Musical Express** Poll Winners Concert" at the Empire Pool, Wembley, Middx.
May [9] *Don't Throw Your Love Away*, their update of a Shirelles song, is the group's third UK #1.
[16] *(Ain't That) Just Like Me* peaks at US #61, and ***Meet The Searchers - Needles And Pins*** is their first US album chart-maker, at #22.
[24] The group makes its debut on ITV's "Sunday Night At The London Palladium".
[28] They begin a two-week US tour at the World's Fair in New York, NY.
June ***It's The Searchers*** hits UK #4.
[13] *Sugar And Spice*, released on Liberty, makes US #44.
July [11] *Don't Throw Your Love Away* reaches US #16, while the live ***Hear! Hear!***, a compilation of early tracks recorded in Hamburg, peaks at US #120.
Aug [8] *Some Day We're Gonna Love Again*, their cover of a Barbara Lewis track, reaches UK #11. Jackson departs for a solo career, signing to CBS, and is replaced by Frank Allen (b. Francis McNeice, Dec. 14, 1943, Hayes, Middx.), ex-Cliff Bennett's Rebel Rousers.
Sept [26] *Some Day We're Gonna Love Again* makes US #34.
Oct [24] *When You Walk In The Room*, another Jackie DeShannon cover, hits UK #3, while ***This Is Us*** makes US #97.
Nov [21] *When You Walk In The Room* reaches US #35.

1965

Jan [9] *What Have They Done To The Rain?*, an anti-nuclear protest song written by Malvina Reynolds, highlighting the group's softer, folk-influenced side, normally restricted to album tracks (and influential on many mid-'60s folk-rock groups), reaches UK #13.
[16] Their revival of the Clovers' *Love Potion #9*, only available in Britain as an album track, hits US #3.
Feb [23] The Searchers guest on NBC-TV's "Hullabaloo" by way of a video clip of *What Have They Done To The Rain.*
[27] *What Have They Done To The Rain?* reaches US #29.
Apr [3] *Goodbye My Love* hits UK #4.
[25] A 12-date twice-nightly UK package tour, with Dusty Springfield, Heinz, the Zombies, special guest star Bobby Vee and others, opens at the Odeon Cinema, Stockton, Cleveland, set to end on April 10th at the Sophia Gardens, Cardiff, South Glamorgan, Wales.
Apr ***Sounds Like The Searchers*** hits UK #8 (and is the group's last UK chart album). ***The New Searchers LP*** peaks at US #112.
[12] The band plays at the "**New Musical Express** Poll Winners Concert" at the Empire Pool, Wembley.
[14] The group appears on ITV's "The Bacharach Sound" with Dionne Warwick, Dusty Springfield and others.
[24] *Bumble Bee*, an update of a LaVern Baker hit, is a US-only release (though it finds UK success as the leading track on an EP), making US #21.
May [8] *Goodbye My Lover Goodbye*, a US re-titling, for copyright reasons, of *Goodbye My Love*, peaks at US #52.
July [14] The group leaves for a month-long US tour.
Aug [7] *He's Got No Love* reaches UK #12.
[14] *He's Got No Love* peaks at US #79.
Oct [23] *When I Get Home* makes UK #35 while ***The Searchers No. 4*** stops at US #149.

1966

Jan [22] P.F. Sloan-penned *Take Me For What I'm Worth*, on which a harder folk-rock style is demonstrated, reaches UK #20.
[26] The group begins a tour of the Far East, Australia and the US, in Hong Kong.
Mar [5] *Take Me For What I'm Worth* peaks at US #76.
[12] A six-date twice-nightly UK tour with bill-topper P.J. Proby and others, begins at the Town Hall, Birmingham, Warks., set to end on the 27th at the Empire Theatre, Liverpool. John Blunt (b. Mar. 28, 1947, Croydon, Surrey) fills in for Curtis, who is suffering from nervous exhaustion. Curtis will not re-join.
May [7] Their cover of the Rolling Stones' *Take It Or Leave It* reaches UK #31.
Oct [22] *Have You Ever Loved Somebody?* makes UK #48 (while Paul & Barry Ryan's version makes #49), the group's last UK chart single.
Dec [10] *Have You Ever Loved Somebody?* peaks at US #94. The group will leave Pye the following year, releasing two singles on Liberty before signing to RCA Records, while Blunt will be replaced on drums by Billy Adamson in December.

1971

Sept [11] *Desdemona* peaks at US #94. ***Second Take*** will be released on RCA the following year while in June 1973, the group will tour the US in the "British Re-Invasion Show", with Wayne Fontana, Herman's Hermits and Gerry & the Pacemakers, before spending the rest of decade playing on the cabaret and club circuits.

1981

Nov [23] Having been signed to Sire Records in 1979 and reached US #191 in March the following year with their comeback album ***The Searchers*** (covering songs by the likes of Tom Petty and Alex Chilton), the group, which has recently released a follow-up, ***Play For Today*** (US title: ***Love's Melodies***), now performs at the "Royal Variety Show" with Adam & the Ants, Lonnie Donegan and Cliff Richard, reunited with the Shadows.

1985

Dec [23] Pender plays his last gig with the group, before leaving to form his own touring band, Mike Pender's Searchers. He is replaced by Spencer James.

1987

May The group begins a successful UK "Solid '60s Silver" tour with Gerry & the Pacemakers and Peter Sarstedt (which will run until June). PRT reissues all the Pye material on album and CD in the UK. In June the following year, the group will take action against Mike Pender's use of the Searchers' name.

1991

Oct [6] The group takes part in the "Biggest '60s Party In Town" at London's Olympia, with the Swinging Blue Jeans, Marmalade, the Tremeloes, the Fortunes, Dave Berry, Dozy, Beaky, Mick & Tich and Freddie & the Dreamers.

1993

Mar [1] Having been signed to Arista Records in 1990 for the one-off album ***Hungry Heart***, the Searchers, still a hot '60s nostalgia booking, embark on a 51-date "Solid Silver Sixties Show 30th Anniversary Tour" with Gerry & the Pacemakers and Billy J. Kramer, at the Beau Sejour Centre, Guernsey, set to end on May 9th at the London Palladium. With Castle Communications' retrospective ***The Complete Collection*** still the most comprehensive anthology available in the UK, Rhino Records issues ***Greatest Hits*** in the US in June.

NEIL SEDAKA

1955

Sedaka (b. Mar. 13, 1939, Brooklyn, New York, NY), a piano student since the age of nine, began to write songs in 1952 with his 16-year-old lyricist neighbor, and Lincoln High School colleague, Howard Greenfield, their first composition being *My Life's Devotion*. While at high school, Sedaka was also chosen as New York City's outstanding classical pianist by Arthur Rubinstein. Impressed by the Penguins' hit, *Earth Angel*, Sedaka and Greenfield now write their first rock'n'roll-influenced song, the doo-wop ballad, *Mr. Moon*, which Sedaka performs with great success at a school talent show. He joins high school vocal group the Tokens, with Hank Medress (who will later co-found another group of that name, and have several hits in the '60s). Also a school colleague and romantic attachment at this time is Carole Klein, who later becomes hit singer/songwriter Carole King.

1957

Sedaka wins a piano scholarship to New York's Juilliard School of Music (at the recommendation of Rubinstein). Studying serious music does not affect his pop interests, and he and Greenfield continue to write regularly, while Sedaka records a one-off single, *Fly, Don't Fly On Me*, for the Philadelphia, PA-based Legion label.

1958

Feb Sedaka releases his own second single, *Laura Lee*, on Decca, but still with no chart success. Songwriters Doc Pomus and Mort Shuman put Sedaka and Greenfield in contact with Don Kirshner and Al Nevins, publishers at Aldon Music in Broadway's Brill Building in New York, who sign them to an exclusive contract, and start placing their songs. The first to be recorded is *Passing Time*, cut by Atlantic all-girl group the Cookies.

Sept Connie Francis' recording of the Sedaka/Greenfield composition, *Stupid Cupid* (originally written for the Shepherd Sisters), reaches US #14 and tops the UK chart.

Dec [1] After Nevins has played Sedaka's demo of *The Diary* to Steve Scholes of RCA, he signs Sedaka to the label as a recording artist.

1959

Feb *The Diary*, Sedaka's first RCA single, reaches US #14.

June [13] The follow-up, *I Go Ape*, a wild rocker, is his UK chart debut, hitting #9, supported by his debut UK tour. It also makes US #42 following a ban by several US radio stations.

June Busy with session work, as well as writing and recording (and still studying at Juilliard), Sedaka plays piano on Bobby Darin's US and UK chart-topper, *Dream Lover*, while his own *Crying My Heart Out For You* fails to score.

Dec *Oh! Carol*, a public display of affection for Carole Klein (to which she responds with the little-heard *Oh! Neil*), hits US #9 and UK #3, and is featured on his debut album, ***Rock With Sedaka***.

1960

May *Stairway To Heaven* hits US #9.

June [18] *Stairway To Heaven* hits UK #8.

Sept Ballad, *You Mean Everything To Me*, reaches US #17 and UK #45, while its uptempo B-side, *Run Samson Run*, makes US #28.

1961

Feb *Calendar Girl* hits US #4.

Mar [4] *Calendar Girl* hits UK #8.

June *Little Devil* reaches US #11 and hits UK #9.

Oct *Sweet Little You* peaks at US #59.

Dec *Happy Birthday, Sweet Sixteen*, one of Sedaka and Greenfield's most enduring songs, hits US #6.

1962

Jan [27] *Happy Birthday, Sweet Sixteen* hits UK #3.

May March-tempo *King Of Clowns*, which will become the official theme of the Ringling Brothers' Barnum & Bailey circus, makes US #45 and UK #23.

Aug [11] Sedaka has his first US chart-topper and first million seller with *Breaking Up Is Hard To Do*, which will hold at US #1 for two weeks. The distinctive gibberish chorus line was conceived after the rest of the song, coming in a flash of inspiration during a sleepless night. Sedaka is touring Britain while the single is on the charts.

Sept [8] *Breaking Up Is Hard To Do* hits UK #7.

Nov *Next Door To An Angel*, almost a clone of *Breaking Up*, hits US #5, and reaches UK #29, where sound-alike follow-ups are generally ill-regarded.

1963

Jan Compilation, ***Neil Sedaka Sings His Greatest Hits***, rounding up major singles from *Oh! Carol* to *Next Door To An Angel*, makes US #55.

Mar *Alice In Wonderland* reaches US #17, but fails to score in the UK (where the Merseybeat boom is just stirring, the subsequent "British invasion" being instrumental in Sedaka's decision to retire from recording during the second half of the '60s).

May *Let's Go Steady Again* reaches US #26.

June [1] *Let's Go Steady Again* makes UK #42.

Aug *The Dreamer* peaks at US #47.

Nov Skeeter Davis, a million seller earlier in the year with *The End Of The World*, hits US #7 with Sedaka's *I Can't Stay Mad At You*.

Dec *Bad Girl* makes US #33. *Sunny* will stop at US #86 the following August with *The World Through A Tear* making US #76 in October 1965.

1966

Feb *The Answer To My Prayer* proves anything but, ending Sedaka's run of hits on RCA. Aware that he is now out of fashion with the pop mainstream, Sedaka gives up recording and live performances at around the same time. He and Greenfield are contracted as staff writers, via Kirshner, for Screen Gems Music.

1968

Sept He signs to the Screen Gems' label, SGC Records in the US, releasing two non-charting singles. Meanwhile, his song *Workin' On A Groovy Thing* takes Patti Drew to US #62. The 5th Dimension's revival of Sedaka's *Workin' On A Groovy Thing* will reach US #20 the following August.

1971

June After the same group has taken Sedaka/Greenfield's *Puppet Man* to US #24 in May the previous year, Tom Jones' cover of *Puppet Man* now reaches US #26 and UK #50. Sedaka visits Britain for the first time in several years, for a four-month tour, mostly of Northern clubs, where his act proves immensely popular.

1972

Jan Tony Christie's version of Sedaka/Greenfield's *Is This The Way To Amarillo* climbs to UK #18. Sedaka signs to Kirshner's new eponymous label and, inspired by the success of friend Carole King's ***Tapestry***, he records ***Emergence***, credited simply as Sedaka. *I'm A Song (Sing Me)* and *Superbird*, from the album, are given strong airplay in the UK and another lengthy tour follows, including a major date at London's Royal Albert Hall. Sedaka moves his wife Leba and children Dara and Marc to London, and sets up a new working base from a flat in Mayfair, though this move splits him from Greenfield as he begins to write with new lyricist, Phil Cody.

June He records the self-produced ***Solitaire*** for Kirshner Records at Strawberry Studios, Stockport, Gtr. Manchester, with the four musicians who will shortly become known as 10cc.

Sept Sedaka performs at London's Royal Albert Hall.

Nov [18] *Beautiful You*, from ***Solitaire***, makes UK #43. Sedaka appears on BBC1-TV's "Top Of The Pops".

Dec [2] A UK reissue of *Oh! Carol*, released on a maxi-single with *Breaking Up Is Hard To Do* and *Little Devil*, reaches UK #19.

1973

Mar [24] *That's When The Music Takes Me*, from ***Solitaire***, makes UK #18.

June [23] *Standing On The Inside*, his first release under a new European recording deal with MGM Records, reaches UK #26.

Sept It is taken from ***The Tra-La Days Are Over***, on MGM, again recorded at Strawberry Studios with 10cc. [29] Extracted UK single *Our Last Song Together*, written as a swan song with Greenfield, makes UK #31.

1974

Feb [23] *A Little Loving*, released on Polydor (which has now absorbed its subsidiary MGM label), reaches UK #34. Meanwhile, Andy Williams' cover of *Solitaire* hits UK #4.

July [20] Sedaka/Cody composition *Laughter In The Rain* reaches UK #15, while the ***Laughter In The Rain*** long-player, this time recorded in Los Angeles, CA, with producer Robert Appere and sessioneers including David Foster, Danny Korthchmar and Russ Kunkel, reaches UK #17.

Aug At a party in the Sedakas' London flat to celebrate the British success of ***Laughter In The Rain***, Sedaka discusses with guest Elton John his current lack of a US recording contract. (His recent UK successes have not been released in the US.) John, a long-time fan, offers a deal to issue the Polydor recordings in North America on his own Rocket label.

Nov Live album, ***Live At The Royal Festival Hall***, recorded with the Royal Philharmonic Orchestra, makes UK #48.

1975

Feb [1] Released on Rocket, *Laughter In The Rain* tops the US chart for a week, and gives Sedaka his second million-selling single, more than 12 years after the first. It is also included on the US album ***Sedaka's Back***, a compilation from the last three UK albums, which reaches US #23 and earns a gold disc for half a million US sales.

Mar *Overnight Success* reaches UK #31, while ***Neil Sedaka Sings His Greatest Hits***, a reissue of the 1963 compilation, peaks at US #161. Sedaka plays in Las Vegas, opening for the Carpenters at the Riviera Hotel, but is asked to leave the show halfway through the two-week engagement when his act starts getting a better response. (The Riviera will invite him back as a headliner.)

Apr [5] Typically bubbly *The Queen Of 1964*, from ***Overnight Success***, makes UK #35, and is Sedaka's final UK hit single.

May Ballad *The Immigrant*, from ***Laughter In The Rain***, which is dedicated to John Lennon (who is currently fighting US authorities to stay in the country), reaches US #22.

June [21] Captain & Tennille's cover of *Love Will Keep Us Together*, originally from ***The Tra-La Days Are Over***, tops the US chart for the first of four weeks and reaches UK #32.

Aug A belated US release of *That's When The Music Takes Me* climbs to US #27.

Oct [11] Uptempo *Bad Blood*, on which Sedaka is joined by Elton John on backing vocals, begins a three-week run at US #1, and is his biggest-selling single, eventually topping 1.4 million domestic units. (It will be deposed by John's *Island Girl*.)

Nov ***The Hungry Years***, a revised version of ***Overnight Success***, and including *Bad Blood*, reaches US #16.

[11] ***Sedaka's Back*** is certified gold by the RIAA.

[25] *Bad Blood* is certified gold by the RIAA.

Dec His re-recording of *Breaking Up Is Hard To Do*, now in a slow ballad format, hits US #8, becoming the only former US #1 to return to the Top 10 in a different version by the same artist.

[18] ***The Hungry Years*** is certified gold by the RIAA.

1976

May *Love In The Shadows* reaches US #16.

[2] Sedaka begins a short UK tour at London's Hammersmith Odeon.

June ***Steppin' Out*** reaches US #26.

July An 18-track TV-promoted compilation, ***Laughter And Tears : The Best Of Neil Sedaka Today***, hits UK #2. Meanwhile, title cut *Steppin' Out* (with Elton John on backing vocals) makes US #36.

Oct His last hit single on Rocket is *You Gotta Make Your Own Sunshine*, which peaks at US #53 as a reissue on RCA of the Kirshner album, ***Solitaire***, makes US #159.

1977

June Newly signed to Elektra Records, his new version of *(Is This The Way To) Amarillo* makes US #44, while his label debut album, ***A Song***, reaches US #59.

Nov On Rocket, ***Neil Sedaka's Greatest Hits***, anthologizing his '70s material, peaks at US #143. A duet with his daughter, Dara, *Should've Never Let You Go*, will reach US #19 in June 1980, his last US singles chart entry, taken from ***In The Pocket***, which peaks at US #135.

1983

Mar [7] Having released ***Now*** in 1981, Sedaka is inducted into the Songwriters Hall of Fame at the 14th annual awards ceremony, held at the Waldorf Astoria Ballroom, New York, also performing a selection of past hits, including *Love Will Keep Us Together* and *The Hungry Years*. (Signing to MCA/Curb Records in 1984 for ***Come See About Me***, Sedaka will issue his autobiography, **Laughter In The Rain**, in 1987, when Polydor releases ***Me And My Friends***).

1995

Nov [11] Having recovered from a bout of diverticulitis in April 1990, Sedaka has performed a UK and US tour each year of '90s thus far, and regularly appears at charity concerts, notably at an American Foundation for AIDS Research benefit in New York in December 1991, after Harry Connick Jr. stormed off after two numbers, apparently disturbed by chatter in the audience. His enduring compositions and recordings still afford regularly released revised compilations, particularly in the UK where ***Timeless - The Very Best Of Neil Sedaka***, a greatest hits anthology issued by Polydor, hit UK #10 on November 9th, 1991, now followed by ***Classically Sedaka*** which reaches UK #23.

BOB SEGER

1964

Seger (b. May 6, 1945, Dearborn, MI), the son of the clarinet-playing leader of the 13-piece Stewart Seger Orchestra, a post-war attraction at the nearby Walled Lake casino resort (but who has left his wife and family in virtual poverty in 1957), has cut an acetate of his self-penned *The Lonely One*, recorded in Max Crook's (the musitron player on Del Shannon's *Runaway*) basement, which a kindly DJ at Ann Arbor, MI's WPAG station played one night in 1961. He has also led his own rock trio, the Decibels, with Eddie "Punch" Andrews and Dave Leone, in high school, before playing full-time in Ann Arbor, with the Town Criers, and now joins Doug Brown & the Omens, the city's leading group, on keyboards. He begins to write songs with vocalist Brown, also recording several demos, paid for by local-based hitmaker Del Shannon, who becomes their publisher. (One of his songs, *Such A Lovely Child*, is recorded by local band the Mushrooms, whose lead singer is future Eagle, Glenn Frey.)

1966

Mar The Omens, under the pseudonym of the Beach Bums, record *The Ballad Of The Yellow Beret* (a parody of S/Sgt. Barry Sadler's US chart-topper, *Ballad Of The Green Berets*) on the Are You Kidding Me? label. The gimmick is a favorite with local college students, but is withdrawn when Sadler sends a telegram threatening a lawsuit.

May The result of a $1,200 recording session is *East Side Story*, Seger's first release under his own name, billed as Bob Seger & the Last Heard (the band being the remnants of the Omens). It is a sizeable hit in Detroit on Hideout Records selling some 50,000 copies, and is picked up for national distribution by Cameo - as is the follow-up, *Persecution Smith*.

Dec Cameo buys out his contract and issues the seasonal rocker, *Sock It To Me, Santa*.

1967

Seger & the Last Heard continue to record for Cameo, cutting *Vagrant Winter* and *Heavy Music Parts 1 & 2*, the latter being a major hit in Detroit but prevented from nationwide success by the sudden demise of Cameo. Brown splits from Seger to pursue his own music while Punch Andrews, who has produced *Heavy Music*, becomes Seger's manager.

1968

Jan Seger re-forms his band as the Bob Seger System and signs to Capitol Records, despite a bigger offer from Motown. His first Capitol single, *2 + 2 = ?*, an anti-war heavy rocker, only finds strong sales in Michigan.

1969

Feb *Ramblin' Gamblin' Man* becomes Seger's US chart debut, reaching #17, while his freshman album, also titled ***Ramblin' Gamblin' Man***, makes US #62.

May *Ivory* peaks at US #97.

1970

Apr After completing work on a second effort, ***Noah***, Seger breaks up the System, which has been increasingly prone to internal strife, and announces that he is quitting music for a year to return to college. (He will enroll, but not stay.) The album does not chart, but from it, *Lucifer* peaks at US #84.

Nov ***Mongrel***, recorded after a short lay-off, with new musicians, peaks at US #171.

1971

Mar Without a band, Seger records the solo, acoustic, singer/songwriter-styled ***Brand New Morning***. He experiments with a new band named STK, including Oklahoma duo Dave Teegarden and Skip "Van Winkle" Knape. (STK is not successful, but its members will form the core of Seger's next stage group.)

Nov *Looking Back* peaks at US #96, after which Seger leaves Capitol. He and Andrews form Palladium Records, which is signed to Warner/Reprise.

1972

Aug His cover of Tim Hardin's *If I Were A Carpenter* makes US #76, taken from his first Palladium album, ***Smokin' O.P.'s*** ("O.P.'s" refers to smoking other people's cigarettes), which makes US #180 and includes a re-make of *Heavy Music*. ***Back In '72***, part-recorded at Muscle Shoals Studios, Muscle Shoals, AL, with guests including J.J. Cale, will peak at US #188 the following March.

1975

May After *Get Out Of Denver* has reached US #80 the previous August (later revived by UK acts Dave Edmunds and Eddie & the Hot Rods), taken from ***Seven/Contrasts***, Seger has re-signed to Capitol after Warner/Reprise has turned down ***Beautiful Loser***. Now issued by Capitol, the album reaches US #131.

Oct *Katmandu*, from ***Beautiful Loser***, makes US #43 (and is a Top 10 hit in Detroit). Seger tours the US with newly-formed backing group, the Silver Bullet Band, featuring Drew Abbott (guitar), Robyn Robbins (keyboards), Alto Reed (saxophones), Chris Campbell (bass) and Charlie Allen Martin (drums). (Band membership will change often over subsequent years, with bassist Campbell the only enduring member. First to go will be drummer Martin, after being injured in a car accident, replaced by Teegarden, who played in STK with Seger.)

1976

Apr The first album to credit the Silver Bullet Band is the performance double, ***Live Bullet***, recorded on stage at Cobo Hall, Detroit, during the previous year's tour, which reaches US #34 during a 140-week chart stay.

June *Nutbush City Limits*, his live cover of Ike & Tina Turner's hit, taken from the double album, reaches US #69.

1977

Jan [23] Seger plays in Tampa, FL, supported by the Patti Smith Group, but loses that act for the remainder of the tour when Smith falls off stage and is badly injured.

Mar ***Night Moves***, featuring the Silver Bullet Band on one side and the Muscle Shoals Rhythm Section on the flip, hits US #8, earning Seger's second consecutive platinum disc. Title track, *Night Moves*, is extracted, and gives Seger his first Top 10 single, hitting US #4.

May *Mainstreet*, also from ***Night Moves***, reaches US #24.

Aug Another track from the album, *Rock'n'Roll Never Forgets*, climbs to US #41.

1978

June A year in the making, the largely self-penned and self-produced ***Stranger In Town*** is released, hitting US #4, and is his third million-selling album, staying on the survey for over two years. It also marks Seger's UK chart debut at #31. The album uses both the Silver Bullet Band and the Muscle Shoals Rhythm Section, and has guest appearances by Eagles' vocalist Glenn Frey (whom Seger has known since they were kids in Detroit and whose first single *Such A Lonely Child* Seger has produced) and Bill Payne of Little Feat.

July *Still The Same*, the first single from the album, hits US #4.

Oct *Hollywood Nights*, also from ***Stranger In Town***, reaches US #12, and is his first UK chart single, peaking at #42.

1979

Jan From the album, the ballad, *We've Got Tonight*, reaches US #13, becoming an enduring career

highlight on US radio.
Feb *We've Got Tonight* peaks at UK #41.
May The final single from the album, *Old Time Rock'n'Roll*, makes US #28.

1980

Mar [19] A US tour to promote the forthcoming ***Against The Wind*** opens in Fayetteville, NC.
May [3] ***Against The Wind***, produced by Bill Szymczyk, the product of almost two years' work, tops the US chart for the first of six weeks during a 110-week chart stay. In the UK, it makes #26 while *Fire Lake*, the first extracted single, hits US #6.
June Title cut, *Against The Wind*, hits US #5.
Oct Third single from the album, *You'll Accomp'ny Me*, reaches US #14.
[3] During a concert by Bruce Springsteen in Ann Arbor, Seger joins him on stage for a duet on *Thunder Road*.
Dec *The Horizontal Bop*, the final extract from ***Against The Wind***, makes US #42.

1981

Feb [25] Seger wins the Best Rock Performance By A Duo Or Group With Vocal category for ***Against The Wind***, at the 23rd annual Grammy Awards.
Oct A second live double album, ***Nine Tonight***, recorded in Boston, MA, and Detroit, hits US #3 and UK #24. From it, a live version of *Hollywood Nights* makes UK #49.
Nov Also from the live album, *Tryin' To Live My Life Without You* hits US #5.

1982

Feb *Feel Like A Number* makes US #48, while a live version of *We've Got Tonite*, from ***Nine Tonight***, peaks at UK #60.

1983

Feb *Shame On The Moon*, written by country performer Rodney Crowell, is Seger's biggest-selling single, hitting US #2. It is taken from ***The Distance***, produced by Seger and Jimmy Iovine over a 14-month period (and originally intended as a double album), which hits US #5 (his sixth consecutive platinum album) and reaches UK #45. On the project, Seger has used new musicians: Russ Kunkel (drums), Waddy Wachtel (guitar) and Roy Bittan from Bruce Springsteen's E. Street Band (piano), alongside bassist Chris Campbell, keyboardist Craig Frost and saxophonist Alto Reed from the current Silver Bullet Band. Drew Abbott leaves the line-up.
[11] ***The Distance*** is certified platinum by the RIAA.
Mar Kenny Rogers and Sheena Easton's cover of *We've Got Tonite* hits US #6 and UK #28, bettering Seger's original in both territories.
Apr With $693,281 in box-office receipts, Seger sets a new house record at the Cobo Arena, Detroit.
May *Even Now*, also from the album, climbs to US #12 and UK #73.
June *Roll Me Away* reaches US #27.
Nov *Old Time Rock'n'Roll*, reissued as a single due to its inclusion in the Tom Cruise movie, "Risky Business", makes US #48. *Understanding*, taken from the soundtrack to the movie "Teachers", will reach US #11 in January.

1986

May [3] *American Storm* reaches US #13, featured on ***Like A Rock*** which hits US #3 and UK #35 and for which, for the first time, Seger has a co-writer, Craig Frost.
[28] ***Like A Rock*** is certified platinum by the RIAA.
June ***Live Bullet***, originally a US #34 in 1976, re-charts to US #135.
July [12] The extracted title song, *Like A Rock*, reaches US #12. (Refusing for many years to allow any of his songs to be used in commercials, and rejecting a number of overtures from General Motors and its advertizing agency to use *Like A Rock*, Seger will eventually relent, permitting the recording to be used to promote the auto company's Chevy Truck models, resulting in a highly successful and long-running blue collar-aimed campaign.)
Sept [20] *It's You*, also from ***Like A Rock***, peaks at US #52.
Nov [29] The last single taken from the album, *Miami*, peaks at US #70. (It will later be used in the NBC-TV series, "Miami Vice".)

1987

Aug [1] *Shakedown*, recorded for the movie "Beverly Hills Cop II" (and originally intended for Frey who is prevented by laryngitis from recording it) gives Seger his first US chart-topper, having been released by MCA, which holds the soundtrack rights. Seger has re-written some of Keith Forsey's original lyrics before recording it.
Dec Jimmy Iovine's Special Olympics benefit album, ***A Very Special Christmas***, to which Seger has contributed his version of *The Little Drummer Boy*, reaches US #20.

1988

Mar [13] Seger receives a star on the Hollywood Walk of Fame.
Aug He makes a guest appearance on Little Feat's newly-released comeback album, ***Let It Roll***, and files for divorce after a brief marriage to Annette Sinclair.

1991

June [6] After ***Beautiful Loser*** has been certified platinum on May 10th 1989, the RIAA now confirms multi-platinum sales of ***Against The Wind*** (four million), ***Live Bullet*** (four million), ***Night Moves*** (five million), ***Nine Tonight*** (three million) and ***Stranger In Town*** (five million), confirming Seger as one of the most popular US rock acts of the last 15 years.
Sept [14] After a five-year album hiatus, ***The Fire Inside***, co-produced with Don Was, Barry Beckett, and long-time cohort Punch, and recorded with the current Silver Bullet Band lineup of Craig Frost, Alto Reed and Chris Campbell, debuts at its US #7 peak.
[21] ***The Fire Inside*** peaks at UK #54.
Oct [5] *The Real Love* reaches US #24.
Nov [8] ***The Fire Inside*** is certified platinum by the RIAA.

1992

Jan [29] Seger is presented with the Governors Award at the second annual NARAS Detroit A&R Showcase, at the Premier Center Nightclub, Detroit.
Apr [12] Seger is voted Motor City Musician Of The Year and ***The Fire Inside*** wins Outstanding National Rock'n'Pop Album, at the first Motor City Music Awards, at the Music Hall Center, Detroit.

1994

July [27] He begins jury duty as foreman of a federal jury in Detroit, trying Louis C. Rossman with bank fraud. Rossman will be found guilty in December.
Oct [18] Seger is inducted into the Hollywood Rock Walk.
Nov [12] Compilation ***Greatest Hits***, including two new tracks, a cover of Chuck Berry's *C'Est La Vie* and *In Your Time*, a self-penned song dedicated to his son Cole, debuts at its US #8 peak.

1995

Feb [4] Reissued *We've Got Tonight* reaches UK #22.
[18] Belatedly released in the UK, ***Greatest Hits*** debuts at its UK #6 peak.
Apr [28] Seger receives the Lifetime Achievement Award at the fourth annual Motor City Music Awards in Detroit, as the RIAA certifies two million sales of ***Greatest Hits***.
May [6] Re-released *Night Moves* makes UK #45.
July [29] A further catalog item *Hollywood Nights* charts for a week at UK #52.
Nov [11] ***It's A Mystery***, Seger's first wholly self-produced effort, debuts at its US #27 peak.

1996

Jan [19] Seger begins his first tour in nearly a decade at the North Charleston Coliseum, Charleston, NC.
Feb [10] *Lock And Load* makes UK #57 in its week of entry.
Apr [18] Seger plays at the Great Western Forum, Inglewood, CA, as he continues his first tour in nine years, backed by longterm Bullets Frost, Reed, Campbell, Chatfield and newcomer drummer Kenny Aronoff.

THE SEX PISTOLS

Johnny Rotten (vocals); **Steve Jones** (guitar); **Sid Vicious** (bass); **Paul Cook** (drums)

1973

Fine Arts graduate and clothing retailer Malcolm McLaren, who has recently changed the name of his Chelsea, London shop from Let It Rock to Too Fast To Live, Too Young To Die, having met schoolfriends Cook (b. July 20, 1956, London) and Jones (b. May. 3, 1955, London) in 1971, begins to take an interest in the band the pair formed in 1972 (which includes friend Wally Nightingale and Del Noone), and, as their part-time manager, integrates bassist Glen Matlock (b. Aug. 27, 1956, Paddington, London), an assistant at the store, into their line-up. Rehearsing throughout the following year as the Swankers, they learn a variety of '60s covers, and also begin to write their own material.

1975

May After the Swankers has made its only public performance, singing three songs at a party above Tom Salter's Café in the King's Road, and with McLaren returned from six months in the US, working as manager for glam-punks the New York Dolls, he decides that Nightingale and Noone will not fit into his scheme for the Swankers. Jones moves to guitar, leaving the band looking for a singer.
June McLaren suggests ex-Television singer Richard Hell (who has already invented a punk look for himself), but the band wants an unknown London vocalist.
Aug John Lydon (b. Jan. 31, 1956, Finsbury Park, London) meets the group at McLaren's shop, now renamed Sex, and is asked to join as singer. He auditions standing next to the shop's jukebox and singing along to Alice Cooper's *School's Out*. The group becomes the Sex Pistols, and Jones christens Lydon "John Rotten", after his catchphrase, "You're rotten, you are."
Nov [6] The Sex Pistols play their first gig at St. Martin's School of Art in London, a performance lasting ten minutes (although Cook will later claim it was 20 minutes), followed by a series of small gigs, mainly at art schools.

1976

Apr [3] They support Joe Strummer's band, the 101ers, at the Nashville Rooms. The group then spends the summer building a cult following in London, playing a novel, volatile, nihilistic brand of seemingly unrehearsed garage rock in a variety of venues, as the seeds of punk rock are sown, masterminded ostensibly by McLaren, who also introduces anti-fashion statements for the band members including bondage clothing, safety-pins through the skin and short, spiked dyed hair.
Aug The Sex Pistols are barred from appearing at the "European Punk Rock Festival" in Mont de Marsan, France, by organizers who dislike their image. (They have already been banned from several London venues, including Dingwalls and the Rock Garden.)
[29] The group plays at the Screen on the Green Midnight Special, Islington, London, supported by the Buzzcocks and the Clash.
Sept [3] The band performs at the Club de Chalet du Lac in Paris. Devoted follower of the band and member of its infamous inner sanctum (dubbed the "Bromley contingent"), Billy Idol, drives to France in his ex-Post Office van with Siouxsie and Steve Severin of the Banshees to see the gig.
[17] They play a concert for inmates at Chelmsford

Prison, Chelmsford, Essex.
[20] The band headlines at the 100 Club punk rock festival, which sees the debuts of Subway Sect and Siouxsie & the Banshees, featuring Sid Vicious (b. John Simon Beverley, May 10, 1957, London, aka John Ritchie) on drums.
The Sex Pistols make their first UK TV appearance singing *Anarchy In The UK* on "So It Goes".
Oct [15] A week after Rotten appears on the cover of music paper **New Musical Express**, the Sex Pistols are signed to EMI Records for a £40,000 advance, following bids by Chrysalis, RAK and Polydor.
Nov [26] *Anarchy In The UK* is released.
[28] The Sex Pistols appear on BBC1-TV's "Nationwide" and ITV's "London Weekend Show".
Dec [1] The group appears on ITV's early evening magazine program, "Today", in place of Queen, who had been scheduled, but pulled out following dental work on Freddie Mercury the previous day. Taunted by interviewer Bill Grundy, they respond with profanities and verbal abuse and make the cover of every newspaper the next day, establishing the group's name across the country.
[5] The "Anarchy In The UK Tour", also featuring the Clash, the Damned and the Heartbreakers, is due to start, but many dates are cancelled. (Only three out of 19 gigs go ahead.)
[7] The Sex Pistols reputation is discussed at EMI's AGM. Chairman Sir John Read apologizes for the group's behaviour.
[18] *Anarchy In The UK* makes UK #38.
[25] In the **New Musical Express**, the Pat Travers Band challenge the Pistols to a jam with Peter Cowling using two bass strings, Travers using three strings and Nicko McBrain using a high hat, snare and cymbal, claiming they could still out-play them.

1977

Jan [12] EMI issues a statement saying it feels unable to promote the Sex Pistols' records in view of the adverse publicity generated over the last two months, even though press reports of their behaviour seem to have been exaggerated. (EMI honors their contract, promising the £40,000 advance. *Anarchy In The UK* sells 55,000 copies before being withdrawn.)
Feb [1] The group begins a European tour in Belgium.
Mar Rotten is fined £40 for possession of amphetamines. Vicious, currently a member of Flowers Of Romance, after auditioning as bass player to replace Matlock, joins, despite his rudimentary playing skills. (Matlock is allegedly dismissed because he "liked the Beatles".) Matlock will form the Rich Kids, with Steve New (guitar) and Rusty Egan (drums).
[10] The Sex Pistols sign to A&M Records on a trestle-table outside Buckingham Palace, at a 7:00 a.m. press conference.
[16] Due to pressure from other label artists and its Los Angeles head office, A&M fires the band, having pressed 25,000 copies of *God Save The Queen*. Much to McLaren's glee, the group has earned £75,000 for its six days with the label.
May The group signs to Virgin Records for £15,000, though the label immediately encounters problems pressing the group's new single, *God Save The Queen*, at the CBS plant when workers threaten to walk out. Jamie Reid's sleeve depiction of the Queen with a safety pin through her mouth causes a furore in the press.
[27] *God Save The Queen* is released, and reportedly sells 150,000 copies in five days, despite being banned from daytime play by BBC Radio 1 and leading chainstores.
June [7] Virgin Records hires a boat called "Queen Elizabeth" for a party on the River Thames. The Sex Pistols perform *Anarchy In The UK* outside the Houses of Parliament, and members of the party are arrested when the boat docks.
[11] *God Save The Queen* hits UK #2, amid claims that the record is out-selling Rod Stewart's chart-topping *I Don't Want To Talk About It*. Virgin Records, trying to buy airtime during "Today" commercial breaks to advertise the record, are turned down.
[18] Rotten, producer Thomas and engineer Bill Price are attacked with razors in the car park of the Pegasus Hotel, Highbury, North London, on their way back to the nearby Wessex Studio.
[19] Cook is set upon by six men wielding knives and an iron bar outside Shepherds Bush underground station. He will have part of his hair shaved after 15 stitches are required.
[21] Rotten is attacked in a brawl at Dingwalls in London.
July [21] The group makes its BBC1-TV's "Top Of The Pops" debut, singing *Pretty Vacant*.
[30] *Pretty Vacant* hits UK #6, while the group tours Scandinavia. McLaren meets film director Russ Meyer to discuss a Sex Pistols film. (Meyer will pull out of the project, which enjoyed the provisional title "Who Killed Bambi?")
Aug [19] The band undertakes an "undercover" UK tour as the Spots (an acronym for Sex Pistols On Tour Secretly) in Wolverhampton, and also plays as the Tax Exiles, Special Guest, the Hampsters and Acne Rabble. Vicious wears a black suit, shirt and tie to appear at Wells Street magistrates court to answer charges of carrying a flick-knife at the 100 Club. With the Clash's Paul Simenon and Mick Jones as defence witnesses, he is fined £125.
Oct [29] *Holidays In The Sun* hits UK #8. The Belgian Travel Service issues a summons claiming the sleeve infringes copyright of one its brochures. (The sleeve is withdrawn from sale.)
Nov [12] The group's first and only original album, the genre-defining ***Never Mind The Bollocks - Here's The Sex Pistols*** enters the UK chart at #1, displacing Cliff Richard's ***40 Golden Greats***. It stays on top for two weeks, before being dethroned by Bread's ***The Sound Of Bread***.
A policewoman sees the album sleeve in a shop window and informs the retailer he is contravening the 1889 Indecent Advertsing Act because of the word "bollocks" on the sleeve. (Magistrates "reluctantly" declare two weeks later that it is not an offence to display the record.) The Sex Pistols sign to Warner Bros. for US distribution.
Dec During the month, police are called to the Ambassador Hotel, Bayswater, London, after complaints from residents about noises coming from a room occupied by Vicious and girlfriend, Nancy Spungen. They are arrested on suspicion of possessing illegal substances, but are released without charge. Listeners to Israeli Radio vote *God Save The Queen* the worst single of the year. In a **Daily Mail** interview, Cook's mum Sylvia admits that she is "making a nice little dining room out of Paul's bedroom. I don't think I really want him back." Aberdeen council meet to decide whether to let the band play at the city's musical hall, while Labour councillor Margaret Williams claims that the group is known to cut up animals on stage and cover themselves in blood.
[15] The band is denied entry into the US two days before a scheduled NBC-TV "Saturday Night Live" appearance. Elvis Costello takes its place. (They had been scheduled to start a US tour at the Leona Theater, Homestead, PA on the 29th.)
[25] The Sex Pistols play their last ever UK gig at Ivanhoe's in Huddersfield, Yorks, a charity performance before an audience mainly made up of children.

1978

Jan [5] The Sex Pistols begin a US tour at the Great Southeast Music Hall, Atlanta, GA, before an estimated crowd of 500.
[10] The band makes its US TV debut on "Variety".
[14] After gigs in Memphis, TN, San Antonio, TX, Baton Rouge, LA, Dallas, TX, and Tulsa, OK, the group plays what will be its last live show, at the Winterland Ballroom, San Francisco, CA. At the fall of the curtain, Rotten says to the 5,000 sellout crowd, "Ha! Ha! Ever get the feeling you've been cheated? Good night." He quits the tour and heads for New York, NY.
[16] Vicious falls through a glass door at their San Francisco hotel, overdoses on drugs and goes into hospital. (He will also overdose on valium and alcohol on a flight to New York.) McLaren returns to London, while Cook and Jones use plane tickets to Rio de Janeiro, Brazil, previously purchased for a planned one-off concert. Virgin declares there will be "no more Sex Pistols releases".
[21] ***Never Mind The Bollocks - Here's The Sex Pistols*** peaks at US #106.
Feb Cook and Jones stay in Rio as guests of "great train robber" Ronald Biggs.
[23] Vicious, currently playing solo gigs at Max's and CBGB's, is arrested with Spungen for possession of drugs in New York.
Apr Cook and Jones play dates with Johnny Thunders at London's Speakeasy club. Vicious also performs as a vocalist with Thunders. After the Sex Pistols split Rotten reverts to his real name, John Lydon, and, having taken a short holiday in Jamaica, returns to the UK and forms a new band with ex-Clash member Keith Levene (guitar), novice bass player Jah Wobble and Canadian Jim Walker (drums), who has played with the Furys, and is recruited after auditions. The quartet, named Public Image Ltd. (PiL), signs to Virgin.
July Virgin refuses to release the single Cook and Jones have recorded with Biggs under the title *Cosh The Driver*. Instead it is released as *No One Is Innocent (A Punk Prayer By Ronnie Biggs)*, as a double A-side with Vicious' version of the standard *My Way*. Vicious plays a farewell gig at the Electric Ballroom, London, under the banner "Sid Sods Off" with the Vicious White Kids - Rat Scabies, Glen Matlock and Steve New.
[25] The formation of Public Image Ltd. is officially announced by Lydon.
Oct [12] Vicious, living in room 100 at the Chelsea Hotel in New York with Spungen, calls police to say that someone has stabbed her. They arrive to find her lying under the bathroom sink in blood-soaked underwear, stabbed to death with a hunting knife. Vicious is arrested, charged with murder and placed in the detox unit of a New York prison. During a four-day spell at Rikers Jail, he will attempt suicide twice. (McLaren eventually bails him out with $50,000 from Virgin.)

1979

Feb [2] Still out on bail, Vicious dies at a New York party from an accumulation of fluid on the lungs caused by a heroin overdose. (His mother will subsequently claim that she provided him with the heroin and was present when he injected himself with it. She claimed she was fearful that he would be arrested if he bought the drug himself.)
The Sex Pistols, McLaren and Virgin go to court in an attempt to resolve the group's financial affairs. The High Court judge appoints a receiver to sort out finances, including money tied up in the movie and album, ***The Great Rock'n'Roll Swindle***, currently in production. He tells those concerned to sort out who owns the name the Sex Pistols and whether Lydon is still under contract to McLaren. (In the course of the week Cook and Jones change sides, joining Lydon/Virgin against McLaren.)
Mar Their revival of Eddie Cochran's *Something Else*, coupled with *Friggin' In The Riggin'*, hits UK #3.
[17] ***The Great Rock'n'Roll Swindle***, a double set of out-takes and jokey songs, hits UK #7 (and will subsequently be edited down to a single album).
Apr *Silly Thing*, a double A-side with Tenpole Tudor's *Who Killed Bambi*, hits UK #6.
July *C'mon Everybody* hits UK #3.
Aug [11] ***Some Product - Carri On Sex Pistols***, containing interviews, commercials and the "Today" interview, but no music, hits UK #6 in its week of entry.
Oct "The Great Rock'n'Roll Swindle" movie premieres. Julien Temple's film is a collection of early Pistols footage and comic situations, with McLaren claiming the whole phenomenon was no more than his inspired hype. Rotten is largely absent from the movie. *The Great Rock'n'Roll Swindle*, a double A-side with Tenpole Tudor's *Rock Around The Clock*, reaches UK #21, while Cook and Jones' new band, the Professionals, make UK #43 with *1-2-3*.
Dec [22] ***Sid Sings*** makes UK #30.

1980

Feb Further Sex Pistols cash-in album, ***Flogging A Dead Horse***, reaches UK #23.
July *(I'm Not Your) Stepping Stone*, reviving the Monkees' hit, makes UK #21.

1986

Jan [13] Lydon, Jones, Cook and Vicious' mother sue McLaren for £1 million. (They will settle out of court.) The official receiver awards the three remaining band members and Vicious' mother £1 million.
July [20] The bio-film, "Sid And Nancy", directed by Alex Cox with Gary Oldman as Sid and Chloe Webb as Nancy, premieres in London. (A video documentary of Sex Pistols' TV footage will appear as the "Buried Alive" video package in 1988.)

1992

Mar [26] ***Never Mind The Bollocks - Here's The Sex Pistols*** is certified platinum by the RIAA.
July [24] UK tabloids report that the group is to re-form to tie in with the release of a greatest hits compilation.
Oct [10] Reissued *Anarchy In The UK* makes UK #33.
[17] ***Kiss This***, a 20-track CD collection including a live bootleg album recorded in Trondheim, Norway, in 1977, debuts at its UK #10 peak.
Dec [12] Reissued *Pretty Vacant* peaks at UK #56.

1996

Mar [18] At a press conference to announce the Sex Pistols' forthcoming comeback tour, Rotten says "We have found a common cause, and it's your money". On the same day the group sends a fax to Princess Diana: "If the Queen doesn't provide the kind of financial settlement you're looking for, the band is prepared to do a benefit concert."
June [3] The Sex Pistols, with Matlock back on bass, begin their first tour in 18 years in London, set to end on July 21st topping the bill on the fourth day of "The Phoenix 1996" festival at Long Marston, Stratford-upon-Avon, Warks., with a six-week US schedule to follow, beginning July 31st in Denver, CO, under the banner "The Filty Lucre Tour".
see also: **PUBLIC IMAGE LTD.**

THE SHADOWS

Hank Marvin (lead guitar); **Bruce Welch** (rhythm guitar); **Brian Bennett** (drums)

1958

Apr [6] Marvin (b. Brian Rankin, Oct. 28, 1941, Newcastle, Tyne & Wear) and Welch (b. Bruce Cripps, Nov. 2, 1941, Bognor Regis, Sussex), having left school in Newcastle, travel to London with their part-time skiffle quintet, the Railroaders, to enter a national talent contest in which they come third. The Railroaders split the following month after the contest. Welch and Marvin remain in London and form the Five Chesternuts, with comedian Charlie Chester's drummer son, Pete, a vocalist and a bass player. One of the group's first appearances is backing comedian Benny Hill on *Gather In The Mushrooms*, at a charity concert at the Town Hall in Stoke Newington, London.
Aug The group records a one-off single for EMI's Columbia label, *Teenage Love*, which leads to an appearance on BBC1-TV's "6.5 Special", but no further success is forthcoming. Welch and Marvin take jobs at the 2I's coffee bar in Soho, London, where they play guitar in the basement club as the Geordie Boys, and operate the orange juice and coca-cola machines.
Sept Marvin, having played a two-week UK tour as temporary guitarist with the Vipers, is seen by Cliff Richard's manager, John Foster, playing at the 2I's. Richard has been offered a British concert tour supporting the Kalin Twins, but his group, the Drifters, has just lost guitarist Ken Pavey and needs a replacement. Foster intended to offer Tony Sheridan the job, but he cannot be found. Marvin is asked to join instead, and insists that Welch joins too. Foster agrees after they play for him at home.
Oct [5] Richard goes on tour backed by a Drifters line-up of Marvin (lead guitar), Welch (rhythm guitar), Ian Samwell (bass) and Terry Smart (drums). Marvin is recruited by the Kalin Twins to play guitar for them too.
[19] As the trek ends, Samwell leaves the Drifters. Fellow 2I's regular Jet Harris (b. Terence Harris, July 6, 1939, Kingsbury, London), a former member of Tony Crombie's Rockers and now on tour backing the Most Brothers, and asked by the Drifters to perform behind the curtain to boost Samwell's hesitant bass playing, is asked by Richard to join.
Nov [14] The Drifters take part in their first studio session at Abbey Road, London, backing Cliff Richard on *Livin' Lovin' Doll* and *Mean Streak*.
[17] Richard and the Drifters open a variety season at the Metropolitan Theatre in the Edgware Road, London. (They follow with a further two weeks at the Chiswick Empire and the Finsbury Park Empire.)
Dec Smart leaves the Drifters to join the Merchant Navy. Harris suggests Tony Meehan (b. Daniel Meehan, Mar. 2, 1943, London), the ex-Vipers drummer, with whom he, Marvin and Welch have all played at the 2I's, as his replacement.

1959

Jan The new quartet plays together on record for the first time on Richard's *Livin' Lovin' Doll*, and backs him at the Free Trade Hall, Manchester, Lancs.
[9] The Drifters audition for EMI at Abbey Road. *Feelin' Fine*, the first track recorded at the session, becomes the group's debut single.
Feb Offered a recording deal in their own right by Columbia's Norrie Paramor, on the strength of their playing with Richard, the Drifters release *Feelin' Fine*, a vocal written by ex-member Samwell (who becomes their manager for ventures independent of Richard). Its B-side, *Don't Be A Fool (With Love)*, written by Marvin and Welch's ex-Chesternuts colleague Chester, is performed by the group on ITV's "Oh Boy!", but fails to chart.
[5] The Drifters sign a contract with EMI to record four sides in the first year with no guarantee of release. If any material is issued, the group will earn a royalty rate of a penny per record, split four ways.
May The group records its first instrumental, *Chinchilla*, for the soundtrack of Richard's film, "Serious Charge".
July *Jet Black*, an instrumental written by Harris, is the second Drifters single. Failing to chart in the UK, it is credited in the US to the Four Jets, since *Feelin' Fine* had to be withdrawn from the American market when Atlantic group the Drifters issued an injunction to prevent duplication of their name. The band decides a permanent change is necessary and adopts the Shadows, suggested by Harris while drinking at the Six Bells pub in Ruislip, Middx.
Dec *Saturday Dance*, another vocal written by Marvin and Chester, is the first single credited to the Shadows, but another non-charter. The group appears with Richard in the pantomime, "Babes In The Wood", in Stockton-on-Tees, Cleveland. During the run, Harris is involved in a car crash, injuring himself and Marvin slightly. Harris is fined £35 and 15 shillings for dangerous driving, failing to display L plates and driving unaccompanied by a qualified driver.

1960

Jan They tour North America with Cliff Richard on the 38-date "The Biggest Show of Stars" package, including Frankie Avalon, Bobby Rydell and Freddy Cannon (during which they will also make their debut on CBS-TV's "The Ed Sullivan Show").
Apr On a UK trek, the group meets singer/songwriter Jerry Lordan, who demonstrates his composition, *Apache*, on the ukelele. They record it with Richard sitting in on bongoes.
June Peter Gormley becomes their full-time manager.
[17] *Apache* is recorded at Abbey Road.
Aug [27] *Apache* hits UK #1 for the first of six weeks, deposing Richard's *Please Don't Tease*. (Danish guitarist Jorgen Ingmann's cover, recorded without hearing the Shadows' version, steals US chart honors.)
Sept [25] The group plays its first "solo" concert at Colston Hall, Bristol, Avon.
Dec [3] *Man Of Mystery*, their version of the theme from the Edgar Wallace movie series, backed with *The Stranger* hits UK #5. *Apache* is voted Record Of The Year in the **New Musical Express**.

1961

Feb [18] *FBI*, credited to manager Gormley because of a publishing wrangle, but a Marvin/Welch/Harris composition, hits UK #4.
Mar The band tours southern Africa, Australasia and the Far East with Richard, and makes its first live recording, a four-track EP, cut at the Colosseum, Johannesburg, South Africa.
June [3] Film theme, *The Frightened City*, hits UK #3, while the band films the movie, "The Young Ones", with Richard, at the Elstree Studios, Elstree, Herts.
Sept [23] Their debut album, ***The Shadows***, featuring new instrumentals and vocals, begins an initial four-week run at UK #1 (and will return to the top spot for a further week on Oct [28]).
Oct [7] *Kon-Tiki* hits UK #1, the week that the Shadows simultaneously hold pole position on the album, single and EP charts (*The Shadows To The Fore*, which includes *Apache*). Meehan leaves during a six-week residency with Richard at Blackpool, Lancs., seeking a move into production, and starts work for Decca as an A&R man. Bennett (b. Feb. 9, 1940, London), an acquaintance from the 2I's, and ex-Marty Wilde's Wildcats and instrumental group the Krew Kats' drummer, is backing Tommy Steele when Welch phones him, and joins the Shadows in time to tour Australia with Richard.
Dec [2] *The Savage*, written by producer Norrie Paramor and taken from the film, "The Young Ones", hits UK #10.

1962

Mar [24] *Wonderful Land*, a Jerry Lordan composition and the first Shadows track with orchestral backing, heads the UK chart for the first of eight weeks, but will be toppled by another instrumental, *Nut Rocker*, by B. Bumble & the Stingers.
Apr Differences between Welch and Harris come to a head, and Harris walks out to pursue a solo career. Brian "Liquorice" Locking, another acquaintance who played with Bennett in the Krew Kats, Vince Taylor's Playboys and Marty Wilde's Wildcats, joins on bass.
[13] The group is belatedly presented with a gold disc for worldwide million-plus sales of *Apache*.
[15] Harris makes his final appearance with the Shadows at the "**New Musical Express** Poll Winners Concert".
[23] Welch collapses on stage at the Queen's Theatre, Blackpool, Lancs. Pete Carter from the Checkmates steps in.
[27] Harris signs to Decca as a solo singer/guitarist, with Jack Good becoming his manager and producer.
May [6] Locking makes his first West End appearance with the group at the "Our Friends The Stars" charity concert.
The group travels to Greece to film "Summer Holiday" (its title theme penned by Welch and Bennett) with Cliff Richard.
June [9] Harris' six-string bass guitar solo version of *Besame Mucho* (with Meehan on drums) reaches UK #22.
Aug [18] *Guitar Tango*, the first Shadows single to feature acoustic guitars, hits UK #4.
[19] Harris makes his live debut at the Princess Theatre, Torquay, Devon, with his backing group the Jetblacks, on a bill with Craig Douglas and Mark Wynter.
[31] The group begin a two-week season at the Olympia, Paris, France.
Sept [15] Harris' second solo single, a revival of *Main Title Theme*, from the '50s Frank Sinatra film, "Man With The Golden Arm", reaches UK #12.

Oct [27] ***Out Of The Shadows***, featuring tracks with Harris, hits UK #1 for the first of three weeks (it will have further runs at the top in November, December and January 1964).

Nov EP *The Boys*, featuring music by the group from the British movie of the same title, tops the UK EP chart. They appear with Richard at the "Royal Variety Show" in London.

1963

Jan [26] The Shadows' *Dance On*, written by vocal group the Avons, hits UK #1, and will be replaced by *Diamonds* the following week, a Lordan composition co-credited to Jet Harris & Tony Meehan (staying on top for three weeks).

Mar [30] *Foot Tapper*, from "Summer Holiday", tops the UK survey for a week, deposing Richard's title song. (It will be the group's final UK #1 single.)

May [3] The Shadows win the Year's Outstanding Score Of A Musical category for "Summer Holiday", at the eighth annual Ivor Novello Awards, held at BBC Television Centre, London.

The Shadows' Greatest Hits, compiling their singles to date, hits UK #2 behind the Beatles' ***Please Please Me***, and will stay in the UK Top 20 for 49 weeks.

[25] Harris and Meehan's second duet, *Scarlet O'Hara*, hits UK #2.

June [29] *Atlantis*, a ballad instrumental with string accompaniment, peaks at UK #2 for two weeks, behind Gerry & the Pacemakers' *I Like It*. The group begins a 16-week summer season, "Holiday Carnival", in Blackpool, Lancs., with Richard.

Aug Pressures of work begin to fray Welch's nerves and he announces that he will leave the group for a desk job in the Shadows' organization, after a tour of Israel and France in October.

[10] The band appears on the 100th edition of ITV's "Thank Your Lucky Stars" with Cliff Richard, the Searchers, Billy J. Kramer, Brian Poole and Alma Cogan.

Sept [28] Harris and Meehan's *Applejack* hits UK #4, but their joint career ends when Harris and girlfriend, singer Billie Davis, are injured in an accident involving their car and a bus. Harris is left in poor physical and mental shape. He leaves Meehan three weeks later on an ITV "Ready Steady, Go!" show, goes home, and reportedly smashes all his guitars.

Oct [12] *Shindig* hits UK #6. Locking, who has become committed to his Jehovah's Witness faith, announces that he is to leave. Marvin and Welch consider recruiting John Paul Jones, bassist with Harris and Meehan's backing group (and later with Led Zeppelin), but settle on ex-Interns bass player, John Rostill (b. June 16, 1942, Birmingham, Warks.). Welch has overcome his nervous problems with medical help, and decides not to quit.

Dec The group films "Wonderful Life" in the Canary Islands with Cliff Richard, while *Geronimo* reaches UK #11, their first single to miss the UK Top 10.

1964

Jan With Harris out of action, Meehan's *Song Of Mexico*, released as by the Tony Meehan Combo, reaches UK #39 (but will be his last hit).

Mar Rostill plays on stage with the Shadows for the first time on a UK tour with Richard.

[8] The Shadows perform at the London Palladium.

Apr [11] *Theme For Young Lovers*, from the ***Wonderful Life*** soundtrack, reaches UK #12. Marvin's 18-month-old twin sons almost drown in his backyard pond, but he saves them with the "kiss of life", a widely-publicized event.

May The group tours Europe while ***Dance With The Shadows*** hits UK #2.

June [6] *The Rise And Fall Of Flingel Bunt*, the Shadows' hardest-rocking single since *The Savage*, hits UK #5.

Aug The band makes its own 25-minute musical comedy film, "Rhythm And Greens", a series of short historical sketches in costume. It is shown in the UK as support to Dirk Bogarde's "King And Country".

Sept [12] Title track, *Rhythm And Greens*, reaches UK #22.

Nov The group peforms three numbers in the "Royal Variety Show", as well as backing Richard.

[22] The Shadows write the score for, and have acting and musical roles in, the Richard-starring pantomime, "Aladdin And His Wonderful Lamp", at the London Palladium, with Arthur Askey and Una Stubbs, which will run for 15 weeks.

1965

Jan [16] *Genie With The Light Brown Lamp*, from the pantomime, makes UK #17.

Mar [6] Ballad, *Mary Anne*, written by Lordan and the first vocal Shadows single since *Saturday Dance*, reaches UK #17.

June [26] The more familiar-sounding instrumental, *Stingray*, makes UK #19, as the Shadows support Richard on another European tour.

July ***The Sound Of The Shadows*** hits UK #4.

Aug [28] Vocal *Don't Make My Baby Blue* (previously recorded by Frankie Laine), hits UK #10 (the last Shadows Top 10 single for almost 13 years).

Dec [21] Frank Ifield's pantomime, "Babes In The Wood", its musical score written (but not performed by) the group, premieres at the London Palladium. ***More Hits!*** a compilation of further hit singles, is the group's first album not to chart in the UK.

[25] *The War Lord*, the theme from the Charlton Heston movie, reaches UK #18.

1966

Apr [2] Vocal *I Met A Girl* reaches UK #22.

May [1] The group takes part in an all-star cast at the annual "**New Musical Express** Poll Winners Concert", at the Empire Pool, Wembley, Middx.

June ***Shadow Music*** hits UK #5.

July [23] *A Place In The Sun*, an instrumental in the *Wonderful Land* mode (and written by Lordan's wife, Petrina) reaches UK #24, while the group is filming "Finders Keepers" with Richard.

Nov [16] Marvin-penned vocal, *The Dreams I Dream*, makes UK #42.

Dec [20] The Shadows-written, Cliff Richard-starring pantomime, "Cinderella", with band members featured as the Brokers Men, and also starring Terry Scott and Hugh Lloyd as the Ugly Sisters, opens at the London Palladium, set to close on April 1st. Puppet likenesses of Richard and the Shadows appear in Gerry Anderson's movie, "Thunderbirds Are Go!", in a nightclub scene as "Cliff Richard Jr. And The Sons Of The Shadows", for which the group writes and performs four tracks, released as an EP.

1967

Apr [30] The group sets out on an eight-week world tour, taking in Spain, Turkey, Japan, Hong Kong, Israel, and Australia.

May [6] *Maroc 7*, the theme from the Gene Barry movie, reaches UK #24. Welch parts from his wife and moves in with Australian singer, Olivia Newton-John.

July ***Jigsaw*** hits UK #8.

Aug The Shadows win the "Split Song Festival", in Yugoslavia, with *I Can't Forget*. They tour Australia and Spain (without Richard).

Sept *Tomorrow's Cancelled* is the first Shadows single since their pre-*Apache* recordings not to chart in Britain.

Oct Bennett releases *Change Of Direction*, with a six-piece group which includes Rostill.

Dec ***From Hank, Bruce, Brian And John***, released, by Shadows standards, somewhat hastily after its predecessor (five months), fails to chart.

[25] The Shadows appear in a UK TV production of the "Aladdin" pantomime.

1968

Jan [1] The group begins a three-week cabaret at the Talk Of The Town club, its first in London without Richard. (After a week, Rostill suffers a minor nervous breakdown and is ordered to rest, while Bennett is ill with appendicitis. Ex-members Locking and Meehan fill in.)

Marvin releases his first solo single, *London's Not Too Far*.

Mar With the current line-up back together, the group tours Japan, while in the UK *Dear Old Mrs. Bell* is released.

May They play a short season at the London Palladium with Tom Jones.

Oct Cliff Richard & the Shadows celebrate their tenth anniversary in the music business with ***Established 1958***, an album which contains equal shares of Shadows-backed Richard vocals and group instrumentals. Welch and his wife are divorced, and he becomes engaged to Olivia Newton-John. It is reported that Welch and Bennett plan to leave the group at the end of the year.

Dec [14] Welch plays his final date with the Shadows, at the end of their London Palladium season. Marvin presents him with an engraved clock.

[19] Following bad feeling and arguments within the group, it is admitted between the quartet that tiredness, disenchantment, and a loss of creativity have set in, and that a split is necessary. They play their last (10th anniversary) show with Richard, at the London Palladium.

1969

Mar Marvin releases the solo single, *Goodnight Dick*, while Bennett plays for seven days in Washington, DC, as Tom Jones' drummer.

May [7] Marvin guests on ITV's "Frankie Howerd At The Poco-A-Poco".

Sept Marvin's duet with Richard on *Throw Down A Line* hits UK #7. Bennett releases ***The Illustrated London Noise***.

Oct With no plans to re-form the group, but attracted by the offer, Marvin, Rostill and Bennett play a short tour of Japan as the Shadows, with keyboards player Alan Hawkshaw, an old friend of Bennett's. A live album is recorded by Japanese EMI/Odeon at Sankei Hall, Tokyo. In the UK, a lengthy version of Richard Rodgers' *Slaughter On 10th Avenue*, recorded earlier without Welch, is released, coupled with Marvin's solo version of the *Midnight Cowboy* theme, but again fails to score.

Nov Marvin's first solo album, ***Hank Marvin***, reaches UK #14.

1970

Mar A second "Cliff and Hank" duet, *Joy Of Living*, reaches UK #25, the theme for a weekly Cliff Richard TV series, on which Marvin is a resident guest, featuring in comedy sketches as well as playing and singing. He declines an invitation by Roy Wood to join the Move.

May [3] The group plays at the annual "**New Musical Express** Poll Winners Concert".

Aug Marvin and Welch (back in action after 18 months) consider setting up as a vocal duo, and invite Australian singer/guitarist/songwriter John Farrar, whom they met on their 1967 tour of Australia when he was in the Strangers, to join them for experimental rehearsals.

Oct ***Shades Of Rock***, a collection of hard-rock oldies recorded earlier in the year by Marvin, Bennett, Hawkshaw and several different bassists, and released as by the Shadows, reaches UK #30.

1971

Jan Having settled as a harmony vocal trio, Marvin, Welch and Farrar debut on Cliff Richard's BBC1-TV show, appearing five times in the series.

Mar The trio, backed by Bennett on drums and Dave Richmond on bass, tours Germany, Switzerland and the Benelux countries, and includes several Shadows tracks in its act due to audience demand.

Apr ***Marvin, Welch And Farrar*** reaches UK #30, and includes *Faithful*. The Welch and Farrar produced Olivia Newton-John single, *If Not For You*, hits UK #7.

Nov Marvin, Welch and Farrar's ***Second Opinion*** is released.

Dec The trio, with Bennett, supports Cliff Richard on a UK tour.

1972

Mar Newton-John breaks off her engagement to Welch, which shatters him emotionally, leading to a reported suicide attempt.
Sept Marvin and Farrar, continuing as a duo and backed by Hawkshaw (keyboards), Rostill and Bennett, tour the Far East with Newton-John and Richard.

1973

Apr Marvin and his wife Carole become Jehovah's Witnesses.
Aug ***Hank Marvin And John Farrar*** fails to chart.
Nov Marvin, Welch, Farrar and Bennett record *Turn Around And Touch Me* as the Shadows, marking Welch's return to working life. (He and Newton-John had reconciled in April, then parted again in June, by mutual consent.)
[26] Rostill, who played in Las Vegas, NV with Tom Jones, but returned to Britain to work, dies from accidental electrocution while playing guitar in his home studio. Welch, who has been writing songs with him, discovers his body when he arrives for a demo session.

1974

Apr ***Rockin' With Curly Leads***, recorded by Marvin, Welch, Farrar and Bennett, with Alan Tarney playing bass, as the Shadows, reaches UK #45. Welch releases *Please Mr. Please*, co-penned with Rostill.
May The group's 11-year-old compilation album, ***The Shadows' Greatest Hits***, is reissued in stereo and re-charts at UK #48.
Aug Bennett joins Georgie Fame's band, the Blue Flames, on drums for a UK tour.
Oct At a charity concert at the London Palladium, the Shadows' appearance (meant as a one-off) prompts BBC-TV boss Bill Cotton Jr. to ask them to represent Britain in the 1975 "Eurovision Song Contest", prompting the group to play a few UK concerts to regain the feel of live performance together. Brian Goode from Peter Gormley's office becomes their manager.

1975

Mar [22] The Shadows perform *Let Me Be The One* in the "Eurovision Song Contest" in Stockholm, Sweden, to a TV audience of 300 million. It is beaten into second place by Dutch group Teach-In, with *Ding-A-Dong*.
Apr [5] *Let Me Be The One* peaks at UK #12 (one place above Teach-In). ***Specs Appeal***, containing the six Eurovision songs from which the UK entry was selected on BBC1-TV, and other new material, reaches UK #30. A demand for more product, following all the recent TV publicity, prompts the recording of a live album at the Olympia Theatre in Paris (intended as this line-up's final concert).
Nov ***Live At The Paris Olympia*** is released.

1976

May *It'll Be Me Babe* is issued. Farrar moves to the US to write produce and write for Olivia Newton-John, while Welch produces Cliff Richard on *Miss You Nights* and *Devil Woman*.
Aug Bennett travels to Russia as Richard's drummer, on a pioneering tour of the USSR by a major Western rock act.

1977

Feb [19] Compilation album, ***20 Golden Greats***, promoted via an acclaimed TV ad involving young lads doing the Shadows' high kicks with cricket bat "guitars", is the group's first UK Top 10 album for nine years, topping the UK chart for the first of six weeks, and becoming the group's biggest seller, with over a million copies sold.
Mar Signed as a soloist to DJM Records (owned by publisher Dick James), Bennett releases the concept album, ***Rock Dreams***, on which Cliff Richard guests.
May The group plays a rapturously-received "20 Golden Dates" UK tour to follow up the hits album, with Alan Jones on bass and Francis Monkman on keyboards
Aug Marvin wins the CBS Arbiter Award for services to British music, with fellow guitarists Joe Brown and Bert Weedon.
Sept ***Tasty***, an album of new Shadows material, is released.
Nov Recruiting several noted guitarists, Marvin issues ***The Hank Marvin Guitar Syndicate***.

1978

Feb Cliff Richard and the Shadows reunite for a series of London Palladium concerts to mark their 20th anniversary, subsequently chronicled on film (for TV) and record as ***Thank You Very Much***.
Apr Bennett releases his second DJM album, ***Voyage***, sub-titled "A Journey Into Discoid Funk".
Aug *Love Deluxe* is released by the Shadows.
Sept The group undertakes a UK tour, with Jones again on bass, and ex-Cliff Richard band member Cliff Hall on keyboards.

1979

Jan *Don't Cry For Me Argentina*, their instrumental version of Julie Covington's #1 hit from the Tim Rice/Andrew Lloyd Webber musical, "Evita", is the Shadows' first Top 10 single since 1965, hitting UK #5.
June *Theme From The Deer Hunter (Cavatina)*, in competition with John Williams' solo guitar version (which makes #13), hits UK #9.

1980

Mar [1] ***String Of Hits***, after several months on the chart, hits UK #1 for the first of three weeks, following a TV ad campaign, while *Riders In The Sky*, a disco-flavored revival of the Ramrods' 1961 hit, makes UK #12. The group's recording contract with EMI expires, and is not renewed when the company fails to agree to the Shadows recording independently and leasing the results. Polydor signs a three-year contract with the band's newly-formed production company, Rollover Records, to release three albums.
Aug Compilation album, ***Another String Of Hot Hits***, makes UK #16, while the group's first Polydor release, a cover of Jean-Michel Jarre's *Equinoxe, Part 5*, reaches UK #50.
Sept ***Change Of Address*** reaches UK #17.

1981

May Their revival of Anton Karas' film theme, *The Third Man*, peaks at UK #44, and is the last Shadows hit single of the decade.
Oct ***Hits Right Up Your Street*** reaches UK #15, following a UK tour to promote the album.

1982

Mar Marvin's solo set, ***Words And Music***, makes UK #66, while the extracted *Don't Talk* reaches UK #49.
Oct Double album, ***Life In The Jungle/Live At Abbey Road***, on which the second disc features a session cut before a live studio audience, reaches UK #24.

1983

May [5] The group is presented with the Special Award For 25 Years In The Music Business at the 28th annual Ivor Novello Awards, held at the Grosvenor House Hotel, London.
Oct ***XXV***, celebrating the group's 25th anniversary, makes UK #34. ***Guardian Angel*** will chart for one week at UK #98 in November the following year.

1986

Mar [29] *Living Doll*, a new charity fund-raising version by Cliff Richard and comedy team the Young Ones of Richard's 1959 chart-topper, featuring Marvin reprising his original guitar contribution, hits UK #1.
May ***Moonlight Shadows*** hits UK #6. ***Simply Shadows*** will make UK #11 on Dec [5] the following year.

1988

Oct Marvin, now living in Australia, will perform at Jean-Michel Jarre's London Docklands open-air concert (a journey which costs the Frenchman a reported £20,000) in October 1988, also guesting on Jarre's UK #52, *London Kid* in January the following year. ***Steppin' To The Shadows*** will reach UK #11 in its week of entry on May [20] the same year with a further compilation, ***At Their Very Best*** reaching UK #12 on Dec [23].

1995

Dec [16] Issued on their own Rollover Record label, ***Reflection*** has hit UK #5 on Oct [27], 1990, followed by ***Themes & Dreams***, UK #21, Nov [23], 1991, Marvin's *We Are The Champions*, featuring Queen's Brian May, UK #66 on Oct [17], 1992, his album ***Into The Light***, UK #18 two weeks later (the same year Harris was banned from driving for three years and fined £120 for drunk driving, at Gloucester City court on May 19th), ***Shadows In The Night***, UK #22, May [15], 1993, Marvin's ***Heartbeat***, UK #17, Dec [25] the same year and ***The Best Of Hank Marvin And The Shadows***, UK #19, Oct [22], 1994. After band members have attended Jerry Lordan's memorial service at London's St. Martin's-in-the-Fields on October 25th earlier this year, Marvin's latest outing, ***Hank Plays Cliff*** now reaches UK #33.
see also: **Cliff RICHARD**

SHALAMAR

Howard Hewett (vocals); **Jody Watley** (vocals); **Jeffrey Daniel** (vocals)

1977

May The group's name is created by producers Dick Griffey and Simon Soussan, to give an identity to *Uptown Festival*, a disco medley incorporating five classic Motown hits, made by session singers and musicians in Los Angeles, CA, which is currently peaking at US #25 and UK #30. It has been released on the Soul Train label, an off-shoot from the Don Cornelius-produced US TV show of the same name, for which Griffey is a talent booker, and is included on ***Uptown Festival***, also cut by sessioneers, which hits US #8 in July.

1978

Nov Having formed his own record label, Solar (Sound Of Los Angeles Records), Griffey has assembled a permanent R&B/disco group to continue as Shalamar, recruiting "Soul Train" dancers Watley (b. Jan. 30, 1959, Chicago, IL), whose godfather is Jackie Wilson, and Daniel (b. Aug. 24, 1955, Los Angeles) and lead singer Gerald Brown. Pairing them with label producer Leon Sylvers III, the dance-oriented ***Disco Gardens*** peaks at US #171.

1979

Jan Co-penned by Sylvers, the extracted *Take That To The Bank* reaches US #79 (R&B #11) and UK #20. Brown leaves and is replaced by Hewett (b. Oct. 1, 1955, Akron, OH), as lead singer.
Nov *The Second Time Around*, from the second Sylvers-produced album, ***Big Fun***, makes UK #45.

1980

Feb *Right In The Socket*, also from the album, peaks at UK #44.
Mar *The Second Time Around* becomes the trio's biggest US success, hitting #9, and selling over one million copies (also topping the US R&B chart, dethroning Michael Jackson's *Rock With You*). ***Big Fun*** makes US #23 and earns a gold disc, Solar's first.
June [13] Daniel marries soul vocalist and star of the Broadway musical "The Wiz", Stephanie Mills. (They will divorce in less than a year.)
Oct *I Owe You One* reaches UK #13.

1981

Feb *Full Of Fire* makes US #55.
Apr *Make That Move* peaks at UK #30.

May Once again helmed by Sylvers III (who is by now creating a Solar sound for other label acts including the Whispers and Dynasty), ***Three For Love*** makes US #40, becoming the group's second gold album. Watley co-writes two tracks and claims on the sleeve notes to "love ... cooking, going to the movies and Michael Jackson". Taken from it, *Make That Move* reaches US #55.
Nov ***Go For It*** peaks at US #115. In addition to four Daniel-penned cuts, it includes a Hewett and James Ingram track, also produced by the pair, *You've Got Me Running*, and features Mills singing on *The Final Analysis*.

1982

May ***Friends*** climbs to US #35, and is Shalamar's third and final US gold album. Extracted from it, *A Night To Remember* makes US #44, while *I Can Make You Feel Good*, the UK excerpt co-penned by Hewett, hits UK #7, and is the first of three consecutive UK Top 10 hits with songs drawn from ***Friends***, which is supported by the "Friends World Tour".
July Co-written and produced by Sylvers, *A Night To Remember* hits UK #5, and is the second dance smash in a run of highly commercial crossover successes.
Sept Premature compilation, ***Greatest Hits***, makes UK #71.
Oct *There It Is* hits UK #5.
Dec Title track, *Friends*, reaches UK #12.

1983

Jan [8] Daniel appears on BBC1-TV show, "Jim'll Fix It", demonstrating the street-dance art of body popping. ***Friends*** peaks at UK #6, having been on the chart for over 40 weeks, while the trio is touring Britain.
July *Dead Giveaway* hits UK #8, taken from ***The Look***, which hits UK #7, its title cut written by Hewett with Stanley Clarke.
Sept *Dead Giveaway* makes US #22, while ***The Look*** reaches US #38.
Nov *Over And Over*, also from ***The Look***, makes UK #23.

1984

Daniel leaves the group, moving to Britain to become the host of a newly-launched C4-TV version of "Soul Train", and to star in the West End in the Andrew Lloyd Webber musical "Starlight Express". Watley also leaves for a solo vocal career, as the Shalamar name continues, with Hewett now joined by Delisa Davis and Micki Free.
Apr Taken from the soundtrack to the film "Footloose", and released on CBS/Columbia, *Dancing In The Sheets* reaches US #17, their most successful US single for over four years, and UK #41, in simultaneous competition with *Deadline USA* (from another movie, "Street Fleet"), which makes UK #52.
Nov [25] Watley takes part in the recording of Band Aid's *Do They Know It's Christmas?* in London.
Dec *Amnesia* peaks at US #73 and UK #61. Shalamar's *Don't Get Stopped In Beverly Hills* is featured in Eddie Murphy's film, "Beverly Hills Cop".

1985

Jan ***Heart Break*** makes US #90, the trio's last album to chart in the US.
Feb *My Girl Loves Me*, from ***Heart Break***, peaks at US #45.
[14] The group begins a short UK tour at London's Dominion Theatre, set to end at the Colston Hall, Bristol, Avon, on March 5th.

1986

Feb Shalamar's *Razzle Dazzle* is featured in the Goldie Hawn movie, "Wildcats". Hewett is arrested outside a Miami shopping centre by FBI agents and charged with four counts of conspiracy to possess cocaine (but is later acquitted).
[25] ***Beverly Hills Cop*** wins Best Album Of Original Score Written For A Motion Picture Or Television Special, at the 28th annual Grammy Awards.
May TV-promoted compilation album, ***The Greatest Hits***, surveying the group's entire chart career, hits UK #5. Meanwhile, a remixed version of their biggest UK hit, *A Night To Remember*, peaks at UK #52, closing the group's UK chart career. Hewett leaves for a solo career, replaced by Sidney Justin, an ex-Los Angeles Rams football player.
Nov [8] Hewett, signed to Elektra, has a minor US hit with *I'm For Real*, on which he is backed by George Duke, Stanley Clarke and Wilton Felder, from his debut solo album, ***I Commit To Love***, which peaks at US #159.

1987

May [2] Signed to MCA as a soloist, Watley hits US #2 for four weeks (behind Cutting Crew's *(I Just) Died In Your Arms* and then U2's *With Or Without You*) with *Looking For A New Love*, which also reaches UK #13, as ***Jody Watley*** hits US #10, and includes a duet with George Michael.
July [11] Watley's *Still A Thrill* makes US #56. Shalamar, now bereft of its hit-making alumni, releases the non-charting ***Circumstantial Evidence***.
Sept [5] ***Jody Watley*** peaks at UK #62.
Oct Watley peaks at UK #55 with *Don't You Want Me*.
Dec [19] *Don't You Want Me* hits US #6.

1988

Mar [2] Now a major US dance/soul star in her own right, Watley wins the Best New Artist category, at the 30th annual Grammy Awards.
Apr [16] Watley's *Some Kind Of Lover* hits US #10.
May Hewett's soul-filled ***Forever And Ever***, including a duet with Dionne Warwick on *Another Chance To Love*, peaks at US #110.
June [4] Watley's *Most Of All* peaks at US #60.

1989

May Hewett contributes *The Ten Commandments Of Love* to the newly-released Richard Perry-produced ***Rock, Rhythm & Blues*** compilation.
[20] Watley hits US #2 with *Real Love* (which has already made UK #31), as her André Cymone-produced album, ***Larger Than Life***, reaches US #16 (and will make UK #39).
June [28] Watley embarks on a US tour in Charleston, NC, set to end on July 27th in Denver, CO.
Aug [26] Watley, with rap inserts from Eric B. & Rakim, hits US #9 and reaches UK #21 with *Friends*.

1990

Jan [6] ***You Wanna Dance With Me?***, a compilation of previously unreleased remixed versions of Watley's hits, makes US #86.
[20] Watley's ballad cut, *Everything*, hits US #4, and peaks at UK #74.
Mar [14] Watley performs at the fourth annual Soul Train Awards at the Shrine Auditorium, Los Angeles.
Apr Daniel, now signed to Epic, releases *She's The Girl*, as the "Jody Watley : Dance To Fitness" video is released.
June [9] Hewett's third solo effort, ***Howard Hewett***, featuring three tracks co-written and produced by ex-Shalamar producer Sylvers, peaks at US #54.
Oct Watley contributes *After You Who* to ***Red Hot + Blue***, an anthology of Cole Porter songs to benefit AIDS education.
Nov [3] ***Rubáiyát***, Elektra's 40th anniversary compilation, to which Hewett has contributed a cover of *I Can't Tell You Why* (subsequently released as a single), makes US #140. (By year's end, Shalamar, still comprising Free, Davis and Justin, return to the recording scene with ***Wake Up***, released on Solar through Epic.)

1996

Feb [13] Largely overtaken by a new generation of R&B stars, Watley and Hewett (her aunt is now married to his brother) have continued to find moderate chart success: Watley's *I Want You* made US #61 on Jan [18], 1992, with ***Affairs Of The Heart*** (with nine of the eleven cuts self-written), shifting away from her dance-diva image, and including six ballads, peaking at US #124 on Feb [8], including the Apr [18] UK #50 and May [16] US #19 peaking *I'm The One You Need*. Her follow-up set, ***Intimacy*** debuted at its US #164 high on Nov [27], 1993, yielding the UK #33 peaking *When A Man Loves A Woman* the following May [21]. Hewett's ***How Fast Forever Goes***, co-produced by Tommy LiPuma and Narada Michael Walden, was released by Elektra in February 1993, while his next set, ***It's Time*** returned him to the chart at US #181 on Feb [25], 1995. With Hewitt signed to Caliber Records in the US and Expansion Records in the UK, MCA now releases the Watley-supervised solo highlights compilation ***Greatest Hits***. (A comprehensive Shalamar retrospective, ***The Collection*** has been issued on CD by Castle Communications in the UK in 1994.)

SHAMEN

Colin Angus (vocals, bass); **Will Sin** (sampling, keyboards)

1987

Sept The band has been formed in 1985 in Scotland by part-time psychiatric nurse and ex-Alone Again Or member Colin Angus (b. Aug. 24, 1961, Aberdeen, Grampian, Scotland), who has been weaned on the music of Pink Floyd, the 13th Floor Elevators and Love, after he left Aberdeen University. Initially including brothers Derek (b. Feb. 27, 1964, Aberdeen) and Keith MacKenzie (b. Aug. 30, 1961, Aberdeen) and Peter Stephenson (b. Mar 1, 1962, Ayr, Strathclyde, Scotland), they have signed to the small Moshka label which has issued two independent singles (*Young 'Til Yesterday* (the previous November) and *Something About You*) and a '60s-influenced debut, ***Drop***, earlier this year. The Shamen now releases *Christopher Mayhew Says*, marking a radical change of direction towards a rock/dance fusion, incorporating sampling and hip-hop rhythms, due not least to the addition of techno whiz Will Sin (b. William Sinnott, Dec. 23, 1960, Glasgow, Strathclyde, Scotland), Angus' friend from Aberdeen.

1988

Apr It is reported that the band is to be dropped from a planned £1 million TV ad campaign for McEwan's Lager, following the group's public comments about the acceptance of drugs and pornography. The company is also apparently unhappy that *Happy Days*, the song to be used in the campaign, is a comment on the Falklands War.
June Signed to the Ediesta label and with the MacKenzies departed, the Shamen, transformed into a fully-fledged techno-dance outfit (from its earlier psychedelic rock beginnings), releases *Jesus Loves Amerika*, showcasing riffling guitars and funky-programmed beats. Angus and Sin, drawn by the burgeoning acid house club scene, relocate to London and spend the summer tripping out at warehouse raves including Dungeons, Phuture, Rip and Spectrum, where they meet future Shamen members "Evil" Eddie Richards and Mr. C.
Nov They release the totally dance-oriented, sequenced and sampled *Transcendental*, on Desire Records, produced by Chicago housemaster Bam Bam, and taken from their second album, ***In Gorbachev We Trust***.

1989

May ***Phorward*** mini-album is released on Moshka, as the band introduces its new "Synergy" plan on a UK tour, incorporating rock gig elements with a club feel, including strobes, projectors and DJs (including Paul Oakenfold, Eddie Richards and Colin Faver), to create a psychedelic, often drug-laced, musical experience.
Oct After much label hopping, the duo settles on the independent One Little Indian, which releases the UK indie hit, *Omega Amigo*.

1990

Mar The Shamen plays a residency at London's T&C 2 Club for their "Synergy" psychedelic music trips, which now incorporate the use of multi-media virtual reality equipment.
Apr *Pro-Gen* is the first Shamen single to feature the rapping DJ Mr. C (aka Richard West), and the first to make the UK chart at #55.
Sept The group's 11th single, *Make It Mine*, makes UK #42.
Nov [3] ***En-Tact***, recorded using state-of-the-art technology, debuts at its UK #31 peak, eventually selling over 100,000 copies.

1991

Apr [20] *Hyperreal*, featuring vocalist Plavka, reaches UK #29. Says Sin: "When we heard (BBC Radio 1 DJ) Simon Bates playing *Hyperreal* every day we knew we'd cracked it."
May [22] Having re-recorded the still in-demand *Pro-Gen*, the duo have travelled to Gomera, Tenerife, to shoot a video. During a filming break, Sin goes swimming, is pulled under by a strong current and drowns. Angus decides to continue with the Shamen, Mr. C being his principal partner in an ever-changing music ensemble based around its leader.
Aug [3] *Move Any Mountain - Pro Gen '91* hits UK #4. The Shamen spends the rest of year taking the "Synergy" follow-up, "Progeny", on the road as its latest live extravaganza.
[31] ***En-tact*** re-charts at UK #45.
Sept [28] ***Progeny*** debuts at its UK #23 peak.

1992

Feb [29] *Move Any Mountain - Pro Gen '91* opens the band's US chart account at #38.
Mar [7] ***En-tact*** climbs to US #138.
Aug [1] *Love Sex Intelligence*, featuring ex-Soul Family Sensation female vocalist Jhelisa Anderson, and Mr. C's rap interjections, hits UK #6.
Sept [19] The group's 15th single release, *Ebeneezer Goode*, widely reported to hail the virtues of the Ecstasy drug, begins a four-week stay at UK #1.
[26] Its parent album, the self-produced ***Boss Drum***, featuring Steve Hillage on guitar, debuts at its UK #3 peak.
Nov [7] *Boss Drum (Remixes)* charts for a week at UK #58.
[14] *Boss Drum* hits UK #4.
Dec [17] The band appears on BBC1-TV's "Top Of The Pops".
[26] *Phorever People* hits UK #5.

1993

Mar [6] *Re:evolution*, narrated by Terence McKenna, debuts at its UK #18 peak.
[8] The group embarks on a 12-date "Progeny V-3.0." UK tour, at the Corn Exchange, Cambridge, Cambs., set to end on the 22nd at the Rivermead Centre, Reading, Berks.
[15] They are featured on BBC2-TV's "Excess Is Not Enough".
May [26] Angus and West are named Songwriters Of The Year at the 38th annual Ivor Novello Awards, at the Grosvenor House Hotel, London.
Nov [13] *The SOS (EP)* reaches UK #14.
[20] ***On Air*** charts for a week at UK #61.

1995

Aug [19] *Destination Eschaton* debuts at its UK #15 peak.
Oct [21] *Transamazonia* peaks at UK #28 in its week of entry.
Nov [4] ***Axis Mutatis*** reaches UK #27 in its week of entry.
[10] Shamen, now comprising Angus, West and new vocalist Victoria Wilson-James, performs an increasingly rare gig at London's Kentish Town Forum, broadcast live over the Internet (at web site : http://www.drci.co.uk/drci/shamen).

1996

Jan [27] They guest on ITV's "It's Not Just Saturday".
Feb [10] *Heal (The Separation)* reaches UK #31 in its week of entry.

THE SHANGRI-LAS

Mary Weiss (lead vocals); **Betty Weiss** (vocals); **Marge Ganser** (vocals); **Mary Ann Ganser** (vocals)

1964

Aug Discovered singing at part-time gigs while still attending Andrew Jackson High School, Cambria Heights, New York, NY, having already been together at the Sacred Heart Grammar School, by George "Shadow" Morton, sisters Betty (b. Elizabeth Weiss) and Mary Weiss, and twins Marge and Mary Ann Ganser, have previously worked briefly with Artie Ripp's Kama Sutra Productions, and recorded *Simon Says*, *Hate To Say I Told You So* and *Wishing Well* for the small Spokane label under the name the Bon Bons, but without chart success. Morton, who has gained the attention of songwriters/producers Jeff Barry and Ellie Greenwich, and promised to deliver them a hit record, has written *Remember (Walkin' In The Sand)* for the group, recorded it as a demo in a Long Island basement studio, and suitably impressed Barry and Greenwich with the result. The duo organizes the signing of both Morton (as a writer and producer) and the newly-renamed Shangri-Las, to Leiber and Stoller's Red Bird label. After coming to an arrangement with Kama Sutra Productions, which still has the girls under contract, Red Bird now releases *Remember (Walkin' In The Sand)*.
Sept [26] Instantly a huge US airplay hit with its offbeat, atmospheric production (including the sounds of ocean and seagulls), *Remember (Walkin' In The Sand)* rockets to US #5, as the group is rushed into a round of TV and live performances for which the older three immediately leave school, leaving Mary Weiss, the youngest, still studying. They also join the bill of a live package at the Brooklyn Fox Theater, New York, with Marvin Gaye, the Searchers and Martha & the Vandellas.
Oct [22] The three-piece group arrives in London for a promotional trip, as the single begins climbing the UK chart. (TV shows "Thank Your Lucky Stars", "Ready Steady, Go!" and "The Eamonn Andrews Show" ban the group from singing their new single, *Leader Of The Pack*.) On the girls' return to the US, Betty Weiss leaves, and sister Mary leaves school to replace her, taking the lead vocal slot. (During the two years of regular road work which follow the initial success, the girls will regularly permutate three out of four, leaving and returning to replace each other, and rarely appearing as more than a trio.)
Nov [21] *Remember (Walkin' In The Sand)* reaches UK #14.
[28] *Leader Of The Pack*, written by Morton, Barry and Greenwich, tops the US chart for one week, becoming a million seller, and the definitive "teen-death" record (storyline: girl meets boy, parents disapprove, boy dies on motorbike). This time the sound effects are of a revving motorbike, brought into the studio by its owner, recording engineer Joey Veneri.
Dec The Shangri-Las take part in Murray The K's "Big Holiday Show" in New York.

1965

Jan Ron Dante, under the name the Detergents, hits with a parody of *Leader Of The Pack* titled *Leader Of The Laundromat*, which reaches US #19, as the Shangri-Las' own follow-up, *Give Him A Great Big Kiss*, climbs to US #18, and the girls' simultaneously-issued revival of the Chantels' *Maybe* makes US #91.
Feb [13] Despite a BBC radio ban because of the nature of its lyric, *Leader Of The Pack* reaches UK #11.
Mar *Leader Of The Pack* (with dubbed audience noise on side two to sound like a live concert by the group) peaks at US #109.
Apr The group tours the US on Dick Clark's "Caravan Of Stars", with Del Shannon, Tommy Roe, the Zombies and others.
May *Out In The Streets* peaks at US #53.
July *Give Us Your Blessings*, a return to the story-song formula (this time with boy and girl both dying), reaches US #29.
Oct *Right Now And Not Later*, an uncharacteristic Motown pastiche, peaks at US #99. Their sophomore album, ***Shangri-Las '65***, is also released.
Dec *I Can Never Go Home Anymore*, a return to the group's expected melodrama (this time a mother dies after a daughter's indifference), hits US #6. The second album is reissued with this as the new title.

1966

Mar *Long Live Our Love* makes US #33.
May *He Cried*, a gender-switched revival of Jay & the Americans' 1961 hit, *She Cried*, returns to melodrama, but peaks at US #65.
July *Past, Present And Future*, a spoken narration by Mary Weiss accompanied by Beethoven's "Moonlight Sonata", peaks at US #59, and will be the group's last US hit. (The Red Bird label folds a few weeks later following the release of ***I Can Never Go Home Anymore***, and the group will move to Mercury Records, which will also lease the back-catalog to compile a ***Greatest Hits*** collection. Further singles, including *The Sweet Sounds Of Summer*, will appear on Mercury, but without chart success. The girls will continue to tour, but for a while are denied the Shangri-Las name because of legal wrangles over its ownership.

1971

After a lengthy hiatus, the trio begins to play oldies tours of the US (though during the year Mary Ann dies of encephalitis). On Nov [18] the following year, *Leader Of The Pack* is reissued in the UK by Kama Sutra which still co-owns its rights, and despite being slightly edited from the original, it hits #3, now unhindered by radio bans. It will be re-released in Britain yet again in July 1976, simultaneously on the Charly and Contempo labels, due to a non-exclusive licensing situation. Combined sales of both releases take it to UK #7.

1989

June [3] Following the January 1984-premiering musical "Leader Of The Pack", based around the songs of Ellie Greenwich, which played at the Bottom Line in Greenwich Village, New York,
the Shangri-Las (minus Marge Ganser who has died of an accidental drug overdose in 1976) reunites for Cousin Brucie's "First Palisades Amusement Park Reunion", at the Meadowlands, East Rutherford, NJ. Also on the bill are Little Anthony, Lesley Gore, Freddy Cannon, the Tokens and Bobby Rydell. (Despite winning a court case which prevents a bogus Shangri-Las from touring, the current official line-up does not comprise any original members, and will continue to appear on nostalgia package tours in the US into the mid-'90s.)

DEL SHANNON

1960

Shannon (b. Charles Weedon Westover, Dec. 30, 1934, Coopersville, MI), having begun singing and playing guitar in high school, then entertained in the Special Services, including several months in the "Get Up And Go" forces radio show in West Germany, when drafted into the military, becomes resident guitarist and vocalist in the band of the Hi-Lo club in Battle Creek, MI, by night, working as a carpet salesman by day. He collaborates on songs with the band's keyboard player, Max Crook, and their promising sound and original material catches the ear of DJ Ollie McLaughlin, on radio station WGRV in nearby Ann Arbor, MI. He introduces Shannon and Crook to Detroit entrepreneurs Harry Balk and Irving Micahnik, who sign Shannon to their Embee Productions, and arrange recording sessions in New York, NY via a deal with Big Top Records. After an unexciting first session, Shannon and Crook write *Runaway*, which is considered by Big Top as commercial enough to be issued as Shannon's first single.

1961

Apr [24] *Runaway* tops the US chart for the first of four weeks. Crook plays the song's instrumental break on a patented high-pitched electronic keyboard called a musitron, and this arresting sound is a major factor in the record's success, which will be repeated worldwide.

July [1] *Runaway* begins a three-week run atop the UK chart, selling half a million copies.

Aug *Hats Off To Larry*, another self-composed song in similar *Runaway* style and arrangement (with a second hook-laden musitron solo by Crook), hits US #5.

Oct *So Long Baby*, an uptempo rocker with the musitron replaced by a kazoo solo, reaches US #28.

[28] *Hats Off To Larry* hits UK #6.

Nov His debut album, ***Runaway With Del Shannon*** is released.

Dec *Hey! Little Girl* makes US #38.

1962

Jan [13] *So Long Baby* hits UK #10.

May [5] *Hey! Little Girl* hits UK #2. The UK B-side is *You Never Talked About Me*, which Shannon sings in a cameo slot in the UK pop/jazz movie, "It's Trad, Dad" (US title: "Ring-A-Ding-Rhythm").

June *Cry Myself To Sleep*, his first recording in Nashville, TN, with vocal backing by the Jordanaires, peaks at US #99.

Sept [16] Shannon begins his first UK tour, with Dion.

Oct [1] Shannon embarks on further UK dates, with Freddy Cannon and Buzz Clifford, at the Ritz, Huddersfield, Yorks.

[6] *Cry Myself To Sleep* reaches UK #29.

[13] Another Nashville recording, *The Swiss Maid*, written by Roger Miller, and featuring Shannon yodelling, makes US #64.

Dec [1] *The Swiss Maid* hits UK #2 (behind Frank Ifield's *Lovesick Blues*).

1963

Feb *Little Town Flirt* hits US #12 and UK #4.

Apr [20] Shannon begins a UK tour with Johnny Tillotson, Dusty Springfield and Jimmie Rodgers in Taunton, Somerset, enthusing to the nation's press about the new music boom sweeping the country, and particularly about the Beatles, whose material he (as a songwriter) rates highly.

May *Two Kinds Of Teardrops* reaches US #50. ***Hats Off To Del Shannon***, a UK compilation of A and B-sides, hits UK #9.

[9] Shannon plays a concert at London's Royal Albert Hall with the Beatles, and suggests covering one of Lennon and McCartney's hits to help give them more exposure in the US.

[18] *Two Kinds Of Teardrops* hits UK #5.

July Returning home, Shannon's version of the Beatles' recent UK chart-topper, *From Me To You*, makes US #77 - the first Lennon/McCartney song to chart Stateside - while ***Little Town Flirt*** reaches US #12.

Sept [21] *Two Silhouettes*, the US B-side of *From Me To You*, is a UK A-side and reaches #23.

Oct [4] Shannon begins another UK tour with Gerry & the Pacemakers and Jet Harris & Tony Meehan, at the Odeon Cinema, Lewisham, London, set to end on November 4th.

Nov Attempting to sever ties with Balk and Micahnik after disagreements over royalties and other business practices, Shannon forms his own label, Berlee Records, and issues the Four Seasons-influenced *Sue's Gotta Be Mine*, which reaches US #71 and UK #21. ***Little Town Flirt***, belatedly released in the UK, makes #15.

1964

Apr [4] *Mary Jane*, a US non-charter, climbs to UK #35.

Aug Shannon moves to New York-based Amy Records for a high-tempo revival of Jimmy Jones' 1960 million seller, *Handy Man*, which makes US #22 and UK #36.

Sept He plays on an all-star bill, with Jan & Dean, Chuck Berry and headliners the Animals, at the Paramount Theater, Brooklyn, New York.

Oct *Do You Want To Dance?*, revived in identical style to *Handy Man*, peaks at US #43.

1965

Jan Shannon hits US #9 after a three-year Top 10 absence with *Keep Searchin' (We'll Follow The Sun)*. ***Handy Man*** is released.

Feb [13] *Keep Searchin' (We'll Follow The Sun)* hits UK #3 (as Peter & Gordon's cover of Shannon's *I Go To Pieces* hits US #9).

[27] Shannon begins a 21-date, twice-nightly UK package tour, with Wayne Fontana & the Mindbenders, Herman's Hermits and others, at the City Hall, Sheffield, S. Yorks, set to close on March 22nd at the Odeon Cinema, Glasgow, Scotland.

Mar *Stranger In Town* reaches US #30 and UK #40.

May *Break Up* peaks at US #95. His tribute album to the country legend, ***Del Shannon Sings Hank Williams*** is released.

June Shannon turns down a request from songwriter Tommy Boyce to record *Action*, the theme song to the new Dick Clark US TV series, "Where The Action Is". (Freddy Cannon makes US #13 with his version in September.)

Sept Titled after the length of the album, ***1,661 Seconds With Del Shannon*** is issued. During the year, Shannon makes a cameo appearance in the movie "Daytona Beach Weekend". The following year, his next album, ***This Is My Bag*** will be released.

1967

Feb [19] Promoting his latest outing, the covers album ***Total Commitment***, Shannon performs at London's Saville Theatre with Chuck Berry. Having moved from Michigan to Los Angeles, CA, and signed a new deal with Liberty the previous year (his revival of Toni Fisher's *The Big Hurt* being his only hit on the label, peaking at US #94 in May 1966), Shannon records extensively for Liberty in the UK, with Andrew Oldham producing. Intended as an album, the completed tracks mostly sit on the shelf for more than a decade.

1969

Oct Having released ***The Further Adventures Of Charles Westover*** the previous July, and leaving Liberty, Shannon is now producing other acts rather than seeking a new deal for himself. His first production success is with the group Smith, whose Shannon-arranged revival of the Shirelles' *Baby It's You* hits US #5.

1970

Nov Shannon has produced Brian Hyland, a long-time friend, on a revival of the Impressions' *Gypsy Woman*, which hits US #3 and becomes a million seller. Shannon's ***Live In England***, a recording of a concert in Manchester, from his UK tour in 1972, will be released in June 1973. Further occasional recordings during the decade will include the Dave Edmunds produced *And The Music Plays On*, also recorded in Britain and issued in October 1974, and a his cover version of the Zombies' *Tell Her No* for Island Records the following May. A second Island single, *Cry Baby Cry*, recorded in collaboration with Jeff Lynne of the Electric Light Orchestra, is released in August the same year. ***And The Music Plays On***, combining the Edmunds-produced title track from 1974 with unreleased tracks cut with Oldham in 1967, will emerge in March 1978, while Shannon is struggling with alcoholism.

1979

Feb [3] He plays a nostalgia show at the Surf Ballroom, Clear Lake, IA, to mark the 20th anniversary of the final performances by Buddy Holly, Ritchie Valens and The Big Bopper. Also playing are the Drifters and Jimmy Clanton (who was on the "Winter Dance Party" tour of 1959).

1982

Jan Something of a comeback album, ***Drop Down And Get Me***, produced by Tom Petty, featuring the Heartbreakers and released on Elektra Records, reaches US #123.

Feb The extracted revival of Phil Phillips' *Sea Of Love* is Shannon's first US Singles chart entry for 15 years, peaking at US #33.

Luis Cardenas, ex-Los Angeles band Renegade, revives *Runaway* at US #83 in October 1986, with Shannon and Donny Osmond taking cameo roles in Cardenas' promotional video.

Performing occasionally during the rest of the decade, Shannon tours Britain in May 1988 on a nostalgic package with his contemporaries Bobby Vee and Brian Hyland.

1990

Feb [3] He performs at the annual Buddy Holly memorial concert in Fargo, ND.

[8] Shannon dies from a self-inflicted gunshot wound, from a .22-caliber rifle at his Santa Clarita Valley, CA home. (Having been prescibed the controversial anti-depressant drug, Prozac prior to his death, his widow will begin litigation against the drug's makers the following year.)

1991

Mar *Rock On!* is belatedly released by Petty's Gone Gator label in the US (and by Silvertone Records in the UK), the fruits of his second collaboration with Petty and Jeff Lynne, recorded shortly before his death. It includes the single, *Walk Away*, written by all three, and featuring their combined efforts at "slapping thighs". (US retrospective label Rhino Records will begin re-issuing early career material on compact disc the following year beginning with ***Greatest Hits***, while UK vault specialist label Castle will bring his '60s hits to CD on ***Looking Back : His Biggest Hits*** in July.)

HELEN SHAPIRO

1961

Jan Having begun writing songs with her primary school friend Susan Heckman at the age of nine and already sung with her brother Ron's Trad Jazz Band at 13, Shapiro (b. Sept. 28, 1946, Bethnal Green, London) is still attending Clapton Park Comprehensive School and taking weekly vocal classes at the Maurice Berman Singing Academy in Baker Street, London, when EMI producer John Schroeder hears her and is impressed by her deep, mature voice and phrasing. He arranges a demo session, recording *The Birth Of The Blues*, and EMI's Columbia label A&R head, Norrie Paramor (who initially refuses to believe he is listening to a 14-year-old girl on the demo), signs her to a recording contract.

May [13] Schroeder has written *Don't Treat Me Like A Child* for her debut and, aided by radio and TV slots (including Saturday night's prime time "Thank Your Lucky Stars"), it hits UK #3.

Aug [12] *You Don't Know*, a mid-tempo Schroeder/Mike Hawker ballad, in contrast to its bouncy teen-beat predecessor, tops the UK chart for the first of three weeks, selling 40,000 copies in a day at its peak. (It also becomes a major hit in many other territories, and worldwide sales will top one million by the end of the year.)

Sept [28] She celebrates her birthday establishing a UK performing record: the first female to make over a dozen radio and TV appearances before the age of 15. This also marks the end of school for her, and the beginning of a schedule of live appearances which takes in a short London Palladium season, and several European tours.

Oct [21] From the same writing team, the teen rocker *Walkin' Back To Happiness*, released with advance orders of 300,000, has hit the UK Top 10, while *You Don't Know* is still resident, and now tops the chart for the first of three weeks, before surrendering to Elvis Presley's *His Latest Flame*.

Dec *Walkin' Back To Happiness* spends a week at #100 on the US chart, regarded as a major achievement for a UK girl singer at this time, with worldwide sales again topping one million. Shapiro is voted Top UK Female Singer in the annual **New Musical Express** Readers' Poll. This success gives her some leeway to follow her own inclinations over material, and she releases a four-track EP of standards, from which *Goody Goody* gains considerable airplay, and tops the UK EP survey.

1962

Jan [15] Her UK tour begins at the Granada Cinema, East Ham, London.

Mar [24] Shapiro just fails to achieve three consecutive UK #1 singles - a feat never achieved by a female performer or a UK act to date - as *Tell Me What He Said*, a US song written by Jeff Barry, peaks at UK #2, held off by the Shadows' *Wonderful Land*.

Apr Her maiden album, ***Tops With Me***, a collection of personal favorite oldies including *Lipstick On Your Collar* and *Will You Love Me Tomorrow?*, hits UK #2. She also has a lead role, opposite Craig Douglas, in the UK pop/jazz movie, "It's Trad, Dad" (US title : "Ring-A-Ding Rhythm"), which is a UK box office success.

May Soundtrack album, ***It's Trad, Dad***, on which she sings *Let's Talk About Love* (a concurrent UK #23) and *Sometime Yesterday*, hits UK #3.

Aug [4] *Little Miss Lonely*, her first ballad on single (and a return to Schroeder/Hawker material) hits UK #8, but will be her last major single success. Meanwhile, she makes a cameo appearance in the Billy Fury film, "Play It Cool", singing *Cry My Heart Out* and *But I Don't Care*.

Oct [27] *Keep Away From Other Girls*, a Bacharach/Hilliard song, originally cut in the US by Babs Tino, makes UK #40.

Nov [9] Shapiro begins another UK tour with Eden Kane and the Vernons Girls as support acts, at the Ritz Cinema, Belfast, Northern Ireland, set to end on December 16th at the Odeon Cinema, Colchester, Essex.

1963

Jan [27] She makes her fourth appearance on ITV's "Sunday Night At The London Palladium".

Feb [2] She begins a further UK trek, opening at the Gaumont Cinema, Bradford, Yorks, set to close on March 2nd at the Gaumont Cinema, Hanley, Staffs. The Beatles are among the supporting acts, and Lennon and McCartney tell her that their song, *Misery*, was written for her, but rejected by Paramor.

[16] *Queen For Tonight* makes UK #33.

Mar [14] Shapiro takes part in the "Top Of The Pops" concert at London's Royal Albert Hall, with Mark Wynter, Craig Douglas and Vince Hill.

Apr ***Helen's Sixteen*** (referring both to her age and its number of tracks) fails to chart.

May [11] *Woe Is Me*, recorded at her first US sessions, in Nashville, TN, the previous month, reaches UK #35. (She also cuts *It's My Party*, though the planned release is cancelled when Lesley Gore's version appears.)

June [28] Shapiro opens a 10-week season at the Aquarium, Great Yarmouth, Norfolk.

July *Not Responsible*, another Nashville recording, is her first single not to chart in Britain.

Nov [2] *Look Who It Is* makes UK #47, while ***Helen In Nashville***, from the sessions earlier in the year, fails to chart.

1964

Jan [25] Her update of Peggy Lee's *Fever* reaches UK #38, her final hit single. She is one of a large generation of immediately pre-beat boom stars whose styles are now out of public fashion.

Mar [7] Shapiro begins a five-week Far East tour of Japan, Malaysia and the Philippines in Hong Kong.

Nov Doctors advise Shapiro not to sing for a month.

1965

Feb [10] She embarks on a nine-day tour of Poland.

May [24] After four unsuccessful singles, Shapiro sings *Here In My Arms* in the "British Song Festival" at the Dome, Brighton, Sussex, but even TV coverage fails to help it score.

July [17] Shapiro guests on the 200th edition of ITV's "Thank Your Lucky Stars", with the Searchers, Dusty Springfield and others.

Sept She is again advised by doctors not to sing before an operation to remove an enlarged thyroid gland.

[24] Shapiro goes into a Harley Street Nursing home for surgery.

1967

May [2] She begins an eight-date twice-nightly UK/Irish tour, headlined by the Beach Boys with Simon Dupree & the Big Sound, Terry Reid with Peter Jay's Jaywalkers, the Nite People and the Marionettes, at the Adelphi Cinema, Dublin, Eire, set to close on May 10th, at the ABC Theatre, Edinburgh, Scotland.

July [24] Shapiro makes her straight-acting theater debut in the farce, "I'll Get My Man" at the Ashton Pavilion, St. Anne's, Lancs.

1968

With UK hits long gone, but still finding plenty of live work, particularly overseas, she switches labels from Columbia to Pye (re-joining John Schroeder, who has made the same move), and has a near-chartmaker with *Today Has Been Cancelled*.

1970

Shapiro begins a successful career in cabaret work and on the London West End stage in musicals like "The French Have A Word For It" and, in 1979, a new production of "Oliver", in which she plays Nancy. During the decade, she also cuts one-off singles for Phoenix, DJM, Magnet and Arista, including Russ Ballard's *Can't Break The Habit*.

1983

Sept Having attended the 50th birthday party of Abbey Road Studios in November 1981,

and newly signed to Oval Records, a label with a reputation for artistic freedom, she records her first album in almost two decades, ***Straighten Up And Fly Right***, with mature versions of standards and personal favorites. The **New Musical Express** gives a rave review to her *Cry Me A River* and BBC Radio 2 plays the album extensively. She showcases the material on stage in a series of dates at Fairfield Halls, Croydon, Surrey. The following year, she will collaborate with jazzman Humphrey Lyttelton and his band, jointly recording ***Echoes Of The Duke***, a tribute to Duke Ellington.

1991

Mar [30] With a 20-track EMI compilation, ***Helen Shapiro 25th Anniversary Album***, celebrating her quarter-century of recording, having been released in 1986 during a decade in which she continued a busy career in cabaret and stage musicals, and began devoting part of her scheduling to gospel concert performances, Shapiro now teams with Cliff Richard for a gospel music event at London's Royal Albert Hall.

SANDIE SHAW

1964

Apr Shaw (b. Sandra Goodrich, Feb. 26, 1947, Dagenham, Essex) is working as an IBM machine operator and singing in her spare time, when she talks her way back-stage at an Adam Faith and the Roulettes one-nighter, impressing them with an impromptu vocal demonstration. Their manager, Eve Taylor, is only marginally enamored, but sees potential in her style, and signs her to a management contract, re-naming her Sandie Shaw.

July After recording demos with producer Tony Hatch, Shaw is signed to Pye Records, and debuts with *As Long As You're Happy*.

Oct [3] Shaw records a Beatles-topped episode of ABC-TV's "Shindig" from the Granville Theatre in Fulham, London, singing her chart-climbing *(There's) Always Something There To Remind Me*.

[24] Her cover of Lou Johnson's US hit, *(There's) Always Something There To Remind Me*, written by Bacharach and David, tops the UK chart where it will stay for three weeks, deposing Roy Orbison's *Oh, Pretty Woman*. Shaw is immediately seen on several UK TV spots and gains as much notoriety from the fact that she always sings barefoot, as from her hit single. (The bare feet are a gimmick dreamed up by Taylor, who predicts that this will be a source of interest for the press. Shaw continues to sing barefoot on stage for several years.)

Dec *(There's) Always Something There To Remind Me*, released in the US on Reprise Records, peaks at US #52 (Johnson's version had made #49 on October 3rd).

1965

Jan [23] Her third single is *I'd Be Far Better Off Without You*, written by Chris Andrews, but several reviewers and DJs note that its B-side, *Girl Don't Come*, is the stronger song, prompting Pye to flip sides with the latter hitting UK #3.

Feb [21] She makes her concert debut, supporting Faith at De Montfort Hall, Leicester, Leics., at the start of a UK tour.

Mar [13] *I'll Stop At Nothing*, written by Andrews for Faith, but given to Shaw instead, hits UK #4, while her maiden album, ***Sandie***, hits UK #3, proving to be her only UK charting long-player.

Apr *Girl Don't Come* makes US #42, her biggest US chart success. She attempts to visit the US for promotion, but is refused a performing visa by US immigration authorities because of the deluge of UK acts currently enjoying Stateside success. She is deemed "not of sufficiently distinguished ability", and a projected season at New York, NY's Paramount Theater is cancelled. Instead, Shaw makes a short promotional visit to Canada.

May [29] Another Andrews composition, *Long Live Love* (rhythmically reminiscent of Tom Jones' *It's Not Unusual*, a UK chart-topper two months earlier, which Shaw had turned down) is her second UK #1, for the first of three weeks.

June She is finally allowed into the US and appears on CBS-TV's "The Ed Sullivan Show", singing *Long Live Love* (which peaks at US #97 two weeks later, and is her final US chart entry). ***Sandie Shaw*** anchors at US #100.

Aug [18] Shaw guests on the premiere of the ITV series, "Ladybirds".

[19] She embarks on a tour of Australasia.

Sept Shaw falls ill with laryngitis for the second time in a month, and cancels live dates.

Oct [6-26] Shaw plays a three-week season at the Paris Olympia, France, with Richard Anthony.

[23] *Message Understood*, also Andrews-penned, hits UK #6.

Nov *Me* is released, but fails to chart. She makes her cabaret debut at London's Savoy Hotel, backed by the Paramounts, faring moderately well through a three-week stint after a disastrous opening night.

Dec [4] *How Can You Tell* reaches UK #21.

1966

Feb [19] *Tomorrow* hits UK #9. She is given the chance to record the theme song to the forthcoming Michael Caine film, "Alfie", as the follow-up, but Taylor rejects it. (The song will be a hit for Cilla Black

in the UK, and Cher in the US.)
[18] Shaw begins a European tour in Bordeaux, France.
Apr Low-priced compilation, ***The Golden Hits Of Sandie Shaw***, anthologizes her hit singles to date.
June [4] *Nothing Comes Easy* reaches UK #14.
July She performs at the "Venice Song Festival" in Venice, Italy.
Sept [24] *Run* peaks at UK #32, during a year in which Shaw concentrates on Europe.
Dec [3] *Think Sometimes About Me* also reaches UK #32.

1967

Jan [21] Shaw sings the first of the "A Song For Europe" entries for the upcoming "Eurovision Song Contest" on "The Rolf Harris Show", as *I Don't Need Anything* charts for a week at UK #50.
Mar She is named as the "other woman" in a widely-publicized divorce case, with the judge delivering a public reprimand.
[30] Shaw performs on BBC1-TV's "Top Of The Pops".
Apr [8] Shaw represents Britain in the "Eurovision Song Contest" in Vienna, Austria, with Bill Martin and Phil Coulter's *Puppet On A String*. The song wins, with 47 points, more than twice as many as the second placed act, Sean Dunphy's *If I Could Choose*, representing Eire. It is the UK's first win after coming second five times.
[29] *Puppet On A String* tops the UK chart, where it will stay for three weeks, eventually selling over 500,000 copies. It also becomes her biggest international success, with sales in West Germany exceeding 750,000, and a worldwide total estimated at four million. The success brings a flood of work offers from all over Europe and elsewhere.
June [14-17] Shaw represents Britain in the second "Bratislava International Festival of Pop Music" in Czechoslovakia.
July [22] Martin and Coulter-penned *Tonight In Tokyo* reaches UK #21.
[26] Shaw begins a cabaret season in Italy followed by a similar stint in the South of France until August 21st.
Nov [11] *You've Not Changed*, written by Andrews, reaches UK #18.
[13] Shaw appears in the "Royal Variety Show" in London.
Dec Despite the year's singles successes, her album, ***Love Me, Please Love Me***, fails to chart.

1968

Feb *Today* reaches UK #27.
[28] Shaw celebrates her 21st birthday with a party in the Chamber of Horrors in Madame Tussaud's, London.
Mar [6] She marries fashion designer Jeff Banks, in London.
Apr *Don't Run Away* is Shaw's first since her debut single not to make the UK Top 50. (*Show Me* in June, and a cover of Nilsson's *Together* in August, will fare similarly.)
Sept She covers Mary Hopkin's debut, *Those Were The Days*, and sings it on BBC1-TV's "Top Of The Pops". The Hopkin version, gaining radio play and promotion, shared with the Beatles' *Hey Jude* and the launch of Apple Records, hits UK #1 while Shaw's remains outside chart ranks.
Nov BBC1-TV musical series, "The Sandie Shaw Supplement", proves popular, and yields ***The Sandie Shaw Supplement***.

1969

Apr [5] *Monsieur Dupont* is a notable, albeit short-lived, UK singles chart comeback, hitting #6.
May [24] *Think It All Over* makes UK #42 (and will be Shaw's last hit single for 15 years).

1970

Feb [23] Shaw attends Prime Minister Harold Wilson's reception for West Germany's Chancellor Willy Brandt, at 10 Downing Street, London. In 1971 she will release two cover singles, Lynn Anderson's *Rose Garden* and Cat Stevens' *Father And Son*, which marks the end of her contract with Pye.

1977

June After five years with no record releases, concentrating on cabaret and overseas work, plus straight theater roles (in Shaw's "St. Joan" and Shakespeare's "Hamlet"), she has signed to CBS Records, which issues *One More Night* and the follow-up, *Your Mama Wouldn't Like It*. (No album is recorded before this deal lapses, and she will disappear from the recording scene for another five years.)

1983

May Having contributed *Anyone Who Had A Heart* to Heaven 17's British Electric Foundation cover versions project, ***Music Of Quality And Distinction*** released the previous April, ***Choose Life***, and the extracted *Wish I Was*, are now released on Palace Records, in association with the World Peace Exposition, is a Buddhist-inspired self-written set. (Shaw is now married to Nik Powell, boss of the Palace record, film and video group.)

1984

May Her revival of the Smiths' first single, *Hand In Glove*, recorded with the group, and released on Rough Trade (to which the band is signed), charts at UK #27. (Smiths' lead singer Morrissey is a long-time Sandie Shaw fan, and has satisfied a personal ambition by working with her and having her record one of his compositions.) On December 19th the following year, Shaw will take part in Carol Aid, an all-star Christmas carol service held at London's Heaven club, to raise money for Band Aid, along with Cliff Richard, Lulu and Chris De Burgh.

1986

June After several years of mainly domestic life, and now signed to Polydor, Shaw's revival of Lloyd Cole & the Commotions' *Are You Ready To Be Heartbroken?* peaks at UK #68, as she undertakes a successful university tour.
July [12-20] She performs during the "Festival Of The Tenth Summer" in Manchester, Gtr. Manchester.

1988

Sept Shaw has signed to Rough Trade for ***Hello Angel***. With musical assistance from George Michael's bassist Deon Estus, the Communards' Richard Coles and the Pretenders' Chrissie Hynde (who plays harmonica on *Nothing Less Than Brilliant*), it features songs written by the Jesus & Mary Chain, Fairground Attraction's Mark Nevin, Clive Langer and Morrissey, with new collaborator Stephen Street. Morrissey and producer Street's song, *Please Help The Cause Against Loneliness*, has previewed the album's release.

1991

May [9] Harper Collins publishes her autobiography, **The World At My Feet**.
Oct [17] Shaw is arrested for failing to provide a breath specimen outside her Harley Street flat in London, and is escorted to Tottenham Court Road police station by P.C. Thomas Nicholls. (In 1992, when the case comes to trial, she accuses Nicholls of sexually assaulting her, but will be fined £100 at Marlborough Street court.)
Dec Shaw's ***Reviewing The Situation*** is her first release on the RPM label. (The following November 14th, and in an unlikely twin-billing, Shaw will perform at London's Mean Fiddler with Dennis Loccoriere, formerly of Dr. Hook.)

1994

Jan [2] Having performed *Gimme Shelter* with Cud for inclusion on a benefit album for the Putting Our House In Order charity, a compilation of twelve versions of the Rolling Stones, classic by various artists, released the previous April, Shaw now hosts the hour-long "Not Fade Away", a 30th anniversary "Top Of The Pops" tribute on Radio One-FM.
Oct [22] She guests on BBC1-TV's "Steve Wright's People Show".
Nov [12] *Nothing Less Than Brilliant* debuts at its UK #66 peak, during a two-week chart stay.
[19] Its parent album ***Nothing Less Than Brilliant*** makes UK #64 in its week of entry.

THE SHIRELLES

Shirley Owens (lead vocals);
Addi "Micki" Harris (vocals);
Doris Coley (vocals); **Beverly Lee** (vocals)

1957

The all-girl vocal quartet is formed as the Poquellos, at high school in Passaic, NJ, by classmates Owens (b. June 10, 1941, Passaic), Harris (b. Jan. 22, 1940, Passaic), Coley (b. Aug. 2, 1941, Passaic) and Lee (b. Aug. 3, 1941, Passaic), initially to sing at school parties and dances, where their speciality piece is the group-composed *I Met Him On A Sunday*. Another schoolfriend, Mary Jane Greenberg, persuades them to audition the song for her mother, Florence Greenberg, who owns the small local label, Tiara Records, which she runs from her front living room.

1958

Jan Greenberg records *I Met Him On A Sunday* with the group at Beltone Studios, but insists on a more commercial-sounding name to put on the release: the Shirelles is the girls' own choice.
Apr With interest in the single building, Tiara, without the resources to promote a national success, leases it to Decca Records.
May *I Met Him On A Sunday* makes US #50. (It will be followed by two more Tiara recordings leased to Decca, *My Love Is A Charm* and *I Got The Message*, but neither will chart.)

1959

May Greenberg forms Scepter Records located at 1674, Broadway, with writer/producer Luther Dixon (whom he has met in an elevator), and the Shirelles are signed as Dixon becomes their producer, and Greenberg their manager.
July Their revival of the Five Royales' ballad (written by lead singer Lowman Pauling), *Dedicated To The One I Love*, stops at US #83. (They first heard the song earlier in the spring when playing at the Howard Theatre, Washington, DC, on a bill with the Five Royales.) Its follow-up, *A Teardrop And A Lollipop*, will fail to score.

1960

Oct After the release of *Please Be My Boyfriend*, *Tonight's The Night*, written by Owens and Dixon, and already recorded by the Chiffons, reaches US #39.
Dec Quartet appears in a Christmas all-star show at Brooklyn's Paramount Theatre, New York, NY, alongside Ray Charles, Dion, Chubby Checker, the Coasters, Neil Sedaka, and many others.

1961

Jan [30] Owing songwriters Goffin and King a favor, Dixon has produced an uptempo string-backed arrangement of their ballad, *Will You Love Me Tomorrow* (with King herself helping with the arrangement and playing drums), which now tops the US chart for the first of two weeks, becoming a million seller, and the first recording by an all-girl group to hit US #1.
Mar *Dedicated To The One I Love* is reissued as a follow-up and this time is a smash, hitting US #3 and becoming the group's second million seller.
[11] *Will You Love Me Tomorrow*, their UK chart debut, hits #4.
Apr [2] Having released its maiden album ***Tonight's The Night***, the group begins a major US tour in Irving Feld's "Biggest Show Of Stars, 1961", debuting in Philadelphia, PA. Also on the bill are Chubby Checker, Fats Domino, the Drifters, Bo Diddley, and others.

June *Mama Said* hits US #4.
[25] They appear at the Hollywood Bowl, in an Alan Freed outdoor spectacular, also starring Brenda Lee, Bobby Vee, Jerry Lee Lewis, and others.
Aug *A Thing Of The Past* halts at US #41, much of its airplay stolen by the B-side, the Goffin and King-penned *What A Sweet Thing That Was*, which peaks at US #54.
Nov *Big John* reaches UK #21, at the same time as Jimmy Dean's *Big Bad John* (a different song) is at US #1. ***The Shirelles Sing To Trumpet And Strings*** is released.

1962

Feb A Bacharach/David song, *Baby It's You* (moulded for the group at Dixon's urging from its original form as *I'll Cherish You*), hits US #8. (A year later, the Beatles will revive it on their debut album, along with a version of *Boys*, the B-side of *Will You Love Me Tomorrow*.)
May [5] *Soldier Boy*, in simple, uptempo C&W style, with a widely applicable lyric, written by Dixon and Greenberg in a few minutes and recorded as rapidly at the end of a session, topping the US chart for the first of three weeks.
June ***Baby It's You*** makes US #59.
[30] *Soldier Boy* reaches UK #23.
July *Welcome Home Baby* reaches US #22. Greenberg turns down Gene Pitney's song, *He's A Rebel*, as a follow-up, when offered it for the Shirelles by publisher Aaron Schroeder. (She is afraid the title will prove controversial in the South, but Phil Spector will record it with the Crystals and take it to US #1.)
Oct *Stop The Music* reaches US #36. (Its B-side, *It's Love That Really Counts*, will later be a UK hit for the Merseybeats.)

1963

Jan Their update of Doris Day's 1958 hit, *Everybody Loves A Lover*, makes US #19. After this, they record without Dixon, who leaves Scepter to work at Capitol, where he forms Ludix Records.
Mar Compilation album, ***The Shirelles' Greatest Hits***, reaches US #19. Their best-selling album, it will stay charted for 49 weeks.
May *Foolish Little Girl* hits US #4, the group's last Top 10 success. By now, the girl-group sound, of which the Shirelles have been the hit-making pioneers, has taken a major hold on the US charts, and competition from groups like the Angels, the Chiffons and Phil Spector's the Crystals, for both songs and chart placings, is intense.
June [1] *Foolish Little Girl* reaches UK #38, their third and final UK hit.
July *Don't Say Goodnight And Mean Goodbye* reaches US #26, while ***Foolish Little Girl*** makes US #68.
Sept *What Does A Girl Do?* peaks at US #53.
Oct Movie-title theme, *It's a Mad, Mad, Mad, Mad World*, peaks at US #92.
Nov [9] The Shirelles begin their first UK tour, with Little Richard and Duane Eddy, at the Regal Cinema, Edmonton, London. Owens and Coley have both married by this time, and are now Shirley Alston and Doris Kenner respectively. (Dionne Warwick, also with Scepter Records, often fills in on stage for one or the other of them during 1963, when family commitments call.)

1964

Jan *Tonight You're Gonna Fall In Love With Me* peaks at US #57. The group is no longer recording for Scepter, having fallen out with Greenberg and the label after discovering that trust fund money from their hit earnings, supposedly theirs at age 21, does not exist. The group attempts to leave but is prevented from signing elsewhere because of extended legal proceedings. (Meanwhile, Scepter will continue to release Shirelles singles regularly, from already-cut material, until the end of the year - though without any great promotion. Dionne Warwick has just broken with *Anyone Who Had A Heart* and is now the label's priority act.)
Apr *Sha-La-La* covered as a bigger success by Manfred Mann, hitting UK #3 in October and US #12 in November, makes US #69.
June [26] The "Dick Clark & His Caravan Of Stars" package tour, featuring the Shirelles, Major Lance, the Crystals, Brian Hyland, the Supremes, Gene Pitney and others, plays at the Fair Grounds Grandstand, Allentown, PA.
Aug *Thank You Baby* reaches US #63.
Nov *Maybe Tonight* peaks at US #88. *Are You Still My Baby?* will stop at US #91 in January, the last Shirelles chart entry for two years.

1967

Aug *Last Minute Miracle*, recorded after legal and other difficulties between the group and Scepter are finally solved, peaks at US #99, and the group signs to Mercury, where *I'll Stay By Your Side* and *There's A Storm Going On In My Heart* both fail to chart. Kenner will leaves the group the following year due to family commitments (she has married again, and is now Mrs. Doris Jackson), leaving the others to continue as a trio.

1969

Feb Newly signed to Bell Records as Shirley & the Shirelles, *Look What You've Done To My Heart* gains some UK airplay (and later some specialist sales as a northern dancefloor favorite), but fails to chart in either the US or UK.
Oct The group appears in Richard Nader's first "Rock'n'Roll Revival Concert" at New York's Felt Forum, alongside Bill Haley & His Comets, Chuck Berry, the Platters, the Coasters, and others.

1972

The trio is signed to RCA, recording ***Happy In Love*** and ***The Shirelles***. Both contain strong cuts (by Bill Withers, Carole King, Marvin Gaye and others), but fail to make significant commercial impact. The following year the group will be featured singing *Soldier Boy* and *Everybody Loves A Lover* in "Let The Good Times Roll", a documentary of the rock revival show, interspersed with vintage performance clips.

1975

Doris Jackson returns to the group to replace Alston, who leaves for a solo career, but is prevented by the other three from billing herself as "Shirley Of The Shirelles". She signs to Prodigal Records and records ***With A Little Help From My Friends***, a collection of oldies on which she is joined by artists associated with the original songs, such as the Drifters (*Save The Last Dance For Me*), the Five Satins (*In The Still Of The Night*), Herman's Hermits (*Silhouettes*) and the Flamingos (*I Only Have Eyes For You*). ***Let's Give Each Other Love***, on RCA, is the group's last album, released in January the following year. Alston will record two further solo albums, ***Lady Rose*** and ***Sings The Shirelles' Biggest Hits***, for the US Strawberry label, both issued in 1977.

1982

June [10] Lacking recording contracts, both Alston and the three-piece Shirelles have continued their performance careers, the latter still popular on nostalgia dates and tours. After a live show in Atlanta, GA, Harris collapses and dies of a heart attack. A memorial service will be held in the group's home town, Passaic.

1989

Sept [14] While the Shirelles have contributed backing vocals to Dionne Warwick's 1983 album ***How Many Times Can We Say Goodbye*** on her cover of *Will You Love Me Tomorrow*, and the group has continued to perform, Shirley Alston Reeves joins forces with members of the Belmonts, the Five Satins, the Jive Five, the Falcons and the Silhouettes, outside the Berklee Performance Center in Boston, MA, in an impromptu doo-wop session to announce the formation of the Doo-Wop Hall of Fame of America.

1991

June [4] The Shirelles take part in "Celebrate the Soul of American Music" at Pantages Theater, Hollywood, CA, to benefit the Thurgood Marshall Scholarship Fund.
July [29] In a ruling against Gusto Records, the sixth US Circuit Court of Appeals upholds an earlier Tennessee court ruling which awards $1 million to the group, Gene Pitney and B.J. Thomas, for outstanding royalties arising from sales of original master recordings.
Aug [9] The group performs at the first of two concerts at "The Apollo R&B Reunion" to benefit the financially distressed theater in Harlem, New York.

1996

Jan [17] With Rhino Records having brought their '60s career highlights to CD with the release of ***Anthology*** and ***Best Of*** compilations with Tomato Records having also issued the twin-CD retrospective ***The World's Greatest Girls Group*** in 1995, and while the Shirelles continue to tour on the oldies circuit, Reeves has received the Lifetime Achievement Award and performed at the opening of the Doo-Wop Hall of Fame of America, held at the Veterans Memorial Auditorium, Providence, RI on May 1st 1993. The Shirelles, already honored at the fifth annual Rhythm and Blues Foundation Pioneer Awards show held at New York's Roseland Ballroom on May 2nd 1994, also singing *Dedicated To The One I Love* for the first time in 17 years, are now inducted into the Rock and Roll Hall of Fame at the 11th annual dinner, held at New York's Waldorf Astoria Hotel.

CARLY SIMON

1964

Apr Sarah Lawrence College-educated Carly (b. June 25, 1945, New York, NY) and older sister Lucy, daughters of Richard L. Simon, co-founder of Simon & Schuster publishers, have formed singing duo the Simon Sisters, playing on the campus circuit and at folk clubs including New York's Gaslight and Bitter End, where they have been seen by record executive Dave Kapp. Kapp signs them to his label, on which they now have a minor hit (US #73) with *Winkin' Blinkin' And Nod*, going on to cut two albums (***The Simon Sisters*** and ***Cuddlebug***), before splitting in 1965 when Lucy gets married and Carly moves to France. Simon returns to the US the following year and meets Bob Dylan's manager, Albert Grossman, who signs her to a management deal in the hope of promoting her as a female Dylan.

1966

Sept Simon records four tracks with producer Bob Johnston, including a version of Eric Von Schmidt's *Baby Let Me Follow You Down*, with revised lyrics by Dylan (which she discussed with him the week before his motorbike accident) and Michael Bloomfield, and members of the Band backing her, but argues with Grossman over her career direction, and the songs are not issued. She meets Jacob Brackman, film critic for **Esquire** magazine, with whom she begins writing songs.

1969

Having spent much of the past two years singing on jingles and making demos, Simon meets Jac Holzman, founder of the Elektra label, via a mutual friend and pop entrepreneur, Jerry Brandt, leading to her signing with the label the following year.

1971

Apr Her maiden album, ***Carly Simon***, produced by Holzman, enters the US chart, eventually reaching #30.
[6] After a Simon performance at the Troubadour in Los Angeles, CA, James Taylor goes backstage to meet her.
July [10] The ballad, *That's The Way I've Always Heard It Should Be*, hits US #10.

1972

Feb [12] *Anticipation* reaches US #13, taken from her sophomore album, ***Anticipation***, also produced by Paul Samwell-Smith and recorded at Morgan Studios in Willesden, North London, which heads to US #30. During the year, she films a cameo role in the movie "Taking Off".
Mar [14] Simon wins the Best New Artist category, at the 14th annual Grammy Awards.
May [6] *Legend In Your Own Time* makes US #50.
Nov [3] Simon marries singer-songwriter James Taylor in her Manhattan apartment. That evening she joins him on stage, where he announces their union.
Dec [8] The still-climbing ***No Secrets*** is certified gold by the RIAA.

1973

Jan [6] Seminal career recording, the self-penned *You're So Vain*, tops the US chart (and will hit UK #3). (The song causes considerable conjecture over the identity of its subject, though it seems unlikely to be backing vocalist, Mick Jagger).
[8] *You're So Vain* is certified gold by the RIAA.
[13] ***No Secrets*** hits US #1 for the first of five weeks, and will also hit UK #3. Showcasing a harder, rock vocal style, it is her first album to be produced by Richard Perry, and will remain her most successful set.
May [26] *The Right Thing To Do* reaches both US and UK #17.
Sept [5] ***Anticipation*** is certified gold by the RIAA.

1974

Jan ***Hotcakes*** hits US #3 and UK #19. Again produced by Perry, it includes backing vocals by husband Taylor, and features their first song written together, *Forever My Love*.
[22] ***Hotcakes*** is certified gold by the RIAA.
Mar [23] *Mockingbird*, a duet with Taylor on Charlie & Inez Foxx's 1963 US #7, hits US #5 and UK #34.
June [22] *I Haven't Got Time For The Pain* peaks at US #14, taken from ***Playing Possum***, again produced by Perry, which hits US #10.

1975

June [21] *Attitude Dancing* reaches US #21.
Aug [9] *Waterfall* peaks at US #78.
Oct [25] *More And More* makes US #94.
Dec [24] Simon goes carol singing with Linda Ronstadt, Joni Mitchell and Taylor in Hollywood, CA.

1976

Jan [17] ***The Best Of Carly Simon*** reaches US #17.
July [17] *It Keeps You Runnin'*, her cover of the Doobie Brothers' hit, makes US #46.
[24] ***Another Passenger***, produced by Ted Templeman and with Brackman as co-writer, reaches US #29.
Dec [18] ***The Best Of Carly Simon*** is certified gold by the RIAA.

1977

Oct [22] *Nobody Does It Better*, co-written by Marvin Hamlisch and Carole Bayer Sager, and issued as the theme to the James Bond movie, "The Spy Who Loved Me", hits US #2, behind Debby Boone's *You Light Up My Life*, having hit UK #7 on Sept [17].
Nov [9] *Nobody Does It Better* is certified gold by the RIAA.

1978

Apr ***Boys In The Trees***, produced by Arif Mardin, hits US #10.
[19] Simon joins Bruce Springsteen, Jackson Browne, the Doobie Brothers and others in petitioning President Carter to end nuclear power in the US. (It precedes her forthcoming involvement in the "No Nukes" project.)
June [24] *You Belong To Me*, written with Doobie Brother Michael McDonald over the telephone, hits US #6.
Aug [7] ***Boys In The Trees*** is certified gold by the RIAA.
Sept [30] Another Simon and Taylor duet, their cover of the Everly Brothers' 1958 US #10, *Devoted To You*, reaches US #36.
Nov [2] Simon guests on *I Live In The Woods* at a concert at Jones Hall, Houston, TX, recorded for the future Burt Bacharach album, ***Woman***.

1979

June ***Spy***, once again helmed by Mardin, with string arrangements by Gene Orloff, reaches US #45, and will be Simon's last for Elektra.
July [14] *Vengeance* peaks at US #48.
Sept [19] Simon joins other anti-nuclear stanced musicians, singing with Graham Nash, John Hall and Taylor, on the first of a five-night series of Musicians United for Safe Energy (MUSE) concerts at New York's Madison Square Garden. The show is recorded for ***No Nukes***, which will reach US #19 in December.

1980

July ***Come Upstairs***, Simon's first for Warner Bros. Records, and largely co-written with its producer, Mike Mainieri, makes US #36.
Oct [4] During a nationwide tour to promote ***Come Upstairs***, Simon collapses with exhaustion onstage in Pittsburgh, PA. (Over the next few years, she develops an increasing fear of live performance.)
Nov [1] *Jessie*, from the album, reaches US #11.
Dec [5] *Jessie* is certified gold by the RIAA.

1981

Sept ***Torch***, a collection of standards from the '20s through the '40s, once again helmed by Mainieri, makes US #50. (During the year, Simon will file for divorce from Taylor, though it will take two years to finalize.)

1982

Aug [7] Written and produced by the Chic Organization's Bernard Edwards and Nile Rodgers, and taken from the film soundtrack to "Soup For One", the jaunty pop/dance departure, *Why*, hits UK #10.
Oct [2] *Why* peaks at US #74.

1983

Aug On Will Powers' UK #17, *Kissing With Confidence*, Simon provides lead vocals on the Lynn Goldsmith-pseudonymous novelty hit.
Sept ***Hello Big Man*** reaches US #69.
Oct [8] Taken from it, *You Know What To Do* makes US #83.

1985

July [20] *Tired Of Being Blonde* peaks at US #70.
Sept ***Spoiled Girl***, her only album for Epic Records, variously produced by Paul Samwell-Smith, Don Was, Russ Kunkel, Arthur Baker and Andy Goldmark, stops at US #88. She also appears in the film "Perfect", in which she tips water over John Travolta.

1986

Nov *Coming Around Again*, her first single for Arista Records, reaches UK #12. Produced by Samwell-Smith, the song is from the soundtrack to the Jack Nicholson/Meryl Streep film, "Heartburn". (Its B-side, *Itsy Bitsy Spider*, features the vocal debut of her daughter.)

1987

Jan [24] *Coming Around Again* reaches US #18.
May [23] ***Coming Around Again***, featuring Bryan Adams, Russ Kunkel and Michael Brecker among others, reaches UK #25, and will do likewise in the US.
June [20] *Give Me All Night* peaks at US #61.

1988

Feb [1] ***Coming Around Again*** is certified platinum by the RIAA.
[20] *All I Want Is You* peaks at US #54.
Aug At the annual Martha's Vineyard Celebrity Auction, one of the featured items is a private performance of a song by Simon in the home of the winning bidder. Simon sings three songs for $26,000 each for two men, unable to outbid each other.
Sept [24] ***Greatest Hits Live*** makes UK #49 (and will peak at US #87). The album has been recorded in front of invited guests at the harbor in Gay Head, Martha's Vineyard, MA, for the HBO-TV special "Carly In Concert - Coming Around Again". Now married to Jim Hart, after her 1983 divorce from Taylor, Simon starts work on the movie soundtrack for "Working Girl".

1989

Apr [15] *Let The River Run*, the theme to "Working Girl", makes US #49.
June Reissued *Why* peaks at UK #56.
Aug **Playboy** reports that Simon has opened an art gallery in New York called Riverrun, and that she is writing two songs with Smokey Robinson for her forthcoming album.
Sept [2] Simon signs copies of her newly-published children's book, **Amy And The Dancing Bear**, at the Bunch O' Grapes book-store in Vineyard Haven, MA.

1990

Feb [21] *Let The River Run* wins the Best Song Written Specifically For A Motion Picture Or For Television category at the 32nd annual Grammy Awards, at the Shrine Auditorium, Los Angeles. (It will also go on to win an Oscar for Best Song and lead to her being commissioned to write the film score for "Postcards From The Edge".)
Apr [15] "Carly In Concert : My Romance" airs on HBO-TV, with guests Michael Brecker and Harry Connick Jr.
May [12] ***My Romance***, a standards-filled progression from ***Torch***, makes US #46.
July [26] ***Greatest Hits Live*** is certified gold by the RIAA.
Nov [10] ***Have You Seen Me Lately?***, her second album of the year, featuring 11 new Simon songs and guests including sister Lucy and Judy Collins, makes US #60.
Simon's second children's book, **The Boy Of The Bells**, is published.

1991

Jan [31] Simon makes a rare television appearance on NBC-TV's "Late Night With David Letterman".
May [4] *You're So Vain*, reissued in Britain to coincide with its extensive TV exposure from a Dunlop Tyres commercial, makes UK #41.
Aug [9] Simon duets with Billy Joel on *You're So Vain*, on the second night of a benefit concert at Indian Field Ranch, Montauk, Long Island.

1992

Mar ***This Is My Life***, the Simon composed and recorded soundtrack to the Julie Kavner-starring movie of the same name, is released. Her next children's book **The Fisherman's Song** will be published by Bantam in July.

1993

Feb [25] The Simon-written hour-long children's opera, "Romulus Hunt", concerning unsuccessful efforts by a son to reunite his divorced parents, premieres at the John Jay Theater, New York, before moving to the Eisenhower Theatre at the John F. Kennedy Center for the Performing Arts in Washington, DC on April 7th. The accompanying album ***Romulus Hunt - A Family Opera***, recorded with Andrew Leeds, Kurt Ollman, Jeff Hairston, Wendy Hill and Luretta Bybee, will be issued by Angel Records in April. (Simon will also contribute music to the American Repertory Theatre's production of "Cakewalk" in Cambridge, MA.)
Sept [14] "Phenom", for which Simon has performed the theme song, premieres on ABC-TV.
Nov [20] Frank Sinatra's ***Duets***, to which Simon has collaborated on *Guess I'll Hang My Tears Out To Dry* and *In The Wee Small Hours Of The Morning*, enters at its US #2 peak, behind Pearl Jam's ***Vs***.

1994

June [1] Simon is inducted into the Songwriters Hall of Fame at the 25th annual ceremony, at the Sheraton Hotel and Towers in New York.
Sept [1] President Clinton plays saxophone as Simon sings *Dream*, at a get together on Martha's Vineyard.
Nov [14] She guests on CBS-TV's "Late Show With David Letterman".
[19] Co-produced by Simon with Frank Filipetti, ***Letters Never Sent***, featuring Rosanne Cash, Dave Stewart, Andreas Vollenweider, Marc Cohn, Carlos Alomar and Otis Redding III among many others, debuts at its US #129 peak.
Dec [17] Simon takes part in the ABC-TV's "Christmas At Home With The Stars".

1995

Feb [28] She sings *You're So Vain*, with Annie Lennox, Melissa Etheridge and Sarah McLachlan, at Clive Davis' annual pre-Grammy bash, at the House of Blues in Los Angeles.
Mar [1] Simon and Tori Amos present the Best Male Rock Vocal trophy to Bruce Springsteen at the 37th annual Grammy Awards, at the Shrine Auditorium. (She reveals at the post-Grammy press conference, that she lived in O.J. Simpson's 360 Rockingham Avenue, Brentwood home for five months in 1976.)
[2] Simon guests on NBC-TV's "The Tonight Show".
[3] She begins her first tour in 15 years (an initial seven-date jaunt), a set combining classic hits and material from ***Letters Never Sent***, to a sellout crowd of 550 at the Galaxy Theater, Santa Ana, CA. (She reveals she has only given 60 concerts in her entire career.)
[25] The tour finishes at the Newport Music Hall, Columbus, OH.
Apr Simon reunites with her sister Lucy (and Richie Havens) to contribute *The Great Mandala* to Peter Paul & Mary's newly released ***Lifelines***. She also performs in the rotunda of New York's Grand Central Terminal for an upcoming Lifetime cable TV special.
May [4] Simon makes a return appearance on the "Late Show With David Letterman".
June [3] She sings *You're So Vain* with Tom Jones at the 16th annual KISS Genesis Fund concert at the Great Woods Center for the Performing Arts in Mansfield, MA.
July [27] Simon opens a series of dates, with Daryl Hall & John Oates in support, at the Mann Music Center in Philadelphia, PA, set to end on August 22nd at the Concord Pavilion, Concord, CA.
Aug [30] Featured in this month's **Vanity Fair**, Simon reunites with former husband James Taylor, for the first time since 1979, at a benefit concert, unofficially coined "Livestock '95", for the Martha's Vineyard Agricultural Society at the society's Fairgrounds in West Tisbury, MA. The 10,000 crowd see the couple perform their own sets and then join together for two numbers.
Dec [5] Arista releases the three-CD boxed-set retrospective, ***Clouds In My Coffee 1965-1995***, covering her recording career at Elektra, Warner Bros., Arista, United Artists and Angel, including her first demo, *Play With Me*, cut in 1965 and other unreleased material.

1996

Jan [21, 23, 25, 27] Simon and Hall & Oates play four shows, in support of the American Indian College Fund, at the Fox Arena, Foxwoods Resort Casino in Ledyard, CT.

PAUL SIMON

1958

Following US chart success with friend Art Garfunkel as Tom & Jerry, Simon (b. Oct. 13, 1941, Newark, NJ), his father Louis a bassist in orchestras on Arthur Godfrey and Jackie Gleason TV shows, his mother Belle a music teacher, and having composed his first copyrighted song, *The Girl For Me* in 1955, cuts the solo single, *True Or False*, for the same label, Big Records, under the name True Taylor. Attending Queens College in New York, NY the following year to study English, he makes money cutting demos for music publishers, having been introduced to contacts by fellow demo-maker, Carole Klein (later Carole King). He also adopts the name Jerry Landis to make more solo singles, the first of which is *Anna Belle*, for MGM Records.

1961

Several singles for Warwick Records, including *I Want To Be The Lipstick On Your Collar* and *Play Me A Sad Song*, also fail commercially, before Simon moves (still, at this time making more money from demo work than his own releases) to Madison Records, where he records as Tico and Tico & the Triumphs.

1962

Jan *Motorcycle* by Tico & The Triumphs peaks at US #99 on Amy Records, which has acquired Madison and Simon's contract. He cuts another two Tico singles for Amy, neither of them hits. (Some songs from this period are credited to Simon/Landis, the Simon being Paul's brother, Eddie.)

1963

Jan Once again billed as Jerry Landis, *The Lone Teen Ranger*, on Amy, reaches US #97. (He also writes and produces for others, including Ritchie Cordell, the Fashions and Dotty Daniels, and begins to play at Greenwich Village clubs like Gerde's Folk City at night, while still plugging songs to publishers during the day. Later in the year, while at law school, he teams up again with Garfunkel, who is completing a Math degree at Columbia University, and they perform folk-style material for the first time as Simon & Garfunkel.

1964

Dropping out of law school, Simon travels to Britain (joined during the summer vacation by Garfunkel), where he plays on the burgeoning folk circuit, and is befriended by London social worker, Judith Piepe, with whom he lodges. He records a solo single for UK independent label Oriole Records, still using the name Jerry Landis, *He Was My Brother*, written about a friend killed during the US civil rights disturbances, credited in the US to Paul Kane, where it is issued by Tribute Records.

1965

Jan After the US commercial failure of the first Simon & Garfunkel album, ***Wednesday Morning, 3 A.M.***, Simon returns to the UK, where, with Piepe, he gains experience on BBC radio, contributing songs to a series of Piepe's commentaries on the daily religious series, "Five To Ten". He also returns to the UK folk circuit, with fellow Americans Tom Paxton, Carolyn Hester and Buffy St. Marie.
May Thanks to his US Columbia contract, Simon is able to record the solo album, ***The Paul Simon Songbook*** (showing Simon and Piepe on the sleeve), for UK CBS. (The album, recorded at Levy Studios in Bond Street, London at a cost of £60, contains solo acoustic versions of several songs which will later re-appear on the next Simon and Garfunkel album. It is not a big seller, and will be deleted at the artist's own request in 1979.) While in Britain, he also works with other singer/songwriters, including Jackson C. Frank and Al Stewart.
Sept Simon writes *Homeward Bound* (a future hit with Garfunkel) dedicated to his girlfriend Kathy Chitty, on the platform of the railway station in Widnes, Cheshire, after playing at the Howff folk club. He also makes his debut on ITV's "Ready Steady, Go!"
Dec When Simon & Garfunkel's ***Sounds Of Silence*** hits the US chart, Simon is contacted by producer Tom Wilson and returns to the US, to re-form the duo (which will have five years of huge international success).

1970

Feb After tensions have arisen between Simon & Garfunkel during the lengthy recording sessions for ***Bridge Over Troubled Water*** the previous year, and with the single and album currently topping charts worldwide, the duo officially splits. Simon agrees to continue as a solo artist on CBS/Columbia, but under his own terms.
Apr Simon teaches a class in songwriting and record-making for one semester at New York University.
Aug [6] He takes part in the 12-hour anti-war "Concert For Peace" at New York's Shea Stadium, 25 years after the bombing of Hiroshima.

1972

Mar [18] The self-penned ***Paul Simon***, partly recorded at Dynamic Studios, Kingston, Jamaica, tops the UK chart for one week and hits US #4. The album, co-produced by Simon & Garfunkel's former co-producer and engineer, Roy Halee, features violinist Stephane Grappelli among its guest musicians. Taken from it, *Mother And Child Reunion*, a track recorded in Jamaica (and, according to Simon, written about a dish of egg and chicken on a menu at the 456 restaurant in Chinatown, New York) hits US #4 and UK #5.
May *Me And Julio Down By The School Yard*, also from the album, reaches US #22 and UK #15.
Aug Ballad *Duncan*, a third single from the album, makes US #52.

1973

May [6] Simon begins his first solo tour since his break with Garfunkel, in Boston, MA.
June The self written-and-produced, ***There Goes Rhymin' Simon***, hits US #2 and UK #4, earning a gold disc.
July From the album, *Kodachrome* hits US #2. Another extract, *Take Me To The Mardi Gras* hits UK #7 (with *Kodachrome* relegated to the B-side in the UK, because of the BBC's refusal to play songs which mention commercial brand-names).
Oct The gospel-styled *Loves Me Like A Rock*, recorded with the Dixie Hummingbirds, hits US #2, also reaching UK #39.
[9] *Loves Me Like A Rock* is certified gold by the RIAA.

1974

Jan Ballad, *American Tune*, based on a recurring chorale from Johann Sebastian Bach's "St. Matthew Passion" and from ***There Goes Rhymin' Simon***, makes US #35.
Apr His performance set, ***Paul Simon In Concert/ Live Rhymin'***, peaks at US #33. It was recorded on tour the previous year, and features some of the guests from the previous studio album. (Simon spends the rest of this year writing and recording.)
June [11] ***Live Rhymin'*** is certified gold by the RIAA.

1975

Oct *Gone At Last*, a gospel-style duet with Phoebe Snow, backed vocally by the Jessy Dixon Singers, reaches US #23, and is a taster for Simon's long-awaited new project.
Nov [17] The still-climbing ***Still Crazy After All These Years*** is certified gold by the RIAA.
Dec [6] ***Still Crazy After All These Years***, a jazz-flavored set recorded with a top drawer session crew including David Sanborn, Bob James and Jeff Beck, and co-produced with Phil Ramone, heads the US chart for a week. (Lyrically, the album contains references to his recently failed marriage - Simon and first wife Peggy are now divorced.)
[13] Extracted Simon & Garfunkel duet, *My Little Town* (also included on Garfunkel's new album), hits US #9.

1976

Jan [24] ***Still Crazy After All These Years*** hits UK #6.
[31] Taken from the album, *50 Ways To Leave Your Lover* reaches UK #23.
Feb [7] *50 Ways To Leave Your Lover* tops the US chart for the first of three weeks

[28] Simon wins the Album Of The Year and Best Male Pop Vocal Performance categories for ***Still Crazy After All These Years***, at the 18th annual Grammy Awards.
Mar [11] *50 Ways To Leave Your Lover* is certified gold by the RIAA.
May [29] Title song, *Still Crazy After All These Years*, reaches US #40, while Simon is on a lengthy international tour to promote the album (which includes a BBC-TV special).

1977

Jan [19] Simon participates in the Inaugural Eve Gala Performance for President-elect, Jimmy Carter.

1978

Jan *Slip Slidin' Away* hits US #5, having made UK #36 on Dec [17]. It is also one of two new songs on the compilation album, ***Greatest Hits, Etc.***, which is a million seller, reaching US #18 and UK #6. (The other new song is *Stranded In A Limousine*.) Simon makes his acting debut as Tony Lacey in Woody Allen's movie, "Annie Hall".
Feb [1] ***Greatest Hits, Etc.*** is certified platinum by the RIAA.
Mar Simon and James Taylor provide guest vocals on Art Garfunkel's revival of *(What A) Wonderful World*, which reaches US #17.
[22] The Rutles' movie, "All You Need Is Cash", in which Simon makes a cameo appearance, airs on NBC-TV. (He will make occasional appearances on NBC-TV's "Saturday Night Live", performing both solo and with Garfunkel (and once with George Harrison) for the late-night comedy show, and will also be best man at producer Lorne Michaels' wedding.) NBC-TV will also air "The Paul Simon Special".
Apr [1] The Philadelphia Furies, a soccer team co-owned by Simon, Peter Frampton, Mick Jagger, and Rick Wakeman, loses its first match of the North America Soccer League 3-0 to the Washington Diplomats.

1979

Feb [15] Simon signs to Warner Bros. Records (partly to have the opportunity to undertake his own movie project), paying CBS $1.5 million to release him from his contract. He also begins a law suit against CBS for non-payment of royalties.
Mar He begins work on the screenplay for his movie, "One-Trick Pony".

1980

Jan Simon devotes most of the first half of the year to the movie, writing the script and songs for the project, and also directs and acts in its production. Upon its completion, Simon embarks on a major US and UK concert tour.
Sept *Late In The Evening*, taken from "One-Trick Pony", hits US #6 and reaches UK #58. The soundtrack album, ***One-Trick Pony***, co-produced with Ramone, and treated by fans and reviewers as a new Paul Simon album, reaches US #12 and UK #17.
Oct [1] "One-Trick Pony" opens in US theaters, and will be only a moderate box-office success. Included are brief appearances by the B-52's and a specially re-formed the Lovin' Spoonful.
[14] ***One-Trick Pony*** is certified gold by the RIAA.
Nov Title song, *One-Trick Pony*, makes US #40.
[6] Simon begins a UK tour at London's Hammersmith Odeon, his first live appearance in Britain for five years. He buys the audience drinks during the dates - a gesture which costs him £1,000 a night.

1982

Mar [15] He is inducted into the Songwriters Hall of Fame, at the 13th annual awards dinner, held at the New York Hilton, New York
Apr [19] Simon & Garfunkel announce a reunion (though it will be mainly for nostalgic live concerts).

1983

Feb *The Blues*, a duet with Randy Newman, makes US #51.
Aug [16] Simon marries long-time girlfriend, actress Carrie Fisher.
Dec ***Hearts And Bones*** peaks at US #35 and UK #17. The set, co-produced with Roy Halee, Russ Titelman and Lenny Waronker, is salvaged from what was to be a new Simon & Garfunkel album on Geffen, and guests include composer Phillip Glass. From it, *Allergies* reaches US #44.

1985

Jan [28] Having begun work on a new album the previous year, which has taken him to South Africa to record both vocal and instrumental groups, Simon joins the all-star line-up for the recording of USA For Africa's *We Are The World*, following the 12th annual American Music Awards.
Feb He begins recording in Johannesburg, South Africa, spending nine days at Ovation Studios, in preparation. (He had been introduced to the type of music he is about to record when New York singer/writer, Heidi Berg, gave him a copy of ***Gumboots : Accordian Jive Hits, Volume II***. He then contacted South African producer, Hilton Rosenthal, who sent him 20 albums of Sowetan music.)

1986

Sept [10] Simon guests on NBC-TV's "Late Night With David Letterman".
Oct [4] Heading to US #3 and multi-platinum sales, the resultant self-produced ***Graceland*** tops the UK chart for the first of five weeks. It is chiefly inspired by South African dance music, both traditional and electric, and features the group Ladysmith Black Mambazo (which, as a result of this exposure, becomes an international act, with Simon later co-producing two of their Warner Bros. albums). (Simon will donate more than $100,000 from his royalties to a charity run by Allan Boesak.) The album also includes contributions from Linda Ronstadt, the Everly Brothers and Los Lobos (who later threaten to sue if their name isn't included on the composer credits). From it, *You Can Call Me Al* hits UK #4, and initially US #44 (but will re-chart at US #23 on re-promotion in mid-1987), its popular promo video clip featuring Chevy Chase.
Nov [21] The RIAA certifies platinum sales of ***Paul Simon*** and ***There Goes Rhymin' Simon***.
Dec Also from the album, *The Boy In The Bubble* reaches UK #26.

1987

Jan [10] Title song, *Graceland*, peaks at US #81.
[30] Simon holds a press conference in London to state that both the ANC and the UN have removed him from their black-lists, originally imposed after he broke the boycott on recording in South Africa.
Feb [9] Simon is named Best International Solo Artist, at the sixth annual BRIT Awards held at London's Grosvenor House Hotel.
[24] In winning the Album Of The Year category, ***Graceland*** gives Simon his 11th Grammy trophy, at the 29th annual Awards ceremony at which he also sings *Diamonds On The Sole Of Her Shoes*.
Mar [21] *The Boy In The Bubble* peaks at US #86.
Apr Simon performs UK dates at the Royal Albert Hall, London, and is picketed by anti-apartheid protesters. Guests on stage include husband and wife Hugh Masekela and Miriam Makeba. (Simon will play in Zimbabwe later in the summer, where the TV film and best-selling home video "The Graceland Concert", will be shot.)
May [23] *You Can Call Me Al* now reaches US #23.
Dec ***Graceland*** heads the **Billboard** Compact Disks Top Pop category, in the magazine's year-end round-up.

1988

Jan [25] He wins the Favorite Male Artist, Pop/Rock, and Favorite Album, Pop/Rock categories, at the 15th annual American Music Awards, held at the Shrine Auditorium, Los Angeles, CA.
Mar While working on a projected Broadway musical with Eddie Palmieri, Simon, after having a conversation in a Los Angeles parking lot in August 1987 with Milton Nascimento, goes to Brazil to record drumming tracks for his forthcoming project, ***The Rhythm Of The Saints***.
[2] With the popularity of its parent project now stretched out over two years, *Graceland* is named Record Of The Year at the 30th annual Grammy Awards.
Apr [4] "Graceland The African Concert" video is certified gold by the RIAA.
Sept [13] John Cougar Mellencamp appears with Paul Simon on NBC-TV's "Coca Cola Presents Live : The Hard Rock".
Nov [12] A 16-track compilation, ***Negotiations And Love Songs, 1971-1986***, reaches UK #17 (and will make US #110).
[24] Simon guests on NBC-TV's "Late Night With David Letterman".

1989

June He embarks on a 15-city tour of Europe and Russia.
July [12] Walt Disney announces at a press conference that their cable network will air the Shelley Duvall-produced "Mother Goose Rock'n'Rhyme", in which Simon will appear as Simple Simon, with Garfunkel as the Rhymeland bartender, among others.
Sept [24] Simon closes the 15th anniversary NBC-TV "Saturday Night Live" special.

1990

Feb [12] Simon, along with Bruce Springsteen and Don Henley, is invited on stage by Sting, backed by Herbie Hancock and Branford Marsalis, for a jam at a fund-raiser for the Rainforest Foundation and the Environmental Media Association in Beverly Hills, CA.
June Part of an international delegation in Czechoslovakia to monitor its elections, Simon participates in a concert in Prague's Old Town Square, in front of an estimated 10,000 people.
Aug [30] He performs a benefit concert at Deep Hollow Ranch, Montauk, NY, for the preservation of Montauk Point Lighthouse, near his Long Island, NY home, singing *Sea Cruise* with Billy Joel.
Sept Simon plays his forthcoming album to a seminar audience at the "Evian Music Festival", organized by his brother, Eddie, in Southampton, NY.
Oct *The Obvious Child*, the rhythm track recorded in the square of the capital city of Salvador in the northeastern state of Bahia, trailering the forthcoming ***The Rhythm Of The Saints***, reaches UK #15.
[20] He plays a gala benefit at Meadowlands, East Rutherford, NJ, to re-elect Bill Bradley to the US Senate. Also appearing are the Hooters and Southside Johnny & the Jersey All-Stars.
[27] Self-produced ***The Rhythm Of The Saints***, based around Brazilian rhythms and musicians, enters the UK chart at #1.
Nov [24] ***The Rhythm Of The Saints*** hits US #4.

1991

Jan [4] Simon begins the North American leg of his "Born At The Right Time" tour at the Tacoma Dome in Tacoma, WA.
[5] *The Obvious Child* peaks at US #92.
[19] He donates at least $15,000 from the proceeds of his Desert Sky Pavilion, Phoenix, AZ, concert, to help get a paid state holiday honoring the Rev. Dr. Martin Luther King Jr.
Mar [16] Simon plays to a sellout crowd of 18,647 at Madison Square Garden, grossing $489,225.
May [12] Simon appears by satellite from the G-Mex, Manchester, Gtr. Manchester, at "The Simple Truth" concert for Kurdish refugees at Wembley Arena, Wembley, performing *You Can Call Me Al, Still Crazy After All These Years* and *Love Me Like A Rock*.
June [3] The 16-date UK leg of his "Born At The Right Time" trek ends at the Scottish Exhibition & Conference Centre, Glasgow, Strathclyde, Scotland.
Aug [8] Simon performs at Billy Joel's benefit at Indian Field Ranch, Montauk.

[15] "Paul Simon Live In Central Park : Born At The Right Time Tour : One Night Only", from the Great Lawn in Central Park, airs live on HBO-TV.
Sept [12] The RIAA certifies two million sales of ***The Rhythm Of The Saints***.
[15] He donates the proceeds from his Starwood Amphitheatre, Antioch, TN concert to the W.O. Smith Nashville Community Music School and Country Music Foundation's Words and Music Program. He also speaks at the Country Music Hall of Fame and Museum in Nashville, at a ceremony in his honor.
Oct [12] Simon performs at the Dome, Tokyo, Japan, during the Far East leg of the "Born At The Right Time" tour, which sees him become the first Western artist to appear in China since the pro-democracy demonstrations of 1989.
Nov [23] ***Paul Simon's Concert In The Park***, recorded on August 15th, charts for a week at UK #60.
Dec [11-12] Simon plays his last shows of the year at the National Auditorium, Mexico City, Mexico, grossing $614,660. (His domestic shows have taken more than $20 million.)

1992

Jan [7] Simon arrives in South Africa for five shows at the invitation of the multi-racial South African Musicians' Alliance, and with the approval of the African National Congress and Nelson Mandela. The radical Azanian People's Organisation (AZAPO) protest the concerts, and the Azanian National Liberation Army claim responsibility for a bomb which goes off at Network Productions, the promoter of the series, in Johannesburg five hours after his arrival in the country. The first date at Ellis Park Stadium, Johannesburg, is the 151st concert of his 27-country "Born At The Right Time" tour, though his opening concerts will suffer from low attendance following threats of violence from black nationalist groups, notably the Azanian Youth Organisation (Azayo), whose leader is arrested on suspicion of terrorism.
[9] He spends much of the day in meetings with the Azanian Youth Organisation to defuse threats of violence against his show, scheduled for the 11th.
[11] ***Paul Simon's Concert In The Park*** makes US #74.
Feb [25] Simon sings *Cool Cool River* at the 34th annual Grammy Awards, held at New York's Radio City Music Hall.
Mar [14] Simon takes part in "Farm Aid V" at the Texas Stadium, Irving, TX.
May [30] He marries singer Edie Brickell in Montauk.
June [3] Simon appears on "MTV Unplugged".
Aug He takes part in the third annual "Back To The Ranch" concert in Montauk, with Waylon Jennings, Kris Kristofferson, Willie Nelson and Johnny Cash.
[30] "Paul Simon's Concert In Central Park" wins the Technical Direction, Video Camera, Miniseries Or Special category, at the annual Emmy Awards, in Pasadena, CA.
Sept [26] He performs at "Hurricane Relief" at the Joe Robbie Stadium, Miami, FL, to help the victims of Hurricane Andrew.
Dec [28] A son, Adrian Edward is born to Paul and Edie.

1993

Jan [20] Simon sings *You Can Call Me Al* at the Tennessee Inaugural Ball in Washington, DC, as a reference to Vice-President Al Gore.
Mar [23] Willie Nelson's ***Across The Borderline***, featuring duets with Simon on *Graceland* and *American Tune*, is released.
Apr [26] He appears at a benefit concert for the Boston Playwright Theater's Derek Walcott.
May [15] Simon guests with Willie Nelson on "Saturday Night Live", also teaming with the country star on the 22nd on CBS-TV's "Willie Nelson : The Bix Six-O".
Oct [23] A three CD/cassette boxed-set career retrospective, ***1964-1993***, peaks at US #173.
Dec [17] ***1964-1993*** is certified gold by the RIAA.

1994

Feb [10] Simon takes part in the "Tibet House Benefit Concert" at Carnegie Hall.
June [10] He participates in an benefit for AMFAR in Dallas, TX.
Aug [1] Paul Simon's fifth annual "Back To The Ranch" benefit is held in Montauk Point.
[17] ***Negotiations And Love Songs 1971-1986*** is certified platinum by the RIAA.
Sept [3] Brickell's ***Picture Perfect Morning***, co-produced by Simon, enters the US chart set to reach #68.
Oct The Rainforest Alliance benefit album ***Earthrise***, featuring Simon's *Under African Skies*, is released on Pyramid Records (US).

1995

Jan [31] The RIAA certifies five million sales of ***Graceland***.
May [31] Simon holds a contest to find an a cappella teenage group to perform in his projected Broadway show, "The Capeman".
Sept [5] The season-opener of US syndicated TV's "Oprah Winfrey", featuring the Simon-penned and sung theme, premieres.
[10] Simon's annual Children's Health Fund benefit concert, launched in 1987 with pediatrician Irving Redlener, takes place at The Paramount, New York, with Annie Lennox, Pete Townshend and Wynton Marsalis also appearing.
Dec [9] Annie Lennox's cover of his *Something So Right*, with Simon guesting, debuts at its UK #44 peak.
see also: SIMON & GARFUNKEL

SIMON & GARFUNKEL

Paul Simon (vocals, guitar); **Art Garfunkel** (vocals)

1953

Simon (b. Oct. 13, 1941, Newark, NJ), the son of Louis Simon, a bass-playing veteran of CBS-TV shows "Arthur Godfrey And His Friends", "The Garry Moore Show" and "The Jackie Gleason Show" and New York, NY session musician, and Garfunkel (b. Arthur Garfunkel, Nov. 5, 1941, Forest Hills, New York) meet at Forest Hills High School in New York and, while in sixth grade, play the White Rabbit and the Cheshire Cat respectively in a production of "Alice In Wonderland". Going on to sing *Sh-Boom* together during assembly at Parsons High School, they begin writing songs together in 1955, registering their copyright of *The Girl For Me* at the Library of Congress for $4.

1957

Nov Having taped a demo of Simon's song, *Hey Schoolgirl*, at Sande's Recording Studio in New York, which has come to the attention of Sid Prosen, who has secured them a one-off deal with Big Records, they adopt the name Tom & Jerry (Garfunkel is Tom Graph and Simon Jerry Landis), and *Hey Schoolgirl* is released. The duo appears on Dick Clark's ABC-TV show, "American Bandstand", performing the single directly after Jerry Lee Lewis sings *Great Balls Of Fire*.

1958

Jan *Hey Schoolgirl* makes US #49, selling 120,000 copies, but will be Tom & Jerry's only chart success, despite further singles on Big, including *Don't Say Goodbye* and *Our Song*, most of which are variations of the Everly Brothers' style and sound. (During the year, Simon also releases the solo single *True Or False*, as True Taylor.)

1959

After high school, Tom & Jerry drift apart. Garfunkel attending Columbia University to study mathematics and architecture, while Simon goes to Queens College to study English. He starts making demo tapes for other singers and cuts further solo singles as Jerry Landis, including *Anna Belle*, on MGM, which is another chart failure. He makes money cutting demos, having been introduced to music publishers by fellow demo-maker, Carole Klein (later Carole King).

1960

Between now and 1963, Simon records several singles for Warwick Records and also writes and produces for others, including Ritchie Cordell, the Fashions and Dotty Daniels. Garfunkel releases two singles under the name Artie Garr on the Octavia and Warwick labels. While at law school, Simon teams up again with Garfunkel (completing a Mathematics degree) and they perform folk-style material for the first time as Simon & Garfunkel.

1964

Oct After Simon has traveled to Britain (joined during the summer vacation by Garfunkel), where he has performed on the folk circuit, Simon & Garfunkel have re-united and are signed by Tom Wilson to CBS/ Columbia Records. Their debut album, ***Wednesday Morning, 3 A.M.***, combining Simon's songs with folk standards like *Go Tell It On The Mountain* and Bob Dylan's *The Times They Are A-Changin'*, is released.

1965

Jan Simon returns to the UK, where he contributes songs to a series of his landlady Judith Piepe's commentaries on the daily BBC radio religious series, "Five To 10". He also returns to the UK folk circuit, with fellow Americans Tom Paxton, Carolyn Hester and Buffy St. Marie.
May Thanks to his US Columbia contract, Simon records the solo album, ***The Paul Simon Songbook***, for UK CBS. (Not a big seller, it contains solo acoustic versions of several songs which will re-appear on the duo's forthcoming album.)
Oct Without informing Simon or Garfunkel, Wilson takes *The Sound Of Silence*, an acoustic track from the debut album, and re-mixes it, adding drums, percussion and stinging electric guitar. The resulting commercial blend is issued as a single. (A similar episode will be recounted in Simon's 1980 movie, "One-Trick Pony".)
Nov The disc has hit #1 in Boston when Simon, living at Al Stewart's house in the UK, is informed by Columbia of the duo's success. He returns to the States and re-unites with Garfunkel for promotional appearances.

1966

Jan [1] *The Sound Of Silence* tops the US chart for the first of two weeks, but struggles in the UK, which is a disappointment to Simon, who regards Britain as a spiritual home.
Feb [14] *The Sound Of Silence* is certified gold by the RIAA.
Mar Their debut album, ***Wednesday Morning, 3 A.M.***, is re-promoted and reaches US #30, while their newly-recorded album, ***Sounds Of Silence***, including the "electric" re-mix of *The Sound Of Silence*, reaches US #21. *Homeward Bound*, dedicated to his girlfriend Kathy Chitty, and written on the platform of the railway station in Widnes, Cheshire, hits US #5, while the Bachelors' cover of *The Sound Of Silence* hits UK #3 (after the original has failed to score - Simon is not amused, as he makes clear in interviews).
Apr *Homeward Bound* is the duo's UK chart debut, hitting #9, while ***Sounds Of Silence*** (with *Homeward Bound* added) reaches UK #13.
June *I Am A Rock*, from the album (and originally recorded solo by Simon on 1964's ***The Paul Simon Songbook***) hits US #3.
July *I Am A Rock* makes UK #17, while the Cyrkle's cover version of Simon's *Red Rubber Ball* hits US #2.
[5] The duo arrives in the UK for a promotional visit, though Simon will contract tonsilitis, and some dates will be cancelled.
Sept *The Dangling Conversation*, a Simon song about deteriorating relationships (and the duo's first track to feature strings), reaches US #25. It fails to chart in the UK, as will the duo's next four US hit singles.

Dec *A Hazy Shade Of Winter* reaches US #13. (The Bangles' 1987 revival will hit US #2.) ***Parsley, Sage, Rosemary And Thyme***, which includes *The Dangling Conversation* and the duo's new arrangement of the traditional *Scarborough Fair/Canticle*, hits US #4.

1967

Mar [18] Simon & Garfunkel begin a short four-date UK tour at London's Royal Albert Hall.

Apr *At The Zoo* reaches US #16, while Harpers Bizarre's cover of Simon's *59th Street Bridge Song (Feelin' Groovy)* (from ***Parsley, Sage, Rosemary And Thyme***), makes US #13 and UK #34.

May [14] They guest on CBS-TV's "The Smothers Brothers Comedy Hour".

June [16] The duo closes the first day of the "Monterey International Pop Festival", at the Monterey County Fairgrounds, Monterey, CA.

Aug *Fakin' It*, with oblique references to Donovan and (instrumentally) the Beatles' *Strawberry Fields Forever*, reaches US #23. Its B-side, *You Don't Know Where Your Interest Lies*, becomes the rarest Simon & Garfunkel CBS track. (After its deletion, it is never re-issued on album or in any other form.) The duo is also commissioned to supply music for the Mike Nichols-directed movie "The Graduate".

Oct [15] They make a return appearance on "The Smothers Brothers Comedy Hour".

1968

Mar [1] They begin another four-date UK tour, at the Odeon Cinema, Manchester, Lancs., set to end on the 9th at the Odeon Cinema, Birmingham, Warks.

[4] The RIAA certifies gold sales of ***Wednesday Morning, 3 A.M.***

[27] ***The Graduate*** is also certified gold by the RIAA.

Apr The angelic *Scarborough Fair/Canticle* reaches US #11. Originally included on ***Parsley, Sage, Rosemary And Thyme***, it is also featured in "The Graduate".

[6] Film soundtrack ***The Graduate***, from the movie which stars Dustin Hoffman and Anne Bancroft, tops the US chart for the first of nine weeks. Alongside incidental music by Dave Grusin, the album features five Simon & Garfunkel tracks, of which *Mrs. Robinson* is the only new song.

May [25] ***Bookends***, compiling fresh Simon compositions with the duo's recent hit singles and a new, fuller version of *Mrs. Robinson*, assumes US pole position from ***The Graduate*** at the beginning of a seven-week run.

June [1] *Mrs. Robinson* tops the US chart for the first of three weeks.

[10] *Mrs. Robinson* becomes the duo's second RIAA-certified gold single.

July *Mrs. Robinson* restores the duo to the UK singles chart, hitting #4, supported by soldout concerts at London's Royal Albert Hall. During their time in Britain, they walk out on BBC1-TV's "Top Of The Pops", when go-go girls dance to their record.

Aug [17] ***Bookends*** begins a five-week run atop the UK survey.

[23] The duo performs at the Hollywood Bowl, Hollywood, CA.

Sept ***Parsley, Sage, Rosemary And Thyme*** is re-released in the UK and reaches UK #13.

Nov Soundtrack album, ***The Graduate***, is released in Britain to tie in with the film's UK release, and hits #3. The duo's debut album, ***Wednesday Morning, 3 A.M.***, is also belatedly issued in the UK, reaching #24.

1969

Feb Four-track EP, *Mrs. Robinson*, hits UK #9.

Mar [12] *Mrs. Robinson* is named Record Of The Year and Best Contemporary Pop Performance Vocal, Duo Or Group, and ***The Graduate*** hailed as Best Original Score Written For A Motion Picture Or A TV Special, at the 11th annual Grammy Awards.

May A new Simon composition, *The Boxer*, hits US #7 and UK #6. The duo follows up with a US tour, between lengthy sessions for the next album, interrupted by Garfunkel's acting commitments.

Nov [30] They host their first television special, the original sponsor, AT&T, having pulled out after realizing the show's political inclinations.

1970

Feb [27] On the eve of its reaching the top, *Bridge Over Troubled Water* is certified gold by the RIAA for one million sales.

[28] Simon-composed ballad, highlighted by Garfunkel's angelic vocal style, *Bridge Over Troubled Water*, hits US #1 for the first of six weeks, becoming the duo's seminal recording legacy.

Mar [7] The landmark album ***Bridge Over Troubled Water*** begins a ten-week stretch atop the US album survey, having already topped the UK chart on February 21st (where it is still at #1 during an initial 13-week run). Written (as ever) by Simon, co-produced by the pair with Roy Halee, and featuring a studio band of Fred Carter (guitar), Hal Blaine (drums), Joe Osborn (bass), Larry Knechtel (keyboards) and strings by Jimmie Haskell and Ernie Freeman, among its tracks is a revival of the Everly Brothers' *Bye Bye Love*, recorded live on tour at a concert in Ames, IA. (Relations between the two have become increasingly strained throughout the reported 800 hours it has taken to complete recording of the album with, among other things, Garfunkel objecting to Simon's song *Cuba Ci, Nixon No*, and Simon becoming frustrated by his partner's film commitment interruptions. By the time the album is released, the duo has effectively split.) Simon agrees to continue as a solo artist on CBS, but on his own terms. Garfunkel's first solo project is acting in Mike Nichols' black-comedy war movie, "Catch 22".

Mar [28] *Bridge Over Troubled Water* begins a three-week run at UK #1, placing the duo in the select company of acts who have simultaneously headed the US and UK singles and album charts.

May From the album, *Cecilia* hits US #4, while folk singer Julie Felix's cover of *El Condor Pasa (If I Could)* (Simon's arrangement of a traditional tune from the Andes) reaches UK #19. Also released this month is "Hair" actress/singer Marsha Hunt's version of *Keep The Customer Satisfied*, which makes UK #41.

June [12] *Cecilia* is certified gold by the RIAA for one million US sales.

[13] ***Bridge Over Troubled Water*** returns to UK #1 for a further four weeks (and will eventually log 41 weeks at the top in eight separate runs over an 18-month period, and spend 304 weeks on the UK survey).

Oct The duo's own version of *El Condor Pasa (If I Could)*, featuring Los Incas, who had played on the same bill as Simon at the Theatre de L'est Parisienne in Paris in 1965, reaches US #18.

1971

Mar [16] Simon & Garfunkel sweep the 13th annual Grammy Awards, as *Bridge Over Troubled Water* is named Record Of The Year, Song Of The Year, Best Contemporary Song, Best Arrangement Accompanying Vocalists and Best Engineered Record, and ***Bridge Over Troubled Water*** is hailed Album Of The Year. (Later in the year, Simon will lead a songwriting workshop at New York University.)

1972

Apr They reunite for a one-off concert in aid of presidential candidate, Senator George McGovern, at New York's Madison Square Garden.

July [29] Compilation album, ***Simon & Garfunkel's Greatest Hits***, including live versions of previously unreleased tracks, hits US #5 and UK #2 (at the start of a 283-week chart tenure).

Oct Taken from the compilation, *For Emily, Whenever I May Find Her* reaches US #53, while its B-side, *America*, makes US #97 and UK #25.

1973

Oct [16] *Bridge Over Troubled Water* is the inaugural disc played on the UK's first commercial radio station, Capital Radio in London.

1975

Oct [19] Simon & Garfunkel reunite to perform on NBC-TV's "Saturday Night Live".

Dec [13] After several years of successful solo careers, the duo have re-teamed to record Simon's *My Little Town*, which is included on the current solo album by each partner, and also hits US #9 as a single.

1977

Oct [18] They appear together, in tuxedos, at the Britannia Music Awards in London where, due to a technical fault with TV cameras, they have to perform *Bookends/Old Friends* for six takes. At the ceremony (a one-off event celebrating the Queen's Silver Jubilee) *Bridge Over Troubled Water* is voted the Best International (Non-UK) Album and Single Released Between 1952 And 1977.

1978

Mar [18] Featured on Garfunkel's ***Watermark***, his re-make of Sam Cooke's 1960 US #12 *Wonderful World*, featuring Simon and James Taylor on guest vocals, reaches US #18.

1981

Sept Garfunkel's ***Scissors Cut*** is released, featuring Simon on the Jimmy Webb-penned *In Cars*.

[19] The duo reunites for a concert in New York's Central Park, after 11 years apart. Over 400,000 attend the performance, which is recorded and filmed for subsequent record release and TV/video showing.

Dec [12] UK compilation, ***The Simon & Garfunkel Collection***, hits UK #4.

1982

Apr [17] Double live set, ***The Concert In Central Park***, released by Geffen Records, hits US #6.

[19] They announce a further reunion, to tour overseas.

May [29] From the live album, the duo's revival of the Everly Brothers' *Wake Up Little Suzie* reaches US #27.

June [8] They open a nine-date European tour (which will end on June 19th before a sellout crowd of 70,000 at Wembley Stadium), at the Hippodrome d'Auteuil in Paris, France. (The tour will reveal the international Simon & Garfunkel audience to be as fervent as ever, but plans for a further US leg will falter as personality rifts again come to a head, and they will return to solo projects.)

July [24] ***The Concert In Central Park*** hits UK #6.

1983

July [19] The duo embarks on another US reunion tour, at the Rubber Bowl in Akron, OH. (It will be a major success and a new Simon & Garfunkel album, ***Think Too Much***, is planned as a follow-up, but they will drift apart during recording and the revamped album will appear as Simon's solo effort, ***Hearts And Bones***.)

1986

May [13] ***The Concert In Central Park*** is certified platinum by the RIAA.

Nov [21] The RIAA certifies multi-platinum sales of ***Parsley, Sage, Rosemary And Thyme*** (three million), ***Bookends*** (two million) and ***Bridge Over Troubled Water*** (five million).

1988

Feb [17] Their "The Concert In Central Park" video is certified gold by the RIAA.

1990

Jan [17] Simon & Garfunkel are inducted into the Rock and Roll Hall of Fame, at the fifth annual dinner, at the Waldorf Astoria Hotel, New York, performing *The Boxer* at the traditional after-dinner jam.

Sept *Scarborough Fair* and *The Sound Of Silence* are named two of BMI's Most Performed Songs Of 1940-1990, as they both surpass the three million mark, and *Bridge Over Troubled Water* and *Mrs. Robinson* are named likewise for surpassing four million performances each.

1991

July [22] The RIAA certifies two million sales of ***Sounds Of Silence***.
Dec [21] Further compilation, ***The Definitive Simon & Garfunkel***, hits UK #8.
[28] Reissued *A Hazy Shade Of Winter*, backed with *Silent Night/Seven O'Clock News*, reaches UK #30.

1992

Feb [15] Reissued, *The Boxer* charts for a week at UK #75.
May [4] The duo reunites for the first time since 1981 at New York's Brooks Atkinson Theatre for a benefit, also featuring the comedy team of Mike Nichols and Elaine May, for Friends In Deed, a non-medical AIDS patient-assisting foundation. A second show will take place on the 11th.
July [8] ***Collected Works***, a three-CD boxed set, digitally remixed by Halee at New York's Hit Factory, combining their five albums together, complete with lyrics and released earlier in the year, is certified gold by the RIAA.

1993

Mar [1] Simon & Garfunkel perform another benefit at the Dorothy Chandler Pavilion, Los Angeles, which raises $1 million for the Children's Health Fund Project. They are backed by actor Steve Martin and Neil Young, for whom they return the favor on *Helpless* and *Only Love Can Break Your Heart*.
Oct [1] A further ten-show reunion stint begins at the Paramount, New York.
Nov [5] They take part in the seventh annual Bridge School benefit at the Shoreline Amphitheatre, Mountain View, CA.
[14] The RIAA certifies six million sales of ***Simon & Garfunkel's Greatest Hits***.
see also: **Art GARFUNKEL, Paul SIMON**

SIMPLE MINDS

Jim Kerr (vocals); **Charlie Burchill** (guitar); **Mike McNeil** (keyboards); **John Giblin** (bass); **Mel Gaynor** (drums)

1978

May Members of Johnny & the Self Abusers, a Glasgow, Strathclyde, Scotland septet featuring three guitarists, who split on the day of release of their first single, *Saints And Sinners*, on Chiswick in November the previous year, have divided according to musical interests to form the '60s-flavored Cuban Heels, and the more contemporary and experimental Simple Minds. Now joined by McNeil (b. July 20, 1958, Glasgow), who has previously played keyboards with a variety of local bands, and Derek Forbes (b. June 22, 1956, Glasgow) (bass) ex-Subs, the band records a six-song demo at Glasgow's CaVa Studios. This comes to the attention of Ian Cranna (then contributor to UK music paper, **New Musical Express**, and later manager of Orange Juice) and Edinburgh, Lothian, Scotland record store owner, Bruce Findlay. The band gigs consistently throughout Scotland, including a residency at Glasgow's Mars Bar.
July [17] Simple Minds debut at Glasgow's Satellite City club, with a line-up of Kerr (b. July 9, 1959, Glasgow), Burchill (b. Nov. 27, 1959, Glasgow), Brian McGee (drums) and Duncan Barnwell (guitar), all one-time Self Abusers.
Nov Barnwell quits as the remaining quintet records another demo at CaVa, subsequently released through the Edinburgh indie label, Zoom (run by Findlay and licensed to Arista Records). The deal gives Arista control of Simple Minds, regardless of their own commitment to Zoom.

1979

Jan The band, now with a settled line-up of Forbes, McNeil, Kerr, Burchill and McGee, begins recording its debut album at the Farmhouse Studios in Amersham, Bucks., enlisting the services of John Leckie, whose production work with Magazine has impressed them
The resulting ***Life In A Day*** reaches UK #30 in its first week of release, spending a further five weeks retreating, while its title track, *Life In A Day*, peaks at UK #62. They spend the rest of the year gigging extensively in the UK and the rest of Europe, with two appearances on BBC2-TV's "Old Grey Whistle Test", including a session shot live at New York's Hurrah club during their first US visit in October, and recording a second, more experimental album.

1980

Jan ***Real To Real Cacophony*** is released. According to one reviewer, it is considered the most uncommercial album ever issued by Arista.
Feb With the album and single *Changeling* failing to chart, Zoom folds, and Simple Minds continue on the main Arista label. Findlay joins business lawyer, Robert White, to form Schoolhouse Management (which will handle Simple Minds' future affairs).
Aug [26] The group supports the Skids at London's Hammersmith Palais.
Sept ***Empires And Dance*** charts for three weeks, reaching UK #41, and impresses Peter Gabriel, who invites the group to open for him on a lengthy European tour.
Oct As *I Travel* fails to score, the band looks for a new record deal.

1981

Feb Arista releases *Celebrate*. Simple Minds have negotiated their departure from Arista, renouncing their rights to back royalties, and sign to Virgin Records.
May [30] Their label debut, *The American*, reaches UK #59.
Aug [22] *Love Song*, from the forthcoming album, makes UK #47.
Sept Simple Minds release two albums, ***Sons And Fascinations*** and ***Sister Feelings Call***, both produced by Steve Hillage, in an unusual double package, initially made available as a limited-edition twin-set, and subsequently released separately.
[17] The group plays at Rock City, Nottingham, Notts., during current UK dates.
[19] The double album peaks at UK #11 during a seven-week stay. McGee quits, citing exhaustion, to be replaced by ex-Zones drummer, Kenny Hyslop.
Nov [14] *Sweat In Bullet* peaks at UK #52.

1982

Jan Two days after recording a new single for April release, the band sets off on a European tour.
Mar [6] Arista releases a compilation of early Simple Minds tracks, ***Celebration***, which makes UK #45.
May [15] *Promised You A Miracle*, from the next album, peaks at UK #13 in an 11-week stay. Hyslop quits, to be replaced first by Mark Ogletree, then Mel Gaynor (b. May 29, 1959, Glasgow), veteran sessioneer for the likes of Tina Charles and the Nolan Sisters.
July [16-18] The group performs during the first "WOMAD" festival at the Royal Bath & West Showground, in Shepton Mallet, Somerset.
Oct [2] ***New Gold Dream (81, 82, 83, 84)***, produced by Steve Walsh with work from all three drummers, although Gaynor's contributions predominate, hits UK #3. (The album confirms Simple Minds' increasing popularity, eventually spending over one year on the UK album survey. The band begins a soldout UK tour.)
[9] *Glittering Prize* reaches UK #16. (Having bought the entire Arista/Simple Minds back catalog, Virgin reissues their first four albums.)
Nov [20] Third single from ***New Gold Dream***, *Someone Somewhere (In Summertime)* makes UK #36, its 12" release including *King Is White And In The Crowd*, a BBC radio/session track recorded for the David Jensen program.

1983

Feb Simple Minds begin to make an impression in the US, where ***New Gold Dream*** begins a 19-week stay on the chart, reaching #69.
Aug The band participates in a U2-headlining open-air rock festival at the Phoenix Park, Dublin, Eire.
Nov Anthemic *Waterfront*, marking the group's first collaboration with producer Steve Lillywhite (who has been introduced to Kerr via mutual friend, U2's Bono), makes UK #13.

1984

Jan *Speed Your Love To Me,* featuring Kirsty MacColl on guest vocals, reaches UK #20.
Feb [18] The Lillywhite-produced ***Sparkle In The Rain*** tops the UK chart at the beginning of a 57-week survey tenure, and begins climbing to US #64.
Mar *Up On The Catwalk* reaches UK #27.
[13] A UK tour is cancelled after Kerr falls ill at the end of the opening night in Birmingham, West Midlands.
May Simple Minds play eight consecutive nights at London's Hammersmith Odeon, tying Elton John's 1982 record. John Giblin replaces Forbes on bass.
[5] Kerr marries Chrissie Hynde, after which Simple Minds support Hynde's Pretenders on a US tour.

1985

May [18] Simple Minds achieve a major breakthrough in the States with the Keith Forsey and Steve Chiff-written *Don't You Forget About Me*, from the soundtrack to US "brat-pack" movie, "The Breakfast Club", topping the chart. Their first release that is not self-penned, it had been rejected by both Billy Idol and Bryan Ferry. It also hits UK #7, spending more than half a year on the UK rankings.
June Soundtrack album, ***The Breakfast Club***, including the Simple Minds cut, and the only album which will feature the hit prior to group compilations, reaches US #17.
July [13] Simple Minds perform at the "Live Aid" benefit spectacular at the JFK Stadium, Philadelphia, PA, dedicating *Ghostdancing* to Amnesty International, an organization for which they tour later in the year.
Aug A consistent seller, *Don't You Forget About Me* re-enters at UK #61.
Nov [2] ***Once Upon A Time***, co-produced by Bob Clearmountain and Jimmy Iovine, debuts at UK #1, and will earn UK platinum status during an 82-week chart stay. (Released through their A&M contract in the US, it will hit US #10 in March 1986.) The typically rousing and anthemic extract, *Alive And Kicking*, hits UK #7.
Dec The band begins an extensive world tour.
[28] *Alive And Kicking* hits US #3.

1986

Jan *Sanctify Yourself* hits UK #10.
[31] ***Once Upon A Time*** is certified gold by the RIAA.
Mar *All The Things She Said* hits UK #9.
[15] *Sanctify Yourself* reaches US #14.
Apr [20] The combined Simple Minds/Rod Stewart soccer XI beat Pepperdine 2-0.
May [31] *All The Things She Said* reaches US #28.
June [22] Simple Minds top the bill at the "Milton Keynes Bowl Pop Festival", Milton Keynes, Bucks.
Aug [12] The final date of their current world tour in Paris, France, is recorded for future live album release.
Nov A live version of *Ghostdancing* reaches UK #13.

1987

June [6] Their third successive UK platinum album, ***Live In The City Of Light***, a double performance set recorded in Sydney, New South Wales, Australia, and Paris, enters the UK chart at #1, and will rise to US #96.
July *Promised You A Miracle* makes UK #19, taken from the live set.

1988

Jan The group plays three sellout shows at Barrowlands, Glasgow, donating £40,000 to underprivileged children.

June [11] The group performs at "Nelson Mandela's 70th Birthday Tribute" at Wembley Stadium, Wembley, Middx., much to the displeasure of Scottish MP Nicholas Fairburn, who describes Kerr and fellow performer Annie Lennox as "left-wing scum". They record *Mandela*, which they pledge not to release, but which is aired on UK radio.

1989

Feb [25] *Belfast Child*, produced by Trevor Horn and based on the traditional song, *She Moved Through The Fair*, tops the UK chart for the first of two weeks. (At 6 minutes 39 seconds, it becomes the second longest UK #1 behind the Beatles' *Hey Jude*.)
Apr *This Is Your Land* reaches UK #13.
May [13] ***Street Fighting Years***, concentrating on non-personal themes including *Belfast*, and ecology and anti-apartheid issues (the title track is dedicated to the Chilean poet and songwriter Victor Jara, who was murdered as a political prisoner), enters the UK chart in pole position, and goes on to peak at US #70.
[15] A lengthy world tour begins in Italy. They will not perform at the scheduled Murrayfield Stadium, Edinburgh date, due to Kerr's objection to the venue's administrators allowing Scottish rugby players to attend the sport's centenary celebrations in South Africa.
July [23] The UK tour leg starts at Roundhay Park, Leeds, W. Yorks., set to end at Wembley Stadium, on August 26th. *Kick It In* reaches UK #15.
Dec *The Amsterdam EP*, including Simple Minds' version of Prince's *Sign Of The Times*, reaches UK #18. Following the end of their world trek, Kerr and Birchill retreat to Amsterdam to begin writing for their next album. A series of personnel upheavals has left the pair as the only permanent nucleus of Simple Minds.

1990

Apr The group parts company with manager, Bruce Findlay.
[16] Simple Minds perform at the "Nelson Mandela - An International Tribute For A Free South Africa" concert at Wembley Stadium.
May Virgin Video releases "Verona", a live performance film lensed on the band's last world tour.
June They enter their own Highland Studio in Scotland to begin recording, with Steve Lipson helming production. The new line-up includes band stalwart Gaynor on drums, Malcolm Foster on bass, and session player Peter Vetesse on keyboards. (Forbes and McGee are now in Propaganda with Michael Mertens and Betsi Miller.)
Oct [12] Virgin Records release ***Themes : Volume 1***, the first of four CD-only mini-box sets, each of which includes four discs devoted to chronologically recalling all of Simple Minds' 12" single releases. ***Themes : Volume 2, ... 3, and ... 4*** will be released, one a week, for the following three weeks.

1991

Mar [30] *Let There Be Love*, trailering its parent album, ***Real Life***, hits UK #6.
Apr [20] ***Real Life***, produced by Stephen Lipson, debuts at its UK #2 peak.
May [11] ***Real Life*** makes US #74.
[23] The North American leg of their "Real Life" world tour opens at the Congress Centre, Ottawa, ON, Canada, set to end on June 19th at the Universal Amphitheatre, Universal City, CA.
June [1] *See The Lights* reaches UK #20.
[14] The group guests on US syndicated TV's "Arsenio Hall".
[29] *See The Lights* makes US #40.
Aug [10] The group opens the UK segment of its tour at Maine Road, Manchester, Gtr. Manchester - the home of Manchester City Football Club. This ten-date leg, supported by the Stranglers and Orchestral Manoeuvres In The Dark, will end on the 24th at the Milton Keynes Bowl.
[23] They guest on BBC1-TV's "Wogan".
[31] *Stand By Love* bows at its UK #13 peak.
Oct [21, 23] Simple Minds play additional UK dates at Wembley Arena.
Nov [2] *Real Life* reaches UK #34.
Dec [30] "Real Live At Barrowlands" airs on BBC2-TV.

1992

Jan [3] Divorced from Hynde, Kerr marries actress Patsy Kensit at Chelsea Register Office. Bridesmaids are Kerr's stepdaughter, Jasmine, 9, and daughter, Natalie, 6.
Oct [17] *Love Song/Alive And Kicking* hits UK #6.
[24] A greatest hits collection, ***Glittering Prize 81/92***, enters the UK chart at #1, where it will stay for three weeks.

1994

Sept [24] The group guests on the inaugural BBC2-TV's "TOTP2".
Dec [6] They play at the WFNX "Miracle On Lansdowne Street" benefit concert at the Avalon, Boston, MA, during a series of acoustic Christmas radio benefits.

1995

Jan [3] The group guests on CBS-TV's "Late Show With David Letterman".
[20] They appear on BBC2-TV's "The O Zone".
[28] *She's A River*, the first single from the band's forthcoming ***Good News From The Next World***, debuts at its UK #9 peak.
Feb [9] The group, now comprising Kerr and Burchill with Foster, Mark Taylor (keyboards/acoustic guitar) and Mark Schulman (drums), embarks on a North American tour at Moore Theater, Seattle, WA, set to end on March 1st at the Center Stage Theatre, Atlanta, GA.
[11] Following a three-year silence, Simple Minds returns with ***Good News From The Next World***, inspired by a trip Kerr took to India and produced by Keith Forsey, which peaks at UK #2 in its week of entry.
[25] ***Good News From The Next World*** debuts at its US #87 high.
Mar [3] They guest on NBC-TV's "The Tonight Show".
[4] *She's A River* makes US #52.
[17] A European tour opens at the Point, Dublin, Eire, set to end at the Omnisports, Rennes, France on May 4th.
Apr [8] *Hypnotised*, featuring Tim Simenon's remixes on CD Volume 1 and live recordings of *Up On The Catwalk, And The Band Played On* and *She's A River* on CD Volume 2, debuts at its UK #18 peak.
June [25] The group takes part in the annual "Glastonbury Festival" at Worthy Farm, Glastonbury, Somerset.

1996

Jan Simple Minds, after 14 years with Virgin, signs with Chrysalis Records worldwide, the first act to do so since the label was folded into the EMI parent. (Two weeks after setting up the deal, manager Clive Banks will sever ties with the group.)

SIMPLY RED

Mick Hucknall (vocals); **Sylvan Richardson** (guitar); **Fritz McIntyre** (keyboards); **Tony Bowers** (bass); **Chris Joyce** (drums); **Tim Kellett** (horns)

1985

Manchester-based new wave band the Frantic Elevators, focused around singer/writer Hucknall (b. June 8, 1960, Denton, near Manchester, Lancs.), an ex-local club DJ and art college student since 1980, who was raised by his father, a barber, and his aunt Nellie, has split in 1984, after releasing several singles on local independent labels, including *You Know What* (Eric's), *Searchin' For The Only One* (Crackin' Up), *Voices In The Dark* (TJM) and *Holding Back The Years (No Waiting)*, between 1979 and 1983. Hucknall has formed a new, more soul-influenced group, Simply Red, named after his distinctive wild mop of red hair, with the initial line-up supplemented by David Fryman, Eddie Sherwood, Ojo and Mog, but which now settles as Hucknall, Richardson, McIntyre (b. Sept. 2, 1958, Birmingham, West Midlands), Kellett (b. July 23, 1964, Knaresborough, N. Yorks.) and ex-Durutti Column members, Bowers (b. Oct. 31, 1956) and Joyce (b. Nov. 10, 1957, Manchester). The group signs a worldwide deal with Elektra Records, after Seymour Stein of US label Sire has shown earlier interest, and begins recording in Amsterdam, Holland, with its new personnel.
July Their debut single, the soul, funk-based *Money's Too Tight (To Mention)*, a cover of the Valentine Brothers 1983 UK #73, reaches UK #13, as the band supports James Brown in concert in London.
Sept *Come To My Aid* makes UK #66.
Oct Their first album, ***Picture Book***, produced by Stewart Levine, and showcasing Hucknall's gifted and distinctive soul vocal range, initially reaches UK #34. (It will climb to UK #2 during a more than two-year stay on the survey.)
Nov Ballad, *Holding Back The Years*, a re-recording of the earlier Frantic Elevators song written by Hucknall at the age of 19 with ex-colleague, Neil Smith, initially stops at UK #51, despite four different format releases.

1986

Mar *Moody Jericho* climbs to UK #53, while the band embarks on its first US tour.
July Reissued *Holding Back The Years* hits UK #2, as worldwide sales top the million mark. ***Picture Book*** reaches US #16.
[12] *Holding Back The Years* tops the US chart for one week.
Aug *Open Up The Red Box* makes UK #61.
Sept [15] They perform live at the third annual MTV Video Music Awards, broadcast simultaneously from the Universal Amphitheatre, Universal City, CA, and the Palladium, New York, NY.
Oct [4] *Money's Too Tight (To Mention)*, reissued as the US follow-up, although originally released in August 1985, reaches #28.

1987

Feb [24] The group sings *Money's Too Tight (To Mention)* at the 29th Grammy awards at the Shrine Auditorium, Los Angeles, CA.
Mar *The Right Thing* reaches UK #11.
[21] Their Alex Sadkin-produced sophomore set, ***Men And Women***, hits UK #2 in its week of entry, and will reach US #31. The album, including songs by Cole Porter, Sly Stone and Bunny Wailer, is banned in Singapore because of "crude lyrics" in *The Right Thing*. Their debut album, ***Picture Book***, picks up renewed sales, and now hits UK #2 as the band adds new members - Aziz Ibrahim (guitar), replacing Richardson, Ian Kirkham (sax) and Janette Sewell (vocals).
May [16] *The Right Thing* reaches US #27.
June *Infidelity*, co-written by Lamont Dozier, reaches UK #31.
July *Maybe Someday* is released.
Dec *Ev'rytime We Say Goodbye*, a Cole Porter revival previously issued by Simply Red as a bonus track on the 12" version of *The Right Thing*, reaches UK #11, and features guest cellist, Eleanor Morris.

1988

Feb [17] The group embarks on a UK tour at the Royal Dublin Society Hall, Dublin, Eire, set to end on March 16th at the National Exhibition Centre, Birmingham, West Midlands.
Mar *I Won't Feel Bad* peaks at UK #68.

1989

Jan Soul ballad, *It's Only Love*, reaches UK #13. UK tabloid **Daily Mirror** publishes an article criticising the supposedly left-wing Hucknall for living as a tax exile in Milan, Italy.
Feb [25] Its parent album, ***A New Flame***, produced by Levine and recorded in Montserrat, West Indies, enters at UK #1, where it will stay for four weeks. It features tracks penned by Hucknall with Lamont Dozier and the Crusaders' Joe Sample. Simply Red,

with new guitarist Heitor T.P. replacing Ibrahim (vocalist Sewell is no longer with the band), embarks on a major world tour.
Mar [25] *It's Only Love* peaks at US #57.
Apr Their re-make of Harold Melvin & the Bluenotes' soul classic, *If You Don't Know Me By Know*, hits UK #2.
June ***A New Flame*** reaches US #22 during a 39-week chart residence.
[28] ***A New Flame*** is certified gold by the RIAA.
July Title track, *A New Flame*, reaches UK #17.
[15] *If You Don't Know Me By Now* hits US #1 for one week, their second US chart-topper.
[19] *If You Don't Know Me By Now* is certified gold by the RIAA.
Oct Swaying ballad, *You've Got It*, makes UK #46.

1990

Feb [21] *If You Don't Know Me By Now* is named Best Rhythm & Blues Song, at the 32nd annual Grammy Awards held at the Shrine Auditorium.
Aug [14] ***Picture Book*** is certified platinum by the RIAA.

1991

Sept [11] Simply Red guests on BBC1-TV's "Wogan".
[28] *Something Got Me Started* reaches UK #11.
Oct [3] Hucknall and Moss are honored at ASCAP's 11th annual London Awards at Claridges for the broadcast success of *Holding Back The Years*.
[12] Featuring newly-recruited drummer Gota and bassist Shaun Ward, the Hucknall-penned ***Stars***, again helmed by Levine, enters the UK chart at #1. (It will become the biggest-selling UK album of the next two years, making five trips to the summit, and achieve platinum sales nine times over, including selling 1.32 million units in its first 14 weeks on sale. Worldwide sales will top nine million.)
Nov [9] ***Stars*** makes US #79, the only major territory where the album does not make a significant impression.
[15] Hucknall guests on NBC-TV's "Late Night With David Letterman".
[23] *Something Got Me Started* reaches US #23.
Dec [1] Simply Red appears at the "Red Hot & Dance" AIDS benefit.
[14] Title cut, *Stars*, hits UK #8.
[18] They guest on syndicated TV's "Arsenio Hall".
[31] The group takes part in ABC-TV's "Dick Clark's New Year's Rockin' Eve '92".

1992

Jan [16] Simply Red embarks on a seven-date UK tour at the Exhibition Centre, Aberdeen, Grampian, Scotland, set to end on the 28th at the Sheffield Arena, Sheffield, S. Yorks.
Feb [12] The group shares the Best British Group award (with KLF) at the 11th annual BRIT Awards, at London's Hammersmith Odeon, at which it also performs live.
[22] Ballad, *For Your Babies*, hits UK #9.
Mar [14] *Stars* makes US #44.
Apr [15] Hucknall is named Songwriter Of The Year, at the 37th annual Ivor Novello Awards, at London's Grosvenor House Hotel.
May Simply Red participates in the 1992 World Music Awards held at the Sporting Club, Monte Carlo, Monaco.
[9] *Thrill Me* makes UK #33.
[13] ***Stars*** is certified gold by the RIAA.
[19] The group begins a short US tour at the Warfield Theatre, San Francisco, CA.
[26] Simply Red guests on NBC-TV's "The Tonight Show".
June [10] They play to a sellout crowd of 6,000 at the first Central Park Summer Stage concert series in New York.
July [11-12] The group performs at Wembley Stadium, Wembley, during the European leg of its tour.
[25] *Your Mirror* debuts at its UK #17 peak.
Aug [1] They play at the "Thurles Feile Festival" in Thurles, Tipperary, Eire.
Sept [17-18] Australian tour opens at the Sydney Entertainment Centre, Sydney, New South Wales, before a sellout crowd of 16,650. The ten-date series will end on October 3rd at the Entertainment Centre, Perth, Western Australia.
Nov [21] Live EP, *Montreux*, recorded at this summer's "Montreux Jazz Festival" in Montreux, Switzerland, and comprising three covers and the Hucknall original, *Lady Godiva's Room*, bows at its UK #11 peak.
[21-23] The group begins a 26-date UK tour at Wembley Arena, including four shows at the Sheffield Arena, which break the house record, grossing £1,140,640 and six at the National Exhibition Centre, Birmingham, which are re-scheduled to February 1993 after Hucknall suffers vocal problems.

1993

Feb [16] With ***Stars'*** worldwide sales currently standing at eight million, and performing the extracted *Wonderland* during the ceremony, Hucknall is named the Best Male Artist with Simply Red hailed Best Group, at the 12th annual BRIT Awards, held at London's Alexandra Palace.
[22-24, 26-28] Simply Red plays its re-scheduled National Exhibition Centre, Birmingham dates.

1993

May [3] Hucknall takes part in James Brown's birthday bash at the Civic Center, Augusta, GA.
[26] Simply Red performs at the "Apollo Theatre Hall Of Fame" concert, set to air on NBC-TV on September 6th.
Nov [23] Hucknall and steeplejack Fred Dibnah "top out" the roof of the new Manchester Arena.
Dec [1] He takes part in the "Concert of Hope" at the Wembley Arena, on a bill with George Michael, David Bowie, Annie Lennox and k.d. lang.

1995

Sept [30] *Fairground* enters at UK #1, selling more than 200,000 copies in its first week on sale.
Oct [21] ***Life*** enters at UK #1. The album, produced by Hucknall and longterm collaborator Levine, has been mostly recorded at Chris Joyce's Manchester studio, with a band line-up comprising Hucknall, Heitor, McIntyre, Joyce and Kirkham, with help from veteran rhythm train Sly & Robbie and Bootsy Collins.
[23] Hucknall guests on NBC-TV's "The Tonight Show", during a US promotional visit.
Nov [25] Again failing to match its European success, ***Life*** makes US #75.
Dec [16] *Remembering The First Time*, including live versions of *Enough* and *A New Flame* on CD1 and remixes by Hucknall/Harrington, Self-Preservation Society, Satoshi Tomiie and Too Precious on the CD2 release, debuts at its UK #22 peak.
[18-20] Simply Red performs at the Wembley Arena.
[29] Hucknall sings *Ding Dong Merrily On High* at the end of BBC2-TV's festive "Knowing Me, Knowing Yule ... with Alan Partridge".

1996

Jan [4] Simply Red begins a month-long series of UK dates at the National Exhibition Centre, Birmingham, set to end on February 5th at the London Arena.
Feb [19] Performing *Fairground*, Simply Red opens the 15th annual BRIT Awards held at London's Earl's Court Exhibition Centre.
[24] *Never Never Love* bows at its UK #18 peak.
Mar [25] They perform at the Dubai Beach Hilton, for a reported £150,000, during festivities for the Dubai World Cup horse race on the 27th in the United Arab Emirates.
Apr [13] Simply Red & White's *Daydream Believer (Cheer Up Peter Reid)*, encouraging the Sunderland soccer team in its promotion push and only available in the area, makes UK #41.
June [10] Recorded as the official theme song for the Euro '96 soccer championship, the band's *We're In This Together* is released by East West.
June [13] The group ends a tour of Europe in Budapest, Hungary.

SIOUXSIE & THE BANSHEES

Siouxsie Sioux (vocals); **John McGeoch** (guitar); **Steve Severin** (bass); **Budgie** (drums)

1976

Sept [20] Bromley, Kent punkette Siouxsie (b. Susan Dallion, May 27, 1957, London), working as a waitress in Chislehurst, Kent, takes part in the "100 Club Punk Festival" in London, with Sid Vicious on drums, Steve Havoc on bass and Marco Pirroni on guitar. Their live set, featuring Siouxsie reciting *The Lord's Prayer*, lasts 20 minutes, and is their last performance as the band splits immediately. (Havoc, staying with Sioux in the newly revamped Banshees (taking its name from Vincent Price's 1970 movie "Cry Of The Banshee"), will revert to the name Steve Severin (b. Sept. 25, 1955, London), Vicious will join the Sex Pistols, and Pirroni will join the Models before becoming Adam Ant's songwriting partner in Adam & the Ants.)
Dec [1] Siouxsie appears with the Sex Pistols on ITV's "Today", telling host Bill Grundy, "I always wanted to meet you", to which Grundy replies: "We'll meet afterwards, shall we?" Kenny Morris joins the Banshees on drums.

1977

Feb [24] Pete Fenton joins on guitar.
July [2] John McKay replaces Fenton.
Oct [20] After a Johnny Thunders & the Heartbreakers' Rainbow Theatre, London gig, at which the Banshees are support act, Siouxsie and Morris, and 999's drummer Pablo LaBritain, are arrested and detained overnight at Holloway Road Police Station. They are fined £20 each for obstruction, and released the following morning.
Nov The band sings *Make Up To Break Up* on its debut UK TV appearance.
[29] They record a session for John Peel's BBC Radio 1 show.

1978

June [9] The group signs to Polydor Records, after intense lobbying by their fans, including a "Sign The Banshees Now!" graffiti campaign.
[21] Siouxsie & the Banshees appear with the Clash, the Sex Pistols and Generation X in Don Letts' film, "Punk Rock Movie". (The group was also filmed for Derek Jarman's "Jubilee", but the clip was never used.)
Sept After much word-of-mouth and media interest, their debut single, *Hong Kong Garden*, hits UK #7.
Oct [11] The band starts its first major UK tour with Sioux persisting with her black leather, heavily made-up, often breast-exposing visual stage presence, with Nico and Human League as support acts.
Dec ***The Scream***, co-produced by the band with Steve Lillywhite, reaches UK #12.

1979

Apr [7] The group plays a charity concert for MENCAP, but is later faced with a £2,000 bill for seat damage.
[28] *The Staircase (Mystery)* reaches UK #24.
July *Playground Twist* makes UK #28.
Sept ***Join Hands*** reaches UK #13.
[7] Morris and McKay walk out on the second night of a 24-date UK tour, and after five days of panic, the others are temporarily joined for the balance of the dates by Budgie (b. Aug. 21, 1957, St. Helens, Lancs.) (formerly with the Slits) on drums, and Robert Smith, on loan from the Cure, on guitar.
Oct [3] Sioux is hospitalized with hepatitis.
[29] *Mittageisen (Metal Postcard)* makes UK #47.

1980

Jan [16] With Smith committed to the Cure, John

McGeoch (moonlighting from Magazine) joins temporarily on guitar.
Apr *Happy House*, produced by the band and Nigel Gray, makes UK #17.
June *Christine* makes UK #24.
July McGeoch joins on guitar full-time.
Aug ***Kaleidoscope***, featuring ex-Sex Pistols guitarist Steve Jones, hits UK #5.
Oct The band tours the US for the first time.
Dec [6] *Israel* climbs to UK #41.

1981

Feb The group embarks on an 11-date UK tour.
Mar Altered Images' *Dead Pop Stars*, produced by Severin, is released in the UK.
June[18] The Banshees play their first Iron Curtain concert in Yugoslavia, before embarking on what they state will be their last UK tour.
[27] *Spellbound* reaches UK #22 and ***Juju*** hits UK #7.
Aug [10] The group plays a charity concert for the Disabled Children's International Games.
[22] *Arabian Nights* reaches UK #32, while the band is on a major 30-date UK tour.
Oct Siouxsie and Budgie have started a spin-off project as the Creatures, recording *Mad-Eyed Screamers*, which reaches UK #24.

1982

Jan [9] Compilation album, ***Once Upon A Time***, reaches UK #21, and is also issued as a video collection. The group tours again in the US.
June [5] *Fire Works* reaches UK #22. Siouxsie contracts laryngitis and is ordered to rest her voice for a year, on the advice of doctors at the Gothenberg Hospital, after being struck down during a Scandinavian tour. She cancels the tour and flies back to London for a second opinion.
Oct [16] *Slow Dive* makes UK #41.
Nov [13] ***A Kiss In The Dreamhouse***, produced by Mike Hedges (and including the band's first recordings with string accompaniment) reaches UK #11. Smith is borrowed from the Cure again for the tour to promote the album when McGeoch falls ill. (Without returning, McGeoch will announce within a few weeks that he has left the group, apparently dissatisfied with Siouxsie's attitude.)
Dec [11] *Melt*, a double A-side with the French-language Christmas song, *Il Est Né Le Divin Enfant*, makes UK #49.

1983

Most of the first half of the year is spent on solo/spin-off projects, as Siouxsie and Budgie record the Creatures album, ***Feast***, while Severin and Smith (who has stayed on as a Banshee in addition to his Cure commitments) form the Glove. Both projects will be released on the Banshees' newly-formed Wonderland Records, licensed to Polydor.
May The Creatures reach UK #21 with *Miss The Girl*.
Aug Their follow-up, *Right Now*, originally recorded by Mel Torme as the B-side to his 1963 *Comin' Home Baby* hit, makes UK #14.
Sept [6] The group plays a concert in Italy for the communist party.
Oct Siouxsie & the Banshees' revival of Lennon and McCartney's *Dear Prudence* proves to be the group's biggest UK single success, hitting #3.
[31] The band plays the first of two concerts at London's Royal Albert Hall (the second on November 1st), which are recorded for a live album release.
Dec Live double set, ***Nocturne***, is the first album release on the new Wonderland label, and reaches UK #29.

1984

Apr *Swimming Horses* makes UK #28.
May Smith leaves to concentrate on the Cure's career and is replaced on guitar by John Carruthers (ex-Clock DVA).
June *Dazzle* reaches UK #33. ***Hyena*** reaches UK #15, as the band appears in a C4-TV special.
July ***Hyena***, released in the US by Geffen Records, becomes the group's first American chart success, at #157.
Nov EP *Overground*, featuring the Chandos Players' string-section, comprising renditions of *Overground* and *Placebo Effect*, makes UK #47.

1985

Oct The band undertakes a month-long UK tour, after two attempts at beginning a new studio album with two different producers, Bob Ezrin and Hugh Jones. Siouxsie spends much of the tour with a leg in plaster, after dislocating a kneecap on stage at London's Hammersmith Odeon.
Nov *Cities In Dust* reaches UK #21.

1986

Jan The group appears in the film "Out Of Bounds".
Mar *Candy Man* reaches UK #34.
May ***Tinderbox***, produced by the band with Steve Churchyard, reaches UK #13.
June [6-7] The band performs at the Hollywood Palladium, Hollywood, CA, during a US tour.
July ***Tinderbox*** makes US #88.

1987

Feb Their up-date of Bob Dylan's *This Wheel's On Fire*, originally a UK hit for Julie Driscoll and the Brian Auger Trinity, reaches UK #14.
Mar Carruthers leaves, to be replaced by John Klein (ex-Specimen), while Martin McCarrick joins on keyboards.
[14] ***Through The Looking Glass***, a set of cover versions of songs by Bob Dylan, Billie Holiday, Magazine, Iggy Pop, Roxy Music and others, debuts at its UK #15 peak.
Apr *The Passenger*, their revival of the Iggy Pop song, makes UK #41, as ***Through The Looking Glass*** peaks at US #188.
July The band makes a one-off live London appearance, at the Finsbury Park "Supertent".
Aug *Song From The Edge Of The World* reaches UK #59.

1988

Aug *Peek A Boo*, revealing a shift in the group's musical direction, peaks at UK #16.
Sept [17] Dance-flavored ***Peepshow*** bows at its UK #20 peak, as the band begins another UK tour.
Oct *The Killing Jar* makes UK #41.
Dec [3] *The Last Beat Of My Heart* peaks at UK #44, as *Peek A Boo* makes US #53 and parent album, ***Peepshow***, on Geffen Records, climbs to US #68.

1990

Mar [3] With a previewing cut *Standing There* having already made UK #53 the previous October, the Creatures' ***Boomerang*** bows at its US #197 peak.
[20] The Creatures make their North American live debut in Toronto, Canada.

1991

Jan Siouxsie wins a libel suit against the **Daily Mirror**, who alleged she had received a "nose job".
June [1] *Kiss Them For Me* reaches UK #32.
[22] ***Superstition***, co-produced by Stephen Hague, debuts at its UK #25 peak.
July [1] The group, now with Budgie and Siouxsie husband-and-wife, plays at London's Town & Country club.
[13] *Shadowtime* bows at its UK #57 peak.
[18] The band embarks on the 21-city "Lollapalooza" alternative acts package tour, with Jane's Addiction, Living Colour, Ice-T, Butthole Surfers, Nine Inch Nails and the Henry Rollins Band, at the Compton Terrace, Phoenix, AZ, set to end on August 29th in Seattle, WA.
Sept [14] ***Superstition*** makes US #65.
Oct [19] *Kiss Them For Me* reaches US #23.
Dec [6] The band plays a sellout date at Clubland, Detroit, MI, during current North American dates.

1992

Mar [17-18] The group's tour, with Wonder Stuff in support, comes to an end with two shows at the Ritz, New York.
May Siouxsie & the Banshees work on new tracks, again with producer Hague, at the RAK and Metropolis studios, resulting in *Face To Face*, to be featured in the movie, "Batman Returns".
July [25] *Face To Face* debuts at its UK #21 peak.
Oct [17] ***Twice Upon A Time - The Singles***, a second hits collection, enters at its UK #26 peak.

1994

Aug [20] Morrissey and Siouxsie's *Interlude* debuts at its UK #25 peak.

1995

Jan [7] *O Baby* debuts at its UK #34 peak.
[21] The group embarks on a 15-date UK tour at the Civic Hall, Wolverhampton, West Midlands, set to end on March 12th at London's Kentish Town Forum.
[28] ***The Rapture***, produced with John Cale and written at Siouxsie and Budgie's chateau near Toulouse, France, where husband and wife have lived for three years, enters the UK chart at its #33 peak.
Feb [18] *Stargazer* charts for a week at UK #64.
Mar [4] ***The Rapture*** debuts at its US #127 peak.
May [19] Following a series of North American dates, Siouxsie & the Banshees play to a crowd of 6,182 at the National Auditorium, Mexico City, Mexico.
July [20] The group takes part in the "Heineken Music Festival" at Roundhay Park, Leeds, S. Yorks.

SIR DOUGLAS QUINTET

Doug Sahm (vocals, guitar);
Augie Meyers (organ); **Jack Barber** (bass);
Johnny Perez (drums); **Frank Morin** (horns)

1964

Performing since the age of six on a steel guitar, Sahm (b. Nov. 6, 1941, San Antonio, TX), having recorded *A Real American Joe* as Little Doug, for Texas label Sarg in 1955, and turned down a chance to join the "Grand Ole Opry" in order to finish school, has spent several years playing in local bar bands around San Antonio, before relocating to California in 1960, and now forms the British Invasion-inspired Sir Douglas Quintet, with the help of Houston, TX-based producer Huey P. Meaux, enlisting Morin (b. Aug. 13, 1946), Meyers (b. May 31, 1940, San Antonio), Barber and Perez (b. Nov. 8, 1942).

1965

May Signed to Meaux's Tribe label, *She's About A Mover*, with a distinctive British-beat Vox organ riff from Meyers, reaches US #13.
July *She's About A Mover* climbs to UK #15.
Aug The similarly-styled follow-up, *The Tracker*, fails to chart.
Nov [5] The group appears on ITV's "Ready Steady, Go!" and gigs during a two-week stay in the UK.

1966

Mar *The Rains Came* reaches US #31, taken from the Tribe-released debut, ***The Sir Douglas Quintet***.
June [24] The band takes part in the "KFRC Presents The Beach Boys Summer Spectacular" at the Cow Palace, San Francisco, CA, with the headliners, Lovin' Spoonful, Chad & Jeremy, the Byrds, Jefferson Airplane and others.
July [8-10] The group plays at the Avalon Ballroom, San Francisco, CA. (As the year progresses, the initial novelty of the Quintet wears off, and with a drug bust in Texas hanging over him, Sahm moves permanently to San Francisco.)
Oct [15-16] Following further dates at the venue in September, the Quintet returns to the Avalon Ballroom, with Big Brother & the Holding Company, reprising the same bill at the same venue for further concerts between May 5-7th the following year.

1968

July Sahm's ***Honkey Blues***, with Morin and Martin Fierro (horns), George Rains (drums) and Wayne Talbert (piano), credited to the Sir Douglas Quintet + 2, is released on Mercury Records Smash imprint.
Oct [17-19] The band plays at the Fillmore West, San Francisco, on a bill with Iron Butterfly.

1969

Jan [17-18] Sahm, with a reconstituted Quintet, featuring Harvey Kagan and Rains alongside original members, play the Winterland Ballroom, San Francisco, on a bill with the Mothers Of Invention.
Mar *Mendocino*, reaches US #27, as its parent album, ***Mendocino***, makes US #81.
Aug *Dynamite Woman* peaks at US #83.

1970

June ***Together After Five*** is popular in Europe, while ***1+1+1=4*** is issued in the US followed by ***The Return Of Douglas Saldana*** the following year, and ***Rough Edges***, their last release on Smash in 1973.

1973

Mar Having broken up the band again to go solo and signed to Atlantic Records (also appearing in the current movie "Cisco Pike"), Sahm's ***Doug Sahm And Band*** makes US #125. Produced by Jerry Wexler and Arif Mardin, it includes contributions by Bob Dylan (*Wallflower*) and Dr. John. The following year, he links with Creedence Clearwater Revival's rhythm section on ***Groover's Paradise*** for Warner Bros. Records. (Sahm will reunite with the quintet's original producer, Meaux, in 1976 to record ***Rock For Country Rollers*** for the Dot label, followed by the performance set, ***Live Love***, released in the US on Meyers' Texas label the following year.)

1981

Feb Having appeared in the 1979 film, "More American Graffiti", Sahm's ***Hell Of A Spell*** has been released on Takoma Records in 1980. The group has re-formed again, with original members Sahm, Meyers and Perez joined by Alvin Crow (guitar, vocals), Speedy Sparks (bass) and Shawn Sahm (guitars, vocals) for the newly issued ***Border Wave***, a new wave-flavored comeback on Takoma (released by Chrysalis in the UK), produced by Craig Leon and Cassell Webb, which makes US #184. (It will be followed by ***Quintessence*** in 1982, ***Rio Mendina*** in 1984 and ***Juke Box Music*** in 1988.)

1994

Mar [29] Having spent much of the '80s touring with the Sir Douglas Quintet (not least in Europe, where they remain a popular draw, and which yielded ***Very Much Alive/Love Ya, Europe***), Sahm formed the Almost Brothers, with guitarist Amos Garrett and ex-Blasters pianist, Gene Taylor, in 1988, and, reunited with Meyers, teams with country singer Freddy Fender and accordionist Flaco Jiminez has assembled the Texas Tornados, releasing ***Texas Tornados*** in August 1990. Sahm's ***Day Dreaming At Midnight***, featuring his son Shawn on guitar and Louie Ortega, formerly of Louie & the Lovers, is now issued on the Elektra Nonesuch American Explorer (US) label.

THE SISTERS OF MERCY

Andrew Eldritch (vocals); **Gary Marx** (guitar); **Ben Gunn** (guitar); **Craig Adams** (bass)

1980

The post-punk, pre-Goth rock alternative band, initially studio bound, is formed in Leeds, W. Yorks., with Oxford University-educated Eldritch (b. Andrew Taylor, May 15, 1959, Ely, East Anglia), Marx (b. Mark Pearman), and a drum machine named Doktor Avalanche. Their debut single, *The Damage Done*, is released on their own, independently-distributed, Merciful Release label. In order to play live, Eldritch and Marx recruit Gunn and Adams, touring as support to Nico, the Birthday Party, the Clash and the Psychedelic Furs.

1982

Apr Their second release, *Body Electric*, issued on the Leeds-based Confederacion Nacional de Trabajo label, sells well to a growing cult following, and gains positive UK music press reviews.
June The band arranges a distribution deal for Merciful Release with York-based Red Rhino Records, part of the independent distribution Cartel network. While touring Britain, the Sisters of Mercy record a BBC Radio 1 session for "The John Peel Show".
Oct Another Leeds group, the March Violets, is signed to Merciful Release, and the bands begin a UK tour together.
Nov A row between the two groups flares up and the Violets leave the label to form their own Rebirth Records. The Sisters Of Mercy release *Alice*, which climbs the UK Independent chart.

1983

Mar *Anaconda* is released.
May A five-track EP, *Reptile House*, tops the UK Independent chart.
June Gunn leaves after disagreements within the band and is replaced by Wayne Hussey (b. Jerry Lovelock, May 26, 1958, Bristol, Avon), who has worked with Pauline Murray, Dead Or Alive and ska-punk group, the Walkie Talkies.
Oct After the release of *Temple Of Love*, the group signs a distribution deal with WEA.

1984

June *Body And Soul* makes UK #46.
Sept [22] The group performs at the first "York Rock Festival" at York Racecourse, York, Yorks., with Echo & the Bunnymen, Spear Of Destiny, the Chameleons and the Redskins.
Oct *Walk Away*, written by Eldritch and Hussey, also makes UK #46.

1985

Feb Previewing their freshman set, *No Time To Cry* peaks at UK #63.
Apr Their debut album, ***First And Last And Always***, reaches UK #14, with strong regional sales in the North of England. More problems arise within the group: Eldritch's lifestyle causes him health problems and Marx, overshadowed by Hussey, refuses to attend sound-checks. On a European tour, Eldritch issues an ultimatum - either Marx leaves or he does, resulting in the latter quitting. A concert at London's Royal Albert Hall in June is filmed (and will be released on video as "Wake" - its title, many assume, alluding to the last Sisters Of Mercy concert). Immediately afterwards the group announces its decision to split. (Hussey and Adams, initially making claim to the Sisters Of Mercy name, will form the Mission, while Eldritch moves to Hamburg, West Germany.)

1986

July [26] Amid legal tangles over the use of the Sisters Of Mercy moniker, Eldritch releases ***Gift***, credited to the Sisterhood, which charts for a week at UK #95.

1987

Oct Eldritch and ex-Gun Club bassist, Patricia Morrison (b. Jan. 14, 1962) return as the Sisters Of Mercy, and *This Corrosion*, from the forthcoming ***Floodland*** album, hits UK #7.
Nov [28] ***Floodland*** debuts at its UK #9 peak, and will hit US #101.

1988

Mar The new Sisters' second single, *Dominion*, reaches UK #13, also taken from ***Floodland***.
June *Lucretia My Reflection* reaches UK #20.

1990

Oct [20] With its new line-up of Eldritch, ex-Gen X and Sigue Sigue Sputnik Tony James (guitar), ex-All About Eve bassist Tim Bricheno (b. July 6, 1963, Huddersfield, W. Yorks.) and drummer Andreas Bruhn (b. Nov. 5, 1967, Hamburg, West Germany), the group's first recording in over two years, *More*, reaches UK #14.
Nov [3] ***Vision Thing*** peaks at UK #11, as the band undertakes a sellout European tour.
[24, 26] The group ends its current live trek with a pair of dates at Wembley Arena, Wembley, Middx.
Dec [15] ***Vision Thing*** climbs to US #136.
[22] *Doctor Jeep* makes UK #37.

1991

June [29-30] The group takes part in the "Rock Am Ring Festival '91" in West Germany.
July [12] "Tune In, Turn On, Burn Out ..." tour, with the Sisters Of Mercy, Public Enemy, Gang Of Four and Warrior Soul, opens at the Poplar Creek Music Theatre, Hoffman Estates, IL. (Like many US tours during the summer, the package will do less than satisfactory business, and the last six dates will be cancelled.)
Aug [25] The group plays at the annual "Reading Festival", Reading, Berks.
Oct Tony James quits the group to pursue a solo career. He faxes the news to the press with a demand for £6,000 in cash, for interviews.

1992

Jan The band works on new material in Denmark's PUK Studios, as they prepare to play their first gig of the year at the home of a lucky fan club member, as part of their "Reptile House" gigs.
Apr [30] The group appears on BBC1-TV's "Top Of The Pops".
May [2] *Temple Of Love (1992)* debuts at its UK #3 peak.
[9] Compilation, ***Some Girls Wander By Mistake***, collecting the first six singles and EPs issued on Merciful Release, hits UK #5.
June [27] The band plays a one-off UK date at the National Exhibition Centre, Birmingham, W. Midlands.

1993

July [31] They support Depeche Mode at the Crystal Palace National Sports Centre, Crystal Palace, London.
Aug [28] Previewing their first career retrospective, *Under The Gun*, featuring one-time Berlin singer Terri Nunn, bows at its UK #19 peak, as they play on the second day of "Reading 93".
Sept [4] Compilation ***Greatest Hits Vol. 1*** debuts at its UK #14 peak.
Dec [20-21] The group plays two dates at London's Brixton Academy, with a performance at Birmingham's National Exhibition Centre the following night.
see also: THE MISSION

SKID ROW

Sebastian Bach (vocals); **Rachel Bolan** (bass); **Dave Sabo** (guitar); **Scotti Hill** (guitar); **Rob Affuso** (drums)

1988

Feb The heavy metal outfit has been formed in New Jersey in 1986 by Bolan (Feb. 9, 1964) and Sabo (b. Sept. 16), who recruit Affuso (Mar. 1, 1963), Hill (b. May 31) and finally, initial lead singer Matt Fallon replacement Bach (b. Sebastian Bierk, Apr. 3, 1968, Bahamas, named Sebastian by his parents after John Sebastian), who has grown up in Humboldt County, CA, and Peterborough, ON, Canada, where he studied at a private school also attended by Prince Andrew (of whom Bach will later say: "He was a fucking asshole"). Performing its first gig with Bach at the Mingles club in South Amboy, NJ, and developing a strong local following, the band is now signed to McGhee Entertainment, which manages fellow New Jerseyites, Bon Jovi, and secures Skid Row a recording contract with Atlantic Records.

Apr [3] Bach's son, Paris, is born on the singer's 20th birthday.

Nov Skid Row embarks on a US stadium tour, opening for Bon Jovi, immediately showcasing Bach's energetic and provocative stage style which, coupled with his long blond mane and good looks, provides a strong central focus and glam-boy appeal.

1989

Feb [11] Their metal-blasting debut album, ***Skid Row***, enters the US chart, set to hit #6 during a 78-week stretch, with domestic sales eventually topping five million.

June [10] The extracted *Youth Gone Wild* peaks at US #99.

Sept [13] The still-climbing *18 And Life* is certified gold by the RIAA.

[23] *18 And Life* hits US #4, as ***Skid Row*** climbs to UK #30.

Nov *Youth Gone Wild* makes UK #42.

1990

Jan [9] Bach appears in Hampden County Superior Court and pleads not guilty to assault charges stemming from a glass-throwing incident at the Civic Center, Springfield, MA, gig the previous December, when he leapt into the crowd to confront the missile thrower.

[22] The band collects the Favorite New Artist, Heavy Metal/Hard Rock trophy, at the 17th annual American Music Awards, held at the Shrine Auditorium, Los Angeles, CA.

Feb [3] *I Remember You* hits US #6, as *18 And Life* climbs to UK #12.

Mar [3, 5-6] The group plays three sellout dates at the Great Western Forum, Inglewood, CA, in support of headliners Aerosmith.

Apr *I Remember You* reaches UK #36.

Dec [31] The group appears on MTV's "New Year's Eve World Party".

1991

Feb [12] Their "Oh Say You Can Scream" video is certified platinum by the RIAA.

May [24] The band embarks on a North American tour, supporting Guns N' Roses, at the Alpine Valley Music Theatre, East Troy, WI.

June [15] *Monkey Business* debuts at its UK #19 peak.

[22] ***Slave To The Grind*** peaks at UK #5 in its week of entry.

[29] ***Slave To The Grind***, its album sleeve designed by Bach's father David Bierk, enters the US chart at #1, as the group plays a sellout show at the Rupp Arena, Lexington, KY.

July [29] The RIAA certifies ***Slave To The Grind*** platinum.

Aug [29] Bach files suit against Springfield Civic Center and concert promoters in Hampden Superior Court, regarding the 1989 glass-throwing debacle.

Sept [14] *Slave To The Grind* debuts at its UK #43 peak.

Nov [2] The group guests on NBC-TV's "Saturday Night Live".

[14] Skid Row plays at the Edinburgh Playhouse, Edinburgh, Lothian, Scotland, with L.A. Guns supporting, during a six-week European tour.

[22] The band performs its London date at the London Arena after Wembley Arena management had banned them following the group's behavior at an earlier Wembley Stadium gig, supporting Guns N' Roses.

[23] *Wasted Time* bows at its UK #20 peak.

Dec [31] Skid Row ends the year with a 6,976 sellout performance, at the Kiefer U.N.O. Lakefront Arena, New Orleans, LA, grossing $139,520.

1992

Jan [11] *Wasted Time* peaks at US #88.

[26] Bach injures his knee during a performance at the "Rock In Rio" festival.

May [6] During its five-month US tour, the band plays at Wings Stadium, Kalamazoo, MI, grossing $82,317. 11 fans are hurt by a bomb thrown as the group is about to start its second number. When they catch the offender, Bach says, "We're gonna screw the guy into the dirt", as well as promising to throw a party for the injured.

June [6] The band appears at the "Earth Pledge Concert" on the Great Lawn of New York's Central Park. (During another June gig at the Memorial Centre, Peterborough, ON, Skid Row, having given away free condoms, upsets the venue's management, who claim that fans try out the prophylactics in the rest-rooms during the concert.)

July [26] Bach marries longtime girlfriend, Maria Aquiar, and says: "Boning, being one of my favorite pastimes, has become a Russian roulette of the '90s. This being a fact, I think it is desirable to find someone loving and kinky enough to satisfy any desire so that you never get bored with each other."

Aug [8] The band's South American tour opens in Buenos Aires, Argentina.

[22] The group performs at the annual "Monsters Of Rock" festival at Castle Donington, Leics.

Sept [5] *Youth Gone Wild/Delivering The Goods* reaches UK #22.

[30] Japanese tour bows at the Sun Plaza, Sendai.

Oct [10] Rarities and flip-side collecting album, ***B-Sides Ourselves***, debuts at its US #58 peak.

Dec [12] The band plays at Hammerjack's, Baltimore, MD, to raise funds in memory of Mike Naprstek, a fan close to the group, who was recently killed in an auto accident.

1993

Mar [16] ***B-Sides Ourselves*** is certified gold by the RIAA.

May [23] Still preparing their first album in two years, group members take part in Celebrity Softball Games at the T.J. Martell Foundation, and Neil Bogart Memorial Fund 1993 Rock 'N Charity Celebration, at the Blair Field, Long Beach, CA.

1994

Jan [16] While singing *Devil's Child* at a gig at New York, NY's Limelight club, Bach receives a call on his cellular phone from his pregnant wife Maria, saying her waters have broken.

1995

Apr [8] ***Subhuman Race***, produced by Bob Rock, enters at its UK #8 peak.

[15] ***Subhuman Race*** debuts at its US #35 peak.

June [6] The RIAA certifies five million sales of ***Skid Row***.

Nov [1] Skid Row begins a six-date tour of the UK at the Barrowlands, Glasgow, Strathclyde, Scotland, set to end on the 9th at London's Brixton Academy.

[18] *Breakin' Down* debuts at its UK #48 peak.

SLADE

Noddy Holder (guitar, vocals); **Dave Hill** (guitar); **Jimmy Lea** (bass, piano, violin); **Don Powell** (drums)

1965

Hill (b. Apr. 4, 1952, Fleet Castle, Devon) and Powell (b. Sept. 10, 1950, Bilston, Warks.) have begun playing in Wolverhampton, W. Midlands-based band, the Vendors, the previous year, with Johnny Howells (vocals), Mickey Marston (guitar) and Dave Jones (bass). They do not record commercially, but make a four-song demo EP (*Peace Pipe*, *Twilight Time*, *It's Too Late* and *Take Your Time*). Now re-named the 'N Betweens, the group records with session drummer Bobby Graham producing. The results, only released in France on Barclay label EPs, include versions of the Sorrows' *Take A Heart* and Rufus Thomas' *Can Your Monkey Do The Dog*. Meanwhile, Holder (b. Neville Holder, June 15, 1946, Walsall, Warks.) is guitarist and backing vocalist in Wolverhampton's Steve Brett & the Mavericks, and plays on their December 1965 Columbia single, *Chains On My Heart*.

1966

July Holder and Lea (b. June 14, 1952, Wolverhampton) join Hill and Powell in the 'N Betweens when the others leave, thus completing the future Slade line-up.

Nov The 'N Betweens cover of the Young Rascals' *You Better Run* is released on Columbia, the group's last release under this name.

1969

Feb After playing mostly covers (Motown, Beatles, ska) on the Midlands club circuit, they move to London. They are seen at Rasputin's club by Chas Chandler, ex-the Animals, who launched Jimi Hendrix's career in Britain. He becomes their manager/producer and, in an attempt to cash in first on the UK skinhead cult, dresses them in boots and braces to complement their short-cropped hair. He also arranges a recording contract with Fontana.

Apr The group releases its only album under the name Ambrose Slade, ***Beginnings***, which includes the extracted single, *Genesis/Roach Daddy*, issued in May.

Oct At Chandler's suggestion, the band shortens its name to Slade for its next Fontana release, *Wild Winds Are Blowing*.

1970

Mar *The Shape Of Things To Come*, their cover of a US #22, 1968 hit by Max Frost & the Troopers, is the band's last Fontana single, and again fails to chart, despite a grand launch to press and media at London's Bag O' Nails club.

Sept Newly signed to Polydor Records, *Know Who You Are* is released.

Nov ***Play It Loud*** is issued.

1971

June *Get Down And Get With It*, their revival of a Bobby Marchan song, best known via Little Richard's version, reaches UK #16.

Nov [14] Its follow-up, *Coz I Luv You*, tops the UK chart, where it will stay for four weeks, as the band plays a pub gig at the Black Prince in Bexley, Kent. It is the first of six UK chart-toppers and a five-year run of foot-stomping pop, glam-rock Top 20 hits, all penned by Holder and Lea. It also launches their distinctive trademark of customized title spellings.

Dec [24] The group plays a Christmas Eve party gig at London's Marquee.

1972

Feb *Look Wot You Dun* hits UK #4.

Apr ***Slade Alive*** hits UK #2 (and will remain on the UK chart for over one year).

May [10] The group begins its first major headlining UK tour, supported by Status Quo, in Bradford, W. Yorks.

July [1] *Take Me Bak 'Ome* tops the UK chart for a week.

Sept [7] The group, in the midst of a US tour, flies back to London to headline the opening of the capitol 's Mile End Road Sundown.

[9] *Mama Weer All Crazee Now* also hits UK #1, where it will remain for three weeks.

Oct *Take Me Bak 'Ome* is Slade's first US chart entry, at #97, while ***Slade Alive*** makes US #158.

[15] Holder injures his arm during a gig in Brussels, Belgium, when a brick is thrown at the band onstage, after power lines blow and equipment goes dead, allegedly through sabotage. He also injures his left leg as he leaves the stage.

Dec *Gudbuy T'Jane* hits UK #2, behind Chuck Berry's *My Ding-A-Ling*.

1973

Jan [7] The group performs at the London Palladium as part of the "Fanfare For Europe" festival to celebrate Britain's entry into the Common Market.

[13] ***Slayed*** tops the UK chart for the first of three

weeks, as *Mama Weer All Crazee Now* peaks at US #76.
Feb ***Slayed*** reaches US #69.
Mar [3] *Cum On Feel The Noize* heads the UK chart for the first of four weeks, confirming Slade as the most successful UK hit singles group in the post-Beatles era.
Apr *Gudbuy T'Jane* makes US #68.
June [20] *Skweeze Me Pleeze Me* begins a three-week run atop the UK survey, while *Cum On Feel The Noize* peaks at US #98.
July [4] Powell is badly injured in a car crash, in which his girlfriend, Angela Morris, is killed. (He will be hospitalized for six weeks, and will suffer memory problems, as a result of his head injuries, for some months. He will return to his drum-kit, when eventually fit.)
Oct [6] ***Sladest*** tops the UK chart for the first of three weeks, and makes US #129. *My Friend Stan* hits UK #2, behind the Simon Park Orchestra's million-selling *Eye Level*.
Dec [15] *Merry Christmas Everybody*, recorded in New York during a US tour, enters the UK chart at #1, staying on top for five weeks. After selling over a quarter of a million copies in its first day, it becomes the group's biggest single, selling over one million domestic copies (and will re-chart every Christmas between 1981 and 1986).

1974

Mar [2] ***Old, New, Borrowed And Blue***, is the band's third consecutive UK #1 album, as the US-only ***Stomp Your Hands, Clap Your Feet*** makes US #168.
Apr *Everyday* hits UK #3.
July *Bangin' Man* also hits UK #3. Slade spends the rest of the year working on its feature film, "Flame".
Oct Hymnal *Far Far Away*, an early taster from the "Flame" soundtrack, hits UK #2.
Dec The soundtrack album, ***Slade In Flame***, hits UK #6, as the movie premieres in Britain. Its title is the fictitious name of a mid-'60s band which Slade portrays in the film (which also stars Tom Conti, Alan Lake and UK DJs Tommy Vance and Emperor Rosko).

1975

Mar *How Does It Feel* reaches UK #15, ending a run of 12 top five hits.
May *Thanks For The Memory (Wham Bam Thank You Mam)* hits UK #7.
July ***Slade In Flame*** makes US #93.
Sept [12] The group's movie, "Flame", has its first US showing, in St. Louis, MO (but, like their singles, it will make little impression in the US).
Dec [6] *In For A Penny* reaches UK #11.

1976

Feb [28] *Let's Call It Quits* also peaks at UK #11.
Mar [27] ***Nobody's Fool*** makes UK #14. The group leaves Polydor for manager/producer Chandler's own label, Barn Records.

1977

Feb [5] Their debut Barn single, *Gypsy Roadhog*, peaks at UK #48.
Apr *Burning In The Heat Of Love* is released.
Nov [11] Their rock medley covers of two early Elvis Presley items, *My Baby Left Me/That's All Right Mama*, reaches UK #32.

1978

Mar *Give Us A Goal*, reflecting Slade's enduring affinity with the UK soccer terraces, is issued.
Nov *Rock'n'Roll Bolero* and ***Slade Alive, Vol. 2*** are released.
[29] The group are the special guests at the "Great British Music Festival", Wembley Arena, Wembley, Middx.
Dec Lea and brother Frankie form the Dummies as a sideline from Slade, releasing three singles, without chart success. The last three Barn singles will be issued the following year, *Ginny Ginny* (May), *Sign Of The Times* (October) and *Okey Cokey* (December), with *Okey Cokey* also reissued a month later by the RSO label. ***Return To Base*** follows in October.

1980

June Slade reappears on another Chandler label, Six Of The Best, which specializes in six-song 12" EPs. Tracks include *Night Starvation* and *When I'm Dancin' I Ain't Fightin'*.
Oct *Slade Alive At Reading 80*, a five-track EP recorded at the year's "Reading Rock Festival", Reading, Berks., and released on Chandler's Cheapskate label, makes UK #44, the group's first singles chart entry for three years.
[19] The band plays at London's Lyceum Ballroom, with up-and-coming Irish rock band U2 on the support bill.
Dec A live version of *Merry Christmas Everybody*, recorded at the "Reading Festival", makes UK #70.

1981

Jan [10] Polydor's TV-advertised collection, ***Slade Smashes***, reaches UK #21.
Feb [21] *We'll Bring The House Down* hits UK #10, the group's first Top 10 hit for six years.
Mar [28] ***We'll Bring The House Down*** reaches UK #25.
Apr [11] *Wheels Ain't Comin' Down* peaks at UK #60.
Oct [10] *Lock Up Your Daughters*, the group's first single in a newly-signed deal with RCA, reaches UK #29.
Nov [28] ***Till Deaf Us Do Part*** makes UK #68.

1982

Mar [19] The group begins an 11-date UK tour at the Apollo Theatre, Oxford, Oxon, set to end on April 2nd at the Colston Hall, Bristol, Avon.
Apr [3] *Ruby Red* peaks at UK #51.
Dec [4] *(And Now The Waltz) C'Est La Vie* makes UK #50, with a live version of their seasonal favorite, *Merry Christmas Everybody*, on the B-side, in competition to Polydor's annual reissue of the original.
[18] The live album, ***Slade On Stage***, makes UK #58.

1983

Sept US heavy metal group Quiet Riot hits US #5 and makes UK #45 with a copy-cat revival of *Cum On Feel The Noize*. (The new wave of US glam-metal bands is much influenced by the pop-metal and gaudy image of UK bands like Slade and Sweet - for whom the US audience was generally unreceptive in the early '70s.)
Dec Slade has produced one of its catchiest and most commercial singles, *My Oh My*, pitched at an ideal tempo for TV-massed swaying and scarf-waving, which it duly receives on BBC1-TV's "Top Of The Pops" and other shows. It hits UK #2, behind the Flying Pickets' *Only You*. ***The Amazing Kamikaze Syndrome*** makes UK #49.

1984

Mar *Run Run Away*, a more rock-oriented follow-up, hits UK #7.
May US album, ***Keep Your Hands Off My Power Supply***, containing *Run Run Away*, reaches US #33.
June Polydor releases another hits compilation, ***Slade's Greats***, which makes UK #89. *Run Run Away* reaches US #20, their biggest US hit.
Aug [18] The US follow-up, *My Oh My*, reaches US #37. Meanwhile, Quiet Riot's second Slade cover, *Mama Weer All Crazee Now*, makes US #51.
Nov *All Join Hands* reaches UK #15.

1985

Feb *Seven Year Bitch* peaks at UK #60.
Apr *Myzsterious Mizter Jones* (a return to title mis-spelling) makes UK #50, as ***Rogues Gallery*** also reaches UK #50.
May *Little Sheila* peaks at US #86.
Dec The TV-advertised ***Crackers : The Slade Christmas Party Album***, reaches UK #34, with the extracted *Do You Believe In Miracles* making UK #54.

1987

Feb *Still The Same* makes UK #73.
May [9] ***You Boyz Make Big Noize*** (a title suggested by the tea lady at the recording studio) charts for a week at UK #98.

1988

Dec Slade returns with a revival of Chris Montez' 1962 hit, *Let's Dance*. (Subsequently the band members go their separate ways - Holder presents a rock revival show on Piccadilly Radio in Manchester, Hill records a solo album, Lea produces heavy metal band Chrome Molly, and Powell becomes an antique dealer. Holder and Hill willl release a one-off single *Crying In The Rain* as Blessings In Disgiuse in November 1989.)

1993

Dec [24] Following the UK #55, December 1990 success of *Merry Christmas Everybody* by the Metal Gurus (the Mission in glam-rock disguise), produced by Holder and Lea, Slade's first three albums have been released on CD for the first time in May the following year. Re-formed, and entering their third decade of chart success, *Radio Wall Of Sound* has reached UK #21 on Oct [26] the same year, with ***Wall Of Hits***, the group's first ever compilation on CD, debuting at its UK #34 peak soon after on Nov [23]. Following the release of ***Emergency!*** and the extracted *Hold On To Love* earlier this year, Slade, now known as Slade II, featuring new vocalist Steve Whalley, play a Christmas Eve show at Stonyhurst in Blackburn, Lancs.

SLAYER

Tom Araya (vocals, bass); **Jeff Hanneman** (guitar); **Kerry King** (guitar); **Dave Lombardo** (drums)

1986

Sept With a mutual interest in demonic thrash-metal, the group has been assembled towards the end of 1981 in Huntington Beach, CA, by Araya (b. June 6, 1961, Chile), Hanneman (b. Jan. 31, 1964, Los Angeles, CA), Lombardo (b. Feb. 16, 1965) and King (b. June 3, 1964, Huntington Beach). Early gigging around southern California has resulted in its first vinyl cut, *Aggressive Protector*, being included on metal specialist indie, Metal Blade Records' 1983 compilation ***Metal Massacre III***, a label which has subsequently released two Slayer albums, its self-produced debut, ***Show No Mercy***, in 1983 (heralded as a seminal speed-metal release, and picked up by Music For Nations in the UK), and ***Hell Awaits***, co-produced with Brian Slagel, issued in May the following year (and licensed to Roadrunner in the UK), both sets indicating a thematic interest in the occult and murder, appropriately fuelled by a relentless hardcore thrash-metal style. Having been signed earlier this year to Rick Rubin's predominantly rap-based Def Jam label in the US, Slayer's Rubin-produced ***Reign In Blood*** is now released, but quickly runs into distribution problems with CBS/Columbia which objects to the Joseph Mengele-referencing *Angel Of Death* lead-in track.
Nov [15] With Geffen Records in the US (and London Records in the UK) having picked up distribution, ***Reign In Blood*** enters the US chart set to make #94, Slayer's first chart showing.

1987

June [13] *Criminally Insane* charts for a week at UK #64.
Aug [6] ***South Of Heaven*** enters the US survey set to reach #57.
(During the year, the band contributes music to the River Phoenix-starring movie soundtrack to "River's Edge".)

1990

Nov [3] Having been moved to Def Jam's Def American spin-off label, ***Seasons In The Abyss***, now dominated by Araya's songwriting and the group's most accessible outing to date, reaches US #40, during a 23-week chart run.

1991

Jan [31] During a US tour with Testament, the group plays at the Aragon Ballroom, Chicago, IL, to a sell-out 4,701 crowd.

May [16] The multi-act metal package "Clash Of The Titans" tour opens at the Starplex Amphitheatre, Dallas, TX, featuring Slayer, Megadeth, Anthrax and Alice In Chains, and will include a sold-out $253,530-grossing show at New York, NY's Madison Square Garden on June 28th.

Oct [26] *Seasons In The Abyss* charts for a week at UK #51.

Nov [5-6] During a seven-date UK visit, Slayer performs a pair of dates at London's Hammersmith Odeon.

[9] Variously recorded in London, California and Florida, the double performance album ***Live - Decade Of Aggression*** bows at its US #55 peak, with a limited edition of 10,000 copies made available in a metal box.

1992

May Lombardo quits the group (and will re-emerge with his new band Grip), to be replaced by ex-Forbidden drummer Paul Bostaph (b. Mar. 4, 1965, Hayward, CA).

Aug [15] Slayer participates in "Super Rock 1992" held at Maimarktgelandi, Mannheim, on a bill with Iron Maiden, Black Sabbath, W.A.S.P. and Helloween.

[22] The group performs at the annual "Monsters of Rock" benefit festival at Castle Donington, on a bill with Iron Maiden, Skid Row, Thunder and W.A.S.P., with all proceeds going to the Nordoff Robbins Music Therapy Centre.

Nov [20] ***Reign In Blood*** and ***South Of Heaven*** are both certified gold by the RIAA, with
Seasons In The Abyss reaching the same certification on April 9th the following year.

1994

Oct [15] The self-written and produced ***Divine Intervention*** debuts at its US #8 peak and UK #15 high.

Dec [6] ***Divine Intervention*** is confirmed gold by the RIAA.

1995

Sept [9] The extracted *Serenity In Murder* charts for a week at UK #50.

Nov The group's first home video "Live Intrusion" featuring concert performances and side-footage is released by American Visuals.

1996

June [11] Moving from thrash metal into a punk direction, ***Undisputed Attitude*** is released on American Recordings.

SLY & THE FAMILY STONE

Sly Stone (vocals, keyboards, guitar); **Freddie Stone** (guitar); **Cynthia Robinson** (trumpet); **Jerry Martini** (saxes); **Rosemary Stone** (vocals, piano); **Larry Graham** (bass guitar); **Greg Errico** (drums)

1967

A DJ on Oakland, CA station KDIA (and KSOL) and record producer (for the Beau Brummels and Bobby Freeman, among others, and as an in-house producer at Autumn Records), Stone (b. Sylvester Stewart, Mar. 15, 1944, Dallas, TX), who made his first recording, *On The Battlefield For My Lord*, at the age of four with his family's group, the Stewart Four, having already played in high-school outfit the Vicanes, and formed the Stoners with Robinson (b. Jan. 12, 1946, Sacramento, CA), has assembled the Family Stone the previous year in San Francisco, CA, including his brother, Freddie (b. June 5, 1946, Dallas), sister Rosemary (b. Mar. 21, 1945, Vallejo, CA), cousin Graham (b. Aug. 14, 1946, Beaumont, TX), Martini (b. Oct. 1, 1943, CO) and Errico (b. Sept. 1, 1946, San Francisco), a loose R&B collective, which has been gigging in bars and clubs around Oakland. Their iconoclastic collision of funk, jazz, rock and anarchic humor, soon tagged "psychedelic soul", extends their following to the city's emergent psychedelic movement. Having released *I Ain't Got Nobody* on the local Loadstone label earlier in the year, the group signs to Epic Records and releases its debut set, ***A Whole New Thing***. The label's David Kapralik also becomes the band's manager and Stone's business partner.

1968

Apr Sly-penned *Dance To The Music* hits US #8.

May ***Dance To The Music*** reaches US #142.

June [21-23] The group plays at the Fillmore West, San Francisco, on a bill with Quicksilver Messenger Service.

July *Life/M'Lady* peaks at US #93.

Aug *Dance To The Music* hits UK #7.

Sept [11] Arriving in London to begin a tour, UK Customs find cannabis in Graham's possession. BBC-TV cancels a scheduled appearance, and a week later the band leaves Britain without having performed.

Oct *M'lady* makes UK #32.

Dec ***Life*** reaches US #195.

[26-29] The group plays the Fillmore West with Steve Miller and Pogo.

1969

Feb [13] The still-climbing *Everyday People* is certified gold by the RIAA.

[15] Sly-written *Everyday People* hits US #1, where it will stay for four weeks.

Mar *Everyday People* makes UK #36, while its B-side, *Sing A Simple Song*, peaks at US #89.

May *Stand!* reaches US #22.

June Sly-produced (as with all their material) ***Stand!*** makes US #13. The extracted *I Want To Take You Higher*, the B-side of *Stand!*, peaks at US #60.

July [3-6] For the first time, rock performers take part in the "Newport Jazz Festival" at Newport, RI. Sly & the Family Stone are featured on the bill with Led Zeppelin, James Brown and others.

Aug The band performs *I Want To Take You Higher* at the "Woodstock Music & Art Fair", Bethel, NY. (Press reports suggest several members of the Family Stone have drug problems, and the band acquires a reputation for failing to show at scheduled gigs.)

Oct [18] *Hot Fun In The Summertime* hits US #2, for the first of two weeks.

1970

Feb [9] The still-rising *Thank You (Falettinme Be Mice Elf Agin)* is certified gold by the RIAA.

[14] *Thank You (Falettinme Be Mice Elf Agin)*, coupled with *Everybody Is A Star*, hits US #1.

June Reissued *I Want To Take You Higher* makes US #38.

Nov Compilation ***Greatest Hits*** hits US #2.

Dec By year's end, the increasingly unreliable Stone has missed 26 of his scheduled 80 live appearances and is in mortgage arrears on the house he has bought in Los Angeles, CA, from John Phillips of the Mamas & the Papas.

1971

Sept [4] **The New York Times** reports that Stone's Hollywood landlord is suing him for $3 million, claiming his building is inundated with "loud, noisy and boisterous persons", and he wants Stone to leave the property.

Nov [8] ***There's A Riot Goin' On*** is certified gold by the RIAA.

[30] *Family Affair*, in the week it will reach the summit, is certified gold by the RIAA.

Dec [4] Seminal soul cut, the Sly-penned *Family Affair*, hits US #1 after three weeks, staying on top for five.

[18] Controversial and critically-revered, ***There's A Riot Goin' On*** also tops the US chart, for the first of two weeks.

1972

Jan *Family Affair* reaches UK #15. Graham leaves the group (to form Graham Central Station) and is replaced by Rusty Allen. Errico also quits to be replaced by Andy Newmark, with saxophonist Pat Ricco also joining. (Graham Central Station will score seven US chart albums and four hit singles between 1974 and 1979, before Graham embarks on a solo career which will see four further album chart successes in the early '80s, and the million-selling soul ballad *One In A Million You* in 1980.)

Mar *Runnin' Away* peaks at US #23, as ***There's A Riot Goin' On*** makes UK #31.

May *Runnin' Away* reaches UK #17 while *Smilin'* peaks at US #42.

July [18] Sly and members of the Family Stone are arrested after police search the group's motor home on Santa Monica Blvd. Two pounds of marjiuana and two vials of dangerous drugs are found.

Nov [25] Despite an impressive bill, including Sly & the Family Stone, Los Angeles radio station KROQ's "The Woodstock Of The West" only attracts 32,000 to its 100,000-seater Memorial Coliseum, Los Angeles.

1973

June Sly-written and produced ***Fresh*** hits US #7.

Aug [17] ***Fresh*** is certified gold by the RIAA.

Sept *If You Want Me To Stay* makes US #12.

[12] *If You Want Me To Stay* is also certified gold by the RIAA.

Dec *Frisky* peaks at US #79, as the band embarks on a US tour, supported by Bob Marley & the Wailers.

1974

June [5] Stone marries Kathy Silva, onstage, before a gig at New York's Madison Square Garden.

Aug ***Small Talk***, picturing Stone, Silva and baby Sylvester Bubb Ali Stewart on the sleeve, reaches US #15, while *Time For Living* makes US #32.

Oct [30] Silva files for divorce.

Nov *Loose Booty* is Sly & the Family Stone's last chart entry at US #84.

[4] ***Small Talk*** is certified gold by the RIAA.

1975

Jan [16] Sly & the Family Stone begin a six-night stand at New York's Radio City Music Hall, though attendances at the eight-date residency are less than one-third full.

Nov ***High On You***, credited as a Stone solo effort, makes US #45. The following January, having moved to the Novato ranch, and facing a $5 million tax bill, Stone will file for bankruptcy, a situation unresolved by the release of ***Heard You Missed Me, Well I'm Back***.

1979

Nov With his drug dependency dogging his now intermittent career, Sly & the Family Stone's ***Back On The Right Track***, their debut album for Warner Bros. Records and first release in three years, makes US #152. He will be featured on his psychedelic soul successor, George Clinton and Funkadelic's ***The Electric Spanking Of War Babies***, released in March 1981, when they also tour together.

1983

Feb [21] Stone guests on NBC-TV's "Late Night With David Letterman", not least promoting his second Warner album ***Ain't But The One Way***, his last of the decade. Stone, persuaded by Bobby Womack to seek treatment for his drug addiction (for which he is arrested for cocaine possession during the year), embarks on a two-month US tour with his soul brother.

1986

Oct Newly signed to A&M Records, his association with the label only yields one single, *Eek-A-Bo-Statik*.
Nov Movie soundtrack, ***Soul Man***, featuring two Stone cuts, including a duet with the Motels' Martha Davis on a cover of Joan Armatrading's *Love And Affection*, peaks at US #138.
[21] The RIAA certifies platinum sales of ***Stand!*** and three million sales of ***Greatest Hits***.
Dec [27] Jesse Johnson's *Crazay*, featuring Sly Stone, makes US #53.

1987

Jan [29] Stone helps launch the "Fight For Literacy Day" in California.
Nov He is arrested by Santa Monica police after failing to pay £2,500 maintenance to his ex-wife and their 14-year old son. He is also charged with possession of cocaine. *Family Affair* is reissued on the CBS dance label imprint, Upfront.

1989

Nov Stone is arrested in Bridgeport, CT, and returned to Los Angeles.
Dec [1] He is sentenced to 55 days in jail, after pleading guilty to a misdemeanor charge of driving under the influence of cocaine.
[14] Stone pleads guilty in Santa Monica to two further counts of possession of cocaine. He is sentenced to spend 9-14 months in a drug rehabilitation center, placed on three years probation, and ordered into an anti-drug program as an alternative to county jail by Superior Court Judge, Robert Altman. Charges stem from arrests in 1986 and 1987.

1993

Jan [12] Following Sony Music's 1992 release of the CD anthology ***Takin' You Higher - The Best Of Sly & the Family Stone***, Sly & the Family Stone are inducted by George Clinton into the Rock and Roll Hall of Fame, at the eighth annual awards dinner, held at the Century Plaza Hotel, Los Angeles. (Stone will shortly thereafter be found living in a Los Angeles' sheltered-housing complex, but will be signed to Avenue Records in 1995 in an attempt to prepare a comeback album.)

THE SMALL FACES

Steve Marriott (vocals, guitar);
Ronnie "Plonk" Lane (bass);
Ian McLagan (organ); **Kenney Jones** (drums)

1965

June The group is formed in London when Lane (b. Apr. 1, 1946, Plaistow, London) and ex-Outcasts drummer Jones (b. Sept. 16, 1948, Stepney, London), who originally met while in the Army cadets and renewed their acquaintance in a Stepney pub, playing in a pub trio with Jimmy Winston (b. James Langwith, Apr. 20, 1945, Stratford, London), and looking for a strong singer or guitarist, find both in Marriott (b. Jan. 30, 1947, Bow, London), whom they meet working in a music shop in East Ham, London. In show business since age 12 as an actor (appearing in the London production of "Oliver", and UK radio and TV plays and shows), he has cut a solo single (*Give Her My Regards*) for Decca Records in 1963. They adopt the name Small Faces, because of their lack of height, and the Mod connotations of "Face". All are R&B fans, and they pitch the group directly at the Mod/R&B scene recently opened up by the Who.
Oct Signed to Decca, their debut is the Ian Samwell-written and produced, *Whatcha Gonna Do About It*, which borrows its rhythm structure from Solomon Burke's *Everybody Needs Somebody To Love*, and adds some sawing pop-art guitar. It reaches UK #14.
Nov [1] Winston leaves, to be replaced by McLagan (b. May 12, 1945, Hounslow, Middx.), who comes recommended via a glowing review in **Beat Instrumental** magazine of his playing in Boz & the Boz People. At the same time, the follow-up single, *I've Got Mine*, just misses the chart, and the group begins live work (notably in a residency at London's West End Cavern club, off Leicester Square) to build a firm following on which to launch subsequent discs.

1966

Mar *Sha La La La Lee*, written by Kenny Lynch and Mort Shuman, hits UK #3.
May *Hey Girl*, which hits UK #10, is the group's first Marriott/Lane-composed chart-maker.
[1] The group takes part in the annual "**New Musical Express** Poll Winners Concert" at the Empire Pool, Wembley, Middx.
June ***The Small Faces*** hits UK #3, during a six-month chart stay.
[10] Marriott collapses while performing on ITV's "Ready Steady, Go!", with the group cancelling the following week's gigs.
July [29] The band performs at the sixth annual "National Jazz & Blues Festival", Windsor, Berks.
Aug [12] The Small Faces begin Radio England's "Swingin' 66" tour with Crispian St. Peters, Wayne Fontana, Neil Christian and Geneveve, at the Odeon Cinema, Lewisham, London, set to end on the 25th at the Gaumont Cinema, Southampton, Hants.
Sept [15] Another Marriott/Lane song, *All Or Nothing*, tops the UK chart for a week (deposing the Beatles' *Yellow Submarine/Eleanor Rigby*).
[25] The group plays a concert at the Regal Cinema, Gloucester, Gloucs., after a 2,000-signature petition to perform there has been presented to them.
Oct [15] They begin a 20-date twice-nightly UK tour with the Hollies, the Nashville Teens, Paul & Barry Ryan, Paul Jones and others, at ABC Cinema, Aldershot, Hants., set to end on November 6th at the City Hall, Newcastle, Tyne & Wear.
Dec *My Mind's Eye*, again written by Marriott and Lane, hits UK #4 (part of its melody is lifted from Christmas carol *Angels From The Realms Of Glory*). Aware that Decca is trying to push a more polished version of the group on record than that seen in its raucous, stomping live gigs, they are amused when Decca releases a rough mix of the single instead of a more polished take - apparently in error.

1967

Mar *I Can't Make It*, although banned by the BBC, reaches UK #26, after which the group announces it is to leave Decca for Andrew Oldham's Immediate label.
[3] The band begins a 32-date twice-nightly UK tour with Roy Orbison, P.P. Arnold, Paul & Barry Ryan and others, at London's Finsbury Park Astoria, set to end on April 9th at the ABC Cinema, Romford, Essex. They pull out of the Leicester De Montfort Hall gig on April 2nd, when Marriott goes down with a virus.
[18] They film a segment for the "Morecambe & Wise" TV show at Elstree, Herts.
May Decca releases a final single, *Patterns*, but, with no promotion from the group, it fails to chart.
[7] The band participates in the annual "**New Musical Express** Poll Winners Concert", at the Empire Pool.
[20-28] The Small Faces tour Sweden.
June Compilation, ***From The Beginning***, on Decca, reaches UK #17.
July *Here Comes The Nice* (with some oblique drug references, in tune with the rock mood of the time) reaches UK #12, and ***Small Faces*** also peaks at UK #12.
[8] Andrew Loog Oldham takes over the group's management from Robert Wace.
Aug [26] They appear at the "Festival Of The Flower Children" at Woburn Abbey, Woburn, Beds.
Sept *Itchycoo Park*, the band's most elaborate and experimental production yet, with phased drums and spacy harmonies, hits UK #3.
[2] The group participates in a TV spectacular to launch color television in West Germany.
Dec [2] They guest on "Jonathan King's Good Evening" TV show.
[11] Marriott is injured a car crash with mild concussion as the group drives to London Airport to fly to Belgium for a TV appearance.

1968

Jan *Tin Soldier*, another complex production, hits UK #9. *Itchycoo Park* is the group's first US hit single, peaking at #16.
[28] The band, currently on tour in Australia, is thrown off an airliner at Melbourne, Victoria, en route from Adelaide, South Australia to Sydney, New South Wales, for alleged drunken behavior with the Who and Paul Jones. After a three-hour delay, they will continue on their way with two security men accompanying them.
Mar ***There Are But Four Small Faces*** makes US #178.
Apr *Tin Soldier* peaks at US #73.
May *Lazy Sunday*, eschewing the psychedelic tendencies of the two previous Lane/Marriott-penned singles, is a loping good-time rocker in Ray Davies/Kinks style, with Marriott vocalizing in an exaggerated cockney accent. Their biggest UK hit since *All Or Nothing*, it hits #2.
June [29] Concept album, ***Ogden's Nut Gone Flake***, tops the UK chart for the first of six weeks. One side features tracks linked by comedian Stanley Unwin, while the album's round cover (representing the lid of the Ogden's tobacco tin) is a selling-point gimmick. The group subsequently refuses to play most tracks from the album when performing live.
Aug *The Universal*, almost free-form in approach, reaches UK #16.
Oct ***Ogden's Nut Gone Flake*** peaks at US #159, as the Small Faces begin a UK package tour with the Who and Joe Cocker.
[19] Peter Frampton of the Herd sits in on guitar at a Small Faces gig, and strikes up a rapport with Marriott. (They begin to make plans to form a new group, which will become Humble Pie; Marriott in particular wants to gain rock credibility, aware of the "teen" tag still attached to the Small Faces, despite their recent progression.)

1969

Jan [14] The group makes its US debut at the Fillmore East, New York.
Feb Marriott leaves and the Small Faces disband. Lane, Jones and McLagan stay together (to link up in June with guitarist, Ron Wood (b. Ronald Wood, June 1, 1947, Hillingdon, Greater London), whose first musical experience has been as a nine-year old with his brothers Ted and Art in their Candy Bison Skiffle Group, and vocalist Rod Stewart (b. Roderick Stewart, Jan. 10, 1945, Highgate, London), and re-launch their career as the Faces).
Mar The final "new" Small Faces single, *Afterglow (Of Your Love)* (coupled with the heavy-rock spoof, *Wham! Bam! Thank You Ma'm*), makes UK #36. Double album, ***The Autumn Stone***, is released at the same time, summarising the group's career via both old and new material.
[8] The group plays its final show at Springfield Theatre, Jersey.

1972

Aug ***Early Faces***, compiled as a cash-in on the success of the Faces, and actually containing Small Faces' Decca tracks, makes US #176. A US reissue of ***Ogden's Nut Gone Flake*** will peak at US #189 the following March.

1976

Jan [3] With the group featured on the front page, the **New Musical Express** announces that the band is to re-form.
[17] *Itchycoo Park* is reissued in the UK, picks up strong airplay, and hits the Top 10 for the second time, at #9.
Apr [3] *Lazy Sunday*, also reissued on the strength of the previous success, makes UK #39.
June Spurred by the interest in the group's old hits, Marriott (who has just disbanded Steve Marriott's All-Stars after a long US tour) re-forms the group, with

Jones and McLagan re-joining, but Lane declining. Rick Wills comes in on bass instead.

1977

Apr [13] The group begins its 11-date reunion tour of the UK with a show at the City Hall in Sheffield, S. Yorks. (The band's resurrection has only been officially announced in March, though they have been rehearsing for some months while contractual wrangles are worked out.)

Aug ***Playmates***, by the new line-up, is released.

Sept A second UK tour is undertaken to promote the album, with Jimmy McCulloch (ex-Paul McCartney's Wings) temporarily recruited on guitar.

1978

May The group splits again after recording the material for a second album. (Jones will join the Who after Keith Moon's death, Wills will move to the US to join Foreigner, McLagan will become a member of the Rolling Stones' augmenting road band, and Marriott will continue to lead R&B groups into the '80s, mostly in small clubs and pubs.)

Sept ***78 In The Shade*** fails to chart, and - unlike the Small Faces material of the '60s - is quickly forgotten.

1983

Sept [20] A benefit concert is held at London's Royal Albert Hall for Ronnie Lane who has been admitted to a Florida hospital for treatment for multiple sclerosis (with the Rolling Stones reportedly helping with his medical bills) in March the previous year. The superstar line-up includes Eric Clapton, Jeff Beck, Steve Winwood and Jimmy Page. (There will be intermittent charity benefits throughout the '80s as Lane continues to battle the disease.)

1991

Apr [20] While McLagan has played in Barking Dogs with Ray Woodbury and Jorge Calderon among others, Marriott has returned to the pub circuit in 1990 with his new band, Steve Marriott & His Packet Of Three. Recently working on new material with Frampton, Marriott dies in a fire in his 16th-century cottage in Arkesden, Essex. His accidental death is from smoke inhalation, having reportedly taken cocaine, valium and a mix of wine and beer.

1996

May [11] New compilation, ***The Decca Anthology 1965-1967***, charts for a week at UK #66.

May [30] McLagan, Wood, Jones and Marriott's mother accept the Lifetime Achievement Award (with Lane too ill to attend) for the Small Faces, at the 41st annual Ivor Novello Awards, held at London's Grosvenor Hotel.

see also: **THE FACES, FOREIGNER, HUMBLE PIE, THE WHO**

SMASHING PUMPKINS

Billy Corgan (vocals, guitar); **James Iha** (guitar); **D'Arcy** (bass); **Jimmy Chamberlain** (drums)

1991

Sept [7] Already a veteran of goth-rock Florida-based band Marked, Corgan (b. Mar. 17, 1967, Chicago, IL), the son of a jazz guitarist father, has formed the Smashing Pumpkins in Chicago in 1987 initially as a duo with D'Arcy (b. D'Arcy Wretzky, May 1, 1968, South Haven, MI), augmented only by a drum machine, making their live debut at the local Avalon club. Having contributed two cuts to an alternative various Chicago artists compilation, ***Light Into Dark*** and cut a one-off *I Am One/Not Worth Asking* for the small Chicago-based Potential indie label in 1989, and a further single, *Tristessa/Honey Spider*, for the seminal Sub Pop company, the group, now fleshed out by Iha (b. Mar. 26, 1968, Elk Grove, IL) and ex-J.P. & the Cats swing ensemble percussionist Chamberlain (b. June 10, 1964, Joliet, IL), has signed with Caroline Records in the US to record its debut album. Having released the included *Siva* in August, the group's first effort, ***Gish***, co-produced by Corgan and Butch Vig, now charts for a week at US #195.

1992

Sept [5] Released in the UK on Virgin Records' associated Hut label, *I Am One*, belatedly extracted from ***Gish***, charts for a week at UK #73.

1993

July [3] *Cherub Rock* bows at its UK #31 peak.

[31] The melodic grunge, rock-based breakthrough set, ***Siamese Dream***, again co-produced by Vig and Corgan and featuring R.E.M.'s Mike Mills on piano, enters at its UK #4 peak.

Aug [14] ***Siamese Dream*** hits US #10.

[23] The group embarks on a European tour, at the Sentrum Scene, Oslo, Norway.

Sept [25] *Today* makes UK #44.

1994

Mar [3] Despite having the week's highest new chart entry, the group is banned from appearing on BBC1-TV's "Top Of The Pops", because of objections to the lyrics of *Disarm*.

[5] *Disarm* debuts at its UK #11 peak.

[14] ***Gish*** is certified gold by the RIAA, with eventual US sales topping 750,000.

Aug [19] The RIAA certifies three million sales of ***Siamese Dream***.

[25] Having become the darlings of this year's "Lollapalooza" US trek, the group headlines the caravan's Aztec Bowl, San Diego State University, CA date, a bill grossing $636,749 from a crowd of 21,707.

Sept [8] The band performs the double-nominated *Disarm*, at the 11th annual MTV Video Music Awards, emceed by Roseanne at New York, NY's Radio City Music Hall.

Oct [22] A collection of B-sides, rarities and live radio performances, ***Pisces Iscariot*** bows at its US #4 peak.

Nov [23] While the group is recording a new album during ten-month sessions held in Chicago and Los Angeles, ***Pisces Iscariot*** is certified platinum by the RIAA.

1995

Apr [10] Demo CDs of new material are stolen from D'Arcy's vacation home.

Aug [25] Smashing Pumpkins play at "Reading '95", near Reading, Berks.

Oct [19] During current US tour dates, the group performs at the Madison Theatre, Peoria, IL, taking $19,200 at the box-office.

[28] *Bullet With Butterfly Wings* bows at its UK #20 peak.

Nov [11] Having entered at its UK #4 high the previous week, and co-produced by Flood, Alan Moulder and Billy Corgan, the Virgin Records-released double-CD, ***Mellon Collie And The Infinite Sadness***, debuts at US #1, as the band performs on NBC-TV's "Saturday Night Live".

1996

Jan [6] *Bullet With Butterfly Wings* reaches US #22.

[17] Corgan inducts Pink Floyd into the Rock and Roll Hall of Fame at its 11th annual dinner held at New York's Waldorf Astoria Hotel, also singing *Wish You Here* with the group at the post-dinner jam.

[27] The band appears on C4-TV's "The White Room".

Feb [1] ***Mellon Collie And The Infinite Sadness*** is confirmed quintuple platinum by the RIAA.

[6-7] Having begun the month with its first shows of the year, a four-night stand at Chicago's Double Door, Smashing Pumpkins now play a pair of dates at the Kezar Pavilion, San Francisco, CA.

Mar [30] *1979* reaches US #12.

May [11] ***Zero*** EP enters at its US #46 Album peak.

[12] Bernadette O'Brien, a 17-year old student from County Cork, dies in Dublin's Mater Hospital, the day after being one of seven people injured when part of the crowd at the Pumpkins' The Point gig begins "body-surfing" near the stage.

[18] *Tonight, Tonight* debuts at UK #8.

June [15-16] The group participates in the Tibetan Freedom Concert in San Francisco, CA, a benefit show organized by the Beastie Boys for the Milarepa Fund.

July [12] The group's keyboard player Jonathan Melvoin dies from a heroin overdose in a Manhattan, NY hotel room after shooting up with drummer Chamberlain, who is himself charged with heroin possession. Other band members are questioned by police and subsequently released. Chamberlain will then be fired by the band.

PATTI SMITH

1971

Feb Smith (b. Dec. 30, 1946, Chicago, IL), having moved with her family from New Jersey to Paris, France, then to London and New York, NY, started a small local newspaper in 1969 before working for **Rock** magazine. Inspired by the work of William Burroughs and Arthur Rimbaud, she has spent much of the following year writing poetry, also meeting Village Oldies record-store clerk Lenny Kaye, who has previously recorded as Link Cromwell (and in 1973 will compile the legendary compilation album, ***Nuggets***, for Elektra records). Smith now invites Kaye to accompany her poetry readings on guitar at live events, not least playing support to Andy Warhol/Velvet Underground follower, Gerard Malanga, at St. Mark's Church, New York. She will also begin writing for rock monthly **Creem** by year's end.

1972

May A professional and personal relationship develops with playwright Sam Shepard (they write the off-Broadway play, "Cowboy Mouth" together), while she works as the opening act for artists at Mercer Art Center for $5 a night. One of the bands she supports is the New York Dolls. Two volumes of her poetry will be published (**Witt** and **Seventh Heaven**) by year's end.

1973

She reunites with Kaye for more readings at Le Jardin in New York, while a piano player, Richard (DNV) Sohl, also joins, the trio playing in an "improv" style. Todd Rundgren's ***A Wizard A True Star*** includes a dedication to Patti Lee Smith, who had earlier nick-named him "Runt".

1974

June Smith records *Hey Joe/Piss Factory* for Robert Mapplethorpe's Mer label. Initially released locally, Sire Records picks it up for nationwide release. (Incongruously, Smith's *Career Of Evil* appears on the newly-released Blue Öyster Cult album, ***Secret Treaties***, not least because she is currently rhythm guitarist's Allen Lanier's girlfriend. After dates at the Whisky, Los Angeles, CA, she recruits new guitar player, Ivan Kral. She plays a three-week stint at New York's CBGB's, and invites the club DJ, Jay Dee Daugherty, to play drums. He stays and the Patti Smith Group is formed.)

1975

Jan [1] Smith participates in the New York poetry project, "New Year's Day Extravaganza", with Yoko Ono at the beginning of a month when the group signs to Arista Records.

1976

Feb [2] Their maiden album, ***Horses***, produced by John Cale, though they have differed over musical direction, with Cale preferring more improvisation, makes US #47. The album includes cover versions of *Gloria* and *Land Of A Thousand Dances*, as well as references to rock icons Jimi Hendrix and Jim Morrison.

Apr A censored version of *My Generation* is released.

May [16-17] The group makes its UK debut at the

Roundhouse, Chalk Farm, London, supported by the Stranglers.

Aug [2] More Smith compositions appear on Blue Öyster Cult's newly-issued ***Agents Of Fortune***.

Oct The Patti Smith Group tours Europe.

1977

Jan [8] ***Radio Ethiopia***, once again capturing the prevailing new-wave rock mood with its socio-political lyrical idealism, makes US #122.

[23] Smith breaks vertebrae in her neck as she falls off stage at a gig in Tampa, FL, where the group is opening for Bob Seger, and she needs 22 stitches.

Sept The full version of *My Generation* is released as a 12" single.

1978

Apr *Because The Night*, co-written with Bruce Springsteen, hits UK #5 and US #13, the first time that Springsteen's name appears in the Top 20 Singles chart. Its parent album, ***Easter***, produced by Jimmy Iovine, reaches UK #16 and US #20.

Aug [27] The Patti Smith Group plays on the final day of the 18th National Jazz Blues & Rock Festival "Reading Rock '78", near Reading, Berks., while *Privilege (Set Me Free)* peaks at UK #72.

1979

Feb Babel, Smith's fifth book of poetry, is published.

May ***Wave*** makes UK #41 and US #18. Produced by long-time friend Rundgren, called in by Arista to encourage her to record again, it will be her last album in nine years. It includes *Frederick* (UK #63), dedicated to future husband, former MC5 guitarist, Fred "Sonic" Smith, and a cover of the Byrds' *So You Wanna Be A Rock'n'Roll Star*.

1980

Mar [1] She marries Smith. Living in Detroit, and raising two children, Jackson and Jesse, she will retreat from the rock world for most of the decade, occasionally emerging for ad-hoc poetry readings.

1988

July Smith comes out of retirement with *People Have The Power* and ***Dream Of Life***, co-produced by Smith and Iovine, and still featuring both Sohl and Daugherty.

[16] ***Dream Of Life*** charts for a week at UK #70, and will make US #65.

1990

June [3] Sohl dies of a cardiac seizure in Long Island, New York, age 37.

1991

May Smith makes a rare public appearance at the Nectarine Ballroom, Ann Arbor, MI, raising $9,000 for the Wellness Networks fight against AIDS. She is joined by Smith, Kaye, Jay Dee Daugherty and Scott Asheton.

1992

Mar [9] The soundtrack album to the Wim Wenders film, "Until The End Of The World", to which Smith has contributed *It Takes Time*, makes US #114.

1993

Apr Having contributed a small essay, "February Snow", to **Interview** magazine's December issue (recalling her dead friends, Andy Warhol, Mapplethorpe and Sohl), her book of short stories, **Wool Gathering**, is published in the US.

July [8] Smith performs in Central Park, New York, as part of the "Summerstage" series.

Dec [25] Having already peaked at UK #65 on Oct [23], 10,000 Maniacs' version of Smith's *Because The Night* reaches US #18.

1995

Apr [8] Following her husband's death from a heart attack the previous November 5th (and having also suffered the loss of her younger brother Todd also in 1994), she takes part in a tribute concert to Fred Smith at the Ark, Ann Arbor, MI.

July [28] She makes an unannounced appearance at a "Lollapalooza" gig in New York, performing a 45-minute set with Kaye and Daugherty.

Sept [14] She participates in the T.J. Martell Foundation 20th anniversary dinner, honoring label boss Clive Davis with the 1995 Humanitarian Award.

Oct [7] Following a performance the day before in Lowell, MA, Smith gives two benefit shows at the Old Cambridge Baptist Church, Cambridge, MA, with Kaye and Thurston Moore backing her in a program of poetry and music.

[24] Female-only compilation ***Ain't Nuthin' But A She Thing'***, with a new cut from Smith, is released in the US.

Nov [2] Smith attends the dedication to her husband at a church in Detroit where a memorial is placed in the building's bell tower.

Dec [7] She begins an eight-date northeastern US tour opening for Bob Dylan, in Danbury, CT.

1996

Jan [9] Soundtrack album ***Dead Man Walking***, including Smith's *Walkin' Blind*, specifically written for the project, is released by Columbia Records (US).

[17] Smith inducts the Velvet Underground into the Rock and Roll Hall of Fame at the 11th annual induction dinner at New York's Waldorf Astoria, also singing *Pale Blue Eyes* at the post-dinner jam.

[25] The **Rolling Stone** Critics Poll names Smith, whose latest prose is published as **The Cruel Sea** and who continues to work on a new album, Most Welcome Comeback.

May [18] Smith makes her first TV appearance in close to two decades on Fox-TV's "Saturday Night Special".

THE SMITHS

Morrissey (vocals); **Johnny Marr** (guitar); **Andy Rourke** (bass); **Mike Joyce** (drums)

1982

Nov Marr (b. John Maher, Oct. 31, 1963, Ardwick, Manchester, Lancs.), a veteran of several Manchester-based bands including Freaky Party, Paris Valentinos, Sister Ray and White Dice, looking for a lyricist for his tunes, has teamed with Morrissey (b. Stephen Patrick Morrissey, May 22, 1959, Davyhulme, Manchester) in May, earlier in the year. The latter, the son of a hospital porter and a librarian, whose book **James Dean Isn't Dead** has been published by locally-based Babylon Books, has also been the UK president of the New York Dolls fan club. (Musically he has played for seven weeks in the Nosebleeds and auditioned to join Slaughter & the Dogs.) Having rejected the names Smithdom and the Smith Family, the pair, always the central creative force in the band, now forms the Smiths, initially recording demos with the Fall's drummer Simon Wolstencroft, before permanently recruiting local musicians Rourke (b. 1963, Manchester), a former schoolfriend of Marr's, and Joyce (b. June 1, 1963, Manchester), and plays its debut gig at hometown venue, the Ritz.

1983

Apr Having made its London debut at the Rock Garden the previous month, and steered by Mancunian entrepreneur Joe Moss, the group signs a one-off single deal with London-based independent label, Rough Trade, after turning down Manchester-based Factory Records, interested in them following popular local gigging. Most early shows have featured Morrissey paying tribute to his various influences/obsessions: a bunch of gladioli, often tucked into the seat of his pants, representing Oscar Wilde, and a hearing aid in tribute to early '50s vocalist Johnnie Ray. He also styles much of his appearance, and hairstyle, on his favorite vocalist - the recently-deceased Billy Fury.

May Their debut single, *Hand In Glove*, benefits from considerable pre-release anticipation, and tops the UK Independent chart.

[18] A group session is broadcast on BBC Radio 1's "John Peel Show", featuring *Miserable Lie*, *Reel Around The Fountain*, *Handsome Devil* and *What Difference Does It Make*.

July The group signs a long-term deal with Rough Trade, in the face of potentially more lucrative offers from major companies, and plays at London's Hammersmith Palais, supporting Altered Images.

Aug [12] After an initial session for BBC Radio 1's "David Jensen Show", the group now records its second series for the program, cutting *Accept Yourself*, *I Don't Owe You Anything*, *Pretty Girls Make Graves* and *Reel Around The Fountain*. **The Sun** newspaper will print a story on the 25th stating that the BBC is in an uproar because of the lyrical content of one of the songs.

Dec Their second single, *This Charming Man*, in a sleeve picturing French actor Jean Marais, is their UK national chart debut and reaches #25, spurred by an appearance on BBC2-TV's "Whistle Test". Already the darling of the UK alternative music media, Morrissey writes an article in the weekly UK rock magazine, **Sounds**, in appreciation of his favorite girl singer, Sandie Shaw.

1984

Jan [1] The group makes its US debut at New York's Danceteria, though further dates will be cancelled when Joyce comes down with chickenpox.

Feb Released to coincide with a 20-date UK tour, the Marr/Morrissey-penned (as will be all Smiths hits) *What Difference Does It Make* reaches UK #12. Its picture sleeve depicts actor Terence Stamp in the film, "The Collector", but when Stamp objects to its use, it is replaced by a similarly-posed picture of Morrissey. (Morrissey, meanwhile, moves from Manchester to London, and contracts laryngitis, which causes the cancellation of some tour dates.)

Mar Their debut album, ***The Smiths***, in a sleeve depicting Joe Dallesandro in Warhol's film "Flesh", hits UK #2. The critically-revered set has been produced by John Porter, following earlier unsuccessful sessions with Troy Tate.

May Backed by the Smiths, Sandie Shaw reaches UK #27 with her version of *Hand In Glove*. Morrissey, although not featured on this release, expresses his admiration both for Shaw and other '60s female singers in the UK music press, which currently regards the Smiths as the darlings of alternative rock.

June *Heaven Knows I'm Miserable Now* is their highest-charting single, hitting UK #10 (despite some major chains' refusal to stock it because of objections to the lyrics of its B-side, *Suffer Little Children*, allegedly after complaints from relatives of victims of Britain's '60s Moors Murderers, Ian Brady and Myra Hindley). ***The Smiths***, released in the US on Sire Records, peaks at #150. The band undertakes another UK tour, and headlines the Greater London Council's "Festival For Jobs".

Sept *William, It Was Really Nothing* reaches UK #17. On a brief US visit, the band plays at the Danceteria in New York.

Nov Live dates in Wales are followed by a tour in Ireland, while the low-priced album, ***Hatful Of Hollow***, a collection of BBC radio session tracks and B-sides, hits UK #7.

1985

Feb *How Soon Is Now?* makes UK #24. (It will subsequently provide the backing for a UK TV jeans commercial, and become heavily sampled in Soho's 1990 hit, *Hippychick*.)

[23] ***Meat Is Murder*** enters the UK chart at #1, displacing Bruce Springsteen's ***Born In The USA***. The group will begin a five-week UK tour the next day, supported by fellow Mancunians, James.

Mar *Shakespeare's Sister* reaches UK #26.

[18] The band's concert at the Apollo Theatre, Oxford,

Oxon, is recorded by the BBC. (A live album is mooted, though the tracks are eventually released on various single B-sides.)
Apr Rourke and Joyce play on *Incense And Peppermints*, the first single by the Adult Net, a band formed as a sideline by Brix Smith, guitarist with the Fall and wife of its leader, Mark E. Smith. (Both will continue to work with the Adult Net on subsequent projects.)
May ***Meat Is Murder*** peaks at US #110.
July The extracted *That Joke Isn't Funny Anymore* makes UK #49.
Oct *The Boy With The Thorn In His Side*, showcasing Marr's familiar jangling guitar work, reaches UK #23.
Dec [17] The group records its last session for the "John Peel Show".

1986

Feb [8] The band appears with New Order and the Fall in the "From Manchester With Love" concert at the Royal Court Theatre, Liverpool, Merseyside, to benefit Liverpool's 48 Labour councillors, currently involved in a rate-capping dispute with the Government.
Apr The band adds a second guitarist, ex-Bluebells and Aztec Camera side-man, Craig Gannon.
June *Big Mouth Strikes Again* reaches UK #26, taken from ***The Queen Is Dead***.
[28] ***The Queen Is Dead*** enters at UK #2, behind Genesis' ***Invisible Touch***.
July [12-20] The Smiths appear during the "Tenth Summer" festival in Manchester.
Aug *Panic* makes UK #11, while ***The Queen Is Dead*** makes US #70.
Nov *Ask* reaches UK #14. Marr is injured in a car crash, forcing the band to cancel an appearance at an Artists Against Apartheid benefit at London's Royal Albert Hall.
Dec Gannon leaves the group.

1987

Jan *Shoplifters Of The World Unite*, despite its controversial lyrics, reaches UK #12.
Feb [7] The group plays what will be its last-ever gig at the "San Remo Festival", San Remo, Italy.
Mar [7] Compilation, ***The World Won't Listen***, enters at UK #2 (behind ***The Phantom Of The Opera*** London cast album). It is announced that the Smiths will sign to EMI Records when its current Rough Trade contract expires.
Apr Originally recorded for a John Peel BBC Radio 1 session, *Sheila Take A Bow* hits UK #10.
[10] The band is featured on C4-TV's "The Tube".
May [30] US #63-peaking double compilation album, ***Louder Than Bombs***, on Sire, is imported into the UK by Rough Trade and, despite its price, bows at its UK #38 peak.
Aug Acoustic guitar-led *Girlfriend In A Coma* reaches UK #13. Unusually for the Smiths (who had once vowed never to get involved with promo videos), it is supported by a video - featuring a solo Morrissey. It fuels speculation that there will soon be no group for EMI to record, as it becomes apparent that Marr and Morrissey are finding it difficult to work together (Morrissey is reportedly upset by Marr's frequent guitar "moonlighting" with Billy Bragg, Bryan Ferry and others, while Marr is concerned with Morrissey's proposed songs selections, saying he didn't form a band "just to play Cilla Black covers"), but several weeks will elapse before the official announcement of a split, despite Morrissey's affirmation in the **New Musical Express** that "Whoever says the Smiths have split shall be severely spanked by me with a wet plimsoul", and the news that Morrissey will sign with EMI as a solo artist.
Oct [10] ***Strangeways, Here We Come*** (referring to the Manchester prison), enters at UK #2, behind Michael Jackson's ***Bad***, and is their final album.
Nov *I Started Something I Couldn't Finish* reaches UK #23, following which Morrissey officially moves to EMI as a solo artist. (Marr will continue working with acts like Bryan Ferry, Paul McCartney and Talking Heads, before becoming involved with the Pretenders, while Rourke and Joyce remain, temporarily, with the Adult Net.)
Dec *Last Night I Dreamt That Somebody Loved Me*, from ***Strangeways***, makes UK #30, while ***Strangeways Here We Come*** reaches US #55.

1988

June [11] With Morrissey's solo career in full swing, Marr plays guitar in Midge Ure's all-purpose back-up band at "Nelson Mandela's 70th Birthday Tribute" at Wembley Stadium, Wembley, Middx.
Sept [17] A live Smiths album, ***Rank*** (recorded in October 1986 at a concert at the National Ballroom, Kilburn, London), enters at UK #2 (and US #77), behind Kylie Minogue's ***Kylie***.
Oct Strange Fruit Records releases a 12" EP featuring the Smiths' May 1983 BBC "John Peel Show" session.
Dec [22] Morrissey, Rourke, Joyce and Gannon re-form to play a last-gasp farewell Smiths gig (without Marr) at the Wolverhampton Civic Hall. To gain entrance, fans must wear either a Smiths or Morrissey T-shirt. (Joyce will continue playing with Morrissey before undertaking work for Julian Cope, Sinead O'Connor, PiL and Suede.)

1989

Apr Marr is announced in the new line-up of Matt Johnson's The The, and is prominent on the act's new album, ***Mind Bomb***, though the liaison will once again prove intermittent, not least because he is so in demand for session work.

1990

May [19] Electronic, an ad hoc teaming of Marr, the Pet Shop Boys' Neil Tennant and New Order's Bernard Sumner, make US #38 with *Getting Away With It*, having made UK #12 in January. (Their debut album, ***Electronic***, will hit UK #2 (on June [8], behind Seal's ***Seal***), and US #109 (Aug [3]) the following summer, yielding the UK #8, *Get The Message* (May [11]), the UK #39 *Feel Every Beat* (Sept [28]), while a second round of recordings will result in the UK #6, *Disappointed*, on July [4], 1992.)
Sept [19] The RIAA certifies gold sales of ***Strangeways Here We Come***, ***Louder Than Bombs*** and ***The Queen Is Dead***.
Oct Marr works with three-piece band, Stex, and will shortly work with Banderas on their debut album.

1991

Mar Joyce (who is currently playing in a re-formed Buzzcocks) says he plans to sue Morrissey and Marr, after discovering that they received 40% each of the group's earnings, while he and Rourke only received a 10% cut.

1995

Mar [4] The Smiths' enduring appeal has seen continued chart action. In 1992, the reissued *This Charming Man* hit UK #8 on Aug [22], ***Best ... I***, the first in a two volume Smiths retrospective compilation, entered the UK chart at #1 on Aug [29] and US #139 on Oct [17], the re-released *How Soon Is Now?* (UK #16, Sept [19], *There Is A Light That Never Goes Out* (UK #25, Oct [31]) and ***Best ... II***, which bowed at its UK #29 peak on Nov [14], one week before *How Does It Feel?* climbed to UK #27. All existing Smiths video clips and UK TV appearances were collected and released as "The Complete Picture" by Warner Reprise Video in December the same year. Acquired by WEA in the UK, the Smiths' entire album back catalog has been released on CD in April 1993. After *Ask* has charted for a week at UK #62 on Feb [18] earlier this year, a further compilation, ***Singles*** now hits UK #5 in its week of entry (and is released in the US on Reprise Records), as ***Meat Is Murder*** (UK #39) and ***The Smiths*** (UK #42) both re-chart.
see also: **MORRISSEY**

SNOOP DOGGY DOGG

1992

May [9] Raised on 21st Street, south of Compton, CA, and given the nickname Snoopy as a baby by his mother, Snoop (b. Calvin Broadus, 1971, Long Beach), also taking his stepfather's last name (whom his mother married during pregnancy), has sung in the Golgotha Trinity Baptist Church choir, but has been subsequently influenced while a teenage member of the Long Beach Insane Crips gang, by local rapper Count Cool Out, and the material produced by N.W.A. and Eric B. & Rakim. One month after graduating from Long Beach Polytechnic High School, Snoop has been arrested for selling cocaine to an undercover agent, serving a year in county jail, during which time he began rapping. After his release, he concentrated on this talent, but returned to jail for several months for violating his probation (and has also been arrested twice more for gun possession). Free again, Snoop has recorded underground demo tapes with a DJ friend, Warren G, selling the cassettes locally. Having borrowed his cousin Tate Doggy Dogg's nickname to become Snoop Doggy Dogg, a tape has also been given to G's brother, N.W.A's Dr. Dre, who has invited Snoop to a recording of the band's ***Niggaz4Life*** album, after which Dre suggests they write and record together. Their first collaboration, *Deep Cover*, is the title song for the movie of the same name, the soundtrack to which, ***Deep Cover***, now enters the US Album chart set to make #166, though the single hits #1 on the US Rap survey, credited to Dr. Dre Introducing Snoop Doggy Dogg.

1993

Feb [13] With most of its lyrics written by Snoop, who is prominently featured as a solo rapper on four cuts, Dre's first solo album ***The Chronic***, its title being slang for marijuana, and hailed as redefining the rap genre, hits US #3.
July [3] *Dre Day*, co-written by Dre, Snoop and Colin Wolfe, hits US #8.
Aug [10] *Dre Day* is certified gold by the RIAA.
[25] Snoop is accused of participating in a murder, driving to a park in the Palms district of Los Angeles, where his bodyguard McKinley Lee allegedly shoots and kills Philip Woldermariam, a member of the By Yerself Hustlers gang, from inside Snoop's Jeep vehicle. Snoop will be released on $1 million bail.
Dec [4] Signed to Dre's hardcore gangsta rap label Death Row, Snoop's first solo single, *What's My Name* debuts at its UK #20 peak.
[11] Snoop's ***Doggystyle***, produced by and featuring Dre and recorded with his Death Row backing rapping aggregate Tha Dogg Pound, simultaneously enters at its US #1 and UK #38 peaks, the first time a debut artist has reached pole position in the US in its first week of release (selling 800,000 copies in that period). The album will eventually sell over four million copies in the US and 140,000 in the UK.

1994

Jan [1] *What's My Name?* hits US #8.
Feb [8] *What's My Name?* is certified gold by the RIAA.
[10] Snoop makes his UK live debut at London's Leicester Square's Equinox, playing a six-track set, though the visit is marred when he is ordered out of the Milestone Hotel, Kensington an hour after checking in, when the management discovers his murder charge. He checks into the Halcyon Hotel in Holland Park. The **Daily Star** tabloid runs a front-page story with the headline "Kick This Evil Bastard Out!". His UK promotion also includes a justified physical attack on Rod Hull's Emu puppet on C4-TV's "The Word".
[12] The follow-up single, *Gin And Juice*, bows at its UK #39 peak.
Mar [26] *Gin And Juice* hits US #8.
Apr [6] *Gin and Juice* is confirmed gold by the RIAA.
[30-**May** 1] Snoop's "The Chronic Tour" plays two shows at London's Brixton Academy.

May [31] The RIAA certifies four million sales of ***Doggystyle***.
Aug [20] *Doggy Dogg World* reaches UK #32 in its week of entry.
Sept [8] Having had a range of clothing featured on "The Goods", MTV's answer to QVC and the Home Shopping Network, Snoop wins the Best Rap Video category at the 11th annual MTV Video Music Awards, held at New York, NY's Radio City Music Hall.
Nov [5] Released by Death Row, the ***Murder Was The Case*** film soundtrack album, built around the title song written and performed by Snoop, and including further collaborations by him with Tha Dogg Pound, enters the US chart at #1. Its accompanying short-form movie has been directed by Dre.
Dec [7] Snoop collects the trophy for Top Male Artist at the fifth annual **Billboard** Music Awards staged at the Universal Amphitheatre, Universal City, and hosted by Dennis Miller and Heather Locklear.

1995

Jan [12] He is charged with possession of marijuana and drug paraphernalia, stemming from a visit to the Lake Charles area of Los Angeles on December 21st the previous year.
[26] Snoop is named Best Rapper in **Rolling Stone**'s 1995 Music Awards (both in the Readers' and Awards' Picks categories).
[30] He wins the Favorite Artist/Rap, Hip-Hop Artist at the 22nd annual American Music Awards held at Los Angeles' Shrine Auditorium. (Snoop will spend much of the rest of the year recording with Tha Dogg Pound, and addressing his various legal problems.)

1996

Feb [20] Snoop is acquitted of murder charges associated with the death of Philip Woldermariam. With the jury deadlocked on the charge of voluntary manslaughter, Judge Paul G. Flynn declares a mistrial.
Mar [18] Prosecutors inform Judge Flynn that they are dropping further litigation in the voluntary manslaughter charges.
[29] Snoop performs at the tenth annual Soul Train Music Awards staged at the Shrine Auditorium.

SOFT CELL

Marc Almond (vocals); **David Ball** (keyboards)

1979

Dec Almond (b. Peter Marc Almond, July 9, 1959, Southport, Lancs.), having left college in Southport and moved to Leeds Polytechnic to study Fine Arts in 1978, has met synthesizer player Ball (b. May 3, 1959, Blackpool, Lancs.), who has a similar interest in Northern Soul music, and with whom he has formed a duo in October, Ball writing music to Almond's theatrical lyrics. With the visual addition of slide and film special effects, handled by Steven Griffith, they become Soft Cell, now playing their first gig at Leeds Polytechnic.

1980

June Their debut four-track EP, *Mutant Moments*, featuring four joint compositions, is recorded in a local studio (the session and pressing of 2,000 copies paid for by Ball).
Sept [6] Coinciding with the release of the EP on its own Big Frock label, Soft Cell plays with great success to a 5,000-plus audience at the "Futurama 2 Science Fiction Music Festival" in Leeds, W. Yorks. The EP, meanwhile, attracts the attention of Some Bizzare Records boss Stevo, who invites the duo (Griffith and the multi-media accessories have now dropped out) to contribute a track to his forthcoming compilation album of new synthesizer-based "futurist" acts. *The Girl With The Patent Leather Face* is recorded on two-track equipment at practically no cost.

1981

Mar Stevo has negotiated a deal for both Soft Cell and Some Bizzare with Phonogram, which includes a £1,000 advance for the duo, and distribution of the compilation ***Some Bizzare Album*** (which makes UK #58). The duo's first Some Bizzare single, *Memorabilia*, produced by Mute Records' boss Daniel Miller, is released, without charting.
July At London's Advision Studios, Soft Cell resurrects the little-known (though long a cult favorite on the Northern Soul circuit) Gloria Jones track, *Tainted Love*, written by ex-Four Preps and Piltdown Men-member Ed Cobb, and produced by Mike Thorne.
Sept [5] *Tainted Love* tops the UK chart for the first of two weeks, and will become the year's biggest-selling single, also hitting #1 in a score of other territories around the world.
Dec [5] *Bedsitter* hits UK #4.
Billboard magazine names Soft Cell New Wave Band Of The Year.

1982

Feb [6] *Tainted Love* re-charts in the UK, reaching #43, and bringing its weeks-on-chart tally to 26.
[20] Typically melodramatic and self-penned, *Say Hello, Wave Goodbye* hits UK #3, as the duo's debut album, ***Non-Stop Erotic Cabaret***, recorded in New York with Thorne, hits UK #5, spurred by a lengthy UK club tour (after which, Ball will return to Leeds for several months, where he will write the music for the next album, leaving Almond to do solo work, for which he becomes Marc & the Mambas, a pseudonym used prior to his Soft Cell days. Keyboards player Annie Hogan assists Almond).
[24] *Tainted Love* is named Best British Single at the first annual BRIT Awards, at London's Grosvenor House Hotel.
June [19] *Torch* hits UK #2, behind Adam Ant's *Goody Two-Shoes*.
July [3] Mini-album, ***Non-Stop Ecstatic Dancing***, featuring New York-recorded dance remixes of several of the duo's tracks, hits UK #6.
[17] *Tainted Love* hits US #8, having been climbing the survey since entering on January 16th. (It will set a new longevity record on the Hot 100, its 43 weeks being the longest consecutive chart run by a single.)
[31] *Tainted Love* charts for the third time in Britain, reaching #50.
Aug [7] ***Non-Stop Erotic Cabaret*** reaches US #22.
[28] *What*, another Northern Soul revival (the original by Judy Street), hits UK #3.
Sept [25] ***Non-Stop Ecstatic Dancing*** makes US #57.
Oct [23] Almond experiments with a different musical direction via ***Untitled***, released under the name Marc & the Mambas. It couples original material with revivals of songs by Jacques Brel, Lou Reed and others, and makes UK #42.
Dec [11] The self-written *Where The Heart Is* reaches UK #21. Marc & the Mambas (Almond, Hogan, bass player Tim Taylor and others) play at London's Theatre Royal, Drury Lane.

1983

Jan ***The Art Of Falling Apart***, recorded in New York the previous September, with co-producer Thorne, hits UK #5. It is packaged with a free 12" Jimi Hendrix tribute disc, containing Soft Cell's versions of *Hey Joe*, *Purple Haze* and *Voodoo Chile*.
Mar *Numbers/Barriers* reaches UK #25, as the duo undertakes another UK tour, while ***The Art Of Falling Apart*** makes US #84. (During the month, Almond and Stevo trash Phonogram's marketing department, leaving the note: "Your marketing will be the death of Soft Cell" after the label has given away free 12" copies of *Tainted Love* with *Numbers*.)
June Ball scores the music for a stage revival of Tennessee Williams' play, "Suddenly Last Summer".
Aug Despite scathing reviews (and a chain-store ban because of allegedly obscene lyrics), the double album, ***Torment And Toreros***, by Marc & the Mambas makes UK #28. Almond's group now includes a string section, all-girl trio the Venomettes (one of whom, Ginny, marries Ball).
Oct Soft Cell's *Soul Inside* reaches UK #16.
Nov Ball releases a solo album, ***In Strict Tempo***, with guest vocals from Genesis P. Orridge of Psychic TV.
Dec Almond and Ball announce the end of Soft Cell as they complete a final album together, and play a last US tour.

1984

Jan [8-10] The duo's final UK live dates are a farewell series at London's Hammersmith Palais. (Almond will immediately embark on a successful solo career, while Ball will form Other People, before joining English Boy And The Love Ranch in 1988.)
Feb *Down In The Subway*, extracted from their final album, makes UK #24.
Mar The final Soft Cell studio set, ***This Last Night In Sodom***, reaches UK #12. *Tainted Love* will chart for the fourth time, making UK #43 the following February before an 11-track Soft Cell compilation, ***The Singles Album***, reaches UK #58 in December 1986.

1990

July Ball re-emerges as one half of the East-West label act, Grid (with Richard Norris), whose modern-dance debut, *Floatation*, makes UK #60. (They will score with a further nine chart singles and two albums - ***Evolver*** (#14, Oct [1] 1994) and ***Music For Dancing*** (#67, Oct [14] 1995).

1991

Mar [23] *Say Hello - Wave Goodbye '91* remix makes UK #38.
May [25] Reissued *Tainted Love*, the duo's most enduring cut, hits UK #5.
June [1] Remixed updates of selected Soft Cell singles by Ball are included on the Soft Cell/Marc Almond Parlophone-issued UK retrospective, ***Memorabilia - The Singles***, which debuts at its UK #8 peak.
see also: **Marc ALMOND**

JIMMY SOMERVILLE

1984

Feb Somerville (b. June 22, 1961, Glasgow, Strathclyde, Scotland) links with Steve Bronski (b. Feb. 7, 1960, Glasgow) and Larry Steinbachek (b. May 6, 1960, London), who evolve an electronic dance music style on their twin synthesizers, to form Bronski Beat in Hackney, London, with Somerville's falsetto vocals the outstanding feature. The trio signs to London Records, via its own Forbidden Fruit label.
June [23] Bronski Beat's pop/dance debut, *Smalltown Boy*, lyrically themed on the alienation felt by a provincial homosexual, hits UK #3.
Oct [6] *Why?* hits UK #6, and its parent album, ***The Age Of Consent***, UK #4.
Dec Somerville announces his intention to leave because of his dislike of the star treatment the band is getting, but is temporarily persuaded to stay.

1985

Jan [19] Their revival of Gershwin's *It Ain't Necessarily So* makes UK #16.
Feb Somerville is fined £50 at London's Bow Street Magistrates' Court for gross indecency.
Mar *Smalltown Boy* is Bronski Beat's only US chart single, at #48.
[4] ***The Age Of Consent***, a reference to UK sex laws, hits US #36.
May [11] Their hi-nrg revival of Donna Summer's *I Feel Love*, in a medley with Summer's *Love To Love You Baby* and John Leyton's *Johnny Remember Me*, hits UK #3. It jointly credits ex-Soft Cell singer Marc Almond, who duets with Somerville. Somerville subsequently leaves to work with keyboardist Richard

Coles (b. June 23, 1962, Northampton, Northants.), an ex-student of the Royal School of Church Music, who has occasionally played on stage with Bronski Beat, and with whom Somerville has worked on a documentary film. They first name themselves the Committee, then discover the moniker is already in use and decide upon the Communards, named after the French dissidents of the 18th Century (1789 to 1794).

Sept Bronski Beat's mini-album, ***Hundreds And Thousands***, consisting mostly of dance remixes of tracks from the first album, makes UK #24. (Bronski and Steinbachek recruit John Jon (Foster), from Newcastle, Tyne & Wear band, Bust, as the replacement Bronski Beat vocalist, and will secure just two further chart singles, *Hit That Perfect Beat* (UK #3 in January the following year) and *Come On, Come On* (UK #20 in April 1986), taken from their only other chart album, ***Truthdare Doubledare***, UK #18 and US #147 in May '86.)

Oct Signed to London Records in the UK, the Communards' debut, *You Are My World*, which establishes their sound, a variation on Bronski Beat's dance-oriented keyboard arrangements, again high-lighting Somerville's falsetto voice, reaches UK #30.

1986

Jan [25] The Communards play on the first of seven dates on the "Red Wedge" tour of Britain, starting at the Apollo Theatre, Manchester, Gtr. Manchester, with Paul Weller and Billy Bragg, in support of the Labour Party. For this and later stage work, the duo recruits its regular backing band of (mainly female) session players.

June *Disenchanted* reaches UK #29.

Sept [13] Their dance-styled revival of Thelma Houston and Harold Melvin's hit, *Don't Leave Me This Way*, featuring Somerville duetting with Sarah-Jayne Morris, who becomes a regular on-stage duettist/backup vocalist, tops the UK chart, where it will stay for four weeks, and is the year's second-biggest UK single, selling 750,000 copies.

Oct ***Communards***, containing the chart singles to date, hits UK #7.

Dec The Communards' *So Cold The Night* hits UK #8, helped by a European tour including major London dates.

1987

Jan ***Communards*** makes US #90.

Feb A re-make of their first single, *You Are My World '87*, makes UK #21.

Mar [7] *Don't Leave Me This Way* is their first US success, reaching #40.

Sept *Tomorrow*, extracted from the forthcoming ***Red***, peaks at UK #23.

Oct [17] The second Communards album, ***Red***, enters at its UK #4 peak.

Nov Their revival of Gloria Gaynor's 1974 UK #2 smash, *Never Can Say Goodbye*, taken from ***Red***, and arranged similarly to *Don't Leave Me This Way*, hits UK #4.

1988

Feb [20] *Never Can Say Goodbye* peaks at US #51, as ***Red*** makes US #93.

Mar *For A Friend*, dedicated to Coles and Somerville's friend Mark Ashton, who has died of AIDS, reaches UK #28.

June Another pro-gay song, *There's More To Love*, reaches UK #20, and proves to be the last Communards success as Somerville contemplates a solo future.

1989

Dec Somerville reaches UK #14 with a re-make of Francoise Hardy's *Comment Te Dire Adieu*.

1990

Jan [20] His version of Sylvester's hi-nrg 1978 UK #8, *You Make Me Feel (Mighty Real)*, hits UK #5.

Feb [3] Somerville's debut solo album, ***Read My Lips***, co-produced by him with Stephen Hague and Pascal Gabriel, reaches UK #29.

Mar [31] *Read My Lips (Enough Is Enough)* makes UK #31.

May [5] ***Read My Lips*** debuts at its US #192 peak.

Oct Somerville, now living in San Francisco, CA, has contributed *From This Moment On*, written for the 1950 stage musical "Out Of This World", but dropped, and subsequently featured in the 1953 version of "Kiss Me Kate", to the newly released ***Red Hot + Blue***, an anthology of Cole Porter songs to benefit AIDS education.

Nov [24] His reggae-tinged cover of the Bee Gees' *To Love Somebody* hits UK #8.

1991

Jan [5] ***The Singles Collection 1984-1990***, comprising material from Somerville's Bronski Beat, Communards and solo phases, hits UK #4.

Aug [10] *Run From Love* debuts at its UK #52 peak.

Dec [1] He performs at the "Red Hot & Dance" AIDS benefit.

[9] Somerville plays a rare London date at the Powerhaus.

1992

Feb [18] He performs at the Fridge, Brixton, London.

Oct Somerville works on new, self-produced, material at Falconer Studios, London.

1993

Apr [5] He is featured on Voice Of The Beehive's cover of the Rolling Stones' *Gimme Shelter*, one of 11 versions of the song recorded to benefit the Putting Our House In Order charity.

Dec [24] Somerville takes part in C4-TV's "Camp Christmas".

1995

Feb [4] *Heartbeat* reaches UK #24.

Mar Following a four-year hiatus, spent mainly travelling to various gay communities around the world, Somerville returns to London.

Apr [15] *Heartbeat* tops the US Hot Dance Music chart.

June [3] *Hurt So Good* reaches UK #15.

[24] ***Dare To Love*** peaks at UK #38 in its week of entry.

Oct [28] *By Your Side* debuts at its UK #41 peak.

Nov [5] Somerville plays at the Opera House, Belfast, Northern Ireland, during a short Irish tour.

SONIC YOUTH

Thurston Moore (vocals, guitar); **Lee Ranaldo** (guitar, vocals); **Kim Gordon** (bass, vocals); **Steve Shelley** (drums)

1981

June [16-24] Together with Josh Baer, art-school gradute Gordon (b. Apr. 28, 1953, Rochester, NY) and her boyfriend, Bethel, CT-raised Moore (b. July 25, 1958, Coral Gables, FL) stage the avant-garde "Noise Festival" at New York's White Columns to showcase alternative acts which have grown out of the late '70s No Wave movement in New York's East Village, with its newly-formed band Sonic Youth, including early keyboardist Ann DeMarinis, drummer Richard Edson and Renaldo (b. Feb. 3, 1956, Glen Cove, NY) in the lineup, taking the stage for the first time on the 18th, its name edited from two unrelated acts, Sonic Rendezvous (formed by ex-MC's Fred "Sonic" Smith) and reggae star Big Youth. The following year, their feedback-laced debut recording, ***Sonic Youth*** EP will be released by Neutral Records, owned by composer/guitarist Glenn Branca, for whom both Moore and Renaldo have previously played.

1984

Aug Following Sonic Youth's first European club tour the previous year with replacement drummer Bob Bert, and two further releases, ***Confusion Is Sex*** and ***Kill Yr. Idols***, Moore sends the band's current six-track demo to the UK-based Doublevision company, an alternative production company run by members of Cabaret Voltaire and Paul Smith. His partners reject the tape, leaving Smith to hawk it independently to London-based labels. With no interest, he subsequently forms his own Blast First label, with UK distribution through Rough Trade, which releases the deliberately discordant six-track album ***Bad Moon Rising*** the following year. (Meanwhile in the US, the indie label Ecstatic Peace has issued ***Sonic Death : Sonic Youth Live***, a performance set which displays the group's preference for using over a dozen differently-tuned guitars.)

1985

Mar With ***Bad Moon Rising*** catching the attention of the alternative music press, the band plays at the ICA in the Mall on a bill with Frank Tovey, before releasing ***Death Valley 69*** EP later in the year. Recruiting permanent drummer Shelley (b. June 23, 1962, Midland, MI) the following year, the group will spurn major label advances, recording three more independently-released albums, ***Evol*** (1986), ***Sister*** (1987), both for SST Records in the US, and the double-set ***Daydream Nation***, which spends one week at UK #99 on Oct [29], 1988, all issued by Blast First in the UK. (In 1986, the group will also score the soundtrack for the art-film "Made In USA", which will be released by Rhino Records in 1995.)

1990

Sept [1] Having released ***The Whitey Album*** under the Madonna-teasing one-off group name Ciccone Youth the previous year (which made UK #63), Sonic Youth's major label debut, having finally signed to Geffen Records' DGC imprint, ***Goo***, co-produced by Ron Saint Germain, Nick Sansano and the band, makes US #96 (having made UK #32 on July [7]), spurred by a near-decade old reputation as the godfathers of noisy, guitar-heavy, alternative modern rock.

1991

Jan [22] A US tour opening for Neil Young & Crazy Horse, reaches the Target Center, Minneapolis, MN, a $243,848-grossing, 12,505-attended sellout.

Nov During the month, the group plays at the fifth annual Bridge School charity benefit on a bill with Tracy Chapman, Willie Nelson, Don Henley, John Lee Hooker, Nils Lofgren and organizer Young, held at the Shoreline Amphitheatre, Mountain View, CA.

1992

July [18] Previewing its second DGC album, *100%* reaches UK #28.

Aug [8] Co-produced by the band with Nirvana collaborator Butch Vig, ***Dirty*** debuts at its US #83 pinnacle.

Nov [7] The extracted *Youth Against Fascism* bows at its UK #52 peak, with *Sugar Kane* entering at its UK #26 high on Apr [3] the following year.

1993

Feb [28] The group embarks on a seven-date US tour at the Aloha Tower, Honolulu, HI, set to end, with a West Coast swing, at the Paramount Theatre, Seattle, WA on March 8th.

1994

May [7] *Bull In The Heather* bows at its UK #24 peak.

[28] Having entered at its UK #10 high the previous week, ***Experimental Jet Set, Trash And No Star***, once again co-produced with Vig, debuts at its US #34 peak.

Sept [10] *Superstar*, coupled with Redd Kross' *Yesterday Once More* and featured on the Carpenters tribute album ***If I Were A Carpenter***, makes UK #45 in its week of entry.

Oct [1] ***If I Were A Carpenter*** makes US #70 in its week of entry.

1995

May [9] Thurston Moore's first solo album ***Psychic*** is released by DGC.

[19] Sonic Youth opens for R.E.M. at the Memorial Coliseum, Portland, OR.

July [4] The alternative music US caravan tour, "Lollapalooza '95", opens at The Gorge, George, WA, with Sonic Youth, Hole, Cypress Hill, Pavement, Sinead O'Connor, Beck, Jesus Lizard and Mighty Mighty Bosstones, a bill grossing $508,750 from 18,500 fans, with the trek set to end on August 15th with the last of two shows at Irvine Meadows Amphitheatre, Irvine, CA.

Oct [10] Including Renaldo in its lineup, the ad-hoc hybrid band the Minus Five's version of *Power To The People*, is featured on the newly-released John Lennon tribute album, ***Peace***.

[14] Co-produced with John Skilet, ***Washing Machine*** bows at its US #58 and UK #39 peaks.

[15] A headlining US tour gets underway at the Coca-Cola Roxy Theatre, Atlanta, GA before a crowd of 1,500.

1996

June [15-16] The band participates in the Tibetan Freedom Concert in San Francisco, CA, a benefit concert organized by the Beastie Boys for the Milarepa Fund.

SONNY & CHER

1957

May Sonny Bono (b. Salvatore Bono, Feb. 16, 1935, Detroit, MI), having moved to Hollywood, CA, in 1954, initially working at the Douglas Aircraft factory on an assembly line, is currently a record-packer at Specialty Records. He writes *High School Dance*, the B-side of Larry Williams' hit, *Short Fat Fanny*, and *You Bug Me Baby*, the flip-side of Williams' *Bony Maronie*, on Specialty. He also pens Don & Dewey's *Koko Joe*, subsequently recorded by the Righteous Brothers. (Sonny later has his own single released by the label, *Wearing Black*, under the name Don Christy, and will become a writer, producer and A&R executive at Specialty.) When Specialty curtails most of its operations in 1960, he will record for two years as Sonny Christie and Ronny Sommers for an assortment of labels, with little commercial success.

1962

May Sonny has co-written *Needles And Pins* with Jack Nitzsche, which is recorded by Jackie DeShannon, and now makes US #84. (It will be an international hit for the Searchers in 1964, topping the UK chart and reaching US #13.) Nitzsche introduces Bono, now working in promotion for Record Merchandising, which distributes Philles, to producer Phil Spector, and he begins to work for him as a general assistant and West Coast promotion man - gaining much knowledge as a producer by witnessing Spector at work in the studio.

1963

Cher (b. Cherilyn Sarkasian La Piere, May 20, 1946, El Centro, CA), having moved to Los Angeles, CA, primarily to act, meets Sonny at Aldo's Coffee Shop, next to radio station KFWB and, through his introduction, becomes a session vocalist for Spector, singing backup for the Ronettes. She also begins to sing as a duo with Sonny, and as Caesar & Cleo they release *The Letter* on Vault Records, arranged by Harold Battiste (with whom they will later work at Atco). Meanwhile, the Righteous Brothers record Bono's song, *Koko Joe*, written in 1957.

1964

Sonny and Cher marry in Tijuana, Mexico, a year after his divorce from Donna Lynn, whom he married in 1954. After much prompting from Sonny (who has signed Charles Greene and Brian Stone as Cher's managers), Spector agrees to record Cher as a solo artist, but only one single is cut: *Ringo I Love You*, on Spector's Annette label, under the pseudonym Bonnie Jo Mason. With borrowed money, Sonny produces a Cher session himself at RCA Studios in Hollywood, but it emerges as another duet after Cher has an attack of studio nerves and asks him to sing with her. Four tracks are recorded, and after sounding out Spector as to their worth, Sonny sells them to Reprise Records (whose Mo Ostin has been contacted by Stone) which issues them under the Caesar & Cleo name as two (initially non-charting) singles, *Baby Don't Go* and *Love Is Strange*. By year's end, the duo also secures the opening slot for Ike & Tina Turner at Los Angeles' Purple Onion.

1965

Apr Atlantic's Ahmet Ertegun, impressed by *Baby Don't Go* and, learning that they have no contract with Reprise, offers a recording deal. They are signed to Atlantic's Atco subsidiary (which does not affect Cher's solo deal with Imperial). They decide to use their own names and debut as Sonny & Cher with *Just You* - again to no initial chart success.

Aug [14] *I Got You Babe*, written and produced by Sonny (and almost issued as the B-side of *It's Gonna Rain*, until he persuades Ertegun otherwise) shoots to US #1, where it will stay for two weeks. Their eye-catching, hippy dress style and long hair immediately bring them notice on TV appearances. (Bono is refused admission to New York's Americana Hotel, because of his mode of dress.)

[31] They arrive in Britain amid much publicity for a first promotional visit. (They also film segments for a future TV special, "Sonny & Cher In London".)

Aug [5] The duo makes its only public UK appearance at the 100 Club in London's Oxford Street.

[6] They appear on ITV's "Ready Steady, Go!".

[26] *I Got You Babe* tops the UK chart for the first of two weeks.

Sept Sonny's solo single, the partially-autobiographical *Laugh At Me*, inspired by an occasion when he was barred entrance to Martoni's restaurant in Hollywood, because of his attire, hits US #10 and UK #9, while the Spector-produced Bonnie & the Treasures' *Home Of The Brave*, with Sonny & Cher on backup vocals, reaches US #77.

[17] *I Got You Babe* is certified gold by the RIAA.

[30] The still-climbing ***Look At Us*** is also certified gold by the RIAA.

Oct *Baby Don't Go*, reissued by Reprise and now credited to Sonny & Cher, hits US #8 and UK #11. *Just You*, re-promoted by Atco, also charts in the US, reaching #20, while their debut album, ***Look At Us***, hits US #2 and UK #7. (Cher also begins a parallel solo career, releasing ***All I Really Want To Do***, produced by Sonny.)

Nov *But You're Mine*, the follow-up to *I Got You Babe*, makes US #15 and UK #17, while Vault reissues *The Letter*, which reaches US #75.

Dec A second solo single by Sonny, *The Revolution Kind*, peaks at US #70.

1966

Feb The Sonny & Cher clothing line comes on sale at department stores throughout the States, including bell-bottom and blouse outfits, and bobcat vests, ranging from $8 to $18.

Mar The duo begins work on their first film, "Good Times", at Paramount Studios. Their revival of *What Now My Love* reaches US #16 and UK #13.

Apr [2] They top the bill at the Hollywood Bowl, with Jan & Dean, the Mamas & the Papas, the Turtles, Otis Redding, Donovan and Bob Lind, with all proceeds going to the Braille Institute.

June *Have I Stayed Too Long* peaks at US #49 and UK #42, taken from ***The Wondrous World Of Sonny And Cher***, which makes US #34 and UK #15.

Aug [26] They make their UK concert debut at a benefit, at the Astoria Theatre, Finsbury Park, London.

Sept [14] Sonny & Cher have a private audience with Pope Paul VI in Rome, Italy.

Oct *Little Man*, in an arresting gypsy-style arrangement by Sonny, reaches US #21 and UK #9.

Nov *Living For You* makes US #87 and UK #44, taken from ***In Case Your In Love***.

1967

Jan [1] They become the first pop duo to ride on a float at the New Year's Day Rose Bowl Parade in Pasadena, CA.

Feb Uptempo *The Beat Goes On* (later revived by Vanilla Fudge) is the duo's last major Atco success, hitting US #6 and reaching UK #29.

Mar [17] They begin a ten-day East Coast US tour.

Apr [7] "Good Times" opens in Chicago, IL. Their soundtrack album, ***Good Times*** is also released.

May *A Beautiful Story* reaches US #53.

[21] They guest on CBS-TV's "The Smothers Brothers Comedy Hour".

June *Plastic Man* peaks at US #74.

Sept *It's The Little Things* makes US #50.

Oct Compilation, ***The Best Of Sonny And Cher***, reaches US #23, as they make a guest appearance on US TV's "The Man From U.N.C.L.E."

Dec They open in cabaret at the Eden Roc Hotel, Miami Beach, FL. (During the year, Bono's solo album ***Inner Views*** is released by Atco.)

1968

Jan Their final Atco hit is *Good Combination*, which reaches US #56.

June The duo appears at the "Soul Together" concert at New York's Madison Square Garden, with Aretha Franklin, the Rascals, Joe Tex, King Curtis and Sam & Dave.

Aug [4] They play at the "Newport Pop Festival" in Costa Mesa, CA, alongside Canned Heat, Steppenwolf, the Grateful Dead, the Byrds, Jefferson Airplane and others.

1969

Mar [4] A daughter, Chastity, is born in Cedars of Lebanon Hospital, Los Angeles, though a second movie, "Chastity" (titled after their baby) will be less successfully delivered.

May [4] They guest on ITV's "This Is Tom Jones".

1970

With hit singles no longer forthcoming, despite sporadic releases as a duo, they move to the cabaret scene, appearing regularly in Las Vegas, NV, in an act which mixes comedy with music. They sign a new recording deal, covering both the duo's and Cher's solo work, with Kapp Records, a subsidiary of MCA.

1971

Aug [1] They begin a highly successful TV series, "The Sonny And Cher Comedy Hour", on CBS-TV, which mixes songs and comedy with star guests, based on the format of the club/comedy act they have perfected.

Dec Bolstered by the popularity of the TV show, *All I Ever Need Is You* hits US #7, while ***Sonny And Cher Live*** makes US #35.

1972

Feb *All I Ever Need Is You* hits UK #8.

Apr *A Cowboy's Work Is Never Done* hits US #8, taken from ***All I Ever Need Is You***, which reaches US #14.

May [6] ***All I Ever Need Is You*** is certified gold by the RIAA.

July [27] ***Sonny And Cher Live*** is also certified gold by the RIAA.

Aug *When You Say Love*, which makes US #32, is taken from a US TV Budweiser beer commercial.

1973

Apr MCA (having absorbed the Kapp label) releases two Sonny & Cher singles during the year, but only *Mama Was A Rock And Roll Singer, Papa Used To*

Write All Her Songs charts, making US #77. It is the duo's last hit together. During the month, the pair also perform at the Fort Wayne Coliseum, IN, grossing $60,000, while ***Live In Las Vegas Vol. 2*** will be issued by year's end.

1974

Jan The final two singles by Sonny & Cher are released by Warner Bros. (taken from the also non-charting ***Mama Was A Rock And Roll Singer, Papa Used To Write All Her Songs***).
Feb [20] Cher files for divorce from Sonny and continues her solo career, with *Dark Lady* already heading to US #1, her fourth solo million-selling single.
Sept [22] "The Sonny Comedy Revue" premieres on ABC-TV, beginning a three-month run until December 29th.

1975

June [26] Sonny and Cher's divorce is finalized. (She will enter into a short-lived marriage with Gregg Allman the following year.)

1976

Feb Following on from a Cher solo TV series on CBS, the network replaces it with a new version of "The Sonny And Cher Show" (which will run until August 29th, 1977). (Sonny will largely retreat from the recording scene, opening a Los Angeles restaurant in 1983 and re-emerging as an actor on both the big-screen and in TV parts during the '80s.)

1987

Nov [14] Sonny & Cher sing *I Got You Babe*, for the first time in ten years, on NBC-TV's "Late Night With David Letterman".

1988

Apr [12] In the same week that Cher wins an Oscar for her role in "Moonstruck", Sonny, recently seen in the movie, "Hairspray", is elected Mayor of Palm Springs, CA, having registered to vote for the first time in his life. (As Cher's star continues to shine in both the film and music arenas, Sonny will become a controversial Mayor, before opening a Palm Springs eaterie in partnership with his fourth wife.)

1991

Sept [10] Pittsburgh-based Bogus Records issues the 16-track ***Bonograph : Sonny Gets His Share***, a compilation of Bono covers by alternative bands.
[22] Sonny plays a record label boss on Fox-TV's "Parker Lewis Can't Lose".
Oct [1] Currently promoting his autobiography, **And The Beat Goes On**, he announces his intention to run for Alan Cranston's senate seat in California.
Nov [4] Sonny is honored at the National Disaster Conference for helping rescue victims of July's Girl Scout bus crash that killed six people near Palm Springs.

1993

May [22] Already revived as a UK #1 for UB40 and Chrissie Hynde in 1985, Sonny & Cher's original and seminal recording of *I Got You Babe*, re-charts at UK #66, following exposure in the Bill Murray movie, "Groundhog Day". Rhino Records in the US brings the duo's hit career to CD with the release of ***And The Beat Goes On : The Best Of Sonny & Cher*** and ***The Atlantic Singles***.

1994

Nov [8] Sonny defeats Democrat Steve Clute 56% to 38% to win California's 44th district congressional seat in the House Of Representatives. (Cher will be quoted in the Washington Post - "Politicians don't work for the people; the system works for the politicians. It's a huge crime to be so greedy and to let the people down and the country fall apart. Politicians are one step below used-car salesmen".)
see also: **CHER**

SOUL ASYLUM

Dave Pirner (vocals, guitar); **Daniel Murphy** (guitar, vocals); **Karl Mueller** (bass, vocals); **Grant Young** (drums)

1984

Aug Sharing the same apartment, Murphy (b. July 12, 1962, Duluth, MN) and Mueller (b. July 27, 1962, Minneapolis, MN), who have also both attended the same Minneapolis high school, have formed Loud Fast Rules at Murphy's sister's home in 1981, where they played their first song, a cover of the Sex Pistols' *Bodies*. Subsequently recruiting ex-high school band, the Shitz' Pirner (b. Apr. 16, 1964, Green Bay, WI) on drums, the group has performed as a post-punk combo in clubs around Minneapolis, while Pirner switched to lead vocals with short-term member Pat Morley replacing him on drums. With the band changing its name to Soul Asylum, Young (b. Jan. 5, 1964, Iowa City, IA) has become the quartet's permanent skinsman in 1983. Signing with the Minneapolis-based indie label Twin Tone Records (for which the Replacements also record), the group now releases its first self-penned album, ***Say What You Will, Clarence ... Karl Sold The Truck***, produced by yet another local outfit, Hüsker Dü's frontman, Bob Mould. Following up with 1986's ***Made To Be Broken*** and ***While You Were Out*** released in March 1988, the group settles into a more mainstream youth-problem themed, mostly Pirner-penned rock groove, which leads to their signing with A&M Records, which issues the Ed Stasium/Lenny Kaye-produced ***Hang Time*** in June the same year.

1990

Sept After Twin Tone has released the remnant EP ***Clam Dip And Other Delights*** the previous year, A&M issues ***Soul Asylum And The Horse They Rode In On***. With its lack of commercial success on the label, relations between the group and A&M sour, with Soul Asylum having to pay $200,000 to break its contract, a debt it will take four years to meet, and a burden which temporarily dissolves the lineup. Impressed by their work thus far, Sony Music's Columbia Records offers the band a new contract in 1991, though label squabbles will result in a two-year gap between releases.

1993

Feb [6] Having entered the chart the previous November, the band's Columbia label debut ***Grave Dancers Union***, produced by Michael Beinhorn and featuring Booker T. Jones, makes US #59, finally matching in sales, the critical praise the band has steadily earned, not least as the media-appointed "best live band in the country" during the '80s.
[19-20, 22-24] The group performs at New York, NY's Beacon Theatre, during a current round of US dates.
June [2] During the group's "MTV Unplugged" program, they are joined by Lulu to sing her 1967 US chart-topper *To Sir With Love*.
[6] Soul Asylum embarks on a 56-date US tour with Spin Doctors and the Screaming Trees at the Coca-Cola Starlake Amphitheatre, Burgettstown, PA, set to end on August 30th at the Aladdin Hotel & Casino, Las Vegas, NV.
July [17] The extracted mid-tempo, homeless-youth/missing-person themed *Runaway Train* initially reaches UK #37.
Aug [17] The still-climbing *Runaway Train* is certified gold by the RIAA.
[28] A cross-format radio smash, the acoustic guitar-led *Runaway Train* hits US #5, also aided by an eye-catching video clip featuring stills of youngsters who have actually run away from home.
Sept [2] The group performs at the tenth annual MTV Video Music Awards, held at the Universal Amphitheatre, Universal City, CA.
[4] *Somebody To Shove* bows at its UK #34 peak.
Nov [20] The re-charting *Runaway Train* hits UK #7.

1994

Jan [29] *Black Gold* debuts at its UK #26 peak, as ***Grave Dancers Union***, which originally entered the UK chart the previous September, finally reaches UK #27.
Feb [23] Pirner and Murphy perform at the "No Nukes On The River" concert at the University of Minnesota in Minneapolis, sharing the bill with Bonnie Raitt.
Mar [1] As its writer, Pirner wins the Best Rock Song category for *Runaway Train* at the 36th annual Grammy Awards, held at New York, NY's Radio City Music Hall.
[23] A five-date UK visit ends at London's Brixton Academy.
[26] Reissued *Somebody To Shove* enters at its UK #32 peak. (During the month, the Generation X-aimed movie "Reality Bites", with Pirner making his acting debut in a film led by his current belle, Winona Ryder, premieres in the US.)
Apr [6] ***Grave Dancers Union*** is certified double-platinum by the RIAA.
Aug [14] Pirner performs a solo set at the alternative "Woodstock II", staged at the original Bethel, NY site.

1995

Apr [6] Soul Asylum is the music guest on CBS-TV's "Late Show With David Letterman".
June [23] The group plays at the 25th annual "Glastonbury Festival" at Worthy Farm, Pilton, Somerset.
[24] With Young having been fired, replaced by ex-Duran Duran session drummer Sterling Campbell, ***Let Your Dime Light Shine***, co-produced by the band with Butch Vig, debuts at its US #6 peak, and will enter at its UK #22 high the following week.
July [15] *Misery* reaches US #20 and bows at its UK #39 pinnacle.
[31] ***Let Your Dim Light Shine*** is certified platinum by the RIAA.
Aug [16-17] The band's "Dimly Lit" US tour gets underway in their hometown with a pair of shows at Midway Stadium, dates grossing $211,170 from 14,078 fans.
Sept [2] The group performs *Back Door Man* with Iggy Pop and *Sweet Jane* with Lou Reed at the Concert for the Hall of Fame held at Cleveland Stadium, OH.
Dec [2] *Just Like Anyone*, backed by their version of Eddie & the Hot Rods' punk nugget *Do Anything You Wanna Do*, (a UK #9 hit in August 1977), charts for a week at UK #52.

1996

Feb [8] The group makes a return visit to the "Late Show With David Letterman".
[17] *Promises Broken*, co-written by Murphy and Jayhawks' bassist Marc Perlman, makes US #63.

SOUL II SOUL

Jazzie B (rap shepherd); **Nellee Hooper** (arranger); **Philip "Daddae" Harvey** (miscellaneous)

1982

North London friends Jazzie B (b. Beresford Romeo, Jan. 26, 1963, London), British-born of Antiguan immigrants, and educated at Holloway Boys Secondary School, London, and Harvey (b. Feb. 28, 1964, London) begin offering their services to the emerging UK dance club scene, making available PAs, sound systems and DJs, under the name created by Harvey, Soul II Soul. Initially travelling to events on public transport, they evolve to a position where they hold their own warehouse raves, mainly at Paddington Dome, under the King's Cross arches, London. Becoming major dance event organizers and providers, their soul collective grows to marketable status.

1985

Hooper, a member of Bristol, Avon mixing crew Massive Attack, and ex-the Wild Bunch Crew, having already cut *The Look Of Love* as a hip-hop number, rents Soul II Soul equipment for a gig in London. When he meets Jazzie B, a furious row erupts over a misunderstanding concerning who should be DJ. The two subsequently become firm friends, and Hooper joins the swelling Soul II Soul ranks. With a keen commercial eye and ear, Soul II Soul begins a fixed Sunday night residence the following year at the Africa Centre, Covent Garden, London, where all their club, event and sound system efforts will develop.

1987

Following a demo recording, featuring the cut *Fairplay*, helmed by Hooper and Jazzie B, who has rejected piano lessons at an early age and concentrates now on creating musical ideas for those around him to perform, Soul II Soul secures a deal with Virgin subsidiary, 10 Records.

1988

May *Fairplay*, featuring Rose Windross on vocals, peaks at UK #63. (As the Soul II Soul collective relocates to the Fridge club, Brixton, London, many of its members are involved in the current pirate local radio station movement, particularly Jazzie B, who hosts a show on the soon-to-be-legal KISS-FM. Soul II Soul has now sprouted offshoot fashion-wear, notably T-shirts and accessories, whose success leads to the opening of two Soul II Soul shops in London, one in Camden, followed by another in Tottenham Court Road.)

Sept Follow-up, *Feel Free*, featuring Do-reen, makes UK #64.

1989

Apr Breakthrough disc, *Keep On Movin'*, hits UK #5. Featuring Soul II Soul fixture Caron Wheeler (b. Jan. 19, 1963, London) on lead vocals, the single mixes a spacious reggae feel with a unique and hall-marking dance shuffle rhythm, which will spawn dozens of imitations over the next two years, and itself provide the distinctive rhythm drive to their own next two hits.

[22] Their debut album, ***Club Classics Volume One***, combining a myriad of dance/reggae/hip-hop/soul elements, is released. Featuring dozens of permanent and temporary Soul II Soul collective members, it will become regarded as a prototype project, and will launch the group (and Jazzie B's oft quoted ethos: "A smiling face, a thumping bass for a happy face") worldwide.

June [24] The extracted, but remixed, *Back To Life (However Do You Want Me)*, again co-written and sung by Wheeler, hits UK #1, becoming a UK summer dance anthem.

July [15] ***Club Classics Volume One*** finally hits UK #1, on its way to multi-platinum success.

Sept [9] Already a US R&B #1, *Keep On Movin* reaches US #11.

Oct [20] *Keep On Movin'* is certified platinum by the RIAA.

Dec [9] Further honing Jazzie B's trademark rhythm section, *Get A Life* hits UK #3. (Wheeler has already left the line-up, and will go on to a successful solo career with RCA in the UK and EMI in the US, beginning with 1990's UK #14, ***UK Blak***.)

[12] *Back To Life (However Do You Want Me)* hits US #4 the same day it is certified platinum by the RIAA, as the album, released in the States as ***Keep On Movin'*** on Virgin America, rises to US #14.

[23] *Keep On Movin'* is named Top Dance Sales 12" single, and the group hailed as Top Dance Sales Artists in **Billboard**'s Year in Music survey.

1990

Jan Increasingly in-demand as producers and arrangers, Jazzie B and Hooper arrange Sinead O'Connor's international chart-topper, *Nothing Compares 2 U*. (They also make contributions to albums by the Chimes, Fine Young Cannibals, Maxi Priest and Neneh Cherry.)

Feb [21] Having been awarded three American Music Awards and four British DMC Dance Awards, Soul II Soul wins the Best R&B Performance By A Duo Or Group With Vocal (for *Back To Life*) and Best R&B Instrumental Performance (for *African Dance*) categories at the 32nd annual Grammy Awards, at the Shrine Auditorium, Los Angeles, CA.

Mar [8] The group is voted Best New Foreign Band in **Rolling Stone** magazine's 1989 Critics Awards.

[14] Soul II Soul nabs the R&B/Urban Contemporary Album Of The Year, Group, Duo Or Band, for ***Keep On Movin'***, R&B/Urban Contemporary Song Of The Year, and Best R&B/Urban Contemporary Single, Group, Duo Or Band, for *Keep On Movin'*, at the fourth annual Soul Train Awards, also held at the Shrine Auditorium.

May [5] Now overseeing two Soul II Soul shops, the Silent Productions company (recording Victoria Wilson-James, Marcia Lewis, Lamya and Jimmy Polo, all for projected release on a proposed new label), Soul II Soul Visions video and film company, a fan club and a talent agency, with their own record company in the pipeline, Jazzie B, Hooper and Daddae launch the second recording phase of Soul II Soul, with *A Dream's A Dream*, featuring Wilson-James, which hits UK #6.

[12] *Get A Life* makes US #54.

June [2] ***Volume II : 1990 A New Decade*** debuts at UK #1, and will make US #21 on the 30th. It once again aggregates a large number of singers, DJs, arrangers and musicians, including South African unit Shikisha, hip-hopper Fab 5 Freddie, UK sax-master Courtney Pine, and female vocalists Kym Mazelle, Razette and Jazzie B's cousin, Marcie Lewis.

July [14] *A Dream's A Dream* makes US #85.

[23] ***1990 - A New Decade*** is certified gold by the RIAA.

[26] The group's US tour begins in Dallas, TX.

Aug [14] The RIAA confirms two million sales of ***Keep On Movin'***.

[18] Jazzie B suffers back injuries in a seven-car pile-up on Interstate 290, as the group is travelling from Detroit, MI to Chicago, IL, for a Poplar Creek Music Theatre concert, that sends 31 people to hospital, causing the cancellation of their North American tour.

Sept [16-17] "The Further Adventures Of Soul II Soul" UK tour begins at the Wembley Arena, Wembley, Middx., set to end on the 26th at London's Brixton Academy. Jazzie B says that after current gigs, the band will stop playing live.

Dec [1] *Missing You*, with vocals from Kym Mazelle, reaches UK #22.

1991

Mar [9] The Peace Choir's *Give Peace A Chance*, which features Jazzie B, makes US #54, while Massive Attack's *Unfinished Sympathy*, produced by Hooper, reaches UK #13.

Apr [7] Jazzie B and Hooper win the DMC World DJ award for Best UK Producer.

[12] Jazzie B launches his new record label, Funki Dred, at the Café Royal, London. A joint venture with Motown, early signings include Kofi and Lady Levi.

Oct [3] Law and Romeo are honored at ASCAP's 11th annual London Awards, at Claridges, for *Back to Life*.

[19] ***Simply Mad About The Mouse***, a collection of new interpretations of Disney classics to which Soul II Soul has contributed *Kiss The Girl*, debuts at its US #160 peak.

Nov [18] Jazzie B and Wheeler are featured on BBC2-TV's "Open Space : Soul Searching".

Dec [2] *Back To Life* is named one of the Most Performed Pop Songs of 1990 and wins BMI's College Radio Award for 1991, at the BMI Awards, at London's Dorchester Hotel.

1992

Apr [11] With Richie Stephens at the mike, *Joy* hits UK #4.

[25] Once again featuring Wheeler, ***Volume III Just Right***, also featuring vocalist Kofi Kari Kari (b. Sept. 11, 1962, London) among a new ensemble, debuts at its UK #3 peak.

May [23] ***Volume III Just Right*** makes US #88.

June [20] A second extract, *Move Me No Mountain*, makes UK #31.

Sept [26] *Just Right* bows at its UK #38 peak.

Oct [28] The group appears on BBC1-TV's "What's That Noise!"

1993

Mar [9] James Brown's first album of the '90s, ***Universal James***, co-produced by Jazzie B, is released.

Nov [6] *Wish* debuts at its UK #24 peak.

Dec [4] ***Volume IV The Classic Singles 88-93***, a UK-only compilation, hits UK #10.

1994

Jan [15] The group takes part in the International Dance Awards, to benefit the Dance Aid trust and the John Grooms Association for the Disabled, at Hammersmith's Labatt's Apollo.

May [30] They perform live on ITV's "21 Years Of Virgin Records".

1995

Feb [20] Hooper is named Best British Producer, for Madonna's *Bedtime Stories*, at the 14th annual BRIT Awards, held at London's Alexandra Palace.

July [22] *Love Enuff* debuts at is UK #12 peak.

Aug [12] ***Volume V - Believe***, with contributions from Wheeler, Pennye Ford and Melissa Bell (b. Mar. 5, 1964, London) among the updated cast of characters, peaks at UK #13 in its week of entry.

Oct [21] *I Care* debuts at its UK #17 peak.

Dec [17] Soul II Soul takes part in "The Greatest Music Party In The World" at the National Exhibition Centre, Birmingham, West Midlands, with Diana Ross, Des'ree, Echobelly and others (set to air on BBC1-TV on Christmas Day).

SOUNDGARDEN

Chris Cornell (vocals, guitar);
Kim Thayil (guitar); **Ben Shepherd** (bass);
Matt Cameron (drums)

1987

June Friends Thayil (b. Sept. 4, 1960, Seattle, WA) and Hiro Yamamoto (b. Apr. 13, 1961), together with future Sub Pop label founder Bruce Pavitt, have moved from Illinois via Olympia, WA, to Seattle in 1982, where bass player Yamamoto has joined his roommate Cornell's (b. July 20, 1964, Seattle) new band the following year, subsequently recruiting Thayil to form Soundgarden in 1984, named after a sculpture in a local park. Replacing early drummer Scott Sundquist with Cameron (b. Nov. 28, 1962, San Diego, CA) in 1986, the group has earned a solid live reputation in the burgeoning Seattle alternative scene, playing a metal/psychedelia-fused brew, highlighted by Cornell's ranting lead vocal. Signed by Pavitt to Sub Pop, the band's first single, *Hunted Down* is now issued, to be followed by two EPs, *Screaming Life*, released in October, and *FOPP*, issued in August the following year. (These Sub Pop recordings will be cited by Kurt Cobain as the reason Nirvana also signed with the label.) Courted by major labels who smell the teen spirit of Seattle's bursting grunge scene, Soundgarden elects to release its debut album ***Ultramega OK*** in November 1988, on the hardcore indie SST label. Following the SST 12" single *Flower* in March 1989, the group finally signs to A&M Records.

1990

Mar [10] Its label debut, ***Louder Than Love***, released the previous September and co-produced with Terry Date, makes US #108.

Oct Following A&M's *The Loud Love EP* in July,

Sub Pop releases the 7" remnant single *HIV Baby/ Room A Thousand Years Wilde*. During the year, sometime Nirvana bassist Jason Everman replaces Yamamoto (who will re-emerge in 1994 as a member of Truly), though Everman's tenure will be short-lived, subsequently making way for long-term recruit Shepherd (b. Hunter Shepherd, Sept. 20, 1968, Okinawa, Japan).

1991

Oct [12] The group performs at the Oakland-Alameda County Stadium, Oakland, CA to a 50,271 crowd on a bill with Metallica, Queensryche and Faith No More.
Dec [9-10, 13] Invited by Guns N' Roses to open for them on a US and European tour, Soundgarden performs at Madison Square Garden, a $1,339,860-grossing, three-night sellout affair.

1992

Feb [29] Once again co-helmed by the group with Date, the critically-revered ***Badmotorfinger*** reaches US #39.
Apr [11] The extracted *Jesus Christ Pose* debuts at its UK #30 peak.
[25] ***Badmotorfinger*** enters at its UK #39 high, with an early limited edition issue including the EP *Somms*.
May [16] European dates supporting Guns N' Roses begin in Dublin, Eire, set to end on June 20th at the Wurzburg Flugplatz Schenkenturm, Germany.
June [20] *Rusty Cage* charts for a week at UK #41.
[27] Pearl Jam members Stone Gossard, Mike McCready and Eddie Vedder together with Soundgarden's Cameron and Cornell have recorded ***Temple Of The Dog***, a tribute album to Seattle band Mother Love Bone's lead singer Andrew Wood who died from a drug overdose in 1990. Released by A&M and credited to Temple Of The Dog, the album now enters the US chart, set to hit #5 on Sept [5].
July [18] The film soundtrack to "Singles", featuring a solo cut by Cornell, enters the US chart set to hit #6.
Nov [21] Soundgarden's *Outshined* spends a week at UK #50.

1993

Jan [20] ***Badmotorfinger*** is certified platinum by the RIAA.
Aug [12] Soundgarden begins a US tour opening for Neil Young, set to close on the 23rd.
Sept Shepherd and Cameron's ad-hoc side band Hater, assembled with Fire Ant's Brian Wood on vocals and John Waterman on bass, releases ***Hater*** on A&M.

1994

Jan The group headlines the "Big Day Out" festival caravan tour in Australia and New Zealand, also featuring Smashing Pumpkins, the Ramones and Teenage Fan Club.
Feb [26] Soundgarden's *Spoonman* bows at its UK #20 peak.
Mar [26] The more mainstream-aimed, glossier outing, ***Superunknown***, a 71-minute set co-produced with Michael Beinhorn, debuts at US #1 have entered at its UK #4 high the previous week. As Shepherd says of the album's musical change of direction: "I don't see us as having any boundaries at all. If you have boundaries, it's obviously some kind of personal complex, and fuck that."
Apr [30] *The Day I Tried To Live* bows at its UK #42 peak.
June [3] A two-month North American headlining tour opens at the Events Center Arena, San Jose State University, CA, grossing $94,395 from 5,043 fans, a trek set to close on August 6th at Molson Park, Barrie, ON, Canada.
Aug [18] The group is forced to postpone a European tour after doctors order Cornell to stop singing until damaged vocal chords heal.
[27] *Black Hole Sun* reaches UK #12.
Sept [8] Soundgarden wins the Best Metal/Hard Rock Video category for "Black Hole Sun" at the 11th annual MTV Video Music Awards, held at New York's Radio City Music Hall.
Oct [18] The RIAA certifies three million sales of ***Superunknown***.

1995

Jan [26] The group is named Best Metal Band in **Rolling Stone**'s 1995 Music Awards (in both the Readers' and Critics' Picks sections).
[28] *Fell On Black Days* debuts at its UK #24 peak.
Mar [1] *Black Hole Sun* is named Best Hard Rock Performance, while *Spoonman* nabs the Best Metal Performance category, at the 37th annual Grammy Awards, staged at Los Angeles, CA's Shrine Auditorium.
Aug [27] The band plays at "Reading '95", near Reading, Berks, before participating in the "Sunstroke Festival" in Eire the following month.
Nov [21] A&M's first multimedia enhanced-CD Plus release is Soundgarden's ***Alive In The Superunknown***.

1996

Mar [3] Lollapalooza organizers announce that Soundgarden will participate in this summer's US caravan tour.
May [18] *Pretty Noose* bows at UK #14.
[21] The stripped down, self-produced ***Down On The Upside*** is released by A&M.

JOE SOUTH

1958

Aug South (b. Joe Souther, Feb. 28, 1940, Atlanta, GA), an accomplished guitarist since the age of 11 and a regular performer on his local Atlanta station, WGST from 1952, has also worked in a country band with steel guitarist Pete Drake at the age of 15, and now has his first success with the novelty recording *The Purple People Eater Meets The Witch Doctor* - a cash-in on two recent million-selling novelty hits by Sheb Wooley and David Seville written by the Big Bopper. It reaches US #47, but proves difficult to follow up, so he begins honing his skills as a songwriter, initially setting poems written by his mother to music.

1961

Aug He becomes a DJ on a country music radio station in Atlanta, but continues to record sporadically. *You're The Reason*, on the Fairlane label, reaches US #87 (eclipsed by Bobby Edwards' US #11 version on Crest).

1962

Nov As a session guitarist on the Atlanta studio scene, he begins to place his own songs with local acts, writing the Tams' *Untie Me*, which peaks at US #60. He also plays guitar on several sessions by Tommy Roe.

1965

Aug South produces his close friend, Atlanta-based singer Billy Joe Royal, who is signed to CBS/Columbia. Royal's debut, South's composition *Down In The Boondocks*, hits US #9 - his first Top 10 success as a writer.
Oct *I Knew You When*, a second South song by Royal, reaches US #14 (while *Down In The Boondocks* makes UK #38). Royal's album, ***Down In The Boondocks***, makes US #96, produced by South, and featuring six of his compositions, including the two hits and Royal's next (US #38) single, *I've Got To Be Somebody*.

1967

Oct While undertaking session work for CBS as a guitarist (not least on Simon & Garfunkel's *The Sound Of Silence*, to which he helps add a rock backing track to the original acoustic arrangement), South continues to work with Royal, writing and producing *Hush*, which Royal now takes to US #52.

1968

Sept *Hush*, covered in a heavier arrangement, by Deep Purple, now hits US #4, South's first million-selling composition. Meanwhile, he signs to Capitol Records as a vocalist, debuting with his own song *Birds Of A Feather*, which is a regional success but does not make the US Hot 100.

1969

Mar South's first album, ***Introspect***, featuring 11 of his own songs, makes US #117. Taken from it, *Games People Play* becomes a major hit, reaching US #12. At the same time, Johnny Rivers' cover of South's *These Are Not My People* (also from the album), reaches US #55.
Apr *Games People Play* hits UK #6, but will be South's only UK success.
July Reissued *Birds Of A Feather* peaks at US #96.
Oct *Don't It Make You Want To Go Home* reaches US #41. It co-credits South's group the Believers, which comprises Tommy South (drums, back-up vocals), Barbara South (keyboards, back-up vocals), Eddie Farrell (bass, back-up vocals) and Pee Wee Parks (back-up vocals).

1970

Feb *Walk A Mile In My Shoes*, also featuring the Believers, reaches US #12, taken from ***Don't It Make You Want To Go Home***, a collection of 14 more of his own songs (including his own versions of *Hush* and *Untie Me*), which climbs to US #60.
Mar [11] South wins two Grammy Awards as *Games People Play* is named Best Contemporary Song and Song of the Year for 1969 at the 12th annual ceremony.
Apr *Children* peaks at US #51.
Oct Compilation ***Joe South's Greatest Hits***, with the cream of tracks from his previous two albums, makes US #125.

1971

Feb Country singer Lynn Anderson's version of *Rose Garden* (from South's ***Introspect***) becomes a million-seller, hitting both US and UK #3. (This will become one of South's most-covered compositions, with Elvis Presley, among many others, also cutting the song.)
Dec *Fool Me* makes US #78, and will be South's last chart single. Though his songs continue to attract a prolific number of cover versions, he drops out of the busy work schedule which has given him such a high profile for two years, feeling a need for rest from the pressures. He is also affected by the death of his brother Tommy - a member of the Believers. (He will not attempt to maintain further commercial success as an artist, and moves to Maui, Hawaii, for three years. Later albums ***So The Seeds Are Growing***, ***A Look Inside***, ***Midnight Rainbows*** and ***To Have, To Hold And To Let Go*** (the latter two on the Island label, to which he moves on returning to the mainland US in 1975) will fail to chart, and he will slip into obscurity. Rhino Records will release ***The Best Of Joe South*** on CD in 1990, followed by Capitol's 1992 issue ***Best Of Joe South***. Working in music publishing into the '90s, South will participate in the 1994 showcase "The American South" held in London and also featuring other notable southern talents including Guy Clark and Allen Toussaint.

SPANDAU BALLET

Gary Kemp (guitar); **Martin Kemp** (bass); **Tony Hadley** (vocals); **John Keeble** (drums); **Steve Norman** (rhythm guitar, sax, percussion)

1976

Gary Kemp (b. Oct. 16, 1959, Islington, London), who was given his first guitar by his parents on his ninth birthday (later playing two songs at his primary school prize-giving day, impressing the attendant Bishop of Stepney who presented him with a tape recorder, which he has subsequently used in writing songs), having failed his "A-level" examinations, assembles power-pop group, the Makers, with Owens Grammar school-friends, Hadley (b. Anthony Hadley, June 2, 1960, Islington), who, having had vocal lessons for some years, won a 1974 talent contest singing Gary Puckett's *Young Girl*, Keeble (b. July 6, 1959, Islington), Norman (b. Mar. 25, 1960, Islington) and Richard Miller.

1979

July Gary Kemp and ex-school-mate Steve Dagger revive the failed Makers under a new name, which becomes Spandau Ballet. Hadley (who featured in a photo-love story, "Sister Blackmail", in the British **My Guy** girls' magazine the previous April), Keeble, Norman and Martin Kemp (b. Oct. 10, 1961, Islington) (later bassist, but who cannot yet play the instrument, and who has excelled at soccer, training with Arsenal Football Club in 1975) all join, while Dagger becomes their manager. (Brothers Martin and Gary have also taken lessons at Anna Scher's children's theater for acting in 1970.)

Nov [17] Inspired by frequent Soho, London, night-clubbing at Blitz, Billy's Le Kilt and Le Beate Route, Spandau Ballet invites 50 friends to an Islington studio to hear new songs.

Dec At a Steve Strange Blitz club party, Island Records boss Chris Blackwell offers to sign the band. Dagger rejects the overture, and hires a lawyer to organize a label of their own.

1980

Mar [7] Setting their own "New Romantic" style, with an emphasis on extravagant clothing, make-up and night-clubbing, Spandau Ballet, now wearing kilts, selects unusual one-off live dates to intrigue the music media, including tonight's gig at the Scala Cinema, London.

[13] The band is filmed at the Scala Cinema for inclusion on a "Blitz Kids" club-scene documentary, on ITV's "20th Century Box".

Apr Having formed its own Reformation label, the group signs a licensing deal with Chrysalis Records.

July [26] The band plays aboard H.M.S. Belfast, a Second World War cruiser moored on the River Thames in London.

Dec [6] Their debut single, *To Cut A Long Story Short*, well marketed, stylishly packaged (as will be all the early releases) and much anticipated after the "buzz" and music press interest surrounding the band, hits UK #5.

1981

Feb [7] *The Freeze* reaches UK #17.

Mar [21] The Richard James Burgess-produced ***Journey To Glory*** hits UK #5.

Apr The band visits the US to spread the "New Romantic" style - playing at New York's Underground club, with a collection of UK fashion designers.

May [9] *Musclebound* hits UK #10.

Aug [1] Danced-aimed *Chant #1 (I Don't Need This Pressure On)*, featuring UK funk outfit Beggar & Co., hits UK #3.

Nov [28] *Paint Me Down*, its video banned by the BBC because it features the group in loin cloths painting each other, makes UK #30.

1982

Jan Gary Kemp and Burgess work on actress/comedienne Pamela Stephenson's EP, *Unusual Treatment*.

Feb [6] *She Loved Like Diamond* peaks at UK #49.

Mar [27] ***Diamond*** reaches UK #15. (Norman and Hadley make the half-time lottery draw at a Tottenham Hotspur vs. Southampton game at White Hart Lane.)

Apr The group begins a UK tour in Edinburgh, Lothian, Scotland.

May [15] *Instinction*, from ***Diamond***, remixed for single release by Trevor Horn, hits UK #10.

Sept BBC1-TV's "The Late Late Breakfast Show", with its group-penned theme, premieres.

Oct [23] *Lifeline*, produced by Swain and Jolley, hits UK #7.

1983

Mar *Communication* reaches UK #12.

Apr [30] The Gary Kemp-penned ballad and career highlight, *True*, begins a four-week stay atop the UK chart in its second week of release.

May [14] Parent album, ***True***, tops the UK chart for a week.

July Now a major live attraction, Spandau Ballet perform at London's Royal Albert Hall, Sadlers Wells Theatre and Royal Festival Hall.

Aug The Gary Kemp-written (as with all the group's hits) *Gold*, extracted from ***True***, hits UK #2, held off the top by KC's *Give It Up*. (The song will be used by BBC-TV as the theme for its Olympics coverage the following year.)

Oct *True* is their belated US chart debut, hitting #4, while ***True*** reaches US #19.

1984

Jan *Gold* makes US #29.

Feb [21] Spandau Ballet wins the Sony Trophy For Technical Excellence, at the third annual BRIT Awards, at London's Grosvenor House Hotel.

Apr *Communication* peaks at US #59.

June *Only When You Leave*, taken from the band's forthcoming album, hits UK #3.

July ***Parade*** hits UK #2, held from the top by Bob Marley's ***Legend***.

Sept *I'll Fly For You* hits UK #9, while *Only When You Leave* makes US #34.

Oct ***Parade*** climbs to US #50 while the extracted *Highly Strung* reaches UK #15.

Nov [25] The group takes part in the all-star session for Band Aid's *Do They Know It's Christmas?*, which will end the year at UK #1, with Hadley taking one of the lead vocal lines.

Dec *Round And Round* reaches UK #18.

[4] The group plays the first of six nights of major concerts at Wembley Arena, Wembley, Middx.

1985

Feb The band sues Chrysalis for release from its contract, claiming that a lack of consistent US success is due to the label's inefficient promotion. (The dispute will mean that no new material can be released by Spandau Ballet until legal matters are resolved.)

July [13] Spandau Ballet appears on the "Live Aid" benefit bill at Wembley Stadium, Wembley.

Nov Chrysalis-released compilation, ***The Singles Collection***, issued without the band's co-operation, hits UK #3, aided by TV promotion - also much to the group's chagrin.

1986

Jan [25] Gary Kemp appears solo on the Labour Party "Red Wedge" UK tour, which opens in Manchester, Gtr. Manchester.

Apr [26] The Kemp brothers and Norman all escape serious injury when their car (driven by Norman) crashes in West Berlin, West Germany.

May Freed from its Chrysalis deal, the group signs their Reformation label to CBS. (The band makes it a condition of the new contract that its records will not be released in South Africa.)

July *Fight For Ourselves* reaches UK #15.

Nov ***Through The Barricades***, recorded in France, hits UK #7, while the ballad title track *Through The Barricades*, hits UK #6.

1987

Feb *How Many Lies*, also from the album, peaks at UK #34.

June The group participates in the TV special, "Ibiza '92", at the Ku Club, Ibiza

[5-6] Gary Kemp appears at the fifth annual "Prince's Trust Rock Gala" at the Wembley Arena.

1988

May The Kemp brothers attend the "Cannes Film Festival", France, where they officially announce that they are to play the notorious '60s London gangland leaders, Ron and Reggie Kray, in the forthcoming movie, "The Krays".

July *Raw* reaches UK #47, the group's first release since early 1987.

1989

Sept *Be Free With Your Love* makes UK #42.

[30] Its parent album, ***Heart Like A Sky***, co-produced with Gary Langan, debuts at its UK #31 peak. (Much to the displeasure of the band, who undertake a UK tour to promote the release, between December 14th and March 6th, 1990, CBS will not release the album in the US, which will ultimately result in termination of the CBS contract.)

1990

Mar Gary Kemp, with Jimmy Somerville and others, participates in Artists Against The Poll Tax. Spandau Ballet becomes inactive as each member views further group projects with differing levels of enthusiasm.

1991

May Martin Kemp starts filming the six-part TV series, "Growing Rich" (and will feature in the sci-fi pic, "Waxwork II : Lost In Time", the following year).

Sept [28] ***The Best Of Spandau Ballet*** debuts at its UK #44 peak. (P.M. Dawn's current international R&B smash, *Set Adrift On Memory Bliss*, heavily samples Spandau's *True*, with Hadley also making an appearance in its promo video clip. Hadley will shortly sign a solo deal with EMI, notching up three UK chart singles over the next two years: *Lost In Your Love* (Mar [14] 1992 - #42), *For Your Blue Eyes Only* (Aug [29] 1992 - #67) and *The Game Of Love* (Jan [16] 1993 - #72), while Gary Kemp will re-emerge playing Whitney Houston's manager in the 1992 hit movie, "The Bodyguard", before releasing his solo debut, ***Little Bruises***, in October, 1995.)

THE SPECIALS

Jerry Dammers (keyboards); **Terry Hall** (vocals); **Neville Staples** (vocals, percussion); **Lynval Golding** (guitar); **Roddy Radiation** (guitar); **Sir Horace Gentleman** (bass); **John Bradbury** (drums)

1977

July The band is formed in Coventry, W. Midlands, by Dammers (b. Gerald Dankin, b. May 22, 1954, India), Golding (b. July 7, 1952, St. Catherine's, Jamaica) and Gentleman (b. Horace Panter) as the Coventry Automatics, who initially attempt to forge a punk/reggae fusion, with only moderate results. When they start to delve back into the rougher pre-reggae Jamaican ska form, the sound gels. The line-up expands to include Hall (b. Mar. 19, 1959, Coventry) and Staples (b. Apr. 11, 1956, Christiana, Jamaica) (initially a roadie) on vocals, a drummer named Silverton, and guitarist Radiation (b. Rodney Byers). They are briefly known as the Coventry Specials before settling on the Special AKA.

1978

June After attracting the attention of Joe Strummer, the band plays UK dates as support act on the Clash's "On Parole" tour. Clash manager Bernie Rhodes also manages the group, moving it to London for rehearsals in Camden Town, which last for many weeks, but which also leads to Silverton leaving. Convinced that this approach is wrong, Dammers splits from Rhodes and takes the band back to Coventry, where new manager Rick Rogers takes over.

1979

Mar Dammers conceives the idea of the group recording on its own independent label. £700 is borrowed to pay for recording the Dammers-penned *Gangsters*, a tribute to Prince Buster's ska classic, *Al Capone*. Bradbury joins on drums, in time to play on the *Gangsters* session. Because the group cannot afford to record a B-side, Golding suggests to his friend, guitarist Noel Davies, that they use the instrumental track, *The Selecter*, which Davies has cut with Bradbury on drums, and local trombonist Barry Jones. (This is credited to "The Selecter", though Davies will not form the actual group until the single is selling.)

Apr Dammers makes use of his art college background to design a label, with the name 2-Tone coming from his black-and-white creation. A deal is cut with Rough Trade in London, which presses 5,000 copies of the single and arranges distribution.

July With the single attracting interest and sales, overtures are made by major record companies. Chrysalis signs the Special AKA, and agrees to accomodate the autonomous 2-Tone label which is to be given a budget and marketed by Chrysalis, in releasing at least six singles a year. All the Special AKA members, and their managers, become 2-Tone directors.

Sept *Gangsters*, taken over by Chrysalis, hits UK #6. Abridging its name to the Specials, the group tours Britain with the newly-formed Selecter, and 2-Tone's other signing, London group Madness. Veteran trombonist Rico Rodrigues (b. Oct. 17, 1934, Jamaica) joins the Specials, while trumpeter Dick Cuthy is added for tour work.

Oct [19] The Specials, Madness and the Selecter embark on the 2-Tone UK tour, at the Top Rank, Brighton, Sussex, as the ska revival, masterminded by Dammers, gets underway.

Nov Their debut album, ***Specials***, produced by Elvis Costello, hits UK #4, while a revival of *A Message To You, Rudy* hits UK #10.

Dec [28] The group performs alongside the Who and the Pretenders at the third of four concerts in aid of the People of Kampuchea, at London's Hammersmith Odeon.

1980

Jan [25] A six-week US tour by the group opens at New York's Hurrah club, set to end with four soldout dates at the Whisky A-Go-Go in Los Angeles, CA, where many fans pose in "2-Tone" black-and-white clothing.

Feb [2] The performance EP, *The Special AKA Live*, containing four revivals of '60s/early '70s ska and reggae hits, plus the original song, *Too Much Too Young* (which captures the airplay), tops the UK chart for the first of two weeks.

June *Rat Race* hits UK #5.

[4] The group embarks on a 13-date "Seaside Specials" tour at Tiffanys, Great Yarmouth, Norfolk, set to close on the 19th at the Guildhall, Portsmouth, Hants., following which the band will tour Japan and Belgium.

July Golding is beaten up after leaving a Modettes gig at the Moonlight club.

Sept [13] A UK autumn tour opens at the Riviera Lido, St. Austell, Cornwall, with 2-Tone act the Swinging Cats as support group.

Oct *Stereotype* hits UK #6, while the band's second album, ***More Specials***, produced by Dammers and Dave Jordan at Horizon Studios, Coventry, hits UK #5. It moves away from the band's ska roots, into what Dammers describes as "lounge music" - much of it coming from his fascination with film soundtracks.

[16] Their UK tour ends in Birmingham, West Midlands, having played a month of English dates, and two in Scotland at Glasgow, Strathclyde and Edinburgh, Lothian. (At a gig in Cambridge, Cambs., Dammers and Hall have been arrested and charged with incitement to violence, after trouble in the audience causes them to stop the show.)

1981

Jan [9] Dammers and Hall are each fined £400 after being convicted of using threatening words and behavior at the Cambridge gig in October.

[17] *Do Nothing*, backed with *Maggie's Farm*, hits UK #4. A proposed US tour is cancelled by Dammers, who is suffering from exhaustion.

Feb "Dance Craze", a concert movie based around the music of the Specials and the 2-Tone stable, is released. The parallel soundtrack album, ***Dance Craze***, featuring songs by the bands appearing in the film, hits UK #5.

July [11] *Ghost Town*, a haunting narrative of urban decay, tops the UK chart for the first of three weeks, its lyric proving topical as riots flare in several British inner-city areas.

Oct [2] The group fragments with vocalists Staples, Hall and Golding leaving to form the Fun Boy Three (they will release two albums and have five UK hit singles before splitting in 1983, with Hall subsequently forming Colourfield, and then the 1990 trio, Terry, Blair & Anouchka. ***Terry Hall : The Collection***, rounding up the highlights from these ventures will be released in 1993, when he forms an alliance with Dave Stewart in the band Vegas). Byers forms his own rockabilly group, Roddy Radiation & the Tearjerkers, while Gentleman also leaves, initially joining a religious sect, and later re-emerging in General Public. Ranking Roger re-forms as Special Beat with Staples, Gentleman and Bradbury, augmented by Bobby Bird (guitar), Sean Flowerdew (keyboards) and singer, Finny. Dammers re-forms the group and reverts to the earlier name of the Special AKA. He, Gentleman and Bradbury remain from the earlier line-up, while Gary McManus (bass), John Shipley (guitar) and three vocalists - Rhoda Dakar (ex-the Bodysnatchers), Stan Campbell (ex-the Selecter) and Egidio Newton (ex-Animal Nightlife) join.

1982

Feb Fellow 2-Tonée Rhoda, listed with the Special AKA, makes UK #35 with *The Boiler*.

Apr Gentlemen quits, leaving Dammers and Brad as the only original members of the nine-piece band. *Racist Friend*, the second release by the new line-up following January's *War Crimes*, will make UK #60 in September the following year.

1984

Apr *Nelson Mandela*, a politically-themed anthem demanding freedom for the ANC leader imprisoned in South Africa, hits UK #9, but will become a global chant throughout the decade at relevant supportive gatherings.

June ***In The Studio*** reaches UK #34. Long in preparation, it carries a purposely ironic title.

Sept *What I Like Most About You Is Your Girlfriend* peaks at UK #51.

[18] C4-TV's documentary on the band "At Home" is broadcast.

1985

Mar The members of Special AKA take part, along with Madness, UB40, General Public and the Pioneers, in recording *Starvation*, a new version of an old Pioneers song, released to raise funds for Ethiopian famine relief. Released on Madness' Zarjazz label, it reaches UK #33.

1986

Apr [23] Dammers forms Artists Against Apartheid in a meeting at Donmar Warehouse, London.

June [28] Dammers and Artists Against Apartheid organize an anti-apartheid concert on Clapham Common in London, featuring Elvis Costello, Peter Gabriel, Boy George, Sade, Sting, Billy Bragg, Hugh Masekela, and others.

1988

June [11] Dammers is the prime mover behind "Nelson Mandela's 70th Birthday Tribute" concert, held at Wembley Stadium, Wembley, Middx., and seen all over the world via TV. Artists performing include Dire Straits, Whitney Houston, Stevie Wonder, Simple Minds, Tracy Chapman, and many others. The Special AKA's *Nelson Mandela* is the show's anthem, and, re-titled *Nelson Mandela (70th Birthday Remake)*, the song is reissued in the UK.

1990

Apr [16] Dammers appears at "Nelson Mandela - An International Tribute For A Free South Africa", a second concert also held at Wembley Stadium.

Oct [24] Hybrid group, Special Beat, comprising Ranking Roger, Staples, Panter, Bobby Bird, Shawn Flowerdew and Finn, embarks on a US tour at the Ritz, New York.

1991

Sept [21] Retrospective collection, ***The Specials Singles***, debuts at its UK #10 peak. The following year, Receiver Records will release ***Live - Too Much Young***, while ***Live At The Moonlight Club*** emerges on the Dover label.

1993

July Dammers, currently running a club at London's Rock Garden, says in **Details** magazine: "I'm going to build a little home studio and stay independent of record companies. The music I'd like to do might sell just a few thousand, but I'll be happy".

Oct [9] *The 2-Tone (EP)*, on which the Specials are one of the featured acts, debuts at its UK #30 peak.

1996

Feb [10] While Hall's solo career has seen *Forever J* chart for a week at UK #67 on Aug [27], 1994, followed by *Sense* at UK #54 peak on Nov [12] (both featured on his debut solo album ***Home***, co-produced by Ian Broudie and featuring guests Nick Heyward and Andy Partridge), and his *Rainbows EP* reach UK #62 on Oct [28], 1995, a re-formed Specials, led by original members Golding, Staples, Panter and Radiation, now bows at its UK #66 peak with its cover of the Wailers' *Hypocrite*. Signed to UB40 lead singer Ali Campbell's Virgin imprint label Kuff Records, their album ***Today's Specials*** will be released in the UK on April 15th as the group undertakes a UK tour, followed June and July dates in the US.

THE SPIN DOCTORS

Chris Barron (vocals); **Eric Schenkman** (guitar); **Mark White** (bass); **Aaron Comess** (drums)

1987

Chris Barron (b. Christopher Barron Gross, Feb. 5, 1968, HI), conceived in 1967 on a boat going to Pearl Harbor, HI, where his father is stationed before going to Vietnam, has spent his childhood in Australia, moving to Princeton, NJ in his teens. Having played in the Dead Alcoholics With Boners while at Bennington College, VT, Barron is now studying music theory at New York, NY's New School College, where he links with fellow course members Schenkman (b. Dec. 12, 1963, MA), son of a cellist father and flautist mother, from Toronto, ON, Canada, where he played with country-punk combo Dead Heroes, and Dallas, TX raised drummer Comess (b. Apr. 24, 1968, AZ), who has studied at the Berklee College of Music in Boston for a year. The trio begins rehearsing together for a gig at Columbia University's frat house with White (b. Mark Burton White, July 7, 1962, New York), bassist for punk/funk band Spade (which also briefly included Comess), the last to join. Coming together during the 1988 Presidential Election, they adopt the moniker Spin Doctors at the suggestion of one of Schenkman's tutors. (Baron and Schenkman will also form the parallel ad-hoc outfit Trucking Company in 1989 with fellow student John Popper (who moonlights from his longterm outfit Blues Traveler).)

1990

Dec After a year of solid gigging and recording early tracks to sell at live shows, the Spin Doctors are signed to Epic Records by Franky LaRocka, which now issues the EP *Up For Grabs*, not least as a marketing ploy to help secure more live work. (It eventually sells in excess of 50,000 copies, its songs appearing on the 1992 released live album ***Homebelly Groove***.)

1991

Manchester, VT radio station WEQX receives immediate listener phone response having played a segment of *Up For Grabs* to promote a local concert featuring the Spin Doctors and other fledgling local acts.

1992

June The band embarks on a US "Horizon Of Rock Developing Everywhere" package tour with Blues Traveler, Phish and Widespread Panic.

Oct [10] The group is the musical guest on NBC-TV's "Saturday Night Live", a breakthrough performance which spurs sales of its debut studio album.

Dec [12] The acerbic, funk-tinged rock outing ***Pocket Full Of Kryptonite*** reaches its 1992 peak at US #26. Once again championed early on by WEQX, album cuts begin filling American album rock playlists.

[26] The extracted *Little Miss Can't Be Wrong*, despite criticisms that the song sounds similiar to mid-'70s Steve Miller and has sexist lyrics, reaches US #17.

[31] The group performs on a bill at New York's Beacon Theatre before appearing later in the night on "MTV Drops The Ball '93" from New York's Roseland Ballroom.

1993

Jan [7] The band is featured on the front cover of **Rolling Stone**.

[19] Spin Doctors gross $32,250 at a US tour gig at the Orpheum Theatre, Minneapolis, MN.

Mar [6] Collecting early live recordings, ***Homebelly Groove*** peaks at US #145.

[16] The band plays at the Boardwalk, Manchester, Gtr. Manchester, during a handful of UK dates.

Apr [10] *Two Princes* hits US #7.

[24] With ***Pocket Full Of Kryptonite*** now hitting its US #3 peak (and already past the two million sales mark) and following non-stop roadwork, the group begins sessions for a album with producer Jim Dickinson at Ardent Studios, Memphis, TN.

June [9] The band embarks on the 50-date "Alternative Nation Tour", sponsored by Apple Computers, opening at Mud Island Amphitheatre, Memphis, TN.

[12] *Two Princes* hits UK #3.

Aug [21] *Little Miss Can't Be Wrong* debuts at its UK #23 peak.

[28] ***Pocket Full Of Kryptonite*** hits UK #2.

Sept [1] The group guests on CBS-TV's "Late Show With David Letterman".

[2] They perform live at the tenth MTV Awards, from the Universal Amphitheatre, Universal City, CA.

Oct [9] *Jimmy Olsen's Blues* debuts at its UK #40 peak.

[23] *Jimmy Olsen's Blues* peaks at US #78.

Nov [27] ***Stone Free : A Tribute To Jimi Hendrix***, featuring the group's *Spanish Castle Magic*, debuts at its US #28 peak.

Dec [4] *What Time Is It?* charts for a week at UK #56.

1994

Feb [25] Following appearances on the 23rd and 24th at the Roger Daltrey 50th birthday concert at New York's Carnegie Hall, singing *I Can't Explain*, the band now backs him on *Substitute* on CBS-TV's "Late Show With David Letterman".

May [4] The group is named the World's Best-selling Rock Newcomers Of The Year at the annual World Music Awards held at the Sporting Club, Monte Carlo, Monaco, set to air on ABC-TV on the 31st.

June [24] The group takes part in the annual "Glastonbury Festival" at Worthy Farm, Glastonbury, Somerset.

[25] *Cleopatra's Cat* peaks at US #84 and debuts at its UK #29 peak.

July [2] ***Turn It Upside Down*** debuts at its US #28 peak.

[9] ***Turn It Upside Down*** hits UK #3 in its week of entry.

[30] *You Let Your Heart Go Too Fast* charts for a week at UK #66, as the group plays the second of two dates at the Jones Beach Theatre, Wantagh, NY.

Aug [6] *You Let Your Heart Go Too Fast* makes US #42.

[14] The group performs at "Woodstock '94" at Winston Farm, Saugerties, NY.

Sept [19] They participate in "Farm Aid VII", at the Louisiana Superdome in New Orleans, LA.

[25] The group ends a short tour with Gin Blossoms at the Blockbuster Pavilion, Charlotte, NC.

Oct [10] Spin Doctors, with Anthony Krizan (b. Aug. 25, 1965, Plainfield, NJ) having replaced Schenkman, open a nine-date UK tour at the City Hall, Newcastle, Tyne & Wear, set to end on the 20th at Leas Cliff Hall, Folkestone, Kent.

[20] The group opens the new HMV superstore in Leeds, S. Yorks.

[29] *Mary Jane* charts for a week at UK #55.

Nov [22] The band embarks on a North American tour with the Rolling Stones before a sellout crowd at Tampa Stadium, Tampa, FL.

Dec [5-6] The group plays two sellout dates on the Canadian swing of its tour, opening for the Stones, at the Olympic Stadium, Montreal, PQ.

1995

Jan [16] They return to the "Late Show With David Letterman".

Feb [2, 4] The group plays before two combined crowds of 141,053, again in support of the Rolling Stones, at the Maracana Stadium, Rio de Janeiro, Brazil.

Mar [12] Barron returns to Princeton High School for a benefit concert to help the school choir raise money for a trip to England and France. The group performs tracks from ***Pocket Full Of Kryptonite***, raising $10,000.

[16] ***Turn It Upside Down*** is certified platinum by the RIAA.

June [3] The group takes part in the 16th annual KISS concert to benefit the Genesis Fund at the Great Woods Center for the Performing Arts in Mansfield, MA.

Aug [22] The RIAA certifies five million sales of ***Pocket Full Of Kryptonite***.

Sept [21] The band and its publishing company Mow B'Jow, files suit seeking $5 million against the Miller Brewing Co., advertising agency Leap Partnership and Trivers/Myers Music in Los Angeles District Court, claiming, among other things, copyright infringement, after a Miller Lite Ice beer commercial has been staged in a bar setting not dissimilar to New York's Nightingales club, a venue closely associated with the band's roots, using a song similar to *Two Princes*.

1996

Widening the group's musical landscape, ***You've Got To Believe In Something***, produced by Danny Kortchmar and Peter Denenberg, is set for summer release.

SPINAL TAP

David St. Hubbins (lead vocal); **Nigel Tufnell** (lead guitar); **Derek Smalls** (bass)

1961

Dec [14] Initially coming together as an early '60s beat group, Smalls (b. Harry Shearer, Dec. 23, 1943, Los Angeles, CA), St. Hubbins (b. Michael McKean, Oct. 17, 1947, New York City, NY) and Tufnell (b. Christopher Guest, Feb. 5, 1948, New York City) make their debut recording *All The Way Home*, at a studio located at the bottom of Squatney Road, London, E18. (St. Hubbins and Tufnell grew up in London's East End, where they were next-door neighbors in Squatney Road at numbers 47 and 48.)

1967

Having formed the psychedelic rock group Spinal Tap, the trio, who will never retain a full-time drummer, perform their first electric set at the "Newport Folk Festival", cranking their amps up to 110 watts. (Their first drummer John "Stumpy" Pepys died in a bizarre gardening accident, while his replacement, Eric "Stumpy Joe" Childs, dies of a melanin overdose just before completion of ***The Sun Never Sweats*** project. Peter "James" Bond takes over, but dies in mysterious circumstances. Mick Shrimpton replaces him, but dies at the end of a Japanese tour, when he spontaneously combusts at the final concert. While attending his funeral, former organist Viv Savage is blown up in a freak natural gas accident. Rick's twin Mick joins, but has trouble getting insurance. During their hard-working career, the group will go through 22 different names - including Intravenus De Milo, Silent But Deadly and Smell The Glove, though the Spinal Tap moniker will prove to be the most enduring.)

1976

In a lean decade during which they become a full-fledged heavy-metal act, but dogged by internal friction and management hassles, the trio's foray into glam/dance, *Tap Dancing*, fails to reverse their commercial misfortunes.

1982

Disheartened and on the verge of a permanent split following a Japanese tour, Tufnell returns to Ealing, Middx., where he becomes an inventor, his creation including the folding wine glass. Smalls returns home to Nilford to look after his father, Donald "Duff" Smalls, while he recuperates from a hernia operation, and to help him with Sani-Fhone, his telephone sanitizing business.

1984

Apr [11] Reunited and signed to Polydor Records, Spinal Tap plays at the Music Machine, Los Angeles

[28] ***This Is Spinal Tap***, released on Polydor, enters the US chart, set to reach #121 during a ten-week run. It is released to tie in with the full-length warts'n'all rockumentary feature film, "This Is Spinal Tap", directed by Marty DiBergi (who will go on to lens "Kramer Vs. Kramer Vs. Godzilla"), distributed by Embassy Pictures, which follows the denim-clad, unwashed group through a disastrous US tour, and features cameo appearances by Rob Reiner and Bruno Kirby. (The movie, though not a box-office smash, will become a seminal video item for the band's burgeoning cult following.) Shortly after the album's release, the group splits however, torn apart by personality conflicts, clashes over musical direction, and lack of commercial reward.

1988

During the band's split, St. Hubbins and his wife Jeanie settle in Pamona, CA, where he receives a stipend from the Parks Department to undertake soccer training with four and five-year-old girls. He also manages the trio Meconium, before touring with Christian rock band, Lambs Blood, between 1988 and 1989, and playing at the "Monsters Of Jesus" festival, while Jeanie runs her two stores, Potato Republic and The Drippery. Meanwhile, Tufnell heads up the TFA (Travel For Animals) company.

1991

Oct [31] With the three members having decided to re-form when meeting up at ex-manager Ian Faith's funeral, Spinal Tap announces a formal re-union. Smalls states: "It was destiny and also because none of us were really making a great amount of money". They sign a management deal with Wendy Goldfinkel (formerly the group's fan club president) of Go Figure Management, and secure a recording deal with MCA Records (who have tendered the lowest bid) following an intense label-bidding war.

1992

Mar [28] *Bitch School* debuts at its UK #35 peak.
Apr [4] After 18 career albums, only one of which has charted (in 1984), ***Break Like The Wind***, variously produced by Danny Kortchmar, Steve Lukather, Dave Jerden and T-Bone Burnett, featuring music guests including Joe Satriani, Jeff Beck and Slash, and using a drum machine which exploded during the sessions, bows at its US #61 pinnacle. (In a **Billboard** special celebrating Spinal Tap's 25th anniversary, tributes from many include one from Ozzy Osbourne: "They've been in the business for 25 years? It's a little too long if you ask me.")
[8] The group is interviewed on TV-AM's "Good Morning Britain" couch.
[10] Following a much-publicized audition for a drummer (a slot reportedly sought by the Monkees' Micky Dolenz and Mick Fleetwood among others), they finally settle on Rick Shrimpton, former house drummer for the "Eurovision Song Contest", and younger twin of Mick Shrimpton, who appeared in "This Is Spinal Tap", to tub-thump on their forthcoming tour.
[11] ***Break Like The Wind*** debuts at its UK #51 peak.
[20] They play *The Majesty Of Rock* at the "A Concert for Life" tribute for Freddie Mercury at Wembley Stadium, Wembley, Middx. They introduce their performance, resplendent in regal outfits, declaring that they will cut short their set by 35 songs "because we know Freddie would have wanted it this way".
[23] The band is featured on Fox-TV's "The Simpsons".
May [1] The group is interviewed on syndicated TV's "The Arsenio Hall Show".
[2] *The Majesty Of Rock* charts for a week at UK #61.
[22] During its most successful US tour to date, Spinal Tap plays at the Riviera Theatre, Chicago, IL, grossing $51,750, before an audience of 2,300.
[29] Curtis Stigers and Nancy Wilson join the band onstage for *Break Like The Wind*, at the group's gig at the Seattle Paramount Theatre, WA.
July [1] Spinal Tap performs two "Canada Day" concerts in one day, the first at the Thunderbird Stadium, University of British Columbia, Vancouver, followed by another at Molson Park, Barrie.
[7-8] The group plays at London's Royal Albert Hall with VJ Martha Quinn presenting the show for an NBC-TV special. (The support act is the veteran folk act, the Folksmen, who made the US Top 70 with *Old Joe's Place* in 1962.)
Oct [31] ABC-TV's In Concert "Halloween Jam At Universal Studios" special, in which the group guests with the Black Crowes, En Vogue, Ozzy Osbourne, Slaughter, AC/DC, Jodeci, Sir Mix-A-Lot and Cracker, airs.
Dec [31] NBC-TV broadcasts the "Spinal Tap Reunion" film, directed by Marty DiBergi's son, Jim, featuring tributes from the likes of Kenny Rogers, Martin Short and Mel Torme.

1993

June Spinal Tap's support act at last year's Royal Albert Hall gig, the Folksmen, perform at the "Troubadours of Folk" festival in Los Angeles, on a bill with Joni Mitchell, Roger McGuinn, Mary-Chapin Carpenter and the Kingston Trio (the latter similarly attired to the Folksmen). (The group's live appearances will be rare in 1993, although later in the year, they will take part in a "Voters For Choice" benefit, at the Civic Center, Santa Monica, CA, because "we heard women would be there".)

THE SPINNERS

Bobbie Smith (vocals); **Phillipé Wynne** (vocals); **Billy Henderson** (vocals); **Henry Fambrough** (vocals); **Pervis Jackson** (vocals)

1961

Aug Raised in the tough Detroit, MI-ghetto of Royal Oak Township, the R&B vocal group, began as the Domingos, which initially comprised tenors Smith (b. Apr. 10, 1936, Detroit), Henderson (b. Aug. 9, 1939, Detroit), C.P. Spencer, baritone Fambrough (b. May 10, 1938, Detroit) and bass singer Jackson (b. May 16), formed at the city's Ferndale High School in 1955, going on to win a local amateur contest at the Gold Coast Theatre. With George Dixon having replaced Spencer and renaming themselves the Spinners after the large chrome hubcap on Smith's 1951 Ford Crown Victoria, the group has served its apprenticeship performing hundreds of gigs at various USO Army bases. An appearance on WJR Detroit's "Make Way For Youth" show has caught the attention of Moonglows' singer/producer Harvey Fuqua's, who has signed them to his Tri-Phi label, an associate of Motown Records, and which now releases *That's What Girls Are Made For*, which hits US R&B #5. It is also the label's first release, and features Fuqua on lead vocals, a role he repeats on the follow-up, *Love (I'm So Glad) I Found You*, which will peak at US #91 in November.

1965

Aug With Edgar 'Chico' Edwards having replaced Dixon and, signed, at Fuqua's instigation, to Motown Records in 1963, they have struggled for commercial acceptance until *I'll Always Love You* now reaches US #35, taken from ***My Pad***, recorded under the guidance of the label's musical director Cholly Atkins. (During their largely hitless decade at Motown, members of the Spinners have been used by the label as road managers, chaperones for the roster's female groups, chauffeurs for the Temptations and the Jackson 5, and even as clerks in the Motown shipping department.)

1967

Apr During another lengthy dearth of chart action (which has only yielded the 1966 US R&B #16 hit, *Truly Yours*), G.C. (George) Cameron, having just left the U.S. Marines, joins the group as lead singer, and ***The Original Spinners*** is released, still on Motown.

1970

Oct After a further period without commercial success, the group has been moved by Motown to its V.I.P. subsidiary, in search of new impetus. The Stevie Wonder-written and produced *It's A Shame* finally makes a breakthrough, reaching US #14.
Nov ***2nd Time Around*** makes US #199.
Dec The group, dubbed the Motown Spinners in Britain to avoid confusion with the well-known Liverpool, Lancs. folk group, the Spinners, makes its UK chart debut, as *It's A Shame* climbs to #20.

1971

Jan Follow-up on V.I.P., again produced by Wonder, *We'll Have It Made*, peaks at US #89. Subsequently, the group leaves Motown in search of a new deal. Both Stax and Avco Embassy are interested, but Aretha Franklin, a long-time friend of the group in Detroit, puts them in touch with Atlantic Records, to which they will sign before the year's end. Prior to this, Cameron has left to pursue a solo career at Motown, replaced by ex-Pacesetters, ex-Afro Kings, Wynne (b. Philip Walker, Apr. 3, 1938, Cincinnati, OH) as lead vocalist.

1972

Nov [18] Songwriter/producer Thom Bell, a classically trained pianist and long-time admirer of the Spinners, has produced sessions with the group, while contracting productions in Philadelphia, PA, for Atlantic. (As the house pianist at the Uptown Theatre in Philadelphia in 1960, Bell first heard them singing *That's What Girls Are Made For*, later recalling: "It was a piece of harmony that was extremely hard to sing. That's what made the sound of the Spinners and made me want to produce them.") Their collaborative debut, the soul ballad, *How Could I Let You Get Away*, has been released, but its B-side, *I'll Be Around*, co-penned by Bell with Phil Hurtt, steals airplay until it is made A-side by default. It now hits US #3 having already become the group's first million-seller, certified gold by the RIAA on October 30th.

1973

Feb [13] Its still-rising follow-up, *Could It Be I'm Falling In Love* is also certified gold by the RIAA.
Mar [3] Co-written by brothers Melvin and Mervin Steals, *Could It Be I'm Falling In Love*, produced again by Bell (as will be all the Spinners' Atlantic output until 1979) and pairing the twin lead vocals of Wynne and Smith, hits US #4.
June [6] Cashing in on their current success, Motown has reissued a 1968 track, *Together We Can Make Such Sweet Music*, which makes US #91. A Motown compilation, ***The Best Of The Spinners***, also peaks at US #124.
July Their debut Atlantic album, ***Spinners***, reaches US #14 while *One Of A Kind (Love Affair)* peaks at US #11. The Spinners also finally re-chart in Britain, as *Could It Be I'm Falling In Love* reaches #11. The change of label has also meant a change of name for the group in the UK, where they are now known as the Detroit Spinners.
July [13] The RIAA confirms gold sales of both *One Of A Kind (Love Affair)* and ***Spinners***.
Sept [15] The Linda Creed-penned, socially-conscienced *Ghetto Child* reaches US #29.
Nov *Ghetto Child* hits UK #7.

1974

Mar [23] *Mighty Love Part 1* makes US #20.
May Its lushly-orchestrated parent set ***Mighty Love*** reaches US #16.
[21] ***Mighty Love*** is certified gold by the RIAA.
June [29] *I'm Coming Home*, taken from the album, reaches US #18.
Oct [26] After the group has been the opening act for Dionne Warwick on a five-week summer theater tour taking in Las Vegas, NV, Bell has suggested a duet between her and the group - not a contractual problem, since Warwick is signed to Atlantic's associate label, Warner Bros. The resulting *Then Came You*, written by Sherman Marshall and Phil Pugh, now tops the US chart for a week - the first #1 hit for either side of the partnership. (After recording the cut, Bell recalls: "Dionne made a face when we finished it. She didn't like it much, but I knew we had something. So we ripped a dollar in two, signed each half and exchanged them. I told her, 'If it doesn't go number one, I'll send you my half'. When it took off, Dionne sent hers back. There was an apology on it.")
Nov [16] *Love Don't Love Nobody* reaches US #15, while *Then Came You* peaks at UK #29.
Dec [18] The still-climbing ***New And Improved*** is certified gold by the RIAA.

1975

Feb ***New And Improved***, which includes the duet with Warwick, hits US #9.
Apr [5] *Living A Little, Laughing A Little*, reaches US #37.
May [24] Ballad *Sadie* makes US #54.
Sept [18] Yet-to-peak ***Pick Of The Litter*** is certified gold by the RIAA.
Oct [4] ***Pick Of The Litter*** hits US #8. It features studio musicians Thom Bell (keyboards), Tony Bell (guitar), Bobby Eli (guitar), Don Murray (guitar), Andrew Smith (drums), Larry Washington (congas) and the MFSB Orchestra, conducted by producer Bell.
[25] Extracted *They Just Can't Stop It (Games People Play)* hits US #5
Nov [14] *They Just Can't Stop It (Games People*

Play) is certified gold by the RIAA.

1976

Feb [7] *Love Or Leave* reaches US #36.
Mar [6] The double album, ***Spinners Live!***, climbs to US #20.
Aug [7] *Wake Up Susan* makes US #56.
Sept [4] ***Happiness Is Being With The Detroit Spinners***, recorded at Sigma Sound Studios, Philadelphia, with the familiar session crew, reaches US #25.
Oct [12] ***Happiness Is Being With The Detroit Spinners*** is certified gold by the RIAA.
Dec [4] R&B swinger *The Rubberband Man*, co-written by Bell and Creed hits US #2 for the first of three weeks (behind Rod Stewart's *Tonight's The Night*). It also reaches UK #16 - the group's first UK hit in two years.
[8] *The Rubberband Man* is certified gold by the RIAA.

1977

Jan [3] A gifted, but always troubled, lead vocalist, Wynne splits from the group immediately following a show at the Circle Star Theatre in California, set on a solo career which will initially yield the Cotillion label-released ***Starting All Over Again***. (Also becoming a Minister of his own church which he calls the Lost Black Sheep, he will go on tour as part of George Clinton's Parliament/Funkadelic troupe.) He is replaced in the Spinners by John Edwards (b. St. Louis, MO), who has often filled in for him for live shows since 1973.
Feb *Wake Up Susan* reaches UK #29.
Apr [16] *You're Throwing A Good Love Away* makes US #43.
May A four-track UK EP, tied in to a UK tour, coupling the earlier hit, *Could It Be I'm Falling In Love*, with three album tracks, makes UK #32.
[21] UK compilation, ***Detroit Spinners' Smash Hits*** (with sleeve notes by Paul Gambaccini), peaks at UK #37, and ***Yesterday, Today And Tomorrow***, the last album to feature Wynne, reaches US #26.
June [10-11] The Spinners take part in the third "Kool Jazz Festival" in San Diego, CA.
Oct [22] *Heaven And Earth (So Fine)* peaks at US #89.

1978

Jan ***Spinners 8***, recorded with Bell in Seattle, WA, and Philadelphia, climbs to US #57.
June A compilation album, ***The Best Of The Spinners***, makes US #115.
Aug [26] *If You Wanna Do A Dance* reaches US #49, the group's last Bell-produced hit single.
The disco-based ***From Here To Eternally***, their final album collaboration with Bell, will peak at US #165 the following June.

1980

Mar [29] Now teamed with producer Michael Zager, their version of the Four Seasons' *Working My Way Back To You*, blended in a medley with *Forgive Me Girl*, a new song of Zager's, hits US #2, while its parent album, ***Dancin' And Lovin'***, climbs to US #32.
Apr [10] *Workin' My Way Back To You/Forgive Me Girl* is certified gold, the group's last, by the RIAA.
[12] *Working My Way Back To You/Forgive Me Girl* becomes their all-time biggest seller in the UK, topping the chart for the first of two weeks.
June *Body Language* reaches UK #40.
July A second medley in similar new-plus-old style, blending a revival of Sam Cooke's *Cupid* with *I've Loved You For A Long Time*, hits both US and UK #4.
Aug ***Love Trippin'***, which includes the *Cupid* medley, makes US #53.

1981

Mar Another medley, *Yesterday Once More/Nothing Remains The Same*, reaches US #52.
Apr ***Labor Of Love*** peaks at US #128. ***Can't Shake This Feelin'*** will peak at US #196 on January 16th the following year with the excerpted *Never Thought I'd Fall In Love* making US #95 on March 6th.

1983

Jan [22] Their revival of the Willie Nelson standard, *Funny How Time Slips Away*, is the group's final US chart single, making #67, while ***Grand Slam*** is their album survey swan song, peaking at US #167.

1984

July [14] Having released two further solo albums, ***Wynne Jammin'*** and ***Phillipé Wynne***, former lead vocalist Wynne dies from a heart attack, while performing his third encore of the night, *Love Don't Love Nobody*, to an audience of 200 at San Franciscos Ivey club. (During the year, the group, still signed to Atlantic, will release the Leon Sylvers III-produced ***Crossfire***, followed by ***Lovin' Feelings*** the following year, after which they will be dropped from the label.)

1988

May [14] Still touring in both the UK and US and appearing regularly at nostalgia events (like the "Rock'n'Roll Special" at Meadowlands, East Rutherford, NJ, with the Righteous Brothers, Frankie Valli & the Four Seasons and Tommy James & the Shondells on August 5th 1986), they now participate in Atlantic Records' 40th anniversary show, at New York's Madison Square Garden, as they continue to tour regularly.

1995

June [24] Having only released ***Down To Business*** on Volt Records in 1989, the group continues to perform on the R&B oldies circuit, with its lineup intact and Fambrough and Edwards sharing lead vocals. Rappin' 4-Tay's *I'll Be Around*, featuring the Spinners, briefly returns them to the UK survey, now debuting at its UK #30 peak, while its original can be found on the comprehensive Harry Weinger-compiled, 30-track, double-CD retrospective, ***A One Of A Kind Love Affair***, released by Rhino Records (US) in 1991 and which includes the previously unreleased *(Oh Lord) I Wish I Could Sleep.*

SPIRIT

Randy California (guitar, vocals);
Jay Ferguson (vocals); **John Locke** (keyboards);
Mark Andes (bass); **Ed Cassidy** (drums)

1966

Dec California (b. Randy Craig Wolfe, Feb. 20, 1951, Los Angeles, CA), his veteran jazz-drumming step-father, the shaven-headed Cassidy (b. May 4, 1923, Chicago, IL), and Locke (b. Sept. 25, 1943, Los Angeles) form Spirits Rebellious in Los Angeles. Locke has played for four years with Cassidy in the New Jazz Trio, while Cassidy and California have been in the Red Roosters in 1965, prior to finding session work in New York, NY. The trio recruits two other ex-Red Roosters and Locke's fellow UCLA students Ferguson (b. John Arden Ferguson, May 10, 1947, Burbank, CA) who has also played in the Oat Hill Stump Straddlers, and Andes (b. Feb. 19, 1948, Philadelphia, PA), also an alumnus of the Marksmen and Western Union (with Ferguson), the following year, when the group shortens its name to Spirit.

1968

Apr Signed to Lou Adler's new Ode label, the group releases ***Spirit***, critically rated as a progressive rock masterpiece, which climbs to US #31 during an eight-month chart stay.
Dec [5-8] Spirit plays at the Fillmore West in San Francisco, CA, on a bill with Jeff Beck.

1969

Mar ***The Family That Plays Together***, produced by Lou Adler with lyrics largely penned by Ferguson, reaches US #22, their highest album chart placing.
[6-9] The group performs again at the Fillmore West, sharing the bill with Ten Years After.
[15] The extracted *I Got A Line On You* peaks at US #25.
June [20] They take part in the "Newport '69 Pop Festival" at San Fernando Valley State College, Devonshire Downs, Northridge, CA.
Oct ***Clear Spirit***, including Locke's instrumental music from the movie "The Model Shop", in which the band also has a cameo, makes US #55.

1970

Mar [21] *1984*, taken from ***Clear Spirit***, reaches US #69.
Sept [12] Newly signed to Epic Records, their label debut, *Animal Zoo*, charts briefly at US #97.

1971

Feb ***The 12 Dreams Of Dr. Sardonicus***, critically regarded as their most accessible work, and co-written by California and Ferguson, makes US #63.
June California leaves for Britain to undertake a solo career, while Andes and Ferguson depart to form Jo Jo Gunne, with Matt Andes (guitar) and Curly Smith (drums), which signs to Asylum Records.

1972

Apr ***Feedback***, recorded by Cassidy and Locke with newly-recruited Texas guitarist Chris Staehely and his bassist brother, Al, reaches US #63, after which Cassidy and Locke also leave, and a totally non-original Spirit tours the US.
May Jo Jo Gunne's *Run Run Run* reaches US #27 and UK #6, its only chart single, taken from ***Jo Jo Gunne***, which makes US #57.
Sept Recovering from nervous exhaustion and an accident when he fell off a horse, California releases the solo album, ***Captain Kopter And The Fabulous Twirlybirds***.

1973

May Jo Jo Gunne's ***Bite Down Hard*** makes US #75, featuring Jimmie Randall on bass in place of the departed Mark Andes.
Aug Compilation album, ***The Best Of Spirit***, peaks at US #120.
Oct [27] *Mr. Skin* stops at US #92.

1974

Jan Jo Jo Gunne's ***Jumpin' The Gunne*** peaks at US #169. Cassidy and California re-form Spirit as a trio, with Barry Keene on bass, and sign to Mercury Records.
Dec Final Jo Jo Gunne album, ***So ...Where's The Show?***, featuring ex-Spirit member Chris Staehely replacing Andes on guitar, reaches US #198.

1975

June Locke has re-joined Spirit for the double album, ***Spirit Of '76***, on Mercury Records, which reaches US #147.

1976

May ***Son Of Spirit*** is released, featuring a returned Andes who has also recruited his brother, Matt, from Jo Jo Gunne.
June [18] ***The 12 Dreams Of Dr. Sardonicus*** is certified gold by the RIAA, six years after its release.
Aug [21] ***Farther Along*** peaks at US #179.
[29] The group plays a reunion concert at Santa Monica, CA, with Neil Young guesting for an encore version of Bob Dylan's *Like A Rolling Stone*.

1977

Apr The group's final Mercury album, ***Future Games (A Magical Kahvana Dream)***, is released, including dialogue from "Star Trek", but not featuring Locke or the Andes brothers, who have departed (Mark Andes to join Firefall and eventually Heart in 1982).

1978

Feb Locke joins Nazareth for a US tour.
Apr Ferguson, having stayed with Asylum as a solo artist after the demise of Jo Jo Gunne, hits US #9 with *Thunder Island*. (It is taken from ***Thunder Island***,

which makes US #72, and will be followed by two further US chart outings, ***Real Life Ain't This Way*** (#86, 1979) and ***White Noise*** (#178, 1982.)

Aug [26] Spirit plays on the second day of the 18th National Jazz Blues & Rock Festival "Reading Rock '78", near Reading, Berks.

1979

Jan Performance set, ***Live***, recorded on stage in West Germany, is released in the US on the group's own Potato label, subsequently issued in Britain on Illegal Records.

Oct [2] Having established his own combo, the Randy California Band, with California, Jack Willowby (drums) and Liberty (bass), begins a UK tour in Preston, Lancs., set to end on the 24th at London's Rainbow Theatre, supporting Ian Gillan's band.

1981

Apr [18] Rhino Records in the US releases Spirit's ***Journey To Potatoland***, a project from the early '70s, rejected by Epic as lacking commercial potential. It reaches UK #40 on Beggars Banquet Records - Spirit's only UK chart entry.

June [16] California and Cassidy, with keyboard player George Valuck, perform on BBC2-TV's "The Old Grey Whistle Test", followed the next night by a one-off gig at London's Hammersmith Odeon. (California's next solo set, ***Euro American*** will be released the following April.)

1984

Feb Spirit reunites as a five-piece, releasing a re-recorded version of *1984*.

Mar ***Spirit Of '84/Dream The Thirteenth Dream***, on Mercury Records, features the reunited line-up on new cuts of old songs *Fresh Garbage*, *I Got A Line On You* and *1984*, augmented by new material. (California's ***Restless*** will emerge in June the following year.)

1989

Apr With California and Cassidy teaming up again for touring the previous year with Mike Nile on bass and Scott Monahan on keyboards, a recording deal with I.R.S. yields ***Rapture In The Chamber***, and ***Tent Of Miracles***, released the following year.

1993

May [4] With Spirit still gigging regularly on the US club circuit, Cassidy, who has also become a lecturer and written **Ed Cassidy's Musicians Survival Manual**, celebrates his 70th birthday with a party at the Troubadour in Los Angeles. Sony Music's Legacy imprint has brought Spirit's Ode highlights to compact disc with the 1991 release of ***Time Circle 1968-1972*** which follows a UK counterpart, ***The Collection***, issued by Castle the previous year.

SPLIT ENZ

Tim Finn (vocals, piano); **Neil Finn** (vocals, guitar); **Phil Judd** (vocals, guitar); **Eddie Rayner** (keyboards); **Wally Wilkinson** (guitar); **Mike Chunn** (bass); **Paul Crowther** (drums); **Noel Crombie** (spoons, design)

1972

Oct The group forms in Auckland, New Zealand, initially as Split Ends, with Tim Finn (b. June 25, 1952, Te Awamutu, North Island, New Zealand), Judd, Chunn, Miles Golding and Michael Howard. Their first tour, around colleges and universities in March of the following year, is followed by a full New Zealand trek, supporting John Mayall. Their first release, a one-off single for Vertigo Records, *For You*, is released in April 1973, after which, in September, the band makes the final of the New Zealand NZBC-TV "New Faces" talent show, giving their startling theatrical image (including bizarre clothes and make-up) nationwide coverage, which also results in their being offered sponsorship by a major brewery to tour on the pub circuit.

1975

Mar The band moves to Sydney, New South Wales, Australia, and changes its name to Split Enz.

May Newly signed to Australian-based Mushroom Records, their debut album, ***Mental Notes***, is given an Antipodean-only release. The group supports Roxy Music in Sydney, which sparks interest from guitarist Phil Manzanera.

1976

May The band relocates to Britain, where Manzanera produces ***Second Thoughts*** (mainly upgraded re-recordings of songs from the first album) which will be licensed to Chrysalis Records for UK release the following year.

1977

May During a US tour Judd leaves and is replaced by Finn's 18-year-old brother, Neil (b. May 27, 1958, Te Awamutu). Wilkinson, Chunn and Crowther also quit to be replaced by Englishmen Nigel Griggs (b. Aug. 18, 1949) and Malcolm Green (b. Jan. 25, 1953), shortly before their third album, ***Dizrhythmia***, co-produced with Geoff Emerick, is released, via a new deal with Chrysalis Records.

Nov The group plays at London's Roundhouse on a bill with XTC and the Cortinas.

1978

Oct Split Enz performs at **Time Out** magazine's "10th Anniversary Concert" in London. During the year, the band tours around the UK, usually as a support act, and records ***Frenzy*** with producer Mallory Earl (only released in Australia and New Zealand by Mushroom until it is licensed to A&M in 1982). Returning to Sydney, Judd re-joins, and *I See Red* hits the Top 10 in their home territory.

1980

Jan Having spent much of the previous year touring, and releasing ***True Colours*** in Australia in September, a fully-rounded pop/rock outing produced by David Tickle, A&M Records offers the group a worldwide contract on the strength of the album. Led by Neil Finn's catchy single, *I Got You*, ***True Colours*** becomes the group's most commercially successful set (eventually selling over 700,000 copies worldwide). Chrysalis releases the early retrospective, ***Beginning Of The Enz***.

Aug *I Got You* reaches UK #12 and US #40. ***True Colours*** is re-released in various gimmick formats, including different color sleeves and the first commercial use of laser-etched vinyl. It peaks at UK #42 and US #40, during a six-month chart run.

1981

May [23] The Neil Finn-penned *History Never Repeats* makes UK #63, taken from the Tickle-produced ***Waiata*** (the Polynesian word for "party", released in Australia by Mushroom as ***Corroboree***) which enters the US chart and is set to reach #45 during a 19-week run.

1982

May [8] ***Time And Tide***, produced by Hugh Padgham, charts for a week at UK #71, and will peak at US #53 in June, while the extracted *Six Months In A Leaky Boat* is banned by the BBC in the event that it might refer to the British fleet preparing to engage Argentina in the Falklands War (even though it was written by Tim Finn about the hardships suffered by New Zealand's first European settlers). Following the album's release, Green leaves.

1983

Mar The group celebrates its tenth anniversary with a concert in Te Awamutu.

Sept Tim Finn's solo album, ***Escapade***, peaks at US #161.

1984

Aug ***Conflicting Emotions***, again helmed by Padgham, with help from Eddie Rayner, its songs independently written by either Neil or Tim Finn, makes US #137.

Dec The band undertakes a tour of Australia and New Zealand.

1985

Tim Finn announces he is leaving the group for a solo career (securing a deal with Virgin Records for whom he will record ***Big Canoe*** the following year). After the Antipodean-only release of the Split Enz mini-album, ***See Ya Round***, Neil Finn and Hester form Crowded House in 1986, a new trio completed by Nick Seymour (which will add Tim Finn at the turn of the decade following his third solo outing, ***Tim Finn*** on Capitol Records).

1993

Mar Following the 1987 A&M release of the retrospective collection, ***History Never Repeats Itself (The Best Of Split Enz)***, a six-disc boxed set (of the group's first five albums plus an extra side of demos, live tracks and rarities), ***Oddz & Endz*** is issued in Australia. A second six-CD boxed set, ***Rear Enz***, containing their last five albums and further rarities, will be released, again only in Australia, in May.

see also: **CROWDED HOUSE**

DUSTY SPRINGFIELD

1961

Sept Convent-educated Springfield (b. Mary O'Brien, Apr. 16, 1939, Hampstead, London), ex-member of UK vocal trio the Lana Sisters, with her brother Dion O'Brien and friend Tim Feild, has formed the Springfields, a folk and country music-based vocal/guitar trio, the previous year. She has adopted the new stage name Dusty Springfield, while Dion becomes Tom Springfield, as they began working the folk club circuit. Signed to Philips Records, the trio's debut, *Dear John*, released in May, is now followed by *Breakaway*, which makes UK #31.

Dec Christmas song, *Bambino*, reaches UK #16. Their debut album, ***Kinda Folksy***, is released, and they are named Best UK Vocal Group in the **New Musical Express** Readers' Poll, on the strength of two minor hits.

1962

June Feild leaves and is replaced by Mike Pickworth, who changes his name to Mike Hurst.

Sept *Silver Threads And Golden Needles*, having failed to chart in Britain, reaches US #20.

Nov *Dear Hearts And Gentle People* is the US follow-up, and makes #95.

1963

Mar *Island Of Dreams* hits UK #5.

Apr *Say I Won't Be There* also hits UK #5, as the group tours Britain supporting US visitors, Del Shannon and Johnny Tillotson.

Aug The Springfields' *Come On Home* reaches UK #31, their last hit.

Sept [24] The group announces that it is to split, and that Dusty Springfield will be signing a solo deal with Philips.

Oct [11] The group plays its farewell concert at the London Palladium. (After the split, Hurst will become a record producer, most notably for Showaddywaddy in the '70s, while Tom Springfield will write such hits as *The Carnival Is Over* and *Georgy Girl* for the Seekers, and in the early '70s will launch Springfield Revival.)

[20] Springfield makes her solo debut at a concert for British troops stationed in West Germany.

Nov [8] She begins her first tour, with the Searchers, Freddie & the Dreamers, Brian Poole & the Tremeloes and Dave Berry, in Halifax, W. Yorks.

1964

Jan Dusty's solo debut, *I Only Want To Be With You*, a change from pop/folk to a more Motown-styled offering, and written by Mike Hawker and Ivor Raymonde, hits UK #4. The Springfields appear in the UK movie, "It's All Over Town" (a cameo slot filmed before their break-up), singing *If I Was Down And Out*, which is also released as a final Springfields single.

[1] *I Only Want To Be With You* is the first record played on the new BBC-TV show, "Top Of The Pops".

[29] Springfield begins a 29-date, twice-nightly UK package tour, with the Swinging Blue Jeans, Bobby Vee and Big Dee Irwin, at the Adelphi Theatre, Slough, Berks., set to end at the Empire Theatre, Liverpool, Lancs., on March 29th.

Mar *Stay Awhile*, in similar style to her debut and written by the same team, reaches UK #13, while *I Only Want To Be With You* makes US #12.

Apr [20] She arrives in the US, following a tour of Australia with Gerry & the Pacemakers.

May Her maiden album, ***A Girl Called Dusty***, showcasing her distinctively husky vocal style, hits UK #6, as *Stay Awhile* reaches US #38.

[10] Springfield makes her debut on CBS-TV's "The Ed Sullivan Show".

July The Bacharach/David-written *I Just Don't Know What To Do With Myself* hits UK #3.

Aug *Wishin' And Hopin'*, another Bacharach/David song (originally the B-side of Dionne Warwick's *This Empty Place*), and taken from Springfield's debut album, hits US #6. (A version by the Merseybeats charts in the UK at the same time.) She briefly visits the States to record tracks in New York.

Oct US-only *All Cried Out* makes US #41.

Nov [14] Springfield embarks on a 21-date UK package tour, with Herman's Hermits, Dave Berry & the Cruisers and Brian Poole & the Tremeloes, at the Granada Theatre, Edmonton, London, set to end on December 6th at the Gaumont Theatre, Hanley, Staffs.

[29] *Losing You*, co-penned by Tom Springfield and Clive Westlake, hits UK #9.

Dec [9] Springfield leaves for a South African tour, stipulating that she will only perform in front of non-segregated audiences.

[14] She sings to a multi-racial audience at a cinema near Cape Town.

[15] Officials from the South African Minister of the Interior serve her with deportation orders, and she leaves South Africa the next day.

1965

Feb *Your Hurtin' Kinda Love* makes UK #37.

Mar [25] Springfield begins a 12-date, twice-nightly UK package tour, with the Searchers, Heinz, the Zombies, special guest star Bobby Vee and others, at the Odeon Theatre, Stockton-on-Tees, Cleveland, set to close on April 10th at the Sophia Gardens, Cardiff, South Glamorgan Wales.

[27] *Losing You* peaks at US #91.

Apr [11] She takes part in an all-star cast at the annual "**New Musical Express** Poll Winners Concert", at the Empire Pool, Wembley, Middx.

[14] Springfield guests on ITV's "The Bacharach Sound", with Dionne Warwick and the Searchers among others.

[21] "The Sound Of Motown", an ITV special featuring the Supremes, Martha & the Vandellas, Stevie Wonder, Smokey Robinson & the Miracles and the Temptations, and hosted by Springfield, airs.

July Uptempo *In The Middle Of Nowhere* hits UK #8.

[30] She goes to a Harley Street specialist to gain a medical ruling on whether she will be fit to open in her summer show next Monday (a six-week engagement at the Winter Gardens, Bournemouth, Dorset, which she pulls out of, with Cleo Laine deputizing for two weeks).

Aug She flies to the Virgin Islands for a complete rest and cancels all engagements.

Sept [17] Springfield appears on "Ready Steady, Go!", her first TV appearance since her illness.

Oct *Some Of Your Lovin'*, a Goffin and King-penned ballad, with vocal backing by Madeleine Bell and Doris Troy, hits UK #8.

Nov ***Everything's Coming Up Dusty***, once again highlighted by a pioneering choice of cover material, hits UK #6.

[8] She appears in the "Discotheque Segment" of the "Royal Variety Show" in London.

Dec [6] Springfield begins a week in cabaret at Mr. Smith's in Manchester.

1966

Feb Uptempo *Little By Little* , featured in the movie "The Corrupt Ones", reaches UK #17.

Apr [28] *You Don't Have To Say You Love Me*, an Italian song (which had been that country's entry for the "San Remo Song Festival") with new English lyrics by Simon Napier-Bell and Vicki Wickham, tops the UK chart, and becomes her all-time best-selling single.

May [1] Springfield appears on a star-studded bill at the annual "**New Musical Express** Poll Winners Concert", at the Empire Pool, Wembley.

July A further Goffin and King ballad, *Goin' Back*, hits UK #10, as *You Don't Have To Say You Love Me* hits US #4.

Aug [18] BBC-TV series, "Dusty", airs for the first time.

Oct Another ballad, *All I See Is You*, hits UK #9 and US #20.

Nov Compilation album, ***Golden Hits***, rounding up her singles successes to date, hits UK #2.

[3] She makes her US night-club debut at Basin Street East, New York, amidst complaints that the support acts, Los Vegas and the Buddy Rich Orchestra, and a host of celebrities introduced to the audience, mean Springfield waits more than three hours to make her debut.

Dec [23] Springfield opens in "Merry King Cole" at the Empire Theatre, Liverpool.

1967

Jan She records two movie-theme songs, *The Corrupt Ones* for "The Peking Medallion" and *The Look Of Love* for the James Bond movie, "Casino Royale".

Mar *I'll Try Anything* reaches UK #13, helped by an appearance on BBC1-TV's "Top Of The Pops" on the 30th, and US #40.

June *Give Me Time* makes UK #24 and US #76.

July [7] Springfield begins a three-week season at New York's Copacabana.

Sept [19] A second series of BBC-TV's "Dusty" comes to a close.

Nov *The Look Of Love*, from "Casino Royale", is her last hit on Philips in the US, reaching #22, while ***Where Am I Going*** peaks at UK #40.

Dec *What's It Gonna Be* reaches US #49, spurred by a performance on US TV's "Operation Entertainment" on the 8th.

1968

Mar Springfield undertakes a three-week engagement at the Venus Club, Baltimore, MD.

May [8] The nine-week "It Must Be Dusty" series airs for the first time on ITV.

[19] Springfield performs at the "Royal Variety" TV show with Tom Jones, Long John Baldry and others.

Aug *I Close My Eyes And Count To Ten* hits UK #4.

Sept *I Will Come To You* is released. Now signed to Atlantic records in the US, she travels to Memphis, TN, to record an album with the label's top Southern session crew.

Nov [24] Springfield guests on CBS-TV's "The Ed Sullivan Show", during a US promotional tour.

1969

Jan *Son Of A Preacher Man*, recorded in Memphis, hits UK #9 and US #10, while ***Dusty ... Definitely*** makes UK #30.

[6] Springfield embarks on a 30-day US college tour.

Mar *Don't Forget About Me* makes US #64, while its B-side, *Breakfast In Bed*, peaks at US #91.

[15] Springfield flies to Berlin, West Germany, to take part in the two day "Festival Du Disque".

Apr ***Dusty In Memphis***, from the Memphis sessions, and recorded in less than a week (later considered to be one of her finest albums) with producers Tom Dowd, Arif Mardin and Jerry Wexler, is released, but is her first album not to chart in Britain.

[28] Springfield guests on ABC-TV's "Joey Bishop Show", followed by a ten-day North American tour, accompanied by King Curtis.

May *The Windmills Of Your Mind*, the theme song from the film, "The Thomas Crown Affair", reaches US #31.

July Her version of Tony Joe White's *Willie And Laura Mae Jones* peaks at US #78.

Sept *Am I The Same Girl*, covering Barbara Acklin's US #79 and Young-Holt Unlimited's US #3 instrumental version *Soulful Strut*, peaks at UK #43.

Nov [30] She appears with David Bowie, Grapefruit and the Graham Bond Organisation, at "Save Rave '69", a benefit show at the London Palladium for the magazine, **Rave**.

Dec *A Brand New Me*, written and produced in Philadelphia, PA, by Gamble and Huff, and taken from ***A Brand New Me***, reaches US #24.

1970

Mar *Silly, Silly Fool* peaks at US #76, her last Hot 100 entry for 18 years.

Sept Her revival of the Young Rascals' *How Can I Be Sure* makes UK #37, and is her last UK hit single for nine years. Permanently relocating to Los Angeles, CA, ***See All Her Faces*** will be released in November the followwing year, with ***Cameo*** being issued on Philips in Britain and Dunhill in the US next May.

1974

Mar *What's It Gonna Be* is her last release for Philips in the UK. (During the year she will record a second (but unreleased) album for Dunhill, ***Longings***, and become an in-demand session singer, not least for Anne Murray, in Los Angeles, before releasing ***Dusty Sings Burt Bacharach And Carole King*** in 1975.)

1978

Feb Attempting a recording comeback, having signed new deals with Mercury in Britain and United Artists in the US, ***It Begins Again***, produced by Roy Thomas Baker, makes UK #41, and includes the extracted *A Love Like Yours*.

1979

Nov Following the May release of ***Living Without Your Love***, *Baby Blue*, on Mercury, reaches UK #61 - her first UK chart single since 1970.

1980

Oct [7] She makes her first New York stage appearance in eight years, at the Grande Finale club. (Signed during the year to 20th Century Records in the US, the deal yields only one single *It Goes Like It Goes*, her version of the Oscar-winning song from the movie, "Norma Rae".)

White Heat, an electronic dance-flavored set will be released in the US-only on Casablanca Records in March 1983. A duet with Spencer Davis re-working the William Bell/Judy Clay hit, *Private Number*, will emerge the following March in the UK on Allegiance Records, with another one-off single *Sometimes Like Butterflies*, released on Peter Stringfellow's Hippodrome label in August 1985.

1987

Aug The beginning of a fruitful relationship which will return her to the spotlight, the Pet Shop Boys have invited Springfield to guest on its single, *What Have I Done To Deserve This?*, which hits UK #2.

Sept She sings guest vocals on Richard Carpenter's single, *Something In Your Eyes*, featuring her guests vocals, is released.

Dec *I Only Want To Be With You* is reissued to tie in with Springfield's brief appearance in a UK soft drink TV commercial. The single is backed by her 1968 recording of *Breakfast In Bed* (which will be a hit in

1988 for UB40 & Chrissie Hynde).

1988

Feb [8] She makes a rare TV appearance with the Pet Shop Boys at the annual BPI Awards ceremony at London's Royal Albert Hall, performing *What Have I Done To Deserve This?*.
[20] *What Have I Done To Deserve This?* hits US #2.
[27] A compilation, ***Dusty - The Silver Collection***, on Philips, reaches UK #14.
Dec Springfield teams with US singer B.J. Thomas to record *As Long As We Got Each Other*, used as the theme to the hit ABC-TV sitcom, "Growing Pains".

1989

Mar *Nothing Has Been Proved*, penned and co-produced by the Pet Shop Boys, and featured in the film, "Scandal", reaches UK #16.
Dec Uptempo *In Private*, also written and co-produced by Tennant and Lowe, reaches UK #14, following an appearance on ITV's "The Dame Edna Experience".

1990

May *Reputation* makes UK #38.
July [7] ***Reputation***, with four tracks written by the Pet Shop Boys, a re-make of the Goffin/King song, *I Want To Stay Here*, and two tracks produced by Dan Hartman, enters at its UK #18 peak.
Nov The extracted *Arrested By You* peaks at UK #70.

1991

June [30] She guests on ITV's "The Dame Edna Experience".
Nov [25] Springfield wins £75,000 in a libel suit brought against TVS television, after the station aired a show with comedian/impressionist Bobby Davro, which portrayed Springfield as a drunk.

1995

June [17] Following the UK #75 peaking *Heart And Soul*, a duet with Cilla Black, on Oct [30], 1993, and another retrospective, ***Goin' Back - The Very Best Of Dusty Springfield***, which hit UK #5 on May [21] the following year, and recovering from cancer, Springfield returns with *Wherever Would I Be*, a duet with Daryl Hall penned by Diane Warren and featured in the movie "While You Were Sleeping", now makes UK #44.
July [8] Newly signed to Columbia Records, her first new album in five years, ***A Very Fine Love***, produced by Tom Shapiro and featuring K.T. Oslin and Mary Chapin Carpenter among its guests, makes UK #43 in its week of entry.
Nov [4] The excerpted *Roll Away* charts for a week at UK #68.

RICK SPRINGFIELD

1970

Springfield (b. Richard Springthorpe, Aug. 23, 1949, Sydney, New South Wales, Australia), the son of an army officer, has led a nomadic military childhood, including some pre-teen years in Britain, and was given a guitar on his 13th birthday, subsequently setting his sights on a career in music. Having completed school, he has played with groups including Rock House (making a visit to entertain troops in Vietnam) and Wackedy Wak in Sydney, and now joins Zoot, which becomes Australia's most successful teen-idol band, with a string of local hits. As a member of this outfit, he records *Speak To The Sky*, which hits #1 in his home country.

1972

Oct [7] After recording his debut solo album for Capitol Records in London, he moves to the States as the extracted, self-penned *Speak To The Sky* becomes a US hit, reaching #14.
Nov Splashing his youthful good looks around the teen media, Capitol tries to make him its answer to Donny Osmond, as his freshman set, ***Beginnings*** makes US #35 (though he will have no further chart albums until 1981).
Dec [9] *What Would The Children Think* makes US #70.

1974

July Leaving Capitol, and newly signed to CBS/Columbia, ***Comic Book Heroes*** is released, including *American Girls* which peaks at US #98 (July [13]). Management and immigration problems (which mean he is not permitted to play live) force him out of active performance, but he remains in the US and attends acting school.

1976

Oct [2] A brief deal with Chelsea Records sees no chart action for ***Wait For The Night*** (which features Nigel Olsson on drums and Dee Murray on bass), but *Take A Hand* makes US #41. He finds TV acting work with Universal in Hollywood, CA, appearing in hit series including "The Rockford Files" and "The Six Million Dollar Man". (TV work will keep his musical career on a back burner, as he also guests in "The Incredible Hulk" and appears regularly in daytime soap "The Young And The Restless".)

1981

Aug [1] Following a deal with Mercury Records in 1978 (material from which will be re-released in 1985), he has signed a new recording contract with RCA. With his popularity cemented by a high TV profile playing Dr. Noah Drake in another soap, "General Hospital", his first RCA hit, the self-penned *Jessie's Girl*, now tops the US chart for the first of two weeks.
[4] *Jessie's Girl* is certified gold by the RIAA.
Sept His debut RCA album, ***Working Class Dog***, hits US #7.
Nov [7] *I've Done Everything For You*, taken from the album and written by Sammy Hagar, hits US #8.
Dec [2] ***Working Class Dog*** is certified platinum by the RIAA.

1982

Feb [13] *Love Is Alright Tonite* makes US #20.
[24] *Jessie's Girl* earns Springfield a Grammy Award, named Best Male Rock Vocal Performance of 1981 at the 24th annual ceremony.
May [11] Still-climbing ***Success Hasn't Spoiled Me Yet*** is certified as his second platinum album by the RIAA.
[22] *Don't Talk To Strangers* hits US #2 for four weeks, behind Paul McCartney and Stevie Wonder's *Ebony And Ivory*, while its parent set ***Success Hasn't Spoiled Me Yet***, produced by Keith Olsen, also hits US #2 (behind Asia's debut effort).
July [3] The extracted *What Kind Of Fool Am I* reaches US #21.
Oct [30] *I Get Excited* makes US #32.

1983

Jan RCA reissues his 1976 Chelsea album ***Wait For Night***, to minor sales at US #159.
[17] He ties (with John Mellencamp) to win in the Favorite Male Artist, Pop/Rock category at the tenth annual American Music Awards held at the Shrine Auditorium, Los Angeles, CA.
Feb He begins filming in Ray Stark's "Hard To Hold" for Universal - his first starring non-TV movie role.
June [18] *Affair Of The Heart* hits US #9, taken from ***Living In Oz***, which reaches US #12 and is his third million-selling album.
Sept [10] *Human Touch*, another cut from ***Living In Oz***, makes US #18.
[30] ***Living In Oz*** is certified platinum by the RIAA.
Dec [3] *Souls* peaks at US #23.

1984

Jan *Human Touch* is his UK chart debut at #23.
Feb ***Living In Oz*** makes UK #41.
Apr *Jessie's Girl* reaches UK #43.
May [5] The first song taken from the soundtrack of the premiering movie "Hard To Hold", in which Springfield stars, is *Love Somebody*, which hits US #5.
June Soundtrack album ***Hard To Hold*** reaches US #16.
July [7] *Don't Walk Away*, another track from the movie, makes US #26.
[10] ***Hard To Hold*** is certified platinum by the RIAA.
Oct [20] *Bop 'Til You Drop*, also from ***Hard To Hold***, reaches US #20.
Dec [8] The B-side of *Bop, Taxi Dancing* (a duet with Randy Crawford), makes US #59.

1985

Jan [12] *Bruce*, one of the songs Springfield originally recorded in 1978 for Mercury, is issued to capitalize on the popularity of its subject matter - an autobiographical piece concerning people mistaking him for Bruce Springsteen. It reaches US #27. Mercury also issues ***Beautiful Feelings***, containing other 1978 tracks with new accompaniment added, which makes US #78.
May [18] *Celebrate Youth*, from his newly-recorded album, reaches US #26.
June ***Tao***, marking a shift in style from guitar-based rock to a more electronic style using drum machines, makes US #21 and UK #68.
[13] ***Tao*** is certified gold by the RIAA.
Aug [17] *State Of The Heart*, another song from ***Tao***, makes US #22.

1988

Apr [2] After an extended absence from recording, Springfield returns with self-penned *Rock Of Life*, which reaches US #22. Its parent album ***Rock Of Life*** makes US #55 and UK #80 (Mar [26]), though several summer concerts will be cancelled due to poor ticket sales. RCA will releases the 12-track CD compilation ***Greatest Hits*** package in September the following year, while Springfield appears in the universally-panned TV pilot "Nick Knight".

1993

Apr [3] With his recording career still on hold, and ongoing acting chores including an appearance as a Vietnam vet on ABC-TV's "Human Target" in July 1992, Springfield, who has begun rehearsals at the Pelican's Retreat in Calabasa, CA in January in preparation for US dates, now performs at the Roxy, Phoenix, AZ, a gig grossing $7,958.

BRUCE SPRINGSTEEN

1965

Having unsuccessfully tried drumming at an early age, Springsteen (b. Sept. 23, 1949, Freehold, NJ), son of a secretary mother Adele and bus-driving father Douglas Springsteen, already influenced by Elvis Presley and Chuck Berry, bought his first guitar at the age of 14 for $18 from a local pawn shop, and began to learn songs from the radio, the first being the Rolling Stones' *It's All Over Now*. Already composing his own songs, Springsteen discovers that his sister Ginny's boyfriend, George Theiss, has a vacancy in his high school band, the Castiles (who take their name from Theiss' use of the soap), and passes two auditions for group manager, 32-year-old Tex Vinyard. With the band practicing every day after school, Vinyard, an unemployed factory worker, secures the Castiles constant gigs at school dances, YMCA parties and clubs around New Jersey areas Red Bank, Long Branch and Asbury Park.

1967

Aug Having recorded two demos, the Springsteen-penned *That's What You'll Get* and *Baby I* on May 22nd, 1966, the Castiles play their final gig at the Broad Street coffee house, Red Bank. Springsteen moves to live in nearby Asbury Park and joins the short-lived trio, Earth. He also begins spending many evenings at the Upstage club, a popular local hangout for aspiring musicians, where he meets Vini Lopez, Southside Johnny and Steve Van Zandt (aka Miami Steve and Little Steven) (b. Nov. 22, 1949).

1969

Springsteen forms a new band, Child, from club members, which changes its name to Steel Mill (which intially features Viny Roslyn on bass), when they realize another Child already exists. Managed by Tinker West, the group begins constant local gigging, and also a mini club-tour of California, which attracts positive press reviews.

1971

Feb Steel Mill splits. (Three members - drummer Lopez, keyboardist Danny Federici (b. Jan. 23, 1950) and bassist Van Zandt will join Springsteen's future backing group, the E Street Band.) Springsteen forms Dr. Zoom & the Sonic Boom, a collection of Asbury Park musicians not currently affiliated to other line-ups. It plays only three dates, as summer performing is seriously interrupted by the Asbury riots.

Sept Springsteen assembles a ten-piece group, the Bruce Springsteen Band, with a horn section and girl singers. After only two dates, the line-up is cut to David Sancious on keyboards, Garry Tallent on bass, Van Zandt (now on guitar), Lopez and Federici, while Asbury saxophonist Clarence Clemons (b. Jan. 11, 1942, Norfolk, VA) also joins.

1972

May Springsteen auditions for aspiring producers Mike Appel and Jim Cretecos and, after returning from an unsuccessful solo trip to California, signs a long-term management contract with Appel's Laurel Canyon Promotion Company, on a car hood in an unlit parking lot. The following day, Appel arranges an audition for Springsteen in front of CBS/Columbia A&R head, John Hammond (for whom he sings *It's Hard To Be A Saint In The City*), who is impressed and arranges a further audition for Columbia colleagues at the Gaslight club, Greenwich Village, New York.

June [9] Despite negotiation difficulties between an aggressive Appel and the label, Springsteen signs a worldwide, ten-year, ten-album CBS deal for an advance of $25,000, with a $40,000 recording budget. Springsteen quickly re-forms the Bruce Springsteen Band (now without Van Zandt) against the wishes of CBS, which sees him as a solo folk performer. Undaunted, Springsteen takes the band into the studio to record his first album in three weeks.

1973

Jan His debut album, ***Greetings From Asbury Park***, is released. Selected as a priority by CBS head Clive Davis, critics are encouraged to think of singer/songwriter/guitarist Springsteen as the new Dylan. Despite a lengthy club tour and a ten-date support role to CBS headliners Chicago (criticized as a misconceived disaster), the album initially only sells 25,000 copies, as relations between the artist's management and CBS worsen.

Feb Springsteen's *Blinded By The Light* disappears without trace.

May While Davis is fired, Springsteen plays at the CBS Records Annual Convention in San Francisco, CA, prior to recording his second album.

Nov His sophomore set, ***The Wild, The Innocent And The E Street Shuffle***, is released. It proves popular with rock critics, who pay particular attention to the ballad, *Asbury Park Fourth Of July (Sandy)*. A six-city club tour fails to ignite sales, even though Springsteen and the band are now seasoned live performers, commonly playing two-hour sets. Ernest Carter replaces Lopez as the backing group are named the E Street Band - after the road where Sancious' mother lives in Belmar, NJ.

1974

Apr [9] The band plays the first of three nights at Charley's club in Harvard Square, Cambridge, MA, one of which is attended by influential rock critic, 26-year-old Jon Landau, who writes for **Rolling Stone** and Boston-based **The Real Paper**, and is suitably impressed.

May [22] After seeing a further date in Cambridge, supporting Bonnie Raitt where he premieres a new song, *Born To Run*, Landau is moved to write: "I saw rock and roll's future - and its name is Bruce Springsteen." The often misquoted sentence immediately sparks intense promotion ideas at CBS, and snowballs into further, similar reviews by other critics. CBS re-promotes the first two Springsteen albums as a long-term friendship develops between the artist and Landau.

Aug [3] Springsteen & the E Street Band open for Anne Murray at the "Schaefer Festival", New York, NY. It is the final gig for Carter and Sancious, who are replaced by drummer Max Weinberg (b. Apr. 13, 1951) and pianist Roy Bittan, whom Springsteen has met while playing at Charley's.

Nov With production indecision delaying the third album, Springsteen asks Landau to help, a role which he unofficially but enthusiastically undertakes.

1975

Feb Landau becomes co-producer of the new album (with a less than happy Appel) and invites Steve Van Zandt to rejoin the backing band to add a rockier edge to current recordings.

Apr UK act the Hollies shorten an earlier Springsteen song to *Sandy*, peaking at US #85.

July [20] Guitarist Miami Steve plays his first gig as a member of the E Street Band.

Oct [11] His third album, ***Born To Run***, immediately hailed as a rock classic, hits US #3. Springsteen and the band begin their first national tour, a 40-date "Born To Run" trek which gains sensational reviews.

[18] Springsteen's first two releases finally chart, ***Greetings*** making US #60 and ***The Wild, The Innocent And The E Street Shuffle*** reaching US #59.

[27] In an unprecedented move, both **Time** and **Newsweek** magazines feature cover stories on Springsteen, while a number of other critics feel that the hype machine is out of control.

Nov At a Los Angeles, CA gig, Springsteen meets Phil Spector. The arrangement of the title track *Born To Run* was credited as a tribute to the producer. Spector invites Springsteen to a Dion session.

[1] *Born To Run* reaches US #23.

[18] Springsteen embarks on his first European tour with the first of two dates at London's Hammersmith Odeon, his debut performances in Britain. As ***Born To Run*** makes UK #36, many people, including Springsteen, are outraged by his record label's pre-gig hype, which features bill posters of the famous (misquoted) Landau review. A theater hoarding announces "At last London is ready for Bruce Springsteen."

Dec Appel tapes three concerts for a planned live album. The only cut which will officially emerge is the festive *Santa Claus Is Coming To Town*, which highlights the live rapport between Clarence Clemons and Springsteen.

1976

Feb [7] Follow-up, *Tenth Avenue Freeze Out*, peaks at US #83. (Van Zandt produces ***I Don't Want To Go Home*** for Southside Johnny & the Asbury Jukes, including Springsteen's song, *The Fever*.)

Mar Springsteen enlists the help of Landau and lawyer Mike Mayer in reviewing his original Appel contract. Appel is seeking to renegotiate a management deal with the artist, who realizes for the first time that he only receives 3½% of wholesale album sales as opposed to Appel's 14%.

Apr The band begins a US tour as Manfred Mann's Earth Band's cover of Springsteen's *Spirit In The Night* peaks at US #97 (it will re-chart a year later to make US #40).

[29] At 3:00 a.m., after a gig in Memphis, TN, Springsteen, Van Zandt and publicist Glen Brunman ask a Memphis cab driver to take them to Elvis Presley's Graceland home. Springsteen climbs over the wall, but a security guard assumes he is just another crank fan and apprehends him.

May [14] Appel's Laurel Canyon company sends Springsteen an outstanding payment cheque for $67,368.78.

July [2] Appel legally informs Springsteen that he must not use Landau as a producer on his fourth album.

[27] Springsteen counters with writs in US district court alleging fraud and breach of trust by Appel.

Aug He plays a one-week engagement in Red Bank, NJ, to earn money during the legal dispute.

Sept He opens another lengthy tour, at the Coliseum, Phoenix, AZ.

1977

Feb [19] Manfred Mann's Earth Band's cover of Springsteen's *Blinded By The Light* tops the US chart (having hit UK #6 six months earlier).

May [28] After several legal flurries, an out-of-court settlement is reached with Appel. He reportedly wins substantial monies, but Springsteen is now free to seek new management and make his own career decisions.

June [1] Springsteen and Landau begin recording under a re-negotiated deal with CBS at Atlantic Studios, Manhattan, NY.

July Always a prolific songwriter, Springsteen gives *Fire* to New York rockabilly Robert Gordon, and *Because The Night* to Jimmy Iovine, who is producing a Patti Smith album in the next door studio. The song, credited as a co-write with Smith, will reach US #13 and UK #5.

1978

May [23] Prefacing the finished album, Bruce Springsteen & the E Street Band return to stage-work at Shea's Buffalo Theatre. The beginning of another lengthy concert series, the performances now extend to three hours, with the inclusion of many cover versions.

June [3] Springsteen plays at the Nassau Veterans Memorial Coliseum, Uniondale, NY, - his first New York appearance in two years.

Self-penned (as with all Springsteen albums), ***Darkness On The Edge Of Town*** is finally released and hits US #5 and makes UK #16.

[27] ***Darkness On The Edge Of Town*** is certified platinum by the RIAA.

July [22] The extracted *Prove It All Night* makes US #33 (he will remain without a UK chart single until 1980).

Sept [23] *Badlands* peaks at US #42.

Dec The Pointer Sisters' cover of *Fire* hits US #2 (and UK #34 in March 1979).

1979

Jan [1] A seven-month tour ends in Cleveland, OH, after 109 shows in 86 cities, all sellouts including dates at New York's Madison Square Garden.

Mar The band enters New York's Power Station Studio to record a new album.

Apr During hi-jinks with comic Robin Williams and Springsteen's girlfriend, Joyce Heiser, Springsteen damages his leg in a motorbike accident at home, forcing him to take a three-month break.

May Tapes for a new album leak out of the studio, aiding increasing pirate/bootleg operations.

June [3] Springsteen & the E Street Band are joined by Rickie Lee Jones and Boz Scaggs for a jam session on-stage at the Whisky A-Go-Go in Los Angeles, at the wedding reception of his lighting man, Mark Brickman.

July Greg Kihn cuts Springsteen's *For You* on his album, ***With The Naked Eye***, while the Knack record his *Rendezvous*.

Aug CBS and Springsteen file suit in Los Angeles against five bootleggers, seeking $1.75 million in damages.

Sept [23] On his 30th birthday, Springsteen performs at the Musicians United for Safe Energy (MUSE) concert at New York's Madison Square Garden, at Jackson Browne's invitation. Springsteen appears on condition that no politicians are present and that photographer Lynn Goldsmith is also barred (Goldsmith had sold private pictures of Springsteen taken during their brief 1978 tour affair). Springsteen is prominently featured on the subsequent ***No Nukes*** triple album and film.

Oct Springsteen enters the studio to work on a new album.

1980

Apr [14] A New Jersey assemblyman proposes that *Born To Run* be declared the official state song.
Nov [8] Trimmed from an original choice of 60 songs, the double album, ***The River***, co-produced by Springsteen, Landau and Van Zandt, tops the US chart for the first of four weeks, and hits UK #2, spending over a year on both surveys.
[3] "The River" tour begins in Ann Arbor, MI, with the live set now extended at some dates to four hours, and including a popular encore medley of Mitch Ryder songs which will remain a long-term live highlight.
Dec [27] The extracted *Hungry Heart*, with the unavailable-elsewhere B-side, *Held Up Without A Gun*, hits US #5 and having made UK #44.
[29, 31] Springsteen plays year-end dates at the Nassau Veterans Memorial Stadium.

1981

Mar [14] *Fade Away* reaches US #20.
[19] After initially postponed dates caused by ill-health, he returns to Britain for his first dates since 1975, opening with two nights in London.
May Gary U.S. Bonds releases ***Dedication*** (US #27 and UK #43) produced by Springsteen and containing four of his songs, including *This Little Girl* (US #11, UK #43) and *Jolé Blon* (US #65, UK #51). Springsteen will also convert backing vocals on the album to live assistance on selected Bonds' dates.
[11] Springsteen finishes a 32-date European tour in Paris, France.
June [27] Title track, *The River*, makes UK #35.
Aug [20] Springsteen gives a concert at the Los Angeles Sports Arena to benefit the Vietnam Veterans of American Foundation and Mental Health Association.
Sept [5] He joins the Pretenders onstage at their Perkins Cow Palace, Pasadena, CA show, on *(Your Love Keeps Lifting Me) Higher And Higher*.
Oct 1975-recorded *Santa Claus Is Comin' To Town* is included on the CBS various artists' sample, ***In Harmony***, released to benefit the Children's Television Workshop and other children's charities. The song becomes a seasonal radio favorite.

1982

Jan [3] Sessions for a new album begin on a four-track, Teac Tascam cassette recorder, at Springsteen's rented Holmdel, NJ home and in the studio.
June [12] Before an audience of 750,000, he participates in a concert rally supporting nuclear disarmament alongside Jackson Browne, Linda Ronstadt, James Taylor and others in New York's Central Park.
July A second Springsteen-produced Gary U.S. Bonds album, ***On The Line***, is issued (US #52, UK #55), including the US #21-peaking *Out Of Work*. UK rocker Dave Edmunds records Springsteen's *From Small Things (Big Things One Day Come)*.
Sept With little fanfare, Springsteen releases ***Nebraska***, a solo set of acoustic compositions recorded with engineer Mike Batlin at the Power Station on his four-track home tape recorder. The original demos also feature new songs including *Working On The Highway*, and the first electric version of future hit, *Born In The USA*.
Oct [9] ***Nebraska*** hits US #3, but no singles will be issued from the work.
[30] ***Nebraska*** hits UK #3.

1983

Springsteen spends the year writing and recording over 100 new songs for selection on his next project. With no live dates, he also spends much of the year driving extensively throughout the States.

1984

Apr Van Zandt leaves the E Street line-up amicably, and sets up Little Steven & the Disciples Of Soul.
May Following a near two-year wait, new material emerges with *Dancing In The Dark*, helped on its way by his first formal video, directed by Brian De Palma, and featuring the actress Courteney Cox. Previously shy of the device, his only previous celluloid promotion has been a live clip of popular number, *Rosalita*.
June [17] New album, ***Born In The USA***, is released, set to become his most successful multi-platinum album and establishing him as one of the most dominant forces in '80s rock music.
[29] The "Born In The USA" tour debuts at the Civic Centre in St. Paul, MN, with Nils Lofgren replacing Van Zandt on guitar. It is Springsteen's first live work since "The River" tour and will take in Europe, Australia, the US, Canada and Japan. It also features his first female backing singer, Patti Scialfa (b. July 29, 1956), ex-Southside Johnny & the Asbury Jukes.
[30] ***Born In The USA*** hits US #2, behind Duran Duran's Reflex, and reaches UK #28.
July [7] ***Born In The USA*** begins a seven-week tenure atop the US chart, during a 139-week survey stay.
Oct [20] *Cover Me* hits US #7, and will reach UK #16.

1985

Jan [19] Title cut, *Born In The USA*, already a popular anthemic live number re-establishing Springsteen's harder rock style, hits US #9.
[28] Having won the Favorite Single, Pop/Rock category, at the 12th annual American Music Awards, held at the Shrine Auditorium, Los Angeles, he contributes a lead vocal to USA For Africa's *We Are The World* benefit disc. (He will also donate a popular live cut, the previously un-released *Trapped*, for the forthcoming USA For Africa album - the track was recorded on August 6th, 1984 at the Meadowlands Arena, East Rutherford, NJ, and is part of extensive live recordings accompanying the "Born In The USA" tour). Meanwhile, *Dancing In The Dark* is re-promoted in the UK, now hitting #4.
Feb [5] Springsteen is featured on an ABC-TV "20/20" special, "The Conscience Of Rock And Roll".
[16] ***Born In The USA*** belatedly tops the UK chart for a week (and will return to pole position for a further four weeks on July [6]).
[26] *Dancing In The Dark* wins the Best Rock Vocal Performance, Male category at the 27th annual Grammy Awards.
Mar Reissued *Cover Me* makes UK #16, as US close-harmony covers band Big Daddy's unrecognizable version of *Dancing In The Dark* makes UK #21.
Apr [13] Ballad, *I'm On Fire*, supported by his first concept-acted video, directed by John Sayles, hits US #6, during a five-month US chart stay.
May [13] Springsteen marries model/actress Julianne Phillips shortly after midnight at Our Lady of the Lake Church, Lake Oswego, OR.
June The tour reaches Britain amid unprecedented ticket demand, with sellouts at 72,000-attended dates at Wembley Stadium, Wembley, Middx.
July [13] Double A-side, *I'm On Fire/Born In The USA*, hits UK #5, as all seven Springsteen albums either re-enter or enter the UK chart simultaneously (***Born To Run*** now makes UK #17, ***The Wild, The Innocent And The E Street Shuffle*** peaks at #33, while ***Greetings*** makes #41).
Aug [3] With its video directed by John Sayles, *Glory Days* hits US #5.
[10] *Glory Days* reaches UK #17.
Sept [13] "I'm On Fire", also directed by Sayles, wins the Best Male Video category with "Dancing In The Dark" named Best Stage Performance Video, at the second annual MTV Video Music Awards, held at Radio City Music Hall, New York.
Oct [2] The "Born In The USA" tour ends at the Memorial Coliseum, Los Angeles.
[26] *I'm Goin' Down* , the sixth extract from ***Born In The USA***, hits US #9.
Nov Springsteen contributes lead vocals to the Artists United Against Apartheid single *Sun City*, and appears in a video alongside its creator, Little Steven Van Zandt (US #38, UK #21).
Dec Festive *Santa Claus Is Coming To Town*, coupled with *My Hometown*, hits UK #9.

1986

Jan [19] Springsteen makes an unannounced appearance at a benefit for laid-off 3M Factory workers in Freehold, NJ.
[25] Still from ***Born In The USA***, *My Hometown* hits US #6.
[27] He wins the Favorite Male Artist, Pop/Rock, Favorite Male Video Artist, Pop/Rock, and Favorite Album, Pop/Rock categories, at the 13th annual American Music Awards, held at the Shrine Auditorium.
Feb Lee Iacocca reportedly offers Springsteen $12 million to license *Born In The USA* for a series of Chrysler commercials. Springsteen rejects the offer.
[10] Springsteen is named Best International Solo Artist at the fifth annual BRIT Awards, held at London's Grosvenor House Hotel.
Mar Always concerned at the quality and quantity of live bootleg recordings, Springsteen has ensured that many of the "Born In The USA" dates have been taped to add to other live recordings of the past ten years for future release. Over 200 album bootlegs are freely available.
Sept [25] Springsteen joins U2 onstage during the group's concert in Philadelphia, PA.
Nov [29] Having performed over 500 shows in the past decade, he releases the personally-compiled, unprecedented five-album live set ***Live 1975 - 1985***, reflecting the performance glory which has so endeared his live act to his dedicated followers. Dominated by his latest stadium concerts, the set includes four never-before-available Springsteen performances: the instrumental *Paradise By The Sea*, his versions of *Because The Night*, *Fire* and the new *Seeds*, taped at Los Angeles' Memorial Coliseum in September 1985. Produced by Landau, Springsteen and Chuck Plotkin and compiled from 21 concerts, it historically enters the US chart at #1 and hits UK #4.
Dec [27] Taken from it, *War*, his cover of Edwin Starr's 1970 US #1 hit, accompanied by a live video, hits US #8, and makes UK #18.

1987

Jan [21] Springsteen performs *Oh, Pretty Woman* with its composer, Roy Orbison, at the second annual Rock and Roll Hall of Fame induction post-dinner jam, at New York's Waldorf Astoria Hotel.
Feb [28] *Fire* makes US #46 and UK #54.
May Live version of *Born To Run* reaches UK #16.
Aug [22] Springsteen joins Levon Helm & His All Stars on *Lucille* and *Up On Cripple Creek*, at the Stone Pony, Asbury.
Sept [30] He participates in the recording of Cinemax's "A Black And White Night" Roy Orbison special, recorded at the Coconut Grove in Los Angeles.
Oct [17] New studio album, the subdued and largely love-themed ***Tunnel Of Love***, co-produced by the artist with Landau and Plotkin, enters the UK chart at #1, while *Brilliant Disguise* reaches UK #20.
[22] Springsteen attends a memorial service for John Hammond at St. Peter's Church in New York, singing Dylan's *Forever Young*.
[31] Springsteen and members of the E Street Band play a halloween gig at McLoone's Rumrunner, Sea Bright, NJ, performing much of the ***Tunnel Of Love*** album for the first time, and an acoustic version of *Born To Run*.
Nov [6] He jams with the Fabulous Greaseband at an open day at a school near his home in Rumson, NJ. They perform *Carol*, *Lucille*, *Stand By Me* and *Twist And Shout*.
[7] ***Tunnel Of Love*** tops the US chart.
[20] Springsteen joins Bobby Bandiera's band on stage at the Stone Pony, singing *Carol*, *Little Latin Lupe* and others.
[21] *Brilliant Disguise*, its promo clip directed by Meiert Avis, hits US #5.
Dec *Tunnel Of Love* makes UK #45.
[7] He performs *Remember When The Music* at a

memorial concert for Harry Chapin at Carnegie Hall, New York, with Paul Simon, Harry Belafonte and others.
[13] At a Madison Square Garden, Paul Simon-organized benefit for homeless children, Springsteen joins Billy Joel, Lou Reed and James Taylor, vocally backing Dion on *Teenager In Love*, before playing an acoustic version of *Born To Run*.

1988

Jan Springsteen plays selected acoustic gigs in aid of the Harry Chapin Memorial Fund, and begins a six-week period of rehearsals with the E Street Band for an upcoming tour.
[20] He inducts Bob Dylan into the Rock and Roll Hall of Fame at the third annual dinner, again held at the Waldorf Astoria Hotel.
Feb [6] *Tunnel Of Love* hits US #9.
[25] The "Tunnel Of Love Express" tour opens Stateside at the Centrum, Worcester, MA, set to end May 23rd.
Mar [2] ***Tunnel Of Love*** wins the Best Rock Vocal Performance, Solo category at the 30th annual Grammy Awards.
Apr [19] The RIAA certifies three million sales of ***Tunnel Of Love***.
[23] Ballad, *One Step Up*, reaches US #13.
May Natalie Cole's cover of a previous Springsteen B-side, *Pink Cadillac*, hits #5 in both the US and UK.
June [11] Springsteen's European tour begins at the Stadio Communale, Turin, Italy.
[21] UK leg of "Tunnel of Love Express" tour opens at Aston Villa Football Club, Birmingham, West Midlands.
July *Tougher Than The Rest* reaches UK #13.
[3] During his second show in Stockholm, Sweden, Springsteen announces the planned Amnesty "Human Rights Now!" tour.
Aug [3] The European leg of his tour ends at the Nou Camp football stadium, Barcelona, Spain.
[30] Phillips files for divorce, following photographic newspaper evidence of a close relationship between Springsteen and backing singer, Patti Scialfa.
Sept [2] Springsteen participates in the opening concert at Wembley Stadium of the "Human Rights Now!" Amnesty International six-week world tour, with Sting, Peter Gabriel, Tracy Chapman and Youssou N'Dour, set to end on October 15th in Buenos Aires, Argentina. Springsteen contributes *I Ain't Got No Home* and *Vigilante Man* to the Woody Guthrie/Leadbelly tribute album, ***Folkways : A Vision Shared***.
Oct *Spare Parts* makes UK #32.

1989

Jan [18] Springsteen sings *Crying* as a tribute to Roy Orbison (who has died the month before), at the fourth annual Rock and Roll Hall of Fame dinner, held at the Waldorf Astoria Hotel.
Feb Video compilation, "Bruce Springsteen - Video Anthology 1978-88", is released. Featuring over 100 minutes of clips up to *Spare Parts*, it is an instant best-seller in the US and UK.
Mar [1] The Springsteens' divorce decree is finalized. (He has reached an out-of-court settlement with Phillips, which reportedly prevents her revealing details of their marriage to the press or in book form.)
[10] Springsteen makes a surprise appearance on-stage with the Mighty Hornets, a local band at Mickey Rourke's Los Angeles club, Rubber, singing *See See Rider*.
[29] The RIAA certifies sales of 350,000 of "Bruce Springsteen - Video Anthology 1978-88".
June [30] Having jammed at Nils Lofgren and Neil Young concerts earlier in the month, Springsteen joins Jackson Browne on stage at Bally's, Atlantic City, for *Stay*, *Sweet Little Sixteen* and *Running On Empty*.
July [6] The RIAA confirms platinum sales of ***Nebraska*** and two million sales of ***The Darkness On The Edge Of Town***.
Aug [11] He joins Ringo Starr on stage at the Garden State Arts Center, Holmdel, NJ, for four numbers (*Get Back*, *Long Tall Sally*, *Photograph* and *With A Little Help From My Friends*) with actor John Candy also making an appearance on tambourine.
Sept [13-14] Springsteen records *Viva Las Vegas* at the One On One Studio in North Hollywood, CA, for ***The Last Temptation Of Elvis***, a benefit album organized by Roy Carr of the **New Musical Express** to raise funds for the Nordoff Robbins Music Therapy charity. His rhythm section comprises Ian McLagan on keyboards, Bob Glaub on bass and Jeff Porcaro on drums.
[22] On the eve of his 40th birthday, Springsteen joins Jimmy Cliff on-stage at the Stone Pony to sing *Trapped*, the Cliff-penned track Springsteen previously contributed to ***We Are The World***.
[23] Springsteen celebrates his birthday at the McLoone's Rumrunner with the E Street Band and Little Steven. Editors of the Springsteen fanzine, **Backstreets**, publish a book on the Boss' 40th birthday.
[29] Springsteen, travelling from Los Angeles on a motorbike, drops in at Matt's Saloon in Prescott, AZ, and jams with the house combo Mile High Band for about an hour, singing *Don't Be Cruel*, *I'm On Fire*, and *Route 66*, among others. (A few weeks later, Springsteen will send Matt's barmaid Brenda Pechanec $100,000 to pay her hospital bills.)
Nov [13] **Newsweek** and **People** both run stories stating that Springsteen has told the members of the E Street Band they are no longer needed.

1990

Jan [17] Springsteen attends the fifth annual Rock and Roll Hall of Fame dinner, at the Waldorf Astoria Hotel, joining the traditional jam at the end of the proceedings, teaming with John Fogerty in an ensemble version of *Long Tall Sally*.
Feb [12] Springsteen joins Jackson Browne, Don Henley and Paul Simon, for a jam at a benefit concert for Sting's Rainforest Foundation and the Environmental Media Association in Beverly Hills, CA. After the show, Springsteen repairs to Los Angeles' China club, where he joins Bruce Hornsby, Henley, Sting and Branford Marsalis for a 45-minute impromptu set.
Mar [1] Springsteen and Bob Dylan join Tom Petty on stage at the latter's Great Western Forum, Inglewood, CA, concert.
[12] The RIAA certifies ***Born In The USA*** as having reached domestic sales of 12 million.
Apr Springsteen and Tom Waits sing *Jersey Girl*, *Stand By Me* (Springsteen) and *Fever* (Waits) at Chuck Plotkin's marriage to Jersey girl, Wendy Brandchaft, at Michael's restaurant, Santa Monica, CA.
June Springsteen gives rap group 2 Live Crew permission to sample *Born In The USA* for their single, *Banned In The USA*.
July [10] ***The Wild, The Innocent And The E Street Shuffle*** is certified platinum by the RIAA.
[25] Scialfa gives birth to their first son, Evan James Springsteen at Los Angeles' Cedars-Sinai Medical Center, weighing in at 7lb. 9oz.
Aug [22] Landau issues a statement answering speculation that Walter Yetnikoff is stepping down as CBS head, concerned that the label would continue to remain committed to Springsteen's career, and that since Sony purchased CBS, he and Yetnikoff had not had a significant conversation in two years.
Oct Springsteen donates $50,000 to the World Hunger Year's Reinvesting in America program.
Nov [16] Springsteen joins Jackson Browne and Bonnie Raitt for an acoustic concert to raise money for the Christic Institute, a non-profit group that is waging a lawsuit accusing the US Government of sanctioning illegal arms sales and drugs trafficking to finance covert operations during the Iran-Contra affair. The concert, which raises more than $600,000, is Springsteen's first official concert appearance since his participation in the Amnesty International World Tour.

1991

Jan [16] Springsteen sings *People Get Ready* with Browne and Darlene Love at the perfunctory post-dinner jam at the sixth annual Rock and Roll Hall of Fame induction ceremonies, again held at New York's Waldorf Astoria Hotel.
[20] Springsteen and Weinberg reunite at McLoone's Rumrunner, taking part in a benefit for local singer, Jim Faulkner, who is recovering from a stroke.
May He drops in on the Smithereens, who are recording in a studio next to him at A&M in Los Angeles.
June [8] Springsteen and Scialfa marry.
[22] ***For Our Children***, a benefit album for the Pediatric AIDS Foundation, to which Springsteen contributes *Chicken Lips And Lizard Hips*, reaches US #31.
Sept Springsteen guests on John Prine's album, ***The Missing Years***.
[5] Following a dismissal motion heard before Superior Court Judge Florence Peskoe in Freehold, NJ, which had resulted in some of the plaintiffs' over-time claims being thrown out, Springsteen settles out of court with two former road crew members, Michael Batlan and Douglas Sutphin, for a reported $350,000.
[26] Springsteen contributes to a Southside Johnny video for *It's Been A Long Time*, at the Stone Pony, with 500 friends and fans. (It will air for the first time on ABC-TV's "In Concert '91" series on November 1st.)
Dec [30] Their second child, daughter Jessica Rae, is born, weighing 8lb. 5oz.

1992

Mar [21] *Human Touch* debuts at its UK #11 peak, previewing the release of two separate albums recorded over the past year. (During the month, Springsteen plays a couple of songs with the Iguanas at the group's gig at the Maple Leaf, New Orleans, LA.)
Apr [4] ***Human Touch*** enters the UK chart at #1, becoming the fastest-selling album to reach pole position - two days - as the simultaneously-released ***Lucky Town*** bows at UK #2, both co-produced by Springsteen, Landau, Plotkin and Bittan.
[9] The RIAA certifies two million sales of ***Greetings From Asbury Park, New Jersey***.
[11] *Human Touch*, backed with *Better Days*, reaches US #16.
[18] ***Human Touch*** debuts at its US #2 peak (behind Def Leppard's ***Adrenalize***), while ***Lucky Town*** comes in at US #3.
May [5] The RIAA certifies gold sales of *Santa Claus Is Coming To Town* and platinum sales of *Dancing In The Dark*.
[6] Springsteen gives a private performance at New York's Bottom Line for Columbia Records staff and executives.
[9] He makes his US network TV debut, and also his first live television performance, playing three songs on NBC-TV's "Saturday Night Live", hosted by actor Joe Pesci.
[28] ***Lucky Town*** and ***Human Touch*** are both certified platinum by the RIAA.
[30] *Better Days* makes UK #34.
June [5] He gives a live radio broadcast from a Los Angeles sound-stage to introduce his forthcoming touring band - Bittan, Shane Fontayne (guitar), Tommy Sims (bass) Zachary Alford (drums), Crystal Taliefero (acoustic guitar/percussion) and Bobby King, Angel Rogers, Carol Dennis, Cleo Kennedy and Gia Ciambotti (vocals).
[15] Springsteen begins the European leg of his world tour at the Globe Arena, Stockholm, Sweden, before a sellout 15,500 crowd.
[27] TV-damning *57 Channels (And Nothin' On)* peaks at US #68. (During the month, Springsteen remixes some material with the Family Stand production team at Green St. Recording Studios in New York.)
July [6, 9-10, 12-13] Springsteen plays five sellout shows at the Wembley Arena, Wembley.
[8] The RIAA certifies four million sales of ***Live 1975 - 1985***.
[23] North American tour begins with the first of 11 dates at the Meadowlands Arena, East Rutherford, NJ, grossing $6,295,707, before sellout crowds totalling 220,902.
Aug [1] *57 Channels (And Nothin' On)* reaches UK #32.
[6] At the first of five Wembley Stadium shows, Springsteen dedicates *Human Touch* to the memory of

Jeff Porcaro, who dies the day before.
Sept [22] Springsteen performs a set at Warner Bros.' Hollywood Studios, Los Angeles, for MTV's "Unplugged" show. (He feels more comfortable playing electric, so the show, set to air on November 11th, is re-titled "Plugged".)
[24-25, 28] He plays three sellout shows at the Sports Arena, Los Angeles, grossing $1,383,590.
Oct [8-9] Concerts at the Shoreline Amphitheatre, Mountain View, CA are re-scheduled to the 21st and 22nd, when Springsteen falls victim to a severe sore throat.
[13] He crosses a picket line to perform at the Tacoma Dome, Tacoma, WA, but despite attempts by the media to paint a poor picture of Springsteen, fans care little.
[15] Springsteen plays the first of three Canadian dates (the other two will be in Calgary and Edmonton) at the Pacific Coliseum, PNE Grounds, Vancouver.
[31] *Leap Of Faith* makes UK #46.
Nov [11] "Bruce Springsteen Plugged", a 24-song set, airs on MTV.
Dec [16] Springsteen ends his 68-date tour before a sellout crowd of 15,710 at the Civic Arena, Pittsburgh, PA. The tour has grossed more than $30 million and has been seen by more than 1 million people.
[27] He guests at a Southside Johnny gig at the Stone Pony, singing *Fever*, and is then joined by Jon Bon Jovi for *Long Long Time* and *We're Having A Party*.

1993

Jan [12] Springsteen inducts Creedence Clearwater Revival into the Rock and Roll Hall of Fame at the eighth annual dinner, held at Los Angeles' Century Plaza Hotel.
Mar [23] He plays a surprise concert at the Count Basie Theatre, Red Bank, NJ, to benefit the theater and the Community Food Bank. (The 1,300 sellout is a warm-up for an upcoming nine-week European tour.)
[31] Springsteen embarks on an 18-date European trek at the Scottish Exhibition & Conference Centre, Glasgow, Strathclyde, Scotland, set to end on May 22nd at the Milton Keynes Bowl, Milton Keynes, Bucks.
Apr [1] He makes his BBC1-TV "Top Of The Pops" debut, live by satellite from Glasgow.
[10] *Lucky Town (Live)* debuts at its UK #48 peak.
[24] ***In Concert - MTV Plugged***, released in Europe to promote his current tour of the continent, and due to be deleted after 90 days of retail, hits UK #4.
June [5] He attends the wedding of Mariah Carey and Tommy Mottola at the St. Thomas Episcopal Church on 5th Avenue in New York.
[25] Springsteen makes his first appearance on the last ever NBC-TV "Late Night With David Letterman" show, singing *Glory Days*.
[26] He performs at a benefit at Madison Square Garden which raises more than $1.5 million for the Kristen Ann Carr Fund.
Dec [25] Having already peaked at UK #65 on Oct [23], 10,000 Maniacs' version of Springsteen's and Smith's *Because The Night* reaches US #18.

1994

Jan [5] His third child with Scialfa, Sam Ryan, is born in Los Angeles.
[14] UK Dare International label are injuncted to prevent the release of ***Prodigal Son***, a 23-cut double CD of early studio material, pre-dating his Columbia contract. (Springsteen and Dare will reach an out-of-court settlement in December.)
[19] Springsteen sings *Come Together* with Axl Rose at the post-dinner jam at the ninth annual Rock and Roll Hall of Fame induction ceremonies at the Waldorf Astoria Hotel.
[27] He sings *Streets Of Philadelphia* at a fundraiser for AIDS Project Los Angeles at the Universal Amphitheatre, Universal City, in the presence of First Lady, Hillary Clinton.
Feb A Curtis Mayfield tribute album ***All Men Are Brothers***, to which Springsteen has contributed his version of *Gypsy Woman*, is released.
Mar [1] He joins Steve Winwood, B. B. King, Bonnie Raitt, Steve Cropper, Don Was and others on a Mayfield medley at the 36th annual Grammy Awards.
[21] Following on from its win at the Golden Globe Awards in January, *Streets Of Philadelphia* wins the Oscar for Best Song at the 66th Academy Awards ceremony, staged at the Dorothy Chandler Pavilion, Los Angeles. (He also performs the song.)
Apr [2] *Streets Of Philadelphia*, written and performed by Springsteen for the Tom Hanks/Denzel Washington movie "Philadelphia", hits UK #2, behind Doop's *Doop*.
[23] *Streets Of Philadelphia* hits US #9.
[26] *Streets Of Philadelphia* is certified gold by the RIAA.
[30] Springsteen joins in an all-star version, including Magic Johnson, Dan Aykroyd, Jim Belushi, Steve Cropper and Woody Harrelson, of *Get On Up* at the end of the opening night of the House of Blues on Sunset Boulevard in Los Angeles.
June [18] Springsteen sings an acoustic version of *Wreck On The Highway* with John Wesley Harding, outside McCabe's Guitar Shop in Santa Monica.
July [16] He performs with Southside Johnny & the Asbury Jukes at the Stone Pony's 20th anniversary celebrations.
Aug [20] Springsteen performs a 90-minute set with Pittsburgh, PA rocker Joe Grushecky at the Marz club in Long Branch, NJ.
Sept [8] He performs *Streets Of Philadelphia*, which wins the Best Video From A Film category, at the 11th annual MTV Video Music Awards, held at Radio City Music Hall.
[20] Springsteen sings *In The Midnight Hour* with John Fogerty at the Emergency Blues benefit concert for cancer victim Jamie Belmony at the House of Blues in Los Angeles.
Oct [17] The RIAA certifies three million sales of ***The River***.
[20] Springsteen and Neil Young back Bob Dylan on an encore of *Highway 61 Revisited* at the latter's Roseland Ballroom, New York concert.
Nov [17] The RIAA confirms four million sales of ***Born To Run***.

1995

Feb [21] Springsteen reunites with the E Street Band at Manhattan nightclub Tramps, for a "Murder Incorporated" video shoot with director Jonathan Demme.
Mar [1] Springsteen opens the 37th annual Grammy Awards, staged at the Shrine Auditorium, with a performance of *Streets Of Philadelphia*, which goes on to win the Song Of The Year, Best Male Rock Vocal Performance and Best Rock Song Written Specifically For Motion Picture Or Television categories.
[6] He sings *Tracks Of My Tears* with Soul Asylum at their Tramps, Manhattan concert.
[11] ***Greatest Hits***, a 16-track compilation featuring two new tracks (*Secret Garden* and *This Hard Land*) recorded with the E Street Band, hits UK #1 in its first week.
[18] ***Greatest Hits*** also debuts at US #1.
[21] Melissa Etheridge's "Unplugged", with Springsteen duetting on *Thunder Road*, premieres on MTV-US.
Apr [5] Springsteen guests on CBS-TV's "Late Show With David Letterman".
[12] He performs at the sixth annual "Rainforest Benefit Concert", held at New York's Carnegie Hall.
[19] The RIAA certifies 15 million sales of ***Born In The USA***.
[22] Ballad *Secret Garden* debuts at its UK #44 peak.
[24] The RIAA ratifies two million sales of ***Greatest Hits***.
May [27] *Secret Garden* makes US #63.
Sept [2] Springsteen sings *Darkness On The Edge Of Town*, *Shake Rattle And Roll* and *She's The One*, backs Bob Dylan on *Forever Young* and Chuck Berry on *Johnny B. Goode* and *Rock And Roll Music*, at the Concert for the Hall of Fame at Cleveland Stadium, Cleveland.
Oct [17] He begins a six-date club swing at the Stone Pony, playing back-up for Joe Grushecky.
[28] Springsteen takes part in the ninth annual Bridge School benefit at the Shoreline Amphitheatre, Mountain View, CA, performing two new songs - *The Ghost Of Tom Joad* and *Sinaloa Cowboys*.
Nov [11] Reissued *Hungry Heart* debuts at its UK #28 peak.
[17] Two days before the taping of Frank Sinatra's 80th birthday tribute, at which he will sing *Angel Eyes*, Springsteen, Sinatra, Dylan and Steve & Eydie gather round a piano for an impromptu sing-song.
[25] Dark, mainly acoustic set, ***The Ghost Of Tom Joad***, recorded at his Thrill Hill studio in Los Angeles, peaks at UK #16 in its week of entry.
[26-27] Springsteen begins his first solo acoustic tour at the Wiltern Theatre, Los Angeles.
Dec [9] ***The Ghost Of Tom Joad*** debuts at its US #11 peak.
[10] Prior to a couple of upcoming concerts at the Beacon Theatre, Springsteen gives a free concert for hunger organizations in New York.
[14] Springsteen makes a return appearance to the "Late Show With David Letterman".

1996

Jan [8] He continues his North American tour with a sellout date at Massey Hall, Toronto, ON, Canada.
[9] Columbia releases the movie soundtrack album to the Tim Robbins-directed "Dead Man Walking", including Springsteen's *Dead Man Walkin'*, written specifically for the project.
Mar [25] Springsteen sings his Oscar-nominated *Dead Man Walkin'* at the 68th annual Academy Awards, held at the Dorothy Chandler Pavilion.
May [4] *The Ghost Of Tom Joad* enters at its UK #26 peak.

SQUEEZE

Chris Difford (vocals, guitar); **Glenn Tilbrook** (vocals, lead guitar); **Jools Holland** (keyboards); **Harry Kakoulli** (bass); **Gilson Lavis** (drums)

1974

Mar Difford (b. Nov. 4, 1954, Greenwich, London) meets Tilbrook (b. Aug. 31, 1957, London) when he answers Difford's ad - "Lyricist seeks musicians for co-writing", placed in a shop window. With the recruitment of Holland (b. Julian Holland, Jan. 24, 1955) and early drummer Paul Gunn, Squeeze is formed in Deptford, London, taking its name from the last Velvet Underground album. More literate than many other upcoming UK new wave rock acts, and earning its performance credentials on the London pub rock circuit, the group goes on to sign to Miles Copeland's BTM label and management company in 1976, by which time Gunn is replaced by ex-tour manager and drummer for Chuck Berry, Lavis (b. June 27, 1951, Bedford, Beds.), and Kakoulli joins on bass.

1977

Jan *Take Me I'm Yours*, scheduled for release by BTM, is withdrawn.
Apr During a gig supporting Eddie & the Hot Rods at a veterinary college in Bournemouth, the band has bottles of blood thrown at them.
July EP *Packet Of Three*, released on Deptford Fun City Records and produced by John Cale, is released, and leads to the group signing a worldwide contract with A&M Records, becoming the company's first "new wave" signing since the Sex Pistols.

1978

Apr *Take Me I'm Yours*, now released on A&M, reaches UK #19, taken from their debut album, ***Squeeze***, also produced by Cale. The band makes its first visit to the US, courtesy of Laker Skytrain's £61 airfare, but has to temporarily change its name to UK Squeeze to avoid confusion with a US outfit called Tight Squeeze. (The band will subsequently complete

eight US tours over the next four years.)
June *Bang Bang* peaks at UK #49.
Aug [27] They appear on the final day of the 18th National Jazz Blues & Rock Festival "Reading Rock '78", near Reading, Berks.
Nov *Goodbye Girl* reaches UK #63.

1979

Mar Their sophomore set, ***Cool For Cats***, once again highlighted by the composing partnership of Difford and Tilbrook, and produced by John Wood, makes #45.
Apr Title cut, *Cool For Cats*, hits UK #2, kept from the top by Art Garfunkel's *Bright Eyes*.
June *Up The Junction* also hits UK #2, this time blocked by Tubeway Army's *Are "Friends" Electric?*
Sept *Slap And Tickle* reaches UK #24.
Oct [4] The group performs on BBC1-TV's "Top Of The Pops".
Nov Festive *Christmas Day* fails to chart.

1980

Mar Shedding their earlier new-wave leanings, ***Argy Bargy***, again produced by Wood, and featuring new bassist John Bentley (b. Apr. 16, 1951, London), makes UK #32. *Another Nail In My Heart* reaches UK #17.
Apr The group begins its fourth US tour.
May *Pulling Mussels From A Shell* reaches UK #44.
July [28] They perform at the "Dalymount Festival", Dublin, Eire, on a bill with the Police and U2.
Aug After returning to Britain, Holland quits the group. (He initially supports the Police on tour and makes a documentary with them for UK TV, which leads him into becoming a co-host of C4-TV show "The Tube" from 1982 to 1987, and thereafter a regular TV celebrity who relies on his droll wit. He will also front his own band, the Millionaires, releasing ***Jools Holland & His Millionaires*** in 1981, before issuing the solo ***Jools Holland Meets Rock'a'Boogie Billie*** in 1984, and host a late '80s US TV rock series, ending the decade as the new host for BBC-TV's "Juke Box Jury" revival.) He is replaced by ex-Ace vocalist/pianist Paul Carrack (b. Apr. 22, 1951, Sheffield, Yorks.)
Nov [30] Squeeze and Elvis Costello perform a benefit concert at the Top Rank club in Swansea, Wales, for the family of Welsh boxer Johnny Owen, who died from injuries sustained during a world-title bout in Las Vegas, NV.

1981

Mar Tilbrook teams Elvis Costello for a one-off single, *From A Whisper To A Scream*.
June [13] *Is That Love* makes UK #35.
[20] ***East Side Story***, co-produced by Costello with Roger Bechirian, reaches UK #19.
[27] ***East Side Story*** makes US #48.
Aug [1] Soulful *Tempted*, with Carrack on lead vocal, reaches UK #41.
Sept [12] *Tempted* makes US #49.
Nov [7] Country-flavored ballad, *Labelled With Love*, hits UK #4. Prior to its release Carrack leaves to join Carlene Carter's band, replaced by ex-Sincero, Don Snow (b. Jan. 13, 1957, Kenya).

1982

May [1] *Black Coffee In Bed*, with guest vocals from Costello and Paul Young, reaches UK #51.
[15] ***Sweets From A Stranger***, co-produced by the band with Phil McDonald, makes UK #37.
June The group tours the US, including sellout dates at New York's Madison Square Garden.
July [10] ***Sweets From A Stranger*** reaches UK #32.
Oct [30] Following the July release of *When The Hangover Strikes*, the Alan Tarney-produced *Annie Get Your Gun* makes UK #43.
Nov The group announces a split and plays what will be its last show with the current line-up at the three-day "Jamaica World Music Festival", at the Bob Marley Performing Centre near Montego Bay, Jamaica.
[13] Compilation album, ***Singles 45's And Under***, hits UK #3.

1983

Feb "Labelled With Love", a musical based on Difford and Tilbrook songs, opens in Deptford. They decide to stay together to write and will go on to work with Helen Shapiro, Billy Bremner (ex-Rockpile), Paul Young and Holland. Lavis joins Chris Rea's band.

1984

July Difford and Tilbrook's ***Difford And Tilbrook***, co-produced by Tony Visconti and E.T. Thorngren, makes UK #47, while *Love's Crashing Waves* makes UK #57.
Dec [24] Tilbrook gatecrashes a Jools Holland gig in a Greenwich pub to perform *Shake Rattle And Roll*, and the idea to re-form Squeeze is mooted.

1985

Jan [14] Squeeze re-unites for a charity gig at a pub in Catford, London. The reunion becomes permanent with the line-up of Difford, Tilbrook, Holland and Lavis, with Keith Wilkinson (b. Sept. 24, 1954, Southfield, Hereford & Worcester) on bass.
Mar *The Last Time Forever* peaks at UK #45.
Sept ***Cosi Fan Tutti Frutti***, produced by Laurie Latham, reaches UK #31 and US #57.

1986

Apr [28] Holland and Lavis (who breaks an arm) are involved in a car crash returning to London from Plymouth, Devon, after performing in a charity concert for a drug and alcohol rehabilitation center.

1987

Aug *Hourglass* reaches UK #17.
Sept [19] ***Babylon And On***, featuring additional keyboard player, ex-Soft Boy Andy Metcalfe, reaches UK #14 and will make US #36. (Squeeze embarks on another successful US tour, spurred by renewed US chart activity, including further sold out Madison Square Garden concerts in New York.)
Oct [17] Taken from it, *Trust Me To Open My Mouth* peaks at UK #72.
Dec [5] *Hourglass* reaches US #15.

1988

Feb [13] *853 5937*, also from the album, makes US #32.
Aug [28] The group headlines the final day at the annual "Reading Rock Festival".
Sept [7] "Hourglass" wins the Best Special Effects and Best Art Direction categories at the fifth annual MTV Video Music Awards, held at the Universal Amphitheatre, Universal City, CA.

1989

Sept [23] Produced by Tilbrook with Thorngren, ***Frank*** makes UK #58 (and will climb to US #113 the following month).
Oct Difford, Tilbrook, Holland, Lavis and Wilkinson embark on another extensive US trek, set to end on December 11th at the Universal Amphitheatre (and during which, A&M drops the band from its roster).

1990

Jan Holland again leaves the group to devote more time to TV work (not least his highly successful BBC2 music showcase, "Later With Jools Holland" which will bow in 1992), replaced by Matt Irving, while Squeeze prepares to support Fleetwood Mac on another US tour.
Apr [7] Newly signed to Copeland's I.R.S. label, the live album, ***A Round And A Bout***, makes UK #50 in its week of entry.
May [5] Holland's third solo set, ***World Of His Own***, climbs to UK #71. (It will be followed by ***The Full Compliment*** in 1991 and ***The A-Z Of Piano*** two years later, all released on I.R.S.)
[30] The group opens as support to Fleetwood Mac on the US leg of "The Mask" tour in Portland, OR, set to end at the Jones Beach Theatre, Wantagh, NY, on August 2nd.
June [23] ***A Round And A Bout*** makes US #163.

1991

Aug [4] The band, newly signed to Reprise Records and now comprising Difford, Tilbrook, Lavis and Wilkinson, performs at the Crystal Palace Bowl, Crystal Palace, London, on a bill with Level 42, Gary Clail, Big Dish and Witness.
Sept [7] ***Play***, produced by Tony Berg and featuring Bruce Hornsby, Michael Penn, Steve Nieve and Spinal Tap, charts for a week at UK #41.
Oct [16-17] Squeeze play at New York's Beacon Theatre, during its current US tour.
[17] The group guests on NBC-TV's "Late Night With David Letterman".
Dec [22-23] The band plays year-end dates at London's Town & Country club.

1992

Feb [1] Compilation ***Singles 45's And Under*** is certified platinum by the RIAA, for one million US sales.
Apr [25] Reissued *Cool For Cats* debuts at its UK #62 peak.
May [23] ***Greatest Hits*** hits UK #6 (as the group supports Bryan Adams on his "Waking Up The Neighbours" UK stadium tour).
June [23-24] The band plays a pair of acoustic gigs at the Town & Country Club, London.
Dec [20-22] In further dates at the Town & Country, the group is joined onstage by ex-Attractions Pete Thomas and Steve Nieve.

1993

Jan Squeeze begins working on new album at the Real World Studios, with Pete Smith producing.
July [24] *Third Rail* debuts at its UK #39 peak.
Sept [11] *Some Fantastic Place* charts for a week at UK #73.
[25] With Carrack back in the line-up, and now joined by Pete Thomas on drums, the band's ***Some Fantastic Place***, once again penned by Difford and Tilbrook, debuts at its UK #26 peak. (The following week it will enjoy a one-week chart stay at US #182.)
Dec [10-11] The group takes part in the "WNEW-FM Christmas Concert" at the Beacon Theatre, New York.
[22-23] Squeeze play two year-end dates at London's Kentish Town Forum.

1994

July [9] They perform an acoustic show at the Beacon Theatre, with Aimee Mann.
[14-17] Squeeze takes part in the annual "Phoenix Festival" at Long Marston, Stratford-upon-Avon, Warks.
Oct Difford and Tilbrook take part in EMI Music's week-long songwriters' workship at the Huntsham Court Hotel in Devon.
Dec [8] The group embarks on an 11-date UK trip at Leeds' Town & Country club, set to end on the 21st the Island, Ilford, Essex.

1995

Feb [11] They appear on BBC1-TV's "The Danny Baker Show".
July [21] Squeeze performs at the "Heineken Music Festival" at Roundhay Park, Leeds.
Aug [22] A&M (US) re-issues the nine-title Squeeze catalog on CD.
Sept [9] *This Summer* debuts at its UK #36 peak.
Nov [18] *Electric Trains* debuts at its UK #44 peak.
[22] Squeeze plays a near sellout date at The Academy, New York, during a brief US visit.
[25] ***Ridiculous*** makes UK #50 in its week of entry. Aimee Mann's ***I'm With Stupid***, featuring guest work by Difford and Tilbrook, will be released in the US the following February.

LISA STANSFIELD

1986

Having met Andy Morris and Ian Devaney in a Rochdale, Lancs. school musical, and started her musical career at the age of 15, winning several local talent contests, Stansfield (b. Apr. 11, 1966, Rochdale), who more recently has been a presenter on ITV's "Razzamatazz" pop show, formed Blue Zone in 1984, with her two friends (once married, Stansfield also lived with Devaney for two years), pooling their financial resources to build their own self-contained studio. Honed as a soul-funk outfit, Blue Zone now signs, via its own fledgling Rockin' Horse label, to Arista Records, and records its debut album, ***Big Thing***, around self-penned pop/dance songs. (Three singles, all featuring Stansfield's lead vocals, *Jackie*, *On Fire* and *Thinking About His Baby*, will be released, though none will chart.)

1989

Apr UK dance production duo, Matt Black and Jonathan Moore (after Morris and Devaney have worked on their previous hit, *Stop This Crazy Thing*), have invited Stansfield to contribute her soulful voice to their own Coldcut's third single, *People Hold On*, a dance-soul composition, which reaches UK #11. Its success confirms the interest being shown in Stansfield as a solo artist by ex-Wham! manager and Big Life owner, Jazz Summers, who signs her. Devaney and Morris continue to back the soulstress with full writing and production support.

Sept Written by Devaney/Morris/Stansfield, but produced as a one-off by the Coldcut team, her debut solo single, *This Is The Right Time*, reaches UK #13, released on Arista via the Big Life label.

Nov [11] Instant airplay favorite, *All Around The World*, hits UK #1 for the first of two weeks, highlighted by Stansfield's soul-filled vocal performance. It will go on to chart-top in over ten other territories.

Dec [2] Her maiden set, ***Affection***, debuts at its UK #2 peak. Entirely written by the ex-Blue Zone trio, and produced (bar the Coldcut track) by Devaney and Morris, who also play all instruments except an additional trumpet on *The Love In Me*, it will go on to sell over four million copies worldwide, and launch the singer as a major new soul star. (Part of her affable image includes the constant donning of a variety of hats on her UK TV appearances.)

1990

Feb [6] Stansfield collects the Variety Club Of Great Britain Recording Artist Of 1989 honor, at their annual awards lunch in London.

[17] *Live Together* hits UK #10.

[18] She is named Best British Newcomer at the ninth annual BRIT Awards, held at London's Dominion Theatre.

[20] Stansfield is presented to the US media at an Arista pre-Grammy Awards dinner, held at the Beverly Hills Hotel, Beverly Hills, CA.

Mar [17] She participates in the "That's What Friends Are For" benefit, alongside label-mates Whitney Houston, Dionne Warwick, the Four Tops and Daryl Hall & John Oates among others, celebrating Arista Records' 15th anniversary' and raising money for AIDS charities.

Apr [2] Stansfield, Devaney and Morris collect the Best Contemporary Song trophy for *All Around The World*, at the 35th annual Ivor Novello Awards lunch, held at London's Grosvenor House Hotel.

[7] *All Around The World* launches her US career, hitting #3 (it will also top the US R&B chart, with Stansfield becoming only the second white artist to achieve that feat).

[18] Stansfield embarks on the UK leg of her "All Around The World" global tour in Liverpool, Merseyside, set to end on May 14th at the Queen Elizabeth Hall, Oldham, Lancs.

[23] *All Around The World* is certified gold by the RIAA.

May [12] ***Affection*** hits US #9 on the day after her first US tour begins.

[19] A UK EP release, *What Did I Do To You*, reaches UK #25.

[30] ***Affection*** is certified platinum by the RIAA, and will go on to sell four million worldwide.

June [22] She is named Best Newcomer at the annual Nordoff Robbins Music Therapy charity awards lunch,, held at the Grosvenor House Hotel.

July [18] Stansfield participates in the annual "Prince's Trust Rock Gala" at the Wembley Arena, Wembley, Middx.

[28] The US follow-up *You Can't Deny It*, reaches US #14.

Sept [18] European dates re-start, set to climax at the Wembley Arena, at the end of October.

Oct [6] The belated US issue of *This Is The Right Time* reaches US #21, while Stansfield contributes her version of *Down In The Depths*, written for the 1936 stage musical, "Red Hot & Blue", to ***Red, Hot + Blue***, an anthology of Cole Porter updates, released to benefit AIDS awareness.

Dec [23] Band Aid II's re-working of *Do They Know It's Christmas?*, with Stansfield as a featured vocalist, hits UK #1.

1991

Jan Stansfield participates in "Rock In Rio II" in Brazil.

Feb [10] Stansfield is named Best British Female Artist at the tenth annual BRIT Awards and, despite a prior request from organizer Jonathan King not to do so, she is the only winner who mentions the Gulf War in her acceptance speech.

[19] She guests on NBC-TV's "Late Night With David Letterman".

Mar [7] Stansfield is hailed Best New Female Singer in the annual **Rolling Stone** Critics' Picks 1990 music awards.

May [2] *All Around The World* is named International Hit Of The Year at the 36th annual Ivor Novello Awards, again held at the Grosvenor House Hotel.

[12] Stansfield appears live at "The Simple Truth - A Concert For Kurdish Refugees", a benefit for Kurdish refugees at Wembley Arena.

July She puts the finishing touches to her sophomore album at her home studio in Rochdale.

Oct [3] Stansfield is honored at ASCAP's 11th annual London Awards at Claridges for *All Around The World.*

[26] *Change* hits UK #10.

Nov [21] She guests on NBC-TV's "The Tonight Show".

[30] Stansfield takes part in the "Red Hot & Dance" AIDS benefit at London's Brixton Academy.

Dec [28] She appears on ITV's "Amnesty International's Big 30 Concert".

[30] Stansfield guests on ITV's "Des O'Connor Tonight".

1992

Jan [7] The still-climbing ***Real Love*** is certified gold by the RIAA.

[11] Ballad, *All Woman*, reaches UK #20.

[18] ***Real Love***, once again co-penned and produced with Devaney and Morris, hits UK #3, as *Change*, remixed by Frankie Knuckles, reaches US #27.

Feb [8] ***Real Love*** makes US #43.

[12] Stansfield is once again named Best Female Artist at the 11th annual BRIT Awards, held at London's Hammersmith Odeon, at which she also performs.

Apr [11] *Time To Make You Mine* reaches UK #14.

[18] *All Woman* makes US #56.

June [6] *Set Your Loving Free* debuts at its UK #28 peak.

[8] Stansfield begins a re-scheduled 12-date British tour at the Bournemouth International Centre, Bournemouth, Dorset, set to end on the 24th at the National Exhibition Centre, Birmingham, West Midlands.

July [20] She embarks on a short US trek at the Pantages Theater, Hollywood, CA, selling out New York's Radio City Music Hall on the 26th.

Sept [17] Stansfield performs at the Music & Entertainment Industry Chapter of the City Of Hope benefit, at the Century Plaza Hotel, Los Angeles.

Dec She wins an injunction against Sovereign Music to prevent them from releasing early recordings as ***Lisa Stansfield In Session***.

[21] Stansfield appears on BBC2-TV's "Dance Energy Christmas House Party".

1993

Jan [2] *Someday (I'm Coming Back)*, featured in the movie, "The Bodyguard", hits UK #10.

Mar [12] She participates in BBC1-TV's "Total Relief : A Night Of Comic Relief" telethon.

June [10] Stansfield appears on BBC1-TV's "Top Of The Pops" promoting her new single.

[26] *In All The Right Places* hits UK #8.

Oct [23] *So Natural* debuts at its UK #15 peak.

Nov [20] ***So Natural*** bows at its UK #6 high.

Dec [11] *Little Bit Of Heaven* enters at its UK #32 pinnacle.

1994

Aug [23] ***No Prima Donna***, a various artists tribute album to Van Morrison, is released including Stansfield's interpretation of *Friday's Child*.

1995

Oct [17] Having contributed *Dream Away*, a duet with hot R&B producer Babyface, for the motion picture "The Pagemaster", Stansfield's *Just To Keep You Satisfied* is included in the newly-released ***Inner City Blues - The Music Of Marvin Gaye*** tribute album.

THE STAPLE SINGERS

Mavis Staples (vocals); **Cleo Staples** (vocals); **Pervis Staples** (vocals); **"Pop" Staples** (vocals); **Yvonne Staples** (vocals)

1956

The group has been formed in Chicago, IL, in 1951 as a family gospel quartet led by former blues guitarist "Pop" Staples (b. Roebuck Staples, Dec. 28, 1915, Winoma, MS), who has relocated to the windy city in the mid-'30s with his wife Oceola, with son Pervis (b. 1935, Chicago) and daughters Mavis (b. 1940, Chicago) who takes a lead vocal role against her father's light tenor and Cleo (b. Cleotha Staples, 1934, Chicago). Now signed to Vee-Jay Records (having recorded for United in 1954 and already released *Will The Circle Be Unbroken* and *I'm Coming Home*), the quintet has its first major US National Gospel chart-topper with *Uncloudy Day*. (Releasing ***Gospel Program*** (1961), ***Hammers And Nails*** (1962), ***Great Day*** (1963), they go on to record for CBS/Epic Records in 1964, and decide to mix gospel with more mainstream R&B music, though social and moral issues will continue to play a large part in their material's lyric content (as showcased on ***Freedom Highway*** (1965) and ***Why*** (1966).)

1967

June [3] Larry Williams-produced *Why? (Am I Treated So Bad)* gives the group its first US Hot 100 single, at #95.

Oct [7] Their cover of Stephen Stills' *For What It's Worth* peaks at US #66, taken from ***For What It's Worth***.

1968

July The group switches to Stax Records, where its first producer is house band guitar-mainstay Steve Cropper, whose purist production values fail to secure chart success.

Aug [27-29] The group plays at the Fillmore West in San Francisco, CA, on a bill with the Grateful Dead, Steppenwolf and Santana. By year's end, their Stax debut, ***Soul Folk In Action*** is released, closely followed by ***We'll Get Over***, both showcasing Mavis' mournful, soulful vocal quality.

1970

Sept [12] Still within the family group, Mavis' solo single *I Have Learned To Do Without You* peaks at US #87, while her solo album ***Only For The Lonely***, which follows last year's maiden effort, ***Mavis Staples***, makes US #188.

1971

Mar The family's first crossover chart album ***The Staple Singers*** makes US #117.
Apr The group tours the US with the Bee Gees. Pervis leaves to serve his US military service, and is replaced by his sister Yvonne (b. 1939, Chicago) - he will not return to the line-up.
[10] Now produced by Al Bell, the group has its first Top 30 single with their cover of Bobby Bloom's *Heavy Makes You Happy (Sha-Na-Boom Boom)*, at US #27. (Bell will continue to produce the group throughout its stay with Stax, until 1974.)
June The Staple Singers' appearances in Ghana, Africa, earlier in the year are included in film "Soul To Soul", which also features Ike & Tina Turner, Wilson Pickett and Santana.
Aug [7] *You've Got To Earn It* peaks at US #97.
Dec [25] *Respect Yourself* hits US #12 and US R&B #2.

1972

Feb Its parent album, ***Beatitude : Respect Yourself*** makes US #19.
June [3] The band tops the US chart with their version of Alvertis Isbell's *I'll Take You There*, earning a gold disc, and set to reach UK #30.
Sept [2] *This World* makes US #38.

1973

Apr [28] *Oh La De Da* makes US #33.
June [30] *Be What You Are* peaks at US #66.
Aug ***Be What You Are*** climbs to US #102. The group is featured in the movie "Wattstax" alongside Isaac Hayes, Rufus Thomas and Richard Pryor.
Dec [19] Set-to-peak *If You're Ready (Come Go With Me)* is certified gold by the RIAA.
[22] The second single from ***Be What You Are***, *If You're Ready (Come Go With Me)*, hits US #9.

1974

Jan [23] The group performs at the annual "Midem Festival", Cannes, France.
Apr [13] *Touch A Hand, Make A Friend* reaches US #23.
June *If You're Ready (Come Go With Me)* makes UK #34.
Sept [7] *City In The Sky* peaks at US #79.
City In The Sky makes US #125.
Dec [21] Their last Stax release, *My Main Man* stops at US #76.

1975

Apr A one-off album on the Milestone label, ***Great Day***, produced by Orrin Keepnews, is released.
Nov [24] The still-climbing *Let's Do It Again* is certified gold by the RIAA.
Dec [27] Newly signed to Curtis Mayfield's Curtom label, and produced by Mayfield, the group achieves its second US #1 with the Mayfield-written *Let's Do It Again*, the title track to the Sidney Poitier/Bill Cosby-starring film, and featured on ***Let's Do It Again*** which climbs to US #20.

1976

Mar [27] Again from ***Let's Do It Again***, *New Orleans* makes US #70.
Oct [16] Now signed to Warner Bros. Records, as the Staples, their label debut ***Pass It On*** peaks at US #155.
Nov [25] The group performs at "The Last Waltz", a celebrity-packed celebration of the Band's final concert at San Francisco, CA's Winterland Auditorium, with Mavis and Roebuck joining the group on *The Weight*. (Remaining with Warner Bros. through to decade's end, the Staple Singers will release ***Family Tree*** (1977) and ***Unlock Your Mind*** (1978) which together yield five US R&B hits. Mavis' will record ***A Piece Of The Action*** (1977) and ***Oh, What A Feeling*** (1979.)

1984

Nov UK band the Kane Gang reaches UK #21 with a cover of *Respect Yourself*, while Talking Head's version of the Staple's *Slippery People* simultaneously makes UK #68. (Ruby Turner's treatment of their *If You're Ready (Come Go With Me)* will also reach UK #30 in 1986.) The Staple Singers have recently signed to the Private label, releasing ***Turning Point*** to be followed by ***The Staple Singers*** in 1985 (their final album of the decade), this pair again yielding five US R&B hits.

1990

Aug Prince's movie "Graffiti Bridge", featuring Mavis in the role of Melody Cool, premieres in the US. (She is also signed as a solo artist to his Paisley Park label which has released her ***Time Waits For No-One*** the previous year.)

1991

Sept [9] British Electric Foundation's ***Music Of Quality & Distinction Volume 2***, on which Mavis is featured, is released in UK.
Dec [13] Mavis performs at the seventh annual Stellar Awards for gospel music at Royce Hall, UCLA, Los Angeles, CA.

1992

Jan [11] Bebe and CeCe Winans' *I'll Take You There*, featuring Mavis Staples, peaks at US #90.
Feb [26] The group is recognized at the Rhythm and Blues Foundation's third Annual Pioneer Awards at New York's Rainbow Room, for which they receive a financial award, for their contribution to the wider recognition of R&B.
June [2] The Staples guest on NBC-TV's "Late Night With David Letterman".
July [4] Pops Staples, currently promoting his solo album ***The Neighborhood***, co-produced by Bonnie Raitt and featuring covers of Jackson Browne's *World In Motion* and the Los Lobos' title track, takes part in BBC-Radio 1's "American Music Festival Blues Day" at London's Crystal Palace Bowl.

1994

Mar [23] The group takes part in "Rhythm Country And Blues - The Concert", benefitting the Country Music Foundation and the Rhythm and Blues Foundation, at the Universal Amphitheatre, Universal City, CA.
Apr [30] They participate in the 25th annual "New Orleans Jazz & Heritage Festival".

1995

Mar [1] Patriarch Pops collects the Best Contemporary Blues Album trophy (for his 1994 album ***Father Father***) at the 37th annual Grammy Awards, staged at Los Angeles' Shrine Auditorium.

RINGO STARR

1970

Feb [22] Raised from the age of three by his step-father and mother, Starr (b. Richard Starkey, July 7, 1940, Dingle, Liverpool, Lancs.), who suffered from pleurisy as a child and took his first job working for British Railways in 1955, was the drummer with Rory Storm & the Hurricanes before playing his first live gig with the Beatles on August 18th, 1962. Having subsequently become a household name as one of the recently split Fab Four (and performed the very occasional lead vocal, notably on *Yellow Submarine*) he has already appeared as a Mexican gardener in "Candy", an Italian/French film adaptation of Voltaire's "Candide", which opened at Kensington's Odeon Cinema, London, on February 20th the previous year, is now featured as Youngman Grand, the adopted son of the world's richest man, Sir Guy Grand (played by Peter Sellers), in "The Magic Christian", which now premieres in New York, NY. (Starr has also guested in NBC-TV's "Rowan & Martin's Laugh-In", on January 27th.)
Apr Released on the Beatles' Apple label, Starr's solo debut, ***Sentimental Journey***, hits UK #7 and US #22, with Starr claiming "I did it for me mum!". The commercial value of being an ex-Beatle going solo is exemplified by this George Martin-produced selection of standards, including *Night And Day* and *Bye Bye Blackbird*. Arrangers on the album include the Bee Gees' Maurice Gibb, Elmer Bernstein, Johnny Dankworth, Les Reed and Quincy Jones.
June [30] Starr flies to Nashville, TN, to begin recording tracks for a forthcoming album.
Oct Nashville album, ***Beaucoups Of Blues***, makes US #65. Using songs commissioned from top C&W writers and produced by pedal steel guitarist, Pete Drake, and engineered by Elvis Presley's guitarist, Scotty Moore, it features top country musicians, including Jerry Reed, the Jordanaires (Elvis Presley's backing vocalists) and Charlie Daniels.
Nov [28] Title cut, *Beaucoups Of Blues*, peaks at US #87.

1971

Apr [25] Starr appears live on BBC1-TV's "Cilla" show.
June [5] The self-penned *It Don't Come Easy*, featuring guitar work from producer George Harrison and Stephen Stills, hits both UK and US #4, as he begins shooting the film "Blindman".
Aug [1] Starr appears with Eric Clapton, Bob Dylan, Billy Preston, Leon Russell and others at the George Harrison-organized "Concert For Bangla Desh" benefit.
[3] *It Don't Come Easy* is certified gold by the RIAA.
Nov [10] Frank Zappa's film, "200 Motels", in which Starr has the dual roles of Larry the Dwarf and Frank Zappa, premieres in New York.
[15] "Blindman", a spaghetti western in which he plays an outlaw called Candy, premieres in Rome, Italy.

1972

May [13] The Harrison-produced *Back Off Boogaloo* hits UK #2 and US #9.
Nov Starr appears as Uncle Ernie in Lou Reizner's all-star album drawn from the Who's ***Tommy***.
Dec [14] "Born To Boogie", a film of T. Rex in concert at Wembley, recorded on March 18th, and Starr's debut as a director, premieres at the Oscar 1 cinema in London.

1973

Apr [12] "That'll Be The Day", in which Starr plays a teddy boy, premieres at the ABC2 cinema, Shaftesbury Avenue, London.
Sept [18] Starr buys Tittenhurst Park from John and Yoko Lennon.
Nov [24] *Photograph*, co-written with Harrison, tops the US chart for one week and hits UK #8. ***Ringo*** hits UK #7 and US #2, produced by Richard Perry, and including ex-Beatle contributions (notably Lennon's *I'm The Greatest*, which features all but Paul McCartney).
Dec [28] *Photograph* is certified gold by the RIAA.

1974

Jan [26] With Harry Nilsson on "shoo-wops", and a kazoo vocal by McCartney, *You're Sixteen*, Starr's cover of Johnny Burnette's 1960 US #8 hit, hits US #1, and UK #3.
[31] *You're Sixteen* is certified gold by the RIAA.
Apr [7] BBC Radio 1 airs Starr's personal musical favorites in "My Top Twelve".
[27] *Oh My My* hits US #5.
Dec ***Goodnight Vienna***, again produced by Perry and using top Los Angeles, CA session men, reaches UK

#30 and US #8.
[9] ***Goodnight Vienna*** is certified gold by the RIAA.

1975

Jan [11] His version of the Platters' 1955 smash, *Only You*, makes UK #28 and hits US #6, his last UK hit single.
Apr [5] *No No Song*, written by Hoyt Axton, hits US #3.
[28] Starr guests on NBC-TV's "The Smothers Brothers Comedy Hour".
July [12] *It's All Down To Goodnight Vienna* makes US #31. Starr appears as the Pope in Ken Russell's film, "Lisztomania".
[17] Starr and his wife Maureen are divorced. (She will die of cancer in 1994.)

1976

Jan [17] Greatest hits album, ***Blast From Your Past***, reaches US #30.
[25] He joins Bob Dylan on stage for his "Night Of The Hurricane II" benefit concert for boxer Ruben "Hurricane" Carter, at the Astrodome, Houston, TX.
Mar [10] Starr signs with Polydor in the UK and Atlantic in the US.
Nov [6] *A Dose Of Rock'n'Roll* reaches US #26.
[13] ***Ringo's Rotogravure***, another all-star session, this time produced by Arif Mardin, makes US #28.
[25] Starr appears with a host of stars performing *I Shall Be Released* at the Band's "The Last Waltz" farewell concert, from the Winterland Ballroom, San Francisco, CA.
Dec He starts shooting "Sextette", Mae West's last film, at Paramount Studios in Hollywood, CA, with Tony Curtis, Timothy Dalton and Keith Moon.

1977

Feb [12] His treatment of Bruce Channel's 1962 US chart-topper, *Hey Baby*, peaks at US #74.
Nov [12] ***Ringo The 4th*** peaks at US #162.
Dec "Scouse The Mouse" is released, with Starr in the title role of this children's story, written by British actor, Donald Pleasence.

1978

Apr [26] TV special, "Ringo", a musical adaptation of "The Prince And The Pauper", narrated by George Harrison, airs on NBC-TV. (Ratings released the following week, show that it finished 53rd out of 65 programs.)
May ***Bad Boy*** peaks at US #129. A collection of cover versions, it includes the Supremes' *Where Did Our Love Go* and Gallagher & Lyle's *Heart On My Sleeve*.

1979

Apr Starr has a life-saving intestinal operation in Monte Carlo, Monaco.
May [19] He teams with McCartney and Harrison to play at Eric Clapton's wedding reception.
June [8] Starr drums on NBC-TV's "Midnight Special".
Sept [3] He appears on Jerry Lewis' annual Muscular Dystrophy telethon.
Nov [28] His Los Angeles home is destroyed by fire.

1980

Feb [18] Starr begins filming "Caveman" in Durango, Mexico, where he meets future wife, actress Barbara Bach.
May [19] Driving to a party in southwest London, Starr and Bach are involved in a serious car smash, less than half a mile from where Marc Bolan has been killed. Although their car is a write-off, they are not seriously hurt.

1981

Apr [27] Starr and Bach marry.
Nov ***Stop And Smell The Roses***, issued on the Boardwalk label, but originally intended for Columbia release as ***Can't Fight Lightning*** (with extra tracks), makes US #98. McCartney and Harrison contribute and Van Dyke Parks produces a new version of *Back Off Boogaloo* for the album, featuring a medley of Beatles and Starr songs.
Dec [12] Starr guests on BBC1-TV's "Parkinson" chat-show, as *Wrack My Brain* makes US #38.

1983

Nov [6-7] Judith Krantz's "Princess Daisy", in which Mr. and Mrs. Starr appear, airs on US TV.

1984

July [4] He guests at two Beach Boys gigs in one day, an afternoon show in Washington, DC, and an evening concert in Miami, FL.
Oct [9] Children's series, "Thomas The Tank Engine And Friends", narrated by Starr, premieres on ITV (and will become a long-running worldwide success).
Nov Mr. and Mrs. Starr appear in Paul McCartney's premiering film, "Give My Regards To Broad Street". Starr's ***Old Wave***, co-produced with Joe Walsh, is released in Canada and Germany only.
Dec [8] Starr guests on NBC-TV's "Saturday Night Live".

1985

Jan [18] "Water", in which Starr guests with Harrison and Clapton, premieres in London.
[22] He becomes a father-in-law when his son, Zak, marries Sarah Menikedes, although he is not aware of it at the time.
Mar [11] Starr films a cameo appearance for Bill Wyman's video, "Willie & The Poor Boys".
Sept [7] He is the first Beatle to become a grandfather when Zak and Sarah have a daughter, Tatia Jayne.
Oct [21] Starr takes part in the Carl Perkins' C4-TV special, "Blue Suede Shoes", with Eric Clapton, Dave Edmunds, Harrison and others, recorded at Limehouse Studios in London. (The program is shown at Christmas and subsequently released on video.)
Dec [9] Starr appears as the Mock Turtle in a US TV production of "Alice In Wonderland".
[14] Starr and son Zak both contribute to the ***Artists United Against Apartheid*** album, from which *Sun City* makes US #38 and UK #21.

1986

Sept [24] The second "Thomas The Tank Engine" series premieres on ITV.

1987

June [5-6] Starr takes part in the "Prince's Trust Rock Gala" at Wembley Arena, Wembley, Middx., singing *With A Little Help From My Friends*, with George Harrison, Elton John and Jeff Lynne.
Sept [26] Starr's co-owned restaurant, the London Brasserie, opens in Atlanta, GA.

1988

Jan [20] He attends the third annual Rock and Roll Hall of Fame dinner, at the Waldorf Astoria Hotel, New York, with Harrison and Yoko Ono, celebrating the Beatles induction.
Feb He appears in a video for Harrison's Beatles-recalling hit, *When We Was Fab*.
Mar [3] Starr and Harrison appear on ITV chat-show, "Aspel & Co."
Aug Reports emanate from US that Starr, Harrison and Lynne are forming a group and intend to tour.
Oct [11] The Starrs begin treatment for an alcohol abuse problem in Tucson, AZ.

1989

Jan The Walt Disney album, ***Stay Awake***, to which Starr has contributed his version of *When You Wish Upon A Star*, is released.
Feb He hosts US syndicated TV's weekly show, "Shining Time Station", playing 18" tall Mr. Conductor, a revamp of his "Thomas The Tank Engine" clips. (The show will be nominated for an Emmy Award.)
Mar [5] He contributes to *Spirit Of The Forest*, an ecology benefit single.
[27] Starr records *Act Naturally* with country star Buck Owens, at Abbey Road Studios in London.
Apr Rhino Records in the US releases the compilation, ***Starrstruck : Ringo's Best 1976-83***.
June [13] Starr joins Bob Dylan on stage at the latter's Les Arenes, Frejus, France, concert.
[20] He announces a comeback tour with his All-Starr Band, comprising Dr. John, Billy Preston, Joe Walsh, Rick Danko, Levon Helm, Nils Lofgren, Jim Keltner and Clarence Clemons, and later that evening guests on NBC-TV's "Late Night With David Letterman".
July [23] Ringo Starr & His All-Starr Band begin a 30-date "Tour For All Generations" North American trek (the first by a Beatle in 13 years), at the Park Central Amphitheater, Dallas, TX, set to end on September 4th at the Greek Theatre, Los Angeles.
[26] Starr succeeds in temporarily blocking the release of a Chips Moman-produced album, because of his dissatisfaction with his own performance. In his lawsuit, Starr contends that the recording quality was not up to standard because Moman brought alcoholic beverages into the sessions. Atlanta's Fulton County Superior Court Judge Clarence Cooper presides over the case.
Aug [11] Bruce Springsteen joins Starr on stage for four numbers (*Get Back*, *Long Tall Sally*, *Photograph* and *With A Little Help From My Friend*) at the Garden State Arts Center, Holmdel, NJ, with actor John Candy also making an appearance on tambourine.
Oct [14-15] Starr gives a party in Cannes, France, to celebrate one year of sobriety.
[30] Starr and his band begin a seven-date Japanese tour at the Rainbow Hall, Nagoya, set to end on November 8th at the Yokohoma Arena.
Nov [15] He testifies in Atlanta to block the release of the 1987 Chips Moman album, and will win a permanent court order blocking its release.

1990

Jan [5] Judge Cooper rules that Moman hands over recordings in exchange for $74,000 in expenses.
Mar [22] Starr, with Lynne, Petty, Walsh and Keltner, records *I Call Your Name*, as part of a John Lennon tribute to be held in Liverpool on May 5th.
Apr [12] Starr dubs the voice of the cartoon Ringo Starr in Fox-TV's "The Simpsons".

1991

May Starr begins work on his debut album for the Private Music label with producer Jeff Lynne.
Aug He continues recording at Conway Recording in Los Angeles, with Don Was producing.
Nov Starr's *You Never Know*, penned by Steve Dorff and John Bettis, and featured in the "Curly Sue" movie, is released on the Giant label.
[26] His 1973 album ***Ringo*** is certified platinum by the RIAA.
Dec [2] *It Don't Come Easy* is recognized for one million US broadcast performances at the annual BMI Awards held at London's Dorchester Hotel.

1992

Apr [2] Starr announces his upcoming tour at a press conference at New York's Radio City Music Hall.
[3] He guests on NBC-TV's "Late Night With David Letterman".
June [2-3] Starr embarks on a world tour at the Sunrise Music Theatre, Sunrise, FL.
[6] *Weight Of The World* charts for a week at UK #74. It is taken from the non-charting ***Time Takes Time***, variously produced by Peter Asher, Lynne, Phil Ramone and Was, and includes contributions from Nilsson, Brian Wilson, Andrew Gold, Jellyfish and Petty, among others.
[25] Starr performs at "Summerfest '92, The Big Encore" at the Marcus Amphitheatre, Milwaukee, WI.
July [2] Scandinavian leg of his tour begins in Gothenberg, Sweden, with Starr leaving his hand-prints in cement at the Celebrities Plaza in the Liseberg Amusement Park.
[6] Starr returns home to play at the Empire Theatre, Liverpool.
[24] The European leg of the tour ends at Foro Italico, Rome, Italy.

Aug [1] US dates resume with a show at Champs de Brionne, George, WA.
Oct [23] Starr sings *With A Little Help From My Friends* with Nils Lofgren, Jimmy Buffett and James Taylor, on the first day of the three-day Ringo Starr Celebrity Weekend benefit, at Loews Ventana Canyon Resort, Tucson, AZ.

1993

Apr [16] Starr joins McCartney on stage for *Hey Jude* at the latter's "Earth Day" concert set, at the Hollywood Bowl, Hollywood, CA.
[24] He debuts his new backing band - the New Maroons, with Benmont Tench (keyboards), Alex Duvall (bass), Was (guitar) and Jonell Masser (vocals), at "Farm Aid VI", held in Ames, IA.
June [6] Starr attends the Pediatric AIDS Foundation's fourth annual picnic in Brentwood, CA.
Sept [7] ***Volume Two : Live From Montreux***, recorded with his All-Starr Band on last year's tour, is released in the US by Rykodisc.

1995

Apr Having reunited with McCartney and Harrison to assemble two new tracks for the forthcoming Beatles' ***Anthology*** project, and appear in the acompanying documentary, Starr has teamed with Stevie Nicks to contribute *Lay Down Your Arms* to the newly-released Harry Nilsson tribute album, ***For The Love Of Harry (Everybody Sings Nilsson)***.
May [25] He guests on CBS-TV's "Late Show With David Letterman".
June [29] A Pizza Hut commercial, featuring Starr as the drummer in a re-formed Monkees with Davy Jones, Mickey Dolenz and Peter Tork, premieres on US TV. (He is paid a reported $500,000.)
July [8] Ringo and his All-Starr Band, now comprising his son Zak, Billy Preston, Felix Cavaliere, Mark Farner, Randy Bachman and John Entwistle, embarks on a US tour at the Star Plaza Theatre, Merrillville, IN. (The last six dates on the tour will be cancelled, after Starr's daughter becomes gravely ill.)
see also: **THE BEATLES**

STATUS QUO

Francis Rossi (guitar, vocals); **Rick Parfitt** (guitar, vocals); **Alan Lancaster** (bass); **John Coghlan** (drums)

1962

Lancaster (b. Feb. 7, 1949, Peckham, London) and friend Alan Key join their Beckenham, Kent comprehensive school orchestra, playing trombone and trumpet respectively, and also form a trad jazz combo. This evolves into a beat group, with Lancaster on bass and Key and his friend Rossi - then calling himself Mike - (b. Apr. 29, 1949, Forest Hill, London) playing guitars. Class-mate Jess Jaworski is talked into trading in his new guitar for a Vox organ, and joins the group when Key quits. With a friend playing drums, they make their live debut at the Samuel Jones sports club in Dulwich. After adding permanent drummer Coghlan (b. Sept. 19, 1946, Dulwich, London), they call themselves the Spectres.

1964

After regular working men's club appearances, local gas-fitter Pat Barlow offers to manage them, and secures the act a Monday night residency at the Café des Artistes in London's Brompton Road. He also arranges a gig on the same bill as the Hollies, which doubles as an audition for a residency as a Butlins holiday-camp group.

1965

They accept a four-month Butlins summer contract. Jaworski decides to continue his education and is replaced by Roy Lynes (b. Nov. 25, 1943, Redhill, Surrey). They also meet Parfitt (b. Richard Harrison, Oct. 12, 1948, Woking, Surrey), who is playing at UK holiday camps. (He will join the group two years later.)

1966

Apr Songwriter Ronnie Scott introduces the group to John Schroeder, Pye Records' recording manager.

1967

Mar Following the release of three singles - *I (Who Have Nothing)*, *Hurdy Gurdy Man*, and *We Ain't Got Nothin' Yet*, the Spectres name-change to Traffic Jam, at the same time as Steve Winwood forms Traffic, and release *Almost But Not Quite There*.
Nov At Barlow's suggestion, the group becomes Status Quo, and is signed to the main Pye label.

1968

Feb *Pictures Of Matchstick Men*, with Parfitt in the group, hits UK #7, while the group is working as Madeleine Bell's backing band, and with Barlow still their part-time manager.
[23] The band plays a four-date tour of Scotland, opening at Glasgow University, Glasgow, Strathclyde.
Apr Follow-up single, *Black Veils Of Melancholy*, is released.
[5] The group begins a 28-date, twice-nightly UK tour with Gene Pitney, Amen Corner, Don Partridge, Simon Dupree & the Big Sound and others, at the Odeon Theatre, Lewisham, London, set to end on May 7th at the Granada Theatre, Walthamstow, London.
June The **New Musical Express** reports that Rossi has been invited to write the title song and incidental music for the French film, "Je", which begins production in August.
Aug [3] *Pictures Of Matchstick Men* reaches US #12 prompting a US tour.
Sept Their debut album, ***Picturesque Matchstickable Messages***, is released. In addition to the singles, it includes covers of the Bee Gees' *Spicks And Specks*, the Lemon Pipers' *Green Tambourine* and Tommy Roe's *Sheila*.
Oct [7] The band returns to the US for ten days of promotional dates.
[12] *Ice In The Sun*, co-written by singer Marty Wilde, hits UK #8 and peaks at US #70. The band is currently promoted with smartly chic outfits.

1969

Jan [24-25] The group takes part in the all-night "Midnite Rave - Part 2", with Love Sculpture, Gun, Joe Cocker, Aynsley Dunbar and others.
Mar [16] A US tour opens in Philadelphia, PA.
Apr Status Quo supports Gene Pitney on a UK tour, as it begins to mix a pop sound with a subsequently-dominant 12-bar blues style.
May Ballad, *Are You Growing Tired Of My Love*, peaks at UK #46.
Oct ***Spare Parts*** fails to chart as the members decide to grow their hair, and permanently switch to a harder musical direction.

1970

July Boogie-tinged *Down The Dustpipe* reaches UK #12, as Lynes quits the band.
Aug ***Ma Kelly's Greasy Spoon*** is released. Blues-based, it includes *Junior's Wailing*, their cover of a song by blues band, Steamhammer, which will become one of the group's most popular live cuts.
Dec *In My Chair*, penned by Rossi and group tour-manager Bob Young (who will co-write many of the group's future hits), reaches UK #21. Its follow-up, *Tune To The Music*, marking the beginning a two-year chart absence, will be issued the following June with their final
Nov Final Pye album, ***Dog Of Two Heads*** released in November.

1972

Jan As the band leaves the label, it begins building a solid cult following on the club circuit, playing a heavier brand of blues and boogie, and signs to Phonogram's new rock subsidiary, Vertigo Records.
May [10] Status Quo begins a UK tour in Bradford, W. Yorks., supporting Slade.
July The group receives critical and popular acclaim performing at the "British Great Western Festival" in Lincoln, Lincs. (and the "Reading Rock Festival", Reading, Berks., in August).

1973

Jan Their self-produced debut Vertigo album, ***Piledriver*** enters the UK chart, set to hit #5. Status Quo has now defined its classic long-haired image onstage initiating a heads-down, no-nonsense rock act, which sets the style and pose for a myriad of UK heavy-metal groups, none of which will be so successful for so long.
Feb *Paper Plane* hits UK #8, as Status Quo tours Australia supporting Slade.
May *Mean Girl*, from the last Pye album, reaches UK #20.
June Pye-released compilation ***The Best Of Status Quo***, peaks at UK #32.
Aug The group performs again at the annual "Reading Rock Festival".
Oct Vertigo-issued single, *Caroline*, written in 1970, hits UK #5.
[27] Self-produced album, ***Hello***, with ex-Herd member Andy Bown guesting on keyboards, enters the UK chart at #1.

1974

May *Break The Rules* hits UK #8 as its parent album, ***Quo***, hits UK #2.

1975

Jan [18] *Down Down*, produced by Roger Glover, becomes Status Quo's only UK singles chart-topper.
Mar [1] ***On The Level*** hits UK #1 for the first of two weeks. Pye releases ***Down The Dustpipe***, featuring 1970-71 material, on its Golden Hour label, which reaches UK #20, as the group embarks on a two-month US tour.
June Three-track live EP, *Roll Over Lay Down*, with *Gerdundula* and *Junior's Wailing*, with sleeve notes by UK DJ John Peel, hits UK #9.

1976

Mar [6] *Rain* hits UK #7.
[20] Its parent album, ***Blue For You***, begins a three-week run at UK #1, helped by Phonogram's marketing deal with Levi's jeans (a Status Quo trademark), which sees the record advertised in 6,000 clothes shops (one of the first sponsorship tie-ups between a commercial product and rock music in the UK).
[28] After an incident at Vienna Airport, Vienna, Austria, Rossi, Parfitt and Lancaster are arrested. Lancaster is charged with assaulting an airport official, and the other two with resisting arrest. They are released on bail.
May [15] ***Status Quo*** is the group's only US chart album, reaching #148 during a seven-week stay.
July [24] The group tops a bill featuring Hawkwind, Curved Air, the Strawbs and Budgie, at Cardiff Castle, Cardiff, South Glamorgan, Wales.
Aug [14] *Mystery Song* hits UK #11.
Oct The Rolling Stones' mobile studio is brought to Glasgow's Apollo Theatre to record three concerts. Tickets for the shows have sold out within hours. Former Herd keyboardist, Andy Bown, joins the live line-up.

1977

Jan [22] *Wild Side Of Life*, reviving Tommy Quickly's 1964 hit, and produced by ex-Deep Purple bassist Roger Glover, hits UK #9. In Vienna, the three Status Quo defendants plead guilty to a reduced charge of obstructing the police, and are fined a total of £3,200.
Mar ***Status Quo - Live*** hits UK #3. The band begins a world tour that will take it to Europe, the Far East, and Australasia.
Nov [19] Their version of John Fogerty's *Rockin' All Over The World*, is released during the UK leg of the tour, hitting UK #3. (When Status Quo performs it on

BBC1-TV show, "Top Of The Pops", Lancaster, now semi-resident in Australia, is substituted by a life-size string puppet, discreetly playing bass in the background.)
Dec [3] ***Rockin' All Over The World***, with Pip Williams co-producing, hits UK #5.

1978

Aug [26] The band makes its only UK appearance of the year, headlining the second day of the 18th National Jazz Blues & Rock Festival "Reading Rock '78", near Reading, Berks. For tax reasons, Status Quo will not reside in the UK throughout the year, touring in Australia and recording new material in Hilversum in Holland for ***If You Can't Stand The Heat***.
Sept *Again And Again* reaches UK #13.
Nov ***If You Can't Stand The Heat*** hits UK #3.
Dec *Accident Prone* makes UK #36, as Status Quo returns to Hilversum for further recording.

1979

Oct *Whatever You Want*, written by Parfitt and Bown, hits UK #4, while its parent album, ***Whatever You Want***, hits UK #3, despite music press criticism of the band's supposed three-chord rock limitations.
Nov [25] The group takes part in **The Sun**/ Goaldiggers Five-A-Side Soccer tournament at the Empire Pool, Wembley, Middx., with Manfred Mann's Earth Band and the Electric Light Orchestra.
Dec Rare ballad, *Living On An Island*, co-penned by Parfitt and Young, reaches UK #16.

1980

Mar Vertigo compilation, ***12 Gold Bars***, hits UK #3.
Oct ***Just Supposin'*** hits UK #4, as the extracted *What You're Proposing* hits UK #2.

1981

Jan [17] *Lies*, backed with *Don't Drive My Car*, reaches UK #11.
Mar [6] Status Quo begins a UK tour in St. Austell, Cornwall.
[7] ***Never Too Late*** hits UK #2.
[28] The extracted *Something 'Bout You Baby I Like* hits UK #9.
June [26] The group is honored with the Silver Clef Award at the sixth annual Nordoff Robbins Music Therapy Centre lunch, in London.
Oct [10] ***Fresh Quota***, a rarities album from the PRT label, spends a week at UK #74.
Dec [26] *Rock'n'Roll*, a ballad from ***Just Supposin'***, hits UK #8.

1982

Mar Coghlan leaves during the recording of a new album in Montreux, Switzerland, to concentrate on his own band, Diesel, to be replaced by Pete Kircher (b. Jan. 21, 1948, Folkestone, Kent), ex-Honeybus and the Original Mirrors.
Apr [17] *Dear John* hits UK #10.
[23] The band begins another British tour.
[24] ***1982*** is the group's fourth UK chart-topping album.
May Status Quo performs a BBC-televised show at the National Exhibition Centre, Birmingham, West Midlands, attended by the Prince and Princess of Wales - with all proceeds going to the Prince's Trust charity. (The show is also recorded for a live album.)
June [26] *She Don't Fool Me* makes UK #36.
Nov [6] *Caroline*, recorded live at the National Exhibition Centre, Birmingham, reaches UK #13.
[27] ***From The Makers Of ...***, a three-album set including a live album from the National Exhibition Centre, as well as a selection of hits on both Pye and Vertigo, hits UK #4.

1983

Sept *Ol' Rag Blues* hits UK #9.
Nov *A Mess Of The Blues* reaches UK #15.
Dec ***Back To Back*** hits UK #9. (During the year, Lancaster, who now only plays with the band on an ad-hoc basis, relocates to Australia.)

1984

Jan Displaying their lightest pop side to date, *Marguerita Time* hits UK #3, as the band begins its UK "The End Of The Road Tour".
June *Going Down Town Tonight*, the fourth single from ***Back To Back***, reaches UK #20.
July [21] The group ends its UK tour topping the bill at Milton Keynes Bowl, Milton Keynes, Bucks., filmed for later video release.
Aug Dutch import album, ***Live At The NEC***, reaches UK #83.
Nov Their revival of Dion's *The Wanderer* hits UK #7. Lancaster quits the line-up.
[25] Parfitt and Rossi contribute to the historic all-star recording of Band Aid's *Do They Know It's Christmas?*.
Dec A second TV-advertised album, ***12 Gold Bars***, reaches UK #12.

1985

May While Parfitt records an unissued solo album, Rossi's duet with Bernard Frost on *Modern Romance (I Want To Fall In Love Again)* makes UK #54.
July [13] Lancaster rejoins Status Quo to perform at the "Live Aid" benefit spectacular at Wembley Stadium, Wembley. They set the tone for the event by opening with *Rockin' All Over The World*. (By the time the group has gone back to the studio, however, Lancaster has taken out an injunction to stop the others playing without him as Status Quo. A ruling eventually sides with Rossi and Parfitt. Kircher also quits the line-up. The group fails to release a single during the year, breaking a run of achieving a Top 20 hit each year since 1973.)

1986

May Status Quo, with a line-up of Rossi, Parfitt, Bown, bassist John Edwards and ex-Climax Blues Band drummer Jeff Rich, re-emerges with the Dave Edmunds-produced *Rollin' Home*, which hits UK #9.
July [11-12] They support Queen for two nights at Wembley Stadium.
Aug *Red Sky* hits UK #19.
[9] The band appears in front of a 200,000 crowd at the "Knebworth Festival", Knebworth, Herts.
Sept ***In The Army Now*** hits UK #7.
Nov *In The Army Now*, penned by German pop-writers Bolland and Bolland, hits UK #2.

1987

Jan *Dreamin'* reaches UK #15.
Aug [29] The group headlines the second day of the annual "Reading Festival".

1988

Apr *Ain't Complaining* makes UK #19. During the month, Quo apologizes to the United Nations for appearing at Sun City, South Africa, and are removed from the cultural register of blacklisted entertainers.
June *Who Gets The Love* peaks at UK #34.
[12] Its parent album, ***Ain't Complaining***, bows at its UK #12 peak.
Sept *Running All Over The World*, a revised jogging version of *Rockin' All Over The World* altered for Sport Aid, reaches UK #17.

1989

Jan *Burning Bridges (On And Off And On Again)*, their 39th consecutive chart single, hits UK #5. In terms of chart achievements, Status Quo are now the most successful UK group ever, leading the Rolling Stones (with 34 hits) and the Hollies (with 31). The band ends a major UK tour, portraying itself as a non-alcohol, non-drug-taking outfit, after recent media reports about their hell-raising past.
Oct *Not At All* makes UK #50.
Dec [2] ***Perfect Remedy*** enters at its UK #49 peak.

1990

Oct *Anniversary Waltz Part 1*, a medley of rock'n'roll standards in non-stop Quo style, hits UK #2.
[20] The compilation album, ***Rockin' All Over The Years***, also hits UK #2 in its week of entry.
Nov [30] The group embarks on a 12-date UK tour at the Newport Centre, Newport, Gwent, Wales, set to end on December 17th at the Brighton Centre, Brighton, East Sussex.

1991

Feb [10] The group is honored with Outstanding Contribution To The British Music Industry at the tenth annual BRIT Awards, at London's Dominion Theatre, and celebrates by disrobing regulation black-tie formal wear to reveal their traditional jeans'n't-shirt uniform.
May [1] Waxworks of Rossi and Parfitt are unveiled at London's Rock Circus in Piccadilly.
June [15] The "1991 World Music Awards", featuring an appearance by Quo, is broadcast on ITV.
July [23] They hold a press conference to announce the forthcoming "Rock 'Til You Drop" tour, at RAF Northolt, Middx., where they also perform after flying in Spitfires.
Aug [28] Quo guests on BBC1-TV's "Wogan".
Sept [7] *Can't Give You More* debuts at its UK #37 peak.
[20] Nordoff Robbins Music Therapy Race Day is held at Newbury. Tiptoes wins the "Status Quo Rock 'Til You Drop Stakes".
[21] Status Quo enters **The Guinness Book Of Records** by playing four venues (Sheffield International Centre, Glasgow Scottish Exhibition & Conference Centre, Birmingham National Exhibition Centre and Wembley Arena) in one day under the banner "Rock 'Til You Drop", performing at the four arenas in a 12-hour period as part of group's 25th anniversary.
Oct [5] "Rockin All Over The UK", a film of the September 21st shows, airs on C4-TV, as ***Rock 'Til You Drop*** hits UK #10 in its week of entry.
Dec [6-8] The group plays at Wembley Arena.

1992

Jan [14] The UK leg of "Rock 'Til You Drop" tour ends at the Bournemouth International Centre, Bournemouth, Dorset.
[18] *Rock 'Til You Drop* bows at its UK #38 peak.
June [7] The group opens the annual Isle of Man TT race with a concert at The Bowl, King George's Park, Douglas, Isle of Man.
[20] A show at Smallbrook, Ryde on the Isle of Wight is cancelled because of poor ticket sales.
Aug [30] The group headlines BBC Radio 1's birthday party at Sutton Park, Birmingham.
Oct [17] Now with Polydor Records, Quo's *Roadhouse Medley (Anniversary Waltz Part 25)* reaches UK #21.
Nov [14] ***Live Alive Quo*** charts for a week at UK #37.
[15] Status Quo embarks on a 13-date German tour at the Rudi Sedimayer Hall, Munich, set to close on December 1st at the Philipshalle, Dusseldorf.
Dec [4] The group begins a 12-date UK trek at the Sheffield Arena, set to end on the 21st at Wembley Arena.

1993

Nov [23] They begin a massive "Just For The Record World Tour" at the Reading Rivermead Centre, coinciding with the publication of Quo's autobiography, inked by Rossi and Parfitt.

1994

May [21] Manchester United Football Club's *Come On You Reds*, produced by Quo and based on *Burning Bridges (On And Off And On Again)* tops the UK chart.
Aug [13] *I Didn't Mean It* reaches UK #21.
Sept [3] ***Thirsty Work*** debuts at its UK #13 peak.
[24] The group is featured on the inaugural BBC2-TV "TOTP2" show.
Oct [22] *Sherri Don't Fail Me Now!* debuts at its UK #38 peak.
Dec [3] Quo's version of the Jennifer Warnes-penned

ballad *Restless*, featuring a 32-piece orchestra, debuts at its UK #39 peak.

1995

May [21] Parfitt is found at the wheel of his Porsche after it leaves the M3 in Surrey. He fails a roadside breath test and police later find a packet of cocaine with a street value of £100. (He will be banned from driving for 18 months, fined £1,000 for drunk-driving and £500 for drug-possession on September 7th.)
Oct [28] The group performs *Rockin' All Over The World* before the Rugby League Cup Final between England and Australia.
Nov [4] *When You Walk In The Room* debuts at its UK #34 peak.
[27] The group embarks on a month-long UK tour at the Apollo Theatre, Manchester, Gtr. Manchester, set to end on December 17th, with the second of two dates at the Wembley Arena.

1996

Feb [17] ***Don't Stop*** bows at UK#2.
Mar [2] Status Quo, backed by its originators the Beach Boys, debuts at UK #24 peak with its 50th chart records - an update of *Fun Fun Fun* - no thanks to BBC Radio's 1FM which refuses to play the chart disc on the grounds that the band is "too old". Quo responds with a writ against 1FM alleging "ageism".
Apr [13] *Don't Stop*, reviving Fleetwood Mac's 1977 smash, reaches UK #35 in its week of entry.

TOMMY STEELE

1956

July Steele (b. Thomas Hicks, Dec. 17, 1936, Bermondsey, London), having served four years as a pantry boy, lift boy and assistant steward for the Cunard shipping line, and having sung semi-professionally while ashore, including stints as guitarist with C&W group Jack Fallon & the Sons Of The Saddle, and a UK tour playing second guitar behind bluesman, Josh White, is singing at the 2I's coffee bar in Soho, London, at the start of a month-long leave the day after his ship has docked, when he is approached by photographer and PR man, John Kennedy, who sees potential in his singing style and youthful looks. Kennedy is working for managers/agents Roy Tuvey and Geoff Wright, who have already spotted Steele, but after disagreements over financial matters, Kennedy splits from them and teams instead with Larry Parnes, who is willing to finance Steele's launch while Kennedy handles management. They persuade him to leave the Merchant Navy and sign to them as a professional (they also promise his parents that if nothing comes of his career within a few months, they will not hold him to any contract).
Aug Kennedy re-names him Tommy Steele, felt to be a "sharper" name than Hicks' own. He launches the singer on the live circuit in ways calculated to gain publicity, performing at high class, high-profile debutantes' balls, and at the plush Stork Rooms in London's West End. It all makes major (favorable) press copy.
Sept George Martin at EMI Records rejects Steele, but Decca A&R man, Hugh Mendl (who auditions Steele in his own office), is enthusiastic, and Steele becomes the label's first rock signing.
Oct His debut recording is *Rock With The Caveman*, written by Steele, with Mike Pratt and Lionel Bart. The backing session musicians are mostly jazz-men, led by saxophonist Ronnie Scott, but credited as "The Steelmen" on the disc.
[15] He makes his UK TV debut performing the single on Jack Payne's "Off The Record" show.
Nov *Rock With The Caveman* reaches UK #13. His earnings shoot up from £7 a week, six months previously, to £700 a week.
[5] He makes his bill-topping debut at the Empire Theatre, Sunderland, Tyne & Wear.
[26] Steele begins a week-long engagement at the Finsbury Park Empire, London.
Dec [7] A bona fide group of Steelmen (including Roy Plummer on guitar and Alan Stewart on saxophone) is put together to back him on stage, and he begins live work in earnest (debuting at London's Finsbury Park Astoria), to fan hysteria reminiscent of that being generated by Elvis Presley in the US. Meanwhile his second single, *Elevator Rock*, fails to chart, when Steele's cover of Guy Mitchell's current US #1 hit, *Singing The Blues*, is rush-released.

1957

Jan Both Mitchell's and Steele's versions of *Singing The Blues* top the UK chart, the latter replacing the former for a week, and then being deposed by it again, and proves to be Steele's biggest UK hit. Meanwhile, his first major cabaret engagement is at London's Café de Paris.
Feb He has a cameo role (as a coffee-bar singer) in the British thriller movie, "Kill Me Tomorrow". A starring role in a semi-autobiographical feature film, "The Tommy Steele Story", is also announced.
Mar Steele also covers Mitchell's follow-up, *Knee Deep In The Blues* (written, like *Singing The Blues*, by Melvin Endsley), but Mitchell hits UK #4 while Steele makes UK #15.
May [3] Rapidly-made low-budget film, "The Tommy Steele Story", premieres in Britain. (It will be a UK box office success, released in the US as "Rock Around The World".)
[20] Steele opens at the Dominion Theatre, London, headlining a variety bill. **The Daily Telegraph** reports : "It may seem a far cry from the 12th century troubadour to Mr. Steele, but the connection is there, though he may appear to some to be no more than a crazy mixed-up minstrel with ants in his pants."
July *Butterfingers*, another Steele/Pratt/Bart song, included in the movie, hits UK #8.
Aug Steele's cover of Andy Williams' *Butterfly* is one of six tracks by various artists on the EP, *All-Star Hit Parade, No. 2*, which reaches UK #15.
Sept Double A-side, *Water, Water/Handful Of Songs*, from "The Tommy Steele Story", hits UK #5. (*Handful Of Songs* is also the theme for his television shows, and for many years will be Steele's signature tune.) He has also written and sung the theme song for another UK film, "The Shiralee", which reaches UK #11.
Oct He begins filming his second movie, "The Duke Wore Jeans". In the UK music paper **New Musical Express** annual Readers' Poll, Steele is named runner-up to Elvis Presley as World Musical Personality.
Nov *Hey You* makes UK #28.
[18] Steele appears in the "Royal Variety Performance" in London, singing *Long Tall Sally*.
Dec He appears in pantomime for the first time, playing in "Goldilocks" in Liverpool, Lancs.

1958

Mar Calypso-flavored *Nairobi*, released while Steele is touring South Africa, hits UK #3.
May *Happy Guitar* reaches UK #20.
June Steele becomes engaged to dancer Anne Donati. Kennedy and Parnes try to keep this quiet, believing it will adversely affect his teen following, but his career has already moved from rock'n'roll singer to versatile family entertainer. (Marty Wilde - another Larry Parnes protegé - arrives on the scene in mid-summer, and Cliff Richard in mid-autumn, with teenage fans switching allegiance to them.)
Aug Steele's cover of Tony Bennett's US hit, *The Only Man On The Island*, reaches UK #16.
Nov [15] Steele and his backing group, the Steelmen, part company.
Dec His treatment of Ritchie Valens' first US release, *Come On Let's Go*, hits UK #10, while Valens' original fails to chart in the UK. Steele begins another pantomime season in "Cinderella".

1959

Aug His version of Freddy Cannon's *Tallahassie Lassie* just out-sells the original in Britain - Cannon reaches UK #17, but Steele makes #16 - while its B-side, *Give Give Give*, also makes UK #28.
Sept Steele tours Australia, earning £100,000 for a ten-week stint.

1960

Jan He stars in the UK comedy film, "Tommy The Toreador", with Sid James and others. From it, the Pratt/Bart/Roy Bennett-penned children's favorite, *Little White Bull*, hits UK #6 and will re-enter on Mar [12] for a further five weeks.
June [18] Steele and Donati marry at St. Patrick's Church, Soho Square, London.
July *What A Mouth*, a pure cockney music-hall song, hits UK #5.
Dec Seasonal *Must Be Santa* makes UK #40.

1961

Aug *The Writing On The Wall*, his cover of a US top five hit by Adam Wade, reaches UK #30, and is Steele's last chart entry. (He will continue to record for Decca for a year, and will cover Brook Benton's *Hit Record*, before switching to Columbia for more sporadic releases. Steele will leave the record world behind him during the early '60s, and become an international star of stage and film musicals. His movie successes will include "Half A Sixpence", "The Happiest Millionaire" and "Finian's Rainbow". He will also triumph on stage in "Half A Sixpence" in London, and on Broadway in 1963/64, at the Old Vic, London, as Tony Lumpkin in "She Stoops To Conquer", and in the self-directed "Hans Christian Andersen" and "Singing In The Rain", at the London Palladium ten and 20 years later - well removed from his ground-breaking role as the prototype UK rock star and teen idol. In 1990 Decca will bring his hits to compact disc on the 20-track ***Tommy Steele's Greatest Hits*** on its Deram label.))

STEELY DAN

Donald Fagen (vocals, keyboards); **Walter Becker** (bass); **Jeff "Skunk" Baxter** (lead guitar); **Denny Dias** (rhythm guitar); **Jim Hodder** (drums)

1969

Fagen (b. Jan. 10, 1948, Passaic, NJ), son of a local accountant and one-time Catskills dance-band singing mother, and Becker (b. Feb. 20, 1950, New York City, NY), who first met as students at Bard's college in upstate New York two years earlier (forming a band with Chevy Chase on drums, alternately calling itself either Bad Rock Group or Leather Canary), leave their studies (only Fagen graduates - in English literature) and begin trying to sell songs they have written while there, with little success. (Fagen later recalls: "We just liked writing funny songs - we were both jazz fans, had begun an interest in Chicago blues and liked the Byrds.") Intent on a career in music, they cut a low-key film soundtrack for an early Richard Pryor movie, "You Gotta Walk It Like You Talk It" (which will not be released on disc until the late '70s). Despite its commercial failure, it leads to another movie project, a dance video starring Becker's mother, for which they are paid $1,500. Continuing to plug self-written songs to Brill Building publishers in New York, Becker and Fagen answer an ad in the **Village Voice** newspaper the following year from guitarist Dias, who is looking for "musicians with jazz chops". They join Dias' band, Demian, and record demos in his basement.

1971

Nov Having sold *I Mean To Shine* for recording on Barbra Streisand's ***Barbra Joan Streisand*** album, through producer Richard Perry, Becker and Fagen have quit Demian earlier in the year to join Jay & the Americans through Kenny Vance, who had produced the "You Gotta Walk It Like You Talk It" soundtrack. Together they sing on Brill Building demos and on the New York live circuit. With the band, they have met producer Gary Katz (a three-year partner in Cloud Nine Productions with Perry) and guitarist Baxter (b. Dec. 13, 1948, Washington, DC), a communications major from Boston University, and a veteran of the bands Ultimate Spinach, the Holy Modal Rounders and briefly in the un-recorded group, Spire. Katz is now offered the house producer's job at ABC-Dunhill Records in Los Angeles, CA. He accepts on condition that Fagen and Becker are hired as staff writers, and all parties agree.

1972

Feb After only four months, the songwriting contract is cancelled and replaced by Dunhill with an offer for Becker and Fagen to record their own compositions. Katz gathers session help from Dias, Baxter, Boston, MA drummer Hodder (ex-Bead Game) and others, including David Palmer (ex-Myddle Class), from Plainfield, NJ, who initially handles vocals.

Mar Their debut single, *Dallas*, is released. The group name Steely Dan is taken from William Burroughs' novel, **The Naked Lunch** (in which it is the name given to a steam-powered dildo), and work begins on a debut album.

1973

Feb Katz-produced ***Can't Buy A Thrill*** reaches US #17, supported by a US tour.

[11] *Do It Again*, taken from it, hits US #6.

Apr Palmer departs (to resurface in the Big Wha-Koo on ABC), and Fagen reluctantly takes over lead vocals.

May [12] *Reeling In The Years*, also from the first album, reaches US #11.

July Steppenwolf's John Kay's second solo album, ***My Sportin' Life***, is released, including Becker and Fagen's *Giles Of The River*.

Sept [1] *Show Biz Kids* peaks at US #61.

Further defining their literate and witty lyrical style and establishing their unique-sounding pop/rock/jazz meld, ***Countdown To Ecstasy***, recorded with session help from Ben Benay (acoustic guitar), Ray Brown (bass), Rick Derringer (slide guitar) and Victor Feldman (vibes), makes US #35, but yields no major hit singles. They tour the US with two backing vocalists, Jenny Soule and Gloria Granola, temporarily in the line-up. (From 1972 to 1974, they will support the Beach Boys, Chuck Berry and Frank Zappa.)

Dec [1] *My Old School*, taken from the album, peaks at US #63.

1974

May Their debut UK tour is interrupted by Fagen's throat infection, and only five of 12 dates are completed, though the visit boosts the newly-released ***Pretzel Logic*** into becoming the band's UK chart bow at #37. (On its return to the US, the band will play a selection of Californian dates.)

June Becker and Fagen-penned (as with all Steely Dan projects) ***Pretzel Logic*** hits US #8.

July [4] Following an Independence Day gig at the Civic Center, Santa Monica, CA, Becker and Fagen retire from live work (for three years).

Aug [3] With little prospect of further work with Steely Dan, Baxter leaves to join the Doobie Brothers (with whom he has toured before), and Hodder also leaves. Jeff Porcaro (b. Apr. 1, 1954, Hartford, CT) replaces the latter, while Michael McDonald (b. Feb. 12, 1952, St. Louis, MO), joins on keyboards (both have augmented the group on tour, with extra vocalist Royce Jones). (Porcaro had been hired to drum on a Becker/Fagen Schlitz commercial at the suggestion of Dias.) Meanwhile, *Rikki, Don't Lose That Number*, written about Rick Derringer who has contributed to the forthcoming ***Katy Lied***, becomes the band's biggest-selling US single, hitting #4.

Nov [2] *Pretzel Logic* makes US #57.

1975

May ***Katy Lied***, including music guests Derringer, David Paich, Chuck Rainey, Wilton Felder and Hal Blaine among others, reaches both US and UK #13. (The near-complete recording was almost ruined by faulty studio equipment - which caused producer Katz to storm out of ABC for Warner Bros.) Following its recording, McDonald also leaves to join the Doobie Brothers, Porcaro returns to sessions (and will eventually form Toto), while Dias leaves to move into session work. They are not replaced: the nucleus of Steely Dan remains Becker and Fagen, using numerous session men on subsequent album recordings.

June [21] *Black Friday*, written about the 1929 stock-market crash, taken from ***Katy Lied***, makes US #37.

Sept Their debut album, ***Can't Buy A Thrill***, belatedly charts at UK #38, as does *Do It Again*, at UK #39.

1976

May [22] ***The Royal Scam*** reaches UK #11, following a European promotional tour.

July [10] ***The Royal Scam*** reaches US #15.

[17] *Kid Charlemagne*, from ***The Royal Scam***, peaks at US #82.

Oct [16] *The Fez*, also from the album, makes US #59.

1977

Jan [22] UK-only release, *Haitian Divorce*, taken from ***The Royal Scam***, reaches UK #17, and is Steely Dan's best-selling UK single.

Mar [31] ABC, irritated by the duo's endless perfectionism in the studio, has set this date for delivery of the next album. Becker and Fagen will miss it by months.

Oct [1] ***Aja*** hits UK #5, becoming the first Steely Dan album to hit the UK Top 10, and the first official Steely Dan release by Becker and Fagen as a duo.

[22] ***Aja*** hits US #3.

1978

Feb [23] The duo wins a Grammy Award for ***Aja***, named the Best-Engineered Non-Classical Recording, at the 20th annual ceremony.

Mar [2] ***Countdown To Ecstasy*** is certified gold by the RIAA.

[11] *Peg*, extracted from ***Aja***, reaches US #11.

June [10] *Deacon Blues*, also from ***Aja***, makes US #19. (Its title will inspire the name for '80s Scottish group, Deacon Blue.)

July [29] *FM (No Static At All)*, taken from the soundtrack to the movie "FM", reaches US #22.

Aug *FM (No Static At All)* makes UK #49.

Oct [14] *Josie*, a final single from ***Aja***, reaches US #26. (During the year, Becker and Fagen also produce jazz album, ***Apogée***, for the Pete Christlieb/Warne Marsh Quintet.)

Dec [7] The still-rising ***Greatest Hits*** is certified platinum by the RIAA.

1979

Jan Double compilation, ***Greatest Hits***, reaches US #30, and makes UK #41. It includes a new song, *Here In The Western World*, and is the first of several Steely Dan compilations.

Mar The reissued *Rikki Don't Lose That Number* makes UK #58.

1980

During a year when Becker is struck by car outside his Upper West Side apartment in Manhattan, suffering a broken leg and other injuries, the duo signs to Warner Bros. Records and begins work on ***Metal Leg***, until it is pointed out that Steely Dan still owes an album to MCA Records, ABC's new owners.

1981

Jan [22] ***Gaucho*** is certified platinum by the RIAA.

[24] Meticulously-assembled ***Gaucho***, still produced by long-time cohort Katz, and released on MCA, hits US #9. Featuring Derringer and Mark Knopfler on guitar and a roundup of top-drawer jazz session players, it also makes UK #27.

Feb [14] *Hey Nineteen*, from ***Gaucho***, hits US #10 (their first US Top 10 hit for six years).

Apr [25] Also from ***Gaucho***, *Time Out Of Mind* makes US #22, and is the duo's final US chart single.

June [21] The duo announces its split, but does not rule out working together as Steely Dan again at some future time. (Each begins work on solo projects: Becker as a producer and Fagen as a solo act.) Shortly thereafter, Fagen's *True Companion* appears on the soundtrack to ***Heavy Metal***.

1982

Feb [24] ***Gaucho*** is named Best Engineered Recording at the 24th annual Grammy Awards.

July [17] Retrospective set, ***Steely Dan Gold***, makes UK #44.

Aug [7] ***Steely Dan Gold*** peaks at US #115.

Oct [30] Fagen's ***The Nightfly***, released on Warner Bros., makes UK #44, and will go on to reach US #11. The album's concept is an account of a night at a fictional jazz radio station, WJAZ, with Fagen as a DJ known as "The Nightfly".

Dec From ***The Nightfly***, *I.G.Y. (What A Beautiful World)* reaches US #26. (Greg Phillinganes' album, ***Pulse***, featuring the Fagen-written and arranged original, *Lazy Nina*, will be released in 1984.)

1985

May Produced by Becker, UK combo China Crisis' album, ***Flaunt The Imperfection*** hits UK #9.

Nov TV-promoted compilation, ***Reelin' In The Years - The Very Best Of Steely Dan***, makes UK #43.

1987

Feb Ex-model Rosie Vela's A&M debut album, ***Zazu***, is released, produced by Katz, who has persuaded both Becker and Fagen to play on it, leading to premature speculation about a reunion.

Oct [10] Another TV-promoted compilation album, ***Do It Again - The Very Best Of Steely Dan***, debuts at its UK #64 peak.

1988

Apr Fagen takes time off from being music editor of US movie magazine, **Premiere**, to release *Century's End*, taken from the movie soundtrack of "Bright Lights Big City". (Other one-off Fagen songs have also appeared on the soundtracks to "The King Of Comedy" and "Arthur 2 : On The Rocks".)

1990

May [21] Becker (who helmed 1989's US #39-peaking Rickie Jones album, ***Flying Cowboys***) produces Fagen tracks at the Hit Factory, New York, again hinting at speculation of a Steely Dan reunion.

June [5] Hodder drowns in Point Arena, CA, at the age of 42.

Aug [24] Organized as an annual event by Fagen at the urging of his girlfriend, Libby Titus, and conceived after he had performed a show with Dr. John at Elaine's restaurant in New York, the first "New York Rock & Soul Revue" is held at the "Evian Music Festival", Southampton, NY.

Sept [4] ***Dead City Radio***, a collection of 17 readings from William Burroughs, which features Fagen, is released by Island.

1991

Mar [1-2] Fagen's second "Rock And Soul Revue II", with Michael McDonald, Boz Scaggs, Phoebe Snow and Charles Brown, takes place at the Beacon Theatre, New York.

May Having overcome the drug-related death of a girlfriend, his own drug addiction and a bout of depression, Becker signs a long-term production deal with Windham Hill Records having also inked a contract with the Triloka label for helming jazz recordings (for the likes of Leeann Ledgerwood, Andy Laverne, Jeff Beal, Jeremy Steig, David Kikosi, Lorraine Feather and Sam Butler).

1992

Feb [8] ***The New York Rock And Soul Revue - Live At The Beacon***, to which Fagen has contributed *Madison Time*, *Green Flower Street*, *Chain Lightning* and *Pretzel Logic* (with Michael McDonald), peaks at

US #170.
Aug [30] The now expanded "New York Rock & Soul Revue" US summer tour plays the New Pine Knob Theatre, Clarkston, MI.

1993

Apr Signed to Irving Azoff's Giant Records (Steely Dan was signed to Azoff's Frontline Management in the early days), Hawaiian resident Becker continues to work at his Maui studio on his debut solo set, co-penning songs with Dean Parks, and using sessioneers John Beasly (keyboards), Fima Ephron (bass) the Lost Tribe group, Ben Perowski (drums) and Adam Rogers (guitar).
June [5] Fagen's sophomore solo set, the Becker-produced ***Kamakiriad*** ("praying mantis" in Japanese), a concept album set in the future about a suicidal man's trip to Flytown, where he has a spiritual re-awakening through music, debuts at its UK #5 peak.
[12] ***Kamakiriad*** hits US #10 in its first week of release.
July [3] The extracted *Tomorrow's Girls* makes UK #46.
Aug [13] After a near 15-year live lay-off, the Becker and Fagen re-formed Steely Dan begins a US tour at the Palace of Auburn Hills, Auburn Hills, MI. (When asked to explain the reunion, Becker quips: "We spent all the money from the last tour. We made 800 bucks each and it's all gone now".)
[24] Steely Dan performs at New York's Madison Square Garden.
Sept [7] Confirming the enduring appeal of Steely Dan's meticulously crafted recordings, the RIAA certifies gold, platinum and multi-platinum sales of ***Pretzel Logic*** (platinum), ***Aja*** (two million), ***Katy Lied*** (platinum), ***Can't Buy A Thrill*** (platinum), ***A Decade Of Steely Dan (The Best Of)*** (gold), ***The Royal Scam*** (platinum) and ***Gold*** (gold).
[8] During the band's sold out three-night stand at Los Angeles' Greek Theatre, Steely Dan is inducted into Hollywood's Rock Walk.
Nov [27] ***Remastered - The Best Of Steely Dan*** makes UK #42.
Dec [7] A four-CD/cassette boxed set career anthology, ***Citizen Steely Dan : 1972-1980***, is released in the US.

1994

Aug [19] Steely Dan embarks on an 18-date US tour at the ThunderDome, St. Petersburg, FL.
Oct Becker's first solo album, ***Whack***, produced by Fagen, is finally released on Giant Records.

1995

Oct [20] Steely Dan guests on CBS-TV's "Late Show With David Letterman".
[28] The performance album ***Alive In America***, the first new Steely Dan album in 15 years, enters at its UK #62 peak.
Nov [4] ***Alive In America*** debuts at its US #40 high.

1996

July [5] Steely Dan embarks on its US summer tour at the North Charleston Coliseum, Charleston, SC, set to end on August 16th-17th at The Gorge, George, WA.

STEPPENWOLF

John Kay (guitar, vocals); **Michael Monarch** (guitar); **Rushton Moreve** (bass); **Goldy McJohn** (organ); **Jerry Edmonton** (drums)

1966

Kay (b. Joachim Krauledat, Apr. 12, 1944, Tilsit, Germany), Monarch (b. July 5, 1950, Los Angeles, CA), Moreve (b. 1948, Los Angeles), McJohn (b. John Goadsby, May 2, 1945) and Edmonton (b. Jerry McCrohan, Oct. 24, 1946, Canada) form, as Sparrow, in Canada. Kay has arrived in Canada in 1958 with his mother and step-father after escaping from East Germany to West Germany ten years earlier, but has moved to New York, NY in 1963 and Santa Monica, CA the following year, where he began performing on the folk-rock scene, subsequently returning to New York where he first met Edmonton. After recording the non-charting single, *Tomorrow's Ship*, for Columbia Records, Sparrow relocate to California where they are noticed playing at a coffee house in Venice Beach resulting in them signing a recording deal with Dunhill Records and, at producer Gabriel Mekler's suggestion, the name is changed to Steppenwolf (taken from the Herman Hesse novel). After some early recordings and gigs, Moreve is replaced on bass by John Russell Morgan.

1968

Jan Their debut album, ***Steppenwolf***, is released, together with a single reviving Don Covay's *Sookie Sookie*. The single does not chart, but the album slowly climbs as the group's hard rock live reputation spreads. (It will hit US #6 when *Born To Be Wild*, the second single extract, becomes a smash.) The set also contains the band's anti-drug song, *The Pusher*, which becomes an on-stage anthem.
July [5] The group plays at the Hollywood Bowl, Hollywood, CA, with bill-toppers the Doors.
Aug [24] *Born To Be Wild*, penned by Jerry Edmonton's brother Dennis (aka Mars Bonfire) and featuring the lyric "heavy metal thunder", hits US #2 for three weeks behind the Young Rascals' *People Got To Be Free*. (It will become the archetypal biker song when used in the film, "Easy Rider", a year later.)
[4] The group performs at the "Newport Pop Festival" in Costa Mesa, CA, alongside Canned Heat, Sonny & Cher, the Grateful Dead, the Byrds, and others.
[9-11] They play at the Avalon Ballroom, San Francisco, CA, sharing the bill with Santana.
Sept [19] *Born To Be Wild* is certified gold by the RIAA.
Nov [27] ***Steppenwolf*** is certified gold by the RIAA.
[30] *Magic Carpet Ride* hits US #3, taken from ***Steppenwolf The Second***, which also hits US #3.
Dec [6] Steppenwolf takes part in the "Quaker City Rock Festival" at the Spectrum, Philadelphia, PA, with the Grateful Dead and Iron Butterfly.
[28] The band appears at the "Miami Pop Festival" in Hallandale, FL, in front of 100,000 people. The three-day bill includes the Grateful Dead, Marvin Gaye, Chuck Berry, the Turtles and Joni Mitchell, among others.

1969

Feb [12] ***Steppenwolf The Second*** is also certified gold by the RIAA.
Mar [25] *Magic Carpet Ride* is certified gold by the RIAA.
Apr ***At Your Birthday Party***, which includes *Rock Me*, hits US #7. Monarch and Morgan leave the band, and are replaced by Larry Byrom (b. Dec. 27, 1948) on guitar and Nick St. Nicholas (b. Klaus Karl Kassbaum, Sept. 28, 1943, Hamburg, Germany) on bass.
[19] *Rock Me*, notable for its lengthy polyrhythmic drum/percussion break, hits US #10. The song also features in the sex-spoof film, "Candy", for which they write and perform material (and which premiered in the US a month earlier).
May [31] *It's Never Too Late* stops at US #51.
June *Born To Be Wild* is the group's only UK chart entry, at #30.
[20] They play at the "Newport '69 Pop Festival" at San Fernando Valley State College at Devonshire Downs, Northridge, CA, on a bill with Jimi Hendrix, Joe Cocker, the Byrds, Creedence Clearwater Revival and others.
Aug ***Early Steppenwolf***, a live recording from 1967 when the group was still known as Sparrow (and including an early marathon 21-minute version of *The Pusher*), reaches US #29. The film "Easy Rider" uses Steppenwolf's *The Pusher* and *Born To Be Wild* as the soundtrack for its opening scenes.
Sept [20] *Move Over* (the first notice of the band's developing concern with political matters) makes US #31.

1970

Jan Politically-oriented cocept album ***Monster*** reaches US #1.
Feb [7] Its title track, *Monster*, makes US #39.
Mar [18] ***Monster*** is certified gold by the RIAA.
May Performance double set, ***Steppenwolf Live***, hits US #7.
[16] *Hey Lawdy Mama* peaks at US #35.
[24] The group embarks on a short UK tour at Fairfield Halls, Croydon, Surrey.
June St. Nicholas leaves, and is replaced by George Biondo (b. Sept. 3, 1945, Brooklyn, New York, NY).
[26] The band appears at the "Bath Festival of Blues and Progressive Music", at Shepton Mallet, Somerset, together with Led Zeppelin, the Byrds, Donovan, Frank Zappa, Santana and others.
July [4] ***Steppenwolf Live*** is certified gold by the RIAA.
Aug [6] Steppenwolf takes part in a 12-hour, anti-war rock festival at New York's Shea Stadium, alongside Paul Simon, Janis Joplin, Johnny Winter and others.
Sept [19] *Screaming Night Hog* climbs to US #62.
Dec ***Steppenwolf 7*** reaches US #19.
[12] *Who Needs Ya* makes US #54.

1971

Apr [10] Another anti-drug song, *Snow Blind Friend*, makes US #60, while the compilation, ***Steppenwolf Gold***, rounding up the hit singles to date, reaches US #24.
[12] The RIAA certifies gold sales of ***Steppenwolf 7*** and, appropriately, ***Steppenwolf Gold***.
May Byrom is replaced on guitar by Kent Henry.
Aug [21] *Ride With Me* peaks at US #52.
Nov ***For Ladies Only*** makes US #54.
Dec [11] The extracted title track, *For Ladies Only*, reaches US #64.

1972

Feb [14] Kay formally announces the group's dissolution in a press conference at the Holiday Inn, Hollywood, CA, explaining: "We were locked into an image and style of music and there was nothing for us to look forward to." (The group has been trapped by its own success, turning over $40 million in disc sales for Dunhill.) The day is declared "Steppenwolf Day" in Los Angeles by Mayor Sam Yorty, commemorating the group's retirement.
May Kay's solo album, ***Forgotten Songs And Unsung Heroes***, on Dunhill, makes US #113, and provides him with his only solo hit single, a revival of Hank Snow's *I'm Movin' On*, which reaches US #52. Edmonton and McJohn form their own band, Manbeast, without notable commercial success.
Aug Steppenwolf album, ***Rest In Peace***, compiled from earlier material, reaches US #62.

1973

Mar Another compilation, ***16 Greatest Hits***, peaks at US #152.
July [14] Kay's second album, ***My Sportin' Life***, anchors the US chart at #200, and includes *Giles Of The River*, composed by Steely Dan's Walter Becker and Donald Fagen.

1974

Feb Kay re-forms Steppenwolf, with McJohn, Edmonton, Biondo and ex-Flying Burrito Brothers' guitarist, Bobby Cochran, and the band is signed to the Mums label.
Oct ***Slow Flux***, on Mums, reaches US #47.
[12] The extracted *Straight Shootin' Woman* is the band's final US chart single, at #29. McJohn is replaced by Wayne Cook.

1975

Oct ***Hour Of The Wolf***, released on Epic and climbing to US #155, regains some of the band's old spirit, though Kay's material is generally considered weaker than his early songs. (The group will dissolve once again in 1978 after the release of ***Skullduggery*** and ***Reborn To Be Wild***, with Monarch joining heavy metal band, Detective, and Kay recording his third solo album, ***All In Good Time***, for Mercury Records in the same year.

1981

July [1] While Kay has re-assembled the band the previous year which will intermittently tour the US as John Kay & Steppenwolf throughout the rest of the decade, early bassist Moreve is killed in a car accident in Los Angeles.

1987

Oct With ***16 Greatest Hits*** having been certified gold by the RIAA the previous December 4th, ***Rock & Roll Rebels***, released on the Qwil label, and credited to John Kay & Steppenwolf, peaks at US #171.

1993

Nov [28] Longtime drummer Edmonton dies in an auto accident near Santa Barbara, CA. (Following the June 1990 release of Kay & Steppenwolf album's ***Rise And Shine*** on I.R.S. Records, and MCA's 1991 compilation ***Born To Be Wild - A Retrospective***, the group, whose lineup varies under Kay's leadership, has continued touring into the mid-90s, including a US package trek earlier this year with Poco, Edgar Winter and Dave Mason. Kay, now living in Tennessee, will publish his autobiography, **Magic Carpet Ride** the following year.)

CAT STEVENS

1966

July Stevens (b. Steven Demetri Georgiou, July 21, 1947, Soho, London), son of a Greek London restaurateur and a Swedish mother, who has begun spare-time singer/songwriting in a folk/rock style, while studying at Hammersmith College, London, the previous year, gigging under the name Steve Adams, is heard performing at the college by ex-Springfields member, now record producer, Mike Hurst. Though he has been planning to leave for the US to work, Hurst is sufficiently excited by the young student's songs and voice to organize a recording session, at which they cut the self-penned, *I Love My Dog*. This impresses Tony Hall at Decca Records, who signs him (now re-named Cat Stevens) as the first act on the new Deram label imprint, designed to be a showcase for progressive young British talent.
Nov [5] His debut single, *I Love My Dog*, reaches UK #28, aided by strong pirate radio airplay.

1967

Feb [4] Highly-commercial, orchestrally-arranged *Matthew And Son* hits UK #2 (behind the Monkees' *I'm A Believer*), and heightens his reputation as a songwriter. (His repertoire is already attracting cover versions - the Tremeloes' first hit without Brian Poole is a version of his *Here Comes My Baby*, at UK #4.)
Mar [31] Stevens embarks on a 25-date UK package tour with the Walker Brothers, Engelbert Humperdinck and the Jimi Hendrix Experience, at Finsbury Park Astoria, London, set to end on April 30th at Granada Cinema, Tooting, London.
Apr [29] *I'm Gonna Get Me A Gun* (publicized by some gun-toting pictures which Stevens will later disown) is another commercially strong combination of unusual lyric and string arrangement, and hits UK #6.
May [13] His entirely self-written debut album, ***Matthew And Son***, hits UK #7.
June [16] Stevens films the "A Spoonful Of Sugar" documentary, due to be aired during the summer, at Stanmore Hospital, Stanmore, Middx., talking to patients.
[17] Former Ikette P.P. Arnold's cover of Stevens' *The First Cut Is The Deepest* reaches UK #18.
Aug [26] *A Bad Night* reaches UK #20.
Nov [17-18] Stevens performs at the Palais de Sports, Paris, France, on a bill with the Spencer Davis Group, Soft Machine, Keith West & Tomorrow and Dantalian's Chariot.
[22] He films the pilot of a show hosted by Alan Freeman, tentatively titled "All Systems Go", as a replacement for "Juke Box Jury".
Dec [15] Stevens guests on BBC1-TV's "Crackerjack".
[23] *Kitty* makes UK #47, as his sophomore effort, ***New Masters***, fails to chart.

1968

Feb *Lovely City* is released, but Stevens is unavailable to promote it having contracted tuberculosis requiring hospitalization. Two more non-charting singles, *Here Comes My Wife* and *Where Are You* are issued while he is convalescing, which complete his Deram contract.

1969

Originally reported to be writing a musical, Stevens spends the last months of his recuperation honing more sensitive and less commercial songs, having intensely disliked the whirlwind pop star trappings of his initial rise to fame.

1970

July Newly signed to Island Records in the UK and A&M in the US, ***Mona Bone Jakon***, produced by ex-Yardbird Paul Samwell-Smith, showcases a new, more serious singer/songwriter style and makes UK #63.
Aug [8] *Lady D'Arbanville*, taken from the album and dedicated to former girlfriend, actress Patti D'Arbanville, hits UK #8.
Sept [12] Jimmy Cliff's cover of the Stevens-written and-produced *Wild World* hits UK #8.
Dec ***Tea For The Tillerman***, again helmed by Samwell-Smith, with cover art by Stevens, also featuring his original version of *Wild World*, reaches UK #20. It has been recorded with his mainstay session musicians, Alun Davies (guitar), John Ryan (bass) and Harvey Burns (drums), with string arrangements by Del Newman.

1971

Apr [10] *Wild World* is his US chart debut, reaching #11, spurring ***Tea For The Tillerman*** to eventually hit US #8 during a 79-week chart run. ***Mona Bone Jakon*** also belatedly charts in the US, at #164.
May Double album, combining his first two albums, ***Matthew And Son/New Masters***, now sells the Deram material in the US, reaching #173.
[12] ***Tea For The Tillerman*** is certified gold by the RIAA.
Aug [14] *Moon Shadow*, from a forthcoming album, makes US #30.
Oct ***Teaser And The Firecat*** hits UK #3 during a 93-week chart tenure, and US #2. Once again the sleeve features his own artwork, and he has also produced a short animated film with the same title as the album, for subsequent screening at gigs.
[16] *Moon Shadow* reaches UK #22.
[18] ***Teaser And The Firecat*** is confirmed gold by the RIAA.
Nov [6] US-only released *Peace Train*, extracted from the album, hits #7.

1972

Jan [29] Also from the album, Stevens' interpretation of Eleanor Farjeon's children's hymn, *Morning Has Broken*, with Rick Wakeman playing piano, hits UK #9.
Feb Compilation, ***Very Young And Early Songs***, is released on Deram in the US, reaching #94.
May [27] *Morning Has Broken* hits US #6. Stevens contributes to the newly-released soundtrack of Hal Ashby's cult movie, "Harold And Maude".
Sept He begins a 31-date North American tour at the Shrine Auditorium, Los Angeles, CA, backed by an 11-piece orchestra (and supported by folk/blues singer Ramblin' Jack Elliott) to a sold-out crowd of 6,500.
Nov ***Catch Bull At Four***, which broadens his instrumentation by using Davies (guitar), Jean Roussel (piano), Alan James (bass) and Gerry Conway (drums), with Stevens himself playing synthesizer on some tracks, hits UK #2.
Oct [12] The still-rising ***Catch Bull At Four*** is certified gold by the RIAA.
[18] ***Catch Bull At Four*** tops the US chart for the first of three weeks.
Dec Stevens performs at London's Royal Albert Hall.

1973

Jan Different singles are extracted from ***Catch Bull*** in the UK and US: *Can't Keep It In* reaches UK #13 (Jan [27]), while *Sitting* reaches US #16 (Jan [13]).
Aug [1] ***Foreigner*** is certified gold by the RIAA.
Foreigner hits both UK and US #3. One side is devoted to *Foreigner Suite*, a long and lyrically-profound piece indicating Stevens' increasing involvement with philosophical and religious concerns. His live appearances dwindle, and he becomes more reclusive and rarely grants interviews.
[25] The extracted *The Hurt* makes US #31, but fails to chart in the UK. He is now living in Brazil, having left Britain for a year's tax exile. The money he would have lost to the UK taxman, he donates to UNESCO and other charities.
Nov [9] He makes his US network TV debut on ABC-TV's "In Concert" show, a 90-minute special taped at the Hollywood Bowl, Hollywood, CA.

1974

Apr [8] The still-climbing ***Buddah And The Chocolate Box*** is certified gold by the RIAA.
[20] ***Buddah And The Chocolate Box*** hits UK #3 and will hit US #2.
June [1] *Oh Very Young*, taken from it, hits US #10, but fails to chart in the UK (where Island does not promote his singles heavily, keen to maintain Stevens as its best-selling album act).
Sept [28] His revival of Sam Cooke's *Another Saturday Night* reaches UK #19.
Oct [12] *Another Saturday Night* hits US #6.

1975

Jan [25] *Ready* reaches US #26.
Aug [23] *Two Fine People*, included on the compilation, reaches US #33, as compilation album ***Greatest Hits***, rounding up his Island/A&M singles, hits US #6, becoming an enduring catalog item.
Sept [27] ***Greatest Hits*** hits UK #2.
Nov He tours Europe with a five-piece backing band, including a Brazilian percussionist, and a female back-up vocal group, performing on an elaborate and specially-constructed stage set.
Dec [11] The UK leg of his tour begins at the Empire Theatre, Liverpool, Merseyside, ending on the 20th at London's Hammersmith Odeon.

1976

Jan [15] The RIAA certifies gold sales of ***Mona Bone Jakon*** and ***Numbers***.
[24] ***Numbers*** reaches US #13, but is his first Island album not to chart in the UK. His most complex and lyrically-involved album, it proves inaccessible to many devotees of his light earlier touch.
Mar [6] *Banapple Gas* makes US #41.

1977

Apr [16] Rod Stewart's cover of the Stevens-penned *First Cut Is The Deepest* reaches US #21.
May [21] *First Cut Is The Deepest* tops the UK chart, as ***Izitso*** reaches UK #18.
June [13] ***Izitso*** is ratified gold by the RIAA.
July [2] ***Izitso*** hits US #7.
[9] *(Remember The Days Of The) Old School Yard*, on which Stevens duets with Elkie Brooks, is his last chart single in the UK, making #44.
Aug [6] *(Remember The Days Of The) Old School Yard* reaches US #33.
Dec [23] Stevens formally embraces Islam on the 16th Muharram, 1398, and changes his name to Yusef Islam.

1979

Feb [10] After the instrumental cut *Was Dog A Doughnut* has peaked at US #70 on Jan [14], the previous year, ***Back To Earth*** reaches US #33. The extracted *Bad Brakes* peaks at US #83. Signalling an exit from international celebrity to a deeply religious private life, Stevens retires from all aspects of making music.

Sept [9] He marries Fouzia Ali at Kensington Mosque, London.

1981

He finances the establishment of, and begins to teach at, a Muslim school in North London. (He also has the Greek flag removed from the sleeve artwork of his ***Greatest Hits***.) Cutting short one of the most successful singer/songwriter careers of the '70s, he officially confirms he has left show business for good, auctions all the trappings of his pop career, including his gold discs, and donates the money to his current work.

1985

Jan [5] Compilation, ***Footsteps In The Dark - Greatest Hits Volume Two***, combining tracks from his nine Island/A&M albums with three additional songs, makes US #165.
July [13] Rumors that Yusef is to appear at "Live Aid", and is even willing to go on stage as Cat Stevens, prove unfounded.

1988

June Following 10,000 Maniacs cover of Stevens' *Peace Train* on last year's ***In My Tribe*** album (which will be re-pressed without the track following Yusef's call for Salman Rushdie's death the following year), Maxi Priest now hits UK #5 with his treatment of *Wild World.*

1989

Feb Yusef endorses Ayatollah Khomeini's call for the execution of **The Satanic Verses** author Salman Rushdie. Los Angeles radio station KFI's Tom Leykis holds a Cat Stevens' record burning session, beginning a more serious boycott by a large number of US radio stations of Stevens' work.

1990

Feb [3] An 18-track anthology, ***The Very Best Of Cat Stevens***, hits UK #4.
June Yusef is barred from entering Tel Aviv, Israel, turned away with his eight-year-old son, Mohammed, as an "undesirable".
Nov Yusef visits Iraq and successfully secures the release of a number of UK Muslims held hostage by the Gulf crisis.

1992

May Yusef refuses to give Levi's permission to use *First Cut Is The Deepest* for a jeans television commercial.
Nov [19] The RIAA certifies three million sales of ***Greatest Hits***.

1993

Mar [2] Yusef, now the President of the Islamic Association of North London, wins undisclosed libel damages in High Court over a **Private Eye** article which claimed he misused £80,000 of charitable funds to buy arms for Afghan rebels. He donates his damages to charity.

1995

Sept [5] After 18 years musical silence, Yusef, living with his wife and five children at the Islamia School he founded in 1983 in the North London suburb of Kilburn, signs copies of his new album in London, the predominantly spoken-word, ***The Life Of The Last Prophet***. (The following February, Yusef will write a letter to the **Irish Times** refuting an earlier claim by reader Stephen J. Place that a purchase of Boyzone's recent cover version of Stevens' *Father And Son* amounts to a show of support for the Islamic faith's death sentence on Rushdie.)

SHAKIN' STEVENS

1968

Stevens (b. Michael Barratt, Mar. 4, 1948, Ely, S. Glamorgan, Wales), one of 12 children, whose chief childhood musical influence has been '50s rock'n'roll records owned by his elder brothers, begins playing on the Cardiff, S. Glamorgan, Wales club circuit with a rock'n'roll revival band, the Sunsets. After gaining a strong reputation on the UK rock revival circuit, Shakin' Stevens & the Sunsets go on to sign a recording contract with EMI's Parlophone label in January 1970, and record ***A Legend***, with producer Dave Edmunds, at Rockfield Studios, Monmouth, Gwent, Wales. It fails to sell, as does their revival of Big Al Downing's *Down On The Farm*, and EMI drops the group. In a second one-off deal, with CBS the following year, ***I'm No J. D.*** is released to equal indifference. Popular as a live attraction in Europe, the group signs to Dutch label Dureco for another album in 1973, and amid many successful European tours, will continue to record for Dutch labels like Dynamo and Pink Elephant until 1976, when their final single, a version of Hank Mizell's *Jungle Rock*, released on Mooncrest, marks the end of the group's career.

1977

Apr Having been selected as one of three actors (with P.J. Proby and Tim Whitnall) signed to play Elvis Presley at various stages of his life in the Jack Good musical "Elvis", on London's West End stage (a musical which will run for 19 months and win a theater award as Best Musical Of 1977), Stevens is signed as a solo act to Track Records, but in spite of his West End success, three singles and a debut solo album, ***Shakin' Stevens***, fail to chart over a 12-month period with the label.

1978

Aug Having become a UK TV regular, alongside Lulu, Alvin Stardust and others, in Good's revival of his late '50s rock show, "Oh Boy", and having featured in Good's "Let's Rock" in the US, and now under the direction of manager Freya Miller, Stevens is signed to the Epic division of CBS, working with producer Mike Hurst. His label debut, *Treat Her Right*, fails to score, as will two follow-ups, his revivals of Jody Reynolds' *Endless Sleep* and Classics IV's *Spooky*.

1980

Mar [22] *Hot Dog*, taken from his debut Epic album, ***Shakin' Stevens Take One!***, finally gives him a UK singles chart debut at #24, while the album makes UK #62. Produced by Hurst (his last work with Stevens), the album features "musical co-ordination" and remixing by Stuart Colman, who also plays bass as part of the eight-man backing group, which includes Albert Lee on lead guitar.
Sept [20] Colman has taken over production on *Marie Marie*, a cover of a song by US rockabilly band, the Blasters, which reaches UK #19.

1981

Mar [28] His pop'n'roll revival of Stuart Hamblen's *This Ole House*, a 1954 UK #1 for Rosemary Clooney, is given a sharp rock arrangement by Colman, and proves to be Stevens' major breakthrough, topping the UK chart for the first of three weeks.
Apr ***This Ole House***, with rock revival band Matchbox guesting, hits UK #2.
May *You Drive Me Crazy*, an original song by Ronnie Harwood, hits UK #2 for four weeks (behind Adam & the Ants' *Stand And Deliver*).
Aug Budget album, ***Shakin' Stevens***, a compilation of early material, makes UK #34.
[1] His update of the Jim Lowe/Frankie Vaughan 1956 hit, *Green Door*, tops the UK chart for the first of four weeks.
Oct Stevens' first slow-tempo hit, reviving Irma Thomas' *It's Raining*, hits UK #10.
Nov [7] ***Shaky***, produced by Colman, and including the three recent hits, tops the UK chart for one week.

1982

Jan [30] *Oh Julie*, his first self-penned hit, heads the UK survey for one week.
May *Shirley*, his revival of an obscure '60s John Fred & His Playboy Band track, hits UK #6.
Sept Uptempo *Give Me Your Heart Tonight* reaches UK #11.
Oct ***Give Me Your Heart Tonight*** hits UK #3.
Nov Stevens revival of one of Jackie Wilson's early R&B-rockers, *I'll Be Satisfied*, hits UK #10.
Dec *The Shakin' Stevens EP*, spotlighting a seasonal revival of Elvis Presley's *Blue Christmas*, hits UK #2, held from the top by Rene & Renato's *Save Your Love.*

1983

Aug Stevens, having switched producers to Christopher Neil, takes a revival of Ricky Nelson's 1959 hit, *It's Late*, to UK #11.
Nov *Cry Just A Little Bit*, an original composition by Bob Heatlie, hits UK #3, while parent album, ***The Bop Won't Stop***, reaches UK #21.

1984

Jan Stevens has teamed with fellow Welsh vocalist Bonnie Tyler, to revive Brook Benton and Dinah Washington's 1960 US Top 10 smash, *A Rockin' Good Way (To Mess Around And Fall In Love)*, which, credited to Shaky & Bonnie, hits UK #5.
Apr *A Love Worth Waiting For* hits UK #2 for two weeks, behind Lionel Richie's *Hello.*
May Stevens' only US chart-maker is *Cry Just A Little Bit*, which reaches US #67.
Sept Dennis Linde's song, *A Letter To You*, hits UK #10.
Nov Compilation, ***Greatest Hits***, anthologizing 18 singles from *Hot Dog* up to date, hits UK #8.
Dec The self-penned *Teardrops* hits UK #5.

1985

Mar *Breaking Up My Heart*, another Heatlie song, reaches UK #14.
Nov Stevens reunites with his original producer, Dave Edmunds, for an update of *Lipstick, Powder And Paint*, a mid-'50s US R&B hit for bluesman, Joe Turner, which makes UK #11. The Edmunds-produced album, ***Lipstick, Powder And Paint***, reaches UK #37.
Dec [28] Heatlie-penned *Merry Christmas Everyone*, produced again by Edmunds, tops the UK chart in Christmas week, his fourth UK #1.

1986

Feb *Turning Away* reaches UK #15.
Nov *Because I Love You*, again produced by Neil, reaches UK #14.
Dec *Merry Christmas Everyone* re-charts, making UK #58.

1987

Aug Stevens' revival of Gary Glitter's *A Little Boogie Woogie (In The Back Of My Mind)* makes UK #12, co-helmed by Mike Leander, Glitter's former producer.
Oct [10] His treatment of the Supremes' 1964 million-seller, *Come See About Me*, reaches UK #24, and marks a reunion with Stuart Colman.
Dec [12] His self-produced (with Carey Taylor) update of Emile Ford's 1959 million seller, *What Do You Want To Make Those Eyes At Me For?*, in an almost identical arrangement, hits UK #5.
[26] ***Let's Boogie***, Stevens' first album after an unusually long hiatus, makes UK #59.

1988

Aug His version of the Detroit Emeralds' mid-'70s soul hit, *Feel The Need In Me*, reaches UK #26.
Oct *How Many Tears Can You Hide?* makes UK #47.
Dec Stevens has a rare ballad hit with a revival of the Bing Crosby/Grace Kelly oldie, *True Love*, at UK #36.
[17] ***A Whole Lotta Shaky*** peaks at UK #42.
[31] As one of the most successful UK performers of the '80s, Stevens appears on the 25th Anniversary edition of BBC1-TV's "Top Of The Pops", singing his first chart-topper, *This Ole House.*

1989

Feb [18] Incongruously produced by Art Of Noise's J.J. Jeczalik, *Jezebel* peaks at UK #58.
May *Love Attack* restores him to the UK Top 30 at UK #28. During the past decade, Shakin' Stevens has accumulated no less than 26 Top 30 hits, unsurpassed by any other act.

1990

Mar The run continues as the Pete Hammond-produced, *I Might*, reaches UK #20.Three further, less successful Hammond-helmed singles during the year - *Yes I Do* (#60), *Pink Champagne* (#59) and *My Cutie Cutie* (#75), together with the Telstar-issued album ***There's Two Kinds Of Music: Rock'n'Roll*** (#65 - Oct [20]), indicate that Shaky's fans may have now grown up.

1995

Apr [9] *I'll Be Home This Christmas*, taken from a seasonal album recorded at Westside Studios, has made UK #34 on Dec [28], 1991, followed by *Radio*, credited to Shaky, which debuted at its UK #37 peak on Oct [10], 1992, before the compilation ***The Epic Years***, bowed at its UK #57 pinnacle on Oct [31]. Hitless since then, Stevens has continued to undertake UK tours each year into the mid-'90s, now appearing at the Empire Theatre, Sunderland in the middle of 14-date UK swing.

AL STEWART

1965

Stewart (b. Sept. 5, 1945, Glasgow, Strathclyde, Scotland), having moved from Scotland with his widowed mother at the age of three, and subsequently attended public school until dropping out, learnt guitar alongside Robert Fripp (later to found King Crimson), and played his first live gigs as lead guitarist in rock/pop band Tony Blackburn (future UK DJ) & the Sabres, in Bournemouth, Dorset, in 1962. Strongly influenced by Bob Dylan, he becomes immersed in modern folk music and starts to write his own songs, now performing at London area folk club venues like Bunjies (where he earns £3 a week for his Friday night residency) and Les Cousins. He also temporarily shares a flat in the East End with a visiting Paul Simon (having also lodged with Sandy Denny and Jackson C. Frank). His first recording, *The Elf*, inspired by his reading J.R.R. Tolkein's **The Lord Of The Rings**, a one-off on Decca Records released in August 1966, will reportedly sell 496 copies.

1967

Sept Signed to CBS Records in the UK, his debut album, ***Bedsitter Images***, is issued, featuring mostly introspective songs for voice and guitar, backed by orchestral arrangements. CBS mounts a concert at London's Royal Festival Hall, presenting Stewart with a complete group and orchestra as back-up. His more usual shows are still one-man affairs, and he becomes a popular fixture on the college circuit, where his self-analytical, sometimes acidic, and occasionally controversial lyrics, are widely appreciated.

1968

July [6] Stewart takes part in the "Woburn Music Festival", Woburn, Beds.
Aug [9-11] He performs at the eighth annual "National Jazz & Blues Festival" at Kempton Park racecourse, Sunbury-on-Thames, Middx.

1969

Jan ***Love Chronicles***, featuring Jimmy Page on guitar, has an 18-minute title track which includes the word "fucking", preventing airplay. It is Stewart's first US release, and his only one on Columbia.
Dec UK music weekly **Melody Maker** votes ***Love Chronicles*** Folk Album Of The Year in its annual survey.

1970

Jan [3] Stewart perfoms at the Queen Elizabeth Hall, London backed by the Third Ear Band, the highlight of an 11-date UK tour set to end on the 27th in Brighton, Sussex.
Apr ***Zero She Flies*** is Stewart's UK chart debut, reaching #40.

1972

Feb ***Orange*** is released, displaying musical influences outside the folk troubadour style of his first three albums, but fails to chart.
May [6] Stewart takes part in the "Bickershaw Festival" near Wigan, Lancs.

1974

Mar Having performed the previous December 23rd at the Alexandra Palace, London, on a bill with Renaissance, Wishbone Ash and Vinegar Joe, Stewart now embarks on his first major US tour accompanied by members of the recently disbanded group, Home.
June ***Past, Present And Future***, a concept album tracing historical events, with inspiration drawn from the book, **The Centuries Of Nostradamus**, fails to chart in the UK, but released via a new US deal with Janus Records, makes US #133.

1975

Apr Catching the ear of FM radio in the States, ***Modern Times*** reaches US #30, supported by a US tour with a backing band comprising Gerry Conway, Pat Donaldson, Simon Nicol and Simon Roussell.

1977

Feb [5] Newly signed to RCA Records in the UK, ***Year Of The Cat***, produced by Alan Parsons (and rejected a year earlier by Virgin boss, Richard Branson, who was offered the album for a £5,000 advance), reaches UK #37. The extracted title track, *Year Of The Cat*, makes UK #31, his only UK chart single. It is also his US singles chart debut and, aided by strong radio airplay, hits #8 (Mar [5]).
[19] ***Year Of The Cat*** hits US #5.
Mar [24] ***Year Of The Cat*** is certified platinum by the RIAA.
May [21] *On The Border*, also from ***Year Of The Cat***, reaches US #42.

1978

Oct [21] A new US label deal with Arista Records precedes ***Time Passages***, also produced by Parsons. It reaches UK #39 (on RCA) and hits US #10. It is another of his albums to eschew romantic songs in favor of time-capsule pieces, concerned with specific historical events.
Dec [9] Its title song, *Time Passages*, hits US #7, during a ten-week spell atop the US AC chart.

1979

Mar [3] *Song On The Radio*, again from ***Time Passages***, makes US #29.
[16] ***Time Passages*** is certified platinum by the RIAA.

1980

Sept [6] ***24 Carrots*** reaches UK #55 and US #37.
Oct [25] Taken from it, *Midnight Rocks* peaks at US #24, and is Stewart's last US chart single. A double album, ***Live/Indian Summer***, consisting of three sides of live material and one from the studio, will make US #110 in December the following year. His next studio project, ***Russians And Americans*** will peak at UK #83 in June 1984, following a performance in May at London's Royal Albert Hall.

1988

May After four years of legal problems which have restricted any output, Stewart releases *License To Steal* on Enigma Records, on which he suggests that lawyers should be subject to limited nuclear warfare. It is taken from ***Last Days Of The Century***. Resident in Los Angeles, CA since 1976, Stewart (who also owns a house in France) will return to the UK in July the following year for a one-off performance at the Cambridge Folk Festival, Cambridge, Cambs.

1995

July Having contributed to ***Rock The World***, a 1990 benefit album raising money for the Phoenix House, London-based rehabilitation center, and promoted the April 1991 EMI-released retrospective collection, ***Chronicles ... The Best Of Al Stewart*** with a 19-date UK tour, his first such venture in 15 years, then completed US dates in June 1992 when a new album, ***Rhymes In Rooms - Al Stewart Live Featuring Peter White*** emerges on Permanent Records in the UK and Mesa in the US, the same label combination has released last year's ***Famous Last Words***, and now issues ***Between The Wars***, a collaboration with Laurence Juber, inspired by the swing-era.

ROD STEWART

1961

Stewart (b. Roderick David Stewart, Jan. 10, 1945, Highgate, London), of Scottish parents who moved to London and gave him a guitar for his 14th birthday, having attended William Grimshaw School, Hornsey, with Ray and Dave Davies and Pete Quaife (who will later achieve success as the Kinks), signs as an apprentice with Brentford Football Club. After three weeks, tired of little more than polishing other players' boots, he quits, heading for Europe, where he becomes a busker with his accomplice, folk singer Wizz Jones (and is deported from Spain for vagrancy). He returns to Britain, becomes a beatnik, and attends CND's Aldermaston marches. Going on to join Birmingham, Warks. R&B band, the Five Dimensions, as vocalist and harmonica player in 1963, he plays throughout the UK, backing singer Jimmy Powell, who records a single for Pye on which Stewart plays blues harp.

1964

Aug Having recently performed the same duties for Long John Baldry & the Hoochie Coochie Men, who have just signed with United Artists Records (Baldry had heard Stewart singing in his distinctive R&B-influenced, raspy style, while waiting for a train at Twickenham station), Decca Records staff producer Mike Vernon sees Stewart perform at London's Marquee club, and signs him to a five-year solo deal.
[6] Stewart makes his UK TV debut on "The Beat Room", with the Hoochie Coochie Men.
Oct His debut single, *Good Morning Little Schoolgirl*, despite an appearance on ITV show "Ready Steady, Go!", fails to chart. The Hoochie Coochie Men split, and Stewart briefly joins the Southampton, Hants.-based band, the Soul Agents.

1965

July Having joined Steampacket earlier in the year, a group formed by Giorgio Gomelsky, with Stewart sharing vocals with Baldry and Julie Driscoll, with Brian Auger (keyboards), Rick Brown (bass) and Mickey Waller (drums) also in the line-up, the group now supports the Rolling Stones and the Walker Brothers on a UK tour, and records an album (which will not be released until the '70s).
Nov Let go by Decca, Stewart signs a solo deal with EMI, releasing *The Day Will Come*, on its Columbia imprint.
[2] "Rod The Mod", a 30-minute portrait of a typical mod, directed by Francis Megahy, airs on UK TV.

1966

Mar Steampacket splits and Stewart joins the Shotgun Express with Peter Bardens (keyboards), Beryl Marsden (vocals), Peter Green (guitar), Dave Ambrose (bass) and Mick Fleetwood (drums).
Oct Steampacket releases the single, *I Could Feel*

The Whole World Turn Around, and appears at the "Richmond Rhythm & Blues Festival", Richmond, Surrey.

Dec Stewart joins the Jeff Beck Group (which includes his future Faces guitarist, Ron Wood), remaining with the band for two years. (Initially prevented by producer Mickie Most from taking a lead-vocal role on A-sides, Stewart will often appear on B-sides, not least on *I've Been Drinking*, the flip-side of Beck's 1968 hit version of the Eurovision song contest entry, *Love Is Blue*.)

1968

Mar Stewart releases the non-charting *Little Miss Understood* on Immediate Records.

1969

Oct Following the release of two Stewart-featured Jeff Beck Group albums, the influential ***Truth*** in 1968, and the recent ***Cosa Nostra - Beck Ola***, and having appeared with the Small Faces at a June gig at Cambridge University, Cambridge, Cambs. (billed as Quiet Melon), Stewart, having left Beck, turns down the chance to join US band, Cactus. He stays in Britain and, together with Wood, joins the Faces (now without the "Small" prefix), who sign to Warner Bros. He also signs a solo deal with Phonogram, and will run his group and individual careers simultaneously until the Faces split. (Stewart is advanced £1,000 to record his solo debut.)

Nov ***An Old Raincoat Won't Ever Let You Down***, comprising a mixture of originals and cover versions, and featuring the Faces, fails to chart in the UK, but makes US #139.

1970

Oct [1] He begins a 28-date US tour at Goddard College, Plainfield, VT. (During the year, Stewart records guide vocals for Python Lee Jackson's *In A Broken Dream*, for which he is paid enough to buy seat covers for his car. When the record is released and becomes a hit, Stewart's vocal has not been replaced, though he receives no credit.)

[3] ***Gasoline Alley***, again highlighted by his distinctively raspy vocal style, reaches UK #62 and US #27.

1971

Aug [14] Stewart's version of the Tim Hardin-ballad, *Reason To Believe*, peaks at US #62, but DJs (the first being in Cleveland, OH) flip the record, and *Maggie May* becomes the airplay-friendly A-side.

Sept [11] *Reason To Believe*, reaches UK #19.

Oct [1] The still-climbing *Maggie May* is certified gold by the RIAA.

[2] Largely self-written and entirely self-produced, ***Every Picture Tells A Story***, tops the UK chart for the first of six weeks, and simultaneously begins a four-week run at US #1. Much of the album's success is due to the self-penned *Maggie May*, which also hits US #1, and featuring Lindisfarne's Ray Jackson on mandolin.

[9] Stewart becomes one of a select number of artists to have a chart-topping single and album in both the UK and US in the same week, as *Maggie May*, now the A-side, begins a five-week stretch at UK #1.

Dec [25] *(I Know) I'm Losing You* reaches US #24.

1972

Mar [11] *Handbags And Gladrags*, written by Mike D'Abo, and produced by Lou Reizner, makes US #42.

July [28] The still-rising ***Never A Dull Moment*** is certified gold by the RIAA.

Sept [2] *You Wear It Well* tops the UK chart.

[16] ***Never A Dull Moment*** hits UK #1 for the first of two weeks, and heads to US #2.

Oct [14] *You Wear It Well* reaches US #13.

[28] Python Lee Jackson's *In A Broken Dream* hits UK #3, having already climbed to US #56.

Dec [9] Double A-side, *Angel* (a Jimi Hendrix cover) and *What Made Milwaukee Famous* (a hit for Jerry Lee Lewis), hits UK #4, as Stewart sings *Pinball Wizard* in a special stage production of "Tommy".

[16] *Angel* makes US #40.

1973

May Re-released *I've Been Drinking*, credited to Jeff Beck & Rod Stewart, reaches UK #27.

Sept [1] Compilation, ***Sing It Again Rod***, tops the UK chart and makes US #31.

[15] His revival of Sam Cooke's *Twisting The Night Away* stops at US #59.

[22] *Oh No Not My Baby*, reviving Manfred Mann's 1964 hit, hits UK #6.

Oct [12] ***Sing It Again Rod*** is certified gold by the RIAA.

Nov [17] *Oh No Not My Baby* makes US #59.

1974

May Stewart guests on the Scotland World Cup Football Squad's newly-released album, ***Easy Easy***, duetting with soccer star Denis Law on *Angel*.

[5] Stewart and Elton John perform a benefit for the Watford Football Club.

Oct [19] *Farewell*, backed with a medley of *Bring It On Home To Me* and *You Send Me*, hits UK #7, as its parent album, ***Smiler***, a self-produced mix of Stewart originals and covers, and featuring music guests Elton John, Ray Cooper and Willie Weeks among others, tops the UK chart, and reaches US #13.

Dec [21] *Mine For Me*, written for inclusion on ***Smiler*** by Paul McCartney (along with Elton John and Bernie Taupin's *Let Me Be Your Car*), peaks at US #91. Stewart signs to Warner Bros. Records after a legal dispute over whether Phonogram or Warner has the rights to his solo releases.

1975

Mar [5] Stewart meets Swedish actress, Britt Ekland, at a party in Los Angeles, CA, and embarks on a highly-publicized love affair. He announces that he is setting up permanent residency in the US, and applying for citizenship.

July Press reports claim that Stewart owes the UK taxman over £750,000. On a trip to Britain, Stewart refuses to leave the international departure lounge to avoid setting foot in the country.

Aug [30] ***Atlantic Crossing*** begins a five-week run atop the UK survey. The set has been produced by Tom Dowd in Muscle Shoals, AL, using the famed rhythm section, which includes Steve Cropper and Donald "Duck" Dunn.

Sept [6] *Sailing*, a ballad penned by Gavin Sutherland, tops the UK chart for the first of four weeks.

Oct [12] Stewart performs what will prove to be his last show with the Faces.

Nov [1] ***Atlantic Crossing*** hits US #9.

[8] *Sailing* makes US #58.

Dec [6] Reviving the Motown classic, *This Old Heart Of Mine*, Stewart hits UK #4 with his first release on Riva Records, set up by his manager, Billy Gaff.

[18] The Faces confirm their official split, leaving Stewart to concentrate on his solo career.

[19] ***Atlantic Crossing*** is certified gold by the RIAA, the same day the **Daily Mirror** runs the headline: "Why Rock Star Rod Is Quitting The Faces".

1976

Jan [31] *This Old Heart Of Mine* makes US #83.

June [19] Compilation album, ***The Best Of Rod Stewart***, makes US #90.

[26] *Tonight's The Night (Gonna Be Alright)* hits UK #5. (The song is mostly banned because of its subject matter, the seduction of a virgin.)

July [10] ***A Night On The Town***, recorded in Los Angeles with top session players David Foster, John Jarvis and the returning Cropper and Dunn, hits UK #1.

Aug BBC1-TV documentary series, "Sailor", adopts *Sailing* as its theme, sung by the crew of H.M.S. Ark Royal. It becomes the unofficial anthem of the Royal Navy.

Sept [18] He sings *The Wild Side Of Life* at the Don Kirshner Rock Awards in the US, as the Stewart-penned *The Killing Of Georgie (Parts 1 and 2)*, a two-part saga about the death of a gay friend in New York, NY, hits UK #2.

Oct [16] *Sailing*, reissued because of the TV documentary, hits UK #3. A television special based on ***A Night On The Town*** airs in the UK.

Nov [13] *Tonight's The Night (Gonna Be Alright)* tops the US chart for the first of eight weeks.

[27] Stewart opens a UK tour at Manchester's Belle Vue.

[30] *Tonight's The Night (Gonna Be Alright)* is certified gold by the RIAA.

Dec [4] ***A Night On The Town*** hits US #2.

[11] *Get Back*, featured in Lou Reizner's film, "All This And World War II", utilizing covers of Lennon/McCartney songs, reaches UK #11.

[18] A reissued *Maggie May* makes UK #31.

1977

Jan [11] Stewart plays an extra date at the Edinburgh Playhouse, Edinburgh, Lothian, Scotland, after cancelling the first of six shows at the Glasgow Apollo, Glasgow, Strathclyde, Scotland, because of 'flu.

Apr [16] His update of the Cat Stevens-penned *First Cut Is The Deepest* reaches US #21.

May [21] Coupled with *I Don't Want To Talk About It* as a double A-side, *First Cut Is The Deepest* begins a four-week run atop the UK chart, holding off the Sex Pistols' *God Save The Queen*.

July [23] *The Killing Of Georgie (Parts 1 and 2)* makes US #30.

Sept [17] Compilation album, ***The Best Of Rod Stewart***, reaches UK #18.

Oct [29] *You're In My Heart (The Final Acclaim)* hits UK #3.

Nov [19] ***Foot Loose And Fancy Free***, once again produced by Tom Dowd and recorded in Toronto, Canada, hits UK #3, as Stewart begins a major tour with a band comprising Jim Cregan (guitar), Gary Grainger (guitar), Billy Peek (guitar), Phil Chen (bass) and Carmine Appice (drums).

1978

Jan [7] ***Foot Loose And Fancy Free*** hits US #2.

[14] *You're In My Heart (The Final Acclaim)* hits US #4.

Feb [8] *You're In My Heart* is confirmed gold by the RIAA.

[18] Hot-rocking *Hotlegs*, coupled with the ballad, *I Was Only Joking* (featuring a reference to *Maggie May*), hits UK #5.

Apr [1] *Hotlegs* reaches US #28.

May [25] ***The Best Of Rod Stewart*** is certified gold by the RIAA.

June [10] Stewart, pursuing his love of soccer, hits UK #4 with *Ole Ola (Muhler Brasileira)*, recorded with the Scottish World Cup Football Squad. (After Scotland fails to qualify for the second round, drawing 1-1 with Iran, it speedily drops down the chart.)

[24] *I Was Only Joking* makes US #22.

Dec [2] Disco-pumping *D'Ya Think I'm Sexy*, written by Stewart and Appice, tops the UK chart. (Songwriter Jorge Benjor will later sue, claiming it is based on his *Taj Mahal*.)

[9] Its parent album, ***Blondes Have More Fun***, once again helmed by Dowd with string arrangements by Del Newman, hits UK #3.

1979

Jan [9] The "Music For UNICEF" concert, to celebrate the International Year Of The Child, takes place in the General Assembly Hall of the United Nations in New York, with Stewart singing *D'Ya Think I'm Sexy?*, donating the royalties from the song to UNICEF. (The following day NBC-TV will air "A Gift Of Song - The Music For UNICEF Concert".)

Feb [10] ***Blondes Have More Fun*** begins a three-week run atop the US survey, the same week that *D'Ya Think I'm Sexy* also hits US #1.

[21] *D'Ya Think I'm Sexy* is certified platinum by the RIAA.

[24] *Ain't Love A Bitch* reaches UK #11.

Apr [6] Stewart marries Alana Hamilton, ex-wife of actor George Hamilton, in Beverly Hills, CA.

May [12] Title cut, *Blondes (Have More Fun)*, peaks at UK #63.
June [9] *Ain't Love A Bitch* reaches US #22.
[21-28] Stewart finishes a four-month US tour with six performances at the Great Western Forum, Inglewood, CA.
Dec [8] ***Rod Stewart's Greatest Hits*** tops the UK chart for the first of five weeks, his seventh UK chart-topping album, and reaches US #22.

1980

Feb [2] *I Don't Want To Talk About It* makes US #46. (Written by Crazy Horse-member Danny Whitten, Everything But The Girl's version will re-chart in the UK in 1988, and Stewart himself will re-record it in 1990.)
July [5] *If Loving You Is Wrong (I Don't Want To Be Right)* reaches UK #23.
Nov [29] ***Foolish Behaviour***, recorded at Los Angeles' Record Plant Studio, and featuring Valerie Carter, Paulinho da Costa and Tony Brock among others, hits UK #4 and US #12. The extracted *Passion* makes UK #17.

1981

Jan [17] The self-penned ballad, *My Girl*, reaches UK #32.
Feb [7] *Passion* hits US #5.
Mar [4] ***Foolish Behavior*** is certified platinum by the RIAA.
[28] *Somebody Special* peaks at US #71.
Nov [14] ***Tonight I'm Yours***, produced and largely written by the singer, hits UK #8. Stewart embarks on his first North American tour in three years, billed as "Le Grand Tour Of America And Canada - Worth Leaving Home For", in Greensboro, NC.
[21] Extracted *Tonight I'm Yours (Don't Hurt Me)* hits UK #8.
Dec [19] *Young Turks*, aided by a gang-dancing video, hits US #5.
[26] *Young Turks* reaches UK #11.

1982

Jan [9] ***Tonight I'm Yours*** US #11.
[28] ***Tonight I'm Yours*** is certified platinum by the RIAA.
Mar [6] Stewart's cover of Ace's hit, *How Long*, makes UK #41, his last chart single for Riva.
[20] *Tonight I'm Yours (Don't Hurt Me)* reaches US #20.
Apr [26] He is mugged in Los Angeles, while standing next to his car.
May [22] *How Long* makes US #49.
July Stewart records Burt Bacharach and Carole Bayer Sager's *That's What Friends Are For* for the Henry Winkler/Michael Keaton film, "Night Shift". (Dionne Warwick & Friends will subsequently take the song to the top of the US chart.)
Nov [13] Double performance album, ***Absolutely Live***, reaches UK #35.
Dec [18] ***Absolutely Live*** makes US #46.

1983

June ***Body Wishes***, co-produced with Dowd (who Stewart thanks for "coming in on the project at the last minute and saved it from going down the toilet") and his first for Warner Bros., hits UK #5 and US #30.
July [2] *Baby Jane* tops the UK chart, as a prelude to a UK tour.
[30] *Baby Jane* reaches US #14.
Sept [10] *What Am I Gonna Do (I'm So In Love With You)* hits UK #3.
Oct [8] *What Am I Gonna Do (I'm So In Love With You)* makes US #35.

1984

Jan [14] *Sweet Surrender* reaches UK #23.
June [16] Now separated from his wife, Alana, Stewart's *Infatuation* makes UK #27, while its parent album, ***Camouflage***, produced by Michael Omartian, hits UK #8 and US #18.
July [28] *Infatuation*, featuring a guitar solo by his old boss, Jeff Beck, hits US #6.
Aug [21] ***Camouflage*** is certified gold by the RIAA.
Sept [1] His revival of *Some Guys Have All The Luck* reaches UK #15.
[18] He performs live at the inaugural MTV Video Music Awards, held at Radio City Music Hall, New York, NY.
Oct [22] The RIAA certifies multi-platinum sales of ***A Night On The Town*** (two million), ***Blondes Have More Fun*** (three million) and ***Footloose And Fancy Free*** (three million).
[27] *Some Guys Have All The Luck* hits US #10.

1985

Jan [12] His update of Free's *All Right Now* peaks at US #72. Stewart headlines two nights at the world's largest rock festival, "Rock In Rio", in Rio de Janeiro, Brazil.
July [20] Stewart has teamed with Beck for a version of the Impressions' *People Get Ready*, from Beck's ***Flash***, which makes US #48.

1986

May [31] *Love Touch*, produced by Mike Chapman, and taken from the Robert Redford/Debra Winger-starring film, "Legal Eagles", reaches UK #27.
July [5] "Rod Stewart and His Very Special Guests and Friends" concert is staged at Wembley Stadium, Wembley, Middx.
[19] *Every Beat Of My Heart* hits UK #2, while ***Every Beat Of My Heart*** produced by Bob Ezrin, hits UK #5, and, titled ***Rod Stewart*** in the US, reaches #28.
Aug [9] *Love Touch* hits US #6.
Sept [20] *Another Heartache*, co-written by Bryan Adams, makes UK #54.
[27] *Another Heartache* makes US #52.
Nov [2-6] Stewart plays four special concerts in Bournemouth, Dorset, and Brighton, East Sussex, in place of postponed shows in late September.
[29] *Every Beat Of My Heart* peaks at US #83.

1987

Apr [4] Reissued for the second time, *Sailing* makes UK #41, with all royalties going to the bereaved families and survivors of the Zeebrugge Ferry Disaster.
July [25] *Twistin' The Night Away*, a new version of his 1973 US #59, used in the Dennis Quaid/Martin Short film, "Innerspace", peaks at US #80.

1988

June [4] ***Out Of Order***, produced by Duran Duran's Andy Taylor and Chic's Bernard Edwards, enters at its UK #11 peak, and will reach US #20. Songwriting assistance comes from Simon Climie, whose *Love Changes Everything* Stewart has previously turned down. The extracted *Lost In You* reaches UK #21.
July [16] *Lost In You* reaches US #12.
Aug [20] *Forever Young* peaks at UK #57.
Sept [7] He performs at the fifth annual MTV Video Music Awards held at the Universal Amphitheatre, Universal City, CA.
Oct [15] *Forever Young* reaches US #12, helped by a video co-starring Stewart's child by current girlfriend, Kelly Emberg.

1989

Jan [30] Stewart, who has yet to win a Grammy, hosts the 16th annual American Music Awards, held at the Shrine Auditorium, Los Angeles.
Feb [25] His "South Of The Border Tour" starts in Mar Del Plata, Argentina.
Apr [1] *My Heart Can't Tell You No*, the third single from ***Out Of Order***, hits US #4, after a four-month chart climb.
[8] 450 fans are injured trying to rush the stage at a concert at Monterrey, Mexico.
May [13] Belated UK release, *My Heart Can't Tell You No*, peaks at #49 as his ex-wife, Alana, applies for increased alimony. A retrospective video collection, "Rod Stewart & the Faces", is released in the UK.
[31] Stewart embarks on a 39-date US tour in New Haven, CT, set to end on July 31st at the Hollywood Bowl, Hollywood, CA.
June [3] Stewart fails to show up for Boston radio station WXKS' birthday concert because of voice problems. DJ Sunny Joe White extracts a promise from Stewart to re-book.
[20] He begins another six-week US concert tour at Columbus, OH, having toured intermittently for over a year.
July [29] *Crazy About Her* reaches US #11.
Aug [5] Stewart fulfills his promise to White, performing a charity concert at the Wang Center, Boston, MA, in aid of the American Cancer Society, in memory of Terry Fox. (*Never Give Up On A Dream* is written about Fox.)
Nov [18] Re-cut with Ronald Isley, another updated version of the Isley Brothers' *This Old Heart Of Mine* makes UK #51.
[25] ***The Best Of Rod Stewart*** hits UK #3 in its week of entry.

1990

Jan [13] Definitive solo and group retrospective boxed-set, ***Storyteller/The Complete Anthology : 1964-1990***, makes US #54.
[16] Charles Falterman, who slipped and fractured his kneecap at a Stewart concert on April 22nd, 1989 in Lafayette, IN, files a lawsuit against the singer, alleging that his kicking soccer balls into the audience caused the crowd to "react almost as an uncontrollable herd of animals".
[27] His Trevor Horn-produced cover version of Tom Waits' *Downtown Train* hits US #3.
Feb [5] ***Storyteller - The Complete Anthology 1964-1990*** is certified gold by the RIAA.
Mar [3] *Downtown Train* hits UK #10, following a performance of the song at the BRIT Awards, held at London's Dominion Theatre.
May [19] ***Downtown Train/Selections From Storyteller***, with extracted cuts from the ***Storyteller*** boxed-set, reaches US #20.
[26] *This Old Heart Of Mine*, the duet revival with Ronald Isley, hits US #10.
Sept Stewart sings *Hot Legs* at a benefit for AIDS Project Los Angeles, at the Wiltern Theatre, Los Angeles.
Nov [13] Patricia Boughton of Utica, MI, files a lawsuit in Oakland County Circuit Court, Pontiac, MI, alleging that she suffered a ruptured tendon in her middle finger and a possible break after Stewart kicked a football into the crowd during a June 22nd concert at the Pine Knob Music Theatre, East Troy, WI. She will receive a $17,000 settlement having claimed that the accident made sex between her and her husband "very difficult" and contributed to the break-up of their 14-year marriage.
Dec [1] *It Takes Two*, an update of Marvin Gaye & Tammi Terrell's Motown classic, now duetted with Tina Turner, mainly for blanket coverage as the latest UK Pepsi commercial theme, hits UK #5. (They will reportedly share £1 million between them for the ad.)
[15] Stewart marries New Zealand model Rachel Hunter in Beverly Hills Presbyterian church. (In a later quote, Stewart says: "I found the girl I want, and it's all up to me now. I won't be putting my banana in anybody's fruit bowl from now on.")

1991

Feb [15] Kelly Emberg, who lived with Stewart from 1985 to 1990, files a $25 million palimony suit in Los Angeles Superior Court.
Mar [23] *Rhythm Of My Heart*, his new album's lead-off track, hits UK #3.
Apr [1] Elton John gatecrashes Stewart's Wembley Arena concert, dressed to look like Stewart's new bride, Rachel Hunter (who has helped John with his make-up).
[6] ***Vagabond Heart***, dedicated to his father, Robert Joseph Stewart (who passed away the previous September), variously produced by Horn, Richard Perry, Patrick Leonard, Stewart and Bernard Edwards, debuts at its UK #2 peak, behind ***Eurythmics' Greatest Hits***.
May [11] ***Vagabond Heart*** hits US #10.
[12] Stewart appears by satellite from Lausanne, Switzerland, in "The Simple Truth" concert for Kurdish refugees at Wembley Arena, Wembley,

singing *Sweet Soul Music* and *Rhythm Of My Heart*.
[18] *Rhythm Of My Heart* hits US #5.
June [1] Stewart opens the UK leg of his "Vagabond Heart" tour at Parkhead Stadium, Glasgow, Scotland. (He will selectively cancel dates when he suffers with a bad throat.)
[28] He receives the Silver Clef Award For Services To Music at the annual Nordoff Robbins Music Therapy luncheon, in London.
[29] *The Motown Song*, with backing vocals provided by the Temptations, hits UK #10.
July [16] ***Vagabond Heart*** is certified platinum by the RIAA.
Aug [17] The 40-city North American leg of the "Vagabond Heart" tour opens at Citadel Hill, Halifax, NS, Canada.
Sept [6] **The Sun** reports that his brother-in-law, Jimmy Bonner, signs him to the Highgate chapter of the British Legion, and that he accepts.
[13-15] Stewart breaks the house record at the Pacific Amphitheatre, Costa Mesa, CA, playing to crowds totalling 46,445, grossing $1,073,922.
[14] *Broken Arrow*, penned by Robbie Robertson, peaks at UK #54.
[21] *The Motown Song* hits US #10.
[24, 26-27] Stewart plays three sellout shows at the Meadowlands Arena, East Rutherford, NJ.
Nov [12-13] He performs to two sellout crowds, totalling 35,786, at the Nassau Veterans Memorial Coliseum, Uniondale, NY, but will postpone dates either side of the event, once again because of a sore throat.
[23] Glass Tiger's *My Town*, on which Stewart provides uncredited vocals, reaches UK #33.
Dec [18-20] Stewart plays year-end dates at Palacio de los Deportes, Mexico City, Mexico, grossing $1,549,233.

1992

Jan [11] Stewart begins the second segment of the North American leg of his "Vagabond Heart" tour, at Freedom Hall, Louisville, KY, as ***Two Rooms - Celebrating The Songs Of Elton John & Bernie Taupin***, to which Stewart contributes *Your Song*, reaches US #18.
[25] *Broken Arrow* reaches US #20.
[27-28] Stewart grosses $1,033,760 at two sellout dates at New York's Madison Square Garden.
Feb [14] "Valentine Vagabond : Rod Stewart Live On Valentine's Day" airs live from the Universal Amphitheatre, on pay-per-view and on the Global Satellite Network.
[29] Antipodean leg of his "Vagabond Heart" tour opens at Western Springs, Auckland, North Island, New Zealand.
Mar [13] Stewart is served with a summons alleging that he assaulted Sydney, Australia newspaper photographer, Geoff Henderson, who snapped him at a Sydney hotel.
Apr [1] A Los Angeles judge refuses to drop an invasion of privacy section of a $25 million lawsuit brought by Stewart against the Canadian tabloid, **News Extra**, which had alleged on July 2nd 1991, that he was conducting extra-marital affairs with his wife's blessing. (During the year, and commenting on his forthcoming autobiography, Stewart claims: "No stone will go unturned, and what crawls out had better run for the hills, as I intend to delve deeply into the numerous stains I've left on the tapestry of life".)
[25] His version of Elton John's *Your Song* coupled with the reissued *Broken Arrow* makes UK #41.
June [2] His fourth child, daughter Renée, is born at Portland Hospital, London.
[6] *Your Song* makes US #48.
Oct [3] Stewart attends the bi-annual Children's Diabetes Foundation benefit at the Beverly Hilton, Los Angeles.
Nov [7] ***The Best Of Rod Stewart And The Faces 1971-1975*** charts for a week at UK #58.
Dec [12] *Tom Traubert's Blues (Waltzing Matilda)*, a second Tom Waits' cover, hits UK #6.

1993

Jan Stewart works on a new album at SARM Studios, London, with Trevor Horn producing.
Feb [5] Reunited for the occasion with Ron Wood, Stewart tapes "MTV Unplugged" at Universal Studios, Universal City, to be broadcast on May 5th. Songs include *Gasoline Alley, Maggie May, Stay With Me, Every Picture Tells A Story* and *Have I Told You Lately*.
[16] Stewart is presented with the Lifetime Achievement Award at the 12th annual BRIT Awards, held at the Alexandra Palace, London, at which he also reunites with the Faces (minus Ronnie Lane) for a one-off performance, singing *Ruby Tuesday* and *Stay With Me*.
[27] His cover of the Rolling Stones' *Ruby Tuesday* reaches UK #11.
Mar [6] While his recently-recorded album, ***Under The Blue Moon***, is shelved, a UK career retrospective, ***Rod Stewart : Lead Vocalist***, compiled by the artist and including five new cuts from the ***Blue Moon*** sessions, hits UK #3, in its week of entry.
[27] ***The Best Of Rod Stewart*** re-charts at UK #44.
Apr [24] His update of *Shotgun Wedding* makes UK #21.
[27] He sings *This Old Heart Of Mine* and duets with Aretha Franklin on *People Get Ready* on her Fox-TV "Aretha Franklin : Duets" special (set to air on May 9th).
May [12] He performs *Have I Told You Lately* at the fourth annual World Music Awards from the Sporting Club, Monte Carlo, Monaco, at which he is also honored with the Lifelong Contribution To The Music Industry Award.
June [12] Warner Bros.-released 15-track ***Unplugged ... And Seated***, from his recent MTV performance, featuring Wood on nine cuts, begins a five-week stay at US #2.
[19] The extracted cover of Van Morrison's *Have I Told You Lately*, dedicated to his wife, hits US #5.
[24] He is featured on BBC1-TV's "Top Of The Pops".
[29] *Have I Told You Lately* is certified gold by the RIAA.
July [3] ***Unplugged ... And Seated*** also hits UK #2, behind Jamiroquai's ***Emergency On Planet Earth***, as *Have I Told You Lately* hits UK #5.
[16] He performs on NBC-TV's "The Tonight Show".
Aug [28] Stewart's "unplugged" version of *Reason To Believe* makes UK #51.
Sept [16] He guests on CBS-TV's "Late Show With David Letterman".
Oct [2] *Reason To Believe* reaches US #19.
Dec [8] Stewart receives the 1993 Tribute To Artistic Excellence award and sings *Having A Party* at the **Billboard** Music Awards.
[9] The RIAA certifies two million sales of ***Storyteller - The Complete Anthology 1964-1990***.
[25] *People Get Ready* climbs to UK #45.

1994

Jan [19] Jeff Beck inducts Stewart into the Rock and Roll Hall of Fame at the ninth annual induction dinner at New York's Waldorf Astoria Hotel. (He is unable to attend because of an earthquake in Los Angeles two days earlier.)
[22] *All For Love*, featuring the trio of Stewart, Bryan Adams and Sting and from the movie "The Three Musketeers", tops the US chart.
[29] *All For Love* hits UK #2.
Feb [2] *All For Love* is certified platinum by the RIAA.
[7] Stewart is presented with the Michael Jackson International Artist Award by Tony Bennett at the 21st annual American Music Awards. He also sings *Maggie May* and *Having A Party*.
[11] He begins a North American tour at the Montreal Forum, Montreal, PQ, Canada.
[12] *Having A Party* reaches US #36.
Apr [5] As Stewart's tour continues, he donates the proceeds of his second concert at the Arrowhead Pond of Anaheim, Anaheim, CA to the American Red Cross Los Angeles Earthquake Relief Fund and the American Red Cross Orange County Disaster Services Fund.
June [27] The RIAA certifies three million sales of ***Rod Stewart's Greatest Hits, Volume I And II***.
Aug [19] Stewart files suit against News Group Newspapers Ltd., after **The Sun** reported in its February 22nd issue that he was suffering from inflammed throat nodules and was unfit to perform.
Dec [31] Tieing in with his latest promotional deal with Pepsi-Cola, which includes a Latin American TV ad campaign, Stewart performs a free New Year's Eve show at Rio de Janeiro's Copacabana Beach, broadcast live on Brazilian TV, before an estimated 3½ million crowd. (He is unable to perform an encore, and is given oxygen to combat exhaustion before being taken away in an ambulance.)

1995

Jan [27] ***Every Picture Tells A Story*** is certified platinum by the RIAA.
Feb [9] The RIAA also confirms two million sales of ***Downtown Train - Selections From Storyteller Anthology***.
Apr [10] Stewart claims he was misunderstood in an interview which reported he was going to retire soon.
May [13] He guests on NBC-TV's "The Tonight Show".
[20] *You're The Star* debuts at its UK #19 peak.
June [17] Written by Tom Petty, *Leave Virginia Alone* makes US #52, as ***A Spanner In The Works*** hits UK #4. In the midst of a current European tour, Stewart breaks the attendance record (83,000) at Wembley Stadium.
July [1] ***A Spanner In The Works*** reaches US #35.
[8] A private jet carrying Stewart is forced to make an emergency landing at Landvetter Gothenburg International Airport, after a bird is sucked into one of its two engines.
Aug [10] ***A Spanner In The Works*** is certified gold by the RIAA.
[19] *Lady Luck* charts for a week at UK #56.
Nov [13] The RIAA certifies three million sales of ***Unplugged ... And Seated***.
Dec [14] Stewart takes part in "The Greatest Music Party In The World" at the National Exhibition Centre, Birmingham.
[15] While renewing their marriage vows in London, the Stewarts are showered by broken glass when a window in their horse-drawn carriage taking them from the church to the hotel reception is smashed by a bodyguard.
[28-30] Stewart finishes a month-long UK tour with dates at Wembley Arena.

1996

Feb [5] He begins another series of US dates, billed as "In The Round" at the Summit, Houston, TX.
Mar [13-14] A pair of gigs at New York's Madison Square Garden are postponed (until May 22nd-23rd) with Stewart suffering from viral laryngitis.
Apr [28] He performs at the 1996 VH1 Honors, a concert held to benefit the human rights' organization, Witness, broadcast live by the cable network in the US.

STING

1971

Having played bass with the Ronnie Pierson Trio on board Princess Cruises liners, and while attending teacher-training college, Gordon Matthew Sumner (b. Oct. 2, 1951, Wallsend, Newcastle, Tyne & Wear) plays in semi-professional jazz-rock combos, Earthrise, Phoenix Jazz Band and the River City Jazz Band. Going on to teach under-nines at St. Paul's First School, Cramlington, Tyne & Wear, Sumner joins the Newcastle Big Band the following year, which makes a locally-distributed album on which he plays bass. He is nicknamed Sting by Newcastle jazz player Gordon Soloman, because of his yellow-and-black-hooped soccer jersey, reminiscent of a bee.

1977

Jan Having joined Last Exit in 1974, singing and playing bass on both sides of the single *Whispering Voices* the following year, Sting now forms the Police, becoming both lead vocalist and bass player. Signing a publishing deal with Virgin, he will pen all of their hits, including 15 Top 20 UK hits and five UK chart-toppers

1979

Nov With many acting roles in television commercials behind him, Sting has filmed a cameo role in "Quadrophenia", based on the Who's album, playing mod character Ace, which now receives its US premiere. Chris Pettit's film, "Radio On", with Sting appearing as Just Like Eddie, will bow in the US the following September during a year when he also appears in the UK TV movie, "Artemis '81".

1981

May "The Secret Policeman's Other Ball", in which Sting performs an acoustic version of the Police hit, *Roxanne*, opens in US cinemas.
[19] Still a member of the Police, Sting is named Songwriter Of The Year at the 26th annual Ivor Novello Awards, held at London's Grosvenor House Hotel.

1982

Apr [29] Sting wins a second Ivor Novello Award, at the 27th annual luncheon held at the same venue, as *Every Little Thing She Does Is Magic* is named Best Pop Song.
June [27] An out-of-court settlement is reached between Sting and Virgin Music over a contract concerning the copyright to Sting's early songs, originally signed in 1977. He is granted a 100% royalty for his next solo album, copyright of his songs are returned to him within 7½ years, and he receives an immediate payment of £200,000.
Aug [11] His first solo outing, a cover of the Vivian Ellis co-penned standard, *Spread A Little Happiness*, from the soundtrack to the TV film, "Brimstone And Treacle", in which Sting also stars as Martin, reaches UK #16. He also records cover versions of *Tutti Frutti* and *Need Your Love So Bad* for A&M's ***Party Party*** soundtrack.
Sept Sting splits from his actress wife, Frances Tomelty.
Nov [10] He guests on NBC-TV's "Late Night With David Letterman".

1984

Feb [28] *Brimstone And Treacle* is named Best Rock Instrumental Performance at the 26th annual Grammy Awards.
Apr [19] He nabs the Best Song Musically And Lyrically and Most Performed Work trophies for writing the Police career highlight, *Every Breath You Take*, at the 29th annual Ivor Novello Awards, again held at the Grosvenor House Hotel.
Nov [25] Sting contributes a vocal lead to Band Aid's historic recording of *Do They Know It's Christmas?* at the SARM Studios, Notting Hill, London.
Dec A film of Frank Herbert's novel, **Dune**, with Sting starring as Feyd Rautha, opens in the US.

1985

Jan With the Police now effectively disbanded, he holds auditions for a new group in New York, looking for top jazz talent.
Feb His backing group the Blue Turtles Band is formed, with Sting (vocals, bass), Darryl Jones (bass), Kenny Kirkland (keyboards), Omar Hakim (drums), Branford Marsalis (various brass, woodwind), Wynton Marsalis (trumpet) and Dollette McDonald and Janice Pendarvis (vocals), which makes its debut at the New York Ritz.
Mar [2] Phil Collins' ***No Jacket Required***, featuring a Sting duet on *Long Long Way To Go*, hits UK #1.
June [29] Sting's *If You Love Somebody Set Them Free* makes UK #26, as his self-penned jazz-flavored debut album, ***The Dream Of The Blue Turtles***, co-produced with Pete Smith at Eddy Grant's Blue Wave Studio in Barbados, and released via a worldwide solo deal with A&M, hits UK #3, spending over one year on the survey. He is also featured on Miles Davis' current album, ***You're Under Arrest***.
July [13] He performs at the "Live Aid" benefit spectacular with Phil Collins and Branford Marsalis in his backing band.
Aug [3] *If You Love Somebody Set Them Free* hits US #3. "The Bride", in which Sting stars as Frankenstein, premieres in the US.
Sept [7] ***The Dream Of The Blue Turtles*** hits US #2.
[13] Sting begins his first solo tour in San Diego, CA. (The film of David Hare's play, "Plenty", with Sting co-starring opposite Meryl Streep and Sam Neill, opens across the US.)
[14] *Love Is The Seventh Wave* makes UK #41.
[21] Dire Straits' *Money For Nothing*, co-written with Mark Knopfler, and highlighted by Sting's unmistakeable vocal intro, tops the US chart (having already hit UK #4).
Oct [26] *Fortress Around Your Heart* hits US #8.
Nov [8] Director Michael Apted's film of Sting and his band before and during his concert tour in Paris, France, titled "Bring On The Night", opens in the US. (The various artists compilation, ***Lost In The Stars***, an anthology of Kurt Weill's work featuring Sting's version of *Mack The Knife*, is released by A&M.)
Dec [28] *Love Is The Seventh Wave* reaches US #17.

1986

Jan [4] The 18-date UK leg of "The Dream of the Blue Turtles World Tour" opens at the Bournemouth International Centre, Bournemouth, Dorset, including six nights at London's Royal Albert Hall, set to end on the 27th at the Brighton Centre, Brighton, East Sussex.
[18] The politically-themed *Russians*, aided by a black and white Godley & Creme video, makes UK #12.
Feb [22] Jazz-tinged *Moon Over Bourbon Street* makes UK #44.
Mar [1] *Russians* reaches US #16.
June [11] The Police reunite at an Amnesty International concert in Atlanta, GA, performing five songs.
[28] Sting takes part in the Jerry Dammers-organized "Artists Against Apartheid" concert on Clapham Common, London, with Elvis Costello, Peter Gabriel, Billy Bragg, and others. Live double album, ***Bring On The Night***, released to accompany the documentary, which has been edited from 350,000' of film, reaches UK #16.
July [21] The Police begin recording for the follow-up to ***Synchronicity***, but abandon the sessions soon after, as Sting insists on pursuing solo music and acting interests.
Nov "A Conspiracy Of Hope" tour, supporting Amnesty International, begins in the US with Sting, Bryan Adams, Bob Dylan, Peter Gabriel, Tom Petty and U2.
[14] ***Conspiracy Of Hope***, again aiding Amnesty International, with contributions from Sting, Peter Gabriel, Elton John and Steve Winwood, is released.

1987

Feb [24] "Bring On The Night" wins the Best Music Video, Long Form category at the 29th annual Grammy Awards.
July Sting joins former musical associate, Eberhard Schoener, in an evening of songs by Bertolt Brecht and Kurt Weill in Hamburg, West Germany. He also plays at the "Umbria Jazz Festival", in Italy, with the Gil Evans Orchestra.
[2] Following the death of his mother, Sting continues recording his second album in Montserrat, which he will dedicate to her.
Oct [24] His sophomore set, ***Nothing Like The Sun***, co-produced with Neil Dorfsman with guests, Andy Summers, Eric Clapton, Knopfler, Rubén Blades and Branford Marsalis, hits UK #1 for one week, at the beginning of a 47-week chart stay, and heads towards US #9 during a one-year tenure and double platinum status.
Nov [21] The extracted *We'll Be Together* makes UK #41.
Dec [5] *We'll Be Together* hits US #7. (Sting contributes *Gabriel's Message* to the Jimmy Iovine-conceived Special Olympics Christmas album, ***A Very Special Christmas***.)

1988

Jan [20] Sting begins a 46-date US tour in Tampa Bay, FL.
Feb [8] ***Nothing Like The Sun*** is named Best British Album at the seventh annual BRIT Awards, at the Royal Albert Hall.
[20] *An Englishman In New York*, written about UK exile Quentin Crisp, stops at UK #51.
Mar [2] ***Bring On The Night***, despite not charting in the US, wins Best Pop Vocal Performance, Male category, at the 30th annual Grammy Awards.
[12] *Be Still My Beating Heart* reaches US #15.
[29] His US tour ends in Portland, OR.
Apr [9] *Fragile* peaks at UK #70. ***... Nada Como El Sol***, a mini-album of Spanish versions of selections from his last album, is released for the South American market. Sting also contributes a cover of George Gershwin's *Someone To Watch Over Me* as the title theme to Ridley Scott's thriller of the same name.
[23] *An Englishman In New York* peaks at US #84.
June [11] Sting opens "Nelson Mandela's 70th Birthday Tribute" concert with *If You Love Somebody Set Them Free* at Wembley Stadium, Wembley, Middx.
Aug Sting plays the title role in Stravinsky's "Soldier's Tale", released on his own Pangæa label. Ian McKellen plays the narrator, and Vanessa Redgrave the devil, accompanied by the London Sinfonietta. Sting also writes the music for the Quentin Crisp documentary, "Crisp City".
Sept Ballad, *They Dance Alone*, from ***Nothing Like The Sun***, written as a human rights protest about Peruvian leader, General Pinochet, fails to chart in the UK. Sting's *Englishman In New York* is used as the title track to the Daniel Day Lewis film, "Stars And Bars". (Sting's own movie appearances in 1988 include "Stormy Monday" and "Julia Julia".)
[2] He joins Bruce Springsteen, Tracy Chapman, Peter Gabriel and Youssou N'Dour on Amnesty International's "Human Rights Now!" six-week world tour.
[7] "We'll Be Together" wins the Best Cinematography category at the fifth annual MTV Video Music Awards, held at the Universal Amphitheatre, Universal City, CA.
Nov A compilation of Sting clips, "The Videos", is released, while he contributes *I Can't Say* to Rubén Blades' current album, ***Nothing But The Truth***.

1989

Mar Sting donates a track to the ecological album, ***Greenpeace Rainbow Warriors***.
Apr He undertakes an international promotional tour of interviews to publicize the plight of the Kayapo Indians to help save their Brazilian rain-forest homeland, resulting in the establishment of the Rainforest Foundation.
[4] Sting collects the Best Song Musically And Lyrically trophy for *They Dance Alone* at the 34th annual Ivor Novello Awards, held at London's Grosvenor House Hotel.
June The press reports that Sting and Paul McCartney are to lead a BBC radio campaign to raise listeners' awareness of environmental issues.
Aug Playboy reports that Sting is to star, with Kris Kristofferson and Peter Coyote, in the movie "Sandino" about the Nicaraguan general assassinated in 1934.
Nov [5] Sting opens in "The Threepenny Opera" at the Lunt-Fontanne Theatre in New York, following its premiere at Washington's National Theatre.
Dec [5] He is a keynote speaker at the second annual Human Rights Award ceremonies, at Faneuil Hall, Boston, MA, where he presents a $30,000 award to four young activists in the Chinese student movement.

1990

Feb [12] Sting, backed by Herbie Hancock and Branford Marsalis, invites Bruce Springsteen, Paul Simon, Jackson Browne and Don Henley on stage for a jam at the Rainforest Foundation and Environmental Media Association fund-raiser in Beverly Hills, CA. After the benefit, Sting, Springsteen, Henley, Marsalis and Bruce Hornsby repair to Los Angeles' China club for a 45-minute impromptu set.
Aug [25] Curious Ben Liebrand-remix update (in Soul II Soul-style) of Sting's *Englishman In New York* reaches UK #15.

1991

Jan [19] Sting hosts NBC-TV's "Saturday Night Live", as *All This Time*, from the forthcoming ***The Soul Cages***, reaches UK #22.
Feb [1] Sting kicks off his "Soul Cages" world tour, with a backing band featuring Dominic Miller (lead guitar) David Sancious (keyboards) and Vinnie Colaiuta (drums), at the Berkeley Community Theatre, Berkeley, CA.
[2] ***The Soul Cages***, co-produced with Hugh Padgham at the Studio Guillaume Tell, Paris, France, and Villa Salviati, Migliarino, Italy, debuts at UK #1.
Mar [9] The second UK extract, *Mad About You*, peaks at UK #56.
[10] His "Rainforest Foundation Benefit Concert" at New York's Carnegie Hall raises $250,000.
[16] *All This Time* hits US #5.
[23] ***The Soul Cages*** hits US #2, behind Mariah Carey's eponymous album.
Apr I.R.S. Books publishes Sting's lyrics, with illustrations by Italian artist, Gligorov.
[8] ***The Soul Cages*** is certified platinum by the RIAA.
[10] Sting performs on "MTV Unplugged".
[20] His European tour leg debuts at the Buddle Art Centre, Newcastle, a set recorded for subsequent album release. The 59-date trek will end on July 14th at an open-air concert at the Milton Keynes Bowl, Milton Keynes, Bucks.
May [4] Title cut, *The Soul Cages*, debuts at its UK #57 peak.
[12] Sting appears by satellite from Holland in "The Simple Truth" concert for Kurdish refugees at Wembley Arena, Wembley, singing *Purple Haze*.
June [1] Sting stars in the first airing of Soviet TV rock show, "Rock Steady" from Moscow, Russia.
[22] Kids collection, ***For Our Children***, to which Sting contributes *Cushie Butterfield*, reaches US #31.
July He performs at the annual "Montreux Jazz Festival", Montreux, Switzerland.
Sept [4] Sting guests on NBC-TV's "Late Night With David Letterman".
[5] He performs a sellout show before 14,233 at New York's Madison Square Garden.
Oct [2] A&M Records lays on a 40th birthday party for him, staged after his first Hollywood Bowl concert, attended by Herb Alpert, Bob Dylan, Don Henley, Jackson Browne, Andy Summers, Joni Mitchell and others. The set is designed to resemble his Newcastle birthplace.
[11-14] Sting plays sellout shows at the Sports Palace, Mexico City, Mexico, grossing $2,745,360.
[24] The RIAA certifies two million sales of ***Nothing Like The Sun***.
Nov [21] He begins the 12-date UK leg of his current tour at the Aberdeen Exhibition & Conference Centre, Aberdeen, Grampian, Scotland, set to end on December 8th at the National Exhibition Centre, Birmingham, West Midlands. (A live concert at the Glasgow Scottish Exhibition & Conference Centre on the 23rd highlights programming on the first day of full-scale high definition (HDTV) television broadcasting in Tokyo, Japan.) A five-track mini-album, ***Acoustic Live In Newcastle***, is released by A&M. (During the year, Sting is also featured on Claudio Abbado's version of ***Peter And The Wolf***, released on Deutsche Grammophon, while the Bob Belden Ensemble issues the jazz tribute album, ***The Music Of Sting Straight To My Heart***.)

1992

Jan [9] Sting is a guest voice on Fox-TV's "The Simpsons".
[11] ***Two Rooms - Celebrating The Songs Of Elton John & Bernie Taupin***, to which Sting has contributed *Come Down In Time*, reaches US #18. (During the month, he buys a 54-acre, 41-room Tudor mansion in the village of Lake, near Amesbury, Wilts., for close to the asking price of £2 million.)
Feb [25] *Soul Cages* is named Best Rock Song at the 34th annual Grammy Awards, held at Radio City Music Hall, New York.
Aug [20] Prior to a church blessing in two days time, Sting and long-time girlfriend Trudie Styler marry at a London registry office. (They already parent three children, Mickey (8), Jake (7) and Coco (2).)
[22] Following the church blessing, they hold a reception at their 16th-century estate in Lake, with the Troggs providing musical entertainment and Summers and Copeland reuniting with Sting on performances of *Message In A Bottle* and *Roxanne*.
Sept [5] *It's Probably Me*, recorded with Eric Clapton for the soundtrack to "Lethal Weapon 3", reaches UK #30.
[22] *All This Time* is honored at the annual ASCAP PRS Awards as one of the most performed songs in 1991.
[27] Sting performs with an all-star line-up at a benefit for leukemia patients in Luciano Pavarotti's horse stables in Modena, Italy, duetting with the opera star on *Panis Angelicus* (subsequently release on ***Pavarotti & Friends*** the following year).
Nov [13] He receives an honorary doctorate of music from the University of Northumbria in Newcastle upon Tyne, from Vice Chancellor, Lord Glenamara, in recognition of his contribution to the arts and his campaigning on ecological issues.

1993

Feb [20] He guests on NBC-TV's "Saturday Night Live", performing two songs and appearing in sketches, with guest host Bill Murray, as *If Ever I Lose My Faith In You* reaches UK #14.
[22-24] Sting plays three warm-up dates for his world tour, scheduled to start in May, at the 1,700 seater Gusman Center, Miami, FL. (Willing to take a support slot opening for the Grateful Dead on early US dates, Sting says: "I want to see this Deadhead phenomenon. I want to see it first-hand.")
Mar [2] He participates in a concert at New York's Carnegie Hall to benefit the world's rain forests with Bryan Adams, Herb Alpert, Tom Jones, George Michael, James Taylor, Tina Turner and Dustin Hoffman.
[13] Co-produced again with Padgham, ***Ten Summoner's Tales***, recorded at Sting's Lake House home studio, enters the UK chart at its #2 peak, behind Lenny Kravitz's ***Are You Gonna Go My Way***.
[27] ***Ten Summoner's Tales*** hits US #2 on its way to platinum sales.
Apr [19-22] Sting performs four dates at the Royal Albert Hall (previously postponed from March) during his world trek.
[24] *Seven Days* debuts at its UK #25 peak.
May [1] *If Ever I Lose My Faith In You* reaches US #17.
[13] He appears on NBC-TV's "The Tonight Show".
June [17] He is featured on BBC1-TV's "Top Of The Pops".
[19] Ballad, *Fields Of Gold* reaches UK #16.
July [24] *Fields Of Gold* climbs to US #24.
Sept [2] Sting performs *If I Ever Lose My Faith* at the tenth annual MTV Video Music Awards, staged at the Universal Amphiteatre, Universal City.
[4] *Shape Of My Heart* charts for a week at UK #57.
[6] Sting takes part in a benefit for Walden Woods at Foxboro Stadium, Foxborough, MA, with Elton John, Don Henley and Melissa Etheridge.
Oct [30] ***Demolition Man***, a 6-track EP - its title track featured in the Sylvester Stallone/Wesley Snipes movie of the same name, peaks at US #162.
Nov [6] *Nothing 'Bout Me* makes US #57.
[20] *Demolition Man* debuts at its UK #21 peak.

1994

Jan [7] Sting embarks on a seven-date UK leg of a world tour at the National Exhibition Centre, Birmingham.
[22] *All For Love*, featuring the trio of Rod Stewart, Bryan Adams and Sting and from the movie "The Three Musketeers", tops the US chart, as Sting performs at the International Centre, Fukuoka, Japan, during the southeast Asia and Australian leg of the tour.
[29] *All For Love* hits UK #2.
Feb [2] *All For Love* is certified platinum by the RIAA.
[11] Sting performs at the "Bushfire Benefit Concert" at Sydney Football Stadium. (Bryan Adams joins him onstage at the end of his set to sing *All For Love*.)
[14] He wins Best British Male Artsist category at the 13th annual BRIT Awards, held at London's Alexandra Palace.
[18] US leg of the world tour commences at the Stephen O'Connell Center, Gainesville, FL.
[26] *Nothing 'Bout Me* debuts at its UK #32 peak.
[28] Sting guests on CBS-TV's "Late Show With David Letterman".
Mar [1] Sting wins the Best Pop Vocal Performance, Male (*If I Ever Lose My Faith In You*) and Best Music Video, Longform ("Ten Summoner's Tales") categories at the 36th annual Grammy Awards, staged at New York's Radio City Music Hall. He also performs *If I Ever Lose My Faith In You*.
[2] He plays four sellout dates before crowds totalling 20,952 at the Paramount, New York.
Apr [9] Sting takes part in the fifth annual "Rainforest Foundation Benefit Concert" held at New York's Carnegie Hall, with Elton John, James Taylor, Aaron Neville, Luciano Pavarotti, Branford Marsalis and Whitney Houston.
[29] The RIAA certifies three million sales of ***Ten Summoner's Tales***.
May [15] Sting is awarded an honorary doctorate of music at Boston's Berklee College of Music at the Hynes Convention Center.
[24] The RIAA certifies three million sales of ***The Dream Of The Blue Turtles***.
[25] Sting wins the Best Song Musically And Lyrically category for *If I Ever Lose My Faith In You* at the 39th annual Ivor Novello Awards, held at London's Grosvenor House Hotel.
June [24] Eric Clapton presents Sting with the Silver Clef Award at the 19th Nordoff Robbins Music Therapy lunch.
Oct [10] Tammy Wynette's duets album, ***Without Walls***, which sees her paired with Sting on an update of *Every Breath You Take*, is released.
[23] Sting takes part in the Stonewall Equality Show at the Royal Albert Hall, the same day that BMI honors *If Ever I Lose My Faith In You* with its Robert Musel Award as the Most Performed Song Of The Year at its annual ceremony held at London's Dorchester Hotel, at which *Every Breath You Take* is also cited for its three millionth broadcast performance.
[29] *When We Dance*, one of two new tracks from his forthcoming hits compilation, debuts at its UK #9 peak.
Nov [9] Sting guests on the "Late Show With David Letterman".
[19] ***Fields Of Gold - The Best Of Sting 1984-1994*** bows at its UK #2 high.
[26] ***Fields Of Gold - The Best Of Sting 1984-1994*** debuts at its US #7 peak.
Dec [17] *When We Dance* reaches US #38.

1995

Feb [11] *This Cowboy Song* debuts at its UK #15 peak.
Apr [12] Sting performs at the sixth annual "Rainforest Foundation Benefit Concert" from Carnegie Hall, with Bruce Springsteen, James Taylor, Elton John, Jon Bon Jovi, Jessye Norman and Geoffrey Oryema.
May [30] Paul Allen's Starwave multi-media company launches Sting's forthcoming CD-ROM ***All This Time***,

as a work-in-progress, at the NARAS Music & Multimedia conference in San Francisco, CA.
[31] ***Fields Of Gold - The Best Of Sting 1984-1994*** is certified platinum by the RIAA.
June [8] Sting makes his first UK appearance in two years, at the annual "Fleadh Festival" in London's Finsbury Park.
Oct [7] He celebrates his birthday at home with George Michael, Jimmy Nail and five pupils from Downside who sing for their proverbial supper.
[14] ***Tower Of Song : The Songs Of Leonard Cohen***, including Sting and the Chieftains' *Sisters Of Mercy*, charts for a week at US #198.
[17] Sting's former accountant, Keith Moore, is found guilty of embezzling £6 million from the singer and sentenced to six years in jail at Southwark Crown Court. During the case, in which Sting was the main prosecution witness, it is revealed that he has 108 bank accounts worldwide.
Nov The film soundtrack to "Ace Ventura : When Nature Calls" is released by MCA Records including a Trevor Horn-produced reworking of the Police hit *Spirits In The Material World* by Sting and Pato Banton. Three jazz covers by Sting, *Angel Eyes*, *My One And Only Love* and *It's A Lonesome Old Town*, also appear on the newly-released soundtrack to the Mike Figgis-directed film "Leaving Las Vegas".
[25] The ***All This Time*** CD-ROM, a twin-disc set including retrospective material and interactive elements, is released.
Dec [17] A son, Giacomo Luke is born to Trudie and Sting in London.

1996

Feb [20] After performing a duet with M People's Heather Small, Sting presents Elton John with the Outstanding Contribution To The British Record Industry at the 13th annual BRIT Awards, held at London's Alexandra Palace.
[24] Sting guests on "Saturday Night Live".
Mar [2] Previewing his new album, *Let Your Soul Be Your Pilot* enters at its UK #15 peak.
[5] Sting attends the launch of the 25th anniversary celebrations of London's Hard Rock Café, performing songs from his new album.
[9] He embarks on a world tour at the 1,200-seat Paridiso Club in Amsterdam, Holland.
[16] Featuring his regular sidemen Dominic Miller (guitar), Kenny Kirkland (keyboards) and Vinnie Colaiuta (drums) and guests including Branford Marsalis, B.J. Cole and the Memphis Horns, ***Mercury Falling***, co-produced with Padgham, peaks at UK #4 in its week of entry, as *Let Your Soul Be Your Pilot* stalls at US #86.
[30] ***Mercury Falling*** bows at its US #5 peak.
Apr [10] He guests again on the "Late Show With David Letterman".
[12] Sting performs at the sixth annual "Rainforest Foundation Benefit Concert" held again at Carnegie Hall.
[13] Tina Turner's ***Wildest Dreams***, featuring Sting among its guests, bows at its UK #4 high.
May [11] *You Still Touch Me* reaches UK #27 in its week of entry, and will debut at US #89 the following week at the start of its chart climb.
June [21] The North American leg of the world tour opens at the Coral Sky Amphitheatre, West Palm Beach, FL.
Dec [5-7, 9-11] Sting's ten-month world tour comes to end with six nights at the Royal Albert Hall.
see also: **POLICE**

THE STONE ROSES

Ian Brown (vocals); **John Squire** (lead guitar); **Gary "Mani" Mounfield** (bass); **Alan "Reni" Wren** (drums)

1983

Brown (b. Ian George Brown, Feb. 20, 1963, Ancoats, Lancs.) and Squire (b. John Thomas Squire, Nov. 24, 1962, Broadheath, Lancs.), having been brought up two doors apart on Sylvan Avenue, Sale, Lancs., and attended Altrincham Grammar School together, have formed the Patrol in 1980, lining-up as Andy Couzens (vocals), Brown (bass), Simon Wolstencroft - ex-the Fall (drums) and Squire (lead guitar), playing local colleges and clubs. Squire and Brown subsequently moved to a Hulme housing estate in central Manchester. The Patrol now changes its name to English Rose, inspired by a Jam track from ***Setting Sons***. Wolstencroft is temporarily replaced by a drummer known only as Wazza. Brown spends much of his time being a "scooter boy", while Squire takes a number of jobs including set-making on a TV adaptation of "The Wind In The Willows".

1984

Hitching around Europe, Brown meets a Scandinavian promoter in Germany who guarantees the band gigs in Sweden. Brown returns to Britain and hastily re-assembles the band with himself now as vocalist, Couzens switched to guitar, Squire, and new members Pete Garner (bass) and drummer Wren (b. Alan John Wren, Apr. 10, 1964, Manchester), whom Squire and Brown have known since the age of 11, fighting with him at the Belle Vue speedway track. Rejecting the name the Angry Young Teddy Bears, they travel to play five gigs in Sweden as the Stone Roses, a combination of their earlier name and the Rolling Stones, their favorite band.

1985

June The Stone Roses perform at the latest of their own middle-of-the-night warehouse parties in Manchester and begin spray-painting the city with the band logo.
Aug The group signs to the small local independent label, Thin Line, which issues the non-charting 12" single, *So Young*, backed with *Tell Me*, produced by legendary Mancunian music figure, Martin Hannett. Further sessions with the producer prove unfruitful.

1986

The band links with manager Gareth Evans, a local club owner. Couzens quits, later to form the High, as the group seeks a more commercial direction, influenced not least by the Creation label group, Primal Scream.

1987

June The Stone Roses release *Sally Cinnamon*, a one-off 12" for the FM Revolver label, which is critically praised, but fails to sell beyond Manchester.
Sept They perform at Sefton Park, Liverpool, Merseyside, on a bill with the La's at a one-day indie-fest. Wren is currently moonlighting as a kissogram, while Garner is replaced by old band friend, Mounfield (b. Gary Michael Mounfield, Nov. 16, 1962, Crumpsall, Gtr. Manchester).

1988

Oct Rough Trade pulls out of an expected label deal, so New Order's Peter Hook-produced *Elephant Stone* is licensed, together with the band, to Andrew Lauder's new Silvertone Records. (Lauder had seen the band at an Anti-Clause 28 gig at Manchester's International.) The Stone Roses are fast becoming the darlings of the alternative music press and late-night UK radio.
Dec The band performs at the Central London Polytechnic with Chameleons' offshoot, the Sun & the Moon.

1989

Feb [23] During a UK tour, which has included dates at Manchester's Hacienda, London's Powerhaus and Hull's Unity club, the Stone Roses perform a much praised gig at the Middlesex Polytechnic, while *Made Of Stone*, written about Brown's hitch-hiking days, hits the UK Independent chart at #4.
May [13] Their critically-revered debut album, ***The Stone Roses***, produced mainly by John Leckie, and featuring 11 Squire/Brown compositions, initially makes UK #32, but will re-chart five times over the next 12 months.
July [29] The group performs before a soldout 6,000 capacity audience at the Empress Ballroom, Blackpool, Lancs., to be followed by European dates and four further sellouts in Japan.
Nov The Stone Roses are heard for only 45 seconds on BBC-TV's arts program, "The Late Show", when the volume of their performance blows BBC studio fuses.
[18] A capacity 8,000 see the band play at London's Alexandra Palace.
Dec [2] Now hailed, together with the Happy Mondays, as pioneers of the new movement bursting from Manchester's rock dance scene, the Stone Roses hit UK #8 with the bass funk-laden *Fool's Gold*, double A-sided with *What The World Is Waiting For*, later to be sampled by Run D.M.C. By coincidence, both the Roses and the Mondays have made their BBC1-TV "Top Of The Pops" debuts on November 30th.

1990

Jan As ***The Stone Roses*** re-enters the UK chart set to peak at #19, the band vents its anger in a growing dispute with old label, FM Revolver, by staging a paint attack inside the company's office, causing £23,000 of damage. The label has made a video without the group's permission or approval, to re-promote *Sally Cinnamon*, which re-enters at UK #46.
Mar [3] ***The Stone Roses*** makes US #89 spurred by college radio support.
[4] At their subsequent fan-attended court case, the band is fined £3,000.
[17] Silvertone begins reissuing the group's three label singles: *Made Of Stone* re-charts at UK #20.
[27] Stone Roses perform to a fanatical 30,000 capacity crowd at Spike Island, Widnes, Cheshire.
[30] *She Bangs The Drums* now makes UK #34.
July [14] After a lengthy recording absence, the newly-issued *One Love* debuts at its UK #4 peak, during a seven-week chart stay.
Sept To the growing displeasure of the band, Silvertone reissues *Fool's Gold/What The World Is Waiting For* (UK #22), in the knowledge that the band is now the most sought after signing for a major label. Months of courting by nearly all the majors will result in Silvertone and the Stone Roses entering into lengthy litigation over their recording and license obligations. Initial moves by Silvertone will prevent the band from even entering a recording studio until well into 1991.

1991

May [20] High Court Judge John Humphries frees the band from its contract, citing it as an "unfair, unjustified and unjustifiable restraint of trade" which was unenforceable. He also grants the band costs, believed to be between £100,000 and £500,000.
Aug Reni appears in Manchester Court charged with threatening behavior and illegal parking. He pleads not guilty. The case is adjourned until November 14th when he will be acquitted.
Sept [14] With Silvertone still mining early recordings, *I Wanna Be Adored* debuts at its UK #20 peak.

1992

Jan [18] *Waterfall* reaches UK #27.
Feb The group splits from manager Gareth Evans.
Mar Newly signed to Geffen Records for a reported $4 million, the band begins work on its label debut with producer Leckie, using the Rolling Stones Mobile Studio in Wales.
Apr [11] Silvertone-issued *I Am The Resurrection* bows at its UK #33 pinnacle.
May [30] *Fools Gold* re-charts for a week at UK #73.
Aug [1] ***Turn Into Stone***, a collection of singles and B-sides, reaches UK #32.
Dec Former manager Gareth Evans files suit alleging that the band owes him £120,000, plus compensation.

1993

Feb Geffen Records issues a statement saying there

have been further delays in recording the much-anticipated Stone Roses label debut.
July Leckie quits the sessions with Paul Schroeder and Simon Dawson taking over, though only Dawson will see the project through.
Dec US Geffen executives John Kalodner and Tom Zutack visit the group at Rockfield Studios in Monmouth, Gwent, Wales to check on their investment.

1994

Mar Their tongue-in-cheek titled, much-anticipated sophomore set, ***Second Coming***, is scheduled for release, but fails to appear.
Nov [7] The group's new single, *Love Spreads,* receives its world premiere on BBC Radio 1FM's "Evening Session".
Dec [3] *Love Spreads* debuts at its UK #2 peak.
[5] Much to the chagrin of the UK's alternative music media, the group conducts its first interview in five years in **The Big Issue**, a magazine sold by and for the homeless.
[17] ***Second Coming*** peaks at UK #4 in its week of entry.

1995

Feb [4] ***Second Coming*** enters at its US #47 high.
Mar [10] Having recently appointed Doug Golstein as their new manager, a court battle with his predecessor, Gareth Evans, set to begin on the 13th, is settled out of court.
[11] *Ten Storey Love Song* debuts at its UK #11 peak.
Apr Robbie Maddix, who has drummed for Errol Brown, Ruby Turner, Terence Trent D'Arby and several Manchester bands including Rebel MC, replaces Wren who has departed the previous month.
[29] *Fools Gold '95* debuts at its UK #25 peak.
May [27] Compilation ***The Complete Stone Roses*** hits UK #4 in its week of entry.
June [2] Squire breaks his collarbone and shoulder blade in a mountain bike accident near San Francisco, during the group's first-ever US tour. (They had completed 11 dates before cancelling the tour, and will also be unable to make a much anticipated appearance at the "25th Glastonbury Festival" at the end of the month.)
Nov [11] *Begging You*, with a Carl Cox remix, bows at its UK #15 peak.
[28] Stone Roses begin a 19-date sellout UK trek (all 53,000 tickets were sold in 24 hours) at the Spa Pavilion, Bridlington, Humberside. (The group's first UK dates in five years, they nearly cause a riot at the Newport Centre, Newport, Gwent, Wales show on December 4th, when Brown takes to the stage wearing a Cardiff City soccer shirt.)

STONE TEMPLE PILOTS

Scott Weiland (vocals); **Dean DeLeo** (guitar); **Robert DeLeo** (bass); **Eric Krez** (drums)

1987

Robert DeLeo (b. Feb. 2, 1966, NJ) meets Weiland (b. Oct. 27, 1967, Santa Cruz, CA) at a Black Flag concert in Long Beach, CA (as Weiland will later recall of the meeting : "It was one of those weird things. You get into a heavy discussion with a total stranger, and you discover that both of you are seeing the same girl."), deciding to form a hard-rock/punk combo together back in their hometown, San Diego, CA. Initially named Mighty Joe Young, they recruit Kretz (b. June 7, 1966, Santa Cruz) after seeing him play at a local club, before Robert's older brother Dean (b. Aug. 23, 1961, NJ) completes the quartet, playing early dates around San Diego. Changing its name to Shirley Temple's Pussy, the band begins gigging around Southern California, before settling on the final moniker, Stone Temple Pilots in 1990, subsequently signing with Atlantic Records in 1992, on the strength of its demo tape and a solid live reputation.

1992

Sept Their sonically aggressive, '70s rock-influenced debut album, ***Core***, produced by Brendan O'Brien, is released.
Nov The group opens for Rage Against The Machine on a four-week US tour.
Dec [31] The band begins a further 40-date US trek, supporting Megadeth.

1993

Mar [25] STP begins its first European tour, at the Berlinloft, Berlin, Germany, set to end on April 8th at Doomroosje, Nijmegen, Holland.
[27] The date rape-themed *Sex Type Thing* bows at its UK #60 peak.
June [18] The group embarks on a 39-date US tour, supported on selected dates by the Butthole Surfers, fIREHOSE and Basshead, at the Jannus Landing, St. Petersburg, FL, set to end on August 15th in Honolulu, HI.
July [3] ***Core*** finally hits US #3. (During the month the band plays at Los Angeles' Castaic Lake concert to benefit the Bohemian Women's Political Alliance and perform at another fundraiser held at the Hollywood Palladium, Hollywood, CA benefitting Rock For Choice.)
Aug [3-4] During current US dates the band plays two sell-out gigs at New York's Roseland Ballroom, in the guise of their teen-heroes, Kiss.
[27-28] STP begins an eight-date tour of England and Germany in London.
Sept [2] The group wins the Best New Artist category for "Plush" at the tenth annual MTV Video Music Awards, held at the Universal Amphitheatre, Universal City, CA.
[11] *Plush* reaches UK #23.
[17] STP performs on CBS-TV's "Late Show With David Letterman".
[18] ***Core*** reaches UK #27.
Oct [23] The group is featured on ABC-TV's "Halloween Jam II" broadcast, from Orlando's Universal Studios, FL.
Nov [20] The group guests on NBC-TV's "Saturday Night Live".
[27] The reissued *Sex Type Thing* debuts at its UK #55 peak.
Dec [8] The band is named Top Modern Rock Act of the Year and *Plush* hailed as the Top Rock Track at the fifth **Billboard** Music Awards staged at the Universal Amphitheatre.
[17] The group guests on NBC-TV's "The Tonight Show".

1994

Jan [27] Stone Temple Pilots are simultaneously voted Best New Band (in the Readers' Picks section) and Worst New Band (by the Music Critics) in **Rolling Stone**'s 1994 Music Awards.
Feb [7] The group wins the Favorite Pop/Rock New Artist and Heavy Metal/Hard Rock New Artist categories at the 21st annual American Music Awards held at the Shrine Auditorium, Los Angeles.
[8] The RIAA certifies sales of three million copies of ***Core***.
Mar [1] *Plush* is named Best Hard Rock Performance With Vocal at the 36th Grammy Awards, staged at New York's Radio City Music Hall.
May [17] The group embarks on a five-date UK tour at the Barrowlands, Glasgow, Strathclyde, Scotland, set to end on the 22nd at London's Brixton Academy.
June [25] Once again overseen by O'Brien and recorded in three weeks during the spring at Southern Tracks studio in Atlanta, GA, ***Purple*** debuts at US #1 having entered the UK survey at its #10 peak the previous week.
July [4] A two-month headlining US tour gets underway at the Kiefer U.N.O. Lakefront Arena, New Orleans, LA, an opening gig grossing $108,577 from 6,253 fans, set to end on September 4th at the Ocean Center, Daytona Beach, FL.
Aug [19-20] The group opens for the Rolling Stones at the Exhibition Stadium, Toronto, ON, Canada.
[20] *Vasoline* bows at its UK #48 peak.
Sept [8] The group performs an acoustic version of *Pretty Penny* at the 11th annual MTV Video Music Awards, emceed by Roseanne, at Radio City Music Hall.
[17] Weiland marries Jannina Castenada.
[19] *Interstate Love Song* begins a record-setting 15-week stay atop the US Album Rock Tracks chart, and will log more than 60,000 radio spins in the US alone by December.
Oct [28] The RIAA certifies sales of three million copies of ***Purple***.
Nov [16] A three-date South American visit begins in Sao Paolo.
[22] Their European tour ends at London's Brixton Academy with a £10 admission.
Dec [10] *Interstate Love Song* charts for a week at UK #53.
[16] STP is once again the music guest on "Late Show With David Letterman".

1995

Apr [8] ***Encomium: A Tribute To Led Zeppelin***, including the band's version of *Dancing Days*, reaches US #17 in its week of entry.
May [15] Having scrapped two weeks of recording sessions in February, Weiland is arrested for heroin and cocaine possession outside Posada Motel in Pasadena, CA.
[16] Weiland and Hole's Courtney Love phone KROQ radio in Los Angeles, with Love reading a message written by him explaining his drug addiction.
[23] Weiland is formally charged with drug possession, facing up to three years in prison, with a court date set for April 9th the following year. (He will plead not guilty at his arraignmemt on June 9th.)
Oct Having temporarily fallen out with his band-mates, and formed the ad-hoc side unit Magnificent Bastards with guitarists Zander Schloss and Jeff Nolan, bassist Bob Thomson and drummer Victor Indrizzo (which has contributed *Mockingbird Girl* to the recent "Tank Girl" soundtrack and a cover of *How Do You Sleep?* to the John Lennon tribute album, ***Peace***), Weiland regroups with Stone Temple Pilots to begin recording the band's third album at Westerly Ranch, Santa Ynez, CA.

1996

Apr [13] Once again produced by O'Brien and released on Atlantic, ***Tiny Music : Songs From The Vatican Gift Shop*** enters at its US #4 peak.
[24] Having cancelled scheduled free concerts in New York, Chicago and Los Angeles, the group issues a statement confirming that Weiland "has become unable to rehearse or appear for these shows due to his dependency on drugs. He is currently under a doctor's care in a medical facility." The band's slot opening for Kiss on the latter's US summer dates is left open.
[29] Weiland is ordered by a Pasadena judge to spend up to six months in a drug rehabilitation center under round-the-clock supervision.

THE STRANGLERS

Hugh Cornwell (vocals, guitar); **Dave Greenfield** (keyboards); **Jean-Jacques Burnel** (vocals, bass); **Jet Black** (drums)

1974

Oct The Guildford Stranglers are formed in Chiddingford, Surrey, originally as a trio comprising chemistry graduate and ex-science teacher Cornwell (b. Aug. 28, 1949, London), one-time jazz drummer and ice-cream salesman, Black (b. Brian Duffy, Aug. 26, 1948, Ilford, Essex) and Burnel (b. Feb. 21, 1952, London), son of French parents, and a history graduate from Bradford University. The group signs with Albion management and Greenfield (b. Mar. 29, 1949, Brighton, Sussex) joins on keyboards the following May, after answering an ad placed by the band as a "soft-rock group" in **Melody Maker**, replacing Swedish guitarist, Hans Warmling. A sax player, recruited at the same time, lasts for just three days, and the band decides to remain a quartet.

1976

Feb [29] After close to a year on the road in minor club gigs, the Stranglers make their major venue debut when they take part in the "Special Leap Year Concert" with Deaf School, Nasty Pop and Jive Bombers, at London's Roundhouse.
May [17] The Stranglers support Patti Smith at the Roundhouse.
[19] A seven-date UK tour begins at Bogarts in Birmingham, West Midlands, set to end on the 28th at the Gaiety Theatre, Leicester, Leics.
July [4] The group plays at the American bicentennial show at the Roundhouse, with the Ramones and the Flamin' Groovies.
Sept They support Patti Smith on a full UK tour (followed by a further UK trek on their own through October and November).
Dec [3] The band signs a recording deal with United Artists, one of the earliest punk/new wave contracts.

1977

Feb [8] Supporting the Climax Blues Band at London's Rainbow Theatre, the band's performance is cut short by a power turn-off after Cornwell reveals his "Fuck" T-shirt on stage. (The Greater London Council has warned the management that its performance regulations would not allow this display.)
Mar The Stranglers record their first live session for "The John Peel Show" on BBC Radio 1, after completing a UK mini-tour.
[5] The group-penned debut single, *(Get A) Grip (On Yourself)*, produced by Martin Rushent, makes UK #44 (after being accidentally omitted from the chart by compilers, BMRB, in its first week of release), while the group is playing live dates in Europe.
Apr The group plays again at London's Roundhouse, with the Jam and Cherry Vanilla.
May Another UK tour begins, lasting into June. Some dates are cancelled when local councils and venue bookers begin banning punk-associated groups.
[7] First album, ***The Stranglers IV : Rattus Norvegicus***, recorded in six days, hits UK #4.
June The band backs Celia Collin, a female singer discovered by its manager, Dai Davies, who has sung live with them at London's Nashville, on a revival of Tommy James & the Shondells' *Mony Mony*, credited to Celia & the Mutations.
[4] After trouble at a Clash gig at the Rainbow Theatre, the Stranglers have seven tour dates cancelled. The Damned, the Jam and the Adverts are also affected by cancellations.
July [9] *Peaches/Go Buddy Go* hits UK #8. (The A-side is banned by the BBC for "offensive lyrics", so the B-side is promoted equally as the group performs the cut on their first major TV appearance, on BBC1-TV's "Top Of The Pops".) Burnel receives call-up papers to complete national service in France. He is ordered to report to the 39th Infantry Division in Rouen, but objects on the grounds that it would "conflict with my commitment to the Stranglers", and escapes the draft by providing proof of his permanent residency in Britain.
Aug [20] *Something Better Change/Straighten Out* hits UK #9.
Sept Banned from appearing at Manchester's Belle Vue Elizabethan Rooms because owners Trust House Forte object to the band, a Stranglers spokesperson says, "Trust House Forte should concentrate on food served up in their motorway cafés before they start worrying about punk".
[1] The Stranglers begin a major UK tour, followed by further European dates.
Oct [15] ***No More Heroes***, again produced by Rushent, hits UK #2. During live dates, a number of Glaswegian councillors attend an Apollo Theatre gig to check on the group's behavior. Cornwell has spotlights shone on them in the stalls and dedicates *Ugly* to them.
[22] *No More Heroes* hits UK #8.
Nov The group plays a short residency at London's Roundhouse, supported by the Dictators and partially recorded for a later live album release. Burnel and Black spend a night in jail in Brighton, East Sussex, after a gig at the Top Rank, charged with obstruction, after trying to help two Dutch Hell's Angels Stranglers fans who had been arrested.
[22] The Stranglers perform on the first night of the three-week "Hope & Anchor Front Row Festival" in Islington, London.

1978

Feb [25] *Five Minutes* makes UK #11.
Mar [16] The group begins its first US tour before moving on to Canada, Iceland, Scandinavia, and back through Europe.
May [20] *Nice'n'Sleazy* makes UK #18.
June [3] ***Black And White***, including *Nice'n'Sleazy*, hits UK #2, supported by UK dates.
Sept [2] Their keyboard-driven revival of Bacharach/David's *Walk On By* makes UK #21, with jazzman George Melly guesting on the B-side cut, *Old Codger*.
Oct The group plays at London's Battersea Park with Peter Gabriel (with strippers performing during *Nice'n'Sleazy*), before beginning a series of one-off shows in London using pseudonyms to beat local council bans.

1979

Mar [10] Live album, ***Live (X Cert)***, from a variety of concert appearances, hits UK #7.
Apr [28] Burnel's debut solo album, ***Euroman Cometh***, makes UK #40 as he undertakes a solo tour.
June The group records a new album in Paris, France, co-producing the tracks with Alan Winstanley (who had engineered previous recordings), and also headlines the Loch Lomond Festival in Scotland.
Aug [18] The Stranglers perform at Wembley Stadium, Wembley, Middx., with AC/DC, Nils Lofgren and headliners, the Who.
Sept [8] *Duchess*, from the forthcoming album, makes UK #14.
Oct [13] ***The Raven***, with initial pressings featuring a 3-D sleeve picture, hits UK #4. Cornwell also releases an album, ***Nosferatu***, in collaboration with Robert Williams.
[27] *Nuclear Device (The Wizard Of Aus)*, taken from ***The Raven***, reaches UK #36, as the band tours Britain.
Dec [8] Four-track EP, *Don't Bring Harry*, makes UK #41.

1980

Jan [7] Cornwell is found guilty of possession of heroin, cocaine and cannabis. He is fined £300, and sentenced to three months' imprisonment in Pentonville Prison, London.
Mar [21] He is sent to Pentonville after losing the appeal against his drug conviction.
Apr [25] Cornwell is released from prison. (The story of his time spent there will be related in his book, **Inside Information**.)
May [29] *Bear Cage* makes UK #36.
June [14] *Who Wants The World* reaches UK #39.
[21] The Stranglers are arrested in Nice, France, after allegedly inciting a riot when a concert at the university is cancelled because a generator has not been supplied for electrical power. (Black will chronicle this event in his book, **Much Ado About Nothing**. The group members will be fined in a Nice court later in the year.)

1981

Feb [7] *Thrown Away* makes UK #42, the group's first release on Liberty Records (as parent company EMI re-names United Artists).
[21] Their self-produced ***Themeninblack***, also on Liberty, hits UK #8.
Nov [14] *Let Me Introduce You To The Family* peaks at UK #42, as the band tours the UK to promote the forthcoming album, ***La Folie***.

1982

Feb [13] A far cry from their punk beginnings, the melodic, waltz-time *Golden Brown*, with an arresting harpsichord arrangement, proves to be the Stranglers' most popular single, hitting UK #2, behind the Jam's *A Town Called Malice/Precious*. (During a show at the Swindon Leisure Centre, the group is angered by a shower of spittle fired in their direction throughout their set. They apprehend the ringleader of the gobbing throng, remove his pants, and use his bare buttocks as tom toms during *Golden Brown*.)
Mar [6] ***La Folie***, which includes *Golden Brown*, makes UK #11.
May [1] Title track, *La Folie*, sung in French by Burnel, makes UK #47.
Aug [21] *Strange Little Girl* hits UK #7, during a 9-week chart stay.
Oct [2] ***The Collection 1977-1982***, a 14-track singles anthology compiled as a final EMI album, makes UK #12. Disagreements with the label in 1982 ensure that the Stranglers will not re-sign to Liberty as their first contract expires (they have tried to move to Phonogram but an EMI injunction prevented it).
Nov The band signs a new recording deal with Epic Records.

1983

Jan [22] *European Female* hits UK #9, while parent album, ***Feline***, their first for Epic, hits UK #4.
Feb The band embarks on a UK tour in support of the album.
Mar [12] *Midnight Summer Dream*, from the album, makes UK #35.
Apr During the month, London's Hammersmith Odeon venue cancels a second concert by the group after the previous night's audience has caused damage to the building.
May [5] *Golden Brown* is named the PRS' Most Performed Work Of 1982, at the 28th annual Ivor Novello Awards luncheon, held at London's Grosvenor House Hotel.
Aug [13] *Paradise*, also from ***Feline***, reaches UK #48.
[27] The group plays at the annual "Reading Rock Festival", Reading, Berks., before embarking on a tour of Europe.
Dec Burnel and Greenfield's ***Fire And Water*** reaches UK #94.

1984

Oct [20] *Skin Deep*, a trailer for the forthcoming album, makes UK #15.
Nov ***Aural Sculpture***, produced by Laurie Latham, makes UK #14.
Dec [15] *No Mercy*, extracted from ***Aural Sculpture***, peaks at UK #37.

1985

Feb [23] *Let Me Down Easy*, also from the album, reaches UK #48. A current UK tour of major venues includes five nights at London's Dominion Theatre.
Sept Cornwell's solo single, *One In A Million*, recorded for Epic's associated Portrait label, is released.

1986

Sept [6] *Nice In Nice*, referring to their June 1980 imprisonment in France, precedes the new Epic album, and reaches UK #30, while a Liberty-released set, ***Off The Beaten Track***, a compilation of rare earlier tracks, makes UK #80.
Nov [1] *Always The Sun* makes UK #30, taken from the Latham-produced ***Dreamtime*** album, which reaches UK #16.

1987

Jan [3] *Big In America*, also from the album, peaks at UK #48.
Mar [21] *Shakin' Like A Leaf* makes UK #58.
May ***Dreamtime*** peaks at US #172.
Aug [30] The group plays on the final day of the

annual "Reading Rock Festival".

1988

Jan [16] After a lengthy absence from recording, the group's revival of the Kinks' *All Day And All Of The Night* hits UK #7.

Feb [20] ***All Live And All Of The Night***, combining onstage recordings from 1987 with the recent, studio-recorded hit single, bows at its UK #12 peak.

May [7] Cornwell, signed solo to Virgin Records, charts for a week at UK #71 with *Another Kind Of Love*, and ***Wolf***, which makes UK #98 for a week on June [18]. During the year, Burnel's debut solo set ***Un Jour Parfait*** is issued.

1989

Feb [4] As part of a current, inexplicable UK trend, *Grip '89 (Get A) Grip (On Yourself)*, a remixed update of their debut, reaches UK #33, issued by EMI.

[18] ***The Singles***, an incomplete EMI anthology, debuts at its UK #57 peak.

1990

Feb [19] The Stranglers undertake their final UK tour with the current line-up, set to last until March 21st. (Cornwell quits after a final concert at London's Alexandra Palace during the summer.)

[24] Their re-make of ? & the Mysterians' *96 Tears* reaches UK #17.

Mar [17] Their tenth album,the appropriately titled***10***, produced by Roy Thomas Baker, reaches UK #15 in its week of entry.

Apr [21] *Sweet Smell Of Success* peaks at UK #65.

1991

Jan [19] *Always The Sun*, a remix of their 1986 UK #30 hit, reaches UK #29.

Feb [2] Epic-released ***Greatest Hits 1977-1990*** hits UK #9.

Mar [30] Reissued *Golden Brown*, originally a 1982 UK #2, debuts at its UK #68 peak.

Aug [10] The group, now with Paul Roberts (b. Dec. 31, 1959, London) on vocals and ex-Vibrator John Ellis (b. June 1, 1952, London) on guitar, supports Simple Minds on their current UK tour, at Maine Road, Manchester.

1992

Apr [10] Cornwell's new band, CCW, with Roger Cook and Andy West, performs a one-off date at Ronnie Scott's (and will release ***CCW featuring Hugh Cornwell*** in July).

June The Stranglers ink a new deal with China Records, recording their new album at Jacobs Studios, with producer Mike Kemp.

Aug [22] *Heaven Or Hell* bows at its UK #46 peak.

Sept [18] The group becomes the first ever to play a rock concert in Dartmoor prison.

[19] With drummer Tikake Tobe having replaced Black, ***Stranglers In The Night***, their first for China, charts for a week at UK #33.

[29] The group embarks on a 12-date "Stranglers In The Night Tour", their first in two years, at the Colston Hall, Bristol, Avon, set to end on October 12th at the Corn Exchange, Cambridge, Cambs.

1993

Feb [4] The band begins an 11-date series at Caird Hall, Dundee, Tayside, Scotland, set to end on the 18th at London's Town & Country club.

May Castle Communications release ***Saturday Night Sunday Morning***, documenting the last original Stranglers gig in August 1990.

June [30] Cornwell plays at London's Subterania club to promote his Transmission Records released solo set, ***Wired***.

Dec [17] The Stranglers play at the Civic Hall, Wolverhampton, West Midlands, during a handful of UK dates.

1994

July [7-10] They take part in the "Heineken Music Festival" at Roundhay Park, Leeds, S. Yorks.

Nov [7] The group begins a four-date mini-tour at the Northwick, Worcester, Hereford & Worcs., set to end on the 12th at London's Shepherd's Bush Empire.

1995

Jan [6] During a short series of dates in the US, the Stranglers play a sellout show at the Great American Music Hall, San Francisco, CA.

May [27] Released on the independent When! label, ***About Time*** debuts at its UK #31 peak.

June [2] The group embarks on an eight-date UK tour at the Colston Hall, Bristol, set to end on the 10th at the Royal Court Theatre, Liverpool, Merseyside.

Nov [30] The Stranglers begin a further 14-date UK swing at Leicester University, set to close on December 16th at the London Forum.

THE STRAY CATS

Brian Setzer (guitar, vocals); **Lee Rocker** (double bass); **Slim Jim Phantom** (drums)

1980

July The trio has been formed the previous year in Long Island, NY, by three former school-friends with a taste for rough-edged ' 50s rockabilly. Early gigs, mostly featuring revivals of Eddie Cochran and Gene Vincent numbers, were on a part-time basis, since Setzer (b. Apr. 10, 1959, Long Island) was also a member of New York rock band, the Bloodless Pharoahs. When the latter group split, he joined Rocker (b. Leon Drucher, 1961) and Phantom (b. Jim McDonnell, Mar. 20, 1961) full-time, rehearsing their own, traditionally-styled, new material. Now visiting Britain, with manager Tony Bidgood, upon arrival in London they find previously-booked gigs and accommodation unavailable. Rather than returning home, they persist in launching themselves on the London club circuit (helped by Keith Altham's PR office, which is also their first London home), where well-received performances quickly attract positive UK music press coverage and record company interest.

Sept [29] They perform at London's Rainbow Theatre as the opening act for Elvis Costello.

Oct With interest from several labels, the group signs to Arista Records UK.

Dec [20] Their debut single, the double bass-heavy *Runaway Boys*, written by Setzer, hits UK #9.

1981

Feb [21] *Rock This Town*, again penned by Setzer, also hits UK #9.

Mar [14] ***Stray Cats***, mostly produced by Dave Edmunds, hits UK #6.

May [23] *Stray Cat Strut* reaches UK #11. (The group will spend much of the rest of the year on tour, selling out in Europe and Australia, and also playing support dates to the Rolling Stones in the States.)

June [27] The Stray Cats, teamed with a credited Edmunds, make UK #34 with a re-make of George Jones' 1964 US Country #3, *The Race Is On*.

Nov [14] *You Don't Believe In Me* peaks at UK #57.

[21] It is taken from the group's second album, ***Gonna Ball***, self-produced in Montserrat with the aid of Hein Hoven, which makes UK #48.

1982

July The band signs a US recording deal with EMI America Records, and embarks on a three-month US tour, in an effort to succeed domestically.

Nov ***Built For Speed***, a US compilation from earlier UK albums, hits US #2 for 15 consecutive weeks, held from the top by Men At Work's ***Business As Usual***, and then Michael Jackson's ***Thriller***.

Dec [1] ***Built For Speed*** is certified platinum by the RIAA.

[11] Bolstered by heavy MTV rotation, *Rock This Town* finally debuts the group on the Hot 100, hitting #9.

1983

Feb [26] *Stray Cat Strut* hits US #3.

May [28] The group co-headlines the first day of the three-day "US '83 Festival" in San Bernardino, CA, with the Clash and Men At Work.

Sept [10] The band's last UK hit single until 1989 is Setzer's *(She's) Sexy And 17*, which makes UK #29. ***Rant'n'Rave With The Stray Cats***, again produced by Edmunds, peaks at UK #51.

Oct [1] *(She's) Sexy And 17* hits US #5, while ***Rant'n'Rave With The Stray Cats*** makes US #14.

[19] ***Rant'n'Rave With The Stray Cats*** is certified gold by the RIAA.

Dec [17] *I Won't Stand In Your Way* reaches US #35.

1984

Feb [18] *Look At That Cadillac* peaks at US #68. The band splits shortly after, as Setzer begins a solo career, staying with EMI America to record ***The Knife Feels Like Justice***.

Mar [20] Phantom marries actress Britt Ekland on his 23rd birthday.

1985

Oct Rocker and Phantom have formed a new trio with David Bowie's ex-guitarist, Earl Slick, naming themselves Phantom, Rocker And Slick. Signed to EMI America, ***Phantom, Rocker And Slick*** makes US #61.

[21] Rocker and Phantom take part in the taping of "Carl Perkins And Friends" at London' s Limehouse Studios, to celebrate the 30th anniversary of *Blue Suede Shoes*.

1986

Jan [1] "Blue Suede Shoes" TV special airs on C4-TV.

Apr Setzer's solo album, ***The Knife Feels Like Justice***, reaches US #45 while Phantom, Rocker And Slick's second and last album, ***Cover Girl*** is released.

Oct Stray Cats' ***Rock Therapy*** makes US #122.

1988

July Setzer, who played Eddie Cochran in the Ritchie Valens biopic, "La Bamba" the previous year, releases the Dave Stewart-produced solo album, ***Live Nude Guitars***, on EMI Manhattan, which makes US #140.

Sept The trio reunites for a 35-date US tour. (Recording sessions for a new album with original producer Edmunds will follow.)

1989

Mar [4] *Bring It Back Again*, the lead-off single from the group's comeback album, makes UK #64.

Apr Reunion album released by EMI, ***Blast Off***, peaks at US #111.

[8] ***Blast Off*** makes UK #58.

Oct [18] The group plays in Las Vegas, NV, during a short US tour.

1991

Oct With Slim Jim reportedly auditioning to be the new Spinal Tap drummer, Setzer is featured playing guitar alongside a granny rocker in a much-aired US TV commercial promoting Budweiser beer.

[31] The group plays at the Ritz, New York, promoting its new Nile Rodgers-produced album, ***Let's Go Faster***, released by Jordan Records.

1992

Oct [6-7] The group plays at London's Town & Country club, during a tour of Europe, promoting its latest album ***Choo Choo Hot Fish***, released by Jordan.

Dec [9] With the Stray Cats inactive once again, Setzer joins Travis Tritt on a version of *Burning Love* at the **Billboard** Music Awards, at the Universal Amphitheatre, Universal City, CA.

1993

Jan Slim Jim' s new blues/rockabilly outfit, Cheap Dates, with Tony Sales, Jeff "Skunk" Baxter, Jamie

James and actor Harry Dean Stanton, makes its debut at the Gate in Los Angeles.
Mar [23] The Paul Rodgers-assembled ***Tribute To Muddy Waters***, featuring fret-work from Setzer, is released on Victory Music.
May An official Stray Cats bootleg, ***Original Cool***, produced by Baxter and featuring the songs of Eddie Cochran, Buddy Holly, Carl Perkins, Gene Vincent and others, is released by Toshiba/EMI in Japan.

1996

May With his former band's '80s highlights available on the CD retrospective ***Back To The Alley - The Best Of The Stray Cats***, Setzer remains the most visible Cat, having formed his own 16-piece orchestra to perform swing versions of rockabilly and pop standards in 1994. Signed to Hollywood Records, ***The Brian Setzer Orchestra*** has debuted at its US #158 peak on Apr [9] the same year, and is now followed by a second set, the jazz-rockabilly fused ***Guitar Slinger***, produced by Phil Ramone for Interscope Records, and featuring three collaborations with ex-Clash front man Joe Strummer.

THE STYLE COUNCIL

Paul Weller (vocals, guitar);
Mick Talbot (keyboards)

1983

Mar [26] After the break-up of the Jam, which he has fronted as lead guitarist and lead singer and for whom he has written 13 UK Top 20 hits including four chart-toppers, Weller (b. John Weller, May 25, 1958, Woking, Surrey), who has also formed his own Respond label in 1981, but recently wound up his **Jamming** magazine, has teamed with Talbot (b. Sept. 11, 1958, London), ex-late-'70s London mod band, the Merton Parkas, and Dexy's Midnight Runners' off-shoot the Bureau, to concentrate on soul/jazz-based music, which is closest to their hearts, and signed to the Jam's former label, Polydor Records as the Style Council. Their debut single, *Speak Like A Child*, now hits UK #4, supported by an appearance on the first broadcast of C4-TV's "The Tube".
May [1] The Style Council plays its first live gig, part of the "May Day Show For Peace And Jobs" at the Empire Theatre, Liverpool, Merseyside.
June [4] *The Money-Go-Round* reaches UK #11. The duo plays another live gig at a festival in Brockwell Park, London, and a week of recording sessions in Paris, France follows.
Aug [20] EP *Paris*, featuring *Paris Match* and *Long Hot Summer*, hits UK #3.
Nov [26] *Solid Bond In Your Heart*, originally planned as the final Jam single, reaches UK #11. (The duo's Solid Bond recording studio, near Marble Arch, London, is named after the cut.) In the US, a mini-album, ***Introducing The Style Council*** (not released in Britain but featuring tracks from early UK singles) peaks at #172.

1984

Jan [2] The Style Council appears at the "Big One" peace show at London's Victoria Apollo Theatre, with part-time collaborator Dee C. Lee (ex-back-up singer with Wham!, and later a solo artist) as a vocalist.
Mar Their debut album, ***Café Bleu***, largely written by Weller, with guests including Tracy Thorn of Everything But The Girl (on a new version of *Paris Match*), hits UK #2, and will stay on the UK chart for 38 weeks.
[12] The Style Council plays its first full UK concert date, at the Gaumont Theatre, Southampton, Hants., followed by seven similar gigs, billed as "Council Meetings".
[25] From the album, *My Ever Changing Moods* hits UK #5.
May *My Ever Changing Moods*, a slightly amended version of ***Café Bleu***, is released on Geffen in the US, and reaches US #56.
June [2] *Groovin'*, a maxi-single, with joint lead tracks *You're The Best Thing* and *Big Boss Groove*, hits UK #5.
[9] The title track from the US album, *My Ever Changing Moods*, is the group's first US hit single, peaking at #29.
July [28] The US follow-up, the soul ballad *You're The Best Thing*, peaks at #76.
Sept [7] Weller appears in a concert at London's Royal Albert Hall, with Wham! and other acts, to benefit the strikers involved in the UK coal-mining dispute.
Oct [20] *Shout To The Top* hits UK #7.
Nov [25] Weller takes part in the recording of Band Aid's *Do They Know It's Christmas?*, at Sarm Studios, London.
Dec *Soul Deep*, inspired by the UK coal-miners strike, reaches UK #24, released under the name the Council Collective, and including guests Jimmy Ruffin and Junior. Royalties go jointly to the support group Women Against Pit Closures, and the widow of taxi driver David Wilkie who was killed during the dispute.

1985

May [18] *The Walls Come Tumbling Down* hits UK #6.
June [8] ***Our Favourite Shop*** tops the UK chart for one week, during a 22-week survey run.
July [13] The Style Council plays on the "Live Aid" benefit bill at Wembley Stadium, Wembley, Middx., as *Come To Milton Keynes* makes UK #23.
Aug [3] ***Internationalists***, released in the US on Geffen, climbs to #123.
Oct [5] *The Lodgers* reaches UK #13.

1986

Jan [25] The "Red Wedge" tour, featuring the Style Council and several other acts with similarly left-wing inclinations (Billy Bragg, Junior, and the Communards), and designed to encourage support among young voters for Britain's Labour Party, opens in Manchester, Gtr. Manchester.
Feb Weller closes his record label, Respond Records, which achieved moderate success for new acts, including Tracie and the Questions.
Apr [12] *Have You Ever Had It Blue*, written for the Julien Temple-directed movie, "Absolute Beginners", makes UK #14.
May [17] A live Style Council album, ***Home And Abroad***, hits UK #8.
Dec Weller and Dee C. Lee are married.

1987

Jan [24] *It Didn't Matter* hits UK #9.
Feb [14] ***The Cost Of Loving***, with guest vocalists Curtis Mayfield and the Valentine Brothers, hits UK #2, behind Paul Simon's ***Graceland***, as the group performs at London's Royal Albert Hall.
Mar [14] *Waiting* peaks at UK #52. The group's 30-minute movie, "JerUSAlem", a satire on the pop world and the Style Council's relationship with it, is released as a cinema support feature, and on home video.
May The group returns to Polydor in the US for ***The Cost Of Loving***, which makes US #122.
Nov [7] *Wanted* reaches UK #11.

1988

May [28] *Life At A Top People's Health Farm* reaches UK #28. Weller and his wife Dee have a son.
July [2] Despite constant rumors of a split, the group's ***Confessions Of A Pop Group*** reaches UK #15, and will make US #174.
[23] *How She Threw It All Away*, taken from it, makes UK #41.

1989

Feb [25] *Promised Land*, their cover of the concurrently-released original by Joe Smooth, reaches UK #27.
Mar [18] A TV-advertised Style Council career retrospective, ***The Singular Adventures Of The Style Council***, debuts at its UK #3 peak.
May [27] A remixed version of *Long Hot Summer*, peaks at UK #48. With the rejection of the Style Council's fifth studio album ***Decades Of Modernism*** by Polydor, the group parts company with the label and splits, with Weller finding himself without a record deal for the first time in his career, also selling his Solid Bond Studios. He will move on to a third critically and commercially successful career phase, beginning a new decade fronting the short-lived Paul Weller Movement before embarking on well-received solo ventures. A Style Council rarities and out-takes collection, ***Here's Some That Got Away*** will reach UK #16 on July [10], 1993 with a second hits compilation, ***The Style Council Collection*** making UK #60 on Mar [2], 1996.
see also: **THE JAM, Paul WELLER**

THE STYLISTICS

Russell Thompkins, Jr. (lead vocals);
Herb Murrell (vocals); **Airrion Love** (vocals);
James Dunn (vocals); **James Smith** (vocals)

1968

The R&B vocal quintet is formed in Philadelphia, PA, when members of two earlier vocal groups, the Percussions, which had included baritones Murrell (b. Apr. 27, 1949, Lane, SC) and Dunn (b. Feb. 4, 1950, Philadelphia) and the Monarchs, which yielded lead vocalist Thompkins (b. Mar. 21, 1951, Philadelphia), tenor Love (b. Aug. 8, 1949, Philadelphia) and bass vocalist Smith (b. June 16, 1950, New York, NY), join forces. Going on to record *You're A Big Girl Now*, written by road manager Marty Bryant and backup band member, Robert Douglas, the single is released the following year on the independent Philadelphia label, Sebring Records, and becomes a local hit.

1971

Feb [13] A year of steady East Coast US sales for the single has attracted the attention of Avco Embassy Records, which has signed the group and reissues *You're A Big Girl Now*, providing their US chart debut at #73.
July The group is teamed with Philadelphia-based producer, Thom Bell, at Sigma Sound Studios, and his songwriting partner, Linda Creed.
[17] Their first collaboration, *Stop, Look, Listen (To Your Heart)*, makes US #39, and establishes the Stylistics' forté: rich, soft-soul ballads, given an extra edge by Thompkins' distinctive high tenor/falsetto vocal phrasing.

1972

Jan [3] Still-climbing *You Are Everything* is certified gold by the RIAA.
[22] *You Are Everything*, again written by Bell and Creed (as is virtually all the group's material for two years), hits US #9, the first of five million-selling singles. (It will be revived as a UK Top 10 hit in 1974 as a Diana Ross and Marvin Gaye duet, as will *Stop, Look, Listen (To Your Heart)*.)
Apr [17] Still-climbing *Betcha By Golly Wow* is certified gold by the RIAA.
May [6] *Betcha By Golly, Wow* hits US #3. The group's debut album ***The Stylistics***, containing the singles to date, reaches US #23.
July [22] Socially-conscious *People Make The World Go Round* peaks at US #25, while *Betcha By Golly, Wow* is the band's first UK hit, at #13.
Oct Following a US coast-to-coast tour, the group visits Britain for the first time, and also tours US bases in West Germany.
Nov [25] *I'm Stone In Love With You*, taken from the second album, hits UK #9. (It will also be a UK Top 10 hit for Johnny Mathis in 1975.)
Dec [9] *I'm Stone In Love With You* hits US #10.
[13] *I'm Stone In Love With You* is certified gold by the RIAA, their third straight million-seller.

1973

Jan ***Stylistics : Round 2*** makes US #32.
Feb [16] ***The Stylistics*** is confirmed gold by the RIAA.
Mar [31] *Break Up To Make Up*, from the second album, reaches UK #34.
Apr [6] Still-climbing *Break Up To Make Up* is certified gold by the RIAA.
[7] *Break Up To Make Up* hits US #5.
June [23] Their revival of the Bacharach/David-penned Dionne Warwick hit, *You'll Never Get To Heaven*, reaches US #23.
[14] ***Stylistics : Round 2*** is certified gold by the RIAA.
July [21] *Peak-A-Boo* climbs to UK #35.
Dec [22] The group's first uptempo hit is Bell and Creed's *Rockin' Roll Baby*, which peaks at US #14. It is extracted from ***Rockin' Roll Baby***, which makes US #66, but is the final album collaboration between the Stylistics and Bell.

1974

Feb [9] *Rockin' Roll Baby* hits UK #6.
May [22] The still-climbing *You Make Me Feel Brand New* is certified gold by the RIAA.
June [15] Belatedly extracted from the third album, and featuring Love's deep baritone lead for much of the song, rather than Thompkins' familiar falsetto, *You Make Me Feel Brand New* is the group's biggest US hit, and their fifth and last million-selling single, hitting #2 for two weeks (behind Bo Donaldson & the Heywoods' *Billy, Don't Be A Hero*).
July Avco have teamed the group with the veteran writing/production team of Hugo (Peretti) and Luigi (Creatore), with arranger Van McCoy, for ***Let's Put It All Together***, which, like subsequent recordings, takes them away from Philadelphia and to Media Sound Studios in New York, and reaches US #14.
Aug [24] Extracted *You Make Me Feel Brand New* repeats its US success by hitting UK #2. (*You Make Me Feel Brand New* had originally been the B-side of an April release, *Only For The Children*.)
[12] ***Let's Put It All Together*** is certified gold by the RIAA.
Sept [14] ***Rockin' Roll Baby*** is, belatedly, the group's first UK chart album, reaching #42.
[21] *Let's Put It All Together*, reaches US #18.
Nov [16] *Let's Put It All Together* hits UK #9.
[23] *Heavy Fallin' Out*, taken from the second Hugo and Luigi-produced album, peaks at US #41. ***Let's Put It All Together*** makes UK #26.
Dec ***Heavy*** reaches US #43.

1975

Feb [15] *Star On A TV Show* makes US #47 and UK #12.
Mar ***Heavy*** has been re-titled ***From The Mountain*** in the UK and given a different sleeve design (both are considered out of keeping with the group's UK image), reaching UK #36.
Apr Compilation ***The Best Of The Stylistics*** reaches US #41.
[19] ***The Best Of The Stylistics*** tops the UK chart for the first of two weeks (and will return to #1 for five weeks in May and two weeks in August), eventually spending 63 weeks on the survey. It is the best-selling album of the year and the biggest seller ever in the UK by a black act.
May [17] *Thank You Baby*, the title track from their forthcoming album, peaks at US #70.
[31] *Sing Baby Sing*, also from the album, hits UK #3.
July ***Thank You Baby*** makes US #72.
Aug [16] Taken from the album, *Can't Give You Anything (But My Love)* tops the UK chart for the first of three weeks, the group's biggest UK hit, and peaks at US #51.
[23] ***Thank You Baby*** hits UK #3 (with ***The Best Of The Stylistics*** lodged at #2).
Dec [13] *Na Na Is The Saddest Word*, taken from it, hits UK #5. ***You Are Beautiful*** reaches UK #26.
[20] ***You Are Beautiful*** makes US #99.

1976

Jan [31] The extracted *Funky Weekend* makes US #76.
Mar [6] *Funky Weekend* hits UK #10.
Apr [4] The group begins an 11-date UK tour, with Brook Benton, at the De Montfort Hall, Leicester, Leics., set to end at Wolverhampton Civic Hall, West Midlands, after two shows at the London Palladium on April 9th-10th.
[17] Title track, *You Are Beautiful*, reaches US #79, and is the Stylistics' last US chart single. (A string of 45s will continue to be major UK hits while making minor or no impression in the US. The split from Bell and subsequent loss of the soft Philly soul sound is cited as a factor for the US decline: under Hugo and Luigi, the group's material has become more brashly orchestrated, and more obviously middle of the road, losing much of the R&B radio market in the US.)
May [22] The band's revival of Elvis Presley's *Can't Help Falling In Love* (written by Hugo and Luigi, with long-time collaborator George David Weiss) hits UK #4.
June [19] Hugo and Luigi have formed their own H&L label, taking the Stylistics with them. ***Fabulous***, the group's last album for Avco Embassy in the UK, makes UK #21.
July [3] ***Fabulous***, their debut set on H&L, makes US #117.
Sept [11] *16 Bars*, extracted from ***Fabulous***, hits UK #7.
Oct [2] A second compilation, ***The Best Of The Stylistics, Vol. 2***, tops the UK chart for one week.
Dec [18] EP *You'll Never Get To Heaven*, coupling the earlier US hit with three later tracks, makes UK #24.

1978

Apr [5] The group opens a UK visit at the London Palladium, previewing ***Love Spell***, their first and only outing for Mercury Records.
[16] Having released ***Wonder Woman*** the previous year, the overnight domination by disco music of the R&B music scene finally puts the Stylistics out of commercial favor in Britain, with their last chart single, *7,000 Dollars And You*, making #24.

1980

Dec After two quiet years of mainly club work, the group has signed to TSOP Records, a division of Gamble and Huff's Philadelphia International label. ***Hurry Up This Way Again*** makes US #127, after a four-year chart absence. (There are no Stylistics hit singles on TSOP. With almost a decade's-worth of mostly ballad-slanted hit repertoire behind them, the Stylistics will continue to command nightclub and occasional TV work all around the world, particularly in the UK, where they will remain frequent cabaret visitors throughout the decade. They will also release ***Closer Than Close*** (1981), ***1982*** (1982) and ***Some Things Never Change*** (1985), and back Glenn Medeiros on his *Me-U=Blue* US #78.)

1996

Jan While the first of a number of CD collections, ***The Greatest Hits Of The Stylistics*** has made UK #34 on Oct [24], 1992, the same year the group's first seasonal album ***Christmas*** has also been released, the Stylistics, who continue to perform annually on veteran R&B package tours (not least appearing at the "Apollo Theatre Hall Of Fame" concert in New York on May 26th, 1994), now reduced to a trio following the departure of both Dunn and Smith, follow their 1993 album ***Love Talk*** with the Preston Glass-produced ***Love Is Back In Style***, issued by Marathon/Bellmark Records.

STYX

Dennis DeYoung (vocals, keyboards); **Tommy Shaw** (lead guitar); **James Young** (guitar); **Chuck Panozzo** (bass); **John Panozzo** (drums)

1964

Latter-day Styx alumni come together in Chicago, IL, as the Tradewinds, comprising neighbors DeYoung (b. Feb. 18, 1947, Chicago), the twin Panozzo brothers (b. Sept. 20, 1947, Chicago) and guitarist Tom Nardini. They play regular gigs on the Chicago bar and club circuit, and shorten their name to TW4 in 1965 to avoid confusion with *New York's A Lonely Town* hitmakers, Trade Winds (actually songwriters Anders and Poncia). In October 1969, the group is based at Chicago State University, where DeYoung and the Panozzos enroll. Nardini leaves, and TW4's new guitarist is fellow student, John Curulewski. Young (b. Nov. 14, 1948, Chicago), who has been playing with a rival band, joins the quartet the following year, and the new line-up begins more musical experiments, with classical/rock fusions, and electronic trickeries, all of which find favor on college dates.

1972

Oct Offered a recording deal by Wooden Nickel Records' Bill Traut, who received a demo tape from the band the previous year, he has re-named the group Styx after the mythological river of the dead. Their first album, ***Styx***, has been issued, but only sells around their live performances.
[14] Their chart debut, *Best Thing* now peaks at US #82, mainly on Chicago-area sales and airplay.

1973

July ***Styx II*** is released, again initially without charting, though DeYoung's song, *Lady*, again picks up local Chicago radio play. The group members quit their day jobs and begin regular touring further afield, to create a wider following.

1974

Feb Their third album, ***The Serpent Is Rising***, peaks at US #192.
Nov Styx's second album of the year, ***Man Of Miracles***, produced by John Ryan, makes US #154.

1975

Mar [8] *Lady*, still the most popular track on the band's home-town airwaves, is given renewed national promotion as a single, and this time hits US #6. In its wake, the parent album, ***Styx II***, reaches US #20, some two years after its release.
May [1] ***Styx II*** is certified gold by the RIAA.
[17] *You Need Love*, taken from ***Man Of Miracles***, peaks at US #88.
Dec Curulewski leaves the band, and a road manager suggests Shaw (b. Sept. 11, 1950, Montgomery, AL) as a replacement, having seen him play guitar with a Chicago group named Ms. Funk. A week after auditioning, Shaw gets the gig.

1976

Mar [27] Newly signed to A&M Records, their label debut, ***Equinox***, peaks at US #58 as US FM radio begins to take notice.
Apr [24] Their first A&M single, *Lorelei*, taken from the album, makes US #27. Derek Sutton becomes the band's manager, restructures its business affairs, and organizes their first nationwide tour.
Aug [25] ***Equinox*** is certified gold by the RIAA.
Nov [27] ***Crystal Ball***, the first album with Shaw, makes US #66
Dec [25] The extracted *Mademoiselle* reaches US #36.

1978

Jan [28] *Come Sail Away* hits US #8.
Feb [25] Issued the previous year, its parent album, ***The Grand Illusion***, hits US #6, and is the group's first platinum album, confirming Styx as a pioneering

force in the media-coined pomp-rock genre.
Apr [22] *Fooling Yourself (The Angry Young Man)*, also from ***The Grand Illusion***, makes US #29.
May The group makes its live UK debut at London's Hammersmith Odeon.
Nov [10] ***Crystal Ball*** is certified gold by the RIAA.
[18] *Blue Collar Man (Long Nights)* reaches US #21, while ***Pieces Of Eight*** hits US #6.

1979

Feb [10] *Sing For The Day* makes US #41.
June [9] *Sing For The Day*'s B-side, *Renegade*, reaches US #16. A US national poll by Gallup reveals that Styx is currently the most popular rock band with 13 to 19-year-olds.
Dec ***Cornerstone*** hits US #2.
[8] DeYoung's rock ballad, *Babe*, tops the US chart for the first of two weeks, and becomes their all-time best-selling single. (The released version is a scarcely-embellished reissue of DeYoung's original demo, which sounds superior to attempted re-recordings.)

1980

Jan [26] *Babe* hits UK #6.
[28] *Babe* is certified gold by the RIAA.
Feb [9] *Why Me* reaches US #26. ***Cornerstone***, their UK chart debut, now reaches #36.
Apr [19] *Borrowed Time* peaks at US #64.
June [20] The group plays again at London's Hammersmith Odeon.

1981

Jan [16] Styx begins a 110-date six-month North American tour in Miami, FL.
[31] *The Best Of Times* makes UK #42.
Feb [7] Its parent set, ***Paradise Theater***, a concept album, hits UK #8.
Mar [21] *The Best Of Times* hits US #3.
Apr [4] ***Paradise Theater*** tops the US chart for the first of three weeks.
May [23] *Too Much Time On My Hands*, also from the album, hits US #9.
Aug [1] *Nothing Ever Goes As Planned* peaks at US #54.
Oct The band begins recording a new album, using solar-powered equipment.

1983

Mar ***Kilroy Was Here***, another concept album, makes UK #67.
[11] The band begins a major venue "Kilroy Was Here" US tour in San Diego, CA, which will continue through the year, with a theatrical stage act built around the album, in which costumed band members have roles and dialogue, in addition to playing the music. (Not everybody rates the idea and some venues fail to sell out.)
Apr [16] *Mr. Roboto* hits US #3, while its parent album, ***Kilroy Was Here***, also hits US #3.
[29] ***Kilroy Was Here*** is certified platinum by the RIAA.
May [16] *Mr. Roboto* is confirmed gold by the RIAA.
June [25] *Don't Let It End*, taken from ***Kilroy Was Here***, peaks at UK #56.
July [2] *Don't Let It End* hits US #6.
Sept [10] *High Time* makes US #48.

1984

May Live double album, the self-produced ***Caught In The Act***, climbs to US #31 and UK #44, following which DeYoung and Shaw will both pursue solo projects for A&M (putting Styx on extended hold for the remainder of the decade). (DeYoung will score with ***Desert Moon*** (US #29 in October) and ***Back To The World*** (US #108 in April 1986), while Shaw will chart with ***Girls With Guns*** (US #50 in 1984) and ***What If*** (US #87 in November the following year.)
June [2] *Music Time*, from the live set, makes US #40.
July [31] ***Best Of Styx*** is certified gold by the RIAA.
Nov [14] The RIAA certifies multi-platinum sales of ***Cornerstone*** (two million), ***Paradise Theater*** (three million), ***Pieces Of Eight*** (three million) and ***The Grand Illusion*** (three million), confirming the group as one of the most successful power rock acts of the pre-MTV era.

1990

Oct [27] Following DeYoung's third solo album, ***Boomchild*** in 1988, and with Shaw, who released ***Ambition*** in 1987 having recently formed Damn Yankees with Ted Nugent, a re-assembled Styx, with Glen Burtnik in Shaw's place, makes US #80 with *Love Is The Ritual*, from their comeback album, the DeYoung-produced ***Edge Of The Century***.
Nov [3] ***Edge Of The Century*** makes US #63.

1991

Mar [16] Styx' *Show Me The Way* hits US #3, fuelled by Gulf War patriotic sentiment. Its chart appearance means that Styx joins an elite club of acts who have secured Top 10 hits under each of the last four US presidents.
June [15] *Love At First Sight* reaches US #25.

1993

May [25-30] With Styx once again inactive, DeYoung makes his theatrical bow, playing Pontius Pilate in a 20th anniversary production of "Jesus Christ Superstar", at the Universal Amphitheatre, Universal City, CA. (He will subsequently make his Broadway debut in the role.)

1995

Sept [23] Following Young's last solo project, ***10 On Broadway***, a collection of show tunes released in July the previous year, the RIAA gold certification of an earlier Styx compilation on October 19th also in 1994, and Shaw's latest solo effort ***Hallucination*** released by Warner Bros. Records in March of this year, a further Styx collection, ***Greatest Hits*** now debuts at its US #138 peak.

1996

May [21] With ***Greatest Hits*** re-charting at US #183 on the 4th, Styx, re-united with the hit-making line-up, embarks on a three-month US tour with Kansas at the Five Seasons Center, Cedar Rapids, MI, set to end on August 17th at the Desert Sky Pavilion, Phoenix, AZ. (John Panozzo will die July 16 from gastrointestinal bleeding linked to excessive use of alcohol.)

SUEDE (LONDON SUEDE)

Brett Anderson (vocals); **Bernard Butler** (guitar); **Mat Osman** (bass); **Simon Gilbert** (drums)

1990

Sept The son of an ice-cream vendor, Anderson (b. Sept. 27, 1967, Haywards Heath, Sussex) has formed Geoff in 1985, initially in the role of guitarist, a Haywards Heath-based quartet, also comprising his schoolfriend and bassist Osman (b. Oct. 9, 1967), lead vocalist Gareth Perry and drummer Danny Wilder. Having recorded two demos, the combo has split up the following year, allowing Anderson and Osman to attend university in London. Forming and dissolving the short-lived outfit, Suave & Elegant, in 1989, the pair placed an ad in the **New Musical Express** looking for a "non-muso" guitarist. Butler (b. May 1, 1970) is subsequently recruited and, using a drum machine, the trio, now named Suede, tapes a number of demos, principally written by Anderson and Butler. A second set of try-out recordings, ***Specially Suede***, contains *Wonderful Sometimes*, which has won London's GLR radio station DJ Gary Crowley's "Demo Clash" weekly contest for five consecutive Sundays during 1990. With the addition of a second guitarist, Anderson's girlfriend, Justine Frischman, Suede signs a seven-album deal with the small Brighton, East Sussex-based independent label, RML, a condition that the band acquiesces to, just to see the release of its debut single, *Be My God* (which features ex-Smiths Mike Joyce on drums). Falling out with the label boss and nullifying the entire deal, a few 12" copies of the single are pressed, though it remains unissued.

1991

Nov Following a year of rehearsals and refocused songwriting (towards an alternative pop/glam rock meld), during which Gilbert (b. May 23, 1965) joins as the band's permanent drummer, Suede records further demos including the tracks *C'Mon C'Mon*, *He's Dead*, *Moving*, *The Drowners* and *To The Birds*, and links with a new manager, Fire Records' head, John Edymann.

1992

Jan Undertaking a formal demo session for Island Records, rock publicist John Best sends selected tracks to **Melody Maker** assistant editor, Steve Sutherland. Frischman quits, and will shortly form Elastica.
Apr [25] Having signed a two-single deal with the independent Nude Records in March, at the instigation of label boss Saul Galpern, Suede achieves the rare distinction of making the front cover of **Melody Maker** without having released any material.
May [23] Their debut single, *The Drowners*, coupled with *To The Birds*, finally emerging on Nude and produced by Ed Buller, bows at its UK #49 peak.
Aug [29] Suede plays in the Radio 1FM Session Tent on the second day of the annual "Reading Festival", near Reading, Berks.
Sept [26] Follow-up, *Metal Mickey*, proves to be the band's chart breakthrough, reaching UK #17, following an auspicious "Top Of The Pops" TV debut. Galpern re-negotiates Nude's contract with the band, securing worldwide distribution via Sony Records. Meanwhile, Suede's cover version of the Pretenders' *Brass In Pocket* is included on the **New Musical Express** compilation, ***Ruby Trax***.
Nov While recording its debut album, the group continues to appear intermittently at low-key UK venues, often too small to contain the ardent and burgeoning fan following which has built up around them, due to overwhelming UK music press adulation.

1993

Feb [16] Performing *Animal Nitrate* at the 12th annual BRIT Awards, at the Alexandra Palace, London, Anderson offends some industry attendees by repeatedly slapping the microphone on his bum, while Osman smashes his bass upon leaving the stage.
[24] A short UK tour, showcasing Anderson's androgynous, Bowielike live persona, begins at the Pyramids, Portsmouth, Hants., set to close on March 1st at the Cambridge Junction, Cambridge, Cambs.
Mar [6] *Animal Nitrate* debuts at its UK #7 peak.
[28] They begin a two-month UK tour at Belfast's Limelight, Northern Ireland, set to end on May 23rd at the Royal Court Theatre, Liverpool, Merseyside.
[29] The band is featured on ITV's "The Beat".
Apr [10] Lyrically directed by Anderson's writing, the group's glam-rock inspired debut album, ***Suede***, enters the UK chart at #1, with the biggest one-week sales by a debut act since Frankie Goes To Hollywood's ***Welcome To The Pleasuredome***.
May [27] They appear on BBC1-TV's "Top Of The Pops" (having had to pull out of an earlier appearance in March when Anderson lost his voice).
[29] The extracted *So Young* debuts at its UK #22 peak.
June [4] The group performs on BBC2-TV's "Later With Jools Holland".
[8] Under the name London Suede (its UK moniker already reserved by a previous US band), the group makes its US TV debut on NBC-TV's "The Tonight Show".
[25] The band performs at the annual "Glastonbury Festival", at Worthy Farm, Pilton, Somerset.
Sept [8] ***Suede*** wins the Mercury Music Prize, at the second annual ceremony in London. (It will go on to amass 69,000 sales in Japan, 42,000 in Germany, 39,000 in Sweden and 37,000 in France, though make little impression in the US.)
Dec [24] The group previews its new single *Stay Together* and two other new tracks, *The Living Dead*

and *My Dark Star*, at "XFM 100.5's Christmas Party" held at London's Kentish Town Forum.

1994

Jan Suede wins Best Band in the annual **New Musical Express** BRAT Awards.
Gilbert is a guest speaker at a House of Commons meeting to call for the lowering of the age of homosexual consent to 16.
[27] Suede is named Hype of the Year in the **Rolling Stone** 1994 Music Awards Critics' Picks.
Feb [8] The band plays its first gig of the year at Worthing Pier, Worthing, W. Sussex, at the start of a four-day UK jaunt.
[26] *Stay Together* debuts at its UK #3 peak.
July Butler quits the band in the middle of recording its second album, and is replaced by 17-year old Richard Oakes (b. Oct. 10, 1976).
Sept Anderson is the first man to appear on the cover of **i-D** magazine in ten years.
[24] *We Are The Pigs* debuts at its UK #18 peak.
Oct [10] Oakes plays his first gig with the band at its album launch at London's Raw club on his 18th birthday.
[22] Still produced by Buller, ***Dog Man Star*** hits UK #3 in its week of entry.
[25] Suede begins an eight-date UK tour at the Town Hall, Middlesbrough, Cleveland, set to end on November 4th at the Corn Exchange, Cambridge, Cambs.
Nov [19] *The Wild Ones*, released in two CD versions - one with *Modern Boys* and *This World Needs A Father*, and the other a 16-minute remix of *Introducing The Band* by Brian Eno and *Asda Town*, marking Oakes' recording debut, bows at its UK #18 peak.

1995

Jan Anderson and Jane Birkin record Les Yeux Fermes for inclusion on an AIDS charity album only available in France.
[24] Suede embarks on an 11-date UK tour at the Apollo Theatre, Oxford, Oxfordshire, set to end on February 6th-7th at the Hammersmith Palais.
Feb [4] The group guests on BBC1-TV's "The Danny Baker Show".
[11] *New Generation* bows at its UK #21 peak.
[14] During the group's sellout show at the Manhattan Center Ballroom, New York, Anderson falls, and will have to use a cane for the rest of its US tour.
May [21] The group plays a benefit concert on behalf of the Friends of the Earth at London's Royal Albert Hall.
June [3] Butler, and former Thieves' singer David McAlmont, hit UK #8 with *Yes*. (Its follow-up, *You Do* will peak at its UK #17 debut on Nov [4].)
July [14] Suede takes part in the annual "Phoenix Festival" at Long Marston, Stratford-upon-Avon, Warks.
Sept [4] They record *Shipbuilding* for the Go! Discs War child charity album ***Help***.
Oct [7] Gilbert is attacked by "redneck homophobic bashers" in Stratford-upon-Avon, and requires stitches for a head wound.

1996

Jan [27] The band, already eclipsed by BritPop pioneers Blur and Oasis, plays a secret gig at London's Hanover Grand, previewing nine new songs and introducing its latest addition, Neil Codling, who is Gilbert's cousin.

DONNA SUMMER

1968

Having sung in her local church choir in Boston, MA as a child, Summer (b. LaDonna Andrea Gaines, Dec. 31, 1948, Dorchester, MA), after singing with a number of Boston, MA-based rock groups including Crow, tests for an understudy part in "Hair" on Broadway, but, after a short time in a road company production, is instead offered a leading role in another production of the musical in Munich, West Germany. She will remain in "Hair" for a year and a half, also undertaking some modeling jobs and studio back-up singing in West Germany. Subsequently offered parts in Vienna Volksoper's productions of "Porgy And Bess" and "Showboat", she relocates to Austria in 1971, and also marries Austrian actor, Helmut Sommer (keeping an anglicized version of his surname after they are divorced).

1973

While performing back in West Germany in the German production of "Godspell", she begins regular work as a session singer at Munich's Musicland Studios, where she meets owner/producer, Pete Bellotte, and his partner Giorgio Moroder, who hears her singing at a Blood Sweat & Tears demo session. She is invited to record for their Oasis label in her own right. *The Hostage*, *Virgin Mary* and *Lady Of The Night* are European hits, but are not released in the US or UK.

1975

She records *Love To Love You Baby*, an erotic love song with a disco beat, and inspired by the success in Europe of the reissued *Je T'Aime ... Moi Non Plus* by Jane Birkin & Serge Gainsbourg. Moroder mixes a 17-minute version with Summer's overtly climactic breathy sighs and groans. It initially fails to score in Europe, but Neil Bogart of US Casablanca Records sees commercial potential in the track, and he licenses and issues the cut in its full version to discos, and in edited form as a single.

1976

Jan [19] Yet to climax, *Love To Love You Baby* is certified gold by the RIAA.
Feb [7] *Love To Love You Baby* hits US #2, behind Paul Simon's *50 Ways To Leave Your Lover* and UK #4.
[14] Summer's maiden album, ***Love To Love You Baby***, reaches US #11 and UK #16. She begins a two-month US tour, and is also divorced from her husband.
[19] *Love To Love You Baby* is certified gold by the RIAA.
May [22] Mixing a ballad intro with a disco mid-section *Could It Be Magic*, based on a Chopin melody and taken from her sophomore album ***A Love Trilogy***, makes US #52.
June [5] ***A Love Trilogy***, her sophomore set, again helmed by Moroder and Bellotte, makes US #21.
[19] *Could It Be Magic* makes UK #40.
[29] ***A Love Trilogy*** is certified gold by the RIAA.
July [24] *Try Me, I Know We Can Make It*, also from ***A Love Trilogy***, peaks at US #80.
Sept [25] ***A Love Trilogy*** reaches UK #41.
Nov [11] Five-track mini-album, ***Four Seasons Of Love***, accompanied by the Munich Machine, reaches US #29, and is certified gold by the RIAA.

1977

Jan [22] The R&B-swaying *Winter Melody*, also from the album, reaches UK #27.
Feb [5] Also taken from it, *Spring Affair* makes US #47.
Mar [19] *Winter Melody* makes US #43.
July [13] ***I Remember Yesterday*** is certified gold by the RIAA.
[23] *I Feel Love*, a disco song built around a mesmeric electronic sequencer rhythm, tops the UK chart for the first of four weeks, eventually selling over half a million copies. It is taken from ***I Remember Yesterday***, which hits UK #3.
Sept [10] *Down Deep Inside*, her theme song from the Nick Nolte/Jacqueline Bisset-starring film, "The Deep", hits UK #5.
Oct [22] Title cut, *I Remember Yesterday*, reaches UK #14, released on GTO Records, the original UK licensee of Summer's recordings, whereas "The Deep" theme is issued on Casablanca, which now takes up new recordings. (For six months, singles are released in competition by both labels.)
Nov [5] ***I Remember Yesterday*** reaches US #18.
[9] *I Feel Love* is certified gold by the RIAA.
[12] *I Feel Love*, extracted as a US single following its UK success, hits US #6.
Dec [3] ***Once Upon A Time*** reaches UK #24.
[9] The still-climbing ***Once Upon A Time*** is certified gold by the RIAA.

1978

Jan [14] *Love's Unkind*, on GTO, and *I Love You*, on Casablanca (and taken from the disco fairytale concept album ***Once Upon A Time***), hit UK #3 and #10 respectively. ***Once Upon A Time*** reaches US #26.
[28] GTO compilation album, ***Greatest Hits***, hits UK #4.
Feb [4] *I Love You* makes US #37.
Mar [18] *Rumour Has It* reaches UK #19.
Apr [15] *Rumour Has It* makes US #53.
[29] *Back In Love Again* reaches UK #29.
May [17] The movie, "Thank God It's Friday", a disco-oriented Casablanca/Motown co-production, in which Summer features as a singer attempting to make the big time, premieres in Los Angeles, CA.
June [24] *Last Dance*, penned by Paul Jabara, who had appeared with Summer in the German production of "Hair", and taken from "Thank God It's Friday", peaks at UK #51.
July [19] Still-climbing *Last Dance* is certified gold by the RIAA.
Aug [12] *Last Dance* hits US #3. (It will earn an Oscar at the 1979 Academy Awards as Best Film Song.)
Oct [19] Still-rising ***Live And More*** is certified platinum by the RIAA.
[26] Set-to-peak *MacArthur Park* is certified gold by the RIAA.
[28] Her disco revival of Jimmy Webb's *MacArthur Park* (originally a 1968 hit for actor Richard Harris) hits UK #5.
Nov [11] *MacArthur Park* tops the US chart, where it will remain for three weeks. It is taken from the studio side of the double album, ***Live And More***, with three sides of Summer recorded in concert at the Universal Amphitheatre, Universal City, CA. The album tops the US chart for one week.
[18] ***Live And More*** reaches UK #16.

1979

Jan [9] The "Music For UNICEF Concert", to celebrate the International Year Of The Child, takes place in the General Assembly Hall of the United Nations in New York, at which Summer sings *Mimi's Song*, donating the royalties from the song to UNICEF. (NBC-TV airs "A Gift Of Song - The Music For UNICEF Concert" the following day.)
[12] She wins the Favorite Female Artist, Disco, Favorite Single, Disco, and Favorite Album, Disco categories, at the sixth annual American Music Awards, held at the ABC-TV Studios, Hollywood, CA.
Feb [15] Summer wins the Best R&B Vocal Performance, Female category for *Last Dance*, at the 21st annual Grammy Awards. *Last Dance* is also named Best R&B Song.
Mar [5] Still-climbing *Heaven Knows* is certified gold by the RIAA.
[10] *Heaven Knows*, from ***Live And More***, and recorded with disco trio, Brooklyn Dreams, makes UK #34.
[17] *Heaven Knows* hits US #4.
Apr [9] *Last Dance* wins an Oscar for Best Original Song at the 51st annual Acacemy Awards.
June [2] *Hot Stuff*, written by Bellotte with Harold Faltermeyer, heads the US survey at the beginning of a three-week run, and reaches UK #11.
[16] ***Bad Girls*** tops the US chart for the first of six weeks, confirming Summer as the queen of disco, and reaches UK #23.
[19] Still-climbing *Bad Girls* is certified gold by the RIAA.
July [14] Title song, *Bad Girls*, tops the US chart for the first of five weeks.
[28] *Bad Girls* makes UK #14.
Aug [1] *Hot Stuff* is certified platinum by the RIAA - her first two-million selling single.
Sept [4] *Bad Girls* is also confirmed platinum by the RIAA.
Oct [13] *Dim All The Lights*, a third single from ***Bad Girls***, reaches UK #29.

Nov [10] *Dim All The Lights* hits US #2.
[17] Double compilation album, ***On The Radio - Greatest Hits - Volumes I And II***, anthologizing Summer's Moroder-helmed hits up to the still-rising Streisand duet, reaches UK #24.
[24] Summer's duet with Barbra Streisand on the Paul Jabara and Bruce Robert-penned *No More Tears (Enough Is Enough)*, begins a fortnight at US #1 (while *Dim All The Lights* is still in the top five).
Dec [1] *No More Tears (Enough Is Enough)* hits UK #3.
[11] *Dim All The Lights* is certified gold by the RIAA.

1980

Jan [5] ***On The Radio - Greatest Hits - Volumes I And II*** tops the US chart for one week. Meanwhile, Summer sues her manager, Joyce Bogart, and husband Neil Bogart's Casablanca Records for $10 million, alleging "undue influence, misrepresentation and fraud". The label releases her from her contract.
[18] Summer collects the Favorite Female Artist, Pop/Rock, Favorite Single, Pop/Rock, and Favorite Female Artist, Soul/R&B trophies, at the seventh annual American Music Awards, held again at the ABC-TV Studios, Hollywood.
Feb [11] *No More Tears (Enough Is Enough)* is certified gold by the RIAA.
[23] *On The Radio*, a new song extracted from the compilation album, and featured in the Jodie Foster-starring movie, "Foxes", peaks at UK #32.
[27] Summer wins the Best Rock Vocal Performance, Female category for the disco single *Hot Stuff*, at the 22nd annual Grammy Awards.
Mar [8] *On The Radio* hits US #5.
[11] *On The Radio* is certified gold by the RIAA.
June [19] Summer is the first act signed by David Geffen to his new Geffen label.
July [5] *Sunset People*, issued only in the UK by Casablanca, reaches UK #46.
[16] She weds Bruce Sudano of Brooklyn Dreams (and former member of Alive 'N Kickin' 1970 *Tighter Tighter* hitmakers), in Los Angeles.
Oct [18] Summer's final Casablanca single, *Walk Away*, makes US #36.
[25] *The Wanderer* makes UK #48.
Nov [8] Its parent album, ***The Wanderer***, makes UK #55.
[15] *The Wanderer*, her Geffen debut, hits US #3, while another Casablanca compilation, ***Walk Away - Collector's Edition (The Best Of 1977-1980)***, climbs to US #50.
Dec [2] *The Wanderer* is certified gold by the RIAA with its parent album receiving the same certification ten days later.

1981

Jan Having become a born-again Christian in 1979, she includes the first lyrics alluding to her new-found faith on ***The Wanderer***, which reaches US #13.
[17] Taken from it, *Cold Love* reaches US #33. (Later born-again pronouncements, in public rather than on record, will cause more controversy - notably when she allegedly nominates gays as sinners and AIDS as a divine ruling, comments she will subsequently refute, but which help to alienate a section of her consumer base.)
[24] *Cold Love* makes UK #44.
Mar [28] *Who Do You Think You're Foolin'*, from the album, makes US #40.

1982

Aug [11] Summer and husband Sudano have a daughter, Amanda Grace.
[14] After a lengthy recording hiatus, during which Geffen has rejected a Moroder/Bellotte double-length set, bringing Quincy Jones in to produce an entirely new album, *Love Is In Control (Finger On The Trigger)* reaches UK #18.
[21] ***Donna Summer***, produced by Jones and featuring a host of top session players, reaches UK #13.
Sept [18] ***Donna Summer*** reaches US #20.
[21] ***Donna Summer*** is certified gold by the RIAA.
[25] *Love Is In Control (Finger On The Trigger)* hits US #10.
Nov [6] From the album, her hymnal revival of Jon & Vangelis' *State Of Independence*, with Summer joined by an all-star chorus including Michael Jackson, Lionel Richie, Kenny Loggins, Dionne Warwick, James Ingram and Stevie Wonder, makes US #41.
[20] *State Of Independence* reaches UK #14.

1983

Jan [15] A remix of *I Feel Love* reaches UK #21.
Feb [26] *The Woman In Me* makes US #33.
Mar [5] *The Woman In Me* peaks at UK #62.
July [23] *She Works Hard For The Money* reaches UK #25.
Aug [6] *She Works Hard For The Money* hits US #3 and makes UK #25, while the album, ***She Works Hard For The Money***, hits US #9, and reaches UK #28. (These releases on Mercury, sister label to Casablanca, are part of a contractual settlement whereby Summer delivers an album owed at the time of severing her former contract. After this, she returns to Geffen.)
[30] ***She Works Hard For The Money*** is certified gold by the RIAA.
Oct [8] *Unconditional Love*, with back-up vocals from UK youngsters Musical Youth, makes US #43.
Nov [19] *Unconditional Love* reaches UK #14.

1984

Jan [28] *Stop, Look And Listen* makes UK #57, as *Love Has A Mind Of Its Own*, duetted with Matthew Ward of gospel group, 2nd Chapter Of Acts, makes US #70.
Feb [28] Summer wins the Best Inspirational Performance category for *He's A Rebel*, at the 26th annual Grammy Awards.
Oct ***Cats Without Claws*** makes US #40 and UK #69.
[13] Taken from it, *There Goes My Baby*, reviving the Drifters' 1960 hit, makes US #21.
Nov [24] *Supernatural Love*, also from ***Cats Without Claws***, peaks at US #75.

1985

Jan [19] Summer takes part in ABC-TV's "50th American Presidential Inaugural Gala".
Feb [26] She nabs her second Best Inspirational Performance trophy for *Forgive Me*, at the 27th annual Grammy Awards. (Summer asks to be released from her Geffen contract, but is turned down, remaining with the label until 1988, and begins spending more time at her farm outside Los Angeles.)

1987

Aug [27] Summer embarks on a US and European tour in Concord, CA - her first US outing since 1983.
Oct [3] Her first single in three years, the Brenda Russell-penned *Dinner With Gershwin*, makes US #48, while its parent album, ***All Systems Go***, peaks at US #122, its disappointing sales resulting in the cancellation of further American dates.
Nov [28] Newly signed in the UK to Warner Bros. Records, *Dinner With Gershwin* reaches UK #13.

1989

Jan [30] *All Systems Go* peaking at UK #54 in January the following year.
Mar [25] The lead-off single from sessions with UK hitmaking songwriting and production team, Stock/Aitken/Waterman (a suggestion mooted by Sudano), *This Time I Know It's For Real*, hits UK #3, as its parent album, ***Another Place And Time***, debuts at its UK #17 peak.
June [3] *I Don't Wanna Get Hurt* hits UK #7.
[24] *This Time I Know It's For Real* hits US #7, as its parent album, ***Another Place And Time***, picked up in the US by Atlantic Records, reaches US #53.
July [11] *This Time I Know It's For Real* is certified gold by the RIAA.
Sept [2] *Love's About To Change My Heart* reaches UK #20.
[23] *Love's About To Change My Heart* stops at US #85.
Nov [25] A fourth extract, *When Love Takes Over You*, peaks at UK #72.

1990

June Now an enthusiastic canvas artist, Summer exhibits her neo-Primitive paintings and lithographs in Beverly Hills, CA. She sells 75 pieces for as much as $38,000 each.
Nov [24] The Warner Bros.-issued ***The Best Of Donna Summer*** reaches UK #24 in its week of entry, while a remixed version of *State Of Independence* makes UK #45.

1991

Jan [19] *Breakaway* peaks at UK #49.
Mar [23] Summer takes part in the "American Music Awards Concert Series" at Yokohama Arena, Yokohama, Japan.
Aug [31] *When Love Cries* stops at US #77.
Nov [30] *Work That Magic* charts for a week at UK #74.

1992

Mar [18] Summer is honored with a star on the Hollywood Walk of Fame, also singing *Friends Unknown*, a song she has written for the occasion.
Oct [19] She performs at the Palais Omnisports Paris Bercy, Paris, France, during European dates.

1993

Oct A two-CD/cassette career retrospective, ***The Donna Summer Anthology***, including a track from her never-released 1981 project, ***I'm A Rainbow***, is released in PolyGram's Chronicles series.
Dec [1] The RIAA certifies two million sales each of ***Bad Girls*** and ***On The Radio, Volume I And II***.
[31] Summer takes part in "Merv Griffin's New Year's Eve Third Annual Special", from his Resorts Casino Hotel, Atlantic City, NJ, which airs on Fox-TV.

1994

June [5] Now resettled in Nashville, TN, Summer sings with the Nashville Symphony during the city's annual "Summer Lights Arts Festival".
Oct [4] ***Christmas Spirit***, her first seasonal collection, is released on Mercury (US).
Nov [12] *Melody Of Love (Wanna Be Loved)*, a new cut taken from a single CD greatest hits ***Endless Summer - Greatest Hits***, an abbreviated version of last year's two-CD anthology, debuts at its UK #21 peak.
[26] ***Endless Summer - Greatest Hits*** makes UK #37 in its week of entry.

1995

Jan [7] *Melody Of Love (Wanna Be Loved)*, written and produced by Clivilles and Cole, now tops the US Dance chart.
Feb [14] Summer guests on CBS-TV's "Late Show With David Letterman".
May [23] She begins a tour of Brazil in Sao Paolo.
July [11] Summer embarks on a US tour at the Nautica Stage, Cleveland, OH.
Aug [4] She plays to a sellout audience of 6,251 at the Universal Amphitheatre, during a month when she splits from Mercury Records.
Sept [9] Reissued *I Feel Love* debuts at its UK #8 peak.
Dec [29] Summer guests on NBC-TV's "The Tonight Show".

1996

Mar [6] She grosses $310,240 from a sellout crowd at New York's Radio City Music Hall, while Angel Records releases a new ballad duet by Summer and Liza Minnelli, *Does He Love You*.
Apr [6] A remix of *State Of Independence* reaches UK #13 in its week of entry.

SUPERGRASS

Gaz Coombes (vocals, guitar); **Mickey Quinn** (guitar); **Danny Goffey** (drums)

1992

Aug Coombes (b. Gareth Coombes), Goffey and his brother Nick (sons of BBC2-TV's "Top Gear" presenter Chris Goffey) have formed the Jennifers with bassist Andy Davies earlier in the year, while Coombes is still attending Wheatley Park Comprehensive School in Oxford, Oxfordshire, which Danny has recently left. Via an approach to fellow Oxford-based combo Ride's management, the group has agreed a one-single deal with London-based indie Nude Records established by Saul Galpern, which now releases its debut single *Just Got Back Today*, though the band's progress and priority at the label is overshadowed by the success of labelmates Suede. With Davies going off to Bristol University, Bristol, Avon, Coombes, continuing to rehearse new numbers with Coffey, not least at Wheatley Cottage in Oxford, subsequently leaves school to take a number of part-time jobs including one as a waiter at a local Harvester restaurant, where he meets Quinn, five years his senior.

1994

Feb The trio of Coombes, Goffey and Quinn, now calling themselves Theodore Supergrass, send a six-track demo, including *Caught By The Fuzz* and *Mansize Rooster* to another Oxford-based band, Radiohead's management team, who like what they hear and contact EMI Records imprint Parlophone, which will sign the band in October.
Aug Local Oxford label Backbeat gets permission from Parlophone to press 1,000 copies of a single *Caught By The Fuzz* to sell at gigs, which the label believes will be an innovative way to build early strong word of mouth. The single, credited simply to Supergrass, becomes record of the week in both the **New Musical Express** and **Melody Maker**, prompting the group to re-record it at Parlophone's request.
Oct [29] Revamped and now released by Parlophone, *Caught By The Fuzz* bows at its UK #43 peak.

1995

Feb [18] With its video clip directed by ex-Jennifer Nick Goffey, *Mansize Rooster* debuts at its UK #20 high, also spurred by a UK tour opening for the Bluetones.
Mar [25] *Lose It* charts for a week at UK #75 as the band undertakes first US club tour with *Caught By The Fuzz* picking up strong reaction from college radio.
Apr During the month, the group performs its first shows in Japan.
May [13] The Kinky Machine/Led Zeppelin influenced *Lenny* hits UK #10 in its week of entry.
[27] Their critically-revered debut album (with the group hailed by **Melody Maker** as "our favourite band in the world ever, ever, ever"), the rapid fire, quirky rock set, ***I Should Coco***, initially peaks at its UK #3 entry position.
June For its performance at the 25th annual "Glastonbury Festival", Worthy Farm, Pilton, Somerset, Supergrass appears onstage wearing Stone Roses masks and using fake Manchester accents, after the Roses has cancelled its headline appearance.
July [15] *Alright*, coupled with *Time*, enters at its UK #2 peak, behind the Outhere Brothers' *Boom Boom Boom*, as the group undertakes a two-month US tour.
[29] ***I Should Coco*** hits UK #1.
Aug [5] Supergrass performs at the "T In The Park" festival, held in Strathclyde Country Park, Hamilton, Strathclyde, Scotland.
Nov [6] The group appears on BBC2-TV's "The O-Zone".
[7] Supergrass is named Best New Act at the **Q** Awards held at London's Park Lane Hotel.
Dec [31] The band is featured on UK-TV's "Jools Hootenanny".

1996

Feb [19] Supergrass is named Best Newcomer at the 1996 BRIT Awards held at London's Earl's Court Exhibition Centre.
[26] Following two shows in Brazil including one at the Hollywood Rock Festival, the band begins a six-date UK tour at Oxford's Apollo Theatre.
Mar [1] Their second of three nights at the London's Astoria Theatre is broadcast live over the Internet in a Vladivar vodka-sponsored event at http://www.good-cleanfun.freud.co.uk.
[8] Supergrass is featured on C4's "TFI"
[9] *Going Out* hits UK #5 in its week of entry.
May [30] Goffey, Coombes and Quinn collect the Best Contemporary Song Trophy for *Alright* at the 41st annual Ivor Novello Awards luncheon, held at London's Grosvenor House Hotel.
Aug [17] Supergrass takes part in the "V96" festival at Hylands Park, Chelmsford, Essex.

SUPERTRAMP

Richard Davies (vocals, keyboards); **Roger Hodgson** (guitar); **John Helliwell** (saxophone); **Dougie Thomson** (bass); **Bob C. Benberg** (drums)

1969

The band is formed in Britain as the result of sponsorship from young Dutch millionaire, Stanley August Miesegaes, known as Sam, whom Davies (b. July 22, 1944) has met in Munich, West Germany, while playing in a band named the Joint. Davies recruits other players through a UK music paper ad, offering a "genuine opportunity" to form a new group, which sees the arrival of bass player Hodgson (b. Mar. 21, 1950, London), Richard Palmer (b. June 1947, Bournemouth, Hants.) (guitar) and Bob Miller (drums). Originally to have been named Daddy, the group follows Palmer's suggestion and takes its name from W.H. Davies' book, **The Autobiography Of A Supertramp**, published in 1910.

1970

Aug Signed to A&M Records, the band, now with Dave Winthrop (b. Nov. 27, 1948, NJ) (saxophone) in its line-up, celebrates the release of ***Supertramp*** with a reception at the Revolution club in London.
[27] Supertramp plays on the second day of the "Isle Of Wight Festival" at East Afton Farm, Godshill, Isle of Wight.
Dec Palmer quits the band after a gig at the Zoom Club, Frankfurt, West Germany.

1971

Jan Miller follows suit after the group returns from an unsuccessful tour of Norway.
July New members, Kevin Currie (drums) and Frank Farrell (bass) (with Hodgson switching to lead guitar) have joined for ***Indelibly Stamped***. Supertramp and sponsor Sam split, with the latter absolving the group of some £60,000-worth of owed equipment and recording costs. The other players also depart, leaving just Davies and Hodgson.

1973

Aug Helliwell (b. Feb. 15, 1945, Todmorden, Lancs.), Thomson (b. Mar. 24, 1951, Glasgow, Strathclyde, Scotland) (both ex-Alan Bown) and Benberg (b. Robert Siebenberg), ex-Bees Make Honey, join the group, with Thomson taking charge of the group's business affairs.

1975

Jan [23] The group begins a ten-date UK tour at the City Hall, Sheffield, S. Yorks, set to end on February 9th at Colston Hall, Bristol, Avon.
Mar [8] *Dreamer*, taken from the album, makes UK #13.
[15] The keyboard-led progressive-pop/rock based ***Crime Of The Century***, written and recorded by the band in Southcombe (a farmhouse in Somerset, in which A&M has installed the band), and produced by Ken Scott, hits UK #4.
May [24] *Bloody Well Right*, also from the album, reaches US #35, supported by their debut US tour, while ***Crime Of The Century*** makes US #38.
Aug [23] The group plays on the second day of the 15th National Jazz Blues & Rock Festival "Reading Rock '75", near Reading, Berks.
Nov [13] The band begins a major 30-date UK tour, with Joan Armatrading, at Colston Hall, Bristol, set to end on December 20th at the Kursaal, Southend, Essex.
Dec [6] ***Crisis? What Crisis?***, again produced by Scott, with the group's now-familiar electric piano rhythm-based tracks, topped by the distinctive and contrasting dual vocals of Hodgson and Thomson, reaches UK #20.

1976

Jan [31] ***Crisis? What Crisis?***, once again co-helmed with Scott, makes US #44 as Supertramp's music becomes staple FM radio material.
Feb During the month, the group performs at London's Royal Albert Hall.

1977

May [14] The self-produced ***Even In The Quietest Moments ...***, with orchestral arrangements by Michel Colombier, reaches UK #12 and US #16.
July [2] Nearly three years after its release, ***Crime Of The Century*** is certified gold by the RIAA.
The band's re-promoted debut album, ***Supertramp***, will make US #158 the following March.
[9] Acoustic-guitar based *Give A Little Bit*, taken from the album, climbs to UK #29, as the group embarks on a 150-date US tour.
[13] Still-climbing ***Even In The Quietest Moments ...*** is certified gold by the RIAA.
[23] ***Even In The Quietest Moments ...*** reaches US #16.
Aug [27] *Give A Little Bit* makes US #15, as the group embarks on an extensive US tour.

1979

Apr [9] The still-climbing ***Breakfast In America*** is certified gold by the RIAA.
[28] The extracted *The Logical Song* hits UK #7.
May [12] ***Breakfast In America***, written by Davies and Hodgson (as with all of the group's hit material to date) and meticulously co-produced by the band with Peter Henderson, hits UK #3, and will become their most successful and enduring album.
[19] ***Breakfast In America*** tops the US chart for the first of six weeks.
June [16] *The Logical Song* hits US #6.
Aug [4] Title cut, *Breakfast In America*, hits UK #9.
Sept [8] *Goodbye Stranger*, also from the album, reaches US #15.
Nov [10] *Goodbye Stranger* makes UK #57.
[29] The group's concert at the Pavilion in Paris, France, is recorded for future album release.
Dec [15] *Take The Long Way Home*, the final extract from ***Breakfast In America***, hits US #10.

1980

May [9] *The Logical Song* is named Best Song Musically And Lyrically, at the 25th annual Ivor Novello Awards, held at London's Grosvenor House Hotel.
Oct [11] Live double set, ***Paris***, recorded at the Pavilion in 1979, hits UK #7.
Nov [8] A live version of the band's early hit, *Dreamer*, taken from ***Paris***, climbs to US #15, as the album hits US #8.
Dec [10] ***Paris*** is certified gold by the RIAA.
[27] Also from the album a live version of *Breakfast In America*, peaks at US #62.

1982

Nov [6] ***Famous Last Words***, once again co-produced with Henderson, hits UK #6, while the extracted *It's Raining Again* makes UK #26. This is Supertramp's last album with Hodgson, who elects on a solo career, leaving the band as a quartet.

[27] ***Famous Last Words*** hits US #5.
Dec [11] *It's Raining Again* makes US #11.

1983

Jan [5] ***Famous Last Words*** is certified gold by the RIAA.
Mar [19] *My Kind Of Lady*, taken from ***Famous Last Words***, reaches US #31.

1984

Oct Hodgson's debut solo album (also for A&M), ***In The Eye Of The Storm***, climbs to UK #70 (and US #46, two months later).
Nov [14] The RIAA certifies four million sales of ***Breakfast In America***.
Dec [8] Hodgson's *Had A Dream (Sleeping With The Enemy)* makes US #48.

1985

May [25] Supertramp's first post-Hodgson album, ***Brother Where You Bound***, a more R&B-rooted affair than earlier efforts, makes UK #20.
July [6] *Cannonball*, taken from it, and written by Davies, makes US #28.
[13] ***Brother Where You Bound*** reaches US #21.
Sept The group undertakes a North American tour to promote the album, beginning in Chicago, IL.

1986

Mar A six-month US tour comes to an end during a month when the band performs at London's Royal Albert Hall.
Oct A 14-track compilation, ***The Autobiography Of Supertramp***, hits UK #9. Hodgson briefly re-joins the group for a short promotional stint.

1987

Oct [31] Supertramp album, ***Free As A Bird***, produced by the band, featuring a full horn section, mixed by Tom Lord-Alge, and recorded at Davies' own Los Angeles studio, peaks at UK #93.
Nov ***Free As A Bird*** stops at US #101, but includes a surprise US Dance-chart hit, *I'm Begging You*. Meanwhile, Hodgson's second solo album, ***Hai Hai***, co-produced with Jack Joseph Puig and featuring Toto members on its guest list, makes US #163, and includes *London*, also released as a single, and a lyrical counterpoint to his earlier composition, *Breakfast In America*. The decade will round out with the release of ***Supertramp Live 88*** in October 1988.

1993

Apr [14] Following the UK #24 peak of a second compilation ***The Very Best Of Supertramp*** on Aug [15] the previous year, and, after Hodgson has recently told KLSX Los Angeles DJ, Cynthia Fox that Supertramp may reunite, with Davies, for a 1994 tour, the group re-assembles at the Entertainment Industry's Foundation for Cities In Schools first fund-raiser, at the Beverly Hilton Hotel, Los Angeles, CA, an event also honoring A&M Records founder, Jerry Moss.

THE SUPREMES

Diana Ross (lead vocals); **Mary Wilson** (vocals); **Florence Ballard** (vocals)

1959

A female R&B vocal trio is formed by Detroit, MI manager, Milton Jenkins, to complement his male group the Primes, later to become the Temptations, onstage, comprising Wilson (b. Mar. 6, 1944, Greenville, MS), Ballard (b. June 30, 1943, Detroit) and Betty Travis. They are joined by Ross (b. Diane Ernestine Ross, Mar. 26, 1944, Detroit), brought in by Paul Williams of the Primes to help fill out the original trio's sound. As the Primettes support the Primes on Detroit club dates, Travis leaves the following year to be replaced by Barbara Martin, before the group dissolves as Ballard's and Martin's parents persuade them to concentrate on high school grades. Wilson and Ross perform as a duo before the quartet re-forms, and is signed briefly to LuPine Records, after Smokey Robinson (a neighbor of Ross) initially fails to interest Motown's Berry Gordy Jr. in the girls, though they complete some studio work for him, backing Marvin Gaye and others.

1960

Dec Martin leaves again as Gordy has decided to sign the group. He requests a name-change, and Ballard chooses the Supremes, initially much disliked by Ross and Wilson. *I Want A Guy* is issued as their first US single, but fails to chart. Its follow-up, *Buttered Popcorn*, with Ballard singing lead, will released in the US on July 21st the following year.

1962

Aug [18] *Your Heart Belongs To Me* is their US chart debut, reaching #95.
Oct [16] The Supremes begin a two-month US Motown Records package tour, with label-mates Marvin Gaye, the Miracles, Mary Wells and Little Stevie Wonder, in Washington, DC.
Nov [19] The Motown package tour begins a further ten-day run in residence at New York's Apollo Theatre in Harlem.

1963

Feb [2] *Let Me Go The Right Way*, written by Gordy, makes US #90, having already marked their debut on the US R&B survey at #26 the previous Dec [29].
Sept [7] *A Breath Taking Guy*, penned by Smokey Robinson, makes US #75.

1964

Jan [11] A Holland/Dozier/Holland song, the uptempo dancer *When The Lovelight Starts Shining Through His Eyes*, is the group's Top 30 breakthrough, reaching US #23.
Mar [21] *Run, Run, Run*, penned by the same trio, peaks at US #93.
June The group begins a US tour on Dick Clark's "Cavalcade Of Stars", alongside Gene Pitney, the Shirelles, the Crystals, Brian Hyland, Brenda Holloway, and others.
Aug [22] Defining both the Supremes' sound and Motown's songwriting and production style, *Where Did Our Love Go* (written by Holland, Dozier and Holland for, but rejected by, the Marvelettes) tops the US chart for the first of two weeks, and is the group's first million seller (though not officially certified, as with much of the label's '60s output).
Sept [13] The trio appears in Murray The K's ten-day "Rock'n'Roll Spectacular" at New York's Fox Theater, Brooklyn, on a bill including Motown labelmates the Temptations, Marvin Gaye, the Miracles and Martha & the Vandellas.
Oct [3] *Where Did Our Love Go* is the Supremes' UK chart debut, at #3.
[9] During the trio's first visit to the UK, they appear on ITV's "Ready Steady, Go!".
[28-29] The group appears in the T.A.M.I. show, a stage spectacular videotaped for US TV and UK movie release, alongside the Rolling Stones, the Beach Boys, Marvin Gaye, James Brown, and others, held at the Civic Auditorium, Santa Monica, CA.
[31] Career highlight, *Baby Love*, also written by Holland/Dozier/Holland, begins a four-week stretch at US #1, becoming a second million seller.
Nov [21] The Supremes become the first all-girl group to hit UK #1, when *Baby Love* tops the UK chart for the first of two weeks.
Dec [12] ***Meet The Supremes*** reaches UK #13.
[19] *Come See About Me*, by Holland/Dozier/Holland, and taken from the album to compete with Nella Dodds' version (a minor US hit on Wand Records), heads the US survey for one week, before being deposed by the Beatles' *I Feel Fine*.
[27] The trio makes its debut on CBS-TV's "The Ed Sullivan Show".

1965

Jan [16] *Come See About Me* replaces the Beatles *I Feel Fine* for a further week at US #1, and is their third consecutive million seller. ***Where Did Our Love Go*** hits US #2, staying charted for 89 weeks.
Feb [6] ***A Bit Of Liverpool***, featuring covers of UK group hits, makes US #21.
[13] *Come See About Me* reaches UK #27.
Mar [20] The Supremes arrive in London to take part in the 24-day Motown package tour, which helps launch the label's identity in Britain (all previous releases having been licensed on UK labels like London, Oriole and Stateside), with labelmates Martha & the Vandellas, the Miracles, the Temptations and Stevie Wonder.
[27] Again the trio deposes the Beatles as Holland/Dozier/Holland's *Stop! In The Name Of Love* replaces Lennon/McCartney's *Eight Days A Week* at US #1, for the first of two weeks.
Apr [17] *Stop! In The Name Of Love*, the first single released on the UK Tamla Motown label, hits UK #6. The trio's characteristic hand-movement choreography for the song is worked out during rehearsals for ITV's "Ready Steady, Go!" ***The Supremes Sing Country, Western And Pop*** makes US #79.
June [12] *Back In My Arms Again* tops the US chart for one week, the trio's fifth consecutive US #1 single and million seller. In the UK, it makes #40 while ***We Remember Sam Cooke***, featuring songs associated with the recently-deceased singer, climbs to US #75.
[28] The group appears on CBS-TV's "It's What's Happening Baby" special.
July [29] The Supremes begin a three-week engagement at New York's Copacabana club.
Sept [4] *Nothing But Heartaches* reaches US #11.
Oct [10] The Supremes appear again on CBS-TV's "The Ed Sullivan Show", introducing *I Hear A Symphony*.
[16] ***More Hits By The Supremes*** hits US #6.
Nov [20] Yet another Holland/Dozier/Holland effort, *I Hear A Symphony* tops the US chart for the first of two weeks (deposing the Rolling Stones' *Get Off Of My Cloud*) and becomes another million seller.

1966

Jan [1] Live album, ***The Supremes At The Copa***, a recording of their club act at New York's Copacabana, reaches US #11.
[8] *I Hear A Symphony* makes UK #39.
Feb [19] *My World Is Empty Without You* hits US #5, and is a further million seller.
Apr [30] ***I Hear A Symphony*** hits US #8.
May [28] *Love Is Like An Itching In My Heart* hits US #9. (Though not a UK hit, it will become a classic dance record on the UK Northern Soul scene in the mid-'70s.)
Sept [10] *You Can't Hurry Love* hits US #1 for a fortnight, selling one million-plus copies. (Phil Collins' 1982 revival of the song will also become a million seller.)
Oct [1] *You Can't Hurry Love* hits UK #3.
[22] ***The Supremes A' Go-Go*** tops the US chart for the first of two weeks, deposing the Beatles' ***Revolver***, the trio's first #1 album.
Nov [19] *You Keep Me Hangin' On* begins two weeks at US #1, its sales again reaching seven figures.
Dec [24] *You Keep Me Hangin' On* hits UK #8.

1967

Jan [6] The Supremes begin recording an album of Disney tunes. (The project is shelved before release, and only *When You Wish Upon A Star* appears.)
[14] ***The Supremes A' Go-Go*** makes UK #15.
Mar [11] *Love Is Here And Now You're Gone* tops the US chart for one week (becoming a further million seller).
[18] ***The Supremes Sing Holland-Dozier-Holland***, which hits US #6.
Apr After Ballard, unhappy about her role in the group, starts to become unreliable, missing concerts in New Orleans, LA and Montreal, PQ, Canada, Cindy

Birdsong (b. Dec. 15, 1939, Camden, NJ) of Patti LaBelle & the Bluebelles is auditioned as a stand-in.
[1] *Love Is Here And Now You're Gone* reaches UK #17.
[29] Birdsong makes her Supremes stage debut at the Hollywood Bowl, Hollywood, CA, at a benefit show for the United Negro College Fund and UCLA School of Music, which also features the 5th Dimension, Johnny Rivers, and others.
May [13] *The Happening*, the theme from the Anthony Quinn film of the same name, becomes the Supremes' tenth US #1 (in 13 releases), for one week.
June [10] *The Happening* hits UK #6.
July [8] ***The Supremes Sing Motown*** (a re-titling of the Stateside album ***The Supremes Sing Holland-Dozier-Holland***) reaches UK #17.
[22] ***The Supremes Sing Rodgers And Hart*** makes US #20. During a Las Vegas, NV club engagement at the Flamingo, Ballard is dismissed from the group and fired from Motown (the label flies her back to Detroit, where she is hospitalized with exhaustion). Birdsong steps in, but Gordy announces that lead singer Ross is to be elevated to featured status in preparation for a solo career, and the group will henceforth be credited as Diana Ross & the Supremes.
Sept [9] *Reflections*, the first release with the new billing (and also one of Motown's first experiments with "progressive" backing-music elements, featuring a characteristically 1967 swirling "psychedelic" intro), hits US #2 (behind Bobbie Gentry's *Ode To Billie Joe*), selling over one million.
[30] *Reflections* hits UK #5.
Oct [21] ***The Supremes Sing Rodgers And Hart*** makes UK #25.
[28] Double compilation album, ***Diana Ross And The Supremes' Greatest Hits***, heads the US survey for the first of five weeks.
Dec [9] *In And Out Of Love* hits US #9.

1968

Jan [6] *In And Out Of Love* reaches UK #13.
[12] A "Tarzan" episode, with the group appearing as nuns, airs on US TV.
[22] The trio plays a short nightclub season at London's Talk Of The Town. Among those who catch the opening of the act are Paul McCartney, Cliff Richard and Michael Caine.
[28] They also appear on ITV's "Sunday Night At The London Palladium", with Tom Jones and Des O'Connor.
Feb [3] TV special, "The Supremes Live At The Talk Of The Town", airs on BBC-TV.
[17] Compilation album, ***Diana Ross And The Supremes' Greatest Hits***, reduced from the US double album to a 16-track single album for the UK, tops the UK chart for the first of three weeks.
[29] Ex-Supreme Ballard marries Thomas Chapman in Detroit.
Mar Ballard signs to ABC Records as a soloist. (She will record two solo singles but neither will sell.)
Apr [27] *Forever Came Today*, the last Supremes single written and produced by Holland/Dozier/Holland (who will leave Motown to set up their own successful Invictus and Hot Wax labels), reaches both US and UK #28.
May [11] A UK-recorded live album, ***Live At The Talk Of The Town***, hits UK #6.
June [15] ***Reflections*** peaks at US #18.
July [6] *Some Things You Never Get Used To*, written and produced by Ashford and Simpson, makes US #30 and UK #34.
[27] ***Reflections*** makes UK #30.
Aug Rumors that Ross is shortly to leave the Supremes are reported in both the US and UK media.
Nov [2] ***Funny Girl***, featuring the group's versions of songs from the stage show, makes US #150.
[19] The Supremes appear before the Queen at the "Royal Variety Performance" in London. Ross performs an unrehearsed between-songs monologue urging racial tolerance, which is rapturously applauded.
[30] *Love Child*, a social conscience-themed song, team-written by Pam Sawyer, Frank Wilson, Deke Richards and R. Dean Taylor, hits US #1 for the first of two weeks, after the trio has premiered the cut on CBS-TV's "The Ed Sullivan Show". It deposes the Beatles' *Hey Jude*, and is another million seller.

1969

Jan [4] ***Live At London's Talk Of The Town*** peaks at US #57.
[11] Their revival of Madeleine Bell's *I'm Gonna Make You Love Me*, duetted with the Temptations, and taken from the two groups' joint album, is a millon seller, hitting US #2 (behind Marvin Gaye's *I Heard It Through The Grapevine)*, as *Love Child* makes UK #15. ***Diana Ross And The Supremes Join The Temptations*** hits US #2.
[25] ***Love Child*** reaches US #14.
Feb [8] ***T.C.B.***, again recorded with the Temptations, and featuring the soundtrack of the two groups' TV spectacular of the same title, heads the US survey for one week.
[15] ***Diana Ross And The Supremes Join The Temptations*** tops the UK chart for the first of four weeks, while ***Love Child*** hits UK #8.
[22] *I'm Livin' In Shame* (said to have been inspired by the Lana Turner film, "Imitation Of Life") hits US #10, as *I'm Gonna Make You Love Me* hits UK #3.
Apr [12] The Supremes' revival of the Miracles' *I'll Try Something New*, again with the Temptations (taken from ***T.C.B.***), makes US #25.
May [10] *I'm Livin' In Shame* makes UK #14.
[17] *The Composer*, penned by Smokey Robinson, reaches US #27.
June [28] *No Matter What Sign You Are* peaks at US #31.
July [12] ***T.C.B.*** reaches UK #11.
[19] ***Let The Sunshine In*** makes US #24.
[26] *No Matter What Sign You Are* climbs to UK #37.
Aug [23] *No Matter What Sign You Are*'s B-side, *The Young Folks*, makes US #69.
Oct [4] Their treatment of the Band's *The Weight*, duetted with the Temptations, peaks at US #46, as a revival of the Miracles' *I Second That Emotion*, again with the Temptations, makes UK #18.
Nov [22] ***Together***, a third set with the Temptations, makes US #28.
Dec [27] *Someday We'll Be Together*, produced and co-written by Johnny Bristol, tops the US chart for one week, and sells over a million. It is the Supremes' 12th and last US #1 (and their last single together before Ross departs for a solo career), and the last #1 of the '60s. It is taken from ***Cream Of The Crop***, the last studio set from the Ross-led line-up, which reaches US #33.
[21] Ross & the Supremes make their last TV appearance together on "The Ed Sullivan Show", singing *Someday We'll Be Together*.
[27] ***On Broadway***, the soundtrack to a Supremes/Temptations TV special, makes US #38.

1970

Jan [14] Diana Ross & the Supremes make their final live appearance together at Las Vegas' Frontier Hotel. (Ross will leave the following day, having introduced her replacement, Jean Terrell (b. Nov. 26, 1944, Texas), the sister of boxer, Ernie Terrell, onstage.)
[17] *Someday We'll Be Together* makes UK #13.
Feb Compilation album, ***Diana Ross And The Supremes Greatest Hits, Volume 3***, continuing the hits anthology from the earlier double album, makes US #31.
[14] ***Together***, with the Temptations once more, reaches UK #28.
Apr [18] The group's billing reverts back to the Supremes for *Up The Ladder To The Roof*, the first release featuring Terrell on lead vocals, which hits US #10. The girls are now working with producer Frank Wilson, who has co-written the song with Vincent DiMirco. *Why (Must We Fall In Love)*, with the Temptations (and featuring Ross), makes UK #31.
May [30] *Up The Ladder To The Roof* hits UK #6.
June Live double album, ***Farewell***, by Diana Ross & the Supremes, a recording of the trio's final concert on January 14th, peaks at US #46.
July ***Right On***, the first album featuring Terrell, reaches US #25.
Sept [5] *Everybody's Got The Right To Love*, from the recent set, makes US #21.
Nov ***The Magnificent 7***, recorded with the Four Tops, peaks at US #113, while the Supremes' ***New Ways But Love Stays*** makes US #68.
Dec [19] From the album, *Stoned Love*, produced and co-written by Frank Wilson, hits US #7, giving the new line-up its first million seller.

1971

Jan [9] Their update of Ike & Tina Turner's *River Deep, Mountain High*, with the Four Tops (from ***The Magnificent 7***), reaches US #14.
Feb [6] *Stoned Love* hits UK #3.
June [19] *Nathan Jones* reaches US #16.
July [3] The duetted *You Gotta Have Love In Your Heart*, taken from it, makes US #55.
[10] ***The Magnificent 7***, with the Four Tops, hits UK #6.
[24] *River Deep, Mountain High* peaks at UK #11, while the Supremes' ***Touch***, with sleeve notes written by Elton John, makes US #85, and ***The Return Of The Magnificent Seven***, again with the Four Tops, climbs to US #154.
Sept [18] *Nathan Jones* hits UK #5 (and will be revived by Bananarama in 1988).
[25] ***Touch*** makes UK #40.
Oct [16] The title cut, *Touch*, peaks at US #71.
Nov [12] The group begins a 13-date UK tour at the Regal Theatre, Edmonton, London, set to end on the 29th at the Dome, Brighton, East Sussex.
Dec [18] *You Gotta Have Love In Your Heart*, with the Four Tops, makes #25 on UK chart.

1972

Jan ***Dynamite***, with the Four Tops, makes US #160.
Mar [11] *Floy Joy*, written and produced by Smokey Robinson, reaches US #16.
Apr [1] *Floy Joy* hits UK #9.
June Birdsong leaves, to devote more time to home and marriage. She is replaced by Lynda Lawrence. ***Floy Joy*** reaches US #54.
[17] From it, another Robinson song, *Automatically Sunshine*, makes US #37.
Aug [5] *Automatically Sunshine* hits UK #10, the group's last Top 10 hit.
Sept [9] *Your Wonderful, Sweet Sweet Love* makes US #59.
Nov [25] *I Guess I'll Miss The Man* (from the Broadway musical, "Pippin") stops at US #85.
Dec ***The Supremes***, written and produced by Jimmy Webb, makes US #129.

1973

May [5] *Bad Weather*, produced and arranged by Stevie Wonder, makes UK #37.
June [9] *Bad Weather* spends a week at US #87. It is the group's last recording to feature Terrell, who leaves shortly after, and is replaced by Freda Payne's sister Scherrie Payne (b. Nov. 14, 1944, Detroit).

1974

July Triple compilation album, ***Anthology (1962-1969)***, reaches US #66.
Sept [28] Reissued in the UK, *Baby Love* makes #12, the group's final UK chart 45. ***The Supremes*** will peak at US #152 the following July. Laurence will subsequently leave, Birdsong will temporarily return with the third slot filled by Susaye Greene, previously a member of Stevie Wonder's Wonderlove backing troupe.

1976

Feb [21] Having hit hard times, including a lost $8.7 million lawsuit against Motown, and separation from her husband, which has left her on welfare, Ballard dies of cardiac arrest at 10:05 a.m., aged 32, at Mount Carmel Mercy Hospital, Detroit. ME Dr. Werner Spitz states that she had ingested an unknown amount of pills and alcohol. (The Four Tops and Marv Johnson will act as pall-bearers at the New Bethel Baptist Church funeral, with the eulogy to be delivered by the

Rev. C.L. Franklin. Ross will be escorted from her limousine by a cordon of bodyguards.)
June [19] ***High Energy*** makes US #42.
Aug [7] The extracted *I'm Gonna Let My Heart Do The Walking* makes US #40 (after the group has been absent from the singles chart for three years).
Dec [25] *You're My Driving Wheel* peaks at US #85, and is their final US chart single. Wilson, the final original member, leaves, and is replaced by Karen Jackson. (Motown sees little commercial potential left in the group, and it will disband. Wilson, who will sue Motown for unpaid royalties, will later perform with new back-up singers as Mary Wilson & the Supremes.)

1977

Sept [17] TV-promoted UK compilation album, ***Diana Ross And The Supremes' 20 Golden Greats***, tops the UK chart for the first of seven weeks. The trio of Mary Wilson, Karen Jackson and Kaaren Ragland, will perform three shows at the London Palladium the following April.

1981

Dec [20] Musical "Dreamgirls", supposedly based on the story of the Supremes, opens on Broadway at the Imperial Theater.

1983

May [16] Wilson and Birdsong are reunited with Ross, as the Supremes, on the Motown 25th anniversary NBC-TV spectacular, singing *Someday We'll Be Together*.
June Now billed as the Supremes with Wilson, the group tours the US on an oldies package trek, with Frankie Valli & the Four Seasons, the Righteous Brothers, the Four Tops and the Association. (The following year, Wilson's **Dreamgirl : My Life As A Supreme**, a book documenting her own history of the group, will be published.)

1986

June ***25th Anniversary*** compilation makes US #112. (Terrell, Payne and Lawrence, who were never in the band together at the same time originally, reunite to tour and record for the Superstar International (US) and Motorcity (UK) labels, as the FLO's (Former Ladies Of The Supremes) and will stay together until February 1993, when Sundray Tucker replaces the departing Terrell.)

1988

Jan [20] Much revered and a staple on US oldies radio stations, the Supremes are inducted into the Rock and Roll Hall of Fame, at the third annual dinner, held at the Waldorf Astoria Hotel, New York. (***Love Supreme***, a further UK-released collection, will make the UK Compilation chart in December, and the re-issued *Stop! In The Name Of Love* will chart for a week at UK #62 on Feb [18], 1989. Wilson will be seriously in an auto accident on January 29th, 1994, when her Jeep Cherokee hits the central barrier on a California highway, also resulting in the death of her 14-year old son.)
see also: **Diana ROSS**

SURVIVOR

Jim Peterik (keyboards, guitar, vocals);
Frank Sullivan (lead guitar, vocals);
Dave Bickler (synthesizers, lead vocals);
Stephan Ellis (bass); **Marc Droubay** (drums)

1978

The nucleus of the hard-rock group is formed in Chicago, IL, after Peterik (b. Nov. 11, 1950), having been in the Ides Of March, whose 1970 US #2 million seller, *Vehicle*, he also wrote, subsequently continuing as a solo artist recording *Don't Fight The Feeling*, teams with Bickler. Sullivan joins the duo after playing with local band, Mariah, and early drummer Gary Smith and bassist Dennis Johnson are recruited before the band starts touring around Chicago and the Pacific northwest, eventually coming to the attention of Scotti Brothers Records, which signs the group the following year.

1980

Mar The Peterik and Sullivan-penned *Rockin' Into The Night* reaches US #43 for Florida rock band, .38 Special.
Apr Survivor's hard rock debut album, ***Survivor***, makes US #169.
May [3] The Peterik-written extract, *Somewhere In America*, peaks at US #70.

1981

Feb Ellis and Droubay join on bass and drums respectively, replacing Johnson and Smith.
May Once again written by Peterik and Sullivan, *Hold On Loosely* gives .38 Special a second hit single, at US #27.
Aug The Peterik-penned theme for the animated movie, "Heavy Metal", which is recorded by Don Felder as *Heavy Metal (Takin' A Ride)*, reaches US #43.
Dec [12] Taken from a forthcoming album, Survivor's *Poor Man's Son* makes US #33.

1982

Jan Their sophomore set, ***Premonition***, makes US #92.
Mar [27] *Summer Nights*, also from the album, makes US #62.
Apr The group begins recording its third album at Rumbo Recorders, Los Angeles, CA, with Peterik and Sullivan co-producing and co-writing. Among the tracks is *Eye Of The Tiger*, which they have written as the theme to Sylvester Stallone's forthcoming third "Rocky" movie. Tony Scotti of their record label has played ***Premonition*** to Stallone, who has indicated that he wants a contemporary, rock-oriented sound with a strong beat, and has given the writers a rough-cut video of the film for inspiration - which provides the key phrase, as Rocky's trainer continually reminds him to "keep the eye of the tiger".
July [24] Rock-pop anthem *Eye Of The Tiger* tops the US chart for the first of six weeks, eventually selling over two million copies to earn a platinum disc.
Aug [14] Survivor's third album, ***Eye Of The Tiger***, hits US #2 for four weeks (behind Fleetwood Mac's ***Mirage***) while the movie's soundtrack album, which includes the single, also makes US #15.
Sept [4] *Eye Of The Tiger* is the band's UK chart debut, hitting #1 for the first of four weeks and eventually selling 800,000 copies. ***Eye Of The Tiger*** also reaches UK #12, while the soundtrack album, ***Rocky III***, makes UK #42.
Sept [21] ***Eye Of The Tiger*** is certified platinum by the RIAA.
Nov [20] *American Heartbeat*, taken from ***Eye Of The Tiger***, reaches US #17.

1983

Feb [12] *The One That Really Matters* peaks at US #74.
[23] Survivor wins the Best Rock Performance By A Duo Or Group With Vocal category for *Eye Of The Tiger*, at the 25th annual Grammy Awards.
Nov ***Caught In The Game*** peaks at US #82.
[5] Its Peterik/Sullivan-penned title track, *Caught In The Game*, stopping at US #77.

1984

July [7] *The Moment Of Truth*, from the film soundtrack to the Ralph Macchio-starring "The Karate Kid", released as a single on Casablanca, makes US #63.
Dec Ex-Cobra vocalist Jimi Jamison (b. Aug. 23, 1951) replaces Bickler as Survivor's lead singer.
[8] *I Can't Hold Back* reaches US #13.

1985

Mar [23] *High On You* hits US #8, during a 17-week chart run.
June [24] The still-climbing ***Vital Signs*** is certified platinum by the RIAA.
July [13] *The Search Is Over* hits US #4, while ***Vital Signs***, the first album to feature Jamison, and including both the current hit and the previous two, reaches US #16 (having steadily climbed the chart since the end of 1984).
Sept [7] *First Night* peaks at US #53.

1986

Feb [1] *Burning Heart*, written by Peterik and Sullivan for the soundtrack to "Rocky IV" hits US #2, for the first of two weeks (behind Dionne Warwick and Friends' *That's What Friends Are For*), while ***Rocky IV***, which again includes *Eye Of The Tiger*, hits US #10.
Mar [1] *Burning Heart* hits UK #5, while ***Rocky IV*** hits UK #3.

1987

Jan [17] *Is This Love* hits US #9, as its parent album, ***When Seconds Count***, co-produced by Sullivan with Ron Nevison, makes US #49.
Mar [28] Follow-up single, *How Much Love*, peaks at US #51.
May [23] *Man Against The World* stops at US #86.

1988

Nov [12] *Didn't Know It Was Love* climbs to US #61, as its parent set, ***Too Hot To Sleep***, spends just two weeks on the US survey, peaking at #187. After a second extract *Across The Miles* peaks at US #74 on Feb [11], 1989, and with its last chart disc,the group, clearly out of vogue, disbands.

1994

Oct [26] Following the release by Scotti Brothers Records in March the previous year of ***Greatest Hits***, containing previously unavailable material, when the band has also reunited with original guitarists Peterik, Sullivan and lead vocalist Bickler (his earlier replacement Jamison having gone on to write the theme music to the hit TV show "Baywatch"), embarking on a spring tour of Canada, followed by US festival and fair dates throughout the summer, the RIAA now certifies two million sales of the group's career-defining hit, *Eye Of The Tiger*.

SWEET

Brian Connolly (vocals); **Andy Scott** (guitar);
Steve Priest (bass); **Mick Tucker** (drums)

1968

Jan Ex-members of Wainwright's Gentlemen, Connolly (b. Oct. 5, 1949, Hamilton, Strathclyde, Scotland) and Tucker (b. July 17, 1949, Harlesden, London) form Sweetshop with Priest (b. Feb. 23, 1950, Hayes, Middx.) and Frank Torpey on guitar. Making their live debut the following month at the Pavilion, Hemel Hempstead, Herts., their first single, *Slow Motion*, is released on Fontana Records in July, while their first radio broadcast, on BBC Radio 1's "David Symonds Show", airs in August. A move to EMI's Parlophone label for *Lollipop Man* the following month sees minimal sales. Two more Parlophone singles, *All You'll Ever Get From Me* and *Get On The Line*, will also fail to chart in 1970, before the label drops the group. In the same year, Torpey is replaced by Scott (b. June 30, 1951, Wrexham, Clwyd, Wales), who has moved to London after his most recent group, the Elastic Band, has split up, and the group abbreviates its name to Sweet.

1971

Jan The group makes its UK TV debut, on the kids pop show "Lift Off". A new recording deal is signed with RCA Records, as Sweet links with producer, Phil Wainman.
May [8] The Wainman-produced Nicky Chinn/Mike Chapman composition, *Funny Funny*, their UK chart

debut, reaches #13.
July [10] *Co-Co* hits UK #2, held off the top by Middle Of The Road's *Chirpy Chirpy Cheep Cheep*.
Oct [2] *Co-Co*, issued on Bell Records, opens their US account, at #91.
Nov [6] *Alexander Graham Bell* makes UK #33.
Their debut album, ***Funny How Sweet Co-Co Can Be*** is released.

1972

Mar [4] *Poppa Joe* reaches UK #11. It begins a series of ChinniChap-penned glam-pop confected UK hits, which makes the band "Top Of The Pops" regulars on BBC1-TV, and encourages its increasingly way-out visual image, with flamboyant glam costumes, make-up and glitter.
May The group is taken to court in Belgium, by a town objecting to an earlier Sweet concert, which involved the use of an allegedly pornographic film clip.
July [1] *Little Willy* hits UK #4. The slight double entendre is exploited by the group (and its audience), especially on live ballroom dates. (Later, for what is considered an overtly sexual stage act, the group is banned from the Mecca dancehall circuit.)
Oct [7] *Wig Wam Bam* hits UK #4, promoted by TV appearances in Native American costumes and warpaint-like make-up.
Nov Compilation ***Sweet's Biggest Hits*** is released by RCA in the UK.

1973

Jan [27] *Blockbuster*, using one of the most familiar riffs in rock music (the same one as David Bowie's *The Gene Genie*, which sits at #2), tops the UK chart for the first of five weeks. Like all Sweet hits, it has a hard-rock, band-composed B-side.
Apr [25] The still-rising *Little Willy* is certified gold by the RIAA.
May [5] *Little Willy* gives the band its biggest US success, hitting #3.
[12] *Hellraiser* hits UK #2, behind Dawn's *Tie A Yellow Ribbon*.
July [28] *Blockbuster* peaks at US #73.
Aug Their third album, ***The Sweet*** makes US #191.
Sept [22] *Ballroom Blitz* enters the UK chart at #2, held off the top by Simon Park Orchestra's *Eye Level*.

1974

Jan [26] *Teenage Rampage* is their third in a row at UK #2, behind Mud's *Tiger Feet* (also written by ChinniChap).
May [25] ***Sweet Fanny Adams*** makes UK #27 - the group's only UK chart album during the '70s. In contrast to the singles, it is entirely self-written. (The band embarks on its first UK tour.)
July [27] *The Six Teens* hits UK #9.
Nov [16] *Turn It Down* makes UK #41.
Dec The group splits from Chinn and Chapman, to write and produce itself, in an attempt to find greater international rock credibility.

1975

Apr [12] The group-penned *Fox On The Run* hits UK #2, behind the Bay City Rollers' *Bye Bye Baby*.
Aug [2] *Action* reaches UK #15.
Sept The band begins a three-month US tour, which heralds its greatest period of Stateside success.
Oct [18] *Ballroom Blitz* hits US #5, a year after its UK success.
[25] ***Desolation Boulevard***, having failed to chart domestically, reaches US #25 with a different track listing including cuts from ***Sweet Fanny Adams***.

1976

Jan [17] *Fox On The Run* hits US #5, their third and last US top five success.
[31] *Lies In Your Eyes*, included on the live album ***Strung Up***, makes UK #35.
Feb [23] *Fox On The Run* becomes the band's second RIAA-certified gold disc.
Apr [17] *Action* makes US #20, while the self-penned ***Give Us A Wink***, recorded in Munich, West Germany, reaches US #27.
May [25] ***Desolation Boulevard*** is confirmed gold by the RIAA.

1977

June [4] ***Off The Record*** makes US #151.
Sept [10] *Funk It Up (David's Song)*, not issued as a UK single, makes US #88. The group retires to Clearwell Castle in Wales to write another album, before recording sessions in France.

1978

Feb [18] After a two-year UK singles chart absence, the band has left RCA following three non-charting singles releases, and signed to Polydor in the UK (and Capitol in the US), for whom *Love Is Like Oxygen*, also featured in the Joan Collins movie "The Bitch", now hits UK #9, spurred by an appearance on BBC1-TV's "Top Of The Pops" on the 16th. Sweet tours Britain for the first time in four years.
June [24] *Love Is Like Oxygen* hits US #8, while its parent album, ***Level Headed***, makes US #52.
Aug [26] Also from the album, *California Nights* makes US #76, the band's final chart single.

1979

June [2] ***Cut Above The Rest*** makes US #151, as Connolly leaves for a solo career. (Priest takes over as lead vocalist, with Gary Moberley joining on keyboards. Connolly will later form the New Sweet, with no other original members.)

1984

Oct Following the release of ***Water's Edge*** (1980) and ***Identity Crisis*** (1981), which marked the dissolution of the band, a retrospective compilation, ***Sweet 16 - It's ... It's ... Sweet's Hits***, released on the UK independent label, Anagram, reaches UK #49.

1985

Feb [16] Also on Anagram, the segued *It's It's The Sweet Mix*, assembled from original hits (*Blockbusters*, *Fox On The Run*, *Teenage Rampage*, *Hellraiser* and *Ballroom Blitz*), makes UK #45. Amid the interest this creates, the group re-forms briefly, with Paul Mario Day (ex-Wildfire) replacing Connolly, and keyboardist Phil Lanzon (ex-Grand Prix).

1991

Oct [18-21] After the the group has re-formed again in 1990 with Scott (who had briefly toured the UK in 1988 with pub-rockers Paddy Goes To Holyhead) and Tucker, adding Mal McNulty (vocals) Steve Mann (keyboards) and Jeff Brown (bass), and releasing ***Live At The Marquee*** on Maze Records, accompanied by a British tour, Sweet now performs at the second "Hemsby '70s & Glam Rock Weekender" held at Pontins Holiday Centre in Hemsby, Norfolk, with Showaddywaddy, Mud, the Glitter Band, Alvin Stardust, Mungo Jerry and the Rubettes. (Capitol Records in the US will release ***The Best Of Sweet*** on CD in May 1993, the same year Connolly (who has only recently discovered that he is the biological brother of actor Mark McManus, who played the lead role in ITV's "Taggart"), billed as Brian Connolly's Sweet, undertakes a December UK tour alongside Mud.)

THE SWINGING BLUE JEANS

Ray Ennis (lead guitar, vocals); **Les Braid** (bass); **Ralph Ellis** (rhythm guitar, vocals); **Norman Kuhlke** (drums)

1958

May The group forms from the nucleus of two Liverpool, Lancs. skiffle groups, who come first and second in a talent contest at Liverpool's Empire Theatre. The four who decide to re-group to play rock'n'roll rather than skiffle are Ennis (b. May 26, 1942, Liverpool), Ellis (b. Mar. 8, 1942, Liverpool), Braid (b. William Leslie Braid, Sept. 15, 1941, Liverpool) and Kuhlke (b. June 17, 1942, Liverpool); they name themselves the Bluegenes.

1961

Mar [21] Holding a regular Tuesday night residency at Liverpool's Cavern club, the Bluegenes host the first appearance of a new group at the club, the Beatles. (They will go on to hold residencies at Liverpool's Mardi Gras and Downbeat clubs the following year, becoming synonymous with these venues, much as the Beatles do with the Cavern.)

1963

July [13] Having changed their name to the more commercial-sounding Swinging Blue Jeans, and one among many from Liverpool to gain a recording contract in the wake of the Beatles' early success, signing to EMI's HMV label, their debut single, *It's Too Late Now*, reaches UK #30.
Sept *Do You Know* is the non-charting follow-up.
[29] The group begins a 13-week series, "Swingtime", sponsored by jeans manufacturers Lybro, on Radio Luxembourg.
Dec [7] The Beatles, appearing on BBC-TV show "Juke Box Jury", vote the group's new single a hit. A raucous revival of Chan Romero's *Hippy Hippy Shake*, it is a long-time stage favorite with the group. The band also appears in an episode of BBC-TV's police drama series, "Z Cars", as a Merseyside beat group, singing *Hippy Hippy Shake*.

1964

Jan [6] The group embarks on a 12-date twice-nightly "Group Scene 1964" UK package tour, with the Rolling Stones, the Ronettes, Dave Berry & the Cruisers and Marty Wilde & the Wildcats, at the Granada Cinema, Harrow, Middx., set to end at Bristol's Colston Hall, Somerset.
[17] The band appears on UK TV's "Ready Steady Go".
[25] *Hippy Hippy Shake* hits UK #2, behind the Dave Clark Five's *Glad All Over*.
Feb [29] They begin a further 20-date twice-nightly UK package tour with Gene Pitney, Billy J. Kramer & the Dakotas and Cilla Black, at the Odeon Cinema, Nottingham, Notts.
Apr [4] *Hippy Hippy Shake* is their US debut, reaching #24.
[18] Their similarly-styled revival of Little Richard's *Good Golly Miss Molly* reaches UK #11.
[26] The group appears at the annual "**New Musical Express** Poll Winners Concert", with the Beatles, the Dave Clark Five and others, at the Empire Pool, Wembley, Middx.
May [9] The band starts a 21-date, twice-nightly UK trek supporting Chuck Berry, with Carl Perkins, the Animals, the Nashville Teens and others, at the Finsbury Park Astoria, London, set to close on the 29th at Southend's Odeon Cinema, Essex.
June [13] *Good Golly Miss Molly* makes US #43, while ***Hippy Hippy Shake*** reaches US #90.
July [4] A more subdued cover of Betty Everett's *You're No Good* hits UK #3.
Aug *Promise You'll Tell Her*, a self-penned but undistinctive number, fails to chart.
[8] *You're No Good* peaks at US #97.
Oct The group's first UK album, ***Blue Jeans A-Swingin'***, is released (the earlier US album having been a compilation of single/EP tracks) but sells poorly.
Dec *It Isn't There* is released.

1965

While continuing to work and tour regularly, the group's music on record loses the pulse of the UK music scene, as it moves on from Merseybeat into a tougher R&B stance. Two singles, *Make Me Know You're Mine* and *Crazy 'Bout My Baby* (with a version of *Good Lovin'*, a million seller for the Young Rascals in 1966, on the B-side), are released, without chart success.

1966

Feb [17] Ellis leaves the group and is replaced by

Terry Sylvester (b. Jan. 8, 1945, Liverpool) from the Escorts, who makes his debut with the band in Bolton, Lancs. Only weeks later, Braid also departs, and another ex-Escort, Mike Gregory, replaces him.
[26] Their revival of Dionne Warwick's *Don't Make Me Over* provides the group's first success for 18 months, reaching UK #31, but the Swinging Blue Jeans will not chart again.

1968

June Following a cover of Herman's Hermits' US hit, *Don't Go Out Into The Rain*, the previous August, and in an effort to re-define the group's image, the follow-up, *What Have They Done To Hazel?*, is credited to Ray Ennis & the Blue Jeans, and released on Columbia (EMI having closed HMV as a pop label). When this fails too, Sylvester leaves (to join the Hollies six months later) and the group splits.

1973

Ennis re-forms the group with a new line-up, to capitalize on the nostalgic success of events like Herman's Hermits/Gerry & the Pacemakers/Searchers "British Re-Invasion" tour of the US. The group finds solid club and cabaret bookings, as well as playing on oldies tours in the UK and Europe (proving particularly popular in Scandinavia). ***Brand New And Faded***, plus a re-make of *Hippy Hippy Shake*, released on the independent Dart label, fail to make much impression. (With a name still striking a chord with adult audiences who were teenagers in 1964, the Swinging Blue Jeans will continue to work as a successful club nostalgia act into the '90s, often as part of package tours such as "The Solid Silver '60s Show" and "The Biggest '60s Party in Town" (both in 1991). In May 1993, EMI will release the career anthology, ***Hippy Hippy Shake : The Definitive Collection***, on CD.

TAKE THAT

Gary Barlow (vocals); **Robbie Williams** (vocals); **Jason Orange** (vocals); **Howard Donald** (vocals); **Mark Owen** (vocals)

1991

July Hand-picked by their manager Nigel Martin-Smith who has determined to assemble a teen-based dance/pop quintet in the mold of New Kids On The Block, he has selected five Manchester, Gtr. Manchester-based singers: Barlow (b. Jan. 20, 1971, Frodsham, Cheshire) whose music career began as a teenager playing the organ on Ken Dodd's UK TV shows and who has seen an early composition, *Let's Pray For Christmas* short-listed in a festive song competition held by BBC1-TV's "Pebble Mill At One", former bank clerk and soccer enthusiast, Owen (b. Mark Anthony Owen, Jan. 27, 1974), Williams (b. Feb. 13, 1974, Stoke-on-Trent, Staffs.) who has played a bit-part in C4-TV's "Brookside" soap series, sold double-glazing in Stoke-on-Trent, and who has also been in the group Cutest Rush with Barlow and Donald (b. Howard Paul Donald, Apr. 27, 1970, Droylsden, Manchester), who has worked as an auto-mechanic, and Orange (b. Jason Thomas Orange, July 10, 1970, Manchester), formerly a member of a break-dancing act, Street Beat. Chosen not least for their youthful good-looks, the group now releases its debut single, *Do What U Like*, written by Barlow and producer Ray Hedges and issued on its own Dance U.K. label. Attracting attention via its risqué video (featuring a beach-located group 'mooning') and showing promise as the first major domestic teen-appeal act of the '90s, the band is signed to RCA Records.

Nov [23] Also co-penned by Barlow, *Promises* bows at its UK #38 peak.

1992

Feb [15] Solely written by him, *Once You've Tasted Love* makes UK #47.

June [27] Their cover of Tavares' *It Only Takes A Minute* proves to be their chart breakthrough, hitting UK #7.

Aug [29] *I Found Heaven* reaches UK #15.

Sept [5] The group's debut effort ***Take That And Party***, mainly written by lead singer Barlow, debuts at its initial UK #5 peak.

Oct [31] EP *A Million Love Songs* hits UK #7.

Dec [6] Take That nabs seven trophies, including Most Fanciable Male for Mark Owen, at the annual **Smash Hits** Readers Poll Party Awards, from London's Olympia Hall, at which they also perform.

[31] While the recently released "Take That And Party" long-form video has already sold over 100,000 units, the quintet appears on Carlton TV's first ITV franchise show, on a New Year's Eve special, which also stars Paul McCartney.

1993

Jan [9] Their cover of Barry Manilow's 1975 ballad smash, *Could It Be Magic*, hits UK #3.

[16] ***Take That And Party*** now hits UK #2.

Feb [16] Take That wins the Best British Single category, for *Could It Be Magic*, at the 12th annual BRIT Awards, held at London's Alexandra Palace.

[20] *Why Can't I Wake Up With You?* debuts at its UK #2 peak, behind 2 Unlimited's *No Limit*.

Mar [13] Orange discusses his sexual fantasies on ITV's "Speakeasy".

[29] "Take That Away", a band documentary, airs on BBC2-TV.

Apr [9] C4-TV airs "Take That And Party" special.

[27] Having test-marketed the band's material in a junior high school gym in Setauket, NY, and prepared a Take That breakfast-cereal box, the group is launched in the US with the release of *It Only Takes A Minute*, and ***Take That And Party***.

June The group begins recording its sophomore album at the Marcus Studios, under the production of Steve Vervier.

July [17] *Pray* debuts at UK #1, with Take That teen-mania sweeping Europe.

[20] Take That donates the proceeds from its Manchester G-Mex concert to a local children's hospital, by way of the Bryan Robson Scanner Appeal.

Sept [28] Hundreds of screaming fans greet the band, as they arrive at **The Sun**'s Wapping building in London, to pen the following day's "Bizarre" column.

Oct [9] *Relight My Fire*, featuring guest vocalist Lulu, enters the UK chart at #1.

[23] Dominated by Barlow compositions, who is emerging as a top drawer pop-writer, ***Everything Changes*** debuts at UK #1, and will nominated for the third Mercury Music Prize (also going on to top three million sales worldwide).

Dec [18] *Babe* enters UK chart at UK #1, but is toppled by Mr. Blobby during Christmas week.

[19] "The O Zone Take That Special" airs on BBC2-TV.

1994

Feb [14] The group performs a medley of Beatles hits to celebrate the 30th anniversary of the Beatles' conquest of the US, at the 13th annual BRIT Awards, at London's Alexandra Palace. They also snare trophies for Best Single (*Pray*) and Best Video ("Pray").

Apr [1] *Everything Changes* debuts at UK #1, making Take That the first group to have four #1s from a debut album, and the first to enter at #1 four times.

May [25] Barlow is named Songwriter Of The Year and *Pray* is voted Best Contemporary Song at the 39th annual Ivor Novello Awards, staged at London's Grosvenor House Hotel.

July [9] *Love Ain't Here Anymore* debuts at its UK #3 peak.

Oct [8] The group guests on BBC1-TV's "Steve Wright's People Show" premiere.

[15] *Sure*, co-penned by Barlow, Owens and Williams, debuts at UK #1.

Nov [24] Take That wins the Best Group category at the inaugural MTV European Music Awards, staged at the Pariser Platz, Berlin, Germany, against the backdrop of the Brandenburg Gate.

[28] They take part in the 67th "Royal Variety Performance" at London's Dominion Theatre, in the presence of H.R.H. the Prince of Wales.

Dec [1] Take That performs at Wembley Arena, in aid of H.R.H. Princess Diana's Concert of Hope charity.

[4] They win the Best British Group and Best Single (*Sure*) categories, and also perform, at the seventh annual **Smash Hits** Poll Winners' Party.

[25] The group presents the Christmas Day edition of BBC1-TV's "Top Of The Pops".

1995

Feb [27] The group premieres its forthcoming single, *Back For Good*, at the 14th annual BRIT Awards, at London's Alexandra Palace, and on BBC Radio's 1FM, as part of the station's awards broadcast.

Mar [31] Take That launches its new album before 200 media representatives at the Bayerische Theaterkademie in Munich, Germany, during its current German tour.

Apr [8] *Back For Good* debuts at UK #1, having sold more than 300,000 copies in its first week, the highest first week tally in ten years.

May [13] Entirely written by Barlow and variously produced by him with Chris Porter, Jervier, Brothers In Rhythm and others, ***Nobody Else*** enters at UK #1.

June [23] Take That receives the Silver Clef Award at the 20th Nordoff Robbins Music Therapy lunch held at London's Intercontinental Hotel.

July [17] It is announced that Williams is quitting the band, leaving Take That as a four-piece. (Williams has announced his intention to leave at the end of the band's forthcoming tour, but is ousted with immediate effect, resulting in legal action between Williams and Martin-Smith.)

[22] The group guests again on "Steve Wright's People Show".

Aug [5] *Never Forget* debuts at UK #1.

[26] The US version of ***Nobody Else***, with an altered track listing and only featuring the four remaining

members on its cover, reaches UK #26 in its week of entry.

Oct [31] Take That guests on CBS-TV's "Late Show With David Letterman".

Nov [11] Career highlighted, the Barlow-penned ballad *Back For Good* hits US #7, released via a new deal with Arista Records.

[18] ***Nobody Else*** makes US #69.

[23] The group wins the Best Live Act category at the second annual MTV Europe Music Awards, staged at Le Zenith in Paris, France.

1996

Feb [13] The group holds a press conference in Manchester, announcing its intention to split following farewell commitments. The 24-hour Childline helpline and the Samaritans report that they are deluged with calls from distraught fans.

[19] The group performs *How Deep Is Your Love* at the 15th annual BRIT Awards held at London's Earl's Court Exhibition Centre, also taking home the trophy for Best Single (*Back For Good*).

[26] Minutes before the trial is due to start, Williams withdraws his lawsuit brought against BMG (UK) to prevent the release of a forthcoming greatest hits package.

Mar [1] *How Deep Is Your Love*, reviving the Bee Gees' 1977 hit, becomes the group's eighth single to debut at UK #1.

Apr [6] ***Greatest Hits***, as expected, debuts at UK #1. (Barlow's solo debut, *Forever Love*, is scheduled for release in July.)

TALK TALK

Mark Hollis (vocals, guitar, keyboards); **Paul Webb** (bass); **Lee Harris** (drums)

1977

Relocated to London having left in his second year of studying child psychology at Sussex University, and inspired by the current UK punk movement, Hollis (b. 1955, Tottenham, London) begins writing songs while his brother, Ed, manager of Eddie & the Hot Rods, secures Hollis studio time, funded by Island Records, keen to hear a demo tape. The company signs Hollis' band, the Reaction, which will release only one single, *I Can't Resist*, the following year, though it affords Hollis the opportunity to record *Talk Talk* (which appears on the Beggars Banquet punk compilation album, ***Streets***). The Reaction folds in 1979, with Hollis largely supported financially by his wife, Flick.

1981

Apr Ed Hollis brings in two musicians he is currently working with to record new demos with brother Mark: drummer Harris and bassist Webb (b. Jan. 16, 1962), friends since schooldays and veterans of a number of Southend R&B bands. They are joined by keyboardist Simon Brenner. Rehearsals on Hollis compositions go well, and Talk Talk is formed while he signs a publishing deal with Island Music, which provides six months' studio money. Keith Aspden leaves his job at Island Music to manage the group.

Sept The group makes its first live appearance in London.

Oct BBC Radio 1 DJ David "Kid" Jensen attends Talk Talk's debut gig, and invites them to record a radio session.

Nov Impressed by demos produced by Rolling Stones producer, Jimmy Miller, EMI Records sign Talk Talk.

1982

Feb [5] While their debut album is completed, the first single, *Mirror Man*, is released.

May [1] Synth-heavy *Talk Talk* makes UK #52, as the band supports label-mates Duran on a UK tour. Both groups are currently using EMI-nominated Colin Thurston as producer.

Aug Talk Talk begins a US visit opening for Elvis Costello & the Attractions.

Sept [4] The synthesizer-based debut album, ***The Party's Over***, with all songs penned or co-penned by Hollis, peaks at UK #21, as the group embarks on its first headlining UK tour.

[11] As *Today* reaches UK #14.

Nov [6] *Talk Talk* peaks at US #75.

[20] ***The Party's Over*** makes US #132.

Dec [4] Re-issued *Talk Talk* now rises to UK #23.

1983

Apr [2] Their only chart record of the year, *My Foolish Friend*, makes UK #57. In what will become a familiar band practice, Talk Talk retreats for an entire year to prepare a new album. Brenner leaves, but his replacement becomes an invisible fourth member: Tim Friese-Green arrives to co-write with Hollis, play keyboards, and produce the new songs.

1984

Jan [28] The anthemic, synthesizer-driven *It's My Life* peaks at UK #46.

Feb Its parent album ***It's My Life*** peaks at UK #46, but repays its £250,000 studio costs by earning a gold disc in every other major European territory.

Apr [21] *Such A Shame* makes UK #49, as the band begins a European tour, with dates in Belgium, Holland, Italy and Germany.

May [19] Spurred by a Steve Thompson US remix, *It's My Life* rises to US #31, topping the **Billboard** Dance chart in the process, while ***It's My Life***, spends five months on the chart, peaking at US #42.

July [7] *Such A Shame* makes US #49.

Aug [11] *Dum Dum Girl* stops at UK #74.

Oct A remix album, ***It's My Mix***, featuring six cuts from the first two Thompson-mixed albums, emerges from EMI Italy and becomes a UK import favorite. Talk Talk will play at the San Remo, Italy, TV festival in January, after which Hollis and the band retreat again to work with Friese-Green on the next project.

1986

Feb [8] Piano-led *Life's What You Make It* is released, and becomes their biggest hit in four years at UK #16.

[15] *Life's What You Make It* makes US #90.

Mar [1] ***The Colour Of Spring*** hits UK #8, their most successful release to date, eventually earning gold status, also peaking at US #58. Written and produced by Hollis and Friese-Green, it features Steve Winwood playing organ on two tracks, and is another substantial European success.

[22] As *Living In Another World* makes UK #48, Talk Talk begins a major world tour.

May [24] Ballad, *Give It Up*, peaks at UK #59.

1987

While a further remix mini-album emerges from EMI Greece, the band retreats to the studio, with Hollis keen to experiment with a more abstract sound and songwriting style. Together with his wife, Flick, and their two children, he also moves from London to rural Suffolk, while Webb and Harris relocate to North London.

1988

Sept Now diverted from EMI's main label to UK Parlophone, the fourth Talk Talk album, ***Spirit Of Eden***, 14 months in the making, is issued, featuring six extended free-form tracks. Confirming its less commercial style, EMI issues a statement that, according to Hollis' wishes, a single will not be extracted.

[24] ***Spirit Of Eden*** bows at its UK #19 peak, as a single, *I Believe In You*, an anti-heroin song, is released, but fails to chart.

Oct Talk Talk announces it will not tour to promote the album due to the complexities of re-producing ***Eden***'s sound, which includes a mini-orchestra and the Chelmsford Cathedral Choir. (Relationships between band and label will deteriorate to the point of legal confrontation the following year, resulting in Talk Talk signing to Polydor Records.)

1990

May Prior to its Polydor debut, EMI has begun remixing and reissuing its Talk Talk catalog: *It's My Life* reaches UK #13 (June [9]) followed by *Life's What You Make It* at UK #23 (Sept [15]).

June [16] EMI-released compilation ***Natural History : The Very Best Of Talk Talk***, hits UK #3, during a five-month chart residence and will eventually sell over one million copies as a strong catalog item. A video collection of the same title is also issued.

1991

Apr [6] A further EMI re-hash, released against the group's wishes, ***History Revisited - The Remixes***, debuts at its UK #35 peak.

Sept [28] ***Laughing Stock***, the group's fifth album, released on Polydor imprint Verve Records, bows at its UK #26 pinnacle, once-again a six-track, improvisational-sounding affair, co-helmed by Hollis and long-term collaborator Friese-Green.

Nov The group serves four writs against EMI, claiming that the band is owed money from unpaid royalties and will win the first round of litigation the following March. The hermit of Mark Hollis will release no new material over the next five years, while early Talk Talk alumni, Webb and Harris will re-emerge with ***Herd Of Instinct*** on the Echo (UK) label in August 1994.

TALKING HEADS

David Byrne (guitar, vocals); **Tina Weymouth** (bass); **Jerry Harrison** (keyboards); **Chris Frantz** (drums)

1974

Sept Having first met in September 1970 as freshmen students at the Rhode Island School of Design, Byrne (b. May 14, 1952, Dumbarton, Strathclyde, Scotland), Weymouth (b. Martina Weymouth, Nov. 22, 1950, Coronado, CA) and her boyfriend, Frantz (b. Charlton Christopher Frantz, May 8, 1951, Fort Campbell, KY), form a trio after Frantz and Weymouth graduate, and move to New York. (Byrne, the son of an electrical engineer, has earlier played in a duo called Bizadi, while at the Maryland Institute College of Art in Baltimore, MD, and Frantz has been in the Beans, who had a residency at New York's Electric Circus in 1970. Since their student days together, the two have also played, between October 1973 and June 1974, in the Artistics, sometimes also known as the Autistics, a Rhode Island quintet playing mainly '60s covers, but also include the Byrne/Franz/Weymouth composition, *Psycho Killer*.)

Oct They begin rehearsing, living together in a Chrystie Street garret on Manhattan's Lower East Side, and obtain day jobs.

1975

May After rejecting names like the Portable Crushers and the Vague Dots, Talking Heads is found in an old issue of **TV Guide**.

June Following an audition for Hilly Kristal, owner of New York's CBGB's club (which stands for "Country, Bluegrass and Blues, and other Music for Urban Gourmets"), the group is given its first gig, supporting the Ramones.

Oct Sire Records boss, Seymour Stein, sees the band and offers a recording deal, which is initially rejected.

Dec Their first TV appearance is in "Rock From CBGB's", on a Manhattan cable network.

1976

Apr Harrison (b. Jeremiah Harrison, Feb. 21, 1949, Milwaukee, WI) sees the band playing in Boston, MA, and expresses his wish to join. (He has been a member of Jonathan Richman and the Modern Lovers from 1970 to 1974, later studying at Harvard, and working in the computer industry in Boston.)

July The group headlines CBGB's bicentennial celebrations concert.
Sept Harrison plays with Talking Heads for the first time, at the Ocean Club in Lower Manhattan, though he does not join immediately, having enrolled in an architecture course at Harvard.
Nov After considering recording offers from Arista, CBS, RCA and Beserkley Records, the trio signs with Stein at Sire.
Dec Their debut single, *Love Goes To Building On Fire*, produced by Tony Bongiovi, is released.

1977

Jan The group plays a mini-tour of the northeastern US, with additional dates in Toronto, ON, Canada, with Harrison joining for dates in Boston and Providence.
Feb Harrison, having completed his Harvard degree, becomes a full-time member, as work on the debut album begins with Bongiovi.
Apr [24] The band begins its first European tour, opening for the Ramones, in Switzerland, France, Holland and the UK.
May [14] Talking Heads play a headlining date at London's Rock Garden, where they are seen by Brian Eno, who develops what will be a lasting professional relationship with Byrne.
June [6] The group supports the Ramones at London's Roundhouse, returning to the US the next day.
[18] Frantz and Weymouth marry in Maysville, KY.
[23] The group supports Bryan Ferry at New York's Bottom Line club.
July Its debut album is completed, despite disagreements between the group and producer, Bongiovi.
Oct While the band is on a 38-day promotional tour of East Coast and Mid-Western clubs and colleges, ***Talking Heads ' 77*** enters the US chart (for a six-month stay), peaking at #97 on Mar [4], 1978.
Dec [2-18] The band plays its first West Coast tour, taking in San Francisco, CA, and Los Angeles, CA.

1978

Jan [9] Talking Heads return to Europe for a 27-day trek of France, Holland, Belgium, West Germany and the UK, this time as headliners. Support acts include XTC in Europe, and Dire Straits in the UK.
[31] The band makes its British TV debut, on BBC2-TV's "The Old Grey Whistle Test".
Feb [25] ***Talking Heads ' 77*** spends a week at UK #60. (The group records in the Bahamas, with Eno producing.)
Mar [11] Edgy, new-wave tinged *Psycho Killer*, originally performed by Byrne and Frantz in the Artistics, is the group's first singles chart entry, at US #92.
May They begin a US tour, before playing in Europe (including one UK show at the Lyceum Ballroom in London).
July [29] ***More Songs About Buildings And Food***, produced by Eno, and once again showcasing the group's quirky new-wave rock edge and Byrne's unique vocal style, reaches UK #21, while the group is on tour in Britain.
Nov ***More Songs About Buildings And Food*** makes US #29.

1979

Feb [10] Their revival of Al Green's *Take Me To The River* reaches US #26.
June After completing a new album, the band embarks on its first Pacific tour, taking in New Zealand, Australia, Japan and Hawaii.
Aug [10] The group plays at the "Dr. Pepper Festival" in New York's Central Park, during current US dates to promote the new album.
Sept [15] The self-penned ***Fear Of Music***, again produced by Eno, reaches UK #33. The group appears at the Edinburgh Festival in Scotland, alongside Van Morrison and the Chieftains. (Touring continues through Europe, with eight more UK dates, until the end of the year.)
Nov [3] ***Fear Of Music*** reaches US #21.
[24] *Life During Wartime (This Ain't No Party ... This Ain't No Disco ... This Ain't No Foolin' Around)* peaks at US #80.
[29] The group plays at the Odeon Cinema, Edinburgh, during its current UK visit.
Dec [23] They are featured on ITV's "South Bank Show".

1980

Jan The group returns home after an exhausting tour, and all four take a rest from Talking Heads projects. Byrne records ***My Life In The Bush Of Ghosts*** with Eno.
July After completing a new album, the band considers touring again, but feels extra musicians are needed to do justice to the new material. Harrison recruits several players with whom he has been working on other projects in New York and Philadelphia.
Aug [23] Talking Heads makes its live debut with the expanded line-up at the "Heatwave Festival" in Mosport Park, Toronto, Canada, along with Elvis Costello, Rockpile, the Pretenders and others. The augmenting musicians are Busta "Cherry" Jones (bass), Donette MacDonald (back-up vocals), Bernie Worrell (keyboards), Steven Scales (percussion) and Adrian Belew (guitar).
[27] The nine-piece band plays again, at Wollman Rink in New York's Central Park. (This and the Canadian gig were designed to be the only showcase for the larger band, but Sire Records agrees to support a tour.)
Dec [1-2] The group plays two UK shows at London's Hammersmith Palais and Odeon, during a European tour, with hot new Irish band U2 as the support act.

1981

Mar [7] *Once In A Lifetime*, spurred by a wildly flailing Byrne in its accompanying video clip, reaches UK #14, while Byrne and Eno's ***My Life In The Bush Of Ghosts*** reaches UK #29 and US #44.
[21] The critically-praised ***Remain In Light***, with lyrics by Byrne and music composed by the group with Eno, and recorded in the Bahamas where the larger line-up has been playing live, reaches US #19 and UK #33.
May [16] *Houses In Motion* makes UK #50. At the end of another major tour, the band members disperse to work on individual projects.
July [18] Frantz and Weymouth's spin-off funk group, the Tom Tom Club (including Weymouth's two sisters sharing vocals, plus Steve Scales on percussion, Alex Weir on guitar and Tyron Downie on keyboards), hits UK #7 with the dance/rock fused *Wordy Rappinghood.*
Sept [22] "The Catherine Wheel", a ballet choreographed by Twyla Tharp, featuring Byrne's music, premieres at the Broadhurst Theater on Broadway, New York (and will be shown in March 1983 on PBS-TV).
Oct [17] Tom Tom Club's *Genius Of Love* peaks at UK #65, while ***The Tom Tom Club*** makes US #23 and UK #78.
Nov Harrison's first solo album, ***The Red And The Black*** is released by Sire.
Dec A concert at the Pantages Theater in Hollywood, CA, is recorded for future release as ***Stop Making Sense***.

1982

Jan *Genius Of Love* by the Tom Tom Club tops the US Disco chart, as Byrne's album of music from "The Catherine Wheel" makes US #104.
Feb The B-52's ***Mesopotamia***, produced by Byrne, is released.
Apr [10] Double album, ***The Name Of This Band Is Talking Heads***, a compilation of live performances and out-takes, reaches UK #22, as the group tours the US and Europe as an eight-piece.
[24] Tom Tom Club's *Genius Of Love* crosses over to make US #31.
May [22] ***The Name Of This Band Is Talking Heads*** reaches US #31.
[26] ***Tom Tom Club*** is certified gold by the RIAA.
July [13] The band plays at the Wembley Arena, Wembley, Middx., with the Tom Tom Club as support act.
Sept [3-5] Talking Heads perform at the three-day "US Festival", financed by Apple Computers founder, Steven Wozniak, in San Bernardino, CA, to 400,000 people, along with Jackson Browne, the Cars, Fleetwood Mac, the Grateful Dead, Eddie Money, Police and Santana, among others.
[11] Tom Tom Club's *Under The Boardwalk* cover reaches UK #22.
Nov [4] While the group is in Nassau, the Bahamas, recording at Compass Point studios, Weymouth gives birth to a son, Robert.

1983

Feb UK trio the Fun Boy Three's ***Waiting***, produced by Byrne, is released.
July Talking Heads' first album in over two years, the self-produced, critically-revered ***Speaking In Tongues*** makes US #15 and UK #21.
Aug The Jonathan Demme-directed movie, "Stop Making Sense", a filmed account of Talking Heads on tour, premieres. It includes Byrne (typically fitted out in an over-sized suit) performing a version of *Psycho Killer*, backed only by a cassette recorder playing its rhythm track.
Sept Tom Tom Club album, ***Close To The Bone***, makes US #73.
Oct [22] Talking Heads' *Burning Down The House* hits US #9, their biggest hit single to date.
Nov [16] ***More Songs About Buildings And Food*** is certified gold by the RIAA.
Dec [17] *This Must Be The Place (Naive Melody)* peaks at US #62.

1984

Jan [28] *This Must Be The Place (Naive Melody)* makes UK #51.
Apr [4] Byrne begins recording a solo album at the One On One Studios in Hollywood, CA.
Oct ***Stop Making Sense***, recorded alongside the filming of a concert at Hollywood's Pantages Theater in December, reaches US #41 and UK #37, where it stays on chart for 81 weeks.
Nov [10] Their cover of the Staple Singers' *Slippery People* peaks at UK #68.

1985

Jan Byrne stages a solo show, illustrating (with slides) a journey across the US, titled "The Tourist Way Of Knowledge", at the New York Public Theater.
June [29] Self-produced ***Little Creatures***, mostly written by Byrne, hits UK #10. Harrison produces Milwaukee's Violent Femmes' ***The Naked Leading The Blind***, while Frantz and Weymouth work on a third Tom Tom Club album.
July [27] ***Little Creatures*** reaches US #20.
Sept Byrne releases the solo set, ***Music For The Knee Plays***, a series of musical vignettes linking longer scenes from Robert Wilson's epic opera, "The Civil Wars".
[13] Byrne shares the prestigious Video Vanguard Award (with Godley & Creme and Russell Mulcahy), at the second annual MTV Video Music Awards, held at Radio City Music Hall, New York.
[17] The RIAA certifies gold sales of ***Fear Of Music*** and ***Remain In Light***.
Nov [2] *And She Was* makes US #54, during a 20-week chart stay.
[30] *Road To Nowhere*, aided by a typically innovative video, brings Talking Heads its only UK Top 10 success, hitting #6.

1986

Mar [17] *And She Was*, its video clip directed by Jim Blashfield, reaches UK #17.
May [3] Some five years after giving the group its first UK chart success, *Once In A Lifetime* peaks at US #91, following its exposure in the film, "Down And Out In Beverly Hills" (although this single is the live version from ***Stop Making Sense***).
July "True Stories", a movie written and conceived by

and starring Byrne, premieres. The ***Sounds From True Stories*** soundtrack from the film performed by Byrne, and a separate album of songs under the title ***True Stories***, performed by Talking Heads, are simultaneously released.
Sept [11] "Wild Wild Life" wins the Best Group Video and Best Video From A Film categories, at the fourth annual MTV Video Music Awards, held at the Universal Amphitheatre, Universal City, CA.
[13] *Wild Wild Life* makes UK #43.
Oct Talking Heads' ***True Stories*** reaches US #17 and hits UK #7.
Nov Byrne, who has recently completed work on the soundtrack to "The Last Emperor" with Ryuichi Sakamoto and Cong Su, premiere's "The Knee Plays", his collaborative work with Robert Wilson, in New York.
[18] ***True Stories*** is certified gold by the RIAA.
Dec [6] The extracted *Wild Wild Life* reaches US #25.
[15] ***Speaking In Tongues*** is certified platinum by the RIAA.

1987

May [16] *Radio Head* bows at its UK #16 peak.

1988

Apr ***Naked***, recorded in Paris with producer Steve Lillywhite (and assistance from guitarist Yves N'Djock and keyboardist Wally Badarou), and then completed in New York, reaches US #19 having already hit UK #3 (Mar [26]), after which the band disperses to work on individual projects.
[11] Byrne wins the Oscar for Best Score for "The Last Emperor", with Ryiuchi Sakamoto and Cong Su.
May Harrison's ***The Casual Gods*** (also the name of his 13-member backing group) makes US #78.
[17] ***Naked*** is certified gold by the RIAA.
Aug [20] *Blind* peaks at UK #59, while Byrne appears live with David Bowie in London.
Sept Tom Tom Club plays a three-week stint at New York's CBGB's, during which Lou Reed and Debbie Harry make special guest appearances. Harrison's *Rev It Up*, taken from ***The Casual Gods***, brakes at UK #90.
Oct Tom Tom Club's third album, ***Boom Boom Chi Boom Boom***, produced by Frantz and Weymouth, is released (following the duo's production work earlier in the year with Bob Marley's son, Ziggy, which resulted in the latter's hit album, ***Conscious Party***, and single, *Tomorrow's People*). The group (with guitarist Mark Roule and keyboard player Gary Posner) undertakes a UK club tour.

1989

Apr Tom Tom Club's ***Boom Boom Chi Boom Boom*** makes US #114.
June [9] Byrne and wife Adele Lutz become parents to a daughter, Malu Valentine.
July [5] PBS-TV airs Byrne's Brazilian music-influenced program, "Ilé Aiyé (The House Of Life)", as part of its "Alive From Off Center" summer season.
[18] Talking Heads makes its first appearance since the 1984 "Stop Making Sense" tour when Byrne and Harrison join Weymouth and Frantz during a Tom Tom Club gig at the Ritz, New York.
Oct [2] Byrne embarks on a solo world tour in Japan with 14 backing musicians, while his album, the Latin-flavored ***Rei Mo Mo***, co-produced with Lillywhite and featuring Latin percussionist Milton Cardona, peaks at US #71 and UK #52 (on the 21st). The album also launches his own Luaka Bop label, distributed through Warner Bros., established to release world music around the globe, notably previously banned records from Cuba.
Nov [1-2] Byrne performs in New York during the US leg of his tour.

1990

June [23] Harrison's Casual Gods' ***Walk On Water*** peaks at US #188.
Aug Frantz, Harrison and Weymouth, waiting for Byrne's next Talking Heads move, participate in a low-key coast-to-coast US tour as part of a CBGB's new wave, but now veteran, retrospective package, also including other acts which played at the seminal venue, including the Ramones and Deborah Harry.
Sept [25] Byrne opens a full lecture series, "Speaking Of Music & Other Things", at the New School For Social Research, in New York.
Oct Byrne contributes *Don't Fence Me In*, written for a never-produced 1934 movie, "Adios, Argentina", and featured in a 1944 Roy Rogers picture, "Hollywood Canteen", to the newly released ***Red Hot + Blue***, an anthology of Cole Porter songs released to benefit AIDS education.
Nov Byrne and Harrison, who will become an increasingly in-demand producer in the '90s, contribute to Bernie Worrell's ***Funk Of Ages*** album.

1991

Mar Byrne and folk veteran, Richard Thompson, perform an acoustic set together for C4-TV's "Rock Steady", at the Town Crier Pub, Pawling in New York.
Apr Byrne releases his third various artists collection of Brazilian music, ***Brasil Classics 3***, this time concentrating on "forro".
June [8-9] Byrne performs in the St. Ann's Church series of concerts, at the Town Hall, Manhattan. (During the month, his second collaboration with Robert Wilson, the instrumental album ***The Forest***, is released by Luaka Bop.)
Sept [10] The soundtrack album to Wim Wenders' new film, "Until The End Of the World", featuring Byrne's *Sax And Violins*, is released.
Oct The group assembles at the Electric Lady studios to record new tracks and remix/re-master old ones, for a forthcoming Talking Heads anthology.
[12] Byrne participates in the "Ban The Dam Jam" benefit at New York's Beacon Theatre.
Dec Much to the disappointment of his former colleagues, Byrne announces the formal dissolution of Talking Heads, in a **Los Angeles Times** report.

1992

Mar [14] Byrne's ***Uh-Oh*** debuts at its UK #26 peak and features backing band guests George Porter, Oscar Salas and Hector Rosado.
[28] ***Uh-Oh*** does so-so at US #125. (During the month, Weymouth and Frantz have to abandon production chores for UK band Happy Mondays in the West Indies, not least due to the behavior of the group's drug-laced frontman Shaun Ryder. Weymouth will later say of the sessions: "They just didn't know how much trouble they were getting into. In the end, we were lucky nobody died.")
Aug [14] Tom Tom Club, promoting its new ***Dark Sneak Love Action*** album, and now comprising Frantz, Weymouth, Roule, and Bruce Martin, guests on NBC-TV's "Late Night With David Letterman".
Sept [4] Byrne plays to a sellout crowd of 2,421 at the Orpheum Theatre, Minneapolis, MN, during his current US tour.
[15] He guests on NBC-TV's "The Tonight Show".
Oct [17] The group single, *Lifetime Piling Up*, makes UK #50.
[22] Ex-Talking Heads band members colectively file suit in a New York federal court charging that EMI Records owes them a $750,000 advance for the current greatest hits compilation.
[24] ***Once In A Lifetime/Sand In The Vaseline***, a double retrospective anthology, debuts at its UK #7 peak.
[31] Re-titled in the US, ***Popular Favorites 1976-1992 : Sand In The Vaseline*** debuts at its US #158 peak, during a two week chart stay.
Nov [29] David Byrne & the Pro Arte Orchestra perform at the Amnesty International concert for Human Rights, at London's Royal Albert Hall, with Alison Moyet and the Balanescu Quartet.

1993

Feb [19] Byrne performs at New York's The Bottom Line with Luka Bloom, Lou Reed and Rosanne Cash.
Sept [20] He participates in WFNX's "10th Birthday Bash" in Boston.

1994

June [11] Returning to a rock base, ***David Byrne***, featuring Mauro Refosco on percussion, Todd Turkisher on drums and Paul Socolow on bass, debuts at its US #139 peak having done the same at UK #44 the previous week.
Aug [4] Talking Heads' ***Stop Making Sense*** is certified for two million sales by the RIAA which will confirm the same double platinum status for ***Little Creatures*** on the 17th.

1995

Sept [15] Luaka Bop releases the film soundtrack album ***Blue In The Face***, including new music from its co-executive producer Byrne, including his unlikely duet with the late Latin star, Selena and Indian artist Vijaya Anand.
Sept [23] Mariah Carey's *Fantasy*, heavily sampling Tom Tom Club's *Genius Of Love*, debuts at its UK #4 peak, set to hit US #1.
Nov Byrne's photo book, **Strange Ritual** is published in the US by Chronicle.

1996

Jan [17] Byrne inducts David Bowie into the Rock and Roll Hall of Fame at the 11th annual dinner held at New York's Waldorf Astoria Hotel.

JAMES TAYLOR

1963

Taylor (b. Mar. 12, 1948, Boston, MA), the second of five children in a musically-talented family, having spent his childhood between Chapel Hill, NC (where his father is dean of the University's medical school), and Milton Academy, Milton, MA, meets Danny Kortchmar in Chilmark, Martha's Vineyard, MA, where they win the local hootenanny contest. The following year, Taylor joins older brother Alex's rock band, the Fabulous Corsairs, but shortly after commits himself to the McLean psychiatric hospital in Belmont, MA, suffering from severe depression. During his ten-month stay there, he begins writing songs. Moving to New York in July 1966, he joins Kortchmar's new band the Flying Machine, which plays on the Greenwich Village club circuit, and signs a record deal with Chip Taylor and Al Gorgoni's fledgling Rainy Day label (named after one of Taylor's songs), releasing the Taylor-penned *Brighten Your Night With My Day* and *Night Owl*, before splitting the following spring.

1968

Nov In an attempt to overcome heroin addiction, Taylor has relocated to London's Notting Hill, and, at Kortchmar's suggestion, takes a demo tape to Apple Records A&R executive, Peter Asher (ex-Peter & Gordon), who signs Taylor to the label.
Dec [6] His debut album, ***James Taylor***, produced by Asher, is released in the UK. Unable to kick his drug habit, Taylor returns to the US, and enters the Austin Riggs Hospital in Stockbridge, MA.

1969

July Taylor makes his live solo debut at Los Angeles, CA's Troubadour, but his career is halted when he breaks both hands in a motorbike accident.
Dec He signs to Warner Bros. Records. and moves to California, to work with Asher on a new album. (Asher becomes his manager and will produce most of his future output.)

1970

Mar ***Sweet Baby James***, with musical contributions from Carole King, Randy Meisner, Red Rhodes and Chris Darrow, enters the US chart, set to hit #3 during a two-year run. Showcasing Taylor's soothing, radio-friendly composition and vocal skills, it establishes the artist as a pre-eminent singer/songwriter act, who

will rarely deviate from this popular style.
Oct [31] *Fire And Rain*, written in three segments, the first in London, the second in a Manhattan hospital room and the third at Austin Riggs, all during 1968, hits US #3, as ***Sweet Baby James*** is certified gold in the US, where his debut album, ***James Taylor***, now reaches #62.
Nov [28] *Fire And Rain* reaches UK #42.
Dec [26] *Carolina In My Mind*, featuring Paul McCartney on bass, peaks at US #67.

1971

Jan [3] Taylor begins recording a new album at Hollywood, CA's Crystal Recording Studios, with Asher once again producing.
[23] ***Sweet Baby James*** hits UK #7, during a 53-week chart stay.
Feb Euphoria Records releases ***James Taylor And The Original Flying Machine - 1967***, which makes US #74.
Mar Taylor stars in Monte Hellman's film, "Two Lane Blacktop", with Dennis Hopper, Warren Oates and the Beach Boys' Dennis Wilson.
[1] Taylor is featured on the cover of **Time** magazine.
[20] *Country Road* makes US #37, as he begins a sellout 27-city US tour.
Apr [6] After a performance by Carly Simon at the Troubadour in Los Angeles, James Taylor goes back-stage to meet her.
May [29] ***Mud Slide Slim And The Blue Horizon*** enters the US and UK charts, set to hit #2 and #4 respectively.
July [31] Carole King-penned *You've Got A Friend*, with Joni Mitchell on backing vocals, tops the US chart for a week.
Sept [13] *You've Got A Friend* is certified gold by the RIAA.
Oct [16] *You've Got A Friend* hits UK #4.
Nov [6] *Long Ago And Far Away*, again featuring Mitchell, makes US #31.

1972

Mar [9] Taylor plays a benefit concert, with many others, raising $300,000 for presidential candidate George McGovern, at the Great Western Forum, Inglewood, CA.
[12] He wins the Best Pop Vocal Performance, Male category for *You've Got A Friend* at the 14th annual Grammy Awards. The song also wins its writer, Carole King, the Song Of The Year trophy.
Nov [3] Taylor marries Carly Simon in her Manhattan apartment. He plays at New York's Radio City Music Hall that evening, and announces the happy event to his audience.
Dec ***One Man Dog***, with contributions from King, Linda Ronstadt, Simon and Taylor's brothers, Alex and Hugh, and sister Kate, hits US #4 and makes UK #27.
[18] ***One Man Dog*** is certified gold by the RIAA.

1973

Jan [13] Ballad, *Don't Let Me Be Lonely Tonight*, featuring Michael Brecker's tenor sax, much of the song recorded in Taylor's house, reaches US #14.
Mar [10] *One Man Parade* peaks at US #67.

1974

Mar [23] Taylor's duet with his wife on Inez & Charlie Foxx's hit, *Mockingbird*, hits US #5.
[30] *Mockingbird* reaches UK #34.
Apr [30] He begins a month-long US tour in Moorehead, MN, set to end at the Nassau Veterans Memorial Coliseum, Uniondale, NY.
May [14] *Mockingbird* is confirmed gold by the RIAA.
June ***Walking Man***, produced by David Spinozza, makes US #13.
July [13] He begins a three-week tour, accompanied by his band, the Manhattan Dirt Riders, and special guest, Ronstadt.
Dec [24] Taylor and Simon join Ronstadt and Joni Mitchell, singing Christmas carols on the streets of Hollywood.

1975

Apr [30] He starts a month-long US tour in Indianapolis, IN, which will end with three nights at New York's Carnegie Hall.
May ***Gorilla***, produced by Russ Titelman and Lenny Waronker, hits US #6.
[30] Taken from it, a cover of Marvin Gaye's 1965 smash, *How Sweet It Is (To Be Loved By You)*, with David Sanborn on saxophone, hits US #5.
July [2] Taylor begins a further month-long US tour to promote ***Gorilla***.
Sept [12] ***Gorilla*** is certified gold by the RIAA.
Nov [8] He makes two short US tours while *Mexico*, with vocal assistance from David Crosby and Graham Nash, makes US #49.

1976

Aug [21] ***In The Pocket***, again produced by Titelman and Waronker, and including the song, *Don't Be Sad 'Cause Your Skin Is Down*, co-written with Stevie Wonder, peaks at US #16.
Sept [18] *Shower The People* reaches US #22.
Oct [19] ***In The Pocket*** is certified gold by the RIAA.
Dec Aware that Taylor is to leave the company, Warner Bros. releases ***Greatest Hits***.

1977

Jan [15] It reaches US #23 (and will become a popular catalog item) as the artist signs to CBS/Columbia Records.
Mar [15] Taylor begins recording a new album at Los Angeles' The Sound Factory, reunited once more with Asher as his producer.
July [26] He ends a 22-date tour of the US at the Pine Knob Music Theatre, Clarkston, MI.
Aug [27] Taylor's first CBS/Columbia set, ***JT***, from which it is extracted, hits US #4.
Sept [10] His cover of Jimmy Jones' 1960 smash, *Handy Man*, hits US #4.
Oct [8] Taylor produces, plays guitar and sings on sister Kate's CBS/Columbia debut, a cover of Betty Everett's 1964 US #6, *It's In His Kiss (The Shoop Shoop Song)*, which makes US #49.
Nov Taylor begins a brief tour of California and Hawaii, including four nights at the Pantages Theater, Hollywood, CA.
Dec [17] *Your Smiling Face* reaches US #20. Country singer George Jones releases a cover of *Bartender's Blues* by Taylor, who has also contributed backing vocals.

1978

Feb [23] Taylor wins his second Best Pop Vocal Performance, Male trophy for *Handy Man*, at the 20th annual Grammy Awards, as Asher is named Best Producer Of The Year.
Mar [18] Taylor has joined Paul Simon to sing on Art Garfunkel's *What A Wonderful World*, which reaches US #17.
[25] *Honey Don't Leave LA*, the third single from ***JT***, and once again featuring the sax work of Sanborn, peaks at US #61.
Apr Taylor and over 40 performers petition President Jimmy Carter to end the US commitment to nuclear power.
May ***Kate Taylor***, produced by brother James, on which he plays and sings, is released.
July CBS/Columbia issues the original Broadway cast album, ***Working***, a musical based on the life of Studs Terkel, which contains three Taylor songs: *Millworker*, *Brother Trucker* (his own versions will appear on ***Flag***) and *Un Mejor Dia Vendra*.
Sept [30] A second duet with Carly Simon, a version of the Everly Brothers' 1958 hit, *Devoted To You*, makes US #36.

1979

Jan [4] Taylor begins recording his second CBS/Columbia album at The Sound Factory.
June [16] The Asher-helmed ***Flag***, including a cover of Lennon/McCartney's *Daytripper*, enters the US chart, set to hit #10.
July [21] Taken from it, *Up On The Roof*, a cover of the Drifters' Goffin/King-penned 1962 smash, hits US #28.
[3] Taylor begins a 25-date US summer tour, including five nights at Los Angeles' Greek Theatre, in Memphis, TN. The tour will close on August 17th at the Greek Theatre, Berkeley, CA.
Sept [19] Taylor performs in the first of five Musicians United For Safe Energy (MUSE) concerts at New York's Madison Square Garden. The shows are filmed and recorded under the ***No Nukes*** banner, and also feature Jackson Browne, the Doobie Brothers and Bruce Springsteen.
Dec Live triple album, ***No Nukes***, featuring two Taylor cuts and further collaborations with the Doobie Brothers, Carly Simon and John Hall, makes US #19.

1980

July [19] The "No Nukes" film documentary premieres in New York.
Aug [3] Taylor undertakes a 23-date US tour in Memphis, TN, set to close on the 30th at the Merriweather Post Pavilion, Columbia, MD.
Sept [5] He begins recording a new album at Los Angeles' Record One studio.
[24] All-star album, ***In Harmony***, recorded for children's PBS-TV show, "Sesame Street", is released, with the Taylor and Simon families featuring on most of the tracks, *Jelly Man Kelly* being co-written with Taylor's daughter, Sarah. (The album will win a Grammy for Best Children's Recording.)

1981

Feb [11] Taylor begins a five-week US tour at the Holiday Star Theatre, Merrillville, IN.
Apr [25] A further 47-date US trek opens at the Greek Theatre, Berkeley, as ***Dad Loves His Work*** hits US #10. The tour, which will include eight sold-out shows at the Savoy, New York, will end on July 4th at the Belmont Race Track, New York.
May [2] *Her Town Too*, a post-divorce themed bitter-sweet ballad, duetted with J.D. Souther, makes US #11. (Souther will also join the first leg of the tour.)
[5] ***Dad Loves His Work*** is certified gold by the RIAA.
June [20] *Hard Times* peaks at US #72.
Sept [4] Singing *Brother Trucker*, Taylor appears as a truck driver in PBS-TV's "Working", slated for broadcast in early 1982.
[11] Taylor begins a 17-date tour of Japan and Australia in Osaka, Japan, set to end on October 10th in Adelaide, Australia.
Oct [13] On his return to the US, Taylor stops off in Hawaii, where he performs a sellout show at the 12,000-seat NBC Arena in Honolulu.

1982

Feb [1] A 30-date US concert series starts at the Front Row Theatre, Highland Heights, OH.
June [9] Taylor appears with Jackson Browne and Linda Ronstadt in a "Peace Week" benefit concert at the Nassau Veterans Memorial Coliseum. (Three days later he will take part in another benefit, in New York's Central Park, in front of some one million people.)
July [14] Taylor begins a further 37-date US tour in Columbia, MD.

1983

Aug [1] Another 25-date US trek begins at the Blossom Music Center, Universal City, CA.

1984

Apr [4] Taylor begins the first of three separate US tours lasting until September, a 23-date series which will end in Dallas, TX.
Aug [1] He begins his second 29-date tour in Cincinnati, OH, with Randy Newman the opening act.

1985

Jan [12] Taylor makes the first of two appearance at the "Rock In Rio Festival", in Rio de Janeiro, Brazil.

Dec ***That's Why I'm Here***, Taylor's first album in four years, and his first self-produced effort, with help from engineer Frank Filipetti, is released. The album, which features guests Joni Mitchell, Don Henley, Graham Nash, Sanborn, the Brecker Brothers and Deniece Williams, reaches US #34. He also duets with Ricky Skaggs on the Christmas song, *New Star Shining*, for the country singer's newly-released album. (During a busy month, Taylor also marries for the second time, to Kathyrn (née Walker).)
[14] A cover of Buddy Holly's *Everyday* peaks at US #61.

1986

Mar [28] Taylor embarks on a four-date UK tour, his first in 15 years, at London's Hammersmith Odeon.
Oct [13] The RIAA certifies three million sales of ***Sweet Baby James***.

1987

Apr [11] A 16-track UK-only compilation, ***Classic Songs***, released by CBS but including a smattering of Warner Bros. highlights, makes UK #53.

1988

Mar ***Never Die Young***, produced by his long-time keyboard player, Don Grolnick, reaches US #25.
Apr [23] *Never Die Young* climbs to US #80.
June Taylor appears in Britain, before embarking on a major US tour during the summer. He is also featured duetting with brother Livingston's *City Lights*, from the latter's newly released ***Life Is Good*** album.

1989

July [6] The RIAA certifies two million sales of ***J.T.***
Sept [11] He plays at a "House The Homeless" benefit concert at Harvard Stadium, Cambridge, MA.

1990

Feb Taylor sings at the Cathedral of St. John the Divine, New York, with Paul Simon, Roberta Flack and Placido Domingo, at a celebration for Czech President, Vaclav Havel.
Oct [21] Taylor ends a five-month US tour before a sellout crowd of 8,725, at the Concord Pavilion, Concord, CA.

1991

Feb Taylor guests on new Atlantic recording artist Marc Cohn's self-titled debut.
May [18] He plays a benefit with Stephen Stills at Toad's Place, New Haven, CT, to pay the campaign debt of unsuccessful US Senate candidate, Toby Moffett.
June [22] ***For Our Children***, the Pediatric AIDS Foundation benefit album, to which Taylor has contributed *Getting To Know You*, reaches US #31.
Oct [2] Taylor performs his new single, *Copperline*, on NBC-TV's "The Tonight Show".
[12] He makes a guest appearance at the "Ban the Dam Jam" benefit at the Beacon Theatre, New York.
[25-27, 29-31] Taylor breaks the house record at The Paramount, New York, selling out six shows and grossing $842,820, before a total crowd of 32,400.
[26] ***New Moon Shine***, once again produced by Grolnick, reaches US #37.
Nov [12] He appears on NBC-TV's "Late Night With David Letterman".
Dec [14] Taylor is the musical guest on NBC-TV's "Saturday Night Live".

1992

Apr [12] "James Taylor : Going Home" premieres on the Disney cable channel.
[16] Taylor wins the Outstanding Male Vocalist category, and is honored with the Hall Of Fame Award, at the Boston Music Awards, held at the Wang Center, Boston.
May [5] He takes part in the "Among Animals - An Evening Of Poetry And Song" benefit for the Fund For Animals, at the 92nd Street Y, New York.
[28] Taylor performs at London's Hammersmith Odeon, his only UK date, during a short European tour.
July [9] He guests again on "The Tonight Show".
Aug [8-9] Taylor grosses $489,164 from two sellout concerts, at the Mann Music Center, Philadelphia, PA, during his latest US tour.
Oct He cancels several dates on his current tour to undergo minor surgery on his vocal chords.
Nov [1] Taylor takes part in Neil Young's annual "Bridge School Benefit" with Elton John, Sammy Hagar and Pearl Jam, before a sellout crowd of 20,000, at the Shoreline Amphitheatre, Mountain View, CA.

1993

Mar [2] He participates in a concert at New York's Carnegie Hall to benefit the world's rain forests, with Bryan Adams, Herb Alpert, Tom Jones, George Michael, Sting, Tina Turner and Dustin Hoffman.
May [25] Taylor performs at the Symphony Hall, Boston, with the Boston Pops Orchestra.
Aug [28] ***James Taylor Live***, a double stage set, bows at its US #20 peak, as Taylor records a duet with Art Garfunkel, reviving the Everly Brothers' *Crying In The Rain*, for Garfunkel's forthcoming ***Up 'Til Now*** album, and continues to work on the opera, "Faust", with Randy Newman.
Sept [24] Taylor guests on CBS-TV's "Late Show With David Letterman".
Nov [13] He appears as the musical guest on NBC-TV's "Saturday Night Live".
[16] ***James Taylor Live*** is certified platinum by the RIAA.

1994

Feb [24] Taylor serenades NASA astronauts on an episode of Fox-TV's "The Simpsons".
Apr [9] He takes part in the fifth annual "Rainforest Foundation Benefit Concert" at New York's Carnegie Hall, with Elton John, Sting, Aaron Neville, Luciano Pavarotti, Branford Marsalis, Tammy Wynette and Whitney Houston.
July [4] Taylor plays an Independence Day concert at the Gorge in George, WA, during a five-month US tour.
Aug [4] The RIAA certifies seven million sales of ***Greatest Hits***.
[5] The RIAA confirms two million sales of ***Mud Slide Slim And The Blue Horizon***.
Oct [3] ***Never Die Young*** is certified platinum by the RIAA, with ***That's Why I'm Here*** reaching the same certification three days later.
[9] Taylor plays a sellout date at the Civic Center, Pensacola, FL, as his US tour continues.
[28] ***Flag*** is also certified platinum by the RIAA.
Dec [13] One million US sales are also confirmed for ***New Moon Shine***.

1995

Jan Taylor contributes *Dream Lover* to Manhattan Transfer's newly released ***Tonin'*** album.
Apr [12] He performs at the sixth annual "Rainforest Foundation Benefit Concert", staged at Carnegie Hall.
May [5] Taylor takes part in the 26th annual "New Orleans Jazz & Heritage Festival" in New Orleans, LA.
[7] He receives an honorary doctorate of music from the Berklee College of Music in Boston.
Aug [30] Taylor performs with ex-wife Carly Simon for the first time since 1979, at "Livestock '95", a benefit concert for the Martha Vineyard's Agricultural Society, at the society's fairgrounds in West Tisbury, MA. They play their own sets, and perform two songs together.
Sept [30] He performs at the opening of the FleetCenter in Boston, singing 13 songs backed by the Boston Pops Orchestra and duetting with Patti LaBelle on *Shower The People*.
Dec Sony (US) releases an Enhanced-CD version of Taylor's ***Greatest Hits Live***, with interactive elements added.

1996

Apr [12] Prior to a US summer tour, Taylor participates in the seventh annual "Rainforest Foundation Benefit Concert" at New York's Carnegie Hall.
July [29] Taylor performs at Tanglewood, Lenox in his home state, during his five-month US tour.

THE TEARDROP EXPLODES

Julian Cope (vocals, bass); **Michael Finkler** (guitar); **Paul Simpson** (keyboards); **Gary Dwyer** (drums)

1978

Nov [15] Named after a **Marvel** comic caption, the psychedelia-influenced Teardrop Explodes has formed in October from the remnants of several Liverpool, Merseyside, bands. Cope (b. Oct. 21, 1957, Bargoed, M. Glamorgan, Wales), ex-the Crucial Three (with Ian McCulloch (later of Echo & the Bunnymen) and Pete Wylie (later of Wah!)), has moved on to the Mystery Girls and the Nova Mob, before joining Finkler and Simpson in A Shallow Madness. The trio, now augmented by Dwyer, plays its first concert as the Teardrop Explodes at Liverpool's seminal alternative music venue, Eric's.

1979

Feb The group's first disc, the EP *Sleeping Gas*, is issued by Zoo Records.
June Simpson leaves to study, and is replaced by Dave Balfe, ex-Lori & the Chameleons, and co-owner of Zoo. *Bouncing Babies* is released.
Aug The Teardrop Explodes, initially managed by Bill Drummond (who will subsequently create KLF), plays at an all-day, open-air concert in Leigh, Gtr. Manchester, with A Certain Ratio, Echo & the Bunnymen, Joy Division and OMD, before an estimated 300-strong audience.
Sept [8-9] The group takes part in the two-day "Futurama Festival" at the Queens Hall, Leeds, W. Yorks.

1980

Feb *Treason (It's Just A Story)*, written by Cope with McCulloch, and produced by Clive Langer and Alan Winstanley, is the group's third single release.
July Alan Gill, ex-Dalek I Love You, replaces Finkler, who leaves to attend college. Zoo signs a distribution deal with Phonogram Records.
Aug The group signs to Phonogram subsidiary, Mercury Records.
Oct [11] Their debut Mercury release, *When I Dream*, reaches UK #47, taken from ***Kilimanjaro***, largely produced by the Zoo production team (aka the Chameleons). Balfe leaves temporarily and is replaced by Jeff Hammer.

1981

Mar [21] *Reward*, added to a reissued ***Kilimanjaro***, with trumpet from "Hurricane" Smith, hits UK #6.
May [23] The group's third single, *Treason (It's Just A Story)*, is remixed, now climbing to UK #18.
June [20] ***Kilimanjaro*** reaches UK #24, during a 35-week chart stay
Aug *Ha, Ha, I'm Drowning* and *Poppies In The Field* are scheduled for release, but Cope objects, and some 30,000 copies are withdrawn.
Oct [3] *Passionate Friend*, written by Cope about McCulloch's sister, Julie, reaches UK #25. Cope reorganizes the band as all but Dwyer depart. Alfie Agius, ex-Interview, briefly joins on bass, while Troy Tate, ex-Shake, arrives on guitar. Balfe rejoins taking Hammer's place (who will later join the Stray Cats), while front-man and lyricist Cope switches from bass to rhythm guitar.
Nov [28] *Colours Fly Away* lands at UK #54.
Dec Club Zoo opens in Liverpool, with support from the band.
[5] Their sophomore effort, ***Wilder***, helmed by Langer & Winstanley, reaches UK #29.

1982

Jan After Agius leaves, ex-Sincero Ron Francois joins

on bass.
Feb [13] ***Wilder*** makes US #176.
Mar Three Teardrop Explodes tracks are featured on the newly released various artists compilation album, ***To The Shores Of Lake Placid***.
June [26] *Tiny Children* makes UK #44.
July Francois and Tate quit, leaving a trio of Cope, Dwyer and Balfe.
[16-18] Cope and Balfe form the one-off La Place De La Concorde, at the three-day WOMAD festival.
Nov [15] Cope splits the band on its fourth anniversary. Balfe joins the Dumbfounding Two, before forming his own management company and the successful Food label, while Dwyer remains, temporarily, with Cope.

1983

Mar [26] The group's final single, *You Disappear From View*, makes UK #41.
Nov Remaining contracted to Mercury Records, Cope returns as a solo artist on *Sunshine Playroom*, which peaks at UK #64, previewing his debut solo set, ***World Shut Your Mouth***.

1990

Apr [14] ***Everybody Wants To Shag The Teardrop Explodes***, collecting rare old material and out-takes, and released on Fontana, peaks at UK #72, featuring the extracted *Serious Danger* and *Count To Ten And Run For Cover*, while a second retrospective, ***Piano*** (comprising the band's Zoo material), will emerge later in the year with ***Live In Concert***, recorded for BBC Radio 1, emerging in December 1993 on the Windsong label.
see also: **Julian COPE**

TEARS FOR FEARS

Curt Smith (vocals, bass);
Roland Orzabal (guitar, keyboards)

1980

Smith (b. June 24, 1961, Bath, Somerset), named by his parents after German actor Curd Jurgens, and Orzabal (b. Roland Orzabal de la Quintana, Aug. 22, 1961, Portsmouth, Hants), having first met at the age of 13 (Smith mistakenly taking his future partner for a French exchange student), when Smith inducted guitar-playing Orzabal into his school band in Bath, join Graduate together, a five-piece pop/ska band, influenced by the current 2-Tone sound, also including Steve Buck, Andy Marsden and John Baker. Signed to Pye's Precision label in the UK, and produced by Tony Hatch, Graduate has a near-hit with *Elvis Should Play Ska*, and cuts ***Acting My Age***, as well as releasing three further singles (which prove most popular in Spain).

1981

Nov After Graduate has split, Smith and Orzabal have stayed together, calling themselves History Of Headaches, and record demos of two Orzabal songs - *Suffer The Children* and *Pale Shelter*, at David Lord's studios in Bath, experimenting with synth-pop. The duo's subsequent name, Tears For Fears, is derived from a chapter heading in Arthur Janov's book, **Prisoners Of Pain**, concerned with Primal Therapy: confronting fears in order to eliminate them (or shedding "tears for fears"), which Orzabal has read in 1978. Demos of their first two songs have caught the attention of Phonogram Records A&R man, Dave Bates, who has signed them to the Mercury label, initially only for the two releases. Their first single, *Suffer Little Children*, is now issued, while Manny Elias (drums) and Ian Stanley (keyboards) join for live work.

1982

Mar *Pale Shelter* is released.
Nov [6] The synthesizer-led *Mad World*, produced by former Adam & the Ants drummer and one-half of the Merrick & Tibbs duo, Chris Hughes, hits UK #3, as the band plays its first UK tour as support act to the Thompson Twins.
Dec The group is named Most Promising New Act Of 1982 in the **Smash Hits** magazine poll, and signs a management deal with Paul King.

1983

Feb [17] Insistent pop smash, *Change*, hits UK #4.
Mar [26] Their debut set, ***The Hurting***, further inspired by Janov's theories, and entirely written by Orzabal (though largely featuring Smith as lead singer) and produced by Hughes, hits UK #1 in its second week on the survey, and will remain charted for 65 weeks.
May [7] *Pale Shelter* is reissued in a remixed version, included on the album, and hits UK #5. Meanwhile, the band's US chart debut comes with ***The Hurting***, which makes US #73.
Aug [27] *Change* is their first US singles chart entry, also peaking at #73.

1984

Jan [14] *The Way You Are* reaches UK #24.
Sept [8] *Mother's Talk*, using a computer sample of strings from a Barry Manilow record, reaches UK #14.

1985

Jan [26] The anthemic *Shout* hits UK #4.
Mar [9] ***Songs From The Big Chair***, also produced by Hughes, and featuring both keyboardist Stanley and drummer Elias, and supposedly inspired by the TV mini-series, "Sybil", hits UK #2. Containing only eight tracks, it will eventually earn triple-platinum status in Britain.
Apr [20] *Everybody Wants To Rule The World* hits UK #2, behind USA For Africa's *We Are The World*.
May The group ends a major headlining UK tour at London's Royal Albert Hall, before setting off on an 18-month world concert trek.
June [8] *Everybody Wants To Rule The World*, written by Orzabal, Smith and Hughes, tops the US chart for two weeks, aided by a heavy-rotation video on MTV, and earns the group a gold disc. (It will become the band's most popular cut on US radio, subsequently cited for two million broadcast performances by BMI in October 1994.)
July [6] *Head Over Heels* makes UK #12.
[13] ***Songs From The Big Chair*** begins a five-week reign atop the US chart, eventually turning quintuple platinum, with sales over five million.
Aug [3] *Shout* hits US #1, becoming their second consecutive chart-topping single.
Sept [7] The band's first two singles, *Suffer The Children* and *Pale Shelter*, are reissued in the UK, charting at #52 and #73.
Oct [19] *I Believe (A Soulful Re-Recording)*, a new version of a track from the album, written by Orzabal specifically with Robert Wyatt in mind (and including the duo's version of his *Seasong* on its B-side), recorded at Smith's insistence, reaches UK #23.
Nov [9] *Head Over Heels* hits US #3.

1986

Feb [10] *Everybody Wants To Rule The World* wins the Best British Single category at the fifth annual BRIT Awards, at London's Grosvenor House Hotel.
[22] *Everybody Wants To Rule The World* re-charts for a week, at UK #73.
Apr [7] Orzabal is named Songwriter Of The Year, at the 31st annual Ivor Novello Awards, held at the Grosvenor House Hotel.
May [24] *Mother's Talk*, belatedly issued as a US single in a remixed version, makes #27.
June [7] *Everybody Wants To Run The World*, a re-written version of *Rule The World*, with lyrics relating to Sport Aid's "Race Against Time", used as the theme tune for Sport Aid Week and the worldwide fun run, raising funds for African famine relief, hits UK #5.
Nov Smith retreats from an exhausting two years to renovate a new house he has bought with his wife, Lynn, while Orzabal does similarly with his wife, Caroline, in Chalk Farm, London.

1987

Jan Orzabal, now recognized as the main creative force in Tears For Fears, and increasingly at odds with Smith, starts work on new material with keyboardist Nicky Holland.

1988

Jan Smith receives substantial damages from UK newspapers the **Daily Star**, **The Sun** and the **News Of The World** over their stories in October 1986 allegedly revealing antics from his schooldays in St. Albans, Herts. (Smith had never even been to St. Albans. He gives the out-of-court settlement to his mother, to buy the council flat in which she lives.)
Feb Smith and Orzabal begin work yet again in London on the ***Big Chair*** follow-up, with David Bascombe, after lengthy sessions with Langer and Winstanley and then Chris Hughes have proved unsatisfactory. The featured musicians are Seattle, WA-born Oleta Adams (who the duo had discovered in the Hyatt Regency restaurant, the Peppercorn Duck club, in Kansas City, MO, on their last US tour.) They will subsequently write and produce songs for her May 1990 debut album, ***Circle Of One***, Manu Katche (drums), Neil Taylor (guitar), Pino Palladino (bass), Carole Steele (percussion) and Simon Clark (keyboards).
June [11] Smith participates in "Nelson Mandela's 70th Birthday Tribute" concert at Wembley Stadium, Wembley, Middx., taking time off from recording the new album.

1989

May [9] *Shout,* some four years after its release, is certified gold by the RIAA.
July [15] Smith, Orzabal and Bascombe oversee the final mix of the new album at London's Mayfair studios.
Sept [16] The first release from the much-anticipated album, the Beatles-celebrating *Sowing The Seeds Of Love*, hits UK #5.
Oct [7] Its parent album, ***The Seeds Of Love***, costing over £1 million to record, enters the UK chart at #1, where it stays for a week.
[28] *Sowing The Seeds Of Love* hits US #2 and ***The Seeds Of Love*** US #8.
Nov [29] ***The Seeds Of Love*** is certified platinum by the RIAA.
Dec [2] *Woman In Chains*, featuring Phil Collins on drums and Adams on vocals, reaches UK #26.

1990

Feb [3] *Woman In Chains* makes US #36, as they tour the US with Deborah Harry as their support act.
[18] The group plays a sellout show at the Meadowlands Arena, East Rutherford, NJ.
Mar [3] *Advice For The Young At Heart* makes UK #36.
[8] The group wins Best Video and Best Album Cover categories in the annual **Rolling Stone** Readers' Picks 1989 music awards.
[24] *Advice For The Young At Heart* peaks at US #89.
June [22] The group performs at the Jones Beach Theatre, Wantagh, NY, during its current North American tour.
Sept [7] "Sowing The Seeds Of Love" wins the Best Special Effects and Breakthrough Video categories, at the seventh annual MTV Video Music Awards, held at the Universal Amphitheatre, Universal City, CA.

1991

Feb [2] Masquerading as Johnny Panic & the Bible Of Dreams, Orzabal and Bascombe debut at UK #70 with *Johnny Panic & The Bible Of Dreams*, a re-recording of a Tears For Fears B-side (from *Advice For The Young At Heart*).
May UK specialist label, Sequel, issues early Graduate material on CD.
Oct It is announced that Orzabal and Smith are to go their separate ways.
Dec [2] *Head Over Heels* is honored for more than one million performances, and *Sowing The Seeds Of Love* is named one of the Most Performed Pop Songs Of 1990 at the BMI Awards at London's Dorchester Hotel.

1992

Feb [29] *Laid So Low (Tears Roll Down)*, from a forthcoming greatest hits album, and penned solo by Orzabal after the break-up, reaches UK #17.

Mar [14] ***Tears Roll Down (Greatest Hits 82-92)*** debuts at its UK #2 peak, behind Madness' ***Divine Madness***.

[22] PolyGram officially confirms that Smith and Orzabal have split. The latter, always the musical core of the unit, will continue under the Tears For Fears moniker, while Smith, now resident in New York, NY is signed to a solo deal with Mercury.

Apr [11] ***Tears Roll Down (Greatest Hits 82-92)*** makes US #53.

[25] *Woman In Chains*, featuring a now co-credited Adams, re-charts for a week at UK #57.

1993

June [5] *Break It Down Again* reaches UK #20.

[19] Tears For Fears first album without Smith, ***Elemental***, recorded by Orzabal with co-producers Tim Palmer and Alan Griffiths at the former's home studio, including the extracted *Break It Down Again* and *Fish Out Of Water*, a thinly veiled post-script dig at his former partner, bows at its UK #5 pinnacle.

July [10] ***Elemental*** debuts at its US #45 peak.

[31] *Cold* charts for a week at UK #72.

Aug [24] Smith releases his debut solo album, ***Soul On Board***, on Mercury.

Sept [25] Tears For Fears' *Break It Down Again* reaches US #25.

Dec [1] ***The Hurting*** is certified gold by the RIAA.

[6] ***Elemental*** is also confirmed gold by the RIAA.

[14] Tears For Fears perform at Wembley Arena.

1995

May [15] The RIAA certifies platinum sales of ***Tears Roll Down*** and five million sales of the group's career highlight, ***Songs From The Big Chair***.

Oct [7] *Raoul And The Kings Of Spain* debuts at its UK #31 peak.

[9] Newly signed to Epic worldwide after an acrimonious split with Mercury (with whom the band has sold 16.5 million records worldwide) over the artwork for its forthcoming album, ***Raoul And The Kings Of Spain*** is now released. Orzabal also starts his own production company, Bread & Buddah, his first signing being Tears For Fears bassist Gail Ann Dorsey.

[11] The group guests on NBC-TV's "The Tonight Show".

[28] ***Raoul And The Kings Of Spain*** debuts at its UK and US #41 and #79 peaks.

TELEVISION

Tom Verlaine (vocals, lead guitar); **Richard Lloyd** (rhythm guitar); **Richard Hell** (bass); **Billy Ficca** (drums)

1973

Dec Bassist/vocalist Hell (b. Richard Myers, Oct. 2, 1949, Lexington, KY) has formed his first group, the Neon Boys, in New York, NY with ex-boarding-school friend Verlaine (b. Thomas Miller, Dec. 13, 1949, Mt. Morris, NJ), who has dropped out of two colleges in South Carolina and Pennsylvania before relocating to New York in 1969 and who re-named himself after the French poet, and drummer Billy Ficca, in 1971, though neither this outfit, nor the subsequent trio, Goo Goo, has lasted. New Jersey guitarist Lloyd, after seeing a Verlaine solo gig, suggests they form a group. Verlaine calls up Hell, Ficca returns from his blues band job, and Television is formed.

1974

Mar Television makes its live debut at New York's Townhouse Theater, and picks up a sufficient following in the New York underground for Verlaine to convince the owner of CBGB's to feature live bands, thus establishing an important base for the city's new wave of music.

Verlaine plays guitar on Patti Smith's first single, *Hey Joe/Piss Factory*, and collaborates with Smith on a book of poetry, **The Night**.

1975

Aug Brian Eno produces demos for the band for Island Records, but the label does not sign them. Hell leaves, replaced by Fred Smith (b Apr. 10, 1948, New York). (Hell will later form the Heartbreakers with ex-New York Doll, Johnny Thunders, before quitting again to form a backing unit, the Voidoids with Marc Bell on drums and Ivan Julian and Robert Quine on guitars, releasing the punk album ***Blank Generation*** in 1977.) Television records *Little Johnny Jewel*, released on its own Ork records in October (named after ex-manager, William Terry Ork), selling enough copies to attract major record company attention. A Television's EP, *Blank Generation*, will be released as a one-off on the Stiff label the following year in the UK, while the group signs a longer term deal with Elektra Records.

1977

Apr [30] *Marquee Moon* reaches UK #30.

May [14] Their debut album, ***Marquee Moon***, a critical success, but with poor sales in the US, is enthusiastically received in Britain, where it makes #28.

[28] The group makes its UK debut at London's Hammersmith Odeon, on a bill with Blondie.

Aug [6] *Prove It* makes UK #25.

1978

Apr [22] *Foxhole* makes UK #36.

[29] Television's second effort, ***Adventure***, hits UK #7, where the punk/new wave explosion is more receptive to its alternative edge.

Aug After just two albums, the group splits, with Smith going on to perform with Blondie, Ficca playing drums with the Waitresses, and Lloyd and Verlaine embarking on solo careers: Lloyd will release ***Alchemy*** in December the following year but career efforts will be hampered by drug-related problems. Verlaine will issue ***Tom Verlaine*** for Elektra in September 1979.

1981

Oct Verlaine's sophomore set, ***Dreamtime***, released through Warner Bros., peaks at US #177 in October 1981. It will be followed by ***Words From The Front*** next May, when Hell also unveils ***Destiny Street*** on the independent Red Star label, with Fred Maher on drums. (Making his film debut in "Smithereens" the following November, Hell will semi-retire from music, and work predominantly as a journalist.)

1985

Nov After a lengthy hiatus, Verlaine has released ***Cover*** on Virgin Records, including the extracted *Five Miles Of You* and *Let Go The Mansion*, the previous September, while Lloyd, having overcome his drug problems, now issues ***Field Of Fire***. He plays well-received comeback gigs (which will result in the performance album ***Real Time*** released in October the following year), but soon returns to obscurity.

1987

Feb Phonogram revives the Fontana label for Verlaine's album, ***Flash Light***. Three singles are released from the album, which spends one week at UK #99.

Mar *Cry Mercy Judge* is released, as Verlaine plays a well-received gig at London's Town & Country club.

1990

Oct Lloyd, recently a featured member of former X leader, John Doe's backing band on his album, ***Meet John Doe***, and Verlaine, who issued ***Wonder*** in April, resume initial discussions about re-forming Television. They will jam with Smith and Ficca in December, and shortly thereafter sign with Capitol Records. While preparing the group's first album in 13 years, Lloyd says "There's a lot of unfinished stuff for us to do".

1992

Apr [6] Verlaine releases his seventh solo album, ***Warm And Cool***, an instrumental work, featuring Smith and Jay Dee Dougherty, recorded at New York's Acoustilog Studio.

June [26-28] The re-formed Television takes part in the three-day "Glastonbury Arts & Music Festival" at Shepton Mallet, Avon, their first UK gig since Hammersmith Odeon in 1978. (They will play several European festivals during the summer, before embarking on a tour of Japan in September, then touring North America until the year's end.)

Sept Their comback album, ***Television***, is finally released by Capitol. Once again, it is warmly received by the music media, but maintains Television's record of never making the Top 200 US album chart, this time with the added kudos of also failing to score in the UK.

Nov [19] They play a one-off UK date at London's Town & Country club.

Dec [8-9] Television performs at the Great American Music Hall, San Francisco, CA, during its US trek. Though the band will be named Comeback Of The Year in **Rolling Stone**'s 1993 Music Awards Critics' Picks, it is dropped by Capitol, and following spring dates in New York, the group dissolves once again.

THE TEMPTATIONS

Eddie Kendricks (tenor vocals); **Otis Williams** (baritone vocals); **Paul Williams** (tenor vocals); **Melvin Franklin** (bass vocals); **David Ruffin** (baritone vocals)

1960

Initially known as the Elgins, the R&B vocal group forms from members of the Primes and the Distants, both based in Detroit, MI. The Primes consisted of Kendricks (b. Dec. 17, 1939, Union Springs, AL) (ex-Cavaliers, who has also formed all-girl group the Primettes to perform with the Primes and who will later become the Supremes), Paul Williams (b. July 2, 1939, Birmingham, AL) and Cal Osborne, and were formed in Birmingham. The Distants included ex-Voice Masters group member Franklin (b. David English, Oct. 12, 1942, Montgomery, AL), ex-Siberians leader Otis Williams (b. Otis Miles, Oct. 30, 1939, Texarkana, TX) who first heard Franklin singing bass on a Voice Masters single recorded for the Anna label and invited him to the Distants, Franklin's cousin, Richard Street (b. Oct. 5, 1942, Detroit), Albert Harrell and Elbridge Bryant. After the Distants have failed to score with *Come On* on Johnnie Mae Matthews' Northern label, Street and Harrell leave (Street will subsequently join the Temptations in 1971) and Kendricks and Williams are invited to join the remaining Distants to form the Elgins. (Kendricks has originally moved to Detroit after forging his brother's signature on an $82 income-tax refund cheque.)

1961

Aug Signed as the Elgins by Berry Gordy Jr. to his new Motown subsidiary, Miracle Records earlier in the year, the group has been re-named the Temptations (a suggestion from Otis Williams) for release of its first single, *Oh Mother Of Mine* which will be quickly followed by *Check Yourself* in November.

1962

Apr *Dream Come True* (released on the Gordy label, where the group will remain throughout its tenure with Motown), is released.

Sept With three non-charting efforts as the Temptations, Gordy renames the group the Pirates for the one-off single *Mind Over Matter*, again to little notice.

1963

Jan The group's fifth single, reverting to the

Temptations name, *Paradise* is released, followed by two more 45s, *I Want A Love I Can See* in March and *May I Have This Dance* in July. Motown's dance arranger, Cholly Atkins, starts teaching the group the synchronized dance-step routines which will highlight their live work, during a year in which they will perform at the Howard Theater, Washington, DC.
Dec Also working part-time at a dairy, Bryant, angry that the group is performing away from Detroit, attacks Paul Williams with a bottle after the group has appeared at the "Motortown Revue, Christmas Show", is immediately fired and subsequently replaced by Ruffin (b. Davis Eli Ruffin, Jan. 18, 1941, Whynot, MS), who has headed for Memphis at the age of 14, joined the Dixie Nightingales for two years after high school, before moving to Detroit, and becoming involved with Motown through his friend, Gwen Gordy, initially helping Pops Gordy build a studio. The Temptations begin working with in-house writer/producer, Smokey Robinson, who knows Franklin and Otis Williams from Northwestern High School.

1964

Apr [11] The Robinson and Robert Rogers' penned song, *The Way You Do The Things You Do*, with Kendricks on lead vocals, is the Temptations' first US hit, making #11.
June ***Meet The Temptations*** reaches US #95.
July [4] *I'll Be In Trouble*, also penned by Robinson, makes US #33.
Sept [13] They appear in Murray The K's "Rock'n'Roll Extravaganza" at New York's Fox Theater, Brooklyn, with Marvin Gaye, Martha & the Vandellas, the Supremes, the Searchers and the Ronettes.
Oct [17] *Girl (Why You Wanna Make Me Blue)*, written by Eddie Holland and Norman Whitfield, and produced by the latter, peaks at US #26.

1965

Mar [6] Ruffin takes over the lead vocal on *My Girl*, co-written (with Ronald White) and produced by Robinson, which tops the US chart for a week, eventually selling a million copies (though, like many '60s Motown hits it will remain officially uncertified), making the Temptations the first male Motown group to have a #1 hit.
[20] In the UK, *My Girl* makes #43, as the group arrives in London to play on the Motown package tour with labelmates, Martha & the Vandellas, the Supremes and Little Stevie Wonder.
Apr [3] *It's Growing* makes UK #49.
May [15] *It's Growing*, a Robinson-Warren Moore song, reaches US #18.
June [5] ***The Temptations Sing Smokey***, which makes US #35.
[28] The group is featured on CBS-TV's "It's What's Happening Baby" special.
Aug [28] *Since I Lost My Baby*, also penned by Robinson and Moore, makes US #17.
Nov [27] *My Baby* climbs to US #13.

1966

Jan [15] *Don't Look Back*, the B-side of *My Baby*, makes US #83.
Feb [5] ***Temptin' Temptations*** reaches US #11.
Apr [2] Robinson's final production for the group, *Get Ready*, makes US #29, and tops the R&B chart.
July [16] *Ain't Too Proud To Beg*, written by Eddie Holland and Whitfield, and produced by the latter, reaches US #13, again topping the R&B survey.
Sept [3] *Ain't Too Proud To Beg* is their first UK Top 30 hit, peaking at #21.
[24] ***Gettin' Ready*** makes US #12.
Oct [1] *Beauty Is Only Skin Deep*, another Holland-Whitfield collaboration, hits US #3 and R&B #1.
Nov [12] *Beauty Is Only Skin Deep* reaches UK #18.
Dec [31] *(I Know) I'm Losing You* hits US #8 and R&B #1, while ***Gettin' Ready*** is the group's first UK chart album, reaching #40.
[23-**Jan** 1] The group takes part in the Motortown Revue at the Fox Theatre in Detroit, with fellow Motown acts Stevie Wonder, Gladys Knight & the Pips, Martha & the Vandellas, Jimmy Ruffin and others.

1967

Jan [14] *(I Know) I'm Losing You* makes UK #19.
Feb [11] Compilation album, ***The Temptations' Greatest Hits***, is the group's first US Top 10 album, peaking at #5.
Mar [11] ***The Temptations' Greatest Hits*** reaches UK #26).
May [20] ***Temptations Live!*** hits US #10.
June [17] Whitfield is now the group's sole producer. *All I Need*, written by Eddie Holland, Frank Wilson and R. Dean Taylor, hits US #8 and R&B #1.
Aug [10] The group debuts at the Copacabana with a two-week stint.
[12] Performance set ***Temptations Live!*** reaches UK #20.
Sept [16] *You're My Everything* hits US #6.
[30] ***With A Lot O' Soul*** hits US #7.
Oct [14] *You're My Everything* reaches UK #26.
Nov [11] *(Loneliness Made Me Realize) It's You That I Need* reaches US #14. (Motown takes out press ads to inform people that a group calling itself "The Fabulous Temptations" have nothing to do with the real Temptations.)
Dec [16] ***With A Lot O' Soul*** makes UK #19.
[17] The Temptations guest on CBS-TV's "The Smothers Brothers Comedy Hour".

1968

Feb [17] Written by Whitfield, Barrett Strong and Roger Penzabene, the ballad *I Wish It Would Rain*, taken from ***Mellow Mood***, hits US #4 and R&B #1.
Mar [9] *I Wish It Would Rain* makes UK #45. (The Whitfield/Strong writing team will provide the group with its next 13 hits.)
[16] ***The Temptations In A Mellow Mood***, which includes a selection of Broadway standards, makes US #13.
June [15] *I Could Never Love Another (After Loving You)* reaches US #13, tops the R&B chart, and peaks at UK #47.
July Ruffin, after pushing for a change in the group's sound to a deeper soul style, leaves and signs to Motown as a solo artist, and is replaced by Dennis Edwards (b. Feb. 3, 1943, Birmingham), who has sung with gospel group the Golden Wonders, and with Motown's the Contours.
[9] The Temptations make their first appearance without Ruffin at the Valley Forge Music Fair, Devon, PA.
Aug [17] ***The Temptations Wish It Would Rain*** (which shows them on the sleeve in a desert wearing Foreign Legion uniforms) also climbs to US #13.
[31] *Please Return Your Love To Me* reaches US #26, and is the last single in the familiar Temptations style.
Sept Ruffin sues Motown for $5 million, alleging that the company has put him in peonage by blocking his ability to make recordings and live appearances.
Dec A ten-day revue begins in Detroit with the Temptations, Stevie Wonder, Gladys Knight & the Pips, Edwin Starr and Bobbie Taylor.

1969

Jan [4] Whitfield's ideas for a different direction for the group first take shape on *Cloud Nine*, which has Edwards on lead vocal, and adopts the "psychedelic soul" style pioneered by Sly & the Family Stone. It hits US #6 and R&B #2 (and will win Motown's first Grammy Award, as Best Group R&B Performance).
[11] The group has teamed with the Supremes on ***Diana Ross & The Supremes Join The Temptations***, which hits US #2. Taken from this is a duetted revival of Dee Dee Warwick's hit, *I'm Gonna Make You Love Me*, which hits US #2, behind Marvin Gaye's *I Heard It Through The Grapevine*.
Feb [8] ***T.C.B.***, the soundtrack to a TV special of the same title, featuring the Supremes and the Temptations, tops the US chart for a week.
[22] *I'm Gonna Make You Love Me* hits UK #3.
Mar [1] ***Diana Ross & The Supremes Join The Temptations*** tops the UK chart, while the group's own album, ***Live At The Copa***, reaches US #15. It is the first album to feature Edwards
[29] *Runaway Child, Running Wild*, once again written by Whitfield and Barrett Strong, with a similar sound to *Cloud Nine* and a further socially-conscienced lyric, hits US #6 and R&B #1. *Get Ready*, not a hit on its original UK release, is reissued, and hits UK #10.
[12] *Cloud Nine* is named the Best R&B Performance By A Duo Or Group, Vocal Or Instrumental Of 1968, at the 11th annual Grammy awards.
Apr [12] A revival of the Miracles' *I'll Try Something New*, duetted with Ross and the Supremes, reaches US #25.
May [3] ***Cloud Nine*** hits US #4.
[10] The band plays at a Masquerade Ball at the White House in Washington, DC, as guests of Tricia Nixon.
June [28] *Don't Let The Joneses Get You Down*, again dealing with social issues, reaches US #20 and R&B #2.
July [12] ***TCB*** reaches UK #11,
Sept [13] The TV soundtrack album, ***The Temptations Show***, peaks at US #24.
[20] ***Cloud Nine*** album makes UK #32.
[27] *Cloud Nine*, belatedly issued in the UK (it was originally considered "too progressive"), reaches UK #15.
Oct [4] A treatment of the Band's *The Weight*, with Ross and the Supremes, and the B-side of the still-climbing of *I Can't Get Next To You*, makes US #46, as *I Second That Emotion*, also with Ross and the Supremes, reaches UK #18.
[18] *I Can't Get Next To You*, which has each member of the group singing lead in succession, tops the US chart for the first of two weeks, eventually selling over a million copies.
Nov [22] ***Together***, with Ross and the Supremes, makes US #28.
[29] ***Puzzle People***, including *I Can't Get Next To You*, hits US #5.
Dec [27] Television soundtrack album, ***On Broadway***, featuring the Temptations and the Supremes performing show tunes, reaches US #38.

1970

Feb [7] *I Can't Get Next To You* reaches UK #13.
[14] ***Together*** reaches UK #28.
[21] ***Puzzle People*** makes UK #20.
[28] *Psychedelic Shack* hits US #7 and R&B #2.
Apr [18] *Why (Must We Fall In Love)*, with Ross and the Supremes, reaches UK #31.
May ***Psychedelic Shack*** hits US #9.
June [27] *Ball Of Confusion (That's What The World Is Today)* is another million seller, hitting US #3 (and R&B #2).
July [11] *Psychedelic Shack* makes UK #33, as the parent album, ***Psychedelic Shack***, reaches UK #56.
Sept Live album, ***The Temptations Live At London's Talk Of The Town***, recorded in the UK, reaches US #21.
Oct [31] *Ungena Za Ulimwengu (Unite The World)*, continuing the formula of recent hits, reaches US #33. Whitfield decides on a change of pace for the next release. *Ball Of Confusion* is the group's highest-placed UK single to date, hitting #7.
Nov Compilation, ***The Temptations' Greatest Hits, II***, reaches US #15.
Dec The group's festive selection, ***Christmas Card***, is released.

1971

Jan [16] ***The Temptations' Greatest Hits, II*** makes UK #35.
Apr [3] With Kendricks on lead vocal, *Just My Imagination (Running Away With Me)*, a slow ballad in the group's traditional soul-harmony style, tops both the US pop and R&B charts, for the first of two weeks, becoming another million seller, and a timeless soul standard.
July ***The Sky's The Limit***, including *Just My Imagination*, makes US #16.
[10] *Just My Imagination (Running Away With Me)*, written by Whitfield and Strong, hits UK #8. (Kendricks leaves for a solo career (like Ruffin, staying with Motown). Paul Williams is also forced to

quit the group because of poor health (he has an alcohol problem and a serious liver complaint). Following the temporary fill-in Ricky Owens, they are replaced by Damon Harris (b. July 3, 1950, Baltimore, MD), and their early colleague, ex-the Distants and the Monitors' Street (b. Oct. 5, 1942, Detroit).)

Aug [21] *It's Summer*, from ***The Sky's The Limit***, peaks at US #51.

Dec [18] *Superstar (Remember How You Got Where You Are)* makes US #18. (By year's end, Kendricks has kicked off his solo career with a week's residence at the Apollo Theatre, Harlem, NY.)

1972

Feb [19] *Superstar (Remember How You Got Where You Are)* peaks at UK #32.

Mar ***Solid Rock*** makes both US and UK #24.

Apr [1] *Take A Look Around*, from ***Solid Rock***, reaches US #30.

May [20] *Take A Look Around* reaches UK #13.

July [15] *Mother Nature* peaks at US #92.

Aug Kendricks is one of the featured artists performing on the very first US-TV "Soul Train" broadcasts.

Dec [2] *Papa Was A Rollin' Stone*, edited from an 11-minutes-plus album track, with Edwards on lead vocal, tops the US chart for a week, selling over a million and becoming another landmark R&B recording. (The instrumental section of the song on the single's B-side will win a Grammy as Best R&B Instrumental.) ***All Directions***, containing the full version, hits US #2.

1973

Jan [27] *Papa Was A Rollin' Stone* peaks at UK #14, and ***All Directions*** at UK #19.

Apr [28] *Masterpiece* hits US #7 and R&B #1, while the album, ***Masterpiece***, also hits US #7.

July [7] *The Plastic Man*, from ***Masterpiece***, peaks at US #40, as the album reaches UK #28.

Aug [17] Paul Williams, in ill health since leaving the group in 1971, though he has continued to supervise the group's choreography, is found dead in his car a few blocks from Motown's offices. (Owing $80,000 in taxes, his Celebrity Boutique failed, and with matrimonial and health troubles, he has shot himself in the head.)

Sept [22] *Hey Girl (I Like Your Style)* makes US #35.

Oct [13] *Law Of The Land*, issued as a single in Britain, but not in the US, makes UK #41.

Nov Triple-compilation album, ***Anthology***, makes US #65.

1974

Jan [26] *Let Your Hair Down* reaches US #27, while its parent set, ***1990***, makes US #19.

Feb [19] They collect the Favorite Band, Duo Or Group, Soul/R&B trophy, at the inaugural American Music Awards, held at the Aquarius Theater, Hollywood, CA.

Mar [2] The group wins Best Group R&B Performance category for ***Masterpiece***, at the 16th annual Grammy Awards.

May [4] *Heavenly* climbs to US #43.

July [13] *You've Got My Soul On Fire* makes US #74 (and is the group's last single to be produced by Whitfield for nearly ten years).

1975

Feb [1] *Happy People*, with new producer Jeffrey Bowen, and co-written by Lionel Richie, makes US #40.

Mar ***A Song For You*** reaches US #13, also becoming their 17th, and last, US R&B chart-topper.

June [7] *Shakey Ground* makes US #26.

Aug [30] *Glasshouse* reaches US #37, as Damon Harris leaves the group to be replaced by Glenn Leonard.

Dec [20] ***House Party*** peaks at US #40.

1976

Jan [31] They nab the Favorite Album, Soul/R&B trophy, at the third annual American Music Awards, held at the Civic Auditorium, Santa Monica, CA.

Feb [28] *Keep Holding On* makes US #54.

June [5] ***Wings Of Love*** flies to US #29.

July [31] *Up The Creek (Without A Paddle)* peaks at US #94.

Oct [23] ***The Temptations Do The Temptations***, on which the group cuts members' own compositions, reaches US #53. After 15 years with Motown, the relationship sours and the increasingly self-sufficient group leaves the label.

1978

Jan [7] Without Edwards, who leaves to go solo, replaced by Louis Price, the Temptations have signed a new deal with Atlantic Records. ***Hear To Tempt You***, produced by Norman Harris and Brian Holland, and mostly written by Ron Tyson (who will join the group in 1983) peaks at US #113. Out of the public eye at a time when new disco acts abound on the charts, the group settles into steady work on the club and cabaret circuits. (Kendricks will sign a solo deal with Arista, before moving to Atlantic in 1980.)

Nov ***Bare Back***, also on Atlantic, makes R&B #46, but fails to cross over.

1980

June [14] Berry Gordy, having lured the Temptations back to Motown, writes and produces their first Top 50 hit in five years, *Power*, which makes US #43, and features Edwards returning to sing lead vocal, replacing Price. Its parent album ***Power*** also reaches US #45.

1981

Oct [3] *Aiming At Your Heart* makes US #67, while its parent album, ***The Temptations***, reaches US #119.

1982

June [5] ***Reunion***, with its accompanying tour seeing the brief return of Ruffin and Kendricks to the line-up, reaches US #37. The extracted *Standing On The Top, Part 1* makes US #66. It is written and produced by, and features, Rick James. (A reunion tour will end with sellout dates at New York's Radio City Music Hall.)

[19] *Standing On The Top, Part 1* makes UK #53.

1983

Apr [16] *Love On My Mind Tonight* peaks at US #88, while ***Surface Thrills*** makes US #159.

May [16] Augmented by a new member, Ron Tyson, a successful writer and producer who has replaced the departing Leonard, the Temptations appear on NBC-TV's "Motown 25th Anniversary" special. They team-up on the show with the Four Tops, trading oldies' medleys, leading to a joint international tour.

1984

May [5] The group, once again minus Ruffin and Kendricks, is reunited with Whitfield for *Sail Away*, which docks at US #54, as ***Back To Basics*** climbs to US #152.

Nov [24] Uptempo chugger, *Treat Her Like A Lady*, with new lead vocalist, Ali-Ollie Woodson (who has replaced Edwards), reaches UK #12.

1985

Feb [9] *Treat Her Like A Lady* peaks at US #48.

Mar [9] ***Truly For You*** makes US #55, having made UK #75.

July [13] Now a regular touring duo, Ruffin and Kendrick (having dropped the "s" at the end of his name, apparently due to the fact that Motown owns the rights to his name, although it will re-appear in the future) appear at the "Live Aid" benefit at the JFK Stadium, Philadelphia, PA.

Oct Having joined Daryl Hall & John Oates at the re-opening of New York's Apollo Theatre in May, the resulting team-effort versions of the Temptations' classics, *The Way You Do The Things You Do* and *My Girl*, reach US #20 and UK #58, as a medley titled *A Nite At The Apollo Live!*. An album of the event, ***Live At The Apollo With David Ruffin And Eddie Kendrick***, makes US #21 and UK #32.

Dec Ruffin and Kendrick contribute to the all-star Artists United Against Apartheid combine, with *Sun City* making US #38 and UK #21.

1986

Feb ***Touch Me*** makes US #146.

May Another anthology collection, with an eight-page booklet, ***25th Anniversary*** climbs to US #140.

Aug ***To Be Continued*** peaks at US #74.

Nov [8] *Lady Soul* makes US #47.

[15] The Temptations appear on NBC-TV show, "227", performing *Get Ready* and *Lady Soul*.

1987

July [11] The Temptations back actor Bruce Willis on his version of *Under The Boardwalk*, which hits UK #2 and will make US #59.

Aug [29] *Papa Was A Rollin' Stone*, given an up-dated remix for the UK dance market, climbs to UK #31.

Nov With Edwards back in the line-up, ***Together Again*** makes US #112 and includes *Look What You Started*, which will make UK #63 the following Feb [6].

Dec Signed as a duo to RCA, Ruffin and Kendricks issue ***Ruffin And Kendricks***, which makes US R&B #60, with an extracted single, *I Couldn't Believe It*, reaching #14 on the US R&B chart. The following year, Ruffin, a long-time substance abuser, will be convicted of cocaine possession.

1989

Jan [18] The Temptations are inducted into the Rock and Roll Hall of Fame by Hall & Oates, at the fourth annual dinner, at New York's Waldorf Astoria Hotel.

Oct [21] *All I Want From You* peaks at UK #71, taken from their current Motown album, ***Special***, variously produced by Larry Hatcher, Keith Andes, Stan Sheppard and Michael Sembello. Edwards has once again left, replaced by Woodson.

1990

Mar As a duo, Kendricks and Edwards release *Get It While It's Hot*, co-penned by Jermaine Jackson, on A&B Records.

Nov [25] Having recently released ***Solid Rock,*** the Temptations take part in CBS-TV's "Motown 30 : What's Goin' On!" special, and have been featured throughout the year singing *Get Ready*, with assistance from Candice Bergen, Delta Burke, Dixie Carter, Jean Smart and Gerald McRaney, helping to promote CBS-TV programs, this new version appearing on the ***Sounds Of Murphy Brown*** album.

1991

Apr [26] Kendrick, Edwards and Ruffin embark on a 15-date UK tour at the Newport Centre, Newport, Gwent, Wales, set to end on May 14th at the De Montfort Hall, Leicester, Leics.

May [14] The Temptations contribute *Shake Your Paw* to jazz label GRP's Garfield tribute album, ***Am I Cool, Or What?***

June [1] Ruffin dies of a drug overdose at the Hospital of the University of Pennsylvania, at 3:55 a.m. He has been brought to the emergency room in a limousine, though the driver does not identify the singer. An FBI check of his fingerprints confirms that it is indeed the Temptation.

[10] Pallbearer Kendrick is arrested at Ruffin's funeral at the New Bethel Baptist Church, Detroit on charges of failure to pay $26,000 in child support to his ex-wife, Patricia (they divorced in 1975). He is arraigned the following day, and held on a $10,000 bond.

Sept [9] The Temptations guest on the premiere of NBC-TV's "The Adventures Of Mark & Brian", having just released the mostly Steve Lindsey-produced ***Milestone***, the group's 50th album.

[21] Rod Stewart's *The Motown Song*, for which the Temptations have provided backing vocals, hits US #10.

Oct [19] Still touring regularly, the Temptations return home to play the Alabama State Fair, in Birmingham, AL.

Nov [1] Kendrick is discharged from Georgia Baptist Medical Center in Atlanta, after a cancerous right lung is removed.
[14] Originally released in November 1982, ***Give Love At Christmas*** is certified gold by the RIAA.
[27] "My Girl" movie, starring Macaulay Culkin, and featuring the Temptations title track, opens throughout the US.
Dec [24] Compilation ***All The Million Sellers*** is certified gold by the RIAA.

1992

Jan [11] The Temptations are inducted into the Image Hall Of Fame, at the 24th NAACP Image Awards, at the Wiltern Theatre, Los Angeles.
Feb [21] Now regularly touring on a shared bill with the Four Tops, the two legendary Motown acts play the Fox Theatre, Detroit.
[22] *The Jones'*, taken from their latest album, ***Milestone***, charts for a week at UK #69.
[29] Reissued *My Girl*, benefitting from the UK premiere of the movie, hits UK #2, behind Shakespear's Sister's *Stay*.
Apr [5-7] The group performs at the Wembley Arena, Wembley, Middx., on a bill with the Four Tops, Edwin Starr, Jimmy Ruffin, the Supremes, Martha & the Vandellas and the Marvelettes.
[11] The group participates in the Grand Opening of Euro-Disney, near Paris, France.
[25] ***Motown's Greatest Hits***, a Temptations collection, hits UK #8.
May [6] The group guests on NBC-TV's "The Tonight Show".
Aug [31] Kendrick files suit in US District Court in Los Angeles, against Motown and Jobete claiming, among other things, they have refused access to his accounts and withheld royalties.
Oct [5] Kendrick dies of lung cancer at Baptist Medical Center-Princeton, Birmingham, one year after having a lung removed.
[30] The Temptations play on the "Giants of Motown" bill at Butlins Southcoast World, Bognor Regis, Sussex, during their latest UK tour.
Dec [7] The group plays at Walt Disney World, Lake Buena Vista, FL, during a current US tour.

1993

Apr [30] Edwards files suit in US District Court in Los Angeles against Motown, charging fraud and breach of contract, seeking compensatory and punitive damages of more than $10 million, over alleged non payment of back royalties. (During the year, Street will leave, replaced by Theo Peoples.)

1994

Sept [20] During a week when the Temptations are awarded their star on the Hollywood Walk Of Fame, a five CD-boxed set retrospective ***Emperors Of Soul***, including new cuts, is released by Motown.

1995

Feb [23] Franklin dies of heart failure at Cedars-Sinai Medical Center, Los Angeles. He will be replaced by Ray Davies (b. Mar. 29, 1940, Sumter, SC). Otis Williams, now the only original member, will continue to lead the group which lines up behind him as Woodson, Tyson, Davis and Peoples, who record a standards album, ***For Lovers Only*** to be released by Motown in January 1996. Dedicated to Franklin, and including *Life Is But A Dream*, his last recording with the group, the album also features Stevie Wonder among its guests.

10cc

Graham Gouldman (vocals, guitar); **Eric Stewart** (vocals, guitar); **Lol Creme** (vocals, guitar); **Kevin Godley** (vocals, drums)

1969

Sept Godley (b. Oct. 7, 1945, Manchester, Lancs.) and Creme (b. Lawrence Creme, Sept. 19, 1947, Manchester), having recently worked as designers for Pan Books on cut-out titles based around films such as "The Railway Children" and "The Charge Of The Light Brigade", sign a contract with ex-Yardbirds manager Giorgio Gomelsky's short-lived Marmalade label and release *I'm Beside Myself*, billed as Frabjoy & Runcible, with Gouldman (b. May 10, 1946, Manchester) and Stewart (b. Jan. 20, 1945, Manchester) playing on the session, bringing together all future members of 10cc for the first time. Each member already has an illustrious music career: All four have been active in Manchester-based bands since the beat scene exploded in 1963. Gouldman, who has already played in the High Spots, the Crevattes and the Planets, joined Whirlwind, which became a house band at the local Jewish Lads Brigade, where he met the Sabres, whose line-up included Neil Levin, his cousin Creme and Godley (who are studying graphic design at art college). Towards the end of 1964, Gouldman, working by day in Bargains Unlimited, a gentleman's outfitters in Salford, Lancs.) dissolved Whirlwind (who had signed to the HMV label, releasing a cover of Buddy Holly's *Look At Me* with the Creme-penned B-side, *Baby Not Like Me* in June) and formed the Mockingbirds in February 1965, with Whirlwind member Steve Jacobsen and Bernard Brasso and Godley (on drums), from the Sabres. (During this period, Stewart was a member of Jerry Lee & the Staggerlees, before joining Wayne Fontana & the Mindbenders in April 1964, who enjoyed success in the UK and US with major hits including *The Game Of Love* and *Um Um Um Um Um Um*.) Signed to the Columbia label, the Mockingbirds began a regular spot as warm-up band for BBC-TV's "Top Of The Pops", transmitted from Manchester. Gouldman's first song for the group, *For Your Love*, was rejected by Columbia, but became a major success for the Yardbirds in April 1965. (Gouldman went on to write a number of other hits, including *Heart Full Of Soul* and *Evil Hearted You* (the Yardbirds), *Bus Stop* and *Look Through Any Window* (the Hollies) and songs for Herman's Hermits, including *East West* and *No Milk Today*. He also began a solo career with Decca in 1966, and wrote a song for the Connie Francis movie, "When The Boys Meet The Girls".) Meanwhile, the Mindbenders split from Wayne Fontana and enjoy a major hit with *A Groovy Kind Of Love* in October 1965. Signed as a songwriter to the US Robbins Music company in 1967, Gouldman also penned *Tallyman*, for Jeff Beck, before releasing three singles and ***The Graham Gouldman Thing*** album for RCA the following year. Having stepped in as a temporary replacement for Bob Lang in the Mindbenders in March 1968, he also wrote the group's last single, *Uncle Joe, The Ice Cream Man*, released in August. Following the Mindbenders' split in November, Stewart and Peter Tattersall have bought the Inter-City recording studio in Manchester, renamed Strawberry by Stewart after the Beatles song, *Strawberry Fields Forever*.
Oct Gouldman spends time in New York as a staff writer for the Kasenatz-Katz production team, which specialises in creating "bubblegum" music for teenagers. He writes and sings lead vocal on *Sausalito (Is The Place To Go)*, as Ohio Express, before returning to the UK where he invests in the Strawberry Studios.
Nov Kasenatz-Katz books Strawberry Studios for three months as the UK branch of its operation. Gouldman and Stewart call in Godley and Creme to help on the sessions, and the fledgling members of 10cc embark on a marathon bout of writing, producing and playing on records which are released worldwide, under different names. Godley and Creme pen *There Ain't No Umbopo*, which is released as by Crazy Elephant, while Gouldman writes and sings on a million seller in France for Freddie & the Dreamers, *Susan's Tuba* (although Freddie will claim that he is the singer on the disc).

1970

Aug With money from their Kasenatz-Katz work, the group re-equips Strawberry Studios, and writes the heavily rhythmic, African-styled *Neanderthal Man*, to test out the new equipment. When Dick Leahy of Philips Records hears the test tape, he offers the group £500 as an advance. The disc eventually sells over two million copies worldwide, hitting UK #2 and US #22, under the group name, Hotlegs. Two further singles and an album, ***Thinks : School Stinks***, fail to successfully follow-up, and a spot on a Moody Blues tour is cancelled when the Moodies' John Lodge goes down with a viral infection.

1971

The four concentrate on writing, producing and playing on a variety of sessions at Strawberry Studios (including records by soccer teams Manchester City and Leeds United, John Paul Joans' hit, *The Man From Nazareth*, and writing the material for ***Space Hymns*** by a central heating salesman from Sheffield, S. Yorks, called Ramases, who believes he is a reincarnation of an Egyptian god). Their most successful venture is in reviving Neil Sedaka's career with work on his albums ***Solitaire*** and ***The Tra La La Days Are Over***, and the singles *That's When The Music Takes Me*, *Standing On The Inside*, *Dimbo Man* and *Our Last Song Together*.

1972

July Having recorded demos of *Donna* and *Waterfall*, Jonathan King, an old friend of Stewart's, signs them to his UK label, naming them 10cc. (For many years, the legend persists that their moniker was inspired by the average male ejaculation: 9cc, adding 1cc to indicate they are above average, though Gouldman will confirm, in 1993, that the name came to King in a dream.)
Oct [21] *Donna*, a Godley & Creme pastiche of '50s US pop, hits UK #2, spurred by the group's debut performance on BBC1-TV's "Top Of The Pops".
Nov Its follow-up, *Johnny Don't Do It*, another '50s pastiche, but a teen-death song, sinks without trace.

1973

June [23] The group's first UK #1 hit is with the jail-riot song, *Rubber Bullets*, despite sparse radio play because of the British Army's controversial use of rubber bullets in Northern Ireland.
Aug [26] 10cc makes its stage debut at the Douglas Palace Lido, Isle of Man, at the beginning of a UK tour.
Sept [15] *The Dean And I* hits UK #10 as parent album, ***10cc***, makes UK #36.
Oct [20] *Rubber Bullets* is the group's US chart debut, peaking at #73.

1974

Feb [18] The group begins its first US tour at Richard's, Atlanta, GA, set to end on April 8th at the Convention Theatre, Indianapolis, IN.
Mar [14] Godley is taken ill and the rest of the tour is cancelled.
May [16] *Rubber Bullets* (written by Godley, Creme and Gouldman) is named Best Beat Song at the 19th annual Ivor Novello Awards, held at London's Grosvenor House Hotel.
[28] A rescheduled US trek begins.
July [13] *Wall Street Shuffle* hits UK #10.
Aug [23] 10cc performs at the annual "Reading Festival", Reading, Berks.
Sept [1] The band begins a UK tour.
Oct [5] *Silly Love* makes UK #24, ***Sheet Music***, continuing the group's innovative writing style with subject matter ranging from a talking bomb to voodoo, hits UK #9, and makes US #81.

1975

Feb They sign to Phonogram Records in a deal reportedly exceeding $1 million.
Mar [5] The group embarks on another UK tour at Leeds University, W. Yorks, set to end on the 26th at the Empire Theatre, Liverpool, Merseyside.
May [3] *Life Is A Minestrone* hits UK #7.
[17] ***The Original Soundtrack*** hits UK #4 [OR #3] and US #15.
June [28] The Gouldman/Stewart-penned *I'm Not In Love* hits UK #1. The group has been reticent about releasing this plaintive, Stewart-sung, ballad, with a multiplicity of overdubbed backing vocals, amounting to 256 voice tracks assembled by three voices recorded 16 times each on a 13-note chromatic scale, but UK airplay forces its release and radio listeners will consistently vote it into all-time Top 10 lists in coming years. (It will also be revived by the Pretenders in 1993.) ***10cc - The Greatest Hits*** hits UK #9.
July The group appears at Cardiff Castle, Cardiff, S. Glamorgan, Wales, supported by Steeleye Span and Thin Lizzy.
[26] *I'm Not In Love* hits US #2 (where it will stay for three weeks, behind three different US chart-toppers).
Oct 10cc begins a third US tour, and appears on Moody Blues' Justin Hayward and John Lodge's ***Blue Guitar***.
[4] ***100cc*** peaks at US #161.
Dec [27] *Art For Art's Sake* peaks at US #83.

1976

Jan [17] *Art For Art's Sake* hits UK #5.
[31] ***How Dare You?*** hits UK #5.
Feb [7] The group begins a 14-date UK tour at the Usher Hall, Edinburgh, Lothian, Scotland, set to close on the 22nd at the Odeon Theatre, Birmingham, West Midlands.
Mar [27] ***How Dare You?*** makes US #47.
Apr [10] *I'm Mandy Fly Me* hits UK #6.
[24] *I'm Mandy Fly Me* peaks at US #60.
May [26] *I'm Not In Love* wins the Most Performed British Work, Best Pop Song and International Hit Of The Year categories at the 21st annual Ivor Novello Awards, at the Dorchester Hotel, London.
Aug [21] The group appears at the "Knebworth Festival", Knebworth, Herts., on a bill topped by the Rolling Stones.
Nov [26] Godley and Creme announce they are quitting the group, not least to develop a new musical instrument - the "Gizmo", a guitar attachment which can hold notes and create orchestral sounds for a long period. They plan to record a single showcasing its effect, but sessions will lead to a triple album and a long-term career as a duo. Gouldman and Stewart carry on with 10cc, and open the Strawberry South Studio in a former cinema in Dorking, Surrey. They become a trio when drummer Paul Burgess joins full time after working on previous tours (but will not add the Moody Blues' Hayward, despite rumors to the contrary).
Dec [23] 10cc appears on BBC1-TV's "Top Of The Pops" performing *The Things We Do For Love*.

1977

Jan [15] 10cc's perky, pop-aimed *The Things We Do For Love* hits UK #6.
Apr [16] *The Things We Do For Love* hits US #5.
[18] *The Things We Do For Love* is certified gold by the RIAA.
May [21] ***Deceptive Bends***, with Stewart and Gouldman playing all of the instruments, hits UK #3.
[28] *Good Morning Judge* hits UK #5. (The group begins a UK tour, adding Stuart Tosh on drums, Rick Fenn on guitar and Tony O'Malley on keyboards.)
June [25] *People In Love* makes US #40, as ***Deceptive Bends*** makes US #31.
Sept [24] *Good Morning Judge* peaks at US #69.
Nov [19] Godley & Creme's triple boxed set, ***Consequences***, featuring Sarah Vaughan and Peter Cook, makes UK #52, while the extracted *Five O'Clock In The Morning* is also released. Another excerpt from ***Consequences*** will later be used in a UK cinema cigarette commercial. The duo's novel guitar attachment, the "Gizmo", featured on the album, also fails to take off, despite promotion as a major new musical innovation.

1978

Jan [7] A live 10cc double album, ***Live And Let Live***, from the May tour, highlighting ***Deceptive Bends*** and Stewart/Gouldman compositions from the classic 10cc era, reaches UK #14.
[21] ***Live And Let Live*** peaks at US #146.
Mar Duncan Mackay joins on keyboards.
Sept [9] Godley & Creme's ***L***, with assistance from Andy Mackay on saxophone, and DJ Paul Gambaccini playing the role of "The Bad Samaritan" on the track *The Sporting Life*, makes UK #47.
[23] 10cc's pop/reggae meld, *Dreadlock Holiday*, hits UK #1 for a week, inspired by Justin Hayward's experience on holiday in the Caribbean.
Oct [7] Its parent album ***Bloody Tourists*** hits UK #3 and makes US #69.
Nov [18] *Dreadlock Holiday* makes US #44.
Dec [22] 10cc plays at the Wembley Conference Centre, Wembley, Middx.

1979

Jan Stewart is involved in a serious auto accident.
Feb [10] *For You And I*, from the John Travolta/Lily Tomlin film, "Moment By Moment", soundtrack, peaks at US #85.
July Gouldman makes UK #52 with *Sunburn*, the title theme to a Farrah Fawcett-starring movie.
Aug Stewart produces Sad Café's newly-released second album, ***Strange Little Girl***.
Nov [10] ***Greatest Hits 1972-1978*** hits UK #5, but stalls at US #188. (Meanwhile, Godley & Creme, now signed to Polydor, releases *An Englishman In New York*, followed by ***Freeze Frame***, featuring Paul McCartney, in November.)

1980

Apr [12] 10cc's ***Look Hear?*** makes UK #35 and US #180. Gouldman releases music from the animated feature album, ***Animalympics*** (and will later produce the Ramones (***Pleasant Dreams***) and Gilbert O'Sullivan) while Stewart writes music for the French film, "Girls" (which yields ***Girls*** on Polydor), and produces Sad Café.

1981

Oct [17] Having completed production for Mickey Jupp's ***Long Distant Romancer*** earlier in the year, Godley & Creme finally find mainstream appeal with *Under Your Thumb*, which hits UK #3.
[24] Its parent album, the self-written and-produced ***Ismism***, reaches UK #29.
Nov 10cc's ***Ten Out Of 10*** is released, its first non-charting album.
Dec Godley & Creme's *Wedding Bells* hits UK #7. Concurrently running an increasingly successful career as music video directors and producers, their work includes clips for Visage, Duran Duran and Toyah (and will also embrace television commercials).

1982

Apr Stewart has been recruited by Paul McCartney to play on the latter's newly-released ***Tug Of War***, and appears in the group line-up for the video of McCartney's hit, *Take It Away*.
Aug [14] *Run Away* is the group's final chart single of the decade at UK #50 (and the only one to chart from 11 releases since *Dreadlock Holiday*.) During the month, Stewart's second solo effort, ***Frooty Rooties*** is issued by Mercury Records.

1983

Apr Godley & Creme's ***Birds Of Prey*** and the extracted *Samson* are released to indifferent reaction. The duo directs three videos from Police's ***Synchronicity*** project (including the award-winning black-and-white-lensed *Every Breath You Take*), moving on to Herbie Hancock's equally trophy-lifting *Rockit* and a brief reunion with Gouldman and Stewart, directing 10cc's *Feel The Love* promo clip.
Oct 10cc's ***Windows In The Jungle*** makes UK #70, after which the group splits. (Stewart will retreat to Bordeaux, France, while Gouldman will re-emerge as one half of Common Knowledge which transforms into Wax, both units formed with Andrew Gold, scoring (as Wax) with *Right Between The Eyes* (UK #60, and US #43 in the spring of 1986) and *Bridge To Your Heart* (UK #12 in August the following year), taken from the UK #59-peaking ***American English*** in September.)

1984

Sept [18] Godley & Creme's innovative "Rockit" video wins the Best Concept Video, Best Special Effects, Best Art Direction, Best Editing, and Most Experimental categories at the inaugural MTV Video Music Awards, held at New York's Radio City Music Hall. (Much of their year is spent directing videos for hot new UK act Frankie Goes To Hollywood, notably clips for *Relax* and *Two Tribes*. They also complete the "Rebellious Jukebox" series for MTV and release their own *Golden Boy*.)

1985

Apr The Godley & Creme-penned *Cry*, produced by Trevor Horn, reaches UK #19 for the duo, aided by their own highly-acclaimed and much-copied pre-morphing video, featuring continuous three-second face changes. (The song will rechart the following year, at UK #66, after being featured in an edition of the NBC-TV show "Miami Vice".) Horn remixes 10cc and Godley & Creme material for ***The History Mix Volume I***. A video of ***History Mix***, compiled from promo clips and others they have directed, is issued in the US.
Sept [13] They share the prestigious Video Vanguard Award, with David Byrne and Russell Mulcahy, at the second annual MTV Video Music Awards, held at Radio City Music Hall.
Oct [5] *Cry* reaches US #16, the duo's only non-10cc US hit. The following year, Godley and Creme will create "Mondo Video", an experimental visual project, to be issued on their own Videola label in 1988.

1987

Sept [19] With Godley & Creme still much in-demand commercials' directors (having recently lensed a NYNEX Yellow Pages TV ad for the US market), the 16-track combination compilation, ***The Changing Faces Of 10CC And Godley And Creme***, combining hits from both camps, hits UK #4 and achieves gold status.

1988

Feb Self-written and produced, Godley & Creme's ***Goodbye Blue Sky***, featuring much harmonica playing by Mark Feltham and Mitt Gamon, and the backing vocals of Londonbeat, is released to critical acclaim, as is *A Little Bit Of Heaven*. By year's end, the pair completes its debut feature film, "Howling At The Moon". (Creme will continue the foray into motion pictures, making his directorial debut in 1992 with "The Lunatic").

1990

Feb [28] Godley, the co-founder of UK environmental organization ARK, begins work on the TV-special, "One World, One Voice", a week-long series of programs about the environment, with contributions from Sting, Peter Gabriel, Lou Reed, Chrissie Hynde, Stewart Copeland, Joe Strummer, Wayne Shorter, Afrika Bambaataa, Laurie Anderson, Johnny Clegg, Dave Stewart, Robbie Robertson and others. The resultant ***One World One Voice*** album, overseen by Godley and Rupert Hine, peaks at UK #27 following its TV broadcast in June.

1991

Sept Gouldman and Stewart reunite as 10cc to record ***Meanwhile***, produced by Gary Katz at the Bearsville

Studios, Woodstock, NY, with Godley and Creme both making contributions, and released the following year.

1995

Feb [16] The band, once again minus Godley & Creme, plays an acoustic set at Lloyds building in the City of London, augmented by Rick Fenn on guitar.
Mar [18] Their acoustic remake of *I'm Not In Love*, featured on its new album ***Mirror Mirror*** which is released on the Japanese Avex label, debuts at its UK #29 peak, during a two-week chart stay.
June Mercury (US) releases ***The Things We Do For Love***, a double CD 10cc anthology.
see also: **Wayne FONTANA & THE MINDBENDERS**

10,000 MANIACS

Natalie Merchant (vocals); **Robert Buck** (guitars); **Steven Gustafson** (bass); **Dennis Drew** (keyboards); **Jerry Augustyniak** (drums)

1981

Jan Based in Jamestown, NY, Gustafson (b. Apr. 10, 1957, Madrid, Spain) and Drew (b. Aug. 8, 1957, Buffalo, NY) join Still Life, whose line-up already includes Buck (b. Aug. 3, 1958, Jamestown), and begin performing local gigs, playing mostly cover versions of late '70s UK new wave acts, including Joy Division and the Gang Of Four. Merchant (b. Oct. 26, 1963, Jamestown), formerly a church choirist who has always had artistic aspirations, and who has met Gustafson in 1980 when he was running the campus radio station, with Drew, at the Jamestown Community College, where she is studying, joins as lead vocalist. The band, augmented by guitarist John Lombardo (b. Sept. 30, 1952, Jamestown), changes its name, mistakenly taking it from a B-movie horror-pic, "2,000 Maniacs". Initially a fluid ensemble including up to 12 members (including a female doctor), the group begins rehearsing in a local rented warehouse space around Jamestown.

1982

Trimmed to a six-piece, 10,000 Maniacs add folk and country influences to their repertoire, and release a five-track EP, *Human Conflict Number Five*, on their own Christian Burial Records. The tracks are recorded as projects for the sound engineering program, at the State University Of New York in Fredonia.

1983

Now including drummer Augustyniak (b. Sept. 2, 1958, Lackawanna, NY), and commuting between London and New York, NY, the band releases its debut album, ***Secrets Of The I Ching***, again on its own US label and distributed via a US East Coast tour. The album is licensed for independent UK distribution and tops the specialist chart, while New York-based Englishman, Peter Leak, becomes the group's manager, securing it a worldwide recording deal with Elektra the following year.

1985

Nov ***The Wishing Chair*** is released. Recorded at Livingstone Studios in London, it is produced by Joe Boyd, and is comprised entirely of songs written by Merchant and Lombardo. Receiving rave critical reviews in both the US and UK, it introduces their literate, alternative folk/rock leanings, led by Merchant's distinctively plaintive vocal style.

1986

July Founding member Lombardo quits, leaving the four remaining males to construct music around Merchant's lyrics. (Lombardo will re-emerge with a debut album on Rykodisc, with guests Augie Meyers and Ronnie Lane, before teaming with Mary Ramsey as John & Mary, releasing ***Victory Gardens*** in 1991 and ***The Weedkiller's Daughter*** in 1993.)

1987

June 10,000 Maniacs tour behind natural musical allies, R.E.M., in the US.
July [29-30] The band performs at the annual "Cambridge Folk Festival", Cambridge, Cambs.
Aug ***In My Tribe***, produced by Peter Asher, is released, and is again highly rated by critics. It tops the US college charts, becoming a campus favorite (and will climb to US #51 in September 1988).
Nov 10,000 Maniacs begin a successful UK tour to promote the album, after which Merchant will contract spinal meningitis.

1988

Feb Merchant performs a solo showcase at London's Donmar Warehouse, preceding a similar low-key set by new Elektra signing, Tracy Chapman.
June [4] *Like The Weather* makes US #68.
July [29-31] The band appears for the second year running at the three-day "Cambridge Folk Festival" at Cherry Hinton Hall, Cambridge.
Oct [1] *What's The Matter Here* peaks at US #82.

1989

Apr The group performs at the "First Earth Day" concert, at Merriweather Post Pavilion, Columbia, MD.
May [20] A second Asher-produced set, ***Blind Man's Zoo***, begins a 12-week US chart stint, during which it peaks at #44.
[27] ***Blind Man's Zoo*** reaches UK #18.
July [11] ***Blind Man's Zoo*** is certified gold by the RIAA.
Aug [10] ***In My Tribe*** is confirmed platinum by the RIAA.
[12] *Trouble Me*, extracted from ***Blind Man's Zoo***, makes US #44, while *Eat For Two*, Merchant's observation on pregnancy, will become a hot Modern airplay track, as the group embarks on a major US tour, after which Merchant will take a year off.
Nov [3] ***Rubáiyát***, Elektra's 40th anniversary compilation, to which the group has contributed a cover of Jackson Browne's *These Days*, makes US #140, as the band performs at London's Royal Albert Hall, during a brief UK visit.

1990

Apr [21] Merchant and R.E.M's Michael Stipe appear at "A Performance For The Planet", at the Merriweather Post Pavilion.
Oct [18] The group's "Time Capsule" tour opens at the Keg Room, Jamestown, where the band got its start, with John & Mary the opening act.
Nov [10] ***Hope Chest***, a re-packaging of tracks from the first two 10,000 Maniacs projects, now released by Elektra, peaks at US #102. Also known as "The Fredonia" set, it collects 14 recordings made between 1982 and 1983, newly remixed by Joe Barbaria.
[26-28] The band performs at London's Town & Country Club.

1991

Apr [20] 10,000 Maniacs take part in the "Earth Day 1991 Concert", at Foxboro Stadium, Foxborough, MA, with Billy Bragg, Jackson Browne, Rosanne Cash, Bruce Cockburn, Bruce Hornsby & the Range, Indigo Girls, Queen Latifah, Ziggy Marley, Willie Nelson and others.
May [18] The group helps organize the clean-up of the polluted Chadakoin River in Jamestown.

1992

Aug [19-23] Merchant performs solo during WEA's annual marketing meeting, at the Ritz Carlton, Chicago, IL.
Sept [19] *These Are Days* peaks at UK #58.
[23] The group performs at New York's Carnegie Hall during a current US tour. (They have to use substitute drummer Max Weinberg for the first month, while Augustyniak recovers from a broken clavicle after being hit by a car while riding his bike.)
[29] The band plays a low-key gig at the Orange Club in Kensington, London.
Oct [10] ***Our Time In Eden***, produced by Paul Fox and featuring Maceo Parker and Fred Wesley on horns, debuts at its UK #33 peak.
[17] ***Our Time In Eden*** bows at its initial US #34 pinnacle.
[31] The group is the musical guest on NBC-TV's "Saturday Night Live".
Nov [5] They appear on NBC-TV's "The Tonight Show".
[19] The band performs on the same network's "Late Night With David Letterman".
Dec [12] 10,000 Maniacs play to a sellout crowd of 3,399 at the Berkeley Community Theatre, Berkeley, CA.
[15] Merchant performs solo, at the piano, on the "Regis & Kathie Lee" syndicated daytime-TV show.
[26] *These Are Days* peaks at US #66.
[31] The group participates in the "MTV Drops The Ball '93" New Year's Eve celebration, broadcast from New York's Roseland Ballroom.

1993

Jan [20] The group sings *These Are Days*, *To Sir With Love* and *Give Them What They Want*, with Stipe, at MTV's "1993 Rock'n'Roll Inaugural Ball" in Washington, DC.
Feb [6] ***Our Time In Eden*** finally reaches US #28.
Apr [10] *Candy Everybody Wants* debuts at its UK #47 peak.
[16] 10,000 Maniacs perform at the "National Earth Day" concert, headlined by Paul McCartney, at the Hollywood Bowl, Hollywood, CA, with proceeds going to PETA, Greenpeace and the Friends Of The Earth, before a sellout crowd of 17,965.
[23] The band embarks on a three-month US tour at the University of Vermont, Middlebury, VT.
[24] *Candy Everybody Wants* peaks at US #67.
May [29-30] They take part in the first annual two-day Laguna Seca Daze, at the Laguna Seca Recreation Area, Monterey, CA.
June [1] 10,000 Maniacs are the featured artist on MTV's "Unplugged" series.
[9] ***Our Time In Eden*** is certified platinum by the RIAA.
[23] They guest again on "Late Night With David Letterman".
Aug [21] *Few And Far Between* peaks at US #95, as Merchant has announced her intention to quit the band, saying that "being in a band for me was like having five husbands. The divorce was pretty amicable".
Oct [23] *Because The Night*, the Bruce Springsteen/Patti Smith song performed on the MTV "Unplugged" show, charts for a week at UK #65.
Nov [6] ***Unplugged*** makes UK #40.
[13] ***MTV Unplugged*** debuts at its US #13 peak.

1994

Jan [11] ***MTV Unplugged*** is certified platinum by the RIAA.
Feb [19] *Because The Night* reaches US #11.

1995

May With Lombardo returning and Mary Ramsey replacing Merchant, the band re-enters the studio to work on a new album.
Aug Ramsey is concussed after being struck on the head by a collapsing lighting truss while performing, causing the cancellation of a number of summer dates.
see also: **Natalie MERCHANT**

TEN YEARS AFTER

Alvin Lee (guitar, vocals); **Leo Lyons** (bass); **Chick Churchill** (keyboards); **Ric Lee** (drums)

1966

Nov The hard rock/R&B-based group has formed in

Nottingham, Notts., as the Jaybirds in August 1965, when Alvin Lee (b. Dec. 19, 1944, Nottingham), already an alumnus of several bands since his 1957 membership of the Jailbreakers, including the Square Caps, Jay Caps, Jay Men and Blues Yard, and Lyons (b. Nov. 30, 1943, Standbridge, Beds.), who have been in a trio of the same name which has played clubs in Hamburg, West Germany, teamed with Ric Lee (b. Oct. 20, 1945, Cannock, Staffs.), from the Nottingham-based group, the Mansfields. Earning their musical spurs on the North of England club circuit, the group has moved to London earlier this year, to play a six-week stint as the stage band for the play, "Saturday Night and Sunday Morning", before backing the Ivy League on tour. Having been contacted by Chris Wright of the Chrysalis management agency, the band is now signed up while Churchill (b. Jan. 2, 1949, Mold, Clwyd, Wales) joins, and the group changes its name to Ten Years After (following a single Marquee gig as the Blues Yard).

1967

Oct Signed via Chrysalis to Decca Records, the band's debut album ***Ten Years After*** is released on the new "progressive" Deram imprint. (The band will release few singles, particularly in Britain, during its album-dominated career.)

1968

Apr Churchill is temporarily sidelined, undergoing a hernia operation in hospital.

May [31] Ten Years After begins a seven-week US tour at the Fillmore Auditorium, San Francisco.

Aug [9-11] The band performs at the eighth annual "National Jazz & Blues Festival" held at Kempton Park racecourse in Sunbury, Middx., on a bill including the Herd, T. Tex, Marmalade, Traffic, Al Stewart, the Incredible String Band, Jethro Tull, Nice, Joe Cocker, Taste and John Mayall among others.

Sept [3-15] The group records their forthcoming ***Stonedhenge*** set at Decca's West Hampstead studios.

[28] Their chart debut, the live album, ***Undead***, recorded at the Klooks Kleek venue during incessant early club work, makes UK #26.

Oct [19] ***Undead*** makes US #115.

1969

Feb [28] Following a January performance at London's Royal Albert Hall, a US tour begins at the Fillmore East in New York.

Mar [1] ***Stonedhenge*** hits UK #6.

[6-9] The group plays the Fillmore West, San Francisco, CA, with Spirit.

Apr [12] ***Stonedhenge*** peaks at US #61.

July [3-6] Ten Years After participates in the "Newport Jazz Festival" at Newport, RI - the only occasion that rock bands play at the event.

[22-24] The band plays at the Fillmore West in San Francisco, CA, on a bill with Ike & Tina Turner.

Aug [15] The band plays at the "Woodstock Music & Art Fair" in Bethel, NY, where Alvin Lee's lightning-guitar technique proves a show-stopper, highlighted by his 11-minute axe trip on *I'm Going Home*, showcased in the subsequent "Woodstock" movie. The group's success in the US is earned through spending eight months per year touring the country.

Oct [4] ***Ssssh***, its cover photo lensed by Graham Nash, hits UK #4 and US #20.

1970

May [2] The extracted *Love Like A Man* peaks at US #98.

[9] ***Cricklewood Green*** hits UK #4 (the band's most successful UK album, staying charted for 27 weeks) and US #14.

Aug [8] *Love Like A Man* is the band's only UK singles chart entry, hitting #10. It couples the studio cut of the song with a long live B-side version, which plays at 33rpm.

1971

Jan [23] ***Watt*** hits UK #5 and makes US #21.

Apr [22-25] The group plays at the Fillmore West, sharing a bill with Taj Mahal, Stoneground and Trapeze.

Sept [18] The group begins its first UK tour in 18 months, at the Coliseum, London.

Nov [13] Now signed direct to Chrysalis Records, ***A Space In Time***, which introduces electronics as a counter to Lee's guitar, charts for a week at UK #36.

[20] *I'd Love To Change The World* reaches US #40, taken from ***A Space In Time***, which is the band's biggest-selling US album (and first for CBS/Columbia), reaching #17, and earning a platinum disc for one million sales.

1972

Feb [5] *Baby Won't You Let Me Rock'n'Roll You* peaks at US #61.

Apr [13] The group begins another North American tour.

May Compilation, ***Alvin Lee And Company***, rounding up early tracks, is released by Deram in the US, and makes #55.

Aug [13] They top the bill at the last night of the annual "Reading Jazz, Blues and Rock Festival", Reading, Berks., their first UK gig since January, and their first British festival appearance since the Isle of Wight in 1970.

Oct [7] ***Rock'n'Roll To The World*** makes UK #27 and US #43.

1974

Jan [13] *Choo Choo Mama* peaks at US #89, ending the band's short run of chart singles. The group's performance double album, ***Recorded Live***, will make UK #36 and US #39 in July.

Feb Lee's ***On The Road To Freedom***, recorded at his newly built home studio in Berkshire and featuring US gospel singer Mylon LeFevre, plus guest players Steve Winwood, Jim Capaldi, George Harrison and Ron Wood, reaches US #138, while Churchill releases the solo, ***You And Me***.

Mar After the greater part of a decade on the road, including 28 lucrative but gruelling US tours, Lee decides that Ten Years After has run its natural course, and dissolves the band. (Churchill will enter into music publishing for Chrysalis, Ric Lee forms a production company, with Lyons also moving on to production, notably for UFO.)

[22] The group plays its final UK concert, at London's Rainbow Theatre.

June Farewell album, ***Positive Vibrations***, makes US #81.

Sept Lee forms Alvin Lee & Co., initially a one-off band to play the gig which is recorded for ***In Flight***, and then as a unit for touring.

1975

Feb Live double album, ***Alvin Lee & Co : In Flight***, reaches US #65.

Apr [5] In an interview in the **New Musical Express**, Lee says that the band will remain indefinitely "inactive", and will only play when they need the money.

July Ten Years After, evidently needing the money, regroups for a one-off farewell US tour (40 dates through July and August).

Aug [18] The Deram retrospective, ***Goin' Home! Their Greatest Hits***, peaks at US #174.

Sept Lee's solo release, ***Pump Iron!***, peaks at US #131. In March the following year, Lee forms another version of Alvin Lee & Co. for a UK/European trek, and to record tracks for an album (which will not be released).

1978

Feb After an inactive year, Lee forms the three-piece Ten Years Later, with Tom Compton on drums, and Mick Hawkesworth on bass, and signs to RSO Records.

July Ten Years Later's ***Rocket Fuel***, credited to Lee, makes US #115. Ten Years Later's ***Ride On***, again credited to Lee, will make US #158 the following June.

1980

May Ten Years Later splits, but Lee has only been off the road for a few weeks before he has assembled the Alvin Lee Band, with Steve Gould (guitar), Mickey Feat (bass) and Compton. Having toured again, ***Freefall***, recorded for Atlantic Records, makes US #198. (Lee, who will release ***RX-5*** in November 1981 featuring ex-Rolling Stone Mick Taylor, will continue to tour with short-lived backing groups throughout the early-mid '80s, including an appearance at the "Reading Festival" in 1983.)

1986

Aug Lee's ***Detroit Diesel***, featuring Lyons and George Harrison, makes US #124.

Nov Ten Years After's 1971 album, ***A Space In Time*** is certified platinum by the RIAA.

1989

Oct [1] After a German promoter has successfully encouraged the original band to re-form for four festivals in West Germany the previous year, a US tour begins as ***About Time***, produced by Terry Manning, and released on Chrysalis, clocks in at US #120.

1991

Dec [8] Still performing into a fourth decade, Ten Years Later plays at London's Town & Country club. (Ric Lee will form the Breakers with Ian Ellis, former lead singer with Savoy Brown.) While a Ten Years After retrospective, ***Essential Ten Years After*** has been released earlier this year, Alvin's next solo recording, ***Zoom*** will be released by Domino Records in 1992, followed by ***I Hear You Rockin'*** for the Viceroy label in 1994.

THE THE

Matt Johnson (vocals, guitar)

1980

July Johnson (b. Aug. 15, 1961, London), his father the landlord of the Two Puddings pub which has played host to David Essex and Long John Baldry among others, having played in bands since the age of 11, including rock combo Road Star, and having left school at 15, has already worked for a music publisher in London where he has met Colin Tucker and John Hyde, with whom he formed the alternative music outfit, the Gadgets. Now teamed with Keith Laws as The The, and through friend (and cartoonist) Tom Johnstone, the duo has enlisted the production help of Wire's Graham Lewis and Bruce Gilbert to record their initial demo. The results interest 4AD indie label boss Ivo Watts-Russell, who releases their debut one-off single, *Controversial Subject*.

1981

Laws loses interest in the project, and Johnson, now with Johnstone and drummer Peter Ashworth, returns to the studio to record two further tracks, *Time Again For The Golden Sunset* and *The River Flows East In Spring*, subsequently taping an entire album, now planned as a solo project for Johnson. He releases the resulting album, ***Burning Blue Soul***, under his own name on 4AD, but will revert to The The for all future releases.

1982

Dec [11] Newly signed to Some Bizzare, label boss Stevo has secured a licensing deal for The The with CBS/Epic Records, which releases *Uncertain Smile* (having scrapped the planned ***The Pornography Of Despair***). Featuring Squeeze pianist Jools Holland, the single now reaches UK #68.

1983

Feb Follow-up, *Perfect*, is released.

Mar The band plays a month-long season at London's Marquee in a group with Marc Almond, Thomas Leer

and Zeke Monkaya.
Sept [17] *This Is The Day* peaks at UK #70, its 12" including cuts from ***The Pornography Of Despair*** sessions.
Nov ***Soul Mining***, based entirely around Johnson's ideas, songs and production, but also featuring Holland, Leer and Monyaka, reaches UK #27, on its way to gold certification.

1984

June 4AD Records re-releases his 1980 solo album, ***Burning Blue Soul***, but with new sleeve artwork by long-time girlfriend, Fiona Skinner. During a period of introspection and songwriting in preparation for his next album, Johnson will contribute a new The The track, *If You Can't Please Yourself, You Can't Please Your Soul*, to the 1985 Some Bizzare compilation, ***Flesh And Bones***.

1986

May *Sweet Bird Of Truth* is issued, though CBS/Columbia fails to promote it (the song's storyline of a US fighter pilot lost in Arab territory is close to current world affairs in Libya). The label is also advised to take down the US flag at its London offices for fear of a Libyan bomb attack. Further problems with a censored sleeve hinder its chart progress.
July Another controversial cut, *Heartland*, reaches UK #29.
Sept Two years in the making, the politically-themed ***Infected*** is released, with a full-length video, and accompanying book, illustrated by Johnson's brother, Andy Dog, who designs all The The covers. Johnson has used 62 musicians, three producers and five video directors, filming in four different countries. With extensive promotion, ***Infected*** reaches UK #14.
Nov [15] The title cut, *Infected*, makes UK #48, both despite Johnson's reluctance to tour behind the project.

1987

Jan [24] *Slow Train To Dawn*, featuring Neneh Cherry on backing vocals, peaks at UK #64.
Mar ***Infected*** makes US #89.
May [23] *Sweet Bird Of Youth* makes UK #55.

1989

Apr [8] *The Beat(en) Generation*, introducing ex-Smith Johnny Marr (b. Oct. 31, 1963, Manchester, Lancs.) as a new member, reaches UK #18, and becomes a hot US college-airplay track.
May [27] ***Mind Bomb***, inspired by Johnson's recent reading of the Bible and the Koran, hits UK #4 in its week of entry, and will make US #138, as The The embarks on a major world tour, its first.
Aug [5] *Gravitate To Me* peaks at UK #63.
Oct [14] *Armageddon Days Are Here* makes UK #70.

1990

Mar [7] The The, comprising Johnson, Marr and ex-ABC's James Filer (bass) and David Palmer (drums), ends its North American tour at the Wiltern Theatre, Los Angeles, CA.
July Prior to summer dates opening for David Bowie on his US tour, The The performs at London's Royal Albert Hall.

1991

Mar [2] EP *Shades Of Blue* makes UK #54. Co-producer Bruce Lampcov and Johnson will collaborate the following year on a new The The album, recording at London's Hit Factory studio.

1993

Jan [16] *Dogs Of Lust* debuts at its UK #25 peak.
[21] The The is featured on BBC1-TV's "Top Of The Pops".
Feb [6] Fourteen years after Johnson's first recordings, ***Dusk***, described by Lampcov as "the Plastic Ono Band without the crap songs", bows at its UK #2 peak, behind Jam's ***Little Angels***, and will make US #142 on the 20th. Less political and more personal than previous efforts, it is supported with a world tour, featuring the current line-up of Keith Joyner, Jared Nickerson, D.C. Collard, Jim Fitting, Palmer and Johnson.
Apr [24] *Slow Motion Replay* reaches UK #35.
June [19] Johnson's 1980 solo album, ***Burning Blue Soul***, now issued on CD, charts for a week at UK #65.
[26] The extracted, *Love Is Stronger Than Death*, reaches UK #39.
Aug [28] The The performs on the second day of "Reading 93", near Reading, Berks.
Nov [20-21, 23-24, 26] The The supports Depeche Mode at five sellout shows at the Great Western Forum, Inglewood, CA.
Dec [16] The The performs at London's Brixton Academy.

1995

Feb [4] After The The's *Dis-Infected* EP has debuted at its UK #17 peak on Jan [15] the previous year, *I Saw The Light* now enters at its UK #31 high.
[25] ***Hanky Panky***, a collection of Hank Williams covers, reaches UK #28 in its week of entry. (Johnson had intended to use guest singers such as Leonard Cohen, Marianne Faithfull, Michael Stipe and Tom Waits on the project, but will reject this in favor of his own interpretations.)

THEM

Van Morrison (vocals, harmonica, sax);
Billy Harrison (lead guitar); **Jackie McAuley** (piano); **Alan Henderson** (bass);
Patrick McAuley (drums)

1963

The group is formed in Belfast, Northern Ireland, with Morrison (b. George Ivan, Aug. 31, 1945, Belfast), having had extensive experience as a member of the Monarchs, Harrison (b. Oct. 14, 1942, Belfast), Henderson (b. Nov. 26, 1944, Belfast), Eric Wrixen (piano) and Ronnie Millings (drums). One of the first R&B/beat groups in a country dominated by conservative "showbands", it builds its reputation as a strong live act during a residency at the R&B club at Belfast's Maritime Hotel.

1964

July Wrixen leaves to join the Wheels, and Millings quits to become a milkman, replaced by the McAuley brothers, Jackie (b. Dec. 14, 1946, Coleraine, Northern Ireland) (piano) and Pat (b. Mar. 17, 1944) (drums). The group moves to London, and signs to Decca Records.
Sept Its debut single, *Don't Start Crying Now*, is released with prominent sales in Belfast.

1965

Feb [13] Aided by "Ready Steady, Go!" TV appearances, *Baby Please Don't Go*, a sharp R&B version of a blues standard, hits UK #8. Like most later Them recordings, it is made with little contribution from the band itself; the producers, Tommy Scott and Bert Berns, back Morrison on vocals, with session-men, including Jimmy Page on guitar, and Peter Bardens on piano. Its B-side, little-played in Britain at the time, is the Morrison-penned *Gloria*, a riff-driven group favorite which frequently develops into a 20-minute jam when played live. It becomes an anthem to the emerging US garage band generation, fitting into their basic repertoire alongside *Louie Louie*. (It will be Them's most enduring number, and one of the most influential records of the '60s, despite its lack of early chart success.)
Apr [24] *Here Comes The Night*, written and produced by Berns (writer of *Twist And Shout* and *Hang On Sloopy*), hits UK #2, Them's biggest, but last, UK chart success. (Berns, an American working in London, cut *Here Comes The Night* the previous November with Lulu, when it made UK #50. He will work extensively with Them, mainly because he is impressed with Morrison as a vocalist. After this hit, he will return to the US to launch his own Bang label, bringing success to the Strangeloves, the McCoys and many others.) The debut album ***(The Angry Young) Them*** is released in Britain, featuring Morrison with various session-men, which causes the disillusioned McAuley brothers to quit and form their own, similar, R&B band, the Belfast Gypsies, with Ken McLeod and Mike Scott. Bardens joins for a while.
[11 The group plays at the annual "**New Musical Express** Poll Winners Concert", at the Empire Pool, Wembley, Middx. Morrison's distinctive vocals are the focus of Them's live appeal, which otherwise suffers from a lack of visual image, due to the ever-changing line-up.
May [28] *Gloria* peaks at US #71, selling mostly in California, where it hits Top 10 in some West Coast cities, while the Morrison-penned *One More Time* is released in the UK.
July [17] *Here Comes The Night* reaches US #24.
Aug *(It Won't Hurt) Half As Much*, written by Berns, is issued in Britain. Harrison leaves to work for the Irish post office, with Joe Boni and Terry Noon joining.
Sept Bardens, Noon and Boni all quit, leaving Morrison and Henderson as the only remaining members.
Sophomore effort, ***Them***, makes US #54.
Oct [1] The group returns to London to recommence ballroom dates with three new Irishmen in the line-up: John Wilson (b. Nov. 6, 1947) on drums, Jim Armstrong (b. July 24, 1944) on guitar and Ray Elliott (b. Sept. 13, 1943) on piano and saxophone, all credited on the recent album release.
Dec [11] *Mystic Eyes*, a Morrison-penned, harmonica-led rave-up taken from the album, makes US #33.

1966

Jan ***Them Again***, mixing R&B standards with originals, is released in the UK.
Apr The band (with Dave Harvey on drums) tours the US, playing mainly California dates, including the Fillmore West in San Francisco, CA, and the Troubadour Club in Los Angeles, CA.
May Aided by the group's live presence, *Gloria* climbs to US #71, but a US cover by the Shadows Of Knight hits US #10. ***Them Again*** reaches US #138.
June Them's return to Britain coincides with the release, on Decca, of a cover of Paul Simon's *Richard Cory*. It fails to sell, and the group splits. Morrison returns to Belfast where he will play gigs with friends, including Eric Bell, later of Thin Lizzy, before flying to the US at Berns' invitation, to sign to Berns' Bang label, and begin a successful solo career. Them will re-group in Los Angeles in 1967 in its final line-up, but with Belfast vocalist Ken McDowell in Morrison's place. Two US albums (***Now And Them*** and ***Time Out, Time In For Them***) on the Tower label, will appear between 1967-68, and the group will continue until the early '70s, re-recruiting some of its earliest members to cut ***In Reality*** (1971). The double album, ***Them Featuring Van Morrison***, a compilation of Decca material, will peak at US #154 in August 1972.

1991

Feb [16] After Henderson has recruited Mel Austin, Billy Bell, Billy Harrison and Eric Wrixen for a short-lived reunion tour and album (***Shut Your Mouth***) in 1979, a reissued *Baby Please Don't Go* peaks at UK #65.
see also: **Van MORRISON**

THIN LIZZY

Phil Lynott (vocals, bass); **Scott Gorham** (guitar); **Brian Robertson** (guitar);
Brian Downey (drums)

1969

The hard-rock-driven group is formed in Dublin, Eire, featuring Lynott (b. Aug. 20, 1951, Birmingham, Warks., the illegitimate son of a Brazilian father and

Irish mother, who at the age of three was sent to live with his grandmother in Crumlin, Dublin, and at 16 joined covers band, Black Eagles, and Downey (b. Jan. 27, 1951, Dublin), who have been at school together, and have played variously or together in Skid Row (whose line-up also included future Thin Lizzy guitarist, Gary Moore), Sugar Shack (whose version of Tim Rose's *Morning Dew* was a success in Northern Ireland), and Orphanage. They have been recruited, initially against Downey's wishes, from Orphanage by guitarist Eric Bell (b. Sept. 3, 1947, Belfast, Northern Ireland), earlier briefly with Them, and early keyboardist Eric Wrixen, and the band begins to play gigs around Ulster, sometimes fly-posted as "Tin Lizzie". (Legend has it that the name came from a character in the **Beano** comic, although it is also thought to be taken from the Ford Model-T car.)

1970

Apr Managed by Brian Tuite and Ted Carroll, the band makes its live debut in Newbridge, Northern Ireland, including two covers of Jimi Hendrix songs (with whom Lynott shares a similar, semi-Afro, hair-style).

Nov Alerted by the group's Irish reputation as a strong live act, Decca's A&R man, Frank Rodgers, spots them supporting Ditch Cassidy in Dublin, and signs the band, already minus Wricksen, to a three-year deal with the label. The trio moves to London to play club gigs, but a UK debut at the Speakeasy club in London proves less than successful.

1971

Apr The band's first album ***Thin Lizzy***, produced by US songwriter Scott English, and recorded in three days, is released by Decca, as the trio tours with Arrival and Worth at poorly-attended dates.

Aug [20] With Chris Morrison having taken over as manager from Tuite, the group releases the four-track EP, *New Day*.

1972

Mar [10] ***Shades Of A Blue Orphanage***, produced by Nick Tauber, featuring Clodagh Simonds on harpsichord and mellotron, and containing nine Lynott-penned songs, is released.

Dec The band supports Slade on a UK tour.

1973

Feb [24] *Whiskey In The Jar*, a guitar riff-driven rock version of a folk tune, is their first UK hit, at #6.

May *Randolph's Tango* is released as the follow-up.

Sept ***Vagabonds Of The Western World*** (not including *Whiskey In The Jar*), produced by Lynott and Tauber, showcasing a heavier rock style, is issued.

Dec [18] The group returns to Northern Ireland for annual Christmas gigs after a short tour of West Germany and Denmark.

[31] Bell storms off stage at a Queen's University, Belfast gig, leaving Lynott and Downey to finish as a duo.

1974

Jan Gary Moore, ex-Skid Row with Lynott, is recruited as Bell's replacement. (He will only stay for four months before leaving to join Jon Hiseman's Colosseum.)

May Guitarists Andy Gee (ex-Steve Ellis' band) and John Cann (ex-Bullitt) are brought in for an already-contracted tour of West Germany.

June Full-time guitarists Brian Robertson (b. Sept. 12, 1956, Glasgow, Strathclyde, Scotland) (who auditions in the same week as a drummer for Slack Alice), and Scott Gorham (b. Mar. 17, 1951, Santa Monica, CA) (who is playing the pub circuit with Fast Buck, when his brother-in-law, Supertramp's Bob Benberg, suggests he should try-out for Lizzy), both join.

Aug [24] The new line-up debuts at the 14th annual "National Jazz, Blues, Folk & Rock Festival", near Reading, Berks. A new recording deal is signed with Phonogram's progressive-rock label, Vertigo, as Chris O'Donnell becomes co-manager.

Oct Debut Vertigo single, *Philomena*, and album, ***Nightlife***, are released. Lynott's book of poems **Songs For While I'm Away**, is also published.

[4] New line-up begins a UK club and college tour at Aberystwyth University, Aberystwyth, Dyfed, Wales.

1975

Mar Already developing a strong drug-dependency, Lynott contracts hepatitis.

June A British tour includes a major headlining gig at London's Roundhouse.

July [12] Thin Lizzy and 10cc headline an open-air festival at Cardiff Castle, Cardiff, S. Glamorgan, Wales.

Aug [23] The group plays on the second day of the 15th National Jazz Blues & Rock Festival "Reading Rock '75", near Reading, Berks.

Sept [27] ***Fighting*** is the group's first chart album, at UK #60, and includes *Still In Love With You*, with guest vocalist Frankie Miller, with the band touring the UK to promote the album.

Nov *Wild One* is released.

Dec The group performs at the "Great British Music Festival", Olympia, London.

1976

Mar [5] Thin Lizzy begin a 15-date UK tour at Sheffield University, S. Yorks., set to end on the 20th at Liverpool Stadium, Merseyside.

May The band embarks on a US tour, "blowing away" headliners Bachman-Turner Overdrive, but the trek is cut short when Lynott once again contracts hepatitis.

July [3] *The Boys Are Back In Town*, from the forthcoming ***Jailbreak*** album, hits UK #8.

[24] *The Boys Are Back In Town* reaches US #12.

Aug [21] The extracted title song, *Jailbreak*, makes UK #31.

Sept [4] ***Jailbreak***, produced by John Alcock, is the band's major breakthrough album, hitting UK #10 in a 50-week chart run, and also marks the band's US chart debut, reaching #18 and earning a gold disc.

Oct [30] *Cowboy Song* is the band's second (and last) US chart single, at #77.

Nov [6] ***Johnny The Fox*** reaches UK #11.

[14-16] The group plays at London's Hammersmith Odeon, during its "Johnny The Fox" tour.

[27] ***Johnny The Fox*** makes US #56.

Dec Robertson severs tendons in his hands following a brawl at London's Speakeasy club, on the eve of a US tour. He is unable to play on the ten-week trek supporting Queen, and Gary Moore returns to replace him.

1977

Feb [5] *Don't Believe A Word*, from ***Johnny The Fox***, reaches UK #12.

Mar [25] An announcement is made that Robertson is leaving the band permanently.

May Moore returns to Colosseum (from which he has been "on loan") and Robertson, having recovered and toured with Graham Parker & the Rumour, deputizing for Brinsley Schwarz, re-joins Thin Lizzy for the recording of ***Bad Reputation*** in Toronto, ON, Canada, despite earlier reports that he would not do so.

Aug [27] The group plays on the second day of the 17th National Jazz Blues & Rock Festival "Reading Rock '77", during a European tour, which also includes a bill-topping date at Dalymount Park, Dublin.

Sept [10] *Dancin' In The Moonlight (It's Caught Me In The Spotlight)*, taken from ***Bad Reputation***, reaches UK #14.

Oct [8] ***Bad Reputation*** hits UK #4.

[20] ***Jailbreak*** is certified gold by the RIAA.

[29] ***Bad Reputation*** makes US #39.

Nov The group embarks on the 27-date sellout UK leg of its "Bad Reputation" tour, ending with two dates at London's Hammersmith Odeon in December.

1978

Mar The group's concert at London's Rainbow Theatre is televised.

May Thin Lizzy embarks on a European tour.

June [24] Performance double album, ***Live And Dangerous***, hits UK #2 (and will stay on the UK survey for 62 weeks). It yields the live medley, *Rosalie/Cowgirl's Song*, which reaches UK #20.

July Robertson plays his last dates with the band at an Ibiza bullring.

Aug Robertson quits again, to form Wild Horses, replaced, once again, by Moore.

Sept ***Live And Dangerous*** makes US #84, supported by another US tour with Mark Nauseet deputizing for Downey, who will spend time with his sick son. (He will re-join for Australian dates and a Christmas show in London.)

1979

Mar [24] *Waiting For An Alibi*, from the group's next album, hits UK #9, as the group embarks on another UK tour.

May [12] ***Black Rose (A Rock Legend)*** is their second consecutive UK #2 album, held from the top by ***The Very Best Of Leo Sayer***. Meanwhile, Moore's solo single on MCA, *Parisienne Walkways*, hits UK #8, featuring Lynott as guest vocalist.

June [16] ***Black Rose (A Rock Legend)*** makes US #81.

July [14] *Do Anything You Want To* reaches UK #14.

[17] Moore is sacked by the band's management during a US tour, and is temporarily replaced by ex-Slik and Rich Kids (and future Ultravox) guitarist, Midge Ure.

[28] The group appears at the "World Series Of Rock" concert at Cleveland Stadium, OH, along with Journey, Ted Nugent and Aerosmith.

Aug Ure, never intended as a permanent guitarist in the band, remains for a tour of Japan after the US visit (while Manfred Mann's Earthband's Dave Flett also joins), before leaving for Ultravox.

[25] Thin Lizzy headlines the second day of the 19th National Jazz Blues & Rock Festival "Reading Rock '79".

Nov [12] Guitarist Snowy White (ex-Pink Floyd's live band, Jonathan Kelly, Peter Green) replaces Ure.

Dec [1] *Sarah* reaches UK #24.

1980

Jan [5] The Greedies' *A Merry Jingle*, a seasonal novelty featuring Lynott and members of the Sex Pistols and the Boomtown Rats, reaches UK #28.

Feb [13] Lynott marries Caroline Crowther, daughter of UK TV personality, Leslie Crowther.

Apr [26] Lynott releases his first solo single, *Dear Miss Lonely Hearts*, which makes UK #32.

May His debut album, ***Solo In Soho***, featuring session players Jimmy Bain (bass), Rusty Egan (drums), Darren Wharton (keyboards) and guests Huey Lewis and Ure, reaches UK #28.

July [12] *Chinatown*, the title track from Thin Lizzy's forthcoming album, reaches UK #21, as Lynott's solo single, *King's Call*, featuring Mark Knopfler on guitar, a tribute to Elvis Presley, makes UK #35.

Oct [11] *Killer On The Loose* hitting UK #10. (Its lyrics cause controversy in the wake of the Yorkshire Ripper killings.)

[18] ***Chinatown*** hits UK #7.

Dec ***Chinatown*** peaks at US #120.

1981

Feb The group embarks on a Scandinavian tour with new member, 18-year old Wharton.

Mar [28] Lynott's solo effort, *Yellow Pearl*, makes UK #56.

Apr TV-promoted compilation, ***Adventures Of Thin Lizzy***, hits UK #6.

May [23] EP *Killers Live*, including *Bad Reputation, Are You Ready* and *Dear Miss Lonely Hearts*, reaches UK #19.

June The group headlines a concert at Milton Keynes, Beds.

Aug [22] *Trouble Boys* peaks at UK #53, as the group sets out on a European tour followed by a UK trek at year's end.

Dec [12] ***Renegade*** makes UK #38, the last album to feature White, who leaves for a solo career (and a spell with Whitesnake), to be replaced by ex-Streetfighters and Tygers Of Pan Tang guitarist, John Sykes.

1982

Jan [23] Lynott's *Yellow Pearl* is reissued, this time climbing to UK #14, having been selected as the new theme tune to BBC1-TV's "Top Of The Pops". It also appears on his second solo album, ***The Philip Lynott Album***.
[20] Lynott appears with Rick Derringer and Charlie Daniels in a UNICEF benefit show at the Savoy Hotel, New York.
Mar [13] *Hollywood (Down On Your Luck)*, from ***Renegade***, peaks at UK #53.
[27] ***Renegade*** makes US #157.
Apr [22] The group begins an eight-date UK tour which will end on May 1st at London's Dominion Theatre.

1983

Mar ***Thunder And Lightning***, the group's final studio set, hits UK #4.
Feb [26] Extracted *Cold Sweat* reaches UK #27.
Apr The group walks off the "Top Of The Pops" set, after turning up two hours late and being verbally abused by the producer.
May [7] The extracted title cut, *Thunder And Lightning*, reaches UK #39, as the band begins a final tour of Europe and Japan, ending with four nights at London's Hammersmith Odeon, with Bell, Robertson and Moore all making cameo appearances.
June ***Thunder And Lightning*** makes US #159.
Aug [6] The band splits, Lynott feeling that it has become predictable and directionless, while a final chart single, *The Sun Goes Down*, peaks at UK #52. Lynott, Downey, and Sykes briefly tour Scandinavia as the Three Musketeers.
[28] Thin Lizzy plays its last UK show, headlining the annual "Reading Festival".
Sept [4] They play their final date at Zeppelinfield, Nuremberg, Germany, as part of the "Monsters Of Rock" European tour.

1984

Feb Lynott forms Grand Slam with Laurence Archer (guitar), Mark Stanway (keyboards) and Downey (who will quit by June to be replaced by Robbie Brennan.) (Gorham will re-appear in 1992 forming 21 Guns with A440 singer, Tommy LaVerdi, and Leif Johannsen and Mike Sturgis, both from a-ha's backing band.)
Dec A double Thin Lizzy album, ***Life - Live***, recorded live before the split, reaches UK #29. Its tracks feature all the ex-Thin Lizzy guitarists in spotlighted roles.

1985

Feb ***Life - Live*** peaks at US #185. Lynott goes solo again to cut *Nineteen*, with Paul Hardcastle producing (but not the same song as the latter's own hit of the same title).
June [8] Moore and Lynott hit UK #5 with *Out In The Fields*.
Sept Dublin Judge Gillian Hussey finds Lynott guilty of a narcotics possession charge, prophetically stating that "as long as he is only using these drugs himself and not giving them to others, he is only destroying himself".

1986

Jan [4] Lynott dies of "heart failure and pneumonia following septacaemia" in Salisbury General Infirmary, Salisbury, Wilts., with his wife Caroline and father-in-law, Leslie Crowther, by his bedside. (Following an overdose, he has been in a coma for eight days.) He is buried in Howth, his grave overlooking Dublin Bay.
May [17] The remaining members of Thin Lizzy re-form for a one-off date at the "Self Aid" concert in Dublin, its act a tribute to Lynott, with Bob Geldof handling vocals. ***Soldier Of Fortune - The Best Of Phil Lynott And Thin Lizzy*** will make UK #55 on Nov [28] the following year.

1996

Jan [20] After *Dedication* has debuted at its UK #35 peak on Jan [26], 1991, previewing the 18-track anthology, ***Dedication - The Very Best Of Thin Lizzy***, which hit UK #8 on Feb [16], the re-released *The Boys Are Back In Town*, originally a 1976 UK #8, also re-charted for a week at UK #63 on Mar [23] the same year. While past alumni of Thin Lizzy performed a one-off reunion, with six former members, at the Civic Hall, Wolverhampton, West Midlands on August 20th, 1994, a further retrospective, ***Wild One - The Very Best Of Thin Lizzy*** now reaches UK #18. Hot Press Books in Eire will publish **My Boy - The Philip Lynott Story**, written by his mother Philomena with Jackie Hayden, on the tenth anniversary of his death.

RICHARD THOMPSON

1972

June Guitarist/singer/songwriter Thompson (b. Apr. 3, 1949, Totteridge, London), already a veteran performer and principal songwriter with Britain's earliest folk innovators, Fairport Convention, which he co-founded in 1967 with Judy Dyble, Ashley Hutchings, Martin Lamble, Ian Matthews and Simon Nicol, leaves the band in January 1971 after writing material for the group's sixth album, ***Angel Delight***. Having completed the album ***Rock On*** with assorted Fairport alumni earlier in the year under the group name Bunch, and signed to Fairport's manager and producer Joe Boyd's production company, Thompson now releases his debut solo album on Island Records, ***Henry The Human Fly***, featuring ex-Bunch singer Linda Peters on vocals, with whom he strikes up a professional and personal relationship, subsequently marrying her.
Oct Richard and Linda join folk outfit the Albion Country Band for three months of UK dates.

1974

Feb Richard and Linda Thompson release the highly-acclaimed ***I Want To See The Bright Lights Tonight***, subsequently touring with ex-Fairport Convention colleague Nicol, billed as the trio Hokey Pokey, and then the five-piece Sour Grapes (between March and May), including a European tour supporting Traffic.

1975

Mar Island releases the duo's ***Hokey Pokey***.
Apr [25] During a UK tour, Sour Grapes perform at London's Queen Elizabeth Hall, where they are joined by Fairport's Dave Mattacks and Dave Pegg, and Steeleye Span's John Kirkpatrick.
Aug The Thompsons, recently converted to the Sufi-Moslem religion, appear at the annual "Reading Festival" in Reading, Berks.
Nov ***Pour Like Silver*** is released, the husband-and-wife team's second album of the year.

1976

May Island issues ***Guitar, Vocal***, a double album collection of Thompson rarities and previously unreleased material. Following a two-month UK tour beginning in April 1977 which will yield their final Island outing, ***Almost Live (More Or Less)***, the duo will sign to Chrysalis Records, releasing ***First Light***, supported by a UK tour, in November 1978.

1979

Feb With backing players Pegg, Kirkpatrick, Sue Harris and Mike Arscott, the Thompsons embark on another UK tour, promoting ***Sunnyvista***, following which Thompson records sessions with Gerry Rafferty, which will not be made public until 1993, though some of the songs are re-recorded for the subsequent ***Shoot Out The Lights*** project.

1981

Sept Having appeared with Linda at one of Fairport Convention's annual reunion concerts in August the previous year, and now returning to a solo career, Thompson releases his second solo effort, the entirely instrumental ***Strict Tempo*** on the Elixir Label.

1982

June With the release of their final collaboration, ***Shoot Out The Lights***, another warmly received critical success, Richard and Linda, their marriage dissolving, make their last live appearance together at the South Yorkshire Folk Festival, Sheffield, S. Yorks. (She will go on to release ***One Clear Moment***, a solo album for Warner Bros. in 1985.)
Dec Thompson issues the live performance set, ***Small Town Romance***.

1983

Sept Now married to US concert promoter Nancy Covey, the Celtic-tinged ***Hand Of Kindness***, still produced by Boyd, and featuring Clive Gregson (former frontman for Any Trouble), Nicol and Dave Mattacks among others, reaches UK #186.

1985

Apr [27] Newly signed to Polydor Records, ***Across A Crowded Room*** becomes his first UK chart album, at #80, having made US #102 on the 13th.

1986

Oct [18] With the Mitchell Froom-produced ***Daring Adventures*** peaking at UK #92 (and US #142), Thompson undertakes UK and US tours with a backing band featuring Gregson and Christine Collister.

1987

Oct ***The Marksman*** is issued by BBC Records, the Thompson-scored soundtrack to a BBC-TV drama series, while ***Live, Love, Larf And Loaf***, an avant-garde, improvisational work with Fred Frith, John French, Henry Kaiser and Thompson, appears before year's end.

1988

Oct [29] Now signed to Capitol Records, his label debut, ***Amnesia***, reaches UK #89, making US #182 in November.

1991

May [25] ***Rumor And Sigh*** debuts at its UK #32 peak.
July [9] Thompson guests on NBC-TV's "Late Night With David Letterman" and then performs at the Ritz, New York, NY.
Oct [11] He is showcased on ABC-TV's "In Concert '91".
[18] Thompson appears on the fourth night of the "Guitar Legends" axe fest held in Seville, Spain.
Sept The Golden Palaminos' ***Drunk With Passion***, prominently featuring Thompson, is released.
Nov [2] He collects the Solo Artist, Songwriter Of The Year and the Life Achievement trophies, at the New Music Awards, New York, NY.

1992

Feb [25] Thompson performs on C4-TV's "Return To The Dome".
Mar [19] During US dates, he plays at the Berklee Performance Center, Boston, MA, sharing the bill with Roger McGuinn.
[24] Thompson performs with David Byrne at an acoustic benefit for the Arts, at the Church of St. Ann and the Holy Trinity, Brooklyn, New York.
June [1] Thompson embarks on a 20-date UK tour at the Bath Forum, set to end on the 26th at Edinburgh's Queens Hall, to promote his latest effort, the critically-praised ***Sweet Talker***.
[9] Jennifer Warnes' ***The Hunter***, featuring Thompson on *Lights Of Louisianne*, is released.
July [18] He plays at the Wolf Trap Farm Park for the Performing Arts, Vienna, VA, supporting Mary-Chapin Carpenter, before a crowd of 7,117.
Aug [14-15] Thompson appears on the "Cropredy Festival" bill, Cropredy, Oxon.
Sept Suzanne Vega's ***99.9°F*** is released, with Thompson guesting on *As Girls Go*.

1993

Apr [30] Thompson duets with Tim Finn at a party to

celebrate the launch of Virgin Radio at London's Piccadilly Theatre.
May [4] US label Rykodisc releases a three-CD/cassette boxed set, ***Watching The Dark : The History Of Richard Thompson***, a 47-track retrospective, from his early recordings with Fairport Convention to the present, which includes three tracks from the never-released 1980 sessions he recorded, with Gerry Rafferty producing.
June [12] Thompson participates in Los Lobos' 20th anniversary concert at the Greek Theatre, Griffith Park, Los Angeles.
July [9] He guests on CBS-TV's "Late Show With David Letterman".

1994

Jan [1] Thompson performs at Ronnie Scott's, with Christine Collier, Pete Thomas and Danny Thompson.
[29] ***Mirror Blue*** reaches UK #23 in its week of entry.
Feb [14] He takes part in the 20th anniversary celebrations of New York's Bottom Line, with Shawn Colvin.
[16] Thompson guests on CBS-TV's "Late Show With David Letterman".
[26] ***Mirror Blue*** debuts at its US #109 peak, as Thompson guests on BBC2-TV's "Later With Jools Holland".
Mar [11] He embarks on a North American tour in Portland, OR.
Oct Capitol releases ***Beat The Retreat - The Songs OF Richard Thompson***, a Thompson tribute album with interpretations of his songs by David Byrne, Beausoleil, Dinosaur Jr., Los Lobos, Shawn Colvin & Loudon Wainwright III, Graham Parker, Bonnie Raitt, R.E.M, Syd Straw & Evan Dando and X, among others.

1995

Jan [20] Thompson embarks on a 27-date UK and Irish tour at the Ulster Hall, Belfast, Northern Ireland, set to end on February 26th at the Theatre Royal, Nottingham, Notts.
June [25] He takes part in the "Jazz & Blues Festival" at the Filene Center for the Performing Arts, Wolf Trap Farm Park, Vienna, VA.
Aug [12] Thompson participates in the annual "Cropredy Festival".
Sept Non-bootleg mail order album, ***Live At Crawley***, is released by Flypaper Records (US).

1996

Apr [20] His latest album, the double-CD ***You? Me? Us?***, comprising one disc of acoustic ballads, the other, a darkly electric set, debuts at its UK #32 peak.
May [4] *You? Me? Us?* makes US #97 in its week of entry.
June [3] Following a recently-completed UK tour, Thompson begins a month-long US trek at the Mann Music Center, Philadelphia, PA, set to end on July 14th at the Summer Nights At The Pier, Seattle, WA.
see also: **FAIRPORT CONVENTION**

THE THOMPSON TWINS

Tom Bailey (vocals, keyboards);
Joe Leeway (percussion); **Alannah Currie** (vocals, saxophone, percussion)

1977

Aspiring classical pianist Bailey (b. June 18, 1957, Halifax, Yorks.), having met friends Leeway (b. Nov. 15, 1957, London) and John Hadd at teacher-training college, initially ignores these associations and forms the Thompson Twins (named after a pair of identical detectives in Hergé's cartoon creation, **Tin Tin**), with guitarists Peter Dodd (b. Oct. 27, 1953) and John Roog in Chesterfield, Derbys. Moving to London in 1978, with Hadd as their agent, they link up with drummer Chris Bell and, equipped with a van and a PA, they begin constant London gigging in pubs and clubs with the pledge that they can play anywhere, anytime (which they do for two years), and are also particularly active for the "Rock Against Racism" cause.

1980

May The group's first release, *Squares And Triangles*, is on its own independent Dirty Discs label.
July [21] The band plays at London's Hope & Anchor pub.
Nov Another independent label, Latent, releases *She's In Love With Mystery*, which becomes a UK Independent chart-topper, while Bailey begins dating Currie (b. Sept. 20, 1959, Auckland, North Island, New Zealand).

1981

Feb The band signs to Arista Records in the UK, with *Perfect Game* issued on the Tee imprint.
June Ex-Japan saxophonist, Jane Shorter, has been recruited to help Bailey, Dodd, Roog and Bell record the group's debut album, ***A Product Of ...***, which includes the extracted *Animal Laugh*.
Aug During an album-promotion tour, Currie joins the band on percussion, while old friend Leeway, until now a roadie, is also invited by Bailey to join, after the group buys him a pair of bongos.
[30] The band performs on the final day of the 21st National Rock Festival "Reading Rock '81", near Reading, Berks.
Sept *Make Believe* is released.

1982

Jan Shorter is fired as ex-Soft Boys bassist, Matthew Seligman, is recruited.
Mar ***Set***, produced by Steve Lillywhite and promoted by live performances, makes UK #48. Taken from it, *In The Name Of Love* becomes a hot US club hit (#1 on the Dance chart) while ***Set***, released in the US as ***In The Name Of Love*** peaks at US #148.
Apr After a successful UK university/college tour, a US visit is offered. Manager Hadd turns it down, also firing Bell, Dodd, Seligman and Roog, leaving the Thompson Twins as a permanent trio creatively led by Bailey. (Seligman will play live with David Bowie, while Bell will join Spear Of Destiny, Specimen and Gene Loves Jezebel.)
May After *Runaway* is released, Arista drops the Tee subsidiary, and releases all future product on its main label.
Oct Their first Arista disc, *Lies*, peaks at UK #67, the first in a string of chart hits, as the group embarks on an extensive UK tour, with Tears For Fears supporting.

1983

Jan The trio-penned *Love On Your Side* hits UK #9.
Mar Proving to be a commercial turning point, ***Quick Step And Side Kick***, written by Thompson, Currie and Leeway, and produced by Alex Sadkin in Nassau, hits UK #2. Released in the US as ***Side Kicks***, it will peak at #34 during a 25-week run.
[26] *Lies* reaches US #30, aided by strong club and dance reaction.
Apr *We Are Detective* hits UK #7, and features Currie's vocals for the first time.
June [4] *Love On Your Side* makes US #45.
July *Watching*, featuring Grace Jones on backing vocals, makes UK #33.
Nov *Hold Me Now*, introducing a firm slow style, hits UK #4.

1984

Feb *Doctor Doctor* hits UK #3.
[25] The group's third album, ***Into The Gap***, co-helmed by Bailey and Sadkin, hits UK #1 for the first of three weeks. (In the US it will stay charted for over a year, and hit #10 after six months.)
Mar *You Take Me Up* hits UK #2.
[18] The band performs at the Birmingham Odeon, West Midlands, during current UK dates.
May [5] *Hold Me Now* hits US #3.
June *Sister Of Mercy* reaches UK #11.
July [21] *Doctor Doctor* reaches US #11, while the group undertakes a world tour.
Oct [2] ***Into The Gap*** is certified platinum by the RIAA.
[6] *You Take Me Up* makes US #44.
Nov *Lay Your Hands On Me* reaches UK #13.
Dec [1] The US-only release, *The Gap*, peaks at #69.

1985

Feb [2] Foreigner's *I Want To Know What Love Is*, featuring keyboard work from Bailey, tops the US chart.
Mar Having toured endlessly for two years, and now writing and producing a new album, Bailey falls sick through exhaustion. Current live work is suspended, and US producer, Nile Rodgers, is recruited to complete the project.
July [13] Bailey recuperates in time for the group's appearance at the "Live Aid" benefit concert in Philadelphia, PA. Madonna joins them for their set, which includes a version of the Beatles' *Revolution*.
Sept [7] The anti-drug-themed *Don't Mess With Doctor Dream* reaches UK #15.
[28] ***Here's To Future Days*** hits UK #5.
Nov [2] From it, *King For A Day* reaches UK #22.
[23] Nearly a year after its UK success, *Lay Your Hands On Me* hits US #6.
[26] ***Here's To Future Days*** is certified gold by the RIAA.
Dec *Revolution* peaks at UK #56.

1986

Feb ***Here's To Future Days*** reaches US #20.
Mar [22] *King For A Day* hits US #8.
Sept [13] *Nothing In Common*, the Thompson Twins' title track for the newly-released Tom Hanks/Jackie Gleason starring movie, makes US #54.
Dec Leeway, frustrated with growing internal friction, quits the group, leaving Bailey and Currie (who has recently been made an Honorary Cultural Ambassador for New Zealand) as the Thompson Twins.

1987

Jan Major tour dates are postponed as Currie goes through serious personal problems, and re-scheduled UK gigs are cancelled.
Mar Following early promotion at the "Montreux Music Festival" in Montreux, Switzerland, their first single as a duo, *Get That Love*, peaks at UK #66.
May [2] ***Close To The Bone***, produced by Rupert Hine, charts for a week at UK #90, and will peak at US #76.
[16] *Get That Love* reaches US #31.
June *Long Goodbye* is their first UK single in five years not to chart.

1988

Apr Currie and Bailey have their first child.
Sept ***Greatest Mixes***, a collection of hits and remixes, peaks at US #175.
Oct A remix of *In The Name Of Love* makes UK #46.

1989

Oct ***Big Trash***, the first fruits of a major new recording contract with Warner Bros. Records, peaks at US #143, while Deborah Harry's debut Sire album, ***Def, Dumb & Blonde***, featuring two cuts co-produced by Bailey, is released.
Nov [18] Extracted from ***Big Trash***, *Sugar Daddy* reaches US #28.

1990

Mar [24] UK-only released Stylus TV-advertised ***The Greatest Hits*** reaches #23, in its week of entry.
Nov AIDS benefit album, ***Red Hot + Blue***, featuring the band's version of the 1956 standard, *Who Wants To Be A Millionaire*, hits UK #6.

1991

Oct [5] *Come Inside* peaks at UK #56.
Nov ***Queer***, a second Warner Bos. effort, is released, the first Thompson Twins album in ten years not to make the UK or US charts. The excerpted *The Saint* will peak at UK #53 on Feb [1] the following year.

1993

July Now recording under a new band name, Bailey and Currie's first cut as Babble, *Chale Jao* is featured on the soundtrack to the Dan Aykroyd-starring movie, "The Coneheads", with their debut album, the ambient-based ***The Stone*** also featuring third member Keith Fernley, released in October by Reprise Records.

THREE DOG NIGHT

Danny Hutton (vocals); **Cory Wells** (vocals); **Chuck Negron** (vocals); **Mike Allsup** (guitar); **Jimmy Greenspoon** (organ); **Joe Schermie** (bass); **Floyd Sneed** (drums)

1968

The group is formed in Los Angeles, CA, by Hutton (b. Sept. 10, 1946, Buncrana, Eire, and raised in the US), an ex-freelance producer and session singer with Hanna-Barbera Productions, who has had a solo hit with the self-penned (and produced) *Roses And Rainbows* (US #73 in 1965). After auditioning unsuccessfully for the Monkees and recording a one-off (unreleased) single (*Thinkin' Bout You Baby*) as Redwood for the Beach Boys' Brother label, he conceives the idea of a rock group with a triple lead singer line-up, and enlists Wells (b. Feb. 5, 1944, Buffalo, NY), whom he has produced for MGM as a member of the Enemies, and Negron (b. June 8, 1942, The Bronx, New York, NY), who has previously recorded as a soloist (without chart success) for CBS/Columbia. The backing quartet of Greenspoon (b. Feb. 7, 1948, Los Angeles), Sneed (b. Nov. 22, 1943, Calgary, AB, Canada), Allsup (b. Mar. 8, 1947, Modesto, CA) and Schermie (b. Feb. 12, 1945, Madison, WI) is assembled from a variety of backgrounds, from Los Angeles session work to country, gospel and backing José Feliciano. The group name derives from an Australian expression: in the outback, the colder the night, the more dogs you sleep beside to share warmth: coldest is a three-dog night.

Nov Signed to Lou Adler's Dunhill label, ***Three Dog Night*** is released (together with *Nobody*), produced by Gabriel Mekler, and mainly comprising cover versions. (The group's forté will always be personalized versions of outside writers' material, which sees the outfit running against the grain of most late '60s/early '70s rock, but results in it being an early champion of writers like Randy Newman, Harry Nilsson, Laura Nyro and Leo Sayer.)

Dec [28] The group appears at the Miami Pop Festival, at the Gulfstream Racing Park, in Hallandale, FL, before a 100,000 crowd, on a bill with Chuck Berry, Fleetwood Mac, Country Joe & the Fish, Joni Mitchell and Canned Heat, among others.

1969

Apr [19] From their debut album, a revival of *Try A Little Tenderness*, based on Otis Redding's 1967 soul version, is the group's first US chart single, at #29.

June [20] Three Dog Night takes part in the "Newport '69" Festival at San Fernando Valley State College, Devonshire Downs, Northridge, CA.

[28] A Harry Nilsson song, *One*, the last single taken from ***Three Dog Night***, hits US #5. During a 62-week chart stay, the album climbs to US #11 and will be the first of 12 consecutive gold albums.

July [23] *One* is certified gold by the RIAA.

Aug [15] ***Three Dog Night*** is also confirmed gold by the RIAA.

Sept [27] The band's version of *Easy To Be Hard* (from the rock musical, "Hair") hits US #4. It is taken from ***Suitable For Framing***, which reaches US #16 during 74 charted weeks.

Nov [29] Also from the album, their treatment of Nyro's *Eli's Coming* hits US #10.

Dec [23] ***Suitable For Framing*** is certified gold by the RIAA.

1970

Jan [16] Recorded on stage in Los Angeles, ***Captured Live At The Forum*** is certified gold by the RIAA on its way to hit US #6.

Mar [28] Bonner/Gordon's gospel-styled *Celebrate* reaches US #15.

July [11] Their revival of Randy Newman's *Mama Told Me (Not To Come)*, previously cut by Eric Burdon as an album track, tops the US chart for the first of two weeks. It is included on ***It Ain't Easy***, produced by Richard Podolor (who had engineered the previous album), which hits US #9.

[14] The RIAA certifies gold sales of *Mama Told Me Not To Come* and ***It Ain't Easy***.

Sept *Mama Told Me (Not To Come)* is the band's UK chart debut, hitting #3.

Oct [17] *Out In The Country*, also from ***It Ain't Easy***, reaches US #15.

1971

Jan [9] *One Man Band*, from the band's forthcoming ***Naturally***, reaches US #19.

Feb ***Naturally*** makes US #14.

Apr [9] The RIAA certifies gold sales of the still-rising *Joy To The World* and the recently peaked ***Naturally***.

[12] The still-climbing compilation ***Golden Bisquits*** is also confirmed gold by the RIAA.

[17] The closing track from ***Naturally***, *Joy To The World*, first presented to the group by its composer, Hoyt Axton, via a rendition in the recording studio, becomes their second US #1 at the start of a six-week run (despite Axton himself reportedly being disappointed by the group's cover). With sales of over two million, it is the biggest-selling single of 1971 in the US, and also the biggest seller both for the group and for Dunhill Records. Meanwhile, ***Golden Bisquits***, rounding up their singles to date, hits US #5.

June *Joy To The World* makes UK #24, the group's second and final UK hit.

July On tour in Europe, the band hears the reggae arrangement of *Black And White* by Greyhound (a UK #6), and determines to record it.

Aug [28] Their treatment of Russ Ballard's song, *Liar* (originally cut by his group Argent) hits US #7.

Oct [13] The still-climbing ***Harmony*** is certified gold by the RIAA.

Dec [18] *An Old Fashioned Love Song*, written by Paul Williams, hits US #4, taken from ***Harmony***, which hits US #8.

[29] *An Old Fashioned Love Song* is certified gold by the RIAA.

1972

Feb [12] Also from the album, *Never Been To Spain*, another Axton song (and later performed live by both Tom Jones and Elvis Presley) hits US #5.

Apr [29] *The Family Of Man* reaches US #12.

July [28] Yet-to-peak ***Seven Separate Fools*** is certified gold by the RIAA.

Sept [16] The group has its third (and final) US #1, and sixth million-selling single (certified on October 2nd), with the racial harmony-themed *Black And White* (written in 1955 by Earl Robinson and David Arkin, in response to the 1954 US Supreme Court ruling banning segregation in US schools). It is included on ***Seven Separate Fools***, which hits US #6.

1973

Jan [13] *Pieces Of April*, written by Dave Loggins, peaks at US #19.

Mar [6] The still-rising ***Around The World With Three Dog Night*** is certified gold by the RIAA.

May Live double album, ***Around The World With Three Dog Night***, recorded on various worldwide tour dates, reaches US #18.

June [20] The group appears on the 20th anniversary special of Dick Clark's "American Bandstand" on ABC-TV, along with Little Richard and Paul Revere & the Raiders.

July [24] Yet-to-peak *Shambala* is certified gold by the RIAA.

[28] *Shambala* hits US #3. Schermie leaves, and is replaced on bass by Jack Ryland. A new keyboards player, Skip Konte, also joins, making the group an eight-piece.

Nov ***Cyan***, ratified gold on October 12th, and including *Shambala*, peaks at US #26.

Dec [1] *Let Me Serenade You*, from ***Cyan***, reaches US #17.

1974

May [25] The group's version of the Leo Sayer chart-topper, *The Show Must Go On*, hits US #4, its final million-selling single, while its parent album, ***Hard Labor***, works its way to US #20.

Aug [10] *Sure As I'm Sittin' Here* makes US #16.

Nov [16] *Play Something Sweet (Brickyard Blues)* peaks at US #33.

1975

Feb Compilation, ***Joy To The World - Their Greatest Hits***, already confirmed gold on January 14th, reaches US #15, and is the last of the group's 12 consecutive gold albums.

July [3] On the opening night of a US tour, Negron is arrested in his hotel room in Louisville, KY, and charged with cocaine possession. (The charge will be dropped in court in October, on the grounds that the warrant used for the arrest was issued on "unfounded information".)

Aug Dunhill is absorbed into parent company, ABC, and the group's first album on the new label, ***Coming Down Your Way***, peaks at US #70.

[16] From it, a Dave Loggins' song, *'Til The World Ends*, is the band's final US singles chart entry, reaching #32.

1976

May ***American Pastime*** peaks at US #123, despite continuing success in live work. Hutton leaves and is replaced by new vocalist, Jay Gruska, while three former members of Rufus - Al Ciner, Ron Stocker and Denny Belfield, join the expanded backing band, as the group becomes more of a cabaret soul revue troupe, but splits before making any further recordings.

1981

June After varied solo work (Hutton has produced new wave bands in Los Angeles, including Fear), Three Dog Night re-forms for live work in the US, around the original vocal nucleus of Hutton, Negron and Wells. ***The Big Chill*** movie soundtrack, featuring *Joy To The World*, will enter the US chart on its way to #17 on Oct [22], 1983.

1993

Dec [7] Having successfully fought a legal battle in August 1989 to continue using the Three Dog Night name for touring, and performed at Superbowl XXV in January 1991, the veteran troupe, now plays consistently on the nostalgia circuit, appearing, for example, at the Champlain Valley Exposition, Essex Junction, VT, with the Grass Roots on September 6th, 1992. Following a return recording on the Passport label released as ***It's A Jungle EP*** earlier this year, a 43-track two-CD/cassette career anthology, ***Celebrate : The Three Dog Night Story***, is now made available in the US by MCA Records.

THUNDER

Danny Bowes (vocals); **Luke Morley** (guitarist); **Mark Luckhurst** (bass); **Gary James** (drums); **Ben Matthews** (guitar)

1989

Bowes (b. Apr. 14, 1960), Morley (b. June 19, 1960) and James (b. Dec. 14, 1960) have already achieved moderate success with UK lite-rock outfit Terraplane in the mid-'80s, issuing the 1986 UK #74-peaking ***Black And White*** and follow-up ***Moving Target*** (1987), but, released from their contract with Epic Records, now form the nucleus of Thunder, enlisting Luckhurst and a second guitarist Matthews (b. July 21, 1963). Impressed by their Bad Company-influenced demo tape of rootsy-rock and power ballads, the group is promptly signed by EMI Records for a UK-only deal.

1990

Mar [21] Its well-received debut album, the blues/rock ***Backstreet Symphony***, produced by Duran Duran's Andy Taylor, debuts at its UK #21 peak, earning a gold disc.
Aug With Thunder performing as the opening act at the annual "Monsters of Rock" festival at Castle Donington, Leics., Whitesnake's David Coverdale encourages Geffen Records A&R chief John Kaldoner to see the band, coinciding with a separate recommendation by Axl Rose in the US to Geffen executive Ed Rosenblatt. Suitably impressed, the label signs Thunder to a US contract following a showcase at New York's Cat Club.
Nov [14] A 21-date UK tour bows at the Colston Hall, Bristol, Avon, set to end at the De Montfort Hall, Leicester, Leics. on December 12th.

1991

Jan [20] Thunder performs at the "Great British Music Weekend" at Wembley Arena, Wembley, Middx.
Mar [2] *Love Walked In* reaches UK #21.
June [29] ***Backstreet Symphony***, largely written by Morley, peaks at US #114.
July [6] The group takes part in the "Rock The Bowl '91" concert at Milton Keynes Bowl, with Z.Z. Top, Bryan Adams and Little Angels.
[13] The extracted *Dirty Love* makes US #55.
Sept EMI issues a CD twin-set, pairing ***Backstreet Symphony*** with ***Backstreet Symphony Live***.
Dec [3] The group begins a further eight-date UK tour at the Ulster Hall, Belfast, Northern Ireland, set to end on the 12th at the De Montfort Hall.

1992

Feb Thunder begins recording its sophomore album, eventually selecting 14 songs from an initial pool of 30.
Aug [20] The band performs on BBC1-TV's "Top Of The Pops".
[22] Thunder makes a second appearance at Castle Donington's "Monsters of Rock" festival on the same day that the homeless-themed *Low Life In High Places*, its promo video clip shot at London's Victoria Dock, reaches UK #22.
[24] The group performs live at the HMV Shop in London's Oxford Street to promote the release of its second album.
Sept [5] ***Laughing On Judgement Day***, with cover art by Storm Thorgerson, debuts at its UK #2 peak, behind Kylie Minogue's ***Kylie's Greatest Hits***.
Oct [1] A 20-date UK tour opens at Belfast Ulster Hall set to close on the 24th at the Plymouth Pavilions, Devon.
[17] *Everybody Wants Her* makes UK #36.
Nov The band begins working on a new single at E-Zee Studios with Morley producing.

1993

Jan Luckhurst splits from the band due to personal differences, to be replaced by Mikael Hogland (b. May 15, 1962).
Feb [11] Thunder appears on BBC1-TV's "Top Of The Pops".
[13] *A Better Man* reaches UK #18.
Apr [5] The group is featured singing *Gimme Shelter* on a newly-released benefit single for the Putting Our House In Order charity with eleven other versions of the song by other artists.
June [6] They play at the Sheffield Don Valley Stadium, Sheffield, S. Yorks., supporting Def Leppard.
[19] EP *Like A Satellite* debuts at its UK #28 peak.

1995

Feb [4] ***Behind Closed Doors*** hits UK #5 in its week of entry.
June [23-25] Thunder plays at Wembey Stadium, supporting Van Halen.
Oct [7] Compilation ***The Best Of Thunder - Their Finest Hour*** debuts at its UK #22 peak.
Dec [2] The group plays at London's Shepherd's Bush Empire, during a round of current UK dates.

TIFFANY

1987

June [23] Tiffany (b. Tiffany Renee Darwish, Oct. 2, 1971, Norwalk, CA), who had impressed producer/manager George Tobin by performing country songs in his office in 1984 at the age of 13, having been signed to his production company, has secured a worldwide recording contract with MCA Records in 1986, and now begins the novel "Tiffany Shopping Mall Tour '87" in Paramus, NJ. It involves three shows each weekend in busy US shopping malls, where Tiffany performs free for passing consumers, an innovative idea which generates enormous media interest. (After the summer break, she will return to high school in Norwalk, to begin her junior year.)
Sept Her maiden album ***Tiffany***, a teen-pop set produced by Tobin, who has chosen all ten cuts, is released and promoted across the US on a "School Spirit Tour" with the Jets.
Oct [8] Tiffany appears on NBC-TV's "The Tonight Show".
Nov [7] First single from the album, a re-make of Tommy James & the Shondells' *I Think We're Alone Now*, tops the US chart for the first of two weeks (knocked off pole position by Billy Idol's version of James & the Shondells' *Mony Mony* on the 21st).

1988

Jan [23] ***Tiffany*** hits US #1.
[30] Despite a lack of shopping malls, *I Think We're Alone Now* tops the UK chart for the first of three weeks, as Tiffany arrives in Britain to great media hoopla.
Feb [6] Lois Blaisch-penned ballad, *Could've Been*, also tops the US survey.
[27] ***Tiffany*** hits UK #5.
Mar Tiffany runs away from problems with her mother, Janie Williams, to live with her grandmother in La Mirada, CA. *Could've Been* hits UK #4.
Apr [2] A court gives Tiffany's aunt a temporary custody order to become the teenager's guardian.
[5] The RIAA certifies four million sales of ***Tiffany***.
[23] *I Saw Him Standing There*, a gender-amending re-make of the Beatles' 1964 US #14 smash, hits US #7.
June *I Saw Him Standing There* hits UK #8. The court issue is resolved: Janie Williams resumes guardianship over her daughter, and royalties already due to Tiffany are placed in trust.
July [16] *Feelings Of Forever* makes US #50 and UK #52, as Tiffany signs a deal to appear on Coco Puffs cereal boxes in the US.
Dec [10] Her sophomore album, ***Hold An Old Friend's Hand***, again helmed by Tobin, is released, set to reach US #17, and *Radio Romance* reaches UK #13.
[17] ***Hold An Old Friend's Hand*** makes UK #56.

1989

Jan [20] ***Hold An Old Friend's Hand*** is certified platinum by the RIAA.
[25] Tiffany is presented with the platinum disc for ***Hold An Old Friend's Hand***, in, where else, a shopping mall in Los Angeles.
Feb *All This Time* makes UK #47.
[11] *All This Time* hits US #6.
Apr [1] *Radio Romance* peaks at US #35.
[4] She sings the national anthem on the opening day of the baseball season at the California Angels' game at Anaheim Stadium, Anaheim, CA.
July [8-9] She plays two sellout shows at the Westbury Music Fair, Westbury, NY, supporting the New Kids On The Block, during their US summer tour.
Sept [12] A Los Angeles Superior Court judge orders Jeff Deane Turner of Santa Cruz, CA, to stay at least 200 yards away from Tiffany. The defendant, described as an obsessed fan, had written numerous letters to the starlet, including one which states "that God wants us to be together".

1990

May Tiffany is featured as the voice of Judy Jetson in "Jetsons: The Movie", and contributes three songs to its soundtrack. She also begins work on her third MCA album with producer Maurice Starr, projecting the teen star, now separated from Tobin and teamed with New Kids On The Block manager Dick Scott, at a more mature audience.
Dec Her third album, ***New Inside***, with New Kid Donnie Wahlberg guesting, and an extracted single, the Diane Warren-penned *Here In My Heart*, are released, but neither charts. Tiffany's star appears to have fallen as quickly as it rose.
[23] Tiffany sings at Fort Campbell, KY, home of the 101st Airborne Division's Screaming Eagles, before a crowd of 4,000 children, whose parents are serving in Saudi Arabia.

1991

Feb [10] Tiffany joins with nearly 100 celebrities in Burbank, CA, to record *Voices That Care*, a David Foster and fiancée Linda Thompson Jenner-composed and-organized charity record, to benefit the American Red Cross Gulf Crisis Fund. Having married Bulmaro Garcia seven months earlier, Tiffany will give birth to a son, Elijah on September 17th, 1992. A new recording *If Love Is Blind* will emerge in Southeast Asia in January 1994.

TLC

Tionne "T-Boz" Watkins (vocals); **Lisa "Left Eye" Lopes** (vocals); **Rozonda "Chilli" Thomas** (vocals)

1991

Feb [28] T-Boz (b. Tionne Watkins, Apr 26, 1970, Des Moines, IA) (who as a child sang *Oh, Sinner, You're Gonna Be Sorry* every Sunday in her mother's church choir) and Left Eye (b. Lisa Nicole Lopes, May 27, 1971, Philadelphia, PA), currently performing as the teen-duo Second Nature, sign a management deal with R&B performer Pebbles' production company Pettibone (she is married to business partner and top R&B co-producer (with Babyface) L.A. Reid) in Atlanta, GA. On July 10th, Pebbles will complete the trio, named TLC after the first initials of the performers' nicknames, by signing Chilli (b. Rozonda Thomas, Feb 27, 1971), the daughter of an absent Indian-born father she has never known, Abdul Tahil Ali, and whose musical experience thus far has been as a member of a talent contest girl group called the Showcase Babydolls, and who is currently a dancer with LaFace act, Damian Dame. With each girl taking a distinctive and equal singing role and with Chilli developing the pop/R&B trio's choreography, Pebbles subsequently signs TLC to Atlanta-based LaFace Records (which is co-owned by Reid and Babyface).

1992

Apr [25] Co-written by producer Dallas Austin and Left Eye though sampling James Brown's *Escapism*, the Average White Band's *School Boy Crush*, Silver Convention's *Fly Robin, Fly*, Bob James' *Take Me To The Mardi Gras* and Kool & the Gang's *Jungle Boogie*, TLC's debut single, *Ain't 2 Proud 2 Beg* hits US #6.
May [15] *Ain't 2 Proud 2 Beg* is certified platinum by the RIAA.
June [27] *Ain't 2 Proud 2 Beg* reaches UK #13.

Aug [15] Co-penned by Reid, Babyface and Daryl Simmons, *Baby-Baby-Baby* hits US #2.
[29] *Baby-Baby-Baby* makes UK #55.
Sept [5] TLC's maiden album, the pop/hip-hop fused ***Ooooooohhh ... On The TLC Tip*** reaches US #14, but will not chart in the UK.
[29] *Baby-Baby-Baby* is certified platinum by the RIAA.
Oct [31] The extracted *What About Your Friends* makes UK #59.
Nov [19] Still-climbing *What About Your Friends* is certified gold by the RIAA.
[21] *What About Your Friends* hits US #7.

1993

Mar [20] *Hat 2 Da Back*, sampling KC & the Sunshine Band's *What Makes You Happy* and L.L. Cool J's *Big Ole Butt*, reaches US #30.
July [24] Written by Prince and taken from the film soundtrack to "Poetic Justice", TLC's *Get It Up* makes US #42.

1994

May [7] Keith Sweat's *How Do You Like It?*, featuring guest vocalist Left Eye, reaches US #48.
June [9] Following a quarrel, Left Eye sets fire to boyfriend and Atlanta Falcons' wide receiver Andre Rison's $2 million Country Club of the South, Atlanta mansion. With the home burnt to the ground, Left Eye is indicted for arson.
Dec [29] Left Eye pleads guilty to the arson charge but, having reconciled with Rison, he has refused to press further charges. She receives a $10,000 fine (plus restitution to the firefighters), five years probation and must undergo alcohol rehabilitation in a halfway house. (Rison's insurance company, Lloyd's of London will also claim $1.3m compensation from Left Eye.) (During the year on the music front, TLC has recorded its follow-up album, supplied the theme song to Nickleodeon-TV's "All That" show, co-starred in the movie "House Party 3", appeared on Queen Latifah's US-TV show "Living Single" and Patti LaBelle's sitcom "Out All Night" and contributed its version of *Sleigh Ride* to the "Home Alone II" film soundtrack.)

1995

Jan [6] *Creep*, produced by Dallas Austin and still climbing the US survey, is already certified platinum by the RIAA.
[21] *Creep* bows at its UK #22 peak.
[28] *Creep* tops the US chart.
Apr [5] The RIAA certifies sales of three million US copies of ***Ooooooohhh ... On The TLC Tip***.
[15] *Red Light Special*, produced by Babyface, hits US #2 and will be certified gold by the RIAA two days later.
[22] *Red Light Special* enters at its UK #18 peak.
June [10] TLC performs *Waterfalls* at the MTV Movie Awards held at Warner Bros., Studios, Burbank, CA.
July [8] *Waterfalls*, produced by the Organized Noize team (whose Rico Wade is T-Boz's neighbor), tops the US chart, spurred by an award-winning special-effects promo clip.
[20] With TLC having left Pebbles' Pettibone management company for its new manager, Hiriam Hicks, Pebbles, now divorced from Reid, files a $10 million lawsuit against LaFace Records in the latest salvo in legal wranglings surrounding the group. Meanwhile, TLC, with *Waterfalls* still the best-selling single in the US and their new album on its way to nine million-plus US sales, files for Chapter 11 bankruptcy.
[29] ***CrazySexyCool***, variously produced by Babyface, Organized Noize, Dallas Austin, Sean "Puffy" Combs, Jermaine Dupri and Left Eye, hits US #3.
[31] *Waterfalls* is certified platinum by the RIAA.
Aug [19] *Waterfalls* hits UK #4.
Sept [7] "Waterfalls" picks up Best Video, Best Group Video, Best R&B Video and the People's Choice of the Year awards at the 12th annual MTV Video Music Awards held at New York's Radio City Music Hall.
[23] ***Crazysexycool*** also hits UK #4.
Oct [7] The RIAA confirms that TLC is now the all-time biggest-selling all-female recording act in the US.
[21] TLC appears on ITV's "Scratchy & Co."
Nov [4] *Diggin' On You*, written and produced by Babyface, bows at its UK #18 peak.
[14] Babyface-produced film soundtrack ***Waiting To Exhale*** is released in the US by Arista, including a new TLC cut, *This Is How It Works*.
Dec [6] TLC collects the Top Artist of the Year, Top R&B Single (*Creep*) and Top R&B Artist trophies at the sixth annual **Billboard** Music Awards broadcast live on Fox-TV from New York's Coliseum.
[30] *Diggin' On You* hits US #5.

1996

Feb [6] The RIAA certifies ***Crazysexycool*** for 9 million US sales, making it the biggest-selling US album ever by an all-female act.
[22] Chilli appears with her newly-found half-brother and half-sister on the US-TV syndicated "Sally Jessy Raphael" talk show having been recently reunited with her biological father, Abdul Tahil Ali (whom she had never met).
[28] TLC lip-synchs to *Waterfalls* at the 38th annual Grammy Awards held at Los Angeles' Shrine Auditorium, at which *Creep* wins Best R&B Vocal Performance, Duo or Group and ***Crazysexycool*** nabs Best R&B Album.
Mar [6] ***Crazysexycool*** is voted Favorite Album at the second annual Blockbuster Entertainment Awards staged at Hollywood's Pantages Theater, CA.

TOAD THE WET SPROCKET

Glen Phillips (vocals, guitar); **Todd Nichols** (guitar, vocals); **Dean Dinning** (bass); **Randy Guss** (drums)

1989

Oct Santa Barbara high school friends Phillips and Nichols have performed together in their hometown in 1988, initially playing regularly at a local bar under the name Glen, before adding Dinning when they are billed as Three Young Studs, finally settling on Toad The Wet Sprocket, named after a Monty Python comedy sketch, when fully augmented by Guss. Having released its debut single, *Reaching For The Sky*, earlier this year on their own Sprockets label, the band has become the first Santa Barbara-based act to be signed up by a major label, after Columbia Records' label executive Don Ienner, during his first month at the company, has seen the band perform at a New York University gig with 12 people in the audience, but has also been impressed by its self-financed ten-track demo album, recorded for $650. With the demo providing the basis for its freshman album, ***Bread And Circus*** is now released. Its follow-up set, ***Pale***, produced by Marvin Etzioni, will be issued the following year having cost $6,500 to produce - both will eventually sell over 50,000 copies in the US.

1991

Aug Produced by Gavin MacKillop, the group's third album ***Fear*** is released, once again showcasing the group's melodic rock songcrafting skills, while will prove initially appealing to a college-based following.

1992

Sept [12] Jangly-guitar, pop-rock breakthrough hit, *All I Want* reaches US #15, benefitting from crossover appeal, breaking from college radio to mainstream formats.
[19] ***Fear*** reaches US #49.
Nov [6] ***Fear*** is certified gold by the RIAA.

1993

Jan [13] A North American tour reaches the Town Pump club, Vancouver, BC, Canada, a gig grossing $4,558 from an audience of 400.
[18] The band appears at the Town Hall in Washington, DC, as part of the Reunion On The Mall, during Inauguration festivities.
[30] *Walk On The Ocean* reaches US #18.
Apr [14] The band plays at the Civic Center, Salem, VA, during its current US tour.
May [22] The group participates in a LIFEbeat CounterAid benefit concert.
Aug [14] The film soundtrack to "So I Married An Axe Murderer", including a new cut by the band, enters the US chart, set to make #88.

1994

Apr Deborah Holland's album, ***Freudian Slip***, including a guest appearance by the band, is released.
June [11] Once again helmed by MacKillop, ***Dulcinea***, a literary reference to Don Quixote, debuts at its US #34 peak.
July [23] The extracted *Fall Down* reaches US #33.
Sept [1] ***Fear*** is certified platinum by the RIAA.
Nov [26] *Something's Always Wrong* reaches US #41.
Dec [1] The band guests on CBS-TV's "Late Show With David Letterman".
[7] The group performs live at the fifth annual **Billboard** Music Awards held at the Universal Amphitheatre, Universal City, CA.

1995

Apr [22] Toad The Wet Sprocket participates in this year's Earth Day events, performing at a benefit concert in Washington.
July [31] ***Dulcinea*** is confirmed platinum by the RIAA.
Aug [22] The ***Empire Records*** film soundtrack is released, including a new cut by Toad.
Sept ***Friends - The Album*** television soundtrack including the band's *Good Intentions*, is issued by Reprise Records in the US.
Oct [28] A John Lennon-tribute album ***Working Class Hero***, including Toad's version of *Instant Karma*, released by Hollywood Records, debuts at its US #94 peak. During the month Sony Music issues the multimedia Enhanced-CD version of ***Dulcinea***, with interactive elements added to music from the original album.
Nov [11] Containing rare cuts, non-album singles, B-sides and soundtrack entries, ***In Light Syrup*** debuts at its US #37 peak.

1996

Jan [5] The group makes a return visit to "Late Show With David Letterman".

THE TOKENS

Hank Medress (tenor vocals); **Jay Siegel** (baritone vocals); **Mitch Margo** (tenor vocals); **Phil Margo** (bass vocals)

1955

The group begins, as the Linc-Tones, at Lincoln High School, Brooklyn, New York, NY, formed by Medress (b. Nov. 19, 1938, Brooklyn) and Neil Sedaka (b. Mar. 13, 1939, Brooklyn), with Eddie Rabkin and Cynthia Zolitin, performing at local hops and dances. Siegel (b. Oct. 20, 1939, Brooklyn) replaces Rabkin the following year, when the group records *I Love My Baby* for the small Melba label, while Sedaka leaves in 1958 to develop his songwriting career, signing to RCA Records as a soloist. Zolitin also departs in 1958, as Medress and Siegel draft in replacements and become Daryl & the Oxfords for a year, with little success.

1959

Dec Margo brothers Phil (b. Apr. 1, 1942, Brooklyn) and Mitch (b. May 25, 1947, Brooklyn) join and the group is re-named the Tokens. The following year, the Margos and Medress write *Tonight I Fell In Love*, a determined effort to create a hit song, recording it privately, before hawking it around New York record companies.

1961

May [8] Sold as a one-off to Morty Kraft's Warwick label, *Tonight I Fell In Love* reaches US #15. The Tokens audition for producer/songwriters Hugo (Peretti) and Luigi (Creatore) at RCA.
Oct The group's RCA debut is a revised version of Paul Campbell's African folk-based *Wimoweh*, one of the group's audition songs, for which Hugo and Luigi, with songwriting partner George Weiss, have written new English lyrics, re-titling it *The Lion Sleeps Tonight*.
Dec [18] *The Lion Sleeps Tonight* tops the US chart for the first of three weeks. Additional vocalist Joseph Venneri joins the group to fill out their sound for live appearances.

1962

Jan *The Lion Sleeps Tonight* reaches UK #11, the group's only UK success. Meanwhile, it signs a production deal with Capitol, independent of its recording contract with RCA, and sets up its own company, Big Time Productions, in New York.
[9] *The Lion Sleeps Tonight* is certified gold by the RIAA.
Mar [3] The follow-up, *B'Wa Nina*, a similar pseudo-African blend, peaks at US #55, while their debut album, ***The Lion Sleeps Tonight***, makes US #54.
Only weeks after the Tokens' hit, Scottish folk/pop singer Karl Denver takes *Wimoweh*, in its traditional form, to UK #4.
July [28] *La Bomba*, their re-working of Ritchie Valens' hit, *La Bamba*, makes US #85.

1963

Mar [30] The group's first major production success is with the Chiffons' *He's So Fine*, which tops the US chart. (Several other Chiffons' production hits will follow.)
Aug [31] *Hear The Bells* peaks at US #94, and is the Tokens' last hit on RCA.

1964

Sept [26] The group forms its own B.T. Puppy label (B.T. standing for Big Time), debuting with the Four Seasons-influenced *He's In Town*, written by Goffin and King, which climbs to US #43. (The Rockin' Berries' cover hits UK #3.) They will also record as the Four Winds, the Buddies and the Coeds (with added girl vocalists) on the B.T. Puppy subsidiary, Swing.

1966

Apr [23] *I Hear Trumpets Blow*, written by the group, reaches US #30, and is its final hit on its own label.
May ***I Hear Trumpets Blow*** peaks at US #148.
Aug The Happenings, a vocal quartet from Paterson, NJ, is signed to B.T. Puppy, and produced by the Tokens on a revival of the Tempos' *See You In September*, which hits US #3. (There will be seven more Tokens-produced Happenings US hits over the next two years, including another #3, *I Got Rhythm*.)

1967

May [27] The Tokens, now signed to Warner Bros. Records, reach US #36 with a revival of the Steve Lawrence/Matt Monro ballad, *Portrait Of My Love*.
Aug [5] *It's A Happening World*, also on Warner, peaks at US #69, while the B.T. Puppy album, ***Back To Back***, offering a side apiece by the Tokens and the Happenings, makes US #134.

1970

Jan [10] After a lean period, the group resurfaces on Buddah Records with *She Lets Her Hair Down (Early In The Morning)*, an adaptation of a Silvikrin TV commercial jingle, which it has also performed. It reaches US #61.
Mar [7] The final Tokens chart single, again on Buddah, is a revival of the Beach Boys' *Don't Worry Baby*, peaking at US #95. The group also records an album for Buddah, ***Both Sides Now***, which includes re-makes of most of its earlier hits.
Oct Medress leaves the group to concentrate on production (which will include a new version of *The Lion Sleeps Tonight* by Robert John, which hits US #3 in March 1972 also becoming a million seller), and begins a new string of successes in collaboration with Dave Appell, producing the Tony Orlando-led group, Dawn. The Tokens continue performing as a trio.

1973

Oct Siegel and the Margo brothers, signed to Atco under the new name of Cross Country, reach US #30 with a harmony update of the 1965 Wilson Pickett hit, *In The Midnight Hour*. (This is their only chart success, and they will split a year later, moving into various production and writing areas, with Phil Margo concentrating on movie work.)

1981

Oct [3] Several years after the group has quietly dissolved, the Margo brothers, Medress and Siegel are reunited for a final reunion/farewell show as the Tokens, at New York's Radio City Music Hall. The following Mar [6], *The Lion Sleeps Tonight*, updated by UK group Tight Fit, with an '80s dance beat, will top the UK chart.

1994

Sept [3] Having been re-formed by Siegel in 1988, not least to cut an updated version of *The Lion Sleeps Tonight* for the Downtown label, the Tokens, have become regulars on the US nostalgia circuit (including an appearance as part of Richard Nader's Original Doo Wop Reunion package in June 1992). The group's most enduring cut, *The Lion Sleeps Tonight (Wimoweh)*, which has also been reworked by R.E.M. for the basis of its *Sidewinder Sleeps Tonite* track featured on the 1993 album ***Automatic For The People*** in addition to its use in projects including the "Dead Calm" and "Ace Ventura Pet Detective" movies and Burger King commercials, is currently included in the movie "The Lion King", and now makes US #51. The Tokens, lining up as Mitch, Phil and Noah Margo, Jay Leslie and Mike Johnson continue its 50-date per year schedule (competing with Jay Siegel's rival East Coast Tokens combo).

THE TORNADOS

Alan Caddy (lead guitar); **George Bellamy** (rhythm guitar); **Roger Lavern** (keyboards); **Heinz Burt** (bass guitar); **Clem Cattini** (drums)

1961

Sept London-based session musicians Caddy (b. Feb. 2, 1940, Chelsea, London), Bellamy (b. Oct. 8, 1941, Sunderland, Tyne & Wear), Lavern (b. Roger Jackson, Nov. 11, 1938, Kidderminster, Worcs.), Burt (b. July 24, 1942, Hargin, Germany) and Cattini (b. Clemente Cattini, Aug. 28, 1939, London) are recruited by independent UK producer, Joe Meek. Cattini, who began playing drums with Teddy Kennedy's Rock'n'Rollers in 1956, and Caddy are ex-members of Johnny Kidd's Pirates, while Burt is a protegé of Meek, who feels his teutonic good looks will give the group's visual image a focus. The producer uses them as session men to back his solo artists on disc, and plans to record them as an instrumental group with a prominent keyboard sound, to challenge the Shadows' guitar-led grip on the instrumental market.

1962

Feb After playing early live dates supporting singer John Leyton, the group becomes Billy Fury's onstage backing unit, playing on recording sessions for Meek behind Leyton, Don Charles, Michael Cox and Alan Klein.
Apr Meek records the Tornados on his instrumental composition, *Love And Fury* (a deliberate reference to their stage "boss"), and signs them to Decca Records. Released as their debut single, it fails to chart.
July They accompany Fury during his summer season at the Windmill Theatre, Great Yarmouth, Norfolk.
Aug Inspired by the recently-launched (July 10th) Telstar communications satellite, Meek writes the instrumental, *Telstar*, tailored to the Tornados' style, with futuristic sound effects.
Oct [4] *Telstar* tops the UK chart for the first of five weeks, eventually selling 910,000 domestic copies.
Dec [22] *Telstar* starts a three-week run atop the US survey, the first single by a UK group to do so. The chart-topping pattern is repeated worldwide, with global sales over five million.

1963

Jan Burt leaves to go solo as a vocalist, using his first name, Heinz, but Meek remains his producer. He is initially replaced on bass by Chas Hodges of the Outlaws, then by Tab Martin.
[26] *Globetrotter*, a Meek tune with a Telstar-clone sound and arrangement hits UK #5, making it one of three instrumentals in the UK top five. (The Shadows' *Dance On* is at #1, with the still-climbing *Diamonds* by Jet Harris and Tony Meehan at #4). ***Telstar***, a US-only release, climbs to #45.
Feb [15] The group joins Larry Parnes' "Your Lucky Stars" tour. Its gold disc for *Telstar* is stolen from the Edmonton Granada cinema dressing room.
Mar Martin leaves to form another Meek-produced group, the Saints (who back Heinz on stage). Brian Gregg, ex-Johnny Kidd's Pirates, replaces him.
[9] *Ridin' The Wind* breezes to US #63. Lavern quits the tour and is admitted to Kidderminster Hospital, with a mystery illness.
Apr *Robot* reaches UK #17, while the group appears in the UK pop movie, "Just For Fun", playing *All The Stars In The Sky*.
May Heinz' first single, *Dreams Do Come True* (later recorded by the Tornados as an instrumental album track) is released, taken from the UK film, "Farewell Performance", in which he also features, and which boasts a score by Meek.
[3] *Telstar* wins the Best Selling British A-Side category, at the eighth annual Ivor Novello Awards, held at the BBC Television Centre, London.
June The soundtrack album, ***Just For Fun***, reaches UK #20. *The Ice Cream Man* reaches UK #18.
July EP *Tornado Rock* is released. A departure from their usual sound, it contains revivals of rock classics *Ready Teddy*, *My Babe*, *Long Tall Sally* and *Blue Moon Of Kentucky*.
Aug Lavern, Bellamy and Gregg leave for solo and session work, and are replaced by Jimmy O'Brien, Brian Irwin and Ray Randell.
Sept Heinz, long an ardent Eddie Cochran fan, hits UK #6 with the tribute song, *Just Like Eddie*, written by Meek.
Oct The Tornados' *Dragonfly* makes UK #41. They appear with Billy Fury on ***We Want Billy!***, recorded live on stage.
Dec *Country Boy* by Heinz makes UK #26, taken from his solo album, ***Tribute To Eddie***. The Tornados finally split with Fury.

1964

Jan The Tornados' first UK album, ***Away From It All***, is released. The once revolutionary sound of the group is now, in the context of Merseybeat and Beatlemania, out of date. Caddy leaves and is replaced by Stuart Taylor from Screamin' Lord Sutch's group. He teams with singer, Don Charles, to form the Sound Ventures production company, to records acts for EMI.
[3] The group undertakes its final engagement with Billy Fury in Amsterdam, Holland.
Feb *Hot Pot* is released, followed by *Monte Carlo* and *Exodus* (released by Decca in April and August.)
Mar Heinz reaches UK #26 with *You Were There*.
Oct On Columbia, Heinz makes UK #39 with *Questions I Can't Answer*.

1965

Jan Also on Columbia, the Tornados release *Granada*.
Feb Cattini, the last remaining original Tornado, leaves to become drummer and leader of Division Two, the touring band behind UK hitmakers, the Ivy

League. (He will move to constant session work, drumming on records by most of the major UK names of the '60s and '70s.)
Mar Heinz makes UK #49 with *Diggin' My Potatoes*. (He will move into cabaret work, before fading from sight and later returning in '70s rock'n'roll revival shows.)
Apr Cattini releases *No Time To Think* as the Clem Cattini Orchestra.
May [21] The band re-forms as Tornados '65, releasing *Early Bird*, named after another communications satellite, on Columbia.
Sept The group records the theme for Gerry Anderson's TV puppet series, "Stingray".

1966

Aug Following two more non-charting singles, *Pop Art Goes Mozart* and *Is That A Ship I Hear?*, the Tornados (who have had fluctuating personnel since Cattini left) disband, members mostly returning to studio session work.

1967

Feb [3] On the eighth anniversary of Buddy Holly's death, Meeks fatally shoots his landlady, Mrs. Violet Shenton, at his 304 Holloway Road flat, before turning the gun on himself.

1991

May After a nine-year legal battle, the group wins back the rights to its own records in the High Court, paving the way for the 1994 UK release of ***Telstar - The Original Sixties Hits Of The Tornados*** on the Music Collection International label.
June [7] The original Tornados line-up reunite for the first time in nearly 30 years, to perform at a Joe Meek tribute at the Lewisham Theatre, Lewisham, London, with Screaming Lord Sutch, Cliff Bennett, the Honeycombs, Mike Berry, Heinz, the Moontrekkers and Danny Rivers.

TOTO

Bobby Kimball (lead vocals); **David Paich** (keyboards, vocals); **Steve Lukather** (lead guitar); **Steve Porcaro** (keyboards, vocals); **David Hungate** (bass); **Jeff Porcaro** (drums, percussion)

1978

The group is formed in Los Angeles, CA, by six noted session-men: brothers Jeff (b. Apr. 1, 1954, Hartford, CT) and Steve Porcaro (b. Sept. 2, 1957, Hartford), sons of jazz percussionist Joe Porcaro, their boyhood friend Paich (b. June 25, 1954, Los Angeles), son of bandleader/arranger Marty Paich, who has previously played in Rural Still Life with Jeff, and Hungate (b. Los Angeles), Lukather (b. Oct. 21, 1957, Los Angeles) and Kimball (b. Robert Toteaux, Mar. 29, 1947, Vinton, LA), with whom the first three have co-performed for several years, behind acts including Jackson Browne, Aretha Franklin and Barbra Streisand, and as backup band on Boz Scaggs' hit albums, ***Silk Degrees*** and ***Down Two Then Left***, in 1976 and 1977. Signed to CBS/Columbia Records, the Toto name is partly a simplification of lead singer Kimball's real surname, and partly in reverence to the dog in "The Wizard Of Oz".

1979

Jan [13] Their debut single *Hold The Line*, written by Paich, hits US #5 while their self-produced debut album, ***Toto***, hits US #9, securing an enthusiastic album-oriented rock live following. Recorded in Hollywood, eight of the ten cuts are written by Paich.
Feb [15] *Hold The Line* is certified gold by the RIAA.
Mar [31] *I'll Supply The Love*, taken from the album, makes US #45, while *Hold The Line* is their UK chart debut, at #14.
Apr ***Toto*** peaks at UK #37.
June [2] *Georgy Porgy*, with guest vocals by soul songstress, Cheryl Lynn, makes US #48.
Dec Hard rock follow-up, ***Hydra***, produced by the band with Tom Knox, makes US #37.

1980

Mar [6] ***Hydra*** is certified gold by the RIAA.
[15] *99*, from the second album, reaches US #26. (All band members will remain highly respected and in-demand writers and session musicians in between Toto projects, and will individually contribute to much of the best-selling mainstream US music of the '80s.)

1982

July Following the self-produced ***Turn Back*** which made US #41 in February the previous year, ***Toto IV*** becomes the group's most successful album, hitting US #4.
[3] From it, *Rosanna* (a tribute to Lukather's girlfriend, actress Rosanna Arquette) stays at US #2 for five weeks, behind Human League's *Don't You Want Me*, then Survivor's *Eye Of The Tiger*.
Sept [25] *Make Believe*, also from ***Toto IV***, reaches US #30.

1983

Feb [5] *Africa*, written by Paich and Jeff Porcaro, tops the US chart for a week and will also hit UK #3.
[23] Toto dominates the 25th annual Grammy Awards, nabbing six trophies: Record Of The Year, Best Vocal Arrangement For Two Or More Voices and Best Instrumental Arrangement Accompanying Vocal (all for *Rosanna*) and Album Of The Year, Best Engineered Recording and Producer Of The Year (the group itself) for ***Toto IV***.
Apr [30] *Rosanna*, reissued in Britain, now reaches #12.
May [7] Ballad, *I Won't Hold You Back*, hits US #10.
July [30] *Waiting For Your Love* peaks at US #73, while *I Won't Hold You Back* makes UK #37.

1984

Apr Hungate leaves, to be replaced on bass by a third Porcaro brother, Mike (b. May 29, 1955, Hartford). Shortly after, Kimball also departs for a solo vocal career, and is replaced by Dennis "Fergie" Fredericksen (b. May 15, 1951). (Hungate will move to Nashville, TN, and become an in-demand session musician, while Kimball will re-emerge in the Frank Farian-masterminded rock group, Far Corporation, which hits with a carbon-copy revival of Led Zeppelin's *Stairway To Heaven* in 1986.)
Dec [22] *Stranger In Town* climbs to US #30, as its parent album, ***Isolation***, will peak at US #42 and UK #67.

1985

Jan [28] The band members are instrumental in helping to record the backing track for the historic USA For Africa recording, *We Are The World*.
The group's wholly instrumental soundtrack album, ***Dune***, for the science-fiction movie of the same name (on which the band is accompanied by the Vienna Symphony Orchestra) stops at US #168.
Feb *Holyanna* peaks at US #71.
[28] ***Isolation*** is certified gold by the RIAA.

1986

Nov The band-produced ***Fahrenheit***, the first album to feature new singer, Joseph Williams (who has previously recorded a solo album for MCA and has been a backing singer for Jeffrey Osborne), makes US #40 and UK #99, and features guest appearances from Miles Davis, Michael McDonald, Don Henley and others.
[22] Taken from it, the ballad *I'll Be Over You*, written by Lukather with Randy Goodrum, reaches US #11.

1987

Feb [14] Paich-penned *Without Your Love*, taken from ***Fahrenheit***, makes US #38. Keyboardist Steve Porcaro quits the line-up and is not replaced, but will continue to contribute in a reduced capacity.

1988

Apr [9] ***The Seventh One***, with an almost identical album cover to their first release, makes UK #73, and will reach US #64. Guest vocalists include Jon Anderson and Linda Ronstadt.
May [7] Consistent with the previous six albums, there is at least one cut named after a woman: *Pamela*, which, extracted as a single, reaches US #22.

1990

Sept [18] After a lengthy period of group silence, Toto, now comprising Paich, Lukather and Jeff and Michael Porcaro, returns with another new lead vocalist, Jean-Michel Byron, and begins a 16-date European tour at the Forest National, Brussels, Belgium, set to end on October 9th at London's Hammersmith Odeon.
[22] Singles anthology, ***Past To Present 1977-1990***, also featuring four new tracks with Byron's vocals, debuts at its US #153 peak.

1991

Aug [9] The RIAA certifies three million sales of Toto IV following the double platinum confirmation of ***Toto*** on November 10th, 1989.
Sept [12] The group plays a one-off UK date at London's Town & Country club.
Oct [7] The RIAA certifies gold sales of *Africa* and *Rosanna*.

1992

Aug [5] Jeff Porcaro dies, age 38, of a heart attack, probably induced, according to his manager Larry Fitzgerald, by an allergic reaction to lawn pesticides, at his Hidden Hills, Los Angeles home. He is survived by wife, Susan, and sons, Miles, Chris and Nico. He is pronounced dead at 8:36 p.m. at the West Hills Medical Center, Los Angeles.
[6] Bruce Springsteen dedicates *Human Touch* to Porcaro in concert, at the first of his five Wembley Stadium shows.
[10] Porcaro's funeral is held at Forest Lawn Memorial Park's Hall of Liberty in Los Angeles. Steely Dan's *Home At Last*, *Deacon Blues* and *Third World Man*, and Jimi Hendrix's *The Wind Cries Mary* are all played at the service.
Sept [3] Contradicting earlier reports, Los Angeles County Coroner Bob Dambacher releases a statement revealing that the autopsy on Pocaro found the cause of death to be a hardening of the arteries, caused by cocaine abuse. Finding no traces of pesticides, the toxicology report found a cocaine level of .21 micrograms/millilitre in his blood, while a cocaine by-product, benzoylecgonine, was also present at 1.5 micrograms/millilitre.)
[27] Toto, with Simon Phillips filling Porcaro's place, plays at London's Brixton Academy during UK dates, as their new album, ***Kingdom Of Desire***, is released in Europe.
Dec [14] The group performs at a benefit at the Universal Amphitheatre, Universal City, CA, with George Harrison, Donald Fagen, Henley, McDonald, Eddie Van Halen and Boz Scaggs, to establish a trust fund for Jeff Porcaro's children.

1993

May [11] ***Kingdom Of Desire***, featuring Jeff Porcaro, is released in the US.
June [3] The group begins its first US tour in seven years in Houston, TX, set to end on the 23rd in Ventura, CA. Toto now comprises lead singer Lukather, Paich, Mike Porcaro and Phillips.

1995

Nov [18] While ***Farenheit*** has been certified gold by the RIAA on October 3rd the previous year, *I Will Remember*, taken from the band's latest album ***Tambu***, charts for a week at UK #64. While ***Farenheit*** has been certified gold by the RIAA on October 3rd the previous year ***Tambu*** will be released by the Sony's Legacy label on June 5th the following year.

TRAFFIC

Steve Winwood (vocals, keyboards, guitar); **Dave Mason** (vocals, guitar); **Chris Wood** (flute, saxophone); **Jim Capaldi** (drums, vocals)

1967

Apr [2] Winwood (b. May 12, 1948, Birmingham, Warks.) leaves the Spencer Davis Group at the height of its success after three years, and forms a new band with three friends from the Midlands, with whom he jammed at Birmingham's Elbow Room the previous year: former Spencer Davis roadie Mason (b. May 10, 1945, Worcester, Worcs.), ex-Locomotive and Sounds Of Blue player Wood (b. June 24, 1944, Birmingham) and Capaldi (b. Aug. 24, 1944, Evesham, Herefordshire), who has played with Mason in the Hellions, and with Winwood in Deep Feeling. Signed to Island Records, they cut a debut single, before retreating to a cottage in the Berkshire village of Aston Tirrold, to rehearse, write and prepare their first album.

July *Paper Sun*, written by all four members, and with a lead vocal by Winwood, hits UK #5.

Sept [2] *Paper Sun* charts for a week at US #94, as the group makes its live debut in Oslo, Norway.

Oct *Hole In My Shoe*, penned by Mason and featuring his lead vocal, hits UK #2. (It will also be a UK #2 hit 17 years later in a spoof revival by Neil, from the "Young Ones" TV series.)

[4] The group embarks on a UK tour, with the Young Rascals, at London's Finsbury Park Astoria.

Dec [16] *Here We Go Round The Mulberry Bush*, the theme from a UK movie of the same title, a romantic teen drama starring Barry Evans and Judy Geeson, hits UK #8. Traffic's *Utterly Simple* is also heard on the film's soundtrack, with contributions from the Spencer Davis Group and others.

[26] The Beatles BBC2-TV fantasy, "Magical Mystery Tour", which features Traffic, airs.

[29] Mason leaves after differences of musical opinion with Winwood, and goes to the US to play initially with Delaney & Bonnie before working solo. He is not replaced, and Traffic continues as a trio.

1968

Jan ***Mr. Fantasy*** hits UK #8.

Mar *No Name, No Face, No Number*, from the album, makes UK #40, and will be the group's last UK chart single.

May Mason re-joins the group to contribute to sessions for a second album.

June ***Mr. Fantasy*** (which has a different track content from the UK release, and includes *Paper Sun* and *Hole In My Shoe*), reaches US #88.

[10] The group plays at the "Zurich Rock Festival" in Zurich, Switzerland, with Jimi Hendrix and Eric Burdon & the Animals.

Aug [11] Traffic takes part in the eighth "National Jazz & Blues Festival" at Kempton Park Racecourse, Sunbury-on-Thames, Middx.

Sept *Feelin' Alright*, from the forthcoming album, is released.

Oct Mason quits for the second time.

Nov ***Traffic*** hits UK #9. Its most-aired track, *You Can All Join In*, is not released as a UK single (though it sells well on import from Europe), but its wide exposure helps boost album sales.

1969

Jan Traffic splits as Winwood leaves to join Eric Clapton, Rick Grech and Ginger Baker in Blind Faith. Keyboard player Wynder K. Frog joins Capaldi, Mason and Wood, and they briefly become Wooden Frog, before splitting after just two months of rehearsal.

[7] Capaldi and Wood both attend Winwood's first gig with Blind Faith, a free concert in London's Hyde Park.

[25] ***Traffic*** reaches US #17.

July Having failed to chart in Britain, ***Last Exit***, recorded as a farewell package before the split, reaches US #19.

1970

Feb After the demise of Blind Faith, and having spent a month with Ginger Baker's Airforce, Winwood records the solo album, ***Mad Shadows***. Capaldi and Wood join the sessions (which are initially produced by Guy Stevens) and, with the results working well, it is decided to make it a Traffic album, which will be released as ***John Barleycorn Must Die***. Meanwhile, a compilation, ***Best Of Traffic***, rounding up their hit singles and tracks from earlier albums, reaches US #48.

May [22-24] The group takes part in the three-day "Hollywood Music Festival" at Newcastle-under-Lyme, near Stoke, Staffs.

June [13] Traffic performs at the "Cincinnati Pop Festival", Cincinnati, OH.

[14] Mason breaks a lengthy spell of solo touring in the US to join Eric Clapton's Derek & the Dominos, for their first UK live shows.

Aug Ric Grech (b. Nov. 1, 1946, Bordeaux, France), an ex-colleague of Winwood's in Blind Faith and Airforce, joins on bass. Mason, signed in the US as a soloist to Blue Thumb Records, reaches US #22 with his debut album, ***Alone Together*** (recorded with help from Capaldi, Leon Russell, Delaney & Bonnie, and others), also earning his first gold disc.

Sept ***John Barleycorn Must Die*** reaches UK #11 and hits US #5, the group's biggest US success. From Mason's album, his solo version of *Only You Know And I Know* (which will be a US Top 20 hit by Delaney & Bonnie a year later) reaches US #42.

Oct [14] *Empty Pages*, from ***John Barleycorn Must Die***, makes US #74.

Dec Mason's *Satin Red And Black Velvet Woman* peaks at US #97.

[21] ***John Barleycorn Must Die*** is certified gold by the RIAA.

1971

Apr The group returns from an inactive winter spent in Morocco, having ostensibly been writing a movie score (for "Nevertheless", starring Michael J. Pollard). Mason has teamed with Mama Cass Elliot, formerly with the Mamas & the Papas, their duet album, ***Dave Mason And Cass Elliot***, making UK #49.

May For new recordings, and in preparation for UK and US tours, the group expands its line-up, adding Ghanaian percussionist, Reebop Kwaku-Baah, and Derek & the Dominos' drummer Jim Gordon (freeing Capaldi for more vocal spotlights). Mason also returns for a few months, and is present for the live recordings which produce ***Welcome To The Canteen***.

June Double compilation album, ***Winwood***, bringing together Spencer Davis Group, Blind Faith and Traffic tracks which feature Winwood on lead vocals, makes US #93, but will remain unreleased in the UK.

Nov ***Welcome To The Canteen*** reaches US #26.

[20] A live single extract, their revival of the Spencer Davis Group's *Gimme Some Lovin'*, with Winwood reprising his lead vocal, peaks at US #68.

Dec Grech leaves (later to join KGB), while Mason quits and Gordon returns to session work in the US.

1972

Jan ***The Low Spark Of High Heeled Boys***, recorded before the break-up of the last line-up (though after Mason's departure) hits US #7.

[22] *Rock'n'Roll Stew (Part 1)* makes US #93. Winwood contracts peritonitis and his illness and recuperation render Traffic temporarily inactive. Capaldi fills the time recording a solo album in Muscle Shoals, AL, while Mason undertakes another solo set.

Feb [7] ***The Low Spark Of High Heeled Boys*** is certified gold by the RIAA.

Apr Capaldi's ***Oh How We Danced*** makes US #82, and the extracted *Eve* peaks at US #91, while Mason's half-studio, half-live album, ***Headkeeper***, reaches US #51.

Nov Muscle Shoals drummer and bassist Roger Hawkins and David Hood, who played with Capaldi at the beginning of the year, are invited to Jamaica to record Traffic's next album, with Winwood, Capaldi, Wood and Kwaku-Baah still in the main line-up.

1973

Mar ***Shoot-Out At The Fantasy Factory*** hits US #6.

[7] ***Shoot-Out At The Fantasy Factory*** is confirmed gold by the RIAA.

May Mason's live solo album, ***Dave Mason Is Alive!***, makes US #116.

June Hawkins and Hood remain with Traffic for a world tour, while keyboard player Barry Beckett is also recruited to fill out the stage sound on tour. Several gigs are recorded for a future live album.

Aug [23] In mid-tour, the group headlines the annual "Reading Festival", Reading, Berks.

Sept After the tour, Kwaku-Baah, Hood, Hawkins and Beckett all return to session work, and the three principals rest for two months.

Nov Bass player Rosko Gee (formerly with Gonzales) joins to augment the trio for selected UK live dates (and will stay for the last year of the group's life).

Dec Live double album, ***Traffic - On The Road***, recorded on the world tour, reaches UK #40 and US #29, while Mason has switched labels to CBS/Columbia and makes US #50 with ***It's Like You Never Left***, which features guest appearances by Graham Nash and Stevie Wonder.

1974

July Compilation of Mason's Blue Thumb recordings, ***The Best Of Dave Mason***, makes US #183.

Aug *It's All Up To You*, a Capaldi solo effort, reaches UK #27.

[24] Traffic makes its final live performance at the 14th annual "National Jazz, Blues Folk & Rock Festival", near Reading, Berks.

Sept ***When The Eagle Flies***, Traffic's final recording, reaches UK #31, and is the group's last UK chart album. Meanwhile, Capaldi's solo set, ***Whale Meat Again***, peaks at US #191.

Nov ***When The Eagle Flies*** hits US #9. They complete a US tour, then decide to split to pursue individual careers.

[5] ***When The Eagle Flies*** is certified as the group's fourth and final gold disc by the RIAA.

Dec Mason's solo album, ***Dave Mason***, on Columbia, reaches US #25 and earns his second gold disc.

1975

Mar [1] Capaldi's solo single, *It's All Right*, makes US #55.

A revised version on Blue Thumb of the compilation album, ***The Best Of Dave Mason***, now titled ***Dave Mason At His Best***, after the substitution of one track, peaks at US #133.

May The group compilation album, ***Heavy Traffic***, makes US #155.

Oct Follow-up anthology, ***More Heavy Traffic***, peaks at US #193.

Nov Capaldi's solo revival of *Love Hurts* hits UK #4 and reaches US #97, where a competing version by UK group, Nazareth, hits US #8. Meanwhile, Mason's album, ***Split Coconut***, with guest appearances by Manhattan Transfer, David Crosby and Graham Nash, reaches US #27. (Both will continue to achieve moderate US chart success as solo acts: Capaldi will make #193 with ***Short Cut Draw Blood*** (Feb 1976), #91 with ***Fierce Heart*** (June 1983) and #183 with ***Some Come Running*** (Jan 1989) followed by one-non charting album, ***Prince Of Darkness*** (1993), while Mason's ***Certified Live*** reaches US #78 (Dec 1976), ***Let It Flow*** makes #37 (July 1977), ***Mariposa de Oro*** peaks at #41 (Aug 1978), ***Very Best Of Dave Mason*** reaches #179 (Nov 1978) while ***Old Crest On A New Wave*** closes his chart account, at #74, in July 1980. The non-charting Mason album ***Two Hearts*** will emerge in 1988.) Winwood will launch a highly successful solo career beginning with ***Steve Winwood*** in July 1977.

1983

July [12] Chris Wood dies of liver failure after a lengthy illness, in London. (A two-CD Traffic retrospective, ***Smiling Phases***, will be released in 1991.)

1994

May [18] Reunited with the lineup of Winwood, Capaldi, Randall Bramblett, Mike McEvoy, Walfredo Reyes and Rosko Gee, Traffic's reunion tour opens in Omaha, NE, set to end September 10th at Jones Beach Theatre, Wantagh, NY.
[21] Their reunion album, ***Far From Home***, debuts at its respective US #33 and UK #29 peaks.
June [14] The group guests on NBC-TV's "The Tonight Show".
Aug [14] Traffic takes part in "Woodstock '94" at Winston Farm, Saugerties, NY.
see also: **BLIND FAITH, THE SPENCER DAVIS GROUP, STEVE WINWOOD**

RANDY TRAVIS

1979

Jan Travis (b. Randy Bruce Traywick, May 4, 1959, Marshville, NC) is already a country-music veteran, having formed a duo with his brother Ricky at the age of ten, moved to Charlotte, NC, when 16, where he won a talent contest at the Country City USA club, and subsequently become one of the venue's regular performers under the wing of its (and Travis' subsequent) manager, Lib Hatcher, when he makes his recording debut for the local Paula Records under his given name, cutting *Dreamin'* and *She's My Woman*, produced by Joe Stamford. The latter inauspiciously opens his US Country chart account at #91, and it will be six more years until he becomes a survey regular.

1981

Travis relocates to Nashville, TN, where he concentrates on songwriting, earning a living initially as a cook and washer-up. Over the next four years he will become a seasoned country performer, again under the guidance of Hatcher, who has by now opened a Nashville club. He will also release his debut album, ***Randy Ray Live At The Nashville Palace*** in 1982, again on the Paula label.

1985

Jan He signs to Warner Bros. Records, and makes his label debut recording *Prairie Rose* for inclusion on the movie soundtrack album, ***Rustler's Rhapsody***.
Mar [7] Travis makes his debut on the legendary "Grand Ole Opry" radio showcase at Opryland, Nashville.
Sept His first solo Warners release, *On The Other Hand*, immediately showcasing Travis' smooth, deep-throated, earthy baritone-vocal quality, initially makes US Country #67.

1986

Feb A second outing, *1982*, hits US Country #6.
July [26] Reissued Paul Overstreet/Don Schlitz-written *On The Other Hand* is the first of many US Country chart-toppers for Travis.
Aug [9] Its parent album, ***Storms Of Life***, which has cost $65,000 to produce, ultimately earning the label $5.2 million in revenue, tops the US Country survey on its way to US #85 and multi-platinum sales status. Heralded as one of the pioneering albums for the new country movement, which will find increasing sympathy from the rock and pop markets, it is produced by Kyle Lehning (who will helm all of his remaining albums this decade), and contains songs and session work from the cream of Nashville's musicians.
Nov [8] *Diggin' Up Bones* also hits the US Country top spot, as Travis wins the Country Music Association's Horizon Award for the Most Promising Newcomer Of The Year, the first of many CMA honors.

1987

Feb The fourth extract, *No Place Like Home*, hits US Country #2.
[24] Travis sings *Diggin' Up Bones* at the 29th Grammy Awards held at Los Angeles' Shrine Auditorium.
May He visits Europe for a US Forces tour, the first time he has been outside his home country.
June [20] ***Always & Forever*** hits US Country #1 for the first of 40 weeks, and will also reach US #19, eventually selling over four million copies. It includes four US Country #1 hits and confirms Travis as the leading new country voice, whose young, handsome country looks boost his success, and belie the maturity of his exceptional voice.

1988

Jan [25] He collects the Favorite Male Artist, Country, Favorite Single, Country, Favorite Video, Country, and Favorite Album, Country trophies, at the 15th annual American Music Awards, held at the Shrine Auditorium, Los Angeles, CA.
Mar [2] Travis wins the Best Country Vocal Performance, Male category for ***Always & Forever***, at the 30th annual Grammy Awards. The ceremony, acknowledging the growing popularity of the new country movement, includes performances by its three brightest stars, Steve Earle, Dwight Yoakam and Travis.
June Travis performs at London's Royal Albert Hall, at the beginning of his first headlining UK tour, as *Forever And Ever, Amen* peaks at UK #55.
Aug [27] ***Old 8 x 10***, featuring a familiar line-up of guest musicians and songwriters, and again produced by Lehning, hits US Country #1, and reaches US #35 and UK #64 (on Aug [6]). Once again, it will spawn country single chart-toppers: *Honky Tonk Moon*, *Deeper Than The Holler* (scribed by Overstreet and Schlitz), and *Is It Still Over?*.
Sept [13] ***Old 8 x 10*** is certified platinum by the RIAA.

1989

Jan [30] Having recently swept the board at another CMA Awards ceremony, Travis wins the Favorite Male Artist, Country, Favorite Single, Country (*I Told You So*), and Favorite Album, Country (***Always & Forever***) categories, at the 16th annual American Music Awards, held at the Shrine Auditorium.
Feb [22] Travis collects his second Best Country Vocal Performance, Male trophy, for the album ***Old 8 x 10***, at the 31st annual Grammy Awards.
Nov [4] *It's Just A Matter Of Time*, his update of Brook Benton's 1959 US #3, recorded initially for producer Richard Perry's labor of love, ***Rock, Rhythm & Blues***, hits US Country #1 in the same week that its other parent album, ***No Holdin' Back***, achieves the same on the Album survey, having already made US #33 and platinum certification.
Dec A US only-issued festive collection of chestnut covers and new country songs, ***An Old Time Christmas***, peaks at US #70, selling over 500,000 copies.
[23] In **Billboard**'s The Year In Music survey, ***Old 8 x 10*** is named Top Country Album, and Travis Top Country Artist.

1990

Jan [17] ***No Holdin' Back*** is certified platinum by the RIAA.
[22] He wins the Favorite Male Artist, Country, Favorite Single, Country, and Favorite Album, Country categories, all for the third consecutive year, at the 17th annual American Music Awards, held again at the Shrine Auditorium.
Apr [1-2, 5] Travis plays three sellout dates at the Patriot Center, Fairfax, VA, grossing $401,596.
May ***Always & Forever*** is voted Country Album Of The Decade by **Billboard** magazine.
[5] Travis contributes *Nowhere Man* to the "John Lennon Tribute Concert", held at the Pier Head Arena in Merseyside, to celebrate the former Beatle's work.
July [30] The RIAA certifies four million sales of ***Always And Forever***.
Oct [8] He co-hosts the "24th Annual Country Music Association Awards" on CBS-TV.
[23] Travis guests on NBC-TV's "Late Night With David Letterman".
Nov [3] His sixth platinum album, ***Heroes And Friends***, reaches US #31. It comprises 12 duets with "artists who have been heroes to me most of my life and over the past few years ... have now become friends", namely Dolly Parton, Willie Nelson, Merle Haggard, Vern Gosdin, Loretta Lynn, B.B. King, George Jones, Kris Kristofferson, Tammy Wynette, Clint Eastwood, Conway Twitty and Roy Rogers.
Dec [4-8] Travis, who spends the best part of every year on SRO tours, performs five consecutive dates at Bally's, Las Vegas, NV. (His $10 million gross in 1990 makes him the most popular country act of the year.)
[22] In **Billboard**'s The Year In Music survey, Travis is once again named Top Country Artist, and ***No Holdin' Back*** is named Top Country Album.

1991

Feb [10] Travis joins with nearly 100 celebrities in Burbank, CA, to record *Voices That Care*, a David Foster and fiancée Linda Thompson Jenner composed-and-organized charity record to benefit the American Red Cross Gulf Crisis Fund. (Travis will participate in several of the US TV networks' "Welcome Home" to the troops celebrations.)
[28] Travis embarks on a US tour in Huntsville, AL, with support act, rising country star, Alan Jackson.
Mar [7] He is named Best Country Artist in the annual **Rolling Stone** magazine Readers' Picks music awards.
[8] Travis issues a statement confirming that he has been living with his manager, Lib Hatcher, for some years, in response to a claim by the **National Examiner** that he is gay.
[9] He guest stars, as himself, on NBC-TV's sitcom "Down Home".
Apr [13] Travis sells out the The Summit, Houston, TX., during the "GMC Truck American Music Tour", grossing $218,356 from an 11,803 crowd.
[27] He participates in ABC-TV's "Celebration Of Country".
May [31] Travis and Hatcher marry at their Maui, HI home.
July [24] ***Heroes And Friends*** is certified platinum by the RIAA.
Aug [15] He sings *Point Of Light* on ABC-TV's "The International Special Olympics All-Star Gala"
Sept [19] He performs *Your Cheatin' Heart* for "Ray Charles : 50 Years In Music", which will air on Fox-TV on October 6th.
[21] ***High Lonesome*** makes US #43 as the new country movement, which he helped establish, becomes dominated by Garth Brooks.
[23] Travis guests on NBC-TV's "The Tonight Show".
Oct [12] He appears with George Jones on HBO-TV's "Influences".
Travis duets with Roy Rogers on the latter's come-back album, ***Tribute***.
[31] ***High Lonesome*** is confirmed gold by the RIAA.
Nov [23] Travis helps the Feed The Children charity distribute food and toys to local beneficiaries at the Someone Cares Mission in St. Louis, MO.
Dec [1] He guests on NBC-TV's "Hot Country Nights".

1992

Feb [14] Travis embarks on the 15-city "GMC Truck American Music Tour" at the Palace of Auburn Hills, Auburn Hills, MI.
[18] The RIAA certifies gold sales of ***An Old Time Christmas*** and three million sales of ***Storms Of Life***.
[25] He appears on NBC-TV's "Late Night With David Letterman".
[27] Having already cameod in the movie, "Young Guns", and TV sitcom "Down Home", Travis guests as a hitch-hiking house painter and aspiring country singer in "Matlock", with Andy Griffith.
Apr [1] Travis participates in the silver anniversary of the Country Music Hall of Fame, from the Grand Ole Opry, set to air on CBS on May 20th. (He became the Opry's 64th member the previous year.)
[29] He performs at the 27th annual Academy of Country Music Awards.
May [1] Travis sells out the new 4,000-seater hall at Grand Palace, Branson, MO.

July [17] He is interviewed with George Jones, Alan Jackson and Vince Gill, on CBS-TV's "Burt Reynolds" show.
Aug [6] Travis plays before a sellout crowd of 3,400 at the Melody Fair Theatre, North Tonawanda, NY, during his current US tour.
[8] Written and recorded specifically for the event, Travis' *Heart To Climb A Mountain* airs over NBC-TV's coverage of the Marathon at the 1992 Olympic Games. (The cut is also featured on the ***Barcelona Gold*** compilation.)
Oct [10] ***Greatest Hits, Vol. 1*** makes US #44.
[17] The concurrently-issued ***Greatest Hits, Vol. 2*** makes US #67.
Dec [3] Travis is honored in Washington by the USO for his work on their behalf.
[8-12] He plays his final dates of the year at Bally's Casino Resort, Las Vegas, NV, having grossed more than $6 million in concert during 1992.
[10] Travis appears on ABC-TV's "Best Of Country '92 : Countdown At The Neon Armadillo".
[14] He guests on NBC-TV's "The Tonight Show".

1993

Feb [16] Travis performs on NBC-TV's "Academy Of Country Music's Hits" special.
Aug [23] He makes a return visit to "The Tonight Show".
Sept [18] ***Wind In The Wire***, Travis' original soundtrack to the TV film of the same name which aired on ABC-TV on August 25th, makes US #121, as he works on the movie "At Risk" in San Francisco, about AIDS in the heterosexual community.

1994

Mar [1] Following his first concerts in 14 months, Travis now plays at the Warner Bros. showcase at the County Radio Seminar in Nashville.
Apr [29] He guests on CBS-TV's "Late Show With David Letterman".
May [3] Travis takes part in the 29th annual Academy of Country Music Awards, from Los Angeles.
[21] ***This Is Me*** reaches US #59.
July [6] ***This Is Me*** is certified gold by the RIAA.
Aug [28] Travis records a commercial in Camarillo, CA for the New Jersey-based Home Loans company.
Sept [3] He returns to the top of the US Country chart, with *Whisper My Name*.
[25] Travis performs at the Northwest Concert Center, Western Washington Fair, Puyallup, WA, during his latest US dates.

1995

Jan [19] He embarks on another round of US dates, at the Broome County Veterans Memorial Arena, Binghamton, NY.
Mar [6] The RIAA certifies platinum sales of ***Greatest Hits, Vol. 1*** and ***Vol. 2***.
Apr [22] ***Come Together : America Salutes The Beatles***, a country tribute album to which Travis has contributed his version of *Nowhere Man*, which he had previously performed at the May 5th, 1990 "John Lennon Tribute Concert", debuts at its US #90 peak.
Sept [2] Travis grosses $160,530 from a show at the Concord Pavilion, Concord, CA, during a series of dates in California.
Nov [7] He hosts a multi-artist concert at Opryhouse, Nashville, TN, to benefit the children's facial deformity treatment charity, Operation Smile.
Dec [12] Travis stars in the CBS-TV movie "A Holiday To Remember" with Connie Sellecca.

1996

Aug [9-11] Travis plays at Bally's Grand Hotel, Atlantic City, NJ, during a series of US dates.

THE TREMELOES

See: **Brian POOLE & THE TREMELOES**

T. REX

Marc Bolan (vocals, guitar);
Steve Peregrin Took (percussion)

1965

Aug [9] Bolan (b. Mark Feld, Sept. 30, 1947, Hackney, London), having formed a skiffle group with Stephen Gould, Melvyn Fields, Helen Shapiro and Susan Singer as Susie & the Hula Hoops, in the summer of 1957 (Shapiro will go on to great solo success in the early '60s, while her cousin, Singer, name-changes to Susan Holliday and records for Columbia with Gould, having one-off success with a version of the Beatles' *Girl* as half of Truth), appeared in a photo-ed piece on mods in the **Evening Standard** in 1961, featured in **Town** magazine in September 1962, photographed by Donald McCullin, and appeared as an extra on ITV children's show, "Five O'Clock Club", has recorded demos under the name Toby Tyler in January and February at Maximum Sound and Abbey Road studios, which have now led to his signing to the Decca label.
Sept [14] Bolan records *The Wizard*, *Beyond The Risin' Sun* and *That's The Bag I'm In* at Decca's West Hampstead studios.
Nov [12] Having changed his performing name from Toby Tyler to Marc Bolan, he performs his first single, *The Wizard*, on ITV's "Ready Steady, Go!".
[23] He makes his second TV appearance on "Five O'Clock Funfair", and will play his first gig at the Pontiac Club in Putney, London, by month's end.

1966

June His second single, *The Third Degree*, is released.
Nov Bolan links with new producer, Simon Napier-Bell (also the Yardbirds' manager), and records a third single, *Hippy Gumbo*, for EMI, plus many other tracks which will only emerge in 1974, after he achieves fame.
Dec [13] He performs *Hippy Gumbo* on ITV's "Ready Steady, Go!", on the same edition which sees Jimi Hendrix make his TV debut.

1967

Mar He signs to Track Records and joins South London psychedelic group, John's Children, as guitarist/harmony vocalist, along with Andy Ellison (vocals), John Hewlett (bass) and Chris Townson (drums).
Apr The group has already been kicked off a Who tour after inciting a riot at the Rheinhalle, Ludwigshafen, West Germany, which resulted in the headline band being unable to appear.
[29] John's Children take part in the "14 Hour Technicolor Dream" at London's Alexandra Palace.
May [19] Bolan makes his final appearance at the John's Children Club, Leatherhead, Surrey.
June [11] A Bolan-placed ad in **Melody Maker** reads:- "Freaky lead guitarist, bass guitarist and drummer wanted for Marc Bolan's new group. Also any other astral flyers like with cars, amplification and that which never grows in window boxes. Phone WIMBLEDON 0697 9am-3pm". Took (b. Stephen Porter, July 28, 1949, Eltham, Kent) and Ben Cartland are the two successful applicants, joining his group which will make its debut in July at the Electric Garden, Covent Garden, London.
Aug [14] Six Bolan songs are featured on the final edition of John Peel's underground show, "The Perfumed Garden", on the pirate station, Radio London. Peel becomes so enamored of the band, that they will always appear with him at his Friday and Saturday night residencies at the Electric Garden (now renamed Middle Earth) and as part of his entourage for club and college bookings.
Oct [30] Tyrannosaurus Rex records a session for Radio 1's "Top Gear", the first group without a record deal to do so.

1968

Feb The duo signs a deal with producer Tony Visconti, with records set for release on EMI's Regal Zonophone label.
Mar [21] They appear at London's Royal Albert Hall, supporting Donovan, in a concert benefitting the Imperial College charity carnival.
May The debut Tyrannosaurus Rex single, *Debora*, reaches UK #34.
June [29] They take part in a free concert in London's Hyde Park, with Pink Floyd, Jethro Tull and Roy Harper.
July ***My People Were Fair And Had Sky In Their Hair, But Now They're Content To Wear Stars On Their Brow***, recorded at Advision Studio, makes UK #15.
[6] The duo takes part in the "Woburn Music Festival", Woburn, Beds. (They will also perform at the Isle of Wight and Kempton Park festivals.)
Aug [9-11] Tyrannosaurus Rex takes part in the eighth "National Jazz & Blues Festival", Kempton Park Racecourse, Sunbury-on-Thames, Middx.
Sept *One Inch Rock* reaches UK #28.
Nov ***Prophets, Seers And Sages, The Angels Of The Ages*** is issued in the UK, as the duo makes its TV debut on "John Peel In Concert".

1969

Jan *Pewter Suitor* is released.
Mar Bolan's book of poetry, **The Warlock Of Love**, is published.
June Third album, ***Unicorn***, reaches UK #12.
Aug *King Of The Rumbling Spires* spends a week at UK #44, and is the group's first record to feature Bolan playing electric guitar.
[6] The group begins a US tour, in a reciprocal arrangement with the Musicians' Union, to allow Bob Dylan to play at the Isle of Wight festival.
Oct Following their poorly-received US trek, Took leaves, and is replaced by Mickey Finn (b. Michael Finn, June 3, 1947, Thornton Heath, Surrey), who has been introduced to Bolan by a mutual friend. Bolan had received 300 replies to his **Melody Maker** ad: "Wanted to work with T. Rex - a gentle young guy who can play percussion, i.e. bongos and drum-kit, some bass guitar and vocal harmony. Photos please. Box 8679."
Nov [21] Tyrannosaurus Rex begins a UK tour at Manchester's Free Trade Hall.

1970

Jan *By The Light Of The Magical Moon* is released by the new duo.
[4] They perform a live concert at the BBC.
[8] Bolan plays guitar on David Bowie's newly released *Prettiest Star*.
Mar ***A Beard Of Stars*** reaches UK #21.
May [25] The duo performs at the Electric Garden, Glasgow, Scotland, at the end of a short Scottish tour.
June [1] Tyrannosaurus Rex takes part in "Pop Extravaganza '70" at the Olympia Hall, London.
Aug Bolan, Visconti, Bowie and Rick Wakeman release an impromptu UK single, *Oh Baby*, under the name Dib Cochran & the Earwigs. It fails to sell, but will later be an in-demand collectors' rarity.
Oct Visconti shifts the label outlet for his productions from Regal Zonophone to Fly Records in Britain. After much urging from his producer, Bolan abbreviates his group name to T. Rex, and releases *Ride A White Swan*, which climbs steadily to hit UK #2 at the year's end.
Nov [28] At a Roundhouse, Dagenham, Essex, gig, the Turtles' Howard Kaylan joins the duo on stage.
Dec [12] Steve Currie (b. May 20, 1947, Grimsby, Lincs.) joins on bass. ***T. Rex*** peaks at UK #13, in a chart residency lasting six months.

1971

Feb [13] *Ride A White Swan*, the group's US chart debut, peaks at #76.
Mar [20] *Hot Love*, introducing a pop/glam rock meld which will characterize his forthcoming string of hits, tops the UK chart for the first of six weeks.
Bill Legend (b. William Fifield, May 8, 1944, Barking, Essex) joins on drums, making his debut in Detroit, MI, at the start of a US tour supporting

Humble Pie and Mountain. (Bolan calls him Legend because he was recruited from the Mickey Jupp-led group of the same name.)
June [5] *Hot Love* peaks at US #72, while ***T. Rex*** edges in at #188.
July [24] *Get It On* tops the UK chart for the first of four weeks, and will become Bolan and T. Rex's biggest international hit.
Aug Compilation album, ***The Best Of T. Rex***, largely composed of tracks by Tyrannosaurus Rex, reaches UK #21.
[28-29] The group takes part in the "Weeley Festival", Weeley, Essex.
Oct ***Electric Warrior***, the first album by the four-piece group, is released.
[19] The group embarks on a UK tour at the Portsmouth Guildhall.
Nov As Bolan decides to leave Fly Records for a new deal, the label issues the album track, *Jeepster* (never intended by Bolan for single release), which leaps to UK #2.
Dec [18] ***Electric Warrior*** begins a six-week reign at UK #1, and will reach US #32. Bolan joins Elton John onstage at Croydon's Fairfield Halls, performing a medley of *Get It On*, *Whole Lotta Shakin'* and *My Baby Left Me*.

1972

Jan [1] Bolan signs a new deal with EMI, allowing him to release records in Britain on his own T. Rex Wax Co. label.
Feb [5] *Telegram Sam*, the first EMI release, tops the UK chart for the first of two weeks.
[10] T. Rex begins its first headlining US tour in Seattle, WA.
Mar [4] *Bang A Gong (Get It On)* is Bolan's biggest US hit, at #10, where the title amendment has been necessary because another group, Chase, has had a Top 30 hit with a different song titled *Get It On* in 1971.
[18] T. Rex plays two soldout concerts at the Empire Pool, Wembley, Middx., to audiences of 100,000, while being filmed by Ringo Starr for the Apple documentary film on the group's success, "Born To Boogie". (This is the first instance of a rock concert at the venue, apart from the annual "**New Musical Express** Poll Winners" concerts.)
May [6] Double album reissue, coupling ***My People Were Fair ...*** and ***Prophets, Seers And Sages*** by Tyrannosaurus Rex, tops the UK chart for a week, while a single-reissue, twinning *Debora* and *One Inch Rock*, hits UK #7.
[13] *Telegram Sam* peaks at #67.
[20] *Metal Guru* ("It's about a car," says Bolan) begins a four-week stay atop the UK chart and ***Bolan Boogie***, on Fly, compiling the hits up to *Jeepster*, begins a three-week tenure at UK #1, as the country is afflicted by "T. Rextasy".
June [9] T. Rex begins a short UK tour at the Birmingham Odeon. (At the start of the Manchester Belle Vue show, a fan breaks his jaw in the rush to get good front row seats.)
[22] Track and Polydor Records are prevented by an injunction from releasing ***Hard On Love***, an album of demo recordings.
July Newly-recorded ***The Slider*** hits #4 in the UK (reputedly selling 100,000 copies in four days), and also becomes the group's most successful US album, peaking at #17.
Sept *Children Of The Revolution* hits UK #2, as the group embarks on a North American trek in Montreal, Canada, supported by the Doobie Brothers, who by tour's end will be the headliners.
Dec [14] The "Born To Boogie" movie, featuring T. Rex, premieres in London. *Solid Gold Easy Action* peaks at UK #3, while another double reissue album, coupling ***Unicorn*** and ***A Beard Of Stars***, charts briefly at UK #44.

1973

Jan [27] Bolan guests on BBC1-TV's "Cilla Black Show", duetting on *Life's A Gas*.
Mar *Twentieth Century Boy* hits UK #3, while ***Tanx*** hits #4, and also reaches US #102.
June *The Groover* hits UK #4 - T. Rex's tenth and final UK top five hit.
July Jack Green and Paul Fenton join the group on additional guitar and drums respectively, and three girl backup vocalists are recruited, including US soul singer, Gloria Jones (b. Sept. 19, 1947, OH), who will become Bolan's girlfriend. (Bolan had met Jones on tour in the US in 1969, when she was appearing in "Hair". In 1972, she had been a house writer for Motown, co-penning Gladys Knight's Grammy-nominated *If I Were Your Woman*, the Jackson 5's *2468*, Diana Ross and Marvin Gaye's *My Mistake Was To Love You* and the Four Tops' *Just Seven Numbers (Can Straighten Out My Life)*, before coming to the UK in the summer of 1972 as a member of the Sanctified Sisters, part of Joe Cocker's backing band.)
[20] The group embarks on a 31-date US tour at the Milwaukee Arena, Milwaukee, WI, set to end on September 2nd at the "Evansville Rock Festival", Evansville, IN.
Aug ***Blackjack*** is issued in the UK under the name Marc Bolan with Big Carrot.
Nov Compilation album, ***Great Hits*** (an anthology from *Telegram Sam* onwards), peaks at UK #32. (Legend quits the group after a tour of Australia.)
Dec *Truck On (Tyke)* reaches UK #12.

1974

Jan [22] The group, now comprising Bolan, Finn, Currie, Green, Fenton and Davey Lutton (drums), embarks on a six-date "Truck Off" tour at Glasgow's Apollo Theatre, set to end on the 28th at Birmingham's Odeon Cinema. The shows are T. Rex's first major UK dates in two years. (Green and Fenton will be dropped from the band at the end of the tour.)
Feb *Teenage Dream* reaches UK #13, the first release on which the group's name is amended to Marc Bolan and T. Rex.
Mar ***Zinc Alloy And The Hidden Riders Of Tomorrow*** reaches UK #12, as Bolan parts company with his long-time producer, Visconti.
Apr Bolan leaves Britain for several months' tax exile in Monte Carlo.
June Tracks recorded as demos in 1966 with Simon Napier-Bell finally gain commercial release in the UK, via Track Records, as ***The Beginning Of Doves***, and the maxi-single, *Jasper C. Debussy*.
July *Light Of Love* reaches UK #22.
Sept The group embarks on another US tour, playing with Black Oak Arkansas, Blue Öyster Cult and Kiss on various dates.
Oct [8] Bolan guests on "Don Kirshner's Rock Concert".
Nov *Zip Gun Boogie*, taken from ***Zip Gun***, makes UK #41.
Dec Dino Dines joins on keyboards.

1975

Feb Finn quits.
July *New York City* restores Bolan to the UK Top 20, reaching #15.
Sept [26] Rolan, son of Bolan and Gloria Jones, is born in London.
Oct *Dreamy Lady* (credited to T. Rex Disco Party) reaches UK #30, as Bolan is offered his own interview slot on ITV's "Today".

1976

Mar ***Futuristic Dragon*** and the extracted *London Boys* make UK #50 and #40 respectively.
July *I Love To Boogie* becomes Bolan's last UK Top 20 hit, reaching #13.
Aug "Rollin' Bolan" airs on ITV, marking the last time Currie and Lutton perform with the band.
Oct *Laser Love* makes UK #41. Bolan performs the song on BBC1-TV's "Top Of The Pops" with Dines (keyboards), Miller Anderson (guitar), Herbie Flowers (bass) and Tony Newman (drums).
Dec [19] They also make up the final touring line-up of T. Rex, accompanying Bolan on a charity date at London's Drury Lane Theatre Royal, filmed for an ITV "Supersonic Christmas Special", in conjunction with the **Daily Mirror** Pop Club.

1977

Jan Bolan and Gloria Jones issue a duet revival of the Teddy Bears' *To Know Him Is To Love Him*, later becoming another collectors' item.
Mar [10] The group embarks on a final tour, with new wave band the Damned supporting.
[20] The final live T. Rex gig takes place at the Locarno in Portsmouth, Hants.
Apr *The Soul Of My Suit* makes UK #42, while ***Dandy In The Underworld***, Bolan's final album to be issued in his lifetime, reaches UK #26. (The album title track will be issued as a quick UK follow-up single.)
Aug *Celebrate Summer* fails to chart in the UK, making it Bolan's second consecutive miss. Meanwhile, he begins a stint as a guest pop journalist, writing a weekly column in **Record Mirror**, and also hosts a series of six weekly Wednesday late-afternoon ITV shows, titled "Marc". Guests include David Bowie (on September 9th), the Boomtown Rats, the Jam and Generation X. (Bolan signs off each week's show with "Keep a little Marc in your heart, see ya next week, same Marc time, same Marc channel".)
Sept [16] After a long night out at a London club, Bolan and Gloria Jones are on their way home when, at 5:00 a.m., their car (driven by Jones) leaves the road at a bend on Barnes Common, London, and crashes into a tree. Jones is badly injured, and Bolan is killed, two weeks shy of his 30th birthday. (The car, a purple Mini 1275 GT had a tyre replaced and its wheels balanced by a Sheen garage three days earlier. It is discovered after the crash that the off-side tyre pressure was 16 pounds, when by law it is required to be 26 pounds, and that two nuts on the off-side front wheel were only finger tight.)
[20] Bolan is cremated at Golders Green Crematorium, London.

1978

Apr *Crimson Moon* is the first posthumous Bolan release and, though it fails to chart, it begins a sequence of reissues and releases comprising previously unheard material which will still be in full flood a decade after his death. (In all, five UK singles will chart posthumously: the EP *Return Of The Electric Warrior* (May 1981 - #50), *You Scare Me To Death* (September 1981 - #51), a reissue of *Telegram Sam* (March 1982 - #69), a medley of hit extracts titled *Megarex* (May 1985 - #72) and *Get It On* (May 1987 - #54). Four albums: ***Solid Gold*** (July 1979 - #51), ***T. Rex In Concert*** (September 1981 - #35), ***You Scare Me To Death*** (November 1981 - #88), ***Dance In The Midnight*** (September 1983 - #83) and ***Best Of The 20th Century Boy*** (May 1985 - #5) - will also be posthumous UK chart entries over the next six years.)

1980

Oct [27] Bolan's first performing partner, Steve Peregrine Took, having spent a royalty cheque on the purchase of morphine and magic mushrooms, chokes to death on a cherry after the mushrooms numb any sensation in his throat.

1981

Apr [28] Currie is killed around midnight when his car veers off the road as he returns to his Val Da Parra, Portugal home.

1985

May A greatest hits package, ***Best Of The 20th Century Boy***, hits UK #5, and an accompanying video collection also confirms Bolan's enduring popularity. Channel 5 video company will release "Marc", a compilation of Bolan's '70s TV appearances, in February 1989, the same year his albums begin to become available on CD in the US.

1995

Oct [7] After *20th Century Boy*, re-released by the

Total Record Company to tie in with its use on a Levis 501 jeans commercial, with royalties going to Bolan's estate, has re-charted at UK #13 on Sept [14], 1991, the Marc Bolan Liberation Front co-organized a 15th anniversary party at Lacey's nightclub on the 16th of that month, with proceeds going to the London Lighthouse AIDS fund and Cancer Research. (The Liberation Front subsequently issued a statement that John Bramley and his Marc On Wax label should be investigated, having enjoyed a ten-year license with EMI to issue product.)
[28] Following Marc Bolan & T. Rex's ***The Ultimate Collection*** UK #4 success on Sept [28], 1991, a further compilation, ***The Essential Collection*** now reaches UK #24 in its week of entry.

TRICKY

1991

Mar [28] Tricky (b. Adrian Thaws), an asthmatic who has been raised by his grandmother since the age of four when his mother died, has grown up in the Bristol, Avon ghetto of Knowle West. Nicknamed Tricky Kid as a teenager, he has been seduced into petty crime, spending four days in prison at the age of 17 for distributing forged £50 notes. Inspired to become a rapper after hearing Slick Rick, but also weaned on his grandmother's Nina Simone records, Tricky has joined the Bristol-based Wild Bunch R&B aggregate, breeding ground for the burgeoning Bristol sound, through his friend and co-member Milo Johnson in late '80s, and has subsequently been invited to join its offspring, Massive Attack's maiden sessions. The group's critically-revered debut album ***Blue Lines***, to which Tricky has contributed three tracks, now makes UK #67.

1994

Feb [5] *Aftermath*, with singer and girlfriend, Martina (whom Tricky met in 1991), charts for a week at UK #69.
Oct [8] Having recently completed the programming for Chante Moore's MCA-released album ***A Love Supreme***, signed with fellow-Bristol act Portishead's Fruit management team and subsequently to Island Records as a solo artist via his own Durban Poison label, and begun recording his debut album with Martina, though she will also continue her studies at Cambridge), two Tricky contributions appear on Massive Attack's sophomore album ***Protection***, which now hits UK #4.

1995

Jan [28] *Overcome* bows at its UK #34 peak.
Mar [4] His 12-track, trip-hop, self-produced debut album, ***Maxinquaye***, including a cover of Public Enemy's *Black Steel* and featuring music guests Martina, Pete Briquette, Alison Goldfrapp, Ragga and Mark Saunders among others, hits UK #3 in its week of entry.
Apr [15] *Black Steel* reaches UK #28 in its week of entry.
June [24] Partly produced by Tricky, who also appears on the track *Enjoy*, Björk's album ***Post*** enters at its UK #2 high and will debut at its US #32 peak the following week.
Aug [5] *The Hell EP*, credited to Tricky Vs. The Gravediggaz, reaches UK #12 in its week of entry.
[26] Tricky takes part in "Reading '95", near Reading, Berks.
Nov [11] *Pumpkin* debuts at its UK #26 peak.

1996

Apr [20] *Poems*, credited to the artist Nearly God - which is also the title of his second album, reaches UK #28 in its week of entry.
May [4] ***Nearly God***, titled after his own media-fed deification, featuring guests, Damon Albarn, Terry Hall, Bjork and Neneh Cherry, debuts at is UK #10 peak.
Aug [18] Tricky takes part in the "V96" festival in Hylands Park, Chelmsford, Essex.

THE TROGGS

Reg Presley (vocals); **Chris Britton** (guitar); **Pete Staples** (bass); **Ronnie Bond** (drums)

1964

Based in Andover, Hants, the group intially forms as the Troglodytes comprising Howard Mansfield (guitar, lead vocals), Dave Wright (guitar), and ex-apprentice bricklayers, Presley (b. Reginald Ball, June 12, 1943, Andover - he will not use the name Presley until 1966) (bass) and Bond (b. Ronald Bullis, May 4, 1943, Andover) (drums), in school band the Emeralds. The following year, Mansfield and Wright leave the group, and are replaced by Britton (b. June 21, 1945, Watford, Herts.) and Staples (b. May 3, 1944, Andover), both ex-Andover group, Ten Foot Five. Staples plays bass, so Presley, with initial reluctance, becomes lead vocalist in Mansfield's place. This new line-up, which rehearses above the Copper Kettle café in Andover High Street, is spotted and signed by the Kinks' manager, Larry Page, after he witnesses their very basic live rendition of the Kinks' *You Really Got Me* (a rawness which will always underpin the Troggs' individuality.)

1966

Feb [11] Having abridged its name to the Troggs, the group's debut single, Presley's song, *Lost Girl*, leased by Page to CBS, is released.
Apr *Wild Thing*, penned by US writer Chip Taylor, and cut (obscurely) in the US by Jordan Christopher & the Wild Ones, is sent to Page by his American publishing associate. The group thinks the lyric corny but, once the heavy, innuendo-laden arrangement is worked out, it is recorded in a rapid session, with an unusual ocarina solo in place of the whistling passage on the US original.
May At the suggestion of **New Musical Express** journalist Keith Altham, Ball changes his name to Reg Presley (which, as anticipated, gets him press notice once the record is climbing), as the single is released via a new deal between Page's production company, Page One, and the Fontana label. Following an initial play on BBC Radio's "Saturday Club", and TV slots on "Thank Your Lucky Stars" and "Top Of The Pops", *Wild Thing* hits UK #2.
July [30] *Wild Thing* tops the US chart for the first of two weeks, eventually selling more than a million copies. Because of a US-rights dispute, it is released there on both the Fontana and Atco labels. The Fontana release shares the same B-side as the UK version, but Atco couples *Wild Thing* with the UK follow-up, *With A Girl Like You*.
Aug [4] Presley's composition, *With A Girl Like You*, cut in slightly lighter, but similar, style to *Wild Thing*, begins a two-week stay atop the UK chart while the group's debut album, ***From Nowhere ... The Troggs***, hits UK #6.
Sept [10] Fontana issues *With A Girl Like You* in the US, but since many of its consumers already own the track from the *Wild Thing* release, it halts at US #29.
Oct [1] The group begins a 33-date, "Star Scene 66" twice-nightly package tour, with the Walker Brothers and Dave Dee, Dozy, Beaky, Mick & Tich, at the Granada Cinema, East Ham, London, set to close on November 13th at London's Finsbury Park Astoria.
[29] The Presley-penned *I Can't Control Myself* hits UK #2 (released on Page's new Page One label), as *Wild Thing* climbs to US #52.
Nov [12] *I Can't Control Myself*, also a dual-label release in the US, makes #43.

1967

Jan Another Chip Taylor song, *Any Way That You Want Me* (also a US hit three years later for Evie Sands), hits UK #8.
Feb [17] The band begins a 28-date UK tour, with Gene Pitney, David Garrick, Sounds Incorporated, the Loot and Normie Rowe & the Playboys, at Finsbury Park Astoria, set to end on March 19th at the Coventry Theatre, Coventry, Warks.
Mar Chanted *Give It To Me*, also Presley-inked, reaches UK #12, while ***Trogglodynamite*** hits UK #10.
Apr [1] Page announces he is imposing a "ban in reverse": he is forbidding the Troggs from playing London dates, because of illegal-drug publicity the city's music venues are receiving. (The date of the ban appears to be significant.)
[3] The group cancels a recording session after Britton announces he is quitting. "I am fed up with the connection between pop groups and drugs. It is so bad now, you cannot move without being searched. My guitar was pulled to pieces last week when we came back from the Continent. It has depressed me and got on my nerves so that I cannot play properly and I'm letting down the group. I can't stand the way people look at you and immediately think that because you're in a group you're drugged to the eyebrows. I'm getting out." (He will change his mind shortly thereafter.)
June *Night Of The Long Grass*, a deliberate change of sound with a hint of psychedelia in lyric and arrangement, and released in favor of the intended *My Lady*, reaches UK #17.
[8] The group leaves Britain for a three-week tour of Sweden.
[30] A High Court injunction prevents the band from engaging anyone other than Page One Records to act as its managers, agents or representatives, after it tries to leave the label.
Aug *Hi Hi Hazel* (a minor UK hit the previous year for soul singer, Geno Washington) peaks at UK #42, while a compilation, ***Best Of The Troggs***, reaches UK #24, the group's last UK chart album.
Nov *Love Is All Around*, a ballad with merely a hint of *Wild Thing*'s jerky rhythm, hits UK #5. (Presley had written the song on a Sunday afternoon after lunch while watching a TV program with the Salvation Army singing about love being all around.) Agent Danny Betesh says that the group will visit Los Angeles in February 1968 to sign a deal to write the title song for a Hollywood movie.
[20] The Troggs win the Del Mar Plata 1967 Award at the annual "Festival of International Records" held in Argentina.

1968

Mar *Little Girl* reaches UK #37, and is the Troggs' last UK chart entry. (The band will continue live work for another year on the UK club and college circuits.)
May [18] *Love Is All Around* hits US #7.
June ***Love Is All Around*** makes US #109.

1969

Presley and Bond both record solo singles, *Lucinda Lee* and *Anything For You* respectively, as Britton releases ***As I Am***. (Staples, whose bass playing has given the group cause for concern, is replaced by Tony Murray, from label-mates, Plastic Penny.)

1972

Following a split from Page, the Troggs, newly signed to Pye, recruit Richard Moore to replace Britton, who moves to Portugal to start his own nightclub. A studio tape made during sessions in their later days at Page One also surfaces in bootleg form, under the title ***The Troggs Tapes***, its main interest being West Country foul language as the group struggles with the attempted creation of a hit. This revives interest in the Troggs, particularly in the US.

1973

Nov [16] The group performs *Wild Thing* on David Bowie's first US TV special, "The 1980 Floor Show", taped earlier at London's Marquee club, and aired on NBC-TV's "Midnight Special".

1975

Jan The Troggs, reunited with Page, cut a revival of the Beach Boys' *Good Vibrations* for his Penny

Farthing label. Reviews are more amused than scathing, but it fails to chart.

Nov The band revival of the Rolling Stones' *(I Can't Get No) Satisfaction* also fails to score.

1976

May The group is on a nostalgia tour of the US when the Sire label releases the compilation, ***Vintage Years***, containing the Troggs' '60s hits.

July Penny Farthing releases ***The Troggs Tapes*** (which capitalizes on the bootleg-tape title, but has nothing to do with it). Rhythm guitarist Colin Fletcher has now made the group a quintet.

Nov [14] While the inherent non-musicality of the Troggs is currently cited as an influence by many punk groups, (Los Angeles band X is reviving *Wild Thing* on disc), the group performs at London's Roundhouse with the Damned and the Flamin' Groovies.

1980

Signed in the US to Basement records, the band releases ***Live At Max's Kansas City***, recorded at the New York club. (With a cult following which is apparently undying, the group will continue regular live work in both the US and UK into the '90s.)

1989

Apr [27] The group appears at a concert at the City Hall, Sheffield, S. Yorks., in aid of the Hillsborough soccer disaster.

1990

Wild Thing is extensively aired on UK TV as the theme for a Lion Bar chocolate ad, and will receive further exposure when used for ITV's "Gladiators" program (re-charting at UK #69 on Oct [30], 1993, with help from gladiator, Wolf. (It also receives added attention in the US, when used in the baseball movie, "Major League", to illustrate Charlie Sheen's character. Real-life pitcher Mitch Williams will then have the nickname "Wild Thing", attached to him.)

1991

Sept The group, now comprising Presley, Britton (who had re-joined in 1978), Peter Lucas (bass) and Dave Maggs (drums), begins work on the new album, ***Athens Andover***, with help from Athens, GA-based R.E.M. members at Jacobs Studio in Farnham, Surrey.

1992

Mar ***Athens Andover*** is released on Essential/Page One Records, prior to the issue of a two-CD retrospective, ***Archeology (1966-1976)*** by Fontana /Mercury Records.

Aug [22] The Troggs are the live band at Sting's wedding reception.

Nov [13] Bond dies, age 51, at Winchester General Hospital, Winchester, survived by his wife and three sons.

1994

June [4] After the Troggs' re-recording of *Wild Thing* has bowed at its UK #69 peak on Oct [30] the previous year, Wet Wet Wet's version of *Love Is All Around*, currently featured in the hit movie "Four Weddings And A Funeral", begins an unbroken 15-week run at the top of the UK charts. (Presley will reportedly spend some of his royalties researching into the corn circle phenomenon.)

July [16] Troggs' compilation ***Greatest Hits***, reaches UK #27 in its week of entry.

Oct [18] Presley wins the Gold Badge award at BASCA's 20th annual awards ceremony at London's Hilton Hotel.

1995

May [23] Presley collects the Best Selling Song, the PRS Most Performed Work and International Hit Of The Year (all for *Love Is All Around*) trophies at the 40th annual Ivor Novello Awards at London's Grosvenor House Hotel.

Nov [29] The Troggs perform their most enduring songs, *Wild Thing* and *Love Is All Around* at a BASCA Songmakers event.

THE TUBES

"Fee" Waybill (vocals); **Bill "Sputnick" Spooner** (guitar); **Vince Welnick** (keyboards); **Rick Anderson** (bass); **Michael Cotten** (synthesizer); **Roger Steen** (guitar); **Prairie Prince** (drums); **Re Styles** (vocals, guitar); **Mingo Lewis** (percussion)

1975

Feb Establishing a reputation as San Francisco, CA's prime theatrical rock band, the Tubes, formed in Phoenix, AZ, in the late '60s by Anderson (b. Aug. 1, 1947, St. Paul, MN), Spooner (b. Apr. 16, 1949, Phoenix) and Welnick (b. Feb. 21, 1951, Phoenix) have been joined by front-man, and ex-drama student Waybill (b. John Waldo, Sept. 17, 1950, Omaha, NE) in 1972 in San Francisco, and, having added Cotten (b. Jan. 25, 1950, Kansas City, MO), Prince (b. May 7, 1950, Charlotte, NC), Steen (b. Nov. 13, 1949, Pipestone, MN) and Styles (b. Mar. 30, 1950), now sign to A&M Records, using the advance to produce even more extravagant stage shows.

Aug Al Kooper-produced debut, ***The Tubes***, featuring the band's anthem, *White Punks On Dope*, peaks at US #113.

1976

June ***Young And Rich***, helmed by Ken Scott, makes US #46.

Aug [14] *Don't Touch Me There*, with Waybill in the guise of glam-rock star "Quay Lewd", peaks at US #61.

1977

June ***The Tubes Now*** reaches US #122.

Nov The group tours Britain for the first time, and a live performance ban in Portsmouth, Hants., after local councillors have seen the band at an earlier date, does not hinder the chart progress of *White Punks On Dope*, which peaks at UK #28.

1978

Mar [4] Live double album, ***What Do You Want From Live***, reaches UK #38.

Apr [15] ***What Do You Want From Live***, makes US #82.

May [9] While on a further UK tour, Waybill falls off stage and breaks a leg, causing the cancellation of seven nights at London's Hammersmith Odeon. The BBC's film of the incident shows him apparently wielding a chainsaw.

Aug [9] The Tubes appear at "Knebworth II" in Knebworth, Herts., on a bill also including Frank Zappa and Peter Gabriel.

1979

Mar The band fills large venues with its outrageously burlesque stage shows, but is unable to translate its live popularity into disc sales. With the Todd Rundgren-produced US #46-peaking ***Remote Control***, they announce that their future emphasis will be along more commercial lines.

May The extracted *Prime Time* makes UK #34 spurred by an appearance on BBC1-TV's "Top Of The Pops" on the 17th.

June ***Remote Control*** reaches UK #40.

1980

Aug The band appears in the Olivia Newton-John/ Gene Kelly-starring movie, "Xanadu". (During the year, they begin recording a follow-up album, ***Suffer For Sound***, but its release is blocked by A&M.)

1981

July Having been dropped by A&M and snapped up by Capitol Records, their label debut, ***Completion Backwards Principle***, produced by David Foster, becomes the Tubes' highest charting album to date, at US #36.

Aug [8] Uncharacteristic ballad, *I Don't Want To Wait Anymore*, makes US #35 and UK #60.

1982

June While the Tubes are touring Britain, a publicity stunt involving young girls dancing on the back of a flat-bed truck in London's Tottenham Court Road results in Waybill's arrest for obstruction.

July The Tubes plays a sellout show at the Oakland Stadium, Oakland, CA, with Journey, Toto, Santana and Gamma, grossing $957,851 from a 57,000 crowd.

Sept A&M releases ***T.R.A.S.H. (Tubes Rarities And Smash Hits)***, comprising hits and out-takes, which peaks at US #148.

1983

May ***Outside Inside***, including guest appearances from Earth, Wind & Fire's Maurice White and the Motels' Martha Davis, reaches US #18 and UK #77.

July [2] The group's first and only US Top 10 hit is *She's A Beauty* at #10.

Aug [20] *Tip Of My Tongue* makes US #52.

Oct [15] *The Monkey Time* peaks at US #68.

1984

Nov Waybill's debut solo set, ***Read My Lips***, recorded at the band's own Sound Hole Studio in San Francisco, makes US #146. A second excerpt, *Piece By Piece* will peak at US #87 the following Mar [16].

1986

Mar ***Love Bomb***, reuniting the group with producer Rundgren, lands at US #87. While PMI will release "The Tubes Video", which captures the band performing *White Punks On Dope* and *Mondo Bondage* among others, in May, the band's energy is now spent, and its members mostly retreat to session work.

1993

Apr [24] After Welnick has replaced Brent Mydland in the Grateful Dead, Waybill, who appeared on Richard Marx's eponymous album in 1988, has contributed *Meeting Half The Way* to the 1990 ***Nobody's Perfect*** film soundtrack. With their career highlights brought to CD with the 1992 release of ***The Best Of The Tubes*** the reunited Tubes return to their home town to perform at the "KUPD U-Fest", at Compton Terrace, Phoenix. They will continue performing as a live band, with Waybill as lead singer, backed by Anderson, Steen and Prince, augmented by keyboardist Gary Cambra and backing vocalists Amy French and Jennifer McFee.

IKE & TINA TURNER

1951

June [9] Ike Turner (b. Izear Luster Turner, Jr., Nov. 5, 1931, Clarksdale, MS), son of Baptist minister Izear Luster Turner, Sr., a self-taught musician who has backed local bluesmen Robert Nighthawk and Sonny Boy Williamson on piano, is a DJ at Clarksdale's WROX station, which leads to recording work with his Kings Of Rhythm band, which he has formed at high school (initially as the Top Hatters). Their *Rocket 88*, recorded at Sam Phillips' Sun Studio in Memphis, with a lead vocal by sax player Jackie Brenston (and credited to him, backed by the Delta Cats (who are the Kings of Rhythm), now hits R&B #1 (and will often be cited as the first rock'n'roll record).

1952

Moving on to a considerable body of session guitar work and production, Ike will play on recordings for B.B. King, Howlin' Wolf (both of whom he recruits for Modern Records in Los Angeles, CA, having become a roving R&B talent scout for the label around the South), Johnny Ace and others, as well as touring with his band, until 1956.

1956

The Kings Of Rhythm have settled into a residency at a club in East St. Louis, MO, where Ike first meets the 17-year old Tina (who at this time is still Annie Mae Bullock, b. Nov. 26, 1939, Brownsville, TN) and her older sister, Alline. Deserted by their mother, and later their father, into the care of relatives before their teens, the sisters have moved to St. Louis to work, and are regulars at R&B clubs. Annie has been singing since childhood in church and junior talent contests, and repeatedly asks Ike if she can sing with his band, but he is not interested. One evening at the club, after the drummer has offered the microphone to her sister, who is unwilling to sing, she takes it and jumps on stage with the group. She and Ike begin dating, and she becomes a regular band vocalist.

1958

Ike and Annie are married and, at Ike's suggestion, she takes the stage name Tina Turner (because, according to Tina, "it reminded him of Sheena the jungle queen from the TV series"). During the year, Tina, who sings at night and works at a hospital during the day, also gives birth to a boy, Craig, parented by one of Ike's backing musicians.

1960

Oct [22] Their first record as Ike & Tina Turner has come about by accident when the session singer booked to record Ike's *A Fool In Love* failed to show, and Tina steps in. Already a US R&B #2 success, *A Fool In Love* is the duo's first crossover hit, now reaching US #27 on the Sue label. Ike's band becomes the Ike & Tina Turner Revue, and three female backing singers, the Ikettes, are incorporated to support Tina, around whom the show's routines revolve - she is now a striking and uninhibited live performer.

Dec [31] *I Idolize You* peaks at US #82 and R&B #5. *It's Gonna Work Out Fine* will be their first US Top 20 hit, reaching #14 (and R&B #2) on Sept [18] the following year, three months prior to the release of their debut album, ***The Soul Of Ike & Tina Turner***.

1962

Jan [27] *Poor Fool* makes US #38 (and R&B #4).

Feb Without Tina, the Ikettes and the band have recorded *I'm Blue (The Gong Gong Song)*, which Ike has leased to Atco and which reaches US #19.

Apr [28] *Tra La La La La* makes US #50.

June [30] *You Should'a Treated Me Right* peaks at US #89 and is the duo's last pop hit for Sue Records (which will also issue two further Ike & Tina Turner albums during the year, ***It's Gonna Work Out Fine*** and ***Don't Play Me Cheap***).

1964

Oct [17] *I Can't Believe What You Say (For Seeing What You Do)* reaches US #95, the duo's only single for the Kent label. A pattern of R&B successes that do not always cross over is developing: the Ike & Tina Turner Revue will be one of the most popular acts of the '60s on the R&B tour circuit, but will only consistently break to wider audiences towards the end of the decade.

1965

Feb They move to Warner Bros. Records on the strength of the recent hit single. No singles chart entries will follow on the label however, but ***Live! The Ike And Tina Turner Show***, a recording of their highly-rated stage act at the Skyliner Ballroom, Fort Worth, TX, makes US #126.

Apr Ike has recorded the Ikettes again for Kent's sister label, Modern, and their *Peaches'n'Cream* climbs to US #36.

Nov The Ikettes' follow-up, *I'm So Thankful*, peaks at US #74.

Dec They film a segment, performing *One More Time* and *It's Gonna Work Out Fine,* for the "TNT Award Show" TV program, with Joan Baez, Bo Diddley, the Byrds, Ray Charles, the Lovin' Spoonful, the Ronettes, Roger Miller, Petula Clark and Donovan.

1966

Jan While moving around in one-off record deals with independent labels like Innis and Pompeii, they meet producer Phil Spector, who offers Ike $20,000 dollars to put Tina under a production contract. (Spector admires Tina's voice, but is underwhelmed by Ike's production of her records, so the payment is part of a condition that Ike will not be involved in the sessions.) Songwriters Jeff Barry and Ellie Greenwich are called in to pen songs, with Spector.

Mar [7] Tina records her vocal on *River Deep, Mountain High* after Spector has already spent over $22,000 creating the "Wall Of Sound" backing track.

June [18] Released on Spector's Philles label, *River Deep, Mountain High* peaks at US #88. (This apparent rejection of what he regards as one of his finest productions is given as a major factor in Spector's shutdown of Philles immediately afterwards, and his semi-retirement from production.)

July By contrast, *River Deep, Mountain High* is a major UK success (the duo's first), hitting #3. Warner Bros. releases an earlier track, *Tell Her I'm Not Home*, in the UK, and this too charts, making #48. After years as an R&B enthusiasts' act in Europe and the UK, the Turners are suddenly considered major stars - despite still being restricted to the R&B circuit in the US.

Sept [23] They begin a 12-date "Rolling Stones '66" UK tour with headliners the Rolling Stones and the Yardbirds, Long John Baldry and others, at London's Royal Albert Hall, set to end on October 9th at the Gaumont Theatre, Southampton, Hants. They also appear on ITV's "Ready Steady, Go!"

Oct ***River Deep, Mountain High***, coupling Spector productions with new Ike Turner-produced versions of oldies by the duo, makes UK #27.

Nov Spector-produced UK (but not released in the US) follow-up from the same sessions as *River Deep*, a revival of a Martha & the Vandellas B-side, *A Love Like Yours*, reaches UK #16.

Dec The group performs during Christmas week at the Galaxy in Hollywood.

1967

Apr [2] Following the February release of ***The Ike & Tina Turner Show Vol. II***, they embark on an eight-day promotional visit of the UK. (During a relatively barren recording period, the only studio release will be ***So Fine*** in 1968.)

1969

Feb *River Deep, Mountain High* is reissued in the UK, and reaches #33.

May The duo signs a two-album deal with Blue Thumb Records, cutting mainly blues-based material, and also a longer-term contract with Minit. A revival of Otis Redding's *I've Been Loving You Too Long* on Blue Thumb peaks at US #68 on May [31], and *I'm Gonna Do All I Can (To Do Right By My Man)*, for Minit, reaches US #98 on May [17], while the Blue Thumb album, ***Outa Season***, makes US #91.

June [20] Ike & Tina Turner perform during the three-day "Newport '69 Festival" at San Fernando Valley State College, Devonshire Downs, Northridge, CA.

Aug [2] *The Hunter*, on Blue Thumb, peaks at US #93, while the live Minit album, ***In Person***, recorded at Basin Street West, reaches US #142.

Oct ***River Deep, Mountain High***, finally released in the US on A&M after three years, peaks at US #102.

Nov A second Blue Thumb album, ***The Hunter***, makes US #176.

[7] The duo once again supports the Rolling Stones on a US tour, which opens in Denver, CO.

1970

Jan [31] Ike's composition, *Bold Soul Sister*, a final 45 for Blue Thumb, peaks at US #59.

Apr [4] Their version of the Beatles' *Come Together* (on Minit) makes US #57.

June ***Come Together*** peaks at US #130.

Aug [29] Their revival of Sly & the Family Stone's *I Want To Take You Higher* is their first hit on Liberty, which has absorbed Minit. It reaches US #34 (and will become a highlight of the Turners' live act). The Ike & Tina Turner Revue guests on prominent US TV shows, including Ed Sullivan's and Andy Williams', and they will also pick up lucrative work in Las Vegas, NV casinos. (By the end of the year Ike has built his own Bolic Sound recording studio in Inglewood, CA.)

1971

Mar [27] An R&B-style revival of Creedence Clearwater Revival's *Proud Mary* is their first US Top 10 hit, at #4, and will become their first million-selling single. It is taken from ***Workin' Together***, which is their biggest-selling album to date in the US, peaking at #25. (Despite a hugely successful European tour, neither single nor album produce similar chart results in UK.)

May [6] *Proud Mary* is certified gold by the RIAA.

June [12] Their treatment of Jesse Hill's *Ooh Poo Pah Doo* (on United Artists, as Liberty Records has now become) reaches US #60.

Sept Performance double set, ***Live At Carnegie Hall/ What You Hear Is What You Get***, reaches US #25.

Dec ***'Nuff Said*** peaks at US #108.

1972

Mar [18] *Up In Heah* makes US #83.

Aug ***Feel Good*** peaks at US #160.

Sept [11] ***Live At Carnegie Hall/What You Hear Is What You Get*** is certified gold by the RIAA, the duo's only album to officially sell over half a million copies in the US.

1973

Nov [17] Tina's composition, the stomping, roots-themed *Nutbush City Limits*, reaches US #22, and hits UK #4. Its parent album, ***Nutbush City Limits*** will peak at US #163 in January the following year, before Tina, on April 22nd, begins filming in the role of the Acid Queen in the Who's film, "Tommy", directed by Ken Russell. *Sexy Ida* will make US #65 the following Dec [7].

1975

June [28] Ike Turner-penned *Baby Get It On* reaches US #88, and is the duo's last hit single together. (Behind the scenes, all is not well with the couple domestically: Tina will later claim to have been regularly beaten and kept a prisoner in the house by her drug-addicted husband.)

Oct On the strength of her performance in "Tommy", Tina has recorded a solo album, ***The Acid Queen***, which peaks at US #155.

1976

July After years of abuse and Ike's blatant infidelity and cocaine addiction, Tina leaves her husband, after a notably bloody beating, with only 36 cents and a Mobil gas card, having run away from the Hilton Hotel in Dallas, TX, where they are performing. (Initially living on food stamps, she will take nothing from their 1978 divorce and, strengthened by her new-found Buddhist faith, will begin to rebuild her life as a mother and entertainer, initially recruiting a band and playing cabaret gigs. Still a far bigger draw in Europe than in the US, she will link with Australian producer Roger Davies in 1979, and move on to considerable solo success in the '80s and '90s.) In the short-term, Ike continues to produce at his studio (where he will be arrested after rigging electronic equipment to make long-distance telephone calls without charge).

Oct [15] The duo officially dissolves its professional partnership after 19 years.

1988

July With his studio having been destroyed by fire in 1982, Ike Turner, sentenced to a year's imprisonment for possession and transportation of cocaine, begins work on ***My Confessions***, an autobiographical set to be released on the Starforce label.

1990

Jan [16] Ike Turner is convicted, in his absence, of driving under the influence of cocaine and being under the influence of cocaine, and sentenced to a four-year prison sentence at the California Men's Colony, San Luis Obispo, CA. The Santa Monica jury is deadlocked on two felony cocaine charges, forcing a mistrial on those counts.

1991

Jan [16] Ike & Tina Turner are inducted into the Rock and Roll Hall of Fame, at the sixth annual dinner, at New York's Waldorf Astoria Hotel, with Phil Spector accepting the award on their behalf.
Sept [3] Ike is released from prison, having served 18 months of a four-year prison term, into the custody of his daughter, Twanna Melby, in Vallejo, CA. He announces his intention of writing his autobiography and relaunching his career.

1992

Oct [20] Ike is interviewed on syndicated TV's "Whoopi Goldberg" show.
Dec While Tina oversees filming of the Walt Disney /Touchstone bio-movie, "What's Love Got To With It?", which documents her years with Ike, her former partner has signed a long-term contract with JRS Records. In an interview with **Variety**, Ike, who has been arrested 11 times, claims that he spent some $11 million on cocaine before kicking the habit during his recent jail stretch. Claiming to be drug-free, he now lives with 30-year old Jeanette Bazzell, and is trying to sell his own TV movie bio-script.
see also: **Tina TURNER**

TINA TURNER

1976

July Turner (b. Annie Mae Bullock, Nov. 26, 1939, Brownsville, TN), the daughter of cotton plantation workers in Nutbush, TN, both of whom deserted her and sister Alline (the pair subsequently moved together to St. Louis, MO, in their teens, where Tina met future husband Ike Turner in 1956 - he was responsible for changing her name), has already achieved considerable success as one-half of the spirited R&B Ike & Tina Turner Revue, in both the secular market in the US and as a cross-over act in Europe, a pairing highlighted by Tina's legendary, foot-stomping, sexy stage antics, and powerful soul vocal style, now leaves Ike after a two-decade professional and private union. Having endured years of abuse and Ike's blatant infidelity and addiction to cocaine, Tina leaves Ike with 36 cents and a Mobil gas card as her only material assets, running away from his final beating at the Hilton Hotel in Dallas, TX. Strengthened by her new-found Buddhist faith and initially living on food stamps, she will take nothing from their 1978 divorce and continue to raise her four children. She is lent money by ex-United Artists label executive, Michael Stewart, who also begins booking cabaret and club dates for her.
Oct [15] Ike and Tina officially dissolve their professional partnership.

1979

Some $500,000 in debt, without a recording contract and working wherever she can (including gigs in Yugoslavia, Poland, Singapore and Bahrain), Turner meets Roger Davies, a young Australian promoter trying to make it in the US music business.

1980

Turner signs a management deal with Davies, who makes changes in her backing band, and books her into less middle-of-the-road-oriented venues (with the occasional Las Vegas stand to pay the bills). Record company interest is minimal, partly because Ike's difficult reputation still taints Tina.

1981

Sept [25] Turner's career prospects brighten again as she supports the Rolling Stones (for whom the Ike & Tina Turner Revue had opened for two tours in the '60s) on their tenth US trek, now opening at the JFK Stadium, Philadelphia, PA. Late in the year, Davies is contacted by Virgin Records in the UK to say that Ian Craig Marsh and Martyn Ware of Heaven 17 and the British Electric Foundation want Tina to sing the Temptations song, *Ball Of Confusion*, on their album of choice revivals, ***Music Of Quality & Distinction Volume 1*** (set for release in April the following year). With its electronic backdrop, it is at odds with her R&B legacy, but the finished track brings her renewed notice as an active vocalist.
Dec [18] Tina supports Rod Stewart at a Great Western Forum, Inglewood, CA concert, broadcast live by satellite around the world.

1982

Apr [9] With Davies earnestly seeking a recording deal for Turner, she begins a concerted comeback at London's Hammersmith Odeon.
Dec Davies promotes a series of Turner showcase dates at the Ritz Hotel, New York, building up a guest list of record industry notables. Having interested Capitol Records, label executives have been prevaricating, when David Bowie resolves the problem. He has just signed to EMI (Capitol's parent company), and its top executives from around the world have been invited to a listening party for his forthcoming ***Let's Dance*** album. When Bowie announces to the party that he is moving on to see his "favorite singer", Tina Turner, label honchos follow, and witness a storming comeback show, resulting in her signing to the company.

1983

Dec Marsh and Ware-produced version of Al Green's *Let's Stay Together* is Turner's first Capitol single, hitting UK #6, her UK profile raised by packed dates at London's The Venue, and an appearance on C4-TV's "The Tube".

1984

Mar [24] *Let's Stay Together* reaches US #26, as various writer-producers, including Rupert Hine and Terry Britten, are recruited to collaborate on a first Capitol album. It is recorded at UK sessions spread over just two weeks, while her revival of the Beatles' *Help!* reaches UK #40.
[27] Turner begins a UK tour at the Coliseum, St. Austell, Cornwall.
Apr She opens as support on Lionel Richie's "Can't Slow Down" tour.
July The first release from the album sessions is *What's Love Got To Do With It?*, written by Britten and Graham Lyle, which hits UK #3.
Aug Her maiden album, the R&B/rock/pop-fused ***Private Dancer*** hits US #3 and UK #2 (and will stay in the US Top 10 until May 1985, and sell over ten million copies worldwide, with half the tally amassed in the US).
[21] The still-climbing *What's Love Got To Do With It* is certified gold by the RIAA.
Sept [1] As the tour with Richie closes, *What's Love Got To Do With It*, tops the US chart for the first of three weeks. It is her first #1 hit, and sets a new record for the length of time between an act's first US Top 100 entry and first #1 record - 24 years. On the same day the single reaches pole position, she seals a deal with Australian director George Miller to appear in his third "Mad Max" movie, with Mel Gibson. (Miller had called offering her a part, unaware of "Mad Max 2" being one of her favorite films). Meanwhile, *Better Be Good To Me*, from ***Private Dancer***, reaches UK #45. (By year's end, she honors a commitment, booked during her lean years, to perform at a series of McDonald's sales conventions.)
[18] Turner performs live at the inaugural MTV Video Music Awards, held at Radio City Music Hall, New York.
Nov [24] Written by Mike Chapman, Nicky Chinn and Holly Knight, *Better Be Good To Me* hits US #5.
Dec Title track, *Private Dancer*, penned by Mark Knopfler with Jeff Beck handling the lead guitar part, reaches UK #26.

1985

Jan She plays at the "Rock In Rio" festival, at Rio de Janeiro, Brazil, along with Rod Stewart, Queen, Whitesnake and AC/DC.
[28] Following the 12th annual American Music Awards, at Los Angeles, CA's Shrine Auditorium, at which she collected the Favorite Female Artist, Soul/R&B, and Favorite Female Video Artist, Soul/R&B trophies, Turner takes part in the recording of USA For Africa's *We Are The World*.
Feb [26] *What's Love Got To Do With It?* wins Record Of The Year, Song Of The Year, and Best Female Vocal Performance, and *Better Be Good To Me* wins Best Female Rock Vocal, at the 27th annual Grammy Awards.
Mar [14] Turner performs at Wembley Arena, Wembley, Middx., as her revival of Ann Peebles' *I Can't Stand The Rain* peaks at UK #57.
[23] *Private Dancer* hits US #7 - her third consecutive US Top 10 hit from the album.
June [1] *Show Some Respect* reaches US #37. (Having appeared as the Acid Queen in Ken Russell's "Tommy" in 1974, her acting career resumes with the premiere of "Mad Max: Beyond Thunderdome". Tina's performance as Aunty Entity is striking, and leads to further film offers. (She reportedly turns down Steven Spielberg's offer of a role in "The Color Purple" three times.) Meanwhile, her European tour is breaking records, and the original eight dates in Germany are extended to 30.)
July [13] She appears on the "Live Aid" benefit bill at the JFK Stadium in Philadelphia, where she duets raunchily with Mick Jagger (of whom Turner manages a deft dance-step aping impersonation).
Aug *We Don't Need Another Hero (Thunderdome)*, from the ***Mad Max : Beyond Thunderdome*** soundtrack, hits UK #3.
Sept [13] "What's Love Got To Do With It" wins the Best Female Video category, at the second annual MTV Video Music Awards, held again at Radio City Music Hall.
[14] *We Don't Need Another Hero (Thunderdome)* hits US #2, behind John Parr's *St. Elmo's Fire*.
Oct A second soundtrack single, *One Of The Living*, reaches UK #55.
Nov *It's Only Love*, a duet with Canadian rocker Bryan Adams (released on his label A&M), reaches UK #29.
[23] *One Of The Living* reaches US #15.
Dec [8] Turner wins an award as Best Actress from the NAACP for her role in "Mad Max: Beyond Thunderdome".

1986

Jan [18] *It's Only Love* makes US #15.
[27] She nabs the Favorite Female Artist, Pop/Rock category, at the 13th annual American Music Awards, held at the Shrine Auditorium.
June [20] Turner participates in the Prince's Trust concert in London, alongside Eric Clapton, Elton John and Bryan Adams.
Aug [28] She receives her star on the Hollywood Walk of Fame, outside Capitol Records' headquarters on Vine Street.
Sept *Typical Male*, from her forthcoming album, reaches UK #33.
[15] "It's Only Love" wins the Best Stage Performance category at the third annual MTV Video Music Awards (at which she also performs), broadcast simultaneously from the Universal Amphitheatre, Universal City, CA, and The Palladium, New York.
Oct [18] *Typical Male* hits US #2, behind Cyndi Lauper's *True Colors*, as ***Break Every Rule***, variously produced by Adams, Britten, Bob Clearmountain, Neil Dorfsman, Rupert Hine and Knopfler, hits UK #2.

Nov *Two People*, also from ***Break Every Rule***, makes UK #43, while the album hits US #4.
[6] ***Break Every Rule*** is certified platinum by the RIAA.

1987

Jan [10] *Two People* reaches US #30.
Mar [4] Turner embarks on her "Break Every Rule" world tour in Munich, West Germany, which will break box-office records in 13 countries. Financial backing is provided by her corporate sponsors, Pepsi-Cola, for whom she films a "live" commercial. ***Break Every Rule*** has now hit #1 in nine territories.
Apr [4] *What You Get Is What You See* reaches UK #30 and US #13.
May [23] *Break Every Rule* peaks at US #74.
June *Break Every Rule* makes UK #43.
Aug US leg of her world trek begins.
Sept [9] The RIAA certifies five million sales of ***Private Dancer***.

1988

Jan [16] On the South American tour leg, Turner plays to 182,000 people in the Maracana Arena, Rio de Janeiro - the largest audience ever assembled for a single performer. (She will enter **The Guinness Book Of Records** for this achievement.)
Mar Live version of Robert Palmer's *Addicted To Love* peaks at UK #71.
[28] "Break Every Rule" world tour comes to a close after 230 dates in 25 countries (playing to three millon fans) in Osaka, Japan.
Apr [2] A double concert album, ***Live In Europe***, hits UK #8 in its week of entry, but will only make US #86.
May "Rio '88" video, featuring live footage filmed in Brazil, is released.

1989

Jan [18] Turner inducts Phil Spector (who had written and produced *River Deep, Mountain High*) into the Rock and Roll Hall of Fame, at the fourth annual dinner at New York's Waldorf-Astoria Hotel.
June She recreates her Acid Queen role in "Tommy" for a Los Angeles charity event, as part of the Who's reunion tour. She also completes the Paris, France/Los Angeles recording of her upcoming album, ***Foreign Affair***.
Sept Anthemic *The Best*, its lead-off cut, spurred by a video clip directed by Lol Creme and written by Mike Chapman and Holly Knight, hits UK #5.
[30] ***Foreign Affair*** enters the UK chart at #1, and will rise to US #31.
Nov [4] *The Best*, featuring an Edgar Winter sax solo, reaches US #15, and will become a natural TV commercials theme for a number of products over the next two years.
[26] Turner celebrates her 50th birthday at the Reform Club with Eric Clapton, Mark Knopfler, Bryan Adams, Duran Duran and others.
[27] *Foreign Affair* is certified gold by the RIAA.
Dec Ballad, *I Don't Wanna Lose You*, hits UK #8.

1990

Jan [6] *Steamy Windows*, penned by Tony Joe White, reaches US #39, set to make UK #13.
Apr [27] Turner opens the European leg of her soldout, 121-date "Foreign Affair" World tour in Antwerp, Belgium.
June [28] She plays at the Palace of Versailles during European dates, becoming the first woman to play there. (Pink Floyd are the only other act to have performed at the venue, in 1988.)
Aug *Look Me In The Heart* makes UK #31.
Sept [26] Turner performs at the Wembley Arena, Wembley, Middx., during her current tour.
Oct *Be Tender With Me Baby* reaches UK #28.
Nov [4] "Foreign Tour" world sojourn ends in Rotterdam, Holland, having been seen by more than three million people.
Dec *It Takes Two*, an update of Marvin Gaye & Tammi Terrell's Motown classic, now duetted with Rod Stewart (although recorded in different parts of the world), mainly for blanket coverage as the latest UK Pepsi commercial theme, hits UK #5. (They will reportedly share £1 million between them for the ad.)

1991

Jan [4] Turner's "The Queen Of Rock Struts Her Stuff" concert in Barcelona, Spain, airs on pay-per-view.
Sept [9] The British Electric Foundation's ***Music Of Quality & Distinction Volume 2***, on which Turner contributes *A Change Is Gonna Come*, is released in the UK.
[28] *Nutbush City Limits (The 90s Version)* reaches UK #23.
Oct [19] Capitol singles-collection, ***Simply The Best***, augmented by three fresh cuts, hits UK #2, behind Simply Red's ***Stars***.
Nov [16] ***Simply The Best*** peaks at US #113.
[26] Turner receives a quintuple-platinum award in London to mark UK sales of 1.5 million for ***Foreign Affair***, and also receives a solid silver CD in honor of her 52nd birthday, from label-boss Rupert Perry.
[30] *Way Of The World* reaches UK #13.

1992

Jan [11] ***Two Rooms - Celebrating The Songs Of Elton John & Bernie Taupin***, to which she contributes *The Bitch Is Back*, reaches US #18.
Feb [15] *Love Thing* debuts at its UK #29 peak.
[25] "The Girl From Nutbush", a Tina Turner television career retrospective is broadcast on BBC1-TV.
Apr [11] Tina participates in the Grand Opening of Euro-Disney near Paris.
June [13] *I Want You Near Me* reaches UK #22.

1993

Jan Currently living in Germany with the 37-year old managing director of EMI Germany, Turner donates $50,000 to help open the Exchange Club-Tina Turner Child Abuse Center in Ripley, TN.
Mar [2] She participates in the concert at New York's Carnegie Hall, to benefit the world's rain forests with Bryan Adams, Herb Alpert, Tom Jones, George Michael, Sting, James Taylor and Dustin Hoffman.
Apr [30] Turner is one of the eight honorees at the sixth annual Essence Awards, at The Paramount, New York, and then guests on NBC-TV's "Late Night With David Letterman".
May [12] Turner is honored with the Outstanding Contribution To The Music Industry, and performs *I Don't Want To Fight*, at the World Music Awards from the Sporting Club, Monte Carlo, Monaco.
[14] She guests on NBC-TV's "The Tonight Show".
[27] She performs her current single on BBC1-TV's "Top Of The Pops".
[29] *I Don't Wanna Fight*, co-penned by Lulu, hits UK #9.
June [6] Her first North American tour in six years, the "What's Love?" trek, kicks off in Reno, NV, supported by Lindsey Buckingham and then Chris Isaak. (Touchstone Pictures premieres "What's Love Got To Do With It?", a movie based on her 1986 best-selling autobiography, **I, Tina** (written with MTV's Kurt Loder), with Angela Bassett playing (and lip-synching) Turner, and Lawrence Fishburne as Ike.)
June [19] The accompanying soundtrack, ***What's Love Got To Do With It***, comprising updated recordings of earlier hits with Ike, plus three new songs, debuts at UK #1.
July [17] ***What's Love Got To Do With It*** reaches US #17.
Aug [14] *I Don't Wanna Fight* hits US #9.
[22] Turner performs the final date of her US tour in Miami, FL.
[28] *Disco Inferno*, reviving the Trammps 1978 US #11/1977 UK #16, hits US #9.
Sept Turner sings at the Australian Rugby League championship game in Sydney, New South Wales, Australia.
[4] *Disco Inferno* reaches UK #12.
Oct [30] *Why Must We Wait Until Tonight* debuts at its UK #16 peak, having done the same in the US the previous week, at #97.
Dec [14] Turner's star is unveiled in an inaugural ceremony with 15 other artists at the "Sidewalk Of The Stars" outside New York's Radio City Music Hall.
[28] Fox-TV airs "Tina What's Love? Live Special", taped in September 1993 in San Bernardino, CA.

1994

Nov [16] ***Simply The Best*** is certified platinum by the RIAA.
[23] ***What's Love Got To Do With It*** is also confirmed platinum by the RIAA.

1995

Jan Capitol releases a three-disc boxed-set anthology ***The Collected Recordings - Sixties To Nineties***.
Nov [18] *Goldeneye*, her title theme to the first Pierce Brosnan-starring James Bond film "Goldeneye", debuts at its UK #10 peak.
Dec [3] VH1 airs its inaugural "Fashion & Music Awards", with a live performance by Turner, singing *Goldeneye* and duetting with Elton John.
[6] She performs live at the 1995 **Billboard** Music Awards, broadcast live on Fox-TV from New York's Coliseum.

1996

Mar [23] *Whatever You Want*, trailering her forthcoming album, reaches UK #23 in its week of entry.
Apr [13] Turner's first entirely new studio album in seven years, ***Wildest Dreams***, featuring duets with Sting and actor Antonio Banderas, bows at its UK #4 high.
July [12] Turner begins the UK leg of her European tour at the International Stadium, Gateshead, Tyne & Wear, set to end on the 24th at Alton Towers.
see also: **Ike & Tina TURNER**

THE TURTLES

Howard Kaylan (lead vocals, saxophone); **Mark Volman** (vocals, violin, saxophone); **Al Nichol** (guitar, piano, vocals); **Jim Tucker** (guitar); **Chuck Portz** (bass); **John Barbata** (drums)

1963

Kaylan (b. Howard Kaplan, June 22, 1947, New York, NY), Nichol (b. Mar. 31, 1946, Winston Salem, NC), Tucker (b. Oct. 17, 1946, Los Angeles, CA) and Portz (b. Mar. 28, 1945, Santa Monica, CA) add saxophone player Volman (b. Apr. 19, 1947, Los Angeles) to their Westchester, Los Angeles high school surf band, the Nightriders, and change their name to the Crossfires. Playing popular surf instrumentals, the new line-up wins several Battle of the Bands competitions, earning a residency at Redondo Beach's Revelaire club, run by KRLA DJ, Reb Foster, followed by another stint at Hollywood's Red Velvet club. (During their time playing as the house band at the Club, they also back the Righteous Brothers, Sonny & Cher, the Coasters, the Drifters and many other acts.) Their debut single is the surf instrumental, *Fiberglass Jungle*, released on the local independent Capco Records, followed by *That'll Be The Day* and *One Potato, Two Potato* for the Lucky Token label.

1964

The "British Invasion" influence (they frequently impersonate UK groups to gain gigs) inspires them to dispense with surf instrumentals, and Volman and Kaylan switch from saxes to vocals. As a change of pace, they sometimes perform folk music dates at high schools as the Crosswind Singers, gradually electrifying their material as the folk-rock style begins to bite nationally.

1965

Apr Promotion men Lee Lasseff (Liberty/United Artists) and Ted Feigen (Columbia), starting up their own White Whale label, approach the group at a gig and offer a recording deal, though a change of name is thought advisable. Manager Reb Foster suggests the Tyrtles (having seen the Byrds around town), but the eventual compromise is the more conventional Turtles.

Sept [18] A driving version of Bob Dylan's *It Ain't Me Babe* hits US #8.
Nov Their debut album ***It Ain't Me Babe*** makes US #98.
[27] The follow-up single, P.F. Sloan's *Let Me Be* (chosen by the band in preference to *Eve Of Destruction*, both of which Sloan has given to the band backstage at the Crescendo club), reaches US #29.

1966

Mar [26] *You Baby*, another Sloan song, reaches US #20.
June [25] *Grim Reaper Of Love*, penned by Nichol and Jim Pons, dies at US #81, while ***You Baby***, recorded hurriedly between tours, fails to chart. Murray, tired of touring, quits the band, to be replaced by John Barbata (b. Apr. 1, 1946, New Jersey), ex-drummer with surf band, the Sentinels, and currently playing drums with Lee Michaels. Portz also leaves shortly afterwards, replaced first by former Californian State Diving finalist of 1961, Chip Douglas, ex-Modern Folk Quartet and currently playing with Gene Clark, and on occasion with the Turtles' touring line-up, then by Pons (b. Mar. 14, 1943, Santa Monica, CA), a founder member of the Leaves.
July [6] The group plays at the Fillmore Auditorium, San Francisco, CA.
Nov [26] *Can I Get To Know You Better?* peaks at US #89.

1967

Feb [12] The group guests on CBS-TV's "The Smothers Brothers Comedy Hour".
Mar [25] *Happy Together*, written by Gary Bonner and Alan Gordon, members of New York group, the Magicians, and acquired when the Turtles are playing New York's Phone Booth club, tops the US chart for the first of three weeks (having been rejected by the Vogues, the Happenings, the Tokens and others).
Apr *Happy Together*, the band's UK chart debut, reaches UK #12.
May [4] *Happy Together* is certified gold by the RIAA.
June [17] Another Bonner/Gordon song, in a romping good-time arrangement, *She'd Rather Be With Me*, hits US #3, and earns the band's second gold disc as ***Happy Together*** reaches US #25.
July *She'd Rather Be With Me* hits UK #4 while the group is on a UK tour. Tucker leaves, and is not replaced.
Sept [30] *You Know What I Mean*, a mid-tempo ballad, reaches US #12.
Dec [23] *She's My Girl*, with a hint of psychedelia, reaches US #14.

1968

Jan Compilation, ***The Turtles! Golden Hits***, is the group's biggest-selling album, hitting US #7.
Mar [30] *Sound Asleep*, the first single produced by the band itself, makes US #57.
Apr [12] ***The Turtles' Greatest Hits*** is certified gold by the RIAA.
July [13] Their treatment of the Nilsson song *The Story Of Rock And Roll* (with the composer on piano), peaks at US #48.
Nov [2] *Elenore* hits US #6 and UK #7 (and will be the Turtles' last UK hit). It is taken from the jokey concept album, ***The Turtles Present The Battle Of The Bands***, which peaks at US #128.
Dec [28] The Turtles take part in the three-day Miami Pop Festival, at the Gulfstream Racing Park, Hallandale, FL.

1969

Mar [1] *You Showed Me*, originally recorded by the Byrds, pre-*Mr. Tambourine Man*, and resurrected by the Turtles on ***Battle***, is extracted to hit US #6.
May [10] The band plays at the White House as guests of Tricia Nixon. (Stories circulate concerning Kaylan and Volman allegedly snorting cocaine on Abraham Lincoln's desk.)
Barbata leaves (later to join Jefferson Airplane) and is replaced by John Seiter (b. Aug. 17, 1944, St. Louis, MO), ex-Spanky & Our Gang.
July [12] *You Don't Have To Walk In The Rain* makes US #51.
Oct [18] *Love In The City* peaks at US #91.
Nov The Kinks' Ray Davies-produced ***Turtle Soup*** reaches US #117.
Dec [20] Judee Sill-penned *Lady-O*, the last official Turtles single, peaks at US #78. (Sill is the first signing to the group's own Blimp production company.)

1970

May Compilation, ***The Turtles! More Golden Hits***, reaches US #146.
June [27] The band refuses to complete the Jerry Yester-produced ***Shell Shock*** because of growing displeasure with White Whale, which retaliates by issuing *Eve Of Destruction* (from the first album) as a single, which now spends a week at US #100, while the band dissolves amid dissension within its own ranks, as well as with the label. Kaylan and Volman (with Pons following), accept Frank Zappa's invitation to join the Mothers Of Invention, first appearing on ***Chunga's Revenge***, billed as the Phlorescent Leech & Eddie, because of a legal restraint against using their real names.

1971

June With Zappa, they record the live set, ***Fillmore East, June 1971***. (Having befriended Marc Bolan when Tyrannosaurus Rex supported the Turtles on a US tour, Kaylan and Volman also assist on Bolan's new T. Rex material, singing backup vocals on the albums ***T. Rex*** and ***Electric Warrior***, and on the hit singles *Hot Love* and *Get It On (Bang A Gong)*.)
Aug [7] At UCLA, Zappa tapes another live recording, ***Just Another Band From LA***, the last to feature Kaylan and Volman, who leave to record as Flo (Volman) and Eddie (Kaylan). The duo also appears in Zappa's movie, "200 Motels".

1972

The Phlorescent Leech And Eddie, released on Reprise, is recorded with Pons, Aynsley Dunbar, Don Preston and Gary Rowles (ex-Love). The duo also sings back-up vocals on John Lennon's ***Some Time In New York City***. With the duo having shortened its name, ***Flo & Eddie*** will be released the following year, while a weekly radio show, "Flo And Eddie By The Fireside", goes into national syndication in the US in 1974.

1975

Jan Double-anthology, ***Happy Together Again : The Turtles' Greatest Hits***, compiled and annotated by Kaylan and Volman, and including rare and unissued material as well as the hits, peaks at US #194. Meanwhile, Flo & Eddie change labels, releasing ***Illegal Immoral And Fattening*** on CBS/Columbia.

1976

Moving Targets is released, including a new version of the Turtles' *Elenore*. Volman and Kaylan buy the rights to the group's name. Nichol moves to Arcata, CA, for the hippy life, while Pons heads the film department of the New York Jets football team, before signing a publishing deal with Chappell in Nashville, TN.

1981

After a period as guest vocalists (notably on albums by Blondie (***Autoamerican***) and Alice Cooper (***Flush The Fashion***), and as producers, the duo releases ***Rock Steady With Flo And Eddie***, on Epiphany, recorded in Jamaica with top reggae artists.

1982

Rhino Records in the US begins a reissue program of the entire Turtles catalogue, releasing all of their albums, including the rare ***Wooden Head***, various compilations and much previously unavailable material - all with full assistance from Kaylan and Volman. A new touring version of the Turtles, based around the duo, hits the road for a successful series of nostalgia gigs, including the "Happy Together" oldies tour across the US with the Buckinghams, the Grass Roots, Mamas & the Papas, and others in April 1985. Two years later, Rhino issues the previously unreleased ***Shell Shock***, abandoned at the end of the group's White Whale career, and will also retail four Turtles hits on 3" CD EPs in 1988.

1989

July Volman and Kaylan sue De La Soul for $1.7 million for sampling part of *You Showed Me*, as the backing track for *Transmitting Live From Mars*, before beginning a radio show as Flo & Eddie on WXRK, New York, the following year.

1995

With the Turtles, still a notable nostalgia act, Sundazed Records (US) releases four of the Turtles' original albums with previously unreleased additional tracks.
see also: **JEFFERSON AIRPLANE, THE MOTHERS OF INVENTION**

BONNIE TYLER

1976

Nov Tyler (b. Gaynor Hopkins, June 8, 1953, Skewen, W. Glamorgan, Wales), having attended Rhydhir School, Neath, W. Glamorgan, Wales, has won a local talent contest at the age of 17, and left her shop job to begin singing in local pubs and clubs in the early '70s. A recurring problem with nodules on her throat is finally cured by an operation, which leaves her with what will become her trademark husky vocal tone. By now a veteran of the South Wales club scene, fronting a band named Mumbles which specializes in covers of raunchy soul material, she is spotted at Swansea, W. Glamorgan's Townman club by producer/songwriters Ronnie Scott and Steve Wolfe, who decide her voice is ideal to record their joint composition, *Lost In France*, also becoming her managers and producers. Signed to RCA Records, *Lost In France* now hits UK #9. Its follow-up, *More Than A Lover* will reach UK #27 the following April.

1978

Jan Airplay favorite *It's A Heartache* hits UK #4.
June [16] Still-rising *It's A Heartache* is certified gold by the RIAA.
[24] Written by Scott and Wolfe, *It's A Heartache* hits US #3.
[27] The still-rising parent album, ***It's A Heartache*** is certified gold by the RIAA.
July [8] Her maiden set, ***It's A Heartache*** reaches US #16.

1979

Mar ***Diamond Cut*** makes US #145.
July *Married Men* (from the movie "The World Is Full Of Married Men" adapted from the Jackie Collins novel) makes UK #35.
Nov Tyler wins the "Yamaha World Popular Song Contest" with *Sitting On The Edge Of The Ocean*.

1981

June After several non-charting singles and the release of ***Goodbye To The Island***, Tyler does not renew her contracts with either Scott and Wolfe or RCA when they expire, signing instead to CBS/Columbia with David Aspden becoming her new manager.

1983

Mar [12] In search of a fuller, rock sound Tyler has teamed with writer/producer Jim Steinman (creator of Meat Loaf's ***Bat Out Of Hell***) whose composition, the melodramatic pop/rock anthem *Total Eclipse Of The Heart* tops the UK chart for the first of two weeks, deposing Michael Jackson's *Billie Jean*.
Apr [16] Steinman-helmed ***Faster Than The Speed Of Night*** tops the UK survey - only the second album by a UK female singer (the first being Kate Bush's ***The Kick Inside***) to do so.

May Title cut *Faster Than The Speed Of Night*, also written by Steinman, peaks at UK #43.
July An update of Creedence Clearwater Revival's *Have You Ever Seen The Rain?* makes UK #47.
Oct [1] *Total Eclipse Of The Heart* begins a three-week stay atop the US chart while ***Faster Than The Speed Of Night*** hits US #4.
[3] *Total Eclipse Of The Heart* is certified gold by the RIAA.
Nov [7] ***Faster Than The Speed Of Night*** is confirmed platinum by the RIAA.

1984

Jan Tyler's duet with Shakin' Stevens on their revival of 1960 US Top 10 duet hit by Brook Benton and Dinah Washington, *A Rockin' Good Way (To Mess Around And Fall In Love)* hits UK #5, but is a one-off collaboration.
[14] Her solo single *Take Me Back* reaches US #46.
Apr [14] *Holding Out For A Hero*, a Steinman song included on the soundtrack of the movie "Footloose", reaches US #34.
Sept [1] *Here She Comes*, from Giorgio Moroder's soundtrack from the revived silent movie "Metropolis", peaks at US #76.

1985

Sept *Holding Out For A Hero* is belated UK success, hitting #2 behind Mick Jagger and David Bowie's revival of *Dancing In The Street*.
Dec Another Steinman composition, *Loving You's A Dirty Job But Somebody's Gotta Do It*, peaks at UK #73, featuring Todd Rundgren as guest vocal duettist.

1986

May [3] Rundgren also contributes vocals to *If You Were A Woman (And I Was A Man)*, which makes US #77, as ***Secret Dreams And Forbidden Fire*** stops at US #106.

1988

May The Desmond Child-produced ***Hide Your Heart*** is released by CBS.
Aug [27] Tyler performs on the second day of the annual "Reading Rock Festival", near Reading, Berks.
Oct Tyler participates, along with a host of other Welsh acting and singing personalities, on the all-star version of Dylan Thomas' **Under Milk Wood**.
Nov She embarks on a tour of the USSR.
[13] Tyler contributes to the ***Rock The World*** benefit album to raise money for the Phoenix House, London-based rehab center.

1991

May Newly signed to the German Hansa label, Tyler releases ***Bitterblue*** (with music guests Nik Kershaw, Moroder and Harold Faltermeyer), while vault specialist label Castle Communications brings her hit catalog to CD with the issue of ***The Collection***.
June [4] Tyler participates in the Mike Batt-conducted Royal Philharmonic Pops Orchestra concert of classic pop numbers at the Barbican Theatre, London, with proceeds going to the Save The Children charity.
Dec [28] *Holding Out For A Hero*, originally a 1985 UK #2 and now used for a Hero Fabergé TV commercial, charts for a week at UK #69. The similarly reissued *Making Love (Out Of Nothing At All)* will make UK #45 in its week of entry on Jan [27], 1996. (Total Eclipse Of The Heart will be revived by Nicki French in 1994, charting for a week at UK #54 on Oct [15] and hitting US #2 the following June [24].

U

V

UB40

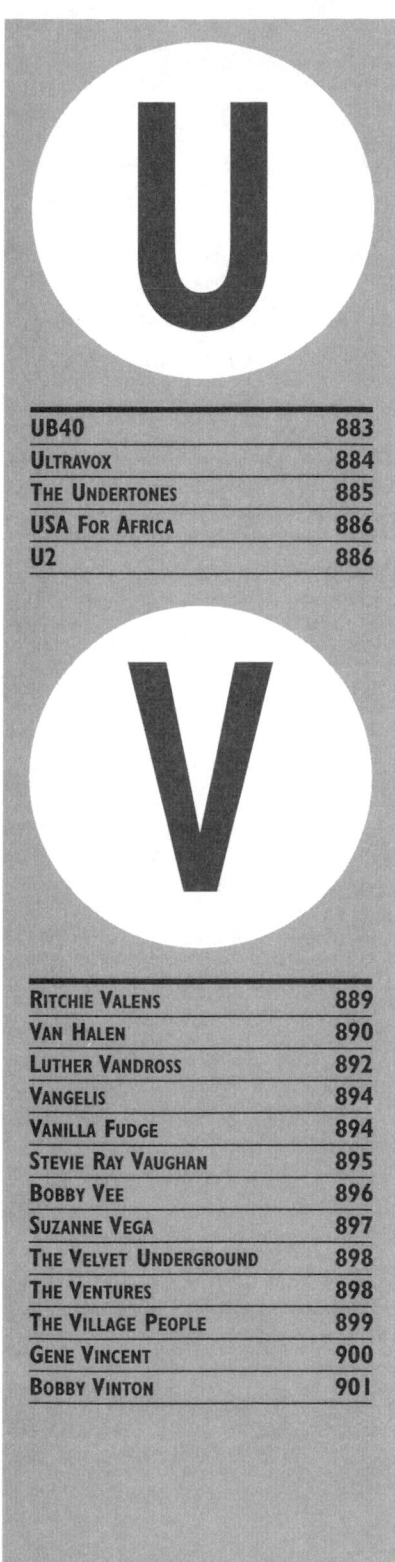

Ali Campbell (lead vocals, rhythm guitar); **Earl Falconer** (bass); **Robin Campbell** (lead guitar, vocals); **Mickey Virtue** (keyboards); **Brian Travers** (saxophone); **Jim Brown** (drums); **Norman Hassan** (percussion); **Astro** (vocals, voice)

1979

Feb After six months of rehearsals, reggae outfit UB40, named after the number of the UK unemployment benefit form, debuts at the Horse and Hounds in King's Heath, Birmingham, W. Midlands, sharing the bill with another new local band, the Au Pairs. Most of the group have known each other for up to ten years, and several have attended art school together. Ali (b. Alastair Campbell, Feb. 15, 1959, Birmingham) and Robin Campbell (b. Dec. 25, 1954, Birmingham), sons of Scottish folk singer, Ian Campbell, have sung with two other brothers in a barber-shop quartet, and been reggae fans since childhood. After only one more gig, percussionist "Yomi" Babayemi is deported to Nigeria by immigration authorities. The group and its manager, ex-encyclopedia salesman Simon Woods, contact local producer, Bob Lamb, an ex-member of Birmingham reggae band the Locomotive (1968 hit-makers with *Rudi's In Love*), who owns an eight-track studio, to make some demos. Before the first sessions, reggae toaster/singer Astro (b. Terence Wilson, June 24, 1957, Birmingham) joins the group, which now also includes Falconer (b. Jan. 23, 1959, Birmingham), Virtue (b. Jan. 19, 1957, Birmingham), Brown (b. Nov. 20, 1957) and Hassan (b. Jan. 26, 1957, Birmingham). Their big break comes when the Pretenders' Chrissie Hynde sees their live show, and offers a support slot on her group's 1979/80 UK tour. Despite major label interest, the group signs to the independent Graduate, run by David and Susan Virr from their record shop in Dudley, W. Midlands. The deal gives them total control, but no advance monies - resulting in debts at the outset of their career.

1980

Apr The A-side of the group's first release is *King* (a dedication to Martin Luther King), but radio favors the catchy B-side, *Food For Thought*. It tops the Independent chart for three months before now hitting UK #4. Recorded in Lamb's studio, it sells over half a million copies. Major record company pressure intensifies during their tour with the Pretenders.

May [1] UB40 begins a 30-date UK tour at Trent Polytechnic, Nottingham, Notts.

July The follow-up, *My Way Of Thinking*, backed with a cover of Randy Newman's ballad *I Think It's Going To Rain Today*, hits UK #6.

[26] UB40 supports Police at the "Rockatta De Bowl", Milton Keynes, Bucks.

Sept Their first album, ***Signing Off***, recorded by Lamb on eight-track, hits UK #2 (staying charted for 71 weeks), its cover nothing more than an enlarged dole benefit application.

Nov *The Earth Dies Screaming* hits UK #10.

Dec UB40 leaves Graduate, apparently due to the label deleting the anti-apartheid song, *Burden Of Shame*, from the South African release of the album, setting up its own DEP International company (licensed through Virgin Records). After concerts in Europe and Ireland, UB40 tours the UK and appears on a Christmas bill at the Birmingham NEC.

1981

June ***Present Arms***, the first album on DEP International, hits UK #2, spending 38 weeks on the survey. Initial pressings come with a free 12" single containing two instrumentals, *Don't Walk On The Grass* and *Dr. X* (a re-working of the album's title track). The tracks are produced by the band's sound engineer, Ray "Pablo" Falconer, brother of bassist Earl. The extracted *Don't Let It Pass You By/Don't Slow Down* makes UK #16.

Sept *One In Ten* hits UK #7. UB40 plays benefit gigs for those arrested during the UK inner-city riots of the summer (which leads to them being banned from venues in some towns), before beginning a major international tour.

Oct ***Present Arms In Dub***, a dub re-working of the album, makes UK #38.

1982

Feb *I Won't Close My Eyes* makes UK #32.

June *Love Is All Is Alright* makes UK #29, and hits #1 in Zimbabwe, for three weeks.

Sept Funk-tinged *So Here I Am* reaches UK #25, as ***The Singles Album***, a collection of the group's Graduate singles, makes UK #17.

Oct ***UB44***, released with a hologram cover, a first in the UK record industry, hits UK #4, despite some negative reviews.

1983

Feb *I've Got Mine* makes UK #45 (their poorest chart position to date).

Mar ***UB40 Live*** reaches UK #44.

Sept [3] *Red Red Wine*, their first UK #1 hit, begins a three-week stay in pole position. (The group claims to have been unaware that the song was a Neil Diamond composition, and had picked it up from Jamaican singer Tony Tribe's 1969 version.)

[24] ***Labour Of Love***, a collection of classic songs given UB40 reggae treatments, hits UK #1, and will stay on the chart for 18 months. It is supported by a short film, similarly titled, directed by Bernard Rose together with latest band recruit, Brian Travers (b. Feb. 7, 1959, Birmingham).

Nov *Please Don't Make Me Cry*, reviving Winston Groovy's original, hits UK #10.

Dec Their cover of Jimmy Cliff's *Many Rivers To Cross* reaches UK #16.

1984

Mar [31] *Red Red Wine* makes US #34, the group's first US hit single in a country traditionally resistant to crossover reggae hits.

Apr *Cherry Oh Baby* reaches UK #12 while ***Labour Of Love*** reaches US #39.

Oct *If It Happens Again*, offered as a comment on Margaret Thatcher, whose Conservative Party is seeking re-election, hits UK #9, while ***Geffrey Morgan*** hits UK #3.

Dec *Riddle Me* peaks at UK #59. The group plays concerts for the Greater London Council, which is (unsuccessfully) fighting off dissolution by the Tory Government. ***Geffrey Morgan*** makes US #60.

1985

Feb UB40 joins Madness, the Special AKA, General Public and the Pioneers to record *Starvation* (with the profits going to the Ethiopian appeal).

May *I'm Not Fooled* peaks at UK #79.

Aug [31] UB40 and Chrissie Hynde's duet on a reggae version of Sonny & Cher's *I Got You Babe*, hits UK #1 for a week, its promo clip filmed by Jonathan Demme at a concert at Jones Beach, Wantagh, NY, during one of UB40's three 1985 US visits.

Sept ***Baggariddim***, consisting of dub versions of tracks from the previous two albums, with toasters Dillinger and Sister V guesting, reaches UK #14. A trimmed-down version in the US, ***Little Baggariddim***, makes #40.

[21] *I Got You Babe* (also included on the mini-album) makes US #28.

Dec *Don't Break My Heart*, taken from the free 12" issued with the album, hits UK #3.

1986

July *Sing Our Own Song*, an expression of solidarity with black activists in South Africa, hits UK #5.

Aug [9] ***Rat In The Kitchen***, featuring US label boss Herb Alpert on guest trumpet, hits UK #8 in its week of entry, and will make US #53.

Oct *All I Want To Do* makes UK #41.

1987

Jan Single *Rat In Mi Kitchen* reaches UK #12.
May *Watchdogs* makes UK #39.
June Live Russian visit rockumentary, "UB40 : CCCP", is released by Virgin Video.
Sept ***CCCP : Live In Moscow*** climbs to US #121.
Oct *Maybe Tomorrow* reaches UK #14. "The Best Of UB40 : Volume 1", a collection of video hits linked by Travers-directed "Fat Family" sketches, becomes a best-seller.
Nov [7] Virgin Records-released TV-advertised ***The Best Of UB40 Vol. 1*** debuts at its UK #3 peak.
Falconer's Volvo turbo goes out of control and hits a wall, killing his brother, Ray. The discovery of twice the legal limit of alcohol in Earl's blood leads to charges.

1988

Feb UB40 guests on the UK #17-peaking Afrika Bambaataa hit, *Reckless*.
June A second UB40/Chrissie Hynde collaboration, their version of reggae standard, *Breakfast In Bed*, hits UK #6, as the band completes the short-film, "Dance With The Devil", featuring Ali Campbell in the lead role as a trickster, and a host of guest artists, including Hynde, Robert Palmer and ITV soap "Crossroads" actor, Paul "Benny" Henry.
July A week before the group's world tour (set to last for 12 months) is due to start, a Birmingham Crown Court judge jails Earl Falconer for six months, on charges relating to the car accident. The band is forced to use a stand-in bassist at short notice.
[11] UB40 performs at "Nelson Mandela's 70th Birthday Tribute" at Wembley Stadium, Wembley, Middx.
[23] Newly-recorded ***UB40***, with a sleeve painting by UK artist Steve Masterson, reaches UK #12 in its week of entry.
Sept *Where Did We Go Wrong* reaches UK #26.
[8] ***Labour Of Love*** is certified platinum by the RIAA.
Oct [15] The band is on a major US tour when *Red Red Wine* (originally a 1984 US #34) hits the top spot. It has been resurrected by a Phoenix, Arizona DJ, who began heavy airplay rotation of the disc following its performance at the Nelson Mandela concert. ***Labour Of Love*** (which contains the single) now reaches US #14, as ***UB40*** makes US #44.

1989

Jan [25] *Red Red Wine* is certified gold by the RIAA.
June *I Would Do For You* makes UK #45.
Nov Their remake of the Chi-Lites' *Homely Girl* hits UK #6.

1990

Feb [3] *Here I Am (Come And Take Me)* makes UK #46, as ***Labour Of Love II*** peaks at US #69.
Apr [14] *Kingston Town* hits UK #4.
May [4-9] UB40 tours Hawaii during North American dates.
[19] ***Labour Of Love II***, arranged and produced by the band, and featuring a sleeve design by Barry Kamen, hits UK #3, proving to be another multi-platinum collection of the band's interpretations of oldies.
July [8-9] UB40 ends a 50-city North American arena tour with two shows in San Diego, CA.
Aug [1] The band is deported from the Seychelles after police discover marijuana in their hotel room. They choose deportation over the other option, a mandatory three-year jail term. (The band will later claim that the drug bust is a set-up.)
[18] *Wear You To The Ball* makes UK #35.
Nov [17] A collaboration with Robert Palmer, covering Dylan's *I'll Be Your Baby Tonight*, hits UK #6.
Dec [1] *Impossible Love* makes UK #47.
[15] *The Way You Do The Things You Do,* reviving the Temptations' 1964 US #11, hits US #6.

1991

Jan [16] *The Way You Do The Things You Do* is certified gold by the RIAA.
Feb [9] EP *The Way You Do The Things You Do* makes UK #49.
June [22] The group plays a one-off UK date at London's Finsbury Park.
[24] The still-climbing ***Labour Of Love II*** is certified platinum by the RIAA.
July [7] UB40 performs at the Pacific Amphitheatre, Costa Mesa, CA, during its current US tour.
[13] *Here I Am (Come And Take Me)* hits US #7.
Aug [10] ***Labour Of Love II*** reaches US #30.
Dec [7] *Groovin'* peaks at US #90.
[26] "UB40 - A Family Affair", filmed at the Finsbury Park gig in June, airs on C4-TV.

1992

Jan The group begins work on a new album at its own Abbatoir Studios in Birmingham, as former secretary, Deborah Banks, files a suit against the band, claiming that the lyrics of *Don't Break My Heart* were based on a poem of hers she had given to former UB40 member Javid Khan.
Apr They launch a range of clothes with Lee Cooper, after the company had used *Homely Girl* for a TV and cinema commercial.
Aug [1] The group makes a rare hometown appearance at Birmingham's Cofton Park.
Dec [19] Reworking their own 1981 UK #7 smash, but now teamed with 808 State, *One In Ten* reaches UK #17. They also contribute to *Wintertime Is On* by the Whole World Band, written by prison inmate Sam Jones (CP1766), former leader of I Level, who is currently serving time at Ford Prison in Sussex, with proceeds going to the Down Syndrome Association and Sickle Cell Society.

1993

June [12] UB40's cover of Elvis Presley's 1962 hit, *Can't Help Falling In Love*, featured on the soundtrack to "Sliver", tops the UK chart. (Originally recorded for the film "Honeymoon In Vegas", it had been bumped in favor of Bono's version.)
July [24] *Can't Help Falling In Love* tops the US chart, as ***Promises And Lies***, UB40's first album of the '90s, debuts at UK #1.
Aug [8] *Can't Help Falling In Love* is certified platinum by the RIAA.
[21] *Higher Ground* bows at its UK #8 peak, as ***Promises And Lies*** hits US #6.
Sept [2] The group guests on NBC-TV's "The Tonight Show".
[28] ***Promises And Lies*** is confirmed platinum by the RIAA.
Dec [11] *Bring Me Your Cup* debuts at its UK #24 peak.

1994

Jan [1] *Higher Ground* makes US #45.
[5-6] UB40 embarks on a 17-date UK and Irish tour at the Cardiff International Arena, Cardiff, S. Glamorgan, Wales, set to end on the 30th at the Point, Dublin, Eire.
Feb [12] The group guests on NBC-TV's "Saturday Night Live".
[14] US tour opens at the Paramount, New York, NY.
Mar [28-29] As the tour winds down, UB40 plays two dates at the Universal Amphitheatre, Universal City, CA.
Apr [2] *C'Est La Vie* debuts at its UK #37 peak.
Aug [21] The group guests on BBC2-TV's "The O Zone".
[27] *Reggae Music* debuts at its UK #28 peak.
[28] A 13 city Pan-Latin American tour opens at the Sports Palace, Mexico City, Mexico, with an 18,253 sellout performance.
Nov [26] ***Labour Of Love - Volumes I And II*** hits UK #5.

1995

May [27] Having established his own Kuff label (through Virgin Records, which also signs the recently reformed Specials), Campbell's debut solo, *That Look In Your Eye* hits UK #5.
June [17] His album ***Big Love***, co-produced with Gerry Parchment and featuring UB40 members and a guest appearance by Rudolph Schenker, hits UK #6 in its entry week, largely indistinguishable from a UB40 album, such is the trademark of his vocal delivery. Its CD booklet includes an essay titled "The Case For Hemp".
July Birmingham secretary Deborah Banks wins her suit, brought against the band and its Fernscan Ltd company in February, after convincing High Court Judge Mr. Justice Harman that *Don't Break My Heart*'s lyrics were based on her poem.
Aug [26] Campbell's *Let Your Yeah Be Yeah* enters at its UK #25 peak.
Nov [1] UB40 guests on CBS-TV's "Late Show With David Letterman".
[4] *Until My Dying Day* bows at its UK #15 peak.
[11] ***The Best Of Volume Two***, including two cuts *Superstition* and *Until My Dying Day*, debuts at its UK #12 peak.
Dec [9] *Somethin' Stupid*, duetted with his wife Kibibi Campbell, bows at its UK #30 peak.

ULTRAVOX

Midge Ure (guitar, lead vocals);
Billy Currie (synthesizer, piano); **Chris Cross** (bass, synthesizer); **Warren Cann** (drums)

1976

July Initially formed as Tiger Lily in 1973 by John Foxx (b. Dennis Leigh, Chorley, Lancs.) and ex-Preston, Lancs. band Stoned Rose member Cross (b. Christopher St. John, July 14, 1952, London), they have recruited Cann (b. May 20, 1952, Victoria, BC, Canada) on drums and Steve Shears on guitar. With Roxy Music as their chief musical inspiration, they performed club dates (including London's Marquee in August of that year), before being joined by Currie (b. Apr. 1, 1952, Huddersfield, W. Yorks.) in October. Demos led to their recording of Fats Waller's *Ain't Misbehavin'* (for an X-certificate film of the same title), coupled with *Monkey Jive*, for the small Gull label in March 1975 (reissued on Dead Good Records in August 1980) and, after trying a series of names, including the Zips, the Innocents, London Soundtrack and Fire Of London, they now settle on Ultravox.
Aug The group signs to Island Records and will spend the rest of the year writing and recording its debut album. First product is *The Wild, The Beautiful And The Damned*, which is featured on an Island sampler album.

1977

Feb Their debut single, *Dangerous Rhythm*, is issued, as the group plays at London's Nashville Room.
Mar ***Ultravox!***, a heavily-synthesized effort, co-produced by ex-Roxy Music keyboardist Brian Eno, is released, and is critically well received.
Aug [27] The group plays on the second day of the 17th National Jazz Blues & Rock Festival "Reading Rock '77", near Reading, Berks.
Oct *Rockwork* and a parent album, ***Ha! Ha! Ha!***, are issued.

1978

Feb *Retro*, a live 4-track EP, is released, as the band travels to West Germany to record with Conny Plank. Prior to the sessions, Shears leaves, to be replaced by Robin Simon, ex-Neo.
Aug [25] The group plays, as special guests, on the opening day of the 18th National Jazz Blues & Rock Festival "Reading Rock '78", and play five consecutive dates at London's Marquee.
Sept Plank-produced ***Systems Of Romance*** is issued.
Dec [26] The original line-up plays its last two UK dates at London's Marquee.

1979

Jan Island Records drops the group.
Mar Returning to Britain after final gigs in the US, and creating his own MetalBeat label, Foxx leaves for a solo career (which will spawn four UK chart albums during the '80s: ***Metamix*** (#18, Feb 1980), ***The***

Garden (#24, Oct 1981), ***The Golden Section*** (#27, Oct 1983) and ***In Mysterious Ways*** (#85, Oct 1985)). Cann works with New Zealand singer, Zaine Griff, while Currie and Simon play with Gary Numan and Magazine respectively, and Cross writes songs with his brother. Apart from Foxx, the members still wish to continue with Ultravox, and look for a new singer and guitarist.

Apr Guitarist/vocalist Ure (b. James Ure, Oct. 10, 1953, Gambusland, Scotland) joins. He has been with Currie and Steve Strange in Visage, and was in Salvation, which eventually became UK teenybop try-outs, Slik. (In 1976, after teaming with the Bay City Rollers' producers, Bill Martin and Phil Coulter, they become brief pop sensations, hitting UK #1 with *Forever And Ever*. Ure left in 1977, teaming with ex-Sex Pistols Glen Matlock in the Rich Kids.) While the group works on new material, Ure stands in for Brian Robertson in Thin Lizzy.

Nov The new line-up plays four UK gigs, starting at Eric's, Liverpool, Merseyside, to prepare for a US tour the following month.

1980

Apr Newly signed to Chrysalis Records, the group's debut single with Ure, *Sleepwalk*, reaches UK #29, while Island issues ***Three Into One***, a compilation of the best of their three albums for the label.

July ***Vienna***, the group's first album to feature Ure's melodramatic lead vocal style, hits UK #3, during a 72-week chart stay, confirming their position as a leading act in the currently fashionable new romantic/rock synthesizer field.

Aug [2] The group begins a UK tour at the Drill Hall, Lincoln, Lincs.

[24] They play at Tiffanys as part of the Edinburgh Rock Festival, Edinburgh, Lothian, Scotland.

Oct Ultravox's *Passing Strangers* peaks at UK #57, as ***Vienna*** is their US debut, at #164.

1981

Jan Grandiose ballad, *Vienna*, penned by all four band members, attracts heavy UK airplay, hitting UK #2, held off the top by Joe Dolce's novelty *Shaddap You Face*.

Mar Island releases the three-track EP, *Slow Motion*, which makes UK #33.

June *All Stood Still* hits UK #8.

Aug *The Thin Wall*, recorded earlier in the year in Germany with producer Plank, reaches UK #14.

Sept ***Rage In Eden*** hits UK #4.

Nov The extracted *The Voice* peaks at UK #16, while ***Rage In Eden*** makes US #144.

1982

June Ure's solo cover (on Chrysalis) of the Tom Rush-penned, Walker Brothers's 1976 UK #7, *No Regrets*, hits UK #9. (During the year, he will also produce Steve Harley, Atrix and Modern Man, while also working with Visage.)

Sept Ultravox reaches UK #12 with *Reap The Wild Wind*.

Oct ***Quartet***, recorded in Montserrat, Leeward Islands, with producer George Martin, hits UK #6.

Nov A second extract, *Hymn*, reaches UK #11.

1983

Mar *Visions In Blue* reaches UK #15.

Apr [30] The group achieves its only US single success with *Reap The Wild Wind*, which makes US #71, while ***Quartet*** peaks at US #61.

June *We Came To Dance* steps to UK #18.

July Ure's *After A Fashion*, featuring Japan bassist Mick Karn, makes UK #39.

Oct ***Monument - The Soundtrack*** hits UK #9.

1984

Feb *One Small Day* reaches UK #27.

Apr The band-produced ***Lament***, recorded at the Musicfest Studio, and featuring guest gaelic vocalist, Mae McKenna, hits UK #8.

May *Dancing With Tears In My Eyes* becomes Ultravox's first UK Top 10 record in three years, hitting #3.

June ***Lament*** climbs to US #115.

July [14] Its extracted title cut, *Lament*, reaches UK #22.

Oct *Love's Great Adventure* reaches UK #12.

Nov Chrysalis issues a retrospective album of its Ultravox recordings, ***The Collection***, which hits UK #2. Ure is approached by Bob Geldof to write a song to be recorded by an all-star band to raise funds for the starving people of Ethiopia.

[25] Co-penned by Ure with Geldof, *Do They Know It's Christmas?* is recorded by the Band Aid aggregation, which Ure has also co-organized. (It will enter the UK chart at #1, and become the country's biggest-selling single.)

1985

Mar [13] Ure receives the Best Selling A-Side trophy (with Geldof), for *Do They Know Its Christmas?*, at the 30th annual Ivor Novello Awards, held at London's Grosvenor House Hotel.

July [13] Continuing his efforts with Geldof to raise money to ease famine in Africa (though receiving less praise than the Irishman), Ure is active behind the scenes in organizing the "Live Aid" spectacular at Wembley Stadium, Wembley, Middx., at which he also performs with Ultravox.

Sept Synth-led as ever, Ure's solo single, *If I Was*, tops the UK chart, as Ultravox takes an extended hiatus.

Oct Ure's ***The Gift*** hits UK #2.

Nov The extracted *That Certain Smile* reaches UK #28.

Dec Ure begins his first solo tour, with Zal Cleminson, ex-Sensational Alex Harvey Band, on guitar, and Kenny Hyslop (with whom Ure has worked in Slik), on drums.

1986

Feb Ure's *Wastelands* makes UK #46.

June His follow-up, *Call Of The Wild*, reaches UK #27.

Oct Ultravox, now minus Cann, releases ***U-Vox***, which hits UK #9, as *Same Old Story* makes UK #31. It will be the band's final album despite each of its last seven albums having made the UK Top 10. (Aside from Ure, Currie will remain most active, going on to release ***Transportation*** on No Speak Records in 1989, and ***Stand Up And Walk*** on the Hot Food label in 1991.)

Nov Ultravox's *All Fall Down* reaches UK #30.

1988

June [11] Ure fronts the house band for "Nelson Mandela's 70th Birthday Tribute" concert, at Wembley Stadium, Wembley.

Sept [10] Ure's ***Answers To Nothing*** reaches UK #30 in its week of entry (and US #88 the following February), as the title track, *Answers To Nothing*, makes UK #49 (and US #95 in March).

Nov His *Dear God* peaks at UK #55.

1991

June [8] Ure headlines the "Cyclone Relief Concert Of Direct Funding To Bangladesh" benefit, at the Fountain Centre, Brentford, Middx.

Aug [31] His *Cold, Cold Heart* reaches UK #17.

Sept [28] Its parent album, ***Pure***, debuts at its UK #36 peak.

Nov [10] He begins a nine-date UK tour at the Symphony Hall, Birmingham, W. Midlands, set to end on the 29th at Leeds University, Leeds, S. Yorks.

1995

June [6] After a reissued *Vienna* has reached UK #13 on Feb [13], 1993 with ***If I Was - The Very Best Of Ultravox & Midge Ure*** debuting at its UK #10 peak on Mar [6], prompting Ultravox to embark on a five-date UK tour at Birmingham Town Hall on May 21st the same year with new lead singer, Tony Feneller, also aimed to tie in with a new album, ***Revelation*** on dsb Records, Ure is now presented with the first Scottish Silver Clef Award at the Roxburgh Hotel, Edinburgh, Lothian, Scotland.

1996

May [25] Ure returns to the UK chart, at #70, with *Breathe*.

THE UNDERTONES

Feargal Sharkey (vocals); **John O'Neill** (guitar); **Damian "Dee" O'Neill** (guitar); **Michael Bradley** (bass); **Billy Doherty** (drums)

1978

June [15] Led by Sharkey (b. Aug. 13, 1958, Londonderry, Northern Ireland) and John O'Neill (b. Aug. 26, 1957, Londonderry), the Undertones were formed by five friends in Londonderry in November 1975, initially playing pop covers in local pubs. By 1977, and influenced by the burgeoning punk movement, the band began to perform its own songs, and made a demo which was rejected by Stiff, Chiswick and Radar Records. After a period of playing regional gigs during which their act and repertoire are finely honed, and having been spotted in a "Battle of the Bands" contest in Belfast, they now make their recording debut at Wizard Studios, for local independent label, Good Vibrations.

Sept Their punk-tinged debut release, *Teenage Kicks*, receives UK airplay from BBC Radio 1 DJ John Peel, which brings A&R interest from UK labels. (Peel will later confess that the cut is his all-time favorite 45.)

Oct [26] The band has flown to London to appear on tonight's BBC1-TV's "Top Of The Pops", as the record climbs the chart. They are still without a manager, so Sharkey negotiates a five-year deal with Sire Records. Sire reissues *Teenage Kicks* (only 7,000 copies were originally pressed on Good Vibrations).

Nov *Teenage Kicks* reaches UK #31 during a six-week chart run, as the band, gigging for the first time outside Northern Ireland, begins its first UK tour with the Rezillos, who split halfway through leaving the Undertones to go it alone.

1979

Feb *Get Over You* makes UK #57.

May [26] *Jimmy Jimmy* is the band's first UK Top 20 hit, at #16, once again showcasing Sharkey's urgently distinctive vocal style.

June [16] Their debut album, the teen-angst themed ***The Undertones***, reaches UK #13, the sleeve inspired by the Who's *My Generation* 1965 debut.

July A re-recorded version of *Here Comes The Summer*, extracted from the album, makes UK #34, as the group undertakes its first US tour, supporting the Clash.

Oct *You've Got My Number (Why Don't You Use It?)* peaks at UK #32.

1980

Jan The band travels to Holland with producer Roger Bechirian to record its sophomore effort.

Apr ***Hypnotised*** becomes their biggest-selling UK album, hitting #6, while the extracted *My Perfect Cousin*, written by Bradley and Damian O'Neill, is their biggest UK hit single, at #9, aided by a UK Subbuteo soccer boardgame-featuring promotional video.

Aug [2] The extracted *Wednesday Week* charts at UK #11.

The Undertones tour the US again, this time as headliners, but remain only cult favorites. A headlining European tour follows.

Oct Dissatisfied with its lack of chart progress outside Britain, the band is freed from its Sire contract, and sets up its own label, Ardeck Records, licensed through EMI.

1981

Apr The group embarks on a major UK tour, including shows at London's Rainbow Theatre and Hammersmith Palais.

May *It's Going To Happen* peaks at UK #18, while its parent album, ***Positive Touch***, recorded in Holland

and reflecting a more sophisticated and mature musical approach, reaches UK #17.
Aug [8] Its rapid UK follow-up, *Julie Ocean*, makes #41.
Sept The group begins a European tour in Finland.

1982

Feb *Beautiful Friend* is issued.
Aug [2] The band performs in New York, during selected US dates.
Oct The psychedelia-influenced *The Love Parade* is released.

1983

Mar With no hit singles to sustain its chart progress, ***The Sin Of Pride*** makes UK #43.
[9] The group begins a 30-date UK tour in Liverpool.
June The Undertones disband, and EMI marks the split by reissuing *Teenage Kicks*, which peaks at UK #60.
Dec A 30-track compilation, ***All Wrapped Up***, issued as a memorial to the band, charts at UK #67. Sharkey, always the group's main focus, joins ex-Depeche Mode and Yazoo writer/keyboardist, Vince Clarke, for the Assembly one-off single, *Never Never*, which hits UK #4, before announcing plans to continue as a solo artist. (The O'Neill brothers will go on to form That Petrol Emotion, with Steve Mack (lead vocals), Reamann O'Gormain (guitar) and Ciaran McLaughlin (drums), releasing ***Manic Pop Thrill*** (1986), ***Babble*** (1987), ***End Of The Millenium Psychosis Blues*** (1988), ***Chemicrazy*** (1990) and ***Fireproof*** in 1993 before disbanding the following year.)

1984

Oct Invited to be the first act on Madness' Zarjazz label, Sharkey has the nutty boys back him on his solo debut, *Listen To Your Father*, which reaches UK #23.
Dec [7] He performs in a benefit concert for Ethiopia at London's Royal Albert Hall, organized by the Save The Children Fund, along with Nick Heyward, Julian Lennon, Mike Rutherford of Genesis and others.

1985

July Newly signed to Virgin Records, Sharkey's label debut, *Loving You*, makes UK #26.
Nov [16] He tops the UK chart for the first of two weeks with *A Good Heart*, written by Maria McKee of US group, Lone Justice. ***Feargal Sharkey***, produced by Dave Stewart of Eurythmics, makes UK #12.

1986

Jan *You Little Thief*, taken from the album (and first promoted in Britain by Sharkey on a live TV slot from a Virgin airliner, flying over London on Christmas Day) hits UK #5.
Feb [6] While Sharkey is touring the UK and performing in Sheffield, his mother, Sybil, and sister Ursula, visiting friends in Londonderry, Northern Ireland, are held at gunpoint for four hours by terrorists, but are eventually released.
Apr *Someone To Somebody* makes UK #64. Sharkey separates from his wife, and moves to Los Angeles, CA, to re-start his career. *A Good Heart* makes US #74 as its parent album, ***Feargal Sharkey***, reaches US #75. *More Love*, Sharkey's first recording for over 18 months, will make UK #44 in January 1988, though its parent album, ***Wish***, will fail to score when issued in April.

1993

Oct [2] Having contributed an acoustic version of *Never Never* to the 1990-released ***Rock The World*** benefit album, to raise money for the Phoenix House, London-based rehabilitation center, Sharkey's *I've Got News For You* has reached UK #12 on Apr [6], 1991 taken from ***Songs From The Mardi Gras*** which debuted at its UK #27 peak two weeks later. Subsequently joining Polydor Records as an A&R executive on September 1st the following year, he will move on to head up a new interactive record label for the multimedia company ESP in December 1994. An Undertones CD-released career retrospective, ***Teenage Kicks***, now makes UK #45.

USA FOR AFRICA

1984

Dec [15] UK all-star group, Band Aid, assembled by Bob Geldof, hits UK #1 with *Do They Know It's Christmas?*, released to raise funds to help feed starving people in Ethiopia and elsewhere in Africa. It sells over three million copies in the UK alone, and Geldof suggests that the music industry, on a worldwide basis, could raise over $500 million.
[20] Inspired by Geldof's efforts, music veteran Harry Belafonte conceives the idea for a US fund-raiser for the same cause, calling management and TV production company head, Ken Kragen, who in turn contacts Lionel Richie.
[21] Richie's wife, Brenda, spots friend Stevie Wonder in their local store and asks him to contact her husband about the idea. Meanwhile, Kragen asks Quincy Jones to produce the project, and the veteran helmer secures the help of Michael Jackson.

1985

Jan While Kragen establishes the United Support of Artists Foundation (with himself as president and Jackson, Richie, Belafonte, Jones and Kenny Rogers on the board of directors), and as major stars are quietly invited to participate, he enlists the financial and organizational abilities of Marty Rogol, who has already run fund-raisers with Harry Chapin and Rogers. Kragen also invites Barrie Bergman, head of large US record retailers Record Bar, to organize a committee, to ensure that all retail profits from any product will go to the USA For Africa fund.
[28] Following the American Music Awards celebrations at 10:00 p.m. (Kragen has decided to record the USA For Africa disc on this night when a healthy aggregation of top acts will be in attendance), 45 artists arrive at the A&M Studios, Hollywood, CA, greeted by a warning from Jones to "check your ego at the door". The song to be recorded, *We Are The World*, has been written by Jackson and Richie in just two hours, following three days of preparation. It is arranged, produced and engineered by Jones, Tom Bahler and Humberto Gatica. Inside the studio, a strip of named tape for each performer has been stuck on the floor forming a semi-circular ensemble. Those chosen for lead vocals will later be grouped close to one of six microphones, as their efforts will be recorded after the choruses have been taped. (Geldof sings as part of the chorus, with a host of stars.) This in turn follows the instrumental tracks, recorded earlier by Jones. The end result features 21 solo vocal segments which are, in order of appearance, Lionel Richie, Stevie Wonder, Paul Simon, Kenny Rogers, James Ingram, Tina Turner, Billy Joel, Michael Jackson, Diana Ross, Dionne Warwick, Willie Nelson, Al Jarreau, Bruce Springsteen, Kenny Loggins, Steve Perry, Daryl Hall, Huey Lewis, Cyndi Lauper, Kim Carnes, Bob Dylan and Ray Charles. Prince has been invited, but fails to show. (He will contribute a song to the subsequent album.) A video team lenses the historic event, resulting in 75 hours of footage, later edited to promote the song. After ten hours, only Richie and Jones remain, putting the final touches to an extraordinary record.
Feb While efforts are made to ship the disc as soon as possible, Kragen decides on CBS/Columbia for its free manufacturing and distribution (all major record companies have offered the same). Meanwhile, Jim Mazza at EMI suggests Kragen organize the release of an album of unissued tracks from selected USA For Africa artists.
Mar [7] 800,000 copies are distributed to record stores nationwide in the US. (Within two days they have been sold, and re-orders are flooding in.)
[23] *We Are The World* enters the US chart at #21.
Apr [1] The RIAA certifies four million sales of *We Are The World*.
[4] Columbia ships 2.7 million copies of ***We Are The World*** in the US. Rush-released, donated cuts are from Springsteen, Prince (*4 The Tears In Your Eyes*), Huey Lewis & the News, Chicago, Turner, the Pointer Sisters, Rogers, Perry, USA For Africa and Northern Lights. (Inspired by USA For Africa, a Canadian effort under the banner Northern Lights has also been organized. The track, *Tears Are Not Enough*, produced by David Foster, features Bryan Adams, John Candy, Corey Hart, Dan Hill, Gordon Lightfoot, Joni Mitchell, Anne Murray, and Neil Young, among others.)
[5] At 3:50 p.m. GMT, over 5,000 radio stations worldwide unite for seven minutes and two seconds, as *We Are The World* is aired.
[13] *We Are The World* hits US #1, where it will stay for four weeks. (It will go on to top the charts in most western territories.)
[20] *We Are The World* begins a two-week stay at UK #1. The USA For Africa Foundation's legal counsel, Jay Cooper, claims that bootleg merchandise, particularly T-shirts, is appearing in many US cities. Authorized merchandisers, Winterland, take measures to clamp down on the pirates.
[27] In its second week of release, ***We Are The World*** hits US #1, where it will stay for three weeks, eventually selling over three million copies in five months.
May [16] An initial cheque for $6.5 million in royalties is handed to Kragen by Columbia executive, Al Teller. Associated and combined sales receipts from the song, album and merchandise, will exceed $50 million.
[25] ***We Are The World*** makes UK #31.
June [10] The first airlift of supplies is flown to Africa for famine relief.
[14] With various local fund-raising efforts still gathering momentum, video distributor RCA/Columbia ships "We Are The World - The Video Event", to swell USA For Africa funds further. Company president Robert Blattner signs an agreement with Richie to ensure that all profits from the $14.95 video are donated directly to the foundation.
[24] The RIAA certifies three million sales of ***We Are The World***.
Sept [13] "We Are The World" wins the Best Group Video and Viewers Choice categories, at the second annual MTV Video Music Awards, held at Radio City Music Hall, New York, NY.

1995

Jan [30] Celebrating the tenth anniversary of the first play of *We Are The World*, radio stations worldwide play the record at noon EST, while Voice of America radio begins a one-hour special focusing on the charity. At this evening's 22nd annual American Music Awards held at the Shrine Auditorium, the last ten minutes of the show honors the song, with a segment presented by Harry Belafonte, Quincy Jones and Kenny Rogers. A total of 7.2 million singles and albums have been sold over the past ten years with the total project amassing $88.1 million, including Hands Across America.

U2

Bono (vocals); **The Edge** (guitar);
Adam Clayton (bass); **Larry Mullen Jr.** (drums)

1976

A Dublin, Eire schoolboy band, featuring Bono (b. Paul Hewson, May 10, 1960, Dublin), The Edge (b. David Evans, Aug. 8, 1961, Wales), Clayton (b. Mar. 13, 1960, Chinnor, Oxon.), Mullen Jr. (b. Oct. 31, 1961, Dublin) and Dick Evans, forms as Feedback, at Mullen's parents' home, in response to Mullen's recruitment note left on a Mount Temple High School notice-board. Playing mainly Beatles and Stones cover versions, at small-time local engagements, the group changes its name to the Hype the following year and, with Evans' departure to form the Virgin Prunes, eventually settles on U2. (Hewson has adopted the name Bono from a billboard, advertising a hearing-aid retailer, Bono Vox.)

1978

Jan [14] "Manager seeks the whereabouts of The Hype after amazing Howth gig. Please ring Brian 450822. (Malahide, Dublin). It was great lads" advertisement appears in a local newspaper. (It has been placed by Clayton in the hope that it would get the band more gigs.)
Mar [18] After playing pub and club gigs in Dublin, U2 wins a talent contest sponsored by the Evening Press and Guinness Harp Lager at the Limerick Civic Week. Still in their final year at school, they win £500, and the chance to audition for CBS Ireland (through contest adjudicator, A&R man Jackie Hayden) at the Keystone Studios.
May [25] Paul McGuinness, manager for the Stranglers and the Greedy Bastards, sees the band play at the Project Arts Centre, Dublin.
Sept Hayden arranges for **Record Mirror** journalist, Chas de Whalley, to record further demos at the Windmill Lane Studios, Dublin, which leads to their signing with CBS Ireland (their UK counterparts do not take up the option).
[18] The band poses backstage after a gig at Dublin's Project Arts Centre, holding gun and pistol replicas.

1979

Sept Having built considerable Irish fan support, following an RTE Radio 2 Irish demo session tape broadcast, U2 finally releases the EP, *U2:3*, featuring *Out Of Control*, *Stories* and *Boy - Girl*. Only available in Ireland, it tops the national chart.
Dec U2 plays its first UK dates to little interest. Miscredited as "V2" at the Hope & Anchor pub in London, only nine people turn up to watch them.

1980

Jan U2 wins five categories in Irish music magazine **Hot Press**' annual poll.
Feb As *Another Day*, produced by Whalley, also hits #1 in Ireland, U2 plays sellout gigs during its "Come Out To Play" Irish tour.
Mar After more promising UK dates, attended by A&R employee Bill Stewart, UK label Island Records signs the band (though it remains on CBS in Ireland).
May Debut Island single, *11 O'Clock Tick Tock*, is released, produced by Martin Hannett.
[22] A UK tour opens at the Hope & Anchor to coincide with the issue of *11 O'Clock Tick Tock*, set to end at the Half Moon, Herne Hill, London, on June 8th.
July [28] The group participates in the Dalymount Festival, Dublin, with the Police and Squeeze.
Aug *A Day Without Me* is issued.
Oct *I Will Follow* is released in both the UK and US.
[19] U2 plays at London's Lyceum Ballroom, supporting Slade.
Nov Their debut album, ***Boy***, produced by Steve Lillywhite, and recorded at the Windmill Lane Studios, is released, hinting at the anthemic rock style which will hallmark much of their work in the '80s. (The boy featured on the front cover is Peter, the brother of Virgin Prunes vocalist, Guggi.) U2 performs its first US dates, a three-week club tour on the East Coast.
Dec Constantly gigging, U2 supports Talking Heads on a UK trek, having recently played in Belgium and Holland.

1981

Feb Prior to embarking on a major US tour, the group headlines at London's Lyceum Ballroom, also appearing on BBC2-TV's "The Old Grey Whistle Test".
Mar ***Boy*** makes US #63.
Apr US tour closes with gigs at New York's Palladium and the Civic Center, Santa Monica, CA. (During the tour, the group is the supporting attraction at a Miss Wet T-shirt night in Dallas, TX.)
June The band returns to the UK to perform at London's Hammersmith Palais.
July *Fire*, recorded during a US tour break at Compass Point Studio, Nassau, Bahamas, is the group's UK chart debut, at #35.
Aug ***Boy*** belatedly reaches UK #52.
Oct [1] U2 begins an 18-date UK tour.
[24] *Gloria* makes UK #55, supported by a video, lensed at Dublin docks.
Nov Its parent album, ***October***, again produced by Lillywhite, and again recorded at the Windmill Lane Studios (their long-term professional base), reaches UK #11 and US #104, as U2 begins a fresh round of US dates.

1982

Jan U2 performs its first Irish tour for over a year, with a finalé at the Royal Dublin Society Hall, Dublin.
Mar [17] U2 plays a St. Patrick's Day gig at The Ritz, New York.
Apr Following a soldout UK tour, *A Celebration* (not available on album) makes UK #47.
June U2 enters Windmill Lane to spend much of the rest of the year recording new material.
Oct During a concert in Belfast, Northern Ireland, Bono introduces a new song, *Sunday Bloody Sunday*. (Written principally by The Edge and Bono, its "peace in Northern Ireland" message becomes a live focal point for the band in coming years, and highlights the group's ongoing socio-political lyrical stance.)

1983

Feb *New Year's Day*, boosted by a snow-bound video, hits UK #10, as its parent album, ***War***, their last with Lillywhite, climbs to US #12. U2 begins a 27-date sellout UK tour.
Mar [12] ***War*** enters the UK chart at #1.
Apr The band begins a two-month US arena tour, while *Two Hearts Beat As One* reaches UK #18.
May [4] Their debut US chart single, *New Year's Day*, makes #53, as remaining US dates draw superlative reviews and large crowds.
[28] U2 takes part in the three-day "US Festival" in San Bernadino, CA.
Aug The group headlines the Irish open-air rock festival, "A Day At The Races", in front of 25,000 people at Dublin's Phoenix Park.
Nov Their first live album, the Jimmy Iovine-produced ***Under A Blood Red Sky***, capturing the band's powerful rock stage presence, is released simultaneously with a similarly-titled video. It hits UK #2, and begins a climb to US #28. Recorded in Boston, MA, Germany, and at the Red Rocks Festival in Colorado, it becomes the most successful live album ever, but does little to off-set the growing number of U2 bootleg recordings.
Dec U2 performs its first gigs in Japan.

1984

Jan [2] The group participates in "The Big One" peace benefit, at London's Apollo Theatre, Victoria.
[28] *I Will Follow* peaks at US #81.
July Bono duets with the writer of *Blowin' In The Wind* and *Leopard Skin Pill Box Hat* at Dylan's concert, at Slane Castle, Eire.
Aug U2 performs the first concerts of a new world tour in New Zealand and Australia. The band also establishes its own Mother Records with McGuinness, to showcase the recordings of unsigned talent (mostly Irish). The label's first release is In Tua Nua's *Coming Thru'*. Run by Fachtra O'Ceallaigh, Mother will also sign, usually on a one-release basis, bands including Cactus World News, Tuesday Blue, Operating Theatre, Painted Word, the Subterraneans and Hothouse Flowers.
Oct [22] Now produced by Brian Eno and Daniel Lanois, who refine the band's innate rawness, a new studio album, recorded in the ballroom at Slane Castle, ***The Unforgettable Fire***, debuts at UK #1 and will reach US #12, as the extracted *Pride (In The Name Of Love)*, dedicated to Martin Luther King Jr., hits UK #3.
Nov [25] Bono contributes an unmistakable lead vocal part to Band Aid's recording of *Do They Know It's Christmas?*, while Clayton plays bass. Both are in London on the UK leg of an on-going tour, including two SRO dates at Wembley Arena, Wembley, Middx. (Bono is also invited by Irish Premier, Garrett Fitzgerald, to join a committee set up to look at the problems of youth unemployment in Eire.)
Dec [15] *Pride (In The Name Of Love)* makes US #33.

1985

Feb [25] U2 begins its first full US arena tour, following soldout European dates, in Dallas, TX.
Apr [1] The group headlines at New York's Madison Square Garden, as **Rolling Stone** magazine honors the group as "The Band Of The '80s".
May Strings-accompanied *The Unforgettable Fire* hits UK #6.
June [22] The band tops the bill at "The Longest Day" concert at the Milton Keynes Bowl, Milton Keynes, Bucks., in a series of summer European festival dates.
[29] U2 returns to Eire to perform in front of a 55,000-strong audience at Dublin's Croke Park.
On the same day, and released as an EP in the US, the four-track ***Wide Awake In America*** enters the US Album chart for just one week. It is then dropped from the survey, because its length is considered too short for the relevant listing, but will be reinstated to the US Album chart in April 1987 when it will resume climbing to its #37 peak.
July [13] Introduced via satellite by Jack Nicholson in Philadelphia, PA, U2 performs at the fund-raising "Live Aid" spectacular at Wembley Stadium, Wembley.
Aug [31] The US import title, ***Wide Awake In America***, comprising two studio outtakes and two live cuts, reaches UK #11.
Nov Bono appears on the Little Steven-organized Artists United Against Apartheid single and video, *Sun City* (UK #21 and US #38), also singing the closing number, *Silver And Gold*, on the accompanying album, recorded with the Rolling Stones' Keith Richard and Ron Wood.
(By year's end, Clayton is banned from driving for two years after pleading guilty to dangerous driving and intoxication in Dublin's Rathgar district.)

1986

Jan Bono is the featured vocalist on Irish folk group Clannad's *In A Lifetime*, which reaches UK #20.
Feb U2 wins Best Band, and Best Live Aid Performance, in **Rolling Stone**'s 1985 Readers' Poll.
Mar The group resumes world touring (which will include performing on Amnesty International's 25th anniversary tour).
May [17] U2 joins other Irish rock acts to play "Self Aid" in Dublin, to raise funds for the unemployed.
June [4] Amnesty International's "A Conspiracy Of Hope" two-week US tour begins, featuring U2, Sting, Peter Gabriel, Bryan Adams and Lou Reed, at the Cow Palace, San Francisco, CA.
Aug The band enters the studio, with Eno and Lanois, to record a new album. (The Edge also records the soundtrack album, ***The Captive***, with Irish diva, Sinead O'Connor.)
Sept [25] U2 is joined on stage by Bruce Springsteen during a concert in Philadelphia.

1987

Feb U2 begins a 110-date arena world tour.
Mar [21] ***The Joshua Tree*** enters the UK chart at #1, selling 235,000 copies in its first week of release, having gone platinum in 48 hours, the fastest-selling album in UK chart history to date. Regarded as a career highlight, the Lanois/Eno-helmed set will confirm U2 as the world's biggest-retailing rock act since Dire Straits. (The album is dedicated to the group's PA, Greg Carroll, who was killed in Dublin in July 1986 while riding a motorbike.)
[27] The group films a video for *Where The Streets Have No Name* in downtown Los Angeles, CA, drawing a crowd of thousands.
[28] *With Or Without You* hits UK #4.
Apr [2] U2 embarks on another world tour, beginning in Arizona.
[25] ***The Joshua Tree*** tops the US chart, where it will stay for nine weeks.
[27] U2 makes the cover of **Time** magazine with the headline: "U2 : Rock's Hottest Ticket".

May [16] *With Or Without You* becomes U2's first US #1 single. With music by U2, and lyrics by Bono, it is an immediate airplay and sales smash, staying in pole position for three weeks.
[27] European leg of their latest world trek opens in Rome, Italy, set to end August 8th in Cork, Eire.
June [13] *I Still Haven't Found What I'm Looking For*, with a video filmed on the streets of Las Vegas, NV, hits UK #6.
Aug [8] *I Still Haven't Found What I'm Looking For* tops the US chart.
Sept [10] The North American leg of the world tour resumes at the Nassau Veterans Memorial Coliseum, Uniondale, NY, the first of 50 dates.
[11] "With Or Without You" wins the Viewers Choice category, at the fourth annual MTV Video Music Awards, held at the Universal Amphitheatre, Universal City, CA.
[12] *Where The Streets Have No Name*, accompanied by the performance video filmed on top of a Los Angeles building, complete with a "Get Back" police presence, debuts at its UK #4 peak.
Nov [7] *Where The Streets Have No Name* reaches US #13. A book **Unforgettable Fire : The Story Of U2**, hits the UK best-seller lists. Written by Eamon Dunphy, it was originally authorized by the band, who later withdrew their support having negotiated unsuccessfully to change the text, which is claimed to be inaccurate.
[18] U2 opens for itself at Los Angeles' Coliseum, as the country/rock outfit, the Dalton Brothers - Alton (Bono), Luke (The Edge), Betty (Clayton) and Duke (Mullen).
Dec The group contributes *Christmas (Baby Please Come Home)* to the newly-released Jimmy Iovine-produced benefit album, ***Special Christmas***.

1988

Jan [23] *In God's Country* makes US #44, after making UK #48 on import.
Feb [8] U2 receives the Best International Group honor at the seventh annual BRIT Awards, held at London's Royal Albert Hall.
[20] ***The Joshua Tree Singles*** package anchors at UK #100.
Mar [2] The band wins the Album Of The Year and Best Rock Performance By A Duo Or Group With Vocal categories, both for ***The Joshua Tree***, at the 30th annual Grammy Awards, held at Radio City Music Hall, New York.
Apr The band works in Los Angeles, recording new album tracks and overseeing post-production of their forthcoming live documentary movie, "Rattle And Hum".
Sept U2 has contributed *Jesus Christ* to the newly released Woody Guthrie/Leadbelly tribute album, ***Folkways : A Vision Shared***, while Bono and The Edge also make contributions to Roy Orbison's comeback album, ***Mystery Girl***.
Oct [8] *Desire* becomes U2's first UK #1 single.
[16] The band performs at the "Smile Jamaica" live TV fund-raiser for the Hurricane Gilbert disaster fund, at London's Dominion Theatre, playing four cuts from ***Rattle And Hum***, joined on stage by Keith Richards and bill-topper, Ziggy Marley.
[22] Double album, ***Rattle And Hum***, produced by Jimmy Iovine (the title taken from U2 song *Bullet The Blue Sky*), capturing live performances from the past two years, and including rare studio cuts, hits UK #1 (again with record ship-out figures).
[27] U2's film "Rattle And Hum" receives its world premiere in Dublin. It was directed by Philip Joanou, whose brief was to "follow the "Joshua Tree" tour and make a film".
Nov [12] ***Rattle And Hum*** tops the US chart.
[26] *Desire* hits US #3.
Dec *Angel Of Harlem*, recorded at the legendary Sun Studios, Memphis, TN, hits UK #9.
The group is featured singing *Maggie's Farm* on ***Live For Ireland***, a newly-released compilation which also features Elvis Costello and Van Morrison, among others.

1989

Jan [10] *Desire* is certified gold by the RIAA.
Feb [11] *Angel Of Harlem* reaches US #14.
[13] The band is once again named Best International Group, at the eighth annual BRIT Awards, at the Royal Albert Hall.
[22] U2 wins the Best Rock Performance By A Duo Or Group With Vocal, for *Desire*, and Best Performance Music Video, for "Where The Streets Have No Name", categories at the 31st annual Grammy Awards.
Apr [22] *When Love Comes To Town*, with blues legend B.B. King, hits UK #6.
[29] *When Love Comes To Town* peaks at US #68.
May [10] Bono and his wife Alisa's daughter Jordan is born.
June [4] Bono joins Bob Dylan on stage in Dublin for encores of *Knockin' On Heaven's Door* and *Maggie's Farm*.
[24] *All I Want Is You* (with U2's version of *Unchained Melody*) hits UK #4, as a 23-date Australian tour, the group's second, opens in Perth, W. Australia.
July [15] *All I Want Is You* peaks at US #83.
Aug [6] Clayton is arrested in the Blue Light Inn car park in Dublin for marijuana possession, and intent to supply the drug to another person.
Sept [1] Clayton's marijuana conviction is waived in exchange for paying £25,000 to the Dublin Women's Aid & Refuge Centre. (Devoted group fan, Paul Matthews, a member of U2 tribute band, the Joshua Trio, will set free 25,000 white butterflies as a parallel gesture to the fine.)
[6] U2 and B.B. King win Best Video From Film category, at the sixth annual MTV Video Music Awards ceremony, staged at the Universal Amphitheatre.
[10] NBC-TV broadcasts its first annual International "Very Special Arts Festival", featuring U2, Kenny Rogers, Mikhail Baryshnikov, Lauren Bacall and Michael Douglas, from the lawn of the White House. The festival celebrates the accomplishments of physically-and-mentally-handicapped artists from around the world.
[12] The band begins a five-week, 19-date Australian tour in Perth, followed by nine further concerts in New Zealand and Japan.
Nov The Edge celebrates the birth of his third child (by his wife, Aislinn), by water-skiing on Lake Liffey with Luke and Matt Goss of Bros.

1990

Feb [6] The Royal Shakespeare Company production, "A Clockwork Orange 2004", an adaptation of Anthony Burgess' controversial novel **A Clockwork Orange**, with music by The Edge, opens in London. (Burgess criticizes the score as being "neo-wallpaper and not music at all".)
[18] For the third consecutive year, U2 nabs the Best International Group trophy, at the ninth annual BRIT Awards, held at London's Dominion Theatre.
Mar [8] Bono is named Best Songwriter, and Sexiest Male Rock Artist, and Adam Clayton is named Best Bassist, in the annual **Rolling Stone** Readers' Picks 1989 music awards.
May [26] The Chimes' soulful cover of *I Still Haven't Found What I'm Looking For* hits UK #6.
June Mullen pens the Eire World Cup soccer team's official theme song.
Sept Bono co-writes *Jah Love*, with Neville Brother Cyril, via fax (for inclusion on a future Nevilles' set).
Oct U2 contributes *Night And Day* to ***Red Hot + Blue***, an anthology of Cole Porter songs, released to benefit AIDS education, and travels to Berlin, Germany, to film a promo clip with director Wim Wenders.
Dec [1] U2's "Night And Day" video is featured in the hour-long TV special, "Red Hot + Blue", on International AIDS Day.
[31] The band's New Year's Eve gig at Dublin's Point Depot is broadcast live throughout Europe.

1991

Mar [18] U2 pays a £500 (Irish) pounds fine, imposed on the Irish Family Planning Association, found guilty of selling condoms illegally at the Virgin Megastore, Dublin. (During the month The Edge buys Oscar Wilde's former family home in Cong, County Mayo, Eire.)
May During a month when The Edge moves in with Clayton following the break-up of his marriage to wife Aislinn, recording for the band's sixth studio album begins at the luxury, £4,000 a day Elsinore on Dalkey mansion in Coliemore Road, Dublin, but sessions will eventually move onto the Hansa Studios in Berlin, Germany.
Aug [8] The Joshua Trio performs at The Edge's 30th birthday bash, with David Bowie, Van Morrison and actor Sean Penn among the guests.
Nov [2] Reflecting a musical shift away from the group's traditional, anthemic rock style, *The Fly* enters the UK chart at #1.
[23] *The Fly* makes US #61.
[30] ***Achtung Baby***, continuing the band's darker and more experimental musical foray, previewed by *The Fly*, debuts at its UK #2 peak, lodged behind Michael Jackson's ***Dangerous***. (Its title comes from a Dick Shawn line in "The Producers" film, which sound engineer Joe O'Herlihy had developed as his pet phrase during the album's recording.)
Dec [1] The group appears at the "Red Hot & Dance AIDS" benefit.
[7] ***Achtung Baby*** debuts at US #1.
[14] *Mysterious Ways* debuts at its UK #13 peak.

1992

Jan [15] The Edge inducts the Yardbirds into the Rock and Roll Hall of Fame, at the seventh annual dinner, held at New York's Waldorf Astoria Hotel.
[25] *Mysterious Ways* hits US #9, its video clip directed by Stephane Sednaoui.
Feb [24] The group guests on BBC1-TV's "Top Of The Pops", live by satellite.
[29] The "Zoo TV Tour", a near-nightly, grand, multi-media experience, opens at the Lakeland Civic Center Arena, FL, before a sellout crowd of 7,251.
Mar [14] *One* hits UK #7.
[17] U2 performs at Boston Garden, Boston, on St. Patrick's Day.
[27] During a concert at the Palace Of Auburn Hills, Auburn Hills, MI, Bono orders 10,000 pizzas to go from Speedy Pizza. An hour later, 100 arrive with three delivery men, who each receive a $50 tip. (During the current tour, the group's hottest merchandise items are the "Achtung Baby" condoms, at $3 for two.)
May [16] With an accompanying video directed by Phil Joanou, *One* hits US #10.
[31] The group performs at London's Earls Court during the European leg of their "Zoo" tour. (They have been joined onstage in Vienna, Austria by Axl Rose, to sing an acoustic version of *Knockin' On Heaven's Door*, while Aerosmith's Steve Tyler and Joe Perry are special guests at their Hippodrome de Vincennes, Paris, France concert.)
June [11] At their Stockholm, Sweden gig, the band is joined onstage by Abba's Benny Andersson and Bjorn Ulvaeus, for a rendition of *Dancing Queen*.
[19] U2 headlines the "Greenpeace Stop Sellafield" campaign concert, at Manchester's G-Mex, with Public Enemy, Big Audio Dynamite II and Kraftwerk.
[27] *Even Better Than The Real Thing* reaches UK #12.
July [18] *Even Better Than The Real Thing (Remix)* hits UK #8.
Aug [11] "Zoo TV Outside Broadcast" tour opens at Giants Stadium, East Rutherford, NJ, set to end on November 25th at the Sports Palace, Mexico City, Mexico, as the "Honeymoon In Vegas" film soundtrack, featuring Bono's version of *Can't Help Falling In Love*, is released.
[29] The band, supported by Public Enemy, becomes only the second act ever (Billy Joel was the first) to perform at Yankee Stadium, New York, one of the venues on the current stadium leg of their sellout "Zoo" tour.

Sept [9] "Even Better Than The Real Thing" wins the Best Group Video, and Best Special Effects categories, at the ninth annual MTV Video Music Awards, held at the Pauley Pavilion, Los Angeles.
[12] *Even Better Than The Real Thing* makes US #32.
[23] U2 is featured on MTV's "Rock The Vote".
Oct [30-31] The band plays to two sellout crowds of 108,357 at Dodger Stadium, Los Angeles.
Nov [29] Fox-TV airs "U2 - Zoo TV", the group's first TV special, directed by Kevin Godley.
Dec [5] *Who's Gonna Ride Your Wild Horses* debuts at its UK #14 peak.
[9] The group wins the Top Album Rock Tracks Artists, Top Album Rock Tracks, Top Modern Rock Tracks Artists, Top Modern Rock Tracks categories, at the third annual **Billboard** Music Awards, held at the Universal Amphitheatre.
[19] *Who's Gonna Ride Your Wild Horses* makes US #35.
(By year's end, the phenomenally successful "Zoo TV" tour has grossed $67 million, putting them third on the all-time box-office list behind the Rolling Stones ($98 million in 1989) and New Kids On The Block ($74.1 million in 1990). During a busy 12 months, the group has also bought the Clarence Hotel, near Dublin's Tony Temple Bar, met with presidential candidate, Bill Clinton, in a Chicago Ritz-Carlton hotel room, while Bono has penned English lyrics to Zucchero and Pavarotti's duet, *Misere*, and also written a screenplay, "Million Dollar Hotel", with Nicholas Klein, its rights bought by Mel Gibson's Icon Productions.)

1993

Jan [20] Clayton and Mullen join R.E.M.'s Michael Stipe and Mike Mills as Automatic Baby, on an acoustic version of *One*, at the "MTV 1993 Rock'n'Roll Inaugural Ball" in Washington, DC.
Feb [16] U2 wins the Best Live Act category, at the 12th annual BRIT Awards, held at London's Alexandra Palace.
[24] The band wins the Best Rock Vocal, Duo Or Group category, at the 35th annual Grammy Awards, staged at the Shrine Auditorium, Los Angeles.
Mar [21] The group nabs the International Entertainer Of The Year trophy, at the 22nd annual Juno Awards, held at the O'Keefe Centre, Toronto, Canada.
May [9-10] The constantly evolving "Zoo" tour, now named "Zooropa '93", opens in Rotterdam, Holland.
[12] The group is named Best Selling Irish Artist Of The Year, at the fifth annual World Music Awards, staged at the Sporting Club in Monte Carlo, Monaco.
June [2] PolyGram Holding Inc., Island's parent company, announces that it is signing U2 to a new long-term deal. (**The New York Post** announces it is worth a reported $200 million, although it is believed to more like $50 to $60 million.)
July [17] A new studio set, ***Zooropa***, recorded during tour breaks in the spring, enters the UK chart at #1. Produced by Eno, Flood and The Edge, and including *The Wanderer*, featuring Johnny Cash on lead vocals, which Bono describes as "... one of the best things we've ever done and I'm not even on it", it will debut at US #1 on the 24th.
Aug [11-12, 20-21] As the group continues its "Zooropa" world tour, they play four nights at Wembley Stadium. (At one of the shows Salman Rushdie wanders onstage.)
[28] The group performs in Phoenix Park, Dublin, during the Irish leg of the "Zooropa" tour.
Sept [2] The Edge performs live at the tenth annual MTV Video Music Awards, at the Universal Amphitheatre.
[8] The RIAA certifies two million sales of ***Zooropa***.
Dec [10] Two-year "Zooropa" tour ends at the Dome in Tokyo, Japan. (A week earlier, Clayton had missed a show in Sydney, New South Wales, Australia, with his roadie Stuart Morgan filling in for him.)
[11] *Stay (Faraway, So Close)*, backed with Bono's duet of *I've Got You Under My Skin* from Frank Sinatra's ***Duets*** album, hits UK #4.

1994

Jan [1] *Stay (Faraway, So Close)* peaks at US #61.
[19] Bono inducts the late Bob Marley into the Rock and Roll Hall of Fame at the ninth annual dinner at New York's Waldorf Astoria.
Feb [1] The group files suit in the High Court against the Performing Right Society, alleging inefficiency, restraint of trade and abuse (in contravention of Article 86 of the Treaty of Rome) of its dominant position in collecting its live performance royalties.
[14] U2's own dance club, the Kitchen, located in the basement of the Clarence Hotel in Dublin, opens.
Mar [1] The group wins the Best Alternative Music Album (***Zooropa***) trophy at the 36th Grammy staged at Radio City Music Hall. Bono states that "We shall continue to abuse our position and fuck up the mainstream". He also presents Frank Sinatra with his Living Legend honor.
[10] U2 is named Best Live Act at the fifth Uno Ano De Rock Awards at Real Madrid's Indoor sports Pavilion.
Apr [9] Bono and Gavin Friday's *In The Name Of The Father*, recorded for the film of the same name, debuts at its UK #46 peak.
May [4] U2 is named the World's Best-selling Irish Recording Artists Of The Year at the annual World Music Awards at the Sporting Club, Monte Carlo, Monaco. (The show will be broadcast on ABC-TV on the 31st.)
[23] The RIAA certifies one million sales of ***Wide Awake In America*** and three million sales of ***Under A Blood Red Sky***.
[25] Bono and the Edge accept a Special Award for International Achievement at the 39th annual Ivor Novello Awards, held at London's Grosvenor House Hotel.
Sept [14] Bono pays $56,000 for Charlie Chaplin's costume worn in the movie "The Great Dictator" to be exhibited in Dublin's Hard Rock Café.
Oct [8] U2 appears, on tape, performing *Can't Help Falling In Love*, at the "Elvis Aaron Presley : The Tribute", an all-star tribute from the Pyramid Arena, Memphis, TN, airing live on US pay-per-view TV.

1995

Feb [15] Their "Zoo TV - Live From Sydney" video is certified gold by the RIAA.
Mar [1] "Zoo TV - Live From Sydney", directed by David Mallet, wins the Best Music Video, Longform category at the 37th annual Grammy Awards, held at Los Angeles' Shrine Auditorium.
May Bantam Press (UK) publishes **At The End Of The World**, chronicling the band's career from 1990 to 1993, written by band intimate Bill Flanagan. (Delacorte Press (US) will publish the book in June.)
June [17] *Hold Me, Thrill Me, Kiss Me, Kill Me*, featured on the movie soundtrack to "Batman Forever", debuts at its UK #2 peak.
July [15] *Hold Me, Thrill Me, Kiss Me, Kill Me* reaches US #16.
Sept [6] The RIAA confirms seven million sales of ***Achtung Baby***.
[11] In a slew of further disc awards, the RIAA certifies platinum sales of ***Boy*** and ***October*** and multi-platinum sales of ***Rattle And Hum*** (five million), ***The Joshua Tree*** (ten million), ***The Unforgettable Fire*** (three million) and ***War*** (four million).
[12] Bono, The Edge and Brian Eno sing *Miss Sarajevo* and *One* at Luciano Pavarotti's War Child charity benefit at Novi Sad Park, Modena, Italy (which will be included on ***Pavarotti & Friends*** released the following March).
Oct [14] ***Tower Of Song : The Songs Of Leonard Cohen***, to which Bono has contributed *Hallelujah*, charts for a week at US #198.
Nov [4] ***Inner City Blues - The Music Of Marvin Gaye***, featuring an electronic duet between Marvin Gaye and Bono on *Save The Children*, makes US #106.
[18] ***Original Soundtracks 1***, credited to the Passengers, a union between U2 and Brian Eno, with guest appearances by Luciano Pavarotti, DJ Howie B and Japanese singer Holi, bows at its UK #12 peak, and includes Bono and Pavarotti on a studio duet of *Miss Sarajevo*.
[23] Bono, picking up the Best Group Award, launches a scathing attack on President Jacques Chirac for his country's nuclear policy ("What a city. What a night. What a mistake. What a wanker you have for President"), at the second annual MTV Europe Awards at Le Zenith in Paris, France.
[25] ***Original Soundtrack 1*** debuts at its US #76 peak.
Dec [2] The Passengers' *Miss Sarajevo* debuts at its UK #6 peak.

1996

Jan [16] With Island Records boss Chris Blackwell and Bono on board (Jimmy Buffett and Bono have been guests at Blackwell's Jamaican estate and at his Pink Sands resort on Harbour Island), Buffett makes an emergency landing of his sea-plane, the Flying Boat, after Jamaican police open fire on the aircraft as it takes off from Montego Bay, Jamaica. An anonymous tip-off had incorrectly identified the plane as carrying drugs. Bullets are lodged in the craft but with no injuries to any party.
Mar [29] U2 accepts a £400,000 offer from the PRS to settle the February 1st, 1994 suit, brought against the organization.
May [9] U2 announces plans for a spring 1997 world tour, promoted by Michael Cohl of Canadian-based Concert Promotions International.
[18] Clayton and Mullen's *Theme From Mission : Impossible*, the Lalo Schifrin-composed music from the original television series, now updated by the pair for the Tom Cruise-starring summer blockbuster movie, begins its US chart climb at #66.
June [15] *Theme From Mission : Impossible* hits UK #7 in its week of entry.

RITCHIE VALENS

1952

At Pacoima Junior High, Valens (b. Richard Stephen Valenzuela, May 13, 1941, Pacoima, CA) builds a solid-body electric guitar (which he will use until success pays for a Fender Stratocaster), after learning to play acoustic Spanish guitar (right-handed, despite being naturally left-handed) two years earlier. Weaned on Mexican music (with Mexican-Indian parents, who have separated, Valens living with his father until his death in 1951, and then being raised by his mother), he has been music-obsessed since an early age - initially focusing on Chicano folk, then R&B, and eventually Little Richard-styled rock'n'roll.

1957

Nov He joins the Silhouettes, a Mexican band which includes a Japanese tenor-sax player, and two Afro-Chicanos. He sings R&B and rock'n'roll numbers with the group around the San Fernando Valley area, and is so popular that he becomes its front-man.

1958

May He auditions for Bob Keene, owner of the Hollywood, CA-based Del-Fi label, after being seen at an American Legion dance in San Fernando, CA, by a Del-Fi talent scout. Keene decides to record him, and the first session at the Gold Star Studios produces *Come On, Let's Go*, for which he has a riff worked out, but no lyrics, so he makes up the words on the spot. Coupled with Leiber & Stoller's *Framed* (also recorded by the Coasters), it is released, with his name shortened to Ritchie Valens.
Aug Valens begins his first US tour, during which he befriends Eddie Cochran, and appears singing *Come On, Let's Go* on Dick Clark's "American Bandstand" TV show.
Nov [29] *Come On, Let's Go* peaks at US #42, during a 13-week US chart run, as he completes the tour. (In the UK, Tommy Steele's cover hits #10). On his return to Los Angeles, CA, Valens records *Donna*, written

for his San Fernando High School sweetheart, Donna Ludwig. For the B-side, Keene suggests updating a traditional "huapango" Mexican wedding song which, sung in Spanish, becomes *La Bamba*.

Dec [5] Valens returns to his old school, to play a concert which is recorded by Keene. He films a cameo slot for Alan Freed's movie, "Go, Johnny, Go", lip-synching on *Ooh My Head*.

[25] After a second "American Bandstand" appearance, he plays a ten-day run with Cochran, Bo Diddley and the Everly Brothers, in Alan Freed's Christmas Show at New York's Loew's State Theater, as both sides of his second single (*Donna* and *La Bamba*) race each other up the US chart, *La Bamba* initially in the lead.

1959

Jan Valens records tracks for an album and joins "The Winter Dance Party" tour through the upper midwest in icy weather.

Feb [3] At approximately 1:00 a.m. after a show at Clear Lake, IA, a plane, chartered by Buddy Holly to fly to the next venue in Moorhead, MN, crashes in a frozen corn field, killing all on board, including Valens, who had persuaded Holly's guitarist, Tommy Allsup, to give up his seat for him. (He will be buried in the San Fernando Mission Cemetery.)

[7] *La Bamba* reaches US #22.

[28] *Donna* hits US #2.

Mar *Donna* charts in the UK at #29 for a week, overtaken by Marty Wilde's cover, which hits #3.

Apr ***Ritchie Valens*** makes US #23.

May [2] *That's My Little Suzie* peaks at US #55.

July [25] *Little Girl* reaches US #92. (Further singles and two albums - ***Ritchie***, made up from the remainder of his unissued studio tapes, including some guitar instrumentals, and ***Live At Pacoima Junior High School***, from the December 1958 concert, will be released by Del-Fi over the following 12 months, but neither will chart. Valens' songs will be covered by many artists, and his influence as a pioneer of "Chicano rock" will endure despite his short career.)

1987

July Taylor Hackford's biopic, "La Bamba", with Lou Diamond Phillips playing Valens, attracts a new audience, and Los Lobos hit US and UK #1 with their interpretation of *La Bamba*, featured on the movie soundtrack, as Rhino Records releases the three-volume set, ***History Of Ritchie Valens***.

Sept ***The Best Of Ritchie Valens*** makes US #100. (Rhino will also release ***The Ritchie Valens Story***, a 16-track CD pairing his hits with rare demos, narrated by his original producer, Bob Keane.)

1990

May [11] After Manuel Velasquez, artist and counsellor for the Community Youth Gang Services, has honored Valens with a mural at Pacoima Junior High in 1985, and Ritchie Valens Recognition Day has been celebrated on May 14th, 1988 at the American Legion Hall in San Fernando, CA, where he had played 30 years earlier, Dick Dale & the Deltones headlined a Ritchie Valens Night at the Country Club, Reseda, CA on May 13th 1989 with proceeds going to the Ritchie Valens Community Talent Service, and the National Hispanic Scholarship programs in music at Pacoima Junior and San Fernando High schools. Today, Valens is posthumously honored with the dedication of a star on the Hollywood Walk of Fame.

VAN HALEN

David Lee Roth (vocals); **Eddie Van Halen** (guitar); **Michael Anthony** (bass); **Alex Van Halen** (drums)

1973

Roth (b. Oct. 10, 1955, Bloomington, IN), who has attended a child-guidance clinic as a child, suffering from hyperactivity, having moved to Pasadena, CA, with his parents in 1972 (his father is a surgeon), joins local rock band, the Red Ball Jets, while Alex Van Halen (b. May 8, 1955, Nijmegen, Holland) and his brother Eddie (b. Jan. 26, 1957, Nijmegen), whose family has moved to Pasadena from Holland in 1965, and who have both learnt to play the piano as kids, have graduated to drums and guitar respectively in high school band the Broken Combs, subsequently playing as Revolver. The Van Halens invite Roth to join their latest outfit, Mammoth, deciding it is cheaper to have him in the band than continue to rent his PA system which they have been doing for $35/weekend. As a heavy-rock covers group, Mammoth plays on the local club circuit before recruiting Snake bassist, Anthony (b. June 20, 1955, Chicago, IL) the following year.

1975

Now established as the loudest and heaviest band in the Los Angeles area, they reject the name Rat Salade, and settle on Van Halen. With a burgeoning live reputation, they open for groups including Santana, UFO and Sparks, mostly at the Gazzari club on Los Angeles' Sunset Strip.

1976

While playing at Los Angeles' Starwood, having been booked there by Rodney Bingenheimer who had in turn seen them on the California bar circuit, Van Halen impresses Kiss bassist, Gene Simmons, who offers to produce a demo tape of live numbers, including *Runnin' With The Devil*, and *House Of Pain*, though it will be rejected by all major labels. A songwriting pattern is emerging with Roth writing lyrics, and the other members creating the music.

1977

Again playing at the Starwood club, Van Halen, led as much by Eddie Van Halen's impressive guitar work as by Roth's outrageously extrovert stage antics, is spotted by Warner Bros. Records' producer, Ted Templeman, who persuades label boss Mo Ostin to sign the band. The contract allows Van Halen to retain full artistic control, and includes paternity insurance clauses.

1978

Feb Their debut album, ***Van Halen***, produced by Templeman, is released, and will hit US #19, during a three-year-plus chart tenure, with sales exceeding two million in its first year alone.

Mar [3] Van Halen embarks on its first US tour at the Aragon Ballroom, Chicago, highlighted by Roth's self-confident front-stage acrobatics, and Eddie's guitar prowess, with contracts insisting that their M&M confectionery provision does not include the brown ones.

[25] Van Halen's cover of the Kinks' *You Really Got Me* makes US #36.

May [20] *Runnin' With The Devil* peaks at US #84 and, supported by a first UK tour behind Black Sabbath, makes UK #52, while ***Van Halen*** rises to UK #34.

1979

Apr ***Van Halen II***, again helmed by Templeman, has taken only six days to record. It will hit US #6 (and UK #23).

[7] The group plays at the California Music Festival at Los Angeles' Memorial Coliseum.

[8] Van Halen begins a ten-month world tour, transporting over 22 tons of equipment. At some gigs, Roth invites all their fans to back-stage parties, as the media concentrates increasingly on alleged drug-taking and wild rock'n'roll celebration.

[13] Roth collapses on stage in Spokane, Washington, DC.

June Van Halen headlines the UK leg of its world tour.

July [14] *Dance The Night Away* reaches US #15. As US dates resume, the group hires lookalikes to parachute into Anaheim Stadium, Anaheim, CA, as a prelude to the gig.

Oct [6] *Beautiful Girls* peaks at US #84.

1980

Apr ***Women And Children First*** hits US #6 and UK #15. Van Halen's annual tour begins, now titled "Invasion".

June Roth breaks his nose and suffers multiple contusions and concussion during the recording of an Italian TV special, colliding with hanging stage lights during the execution of a flying squirrel leap.

[28] *And The Cradle Will Rock* makes US #55.

1981

Apr [11] Eddie Van Halen marries actress Valerie Bertinelli.

May ***Fair Warning*** hits US #6, and makes UK #49.

1982

Apr [17] *(Oh) Pretty Woman*, reviving Roy Orbison's 1964 US and UK #1 hit, reaches US #12.

May Their fifth album, ***Diver Down***, is released set to hit US #3 and UK #36.

June Van Halen hires Francis Ford Coppola's soundstage at Zoetrope Studios, to try out its new touring sound system.

July [3] *Dancing In The Street* makes US #38.

Sept [3-5] Their "Hide Your Sheep" tour begins at Steve Wozniak's three-day "US Festival" in San Bernardino, CA.

Oct [22] "Van Halen Day" is declared in Worcester, MA.

1983

Feb In place of a cancelled UK visit, Van Halen embarks on its first South American tour, playing Uruguay, Venezuela, Brazil and Argentina.

Apr [3] Michael Jackson's *Beat It*, featuring acclaimed fret work from Eddie Van Halen, hits US #1. (Eddie completed the session work free of charge, as a favor.)

May [28] The band is paid $1 million (the largest fee ever) to play a single concert, at the second "US Festival" in San Bernardino. The organizers need an audience of 750,000 to break even - but only 300,000 show.

Dec [31] ***1984*** is released on New Year's Eve, at the band's insistence.

1984

Feb ***1984*** hits US #2 and UK #15 (despite a ban in some UK outlets due to a baby-smoking cover shot). Becoming another multi-platinum smash, it marks the band's first major use of synthesizers and includes a live favorite from 1976, *House Of Pain*.

[25] *Jump*, group-penned, tops the US chart for the first of five weeks. The promotional video, according to Roth, cost $6,000 to record on 16mm home equipment.

Mar Despite the BPI imposing a £6,000 fine on UK Warner Bros. for hyping the single, *Jump* hits UK #7.

[21] Kurt Jefferies of Phoenixville, PA, wins a "Lost Weekend With Van Halen" competition, out of more than one million entrants.

Apr [3] *Jump* is certified gold by the RIAA.

May *Panama* stops at UK #61.

June [2] *I'll Wait* reaches US #13.

Aug Van Halen plays at the annual "Monsters Of Rock" festival at Castle Donington, Leics.

[18] *Panama* makes US #13.

Sept UK act Aztec Camera's acoustic-ballad version of *Jump* is featured as the B-side to its UK #34 hit *All I Need Is Everything*.

[18] Van Halen wins the Best Stage Performance Video category for "Jump", at the inaugural MTV Video Music Awards, held at Radio City Music Hall, New York, NY, hosted by Dan Aykroyd and Bette Midler.

Oct As president of his own "Jungle Studs" club, Roth plans a trip to Papua New Guinea.

Nov [24] *Hot For Teacher* makes US #56.

1985

Feb Always the central focus of the band Roth, still

officially in the Van Halen line-up, has released his debut solo single, with the help of the Beach Boys' Carl Wilson, a cover of their seminal *California Girls*. Spurred by a predictably babe-filled video, it hits US #3 and UK #68.
Apr [1] Roth quits the band to go solo.
June [1] A long-time Al Jolson fan, Roth's medley of *Just A Gigolo* and *I Ain't Got Nobody* reaches US #12.
Sept [13] Ted Templeman has bet Roth that he can't drive his 1951 Mercury Lowrider from Los Angeles to New York, NY in three days, in time for the second annual MTV Video Music Awards. In typical Roth style, he now arrives, minutes before the show is due to start at Radio City Music Hall.

1986

Feb Eddie and Alex ignore Warner Bros.' advice not to use the Van Halen name with Roth gone, having recruited Sammy Hagar (b. Oct. 13, 1947, Monterey, CA) as his replacement. (Ex-Montrose singer/guitarist Hagar is already a chart veteran as a solo artist, logging nine US hit albums since leaving Montrose in 1975, and will include his biggest single success, *I Can't Drive 55*, in Van Halen's future live repertoire.)
Apr [26] The group's ***5150***, the first to feature Hagar, tops the US survey for the first of four weeks. It is titled after New York's Police code for the criminally insane, and the name of Eddie Van Halen's own recording studio, where it was recorded.
May [17] *Why Can't This Be Love* hits US #3.
June *Why Can't This Be Love* hits UK #8, as parent album, ***5150***, reaches UK #16.
July Roth releases further cover versions on the mini-album ***Eat 'Em And Smile***, which hits US #4 and UK #28, and includes Sinatra's *That's Life*.
[19] Van Halen's *Dreams* makes US #22 and peaks at UK #62.
Aug [30] Roth's *Yankee Rose* reaches US #16, as he begins a ten-month tour at Hampton, VA, with a band comprising Steve Vai (guitar), Billy Sheehan (bass) and Gregg Bissonette (drums).
Sept [15] The band performs live at the third annual MTV Video Music Awards, broadcast simultaneously from the Universal Amphitheatre, Universal City, CA, and The Palladium, New York.
Oct [4] Van Halen's *Love Walks In* makes US #22.
[18] Roth's *Goin' Crazy* makes US #66.
Dec [6] *That's Life* peaks at US #85.
[20] Linda Duke claims she suffers "acoustic trauma" at Roth's Great Western Forum concert in Inglewood, CA, resulting in litigation.

1987

Mar [14] Hagar's solo single, *Winner Takes All*, from the Sylvester Stallone movie, "Over The Top", peaks at US #54.
[27] Hagar makes his live debut with Van Halen in Shreveport, LA.
June Hagar continues a parallel solo career with ***Sammy Hagar***, which makes US #14 and UK #86. From it, *Give To Live* reaches US #23, while *Eagles Fly* will perch at US #82.

1988

Jan While vacationing on Turtle Island off the Australian coast, Eddie Van Halen suffers heat-stroke from the 105°F temperature, having also been bitten by a mosquito.
Feb Roth's third solo album, ***Skyscraper*** (featuring a front-cover photograph of him hanging on to the side of a mountain) is released, hitting US #6 and UK #11.
Mar The extracted *Just Like Paradise* hits US #6 and UK #27.
May His follow-up, *Stand Up*, makes US #64.
[27] Van Halen returns to live work after a two-year break, opening its "Monsters Of Rock" tour at the Alpine Valley Music Theatre, East Troy, WI. Featuring four other heavy metal acts (the Scorpions, Dokken, Kingdom Come and Metallica), it is the most ambitious HM package tour ever staged. With 250,000 watts of sound at 20 all-day festival concerts, the events are mostly under-attended, and some lose money.
June [4] Van Halen album, ***OU812***, produced by long-time band associate, Donn Landee, and featuring Hagar's lyrics and vocals, reaches UK #16 in its week of entry.
[25] ***OU812*** tops the US chart.
Aug The first single from the album, *Black And Blue*, reaches US #34.
Sept [3] Roth's *Damn Good/Stand Up* makes UK #72.
[10] Van Halen's *When It's Love*, hits US #5 and UK #28.
[29] The band begins a 45-city US tour, in support of ***OU812***.
Oct The group is awarded the Gold Ticket for playing to over 100,000 fans at New York's Madison Square Garden.
Nov Roth returns to the UK for selected dates, including Wembley Arena, Wembley, Middx., as *California Girls* is reissued.
Dec [10] Van Halen's *Finish What Ya Started* reaches US #13.

1989

Jan [18] The RIAA certifies three million sales of ***OU812***.
Feb [22] The RIAA also confirms three million sales of ***Diver Down***.
Mar [18] *Feels So Good* reaches US #35.
Oct [15-16] Eddie Van Halen and Anthony participate in the first World Music Invitational Pro/Am celebrity golf tournament, at Stonebridge Ranch in Dallas, TX.

1990

Jan [23] Van Halen's "Live Without A Net" video is certified by the RIAA for 100,000 sales.
Apr [21] The group plays at the opening night of its recently-purchased 350-seater Cabo Wabo Cantina restaurant and bar, in Cabo San Lucas, Mexico.
July [5] The RIAA certifies four million sales of ***Van Halen II***.
Dec [17] The group files a federal law suit against rap act, 2 Live Crew, alleging they used a riff from *Ain't Talkin' 'Bout Love* for their *The Funk Shop* without permission. They are seeking $300,000 for copyright infringement and unfair competition.

1991

Jan [19] Roth's *A Lil' Ain't Enough*, from his forthcoming album, makes UK #32.
[26] ***A Little Ain't Enough*** enters the UK chart at its #4 peak.
Feb [16] ***A Little Ain't Enough*** reaches US #18.
[22] Roth's 32-date European leg of his world tour opens in Glasgow, Strathclyde, Scotland.
Mar [16] Wolfgang, a son to Eddie and Valerie Van Halen, is born at St. John's Hospital, Santa Monica, CA.
Apr [26] Roth's North American leg of his world tour opens at the Centrum, Worcester, MA.
June [18] Alex Van Halen is inducted into the Hollywood Rock Walk with Ginger Baker and Carmine Appice.
[22] Van Halen's *Poundcake* charts for a week at UK #74.
[29] ***For Unlawful Carnal Knowlege*** debuts at its UK #12 peak.
July [6] ***For Unlawful Carnal Knowledge*** bows at US #1, making Van Halen the first act to hit #1 with three consecutive studio albums since Madonna. (The Rolling Stones were the last previous group to do it.)
Sept [8] The group performs live at the eighth annual MTV Video Music Awards ceremony, staged again at the Universal Amphitheatre.
[13-14] Van Halen plays two sellout shows at the Shoreline Amphitheatre, Mountain View, CA, during its current US tour, grossing $990,762.
Oct [19] *Top Of The World* charts for a week at UK #63.
Nov [23] *Top Of The World* reaches US #27.
Dec [4] The group plays a free concert at the Dallas Alley entertainment complex, after promising they would do so at the 1988 "Texxas Jam" show.

1992

Jan [27] The band collects the Favorite Album, Heavy Metal/Hard Rock trophy, at the 19th annual American Music Awards, held at the Shrine Auditorium, Los Angeles.
Feb After saying guitar picking isn't as hard as brain surgery on an MTV interview, Eddie Van Halen receives a letter from Massachusetts General Hospital neuro-surgeon, Dr. Jim Schumacher, offering neuro-surgery technique in exchange for guitar lessons.
[25] Van Halen wins Best Hard Rock Performance With Vocal category for ***For Unlawful Carnal Knowledge***, at the 34th annual Grammy Awards, from New York's Radio City Music Hall.
Mar [7] Hagar wins the Outstanding Male Vocalist category, at the 15th Bay Area Music Awards, from the San Francisco Civic Auditorium.
[28] *Right Now* makes US #55.
Apr [9] 19-year old Sean Pierce is arrested while walking home in Fort Smith, AR, and charged with "violating a statute against wearing a smutty shirt", after buying a ***For Unlawful Carnal Knowledge*** T-shirt the day before, at a concert in Little Rock, AR. The band phones Pierce and offers to pay his fine should he be convicted on June 18th.
May [12, 16] As the US leg of the "For Unlawful Carnal Knowledge" tour winds down, Van Halen plays two sellout shows at the Great Western Forum, before combined crowds of 31,692.
June The McNutt family, former residents of Tulsa, OK, bring a $2.068 million lawsuit against the band and Warner Bros., for emotional distress caused as a result of the group allegedly including their home telephone number amidst a scrawl of graffiti on the cover of ***For Unlawful Carnal Knowledge***. The number had previously belonged to Steve Ripley, a friend of Eddie Van Halen's.
July Copyright holders of the song *Right Now Collection* (Thomas Chaffee, Jeff Crossberg and Todd Sucherman from Illinois), file an infringement lawsuit against the band, claiming their title to be too similar to Van Halen's *Right Now* cut, from the recent album.
Aug [20] Syndicated radio network Westwood One broadcasts from the Cabo Wabo Cantina, with Hagar and Anthony hosting a three-hour show combining live entertainment and excerpts from the group's arena tour.
Sept [9] "Right Now" wins the Best Video, Best Direction, and Best Editing categories, at the ninth annual MTV Video Music Awards, held at the Pauley Pavilion, Los Angeles.
Nov [1] Hagar participates in Neil Young's sixth annual "Bridge School Benefit" from the Shoreline Amphitheatre.
Dec [14] Eddie Van Halen takes part in a benefit at the Universal Amphitheatre, to establish an education trust fund for Jeff Porcaro's children. (Porcaro, the legendary session drummer and founder member of Toto, had died the previous August.)

1993

Mar [8] Hagar is named Outstanding Male Vocalist, at the 1993 Bay Area Music Awards held at the Bill Graham Civic Auditorium, San Francisco.
[13] Van Halen's first live album, the 24-track, two-hour double CD, ***Right Here, Right Now*** bows at its US #5 peak (having done likewise a week earlier at UK #24). Its title cut is currently being used as a TV commercial theme by Pepsi.
[27] *Jump (Live)* debuts at its UK #26 peak.
[30] The first leg of the group's "Right Here Right Now World Tour" opens at the Olympiahalle, Munich, Germany.
Apr [16] Roth is arrested in New York's Washington Square Park for allegedly buying a $10 bag of marijuana.
[25] The UK segment of the tour, their first UK dates in nine years and the first with Hagar, opens at the National Exhibition Centre, Birmingham, W. Midlands.
Sept [20] The RIAA certifies two million sales of ***Right Here, Right Now***.
Nov [5] Hagar takes part in the seventh annual "Bridge School Benefit", at the Shoreline Amphitheatre, while Eddie Van Halen backs Simon & Garfunkel on *Sounds Of Silence* on guitar.

1994

Feb [19] Roth's *She's My Machine* charts for a week at UK #64.
Mar [26] Roth's ***Your Filthy Little Mouth*** debuts at its US #78 peak, during a two-week chart stay, having hit UK #28 the week before.
Apr [2] Hagar's ***Unboxed*** debuts at its US #51 peak.
May [28] Roth's *Night Life* charts for a week at UK #72.
July [11] The RIAA certifies seven million sales of ***1984*** and eight million sales of ***Van Halen***.
Aug [4] Two million sales of ***Fair Warning*** and three million sales of ***Women And Children First*** are also certified by the RIAA.
[17] The RIAA additionally certifies five million sales of ***5150*** and three million sales of ***For Unlawful Carnal Knowledge***, confirming the group as one of the biggest-selling rock acts of the past 15 years.
Oct [8] Hagar performs at "Elvis Aaron Presley : The Tribute", an all-star musical tribute from the Pyramid Arena, Memphis, TN, broadcast live on US pay-per-view TV.

1995

Jan [21] *Don't Tell Me* debuts at its UK #27 peak.
Feb [4] ***Balance***, recorded at Eddie's 5150 studio and produced by Bruce Fairbairn, bows at its UK #8 peak.
[11] ***Balance*** debuts at US #1.
Mar [11] The group embarks on a major US tour at Pensacola Civic Center, Pensacola, FL. (Warner Bros. establishes a dedicated Van Halen Web information site at http://www.vanhalen.warnerrcrds.com/Balance.)
[29] The RIAA certifies two million sales of ***Balance***.
Apr [1] *Can't Stop Lovin' You* debuts at its UK #33 peak.
[7] A loaded Beretta semi-automatic pistol is seized from Eddie Van Halen's carry-on luggage at Burbank Airport. He is detained, forcing the postponement of concerts in the San Francisco bay area.
[20] Eddie pleads no contest to the April 7th incident. He is fined $300 and placed on probation for a year.
May [24] Van Halen begins the European leg of its tour in Paris, France.
June [10] *Can't Stop Lovin' You* reaches US #30.
[23-25] The group performs three dates at Wembley Stadium, supporting Bon Jovi.
Aug [19] *Not Enough* debuts at its US #97 peak.
Oct [15] Van Halen's seven-month tour winds down before a 15,400 sellout audience at the Irvine Meadows Amphitheatre, Irvine, CA.
Dec [8] Taped at the August 19th concert at the Molson Amphitheatre, Toronto, ON, Canada, and already broadcast on Canadian pay-per-view on November 10th and 16th, the band's first pay-per-view concert airs on US TV, priced at a modest $9.95.

1996

May Van Halen contributes *Humans Being* to the soundtrack of the movie "Twister".
June [28] After the group has announced two days earlier that Hagar has left the lineup, following an invitation by the band to former lead singer Roth to record a new track for inclusion on a forthcoming greatest hits album, Hagar issues a statement saying the split is "a devastating, backstabbing. I-don't-get-it, real big disappointment". Roth is strongly rumored to be his permanent replacement, though Van Halen confirms that it will undertake auditions for its new vocalist.

LUTHER VANDROSS

1973

Learning the piano from the age of three, Vandross (b. Luther Ronzoni Vandross, Apr. 20, 1951, New York, NY), his father a crooner, his mother a gospel singer and his sister Patricia a member of '50s group, the Crests, having been influenced by the soul music of the early '60s and inspired to embark on a music career at the age of 13 having attended a Dionne Warwick concert ("It formed my whole life"), has assembled his first group with friends, guitarist Carlos Alomar and Robin Clark, while still attending William Howard Taft High School in the Bronx, New York, which becomes Listen My Brother, a musical theater workshop that performs at the Apollo Theatre, Harlem. Subsequently appearing on the first episode of TV show, "Sesame Street", he studies music briefly after the group breaks up in the early '70s, and disappears into a succession of day jobs. He then spends two semesters at Western Michigan, and has also worked as an S&H Green Stamp defective-merchandise clerk.

1974

Alomar, working with David Bowie, invites Vandross and Clark to Philadelphia, PA's Sigma Sound Studios for the recording of the album, ***Young Americans***. Bowie is impressed with the pair, and invites Vandross to arrange all the vocal parts. He also sings backing vocals on most of the tracks, as well as contributing the song, *Fascination*.

1975

Apr Vandross and Clark join Bowie on the "Young Americans" tour, with Vandross also becoming the opening act. Vandross' *Everybody Rejoice (A Brand New Day)* is included in the forthcoming movie, "The Wiz" (the song will later be used in a Kodak commercial). Bowie introduces Vandross to Bette Midler, for whom he performs vocals on her album, ***Songs For The New Depression***. (Producer Arif Mardin will later use Vandross for sessions with Ringo Starr, Carly Simon, Chaka Khan, Donna Summer, Barbra Streisand and the Average White Band.)

1976

June Newly signed, as the leader of Luther, to Cotillion Records, Vandross releases ***Luther***, which yields two US R&B hits (*It's Good For The Soul* at #28, and *Funky Music (Is A Part Of Me)* at #34), though its style does not mesh with the disco flavor of the times.

1977

Apr A second and final "Luther" set, ***This Close To You***, is released, before the combo is dropped by Cotillion. Without a recording contract, Vandross earns a living as a much in-demand session vocalist, arranger and jingles singer (some of his credits include AT&T, Burger King, Kentucky Fried Chicken, Pepsi-Cola, Seven-Up, the US Army, and Miller Beer, featuring an all-star choir of Ashford & Simpson, Roberta Flack and Teddy Pendergrass.

1978

June Quincy Jones enlists Vandross' vocals for his album, ***Sounds ... And Stuff Like That!!*** He duets with Patti Austin on *I'm Gonna Miss You In The Morning*, and Gwen Guthrie on *Takin' It To The Streets*.
Dec He also sings back-up vocals on Chic's *Le Freak*, and Sister Sledge's *We Are Family*.

1979

Nov Vandross arranges the vocals on Barbra Streisand and Donna Summer's smash, *No More Tears (Enough Is Enough)*. (By the end of the decade, Vandross has also been voted MVP Background Singer, three years in a row, for his commercials work.)

1980

May Vandross is the featured lead vocalist for the newly-released debut album, ***The Glow Of Love***, by disco group Change, which will earn a gold disc, notably on the group's two early hits, *Searchin'* and *The Glow Of Love*.
Dec Vandross signs a solo recording contract with Epic Records, in a deal which allows him self-production freedom.

1981

Apr Vandross' composition, *You Stopped Lovin' Me*, sung by Roberta Flack, is featured on the film soundtrack to "Bustin' Loose".
Sept ***Never Too Much***, Vandross' first solo album, reaches US #19. Self-produced, it includes six self-penned numbers, and a cover of Bacharach & David's *A House Is Not A Home*, and immediately confirms the talent hinted at during his earlier back-seat collaborations.
Oct [24] Its title cut, *Never Too Much*, tops the US R&B chart.
Nov [28] Vandross has his first solo crossover hit with *Never Too Much* reaching US #33.

1982

Feb [20] He performs *Never Too Much* on NBC-TV's "Saturday Night Live".
Aug Vandross finishes production on Aretha Franklin's ***Jump To It***, as he performs at the "Budweiser Superfest", held at the Rose Bowl, Pasadena, CA, with Stevie Wonder, Aretha Franklin, Quincy Jones, Patti Austin, James Ingram, Ashford & Simpson, Third World and Frankie Beverly & Maze.
Oct His soul-drenched sophomore effort, the self-helmed, mostly self-penned ***Forever, For Always, For Love*** is released, and will reach US #20.
Dec [4] Vandross makes US #55 with *Bad Boy/Having A Party*.

1983

Mar [7] ***Forever, For Always, For Love*** is certified as his first platinum disc by the RIAA.
Nov He produces Dionne Warwick's ***How Many Times Can We Say Goodbye*** (UK title: ***So Amazing***).
[12] His duet with Warwick on the ballad title track, *How Many Times Can We Say Goodbye*, makes US #27.
Dec [24] ***Busy Body*** enters the US chart, and is set to reach #32. It has been co-produced with session bassist, Marcus Miller, who also contributed to Vandross' first two outings.

1984

Jan While his first two albums have remained hot import titles, ***Busy Body*** makes UK #42.
May [12] *Superstar*, a soulful reworking of the Leon Russell classic, peaks at US #87.

1985

Jan [2] ***Busy Body*** is certified platinum by the RIAA.
Apr [6] ***The Night I Fell In Love*** reaches UK #19 in its week of entry, and will make US #19.
May [25] *'Til My Baby Comes Home* reaches US #29.

1986

Sept [20] The uptempo *Give Me The Reason*, from the movie, "Ruthless People", makes US #57.
Nov ***Give Me The Reason*** enters the UK chart, set to hit UK #9 during a one-year chart tenure.
[29] ***Give Me The Reason*** tops the US R&B chart, and will reach US #14.
Dec [8] ***Never Too Much*** is certified platinum by the RIAA.

1987

Jan [17] *Stop To Love* tops the US R&B survey.
Feb [14] *Stop To Love* reaches US #15.
[24] Vandross sings *Give Me The Reason* at the 29th annual Grammy ceremonies. He is nominated in the Best R&B Vocal, Male category, but is pipped by James Brown.
Mar [23] Vandross and Dionne Warwick co-host the first annual Soul Train Music Awards, at the Hollywood Center Television Studios, Hollywood, CA, at which he also wins the Album Of The Year, Male category.
Apr He produces *It's Hard For Me To Say* for Diana Ross' newly-released ***Red Hot Rhythm & Blues*** album.
May [9] Vandross' duet with Gregory Hines, *There's*

Nothing Better Than Love, makes US #50, and tops the US R&B chart.
June [8] Vandross' session drummer, Yogi Horton, leaps to his death from a 17th-floor hotel window, having allegedly told his wife he is tired of living in Vandross' shadow.
[18] Vandross cancels two sellout concerts in Phoenix, AZ as a protest to Governor Mecham's rescinding of the Martin Luther King public holiday.
July [18] ***Forever, For Always, For Love*** belatedly reaches UK #23.
Sept [5] ***Never Too Much*** makes UK #41.

1988

Jan On its second reissue, *Give Me The Reason* reaches UK #26.
[25] He collects the Favorite Male Artist, Soul/R&B trophy, at the 15th annual American Music Awards, held at the Shrine Auditorium, Los Angeles.
Mar [5] ***Give Me The Reason*** now hits UK #3.
May *I Gave It Up (When I Fell In Love)* reaches UK #28.
July *There's Nothing Better Than Love* peaks at UK #72.
Sept [28] Vandross begins a three-month "The Heat" US tour, with Anita Baker in Washington, DC.
Oct [29] ***Any Love***, again co-produced and written with Miller (who is now his long-term collaborator), enters the UK chart at #3, and hits US #9.
Nov [12] The extracted title track, *Any Love*, makes US #44 and UK #31. (Both single and album, his fifth straight platinum seller, will go on to top the US R&B chart.)
Dec [19] ***Any Love*** is certified platinum by the RIAA.

1989

Jan [3] Vandross sings *Love Won't Let Me Wait*, a cover of Major Harris' 1975 US #5, on the first edition of syndicated TV's "The Arsenio Hall Show".
Feb *She Won't Talk To Me* makes UK #34.
[22] Vandross sings *She Won't Talk To Me* at the 31st Grammy Awards, held at the Shrine Auditorium.
Mar [18] *She Won't Talk To Me* reaches US #30.
[31] Vandross performs at Wembley Arena, Wembley, Middx., during a ten-day stint, attended by 115,000 people.
Apr *Come Back* makes UK #53.
Oct Remixed *Never Too Much* reaches UK #13.
Nov [11] Double compilation set, ***The Best Of Luther Vandross - The Best Of Love*** debuts at its UK #14 peak.

1990

Jan [13] *Here And Now* makes UK #43. (Vandross has sung the song at the wedding, broadcast live, of Sharyn Gillyard and Michael Haynes, of New York, who had won WBLS' "Wedding Of A Lifetime" contest.)
[22] Vandross wins the Favorite Male Artist, Soul/R&B category, at the 17th annual American Music Awards, held at the Shrine Auditorium.
[27] ***The Best Of Luther Vandross - The Best Of Love***, reaches US #26.
Feb [5] The RIAA certifies two million sales of ***The Night I Fell In Love***.
Mar [14] Vandross wins Best R&B/Urban Contemporary Single/Male category for *Here And Now*, at the fourth annual Soul Train Awards, at the Shrine Auditorium, also co-hosting the event with Patti LaBelle and Dionne Warwick.
Apr [6] The still-climbing *Here And Now* is certified gold by the RIAA.
[21] *Here And Now* hits US #6, remarkably his first Top 10 US hit.
May [24] The RIAA certifies platinum sales of "Live At Wembley" video and two million sales of ***Give Me The Reason***.
June [12] Vandross guests on NBC-TV's "The Tonight Show".
July [18, 20-21] During his current US tour, Vandross plays three sellout shows at the Westbury Music Fair, Westbury, NY.
Aug [24] He plays the first of seven sellout shows at the Fox Theatre, Detroit, MI.
Nov Whitney Houston's, ***I'm Your Baby Tonight***, featuring the Vandross produced *Who Do You Love?* is released.
Dec [1] He is named Best Male Artist for ***The Best Of Luther Vandross***, at the 23rd annual NAACP Image Awards, at the Wiltern Theatre, Los Angeles.

1991

Feb [10] Vandross joins with nearly 100 celebrities in Burbank, CA, to record *Voices That Care*, a David Foster and fiancée Linda Thompson Jenner composed-and-organized charity record, to benefit the American Red Cross Gulf Crisis Fund.
[20] Vandross collects the Best R&B Vocal Performance, Male trophy for *Here And Now*, at the 33rd annual Grammy Awards, at New York's Radio City Music Hall.
Mar [12] Vandross co-hosts the fifth annual Soul Train Music Awards staged at the Shrine Auditorium.
May [18] *Power Of Love/Love Power*, the latter previously a 1968 US #22 for the Sandpebbles, makes UK #46.
[25] ***Power Of Love*** hits US #7 and debuts at its UK #9 peak.
June [14] "Luther Vandross Day" is declared in Los Angeles.
[29] *Power Of Love/Love Power* hits US #4.
July [30] Vandross guests on an "Arsenio Hall" special, devoted to Patti LaBelle.
Sept [11] He embarks on a 14-week, 55-date North American tour in Hampton, VA.
Oct [2-3, 5-6] Vandross plays four sellout shows at New York's Madison Square Garden, grossing $1,499,390.
Nov [2] *Don't Want To Be A Fool* hits US #9.

1992

Jan [3] Vandross files suit in Los Angeles Superior Court, Santa Monica, against Sony Entertainment (Epic's parent company), citing the California Labor Code section 2855, that states personal service contracts cannot exceed seven years.
[7] He takes part in the recording of the Jeffrey Osborne-penned *The Heart Of A Hero*, recorded by an all-star cast in Los Angeles, to raise money for AIDS research.
[11] Vandross wins the Best Male Vocalist and Best Album category at the 24th annual NAACP Image Awards, at the Wiltern Theatre, Los Angeles.
[18] ***The Rush*** debuts at its UK #53 peak.
[25] ***The Rush*** climbs to US #73.
[27] He collects the Favorite Album, Soul/R&B, and Favorite Male Artist, Soul/R&B trophies, at the 19th annual American Music Awards, held again at the Shrine Auditorium.
Feb [25] Vandross collects the Best R&B Song, for *Power Of Love/Love Power*, and Best R&B Vocal Performance, Male (for ***Power Of Love***) trophies at the 34th annual Grammy Awards, from Radio City Music Hall, New York, at which he also sings *Power Of Love/Love Power* with Aretha Franklin.
Mar [12] He wins the R&B/Soul Album Of The Year, Male category, at the sixth annual Soul Train Music Awards, held at the Shrine Auditorium.
June [13] *The Best Things In Life Are Free*, a duet with Janet Jackson from the movie, "Mo' Money", hits US #10.
July [18] Vandross attends Whitney Houston and Bobby Brown's nuptuals in Mendham, NJ.
Aug [29] *The Best Things In Life Are Free* hits UK #2, behind Snap's *Rhythm Is A Dancer*.
Sept [24] He performs at the "Jean Paul Gaultier In LA" fashion benefit for AMFAR AIDS Research, at the Shrine Auditorium.
[26] Vandross makes a guest appearance on NBC's "Out All Night".
Oct [8] The RIAA certifies two million sales of ***The Best Of Luther Vandross - The Best Of Love***.

1993

Jan [17] Vandross sings *Stand By Me* at "An American Reunion : The People's Inaugural Celebration", from the Lincoln Memorial in Washington, DC, joined part way through by Ben E. King.
Mar [9] He co-hosts the seventh annual Soul Train Music Awards, with Natalie Cole and Patti Labelle, at the Shrine Auditorium.
May [16] Vandross is featured on BBC2-TV's "The O Zone".
[21] The RIAA certifies two million sales of ***Power Of Love***.
[22] *Little Miracles (Happen Every Day)*, the lead-off track from his new ***Never Let Me Go*** album, bows at its UK #28 peak, as he currently tours Europe.
June [12] *Little Miracles (Happen Every Day)* makes US #62, as ***Never Let Me Go*** debuts at its UK #11 peak.
July [3] ***Never Let Me Go*** hits US #6.
Aug [23] ***Never Let Me Go*** is certified platinum by the RIAA.
Sept [10] Vandross embarks on a major US tour at the Mobile Civic Center, Mobile, AL, set to end on November 18th at the Hersheypark Arena, Hershey, PA.
[18] *Heaven Knows* debuts at its UK #34 and US #94 peaks.
Nov [29-30, **Dec** 2] Vandross plays at Wembley Arena, during his latest UK visit.
Dec [4] *Love Is On The Way* debuts at its UK #38 peak.

1994

Jan [5] Vandross is named Outstanding Male Artist at the NAACP 26th annual Image Awards held in Pasadena, CA.
Feb [7] He wins Best Male Artist Soul/R&B category at the 21st annual American Music Awards, staged at the Shrine Auditorium.
Apr [22] Vandross performs at the seventh annual **Essence** Awards from the Paramount, New York, set to end on Fox-TV on June 6th.
Sept [13] He makes his only UK appearance of the year, at London's Royal Albert Hall.
[17] Updating the 1981 Lionel Richie/Diana Ross chart-topper, his duet with Mariah Carey on *Endless Love*, debuts at its UK #3 peak.
Oct [1] *Endless Love* hits US #2, behind Boyz II Men's *I'll Make Love To You*, as an album of his favorite covers, simply titled ***Songs*** enters the UK chart at #1.
[8] ***Songs*** debuts at its US #5 peak.
[30] Vandross takes part in the "Gala For The President" at the Ford Theatre in Washington, in the presence of President Clinton. (ABC-TV will air the show on December 7th.) (In this month's **Details** magazine, Vandross claims that his current diet is the ninth time he has "lost, gained, and lost in excess of 120 pounds. An entire person, nine times. I lost the Osmond Brothers! Wait, let me pick a black group ... the Jacksons!")
Nov [23] ***Songs*** is certified platinum by the RIAA.
[28] He guests on CBS-TV's "Late Show With David Letterman".
Dec [3] His cover of Stephen Stills' *Love The One You're With*, backed with *Give Me The Reason*, recorded live at Wembley, and Gregg Diamond's Bionic Boogie's *Hot Butterfly* with Vandross on lead vocals, reaches UK #31.

1995

Jan [28] *Always And Forever*, reviving Heatwave's 1978 UK #9 and US #18, peaks at US #58.
Feb [4] *Endless Love* re-charts at UK #55.
[11] *Always And Forever* reaches UK #20.
Apr [15] Updating McFadden & Whitehead's 1979 hit, *Ain't No Stopping Us Now* debuts at its UK #22 peak.
[22] *Love The One You're With*, coupled with *Going In Circles*, enters at its US #95 high.
May [31] Vandross begins another round of US dates at the Summer Pops Bowl Amphitheatre, San Diego, CA.
June [3] He is named Top R&B Artist (Male) at the Inaugural Blockbuster Entertainment Awards, held at Hollywood's Pantages Theater. (CBS-TV will broadcast the event on June 6th.)

Nov [11] Reissued *Power Of Love/Love Power* debuts at its UK #31 peak, as Vandross appears on BBC1-TV's "National Lottery Live" program.
[25] ***Greatest Hits 1981-1995***, a UK-only compilation including a new Jimmy Jam & Terry Lewis production, *The Thrill I'm In*, reaches UK #12 in its week of entry.
Dec [14] Vandross guests on NBC-TV's "The Tonight Show".
[16] His reissued duet with Janet Jackson, *The Best Things In Life Are Free (Remix)* debuts at its UK #7 peak.
[20] He goes on America OnLine to respond to cyber-fans.
[23] *Every Year, Every Christmas* debuts at its UK #43 peak.
[30] Seasonal collection, ***This Is Christmas***, including seven original compositions, reaches US #28.

1996

Jan [30] Vandross is once again named Favorite Male Artist, Soul/R&B at the 23rd annual American Music Awards held at the Shrine Auditorium.
July [5-6] He performs at the Louisiana Superdome, New Orleans, LA, during a ten-date US summer tour.

VANGELIS

1968

Nov Vangelis (b. Evangelos Papathanassiou, Mar. 29, 1943, Volos, Greece), having been a keyboards prodigy in his youth, and a student at the Academy of Fine Arts in Athens, Greece, studied classical music under Aristotelis Coudourof, having been a member of Greek pop group Formynx in the early '60s, has teamed with vocalist Demis Roussos (b. June 15, 1947, Alexandria, Egypt) and drummer Lucas Sideras (b. Dec. 5, 1944, Athens) as Aphrodite's Child, moving to France to escape the Greek Colonels' right-wing coup, where the trio has come to the attention of Pierre Sberre, of French Philips Records, and signed to the label. After spending three months at the top of the French chart, and hitting the Top 10 in most European countries, Aphrodite's Child's *Rain And Tears*, sung in English by Roussos, and using Vangelis' arrangement of a 17th-century German tune by Johann Pachelbel, now reaches UK #27. (Further European hits, *It's Five O'Clock* and *Break*, will follow for the trio, but they fail to chart in the US or UK.)

1972

Aphrodite's Child splits, following the release of its fourth album, the concept project, ***666***. (Roussos begins a solo vocal career, which will find considerable international success.) Vangelis, who has already released two solo albums in 1971, ***The Dragon*** and ***Hypothesis***, remains in Paris, and writes music scores for a number of wild-life shorts directed by French film-maker, Frédérick Rossif, and released collectively as ***L'Apocalypse Des Animaux***.

1974

Signed to Vertigo Records, Vangelis moves to Britain, building his own Nemo recording studio in London's West End and releasing ***Earth***. Concentrating exclusively on synthesizer compositions, he will switch to RCA Victor Records the following year.

1976

Jan The largely electronic instrumental, ***Heaven And Hell***, also featuring the English Chamber Choir, is Vangelis' first solo chart entry, making UK #31.
Mar Vangelis plays a one-off Royal Albert Hall, London concert, with two percussionists, six African congo players, bass guitar, a singer doubling on harp, the English Chamber Choir, and conductor/pianist David Bedford and 60-plus girl students on tympani and kettledrums. (Uncomfortable in the public eye, Vangelis will rarely perform live.)
Oct ***Albedo 0.39***, sampling the historic voices of US astronauts landing on the moon, reaches UK #18.

1979

After two further albums for RCA, ***Spiral*** (1977) and ***Beauborg*** (1978), Vangelis moves to Polydor Records for ***China***. Several of its oriental themes will be used extensively on a number of Far-Eastern related TV documentaries in the future).

1980

Feb Vangelis has teamed with Jon Anderson, lead singer of Yes (with whom he has maintained a close acquaintanceship since 1974, when he was mooted as their keyboards replacement for Rick Wakeman), to record a voice/synthesizer project for Polydor. The duo's *I Hear You Now* hits UK #8.
[16] Its parent album ***Short Stories*** hits UK #4.
July ***Short Stories*** peaks at US #125.
Sept *I Hear You Now* makes US #58.
Nov His latest solo project, ***See You Later*** is released by Polydor.

1981

June Having been commissioned by film producer, David Puttnam, to compose the score for "Chariots Of Fire", Vangelis' soundtrack album, ***Chariots Of Fire***, hits UK #5, remaining on the survey for 97 weeks. Entirely instrumental, the main title theme from "Chariots Of Fire" also becomes Vangelis' first solo hit single, reaching UK #12.
July Used as the theme for Carl Sagan's BBC1-TV series, "Cosmos", Vangelis' *Heaven And Hell, Third Movement* climbs to UK #48 (on BBC Records).
Sept Jon & Vangelis' follow-up effort, ***The Friends Of Mr. Cairo*** climbs to US #64.

1982

Jan Jon & Vangelis' *I'll Find My Way Home* hits UK #6.
Feb [13] ***The Friends Of Mr. Cairo***, hits UK #6. (One of its tracks, *State Of Independence*, which fails to chart, will be covered by Donna Summer, making UK #14 and US #41.)
Apr [8] ***Chariots Of Fire*** is certified platinum by the RIAA.
[17] Vangelis' soundtrack album, ***Chariots Of Fire***, tops the US chart for the first of four weeks, after the music has won an Oscar for Best Original Score, at the 54th annual Academy Awards. It earns a platinum disc for sales of over a million.
May [8] The main title theme, *Chariots Of Fire*, also tops the US chart for a week (after climbing the Hot 100 for 21 weeks), and becomes a million seller. It also re-enters the UK chart, reaching #41.
June Jon & Vangelis' *I'll Find My Way Home* makes US #51. (During the year, Vangelis completes the soundtrack to "Blade Runner", which will remain unreleased until 1994.)

1983

Aug Jon & Vangelis' *He Is Sailing* reaches UK #61, as the duo's ***Private Collection*** climbs to UK #22 and US #148. (During the year, Vangelis composes and records his next film soundtrack project for "The Bounty", which will also remain unissued.)

1984

May ***Chariots Of Fire*** re-charts at #39.
Aug Compilation, ***The Best Of Jon And Vangelis***, reaches UK #42, while the reissued *State Of Independence*, also included on the retrospective, makes UK #67.
Oct Self-composed, arranged, played and produced (as are all his solo albums), ***Soil Activities***, once again a collage of electronic and orchestral textures, makes UK #55. A further solo effort ***Mask***, written and performed for the film of the same name, will peak at UK #69 the following March, the same month his ***Rhapsodies*** is also released.

1987

Feb Vangelis is cleared in a UK court by Mr. Justice Whitford of using Stavros Logarides' melody of *City Of Violets* for his own *Chariots Of Fire*.
May ***Opera Sauvage***, recorded almost ten years previously for the Rossif nature films, and now helped by the exposure of two tracks in US beer commercials, reaches #19 on the US CD survey.

1988

Sept *Chariots Of Fire* gains yet another lease of life in the UK, when Vangelis' original version is used as the theme for BBC-TV coverage of the Seoul Olympic Games.
Nov ***Direct***, Vangelis' first album for Arista Records, which promotes the album as New Age music in the US, is released.

1989

July [29] ***Themes***, a 14-track Polydor compilation, reaches UK #11. It includes the first commercial release of highlights from his soundtrack scores to "Blade Runner", "Missing" and "Mutiny On The Bounty". Subsequently signed to East West Records in the UK, his label debut ***City***, also the latest Vangelis film soundtrack, will be released the following November.•

1991

Apr Reunited with Anderson, ***Page Of Life*** emerges on Arista.
July Vangelis is featured on the newly-released various artists ***Polar Shift : A Benefit For Antarctica*** charity album.

1992

Oct [24] ***1492 - Conquest Of Paradise***, his score to the current Gerard Depardieu-starring movie, debuts at its UK #33 peak.
[31] The extracted *Conquest Of Paradise* bows at its UK #60 pinnacle.

1994

June [18] Critically regarded as one of his finest soundtrack works, ***Blade Runner*** has finally been released and reaches UK #20 in its week of entry. During the year, he will complete his latest soundtrack work for the film "Bitter Moon".

1996

Mar [2] ***Voices*** bows at its UK #58 peak.
Apr [20] ***Portrait (So Long Ago, So Clear)*** reaches UK #14 in its week of entry.

VANILLA FUDGE

Mark Stein (vocals and organ);
Vince Martell (guitar); **Tim Bogert** (bass);
Carmine Appice (drums)

1966

Dec Bogert (b. Aug. 27, 1944, Richfield, NJ) and Stein (b. Mar. 11, 1947, Bayonne, NJ), who have been playing in Rick Martin & the Showmen, have formed their own group, the Pigeons, earlier in the year with Martell (b. Nov. 11, 1945, New York, NY) joining as lead guitarist, and Appice (b. Dec. 15, 1946, New York) replacing the original drummer. Now signed to Atlantic Records, which renames the combo Vanilla Fudge, the quartet is one of the few East Coast groups to join ranks with the acid-rock West Coast movement, with a style it will describe as "psychedelic-symphonic rock" (a central element of which is slowed-down rearrangements of other artists' hit singles).

1967

July [22] The group makes its New York debut at the Village Theater (soon renamed the Fillmore East) with the Byrds and the Seeds, as their debut single, a version of the Supremes' *You Keep Me Hangin' On*, peaks at US #67.
Aug [10-13] The band plays at the Avalon Ballroom, San Francisco, CA, with Canned Heat and Moby Grape.
Sept [13] *You Keep Me Hangin' On* reaches UK #18. Their debut album, ***Vanilla Fudge***, hits US #6 (and

will make UK #31 two months later). It includes elongated versions of the Beatles' *Eleanor Rigby* and *Ticket To Ride*, and Cher's *Bang Bang*.

1968

Mar [2] *Where Is My Mind* peaks at US #73.
Apr [6] ***The Beat Goes On*** reaches US #17. A concept set, it is ambitiously presented as a musical record of the past 25 years, its title track professing to include the entire history of music in 12 minutes playing time.
July ***Renaissance*** makes US #20.
[23] ***Vanilla Fudge*** is certified gold by the RIAA.
Aug [31] *You Keep Me Hangin' On* now hits US #6.
Sept [14] The band plays at the Hollywood Bowl, Hollywood, CA, on a bill with Jimi Hendrix, Soft Machine and Eire Apparent.
Oct [26] *Take Me For A Little While*, from the album, reaches US #38.
Dec [28] Also from ***Renaissance***, a cover of Donovan's *Season Of The Witch* peaks at US #65.

1969

Mar ***Near The Beginning*** (one side recorded in the studio, the other live) makes US #16.
[29] The extracted *Shotgun* peaks at US #68.
July Vanilla Fudge takes part in the three-day "Seattle Pop Festival" at Woodenville, WA, with the Byrds, the Doors and Led Zeppelin, among others.
Oct ***Rock And Roll*** makes US #34.

1970

Internal dissent leads the group to disband. Appice and Bogert form the heavy-metal band, Cactus, before joining Jeff Beck in Beck, Bogert & Appice. Stein forms Boomerang, before working with Alice Cooper and Tommy Bolin, while Martell, after linking with the Good Rats leaves the music world.

1988

May [14] Having already re-formed twice this decade, once in 1982 (when ***Greatest Hits*** was released) and again in 1984, when they signed to Atco Records for ***Mystery***, Vanilla Fudge reunites once more to participate in Atlantic Records' 40th Anniversary celebration, at New York's Madison Square Garden.

STEVIE RAY VAUGHAN

1972

Having recently seen Cream, and heavily influenced by an Albert King tape, 14-year-old Vaughan (b. Oct. 3, 1954, Dallas, TX), the son of an asbestos plant worker, and a secretary at a ready-mix cement factory, picked up a guitar for the first time in 1968. Hooked on blues, he has played for local school outfits, including the Chantones, Nightcrawlers and Blackbird. After dropping out of high school in his senior year, Vaughan now follows his older brother, Jimmie (b. Mar. 20, 1949, Dallas), to Austin, TX. Jimmie has left home in 1966 to tour with the Chessmen, and will tutor his brother, and invite him to join several bands during Stevie's Austin apprenticeship. (Jimmie will go on to form the Fabulous Thunderbirds in 1979, with vocalist Kim Wilson.) Performing consistently on the Texas club circuit, Vaughan will join Austin blues outfit, the Cobras, before forming the similarly-inclined Triple Threat, with Lou Ann Barton, in 1977.

1981

Taking its name from the Otis Rush blues track, Vaughan recruits Tommy Shannon, a veteran of Johnny Winter's band circa 1970, on bass, and Chris Layton on drums, to form Double Trouble, after Triple Threat disbands. (The Rolling Stones' Mick Jagger will see a video of the group in concert, which will lead to a New York nightclub appearance at his request.)

1982

Now augmented by keyboardist Reese Wynans, Double Trouble is signed to Epic Records by A&R veteran talent scout, John Hammond, who has seen them performing at the annual "Montreux Jazz Festival" in Montreux, Switzerland. Vaughan also comes to the attention of David Bowie, who invites him to make a major guitar contribution to his current Nile Rodgers-produced recording of ***Let's Dance***.

1983

July Always projected as Stevie Ray Vaughan & Double Trouble, their debut release, ***Texas Flood***, recorded after Jackson Browne offered them free studio time, begins its US chart ascendancy to #38, ultimately selling over 1,000,000 copies, spurred by near constant cross-country touring, which the band will maintain throughout its history.
Aug Vaughan performs at the annual "Reading Festival", Reading, Berks.

1984

Feb [28] Stevie Ray Vaughan & Double Trouble feature prominently in the 26th annual Grammy Awards, with (unsuccessful) nominations in the Best Rock Instrumental (*Rude Mood*), and Best Traditional Blues Recording (***Texas Flood***) categories.
June Their sophomore album, ***Couldn't Stand The Weather***, displaying a tougher edge than its predecessor, begins a US chart climb to #31, where it will become his first platinum album. It includes the first of two cover versions he will perform of Jimi Hendrix' *Voodoo Chile*, which will receive a Grammy nomination.
Dec By year's end, Vaughan is voted Best Electric Blues Player, while the recent album is confirmed Best Guitar Album, in **Guitar Player** magazine. He is also named Entertainer Of The Year and Instrumentalist Of The Year by the Blues Foundation.

1985

Feb [26] Stevie Ray Vaughan & Double Trouble share the award (with Sugar Blue, Luther Johnson and others) for Best Traditional Blues Recording, at the 27th annual Grammy Awards, for their contribution of the track, *Flood Down In Texas*, to the Atlantic blues collection, ***Blues Explosion***.
Oct The jazz-tinged third album, ***Soul To Soul***, is released, set to make US #34 and receive a gold disc. (During their album-supporting US tour, Vaughan will be voted Best Electric Blues Player by **Guitar Player** magazine, and receive another Grammy nomination for Best Rock Instrumental, for the extract *Say What*.)

1986

Feb [15] They perform on NBC-TV's "Saturday Night Live". (During a year of continued live performing, including a return to the "Montreux Jazz Festival", Vaughan, suffering from an ongoing drug and alcohol abuse problem, falls off stage in London, and spends a month in rehabilitation in an Atlanta, GA hospital. He will also complete co-production of Lonnie Mack's comeback album, ***Strike Light Lightning***.)

1987

Feb Double performance album, ***Live Alive***, peaks at US #52, featuring the Grammy-nominated track, *Say What*.
May Vaughan's interpretation of the Chantays' *Pipeline* is featured in the newly-released movie soundtrack to "Back To The Beach", and will receive a Grammy nomination for Best Rock Instrumental, at the 30th annual Awards ceremony, held next year.

1989

July Fifth Epic album, ***In Step***, produced by Jim Gaines, and Vaughan's first studio effort in four years, begins its gold sales rise to US #33.
[15] ***In Step*** brings Vaughan his UK chart debut, at #63.
Oct [25] Vaughan & Double Trouble begin a US arena tour, with Jeff Beck, at the Northrop Memorial Auditorium, Minneapolis, MN. (By year's end, Vaughan has been inducted into **Guitar Player** magazine's "Gallery Of The Greats".)

1990

Feb [21] ***In Step*** wins the Best Contemporary Blues Recording category at the 32nd annual Grammy Awards, held at the Shrine Auditorium, Los Angeles, CA.
Mar [14] Vaughan is named Musician Of The Year and Musician Of The Decade, at the ninth annual Austin Music Awards, held at the Palmer Auditorium, Austin.
June [8] Vaughan & Double Trouble begin their North American "The Power And The Passion Tour" with Joe Cocker, at the Shoreline Amphitheatre, Mountain View, CA, set to end on July 22nd in Vancouver, BC, Canada.
[17] An all-star bill, featuring Vaughan, Joe Cocker, B.B. King and Dr. John, plays a sellout show at the Starplex Amphitheatre, Dallas, as part of the "Benson & Hedges Blues '90 Festival".
July He completes recordings of a forthcoming album, ***Family Style***, with his brother Jimmie, produced by Nile Rodgers at studios in Memphis, TN, Dallas and New York.
Aug [27] During a US tour, Vaughan is killed when the Bell 206 helicopter in which he is traveling to Chicago, IL, following a concert at the Alpine Valley Music Theatre, East Troy, WI, which ended with a jam including Vaughan, his brother Jimmie, Eric Clapton, Robert Cray, Buddy Guy and Phil Palmer, crashes, in thick fog, into the side of a man-made ski hill. (Also killed are Clapton's agent, Bobby Brooks, his bodyguard, Nigel Browne, the tour manager, Colin Smythe and the pilot, Jeffrey Brown.)
[31] At his memorial service held in the Laurel Land Memorial Park, Oak Cliff, Dallas, Jackson Browne, Bonnie Raitt and Stevie Wonder sing *Amazing Grace*.
Sept ***Couldn't Stand The Weather*** becomes Vaughan & Double Trouble's first RIAA-certified million seller, six years after release.
[22] Previously charting ***In Step*** makes US #75.
[26] ***Couldn't Stand The Weather*** is certified platinum by the RIAA.
Oct [20] ***Family Style*** makes UK #63 in its week of entry.
Nov [10] The Vaughan Brothers album, ***Family Style***, hits US #7. It features Jimmie singing a rare vocal on one cut, while Stevie had recorded the lead on the remaining songs.
[19] ***Family Style*** is confirmed platinum by the RIAA.
[24] The Vaughan Brothers' *Tick Tock* peaks at US #65.

1991

Feb [15] "Pride And Joy" video is certified platinum by the RIAA.
[20] *D/FW*, a track from ***Family Style*** in named Best Rock Instrumental Performance, and ***Family Style*** wins the Best Contemporary Blues Recording category for the Vaughan Brothers, at the 33rd annual Grammy Awards, staged at New York's Radio City Music Hall.
Mar [20] Vaughan is posthumously honored by the local music community at the annual Austin Music Awards.
Nov [23] ***The Sky Is Crying***, collected from previously unissued material, debuts at its US #10 peak.

1992

Jan [22] The Fender Guitar company issues a Stevie Ray Vaughan "signature" model of their famous Stratocaster, in honor of the late guitarist, on the same day his 1983 debut set, ***Texas Flood*** is certified platinum by the RIAA.
July [22] Vaughan's mother, Martha, and brother, Jimmie, file suit in the Cook County Circuit Court, Chicago, against Omniflight Helicopters Inc., stating that they "knew, or should have known, that poor visibility precluded safe flying conditions".
Aug [11] ***Soul To Soul*** is certified platinum by the RIAA.
Oct [3] A memorial to Vaughan is unveiled in Austin.
[24] ***In The Beginning***, a retrospective of his earliest work, debuts at its US #58 peak.
Nov A memorial to Vaughan, sculpted by Ralph Helmick is unveiled on the shores of Town Lake in Austin.

1993

Feb [24] Brother Jimmie collects the Best Rock Instrumental trophy for his brother's *Little Wing*, and the Best Contemporary Blues Album statuette for ***The***

Sky Is Crying, at the 35th annual Grammy Awards, held at the Shrine Auditorium, Los Angeles.

1995

June [6] Following its platinum certification of ***Live Alive*** on December 5th the previous year, the RIAA now confirms two million sales of ***In Step*** and ***The Sky Is Crying***.
Oct [13] "Live At The Mocambo" video is certified platinum by the RIAA for sales of 100,000.
Nov [18] Compilation set ***Greatest Hits*** reaches US #39.

BOBBY VEE

1959

Feb [3] Inspired by Buddy Holly's *That'll Be The Day*, Vee (b. Robert Thomas Velline, Apr. 30, 1943, Fargo, ND) has formed the Shadows at Central High School in Fargo the previous year, with brother Bill, Bob Korum and Jim Stillman, playing mainly instrumentals, mixed with a few Holly tunes, and self-penned vocal items by Vee. The Shadows now answer a request over local radio station, KFGO, for a group to fill in on the visiting "Winter Dance Party" one-night show in Fargo (which Holly, the Big Bopper and Ritchie Valens, who all died in a plane crash in the early hours, would have played). They appear second on the program, performing *Bye Bye Love* and *Long Tall Sally*, wearing matching outfits, which they bought that afternoon.
[14] Local promoter Bing Bingstrom, who was in the "Winter Dance Party" audience, has offered to find the Shadows some paying gigs, their first being a Valentine Day dance, earning $60.
June [1] The group pays $500 to record its own session at Soma Records' Studio, Minneapolis, and cuts the Vee-penned *Suzie Baby*, and the group instrumental, *Flying*.
July Soma issues the single, to major success in Minneapolis and surrounding areas. The group tours radio stations around Iowa and North Dakota, and sales spread. After a San Diego, CA station starts to play it, *Suzie Baby* attracts the attention of Liberty Records, which buys the master, and releases it nationally. The band experiments by adding a pianist to expand the live sound, and hires Bob Zimmerman, who is spending the summer in Fargo. (He calls himself Elston Gunn at the time - the name will later change to Bob Dylan.) He plays two gigs with the Shadows, but his repertoire provokes a compatibility problem. He is paid $30 and asked to leave.
Sept [19] *Suzie Baby* peaks at US #77. Liberty signs both the group, and Vee, to a separate solo deal. (The label will do little on record with the group, which will back Vee on tour until 1963.)

1960

Apr [16] Pairing him with producer Snuff Garrett, Liberty has Vee cover Adam Faith's recent UK chart-topper, *What Do You Want?* (which is also in Holly-influenced style), which peaks at US #93.
Oct [22] After an album session at Norman Petty's studio in Clovis, NM (where most of Holly's hits had been recorded), Garrett has persuaded Vee (against the singer's wishes) to cover the Clovers' R&B oldie, *Devil Or Angel*. Originally the B-side, but flipped by a Pittsburgh radio station, it becomes his first major success, hitting US #6. (The other cut, a similar revival of Ivory Joe Hunter's *Since I Met You Baby*, has peaked at US #81 on Sept [17]).
Dec [23] He begins a week's engagement at New York's Brooklyn Paramount Theater, in Clay Cole's "Christmas Rock'n'Roll Show", alongside Neil Sedaka, Dion and Bo Diddley, among others.

1961

Jan [9] Garrett is offered material from Don Kirshner's Brill Building Aldon Music stable for Vee, and *Rubber Ball*, co-written by Gene Pitney, hits US #6, becoming his first million seller.
Feb *Rubber Ball* is his UK chart debut, hitting #4, after holding off a Top 10 cover version by the more-established Marty Wilde.
Mar [13] A John D. Loudermilk song, *Stayin' In*, makes US #33.
[20] The B-side revival of the Crickets' (post-Buddy Holly) *More Than I Can Say*, peaks at US #61. He has his first album chart success with his second album, ***Bobby Vee***, which reaches US #18.
May *More Than I Can Say*, promoted as a UK A-side, hits UK #4.
June [12] *How Many Tears*, the first of a run of Carole King/Gerry Goffin songs recorded by Vee, makes US #63.
[25] He appears on Alan Freed's outdoor rock show at the Hollywood Bowl, Hollywood, CA, together with Jerry Lee Lewis, Brenda Lee, the Shirelles, and others.
Sept [18] Goffin and King's *Take Good Care Of My Baby* becomes Vee's all-time most successful single, topping the US chart for the first of three weeks, and selling over a million. Meanwhile, *How Many Tears* hits UK #10.
[30] 2,000 teenage fans, members of the California Racquet Club in Cheviot Hills, Los Angeles, CA, fete the singer on "Bobby Vee Afternoon".
Nov ***Bobby Vee Sings Hits Of The Rockin' '50s*** peaks at US #85.
Dec [25] *Run To Him*, penned by Goffin with Jack Keller, hits US #2 (behind the Tokens' *The Lion Sleeps Tonight*).

1962

Jan Despite a universal thumbs-down from the "Juke Box Jury" panelists on BBC-TV, *Run To Him* hits UK #6. (For a while it is available in Britain on two labels, as London Records' UK licensing agreement with Liberty runs out, and the US label releases it through EMI.)
[20] Its B-side, Goffin/King's *Walkin' With My Angel*, making US #53.
Feb ***Take Good Care Of My Baby*** makes US #91, and hits UK #7, as Vee appears on UK national radio ("Easy Beat") and TV ("Thank Your Lucky Stars").
[9] Vee begins a 15-date, twice-nightly UK tour with Tony Orlando, Clarence "Frogman" Henry, the Springfields and others, at the Doncaster Gaumont, Yorks, set to end on the 25th at the Winter Gardens, Bournemouth, Dorset.
Mar *Please Don't Ask About Barbara* peaks at UK #29, while ***Hits Of The Rockin' '50s*** reaches UK #20.
Apr [7] *Please Don't Ask About Barbara* reaches US #15. (The B-side, *I Can't Say Goodbye*, has already peaked at US #92 on Feb [24].)
July [7] *Sharing You*, a Goffin/King song in similar style to *Run To Him*, reaches US #15 and UK #10.
Aug ***Bobby Vee Meets The Crickets*** (Holly's ex-backing group, at this point consisting of Sonny Curtis, Jerry Allison, Glen D. Hardin and Jerry Naylor, is also recording for Liberty) makes US #42, while ***A Bobby Vee Recording Session*** peaks at US #121. Vee appears in a cameo slot, singing *At A Time Like This* (which he has recorded in the UK at EMI), in the Billy Fury-starring film, "Play It Cool".
Oct [13] *Punish Her* reaches US #20. (The B-side, *Someday (When I'm Gone From You)*, taken from the album with the Crickets, made US #99 on Sept [29].)
Nov ***Bobby Vee Meets The Crickets*** is his most successful album in Britain, hitting #2, behind the UK Shadows' ***Out Of The Shadows***. Vee undertakes a lengthy UK tour with the Crickets.
Dec Compilation album ***Bobby Vee's Golden Greats***, reaches US #24, while the seasonal ***Merry Christmas From Bobby Vee*** makes US #136. *A Forever Kind Of Love*, recorded in Britain during the summer with producer Norrie Paramor, reaches UK #13.

1963

Feb [2] *The Night Has A Thousand Eyes*, from the movie "Just For Fun" (in which he has a cameo role, singing two songs), hits US #3, and becomes another million seller. ***A Bobby Vee Recording Session*** hits UK #10.
Mar *The Night Has A Thousand Eyes* hits UK #3.
Apr ***The Night Has A Thousand Eyes*** makes US #102.
May Compilation, ***Bobby Vee's Golden Greats***, hits UK #10.
[11] *Charms* reaches US #13.
June ***Bobby Vee Meets The Ventures***, pairing the singer with Liberty's top guitar instrumental group, makes US #91.
July [20] *Be True To Yourself* reaches US #34. (The B-side, *A Letter From Betty*, peaks at US #85.) *Bobby Tomorrow*, a reversal of *Charms*, which is relegated to a UK B-side, makes UK #21, his last UK hit single.
Oct ***The Night Has A Thousand Eyes*** reaches UK #15.
Nov [8] He begins a US tour with Dick Clark's "Caravan of Stars" package, in Teaneck, NJ, sharing the bill with Brian Hyland, the Ronettes and Little Eva, among others.
Dec [14] *Yesterday And You (Armen's Theme)* climbs to US #55. (The B-side, *Never Love A Robin*, perches at US #99 on the 28th.)
[28] Vee marries Karen Gergen at the Holy Rosary Catholic Church in Detroit Lakes, MI.

1964

Feb [8] *Stranger In Your Arms* peaks at US #83.
[29] Vee begins a 29-date, twice-nightly UK package tour with Dusty Springfield, the Searchers and Big Dee Irwin at the Adelphi Cinema, Slough, Berks., set to close on March 29th at the Liverpool Empire, Liverpool, Lancs.
Apr [4] *I'll Make You Mine* makes US #52.
[11] On tour again in Britain, Vee appears on the BBC radio show, "Saturday Club", with the Searchers, Adam Faith and Gerry & the Pacemakers.
June ***Bobby Vee Sings The New Sound From England!***, featuring Merseybeat arrangements, and recent UK hits (plus *She's Sorry*, written as a straight imitation of the Beatles' *She Loves You*), reaches US #146, as Vee tours the US with the Rolling Stones.
July [11] *Hickory, Dick And Doc* climbs to US #63.

1965

Jan [9] *(There'll Come A Day When) Ev'ry Little Bit Hurts* peaks at US #84 (its B-side, *Pretend You Don't See Her*, having peaked at US #97 on Dec [5]).
Feb [6] *Cross My Heart* peaks at US #99. It is his last single with producer Garrett (its B-side is titled *This Is The End*) as the two cease working together by mutual consent.
Mar [25] Vee begins a 12-date, twice-nightly UK package tour, with Dusty Springfield, the Searchers, Heinz, the Zombies and others, at the Odeon Cinema, Stockton, Cleveland, which will end on April 10th at the Sophia Gardens, Cardiff, S. Glam, Wales.
June [5] *Keep On Trying*, recorded in the UK with producer George Martin, peaks at US #85.

1966

July [30] *Look At Me, Girl* makes US #52.

1967

Sept [9] Folk-tinged ballad *Come Back When You Grow Up*, produced by Dallas Smith, and pairing Vee with the Strangers, hits US #3, and is his final million seller (and first to be certified).
Oct ***Come Back When You Grow Up*** reaches US #66.
[16] *Come Back When You Grow Up* is certified gold by the RIAA.
Dec [16] A cover version of Kenny O'Dell's *Beautiful People* makes US #37 (one place ahead of the original).
[20] Vee guests on BBC-TV's "Juke Box Jury".

1968

Mar [16] *Maybe Just Today* reaches US #46.
May [25] A medley of two oldies, Smokey Robinson's *My Girl* and Goffin/King's *Hey Girl*, makes US #35, while ***Just Today*** peaks at US #187.
Sept [14] *Do What You Gotta Do*, reviving the Four Tops hit, makes US #83.
Dec [28] *I'm Into Lookin' For Someone To Love Me* peaks at US #98.

1970

Dec [5] After *Let's Call It A Day Girl* has made US #92 on Aug [2], and with Liberty Records having become United Artists Records, *Sweet Sweetheart* peaks at US #88, Vee's last US chart entry.

1972

In a conscious effort to break from his earlier style and image, Vee releases ***Nothing Like A Sunny Day***, under his real name, Robert Thomas Velline. A laid-back country/rock-styled package, along the lines of Rick Nelson's Stone Canyon Band material, it features a small combo backing (including legendary pedal steel guitarist, "Red" Rhodes), while among its tracks is a slowed-down re-creation of *Take Good Care Of My Baby*.

1980

May Compilation, ***The Bobby Vee Singles Album***, hits UK #5, confirming the nostalgic appeal of his early '60s recordings.

1992

Dec [5] Having continued to tour on nostalgia package tours throughout the '80s, often with Del Shannon, Rick Nelson and Brian Hyland and making an annual appearance at the "Buddy Holly Memorial" concert held in either Fargo or Clear Lake, Vee, whose career highlights have been brought to compact disc in 1990 with the EMI-released ***Bobby Vee***, and who has established his own Rockhouse label issuing ***UK Tour '90*** in the same year, now participates in "The Giants Of Rock'n'Roll", with Little Richard, Lloyd Price, Duane Eddy, Johnny Preston, Chris Montez and Little Eva, at the Wembley Arena, Wembley, Middx., as a cassette of newly-recorded material is released as ***The Last Of The Great Rhythm Guitar Players***.

SUZANNE VEGA

1977

Singer/songwriter/acoustic guitarist Vega (b. Aug. 12, 1959, New York, NY), having grown up in a Hispanic neighbourhood of New York, has been encouraged by her Puerto Rican stepfather, a novelist, to attend the New York High School of Performing Arts (of "Fame" fame) where she studies dance and begins composing songs in 1975. Having also attended New York's Barnard College, she is now working as an office receptionist during the day, performing her own compositions on the Greenwich Village folk circuit, including gigs at Folk City, the Speakeasy and the Bottom Line. Subsequently meeting lawyer, Ron Fiernstein, and engineer, Steve Addabbo, they offer to manager her, together forming the publishing units, Waifersongs and AGF Music Ltd in 1983.

1984

July A **New York Times** review of a recent performance describes Vega: "one of the most promising talents on the New York City folk circuit".
Dec Encouraged by increasingly glowing notices, A&M Records signs her to a worldwide recording deal.

1985

Jan She begins three months of taping ten of her own compositions for her first album, at New York's Celestial Studios.
Apr Her self-penned maiden album, ***Suzanne Vega***, introducing her literate and sensitive songwriting and vocal style, is released to universal critical acclaim, as she becomes regarded as the first of a new generation of female folk stars of the late '80s. Produced by Addabbo and ex-Patti Smith guitarist Lenny Kaye, the album will spend 27 weeks on the chart, climbing to US #91, and will achieve double gold status in the UK (where it reaches #11).
May With UK reaction breaking faster, Vega takes her band, including Marc Shulman (guitar), Sue Evans (drums), Mike Visceglia (bass), Anton Sanko (keyboards) and Stephen Ferrare (percussion) on a European tour, including a performance at London's Royal Albert Hall.

1986

Jan From the debut album, *Small Blue Thing* peaks at UK #65.
Mar *Marlene On The Wall* is her first major chart single, reaching UK #21.
June [26] She appears at the "Prince's Trust Rock Gala" at the Wembley Arena, Wembley, Middx.
July [12] A new recording, *Left Of Center*, makes UK #32, with the help of one of the earliest CD single release formats. With Joe Jackson featured on piano, the song is included on the current John Hughes film soundtrack, ***Pretty In Pink***, but will not appear on a Vega studio release.
Aug The Smithereens' ***Especially For You***, for which Vega has co-written and duetted on *A Lonely Place*, is released.
Nov [18-19] As a climax to a successful year touring in Europe (and on the larger US folk circuit), Vega plays selected UK venues including two soldout dates at London's Royal Albert Hall, which are filmed for a BBC-TV showing and later video release.

1987

Feb While writing songs for her second album, Vega contributes two compositions to a forthcoming Philip Glass album, ***Songs From Liquid Days*** - one will be sung by Janice Pendarvis, the other by Linda Ronstadt.
May [9] ***Solitude Standing***, again produced by Addabbo and Kaye, will benefit from the international success of *Luka*, debuts at UK #2, behind Curiosity Killed The Cat's ***Keep Your Distance***, and will reach US #11. Vega begins an 11-month "Suzanne Vega World Tour 87", beginning in the UK and Eire (travelling to the US and Canada in July and August, including sold-out nights at New York's Carnegie Hall, and returning to Europe in the autumn, following her first visits to Japan and Australia).
June The child abuse-themed *Luka*, featuring Shawn Colvin on backing vocals, reaches UK #23.
July A cappella, *Tom's Diner*, makes UK #58.
[15] ***Solitude Standing*** is certified gold by the RIAA.
Aug [22] *Luka* becomes her first major US hit, peaking at #3, and earning a Grammy nomination.
Sept [12] *Solitude Standing*, with a Jonathan Demme-directed video, peaks at US #94.

1988

Aug UK CD-only EP is released, featuring *Luka* and *Left Of Center*.
Sept [7] "Luka" wins the Best Female Video category, at the fifth annual MTV Video Music Awards, held at the Universal Amphitheatre, Universal City, CA.
Oct Vega has contributed the title track to the newly-released Disney compilation, ***Stay Awake***, for A&M Records.

1989

July She begins writing and rehearsing her third album, with beau Anton Sanko, using a makeshift studio, assembled in their apartment.

1990

Feb Hugh Padgham mixes the album in New York.
Apr [28] ***Days Of Open Hand***, recorded at New York's Skyline Studios, with a band comprising Sanko, Visceglia, Shulman and Frank Vilardi (drums), hits UK #7 in its week of entry.
May [19] *Book Of Dreams*, with Colvin again featured on backing vocals, peaks at UK #66, as ***Days Of Open Hand*** makes US #50.
June [9] D. A. Pennebaker's film documentary on Vega airs on VH1, and subsequently on BBC2-TV.
[11] Vega begins a North American tour in Washington, DC.
Aug [11] UK remixers DNA hit UK #2 for three weeks with *Tom's Diner*. The sampling duo have "borrowed" the cut, adding a repetitive dance rhythm track, releasing it initially as a bootleg, only to have it signed up by A&M (with whom Vega is still contracted). She is reported to be initially appalled, though the DNA hit will out-perform all of her own original material from her current album.
Oct [2] Vega begins the second leg of her North American tour in Atlanta, GA, at the conclusion of a European tour.
Dec [22] *Tom's Diner* hits UK #5.

1991

Feb [26] She lectures at the New School for Social Research, in New York.
Mar Vega sings *Who By Fire*, at the 20th annual Juno Awards, held at the Queen Elizabeth Theatre, Vancouver, BC, Canada.
May [18] ***Deadicated***, a collection of Grateful Dead covers, to which Vega has contributed *China Doll* and *Cassidy*, reaches US #24.
July [26-28] Vega takes part in the three-day "Abbot Ale Cambridge Folk Festival" in Cambridge, Cambs.
Sept [24] Various artists collection, ***Tom's Album***, comprising entirely of unusual cover versions of the Vega cut, *Tom's Diner*, is released.

1992

July [12] Vega appears at the Woody Guthrie Tribute, as part of the Central Park "Summer Stage '92" concert series in New York.
Aug [22] *In Liverpool* debuts at its UK #52 peak.
Sept [19] ***99.9F***, marking a departure from her normal folk material, now with a dance edge, bows at its UK #20 peak.
[27] Vega performs at a benefit concert for leukemia patients, in Luciano Pavarotti's horse stables in Modena, Italy.
Oct [3] ***99.9F*** makes US #86.
[24] Title cut *99.9F* debuts at its UK #46 peak.
Nov [27] Vega guests on NBC-TV's "Late Night With David Letterman".
Dec [26] *Blood Makes Noise* peaks at UK #60.

1993

Feb [19] Vega appears on NBC-TV's "The Tonight Show".
Mar [6] *When Heroes Go Down* charts for a week at UK #58.
[11] She plays a sellout show at the Academy, New York, during her current North American tour. (During the month, ***Pavarotti & Friends***, featuring Vega, and recorded last year at the benefit concert for the Berloni Foundation, is released.)
Apr [1] Vega begins a 15-date UK concert series at the Poole Arts Centre, set to end on the 18th at the Fairfield Halls, Croydon, Surrey.

1994

Feb [2] Vega takes part in "In My Own Words : A Bunch Of Songwriters Sittin' Around Singing" at the Bottom Line, New York, as part of its 20th anniversary celebrations.

1995

Mar [17] Vega marries Mitchell Froom in Radio City Music Hall.
Apr Columbia Records (US) releases Vega's duet with John Cale on *The Long Voyage*, written and produced by Hector Zazou.
Aug Following the birth of her first child, Vega returns to the studio to complete her next A&M album.
Oct [14] ***Tower Of Song : The Songs Of Leonard Cohen***, including Vega's version of *Story Of Isaac*, charts for a week at US #198.

1996

Jan [9] ***Dead Man Walking***, featuring Vega's *Woman On The Tier*, is released in the US, while another new cut, *Caramel*, will be included on the May released soundtrack ***The Truth About Cats And Dogs***, with her first album in four years scheduled for summer release.

THE VELVET UNDERGROUND

Lou Reed (vocals, guitar); **Sterling Morrison** (bass, guitar); **John Cale** (bass, keyboards, viola, vocals); **Nico** (vocals); **Maureen Tucker** (drums)

1964

The classically-trained Cale (b. Dec. 4, 1940, Garnant, Dyfed, Wales), in New York, NY on a Leonard Bernstein scholarship, has been performing in avant-gardist La Monte Young's ensemble, the Dream Academy, when he meets Reed (b. Louis Firbank, Mar. 2, 1943, Freeport, Long Island, NY) at a party. Reed plays Cale demos of his songs (including *The Ostrich*), and the two decide to form a band. Reed brings in Morrison (b. Holmes Sterling Morrison, Aug. 29, 1942, East Meadow, Long Island), who he met while both were studying creative writing at Syracuse University, while Cale adds his neighbor, Angus MacLise, on percussion. They play mostly free gigs under a variety of names and, as the Primitives, release several singles for Pickwick Records (for whom Reed has become a contracted songwriter). (The Velvet Underground, a name suggested by MacLise, is taken from the title of a pornographic paperback.)

1965

July Reed Cale and Morrison record demos at Cale's apartment at 56, Ludlow Street, New York. Mutual friends subsequently draw them to the attention of pop-art protagonist, Andy Warhol, who becomes the group's manager following a gig at Greenwich Village's Café Bizarre, and who will direct them towards a number of increasingly avant-garde multi-media showcases. He decides that Nico (b. Christa Päffgen, Oct. 16, 1938, Cologne, Germany), who is singing at the Blue Angel Lounge, New York, should join the group. The rest of the band are less enthusiastic, and MacLise abruptly leaves for Nepal. (He will die there of malnutrition, in 1979, aged 41.) He is replaced by computer operator and sometime drummer, Tucker (b. 1945, NJ).

Nov [11] The Velvet Underground plays as the opening act for the Myddle Class at a high school dance in Summit, NJ.

1966

During the year, the group performs a further residency at the Café Bizarre, becomes the house band for Warhol's Factory arts collective in New York, and are integrated as the musical component of his multi-media show, "The Exploding Plastic Inevitable". The band also signs to MGM's Verve label and makes a cameo appearance in the movie, "Hedy The Shoplifter".

1967

Jan [2-14] The Velvet Underground performs at the Scene in New York. (Later in the month, the group plays a week-long series of concerts at the "Montreal World Fair", Montreal, PQ, Canada.)

Mar Subsequently regarded as a seminal and influential recording, their debut album, ***The Velvet Underground And Nico***, is released, reaching US #171. Produced by Warhol, it features a distinctive sleeve, depicting a peeled-off banana created by Warhol as a screenprint. The album is highlighted by Reed's dark, amoral lyrical stance (not least on the much-heralded cut, *Heroin*) and Nico's gothic vocal style. (With the album will go the quote : "hardly anybody bought it, but everyone who did formed a band ...") Reed subsequently takes control of the band as Nico leaves, and Warhol's services also end. (Nico's solo career will begin with a collection of covers for ***Chelsea Girls***, followed by ***The Marble Index*** (1968), ***Desertshore*** (1971), ***The End*** (1974), ***Drama Of Exile*** (1981), ***Do Or Die*** (1983), some of which are produced by Cale, and five live albums, during the remainder of the '80s.)

1968

Jan Typically eclectic, ***White Light, White Heat***, recorded in a day at the end of a tour, charts for two weeks at US #199.

Mar Clashes between Reed and Cale come to a head, and Cale leaves. Bassist Doug Yule, ex-Boston folk-rock groups Eden's Children and the Grass Menagerie, replaces him.

Oct [18-20] The group plays at the Avalon Ballroom, San Francisco, CA.

1969

Apr The more pastoral ***The Velvet Underground***, recorded in Los Angeles, is released. Atlantic Records subsequently signs the band after they leave MGM.

1970

June The group returns to New York for a month's residency at Max's Kansas City club. Tucker is pregnant, so Yule's brother, Billy, deputizes. ***Loaded*** is released, including Reed's much-praised *Sweet Jane*, though he complains that the album has been remixed without his knowledge. The band tours the East Coast with Yule on lead vocals with singer, Walter Powers, added to the line-up.

Aug [23] After playing his last gig with the group at Max's Kansas City, Reed's parents pick him up and take him home to Freeport, Long Island, where he will stay for next two years, working as a typist in his father's accountancy firm for $40 a week.

1971

Mar Willie Alexander joins the band in place of Morrison, who leaves to teach medieval literature at the University of Texas in Austin, before working as a tugboat captain out of Houston, TX for a while. Tucker also quits shortly thereafter, and moves to Phoenix, AZ, to raise a family (and will re-emerge in 1982 with the Spy Records-released, ***Playing Possum***, and the 1986 EP, *MoeJadKateBarry*). Yule will keep the Velvet Underground name (until 1973), recording ***Squeeze***, an almost solo effort, released only in the UK. (He will join West Coast band American Flyer, in the mid '70s.)

Oct [20] The group embarks on an eight-date UK tour at Birmingham University, Birmingham, W. Midlands, set to end the 28th, at Bristol University, Bristol, Avon.

1974

Feb Following Atlantic's 1972 release of ***Live At Max's Kansas City***, taken from fan Brigit Polk's cassette recording of the group's last gig with Reed, the double performance album, ***1969 - The Velvet Underground Live***, recorded in California and Texas, is released on Mercury, contains previously unrecorded songs. Reed, Cale and Nico play an impromptu "reunion" concert in Paris, France, which is filmed.

June [1] Nico joins Cale, Kevin Ayers and Brian Eno for a London concert (recorded for ***June 1st, 1974***).

Dec [13] She performs at Rheims Cathedral with Tangerine Dream.

1985

Mar ***V.U.***, a remixed album of previously unissued material from 1968-69 released by Polydor, makes US #85 and UK #47. Polydor UK will release the Velvet Underground box set, ***Another View*** in May the following year.

1988

July [18] Nico, having spent several years living in Manchester, Gtr. Manchester, with poet John Cooper Clarke, dies of a brain haemorrhage, having fallen off her bicycle while on holiday in Ibiza.

1989

Sept Tucker releases ***Life In Exile After Abdication***. (She has been working at a Georgia Wal-Mart discount-store warehouse, and has asked for leave to record the album, and quits when she is refused permission.) Lou Reed and Sonic Youth guest on the album, which magician Penn Jellette, of Penn and Teller, helps with finance for the project on the 50 Skidillion Watts label.

1990

June [15] The original group plays together for the first time since 1969, as they attend the opening of the Cartier Foundation's Andy Warhol retrospective at Jouy en Josas, outside Paris, and perform *Heroin*.

1991

Nov The original Velvets record together on *I'm Not*, for Maureen Tucker's new ***I Spent A Week There The Other Night*** album.

Dec [9] Imaginary Records releases the five-album boxed-set, ***The Imaginary Box***, which includes a various artists covers album - ***Heaven & Hell : A Tribute to the Velvet Underground***.

1992

Dec Reed and Morrison join Cale at the latter's New York University show, performing *Style It Takes* and *Forever Changed*.

1993

Jan [19] Cale appears on NBC-TV's "The Tonight Show" to promote his latest solo album. He tells host, Jay Leno, that the remaining Velvets plan to formally re-unite. When pressed for a reason, Cale responds: "Money".

June [6] A re-formed Velvet Underground play at the Wembley Arena, Wembley, Middx., following two shows at the Playhouse, Edinburgh, Lothian, Scotland, on the 1st and 2nd, and the Forum, London, on the 5th.

Nov [13] Two-CD set ***Live MCMXCIII***, recorded in Paris, charts for a week at UK #70 and US #180.

Dec [18] Tucker denies comments made by Reed that his clash with Cale has caused the band to split.

1994

Jan [27] The Velvet Underground is named Comeback Of The Year in **Rolling Stone**'s 1994 Music Awards Critics' Picks.

Mar [12] *Venus In Furs* charts for a week at UK #71.

Nov [18] The band reunites again, this time minus Reed, at the Andy Warhol Museum in Pittsburgh, PA, for their first US concert since 1968.

1995

Aug [30] Morrison dies of non-Hodgkin's lymphoma in Poughkeepsie, NY.

Sept [2] Reed dedicates *Sweet Jane* to Morrison at the Concert for the Rock and Roll Hall of Fame at Cleveland Stadium, Cleveland, OH.

[26] A definitive 75-track five-CD retrospective boxed set ***Peel Slowly And See*** is released.

1996

Jan [17] The Velvet Underground is inducted into the Rock and Roll Hall of Fame at the 11th annual induction dinner, and sing *Last Night I Said Goodbye To My Friend*, written a few days earlier and dedicated to Morrison.

see also: **John CALE, Lou REED**

THE VENTURES

Nokie Edwards (lead guitar);
Don Wilson (guitar); **Bob Bogle** (guitar, bass);
Howie Johnson (drums)

1960

Jan Wilson (b. Feb. 10, 1937, Tacoma, WA) and Bogle (b. Jan. 16, 1937, Portland, OR), working as tuckpointers (mortar removers) for a building construction company in Seattle, WA, have started playing as a duo at local dances and hops the previous year, and now recruit Edwards (b. May 9, 1939, WA), initially on bass, and Johnson (b. 1938, WA), the quartet naming itself the Versatones, with Wilson's mother, Josie, as manager.

Feb After nailing down tracks at Custom Recorders in Seattle, they release *Cookies And Coke*, on their own Blue Horizon label.

Apr Their second Blue Horizon single, a version of Johnny Smith's *Walk Don't Run*, which Bogle has first heard performed by Chet Atkins on the album ***Hi-Fi In Focus***, is pressed in small quantities, with the group having changed its name to the Ventures (simply from undertaking its new "venture"). They take the disc to the Fleetwoods' manager, Bob Reisdorff, who runs the local Dolton label. He turns it down, so they try DJ acquaintance, Pat O'Day, who has a show on KJR in Seattle, and he plays it after each news bulletin. Reisdorff, hearing the song on the radio, reconsiders and buys the master of *Walk Don't Run*, and signs the group (in a deal carefully negotiated by Josie Wilson, which gives the group artistic control over its releases via Blue Horizon Productions, with Reisdorff and Wilson named as joint producers).

Sept [3] Released nationally, *Walk Don't Run* hits US #2 (behind Elvis Presley's *It's Now Or Never*) and becomes a million seller. Because Dolton is marketed nationally by Liberty Records, the Ventures' recording operations are moved to Los Angeles, CA, where Liberty has its studios, and the group cuts a debut album, mainly consisting of versions of other acts' instrumental hits.

Oct *Walk Don't Run* hits UK #8, in a close race with a UK cover version by the John Barry Seven.

Dec [31] Their revival of the '30s standard, *Perfidia*, given the same instrumental guitar treatment as *Walk Don't Run*, reaches US #15.

1961

Jan Their debut album, ***The Ventures***, reaches US #11, while *Perfidia* hits UK #4.

Mar [6] *Ram-Bunk-Shush*, a 1957 hit for R&B organist Bill Doggett, reaches US #29 and UK #45.

May [15] Another updated oldie, *Lullaby Of The Leaves*, peaks at US #69 and UK #43 (the Ventures' last UK chart entry).

June [25] The Ventures take part in the "Alan Freed Spectacular" at the Hollywood Bowl, Hollywood, CA, with Brenda Lee, Bobby Vee, B.B. King, the Shirelles, and others.

Aug ***Another Smash!!!*** reaches US #39.

Sept [11] *(Theme From) Silver City*, played with Hank Levine's orchestra, makes US #83.

Nov [20] *Blue Moon*, recently a vocal million seller by the Marcels, is put through its guitar paces to US #54.

1962

Mar ***Twist With The Ventures***, containing instrumental versions of Twist dance-craze hits, reaches US #24. (It is the first and most successful of a quick series of Ventures albums intended as music for dancing to: ***The Ventures Twist Party Volume 2***; ***Mashed Potatoes And Gravy*** and ***Going To The Ventures Dance Party!***)

Sept [15] *Lolita Ya-Ya*, the theme from the film, "Lolita", makes US #61. Meanwhile, following an car accident, Johnson, although not physically injured, feels the need to rest, and leaves the group. (He will die in 1988.) He is replaced on drums by Mel Taylor (b. New York, NY).

1963

Feb [23] Historically notable for being the first single recording to use fuzz-box guitar, *The 2,000lb Bee* peaks at US #91.

Feb ***The Ventures Play Telstar And The Lonely Bull***, which contains covers of those two and several more instrumental hits, is the group's biggest-selling album, hitting US #8, and earning a gold disc for half a million sales. Edwards, who has been sharing lead guitar on record and stage for some time, officially takes over on lead, with Bogle switching to bass.

June *Surfing*, a cash-in on the current California surf instrumental boom (which has gained much of its original inspiration from the Ventures), reaches US #30. The group has also teamed with Liberty artist, Bobby Vee, for the part-vocal, part-instrumental ***Bobby Vee Meets The Ventures***, which peaks at US #91.

July The Blue Horizon Productions contract clause expires, and Josie Wilson drops out of production, with the group losing automatic creative control over its releases.

Oct ***Let's Go!***, headed by a cover of the Routers' hit, makes US #30.

1964

Mar The last Ventures album produced by Reisdorff, ***The Ventures In Space***, combining original material with versions of science-fiction movie themes, reaches US #27. (Keith Moon of the Who will later nominate this as one of his favorite albums.)

Aug [22] The Ventures' new, updated arrangement of *Walk Don't Run*, now under the title *Walk Don't Run '64*, with ideas borrowed liberally from the Chantays' *Pipeline*, and other surf instrumentals, hits US #8. ***The Fabulous Ventures***, with new producer Dick Glasser, makes US #32.

Nov [28] Their update of Richard Rodgers' *Slaughter On 10th Avenue* makes US #35, taken from ***Walk Don't Run, Vol. 2*** (also featuring *Walk Don't Run '64*), which stops at US #17.

1965

Feb [13] *Diamond Head*, another surf-style instrumental, makes US #70.

Apr ***The Ventures Knock Me Out!*** reaches US #31.

Aug Live set, ***The Ventures On Stage***, recorded at concerts in Japan and the US, peaks at US #27. (The group's first visits to Japan coincide with the first mass availablity of electric guitars in Japan, and the Ventures become the model guitar group in the Orient. Over the next ten years, although little of it will feed back to the West, the group runs a parallel career in Japan, where its popularity is on a par with the Beatles'. Regular tours and dozens of albums, recorded specifically for the Japanese market, keep a vast demand satisfied. Their collaboration with Japan's emerging pop culture is such that the Ventures write many tunes designed for Japanese writers to add lyrics in their own language.)

Sept ***Play Guitar With The Ventures*** is an instructional album, with four tunes (including *Walk Don't Run*) repeated over with lead, rhythm or bass guitar parts missing, and the instructions to enable the apprentice guitarist to fill the part with his own instrument, and play along with the Ventures. The album makes US #96, during a 13-week chart stay.

Nov Joe Saraceno takes over as the group's producer for ***The Ventures A Go-Go***, an anthology of instrumental dance tunes, which reaches US #16.

Dec The seasonal ***Christmas With The Ventures*** is released.

1966

Mar [26] Having recently released ***Where The Action Is***, the group competes with Johnny Rivers on *Secret Agent Man*, the theme from the CBS-TV series, "Secret Agent" (a re-titling of the UK series "Danger Man"), starring Patrick McGoohan. Rivers' vocal version hits the US Top 10, while the Ventures' cut now makes US #54.

Apr The group cashes in on another TV craze with ***The Ventures/Batman Theme***, which makes US #42.

1967

Apr The band explores the current vogue for psychedelic sounds with a mainly cover-version dominated set, ***Guitar Freakout***, which reaches US #57.

Oct ***Golden Greats By The Ventures*** (not a compilation of their own, but a collection of other acts' hits) reaches US #50 and, in a 44-week chart stay, earns another gold disc.

1969

May [10] After Edwards has left for a solo career the previous June, replaced on lead guitar by Jerry McGee, the Ventures hit US #4 with *Hawaii Five-0*, the theme from the police TV series, starring Jack Lord, which becomes another million seller. The group is now a quintet, having added keyboard player, Johnny Durrill (ex-the Five Americans).

June ***Hawaii Five-0*** reaches US #11.

July [19] Their treatment of Percy Faith's 1960 million seller, *Theme From A Summer Place*, taken from the album, peaks at US #83, and is the group's last chart single.

1970

Jan ***Swamp Rock*** reaches US #81.

May [19] ***Golden Greats By The Ventures*** and ***The Ventures Play Telstar, The Lonely Bull And Others*** are certified gold by the RIAA.

Nov The double album, ***The Ventures' 10th Anniversary Album***, makes US #91. ***Hawaii Five-0*** will be certified gold by the RIAA on July 21st the following year.

1972

Mar While Edwards has returned to the fold following McGee's departure to join Delaney & Bonnie's band, ***Joy/The Ventures Play The Classics*** peaks at US #146, the last Ventures US chart album.

1981

With an estimated career sales tally of some 30 million discs, and after many years concentrating on their still-buoyant Japanese appeal, the Ventures, its line-up reverted to the quartet of Bogle, Wilson, Edwards and Taylor, record *Surfin' And Spyin'* (written by Charlotte Caffey of the Go-Go's). It is distributed mainly around the Californian surf music revival circuit, where they play live shows to huge acclaim. (A mainstay on the nostalgia circuit, the group is inducted into the Northwest Area Music Association's Hall Of Fame in April 1990 when EMI (US) releases ***Walk Don't Run : The Best Of The Ventures***, while a trusty 27-track CD retrospective, ***The Ventures Collection***, has already been issued in 1986 in the UK by Castle Communications.)

THE VILLAGE PEOPLE

Victor Willis (lead vocals); **David Hodo** (vocals); **Felipe Rose** (vocals); **Randy Jones** (vocals); **Glenn Hughes** (vocals); **Alex Briley** (vocals)

1977

Mar The group is formed by Jacques Morali, a French producer working in the US, after seeing costumed young men in New York gay discos. He conceives the idea of Village People visually representing six American male stereotypes: the cowboy, the Indian, the policeman, the biker, the G.I. and the construction worker. Beginning with go-go dancer Rose (b. Jan. 12, 1954), he hires actor/singers to perform his tailor-made disco songs behind lead singer, Willis, recruiting Hodo (b. July 7, 1947), Jones, Hughes (b. July 18, 1950, The Bronx, New York, NY) and Briley (b. Apr. 12, 1951). The name represents Greenwich Village, New York, from which the inspiration has come. Via his Can't Stop Productions, Morali signs the group to Casablanca Records in the US, and Mercury/ Phonogram for the rest of the world, and will produce and co-write (either with Willis and Henri Belolo, or Phil Hurtt and Pete Whitehead) all of its material.

Oct Their debut album, ***Village People***, reaches US #54 during an 86-week chart stay.

Dec A disco hit in the US, the group's first single, *San Francisco (You've Got Me)*, makes UK #45.

1978

May The group is heard on the soundtrack of the Casablanca/Motown-produced disco movie, "Thank God It's Friday", singing the gay anthem, *I Am What I Am*, and *Hollywood*.

Aug [26] The group performs in Ontario, Canada, at the first Canada Jam festival, before 80,000 people, sharing the bill with the Commodores, Kansas, Earth, Wind & Fire, Dave Mason and the Atlanta Rhythm Section.
Sept [2] Unabashed disco/pop cut, the super-camp *Macho Man*, reaches US #25 and, despite its self-conscious (a tongue-in-cheek feature of subsequent singles also) gay idiom, will sell over a million copies. The album, ***Macho Man***, makes US #24, staying charted for 69 weeks.
[18] ***Village People*** is certified gold by the RIAA.
Oct [30] *Macho Man* is confirmed gold by the RIAA.
Dec [13] The still-rising follow-up album ***Cruisin'*** is ratified platinum by the RIAA.
[26] ***Macho Man*** is certified platinum by the RIAA.

1979

Jan [6] *Y.M.C.A.*, a disco smash with the ultimate camp lyric, tops the UK chart for the first of three weeks, selling 150,000 copies in one day at its retail peak, with eventual UK sales of almost 1,300,000 (one of Britain's top 25 all-time best-sellers to date).
[25] Yet-to-peak *Y.M.C.A.* is certified platinum by the RIAA.
Feb [3] *Y.M.C.A.* hits US #2.
Cruisin', which includes *Y.M.C.A.*, hits US #3 and reaches UK #24.
Mar [15] *In The Navy* is confirmed gold by the RIAA.
Apr [4] The still-climbing ***Go West*** is certified platinum by the RIAA.
May [19] *In The Navy* (which the US Navy considers using as a recruitment song until its full implications are pointed out) hits US #3, again selling over a million, and UK #2.
Go West, featuring *In The Navy*, hits US #8 and reaches UK #14.
July [7] Its title track, *Go West*, reaches US #45 and UK #15.
Sept Scottish comedian (and one-time folk singer) Billy Connolly makes UK #38 with a parody version of *In The Navy*, retitled *In The Brownies*.
Dec [15] *Ready For The '80s* peaks at US #52, ironically the group's final US hit single, while the double album, ***Live And Sleazy***, coupling a live album with a studio set, makes US #32. Willis leaves, and is replaced as lead singer by Ray Simpson (b. Jan. 15, 1952, New York), brother of Valerie Simpson (of writer/producer/performer duo, Ashford & Simpson).

1980

Sept *Can't Stop The Music* reaches UK #11, while the group co-stars with Valerie Perrine and Bruce Jenner in the movie of the same title. The soundtrack album, ***Can't Stop The Music***, featuring further Village People contributions, hits UK #9 and US #47.

1981

Aug The group has signed to RCA Records but ***Renaissance***, an attempt to change its visual image, with the stereotype macho men disappearing in favor of smooth, New Romantic types, peaks at US #138, the band's last US chart entry.

1982

Simpson leaves and is replaced by Miles Jaye (who will in turn go on to a successful R&B career in the mid '80s). With the fading of disco as a major commercial pop genre, the group loses its commercial appeal on disc, but as a performing unit with an ever-changing lineup, will continue to tour throughout the decade. *Sex Over The Phone*, taken from an album of the same name, will provide one last gasp at UK #59 in February 1985 with a ***Greatest Hits*** package bringing the Village People hits to compact disc in 1988.)

1994

May [28] After Morali has died of complications from AIDS, in Paris, France, at the age of 44 on November 15th, 1991, and with Village People still performing at nostalgia events into a new decade, the Pet Shop Boys' cover of *Go West* has hit UK #2 on Sept [18], 1993, helping to bring remixed material of the group's highlights back to the UK chart: *Y.M.C.A. '93 (Remix)* has reached #12 on Dec [4], 1993, preceding ***The Best Of Village People*** which charted for a week at #58 on Dec [18], while *In The Navy - 1994 Remixes* now debuts at its #36 peak.

GENE VINCENT

1956

Mar Vincent (b. Vincent Eugene Craddock, Feb. 11, 1935, Norfolk, VA), having left the US Navy with a serious leg injury, after a motorcycle accident as a despatch rider in May 1955 (his broken bones do not heal properly, because of too-rapid use, and he spends several months in hospital with his leg still in a plaster cast at year's end), married to 15-year old Ruth Ann Hand last month on February 11th (a union which will prove short-lived), hangs out at his local WCMS radio station, and occasionally sits in with the house band, the Virginians. Among the songs he sings is *Be-Bop-A-Lula*, purchased for $25 from fellow hospital patient, Donald Graves. WCMS DJ, "Sheriff" Tex Davis, notices the young singer, and arranges for him to make a demo tape containing that song, *Race With The Devil* and *I Sure Miss You*.
Apr Davis sends the demo to Ken Nelson of Capitol Records, who is on the look-out for another Elvis Presley. Vincent is signed to the company, after entering the label's "Elvis Soundalike Sweepstakes".
May [4] Nelson arranges for a recording session at Owen Bradley's Nashville, TN studio, using the same demo band: guitarists Cliff Gallup and Willie Williams, bass player Jack Neal and drummer Dickie Harrell, who become the Blue Caps, taking their name from President Eisenhower's favorite blue golf cap. The three demo songs are re-recorded, adding *Woman Love*.
June *Woman Love* is the first Gene Vincent & the Blue Caps release, but its B-side, *Be-Bop-A-Lula*, is the one to enter the US chart.
[4] Vincent & the Blue Caps play their first live gig, at Myrtle Beach, NC.
July [28] They make their first US national TV appearance on NBC-TV's "Perry Como Show".
Aug [2] *Be-Bop-A-Lula* hits US #7, bringing a sudden demand for extensive live work.
Woman Love is banned in the UK by the BBC, because of its suggestive lyrics, but *Be-Bop-A-Lula* climbs to UK #16.
Sept Williams quits the Blue Caps and is replaced by Paul Peek in time for a two-week residency in Washington, DC.
Oct ***Blue Jean Bop*** reaches US #16 (Vincent's only US album chart entry).
[25] The follow-up single, *Race With The Devil*, peaks at US #96 and makes UK #28. The strain of performing aggravates Vincent's leg (still in a plaster cast), but he ignores medical advice to slow down, and will go to Hollywood with the Blue Caps to film a slot performing *Be-Bop-A-Lula* for the movie, "The Girl Can't Help It". (The bottom of his plaster cast is disguised as a shoe by the studio's make-up department.)
Nov [8] *Blue Jean Bop* climbs to US #49, and makes UK #16.
Dec Gallup, who left the Blue Caps before the Hollywood movie, but returned to play on the recording of a second album, leaves for good, taking his influential and original guitar sound with him. (The line-up changes frequently, and there will be six different versions of the Blue Caps in two years.)

1957

Jan Vincent spends three weeks in a Norfolk hospital for treatment to his injured leg. He is also prevented from live work while a legal wrangle over his management is cleared up.
June He has a metal leg brace (which he will wear for the rest of his life) fitted, in place of his plaster cast. The new touring version of the Blue Caps (with drummer Harrell the only original) proves successful, with new lead guitarist Johnny Meeks.
Oct [5] *Lotta Lovin'*, coupled with *Wear My Ring*, climbs to US #13, as he makes an ecstatically-received tour of Australia, with Eddie Cochran and Little Richard.

1958

Jan [13] *Dance To The Bop* reaches US #23, after being performed on CBS-TV's "The Ed Sullivan Show". (It will be Vincent's last US hit.)
Mar Vincent and the band appear in the teen movie, "Hot Rod Gang" (UK title: "Fury Unleashed"). They record in Hollywood, with Vincent's friend (since touring together twice in 1957) Eddie Cochran moonlighting on (uncredited) backing vocals on the sessions.
Apr Vincent begins a US West Coast tour, which is followed by a 40-date trip around Canada. Vincent has trouble holding his group together, due to the exhausting pace on and (allegedly) off-stage, which has players constantly leaving to rest or keep themselves from going crazy. These worries, and a growing list of non-hit records take their toll on Vincent (who becomes increasingly moody and unreliable - particularly to DJs and the media - and begins to drink heavily).
Nov After a year without hits and with only low-paid Los Angeles, CA live gigs, the Blue Caps split, when Vincent abandons his group in mid-tour because he is unable to pay them three weeks' back wages. The Musicians Union withdraws his union card, and he moves with his new wife, Darlene Hicks, to the northwest, playing local gigs with pick-up bands.

1959

June Vincent meets and works with guitarist Jerry Merritt. With a new band, they play one of the first-ever rock tours of Japan, where they are enthusiastically welcomed.
Aug Regaining his card, Vincent returns to Los Angeles and records ***Crazy Times***, with Merritt on guitar, and session-men, including Sandy Nelson on drums and Jackie Kelso on saxophone. The album meets little success at a time when the US record industry is looking for clean, inoffensive pop stars. After more low-key live work, he moves to Europe, at the invitation of promoter Larry Parnes, and UK TV producer, Jack Good.
Dec [5] Vincent arrives in the UK, where his reputation remains high despite three years without hits, and receives an enthusiastic welcome from fans at London airport.
[6] He makes his UK live debut at the Tooting Granada, London, as a guest on Marty Wilde's show.
Vincent also appears on the UK TV rock show, "Boy Meets Girls", headlined by Wilde. In the US Vincent was urged to tone down his image, but TV producer Jack Good persuades him to dress entirely in black leather, and to emphasise his limp. Good gives him a residency on "Boy Meets Girls", and the image of the tortured black-leather rock rebel is created. He plays to a rapturous reception at the Paris Olympia, France, and well-received dates at military bases in Germany.

1960

Jan *Wild Cat* makes UK #21. Vincent plays a 12-date UK tour. Eddie Cochran flies to the UK, at Parnes' invitation, to co-headline a 12-week tour with him.
[16] Vincent and Cochran appear together on "Boy Meets Girls".
Feb While touring in Scotland, Vincent has a kilt and tam o'shanter made in Craddock tartan.
Mar [14-20] Vincent and Cochran headline a package at the Liverpool Empire, Liverpool, Lancs.
[19] *My Heart* reaches UK #16.
Apr [17] The car taking Vincent and Cochran to London Airport, at the end of their UK tour, in Bristol, Somerset, crashes, killing Cochran. With a broken collarbone, broken ribs and further damage to his leg, Vincent also suffers psychologically from the death of his closest professional friend.
May [11] After a short spell in hospital and a rest in the US, Vincent returns to Britain to make his first UK recording, at EMI's Abbey Road Studios, in London.

Backed by the Beat Boys (with Georgie Fame on piano), he cuts *Pistol Packin' Mama.*

June [12] Vincent cancels a UK variety tour and upcoming Blackpool summer season and flies back to New York, claiming he had a telegram telling him that his 18-month old daughter Melody had died from pneumonia. It subsequently transpires that Vincent has made up the whole story.

July *Pistol Packin' Mama* reaches UK #15 as ***Crazy Times*** peaks at UK #12 (his only UK chart album).

1961

May He tours South Africa for the first time, playing with the Mickie Most Band.

July To coincide with another UK visit, *She She Little Sheila*, recorded in 1959 at the ***Crazy Times*** sessions, reaches UK #22.

Sept *I'm Going Home*, taped in London with backing by the UK group, Sounds Incorporated, makes UK #36 (his last UK chart single, despite impressive ongoing live form).

1962

Mar [31] He begins a UK tour with Brenda Lee at the Brighton Essoldo, Brighton, Sussex, and performs *Spaceship To Mars*, accompanied by Sounds Incorporated (and dressed wholly in white, rather than his customary all-black leathers), in the UK pop movie, "It's Trad, Dad!" (US title: "Ring-A-Ding-Rhythm".)

July [1] Vincent stars at Liverpool's Cavern club, on a bill featuring up-and-coming local group, the Beatles.

Nov [21] He begins another UK trek with Adam Faith, set to end on December 9th at the De Montfort Hall, Leicester, Leics.

1963

Apr [22] His recording contract with Capitol expires, and is not renewed. His last recording, at Abbey Road, with Charles Blackwell's orchestra, is an inferior remake of *Be-Bop-A-Lula*.

1964

Mar [20] He begins a UK tour, with Carl Perkins, on a package headlined by the Animals.

Oct ***Shakin' Up A Storm***, recorded in London, is issued on EMI's Columbia label.

Dec [31] Vincent flies back to the US to spend New Year with his parents.

1965

Mar [17] He enters the Royal National Ear, Nose & Throat Hospital, Gray's Inn Road, London for an emergency operation.

July He begins a three-month UK seaside summer season, at South Pier Theatre, Blackpool, Lancs., backed by UK group, the Puppets.

Dec Vincent is ordered to pay £675 to manager Don Arden for breach of contract.

1966

July He records in a country style for Challenge Records in Los Angeles. (***Bird-Doggin'*** will be released in the UK only, in 1967.)

1969

Sept [13] Vincent performs at the Toronto Rock'n'Roll Festival, Toronto, ON, Canada, with several of his contemporaries, and newer acts like the Doors and John Lennon's Plastic Ono Band, but is overshadowed by performances from Chuck Berry and Jerry Lee Lewis. He returns for more British dates, backed by the Wild Angels, and is the subject of a BBC-TV documentary, "The Rock'n'Roll Singer".

1970

Feb The critically-revered ***I'm Back And I'm Proud***, mixing rock and country, is released on the Dandelion label, run by life-long Vincent fan and UK BBC radio DJ, John Peel.

Apr He signs in the US to Kama Sutra Records, and records two country albums, ***Gene Vincent*** and ***The Day The World Turned Blue***, which are well reviewed, but sell poorly. His personal life declines in keeping with his lack of commercial success, with ever-present management and ex-wife problems causing constant depression, accentuated by heavier drinking, which adversely affects his previously consistent stage form. His fourth wife leaves him.

Sept [1] He records five songs at the BBC Radio studios in Maida Vale, London, with backing by UK band, Kansas Hook, before embarking on what will be a chaotic UK tour.

[12] Having returned to the US to scrape some money together, Vincent dies in hospital in Newhall, CA, from a bleeding ulcer, aged 36. The most eloquent tribute - apart from covers of *Be-Bop-A-Lula* by major artists like John Lennon, and widespread aping of his leather-clad tough rocker image - will be Ian Dury's 1977 song, *Sweet Gene Vincent*. A career retrospective, ***The Best Of Gene Vincent & His Blue Caps***, will be released on CD in 1988, with an alternative selection made available in 1991 by Capitol Records in the US with ***Gene Vincent***.

BOBBY VINTON

1960

Vinton (b. Stanley Robert Vinton, Apr. 16, 1935, Canonsburg, PA), the son of a band leader, having formed his own big band in high school (he drops his first name because of confusion over which Stanley Vinton Band, his or his father's, was wanted for bookings), played trumpet while at Duquesne University, in the Hi-Lites, with Mike Lazo and Gene Schachter, who became the Tempos. Posted to Fort Dix, KY (and then Dix, NJ), in the US Army, he continues to play in the Tempos, now a military band with two new recruits, before putting together a group of his own, once he is out of the service. They play a gig on Arthur Godfrey's "TV Talent Scouts", which leads to slot on "The Fall Edition Of The Biggest Show Of Stars For 1960" US tour, providing the musical accompaniment for Chubby Checker, Brenda Lee, Fabian and Jimmy Clanton, before securing an engagement as both a back-up unit and featured outfit on a Dick Clark "Caravan Of Stars" US trek. On a concert stop in Pittsburgh, PA, Vinton records a single for local DJ, Dick Lawrence, who intends to place it with a label. Epic Records passes on the disc, but is interested in Vinton's band, and he is signed to a two-album contract by Jim Fogelsong, which yields ***Dancing At The Hop*** and ***Bobby Vinton Plays For His L'il Darlin's*** (1961).

1962

Apr With neither band album having sold, Vinton is to be dropped, but still owes the label two single sides. In favor of a band arrangement, he records a country-style version of a song found on a demo, *Roses Are Red*, co-penned by Paul Evans and produced by Bob Morgan, and *Mr. Lonely* (written while he was in the army). To promote the record, Vinton drives around with copies of the single to sell directly to shops, and gives away roses to radio stations.

July [14] *Roses Are Red* tops the US chart, where it will stay for four weeks, eventually selling over three million copies (Epic's first #1 hit), and Vinton's recording contract is renewed. Although he will do further big-band work, and continue to play trumpet at live gigs, on disc he will stick to the middle-of-the-road vocal slot which *Roses Are Red* has established for him.

Aug [13] *Roses Are Red* is certified gold by the RIAA (multi-certifications are not currently used).

[25] *Roses Are Red* reaches UK #15, beaten by a cover version from the UK's Ronnie Carroll, which hits #3. During the month, Vinton also headlines at the Fox Theater, Brooklyn.

Sept ***Roses Are Red*** hits US #5, while Vinton visits the UK.

[29] *I Love You The Way You Are*, a 1960 recording which Lawrence has dusted off and sold to Diamond Records after the success of *Roses Are Red*, reaches US #38.

Oct [6] *Rain Rain Go Away*, from ***Roses Are Red***, reaches US #12, while he tours New Zealand with Gene Pitney.

1963

Jan ***Bobby Vinton Sings The Big Ones*** peaks at US #137.

[19] Double A-side, *Trouble Is My Middle Name/Let's Kiss And Make Up*, makes US #33 and UK #38.

Apr [27] His revival of Johnnie & Joe's *Over The Mountain (Across The Sea)* reaches US #21.

July [6] *Blue On Blue*, submitted by Burt Bacharach for Vinton, hits US #3, and earns him his second gold disc.

Sept [21] *Blue Velvet*, previously a 1951 US #16 hit for Tony Bennett, now arranged by Bacharach and recorded in Nashville, TN, with stellar musicians including Floyd Cramer, Charlie McCoy and Grady Martin, tops the US chart for the first of three weeks, becoming another million-seller. ***Blue Velvet***, on which all the songs are concerned with the color blue, hits US #10.

Dec [7] The Beatles, appearing on BBC-TV's "Juke Box Jury", vote Vinton's new single, *There! I've Said It Again*, a miss. (Eight weeks later, the group's *I Want To Hold Your Hand* will knock the song off the top of the US chart, marking the beginning of the Beatles' dominance of the American pop scene.)

Vinton stars in the movie, "Surf Party", with Jackie De Shannon and Patricia Morrow, and appears on NBC-TV's "The Tonight Show". (Previously overseen by Alan Bregman while living in Los Angeles, Allen Klein now becomes his manager, as Vinton moves to New York where, performing at the Copacabana club, Klein has arranged for a Times Square billboard to hail "Bigger Than Life - Bobby Vinton".)

1964

Jan [4] *There! I've Said It Again*, his update of Vaughn Monroe's 1945 US #1, recorded by Vinton in one take, begins a four-week run at US #1 (holding the Kingsmen's *Louie Louie* at #2). It earns Vinton's fourth gold disc, as he begins a two-week residency at the Town & Country Club, Brooklyn, NY.

[18] *There! I've Said It Again* makes UK #34 - his second and final UK hit of the decade.

Mar [8, 22] Vinton guests on CBS-TV's "The Ed Sullivan Show".

[28] *My Heart Belongs To Only You*, reviving June Christy's 1953 US #22, hits US #9, as ***There! I've Said It Again***, containing both the title track and the new single, hits US #8.

June [20] *Tell Me Why*, a remake of Eddy Howard's 1949 US #25 hit, and subsequently charted by the Four Aces (US #2) and Eddie Fisher (US #4) in 1952, reaches US #13.

Aug ***Tell Me Why*** climbs to US #31.

Sept [12] *Clinging Vine* reaches US #17.

Nov Compilation album, ***Bobby Vinton's Greatest Hits***, reaches US #12, earning a gold disc for half a million sales.

Dec [12] The self-penned *Mr. Lonely*, originally recorded alongside *Roses Are Red*, and used as a track on the album of that title, has been belatedly released, after an earlier cover version by Buddy Greco has failed, and tops the US chart for a week, becoming another million seller.

1965

Feb ***Mr. Lonely*** reaches US #18.

Apr Vinton re-records *Don't Go Away Mad* in London, under the direction of Mickie Most.

[10] His remake of Lee Andrews & the Hearts' 1957 doo-wop classic *Long Lonely Nights*, reaches US #17.

June [5] *L-O-N-E-L-Y* reaches US #22.

[26] Having been temporarily refused a UK work permit (a retaliation against visa restrictions imposed on UK artists by US authorities), papers are finally issued allowing Vinton to appear on BBC-TV's "Juke Box Jury".

July ***Bobby Vinton Sings For Lonely Nights*** makes US #116.

Aug [7] *Theme From Harlow (Lonely Girl)*, from the Carroll Baker-starring movie, "Harlow", peaks at US #61.

Oct [16] Protest song, *What Color (Is A Man?)*, makes US #38.

1966

Jan [15] *Satin Pillows*, which sees Vinton return to his most romantic style, reaches US #23.

Feb ***Satin Pillows And Careless*** makes US #110.

Mar [19] His cover of Ken Dodd's UK million seller, *Tears*, peaks at US #59.

May [28] *Dum-De-Da* makes US #40.

Aug [20] *Petticoat White (Summer Sky Blue)* peaks at US #81.

Dec [12] ***Bobby Vinton's Greatest Hits*** is certified gold by the RIAA.

1967

Jan [7] *Coming Home Soldier* reaches US #11.

Apr [1] His version of the traditional sing-a-long *For He's A Jolly Good Fellow* makes US #66.

May [27] *Red Roses For Mum* wilts at US #95.

Nov [18] *Please Love Me Forever*, a Billy Sherrill-produced remake of Tommy Edwards' 1958 US #61 charter, revived to US #12 by Cathy Jean & the Roommates in 1961, and reprising Vinton's *There! I've Said It Again*-style, hits US #6.

1968

Feb [10] *Just As Much As Ever* (a US #32 hit for Bob Beckman in 1959) reaches US #24, as ***Please Love Me Forever*** makes US #41.

Apr [20] Vinton's revival of Bobby Vee's 1961 chart-topper, *Take Good Care Of My Baby*, makes US #33.

June ***Take Good Care Of My Baby*** makes US #164.

Aug [24] Another revived 1961 Goffin/King song, *Halfway To Paradise*, a US #39 for Tony Orlando and UK #3 for Billy Fury, reaches US #23.

Dec [14] Vinton's update of *I Love How You Love Me* (a 1962 Phil Spector-produced US #5 hit by the Paris Sisters) hits US #9.

[19] *I Love How You Love Me* is certified gold by the RIAA, his sixth million-seller. (During the year, Vinton loses out on recording *Raindrops Keep Falling On My Head* by asking for too much money. He does, however, appear in the John Wayne movie, "Big Jake", and "The Train Robbers".)

1969

Feb ***I Love How You Love Me*** reaches US #21.

May [3] Another updated oldie, the Teddy Bears' hit, *To Know You Is To Love You*, makes US #34.

June ***Vinton*** peaks at US #69.

July [12] *The Days Of Sand And Shovels* stops at US #34.

1970

Jan ***Bobby Vinton's Greatest Hits Of Love*** peaks at US #138.

Mar [14] His version of *My Elusive Dreams* (a country duet hit for David Houston and Tammy Wynette) makes US #46.

Apr ***My Elusive Dreams*** peaks at US #90.

Aug [1] *No Arms Can Ever Hold You*, originally a US #23 for Georgie Shaw in 1955, and subsequently bringing success for Pat Boone (US #26 - 1955), the Gaylords (US #67 - 1955) and the Bachelors (UK #7 and US #27 - 1965), peaks at US #93.

1972

Apr [29] *Every Day Of My Life*, reviving the McGuire Sisters' 1956 US #37 original, reaches US #24, as ***Ev'ry Day Of My Life*** makes US #72.

Aug [19] His treatment of Brian Hyland's 1962 original, *Sealed With A Kiss*, reaches US #19, its parent album, ***Sealed With A Kiss***, peaking at US #77, while ***Bobby Vinton's All-Time Greatest Hits*** makes US #119. After selling more than 30 million records, Epic drops him from the label. A final Epic remnant, *But I Do*, will make US #82 on Feb [3] the following year.

1974

Nov [16] Vinton has signed a new recording deal with ABC Records, and returned to his original producer, Bob Morgan, who is currently working in real estate. The result is his first million-selling single for six years, *My Melody Of Love* (partly sung in Polish - a bow to his own ancestry), and turned down by seven labels, which hits US #3. The ABC issued album, ***Melodies Of Love***, reaches US #16.

Dec ***With Love*** makes US #109.

[5] The RIAA certifies gold sales of *My Melody Of Love* and ***Melodies Of Love***.

[29] Vinton makes his venue debut at Carnegie Hall, New York.

1975

Jan [18] Chicago Mayor Richard Daley declares "Bobby Vinton Day", making him an honorary citizen, and awards him the city's Certificate Of Merit. In the evening, he plays before a 20,000 sellout crowd at Chicago Stadium, where he is crowned "The Polish Prince". (Soon after, Zbigniew Dembowski, the Polish consul-general in New York, hosts a ball in his honor at the consulate.)

Vinton begins a syndicated weekly musical variety show on US TV (which will air until 1978.)

Apr [19] *Beer Barrel Polka*, a disco-styled revival of Will Glahe's 1939 US chart-topper and the Andrews Sisters' 1939 US #4, backed with *Dick And Jane*, makes US #33.

July [12] Vinton's remake of Elvis Presley's *Wooden Heart* peaks at US #58, as ***Bobby Vinton Sings The Golden Decade Of Love***, released by Epic, and featuring songs from the '50s, climbs to US #154. Meanwhile, the ABC album, ***Heart Of Hearts***, reaches US #108.

1976

Jan [24] ***The Bobby Vinton Show*** makes US #161.

May [8] *Moonlight Serenade*, reviving Glenn Miller's 1939 US #3, stops at US #97.

June [12] Vinton's version of *Save Your Kisses For Me*, a cover of Brotherhood Of Man's UK million seller (and winner of the 1976 "Eurovision Song Contest"), peaks at US #75. *Only Love Can Break A Heart* will make US #99 on June [4] the following year, as ***The Name Is Love*** makes US #183. In 1978, Duquesne University will award Vinton an honorary doctorate of music.

1980

Jan [12] After another quiet period, Vinton, now signed to the Tapestry label, makes US #78 with *Make Believe It's Your First Time*, his final US chart outing. In 1986, his version of *Blue Velvet* will be used as the theme for the movie of the same title, and three years later Sergiusz Mikulicz, head of Poland's radio and TV ministry, will approve the playing of Vinton's *Santa Must Be Polish* on state radio in December.

1990

Oct Vinton unexpectedly hits UK #2 (though widely touted as #1 on UK's Network Singles chart) as *Blue Velvet*, in its original 1963 form, benefits from UK TV commercial exposure for Nivea face cream. Vinton subsequently cuts *What Did You Do With Your Old 45s* on a new album, ***Timeless***, and updates his own *Mr Lonely (Letter To A Soldier)*, on Curb Records.

Nov [17] *Roses Are Red (My Love)* reissue peaks at UK #71.

[24] A hastily-packaged Epic album, ***Blue Velvet***, makes UK #67.

1996

Apr [13] Living in semi-retirement in California, and still earning considerable income from occasional US cabaret engagements, Vinton, having duetted on *I Know What It Is To Be Old* with the 96-year old veteran comedian on George Burns' ***As Time Goes By*** in 1992, has opened the Bobby Vinton Blue Velvet Theater in Branson, MO in June the following year (the original opening was delayed after the building had fallen down a week into construction), and released ***Kissin' Christmas***, an album of all-new recordings, Vinton returns to the US chart for a week at #199 with ***16 Most Requested Songs*** on the strength of a promotion on the QVC home-shopping network.

W

JOHN WAITE

1975

Waite (b. July 4, 1954, Lancaster, Lancs.) is already a veteran of a number of bands when he is invited by the manager of UK rock act the Babys, which already includes guitarist Mike Corby (b. July 3, 1955, UK), guitarist Wally Stocker (b. Mar. 17, 1954, London) and drummer Tony Brock (b. Mar. 31, 1954, Bournemouth, Dorset) to join the group as its bassist, vocalist and co-songwriter. Waite, who has played bass, harmonica and sung vocals since he was 14, has formed the short-lived outfit Graf Spee whilst studying graphic design at Lancaster Art College before briefly relocating to West Hampstead to live in a 10' x 8' room, during which he is a three-month recruit of rock unit England, having left Lancaster wrongly accused by the local police of involvement in a jewel robbery. After a brief stint in another rock outfit, the Boys, based in Cleveland, OH, at the instigation of an England colleague, Waite has returned once again to London and, having joined the Babys, fronts an expensive Mike Mansfield-directed promo video which, even without a traditional audio demo tape, secures the group a lucrative (Waite describes it as "elephant dollars") contract with Chrysalis Records.

1976

During its five-year history, Waite will co-write and sing on the majority of Babys' hits which are projected firmly at the American market (they will only make UK #45 in February 1978 with *Isn't It Time*). While personnel changes will see Jonathan Cain (b. Feb. 26, 1950, Chicago, IL) replace Corby in 1977 and Ricky Phillips join as a main bassist allowing Waite to feature more prominently up front in 1979, the Babys will garner eight US chart singles (1977's *If You've Got The Time* #88 and their biggest hit, the power ballad *Isn't It Time* #13, 1978's *Silver Dreams* #53, 1979's *Every Time I Think Of You* #13 and three final entries in 1980, *Back On My Feet Again* #33, *Midnight Rendezvous* #72 and *Turn And Walk Away* #42. US album successes begin with ***The Babys*** #133 and ***Broken Heart***, both released in 1977, 1979's ***Head First*** #22, 1980's ***Union Jacks*** #42 and the final ***On The Edge*** #71. (Many producers will cut their teeth on these projects, including Ron Nevison and Keith Olsen.)

1980

Dec [9] The day after John Lennon's murder in New York, Waite, performing with the Babys in Cincinnati, OH on the group's farewell US tour, is pulled off stage by a member of the audience, damaging the cartilage in his knee and forcing him to complete his last Babys project on crutches.

1981

With the Babys officially split (Cain will travel on to Journey, Stocker will join Air Supply) and the retrospective ***Anthology*** peaking at US #138, Waite returns to the UK and spends six months writing songs at his Lake District home, recently bought with his girlfriend.

1982

July Still signed to Chrysalis, Waite's debut solo album ***Ignition***, recorded in New York, is released, set to reach US #68, where he, both as a solo artist and group member, will remain most popular.

1984

July Following a period of semi-retirement, Waite, newly signed to EMI America, issues ***No Brakes***, co-produced with David Thoener and Gary Gersh. It will eventually hit US #10, and is released at a time when Waite is appearing as a hairdresser in the hit ABC-TV series "Paper Dolls", co-starring Morgan Fairchild.
Sept [22] The extracted ballad *Missing You*, featuring Waite's powerful rock vocal over an Andy Summers' recalling rhythm-guitar pick, co-written by Waite about his relationship with his Lake District belle, hits US #1 and will also hit UK #9.
Nov *No Brakes* peaks at UK #64, his first and only native album score as either a solo or group act, while the US follow-up *Tears* makes US #37.

1985

Feb The third extract *Restless Heart* peaks at US #59.
Apr Resurrected from his debut album and now featured in the movie soundtrack to "Vision Quest", *Change* makes US #54.
Sept As Waite embarks on a lengthy US tour, ***Mask Of Smiles*** begins a chart rise to US #38.
[28] Its lead-off single *Every Step Of The Way* reaches US #25.
Nov *Welcome To Paradise* peaks at US #85.

1986

July [17] While he is recording a new album at the Right Track Studios, New York, with producer Frank Fillipetti, *If Anybody Had A Heart*, chosen for the "About Last Night" Rob Lowe/Demi Moore-starring movie soundtrack compiled by Bones Howe, makes US #76.
Aug [22-24] John Waite & the No Brakes Band play at the three-day 24th annual "Reading Festival", Reading, Berks.

1987

Aug [1] Co-written with Bon Jovi collaborator Desmond Child, *These Times Are Hard For Lovers* peaks at US #53, while its parent album ***Rover's Return***, named after the pub featured in Waite's favorite ITV soap opera "Coronation Street", climbs to US #77, with Maria Vidal the featured guest vocalist.
Oct [10] Extracted *Don't Lose Any Sleep* peaks at US #81. Without a major hit since 1984, Waite leaves EMI America.

1988

Oct Reunited with ex-Babys Phillips (bass) and Cain (keyboards), Waite forms a rock supergroup with Cain's Journey colleague, guitarist Neal Schon (b. Feb. 27, 1954, San Mateo, CA). Together with drummer Dean Castronova, Bad English, based around a hard rock AOR Waite vocal-led style, signs to CBS/ Columbia Records to cut its debut album.

1989

Aug [26] Bad English's chart debut, the rock-driven *Forget Me Not* makes US #45.
Nov [11] Power ballad, *When I See You Smile*, written by Diane Warren and highlighted by Waite's soaring rock vocal, hits US #1 for the first of two weeks, while their debut album ***Bad English***, produced by Richard Zito, climbs to US #21 and platinum certification.

1990

Mar [10] *Price Of Love*, co-written by Waite and Cain, hits US #5.
[21] The group embarks on a major US tour, supporting Whitesnake, in Pensacola, FL.
Apr [28] A fourth extract *Heaven Is A Four Letter Word* peaks at US #66.
June [29] Its US tour comes to an end in Weedsport, NY.
Aug [18] *Possession* reaches US #21.

1991

Sept The group's follow-up set, the aptly titled ***Backlash*** peaks at US #72, yielding only the US #42 *Straight To The Heart*. Bad English's short career ends the following year with Waite going on to work with hard-rock outfit Vandenberg (with Phillips and Castronovo working with David Coverdale and Jimmy Page and Schon forming Hardline).

1995

Mar After a reissued *Missing You* has debuted at its UK #56 peak on Feb [13], 1993, Waite releases his first solo album of the '90s, ***Temple Bar***.

TOM WAITS

1971

July Having joined the Systems soul group at high school, which he dropped out of at the age of 16 to work at Napoleon's Pizza House, Waits (b. Dec. 7, 1949, in the back of a taxi cab in the parking lot at Murphy Hospital, Pamona, CA) sang and played professionally in his late teens and early 20s on the accordion and piano in San Diego, CA, and Los Angeles, CA bars and dives. The singer/songwriter/pianist, now a popular local performer on the Los Angeles blues and rock club circuit, is spotted by his future manager, Herb Cohen, performing at the famous Los Angeles Troubadour haunt, playing his own subterranean brand of songs on "Amateur Hoots Nights". He now records a number of Robert Duffey-produced demos through December (which will emerge in 1991 on ***The Early Years***, via Bizarre Records (US) and Edsel (UK)), which leads to his signing to David Geffen's Asylum Records.

1973

May His debut album, ***Closing Time***, produced by Jerry Yester, is released, arousing critical acclaim and modest sales, and prompts opening live slots for the likes of Charlie Rich and Frank Zappa, which are mostly ill-received.

1974

Jan Waits has teamed with producer Bones Howe for his newly-released sophomore effort, ***The Heart Of Saturday Night***. The self-penned, raconteurial tracks reveal a hardened, whiskey-soaked, throaty vocal-style, confirming his legendary beatnik lifestyle of "liquor, girls, liquor and more liquor".

June Labelmates the Eagles' ***On The Border***, including a cover of Waits' *Ol' 55*, is released, set to reach US #17. It becomes Waits' first compositional success, though he will later claim "the only good thing about an Eagles LP is that it keeps the dust off your turntable".

1975

Nov Waits, after five years living in different motels, has settled on a permanent residence at the Tropicano Motel in West Hollywood, CA, where he has a piano installed in the kitchen. He releases the double album, ***Nighthawks At The Diner***, recorded live in the studio before an invited audience, which enters the US chart at #164, and, by year's end, has the word "nighthawk" tattooed on his right arm.

1976

June On his first ever visit to the UK, he performs at Ronnie Scott's jazz club, in London.

Nov The Howe-produced ***Small Change*** makes US #89, spurred by constant US touring. Continuing his highly literate documentary of bottom-line Americana, it features a mixture of original jazz blues with lush "bad lives and broken heart" ballads.

1977

Oct ***Foreign Affairs***, featuring *I Never Talk To Strangers*, a wry, bar-stool located, duet ballad with Bette Midler, makes US #113. With string arrangements by Yester, Waits is backed by Jim Hughart (bass), Shelly Manne (drums) and Lew Tabackin (tenor sax).

1978

June Waits begins an acting career with a bit part in Sylvester Stallone's premiering "Paradise Alley".

Nov ***Blue Valentine***, recorded on a two-track tape during six days with Howe at the desk (and featuring some-time girlfriend, Rickie Lee Jones, on the back cover), peaks at US #181, but once again, garners substantial critical praise.

1979

Apr [21] He performs at the London Palladium.

1980

Oct Waits has recorded his final album for Asylum, ***Heartattack And Vine***, which charts at US #96. It features *Jersey Girl*, which will become an integral part of Bruce Springsteen's live sets throughout the decade. Waits is quoted as saying: "I'm so broke I can't even pay attention."

1981

Dec [31] He marries Irish playwright, Kathleen Brennan, whom he met while working on the soundtrack to the Francis Ford Coppola film, "One From The Heart", at the Always and Forever Wedding Chapel, Manchester Boulevard, Los Angeles.

1982

June After 18 months' work, his soundtrack album, ***One From The Heart***, featuring Crystal Gayle, is released through CBS/Columbia. It is Waits' final work with producer Bones Howe, and also marks the end of a certain musical style for the songwriter, not least in the area of lushly-orchestrated ballads. The soundtrack receives an Oscar nomination.

1983

Mar Having made various cameo acting appearances since 1978, including "Wolfen", "Stone Boy" and "One From The Heart", Waits now features in "The Outsiders", with Matt Dillon, followed by Coppola's "Rumblefish". Asylum releases three compilations during the year: the double set, ***The Asylum Years***, ***Bounced Check***, which includes the previously unreleased *Mr. Henry*, and ***Anthology***.

July Rickie Lee Jones 10" mini-album, ***Girl At Her Volcano***, including the Waits' composition, *Angel Wings*, reaches US #39.

Oct Waits' daughter, Kellesimone, is born. His debut for Island Records, the self-produced ***Swordfishtrombones***, makes US #167 and UK #62, the first of three concept albums loosely based around *Frank's Wild Years*, a featured track, which marks a serious change of musical direction which Waits describes as "sounding like a demented parade band".

1985

June Having appeared in another cameo role in Coppola's film, "The Cotton Club", and contributed a cover version of *What Keeps Man Alive* to an A&M released Kurt Weill tribute album, ***Lost In The Stars*** the previous year, Waits moves from Los Angeles to New York, NY, claiming "it's a great town for shoes".

Sept The Waits' son, Casey Xavier, is born. Waits' first-choice name, Senator Waits, is rejected by Kathleen.

Oct He undertakes a sold-out US and European tour to promote his second Island album, the self-penned and produced ***Raindogs***, which makes UK #29 and US #181. Guest musicians on the release include Keith Richards (whom Waits claims is "a relative I met in a lingerie shop"), while boxing legend, Jake La Motta, appears in the video for the single, *Downtown Train*.

1986

June His musical, "Frank's Wild Years", written with his wife, opens at the Steppenwolf Theater Company in Chicago, IL, and later moves to New York. He also plays a jail-breaking, unemployed disc jockey in his first starring role, in the black and white film, "Down By Law".

1987

Sept [5] ***Frank's Wild Years***, featuring many songs from the musical and completing the trilogy started in 1983, reaches UK #20 in its week of entry, and will make US #115.

[30] "A Black And White Night", a club concert at which Roy Orbison is backed by a cast of star admirers, including Waits, takes place at the Coconut Grove, Ambassador Hotel in Los Angeles.

Nov Waits visits the UK to perform songs from the musical and others, at sellout concerts, including London's Dominion Theatre, which receive ecstatic reviews.

1988

Oct ***Big Time***, recorded live in Berlin, West Germany, Dublin, Eire, Los Angeles, San Francisco, CA, and Stockholm, Sweden, with backing musicians Michael Blair (drums), Ralph Carney (saxophone), Greg Cohen (bass), Marc Ribot (guitars) and Willie Schwarz (keyboards), peaks at US #152, and spends a week on the UK chart at #84 (Oct [8]). (The "Big Time" performance movie also premieres.)

Nov ***Stay Awake***, a Disney compilation of kids' favorites, to which he has contributed *Heigh-Ho (The Dwarfs' Marching Song)*, makes US #119. He begins work on a new film project in Montana (which follows his successful portrayal of a dying street-bum in the Nicholson/Streep movie, "Ironweed"). Looking to the future, Waits insists that his gravestone epitaph read: "I told you I was sick."

1989

Waits sings the end title theme to the Al Pacino/Ellen Barkin thriller, "Sea Of Love", reviving Paul Phillips' 1959 US #2, and continues his acting career, starring in "Cold Feet" with Keith Carradine and Sally Kirkland.

1990

Jan [27] Waits has his biggest success as a writer when Rod Stewart hits US #3 with *Downtown Train* (also currently covered by Everything But The Girl).

Mar [3] Stewart's *Downtown Train* hits UK #10.

Apr [10] Waits' lawsuit against Frito-Lay and Tracy-Locke for using a Waits-soundalike in radio ads for Doritos chips begins. A Los Angeles jury will award Waits $2,475,000 in punitive damages. Waits comments: "Now by law I have what I always felt I had . . . a distinctive voice."

June [1] Thrash-jazz trio Primus' ***Sailing The Seas Of Chease***, with Waits featured as the voice of the cat on *Tommy The Cat*, enters the US chart set to make #116.

Dec [31] He performs a sellout New Year's Eve concert at the Orpheum Theatre in San Francisco, where he now lives.

1992

May [30] Having recently contributed to the movie soundtrack to "Night On Earth", Waits plays an hour-long benefit concert, on a bill also featuring Fishbone, at the Wiltern Theatre, Los Angeles, to show support in rebuilding the riot-torn sections of the city.

Sept [19] ***Bone Machine***, co-produced with his wife, and featuring Keith Richards, David Hidalgo and Les Claypool, debuts at its UK #26 peak.

[26] ***Bone Machine*** enters at its US #176 high, during a three week chart stay.

Oct [9] He performs on syndicated TV's "The Arsenio Hall Show". (During the year, Waits has written the score for an "Alice In Wonderland" stage show in Hamburg, Germany, and cut a version of *Brother Can You Spare A Dime* to support the national fund-raising day of action by the National Coalition for the Homeless in the US. His acting career continues to blossom, with roles in "Bram Stoker's Dracula" (in the part of Renfield), having also appeared in "The Fisher King", "At Play In The Fields Of The Lord" and "Queen's Logic".)

1993

Feb [24] Waits wins his first Grammy, as ***Bone Machine*** is named Best Alternative Music, at the 35th annual Grammy Awards, held at the Shrine Auditorium, Los Angeles.

Mar [29] He sues his music publishers, Third Story Music, in the Los Angeles Superior Court, claiming that they violated a 1980 ammendment to his 1977 contract, stating they "may not grant the rights to use a composition in commercials ... without (Waits') consent ...". Third Story has recently licensed *Heart-attack And Vine* for a UK Levi Jeans commercial (re-cut by Screamin' Jay Hawkins) and *Ruby's Arms* for a

French Williams Gel commercial. Third Story countersues.
Nov [20] Waits' ***Black Rider***, written with Robert Wilson and William Burroughs, debuts at its UK #47 and US #130 peak.
Dec His collaborative avant-garde theatrical opera-piece "The Black Rider", on which the album has been based, enjoys a two-week run at New York's Brooklyn Academy.

1995

June [6] Also featured in the cult film, alongside Harvey Keitel, William Hurt and Ashley Judd among others, the soundtrack to "Smoke", including a new cut by Waits, is released in the US.
Sept [12] Holly Cole's ***Temptation***, entirely comprised of her interpretations of Waits' material, is issued in the US by Blue Note Records. (It follows Sarah McLachlan's reading of Waits' *Ol' 55* on the January release of the soundtrack to "Boys On The Side", and precedes Meat Loaf's treatment of his early chestnut, *Martha*, which will emerge on Loaf's November-released ***Welcome To The Neighborhood***).
Dec [2] ***Music From The Motion Picture 12 Monkeys***, including the fresh Waits' track *Earth Dies Screaming*, is released.
[23] A one-page apology ad appears in this week's **Billboard** magazine in which the Levi Strauss company expresses regret for using Screamin' Jay Hawkins' version of Waits' *Heart Attack And Vine* without authorization for a Levi's 501 jeans commercial campaign (titled "Procession") broadcast in 17 countries between January and June 1993. Levi's claims it was "unaware of Mr. Waits' objections to such usage of his composition".

1996

Jan [9] While Waits completes work on his next album, due in the summer, Columbia Records (US) releases ***Music From And Inspired By The Motion Picture Dead Man Walking***, including his *Fall Of Troy* and *Walk Away*, both written specifically for the project.

JR. WALKER & THE ALL-STARS

Jr. Walker (saxophone, vocals);
Willie Woods (guitar); **Vic Thomas** (organ);
James Graves (drums)

1961

Four high-school friends form a jazz/R&B-styled band to play the South Bend, IN club circuit. The group's leader is the ex-construction worker, and Earl Bostic-influenced saxophonist, Walker (b. Autry DeWalt Jr. 1931, Blythesville, AR, not in 1942, a legend perpetuated by his record label during his early career), called Junior by his stepfather, while the backing combo's name arises from an occasion when, as they perform a jazz number at a club, a customer shouts out: "these guys are all stars". Noticed by Johnny Bristol at a club date the following year, he recommends them to ex-Moonglow, Harvey Fuqua, in Detroit, MI, who signs Walker and the All-Stars to his Harvey label, and releases three of the band's instrumental singles during 1962. After Fuqua's labels are absorbed into Berry Gordy's Motown conglomerate, Jr. Walker & the All-Stars are re-signed by Gordy, and placed on the Soul label in 1964.

1965

Jan Playing a benefit show in Benton Harbor, MI, Walker sees two teenagers performing an unfamiliar dance, which they call the Shotgun. Walker pens a booting dance tune with that title in his motel room, and records it back in the studio in Detroit.
Mar [13] An immediate success, *Shotgun* tops the US R&B chart for the first of four weeks.
Apr *Shotgun* crosses over to hit US #4, becoming a million seller.
July A celebration of another dance, *Do The Boomerang* reaches US #36.
Aug His first Soul album, ***Shotgun***, peaks at US #108.
Sept *Shake And Fingerpop*, in a similar dance groove to the first two singles, reaches US #29.
Nov The B-side of *Shake And Fingerpop*, the slow, more jazz-influenced *Cleo's Back*, wholly instrumental, unlike the previous hits, peaks at US #43.

1966

Feb Another instrumental in almost identical style, *Cleo's Mood* reaches US #50.
Mar [15] *Shotgun* is nominated for Best R&B Recording Of 1965, at the eighth annual Grammy Awards, but is beaten by James Brown's *Papa's Got A Brand New Bag*.
Apr ***Soul Session*** peaks at US #130.
June *(I'm A) Road Runner*, produced by Holland/Dozier/Holland, reaches US #20.
Aug [8-13] The group plays at the Beach Club in Myrtle Beach, SC.
Sept Their revival of Marvin Gaye's *How Sweet It Is (To Be Loved By You)* reaches US #18, and also debuts Walker on the UK chart, at #22. ***Road Runner*** peaks at US #64.
Dec Their treatment of another Motown classic, Barrett Strong's *Money (That's What I Want) Part 1*, makes US #52.

1967

Mar *Pucker Up Buttercup*, a return to *Shotgun* style, reaches US #31.
Aug *Shoot Your Shot* makes US #44.
Oct ***"Live!"*** peaks at US #119.

1968

Jan Their remake of the Supremes' *Come See About Me*, mellower than is usual for the troupe, reaches US #24.
Aug [2] Walker & the All Stars begin a three-week UK tour at the California Ballroom, Dunstable, Beds., to be followed by other European dates in France, Germany, Belgium and Holland.
Oct *Hip City, Pt. 2* makes US #31.
Dec [28] The group plays at the "Miami Pop Festival", at the Gulfstream Racing Park in Hallandale, FL, alongside Chuck Berry, Marvin Gaye, Three Dog Night and Fleetwood Mac, among others.

1969

Feb ***Home Cookin'*** peaks at US #172, while its extracted title track, *Home Cookin'*, makes US #42.
May A reissue of *(I'm A) Road Runner* reaches UK #12.
Aug ***Greatest Hits***, a compilation of hit singles to date, makes US #43, while a new single, *What Does It Take (To Win Your Love)*, with a lengthy, distinctive sax intro from Walker, is the group's biggest success since *Shotgun*, hitting US #4, and selling over a million (having topped the US R&B survey on July 19th).
[8-10] The group performs at San Francisco's Fillmore West.
Nov *What Does It Take (To Win Your Love)* reaches UK #13.
Dec *These Eyes*, a cover of a hit by Canadian rock band, Guess Who, reaches US #16, as the group starts a production liaison with Johnny Bristol.

1970

Feb ***What Does It Take To Win Your Love*** makes US #92.
Mar *Gotta Hold On To This Feeling*, from the album, reaches US #21.
Aug *Do You See My Love (For You Growing)* makes US #32.
Oct ***A Gasssss*** peaks at US #110.

1971

Jan Their revival of Neil Diamond's *Holly Holy* peaks at US #75.
Aug ***Rainbow Funk*** makes US #91.
Sept *Take Me Girl, I'm Ready*, extracted from the album, makes US #50.

1972

Jan *Way Back Home* makes US #52.
Feb ***Moody Jr.***, Walker's final US album chart entry, peaks at US #142.
June Atmospheric and semi-instrumental *Walk In The Night* makes US #46.
Sept [8] The group takes part in the "Jazz & Blues Festival", Ann Arbor, MI, a tribute to blues pianist Otis Spann, alongside Muddy Waters, Howlin' Wolf, Bobby Bland and others.
[23] *Walk In The Night* reaches UK #16.

1973

Feb *Take Me Girl, I'm Ready*, belatedly issued in the UK, reaches #16, as the new set, ***Peace And Understanding Is Hard To Find***, is released.
July Another belated release, *Way Back Home*, makes UK #35.

1977

Feb [9] Following the release of the disco-aimed, Brian Holland-produced ***Hot Shot*** the previous July, Walker participates in ABC-TV's "American Bandstand's 25th Anniversary Special", as part of an all-star house band, including Chuck Berry, Johnny Rivers and Steve Cropper of Booker T. & the MG's. (During the year he will release ***Sax Appeal*** and ***Whopper Bopper Show Stopper***, followed by ***Smooth*** in 1978.)

1981

Sept Signed to Norman Whitfield's Whitfield label, Walker has released ***Back Street Boogie*** in 1979. Foreigner's *Urgent*, featuring a blistering sax solo from Walker, now hits US #4, as Walker continues what he does best - playing live.

1983

May [16] Walker performs *Shotgun* at the 25th anniversary Motown special. Walker's son, Autry DeWalt III, becomes the All-Stars drummer as the combo, re-signed to Motown, releases ***Blow The House Down***, its last new recording of the decade.

1995

Nov [23] Having received the Pioneer Award at the sixth annual Rhythm and Blues Foundation ceremonies held at the Hollywood Palladium, Hollywood, CA on March 2nd earlier in the year, Walker dies of cancer in Battle Creek, MI. (The group's career is brought together in a 41-track two-CD compilation, ***Nothin' But Soul - The Singles 1962-1983***.)

THE WALKER BROTHERS

Scott Engel (vocals); **John Maus** (vocals);
Gary Leeds (drums)

1964

Aug The trio comes together in Los Angeles, CA, after Leeds (b. Sept. 3, 1944, Glendale, CA), drumming for P. J. Proby, befriends Engel (b. Noel Scott Engel, Jan. 9, 1944, Hamilton, OH) and Maus (b. Nov. 12, 1943, New York, NY) when they are playing bass and lead guitar with the Dalton Brothers, the resident band at Gazzari's club on Sunset Boulevard, Los Angeles. Leeds, a drummer since his early teens, studied at the Aerospace Technology School in New York (having to quit after a leg injury), co-founded the *Dirty Water* chartmakers the Standells in Los Angeles in 1963, but left after the first two singles to join first Johnny Rivers, and then P.J. Proby, and visited Britain during Proby's launch on a Jack Good TV show. Engel, having made some solo singles for minor California labels in his teens, and learned double bass at high school, majored in music, and switched to electric bass to join instrumental group, the Routers, playing on its 1963 hit, *Let's Go*, and follow-up, *Make It Snappy*. Maus, a child actor at the

age of 12 in the TV series, "Hello Mum", with Betty Hutton, moved to the West Coast, already playing under the pseudonym John Stewart, and teamed up with Engel after being cast as brothers in a TV play.
Oct They make their first recordings with producers Jack Nitzsche and Nik Venet (ex-Capitol Records, to which the Dalton Brothers were contracted). Four titles are recorded, and a deal signed with Mercury Records' Smash label. They appear in a cameo slot in the teen movie, "Three Hats For Lisa", but Leeds is keen to return to the UK, having seen the potential for success while touring with Proby. Jack Good also advises the trio to launch itself in London.

1965

Jan [20] The group appears on ABC-TV's "Shindig".
Feb [18] The trio arrives in Britain, with a $10,000 loan from Gary's father.
Mar US-recorded uptempo effort, *Pretty Girls Everywhere*, with Maus on lead vocal, is their debut single.
[13] A short article about the Walker Brothers, written by Chris Welch, appears in **Melody Maker**, after the group walked into the newpaper's offices and button-holed the writer, talking about its connection to P.J. Proby.
[26] The group makes its UK TV debut on "Ready, Steady, Go!" (After a couple of months going nowhere, they link up with Barry Clayman and Maurice King as managers, and impress Johnny Franz, an A&R man at Mercury's UK counterpart, Philips Records.)
May [22] They make their first live UK appearance at the Odeon Cinema, Leeds, W. Yorks., deputizing for the Kinks.
June Dramatic ballad, *Love Her*, updating a Barry Mann/Cynthia Weil-penned Everly Brothers B-side, reaches UK #20. Another of the tracks made with Venet in sessions in Los Angeles (during which the Rolling Stones dropped in), with Nitzsche's arrangement, it establishes the trio's lush, orchestrally-backed style, highlighting Engel's rich lead vocals. The Walker Brothers begin to play live in the UK, with Engel and Maus laying aside bass and guitar to front the act on vocals, and a backing band, the Quotations, is formed around Leeds.
Sept [23] Amid regular slots on "Ready Steady, Go!", *Make It Easy On Yourself*, their treatment of Jerry Butler's 1962 US #20, which Franz produces in similar style to that established by *Love Her*, tops the UK chart. The Walker Brothers become major teen favorites, constantly pictured in magazines, and subject to hysterical female audiences at live gigs.
Dec [4] *Make It Easy On Yourself* reaches US #16. A show at London's Finsbury Park Astoria is their last before UK work permits are renewed.

1966

Jan *My Ship Is Coming In*, a cover of US soul singer Jimmy Radcliffe's original, hits UK #3, while their debut album, ***Take It Easy With The Walker Brothers***, hits UK #4. Leeds, who for contractual reasons cannot sing or play on the trio's records, signs as a solo singer to CBS/Columbia.
Feb [12] Leeds makes his solo debut on ITV's "Thank Your Lucky Stars", promoting *You Don't Love Me*, issued on CBS under the name Gary Walker, which reaches UK #26.
[19] *My Ship Is Coming In* peaks at US #63.
[27] Trio appears on ITV's "Ready Steady, Go!", broadcast live from La Locomotive club in Paris, France.
Mar [17] *The Sun Ain't Gonna Shine Anymore*, originally recorded in 1965 by Frankie Valli of the Four Seasons, tops the UK chart for the first of four weeks.
[19] Leeds is kidnapped by students raising money for the Harrow Technical College Rag Fund. He is taken to a tube station at 4:00 a.m. and left to be collected - four days later he hands over £50 to the charity.
[25] The trio begins a 31-date, twice-nightly UK tour with Roy Orbison, Lulu and others, at London's Finsbury Park Astoria, set to end on May 1st at the Coventry Theatre, Warks.
[29] Engel and Maus are concussed, as the group is mobbed entering their hotel in Chester, Cheshire. They are unable to perform the next night in Wigan, Lancs.
Apr [3] The group spends two hours in a Leeds police station, before being escorted to a gig.
May [1] The Walkers perform at the annual "**New Musical Express** Poll Winners Concert", at the Empire Pool, Wembley, Middx.
[21] *The Sun Ain't Gonna Shine Anymore* peaks at US #13, their last US hit single. Capitol Records in the UK releases *I Only Came To Dance With You*, credited to Scott Engel & John Stewart, actually a relic of their days in the Dalton Brothers.
June Another Gary Walker solo release, *Twinkie Lee*, reaches UK #26.
[12] The group makes its London Palladium debut.
July [8] "Ready Steady, Go!" airs a special on the group.
Aug *(Baby) You Don't Have To Tell Me* reaches UK #13.
[15] Scott is found unconscious in his gas-filled apartment.
Sept ***Portrait*** hits UK #3.
Oct Their revival of Gene McDaniels' *Another Tear Falls* reaches UK #12.
[1] The group begins a 33-date, twice-nightly tour with the Troggs, Dave Dee, Dozy, Beaky, Mick & Tich and others, at the Granada Cinema, East Ham, London, set to close on November 13th at London's Finsbury Park Astoria.
Dec *Deadlier Than The Male* (the theme from the film of the same title) peaks at UK #34. EP *Solo Scott - Solo John* displays the two vocalists' individual talents. Engel and Maus are growing increasingly irritated by each other's company, both off-and-onstage, with the consequent pressures starting to pull the trio apart as hit singles lessen in impact. (During the month, Scott disappears on the eve of an Australian tour and enters the Quarr Monastery on the Isle of Wight, but when fans find out, he has to leave.)

1967

Jan [20] Engel is placed under sedation after the plane the group is taking to Australia returns to Heathrow Airport having developed engine trouble. A tour of Australia and the Far East with Roy Orbison, the Yardbirds and others, follows, opening at Sydney Stadium, Sydney, New South Wales, Australia, during which 17 teenage girls are taken to hospital after collapsing in the 90°F heat.
Feb Their cover of Lorraine Ellison's *Stay With Me Baby* reaches UK #26.
Mar [31] The trio embarks on what will be its last UK tour, a 24-date package with Cat Stevens, Jimi Hendrix and Engelbert Humperdinck, at London's Finsbury Park Astoria, set to end on April 30th at the Tooting Granada, London.
Apr ***Images*** hits UK #6.
[2] The group tops the bill on ITV's "Sunday Night At The London Palladium".
May [3] At the end of a concert at Tooting Granada, London, they announce their intention to split, because of growing internal friction.
[14] Fans of the trio march from Baker Street station to the Maida Vale apartment of manager, Barry Clayman, where Maus has been living, to protest at the break-up of the group.
June The **New Musical Express** reports that Maus has been invited to write four songs and incidental music for Franco Zefferelli's movie, "Romeo And Juliet".
[4] Maus plays a solo date at the Olympia, Paris, while the Walker Brothers' revival of the Ronettes' *Walking In The Rain* reaches UK #26.
[25] Leeds joins a star-studded team of backing vocalists at the recording of the Beatles' *All You Need Is Love*, on the "Our World" TV show.
July [25] Engel is taken to St. John & Elizabeth Hospital, London, suffering from head injuries after a fall in Regent's Park.
Aug Maus has the first post-Walker Brothers solo hit. Released under the name John Walker, *Annabella* reaches UK #24. (He will not be able to maintain his UK chart profile, and will return to California. Leeds will drop completely out of sight, but will continue to reside in Britain.)
Sept Engel visits Moscow for two weeks to study Russian culture, and is invited to perform in Cuba by the Castro government.
Oct Compilation, ***The Walker Brothers' Story***, hits UK #9, but its sales are overshadowed by Engel's first solo album ***Scott***, credited to Scott Walker, which hits UK #3.
Dec [3] Former group members begin a Japanese tour, but as three solo acts on the same bill, not as a trio.
[25] Engel guests on ITV's "Down At The Old Bull And Bush" with the Bachelors, Kiki Dee, Tommy Bruce, Kim Cordell, Bud Flanagan and Kenneth McKellar.

1968

Jan *Jackie* by Scott Walker, a dramatic reading of Jacques Brel's song, with a controversial lyric which guarantees it little airplay, reaches UK #22.
Apr Leeds' new band, Rain, comprising John Lawson (bass), Joey Molland (lead guitar) and Paul Crane (rhythm guitar), embarks on its first UK tour with the Kinks, the Tremeloes and the Herd.
May [18] ***Scott 2***, like its predecessor a mixture of songs by an eclectic batch of choice composers, with a large proportion of Jacques Brel numbers, tops the UK chart, replacing Bob Dylan's *John Wesley Harding*.
June *Joanna*, a romantic ballad by Scott Walker, which he himself professes to dislike, is his biggest UK solo hit, at #7.
July [26] Scott and Gary reunite for a one-off tour of Japan.
Oct [4] Now recovered from catching typhoid in Tunisia, Engel embarks on a 14-date UK solo tour, with the Love Affair, the Paper Dolls and others, at the Finsbury Park Astoria, set to end on the 20th at the Coventry Theatre, Warks.

1969

Jan [10] Maus is injured in a car crash.
Mar A Scott Walker weekly TV show on BBC1, mostly a straight showcase for his singing, begins a two-month run.
Apr ***Scott 3*** hits UK #3.
July *Lights Of Cincinnati* is Engel's last solo hit single as Scott Walker. It reaches UK #13, but ***Scott Walker Sings Songs From His TV Series***, with a strong MOR slant, hits UK #7. (Scott Walker will follow his "brothers" out of the charts, despite recording albums regularly, and will spend most of his time in seclusion, making live appearances with little notice once or twice a year. His non-charting albums will be ***Scott 4*** and ***'Til The Band Comes In***, self-penned under the name Noel Scott Engel, in 1970; the film-theme set, ***The Moviegoer***, in 1972; ***Any Day Now***, anthologizing favorite songwriters, in 1973; and two country-tinged sets for CBS: ***Stretch*** and ***We Had It All***, in 1974.)
Sept Maurice King sues Engel, alleging breach of contract.

1975

Jan Leeds releases *Hello How Are You*, produced by the Hollies' Allan Clarke, on United Artists.
Aug Against all expectations, the trio reunites, and signs to GTO Records in the UK.

1976

Feb Their treatment of Tom Rush's *No Regrets*, performed in the trio's traditional dramatic style, hits UK #7, and the newly-recorded album, ***No Regrets***, makes UK #49.
Sept *Lines*, and its parent set, ***Lines***, are released.

1978

July The Walker Brothers' final album, ***Nite Flights*** is issued, breaking new ground by containing material written entirely by the trio and is more avant-garde in approach and arrangement than any previous group album. It includes the extracted *The Electrician*, written by Engel.

1984

Mar [31] Scott Walker solo set, ***Climate Of Hunter***, featuring Peter Van Hooke on drums, Brian Gascoigne on keyboards and Mo Foster on bass, released by Virgin Records, peaks at UK #60, though the singer himself remains in typical seclusion.

1985

Engel, now signed to Fontana via an optimistic six-album deal, begins work on the planned ***Abandoned*** album with the same session crew, subsequently recording with producers Brian Eno and Daniel Lanois, though the project will be ultimately shelved.

1987

July While Leeds is now a motorcycle courier living in Essex, and Maus has finally quit the UK, after an abortive tour with Screaming Lord Sutch, the previous year, Engel appears in the UK black-and-white TV and cinema commercial for Britvic soft drinks, in a cameo role as his '60s persona. Also in the ad are '60s contemporaries, Sandie Shaw, Georgie Fame, Dusty Springfield and Dave Dee, among others.

1995

May [20] After the Walker Brothers' ***After The Lights Go Out - The Best Of 1965-1967***, and the Engel solo album, ***Boy Child - The Best Of 1967-1970*** have been released in the UK on Fontana in August 1990, when a reappraisal of the trio's career becomes fashionable, Scott has renegotiated a new solo deal with Fontana in March the following year, though he has spent much of the next three years studying art at Byam Shaw College. Following the success of a further CD collection, ***No Regrets - The Best Of The Walker Brothers 1965-1976*** which hit UK #4 on Feb [8], 1992, Scott's comeback album, ***Tilt***, now reaches UK #27 in its week of entry.

JOE WALSH

1969

Nov Walsh (b. Nov. 20, 1947, Wichita, KS), having been raised in New Jersey and played clarinet in junior high, then rhythm guitar in the G-Clefs, a duo playing Ventures' instrumentals, subsequently joining the Beatles-styled the Nomads, has begun studying at Kent State University, OH in 1965, and now joins campus band the Measles, who become local favorites. When they split, Walsh is asked to join Cleveland, OH-based the James Gang to replace guitarist Glenn Schwartz, who has left to play with Pacific Gas & Electric. The group, comprising Walsh, Tom Kriss on bass and vocals and Jim Fox on drums and vocals, now makes US #83 with ***Yer' Album***.

1970

Jan Dale Peters replaces Kriss.
May The James Gang, having opened for the Who in Pittsburgh, PA in 1969, is invited to support the band on its European tour.
[4] Walsh witnesses the killings of four students on Kent State campus. (In 1988, Walsh will campaign to erect a memorial for them.)
Sept *Funk #49* peaks at US #59 as ***James Gang Rides Again*** reaches US #20, earning a gold disc.

1971

June *Walk Away* makes US #51 as ***Thirds*** reaches US #27 and earns another gold disc.
Sept Live ***James Gang Live In Concert*** enters the US chart, and becomes the group's third gold disc, reaching US #24.
Oct *Midnight Man* peaks at US #80.

1972

Jan Walsh quits the James Gang and, turning down an invitation from Steve Marriott to join Humble Pie, leaves industrial Cleveland for the open air of Boulder, CO.
Mar Walsh forms the Barnstorm trio with Kenny Passarelli on bass and Joe Vitale on drums, signed to Dunhill Records.
Oct The Bill Szymczyk-produced ***Barnstorm***, recorded at Caribou Studios and credited as a Joe Walsh solo, makes US #79.
Nov Keyboards player Rocke Grace joins as the group begins major US tour, much of it as support act to Stephen Stills.

1973

Feb Compilation ***The Best Of The James Gang Featuring Joe Walsh*** makes US #79.
Apr Walsh moves from Boulder to Studio City, Los Angeles, CA.
June Tom Stephenson has replaced Grace as ***The Smoker You Drink, The Player You Get***, including the live favorite *Rocky Mountain Way*, is released, set to hit US #6 and earn Walsh's first solo gold disc.
Oct *Rocky Mountain Way* reaches US #23 and UK #39.
Dec James Gang compilation ***16 Greatest Hits***, featuring Walsh, peaks at US #181. ***Barnstorm*** splits after touring for most of the year.

1974

Jan Walsh solo *Meadows* peaks at US #89. He will spend much of the year working on ***So What*** and also play on sessions for the Eagles, B.B. King, Rod Stewart and Stephen Stills.
Feb The James Gang has a final hit at US #54 with *Must Be Love*.
Dec Walsh has produced Dan Fogelberg's new released ***Souvenirs***.

1975

Jan ***So What***, including five tracks recorded with Barnstorm begins a rise to US #11, earning Walsh a second gold disc.
Mar *Turn To Stone* peaks at US #93.
June [21] Walsh plays on the "Midsummer Madness" bill at Wembley Stadium, Wembley, Middx, with the Beach Boys, the Eagles and Elton John.
Dec [20] He replaces Bernie Leadon in the Eagles. He makes an early but enduring impression with a lengthy guitar lead on the title cut for forthcoming ***Hotel California***.

1976

Apr Walsh's live solo ***You Can't Argue With A Sick Mind*** reaches US #20 and UK #28. An EP combining *Rocky Mountain Way* with *Turn To Stone*, *Meadows*, *Walk Away* and the title track, will make UK #39 in July the following year.

1978

June Still an Eagle but newly signed to Asylum Records, he continues his solo career with the satirical, rock-lifestyle themed *Life's Been Good* reaching US #12 and UK #14 as its parent album ***But Seriously, Folks ...*** , produced by Szymczyk and featuring his current band colleagues, hits US #8, earning Walsh his first platinum disc, and reaches UK #16.
Nov ***The Best Of Joe Walsh***, including James Gang tracks, makes US #71.

1979

Sept [22] Walsh announces he will run for president in 1980.

1980

July Walsh's *All Night Long*, from the soundtrack album for John Travolta-starring movie "Urban Cowboy", reaches US #19.

1981

July With the Eagles no longer active, Walsh's *A Life Of Illusion* makes US #34 as he switches to the main Warner Bros. label for the self-produced US #20 ***There Goes The Neighborhood***, which features Russ Kunkel, David Lindley and Joe Vitale among top session players.

1983

July *Space Age Whiz Kids* makes US #52.
Aug ***You Bought It - You Name It*** makes US #48. Producing Ringo Starr's ***Old Wave*** the following year, Walsh's ***The Confessor*** will peak at US #65 in July 1985.

1987

Aug ***Got Any Gum?*** peaks at US #113.
Sept [19] Walsh participates in the "Farm Aid II" benefit with John Cougar Mellencamp, Neil Young, Lou Reed and others at the University of Nebraska's Memorial Stadium, NE.

1990

Feb Walsh begins the new decade working as a DJ on New York's KROQ on Friday nights.
Nov Walsh is a member of ad-hoc outfit, the Best, an aggregation of John Entwistle, Jeff "Skunk" Baxter, Keith Emerson, Simon Phillips and singer Rick Livingstone, which plays at the Yokohama Arena, Yokohama, Japan.
Dec [4] Walsh is featured playing guitar on *School Days* from the ***The Simpsons Sings The Blues*** album. (During the year, Walsh reunites with his James Gang colleagues, Jim Fox and Dale Peters for "The Class Of 1970" TV special in Cleveland.)

1991

May Walsh releases ***Ordinary Average Guy*** on the new Pyramid Records label.
[19] He performs two acoustic benefit concerts in his home town, Wichita, to raise funds for the area's tornado relief fund.
Aug Walsh is featured on Bob Seger's newly-released ***The Fire Inside***.
Nov [23] He takes part in the "Rock Against Hunger" benefit at the Count Basie Theater, Red Bank, NJ, with Rick Derringer, Southside Johnny & the Asbury Jukes and others.

1992

Mar [14] A sometime member of Ringo Starr's All Star Band, Walsh, who has recently issued ***Songs For A Dying Planet***, performs solo at "Farm Aid V", where he is joined by Bonnie Bramlett.

1993

Mar [26] Walsh and fellow former-Eagle Glenn Frey perform before a sellout crowd at the Sunrise Musical Theatre, Sunrise, FL, on a twin-billed US tour. While the solo retrospective ***Look What I Did : The Joe Walsh Anthology*** will be released the following year, Walsh will reconvene with the reformed Eagles for a highly successful album and lengthy world tour, projects beginning in 1994.
see also: THE EAGLES

WAR

Lonnie Jordan (keyboards, vocals);
Howard Scott (guitar, vocals); **Charles Miller** (saxophone, clarinet); **B.B. Dickerson** (bass, vocals); **Harold Brown** (drums, percussion);
"Papa Dee" Allen (keyboards, vocals);
Lee Oskar (harmonica)

1969

June The group has been formed from the remnants of early '60s Long Beach, CA group, the Creators, who became Night Shift, and were successful on the local circuit. As Night Shift, Jordan (b. Leroy Jordan, Nov. 21, 1948, San Diego, CA), Scott (b. Mar. 15, 1946, San Pedro, CA), Miller (b. June 2, 1939, Olathe, KS) and Brown (b. Mar. 17, 1946, Long Beach), with bassist Peter Rosen, are backing football star turned soul singer, Deacon Jones, when they are noted by former Animals lead singer, Eric Burdon, harmonica player Oskar (b. Oskar Levetin Hansen, Mar. 24, 1946,

Copenhagen, Denmark) and producer, Jerry Goldstein, who are looking for a blues-based black band to accompany Burdon. Burdon, Oskar and the band now meet at Goldstein's home, and decide to work together with Goldstein as producer. The name War is chosen because it is in stark contrast with current peace preoccupations in music, and therefore memorable. Shortly after, Rosen dies from a drug overdose, and ex-Creators bassist, Dickerson (b. Morris Dickerson, Aug. 3, 1949, Torrance, CA) replaces him, while Allen (b. Thomas Allen, July 18, 1931, Wilmington, DE) also joins on keyboards, to make it a seven-piece instrumental unit. Burdon is already signed to MGM, and the new team continues with the label.

1970

July War, in Europe following a US tour, jams with Jimi Hendrix at an impromptu session at Ronnie Scott's jazz club in London.

Aug Its debut album, ***Eric Burdon Declares War***, reaches US #18. Taken from it, the group-composed *Spill The Wine* hits US #3. The album also contains musical tributes to Roland Kirk and Memphis Slim, and a version of John D. Loudermilk's much-revived *Tobacco Road.*

Oct ***Eric Burdon Declares War*** makes UK #50.

1971

Jan *They Can't Take Away Our Music* reaches US #50. It is taken from the double album, ***The Black Man's Burdon***, which again displays a powerful fusion of soul, funk, r&b and rock, and makes US #82.

Feb ***The Black Man's Burdon*** makes UK #34, and another European tour follows, but Burdon drops out, exhausted, and returns to Los Angeles, CA. The band completes all contracted dates on its own and, at tour's end, it is decided not to continue the partnership with Burdon. The group's manager, Steve Gold, negotiates a new recording deal with United Artists Records.

May ***War***, their debut without Burdon, peaks at US #190.

June [30] The band plays the Hollywood Bowl in United Artists' "99 Cent Spectacular", a low entry-price showcase for the label's new acts.

Sept *All Day Music*, written by Goldstein and the band, makes US #35.

1972

May *Slippin' Into Darkness* reaches US #16, during a 22-week chart stay, and will sell over a million copies. The track is an edited version of a cut on ***All Day Music***, which also reaches US #16.

June [26] The RIAA certifies gold sales of *Slippin' Into The Darkness* and ***All Day Music***.

Aug [19] The group plays on the first edition of NBC-TV's "Midnight Special", performing *Slippin' Into Darkness*.

Dec [13] The still-climbing ***The World Is A Ghetto*** is certified gold by the RIAA.

1973

Jan *The World Is A Ghetto* hits US #7, subsequently becoming another million seller.

Feb [17] ***The World Is A Ghetto***, written by the band, and produced by Goldstein (he and the group have formed their own Far Out production company, which leases all recordings to UA), tops the US chart for the first of two weeks. It includes a ten-minute version of the title track, and the 13-minute cut, *City, Country, City*.

Mar [2] *The World Is A Ghetto* is certified gold by the RIAA.

[6] The still-climbing *Cisco Kid* is also confirmed gold by the RIAA.

Apr *The Cisco Kid*, from the album, hits US #2.

Sept *Gypsy Man* hits US #8, taken from ***Deliver The Word***, which hits US #6.

[11] ***Deliver The Word*** is certified gold by the RIAA.

1974

Jan Also from ***Deliver The Word***, *Me And Baby Brother* reaches US #15.

Mar [13] The still-rising ***War Live!*** is ratified gold by the RIAA.

May Live double album, ***War Live!***, reaches US #13.

July Instrumental track, *Ballero*, taken from the performance set, climbs to US #33.

1975

July [25] Yet-to-peak ***Why Can't We Be Friends?*** is certified gold by the RIAA.

Aug ***Why Can't We Be Friends?*** hits US #8, while the title track *Why Can't We Be Friends?* hits US #6. (The song is beamed into space to US and Russian astronauts during the summer 1975 link-up in Earth orbit.)

[19] *Why Can't We Be Friends?* is confirmed gold by the RIAA.

Nov Sparse Latin-phrased funk track, *Low Rider*, also from ***Why Can't We Be Friends?***, hits US #7.

1976

Feb The group has signed a new deal for UK distribution with Island Records, and *Low Rider* is its UK chart debut, reaching #12.

July *Me And Baby Brother*, belatedly issued in Britain as a follow-up, reaches UK #21, while Oskar sees solo success with the US #29 album, ***Lee Oskar***. (Two further solo albums, ***Before The Rain*** (US #86) and ***My Road Our Road*** (US #162) will chart in 1978 and 1981.)

Sept *Summer* hits US #7. The group writes and performs the music for Krishna Shah's movie, "The River Niger", starring Cicely Tyson and James Earl Jones.

[14] *Summer* is certified gold by the RIAA.

Oct Compilation, ***Greatest Hits***, rounding up all the successful singles, hits US #6, becoming the band's biggest-selling album. Meanwhile, War and United Artists are at loggerheads (or experiencing "philosophical differences", as the press release quote) over matters of marketing the band's music. The agreed solution is that the band's production company will move elsewhere, but will deliver a final album to UA, to be a departure from the mainstream, for release on its subsidiary Blue Note jazz label.

1977

Jan ***Love Is All Around***, a collection of early tracks recorded with Burdon in 1969 and 1970, and released by ABC, peaks at US #140.

[6] ***Greatest Hits*** is certified platinum by the RIAA.

Aug *L.A. Sunshine*, the rare appearance of a single on Blue Note (and a sampler for their new album) peaks at US #45.

[10] ***Platinum Jazz*** is confirmed gold by the RIAA.

Sept Double album, ***Platinum Jazz***, the set owed to UA, makes US #23.

Nov [28] The still-rising ***Galaxy*** is certified gold by the RIAA.

1978

Feb With the band's Far Out Productions having signed a new deal with MCA Records, the first release, ***Galaxy***, reaches US #15, while its title track, *Galaxy*, makes US #39 and UK #14. Alice Tweed Smyth joins on additional vocals.

Apr *Hey Senorita*, from ***Galaxy***, climbs to UK #40. Dickerson leaves, and is replaced on bass by Luther Rabb.

Aug War's soundtrack album for "Youngblood", a film depicting ghetto gang warfare, reaches US #69.

1979

May ***The Music Band*** peaks at US #41, earning War its final gold album, as the group adds Pat Rizzo on horns and Ron Hammond on percussion.

July [21] ***The Music Band*** is certified gold by the RIAA. ***The Music Band 2*** will climb to US #111 the following January.

1982

Apr Newly signed to RCA Records, ***Outlaw*** reaches US #48, as *You Got The Power*, taken from the album, makes US #66 and UK #58. Smyth leaves.

July Title cut, *Outlaw*, peaks at US #94. The RCA follow-up album ***Life (Is So Strange)*** will reach US #164 in July the following year.

1985

Apr *Groovin'*, their revival of the Young Rascals' 1967 chart-topper, leased by the band and Goldstein to UK independent R&B music label, Bluebird Records, makes UK #43, as the group releases ***Raw War***.

1987

July Goldstein launches the band's own Lax label in Britain, with its first release an updated remix of *Low Rider* on 12" single, which peaks at UK #98, as ***The Best Of War ... And More*** stops at US #156.

1988

Aug [30] Allen dies of a cerebral haemorrhage, while on tour.

1995

Oct [13] After *Low Rider (On The Boulevard)*, remixing their 1975 US #7 hit with Latin Alliance, and including samples of Santana's *Evil Ways*, has made US #54 on Sept [7], 1991, and Rhino Records (US) has begun reissuing the War catalog on CD in 1993, ***Best Of War ... And More*** has been certified gold by the RIAA on July 1st 1994, with a new War title, the critically-revered ***Peace Sign***, featuring José Feliciano and Lee Oskar among others, charting for a week at US #200 on July [23] the same year. Following the issue of a 32-track twin-CD ***War Anthology 1970-1994***, produced and remastered by Avenue Records president Jerry Goldstein, released last November, War, now comprising Jordan, Brown, Sal Rodriguez, Tetsuya "Tex" Nakamura, Ronnie Hammon, Charles Green, Howard Scott, Kerry Campbell and Rae Valentine, performs at the Fox Theatre, Detroit, MI, on a bill with the Average White Band and Larry Graham & Graham Central Station.

see: **THE ANIMALS**

JENNIFER WARNES

1968

Nov [17] Warnes (b. Jennifer Jeane Warnes, Mar. 3, 1947, Seattle, WA), having been raised in Orange County, CA, has made her professional debut in 1956 while still at high school, wrapped in the US flag, singing *The Star Spangled Banner*, accompanied by 300 accordions. Following secondary education at a convent, she has worked at the Bun & Cone hamburger stand, on Commonwealth Street in Fullerton, CA, before becoming a sales assistant at the local Shades & Blinds store. Warnes, billed as Jennifer Warren, now makes the first of many regular appearances on CBS-TV's weekly "The Smothers Brothers Comedy Hour", singing a song with fellow guest Donovan. One of the show's writers, Mason Williams, subsequently invites Warnes to duet with him on *Cinderella Rockefella* for his album, ***The Mason Williams Ear Show***.

[22] A West Coast production of "Hair", in which Warnes stars as Sheila, opens at Los Angeles, CA's Aquarius Theater.

Dec Signed to the Decca Records imprint Parrot as Jennifer Warren, Warnes releases her maiden effort, ***... I Can Remember Everything***, an 11-track set of covers produced by Martin Cooper.

1969

Apr Warnes releases her sophomore Parrot effort, ***See Me, Feel Me, Touch Me, Heal Me!***, featuring guests Martin Cooper, Al Capps and Williams, and including "Hair" extracts *Easy To Be Hard/Let The Sunshine In*.

1972

By now a veteran of the Los Angeles folk scene, notably singing Canadian poet Leonard Cohen's songs, and newly signed to Reprise Records, her label debut, ***Jennifer***, is released, produced by John Cale, and featuring songs by Jackson Browne, Jimmy Webb, Donovan and Barry Gibb.

1977

May Newly signed to Arista Records, and showcasing her gifted and sensitive vocal phrasing, ***Jennifer Warnes***, produced by Jim Ed Norman and Jim Price, and featuring top-flight session help from Kenny Edwards, Jay Graydon, Nicky Hopkins and Jim Horn, among others, makes US #43. It will yield two US chart hits, the Pete McCann-penned extract, *Right Time Of The Night*, which hits US #6 the following March and *I'm Dreaming*, which makes US #50 in September.

1979

Aug ***Shot Through The Heart***, co-produced with Rob Fraboni, makes US #94, and includes a further set of choice AC covers.
Nov *I Know A Heartache When I See One* reaches US #19.

1980

Jan Her revival of Dionne Warwick's 1963 Bacharach/David-penned hit, *Don't Make Me Over*, peaks at US #67.
Apr [14] The David Shire/Norman Gimbel-penned ballad, *It Goes Like It Goes*, from the Sally Field-starring film "Norma Rae", sung by Warnes, wins an Oscar for Best Original Song, at the annual Academy Awards.
May *When The Feeling Comes Around* makes US #45.

1982

Jan With *One More Hour*, written by Randy Newman for his score for the movie "Ragtime", and sung by Warnes, having received an Oscar nomination the previous year, *Could It Be Love*, one of three new tracks from the otherwise retrospective Arista collection, ***The Best Of Jennifer Warnes***, now makes US #47.
Apr [13] Warnes guests with James Taylor on PBS-TV's "America Playhouse : Working".
Nov [6] Written by Will Jennings, Jack Nitzsche and Buffy Saint-Marie, *Up Where We Belong*, a Warnes duet with Joe Cocker from the Richard Gere-starring film, "An Officer And A Gentleman", tops the US chart, where it will stay for three weeks.

1983

Feb [12] *Up Where We Belong* hits UK #7.
[23] *Up Where We Belong* is named Best Pop Performance By A Duo Or Group With Vocal Of 1982, at the 25th annual Grammy awards.
Apr [11] Cocker and Warnes perform *Up Where We Belong* at the Academy Awards, at which it wins the Oscar for Best Original Song.
Nov *All The Right Moves*, her duet with Chris Thompson, from the movie of the same name, peaks at US #85.

1987

Feb Warnes, the first signing to the new Cypress label, has released the critically-acclaimed ***Famous Blue Raincoat***, featuring only Leonard Cohen songs (including a duet with the folk veteran on *Joan Of Arc*), and self-produced with Roscoe Beck, which makes US #72. (Costing $106,000 to record, it will sell over one million copies worldwide, though the artist will receive no royalties, ultimately resulting in a split from the label.)
July Warnes duets with country singer Gary Morris on *Simply Meant To Be*, penned by Henry Mancini with George Merrill and Shannon Rubicam (the husband-and-wife writers of Whitney Houston's *I Wanna Dance With Somebody* and *How Will I Know*), for the Bruce Willis/Kim Basinger film, "Blind Date".
[25] *First We Take Manhattan* spends a week on the UK chart, at #74.
Aug [15] ***Famous Blue Raincoat*** makes UK #33, during an 11-week run.
Sept [30] "A Black And White Night", a club concert at which Roy Orbison is backed by a cast of star admirers, including Warnes, takes place at the Coconut Grove, Ambassador Hotel in Los Angeles.
Nov [28] Warnes' duet with Bill Medley, *(I've Had) The Time Of My Life*, from the film "Dirty Dancing", tops the US chart, and hits UK #6.

1988

Mar [2] *(I've Had) The Time Of My Life* wins the Best Pop Performance By A Duo Or Group With Vocal category at the 30th annual Grammy Awards.
Apr [11] *(I've Had) The Time Of My Life* wins the Oscar for Best Original Song, the third Warnes-sung tune to do so.

1991

Jan [26] Reissued *(I've Had) The Time Of My Life* hits UK #8.
Feb Currently signed to Private Music, Warnes' latest guest appearance is on UK songstress Tanita Tikaram's newly-released third album, ***Everybody's Angel***.
Mar During the month, Warnes sings *Joan Of Arc* at the induction of Leonard Cohen into the Juno Hall of Fame, at the 20th annual Juno Awards, from the Queen Elizabeth Theatre, Vancouver, BC, Canada.
June [22] ***For Our Children***, to which Warnes and Jackson Browne have contributed their version of the Beatles' *Golden Slumbers*, reaches US #31.

1992

Aug Selections from her first two Decca albums are collected for the John Tracy-compiled ***Just Jennifer***, released in the UK on the Deram imprint.
Sept Private Music issues ***The Hunter***, Warnes first album in five years. Co-produced with C. Roscoe Beck and Elliot Scheiner, it includes songs by Mike Scott, Donald Fagen, and Todd Rundgren among others, and guest musicians including Lenny Castro, Fagen, Eric Johnson,Van Dyke Parks and Richard Thompson.

WARRANT

Jani Lane (vocals); **Erik Turner** (guitar); **Joey Allen** (guitar); **Jerry Dixon** (bass); **Steven Sweet** (drums)

1984

Turner (b. Mar. 31, 1964) and Dixon (b. Sept. 15, 1964) form Warrant in Los Angeles, CA, initially recruiting vocalist Adam Shore. He is replaced by Lane (b. Johnny Lane, Feb. 1, 1964), raised in Cleveland, OH, who begun playing in clubs at age 11 under the name Mitch Dynamite, while Sweet (b. Oct. 29, 1965), having fronted rock outfit, Plain Jane, with Lane, gigging by night and packaging porn movies by day, is enlisted on drums. Allen (b. June 23, 1964), who has already been in the Orange County, CA-based band Rebellious Youth with Turner, is the last to join. Building a strong regional following at Los Angeles clubs, the hard-rock outfit, having landed one cut on the ***Game Of War*** soundtrack, signs to CBS/Columbia Records in 1988.

1989

Mar [4] Their debut album, ***Dirty Rotten Filthy Stinking Rich***, enters the US Album chart, set to hit #10, staying charted for more than a year, and earning two platinum sales awards.
July [8] The extracted *Down Boys* peaks at US #27.
Sept [23] *Heaven* hits US #2, earning a gold disc for 500,000 sales.
Nov [11] A further excerpt, *Big Talk*, reaches US #93.
Dec [10] During a US tour supporting Mötley Crüe, Warrant plays a sellout at the Meadowlands Arena, East Rutherford, NJ, grossing $373,883.

1990

Mar [3] The fourth cut from their debut album, *Sometimes She Cries*, makes US #20.
Sept [29] Warrant's sophomore album, the Beau Hill-produced ***Cherry Pie***, with a busty diner-waitress sleeve, enters the US survey, where it will hit #7, earning two further platinum discs.
Nov [3] Lane-penned glam-metal title cut *Cherry Pie*, spurred by a risqué video, hits US #10.
[17] *Cherry Pie* peaks at UK #59.
Dec [31] The band ends the year at the Long Beach Convention & Entertainment Center, CA, before a 13,650 sellout crowd, supporting Poison.

1991

Jan [12] A five-month US tour closes at the Arena, Rushmore Plaza Civic Center, Rapid City, IA, grossing $134,922.
Feb [22] Warrant performs a concert for 3,000 members of the armed forces and their teenage kids, at McGuire Air Force Base, NJ.
[23] *I Saw Red*, also written by Lane, hits US #10.
Mar [4] Lane fractures two ribs while singing *Cherry Pie* during a show in Birmingham, W. Midlands, causing the cancellation of the rest of its UK tour.
May [18] *Uncle Tom's Cabin* peaks at US #78.
[31] The group's summer tour opens in Bismarck, ND.
July [20] *Blind Faith* climbs to US #88.
[27] Lane (currently appearing as Vol, a heavy-metal rocker, in the movie "High Strung"), marries TV spokesmodel Bobbie Brown in Los Angeles.
Sept [2] Kylie Josephine is born to Joey and Kathy Allen.
[3] *Cherry Pie* re-enters the UK survey, on its way to #35.
Nov [28] Dixon marries model, Susan Ashley, in Maui, Hawaii.

1992

Mar [28] *We Will Rock You* peaks at US #83.
Sept [12] ***Dog Eat Dog*** debuts at its US #25 peak, making UK #74 the following week.
Nov [8] During current US dates, the band plays at the Toledo Sports Arena, OH.

1993

Feb [5] The group plays a sellout show at the Backstage, Houston, TX, during its current club tour.
Mar With grunge-metal having eclipsed the '80s glam-rock style so epitomized by Warrant, Lane, slated to appear in the movie, "Hotel Oklahoma", with David Keith and Ray Sharkey, quits the band to pursue a solo career, but will return to the fold at the end of 1994.

DIONNE WARWICK

1960

After singing in the New Hope Baptist church choir in nearby Newark, NJ, from the age of six, Warwick (b. Marie Dionne Warrick, Dec. 12, 1940, East Orange, NJ), daughter of the Chess Records' gospel promotion department head, is a regular performer, playing piano with the Drinkard Singers gospel group, and is managed by her mother. She forms the Gospelaires, with sister Dee Dee, cousin Cissy Houston and friend Doris Troy, and they sing in churches throughout New York and New Jersey. Warwick enrolls at the Hartt College of Music in Hartford, CT, and to pay for her tuition, the Gospelaires work as back-up singers at the Apollo Theater, Harlem, New York, and on New York studio pop and R&B recording sessions.

1961

July While working with the Gospelaires on a Leiber/Stoller-produced session for the Drifters', Warwick is first heard by composer, Burt Bacharach, and then-partner, Bob Hilliard, whose song *Mexican Divorce*, the Drifters are cutting. Later, on a break from college, Warwick contacts Bacharach, who invites her to become the regular singer on demos he and lyricist partner, Hal David, are making of their songs.

1962

Via demos made for Scepter Records' group the Shirelles, Warwick begins regular studio back-up work for the label's acts, including Chuck Jackson and Tommy Hunt, and is signed to Scepter as a solo vocalist, with Bacharach and David as writers and producers.

1963

Jan Having left college, her solo recording debut, *Don't Make Me Over*, written (as will be virtually all her Scepter output) by Bacharach and David, reaches US #21.
Apr *This Empty Place* peaks at US #84 (its B-side is *Wishin' And Hopin'*, later successfully revived by Dusty Springfield and the Merseybeats). Marlene Dietrich introduces Warwick on her debut at the Olympia Theatre in Paris, France.
Aug *Make The Music Play* makes US #81.

1964

Feb *Anyone Who Had A Heart* hits US #8, while in the UK it makes #42, eclipsed by Cilla Black's #1 cover version.
May *Walk On By*, rush-released in the US and UK to pre-empt cover versions, and promoted by Warwick on UK TV shows during a promotional visit, marks her UK breakthrough, hitting #9.
[30] Warwick makes her British TV debut on the BBC-TV's "Top Of The Pops", during a week-long radio and promotional tour.
June [13] *Walk On By* hits US #6, becoming her first international million seller,
[20] ***Presenting Dionne Warwick*** reaches UK #14.
Aug *You'll Never Get To Heaven (If You Break My Heart)*, which will later be revived by the Stylistics, reaches UK #20.
Sept *You'll Never Get To Heaven (If You Break My Heart)* makes US #34, while its B-side, *A House Is Not A Home* (the theme from the movie of the same title) peaks at US #71, in competition with a version by Brook Benton.
Oct *Reach Out For Me* reaches UK #23.
Nov *Reach Out For Me* stops at US #20, as ***Make Way For Dionne Warwick*** peaks at US #68.
[9] While on a UK tour, Warwick is slightly injured in an car accident in Glasgow, Strathclyde, Scotland, causing the cancellation of tour dates.
[28] She makes her second appearance on the ITV show, "Thank Your Lucky Stars", with the Isley Brothers.
Dec [1] She flies back to the US after recording an album at Pye's London studios with Bacharach. (Warwick is named Top Selling Female Vocalist Of The Year by NARM.)

1965

Mar ***The Sensitive Sound Of Dionne Warwick*** peaks at US #107.
[29] Warwick begins a two-week stint in cabaret at London's Savoy Hotel.
Apr *Who Can I Turn To*, from the musical, "The Roar Of The Greasepaint - The Smell Of The Crowd", peaks at US #62.
[2] Warwick guests on the first ever "Ready Steady, Goes Live!"
[10] She is a guest panelist on BBC-TV's "Juke Box Jury".
[14] Warwick appears on the ITV show, "The Bacharach Sound", with Dusty Springfield, the Searchers and others.
May [1] An uncharacteristic uptempo R&B single, *You Can Have Him*, peaks at US #75, having reached UK #37 on Apr [17].
June [28] Warwick guests on CBS-TV's "It's What's Happening Baby" special.
Aug *Here I Am*, from the Bacharach/David-penned soundtrack of the movie "What's New Pussycat?", makes US #65. (Its B-side is Warwick's original recording of *(They Long To Be) Close To You*, which will be a million seller five years later for the Carpenters.)
Sept [16] "The Divine Dionne Warwick" special airs on ITV.
Nov *(Here I Go Again) Looking With My Eyes* peaks at US #64.

1966

Jan *Are You There (With Another Girl?)* makes US #39.
Feb *Here I Am* makes US #45.
May Live album, ***Dionne Warwick In Paris***, recorded on stage at the Olympia, peaks at US #76, while *A Message To Michael*, a gender-switched revival of Bacharach/David's hit by both Lou Johnson and Adam Faith (as *A Message To Martha (Kentucky Bluebird)*), hits US #8.
June Compilation album ***Best Of Dionne Warwick*** hits UK #8.
Aug *Trains And Boats And Planes* (a 1965 UK success for Bacharach himself, and a US and UK hit by Billy J. Kramer) reaches US #22.
Nov *I Just Don't Know What To Do With Myself*, an album cut covered as a UK hit by Dusty Springfield in 1964, reaches US #26.

1967

Jan *Another Night* makes US #49, as Warwick begins a four-month European tour.
Feb ***Here, Where There Is Love*** reaches US #18 and UK #39, and becomes Warwick's first RIAA certified gold album. It contains her version of *Alfie*, the film theme which has hit for Cher and Cilla Black the previous year.
June Originally billed to sing at the "Monterey International Pop Festival", the management of San Francisco's Fairmont Hotel, where she is currently appearing, refuses to let her perform, saying it will damage her drawing power in the city.
On Stage And In The Movies peaks at US #169.
[10] Warwick appears at the two-day "Fantasy Faire And Magic Mountain Music Fest" in Mt. Tamilpais, CA, before an audience of 15,000. She is billed alongside the Miracles and several of California's new breed of rock bands, including the Doors and Jefferson Airplane.
July After strong airplay as an album track, *Alfie* reaches US #15, while its B-side, *The Beginning Of Loneliness*, peaks at US #79. She makes her West Coast cabaret debut at the West Side Room, Los Angeles, CA.
Sept *The Windows Of The World* makes US #32.
Nov ***The Windows Of The World*** reaches US #22.
Dec From the album, *I Say A Little Prayer* hits US #4.

1968

Jan ***Dionne Warwick's Golden Hits, Part One*** hits US #10.
Feb *I Say A Little Prayer*, with its B-side movie theme, *(Theme From) Valley Of The Dolls*, penned by André and Dory Previn, recorded at the suggestion of the film's star, Barbara Parkins, becomes Warwick's biggest double-sided chart-maker of her career, and a million seller in the US alone. Issued in the UK as an A-side, *(Theme From) Valley Of The Dolls* reaches #28.
[15] *I Say A Little Prayer* is certified gold by the RIAA.
Apr ***Valley Of The Dolls*** hits US #6, and eventually earns a gold disc.
May Still recording Bacharach/David material, *Do You Know The Way To San José*, taken from the album, hits US #10, while its B-side, *Let Me Be Lonely*, peaks at US #71.
June ***Valley Of The Dolls*** hits UK #10, as *Do You Know The Way To San José* hits UK #8.
Sept *Who Is Gonna Love Me?* makes US #33. Its B-side revives Warwick's original *(There's) Always Something There To Remind Me* (a 1964 hit for Sandie Shaw and Lou Johnson), and peaks at US #65.
Dec *Promises Promises*, from Bacharach/David's Broadway musical of the same title, reaches US #19.

1969

Jan ***Promises Promises*** reaches US #18.
Feb [24] ***Dionne Warwick's Greatest Hits*** is certified gold by the RIAA.
Mar *This Girl's In Love With You*, from ***Promises, Promises*** (and a gender-switch revival of Herb Alpert's million seller of the previous summer), hits US #7.
[12] *Do You Know The Way To San José* wins Best Contemporary Pop Vocal Performance, Female, at the 11th annual Grammy Awards.
May ***Soulful***, recorded in Memphis, TN, with producer Chips Moman, reaches US #11.
June *The April Fools*, the title theme from the Jack Lemmon/Catherine Deneuve film, makes US #37. Warwick makes her own film acting debut in "Slaves", a historical drama, opposite Stephen Boyd and Ossie Davis, also recording the movie's theme song. (The next time she acts will be in a guest-starring role with Isaac Hayes, in an episode of "The Rockford Files".)
Sept ***Dionne Warwick's Greatest Motion Picture Hits*** makes US #31, while *Odds And Ends* reaches US #43.
Nov Her treatment of the Righteous Brothers' *You've Lost That Lovin' Feelin'* reaches US #16.
Dec Compilation, ***Dionne Warwick's Golden Hits, Part 2***, reaches US #28.

1970

Feb *I'll Never Fall In Love Again*, from "Promises Promises" (a UK hit for Bobbie Gentry in 1969), hits US #6.
Mar [1] CBS-TV's "The Ed Sullivan Show - The Beatles Songbook", on which Warwick sings *We Can Work It Out* and *A Hard Day's Night*, and duets with Peggy Lee and Paul McCartney (whose contribution has been spliced in from an earlier show) on *Yesterday*, airs.
Apr [13] Warwick makes a sole European appearance at London's Royal Albert Hall.
May *Let Me Go To Him* makes US #32.
June Compilation albums, ***Greatest Hits Vol. 1*** and ***Greatest Hits Vol. 2***, reach UK #31 and #28 respectively, while *I'll Never Fall In Love Again* peaks at US #23.
Aug *Papier Maché* stops at US #43.
[6] The RIAA certifies gold sales of ***Here Where There Is Love*** and ***Valley Of The Dolls***.
Nov *Make It Easy On Yourself*, a revival of Bacharach/David's 1962 hit for Jerry Butler, makes US #37.
[9] Warwick takes part in the "Royal Variety Performance" in London.
[26] She appears in an NBC-TV special, with Andy Williams, the Supremes, Bobbie Gentry, Henry Mancini, Burl Ives, Tennessee Ernie Ford and Pearl Bailey.

1971

Jan ***Very Dionne*** makes US #37 while, taken from it, *The Green Grass Starts To Grow* reaches US #43.
Mar [16] Warwick receives her second Grammy, as *I'll Never Fall In Love Again* is named Best Contemporary Vocal Performance, Female, at the 13th annual Grammy Awards.
Apr *Who Gets The Guy* makes US #57.
Aug *Amanda*, from the soundtrack, ***The Love Machine***, peaks at US #83, and is Warwick's last hit single on Scepter, as she is now signed to Warner Bros.
Dec Double album, ***The Dionne Warwicke Story***, featuring live versions of her hits, makes US #48. (A numerologist advises Warwick to suffix an "e" (for husband Bill Elliot) to her name, to bring her luck. For a short period, she changes the spelling of her surname on all billing, to include the extra "e" in Warwicke, but will revert back to its original form in 1975.) (Elliot, who she married in the early '60s, and by whom she has two sons, Damon and David, will die in the early '70s.)
[23] ***The Dionne Warwicke Story*** is certified gold by the RIAA.

1972

Mar ***Dionne***, her label debut for Warner Bros., makes US #54, while the extracted *If We Only Have Love* peaks at US #84. This hit marks the end of her long collaboration with Bachararch and David, who will no longer write for her, as they also split professionally. Warwick sues the duo, alleging the breach of a contractual obligation.
Apr ***From Within***, featuring reissued Scepter material, makes US #169.

1973

Feb Her second Warners album, ***Just Being Myself***, teaming her with Holland/Dozier/Holland peaks at US #178 and, like most of Warwick's Warner albums, fails to yield a hit single. (Her vocals are added to tracks already used by Freda Payne and Honey Cone.)

1974

Oct [8] The still-climbing *Then Came You* is certified gold by the RIAA.

[26] After R&B vocal group the Spinners has been the opening act for Dionne Warwick on a five-week summer US theater tour, producer Thom Bell has suggested a duet between Warwick and the group. The resulting *Then Came You*, written by Sherman Marshall and Phil Pugh, now tops the US chart for a week - the first #1 hit for either side of the partnership. (After recording the cut, Bell recalls: "Dionne made a face when we finished it. She didn't like it much, but I knew we had something. So we ripped a dollar in two, signed each half and exchanged them. I told her, 'If it doesn't go number one, I'll send you my half'. When it took off, Dionne sent hers back. There was an apology on it.")

Nov *Then Came You* reaches UK #29.

1975

Feb Warwick performs at London's Royal Albert Hall.

Mar ***Then Came You***, including the duet with the Spinners, peaks at US #167. ***Track Of The Cat***, produced by Bell, and mostly written by him and Linda Creed, will make US #137 the following January with the extracted *Once You Hit The Road* peaking at US #79 in February.

1977

Mar The live double album recorded at the Fox Theatre, Atlanta, GA, ***A Man And A Woman***, on which Warwick duets with Isaac Hayes, released on his Hot Buttered Soul label, makes US #49, and coincides with the opening of a joint US tour by the pair. (They will also shortly appear together in an episode of NBC-TV's "The Rockford Files".)

1979

Jan Following the non-charting ***Only Love Can Break A Heart*** and ***Love At First Sight***, marking the end of relationship with Warner Bros., Warwick signs to Arista Records while also completing her masters degree in music.

Oct *I'll Never Love This Way Again* hits US #5. It is taken from her debut Arista album, ***Dionne***, produced by labelmate Barry Manilow, which reaches US #12 during a one-year plus chart stay.

[19] *I'll Never Love This Way Again* is certified gold by the RIAA.

1980

Feb *Déjà Vu*, also from ***Dionne***, reaches US #15.

[27] Warwick wins the Best Pop Vocal Performance, Female, for *I'll Never Love This Way Again*, and Best R&B Vocal Performance, Female, for *Déjà Vu*, categories at the 22nd annual Grammy Awards.

Mar [11] ***Dionne*** is certified platinum by the RIAA.

Apr *After You*, the theme of the film of the same title, also produced by Manilow, peaks at US #65.

Sept Warwick hosts the first season of the US syndicated-TV pop show, "Solid Gold". (She refuses to return for the second season, unwilling to co-host with country singer, Tanya Tucker. She returns though, in 1984 through to 1986.)

Oct The Steve Buckingham-produced ***No Night So Long***, and the extracted title track, the Richard Kerr/Will Jennings-penned *No Night So Long*, both reach US #23.

Dec [13] *Easy Love*, also from the album, peaks at US #62.

1981

July Double album, ***Hot! Live And Otherwise***, which has three live sides (recorded at Harrah's in Reno, NV) and one studio-recorded side, makes US #72. Taken from it, the Michael Masser-produced *Some Changes Are For Good* peaks at US #65.

1982

June ***Friends In Love*** makes US #83, while the title song, *Friends In Love*, a duet with Johnny Mathis, reaches US #38.

Dec ***Heartbreaker***, produced by the Bee Gees' Barry Gibb with Albhy Galuten and Karl Richardson, and mostly co-written by Gibb (apart from the revived oldie, *Our Day Will Come*) reaches US #25 and hits UK #3, while the title track, *Heartbreaker*, written by the Bee Gees, and featuring Barry Gibb on backing vocals, hits UK #2.

1983

Jan *Heartbreaker* hits US #10 while its UK follow-up, the Bee Gees-penned ballad, *All The Love In The World*, hits UK #10.

Feb *Yours*, another brothers Gibb composition, peaks at UK #66.

Apr *Take The Short Way Home*, written by Gibb and Galuten, is Warwick's 50th US hit single, making US #41.

May A UK-only compilation, ***The Collection***, reaches UK #11.

June The reissue of *I'll Never Love This Way Again*, taken from ***The Collection***, peaks at UK #62.

Nov ***So Amazing*** makes UK #60.

Dec ***How Many Times Can We Say Goodbye*** (the US title of ***So Amazing***), produced by Luther Vandross, peaks at US #57, as the title song, *How Many Times Can We Say Goodbye*, a duet with Vandross, reaches US #27.

1984

Nov Stevie Wonder's soundtrack album, ***The Woman In Red***, featuring Warwick, hits US #4 and UK #2.

1985

Jan [28] Warwick takes part in the recording of the all-star charity single, *We Are The World*, by USA For Africa, which will top charts throughout the world.

Feb ***Without Your Love***, containing duets with Barry Manilow, Glenn Jones and Stevie Wonder, and reuniting her with Burt Bacharach, peaks at UK #86.

Mar In the US, the album is given the alternative title, ***Finder Of Lost Loves***, and peaks at US #106.

Nov *That's What Friends Are For*, written by Bacharach and his wife, Carole Bayer Sager, for the 1982 film, "Night Shift", and originally sung by Rod Stewart, is revived, initially to provide a duet for Warwick and Stevie Wonder. When it is decided to donate its profits to the American Foundation for AIDS Research, Warwick first asks Gladys Knight, and then Elton John, to add vocal parts. The song is released as a single, credited to Dionne Warwick & Friends, and reaches UK #16.

Dec ***Friends*** reaches US #12.

[12] She receives a star on Hollywood's Walk of Fame.

1986

Jan [15] The still-climbing *That's What Friends Are For* is certified gold by the RIAA.

[18] *That's What Friends Are For* begins a four-week stay at US #1. All company and artists' profits from it are given to AIDS charities, as it becomes the year's best-selling single in the US.

[25] *That's What Friends Are For* tops the US R&B chart.

Feb [25] Warwick presents her cousin, Whitney Houston, with the trophy for Best Pop Vocal Performance, Female, at the 28th annual Grammy Awards. (She announces the setting up of the Warwick Foundation to find a cure for AIDS.)

Mar [11] ***Friends*** is certified gold by the RIAA.

[29] *Whisper In The Dark*, also from ***Friends***, peaks at US #72.

1987

Feb [24] *That's What Friends Are For* wins the Song Of The Year, and Best Pop Performance By A Duo Or Group With Vocal categories at the 29th annual Grammy Awards, staged at the Shrine Auditorium. Warwick, Stevie Wonder and Gladys Knight, accompanied by Burt Bacharach on the piano, sing the song on the telecast.

Mar Warwick co-hosts the inaugural Soul Train Music Awards with Luther Vandross, at the Hollywood Center television studios.

Aug *Love Power*, a duet with Jeffrey Osborne, peaks at UK #63.

[29] *Love Power* reaches US #12. Its parent album, ***Reservations For Two***, containing duets with Kashif, Howard Hewett (ex-Shalamar), Osborne, Smokey Robinson and June Pointer of the Pointer Sisters, makes US #56.

Sept [23] The city of New York honors Warwick for her work in raising $1 million for AIDS research.

Nov [21] *Reservations For Two*, taken from the album of the same title, and duetted with Kashif, peaks at US #62.

1988

Sept Warwick tapes *Champagne Wishes And Caviar Dreams*, the theme for the sixth season of Robin Leach's syndicated-TV show, "Lifestyles Of The Rich And Famous".

1990

Jan [14] TV show, "Dionne And Friends", premieres on US cable stations.

[20] A 12-track Arista compilation, ***Greatest Hits 1979-1990***, peaks at US #177.

[27] A UK-only collection, ***Love Songs***, hits UK #6.

Feb Motown releases *Forgotten Eyes*, a benefit single featuring 100 artists, including Warwick. (All proceeds from the record will go to benefit Retinitis Pigmentosa International.)

Mar Melba Moore's *Lift Up Every Voice And Sing*, on which Warwick guests with Anita Baker, Bobby Brown, Howard Hewett, Freddie Jackson, Jeffrey Osborne, and Stevie Wonder, to benefit the NAACP United Negro College Fund, and sickle cell anemia research, is released on Capitol.

[14] Warwick co-hosts the fourth annual Soul Train Awards, at the Shrine Auditorium, Los Angeles, with Patti LaBelle and Luther Vandross.

[17] She joins her Arista labelmates in the company's "That's What Friends Are For" 15th anniversary concert at New York's Radio City Music Hall, which will raise more than $2 million, the proceeds going to the Gay Men's Health Crisis and other AIDS organizations.

July [19-21] Warwick performs at the Greek Theatre, Los Angeles, with Johnny Mathis.

Sept [15] ***Dionne Warwick Sings Cole Porter*** peaks at US #155.

Nov [4] She takes part in "Women In Concert" benefit with the Roches and the Judds at the Academy of Music, Philadelphia, PA.

[17] Warwick is honored at the Big Sisters Guild of Los Angeles' fourth annual gala fund-raiser, titled "Dionne, Sisters & Friends", at the Bonaventure Hotel, Los Angeles.

Dec [1] She is given the Key Of Life Award at NAACP's 23rd annual Image Awards, at Los Angeles' Wiltern Theatre.

1991

Mar [12] Warwick co-hosts the fifth annual Soul Train Music Awards, held again at the Shrine Auditorium.

June [15] She appears at a Los Angeles benefit, organized by Robert Townsend, for the family of the late David Ruffin, with Gladys Knight and Stevie Wonder.

Dec [13] Warwick performs at the seventh annual Stellar Awards for gospel music at UCLA's Royce Hall, Los Angeles.

1992

Jan [20] She is honored with the Humanitarian Award

at the 50th anniversary CORE "Living the Dream 1992 Awards Dinner" at the Sheraton Center Hotel & Towers, New York.

Mar [11-14] Warwick and Johnny Mathis perform at New York's Radio City Music Hall, New York, grossing $715,165.

May She attends a service at the First African Methodist Episcopal Church in Los Angeles, immediately after the riots.

[2] Warwick receives the DIVA Award at the second annual "Divas : Simply Singing!" benefit for the Minority AIDS Project, at the Masonic Temple, Los Angeles.

[25] She embarks on a ten-date UK tour at St. David's Hall, Cardiff, S. Glamorgan, Wales, set to end on June 4th at London's Hammersmith Odeon.

June [5] Warwick is bestowed with the Humanitarian Award at the 22nd annual Nosotros Golden Eagle Awards (dedicated to raising the image of Latinos in the media) at the Beverly Hilton, Los Angeles.

[12] She sings *That's What Friends Are For* with Whitney Houston, at Clive Davis' "Man Of The Year" tribute, at the Friars Club, Waldorf Astoria Hotel, New York, despite having earlier collapsed at Los Angeles International Airport, suffering from a chronic back problem.

July [16] Warwick leads an all-star tribute to retiring NAACP chief, Benjamin Hooks, at the 83rd annual convention of the NAACP in Nashville, TN.

[28] On tour with Burt Bacharach, Warwick performs at the New Pine Knob Music Theatre, Clarkston, MI.

Sept [16] She sings *Amazing Grace* at a fund-raiser for presidential candidate, Bill Clinton, at Ted Field's Beverly Hills estate.

Oct [23-25] Warwick performs at Caesar's Palace, Las Vegas, NV.

Nov She participates at a Celebrity Theatre, Anaheim, CA, benefit to raise money for the Los Angeles Minority Aids Project.

[1] Warwick guests on the Nancy Wilson-hosted "Family Night", an all-star benefit at UCLA's Royce Hall, for the National Council of Negro Women.

Dec [26] She participates in the "Lou Rawls Parade of Stars" annual telethon in Los Angeles, which raises $11 million for the United Negro College Fund.

1993

Jan [17] Warwick takes part in "An American Reunion : The People's Inaugural Celebration", at the Lincoln Memorial, Washington, DC, as the first single, *Sunny Weather Lover*, from her forthcoming album, ***Friends Can Be Lovers***, marking a reunion for the singer with Bacharach & David, who themselves have not written together for over 20 years, is released.

May [24] She sings Bacharach and David songs, at the 10th annual ASCAP Pop Awards dinner, at the Beverly Hilton Hotel, Beverly Hills, CA.

June [4-5] Warwick performs at the Ohio Theatre, Columbus, OH, during current US dates.

1994

Feb [19] Currently in the spotlight as the hostess of US-TV infomercials for the "Psychic Friends Network" (for which she reportedly earns a seven-figure annual sum), she nevertheless takes part in the "Jackson Family Honors" from the MGM Grand Hotel in Las Vegas, NV, a much hyped and troubled event.

[23] Warwick attends a Judiciary juvenile justice sub-committee hearing in Washington, DC, calling gangsta rap "pornography".

Mar [4-6] She performs a three-day stint at Caesar's Palace in Las Vegas.

Aug [12] Warwick expresses sympathy and support for long-time friend, the currently beleaguered O. J. Simpson, on US syndicated TV's "Geraldo" show.

Nov [8] Arista Records releases her 13th album for the label, a collection of Brazilian songs titled ***Aquarela Do Brasil***. (She intends to re-locate to Brazil permanently by year's end.)

1995

Jan [10] Warwick sings at a tribute to Ella Fitzgerald held at the Universal Amphitheatre, Universal City.

Mar [23] She performs the first of five Euro-dates, with Bacharach accompanying her, in Paris, France.

THE WATERBOYS

Mike Scott (vocals, guitar); **Anthony Thistlethwaite** (saxophone, multi-instrumentalist)

1981

June Having run a fanzine, **Jungleland** in 1977-78, inspired by the Bruce Springsteen song, for which he has interviewed the Clash and the Only Ones, among others, Scott (b. Dec. 14, 1958, Edinburgh, Lothian, Scotland), a veteran of unsuccessful UK bands including DNV, Funhouse, and Another Pretty Face, who were signed to Virgin Records for four months in 1980, now relocates from his native Edinburgh, where he has studied English and Philosophy at Edinburgh University, to London, and conceives his latest project, the Waterboys (which will always revolve around his songwriting and creative vision), signing to the fledgling Ensign label.

Dec Scott begins recording the debut album (which will only feature sessioneers Kevin Wilkinson, Ray Massey, Norman Rodger, Nick Linden and Steven Tayler on one track, the rest entirely recorded by Scott), at the Redshop Studio, London, moving on to the Farmyard Studio, Little Chalfont, Bucks. in May '92. Sax player Thistlethwaite (b. Aug. 31, 1955, Leicester, Leics.) will also join the sessions, and perform with Scott in the short-lived side combo, the Red & the Black in London the following year.

1983

Mar The Rupert Hine-produced *A Girl Called Johnny*, written by Scott about Patti Smith, whom he met in London in 1978.

Apr Having answered an ad placed by Scott in **Sounds**, looking for a "guitarist into Iggy Pop", keyboardist Karl Wallinger (b. Oct. 19, 1957, Prestatyn, Clwyd, Wales) joins the Waterboys, in time to contribute to the second album recording sessions. He has previously worked at a music publishers and served in indie outfits, the Invisible Body Club and Out.

May The Waterboys make their TV debut on BBC2-TV's "The Old Grey Whistle Test".

July Scott-penned ***The Waterboys*** is released.

1984

Feb The Waterboys make their live debut in Batschkaap.

June [18] The celtic-rock tinged ***A Pagan Place***, featuring current Waterboy Kevin Wilkinson on drums, makes UK #100. It is entirely written and produced by Scott, and attracts much critical praise.

Dec Having toured the UK and rest of Europe throughout the year, the group now supports U2 on its US trek.

1985

Jan Scott, staying at New York, NY's Gramercy Hotel, begins writing what will become *The Whole Of The Moon*, while drinking at the hotel bar, after his girlfriend asks him if it is difficult to write a song. He responds by inking the first verse and chorus on the back of an envelope. (The rest of the song will take him another four months to complete.)

Mar The band, now augmented by ex-In Tua Nua Irish fiddle player Steve Wickham (who will become a fulltime member in September), begins recording a new album at the Townhouse Studio in London, although the bulk of the five month sessions will take place at Park Gates studio in Hastings, Sussex and London's Livingstone studio. It becomes apparent during recording that Wallinger, himself full of creative energy, wants an increasingly active role. In addition to songwriting, he also co-arranges tracks, and becomes a multi-instrumentalist on the project.

Oct Their third album, ***This Is The Sea***, is released, set to make UK #37, a critical and commercial breakthrough, as the group sets off on European and US tour dates through the end of the year.

Nov The extracted, anthemic track, *The Whole Of The Moon*, reaches UK #26, in the same month Wallinger announces his departure fom the band after a show in New York, "pregnant with World Party" as Scott will later indicate. (World Party, over which Wallinger will have complete creative control, will also sign with Ensign.)

1986

Jan [23] At Wickham's invitation, Scott has moved to Dublin, Eire earlier in the month and now begins recording the next Waterboys album at the city's Windmill Lane Studios, but will scrap the project in favor of a new folk-rock "raggle-taggle" direction, such is his interest in Irish celtic and gaelic music.

Apr The band tours Eire and the UK, with Thistlethwaite alternating between saxophone and mandolin. (During the spring, the Waterboys debut their new sound on C4-TV's "The Tube".)

May The group continues touring, appearing at a number of summer festivals around Europe.

Dec Scott begins fresh recording sessions in San Francisco, CA with Bob Dylan's former producer Bob Johnston.

1987

May While the group will spend much of the year recording some 60 songs back at the Windmill Lane Studios, they perform a show on board Sirius, a Greenpeace ship docked in Dublin's harbour.

Oct During the month, the Waterboys play two shows in support of the Irish Green Party at Dublin's Olympic Ballroom.

1988

Apr The band completes recording the second half of its next album in the dining room at Spiddal House, County Galway, Eire.

Oct [29] The resulting ***Fisherman's Blues*** reaches UK #13 in its week of entry, and will make US #76 during a half-year chart stay. The album includes an update of Van Morrison's *Sweet Thing*, a track titled *World Party*, which will become a popular US college cut, and the Scott-penned *Strange Boat*, which will subsequently be recorded by Tom Jones.

Dec [15] The group's first full tour in over two years begins at City Hall, Cork, Eire.

1989

Jan The title track, *Fisherman's Blues*, makes UK #32.

Feb The full raggle-taggle Waterboys line-up undertakes further live UK dates with the Saw Doctors opening.

June County Clare, Eire-based accordion player Sharon Shannon joins the group.

July *And A Bang On The Ear* peaks at UK #51.

Sept Still based on the west coast of Eire, Scott produces an unreleased album by traditional celtic players, Steve Cooney and Seamus Begley, recorded in a pub in Dingle Bay.

Oct The band embarks on its first US tour in four years.

1990

Feb Recording by Scott and Thistlethwaite, now augmented by Wickham, Trevor Hutchinson (double bass), Colin Blakey (flute, organ, who joined in December 1988), Noel Bridgeman (drums, who joined in June the previous year) and Shannon.

June Scott marries Irene Keough in Dublin (she was the studio manager at the Windmill Lane complex). A dance update of *The Whole Of The Moon* by Little Caesar peaks at UK #68.

July Wickham leaves the group following completion of album sessions and will join Dublin folk unit, the Texas Kellys. Shannon, Blakey and Bridgeman also leave.

Sept[15] The Waterboys, having already played opening shows in Scotland the previous month, embark on a further ten-date UK tour at the Guildhall, Preston, Lancs., focused in a rock direction with the

live line-up of US drummer Ken Blevins, Hutchinson, and helmsmen Scott and Thistlethwaite. The tour will end on the 29th at London's Highbury Fields.
[29] Co-produced by Scott and Barry Beckett, ***Room To Roam*** hits UK #5.
Nov [10] ***Room To Roam*** peaks at US #180.
Dec [7] The group plays at the Symphony Hall, Phoenix, AZ, during its current US tour.
[31] The Waterboys plays what will prove to be its final gig at the Leisureland in Galway, Eire.

1991

Apr [13] In a period of hip reappraisement of the band (during the year, the group is featured in the TV documentary, "Bringing It All Back Home", a five-part look at the roots of Irish music and the role America has played in its history), *The Whole Of The Moon*, originally a 1983 UK #26 and reissued as a trailer to a greatest hits package, ***Best Of The Waterboys '81-'90***, hits UK #3.
May [11] ***Best Of The Waterboys '81-'90*** debuts at its UK #2 peak, behind Eurythmics' ***Greatest Hits***.
June [8] *Fisherman's Blues*, originally a 1989 UK #32, charts for a week at UK #75.
Aug Scott makes a surprise appearance at the "Feile Festival" at the Semple Stadium, Thurles, Co. Tipperary, joining the Saw Doctors onstage.
Sept [1] Scott makes his first ever solo appearance at the Abbey Theatre, Dublin, in a benefit for the "Yeats International Festival", singing four W.B. Yeats poems set to music.
[7] He makes a second solo appearance at "The West's Awake Festival" in Tuam, Co. Galway.
[28] Relocating to New York, Scott will begin auditioning for a new Waterboys line-up.
Dec His long standing professional association with Thistlethwaite ends.

1992

Jan Scott begins recording a new Waterboys album at New York's Right Trade Studios, sessions which will last until August.
Apr [15] *The Whole Of The Moon* is named Best Song Musically And Lyrically, at the 37th annual Ivor Novello Awards, held at London's Grosvenor House Hotel.
Nov During the month, Scott performs two informal shows at Cafe Sin E, in New York.

1993

May [22] *The Return Of Pan* reaches UK #24.
June [5] The Scott-penned Waterboys album ***Dream Harder***, with cover art by musical contributor, Jules Shear's wife Pal Shazar, debuts at its UK #5 peak, and will stop at US #171 on the 12th.
July [24] *Glastonbury Song* debuts at its UK #29 peak.
Aug Having failed to find new band members, Scott leaves New York, effectively bringing the Waterboys concept to a close.
Sept [25] ***Sweet Relief***, a tribute album for singer/songwriter Victoria Williams, featuring the Waterboys' *Why Look At The Moon*, makes US #131. (She has been diagnosed with multiple sclerosis in 1992.)

1994

June [24] Scott makes a surprise appearance at the annual "Glastonbury Festival", Pilton, Somerset, when he wanders onstage during Ian McNabb's set, to sing *Preparing To Fly*.

1995

July Having performed solo dates in the UK, Eire and the rest of Europe between January and April, and bought back the masters of his solo album (already released in the US) from Geffen Records, Scott relocates to London and signs with Chrysalis Records.
Sept [30] His debut album, ***Bring 'Em All In***, recorded in the basement of Universal Hall, reaches UK #23 in its week of entry, previewed by *Bring 'Em All In* which made UK #56 for one week on Sept [16], also yielding *Building The City Of Light* which will enter for a week at UK #60 on Nov [11].
see also: **WORLD PARTY**

MUDDY WATERS

1943

Given his nickname as a child playing in a muddy creek, Waters (b. McKinley Morganfield, Apr. 4, 1915, Rolling Fork, MS), raised on the Stovall Plantation near Clarksdale, MS, where his parents were sharecroppers on the Mississippi Delta, and where he was raised by his grandmother after his mother died when he was three, took up the harmonica at the age of eight, only graduating to the guitar in his mid-teens, much influenced by the music of Robert Johnson and Son House. Having already recorded two songs, *I Be's Troubled* and *Country Blues* in 1941 for a folk/blues anthology assembled by Library of Congress archivist Alan Lomax, and earning a living by driving a truck for a venetian-blind manufacturer, Waters now heads for Chicago, IL, where he is introduced by fellow blues-man, Big Bill Broonzy, to the South Side clubs and bars, where he begins to develop a strong local reputation, backing the likes of Sonny Boy Williamson, while also taking a job at a paper mill.

1946

Having taken to playing the electric guitar two years earlier, performing in a band with fellow guitarist Claude Smith, harmonica player Jimmy Rogers and pianist Eddie Boyd, Waters' first label recordings are for Columbia Records Okeh imprint under the supervision of producer Lester Melrose (but which not emerge until 1981 on the album ***Okeh Chicago Blues***).

1947

Chicago-based Leonard and Phil Chess sign Waters to their Aristocrat Records label, where he begins work as a sideman for other artists, notably on Sunnyland Slim's *Fly Right Little Girl* and *Johnson Machine Gun* and on bassist Big Crawford's *Little Anna Mae* and *Gypsy Woman*.

1948

Sept Waters' first solo material emerges, featuring Crawford on bass: *I Can't Be Satisfied* coupled with his US R&B chart debut, *(I Feel Like) Going Home*, which now makes #11 on the specialist survey, his innovative electric guitar style meshed with Delta blues proving a popular selection on jukeboxes and in stores. Staying with Crawford in the studio (for further sides including 1949's *Screamin' And Cryin'*, followed by *Rollin' And Tumblin'*), Waters begins playing a riveting harder, brasher blues style in the clubs, backed by Rogers, drummer/guitarist Leroy Foster and harmonica player Little Walter Jacobs.

1950

May Waters' first single on Chess (re-named from Aristocrat) is *Rollin' Stone* (subsequently the name inspiration for the Rolling Stones), which features the group he will use on many of his ground-breaking releases over the next decade - Little Walter (harmonica), Otis Spann (piano) and Jimmy Rogers (second guitar); bass player and composer, Willie Dixon, will be another regular in the line-up, with Elgin Evans on drums.

1951

Jan Waters' second major national US R&B success is *Louisiana Blues* which hits #10. (Over the next five years, he will have a further 13 US R&B hits: *Long Distance Call, Honey Bee, Still A Fool* (all this year), *She Moves Me* (1952), *Mad Love* (1953), *I'm Your Hoochie Coochie Man, Just Make Love To Me* and *I'm Ready* (all in 1954), the much-revered *Mannish Boy, Sugar Sweet* (both in 1955), *Trouble No More, Forty Days & Forty Nights* and *Don't Go No Farther* (all in 1956), a body of work which will be critically regarded as some of the finest blues recording ever made.)

1958

With *Close To You* becoming his final R&B hit, and Chess releasing his first album, ***The Best Of Muddy Waters***, Waters, on his first UK tour, makes a big impression on white London blues-men, Cyril Davies and Alexis Korner, who will be pioneers of Britain's emergent R&B movement. (By the end of the decade, the mass black American audience for the blues will largely disappear, favoring the more sophisticated R&B/soul styles. Waters will be able to avoid the limbo into which many US blues-men are cast thanks to marketing initiatives by Chess, who successfully project him as an albums artist, selling increasingly to white audiences.)

1961

Sept His electric live set, ***Muddy Waters At Newport***, released by Chess in the US and Pye Records in the UK, recorded the previous year, introduces him to a wider audience.

1963

Oct [18] Waters plays at the "American Negro Blues Festival" at the Fairfield Halls, Croydon, Surrey, on a bill with Memphis Slim, Sonny Boy Williamson and Willie Dixon.

1964

May ***Muddy Waters Folk Singer***, a solo acoustic album, gives him a new folk following. Waters is also currently championed by UK R&B/beat groups, including the Rolling Stones and the Yardbirds, and reissued albums of his '50s singles start selling to a new generation of fans.

1965

June [17-20] Waters takes part in the first "New York Folk Festival" at Carnegie Hall, New York.
Nov [24-27] He performs at the "Blues Bag" showcase at the Café Au Go Go in New York's Greenwich Village, on a bill with Blues Project, John Lee Hooker and Otis Spann.

1966

Apr Waters makes his first Los Angeles, CA, appearance in ten years, at the Troubadour.
Oct [22] He takes part in "Jazz Expo '68" at London's Hammersmith Odeon, promoting ***The Real Folk Blues*** recently issued by Chess.
Nov [4-6] He performs at the Fillmore West, San Francisco, CA, sharing the bill with the Quicksilver Messenger Service. (***More Real Folk Blues*** and the soul-aimed ***Muddy, Brass and the Blues*** will be released by Chess the following year.)

1968

Sept [2] Waters appears at the three-day "Sky River Rock Festival and Lighter-Than-Air Fair", in Sultan, WA, with Santana, the Grateful Dead, Country Joe & the Fish and the Youngbloods, among others.
Nov Following the May release of ***The Super Blues Band***, recorded with Bo Diddley and Howlin' Wolf, the first of two controversial "psychedelic" albums, ***Electric Mud***, recorded for the Cadet Concept label, reaches US #127 his first album chart showing in the US, to be followed by ***After The Rain***.

1969

Oct Issued by Chess, ***Fathers And Sons***, a partly-live double set, featuring white US blues-men Paul Butterfield and Mike Bloomfield, climbs to US #70.

1972

Mar [14] ***They Call Me Muddy Waters*** wins the Best Ethnic Or Traditional Recording category at the 14th annual Grammy Awards.
July ***The London Muddy Waters Sessions*** is released.
Sept [9] Waters takes part in the "Ann Arbor Jazz & Blues Festival", Ann Arbor, MI.

1973

Mar [3] ***The London Muddy Waters Session*** nabs his second Best Ethnic or Traditional Recording trophy at the 15th annual Grammy Awards.

Oct [11] A serious car accident in which three people are killed, forces Waters into semi-retirement for two years.

1976

Feb [28] ***The Muddy Waters Woodstock Album*** wins the Best Ethnic Or Traditional Recording category, at the 18th annual Grammy Awards. Waters leaves Chess, subsequently suing its publishing company for substantial back royalties he claims are unpaid.

Nov [25] His first major live appearance following his accident is at the Band's farewell "Last Waltz" concert, at the Winterland Ballroom in San Francisco, where he performs *Mannish Boy*.

1977

Mar Blues-rock musician Johnny Winter and partner Steve Paul have signed Waters to their Blue Sky label, with Winter producing Waters on ***Hard Again***, recorded at The Schoolhouse, Boston, MA, which makes US #143.

1978

Feb [23] ***Hard Again*** wins his fourth Best Ethnic Or Traditional Recording trophy at the 20th annual Grammy Awards.

[25] A second Winter-produced set, ***I'm Ready*** enters the US chart set to make #157.

Aug Waters is invited to play at a White House picnic, organized by President Jimmy Carter.

1979

Jan His third Blue Sky set, ***Muddy Mississippi Waters Live***, is released.

Feb [15] ***I'm Ready*** is named Best Ethnic Or Traditional Recording at the 21st annual Grammy Awards.

1980

Feb [27] Recognition for Waters' dominance of the blues genre is confirmed, as he collects his sixth Grammy, for Best Ethnic Or Traditional Recording, for ***Muddy "Mississippi" Waters Live***, at the 22nd annual Awards, during a month when he is also inducted into the Blues Foundation. A final Winter-produced Blue Sky album, ***King Bee*** will peak at US #192 in May the following year, as the pair continue to tour together.

1983

Apr [30] Having last performed live the previous June at an Eric Clapton show, Waters dies of a heart attack in his sleep at home in Chicago.

1987

Jan [21] His legend as a blues pioneer is confirmed with his posthumous induction into the Rock and Roll Hall of Fame, at the second annual dinner held at New York's Waldorf Astoria Hotel.

Mannish Boy will make UK #51 in July the following year, through exposure on a Levi 501 jeans TV commercial.

1992

Feb [25] Waters is honored with NARAS' 1992 Lifetime Achievement Award at the 34th Grammys, in New York.

May [8] City officials in Rolling Fork, MS, dedicate the monument - "Muddy Waters, master of the blues, was born McKinley Morganfield in 1915, near Rolling Fork. His special technique and interpretation powerfully influenced the development of Delta blues music."

1993

Mar [23] Following the 1989 release of the comprehensive boxed-set retrospective ***The Chess Box***, Victory Music releases ***Tribute To Muddy Waters***, a celebration of Waters' work by a number of notable guitarists (including Jeff Beck, Slash, Gary Moore, Santana, Dave Gilmour and Brian May), assembled by Paul Rodgers, who sings lead on all the tracks, backed by a house band of Jason Bonham (drums), Pino Palladino (bass) and Ian Hatton (guitar).

BERT WEEDON

1956

Weedon (b. May 10, 1921, East Ham, London), having begun to play classical guitar at the age of 12, made his first public appearance at East Ham Town Hall in 1939, and during the Second World War and early post-war years played widely with dance bands, and with a jazz group fronted by Stephane Grappelli and Django Reinhardt, now becomes resident guitarist with UK's BBC Showband, led by Cyril Stapleton, and begins regular radio sessions. He signs to EMI's Parlophone label as a solo artist, and his recording debut, *Stranger Than Fiction*, is released as a 78rpm single.

1957

He starts to become an in-demand session player on the expanding UK recording scene, backing UK stars and US visitors including David Whitfield, Alma Cogan, Frank Sinatra, Nat "King" Cole and Judy Garland. With the UK rock'n'roll movement growing, he also works with Marty Wilde, Laurie London and Cliff Richard, among many others. Five more solo guitar singles are released by Parlophone, but none charts.

1959

June Signed to the new Top Rank label, his cover of the Virtues' US rock instrumental hit, *Guitar Boogie Shuffle* (an upbeat update of Arthur Smith's 1945 country tune, *Guitar Boogie*) hits UK #7. (The Virtues' version making UK #24.)

Nov Following the self-penned *Teenage Guitar*, *Nashville Boogie* makes UK #29.

1960

Mar *Big Beat Boogie*, coupled with a cover of Percy Faith's hit, *Theme From A Summer Place*, peaks at UK #37.

June *Twelfth Street Rag* makes UK #47.

July ***King Size Guitar*** reaches UK #18.

Aug The Shadows' version of the Jerry Lordan composition, *Apache*, tops the UK chart, while Weedon's less dramatic rendition peaks at UK #24. (Weedon has actually recorded it first, but EMI, which markets Weedon's Top Rank label and the Shadows' Columbia, has backed the group's version for major promotion.) The Shadows have composed *Mr. Guitar* for Weedon and acknowledge the debt they - and almost all other guitarists in the UK - owe to Weedon, who has been the major role model during the '50s, and whose **Play In A Day** teach-yourself guitar booklet is used by almost every newcomer to the instrument. (The booklet, seldom out of print, will become a far more significant memorial of Weedon's influence than any of his recordings, and will be sequelled by **Play Every Day**.)

Nov *Sorry Robbie* (with hints of a traditional Scottish air, hence the title) reaches UK #28.

1961

Feb The self-written *Ginchy* reaches UK #35.

May *Mr. Guitar*, written by the Shadows, makes UK #47, and is Weedon's last UK singles chart entry.

Nov He moves to EMI's HMV label. He will record 14 singles between now and 1967, but none will chart, though both *Some Other Love* and *South Of The Border* in 1962 come close.

1962

Nov [16] Weedon headlines a show at Croydon, Surrey's Fairfield Halls, supported by B. Bumble & the Stingers, Johnny Kidd, Tommy Bruce, Michael Cox and Vince Eager.

Dec [30] He performs on ITV's "Sunday Night At The London Palladium". Still doing regular session work, as well as making concert appearances in Europe, he will be a familiar face during the next five years on other UK TV variety and children's shows, and in a long-running series of his own.

1963

Feb [1] Weedon gives a show in the window of a garage showroom in Salisbury, Wilts., for the children of two mechanics who repaired his broken windshield.

May [9] He takes part in "Pops For Everyone" at London's Royal Albert Hall, with Susan Maughan, Clinton Ford and others, broadcast on the BBC Light Programme. (His final single for HMV in June 1967, a re-make of *Stranger Than Fiction*, will be his last release for three years.)

1970

He signs to the MOR budget label, Contour Records, eschewing singles for "theme" albums, like ***The Romantic Guitar Of Bert Weedon***, ***The Gentle Guitar Of Bert Weedon*** and ***Bert Weedon Remembers ...***, variously comprised of Nat "King" Cole and Jim Reeves hits.

1971

Rockin' At The Roundhouse, recorded after he is a surprise show-stealer at a vintage rock'n'roll revival concert at London's Roundhouse, includes some of his old hits plus rock guitar standards, including the Ventures' *Walk Don't Run* and Duane Eddy's *Shazam* and *40 Miles Of Bad Road*. Sales of this and other Contour albums are huge (all in six figures), though as budget releases, they are excluded from the UK chart.

1976

Nov [20] Weedon records ***22 Golden Guitar Greats*** for Warwick Records which, promoted via a TV campaign, strikes a nostalgic chord with British audiences, and tops the UK chart for one week, his biggest vinyl success. (Weedon will remain a steady seller in the nostalgia market, occasionally dipping back into rock - as on *Rockin' Guitars*, a 1977 single with a medley of six rock classics, on Polydor - and will continue to release albums at an average rate of two a year into the '80s. By the mid-'80s, he will have appeared on more than 5,000 TV and radio programs, including, finally, a well-deserved tribute on ITV's "This Is Your Life".)

PAUL WELLER

1990

Nov [5] Having already formed and fronted successful UK acts the Jam (from 1976-1982) and the Style Council (from 1983-1989), and following the rejection of the latter's fifth studio album ***Decades Of Modernism*** by Polydor Records, Weller (b. John Weller, May 25, 1958, Woking, Surrey) has formally announced the dissolution of the Style Council in March, finding himself without a record deal for the first time in his career, having also sold his Solid Bond Studios. He now assembles the Paul Weller Movement with ex-Style Councillor Steve White on drums and returns to live performance with an 11-date low-key European tour.

[23] A nine-date sold-out UK university tour opens at Leeds University, Leeds, S. Yorks., set to end on December 4th at Leicester University, Leicester, Leics.

1991

Apr [10] A further 14-date "Live Part 2" UK trek begins at London's Subterania, set to end at the Royal Court Theatre, Liverpool, Merseyside, on the 27th. (The Brixton Academy, London concert is filmed for home video release in August 1991.)

May [13] Weller is interviewed and performs on C4's "The Jonathan Ross Show".

[18] *Into Tomorrow*, released on his own Freedom High Record label, debuts at its UK #36 peak. Dee C.

Lee's project Slam Slam's ***Free Your Feelings*** is released, featuring seven Weller-penned tracks.
[18] Paul Weller Movement's *Into Tomorrow* debuts at its UK #36 peak.
Nov [17] Weller contributes *Don't Let Me Down* to the newly-released ***Revolution No. 9***, a collection of Beatles cover versions released to aid the Oxfam Cambodian Aid Appeal. (The Sunday release date is in response to the UK's arcane trading laws.) (During the month, Weller embarks on his first world tour in Japan, with a new band line-up comprising Steve White (drums), Camille Hands (bass), Helen Turner (keyboards), Jacko Peake (saxes and flute) and Zeke Manyika, ex-Orange Juice, on percussion. All have been previous honorary Style Councillors.)
Dec [4] The US leg of a world tour sees the Movement play five consecutive nights at the Variety Arts Centre in Los Angeles, CA, before finishing with a sell-out show at the Ritz, New York, NY on December 12th.
[18] The Movement plays a one-off London date at the Kilburn National.

1992

Jan Weller begins on his self-financed solo debut at Swanyard and Comfort Place studios with producer Brendan Lynch. He plays the majority of instruments, with White on drums and featuring Peake, Marco Nelson on bass and Carlene Anderson of the Young Disciples, ex-Blow Monkey Dr. Robert and Dee C. Lee as backing vocalists. Sessions lead to a deal with Japanese label Pony Canyon, allowing the album to be mixed and completed for a Japanese release in April.
June [21] Having signed a new UK contract with Go! Discs, Weller embarks on a six-date UK mini-tour at London's Subterania, which will include four London club dates, and witness a Style Council reunion at London's T&C 2 club with Lee and Mick Talbot joining the band for a rendition of Marvin Gaye's *What's Goin' On.*
July [27] Following a sell-out arena tour of Japan, a short North American visit sees Weller play at the Greek Theatre, Los Angeles, where he is joined onstage by former Small Face Ian McLagan to perform *Bullrush.*
Aug [20] Previewing his first strictly solo album, *Uh Huh Oh Yeh* is performed live on BBC1-TV's "Top Of The Pops".
[22] *Uh Huh Oh Yeh* reaches UK #18.
Sept [12] ***Paul Weller*** debuts at its UK #8 peak.
Oct [7] He embarks on a six-date UK tour at the Barrowlands, Glasgow, Strathclyde, Scotland, set to end on the 13th at London's Royal Albert Hall.
[10] *Above The Clouds* debuts at its UK #47 peak.
[13] His latest European jaunt ends at London's Royal Albert Hall.
Nov [25] During his current North American visit, Weller plays before a sellout crowd at the Irving Plaza, New York, a bill grossing $16,128.

1993

Jan [16] He guests on C4's "Saturday Zoo" premiere, performing *Bullrush/Magic Bus.* (He will make a return visit in March.) Despite not charting, his solo debut becomes his biggest-selling to date in the US.
Feb Weller begins working on a new album at Battery Studios, with Ollie Dagois producing.
Mar [11] He plays at London's Town & Country club in the week before its closure. Amid rumors that he is to re-form the Jam, Weller will be the music guest on NBC-TV's "The Tonight Show", performing *Uh Huh Oh Yeh* during a short North American tour at the end of the month.
July [9] He appears on BBC2-TV's "Later With Jools Holland" with new bassist Yolanda Charles (ex-Raw Stylus) who has replaced Camille Hinds. The current **Big Issue** magazine for London's homeless, includes an interview with Weller and is sold with a free flexidisc of *The Loved.*
[17] *Sunflower* bows at its UK #16 peak.
Aug [28] A two-part "Paul Weller Documentary" airs on Radio 1.
Sept [4] Title cut *Wild Wood* debuts at its UK #14 peak.
[10] Weller performs a free live set at London's Oxford Street HMV store, with his new backing guitarist Steve Craddock, ex-Ocean Colour Scene.
[11] ***Wild Wood***, featuring a similar session crew to his last outing with Talbot and Steve Craddock also added, enters at its UK #2 high. Again produced by Lynch and Weller and recorded at The Manor, Shipton-on-Cherwell, Oxfordshire, it initially charts for 26 weeks, selling over 350,000 copies.
Oct [20] Weller opens a new 650-capacity venue King's College, London. A short world tour begins with an eight Japanese dates, followed by a 12-concert UK venue tour finishing in December with shows in Europe and the US.
Nov [13] EP *The Weaver* bows at its UK #18 peak.
Dec Weller donates £20,000 to Horsell Common Muslim Cemetery in his hometown of Woking, a place he wrote about in his track *Amongst Butterflies*, from his debut album.
[14] Weller takes part in the "WEQX Holiday Concert For The Hungry" in Latham, NY.

1994

Jan ***More Wood***, a Japanese-only release containing UK B-sides and unreleased tracks, is issued.
[20] On the fifth birthday celebration of the Acid Jazz label at Ealing Film Studios, Weller jams onstage with ex-Small Face Kenney Jones, James Taylor and Mother Earth (with whom Weller has guested on their recent releases) for the filming of the "History Of Acid Jazz".
Feb [26] Weller begins a ten-date tour of the UK and Eire at Dublin Stadium, set to end on March 13th at the Apollo Theatre, Oxford, Oxfordshire. (It is Weller's first to Ireland since 1978 with the Jam.) Seven European dates will follow.
Mar MTV (Europe) films tonight's gig at Wolverhampton Civic Hall for subsequent broadcast. It will also used for a forthcoming video release "Live Wood".
Apr [9] EP *Hung Up*, including Kosmos (Lynch Mob bonus beats mix), debuts at its UK #11 peak.
[25] ***Wild Wood*** is re-released, with *Hung Up* included, and peaks at UK #18, while a compilation album ***Volume Nine***, to which Weller has contributed his cover of Tim Hardin's *Black Sheep Boy* is issued.
May [3] A 12-date US tour to coincide with the release of ***Wild Wood*** begins at the Avalon, Boston, MA.
[25] Weller wins the Outstanding Contemporary Song Collection (a new category) at the 39th annual Ivor Novello Awards at London's Grosvenor House Hotel.
June [10] A ten-date German arena tour begins with Weller opening for German artist Herbert Groenemeyer.
[25] He plays an electric performance at the "Glastonbury Festival For Contemporary Artists", Pilton, Somerset, second on the bill to Elvis Costello.
July [16] Weller headlines "The Phoenix 1994" festival at Long Marston, Stratford-upon-Avon, Warks.
Aug [1] Opening a summer season of films "Punk And Beyond" organized by the **New Musical Express** and the National Film Theatre at London's South Bank, Weller's career documentary "Highlights And Hang Ups", directed by associates Pedro Romhanyl and Jam biographer Paolo Hewitt, receives its only public showing. It will be released three months later on home video.
Sept [6] Indian Vibes, featuring Weller on guitars, Gerrard Farrell on sitar, Marco Nelson on bass and Crispin Taylor on drums, releases *Mathar*, produced by Lynch, on Virgin Records.
[10] **New Musical Express** issues a free 7" vinyl containing three unreleased tracks, including mixes of *Wild Wood* by dance outfit Portishead and *Sunflower* by Brendan Lynch.
[13] Nominee Weller performs at the annual Mercury Music Prize Awards held at London's Savoy Hotel.
[24] ***Live Wood***, recorded at four European concerts earlier in the year, bows at its UK #13 peak.
Nov [5] *Out Of The Sinking*, from his forthcoming ***Stanley Road*** including a cover of the Beatles' *Sexy Sadie*, peaks at its UK #20 debut.
[19] Following tours in Japan and Europe a 12-date major venue UK tour commences with stand-in bassist Dr. Robert and guests including Lynch, Peake and ex-Suede Bernard Butler on the second of three sold-out dates at London's Royal Albert Hall.
Dec [15] Weller guests at a Primal Scream concert at London's Shepherd's Bush Empire.

1995

Jan Eight weeks of recording at The Manor begin, with producer Lynch.
Feb [27] Having been similarly hailed at last month's NME Brat Awards, Weller is named Best Male Solo Artist at the 13th annual BRIT Awards staged at London's Alexandra Palace.
Apr PolyGram's ***18 Original Hits By 18 Unoriginal Artists***, to which Weller has contributed his treatment of Traffic's *Feelin' Alright*, is released in the UK.
[17] He appears on C4's "White Room" performing three numbers, including *Talk Tonight.*
May [6] EP *The Changing Man* debuts at is UK #7 peak, marking Weller's 17th Top 10 career hit, and his first Top 10 single since *It Didn't Matter* with the Style Council in January 1987.
[13] ***Stanley Road***, named after the road in which Weller lived in as a child in Woking, with sleeve design by Peter Blake, and featuring Steve Winwood, Oasis' Noel Gallagher, Carleen Anderson and Talbot among its guests, enters the UK chart at #1.
[25] Weller performs a one-off gig at London's 100 Club as a warm-up for the summer festivals with a guest appearance by Gallagher. **The Sun** prints an article about Weller's alleged current involvement with Paul McCartney's daughter Mary, since his split with his wife Lee.
June [3] Weller returns to BBC2's "Later With Jools Holland".
[17] He takes part in the "Halfway Festival" near Amsterdam, Netherlands.
July [16] Weller headlines the Sunday night at "The Phoenix 1995" festival at Long Marston.
[22] *You Do Something To Me* bows at its UK #9 peak.
Aug He takes part in the "Feile '95 Festival" at the Semple Stadium, Thurles, Co, Tipperary, Eire.
[5] Weller headlines the Saturday night show at the "T In The Park" festival at Strathclyde Country Park in Hamilton, Strathclyde.
Sept [4] He records *Come Together* for Go! Discs' War Child benefit album ***Help***.
[14] Weller hosts "Radio Woking", a two-hour show on London's GLR Radio, with Dee C. Lee, Dr. Robert and Talbot.
[30] *Broken Stones* debuts at its UK #20 peak.
Nov [24] He performs at Braintree Towerlands Arena - the first time a rock event is held at the venue.

1996

Feb [19] Weller is named Best Male Artist for the second consecutive year at the 14th annual BRIT Awards, held at London's Earl's Court Exhibition Centre.
Mar [19] A re-recorded version of *Out Of The Sinking* reaches UK #16 in its week of entry.
see also: **THE JAM, THE STYLE COUNCIL**

WET WET WET

Marti Pellow (vocals); **Graeme Clark** (bass); **Neil Mitchell** (keyboards); **Tom Cunningham** (drums)

1982

Clark (b. Apr. 15, 1966, Glasgow, Strathclyde, Scotland), Cunningham (b. June 22, 1965, Glasgow) and Mitchell (b. June 8, 1967, Helensborough, Strathclyde), having formed a group while attending Clydebank High School, Glasgow, approach Mark McLoughlin (b. Mar. 23, 1966, Clydebank, Strathclyde) to front their band as vocalist and, as the Vortex Motion, play Clash cover versions, with its first gig at

Clydebank Community Centre. McLoughlin changes his name to Marti Pellow, and the group settles on Wet Wet Wet as a name, taken from a line in the Scritti Politti song, *Getting Having And Holding*, and changes its musical style to a pop/soul fusion.

1984

Dec Having gigged locally in Scotland all year, the group meets Elliot Davis, who becomes its manager. Together they establish their own label, The Precious Organisation, and record a demo tape, which they send to major record companies in London.

1985

From their demo alone, nine major companies compete to sign them. Dave Bates, A&R at Phonogram, wins, but only after guaranteeing that the manager will receive a monthly supply of Whiskas cat food - a small gesture of faith. Phonogram proposes a string of producers, including Stephen Hague and John Ryan, who do not suit the band's white soul aspirations, but eventually allows the group to record a session with its choice, Al Green production maestro, Willie Mitchell.

1986

Jan Their debut television performance is on C4-TV's "The Tube".
[17] The group begins a six-date tour at Liverpool University, Liverpool, Merseyside, their first gigs outside Scotland.
June The band records several tracks with Mitchell in Memphis, TN. Despite creative satisfaction on both sides, Phonogram refuses to use material for their debut album. Increased promotional work includes sessions for Glasgow's Radio Clyde, and an appearance at London's Royal Albert Hall for a Greenpeace charity concert.

1987

Apr The group and management have insisted that a remixed demo of *Wishing I Was Lucky* be released as a debut cut, which now hits UK #6, with Phonogram conceding defeat on trying to force production ideas on the group.
June Prior to its own headline tour, the band undertakes a supporting role on Lionel Richie's UK dates.
Aug Pop/soul tinged *Sweet Little Mystery* hits UK #5.
Oct [3] Their debut album, ***Popped In Souled Out***, recorded in April with another American producer, Michael Baker, and with "fifth" member Graeme Duffin supplying all of the rhythm and lead guitar work (the band is otherwise bereft of guitarists), enters the UK chart at #2 (hitting UK #1 on Jan [16], 1988).

1988

Feb *Angel Eyes (Home And Away)* hits UK #5.
[8] The group wins the Best British Newcomer category, at the seventh annual BRIT Awards, held at London's Royal Albert Hall.
Mar The group travels to New Orleans, LA, to film the video for *Temptation*, which reaches UK #12.
May [21] Wet Wet Wet's re-make of the Beatles' *With A Little Help From My Friends*, from ***Sgt. Pepper Knew My Father***, a benefit album released to raise funds and awareness for the Childwatch charity, tops the UK chart, as a double A-side with Billy Bragg's *She's Leaving Home*. (It is the only instance of two covers of the same Beatles song topping the charts - Joe Cocker's version hit the summit in November 1968.)
During the month, the group is named HMV Music Therapy Newcomer's Award Winner.
June [5-6] As plans to release an EP of the Mitchell Memphis sessions are shelved, the group maintains a high profile, taking part in the sixth annual "Prince's Trust Rock Gala" at the Royal Albert Hall, London, singing *Twist And Shout*.
[11] They perform *Wishing I Was Lucky* at "Nelson Mandela's 70th Birthday Tribute" concert at Wembley Stadium, Wembley, Middx, while undertaking more sold out UK dates.
[25] *Wishing I Was Lucky*, on the newly re-activated Uni label, peaks at US #58. Both Van Morrison and Squeeze reach out-of-court settlements when lyrics are "found" in *Sweet Little Mystery*, from Morrison's *Sense Of Wonder* and *Angel Eyes* and Squeeze's *Heartbreaking World*.
July ***Popped In Souled Out*** peaks at US #123.
Nov [19] ***The Memphis Sessions***, an eight-cut album from the original Willie Mitchell sessions, hits UK #3 in its week of entry.

1989

Apr [19] The group participates in the seventh annual "Prince's Trust Rock Gala" at the London Palladium, with Paula Abdul, Erasure, Debbie Gibson, T'Pau and others.
Oct *Sweet Surrender* hits UK #6.
Nov [11] Self-penned third album, ***Holding Back The River***, debuts at UK #2, behind Chris Rea's ***The Road To Hell***.
Dec Ballad *Broke Away* reaches UK #19.

1990

Mar *Hold Back The River*, written about alcohol abuse, makes UK #31.
May [5] Wet Wet Wet sing *I Feel Fine* at the "John Lennon Tribute Concert" at the Pier Head Arena, in Merseyside, to celebrate the songs of Lennon. (Proceeds go to the John and Yoko-established Spirit Foundation.)
June [3] They participate in "The Big Day", a festival broadcast from various locations in Glasgow, airing live on C4-TV.
July [18] The group takes part in the eighth annual "Prince's Trust Rock Gala" at the Wembley Arena, Wembley.
Aug Double A-side, *Stay With Me Heartache/I Feel Fine*, reaches UK #30.

1991

Sept [14] *Make It Tonight* debuts at its UK #37 peak.
Nov [2] *Put The Light On* bows at its UK #56 pinnacle.
[22] The group takes part in BBC-TV's "Children In Need" charity appeal.
Dec [9] They play a one-off London date at the Subterania.

1992

Jan [25] *Goodnight Girl*, prominently used in ITV's "Coronation Street" Christmas disco broadcast, begins a four-week stay at UK #1.
Feb [8] ***High On The Happy Side***, paired with a free eight-track ***Cloak And Dagger*** album, credited to Maggie Pie & the Imposters, featuring the group's favorite cover versions, enters the UK chart at #1, where it will stay for two weeks.
Mar [2] Wet Wet Wet embarks on a 16-date "High On The Happy Side" UK tour at the Apollo Theatre, Manchester, set to end on the 25th at the National Exhibition Centre, Birmingham.
[28] *More Than Love* reaches UK #19.
July [7-8] The group plays at the Wembley Arena, as part of its 15-date "Lip Service" tour.
[13] They perform a free concert on the Isle Of Arran, broadcast live on BBC Radio 1.
[18] The dance-based *Lip Service* reaches UK #15.
Sept [5] The band performs at Edinburgh Castle.
Nov [3] They play a benefit for the Nordoff Robbins Music Therapy Centre, at London's Royal Albert Hall, with a 40-piece orchestra backing them.

1993

Apr [17] The group guests on BBC1-TV's "Going Live".
[26] They unveil a plaque at the Nordoff Robbins Music Therapy Centre to mark the dedication of the Wet Wet Wet Library.
May [3] "Live At The Royal Albert Hall", from the November 1992 concert, airs on C4-TV.
[8] *Blue For You/This Time (Live)*, from the forthcoming Royal Albert Hall live album, bows at its UK #38 peak.
[29] Performance set ***Wet Wet Wet Live At The Royal Albert Hall***, its royalties going to the Nordoff Robbins Music Therapy charity, debuts at its UK #10 peak.
July Wet Wet Wet signs a two-year deal to sponsor Clydebank Football Club.
Nov [13] *Shed A Tear* reaches UK #22.
[20] ***End Of Part One (Their Greatest Hits)*** debuts at its UK #4 high.
[24] A nine-date "Their Greatest Hits Tour 1993 End Of Part One" opens at the International Arena, Cardiff, S. Glamorgan, Wales, set to end on December 11th at the Wembley Arena.

1994

Jan [5] The group guests on ITV's "Des O'Connor Tonight" show.
[15] *Cold Cold Heart* reaches UK #20.
June [4] Their treatment of the Troggs' 1967 UK #5 and 1968 US #7 hit, *Love Is All Around*, featured in the movie "Four Weddings And A Funeral", begins an unbroken 15-week stay at UK #1 (one shy of Bryan Adam's record), eventually selling over one million domestic copies.
Sept [15] As *Love Is All Around* drops off the top, manager Elliot Davis rings Phonogram MD Howard Berman from the US to get the label to delete the record. (It will ultimately top the charts in 14 countries.)
Oct [1] *Love Is All Around* makes US #41.
[8] They perform *It's Now Or Never* at the "Elvis Aaron Presley : The Tribute", an all-star music event staged at the Pyramid Arena, Memphis, TN, broadcast live on pay-per-view TV in the US.

1995

Apr [1] *Julia Says* hits UK #3.
[22] ***Picture This*** debuts at UK #1.
May [23] *Love Is All Around* is named PRS Most Performed Work, Best Selling Song and International Hit Of The Year at the 40th annual Ivor Novello Awards held at London's Grosvenor House Hotel.
June [10] The group guests on BBC1-TV's "Steve Wright's People Show".
[24] *Don't Want To Forgive Me Now* hits UK #7, as they play the last of three dates at the Sheffield Arena, grossing £577,550.
July [25] Wet Wet Wet plays the inaugural gig at the new 19,500 seater Manchester Arena, Gtr. Manchester. Following the band's 25-date UK tour, it will embark on 12-country trek, taking in Europe, Southeast Asia, South Africa, Australia and the US.
Oct [7] *Somewhere Somehow* hits UK #7.
Nov [24] The group begins a five-date UK tour at the Cardiff International Arena.
Dec [9] *She's All On My Mind* reaches UK #17.

1996

Mar [30] *Morning* enters the UK chart at #16.

WHAM!

George Michael (vocals); **Andrew Ridgeley** (guitar)

1979

Michael (b. Georgios Kyriacos Panayiotou, June 25, 1963, Finchley, London) and Ridgeley (b. Jan. 26, 1963, Windlesham, Surrey), having met on the first day of term at Bushey Meads Comprehensive School in 1975, form the ska-based band, the Executive, together with Ridgeley's brother, Paul, David Austin and Andrew Leaver, which gigs locally, but disbands within 18 months. Concentrating for the next two years on songwriting and rehearsing demos at home, the duo has already written *Careless Whisper* and *Club Tropicana* as the decade turns. Ridgeley remains unemployed, while Michael has several casual jobs, as both enjoy the hectic London nightclub scene, where they create the Wham! name and image, and are inspired to write *Wham Rap! (Enjoy What You Do?)*.

1982

Jan Hiring a Portastudio for £20, Wham! records demos of *Wham Rap!*, *Come On!*, *Club Tropicana* and *Careless Whisper* in Ridgeley's parents' front room. Record companies are universally uninterested. The duo is, however, introduced to ex-Phonogram employee, Mark Dean, who recently established the small dance-based label, Innervision. Through a loan-arrangement with CBS, he offers Wham! a contract which will later prove highly restrictive.
Apr Wham! signs a publishing deal with the Morrison/Leahy Music Group. Club appearances to promote their debut single, *Wham Rap!*, with new girl recruits Shirlie Holliman and Mandy Washburn (soon replaced by Diane Sealey (Dee C. Lee)), fail to lift it into the UK Top 100.
Oct *Young Guns (Go For It)* enters the UK chart, but will take two months to hit UK #3, helped by a memorable dance performance on BBC1-TV's "Top Of The Pops".

1983

Feb Re-release of *Wham Rap! (Enjoy What You Do?)* hits UK #8. Wham! is joined by session players Dean Estus, Robert Anwai and Anne Dudley, to record *Bad Boys*, the first release written solely by Michael.
May *Bad Boys* hits UK #2, accompanied by a black and white video, which Michael later describes as the lowest point in Wham!'s career.
July Experiencing serious difficulties with Innervision, Wham! seeks management assistance from pop entrepreneur, Simon Napier-Bell.
[9] The self-penned, pop/dance filled debut album, ***Fantastic***, co-produced by Michael with Steve Brown, enters the UK chart at #1, while its fourth single, *Club Tropicana*, hits UK #4. Michael assumes control of Wham!'s musical elements, particularly writing and producing, while Ridgeley concentrates on style, image, visuals and direction.
Aug The first Wham! concert tour is announced, sponsored by Fila sportswear. Prior to its start, Michael flies to Muscle Shoals Studios in Muscle Shoals, AL, to record a solo version of *Careless Whisper*, with Jerry Wexler. Sessions are instructive but unsuccessful, and Michael decides to re-record the song in London with the help of keyboardist, Andy Richards, for later release. *Bad Boys*, poorly promoted, peaks at US #60.
Oct Dee C. Lee leaves to join the Style Council, replaced by singer/dancer Pepsi (later to realize success with co-backing performer, Shirlie). The "Club Fantastic" tour is launched in Aberdeen, Scotland, while Wham!'s solicitor, Tony Russell, informs Innervision boss Mark Dean, that the duo is seeking to break its contract.
Nov With a major legal battle looming, Innervision releases a mix of album cuts, titled *Club Fantastic Megamix*. Although Wham! denounces the single in the UK press, it climbs to UK #15.

1984

Jan Wham! visits Japan on a promotional tour.
Mar [22] Released from their wrangle with Innervision, Wham! signs to Epic Records. Michael is busy writing and producing new songs, one of which, *Wham! Shake*, is rejected by Ridgeley.
June [2] First Epic release, *Wake Me Up Before You Go Go*, inspired by a note Ridgeley left lying in his bedroom, but written by Michael, hits UK #1, confirming Wham! as Britain's leading mid-'80s teen pop sensation.
Michael flies to Miami, FL, to shoot a solo video clip for *Careless Whisper*, while Ridgeley receives much-publicized plastic surgery to his nose.
Aug [18] *Careless Whisper*, released in the UK as a solo effort by Michael, despite a co-writing credit with Ridgeley, hits UK #1 for the first of three weeks, and is Epic's first UK million seller, earning a platinum disc. Michael dedicates the ballad to his mother and father, "five minutes in return for 21 years". It will top charts around the world over the next six months.
Sept Michael and Ridgeley, in the South of France to record a second album, with Michael assuming full responsibility in all areas, and Ridgeley providing quality control, advice and guitar-work, meet Elton John, and develop a long-term friendship.
[7] The duo performs at the final "Five Night For The Miners" charity concert on a bill with Paul Weller, Ben Elton, Alexei Sayle and Rik Mayall.
Nov [17] In its tenth week of release, *Wake Me Up Before You Go Go* tops the US Hot 100 in the same week that the duo's sophomore effort, ***Make It Big***, arranged, written and produced by Michael (and including *Careless Whisper*) hits UK #1. ***Fantastic*** also charts at US #83.
Dec A world tour starts at the Whitley Bay Ice Rink, Whitley Bay, Northumberland. Michael is featured singing on Band Aid's Christmas chart-topper, *Do They Know It's Christmas?*, which prevents Wham!'s own *Last Christmas* from hitting the top spot.

1985

Jan Double A-sided *Last Christmas* is flipped with *Everything She Wants*, holding the UK #2 position for another four weeks, and earning a platinum disc. Their World tour continues throughout Australia, Japan and US.
Feb [11] Wham! wins Best British Group category at the fourth annual BRIT Awards, at London's Grosvenor House Hotel.
[16] *Careless Whisper* tops the US chart at the start of a three-week run, credited to "Wham! featuring George Michael".
Mar [2] ***Make It Big*** hits US #1 for the first of three weeks, eventually selling over five million US copies alone.
[13] An emotional Michael receives the prestigious Songwriter Of The Year trophy, from Elton John at the 30th annual Ivor Novello Awards, held at the Grosvenor House Hotel, the youngest-ever recipient. *Careless Whisper* also wins the Most Performed Work category.
Apr Wham! is the first western pop group invited to perform live in China, following lengthy negotiations between Napier-Bell and the Chinese Government.
[7] Wham! plays at the 10,000-seater Workers' Gymnasium in Beijing.
May [25] *Everything She Wants* hits US #1 for the first of two weeks. Michael, becoming increasingly independent musically, performs duets with Smokey Robinson and Stevie Wonder at a Motown Records celebration in New York.
July While Ridgeley fund-raises and performs backing vocals, Michael sings *Don't Let The Sun Go Down On Me*, to Elton John's piano accompaniment, at "Live Aid" at Wembley Stadium, Wembley, Middx., following which, Wham! undertakes a stadium tour of the US.
Aug *Freedom* hits US #3, breaking a run of three consecutive US chart-toppers.
Nov [30] *I'm Your Man* tops the UK chart, while Michael is also featured as the backing vocalist on Elton John's current UK #3 hit, *Nikita*. Privately, Michael and Ridgeley, still very close friends, decide that Wham! will split in 1986.
Dec [21] Michael features on four Top 20 records in the UK Christmas chart: *I'm Your Man*, the re-entered *Last Christmas* (UK #6), Band Aid's *Do They Know It's Christmas?* and as backing vocalist on Elton John's *Nikita*.

1986

Jan [27] Wham! wins the Favorite Video, Duo Or Group, Pop/Rock category, at the 13th annual American Music Awards, held at the Shrine Auditorium, Los Angeles.
Feb [1] *I'm Your Man* hits US #3.
[10] The duo is honored for their Outstanding Contribution To British Music at the fifth annual BRIT Awards, at the Grosvenor House Hotel.
Apr Michael releases a second solo single, the ballad, *A Different Corner*, which hits UK #1 and US #7. It coincides with the official announcement that Wham!, at the peak of its commercial success, is to dissolve, having achieved far more than its original aims. They simultaneously dissolve management links with Napier-Bell.
[28] "Wham! The Video" is certified gold by the RIAA.
June [28] The final Wham! single is a four-track EP, featuring the double-A billed *The Edge Of Heaven/Where Did Your Heart Go*. It tops the UK chart in the same week as Wham!'s farewell concert, "The Final", is performed in front of 72,000 fans at Wembley Stadium.
[19] ***The Final***, a best of compilation, hits UK #2, behind Madonna's ***True Blue***.
Aug The US postscript, the greatest hits package, ***Music From The Edge Of Heaven***, hits US #10. Michael actively pursues a solo career, while Ridgeley concentrates on a future of semi-retirement, unsuccessful motor racing and acting. Both continue solo contracts with Epic Records.
Oct [8] ***Music From The Edge Of Heaven*** is certified platinum by the RIAA.
Nov [1] *Where Did Your Heart Go*, written and originally recorded by Was (Not Was), makes US #50.
Dec Re-promotion of ***The Final*** as a boxed set, complete with Wham! pencil, paper pad and poster, revives its UK chart fortunes for the festive season, as *Last Christmas*, reissued a second time, makes UK #45. Their "Wham! In China : Foreign Skies" will be certified gold by the RIAA on April 3rd the following year, with ***Fantastic*** reaching the same certification on August 9th, 1989.

1991

Jan After Ridgeley has made his recording comeback with the debut solo, ***Son Of Albert*** (US #130 in May 1990) with the extracted *Shake* peaking at US #77 and UK #58 in the same month, Wham! reunites briefly at George Michael's "Rock In Rio" festival performance in Rio de Janeiro, Brazil, when he is joined onstage by his still-best friend Ridgeley, for several numbers.

1994

Oct [7] With Michael and Ridgeley having sued Sony Music Entertainment in December 1992, claiming £1.3 million in unpaid royalties - £958,000 from Wham! recordings and £386,000 from Michael's ***Faith*** album, the RIAA has certified platinum sales of *Careless Whisper* and *Wake Me Up Before You Go Go* on May 5th the same year, and now add to Wham!'s career haul, confirming six million sales of ***Make It Big***.
see also: **George MICHAEL**

BARRY WHITE

1960

Sept [25] Released from jail on August 28th after a three-month sentence for stealing 300 tires from a local car dealer, White (b. Sept. 12, 1944, Galveston, TX), having lived since infancy in East Side Los Angeles, CA, singing and playing organ in a church choir and learning a variety of instruments in his early teens, after troubles in high school which resulted in his attending the Reese school, a center for incorrigible youth, is invited by four high school friends to join Los Angeles R&B quintet, the Upfronts, and sing bass on their second single for Lummtone Records.

1964

Feb Having earned $100 for providing handclaps on his first session, for a single called *Tossing An Ice Cube* in 1961, and formed the Atlantics in 1963, releasing *Home On The Range* and *Let Me Call You Sweetheart* before forming the Majestics with Carl Carlton, and recording for the Linda label, White arranges Bob & Earl's *Harlem Shuffle*, for the Rampart label, which makes US #44. He also plays keyboards on many small label R&B recording sessions, while performing solo in Los Angeles clubs.

1965

Under the name Barry Lee, White releases two singles, *Man Ain't Nothing* and *Make It*, on the Downey and Veep labels respectively.

1966

Jan Earl Nelson of Bob & Earl reaches US #14 under the pseudonym Jackie Lee, with *The Duck*, and White tours with him as drummer and road manager.
Mar Having heard White's demos, Bob Keene, at Keene Records, hires him for $40 a week to be an A&R man for his Mustang and Bronco labels. His first job is to secure a release from their contract for dissatisfied group, the Versatiles. (They will go on to become the 5th Dimension.) He will also play on the Bobby Fuller Four's *I Fought The Law*. Keene and Larry Nunes are looking for a girl singer, and at White's suggestion, sign Felice Taylor, whose *It May Be Winter Outside* makes US #42, and *I Feel Love Comin' On* reaches UK #11. (Also cutting his own *All In The Run Of A Day* for Bronco, White pens and produces Viola Wills' *Lost Without The Love Of My Guy*.)

1968

While still working for Mustang, White discovers the female vocal trio, Love Unlimited (sisters Glodean and Linda James, and Diane Taylor) from San Pedro, CA. He becomes their manager and producer, as he moves towards independent production.

1972

May Having signed Love Unlimited to Uni Records with the help of his associate, Larry Nunes, White has produced *Walkin' In The Rain With The One I Love*, which reaches #14 in both the US and UK, and sells over a million copies. (His own voice is heard in the "telephone break" midway through the disc.) The trio's ***Love Unlimited*** album makes US #151. He also launches, with Nunes, his own production company, Soul Unlimited Productions (originally MoSoul, which was felt too similar to Motown).
Dec White signs himself, his production house, and Love Unlimited, to the newly re-launched 20th Century Records.

1973

June White records under his own name as a soloist for the first time, in a variation of Isaac Hayes' style of deep, intimate R&B vocals accompanied by lush orchestral arrangements, a blend which will become his trademark. His debut album, ***I've Got So Much To Give***, reaches US #16, while the extracted *I'm Gonna Love You Just A Little More, Baby* hits US #3 and makes UK #23.
[6] *I'm Gonna Love You Just A Little More, Baby* is certified gold by the RIAA.
Sept Title song, *I've Got So Much To Give*, reaches US #32.
Nov [6] *I've Got So Much To Give* is also certified gold by the RIAA.
Dec Love Unlimited's revival of Felice Taylor's *It May Be Winter Outside* peaks at US #83.

1974

Jan White's second self-penned and-produced album, ***Stone Gon'***, reaches US #20, as the extracted *Never, Never Gonna Give You Up* hits US #7.
Feb *Never, Never Gonna Give You Up* reaches UK #14, while Love Unlimited's ***Under The Influence Of ...*** hits US #3, and goes gold. The trio's *It May Be Winter Outside* is its second and final UK hit single, reaching #11.
[7] The RIAA certifies gold sales of *Never, Never Gonna Give You Up* and ***Stone Gon'***.
[9] Also taken from the Love Unlimited album is the instrumental cut, *Love's Theme*, a dance piece played by a White-conducted 40-piece orchestra. On the album it serves as the lengthy (eight minute) introduction to the trio's vocal track, *I'm Under The Influence Of Love*, but, popular with disco DJs, White has released it as a single with the musicians credited as the Love Unlimited Orchestra, and it tops the US chart, earning a gold disc, and hits UK #10.
Mar White's *Honey Please, Can't Ya See* makes US #44, while his album, ***Stone Gon'***, reaches UK #18.
Apr ***Rhapsody In White***, an instrumental set by the Love Unlimited Orchestra, featuring *Love's Theme*, hits US #8 and makes UK #50.
May Love Unlimited's *I'm Under The Influence Of Love*, the vocal "sequel" to *Love's Theme* (and another song originally recorded by White with Felice Taylor) peaks at US #76.
June Title track, the Love Unlimited Orchestra's *Rhapsody In White*, makes US #63.
July [4] White marries, for the second time, to Glodean James, a member of Love Unlimited.
Aug ***Together Brothers***, the soundtrack to the film of the same title, performed by the Love Unlimited Orchestra (which currently includes saxophonist Kenny Gorelick, aka Kenny G), and including two vocal tracks by White and Love Unlimited, reaches US #96.
Sept [11] The still-climbing *Can't Get Enough Of Your Love* is certified gold by the RIAA.
[19] Still-to-peak ***Can't Get Enough*** is also confirmed gold by the RIAA.
[21] White's *Can't Get Enough Of Your Love, Babe* hits US #1 for a week and UK #8.
Oct [26] ***Can't Get Enough*** tops the US chart for a week, becoming his biggest-selling album.
Nov ***Can't Get Enough*** is also White's biggest commercial success in the UK, where it hits #4.
Dec [7] *You're The First, The Last, My Everything*, taken from ***Can't Get Enough***, tops the UK chart for the first of two weeks. Love Unlimited Orchestra's ***White Gold*** reaches US #28, as ***In Heat***, credited simply to Love Unlimited, makes US #85.
[18] The still-rising uptempo *You're The First, The Last, My Everything* is certified gold by the RIAA.

1975

Jan *You're The First, The Last, My Everything* hits US #2 (his fourth gold single) behind Elton John's *Lucy In The Sky With Diamonds*, while Love Unlimited's *I Belong To You* reaches US #27, and is the trio's final hit single.
Apr White's *What Am I Gonna Do With You?* hits UK #5 and US #8, while the Love Unlimited Orchestra instrumental track, *Satin Soul*, makes US #22.
May White performs at London's Royal Albert Hall.
June Having already been confirmed gold on April 8th, ***Just Another Way To Say I Love You*** reaches US #17 and UK #12.
[14] The extracted *I'll Do For You Anything You Want Me To* reaches UK #20.
[21] *I'll Do For You Anything You Want Me To* makes US #40.
Dec Compilation album, ***Greatest Hits***, reaches US #23 and UK #18.

1976

Jan *Let The Music Play* hits UK #9 and reaches US #32.
[31] He collects the Favorite Male Artist, Soul/R&B trophy, at the third annual American Music Awards, held at the Civic Auditorium, Santa Monica, CA.
Feb Love Unlimited Orchestra instrumental album, ***Music Maestro Please***, makes US #92.
Mar White's ***Let The Music Play*** reaches UK #22.
[9] ***Greatest Hits*** is certified gold by the RIAA.
Apr *You See The Trouble With Me* hits UK #2 (held from the top by Brotherhood Of Man's *Save Your Kisses For Me*), as ***Let The Music Play*** makes US #42.
July *Baby, We Better Try To Get It Together* peaks at US #92.
Sept *Baby, We Better Try To Get It Together* reaches UK #15.
Nov Love Unlimited Orchestra's ***My Sweet Summer Suite*** peaks at US #123, and is the group's last chart album, while the title track, *My Sweet Summer Suite*, makes US #48.
Dec White's *Don't Make Me Wait Too Long* reaches UK #17 as ***Is This Whatcha Wont?*** peaks at US #125.

1977

Feb The Love Unlimited Orchestra's US singles chart swan-song is *Theme From King Kong*, a disco variation of the movie theme, which peaks at US #68.
Mar *I'm Qualified To Satisfy* makes UK #37. Love Unlimited's ***He's All I've Got*** (on White's own new Unlimited Gold label) peaks at US #192.
Apr Compilation, ***Barry White's Greatest Hits Vol. 2***, reaches UK #17.
Oct *It's Ecstasy When You Lay Down Next To Me* makes UK #40.
[18] The still-climbing *It's Ecstasy When You Lay Down Next To Me* is certified gold by the RIAA.
Nov *It's Ecstasy When You Lay Down Next To Me* hits US #4, becoming his fifth and final solo gold single. It is taken from ***Barry White Sings For Someone You Love***, which hits US #8, and is also a million seller, earning a platinum disc on the 15th.

1978

June *Oh What A Night For Dancing* reaches US #24.
Dec ***Barry White The Man*** makes US #36 during a six-month chart stay while the extracted *Your Sweetness Is My Weakness* peaks at US #60, his last US hit single.
[22] ***Barry White The Man*** is ratified platinum by the RIAA.

1979

Jan White's revival of Billy Joel's 1978 hit, *Just The Way You Are*, reaches UK #12 (but is not issued as a US single).
Feb ***The Man*** (including *Just The Way You Are*) makes UK #46.
Apr *Sha La La Means I Love You* peaks at UK #55.
May White moves to his own Unlimited Gold label (which he has signed to CBS Associated Labels for distribution) with ***The Message Is Love***, which peaks at US #67.
[29] ***The Message Is Love*** is certified gold by the RIAA.
Sept ***I Love To Sing The Songs I Sing***, a swan-song release from 20th Century, makes US #132.

1980

Apr [11] White receives an honorary degree in Recording Arts And Sciences from UCLA's Faculty club.
Aug ***Barry White's Sheet Music*** makes US #85. Its follow-up, ***Change*** will peak at US #148 in October 1982, while in the interim year he will release his first duet album with his wife, ***Barry And Glodean*** and the non-charting album ***Beware!***.

1983

May [24] Currently promoting ***Dedicated***, White instead offers tips on camping as a guest on NBC-TV's "Late Night With David Letterman".
Aug [21] He takes part in the "First Annual Gospel Festival" in Jerusalem, Israel, with Grover Cleveland, Andrae Crouch and Shirley Caesar.

1984

Marvin Gaye tells **Billboard** that White is scheduled to produce his new album, starting on April 2nd, though White professes to know nothing about it. (Gaye is killed by his father on April 1st.) A UK-only TV-promoted compilation, ***Heart And Soul***, anthologizing White's major hits of the '70s, will reach UK #34 in December the following year.

1987

Oct After a rest from recording, during which he has updated his home studio R.I.S.E. (Research In Sound Excellence) in Sherman Oaks, CA, to state-of-the-art '80s specifications, White has signed a new recording deal with A&M Records. With a fresh group of musicians - keyboard players Jack Perry and Eugene Booker (White's god-son) and guitarist Charles Fearing (ex-Ray Parker Jr.'s Raydio), ***The Right***

Night And Barry White makes UK #74.
Nov ***The Right Night And Barry White*** peaks at US #159, while *Sho' You Right*, taken from the album, reaches UK #14.

1988

Jan A remixed issue of *Never Never Gonna Give You Up* makes UK #63.
Apr White performs at the Royal Albert Hall, during a visit to London.
July [16] A further UK compilation, ***The Collection***, a new anthology of White's 20th Century label singles, hits UK #5, as he plans a full UK tour.
Dec ***The Man Is Back!***, and the featured *Super Lover*, are released.

1990

Mar [14] White joins El DeBarge, James Ingram and Al B. Sure! at the fourth annual Soul Train Music Awards, held at the Shrine Auditorium, Los Angeles, singing *The Secret Garden*, a track which features the four soloists from Quincy Jones' ***Back On The Block***.
May [18] White guests on NBC-TV's "Late Night With David Letterman".
[25] Having completed a European tour, including six sold-out UK dates for 70,000 fans in Britain in April, White embarks, with the 30-piece Love Unlimited Orchestra, on a world tour (his first since 1983) in St. Louis, MO, the US leg set to end on August 1st in San Carlos, CA.
June [16] ***The Man Is Back!*** peaks at US #143.
Oct [15] White performs at the Wembley Arena, Wembley, Middx., during a further four-date UK visit.

1991

Feb [23] Re-promoted compilation, ***The Collection***, reaches UK #28.
Nov [8] White guests on syndicated TV's "The Arsenio Hall Show", when fellow guest Earvin "Magic" Johnson reveals he is HIV positive.
[30] His second album of the decade, ***Put Me In Your Mix***, makes US #96.

1992

Jan The Isaac Hayes/White-duetted *Dark And Lovely (You Over There)* is released.
Mar [1] White begins an eight-date sellout UK tour at the Nottingham Royal Centre, set to end on the 12th at London's Hammersmith Odeon.
July [11] ***The Collection*** charts for another week at UK #40.

1993

Feb [22] PolyGram releases a definitive White-assembled three-CD/cassette boxed set, ***Just For You***.
Apr [29] White's silky voice guests on Fox-TV's "The Simpsons".
June [5] He takes part in KISS Radio's all-star annual anniversary concert, at the Great Woods Center for the Performing Arts, Mansfield, MA.
July [31] ***The Collection*** charts at UK #42.

1994

Mar [15] Currently completing a new Jimmy Jam/Terry Lewis-produced album, White is presented with the Heritage Award for career achievement by Magic Johnson, at the eighth annual Soul Train Music Awards at the Shrine Auditorium.
Sept [10] Edie Brickell's *Good Times*, featuring an uncredited but unmistakable White on guest vocal, peaks at US #60.
Nov [7] White guests on CBS-TV's "Late Show With David Letterman".
Dec [10] *Practice What You Preach* reaches US #18, his first Top 20 US hit since 1977.
[15] *Practice What You Preach* is certified gold by the RIAA.

1995

Jan [9] White guests on NBC-TV's "The Tonight Show".
[21] *Practice What You Preach*, coupled with *Love Is The Icon*, debuts at its UK #20 peak.
Feb [11] The critically well-received ***The Icon Is Love*** makes UK #44 in its week of entry.
[14] White provides NBC-TV with its Valentine's Day promo spots.
Mar [13] White wins the Best R&B/Soul Album of the Year, Male (***The Icon Is Love***) and Best R&B/Soul Song Of The Year (*Practice What You Preach*) categories at the ninth annual Soul Train Music Awards, held at the Shrine Auditorium.
[16] White begins on a UK tour at the International Arena, Cardiff, S. Glamorgan, Wales.
Apr [8] *I Only Want To Be With You* debuts at its UK #36 high.
[22] *Come On* bows at its US #87 peak.
[28] White becomes the first westerner to perform at the Safari Park Garden Theatre, Nairobi, Kenya.
June [2] White's first US tour in many years opens in Birmingham, AL.
July [31] The RIAA certifies two million sales of ***The Icon Is Love***.
Nov [2] White is inducted into the Soul Train Hall of Fame at the 25th Soul Train Anniversary, staged at the Shrine Auditorium. White is unable to attend after being admitted to a Las Vegas hospital, suffering from exhaustion. (The show airs on CBS-TV on November 22nd.)
[19] ***The Icon Is Love*** finally reaches US #20.

1996

Apr [27] Once again featured in a Quincy Jones assembled R&B team, this time alongside Babyface, Tamia and Portrait, *Slow Jams* makes US #68.
June [18] White performs at New York's Madison Square Garden, during his latest US tour.

WHITESNAKE

David Coverdale (vocals); **Bernie Marsden** (guitar); **Neil Murray** (bass); **Aynsley Dunbar** (drums)

1976

Mar Rock vocalist Coverdale (b. Sept. 22, 1949, Saltburn-by-the-Sea, Cleveland), the son of a steel-worker, leaves Deep Purple following a disastrous UK tour, after which the band itself dissolves. Contractual ties make it impossible for him to work live or record solo in Britain during the foreseeable future, so he moves to West Germany with his family, writing material for future use, while legal complexities are being untangled.

1977

May His debut solo album, ***Whitesnake***, a set of rock ballads, is released in a snakeskin-style sleeve, but fails to impress in a UK market currently dominated by the punk explosion. (Coverdale, still in West Germany, has recorded his vocals in Munich over backing tracks cut in the UK.)

1978

Jan His enforced exile over, Coverdale returns to Britain to form a band to promote his second solo album, ***Northwinds***, again recorded in both London and West Germany, recruiting the sessioneers who have provided his backing tracks: ex-Juicy Lucy guitarist Micky Moody (b. Aug. 30, 1950), ex-Babe Ruth guitarist Marsden, Murray (bass), Brian Johnston (keyboards) and David Dowle (drums).
Feb [23] As David Coverdale's Whitesnake, the band begins its debut UK tour at Nottingham's Sky Bird club.
June With Pete Solley replacing Johnston on keyboards, the band records the four-track EP, *Snake Bite*, highlighted by a revival of Bobby Bland's 1974 soul classic, *Ain't No Love In The Heart Of The City* (which will become a Coverdale stage favorite). Released by EMI International, at budget price on white vinyl, the EP is the band's chart debut, reaching UK #61.
Aug Coverdale's ex-Deep Purple colleague, Jon Lord (b. June 9, 1941, Leicester, Leics) joins on keyboards, replacing Solley, who is not keen to tour (and will go on to become a successful producer).
Sept *Lie Down (A Modern Love Song)* taken from the band's forthcoming album, is released.
Oct [26] Lord plays his first gig with Whitesnake at Newcastle, Tyne & Wear, on a tour to promote the first full group album.
Nov ***Trouble*** makes UK #50.
[23] The tour ends at London's Hammersmith Odeon, and is recorded for a live album.

1979

Mar *Time Is Right For Love*, from ***Trouble***, is issued in the UK to tie in with a headlining charity show (at London's Hammersmith Odeon on March 3rd, in aid of the Gunnar Nilsson Cancer Treatment Campaign). Much of the first half of this year is spent touring overseas.
July Ex-Deep Purple drummer Ian Paice (b. June 29, 1948, Nottingham, Notts.) replaces Dowle.
Aug [26] The band plays on the final day of the 19th National Rock Festival "Reading Rock '79", near Reading, Berks.
Oct ***Love Hunter*** (still featuring Dowle) reaches UK #29, its sleeve illustrating a naked woman astride a gigantic snake, which is over-stickered in some territories, including the US.
Nov *Long Way From Home*, a 33rpm maxi-single, also including two live tracks, peaks at UK #55.

1980

Mar The band plays its first tour of Japan, where the performance album, ***Live At Hammersmith***, recorded in 1978, is first released.
May *Fool For Your Loving*, a new Coverdale/Moody/Marsden composition, becomes the first major Whitesnake hit single, reaching UK #13.
June [24] The band plays at the Hammersmith Odeon (again recorded for album use), on a UK tour to support ***Ready An' Willing***, which hits UK #6.
July Taken from the album, *Ready An' Willing (Sweet Satisfaction)* makes UK #43.
Aug [24] The band headlines the final day of the 20th National Rock Festival "Reading Rock '80".
Sept Released on the Mirage label, ***Ready An' Willing*** marks the group's US chart debut, peaking at #90, while *Fool For Your Loving* makes US #53.
Oct Whitesnake develops its initial US success with several months of touring, opening for AC/DC, Jethro Tull, and other major rock acts.
Nov A live version of *Ain't No Love In The Heart Of The City*, from the June Hammersmith Odeon show, makes UK #51, while the double live set, ***Live In The Heart Of The City*** (combining both the 1978 and 1980 Hammersmith Odeon gigs), hits UK #5, selling over 300,000 copies in Britain alone.

1981

Jan ***Live In The Heart Of The City*** (released in the US as a single album, featuring just the 1980 gig) peaks at US #146.
May ***Come An' Get It*** hits UK #2 while, from it, *Don't Break My Heart Again* reaches UK #17.
June ***Come An' Get It*** makes US #151 while a second extract, *Would I Lie To You*, makes UK #37. On another UK tour to promote the album, the band sells out five nights at the Hammersmith Odeon.
Aug The band headlines the "Monsters Of Rock" festival at Castle Donington, Leics. (completing its UK live work for the year, before returning to the recording studio, where sessions will be abandoned).
Oct After a tour of West Germany leads to friction within the band, Whitesnake is put on indefinite hold. Coverdale also devotes time to nursing his sick daughter. Lord completes a solo album, while Murray and Paice play with Gary Moore (and will later join his band).

1982

Coverdale re-assembles Whitesnake without Marsden, Murray and Paice. He invites Cozy Powell (b. Dec.

29, 1947, Cirencester, Gloucs.) (drums) to join, while Lord and Moody remain, and recruits Mel Galley (b. Mar. 8, 1948) (guitar) and Colin "Bomber" Hodgkinson (b. Oct. 14, 1945) (bass). The previous year's unfinished recordings are salvaged, with Coverdale re-recording the vocals, and Galley over-dubbing fresh guitar parts.

Feb [27] The reissued 1978 album ***Northwinds*** charts for a week at UK #78.

Nov *Here I Go Again*, from the forthcoming album, makes UK #34.

Dec ***Saints'n'Sinners***, comprising the revamped tracks from a year earlier, hits UK #9.

1983

Aug The band again bill-tops the "Monsters Of Rock" festival, at Castle Donington, its only live UK appearance of the year (which is filmed by EMI for release on home video). *Guilty Of Love*, from an in-progress studio album, produced by Eddie Kramer, and released to tie in with the festival appearance, reaches UK #31. (Shortly after, Coverdale will fire his producer and re-cut all of the remaining album vocals. The strain will prove too much, and he will collapse from exhaustion.)

Nov Moody leaves the band prior to an end of year tour, and Hodgkinson follows him. The latter is replaced by a returning Murray, while the new guitarist is ex-Thin Lizzy and Tygers Of Pan Tang member, John Sykes (b. July 29, 1959).

1984

Jan *Give Me More Time*, from the forthcoming album, reaches UK #29.

Feb ***Slide It In*** hits UK #9, as the group opens a 17-date tour of Britain in Dublin, Eire (ending with a show at Wembley Arena, Wembley, Middx.).

Mar While on tour in West Germany, Galley breaks his arm.

Apr *Standing In The Shadow*, taken from ***Slide It In***, makes UK #62.

May Lord leaves to join the re-forming Deep Purple.

July With a change of US label to Geffen Records, ***Slide It In*** reaches US #40, as Whitesnake tours the US, supporting Dio.

Aug The group performs in Japan, with Richard Bailey filling Lord's keyboards slot on stage. Another US tour follows, supporting Quiet Riot.

1985

Jan Whitesnake participates in the world's largest rock festival, "Rock In Rio", in Rio de Janeiro, Brazil.

Feb *Love Ain't No Stranger*, from ***Slide It In***, makes UK #44.

Oct Whitesnake starts work on a new album with producer, Mike Stone, in Vancouver, BC, Canada. Coverdale, Murray and Sykes are joined by Aynsley Dunbar (b. Jan. 10, 1946, Liverpool) on drums, and Don Airey on keyboards.

1986

Jan Sykes leaves the album sessions to fly home when his former Thin Lizzy colleague, Phil Lynott, dies. Coverdale, meanwhile, is having major problems with his voice, caused by an abcessed sinus infection, which bring the sessions to a halt. Stone suggests a substitute vocalist, and is fired for his trouble.

Apr With a deviated septum diagnosed, Coverdale is forced to have an operation, and rest his voice.

Aug Coverdale returns to the studio with new producer, Keith Olsen, to finish the album. Dutch guitarist Adrian Vandenburg (b. Jan. 31, 1954, Holland) and keyboardist Bill Cuomo help out, along with Mark Andes and Denny Carmassi from Heart.

1987

Apr [11] Finally completed, ***Whitesnake 1987***, co-penned by Coverdale and Sykes, hits UK #8 in its week of entry, while the extracted *Still Of The Night* reaches UK #16. Touring to promote the album, Coverdale puts together a new line-up of Whitesnake, retaining Vandenburg on guitar, and adding Vivian Campbell (guitar), Rudy Sarzo (b. Nov. 9, 1952, Havana, Cuba) (bass) and Tommy Aldridge (b. Aug. 15, 1950, Nashville, TN) (drums).

June ***Whitesnake 1987*** hits US #2, becoming the band's first million-plus selling disc. Regarded as an AOR classic, it will ultimately sell over ten million copies worldwide.

[20] Whitesnake plays at the "10th Annual Texas World Music Fest", with Boston, Aerosmith, Poison and others, at the beginning of a world tour.

July [18] *Still Of The Night* makes US #79 while the rock ballad, *Is This Love*, a Coverdale/Sykes composition, also from the album, hits UK #9.

Aug The group begins a US tour supporting Motley Crue.

Sept [11] They perform at the fourth annual MTV Video Music Awards, held at the Universal Amphitheatre, Universal City, CA.

[15] The RIAA certifies three million sales of ***Whitesnake 1987***.

Oct [10] *Here I Go Again*, originally a track on the 1982 album, ***Saints'n'Sinners*** (and a UK #34 hit single at the time), now re-cut with a new backing track under Coverdale's vocal (during the late 1986 album sessions, at Geffen Records' suggestion), tops the US chart for a week.

[30] The group begins a headlining US tour, set to close on December 6th.

Nov Re-recorded *Here I Go Again* hits UK #9.

Dec [19] *Is This Love* hits US #2 (unable to dislodge George Michael's *Faith*). Coverdale co-stars in the song's promo video with actress, Tawny Kitaen.

1988

Jan [29] The Whitesnake video "Trilogy" is certified platinum by the RIAA.

Feb *Give Me All Your Love*, a re-recorded version of a track from the album, featuring the new band, reaches UK #18.

Mar [19] *Give Me All Your Love* makes US #48.

Aug [12] A further video release "Fourplay" is certified gold by the RIAA.

Dec [7] Coverdale announces that Campbell is no longer in the band, reportedly due to "musical differences". No replacement is announced, but the remaining quartet begins recording an album for mid-1989 release at Coverdale's home in Incline Village, Lake Tahoe, NV. Vandenburg injures his wrist while practicing the piano, with Steve Vai (b. June 6, 1960, Long Island, NY) filling in for him.

1989

Feb [17] Coverdale marries Kitaen in Bel Air, CA.

May [2] Vai officially joins the band.

June Tour dates are cancelled when Coverdale develops laryngitis.

Nov [14] Coverdale guests onstage at an Aerosmith London date, at the Hammersmith Odeon, duetting on *I'm Down*.

[25] Produced by long-time associate, Keith Olsen, and mixed by Mike Clink, ***Slip Of The Tongue***, featuring nine Coverdale/Vandenburg compositions, hits UK #10, and will hit US #10.

Dec An updated re-recording of their 1980 UK #13, *Fool For Your Loving* makes UK #43.

[23] *Fool For Your Loving* makes US #37.

1990

Jan [17] ***Slip of The Tongue*** is certified platinum by the RIAA.

Feb [2] Whitesnake, now comprising Coverdale, Vai, Vandenburg, Rudy Sarzo and Aldridge, begins its latest world trek, opening in Fairfax, VA.

Mar [10] *The Deeper The Love* reaches US #28.

May [26-27] The group performs at the Alpine Valley Music Theatre, East Troy, WI, with Skid Row, Great White, Bad English and Hericane Alice, as part of the "World Series Of Rock '90".

June [2] *Now You're Gone* peaks at US #96.

July The ***Days Of Thunder*** movie soundtrack, including Coverdale's *Last Note Of Freedom*, is released.

Aug [18] The group headlines the "Monsters Of Rock" festival at Castle Donington.

Sept [1] The band appears at the "Super Rock '90" festival in Mannheim, Germany, with Aerosmith, Poison, Queensryche and others. (By year's end, it will become apparent that Coverdale has dissolved the group, in favor of pursuing a solo career, confirmed when he appears as a solo act at the "Great British Music Weekend" held at Wembley Arena, Wembley, Middx., on January 20th the following year.)

1992

July [24] The RIAA certifies two million sales of ***Slide It In***.

Sept Coverdale and Jimmy Page, having begun writing together at the former's Lake Tahoe, CA home earlier in the year, begin working on a combined project at Abbey Road Studios, with Mike Fraser producing.

1993

Mar [27] ***Coverdale/Page*** debuts at its UK #4 peak, and will do likewise at US #5 on Apr [3].

July [3] The extracted *Take Me For A Little While* bows at its UK #29 peak.

Oct [23] A further single, *Take A Look At Yourself*, charts for a week at UK #43.

1994

July [16] Whitesnake's ***Greatest Hits*** debuts at its UK #4 peak.

Aug [6] Reissued *Is This Love*, coupled with *Sweet Lady Luck*, bows at its UK #25 high, as ***Whitesnake's Greatest Hits*** enters at its US #161 pinnacle, during a two week chart stay. Its success prompts Coverdale to re-assemble the group with Vandenburg, Rudy Sarzo, Warren De Martini and Dennny Carmassi for a European tour.

1995

Feb [10] The RIAA certifies eight million sales of ***Whitesnake 1987***.

Nov [7] ***Greatest Hits*** is certified gold by the RIAA.

see also: **DEEP PURPLE, JOURNEY**

WHITE ZOMBIE

Rob Zombie (vocals); **J.** (guitar);
Sean Yseult (bass); **Ivan de Prume** (drums)

1991

Comic-book collector Zombie (b. Robert Straker, 1966) first met female bassist Yseult (b. 1966) at New York, NY's CBGB club in 1985, subsequently recruiting de Prume and early guitarist Tom Guay to form the Black Sabbath-influenced White Zombie, its name taken from the title of a Bela Lugosi-starring horror flick. Playing hardcore, primal, heavy metal, the group has recorded *Psycho Head Blowout*, an EP released on its own Silent Explosion label in 1987, followed by its first full-length set, 1988's ***Soul Crusher***. With guitarist John Ricci replacing Guay, the group has been signed to Caroline Records for the Bill Laswell-produced ***Make Them Die Slowly***, issued the following year, along with another EP led by their version of Kiss' *God Of Thunder*. With J. (b. Jay Yuenger, 1967, Chicago, IL) joining in place of Ricci in 1990, the band is now signed to Geffen Records on the strength of its growing underground cult following.

1993

Mar [26] White Zombie performs at the Huntington Theatre, Las Vegas, NV, during a round of US dates.

June [27] The group embarks on a six-date US tour at Roberts Stadium, Evansville, IN, set to end on July 3rd at the Hara Arena, Dayton, OH.

Oct [30] Their darkly-themed, uncompromisingly satanic label debut, ***La Sexorcisto : Devil Music Vol. 1***, highlighted by Zombie's ranting lead vocal, released the previous year and produced by Andy Wallace,

makes US #26, spurred not least by the band's relentless, highly theatrical concert schedule.
Dec [10] Current US dates reach the Hollywood Palladium, Hollywood, CA, with Phil Buerstatte having replaced longtime drummer de Prume.
[11] With the MTV cartoon duo having inadvertently promoted White Zombie's last album earlier in the year, Beavis & Butt-head's ***The Beavis & Butt-head Experience*** album, including the group's *I Am Hell*, enters the US chart, set to hit #6.

1994

Feb [8] ***La Sexorcisto : Devil Music Vol. 1*** is certified platinum by the RIAA. (During the year, ex-Testament member John Tempesta will become the group's third drummer, replacing Buerstatte.)

1995

Apr [29] Co-produced by the group with Terry Date, ***Astro Creep : 2,000 Songs Of Love, Destruction And Other Synthetic Delusions Of The Electric Head*** debuts at its US #6 peak.
May [27] ***Astro Creep : 2,000 Songs Of Love, Destruction And Other Synthetic Delusions Of The Electric Head*** enters at its UK #25 high.
June [19] ***Astro Creep : 2,000 Songs Of Love, Destruction And Other Synthetic Delusions Of The Electric Head*** is certified platinum by the RIAA.
May [9] A three-month US tour begins at the Grand Ballroom, Phoenix Civic Plaza Convention Center, Phoenix, AZ, a show grossing $72,424 from 3,578 metal fans.
[20] *More Human Than Human* bows at its UK #51 peak.
July [14] The group "blows the lid off the dump", appearing on CBS-TV's "Late Show With David Letterman".
Aug [27] The band participates in "Reading '95", near Reading, Berks.
Sept [7] The group performs *More Human Than Human* and collects the Best Hard Rock Video trophy (for "More Human Than Human") at the 12th annual MTV Video Music Awards, held at New York's Radio City Music Hall.
Oct [28] Its second US trek of the year gets underway at the Irvine Meadows Amphitheatre, Irvine, CA, before a crowd of 8,967.

1996

May [18] *Electric Head Pt. 2 (The Ecstasy)* bows at UK #31.
June [28] The group begins a two-month US tour at the Lawrence Joel Memorial Coliseum, Winston-Salem, NC, set to end on August 28th at Knickerbocker Arena, Albany, NY.

THE WHO

Pete Townshend (guitar); **Roger Daltrey** (vocals); **John Entwistle** (bass); **Keith Moon** (drums)

1959

Having broken his first guitar at the age of 13 when his grandmother complained about the noise coming from the living room, Townshend (b. Peter Dennis Blandford Townsend, May 19, 1945, Chiswick, London), Entwistle (b. John Alec Entwistle, Oct. 9, 1944, Chiswick) and Phil Rhodes form the Confederates (also known as the Aristocrats and the Scorpions) while still at Acton County Grammar School. Townshend comes from a musical background (his father, Cliff, was a sax-playing member of RAF dance band the Squadronaires, and his mother a singer with the Sidney Torch Orchestra) and is determined to become a pop star, spending most of his time learning to play the guitar. Entwistle is an accomplished musician, studying piano and playing french horn with the Middlesex Youth Orchestra. Leaving school in 1961, Townshend goes to art college - the classic training ground for '60s British rock stars - while Entwistle becomes a civil servant.

1962

Daltrey (b. Roger Harry Daltrey, Mar. 1, 1944, Hammersmith, London), an ex-pupil of Acton County Grammar School, invites Entwistle to join his band, the Detours. Townshend soon follows on rhythm guitar, leaving Daltrey to switch to vocals. Semi-professional drummer, Doug Sandom, who is ten years older than the others, also joins.

1963

During the year, the group supports a wide range of artists, from Wee Willie Harris to the Rolling Stones, with material ranging from covers of James Brown to Bo Diddley.

1964

The band meets freelance publicist, Pete Meaden, who introduces them to the burgeoning world of "mod" in London (a youth cult reaction to "rockers", who revelled in motorbike oil and rock'n'roll, mods are polar opposites, dressing and behaving well, holding steady jobs, riding scooters but also indulging in drugs). Meaden moulds them into *the* mod band, as Sandom leaves and various drummers fill in. During a gig at London's Oldfield pub, a drunk man, dressed completely in ginger, jumps onstage and sits in on drums during an interval. His wild style clicks with the band and Moon (b. Keith John Moon, Aug. 23, 1947, Wembley, Middx.), a former Carroll Levis discovery, becomes their permanent drummer. Meaden changes their name to the High Numbers (a mod term for style), and secures a one-off single deal with Fontana Records.
July *I'm The Face*, a re-write of Slim Harpo's *Got Love If You Want It*, with lyrics by Meaden, is released on Fontana.
Sept Director Kit Lambert, looking for a band to appear in a film, goes to a High Numbers gig. He and his partner, Chip Stamp (brother of actor Terence), take up the group's management, paying off Meaden with £500. They make a promo film of a gig and work on the band's style. The abiding image of the group destroying its equipment originates at its regular venue, the Railway Hotel, Harrow, Middx., where the ceiling is so low that Townshend's swinging-guitar style takes chunks out of it, until one evening the top of his guitar neck disappears, leading to complete destruction of the instrument, with crowds arriving weekly to witness the mayhem.
Nov Lambert changes the group's name to the Who (a name they had used before), as he is worried that posters featuring the High Numbers give the image of advertising a bingo session. The group begins a Tuesday night residency at the Marquee club, as the Who-Maximum R&B.

1965

Jan The group's demo is rejected by EMI, but expatriate American producer, Shel Talmy, shows interest, and secures a contract with Brunswick. His reputation is based on his hits with the Kinks, and his hard-edged, raw production sound. Townshend's *I Can't Explain* is selected for a single release, and Talmy augments the Who with leading session man, Jimmy Page, to bolster Townshend's guitar, and the Ivy League, to provide high backing voices.
Feb The group makes its US vinyl debut with the release of *I Can't Explain* on Decca Records.
Apr [2] The band makes its first radio appearance on the BBC's "The Joe Loss Pop Show".
[17] Two months after its release, *I Can't Explain* hits UK #8, having already peaked at US #93 on the 3rd.
May [21] The group performs *Anyway Anyhow Anywhere* on ITV's "Ready Steady Goes Live!"
July [3] *Anyway Anyhow Anywhere* hits UK #10, described by Townsend as "anti-middle age, anti-boss class and anti-young marrieds". Its melange of feedback causes US label, Decca, to return the master-tape claiming it to be faulty. ITV's "Ready Steady, Go!" adopts the number as its theme tune.
Aug [6] The Who plays on the opening day of the fifth annual "National Jazz & Blues Festival" with Manfred Mann, Rod Stewart and the Yardbirds, at the Richmond Athletic Ground, Richmond, Surrey.
Nov [19] The Who performs at the "Glad Rag Ball" at the Empire Pool, Wembley, Middx.
[27] The Townsend-penned *My Generation* hits UK #2. Endearing itself to its angst-filled, youthful subject matter, the song becomes a landmark recording in rock history, though *The Carnival Is Over* by the Seekers prevents it from reaching UK #1. Daltrey threatens to leave the group after onstage bust-ups and Boz Burrell (later of Bad Company) is lined-up to take over, but Daltrey stays. He is quoted as saying: "When I'm 30 I'm going to kill myself, 'cos I don't ever want to get old".
Dec Its first album, ***My Generation***, hits UK #5. Following the Beatles' and the Rolling Stones' debuts, it becomes the final piece of the triumvirate of exported British rock music currently invading international markets.
[9] ABC-TV's "Shindig Goes To London", featuring the Who performing *Anyway Anyhow Anywhere* at the "National Jazz & Blues Festival" in August, airs.

1966

Jan [5] The group appears on the first BBC-TV "The Whole Scene Going" teenage magazine series.
Feb [4] They play the first of six concerts over the weekend, as a rehearsal for the group's first bill-topping UK tour starting March 25th, with the Fortunes, the Merseys and Screaming Lord Sutch.
[12] *My Generation* peaks at US #74.
Mar Townshend produces the Cat's *Run Run Run* on Reaction.
[9] Polydor Records is served with an injunction, preventing any more copies of *Substitute* being sold or distributed, until the court hears a complaint from the group's former recording manager, Shel Talmy. Polydor circumvents the injunction by pressing a new B-side to *Substitute*, namely *Waltz For A Pig*, performed by session musicians under the name of the Who Orchestra.
[18] The injunction lifted, Polydor reverts to the original B-side.
The group breaks with Brunswick, and signs to Robert Stigwood's newly-formed Reaction label.
Apr [1] The group stars in "Ready Steady, Allez-Oops!" from the Locomotive in the Moulin Rouge, Paris, France.
[4] A judge grants an injunction restraining the group from recording for the time being.
[14] The Who embarks on a UK tour with the Spencer Davis Group at the Gaumont, Southampton, Hants.
[16] *Substitute*, on Reaction, hits UK #5, while the Brunswick-released *A Legal Matter* makes UK #32. Talmy, represented by Quentin Hogg, sues the group (and gains a royalty on the Who's next five years of recorded output).
May [1] The Who performs at the annual "**New Musical Express** Poll Winners Concert" at the Empire Pool, Wembley, Middx.
[20] Townshend and Daltrey go on stage at the Rikki Tik club, Newbury, Berks., with a stand-in bassist and drummer, when Entwistle and Moon fail to show up. When they arrive during the show, Townshend hits Moon over the head with his guitar during *My Generation*, causing a black eye and a cut on his leg, which requires three stitches. Moon informs the press that he and Entwistle are going to leave to form a duo. He rests in a London nursing home, but will re-join the Who a week later.
July Allen Klein and Andrew Oldham take over the band's management.
[30] They perform on the second day of the sixth annual "National Jazz & Blues Festival", Windsor, Berks., with the Yardbirds, Chris Farlowe and the Move.
Sept [7] A tour of UK one-nighters starts at the Ipswich Gaumont, Ipswich, Suffolk.
[10] Brunswick-released *The Kids Are Alright* makes UK #41.
Oct [1] *I'm A Boy* hits UK #2. The group also appears on an ITV "Ready Steady, Go!" special.

Nov The "Ready Steady, Go!" performance is re-recorded in the studio, and released on the Who's only EP, *Ready Steady Who*, as a tribute to the program. Tracks include *The Batman Theme*, *Bucket T*, and a cover of the Beach Boys' *Barbara Ann*. Brunswick, meanwhile, releases *La La La Lies*, though neither disc charts.

Dec ***A Quick One*** hits UK #4 (and US #67 in May 1967, released as ***Happy Jack***). Townshend breaks with musical convention, pre-dating ***Sgt. Pepper***, by linking songs into a mini-opera called ***A Quick One While He's Away***, laying the ground for their grand opus, ***Tommy***.

1967

Jan [21] *Happy Jack* hits UK #3.

[29] The group performs at London's Saville Theatre, with Jimi Hendrix.

Mar [25] The Who makes its US stage debut as part of Murray The K's 10-day Easter show, "Music In The 5th Dimension", at the RKO Radio Theater, New York.

Apr [8] The Who begins a 12-day tour of West Germany.

May [20] *Pictures Of Lily*, inspired by a picture of vaudeville star, Lily Bayliss, hanging on a wall in Townshend's girlfriend's house, hits UK #4, released on the newly-formed Polydor imprint, Track (run by Lambert and Stamp).

[29] Moon collapses during a recording session and is rushed to St. George's Hospital. (It is announced that he will be unable to play for at least two weeks, and for UK dates Julian Covey deputizes on drums.)

June [3] *Happy Jack* reaches US #24.

[18] The Who plays at the "Monterey International Pop Festival", at the County Fairgrounds, Monterey, CA.

[25] Moon takes part in the live recording of the Beatles' *All You Need Is Love*, on the "Our World" global TV show.

[30] The group records *The Last Time* and *Under My Thumb*, as a tribute to the Rolling Stones. With Entwistle honeymooning on the QE2, Townshend plays bass.

July [14] The band begins its first US tour, as support to Herman's Hermits and the Blues Magoos in Seattle, WA, set to end on September 8th.

Aug [5] The group's covers of the Rolling Stones' *The Last Time/Under My Thumb*, released as a gesture of support to the imprisoned Mick Jagger and Keith Richard, makes UK #44, as *Pictures Of Lily* peaks at US #51.

Sept [17] The Who appear on CBS-TV's "The Smothers Brothers Comedy Hour". Moon sets a flash powder explosion in his drum kit, not realizing the technical crew had already done so. The resultant explosion leaves Townshend with singed hair and damaged ears and Moon with a cut on his leg caused by a broken cymbal. Fellow guests, Bette Davis and Mickey Rooney, look on in disbelief.

Oct [25] The Who begins a UK tour at the City Hall, Sheffield, Yorks., with the Tremeloes, Traffic, Herd and Marmalade.

Nov [18] *I Can See For Miles* hits UK #10.

[19] The group plays at the Hollywood Bowl, CA, during a US tour.

[25] *I Can See For Miles* hits US #9, the group's first US Top 10 success.

1968

Jan ***The Who Sell Out***, with tracks linked by commercial radio ads, reaches UK #13 and US #48.

[28] A plane carrying the Who, the Small Faces and Paul Jones lands in Melbourne, Australia, en route from Adelaide to Sydney, and delayed for three hours, amidst allegations of drunkenness and unruly behavior. The journey continues with two security men on board.

Feb [21] The Who begins a six-week US tour in San Jose, CA, set to end on March 30th, at the Westbury Music Fair, Westbury, NY.

[22-24] They play at the Fillmore West, San Francisco, CA and become the highest-paid act ever at that venue.

Mar While in Los Angeles, they record a "Little Billy" jingle at the Gold Star Studios for the American Cancer Society, for broadcast on radio stations, dissuading children from taking up smoking.

May [4] *Call Me Lightning*, scrapped as a UK single release, makes US #40.

July [13] *Dogs* reaches UK #25. Townshend becomes enamored of the teachings of Meher Baba, an Indian Perfect Spiritual Master, which will profoundly alter his life, and his writing of ***Tommy***.

Aug [7] The Who takes part in the "Schaefer Music Festival" in New York's Central Park.

[13-15] The group again performs at the Fillmore West.

[24] Moon drives his Lincoln car, into the Holiday Inn swimming pool in Flint, MI, after a raucous birthday party.

Sept [28] *Magic Bus* makes US #25.

Oct ***Magic Bus, The Who On Tour*** reaches US #39.

Nov [9] *Magic Bus* makes UK #26.

[8] They begin a UK tour with Joe Cocker & the Grease Band, the Crazy World Of Arthur Brown and the Mindbenders, at the Granada Theatre, Walthamstow, London.

Dec [11-12] The group takes part in the filming of "The Rolling Stones Rock And Roll Circus".

1969

Apr [26] *Pinball Wizard* hits UK #4. It is released as a curtain-raiser to the rock opera, ***Tommy***, which BBC Radio 1 DJ Tony Blackburn describes as "sick".

May Conceived and written by Townsend, the Who's concept album ***Tommy*** is given a press launch at Ronnie Scott's club, with the Who performing the double album in full. Revered by critics as a landmark recording, the album chronicles the story of a deaf, dumb and blind boy, and pinball genius, who is elevated to prophet status, and then turned on by his followers.

[24] *Pinball Wizard* reaches US #19.

June ***Tommy*** hits UK #2 and US #4. The Who begins a major US tour, performing the opera in its entirety.

The Who opens "The Magic Circus" in Hollywood Palladium, with Poco and the Bonzo Dog Doo Dah Band.

July [2] Thunderclap Newman's era-defining *Something In The Air*, produced by Townshend, tops the UK chart.

[5] They play the last night of the "Pop Proms" at the Royal Albert Hall, sharing the bill with Chuck Berry. (Fans storm the stage, leading to a ban on rock music at the venue.)

Townshend also writes an unreleased tribute to the recently deceased former Rolling Stone, Brian Jones, *A Normal Day For Brian, A Man Who Died Everyday*.

Aug [9] They take part in the ninth "National Jazz & Blues Festival" at Plumpton Racecourse, near Lewes, Sussex, with Yes, King Crimson and the Strawbs.

[16] The Who's performance at the "Woodstock Music & Art Fair", Bethel, NY, is critically regarded as one of its greatest, capturing the spirit of a generation.

[18] ***Tommy*** is certified gold by the RIAA.

[23] *I'm Free* reaches US #37.

[31] They perform with Bob Dylan at the "Isle Of Wight" festival at Woodside Bay near Ryde, Isle of Wight, using one of the largest sound systems ever erected in the UK, with a notice on the speakers warning the audience not to come within 15 feet.

Sept [29] They begin a week of concerts at the Fillmore East, New York.

Oct [5] The group appears on CBS-TV's "The Ed Sullivan Show".

Dec [14] The band performs "Tommy" with the National Opera House at the London Coliseum.

1970

Jan Moon, a non-driver, accidentally runs over and kills his chauffeur, Neil Boland, when trying to escape from a group of skinheads outside a club in Hatfield, Herts.

May [16] *The Seeker* reaches UK #19.

[23] *The Seeker* makes US #44.

June ***Live At Leeds***, recorded at the University on February 14th, hits UK #3 and US #4.

[7] They perform "Tommy" at New York's Metropolitan Opera House.

Aug [6] ***Live At Leeds*** is certified gold by the RIAA.

[15] Taken from the live album, a cover of Eddie Cochran's classic, *Summertime Blues*, reaches UK #38 and US #27.

[29] They perform at the third annual "Isle Of Wight" festival in Godshill, Isle of Wight.

Nov [28] *See Me, Feel Me* reaches US #12.

1971

Aug [14] Rock anthem, *Won't Get Fooled Again*, hits UK #9.

[31] During a US tour, security guard George Byrington is stabbed to death at the Who's concert at Forest Hills, New York.

Sept [16] The still-climbing ***Who's Next*** is certified gold by the RIAA.

[18] ***Who's Next*** becomes their first UK chart-topper, also hitting US #4, as *Won't Get Fooled Again* reaches US #15.

Oct Entwistle is the first group member to achieve solo success, with ***Smash Your Head Against The Wall*** at US #126.

Nov [4] The band inaugurates new rock venue the Rainbow, Finsbury Park, London, performing the first of three nights.

Dec [11] *Let's See Action* reaches UK #16.

[18] *Behind Blue Eyes* makes US #34. A greatest hits album, ***Meaty Beaty Big And Bouncy***, also hits UK #9 and US #11.

1972

Mar [19] The Who are the cover story of **The Observer** color supplement.

May Moon, with Elton John, jams onstage with the Beach Boys, during their UK visit at a Crystal Palace gig, in London.

July [22] *Join Together*, the group's only release of the year, hits UK #9.

Aug Moon appears as a nun in Frank Zappa's film, "200 Motels".

Sept [9] *Join Together* reaches US #17.

[18] They top the bill at the open-air "Rock At The Oval" concert at the Kennington Oval, London, with the Faces, Mott The Hoople, Atomic Rooster, Quintessence and others.

Oct Townshend's first solo album, ***Who Came First***, reaches UK #30 and US #69.

[23] "That'll Be The Day", in which Moon plays J. D. Clover, a drummer with a group backing Billy Fury, goes into production.

[28] The United States Council For World Affairs adopts *Join Together* as its anthem.

Nov Entwistle's second solo album, ***Wistle Rymes***, peaks at US #138.

Dec [9] An all-star cast performs a fully-orchestrated "Tommy", with the Who, at the Rainbow. Lou Reizner's all-star cast version of ***Tommy***, with orchestration, featuring Rod Stewart, Steve Winwood, Peter Sellers, and with Daltrey in the central role, hits US #5.

1973

Jan [13] *Relay* makes US #39. Masterminded by Townshend, Eric Clapton makes his comeback, at the Rainbow, following his heroin addiction.

[27] *Relay* reaches UK #21.

Apr Daltrey has opened a barn studio where one of his first clients is singer/songwriter, Leo Sayer, who has co-written songs with Dave Courtney for Daltrey's debut solo album, ***Daltrey***, which reaches US #45.

May Daltrey's *Giving It All Away* hits UK #5 and US #83.

[26] ***Daltrey*** debuts at its UK #6 peak.

June Entwistle latest solo effort, ***Riger Mortis Sets In***, reaches US #174.

Sept Daltrey's *I'm Free* reaches UK #13.

Oct [20] The Who's *5:15* makes UK #20.

[29] Based on advance sales, ***Quadrophenia*** is

certified gold by the RIAA.
Nov Townshend-conceived follow-up rock opera double set, ***Quadrophenia***, hits #2 in both the UK and US. Inevitably compared with ***Tommy***, it relates the story of Jimmy, an adolescent mod on a spiritual search. The use of sound effects on the album created problems as most FX libraries keep only mono recordings, forcing the Who to re-record every effect, including bribing the driver of a UK rail train to blow his whistle when leaving Waterloo Station.
Nov [20] Moon collapses during a concert at the Cow Palace, San Francisco, CA, after his drink is spiked with horse tranquiliser. 19-year-old audience member Scott Halpin, volunteers to replace him on drums for the remaining three numbers.
Dec [2] The group is arrested in Montreal, PQ, Canada, and spends six hours in a cell after wrecking a hotel suite, agreeing to pay £1,400 compensation in return for the management not pressing charges.
[29] *Love, Reign O'er Me* peaks at US #76.

1974

Feb [9] *The Real Me* reaches US #92.
Mar [1] Daltrey celebrates his 30th birthday by not killing himself.
Apr Shooting begins on a film version of "Tommy", directed by Ken Russell and starring the Who with Oliver Reed, Ann-Margret, Jack Nicholson and Elton John, among others.
[14] Townshend makes his live solo debut, at London's Roundhouse.
May [10] 80,000 tickets for the Who's Madison Square Garden, New York concert are sold in eight hours.
[18] The group tops the bill at an open-air concert at the Charlton Athletic Football Club, Charlton, London, supported by Lou Reed, Bad Company and Humble Pie. It will be broadcast on BBC2-TV's "2nd House" on October 5th.
June The Lambert/Stamp partnership breaks up, and Bill Curbishley unofficially takes over as manager. (Lambert will die after a fall at his mother's house in Fulham, London, in April 1981.)
Oct ***Odds And Sods*** hits UK #10 and US #15, a collection of unreleased material compiled by Entwistle. Moon appears in the film, "Stardust", the follow-up to "That'll Be The Day".

1975

Feb [21] Entwistle starts a five-week US tour with his band, Ox, in Sacramento, CA.
Mar Film soundtrack album, ***Tommy***, makes UK #21, as Entwistle's ***Mad Dog*** peaks at US #192.
May Moon releases his only solo album, ***Two Sides Of The Moon***.
Apr Daltrey wins the American ABC Interstate Theatres' "New Star Of The Year" award, for his role in "Tommy". (Previous recipients have included Warren Beatty, Paul Newman, Dustin Hoffman and Steve McQueen.)
Aug Daltrey stars in the title role of Ken Russell's film, "Lisztomania".
[14] Daltrey's ***Ride A Rock Horse*** reaches UK #14 and will make US #28.
Oct ***The Who By Numbers*** hits UK #7 and US #8. Moon becomes a UK "lollipop man", to promote a road-safety campaign for a zebra crossing, outside Battersea Primary School.
[3] The group opens an 11-date UK tour, at Stafford's New Bingley Hall.
Nov Daltrey's *Come And Get Your Love* makes US #68.
Dec [10] ***The Who By Numbers*** is certified gold by the RIAA.

1976

Feb [14] The Who's *Squeeze Box* reaches US #16.
[28] *Squeeze Box* hits UK #10.
Mar [9] A US tour is postponed when Moon collapses during a performance at the Boston Garden, Boston, MA.
May [31] The group's "Who The Put The Boot In" concert at Charlton Athletic Football Club, with Little Feat, the Sensational Alex Harvey Band and the Outlaws, enters **The Guinness Book Of Records**, as the loudest performance (at 120 decibels) by a rock group.
June The Who is the first recipient of the Nordoff Robbins Music Therapy Centre Silver Clef Award.
Oct Compilation album, ***The Story Of The Who***, hits UK #2.
[9-10] The Who plays the Oakland-Alameda County Stadium, Oakland, CA, sharing the bill with the Grateful Dead.
[22] The group ends its re-scheduled North American tour at Maple Leaf Gardens, Toronto, ON, Canada. (It will be Moon's last concert in North America.)
Nov [20] *Substitute*, re-released in the wake of the recent collection, hits UK #7. (During the year, Sony embarks on an ad for hi-fi components, with the legend : "It's like having Keith Moon in the room. Only safer".)

1977

Feb Townshend is involved in a scuffle with a photographer at London's Speakeasy, after he tried to photograph him in conversation with Sex Pistols' Paul Cook and Steve Jones.
May Daltrey's *Written On The Wind* makes UK #46.
June [4] His ***One Of The Boys*** peaks at its UK #45 peak.
Sept [17] ***One Of The Boys*** makes US #46.
Oct Townshend's collaboration with Ronnie Lane, ***Rough Mix***, makes UK #44 and US #45, as Daltrey's *Avenging Annie* peaks at US #88.
Dec [15] The band plays the first of two "behind closed doors" concerts for its fan club members, at Shepperton TV studios, Shepperton, Middx., filmed for subsequent use in the "The Kids Are Alright" film documentary.

1978

Aug *Who Are You* reaches UK #18.
[5] Pete Meaden commits suicide.
Sept [8] Keith Moon dies of an overdose of Heminevrin, prescribed to combat alcoholism, in the same Park Street, London apartment as Mama Cass had died four years earlier. **The Times** obituary describes Moon as being "among the most talented rock'n'roll drummers in contemporary music". ***Who Are You*** hits UK #6 and US #2.
[20] ***Who Are You*** is certified gold by the RIAA.
Nov [4] *Who Are You* reaches US #14.

1979

Jan Despite the group's claim that Moon is irreplaceable, ex-Small Faces and Faces drummer, Kenney Jones (b. Sept. 16, 1948, London), takes over, beginning a three-month crash course learning Who material. John "Rabbit" Bundrick (b. Texas) is unofficially added to the line-up, on keyboards.
May [2] The new line-up makes its debut at the Rainbow Theatre, as the film, "Quadrophenia", premieres. Based on the original album, it is directed by Franc Roddam, and features Phil Daniels and a cameo role by Sting.
June ***The Kids Are Alright***, a compilation of live cuts tying in with the documentary feature film of the same name, directed by the Who, makes UK #26 and hits US #8.
July [21] *Long Live Rock* peaks at UK #48 and US #54.
Aug [18] The Who plays at Wembley Stadium, Wembley, on as bill with AC/DC, Nils Lofgren and the Stranglers.
Sept The group is awarded the Gold Ticket for playing to over 100,000 fans at Madison Square Garden.
Oct Soundtrack album, ***Quadrophenia***, reaches UK #23 and US #46. Daltrey appears in the horror film, "The Legacy".
[5] ***The Kids Are Alright*** is certified platinum by the RIAA.
Nov [3] *5:15* makes US #45.
Dec [3] A concert at the Riverfront Coliseum, Cincinnati, OH, turns to disaster when 11 members of the audience are trampled to death after a stampede to claim unreserved seats.
[28] The group plays at the "Concert For Kampuchea", at London's Hammersmith Odeon.

1980

Apr Townshend's solo cut, *Rough Boys*, reaches UK #39, as the High Numbers' *I'm The Face* now makes UK #49.
[30] The film, "McVicar", with Daltrey in the title role, premieres in London.
May Townshend's ***Empty Glass*** makes UK #11 and hits US #5.
June His *Let My Love Open Your Door* peaks at UK #46.
Aug [11] ***Empty Glass*** is certified gold by the RIAA.
Sept [20] The soundtrack album, ***McVicar***, makes UK #39 and will reach US #22, while the extracted *Free Me* climbs to UK #39 and US #53. Townshend's *Let My Love Open Your Door* hits US #9.
Oct Daltrey's ballad, *Without Your Love*, makes UK #55 and US #20, as Townshend's *A Little Is Enough* peaks at US #72. Virgin Records re-releases the long-deleted album, ***My Generation***, which reaches UK #20.
Nov *Rough Boys* peaks at US #89.

1981

Mar ***Face Dances***, the first Who album to be recorded by the new line-up, and produced by Bill Szymczyk, hits UK #2 and US #4.
May [9] *You Better You Bet* hits UK #9 and US #18.
July [11] *Don't Let Go The Coat* makes UK #47 and US #84.
Sept [18] ***Face Dances*** is certified platinum by the RIAA.
Oct Entwistle's ***Too Late The Hero*** reaches US #71.

1982

Mar A Daltrey compilation, ***Best Bits***, peaks at US #185.
Apr [29] The Who is honored for its Outstanding Contribution To British Music, at the 27th annual Ivor Novello Awards, held at London's Grosvenor House Hotel.
July Townshend's ***All The Best Cowboys Have Chinese Eyes*** makes UK #32 and US #26.
Aug Townshend's *Uniforms (Corps D'Esprit)* climbs to UK #48.
Sept [9-10] The band performs at the National Exhibition Centre, Birmingham - its only UK dates of the year.
The final Who studio album, ***It's Hard***, reaches UK #11 and hits US #8, as the group embarks on its final North American tour, with the Clash in support, at the Capital Centre, Landover, MD.
Oct [30] *Athena* makes UK #40 and US #28.
Nov [3] ***It's Hard*** is certified gold by the RIAA.
Dec [17] The group performs the last gig of its North American farewell tour at Maple Leaf Gardens, Toronto, an event filmed for television.

1983

Jan [15] *Eminence Front* makes US #68.
Feb [8] Townshend receives a Lifetime Achievement Award, at the second annual BRIT Awards, held at the London's Grosvenor House Hotel.
Mar Townshend's solo album of Who demos and unfinished work, ***Scoop***, reaches US #35.
Dec [16] The Who officially splits.

1984

Mar Daltrey's ***If Parting Should Be Painless*** peaks at US #102, with the excerpted *Walking In My Sleep* making UK #62 and US #56.
Nov ***Who's Last***, documenting the Who's final concert, makes UK #48 and US #81.

1985

July [13] The Who re-forms for a one-off appearance at the "Live Aid" benefit concert at Wembley Stadium.

Oct Daltrey's *After The Fire* makes UK #50 and US #48.
Nov Daltrey's ***Under A Raging Moon*** makes UK #52, while Townshend's ***White City*** reaches UK #70 and US #26.
Dec Townshend has contributed to the Artists United Against Apartheid album, with its extracted single, *Sun City*, making US #38 and UK #21 while Daltrey performs US solo dates, including one at Madison Square Garden, supporting Big Country.

1986

Jan [11] Daltrey's *Let Me Down Easy* peaks at US #86.
[18] Townshend's *Face The Face* reaches US #26.
[22] His ***White City*** is certified gold by the RIAA.
Mar Daltrey's ***Under A Raging Moon*** makes UK #43.
Nov ***Pete Townshend's Deep End Live!*** makes US #98.

1987

Apr [4] Townshend's ***Another Scoop*** charts for one week, at US #198.
July Daltrey solo set, ***Can't Wait To See The Movie***, is released.

1988

Feb [8] The Who is honored for its Outstanding Contribution To British Music, at the seventh annual BRIT Awards, held at London's Royal Albert Hall. *My Generation* duly re-charts in the UK at #68.
Mar [19] A greatest hits collection ***Who's Better, Who's Best***, hits UK #10 in its week of entry, accompanied by the release of a similar video package.

1989

Jan [18] Townshend inducts the Rolling Stones into the Rock and Roll Hall of Fame, at the annual dinner, held at New York's Waldorf Astoria Hotel.
Apr Daltrey completes work as the street singer in a forthcoming film of Bertolt Brecht's "The Threepenny Opera".
June [21] The group plays a warm-up show for "The Kids Are Alright Tour : 1964-1989" at Glen Falls, NY, with additional musicians, Steve "Boltz" Bolton (lead guitar), Bundrick (keyboards) and Simon Phillips (drums).
[24] Entwistle, Townshend and Daltrey reunite to play in Toronto, the scene of their last concert in 1982, at the start of a soldout 25-city North American reunion tour. The performances include songs from Townshend's US #58 album, ***The Iron Man*** (based on Poet Laureate Ted Hughes' children's story, and featuring John Lee Hooker *(Iron Man)*, Nina Simone (*The Dragon*), Daltrey and Entwistle), and two new tracks with the Who line-up.
[27] "Tommy" is performed at New York's Radio City Music Hall, in aid of the Nordoff Robbins Music Therapy charity - its first performance in 19 years.
July [3] The Who plays the last of four sellout shows at Giants Stadium, East Rutherford, NJ, which have grossed $5,243,672.
Aug [17] Townshend smashes his hand during a concert at the Tacoma Dome, WA, and is treated for cuts on his finger and palm at Tacoma's St. Joseph Hospital, after injuring himself doing a windmill-guitar riff during *Won't Get Fooled Again*.
[24] The Who performs "Tommy" at the Universal Amphitheatre, Universal City, CA, with Elton John (the Pinball Wizard), Steve Winwood (the Hawker), Patti LaBelle (the Acid Queen), Phil Collins (Uncle Ernie) and Billy Idol (Cousin Kevin), in aid of charity.
[30] During a concert at the Oakland-Alameda County Coliseum, Townshend presents a $10,000 cheque to hard-of-hearing fellow musician Kathy Peck's non-profit organization, Hearing Education Awareness of Rockers.
Sept [3] The reunion trek ends at the Cotton Bowl, Dallas, TX.
Oct [23-24, 26-27] The band plays four concerts at the Wembley Arena, Wembley.

1990

Jan [17] The Who are inducted into the Rock and Roll Hall of Fame by U2's Adam Clayton, at the fifth annual induction dinner, held at the Waldorf Astoria Hotel.
Feb [5] "The Who Live Featuring Tommy" video is certified platinum by the RIAA.
Mar [20] "Who's Better, Who's Best" video is certified gold by the RIAA.
[29] Compilation ***Join Together*** makes UK #59 in its week of entry.
Apr [14] ***Join Together*** debuts at its US #188 peak, during a two-week chart stay.
July [26] Daltrey wins an approximate £155,000 settlement after suing the Home Farm, who he claims were responsible for the deaths of up to 500,000 fish, at his Iwerne Springs trout farm in Dorset, in August 1986.
Nov [19] Daltrey co-stars in the made-for-TV movie, "Forgotten Prisoners : The Amnesty Files", on the TNT cable network (and is also scheduled to appear in the movie, "The Teddy Bear Habit" with Sam Waterston).

1991

June [12] Townshend receives the Living Legend Award, at the third annual International Rock Awards, at London's Docklands Arena.
Aug Having contributed vocals to the Rock Aid Armenia fund-raising cut, *Rock And Roll*, released on Music for Nations, also featuring John McEnroe and Pat Cash (guitars), Steve Harris (bass), Nicko McBrain (drums) and Andy Barnett (slide guitar), in July, Daltrey works on a solo album at Abbey Road Studios, with Gerald McMahon producing.

1992

Jan [11] ***Two Rooms - Celebrating The Songs Of Elton John & Bernie Taupin***, to which the Who has contributed *Saturday Night's Alright (For Fighting)*, reaches US #18.
Feb The Chieftains, featuring Daltrey on vocals, release a cover of the Who's *Behind Blue Eyes*. Daltrey's latest solo album, ***Rocks In The Head*** will be released by Atlantic later in the year.

1993

Feb Townshend is honored by the Very Special Arts, a foundation for the disabled, for "Tommy", at Sardi's Restaurant, New York.
[8] The RIAA certifies a slew of Who albums - ***Greatest Hits*** (two million), ***Hooligans*** (gold), ***Live At Leeds*** (two million), ***Meaty Beaty Big And Bouncy*** (platinum), ***Quadrophenia*** (platinum), ***The Who By Numbers*** (platinum), ***Tommy*** (two million), ***Who Are You*** (two million), ***Who's Better, Who's Best*** (gold) and ***Who's Next*** (three million).
Apr [22] "Tommy", which had been performed by the La Jolla Playhouse during the summer of 1992, at the Mandell Weiss Theatre, La Jolla, CA, and directed by Des McAnuff, opens on Broadway at the St. James Theatre. (To mark the beginning of the group's 30th anniversary as a group, MCA in the US releases a re-mastered CD of the 1969 album, ***Tommy***, on one disc.)
June [6] Already a box-office smash, "Tommy" the musical nabs three Tony Awards at the annual drama awards in New York.
[7] Townshend attends the ground-breaking ceremony of the Rock and Roll Hall of Fame in Cleveland, OH.
[17] He guests on NBC-TV's "Late Night With David Letterman", smashing his guitar for good measure.
July [3] Townshend's ***Psychoderelict***, released on Virgin in the UK, and Atlantic in the US, featuring new compositions interspersed with dialogue spoken by actors, debuts at its US #118 peak.
[31] The original-cast recording of ***The Who's Tommy*** bows at its US #114 peak.

1994

Feb Townshend receives the Silver Clef Award at the sixth annual Nordoff Robbins Music Therapy Foundation Silver Clef Dinner & Auction at New York's Roseland Ballroom.
[23-24] "Daltrey Sings Townshend", an event celebrating Daltrey's 50th birthday, with Daltrey, Townshend, Entwistle, the Spin Doctors, Alice Cooper, Lou Reed, Sinead O'Connor, Eddie Vedder, the Chieftains, 4 Non Blondes and the Juillard Orchestra, is held at New York's Carnegie Hall.
[25] Daltrey sings *Substitute* with the Spin Doctors on CBS-TV's "Late Show With David Letterman".
Mar [1] The ***Tommy*** original cast recording wins Best Musical Show Album at the 36th Grammy Awards at New York's Radio City Music Hall.
July [16] ***30 Years Of Maximum R&B***, an 80-track four-CD/cassette boxed set retrospective, spanning the group's career from its early days as the High Numbers up to the 1991 cover of Elton John's *Saturday Night's Alright For Fighting*, makes UK #48 in its week of entry.
[23] ***30 Years Of Maximum R&B*** charts for a week at US #170.
Sept [11] Daltrey currently on a US solo tour promoting ***A Celebration : The Music Of Pete Townsend And The Who***, performs at the Mann Music Center, Philadelphia, PA. (In response to Johnny Depp's trashing of a New York hotel room, Daltrey, staying in the same hotel, says: "On a scale of 1 to 10, I give him a 2, because it took so bloody long. The Who could've done the job in one minute".)

1995

Mar [2] Remastered, remixed and repackaged, ***Live At Leeds*** is issued on CD in the US. At 77 minutes, it is twice its original length, and includes eight previously-unreleased songs from the 1970 performance. It precedes MCA's reissue of the entire Who catalog.
[4] ***Live At Leeds*** makes UK #59 in its week of entry.
Nov [5] Daltrey plays the part of the Tin Man in an all-star cast performance of "The Wizard Of Oz" at New York's Avery Fisher Hall, with the proceeds benefitting the Children's Defense Fund.

1996

Mar [17] Produced by Brian Christian (the engineer on Pink Floyd's ***The Wall*** among others), with full creative input from Townsend, the CD-ROM ***Pete Townsend Presents Tommy : The Interactive Adventure*** is released in the US by Interplay. In the same month, a remastered and remixed original ***Tommy*** also hits US stores, while a London production of its musical opens in the West End.
June [29] Townshend is joined by Daltrey, Entwistle and Zak Starkey to perform "Quadrophenia" at the "MasterCard Masters of Music Concert for the Prince's Trust" at London's Hyde Park.

KIM WILDE

1980

Wilde (b. Kim Smith, Nov. 18, 1960, Chiswick, London), daughter of '50s UK hitmaker, Marty Wilde, has been singing backing vocals on her father's live appearances since leaving art school, when she records a demo with her brother, Ricky, who has a production deal with Mickie Most's RAK Records. Most, attracted by her vocal skill and visual appeal, signs her to his label, while her mother, Joyce Smith, ex-the Vernons Girls, becomes her manager. Most reportedly puts £250,000 of RAK's money into launching and developing Wilde as a major pop act.

1981

Mar Her debut single, *Kids In America*, an uptempo pop number written by Ricky and co-produced by him and Marty, hits UK #2, for two weeks.
May *Chequered Love*, hits UK #4. Wilde does no UK touring to promote this and other early singles, relying instead on videos and TV appearances, stating candidly that she will need to strengthen her voice to make a satisfactory live performance with a band.
July Her maiden album, ***Kim Wilde***, mostly written by her brother and including the two earlier singles, hits UK #3, during a three-month chart stay.
Aug Taken from it, double A-side, *Water On Glass/Boys*, reaches UK #11.
Dec *Cambodia* reaches UK #12.

1982

Mar She announces in a magazine interview a desire to write her own material, but for the moment continues to cut her brother's songs.

May *View From The Bridge* reaches UK #16 as her sophomore set, ***Select***, reaches UK #19.

Aug RAK announces that in 18 months, Wilde has sold over six million discs worldwide - more than her father achieved during his 14-hit UK (just two in the US) chart career.

[14] *Kids In America*, following a deal with EMI America, makes US #25, as ***Kim Wilde*** peaks at US #86.

Oct *Child Come Away* makes UK #43, while Wilde begins a European tour which includes sellout dates. (In Germany, her glamorous image sees her nicknamed "The Bardot Of Rock".)

Dec She appears on ITV's "Razzamatazz" Christmas special, filmed at London's Stringfellows club.

1983

Feb [8] Wilde is named Best British Female Artist, at the second annual BRIT Awards, held at London's Grosvenor House Hotel. (She soon moves from the family home to a flat in London.)

Aug *Love Blonde* reaches UK #23.

Nov *Dancing In The Dark* peaks at UK #67, as ***Catch As Catch Can*** spends a week at UK #90.

1984

May Wilde signs a new contract with MCA Records.

Nov Her label debut, *The Second Time*, reaches UK #29, its parent album, ***Teases And Dares***, peaking at UK #66.

Dec *The Touch* makes UK #56.

1985

Feb [9] Her US MCA debut is Marty and Ricky's *Go For It*, which peaks at US #65, while ***Teases And Dares*** makes US #84.

Apr The rockabilly-flavored *Rage To Love*, remixed by Dave Edmunds, reaches UK #19.

May RAK releases a retrospective singles collection, ***The Very Best Of Kim Wilde***, which peaks at UK #78.

1986

Aug [29] A Kim Wilde mini-dress is sold at Christie's Rock Memorabilia auction in London, for £400.

Nov ***Another Step*** charts briefly at UK #73, as she completes dates in Europe.

Dec Wilde's version of the Supremes' 1966 million seller, *You Keep Me Hangin' On*, hits UK #2, and is a major success throughout the rest of Europe.

1987

Apr Wilde is featured on the Ferry Aid single, *Let It Be*, for the victims of the Zeebrugge ferry disaster, which hits UK #1. She also sings at an AIDS benefit concert at Wembley, performing Elton John's *Sorry Seems To Be The Hardest Word*, with Marty and Ricky Wilde.

May Wilde duets with UK soul singer, Junior, on *Another Step (Closer To You)*, which hits UK #6.

June [6] With heavy airplay and rotation on MTV, *You Keep Me Hangin' On* tops the US chart for one week, making Wilde only the fifth UK female artist to achieve a US #1. She gets a telex from Lamont Dozier, one of the song's writers, congratulating her. ***Another Step*** makes US #40.

Aug *Say You Really Want Me*, accompanied by a controversial video which eliminates Wilde's girl-next-door image, and is banned by ITV's "Get Fresh" for being too sexy, reaches UK #29, despite its talented production team of Rod Temperton, Richard Rudolph and Bruce Swedien.

[15] *Say You Really Want Me* makes US #44.

Sept The reissued ***Another Step***, in a new sleeve and with a bonus record of singles remixes, reaches UK #73.

Dec A teaming with comedian Mel Smith (as Mel & Kim), on a remake of Brenda Lee's *Rockin' Around The Christmas Tree*, with all proceeds going to the Comic Relief charity, hits UK #3.

1988

May *Hey Mr. Heartache*, written by Wilde with regular guitar side-man, Steve Byrd, and recorded at the family's home studio in Hertfordshire, reaches UK #31.

July Wilde supports Michael Jackson in Europe on his 1988 "Bad" world tour.

Aug Dance-styled *You Came* hits UK #3.

Oct *Never Trust A Stranger* hits UK #7.

[22] *You Came* makes US #41, as ***Close*** peaks at US #114.

Dec Ballad, *Four Letter Word*, hits UK #6.

1989

Feb [4] ***Close***, co-produced by Ricki with Tony Swain, and featuring Junior on backing vocals, hits UK #8, eight months after charting.

Mar *Love In The Natural Way* reaches UK #32.

1990

Apr Co-written by Kim and Ricky, *It's Here* makes UK #42.

May [26] Its parent album, ***Love Moves***, again produced by her brother, and with all tracks co-penned by Kim, reaches UK #37 in its week of entry.

June The extracted *Time* peaks at UK #71, as US hits continue to prove elusive.

Nov [13] She contributes to the ***Rock The World*** benefit album, to raise money for the Phoenix House, London-based rehabilitation center.

1992

Apr [24] Wilde guests on BBC1-TV's "Wogan" show.

May [9] *Love Is Holy* reaches UK #16.

[14] Wilde performs at the third annual World Music Awards, at the Sporting Club, Monte Carlo, Monaco.

[30] ***Love Is***, co-produced by Rick Nowels, debuts at its UK #21 peak.

July [4] *Heart Over Mind* reaches UK #34.

Sept [19] *Who Do You Think You Are?* makes UK #49.

1993

July [17] Following appearances on BBC1-TV's "Top Of The Pops" and BBC2-TV's "The O Zone", Wilde's version of the Bee Gees-penned *If I Can't Have You*, a 1978 US #1/UK #4 for Yvonne Elliman, reaches UK #12.

Sept [25] Compilation ***The Singles Collection 1981-1993*** debuts at its UK #11 peak.

Nov [13] *In My Life* charts for a week at UK #54.

1995

Mar [9] Wilde performs at Stevie Wonder's live Ronnie Scott's show, broadcast on BBC Radio 1FM.

Oct [14] *Breakin' Away* debuts at its UK #43 peak, during a two-week chart stay.

1996

Feb [10] *This I Swear* makes UK #46 in its week of entry.

MARTY WILDE

1957

Oct South London timber yard laborer Wilde (b. Reginald Smith, Apr. 15, 1939, Greenwich, London) has been spotted singing in London's Condor club, under the name Reg Patterson (though he is also currently performing as a member of UK rockabilly group, the Hound Dogs) by Lionel Bart, who introduces the teenager to impresario Larry Parnes. Parnes signs him and renames him Marty Wilde (in keeping with Tommy Steele and his later signings - a "soft" forename, with a "hard" surname). Now inking a record deal with the Philips label, his debut release, a cover of Jimmie Rodgers' US hit, *Honeycomb*, sets a pattern of recording cover versions of US originals. *Honeycomb* fails to chart, as will the next two releases, but Wilde gains teen popularity performing live one-night stands around the country.

[18] He makes his UK TV debut, singing *Honeycomb*, on Jack Payne's "Off The Record".

1958

June [15] Wilde is a featured act on the premiere of the ITV pop show, "Oh Boy!", broadcast live from the Hackney Empire, London. (He will also appear on the last show, broadcast on May 30th, 1959.)

Aug *Endless Sleep*, a cover of Jody Reynolds' US top five hit two months earlier, is his UK chart debut, hitting UK #4.

1959

Apr His version of Ritchie Valens' *Donna* hits UK #3 (while the original reaches UK #29), boosted by exposure as a resident on Jack Good's "Oh Boy!", as well as by a current UK tour. He has hired a backing group, the Wildcats (Big Jim Sullivan and Tony Belcher on guitars, Brian "Liquorice" Locking on bass and Brian Bennett on drums), for regular support on live dates.

[16] Wilde is found medically unfit for National Service. Doctors send him to a foot specialist immediately after his examination. **The Daily Telegraph** reports that "it is well known that Wilde has suffered from defective feet, including fallen arches and severe corns, for some years."

June [23] He takes part in the "Oh Boy" segment at the "Royal Variety Performance" in London.

July *A Teenager In Love* storms the UK Top 10 as *Donna* leaves it, set to hit UK #2, and wins a three-cornered chart fight with competing versions by Craig Douglas and Dion & the Belmonts (the original), both of which make the Top 30.

Sept [12] Wilde begins a run as host of the TV rock show "Boy Meets Girls" (which will provide a UK showcase for Eddie Cochran, Gene Vincent and UK guitarist, Joe Brown).

Nov *Sea Of Love*, his cover of the US million seller by Phil Phillips, hits UK #3.

Dec [2] He marries Joyce Baker, a member of TV vocal group, the Vernons Girls, in London.

1960

Jan His self-written *Bad Boy* hits UK #7.

Feb [22] *Bad Boy* makes US #45. He tours the US to capitalize on this success, but will have no further US hits. On his return, UK sales are also in decline, with his recent marriage and increasing involvement in acting, plus the rise of Cliff Richard as the UK's major teen idol, cited as factors.

Mar *Johnny Rocco* reaches UK #30.

May *The Fight* makes UK #47.

Nov [18] His wife, Joyce, gives birth to a daughter, Kim.

1961

Jan *Little Girl*, recorded in New York, reaches UK #16.

Feb A rush-released cover of Bobby Vee's *Rubber Ball*, despite being beaten by the original, hits UK #9. Wilde stars in the London production of "Bye Bye Birdie" (and will appear in the action movie, "The Hellions"). His former backing group, the Wildcats, change their name to the Krew Kats, and record as an instrumental group.

July *Hide And Seek* makes UK #47.

Nov The self-penned *Tomorrow's Clown* reaches UK #33.

1962

Mar [11] Wilde begins a UK tour of one-nighters, his first in two years, but will collapse from exhaustion during the trek.

June His rocking revival of Frankie Laine's *Jezebel* reaches UK #19.

Nov [1] Wilde's switch from Philips to Columbia Records becomes effective, under recording manager Norman Newell, and musical director John Barry.

[3] *Ever Since You Said Goodbye* reaches UK #31, and is Wilde's final UK hit single.

1964

Jan [6] Wilde begins the "Group Scene 1964" UK tour, supporting the Rolling Stones, along with the Ronettes and Johnny Kidd, set to end on the 27th at Colston Hall, Bristol, Somerset.
[12] UK musical comedy film, "What A Crazy World", with Wilde, Joe Brown, Susan Maughan, Freddie & the Dreamers and Harry H. Corbett, opens in North London.
Dec [26] Wilde bows as Prince William in the pantomime, "Once Upon A Fairytale", at the Gaumont Theatre, Doncaster, S. Yorks., with Lulu.

1965

Apr He forms the Wilde Three, a vocal trio also including his wife, Joyce, and singer/guitarist Justin Hayward (who will later join the Moody Blues), recording, among others *Since You've Gone* and *I Cried* for Decca.

1969

Aug Having enjoyed success as a writer penning both Status Quo's *Ice In The Sun* and the Casuals' *Jesamine*, with partner Ronnie Scott the previous year, and now signed again to Philips, Wilde's bouncy *Abergavenny* is released under his own name (from ***Diversions***) in the UK but, issued in the US by Heritage Records, under the pseudonym Shannon, it makes #47.

1973

He records for the Magnet label also releasing ***Good Rocking, Then And Now***, under his own name, and under the pseudonyms Shannon and the Dazzling All Night Rock Show.

1977

Feb [13] Wilde embarks on a 15-date "Rock'n'Roll Road Show" UK tour, with Bert Weedon at Central Hall, Chatham, Kent, set to end on the 27th at the New Theatre, Hull, Humberside.

1981

He returns to the pop scene as co-songwriter and producer (with his son Ricky) for his daughter Kim Wilde's solo career. He will go on to sign to Kaleidoscope Records in 1982, reviving Roy Orbison's *In Dreams* and Don Gibson's *Sea Of Heartbreak*, and will make occasional appearances as a nostalgia celebrity, not least joining his son and daughter on stage at Wembley Arena, Wembley, Middx., in April 1987 for an AIDS benefit concert, singing Elton John's *Sorry Seems To Be The Hardest Word*.

DENIECE WILLIAMS

1967

Having grown up in a religious environment, singing in the gospel choir at a local church, Williams (b. Deniece Chandler, June 3, 1951, Gary, IN), working in a record store while still at Tolleston High School, sings (on the recommendation of the store owner) for a rep from the provincial Chicago record label, Toddlin' Town, which signs her and releases *Love Is Tears*, the first of a number of singles, with only limited local success. Attending Baltimore Morgan State College in 1969, she becomes a nurse, moonlighting as a nightclub singer. She then enrolls at Purdue University, marries and will have two children, Ken and Kevin.

1971

Stevie Wonder hears her Toddlin' Town recordings and invites Williams to Detroit to audition for his backing vocal group, Wonderlove. She gigs with them for a month but gets homesick and returns to work at Chicago's Mercy Hospital. Wonder persists and Williams becomes a permanent member of Wonderlove, contributing on the support spot of the Rolling Stones' 1972 tour. During the next three years, she also contributes Wonderlove vocals to Wonder's albums, ***Talking Book*** (1972), ***Innervisions*** (1973), ***Fulfillingness' First Finale*** (1974) and ***Songs In The Key Of Life*** (1976).

1975

Nov Williams leaves Wonderlove to settle in California and concentrate on a solo career. Writing and recording demos, a tape comes to the attention of Earth, Wind & Fire leader, Maurice White, who arranges her signing to CBS/Columbia Records.

1976

Nov Her maiden album ***This Is Niecy*** is released, showcasing her distinctive high-pitched vocal style. Produced by White, it immediately scores in soul circles (US #33) and her first hit single *Free* follows at US #25. She embarks on a six-month period of touring, supporting Earth, Wind & Fire at major US and UK venues.

1977

Mar [9] ***This Is Niecy*** is certified gold by the RIAA.
May [7] *Free*, co-penned with Susaye Green, Hank Redd and Nathan Watts, hits UK #1 for the first of two weeks, spurring ***This Is Niecy*** to UK #31.
Aug *That's What Friends Are For* hits UK #8, with Williams performing at a "Royal Command Performance" before H.R.H. the Prince of Wales.
Nov Her second album ***Songbird*** makes US #66 as *Baby Baby My Love's All For You* reaches UK #32.

1978

Apr Williams has teamed with her childhood heartthrob, Johnny Mathis, to record the ballad duet *Too Much Too Little Too Late* which hits UK #3. Williams and Mathis perform the song in the presence of H.R.H. the Prince of Wales and Princess Anne in a concert in aid of the World College Fund, as she makes an extensive UK promotion visit including a live spot on BBC1-TV's "Val Doonican Show".
June [3] *Too Much Too Little Too Late* tops the US chart, providing a first ever chart-topper for Mathis with his first duet.
July ***That's What Friends Are For***, entirely comprising Mathis/Williams duets, reaches US #19 and UK #16. It includes their follow-up cover of Gaye/Terrell classic *You're All I Need To Get By*, which makes US #47 and UK #45. Compositions by Williams now begin to be covered by acts which will include Frankie Valli, the Whispers, the Emotions and Merry Clayton.

1979

Jan [12] She wins the Favorite Single, Soul/R&B category (with Johnny Mathis) at the sixth annual American Music Awards held at the Civic Auditorium, Santa Monica, CA.
Aug Williams has signed to Maurice White's new ARC label (through Columbia) and ***When Love Comes Calling***, co-produced by David Foster and Ray Parker Jr., makes US #96. *I've Got The Next Dance* peaks at US #73, though Williams will have no further UK chart action for five years.

1981

Aug Written and produced with veteran soul producer Thom Bell, a new mature soul direction is realized on ***My Melody*** which reaches US #74, the extracted ballad *Silly* making US #53.

1982

Apr A second Bell collaboration ***Niecy*** reaches US #20, aided by her biggest hit for six years, a remake of the Royalettes' 1965 hit *It's Gonna Take A Miracle* which hits US #10. Returning to mainstream Columbia, ***I'm So Proud*** will peak at US #54 in April the following year, during a 19-week chart run.

1984

Jan Williams reunites with Mathis to record two further duets, a cover of Major Harris' *Love Won't Let Me Wait* and a new song, *Without Us*, which becomes the popular theme tune to the top-rated US TV series "Family Ties".
Feb The "Footloose" film soundtrack, containing a Williams cut, tops the US chart and hits UK #7.
May [26] The extracted *Let's Hear It For The Boy*, written by Dean Pitchford and Tom Snow, hits US #1 and will hit UK #2, becoming an international smash. It has taken Williams only 20 minutes to record.
June Hastily-prepared ***Let's Hear It For The Boy*** reaches US #26, while a second single from the album, *Next Love* peaks at US #81. ***Hot On The Trail***, produced by Greg Mathieson, will be released in July the following year, with her first full gospel set, ***From The Beginning*** emerging in 1986 on the specialist Sparrow label.

1987

Feb [24] Williams wins the Best Soul Gospel Performance, Female of 1986 with *I Surrender All* and, with Sandi Patti, Best Gospel Performance by a Duo or Group, Choir or Chorus of 1986 with *They Say* at the 29th annual Grammy awards. (Williams' chart success will move back to the specialist R&B/gospel markets with the release of ***Water Under The Bridge***.)

1988

Mar [2] *I Believe In You*, from ***Water Under The Bridge***, wins the Best Gospel Performance, Female category at the 30th annual Grammy awards.
July Returning again to her gospel roots, she releases the inspirational album ***So Glad I Know*** again on the Sparrow label.
Oct [29] *I Can't Wait* peaks at US #66, taken from the George Duke/Monte Moire-produced R&B set ***As Good As It Gets***.

1994

June Following the 1990 Columbia release of a ten-track compilation, ***Change The World***, and Williams' first foray into the children's market with the Jay Gruska co-produced ***Lullabies to Dreamland***, released on Word Records the following year, and with the RIAA having certified her pop career highlight *Let's Hear It For The Boy* platinum on May 5th 1992, Sparrow now releases a round-up of Williams' gospel highlights, ***Greatest Gospel Hits***.

HANK WILLIAMS

1935

Born into a poor sharecropper's family and raised by his mother from the age of six when his father began long-term care at a veterans' hospital for a wound received during the Great War, Williams (b. Hiram Williams, Sept. 17, 1923, Mount Olive West, Butler County, AL), son of Elonzo and Lillian Williams and sister to Irene, learns the rudiments of blues music from an itinerant black street-singer, Tee-Tot (Rufus Payne), in Greenville, AL. He also wins first prize in a songwriting contest with *WPA Blues*. Moving with his family to Montgomery, AL, in 1937, he makes appearances on country radio stations WCOV and WSFA, where he is dubbed "The Singing Kid". He also forms his first group with Smith "Hezzy" Adair, as Hank & Hezzy's Driftin' Cowboys, and begins a long apprenticeship playing the tough honky-tonk circuit. From 1938, he will spend a number of years drifting from job to job, working in a rodeo, for a traveling medicine show, and in the shipyards of Mobile, AL, where he meets his future wife Audrey Mae Sheppard. He makes his first recording, *I'm Not Coming Home Anymore*, at Griffins Radio Shop in Montgomery in 1942.

1944

Dec [15] Hank and Audrey marry at a filling station in Andalusia, Alabama, and she becomes a singing member, and sometime double-bass player in his regular touring outfit, the Drifting Cowboys, and also his manager.

1946

Sept [14] Williams and wife travel to Nashville, TN, to meet songwriter Fred Rose, of the famed Acuff/Rose publishing house, which he had formed in 1942 with country star, Roy Acuff. Williams signs a songwriting agreement, and offers demos to singer, Molly O'Day, who scores hits with *Six More Miles* and *When God Comes And Gathers His Jewels*, which begin to establish Williams' name.

Dec [11] With Oklahoma group, the Wranglers, he records *Wealth Won't Save Your Soul* and *When God Comes And Gathers His Jewels* for Al Middleman's Sterling Records which, although not successful, leads him to cut four more songs for the label.

1947

Jan Sterling releases *Calling You*, backed with *Never Again (Will I Knock On Your Door)*.

Mar [6] As a result, Rose secures the interest of the newly-formed MGM Records, which signs Williams to the label.

Aug [9] *Move It On Over* becomes the first of his 36 Top 10 US Country chart successes, crossing over to hit #4.

1948

Apr The Alabama Journal reports that *Move It On Over*, Williams' 1947 MGM debut recording, has now sold over 100,000 copies.

Dec [22] Williams records one of his biggest hits, *Lovesick Blues*, at the Herzog Studio, Cincinnati, OH. The song originates from the 1922 musical "Oooh Ernest!"

1949

May [7] *Lovesick Blues* tops the US Country chart (the first of eleven such #1s), and crosses over to reach US #24. (It also tops **Billboard**'s Folk Record chart for 16 weeks.)

[26] Randall Hank Williams is born in Shreveport, LA.

June [11] Williams makes his debut at the "Grand Ole Opry" in Nashville, and receives an unprecedented total of six encores. (The Opry had originally been established by radio station WSM as the WSM Barn Dance, on November 28th, 1925. It became the Grand Ole Opry in 1927, when WSM became an NBC affiliate, and followed a highbrow Musical Appreciation Hour. Station director George D. Hay made the announcement: "For the past hour we have been listening to music taken largely from Grand Opera but from now we will present the Grand Ole Opry." The name stuck, giving country listeners a certain pride in their own definition of their music, and thus the Ryman Auditorium inherited a new name.) Williams tours US bases in West Germany, later in the year, as part of an Opry package.

1950

Jan He begins a series of recordings as Luke the Drifter. With songs that consist of moral monologues, including *Men With Broken Hearts*, *The Funeral* and *Be Careful Of Stones That You Throw*, the pseudonym is adopted by MGM to clearly differentiate these releases from Williams' usual material.

1951

Apr *Cold Cold Heart* reaches US #27. (Tony Bennett will top the pop charts with a cover version, later in the year. Other songs become pop hits for Jo Stafford (*Jambalaya*) and Joni James (*Your Cheatin' Heart*).

May [21] Williams is admitted to the North Louisiana Sanitarium, suffering from acute alcoholism. He has regularly resorted to alcohol and narcotics to ease severe back pains, which are now analysed as a birth defect, spina bifida occulta.

Aug [15] He joins one of the largest variety treks ever mounted in the US: the Hadacol Tour (promoting a medicinal compound), appearing alongside celebrities such as Bob Hope, Jack Benny, Jimmy Durante and Milton Berle.

Sept *Hey Good Lookin'* reaches US #29.

1952

Jan [29] He performs at the Mosque, Richmond, VA, in a state of near collapse, due to the combined effects of drink and drugs.

May [29] Hank and wife Audrey divorce.

Aug [17] Williams is arrested for drunken behavior at the Russell Hotel, Alexander City, AL.

Sept [20] To restore his live credibility, he begins the first of weekly Saturday night appearances on the Louisiana Hayride, for a fee of $250 a week. *Jambayala* reaches US #20.

Oct [18] He marries Billie Jean Jones in Minden, LA.

[19] The couple repeat their wedding vows twice, for a paying public, after the 3:00 p.m. and 7:00 p.m. shows that Williams performs at the Municipal Auditorium, New Orleans, LA.

[31] He is admitted to hospital in Shreveport, suffering from acute alcohol intoxication.

Dec [11] Discharging himself from hospital, he is arrested and imprisoned for drunken behavior. Despite being in a rapidly deteriorating condition, Williams fulfills many live engagements, meeting hostile crowds who are appalled by his drunkeness. The ominously-titled *I'll Never Get Out Of This World Alive* reaches US #20.

[30] He flies to Charleston, WV, for a gig, but bad weather grounds his flight in Knoxville, TN.

[31] 17-year-old Charles Carr drives Williams' Cadillac from Montgomery, as they set out for a New Year's Day gig at the Memorial Auditorium, Canton, OH. Highway patrolman, Swann Kitts, books Carr for speeding near Rutledge, TN, and suggests to the driver that his back-seat passenger looks dead. Carr continues driving.

1953

Jan [1] At 5:30 a.m. Carr stops for directions in Oak Hill, WV. Outside a Pure Oil service station, he realizes Williams' body feels cold, and calls police patrolman, Howard Jamey, who confirms the death. A piece of paper is clutched in Williams' right hand. It reads "We met, we lived and dear we loved, then comes that fatal day, the love that felt so dear fades away. Tonight love hathe (sic) one alone and lonesome, all that I could sing, I love you you (sic) still and always will, but that's the poison we have to pay." An autopsy, conducted at Oak Hill Hospital, gives the cause of death as heart failure. At the time of his death, age 29, Williams is the most successful artist in country music history. At Canton Memorial Auditorium, a spotlight is shone on the stage curtain as a weeping audience listen to the Drifting Cowboys perform *I Saw The Light*, behind the drapes.

[4] Williams' funeral service is held at the City Auditorium, Montgomery. Roads leading into the city are choked as 20,000 mourners throng the streets. Williams leaves no will, and for the next 20 years his estate will be wrangled over by his mother and his two wives, who will both begin touring as Mrs. Hank Williams. Billie Jean removes herself from the estate squabbles, after receiving a $30,000 settlement from Williams' mother, Lilly.

[6] A girl, Jett Williams, is born to Nashville secretary, Bobbie Jett. Upon reaching adulthood, Jett will claim, with legal success, that she is Williams' illegitimate daughter, and has a claim over her late father's estate (much to the chagrin of Hank Jr.). (Williams' second wife, Billie Jean, will marry country singer, Johnny Horton in 1954 (who will die in a car crash in 1960).)

Feb [21] *Kaw-Liga* begins a record-breaking 13-week run atop the US Country chart and makes US #23.

Mar [7] It is knocked off the Country top spot by one of Williams' most revered recordings, *Your Cheatin' Heart*, which also makes US #25.

June [6] *Take These Chains From My Heart* becomes Williams' fourth US Country chart-topper of a year which sees him head the survey for 24 weeks.

1961

Nov [3] Williams becomes the first artist inducted into the Country Music Hall of Fame.

1964

A film biography is released called "Your Cheatin' Heart", with George Hamilton in the title role. It is later withdrawn, after Billie Jean sues and wins a libel case claiming the film depicts her as a lewd woman. Hank Williams Jr. sings his father's songs for the screen biography, and will later become a major force in country music in his own right.

1965

Aug [14] ***Father And Son*** peaks at US #139. Hank Jr.'s vocals are dubbed in with those of his father, to create a duet effect. A second 'collaboration', ***Songs My Father Left Me*** will peak at US #164 on July [5] 1969, with Hank Jr. adding music to lyrics written by his father. On the 11th of the previous month, the RIAA will have certified gold sales of ***Hank Williams' Greatest Hits*** and ***Your Cheatin' Heart***.

1987

Jan [21] Having been honored with the Pioneer Award from the Academy of Country Music in 1973, and with *Your Cheating Heart* inducted into the NARAS Hall Of Fame, at the 25th annual Grammy awards on February 23rd 1983, Williams is posthumously inducted into the Rock and Roll Hall of Fame, at the second annual dinner, held tonight at New York's Waldorf Astoria Hotel.

1988

Mar [2] Williams is honored by the NARAS at the 30th annual Grammy Awards with a Lifetime Achievement Award, noting that Williams was "a pioneering performer, who proudly sang his songs so honestly and openly, capturing completely the joys and sorrows and essence of country life, and whose compositions helped create successful careers for various singers who followed him".

1990

Feb [21] *There's A Tear In My Beer*, a posthumous collaboration with Hank Williams Jr. (which was promoted via an ingenious video, which brings the "ghost" of Williams Sr. to the modern day Williams Jr.), wins Best Country Vocal Collaboration, at the 32nd annual Grammy Awards, held at the Shrine Auditorium, Los Angeles, CA.

Dec Polydor Records releases a comprehensive boxed set of Williams' work, the 84-song, ***The Original Singles Collection ... Plus***.

1991

Sept [17] Hank Williams Jr. unveils a life-size bronze statue of his father, erected in the Montgomery city car park, on what would have been the country legend's 68th birthday.

1992

July A New York appeals court rules that Jett Williams, his illegitimate daughter, is entitled to share royalty income (estimated at $1 million a year) with her father's wife, Billie Jean Williams Berlin, and Hank Jr.

Sept *Your Cheatin' Heart* (#7), *I'm So Lonesome I Could Cry* (#8) and *Lovesick Blues* (#10) give Williams three entries in the Top 10 most popular country songs of all time, as voted by readers of **Country America** magazine.

1993

Jan [23] ***The Best Of Hank And Hank***, a compilation pairing pere et fils, charts for a week at US #179.

Feb [23] A selection of Williams' 1949 radio broadcasts, including seven never-before released tracks, are issued by PolyGram, as ***Health And Happiness Shows***.

1994

Mar [4] ***Greatest Hits*** is certified platinum by the RIAA

1995

Apr [18] Following The The's 1994 tribute album to Williams, ***Hanky Panky***, Mercury Records (US) releases a 16-track covers tribute set ***Alone And Forsaken***.

July Mercury issues the ultimate Williams boxed set, ***Hank Williams : The Collectors' Edition***, featuring all 169 songs recorded for MGM and Sterling between 1946 and 1952.

1996

May [2] With his celebrity stronger than ever some 43 years after his death, a two act musical production "Lost Highway : The Music And Legend Of Hank Williams" premieres at Nashville's Ryman Auditorium, with the hero played with disarming accuracy by Jason Petty.

JACKIE WILSON

1950

Wilson (b. Jack Wilson, June 9, 1934, Detroit, MI), while at high school in Detroit, wins the American Amateur Golden Gloves Welterweight boxing title, having also boxed at the Brewster Center and CYO (though never turning professional) by posing as an 18-year-old under the name Sonny Wilson. He is set for a boxing career, but his mother persuades him to finish studying at the Highland Park High School, and develop his singing talent instead. He joins the Ever Ready Gospel Singers, and sings with R&B quartet, the Thrillers (alongside Hank Ballard), once he completes school, and goes to work at a car-assembly plant.

1951

Wilson is discovered in a talent show at Detroit's Paradise Theater, by Johnny Otis, a scouting talent for the King label (who also finds Little Willie John). He mentions Wilson to Billy Ward, vocal teacher and leader of successful doo-wop, group Billy Ward & the Dominoes. Ward notes Wilson's vocal talent, and later hires him as a back-up singer. (In the meantime, Wilson records *Danny Boy* and *Rainy Day Blues*, as Sonny Wilson, for Dizzy Gillespie's Dee Gee label.)

1953

Apr Wilson's own idol, Clyde McPhatter, the Dominoes' lead singer, is fired from the group (and will shortly form the Drifters), and Ward invites Wilson, who has toured with the group, to replace him as lead tenor vocalist. (Wilson has heard a rumor that McPhatter may be leaving the band, and has hustled an audition at the Fox Theater.) He will sing lead on two years' worth of the group's recordings on the King and Federal labels, one of which, *Rags To Riches*, hits R&B #3 in early 1954.

1956

June After leaving King/Federal, and recording briefly for Jubilee, Ward & the Dominoes are signed to Decca Records.

Sept Wilson sings lead on *St. Therese Of The Roses*, the Dominoes' first Decca single, and the group's first US pop chart hit, peaking at #13, though it proves to be his last recording with the group.

1957

Despite the Dominoes' popularity, and his own high status among his peers (Elvis Presley raves about his stage performance of *Don't Be Cruel* on the preserved tape of the December 1956 Sun Records Presley/Carl Perkins/Jerry Lee Lewis jam session), Wilson is feeling stifled as an individual primarily since, because of the group's billing, and the fact that he sings lead, audiences believe him to be Ward. Encouraged by Al Green, a Detroit publisher and agent who has been introduced to the artist through Wilson's cousin, Roquel "Billy" Davis, and becomes his manager, Wilson leaves to go solo, and signs to Brunswick Records, a Decca subsidiary, to work with producer/orchestra leader Dick Jacobs in New York, as part of a deal which would also bring LaVern Baker to the label. However, when Green dies in December, Baker is still contracted to Atlantic.

Sept [8] Wilson's solo career begins with the release of the uptempo *Reet Petite (The Finest Girl You Ever Want To Meet)* (co-written by Berry Gordy Jr., the future founder of Motown, and who had met Wilson in a Detroit boxing gym, and Tyran Carlo, a pseudonym for Wilson's cousin, Billy Davis), on Brunswick.

Nov [23] *Reet Petite* peaks at US #62.

1958

Jan *Reet Petite* hits UK #6.

June [7] In contrast, but also penned by Gordy/Carlo, Wilson's dramatic ballad, *To Be Loved*, makes both US and UK #23.

Oct [4] The Gordy-written *We Have Love* peaks at US #93.

Wilson's first album, ***He's So Fine***, is released (though he will not have a US chart album until 1962).

Dec [15] *Lonely Teardrops* tops the US R&B chart for the first of seven weeks - both his and writer Gordy's first chart-topper.

[25] Wilson begins a ten-day residency in "Alan Freed's Christmas Rock'n'Roll Spectacular", at Loew's State Theater, Manhattan, New York, alongside 16 other acts, including Chuck Berry, Cochran, Bo Diddley and the Everly Brothers.

1959

Feb [14] *Lonely Teardrops* is Wilson's first US Top 10 hit, at #7, selling over a million copies, also earning him his first gold disc.

Mar He headlines a show at Brooklyn's Fabian-Fox Theater, with Fats Domino, Duane Eddy and Bobby Darin.

Apr [22] Freed's film, "Go Johnny Go", in which Wilson appears singing *You Better Know It*, premieres in the US.

May [9] *That's Why (I Love You So)* reaches US #13.

Aug [8] *I'll Be Satisfied* (which UK rocker Shakin' Stevens will revive in 1982) reaches US #20, his last hit to be penned by Gordy and Carlo, amid an acrimonious bust-up.

Sept On Labor Day, Wilson headlines an Alan Freed show at the the Fox Theater.

Oct [17] *You Better Know It* (premiered earlier in the year in "Go Johnny Go") makes US #37, and spends a week at US R&B #1.

1960

Jan [16] *Talk That Talk* reaches US #34. Wilson is now managed by Nat Tarnopol, former assistant to the late Al Green, who steers both his recordings and live performances (which include engagements at major Hollywood, CA, Las Vegas, NV, and New York nightclubs) towards the majority, white, middle-class audience.

May [14] Wilson's second million seller is the double A-side, *Night* (which hits US #4, an almost operatic rendition of a ballad set to the melody of *My Heart At Thy Sweet Voice*, from Camille Saint-Saens' "Samson And Delilah") and *Doggin' Around*, a blues groover, which reaches US #15. *Doggin' Around* also hits US R&B #1 for three weeks, and is issued as a UK A-side, with *The Magic Of Love* on the B-side, the classical adaptation of *Night* being felt likely to fall foul of a BBC ban (academic, since it fails to sell in the UK).

Aug [22] Another double A-side, *(You Were Made For) All My Love*, reaches US #12, while *A Woman, A Lover, A Friend* (its melody based on the Hank Ballard-penned 1953 Royals hit, *I Feel So Blue*) makes US #15, and R&B #4 for four weeks. He also releases one of his most acclaimed albums, ***Jackie Sings The Blues***.

Sept *(You Were Made For) All My Love* reaches UK #33.

Dec [3] *Alone At Last*, its melody based on Tchaikovsky's "Piano Concerto #1 in B flat", hits US #8.

[10] The B-side, *Am I The Man*, makes US #32.

[24] *Alone At Last* makes UK #50, and will be Wilson's last UK chart entry for over eight years. He is voted Entertainer Of The Year by **Cash Box** magazine.

1961

Feb [6] *My Empty Arms*, another classical adaptation (from Leoncavallo's "On With The Motley") hits US #9, its B-side, *The Tear Of The Year*, having made US #44 on Jan [30]. The latter is reissued as a UK A-side after *My Empty Arms* is deleted at the time of release, for similar reasons to those affecting *Night*.

[15] Wilson is shot by Juanita Jones, a female fan, who invades his New York apartment and demands attention. Her gun, with which she has threatened to shoot herself, goes off as he tries to disarm her, and leaves him with a stomach wound, and a bullet lodged in his back. He is rushed to Roosevelt Hospital.

Mar [27] *Your One And Only Love*, B-side of the still-climbing *Please Tell Me Why*, stops at US #40.

[31] Wilson is discharged from hospital, with the bullet still lodged in a not dangerous, but not easily-operable, spot in his abdomen.

Apr [17] *Please Tell Me Why* reaches US #20.

June [12] *Lonely Life*, the B-side of the still-climbing *I'm Coming Back To You*, makes US #80.

July [10] *I'm Coming Back To You* reaches US #19.

Sept [18] *Years From Now* stops at US #37.

Oct [16] Its flip-side, *You Don't Know What It Means* (co-written by Wilson), peaks at US #79.

Nov [13] *The Way I Am* makes US #58.

[27] Its B-side, *My Heart Belongs To Only You*, climbing to US #65.

1962

Jan [21] Wilson appears on CBS-TV's "The Ed Sullivan Show".

Feb [3] *There'll Be No Next Time*, the B-side of the yet-to-peak *The Greatest Hurt*, makes US #75.

[17] *The Greatest Hurt* reaches US #34.

Apr [21] *I Found Love*, a duet with Linda Hopkins (who he'd discovered at the Baby Grand Manhattan), co-written by Wilson and Alonzo Tucker, peaks at US #93.

May [19] *Hearts* makes US #58.

July [28] *I Just Can't Help It*, also by Wilson/Tucker, peaks at US #70.

Oct [13] *Forever And A Day* makes US #82.

Nov ***Jackie Wilson At The Copa***, recorded at New York's Copacabana, is Wilson's first US chart album, reaching #137.

1963

Apr [13] Wilson/Tucker-penned *Baby Workout*, a strong R&B dance performance with big band-type arrangement, in contrast to his ballads, hits US #5.

May [4] *Baby Workout* tops the US R&B chart for the first of three weeks, while ***Baby Workout*** reaches US #36.

June [22] His revival of Faye Adams' *Shake A Hand*, in another duet with Linda Hopkins, greets US #42.

Aug [10] *Shake! Shake! Shake!*, continuing the dance groove of *Baby Workout*, reaches US #33.

Oct [12] *Baby Get It (And Don't Quit It)* makes US #61.

1964

May [23] *Big Boss Line* peaks at US #94.

Aug [29] *Squeeze Her - Tease Her (But Love Her)* climbs to US #89. A return to middle-of-the-road ballads with the traditional Irish paean, *Danny Boy*, will peak at US #94 the following March, with *No Pity (In The Naked City)*, Wilson's last hit to be co-written with Tucker, making US #59 in August and *I Believe I'll Love One* creeping to US #96 in October.

1966

Jan [15] *Think Twice*, a duet with LaVern Baker, on a revival of Brook Benton's 1961 hit, reaches US #93.

Dec [10] Carl Davis-produced *Whispers (Gettin' Louder)*, written by Barbara Acklin, then secretary in Davis' Chicago, IL office, and cut in the Windy City rather than New York, moves Wilson into the emerging soul field, and reaches US #11. (Davis will continue as Wilson's producer.)

1967

Jan ***Whispers*** makes US #108.
Feb [25] *Just Be Sincere* reaches US #91.
Mar [18] Its B-side, *I Don't Want To Lose You*, peaks at US #84.
May [20] *I've Lost You* stops at US #82.
Oct [7] Wilson finally scores his third million-selling single with *(Your Love Keeps Lifting Me) Higher And Higher*, using the Motown session crew, which hits US #6 (and tops the R&B chart for a week).
Dec [23] *Since You Showed Me How To Be Happy* reaches US #32, as ***Higher And Higher*** makes US #163.

1968

Mar [9] His treatment of Jerry Butler and the Impressions' *For Your Precious Love*, on which Wilson sings with Count Basie's band, reaches US #49.
May [25] *Chain Gang*, also with Basie, peaks at US #84.
June Wilson/Basie collaboration, ***Manufacturers Of Soul***, including the two hit singles, peaks at US #195.
Sept [7] Swinging number, *I Get The Sweetest Feeling*, co-written by arranger Van McCoy, reaches US #34.
Nov [16] His revival of the standard *For Once In My Life* peaks at US #70.

1969

June Unsuccessful in the UK on its original release, *(Your Love Keeps Lifting Me) Higher And Higher* reaches UK #11 - Wilson's first UK chart entry since *Alone At Last*, in 1960.
Nov [29] He participates in Richard Nader's second "Rock'n'Roll Revival" concert, also starring Gary U.S. Bonds and Bill Haley & His Comets, among others, at New York's Madison Square Garden.

1970

May [16] *Let This Be A Letter (To My Baby)* peaks at US #91. *(I Can Feel Those Vibrations) This Love Is Real* will make US #56 on Feb [6] the following year, *Love Is Funny That Way* will climb to US #95 on Dec [11] before *You Got Me Walking*, written by Eugene Record of the Chi-Lites, peaks at US #93, Wilson's final US chart single, on Mar [11], 1972. A reissue of *I Get The Sweetest Feeling* will hit UK #9 in September the same year. ***Beautiful Day***, recorded after Davis brings in Detroit writer, Jeffrey Perry, will be released in 1973.

1975

May The double A-side reissue of *I Get The Sweetest Feeling/Higher And Higher* reaches UK #25.
Sept [29] Wilson has a heart attack, while singing *Lonely Teardrops*, at Dick Clark's "Good Ol' Rock'n'Roll" revue at the Latin Casino in Cherry Hill, NJ. Hitting his head as he falls, he lapses into a four-month coma, suffering severe brain damage due to oxygen starvation. (He is hospitalized, and will recover consciousness, but with all faculties, including speech and walking, impaired. Barry White and the Spinners will be among those who perform benefits to raise money for his care, though the $60,000 raised actually goes to the IRS, who Wilson owes $300,000.)

1978

Mar [15] Wilson's *That's Why (I Love You So)* is included on the newly-released soundtrack of the movie, "American Hot Wax", based on the life of DJ Alan Freed, which premieres in the US.

1984

Jan [21] Wilson dies in Mount Holley, NJ, having been immobile and in permanent care since his heart attack. His funeral is held at Chrysler Drive Baptist Church, in Detroit, where Wilson once sung gospel music. The Four Tops, the Spinners and Berry Gordy Jr. all attend.

1986

Dec [27] Wilson's first single, *Reet Petite*, reissued in the UK and promoted via an inventive model-animation video, dethrones the Housemartins' *Caravan Of Love* to top the UK chart at Christmas, for the first of four weeks, 29 years after its original release, this time selling over 700,000 copies.

1987

Jan [21] Three years to the day since his death, Wilson is inducted into the Rock and Roll Hall of Fame, at the second annual ceremony, held at New York's Waldorf Astoria Hotel.
Mar A third UK reissue of *I Get The Sweetest Feeling* is the follow-up to *Reet Petite*, and hits UK #3.
July *Higher And Higher* reaches UK #15. Rhino Records (US) will bring his greatest hits to compact disc with the 1994 release of ***The Very Best Of Jackie Wilson***, following a more substantial retrospective, the three-volume, 72-song boxed set ***Mr. Excitement!***

WILSON PHILLIPS

Chynna Phillips (vocals);
Carnie Wilson (vocals); **Wendy Wilson** (vocals)

1973

Carnie Wilson (b. Apr. 29, 1968, Los Angeles, CA), who has already made her vocal debut at the age of two, on the Beach Boys' *This Whole World*, from their ***Sunflower*** album, her sister Wendy (b. Oct. 16, 1969, Los Angeles), daughters of Beach Boy Brian Wilson and his ex-wife, Marilyn Rovell, record their first (unreleased) song together, *Take Me Out To The Ballgame*, as the Satellites, with childhood friend Chynna Phillips (b. Feb. 12, 1968, Los Angeles), daughter of the Mamas & the Papas' singers John and Michelle Phillips. The three girls will remain friends, and all attend Santa Monica Montessori school.

1986

Owen Vanessa Elliot, daughter of the late Mamas & the Papas' singer, Cass Elliot, having been raised in Northampton, MA, by her aunt, Leah Kunkel, a singer in her own right, goes to California to seek acting work, where she links with her cousin, Chynna, who is already gaining acting roles, including parts in the movies "Some Kind Of Wonderful", "Caddyshack II", "Say Anything", and most notably will star as Roxanne Pulitzer in the TV movie "Roxanne : The Prize Pulitzer". Together, they start looking at a career in music, and hit upon an idea to record an anti-drug single, featuring the offspring of '60s musicians. Phillips contacts the Wilson sisters, who suggest recording a song, *Dog And Butterfly*, written by another pair of Wilson sisters (Ann and Nancy, of Heart), which they practice with Elliot.

1987

The foursome take their demo to veteran producer, Richard Perry, who, after hearing them harmonize on a version of Stevie Nicks' *The Wild Heart*, points them to the studio. It becomes clear that Elliot's vocals do not gel in the unit, and her cousin asks her to leave them as a trio. (Elliot will subsequently be snapped up by MCA for a solo deal.) Perry continues to demo the girls, enlisting the songwriting assistance of Glen Ballard.

1988

Perry hawks the un-named trio's demo around Los Angeles record labels, though only SBK production company, through Charles Koppelman and Artie Mogull, shows enthusiasm, and finances further recordings. Subsequent interest from companies, including MCA and Warner Bros., is rejected by the singers, who also extricate themselves from Perry. He has tried to project them in a Pointer Sisters direction, and through a deal will receive over $200,000 on royalty points from their debut album. New SBK offshoot, SBK Records, enters the bidding arena, and signs the trio, installing Ballard as producer of album tracks to be recorded at Studio Ultimo in Los Angeles, which will be finished by spring '90. (During this period, Phillips will meet up with her father for the first time in eight years, while at the 1989 Capitol Records Grammy Awards party, the Wilson sisters will also meet up with their father for only the second time in eight years, a reunion not planned by Brian Wilson's constant companion, Eugene Landy.)

1990

Apr [24] Wilson Phillips (they have finally settled on their band name after rejecting 40 others including Gypsy and Leda) make their network TV debut on NBC-TV's "Late Night With David Letterman".
May [27] The week-long 19th "Tokyo Song Festival" begins in Tokyo, Japan, with the group winning the event's Grand Prize with their performance of *Hold On*. This is followed by a promotional tour of Japan and Australia.
June [9] Following a carefully orchestrated marketing plan by SBK promotion man, Daniel Glass, their airplay-friendly, close-harmonizing debut smash, *Hold On*, written by Phillips and Ballard with additional lyrics by Carnie Wilson, hits US #1, having already been certified gold by the RIAA on May 22nd. (25 years earlier, to the day, the Beach Boys were at #1 with *Help Me Rhonda*.)
[30] *Hold On* hits UK #6.
July [6] The trio begins a 35-city US tour, supporting Richard Marx, at the Concord Pavilion, Concord, CA.
[16] The trio guests on the premiere of ABC-TV's "Into The Night Starring Rick Dees".
Aug [4] Their maiden album, ***Wilson Phillips***, with six of the ten songs written or co-written by Wilson Phillips, and featuring contributions from Joe Walsh, Little Feat's Bill Payne and Toto's Steve Lukather, hits US #2, after a steady rise, on its way to five million US sales, but proves unable to penetrate MC Hammer's grip on the pole position with ***Please Hammer Don't Hurt 'Em***. (***Wilson Phillips*** has already hit UK #7 on July [7]). It will also sell a further two million copies worldwide.
Sept [14] One-day prior to peaking, *Release Me* is certified gold by the RIAA.
[15] *Release Me*, also hits US #1, having peaked at UK #36 on Aug [25].
Oct Wilson Phillips have to cancel tour dates as Phillips undergoes minor throat surgery.
Nov [2] During a promotional trip to the UK, Wilson Phillips appears on BBC1-TV talk show, "Wogan".
[17] *Impulsive*, penned by Steve Kipner and Clif Magness, makes UK #42.
[26] The trio wins the Hot 100 Single category, with *Hold On*, at the 1990 **Billboard** Music Awards show, in Santa Monica, CA.
Dec The trio turns down a support slot on Michael Bolton's planned 1991 Spring tour.
[16] They perform at radio station Power 99's "Toys For Tots" benefit, at the Omni, Atlanta, GA.
[22] *Impulsive* hits US #4, as **Billboard** magazine confirms the band as Top Singles Act and Top Pop Singles Artist - Duo Or Groups. Wilson Phillips end the year with 27 consecutive weeks in the US Top 10 Album chart, an achievement not bettered since the Supremes in 1967, with their ***Greatest Hits***.
[31] The group performs on MTV's "New Year's Eve World Party", from the Ritz, New York, NY.

1991

Jan [9] "Wilson Phillips" video is certified gold by the RIAA.
[28] Wilson Phillips sing an acoustic medley of their hits at the 18th American Music Awards, at the Shrine Auditorium, Los Angeles.
Feb [5] The trio appears on NBC-TV's "The Tonight Show".
[20] Wilson Phillips are beaten out in all four categories in which they have been nominated, at the 33rd annual Grammy Awards, at New York's Radio City Music Hall.

Apr [16] The RIAA confirms five million sales of ***Wilson Phillips***.
[20] The fourth extract from their debut album, *You're In Love*, tops the US chart.
May [18] *You're In Love* reaches UK #29.
June [1] Their debut album completes a one-year stay in the US Top 10 Album chart.
Aug [3] *The Dream Is Still Alive* reaches US #12.

1992

Jan [11] ***Two Rooms - Celebrating The Songs Of Elton John & Bernie Taupin***, to which Wilson Phillips has contributed *Daniel*, reaches US #18.
[21] The trio performs at the Palais des Festivals, Midem, France, during the annual music industry festival.
May [22] Wilson Phillips guest on BBC1-TV's "Wogan" show.
[23] *You Won't See Me Cry* debuts at its UK #18 peak.
June [13] Their sophomore effort, ***Shadows And Light***, once again produced by Ballard and co-written with him, bows at its UK #6 pinnacle.
[20] ***Shadows And Light*** debuts at its US #4 peak.
[27] *You Won't See Me Cry* reaches US #20.
July [1] Phillips takes part in a fund-raiser for the Hollywood Women's Political Committee, raising over $350,000.
[14] The trio performs the national anthem at Major League Baseball's 63rd All-Star Game at Jack Murphy Stadium, San Diego, CA.
[23] Wilson Phillips guest on "The Tonight Show", as ***Shadows And Light*** is certified platinum by the RIAA.
Aug They cancel a US tour scheduled to begin on the 17th, reportedly due to poor ticket sales.
[22] *Give It Up* debuts at its UK #36 peak.
Sept [19] *Give It Up* reaches US #30.
Oct Carnie duets with Robert Palmer on *Baby It's Cold Outside*, from the latter's newly-released album of oldies, ***Ridin' High***, and also sings live at his Royal Albert Hall, London show.
[10] Wilson Phillips perform at the KISS Radio "Fall Fest" on Boston Common, Boston, MA.

1993

May [22] The Wilson sisters help out at record store counters in Los Angeles to benefit LIFEbeat's CounterAid, a one-day fund-raiser for people with HIV/AIDS, as they prepare for a new album, set to be released in 1994.
Dec [25] Carnie and Wendy Wilson's festive collection ***Hey Santa!*** debuts at its US #116 peak.

1995

Sept [4] Carnie's new daytime talk show premieres on independent TV stations throughout the US, but will be cancelled the following year.
[9] Chynna Phillips marries actor William Baldwin in Southampton, NY.
Nov [7] Chynna's first solo album, ***Naked And Sacred***, overseen by Rick Nowels and Billy Steinberg, is released in the US, while Carnie and Wendy back their father on *Do It Again*, from his ***I Just Wasn't Made For These Times*** project.

JOHNNY & EDGAR WINTER

1968

Albino guitarist/vocalist Johnny Winter (b. John Dawson Winter III, Feb. 23, 1944, Leland, MS), who cut his first single, *Schoolday Blues*, on the Dart label in Texas in 1959, as Johnny & the Jammers, was raised in Beaumont, TX, with his younger brother, Edgar (b. Dec. 28, 1946, Beaumont), the pair playing in a number of southern States' blues/rock club outfits during their teenage years. After several years playing Chicago, IL clubs in groups like Black Plague (with brother Edgar) and Gene Terry & the Down Beats, Johnny now forms his own group, with brother Edgar on keyboards, Tommy Shannon on bass and John Turner on drums. They are recruited as the regular group at New York's Scene, after owner, Steve Paul, reads an effusive article about Johnny's blues-guitar playing in **Rolling Stone** magazine. Paul also becomes Johnny's manager.

1969

Feb Johnny signs to CBS/Columbia Records, on a five-year, $300,000 contract.
May Imperial Records releases a one-off album, ***The Progressive Blues Experiment***, which makes US #49. Recorded some time earlier, it is released in competition with the first Columbia album.
June Columbia debut, ***Johnny Winter***, reaches US #24.
[20] He takes part in the three-day "Newport '69 Festival", at San Fernando Valley State College, Devonshire Downs, Northridge, CA.
[27] Johnny Winter plays at a festival at the Mile High Stadium, Denver, CO, before 50,000 people.
July [3] He participates in the "Newport Jazz Festival" in Newport, RI.
Aug [30] Johnny plays to 120,000 people at the three-day "Texas International Pop Festival" at the Dallas International Motor Speedway, Dallas, TX.
Oct ***The Johnny Winter Story***, a compilation of early tracks cut during his days in Chicago, and released by GRT Records, peaks at US #111.

1970

Jan His second Columbia album, ***Second Winter***, makes US #55.
[24] A revival of Chuck Berry's *Johnny B. Goode*, taken from it, peaks at US #92. (The album is a double, but only three sides contain music, the fourth is blank.)
Apr [17] Johnny tops London's Royal Albert Hall bill, with Flock and Steamhammer.
May ***Second Winter*** is his UK chart debut, at #59.
[4] Johnny supports Jimi Hendrix at the "Holding Together" benefit for Timothy Leary, at New York's Village Gate.
June After appearing on his brother's album, ***Second Winter***, Edgar signs to CBS/Columbia, and ***Entrance***, featuring Edgar on almost all instruments, peaks at US #196.
[26] Johnny performs at the "Bath Festival of Blues & Progressive Music", Shepton Mallet, Somerset.
July [3-5] Johnny plays at the three-day, second "Atlanta International Pop Festival", at the Middle Georgia Raceway near Byron, GA, before an estimated 200,000 crowd, on a bill with Jimi Hendrix, Jethro Tull, B.B. King and others.
Aug [6] Johnny participates in an anti-war, 12-hour festival, at New York's Shea Stadium, alongside Paul Simon, Janis Joplin, Steppenwolf and many others.
Oct ***Johnny Winter And***, featuring Edgar and Rick Derringer's group, the McCoys, as backup band, peaks at US #154.
Nov ***Johnny Winter And*** reaches UK #29.

1971

May Live album, ***Johnny Winter And/Live***, consisting mainly of rock and R&B standards, played by the same line-up as the previous album, reaches US #40 and UK #20.
[1] A cover of the Rolling Stones' *Jumpin' Jack Flash* makes US #89. (Johnny's increasing heroin dependency forces him out of action for a period, following an early 1971 tour.)
June Edgar has formed the brass-based group, White Trash, featuring Floyd Radford (guitar), Bobby Ramirez (drums), George Sheck (bass), Mike McLellan (trumpet, vocals), Jon Smith (saxophone) and Jerry La Croix (lead vocals, saxophone), whose debut album, ***Edgar Winter's White Trash***, peaks at US #111.
[27] Edgar takes part in the final Fillmore East concert with the Allman Brothers, the Beach Boys, Country Joe, the J. Geils Band and Mountain.

1972

Feb *Keep Playin' That Rock'n'Roll*, by White Trash, makes US #70.
May White Trash's double live album, ***Roadwork***, reaches US #23, while an extracted revival of Otis Redding's *I Can't Turn You Loose* peaks at US #81. (Edgar disbands White Trash shortly afterwards to form rock band, the Edgar Winter Group, which includes Ronnie Montrose (guitar), Chick Ruff (drums) and Dan Hartman (bass).)
June [9] Johnny leaves the River Oaks Hospital, after nine months of treatment for heroin addiction.
July [24] White Trash's drummer, Bobby Ramirez, is killed in a brawl in a Chicago bar.

1973

Jan ***They Only Come Out At Night***, the first album by the Edgar Winter Group, produced by Derringer, hits US #3, eventually earning two platinum discs.
Apr Johnny Winter returns to record, with the appropriately-titled ***Still Alive And Well*** reaching US #22.
May [26] *Frankenstein*, an instrumental by the Edgar Winter Group, tops the US chart for a week. It had originally been the B-side of *Hangin' Around*, until airplay prompted Columbia to turn the single over. The title, *Frankenstein*, has been derived from the fact that the track has been heavily cut, patched and edited from its original master.
June *Frankenstein* reaches UK #18.
[19] *Frankenstein* is certified gold by the RIAA.
July [15] Edgar Winter performs at the White City, London, with Sly & the Family Stone, Canned Heat, Lindisfarne, Barclay James Harvest and the JSD Band.
Oct *Free Ride*, also from ***They Only Come Out At Night***, reaches US #14, and features a driving acoustic guitar. (It will be the band's last major hit. Montrose will leave to form his own, eponymous group, and will be replaced first by Jerry Weems, then by the group's producer, Derringer.)

1974

Jan Edgar Winter Group's *Hangin' Around* peaks at US #65.
[28] ***Johnny Winter Live*** is certified gold by the RIAA.
Feb [13] Johnny jams with Stevie Wonder and Dr. John at the opening of New York's Bottom Line club.
Apr His album, ***Saints And Sinners***, makes US #42.
June 96 people are arrested after trouble in the audience during an Edgar Winter concert at the Omni in Atlanta, GA.
July [18] The still-climbing ***Shock Treatment*** is certified gold by the RIAA.
Aug Edgar's ***Shock Treatment***, with Derringer on lead guitar, reaches US #13, while the solo cut, *River's Risin'*, makes US #33.
Nov *Easy Street*, by the Edgar Winter Group, peaks at US #83.
Dec [18] ***Roadwork*** is certified gold by the RIAA.

1975

Jan Johnny's ***John Dawson Winter III*** makes US #78, his first release on the new CBS-distributed Blue Sky label.
July ***Jasmine Nightdreams***, a solo album by Edgar, also on Blue Sky, makes US #69.
Nov ***The Edgar Winter Group With Rick Derringer*** peaks at US #124.

1976

Apr Johnny's ***Captured Live!*** makes US #93, as Hartman and Derringer leave Edgar's group. (Hartman will become first a disco artist, scoring a major hit with *Instant Replay*, then a successful solo performer with more mainstream material like *I Can Dream About You*, and a producer, for James Brown and others.)
July The Winter brothers combine for ***Together***, a collection of live tracks and revivals, which makes US #89.

1977

Mar Johnny, having signed Muddy Waters to his Blue Sky label, has produced the blues legend on ***Hard***

Again, which makes US #143, (and will win a Grammy Award for Waters) and will do the same for its follow-up, ***I'm Ready***, which peaks at US #157 the following March), also tours as a member of his group.
Sept Johnny returns to his roots for ***Nothin' But The Blues***, which peaks at US #146, while Edgar issues ***Recycled***. Johnny's ***White, Hot And Blue*** will make US #141, his last US chart entry for six years, in September the following year. Edgars's last recording of the decade, ***The Edgar Winter Album*** will emerge in 1979.

1981

After Johnny has recruited a new band, including Jon Paris (bass) and Bobby Torello (drums), for last year's ***Raisin' Cain***, Edgar's ***Standing On Rock*** will be his last album for nine years. He will concentrate on session work, for Meat Loaf, Dan Hartman, Bette Midler and others.

1984

Aug Johnny's blues-phrased ***Guitar Slinger***, on independent blues label, Alligator Records, peaks at US #183 and will be nominated for a Grammy Award. ***Serious Business***, also on Alligator, will make US #156 in October the following year, with ***Third Degree*** being released in 1986, the same year the RIAA certifies two million sales of Edgar's 1973 album ***They Only Come Out At Night***, on November 21st.

1987

Sept [12-13] Johnny plays at the 15th "San Francisco Blues Festival" in San Francisco, CA.

1988

Nov [5] He ends a 23-date US tour at the "Riverwalk Blues Fest" in Fort Lauderdale, FL, part of the live promotion for his new album, ***Winter Of '88***, released on Voyager Records, through MCA, and which marks a musical return to rock'n'roll. Edgar will be featured playing sax on Tina Turner's *The Best* which reaches US #15 and UK #5 the following October, the same year he releases his second album of the decade, ***Mission Earth***, issued by Rhino.

1990

Apr [18] Johnny embarks on major US tour in Columbus, OH, while Edgar continues to tour with Rick Derringer, notably in Japan, a visit which will yield the unauthorized performance album ***Live In Japan***, released by Cypress Records.

1991

Mar [19] Edgar and Derringer file suit against Cypress Records in New York's US District Court for allegedly releasing an album, recorded on January 24th, 1990 in Japan, without their permission.
May [31] Johnny embarks on a four-city "Benson & Hedges Fourth Annual Blues Tour", in Los Angeles, CA., promoting his recent ***Let Me In*** release.
Sept He is featured on John Lee Hooker's newly-released Charisma debut, ***Mr. Lucky***.
Oct [8] Johnny performs a one-off London date at the Town & Country club.

1992

Mar [21] Johnny and Edgar perform together for the first time in 15 years, at the Sting club in New Britain, CT.
Oct [16] Johnny sings *Highway 61 Revisited* at the Bob Dylan anniversary tribute, from New York's Madison Square Garden, as he embarks on a US tour through November, promoting his latest album, ***Hey, Where's Your Brother?***.

1993

Jan [30] Johnny sells out the Vic, Chicago, IL, during current US dates.
Apr [17] Johnny and Edgar, currently on a US tour with Poco, John Kay & Steppenwolf and Dave Mason, perform at the USF Soccer Field, University of South Florida, Tampa, FL. Edgar will release his first sanctioned album of the decade, ***Not A Kid Anymore*** for Intersound Records in 1994 while his brother's ***White Lightning : Live At The Dallas International Motor Speedway*** will emerge in the same year on Magnum Music.

STEVE WINWOOD

1974

Dec Hammond organist and vocalist Winwood (b. May 12, 1948, Birmingham, Warks.), who played in the Ron Atkinson Band at the age of eight, with his father and brother Muff, already a prodigious veteran of the Spencer Davis Group, which he joined at age 15 as vocalist, guitarist and keyboardist, has gone on to form Traffic in April 1967 and, between two incarnations of the outfit, has also been a member of Blind Faith and Ginger Baker's Airforce. His first solo album would have been ***Mad Shadows*** in 1970, but it was eventually released as Traffic's ***John Barleycorn Must Die***, after Jim Capaldi and Chris Wood helped him record it, and Traffic re-formed. Under his own name in June 1971, the double album, ***Winwood***, a compilation of tracks featuring him with his previous bands, made US #93. After Traffic has dissolved following a US tour in support of ***When The Eagle Flies***, Winwood now retires home to Gloucestershire, where he builds his own Netherturkdonic Studio. (He will spend the next two years quietly writing and rehearsing, while also working on sessions for others, notably fellow Island label acts, including Sandy Denny, the Sutherland Brothers and Toots & the Maytals.)

1976

Oct Winwood has joined Michael Shrieve to guest on Stomu Yamashta's ***Go***, which makes US #60. He also appears with Yamashta in a concert at London's Royal Albert Hall.

1977

July His solo album, ***Steve Winwood***, released just as punk is getting into its commercial stride in the UK, dismissed by some reviewers as passé, reaches UK #12.
Oct ***Steve Winwood*** makes US #22.

1978

While not active in live work, he decides to cut an album on which he will fill every role, playing all instruments, singing, producing and engineering. (It will take over two years to complete the resulting ***Arc Of A Diver***.)

1981

Jan ***Arc Of A Diver***, with music by Winwood and varied lyrical contributions from Will Jennings, Vivian Stanshall and George Fleming, reaches UK #13, while the extracted *While You See A Chance*, Winwood's first solo single, makes UK #45. His contract with Island has expired, and the album's success enables him to negotiate a new deal on favorable terms, including retrieving all the publishing rights to his earlier material.
Apr ***Arc Of A Diver*** hits US #3 as *While You See A Chance* hits US #7.
June US follow-up single, the title song, *Arc Of A Diver*, reaches US #48.
[26] ***Arc Of A Diver*** is certified platinum by the RIAA.
Nov *There's A River*, the last extract from the album, is released.

1982

Aug ***Talking Back To The Night***, recorded in a similar fashion (though in less time) as the previous album, with Winwood playing everything, but collaborating on the songs with Jennings, who moved from Nashville to the UK to co-write, hits UK #6.
Sept *Still In The Game* makes US #47, as parent album, ***Talking Back To The Night***, reaches US #28.
Oct The synthesizer-driven *Valerie*, from the album, makes UK #51.
Nov *Valerie* peaks at US #70.

1983

Apr [30] His manager, Andy Cavaliere, dies in New York after a heart attack, aged 36.
Sept [20] He appears at the ARMS benefit concert for the multiple sclerosis-suffering, former Faces member, Ronnie Lane, at London's Royal Albert Hall, alongside Eric Clapton, Jeff Beck, Jimmy Page and others. (He also undertakes a short US tour with this charity line-up.) During the year, Winwood contributes songs to the soundtrack album, ***They Call It An Accident***.

1986

Feb With his marriage to first wife, Nicole, in difficulties (the couple will divorce during the year), Winwood moves to New York, and, renouncing one-man recording, assembles ***Back In The High Life***, with producer Russ Titelman and local musicians. Five of its eight songs are again collaborations with Jennings.
July *Higher Love*, featuring guest vocals from Chaka Khan, reaches UK #13.
[9] ***Back In The High Life*** hits UK #8.
Aug [30] *Higher Love* tops the US chart for a week.
Sept ***Back In The High Life*** hits US #3 while *Freedom Overspill*, also from the album, peaks at UK #69.
Oct James Brown's ***Gravity***, to which Winwood has contributed a duet, is released.
Nov [22] *Freedom Overspill* reaches US #20.

1987

Jan [24] *Back In The High Life Again* peaks at UK #53.
Feb [24] *Higher Love* wins the Record Of The Year and Best Pop Vocal Performance, Male categories at the 29th annual Grammy Awards. (Recent recordings complete his Island contract and, with the singer a hot property following his 1986 successes, the label is outbid. He signs a new deal with Virgin Records, reportedly worth $13 million, and carrying a royalty rate of 18%.)
Apr [18] *The Finer Things* hits US #8.
Aug [15] *Back In The High Life Again* reaches US #13.
Oct In the UK, Island reissues, from its forthcoming retrospective compilation, the Winwood/Jennings composition, *Valerie* (a minor hit in late 1982, but subsequently remixed), which reaches UK #19.
Nov [7] Island collection, ***Chronicles***, reaches UK #12 in its week of entry and will make US #26.
Dec [19] Reactivated *Valerie* hits US #9.

1988

Jan [12] The RIAA certifies three million sales of ***Back In The High Life***.
Mar [12] *Talking Back To The Night*, extracted from ***Chronicles***, makes US #57.
May [29] ***Chronicles*** is confirmed platinum by the RIAA.
June *Roll With It*, the title song from his first album for Virgin, makes UK #53. Winwood promotes the album with an appearance at the "Montreux Rock Festival" in Montreux, Switzerland, which is televised worldwide.
July [2] The rock/pop/R&B fused ***Roll With It***, recorded in Dublin, Eire, and Toronto, ON, Canada and co-produced by Winwood and Tom Lord-Alge, hits UK #4 in its week of entry. Most of the songs are Winwood/Jennings collaborations, with *Hearts On Fire* co-written with Jim Capaldi, ex-Traffic.
[7] Winwood begins a two-month, brewery-sponsored US tour, backed by a band recruited in Nashville, TN, followed by dates in Europe.
[30] *Roll With It* begins a four-week stay at US #1, the longest tenure of the year.
Aug [20] ***Roll With It*** also hits US #1 for one week.
Oct [29] The extracted ballad, *Don't You Know What The Night Can Do?*, helped by its exposure on a Michelob beer TV commercial, hits US #6.
Nov [28] The RIAA certifies two million sales of ***Roll With It***.

1989

Jan [28] *Holding On* reaches US #11.
Apr [22] *Hearts On Fire* peaks at US #53.
Aug [24] Having participated in the first stage production in 1972, Winwood plays the Hawker in a charity production of Pete Townshend's "Tommy", at the Universal Amphitheatre, Universal City, CA, with Elton John as the Pinball Wizard, Patti LaBelle as the Acid Queen, Phil Collins as Uncle Ernie and Billy Idol as Cousin Kevin.

1990

Nov [17] The self-produced ***Refugees Of The Heart***, co-penned with Jennings (with one cut co-written with Jim Capaldi) reaches UK #26 in its week of entry.
Dec [8] ***Refugees Of The Heart*** reaches US #27.
[17] ***Refugees Of The Heart*** is certified gold by the RIAA.
[22] *One And Only Man* reaches US #18.

1991

Mar [22] Winwood takes part in the American Music Awards Concert Series, at the Yokohama Arena, Yokohama, Japan.
Apr [12] He guests on NBC-TV's "Late Night With David Letterman".
[29-30] Winwood embarks on a US tour at the Seattle Center Arena, Seattle, WA, sharing most dates with Robert Cray, but also being supported by Roger McGuinn and Warren Zevon.
July [12-13] He plays sellouts shows at the Jones Beach Theatre, Wantagh, NY, with Joe Cocker.

1994

Mar [1] Winwood performs a Curtis Mayfield tribute with Bruce Springsteen, Bonnie Raitt, B.B. King, and others, at the 36th annual Grammy Awards, staged at New York's Radio City Music Hall.
[2] He attends the fifth annual Rhythm and Blues Foundation Pioneer Awards at the Roseland Ballroom, New York.
May [18] Having been a prime mover behind its reunion album ***Far From Home***, Winwood and a reunited Traffic, comprising Jim Capaldi, Randall Bramblett, Mike McEvoy, Walfredo Reyes and Rosko Gee, open their US tour in Omaha, NE, set to September 10th at Jones Beach Theatre, Wantagh, NY.

1995

Mar [21] Winwood sings ***Arc Of A Diver*** at Vivian Stanshall's memorial service at St. Patrick's Church in London's Soho Square, the same day Island releases a four-CD boxed-set retrospective ***The Finer Things***, chronicling Winwood's career from the Spencer Davis Group, Blind Faith, Traffic, fusion experiments with Stomu Yamashta's Go, his work with Winwood/Kanaka/Amao and subsequent solo highlights with both Island and Virgin.
Oct Winwood, together with brother Muff and Spenver Davis, accepts three awards which confirm two million broadcast performances of *Higher Love*, *The Finer Things* and *While You See A Chance* at the annual BMI Awards held at the Dorchester Hotel, London.
Nov [17] Following his contribution to Paul Weller's May-released ***Stanley Road*** album, the soundtrack to the Steven Spielberg animated feature, "Balto", featuring Winwood's *Reach For The Light*, is now released in the US.
see also: **BLIND FAITH, THE SPENCER DAVIS GROUP, TRAFFIC**

WISHBONE ASH

Martin Turner (vocals, bass); **Andy Powell** (guitar); **Ted Turner** (guitar); **Steve Upton** (drums)

1969

Nov [10] Veterans of mid-60s Torquay, Devon-based band the Empty Vessels, Martin Turner (b. Oct. 1, 1947, Torquay) and Upton (b. May 24, 1946, Wrexham, Wales), the latter also ex-Scimitars, have relocated to London with their guitarist Glen Turner to form Tanglewood in the spring of this year. After seeing the band perform in July at London's Hampstead Country Club, opening for the Yardbirds' Keith Relf, the combo has become the first band to be managed by Miles Copeland who, with Turner leaving, places a classified ad in **Melody Maker**, which yields the unrelated ex-King Biscuit member Ted Turner (b. David Alan Turner, Aug. 2, 1950) and ex-Decoys and ex-Sugarband guitarist Powell (b. Feb. 8, 1950). Impressed by their respective talents, the band decides to recruit both, giving the newly-named Wishbone Ash an unusual twin-lead guitar sound. Musically influenced by the Yardbirds, the group now makes its live debut at Dunstable Civic Hall, Beds., opening for Aynsley Dunbar's Retaliation. Following several months on the UK college and club circuits, the band is signed to MCA Records in London in the summer of 1970.

1971

Jan The group's six-track debut album, produced by Derek Lawrence, ***Wishbone Ash*** makes UK #34 during a two-week chart stay. It introduces a ground-breaking progressive form of instrumental-heavy, harmonic rock, sprinkled with historical lyrical themes
Oct Including four instrumental cuts, ***Pilgrimage*** reaches UK #14 and US #169, where it has been released by Decca Records. (During its ten-year plus chart career, the group will never score a chart single in either the UK or US, relying solely on its loyal following for albums sales.)
[30] John Lennon's ***Imagine***, featuring Ted Turner on *Crippled Inside*, tops the UK and US charts.

1972

May [20] Career highlight album, the mystically-themed ***Argus***, with distinctive cover art by Hipgnosis and reflecting a folk-rock leaning, enters the UK chart, set to hit # 3 during a 20-week chart ride, and also climbs to US #44.

1973

May [26] Written in a cottage in North Wales, ***Wishbone Four***, now released worldwide by MCA, enters the UK survey set to make #12, and hit US #44.
Dec MCA releases the performance double album, ***Live Dates***.

1974

May Ted Turner quits the group to follow a spiritual path, to be replaced by ex-Home guitarist Laurie Wisefield.
Dec Recorded in Miami, FL, where the group has spent the year in tax-exile, ***There's The Rub***, produced by Bill Szymczyk, reaches UK #16 and US #88.

1975

Aug [24] The band headlines the final day of the 15th National Jazz Blues & Rock Festival "Reading Rock '75", near Reading, Berks. (During the year, the group relocates to Connecticut.)

1976

Apr Produced by Tom Dowd, the critically-panned ***Locked In*** makes UK #36 and US #136 (where it is the first of two albums for Atlantic Records).
Dec Still popular on the UK college/university tour circuit, their second album of the year, ***New England*** peaks at UK #22 and US #154.

1977

Nov Returned to a global deal with MCA, ***Front Page News*** climbs to US #166, its final US chart album of the decade, and UK #31, supported by a UK tour including a sellout date at the Wembley Empire Pool, Wembley, Middx.

1978

Nov [11] Out of vogue in the UK following the insurgence of punk, ***No Smoke Without Fire*** makes UK #43. The following month, the group performs sellout dates in Japan, recorded for future release as ***Live In Tokyo***.

1980

Feb Largely written by Wisefield, ***Just Testing*** makes UK #41 before peaking at US #179 in March. During the year, founding member Martin Turner leaves the band to concentrate on production, to be temporarily replaced by ex-Uriah Heep and Roxy Music's John Wetton.

1981

May ***Number The Brave***, featuring guest vocalist Claire Hammill, stops at UK #61. (By year's end, Wetton will have moved on to join Asia, with Wishbone Ash, now managed by John Sherry, recruiting ex-Spiders From Mars bassist Trevor Bolder.)

1982

Jan A US-only MCA compilation, ***Hot Ash*** peaks at US #192, its final US chart showing.
Oct Newly signed to AVM Records, ***Twin Barrels Burning*** ends Wishbone Ash's chart career, reaching UK #22. With Bolder also lasting a year, ex-Trapeze bassist Mervyn Spence is recruited, though he too will only make it through one album, albeit two years in the making, 1985's hard-rock outing ***Raw To The Bone***, released by UK heavy-metal indie label Neat Records, following its issue in Germany in 1984.

1987

Dec Urged by their first manager to re-form, the original members, Martin and Ted Turner, Powell and Upton have reunited and signed a new long-term deal with Copeland's I.R.S. Records, which now releases the all-instrumental ***Nouveau Calls***. Its follow-up album, ***Here To Hear*** will be issued in August 1989.

1991

Apr With Upton departed from the lineup, he has been replaced by two drummers, Ray Weston and Robbie France, and with the group also augmented by keyboardist Dan Gillogly, Wishbone Ash's first album of the decade, ***Strange Affair*** is issued by I.R.S. Shortly after its release, Martin Turner quits the group, to be replaced by Andy Pyle.

1994

Aug With the group still touring, now minus Ted Turner (leaving Powell as the only original member, alongside newcomers guitarist Roger Filgate and bassist/singer Tony Kishman) and recording a new album with producer Elliot Scheiner, and following the US-only release of the retrospective double-CD, ***Time Was*** by MCA the previous year, Griffin Records (US) now issues ***The Ash Live In Chicago***, originally brought to compact disc by Permanent Records in the UK two years earlier. The Wishbone Ash Fan Club has held its first convention in Birmingham, West Midlands in May, celebrating the group's 25th year.

BILL WITHERS

1970

Withers (b. July 4, 1938, Slab Fork, WV), having spent nine years in the US Navy, before working as an auto mechanic for Ford and IBM, while writing songs in his spare time, has moved to California in 1967, taking a day job at the Lockheed Aircraft Corporation. He slowly saved $2,500 to pay for studio time to make demos of his songs, but received scant response. Now working in a factory manufacturing jumbo jet toilet seats, and learning the guitar, he meets Booker T. Jones, ex-Booker T. & the MG's, and now recording, writing and producing in Los Angeles, CA, for A&M Records. Jones, impressed by Withers' latest material, helps him secure a recording deal with the A&M-distributed Sussex Records.

1971

June [26] On the release date of his first album, Withers makes his first professional live appearance, in Los Angeles.
Sept Withers' debut album, the soul-drenched ***Just As I Am***, produced by Jones, climbs to US #39, as the extracted, self-penned ballad, *Ain't No Sunshine*, hits US #3.
[21] *Ain't No Sunshine* is certified gold by the RIAA.
Dec *Grandma's Hands*, also from the album, makes US #42.

1972

Mar [14] *Ain't No Sunshine* wins the Best R&B Song category at the 14th annual Grammy Awards.
June [20] The still-climbing *Lean On Me* is certified gold by the RIAA.
July [8] Co-produced with studio musicians Ray Jackson, James Gadson, Melvin Dunlap and Benorce Blackman, the self-penned ***Still Bill*** hits US #4, while the extracted self-written *Lean On Me* hits US #1 for the first of three weeks.
Sept [7] ***Still Bill*** is confirmed gold by the RIAA.
Oct Also from the album, *Use Me* hits US #2. Meanwhile, *Lean On Me* is his UK chart debut, reaching #18. (*Ain't No Sunshine* did not chart in the UK, though Michael Jackson's current cover hits UK #8.)
[12] *Use Me* becomes his third RIAA certified gold single.

1973

Jan *Let Us Love* makes US #47.
Mar *Kissing My Love* reaches US #31.
June The performance double album, ***Bill Withers Live At Carnegie Hall***, makes US #63.
July *Friend Of Mine* peaks at US #80. (During the year Withers and his actress wife, Denise Nicholas (currently starring in the ABC-TV series "Room 222"), become parents for the first time.)

1974

May ***'Justments*** (a title based on a phrase frequently used by his grandmother, who partially raised him), featuring José Feliciano, reaches US #67, while the excerpted *The Same Love That Made Me Laugh* reaches US #50.

1975

Jan *Heartbreak Road* peaks at US #89.
May Compilation set ***The Best Of Bill Withers***, peaks at US #182. This is his last release on Sussex, with which he is now in legal dispute. Soon afterwards, Sussex folds, and Withers signs a new deal with CBS/Columbia Records (which will also purchase his earlier Sussex material for reissue).
Dec His Columbia debut album, ***Making Music***, makes US #81.

1976

Feb *Make Love To Your Mind*, from ***Making Music***, reaches US #76.
Nov ***Naked And Warm*** peaks at US #169.
Dec Mud hit UK #7 with a cover of *Lean On Me*.

1978

Feb Having peaked at US #39 the previous December, ***Menagerie*** reaches UK #27 while, from it, *Lovely Day* reaches US #30, and hits UK #7.
May [18] ***Menagerie*** is certified gold by the RIAA.

1979

Apr ***'Bout Love***, featuring top session help from Russ Kunkel (drums), Jerry Knight (bass) and Ralph MacDonald (percussion), among others, peaks at US #134.

1981

May With Withers' own recording career quiet, he is an eagerly-sought guest vocalist, as Grover Washington Jr.'s *Just The Two Of Us*, written by and featuring Withers on vocals, hits US #2 (behind Sheena Easton's *Morning Train (Nine To Five)*), and is a million seller. The compilation, ***Bill Withers' Greatest Hits*** (which includes *Just The Two Of Us*), peaks at US #183.

1982

Feb [24] *Just The Two Of Us* wins the Best R&B Song category at the 24th annual Grammy Awards.

1985

June After Ralph McDonald's *In The Name Of Love*, with Withers on guest vocal, has made US #58 the previous October, Withers' first new solo material in seven years sees *Oh Yeah!* peak at UK #60, taken from the largely self-produced and self-written set, ***Watching You, Watching Me***, which includes guests David Foster, Phil Perry, Greg Phillinganes and Ernie Watts, and reaches UK #60.

1987

Mar [21] A revival of Withers' song, *Lean On Me*, by Sacramento, CA-based quintet, Club Nouveau, tops the US chart (earning a gold disc) and hits UK #3. Withers sends a telegram to the group, thanking and congratulating them.

1988

Mar [2] *Lean On Me* wins the Best R&B Song category at the 30th annual Grammy Awards.
Sept *Lovely Day*, remixed with new instrumental and rhythmic additions by Dutch DJ, Ben Leibrand, hits UK #4.
[17] ***His Greatest Hits*** package also re-charts, making UK #90.
[18] On the strength of his remixed hit, Withers travels to the UK to play at London's Hammersmith Odeon, where he is introduced on stage by his son, Todd.
Dec Withers returns to Britain for a full national tour, as a reissue of *Ain't No Sunshine* is released.

1992

Aug [8] Withers takes part in the "Summer Jazz Explosion '92" at the Valley Forge Music Fair, Devon, PA.
Oct [16-17] He appears at a pair of tribute concerts for Eddie Kendricks, organized by Bobby Womack, at the Strand Theater, Redondo Beach, CA, with Lou Rawls, Al Green, Chaka Khan, Ike Turner and others, raising $25,000 for his survivors.

1995

Nov [2] Withers is inducted into the Soul Train Hall of Fame at the 25th Soul Train Anniversary, staged at Los Angeles' Shrine Auditorium. The show, which will air on CBS-TV on the 22nd, will also see Withers sing *Lean On Me*. Having signed to Atlantic Records in 1993, Withers' first album of the '90s has yet to emerge.

WIZZARD

Roy Wood (vocals, guitar); **Rick Price** (bass); **Hugh McDowell** (cello); **Nick Pentelow** (saxophone); **Mike Burney** (saxophone); **Bill Hunt** (keyboards, french horn); **Keith Smart** (drums); **Charlie Grima** (drums)

1972

July Wood (b. Nov. 8, 1947, Birmingham, Warks.), having embarked on a new venture with guitarist Jeff Lynne (b. Dec. 30, 1947, Birmingham), after their group, the Move, has enjoyed its last hit (UK #7 in May) with *California Man*, originally titled the Wood-Lynne project but now called the Electric Light Orchestra, which hits UK #9 with its first single, *10538 Overture*, loses interest in the concept, and announces the formation of his new group, Wizzard.
Aug [5] Wizzard debuts at the "London Rock'n'Roll Festival" at Wembley Stadium, Wembley, Middx., on a mis-matched bill with Chuck Berry, Bill Haley, Billy Fury, Gary Glitter and Heinz, to name but a few, followed shortly thereafter by an appearance at the annual "Reading Festival", Reading, Berks.

1973

Jan The group's debut single, *Ball Park Incident*, hits UK #6. The Move's contract with EMI/Harvest officially has two years left to run, but the company continues with both splinter groups.
Apr Wood has written, produced and played on *Farewell*, a newly-released single by UK children's TV presenter, Ayshea.
May [19] The Wood-penned *See My Baby Jive* tops the UK chart for the first of four weeks, as Wood's multi-colored hair and clothes become synonymous with Wizzard's image.
June ***Wizzard Brew*** reaches UK #29.
Aug Wood solo, *Dear Elaine*, reaches UK #18. (Its B-side, *Songs Of Praise*, was short-listed as a candidate for the previous year's UK "Eurovision Song Contest" entry.)
Sept [22] *Angel Fingers* tops the UK chart for a week. Wood's solo album, ***Boulders***, reaches UK #15.
Nov ***Boulders*** peaks at US #173. (Wizzard will never again achieve US chart success.)
Dec Harvest celebrates Christmas with Wizzard's *I Wish It Could Be Christmas Everyday*, which hits UK #4, and Wood's *Forever*, which hits UK #8. (*I Wish It Could Be Christmas Everyday* will seasonally re-chart in 1981 (#41) and 1984 (#23).)

1974

Jan Wood begins the year in poor health, with the demands of touring and recording leading to ulcers, and he is advised to slow down.
May Newly signed to Warner Bros. Records, Wizzard's label debut, *Rock'n'Roll Winter (Looney's Tune)*, hits UK #6.
July Wood's solo cut, *Going Down The Road*, reaches UK #13.
Aug *This Is The Story Of My Love (Baby)* makes UK #34, as ***Introducing Eddy And The Falcons*** reaches UK #19. Each track on the album is in the style of a '50s rock'n'roll hero: Gene Vincent, Duane Eddy, Cliff Richard, Del Shannon, etc.
Nov Wizzard begins a US tour.

1975

Jan *Are You Ready To Rock*, featuring Wood's favorite new instrument - the bagpipes, hits UK #8.
May Wood's solo cut, *Oh What A Shame*, on the Jet label, reaches UK #13.
Oct Wizzard's management refuses to finance a second US tour, and the band splits.
Nov Wood's second album, ***Mustard***, is released, featuring vocal contributions from Phil Everly and Wood's girlfriend, Annie Haslam (it will subsequently be repackaged as ***Roy Wood The Wizzard***).

1976

Jan Wood signs to EMI/Harvest, Warner and Jet at the same time, with little idea which he is most bound to. He also has managerial difficulties.
Mar On Jet, *Indiana Rainbow*, credited to Roy Wood's Wizzard, is drawn from the planned ***Wizzo*** (which will never be released).
Oct [2] The Beach Boys cover of *It's OK*, on which Wood and two other members of Wizzard had played during a break in their 1974 US tour, reaches US #29.

1977

Apr Wood re-emerges with the Wizzo Band for ***On The Road Again***, which features contributions from Led Zeppelin's John Bonham, Andy Fairweather-Low and original Move vocalist, Carl Wayne. The album is deleted soon after release, and the band dissolves. Wood will write and produce for other acts, including Darts, and forms a live band, the Helicopters, as well as releasing several non-charting singles.
Sept Warner Bros. releases Roy Wood's Wizzo Band's ***Super Active Wizzo***, featuring Wood with the new line-up of Bob Wilson (guitar), Rick Price (pedal

steel, guitars), Paul Robbins (vocals, keyboards), Graham Gallery (bass), Billy Paul (saxophones) and Dave Donovan (drums).

1981

Aug [29] Wood performs on the second day of the 21st National Rock Festival "Reading Rock '81", near Reading, Berks.

1982

July Following the 1979 release of the Wood solo album, ***On The Road Again*** in the US and Germany, Speed Records has issued a compilation album of Wood's work with the Move and beyond, ***The Singles***, which reaches UK #37. The following year Wood will contribute his version of *Message In A Bottle* to ***Arrested***, a collection of Police covers, performed by various rock musicians and the Royal Philharmonic Orchestra.

1986

Mar Having signed to Legacy Records the previous year, Wood joins other Birmingham musicians, including Robert Plant, the Electric Light Orchestra and the Moody Blues, for a "Heartbeat '86" benefit gig.

Nov He helps out Doctor & the Medics on their version of Abba's first hit, *Waterloo*, which makes UK #45. His final new album of the decade, ***Starting Up***, will be released in February 1987 on Legacy.

1995

Dec [23] Following the 1990 UK CD release of ***The Best Of Roy Wood & Wizzard*** on the Action Replay label, and having undertaken the occasional UK tour including a 19-date trek in April, 1993, Wood's re-recorded *I Wish It Could Be Christmas Everyday*, now credited to the Roy Wood Big Band, debuts at its UK #53 peak.

see also: **THE ELECTRIC LIGHT ORCHESTRA, THE MOVE**

BOBBY WOMACK

1959

R&B vocal quintet, the Womack Brothers, consisting of Bobby (b. Mar. 4, 1944, Cleveland, OH), Cecil, Curtis, Harris and Friendly Jr., become popular favorites on the gospel circuit and, while touring, meet Sam Cooke & the Soul Stirrers. While continuing his career with his brothers, Bobby Womack is recruited by Cooke as a guitarist in his backing band, in June of the following year, before the Womacks sign to Cooke's own SAR label in 1961, as the Valentinos and then the Lovers.

1962

Sept [29] The Valentinos' *Lookin' For A Love* is an R&B hit, and charts at US #72. It is quickly followed by *I'll Make It Alright*, which peaks at US #97 the following year on Mar [30], their chart success prompting a support slot on a James Brown US tour.

1964

July *It's All Over Now* is the Valentinos' final chart entry together at US #94. Written by Bobby, it will later become a worldwide smash for the Rolling Stones (at UK #1 and US #26), with whom Bobby will develop a long-term relationship.

1965

Feb Following the murder of Sam Cooke in December 1964, Bobby marries his widow, Barbara. He embarks on an unsuccessful stint on the Him label, and begins a busy period of session work. As a guitarist, he will contribute to recordings for artists including King Curtis, Ray Charles, Joe Tex, Wilson Pickett, the Box Tops, Aretha Franklin, Dusty Springfield and Janis Joplin.

1966

As a songwriter, Womack begins writing hits for Wilson Pickett, who will cover 17 Womack songs over three years, including *I'm A Midnight Mover* (US #24), *634-5789* (US #13) and *I'm In Love* (US #45).

1968

Sept Following brief stints at Chess and Atlantic, Womack signs to the Minit label for his first solo success at US #52 with *Fly Me To The Moon*, taken from his debut solo album, also titled ***Fly Me To The Moon***, which makes US #174.

1969

Jan His R&B cover of the Mamas & the Papas classic, *California Dreamin'*, also from the album, makes US #43.

Dec *How I Miss You Baby* peaks at US #93.

1970

May *More Than I Can Stand* (US #90) is his final Minit hit. Divorce from Barbara coincides with his meeting R&B superstar, Sly Stone. Together, they become immersed in a drugs and groupie wilderness, which will dominate their lives throughout much of the '70s.

1971

May A one-off live recording, ***The Womack Live*** (actually recorded some three years earlier at the California Club, Los Angeles, CA), is released on United Artists' subsidiary, Liberty, and peaks at US #188.

1972

Jan His debut single for UA, *That's The Way I Feel About Cha*, makes US #27, and promotes sales for the simultaneously-released ***Communication***, which reaches US #83.

June *Woman's Gotta Have It* reaches US #60, as ***Understanding*** makes US #43.

Sept A cover of Neil Diamond's *Sweet Caroline (Good Times Never Seemed So Good)* charts at US #51.

Dec Its B-side, *Harry Hippie*, a popular Womack live number, makes US #31.

1973

Jan ***Across 110th Street***, his soundtrack to the Anthony Quinn-starring film of the same name, makes US #50, while the title track, *Across 110th Street*, reaches US #56.

Feb [14] *Harry Hippie* is certified gold by the RIAA.

July Beginning a trilogy of albums which will all be recorded in Memphis, TN, ***Facts Of Life*** achieves US #37, and includes *Nobody Wants You When You're Down And Out*, which reaches US #29.

1974

Mar His new Memphis album, ***Lookin' For A Love Again***, reaches US #85, with the title song, *Lookin' For A Love*, giving Womack his biggest career success, hitting US #10.

Apr [8] *Lookin' For A Love* is certified gold by the RIAA.

June He produces long-time friend, Rolling Stone Ron Wood's debut album, ***Now Look***, which peaks at US #118.

July *You're Welcome, Stop On By* makes US #59.

Dec The UA-released ***Bobby Womack's Greatest Hits***, which peaks at US #142.

1975

May *Check It Out* peaks at US #91, during a three-week stay on the survey. Taken from ***I Don't Know What The World Is Coming To***, it is his final UA chart single.

1976

Jan ***Safety Zone***, panned by critics, peaks at US #147.

Mar [6] Womack plays London's Hammersmith Odeon, during a short UK tour.

May Final United Artists album, ***B.W. Goes C&W***, is released. The label drops Womack after his attempt to go country (the original working title of the album is, according to Womack, ***Move Over Charley Pride And Give Another Nigger A Chance***).

Sept He signs a new deal with CBS/Columbia, which releases his final Memphis recording, ***Home Is Where The Heart Is***.

1978

July ***Pieces***, the second CBS/Columbia effort, is released. The murder of his brother, Harry, compounds Womack's depression, as he retreats further into drugs. (He will release his final album of the decade, ***Roads Of Life*** on Arista Records the following year.)

1980

Nov With Womack currently without a contract, Crusader Wilton Felder has enlisted him for lead vocal on *Inherit The Wind*, which reaches UK #39.

1981

Dec Recovered from his narcotics addiction, Womack returns triumphantly with ***The Poet***, released on the small California soul label, Beverly Glen. It becomes a best-selling R&B album, and reaches US #29.

1982

Womack takes label owner, Otis Smith, to court, claiming that he is receiving no royalties. Insisting throughout his career that, like James Brown and many other black artists, he has been short-changed, tempers flair, as Womack punches Smith in the courtroom.

1984

Apr With legal wrangles finally over, Womack is free to release the second part of his Poet project, ***The Poet II***. Via a one-off album deal with Motown, it reaches US #60, and becomes his first UK album chart entry, at #31.

June As Womack undertakes a major US tour, the extracted duet, *Love Has Finally Come At Last*, with Patti LaBelle, peaks at US #88, while *Tell Me Why* makes UK #60.

Dec He organizes a benefit concert for Sly Stone, now seeking rehabilitation, and visits the UK for a mini-tour. (His brother, Cecil, begins scoring hits as one-half of Womack & Womack, with his wife, Linda. As Sam Cooke's daughter, she now becomes Bobby Womack's sister-in-law, having previously been his step-daughter.)

1985

Feb Womack renews his connection with Felder for the latter's second album, ***Secrets***, which makes US #91 and #77 in the UK, where Womack unites with Altrina Grayson for *(No Matter How High I Get) I'll Still Be Lookin' Up To You*, which reaches UK #63.

Sept Having signed a million-dollar recording contract with MCA Records worldwide, the first release, the soul-drenched ***So Many Rivers***, reaches UK #28.

Oct *I Wish He Didn't Trust Me So Much*, taken from the album, peaks at UK #64.

Nov ***So Many Rivers*** makes US #66.

Dec [10] Womack guests on NBC-TV's "Late Night With David Letterman".

[14] Artists United Against Apartheid, comprising 49 artists, including Womack, makes US #38 and UK #21, with *Sun City*.

1986

June The Rolling Stones have invited Womack to contribute guitar and vocals to their newly-released album, ***Dirty Work***, his most prominent contribution being as co-vocalist with Jagger on *Going Back To Memphis*.

July ***Womagic*** is released.

1987

Nov Having recently recorded a cover version of UK band Living In A Box's *Living In A Box*, the album,

Womagic, is deleted and replaced by a new album, ***The Last Soul Man***, including the single, two other new cuts, and the majority of the tracks from ***Womagic***.

1989

May Reunited with his brothers, ***Save The Children***, is released by Solar Records in the US.
Aug Womack guests with Ben E. King, Wilson Pickett, Don Covay, Darlene Love, Mavis Staples and Ellie Greenwich on *What Is Soul?*, from Paul Shaffer's ***Coast To Coast*** album. (He will also guest on *Want Of A Nail*, from Todd Rundgren's newly-released ***Nearly Human***.)
Dec *Ain't Nothin Like The Lovin' We Got*, a duet with Shirley Brown, is released, followed by *Save The Children* in January.

1990

June [22] Womack, a regular visitor to the UK, plays London's Hammersmith Odeon.
Oct [3] He performs at London's Town & Country club, as part of the "Soul Seduction Tour".

1991

July [22] Again touring the UK, Womack plays the famed Hackney Empire, in London's East End.
Sept [7] Womack sings *If You Think You're Lonely Now* at CBS-TV's "Party For Richard Pryor" special, which will air November 23rd.

1992

Apr He takes part in the 23rd annual "New Orleans Jazz & Heritage Festival", New Orleans, LA.
May [31] "Cue The Music" International AIDS Days concert, to which Womack has contributed, airs on ITV.
Sept [16] He begins a seven-date UK tour, at the Apollo Theatre, Manchester.
Oct [16-17] Womack organizes two tribute concerts for Eddie Kendricks at the Strand Theater, Redondo Beach, CA, with Lou Rawls, Al Green, Bill Withers, Chaka Khan, Ike Turner and others, raising $25,000 for his survivors.

1993

Mar [25] Womack appears on BBC1-TV's "Top Of The Pops" with Lulu, duetting with her on her current single, *I'm Back For Me*, which debuts at its UK #27 peak on April 3rd.
Apr A career retrospective, ***Lookin' For A Love (1968-1975)***, is released, on the Razor & Tie Music label (US).

1994

Aug [13] Womack, currently on a US tour with the Isley Brothers, plays to a 6,180 sellout crowd at the Greek Theatre, Los Angeles.
Oct Womack's 33rd album, ***Resurrection***, is released on Ron Wood's Slide label, featuring guests Rod Stewart, Stevie Wonder, Brian May and various members of the Rolling Stones.

1995

Jan [20] During his latest round of US dates, Womack performs at the Fox Theatre, Detroit, MI.
May [13] *It's A Man's Man's Man's World*, featuring Tracy, charts for a week at UK #73.

1996

Feb [29] Womack receives a Pioneer Award at the eighth annual Rhythm and Blues Foundation ceremony held at Los Angeles' Hollywood Palladium.

STEVIE WONDER

1960

Weaned on the music of Ray Charles, and blind since birth (when he was administered too much oxygen while in an incubator), Wonder (b. Steveland Judkins, May 13, 1950, Saginaw, MI), who has learnt to play the piano, drums and harmonica by the age of seven, and begun writing songs at eight, and is a member of the Whitestone Baptist Church Choir, Detroit, MI, with his mother, four brothers and sister, is recommended by friend, John Glover (with whom he has formed a duo) to Glover's cousin, Gerald White, brother of Miracles member Ronnie White, who takes Wonder to meet Motown Records' president, Berry Gordy, and producer, Brian Holland. Gordy signs the ten-year-old child prodigy to a long-term contract with the Tamla label.

1962

Aug [16] His first single, credited to Little Stevie Wonder, *I Call It Pretty Music (But The Old People Call It The Blues)*, featuring Marvin Gaye on drums, is released.
Oct [16] Wonder, after making his live debut at Detroit's Latin Quarter club, begins a two-month Motown Records package tour in Washington, DC, with Marvin Gaye, the Miracles, the Supremes and Mary Wells.

1963

May [21] A Stevie Wonder concert is recorded in Detroit for the forthcoming ***12 Year Old Genius*** album.
Aug [10] His fourth single, *Fingertips - Pt. 2*, recorded at Chicago's Regal Theater, eventually selling over a million copies, tops the US chart for the first of three weeks, and is the first live record to do so.
[24] ***Recorded Live - The 12 Year Old Genius*** tops the US chart, as Wonder becomes the first artist to simultaneously top the Hot 100, R&B Singles and Album surveys. Meanwhile, he enrolls at the Michigan School for the Blind in Lansing, MI, now unable to continue at Fitzgerald School in Detroit, because of his success.
Nov [2] *Workout Stevie, Workout* reaches US #33.
Dec [26] Wonder visits the UK for promotional spots on the ITV shows "Ready Steady, Go!" and "Thank Your Lucky Stars".

1964

Feb [5] Wonder appears on CBS-TV's "The Ed Sullivan Show".
Apr [18] *Castles In The Sand* makes US #52.
July [25] *Hey Harmonica Man* reaches US #29. Wonder drops his "Little" prefix. He makes his movie debut in the teenpix, "Bikini Beach" and "Muscle Beach Party".

1965

Mar [18] Wonder and other Motown artists fly to London, for the recording of ITV's hour-long "The Sound Of Tamla Motown" show.
[20] The Motown review opens a 21-date, twice-nightly UK package tour, at the Finsbury Park Astoria, London, with Wonder, Martha & the Vandellas, the Miracles, the Supremes and the Temptations, with special UK guest stars, Georgie Fame & the Blue Flames, set to end on April 12th at the Guildhall, Portsmouth, Hants.
Oct [2] *High Heel Sneakers* makes US #59.

1966

Jan [21] Wonder flies to London for his third UK tour.
Feb [12] *Uptight (Everything's Alright)* hits US #3 and R&B #1, selling over a million (though Motown's best-sellers throughout the decade will remain officially uncertified).
Mar *Uptight*, his UK chart debut, reaches UK #14.
May [14] *Nothing's Too Good For My Baby* reaches US #20.
June ***Up Tight Everything's Alright*** is released, making US #33.
Sept [3] His revival of Bob Dylan's *Blowin' In The Wind*, duetted with Henry Cosby, hits US #9 and makes UK #36.
Nov Wonder begins a three-week European tour at the Titan club, Rome, Italy.
Dec [23-**Jan** 1] Wonder takes part in the Motortown Revue at the Fox Theatre, Detroit, with the Temptations, Martha & the Vandellas, Gladys Knight & the Pips, Jimmy Ruffin, and other Motown acts.
[24] *A Place In The Sun* hits US #9.

1967

Jan *A Place In The Sun* reaches UK #20.
Feb ***Down To Earth*** enters the US chart, rising to #92.
Apr [1] *Travlin' Man* makes US #32. (Its B-side, *Hey Love*, will make US #90 on May [27].)
July [29] *I Was Made To Love Her* hits US #2, and becomes a million seller.
I Was Made To Love Her hits UK #5 while its parent album, ***I Was Made To Love Her***, will make US #45.
Nov [4] *I'm Wondering* reaches US #12 and UK #22.

1968

Jan Wonder graduates from Michigan State School for the Blind.
Apr ***Greatest Hits*** is released, and will make US #37.
May [25] *Shoo-Be-Doo-Be-Doo-Da-Day* hits US #9, and makes UK #46.
Aug [17] *You Met Your Match* reaches US #35.
Sept ***Stevie Wonder's Greatest Hits*** makes UK #25.
Nov [9] Wonder, credited as Eivets Rednow, reaches US #66 with *Alfie*, a piano instrumental. (He also records an instrumental album under this moniker, a reversal of his own name.)
Dec [28] His updating of the standard, *For Once In My Life*, hits US #2, behind Marvin Gaye's *I Heard It Through The Grapevine*, and is another million seller.

1969

Jan *For Once In My Life* hits UK #3, as its parent album, ***For Once In My Life***, heads for US #50.
Mar [7] He embarks on an 18-day UK concert tour.
[22] *I Don't Know Why* makes US #39.
Apr *I Don't Know Why* reaches UK #14.
May [5] Wonder meets President Nixon at the White House, and is presented with the President's Committee on Employment of Handicapped People's "Distinguished Service Award".
July [26] *My Cherie Amour*, B-side of *I Don't Know Why*, hits US #4, and tops a million sales.
Aug *My Cherie Amour* hits UK #4, as parent album, ***My Cherie Amour***, rises to US #34.
Dec [13] *Yester-me, Yester-you, Yesterday,* written three years earlier by Ron Miller and Bryan Wells, hits US #7 and UK #2, as ***My Cherie Amour*** reaches UK #17.

1970

Jan [10] Wonder is awarded the 1969 Show Business Inspiration Award by Fight For Sight, which promotes research into eye diseases.
Mar [7] *Never Had A Dream Come True* reaches US #26 and hits UK #6.
Apr ***Stevie Wonder Live*** makes US #81.
Aug [8] Co-penned by Wonder, *Signed Sealed Delivered I'm Yours* hits US #3, and reaches UK #15 as parent album, ***Signed Sealed And Delivered***, is released, set to make US #25.
Sept [14] Wonder marries Syreeta Wright, a former secretary at Motown Records, for whom he will co-write and produce several hits.
Nov [28] *Heaven Help Us All* hits US #9, and reaches UK #29.

1971

May [1] *We Can Work It Out*, a revival of the Lennon/McCartney song, reaches US #13 and UK #27.
[13] On his 21st birthday, Wonder receives all his childhood earnings. Despite having earned in excess of $30 million, he receives only $1 million. (His re-negotiations with Motown result in the formation of the autonomous Taurus Productions and Black Bull Publishing companies.)
Where I'm Coming From, written by Wonder and Syreeta, peaks at US #62.
July [3] *Never Dreamed You'd Leave In Summer* makes US #78.
Aug [17] Wonder sings at the funeral of the legendary King Curtis, fatally stabbed in New York City, NY.
Oct [16] *If You Really Love Me*, again written with

Syreeta, hits US #8.
Nov ***Greatest Hits, Vol. 2*** makes US #69.

1972

Jan [13] Wonder begins a UK tour at London's Hammersmith Odeon, set to end on February 2nd at the Manchester Odeon, Gtr. Manchester.
Feb *If You Really Love Me* reaches UK #20, while ***Greatest Hits Vol. 2*** makes UK #30.
Mar ***Music Of My Mind***, recorded with synthesizer specialists, Robert Margouleff and Malcolm Cecil, reaches US #21.
June [3] Wonder begins a 50-date, eight-week North American trek, as support to the Rolling Stones in Vancouver, BC, Canada.
July [22] *Superwoman (Where Were You When I Needed You)* reaches US #33.
Aug [30] Wonder joins John and Yoko Lennon for "One On One", a benefit for Willowbank Hospital, at New York's Madison Square Garden.
Sept [30] *Keep On Running* peaks at US #90.
Nov The self-penned and produced ***Talking Book***, featuring Jeff Beck, Ray Parker Jr. and Deniece Williams, among others, hits US #3.

1973

Jan [27] *Superstition*, originally written for Jeff Beck, tops the US chart (his first single to do since 1963), selling over a million, and reaches UK #11.
Feb ***Talking Book*** reaches UK #16.
May [19] *You Are The Sunshine Of My Life* tops the US chart, becoming another million seller.
June *You Are The Sunshine Of My Life* hits UK #7.
Aug Rufus' *Tell Me Something Good*, Wonder-inked, hits US #3.
[6] While travelling from Greenville, NC, to Durham, NC, during a US tour, Wonder is seriously injured when his car crashes into a logging truck near Winston-Salem, NC. (He suffers multiple head injuries, and lies in a coma for four days. His head injuries will rob him of his sense of smell.)
Sept ***Innervisions***, written, produced and arranged by Wonder (as with all subsequent material) hits US #4, selling over a million, and UK #8.
[25] Wonder makes his first post-accident appearance, jamming on *Honky Tonk Women* with Elton John, at the Boston Garden, MA.
Oct [13] *Higher Ground* hits US #4 and reaches UK #29.
Nov [9] Wonder receives the Nederlands' Edison Award for ***Talking Book***.

1974

Jan [12] *Living For The City* hits US #8 and UK #15.
[20] Wonder gives his first full concert since his accident at the annual Midem festival in France.
Feb [13] He jams with Johnny Winter and Dr. John at the opening of the new Bottom Line in New York.
[19] He collects the Favorite Male Artist, Soul/R&B, and Favorite Single, Soul/R&B trophies, at the inaugural American Music Awards, held at the Aquarius Theater, Hollywood, CA.
Mar He plays his first US concert since his car smash at New York's Madison Square Garden, where he is joined on stage by Roberta Flack, Eddie Kendricks, Sly Stone and Wonderlove, and also sells out concerts at the Rainbow Theatre, London.
[2] Wonder wins four categories: Best Pop Vocal Performance, Male (for *You Are The Sunshine Of My Life*), Best R&B Song and Best R&B Vocal Performance, Male (both for *Superstition*), and Album Of The Year (for ***Innervisions***), at the 16th annual Grammy Awards.
[23] He announces: "I will quit in 1976", stating that he will undertake a two-year program, working with children in Ghana.
May *He's Misstra Know It All* hits UK #10.
June [1] *Don't You Worry 'Bout A Thing* reaches US #16.
Sept [19] ***Fulfillingness' First Finale*** tops the US chart for the first of two weeks, and hits UK #5.
[13] Wonder begins a US tour at the Nassau Veterans Memorial Coliseum, Uniondale, NY.
Nov [2] *You Haven't Done Nothin'*, with the Jackson 5 on backup vocals, hits US #1 and UK #30.
[22] "Stevie Wonder Day" is declared in Los Angeles, CA.

1975

Feb [1] *Boogie On Reggae Woman* hits US #3 and UK #12.
[18] He wins the Favorite Male Artist, Soul/R&B category, at the second annual American Music Awards, held at the Civic Auditorium, Santa Monica CA.
Mar [1] Wonder again wins four Grammys: Best Pop Vocal Performance, Male and Album Of The Year (both for ***Fulfillingness***), Best R&B Vocal Performance, Male (for *Boogie On Reggae Woman*), and Best R&B Song (for *Living For The City*), at the 17th annual Awards ceremony.
[6] Wonder is awarded the NARM Presidential Award "in tribute to a man who embodies every facet of the complete musical artist: composer, writer, performer, recording artist, musician and interpreter through his music of the culture of his time..."
Apr [5] Minnie Riperton's *Lovin' You*, written by Wonder, tops the US chart. Having recently moved to Manhattan, Wonder and new companion, Yolanda Simmons, parent a daughter, Aisha Zakia.
May [10] Wonder headlines a concert in front of 125,000 people at the Washington Monument to celebrate "Human Kindness Day", before performing in Jamaica with Bob Marley & the Wailers.

1976

Jan [25] Wonder joins Bob Dylan and Isaac Hayes for the "Night of the Hurricane II" benefit show for convicted murderer, boxer Ruben "Hurricane" Carter, in the Houston Astrodome, Houston, TX.
The Stevie Wonder Home For Blind and Retarded Children opens, confirming ongoing personal interest in a wide number of charity and human rights causes.
Apr [14] Wonder and Motown Records announce the signing of a $13-million-dollar contract renewal - the largest negotiated in recording history to date.
Oct [16] Critically-revered as his most rounded work, the double set opus, ***Songs In The Key Of Life***, also including a free four-track EP, debuts at US #1, where it will stay for 14 weeks, and hits UK #2.

1977

Jan [22] *I Wish* hits US #1 and UK #5, and is another million seller.
[31] Wonder nabs the Favorite Male Artist, Soul/R&B, and Favorite Album, Soul/R&B categories, at the fourth annual American Music Awards, held at the Santa Monica Civic Auditorium.
Feb [19] Wonder is named Producer Of The Year, ***Songs In The Key Of Life*** wins Album Of The Year and Best Pop Vocal Performance, Male, and *I Wish* is named Best R&B Vocal Performance, Male, at the 19th annual Grammy Awards. (During the month his Stuyvesant Square, New York house is raided by police who confiscate three illegal Taser guns, able to stun victims with a 50,000-volt shock.)
May [21] *Sir Duke*, a tribute to Duke Ellington, is a further million seller, topping the US chart, and hitting UK #2, behind Deniece Williams' *Free*.
Sept *Another Star* makes UK #29.
Oct [8] *Another Star* reaches US #32.

1978

Jan [16] He scoops the Favorite Male Artist, Soul/R&B, and Favorite Album, Soul/R&B trophies, at the fifth annual American Music Awards, held again at the Santa Monica Civic Auditorium.
[21] *As* makes US #36.

1979

Feb [10] *Pops We Love You*, a tribute to Berry Gordy's father on his 90th birthday, with Wonder, Diana Ross, Marvin Gaye and Smokey Robinson, reaches US #59 and UK #66. The compilation, ***Looking Back***, makes US #34.
Apr The Wonders become parents to daughter, Kita Swan Di.
[27] Wonder makes a surprise appearance, performing *Sir Duke*, at a Duke Ellington tribute, at UCLA's Royce Hall, Los Angeles.
Nov Double album, ***Journey Through The Secret Life Of Plants***, hits UK #8.
Dec [2] Wonder, accompanied by the National Afro-American Philharmonic Orchestra, performs material from ***Journey Through The Secret Life Of Plants*** at New York's Metropolitan Opera House.
[22] *Send One Your Love* hits US #4 and UK #52, as parent album, ***Journey Through The Secret Life Of Plants***, the soundtrack for a documentary film of the same title, hits US #4.

1980

Feb *Black Orchid* peaks at UK #63.
Mar [22] *Outside My Window* makes US and UK #52.
Sept [1] Wonder returns for a UK tour after a six-year absence, including six sold-out Wembley Arena, Wembley, Middx. dates.
Oct Marley-inspired *Master Blaster (Jammin')* hits UK #2, behind the Police's *Don't Stand So Close To Me*.
Nov ***Hotter Than July***, dedicated to Martin Luther King Jr., hits US #3 and UK #2. (Wonder will conduct a campaign to have King's January 15th birthdate celebrated as a US national holiday. After marches on Washington in 1981 and 1982, he will have his wish granted in 1986.)
Dec [6] *Master Blaster (Jammin')* hits US #5.

1981

Jan *I Ain't Gonna Stand For It* hits UK #10.
Feb [3] ***Hotter Than July*** is confirmed platinum by the RIAA, his first officially certified disc.
Mar [7] *I Ain't Gonna Stand For It* reaches US #11.
May [9] Ballad, *Lately*, makes US #64, but hits UK #3.
June Wonder contributes to gospel singer Andrae Crouch's *I'll Be Thinking Of You*.
Aug *Happy Birthday* hits UK #2, behind Shakin' Stevens' *Green Door*.
[15] Wonder gives his ***Hotter Than July*** gold disc to Tami Ragoway, whose boyfriend had been shot and killed returning home after Wonder's concert at the Great Western Forum, Inglewood, CA.

1982

Jan [25] He is presented with the Special Award of Merit and the Favorite Male Artist, Soul/R&B trophy, at the ninth annual American Music Awards, held at the Shrine Auditorium.
Mar [20] *That Girl* hits US #4 and makes UK #39.
Apr [24] *Ebony And Ivory*, a duet with Paul McCartney recorded in Montserrat, Leeward Islands, tops the UK survey for the first of three weeks.
May [15] *Ebony And Ivory* heads the US chart, selling over a million, as ***Stevie Wonder's Original Musiquarium I*** hits UK #8. It is a compilation album, spiced with new tracks.
June [6] Wonder participates in the "Peace Sunday : We Have A Dream" anti-nuclear rally at the Rose Bowl, Pasadena, CA, with Jackson Browne, Crosby, Stills & Nash, Bob Dylan, Linda Ronstadt and others.
[26] *Do I Do* hits UK #10, while ***Stevie Wonder's Original Musiquarium I*** hits US #4.
July [9] ***Stevie Wonder's Original Musiquarium I*** is certified gold by the RIAA,
[10] *Do I Do* reaches US #13.
Oct [16] *Ribbon In The Sky* makes US #54 and UK #45.
Dec [4] *Used To Be*, a duet with labelmate, Charlene, reaches US #46.

1983

Mar [7] His two children, Aisha and Keita, accept Wonder's induction award to the Songwriters Hall of Fame at the 14th annual ceremony, held at the Waldorf Astoria Ballroom, New York.
May [7] Wonder plays tennis while hosting NBC-TV's "Saturday Night Live".
[16] He sings ***My Cherie Amour*** and ***You Are The***

Sunshine Of My Life at the 25th Motown Anniversary Show.
Aug Wonder sings on, and co-writes, Gary Byrd's *The Crown*, which hits UK #6 as a 12"-only single.

1984

Jan He guests on Elton John's *I Guess That's Why They Call It The Blues*.
June Wonder begins a UK and European tour.
Sept [8] *I Just Called To Say I Love You* (taken from the soundtrack album, ***The Woman In Red***, which hits US #4 and UK #2) tops the UK chart for the first of six weeks, selling more than a million copies - it is Wonder's first solo UK #1, and one of the ten best-selling UK singles of all time.
Oct [13] *I Just Called To Say I Love You* begins the first of three weeks at US #1.
Nov [8] *I Just Called To Say I Love You* is certified gold by the RIAA.
[10] Chaka Khan's US #3 hit, *I Feel For You*, featuring Wonder's trademark harmonica playing, tops the UK chart, while Wonder's UK-only compilation, ***Love Songs - 16 Classic Hits***, reaches UK #20.
Dec *Love Light In Flight* makes UK #44.
[24] Wonder is given the key to the city of Detroit. (He will later announce plans to run for Mayor.)

1985

Jan Self-explanatory single, *Don't Drive Drunk*, peaks at UK #62.
[28] Wonder participates in the historic recording of USA For Africa's *We Are The World*.
Feb [2] *Love Light In Flight*, also taken from ***The Woman In Red***, reaches US #17.
Mar [25] *I Just Called To Say I Love You* wins the Oscar for Best Song, at the annual Academy Awards ceremony. Wonder dedicates the award to Nelson Mandela.
[26] South African radio stations ban the playing of all Wonder's records, in response to his Mandela tribute.
July Wonder plays harmonica on Eurythmics' *There Must Be An Angel (Playing With My Heart)* UK chart-topper. (He has also recently featured on *I Do Love You*, a song he also wrote for inclusion on the Beach Boys' ***The Beach Boys***.)
Sept *Part-Time Lover* hits UK #3 as parent album, ***In Square Circle***, hits UK #5. He writes and plays on *She's So Beautiful*, with a vocal by Cliff Richard, for the album of Dave Clark's "Time" stage musical. Released as a Richard single, it reaches UK #17.
Oct ***In Square Circle*** hits US #5.
Nov [2] *Part-Time Lover* becomes the first single to top the US pop, R&B, adult contemporary and dance/disco charts. *Go Home* peaks at UK #67.
Dec *I Just Called To Say I Love You* re-enters the UK chart, at #64.
[4] The RIAA certifies two milion sales of ***In Square Circle***.

1986

Jan [15] To celebrate the first observance of Martin Luther King Jr.'s birthday as a US national holiday, Wonder organizes concerts in Washington, New York, and Atlanta, GA.
[18] Wonder joins Elton John and Gladys Knight as Dionne Warwick's "Friends" on the US chart-topping (and UK #16) *That's What Friends Are For*.
[27] He nabs the Favorite Male Video Artist, Soul/R&B, and Favorite Male Artist, Soul/R&B categories, at the 13th annual American Music Awards, held at the Shrine Auditorium.
Feb [1] *Go Home* hits US #10.
[25] ***In Square Circle*** wins Best R&B Vocal Performance, Male, at the 28th annual Grammy Awards.
Apr [12] Ballad, *Overjoyed*, reaches US #24 and UK #17.
June [17] Wonder begins a US tour to promote ***In Square Circle*** in Seattle.
[21] *Land Of La La* peaks at US #86.
July [31] He is nominated for an Emmy for his appearance in NBC-TV's top-rated "The Cosby Show".
Sept Wonder is awarded the Gold Ticket for playing to over 100,000 fans at New York's Madison Square Garden.

1987

Jan *Stranger On The Shore Of Love* peaks at UK #55.
Feb Wonder announces a boycott of the state of Arizona, until Governor Evan Meacham reinstates Martin Luther King Jr.'s birthday as a state holiday. (Several other artists support his boycott.)
[24] Wonder shares a win in the Best Pop Performance By A Duo Or Group With Vocal category with Dionne Warwick, Elton John and Gladys Knight, for *That's What Friends Are For*, at the 29th annual Grammy Awards. He also sings the song with Warwick and Knight, accompanied by Burt Bacharach on piano.
Mar Wonder records the anti-drug song, *Don't Pass Go*, in an audio-visual experiment, linking Nile Rodgers in a New York studio, with Quincy Jones and Wonder in his own Wonderland Studio, 3,000 miles away, in Los Angeles.
[23] He is presented with the Heritage Award, at the inaugural Soul Train Music Awards, held at the Civic Center, Santa Monica, CA.
Aug Wonder begins a UK and European tour.
Sept During an eight-day stint at the Wembley Arena, Wembley, Middx., fan Barry Betts answers Wonder's request to help courier a tape of a new song, *Get It*, to Michael Jackson in Los Angeles.
Oct *Skeletons* peaks at UK #59.
Nov [28] ***Characters***, including the duet, *Get It*, with Jackson and other guests, B.B. King, Stevie Ray Vaughan and Junior, debuts at its UK #33 peak, as *Skeletons* tops the US R&B chart.
Dec [5] *Skeletons* reaches US #19 and hits R&B #1, having faltered at UK #59. ***Characters*** reaches US #17.
[19] ***Characters*** tops the US R&B rankings.

1988

Jan [8] ***Characters*** is certified platinum by the RIAA.
Feb [20] *You Will Know* peaks at US #77.
Mar [5] *You Will Know* tops the US R&B chart.
May Wonder begins a European tour.
[28] *Get It*, with Michael Jackson, makes US #80 and UK #37.
June [4] Wonder/Julio Iglesias duet, *My Love*, peaks at US #80, his last US Hot 100 single of the decade.
[11] Wonder, despite having synthesizer programs stolen prior to the gig, plays at "Nelson Mandela's 70th Birthday Tribute", at Wembley Stadium.
Aug Wonder's duet with Julio Iglesias, *My Love* hits UK #6 as he plays an eight-date series of concerts at New York's Radio City Music Hall, previewing a full-length US tour. (During the year, he is honored by the United Nations' Special Committee Against Apartheid for his commitment to the "upliftment of the oppressed and downtrodden of the world".)

1989

Jan [18] At the age of 38, Wonder is inducted into the Rock and Roll Hall of Fame, at the fourth annual dinner, held at New York's Waldorf Astoria Hotel.
Apr Wonder confirms his backing for the proposed Rhythm Radio Group, pitching for a new station franchise in London.
May He begins a European tour, including soldout dates at major UK venues and stadium dates in Eastern Europe.
[13] Wonder celebrates his 39th birthday, onstage at Wembley Arena, joined by Paul Young during an encore. The belated release of *Free*, from ***Characters***, makes UK #49.
June Wonder becomes the first Motown act to play in Eastern bloc countries, also donating royalties from ***Characters*** to the Polish Foundation for the Handicapped.
[17] Wonder sings *Happy Birthday* at the centenary celebration of the Eiffel Tower in Paris, France.

1990

Jan [6] Wonder plays at the Great Western Forum, to raise funds for the Inner City Foundation for Excellence in Education.
[15] He donates the proceeds of his concert at the Beacon Theatre, New York, to aid the homeless.
Feb [21] Wonder sings *We Can Work It Out* in a tribute to Paul McCartney, being honored with a Lifetime Achievement Award, at the 32nd annual Grammy Awards.
Apr [3] Los Angeles Urban League honors Wonder with the Whitney M. Young Jr. Award, given to individuals who have made significant contributions in advancing civil and human rights for African Americans, and other minorities.
[23-24] He guests with Patti Austin, James Taylor, Phoebe Snow and Take 6 for "Special Olympics Africa" at Carnegie Hall, New York.
Aug [31] Wonder sings *Amazing Grace* with Bonnie Raitt and Jackson Browne, at the memorial service for Stevie Ray Vaughan in Oak Cliff, Dallas, TX.
Oct [26] Whitney Houston presents Wonder with the Carousel of Hope Award from the Children's Diabetes Foundation, at a benefit at the Beverly Hilton Hotel, Los Angeles.
Nov [15] Wonder is honored by Recording Artists Against Drunk Driving, receiving its Honorary Global Founder's Award for *Don't Drive Drunk*.
[25] Wonder participates in CBS-TV's "Motown 30 : What's Goin' On!" special.
Dec [23-24] Wonder performs at the Dome, Tokyo, Japan.

1991

Mar Spike Lee commissions Wonder to pen the soundtrack for his new movie, "Jungle Fever", causing him to put on hold his own ***Conversation Pieces*** album.
May [11] Wonder adds his autograph to a $12,000 Young Chang grand piano, being auctioned at the Peabody Hotel, Orlando, FL, to raise money for the Give Kids The World charity foundation.
[28] He guests on syndicated TV's "The Arsenio Hall Show".
He films a video for *Chemical Love* at Hale House, a Harlem-based program that assists babies born addicted to drugs or with AIDS.
June [3] "Jungle Fever" receives its New York premiere.
[8] Wonder receives the Diamond Award for Excellence at the first IAAAM '91 Celebration of African American Music Month, at the Wyndham Franklin Plaza Hotel in Philadelphia, PA, as the Wonder written-and-performed soundtrack album, ***Music From The Movie Jungle Fever***, charts for a week at UK #56.
[14] Wonder receives the second annual Nelson Mandela Courage Award, in Los Angeles.
[15] He appears in a Los Angeles benefit, organized by Robert Townsend, for the family of the late David Ruffin, with Gladys Knight and Dionne Warwick.
July [10] The still-climbing ***Music From The Movie Jungle Fever*** is certified gold by the RIAA.
[13] ***Music From The Movie Jungle Fever*** reaches US #24.
[27] *Gotta Have You*, from ***Music From The Movie Jungle Fever***, peaks at US #92.
Aug Wonder contributes to a video of Marvin Gaye's *Mercy Mercy Mercy*, a tie-up between Motown and the Audubon Society, to increase awareness of the nation's environmental problems.
Sept [7] He sings *These Three Words* at "Party For Richard Pryor" special, in Beverly Hills. (CBS-TV will air the show on November 23rd.)
[19] He sings *Hallelujah I Love Her So* and duets with Ray Charles on *Living For The City*, on Fox-TV's "Ray Charles : 50 Years In Music", filmed in Pasadena, to benefit the Starlight Pavilion Foundation. (The show will air on October 6th.)
Oct Wonder is featured on the cover of **Ebony Man** magazine.
[12] *Fun Day* charts for a week at UK #63.
Nov [11] He performs at a benefit for former Motown singer, Mary Wells, at the Celebrity Theater, Los Angeles, with Natalie Cole, Dionne Warwick, Isaac

Hayes and others.
[15] Wonder gives another benefit concert in Chicago, IL, for his former employee, Theresa Kyles, and her husband Dwain, whose unborn child will need a heart transplant shortly after birth.

1992

Apr [9] Wonder makes his final appearance on NBC-TV's Johnny Carson-hosted "The Tonight Show", singing *I'll Be Seeing You.*
[12] ***Music From The Movie Jungle Fever*** is named Outstanding National R&B Album, at the Motor City Music Awards, Detroit.
[28] Wonder participates in Quincy Jones' all-star recording of ***Hallelujah!***, a contemporary version of Handel's "The Messiah", at A&M Studios, Hollywood.
May [16] His "European Natural Wonder" tour opens in Switzerland.
June [2-3] He performs at the Wembley Arena, during the tour's UK leg.
July [18] Wonder attends the wedding of Whitney Houston and Bobby Brown in Mendham, NJ.
[21] He is made an Honorary Courtier to traditional Cameroon ruler, Fon Agwafor III, during a week-long visit.
Aug [17] A San Francisco appeals court upholds a prior jury verdict, confirming that Wonder did not steal *I Just Called To Say I Love You* from Lloyd Chate, a Los Angeles songwriter.
Oct [16] Wonder performs *Blowin' In The Wind* at the Bob Dylan anniversary tribute concert, at New York's Madison Square Garden.
Dec [3] He is honored with the National Academy of Songwriters' Lifetime Achievement Award, at the seventh annual "Salute To The American Songwriter", at the Wilshire Ebell Theatre, Los Angeles, with the proceeds going to benefit NAS educational programs.

1993

Jan [15] Wonder performs at breakfast at the America West Arena in Phoenix, AZ, before 17,000 people, to celebrate Arizona having its first Martin Luther King Jr. public holiday.
[16] He wins the Male Artist category, at the 25th annual NAACP Image Awards, held at the Pasadena Civic Auditorium, Pasadena, CA.
June [2] Wonder performs a medley of Motown songs in honor of Berry Gordy Jr., who receives the Abe Olman Publishers Award, at the 24th annual Songwriters Hall of Fame dinner and induction ceremonies, held at the Sheraton New York Hotel.
[6] He takes part in a benefit for the late, great keyboardist, Richard Tee, at the Club Tatou in Beverly Hills, CA, with proceeds going to the Humantics Foundation.

1994

Feb [7] Wonder presents the Award of Merit to Whitney Houston, at the 21st annual American Music Awards, staged at the Shrine Auditorium.
June [6] He donates his harmonica to Hard Rock Café GM Mike Kneidinger in Washington, after performing at the 20th anniversary celebration for the Duke Ellington School of the Arts. While in town, he also receives the 1994 Diamond Award for Excellence at the International Association of African-American Music conference.
[26] Wonder joins Prince onstage, at the latter's Glam Slam club in Minneapolis, MN, to sing *Maybe Your Baby.*
Aug [5] He performs at Monaco's Red Cross Ball.
Dec [10] Frank Sinatra's ***Duets II***, to which Wonder and Gladys Knight have performed on *For Once In My Life*, hits US #9.
[16] Wonder plays at PanaFest in Accra, Ghana, playing an untuned piano.
[31-**Jan** 1] He performs two sellout New Year's shows at the Fox Theatre, Detroit.

1995

Jan [3] Wonder begins his first full US tour in many years, at the Wang Center, Boston, a 28-song greatest hits selection featuring six musicians, four singers and an orchestra, under the collective banner he "Natural Wonder/Charge Against Hunger Tour".
[10] He performs at a tribute concert for Ella Fitzgerald at the Universal City, Universal Amphitheatre.
[12] Wonder gives his first concert in Arizona, at the Grady Gammage Memorial Auditorium In Phoenix, in nine years, following the repeal of the Martin Luther King Jr. Holiday.
Feb [25] *For Your Love* debuts at its UK #23 peak.
Mar [9] Wonder's lunchtime performance at Ronnie Scott's in London, with guests Marcella Detroit, Simon Climie, Brian Kennedy, Julia Fordham, Kim Wilde, Michelle Gayle and others, is broadcast live on BBC Radio 1FM's Simon Mayo show.
[11] He duets with Des'ree on C4-TV's "The White Room".
[25] *For Your Love* makes US #53, as ***Conversation Peace*** hits UK #8 in its week of entry.
Apr [8] ***Conversation Peace*** debuts at its US #16 peak.
May [3] Wonder takes part in the seventh annual World Music Awards held at the Sporting Club in Monte Carlo, Monaco. (The show will air on ABC-TV on the 30th.)
June [12] ***Conversation Peace*** is certified gold by the RIAA.
July [22] *Tomorrow Robins Will Sing* charts for a week at UK #71.
Aug [25] Visiting the town of Dimona, Israel, Wonder is given a brass plaque, inscribed in Braille, by Elisheva Bat-Israel, a member of the so-called Black Hebrews and a former Motown backup singer. He is also given a humanitarian award from the small African community of Hebrew Israelites.
Oct Wonder attends the Million Man March in Washington.
Nov [2] He is inducted into the Soul Train Hall of Fame at the 25th Soul Train Anniversary, staged at the Shrine Auditorium, at which he also performs a medley of *Sir Duke*, *Superstition*, *Overjoyed*, *For Your Love* and *Do I Do*. (The show will air on CBS-TV on the 22nd.)
[21] A Two-CD, 24-song live set, ***Natural Wonder***, recorded during his recent world tour with the Tokyo Symphony Orchestra, conducted by Dr. Henry Panion III, is released.
Dec [6] Wonder performs *Paradise* with Coolio at the sixth annual **Billboard** Music Awards, held at New York's Coliseum, broadcast live on Fox-TV. (The song also collects the Single Of The Year nod.)
[31] He guests on C4-TV's "The White Room New Year Special".

1996

Jan [17]. Wonder sings *I Heard It Through The Grapevine* with Joan Osborne and *Fever* with Little Willie John's son Keith at the post-dinner jam at the 11th annual Rock and Roll Hall of Fame Awards induction dinner, at New York's Waldorf Astoria Hotel.
Feb [26] He performs at the MusiCares "Person Of The Year" dinner at Los Angeles' Century Plaza Hotel.
[28] Wonder receives the Lifetime Achievement Award at the 38th annual Grammy Awards held, at the Shrine Auditorium, having watched a tribute to him performed by D'Angelo and Tony Rich. *For Your Love* is also named Best R&B Vocal Performance, Male and Best R&B Song (while rap star Coolio's *Paradise*, a 1995 US #1 firmly based on Wonder's *Pastime Paradise* from ***Songs In The Key Of Life***, is voted Best Rap Solo Performance).

WORLD PARTY

Karl Wallinger (vocals, guitar, keyboards)

1983

Apr Having drifted through a series of bands, including Zero Zero, Invisible Body Club and funk outfit Out, Wallinger (b. Oct. 19, 1957, Prestatyn, Clwyd, Wales), primarily a keyboardist, answers an ad in **Sounds**, posted by the Waterboys' Mike Scott, looking for a guitarist who is "into Iggy Pop". Auditioning successfully, Wallinger joins the line-up in time for its UK TV debut on BBC2-TV's "The Old Grey Whistle Test", and will record and perform with the band for two albums. Wallinger, the youngest of four children, whose first group experience was in Quasimodo in 1976, with pre-Alarm members, has moved to London in the late '70s, and worked for ATV/Northern Songs music publishers as a royalties analysis clerk, before becoming the musical director of the (then Tracey Ullman-starring) "Rocky Horror Picture Show", in the West End.

1986

Wallinger leaves the Waterboys, frustrated in his desire for complete creative control, and forms World Party, based entirely around his own ideas, songs, musical and production skills. "Pregnant With World Party," as Scott will later claim, Wallinger is invited to retain links with Ensign Records, to whom the Waterboys are contracted, and moves from London to the rural escapism of his Woburn, Beds. home, the Old Rectory, where he establishes his own studio to record the debut album.

1987

Feb Ecology awareness-promoting *Ship Of Fools* makes UK #42.
Mar [28] Edited from over two hours of songs, including unreleased versions of Prince's *Pop Life* and John Lennon's *Across The Universe*, World Party's debut album, ***Private Revolution***, heavily themed on environmental issues, and on which Wallinger produces and plays all instruments (except saxophone by Waterboy Anthony Thistlethwaite, violin by new Waterboy Steve Wickham, and vocal help from labelmate, Irish singer Sinead O'Connor), makes UK #56 and US #39, where the act is an instant success, particularly on the college circuit.
Apr [25] With its extended US title, *Ship Of Fools (Save Me From Tomorrow)* reaches US #27.
May World Party undertakes extensive UK, European and US tours, which will take up the rest of the year.

1988

Jan Three Wallinger-assisted tracks appear on O'Connor's newly-released debut album, ***The Lion And The Cobra***.

1989

Mar [6] Wallinger joins Peter Gabriel, Annie Lennox, The Edge and others for the ***Greenpeace - Rainbow Warriors*** album launch, in Moscow, USSR.
While meticulously recording his second World Party album, Wallinger inks a management agreement with Cavallo, Ruffallo & Fargnoli, the US team which handles Prince.

1990

May [17] World Party guests on NBC-TV's "Late Night With David Letterman".
[26] The critically revered and ecology-heavy, ***Goodbye Jumbo*** makes UK #36, and begins a slow US chart rise as World Party, with a current touring line-up of Dave Catlin-Birch (guitar), Guy Chambers (keyboards), Max Edie (synthesizers) and Chris Sharrock (drums), sets off on a series of four alternate European and US live treks. Featuring O'Connor on backing vocals for *Sweet Soul Dream*, the album, once again edited from 70 minutes of music onto a 53 minute, 38 second set, also includes appearances from Jeff Trott, Chris Whitten and Steve Wickham.
July [7] The extracted world-saving *Message In The Box*, which World Party will perform live at the forthcoming MTV Video Music Awards, reaches UK #39.
Aug [18] ***Goodbye Jumbo*** makes US #73.
Sept [15] *Way Down Now* peaks at UK #66.
Oct [9] The band embarks on a ten-date UK tour, at

Queens Hall, Edinburgh, Lothian, Scotland, set to end on the 21st at the Victoria Rooms, Bristol, Avon.
Nov [10] The group guests on NBC-TV's "Saturday Night Live".
Dec [6] World Party participates in the "Reims Music Festival", Reims, France.

1991

June A nine-track World Party EP, *Thank You World*, including a cover version of the Beatles' *Happiness Is A Warm Gun*, makes UK #68.

1993

Apr [17] *Is It Like Today?* reaches UK #19.
[30] World Party performs at Virgin Radio's celebratory launch-day bash, at London's Piccadilly Theatre.
May [8] After a typically studio-intensive hiatus, ***Bang!*** debuts at its UK #2 and US #126 peak. Co-produced by Wallinger and Steve Lillywhite, it has been recorded at Wallinger's home studio (Seaview, which he bought in 1988), with musical help from touring band members Catlin-Birch and Sharrock.
[15] An eight-date UK tour opens at Barrowlands, Glasgow, Strathclyde, Scotland, set to end on the 25th at London' Kentish Town Forum.
July [17] *Give It All Away* makes UK #43.
Oct [9] *All I Gave* reaches UK #37.
Nov [3] The group performs a sole London date at the Brixton Academy.

1994

June [24] World Party plays on the opening day of the annual "Glastonbury Festival", Worthy Farm, Pilton, Somerset.

1995

July [24-29] Having penned the score for the movie "Reality Bites" last year, Wallinger now attends the five day "Real World Recording Week"at Peter Gabriel's Box studios.
see also: **THE WATERBOYS**

X

Y

Z

XTC

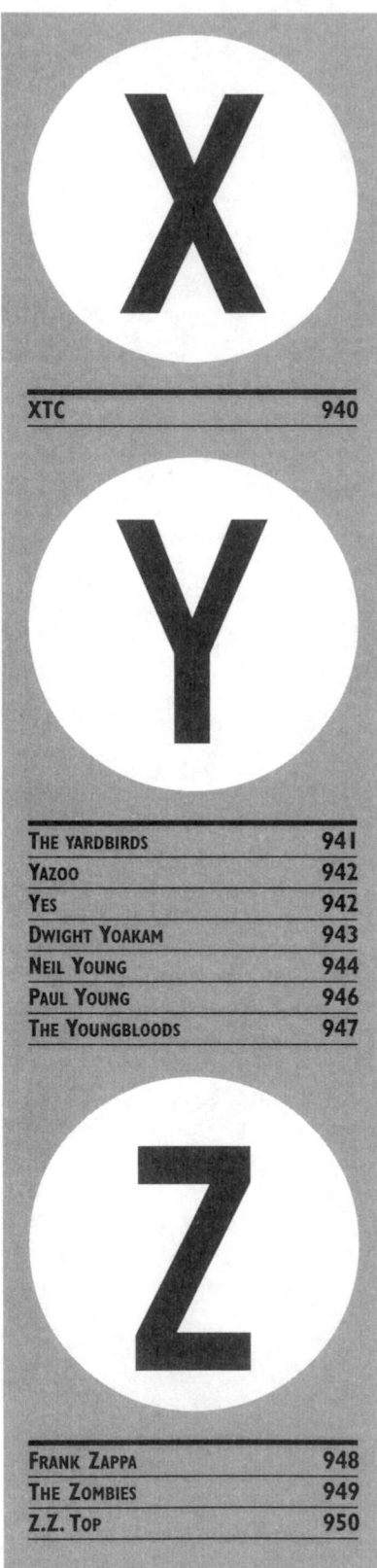

Andy Partridge (guitar, vocals); **Colin Moulding** (bass, vocals); **Dave Gregory** (keyboards); **Terry Chambers** (drums)

1977

Sept Partridge (b. Nov. 11, 1953, Malta), Moulding (b. Aug. 17, 1955, Swindon, Wilts.) and Chambers (b. July 18, 1955, Swindon), all ex-members of the Swindon-based Star Park rock band, who having changed their name to Helium Kidz at the height of the punk boom, are joined by ex-King Crimson keyboard player, Barry Andrews (b. Sept. 12, 1956, West Norwood, London). Having played club dates in London during the summer (including a gig at the Hope & Anchor in July), and earlier auditioned for CBS Records, XTC have signed to Virgin Records (with Partridge and Moulding inked to Virgin Publishing for song copyrights), which now releases their debut EP, *3-D*.

1978

Jan ***White Music***, recorded in one week and largely written by Partridge, makes UK #38, as the band is linked to the currently popular UK new wave movement. (During the month, Partridge's parents appear on the ITV quiz show "Mr and Mrs".)
Feb *Statue Of Liberty* is released.
May *This Is Pop*, produced by Robert John "Mutt" Lange, is released.
Nov *Go 2*, helmed by Martin Rushent, reaches UK #21, including the extracted *Are You Receiving Me?*.

1979

Jan Andrews quits the band on its return from a ten-date US mini-tour. (He teams with Robert Fripp to form the League Of Gentlemen, before joining Shriekback, and recording as a soloist for Virgin.) His is replaced by long-time band friend, Dave Gregory.
May *Life Begins At The Hop* peaks at UK #54.
July The band tours Australia, New Zealand and Japan.
Aug Third album, ***Drums And Wires***, a firm pop/rock set showcasing Partridge's sharp lyrical wit, and produced by Steve Lillywhite, makes UK #34, as XTC begins a brief UK tour.
Nov *Making Plans For Nigel*, written by Moulding, reaches UK #17.

1980

Feb Partridge releases the John Leckie-produced solo set, ***Takeway/The Lure Of Salvage***, under the name of Mr. Partridge. ***Drums And Wires*** climbs to US #176.
Mar *Wait Till Your Boat Goes Down* is released.
Sept Double A-side, *Generals And Majors/Don't Lose Your Temper*, makes UK #32, while ***Black Sea***, again produced by Lillywhite, reaches UK #16.
Oct *Towers Of London* makes UK #31.
Nov *Take This Town*, from the "Times Square" movie soundtrack, is released.

1981

Feb [21] *Sgt. Rock (Is Going To Help Me)* reaches UK #16, while ***Black Sea*** reaches US #41.
Mar *Respectable Street* fails to chart, partly due to its ban on BBC radio for a reference to Sony, as the group begins a tour of Venezuela, and will also visit the US, Middle East, South-East Asia and Australia.

1982

Feb [20] The Partridge-written *Senses Working Overtime*, their biggest success, hits UK #10.
[27] Critically-revered double album, ***English Settlement***, produced by Hugh Padgham, hits UK #5.
Mar Partridge collapses from exhaustion on stage in Paris, France.
Apr [10] *Ball And Chain* peaks at UK #58. Partridge collapses again (with a stomach ulcer), having given himself less than a month to recover from his earlier illness. He later claims it is "a phobia about being in front of people". A tour is cancelled, and Chambers leaves.
May *No Thugs In Our House* is released.
[22] ***English Settlement*** makes US #48.
Nov [20] While Partridge has announced that the band will never play live again, the compilation, ***Waxworks - Some Singles (1977-1982)***, peaks at UK #54 (initially released with a free companion B-sides collection, ***Beeswax***.)

1983

May Bob Sargeant-produced *Great Fire* is released, followed by *Wonderland* in July.
Aug ***Mummer***, featuring songs written during Partridge's convalescence, makes UK #51. Pete Phipps (ex-Glitter Band) plays drums on tracks on which Chambers does not appear. A refusal to promote the album with live work causes friction between band and label.
Oct *Love On A Farmboy's Wages* makes UK #50.
Nov XTC, guised as the Three Wise Men, releases *Thanks For Christmas*. Partridge begins producing other acts, including Peter Blegvad (ex-Slapp Happy).

1984

Mar ***Mummer***, released by Geffen, makes US #145.
Oct Co-produced by the band with David Lord, ***The Big Express*** makes UK #38 and US #178 with *All You Pretty Girls* peaking at UK #55.

1985

Apr Mini-album ***The Dukes Of Stratosphear: 25 O'Clock*** is released by the group's '60s psychedelic alter-ego outfit, the Dukes Of Stratosphear.

1986

June Virgin releases ***The Compact XTC***, an 18-track singles retrospective.
Oct ***Skylarking***, produced by Todd Rundgren at his own Woodstock, NY studio, and the Tubes' Soundhole Studios in San Francisco, CA, peaks at UK #90. It will spend over six months on the US chart, reaching #70.

1987

Aug A second Dukes Of Stratosphear project, ***Psonic Psunspots***, and CD-only compilation ***Chips From The Chocolate Fireball***, are released. Remaining a trio, they continue to work as a studio band only, releasing both XTC and alias issues, including Partridge's singles as Buster Gonad and the Jolly Josticles.

1989

Feb *Mayor Of Simpleton* makes UK #46.
Mar [11] Paul Fox-produced ***Oranges And Lemons***, once again much favored by music critics, reaches UK #28 and makes US #44, the group's most successful US album to date.
May [20] *The Mayor Of Simpleton* peaks at US #72.

1990

Nov The Partridge-produced *Hands Across The Ocean*, released by the Mission, reaches UK #28. (Still in demand at the studio desk, he will also helm for the Lilac Time, while Gregory produces an album for Cud, both in 1991.)

1992

Apr [18] *The Disappointed* makes UK #33.
May [9] XTC's first album of the '90s, the Gus Dudgeon co-produced ***Nonsuch***, featuring Fairport Convention's Dave Mattacks, and displaying a greater emphasis on orchestration and keyboards, enters at its UK #28 high.
[16] ***Nonsuch*** debuts at its US #97 peak.
June [13] *The Ballad Of Peter Pumpkinhead* charts for a week at UK #71. (By year's end, the band's official biography "Chalkhills And Children", written by Chris Twomey, will be published by Omnibus Press.)

1993

Aug Partridge has teamed with Martin Newell, ex-Cleaners From Venus and lyricist for Captain Sensible, to release ***The Greatest Living Englishman***, issued on the Pipeline label in the US.

1994

June Partridge collaborates with ambient innovator Harold Budd for the album ***Through The Hill***, released on All Saints Records. XTC contributes *Cherry In Your Tree* to ***Carmen Sandiego : Out Of This World***, the band's first recording in two years.
Nov Night Tracks Records issues the archive album ***Drums And Wireless : BBC Radio Sessions 1977-1989***.

1995

Oct Thirsty Ear Records (US) releases ***A Testimonial Dinner : The Songs Of XTC***, a various artists tribute album, with covers by Crash Test Dummies, Rembrandts, They Might Be Giants, Joe Jackson and alter-ego the Dukes of Stratosphear.

THE YARDBIRDS

Keith Relf (vocals, harmonica);
Paul Samwell-Smith (bass); **Jeff Beck** (guitar);
Chris Dreja (guitar); **Jim McCarty** (drums)

1963

May Relf (b. Mar. 22, 1943, Richmond, Surrey), Samwell-Smith (b. May 8, 1943, Richmond), Dreja (b. Nov. 11, 1945, Surbiton, Surrey), McCarty (b. July 25, 1943, Liverpool, Lancs.) and Tony "Top" Topham (b. 1947), having been in local groups in the burgeoning London-area R&B scene (McCarty and Samwell-Smith have been in the Country Gentleman in 1962, which has split after playing pubs and school dances), come together at the Kingston Art School, Kingston, Surrey, initially as the Metropolitan Blues Quartet. They gig at pubs and clubs in the local Richmond area, before moving on to dates at Eel Pie Island, the Railway Hotel, Harrow, Middx., and larger London clubs, including Studio 51, soon taking over the residency from the now too-popular Rolling Stones at Giorgio Gomelsky's Crawdaddy club. Topham leaves to return to college, and is replaced by Eric Clapton (b. Eric Clapp, Mar. 30, 1945, Ripley, Surrey) who knew Relf at art school. The Yardbirds name, found in a Jack Kerouac book, is suggested by Relf.
Dec The group is recorded backing Sonny Boy Williamson on his UK tour.

1964

Feb Gomelsky, now managing the group, takes band demos, recorded at R.G. Jones Studios, to various labels. Rejected by Decca, which feels that it already has too many R&B acts, the group signs to EMI's Columbia label, and cuts three songs at its first recording session.
[28] They play the first "Rhythm & Blues Festival" at the Town Hall, Birmingham, Warks.
May Playwright Lord Ted Willis calls the Yardbirds' type of music a "cheap candyfloss substitute for culture" in the House of Lords. The band subsequently goes round to his house in Chislehurst, Kent, and plays in his back garden, while Willis sunbathes with his wife Audrey and two children John and Sally.
Sept After making a promotional visit to the US to make a film for their debut single, a revival of Billy Boy Arnold's *I Wish You Would*, released in the UK in June, Relf suffers a collapsed lung, brought on by his asthma condition.
Oct Despite a BBC ban, a revival of Don & Bob's R&B standard, *Good Morning Little Schoolgirl* makes UK #44.
Dec Their debut album, recorded live at the Marquee club in London, ***Five Little Yardbirds***, is released, including a show-stopping rendition of Howlin' Wolf's *Smokestack Lightning*.
[24] The group opens in "The Beatles Christmas Show", at London's Hammersmith Odeon.

1965

Mar *For Your Love*, written by Graham Gouldman, is the group's first major hit, at UK #3.
[13] Clapton leaves, apparently dissatisfied with the group's musical direction. He joins John Mayall's Bluesbreakers, and Jeff Beck (b. June 24, 1944, Wallington, Surrey), from the Tridents, replaces him within two weeks.
Apr [30] The group begins a 21-date, twice-nightly UK package tour, supporting the Kinks, with Goldie & the Gingerbreads and others, at the Adelphi Cinema, Slough, Berks., ending on May 23rd at the Gaumont Cinema, Derby, Derbys.
June *Heart Full Of Soul*, also written by Gouldman, hits UK #2.
[3] *For Your Love* hits US #6, while their ***For Your Love*** album, including *My Girl Sloopy*, *Putty (In Your Hands)*, a re-working of *Money*, *Sweet Music* and others, reaches US #96.
[20] The group supports the Beatles at the Olympia, Paris, France.
July [17] The band fails to turn up for a gig at the Birdcage, Southampton, Hants., leaving the promoter to announce his intention to ban them from nearly 50 clubs in South-East England.
Aug [6] The Yardbirds play on the opening day of the "National Jazz & Blues Festival" at the Athletic Ground, Richmond.
Sept [2] The group's scheduled visit to New York to start a TV and radio tour is delayed because of work-permit problems. (They had visited the US earlier in the year, although the UK Musicians' Union had not allowed them to play. They had, however, played some low-key dates on the quiet, and recorded *The Train Kept A-Rollin'* at the famed Sun Studios in Memphis, TN.)
[18] The Yardbirds finally begin a ten-day US tour, at McCormack's Palace, Chicago, IL.
[23] They sing *Heart Full Of Soul* on ABC-TV's "Shindig" (a broadcast also featuring Raquel Welch singing *Dancing In The Street*).
[25] *Heart Full Of Soul* hits US #9.
Oct Double A-side, *Evil Hearted You/Still I'm Sad*, hits UK #3.
Nov [18] The group begins a 16-date, twice-nightly UK tour, with Manfred Mann, Paul & Barry Ryan, Inez & Charlie Foxx and others, at the ABC Cinema, Stockton, Cleveland, set to end on December 6th at Slough's Adelphi Cinema.
[22] They miss the first show at Bradford's Gaumont Cinema, after being stranded with a puncture on the M1 motorway, during a blizzard.
Dec [11] *I'm A Man* reaches US #17, while ***Having A Rave Up With The Yardbirds***, including tracks from the UK live album, makes US #53.
[15] The group begins a six-week US tour.

1966

Jan Fontana in the UK releases ***The Yardbirds With Sonny Boy Williamson***, recorded live in December 1963. The group splits with Gomelsky, after a disagreement over an appearance at the "San Remo Song Festival", San Remo, Italy, as Simon Napier-Bell becomes its new manager.
Mar *Shapes Of Things*, recorded at Chess Studios in Chicago, IL, hits UK #3.
Apr [1] The group stars in "Ready Steady, Allez-Oops!", from the Locomotive in the Moulin Rouge, Paris.
[9] Beck collapses on stage during a gig in Marseilles, France. He is admitted to hospital with suspected meningitis. It is a false alarm however, and he resumes playing with the band on the 16th in Southport, Lancs.
May [1] The Yardbirds take part in the annual "**New Musical Express** Poll Winners Concert", at the Empire Pool, Wembley, Middx.
[14] *Shapes Of Things* reaches US #11.
Relf's first solo effort, a cover of Bob Lind's *Mr. Zero*, is released.
June Samwell-Smith leaves for a career as a producer. Dreja moves to bass, while UK session guitarist Jimmy Page (b. Apr. 9, 1944, London) joins to share lead duties with Beck replaced.
[18] *Over Under Sideways Down* hits UK #10.
[21] Page makes his debut with the band at the Marquee in London.
Aug [5] The group joins "Dick Clark's Caravan of Stars" US tour in Minneapolis, MN, set to end September 4th in Honolulu, HI. (Beck will freak out on tour, with Page becoming sole lead guitarist for the remainder of the trek.)
[13] *Over Under Sideways Down* reaches US #11, while the band's first studio album, ***Yardbirds***, makes UK #20.
[22] The group guests on Dick Clark's "Where The Action Is" TV show.
Sept ***Over Under Sideways Down*** makes US #52.
[23] The Yardbirds begin a 12-date "Rolling Stones '66" tour with the Rolling Stones, at London's Royal Albert Hall, set to close on October 9th at the Gaumont Theatre, Southampton, Hants.
Oct [23] They play at the Fillmore Auditorium, San Francisco.
[28] The group embarks on another Dick Clark tour. Beck departs after the first two gigs, to form a band with Rod Stewart, Ron Wood and Aynsley Dunbar. The group continues as a four-piece. *Happenings Ten Years Time Ago* makes UK #43.
Dec [31] *Happenings Ten Years Time Ago* reaches US #30.

1967

Jan Columbia pairs the band with producer Mickie Most (but there will be no more UK hits), for their first recordings as a four-piece. Napier-Bell sells his interest in the band to Peter Grant.
[22] The group begins a tour of Australasia and the Far East, with Roy Orbison and the Walker Brothers, at the Sydney Stadium, Australia.
May [8] The Yardbirds appear at the "Cannes Film Festival" to coincide with their appearance in the film, "Blow Up", playing *Stroll On*.
[20] The Most-produced *Little Games* makes US #51.
June [17] ***The Yardbirds' Greatest Hits*** reaches US #28.
Aug [26] ***Little Games*** makes US #80.
Sept [2] A cover of Manfred Mann's UK hit, *Ha Ha Said The Clown*, reaches US #45.
Nov [18] *Ten Little Indians*, written by Harry Nilsson, peaks at US #96. The group successfully blocks the release of ***Little Games*** in the UK, though it appears in the US despite their opposition.
Dec The band performs at New York's Madison Square Garden, supporting the Young Rascals. (McCarty does not tour with the band, having suffered a breakdown.)

1968

Jan The band enters the studio for the last time, to cut the single, *Goodnight Sweet Josephine*.
Mar [22] The group begins another US tour, set to end on April 28th, followed by a short visit to Japan.
[30] The Yardbirds allow recording of a US gig at Anderson Theater, New York, for possible release as a live album by their US label, Epic, but retain final approval of the project. (On hearing the tapes, they convince the label not to issue the set. Years later, Page successfully halts its planned release in 1971, as ***Live Yardbirds! Featuring Jimmy Page***.)
July [7] The group splits following a final gig in Luton, Beds., their legacy regarded as pivotal in rock history. (To fulfill prior commitments, Page and Dreja put together the New Yardbirds. Terry Reid and B. J. Wilson both turn them down, but Reid recommends a young singer from Birmingham, Robert Plant. Plant in turn suggests drummer John Bonham. Prior to their first recording session, which will lead to the establishment of Led Zeppelin, John Paul Jones is recruited, as Dreja leaves to pursue a successful career in commercial photography. Relf and McCarty form Together, which in turn becomes Renaissance, with Relf's sister, Jane, Louis Cennamo (bass) and John Hawken (keyboards). McCarty will then form Shoot in 1970, and join Illusion in 1977, with Relf going on to join Medicine Head and then Armageddon in 1975, but will die on May 14th, 1976, electrocuted while playing guitar at home. Dreja, McCarty and Samwell-Smith will reunite for gigs in June 1983 at the Marquee club, London: augmented by John Fiddler as lead vocalist,

they form Box Of Frogs, and sign to Epic Records. McCarty will join Eddie Phillips (ex-Creation), Ray Phillips (ex-Nashville Teens), Don Craine and Keith Grant (ex-Downliners Sect) to form the British Invasion All-Stars in 1989, releasing ***Regression***.)

1970

Oct Compilation, ***The Yardbirds Featuring Performances By Jeff Beck, Eric Clapton, Jimmy Page***, peaks at US #155.

1992

Jan [15] The Yardbirds are inducted into the Rock and Roll Hall of Fame, at the seventh annual dinner, at New York's Waldorf Astoria Hotel, while anthologist Phil Cohen completes work on the four-CD Yardbirds boxed-set retrospective, to be released by Charly Records in the UK in April (an update of a seven album Charly collection, ***Shapes Of Things***, issued in 1983).

see also: **Jeff BECK, Eric CLAPTON, LED ZEPPELIN**

YAZOO

Alison Moyet (vocals); **Vince Clarke** (keyboards)

1982

Jan Keyboards/synthesizer whizz Clarke (b. July 3, 1960, Basildon, Essex), having left Depeche Mode after writing three hit singles, and much of the group's first album, is looking for a singer to work with when he answers an ad placed by "Alf" Moyet (b. Genevieve Alison Jane Moyet, June 18, 1961, Billericay, Essex) for a "rootsy blues band". Moyet has been a vocalist with Southend, Essex R&B acts, including the Vicars and the Screaming Abdabs.

May The Clarke-penned *Only You*, released on Daniel Miller's independent Mute label, which also handles Depeche Mode, hits UK #2, blending Clarke's keyboard expertise with Moyet's distinctively soulful vocal.

July Clarke-penned follow-up *Don't Go* hits UK #3.

Sept [4] Yazoo tours the UK to promote its debut album, ***Upstairs At Eric's***, a reference to co-producer Eric C. Radcliffe, which hits UK #2 in its first of 63 charted weeks. The duo also launches itself Stateside, with a New York performance.

Oct [16] *Situation* (the UK B-side of *Only You*), remixed by François Kervorkian, makes US #73, where the pair has to go under the name Yaz, because a small record company has already registered the name Yazoo.

Nov ***Upstairs At Eric's*** peaks at US #92.

Dec *The Other Side Of Love* reaches UK #13.

1983

Feb [8] The duo wins the Best British Newcomer category, at the second annual BRIT Awards, held at London's Grosvenor House Hotel.

Mar [19] *Only You* peaks at US #67.

June *Nobody's Diary*, Moyet's first composing success, hits UK #3. It is announced that Yazoo will break up after completion of a second album, which is currently being recorded. (Both will go on to continued success: Moyet as a solo performer for CBS/Columbia, and Clarke as the instrumental half of two further Mute duos, the short-lived Assembly, and the enduring Erasure.)

July [16] Recorded at the Blackwing Studios, London, and again co-helmed by Radcliffe, ***You And Me Both*** enters the UK chart at #2 (behind Wham!'s ***Fantastic***), before rising to hit #1 the following week.

Sept ***You And Me Both*** makes US #69.

Dec [10] The Flying Pickets' a cappella treatment of *Only You* begins a five-week stay atop the UK chart. ***Upstairs At Eric's*** will be certified platinum by the RIAA on February 22nd 1989 while a remix of *Situation* will reach UK #14 on Dec [15] the following year.

see also: **DEPECHE MODE, ERASURE, Alison MOYET**

YES

Jon Anderson (vocals); **Steve Howe** (guitar); **Tony Kaye** (keyboards); **Chris Squire** (bass); **Bill Bruford** (drums)

1968

June Anderson (b. Oct. 25, 1944, Accrington, Lancs.) meets Squire (b. Mar. 4, 1948, London) in a club in Soho, London. The former has worked in beat group, the Warriors, who released a single for Decca in 1964, and has cut two solo singles for Parlophone in 1967, while Squire has been in Syn, which has recorded for Deram. They are joined by Kaye (b. Jan. 11, 1946, Leicester, Leics.) ex-Federals, Bruford (b. William Scott Bruford, May 17, 1948, London) ex-Savoy Brown, and guitarist Peter Banks (b. July 7, 1947, Barnet, Herts.) also ex-Syn, to form Yes. The group will receive early exposure, performing live on BBC Radio DJ John Peel's "Top Gear" broadcast.)

Nov [26] They open Cream's farewell concert at London's Royal Albert Hall, which subsequently leads to a residency at London's Marquee club.

1969

Apr [21] Yes supports Janis Joplin again at the Royal Albert Hall.

[25-26] The group performs in cabaret at the "Montreux TV Festival", Montreux, Switzerland.

June Signed to Atlantic Records, *Sweetness* is the band's first release.

Nov Its debut album, ***Yes***, featuring re-workings of the Beatles' *Every Little Thing* and the Byrds' *I See You*, is released.

1970

Feb [7] Yes supports the Nice at London's Royal Festival Hall.

Mar Banks (who will go on to form Flash) is replaced by guitarist, Steve Howe (b. Apr. 8, 1947, London), who has played with the Syndicats, the In Crowd, Tomorrow and Bodast.

[21] Howe makes his first London appearance with the band at London's Queen Elizabeth Hall.

Aug ***Time And A Word*** makes UK #45.

1971

Apr ***The Yes Album***, produced by Eddy Offord, hits UK #7, and is their US chart debut at #40, establishing Yes as a pioneering act in the burgeoning progressive-rock field.

Aug Kaye leaves to form Badger, replaced by the classically-trained Rick Wakeman (b. May 18, 1949, London), ex-Strawbs, who adds a more flamboyant keyboard style.

Sept [30] The group begins a 23-date UK tour at the De Montfort Hall, Leicester, Leics., with Wakeman making his live debut with the band, set to end on October 28th at the Guildhall, Southampton, Hants.

Dec [4] *Your Move* makes US #40, as ***Fragile*** hits UK #7 and US #4. It is the group's first album to feature the artwork of Roger Dean, who creates the Yes logo, and the distinctive sci-fi fantasy style of future sleeves.

1972

Jan [14-15] Yes plays two nights at London's Rainbow Theatre.

Feb [15] The group begins its third US tour, in Providence, RI.

Mar [10] ***Fragile*** is certified gold by the RIAA.

Apr [15] *Roundabout* reaches US #13.

Aug Bruford quits to join King Crimson, and is replaced by ex-Plastic Ono Band and Happy Magazine drummer, Alan White (b. June 14, 1949, Pelton, Durham).

Sept [9] The group's revival of Paul Simon's *America* makes US #46, as the critically-revered ***Close To The Edge*** hits UK #4 and US #3.

Oct [30] ***Close To The Edge*** is certified gold by the RIAA.

Dec [16] *And You And I (Part II)* makes US #42.

1973

Feb Wakeman's solo keyboard outing, ***The Six Wives Of Henry VIII***, hits UK #7 and US #30.

Mar [17] The RIAA certifies gold sales of ***The Yes Album*** and ***Yessongs***.

May The ambitious three-album set, ***Yessongs***, drawn from live performances from the previous year, hits UK #7 and US #12. (A movie of the same title also premieres the following year.)

Dec ***Tales From Topographic Oceans*** becomes the first album to qualify for a gold disc, on ship-out sales.

1974

Jan [5] The studio double album, ***Tales From Topographic Oceans***, based on the Shastric scriptures, tops the UK chart for the first of two weeks, and hits US #6.

Feb [8] ***Tales From Topographic Oceans*** is certified gold by the RIAA.

[18] Yes plays the first of two nights at New York's Madison Square Garden.

Apr [19] The band announces plans for each member to release a solo album.

May [25] Wakeman's solo effort, ***Journey To The Centre Of The Earth***, tops the UK chart and hits US #3.

June [8] Wakeman announces he is leaving the band. (After being treated in hospital for suspected coronary disease the following month, he will continue a successful solo career with ***The Myths And Legends Of King Arthur And The Knights Of The Round Table*** (UK #2 and US #21, 1975), his music for the 1976 Innsbruck Winter Olympics, ***White Rock*** (UK #14 and US #126), ***No Earthly Connection*** (UK #9 and US #67, also in 1976), ***Criminal Record*** (UK #25 and US #128 in 1977), ***Rhapsodies*** (UK #25 and US #170 in 1179), ***1984*** (UK #24 in 1981), ***Beyond The Planets***, recorded with Kevin Peak (UK #64, 1984) and the May [16], 1987 UK #94-peaking ***The Gospels***.)

Aug [18] Ex-Refugee member, Patrick Moraz (b. June 24, 1948, Morges, Switzerland), replaces Wakeman.

Sept [4] ***Journey To The Centre Of The Earth*** is certified gold by the RIAA.

Nov ***Relayer*** hits UK #4 and US #5, including *The Gates Of Delirium*, based on Tolstoy's **War And Peace**, on side one.

Dec [18] ***Relayer*** is certified gold by the RIAA.

1975

Mar ***Yesterdays***, including tracks from the first two albums, reaches UK #27 and US #17.

Aug [23] Yes headlines the second day of the 15th National Jazz & Blues Festival "Reading Rock '75", near Reading, Berks.

Oct [20] ***The Six Wives Of Henry The VIII*** is certified gold by the RIAA.

Nov Solo albums by Howe (***Beginnings*** - UK #22 and US #63) and Squire (***Fish Out Of Water*** - UK #25 and US #69), both enjoy chart success, as Yes takes much of the year off from group activities.

1976

Mar White makes UK #41 with ***Ramshackled***.

Apr Moraz's solo album, ***Patrick Moraz***, makes UK #28 and US #132.

July Anderson's ***Olias Of Sunhillow*** hits UK #8 and US #47.

Dec [3] Wakeman re-joins the band, taking Moraz's place. (After releasing the UK #44 ***Out In The Sun*** the following year, Moraz will join the Moody Blues.)

1977

Aug [2] The still-climbing ***Going For The One*** is certified gold by the RIAA.

[13] Retreating to a more straightforward rock style, ***Going For The One*** tops the UK chart for the first of two weeks, and hits US #8, while the group plays a week of sell-out performances at Madison Square Garden, the Coliseum, New Haven, CT, and the Boston Garden, Boston, MA.

Sept *Wonderous Stories* hits UK #7.

Nov *Going For The One* reaches UK #24.

1978

Sept *Don't Kill The Whale* makes UK #36 as its parent album ***Tormato***, hits UK #8 and US #10.
Nov [8] ***Tormato*** is certified platinum by the RIAA.

1979

Nov Howe's second solo album, ***Steve Howe Album***, reaches UK #68 and US #164.

1980

Feb Anderson has teamed with Greek keyboardist, Vangelis Papathanassiou, as Jon & Vangelis, for *I Hear You Now*, which hits UK #8, its parent album, ***Short Stories***, hitting UK #4.
Mar In an unexpected move both Anderson and Wakeman leave the band, after an attempt to record a new album is abandoned.
May ***Jon & Vangelis*** makes US #125.
[18] The two members of Buggles, Trevor Horn (b. July 15, 1949) (vocals and guitar), and Geoff Downes (keyboards), join Yes.
Aug The first release with the new line-up, ***Drama***, hits UK #2 and US #18. (One of the tracks, and US single *Into The Lens*, is later re-recorded by Buggles as *I Am A Camera*.)
Sept Jon & Vangelis' *I Hear You Now* peaks at US #58.
[4-6] The group sells out more shows than any other band in history, when it plays three nights at New York's Madison Square Garden.
Nov Anderson's solo, ***Song Of Seven***, reaches UK #38 and US #143.

1981

Jan A double live set, ***Yesshows***, recorded between 1976 and 1978, reaches UK #22 and US #43.
Apr [18] The group's break-up is confirmed when Squire and White join ex-Led Zeppelin members Robert Plant and Jimmy Page in rehearsals, sessions which eventually come to nothing. (Buggles will re-form, with Downes going on to form Asia with Howe.)

1982

Jan Jon & Vangelis' *I'll Find My Way Home* hits UK #6.
Feb [13] Jon & Vangelis' ***The Friends Of Mr. Cairo*** hits UK #6, and peaks at US #64.
June *I'll Find My Way Home* makes US #51, as Anderson's solo release, ***Animation***, makes UK #43 and US #176.
Sept The retrospective set, ***Classic Yes***, peaks at US #142 as Squire and White form a new band, Cinema, inviting both Kaye and South African guitarist, Trevor Rabin (b. Jan. 13, 1954, Johannesburg, South Africa), to join. They cut several tracks with Rabin on vocals but, dissatisfied with the results, the group approaches Anderson to join, eventually realising that a new Yes has been formed, and abandoning the Cinema name.

1983

Apr Wakeman's soundtrack to "Gole!", the official FIFA 1982 World Cup film, is released.
July *He Is Smiling*, by Jon & Vangelis, peaks at UK #61, while the duo's ***Private Collection*** reaches UK #22 and US #148.
Oct Yes' comeback single, *Owner Of A Lonely Heart*, released on Atlantic subsidiary, Atco, reaches UK #28. It takes a new direction musically, abandoning their "pomp-rock" tradition in favor of a more modern pop/rock sound, as defined by producer Horn, who nevertheless decides against re-joining the band.
Nov ***90125***, named after its international catalog number and helmed by Horn, reaches UK #16, and hits US #5.

1984

Jan [17] ***90125*** is certified platinum by the RIAA.
[21] *Owner Of A Lonely Heart* tops the US chart becoming an enduring FM radio favorite.
Mar *Leave It* reaches UK #24.
Apr [21] *Leave It* also peaks at US #24, the band having filmed 19 different cuts for its accompanying video.
July [14] *It Can Happen* reaches US #51.
Aug Jon & Vangelis' *State Of Independence* (later to fare better as a Donna Summer cover version) peaks at US #67, as a compilation, ***The Best Of Jon And Vangelis***, makes UK #42.

1985

Feb [26] Yes wins the Best Rock Instrumental Performance category for *Cinema*, a track from ***90125***, at the 27th annual Grammy Awards.
Dec Anderson releases the seasonal ***Three Ships***, featuring a mix of new songs with traditional carols, as ***9012 Live : The Solos*** climbs to US #81.

1986

Mar ***9012 Live : The Solos*** makes UK #44.
May Anderson, recently featured on Mike Oldfield's ***Shine***, contributes vocals to Tangerine Dream's ***Legend***, which makes US #96.
July [12] GTR, a five-piece UK rock band with Steve Howe, ex-Genesis guitarist Steve Hackett and Max Bacon, reaches US #14 with *When The Heart Rules The Mind*. Parent album, ***GTR***, reaches US #11.

1987

Oct [3] *Love Will Find A Way* peaks at UK #73.
[17] The new Yes album, this time without Horn, ***The Big Generator***, reaches UK #17 and will make US #15.
[20] Yes begins a two-month US tour at the Civic Center, Peoria, IL.
Nov [28] *Love Will Find A Way* reaches US #30.

1988

Feb [6] *Rhythm Of Love* makes US #40.
Apr [29] ***Big Generator*** is certified platinum by the RIAA.
Aug Anderson's solo set, ***In The City Of Angels***, is released by Atlantic Records.
Nov Anderson joins Steve Harley and Mike Batt on the charity single, *Whatever You Believe*.

1989

June During legal wrangles between various ex-members over who owns the Yes name, Anderson, Bruford, Wakeman & Howe's *Brother Of Mine* peaks at UK #63.
July ***Anderson Bruford Wakeman Howe*** reaches UK #14 and US #30.
[29] Anderson, Bruford, Wakeman & Howe, playing an "Evening of Yes Music", begin a 36-date US tour, at the Mud Island Amphitheater, Memphis, TN, set to end on September 11th in Concord, CA.
Aug [30] ***Anderson Bruford Wakeman And Howe*** is certified gold by the RIAA.

1990

Mar [23] ABWH gross $325,665 at a sellout show at Madison Square Garden, during a further US trek.

1991

Apr [12-13] A fully re-formed Yes, having settled their legal disputés, and currently including Howe, Kaye, Anderson, Squire, White, Rabin, Bruford and Wakeman (who has recently written the score for Lon Chaney's reissued 1925 classic movie, "Phantom Of The Opera"), embarks on the "Yesshows '91 : Round The World In 80 Dates" tour, opening at the Trump Taj Mahal, Mark Ettis Arena in Atlantic City, NJ, before two sellout crowds totalling 9,700.
May [11] ***Union*** debuts at its UK #7 peak.
[25] ***Union*** reaches US #15.
June [22] *Lift Me Up* peaks at US #86.
[28-30] The group plays at the Wembley Arena, Wembley, Middx, during the UK leg of its world tour.
July [2] ***Union*** is certified gold by the RIAA.
[15] Yes sells out Madison Square Garden, during the North American segment of the tour.
[23] Howe's first solo album in 11 years, ***Turbulence***, with help from Bruford and Billy Currie, is released in the US on the Relativity label.
Sept [30] ***Yesstory***, an abbreviated release of a comprehensive CD boxed set, is released.

1992

July Yes is signed to a new recording deal with JVC's record division, Victory Music, by Phil Carson, who has worked at record labels with the group since their inception in 1969.

1993

Sept ***Symphonic Music Of Yes***, featuring Anderson, Bruford and Howe, is released in the US, on RCA Records.

1994

Apr [2] ***Talk***, the new Yes album, with reunited Yes line-up comprising Anderson, Rabin, Squire, Kaye and White, reaches UK #20 in its week of entry.
[9] ***Talk*** debuts at its US #33 peak.
June [2] A US tour opens in Binghamton, NY, set to end on September 10th at New York's Madison Square Garden.
Nov Compton's New Media releases the interactive CD-ROM ***Yes : Active***. (During the year, Anderson will also have two solo projects released, ***Change We Must*** by EMI and the new-age phrased ***Deseo*** on Windham Hill.)
see also: **KING CRIMSON, THE MOODY BLUES**

DWIGHT YOAKAM

1978

Weaned on the honky-tonk country music of the Buck Owens era, Yoakam (b. Oct. 23, 1956, Pikeville, KY), having begun playing as a teenager in southern Ohio (where he will study history and philosophy at Ohio University), has tried, unsuccessfully, to settle into the Nashville, TN-country scene in the mid-'70s, and now relocates to Los Angeles, CA, where, as a roots country singer/songwriter/guitarist, he begins playing local club dates, opening for the likes of Los Lobos, while working days as a truck driver, also working on a loading dock and delivering packages. Short recording contracts, first with Oak Records and then Enigma, will fail to garner commercial success. Rarely seen sans a cowboy hat as a performer, he buys his first one, a buff-colored number, for $75 from Manuel's in Hollywood.

1986

Mar [1] Having recorded an independently-released EP two years earlier, comprising *Ring Of Fire*, *Miner's Prayer*, *It Won't Hurt* and *South Of Cincinnati*) and resisted a return to country's Nashville headquarters (a conscious effort which will see him regarded as a long-term genre outsider), and newly signed to the re-activated Reprise Records, Yoakam enters the US Country chart with a cover of Johnny Horton's *Honky Tonk Man* which will hit #3.
Apr [19] His largely self-penned label debut album ***Guitars, Cadillacs, Etc., Etc.***, produced by Pete Anderson and showcasing his earnest honky-tonk country leanings (which he dubs "California Honky Tonk"), which will also attract a non-country audience, particularly in the UK, enters the US chart on its way to #61, and will become his first platinum sales disc.
May ***Guitars, Cadillacs, Etc., Etc.*** makes UK #51.

1987

Feb [24] Yoakam sings *Guitar, Cadillacs* at the 29th Grammy Awards held at the Shrine Auditorium, Los Angeles.
July His sophomore album, ***Hillbilly Deluxe***, peaks at US #55 and confirms Yoakam's position, along with Randy Travis, as a pioneer of the burgeoning "new country" scene. With a cover sleeve once again depicting the permanently Stetsoned artist in a country-stud pose, the album, again helmed by Anderson, has been recorded in Los Angeles, as Yoakam continues to shun Nashville.
Oct [21] ***Hillbilly Deluxe*** is certified gold by the RIAA.

1988

Sept ***Buenas Noches From A Lonely Room*** peaks at US #68 having made UK #87 on Aug [13].
Oct [15] *Streets Of Bakersfield*, a duet with childhood hero, Buck Owens, becomes Yoakam's first US Country chart-topper, and leads to them performing concerts together. (The cut will also win a **Music City News** Country Award for Best Vocal Collaboration, the following year. Still ignored by Nashville's country establishment, it is only Yoakam's second country trophy (the first being voted Top New Male Artist by the Academy of Country Music in 1986). By contrast, his contemporary, Randy Travis, has already accepted over 20 prestigious awards, during the same period.)

1989

Jan *I Sand Dixie* is his second US Country chart-topper, and his eighth Top 10 success on the specialist survey.
[4] ***Buenas Noches From A Lonely Room*** is certified gold by the RIAA.
Feb [22] Yoakam sings *You Don't Know Me, But You Don't Like Me* with Buck Owens at the 31st Grammy Awards, staged at the Shrine Auditorium.
May [10] ***Guitars, Cadillacs, Etc., Etc.*** is certified gold by the RIAA.
Nov ***Just Lookin' For A Hit*** makes US #68.

1990

Nov [17] Still produced by Anderson, the rockier-edged ***If There Was A Way***, featuring Patty Loveless among its guests, begins a 75-week US chart stay, during which it will make #96 (May [25] 1991), and will nab his second platinum sales award.
[30] Yoakam guests on NBC-TV's "Late Night With David Letterman".

1991

May [18] ***Deadicated***, a collection of Grateful Dead covers to which Yoakam has contributed *Truckin'*, reaches US #24.
June [14] Yoakam plays before a sellout crowd of 53,597, supporting the Grateful Dead, at Robert F. Kennedy Stadium, Washington, DC.
Dec [14] He makes a guest appearance on CBS-TV's "P.S. I Luv You".

1992

May [16] Yoakam performs at the Gene Autry Western Heritage Museum in Los Angeles, CA, as part of a tribute, hosted by Dennis Weaver, to singing cowboys and cowgirls.
Sept [26] The ***Honeymoon In Vegas*** soundtrack, to which Yoakam has contributed his version of *Suspicious Minds*, reaches US #18.
[27] Yoakam performs a rare European date at London's Hammersmith Odeon, as part of a promotional visit to plug his Europe-only compilation release, ***La Croix de L'Amour***, which also includes four previously unreleased cuts.
Oct [26] The TNN cable web airs "Hats Off To Minnie - America Honors Minnie Pearl", with Yoakam one of the featured contributors.

1993

Jan [6] ***If There Was A Way*** is certified platinum by the RIAA.
Mar [26] Yoakam guests on NBC-TV's "The Tonight Show".
Apr [2] He makes his acting debut with Sally Kirkland at the MET Theater in Los Angeles in Joseph G. Tidwell III's play "Southern Rapture", directed by Peter Fonda.
[24] Yoakam takes part in "Farm Aid VI" in Ames, IA, as his sixth album, the Anderson-helmed ***This Time***, reaches US #25.
May [13] He guests on "Late Night With David Letterman".
[14-15] Yoakam embarks on a US tour, his first in four years, at Holiday Star Theatre, Merrillville, IN.
Sept [29] He performs on CBS-TV's "27th Annual Country Music Association Awards".

1994

Jan [1] *Fast As You* peaks at US #70.
Mar [1] Yoakam wins the Best Male Vocal, Country category for *Ain't That Lonely Yet* at the 36th annual Grammy Awards, held at New York's Radio City Music Hall.
Apr [9] Yoakam guests on NBC-TV's "Saturday Night Live".
[12] ***Hillbilly Deluxe*** is certified platinum by the RIAA.
Aug [31] The RIAA also confirms two million sales of ***This Time***.
Oct [8] Yoakam sings *Mystery Train* at "Elvis Aaron Presley : The Tribute", an all-star music event at the Pyramid Arena, Memphis, TN, broadcast live on pay-per-view TV in the US.
Nov [16] His 1989 album ***Just Lookin' For A Hit*** is certified platinum by the RIAA.

1995

June [10] Performance set ***Dwight Live*** enters at its US #56 high.
Nov [18] Still helmed by his longterm collaborator Anderson, ***Gone*** debuts at its US #30 peak.
Feb [1] Yoakam makes a return visit to "Late Show With David Letterman".

1996

Feb [28] An event favorite, he performs at the 38th annual Grammy Awards, held at the Shrine Auditorium, prior to setting off on a world tour beginning in Japan, scheduled to reach the US in May.
July [5] Yoakam plays a home-state gig at the Freedom Hall, Louisville, during his four-month US summer tour.

NEIL YOUNG

1965

Having spent three years performing on the Canadian and border folk club circuit, as the Shadows-influenced Neil Young & the Squires which has released its first single *The Sultan/Aurora* in September 1963, during which time he met fellow musician, Stephen Stills, Young (b. Nov. 12, 1945, Toronto, ON, Canada), who grew up in Winnipeg, MB, Canada, and played in a number of high-school combos, including the Classics, the Stardusters and the Jades, drives to Los Angeles, CA in his 1953 Pontiac hearse, to link with Stills. This follows a one-disc stint with Detroit, MI band, the Mynah Birds, a pop/soul outfit which folded when lead singer Ricky James Matthews (later known as Rick James) was arrested for draft evasion. The band's bassist, Bruce Palmer, accompanies Young on his relocation to the Golden State, which will result in their joining Buffalo Springfield, formed by Stills with Richie Furay and Dewey Martin in March 1966.

1969

Jan After Buffalo Springfield has played its final gig in Long Beach, CA on May 5th the previous year, Young has signed with Joni Mitchell's manager Elliot Roberts and inked a recording deal with Reprise Records as a solo artist, and now releases his freshman album, the orchestral-based ***Neil Young***, with session help from Jack Nitzsche and Ry Cooder.
May With a hastily-formed backing band, Crazy Horse (Danny Whitten on guitar, Ralph Molina on drums, Billy Talbot on bass and producer/arranger Nitzsche), Young releases the follow-up, ***Everybody Knows This Is Nowhere***, which showcases his guitar skills, and begins a long climb to US #34.
July [25] Young plays his first concert with Crosby, Stills & Nash at New York's Fillmore East. He is asked to join the trio, initially for live work (but will record with them periodically over the next 20 years).

1970

Mar CSN&Y release their debut, ***Déjà Vu***, which will become the year's best-selling US album, and confirm each member as a rock superstar.
July [25] *Cinnamon Girl*, by Young and Crazy Horse, rises to US #55, in the wake of CSN&Y's popularity. Young is working on the soundtrack to the movie "Landlord", and is also having a studio installed underneath his Topanga Canyon, CA home. He pens *Ohio* for CSN&Y, inspired by the recent Kent State University killings.
Sept Although continuing to tour with CSN&Y, Young releases the self-penned solo album, ***After The Goldrush***, which hits US #8 and UK #7. The Young/David Briggs/Kendall Pacios set features Crazy Horse members, as well as Nils Lofgren and Stills, and firmly establishes the singer/guitarist as a major critical and commercial success in his own right (eventually going double platinum in the US).
Dec [12] *Only Love Can Break Your Heart* reaches US #33.

1971

Jan [6] Young returns to Canada to perform at the Queen Elizabeth Theatre, Vancouver, BC.
Apr [10] *When You Dance I Can Really Love* peaks at US #93.
Aug Young, still touring with CSN&Y, begins work on scoring music for his movie "Journey Through The Past." He also splits from wife, Susan, and begins a relationship with the actress, Carrie Snodgress.

1972

Mar [11] His fourth solo album, ***Harvest***, hits US #1 for the first of two weeks, and tops the UK chart in the same week. An acoustic set, well received by critics and consumers alike, it includes the global hit, *Heart Of Gold*, the anti-redneck warning *Southern Man* (which will prompt Lynyrd Skynyrd to respond with *Sweet Home Alabama*), and the London Symphony Orchestra-backed ballad *A Man Needs A Maid*, written about Snodgress. The album, variously co-produced with Elliot Mazer, Henry Lewy and Nitzsche, also features Crosby and Nash, and will remain a strong catalog item, eventually logging over three million US sales.
[18] The easy-paced harmony-filled *Heart Of Gold*, featuring Linda Ronstadt and James Taylor on backing vocals, tops the US chart for the first of three weeks, and will prove to be his most enduring radio success. It also hits UK #10.
Apr [21] *Heart Of Gold* is certified gold by the RIAA.
June [3] *Old Man* reaches US #31.
July [29] In a one-off union with Graham Nash, *War Song* peaks at US #61.
Nov Double album, ***Journey Through The Past***, chronicling live recordings with Buffalo Springfield, CSN&Y, the Stray Gators and Crazy Horse, is released, and will make US #45, the only new song being side four's *Soldier*.
[18] Crazy Horse guitarist, 29-year-old Whitten, dies from a heroin overdose.

1973

Jan [5] Young begins a three-month, 65-city US tour with the Stray Gators.
[23] He stops in the middle of a New York concert, to announce that an accord had been reached for Vietnam peace.
Mar The band plays a sold-out date at New York's Carnegie Hall.
Apr [8] His autobiographical documentary film, "Journey Through The Past", premieres to mixed reactions at the "American Film Festival" in Dallas, TX.
Aug [20] Young begins recording the tracks for his future ***Tonight's The Night*** with the new Crazy Horse line-up of Molina, Talbot, Lofgren and Ben Keith.
Sept [20] Young & Crazy Horse open the first of four nights at Los Angeles' Roxy Theater.
Oct ***Time Fades Away***, featuring further collaboration with guests David Crosby and Graham Nash, begins a rise to US #22 and UK #20.

Nov [3] Young embarks on a UK tour at the Palace Theatre, Manchester, Gtr. Manchester, set to end on the 10th at London's Royal Festival Hall, with support act the Eagles.
Dec [7] ***Time Fades Away*** is confirmed gold by the RIAA.

1974

June Young is persuaded to reunite with CS&N to embark on a major US tour, which will gross $8 million.
Aug [3] CSN&Y top the bill, comprising the Beach Boys, Joe Walsh, Jesse Colin Young and the Band, in their last '70s gig together.
[17] *Walk On* peaks at US #69, as its parent album, ***On The Beach***, described by **Rolling Stone** as among the "most despairing albums of the decade", is released, reaching US #16 and UK #42, including the subsequently Young-favored nine-minute *Ambulance Blues*.
Sept [23] ***On The Beach*** is confirmed gold by the RIAA.

1975

Mar [23] Young performs an all-star benefit concert (SNACK - Students Need Athletics Culture & Kicks) at San Francisco's Kezar Stadium to raise funds to make up the shortfall in the city's school system budget. A 60,000 crowd contributes $200,000.
July Dedicated to Danny Whitten, and late CSN&Y roadie, Bruce Berry, ***Tonight's The Night*** is issued. Recorded "live" in the studio, with no overdubbing, it will reach US #25 and UK #48.
Oct [13] Young undergoes a successful throat operation.
Dec Young's ***Zuma*** reaches UK #44 and US #25. Its closing song unites CSN&Y on *Through My Sails*.

1976

May [3] Young performs in Nagoya, Japan during Far Eastern dates.
Oct Young has teamed with Stills to release ***Long May You Run***, reaching US #26 and UK #12. With five Young songs, and four by Stills, they are backed by the Stills-Young band: Joe Lala, Jerry Aiello, George Perry and Joe Vitale.
Nov [25] Young takes part in the Band's farewell, "The Last Waltz" Thanksgiving Day concert, at San Francisco's Winterland, singing *Helpless* with Joni Mitchell, and joining an all-star cast on *I Shall Be Released*, directly after concluding a six-week US tour.

1977

Jan [12] The RIAA confirms gold sales for ***Long May You Run***.
July ***American Stars'n'Bars*** reaches US #21 and UK #17. It includes unissued studio tracks from the past three years, and vocal spots by Emmylou Harris, Linda Ronstadt and Nicolette Larson.
Oct [11] ***American Stars'n'Bars*** is certified gold by the RIAA.
Nov [11-13] Young celebrates his 32nd birthday performing with the 24-piece Gone With The Wind band, at the "Miami Music Festival Of The Arts" in Miami, FL, in front of 125,000 people.
Dec Three-disc retrospective, ***Decade***, makes US #43 and UK #46, selecting Young's work from Buffalo Springfield, CSN&Y and solo material. (It will earn a platinum disc in the US on December 22nd, 1986 a rare achievement for a triple album.)

1978

Oct As the largely acoustic, pastoral-themed ***Comes A Time***, produced with help from David Briggs, Ben Keith and Tim Mulligan, hits US #7 (earning gold status from the RIAA on the 11th) and UK #42, Young and Crazy Horse embark on a major "Rust Never Sleeps" tour. It has replaced the earlier project, "Human Highway", a live documentary film, including Cleveland-based new-wave act Devo, co-directed by Young and Dean Stockwell (under the name Bernard Shakey).
Nov He plays soldout dates at New York's Madison Square Garden.

1979

Mar [3] With a harmony vocal by Nicolette Larson, *Four Strong Winds*, written by Ian Tyson, peaks at US #61 and UK #57.
July [11] Young's concert film, "Rust Never Sleeps", premieres in Los Angeles. It is directed by Young, as Bernard Shakey, and is released simultaneously with the album, ***Rust Never Sleeps***, which will hit US #8 and UK #13. One side of the album is electric, the other features acoustic numbers, all backed by the latest Crazy Horse line-up, Lofgren (guitar), Keith (pedal steel and keyboards), Bruce Palmer (bass), Molina (drums) and Joe Lala (percussion).
Nov [3] The title cut, *Rust Never Sleeps (Hey, Hey, My My (Into The Black))*, including a lyrical reference to Johnny Rotten, peaks at US #79.
Dec Live double set, ***Live Rust***, reaches US #15 (securing another platinum award) and UK #55, as New York magazine **The Village Voice** names Young "Artist of the Decade".

1980

Feb [7] The RIAA confirms platinum sales for ***Rust Never Sleeps***.
Nov Dispensing with Crazy Horse and recruiting top session help, including Levon Helm, Young's ***Hawks And Doves*** reaches US #30 and UK #34.

1981

Nov In an unpredictable R&B groove, Young's 17th album, ***Re-ac-tor***, reaches US #27 and UK #69, and is his last for Reprise label.

1982

Jan [16] *Southern Pacific* peaks at US #70 as "Human Highway", Young's latest movie project, starring Dean Stockwell, Russ Tamblyn and Devo, premieres.
Apr [9] Young performs on a bill with Jethro Tull, the Michael Schenker Group, King Crimson, Melanie and others at the fifth "Golden Summernight Concert" held in Wiesbaden, Rheinwiesen, West Germany.
Aug Young and Crazy Horse begin European and Australian tours.

1983

Jan ***Trans***, his first set for Geffen Records, a techno-pop effort recorded in Hawaii, reaches US #19 and UK #29.
Feb [12] *Little Thing Called Love* peaks at US #71.
Mar [4] Young collapses from exhaustion during his current US tour.
Sept An unexpected rockabilly outing, ***Everybody's Rockin'***, credited to Neil Young & the Shocking Pinks, makes US #46 and UK #50.
Dec The David Geffen Co. seeks $3 million in punitive and exemplary damages, plus compensation, from Young, in a Los Angeles Superior Court. The suit alleges that Young provided albums "which were not commercial in nature, and musically uncharacteristic of Young's previous records".

1985

July [13] Young performs at the JFK Stadium, Philadelphia, PA end of the "Live Aid" benefit spectacular.
Sept ***Old Ways***, a country-inflected set, makes US #75 and UK #39.

1986

Aug Uncompromisingly hard-edged rocking opus, ***Landing On Water***, makes US #46 and UK #52, as his genre travels continue, much to Geffen's dissatisfaction.
Oct [13] The RIAA confirms two million sales for ***After The Gold Rush*** and a million sales for ***Everybody Knows This Is Nowhere***.
Dec [22] ***Decade*** is certified platinum by the RIAA.

1987

July Credited to Young & Crazy Horse, co-produced with veteran collaborators, Briggs and Nitzsche, ***Life*** peaks at US #75 and UK #71.
Sept [19] Young participates in the "Farm Aid II" benefit, with John Cougar Mellencamp, Joe Walsh, Lou Reed and others, at the University of Nebraska's Memorial Stadium.

1988

Feb [17] ***Live Rust*** is confirmed platinum by the RIAA.
May Dropped by a despairing Geffen, and newly signed to the re-activated Reprise label, Young's ***This Note's For You***, recorded with the nine-piece Bluenotes, makes US #61 and UK #56.
July [7] The accompanying video for the corporate sponsorship-attacking title cut, *This Note's For You*, featuring a Michael Jackson-lookalike with hair on fire (referencing Jackson's Pepsi commercial accident), is initially banned on MTV. Young declares the decision "spineless".
Nov After a 14-year gap, Young reunites with CS&N to record ***American Dream***, which will reach US #16 in 1989.

1989

Mar A various artists album, ***The Bridge : A Tribute To Neil Young***, an album of Neil Young songs with a portion of the proceeds going to the Bridge School, a San Franciscan special-education facility, is released.
Aug At the end of a set at the Greek Theatre, Los Angeles, Young is joined by Crosby and Nash, to perform *Ohio*.
Sept [6] In an extraordinary reversal, "This Note's For You" is named Best Video Of The Year, at the sixth annual MTV Video Music Awards ceremony, staged at the Universal Amphitheatre, Universal City, CA.
[30] Young performs *Rockin' In The Free World* on NBC-TV's "Saturday Night Live".
Oct The critically-revered ***Freedom***, co-produced with Niko Bolas, and including three cuts issued earlier in the year on the Japanese-only five-track mini-album, ***Eldorado***, reaches US #35.

1990

Feb [21] ***Freedom*** is confirmed gold by the RIAA.
Mar [8] ***Freedom*** is named the **Rolling Stone** 1989 Critics' Choice for Best Album.
Apr [16] Young participates in the "Nelson Mandela - An International Tribute To A Free South Africa" concert at Wembley Stadium, Wembley, Middx.
Oct [6] The rock-fired ***Ragged Glory***, featuring Crazy Horse, makes US #31 and UK #15.
[26] Young is joined by Elvis Costello, Jackson Browne, Edie Brickell, Chris Isaak and Steve Miller at his fourth annual Bridge School benefit, held at the Shoreline Amphitheatre, Mountain View, CA.

1991

Jan [22] His "Ragged Glory" world tour, with support acts Sonic Youth and Social Distortion, opens to a sellout crowd of 12,505 at the Target Center, Minneapolis, MN.
Apr [1-3] Young's concerts at the San Diego and Los Angeles Sports Arenas are postponed when Young suffers an ear infection. (Later in the year, drunken fans protest at New York's Beacon Theatre, wishing to hear his earlier classic material, while Young insists on playing new songs.)
Nov [2] ***Weld***, a three-disc set including the 35-minute *Arc*, debuts at its UK #20 peak.
[3] Young joins the Grateful Dead on Bob Dylan's *Forever Young*, at a tribute concert for the late Bill Graham, in San Francisco, CA.
[9] ***Weld*** bows at its US #154 peak, Young's first album in 22 years not to crack the US Top 100.

1992

Jan [15] Young inducts the Jimi Hendrix Experience into the Rock and Roll Hall of Fame, at the seventh annual dinner, held at New York's Waldorf Astoria Hotel.

Feb [13-15, 17-19] He performs six sellout shows at New York's Beacon Theatre, grossing $500,040.
Mar [14] Young takes part in "Farm Aid V", at the Texas Stadium, Irving, TX.
July He belatedly receives his school diploma from Lakehead University, Ontario, Canada.
Sept [15] Young continues his US tour, playing to an SRO crowd at the Red Rocks Amphitheatre, Morrison, CO.
Oct [16] He sings *Just Like Tom Thumb's Blues* and *All Along The Watchtower* at the Bob Dylan 30th anniversary celebration, from New York's Madison Square Garden.
Nov [1] Young's sixth annual Bridge School benefit, with Elton John, Sammy Hagar, James Taylor and Pearl Jam, at the Shoreline Amphitheatre, grosses $434,210 from its 20,000 sellout crowd.
[14] 20 years after the release of ***Harvest***, Young has recorded its sequel, ***Harvest Moon***. Co-produced with Ben Keith, and written and recorded in similar style to the earlier ground-breaking set, it debuts at its US #16 and UK #9 peak.
[21-22] Still touring, Young plays to a combined sellout crowd of 5,614, at the Orpheum Theatre, Minneapolis, MN.
Dec [5] Young guests on NBC-TV's "Saturday Night Live".

1993

Jan [23] ***Lucky Thirteen***, a one-hour retrospective from Young's five-album experimental efforts while at Geffen, including a live version of *This Note's For You*, charts for a week at UK #69.
Feb [27] *Harvest Moon* debuts at its UK #36 peak.
Mar [1] Young plays a solo set at the Los Angeles Children's Health Project benefit, at the Dorothy Chandler Pavilion, during which he also backs Simon & Garfunkel on electric guitar for *Sounds Of Silence*, in addition to contributing backing vocals, along with actor, Steve Martin.
[8] ***Harvest Moon*** is named Outstanding Album at the 1993 Bay Area Music Awards, at the Bill Graham Civic Auditorium, San Francisco.
May [22] He guests on CBS-TV's "Willie Nelson The Big Six-O" birthday celebrations.
June [26] ***Unplugged***, from his MTV "Unplugged" showcase earlier in the year, the third Young title to be issued in eight months, including an emotive reading of his 1972 song, *Needle And The Damage Done*, debuts at its UK #4 peak, and will do likewise at US #23 on July [3].
July [3-4] He performs at the Torhout and Wechter festivals in Belgium on successive days, before returning to the US to embark on a tour, which will see him backed by Booker T. & the MG's.
[17] *The Needle And The Damage Done* charts for a week at UK #75.
Sept [2] He performs *Rockin' In The Free World* with Pearl Jam at the tenth annual MTV Video Music Awards held at the Universal Amphitheatre, Universal City, CA.
Oct [30] *Long May You Run (Live)* charts for a week at UK #71.
Nov [5] At his seventh annual Bridge School benefit held at the Shoreline Theater, Mountain View, CA, Young performs *Rockin' In The Free World* with the entire bill to close the show.
[16] The RIAA confirms gold status for ***Unplugged***.

1994

Jan [22] The film soundtrack to "Philadelphia" including Young's haunting ballad, *Philadelphia* enters the US chart set to reach #12.
Mar [20] ***Harvest Moon*** is named album of the year at the 23rd annual Juno Awards held at Toronto's O'Keefe Centre.
[21] Young performs the nominated *Philadelphia* at the 66th annual Academy Awards held at Los Angeles' Dorothy Chandler Pavilion, losing out to soundtrack-mate Bruce Springsteen's *Streets Of Philadelphia* for Best Song From A Motion Picture.
Apr [5] Nirvana's lead singer Kurt Cobain shoots himself in his Seattle, WA, garage apartment. A suicide note found when the body is discovered three days later quotes Young's *My My, Hey Hey (Out Of The Blue)* - "It's better to burn out than fade away".
[9] *Philadelphia* debuts at its UK #62 peak.
June [27] ***Harvest Moon*** is certified for four million sales by the RIAA.
Aug [27] Its title track written about Cobain's death, ***Sleeps With Angels*** debuts at UK #2, behind ♀'s ***Come***.
Sept [3] ***Sleeps With Angels***, released with no promotion or accompanying tour, debuts at its US #9 peak.
Oct [20] He jams with Springsteen backing Bob Dylan at the latter's concert at the Roseland Ballroom, New York, on an encore of *Highway 61 Revisited*.

1995

Jan [12] Eddie Vedder inducts Young into the Rock And Roll Hall Of Fame at the tenth annual dinner held at New York's Waldorf Astoria Hotel, singing *Fuckin' Up* together at the perfunctory after dinner jam, with Young also performing *Act Of Love* backed by Crazy Horse.
[14-15] Young performs at two Pearl Jam-headlining Voters For Choice benefits held at Constitution Hall, Washington, DC.
Feb [6] He joins Pearl Jam on stage in Seattle performing *Peace And Love*.
July [8] Recorded in Seattle, WA, in February, ***Mirror Ball***, a collaborative effort by Young backed by Pearl Jam who back him on nine of the 11 Young compositions, enters the UK chart at its #4 peak.
[15] ***Mirror Ball*** bows at its US #5 peak.
Aug [8] Young's 13-year old film "Human Highway" is finally released on home video (and laserdisc) in the US.
[27] Young performs at the annual "Reading Festival", Reading, Berks.
Sept Young and his longtime manager Elliot Roberts form Vapor Records to release music of their own choosing (Jonathan Richman will reportedly be its first signing), while Young has also recently bought a 30% interest in Linotech, a division of Lionel Trains.
[12] The RIAA confirms gold sales for ***Mirror Ball***.
Oct [1] Young makes his annual appearance at Farm Aid (VIII) held at the Cardinal Stadium, Kentucky Fair & Expo, Louisville, KY, also featuring Hootie & the Blowfish, Dave Matthews Band and founder Willie Nelson among others.
[28] He hosts the ninth annual Bridge Benefit at the Shoreline Amphitheatre, featuring Springsteen, Hootie, the Pretenders, Beck, Blind Melon, Emmylou Harris and Daniel Lanois.

1996

Feb [13] The soundtrack to "Dead Men Walking", featuring Young's music and William Blake poetry read by Johnny Depp, becomes the first release on Young's Vapor label.
June [20] Young begins a tour of Europe at the Hallenstadion, Zurich, Switzerland.
July [19] He tops the bill on the second day of "The Phoenix 1996" festival at Long Marston, Stratford-upon-Avon, Warks.
see also: **BUFFALO SPRINGFIELD, CROSBY STILLS NASH & YOUNG**

PAUL YOUNG

1979

Sept While serving an apprenticeship at a Vauxhall car plant, Young (b. Jan. 17, 1956, Luton, Beds.), having been encouraged by his parents, Doris and Tony, to play piano at school (at the age of 14 changing to learn the bass), has played in two local bands, one of which is the locally-popular Kat Kool & the Kool Kats. The vocalist now forms the rock group, Streetband, with Roger Kelly, John Gifford, Mick Pearl and Vince Chaulk (from Mr. Big), which signs to Logo Records and will reach UK #18 with the novelty, Chaz Jankel-produced hit, *Toast* (actually the B-side of *Hold On*) in November the following year. After releasing two albums (***London*** and ***Dilemna***), the Streetband now splits, with Young taking Gifford and Pearl on to form the eight-piece Q Tips, devoted to performing '60s influenced R&B, led by his natural blue-eyed soul vocal.

1980

Jan Gaining a strong reputation as a live combo, the Q Tips open for US band, the Knack, at London's Dominion Theatre.
May After releasing *SYSLJFM (The Letter Song)* on the Shotgun label, the group signs to Chrysalis.
Aug [30] ***Q Tips*** charts for a week at UK #50. (This will be band's only chart appearance, despite a string of covers including *Tears Of A Clown* and *Love Hurts*.)

1982

Sept After playing over 700 gigs in two years, the band quits, following the release of ***Live At Last***. Young signs a solo deal with CBS/Columbia.
Nov His debut single, *Iron Out The Rough Spots*, is released, as a production association with Laurie Latham is established.

1983

Jan He releases an unsuccessful cover of Nicky Thomas' hit, *Love Of The Common People*, and assembles a backing group called the Royal Family, with ex-Q Tips and songwriting partner, Ian Kewley (keyboards), Mark Pinder (drums), Pino Palladino (bass), Steve Bolton (guitar) and backing vocalists Maz and Kim (nicknamed the Fabulous Wealthy Tarts).
July [23] His cover of Marvin Gaye's *Wherever I Lay My Hat (That's My Home)*, having been nominated **New Musical Express**' Single Of The Week, tops the UK chart for the first of three weeks.
Sept [17] His debut album, ***No Parlez***, featuring his first three singles and covers, including Joy Division's *Love Will Tear Us Apart*, also hits UK #1, as Young begins his first headlining solo UK tour with the Royal Family.
Oct *Come Back And Stay* hits UK #4.
[29] *Wherever I Lay My Hat (That's My Home)* makes US #70.
Nov *Love Of The Common People* is re-released, now hitting UK #2.

1984

Jan He completes an eight-city US tour.
Feb [21] Young is named Best British Newcomer, at the third annual BRIT Awards, at London's Grosvenor House Hotel.
Mar [17] He takes part in the second annual "Prince's Trust Rock Gala", at London's Royal Albert Hall.
Apr ***No Parlez*** makes US #79.
[7] The extracted *Come Back And Stay* reaches US #22.
June [30] *Love Of The Common People* makes US #45. Non-stop touring takes in Australia and Japan, as ***No Parlez*** heads towards world sales of seven million.
July ***No Parlez*** achieves triple-platinum status in UK.
Aug Young's voice goes for a second time, and a two-month rest is ordered. An early retrospective, ***Streetband Featuring Paul Young***, is released on Cambra Records.
Sept The Fabulous Wealthy Tarts leave the Royal Family, as does guitarist Bolton. A new singing soul trio is added to the backing group: George Chandler, Tony Jackson and Jimmy Chambers.
Nov A UK tour begins as his cover of Ann Peebles' *I'm Gonna Tear Your Playhouse Down* hits UK #9.
[25] Young contributes a lead vocal line to Band Aid's historic recording of *Do They Know Its Christmas?*, at the SARM Studios, Notting Hill, London.
Dec *Everything Must Change* is his first self-penned hit (with Kewley) at UK #9.

1985

Feb [11] Young wins the Best British Male Artist category at the fourth annual BRIT Awards, staged at London's Grosvenor House Hotel.
Mar *Every Time You Go Away* hits UK #4.

Apr [6] His sophomore album, ***The Secret Of Association***, again helmed by Latham, and including covers of Tom Waits' *Soldier's Things* and Billy Bragg's *Man In The Iron Mask*, hits UK #1, and will climb to US #19.
July [27] Young's cover of Hall & Oates' *Every Time You Go Away* tops the US chart for one week. *Tomb Of Memories* makes UK #16, as he prepares for a six-month world tour.
[13] Young duets with Alison Moyet, singing *That's The Way Love Is*, at the "Live Aid" benefit concert at Wembley Stadium, Wembley, Middx.
Aug [13] ***The Secret Of Association*** is certified gold by the RIAA.
Nov [2] *I'm Gonna Tear Your Playhouse Down* peaks at US #13.

1986

Jan [11] *Everything Must Change* peaks at US #56.
Feb [10] Young wins the Best British Music Video category for "Every Time You Go Away", at the fifth annual BRIT Awards, held at the Grosvenor House Hotel.
June [20] Young participates in the fourth annual "Prince's Trust Rock Gala" at the Wembley Arena, with Paul McCartney, Elton John, Tina Turner and Phil Collins.
Oct Increasingly concentrating on his own compositions, *Wonderland*, from a forthcoming album, peaks at UK #24.
Nov ***Between Two Fires***, produced by Young, Kewley and Hugh Padgham, hits UK #4, and peaks at US #77, with the extracted *Some People* making UK #56.
Dec [13] *Some People* peaks at US #65.

1987

Feb Young moves to Jersey for tax purposes, as a third extract from ***Between Two Fires***, *Why Does A Man Have To Be Strong*, reaches UK #63, and heralds an 18-month period of relative inactivity, Young devoting much of his time to his young daughter, who he names Levi, after the Four Tops' lead singer.
June [5] Young takes part in the fifth annual "Prince's Trust Rock Gala", at Wembley Arena, duetting with Phil Collins on *You've Lost That Lovin' Feelin'*.

1988

June [11] He sings a cover of Crowded House's hit, *Don't Dream It's Over*, at "Nelson Mandela's 70th Birthday Tribute" at Wembley Stadium.

1990

Jan [17] *Everytime You Go Away* is finally certified gold by the RIAA.
May His revival of the Congregation's 1971 UK #4, *Softly Whispering I Love You*, reaches UK #21.
June His fourth solo album, ***Other Voices***, comprising only cover versions, and variously produced by Warne Livesey, Martin Page, Nile Rodgers, Pete Wingfield and Peter Wolf, hits UK #4 and will make US #142 on Sept [15].
July *Oh Girl*, reviving the Chi-Lites 1972 classic, reaches UK #25.
Sept [4] Young guests on NBC-TV's "The Tonight Show".
Oct [6] *Oh Girl* returns Young to US prominence, hitting #8, as MC Hammer's re-make of another Chi-Lites' classic, *Have You Seen Her?*, is also charting. *Heaven Can Wait* peaks at UK #71.
Nov [21] He performs at the National Arts Centre, Ottawa, ON, Canada, to end his latest North American tour.
[28] Young begins a 15-date UK series at City Hall, Sheffield, S. Yorks., set to end on the 17th at London's Town & Country club.

1991

Jan [12] *Calling You* debuts at its UK #57 peak.
May [11] Zucchero's *Senza Una Donna (Without A Woman)*, with Young on vocals, hits UK #4.
Aug [10] *Both Sides Now*, pairing Young with Irish group, Clannad, and featured in the movie "Switch", charts for a week at UK #74.
Sept [14] CBS hit retrospective, ***From Time To Time - The Singles Collection***, enters at UK #1.
Nov [2] *Don't Dream It's Over*, covering Crowded House's original, reaches UK #20.
Dec [19-20] Young plays two dates at London's Hammersmith Odeon.

1992

Mar [21] His update of Jimmy Ruffin's 1966 soul smash, *What Becomes Of The Brokenhearted*, from the movie "Fried Green Tomatoes", reaches US #22.
Apr [20] Young joins Queen on *Radio Ga Ga* at the Freddie Mercury tribute "A Concert For Life" at Wembley Stadium.

1993

Jan Young works on a new album with early production collaborator Laurie Latham, at The Hit Factory.
Oct [9] *Now I Know What Made Otis Blue* reaches UK #14.
[23] Largely produced by Don Was and featuring top-drawer US session players including Jeff Porcaro playing on one his last albums before his death, ***The Crossing***, dedicated to him, debuts at its UK #23 peak. (It will not be released in the US.)
Dec [4] Having recently contributed *I'm Your Puppet* to Elton John's ***Duets*** album, Young now makes UK #42 with *Hope In A Hopeless World*, written by Bob Thiele and Phil Roy.

1994

Apr [30] *It Will Be You*, again penned by Thiele and Roy, reaches UK #34.
Aug [28] Young performs at the "Whitbread Hop Farm Summer Music Festival".
Nov [26] Comprising Young's interpretations of 15 classic soul songs, ***Reflections*** makes UK #64. (During the month, Young participates in the recording of Music Relief's *What's Going On* benefit single to aid Rwandan refugees.)

THE YOUNG RASCALS

See: THE RASCALS

THE YOUNGBLOODS

Jesse Colin Young (guitar, bass, vocals);
Jerry Corbitt (guitar, vocals);
Banana (keyboards, guitars); **Joe Bauer** (drums)

1964

Young (b. Perry Miller, Nov. 11, 1944, New York, NY), is working as a folk singer in New York, when he meets singer/writer Bobby Scott, who helps him strike a one-off deal with Capitol Records to record the solo album, ***The Soul Of A City Boy***. Moving to Boston, MA, the following year, Young plays the club circuit, releasing his follow-up album, ***Youngblood***, on Mercury Records. He subsequently teams with Corbitt (b. Tifton, GA), to form the Youngbloods, signed to the same label for the release of *My Babe*, before Banana (b. Lowell Levinger III, 1946, Cambridge, MA), from the Trolls, and ex-jazz drummer Bauer (b. Sept. 26, 1941, Memphis, TN) round out the quartet.

1966

The group performs as the house band at New York's Café A-Go-Go, signing to RCA Records after Young has cleared his Mercury contract. (Mercury will release ***Two Trips***, made up of existing recordings, in 1970.)

1967

Feb [11] *Grizzly Bear*, taken from the group's eponymous debut RCA album, peaks at US #52.
Apr ***The Youngbloods***, including the group's trademark song, the era-defining, Dino Valenti-penned *Get Together*, peaks at US #131.
June [15-18] The band plays at the Avalon Ballroom, San Francisco, CA.
Oct [14] *Get Together* makes US #62, as ***Earth Music*** is released. Corbitt leaves for a solo career, and the group continues as a trio and moves to Marin County, CA.

1968

May [24-26] The Youngbloods play one of several stints at the Avalon Ballroom, San Francisco, during the year, with Hourglass and Kaleidoscope.
Sept [2] The group appears at the three-day "Sky River Rock Festival and Lighter-Than-Air Fair", in Sultan, WA, with Santana, the Grateful Dead, Muddy Waters and Country Joe & the Fish, among others, including Valenti as a soloist.

1969

Aug [31] The band participates in the "New Orleans Pop Festival", New Orleans, LA.
Sept [6] *Get Together*, reincarnated as the theme for the National Council of Christians and Jews, now becomes a major seller, hitting US #5. The group is scheduled to perform the song on NBC-TV's "Tonight" show, but walks off the set, unhappy with the technical arrangements. ***Elephant Mountain***, including the popular live numbers, *Darkness Darkness* and *Sunlight*, makes US #118.
Oct [7] *Get Together* is certified gold by the RIAA.

1970

Mar In the UK, where the Youngbloods have made no impact, *Get Together* is covered by the Dave Clark Five, as *Everybody Get Together*, and hits #8.
May [16] *Darkness, Darkness* peaks at US #86.
June The group signs to Warner Bros. in a new deal, which allows the formation of its own Raccoon imprint.
Oct RCA starts re-packaging the group's earlier work with ***The Best Of The Youngbloods***, which reaches US #144.
Nov Their first Raccoon album, ***Rock Festival***, a mixture of live and studio material, reaches US #80.

1971

Mar Michael Kane joins on bass, allowing Young to revert to guitar.
Aug ***Ride The Wind***, consisting of material recorded live in New York in 1969, reaches US #157. ***Sunlight***, another compilation of earlier RCA tracks, makes US #186.
Dec ***Good'n'Dusty***, consisting of oldies covers, reaches US #160.

1972

Apr Young's solo set, ***Together***, reaches US #157. Banana releases ***Mid Mountain Ranch*** (as Banana & the Bunch), while Bauer issues the experimental ***Moonset***. Bauer and Banana will team with Kane to form the band, Noggins, which will release ***Crab Tunes***. Young will produce solo albums for Michael Hurley. Among Corbitt's future production efforts will be Don McLean's debut, ***Tapestry***).
Dec The last group album, ***High On A Ridgetop***, peaks at US #185.

1973

Dec Young solo effort, ***Song For Juli***, makes US #51. It has been released on Warner Bros., following the dissolution of the Raccoon label.

1974

Feb A reissue of Young's 1964 album, ***The Soul Of A City Boy***, peaks at US #172. Though scoring no further chart singles, Young will have a consistently successful US solo chart career, with a string of hit albums: ***Light Shine*** (#37, June 1974); ***Songbird*** (#26, May 1975); ***On The Road*** (#34, May 1976); ***Love On The Wing*** (#64, April 1977); ***American Dreams*** (#165, December 1978).

1979

Sept [19-23] Young appears with Bruce Springsteen, Jackson Browne, the Doobie Brothers and others, in the anti-nuclear MUSE (Musicians United for Safe Energy) concerts at New York's Madison Square Garden (later documented on album and film as ***No Nukes***). (Banana will re-emerge in the short-lived Bandits, in 1984, before opening a hang-gliding store in the late '80s, while Young will re-record *Get Together* for the soundtrack to the film, "1969", in 1988, the year Bauer dies. Rhino Records in the US will bring Young's solo highlights to compact disc with the 1991 release, ***The Best Of Jesse Colin Young : The Solo Years***.)

FRANK ZAPPA

1956

Conversely influenced in his teens by doo-wop recordings of the '50s and the music of Stravinsky, Stockhausen and avant-garde classical composer, Edgar Varése, Zappa (b. Francis Vincent Zappa, Dec. 21, 1940, Baltimore, MD), having moved with his second-generation Sicilian Greek parents and three siblings to California in 1950, and begun to write songs and play drums and guitar in high school bands, meets Don Van Vliet (b. Jan. 15, 1941, Glendale, CA) (later known as Captain Beefheart) at Antelope Valley High School in Lancaster, CA, forming the Black-outs, which turns into Joe Perrino & the Mellotones, and then the R&B-based outfit, the Ramblers. Graduating in June 1958 by which time he is proficient on a number of instruments (though favoring the guitar), and following six-months of music study at the Chaffey College in Alta Loma, CA, Zappa begins to play with various bands gigging around the local bar circuit, before writing the soundtrack for the B-movie, "The World's Greatest Sinner", in 1960.

1962

Zappa and Ray Collins, a member of East Los Angeles' doo-wop group, Little Julian Herrera & the Tigers, write *Memories Of El Monte*, a tribute song to doo-wop, recorded by the Penguins. Released on Art Laboe's Original Sound label (for which Zappa currently undertakes regular work), it becomes a classic of the genre.

1963

The fees from another B-movie soundtrack score, the western, "Run Home Slow", enable Zappa to finance and establish his own Studio Z in Cucamonga, CA. It has already been equipped with specially-designed five-track recording equipment by Zappa's electronics-expert friend, Paul Buff. He continues to gig with local bands, including the Masters and the Soul Giants, which also record one-off singles at Studio Z.

1964

Studio Z is closed down after Zappa is detained and given a ten-day jail sentence in San Bernardino Prison (with three years probation). (He has been arrested after cutting, for a much-needed $100, a mock-pornographic tape for a vice squad officer posing as a used-car salesman.) He moves to Los Angeles, CA, and assembles a new group, the Muthers, from the remains of the Soul Giants, a lineup featuring himself on guitar and vocals, Collins (vocals), Roy Estrada (bass), Dave Coronada (saxophone) and Jimmy Carl Black (drums).

1965

The group is offered a management contract by Herb Cohen, and begins a residency at the Whisky A-Go-Go club in Los Angeles, its name amended to the Mothers, and finally extended to the Mothers Of Invention the following year, when the band is signed by producer Tom Wilson to MGM's jazz/R&B Verve label to record its debut album, ***Freak Out!***. Initially becoming a popular live draw on both coasts (and subsequently throughout the rest of the US and Europe), the Mothers Of Invention, distinguished by Zappa's ever-changing musical vision, biting lyrical satire and a flexible roster of musicians which will prove to be the training ground for a number of subsequently prominent solo performers, will release nine genre-switching US chart albums before Zappa disbands the ensemble at the end of the decade.

1968

June The largely instrumental, orchestrally-built sound collage, ***Lumpy Gravy***, the first album released under Zappa's own name (though the group is still an active unit), peaks at US #159.

1969

Apr The group compilation, ***Mothermania/The Best Of The Mothers***, makes US #151. Compiled by Zappa, it fulfills the band's contractual obligation to Verve. He launches his own Bizarre/Straight Records in partnership with manager Cohen, licensed to Warner Bros. (He will also begin producing a number of acts including Beefheart, the GTO's, Wild Man Fischer and Alice Cooper.)

May Zappa begins to lecture on the US college circuit, speaking in New York, Los Angeles and elsewhere, often on unlikely themes such as "Pigs, Ponies and Rock'n'Roll".

Aug [20] He disbands the Mothers Of Invention (whose line-up had recently included Lowell George) at the end of a short tour of Canada, reportedly "tired of playing for people who clap for all the wrong reasons" (and also because of the heavy expense of keeping the large aggregate on the road). He also moves back to Los Angeles and marries his second wife, Gail (who will be the mother of Zappa's sons, Dweezil and Ahmet Rodan, and daughters, Moon Unit and Diva).

Dec ***Hot Rats***, released under Zappa's own name on Bizarre, and featuring guest appearances by Beefheart and violinist, Jean-Luc Ponty among others, makes US #173.

1970

Mar ***Hot Rats*** hits UK #9, as the Mothers Of Invention's mostly-instrumental ***Burnt Weeny Sandwich*** reaches US #94 and UK #17.

May [11] A re-formed Mothers Of Invention, featuring Zappa and keyboardist Ian Underwood, with newcomers George Duke (keyboards), Jim Pons (bass) and Aynsley Dunbar (drums), with ex-Turtles Howard Kaylan and Mark Volman sharing vocals, play at the Fillmore East in New York.

[15] They premiere the Zappa-conceived ***200 Motels***, recorded with Zubin Mehta and the Los Angeles Philharmonic Orchestra.

Dec Zappa's solo album, ***Chunga's Revenge***, featuring a number of recent Mothers, peaks at US #119 and UK #43.

1971

Feb [8] Zappa is forced to cancel a UK concert at London's Royal Albert Hall with the Royal Philharmonic Orchestra after venue officials have declared the libretto "200 Motels" (the score to which was to have been featured) to be obscene, and refuse to allow its performance. Undaunted, Zappa makes the movie "200 Motels", a fictionalized "documentary" of the Mothers, at UK's Shepperton Studios, with guest appearances by Ringo Starr and Keith Moon of the Who, among others. (Critical and audience response to the film will be muted.)

June [6] John Lennon and Yoko Ono jam on stage with Zappa at the Fillmore East in New York. (Lennon's first stage appearance since 1969, the show is recorded for subsequent release by the ex-Beatle as ***Some Time In New York City***.)

Nov The double soundtrack album, ***Frank Zappa's 200 Motels***, a one-off release on the United Artists label, reaches US #59.

Dec [10] At a concert by the band at London's Rainbow Theatre, Zappa is pushed off the stage into the orchestra pit, by 24-year old Trevor Howell, the jealous boyfriend of an ardent female Zappa fan. He breaks a leg and ankle in several places, and suffers a fractured skull. (Recuperation will involve nine months in a wheelchair, and three more in a surgical brace.)

1972

Sept Still featuring assorted Mothers members, Zappa's five-track instrumental, solo-credited set, ***Waka/Jawaka - Hot Rats***, peaks at US #152.

1973

Dec The Mothers', now comprising Zappa, Ponty, Bruce & Tom Fowler, Ruth Underwood, Duke and Ralph Humphrey, have released ***Over-Nite Sensation***, the first recording on Zappa's newly-formed DiscReet label, which makes US #32.

1974

July Having permanently disbanded the group, Zappa's solo career resumes in earnest with ***Apostrophe***, prominently featuring guest, ex-Cream bassist Jack Bruce among several Mothers alumni, hitting US #10 (his only US top 10 disc).

Nov The extracted *Don't Eat The Yellow Snow* makes US #86.

1975

Aug In an out-of-court settlement, Zappa regains ownership of all of the masters originally recorded for Verve, plus a $100,000 cash payment for unpaid royalties.

Nov Mixing live and studio material and variously credited to the Mothers, Captain Beefheart and Zappa, ***Bongo Fury*** makes US #66.

1976

Apr [7] ***Apostrophe*** is certified gold by the RIAA.

Aug Grand Funk's ***Good Singin', Good Playin'***, produced by Zappa, reaches US #52.

Nov Zappa's current US tour, including Halloween dates in New York, is augmented by the horn-playing Brecker Brothers.

Dec ***Zoot Allures***, a collaboration with drummer, Terry Bozzio, makes US #61.

1977

Nov In further litigation, Zappa sues ex-manager Cohen and Warner Bros., with whom he has severed distribution ties, for $10 million, in an attempt to gain full control of all relevant archive material.

1978

May A live double album, ***Zappa In New York***, reaches US #57 and UK #55.

Aug [9] Zappa appears at the Knebworth II festival, Knebworth, Herts., on a bill with Peter Gabriel, the Tubes and others.

Nov The entirely instrumental ***Studio Tan*** reaches US #147, the first of three instrumental albums delivered by Zappa to Warner Bros. to fulfill contractual obligations, all released on his DiscReet imprint.

1979

Feb A second instrumental set, ***Sleep Dirt***, peaks at US #175.

Mar The first release on his new label Zappa Records (licensed to CBS/Columbia), the double album, ***Sheik Yerbouti***, its title a play on KC & The Sunshine Band's 1976 US chart-topper, *Shake Your Booty*, reaches US #21 and UK #32 and includes guest musicians Adrian Belew (guitar), Pat O'Hearn (bass), Bozzio and keyboardist Peter Wolf.

May *Dancin' Fool*, a disco parody taken from ***Sheik Yerbouti***, makes US #45.

June The instrumental ***Orchestral Favorites***, Zappa's final release on DiscReet, reaches US #169.

Oct ***Joe's Garage, Act I***, featuring vocalist Ike Willis,

Wolf and rhythm guitarist Warren Cucurillo among others, reaches US #27 and UK #62.

1980

Jan The double-album follow-up, ***Joe's Garage, Acts II & III*** including guitar guest Steve Vai, reaches US #53 and UK #75. Zappa's concert/animation mixed movie, "Baby Snakes" also premieres.
June [17-18] Zappa performs two dates at the Wembley Arena, Wembley, Middx., during a European visit.

1981

Apr A Zappa-organized and hosted concert heralding the work of his early influence Varése takes places in New York.
May Another live double album, ***Tinsel Town Rebellion***, baptizing Zappa's new Barking Pumpkin label, reaches US #66 and UK #55.
Oct The right-wing attacking double set, ***You Are What You Is***, reaches US #93 and UK #51.
[31] Zappa plays at New York's Palladium, with a band comprising Ray White, Tommy Mars, Scott Thunes, Ed Mann, Chad Wackerman, Bobby Martin and Vai.

1982

Apr The mail-order only ***Shut Up 'n Play Yer Guitar*** is released, a triple album set of guitar highlights from his career thus far.
June Once again featuring Vai, ***Ship Arriving Too Late To Save A Drowning Witch*** reaches US #23 and UK #61.
Sept The excerpted *Valley Girl*, featuring his daughter, Moon Unit, rapping in the artificial dialect and idioms of San Fernando Valley's spoiled-stupid female teens, reaches US #32.

1983

Feb [9] Zappa conducts the San Francisco Music Players at the city's War Memorial Opera House, in works by Varése, and Anton Webern.
May ***The Man From Utopia*** makes US #153 and UK #87.
While Zappa continues litigation against Warner Bros. for misleading accounting, having successfully won the rights to his entire back catalog, his wife, Gail, also his manager, launches the Barfko-Swill mail-order label.
Oct [31] Zappa performs on NBC-TV's "Late Night With David Letterman".

1984

Apr Conceived by composer/conductor Pierre Boulez, ***Boulez Conducts Zappa/The Perfect Stranger*** is released in the US.
Sept [24-25] He plays a pair of gigs at London's Hammersmith Odeon.
Oct ***Them Or Us***, featuring Johnny 'Guitar' Watson among its guests, makes UK #53.

1985

Mar ***Thing Fish***, a 21-track double album including guest musicians Vai and Watson alongside assorted ex-Mothers, is issued.
June Through his wife's Barfko-Swill mail-order label, Zappa releases a seven-album boxed set containing remixed versions of five Verve archive albums, plus a "Mystery Disk" of previously unreleased material from the early to mid '60s.
Sept Zappa appears before the Senate Commerce, Technology & Transportation Committee in Washington, DC, challenging the right-wing Parents' Music Resource Center pressure group, and denouncing the planned labeling of albums.

1986

Jan Including excerpts from the September hearings, ***Frank Zappa Meets The Mothers Of Prevention*** peaks at US #153.
Mar Zappa makes a cameo appearance in NBC-TV's "Miami Vice".

1987

Feb Comprising eight instrumental cuts, ***Jazz From Hell*** is released by Barking Pumpkin (currently licensed to Capitol/EMI).
June He is relieved of his role as guest host on US TV's "The Late Show", after a disagreement with producers over the choice of guests.

1988

Mar [2] Zappa wins the Best Rock Instrumental category for ***Jazz From Hell***, at the 30th annual Grammy Awards.
Apr A modest six double-CD series collectively titled ***You Can't Do That On Stage Anymore***, comprising live highlights assembled by Zappa, is released in the US.
Aug During his "Broadway The Hard Way" tour, Zappa provides voter-registration booths in theater lobbies, to mobilize the youth vote. He gets 11,000 new voters, but loses $400,000 on the tour. (By year's end, he will also perform in the Soviet Union.)
Dec Another extended live album, ***Broadway The Hard Way*** is released, documenting what will prove to be his final world tour. (His autobiography, ***The Real Frank Zappa Book*** will be published the following year by Poseidon Press.)

1990

Jan [22] Zappa meets with Czech president, Vaclav Havel, in Prague, the Czech Republic, who appoints him Trade & Culture Emissary.
Feb [26-28] Zappa guest hosts "Frank Zappa's Wild Wild East" talk show on the cable-TV Financial News Network's "Focus" series. He interviews Havel for the program and subsequently reports: "He told me he liked my records, especially ***Bongo Fury***."

1991

Aug An eight-CD bootleg collection, ***Beat The Boots!***, is released on the Foo-eee label, adding to ***The Best Band You Never Heard*** and ***Make A Jazz Noise Here***, both released earlier in the year by what is now considered rock music's most prolific artist.
Sept [17-19] Frankfurt's Ensemble Modern introduces Zappa's "The Yellow Shark" at the Alte Oper, during the "Frankfurt Festival '92". Zappa pulls out of the show on the 18th, due to illness, and flies back to Los Angeles.
Nov [7] Zappa's children, Moon and Dweezil, announce in New York, NY that their father is battling prostate cancer, and is canceling a four-night tribute ("Zappa's Universe") to honor his 50th birthday, and also today's scheduled interview on CNN's "Showbiz Today".

1993

Aug Zappa's latest offering, ***Yellow Shark***, is released by Barking Pumpkin. Zappa still helms, together with his wife, a dizzying array of businesses, which, in addition to Barking Pumpkin Records and Barfko-Swill Merchandising, includes Intercontinental Absurdities, Munchkin Music, Honker Home Video, and Why Not?. (A hotline telephone number, (USA) 1-818-PUMPKIN, also provides up-to-the-minute news on Zappa.)
Dec [4] Zappa succumbs to prostate cancer at his Los Angeles home after a two-year battle with the disease.

1994

Mar [1] The collectively credited Zappa's Universe Featuring Steve Vai wins the Best Rock Instrumental for *Sofa* at the 36th annual Grammy Awards held at New York's Radio City Music Hall.

1995

Apr [18] Having bought the rights to his entire back catalog from Gail Zappa and the Zappa Family Trust the previous October, Relativity Records (US) assaults the market with the first batch of the entire reissue of Zappa's 53 newly-remastered albums, all scheduled to hit the stores within the next 26 days. This follows his wife's recent mail-order issue of Zappa's final work, completed just prior to his death, ***Civilization Phaze III***, available on 1-800-PUMPKIN.
Aug [19] Relativity releases ***Strictly Commercial: The Best Of Frank Zappa***, a 19-song collection spanning 22 years, compiled by Jill Christiansen. Also during the month, the city council in the Lithuanian capital of Vilnius approves the erection of a two-metre high statue of the locally popular Zappa in its central park. The erection ceremony is scheduled for December 16th.
Sept [2] ***Strictly Commercial: The Best Of Frank Zappa*** enters the UK chart at its #45 high.

1996

Feb [28] ***Civilization Phaze III*** is named Best Recording Package, Boxed Set at the 38th annual Grammy Awards held at Los Angeles' Shrine Auditorium.
see also: **THE MOTHERS OF INVENTION**

THE ZOMBIES

Colin Blunstone (vocals);
Rod Argent (keyboards); **Paul Atkinson** (guitar);
Chris White (bass); **Hugh Grundy** (drums)

1963

Mar The Zombies are formed by Argent (b. June 14, 1945, St. Albans, Herts.), Blunstone (b. June 24, 1945, Hatfield, Herts.), Grundy (b. Mar. 6, 1945, Winchester, Hants.) and Atkinson (b. Mar. 19, 1946, Cuffley, Herts.), while still at St. Albans Grammar School. Their original bass player, Paul Arnold, leaves to concentrate on exam work (and will later qualify as a doctor), and is replaced by White (b. Mar. 7, 1943, Barnet, Herts.) in September, as the group begins rehearsing and writing its own material, in a room over a store owned by White's father. They begin playing local gigs at colleges and rugby clubs, making their first major public appearance at Watford Town Hall, Herts., traveling to gigs in an old red and white ice-cream van.

1964

Jan The group wins a "Herts Beat" competition for the region's new bands, organized by London newspaper, **The Evening News**, its prize an audition with Decca Records.
June Decca signs the group to a three-year recording contract, more on the strength of Argent's and White's original material than its carefully-prepared demo of the standard, *Summertime* (which will be re-recorded for their first album).
July They leave school (with 50 GCE "O-level" and "A-level" passes between them) and turn professional, signing with manager, Tito Burns, as their debut single, *She's Not There*, is released in the UK.
Sept *She's Not There*, distinguished by a minor-key, subtle jazzy arrangement, and Blunstone's breathy vocal, gains wide airplay and reaches UK #12. (Argent has written the song after being challenged by Decca producer, Ken Jones, to write a hit record.)
Oct Follow-up, *Leave Me Be*, written by White in identical style but lacking a commercial hook, is released.
Dec [12] *She's Not There* hits US #2, and sells over one million copies, bringing offers of US work.
[25] After a three-day wrangle with US immigration authorities, who initially ban the group from playing (despite an international union agreement) because of concern over the number of UK groups "invading" the US to work, the Zombies play ten days of New York concerts, as part of "Murray The K's Christmas Show", alongside the Shangri-Las, the Nashville Teens, the Shirelles and others. The rest of the proposed tour is cancelled.

1965

Feb [27] *Tell Her No* hits US #6 and UK #42, but is the last Zombies UK hit single.
Mar ***The Zombies*** makes US #39.
[25] The group begins a 12-date, twice-nightly UK package tour, with Dusty Springfield, the Searchers, Heinz, special guest Bobby Vee and others, at the Odeon Cinema, Stockton, Cleveland, set to end on April 10th at the Sophia Gardens, Cardiff, S. Glamorgan, Wales.
Apr [24] *She's Coming Home* makes US #58, as the band tours the US for the first time, supporting Herman's Hermits on a 34-day Dick Clark "Caravan Of Stars" trek. Meanwhile ***The Zombies - Begin Here*** is released in Britain.
July [10] *I Want You Back Again* peaks at US #95.
[15] A 25-day US tour with the Searchers opens in Chicago, IL.

1966

Feb [10] "Bunny Lake Is Missing", a movie starring Laurence Olivier/Keir Dullea, in which the group makes a cameo appearance singing *Nothing Is Changed*, *Remember You* and *Just Out Of Reach*, premieres at London's Leicester Square Odeon.
June *Indication* is released. Despite plenty of still-lucrative touring work, mainly in Europe, and the Far East (Japan and The Philippines, where occasional hits are still coming), the group is disenchanted with Decca over a lack of development of its recording career, and the label's reluctance to support another album.

1967

Mar Their revival of Little Anthony & the Imperials' *Goin' Out Of My Head* is the group's tenth, and final, Decca release.
June The group's contract with Decca expires, with no interest in re-signing from either side. The band signs to CBS/Columbia, where more artistic freedom is promised, and the label and group co-finance the recording of the concept album, ***Odessey And Oracle*** (an apparent mis-spelling of the first word by its sleeve designer), produced by Argent and White.
Sept *Friends Of Mine* is the first single from the CBS sessions, followed by *Care Of Cell 44*.
Dec The group splits, spurred by Blunstone and Atkinson, who are both wearied by a lack of acceptance, particularly in the UK. Blunstone leaves the music business for an insurance office job, but will decide to return as a soloist within the year.

1968

Apr The positively-reviewed ***Odessey And Oracle***, and single, *Time Of The Season*, are released by CBS despite the group's demise. (The album is not scheduled for US issue, until Blood, Sweat & Tears' leader, Al Kooper, who also records for CBS, badgers the label into doing it justice. Kooper contributes a sleeve note to the US release, which is hesitantly retailed on its subsidiary, Date label, normally reserved for soul releases.)
June US group, the People, reaches US #14 with White's song, *I Love You*, originally cut by the Zombies as the B-side of the non-charting *Whenever You're Ready*, in 1965. This prompts a reissue of the original as a US A-side.

1969

Jan Blunstone, signed to Deram, has recorded a new version of the original Zombies' hit, *She's Not There*, with a baroque string arrangement, under the pseudonym, Neil MacArthur, which reaches UK #34.
Mar [29] Following a gradual build-up of radio support (which will become huge, and translate into nationwide sales), *Time Of The Season* hits US #3, and will become the group's second million seller. Offers from the US flood in for a Zombies re-formation, including a deal offering $20,000 for a single concert. All are resisted, though Argent does agree, while in the process of assembling his own new band, Argent, to some further recordings as the Zombies (with an interim group comprising himself (vocals, keyboards), Jim Rodford (bass), Hugh Grundy (drums) and Rick Birkett (guitar), with Chris White co-producing) to complete a planned album of unreleased material (which fails to appear).
Apr ***Odessey And Oracle*** makes US #95.
[11] *Time Of The Season* is certified gold by the RIAA. (An enduring radio favorite, it will be honored for two million broadcast performances by the BMI at its annual awards in 1994.)
May Recently-completed, *Imagine The Swan*, is issued as a US single.
July *If It Don't Work Out*, another recent "Zombies" track, completed by Argent (originally cut as a demo for Dusty Springfield), is their final US single. Several bogus groups are touring North America under the Zombies' name, cashing in on *Time Of The Season*'s success; these are eventually litigated to a halt. The group itself has now split for solo pursuits: Atkinson and Grundy will work in A&R for CBS, Blunstone will return as a successful soloist, White and Argent become partners in production, while the latter also founds the successful '70s band, Argent, before linking with co-producer, Peter Van Hooke, in the '80s (not least on Tanita Tikaram's maiden album.)

1991

With *Time Of The Season* recently included on the soundtrack to the Robert De Niro/Robin Williams-starring movie, "Awakenings", a re-formed Zombies, comprising Blunstone, White, Grundy and Sebastian Santa Maria, release a new studio album, ***New World***, on Essential Records, in the UK. (In 1995, Transluxe Records (US) releases 15-track ***Greatest Hits Greatest Recordings***, including an interview with Argent and a 12-page booklet, while Epic/Legacy (US) releases ***It's The Time Of Colin Blunstone - Some Years***.)

Z.Z. TOP

Billy Gibbons (guitar, vocals);
Dusty Hill (bass, vocals); **Frank Beard** (drums)

1967

Gibbons (b. Dec. 16, 1949, Houston, TX), having received a Gibson Melody Maker guitar and a Fender Champ amplifier for his 14th birthday, has formed a succession of local Houston bands, including the Saints, the Coachmen and the Ten Blue Flames. Meanwhile, Hill (b. May 19, 1949, Dallas, TX), hanging out mainly in blues clubs in the early '60s, became a friend of guitar great, Freddie King, and joined East Dallas band, the Deadbeats, with his older brother, Rocky. Beard (b. June 11, 1949, Frankston, TX), having married his Irving High School sweetheart at a shotgun wedding at age 15 (the union soon dissolved), has taken up drumming in 1964. The Hill brothers now form the Warlocks, releasing one-off singles on the Paradise and Ara labels, eventually recruiting Beard, while Gibbons forms the Moving Sidewalks, with Lanier Gregg (bass) and Dan Mitchell (drums), a psychedelic band which has local hits with *99th Floor* and *Need Me*, on Tantara, and are then picked up by Wand.

1968

The Warlocks changes its name to American Blues (and will record two albums - ***The American Blues Is Here On Karma*** and ***The American Blues Do Their Thing***, for Uni Records).
June The Moving Sidewalks open for the Jimi Hendrix Experience, having released ***Flash***.

1969

As both bands split, Gibbons auditions for members for a new southern-boogie rock band, Z.Z. Top (having rejected the names Z.Z. Hill and Z.Z. Brown, the permanent name was inspired when Gibbons passed by a barn, seeing the "Z" beams on a pair of open hay-loft doors). Beard is enlisted (through bassist Billy Etheridge, who soon leaves) as drummer and, via him, Hill joins. Gibbons has also linked with promotion man, Bill Ham, who becomes the band's long-term manager and producer. Z.Z. Top releases its debut single, *Salt Lick*, on the small Scat label.

1970

Feb [10] The group plays its first ever gig in Beaumont, TX.
With a US-only deal signed with London Records, which reissues *Salt Lick*, Z.Z. Top records its debut, ***Z.Z. Top's First Album***, and extracted single *Shakin' Your Tree*, which both fail to sell beyond Texas. The band begins a seven-year period of near non-stop touring, which will provide the base for increased sales in coming years. (It will open for many acts, including Janis Joplin, Humble Pie, Ten Years After and Mott The Hoople, as well as opening on an all-black revue with Muddy Waters, Freddie King and Howlin' Wolf.) Early dates focus strongly in the Texas, Louisiana and Mississippi areas, where it develops a large cult following. In 1971, Ham will book Z.Z. Top into more than 300 venues.

1972

May Self-penned, as with all of the group's albums, ***Rio Grande Mud*** makes US #104, as the band supports the Rolling Stones on a US visit.
July [8] *Francene* makes US #69. The band attracts an audience of 80,000 to its "Z.Z. Top's First Annual Texas Size Rompin' Stompin' Barndance Bar-B-Q" at the University of Texas, Austin, TX.

1973

Aug [10] The group embarks on a 17-date US tour at the Warehouse, New Orleans, LA, set to end at Salem Civic Center, Salem, VA, supporting the release of ***Tres Hombres***, which will hit US #8 and earn an RIAA certified gold disc on May 23rd the following year.

1974

June [29] Documenting the famed "Best Little Whorehouse in Texas", *La Grange* makes US #41.
July Z.Z. Top plays to an 80,000 crowd at Texas Memorial Stadium, Austin, TX, on a bill with Bad Company, Santana and Joe Cocker.

1975

May Now heading towards a no-frills hard rock sound, the half-studio, half-live album (recorded at The Warehouse in New Orleans) ***Fandango!*** hits US #10, as **Newsweek** magazine reports that Z.Z. Top has outdrawn Elvis Presley in Nashville, TN, and broken Led Zeppelin's attendance record in New Orleans, LA, during its current world tour.
June [27] The RIAA certifies ***Fandango!*** gold.
July Their debut UK chart entry, ***Fandango!***, climbs to UK #60.
Sept [6] From the album, *Tush*, the band's future long-term live encore, reaches US #20.

1976

"Z.Z. Top's Worldwide Texas Tour" including 100 US dates and their first concerts in Europe, Australia and Japan, is undertaken. Renowned for touring excess, 75 tons of equipment are transported together with a Texas State-shaped stage, and live buffalo, steer and snakes (among $140,000 worth of Texas livestock). The trek will gross over $10 million, despite the cancellation of its European leg.
Nov [13] *It's Only Love* makes US #44.

1977

Feb ***Tejas*** (Spanish for Texas) rises to US #17 having already been certified gold by the RIAA on January 18th. Exhausted from the tour, the band begins a two-year vacation: Beard visits the Caribbean and back-packs around the world, Hill goes sailing in the Pacific, and scuba-diving in Mexico, and Gibbons travels to Europe and Madagascar, and joins a Buddhist prayer group in Tibet.
Apr [23] B-side of *It's Only Love*, *Arrested While*

Driving Blind makes US #91.

1979

Nov After an interim album, ***The Best Of Z.Z. Top***, has made US #94 in February the previous year (already certified gold by the RIAA on December 30th 1977), their final release on the London label, the band has signed to Warner Bros. Records. Both Gibbons and Hill have stopped shaving, and now sport long beards, unlike the clean-shaven Beard. The front-men will develop these growths as the beards become integral to Z.Z. Top's image for the next ten years. As Warner Bros. reissues all of Z.Z. Top's London albums, the new ***Deguello*** (Spanish for "beheading") peaks at US #24. It features the Wolf Horn section - actually Beard (alto sax), Hill (tenor sax) and Gibbons (baritone sax).

1980

Mar [15] As serious touring resumes, *I Thank You* makes US #34.
July [12] *Cheap Sunglasses* stalls at US #89.

1981

Aug ***El Loco*** (Spanish for "The Crazy") makes UK #88, and will make US #17.
Oct [10] *Leila* makes US #77.
[22] ***El Loco*** is confirmed gold by the RIAA.

1983

Apr Adding synthesizers to their familiar Texan boogie-rock style, ***Eliminator***, recorded at Ardent Recording Studios in Memphis, is released, and will hit US #9 during a 183-week chart tenure, and UK #3 during a 135-week survey stay. (The real Eliminator is a 1933 Ford three-window coupe, much featured in the album's promo video clips.)
May [21] Primed for MTV airplay, the band releases an accompanying video to the current single, *Gimme All Your Lovin'*. The first of a memorable trilogy, directed by Tim Newman, it features common Z.Z. Top images, like stocking-clad babes, heroic story-lines and the striking Z.Z. Top car and keyring. Hot video rotation spurs the single to US #37.
Aug [27] Second in the trilogy, *Sharp Dressed Man* makes US #56, as *Gimme All Your Lovin'* makes UK #61.
Nov [19] The first of many awards, "Gimme All Your Lovin'" receives **Billboard**'s Best Group Performance Video trophy, at a ceremony in Pasadena, CA.
Dec *Sharp Dressed Man* makes UK #53.

1984

Mar As the worldwide "Eliminator" tour sells out, *TV Dinners* peaks at UK #67.
May [11] ***Deguello*** is certified platinum by the RIAA.
July [21] *Legs* hits US #8 (and will subsequently be used for a Leggs pantyhose TV commercial).
Sept [18] Z.Z. Top wins the Best Group Video ("Legs") and Best Direction ("Sharp Dressed Man") categories at the inaugural MTV Video Music Awards, held at Radio City Music Hall, New York, NY, hosted by Dan Aykroyd and Bette Midler.
Nov *Gimme All Your Lovin'*, reissued in the UK, hits #10.

1985

Jan [1] Hill accidentally shoots himself in the stomach (but will recover after surgery).
[19] *Sharp Dressed Man*, again re-released, makes UK #22.
Mar *Legs* reaches UK #16.
July Now a UK chart fixture, Warner Bros. assembles the EP, *Summer Holiday*, including *Tush*, *Got Me Under Pressure*, *Beer Drinkers & Hellraisers* and *I'm Bad, I'm Nationwide*, which makes UK #51.
Nov ***Afterburner*** repeats the ***Eliminator*** formula, and heads towards US #4 (and triple-platinum certification) and UK #2.
Dec [3] The group's "Afterburner Tour" opens in Toronto, ON, Canada, the first engagement in a non-stop 212-date worldwide venture, with increased tonnage and special effects.
[14] From the new album, *Sleeping Bag* hits US #8 and UK #27, aided by a Steve Barron-directed video clip.

1986

Feb *Stages* makes UK #43.
Mar [8] *Stages* reaches US #21.
May [17] Ballad, *Rough Boy*, rises to US #22, and reaches UK #23.
Aug [30] *Velcro Fly* (with a promo film directed by Danny Kleinman, and choreography by Paula Abdul, which will win the MTV Best Choreography Award) reaches US #35, and peaks at UK #54.
Sept [12] The group begins its 29-date European leg of the world tour in Stockholm, Sweden.
[15] "Rough Boy" wins the Best Art Direction category at the third annual MTV Video Music Awards, broadcast simultaneously from the Universal Amphitheatre, Universal City, CA and the Palladium, New York.
Oct [23] At the end of European dates, Z.Z. Top completes a fourth soldout date at Wembley Arena, Wembley, Middx. (By year's end the band will be named the top grossing act of the year with $26,590,345 grossed from 134 shows. During the year they will also become Official Texas Heroes alongside the likes of Davy Crockett, be baptized as admirals in the Texas Navy and be individually named deputies in the Texas counties of Hall, Dallas, Ector and Bell.)

1987

Jan [12] **Pollstar** names Z.Z. Top the #1 concert draw of 1986.
Mar [21] "Afterburner" tour ends in Honolulu, HI, with 40 pounds of confetti blasted into the audience, leaving the band free to resume its vacation.
Oct [10] Z.Z. Top announces that it has made an advance booking for the first passenger flight to the Moon.

1988

The group spearheads a drive to raise $1 million for a permanent Muddy Waters exhibit, at the Delta Blues Museum in Clarksdale, MS. They will also unveil the "CadZ.Z.illa" automobile, designed with Larry Erickson, at Chevy's in New York, the following year.

1990

June [23] *Doubleback*, from the movie, "Back To The Future Part III", makes US #50.
Sept [19] ***Eliminator*** is RIAA-certified for seven million sales, one of the best-selling albums of the previous decade.
Oct [2] "Recycler" world tour opens at PNE Pacific Coliseum, Vancouver, BC, Canada, before a sellout crowd of 13,500.
[20] The group plays a benefit for the Texas Special Olympics at the Cotton Bowl, Fair Park, Dallas, with the Steve Miller Band, Santana and Colin James, grossing $1,715,688 from the 74,100 sellout crowd.
Nov [17] ***Recycler*** hits US #6.

1991

Jan [4] Z.Z. Top continues its North American tour, at the Kiefer U.N.O. Lakefront Arena in New Orleans, supported by the Black Crowes.
[5] The group is honored before its Mid-South Coliseum, Memphis sellout gigs, at a reception given by Governor Ned Ray McWherter, for its help in raising money for the Delta Blues Museum in Clarksdale.
[16] The group inducts Jimmy Reed into the Rock and Roll Hall of Fame, at the sixth annual dinner, held at New York's Waldorf Astoria Hotel.
Feb [23] *Give It Up* gives it up at US #79.
Apr [13] *My Head's In Mississippi* enters at its UK #37 peak.
May [4] Governor Ann Richards declares "Z.Z. Top Day" in Texas, honoring the group for "bringing the powerful beat of Texas boogie to enthusiastic audiences across the globe".
July [6] The European leg of the "Recycler" tour, which began on June 5th, ends at "Rock The Bowl '91" at the Milton Keynes Bowl, Milton Keynes, with Bryan Adams, Thunder and Little Angels.
Sept [27] The group plays before a sellout crowd of 8,960 at the Sports Palace, Mexico City, Mexico. (During the year, the band will gross more than $25 million from more than 100 shows in North America.)

1992

Apr [18] A cover of the Doc Pomus/Mort Shuman-penned, *Viva Las Vegas*, hits UK #10.
May [9] An 18-track retrospective, ***Greatest Hits***, hits UK #5.
[30] ***Greatest Hits*** hits US #9.
June [10] Publisher and songwriter Bernard Besman's La Cienega Music Co. files a $5 million suit in US District Court, Los Angeles, claiming *La Grange* infringes John Lee Hooker's 1948, *Boogie Chillen*. (The lawsuit will be dismissed on November 23rd.)
[27] Reissued *Rough Boy* makes UK #49.
July The group signs a reported $30 million, five-album deal with RCA Records.
Nov [18] Z.Z. Top are honored with the Silver Clef Award, at the fifth annual Silver Clef Award Dinner And Auction, to benefit the Nordoff Robbins Music Therapy Foundation.
Dec [30] The band files a $115 million suit against Mitsubishi Motor Sales, and Gray Advertising, alleging copyright infringement over use of the group's signature song, *La Grange*, for a series of US TV commercials, which ran between 1990-1991.

1993

Jan [30-31] Beard races his car as part of the Z.Z./Pro Technik Racing Team, at the Rolex 24 Hour race in Daytona, FL.
Mar [23] Gibbons contributes fret work to the Paul Rodgers assembled ***Tribute To Muddy Waters*** album, released on Victory Music.
June The group performs at Milwaukee's Marcus Amphitheater to cap off a week of events to celebrate the 90th anniversary of the Harley Davidson company.

1994

Jan [12] In one of its more unlikely appearances, Z.Z. Top performs on ITV's "Des O'Connor Tonight".
[17] ***Greatest Hits*** is certified for two million sales by the RIAA.
[29] *Pincushion* debuts at its UK #15 peak.
Feb [5] Z.Z. Top's long-awaited RCA label debut, ***Antenna***, debuts at its US #14 peak.
Mar [4] The band is the music guest on CBS-TV's "Late Show With David Letterman".
Apr [30] A US tour gets underway at the Hirsch Memorial Coliseum, Shreveport, LA, a bill grossing $229,500 from 10,200 fans, set to climax on November 6th with the second of two nights at The Summit, Houston.
May [7] *Breakaway* charts for a week at UK #60.
June [1] ***Antenna*** is certified platinum by the RIAA.
Aug [17] The RIAA confirms multi-platinum sales awards for ***The Best Of Z.Z. Top*** (two million) and ***Afterburner*** (four million).
Nov [22] ***One Foot In The Blues***, a collection of previously unreleased Z.Z. Top blues treatments recorded over the past 20 years, is released.

1995

Feb [15] The group's lawyers file a trademark infringement suit against Steridyne Corporation, makers of a $100 gel-filled mattress bed-sore product named the ZZ Topper.

1996

Feb [15] The group conducts its first Internet chat on America OnLine.

ACKNOWLEDGMENTS

Among a vast source of newspapers, magazines, books, print and broadcasting archives, the following proved particularly useful during research:

US: Amusement Business, Billboard, Boston Globe, Circus, Details, Discoveries, Entertainment Weekly, Goldmine, Hollywood Reporter, Ice, Interview, Musician, New York Times, People, Performance, Premiere, Pulse, Radio & Records, Rolling Stone, Spin, TV Guide, USA Today, Variety, wire reports.

UK: Disc & Music Echo, Kerrang!, Melody Maker, Music & Media, Mojo, New Musical Express, Q, Record Business, Record Collector, Record Mirror, Record Retailer, RPM, Select, Smash Hits, Time Out, Vox, Zig-Zag.

Books: Joel Whitburn's indispensable range of US chart books, including **Top Pop Singles 1955-1993**, **Top Pop Albums 1955-1992**, **The Guinness Book Of British Hit Singles and Hit Albums** (Paul Gambaccini, Tim Rice, Jonathan Rice), **The Billboard Book Of Number One Hits** (Fred Bronson), **Screenworld**, **Theatre World**, **The Complete Directory To Prime Time Network TV Shows** (Tim Brooks, Earle Marsh); a myriad of CD booklets and album sleeves. We would also like to thank all the music books that credit or do not credit **The Encyclopedia of Rock Stars** as a reference source.

The authors would like to thank the following: Russell Ash; Peter Compton, Barry Lazell and all at MRIB; Christopher Davis, Phil Gilderdale, Susannah Marriott and all at Dorling Kindersley in London and New York; Angela Corio at the RIAA; Kim Bloxdorf at Record Research; Tim Barnes, Stephen Barrett, Damian Dillon, Bonnie Fantasia, Pete Frame, Mike Scott, Peter Viney, Nicholas Warburton.

Special thanks to: Linda and Christiaan Rees and Britt de Bie, without whom...

Publisher's Acknowledgments: Dorling Kindersley would like to thank Nell Graville and Sanchia O'Hara for editorial assistance; Johnny Pau and Kylie Mulquin for design assistance; James Clarke for picture research.

Picture Credits: The publisher would like to thank the following for their kind permission to reproduce the photographs.
t= top, b= bottom, a= above, c= centre, l= left, r= right.
All Action : Justin Thomas 2 cla, 15 clb. **Archive Photos** : 7 tl. **Ronald Grant Archiv**e : 14 cra. **London Features International** : 9 cb, 12 ca. **Pictorial Press** : 7 ca, 7tr, 8 bc, 11 tr, 14cla, / J. Mayer 2 bl, R. Verhorst 15 ca, back cover cr. **Redferns** : 15 br, / Glenn A. Baker Archive 3 cl, 6 cr, 7 crb, back cover tl, back cover cla. Dave Ellis 3 br, 10 bl, Mick Hutson 3 tr, 3 cr, 13 br, 15 tl, Astrid Kirchher 5 cla, B. Levine 9 br, John Marshall 15 tr, Michael Ochs Archive 2 br, 6 bl, 7 cb, 7 bc, 8 cr, 9 cla, 9 tc, 9 cra,10 tc, RB 6 tc, David Redfern 2 tr, 3 bl, 8 tr, 9 bl, 10 cra, 11 clb, 11 c, 13 ca, back cover bl, Ebet Roberts 13 clb, back cover tr. **Retna** : 13 tr, Chris Carrol 12 bl, David Corrio 12 c, King Collection 10 bc, David McGough 12 bl, Neil Preston 13 tl, 14 br, Michael Putland 11 br, James Shrive 13 bc, Paul Slattery 11 cra. **Rex** : 2 cra, 10 br. **Topham Picturepoint** : 3 tl.

FINAL NOTE
In dispelling some myths, we hope not to create new ones. If you are included in this book (or think you ought to be) and would like to correct, corroborate or contribute further information for subsequent editions, or if you are a particular devotee of a certain act with a detailed knowledge of its career and would like to contact the authors, please do so at:

P.O. Box 173, Barnstable, Massachusetts 02630, USA

Charts

Where a specific chart peak date is given, it always refers to the relevant week ending on Saturday, a practice not generally observed by chart compilers in the 50s and 60s.

Gold and platinum awards
You may often see references to these honors, which confirm a particular sales level achieved either by a single, album or music video collection.

In the US: these sales certifications have been confirmed regularly since March 1958 when the RIAA (Recording Industry Association Of America) began issuing gold awards for singles and albums sold only in the United States (though a significant number of record labels, most notably Motown, did not submit records for certification until the 70s). The sales criteria for these discs has changed over the years: up to 1988, a gold single had to sell at least one million copies in the US; this mark was decreased to 500,000 on January 1st, 1989. Platinum singles, a level introduced on January 1st, 1976, required a minimum sale of two million units, though this was also modified, down to one million sales, on January 1st, 1989.

Up to 1974, a gold album needed to shift $1 million in sales at manufacturer's wholesale prices, with an additional requirement set on January 1st, 1975 that an album must also sell a minimum of 500,000 copies. From January 1st the following year, the RIAA introduced platinum awards for which a one million unit sales plateau had to be reached.

Music video collections in the US are certified as platinum with 100,000 units sold and as gold with 50,000 sold.

At the beginning of 1985, the organization instituted multi-platinum honors, which merely multiplies each million-sale achievement for a specific single, album or video collection. All these standards exist today.

In the UK: a comprehensive record sales certification system has not operated for the same period of time in Britain, where sales awards were introduced in 1976 by the BPI (British Phonographic Industry). Current silver, gold and platinum awards levels, now verified on a weekly basis, are:

Singles:
- silver: 200,000 (250,000 before January 1st, 1989)
- gold: 400,000 (500,000 before January 1st, 1989)
- platinum: 600,000 (1,000,000 before January 1st, 1989)

Albums:
- silver: 60,000
- gold: 100,000
- platinum: 300,000

Multi-platinum sales levels (at multiples of the platinum plateau) are also confirmed in the UK for both singles and albums.

The international record labels body, IFPI (International Federation Of The Phonographic Industry) began confirming "Platinum Europe" albums sales awards on July 11th, 1996 (backdated for any album released by a member company since January 1st, 1994), with a one million pan-European sales achievement required for certification.